CONGRESSIONAL QUARTERLY

Almanac®

103rd CONGRESS
2nd SESSION 1994

VOLUME L

Congressional Quarterly Inc.

1414 22nd Street N.W.
Washington, D.C. 20037

CONGRESSIONAL QUARTERLY
1994 ALMANAC

Chairman	Andrew Barnes
Vice Chairman	Andrew P. Corty
Editor and Publisher	Neil Skene
Executive Editor	Robert W. Merry

Managing Editor	Mark Willen
Assistant Managing Editors	John R. Cranford, Rose Gutfeld
Political Editor	Ronald D. Elving

News Editors
Martha Angle, Stephen Gettinger, Jackie Koszczuk, Anne Q. Hoy, Deborah McGregor, Cathy Shaw

Copy Desk Chief	Marileen C. Maher
Art Director	Patt Chisholm

Senior Writers
Rhodes Cook, George Hager, Alissa J. Rubin, Pat Towell

Reporters
Jennifer Babson, Bob Benenson, Donna Cassata, David S. Cloud, Carroll J. Doherty, Beth Donovan, Karen Foerstel, Colette Fraley, Allan Freedman, K. Daniel Glover, Juliana Gruenwald, Jon Healey, Elizabeth Helfgott, David Hosansky, Holly Idelson, Jeffrey L. Katz, Steve Langdon, David Masci, Victoria A. Needham, Paul Nyhan, Elizabeth A. Palmer, Jeanne Ponessa, Jonathan D. Salant, Richard Sammon, Andrew Taylor, Annie Tin, Robert Marshall Wells

Copy Editors
Ron Brodmann, Susan Carroll, Elaine Dwyer Goheen, Will Heyniger, Kelli A. Logan, Charles Southwell, Lisa Clagett Weintraub, Eric Weissman

Editor	Jan Austin
Production Editor	Melinda W. Nahmias
Indexer	Carr Research Group

Graphic Artist	Marilyn Gates-Davis
Systems Editor/ Computer Journalism	Thomas H. Moore

Researchers
Eugene J. Gabler (Senior Researcher), Alan Greenblatt, Mark T. Kehoe, Philip Marwill, Sondra J. Nixon, Rebecca H. Patterson

Editorial Assistants
Bonnie L. Forrest, Spencer Freedman, Micaele Sparacino

Congressional Monitor/ Editor	Larry Liebert
Editor, New Media	David Rapp
CQ Researcher Editor	Sandra Stencel

Associate Publisher	John J. Coyle
Marketing and Sales Director	Edward S. Hauck
Advertising Director	Robert G. Wallace
Fulfillment Director	Judith Stachnik
Creative Services Manager	Donna Colona
General Manager, Books	Patrick Bernuth
Editorial Director for CQ Directories	Robert E. Cuthriell
Books Editorial Director	David R. Tarr
Books Marketing Director	Kathryn C. Suarez
Controller and Director of Corporate Services	Martha Ellis Kelley
Director of Technology	Ronald Knott
Director of Administrative Services	Linda M. Zappasodi
Human Resources Director	Lynne Breger Tag
Library Director	Kathleen Walton
Director, Editorial Development	George Codrea
Managing Editor, CQ Online	Randy Lilleston
Production Manager	I. D. Fuller
Founder	Nelson Poynter (1903-1978)

Congressional Quarterly, Inc.

Congressional Quarterly Inc. is a publishing and information services company and a recognized leader in political journalism. For half a century, CQ has served clients in the fields of news, education, business and government with timely, complete unbiased information on Congress, politics and national issues.

At the heart of CQ is its acclaimed publication the Weekly Report, a weekly magazine offering news and analyses on Congress and legislation. The CQ Researcher (formerly Editorial Research Reports), with its focus on current issues, provides weekly balanced summaries on topics of widespread interest.

Congressional Quarterly Inc. publishes the Congressional Monitor, a daily report on Congress and current and future activities of congressional committees, and several newsletters, including the Congressional Record Scanner and the CQ FaxReport.

Congressional Quarterly Inc. also publishes a variety of books, including political science textbooks, under the CQ Press imprint and public affairs paperbacks to keep journalists, scholars and the public abreast of developing issues and events. CQ Books publishes information directories and reference books on the federal government, national elections and politics, including the Guide to the Presidency, the Guide to Congress, the Guide to the U.S. Supreme Court, the Guide to U.S. Elections, Politics in America, the Federal Regulatory Directory and Washington Information Directory. The CQ Almanac®, a compendium of legislation for one session of Congress, is

published each year. Congress and the Nation, a record of government for a presidential term, is published every four years.

Washington Alert, Congressional Quarterly's online congressional, regulatory and state tracking service, provides immediate access to both proprietary and public databases of legislative action, votes, schedules, profiles and analyses.

What You Will Find in This Book

This is the 50th edition of the Congressional Quarterly Almanac, an annual book that chronicles the course of major legislation and national politics.

Drawing on reporting and writing done throughout the year by the staffs of the Congressional Quarterly Weekly Report and the Congressional Monitor, the Almanac organizes, distills and cross-indexes for permanent reference the full year in Congress and in national politics. The current volume covers the second session of the 103rd Congress.

The following are the major elements of the volume:

● **Inside Congress.** The first chapter gives an overview of the year in Congress. It includes statistical information on the session and stories on legislation governing Congress as a whole, such as campaign finance and lobbying disclosure. This year the section chronicles the legislative setbacks that preceded the Democrats' defeat in the Nov. 8 elections and gives a detailed picture of Republicans' preparations to take control of both chambers in the 104th Congress.

● **Legislative Chapters.** The next nine chapters cover legislative action during the session on economics and finance, government and commerce, social policy, defense and foreign policy.

● **Appropriations.** Chapter 11 contains separate stories detailing the substance and legislative history of each of the 13 regular fiscal 1995 appropriations bills, as well as an overview of the appropriations process in 1994.

● **Political Report.** Chapter 12 details the stunning Republican victory in the Nov. 8 elections, which gave the GOP control of both chambers of Congress for the first time in 40 years.

● **Appendixes.** The volume also includes appendixes on the following topics:

▶ **Glossary.** A 12-page glossary of terms used in Congress.

▶ **Congress and Its Members.** Membership lists for all committees and subcommittees, characteristics of Congress, and a description of the legislative process.

▶ **Vote Studies.** Studies of presidential support, party unity, conservative coalition, and freshmen patterns, as well as the key votes of 1994.

▶ **Texts.** Key presidential and other texts.

▶ **Public Laws.** A complete listing of public laws enacted during the session in the order they were signed by the president.

▶ **Roll Call Votes.** A complete set of roll call vote charts for the House and Senate during the session.

"By providing a link between the local newspaper and Capitol Hill we hope Congressional Quarterly can help to make public opinion the only effective pressure group in the country. Since many citizens other than editors are also interested in Congress, we hope that they too will find Congressional Quarterly an aid to a better understanding of their government.

"Congressional Quarterly presents the facts in as complete, concise and unbiased form as we know how. The editorial comment on the acts and votes of Congress, we leave to our subscribers."

Foreword, Congressional Quarterly, Vol. I, 1945
Henrietta Poynter, 1901-1968
Nelson Poynter, 1903-1978

Errata: 1993 CQ Almanac

p. 140, More Budget Cuts ("Reinventing Government"), col. 1, fourth paragraph. As approved by the House, HR 3400 would have cut over five years:
- $32.5 billion by reducing the federal work force.
- $2.6 billion through rescissions.
- $2 billion in other "reinventing government" savings.

p. 184, China Trade Status, col. 1, seventh paragraph. China gained most-favored-nation status in 1980 as part of a trade agreement.

p. 248, Energy Laboratories, col. 2, eighth paragraph under Energy Lab headline. The Senate passed the bill (S 473) on Nov. 20.

p. 569, Defense Appropriations, col. 1, first paragraph. The measure was the fiscal 1994 spending bill.

SUMMARY TABLE OF CONTENTS

CHAPTER 1 — INSIDE CONGRESS 3
CHAPTER 2 — ECONOMICS & FINANCE 67
CHAPTER 3 — GOVERNMENT/COMMERCE. 143
CHAPTER 4 — SCIENCE & TECHNOLOGY/COMMUNICATIONS 203
CHAPTER 5 — ENVIRONMENT/ENERGY 227
CHAPTER 6 — LAW & JUDICIARY 273
CHAPTER 7 — HEALTH/HUMAN SERVICES 319
CHAPTER 8 — EDUCATION/LABOR/HOUSING/VETERANS 383
CHAPTER 9 — DEFENSE 421
CHAPTER 10 — FOREIGN POLICY 445
CHAPTER 11 — APPROPRIATIONS. 475
CHAPTER 12 — POLITICAL REPORT 561

APPENDIXES

Glossary 3-A
Congress and Its Members 3-B
Vote Studies 3-C
Text. 3-D
Public Laws 3-E
Roll Call Votes
    House. 2-H
    Senate 2-S

INDEXES

Bill Number Index 3-I
Roll Call Vote Index 4-I
General Index. . . . . XX-I

TABLE OF CONTENTS

Chapter 1 — Inside Congress

The Year in Review

103rd Congress: An Overview 3

    2nd Session at a Glance 5

    Public Laws 6

    Leadership — 103rd Congress....................... 7

    Filibusters... 9

    What Passed, What Didn't 10

    Membership Changes.............................. 12

Preparing for the Next Congress

Organizing the 104th Congress 14

    Leadership — 104th Congress...................... 15

    House Republican Leadership Races................ 16

    House Democratic Leadership Races 17

Republicans Lay Out New Rules 18

    Restructuring House Committees................... 19

    Rules Changes.................................... 20

GOP's 'Contract With America' 22

Legislation, Regulation

Congressional Reform 27

Workplace Compliance 28

Clinton Legislative Strategy.......................... 29

Campaign Finance Overhaul......................... 32

FEC Spending Regulations 35

Lobbying Disclosure................................. 36

    Gift Rules 41

Ethics

Rostenkowski Indictment............................. 43

Packwood Investigation 49

Other Ethics Cases................................. 50

Gingrich Investigation............................... 54

Departures

Democratic Departures 55

O'Neill Death....................................... 59

Nixon Death.. 60

Other

Delegate Voting..................................... 61

Nation of Islam Condemnation....................... 62

Congressional Pay Freeze 63

Chapter 2 — Economics & Finance

Budget

Budget Overview.................................... 67

Clinton Budget..................................... 68

    Budget Glossary 69

    Highlights 70

    Economic Assumptions 74

    Budget by Agency................................ 75

    Budget by Function 76

Budget Resolution.................................. 81

Balanced-Budget Amendment 85

Budget Process Reform............................. 87

    'A to Z' Plan 88

Entitlement Reform Panel 90

    Rivlin Memo...................................... 91

Deficit Reduction................................... 92

Tax Simplification 93

Banking

Interstate Banking & Branching 93

    Provisions.. 96

Community Development Lending 100

    Provisions....................................... 102

Fair Trade in Financial Services..................... 107

Whitewater

Whitewater Investigation 108

    Fiske Letter 110

    Chronology of White House-Treasury Contacts........ 112

Other Banking and Finance

Secondary Loan Market 116

Other Banking Legislation.......................... 116

Fair Credit Reporting 117

Insurance Redlining 119

Other Securities-Related Legislation 120

Trade

Export Administration Act........................... 121

GATT Implementation 123

    History... 125

    Highlights of GATT Accord 129

    Provisions...................................... 131

China MFN Status 137

Export-Import Bank................................ 138

OPIC Reauthorization.............................. 138

Nominations...................................... 138

Chapter 3 — Government/Commerce

Government

'Reinventing' Government 143
Federal Procurement Overhaul. 144
   Provisions. 146
Federal Worker Buyouts 147
Unfunded Federal Mandates. 150
Other Federal Workers Legislation 152
Other Government Operations Bills. 154
Disaster Legislation 155
Federal Land Payments. 156
Other Government-Related Legislation 156

Transportation

Maritime Reuthorization. 158
Fishermen's Protection Act. 160
Coast Guard Reauthorization 161
   Omnibus Maritime Bill 162
Maritime Commission. 164
Maritime Heritage Program. 164
National Highway System 165
   Earthquake-Damaged Bridges 167
FAA Reauthorization. 168

Trucking Deregulation 170
Other Transportation Legislation 171

Commerce

Bankruptcy Code Overhaul. 175
   Provisions. 176
Product Liability 178
   Legislative History. 179
Toy Safety 179
Small-Plane Liability. 180
FTC Reauthorization. 181
Baseball Antitrust 182
Insurance Antitrust 183
Patent Bills. 184
Small Business Administration Reauthorization. 185
Other Small-Business Legislation. 186
Aid to Depressed Regions. 187
Other Commerce-Related Legislation 189

Agriculture

Protection for New Plant Varieties. 190
Agriculture Department Reorganization 191
Crop Insurance Overhaul. 194
Other Agriculture-Related Legislation 197

Chapter 4 — Science & Technology/Communications

Communications

Telecommunications Regulation. 203
   Bills Compared 209
   Senate Bill Provisions. 213
Wiretapping 215
Satellite Home Viewer Act. 216
Telemarketing Fraud. 217
FCC Reauthorization. 218

Science & Techonology

NASA Reauthorization 218
NOAA Reauthorization 219
Other Science-Related Legislation. 220
Competitiveness Programs 221
Energy Research Laboratories 223

Chapter 5 — Environment/Energy

Environment

California Desert Protection 227
Superfund Reauthorization 231
Mining Law Rewrite 236
Safe Drinking Water. 238
Clean Water Law. 241
   Corps Water Projects. 242
EPA Cabinet Status 243
Risk Assessment Initiative. 244
Montana Wilderness. 245
Idaho Wilderness. 247
National Park Management. 247
   Endangered Species Act 248
National Park Concessions 249
Park User Fees 251
'American Heritage Areas'. 252

Steamtown National Historic Site 252
Presidio Management. 253
Other National Park Legislation 254
Pacific Northwest Timber Feud 256
Marine Mammal Protection. 257
   Rhinoceros and Tiger Conservation Fund. 258
Fishing Law Reauthorization. 259
Interstate Transport of Solid Waste 261
   Waste 'Flow-Control' Legislation 262
Radioactive Waste 263
Environmental Technology. 263
Radon Disclosure Bill. 264
Other Environmental Legislation. 265

Energy

Strategic Petroleum Reserve 267
Other Energy-Related Legislation. 268

Chapter 6 — Law & Judiciary

Legislation

Omnibus Crime Bill.................................. 273
  Assault Weapons Ban 276
  Evolution of the Crime Bill...................... 281
  Crime Trust Fund 283
  'Brady 2'...................................... 284
  Provisions..................................... 287
Immigration Law 294
Independent Counsel 295

Provisions.. 297
Other Law-Related Legislation 298
Judicial Appointments Confirmed 300
Supreme Court
Breyer Appointment............................... 303
  Vital Statistics 305
  Past Opinions 306
Supreme Court Cases 310
Congressional Term Limits 314

Chapter 7 — Health/Human Services

Health Care Reform

Overview.. 319
  Chronology..................................... 321
  Clinton Plan Highlights.......................... 322
Committee Phase 324
  House Education and Labor 324
    'Single Payer' System........................ 326
  House Ways and Means 329
    Bill Highlights.............................. 332
  House Energy and Commerce 335
  Senate Labor and Human Resources 336
  Senate Finance 338
    Dole Plan Highlights 340
  Other Committees.............................. 343
    Clinton, Committee Bills Compared............. 346
Leadership Phase 348
  Gephardt Bill Highlights........................ 349
  Mitchell Bill Highlights 351
  Clinton, Leadership Bills Compared................. 352
  Compromise Bill Highlights 354

Abortion
Abortion Clinic Access............................ 355
  Other Abortion Legislation 356
Other Health Legislation
Dietary Supplements 357
Minority Health Programs 358
Aid for Disabled 359
Tobacco Industry Controversy 359
Veterinary Drug Use.............................. 360
Other Health-Related Legislation 361
Welfare
Welfare Reform................................... 364
Social Security Independence....................... 366
Domestic Worker Tax............................. 368
Head Start Reauthorization........................ 369
  Provisions..................................... 371
Child Nutrition................................... 373
Child Support Enforcement........................ 375
Food Stamps 376
Holocaust Victims' Benefits....................... 377
Indian Independence 377
Other Indian Legislation.......................... 378

Chapter 8 — Education/Labor/Housing/Veterans

Education

Elementary and Secondary Education Act............. 383
  Provisions..................................... 392
Goals 2000: Educate America Act................... 397
  Provisions..................................... 398
'School to Work' Program......................... 400
Other Education-Related Legislation 401
Labor
Striker Replacement Bill 402
OSHA Overhaul.................................. 403
Underfunded Pensions............................ 403
Other Pension-Related Legislation 404
Retraining Initiative............................... 405
Other Labor-Related Legislation 406

Housing
Housing Reauthorization 408
  Narrow Housing Bill 410
HUD Property Disposal 411
Homeless Assistance 411
Flood Insurance Program 411
Veterans
Persian Gulf Syndrome 412
  Provisions..................................... 413
Women Veterans/Medical Construction 414
VHA Exemptions................................. 416
Other Veterans Legislation 416

Chapter 9 — Defense

Defense Legislation
Defense Authorization 421
   Provisions.. 428
B-2 Bomber Production........................ 432
C-17 Cargo Plane Construction 433
Women in the Military 435
Base Closings 435

Chemical Weapons Treaty............................ 437
Arms Cuts 438
Nominations, Promotions
Perry Confirmation 438
Halperin Withdrawal 439
Military Promotions.................................... 439

Chapter 10 — Foreign Policy

Foreign Policy
Changing World Order........................... 445
War in Bosnia 446
Haiti Occupation 449
Foreign Aid Reform 452
State Department Authorization............. 454
Intelligence
Intelligence Authorization..................... 458
   NRO Undercover Office Complex.................. 461

Ames Spy Case.. 463
   Ames Interview Excerpts 464
Bilateral, Other Issues
Russian Aid 466
Vietnam Trade Embargo Ends 467
Iran-Contra Probe Concluded....................... 468
Other Foreign Policy Legislation 469
Foreign Policy Appointments 471

Chapter 11 — Appropriations

Fiscal 1995 Appropriations
Appropriations Overview 475
   Mileposts 476
Agriculture 477
   Chart... 478
   The Fight Over Food Stamps 480
Commerce, Justice, State..................... 483
   Chart... 484
Defense.. 488
   Chart... 489
   Provisions.. 495
District of Columbia 498
   Chart... 499
   Fiscal 1996 D.C. Authorization 500
Energy and Water................................ 502
Foreign Operations.............................. 505
   Chart... 506
Interior 513
   Chart... 514
   The Art Debate 516

Grazing Fees 518
Labor, HHS, Education 519
   Chart.. 520
Legislative Branch..................................... 524
   Chart.. 525
Military Construction 527
   Chart.. 528
Transportation.. 530
   Chart.. 531
Treasury, Postal Service 536
   Chart.. 537
VA, HUD, Independent Agencies 541
   Chart.. 542
   Revamped Space Station 545
Supplemental Appropriations
Emergency Supplemental 548
   Chart.. 549
   Provisions.. 551
Spring Supplemental 557

Chapter 12 — Political Report

Election 1994
Election Overview 561
   Midterm Ballot-Box Revolutions.................. 562
   Election Highlights................................ 563
   Republican Surge 564
Senate Races..................................... 565
   Senate Membership — 104th Congress............ 567
   Newcomers List................................... 568
House Races....................................... 570
   House Membership — 104th Congress 572

Defeated Incumbents 574
Governors' Races 578
   Governors List....................................... 581
Changing South... 582
Ballot Initiatives....................................... 583
1994 Election Results.................................. 584
Other
Redistricting... 591
House Special Elections............................... 592

Appendixes

Glossary 1-A

Congress and Its Members

The Legislative Process in Brief........................ 3-B
List of Members — 103rd Congress, 2nd Session 6-B
Senators' Committee Assignments 8-B
Representatives' Committee Assignments 10-B
Pronunciation Guide.................................. 15-B
Capitol Hill Map 16-B

Vote Studies

Presidential Support.................................. 3-C
   Leading Scorers 5-C
Party Unity.. 6-C
   Leading Scorers 8-C
Conservative Coalition 9-C
   Leading Scorers 10-C
Voting Participation 11-C
Key Votes... 13-C
   House 13-C
   Senate.. 21-C
Background Material
  Presidential Support
    Definitions and Data........................... 29-C
    List of Votes.................................. 30-C
    Individual Members' Scores 32-C
  Party Unity
    Definitions and Data........................... 35-C
    List of Votes.................................. 36-C
    Individual Members' Scores 37-C
  Conservative Coalition
    Definitions and Data........................... 40-C
    List of Votes.................................. 41-C
    Individual Members' Scores 42-C
  Voting Participation
    Individual Members' Scores 45-C
  Key Votes
    Individual House Members' Scores 48-C
    Individual Senators' Scores..................... 54-C

Text

State of the Union Address 3-D
   Republican Response................................ 8-D
Packwood Diaries Court Decision 10-D
Delegate Voting Court Decision....................... 11-D
Lifting of Vietnam Embargo 12-D
Rostenkowski Repayment 13-D
Mitchell Supreme Court Withdrawal 14-D
Nixon Funeral 16-D
Breyer Hearings 17-D
Clinton on Crime Bill 26-D
Haiti Invasion Plan 27-D
Haiti Agreement 29-D
Clinton's Election Response 33-D
Gingrich's Election Response 35-D
Dole's Election Response 38-D
GOP 'Contract With America' 39-D
Dole, White House on GATT 53-D
Gingrich Acceptance Speech 57-D
Presidential Agenda................................. 60-D
   Republican Response............................. 61-D

Public Laws 1-E

Roll Call Votes

House 2-H
Senate 2-S

Indexes

Bill Number Index.................................... 3-I
Roll-Call Votes Index 4-I
General Index 11-I

## Chapter 1

INSIDE CONGRESS

The Year in Review

103rd Congress: An Overview 3

   2nd Session at a Glance 5

   Public Laws 6

   Leadership — 103rd Congress 7

   Filibusters 9

   What Passed, What Didn't 10

   Membership Changes 12

Preparing for the Next Congress

Organizing the 104th Congress 14

   Leadership — 104th Congress 15

   House Republican Leadership Races 16

   House Democratic Leadership Races 17

Republicans Lay Out New Rules 18

   Restructuring House Committees 19

   Rules Changes 20

GOP's 'Contract With America' 22

Legislation, Regulation

Congressional Reform 27

Workplace Compliance 28

Clinton Legislative Strategy 29

Campaign Finance Overhaul 32

FEC Spending Regulations 35

Lobbying Disclosure 36

   Gift Rules 41

Ethics

Rostenkowski Indictment 43

Packwood Investigation 49

Other Ethics Cases 50

Gingrich Investigation 54

Departures

Democratic Departures 55

O'Neill Death 59

Nixon Death 60

Other

Delegate Voting 61

Nation of Islam Condemnation 62

Congressional Pay Freeze 63

CONGRESSIONAL OVERVIEW

Democratic Stronghold Ends Along With 103rd Congress

*Most of Clinton's major initiatives die on the vine
as Republicans erect roadblocks in House, Senate*

Nineteen ninety-four brought an end not only to the 103rd Congress but also to 40 years of Democratic control of the House.

A year that began with President Clinton and his party's congressional leaders vowing to transform the health care system and fulfill voters' faith in Democratic control of government ended with their legislative agenda in tatters and their electoral supporters in full retreat.

The voters retaliated Nov. 8, giving control of both chambers to the Republicans for the first time since 1955. The elections swept out the House Speaker, Thomas S. Foley, D-Wash., along with legislative powerhouses such as House Ways and Means Committee Chairman Dan Rostenkowski, D-Ill., while no Republican incumbent was defeated in the House or Senate.

The centerpiece of a year of legislative setbacks and political fiascoes was the failure of Clinton's top priority, his health care initiative. Clinton and his supporters had trumpeted the proposal, unveiled in 1993, as the test of his effectiveness in Congress, yet it never got so far as a vote in either chamber. Its travails sucked the wind out of Clinton's standing and elbowed out other legislative initiatives, including welfare reform.

Congress' image suffered with the May 31 indictment of Rostenkowski, one of its most powerful members, on charges of embezzlement, fraud and coverup. At year's end, five members stood under criminal indictment, the most since the 1980 Abscam scandal snared seven members. And a two-year effort to overhaul Congress' own procedures ran aground, thwarted by lack of interest from leaders, skepticism from Republicans and behind-the-scenes opposition from senior members. *(Ethics, p. 50; congressional reform, p. 27)*

The Congress ended Dec. 1, after a three-day lame-duck session during which it handed Clinton a belated bipartisan victory, approving a bill to implement a new global trade accord under the General Agreement on Tariffs and Trade (GATT). The functional and inglorious end, however, had come Oct. 8 when Democrats, having seen their legislative program blocked at every turn by a Republican Party confident of its election prospects, gave up and sent members home for a month of campaigning.

In the preceding weeks, numerous measures, some of which began the year with broad bipartisan support, fell victim to partisan disagreement or other problems and had to be abandoned. Among them were bills dealing with health care, campaign finance, lobbying disclosure, telecommunications and toxic waste cleanup. Many smashed into procedural roadblocks erected by Republicans who grew bold in proclaiming the virtues of gridlock.

"There's no making it smell like a rose. It is a disastrous ending to the Congress. And it makes even more likely the electoral earthquake that many of us sense is occurring this year," said Thomas E. Mann, director of governmental studies at the Brookings Institution.

Wrap-up assessments for the two-year Congress from the principals fell into familiar patterns. Clinton, in an Oct. 7 news conference, saw progress while acknowledging that much of his agenda had been ignored.

"Congress has done well on the economy, on crime, on tax fairness, on education and training, on trade, on loans for the middle class, on family leave, on reinventing government," he said. "Congress has not done well on political reform, on environmental legislation, on health care and on an unprecedented record of using the filibuster and other delaying tactics to try to keep anything from being done."

Senate Majority Leader George J. Mitchell, D-Maine, whose retirement was clouded by the failure of the health care initiative he had pushed, was direct in blaming Republicans for base political motives in opposing legislation. "They are engaged in a cynical effort to discredit the Congress, and then [they] travel around the country and persuade people that Congress won't work and they should be put in charge," he said.

Senate Minority Leader Bob Dole, R-Kan., responded: "We don't make any apologies for trying to protect the American taxpayers from bad legislation."

House Republicans spent the fall not only blocking Democratic initiatives but also thinking about what they would do if they were put in charge. On Sept. 27, more than 300 GOP incumbents and challengers gathered on the Capitol steps to unveil their "Contract With America." Part campaign tool, part ideological manifesto, the 10-point plan outlined

bills the GOP promised to tackle in the first 100 days if it won the 40 seats needed to gain control of the House. The brain-child of House Minority Whip Newt Gingrich, R-Ga., it not only served as a way to nationalize the House elections, it also became the marching orders for the House in the 104th Congress when Gingrich became Speaker on Jan. 4, 1995. *(Contract, p. 22)*

The 103rd Congress was the last hurrah for many law-makers who had dominated the Capitol for years. In addition to Foley, Rostenkowski and Mitchell, departing members included:

● Robert H. Michel, R-Ill., House Republican leader since 1981, who retired having set a record for serving 38 years without ever being in the majority.

● Jamie L. Whitten, D-Miss., who retired having served a record 53 years in the House. Whitten had lost his Appropriations Committee chairmanship in the previous Congress due to illness.

● House Judiciary Committee Chairman Jack Brooks, D-Texas, second in seniority to Whitten, who was defeated.

● House Education and Labor Committee Chairman William D. Ford, D-Mich., who retired.

● Senate Banking Committee Chairman Donald W. Riegle Jr., D-Mich., who retired.

● Senate Budget Committee Chairman Jim Sasser, D-Tenn., who was defeated. Sasser had been running to replace Mitchell as Democratic leader. *(Departures, p. 55)*

Political Scientists' Views

The headlines greeting the pre-election departure of Congress were extraordinarily harsh. "Dysfunctional Congress Collapses," read the Oct. 7 Baltimore Sun. An editorial in The Washington Post the same day was headlined: "Perhaps the Worst Congress."

But political scientists were, by and large, more generous in their assessments.

"My initial reaction is that they did quite a lot," said Nelson W. Polsby of the University of California at Berkeley. Jon R. Bond, a professor at Texas A&M University, called it "an extraordinarily productive Congress doing things that the public wanted done — but not getting credit for it." Norman J. Ornstein, resident scholar at the American Enterprise Institute, said the Congress was "surprisingly productive — and remarkably contentious."

Not every scholar, of course, was impressed. Paul C. Light, a professor at the University of Minnesota, called it "a grand disappointment. . . . It's been a mean Congress, saying a lot of things that muddied public understanding." And Ronald M. Peters, director of the Carl Albert Center for Congressional Research and Studies at the University of Oklahoma, said the Congress gave "sort of a middling performance."

One less impressionistic assessment came from David R. Mayhew, a professor of government at Yale University, whose 1991 book, "Divided We Govern," included a widely quoted method for weighing the legislative achievements of postwar Congresses.

Mayhew's initial reading of the 103rd Congress: "Relatively productive. . . . It's good, it's respectable."

Mayhew's method relied on a close reading of year-end wrap-up articles in major newspapers, buttressed by assessments by scholars in different fields. On average, he found, each postwar Congress has produced about 12 measures that qualified as "important enactments."

Based on his reading of journalists' articles in November 1993, he made a preliminary determination that six, perhaps

seven, laws from the first session of the 103rd Congress would qualify. The North American Free Trade Agreement (NAFTA) and Clinton's deficit-reducing reconciliation bill were judged "historically important." Other important laws included family and medical leave, the "motor voter" plan for voter registration, the inauguration of the National Service corps, the Brady handgun-control bill, and possibly the Hatch Act revisions.

For the second session, Mayhew said he was looking at the crime bill, an interstate branch banking bill and GATT, plus perhaps the Goals 2000 bill that set education standards.

"I think with five years' perspective, we'll say this is an average first Congress for a president," he said. "On balance, they usually do more."

In comparing the 103rd with the initial Congresses of prior administrations, Mayhew said: "It's like Truman's first Congress, or Carter's first, maybe a little bigger than Kennedy's first. Once you step back and look, you wonder whether it adds up to more than Bush's first Congress — which had the Clean Air Act, immigration, the budget deal, the Americans With Disabilities Act. . . . I don't think it's in a class with Ronald Reagan's first Congress."

Other scholars argued that the bills that did not make it to enactment were also worth considering — either as opportunities lost or as progress toward solving a problem.

"If we're going to judge a Congress in terms of what it did, you often have to look at what groundwork was laid, what basic decisions were agreed to in preparation for passage next year," said Ornstein. "The telecommunications bill died an ignominious death. But if you leave it at that, you miss something. That bill established a basic approach of deregulation, developed a remarkably broad bipartisan coalition."

Some political scientists also warned that an exclusive focus on specific legislation could yield a shallow portrait. "If one were to simply score Congress on what it gets done, this one may not look too bad," said Peters. "But if you look at it against expectations and opportunities, it doesn't look too good. And a third way [to judge it] is in terms of public mood. There you have to say it hasn't done too well."

Democratic Priorities Founder

Democrats had entered the second session with high hopes for their party. Laws enacted on budget, trade and social policy during the first session set up brave talk about remaking the health care system, welfare, political campaigns, telecommunications policy, mining law and more. Helping their prospects were signs of a rebounding economy and rising approval ratings for Clinton; he went over 60 percent in a January NBC/Wall Street Journal poll.

In his State of the Union speech, Clinton tried to capitalize on these expectations. Proclaiming that the first session "broke gridlock" as the result of "the most successful teamwork between a president and a Congress in 30 years," he called on Congress to tackle three priorities: health care, welfare and crime. *(Text, p. 3-D)*

None turned into a triumph for Clinton or for the Democratic leadership. Congress took no action on welfare, which was eclipsed by the massive effort to overhaul health care. The crime bill was enacted, but in a spirit of rancor that bloodied Clinton and ended any lingering hope of passing a health care bill in 1994.

Democrats' Declining Fortunes

For months, Democratic leaders had pointed toward the summer as the time when the heavy lifting on health care

would be done on the House and Senate floors. But no committee had produced a bill that could command the necessary votes. One major panel, the House Energy and Commerce Committee, gave up trying entirely despite months of work by Chairman John D. Dingell, D-Mich., and Health Subcommittee Chairman Henry A. Waxman, D-Calif.

After weeks of delays, congressional leaders went to the White House on July 21 to tell Clinton formally that his plan was in trouble and that he would have to make major concessions just to find a bill that could make it to the floor. Clinton gave the go-ahead to slow down the pace of key provisions and to look for common ground, but the necessary breakthroughs could not be found. The two majority leaders, Mitchell in the Senate and Missouri Democrat Richard A. Gephardt in the House, unveiled their own bills, watered-down versions of the Clinton plan, but they inspired little enthusiasm.

Senate floor debate on the health care bill began Aug. 9, but the only votes came on perfunctory amendments. On Aug. 11, front-page attention was jerked elsewhere as a mammoth anti-crime bill, supported by Clinton and the Democratic leadership, was blocked in the House by an odd alliance of conservative pro-gun rights Democrats, anti-death penalty liberals and Republicans of every stripe.

The stunning setback on the crime bill prompted some House Democrats to voice the previously unthinkable: They could end up looking so bad by November that they would lose control of the House for the first time in 40 years. "It was said in there — we won't be the majority if we don't deliver," said Philip R. Sharp, D-Ind., after emerging Aug. 12 from a glum Democratic Caucus meeting.

The White House, sensing danger, on Aug. 9 all but deposed the chairman of the Democratic National Committee, David Wilhelm, and put former California Rep. Tony Coehlo in charge of limiting the Democrats' losses in November.

Other issues on Clinton's legislative agenda also faced difficulties in August. House and Senate negotiators failed to reach a final agreement on a lobbying disclosure and gift ban bill, which leaders had hoped to at least unveil if not clear before the recess. And while the House Ways and Means Committee finished work on a GATT bill Aug. 17, they left some of the toughest issues unresolved. The same committee on Aug. 19 approved its portion of a bill to overhaul the superfund hazardous waste cleanup law, but it, too, faced difficulties.

Meanwhile, on the health care front, the hoped-for coup de grace to gridlock — a complete overhaul of the nation's health care system — seemed on the verge of becoming victim to a coup d'etat. Conservative Democrats were conspiring with moderate Republicans to defeat the House leadership's health care bill, and the leaders backed away from their plan to pass a bill by Aug. 19, indefinitely postponing even bringing the matter to the floor.

The stated reason was the need to wait for cost estimates of each bill. But as Rostenkowski, a legendary nose-counter, said, "It's whispered by the lower echelons of the leadership that we don't have the votes, and we don't know what we can put together to get the 218 votes."

The usually sacrosanct August recess, important to congressional families and crucial to campaigns, was originally scheduled to start Aug. 13, but members were told they could not leave until decisions were made on how to proceed with health care. Some members complained that the leadership kept delaying delivery of the final version of the health care bill. "They're saying what Casey Stengel said when he came out of the dugout: 'Does anybody here know how to play this

2nd Session at a Glance

President Clinton became the first president since 1853 to not veto a single bill during an entire Congress. The last president to do so was Millard Fillmore, the nation's 13th president, in the 32nd Congress (1851-53). President Jimmy Carter did not veto a bill in 1979, but on Jan. 2, 1980, he vetoed a bill that had been cleared in 1979.

During the second session of the 103rd Congress, there were 3,103 bills and resolutions introduced, compared with 6,721 in 1993 and 4,258 in 1992. A total of 465 bills cleared by the 103rd Congress became public laws (210 in the first session). Clinton signed all but two of them; President George Bush signed the first two before leaving office on Jan. 20, 1993. *(Public laws, p. 6)*

After a brief lame-duck session to consider the General Agreement on Tariffs and Trade (GATT), the second session of the 103rd Congress officially ended at 9:14 p.m. on Dec. 1 when the Senate adjourned sine die. The House had adjourned sine die at 9:10 p.m. on Nov. 29. Before the election, the House adjourned at 12:05 a.m. on Oct. 8 and the Senate at 5:11 p.m. the same day.

Convened on Jan. 25, 1994, the second session of the 103rd Congress lasted 311 days — 14 days shorter than the 325 days of the first session, but 30 days longer than the 281 days of the second session of the 102nd Congress.

The Senate was in session for 138 days and the House for 123 in 1994, compared with 153 and 142 days, respectively, for the first session of the 103rd. During the second session of the 102nd Congress, the Senate met for 129 days (the fewest since 1956) and the House for 126 days (the fewest since 1984).

During 1994, the House took 507 roll call votes and quorum calls, 108 fewer than in the previous year. The Senate took 329 roll call votes, 66 fewer than in 1993. *

Recorded Votes

Year	House	Senate	Total
1994	507	329	836
1993	615	395	1,010
1992	488	270	758
1991	444	280	724
1990	536	326	862
1989	379	312	691
1988	465	379	844
1987	511	420	931
1986	488	359	847
1985	482	381	863
1984	463	292	755
1983	533	381	914
1982	488	469	957
1981	371	497	868
1980	681	546	1,227
1979	758	509	1,267
1978	942	520	1,462

* Figures are for roll call votes and quorum calls in each chamber. In previous years (through 1987), tabulations in the House were for roll call votes only, and, in the Senate, en bloc treaty votes were counted just once.

game?' " said Rep. Pat Williams, D-Mont.

House leaders soon decided to delay action on health care until September.

While the Senate waited for the House to revive the crime bill, it continued debating a health care bill drafted by Mitchell, but the measure clearly lacked the votes to pass. Members began examining a proposed compromise from a bipartisan group of moderates, whose stripped-down bill fell far short of Clinton's original demand for universal coverage.

A long, hard week of negotiations that included two all-night sessions produced a new compromise agreement on the crime bill in the early hours of Aug. 21, and the House held a rare Sunday session to act on it. In the House, 188 Democrats and 46 Republicans voted for the crime bill, sending it to the Senate, where Republicans made a last-ditch effort to kill it on grounds of pork barrel spending and restrictions on guns.

The Senate cleared the crime bill Aug. 25, but it did so in an atmosphere of partisan bickering that helped sound the death knell for the health care bill.

Many Republicans insisted that they had been fighting a great ideological battle over which party was tougher on crime, but some conceded that partisan politics was also a motivator. "We see that clearly the president effectively is diminished in the eyes of the American people. That gives us an advantage in the upcoming election," Sen. John McCain, R-Ariz., said in an interview. "The Democrats in 1992 basically blocked the entire Bush agenda. We are doing no less in my view."

Finally, on Aug. 25, Congress began its long-delayed summer recess.

A day later, on Aug. 26, Mitchell scrapped his own health care plan, conceding that comprehensive action would not come in 1994. He continued intensive talks with a bipartisan group of moderates led by Sens. John H. Chafee, R-R.I., and John B. Breaux, D-La., but their search for an "incremental" plan proceeded only in fits and starts. A month later came Mitchell's public acknowledgment that the whole effort was officially dead.

The Final Weeks

By Sept. 30, Mitchell was forced to announce that the Senate would return after the elections for a lame duck session — not because of GOP obstructionism, but because one of his Democratic chairmen, Ernest F. Hollings of South Carolina, refused to allow a vote on GATT. An ardent foe of GATT, the Commerce, Science and Transportation Committee chairman announced Sept. 28 that he would exercise his right under the rules that governed congressional consideration of trade agreements to hold the bill in his committee for 45 legislative days.

After several days of public posturing and private negotiations, the two sides agreed that the Senate would return to take up GATT on Nov. 30, in the first lame-duck session in a dozen years. That meant Clinton and fellow Democrats were robbed of the chance for a much-needed legislative victory

Public Laws

A total of 255 bills cleared Congress in 1994 and became public laws. Following is a list of the number of public laws enacted since 1972:

Year	Public Laws
1994	255
1993	210
1992	347
1991	243
1990	410
1989	240
1988	471
1987	242
1986	424
1985	240
1984	408
1983	215
1982	328
1981	145
1980	426
1979	187
1978	410
1977	223
1976	383
1975	205
1974	402
1973	247
1972	383

before the Nov. 8 elections.

Upon hearing of the Senate delay, House Democrats told their leaders in a caucus that they would rather postpone the politically sensitive vote until after the elections, too.

In what became an increasingly common scene in the final weeks, Democratic lawmakers paraded before the television cameras announcing the demise of everything from new campaign finance regulations to the rewrite of a 122-year-old mining law. As the clock ticked on, efforts to revise low-income housing programs, revamp the superfund hazardous waste cleanup law and reorganize Congress all lay moribund. Clinton even had trouble winning approval of his nominations: Sen. Jesse Helms, R-N.C., stalled the appointment of Robert Pastor as ambassador to Panama.

In the final week of Congress, Democrats pinned their hopes for institutional redemption and political survival on a pair of bills that would make their lives tougher: stricter lobbying rules and a bill to apply important labor laws to Congress. Most agreed that if they could pass these measures, they would have some evidence that they had heard the voters' 1992 clarion call for reform.

But Democrats could not get past roadblocks set up by Senate Republicans. In two separate votes, the Senate failed to cut off a GOP-led filibuster against the conference report on the lobbying disclosure bill. The effort to subject Congress to the same labor laws that applied to private sector companies was blocked by a single senator.

Veteran Democrats complained that GOP leaders had taken partisanship to a new low. "In the 210 years in the history of the United States Senate, never — until last week — has there been a series of filibusters on taking a bill to conference," said Mitchell, speaking of a successful Republican maneuver to kill a campaign finance bill. "This has been total obstructionism." *(Filibusters, p. 9)*

Republicans exulted in their newfound ability to stymie the Democratic majorities in both chambers. Senate Minority Leader Dole summed up the Republican attitude before the Senate voted to kill the lobbying disclosure bill: "We ought to forget about this bill. We ought to forget about this Congress as quickly as we can and go home. The American people don't want any more laws."

House Republicans found ways to mimic their Senate colleagues, even though they did not have the power to filibuster legislation. On Oct. 4, they tied the House in knots, demanding votes on every conceivable procedural question throughout daylong consideration of a bill to protect California desert lands. Democrats worked hard to pass the measure in part to boost the fortunes of Sen. Dianne Feinstein, D-Calif., who was in a close re-election campaign and had been a prime sponsor of the measure. Taking up the GOP cause in the Senate, Malcolm Wallop, R-Wyo., brought the chamber to a halt Oct. 7 with a procedural ploy that forced the line-by-line reading of the desert bill.

The House finally adjourned at 12:05 a.m. on Oct. 8, having

salvaged only a quarter-loaf by changing its rules to apply labor laws to its own members — but leaving House employees without access to federal courts, a key element of the effort to end Congress' exemption from the laws. The Senate left at 5:11 p.m. on Oct. 8, after finally overcoming the GOP filibuster against the California desert bill.

Gingrich's High Profile

Looming over the final days of the regular session was Newt Gingrich. The Republican whip was clearly the dominant figure in the turbulent final days, presaging his ascension to the Speakership for the next Congress.

Gingrich was able to exercise a striking degree of control over the legislative agenda of a body dominated by the opposite party. Fans said he almost single-handedly forced Democratic leaders to abandon their rush to pass the bill implementing GATT, warning that unresolved GOP concerns could sink it. They gave him credit for mounting a whirlwind campaign of outside pressure that wounded the lobbying disclosure bill enough to allow Senate colleagues to kill it. And they hailed him as an engineer of the August floor blockade of the crime bill.

"What Newt has done is to bolster the confidence of the minority," said Sherwood Boehlert, R-N.Y., one of the moderates who helped elect Gingrich as whip over a more moderate GOP rival, Edward R. Madigan, R-Ill., in 1989 in hopes that Gingrich would do exactly this sort of thing. Gingrich's tactics forced "a harsh realization on the part of the majority that they're no longer contending with a weak and ineffectual minority," Boehlert said.

Brookings Institution visiting scholar Charles O. Jones said Gingrich capitalized on Democratic blunders, Clinton's declining support and broad resentment of the Democrats' iron-fisted control of House procedures to rally enough votes to back down Democratic leaders on key issues. John J. Pitney Jr., associate professor of government at Claremont McKenna College in California, said, "I think he has one thing working in his advantage that no Republican leader in 40 years has really had, and that's the prospect that he could become Speaker," said Pitney.

But some House Democrats rejected the notion that Gingrich had anything approaching control of the chamber in its final days. "That's stupid," said Barney Frank, D-Mass. "He had an impact only when he had significant Democratic defections," as on the crime bill and GATT.

Gingrich may have come close to appearing a little too ready to take over from Minority Leader Michel for some. Early in the session's final week, Gingrich suddenly seemed to switch from GATT vote counter to party policy-maker when he told Democratic leaders to postpone the vote. Gingrich had not cleared the change with his leader. "I was caught unaware, I must say," Michel said.

Brief Lame-Duck Session

The lame-duck session to consider GATT was one of the briefest on record. It went entirely according to script.

The House convened Nov. 29 to debate the GATT bill and vote on it, leaving at 9:10 p.m. the same day. In the emotional high point of the day, Speaker Foley, who had been defeated at the polls, let retiring Republican leader Michel wield the Speaker's gavel (which he used to ram through a resolution honoring Foley).

The Senate spent two days on GATT, clearing the bill easily and adjourning at 9:15 p.m. on Dec. 1 to bring the curtain down on the Congress.

103rd Congress Leadership

Senate

President Pro Tempore — Robert C. Byrd, D-W.Va.
Majority Leader — George J. Mitchell, D-Maine
Majority Whip — Wendell H. Ford, D-Ky.
Secretary of the Democratic Conference — David Pryor, D-Ark.

Minority Leader — Bob Dole, R-Kan.
Assistant Minority Leader — Alan K. Simpson, R-Wyo.
Chairman of the Republican Conference — Thad Cochran, R-Miss.
Secretary of the Republican Conference — Trent Lott, R-Miss.

House

Speaker — Thomas S. Foley, D-Wash.
Majority Leader — Richard A. Gephardt, D-Mo.
Majority Whip — David E. Bonior, D-Mich.
Chairman of the Democratic Caucus — Steny H. Hoyer, D-Md.

Minority Leader — Robert H. Michel, R-Ill.
Minority Whip — Newt Gingrich, R-Ga.
Chairman of the Republican Conference — Dick Armey, R-Texas
Chairman of the Republican Policy Committee — Henry J. Hyde, R-Ill.

Although some members and aides scrambled to find ways to resuscitate other legislation in the lame-duck session, no other significant legislative business was transacted.

Leadership Changes

Congressional teamwork took a severe blow early in the year when Mitchell stunned his colleagues March 4 by announcing that he would not run for re-election in November. The news robbed Clinton of his biggest asset in the Senate and set off a wide-open scramble to succeed Mitchell, the first major leadership competition among Senate Democrats since 1988. (Departures, p. 55)

Clinton's boosters put a brave face on Mitchell's action, saying it could free him from political pressures and time-consuming campaign demands. "I don't have any reason to believe it will impede the successful completion of our agenda," said one White House official. "If this means he has more time to work on our stuff, in a selfish way we benefit from it."

But others said his lame-duck status would reduce his leverage. Alan K. Simpson of Wyoming, assistant GOP leader, said Mitchell's impending departure and the power struggle to succeed him would inevitably be disruptive. "It will affect everything," Simpson said. "He was the steady, the gyroscope between the White House and the Senate."

Mitchell gave no indication of his future plans. "This is the right time for me to consider other challenges and to give someone else the chance to serve," Mitchell said in a March 4 statement on Maine television.

Barely a month later, Mitchell was considered the front-runner for a Supreme Court appointment when Harry A. Blackmun on April 6 announced he would retire. (*Breyer*, *p. 303*)

But on April 12, Mitchell again surprised his colleagues by announcing that he would not seek to replace Blackmun. Mitchell said he was afraid that being a court nominee would hurt his ability to effectively push health care and other legislation as majority leader. "I believe there exists a rare opportunity to achieve comprehensive, meaningful reform of our health care system this year," Mitchell said at a news conference. "I don't think that opportunity is going to come along again at any time in the future if we don't seize it this year."

Although he and Clinton said they did not discuss possible future vacancies, Mitchell made plain his continuing interest in serving on the court. And Clinton made it clear that he was grateful for Mitchell's continuing help in the Senate. Clinton thanked him "for his willingness to forgo a great personal opportunity, in anticipation of an enormous struggle with an uncertain result."

"It is a very major gesture on his part," said Sen. Dianne Feinstein, D-Calif. "It provides a stability to the body for the rest of the year."

Mitchell's name also was floated for the vacant job of commissioner of Major League Baseball. Mitchell confirmed that he had discussions about the job, but said, "No position has been offered to me."

The race to fill Mitchell's shoes turned, by mid-April, into a two-man contest between Tom Daschle, D-S.D., and Sasser. But Sasser's defeat in November ended that race, and on Dec. 2 Daschle won a one-vote victory over late challenger Christopher J. Dodd, D-Conn. (*104th Congress, p. 14*)

Appropriations Chairman

On the House side, a key vacancy opened when the declining health of Appropriations Committee Chairman William H. Natcher of Kentucky led to a race to succeed him.

During the weekend of Feb. 6, Natcher — who had lost weight and needed assistance getting around — checked into the hospital complaining of exhaustion. He was released and returned to work to maintain his lifetime record of never missing a vote on the floor. Less than two years before, Natcher had replaced another aging and ailing chairman, Whitten.

Almost immediately, two top committee Democrats — Neal Smith of Iowa and David R. Obey of Wisconsin — began sounding out colleagues about succeeding Natcher. The maneuvering opened a protracted power struggle within one of the House's most important committees — a battle that posed a serious challenge to the seniority system and distracted Democrats for weeks.

Smith, age 73 and a 35-year veteran of the House, was next in line to succeed Natcher and thus had the weight of the seniority system behind his candidacy. Obey, 55 and in his 12th full term, was the No. 5 Democrat on the committee. In most previous cases where the House broke with seniority, chairmen had been hobbled by infirmities.

Natcher struggled valiantly to preserve his voting record and his chairmanship, going to and from the hospital as he was able, but it became clear that he would not be able to do so on March 3, when he missed the first roll call vote of his 40-year career in the House.

Democratic leaders announced that the election of an acting chairman would, for all practical purposes, determine the succession once and for all. They ruled that if Natcher recovered, he would have to win a vote of the caucus to reclaim his position, and that no second election would be held if he died or retired. The transition plan was modeled on an arrangement made in 1991, when Parkinson's disease debilitated Natural Resources Committee Chairman Morris K. Udall of Arizona. The committee's No. 2 Democrat, George Miller of California, was given the power to run the committee and became chairman without contest after Udall resigned.

Natcher died March 29, less than a week after the Appropriations Committee chairmanship had been filled. (*Natcher, p. 58*)

Obey was elected over Smith on March 23 on a 152-106 vote of the House Democratic Caucus. Obey was the youngest person to take control of Appropriations since 1919, when a 52-year-old became chairman.

Smith's fate had been sealed March 21, when the Democratic Steering and Policy Committee nominated Obey for acting chairman. Smith lost decisively even though the 35-member leadership panel traditionally followed seniority in making its recommendations to the caucus. The vote was 18-7 when committee officials stopped counting ballots because Obey had won a majority. Despite that setback, Smith headed into the caucus claiming he had commitments from 137 members — a bare majority of Democrats.

Obey brought a feisty brand of leadership to a committee that had long prided itself on legislating with little fanfare. Of late, however, the panel had been defending against attacks from critics and writhing under fiscal constraints.

After the caucus vote, Smith attributed Obey's victory to his style, suggesting that it appealed to Democrats who had high — even unrealistic — expectations of their leaders. "There's a feeling here that we need somebody that's magic, like Sam Rayburn, to take over," Smith said. "It's not like the days of Sam Rayburn," the Texan who was Speaker a generation earlier.

But many Democrats said Obey seemed better equipped to lead the panel in an increasingly partisan House. "Democrats in the House are thinking about a very partisan, nasty Republican approach," said Frank. "David Obey's combat skills are more highly valued today than they would have been 10 years ago."

In the immediate aftermath of his election, Obey seemed to take pains to dampen expectations — or fears — of a revolution. "The committee will still operate in the tradition set by Bill Natcher," he said. Indeed, for all their many differences of style and outlook, Obey had been in sympathy with Natcher on some key premises about how appropriations bills should be written.

In particular, Obey supported Natcher's resolute opposition to earmarking — the congressional practice of requiring federal agencies to provide a specific level of funding for a favored project or program. In 1993, as chairman of the Foreign Operations Subcommittee, Obey waged a largely successful battle to keep his bill clean of earmarks.

The race caused a bitter split within the Democratic Caucus, largely along generational lines. Some younger black members — including Cynthia McKinney of Georgia and Albert R. Wynn of Maryland — backed Obey. That prompted a harshly worded memo from William L. Clay of Missouri, who hoped to chair the Education and Labor Committee, where he was second in seniority to the retiring Ford, in 1995. "The cavalier manner" in which some blacks endorsed Obey, Clay wrote in the Feb. 22 memo, "is appalling. The willy-nilly excuses offered for promising to support a candidate in violation of the rule of seniority is not in the permanent interest of black legislators or the broader black community."

The succession struggle stirred particularly bitter feelings between Obey and one of the committee's most formidable

power brokers — Defense Appropriations Subcommittee Chairman John P. Murtha of Pennsylvania, an old-school conservative Democrat who had little in common with Obey ideologically or stylistically.

Murtha had ambitions of his own to become Appropriations chairman, his friends said, but decided against a run and instead worked hard to elect Smith. When he nominated Smith to Steering and Policy, Murtha launched an unusually pointed personal attack on Obey, who as a member of the leadership panel was in the room. If this was an attempt to goad Obey into one of the eruptions for which he was renowned, it did not work; Obey remained silent. Obey later said, "I don't respond to smears."

The two adversaries declared a truce after the caucus vote and had a talk about budget matters within an hour after Obey's election.

Smith was defeated for re-election Nov. 8. Obey became the ranking Democrat on the Appropriations Committee when Democrats were relegated to the minority for the 104th Congress.

Ways and Means Chairman

The House's other most powerful chairmanship also turned over, when Sam M. Gibbons, D-Fla., assumed the gavel of the Ways and Means Committee on May 31 after Dan Rostenkowski, its chairman since 1981, was indicted on criminal charges. Gibbons became acting chairman automatically, under Democratic Caucus rules that required a chairman to step aside temporarily while under indictment. *(Rostenkowski, p. 43)*

The transfer came at a difficult time, when Ways and Means was struggling to mark up the health care bill. Its agenda also included the welfare reform effort and legislation to implement the GATT trade agreement.

The impending ascension of Gibbons, more of a survivor than a leader, had sent some Democrats scrambling for an alternative during the weeks of rumors leading up to Rostenkowski's indictment. Some members looked to Majority Leader Gephardt, a committee veteran, to step in as interim chairman. But Gephardt defused the situation by holding a news conference May 25 to declare he would not

Continued on p. 12

Democrats Decry GOP Filibusters

New pages were added to Congress' history of obstructionism as time ran short in the 1994 session. The principal venue was the Senate, where Republicans found new ways to filibuster Democrats' legislative priorities. The delays centered on procedural moves required to reach a final agreement on a bill once it had passed both chambers.

A prime target was the campaign finance bill (S 3), which was high on the agenda of President Clinton and the Democratic leaders.

Senate Republicans filibustered a usually routine motion to disagree with the House, and after the Senate voted to impose cloture Sept. 22, Republicans began an all-night talkathon to use up the full 30 hours of debate left. At 1:45 p.m. on Sept. 23, the Senate voted 93-0 to disagree with the House amendments. That merely cleared the way for the procedural move on the next two procedural motions, and another filibuster began.

The Senate historian and parliamentarian said they could find no precedent for filibusters on those procedural motions. "In the 210 years in the history of the United States Senate, never — until last week — has there been a series of filibusters on taking a bill to conference," said Majority Leader George J. Mitchell, D-Maine. "This has been total obstructionism."

Republicans replied that they were merely trying to call attention to a bill that was bad public policy. With time running out, the bill was abandoned Sept. 30 when a fifth cloture vote failed. *(Campaign finance, p. 32)*

House Republicans found ways to mimic their Senate colleagues. On Oct. 4, they tied the House in knots, demanding 12 votes on every conceivable procedural question throughout daylong consideration of a bill to protect California desert lands — a measure considered important to the re-election chances of Sen. Dianne Feinstein, D-Calif. Democrats finally strong-armed the bill through the House. *(California desert, p. 227)*

Back in the Senate, Malcolm Wallop, R-Wyo., brought the chamber to a halt Oct. 7 by requiring the line-by-line reading of the desert bill. But his colleagues were reluctant to kill the bill, and it passed Oct. 8 after cloture was invoked.

Altogether, there were 22 cloture votes in the Senate in the second session. That was up slightly from the 20 cloture votes taken in the first session, although it fell short of the record of 28 taken in 1992.

Following are the cloture votes cast, with successful motions in **bold**:

Date	Bill	Bill/Nomination Description	Vote
March 15	S 4	Competitiveness Bill	56-42
March 24	HR 3345	Federal Worker Retirement Buyout	58-41
March 24	**HR 3345**	**Federal Worker Retirement Buyout**	**63-36**
March 26	**HR 1804**	**Education Goals 2000**	**62-23**
May 24		**Derek Shearer Nomination**	**63-35**
May 24		Sam Brown Jr. Nomination	54-44
May 25		Sam Brown Jr. Nomination	56-42
June 28	S 687	Product Liability	54-44
June 29	S 687	Product Liability	57-41
July 12	S 55	Striker Replacement	53-47
July 13	S 55	Striker Replacement	53-46
Aug. 25	**HR 3355**	**Crime Bill**	**61-38**
Sept. 22	**S 3**	**Campaign Finance**	**96-2**
Sept. 23	**S 21**	**California Desert Protection**	**73-20**
Sept. 27	S 3	Campaign Finance	57-43
Sept. 30	S 3	Campaign Finance	52-46
Oct. 3		Ricki Tigert Nomination	63-32
Oct. 4		**H. Lee Sarokin Nomination**	**85-12**
Oct. 5	**HR 6**	**Elementary and Secondary Education**	**75-24**
Oct. 6	S 349	Lobbying Disclosure/Gift Ban	52-46*
Oct. 7	S 349	Lobbying Disclosure/Gift Ban	55-42*
Oct. 8	**S 21**	**California Desert Protection**	**68-23**

* Sixty votes were required to invoke cloture in most cases. These votes, because they involved changes in the Senate rules, required two-thirds of those voting (66 in the Oct. 6 vote, 65 in the Oct. 7 vote).

Assessing the 103rd Congress...

The following list, compiled by Congressional Quarterly's editors, shows major legislation that was enacted — or that died — in the 103rd Congress. The listing of legislation not enacted was relatively selective; without a relatively high cutoff point, it could have been almost infinite.

Criteria for this list included:

● *Did the legislation have the potential to make a great impact on the nation and on the lives of Americans?*

● *Would it represent a significant shift in policy?*

● *Would it change the way a significant sector of the economy operated?*

● *Did members in both chambers expend a significant amount of effort to move it through the legislative process?*

● *Was it controversial?*

● *Would the measure be worth consideration in the context of a long-term discussion of what this Congress did?*

In all cases, considerations were based on the final form of the bill or the form it was in when last acted upon, rather than on significant elements that may have been dropped along the way.

Bills are listed alphabetically and by year of action.

Legislation Enacted

1993

Aid to Russia (PL 103-87). Congress helped President Clinton meet his foreign policy priority of bolstering Russian President Boris N. Yeltsin when it voted $2.5 billion in aid to the former Soviet republics as part of the fiscal 1994 foreign operations spending bill. *(1993 Almanac, p. 509)*

Brady Bill (PL 103-159). After seven years of debate, Congress cleared legislation requiring a five-day waiting period and background check before the purchase of a handgun. *(1993 Almanac, p. 300)*

Deficit Reduction (PL 103-66). Passed by a single vote in each chamber, the 1993 budget-reconciliation bill included about $250 billion in taxes, $179 billion in entitlement and appropriations cuts and $60 billion in debt interest payments. *(1993 Almanac, p. 107)*

Earned-Income Tax Credit (PL 103-66). Congress expanded the program as part of the 1993 budget-reconciliation bill. The credit was a tax break for poor working families; those who owed no taxes received the credit as a check from the government. Clinton had sought a bigger increase. *(1993 Almanac, pp. 120, 131)*

Family and Medical Leave (PL 103-3). The law, which required employers to provide unpaid leave to workers, was one of the first enacted by the new Congress. President George Bush had vetoed it in 1990 and in 1992. *(1993 Almanac, p. 389)*

Gays in the Military (PL 103-160). Early in his administration, Clinton tried to lift the ban on gays in the military, but Congress overrode his plan and instead codi-

fied the status quo in an amendment to the fiscal 1994 defense authorization bill. *(1993 Almanac, pp. 433, 454)*

Hatch Act (PL 103-94). The bill, blocked in the past by Republican presidential vetoes, relaxed the off-duty restrictions on political activities by federal workers. *(1993 Almanac, p. 201)*

'Motor Voter' (PL 103-31). The law, which eased voter registration by linking it with the driver's license process, was blocked for five years by Republicans who said it would impose an unfair burden on states and give Democrats an advantage. *(1993 Almanac, p. 199)*

NAFTA (PL 103-182). Clinton's first big bipartisan victory came on the North American Free Trade Agreement, which lowered most trade barriers with Mexico. *(1993 Almanac, p. 171)*

National Service (PL 103-82). Though the program was much smaller than requested, Congress gave Clinton a victory when it set up a system to provide education assistance to individuals who performed community service. *(1993 Almanac, p. 400)*

Radio Spectrum Auctions (PL 103-66). The 1993 reconciliation bill called for auctioning radio spectrum licenses to businesses that sold access (such as cellular phone companies), overturning a longstanding policy of awarding licenses through lottery or merit reviews. *(1993 Almanac, p. 127)*

Student Loans (PL 103-66). Under the 1993 reconciliation bill, Congress set up a system to phase in direct federal loans to students, cutting back the banks, guarantee agencies and secondary markets that had traditionally supplied student loan funds. *(1993 Almanac, p. 410)*

Thrift Bailout (PL 103-204). Hoping to finally close out the savings and loan debacle of the 1980s, Congress provided $18.3 billion for the Resolution Trust Corporation, ending a two-year stalemate during which Congress refused to come up with more funds. *(1993 Almanac, p. 150)*

1994

Abortion Clinic Access (PL 103-259). The law made it a federal crime to use force or the threat of force to intimidate women entering abortion clinics. *(Story, p. 355)*

Bankruptcy (PL 103-394). Reacting to a big increase in filings, Congress — in the closing days of the session — cleared this bill to amend the 1978 Bankruptcy Code to streamline proceedings and establish a special commission to recommend future changes. It aimed to strike a better balance between the needs of creditors and debtors. *(Story, p. 175)*

California Desert (PL 103-433). In its last act before the Oct. 8 adjournment, the Senate cleared the most sweeping land conservation measure since 1980, a bill protecting nearly 8 million acres as wilderness and creating

...What Passed and What Didn't

three national parks. *(Story, p. 227)*

Crime Bill (PL 103-322). With crime a big public concern and a Clinton administration priority, Congress enacted a $30.2 billion measure to toughen penalties, increase prevention programs, build more prisons, hire more police officers and ban assault weapons. *(Story, p. 273)*

GATT (PL 103-465). Returning in late November for a lame-duck session, Congress cleared a bill to implement the new world trade agreement strengthening the General Agreement on Tariffs and Trade. *(Story, p. 123)*

Goals 2000 (PL 103-227). Congress embraced one of Clinton's key "human investment" initiatives in clearing a $400 million bill establishing for the first time national education standards. Other initiatives included a revision of the preschool Head Start program (PL 103-252). *(Goals 2000, p. 397; Head Start, p. 369)*

Independent Counsel (PL 103-270). Eighteen months after the 1978 independent counsel law had lapsed, Congress reauthorized the procedure in the midst of the Whitewater investigation. *(Story, p. 295)*

Intelligence Reauthorization (PL 103-359). Responding to the Aldrich H. Ames spy case, Congress put the FBI in charge of counterintelligence and approved a sweeping review that could challenge the very existence of the CIA. *(Story, p. 458)*

Interstate Banking (PL 103-328). After years of struggle, Congress made it possible for banks to set up nationwide branch networks. *(Story, p. 93)*

Procurement Reform (PL 103-355). A key part of Clinton's "reinventing government" initiative, the law aimed to streamline federal purchasing by encouraging agencies to buy more items off the shelf. Congress also cleared bills to reorganize the Agriculture Department (PL 103-354) and provide cash "buyouts" to federal workers who retired early (PL 103-394). *(Procurement, p. 144; Agriculture, p. 191; buyouts, p. 147)*

Technology Reinvestment (PL 103-337). The centerpiece of Clinton's "defense conversion" efforts, the defense authorization bill included $575 million for projects ranging from shoring up bridges to developing solar energy systems that were designed to help contractors diversify into civilian markets. *(Story, p. 421)*

Legislation Not Cleared

1993

Economic Stimulus Package (HR 1335). Handing Clinton his first major defeat, Senate Republicans killed a $16.3 billion package that contained public works projects, summer jobs, social programs for the poor and high-technology purchases for the federal government. *(1993 Almanac, p. 706)*

1994

Balanced Budget (S J Res 41, H J Res 103). Both chambers defeated a proposed constitutional amendment after highly emotional debates. Had it been ratified, the amendment would have required that by fiscal 1999 at the earliest, the federal government would have had to balance its budget annually unless three-fifths of the House and Senate voted to lift the requirement. *(Story, p. 85)*

Campaign Finance (S 3). Felled by a mainly Republican filibuster, the measure would have set up a system to set limits on congressional campaign spending. The issue was thought to be dead for years to come. *(Story, p. 32)*

Congressional Compliance (HR 4822). The House passed a measure that would have ended Congress' exemption from federal workplace laws and later wrote many of the changes into its own rules. But the Senate never acted on the measure. *(Story, p. 28)*

Congressional Reform/Reorganization (HR 3801, S Res 227, S Res 228, S 1824). Opposition by senior members killed efforts to streamline committee and legislative procedures in the Senate. A House version never made it out of committee. *(Story, p. 27)*

Health Care Reform (HR 3600, S 2351). A sweeping effort to restructure the nation's health care system, Clinton's top legislative priority, foundered. A bipartisan proposal to make incremental changes came too late to win majority support. *(Story, p. 319)*

Lobbying Disclosure/Gift Ban. (S 349). A bill to require more disclosure of lobbying efforts and to limit gifts to members was one vote shy of enactment when Republicans and conservatives blocked it, arguing that it would prevent religious groups from organizing grassroots efforts. *(Story, p. 36)*

Mining Law Overhaul (HR 322, S 775). The administration suffered a defeat when a two-year effort to impose new royalties and environmental standards on companies that extracted valuable minerals from federal lands collapsed under opposition from the mining industry. *(Story, p. 236)*

Safe Drinking Water (HR 3392, S 2019). Despite last-minute efforts, the House and Senate failed to resolve differences over a measure to create a $3.6 billion revolving loan fund to help states meet environmental standards set by the 1974 Safe Drinking Water Act. *(Story, p. 238)*

Superfund (HR 3800, S 1834). Having failed to overcome GOP opposition, the administration in early October abandoned a bill to overhaul the law that required companies to pay for cleanups of the worst hazardous waste sites. *(Story, p. 231)*

Telecommunications (S 1822, HR 3626). The legislation, which would have rewritten the Communications Act of 1934 to promote competition in the telephone and cable markets, failed in the face of opposition from the regional Bell telephone companies. *(Story, p. 203)*

Membership Changes, 103rd Congress

HOUSE

Member, District	Party	Died	Resigned	Successor	Party	Elected	Sworn In
Les Aspin, Wis. (1)	D		1/20/93	Peter W. Barca	D	5/4/93	6/8/93
Leon E. Panetta, Calif. (17)	D		1/21/93	Sam Farr	D	6/8/93	6/16/93
Mike Espy, Miss. (2)	D		1/22/93	Bennie Thompson	D	4/13/93	4/20/93
Bill Gradison, Ohio (2)	R		1/31/93	Rob Portman	R	5/4/93	5/5/93
Paul B. Henry, Mich. (3)	R	7/31/93		Vernon J. Ehlers	R	12/7/93	1/25/94
Glenn English, Okla. (6)	D		1/7/94	Frank D. Lucas	R	5/10/94	5/17/94
William H. Natcher, Ky. (2)	D	3/29/94		Ron Lewis	R	5/24/94	5/26/94
James M. Inhofe, Okla. (1) [1]	D		11/15/94	Steve Largent	R	11/8/94	11/29/94
Dean A. Gallo, N.J. (11)	R	11/6/94		Not replaced			

SENATE [2]

Member, State	Party	Resigned	Lost Election	Successor	Party	Elected	Sworn In
Lloyd Bentsen, Texas	D	1/20/93		Bob Krueger [3]	D		1/21/93
Bob Krueger, Texas	D		6/5/93	Kay Bailey Hutchison	R	6/5/93	6/14/93
David L. Boren, Okla.	D	11/15/94		James M. Inhofe	R	11/8/94	11/17/94
Harlan Mathews, Tenn. [4]	D	12/2/94		Fred Thompson	R	11/8/94	12/9/94

[1] Inhofe was elected to fill the unexpired portion of the Senate term of David L. Boren.

[2] Richard C. Shelby, Ala., switched from the Democratic Party to the Republican Party on Nov. 9, 1994.

[3] Krueger was appointed Jan. 5, 1993, to fill the seat that would be vacated when Bentsen officially assumed the position of Treasury secretary. The interim appointment was until the remainder of the term was filled in a special election. Krueger ultimately lost a June 5, 1993, runoff election to Hutchison.

[4] Harlan Mathews' term expired Dec. 2, when the Tennessee secretary of State certified the Nov. 8 election of Fred Thompson.

Continued from p. 9

do so. "I think in a way it's an insult to the chairman and the members of the committee that I or someone else from the leadership would have to go to the committee so the committee could finish its work on health care," he said.

One member who did eye a challenge to Gibbons was Robert T. Matsui, D-Calif. Although he was only eighth-ranking on the committee, some members admired his energy and organizational skills. A more senior member, Charles B. Rangel, D-Calif., backed Gibbons and the seniority system, but said he might jump into the race if Matsui did. However, neither member contested Gibbons' ascension once the indictment occurred.

Gibbons took the gavel without a long record of legislative achievements or the full confidence of committee members. Some said that while Gibbons was hard-working and fair, he could be doctrinaire, blunt and short-tempered. "There's no doubt in my 32 years and with my very direct manner, I have offended a few people," Gibbons said in an interview with the St. Petersburg (Fla.) Times.

In his many years on the Hill, Gibbons had his share of ups and downs, including unsuccessful attempts to seize power earlier in his career. He took on Majority Whip Thomas P. O'Neill Jr., D-Mass., for the job of majority leader in 1973 and earned O'Neill's permanent enmity. When the chairmanship came open at Ways and Means in 1981, it was O'Neill who urged Rostenkowski to take the job, denying it to Gibbons.

But Gibbons had worked hard in later years, particularly as Rostenkowski's legal problems mounted, to prove that he could handle the chairmanship. He said he was prepared to put aside his personal views to pass legislation, as he had done frequently as chairman of the Ways and Means Trade Subcommittee on bills that offended his free-trade principles.

Membership Changes

Several new members joined Congress in the second session, all of them Republicans.

Natcher was replaced by Ron Lewis, a Baptist minister and religious-bookstore owner who equated a vote for his opponent with a vote for Clinton and his policies. In a portent of the GOP sweep that came in the fall, he won 55 percent of the vote on May 24 to become the first Republican to represent the district since the end of the Civil War. He was sworn in May 26.

Two weeks before, on May 10, Republican Frank D. Lucas won election in Oklahoma to fill the seat of Democrat Glenn English, who resigned Jan. 7 to become head of a lobbying group. Lucas was sworn in May 17.

Rep. Dean A. Gallo, R-N.J., who was not running for re-election, died on Nov. 6 in Denville, N.J. He was 58.

Gallo, who was diagnosed with prostate cancer in 1992, was first elected to Congress in 1984 after serving eight years in the state Assembly (two as minority leader). A member of the Appropriations Committee, Gallo was the only New Jersey member to serve on one of the "money panels" (Appropriations or Ways and Means). One focus of his attention was the massive Passaic River flood control project in northern New Jersey. In the 103rd Congress, Gallo was co-chairman of the Northeast-Midwest Congressional Coalition.

Gallo was not replaced in the 103rd Congress.

A series of shifts that took place after the Nov. 8 election affected the lame-duck session.

The day after the election, Alabama Democratic Sen. Richard C. Shelby announced that he was switching to the Republican Party.

Sen. David L. Boren, D-Okla., left his seat after the election to become president of the University of Oklahoma. Boren was named to the job April 27, with the position effective after the end of the Congress. Boren resigned Nov. 15, and his successor, Oklahoma Republican Rep. James M. Inhofe, who won the November election over Democratic Rep. Dave McCurdy, was sworn in Nov. 17, in time to vote on the GATT legislation and get a leg up on seniority over other freshmen.

Inhofe's House seat was filled by Steve Largent, R-Okla., who was sworn in Nov. 29, also in time to vote in the lame-duck session.

Administrative Changes

Even before Congress convened in January, internal problems surfaced when the House's first professional administrator abruptly quit. Leonard P. Wishart III, a retired Army lieutenant general who had been hired in 1992 to reform the House's scandal-ridden patronage system, announced his resignation from the post of director of non-legislative and financial services in a Jan. 10 letter to House leaders, effective Jan. 21.

Wishart's letter left his reasons vague, although he referred to a July 27, 1993, meeting with the two parties' leaders, which came after he reportedly threatened to resign. At that time, Speaker Foley said Wishart had been reassured that he had all operating authority.

But in his letter, Wishart wrote: "I have become convinced that the situation which existed then is not likely to change. The difficulties I encountered last summer have persisted." He said the leaders had tried to create "a truly nonpartisan administrative structure. Unfortunately, I believe others have different agendas and my usefulness to you is at an end."

The position was created by the House on April 9, 1992, in the midst of controversy over overdrafts at the House bank and embezzlement at the House Post Office. *(1992 Almanac, p. 55)*

Wishart supervised a budget of more than $14 million and more than 600 employees. He had several run-ins with the House Administration Committee, headed by Charlie Rose, D-N.C. The legislation creating Wishart's job included a list of tasks that he was to be in charge of, but Rose argued that it implicitly gave his panel the power to alter the list and was not binding on the current Congress. Wishart was not allowed to assume several operations within the clerk's office, including the photography office and the telephone system, as well as the chamber's computer system, which had 254 employees.

Rose had argued that the computer system was a legislative function that needed to remain under the direct control of members. The House Administration Oversight Subcommittee split along party lines on the issue, with Republicans supporting Wishart. In a letter to Republican leaders in November 1993, lead committee Republican Bill Thomas, Calif., complained, "The transfers [to Wishart] have appeared to bog down as they have gotten closer to Chairman Rose's power base." An aide denied that Rose was trying to protect his power.

Wishart was replaced on a temporary basis by Randall Medlock, his deputy.

When Republicans won the November elections, they eliminated the post of director, creating a new office called chief administrative officer of the House, to be nominated by the Speaker and elected by the full House. The new position was placed directly under the Speaker, rather than reporting to the House Administration Committee.

Staff Cuts

The House Administration Committee angered Republicans on another front, when it moved unilaterally to meet budget-cutting goals not by eliminating staff, but by a series of changes that included "privatizing" the House's restaurants.

In the fiscal 1994 legislative branch appropriations bill (PL 103-69), Congress was ordered to reduce its staff by at least 4 percent by the end of fiscal 1995, with at least 2.5 percent coming in fiscal 1994. That meant, the House panel calculated, that 284 full-time staff positions would have to disappear in 1994. *(1993 Almanac, p. 646)*

At a March 9 committee meeting, Rose and committee member Clay cut short a discussion of options and offered a plan that they said would eliminate 319 full-time positions — 180 of them from turning the House's restaurant operations over to a private contractor. The plan also counted 86 positions eliminated from four select committees that were abolished in early 1993. The director of non-legislative and financial services was directed to cut another 53 positions from his own staff or the staffs of the clerk and the sergeant at arms offices.

Senior committee Republicans Thomas and Pat Roberts, Kan., protested that they had not been consulted. But the plan was approved on a 12-7 vote that reflected party lines. "This kind of sacrifice is sort of a gimmick," said Roberts. He said he doubted whether the plan would achieve any real savings, and he said he thought members who had voted to reduce the size of the legislative branch would be surprised to learn that they did not need to cut any staff positions.

The resolution did not need the approval of the full House.

Committee Funding

Republicans were frustrated again when they tried, as they frequently had in other years, to increase their share of funding for committee aides.

The House on March 22 adopted, 250-172, an annual committee funding resolution (H Res 369) that gave $50.1 million to 21 House committees to support investigative staff and other operations. The bill made a 2 percent reduction from the previous year by cutting the budget of every committee under the House Administration Committee's jurisdiction. The committee had adopted the resolution March 9 by a 12-7 party-line vote. *(Vote 80, p. 24-H)*

Before adopting the resolution, Democrats defeated, 172-251, a Republican motion to recommit the bill to committee in order to reduce its funding level to $47.2 million and give a third of the funds to the minority party. *(Vote 79, p. 24-H)*

Republicans said the bill used a "bogus baseline" for calculating its numbers because it counted the money saved by eliminating the four select committees and the Joint Committee on the Organization of Congress, which had occurred in 1993.

The committee funding bill provided less than half the money for committee operations. It did not reflect funds for a base staffing level of 30 employees for standing committees, and it did not provide funds for the Budget or Appropriations committees, which were funded through other accounts. *(Background, 1991 Almanac, p. 548)* ∎

Preparations Begin for 104th Congress

With a new Republican era in Congress just weeks away, triumphant Republicans and vanquished Democrats assembled their respective troops on Capitol Hill in early December to organize for the first session of the 104th Congress.

It was an exhilarating time for Republicans on both sides of the Capitol, but the real drama took place in the House, where the heir apparent as Republican leader, Newt Gingrich of Georgia, had staged a conservative revolution, gaining GOP control for the first time in 40 years. *(Elections, p. 561)*

The new House would have 86 new members, all but 13 of them Republicans. The newcomers largely shared Gingrich's anti-government fervor and had no stake in the old ways of Congress. These were not garden-variety conservatives, but men and women with a mission: They were coming to Washington as the wrecking crew for the Great Society, and they were eager to get organized for the task.

Senate Republicans, while enormously pleased, were a bit more sober about their new majority status. Many of them had been there before — Republicans controlled the chamber from 1981 through 1986 — and they knew the difficulty of building the coalitions they would need to succeed with their agenda. Even after picking up an extra seat with the party-switch by former Democrat Richard C. Shelby, R-Ala., who announced his defection Nov. 9, Senate Republicans had a relatively slim 53-47 majority that was far from filibuster-proof.

For Democrats, the task of organizing was largely one of adjusting to their stunning reversal of fortune. The trauma was much greater in the House, where politics were more partisan and where Democratic members had virtually no personal experience of serving in the minority. In the Senate, where the rules and customs required more bipartisanship and the Republicans had been in control just eight years earlier, the change was less of a shock.

Senate Republicans went into the meetings with Bob Dole, R-Kan., solidly in control, but there was a tight race for the No. 2 spot. Trent Lott of Mississippi narrowly edged out Alan K. Simpson of Wyoming for majority whip. House Republicans were eager to hand over power to Gingrich, but it took them awhile after the election to sort through the choices for the next level of the leadership. By December, however, it was clear that Dick Armey, R-Texas, who had been conference chairman in the 103rd Congress, would face no opposition to become majority leader.

House Democrats saw their leader, Speaker Thomas S. Foley, D-Wash., defeated in the November elections. Senate Democrats faced a scramble because their leader, George J. Mitchell of Maine, had retired, and one of the two candidates to succeed him, Jim Sasser of Tennessess had been defeated in November.

House Republicans

Having spent the last generation stranded in the minority, House Republicans at last were in a position to realize their dreams of making far-reaching changes in House operations when they met in Washington Dec. 5-7. In three days of party caucuses, they began the task of transforming themselves into a governing party. They also endorsed a series of sweeping institutional reforms.

Choosing the Leadership

The caucuses opened Dec. 5 with a raucous endorsement of Gingrich as the choice for Speaker and the election of Armey as the next majority leader. The GOP then used elections to settle six lower leadership races, balancing the Southern tilt at the top with geographical diversity below and including two women. In the most important of the contested positions, Tom DeLay of Texas emerged as the party's whip, its No. 3 position.

Cheers of "Newt! Newt! Newt!" greeted Gingrich, who accepted news of the nomination from a trio of members picked to highlight the diversity of the party: Henry Bonilla of Texas, one of three Hispanic Republicans; Nancy L. Johnson, Conn., a moderate; and Brian P. Bilbray, Calif., a freshman.

In an emotional speech that combined the fervor of a political rally with the dryness of a history lecture, Gingrich compared the challenges faced by the House Republicans with President Franklin D. Roosevelt's quest for a New Deal after the Depression. Gingrich conceded that the first GOP majority in the House in 40 years was doing the best it could to adjust to the responsibility of being in control. "Let's not kid each other. We're drowning," Gingrich said. "We're doing everything we can to keep us moving in the right direction." *(Text, p. 57-D)*

In rounding out the leadership slate, Republicans chose a team that reflected their emergence as a national party and the activist conservative style established by Gingrich and Armey.

DeLay won the most heated contest, a three-way race for whip, with surprising ease. He amassed 119 votes on the first secret ballot by aggressively courting incumbents and incoming freshmen. His collegial demeanor appealed to members who were aware that their party occasionally would need Democratic votes to pass legislation. "My part [of the leadership] is to organize coalitions, put things together, count those votes and listen to the members to make sure that the strategy is right," DeLay said.

An able fundraiser, DeLay campaigned throughout the country for Republican candidates and tapped a deep network of political and business contacts to reach members. The field work and connections paid off, especially among the freshman members.

DeLay immediately tapped Dennis Hastert of Illinois, his campaign manager, to be the chief deputy whip. He vowed that the rest of the whip's team would cover the rest of the country.

Robert S. Walker of Pennsylvania, who had Gingrich's vote but not an official endorsement, came in second with 80 votes, and Bill McCollum of Florida finished third with 28.

John A. Boehner, Ohio, defeated Duncan Hunter, Calif., for the post of conference chairman in what was seen as a victory for the party's newer members. Although Hunter was a year younger than Boehner, he came to Congress in 1981. Boehner arrived 10 years later, establishing himself as a critic of congressional pay raises and a leader of the junior Republicans who forced Democrats to disclose the names of members who bounced checks in the House bank.

C. Christopher Cox, Calif., was elected Policy Committee chairman. The only lawyer in the House leadership, Cox defeated Jim Kolbe of Arizona, who entered the race late. Cox, first elected in 1988, also was a member of the conference's newer wing. Although he was considered less combative than his colleagues, Cox said he endorsed the confrontational style espoused by Gingrich. "I hope, frankly, that our leadership is bold and that we resist timidity at every opportunity," Cox said.

In an uncontested race, the conference re-elected Bill Paxon, N.Y., as chairman of the National Republican Congressional Committee.

Perhaps the biggest surprise during the GOP's organizational meetings was the election of two women, Susan Molinari of New York and Barbara F. Vucanovich of Nevada, to leadership posts. It was the first time that two women from the same party had been in the leadership together.

Molinari, the only one of the elected leaders who was considered a moderate, beat Cliff Stearns, Fla., for the post of Republican Conference vice chair, despite attempts by groups opposing abortion to defeat her. The National Right to Life Committee sent a letter Dec. 1 to all Republicans outlining what it called Molinari's "activism" on the issue. Molinari vowed not to use her position to advocate abortion rights.

Vucanovich was the surprise winner for conference secretary over Tim Hutchinson, Ark., who was elected in November to his second term. Vucanovich, first elected in 1982, had been concerned that the trend toward newer members would work against her. And she fought what she considered the media's insistence that only one woman would win a GOP leadership race. "People in our conference do realize we need balance in the leadership," Vucanovich said.

Organizing Committees

On Dec. 7, the Republican Conference overwhelmingly ratified a slate of new committee chairmen proposed by Gingrich, with no one offering a challenge. Two days later the Republican Steering Committee (formerly the Committee on Committees) filled most of the committee vacancies, in some cases adding more GOP members than originally planned in order to accommodate Democratic requests that they be given more slots. Freshmen got an unusual share of plum assignments. Seven of the 11 vacancies on Appropriations, three of 10 open seats on Ways and Means, and nine of 10 Commerce positions went to first-term representatives. Many of the coveted spots went to freshmen who had ousted Democratic incumbents and were expected to face tough races in two years.

Under a term-limit proposal that Republicans vowed to put in place at the start of the new Congress, the new chairmen would be able to hold their posts for no more than six years. At the same time, the committee chairs' power got a small boost when the GOP agreed to do away with subcommittee staffs and give the chairman, not the subcommittee chairmen, the power to hire all majority staff members. Chairmen also got the right to name subcommittee chairmen, who were to be limited to three terms.

Gingrich passed over the senior Republicans on three crucial committees — Appropriations, Commerce (formerly Energy and Commerce) and Judiciary — to anoint more vigorous and assertive conservatives as chairman. Not since the days of dictatorial "Uncle Joe" Cannon at the turn of the century had the House allowed a Speaker to dictate the choice of committee chairmanships in the way that Gingrich did.

Perhaps the most telling choice Gingrich made was that of Robert L. Livingston, La., as chairman of the Appropriations Committee. The panel's ranking Republican, Joseph M. McDade, Pa., was under federal indictment on corruption charges and was ordered to step aside until the case against him was resolved. Gingrich passed over three other Republicans with more seniority than Livingston: John T. Myers, Ind.; C. W. Bill Young, Fla.; and Ralph Regula, Ohio. Myers irked Republicans in 1993 when he actively lobbied against the conservative Penny-Kasich proposal to cut government spending. *(1993 Almanac, p. 144)*

A big loser in the Gingrich selections was Carlos J. Moorhead of California, who was passed over for chairman at both Commerce and Judiciary. Gingrich tapped the more aggressive Thomas J. Bliley Jr. of Virginia for Commerce

104th Congress Leadership

Senate

President Pro Tempore — Strom Thurmond, S.C.
Majority Leader — Bob Dole, Kan.
Majority Whip — Trent Lott, Miss.
Chairman of the Republican Conference — Thad Cochran, Miss.
Secretary of the Republican Conference — Connie Mack, Fla.

Minority Leader — Tom Daschle, S.C.
Minority Whip — Wendell H. Ford, Ky.
Secretary of the Democratic Conference — Barbara A. Mikulski, Md.

House

Speaker of the House— Newt Gingrich, Ga.
Majority Leader — Dick Armey, Texas
Majority Whip — Tom DeLay, Texas
Chairman of the Republican Conference — John A. Boehner, Ohio
Chairman of the Republican Policy Committee — Christopher Cox, Calif.

Minority Leader — Richard A. Gephardt, Mo.
Minority Whip — David E. Bonior, Mich.
Chairman of the Democratic Caucus — Vic Fazio, Calif.

and the widely respected Henry J. Hyde of Illinois for Judiciary.

But Gingrich also blessed the elevation of two moderates, Benjamin A. Gilman, N.Y., to chair Foreign Affairs, and Bill Goodling, Pa., to chair Economic and Educational Opportunities (formerly Education and Labor), signaling that lethargy was a bigger liability than what passed for liberalism in the GOP.

In further proof of his flexibility, Gingrich named Gerald B. H. Solomon, N.Y., to chair the Rules Committee. Although Solomon was in line for the position, the choice surprised many who thought Gingrich would seek revenge against Solomon, who in 1993 had mounted a short-lived challenge to Gingrich for the top GOP leadership position upon the retirement of Minority Leader Robert H. Michel, R-Ill.

House Democrats

Still reeling from the Election Day loss of more than 50 Democratic-held seats, including Foley's, House Democrats gathered Nov. 30 and elected veteran leaders with a liberal record: Richard A. Gephardt of Missouri as minority leader, David E. Bonior of Michigan as whip, Vic Fazio of California as caucus chairman and Barbara B. Kennelly of Connecticut as vice chairman.

The resounding rejection of Southern conservatives Charlie Rose of North Carolina for minority leader and Charles W. Stenholm of Texas for whip raised concerns that unhappy conservative Democrats might bolt and join the Republican ranks. "If we're rejected at every turn, that makes it difficult to survive as a Democrat in the South," said Nathan Deal of Georgia. But no House members switched in 1994.

Leadership Contests

The 53-year-old Gephardt, who had served as majority leader since 1989, moved quickly after the Nov. 8 elections to solidify his support. Although Gephardt spent the night before the caucus election in Bethesda Naval Hospital stricken with gallstones, he returned to the Capitol the next day for an hourlong speech and questions from members. He then underwent surgery Dec. 1 to have his gallbladder removed. His hospital stay combined with the Republican organizational meetings set for Dec. 5-7 forced the Democrats to postpone the remainder of their caucus meetings until Dec. 13-14.

Rose portrayed Gephardt as too closely aligned with the White House, noting that his former staffers had become part of the White House inner circle. The House Administration Committee chairman argued that Gephardt was part of the leadership that led Democrats to election defeats.

But Gephardt got his commitments from lawmakers before Rose formally announced his candidacy, and he benefited from experienced leadership. He also stressed many of the points being voiced by disenchanted Democrats, including the call for an inclusive leadership and the promise to develop a separate agenda in the House and then work with the Senate and White House. Rose good-naturedly suggested that Gephardt had borrowed his speech. Gephardt won handily, 150-58.

With Gephardt in what seemed an unassailable position from the outset, conservative Democrats had pinned their hopes for representation in the minority leadership on Stenholm and his long-shot challenge of Bonior for Democratic whip. The contest for the No. 2 job in the Democratic leadership presented a clear choice on ideology and style.

The eight-term Stenholm was a leader of the "Boll Weevil" group of Southern Democrats who had backed former President Ronald Reagan's economic program. He favored passage of a constitutional amendment requiring a balanced budget, a leading item on the Republican agenda. Stenholm believed his party should support a number of Republican proposals and think carefully before challenging the GOP. "When we differ with Republicans, we better be on the side of the angels," he said.

Bonior, the party's majority whip in the 103rd Congress, was a nine-term pro-labor liberal Democrat who strongly supported legislation guaranteeing workers unpaid family and medical leave, opposed the use of U.S. military force in the Persian Gulf and had recently blasted a Republican questionnaire to prospective House employees as smacking of "McCarthyism." The survey questioned individuals about their religious preference, beliefs on abortion and views on various Republicans.

Bonior succeeded because the November elections had left the caucus more liberal and because he, like Gephardt, promised to include all. He also had moved quickly after the elections to round up his support. He prevailed 145-60.

The widely held view was that if anyone in the leadership had to pay for the devastating Election Day losses, it would be the head of the Democratic Congressional Campaign Committee. But Fazio, who had held that post, triumphed for the caucus

HOUSE LEADERSHIP RACES

Outcome of Dec. 5-6 balloting for Republican leadership positions:

Position: Majority Whip.
Result: Tom DeLay 119
Robert S. Walker 80
Bill McCollum 28

Position: Republican Conference chairman.
Result: John A. Boehner 122
Duncan Hunter 102

Position: Republican Policy Committee chairman.
Result: Christopher Cox 148
Jim Kolbe 77

Position: Vice chairman of Republican Conference.
Result: Susan Molinari 124
Cliff Stearns 100

Position: Secretary of Republican Conference.
Result: Barbara F. Vucanovich . .138
Tim Hutchinson 90

chairmanship, 149-57, over Kweisi Mfume of Maryland, who was retiring as chairman of the Congressional Black Caucus.

Kennelly, a deputy majority whip, edged out Louise M. Slaughter in a close race. The Kentucky-born Slaughter, who had represented her New York state district since 1987, unified Southern lawmakers and liberals in her challenge but fell three votes short, 93-90.

Committee Assignments

House Democrats made committee assignments Dec. 13-15, falling back on the venerable rule of seniority in deciding who would be called upon to pay the price of the Democratic defeat at the polls. While the Republicans handed out plum committee assignments and even subcommittee chairmanships to their freshmen, the Democrats dropped their most junior members — many of them women, blacks and Hispanics — from the Appropriations and Ways and Means committees. Republicans had cut the Democratic slots on those three panels by 39 percent, from 70 to 43. Seniority also was the rule of the day when the Democrats chose their ranking members.

The caucus ratified ranking minority members for every committee except Select Intelligence and ethics. The picks, made by the Steering Committee, were almost a mirror image of the Democrats who chaired the panels during the 103rd Congress.

But Gephardt did throw one man overboard: Rose, who had challenged him for the leadership post, was replaced as the top Democrat on the Oversight Committee. Rose had chaired its predecessor, the House Administration Committee, since 1991. He was succeeded by Caucus Chairman Fazio, a veteran lawmaker who knew the inner workings of the House and had close ties to the leadership.

The Democrats created several new leadership positions, which gave Gephardt a chance to bring more women and minorities into the upper echelons of the caucus. Jose E. Serrano of New York, the outgoing chairman of the Hispanic Caucus, was named a vice chairman of the Steering Committee. Patricia Schroeder of Colorado and Slaughter joined the leadership advisory group. Rosa DeLauro of Connecticut became a chief deputy whip. Another whip's spot went to John Lewis of Georgia, while Mfume shifted from the Congressional Black Caucus to the Policy Committee.

Some lawmakers — including Bill Richardson of New Mexico and Cardiss Collins of Illinois on Commerce — agreed to take a leave of absence to free vacancies for other members. Bonior bowed off the Rules Committee, allowing Tony P. Hall of Ohio to stay. But no one was willing to forgo a spot on Appropriations or Ways and Means, even temporarily. Carrie P. Meek of Florida, who lost her Appropriations seat, said she considered making a stronger case that the Democrats should protect minority members of committees but decided against the effort. "I'd rather be a team player," she said.

Senate Republicans

On the Senate side, the victorious Republicans selected their leadership for the coming year in a closed caucus Dec. 2.

Dole was unopposed as the new majority leader, a job that he had held in 1985-86.

But in filling the No. 2 GOP leadership post, Republicans rejected business as usual. Lott won the job of majority whip, edging out Simpson by just one vote. Simpson had held the No. 2 job for a decade. The 27-26 vote was a milestone for the strongly partisan conservative wing of the party, and the narrowness of the vote was emblematic of the divide between moderate Republicans and the GOP right.

The close vote notwithstanding, the message to Dole and the rest of the leadership was the desire for a bolder style in pushing the party's agenda. To some, it also indicated a swing to the ideological right in the Senate, similar to the forces that were shaping the House under Gingrich.

It also was a potential migraine for Dole, who did not have the kind of close relationship with Lott that he shared with Simpson. Dole, with his eye on the White House in 1996, faced the prospect of having to leave the Senate in Lott's care while he campaigned for president. Lott had made no secret of his desire for the majority leader's job, and he was an ally of Sen. Phil Gramm of Texas, who was aggressively seeking the GOP presidential nomination.

In the House, where Lott served from 1973 to 1989, his personal conservatism was tempered by his track record as a loyalist to the party leader. He worked closely with the Republican mainstream when he was House whip under Minority Leader Robert H. Michel of Illinois. Lott was often torn between Michel, who worked closely with Democrats to pass legislation, and a group of rebel conservatives led by Gingrich, with whom Lott had more in common philosophically.

After Lott's selection, he and Simpson emerged from a Senate conference room with their arms linked and took pains to appear united, though the race was acidic for a leadership contest. Simpson said of Lott, "He's going to be a wonderful, vigorous link to the very vigorous House." Lott called Simpson a "class guy."

Mindful of pervasive angst about the Dole-Lott combination, Lott praised Dole, who had publicly supported Simpson in the race. "There won't be a separate agenda," Lott said. "I'm going to ride shotgun for the leader." Nevertheless, Lott's election was expected to push Dole further to the right to reflect the caucus. "The Republican center of gravity has shifted right," said Burdett Loomis, a political scientist at the University of Kansas.

The race between Lott and Simpson, the only leadership contest on the Republican side in the Senate, had taken shape in mid-November after the GOP electoral sweep. The election results convinced Lott and others that conservative senators would be receptive to a change in leadership reflecting the voters' show of confidence in the conservative agenda.

Simpson was unhappy that Lott, who had promised not to challenge him, got into the race after all. Simpson began the race with a significant number of commitments, but Lott was able to draw heavily on contacts made in his days in the House. He won support from at least half the 18 senators who served with him in the lower chamber. In the meantime,

HOUSE LEADERSHIP RACES

Outcome of Nov. 30 voting for **Democratic** *leadership positions:*

Position: Minority leader.

Result: Richard A. Gephardt .150
Charlie Rose 58

Position: Minority whip.

Result: David E. Bonior 145
Charles W. Stenholm . .60

Position: Chairman of Democratic Caucus.

Result: Vic Fazio 149
Kweisi Mfume 57

Position: Vice chairman of Democratic Caucus.

Result: Barbara B. Kennelly . .93
Louise M. Slaughter . .90

Gramm worked the 11 freshman senators on Lott's behalf.

Some moderates considered Lott's entry into the race an unwelcome and premature infusion of presidential politics into Senate business. Said Nancy Landon Kassebaum, R-Kan., who voted for Simpson: "At this juncture, the '96 race was not something anyone wanted to get caught up in here." Lott's jump from secretary of the Republican Conference to the No. 2 leadership job also bumped him ahead of others in line, including fellow Mississippian Thad Cochran, who was conference chairman, and Don Nickles of Oklahoma, who chaired the Policy Committee.

Some senators, especially those seeking to move up the ladder, were privately displeased by what they saw as Lott's show of ambition. "This is just a little bit of ego, and I don't think it's sitting well," said Dave Durenberger, R-Minn., who was retiring. "There are a number of people on the more conservative side of the caucus who consider themselves majority leader material. None of them considered doing what Trent Lott did. There are just a number of people who are unhappy with one guy stepping out of line."

It was a shadow of the jolt that the seniority system had taken in the House when the Republican Conference on Dec. 2 chose Ted Stevens of Alaska to be chairman of the Rules Committee, bypassing John W. Warner of Virginia, who had more seniority but had not held the party leadership role on the committee, as Stevens had.

Senate Democrats

On the other side of the aisle, Senate Democrats had their own battle to succeed retiring Majority Leader George J. Mitchell of Maine as the new Democratic leader. In secret balloting Dec. 2, Tom Daschle, S.D., scored a razor-thin victory to become the next Senate minority leader.

For the other two party elected posts, the caucus re-elected Wendell H. Ford of Kentucky as whip, and Barbara A. Mikulski of Maryland ran unopposed to replace Arkansas' David Pryor as the secretary of the Democratic Conference.

More than anything else, Daschle's 24-23 victory was a tribute to his tenacity. He jumped into the race shortly after Mitchell announced his retirement March 4 and kept at it for eight months, first against Jim Sasser of Tennessee and then — after Sasser's re-election defeat Nov. 8 — against the latecomer Christopher J. Dodd, Conn.

The race proved to be a struggle right to the finish. Following the secret balloting, Pryor announced to the senators that they had deadlocked 23-23. The tie was broken when Pryor announced that the lone proxy vote — cast by Ben Nighthorse Campbell of Colorado — had gone to Daschle. (Campbell jumped to the Republican Party on March 3, 1995.)

Supporters portrayed Daschle as the perfect person to lead the party into the brave new political world created by the Republican landslide. "He presents a youthful image of change, which is something we need right now," said John Kerry of Massachusetts.

But even as Daschle was taking his victory lap, some of his colleagues were questioning whether he was tough enough to

avoid being steamrollered by the increasingly conservative Republican leadership. Part of that doubt stemmed from Daschle's light legislative résumé. Although he had served with Mitchell as co-chairman of the Democratic Policy Committee, he had never chaired a major committee or managed a bill on the floor.

With some exceptions, Daschle received his support from younger senators and those from outside the East. For the most part, Dodd won the backing of the Democratic Old Bulls, such as Appropriations Committee Chairman Robert C. Byrd of West Virginia.

In an apparent effort to dispel doubts that he would be a strong, independent leader, Daschle used his post-victory news conference to put some distance between Senate Democrats and the White House. "My first responsibility is to my caucus," he said. "I believe that it's important for us to create our own identity. . . . We will not be led by the [Clinton

administration]; we will not view ourselves as an extension of them. But I think to the degree we can, we certainly have every interest in working closely with them."

That pledge represented a marked departure from the leadership of Mitchell, who had carried the water for the Clinton administration for two years.

Daschle, who emphasized the importance of improving the party's public relations, named supporter John D. Rockefeller IV of West Virginia to serve as chairman of a new party committee on technology and communications. Daschle placed other allies in key party posts, as well: Harry Reid of Nevada to replace Daschle as co-chairman of the Democratic Policy Committee; Kerry of Massachusetts to chair a strengthened Steering Committee; and Byron L. Dorgan of North Dakota as an assistant floor leader. He reappointed John B. Breaux of Louisiana, another supporter, as chief deputy whip. ∎

Republicans Lay Out New Hill Rules

Incoming Speaker Newt Gingrich, R-Ga., began to remake the House immediately after the November elections, centralizing power in the Republican leadership and sweeping away the vestiges of 40 years of Democratic rule.

More than any other congressional leader in recent times, Gingrich took personal control. He set out to break down many of the established fiefdoms in the House, replacing them with a power structure loyal to him and dedicated to carrying out the "Contract With America," the GOP's manifesto for reforming the institution and redirecting the nation's domestic policy. He pledged that the House would vote on the 10 elements in the contract within the first 100 days of the 104th Congress.

Gingrich quickly set up a 10-member transition team, headed by Republican Jim Nussle of Iowa, to help him draw up proposals to consolidate committees, redistribute power and slash staff. As a result, in three days of party caucuses Dec. 5-7, Republicans endorsed a series of sweeping institutional reforms proposed by the leadership, along with a slate of candidates for committee chairmanships. The rules changes were to be ratified when the House convened Jan. 4. (*Rules changes, p. 20*)

Changing House Committees, Rules

House Republicans endorsed a leadership plan, unveiled Dec. 2, to reshape the committees by eliminating three panels, altering the jurisdiction of others and giving many committees new names.

The transition team had considered, and shelved, proposals for more radical restructuring as senior Republicans, who had waited professional lifetimes to run the committees, objected. Some analysts said Gingrich had lost a rare opportunity to transform Congress' political culture by going further to weaken the links between congressional committees, their constituent industries and federal agencies. Sensitive to suggestions that they backed away from more ambitious reform, Republican leaders defended their plan as more dramatic than anything the Democrats could accomplish — especially when viewed in tandem with other changes planned for committee operations.

The three committees put on the chopping block were the panels on Post Office and Civil Service, District of Columbia, and Merchant Marine and Fisheries. Their elimination promised to bring the House system more in line with the Senate, which had no Merchant Marine panel and had elimi-

nated its Post Office and D.C. committees in 1977. (*1977 Almanac, p. 781*)

Those committees were relatively painless losses for Republicans because they served constituencies, such as postal and maritime unions and the overwhelmingly Democratic city of Washington, D.C., that had few links to the GOP. Republicans found it harder to kill panels nearer and dearer to their party's heart. They quickly dropped a plan to abolish the Small Business Committee in the face of complaints from Kansas Republican Jan Meyers, who was in line to be chairman, and small-business lobbyists who had been key GOP allies in the health care debate.

The plan made relatively minor changes in other committees' jurisdictions. Some, however, cut into established power centers. The Energy and Commerce Committee was to lose some of its jurisdiction as well as the first two words of its title. The House Administration Committee was to turn into a small panel renamed the House Oversight Committee under the direct thumb of the leadership, ending its history as an independent base for chairmen to do favors for members.

A number of other committees were renamed to reflect Republican views. The Education and Labor panel got the new name of Economic and Educational Opportunities. Armed Services became National Security. Natural Resources became just Resources. (*Committees, p. 19*)

● **Chairmen's terms.** In an effort to prevent the committees from becoming separate power centers, as they had under such Democratic giants as Dan Rostenkowski, Ill., and John D. Dingell, Mich., Republicans called for six-year term limits for committee chairmen. The result was expected to be a more fluid committee system in which chairmen would come and go with far more regularity than in the past. A junior member would not have to worry about crossing a chairman who would be gone in a few years. Some analysts also saw it contributing to breaking the ties between committees and their constituencies.

● **Proxy voting.** Republicans agreed to eliminate absentee votes in committee. By gathering proxy votes, well-prepared Democratic chairmen had routinely been able to defeat GOP amendments, even when few Democrats showed up. Proxy voting was already prohibited on the Appropriations Committee and the Rules Committee.

Republicans argued that forcing members to be in the

New Names, Sizes for House Panels

House Republicans' new committee structure, announced Dec. 2, 1994, and modified in the early days of the 104th Congress:

Agriculture

| New size: | 27R | 22D |
| Old size: | 27D | 19R |

Jurisdiction: Added food inspection.

Appropriations

| New size: | 32R | 24D |
| Old size: | 37D | 23R |

Jurisdiction: No change.

Banking and Financial Services *(formerly Banking, Finance and Urban Affairs)*

| New size: | 27R | 22D | |
| Old size: | 30D | 20R | 1 Independent |

Jurisdiction: Added primary jurisdiction over Glass-Steagall Act, which governed securities activities of banks.

Budget

| New size: | 24R | 18D |
| Old size: | 26D | 17R |

Jurisdiction: No change.

Commerce *(formerly Energy and Commerce)*

| New size: | 25R | 21D |
| Old size: | 27D | 17R |

Jurisdiction: Subtracted railroads and inland waterways (to Transportation and Infrastructure); Trans-Alaska Pipeline (to Public Lands and Resources); primary jurisdiction over Glass-Steagall Act (to Banking and Financial Services); food inspection (to Agriculture); energy research and development (to Science).

Economic and Educational Opportunities *(formerly Education and Labor)*

| New size: | 24R | 19D |
| Old size: | 24D | 15R |

Jurisdiction: No change.

Government Reform and Oversight *(formerly Government Operations)*

| New size: | 27R | 22D | |
| Old size: | 25D | 16R | 1 Independent |

Jurisdiction: Added all matters formerly handled by Post Office and Civil Service and District of Columbia committees.

House Oversight *(formerly House Administration)*

| New size: | 7R | 5D |
| Old size: | 12D | 7R |

Jurisdiction: Administrative duties reduced.

International Relations *(formerly Foreign Affairs)*

| New size: | 23R | 19D |
| Old size: | 26D | 18R |

Jurisdiction: No change.

Judiciary

| New size: | 20R | 15D |
| Old size: | 21D | 14R |

Jurisdiction: No change.

National Security *(formerly Armed Services)*

| New size: | 30R | 25D |
| Old size: | 33D | 22R |

Jurisdiction: Added merchant marine (from Merchant Marine and Fisheries).

Resources *(formerly Natural Resources)*

| New size: | 25R | 20D |
| Old size: | 24D | 15R |

Jurisdiction: Added fisheries and endangered species (from Merchant Marine and Fisheries); Trans-Alaska Pipeline (from Energy and Commerce).

Rules

| New size: | 9R | 4D |
| Old size: | 9D | 4R |

Jurisdiction: No change.

Science *(formerly Science, Space and Technology)*

| New size: | 27R | 23D |
| Old size: | 33D | 22R |

Jurisdiction: Added energy research and development (from Energy and Commerce).

Select Intelligence

| New size: | 9R | 7D |
| Old size: | 12D | 7R |

Jurisdiction: No change.

Small Business

| New size: | 22R | 19D |
| Old size: | 27D | 18R |

Jurisdiction: No change.

Standards of Official Conduct

| New size: | 5R | 5D |
| Old size: | 7D | 7R |

Jurisdiction: No change.

Transportation and Infrastructure *(formerly Public Works and Transportation)*

| New size: | 33R | 28D |
| Old size: | 38D | 25R |

Jurisdiction: Added Coast Guard (from Merchant Marine and Fisheries); railroads and inland waterways (from Energy and Commerce).

Veterans' Affairs

| New size: | 18R | 15D |
| Old size: | 21D | 14R |

Jurisdiction: No change.

Ways and Means

| New size: | 21R | 15D |
| Old size: | 24D | 14R |

Jurisdiction: No change.

House Rules Changes Open the Process . . .

The following are rules changes drafted by House Republicans during their caucuses in November 1994 and adopted on the opening day of the 104th Congress.

Committees

- **Committees eliminated.** Three committees were abolished: District of Columbia, Merchant Marine and Fisheries, and Post Office and Civil Service. Several other committees were renamed.
- **Jurisdictions.** The jurisdiction of the Post Office and Civil Service Committee and the District of Columbia Committee was transferred to the Government Reform and Oversight Committee. Matters handled by the Merchant Marine and Fisheries Committee were split between three other committees.

Several issues formerly handled by the Energy and Commerce Committee were parceled out to other committees.
- **Staff cuts.** The rules cut the total number of committee staff by one-third compared to the levels in the 103rd Congress.
- **Subcommittee limits.** With three exceptions, no committee was allowed more than five subcommittees. The exceptions were Appropriations (13), Government Reform and Oversight (7) and Transportation and Infrastructure (6).
- **Subcommittee staff.** Staff hiring was to be controlled by committee chairmen. Subcommittee chairmen and ranking minority members no longer had authority to hire one staffer each.
- **Assignments.** Members could serve on no more than two standing committees and four subcommittees, except for chairmen and ranking members, who could serve ex officio on all subcommittees. Exceptions to the membership limit had to be approved by party caucuses and the House.
- **Proxy voting.** The rules prohibited the practice of allowing a chairman or other designee to cast an absent member's vote in committee. Several committees had long had such a ban.
- **Published votes.** Committees were required to publish the members voting for or against all bills and amendments.
- **Rolling quorums.** Chairmen could no longer hold open a vote in committee indefinitely, allowing members to show up at their convenience to vote.
- **Open meetings.** Committees and subcommittees were barred from closing their meetings to the public, except when an open meeting would endanger national security, compromise sensitive law enforcement information, or possibly degrade, defame or incriminate any person. Closing a meeting under those exceptions would require a majority vote of the committee. Immediate past rules allowed a committee to vote to close its meetings without specifying the circumstances.
- **Broadcast coverage.** Committees were required to allow radio and television broadcasts, as well as still photography, of all open meetings.
- **Budget estimates.** Bills that increased spending on existing programs had to contain a cost estimate that showed the existing cost of the programs. The rule formalized a practice common in most committees.
- **Multiple referrals.** The Speaker could no longer send a bill to more than one committee simultaneously for consideration. The Speaker was allowed to send a bill to a second committee after the first was finished acting, or he could refer parts of a bill to separate committees.

Term Limits

- **Speaker.** The Speaker could serve no more than four consecutive two-year terms.
- **Committee, subcommittee chairmen.** Chairmen of

room while legislation was being drafted would help accomplish their larger goals of breaking down the committee system and improving accountability in the House.
- **Administration.** Republicans eliminated the Office of the Doorkeeper, transferring its functions to the sergeant at arms.

They created a new position of chief administrative officer to run printing, facilities, financial records, procurement and general support services. Gingrich named Scot M. Faulkner, a management consultant and personnel director of Ronald Reagan's 1980 presidential campaign, to the post. The new job replaced the post of director on non-legislative and financial services, created in 1992 to restructure the House's two-century-old patronage system in the wake of scandals over the House bank and Post Office.

To oversee House operations, the Republicans upgraded the House inspector general's office from three to 11 people, with regular audit reports to be made public.
- **Staff cuts.** Republicans agreed to cut committee staff by one-third but rejected an effort by some freshmen to reduce members' personal staff from 18 to 16 slots. The cuts meant big staff losses for Democrats, but the GOP gained staff positions, compared with what it had had in the minority.
- **Supermajority for tax increases.** Republicans also endorsed a precedent-setting rule aimed at making it difficult for Congress to increases taxes. The rule required a three-fifths majority in the House for any bill containing an increase in income tax rates. The original language was broader, applying to any legislation "that increases revenues," but that wording was dropped when Republicans became concerned about unintended consequences, such as the potential effect on a capital gains tax cut, which Republicans insisted would increase revenues.
- **Franking.** Gingrich quietly urged several freshmen to try to abolish taxpayer-funded mailings during election years. Use of the frank had become a potent symbol of the power of entrenched incumbency. But the proposal by freshman-elect Jon Christensen, R-Neb., was withdrawn during the party caucuses when it became clear that some incumbents and freshmen, particularly those from the West, considered the proposal too draconian. Members already were barred from sending franked mail 60 days before an election.

Preparing for New Role

During a two-day strategy session Dec. 15-16, Republicans got a glimpse of what it would be like to run the House — presiding over its committees, setting the legislative agenda, calling the shots on the floor. To aid their efforts, they staged a dry run of opening day procedures — complete with David Dreier, R-Calif., playing the role of House Democratic leader Richard A.

. . . But Strengthen the Reins of Power

committees and subcommittees could hold their positions for no more than three consecutive terms. The limits began with the 104th Congress.

● **Budget, Intelligence committees.** Members could serve on the Budget Committee for four terms during any six Congresses. Previously, members were limited to three terms in any five Congresses. For the Select Intelligence Committee, members could serve up to four terms in any six successive Congresses. The chairman and ranking minority member could serve in one additional Congress if they began their terms in the preceding Congress. Previously, members were limited to three terms.

Floor Procedures

● **Supermajority for tax increases.** A three-fifths majority of members voting was required to pass any bill, amendment or conference report containing an increase in income tax rates.

● **Retroactive tax increases.** No retroactive tax increases that took effect prior to the date of enactment of the bill that required them were allowed.

● **Delegate voting.** Delegates from the District of Columbia, Guam, the Virgin Islands and American Samoa, and the resident commissioner of Puerto Rico, could no longer vote in or preside over the Committee of the Whole, which the House entered into when it was amending a bill on the floor. The Democrats had permitted delegates to vote under such circumstances. Delegates could continue to vote in committees.

● **Verbatim Congressional Record.** Members could no longer delete or change remarks made on the floor in the Congressional Record except for technical or grammatical corrections. Remarks inserted through unanimous consent to revise and extend a speech would appear in the record in a different typeface.

● **Roll call votes.** Automatic roll call votes were required on bills and conference reports that made appropriations and raised taxes. The annual budget resolution and its conference report would have a mandatory roll call as well.

● **Appropriations amendments.** Members were guaranteed the right to offer so-called limitation amendments, which specified that no funds be spent for a particular purpose, without having to defeat a motion to end amendments — unless the majority leader offered that motion.

● **Motions to recommit.** The minority leader or his designee was guaranteed the right to offer a so-called motion to recommit with instructions on a bill under consideration in the House. Such a motion enabled the minority to propose changes, and the vote was on sending the bill back to committee to make those revisions.

● **Commemoratives.** Commemorative legislation could not be introduced or considered.

Administration

● **Administrative offices.** The Office of the Doorkeeper was abolished, its functions transferred to the sergeant at arms. A new position of chief administrative officer (CAO) was created, replacing the director of non-legislative services. The CAO was to be nominated by the Speaker and elected by the full House.

● **House audit.** The House inspector general was instructed to complete an audit of the financial records of the House while it was under the control of the Democrats. He could contract with a private accounting firm to perform the audit, if necessary.

● **Legislative service organizations.** Funding for so-called legislative service organizations, the 28 caucuses in the House that received office space and budgets to operate in the House, was abolished.

Gephardt of Missouri. The run-through was part of an effort to make sure that Republicans' opening day message to the public — that they were changing Congress root and branch — did not get muddled.

In another sign of the changing times, GOP freshmen attended an orientation session Dec. 8-11 in Baltimore, sponsored by the Heritage Foundation and Empower America. The foundation had planned to hold the sessions in Annapolis, Md., but switched to a larger hotel in Baltimore to accommodate the large freshman class. Harvard University, which had sponsored a freshman orientation session for 22 years that was popular with Democrats, canceled its 1994 session due to lack of interest.

Senate Republicans Try To Keep Up

Moving to keep in step with their hard-charging House counterparts, Senate Republican leaders under Bob Dole of Kansas set up "working groups" to speed action on top legislative priorities. Like the House, Dole said, the Senate would remain in session through January — forgoing its tradition of adjourning until after the president's State of the Union Address in late January. Dole said the first issue before the Senate when it convened would be a bill making Congress

comply with laws it imposed on others. Similar legislation (HR 4822) had been blocked on the Senate floor by Republican objections in October. Next was to be a bill prohibiting Congress from imposing mandates on states without providing money to pay for them.

Although Senate Republicans had not campaigned on the 10-point "Contract With America," which became the road map for House Republicans' first 100 days in office, their working groups covered similar issues.

Senate Republicans also began looking at institutional reforms, though at a slower pace than the House. The Senate GOP conference Dec. 2 adopted a non-binding resolution to cut $200 million from the $2.4 billion legislative branch budget, including a 15 percent reduction in committee staff, a 25 percent cut in the General Accounting Office and the elimination of the Office of Technology Assessment.

In an effort to coordinate their agendas, incoming Senate GOP leaders and committee chairmen met with their House counterparts Dec. 2. And Dole made a rare appearance before the House Republican Conference on Dec. 7, where he underscored the importance of cooperation. But, he told reporters afterward, "I did hint in there that there might be some rare times we don't agree." ∎

GOP's 'Contract With America'

Six weeks before the Nov. 8 election, House Republican leaders took a bold gamble: Standing before TV cameras on the Capitol lawn, they unveiled a 10-point campaign manifesto, their "Contract With America," which some 350 Republican House members and candidates proceeded to sign. (*Text, p. 39-D*)

The Sept. 27 event, spearheaded by Minority Whip Newt Gingrich, R-Ga., was aimed at creating a high-profile national platform from which Republicans could attack the Democratic Congress and present their own priorities. With their election victory, the contract was transformed into the agenda for House Republicans' first 100 days in office.

The 10 draft bills that made up the contract were an ambitious attempt to restructure the role of the federal government. They embodied the GOP view that less could be more. They called for tougher law enforcement, welfare reform, a strong national defense, a rollback of government regulations and "pro-family" legislation. Drafters steered clear of controversial social issues such as abortion and some of the most complex legislative matters such as health care. Republicans promised only that the House would vote on the proposals, not that they all would pass or be enacted.

Democrats immediately attacked the contract as an exercise in election year politics that ignored the serious potential for expanding the deficit. And some aspects of

the plan lacked universal support even within the GOP. Opposition to term limits, for example, was obvious from the beginning. In the Senate, GOP leaders rejected entreaties to sign the House contract, opting instead to advertise their "Agenda for the Republican Majority" at a separate event Sept. 21.

The proposals also posed major potential budget problems. According to Gingrich and other House Republicans, the entire package — chiefly potential revenue losers such as a $500-per-child tax credit and a cut in the capital gains tax — was likely to cost up to $148 billion over five years. Under a strict reading of budget rules, not only did those cuts have to be offset — they had to be offset by tax increases or cuts in entitlement spending, such as Medicare or farm programs. Cuts in discretionary spending programs would not count. Republican leaders said they would reduce spending by $176 billion, but they did not say how.

In the preface to the contract, Republicans promised that on the first day of the 104th Congress, they would act to change internal procedures, such as reducing committee staffs and ending proxy voting, and move to end congressional exemptions from various laws.

Following is a summary of each bill and the political landscape in which it lay:

The Budget

Pass a constitutional amendment requiring the federal budget to be balanced every year beginning in 2002 or the second fiscal year after ratification, whichever was later. Enact a line-item veto giving the president authority to veto individual items in a spending bill without vetoing the entire measure.

● **Balanced-budget amendment.** Proponents had tried repeatedly to win congressional approval for a balanced-budget amendment, but they had fallen short of the two-thirds majority needed in both chambers. After winning congressional endorsement, a constitutional amendment also had to be ratified by three-fourths of the states.

The contract specified that the amendment would include a provision barring tax increases unless they were approved by three-fifths of the full membership of each chamber. The requirement for a balanced budget could be suspended by a three-fifths vote of the House and Senate, or during time of war or serious national security threat.

Of all the items included in the contract, the balanced-budget amendment was thought to present House GOP vote counters with perhaps their easiest job. In 1994, proponents had lost by only 12 votes in the House and four votes in the Senate. Confident of passage, they made the amendment the first item on their agenda. (*Balanced-budget amendment, p. 85*)

Supporters of the amendment said it was the only way to force Congress to balance the budget, something it had been unable to do under existing budget procedures. Opponents countered that it could result in a budgetary stalemate that would transfer budget decision-making from Congress to the courts and threaten entitlement programs such as Social Security and Medicare. They also warned that it would severely

limit Congress' ability to raise taxes to shrink the deficit.

Although Republicans asserted that balancing the budget would cost nothing, most budget analysts said it would require $700 billion to $800 billion in spending cuts and/or tax increases over five years. The White House denounced the GOP plan, saying it would cost $743 billion to balance the budget over five years, or $1.2 trillion over seven years.

● **Line-item veto.** The contract proposed a separate bill to give the president permanent, line-item veto authority, which could be used to strike individual spending items in appropriations bills or targeted tax breaks in tax bills. The vetoed items would be stricken automatically unless a majority of the House and Senate voted within 20 days to disapprove. If the president vetoed that disapproval, Congress would have to muster a two-thirds vote of both houses to override him.

Unlike the balanced-budget amendment, this proposal required a simple majority to pass.

Republicans in both chambers had long supported a line-item veto as a means of weeding out pork barrel projects from appropriations bills. While Clinton supported the line-item veto — a power he wielded as governor of Arkansas — the power of the purse was a zealously guarded prerogative of Congress. As a result, this element of the contract — which meant a big shift of power from the legislative to the executive branch — was viewed as highly controversial.

A Republican plan for a line item-veto had fallen only seven votes short in the House in July, when it was offered as an amendment to a so-called expedited rescissions bill (HR 4600). But in the Senate, where a filibuster against the bill was possible, supporters admitted early on that they probably would fall short of the 60 votes needed to end debate. (*Budget reform, p. 87*)

Crime

Shift federal spending for crime prevention programs to prison construction and police hiring. Make it more difficult for death row inmates to appeal their sentences. Set mandatory minimum sentences for certain crimes involving guns.

Republicans wanted to refight several key battles that they had lost during consideration of the 1994 omnibus crime bill (PL 103-222). In particular, the contract proposed to strip much of the law's spending for social programs to prevent crime; add more stringent punishments, including limits on death row appeals; and allow prosecutors to use evidence obtained in some searches conducted without warrants. *(Crime bill, p. 273)*

Democrats had used their majority status to squelch many of these proposals on party-line votes in committee and with the help of advantageous rules for floor debate.

The contract proposed to:
● Revoke about $5 billion dedicated to crime prevention spending and transfer the money to prison construction, local law enforcement and, potentially, some police-related prevention programs.
● Eliminate the existing grant programs for police hiring ($8.8 billion), drug courts ($1 billion) and crime prevention ($4 billion) and replace them with a $10 billion block grant program. These grants were intended primarily for police hiring, equipment and overtime.
● Allow local officials to use the funds allocated under the crime bill for sports leagues or other prevention activities for youths, provided that police organized or participated in the pro-

gram. The grants could not be used for drug courts. The changes would not affect authorizations for drug treatment for prisoners or for prosecuting and deterring crimes against women.
● Replace the $7.9 billion prison construction grant program with a $10.5 billion program. Requirements for states to qualify for the money would be more stringent than those in the existing law, putting more pressure on states to adopt strict "truth in sentencing" laws.

The GOP proposals were not expected to change the overall cost of the crime law, which was estimated at $30 billion over six years.
● Revive language, which had been approved as part of the Senate crime bill, setting mandatory minimum sentences for serious crimes involving a gun. The provision, which effectively would have federalized a vast number of street crimes, had strong appeal for many lawmakers who said violent crimes were not being severely punished.

But the proposal also drew strong criticism from those who said the federal government did not have the resources to prosecute such crimes and would be improperly intruding on state police authority.

Other key elements of the GOP crime proposal were mandatory restitution for crime victims and a so-called good faith exception to the exclusionary rule, which generally prohibited courtroom use of evidence obtained in illegal searches. Republicans proposed to create an exception when police obtained evidence without a warrant but were acting on an "objectively reasonable" belief that the search would not violate constitutional guarantees against unreasonable search and seizure.

Welfare

Discourage illegitimacy and teen pregnancy by prohibiting cash welfare benefits for mothers under 18 with children born out of wedlock. Cap welfare spending. Allow states to end a family's welfare benefits after two years.

The contract's welfare proposal was the last and most nettlesome plank for Republicans to agree on. The drafters eventually struck a balance between moderates who wanted to require welfare recipients to work for their benefits (HR 3500) and conservatives who focused on denying any cash benefits to young mothers (S 2134, HR 4473).

The compromise was to bar benefits under Aid to Families with Dependent Children (AFDC), the main federal-state welfare program, to children born to unwed mothers under age 18, while giving states the option to extend the prohibition to those under age 21. The GOP bill also proposed to cap the spending growth of several welfare programs, while consoli-

dating 10 nutrition programs, including food stamps, into a discretionary block grant to the states.

The proposal was more stringent and more sweeping than one President Clinton had unveiled in June. Clinton wanted to impose time limits on AFDC benefits as a way to encourage recipients to get jobs. The GOP plan, by contrast, raised a more basic question — whether to provide any welfare benefits at all to young unwed mothers. *(Welfare, p. 364)*

Under the contract, the money that otherwise would have gone to these young mothers was to go to states in block grants, to promote adoption and operate orphanages and residential group homes for unwed mothers.

States would be required to terminate AFDC payments to families who had received welfare benefits for five years, and they would have the option in some circumstances to end the benefits after two years.

Children and Families

Increase penalties for child pornography and criminal sexual conduct involving children. Grant families a $500 tax credit for caring for an elderly parent or grandparent. Grant families adopting a child a $5,000 tax credit.

Republicans proposed to use tax incentives and stiffer criminal penalties to encourage better treatment of children and the elderly while avoiding what they regarded as the

Democrats' penchant for creating new federal programs and services. The plan included federal school vouchers to give parents more choice in their children's education, stronger child support payment laws and stiffer penalties for sex crimes against minors.

The plan included a $500 tax credit to take care of an elderly parent at home and a $5,000 tax credit for adopting a child. According to GOP staff estimates, those initiatives

would cost $8 billion and $1 billion, respectively. The contract did not spell out how the costs would be offset.

The contract called for stiffer federal prison sentences for sexual offenses against children, including minors in federal custody. Under the proposal, the minimum sentences for such offenses would be increased to three years, from the existing minimum of one to three years. The minimum for child prostitution offenses would also be three years; existing law provided a maximum sentence of 10 years, but no minimum. The plan also proposed stiffer penalties for the use of a computer in the shipment of child pornography.

The measure encouraged the development of uniform national child support court orders. Supporters said this could make it easier for government agencies to track parents who moved across state lines while owing child support payments. Under existing law, enforcement of such orders often was hampered by inconsistent state laws. Non-custodial parents who received state aid would be required to participate in state job-search program if they owed child support payments.

Tax Cuts

Enact a $500 per child tax credit and a tax credit to ease the "marriage penalty." Create a new "American Dream Savings Account" IRA.

A centerpiece of the Republican contract was a set of proposed middle-class tax cuts, dubbed the American Dream Restoration Act. They were:

● An additional $500 per child tax credit to families earning up to $200,000 a year. Republican staff estimates put the cost at $107 billion in lost revenue over five years. The credit was to be nonrefundable, meaning that families too poor to owe taxes would not receive it in the form of a check, as they did with the earned-income tax credit.

● A new tax credit to ameliorate the effect of the so-called marriage penalty, which could result in married couples' paying higher income taxes than unmarried people living together. The amount of the credit was not specified, but the bill would authorize up to $2 billion worth of credits annually.

● A new type of individual retirement account — the American Dream Savings Account — to which individuals could contribute up to $2,000 annually. Republicans estimated that the change would bring in $5 billion. That was because the account would be "back-ended": Individuals would pay taxes on the amount deposited, but not on the interest when it was eventually withdrawn, if the money was used for retirement, a first home, advanced education or medical costs. And, within two years of enactment, individuals could cash out their existing IRAs and pay the tax due on them without any penalty if the money was put into the new type IRA.

The GOP proposal for tax cuts threatened to cause more competition than controversy between the parties. The ground was fertile for a tax-cut bidding war, such as the one that took place in 1981, when President Ronald Reagan's proposal to cut taxes set off exactly that kind of one-upmanship.

Unlike in 1981, however, lawmakers were constrained by budget rules that required them to offset any tax cuts by raising another tax or by a commensurate cut in entitlement programs. House Republicans were mulling over ways to loosen the rules to make it easier to pay for tax cuts with future reductions in discretionary spending. Democrats opposed any changes in the rules, and Senate Republicans, as well as many Wall Street analysts, viewed such changes warily.

National Security

Protect defense from spending cuts aimed at financing social programs. Resume efforts to build an anti-missile defense system. Restrict the United Nations' ability to command U.S. troops. Cut U.S. funding of U.N. peacekeeping missions.

● **Defense spending.** The contract called for restoring the so-called fire walls that had divided discretionary spending into three categories — defense, domestic and international programs — in fiscal 1991-93. The aim was to prevent Congress from raiding defense to pay for domestic programs.

The contract also called for the creation of a 12-member blue-ribbon commission to recommend by May 1, 1996, changes in U.S. force structure and any funding increases needed to eliminate shortfalls. In documents detailing the budgetary impact of the contract, House Republicans maintained that defense could be strengthened at "no cost."

In addition, the panel was to issue within 90 days recommendations for supplemental defense funding to restore the combat readiness of units lagging because funds were diverted late in fiscal 1994 to pay for unplanned deployments to Haiti and Rwanda.

● **Anti-missile defense.** The only program Republicans specifically singled out for greater emphasis was anti-missile defense. The contract called for the deployment of systems that could provide "highly effective" defenses of U.S. territory and of U.S. forces abroad.

● **U.N. peacekeeping.** The contract called for tough new restrictions on the president's ability to deploy U.S. troops to multinational peacekeeping operations.

It sought to cut off funds for any Pentagon units that came under the "operational control" of a foreign commander. Operational control was a military term that referred to a commander's authority to assign tasks and objectives to a unit. The proposal offered an escape hatch for the president if he could certify that putting U.S. forces under the command of a foreign officer was necessary to protect "the vital national security interests of the United States."

The idea of requiring U.S. commanders for U.S. troops, which had broad appeal in Congress, was partly a response to the 1993 peacekeeping debacle in Somalia, where 18 U.S. Army Rangers were killed in a botched raid on the headquarters of a local warlord. While the doomed U.S. forces ostensibly were carrying out a U.N. mission, however, they actually were under the Pentagon's command. The administration staunchly opposed the GOP proposal, arguing that it would infringe on the president's responsibilities as commander in chief.

The draft bill also proposed to cut the U.S. share of funding for U.N. peacekeeping to 25 percent from its existing level of 31.7 percent. Congress already had mandated that reduction, beginning in fiscal 1996, in the biennial State Department authorization bill (PL 103-236). The contract also

called for reducing the annual U.S. payment by the amount spent by the Pentagon to provide logistics and other support for U.N. operations.

The proposal also placed limits on intelligence sharing between U.S. spy agencies and the United Nations.

In addition, the bill called for several East European nations to be invited to join NATO within the following five years.

Senior Citizens

Permit senior citizens to earn more income without losing Social Security benefits. Repeal the 1993 increase in the amount of Social Security benefits subject to income tax. Grant tax incentives to encourage the purchase of long-term care insurance.

The contract contained a variety of changes in the tax code to decrease the federal tax burden on seniors. Among Republicans, the most popular was a proposal to repeal a provision of the 1993 budget-reconciliation law (PL 103-66) that required individuals with incomes of more than $34,000 and couples with incomes of more than $44,000 to pay taxes on 85 percent of their Social Security benefits. Previously, the tax was on 50 percent of benefits. The 1993 law allowed people with incomes below a threshold level to continue paying at the 50 percent rate. (*1993 Almanac, p. 107*)

Republicans also proposed to raise the Social Security earnings limit, increasing the amount that senior citizens between the ages of 65 and 69 could earn — from $11,160 to $30,000 — without losing any benefits. The American Association of Retired Persons (AARP) estimated that 10 percent of senior citizens between 65 and 69 had earnings that resulted in a drop in benefits.

The House contract also proposed that senior citizens be allowed to make tax-free withdrawals from their IRAs, 401(k) plans and pension funds to buy long-term care insurance. The AARP estimated that a relatively small number of senior citizens — mostly the more affluent — would benefit from such a change.

Other proposed tax cuts would allow life insurance policies to pay accelerated death benefits for individuals who were terminally ill or permanently confined to a nursing home and reduce the cost of long-term care insurance by making it a tax-free fringe benefit like health insurance.

The GOP staff on the House Budget Committee estimated the cost of all of the provisions to be $25.1 billion over five years: $17 billion for phasing out the 1993 Social Security tax increase, $6.8 billion for raising the earnings limits and $1.3 billion for instituting the long-term care plan.

Capital Gains, Unfunded Mandates

Reduce the capital gains tax and index it to inflation. Limit unfunded mandates on state and local governments. Require federal agencies to assess the cost of each federal regulation.

● **Capital gains tax.** Republicans proposed to allow individuals to exclude from their taxes 50 percent of their capital gains — their profits from sales of stocks, bonds, real estate, art, etc. Under existing law, the entire gain was taxed.

The effect would be to drop the maximum tax rate on capital gains from 28 percent to 19.8 percent. Capital gains generally would receive the favorable rate only if the item had been held for at least one year.

The contract also proposed that individuals be allowed to adjust their gains to account for inflation before they determined their taxes.

Another capital gains provision would allow homeowners who sold their houses at a loss to deduct up to $3,000 of that loss annually from their taxable incomes.

To enact these changes, House Republicans wanted to find an escape hatch from the 1990 budget rules that required tax cuts to be paid for by raising another tax or cutting entitlement programs. Many Republicans were on record opposing any tax increases, and many had also promised to avoid any cuts in Social Security or Medicare, the two richest entitlement programs.

One option — albeit one that drew heat from the White House — was to change the way congressional tax estimators at the Joint Committee on Taxation gauged the revenue effects of a capital gains tax cut. Under existing methods, preliminary estimates showed the GOP plan increasing revenues in the first two years after enactment, but losing $120 billion over 10 years. Republicans disagreed, claiming it would raise revenues by stimulating investors' behavior, prompting them to buy and sell more, and thereby stimulating the overall economy.

● **Unfunded mandates.** The unfunded mandates bill essentially proposed to bar Congress from imposing new requirements on state and local governments without also providing the money to pay for them.

The Congressional Budget Office (CBO) would be required to analyze any committee-approved bill that created a mandate on state or local governments of more than $50 million. The committee then would have to identify spending cuts to cover the cost of the mandate. Any mandate that was not accompanied by a CBO analysis and spending offset proposals would be subject to a point of order on the floor.

CBO also would have to analyze the economic impact of any legislation that would impose more than $200 million in unfunded mandates on the private sector.

Drafters added a new provision to bar federal agencies from enforcing mandates that were not accompanied by federal funding.

● **Regulatory relief.** The contract required the Office of Management and Budget (OMB) and CBO to issue reports projecting the cost of federal regulations on the private sector. Such regulations then would be restricted so that their cost eventually would be brought down to a level of 5 percent of the gross domestic product.

In addition, the proposal directed the House and Senate Budget committees to allocate to each congressional committee a two-year regulatory threshold. Any committee that approved legislation exceeding its regulatory allocation would face legislation barring the corresponding agency from issuing regulations.

The proposal also required federal agencies to complete a regulatory impact analysis when drafting any rule that affected more than 100 people and cost more than $1 million. The legislative language listed 23 specific criteria the agen-

cies would have to follow before implementing any new federal rules, which included explaining the "necessity" and "appropriateness" of the rule, estimating its reach and cost, stating whether and how any rule might alter legal precedent and demonstrating that the rule was cost-effective.

● **Risk assessment, property rights.** Under the contract proposal, federal agencies would be required to assess the costs and benefits of all regulations that would cost an individual $1 million or that would affect more than 100 people. Landowners who, because of federal regulations, could not use their property as they had been accustomed to were to be compensated.

Tort Reform

Allow judges to require losers in lawsuits to pay the lawyers' fees of both sides. Limit the non-economic and "punitive" damage awards in product liability and medical malpractice lawsuits. Prohibit joint liability.

The GOP tort reform proposal aimed to discourage frivolous lawsuits and limit liability for sellers and manufacturers.

● **Product liability.** The proposal called for new federal and state standards in product liability cases. The cornerstone was a proposal to limit punitive damage awards. Claimants would have to establish that the harm was the direct result of malicious conduct, and awards would be limited to three times the plaintiff's award for monetary losses. In cases involving minor injuries, awards would be capped at $250,000.

Republicans also proposed to prohibit so-called joint liability for damages such as pain and suffering. Under existing law, one co-defendant could be held liable for an entire damage award if the other co-defendants could not pay. The proposal would limit liability to the defendant's share.

Moreover, retailers would be liable only for damages caused by their own actions — not for selling a defective product. However, sellers could still be liable if the manufacturer could not be brought to court or cover damages.

● **Loser pays.** The measure aimed to discourage frivolous lawsuits by applying the "loser pays rule" in federal suits brought by residents of different states. Since most civil suits were filed in state court, the provision had limited scope. The person who lost a case would have to pay the winner's attorneys' fees. Payments, however, could not exceed the loser's attorneys' fees.

The proposal also sought to:

● Tighten the rules on "expert" testimony by making it inadmissible unless it was based on "scientifically valid" reasoning. Such experts could not accept a contingency fee or a share in monetary damage awards.

● Limit "strike" lawsuits, which were filed by class-action attorneys on behalf of shareholders whose stock purchases had failed to live up to their expectations. The language would require a court-appointed trustee in each suit to ensure that attorneys acted in the best interest of shareholders. Plaintiffs would be limited to five strike suits every three years.

Term Limits

Limit House members to six years (an alternative plan would allow 12) and limit senators to 12 years.

Republicans who signed the contract pledged only to support a floor vote on a term limits amendment, not necessarily to back the proposal itself. Those who did support term limits were split between a 12-year limit for House members and a six-year cutoff.

Moreover, Republicans were divided over whether to pursue a legislative option, which required a majority vote and a presidential signature, or a constitutional amendment, which required a two-thirds vote and ratification by the states.

Term limits movements had been flourishing in the states, 22 of which had adopted some limits on the tenure of their federal lawmakers. *(Initiatives, p. 583)*

But those restrictions were under a legal cloud, with some courts ruling that the Constitution laid out the sole requirements for congressional service. The Supreme Court on Nov. 29 heard a case involving Arkansas' congressional term limits, and it was expected to rule on the case in 1995. If the justices struck down the limits, a constitutional amendment would be needed. *(Term limits, p. 314)* ∎

Hill Reforms Stall at Session's End

Despite repeated vows by Democratic leaders to make the 103rd a "reform Congress," efforts to improve Congress' image by revamping the way it did business ran aground in the second session, the victim of partisan bickering and opposition from senior members who stood to loose power.

A House-Senate panel, the Joint Committee on the Organization of Congress, had made a series of recommendations in 1993 on how to improve the operations of Congress. The suggested changes ranged from shifting to a two-year budget cycle, to reducing the number of committee assignments and Senate filibusters, to ending congressional exemptions from various workplace laws. *(1993 Almanac, p. 21)*

While academics criticized the proposals for offering little to streamline committee jurisdictions, reduce committee assignments or smooth floor procedures, the panel's suggestions proved too controversial for members of Congress. With little public pressure in evidence, most of the proposals never made it to the floor of either chamber for a frontal test of their popularity.

The proposal that emerged as the most popular with members was one that would have made Congress subject to laws such as the Occupational Safety and Health Act and the Fair Labor Standards Act. Over the years, Congress had exempted itself because, leaders said, it would violate the Constitution's separation of powers doctrine to have executive branch agencies snooping into legislative offices.

But members grew tired of complaints that they did not have to live by the laws that governed other businesses, and support mushroomed for plans to establish a separate office to oversee Congress and its agencies. The House passed a bill Aug. 10 to do so, but the measure languished in the Senate. On Oct. 7, the House did what it could without Senate action: It passed a rules change that required the House to apply the laws to its own members. The rules change, however, did not allow aggrieved employees to go to court. *(Workplace compliance, p. 28)*

Some members said splitting off the exemptions measure deprived the larger package of its impetus, allowing more controversial in-house changes to languish and die. Several leaders of the Joint Committee tried to bring their proposals to the floor as amendments to other measures, but they were blocked with procedural tactics. Senior senators said they would fight long and hard against several of the proposals.

Senate Action

The Senate Rules Committee approved a bill and two Senate resolutions — all of them sponsored by Committee Chairman Wendell H. Ford, D-Ky. — but the old bulls who dominated the panel showed a distinct dislike for many of the changes recommended by the Joint Committee.

● **Two-year budget, congressional compliance.** On June 9, the Senate Rules Committee approved a bill (S 1824 — S Rept 103-297) to institute a two-year congressional budget cycle and to take steps toward applying health and safety laws to Congress. The vote was 12-0. But first, the committee approved, 13-3, an amendment by Appropriations Committee Chairman Robert C. Byrd, D-W.Va., removing appropriations from the two-year plan.

Byrd, a staunch guardian of Senate traditions, said budgeting already was an imprecise art, beginning more than a year in advance; a two-year spending cycle would require

many more revisions. Also, he said, agencies should have to justify their expenditures each year.

S 1824 also contained provisions to end Congress' exemption from worker protection laws. But the committee approved, 12-3, an amendment by Thad Cochran, R-Miss., requiring the General Accounting Office to study the impact of bringing Congress under such laws before any actual changes could be made.

● **Floor procedures.** On June 16, the Rules Committee approved an in-house resolution to streamline Senate floor procedures (S Res 228).

During the debate, the committee approved, 7-2, an amendment by Byrd to make it more difficult to add unrelated riders to appropriations bills. Amendments that changed legislative language rather than funding would be declared out of order. To overturn a parliamentary ruling that an amendment was not germane would require 60 votes. Under existing procedures, only a majority was needed to overturn a germaneness ruling.

Byrd complained of a "preponderance of amendments to appropriations bills." He said senators could get 60 votes to consider non-germane amendments, especially if they concerned provisions that came from the House.

S Res 228 also contained a provision to block members from filibustering motions to proceed to a bill. Supporters of the provision said the minority would retain the right to filibuster the bills when the Senate was actually considering them. Opponents countered that the ability to block floor consideration was one of the few ways the minority could influence the floor agenda.

There was no debate on this section during the markup.

At Byrd's suggestion, the committee voted 8-1 to remove a section of S Res 228 that would have charged to individual members' time limits any time spent in quorum calls once cloture had been invoked. Byrd said many quorums were called for legitimate reasons and that individual members should not have their remaining debate time shortened.

● **Committee procedures.** On June 16, the Rules Committee approved, 9-0, another resolution (S Res 227) to shave the number of seats on most standing committees. The measure also specified that senators would be barred from serving on the Finance and Appropriations committees at the same time or on the Foreign Relations and Armed Services committees concurrently. Members approved by voice vote an amendment by Daniel K. Inouye, D-Hawaii, to allow members to take seats on the Indian Affairs Committee without affecting committee assignment limitations.

Senate Floor Action

The Senate took up none of the committee-approved bills.

Anticipating that the recommendations they had developed in the Joint Committee would not make it to the Senate floor, David L. Boren, D-Okla., and Pete V. Domenici, R-N.M., attempted Sept. 29 to force the issue. They offered the full package of Joint Committee proposals to streamline committee and legislative procedures as an amendment to the fiscal 1995 District of Columbia appropriations bill (HR 4649).

But at the urging of Byrd, who opposed key sections of the package, the Senate refused to waive Senate budget rules and make the Boren-Domenici amendment in order. "How long until we act? How long?" asked Boren. The Senate rejected

his attempt on a vote of 58-41; 60 votes were needed to waive budget rules. *(Vote 313, p. 54-S; appropriations, p. 498)*

House Committee Action

The House Rules Committee began work on its version of the Joint Committee recommendations (HR 3801) on Aug. 4 and continued the session on Sept. 21. But the panel was unable to reach a final agreement on the bill, which went no further.

During the Aug. 4 markup, members considered a draft substitute by Rules Committee Chairman Joe Moakley, D-Mass., that dropped the plan for a two-year appropriations cycle. Moakley proposed to:

● Trim from five to four the number of subcommittee assignments for any House member and, more significantly, make it more difficult for members to get waivers that would allow them to join additional panels.

● Allow private citizens to be tapped for fact-finding panels in the initial stages of House ethics investigations.

● Require two-year budget resolutions and multiyear authorizations.

● Require House disclosure of legislative earmarks, site-specific funding that was directed to members' favored projects.

● Merge the Joint House-Senate committees on Printing and the Library into a single committee.

When members resumed the markup Sept. 21, they considered only one amendment before recessing. The committee approved, 7-4, an amendment by Butler Derrick, D-S.C., to delete the requirement for a two-year budget cycle. Moakley adjourned the markup because of a series of roll call votes that took members away from the session. The markup never resumed, effectively killing the overhaul for the remainder of the year. ■

Workplace Compliance Bill Blocked in Senate

Efforts to pass legislation that would have subjected Congress to the same labor laws that governed private sector companies encountered last-minute blocks in the Senate. Although the legislation died at the end of the Congress, the House voted to change its own rules to make the House subject to the compliance requirements.

House Committee Action

On July 28 and 29 respectively, two House committees — Administration and Rules — marked up a bill (HR 4822) aimed at applying 10 prominent labor laws to Congress. The Rules panel approved the measure by voice vote (H Rept 103-650, Part 1), while the Administration Committee approved the bill by a vote of 19-0 (H Rept 103-650, Part 2).

The bill proposed to bring Congress under the coverage of a host of labor and worker protection laws, and to establish a bicameral Office of Compliance to supervise the laws in Congress and in related entities such as the Library of Congress and the Government Printing Office.

During its markup, the House Administration Committee voted 11-8 to strike language in the bill that would have applied the Freedom of Information Act to Congress. The panel also approved an amendment to clarify that the institution, not individual members, would be held liable for violations of the labor laws.

As approved by the two committees, HR 4822 contained provisions to apply the following laws to Congress:

● Fair Labor Standards Act of 1938, the federal statute dealing with minimum wage and mandatory overtime for employees who worked more than 40 hours a week, amended in 1989 to extend some provisions to the House (PL 101-157).

● Americans With Disabilities Act of 1990 (PL 101-336), which prohibited workplace discrimination against disabled people.

● Civil Service Reform Act of 1978 (PL 95-454), which codified the rights of federal employees to join labor unions and bargain collectively.

● Occupational Safety and Health Act of 1970 (PL 91-596), which set safety regulations for workplaces.

● Civil Rights Act of 1964 (PL 88-352), which prohibited discrimination in employment on the basis or race, color, religion, sex or nationality.

● Age Discrimination in Employment Act of 1967 (PL 90-202), which prohibited workplace discrimination against people age 40 and older.

● Family and Medical Leave Act of 1993 (PL 103-3), which set criteria for unpaid parental and disability leave.

● Employee Polygraph Protection Act of 1988 (PL 100-347), which restricted the use of polygraph tests of employees by employers.

● Worker Adjustment and Retraining Notification Act of 1988 (PL 100-379), which required a 60-day notice of a plant shutdown or large layoffs of permanent workers.

The bill called for an Office of Compliance in the legislative branch to issue regulations and enforce the workplace laws for both chambers. The compliance office was to be overseen by a board of eight directors evenly divided between House and Senate appointees. The office would determine whether non-salaried congressional employees were eligible for overtime or should be compensated with time off for hours worked over 40 in a week.

The bill provided a four-part process for filing grievances on alleged violations of the law. The steps were counseling, mediation, formal administrative hearings and, if either an employee or a member was dissatisfied with the results, judicial review of the situation.

House Floor Action

The House took up the bill Aug. 10 and passed it overwhelmingly, 427-4. *(Vote 390, p. 116-H)*

During the debate, the House approved by voice vote an amendment by first-termer Karan English, D-Ariz., to prohibit the personal use by members or staff of frequent flier travel awards that accrued from official travel.

Members also approved, 374-57, an amendment by Leslie L. Byrne, D-Va., to require that any "standard benefits package" approved as a part of a health care bill apply to members of Congress.

In other action, the House by voice vote:

● Rejected an amendment that would have required congressional employees to complete an administrative review of complaints before filing a lawsuit in federal court.

● Approved an amendment to require the Office of Compliance to report annually on the demographics of congressional employees.

● Approved an amendment allowing former members and staff to be on the board of the compliance office, but barring former members from serving as executive director. The bill prohibited lobbyists from serving on the board.

● Rejected an amendment that would have decreased the time for congressional compliance with certain labor laws from one year to six months after enactment.

● Approved an amendment to require that meetings of the

board of the compliance office be open to the public. The bill already required decisions of the board to be made available to the public.

Senate Committee Action

On Sept. 20, the Senate Governmental Affairs Committee approved, 8-0, an amended version of the House bill (HR 4822 — S Rept 103-397). The committee approved, 8-2, an amendment by Joseph I. Lieberman, D-Conn., to allow congressional employees to take claims to a federal appeals court after a counseling process but before they had completed internal administrative processes.

Although the bill appeared to have wide, bipartisan support in the Senate, it never made it to the floor. Some senior senators voiced concerns about the court-review process, and others maintained that the bill would violate the separation of powers doctrine of the Constitution. Trent Lott, R-Miss., blocked a move to take up the bill on Oct. 6, saying he was doing so for another, unidentified member of his party.

Charles E. Grassley, R-Iowa, a strong backer of the legislation, said the last-minute objection amounted to a "shenanigan that will not be understood by the people in the mainland. . . . It's just a question of time until this becomes law. We can't continue to have two sets of laws, one for Pennsylvania Avenue and one for Main Street America."

House Rules Change

With the bill snagged in the Senate, the House on Oct. 7 voted overwhelmingly to approve a resolution (H Res 578) that amended House rules to include much of the language in the House-passed version of HR 4822. The vote was 348-3. (Vote 505, p. 150-H)

The House Rules Committee had reported the resolution to the floor earlier the same day on a party-line 6-3 vote.

"Because the Senate may not act on HR 4822 does not mean we should deprive House employees of the protections they deserve," said Rules Committee Chairman Joe Moakley, D-Mass.

The House rules change was designed to let members tell constituents they had done what they could to address a common voter complaint: that Congress imposed laws on others that it was not willing to live by. It also allowed freshmen to say they delivered on a key "reform" even though more sweeping proposals to alter Congress' operations ran aground.

The move did not entirely satisfy the bill's sponsors. In an Oct. 5 letter to Speaker Thomas S. Foley, D-Wash., Christopher Shays, R-Conn., and Dick Swett, D-N.H., referred to the resolution as a "halfway measure [that] would undermine efforts to do the job right in the 104th Congress next January."

Nonetheless, as the clock ticked down on Oct. 7, Shays argued in favor of adopting the new rule. "It's sad that we have to do it by rule," he said, but he expressed hope that the House action would shame the Senate into passing the stalled legislation.

David Dreier, R-Calif., protested that the rules charge was "designed to kill meaningful reform . . . designed to fool the American people into believing we live by the same rules as everyone else."

Using the House rules approach effectively nullified a section of HR 4822 that would have allowed any of the roughly 40,000 congressional employees to take employment grievances straight to federal court. The resolution provided only an internal administrative review and mediation process, the results of which could be appealed to the directors of a compliance board for a final decision.   ■

Clinton's Legislative Strategy Falters

On a chilly morning in early February, President Clinton invited the Democratic congressional leaders to the White House to plot strategy for passing his health care plan. Still brimming with early-session optimism, senior House members sitting around the table in the Cabinet Room reassured him that they could get the bill through their chamber. But they told him not to expect any Republican support — and not to try for any, according to aides present.

One of the senators at the meeting pointed out that the situation was different in the Senate. Daniel Patrick Moynihan, D-N.Y., reminded the group that any health care measure would need a filibuster-proof 60-vote majority to pass in the upper body. The implication, left unstated by Moynihan, was that Clinton should seek to compromise with Republicans, not freeze them out.

But Clinton and his congressional allies did not pick up on Moynihan's point. The decision to forgo a bipartisan, less confrontational approach to health care prefigured a year of legislative setbacks and political fiascoes that contributed heavily to the rout of the Democrats in the midterm elections. Indeed, many Republican challengers ousted incumbent Democrats by advertising how often the Democrat had voted for Clinton's legislative initiatives.

In the end, Congress voted for Clinton's policies 86.4 percent of the time, the same presidential success score as 1993, but saw few important bills emerge. (Vote study, p. 3-C)

Clinton was left facing the arrival of the first Republican Congress in 40 years — a predicament that was, in many ways, of his own making. The fact that the congressional elections became so powerfully nationalized focused attention on the president's governance and made his re-election chances for 1996 seem slim. (Elections, p. 561)

Looming over the legislative wreckage was the health legislation, which was officially abandoned Sept. 26 but had been strangling quite publicly at the end of a rope throughout the summer. (Health reform, p. 319)

The inglorious demise of Clinton's health care initiative had far wider effects than were immediately realized. Even before the bill died, it had crowded out other priorities, causing delays in getting legislation to Capitol Hill and consuming lawmakers' time and effort on an ultimately fruitless exercise. More damaging to the administration, Republicans emerged from the health care debate more convinced than ever that they could profit politically by obstructing Clinton's agenda.

The 103rd Congress adjourned without passing most of Clinton's second-year agenda. Even his successes, such as passage of the crime bill, frequently were overshadowed by rancorous partisanship on Capitol Hill that worsened as the year unfolded. Clinton's major victory, the implementing legislation for a new global trade accord under the General Agreement on Tariffs and Trade (GATT), was delayed until the lame-duck session — too late to help in the November elections.

"One of the fascinating things that developed was that the public came to believe that Clinton couldn't make govern-

ment work, and that feeling became a self-fulfilling prophecy as Republicans fueled it," said Thomas E. Mann, a scholar at the Brookings Institution.

Administration officials maintained that they had a modestly successful year, citing as accomplishments the crime bill, approval of the GATT bill, several education measures and a bill overhauling federal procurement practices. They blamed most of their difficulties on end-of-session Republican obstructionism. By then, said chief White House lobbyist Patrick J. Griffin, "Darkness took hold of these guys. Everything on the table became something they wanted to kill because we wanted it."

State of Union

The breakdown at the end of the 103rd Congress was all the more striking because at the end of the first session, Clinton appeared to have hit his stride. The 1993 session ended for him with a series of major victories on trade, budget policy and gun control. Early assessments of the administration's 1993 budget plan, pushed through Congress without a single Republican vote, showed the deficit dropping below $200 billion for the first time in years. Lobbying hard late in the session, Clinton had saved an almost lifeless North American Free Trade Agreement (NAFTA), employing a bipartisan majority that appeared to offer him a blueprint for future legislative triumphs. *(1993 Almanac, p. 30)*

Clinton tried to capitalize on his opportunities with a Jan. 25 State of the Union address whose tone modulated from a swaggering veto threat on health care that stirred partisan Democrats, to a discussion of family values that replayed Republican themes, to straight talk to all citizens about their role in the renewal of America.

"What is the state of our union?" Clinton asked in a speech that lasted more than an hour. "It is growing stronger, but it must be stronger still." *(Text, p. 3-D)*

Clinton's speech, both in style and substance, left many politicians and commentators reaching for comparisons to Ronald Reagan — the president whose legacy Clinton was dedicated to overturning. Resorting to gimmicks and theatrics that were unmistakably Reaganesque, Clinton brandished a pen in a "make-my-day"-style veto threat. The White House had an honored New York policeman in the audience to be singled out for praise. Clinton read a poignant letter to his wife from someone who had lost his health insurance.

"He is surpassing Ronald Reagan as the great communicator," said Rep. Henry Bonilla, freshman Republican and former television anchorman from Texas.

Even more remarkable were the Reaganesque strains in Clinton's rhetoric. House GOP Whip Newt Gingrich of Georgia said Clinton's talk about the decline of the family, the failings of the welfare system and the need to get tough on crime sounded like a speech Gingrich himself could have given.

But there was plenty to rile Republicans. Clinton began with a proud litany of the bills that Congress had enacted in 1993, noting that they were "all signed into law with no vetoes." He boasted about the economic recovery, attributing it to his economic program — although many experts said the turnaround began before Clinton took office.

Giving a new push to welfare reform, Clinton promised to submit his plan in the spring. "I know it will be difficult to tackle welfare reform in 1994 at the same time we tackle health care," Clinton said. "But let me point out, I think it is inevitable and imperative."

On health care, he squarely confronted GOP critics. Citing the millions of Americans who had no health insurance or had

lost it unexpectedly, Clinton said, "If any of you believe there's no crisis, you tell it to those people, because I can't." The partisan climax came when Clinton held up a pen and declared: "If you send me legislation that does not guarantee every American private health insurance that can never be taken away, you will force me to take this pen, veto the legislation, and we'll come right back here and start all over again."

Clinton also drew the line on defense, declaring, "We must not cut defense further." While Republicans stood and cheered, Democratic liberals sat in silence.

Responding to growing public concern about crime, Clinton gave a pitch for tough anti-crime legislation. He endorsed a Senate-passed proposal to impose mandatory life sentences on people who committed three violent crimes — a policy opposed by many Democrats, including House Speaker Thomas S. Foley of Washington.

Clinton closed the speech with an emotional acknowledgment of the limits of government action in confronting the thorny problems he had laid on Congress' doorstep. "The American people have got to want to change from within if we are to bring back work and family and community," he said, invoking concepts that Republicans frequently used to criticize Democratic policies.

GOP Response: Confrontation

Despite the overture, Senate Minority Leader Bob Dole, R-Kan., took a tough partisan line in the official Republican response to the address. *(Text, p. 8-D)*

"Far more often than not, the president and his Democrat majority have taken what we believe is the wrong fork in the road, not just on one or two matters of policy, but on their entire approach to government," Dole said.

Dole had been taking an increasingly confrontational line on health care, a shift from 1993, when a chorus of conciliation rose from GOP ranks after the president unveiled his health care plan.

Dole's comments heralded a shift in GOP tactics that lasted throughout 1994: Instead of merely voting against Clinton-backed bills, Republicans gradually grew bolder about using parliamentary maneuvers to block action entirely. Furthermore, Republicans had success at sullying the administration's message at key moments. In the most notable example, obstruction-minded Republicans and conservative Democrats held up passage of the crime bill in August, forcing the administration to trim $3 billion in spending from the bill, labeled "pork" by Republicans, in order to win House approval.

Clinton's Agenda

Clinton had helped assure a fractious legislative session with his long legislative wish list, led by health care, welfare reform and crime legislation — highly charged issues on which there was little or no agreement about solutions. He also called on Congress to enact lobbying restrictions, public financing for congressional campaigns and other measures that responded to voter outrage about the Washington political culture. Behind these, were numerous other bills, such as the rewrite of telecommunications law and several significant environmental measures.

In the end, almost none of it got done.

By virtue of the sheer volume of what Clinton had proposed, his approach to working with Congress appeared somewhat haphazard, with members having trouble knowing what his priorities were.

Even more damaging, some lawmakers said, was the

length of time it took the administration to get major bills to Capitol Hill. Delays often arose as the administration hashed out its proposals in private and left little time for Congress to debate complicated and controversial measures.

The health care bill had not surfaced until late October 1993. A bill to overhaul the superfund, the nation's troubled hazardous waste cleanup law, did not arrive until February. Welfare reform arrived in June, too late for action in a committee at the heart of the health care debate.

In a midyear course correction to try to rebuild his legislative standing, Clinton on June 27 announced that Leon E. Panetta, former chairman of the House Budget Committee, would switch from director of the Office of Management and Budget (OMB) to White House chief of staff. Panetta replaced Thomas F. McLarty III, the former head of an Arkansas energy company and a childhood friend of Clinton's, in mid-July. Panetta's OMB job was filled by his deputy, Alice M. Rivlin, former head of the Congressional Budget Office.

The change did not salvage Clinton's agenda.

"You had a situation where the administration was slow getting off the blocks. They didn't get their legislative initiatives up on the Hill. They thought they should work out everything on an interagency basis, and Congress would salute and it would sail through," said Rep. Ron Wyden, D-Ore. "You've got to get some product to the Hill earlier because if you don't, when you have the inevitable political battles, you don't have much time."

Administration officials contended that the problem was not their slowness in getting bills to Congress; it was the relative shortness of the session. Lawmakers ended the regular session Oct. 8 — one of the earliest adjournments in recent years. "It was a lot to do in a short period," said Griffin.

But one of the reasons Congress left so early was that many Democrats wanted to get home to campaign, sensing that the political tide was running against them.

Whitewater

Throughout the winter and spring, Clinton's position had been eroded by the drip of news accounts on the president and his wife's investments in the 1980s in the Whitewater Development Co. in Arkansas, which involved a tangled web of political and financial relationships. *(Whitewater, p. 108)*

With Clinton's encouragement, Attorney General Janet Reno on Jan. 20 appointed Robert B. Fiske Jr. as special counsel to investigate the president's involvement. But that did not quell GOP demands for a separate congressional investigation. In March, under intense pressure from Republicans, both chambers passed resolutions calling for hearings. After much wrangling, including a series of party-line votes in the Senate in June, Democrats succeeded in limiting the hearings to a narrow "Washington" sliver of the controversy, exploring a host of potentially improper contacts between White House staff aides and banking regulators.

The House and Senate Banking committees held two weeks of hearings in late July and early August. No evidence was produced to indicate that any Clinton administration official tried to derail a probe by banking regulators into the Madison Guaranty Savings and Loan, which was at the center of the controversy. But the hearings uncovered details of a number of improper contacts, evasive testimony before Congress by administration officials and a widespread Whitewater political damage-control effort within the White House.

The highest ranking casualty of the affair was Deputy Treasury Secretary Roger C. Altman, who had been acting head of the Resolution Trust Corporation, which conducted

the original investigation into the Whitewater-Madison link. Altman resigned Aug. 17 after it became apparent that he had lost the confidence of some key congressional Democrats.

On Aug. 5, a three-judge federal panel replaced Fiske with independent counsel Kenneth W. Starr.

Legislative Setbacks

Then came a series of major legislative setbacks. On Aug. 11, Clinton's vulnerability in Congress was writ large when, despite heavy White House pressure, 58 Democrats deserted him to help Republicans keep the crime bill off the House floor. Republicans complained that the bill was too weak and contained too much social-program spending.

Clinton went on the road, flying to Minnesota Aug. 12 to take his case to the people. Surrounded by uniformed police officers and American flags, he blamed special interests — particularly the gun lobby — for the setback on the crime bill. In the end, the bill was rescued with relatively modest changes, but at the cost of a rancorous battle in the Senate that set the tone for the remainder of the session.

The energy and time that congressional leaders had to spend rescuing the crime bill left nothing for the far messier health care fight, and by the time Congress left for its belated summer recess, there was little prospect for Clinton's health plan.

The health care debate proved Clinton's undoing in more ways than one. The strategy of depending on Democratic votes alone to pass the legislation proved to be unworkable.

Despite months of negotiations by leaders in both chambers, Democrats could not agree among themselves about the contents of a bill. Clinton had worked hard to craft hybrid legislation that would use the market to contain health care costs, but Democratic centrists saw too much government involvement and found it too complicated to explain to the public.

"The health care debate did much more damage to this president than many realize," said Will Marshall of the centrist Progressive Policy Institute, an arm of the Democratic Leadership Council. "It defined the administration in conventional liberal terms, but it also crowded out other, very important, measures that could have helped consolidate his credentials as New Democrat reformer."

The long, slow death of health care legislation not only crippled the administration, it emboldened Clinton's opponents. From the beginning, Republicans such as Sen. Phil Gramm of Texas had argued that their party would earn political points by obstructing Clinton initiatives. As other Republicans saw the public recoiling from Clinton and the Democrats' health care plan, it seemed to galvanize them in opposition.

"There was a lot of pent-up frustration and red-hot hostility," said Rep. Fred Grandy, R-Iowa. "It was as if we were spoiling for a fight for so long that we were spilling out of our party caucuses and into the streets."

As the session drew to a close with numerous major bills still awaiting action, Clinton was essentially powerless to prevent Republicans and some renegade Democrats from stopping the legislation. Major bills dealing with campaign finance, lobbying disclosure, telecommunications and toxic waste all died in the waning days. Clinton and his advisers made little public effort to save them, nothing like the public relations onslaughts that Clinton had used to save NAFTA, for example.

"Clinton's style was thwarted by having that jam up at the end. He had promoted this campaign-style of governing. . . . and that style is neutralized when the president can't take to the road because you've got too much to campaign for," said Brookings Institution visiting scholar Charles O. Jones.

Reaction to Election

After the bloodbath for Democrats in the November elections, Clinton sounded sobered by the year. In a Nov. 9 news conference, he suggested that the voters wanted a smaller, less intrusive government and less of what he characterized as political arrogance. The voters, he indicated, were saying: "We don't think government can solve all the problems. And we don't want the Democrats telling us from Washington that they know what is right about everything." *(Text, 33-D)*

Clinton conceded that the American people had formed a perception that his health care program "looked like a government program . . . injecting the government more into health care."

And the president seemed to accept a significant portion of the GOP critique of government — that it was too big and cumbersome, too meddlesome in people's lives and not particularly functional in some areas where it should be helping people. "I agree with much of what the electorate said yesterday," said the president.

But he ended the year without any public plan of action for the new era that was about to dawn with the Republican takeover in the 104th Congress. ∎

Campaign Finance Overhaul Dies

Legislation to limit spending on congressional campaigns and provide candidates with partial public funding died near the end of the 103rd Congress. It was a major defeat for President Clinton and Democratic congressional leaders, and it spelled the end of a long effort to change the system by which congressional campaigns were funded.

For more than a decade, Democrats had advocated a formula that offered public funding, coupled with spending limits, as the best way to reform the campaign finance system. But most Republicans choked on the concept, attacking it as a design to protect fundraising and the incumbency advantages that Democrats enjoyed.

The legislation (S 3) was killed Sept. 30, when Senate Democrats for the second time in a week failed to shut off a GOP-led filibuster that was blocking them from taking the Senate-passed version of the bill to a conference with the House. Speaker Thomas S. Foley, D-Wash., called it "the worst case of obstruction by filibuster by any party that I've ever seen in my 30 years in Congress."

Democrats, however, had set the stage for defeat by waiting until the eleventh hour to come up with a compromise version of a bill they had previously maintained would be a top priority in Clinton's first two years.

Indeed, the long history of the legislation was rich with evidence that many Democrats in both chambers shared GOP objections to establishing a system that would provide congressional candidates with federal subsidies. Other Democrats, particularly in the House, were deeply, if privately, opposed to an overhaul of the financing system that had protected their seats and majority status for years.

In the end, it was the inability of Democrats to iron out their internal differences that delayed the 1993-94 bill so long that it became vulnerable to procedural snags.

Some supporters of the legislation criticized Clinton, who had campaigned on the issue but brought little pressure to bear on it in 1994. "After promising to change Washington in the 1992 election, the failure of President Clinton and the 103rd Congress to clean up the system will only deepen the cynicism citizens now feel about elected officials," said Fred Wertheimer, president of Common Cause, a principal force behind the bill.

While the White House declared it would revisit the issue in the 104th Congress, many supporters said it was the end of the effort, regardless of which party controlled Congress in 1995.

Background

The death of a bill that Democrats had worked aggressively to pass in one form or another since 1987 raised fundamental questions about the future of the traditional Democratic formula for campaign finance reform. For years, Democrats had advocated partial public funding of candidates who promised to abide by spending limits — a system used by presidential primary candidates since 1976. *(1976 Almanac, p. 459)*

Legislation based on that model died of Republican filibusters (with the help of a few Democrats) in 1987 and again in 1989. In 1992, Democrats managed to clear a similar bill, but the task was made easier by the knowledge that President George Bush would not allow the measure to become law. *(1992 Almanac, p. 63)*

During his 1992 presidential campaign, Clinton harshly criticized Bush for vetoing the measure and vowed to sign a similar bill if elected. Clinton presented his own plan May 7, 1993, although he soon turned to other matters on his domestic agenda. The fact that a campaign finance bill might actually become law, however, made it much more difficult for Democrats to reconcile their differences.

The Senate passed its bill (S 3 — S Rept 103-41) June 17, 1993, on a 60-38 vote, the bare minimum needed to break a Republican-led filibuster. Passage came after three weeks of dilatory debate and two unsuccessful cloture votes.

Majority Leader George J. Mitchell, D-Maine, got the bill out of the Senate only by bargaining away almost all public funding of congressional campaigns. It was replaced by a plan to impose a steep new tax on campaigns that rejected spending limits, a tax most election lawyers said was unconstitutional. The bill also included a ban on contributions to federal campaigns by political action committees (PACs), which were strongly opposed by Senate Republicans.

The House did not tackle the issue for another five months. Democrats finally resorted to heavy leadership lobbying to produce a bill (HR 3 — H Rept 103-375, Part 1) much like the one endorsed by Clinton. The bill was approved Nov. 22 on a 255-175 vote, but a switch of just seven votes on the rule bringing the bill to the floor would have killed it. In preparation for conference, the House then passed S 3 by voice vote, substituting its own text.

The bill provided for public funding of campaigns up to one-third of the spending limit, with aggregate caps on PAC money and on contributions of more than $200.

Because of the skittishness of conservative Democrats over public funding, the House bill did not specify where the revenues to support the funding would come from. Even then, Foley personally had to work the floor a day into the 1993 Thanksgiving recess to win the votes needed to bring up the bill. *(1993 Almanac, p. 37)*

Negotiations Stall

In his Jan. 25 State of the Union address, Clinton called on lawmakers "to finish the job both houses began last year by passing tough and meaningful campaign finance reform." But he did not suggest how Democratic leaders might overcome their differences, or how they might get enough Senate Republicans on board to break a filibuster. *(Text, p. 3-D)*

In fact, the two chambers had passed radically different bills, and the need to maintain the fragile coalitions that had enabled them to pass legislation at all restricted the leaders' ability to negotiate on key provisions that were in fundamental disagreement. *(Provisions, 1993 Almanac, p. 42)*

The principal areas of disagreement were:

● **Incentives.** The House and Senate bills offered vastly different incentives to encourage candidates to comply with federal spending limits. The House approach was to provide up to one-third public funding to complying candidates. The Senate bill initially contained a 25 percent public funding incentive, but that was dropped in favor of a new 35 percent tax on all receipts of campaigns that rejected spending limits. Under the Senate bill, public funding was to be provided only after an opponent exceeded the spending limit.

● **PACs.** The Senate bill proposed to ban political action committee (PAC) contributions for all federal candidates. If that ban were found unconstitutional — something many legal scholars said was likely on grounds that it would infringe on free speech — then the maximum PAC contribution to any federal candidate in any election would drop to $1,000 from the existing limit of $5,000. Moreover, congressional candidates could raise no more than an aggregate of 20 percent of the spending limit from PACs. In addition, the Senate bill banned so-called leadership PACs, which enabled members to give substantial sums to one another.

The House bill contained no PAC ban. That meant retaining both the existing donation limit of $10,000 per election cycle and the leadership PACs.

● **Funding.** The House bill contained no funding mechanism, and it was not to become effective until one was enacted. The Senate proposed to fund the limited benefits in its bill with revenues raised by the controversial tax on noncomplying campaigns. The bill also called for a tax on lobbying expenses to fund benefits, but those revenues had been earmarked for deficit reduction in the 1993 budget-reconciliation bill (PL 103-66). *(1993 Almanac, p. 107)*

● **Constitutional issues.** It was the Senate bill, with its penalty tax and its PAC ban, that raised a constitutional controversy.

But the House bill, too, had potential problems. All spending limits were to be lifted and benefits maintained if a House candidate faced an opponent who raised or spent more than 25 percent of the spending limit; all contribution limits were to be lifted if an opponent gave more than $25,000 to his or her own campaign. Both of these thresholds were considered so low as to make it impossible for a candidate to opt out of the system, even though the Supreme Court had said the system must be voluntary.

● **'Soft money.'** Although the House bill contained a handful of exemptions not included in the Senate bill, both bills substantially restricted the use of "soft money" — funds raised outside federal guidelines to influence federal elections.

● **'Bundling.'** The Senate bill banned all "bundling" — in which a group or individual gathered checks from separate individuals and presented them together to a campaign — on the grounds that it could give undue influence to the bundler.

The House bill included an exemption to permit bundling by EMILY's List, a group that gathered checks from like-minded donors for Democratic women candidates.

● **Separate rules.** When Congress cleared the 1992 campaign finance bill, House and Senate Democrats had shunned compromise, opting instead to simply staple their two bills together. Many House Democrats were looking to the stapler again. "The solution is simple," said Sam Gejdenson, D-Conn., the House leadership's point man on the issue. "The Senate has its rules. We have ours."

But in the Senate, that strategy threatened to result in a filibuster. Seven Republicans had provided pivotal votes to pass the bill in 1993, but they promised in a public letter at the time not to do so again unless the House and Senate were brought under similar rules.

No Breakthroughs

House leaders put off appointing conferees while they tried to negotiate a compromise package outside the confines of a normal conference. They chose this tactic because once conferees were appointed, the conference committee would have to be able to file a report within 20 days or Republicans could begin offering embarrassing motions to instruct the negotiators on a variety of issues.

By spring, they reportedly had reached agreement on the use of soft money and independent expenditures (spending directed for or against a candidate by an independent group). These were issues on which their differences had been minor. They also moved toward a compromise that would permit EMILY's List to continue soliciting and bundling contributions for women candidates.

The biggest obstacles to full joint agreement remained public funding and PACs. It appeared impossible to get the necessary number of Senate votes for any system that included significant public funding. And Senate Republicans had dug in to support the elimination of PACs, while House Democrats depended heavily on PAC funding.

Progress was slowed further by the fact that Democratic leaders — particularly House Majority Leader Richard A. Gephardt, D-Mo., who took charge of negotiations — were tied up in the futile effort to move a health care bill.

Some supporters of the legislation hoped that the May 31 indictment of House Ways and Means Committee Chairman Dan Rostenkowski, D-Ill., would unleash a wave of reform sentiment. But most of the charges against Rostenkowski involved official funds, not campaign accounts, and the tie to the legislation was weak. *(Rostenkowski, p. 43)*

In an effort to prod negotiations forward, Democratic leaders met July 27 with the lead negotiators for the House and Senate bills. David L. Boren, D-Okla., chief Senate sponsor, suggested phasing in PAC limits so they would not begin until the 1998 election cycle. Boren said House members offered no immediate reaction.

Democratic leaders also crafted a plan to pay for federal matching funds for candidates who complied with spending limits, by raising money from PACs and lobbyists rather than taxpayers. The Congressional Budget Office reportedly said the working draft would cost $239 million per election cycle, and leaders planned to raise the money through a PAC registration fee, voluntary taxpayer contributions, fees on lobbyists and foreign agents, and an increase in the tax paid by campaigns on interest and dividends.

Gejdenson suggested that the House might go along with tougher PAC limits if the Senate would consider adopting the House's cap on individual contributions.

Republicans were not directly involved in the efforts to draft final versions of the bill. "The Democrats are arguing among themselves," said Republican Rep. Robert L. Livingston of Louisiana.

On Aug. 3, Foley declared: "I do believe very strongly that we will not leave this Congress this year without enacting campaign finance reform." But with the leadership embroiled in other disputes — a sudden crisis over the omnibus crime bill added to the continuing obsession with health care legislation — no conference convened by the time members began a delayed summer break Aug. 25.

End Game

The logjam over PACs was finally broken Sept. 29, when House and Senate Democratic leaders unveiled a plan they hoped a conference committee would rubber-stamp and send to both chambers. The two sides agreed to bring the limit on PAC contributions down to $6,000 from $10,000.

With an eye to keeping the votes of two crucial Senate Republicans, Democrats indicated they would accept an amendment drafted by John McCain, R-Ariz., to ban candidates from using campaign contributions to enhance their lifestyle, and another amendment by James M. Jeffords, R-Vt., aimed at disclosing labor union spending and providing Republicans with a fund to counter those efforts.

But with the Oct. 7 target date for adjournment fast approaching, Senate Republicans found a new weapon. They began a filibuster against the procedural steps that usually were a routine part of convening a conference.

On Sept. 22, the Senate voted 96-2 to cut off debate by invoking cloture on the first step, a motion to disagree with the House's amendments to the bill. Republicans then insisted on using up all the time available for debate on the motion itself, talking straight through the night and through most of Sept. 23 before the Senate voted 93-0 to disagree with the House. *(Votes 303, 304, pp. 52-S, 53-S)*

Republicans then mounted a filibuster against the next procedural hurdle, a motion to go to conference, and advertised the fact that they had enough further procedural moves to bring the Senate to a halt for weeks. Mitchell was outraged, calling the effort "total obstructionism" that was unprecedented in the history of the Senate. *(Filibusters, p. 9)*

Mitch McConnell of Kentucky, leader of the GOP talkathon, was unapologetic. "Gridlock is making a comeback," he said. "The American people are begging us to stop [the campaign finance bill]."

The effort stalled there. Two votes to invoke cloture on the motion to request a conference fell well short of the 60 votes required to shut off debate. On Sept. 27, the motion lost 57-43. The coup de grace came Sept. 30 when six Democrats joined Republicans in the 52-46 vote. *(Votes 309, 314, pp. 53-S, 55-S)*

Mitchell and Minority Leader Bob Dole, R-Kan., immediately rose to sound bitter and partisan post-mortems. "Republican obstructionism" killed the bill, Mitchell said as he announced there would be no more action on campaign finance in 1994. "Republicans are proud to stand with taxpayers and against the public financing of congressional campaigns," responded Dole.

The defeat was a bitter pill for Mitchell in his final days as Senate leader. Since assuming the post in 1988, he had condemned the "money chase" that he said polluted the political process. "This system stinks," he said Sept. 30. Foley, too, had been a career-long believer in public funding of campaigns.

Republicans seemed unfazed by allegations that they were causing gridlock. "I make no apologies for killing this turkey of a bill," McConnell said.

Highlights of Deal

The compromise that Democrats expected to put in a conference report, had they been able to go to conference, included provisions to:

● **Voluntary spending limits.** Set state-by-state limits for Senate campaigns in the 1996 elections ranging from $1.2 million to $5.5 million for general elections, with lower limits for primaries. Set a uniform limit for House campaigns of approximately $675,000 (once inflation was factored in) for 1996. Limits would rise for candidates who won a primary with a margin of less than 20 percent and for those forced into runoff elections.

● **Benefits.** Offer Senate candidates a 50 percent discount for television broadcast time as an inducement to comply with spending limits. Complying House candidates could receive vouchers for advertising and postage costs up to one-third of the spending limit and funds to counter opponents who exceeded the spending limits. Candidates for either chamber could receive funds to respond to independent expenditure campaigns.

● **PACs.** Limit the amount political action committees could give to federal candidates to $6,000 per election cycle, down from the existing limit of $10,000. A maximum of $5,000 could be given for a primary. Total PAC contributions could amount to no more than one-third of the spending limit for House candidates, 20 percent for Senate candidates.

● **Leadership PACs.** Starting in 1997, bar members from having their own PACs as a way of making contributions to other candidates.

● **Bundling.** Bar individuals and committees connected with corporations, trade associations and labor unions from collecting and forwarding individual donations to federal candidates. (EMILY's List could have continued.)

● **Personal use.** Prohibit present and former candidates from spending campaign funds for any use that conferred a personal benefit.

● **Soft money.** Prohibit national or state parties from raising funds outside federal restrictions, with some exceptions.

● **Individual contributions.** Increase the amount an individual could contribute to candidates, political parties and PACs to $60,000 per election cycle from the existing cap of $25,000 per year.

● **Franked mail.** Prohibit senators and House members who became candidates for the Senate from sending mass mail using the franking privilege in the year of the election.

● **Minors.** Bar dependents below voting age from making contributions to federal candidates.

● **Financing.** Raise revenue from a variety of sources to finance the program, estimated by the Congressional Budget Office to cost $168 million over five years. The agreement included proposals to:

• Allow taxpayers to add $5 ($10 for those filing jointly) to their annual federal income tax bills.

• Require PACs to pay a 5 percent fee on annual receipts.

• Require candidates who rejected spending limits and public funding to pay a 35 percent tax on spending in excess of the expenditure limit.

• Require candidates' committees to pay a 35 percent tax on investment income instead of the existing 15 percent.

• Require that lobbyists pay a new annual registration fee of $500.

• Increase registration fees for foreign agents.

• Eliminate the tax deduction available to lobbyists and businesses for meals and entertainment expenses that involved officeholders or federal employees. ■

FEC Adopts Spending Regulations

Fifteen years after Congress outlawed the practice, the Federal Election Commission (FEC) adopted regulations to stop congressional candidates from spending campaign dollars on personal needs.

The new regulations, which the commission approved Dec. 1 to go into effect in early 1995, barred candidates from dipping into their campaign coffers to pay bills that would have existed whether or not they had run for office. Included were home mortgage payments, tuition for family members, club memberships and tickets to sporting events. If a third party paid any of those expenses to aid a candidate, such payments would have to be reported as campaign contributions subject to the applicable limits.

In the past, the FEC had given candidates wide latitude to decide which expenses were campaign-related and which were purely personal. That approach enabled members of Congress to subsidize their lifestyles with infusions of campaign cash for cars, travel, entertainment and meals, said Fred Wertheimer of Common Cause, an advocacy group critical of congressional ethics. "Members of Congress have had a free ride on this issue for years, with no enforcement, and as a result the abuses have become very widespread. Hopefully, this will reverse that practice," he said.

Congress barred the conversion of campaign dollars to personal use in 1979, but the FEC had never adopted regulations defining "personal use." The House and Senate adopted their own rules for incumbents, allowing the use of campaign funds for any "political expense" by House members or "officially connected expense" by senators. *(1979 Almanac, p. 558)*

No Ban on Salaries

Absent from the new regulations was a ban on candidates' use of campaign funds to pay themselves a salary. Such a prohibition would have affected only challengers, as members of Congress already were prohibited by law from drawing any salary beyond their congressional pay.

The commission's lawyers proposed the salary ban, saying it was needed to prevent challengers from circumventing the law against using campaign contributions for personal needs. But Chairman Trevor Potter, a Republican appointee, said salaries should be allowed, to enable people who were not wealthy to run for Congress. He said that because challengers' campaigns tended to be strapped for cash, they would be unlikely to spend their scarce contributions on personal needs.

Commissioner Joan D. Aikens, also a Republican, noted that the overwhelming majority of comments that the FEC received on the proposed regulations favored salaries for non-incumbent candidates.

The six-member commission deadlocked on the proposed ban, with three Democrats voting for it and three Republicans voting against it. Because four votes were required to adopt any proposed regulation, the ban was dropped from the new rules.

Potter then proposed letting candidates use campaign funds to pay themselves salaries no greater than the ones they received before entering the race. That proposal also fell, 3-3, with Republicans supporting it and Democrats opposing.

With no clear regulatory guidance, challengers who paid themselves salaries were unlikely to be stopped by the FEC, although they could wind up in court.

The FEC had tried throughout the 1980s to decide the issue but had been unable to break the deadlock.

The latest effort had begun in August 1993, when the commission announced its intention to adopt rules governing the use of campaign funds for personal expenses. The impasse was not likely to be broken until the commission's membership changed; one Republican and one Democrat were up for reappointment in April 1995.

Lawyers for the Republican and Democratic parties urged the FEC not to adopt any regulations on personal use. Outgoing Rep. Fred Grandy of Iowa, the top Republican on the House ethics committee, said there was no evidence of widespread abuses in the House, but added that it always helped to clarify the rules.

Although he was disappointed on the salary question, Potter still called the new regulations "a huge step forward" in the FEC's efforts to stop candidate abuses. He said the regulations would make the lines between legitimate campaign expenses and personal uses a lot clearer.

Expenses Not Allowed

The regulations provided the same standard for incumbents and challengers alike. In addition to the general standard, the regulations listed specific personal expenses that could not be funded by a campaign. The list included:

- Household food, rent, mortgage payments, utility bills and supplies.
- Funeral expenses.
- Clothing, other than campaign handouts such as T-shirts and caps.
- Tuition payments.
- Tickets to entertainment events that were not part of a specific campaign or officeholder activity.
- Membership dues, tips and fees at clubs, recreation centers and other non-political organizations, unless they were part of a fundraising event at the club or center.

Wertheimer and Elizabeth Hedlund of the Center for Responsive Politics, another public-advocacy group active on campaign finance issues, said more work was needed to guard against abuses. For example, Hedlund criticized the commission's decision to allow members of Congress to use campaign funds to pay their spouses' expenses on official trips — something they could not do with taxpayer funds. "We see this as a gift to Congress," she said.

Wertheimer said the new rules would be no more effective in stopping abuses than the existing law if the FEC did not actively enforce them. He also called on Congress to pass a new law banning its members from using campaign funds for their official duties, a loophole that he said opened the door to more abuses.

The new regulations applied to presidential candidates as well. Those campaigns already were covered, though, by separate laws and regulations governing the use of public financing.

Yearlong Process

The writing of the regulations was a yearlong process, closely watched by members of Congress even if they were reluctant to comment publicly on an issue weighted with self-interest.

The FEC held six hours of hearings Jan. 12 on draft regulations that had been published Aug. 30, 1993.

The hearings followed on news stories such as a Los Angeles

Times report that Sen. Daniel K. Inouye, D-Hawaii, used campaign contributions to buy meals totaling $545 at a hotel in Jakarta, Indonesia, or a story in The Wall Street Journal noting that Rep. Curt Weldon, R-Pa., bought a $5,100 vintage firetruck with campaign funds. Reps. Michael A. Andrews, D-Texas, and Duncan Hunter, R-Calif., paid their House gym dues with campaign money, according to various news accounts.

In the August draft regulations, the commission proposed prohibiting the use of campaign money for any expense "that would exist irrespective of the candidate's campaign or responsibilities as a federal officeholder."

During the public hearing, interest groups and private lawyers found fault with the proposed standard. Even FEC Chairman Potter suggested that any general standard would be insufficient. He related a story of a House member who bought his wife a fur coat so she could "mingle" with upscale constituents. "It's very easy to come up with a political explanation for almost any expenditure," Potter said.

Campaign lawyers Republican Jan Baran and Democrat Robert Bauer said that such a vague standard or anything short of an absolute, exhaustive list of barred expenditures would cause "endless second-guessing." Bauer, for instance, pointed out that a vacation to recuperate from the exhaustion of a campaign or psychotherapy to recuperate from the stress might meet the FEC standard, although, he said, few would find them acceptable uses of campaign funds.

A revised draft of the regulations went to commissioners May 5. It would have forbidden campaigns from paying a salary to candidates. The regulations continued to leave much to the candidates' discretion but included a litany of specific expenses that would be illegal.

The FEC held another six-hour hearing May 19 and ordered its staff to write a new draft.

In the next round, the July 27 draft, the commission proposed transferring much of the responsibility for determining what constituted personal use to the House and Senate ethics committees. But after critics such as Wertheimer and Hedlund protested that this would let abuses continue, the commission changed its proposal for its Aug. 11 meeting, keeping such determinations for itself.

Supreme Court Rejects Case

The Supreme Court considered and then rejected an appeal brought by the FEC against a 1993 court ruling concerning its composition. In that decision by the D.C. Circuit Court of Appeals, the lower court ruled that the commission had violated the constitutional separation of powers by including two non-voting congressional staff members in its deliberations. *(1993 Almanac, p. 76)*

The FEC voted to exclude the two members but asked the Supreme Court to rule that past FEC decisions were still valid. The court accepted the case, *FEC v. the National Rifle Association Political Victory Fund*, on June 20.

In a 7-1 decision handed down Dec. 6, the Supreme Court rejected the appeal on technical grounds, ruling that the agency lacked authority to appeal the matter to the Supreme Court. Chief Justice William H. Rehnquist, writing for the majority, said the law establishing the FEC did not give the agency authority for such appeals. He said that only the solicitor general had such authority.

The decision left the 1993 ruling in place and left a legal cloud hanging over similar court challenges of FEC actions. The court did not speak to the merits of the constitutional challenge. ∎

Lobbying Disclosure Bill Dies

Legislation to revamp lobbying disclosure requirements and tighten gift rules for members of Congress (S 349) went through a tortuous life-and-death struggle during 1994. In the end, the bill fell victim to election-year pressures and disintegrating support from members.

During the 103rd Congress, both chambers passed versions of the legislation by wide margins, beginning in 1993, when the Senate passed its lobbying bill (S 349), and continuing through 1994, when the House acted on a bill that contained lobbying and gift provisions (HR 823). The Senate re-entered the fray in May, passing a free-standing measure to toughen gift rules (S 1935). All three bills then went to conference.

But the apparent support for the lobbying and gift ban legislation masked a deep ambivalence among many members of Congress about toughening gift rules and among lobbyists and organizations that would have had their activities scrutinized far more closely under the proposed rules.

Controversy over the gift rules prevented House and Senate conferees from reaching agreement until Sept. 26. By then, the bill was vulnerable to end-of-session procedural ploys. Republicans mounted a campaign against the conference report on the bill, saying it contained provisions that could require grass-roots lobbying organizations to disclose information about their contributors that could deter citizen involvement in politics.

The House adopted the conference report, but only after Democratic leaders scrambled to prevent opponents from using a procedural move to block its consideration. With support weakening, the bill ultimately died in the Senate, after supporters failed on two end-of-session votes to shut off a Republican-led filibuster.

Bill sponsors accused the Republicans of ginning up objections to kill the measure in order to deny the Democrats and President Clinton a victory. They said some members of both parties joined the effort to preserve their ability to accept gifts from lobbyists. Republicans responded that they had raised objections about the bill earlier but had been ignored.

The defeat killed the last remaining item on the Democratic list of political reforms backed by Clinton, none of which passed.

The final version of the bill would have required nearly anyone spending money or being paid to lobby Congress or the executive branch to register with a new federal agency, called the Office of Lobbying Registration and Public Disclosure, and to report on how much they made, what issues they followed, and how they spent their money.

The new gift rules would have prohibited lobbyists from giving members and staff almost anything except campaign contributions. Rules on gifts from non-lobbyists would have been less restrictive. *(Gift rules, p. 41)*

Background

Congress had considered lobby disclosure proposals since the late 1800s. Passage of the Foreign Agents

Registration Act of 1938 and the Federal Regulation of Lobbyists Act of 1946 did little to put the issue to rest; both laws long had been considered ineffective. The Justice Department in 1983 called the 1946 law unenforceable, and registration came to be viewed as voluntary by lobbyists.

President Harry S Truman appointed a commission to reform lobbying laws in 1948. Nothing happened. Likewise, efforts in the 1950s failed. One or both chambers passed lobbying bills in 1967, 1976 and 1978, but each time Congress failed to agree on how much disclosure to require of whom — mainly whether to require registrants to disclose so-called grassroots activities aimed at drumming up public support and the names of lobbying groups' big contributors.

Both issues emerged again in 1994 and helped kill the lobbying bill yet another time.

Clinton helped put the issue of lobbying reform on the front burner early in his administration by railing against the influence of lobbyists. In a speech to Congress on Feb. 17, 1993, he called on lawmakers to "deal with the undue influence of special interests" by expanding lobbyist registration and disclosure requirements. But he expended almost no political capital to get a bill through Congress.

Carl Levin, D-Mich., chairman of the Senate Governmental Affairs Subcommittee on Oversight, had been leading the effort in Congress to revamp lobbying laws. Levin had been studying the issue since the Wedtech contracting scandal in 1987.

1993 Action

Under the lash of public outrage over members' perquisites, the Senate in 1993 gave overwhelming approval to a far-reaching overhaul of lobbying disclosure rules. But the House version of the bill stalled in a dispute that resurfaced again in 1994: how to limit the gifts and other financial benefits that lobbyists and their clients could bestow on members of Congress.

The Senate passed its bill (S 349), sponsored by Levin, 95-2, on May 6. Under pressure from public interest groups and editorial writers, the Senate included a floor amendment that required lobbyists to disclose gifts and other financial benefits worth more than $20, including meals and entertainment, given to members and staff.

Senators also approved, 98-1, a non-binding call to bring relatively lax congressional gift rules in line with the stricter executive branch limits before the end of 1993. The amendment was offered by Frank R. Lautenberg, D-N.J.

Under existing rules, Congress allowed an unlimited number of gifts worth less than $100 and no more than $250 worth of gifts with values of $100 or more. Most meals and travel did not count toward the caps. The executive branch barred employees from taking gifts worth more than $20 from anyone interested in their agency's work and limited total gifts from any such person to $50 a year; meals counted toward the limits, and travel was subject to a strict approval process.

Lautenberg subsequently introduced a separate gift bill (S 885). He sought to go beyond requiring disclosure to ban law-

---

BOXSCORE

Lobbying Disclosure and Gift Ban — S 349 (HR 823, S 1935). The bill sought to revamp lobbying disclosure laws and tighten gift rules for members and staff.

Reports: S Rept 103-37, S Rept 103-255; conference report H Rept 103-750.

KEY ACTION

March 24 — House passed S 349, revised, 315-110.

May 11 — Senate passed S 1935, 95-4.

Sept. 26 — House-Senate conferees reach agreement on S 349.

Sept. 29 — House agreed to conference report, 306-112.

Oct. 6-7 — Senate twice failed to cut off filibuster, 52-46, 55-42.

---

makers and staff from accepting gifts of $20 or more each, or $50 in the aggregate, from a single source.

In the House, Democratic freshmen took up the cause, demanding stricter gift limits than senior members from both parties said were necessary. The dispute stalled plans by the House Judiciary Subcommittee on Administrative Law and Government Relations to mark up its own lobbying disclosure bill. Instead, a bipartisan task force was set up to study the issue.

In the final days of the 1993 session, the task force came up with a sweeping agreement to ban all meals, entertainment, gifts and travel provided to members and their staffs by lobbyists and lobbying organizations. But the proposal also contained a lengthy list of exceptions.

On Nov. 22, the Judiciary subcommittee, chaired by John Bryant, D-Texas, approved the gift ban agreement as part of its lobbying disclosure bill (HR 823). While the bill banned most gifts from lobbyists to members and staff, it included a variety of exceptions, such as allowing a lobbyist's client to pay for meals and entertainment and allowing members to accept free transportation and accommodations tied to charity functions.

Except for the gift provisions, the bill, approved 10-0, was almost the same as the Senate-passed measure. (1993 Almanac, p. 50)

Support for the gift provisions in the House bill was never firm, however. Although Republican Whip Newt Gingrich of Georgia participated in the talks that produced the bill, he later denied that he had ever agreed to the gift language. Common Cause blasted the bill for having too many exceptions. And freshman supporters quickly began agitating for tougher rules.

House Action

As the 1994 session began, Speaker Thomas S. Foley, D-Wash., hoped to bring the bill to the House floor with bipartisan support for the gift provisions. But in early March, House Republicans turned against what had been billed as a bipartisan compromise. Key Republicans argued that meals, entertainment and other gifts should be disclosed — not banned. Bryant tried to win support for the bill from the GOP Policy Committee on March 9. "It got a chilly reception," said Robert L. Livingston, R-La., afterward. "The Bryant compromise just doesn't make sense — it's half a loaf. The day it passes, we'll be open to criticism. Disclosure takes care of the problem."

Meanwhile, on the other side of the Capitol, Lautenberg and Paul Wellstone, D-Minn., had won grudging agreement from the Senate leadership to hold a vote by May 4 on a new bill that would impose a strict gift ban. The lobbying bill the Senate had passed in 1993 required only disclosure of gifts. Freshmen Democrats who had led the 1993 drive to include gift limits in the House bill — Ohio's Eric D. Fingerhut and Utah's Karen Shepherd — joined in the effort and were pushing to toughen the House bill.

The breakdown of the compromise on the gift provisions presented House leaders with a quandary. "In both caucuses,

you have sizable numbers who don't want to do anything," said Bryant. That made losing on the floor a real possibility.

But after months of hesitation, Democratic leaders took the gamble. With an unexpected gap in the legislative calendar on the eve of a two week recess, they sped the legislation to the House floor the week of March 21. The prospect of bringing home a newly passed "reform" bill enabled them to overcome internal objections and quash protests from Republicans that they were being steamrollered.

House Floor Action

After surviving a key procedural test, a revised version of the lobbying disclosure bill (S 349) sailed to passage March 24 on a 315-110 vote. *(Vote 90, p. 28-H)*

The lobbying provisions — virtually identical to the Senate bill that passed in 1993 — never generated much controversy. They required anyone paid to lobby members of Congress, their staffs or senior executive branch officials to register at a new Office of Lobbying Registration and Public Disclosure.

It was the gift ban that drew objections. Although opposition had come from both sides of the aisle, the floor debate was starkly partisan, an atmosphere fueled by intense maneuvering over the details of the gift ban and over which party would get credit. "Do you folks want to join us in making it against the law for a lobbyist to buy a free meal for a member of Congress or not?" Bryant demanded, looking at Republicans.

The procedural test came as the result of the unusual route Democratic leaders chose in bringing the bill to the floor. On March 23, they tried to get consent to bring the bill up the following day under suspension of the rules, a procedure that required a two-thirds vote for the bill rather than a simple majority. Republicans objected. They complained that the bill had not been considered by the full Judiciary Committee and that the procedure — usually reserved for non-controversial measures — prohibited amendments and allowed each side only 20 minutes for debate.

That objection required the House to approve a rule for floor debate that allowed the bill to be considered under suspension.

Democrats said they were faced with a choice between a good, though imperfect bill, or none at all. Virtually every Democrat who spoke in behalf of the bill cited a need to assuage public concern about the influence of special interests on Congress. "There is in some quarters of public opinion a belief — I think a wrong belief — that we are unduly influenced by the provision of meals or entertainment," said Foley in an unusual floor statement supporting the rule.

Republicans argued strenuously against the process that denied them a chance to amend the bill. They also argued that full disclosure of gifts, meals and travel payments by lobbyists was preferable to a complex set of rules to restrict activities that Democrats and Republicans said were not improper. "It sets up certain criteria that leave us vulnerable to charges for totally innocent situations," said Tom DeLay, R-Texas. "I do not think we should legislate on the basis of public perception," said Hamilton Fish Jr., R-N.Y., "particularly when it is legislation as ill-conceived and as flawed as this."

But public perception seemed to be the order of the day. The rule, which needed a simple majority for approval, won on a 221-202 vote, with the help of nine Republicans. When the bill came up for final passage, 16 Democrats and 101 Republicans who had voted against the rule switched to vote for the bill. Twenty-four Democrats who supported the rule opposed the bill. *(Vote 89, p. 28-H)*

The House-passed bill included several minor amendments to the version approved by Bryant's Judiciary subcommittee in 1993. One was designed to enhance disclosure of lobbyists retained by foreign interests; another established that if a person retained a lobbyist on behalf of another person or entity, both parties would be considered the lobbyist's clients.

Bill Highlights

Following are highlights of the House bill:

● Registration would be required for any organization that spent or received more than $2,500 from all clients it lobbied for or more than $1,000 from any single client in half a year.

● Lobbying contacts were defined as any communications with congressional members, aides or high-level executive branch officials with regard to legislation or official actions, including money spent on grass-roots campaigns.

● Any organization that employed a lobbyist would have to file a report covering all its lobbying activities.

● Reports were required twice a year specifying clients, lobbyists, amounts spent or received, issues involved, agencies and committees contacted, and interests of foreign affiliates.

● Registered lobbyists would be barred from providing meals, entertainment or gifts to members directly or indirectly.

● Companies, unions or other groups that employed a lobbyist could pay for members' travel to political events, conventions, retreats, symposiums and receptions, including meals and entertainment, so long as it was disclosed and funding was available to all of those invited.

● A company or union that employed a lobbyist could provide meals and entertainment for a member as long as a company or union official who was not a lobbyist was present.

Common Cause President Fred Wertheimer said the bill failed "to bring to an end the discredited system of special-interest financed perks for members." An editorial in The New York Times pronounced: "The reason for the House's timidity is depressingly clear. Many House members have grown accustomed to life on the dole."

Gift Bill: Senate Committee

The Senate Governmental Affairs Committee gave voice vote approval April 26 to a separate bill (S 1935 — S Rept 103-255) sponsored by Levin to clamp down sharply on members' ability to accept free meals, entertainment and vacationlike junkets. "People believe that we are simply too cozy with paid lobbyists," said Levin. "This is very strong medicine."

Levin's measure was the strictest gift proposal approved in any forum at least since the latest debate on the issue had begun in mid-1993, and probably ever. It proposed to bar members and staff from accepting just about anything from lobbyists unless they were verifiable friends or family. Most gifts from anyone else would have to be worth less than $20 unless unrelated to official position.

Members still could accept invitations to some events and free trips, but only if they were related to official duties and did not include free recreational activities. Trip costs would have to be disclosed in detail.

Gone would be the free meals that lobbyists and others bought for members and their staffs — a practice pervasive enough that local restaurateurs unsuccessfully petitioned senators to relax the bill's meal restrictions lest their livelihoods be threatened. However, meals would be allowed if a non-lobbyist employee attended.

Though they praised him for trying, several members lam-

basted Levin's bill before voting for it. Robert F. Bennett, R-Utah, proposed raising the $20 ceiling on non-lobbyist gifts to the existing limit of $100. But Levin protested: "We could get two tickets to Redskins games every weekend. . . . I think that's wrong." The amendment was defeated by voice vote.

Ted Stevens, R-Alaska, said the bill "is going to harm this town" by blocking people from spending money on members and aides. "The Kennedy Center will fold up if they don't buy these tickets," he said. "You are going to close 90 percent of the restaurants in Washington."

Sam Nunn, D-Ga., complained that the bill would bar travel for charity golf matches, which frequently were financed by corporations. "If we're barring that, are we saying that there was something wrong with that to begin with?" Nunn asked. He argued that members should be allowed to accept whatever they wanted as long as they disclosed it.

But it seemed clear that the critics were in no mood to fight Levin actively by actually pushing their own proposals.

Lautenberg-Wellstone Alternative

Committee action on Levin's proposal came as the result of concerted pressure by Lautenberg and Wellstone, who had been threatening to offer their own gift ban bill (S 1935) as an amendment to any pending bill on the Senate floor. They relented March 17 after they secured an agreement giving the committee until April 27 to mark up the measure and guaranteeing that the Senate would begin considering it by May 4. That deadline prompted Levin, the original sponsor of the lobbying bill, to draft his own gift proposal.

Lautenberg and Wellstone wanted to force a vote on the gift issue so that the Senate's position would be clear when the lobbying disclosure bill went to conference.

Crafted with the help of the public interest lobby Common Cause, their proposal was based on the House bill but sought to remove or tighten several of the exceptions. Clients could not buy meals and entertainment for members, for example. Golfing trips would be prohibited. It would bar lobbyists from making any charitable contributions in a member's behalf and tighten the friendship exemption. Lobbyist-financed conferences for members also would be prohibited. Lobbyists still could provide travel for speaking engagements, but only if the trip was disclosed in advance in the Congressional Record and publicly detailed later by the lobbyist.

Levin said he wanted to avoid a floor vote and go straight to conference using his bill as the Senate's position on gifts, but Lautenberg and Wellstone, as well as cosponsor Russell Feingold, D-Wis., said they were not sure they wanted to relinquish their rights to a floor debate.

The three senators were particularly worried about a provision in Levin's bill that would allow meals and entertainment in a member's home state from anyone but lobbyists, within higher limits to be set later. They also said they were not sure it was wise to allow gifts from friends to be unlimited in value. And they wanted to make sure the issue was addressed to their satisfaction in conference and not knocked out of the bill later on procedural grounds.

For his part, Levin disliked some aspects of the Lautenberg-Wellstone approach. Levin's main problem with the bill, said the Oversight subcommittee's staff director, Linda J. Gustitus, was that it would, in effect, put the executive branch in charge of policing congressional gift matters. Levin also did not want want lobbyists responsible for disclosing what members received. In addition, Levin opposed treating a business that employed a lobbyist differently from one that did not.

Levin proposed to rewrite Senate and House gift rules, dictating what members could not accept and what they had to disclose, leaving enforcement in the hands of the two ethics committees. The House bill and the Lautenberg-Wellstone proposal, by contrast, sought to supplement existing rules with a new law laying out what lobbyists and their clients could not give and what they had to disclose, giving the executive branch an enforcement role. "I believe the responsibility in this area should be on us," Levin told his colleagues.

Gift Bill: Senate Floor

Despite deep disagreements, the Senate on May 11 passed S 1935 by a vote of 95-4. It was a much stricter gift bill than anyone had thought possible when the latest debate began in 1993. "My head is bloodied and bowed," said J. Bennett Johnston, D-La., a leading opponent, as he walked into the Senate chamber to vote for final passage. *(Vote 107, p. 19-S)*

Levin said, "We have taken a major step to break the excessively cozy relationship between us and lobbyists. This represents a real significant change in the atmosphere here."

But Mitch McConnell, R-Ky., the measure's leading opponent, countered: "This bill will make a lot of honest, highly ethical people into crooks," because it is "riddled with traps, lined with legalistic punji sticks poised to impale the careers of anyone who has the misfortune of falling into one by accident."

Debate on the bill, often anguished and angry, took place May 4-6. A vote on final passage was put off until May 11 under an agreement that blocked further substantive amendments and delayed disposition of one unrelated to the substance of the measure until after some senators return from a trip to South Africa.

On the key vote of the debate, the Senate on May 5 defeated, 39-59, a much more lenient alternative, drafted by McConnell, vice chairman of the Ethics Committee, and Johnston. The McConnell-Johnston proposal would have allowed virtually unlimited free meals and unlimited gifts worth less than $75, down from the $100 threshold under existing rules. All but four of 26 members up for re-election voted against the amendment. *(Vote 101, p. 18-S)*

Johnston spent much of the week lobbying members on the amendment, which was cosponsored by Republican Leader Bob Dole of Kansas and opposed by Majority Leader George J. Mitchell, D-Maine. Johnston and his allies argued that the Levin bill was insulting because it implied that members could be bought for the price of a dinner. At one point, Johnston complained that he would not be able to go to a charity opera ball. Responded Wellstone: "You can go to any opera you want to. You pay for it, just like regular people pay for it when they go to the opera. It's that simple."

After defeating the alternative, senators voted 90-3 to strip even the $20 exemption for gifts from non-lobbyists from the Levin bill. "I don't want to get into determining whether something is worth $20," said Dale Bumpers, D-Ark., a supporter of the more lenient alternative, as he offered the amendment to make the original measure even stricter. *(Vote 102, p. 18-S)*

The opponents' last serious run at the bill came late May 5. Frank H. Murkowski, R-Alaska, proposed allowing free travel and lodging expenses for members who participated in charity events. Many members regularly attended corporate-backed golf and tennis tournaments or ski trips that raised money for needy causes by charging lobbyists and others fees to play with notable pols and other renowned individuals.

These and other trips, the frequent grist for television exposés, were denounced on the floor as the main cause of

the problem that the bill was meant to address. "It was fun while it lasted, but its time has past," said Lautenberg.

Murkowski's amendment was rejected, 37-58. *(Vote 105, p. 19-S)*

As the hours dragged May 5, senators seemed willing to accept any new restrictions: They approved, 66-29, another Murkowski amendment to bar campaign contributions from lobbyists and political action committees. By voice vote, they adopted an amendment by David L. Boren, D-Okla., and John McCain, R-Ariz., to increase from one year to two years the post-employment lobbying restrictions on top appointed and elected officials. By 34-59, however, the Senate rejected an amendment by Conrad Burns, R-Mont., to cut members' salaries 15 percent. *(Votes 104, 103, p. 18-S)*

Under a package of uncontested amendments adopted late May 5, a perishable item (though technically banned) could be donated to charity or "shared within the recipient's office" if "it is not practicable to return." This appeared to allow members and their staffs to consume over-the-transom baskets of fruit.

A ban in the original bill on charitable contributions made in lieu of speaking fees was relaxed to apply only to lobbyists. That meant leaving the existing practice effectively unchanged because such donations generally were made by interest groups, not lobbyists. Lobbyist contributions to members' legal defense funds also were banned.

Meals and entertainment provided by non-lobbyists in members' home states would be subject to separate limits to be established later for each chamber. Also exempt would be free attendance at certain widely attended events where an official was speaking or "performing a ceremonial function appropriate to his or her official position." Members and staff could not accept "entertainment collateral to the event."

All gifts from relatives and friends were to be exempt, though another uncontested change required Ethics Committee approval of a friend's gift worth more than $250. Another change would allow either chamber's ethics committee to waive the gift ban "in an unusual case."

Under the bill, gift-giving from friends would have to be clearly motivated not by an official's position but by friendship (taking into account the history of the relationship and whether gifts have been exchanged in the past). Nor could such gifts be used as the basis for a tax deduction or for a business reimbursement request.

Conference

The next step was for House and Senate negotiators to craft a compromise bill, working from the two chambers' lobbying bills plus the Senate gift ban measure.

Levin and Bryant took the lead. Again, the most difficult issue was the gift ban. The Senate's near-total ban was not popular in the House. Bryant worried about antagonizing a bloc of members who only grudgingly accepted more lenient restrictions and could kill the bill by joining forces with members who opposed the measure. In the Senate, a determined group of gift-limit supporters said they would fight any bill not deemed restrictive enough.

The rewrite of lobbying disclosure requirements was considered almost routine.

After several months without progress, Democratic leaders from both chambers began trying to prod things along in late July, meeting with Levin and Bryant. "The Democrats are arguing among themselves," said Livingston; Republicans were not involved in the negotiations. Signaling a desire to

compromise, Speaker Thomas S. Foley, D-Wash., told reporters Aug. 2 that the House would be willing to move toward the stricter Senate bill as long as there was "some give on both sides."

The Compromise

Levin and Bryant finally unveiled their compromise Sept. 22. The following day, they presented it to House and Senate conferees. Three days later, on Sept. 26, conferees approved the compromise bill (S 349 — H Rept 103-750).

Nearly anyone spending money or being paid to lobby Congress or the executive branch would be required to register with a new federal agency and report on how much they made, what issues they followed and how they spent their money. Firms or people who spent less than 10 percent of their time lobbying or who made less than $2,500 lobbying in a six-month period would be exempt.

Lobbyists would be prohibited from giving members and staff almost anything except campaign contributions, tickets to fundraisers and other political events, and modest food items such as coffee and doughnuts.

Gifts from non-lobbyists would be subject to somewhat less restrictive limits. Allowed from non-lobbyists would be food and refreshments worth less than $20, meals and entertainment worth more if they took place in the member's home state and contributions to legal defense funds.

Private interests still could subsidize travel for speaking engagements, fact-finding trips and other events related to official duties. But substantially recreational trips — including the popular charity golf tournaments and the like — would be banned. So would entertainment collateral to the trip's main purpose.

Gifts based on certain personal and family relationships were exempt from the rules.

The gift provisions were based largely on the stricter Senate bill. Bryant and Levin adopted some more stringent provisions from the House bill, including an enforcement mechanism that gave the executive branch a role. Under the Senate bill, only the ethics committees would have had enforcement power. Under the compromise, the Office of Lobbying Registration and Public Disclosure, the new agency created to implement the law, would be responsible for investigating lobbyists alleged to have given improper gifts, while the ethics committees would investigate members alleged to have accepted them.

Lobbyists found to have violated any provision of the law would face fines of up to $200,000.

Bryant and Levin dropped more stringent Senate proposals in only a few cases, including provisions that would have barred members from taking a family member on free trips and stopped private groups from subsidizing issue retreats for congressional groups. Also dropped was a controversial provision from the House bill that could have made it more difficult for prosecutors to charge members with taking illegal gratuities, a criminal offense akin to bribery.

Enactment Expected

Both opponents and supporters of the gift rules predicted the bill would be sent to Clinton's desk, fulfilling one of his campaign priorities. "There's always uncertainty at the end of the session," said Levin, but "the odds are good that we will get this through."

A few members voiced opposition to the compromise. House Minority Leader Robert H. Michel, R-Ill., expressed skepticism about the gift provisions on the floor Sept. 23. "From what I've learned so far, I just don't think it's the

Proposed Restrictions on Gifts

House and Senate conferees agreed Sept. 22 on new proposals to restrict the gifts members and staff could accept from lobbyists and others. The rules were part of the conference agreement on the lobbying disclosure bill (S 349 — H Rept 103-750). Following are key differences between existing law and rules approved by conferees:

In General
Existing: No limits on gifts worth less than $100; no more than $250 a year in bigger gifts from anyone but relatives, unless ethics panel approved.
Conference: Virtually no gifts from lobbyists. Gifts from non-lobbyists also would be substantially restricted, but not as stringently. Exempt from the rules would be gifts based on personal relationships (in the case of non-lobbyists) or close personal friendships (in the case of lobbyists) or family ties (in either case); personal, non-family gifts worth more than $250 would require an ethics committee waiver. Also exempt would be gifts between members and employees.

Free Travel and Lodging
Existing: Allowed for speeches, fact-finding trips and other events. Member was required to disclose trip but not cost. A family member could travel.
Conference: Similar, except: The trip would have to be related to official duties; lobbyist could not pay; substantially recreational trips would be banned; entertainment collateral to the event also would be banned unless everyone participated; and the cost of the trip would be disclosed. Political groups could provide travel for campaign and fundraising events. Also exempt would be meals and lodging in non-lobbyists' homes.

Travel and Lodging for Charity Events
Existing: Free trips for golf, tennis and ski outings to raise money for charity allowed.
Conference: Such trips would be banned.

Meals and Entertainment
Existing: In most cases, meals were exempt from gift limits; entertainment was subject to the $100/$250 gift limits.
Conference: Lobbyist meals and entertainment would be banned except for things such as coffee and doughnuts. Lobbyists could pay for tickets to political fundraising events. In most cases, food and refreshments from non-lobbyists would be limited to $20, and entertainment would be banned. Meals and entertainment provided by a non-lobbyist in the member's home state would be subject to higher limits.

Events To Honor Members, Subsidized Conferences
Existing: Private interests could finance parties honoring members or conferences for congressional groups.
Conference: Lobbyist could not subsidize the cost.

Charitable Contributions in Lieu of Honoraria
Existing: Allowed; member had to disclose.
Conference: Lobbyists could not contribute.

Contributions to Legal Defense Funds
Existing: In the House, up to $5,000 from each person annually; in the Senate, up to $10,000. Member had to disclose.
Conference: Lobbyists could not contribute.

Charitable Foundations Established by Members
Existing: Members could solicit unlimited donations to their own charity foundations.
Conference: Lobbyists could not contribute.

Exceptions
Existing: Numerous items, most of them not usually considered gifts, were exempt.
Conference: Similar, but explicitly included books and other information materials; campaign contributions; free attendance provided by sponsors of certain "widely attended" events; other non-controversial items based on executive branch gift rules; benefits related to non-government activities as long as customary and not offered or enhanced because of official position; home-state products provided for promotion; and inexpensive things like T-shirts. An unsolicited perishable item could be donated to charity or destroyed if it were not practicable to return. The bill also would give the ethics committees authority to waive the rules "in an unusual case."

proper approach to take," he said.

But other opponents predicted flatly that it would pass. "I don't think you're going to see too many brave soldiers" vote against the bill, said Livingston. Added McConnell: "I made my case, and I lost. I'm going to vote for it, but I think it's going to be a nightmare. My assumption is it's going to pass."

Public interest groups and members who had been fighting for a strict gift bill since early 1993 were giddy over the provisions, which they said exceeded their most optimistic expectations. "When I think of where we started and where we ended up, I'm delighted," said Wellstone. "It's a huge, huge step forward. It's a sea change."

Said Wertheimer of Common Cause: "It's a major achievement in the fight to end the practice of special interests paying for the lifestyles of members of Congress."

Final Action

The conference agreement appeared headed for easy passage until Republicans began raising objections about the bill's effect on grass-roots lobbying. Those objections centered on the bill's lobbying disclosure provisions, an area that had been largely non-controversial until late in the session.

The House agreed to the conference report Sept. 29 by a vote of 306-112. But the comfortable margin disguised a fierce political battle in which the Republican leadership nearly derailed the measure on a procedural vote, capitalizing on many members' desire to scuttle the gift ban without having to go on record against it. *(Vote 451, p. 134-H)*

Ninety-three members who eventually voted for the bill on final passage tried to prevent it from coming to the floor by voting against the rule for debate. The rule was approved 216-

205 after hanging in the balance for several minutes while Democratic leaders twisted arms. *(Vote 449, p. 134-H)*

"This bill says no to the freebie-seeking members . . . a small minority of this House that create a bad impression for the rest of us," said Bryant.

Only a few members were willing to publicly mourn the demise of the free lunch with lobbyists and the expense-paid trip to a resort. "I think it's silly. It's demeaning . . . the idea that somebody can influence me with a lunch," said Charles Wilson, D-Texas, who voted against the measure. He acknowledged, "It will make life a little less gentle."

Republican Whip Gingrich led the last-minute effort to block the bill from the floor, which caught Democratic leaders off guard. Gingrich and several other Republicans contended that the bill would infringe on the rights of religious groups to lobby Congress by forcing them to disclose grassroots efforts.

Their target was language that called for disclosure of the name, address and place of business of "any person or entity other than the client" who paid for someone to lobby on his behalf. Conferees had included the provision, which the House had passed in its version of the bill in an effort to get at the increasingly common tactic of Washington lobbyists urging constituents to call lawmakers on particular issues.

The bill, Gingrich claimed, "threatens the American people's right to be active citizens." He charged that the administration would fill the directorship of the new Office of Lobbying Registration and Public Disclosure with a "secular, anti-religious liberal" who, he said, could use registration information to squelch religious viewpoints. The Christian Coalition, a conservative group that lobbied on social issues, issued a statement saying the bill amounted to a "gag rule" on religious organizations.

Gingrich denied that he had waited until the last moment to kill the bill, saying he had made his objections to the grass-roots provision known during the conference. Gingrich said he had not called attention to the provisions when the House passed the bill, because he said he was not paying attention.

Bryant pointed out that the bill specifically exempted church groups from having to disclose their communications with members as long as outside lobbyists were not orchestrating the effort. He produced letters endorsing the bill from several religious groups, including the U.S. Catholic Conference, the Religious Action Center of Reform Judaism and the Baptist Joint Committee. He accused opponents of the gift ban of ginning up the issue "to protect the desire of many members . . . to keep on playing free golf and keep on getting free baseball tickets."

One reason Democrats had to scramble to save the rule was that several members of the Congressional Black Caucus decided to vote against it as a reminder to Democratic leaders not to take their support for granted. Caucus Chairman Kweisi Mfume, D-Md., said the move had nothing to do with the lobbying bill. Indeed, Mfume and several other caucus members switched their position from no to yes in the waning moments of the procedural vote.

Senate Kills the Bill

After its near-death experience in the House, the conference report was easy pickings for opponents in the Senate.

In two separate votes, the Senate failed to cut off a Republican-led filibuster against the conference report. In the first vote Oct. 6, 10 Democrats joined 36 Republicans in voting against the cloture motion, which failed 52-46. Because the bill included a change in Senate rules, it required a two-

thirds vote of those present to pass, or 66 votes in this instance. In another vote the following day, the motion failed 55-42. *(Votes 322, 325, p. 96-H)*

Following the first vote, bill opponent Malcolm Wallop, R-Wyo., emerged from the Senate chamber to a round of applause from a group of lobbyists assembled there, many of them bearing stickers calling on senators to vote down the cloture motion. Clinton cited the Wallop incident in a news conference Oct. 7, saying, "There is something wrong when a senator can filibuster this bill and walk off the floor and be cheered by lobbyists."

Opposition grew exponentially among Republicans in the days before the cloture vote as outside groups, many of which would have been forced to disclose their lobbying activities for the first time, began to voice objections about the bill's scope. In particular, they said it could require grass-roots lobbying organizations to disclose information about their contributors that would chill citizen involvement in politics.

Levin and William S. Cohen, R-Maine, disputed that interpretation in an Oct. 6 letter to Minority Leader Dole. The provision was intended to prevent organizations from avoiding the disclosure requirements by having someone else pay a lobbyist's expenses, they said. "We believe that it is a misinterpretation to suggest that disclosure is required if a member simply contributes to the lobbying organization," they wrote.

Despite such protestations, opposition intensified as interest groups as diverse as the American Civil Liberties Union, the Humane Society of the United States and the National Right to Life Committee came out against the bill on the grounds that the disclosure requirements could prove burdensome and deter efforts to lobby on legislation. "They know that under this legislation, their members' names will be reported," said Don Nickles, R-Okla.

Majority Leader Mitchell called that assertion "a fictional objection" that senators were using "to change their position." He said the opposition to the bill that lawmakers had cited was an example of "the recent technique of urging one's supporters to call, then citing the calls as a reason to change their position . . . a most transparent technique."

Several grass-roots organizations, including Public Citizen, Common Cause and Ross Perot's United We Stand America, endorsed the bill. "There is nothing in the bill that infringes on our members' rights to communicate with their elected or hired government officials, and nothing would require us to report our membership lists or our members' volunteer activities," said a statement issued by United We Stand America.

Levin asserted that it was the Republican strategy "to stop us from doing anything significant in the way of reform, trying to persuade the public that Congress can't reform itself."

Republicans were clearly nervous about being held responsible for killing a measure that had as one of its goals toughening rules against members' accepting gifts from lobbyists. Several Republicans said the Senate could pass the gift prohibitions as a rules change, pointing out that it could be done without involving the House. But that would have required throwing out sections of the bill toughening the existing loophole-ridden laws on lobbyist disclosure, and Democrats refused to consider the move.

Mitchell made a last-ditch effort Oct. 7 to save the bill by trying to bring up a resolution to excise entirely the disputed provisions on grass-roots lobbying. But that required unanimous consent. Several Republicans objected, saying they had not had time to study the matter. Dole said that perhaps he had not studied the bill enough the first time around and that it would be better to revisit it in the 104th Congress. ∎

Rostenkowski Indicted, Defeated

Rep. Dan Rostenkowski, D-Ill., one of the most powerful members of Congress because of his position as chairman of the House Ways and Means Committee, was indicted on embezzlement, fraud and cover-up charges May 31. He declared his innocence, challenged the constitutionality of the indictment and vowed to reclaim his chairmanship, which party rules required him to relinquish while the charges were pending. But for the voters of his overwhelmingly Democratic district in Chicago, the favors Rostenkowski had done for them were not enough; he was soundly defeated in November by a little-known candidate who ran a low-profile campaign.

The indictment was the product of a high-profile investigation into the House Post Office that began in 1991. It came after Rostenkowski walked away from plea negotiations that had been going on with federal prosecutors for weeks. The 17-count indictment said Rostenkowski embezzled or misused $724,000 in public and campaign funds by paying employees House funds for personal tasks and other non-official purposes, by procuring cars for his family with House and campaign funds, by buying things for himself and associates with his official stationery account and by pocketing cash from phony stamp purchases. He also was accused of obstruction of justice for allegedly telling a witness to keep information from the prosecutors.

"I have always fought for what I believe in," Rostenkowski said in a statement issued May 30. "I strongly believe that I am not guilty of these charges and will fight to regain my reputation in court. That is a far more attractive option than pleading guilty to crimes that I did not commit."

Rostenkowski's attorneys argued that the indictment should be dismissed because it violated the Constitution's separation of powers doctrine. They said it violated the Speech or Debate Clause, which barred prosecutions based on members' legislative acts, and the Rulemaking Clause, which gave each chamber of Congress the power to make and enforce its own rules.

A federal judge in Washington upheld the indictment Oct. 14. An appeal was pending at the end of the year.

The indictment was one of a series of events that undid Democrats in 1994. It was one of many obstacles that derailed President Clinton's health care overhaul proposal, since it took the gavel out of Rostenkowski's hands at a crucial time for the House committee with the biggest role in that issue. (The committee eventually did produce a bill under acting Chairman Sam M. Gibbons, D-Fla., but neither it nor the versions produced by other key committees ever made it to the floor.) *(Health reform, p. 319)*

Some House Republicans demanded a probe by the House Committee on Standards of Official Conduct into the post office affair in general and Rostenkowski in particular, but Democrats on the ethics panel successfully resisted. The Justice Department had asked the committee to delay its probe.

Background

The case against Rostenkowski grew out of allegations in 1991 of drug dealing and embezzlement by low-level clerks at the House Post Office. Using that case as a wedge, prosecutors dug deep into the House's patronage and expense allowance systems. They began focusing on Rostenkowski in mid-1992. *(1992 Almanac, p. 47)*

The indictment was a long time in coming but had been widely expected since at least July 19, 1993, when former House Postmaster Robert V. Rota pleaded guilty in federal court to helping certain members, including Rostenkowski, illegally convert taxpayer-financed stamps and stamp vouchers to cash. Court documents also implicated former Rep. Joe Kolter, D-Pa., who was indicted Oct. 18 on charges of stealing more than $40,000 from taxpayers through stamp and stationery purchases. Kolter pleaded innocent on Oct 28. *(1993 Almanac, p. 64; Kolter, p. 53)*

Repayments Made

Early in the year, Rostenkowski reimbursed the government $82,095, acknowledging that taxpayer funds might have been used improperly to purchase items at the House office supply store for his own use.

In a statement issued Feb. 10, Rostenkowski said that the money covered items he procured though his expense account from the House office supply store. Rostenkowski said he decided to repay the House "for all sums arguably due" after he reviewed several years' worth of purchases to see if they comported with House expense account rules, which he asserted were ambiguous, flexible and ever-changing. He said he could not document all the purchases, and "erred on the side of reimbursing the government for any item which even my fiercest political adversary could question." He said the purchases were related to official activities in many cases, leaving the impression that in at least some cases, they were not.

"This reimbursement is clearly not an admission of wrongdoing but rather a sign . . . that he is trying to do the right and honorable thing," said Robert S. Bennett, Rostenkowski's attorney.

Over the weekend of Feb. 12-13, Bennett released copies of correspondence between Rostenkowski and House Administration Committee Chairman Charlie Rose, D-N.C., explaining the repayments. Rostenkowski said that many of the items — including clocks, china, books, luggage and furniture — had been used for official purposes but that he could not find records to prove it. Some items, he said, were used as gifts to officials, and he said he was not aware that this violated House Administration Committee rules.

Rostenkowski conceded that "there were some purchases by myself or others of items for personal use." He said he had relied on inadequate office procedures to make payments for them.

Rostenkowski issued three reimbursement checks to the Treasury in early January and early February. Somewhat more than half the money came from campaign funds, while the rest came from personal funds.

The purchases were made at a members- and staff-only store in the Longworth Building that provided members with all necessary office supplies. Until 1992, it stocked a range of more expensive items, including leather goods, crystal, candlestick holders and pewter. Members could order bigger items, including office chairs, Capitol china, luggage and whatever else they felt they needed to run their office. House leaders scaled back the store's inventory in response to the 1992 controversy over perks sparked by the House bank overdraft scandal. *(1992 Almanac, p. 23)*

House regulations allowed members to buy non-official items through their expense accounts, but they were supposed to repay the House (plus a 10 percent surcharge) after

they deduced from their monthly statements what was official and what was not. General Accounting Office auditors in fiscal 1988-90 checked whether the supply service was following House rules related to personal purchases and reported no "material weaknesses."

Records showed the store reported revenues of $8 million to $10 million annually in those years — enough for about $20,000 per member, though committees and other offices used the store, too. In the six years covered by the $82,000 reimbursement, 1988-93, House records showed that Rostenkowski spent more than $100,000 at the store.

Congressional Response

After Rostenkowski's reimbursement was disclosed, Democratic and Republican leaders agreed to have their staffs look into what role, if any, House officers and employees played in arranging the repayment.

Leadership aides met during the week of Feb. 14 with Bennett, who told them that Rostenkowski had consulted only with House Administration Committee staff about how to make such a repayment.

Republicans, who had complained about the pace of the investigation since the Clinton administration took over the task begun in the Republican administration of President George Bush, raised questions about the repayments. Minority Whip Newt Gingrich, R-Ga., demanded more information. House Administration Committee Chairman Rose refused to make his aides available to Gingrich's staff, but said he would meet with Gingrich personally to answer his questions, such as why he did not advise Rostenkowski to pay the House rather than the Treasury and why House leaders were not informed.

Republican Ernest Jim Istook Jr. of Oklahoma pressed the case for an investigation on the House floor. In August 1993, he had sponsored a resolution (H Res 238) to require the Committee on Standards of Official Conduct to investigate allegations that the post office gave members cash for stamps and through other improper transactions. It directed the committee to determine which members Rota implicated and whether they were under investigation by the Justice Department — facts the department was supposed to hold in confidence. Under House rules, Istook had the power to bring the resolution to the floor with two days' notice.

Istook announced Feb. 11 that he intended to call up the resolution Feb. 23. Majority Leader Richard A. Gephardt, D-Mo., drafted an alternative that called for an ethics committee inquiry only if the Justice Department did not object.

The Justice Department had several times objected that a congressional inquiry could impede its investigation. On Feb. 23, U.S. Attorney Eric H. Holder Jr., who was heading the inquiry, sent a letter to House leaders urging them to postpone an investigation. Holder said, "My request is all the more urgent now, as this important investigation is in its final stages and will be concluded in the near future."

Istook agreed Feb. 23 to postpone action on the resolution for at least a week so that leaders could try to reach a compromise. They could not, and on March 2 the House voted 238-186 to kill the Istook resolution by tabling it. *(Vote 37, p. 12-H)*

The action came after the House adopted, by a largely party-line vote of 241-184, a resolution (H Res 375) offered by Majority Leader Gephardt directing the committee to continue to consult with the U.S. attorney and to proceed with its own investigation only when it determined that "a committee inquiry would no longer interfere with the criminal investigation." No Republicans voted for the Gephardt resolution; 11 Democrats voted against it. *(Vote 36, p. 12-H)*

The floor debate was relatively subdued. Republicans argued that the unresolved case was damaging the image of the institution and that the House had an obligation to police itself. "Inaction does nothing to stop the erosion of public respect for this body," said Jim Bunning, R-Ky., a member of the ethics committee. "A three-year-old scandal is lying rotting at the heart of this House, and we need to clean it up."

Democrats did not disagree with the contention that the House could and should police its members, but they argued that doing so immediately threatened to undermine criminal proceedings. Several members cited the 1989 felony convictions against former Marine Lt. Col. Oliver L. North in the Iran-contra case that were overturned a year later because they were tainted by a highly publicized congressional inquiry. *(1990 Almanac, p. 534)*

"If I were interested in protecting a Democrat who is the target of an investigation, I would do precisely what you are trying to do," said William J. Hughes, D-N.J., to Republicans. "Because that would be the way to compromise a criminal investigation and have him walk."

Primary Election

In the face of all the bad publicity, Rostenkowski's hopes for political survival in the March 15 primary depended largely on the number of people running against him. He waited late in the campaign to put his Chicago operation into gear, taking until Valentine's Day to get phones installed in his campaign office. He depended largely on a $1 million media campaign.

Running against him were: Dick Simpson, a political science professor, former alderman and guru to Chicago's political insurgents, who got 43 percent of the vote challenging Rostenkowski in the 1992 primary; John Cullerton, a Democratic "regular" who represented Rostenkowski's ward in the Illinois senate; Mike Wojick, an alderman who had been redistricted out of his ward; and John F. McCarthy, a follower of Lyndon H. LaRouche.

To underscore Rostenkowski's value to him in Congress, Clinton traveled to Chicago Feb. 28 to give the veteran Democrat a boost for the primary election. Clinton shied away from an outright endorsement, but he warmly praised the embattled chairman. "Had it not been for his leadership last year, we would not have done the things which were done which have got this economy on the right course," Clinton said. "And we would not be able to do the things that we have to do to meet our obligations to the future in health care, welfare reform and many other areas."

Rostenkowski won a surprisingly easy victory, getting 50 percent of the vote. Finishing second was Cullerton, with 30 percent. Simpson was held to 14 percent.

Rostenkowski had been held to 57 percent in the 1992 general election by a little-known opponent who had legally changed his name to Elias R. "Non-Incumbent" Zenkich. But Zenkich got only 21 percent of the vote in 1994's five-way GOP race. The winner was attorney Michael Patrick Flanagan, a former Army captain, who got 39 percent.

Plea Negotiations

In May, reports surfaced that Rostenkowski's attorney, Bennett, was engaged in plea negotiations — perhaps to save Rostenkowski's chairmanship. Under Democratic Caucus rules, Rostenkowski would have to step down if accused or convicted of a felony punishable by two years' imprisonment or more.

Republicans raised a cry against a possible "sweetheart" deal. "If a bargain is cut which is seen by the country as an effort to keep the Clinton administration's health care leader in charge of the markup — I think the public outcry will make

it virtually impossible for that to happen," said Gingrich. The fact that Bennett had recently been retained by Clinton to defend the president in a sexual harassment suit would compound the appearance of favoritism, Gingrich added.

On May 30, with Washington abuzz with rumors of his impending indictment, Rostenkowski issued a statement declaring that he would fight to the end: "Federal prosecutors threaten to indict me if I fail to plead guilty to a series of crimes I did not commit. I will not make any deals with them. I did not commit any crimes. My conscience is clear, and my 42-year record as an elected official is one I am proud to once again run on.

"I have always fought for what I believe in. I strongly believe that I am not guilty of these charges and will fight to regain my reputation in court. That is a far more attractive option than pleading guilty to crimes that I did not commit.

"If I'm indicted, I will fight in court. I will present a compelling case to the jury, which will, I am confident, find me not guilty. As one who has regularly gone to the voters and asked for their support, I have no hesitation about making a similar case to a jury of my peers. . . . "

Rostenkowski said he would relinquish his Ways and Means chairmanship but remain active in committee deliberations. He vowed to fight for a 19th term in office.

Indictment Announced

On May 31, Holder announced in Washington at a news conference carried live on CNN and Chicago television that Rostenkowski had been indicted on 17 criminal charges. Prosecutors accused the Chicago Democrat of misusing more than $700,000 in public funds and campaign money over the course of two decades. Prosecutors said Rostenkowski padded his payroll with no-show employees, stole cash from the House Post Office, used public and campaign funds to buy cars for himself and his family, charged expensive gifts for friends and associates to his stationery account and tried to obstruct the inquiry against him.

"The allegations contained in today's indictment represent a betrayal of the public trust for personal gain," Holder said. "In essence, this indictment alleges that Congressman Rostenkowski used his elective office to perpetrate an extensive fraud on the American people."

"This is not, as some have suggested, a petty matter," he added, rejecting suggestions by House Democrats that the case was based on shifting ethical standards. "This was not conduct that was ever acceptable."

Though long anticipated, the indictment stunned Rostenkowski supporters and critics alike, for it accused him more directly and in more detail than expected. "I'm pained and shocked by the breadth and the severity of the allegations," said Rep. Charles B. Rangel, D-N.Y., a Ways and Means ally.

The indictment's particulars were as sensational as the amount of money involved: One alleged "ghost employee," a former Rostenkowski son-in-law named Roger Kopacz, supposedly was required to give his $10,400 salary back to the congressman "as cash kickbacks." Other employees allegedly were paid by public funds to renovate his house, to keep his insurance company's books and to mow grass at his Wisconsin summer home.

Rostenkowski also allegedly obstructed justice by instructing another employee who did no official work not to tell investigators about personal chores he had done.

If convicted of all charges, Rostenkowski was likely to face up to six years in prison under sentencing guidelines that included enhanced penalties for crimes involving obstruction of justice.

On June 2, Rostenkowski parted company with Bennett, the lawyer who had conducted the plea bargaining, replacing him soon afterward with an experienced trial lawyer, Dan K. Webb.

The deal that Rostenkowski turned down, according to those close to the case, would have given him about six months in jail and a $150,000 fine (minus the $82,095 he had previously reimbursed for stationery purchases and minus the value of cars that would have been repossessed). As part of the deal, prosecutors would have stopped pursuing cases against his aides.

The 43-year-old prosecutor in the spotlight, Holder, had been named in the summer of 1993 by Clinton to become U.S. attorney for the District of Columbia. He was sworn in in October of that year, and plunged into the politically sensitive case. A graduate of Columbia Law School, Holder worked from 1976 to 1988 at the Public Integrity Section of the Justice Department, which was responsible for weeding out governmental corruption. During that time, he participated in the prosecution of a Philadelphia judge, an assistant U.S. attorney in New York and a number of other politicians and government officials. He was nominated in 1988 by President Ronald Reagan as an associate judge of the District of Columbia's Superior Court. Over the next five years, he presided over hundreds of criminal trials.

Summary of Indictment

According to figures cited in the indictment, Rostenkowski misused $688,000 in public funds and $56,267 in campaign funds, for a total of $724,267. The figures came from the following allegations of misuse:

Ghost employees	$529,200
Stationery store items	$42,200
Stamps for cash	$49,300
(House funds $21,300;	
campaign and PAC funds $28,000)	
Vehicle purchases	$101,767
(House funds $73,500;	
campaign funds $28,267)	
Garage fees	$1,800

Rostenkowski's alleged crimes and the evidence against him could be divided into four areas:

● **Ghost employees.** The government said Rostenkowski padded his payroll with so-called ghost employees, people who did little or no official work. Most allegedly were paid public funds for personal, business or campaign services provided to Rostenkowski and his family.

Rostenkowski allegedly maintained close personal control over his payroll and instructed House finance officials not to disclose information about it to his aides. He placed some individuals on his payroll at irregular intervals, the government said, and he arranged to have the same payroll counselor oversee his account for more than a decade, in violation of a two-year rotation policy.

Several of the alleged ghost employees, it was claimed, were required to return their pay to Rostenkowski's Chicago district office manager, who supposedly paid them "substantially smaller" sums as they performed services for Rostenkowski.

The indictment listed 14 people paid a total of $529,200 over varying periods of time between July 1971 and July 1992 as doing little or no official work. Cited only by number, the employees were identified on June 1 by the Chicago Sun-Times. All but a few of the 14 said they did official work for their pay, sometimes at home.

The following are allegations in the indictment, along with identifications from the Sun-Times:

1. Anthony Ramirez got $20,000 for taking pictures of Rostenkowski family weddings and Wisconsin summer home parties and fund-raising dinners.

2. Harold Joseph Wills got $3,600 for personal services, including engraving gifts, while he was a full-time House sergeant at arms employee.

3. Robert B. Sulski, son of a family friend, got $3,200 as a gift to be used for college expenses.

4. Joseph J. Sodini, Rostenkowski's godson, got $1,500 for mowing the grass at Rostenkowski's Wisconsin vacation home in the summer of 1976.

5. James Nedza, son of former Illinois state Sen. Edward A. Nedza, got $48,400 for no official work over the same three years that two Rostenkowski daughters received $48,000 while on Sen. Nedza's payroll.

6. Roger Kopacz, a former son-in-law, got $10,400 for no official work shortly before marrying into the family but allegedly was required to pay the money back to Rostenkowski as "cash kickbacks."

7. Robert Russo, a tenant in a Rostenkowski family building, got $90,000 over a 10-year period. During that time, the indictment said, he spent one night every two weeks cleaning Rostenkowski's political and district offices; his wife cleaned Rostenkowski's home but received no direct compensation.

8. Sophie Palasz, another Rostenkowski tenant, got $6,800 for no official work.

9. John Kardasz got $53,600. He did little official work, but he did construction maintenance work for the family, including overseeing the renovation of Rostenkowski's home.

10. Patricia Kardasz, John's wife, got $121,400 for little or no official work.

11. Donna Burton got $61,000 for little or no official work. She did bookkeeping work for Rostenkowski's insurance company.

12. Lucille Dudzinski, wife of a Chicago precinct captain and another Rostenkowski tenant, got $32,500 for little or no work.

13. Charles Timothy Friedman Jr., a full-time employee in the House doorkeeper's office, got $21,100. He did little or no official work for Rostenkowski but performed personal services such as picking up his laundry, driving his family members around Washington and working at campaign events.

14. Barbara Koziol got $55,700. She did little or no work. The money primarily covered the rent on space in a building she co-owned that Rostenkowski used in part for his campaign.

"From the standpoint of my clients, with the exception of one whose memory has been affected by age, all say they did substantial official work," said James M. Cole, a lawyer who represented eight of the 14 alleged no-shows and who was being paid by Rostenkowski's campaign.

Nancy Panzke, Rostenkowski's Chicago office manager, also refused to back up the charges. Without naming her, the indictment said the manager maintained a supply of cash from several of the employees' paychecks and gave them "substantially smaller dollar amounts than the checks themselves." Panzke's lawyer, Nancy Luque, who also was being paid by Rostenkowski's campaign, acknowledged the existence of a cash payment system, but said that "every penny was paid to the employees." She said Panzke had not short-changed the employees or paid them for non-official work.

The government faced possible statute-of-limitations challenges because the payments involved in nine of the charges were more than five years old, and four more involved at least some payments over the five-year limit.

● **Stationery store purchases.** Rostenkowski was accused of spending about $42,200 in taxpayer funds for items at the House stationery store that he or his family gave away as gifts or kept for personal use. This included items for which Rostenkowski had reimbursed the government $82,095 early in the year.

Mentioned in the indictment were:

● About 60 armchairs hand-painted with a picture of the Capitol and inscribed with Rostenkowski's name. They cost $379 each, for a total of about $23,000. He reportedly gave some of these to friends and supporters.

● About 60 crystal sculptures of the Capitol costing a total of $12,000. He acknowledged giving some of these away.

● About 250 pieces of fine china costing about $5,000. Most of these allegedly were wedding presents.

● Twenty-six pieces of luggage that cost $2,200 and were ordered by Rostenkowski and his wife.

There was no dispute that Rostenkowski had bought such items at the store; he had admitted as much in giving back funds to the government. But Rostenkowski's letter accompanying the repayments showed that he could argue that some improper purchases were inadvertent, and that ambiguous House rules could have left members with the impression that they could give gifts from the store.

● **Stamps for cash.** The indictment alleged that Rostenkowski pocketed at least $49,300 in cash from the House Post Office through sham transactions made to look like stamp purchases. Rostenkowski allegedly worked the scheme with former Postmaster Rota. The congressman supposedly got cash in three ways: First, in 1978-87, he traded stamps he previously procured with House expense vouchers for cash; the indictment detailed seven such transactions worth $11,500. Second, in 1989-91, he traded stamps or stamp vouchers for cash; the indictment said $9,800 was taken in this period. Third, in 1989-90, he cashed $28,000 in checks from his campaign and political action committee (America's Leaders Fund) and reported them as postage purchases on Federal Election Commission reports.

The indictment alleged previously unknown details about the stamp scam: Rota supposedly gave Rostenkowski a computer-generated list so he could compare his annual stamp purchases with those of other members. (Records showed Rostenkowski bought more stamps than any other member in recent years.) Rostenkowski supposedly promised to pay Rota's legal bills the day after Rota resigned in March 1992. "Rostenkowski then instructed Rota, 'Remember — I always got my stamps,'" the indictment said. Rota, it added, then falsely denied knowing of the scheme to congressional investigators. Thereafter, Rostenkowski aide Virginia C. Fletcher supposedly drove Rota to a pay telephone in Virginia for a long-distance phone call with Rostenkowski. The indictment did not say what they discussed.

Observers said that depending principally on Rota's testimony could cause problems for prosecutors. At least twice in previous years, he had told separate sets of investigators that he knew of no members taking cash from the post office. "He is a cross-examiner's dream," said one defense attorney involved in the case.

There were potential corroborating witnesses, such as James C. Smith, a patronage employee allegedly placed in the job of overseeing the post office's stamp supply at Rostenkowski's request. Smith had a grant of immunity from prosecutors in return for his testimony. Former Rostenkowski Chief of Staff Joanna G. O'Rourke had pleaded guilty to two misdemeanors in 1993 and was cooperating with the authorities.

Investigators had determined from voucher numbers and typewriter analysis that some of the vouchers suspected of being phony came from a supply kept in the post office, not

from Rostenkowski's office supply.

● **Family vehicles.** Rostenkowski obtained personal ownership and clear title to a series of seven vehicles for himself and his family from Wil-Shore Motor Sales in suburban Chicago by paying the dealership $73,500 in House funds and $28,267 in campaign funds — a total of $101,767.

The only personal payment made by Rostenkowski and his family on a Wil-Shore debt of more than $100,000 was $5,294 from a daughter, the government said. The indictment said Rostenkowski had an account at Wil-Shore that allowed him to take lien-free title to cars without down payment, promissory notes or interest.

The House funds came in the form of 70 monthly payments of $1,050 each made on "fraudulent lease agreements" filed with the House Finance Office. The leases were supposedly for "mobile district offices," but the government said the vans became Rostenkowski's personal property and "were seldom if ever used for official purposes." He also allegedly used $1,800 in taxpayer funds to garage one of his vans for 18 months in a three-year period.

To prove that Rostenkowski committed a crime, prosecutors would have to show that he set up the whole scheme just to get free cars. Key to the case were the titles. The Chicago Sun-Times reported that the title applications for three supposedly leased cars specifically asked if they were leased. The answer "no" was checked each time, and the leases bore Rostenkowski's signature. But Rostenkowski's former lawyer, Stanley M. Brand, dismissed that fact as insignificant. "A title is an accident of convenience," he said.

Strengths, Weaknesses

Rostenkowski's fate rested on the considerable strengths and numerous weaknesses of the sweeping case against him.

Defense and prosecution lawyers sized up its strengths this way: It rested on a devastatingly simple case of alleged graft, free of complex legal theories that could confuse a jury. Yet it was rich in understandable detail. Prosecutors decided against pursuing some areas they investigated, such as renting family-owned property to the House and Rostenkowski campaign. Likewise, they did not pursue a tax case. Nevertheless, the indictment had 17 counts, so some could stick even if a jury rejected most of the case.

Moreover, there appeared to be little dispute about what happened on some charges — that he bought gifts with House funds or that the titles to government-leased cars were in his name. The only question was whether those facts constituted crimes. Finally, a web of documents and circumstances appeared to bolster the accusation leveled by the case's star witness, former House Postmaster Rota, who claimed Rostenkowski embezzled stamp funds.

The weaknesses: Many prosecution witnesses were openly hostile to the government's case and disputed the charges; others could have their credibility attacked because, like Rota, they cut deals with prosecutors to avoid lengthy prison terms. All but a few of the so-called ghost employees denied publicly that they did little or no official work. Another key witness, a Chicago car dealer, had died. Numerous counts included conduct that was many years old, leaving wide swaths of the indictment vulnerable to statute-of-limitations challenges.

Also, rules governing the accounts Rostenkowski was charged with misusing had changed over the years and sometimes seemed less than precise, complicating the government's ability to prove criminal intent, a required element in any conviction. Compounding that problem was the lack of a clear motive explaining why a powerful man with vast resources at his disposal would steal.

Reaction From Members

The indictment exacerbated Congress' image problem at a time when majority Democrats were already jittery over their election prospects in November. Some saw it as a bonanza for Republicans. "It's an indictment of the system, not just the individual," said New York Rep. Bill Paxon, chairman of the National Republican Congressional Committee. "You have an unbroken string of Democratic scandals."

But others saw potential for the indictment to tar the entire House, endangering everyone. "The institution loses more than the Republicans gain," said Rep. Jim Ross Lightfoot, R-Iowa.

Democrats hoped that voters would be able to discriminate. "I'm not sure the story comes as a bolt of revelation about Congress," said Democratic pollster Geoff Garin. "People who hate Congress may hate Congress more. But many people will take it as a story about one man."

GOP Whip Gingrich dampened the desires of some Republicans to force an immediate ethics committee inquiry, saying on television June 1, "I would be very opposed to the ethics committee getting in the way of a criminal trial."

So the Republicans pressed for the release of thousands of documents from the House Administration Committee's 1992 probe — a bitterly partisan undertaking that produced separate reports on the matter. After U.S. Attorney Holder said June 9 that he no longer objected, the Democrats backed a GOP release resolution (H Res 450) and it passed 399-2. *(Vote 228, p. 68-H)*

Members disregarded assertions by Al Swift, D-Wash., a member of the task force that ran the inquiry, that witnesses were given confidentiality pledges. A GOP panel member, Pat Roberts of Kansas, insisted that no confidentiality pledges were made. "You will be amazed at how little useful stuff is in it," said Bill Thomas, R-Calif., a task force member.

The House released 3,293 pages of secret transcripts from its 1992 internal probe on July 7. As expected, they contained no major revelations but provided details backing up the investigation's finding that the mismanaged mail operation's top officials were bent on pleasing certain members by doing special favors that sometimes had little to do with official mail delivery.

Among the new details were statements from mailroom workers that top postal officials were especially eager to please Rostenkowski, dispatching workers to help answer his office phones and stamp his name on calendars to be mailed to constituents.

On June 30, Rep. Christopher Shays, R-Conn., filed an official ethics complaint against Rostenkowski based on the indictment. Pressured by Republicans to at least open a preliminary inquiry, an ethics panel delegation met with U.S. Attorney Holder for an hour Aug. 11 to see if there was anything that could be investigated without interfering with the prosecutors. The answer was no.

The House ethics committee on Aug. 17 voted again to defer investigating Rostenkowski, again at the request of federal prosecutors who argued that an internal probe would interfere with their case. The decision was approved by voice vote in a two-hour, closed-door meeting. Ranking Republican Fred Grandy of Iowa said one member voted "nay," but he declined to say who.

Indictment Survives Challenge

Rostenkowski pleaded innocent to graft charges June 10 as his attorney previewed a tough defense strategy based at least in part on challenging the government's notion of what constituted an official expense. "I will wash away the mud

that has been splashed on my reputation," a scowling Rostenkowski told reporters after arraignment in Washington before U.S. District Judge Norma Holloway Johnson.

Webb, Rostenkowski's attorney, told reporters that the charges raised "serious constitutional concerns" because the government was interfering with congressional prerogatives. "Who determines whether or not certain expenditures are official?" Webb said. "The Constitution says that is determined by Congress." He called the indictment "a gross distortion of the true facts."

Webb called charges that Rostenkowski put no-show workers on his payroll "overblown and distorted." Rostenkowski "at no time put anyone on his congressional payroll with knowledge and intent that they would perform no services" for his office, he said. Of the stationery store, he said, "Who's going to define what is official? Congressmen themselves ought to use their best judgment. Where's the line drawn? You can't criminalize where that line is."

Arguments Rejected

Taking an aggressive tack, Rostenkowski's lawyers on Aug. 5 asked a judge to dismiss the entire indictment against him on separation-of-powers grounds — including an obstruction count that the judge had suggested did not invite constitutional challenge.

Rostenkowski's lawyers argued in court papers that the charges violated constitutional provisions giving Congress the power to make and enforce its own rules and shielding members from prosecutions based on legislative acts. They also said House rules on office budgets and campaign funds were so vague and gave members so much discretion that the case was "ill-suited for judicial resolution." They also asked Judge Johnson to cull grand jury records for improper evidence and to order prosecutors to turn over additional information about the case.

Rostenkowski's challenge was similar to one previously raised by Rep. Joseph M. McDade, R-Pa., who was charged with accepting gifts from contractors for official favors. The Supreme Court dismissed McDade's claim in early 1995. *(McDade, p. 51)*

At a July 6 hearing, Johnson had told Webb that she assumed that not all counts would be challenged on constitutional grounds. "I feel certain that on one at least, you will not be able to," she said, apparently referring to the obstruction count in informing Webb that she might allow any unchallenged count to proceed ahead of the others.

Rostenkowski's legal team argued that the entire indictment violated the Constitution's Speech or Debate Clause. "Because proof at trial will inevitably require the Justice Department or the congressman or both to explore his legislative activities, the court should dismiss the indictment," the lawyers wrote.

As for the obstruction count, they argued that prosecutors would have to submit proof about Rostenkowski's lengthy "legislative tenure" to show that he knew that House rules prohibited payment for engraving services to the witness in question.

The 16 other counts should be dismissed, they argued, because they represented a "non-justiciable" dispute — a legal concept meaning the matter was "ill-suited to judicial resolution." His lawyers asserted that the House rules were too vague for the courts to adjudicate: "There are no discoverable and manageable standards for determining whether the congressman's use of clerk hire and official expense allowances funds was within the ambiguous confines of the vague and discretionary standards of House rules."

The rules said members must use staff for official purposes but did not say what that meant, the lawyers said. As for official budgets, the lawyers cited a reference in House documents saying they should be used for expenses that, "in the member's best judgment," are needed for official duties. Adding to the confusion, they said, "the House rules are transient and continue to change."

The 16 non-obstruction counts were based on alleged rules violations, the lawyers said, and so violated the Rulemaking Clause, which gave each chamber the power to make and enforce its rules. "The indictment thus seeks to convert, through crafty pleading, alleged violations of House rules . . . into violations of federal criminal statutes," the lawyers wrote.

In papers filed Sept. 2, lawyers working for Holder argued that Rostenkowski was claiming, "in effect, that the Constitution places the whole question of whether he systematically looted the public treasury beyond the reach of the criminal law."

"The high principles he invokes," they added, "simply have nothing to say about common thievery. Certainly none creates the virtual license to steal that the congressman has imagined for himself."

As for Rostenkowski's Speech or Debate Clause argument, prosecutors claimed that the indictment was far removed from the legislative process — speeches, committee deliberations and the like. "His argument here is really a pitch for virtually absolute legislative immunity for any acts, even administrative ones, that are at all connected to his official (not legislative) duties," they said.

Judge Johnson rejected Rostenkowski's arguments Oct. 14. Johnson concluded that "the indictment charges defendant with crimes that the Speech or Debate Clause has not been held to protect." Thus, Johnson added, "the court concludes that the indictment does not violate the Constitution."

Johnson also rejected Rostenkowski's argument that he was protected under the Rulemaking Clause. "To hold otherwise would mean granting defendant a wholesale immunity from prosecution merely because his status as a member of Congress affords him certain immunities," Johnson wrote.

Rostenkowski's attorneys filed an appeal with the U.S. Court of Appeals for the District of Columbia Circuit on Oct. 25. It was pending at year's end.

November Defeat

On Nov. 8, Rostenkowski was defeated by a virtually unknown political newcomer, Michael Patrick Flanagan, a Republican who did not even hold a press conference until five days before the election. Rostenkowski managed 45 percent of the vote in a district so Democratic that for decades a primary win had been considered tantamount to election.

"It was a good campaign, even if it was only five days," said Flanagan, an attorney and Army veteran.

In contrast to the heavy media attention and high-profile display of Rostenkowski's clout in the competitive primary campaign, no one paid much attention to the race until GOP polls the week before Election Day showed the 18-term incumbent in trouble. Help that had been promised by Chicago Mayor Richard M. Daley, who rallied the troops for Rostenkowski in the primary, never materialized.

A $55,000 infusion from the Republican National Committee enabled Flanagan to advertise in what was a low-profile campaign on both sides. Rostenkowski's only campaign mailing called Flanagan a "radical right-winger" and asked for a chance to clear his name of the criminal charges. Flanagan defeated Rostenkowski in both the city and the suburban parts of the district. ∎

Packwood Ethics Probe Continues

The Senate Ethics Committee continued its probe of sexual harassment charges leveled against Sen. Bob Packwood, R-Ore., with no resolution.

The ethics panel had begun investigating charges of sexual misconduct against Packwood on Dec. 1, 1992. A few days earlier, The Washington Post had detailed the sexual harassment allegations. At least 21 women agreed to cooperate with the Ethics Committee in its probe. Packwood first denied the allegations, then apologized for any misconduct and said he was dealing with a potential problem with alcohol.

The investigation was derailed for the first quarter of 1994 while the Ethics Committee went to court to force Packwood to turn over his personal diaries. Packwood had initially allowed the panel to review transcripts and to copy relevant entries. But he balked after committee lawyers discovered entries from 1989 indicating to them that he might have improperly solicited job offers for his estranged wife from lobbyists and other associates — possibly in exchange for official favors — while in divorce court trying to minimize his alimony payments.

The committee approved a subpoena for all post-1988 diary tapes and transcripts Oct. 20, 1993. The Senate voted 94-6 on Nov. 2 to ask the courts to force Packwood to comply. Federal prosecutors began investigating the job offers shortly thereafter. As the issue moved to court, the committee learned from Packwood's diary transcriber that Packwood had altered some entries after realizing the journals might be subpoenaed. *(1993 Almanac, p. 55)*

Court Battle Over Diaries

Packwood began 1994 touring his home state, drawing small groups of protesters, and announcing that he would no longer consider resigning his seat. It was his first public tour of Oregon in months.

Back in Washington, Senate lawyers Jan. 4 filed their final legal brief in federal court in support of a request for an order forcing Packwood to comply with the Senate Ethics Committee subpoena for his diaries. On Jan. 24, U.S. District Judge Thomas Penfield Jackson upheld the subpoena. In his ruling, Judge Jackson rejected Packwood's three main legal arguments — that the subpoena was overly broad and that it violated his privacy and self-incrimination rights under the Fourth and Fifth Amendments.

Jackson declared that the subpoena was not too broad: "This court . . . has no authority to restrict the scope of the Ethics Committee's investigation." He said the panel had broad powers similar to a grand jury's. He called Packwood's contention that the committee could demand only entries relevant to its probe "manifestly impracticable" in that it would give the probe's subject the power to decide what evidence could be used.

Jackson ruled that Packwood's privacy rights under the Fourth Amendment's ban of "unreasonable searches and seizures" were outweighed by the committee's need to examine the documents as part of its constitutional duty to police the Senate. He said the committee had met the standard of "reasonableness," citing its plan to allow Packwood to mask certain private entries.

Jackson said Packwood's lawyer had relied on an outdated Supreme Court case to argue that the Fifth Amendment's bar against compelled self-incrimination covered private papers. Jacob A. Stein had cited a 108-year-old

case, *Boyd v. United States*, in which the court found that seizing a man's private papers was the same as forcing him to testify against himself. Stein argued that later cases had rejected that notion only with respect to business documents, not private papers. "The Supreme Court has largely repudiated the expansive language of *Boyd*," Jackson said.

Packwood appealed the decision and sought a stay of the order to turn over the diaries until the case could be heard. His lawyers argued that the appeal would be moot if he was forced to turn over his diaries before it was heard. What is more, they argued, turning over the diaries would cause Packwood "irreparable harm" that could not be reversed even if his appeal succeeded.

"The Senate committee would have as complete an inventory of Senator Packwood's daily activities as it was possible for him to maintain," Packwood's lawyers said in court papers. "Once delivered, it cannot be recalled."

Arguing against a stay, lawyers for the Ethics Committee argued that Packwood was unlikely to succeed on the merits of his case and that the committee would be hampered by further delay.

"Issuance of a stay . . . would severely burden the committee's ability to perform its constitutional duties," Senate lawyers argued in papers filed with the court.

On Feb. 18, a three-judge panel of the U.S. Court of Appeals for the District of Columbia Circuit ruled against Packwood, saying he had "not satisfied the stringent standards required for a stay pending appeal."

One week later, on Feb. 25, Packwood took his request for a stay to the U.S. Supreme Court. Once again, he lost. Chief Justice William H. Rehnquist rejected Packwood's request March 2.

"The criteria for deciding whether to grant a stay are well established," Rehnquist said. "An applicant must demonstrate: (1) a reasonable probability that four Justices would vote to grant certiorari; (2) a significant possibility that the Court would reverse the judgment below; and (3) a likelihood of irreparable harm, assuming the correctness of the applicant's position, if the judgment is not stayed. . . . Because this matter is pending before the Court of Appeals, and because the Court of Appeals denied his motion for a stay, applicant has an especially heavy burden.

"Applicant raises three challenges to the enforcement of the subpoena. First, he contends that the subpoena is impermissibly broad. . . . Because resolution of applicant's claim would entail a factbound determination of the nature and scope of respondent's investigation, I do not think his claim raises an issue on which four members of the Court would grant certiorari. . . . Moreover, whatever merit applicant's argument may have had initially, it has been seriously undermined by the evidence, presented to the District Court, that his diary transcripts and tapes have been altered. . . .

"Applicant next asserts that the subpoena violates his Fourth Amendment right to privacy. The District Court . . . . balanced applicant's privacy interests against the importance of the governmental interests. The Court concluded that the latter outweighed the former. . . . Because this claim thus also involves only a factbound determination, I do not think certiorari would be granted to review it.

"Finally, applicant argues that the subpoena violates his Fifth Amendment protection against self-incrimination. . . .

We recently denied a petition for certiorari raising this precise issue. . . . Our recent denial demonstrates quite clearly the unlikelihood that four Justices would vote to grant review on this issue."

On March 14, Packwood finally dropped his challenge to the subpoena. "While I am disappointed in and disagree with the court's decision, I will nonetheless abide by it," he said.

The process agreed upon by both sides provided for the taped diaries and typed transcripts to be reviewed by former Solicitor General Kenneth W. Starr, who was appointed a special master in the case. FBI experts would copy the diaries in a way that protected the originals for possible testing later to see if Packwood tried to obstruct the Ethics Committee's inquiry. The FBI would be barred from reading the transcripts or listening to the tapes to avoid aiding the Justice Department's separate criminal probe of Packwood. Starr would provide copies of the diaries to Packwood, who could mask medical and family matters. Starr would then review Packwood's work and give him 24 hours' notice before handing the papers over to the Ethics Committee.

Committee Expands Probe

The battle for the diaries over, the Ethics Committee resumed its investigation in May. Signaling a formal expansion of the probe, the panel began issuing subpoenas for documents and testimony concerning the suspicions that Packwood improperly solicited job offers for his estranged wife. Ethics lawyers questioned Georgie Packwood on July 21. She told The Oregonian newspaper in Portland that she was asked about six possible job offers in addition to the four made public in 1993. She said none of the six new offers ever materialized.

Mrs. Packwood had said she got unsolicited job offers from lobbyists and others while the couple were getting divorced in 1990. Sen. Packwood cited the offers as evidence of her earning potential to minimize his alimony payments.

Sen. Packwood had said he did nothing improper related to the job offers.

The Ethics Committee did not complete its investigation in 1994. The committee staff spent much of the remainder of the year reviewing Packwood's written diaries. The process was lengthy because of Packwood's ability to censor certain personal entries, subject to review by independent arbiter Starr. The process became more complicated when it came to the tapes themselves.

Despite his problems, with the Republican takeover of Congress in November 1994, Packwood was slated to become chairman of the Finance Committee — one of the most powerful positions in the Senate — in the 104th Congress. ∎

Misconduct Charges Plague Members

High-publicity investigations of Rep. Dan Rostenkowski, D-Ill., and Sen. Bob Packwood, R-Ore., were just part of a recurring series of congressional ethics problems that continued in 1994. At year's end, five members stood under indictment, and several former members were in trouble with the law. One senator was acquitted of felony ethics misconduct charges. Several cases left over from 1993 were resolved. *(Rostenkowski, p. 43; Packwood, p. 49)*

The cluster of criminal charges was not as big as the 1980-82 Abscam case, when an FBI undercover operation led to the bribery convictions of six House members and one senator. But coming after the 1992 House bank imbroglio, the continuing series of ethics problems served as fodder for attacks on Congress as a well of corruption.

The members under indictment were: Rostenkowski; Rep. Mel Reynolds, D-Ill.; Joseph M. McDade, R-Pa.; Walter R. Tucker III, D-Calif.; and Sen. Dave Durenberger, R-Minn. The acquitted senator was Texas Republican Kay Bailey Hutchison, who was cleared Feb. 11.

Only Rostenkowski was defeated in November. Durenberger retired. The others were to return for the 104th Congress.

Ethics investigations continued to be the focus of partisan skirmishing in the House, where a former member and campaign opponent brought accusations against Newt Gingrich, R-Ga., the Republican whip who was slated to become Speaker when Republicans took control of Congress in 1995. The Committee on Standards of Official Conduct was unable to resolve the complaints against Gingrich, which carried over into the new Congress. *(Gingrich, p. 54)*

Durenberger Re-indicted

A federal grand jury in Washington re-indicted Sen. Durenberger on Feb. 25 on charges that he fraudulently billed the Senate for his use of a Minneapolis condominium he secretly owned.

The two felony charges — one count of conspiring to make $3,825 in false claims to the Senate for stays in his condominium and one count of actually making the false claims — were identical to charges that were thrown out by a federal judge Dec. 3, 1993. *(1993 Almanac, p. 68)*

The charges against Durenberger carried penalties of up to 10 years in prison and a $500,000 fine.

In the original case, heard in St. Paul, Minn., U.S. District Judge Warren K. Urbom had ruled that the Justice Department's lawyers had tainted the case by presenting material to the grand jury that came from the Ethics Committee's 1990 proceedings against the senator for financial improprieties. That, the judge said, violated a constitutional provision barring prosecutions of members of Congress based on lawmakers' official speeches.

"There were no grounds the first time, and there are no grounds this time," Durenberger said at a Feb. 25 news conference. "I am absolutely confident that I will be exonerated in a trial, and I look forward to vindication."

The Senate had denounced Durenberger in 1990 for a larger set of condo reimbursements and for other financial transactions. He did not fight the discipline and apologized to the Senate. *(1990 Almanac, p. 98)*

The first case included indictments against Michael C. Mahoney, a Minnesota attorney who advised Durenberger on the matter, and Paul P. Overgaard, the senator's friend and 1978 campaign manager. Those indictments were dismissed at the Justice Department's request Dec. 29, 1993. The two men were not re-indicted Feb. 25.

Durenberger pleaded innocent March 10. He again asked to have the case thrown out on separation of powers grounds, but U.S. District Judge Stanley S. Harris refused July 8. He appealed to the U.S. Court of Appeals for the District of Columbia Circuit.

Durenberger announced in September that he would not seek re-election in 1994.

Hutchison Exonerated

Sen. Hutchison was exonerated of criminal ethics charges by a judge Feb. 11, concluding a legal saga that began within days of her special election victory in June 1993. Hutchison had been charged with five counts of misusing Texas state workers and equipment for personal and political gain while she was state treasurer. *(1993 Almanac, p. 69)*

Just as a state court jury in Fort Worth prepared to hear the case against Hutchison, Judge John Onion Jr. ordered a directed verdict of not guilty before a single piece of evidence was presented. Onion, who had moved the trial to Fort Worth from Austin, told the jury to find Hutchison innocent after prosecutors indicated they were not prepared to go forward. The abrupt conclusion came shortly after Onion refused to indicate whether he would allow the prosecutor, Travis County District Attorney Ronnie Earle, to submit as evidence phone and computer records that were gathered in a raid of Hutchison's office five days after her election.

Hutchison had been accused of asking state workers to run errands for her and to handle political scheduling and correspondence using state equipment. She was also accused of tampering with state records related to the case when she learned of the investigation.

Hutchison said the court case was a political vendetta by Democrats dismayed by her landslide election to fill the unexpired term of Lloyd Bentsen, who left the Senate to become secretary of the Treasury.

Hutchison was first indicted Sept. 27, 1993, but the initial charges were dismissed because one grand juror involved was later found to have been ineligible. She was re-indicted on the same charges Dec. 8, 1993. Onion dismissed the re-indictment as too vague, but he accepted an amended version in early January 1994.

Tucker Indicted

Rep. Tucker was indicted in Los Angeles on Aug. 11 on federal charges of soliciting and accepting $30,000 in bribes while serving as mayor of Compton, Calif., and of failing to report the funds on his federal income tax returns.

The 10-count indictment alleged that Tucker received $30,000 in bribes in 1991 and 1992 from a company that wanted to build a trash incineration plant. Tucker allegedly later demanded another $250,000 from the company, according to the indictment.

"I unequivocally and categorically deny all charges that have been brought against me," Tucker said in a statement. He pleaded innocent Aug. 22 and was re-elected in November with 78 percent of the vote over a Libertarian challenger. He was first elected to represent the 37th District in 1992.

The indictments followed a two-year investigation of Compton officials by the FBI. News reports said the investigation included videotaped meetings in which Tucker appeared to take money from an undercover agent in exchange for putting items on the City Council agenda.

If convicted under any of the eight extortion charges, Tucker would face a prison term of up to 20 years and a $250,000 fine. The income tax charges both carried maximum penalities of three years in prison and a $100,000 fine.

Reynolds Indicted

A Cook County, Ill., grand jury on Aug. 19 indicted Rep. Reynolds on sexual assault and other charges stemming from his alleged relationship with a girl, then 16 years old, who worked on his 1992 campaign. On Oct. 3, a Cook County grand jury indicted Reynolds on another charge, harassment of a witness.

In the first action, Reynolds was charged with three counts of child pornography, one count of solicitation of child pornography, one count of criminal sexual assault, eight counts of aggravated criminal sexual abuse of a child, five counts of obstructing justice and one count of communicating with a witness with intent to deter the witness from testifying truthfully before the grand jury. The probe was conducted by the Cook County state's attorney's office and Chicago police.

A conviction on the sexual assault charge called for a minimum sentence of four years, according to a spokesman for the Cook County state's attorney.

The 42-year-old congressman discussed the impending indictment at an Aug. 11 news conference and denied any wrongdoing. "I have been the victim of scurrilous and vicious lies," he said. "I emphatically, categorically deny any and all allegations made by a sick and disturbed woman." Reynolds, an African-American, charged that the investigation was racially motivated.

The indictment alleged that Reynolds engaged in a sexual relationship with the campaign worker from June 1992, when she was 16, to September 1993. Prosecutors alleged that Reynolds, in June of 1994, requested that the victim obtain "lewd photographs of another girl who was age 15." The age of consent in Illinois was 17. The indictment also alleged that Reynolds "induced the victim to provide false information to police and leave the state" and that he gave false information to authorities.

Reynolds denied he ever engaged in sexual relations with the young woman. He pleaded innocent Sept. 12.

In the second indictment, state prosecutors charged Reynolds with harassing a witness, saying that he had told his accuser that she could be jailed for her actions. Also on Oct. 3, William P. Davis, the director of news affairs for the Chicago Police Department, was indicted on charges of giving Reynolds information about the case. Another man, Edward McIntyre, was indicted on obstruction of justice charges for allegedly pressuring Reynolds' accuser to leave the state.

Reynolds won re-election in November without an opponent.

McDade's Appeal Rejected

A panel of the 3rd U.S. Circuit Court of Appeals on June 15 refused to dismiss a corruption indictment against Rep. McDade, the ranking Republican on the House Appropriations Committee. He appealed to the Supreme Court, but on March 6, 1995, the court turned down his appeal without comment — clearing the way for a trial.

McDade, who had steadfastly denied wrongdoing, was indicted in May 1992 on racketeering, conspiracy and illegal gratuity charges. He appealed his indictment, maintaining that the charges violated the Constitution's Speech or Debate Clause, which said, "for any speech or debate in either House," members "shall not be questioned in any other place." The clause had long been held to reach all acts related to legislative functions, including committee work. *(1992 Almanac, p. 53; 1993 Almanac, p. 72)*

The three-judge appeals panel in Philadelphia, in a 2-1 decision, declined to take a broad view of the constitutional immunity afforded members of Congress. It rejected arguments by lawyers for McDade and the House that the charges

violated the Speech or Debate Clause.

McDade and House lawyers argued that prosecutors violated the clause by including in the charges information about McDade's status as the ranking Republican on the Small Business Committee (for a time in the 1980s) and on the Appropriations Defense Subcommittee. The information was meant to bolster the prosecution's case that McDade traded the influence flowing from his posts for free travel and gifts from contractors.

Writing for himself and Judge William G. Bassler, Judge Samuel A. Alito Jr. rejected arguments that the clause always covered committee status: "This language confers rights on members of Congress in their capacity as members; it makes no reference to membership on a congressional committee or to any other position held within Congress. Consequently, we see no textual basis for arguing that a member of Congress may obtain greater protection under the Speech or Debate Clause by becoming a member of a congressional committee or attaining a leadership position." Judge Anthony J. Scirica dissented, but only on a relatively minor point.

The appeals court also rejected arguments by House lawyers that McDade's office could not constitute a criminal enterprise under the Racketeer Influenced and Corrupt Organizations Act (RICO). The judges indicated that even a committee could be considered an enterprise under RICO.

While Republicans did not make McDade step aside from his position as their leader on the Appropriations Committee in the 103rd Congress (as Democratic Caucus rules would have required for a Democrat under indictment), they denied him the committee's chairmanship when they organized for the 104th Congress. (104th Congress, p. 14)

Rose Pays Fine

Rep. Charlie Rose, D-N.C., settled a five-year-old lawsuit Oct. 27 by paying a $12,500 civil fine to the Justice Department. Rose had been accused of failing to disclose loans from 1979-85 totaling well over $100,000. Some of the money was improperly taken from his campaign committee, according to the House ethics committee, which rebuked him in 1988 for making false financial statements.

The Justice Department had sought fines of $30,000, as allowed under the Ethics in Government Act.

Rose had gone to court to block the government's suit, filed in May 1989, on constitutional grounds, but a panel of the U.S. Court of Appeals for the District of Columbia Circuit on July 12 rejected arguments by Rose and House lawyers that the civil suit violated the Constitution's separation of powers doctrine. One month later, Rose asked his attorney to try to negotiate a deal with the Justice Department to settle the lawsuit.

Rose was the chairman of the House Administration Committee, which oversaw campaign finance laws, and he was in charge of numerous efforts to improve the House's scandal-tarred image. He ran an unsuccessful effort for the leadership of House Democrats in 1994, and he lost his committee leadership post in the reorganization of the Republican-led Congress. (104th Congress, p. 14)

In his appeal, Rose argued that the suit violated the Constitution's separation of powers doctrine because the Justice Department relied on his statements to the House Committee on Standards of Official Conduct and because the panel already had investigated and rebuked him for the same false statements.

In Rose's case, the ethics committee concluded in 1988 that he had improperly borrowed almost $64,000 from his campaign account, pledged $75,000 in campaign funds to secure a personal loan and failed to disclose the loans from his campaign and various banks on his financial statements. The panel rejected Rose's assertions that the money from his campaign account was meant to repay prior unreported loans from Rose and his father to the campaign during his first successful run for Congress in 1972. (1988 Almanac, p. 40)

After reviewing the ethics report, which contained numerous pages of Rose's testimony, the Justice Department sued him for "knowingly and willfully" filing inaccurate financial statements and sought fines of $30,000. The department acted despite pleas from the ethics committee not to proceed because it had concluded that Rose's misdeeds were not knowing and willful.

With backing from House lawyers, Rose argued that members' statements to the ethics committee were protected by the Speech or Debate Clause, and therefore the department violated the clause by basing the suit on its reading of his testimony. Rose also asserted that, under the separation of powers doctrine, the Justice Department could not pile its own punishment on top of that meted out by the ethics committee.

On July 12, a three-judge panel of the U.S. Court of Appeals for the District of Columbia Circuit unanimously rejected his arguments, upholding a district judge's 1992 ruling. Writing for the panel, U.S. Circuit Judge James L. Buckley noted that Congress had given the Department of Justice the authority to enforce the Ethics in Government Act. "In bringing this action," Buckley wrote, "the DOJ was fulfilling its constitutional responsibilities, not encroaching on Congress's."

As for Rose's other argument, Buckley concluded that "Rose's testimony is not protected by the Speech or Debate Clause because it is unrelated to legislative matters."

Kennedy Cleared

The Senate Ethics Committee on Oct. 13 announced that it had decided in June not to investigate a former aide's allegations that Sen. Edward M. Kennedy, D-Mass., had harassed a female staff member and used illegal drugs.

Former Kennedy aide Richard E. Burke made the suggestions in the controversial 1992 book "The Senator — My Ten Years with Ted Kennedy." In a statement dated Oct. 13, the committee said its six members unanimously decided in June not to open a formal investigation into Burke's charges.

The Ethics Committee routinely looked into published allegations of wrongdoing by members but rarely made a public announcement unless it found grounds for the charge. The statement in the Kennedy case came after a conservative media watchdog group, Accuracy in Media (AIM), quoted Burke as saying the committee had received sworn statements alleging harassment from women who had worked for Kennedy.

In its statement, the committee not only denounced the charges but also criticized Burke. "Contrary to statements attributed to Mr. Burke, the committee did not receive complaints by women who claimed to have been sexually harassed by Sen. Kennedy," the panel said. The committee said it had interviewed "Burke and others and found no basis for his allegations nor anyone who could substantiate those allegations."

A spokeswoman for Kennedy, who was in a tough re-election race, called Burke a "discredited and disgruntled former staffer."

A day after the committee statement was released, Burke blamed AIM, saying he had only informed the group that he

had been subpoenaed by the Ethics Committee after being contacted by AIM's chairman.

Frost Case Dismissed

The House Committee on Standards of Official Conduct announced Nov. 29 that it had dismissed a complaint brought by Dallas County GOP Chairman Robert Driegert over congressional redistricting work for the 1992 elections done by the staff of Martin Frost, D-Texas.

In a letter to Frost, committee Chairman Jim McDermott, D-Wash., and ranking Republican Fred Grandy of Iowa wrote: "The committee accepts your statement that you were unaware of the prohibition on utilizing official funds for activities relating to redistricting and is of the opinion that you could have reasonably relied on House approvals for related activities in forming your belief that the expenditures were properly made."

Frost said he would reimburse the Treasury for any money spent on redistricting.

Ex-Rep. Kolter Indicted

Former Rep. Joe Kolter, D-Pa. (1983-93), was indicted Oct. 18 on five counts stemming from the House Post Office investigation, including conspiracy and embezzlement of more than $40,000. Kolter pleaded innocent Oct. 28.

The charges were similar to some of those filed against Rep. Dan Rostenkowski, D-Ill., and stemmed from the same investigation. *(Rostenkowski, p. 43)*

U.S. Attorney Eric H. Holder Jr. said in a statement that the Kolter indictment "demonstrates our office's continuing commitment to hold accountable all those connected to the House Post Office who have engaged in criminal conduct." Eight individuals, including former House Postmaster Robert V. Rota and former top Kolter aide Gerald W. Weaver II, had been convicted on charges related to the scandal.

Kolter was accused of billing $33,000 worth of personal House Stationery Store purchases to official accounts and converting $11,000 worth of postage stamps into cash for his own use. The indictment stated that Kolter instructed Rota to convert vouchers and stamps into cash over a six-year period.

The indictment alleged that Kolter purchased 40 watches and clocks at a cost of $4,300; more than 30 Mont Blanc pens, worth $3,300; more than 650 pieces of china and glassware, worth $21,000; about 30 pieces of luggage, worth $2,000; two 20-inch gold necklaces, worth $220 each; and approximately 40 wooden boxes picturing the Capitol at a cost of $28 each.

Kolter served from 1983 to 1993; he was defeated in a four-way primary in 1992.

Ex-Rep. Perkins Pleads Guilty

Former Rep. Carl C. Perkins, D-Ky. (1985-93), pleaded guilty Dec. 20 to three federal felony charges stemming from overdrafts at the defunct House bank, false reports filed with the Federal Election Commission (FEC) and omissions on his 1990 financial disclosure statement.

Perkins faced a maximum sentence of 40 years in prison and a $1.5 million fine. On March 13, 1995, he was sentenced to 21 months in prison, as well as ordered to serve three years' probation, to perform 250 hours of community service and to complete any alcohol treatment program required by his probation officer.

Perkins, who represented Kentucky's 7th District from 1985 to 1993, pleaded guilty to one count of bank fraud for his involvement in a check-kiting scheme from April 1990 through July 1990 that involved several financial institutions, including the House bank.

His father, Carl D. Perkins, had served as a Kentucky Democrat in the House from 1949 to his death in 1984 and had been chairman of the Education and Labor Committee from 1967.

Ex-Rep. Hubbard Pleads Guilty

Former Democratic Rep. Carroll Hubbard Jr. of Kentucky (1975-93) pleaded guilty April 5 to charges that he misused congressional employees, violated federal election laws and obstructed justice. Hubbard was sentenced Nov. 9 to three years in prison for three felony convictions. U.S. District Judge Louis Oberdorfer of the District of Columbia Circuit also ordered Hubbard to pay $153,000 in restitution. He said Hubbard had "obviously and seriously jeopardized" public confidence in government.

Hubbard's wife, Carol Brown Hubbard, pleaded guilty to a misdemeanor charge April 5 in connection with the case and was put on probation.

The case grew out of the Justice Department's investigation of members' House bank overdrafts, although the charges against Hubbard related only indirectly to his use of the bank.

Hubbard admitted falsifying his campaign reports by concealing numerous disbursements to himself and others, including some that were secretly funneled into his wife's 1992 campaign for a House seat. Both Hubbards lost in the primary. Hubbard also admitted stealing government property by having House employees work on his and his wife's campaigns and perform personal tasks. Mrs. Hubbard admitted aiding and abetting this theft. Finally, Hubbard admitted obstructing justice by staging a burglary at one of his Kentucky offices to make it look as if his House bank and campaign records had been stolen and directing an employee to shred documents that had been subpoenaed.

'Ghost Voting'

House Democratic and Republican leaders on May 18 moved to quash rumors of "ghost voting" by members, saying there was no basis for an investigation. "There is no evidence of any voting irregularity of any kind," said Speaker Thomas S. Foley, D-Wash.

Foley and Minority Leader Robert H. Michel, R-Ill., acknowledged looking into rumors that one member might have used the voting cards of other members to record votes for them on the House's electronic voting system.

Having one member vote on the floor for others was a violation of House rules. In 1987, Austin J. Murphy, D-Pa., was reprimanded for several instances of misconduct, including allowing someone else to vote for him. *(1987 Almanac, p. 29)*

Richard W. Pombo, R-Calif., said in a May 18 statement that in February he saw several of the voting cards in the possession of one member and reported it to Michel. "I saw a member drop on the floor what appeared to be a number of voting cards," Pombo's statement said. He did not allege that he saw a member use the voting cards.

On May 17, Michel obtained electronic voting records for two days, one each in February and March, according to a GOP aide.

The following morning, Minority Whip Newt Gingrich, R-Ga., hinted that a scandal was about to the rock the House,

although he declined to provide details. That same morning, Chief Deputy Whip Robert S. Walker, R-Pa., alluded to ghost voting during a floor speech. Walker had introduced legislation May 4 to make ghost voting a crime.

But a few hours later, Michel and Foley separately said there was no basis for an investigation. Foley said May 19 that many members had multiple voting cards because they had been issued replacements for cards that had been temporarily misplaced. Sometimes, he said, members took several cards to the floor to discover which one had been activated for voting. ∎

Incoming Speaker Gingrich Focus of Investigation

The House ethics committee was unable to conclude its hottest case, an investigation of Newt Gingrich, R-Ga., the next Speaker, and carried the matter over to the 104th Congress.

On Nov. 29, the outgoing leaders of the Committee on Standards of Official Conduct, Chairman Jim McDermott, D-Wash., and ranking Republican Fred Grandy of Iowa, said the panel did not have enough information to decide whether Gingrich violated House rules in soliciting tax-deductible contributions for a college course he taught.

The original complaint against Gingrich was filed Sept. 7 by his opponent in the November election, former Rep. Ben Jones, D-Ga. It contended that Gingrich had improperly used funds donated to a political action committee, GOPAC, which he headed, to support a controversial college course Gingrich taught. In January 1995, Jones amended his complaint to include a controversial book deal that Gingrich signed in December.

Gingrich called Jones' complaint "nonsense" and said it was politically motivated.

In response to the Jones complaint, the Committee on Standards of Official Conduct on Oct. 31 sent Gingrich a letter asking for information to determine whether the course was aimed at helping Republican candidates. The panel also wanted to know why Gingrich did not inform it of the college course's ties to GOPAC when he requested permission to undertake the course in 1993.

The committee met during the short lame-duck session in November, but it was unable to resolve the issue.

On Dec. 8, House Democratic Whip David E. Bonior of Michigan called for an independent counsel to investigate the case. "For the past 15 years, this is exactly the same way similar situations have been handled, for Democrats and Republicans," said Bonior. "In nearly every single high-visibility ethics case since 1979, the ethics committee has retained outside counsel to investigate the charges."

Carrying over the case to the next Congress put Gingrich in the uncomfortable position of being able, as Speaker, to select his party's members for a panel that would judge his case. To avoid the appearance of favoritism, Gingrich and Democratic leaders agreed to begin the 104th Congress with a reduced panel of five members from each party, all of whom had served on the committee in the 103rd Congress.

The media attention to his behavior was uncomfortable for Gingrich for another reason: He had filed the ethics complaint against Democratic Speaker Jim Wright of Texas, who resigned in 1989 after the ethics committee accused him of violating rules through a lucrative book deal and a business relationship with a hometown real estate developer. *(1989 Almanac, p. 36)*

College Course

At the heart of Jones' complaint was a college course that Gingrich taught, "Renewing American Civilization." Jones suggested that the course was a partisan political exercise that, under tax law, should have been kept free of partisan influence, and that GOPAC improperly helped raise money for it.

Gingrich had decided in early 1993 to teach the class, and Kennesaw State College in Georgia expressed an interest in hosting it. The college's tax-exempt foundation was to be the recipient of contributions to pay for the course.

To run the course, a longtime Gingrich associate, Jeffrey A. Eisenach, left his position as executive director of GOPAC. But Eisenach retained close ties to GOPAC. His consulting firm, Washington Policy Group, took on GOPAC as a client even as he was raising money through tax-deductible contributions to fund Gingrich's course.

In the fall of 1993, when controversy arose over Gingrich's course, the Georgia Board of Regents voted to stop elected officials from teaching courses at state colleges. Gingrich moved the course to private Reinhardt College, and it was made available to other groups and some GOP organizations by satellite or on video. Its financing was taken over by the Progress and Freedom Foundation, incorporated as a tax-exempt corporation in Washington in April 1993 and headed by Eisenach.

Jones asked the ethics committee whether the Progress and Freedom Foundation had tilted too far toward the Republicans. Federal law required such foundations to be nonpartisan, and some groups had lost their tax-exempt status for training political operatives of just one party. According to the Atlanta Journal-Constitution, Gingrich had stated that he hoped his course would help mold debate in the 1996 presidential campaign and help recruit 200,000 grass-roots workers nationwide.

Of the $1.5 million spent by the foundation between April 1993 and December 1994, 43 percent, or $632,115, went for "Renewing American Civilization" and a weekly call-in show, "Progress Report," that Gingrich hosted on National Empowerment Television, a cable network.

Jones maintained that the majority of donors were merely looking for a way to contribute to Gingrich in excess of federal campaign limits. In addition, Jones said Gingrich improperly used his Washington office for the project by involving two of his congressional press secretaries and using government equipment and stationery.

GOPAC Executive Director Lisa B. Nelson said the committee followed "campaign finance law to the letter." A spokesman for the Gingrich campaign dismissed the suit as a "scurrilous smear," adding that "this was filed for political gain."

GOPAC Background

GOPAC was a political action committee founded by former Delaware Gov. Pierre S. "Pete" DuPont IV in 1979 as a way to help elect state and local Republicans to office. The idea was to groom a GOP farm team that would be available to run for Congress later. Gingrich took over GOPAC in 1986. Past and present GOPAC employees were involved in Gingrich's other endeavors, and many GOPAC contributors had helped fund them.

Unlike most other political action committees, GOPAC made very few contributions directly to candidates. Instead, the group concentrated on education and training programs for candidates. "The theory was to teach them to fish instead

of giving them a fish," said Eisenach.

Much of the controversy centered on the secrecy of GOPAC's contributor lists. Under Federal Election Commission (FEC) rules, a group that gave money to both federal and state candidates had to indicate which percentage went to federal candidates and disclose only that amount. However, if money was spent to help both federal and state candidates using activities such as a "get out the vote" drive, all of the expenditures had to be reported to the FEC, although the sources of those contributions did not have to be disclosed.

GOPAC maintained that 90 percent of its money was spent for state and local campaigns, and that therefore it did not have to disclose most of its contributors to the FEC. As a result, while GOPAC reported spending $3,954,645 between Jan. 1, 1993, and Dec. 31, 1994, the group revealed the source of only 12 percent of that money, or $477,208.

The election commission sued GOPAC in U.S. District Court, claiming that the committee spent money on the 1990 congressional campaigns and therefore should have registered and filed disclosure statements then instead of two years later. The issue was when GOPAC should have started filing statements with the FEC, not whether the group should disclose a greater percentage of its contributors than it did.

Following the Republican victory in November, GOPAC Executive Director Nelson said the committee would release the names of all future contributors.

Book Deal

Two weeks before he was to be sworn in as Speaker, Gingrich signed a deal with the publishing company HarperCollins to write one book and edit another. His advance: $4.5 million. Immediately, the deal was attacked by Democrats, and some Republicans as well, who believed Gingrich was cashing in on his office.

What caused the flap was that the owner of HarperCollins was media mogul Rupert Murdoch, who also owned Fox Broadcasting Co. and who spent $135,881 to lobby Congress in 1994 in favor of deregulating the broadcasting industry. Deregulation would allow Fox to own more TV stations and gain more flexibility in using the broadcast spectrum.

Gingrich initially defended the book deal, saying it was similar to Vice President Al Gore's arrangements. Gore had earned almost $1 million in advances and royalties from his book, "Earth in the Balance." After a week of controversy, Gingrich agreed to forgo the advance, agreeing instead to accept $1 plus royalties. Murdoch said Gingrich would receive a 15 percent royalty for each hardcover book sold and 10 percent for each paperback and audiocassette sold.

The controversy subsided until the New York Daily News reported Jan. 12, 1995, that Murdoch met with Gingrich while negotiations were under way on the book deal. Gingrich said he was unaware that Murdoch owned HarperCollins; both men said the book deal never came up during their meeting. ∎

Democratic Titans Pass From Scene

The rout that swept the Democrats out of power Nov. 8 took with it a string of prominent Washington figures — chief among them Thomas S. Foley, D-Wash., the first House Speaker to be defeated since 1862. Several other powerful lawmakers, including the Senate majority leader and the House minority leader, retired. Death took two members of the House. *(Elections, p. 561)*

In all, seven of the 10 most senior Democrats in the House during the 103rd Congress were gone after 1994.

In addition to Foley, the following members ended their careers with the Congress:

● Sen. George J. Mitchell, D-Maine, the Democratic majority leader since 1989, who retired. He had led his colleagues to numerous victories over President George Bush but was less successful in delivering President Clinton's program into law. He helped Clinton win most of his economic package and two major trade agreements but ran aground with his, and Clinton's, top priority: a major restructuring of the nation's health care system. Mitchell had served since 1980. *(Health care, p. 319)*

● Rep. Robert H. Michel, R-Ill., the House minority leader since 1981, who retired. He left having served the longest (38 years) without ever having been in the majority. On Nov. 29, in the lame-duck session, Foley allowed Michel to wield the Speaker's gavel he had so long been denied and preside over the House for a few minutes. The senior Republican in the House, Michel had served since 1957. *(Retirement announcement, 1993 Almanac, p. 19)*

● Rep. Jamie L. Whitten, D-Miss., who served a record 53 years in the House before retiring. The chairman of the Appropriations Committee throughout the administrations of Ronald Reagan and George Bush, he had been stripped of his gavel because of illness. He had served since 1941. *(Record, 1991 Almanac, p. 12; chairmanship, 1992 Almanac, p. 22)*

● Rep. William H. Natcher, D-Ky., the chairman of the Appropriations Committee after Whitten, who died March 29. He had served since 1953. *(Natcher, p. 58)*

● Rep. Dan Rostenkowski, D-Ill., the chairman of the Ways and Means Committee since 1981, who was defeated by an unknown who campaigned against entrenchment and corruption. On May 31, Rostenkowski had been indicted on embezzlement, fraud and cover-up charges and forced by Democratic Caucus rules to step aside as chairman. He had served since 1959. *(Rostenkowski, p. 43)*

● Rep. Jack Brooks, D-Texas, the second-senior member of the House and the chairman of the Judiciary Committee since 1989, who was defeated. He had served since 1953.

● Sen. Jim Sasser, D-Tenn., the chairman of the Budget Committee since 1991, who was defeated. He had been running against Tom Daschle, D-S.D., to succeed Mitchell as his party's leader in the Senate. He had served since 1977. *(104th Congress, p. 14)*

● Sen. Donald W. Riegle Jr., D-Mich., chairman of the Senate Banking Committee since 1987, who retired. He had been weakened by a 1991 reprimand for his activities in behalf of savings and loan magnate Charles H. Keating Jr. He had served since 1976. *(1991 Almanac, p. 26)*

● Rep. William D. Ford, D-Mich., chairman of the Education and Labor Committee since 1991, who retired. He had served since 1965.

● Rep. Neal Smith, D-Iowa, a longtime Appropriations subcommittee chairman, who was defeated. He had lost a bid to succeed Natcher as chairman of the committee. He had served since 1959.

Foley's Fall

Foley was a surprise loser and one of the last Democrats to concede defeat, getting 49.5 percent of the vote to his challenger's 50.5 percent. On Nov. 9, Foley extended a hand of help to the victorious George Nethercutt, 50, a Spokane lawyer and former Spokane County GOP chairman.

"I know the thrill of election as well as the honor of service. We understand the thrill George Nethercutt and his family are feeling," Foley said in an emotional but controlled farewell from Spokane. "It is finally my hope that we will have with this new Congress an opportunity to see a new spirit of bipartisanship. ... Despite what some might think, the overwhelming membership of Congress, Republicans and Democrats, are wonderful, upstanding, talented people."

Such characteristic graciousness, rooted in reverence for the House, was what most worked against Foley in the hard-fought race. The same trait, too, had thwarted him as he struggled to balance his dual role as the institutional leader of the House against his partisan position as the congressional torchbearer of his party.

"His own personal decency is what ultimately prevented him from winning this race," said Tony Coelho, a former Democratic whip who resigned from the House in 1989 in the face of questions about his investments. "In many ways, that is the most graceful way to go out. He would not want to end up as minority leader."

No single misstep toppled Foley. Instead, Nethercutt was able to paint Foley's long career as the profile of an entrenched and worn politician. He pounced on Foley for challenging the constitutionality of a term limit initiative approved by Washington voters in 1992. While Foley maintained that he only wanted to preserve the integrity of the House, Nethercutt made much of the image: career politician locked in a litigious relationship with his voters. The National Rifle Association, Foley's longtime ally, also trained its sights on the Speaker for supporting a ban on military-style assault weapons.

Foley's sprawling 5th District had long favored Republican positions. Foley previously had always navigated to victory, though he won only 48 percent of the vote in a three-way contest in 1978 and 52 percent of the vote two years later.

A Vigorous Defender

From Foley's first candidacy in 1964, a race reluctantly pursued at the urging of his former boss and political mentor, the late Sen. Henry M. "Scoop" Jackson, to his defeat, Foley consistently displayed a distaste for the nastiness in American politics. When then-Majority Leader Foley was chosen as Speaker in June 1989 (during the 101st Congress) after the resignation of Jim Wright of Texas, his reserved and cool style was seen as the antidote to Wright's roughshod partisanship.

In the 102nd Congress, however, as the scandal involving members' overdrafts at the House bank unraveled, Foley's measured quality looked to panicked colleagues like indecision. Members blamed him for failing to anticipate the outrage of the electorate. Foley survived the storm. He reacted by pushing reforms of House procedures and asserted himself more directly to project a Democratic legislative agenda. Moreover, he proceeded to politic for his own job, lining up the support of key chairmen and campaigning in behalf of members senior and junior alike. He was re-elected Speaker for the 103rd Congress without opposition in the Democratic Caucus.

Clinton's election further invigorated Foley and strengthened his support. His colleagues had often bristled at his laid-back style and tendency to seek conciliation during Bush's presidency.

Foley pledged to see Clinton's program to enactment. At the outset, he succeeded in pushing the president's politically hazardous economic program to passage in the House.

But even an energized and assertive Foley was not immune to criticism. Throughout the early months of 1993, many Democrats, including some who previously had chastised him as unwilling to lead, chafed at being pushed and shoved. Republicans railed against the leadership's use of "closed" rules to limit floor debate and amendments on legislation. Nonetheless, Foley rallied the House to enact Clinton's budget proposal, the "economic stimulus" package and the North American Free Trade Agreement (NAFTA).

Foley's steady climb to the pinnacle of his party came without the kind of vaunting ambition usually associated with such success. In 1974, he chaired the Democratic Study Group, which was the strategy and research arm of liberal and moderate Democrats. The next year, he became Agriculture Committee chairman in unusual circumstances. His predecessor, the elderly and conservative W.R. Poage, D-Texas, was targeted for removal by the huge bloc of reform-minded "Watergate baby" Democrats. Ever the institutionalist, Foley backed Poage; but when he was unseated anyway, the insurgents promoted Foley over several more senior members.

Foley continued to rise within Democratic ranks, becoming chairman of the caucus in 1977. After the 1980 election, the whip's job opened up. Then-Speaker Thomas P. O'Neill Jr., D-Mass., facing an adversarial relationship with newly elected President Reagan, was looking for a successor with parliamentary skills. Rostenkowski, then the chief deputy whip, was first in line, but when he decided to take over Ways and Means instead, Foley was picked.

When O'Neill announced his plan to retire at the end of the 99th Congress, Foley did not seem to be guaranteed the majority leader's spot, but no challenger emerged. The same dynamic was apparent when, in 1989, Foley rose without opposition to the speakership.

Lynne P. Brown, a political scientist at New York University and a former Foley staff member, said O'Neill's "very good political sniffer" stood in contrast to the cerebral overlay of Foley's political instincts. O'Neill often said, Brown noted, that "the real problem with Foley was that he had too many hands — on the one hand, on the other."

Foley himself once conceded: "I think I am a little cursed with seeing the other point of view and trying to understand it."

Other Defeated Speakers

Foley's defeat marked only the third time that a sitting Speaker had been denied re-election, according to the House historian, Raymond W. Smock. The previous defeats came in 1860 and 1862.

The first to lose, William Pennington, shared (with Henry Clay in 1811) the distinction of having been elected Speaker as a freshman. But he presented a dramatic contrast to "the Great Compromiser" Clay or the erudite Foley.

Pennington, the former Whig governor of New Jersey, went to Congress as a member of the new Republican Party. The House, riven by the slavery issue, deadlocked on its choice for a Speaker for eight weeks in 1859, turning to the freshman in desperation on the 44th ballot. "Unlike Clay, Pennington was chosen in spite of his credentials and avowed policies, and not because of his abilities and views," scholar Ronald M. Peters Jr. wrote in "The American Speakership."

The experiment was not a success. Pennington "is said to have bragged in early life that he would get along with as lit-

tle study as possible," according to a 1934 biography. "As a newcomer he was totally unfamiliar with the procedure, and many were the stories told of his ignorance."

Pennington was defeated by a narrow margin in 1860. He died two years later, apparently from an accidental overdose of morphine.

Pennington's successor, Galusha A. Grow, also lost at the polls. Elected in 1850 as a Democrat, he became a Radical Republican as a protégé to fellow Pennsylvanian Thaddeus Stevens. He was elected Speaker after Abraham Lincoln became president, although Stevens, as chairman of the Ways and Means Committee, ran the House. Grow pushed through the Homestead Act, which gave free land to settlers, but lost badly in 1862 when his district was redrawn and the Civil War's push toward Pennsylvania made the war less popular there.

In 1894, at age 71, Grow was re-elected to the House. He served nine years, according to a 1932 biography, "as a veritable Nestor," referring to the wise old counselor of Homer's "Iliad."

Mitchell Retires

Mitchell's March 4 announcement that he would not run for re-election stunned his colleagues. To them, he had been an adroit and effective leader who was vital to any chances of enacting their program. He had been elected leader in 1988 and was expected to win re-election.

"This is the right time for me to consider other challenges and to give someone else the chance to serve," he said in his announcement made on Maine television.

He declined comment on reports that he was being considered for the vacant job of commissioner of Major League Baseball. A former federal judge, Mitchell also had been mentioned as a possible nominee to the Supreme Court.

Although his decision came as a surprise, some associates had seen signs that the demands of being majority leader — the job of taming 99 strong personalities into a disciplined legislative body — had begun to take its toll on Mitchell.

"He was getting worn down," said Christopher J. Dodd, D-Conn. "The prospect of six more years of doing that is a long commitment."

While Mitchell clearly enjoyed having more power to enact legislation when he was working with a Democratic president, in many ways he got more personal glory while George Bush was president and he was top dog among Democrats in Washington. He relished the role of opposition spokesman, and his tough partisan rhetoric seemed to get under Bush's skin. Bush aimed some harsh words at Mitchell in a magazine interview after the president was ousted from the White House. "Mitchell's purpose, his goal, was simply to bring my presidency down, and to some degree he deserves credit for that," Bush said.

Mitchell won the leadership post in 1988, handily beating J. Bennett Johnston of Louisiana and Daniel K. Inouye of Hawaii. *(1988 Almanac, p. 30)*

In his first Congress as leader, he achieved something he had declared his No. 1 legislative priority when he arrived in the Senate in 1980: legislation to clean up the nation's air. He worked with Bush to reauthorize the law in the 102nd Congress but then pushed Bush into vetoing legislation on family leave, voter registration, abortion counseling, campaign finance and trade with China.

In the 103rd Congress, Mitchell could claim credit for pushing through Clinton's deficit-reduction package without benefit of a single Republican vote and for working with Republicans to approve NAFTA. In early 1994, Congress also enacted legislation undoing Bush's vetoes on family leave, voter registration and political rights of federal workers.

But the end of the Congress proved bitterly disappointing. A campaign finance bill that Democrats had long sought was killed by Republicans, and Mitchell was powerless in the closing days of the regular session to move other major legislation. The biggest failure was the stillborn effort to revise the nation's health care system — a goal that Mitchell had hoped to make the crowning achievement of his last year in office.

Eyeing Supreme Court Post

Talk of Mitchell as a potential Supreme Court justice had seemed irrelevant until April 6, when Justice Harry A. Blackmun announced that he would retire. *(Breyer, p. 303)*

Speculation immediately turned to Mitchell, and the White House did little to quell it. Mitchell seemed to offer Clinton an appealing combination of traits. Mitchell had real-life experience as a prosecutor and judge, as well as a legislator. His ideological credentials on such issues as abortion and the death penalty were indisputably liberal. Moreover, his ability to work for consensus suggested that he could lead and cajole fellow justices in the direction Clinton wanted.

At a time when Clinton could ill afford to spend political capital on a protracted nomination fight, Mitchell seemed like the dream candidate. After his name was floated, Mitchell won praise on both sides of the aisle and seemed assured of easy confirmation. "He's the only progressive, pro-choice person who could make it through the Republican minefield up here," said Sen. Tom Harkin, D-Iowa.

Minority Leader Bob Dole, R-Kan., seemed to signal as much. "I think President Clinton couldn't do any better," he said.

But a Mitchell nomination would have been fraught with political and legal complications. A key question was whether sending Mitchell through the confirmation process would hamper the health care bill. And if the demands of confirmation had required Mitchell to step down as leader before the end of the year, it would have complicated and intensified the competition among Democrats to succeed him as leader.

Mitchell also faced a potential obstacle in the Constitution, which prohibited a lawmaker from accepting a federal job if, during the member's term, Congress had voted to increase the pay for the office — as it had during Mitchell's tenure.

Mitchell boosters had argued that those problems could have been addressed — by, for example, delaying the vote on his confirmation, postponing his swearing-in to the court and lowering the salary for his seat.

Mitchell ended the speculation April 12 with another surprise announcement, this time taking himself out of the running for the court seat.

Mitchell said he was afraid that being a court nominee would hurt his ability to effectively push health care and other legislation as majority leader. "I believe there exists a rare opportunity to achieve comprehensive, meaningful reform of our health care system this year," Mitchell said at a news conference. "I don't think that opportunity is going to come along again at any time in the future if we don't seize it this year."

At an hourlong meeting with Clinton on April 11, shortly after Clinton and White House aides met to discuss his nomination, Mitchell asked him not to consider him for the post. "I told the president that I felt that a nomination to the Supreme Court at this time could affect my ability to serve as majority leader," Mitchell said at his news conference. "I think it is going to require every bit of energy and effort and concentration that I have to pass [health care legislation] and the other

important measures" on the Senate agenda.

Clinton confirmed that Mitchell had been on the brink of nomination. Clinton thanked the senator April 12 "for his willingness to forgo a great personal opportunity, in anticipation of an enormous struggle with an uncertain result." Although he and Clinton said they did not discuss possible future vacancies, Mitchell made plain his continuing interest in serving on the court if another opportunity came.

The speculation about Mitchell as baseball commissioner also came to naught in 1994. Although he was open about his interest in the top baseball job, a strike by baseball players that wiped out the World Series and dragged on into the following spring left that post vacant.

Natcher Dies

With Natcher's death, the House lost its last link to a bygone political era — a time when members campaigned and legislated largely on their own, with nothing like the retinue of aides and handlers and the immense re-election budgets that had become the rule.

Natcher, 84, who had been ailing for much of the year, died of heart failure at Bethesda Naval Hospital the evening of March 29. He was buried April 6 in Bowling Green, Ky.

Natcher was best known by the time of his death for a record without precedent: He had voted at every opportunity — 18,401 roll calls — until illness brought him down. His struggle to maintain that record created a drama that gripped the House in early March.

Clinton, who had visited Natcher in the hospital a few weeks earlier to give him the Presidential Citizens Medal, said the citation that accompanied the medal offered a fitting remembrance for Natcher's career: "Few legislators in our history have honored their responsibilities with greater fealty or shunned the temptations of power with greater certainty than William Huston Natcher."

In a Congress increasingly populated by aggressive, telegenic legislators adept at snappy sound bites, the 20-term congressman from central Kentucky was a throwback: a courtly, diligent lawmaker who drew little attention to himself and avoided most of the trappings thought to be indispensable to a modern member of Congress.

Unlike many of his colleagues in an age of expanding staffs, Natcher had only a handful of people on his office payroll, all women, whom he referred to as his "ladies." He kept details of his voluminous legislative work in his head, where he also had stored Roberts Rules of Order, memorized when he was a law student in the 1930s. He had no press secretary, and though he extended his usual courtliness to reporters, he rarely granted formal interviews.

He ran his campaigns for next to nothing, with no television advertising and no financial contributions from others. In 1990, when his Republican challenger shelled out nearly $145,000, Natcher spent $6,766 of his own and won two-thirds of the vote. Two years later, he cut his spending slightly — to $6,624 — and won with 61 percent.

"Some people are spending $1 million on House races," Natcher once lamented. "That's wrong. It's morally wrong. I don't believe they can really represent their people if they are taking money from these groups [political action committees]."

Despite his prominent role in Congress — as chairman of two Appropriations subcommittees, then as chairman of the full committee — Natcher eschewed publicity and kept much to himself. In Washington, he withdrew habitually to make a record of the day's events in his diary, 54 volumes of which he sent to the Government Printing Office to be bound at his expense, with plans to release them after his death. In his district, he campaigned without an entourage, refusing reporters' requests to accompany him.

Natcher issued one news release a year: It announced the record he continued to set for perfect attendance at roll calls on the floor.

End of the Vote String

Natcher's struggle to maintain that record created the sort of fuss in his final days that he always abhorred. But he and the House went to extraordinary lengths to keep his string alive. On March 1, the House canceled its votes to enable Natcher to stay in the hospital for medical treatment. On March 2, he was brought to the Capitol by ambulance and wheeled into the House chamber four times on a gurney to vote. On March 3, however, he was unable to return, and he missed four votes. He did not return to Congress.

His last day of votes was dramatic. About two dozen reporters watched as Natcher, looking gaunt and frail and accompanied by four medical attendants, was wheeled from his committee office to the nearby House chamber. Two aides wheeled him onto the floor, where he cast his vote by handing in a green card, signifying a "yes" vote, instead of the usual electronic method.

Although he was hooked up to oxygen and intravenous tubes, the courtly chairman was dressed as usual in a three-piece suit with a vest. His last vote was cast just before 8 p.m. on a resolution relating to an ethics investigation of the House Post Office scandal. After voting, he spoke briefly with Foley and other members before being wheeled back to his office.

Natcher cast his first legislative vote Jan. 21, 1954, to approve the building of the Air Force Academy in Colorado. He first won office Aug. 1, 1953, in a special election, but Congress adjourned before he could be sworn in.

For years, acknowledging the burden he had imposed on himself, Natcher warned other members not to try to follow in his footsteps. "Having a perfect voting record was the worst mistake he ever made," said Brooks, who had served in the House a year longer than Natcher.

Appropriator and Parliamentarian

Natcher became a member of the Appropriations Committee his second year in the House, and he helped set the standard of collegiality that for decades defined the panel. As chairman of the District of Columbia subcommittee for 18 years, he was known as "the mayor of Washington" before the District got home rule. He went on to chair the far more influential Subcommittee on Labor, Health and Human Services, and Education. In December 1992 he became chairman of the full Appropriations Committee, when House Democrats formally removed Whitten because of ill health.

As chairman of the Appropriations subcommittee that funded health, education and social service programs, Natcher was reluctant to earmark money for members' pet projects, seeing that practice as eating into the amount of money available for broad-based social programs.

With his exacting nature, Natcher could come across as flinty, and members were loath to cross him, because he was reputed to forget no slight. But colleagues respected his calm evenhandedness and firm command in the heat of legislative battle. He was often called to sit in the Speaker's chair to preside over the House during contentious floor debates. After Natcher's handling of the potentially raucous House debate over immigration legislation in 1986, his colleagues gave him a standing ovation for nearly a minute.

"Bill Natcher runs the House as a parliamentarian better than anyone I've ever seen," Speaker O'Neill once said.

Whitten Retires

Whitten announced April 5 that he would not run for re-election in 1994 after 53 years in Congress, the longest service in the history of the House. While Whitten ended his career with little of the power he had wielded as chairman of the Appropriations Committee, he had been able to channel billions of dollars in federal aid to his poor, rural district in northern Mississippi.

"It is not how long you serve, but how well you serve," Whitten said in announcing his retirement. "I've been proud of all we have been able to do for our district and our state as a result of my position on Appropriations."

Elected in a 1941 special election, Whitten began his career the month before the Japanese attack on Pearl Harbor and was on the House floor the day President Franklin D. Roosevelt gave the "Day of Infamy" speech that sent the nation into World War II.

Whitten's career provided a case study in the assets and liabilities of longevity in the House. He accrued tremendous power and brought extensive benefits to his district, but he increasingly seemed like an anachronism. He was one of the last survivors of the era in which the House was dominated by conservative Democratic committee chairmen from the "Solid South."

A product of that political culture, Whitten adapted to changing times. In 1954, he denounced the Supreme Court's school desegregation decision for starting the nation "on the downhill road to integration and amalgamation and ruin," and in 1956 he signed the Southern Manifesto defending segregation.

But as Whitten rose in the House, he left his segregationist rhetoric behind and followed the majority of his party in supporting civil rights legislation and social programs such as food stamps.

He won a seat on Appropriations in 1943 and became chairman of the Agriculture Subcommittee in 1949. He became the unsurpassed master of federal farm programs and was known as the "permanent secretary of Agriculture." But he found himself at odds with the Zeitgeist in 1975, when the growing ranks of environmentalist liberals plotted to oust him from the agriculture chair. He kept his post by agreeing to give up power over environmental and consumer issues.

Ironically, it was Whitten who, as chairman of the full committee from 1979 until 1992, tried to keep the spirit of the New Deal alive. Whitten advocated government pump-priming of the economy when liberals were thrown on the defensive by President Ronald Reagan.

Soon after he set the record for House service on Jan. 6, 1992, he was hospitalized, reportedly after a stroke. In mid-1992, he allowed Natcher to run the panel as acting chairman, but he refused to give up his title until his colleagues forced him to in late 1992.

In a painful reminder of his diminished clout, the House in 1992 voted by a wide margin to slash funding for the Advanced Solid Rocket Motor, a project in his First District, which he had dominated and assisted for a half-century.

Many of the highways in his district, including the Natchez Trace Parkway, were paved and connected at Whitten's direction. The most spectacular monument to his power was the Tennessee-Tombigbee Waterway, a huge public works project two decades in the making that cut through his district to create a new link to the Gulf of Mexico.

Whitten was succeeded by Roger Wicker, the first Republican to represent the district since Reconstruction. ■

Old-Style Politician O'Neill Helped Define New Era

Until the day he died, Jan. 5, former House Speaker Thomas P. O'Neill Jr. seemed an anachronism — a throwback to times when big-city ward bosses were a real force on Capitol Hill. But in fact, the cigar-smoking, disheveled deal-maker was a midwife at the birth of the contemporary House. His decade as Speaker left a legacy that rewrote how the House was run, the Speaker's role in American politics and relations between the parties in the House.

As Speaker from 1977 until he retired from Congress in 1987, the Massachusetts Democrat helped consolidate the vast institutional changes of the post-Watergate era that decentralized power in the House and made it a more open institution.

The O'Neill years also transformed the speakership itself from an outpost of insider maneuvering to a platform for national political leadership. And he wore a partisan mantle that previous Speakers had rarely donned.

"Tip O'Neill was the nation's most prominent, powerful and loyal champion of working people," President Clinton said after O'Neill died, at age 81, of cardiac arrest in Boston.

It was the end of a life filled with paradox and irony. A man who found his political truths in anecdotes, O'Neill led a generation of politicians who parceled thoughts in sound bites. The embodiment of New Deal liberalism, he reached the height of power just as his views were falling out of favor. The man who coined the phrase "all politics is local" became the House's most famous national figure. He presided over a period of great change, but he changed little himself.

"He really was a transitional figure in the emergence of the modern Congress," said Lynne P. Brown, a political scientist at New York University. "He helped usher in a new age in the House without ever being a new age politician."

The Climb and Dissent

O'Neill's was a life almost entirely devoted to politics. He was elected to the Massachusetts House in 1936 at the age of 24. He served there until he was elected to Congress in 1952.

He got ahead in Washington not in the fashion of self-promoting, impatient baby boomers but in the old style: He rose gradually up the leadership ladder with help from powerful patrons such as Massachusetts Democrat John W. McCormack, who was Speaker from 1962 to 1971.

O'Neill got his first ticket to the inner sanctum in his second term. He won a place on the Rules Committee, where he served the leadership loyally for years. He distinguished himself from other party regulars in 1967, when he broke with President Lyndon B. Johnson and opposed the Vietnam War — a stance that endeared him to younger liberals who became supporters of his later rise to power.

O'Neill was lifted onto the leadership ladder in 1971, when he was appointed whip. He unexpectedly jumped up a rung in 1973, after House Majority Leader Hale Boggs of Louisiana died in a plane accident in Alaska. He became Speaker without opposition after Carl Albert of Oklahoma retired in 1977.

Although O'Neill was remembered with almost universal fondness, his reign as Speaker was hardly an unmitigated love fest. He infuriated Republicans, alienated conservative Democrats, frustrated younger members and found himself

crosswise with a president of his own party.

His first year as Speaker went like gangbusters, as he pushed President Jimmy Carter's energy bill through the House and persuaded reluctant colleagues to adopt a landmark ethics code. But he spent most of the next few years presiding over the rocky intraparty relations between House Democrats and Carter, whom O'Neill regarded as ignorant about the ways of Washington.

He suffered under President Ronald Reagan, when liberal politicians were driven into retreat. Many in his rank and file viewed O'Neill as a liability. In 1984, junior Democrats talked darkly of mutiny against O'Neill. Democrats' political fortunes soon improved, and so did O'Neill's. By the time he retired, deep wounds within his party had healed, and O'Neill re-emerged as a popular figure.

Making the New Ways Work

O'Neill presided over a House whose power structure had been virtually remade in the years before he became Speaker. A series of major changes in the early to mid-1970s gave more power to junior Democrats, broke up the oligarchy of committee chairmen and opened the House to more public scrutiny. Although O'Neill was not the principal architect of those changes, he had an important role in making the transition from the old ways of doing things to the new.

"Tip inherited an institution that was already reformed, and he had to make it work," said Ronald M. Peters Jr., director of the Carl Albert Congressional Research and Studies Center at the University of Oklahoma.

One way he made it work was the politics of inclusion. O'Neill oversaw the expansion of the whip organization, previously a small leadership group that grew to include more than one-third of the Democratic Caucus. Junior members and the caucus played a strong role.

A more visible legacy of the O'Neill years was the very visibility of the speakership. When he retired, O'Neill was famous enough that major corporations, such as American Express, wanted to put him in advertisements. O'Neill's predecessors did not have the exposure made possible by television's rise during his reign. But politics, more than technology, was the source of O'Neill's celebrity.

He was thrust into the role of media star by the 1980 elections, which handed the White House and the Senate to Republican control and left O'Neill as the top spokesman for Democrats. He was an unlikely candidate for the job because his disheveled appearance and garbled syntax were an affront to the aesthetics of television. But his lack of traditional telegenic qualities may, in the end, have worked in his favor.

"People are used to seeing blow-dried politicians, and Tip O'Neill came across on TV as more genuine," said John J. Pitney Jr., a political scientist at Claremont McKenna College in California.

O'Neill also contributed to increased partisanship in the House. Some of the Democratic leadership practices that most infuriated House Republicans had roots in O'Neill's tenure. He stepped up the practice of imposing strict limits on what amendments could be offered to bills on the floor. He skewed the party ratios on key committees to pad Democrats' advantage.

He could be a nasty adversary. O'Neill once said of Reagan, "He's cold. He's mean. He's got ice water for blood." At one point in 1984, O'Neill's attack on Republican Rep. Newt Gingrich of Georgia was so intemperate that he became the first Speaker since 1797 to have his words stricken from the Congressional Record as a violation of decorum.

O'Neill's friend and golfing buddy, Republican Leader Robert H. Michel of Illinois, mourned O'Neill's death as the passing not just of a friend but of a style of politics they shared: "It is a kind of politics that, I am sorry to say, is fast disappearing in this country, one in which partisan fervor and personal good will can — in fact, must — coexist and in which the heated controversies over specific policies never transcend the ultimate affection for individuals." ∎

Nixon Legacy: Power Struggles And Policy Breakthroughs

Former President Richard M. Nixon, one of the most controversial figures of the century, died April 22 in New York City. He was buried April 27 at the Richard Nixon Library in Yorba Linda, Calif. Nixon was the nation's 37th president and the first to resign. He served from Jan. 20, 1969, to Aug. 9, 1974.

Discussions of Nixon's presidency usually began with Watergate and his forced resignation, moving on to his foreign policy breakthroughs with China and the Soviet Union. But just as enduring a legacy may be found in the power relationship of the president and Congress, which 20 years later clearly showed the marks of Nixon's time in office.

Nixon's vision of his office fit the pattern that historian Arthur M. Schlesinger Jr. described as "the imperial presidency." Congress reacted by expanding its own influence into areas previously reserved for the executive, including war powers and budget policy.

Conflict between the two branches was evident from the start of Nixon's presidency. Nixon had won a three-way race for the White House in 1968 with only 43 percent of the vote (the same circumstance and vote share that Bill Clinton would have in 1992). And as he took office with this limited mandate, he had a Democratic Congress to work with and the challenge of Lyndon B. Johnson's Vietnam and Great Society policies to address.

Nixon reacted to those perilous circumstances with bold, sometimes compulsive, grabs for power. In both foreign and domestic policy, Nixon viewed himself and his office as preeminent, even above the law. "I had thrown down a gauntlet to Congress, the bureaucracy, the media, and the Washington establishment," Nixon recalled in his memoirs, "and challenged them to epic battle."

Congress responded in kind. Roughed up by Nixon's politically sharp elbows, Democrats on Capitol Hill reacted warily even to innovative Nixon initiatives on issues such as welfare reform and health care.

During his first term (1969-1973), the tug of war between the legislative and executive branches essentially ended in a draw. Nixon generally received what he wanted in foreign affairs and national security, while Congress succeeded in strengthening some domestic programs that it held dear.

But during Nixon's abbreviated second term (1973-1974), Congress clearly gained the upper hand. Nixon often had sought advantage through the element of surprise, announcing polices to Congress at the same time he announced them to the nation via television. Where he could, Nixon acted unilaterally.

Nixon lost that latitude as the lengthening shadow of Watergate darkened his presidency. Congress responded by expanding its staff and supporting bureaucracy and by passing laws to limit the powers of the president.

War Powers

The most striking example of congressional assertion in foreign policy was the War Powers Resolution. Designed to

force the president to seek congressional approval for any extended military involvement, it passed over Nixon's veto in 1973. The measure set a 60-day limit on the commitment of U.S. troops abroad without congressional consent. It permitted Congress at any time by concurrent resolution to direct the president to disengage troops involved in an undeclared war. *(1973 Almanac, p. 905)*

The measure was spurred by Nixon's April 1970 military "incursion" into Cambodia. Congress had not been consulted, and even some supporters of the president were disturbed at the procedure. Congress for the first time that spring took action to stop a U.S. military action in the Vietnam War, passing and forcing Nixon to sign legislation that halted the bombing of Cambodia in August 1973.

Nixon argued that the War Powers Resolution was both dangerous and unconstitutional. He argued that its major provisions would "take away, by a mere legislative act, authorities which the president has properly exercised under the Constitution for almost 200 years."

But both houses voted to override his veto.

Budget and Staff

It was not long before Congress reasserted itself on the domestic front as well.

The Congressional Budget and Impoundment Control Act of 1974 created a new budget process that specifically restricted the president's power to withhold funds already appropriated by Congress. This "impoundment" power had been used by earlier presidents, but when Nixon began using it openly to flout legislative decisions he disagreed with, Congress stripped it away. *(1974 Almanac, p. 145)*

Nixon argued that he was withholding funds only as a financial management technique, primarily to slow inflation through temporary reductions in federal spending. Congressional Democrats argued that impoundments imposed Nixon's priorities in defiance of laws passed by Congress.

The new budget procedures were a marked departure from the haphazard ways that Congress had customarily revised presidential budget proposals. Lacking any structured budget review system, Congress traditionally had acted on presidential funding proposals in many separate measures — usually voting to increase program spending — without pausing to consider the effects they would have on total spending, taxes and the resulting budget balance.

The 1974 budget law changed that by setting up House and Senate Budget committees, advised by a staff of experts, to analyze the president's budget and recommend a fiscal policy to Congress. It also created an independent Congressional Budget Office, for the first time giving Congress a capacity to make its own economic forecasts, deficit estimates and program cost projections.

The new budget law had dramatic side effects. As the number of congressional committees increased, so, too, did the size of congressional staff.

Campaign Reform

Probably the most direct outgrowth of Watergate was the quick and dramatic overhaul of the nation's campaign finance laws. *(1974 Almanac, p. 611)*

Substantial individual and corporate donations had been at the center of the Watergate scandal, as largely unreported private contributions financed the illegal activities of the 1972 Nixon re-election campaign (the Committee to Re-elect the President). With disclosure of these contributions came calls for sweeping campaign finance reform.

The 1974 law tightened disclosure requirements, set low contribution limits for all campaigns for federal office, established public financing for presidential primary and general-election campaigns, and created the Federal Election Commission to enforce the law.

The bill passed the House just hours before Nixon announced, on Aug. 8, 1974, that he would resign from the presidency as of noon the next day.

Congress tinkered with the law in 1976 to meet Supreme Court objections. But that year's presidential campaign was conducted in an environment almost totally different from four years earlier, when there were loose, largely unenforceable controls on campaign money.

Another aspect of Watergate spawned the creation of independent counsels to investigate allegations of wrongdoing in the executive branch. The process was inspired by the firing of special counsel Archibald Cox on Nixon's orders in October 1973 (after Nixon refused to turn over tapes that Cox requested). The event, dubbed the "Saturday Night Massacre," resulted not only in the sacking of Cox but in the resignation of Attorney General Elliot L. Richardson and the firing of his deputy, William D. Ruckelshaus, for refusing to carry out the presidential dictum.

The barrage of criticism that followed ultimately led to passage of an independent counsel statute in 1978 as part of the Ethics in Government Act. The statute was based on the idea that there was at least a perceived conflict of interest when the attorney general investigated top officials in the executive branch. The law required the attorney general to consider credible allegations against top officials, and if there were grounds to proceed, to ask a special three-judge panel to appoint an independent counsel to carry out the investigation and any related prosecution.

The law was reauthorized in 1982 and 1987, but it lapsed in late 1992 due to Republican opposition. It was reauthorized in 1994. *(Independent counsel, p. 295; 1978 Almanac, p. 835)* ∎

Delegates' Voting Shows Little Impact

A two-year experiment with allowing delegates to vote on the House floor came to an end with the close of the 103rd Congress. The results: The five delegates (all Democrats) voted less often than regular representatives, and their votes seldom affected the business of the House. Still, House Republicans, who saw the procedure as vote-padding by Democrats, planned to change House rules Jan. 4, 1995, to end it.

At the start of the 103rd Congress, the Democratic majority gave the resident commissioner from Puerto Rico and the delegates from American Samoa, the District of Columbia, Guam and the Virgin Islands the right to vote when the House was considering bills for amendment in the Committee of the Whole, a parliamentary framework that expedited action. *(1993 Almanac, p. 3)*

To fend off charges that delegate voting was unconstitutional, the rule stipulated that if the delegates' votes were decisive, there would be an automatic revote in which they would not participate. Citing that provision, the U.S. Court of Appeals for the District of Columbia Circuit upheld the procedure Jan. 25, 1994.

Of the 404 times that delegates were eligible to vote during the 103rd Congress, only three times — all in 1994 — did their votes prove decisive, triggering an automatic revote.

Twice the outcome was reversed.

The three votes:

● On March 17, an amendment to a proposed balanced-budget constitutional amendment (H J Res 103), which would have made it difficult to raise taxes, was rejected 213-215. All of the delegates voted "nay"; on the revote, the amendment was adopted 211-204. *(Votes 62, 63, p. 20-H)*

● On June 23, an amendment to protect fiscal 1995 appropriations for the National Endowment for the Arts (HR 4602) was adopted 218-214. Four delegates voted "yea" and one did not vote; on the revote, the amendment lost 210-216. *(Votes 268, 269, p. 80-H)*

● On June 24, an amendment to the fiscal 1995 Commerce, Justice, State appropriations bill, which would have eliminated a program to create a global network of schoolchildren collecting environmental data, was rejected 190-192. Three delegates voted "nay" and two did not vote; on the revote, the amendment failed again on a 184-184 tie vote. *(Votes 277, 278, p. 82-H)*

In 1993, Republicans repeatedly used procedural moves to force optional separate votes that excluded the delegates, but they demanded only one such revote in 1994.

Low Participation Rates

In 1994, the delegates voted 81 percent of the time on the 215 votes for which they were eligible, compared with 95 percent for the full House. In 1993, the delegates voted 79 percent of the time out of 189 opportunities, compared with 96 percent for the full House.

Delegate Eleanor Holmes Norton, D-D.C., who masterminded the rules change permitting delegate voting, protested the impending loss of the privilege. "It may mean very little to the Republicans who have proposed to take it away, but it meant something close to everything to my constituents," she said. The District's budget depended on an annual appropriations bill, and Congress could overturn its laws. Norton voted 97 percent of the time.

The other delegates, with the exception of Ron de Lugo, D-V.I., who posted a 95 percent score, all scored well below average. Robert A. Underwood, D-Guam, blamed his lower than average score of 77 percent on the distance between Washington and his home island. Eni F. H. Faleomavaega, D-American Samoa, voted 56 percent of the time, and the resident commissioner of Puerto Rico, Democrat Carlos Romero-Barceló, voted 81 percent of the time.

Appeals Court Ruling

The Jan. 25 decision of the U.S. Court of Appeals for the District of Columbia Circuit reaffirmed a ruling handed down by U.S. District Judge Harold H. Greene in March 1993 upholding the voting procedure. But the appeals court issued a pre-emptive warning to those who might want to expand delegate voting privileges. *(1993 Almanac, p. 75)*

Judge Laurence H. Silberman, writing for the unanimous three-judge panel, said the House had come "perilously close" to violating the Constitution in instituting the procedure. It would be "blatantly unconstitutional" to allow anyone who is not a full member of the House the right to a real vote, Silberman wrote.

Angered by the rules change and noting that it had given the Democrats five extra votes because all the delegates were from that party, House Republicans went to court to challenge it on constitutional grounds. They said the delegate votes diluted the power of House members.

Judges Greene and Silberman both cited the automatic revote provision as crucial to their decisions. Silberman said

that made the delegates' votes "largely symbolic."

Silberman's opinion also seemed to lay to rest any residual concern about delegates' participation in committees on an equal footing with members. He found proof of delegate voting in committees as far back as 1840. "The territorial delegates, representing those persons in geographical areas not admitted as states . . . always have been perceived as would-be congressmen who could be authorized to take part in the internal affairs of the House without being thought to encroach on the privileges of membership," he wrote. ■

House Resolution Condemns Nation of Islam

The House on Feb. 23 overwhelmingly approved a resolution condemning a 1993 speech by an aide to Nation of Islam Leader Louis Farrakhan, despite some lawmakers' concerns that the action violated the spirit of constitutional free speech protections.

The resolution (H Res 343), approved 361-34 (with 29 more members voting "present"), denounced Khalid Abdul Muhammad for making a "racist, anti-Catholic, anti-Semitic speech" on a college campus in November 1993. *(Vote 29, p. 10-H)*

"When free speech is abused in a vile and vicious way to promote hatred and to incite murder on a gigantic scale, it is the duty of responsible legislative bodies to condemn such speech in clear and certain terms," said Tom Lantos, D-Calif., principal sponsor of the resolution.

In the wake of Muhammad's comments, the Congressional Black Caucus distanced itself from the Nation of Islam, and caucus Chairman Kweisi Mfume, D-Md., backed away from efforts to work with the black nationalist group. Of the House's 38 African-American members, 20 voted for the resolution condemning Muhammad, 11 voted against, four voted present, and three did not vote.

After the vote, Farrakhan issued a statement offering to testify before Congress on his group's views.

Charles B. Rangel, D-N.Y., a senior member of the black caucus, objected that the resolution circumvented the committee process. "If we are going to root out bigots, racists and anti-Semites, I regret it took me 23 years to find out you could do this without going through regular procedures," he said. But during floor debate, Rangel supported the resolution, saying, "Nobody in this House should walk away where there is any doubt in anybody's mind that the U.S. Congress finds these types of remarks . . . repugnant."

Don Edwards, D-Calif., chairman of the Judiciary Subcommittee on Civil and Constitutional Rights, agreed that Muhammad's remarks were "disgraceful" but warned, "we're doing the Constitution real damage" by putting Congress in the position of condemning speech. "We are making a national and international hero out of this scoundrel who has uttered these disgraceful, awful things," Edwards said. "He will be the only person in world history, to the best of my knowledge, whose speech has been officially condemned by the U.S. Congress."

The Senate on Feb. 2 voted 97-0 to condemn the speech, in a sense-of-the-Senate amendment to an education bill (S 1150). *(Vote 19, p. 5-S)*

Controversial Speech

Three weeks before the House vote, the black caucus had yanked back an olive branch it had extended to the Nation of

Islam in the fall of 1993.

In September 1993, Mfume had invited Farrakhan to address the black caucus' annual legislative conference and announced a "covenant" between the two groups to work together on strengthening the black community. It was part of a tentative rapprochement between Farrakhan and mainstream black leaders, who for years had kept the Nation of Islam at arm's length. *(1992 Almanac, p. 18)*

Under pressure from other African-American lawmakers, Mfume held a news conference Feb. 2, 1994, to make clear that the caucus had no official relationship with the Nation of Islam and to back away from his "covenant" statement.

The controversy stemmed from a speech Farrakhan's spokesman, Muhammad, gave in November 1993 at Kean College in Union, N.J., in which he called Jews "bloodsuckers of the black nation," called the pope a "no-good . . . cracker" and urged South African blacks to murder all the country's whites. The speech came to national attention Jan. 16, when the Anti-Defamation League of B'nai B'rith bought a full-page ad in The New York Times to denounce the speech and reprint excerpts.

At first Farrakhan said nothing to rebuke his spokesman.

Later he denounced the speech as "repugnant" but coupled the condemnation with his own anti-Jewish rhetoric and criticism of blacks in Congress and other public officials. "He did not extend an olive branch to the Jewish community or to the Congressional Black Caucus," said Rep. John Lewis, D-Ga., a black veteran of the civil rights movement. "Rather than try to heal some of the wounds, he may have opened some more."

After meeting with the black caucus Feb. 2, Mfume said members wanted him to make clear that the caucus had never formally voted to establish the "covenant" he had proclaimed.

Mfume condemned the speech but said Congress should not be "selective" in its rebukes. Mfume twice tried to add a provision criticizing a racial joke by Sen. Ernest F. Hollings, D-S.C., but was prevented by parliamentary restrictions. Hollings in December 1993 was quoted as saying that African leaders went to conferences in Europe to "get a good square meal" rather than "eating each other." Hollings subsequently apologized.

The day after Mfume's news conference, Farrakhan announced that he had stripped his spokesman of official duties because of the speech. ∎

Lawmakers See Writing on Wall, Freeze Congressional Pay

For the second consecutive year, Congress denied itself a pay raise, keeping the 1995 salary for all members (except leaders, who earned more) at $133,600. In July, a federal appeals court upheld the constitutionality of the procedure that had raised congressional pay to that level.

Salaries had been scheduled to increase to $137,000 under provisions of the 1989 congressional pay law (PL 101-194). *(1989 Almanac, p. 51)*

The increase was blocked in September not by congressional leaders, but by a lone House Republican, Jim Ross Lightfoot of Iowa. His threat to make the House take a nonbinding procedural vote on the Treasury-U.S. Postal Service funding bill (HR 4539) was enough, coming soon before the November elections, to doom the pay raise. Leaders of both parties agreed to keep in the bill a provision blocking the raise, a provision they previously had agreed to drop. *(Appropriations, p. 536)*

In 1993, after President Clinton proposed scrapping a cost of living allowance (COLA) for federal workers, Congress quickly dropped one for its own members. For fiscal 1995, other federal workers got raises that averaged 2.6 percent nationwide. *(1993 Almanac, p. 12)*

Enter Lightfoot

Lightfoot seized the issue from his post as ranking Republican on the House Treasury-Postal Appropriations Subcommittee, which considered the congressional COLA during deliberations Sept. 20. Lightfoot's action capped a complex legislative dance on the issue, which was injected into the spending bill by Steny H. Hoyer, D-Md., who chaired the House Treasury-Postal Appropriations Subcommittee.

Hoyer, whose district in the Washington suburbs was home to many federal workers, wrote a provision into the spending bill to give federal employees an average raise 1 percent higher than recommended in Clinton's budget. Accompanying the provision for federal workers was low-profile language to block the congressional COLA. Hoyer said he added the language as a way to insulate his federal pay

raise from attacks that it would trigger a higher COLA for Congress.

However, after Clinton agreed in August to embrace Hoyer's higher pay increase, the provision no longer was needed in the Treasury-Postal bill, and House and Senate conferees made plans to drop it, along with the language to block the congressional pay raise.

But Lightfoot, a low-key member who usually fit in well with the get-along-go-along atmosphere of the Appropriations Committee, wrote to House leaders in July to inform them that he would seek to block the congressional COLA. When Hoyer and others, with support from House leaders from both parties, produced a tentative version of the Treasury-Postal conference agreement that preserved the COLA, Lightfoot vowed Sept. 19 that he would make a motion to instruct the House conferees to drop the pay raise. The next day, the conferees met and reluctantly killed the raise themselves.

"There is not a chance of a snowball in Haiti that this bill will go anywhere unless [the COLA] is dropped," said Appropriations Committee Chairman David R. Obey, D-Wis. Lightfoot said, "In the last-minute legislative rush, it would have been utterly irresponsible to let a pay raise for Congress sneak through when it was in our power to stop it." Speaker Thomas S. Foley, D-Wash., and Minority Leader Robert H. Michel, R-Ill., supported the COLA.

Democrats said Lightfoot grabbed the issue for political gain. Republicans said it was Hoyer's fault for creating the issue in the first place. "Lightfoot did not submarine the COLA. Hoyer submarined the COLA," said House Minority Whip Newt Gingrich, R-Ga. "It is Hoyer who wrote it in. It is Hoyer who broke the [1989] agreement. And it is Hoyer who did it in order to have leverage for his re-election. Lightfoot refused to let him take it out."

Court Backs Pay Raise

On July 29, a federal appeals court rejected a constitutional challenge to the most recent congressional pay increase.

Rep. John A. Boehner, R-Ohio, had filed suit in October 1992 along with 27 other members and more than 100 congressional candidates. They sought to block a 3.2 percent COLA for members of Congress and other high government

officials, including judges, that went into effect Jan. 1, 1993. *(1992 Almanac, p. 58)*

The plaintiffs argued that the COLA violated the 27th Amendment to the Constitution. Drafted by James Madison in 1789, approved by Congress that year but not ratified until 1992, the amendment stated: "No law varying the compensation for the services of the senators and representatives shall take effect until an election of representatives shall have intervened."

U.S. District Judge Stanley Sporkin dismissed the case Dec. 16, 1992, but Boehner appealed. A three-judge panel of the U.S. Court of Appeals for the District of Columbia Circuit upheld Sporkin's decision. The panel rejected Boehner's claim that the automatic COLA violated the spirit of the Madison amendment. The appeals court ruled that the annual raises specified by the 1989 law did not go into effect until after the election of 1990 and the seating of a new Congress, and were therefore constitutional. ∎

Chapter 2

ECONOMICS & FINANCE

Budget
Budget Overview.................................... 67
Clinton Budget.................................... 68
   Budget Glossary 69
   Highlights 70
   Economic Assumptions 74
   Budget by Agency............................. 75
   Budget by Function 76
Budget Resolution................................ 81
Balanced-Budget Amendment 85
Budget Process Reform........................... 87
   'A to Z' Plan 88
Entitlement Reform Panel 90
   Rivlin Memo 91
Deficit Reduction................................. 92
Tax Simplification 93

Banking
Interstate Banking & Branching 93
   Provisions.................................... 96
Community Development Lending 100
   Provisions................................... 102
Fair Trade in Financial Services..................... 107

Whitewater
Whitewater Investigation 108
   Fiske Letter 110
   Chronology of White House-Treasury Contacts........ 112
Other Banking and Finance
Secondary Loan Market 116
Other Banking Legislation.......................... 116
Fair Credit Reporting 117
Insurance Redlining 119
Other Securities-Related Legislation 120
Trade
Export Administration Act.......................... 121
GATT Implementation 123
   History...................................... 125
   Highlights of GATT Accord 129
   Provisions................................... 131
China MFN Status 137
Export-Import Bank 138
OPIC Reauthorization............................. 138
Nominations.................................... 138

Clinton, Congress Hold the Line On Major Deficit Reduction

*Fiscal 1995 budget action focuses on first real drop
in discretionary spending in 25 years*

With the pain of enacting a $433 billion deficit-reduction bill in 1993 a recent memory and the effects of the legislation still making their way through the economy, President Clinton and Congress opted to take a year off from major deficit reduction.

Instead, Congress' budget activity consisted mainly of coming to terms with the first year-to-year drop in real discretionary spending since 1969. With less to spend in fiscal 1995 than in 1994, lawmakers faced the sort of zero-sum game that deficit hawks had long advocated, in which most moves to spend money on new programs required scaling back or killing old ones.

Clinton set the tone in February, when he sent Congress a $1.52 trillion budget that mainly sought to rearrange some discretionary spending to make room for "investments" in such areas as education, job training and health care. The year before, Clinton had proposed to cut the deficit by nearly $500 billion over five years and asked Congress for $16 billion in one-year spending increases for investment priorities. In 1994, the White House sought about $25 billion in one-year spending cuts and fiscal 1995 investment spending of less than $14 billion.

"The real purpose of this budget is to stay on track with what was done last year," said White House budget director Leon E. Panetta.

Congress largely went along, tinkering a bit with Clinton's investment priorities and approving a fiscal 1995 budget resolution (H Con Res 218) that cut just $13 billion more over five years than Clinton had requested.

That turned out to be the high-water mark for deficit reduction in 1994.

Although lawmakers continued to talk throughout the year about further spending cuts, they took little concrete action. With interest in specific remedies waning, most of the debate was over general cures, such as the balanced-budget amendment and various proposals to change the budget process.

Solid majorities in both the House and Senate voted in March to change the Constitution to require a balanced budget, but neither chamber mustered the two-thirds majority required to pass a constitutional amendment (S J Res 41, H J Res 103). In fact, in their budget resolutions passed the same month, neither the House nor the Senate laid out five-year plans that came anywhere close to balancing the budget.

Later in the year, a trio of deficit hawks — Charles W. Stenholm, D-Texas, Timothy J. Penny, D-Minn., and John R.

FISCAL 1995 BUDGET

Clinton's Budget. President Clinton sent Congress a $1.52 trillion fiscal 1995 budget that was as modest as the preceding year's had been ambitious. . p. 68

Budget Resolution. Congress agreed on a hold-the-line budget that largely followed Clinton's lead. . . . . p. 81

Balanced-Budget Amendment. Efforts to pass a constitutional amendment failed in both chambers. . . . . p. 85

Budget Process Reform. The House endorsed a series of budget changes, but Senate inaction killed the measures. . . . . . . p. 87

Kasich, R-Ohio — succeeded in getting the House to vote on a series of proposed changes in the budget process. While House Democratic leaders were unenthusiastic about the proposals, they agreed to hold the votes in an effort to undercut support for something they dreaded even more: an "A to Z" plan that would have set aside at least a week of House floor time for debates and votes on an undetermined package of spending cuts. In the end, A-to-Z supporters fell 14 signatures short of the 218 they needed to force the plan to the floor.

With discretionary spending — the funding over which Congress had annual control — already declining in real terms, there was a growing sense that the only way to make serious progress against the deficit was to go after entitlement programs, such as Social Security, Medicare, farm programs and welfare, which made up half of all federal spending.

But lawmakers were not ready to risk the political danger associated with cutting these programs. In July, for example, the House soundly rejected a proposal by Stenholm to set a strict cap on entitlement spending and enforce that with automatic spending cuts. In its last budget vote of the year, the House agreed overwhelmingly not even to debate ideas for cutting entitlements.

The year ended on a low note for deficit hawks. In an internal memo that was subsequently leaked to the press by a Republican operative, White House budget director Alice M. Rivlin laid out options for a new round of deficit cuts. The Oct. 3 memo outlined five possible budget paths, ranging from doing nothing new to balancing the budget.

Although it contained little that students of the budget had not heard dozens of times before, the memo sparked a political furor in the weeks before the election. Republicans seized on it to accuse Democrats of a secret agenda to raise taxes and cut Social Security. Democrats in the White House and Congress quickly ran from the memo and disavowed its most controversial contents.

The memo flap overshadowed a carefully prepared White House political offensive that centered on new deficit numbers. At a speech in Cleveland on Oct. 24, Clinton announced that the 1994 deficit had plummeted from initial estimates of some $300 billion when he took office to $203 billion — proof, he said, that the huge deficit-reduction package he pushed through Congress his first year in office was working. *(1993 Almanac, p. 107)* ∎

Clinton's Modest Fiscal 1995 Plan

President Clinton sent Congress a $1.52 trillion fiscal 1995 budget Feb. 7 that was as modest as the preceding year's sweeping economic plan had been ambitious — a follow-up proposal that filled in the outlines of the deficit reduction Congress mandated in 1993 and asked for a second, smaller installment of Democratic "investment" spending.

The White House argued that it was necessary to give the economy time to digest the 1993 package before initiating major new cuts. So, with a politically costly battle looming over health care reform and the deficit looking better than it had in years, Clinton elected to propose no broad new fiscal initiatives and called for no new deficit reduction.

Indeed, under the deficit-reduction agreement that Clinton and Congress had reached in 1993, the president's options were sharply limited. Unless he was willing to propose drastic cuts in some areas, he could do little more than offer modest shifts in spending to fund the priorities he had set during his 1992 campaign. The budget contained more money for schools, the homeless, children, police, research scientists, highway builders and other programs — but not very much of it. And the projected funds — some $13.4 billion in new domestic "investment" spending — would be available only if Congress agreed to make room under the tight cap on discretionary spending by cutting funds from long-favored programs.

To pay for its new spending priorities, the administration proposed about $25 billion in one-year spending cuts. The budget called for terminating some 115 federal programs and cutting back another 200 or more, including dozens that immediately provoked opposition from Democrats. In a lengthy list of detailed cuts that Republicans charged had been lifted from the budgets of Presidents Ronald Reagan and George Bush, Clinton proposed to slash such Democratic standbys as public housing, mass transit operating subsidies and the Low-Income Home Energy Assistance Program (LIHEAP), which helped the poor pay their utility bills.

Carrying out a promise made in his State of the Union address Jan. 25 to "draw the line" against further defense cuts, Clinton requested $263.7 billion in budget authority for defense. The previous year, the administration had projected $261.1 billion in overall defense spending for fiscal 1995, continuing a long-term reduction. Since then, however, the administration had promised to cover some of the unanticipated costs that were straining the defense budget. About $1.1 billion of the increase was to cover military pay raises required by Congress. *(Text, p. 3-D)*

Many of the spending cuts in Clinton's budget had been included in proposals offered in 1993 by deficit hawks — Timothy J. Penny, D-Minn., and John R. Kasich, R-Ohio, in the House, and Bob Kerrey, D-Neb., and Hank Brown, R-Colo., in the Senate. The difference was that they proposed using some or all of their cuts to further reduce the cap on discretionary spending, whereas the White House wanted to use the cuts to meet the cap and free up a little extra spending room for its investments.

But Penny expressed grudging appreciation for what the administration was trying to do. "I've been pulling my punches" in criticizing the new Clinton budget, Penny said, "because I like the pay-as-you-go implications" of the White House's push to cut some spending programs to pay for its investment priorities. "I think it's very healthy for us to face those choices."

Background

The rules that guided the fiscal 1995 budget had been set in 1990 after a congressional-White House budget summit; they were revised in 1993 as part of a huge budget-reconciliation bill (PL 103-66) that was expected to yield $433 billion in deficit reduction over five years. The budget rules set specific caps on discretionary spending, the one-third of the federal budget over which lawmakers had direct control each year.

Originally, the caps were intended to last for five years, through fiscal 1995. However, as part of the 1993 deficit-reduction bill, Congress tightened them and extended them through fiscal 1998. As a result, discretionary spending for fiscal 1995 was set to decline in inflation-adjusted terms for the first time since 1969. *(1990 Almanac, p. 129; 1993 Almanac, p. 107)*

The same budget laws included pay-as-you-go rules for taxes and for entitlement spending for programs such as Social Security, Medicare and federal retirement. Any increase in entitlement spending had to be offset by tax increases or cuts in other entitlement programs — but only if the increase was a result of specific congressional action. Increases due to economic conditions or other causes beyond lawmakers' control were not covered.

In his first budget, which laid out many of the changes that were enacted in the reconciliation bill, Clinton had proposed to cut the deficit by nearly $500 billion over five years and asked Congress for $16 billion in one-year spending increases for its investments. The fiscal 1994 budget was a highly partisan affair. Republicans bitterly fought the plan as a job-killer and a sure ticket to another recession. Not a single Republican in either chamber voted for that budget in committee or on the floor. *(1993 Almanac, p. 102)*

Good News on the Deficit

Democrats complained about Clinton's proposed cuts for fiscal 1995, but their grumbling was drowned out for the moment by rejoicing over some of the best deficit forecasts in years.

The budget projected a fiscal 1995 deficit of $176.1 billion, the smallest in five years and the third consecutive drop since the record high of $290.4 billion, set in 1992. (The White House predicted an even smaller 1995 deficit — $165.1 billion — if the effects of its health care reform plan were factored in.)

Both the White House's Office of Management and Budget (OMB) and the Congressional Budget Office (CBO) ascribed most of the dramatic drop — from a projection of more than $300 billion just a year before — to the tax increases and spending cuts enacted in 1993. A smaller piece of the reduction came from lower interest rates, which Democrats claimed were propelled in part by the effect the plan had on the financial markets.

Republicans saw it differently, however, arguing that Democrats inherited an improving economy and falling interest rates that would have helped push the deficit down with or without the Clinton plan. Republicans attacked Clinton's latest budget for its increase in appropriated domestic spending and for failing to take on spending for

entitlement programs.

"Some real significant issues could have been taken on, and they didn't take them on," said House Budget Committee ranking Republican John R. Kasich of Ohio. "They ducked."

Pete V. Domenici of New Mexico, ranking Republican on the Senate Budget Committee, criticized Clinton's proposal as an "MIA budget" for items he said were missing in action. Domenici said the budget failed to reflect the impact of Clinton's enormous health care reform proposal, ignored the costs of his upcoming welfare reform plan and offered no way to pay for the recently concluded revisions to the General Agreement on Tariffs and Trade (GATT), which he said would cost $11 billion (later changed to $12 billion).

Panetta later countered that the administration had included those health care items that represented direct savings to or spending by the federal government, and that it planned to work out ways to fully pay for welfare reform and the GATT agreement later on.

Economic Assumptions

The economic assumptions underlying Clinton's budget were in line with those of most outside economists, although CBO was fractionally less sanguine than the administration on most economic indicators, as was the Blue Chip consensus forecast of 51 private economists, often cited as a comparative yardstick.

The administration forecast 3 percent growth in the gross domestic product (GDP), the broadest measure of the nation's economy, in 1994 and 2.7 percent growth in 1995. That was about the pace at which most economists believed the economy would grow if it were performing at its optimal level. The administration assumed that inflation would increase modestly as the economy continued to grow and that unemployment would continue to decline. Finally, the budget assumed a slight increase in short-term interest rates.

Administration economists could point to a good forecasting track record, having predicted fairly accurately a year before the course the economy would take in 1994. The Clinton administration had correctly forecast the 1993 growth rate (preliminary estimates were 2.8 percent), and it had underestimated slightly the decline in inflation, unemployment and interest rates.

CBO Scores Health Care Plan

The day after Clinton released his budget, CBO Director Robert D. Reischauer unveiled a long-awaited CBO analysis of the president's health plan. Reischauer said the Clinton proposal held "the promise of reducing the deficit in the long term," but he put the turnaround date much further into the future than Clinton did. While the White House said its health care plan could start cutting the deficit almost immediately, producing $59 billion in savings by 2000, Reischauer said the plan instead would add some $74 billion to the deficit over the same period before finally beginning to cut spending sometime after 2004.

At a hearing before the House Budget Committee, Panetta parried Republican criticism of the administration's health care reform proposal by insisting that CBO and OMB often had estimating differences and always worked them out. He said he hoped the dispute over the numbers would not divert Congress from its larger goal of passing a health plan, because if Congress ever wanted to get control of the deficit it had to attack health costs. "You damn well better support a health care reform bill that controls costs," Panetta warned members. ∎

Budget Glossary

Appropriations: The process by which Congress provided budget authority — usually through the passage of 13 separate appropriations bills.

Budget authority: The authority for federal agencies to obligate money. The congressional Appropriations committees provided this.

Budget outlays: Money actually spent in a fiscal year, as opposed to money that was appropriated. One year's budget authority could result in outlays over several succeeding years, and the outlays in any given fiscal year resulted from a mix of budget authority from that year and from prior years.

Discretionary cap: An annual limit on all discretionary spending, expressed as separate numbers for budget authority and outlays.

Discretionary spending: Programs that Congress could finance as it chose through appropriations. Most of the apparatus of the federal government and almost everything the government did except pay "entitlement" benefits to individuals was funded by discretionary spending. Examples included the courts, the military and activities from space exploration to child nutrition. Roughly one-third of all federal spending fell into this category.

Entitlements: Programs whose eligibility requirements were written into law. Any individual or other entity that met those requirements was *entitled* to the money, which the government had to spend until Congress changed the law. Examples included Social Security, Medicare, Medicaid, unemployment benefits, food stamps and federal retirement. While some entitlements were provided through the appropriations process, appropriators had little or no control over the money.

Fiscal 1995: Oct. 1, 1994, through Sept. 30, 1995.

Mandatory spending: Made up mostly of entitlements, mandatory spending also included interest on the national debt. Altogether, mandatory spending accounted for about two-thirds of all federal spending.

Pay-as-you-go rule (PAYGO): This rule required that all tax cuts, new entitlement programs or expansions of existing entitlement programs be budget-neutral — offset either by additional taxes or cuts in existing entitlement programs.

Rescissions: The cancellation of previously appropriated budget authority. This was a commonly used way to save money that already had been appropriated, but which either the president or Congress wanted to cancel. A rescissions bill had to be passed by Congress and signed by the president.

Revenues: Taxes, user fees and most other receipts paid to the federal government. Some receipts and user fees showed up as "negative outlays," however, and did not count as revenue.

Sequester: The cancellation of spending authority as a disciplinary measure to correct spending above pre-set limits. Appropriations that exceeded the annual spending "cap" could trigger a sequester that would cut all appropriations by the amount of the excess. Similarly, tax cuts or new or expanded entitlement spending that were not offset under pay-as-you-go rules would trigger a sequester of non-exempt entitlement programs.

Highlights of President's Budget

The following is a summary of the revenue and spending proposals contained in President Clinton's fiscal 1995 budget. The spending proposals are organized by broad program categories, known as functions. The budget is presented in "budget authority" (BA) and "outlays." Budget authority is the amount of new federal commitments that agencies could make during a fiscal year. Outlays are the actual spending that would occur in fiscal 1995; some of outlays are the result of budget authority appropriated in previous years.

The following summaries of budget functions refer to outlays, unless otherwise designated:

Revenues

Having pushed through a massive tax increase on upper-income earners in 1993, Clinton for the most part was prepared to leave the tax code alone in the fiscal 1995 budget. The only new taxes he proposed were intended to help finance his health care reform bill.

The largest was a 75 cents-a-pack increase in the federal excise tax on tobacco products, for a total tax of 99 cents. That was projected to bring in an estimated $12 billion in fiscal 1995 and about $11 billion annually in subsequent years.

Clinton also sought to assess corporations with 5,000 or more employees a tax equal to 1 percent of total payroll if they chose to provide health care insurance directly. (All other employees would have been required to go through a government-sponsored health "alliance.") The assessment, which would have begun Jan. 1, 1996, would have brought an estimated $3.8 billion in 1996 and about $5 billion a year thereafter. This was to help fund academic medical centers, which at the time were funded through Medicare.

In addition, Clinton proposed that employees who received certain health benefits through so-called cafeteria plans be required to include them in their annual incomes for the purpose of calculating taxes owed, beginning Jan. 1, 1997. That would have brought in $5.3 billion in 1997 and more than $8 billion a year thereafter.

Altogether, Clinton's health care funding proposals would have brought in $11.6 billion in 1995 and progressively more in later years. In a setback for the White House financing plan, the Congressional Budget Office said Feb. 8 that Clinton should include mandatory health premiums paid by employers as receipts in the federal budget. Clinton wanted them treated off-budget as a strictly private transaction.

Clinton was willing to let several popular but expensive tax provisions expire at the end of the year, rather than risk generating a tax bill by proposing to extend them. These included the targeted jobs tax credit, which subsidized the hiring of disadvantaged workers, and the employer exclusion for educational assistance provided to employees. Administration officials notified companies that claimed these and other tax breaks that it would seek to renew them in 1995 and make them retroactive.

The budget did include a proposed $1.5 billion increase in various user fees, which the federal government charged for specific services. Perhaps the most controversial was a plan to require miners to pay an 8 percent royalty for the extraction of hard-rock minerals from federal lands. Legislation to impose royalties had passed both the House and Senate and awaited conference. *(Mining law, p. 236)*

The most lucrative proposal was to increase several existing fees on securities transactions. Clinton proposed to increase the fee on the sale of all U.S. exchange-listed securities from 1/300th of 1 percent of the sale amount to 1/250th, and to expand the fee to cover all over-the-counter securities transactions. The existing $150 registration fee imposed on investment advisers was to be changed to an annual fee determined by the volume of assets the individual managed. These and other securities proposals were projected to bring in $378 million annually.

The budget included a proposed increase in the fee that industries paid to the Food and Drug Administration to apply for approval of a new drug or other product — expected to raise $338 million in fiscal 1995 and more than $350 million a year thereafter. It also included a $600-a-year licensing fee for gun dealers; the existing fee was $90 for a three-year license.

Agriculture

As it had for decades, the federal government maintained an extensive regime of programs that promoted the production, marketing and safety of agricultural products. Yet agriculture took up just a small proportion of the Agriculture Department's resources, which were shared by programs in such areas as nutrition, housing, economic development, trade, forestry and environmental conservation.

Of the $60.3 billion in outlays projected for the Agriculture Department, $12.8 billion (21.2 percent) went directly to farm programs and associated agricultural and economic research. That was down from $16.9 billion in expected outlays for fiscal 1994. The 24 percent decline was one of the largest drop-offs of any federal budget category.

However, the decrease was not the outcome of a Clinton administration assault on agriculture programs; it was mainly the result of chance. Most of the spending reduction came from the farm income and crop-price support programs funded through the Agriculture Department's Commodity Credit Corporation. The massive Midwest floods that inundated thousands of acres of farmland during the summer of 1993 had sharply reduced the harvests of certain feed grain crops, especially corn. Market prices went up, which in turn reduced the amounts of subsidies that the department had to pay to farmers.

The budget proposal anticipated passage of a sweeping reform of federal crop insurance, under which the government would subsidize inexpensive disaster insurance for farmers. Such coverage would be required for farmers who participated in federal farm programs, and supplemental disaster aid would be denied to farmers living in areas where crop insurance was provided. The budget credited a net $500 million savings from the crop insurance program changes and reductions in disaster aid spending.

One program in the agriculture account that was singled out for a big cut was the Emergency Food Assistance Program, which was slated to shrink to $40 million from $124 million in fiscal 1994.

The food giveaway program was founded in the early 1980s with the dual mission of providing food to emergency shelters and reducing then-large farm-product surpluses. However, the surpluses had since disappeared, and the Agriculture Department had spent millions of dollars annually to purchase commodities off-the-shelf to give to the needy. Under the fiscal 1995 budget, the program still could distribute food products contributed by other Agriculture programs, but it would be barred from making its own food purchases.

The budget provided the various federally funded agriculture research programs with $1.17 billion, up slightly from $1.16 billion in fiscal 1994. But there were shifts within that area. For example, Clinton wanted to cut budget authority for special research grants to $44.8 million from $87.1 million; this program long had been used by members to earmark grants to colleges and research centers in their districts.

Clinton also proposed to cut out all funding for the buildings and facilities fund of the Cooperative State Research Service. When Clinton made that same request in 1993, Congress instead boosted funding from $52.1 million in fiscal 1993 to $56.9 million in fiscal 1994.

Commerce, Community Development

The budget appeared to contain a big cut in spending for commerce, housing credit, and community and regional development. Overall, outlays for these broad categories of spending were down significantly, from $9.8 billion in fiscal 1994 to $3.7 billion in fiscal 1995.

But one apparent quirk in the budget came from residual effects of the 1980s financial crisis, which caused more than 2,000 banks and savings and loan associations to fail at great cost to taxpayers and to the self-financing deposit insurance funds maintained by the federal government.

The government expected to collect $11.1 billion more in sales of assets acquired from failed banks and thrifts and from deposit insurance premiums than it intended to spend to close failed institutions.

That huge total of "negative outlays," with its salutary effect on the deficit, was a small bright spot in the otherwise gloomy news from the debacle in the financial industry. It also tended to hide spending on related activities.

When the effects of deposit insurance spending were discounted, outlays for commerce and housing credit activities increased to $5.6 billion in fiscal 1995 from $3.8 billion in fiscal 1994. The increase was almost entirely accounted for by a $1.5 billion increase in federal payments to the quasi-independent Postal Service, to $3.4 billion in fiscal 1995, to cover nonprofit mail subsidies and civil service pensions and benefits.

And in broad terms, spending for community and regional development programs would have declined slightly, from $9.3 billion in fiscal 1994 to $9.2 billion in fiscal 1995. That was entirely due, however, to a budgeted decline in outlays for natural disaster assistance to $1.6 billion in fiscal 1995. Outlays for direct disaster payments through the Federal Emergency Management Agency and the National Flood Insurance program and for loans through the Small Business Administration totaled $2.9 billion in fiscal 1993 and were expected to total $2.4 billion in fiscal 1994.

● **Commerce research and development.** Clinton requested $935 million in new budget authority for the Commerce Department's research arm, the National Institute for Standards and Technology, up from $520 million.

The Advanced Technology Program, the focal point of Clinton's effort to accelerate the commercialization of broad-based, high-risk technologies, was to rise to $449.8 million, up from $247.6 million in fiscal 1994. In 1993, as a pilot program, it received $61 million. Manufacturing Extension Partnerships and other technology outreach programs were boosted to $67.5 million, up from $39.8 million.

Though building the nation's "information superhighways" was primarily a private-sector activity, Clinton requested $100 million for grants to help link classrooms, libraries and clinics to broadband computer networks, an increase of $74 million in budget authority from fiscal 1994.

● **Community development.** Discounting disaster aid, spending under the community and regional development function was projected to increase by $691 million, as follows:

Clinton requested $4.4 billion in fiscal 1995 budget authority for Community Development Block Grants, unchanged from the year before. States and localities had discretion over how these grants were spent, but they were intended to promote economic development and affordable housing and to eradicate urban blight. The administration proposed to set aside $200 million of the money for the new Neighborhood LIFT initiative, for retail, commercial or mixed-use development projects in neighborhoods.

The administration also proposed creating community development programs targeted to special projects, including: $500 million in budget authority to revitalize empowerment zones and enterprise communities, $150 million to strengthen community-based organizations and $150 million in economic revitalization grants to help finance projects under the Section 108 loan guarantee program for economic development.

Clinton also called for $100 million in new budget authority for a new program to meet the housing and infrastructure needs in the colonias, impoverished communities near the U.S.-Mexico border. The money was to be matched by Texas, New Mexico, California and Arizona.

● **Area and regional development.** Clinton wanted to increase budget authority for water and waste disposal projects to $136 million in fiscal 1995 from $116 million in fiscal 1994. The increase was significant because of the long time line for building such projects. New budget authority for water and waste disposal grants was to increase to $525 million in fiscal 1995 from $500 million.

The budget also called for a large increase in the guaranteed loan program for businesses and industries outside metropolitan areas. It included $11 million in budget authority in fiscal 1995, up from $2 million in fiscal 1994. The Agriculture Department said the increased demand for the program was due to lower interest rates, nationwide

economic recovery and enterprise zone initiatives.

● **Small Business Administration.** The budget proposed a slight increase in outlays to subsidize the cost of business loans from the Small Business Administration, to $431.6 million in fiscal 1995 from $417.6 million in fiscal 1994. But it presumed a significant shift in the composition of those loans. Direct loans — expected to total almost $137 million in fiscal 1994 — were to be eliminated, while the volume of guaranteed loans was to grow to $11.9 billion in fiscal 1995 from $8.4 billion the previous year.

Defense

Defense spending in Clinton's budget totaled $270.7 billion in outlays, $9.1 billion less than in fiscal 1994, or a 5.2 percent decrease. Clinton sought $263.7 billion in new budget authority, $2.8 billion more than Congress appropriated for defense in fiscal 1994. Allowing for inflation, however, the fiscal 1995 request represented 0.9 percent less purchasing power.

Most of the new budget authority — $252.2 billion — was for the Defense Department. By the Clinton administration's analysis, President George Bush's projected budget for the Defense Department in fiscal 1995 would have required $258.5 billion in budget authority — $6.3 billion more than Clinton's request.

Clinton's request was $4.1 billion higher than projected early in 1993. About $1.1 billion of that increase was to pay for an additional year's cost of the 2.2 percent military pay raise Congress added to the fiscal 1994 defense appropriation bill.

However, Clinton did not increase his budget request to take account of the fact that inflation had driven up prices faster than the administration assumed it would the previous year. If he had allowed the Pentagon to budget for 2.5 percent inflation, rather than the previously assumed rate of 2.3 percent, Clinton would have had to add an additional $1.6 billion to the fiscal 1995 request.

In addition to Defense Department funding, the budget request included $10.6 billion for defense-related programs conducted by the Energy Department. More than half that amount — $5.4 billion — was earmarked for radioactive and toxic waste management at defense nuclear facilities, including cleaning up old waste dumps. Energy's defense budget also contained $3.3 billion for nuclear weapons-related activities, including research on ways to verify the reliability of warheads already in the inventory without conducting nuclear test explosions.

The remaining $1.9 billion was for other activities, including development of nuclear reactors to power Navy warships.

Besides the funds for the Defense and Energy departments, the defense budget included $914 million for various other programs, such as the Transportation Department's maintenance of a "ready-reserve fleet" of cargo ships.

The administration presented its Pentagon budget request as an implementation of the "bottom-up review," an assessment of U.S. defense requirements that was orchestrated by former Defense Secretary Les Aspin and unveiled in September 1993. That analysis was based on the assumption that U.S. forces should be adequate to wage major wars in two widely separated regions, each on the scale of the 1991 war with Iraq. It concluded that U.S. forces should include about 1.45 million active-duty personnel, highly trained and equipped with high-tech weaponry.

Toward that end, Clinton's Pentagon request broke down, in broad spending categories, as follows:

● **Readiness.** The pre-eminence the administration accorded to preserving "readiness" was reflected in the $92.9 billion request for operations and maintenance (O&M). The proportional emphasis on readiness was even greater than it looked: Not only was the request $4.9 billion more than Congress appropriated for fiscal 1994, but it also applied to a smaller combat force, meaning that the readiness spending "per battalion" or "per ship" was higher.

The amount earmarked for major overhauls of ships, planes and vehicles was increased by 20 percent, though fewer weapons would be in service with the smaller force.

● **Military Personnel.** The $70.5 billion requested for military per-

sonnel costs marked a slight decline from the $70.8 billion appropriated for fiscal 1994, reflecting a reduction in the number of active-duty military personnel to 1,526,000. The request anticipated a 1.6 percent pay raise for military personnel. Under Clinton's plan, the decline in personnel was to start leveling off in fiscal 1996.

● **Procurement.** The procurement budget dropped to $43.3 billion, $1.2 billion less than was provided in fiscal 1994 and less than one-third the size of the annual procurement budget in the mid-1980s in inflation-adjusted terms.

Defense Secretary William J. Perry said Feb. 7 that a limited procurement budget was acceptable for the near future because the services had built up such large inventories of modern equipment during the 1980s. But he warned that procurement funding would have to start increasing in fiscal 1997 to maintain the force of 1.45 million personnel projected by Clinton.

Most of the production lines that Clinton assumed would be shut down had been slated for closure, such as the F-16 fighter line. Previously unannounced terminations included several Navy variants of the Army's Blackhawk helicopter.

The administration justified its requests for some programs, at least in part, as a means of preserving militarily critical manufacturing capabilities that otherwise would atrophy. The most notable example of this was the request for $2.5 billion in new budget authority and the transfer of $1.2 billion previously appropriated to provide the $3.7 billion needed for a nuclear-powered aircraft carrier.

Other major procurement requests included:
● $2.9 billion for three Navy *Arleigh Burke*-class destroyers.
● $2.7 billion for six Air Force C-17 cargo planes.
● $1.2 billion for 24 Navy F/A-18 fighters.
● $331 million to upgrade early versions of the Army's M-1 tank and Bradley armored troop carrier.

● **Research.** The administration's emphasis on leveraging U.S. forces with technology undergirded the $36.2 billion request for research and development (R&D). In real terms, Perry said, the administration was seeking higher R&D budgets than were provided during the 1970s, when the Pentagon developed the generation of weapons that armed U.S. forces in the 1991 war with Iraq.

The budget also boosted funding for basic and exploratory research — as opposed to funding linked to developing particular weapons — even faster than R&D as a whole. This included $2.1 billion earmarked to encourage the development of "dual-use" technologies with both civil and military applications.

The request was to continue developing several types of sophisticated new weapons, earmarking:
● $2.5 billion for the Air Force's F-22 fighter.
● $525 million for the Army's Comanche armed helicopter.
● $507 million to develop a new generation of submarines.
● $3.0 billion (plus $273 million in procurement funds) for anti-missile defenses, with a heavy emphasis on relatively early deployment of defenses against short-range (or "theater") ballistic missiles.

● **Other Programs.** The $8.4 billion requested to construct military facilities and family housing was nearly $1.2 billion less than in fiscal 1994. It included nearly $2.7 billion for activities related to the closure of superfluous military bases.

Education

Under Clinton's budget, spending for education, training and social service programs was to rise to $53.5 billion in fiscal 1995, a 5.4 percent jump to fund Clinton's initiatives for preschoolers and disadvantaged students, school reform efforts and job training. Those initiatives also were to benefit from more than $600 million saved by eliminating 33 Education Department programs.

Even with the cuts, Clinton wanted Education Department spending on domestic discretionary programs to increase by 7 percent in budget authority, compared with an increase of less than 1 percent for the rest of the government. With entitlement programs, the department's budget was to grow to $31.7 billion in new budget authority.

The department wanted to increase spending for elementary and secondary school programs by $1.7 billion to $11 billion in budget authority.

The biggest chunk of the new money was to bulk up the Chapter 1 program for disadvantaged students, which was to increase by $667 million, to $7.6 billion, most of it for grants to local school districts. Also getting significant increases were school safety and anti-drug programs ($188 million more, for a total of $660 million) and the Goals 2000 proposal, aimed at increasing education standards in core subjects, which was to get $700 million in its first full year of operation.

The budget also increased the maximum size of Pell grants for postsecondary students by $100, to $2,400, bringing grants back up to the 1992 level.

The total number of students receiving postsecondary aid under all programs was to increase slightly to 6.7 million, at a total cost of $11.2 billion, up about $800 million over fiscal 1994. The percentage of student borrowers getting loans directly from the government was to increase to 40 percent in academic year 1995-96, from 5 percent, under the department's recently revamped loan system.

To save $72 million, the department proposed killing State Student Incentive grants, which encouraged states to offer need-based grants. The department contended that the program, begun in 1972, had fulfilled its goal because all states offered such grants. The administration requested no money for the federal contribution to the revolving fund from which institutions made Perkins Loans, saving $158 million.

The administration proposed killing a slew of other Education Department programs, including more than $40 million in library programs, $35 million for consumer and homemaking education and $39 million for immigrant education grants.

The administration also wanted to retool so-called impact aid programs, which provided money to school districts that educated students connected to federal facilities, such as military bases. The proposal cut the cost of the programs by $48.2 million.

A joint venture between the Education and Labor departments got a total of $300 million in budget authority (split evenly) for the proposed School-to-Work Opportunities Act, aimed at helping students make the transition from high school to the working world.

Other requests for increased funds for Labor Department training programs included:
● $347 million in budget authority for dislocated worker programs, for a total of $1.5 billion. Existing programs for employees displaced by trade pacts, defense cuts and environmental programs were to be consolidated and expanded.
● $200 million for one-stop-shopping career centers. Funded at $50 million in fiscal 1994, these centers gave workers a single place to visit for an array of federal jobs programs, including career counseling, job opportunities and training information.
● $116 million for the Job Corps program, for a total of $1.2 billion, to provide vocational training and job placement for youths.

For social service programs, Clinton proposed a $700 million increase in Head Start, raising spending to $4 billion in fiscal 1995. The administration said it would spend at least $240 million of the increase on improving the quality of local programs, which provided low-income preschoolers with early education, health, nutrition and social services. It said the funding would enable the program's enrollment to grow from 750,000 in fiscal 1994 to 840,000 and that the additional funds would permit Head Start providers to offer more full-day and full-year service to families who needed them.

The budget called for consolidating three programs dealing with runaway and homeless youths, and increasing spending on them from $63 million in fiscal 1994 to $69 million.

Budget authority for the Community Services Block Grant was to be cut from $464.2 million in fiscal 1994 to $434.6 million in fiscal 1995. The budget did not include funding for several discretionary programs among community services, such as emergency homeless assistance and national youth sports.

Among entitlement programs, funding for the Job Opportunities and Basic Skills Training Program (JOBS) was to increase from $1.1 billion in fiscal 1994 budget authority to $1.3 billion. States used JOBS funding for education and training programs designed to help move welfare recipients into the work force.

Payments to states for foster care and adoption assistance were to increase by $448 million, to $3.4 billion in fiscal 1995. The funding

would serve an average of 256,000 children a month.

Clinton's National Service initiative was to get $861 million, up $284 million.

Energy

Energy programs, particularly those that split atoms, got a smaller share of the federal budget under Clinton's proposal. Outlays for energy were to drop 8.5 percent, from just under $5 billion in fiscal 1994 to $4.56 billion in fiscal 1995.

Continuing a shift in emphasis that started with Clinton's first budget, the 1995 proposal boosted spending on energy efficiency and renewable resources largely at the expense of fossil and nuclear energy.

The budget provided a 27 percent increase for energy efficiency and conservation programs, raising spending in those areas to $743 million. Renewable energy programs, such as solar and geothermal power, also were slated for increases.

Spending on fossil energy research and technology programs dropped 2 percent, to $731 million. Within the fossil energy program, the budget increased for natural gas but plummeted for clean coal programs.

Virtually all nuclear reactor research programs were to end, including a controversial program that the administration resisted cutting in 1993: actinide recycling, which was designed to turn plutonium into a less radioactive substance. The Energy Department noted that the United States was urging other countries not to use plutonium as a source of civilian power.

One nuclear reactor program slated for continued support was the development of an advanced light-water reactor, a safer and more efficient version of the existing generation of plants. The program received $51 million in budget authority in fiscal 1995.

In contrast to nuclear reactor programs, the budget for nuclear waste increased dramatically. The Energy Department proposed to move off budget a portion of the Nuclear Waste Fund, which collected fees from power companies to pay for the disposal of spent nuclear fuel rods. Half that money was to be spent on studies at Yucca Mountain, Nev., the proposed long-term disposal site, and on the development of waste containers.

Savings proposed by the administration included the privatization of some of the naval petroleum and oil-shale reserves. The administration proposed, for example, to offer to the private sector its interest in the Elk Hills oil and natural gas field near Bakersfield, Calif., saving about $200 million in fiscal 1995 that would have gone to operate the field. The administration also was counting on saving $106 million from the uranium enrichment program, mainly by canceling a related project called the Atomic Vapor Laser Isotope Separation program.

Loans for rural electric and telephone service — at the time under the Agriculture Department's Rural Electrification Administration but slated for conversion to a new Rural Utilities Service under the Clinton administration's reorganization plan — declined slightly. Direct and guaranteed private loans to electric utilities decreased slightly to $1 billion, from $1.025 billion; telephone loans decreased to $354 million, from $418 million; and the rural telephone bank decreased to $175 million, from $200 million.

Environment

In line with his promise to emphasize environmental safeguards, Clinton proposed significant spending increases for fiscal 1995 in targeted areas, notably operations of the Environmental Protection Agency (EPA).

Overall, fiscal 1995 outlays for environment and natural resources totaled $21.8 billion, a decrease of $468 million from fiscal 1994. That figure represented a shift away from building expensive dams and other construction projects at the Bureau of Reclamation and U.S. Army Corps of Engineers.

Clinton requested increases in what he called the "high-priority" areas: conservation and land management, such as protecting wetlands; recreation programs, such as national park operations; pollution control, such as more money to enforce the 1990

Clean Air Act; and other natural resource activities.

The budget also assumed that Interior Secretary Bruce Babbitt would charge higher grazing fees and Congress would impose, for the first time, royalties for the extraction of gold, silver and other hard-rock minerals.

Clinton sought congressional approval to charge higher entrance and user fees at national parks. Congress rebuffed a similar request in 1993. Roger G. Kennedy, director of the National Park Service, said no decisions had been made about where to charge higher fees or by how much, but the plan was to raise $32 million. Most of the money was to be pumped back into the parks to pay for a backlog of repairs and maintenance.

After tallying up the money directed to Clinton's "investments," the Office of Management and Budget estimated that spending authority for environment and natural resources actually would increase by 5 percent to $35.2 billion.

A key indicator of Clinton's commitment to the environment was his proposal to increase spending for EPA's daily operations by 13 percent, to almost $3.1 billion. In 1993, Clinton was criticized by environmentalists for reducing the EPA budget. EPA Administrator Carol M. Browner said the money would allow the agency to step up its enforcement of environmental laws already on the books and clean up more toxic waste sites under the superfund and leaking underground storage tank programs.

Clinton also proposed paying for some of the environmental initiatives he announced in 1993, including $283 million to be spent by the EPA, Energy Department and other agencies to reduce so-called greenhouse gases such as carbon dioxide. The money was to be used to urge industries to voluntarily adopt energy saving programs.

The budget included a slight increase, to $1.5 billion, to carry out the superfund program to help clean up toxic waste sites. Polluters also paid into the fund. The request did not assume changes the administration proposed to Congress to overhaul the superfund program and encourage faster settlements by polluters who were liable for cleanup costs.

To meet the demands of states clamoring for more money to comply with environmental mandates, Clinton proposed increased spending for water and drinking water programs.

The budget called for $1.6 billion — a $360 million increase — in new budget authority for fiscal 1995 for a revolving loan fund to provide money to build sewage treatment plants and $700 million — a $101 million increase — for another fund to pay for the construction of drinking water treatment facilities.

The budget allowed the EPA to hire 793 new employees, mostly by shifting money spent on outside contractors and converting them into in-house positions.

By contrast, the Interior Department stood to lose 1,377 positions to comply with the Clinton plan to reduce the federal work force.

The $7.2 billion in outlays requested for Interior was essentially the same as the department's fiscal 1994 budget. But funds were shifted to expand the Clinton administration's efforts to protect entire ecosystems instead of separately tending to land, water and endangered species.

For example, $59 million in new budget authority was earmarked for the Everglades in South Florida, with most of the money coming from Interior's National Park Service. The money was to be used to acquire land, operate parks and preserves, recover endangered species such as the Florida panther and protect habitat.

Other ecosystem management projects focused on the Anacostia River in the Washington, D.C., area and Prince William Sound in Alaska.

The budget also followed through on Clinton's promise to direct more money to the Pacific Northwest, which suffered massive job losses because of a protracted legal dispute over protection of the northern spotted owl. The budget called for $372 million for worker retraining, loans to businesses, ecosystem restoration and watershed planning in Northern California, Oregon and Washington. The Interior, Agriculture, Labor and other departments spent $302 million in fiscal 1994 on this effort.

In a related action, the proposed budget included enough money to cut about 4.6 billion board feet of timber in fiscal 1995 — about the same as the previous year. Timber harvests, especially in the Pacific

Continued on page 78

Administration Economic Assumptions

(Calendar years; dollar amounts in billions) [1]

	Actual 1992	Projections						
		1993	1994	1995	1996	1997	1998	1999
Gross domestic product								
Dollar levels:								
Current dollars	6,038	6,371	6,736	7,118	7,522	7,950	8,400	8,870
Constant (1987) dollars	4,986	5,126	5,284	5,433	5,579	5,725	5,873	6,021
Implicit price deflator (1987 = 100), annual average	121.1	124.3	127.5	131.0	134.8	138.9	143.0	147.3
Percent change, fourth quarter over fourth quarter:								
Current dollars	6.7	5.0	5.8	5.6	5.7	5.7	5.7	5.6
Constant (1987) dollars	3.9	2.3	3.0	2.7	2.7	2.6	2.6	2.5
Implicit price deflator (1987 = 100)	2.8	2.6	2.7	2.8	2.9	3.0	3.0	3.0
Percent change, year over year:								
Current dollars	5.5	5.5	5.7	5.7	5.7	5.7	5.7	5.6
Constant (1987) dollars	2.6	2.8	3.1	2.8	2.7	2.6	2.6	2.5
Implicit price deflator (1987 = 100)	2.9	2.6	2.6	2.8	2.9	3.0	3.0	3.0
Incomes								
Personal income	5,145	5,385	5,691	6,016	6,365	6,746	7,148	7,551
Wages and salaries [2]	2,973	3,083	3,261	3,442	3,636	3,849	4,071	4,293
Corporate profits before tax	395	447	508	531	555	573	595	631
Consumer Price Index (all urban) [3]								
Level (1982-84 = 100), annual average	140.3	144.5	148.6	153.3	158.3	163.6	169.2	174.9
Percent change, fourth quarter over fourth quarter:	3.1	2.8	3.0	3.2	3.3	3.4	3.4	3.4
Percent change, year over year	3.0	3.0	2.8	3.2	3.3	3.3	3.4	3.4
Unemployment rate, civilian (percent) [4]								
Fourth-quarter level	7.3	6.7	6.4	6.0	5.8	5.6	5.5	5.5
Annual average	7.4	6.8	6.5	6.1	5.9	5.7	5.5	5.5
Federal pay raises, January (percent) [5]	4.2	3.7	——	1.6	2.2	2.5	2.5	2.5
Interest rates (percent) [6]								
91-day Treasury bills	3.5	3.0	3.4	3.8	4.1	4.4	4.4	4.4
10-year Treasury notes	7.0	5.9	5.8	5.8	5.8	5.8	5.8	5.8

[1] *Based on data available as of December 1993.*

[2] *Not counting health care overhaul. The administration's health care bill was assumed to increase wages and salaries by $23 billion in 1997, $35 billion in 1998 and $47 billion in 1999.*

[3] *CPI for urban consumers. Two versions of the CPI were published. The index shown here was that currently used, as required by law, in calculating automatic adjustments to individual income tax brackets.*

[4] *Percent of civilian labor force, excluding armed forces residing in the United States. Pre-1994 basis. The introduction of a new labor force questionnaire in January 1994 may have resulted in higher unemployment rates than those shown in the table.*

[5] *In January 1994, military personnel received a 2.2 percent pay increase.*

[6] *Average rate on new issues within period.*

SOURCE: President's fiscal 1995 budget

Budget Authority, Outlays by Agency

(Fiscal years; in millions of dollars †)

AGENCY	BUDGET AUTHORITY			OUTLAYS		
	1993 actual	1994 estimate	1995 proposed	1993 actual	1994 estimate	1995 proposed
Legislative Branch	$2,630	$2,673	$2,910	$2,406	$2,755	$2,912
The Judiciary	2,613	2,829	3,199	2,628	2,872	3,078
Executive Office of the President	236	186	190	194	193	188
Funds Appropriated to the President	24,838	10,978	11,326	11,245	11,383	11,149
Agriculture	67,857	65,268	61,657	63,144	64,931	60,254
Commerce	3,159	3,575	4,229	2,798	3,234	3,625
Defense — Military	267,402	248,966	252,153	278,574	267,484	259,295
Defense — Civil	29,883	30,599	30,596	29,266	30,980	30,872
Education	31,471	28,839	31,684	30,290	28,738	29,657
Energy	17,721	16,760	15,907	16,942	17,206	15,676
Health and Human Services, except Social Security	286,597	327,580	334,946	282,779	316,615	341,615
Health and Human Services, Social Security	300,090	316,174	332,021	298,349	314,663	330,529
Housing and Urban Development	26,468	25,635	27,465	25,181	25,535	27,742
Interior	6,880	7,515	7,109	6,796	7,240	7,161
Justice	10,491	10,269	12,837	10,170	10,817	11,343
Labor	46,892	38,646	36,045	44,651	37,111	33,962
State	5,321	5,684	5,284	5,244	5,785	5,393
Transportation	39,971	37,693	40,768	34,457	36,687	37,274
Treasury	300,506	310,139	328,737	298,804	309,268	327,698
Veterans Affairs	36,019	36,528	37,823	35,487	37,919	38,115
Environmental Protection Agency	6,737	6,423	6,915	5,930	6,539	6,663
General Services Administration	604	552	1,567	743	1,048	852
National Aeronautics and Space Administration	14,310	14,468	14,301	14,305	14,183	14,411
Office of Personnel Management	39,345	40,204	42,103	36,794	38,101	40,160
Small Business Administration	1,177	742	809	785	604	478
Other independent agencies	24,050	39,010	19,433	-10,047	15,172	4,907
Allowances			2,979			1,949
TOTAL	**$1,473,557**	**$1,504,701**	**$1,536,981**	**$1,408,205**	**$1,483,829**	**$1,518,945**
On budget	1,204,431	1,219,782	1,238,035	1,141,618	1,202,953	1,223,582
Off budget	269,126	284,919	298,945	266,587	280,876	295,364

† Figures may not add to totals due to rounding; undistributed offsetting receipts not included above.

SOURCE: President's fiscal 1995 budget

Fiscal 1995 Budget by Function

(Figures for 1994 and 1995 are estimates; in millions of dollars †)

	BUDGET AUTHORITY			OUTLAYS		
	1993	1994	1995	1993	1994	1995
NATIONAL DEFENSE						
Military defense	$ 267,194	$ 248,967	$ 252,153	$ 278,561	$ 267,360	$ 259,228
Atomic energy defense activities	12,059	10,877	10,598	11,017	11,184	11,497
Defense-related activities	1,823	1,074	914	1,508	1,280	1,001
TOTAL	281,076	260,918	263,666	291,086	279,824	270,725
INTERNATIONAL AFFAIRS						
International security assistance	5,475	4,499	−913	7,631	6,747	1,973
International development/humanitarian assistance	7,007	7,551	−1,127	5,413	7,325	4,294
Conduct of foreign affairs	4,327	4,619	3,700	4,325	4,742	3,793
Foreign information and exchange activities	1,248	1,358	1,449	1,352	1,405	1,404
International financial programs	14,275	805	484	−1,896	−1,251	−1,057
International cooperation	—	—	15,164	—	—	7,390
TOTAL	32,333	18,831	18,757	16,826	18,968	17,798
GENERAL SCIENCE, SPACE AND TECHNOLOGY						
General science and basic research	4,173	4,600	4,281	3,938	4,445	3,893
Space flight, research and supporting activities	13,064	12,915	13,029	13,092	12,833	13,048
TOTAL	17,236	17,515	17,310	17,030	17,279	16,941
ENERGY						
Energy supply	7,404	3,479	3,230	3,286	3,743	3,206
Energy conservation	561	673	961	521	586	743
Emergency energy preparedness	60	216	144	336	279	242
Energy information, policy and regulation	240	373	384	176	380	373
TOTAL	8,264	4,741	4,720	4,319	4,988	4,564
NATURAL RESOURCES AND ENVIRONMENT						
Pollution control and abatement	6,908	6,568	7,115	6,061	6,667	6,816
Water resources	4,801	5,301	4,028	4,258	5,596	4,615
Conservation and land management	4,775	4,837	5,009	4,777	4,772	4,944
Recreational resources	2,604	2,719	2,670	2,620	2,655	2,754
Other natural resources	2,547	2,740	2,774	2,522	2,595	2,688
TOTAL	21,636	22,163	21,596	20,239	22,285	21,817
AGRICULTURE						
Farm income stabilization	16,464	13,366	10,176	17,799	14,162	9,950
Agricultural research and services	2,660	2,721	2,795	2,643	2,705	2,846
TOTAL	19,124	16,087	12,972	20,443	16,868	12,795
COMMERCE AND HOUSING CREDIT						
Mortgage credit	2,302	2,630	1,758	1,554	−388	−477
Postal Service subsidy (on budget)	161	130	130	161	130	130
Postal Service (off budget)	2,239	4,282	5,349	1,441	1,748	3,259
Deposit insurance	2,462	18,745	859	−27,957	−3,285	−11,097
Other advancement of commerce	2,743	2,405	3,184	2,077	2,298	2,704
TOTAL	9,906	28,191	11,281	−22,725	504	−5,482
(On budget)	(7,667)	(23,909)	(5,932)	(−24,166)	(−1,245)	(−8,741)
(Off budget)	(2,239)	(4,282)	(5,349)	(1,441)	(1,748)	(3,259)
TRANSPORTATION						
Ground transportation	26,446	25,281	26,633	21,251	23,380	24,305
Air transportation	10,396	9,694	10,103	10,049	10,103	10,049
Water transportation	3,287	3,628	4,692	3,423	3,783	3,690
Other transportation	299	315	331	281	315	324
TOTAL	40,428	38,918	41,759	35,004	37,582	38,368
COMMUNITY AND REGIONAL DEVELOPMENT						
Community development	4,848	4,591	5,724	3,681	4,311	4,878
Area and regional development	2,919	3,129	2,963	2,443	2,538	2,662
Disaster relief and insurance	2,387	637	633	2,927	2,434	1,614
TOTAL	10,154	8,357	9,319	9,051	9,282	9,154
EDUCATION, TRAINING, EMPLOYMENT, SOCIAL SERVICES						
Elementary, secondary and vocational education	14,214	14,677	16,558	13,481	15,252	14,918
Higher education	14,759	11,503	12,414	14,483	10,575	11,828
Research and general education aids	2,119	2,158	2,340	2,040	2,219	2,301
Training and employment	7,347	7,946	9,189	6,700	7,136	7,724
Other labor services	933	957	1,062	948	952	1,036
Social services	13,387	16,127	16,133	12,360	14,660	15,717
TOTAL	52,760	53,368	57,696	50,012	50,793	53,524

Fiscal 1995 Budget by Function

(Figures for 1994 and 1995 are estimates; in millions of dollars †)

	BUDGET AUTHORITY			OUTLAYS		
	1993	1994	1995	1993	1994	1995
HEALTH						
Health care services	$ 95,638	$ 102,506	$ 103,282	$ 86,860	$ 98,969	$ 108,983
Health research and training	11,161	11,632	13,474	10,794	11,336	12,401
Consumer and occupational health and safety	1,817	1,937	1,654	1,762	1,947	1,693
TOTAL	108,616	116,075	118,410	99,415	112,252	123,077
MEDICARE	124,757	150,583	156,135	130,552	143,651	156,228
INCOME SECURITY						
General retirement and disability insurance	5,678	6,245	6,149	4,347	5,203	5,241
Federal employee retirement and disability	61,625	63,546	65,740	60,047	62,257	64,408
Unemployment compensation	38,164	29,195	25,442	37,802	29,210	25,453
Housing assistance	21,177	20,729	21,702	21,548	23,840	25,396
Food and nutrition assistance	39,016	39,963	40,721	35,148	38,183	38,443
Other income security	49,154	55,521	61,974	48,366	55,933	62,499
TOTAL	214,815	215,198	221,729	207,257	214,626	221,440
SOCIAL SECURITY	306,338	321,964	338,660	304,585	320,460	337,168
(On budget)	(6,248)	(5,790)	(6,639)	(6,236)	(5,796)	(6,639)
(Off budget)	(300,090)	(316,174)	(332,021)	(298,349)	(314,663)	(330,529)
VETERANS BENEFITS AND SERVICES						
Income security	18,123	18,615	19,059	17,758	19,801	18,959
Education, training and rehabilitation	675	985	1,140	826	1,170	1,196
Housing	1,181	42	513	1,299	212	637
Hospital and medical care	15,235	16,036	17,157	14,812	15,842	17,413
Other benefits and services	1,043	1,057	1,080	1,025	1,104	1,042
TOTAL	36,259	36,736	38,949	35,720	38,129	39,247
ADMINISTRATION OF JUSTICE						
Federal law enforcement activities	6,751	6,872	6,989	6,674	6,843	6,725
Federal litigative and judicial activities	5,486	5,922	6,384	5,336	6,151	6,283
Federal correctional activities	1,937	2,220	2,598	2,124	2,482	2,856
Criminal justice assistance	1,006	859	2,988	822	1,002	1,467
TOTAL	15,180	15,873	18,960	14,955	16,479	17,331
GENERAL GOVERNMENT						
Legislative functions	2,109	2,114	2,323	2,124	2,169	2,318
Executive direction and management	254	254	299	197	254	271
Central fiscal operations	7,254	7,580	7,631	6,976	7,578	7,558
General property and records management	763	740	1,760	1,005	1,324	1,038
Central personnel management	178	177	171	182	162	167
General-purpose fiscal assistance	1,919	2,158	2,170	1,935	2,158	2,172
Other general government	1,503	1,291	1,045	1,329	1,346	984
Deductions for offsetting receipts	−739	−691	−700	−739	−691	−700
TOTAL	13,240	13,623	14,701	13,009	14,299	13,807
NET INTEREST						
Interest on the public debt	292,502	298,505	310,906	292,502	298,505	310,906
Interest received by on-budget trust funds	−55,537	−56,772	−57,191	−55,537	−56,772	−57,191
Interest received by off-budget trust funds	−26,788	−29,073	−31,669	−26,788	−29,073	−31,669
Other interest	−11,356	−9,212	−9,211	−11,387	−9,212	−9,211
TOTAL	198,822	203,448	212,835	198,811	203,448	212,835
(On budget)	(225,610)	(232,521)	(244,504)	(225,599)	(232,521)	(244,504)
(Off budget)	(−26,788)	(−29,073)	(−31,669)	(−26,788)	(−29,073)	(−31,669)
ALLOWANCES	—	—	124	—	—	205
UNDISTRIBUTED OFFSETTING RECEIPTS	−37,386	−37,887	−42,597	−37,386	−37,887	−42,597
(On budget)	(−30,970)	(−31,425)	(−35,841)	(−30,970)	(−31,425)	(−35,841)
(Off budget)	(−6,416)	(−6,463)	(−6,756)	(−6,416)	(−6,463)	(−6,756)
TOTAL	$ 1,473,557	$ 1,504,701	$ 1,536,981	$ 1,408,205	$ 1,483,829	$ 1,518,945
(On budget)	(1,204,431)	(1,219,782)	(1,238,035)	(1,141,618)	(1,202,953)	(1,223,582)
(Off budget)	(269,126)	(284,919)	(298,945)	(266,587)	(280,876)	(295,364)

† Figures may not add due to rounding.

SOURCE: President's fiscal 1995 budget

Continued from page 73

Northwest, had decreased steadily since the mid-1980s.

Clinton also proposed spending $708 million in the Interior Department, EPA and Army Corps of Engineers to implement his plan to protect wetlands. The Agriculture Department was to receive $283 million for its wetlands reserve program to remove up to 300,000 acres of wetlands from agriculture production.

Health, Medicare

The president refrained from proposing major changes in health programs in his 1995 budget in anticipation of passage of a sweeping bill to overhaul the nation's health care system later the year. Pending that outcome, the budget projected that spending for all government health programs except Medicare would rise to $123.1 billion in fiscal 1995, up from $112.3 billion in fiscal 1994. Spending for Medicare, the federal insurance program for the elderly and the disabled, was expected to rise to $156.2 billion, up from $143.7 billion.

In 1993, Congress had enacted deep cuts in both Medicare and Medicaid, the federal-state health insurance program for the poor, and those cuts continued to reduce payments to doctors and hospitals in fiscal 1995.

As part of the administration's effort to reduce government spending, the budget froze or cut 86 discretionary health programs, including that of the Centers for Disease Control and Prevention, whose epidemiologists tracked the outbreak and prevention of communicable disease. Spending rose only for programs that promoted disease prevention and children's health, both well-established priorities for the Clinton administration.

● **Health care overhaul.** Most of the financial effects of Clinton's health care overhaul plan were not expected to be felt until the late 1990s. However, the budget included about $3.5 billion for start-up programs in fiscal 1995; the Public Health Service was to receive about $1.1 billion of those funds to increase access to health care services for the poor. Some cuts also were to begin, including a $2.1 billion reduction in Medicare spending.

The administration's budget omitted the financial effects of both Clinton's proposed insurance premiums on employers and individuals, and the subsidies he wanted the government to provide to help poor people and small employers pay for their coverage.

● **Discretionary spending.** Discretionary spending, the amount that Congress controlled from year to year, represented only a fraction of the government's health spending. It paid for the public health programs that provided medical services to the poor, the research done at the National Institutes of Health (NIH), and much of the government's AIDS research and prevention.

The Clinton budget cut spending for the Indian Health Service and the Centers for Disease Control by 4.5 percent and 4 percent respectively. However, it increased spending for an array of programs that featured prevention. Family planning received $199 million, a 10 percent increase. Child immunizations received $888 million, a 28 percent increase. AIDS research and prevention increased to $2.7 billion, a 6.8 percent increase. And substance abuse treatment and prevention rose to $1.96 billion, a 17 percent increase.

● **Health research.** Although NIH spending totaled $11.5 billion, a 4.7 percent increase over fiscal 1994, a number of individual institutes' funding remained nearly level, except for spending related to AIDS and breast cancer, which were to receive $383 million.

The AIDS research office was slated to receive $1.4 billion in new budget authority, making it second only to the National Cancer Institute in funding among the agency's 23 institutes and offices. Funding the new AIDS office also caused cuts in related institutes, such as the National Institute on Drug Abuse and the National Institute for Allergy and Infectious Diseases.

The administration's Human Genome Project, a multi-year effort to decode the chemical building blocks determining genetic inheritance, got a 21.7 percent increase to $241 million, including both NIH and Energy Department programs.

● **Medicare.** In fiscal 1995, Medicare was expected to serve nearly 37 million people and cost $156.2 billion. Of that, $112 billion was for

Medicare Part A, which paid hospital bills, and $64.2 billion was for Medicare Part B, which paid doctor bills. The Part B costs were offset in part by beneficiaries who shouldered at least 25 percent of the cost of doctor services.

The 1995 Part B budget also reflected a $2 billion reduction that would occur if Clinton's health care overhaul were put into place. The savings were to come from new, higher co-insurance payments by beneficiaries for lab services and a reduction in payments for hospital outpatient services, in addition to Part B reductions stipulated by the 1993 budget agreement.

● **Medicaid.** Medicaid was expected to serve 36 million lower-income Americans at a cost to the federal government of $96 billion in fiscal 1995. Although the federal cost represented an 11 percent increase in funding over 1994, it also reflected a substantial reduction in the rate of growth in the program, which had ballooned in recent years, rising an average of 25 percent annually.

● **Abortion.** The budget allowed federal funding of abortion, but it left open the possibility of restrictions by noting that the administration expected to frame its exact policy with Congress in the course of shaping the health care overhaul bill.

Income Security

Clinton proposed large increases for several income security programs that provided a social safety net. Overall, spending on income security was to increase from $214.6 billion to $221.4 billion.

Spending on homeless assistance, food for low-income mothers and children, and nutrition education were to increase. However, some programs were slated for cuts, namely funding for public housing, housing for the elderly and low-income energy assistance.

Meanwhile, Social Security spending was to increase from $320.5 billion to $337.2 billion, including a projected 3 percent cost of living increase.

● **Housing.** Reducing homelessness was the top priority for Henry G. Cisneros, secretary of Housing and Urban Development. He proposed consolidating several programs for the homeless, including those under the Stewart B. McKinney Homeless Assistance Act of 1987 (PL 100-77), into a new account known as Homeless Assistance Grants. Budget authority under the McKinney Act was to increase to $1.1 billion in fiscal 1995 from $823 million the previous year.

The budget also included $514 million in five-year rental certificates to help move 15,000 homeless families into subsidized private housing. Clinton wanted to add 70,000 housing units to the subsidized rental stock for $2.7 billion, compared with 32,000 units added in fiscal 1994 for $1.1 billion. And he wanted to consolidate HUD's major rental assistance programs.

Improving public housing was Cisneros' second priority, but the administration proposed cutting those programs. Operating subsidies, which generally were the difference between tenants' rent and what it cost to maintain the buildings, were reduced to $2.5 billion in fiscal 1995 budget authority, $124.8 million less than in the previous year. The budget contained $2.8 billion for modernizing public housing developments, a $314 million reduction. And grants to improve some of the nation's most dilapidated public housing units dropped to $500 million in fiscal 1995 budget authority, a $278 million decrease from the previous year.

To encourage home ownership, the administration requested $100 million for the National Homeownership Trust to help low- and moderate-income, first-time buyers with down payments, closing costs and interest rates. The program had not previously been funded. Clinton wanted to reduce the HOME Investment Partnerships program, which provided matching grants to states and localities to expand affordable housing. The proposal cut HOME's budget authority to $1.1 billion, $175 million less than during the previous year.

Another program that felt the budgetary sting was the Section 202 program that provided grants to groups that developed housing for the elderly. Clinton requested $150 million in construction and rental assistance for 1,156 units of housing for the elderly in fiscal 1995, down from $1.2 billion for 9,000 units the year before.

Several programs to promote fair housing and combat discriminatory practices were to be enlarged. The most prominent addition was

$149.1 million in budget authority for a new program to provide counseling grants to help families move out of poverty-stricken areas.

● **Nutrition.** The special supplemental food program for Women, Infants and Children (WIC) was to be increased from $3.2 billion in fiscal 1994 to $3.5 billion in fiscal 1995. The program helped low-income women buy nutritious food for themselves during pregnancy and for their children under age 5. The increase was expected to allow the program to serve an average of 7.2 million people monthly in fiscal 1995, up from 6.5 million the previous year. The administration said about 7.5 million people would be served in 1995 if the program were fully funded.

The administration assumed $25.2 billion in outlays for the food stamp program in fiscal 1995, which was expected to serve an average of 27.3 million people each month. That was down slightly from the $25.5 billion in outlays the previous year, which served about 27.4 million people.

Spending on child nutrition programs, which provided free or reduced-price meals for students and some elderly adults, was to increase from $7.3 billion to $7.7 billion. The administration also proposed increasing funding for nutrition education and training within the Child Nutrition Program, from $12.9 million in fiscal 1994 to $32.5 million in fiscal 1995.

● **Low-Income Home Energy Assistance Program (LIHEAP).** Outlays were slated to decrease from $2.1 billion in fiscal 1994 to $791 million in fiscal 1995 for LIHEAP, which gave states grants to help low-income households with heating and cooling costs, weatherization and emergency energy assistance. The administration said it was better to assist low-income households through broader programs than through those targeted at a special need.

● **Unemployment compensation.** The budget assumed a decline in spending for unemployment compensation from $29.2 billion in fiscal 1994 to $25.5 billion in fiscal 1995.

● **Other income security.** The Supplemental Security Income program, which helped the aged, blind and disabled, was set to increase from $26.7 billion in fiscal 1994 to $28.5 billion in fiscal 1995. The increase included a projected 3 percent cost of living adjustment. Outlays for the earned-income tax credit, which gave a tax break to the working poor, increased from $10 billion in fiscal 1994 to $15.8 billion in fiscal 1995.

The budget made no provisions for overhauling welfare in fiscal 1995, one of Clinton's stated legislative goals. The administration said welfare changes would not add to the deficit. The budget included $16.9 billion in budget authority for Aid to Families With Dependent Children, up from $16.4 billion in fiscal 1994.

Payments to states for child-care assistance would increase from $893 million in fiscal 1994 to $1.1 billion in fiscal 1995.

International Affairs

The administration maintained that its international affairs budget was the first crafted specifically to address the foreign policy challenges of the post-Cold War era. But one thing had not changed. As in past years, the squeeze on international funding had left little room for new initiatives.

The budget anticipated $17.8 billion in outlays for overseas programs in fiscal 1995, nearly $1.2 billion less than the year before. The international affairs budget funded bilateral and economic assistance programs, U.S. contributions to a host of international organizations and operating expenses for the State Department and other agencies.

State Department officials insisted that the outlay level painted a deceptively gloomy picture of the budget. The department calculated available spending in new budget authority rather than in outlays.

The administration requested $20.8 billion in new budget authority, a modest $44 million increase over fiscal 1994. Secretary of State Warren Christopher, who had conducted an unusually public campaign for more funding, said he was pleased with the outcome.

As part of its broader effort to revamp the foreign aid program, the administration scrapped traditional budget categories such as military and economic aid. Instead, it asked for funds to support broad objectives, such as promoting peace and advancing diplomacy. But beyond the new budgetary architecture, it was clear that the administration would be hard pressed just to keep up with its international commitments.

The budget included a significant boost in funding for U.S. contributions to multilateral development banks such as the International Monetary Fund and World Bank. Clinton sought $2.1 billion in new budget authority for fiscal 1995, an increase of more than $600 million over the level Congress appropriated for fiscal 1994. The request was nearly identical to the $2 billion Clinton had requested the year before, but Congress had trimmed about $450 million.

That had been a recurring pattern, and as a result, the United States had fallen behind by an estimated $819 million in promised support for the banks. A portion of the requested increase for those institutions — $87 million — was to be used to begin repaying those arrearages.

Clinton also sought $1.3 billion in budget authority for assessed contributions to U.N. peacekeeping operations — an increase of about $800 million over the level Congress approved the year before. Under a longstanding formula, the United Nations assessed the United States about 31 percent of the cost of such missions. The administration had requested more than half that money, $670 million, in the form of a fiscal 1994 supplemental appropriation, but the Senate Appropriations Committee dealt the administration a setback when it declined to attach the supplemental request to a multi-billion dollar relief package for California earthquake victims

In addition, Clinton proposed to draw $300 million from the Pentagon's budget to pay for U.N. peacekeeping missions.

In keeping with its new, goal-oriented strategy for providing aid abroad, the administration requested more resources to address global problems such as rapid population growth and environmental degradation. The budget included $585 million for international family planning programs, an $83 million increase over fiscal 1994.

The shrinking pool of traditional bilateral assistance was reserved primarily for a handful of countries — Israel, Egypt and the former Soviet bloc countries. Under the budget category of "promoting peace," the administration sought $3 billion in aid for Israel and $2.1 billion for Egypt, the same amounts as in recent years.

It also requested $75 million to back economic development activities in the West Bank and Gaza Strip, part of a multi-year program to support the 1993 peace accord between Israel and the Palestine Liberation Organization.

Clinton requested $900 million for the former Soviet republics, a significant reduction from the massive $2.5 billion aid package for those countries, which Congress approved for fiscal 1994. In addition, he sought $380 million for Central and Eastern Europe, the same level as in fiscal 1994.

Justice

Clinton largely followed through on his promise to make crime-fighting a top domestic priority, requesting $17.3 billion for fighting crime and related law and judicial activities, about $850 million more than outlays for fiscal 1994. Virtually all that increase, $698 million, was to go to finance elements of Clinton's proposed anti-crime package — notably his pledge to put 100,000 new police officers on the nation's streets.

The money was to go into a new "crime control fund," paralleling a proposed anti-crime trust fund in the Senate-passed crime bill (HR 3355) pending in the House.

Clinton wanted to obligate $2.4 billion in new budget authority for the fund, with an additional $21.3 billion over the four subsequent years. That corresponded with the Senate proposal to allocate $22.3 billion over five years to new anti-crime initiatives.

Clinton wanted $1.7 billion of the money in the crime fund to go toward the first phase of the cops-on-the-beat grant program. Attorney General Janet Reno said the money would enable localities to begin hiring as many as 50,000 of the 100,000 promised new police officers.

An additional $100 million was to go toward implementing the

Brady bill (PL 103-159), most of it in the form of aid to states to help them update and computerize their criminal records and conduct the required background checks for would-be handgun purchasers. That was half of what the law authorized for fiscal 1995.

Those increases were somewhat offset by cuts in an existing anti-crime grant program. The administration wanted to cut $374.5 million from the Byrne grant program, eliminating formula block grants that helped states fight crime and drugs. But the budget doubled discretionary grants under this program to $100 million. And the administration also proposed increasing by $69 million, to $172.2 million, existing grants to prevent and handle juvenile crime.

Spending for federal prisons increased 17 percent under the Clinton budget, to a total of $2.6 billion in fiscal 1995 spending authority. His request included a little more than $100 million to activate new prisons and provide close to 9,700 new inmate beds. The budget also included $82.7 million for new prison construction to provide 4,200 new prison slots, although the overall budget request for construction and repairs was down about $80 million from fiscal 1994 appropriations.

Immigration, like crime, was attracting public attention and a corresponding emphasis in the budget. The budget for the Immigration and Naturalization Service rose about $100 million over fiscal 1994 appropriations, to a requested $1.15 billion in new spending authority. Immigration-related fees were expected to bring in about $680 million, adding to the agency's overall budget.

Within the proposed new crime-control fund, $300 million was to go for initiatives to decrease illegal immigration, including expanded border controls and expedited deportation of criminal aliens. And the president sought an additional $98 million in budget authority for other immigration initiatives to streamline the backlogged asylum application process and to promote naturalization for legal aliens who qualify.

Even so, the Justice Department was not immune to overall budget pressures, and many programs faced cuts or stay-even budgets outside select new initiatives.

According to the Justice Department, Clinton's budget meant eliminating the equivalent of 650 full-time positions in fiscal 1995, for projected savings of $65 million plus $33 million in administrative savings. The FBI was one of the departments slated to lose personnel, but administration documents said all the reductions were to be among support staff and that the overall number of active agents would remain the same.

Science, Space, Technology

In the aftermath of the repudiation of costly "big science" projects in fiscal 1994, when Congress killed the superconducting super collider and Clinton scaled down the National Aeronautics and Space Administration's space station, the president's fiscal 1995 science budget emphasized private sector cooperation and smaller-scale initiatives that promised quicker benefits to the work force and the economy.

For example, the number of cooperative research ventures between federal laboratories and the private sector was to jump by 453, to 3,211. The number of programs to transfer government technology to the private sector was to increase by 57 percent, to 865. And while NASA had to struggle with budget cuts overall, its new mission was to produce fast-starting, low-budget space projects that had immediate commercial value.

In a budget climate where an increase to account for inflation was considered good news, science fared rather well. The narrowly defined budget-function category of "general science, space and technology," which included the National Science Foundation, Energy Department general science programs and NASA — but not defense research and development, the National Institutes of Health (NIH) or Commerce Department research — declined to $16.9 billion in outlays, down $338 million from the fiscal 1994 level of $17.3 billion. Governmentwide, the budget produced $69.9 billion in outlays for R&D in fiscal 1995. That figure was up 2.6 percent from the 1994 fiscal year figure of $68.1 billion.

The mix between defense and civilian research was not to change

significantly, despite Clinton's goal upon taking office of boosting civilian research until it reached parity with defense R&D spending, which accounted for some 53 percent of the research budget.

The Defense Department got $36.9 billion in budget authority for R&D programs, up $1.4 billion or 4 percent from fiscal 1994. The Energy Department, which conducted research on nuclear weapons, was to receive about the same research funding at $6 billion.

White House Science Adviser John H. Gibbons said the administration hoped to achieve parity between civilian and defense research by 1998.

● **Commerce.** The Commerce Department was to get the largest percentage increase in funding of all the research agencies. Clinton requested $4.2 billion in new budget authority, an increase of about $650 million, or 18 percent, from fiscal 1994.

● **Life sciences.** The NIH, the government's largest fount of basic research, was to receive a 5 percent increase, but the extra money was to go largely toward a new Office of AIDS Research that was created in 1993.

● **Physical science.** The National Science Foundation, which supported nearly half of all non-biomedical basic research at academic institutions, was to receive $3.2 billion in budget authority, a $182 million increase over fiscal 1994.

Global change research reaped the biggest increase, up 46 percent to $208 million in fiscal 1995 budget authority. High-performance computing and communications research was to rise 23 percent, to $329 million.

As had typically happened in past budget requests, Clinton asked for a huge cut — 50 percent — in academic research facilities, which were to be funded at a level of $55 million. Congress was fond of this category, however, and lawmakers annually appropriated nearly double that amount.

● **Space programs.** For NASA, however, Clinton requested the agency's first year-to-year budget reduction in more than two decades. The administration wanted to cut NASA's budget authority from $14.6 billion in fiscal 1994 to $14.3 billion.

That meant the space shuttle program, for which Clinton requested $3.3 billion in new budget authority, would have to take a $225.3 million hit. NASA planned eight shuttle flights in fiscal 1995, compared with nine flights budgeted in fiscal 1994.

Congress' cancellation in fiscal 1994 of the Advanced Solid Rocket Motor program, for a fiscal 1995 savings of $289 million, helped compensate for much of that reduction.

The redesigned space station program, which included new cooperation from Russia, was to receive $2.1 billion in budget authority, up from $1.95 billion in fiscal 1994.

The budget cuts meant a reduction of more than 3,000 civil service workers, mostly at NASA installations involved in the space station program — Johnson Space Center in Houston, Kennedy Space Center in Cape Canaveral, Fla., and Marshall Space Flight Center in Huntsville, Ala. NASA officials said the reductions would be achieved through retirements and other measures rather than through layoffs.

Mission to Planet Earth, a series of Earth observation satellites and a favorite program of Vice President Al Gore, got a boost of $214 million to $1.2 billion in budget authority.

NASA science programs fared well, rising by $45 million in budget authority to $1.8 billion. The administration proposed a new Mars Surveyor program, at a level of $78.4 million, which the agency hoped would typify its new goal of faster, cheaper projects that yielded quick results.

In that same vein, a NASA program, then a year old, that focused on industry-led research projects into advanced technologies received $67 million in new budget authority, a 60 percent increase.

Transportation

The administration again proposed to spend more on highways, railroads and mass transit programs despite the tightening federal budget. Clinton requested a 2 percent increase in total outlays for transportation programs, to $38.4 billion. More than half the money was to come out of the Highway Trust Fund, a pot that was filled by federal gasoline tax revenues.

To make room for more spending, the Transportation Department again proposed to cut money for highway "demonstration" projects, subsidies for rural airports and university aviation programs. Those programs started in Congress, and the first two still had strong support there.

The main additions to the budget were new subsidy programs for U.S. shipping lines and shipyards. The shipping line subsidy program was to cost $1 billion over 10 years and be paid for by a 150 percent increase in the tonnage duties paid by all oceangoing cargo vessels. The shipyards were to benefit from a new, $500 million guaranteed loan program for ship buyers and yard owners, costing taxpayers $54 million in subsidies in the first year.

For highways, the administration proposed to allow nearly $20 billion in spending from the Highway Trust Fund.

The budget included rescissions of $488 million in budget authority from demonstration projects funded by previous appropriations bills. It also delayed spending on other highway programs, including demonstration projects launched by the 1991 surface transportation law (PL 102-240).

Mass transit spending climbed again by 2 percent, to $3.8 billion, fueled mainly by a large increase in grants for long-term improvements to existing bus and rail services. The proposed total budget authority was slightly less than $5 billion, with $2 billion of that amount slated for capital investments in urban areas.

However, the administration asked for substantial cuts in programs to help cities run and expand their bus and rail lines. The budget authority for operating assistance was cut by 25 percent, to $600 million, and by 57 percent for new transit projects, to $400 million. Discretionary grants to buy buses or build terminals were to be cut by 8 percent, to $327 million.

The administration did not apply the same budgetary thinking to Amtrak, the government-owned passenger rail corporation. Amtrak was to receive a 10 percent increase, to $536 million, for operating expenses and retirement payments, and a 29 percent increase, to $252 million, for capital investments.

One new venture proposed by the Federal Transit Administration was a $30 million program called the Livable Communities Initiative. The program was to aid communities that adopted regulations encouraging the use of mass transit.

Clinton sought to boost the Transportation Department's efforts in research and high-technology development. Among other proposals, he requested $289 million in budget authority for a high-tech approach to reducing highway congestion, a 35 percent increase; $32.5 million to develop high-speed rail technology, almost 10 times more than was appropriated in fiscal 1994; and $45.7 million to use a satellite-based mapping system developed by the Defense Department in civilian transportation.

One high-tech program on the chopping block was the development of a magnetic-levitation train, which would travel at extremely high speeds on a cushion of air. The administration proposed no money for this project in fiscal 1995, and it wanted to rescind $17 million of the $20 million appropriated the previous year.

For aviation programs, spending was to dip slightly to less than $8.7 billion, although budget authority grew slightly to $8.8 billion. Airport improvement grants, Federal Aviation Administration (FAA) operations and aviation research received roughly the same budget authority as in fiscal 1994, but the FAA's budget authority for equipment purchases would increase 7 percent, to $2.3 billion.

Coast Guard spending was to dip by 5 percent, to $3.5 billion, although its budget authority grew 4 percent, to $3.7 billion. Almost all the increase in budget authority was for capital investments, including the renovation or replacement of nine classes of boats and the continued development of a better system to manage vessel traffic.

Among the programs to be cut was the National Highway Traffic Safety Administration, whose budget authority fell $21 million, or 7 percent. The cut stemmed from the end of grant programs that encouraged states to toughen their laws on seat belts, motorcycle helmets and drunken driving.

Boating safety grants to states also were to be eliminated, as were the subsidies for freight rail lines, saving more than $63.6 million.

Veterans Affairs

The budget estimated total spending of $39.2 billion in outlays for veterans programs, an increase of $1.1 billion above the fiscal 1994 level.

Clinton called for a substantial spending increase of $1.6 billion for veterans' health care, to $17.4 billion. This included $1 billion for a new investment fund, which was to be established under the administration's comprehensive health care overhaul proposal to help the Department of Veterans Affairs (VA) make the transition to the new health care system.

The budget included $636 million for the construction and expansion of VA hospitals and other health-related facilities, down from $692 million in fiscal 1994.

The administration estimated spending nearly $17.4 billion to pay compensation and pension benefits to veterans and their dependents. This was slightly less than the $19.8 billion provided in fiscal 1994, but that was due mainly to the fact that the VA had to make 11 instead of the usual 12 monthly payments to beneficiaries in fiscal 1995. The first payment was always issued Oct. 1, the first day of each fiscal year. But since that day fell on a Saturday in 1994, the payment instead was to be issued Sept. 30 (fiscal 1994), the last business day before Oct. 1.

Overall funding for the GI Bill of Rights and related veterans education programs in Clinton's budget was $1.3 billion, an increase of $102 million over the previous year's level. The increase was the result of continued military downsizing, which was expected to increase the pool of veterans eligible for educational benefits   ■

Congress' Budget Mirrors Clinton Plan

Congress completed work on its own fiscal guidelines for the year on May 12, adopting a hold-the-line fiscal 1995 budget resolution (H Con Res 218) that largely followed the proposal President Clinton had submitted in February and complied with his request that Congress take a year off from major deficit-reduction efforts.

The chief difference between the original House and Senate versions of the $1.5 trillion budget resolution (H Con Res 218, S Con Res 63) was an extra $26.1 billion in unspecified spending cuts approved by the Senate. In the end, the House and Senate agreed on an extra $13 billion in outlays to be taken out of appropriations over five years — $500 million of it in fiscal 1995. While the first-year cut was comparatively small, it added another hardship to what appropriators already

had said was going to be a difficult year for them.

Ultimately, it was the appropriators who would have the job of deciding on the program cuts; their only obligation to the budget was to abide by the overall cap of $540.6 billion for discretionary spending in fiscal 1995. The budget resolution did make detailed recommendations — according to Senate Budget Committee Chairman Jim Sasser, D-Tenn., it called for cutting or terminating more than 300 federal programs — but those details were merely advisory.

What worried the appropriators were the tight overall constraints on discretionary spending, the one-third of the federal budget over which they had unfettered control. (The rest of the budget consisted of mandatory spending for entitlement programs such as Social Security and Medicare, and

interest on the federal debt.)

Under budget caps agreed to as part of the 1993 reconciliation bill, discretionary outlays already had been set to decline for the first time since 1969 — from $546.8 billion in fiscal 1994 to $541.1 billion in fiscal 1995. The $500 million in additional 1995 cuts required by the budget resolution brought that to $540.6 billion. According to an analysis by the Congressional Budget Office (CBO), that meant that 1995 outlays would fall about $13 billion below the amount needed to keep 1994 programs even with inflation and population growth.

In addition, while Clinton sought to stay within the caps, he also wanted about $13 billion in new domestic "investment" spending for such purposes as education, health care and child nutrition — a request that could be fulfilled only by cutting even more from other programs.

Finally, CBO found that, by its accounting, the president's budget actually had exceeded the 1995 caps by $3.1 billion. Because Congress lived by CBO rules, appropriators had to squeeze at least another $3.1 billion out of Clinton's 1995 appropriations proposals.

Background

Like Clinton's budget, Congress' fiscal blueprint was confined mainly to filling in the outlines of the deficit reduction that Congress had mandated in 1993. It contained no provisions for a new budget-reconciliation bill to align taxes and entitlement spending with deficit-reduction goals. It focused instead on rearranging spending within the discretionary part of the budget.

The 1993 package of spending cuts and hefty tax increases (PL 103-66) had been extraordinarily controversial. In the end, after intensive lobbying by Democratic leaders and by Clinton himself, the bill had cleared without a single vote to spare in either chamber. Republicans still were seeking ways to repeal some of the 1993 tax increases. *(1993 Almanac, p. 107)*

The 1993 package was expected to yield $433 billion in new deficit reduction over five years. (The bill originally was projected to cut the deficit by $496 billion, but CBO had since calculated the savings at $433 billion.)

Democratic leaders said that was enough for the economy to digest at one time and noted that the projected deficit for 1995 had fallen to $175.3 billion — the result of the reconciliation bill savings and improvements in the economy. That would be the lowest deficit in dollar terms in six years. Measured against the size of the economy, it would amount to 2.5 percent of the gross domestic product (GDP), the lowest in 16 years. The average size of the deficit since 1982 had been 4.4 percent of GDP. "I think whatever anyone could say in the past about the possibility of taking deeper spending cuts, there is no question now that we are at the bone," said Speaker Thomas S. Foley, D-Wash., during the House debate on the budget.

But deficit hawks stressed that after bottoming out at $173.1 billion in 1996, the deficit was projected to begin climbing again, topping $200 billion by 1999. The White House argued that its health care reform proposal would take

---

BOXSCORE

Fiscal 1995 Budget Resolution — H Con Res 218 (S Con Res 63). The $1.5 trillion budget resolution provided the parameters for Congress' fiscal decisions for the year.

Reports: H Rept 103-428, S Rept 103-238; conference report H Rept 103-490.

KEY ACTION

March 11 — House passed H Con Res 218, 223-175.

March 25 — Senate passed H Con Res 218, 57-40, after substituting the text of S Con Res 63.

May 5 — House adopted the conference report, 220-183.

May 12 — Senate adopted the report, 53-46.

---

care of that, bringing health care spending under control and eventually pushing the deficit down significantly. But a CBO analysis suggested that would not begin to happen until after 2004.

The budget was a concurrent resolution setting broad tax and spending priorities for Congress. It did not become law and therefore did not require the president's signature.

House Committee

Voting along strict party lines, the House Budget Committee on March 3 approved a slightly modified version of Clinton's budget (H Rept 103-428). The vote was 26-17, with Democrats unanimous in their support.

The committee tinkered with Clinton's plans to rearrange spending under the fiscal 1995 discretionary limit, imposing some of its own priorities while getting rid of the $3.1 billion excess that CBO had found in Clinton's budget proposal. The Budget Committee ordered 36 separate cuts, including trims of $225 million from defense and $115 million from foreign aid.

The committee also partially restored some cuts that Clinton had proposed, adding back $494 million for the Low Income Home Energy Assistance Program (LIHEAP), which helped low-income people pay utility bills, and $100 million for mass transit operating subsidies.

Republicans Offer Alternative

For the second year in a row, the committee's Republicans, led by John R. Kasich of Ohio, coalesced behind an ambitious alternative budget that included scores of cuts, many of them highly detailed. In 1993, Kasich had had to overcome considerable opposition from Republicans who feared that such a move would shift attention from their attacks on Clinton's budget and tie them up defending their own proposals. In 1994, there was much less internal GOP opposition. "Even some of the most cantankerous people" went along with the program, said David L Hobson, R-Ohio, a Kasich ally.

Kasich said the GOP alternative offered much deeper deficit reduction over five years than Clinton's plan did, while offsetting about a third of the tax increases. The plan included a tax credit of $500 per child for families with incomes of less than $200,000 a year.

Kasich's proposal still envisioned deficits rising after 1996, however, and hitting $176.1 billion in 1999. Kasich conceded that one reason his proposal did not balance the budget was that Republicans had not yet solved the problem of out-of-control health care costs. Further, Kasich said that it might not be realistic to try to balance the budget in less than 10 years.

In a mirror image of their final vote on the budget resolution, Democrats lined up unanimously in the "no" column to defeat the GOP alternative, 17-26.

Committee Democrats united with Republicans to reject a tough proposal by Charles W. Stenholm, D-Texas, that would have eliminated annual cost of living adjustments (COLAs) for all federal retirees and Social Security beneficiaries in 1996 and 1998. The vote was 8-32. Stenholm, chief House

sponsor of a proposed balanced-budget amendment to the Constitution (H J Res 103), said his COLA proposal would save $67.3 billion by 1999 and represented the sort of action Congress would have to find the courage to take if it really intended to balance the budget. Stenholm drew votes from only two other Democrats and five Republicans. *(Balanced-budget amendment, p. 85)*

In other action during the March 3 markup, the Budget Committee:

● Barely rejected, by a vote of 21-22, a Republican amendment to add a GOP welfare-reform plan to the budget resolution. Four Democrats — Stenholm, Glen Browder of Alabama, Bill Orton of Utah and Mike Parker of Mississippi — crossed party lines to join the Republicans.

● Voted 26-17 to approve a sense-of-the-Congress amendment that lawmakers ought to appropriate money to help state governments cope with the huge costs caused by illegal immigration. The committee opted for this amendment over a more aggressive proposal that would have declared that the federal government should fully reimburse the states for those costs.

● Voted by voice to approve a sense-of-the-Congress amendment that said emergency spending provisions repeatedly had been used to provide appropriations spending above the discretionary caps, and that the process should be replaced by a reserve fund that would set aside 1 percent of annual outlays for emergencies. The amendment also said that emergency needs that exceeded the 1 percent fund should be met by cutting other spending.

House Floor

After rejecting conservative alternatives that called for further deficit reduction and liberal proposals for deeper cuts in defense spending, the House voted, 223-175, on March 11 to adopt the budget resolution as it had been crafted by the committee. *(Vote 56, p. 18-H)*

Earlier, the House rejected four substitute proposals:

● **Kasich substitute**. The House on March 11 defeated, 165-243, the chief GOP alternative budget, offered by Kasich. In addition to scores of spending cuts, the Kasich plan included tax cuts, an increase in defense spending above the Clinton level, and Republican proposals for reform of welfare and health care. It would have reduced the deficit by an additional $147.5 billion over five years. *(Vote 55, p. 18-H)*

● **Congressional Black Caucus substitute**. Also on March 11, lawmakers defeated, 81-326, a package introduced by Congressional Black Caucus Chairman Kweisi Mfume, D-Md. The plan sought to create jobs by cutting defense spending authority by $175.1 billion over five years and distributing the savings primarily to a wide array of domestic programs, including education, job training, health and transportation. The Mfume substitute also proposed to increase funding for certain foreign aid programs, and it would have imposed a 20 percent federal tax on the sale of handguns, assault weapons and ammunition. Mfume maintained that the deficit under his substitute would be $1.8 billion lower than that in the House Budget Committee version. *(Vote 54, p. 18-H)*

● **Frank substitute**. The previous day, the House defeated, 105-313, a budget plan offered by liberal Barney Frank, D-Mass. Unlike the other substitutes, Frank's took aim at just one item in the budget, proposing to strip $2.4 billion in budget authority from Clinton's 1995 defense spending proposal. Frank said Clinton had added the money for military pay raises despite having signaled in the fiscal 1994 budget plan that he would push the defense budget no higher. Frank

argued that the military budget should have to absorb extra spending demands just as domestic programs did. *(Vote 51, p. 16-H)*

● Solomon substitute. Also on March 10, the House defeated, 73-342, a hard-line package offered by Gerald B. H. Solomon, R-N.Y. It was a collection of deficit-reduction ideas culled from Kasich's plan and several others with the intention of offering a proposal that actually would balance the budget. *(Vote 52, p. 16-H)*

Solomon said his package would cut $698 billion from the deficit by 1999, almost five times the size of the deficit reduction in Kasich's plan. That would have been more than enough to bring the budget into balance, but at a significant cost: Among Solomon's cuts were the elimination of all agricultural subsidies except those for dairy farmers; a 50 percent cut in all job-training funds; and a cut of $140 billion over five years in Medicare.

The Solomon proposal drew heavy criticism from farm-state Democrats, who said it would throw thousands of farmers into bankruptcy. But Democrat Timothy J. Penny of Minnesota, who supported Solomon's plan, warned that it would "convey to the public just how painful and far-reaching the cuts would be" to balance the budget. And supporter Dick Zimmer, R-N.J., called on fellow supporters of the balanced-budget amendment to back the plan. "Those of us who advocate a balanced budget have a moral responsibility to get specific and show how it can be done," Zimmer said.

Senate Committee

In the Senate, the Budget Committee voted 13-8 on March 17 in favor of a budget (S Con Res 63 — S Rept 103-238) that cut an additional $43.2 billion in spending authority and $26.1 billion in outlays over five years. One Republican, Charles E. Grassley of Iowa, crossed party lines to vote yes with the Democrats. The budget otherwise largely tracked Clinton's proposal.

Committee Chairman Sasser voted for the committee budget, although he first tried to win support for a stay-the-course draft budget resolution similar to that approved by the House. He argued that Congress had done as much as was prudent in 1993. "The economy is presently absorbing as much deficit reduction . . . as we can safely administer," Sasser said.

But Republicans and a handful of the committee's Democrats disagreed. "We ought to take an opportunity when the economy's strong to do something about the deficit," argued ranking committee Republican Pete V. Domenici of New Mexico. "The fact is, what has worked is we had a significant package of deficit reduction last year," said Kent Conrad, D-N.D. "That tells me we ought to stay the course and more."

Conrad and three other Democrats — Jim Exon of Nebraska, Frank R. Lautenberg of New Jersey and Paul Simon of Illinois — joined the panel's nine Republicans in voting to add the cuts to Sasser's draft budget. The committee approved the amendment, offered by Exon and Grassley, by a vote of 13-8.

The committee voted, 9-12, along party lines to reject a substitute budget offered by Domenici that would have cut an additional $322 billion over five years, largely by taking a $180 billion cut out of non-defense appropriations and by using Clinton's proposed savings in Medicare and Medicaid not to pay for health care reform, as Clinton wanted to do, but to reduce the deficit.

The amendment also would have given a $500-per-child

tax credit to middle- and upper-income families, indexed the capital gains tax for inflation and provided $33 billion more in savings through overhauling the welfare system, among other provisions.

Domenici stressed that the GOP substitute would go much further than Clinton proposed in cutting the deficit while returning some of the benefits of spending cuts to taxpayers in the form of reduced taxes. But Sasser charged that the plan was little more than a proposal to "cut taxes now, increase deficits later and make the poor and the middle class pay for it."

Republicans dropped earlier plans to offer a second substitute amendment to balance the budget by 1999, after concluding that the cuts they would have to propose were too tough to make without bipartisan cover in an election year.

As approved by the committee, the budget resolution stuck with Clinton's priorities in all but a handful of areas. For instance, the panel recommended restoring most cuts Clinton sought to make in the LIHEAP program and in mass transit operating subsidies. To offset these add-backs and provide enough additional savings to meet the spending ceiling for 1995, the committee suggested delaying spending on some programs, cutting some of Clinton's additions and reducing federal agency overhead spending, which Clinton already had ordered cut, by an additional 3 percent.

The committee rejected nearly 20 amendments, chief among them a proposal by Domenici to restore a "fire wall" that had been in place from fiscal 1991-93 to protect defense spending from raids to finance non-defense spending programs. "We need to protect ourselves from our own insatiable tendencies to take from defense and spend somewhere else," Domenici said. Democrats countered that defense should compete for resources along with all other priorities. The amendment failed on a 10-11 vote.

Senate Floor

The full Senate adopted H Con Res 218 by a vote of 57-40 on March 25, after substituting the text of the Budget Committee's measure. Before the final vote, the Senate beat back repeated attempts to shield defense from the additional cuts that had been ordered by the committee. *(Vote 82, p. 14-S)*

"It's bizarre," said a frustrated Armed Services Committee Chairman Sam Nunn, D-Ga., who fought in vain to spare defense in a series of votes he called "devoid of logic." Defense made up about half of all discretionary spending, and Nunn said he expected that as much as 60 percent of whatever cuts Congress finally accepted would come from the defense budget. Nunn warned that, although the budget resolution locked in only the overall amount of the fiscal 1995 cuts, the remaining four years' worth of reductions were likely to set an informal benchmark for future budgets. He said he feared that "in defense, it will be close to binding."

But staunch defense hawks said they would risk defense cuts if that was the price of another shot at the deficit. Exon, a chief sponsor of the additional cuts, said the resulting fiscal 1995 reduction in defense probably would amount to less than $1 billion out of the Pentagon's budget of some $271 billion. "Is there anybody in their right mind who thinks they can't find that much? Of course they can," he said.

Although Sasser had predicted that the cuts might be eliminated on the Senate floor, a sounding of Democrats early in the week apparently turned up insufficient zeal to do so, and there was no direct attempt to restore the spending.

The $26.1 billion in outlays the Senate voted to cut from appropriations over five years was less than 1 percent of the $2.7 trillion in discretionary spending projected for 1995-99.

The first-year cut was $1.6 billion in outlays, barely 0.3 percent of all discretionary spending for 1995.

But the White House reacted with alarm, citing concerns about the potential effect of the cuts on Clinton's "investment" spending plans and on defense. Clinton had vowed not to accept additional cuts in defense programs.

Efforts To Protect Defense Fail

Before completing work on the budget resolution March 25, the Senate spent four days working its way through dozens of amendments, including at least four aimed directly at changing the additional deficit cuts. Not one of the votes to shield defense was close:

● By a vote of 35-63, the Senate rejected an amendment by Domenici that would have shifted $20 billion of the $26.1 billion in cuts out of discretionary spending and into mandatory programs, chiefly Medicare and veterans' benefits. *(Vote 72, p. 13-S)*

"I made a mistake" by voting for the discretionary cuts in committee, Domenici confessed, urging his colleagues to avoid putting defense spending at risk.

But by trying to shift the cuts to Medicare, Domenici tangled with the Clinton administration, which wanted to save further cuts in Medicare and Medicaid to finance an extension of health care benefits. John D. Rockefeller IV, D-W.Va., said that while the amount seemed small, "every dime, every dollar . . . is enormous in health care reform." If the Senate adopted Domenici's amendment, he warned, "we're not going to do health care reform."

Even conservative Republican defense hawks abandoned Domenici. Domenici said the vote showed that even his fellow Republicans would rather vote for vague, unspecified cuts in appropriations than for specific cuts in programs such as Medicare. "It's always easier to vote when there are no specific cuts that you are voting on," Domenici said.

Shortly before giving final approval to the budget, the Senate adopted by voice vote a non-binding sense-of-the-Senate amendment by Domenici and Nunn supporting a cap on entitlements, once a health care overhaul had been enacted.

● By a vote of 28-70, the Senate rejected a motion by Charles S. Robb, D-Va., to send the budget resolution back to committee with instructions to make the extra savings without cutting defense. *(Vote 79, p. 14-S)*

● By a vote of 34-64, the Senate rejected an amendment by Trent Lott, R-Miss., that would have ordered the $26.1 billion in discretionary cuts to come from non-defense programs. Lott, however, would have added $20 billion in mandatory cuts, which drew the same criticism as Domenici's amendment for complicating plans to overhaul health care. *(Vote 69, p. 12-S)*

● By a vote of 33-65, the Senate rejected an amendment by Christopher J. Dodd, D-Conn., to shift $30.5 billion over five years to special education programs for students with physical or mental disabilities. Dodd would have paid for the shift by cutting the intelligence budget, canceling the Pentagon's Milstar satellite communications system, designed for use during a nuclear war, and canceling and recapturing about half the $26.1 billion in extra deficit reduction ordered by the Budget Committee. *(Vote 67, p. 12-S)*

Conference/Final Action

After weeks of wrangling over the Senate's extra $26.1 billion in spending reductions, House and Senate conferees reached a compromise (H Rept 103-490), agreeing to cut $13

billion below the budget caps in stages through 1999. The House adopted the conference report by a vote of 220-183 on May 5. The Senate followed suit May 12, approving the budget, 53-46. *(House vote 161, p. 48-H; Senate vote 113, p. 20-S)*

Budget negotiators arranged for the reductions to start gradually, cutting $500 million below the appropriations spending cap for fiscal 1995. In 1996, however, the cuts were to accelerate dramatically, slicing $5.4 billion from that year's $548.1 billion spending cap. The rest of the cuts — $7.1 billion — were to be taken from the spending limits in 1997-99.

Reaching a Compromise

Before the conference got started, Kasich tried to get the House to instruct its conferees to accept the full $26.1 billion in Senate cuts. But, haunted by fears of further reductions in the defense budget and pushed hard by the White House to say no, the House rejected the non-binding motion April 14 by a vote of 202-216. However, the closeness of the vote seemed to ensure that Congress would adopt some portion of the Senate cuts. *(Vote 112, p. 34-H)*

The White House lobbied hard to win the procedural vote. Clinton warned members in a letter that the size of the Senate cuts posed "a threat to our national security." The turning point reportedly came the day before the procedural vote at an 8 a.m. meeting with 40 House Democrats, in which Secretary of Defense William J. Perry, Joint Chiefs of Staff Chairman Gen. John M. Shalikashvili, national security adviser Anthony Lake and other senior defense officials underscored Clinton's warning that the cuts posed a serious threat to defense and had to be stopped.

The conference opened April 20, with Senate negotiators expected to offer to give up half the cuts. But the negotiations were immediately put on hold when Domenici, the Senate's chief GOP negotiator, reversed his support for the Senate-passed cuts, citing his concern that they would fall too heavily on defense. As angry backers of the Senate cuts denounced him, Domenici went on a vote-counting mission to see if he could round up enough Republicans to make up for the Democrats who were likely to vote against the budget if all the cuts were dropped. "I can't for the life of me understand why someone on my side of the aisle would want to split our ranks," said Grassley.

But Sasser and Domenici could not find the votes to drop all the cuts, and in the end they agreed to accept half of them.

In an unrelated matter settled by the budget resolution, the Senate opted to stick with a Senate budget rule that required that cuts in taxes or increases in entitlement spending be deficit-neutral over 10 years, instead of the five years stipulated when the rule originally was imposed as part of the package that grew out of the 1990 budget summit.

The Treasury Department tried to roll the requirement back to five years, because the 10-year rule made it harder to find offsets for tariff revenue that the government anticipated losing because of lower trade barriers expected to result from the latest revisions of the General Agreement on Tariffs and Trade (GATT). The administration already was having trouble finding offsets for the five-year GATT cost of about $12 billion; the 10-year requirement meant offsets of $40 billion or more. ∎

Balanced-Budget Amendment Dies

After much public debate and private lobbying, the Clinton administration and Democratic leaders solidified the opposition to a proposed balanced-budget amendment to the Constitution, resulting in the defeat of the measure in both the House and Senate.

After failing to win adoption of a similar amendment in 1992 and failing to bring the proposal to the floor of either chamber in 1993, proponents had hoped election year pressures would turn the tide in their favor in 1994. However, by raising the specter of cuts to Social Security and giving wavering Democrats enough political cover, opponents managed to defeat the measure (S J Res 41, H J Res 103).

The proposed constitutional change — offered by Paul Simon, D-Ill., in the Senate and Charles W. Stenholm, D-Texas, in the House — stated that "total outlays for any fiscal year shall not exceed total receipts for that fiscal year" unless three-fifths of the House and Senate voted to lift the requirement. The requirement would have taken effect in fiscal 1999 at the earliest. Under the Constitution, an amendment had to be passed by a two-thirds majority in the House and Senate and then be ratified by at least three-fourths of the states (38). The resolution gave the states seven years to complete the task.

BOXSCORE

Balanced-Budget Amendment — S J Res 41, H J Res 103. The resolutions would have approved a constitutional amendment requiring a balanced federal budget, except when three-fifths of both chambers voted to lift the requirement.

Report: S Rept 103-163.

KEY ACTION

March 1 — Senate rejected S J Res 41, 63-37, four votes shy of the two-thirds majority required.

March 17 — House rejected H J Res 103, 271-153, 12 votes short of the necessary two-thirds majority.

The defeat of the amendment was a study in legislative tactics. In each chamber, opponents offered a watered-down version that would have required a balanced budget but effectively put Social Security off limits, making it far more difficult to actually achieve balance.

Neither of the substitute amendments passed, but Democrats were able to vote for them and against the Simon or Stenholm amendments and claim they supported a balanced budget. Enough did that to block the balanced budget drive in the Senate by four votes and in the House by 12 votes.

Background

Growing public concern about the deficit and Congress' perceived inability to address it had made the balanced-budget amendment a popular idea among lawmakers in both parties. Because the amendment required a balanced budget without specifying how that would be achieved, it gave members a chance to vote against the deficit without offending voters by proposing specific spending cuts or tax increases.

In 1992, a similar resolution fell nine votes short in the House and was blocked by a filibuster in the Senate. Ten years earlier, in 1982, the Senate passed a balanced-budget amendment, only to see it fall 46 votes short in the House. Similar pro-

posals made it to the Senate floor in 1986 and the House floor in 1990, but in both cases failed to win a two-thirds majority.

The Senate Judiciary Committee had approved Simon's resolution (SJ Res 41 — S Rept 103-163) by a vote of 15-3, on July 22, 1993, although with time growing short at the end of the session, Senate leaders postponed a vote until early in 1994. Stenholm had introduced the House resolution in February 1993, but it saw no action that year. *(1993 Almanac, p. 145; 1992 Almanac, p. 108)*

The renewed debate came at a time when the deficit seemed more tamable than it had in years, at least in the short run. On Jan. 27, the Congressional Budget Office had released projections showing the deficit falling steadily from $223 billion in fiscal 1994 to $166 billion in fiscal 1996 — although the red ink was expected to begin increasing again after that. Many who opposed the amendment said they were convinced that the deficit had come under control because of the budget-reconciliation act passed in 1993 and said they did not want to hurt the economy by forcing deeper cuts too quickly. *(1993 Almanac, p. 107)*

Senate Floor

The Senate rejected the balanced-budget amendment March 1 by a margin of 63-37, four votes shy of the two-thirds majority required for passage. *(Vote 48, p. 9-S)*

Unable to muster the 34 votes needed for an outright defeat of the resolution, sponsored by Simon and Orrin G. Hatch, R-Utah, Democratic opponents had siphoned votes by putting forward a milder version that also failed but that let wavering lawmakers go on record as favoring a balanced budget. The alternative amendment had the attraction of protecting Social Security, enabling members to claim that by voting for it and against Simon's resolution they were defending that politically sensitive program from possible cuts.

In the end, seven senators — all of them Democrats — tipped the balance by voting for the alternative and against Simon.

With a Democrat in the White House who felt his domestic agenda was being threatened, the Senate debate had more overt partisan characteristics than in past years. Opposition was spearheaded by Majority Leader George J. Mitchell, D-Maine, and Appropriations Committee Chairman Robert C. Byrd, D-W.Va. Extensive lobbying by the White House bolstered their efforts.

Byrd, a fierce defender of congressional prerogatives and a champion of domestic spending programs, had almost single-handedly turned the tide against the amendment in 1992 when adoption appeared certain.

"Some [senators] made campaign promises to vote for the balanced-budget amendment," he said in 1994. "They say to me, 'I know it's a bad idea, but I made a campaign promise.' Well, that's just too bad."

Byrd was one of the most powerful members of the Senate because his ironhanded control of the appropriations process could mean the difference between success and failure for a member seeking funding for a home-state project — although Byrd said that his efforts stopped short of telling colleagues that pet projects in their states might not be funded if they opposed him.

The partisan pressure showed in the end as Democrats provided 34 of the 37 votes to kill Simon's amendment. Four Democrats and one Republican who voted for the amendment in 1986 modified their positions and opposed the Simon version: Democrats Tom Harkin, Iowa; J. Bennett Johnston, La.; Claiborne Pell, R.I.; and David Pryor, Ark.; and Republican Ted Stevens, Alaska.

Only five of the 15 Democrats who served under Byrd on the Appropriations Committee crossed him by voting for Simon's plan.

President Clinton did his best to give political cover to the opponents. "I know it's politically popular, but I don't think it's good policy," he said of the amendment, adding that allowing a minority in Congress to determine when the government could borrow money was "a recipe for total paralysis."

But senators who switched positions still scrambled to explain themselves. Harkin took the Senate floor immediately after the vote to say that when he voted for the amendment in 1986, "I was pulled in that direction" by "what I had seen President [Ronald] Reagan do to this country." His "conscience compelled" him to vote against Simon's amendment this time, he said, because it did not protect Social Security. Harkin was among the senators who took refuge in the alternative balanced-budget amendment.

The Reid Amendment

Sponsored by Harry Reid, D-Nev., the alternative included a number of provisions that would have made it more likely that Congress would continue to run a deficit. The proposal exempted Social Security, which meant that the annual surplus in Social Security payroll collections could no longer have been used to lower the deficit. The Reid amendment also would have allowed the creation of a separate capital budget to permit borrowing for highways and other capital improvements.

Reid's plan was defeated 22-78; all but five Republicans refused to support the measure. *(Vote 47, p. 9-S)*

The amendment, however, proved to be a powerful political wedge in the debate. Two of the senators Simon was counting on unexpectedly voted instead for Reid: Harlan Mathews, D-Tenn., a cosponsor of Simon's amendment, and Pell, who voted for the balanced-budget amendment in 1986. Mitchell denied that he had any role in crafting the Reid amendment. "It's not my doing," he said. But he had been instrumental in working out an agreement that reduced the debate to a showdown between the two plans.

Taking no chances that constituents would misinterpret their votes, 15 lawmakers voted for both amendments.

House Floor

With Democratic freshmen voting overwhelmingly against the idea, the House defeated its version of the balanced-budget amendment March 17 by a vote of 271-153 — 12 votes short of the two-thirds majority needed. The measure received fewer votes than it had in 1992, when the House rejected a balanced-budget amendment by a vote of 280-153. *(Vote 65, p. 20-H)*

The Senate's defeat of the Simon amendment had led to speculation that House members would view this as a free vote, knowing that the amendment had no chance of being sent to the states for approval in 1994. But House leaders warned rank-and-file lawmakers, particularly freshmen, against going on record in favor of the amendment now if they planned to vote no in 1995 or 1996 when it counted.

Stenholm had forced his proposal to the floor using the same tactic he employed in 1992. First, he introduced his own king-of-the-hill rule (H J Res 103), which allowed a floor debate on a series of alternative balanced-budget amendments; the last version adopted was to be submitted for a final vote, requiring a two-thirds majority. Next, Stenholm gathered the 218 signatures needed on a discharge petition that allowed him to bypass the Rules Committee and bring the rule and the balanced-budget amendment directly to the

floor. Once on the floor, his king-of-the-hill rule was adopted 387-22 on March 16. *(Vote 59, p. 20-H)*

The rule allowed for votes on four different balanced-budget amendments. That gave lawmakers from both parties plenty of opportunity to go on record in support of the politically popular concept of balancing the budget. But it also gave the leadership a vehicle for derailing Stenholm's support.

● **Kyl.** The first vote was on a substitute offered by Jon Kyl, R-Ariz. Designed to clamp down on spending, it said that outlays could not exceed receipts or 19 percent of the gross national product. It was rejected March 16 by a vote of 179-242. *(Vote 60, p. 20-H)*

● **Barton-Tauzin.** The next vote came on a GOP substitute offered by Joe L. Barton, R-Texas, and W. J. "Billy" Tauzin, D-La. Their amendment would have prohibited a deficit but also barred Congress from raising taxes at a rate that exceeded the rate of increase in national income, except by a three-fifths vote of the Congress.

Republicans refused to vote for Stenholm's version unless given a chance to bring their amendment up for a vote. And the political attractiveness of opposing tax increases was demonstrated when the House endorsed the Barton-Tauzin plan by a 211-204 vote. *(Vote 63, p. 20-H)*

● **Wise.** The third option, drafted with the blessing of Democratic leaders, was offered by Bob Wise, D-W.Va., a one-time supporter of Stenholm's amendment. In a reprise of the tactic used in the Senate, Wise's less stringent alternative provided a refuge for wavering Democrats, particularly freshmen, who had substantive problems with Stenholm's approach or wanted political cover to vote against it.

In addition to permitting Congress to borrow for capital projects, the Wise proposal would have excluded surplus Social Security payroll tax receipts from the deficit calculation, making the deficit much bigger and the budget harder to balance.

Wise and cosponsor David Price, D-N.C., argued that Stenholm's version was flawed, mainly because it would prohibit Congress from borrowing money to pay for building highways, bridges and other projects with long-term economic benefits. Arguing that not allowing deficit spending on such projects would be short-sighted and a drag on economic growth, Wise said, "If we're going to pass a balanced-budget amendment, we're going to need a solid growth policy."

Stenholm argued that the Wise substitute was a balanced-budget amendment in name only. Allowing Congress to borrow to pay for capital projects would tempt Congress to stretch the definition of capital spending and never get around to eliminating the deficit. "I do not believe we should enshrine the concept of capital budgeting in the Constitution when we do not even agree on what it means," he said.

The Wise amendment was soundly defeated on a 111-318 vote. *(Vote 64, p. 20-H)*

● **Stenholm.** The Stenholm amendment was then adopted by voice vote, superseding the Barton-Tauzin version. But when it was submitted for a final vote, Stenholm's resolution fell 12 votes short of the necessary two-thirds majority. The Wise amendment had siphoned off enough Democratic votes to help ensure its defeat. Sixty-four lawmakers, all Democrats, voted for Wise's version and against Stenholm's. ■

House Passes Budget Reform Bills

Given Congress' lack of appetite for large-scale spending cuts in 1994, deficit hawks turned instead to efforts to reform the budget process. The House passed bills to institute a modified line-item veto, limit entitlement spending, bar the use of automatic inflation adjustments when budgeting for the upcoming year and prohibit Congress from including non-emergency spending in emergency spending bills.

"We start from the premise that we will never completely control federal spending until we get the budget process under control," said Timothy J. Penny, D-Minn. Penny was one of a trio of House deficit hawks pushing the legislation. The others were Charles W. Stenholm, D-Texas, and John R. Kasich, R-Ohio.

Stenholm had won agreement early in the year from House Democratic leaders to take up the budget process changes in exchange for his support of the 1995 budget resolution, which contained virtually no new deficit reduction. The leadership renewed that pledge in mid-June in a successful effort to stave off a marathon House floor session on "A to Z" spending cuts before the session ended. *(Budget resolution, p. 81; A-to-Z, p. 88)*

The Senate did not take up any of the House-passed budget-process bills, leaving them to die at the end of the 103rd Congress. Indeed, the Senate was never expected to act, a fact that made the House votes largely symbolic. Still, House bill sponsors argued that the votes made adoption of the same measures virtually automatic in the House in 1995, increasing pressure on the Senate to act.

Expedited Rescissions

Building on a proposal that it passed in 1993, the House voted to strengthen the president's existing authority to propose to rescind, or cut, individual items from appropriations bills. The House passed the expedited rescissions bill (HR 4600), known popularly as a modified line-item veto, on July 14 by a vote of 342-69. It was the third time in as many years that the House had endorsed such a bill. *(Vote 329, p. 98-H)*

But first, rejecting protests by senior Democrats that they were shifting too much power from Congress to the White House, members agreed to substantially toughen the earlier legislation.

Under existing law, Congress could ignore a presidential request to cancel, or rescind, previously appropriated spending. The request went into effect only if a majority in both chambers approved it; if Congress ignored it, it expired after 45 days.

The 1993 House bill (HR 1578), which passed by a vote of 258-157, would have changed existing law to require Congress to vote on presidential rescissions proposals, which still would have gone into effect only if approved by a majority of both the House and Senate. The measure was good only for what backers called a two-year "test drive," after which Congress could either renew it or junk it. *(1993 Almanac, p. 146)*

As reported by the Rules Committee, HR 4600 (H Rept 103-557, Part 1) differed little from the 1993 bill; its main purpose was to reiterate the desire of the House for action. Stenholm proposed to strengthen the bill, making the procedures permanent and allowing the president to devote the results of any

House Democratic Leaders Block 'A to Z' Plan

Democratic leaders managed to quash an attempt to shut down all other business in the House and devote at least 56 hours — the equivalent of seven eight-hour days — to debating and voting on members' proposals for spending cuts. In the end, sponsors of the controversial "A to Z" plan fell 14 short of the 218 signatures they needed to bypass the committee process and bring the bill directly to the floor. But the once-obscure plan gained surprising momentum before it died.

The bill itself (HR 3266) was a shell waiting to be filled with spending-cut amendments, accompanied by a rule that provided for 56 hours of floor debate. If chief A-to-Z sponsors Robert E. Andrews, D-N.J, and Bill Zeliff, R-N.H., had gotten the necessary signatures, they would have been able to strip leaders of control of the floor for a week or more and handed over management of spending-cut votes to four junior House members.

Zeliff, Andrews and other backers said the legislation was an expression of the frustrations they felt at being regularly blocked from offering spending-cut amendments by restrictive floor rules and committee procedures that excluded their proposals.

But Democratic leaders said that bypassing those safeguards could force the House to take hasty votes on major proposals with very little time to consider the implications.

Angry appropriators saw themselves as the chief targets of A-to-Z, despite the fact that the process would have allowed amendments to reduce authorizations and cut entitlement programs as well as appropriations. "If they're so frustrated, then why aren't they out offering amendments on appropriations bills?" said David Price, D-N.C., who noted that most appropriations bills were coming to the floor with open rules that allowed almost unlimited amendments to strike spending.

Appropriations Committee Chairman David R. Obey, D-Wis., fought back by introducing his own version of A-to-Z, which allowed only amendments that cut a project in the district of the member offering the cut. Obey called his measure the "Anti-Hypocrisy Deficit Reduction Act of 1994."

The plan's largely Republican backers (167 of the 204 members on the discharge petition were Republicans) styled themselves as underdogs fighting an autocratic, out-of-touch House leadership, and they deftly played on that argument in building support outside Congress. Rush Limbaugh and other conservative radio talk show hosts devoted air time to the cause. The Wall Street Journal kept up a steady fire of editorial support for A-to-Z, capitalizing on new House rules that made the previously secret names on discharge petitions publicly available.

Despite the heavy outside pressure, however, Democratic leaders stopped A-to-Z's progress with an alternative plan agreed to June 17 with a group of conservative Democrats led by Bill Orton of Utah. House Majority Leader Richard A. Gephardt, D-Mo., followed up with a letter stating that the House would hold at least eight votes on spending cuts and budget process changes before the August recess.

House leaders had made similar promises earlier in the year to deficit-hawk Charles W. Stenholm, D-Texas. Gephardt told Orton the votes would occur before the August recess, but that timetable slipped, too. By the end of the session, the House had voted on bills to institute a modified line-item veto, limit entitlement spending, bar the use of automatic inflation adjustments when budgeting for the upcoming year, and prohibit Congress from including non-emergency spending in emergency spending bills.

The House declined to debate and vote on a sense of Congress resolution on cutting entitlements. And it never took up proposed "lockbox" requirements that would have devoted cuts in appropriations bills to deficit reduction, instead of freeing up the money to be spent elsewhere, as was the case at the time. *(Budget reform, p. 87)*

rescissions to deficit reduction, rather than freeing the money to be spent elsewhere. In its most controversial expansion of presidential powers, the amendment included presidential authority to reach inside tax bills as well as appropriations bills to pull out targeted tax breaks and ask Congress to cancel them. Stenholm's amendment was adopted by a vote of 298-121. *(Vote 328, p. 98-H)*

However, the House rejected, 205-218, an even tougher line-item veto proposal by Gerald B. H. Solomon, R-N.Y., and House Minority Leader Robert H. Michel, R-Ill. Under their amendment, the president's veto of a spending item or a targeted tax break would have gone into effect unless both chambers turned it down. *(Vote 327, p. 98-H)*

As it had done twice before, the Senate let the rescissions bill languish without action. The adamant opposition of Senate Appropriations Committee Chairman Robert C. Byrd, D-W.Va., who was unwilling to cede additional authority over spending bills to the White House, was enough to kill the legislation in the 103rd Congress.

Limiting Entitlement Spending

In a series of lopsided votes, the House passed a bill (HR 4604) to set limits on entitlement spending for Medicare, farm programs, welfare, food stamps, and the like, and require spending cuts or other action if those ceilings were breached. But members insisted on putting Social Security, which made up 44 percent of all entitlements, strictly off limits.

The House passed the entitlement control measure July 21 by a vote of 316-107 after first rejecting a substitute plan that would have kept Social Security on the chopping block. The House also voted to bar Congress from increasing Social Security taxes to offset other entitlement spending. *(Vote 346, p. 104-H)*

The bill — which the Rules Committee had approved by voice vote July 14 (H Rept 103-602, Part 1) — required the president to set overall targets for fiscal 1994-97 entitlement spending. If spending exceeded the target by more than 0.5 percent in any year, the president would have to propose to make up some or all of the gap with spending cuts, tax increases or both. Alternatively, he could recommend increasing the targets. Congress would have to produce at least as much deficit reduction as the president had, and it would have to vote separately if it chose to increase the targets.

As passed by the House, the requirements in HR 4604 were virtually identical to provisions that had been enacted as part of Clinton's 1993 deficit-reduction package, except that the earlier plan did not protect Social Security. The 1993 provi-

sions were only a change to House rules, however; they did not affect the Senate. (Clinton had issued an executive order imposing the same requirements on the White House.)

In practice, economic growth had helped keep entitlement spending below the limits set in 1993. Entitlement spending was expected to remain below the targets, and neither the 1993 rule nor the new proposal was likely to require cuts anytime soon.

Republicans, led by Kasich, proposed an alternative that would have required Congress and the White House to set new entitlement limits each year, putting caps on individual entitlement programs except Social Security and automatically cutting back any program that exceeded its limit. The House rejected that plan, 194-233. *(Vote 343, p. 104-H)*

Stenholm proposed the toughest alternative of all, a plan to set limits from 1996 through 2000 low enough to force as much as $150 billion in cuts from projected entitlement spending, backed up by strict automatic spending cuts in all entitlements (including Social Security) if Congress did not otherwise move to keep spending below the caps. Stenholm's substitute failed 37-392. *(Vote 344, p. 104-H)*

The House then voted, 424-0, to prohibit any move to increase the Social Security payroll tax to help fill the gap if entitlement spending ever exceeded pre-set limits. *(Vote 345, p. 104-H)*

Critics argued that Congress had kept Social Security in the black by sharply raising the payroll tax while leaving the overall tax burden about the same, effectively shifting resources from the rest of the budget to Social Security. They said that fact, along with the program's sheer size — at a projected $335 billion in 1995, it was expected to account for 22 cents out of every dollar the government spent — should make Social Security a candidate for cutbacks along with other entitlements.

But defenders argued that Social Security should remain off-limits from any entitlement-control legislation because it was self-financed by the payroll tax and ran a huge surplus every year.

Further Steps Rejected

An attempt at the end of the session to take up a non-binding sense of Congress resolution (H Con Res 301) urging entitlement cuts failed when the House voted overwhelmingly Oct. 5 not even to debate the issue. In a lopsided 83-339 vote, the House rejected a rule that would have cleared the way for debate and votes on declaring that trends in spending for entitlements were unsustainable and offering three general ways to cut back. *(Vote 483, p. 142-H)*

"While everyone talks about it, nobody really wants to be on record about doing anything about it," said Bill Orton, D-Utah, who sponsored the resolution. Orton's package would have given House members a chance to signal whether they favored cutting entitlements by means-testing (based on income), by limiting cost-of-living adjustments or by raising the minimum age for entitlements targeted at senior citizens. The death of the rule allowed the House to avoid voting on any of those ideas.

Orton had gotten House leaders to set aside floor time for his resolution as part of a deal to block A-to-Z, and much of the opposition to his resolution came from angry A-to-Z backers, who blamed him for stopping their momentum. Chief cosponsor Bill Zeliff, R-N.H., called Orton's proposal a sham designed to do nothing more than provide political cover. "I want to play the game where we're playing hardball," said Zeliff, who charged that Orton's sense of Congress approach was "phony."

Baseline Budgeting

On Aug. 12, the House gave voice vote approval to a third budget-process bill (HR 4907) — this one requiring that the amounts budgeted for discretionary spending programs in the new fiscal year be compared with the amounts provided the previous year, without adjusting for inflation. The change was to apply to the annual budgets of both the president and Congress. It was at odds with existing practice, which was to compare new budget figures with a "current services" baseline that showed what it would cost to continue a program at its existing level after taking inflation into account.

The original bill — which had been reported Aug. 9 by the Rules Committee (H Rept 103-688, Part 1) — would have permitted budgets to show both the old inflation-adjusted baseline and the new "freeze" baseline. But before passing the bill, the House voted 247-171 to adopt an amendment, sponsored by Penny, Kasich and Stenholm, that allowed only the freeze baseline. *(Vote 395, p. 120-H)*

Kasich and others argued that the move was essential in reforming a pro-spending bias in Congress' budget procedures that allowed lawmakers to increase spending for a program while counting the move as a cut because the amount was below the inflation-adjusted baseline.

Penny rejected arguments that the amendment would merely change the way the budget was presented. "By changing our budget baseline, we change the terms of the debate; we remove the spending bias," he said.

Defenders argued that the inflation baseline represented vital information — how much it would cost in inflation-devalued dollars to buy the same amount of goods and services a given program was providing the year before. No matter what Congress did to the law, they said, congressional committees would continue to need that information and would find a way to get it.

John M. Spratt Jr., D-S.C., sponsor of the underlying bill, offered an amendment to allow both baselines — essentially the original proposal. "The current services baseline won't go away," he said. "It is something that we cannot uninvent." Under a king-of-the-hill procedure, Spratt's amendment came last and, if adopted, would have prevailed. But it was rejected, 170-243. *(Vote 396, p. 120-H)*

Emergency Spending Rules

On Aug. 17, the House again sided with the deficit hawks, voting 406-6 to pass a bill (HR 4906) to modify the way Congress handled emergency spending for floods, earthquakes, wars and the like. The bill barred Congress from mixing emergency spending, which had special treatment under budget rules, with non-emergency add-ons. *(Vote 403, p. 122-H)*

Critics said the ability to mix the two types of spending encouraged lawmakers — especially senators — to load up fast-moving emergency bills with pork barrel items, often making it impossible to trim the pork without voting to kill the entire emergency bill. "The message here is, keep it clean, don't load it up with riders," said Kasich, who had joined with Penny and Stenholm to toughen the bill.

The original, leadership-backed bill, sponsored by Spratt, would have slightly strengthened existing law by lowering from 25 to 10 the number of members required to trigger a floor vote to remove a non-emergency spending provision from an emergency bill. That version, which the Rules Committee had reported by voice vote Aug. 9 (H Rept 103-687), did not bar the mixing of emergency and non-emergency spending, and critics complained that it would have

made virtually no change in existing procedures.

Although he pointed out that Senate inaction would doom the bill, Appropriations Chairman David R. Obey, D-Wis., brought numerous appropriators to the floor to fight the deficit hawks. Obey argued that a flat ban on mixing emergency and non-emergency spending would block the committee from expediting emergency money by adding it to regular spending bills, as he said the panel recently had done by adding emergency relief funds for Rwanda to the 1995 foreign operations appropriations bill. *(Appropriations, p. 505)*

Nonetheless, in the key test during the Aug. 17 floor debate, the House voted, 322-99, to adopt the ban outlined in the Kasich-Penny-Stenholm amendment. *(Vote 402, p. 120-H)*

Although Spratt had the right under a king-of-the-hill debate rule to offer the original language again as an amendment after the vote on Kasich-Penny-Stenholm, he said the size of the vote for his rivals' proposal showed that he did not have a chance of prevailing, and he declined to bring up his amendment.

Supporters saw the outcome, combined with the votes on the other budget process bills, as signaling a growing commitment to tightening budget rules. "These reforms have momentum behind them," said Penny. Others suggested, however, that members knew the Kasich-Penny-Stenholm measure was a free vote, because it was highly unlikely to see the light of day in the Senate. "People are voting for this because they say, 'Hey, it's not real,' " said one senior House aide.

The House declined to take the potentially more painful step of requiring Congress to find ways to pay for emergency spending, rather than adding it to the deficit as it did under existing law.

An amendment by Michael N. Castle, R-Del., would have eliminated emergency spending authority from budget law and instead required Congress to appropriate a reserve fund at the beginning of the year big enough to pay for any emergencies. Castle suggested that the recent annual average of about $5 billion a year for emergencies would be sufficient, but critics noted that Congress already had spent more than $11 billion in 1994 for various emergencies. Castle said such excess spending could be taken care of by cutting other spending or passing a bill to undo the new restriction, but the House voted down his proposal, 184-235. *(Vote 401, p. 120-H)*

Sam Johnson, R-Texas, took a slightly different tack, proposing to pay for emergencies by reducing the amount available the following year for discretionary spending by an equivalent amount. Critics charged that a drafting error in Johnson's amendment meant that it would actually require two cuts — one in the current year and another in the second year. Johnson's amendment was rejected, 160-258. *(Vote 400, p. 120-H)* ∎

Entitlement Commission Closes Its Doors

Undercut by campaign rhetoric and overtaken by events, a bipartisan commission on entitlement reform closed shop Dec. 14 with a stern warning about the future of Social Security, Medicare and other major federal benefit programs — but with no plan of action.

The 32-member Bipartisan Commission on Entitlement and Tax Reform had convened in June with a mandate from President Clinton to get Democrats and Republicans to outline ways to curb the relentless growth in entitlements, which accounted for almost half of all federal spending. Co-chairing

the panel were Sens. Bob Kerrey, D-Neb., and John C. Danforth, R-Mo.

The panel's final product was a letter urging Congress and the Clinton administration to take a more long-term view of tax and spending proposals. Although its members and staff provided dozens of suggestions for ways to restrain the explosive growth of benefit programs, they were unable to build a broad consensus of support for any of them. Moreover, the commission found itself eclipsed as the budget spotlight shifted to plans for tax and spending cuts by House Republicans and the administration, inspired by the Nov. 8 elections, which both parties interpreted as a call for less government.

Speaking at a final news conference, Danforth said, "There's a great irony that, at exactly the same time on the same day that the commission reached [its] conclusion, Congress and apparently the president are now proceeding pell-mell to consider tax legislation aimed not at the long view, aimed not at the future of this country, aimed not at the results with respect to our grandchildren and our great-grandchildren, but rather with respect to who can scramble ahead . . . to keep their political head above water."

Background

Created by executive order in late 1993, the commission was made up of 24 sitting or former members of Congress, three sitting or former state and local officials, two bankers, two budget activists and one labor leader. The panel grew out of a desperate, last-minute drive by Clinton to get Kerrey to support the controversial 1993 deficit-reduction package (PL 103-66). Kerrey suggested the commission, although he insisted that it was not a condition for the vote he finally cast for the Clinton plan, enabling the president to eke out a bare, one-vote win. *(1993 Almanac, p. 107)*

The obvious potential targets were the four biggest entitlements — Social Security, Medicare, Medicaid and federal retirement programs. Together they accounted for more than 75 percent of the annual $730 billion in entitlement spending. But there were compelling political reasons to shy away from cutting any of them.

Outside Pressure and Internal Dissension

The group held its opening session June 13. By August, when the commission issued an interim report, pressure from outside groups and dissension among the commission's members clearly had taken a toll. Just getting agreement to a series of interim findings that described the problem and laid out a vague course of action provoked serious internal debate, Kerrey said. On Aug. 8, the panel voted 30-1 with one abstention to approve the report.

The report noted that entitlements and interest on the national debt consumed more than 61 cents of every dollar the federal government spent, more than twice the figure of 30 years before. By 2003, this "mandatory" spending was expected to require 72 cents out of every dollar, and if no changes were made before 2012, interest and entitlements would consume all the taxes the federal government collected.

"Both Republicans and Democrats are saying, 'Tone it down,' " Kerrey said four days before the findings came up for a vote. Indeed, by the time the panel voted, drafters had dropped language stating that "spending must be reduced, revenues raised, or a combination of both" to fix Social Security and Medicare.

Several panel members warned that they would not support any move to raise taxes. But several others signaled that they were just as concerned about protecting entitlements from damaging cuts. They bristled at what they said was the

vilification of programs that had lifted the nation's elderly out of poverty and given them longer lives. Entitlements such as Social Security and Medicare have done "unqualified and extensive good," said Rep. John D. Dingell, D-Mich.

Commission member Richard L. Trumka, president of the United Mine Workers, said he voted against the findings in part because they lumped all entitlements together without noting that fast-growing health care spending was the chief contributor to deficit problems.

"We are on a course toward national bankruptcy, and we recognized that today," said Danforth. For the commission to declare that and then do nothing to try to change it "would be unconscionable," he said.

No Consensus for Specific Proposals

On Dec. 9, Kerrey and Danforth outlined their proposals for change, which relied chiefly on spending cuts to achieve their goal of preventing runaway growth in entitlements. But the magnitude of the proposed Social Security cuts — from 33 percent to 50 percent of benefits for future beneficiaries — immediately drew howls of protest from interest groups such as organized labor and the American Association of Retired Persons.

The Kerrey/Danforth plan proposed to:

● Phase in an increase to 70 in the age for retirement with full Social Security benefits and index increases in Social Security benefits to the average growth in wages, rather than the Consumer Price Index. Wages had recently been growing more slowly than inflation.

● Create new benefit cuts in Medicare, the program of federally subsidized health care for senior citizens. Under existing law, seniors were eligible for Medicare at age 65; the Kerrey/Danforth plan sought to raise that to age 70 with a lengthy phase-in that would allow those who were at least 56 years old at the time to retain their eligibility for Medicare at age 65. The plan called for Medicare Part B premiums for physician and outpatient services to be indexed to overall Medicare program costs, and the Part B deductible to be raised from $100 to $300.

The plan called for a new $60 per month premium for Medicare Part A, which covered hospitalization; the proposal did not apply to poorer beneficiaries. Payments to Medicare providers also would be cut.

● Cut entitlement programs besides Social Security, Medicare and federal pensions by 10 percent, and then allow the programs to grow with inflation and population growth. Affected programs were to include food stamps, welfare, veterans' pensions, farm subsidies and unemployment compensation.

● To soften the effects of benefit cuts on younger taxpayers, cut the 6.2 percent Social Security withholding tax by 1.5 percent and require that the money be put into accounts modeled after Individual Retirement Accounts.

● Limit income-tax deductions for taxpayers with incomes of $91,850 or more.

With Republicans preparing to take control of Congress in the wake of their party's landslide in November, there was a sense among panel members that the commission had lost much of its utility in the new political landscape. Fully one-third of commission members did not show up for the Dec. 9 session.

Only a handful of commissioners indicated that they could support the Kerrey-Danforth plan, while unions and interest groups representing the elderly organized opposition to it. With several commissioners complaining that the panel had not studied the cumulative effect of the various proposals,

White House Memo Sparks Furor

After a year marked by verbal broadsides but little action on the deficit, a leaked White House memo on options for deficit reduction created a furor that sent lawmakers and the administration scurrying even further from hard deficit choices.

The candid 11-page discussion by White House budget director Alice M. Rivlin, leaked shortly before the November elections, contained almost nothing that students of the budget had not heard dozens of times before. But the fact that the secret Oct. 3 memo — marked "for handout and retrieval in meeting" — attached Rivlin's name to politically volatile options for taxes and Social Security provoked sharp Republican accusations and a pitched battle for political advantage. Within days, all sides had backed away from tough budget choices in ways that seemed to sharply narrow options for future deficit reduction.

Under withering fire from Republicans for privately mulling options such as raising taxes, cutting Social Security and limiting the home mortgage interest deduction, Democrats ran from the memo.

"I do not support cuts in Social Security, and I believe any savings we achieve in the Medicare program should be used in health care," said President Clinton. Said Robert D. Reischauer, director of the Congressional Budget Office: "The most significant negative repercussion of this event is that it has caused the administration to issue statements that reduce its political flexibility in dealing with the deficit."

Rivlin's memo laid out five different budget paths, ranging from doing nothing new to balancing the budget. Balancing the budget by 2000, she noted, would require $689 billion in new deficit reduction over the next five years, while merely holding the deficit steady at the $168 billion level forecast for 1995 would require $184 billion in new cuts over five years. The 1993 deficit plan, by comparison, cut the deficit by $433 billion over five years.

Rivlin said the administration's key priorities were to increase public investment, reduce the deficit, provide universal health coverage and slow the growth of health care costs, make sure the Social Security system remained solvent and "cut taxes, especially for middle-class working families." But, she added, "we cannot do *any* of these things without freeing resources that are now devoted to other things."

Kerrey and Danforth switched tacks.

At the final session Dec. 14, the chairmen offered a letter to Clinton and congressional leaders with a more general set of recommendations. Their letter called for Congress to consider the 30-year effect of any major tax or spending proposal, not the five-year perspective required by existing budget law. It also urged Congress to put Social Security, Medicare and other entitlements on stable financial footing so that they would not increase the deficit in the long term.

Attached to the letter were the Kerrey-Danforth proposal and a handful of alternatives developed by other commissioners, including one that Sen. Alan K. Simpson, R-Wyo., pledged to introduce in the next Congress. Kerrey empha-

sized, however, that a vote for the letter was not an endorsement of any of the suggestions.

Six Democrats on the commission voted against sending the letter. Two members took no position: Rep. Bill Archer, R-Texas, and Sen. Daniel Patrick Moynihan, D-N.Y.

Symbolizing the distance between the commission and the incoming congressional leadership, the final meeting was skipped by Archer, the incoming chairman of the Ways and Means Committee; Sen. Pete V. Domenici, R-N.M., the incoming chairman of the Senate Budget Committee; and Sen. Thad Cochran, R-Miss., the chairman of the Senate Republican Conference.

Aides said the Republican leaders in Congress might be receptive to some of the commission's suggestions as they cast about for budget cuts, but they were more interested in forcing fiscal discipline through a constitutional amendment requiring a balanced budget.

Thomas H. Kean, the president of Drew University in New Jersey and the state's former Republican governor, said the commission was undermined by statements from both the administration and the new congressional leadership that no action on entitlement programs was necessary at this point. Incoming House Speaker Newt Gingrich, R-Ga., and White House Chief of Staff Leon E. Panetta both said categorically that no changes in Social Security benefits were being considered for 1995.

Kerrey put it this way: "There is no crisis now. That's the problem." ∎

Deficit-Reduction Efforts on Track

The federal government closed its books on fiscal 1994 showing less red ink than in any of the previous four years and significantly less than had been expected just 10 months earlier.

The good news was attributed in large part to major deficit-reduction efforts in 1990 and 1993. But a big drop in the actual 1994 deficit from early forecasts was the result of a buoyant economy. In fact, Congress did nothing new in fiscal 1994 that was intended to shrink the deficit appreciably.

For fiscal 1994, which ended Sept. 30, the federal government collected $1.258 trillion in taxes, customs duties and other receipts, and it spent $1.461 trillion. Both were record amounts. The resulting deficit was $203.2 billion, the lowest it had been since fiscal 1989.

Trending Smaller

Not only was the deficit on a clear downward path, but it also was smaller in fiscal 1994 than it had been in six of the preceding 10 years, having peaked at $290.4 billion in fiscal 1992.

The deficit's decreasing size was even more noticeable when measured as a share of the size of the economy. As a percentage of gross domestic product (the total value of goods and services produced in the United States), the deficit reached its second-lowest point in more than a decade.

At 3.1 percent of GDP, the deficit by this measure was well below the levels of 1990-94. In that period, the deficit as a share of GDP ranged from 4.0 to 4.9 percent. Only once since 1981 had the deficit been smaller as a percentage of the economy than it was in 1993: In 1989, the deficit was measured as 2.9 percent of GDP.

Many economists — including some who did not object to the government running a deficit and some who thought Congress needed to do a much better job of controlling the red ink — viewed the deficit's relationship to the overall economy as a more notable measure than its absolute size.

Expressing the deficit as a percentage of GDP indicated in a positive and negative sense how much effect the deficit had on the economy as a whole. First, it showed how much stimulus the excess government spending over revenues might be providing. Second, with the deficit serving as a rough proxy for the amount of borrowing done by the government, it provided a measure of the degree to which the government was limiting credit availability by sopping up money that could be invested elsewhere.

For those economists who did not flatly oppose some federal government indebtedness, an oft-cited benchmark goal for the deficit was about 2 percent of GDP. The 3.1 percent level reached in 1994 was still well above that goal, however.

As measured against the size of the economy, receipts in fiscal 1994 equaled 19 percent of GDP, somewhat larger than in previous years. Outlays were 22 percent of GDP, somewhat smaller than in the recent past. Both figures, however, were within the historic range of the post-World War II era.

What Happened in 1994

The best news in fiscal 1994 was that strong economic growth pushed the deficit downward. But that good news disguised a threat that was likely to swell the deficit in later years — the promise of higher interest rates and a bigger bill to pay on the government's borrowing.

Following the 1990-91 recession and a two-year period of stagnant growth, the economy took off in 1993 and continued stronger than anticipated in 1994.

The result was somewhat larger than expected revenue collections in 1994, though no sizable reduction in spending for social programs. Also, the residual cost of the savings and loan bailout of the early 1990s and a companion rise in bank failures turned out to be somewhat smaller in 1994 than anticipated.

Overall, deficit forecasts for the year became smaller as the year progressed. *(Table, this page)*

The only dark spot on this otherwise sunny horizon was interest rates. As the economy grew, it was expected that interest rates would rise because of an increased demand for borrowing, as well as efforts by the Federal Reserve Board to prevent overheating and a surge in inflation. There was even a slight uptick in expected interest rate costs to the government noted by the Congressional Budget Office in its August 1994 review of the budget. ∎

Fiscal 1994 Deficit Projections *(in billions)*	
Bush, January 1993	$292.4
Clinton, January 1994	234.8
CBO, January 1994	223.0
Clinton, July 1994	220.1
CBO, August 1994	202.0
Actual, Sept. 30, 1994	**$203.2**

SOURCES: Office of Management and Budget, Congressional Budget Office

Senate Does Not Consider Tax Code Simplification

The House on May 17 passed legislation designed to simplify the tax process for both taxpayers and the Internal Revenue Service by making more than 100 changes to the tax code. The bill died at the end of the session, however, because the Senate did not act on it.

The House bill (HR 3419), passed by voice vote, contained provisions aimed at simplifying laws relating to individuals, pensions, partnerships, international operations of U.S. corporations, tax-exempt bonds, estates and gifts, and a variety of other tax matters.

The provision with the broadest potential impact on consumers was a plan to permit taxpayers to pay their taxes with credit cards. Congress paved the way for this change with a provision included in a separate bill revising the bankruptcy code. That bill, which was enacted (HR 5116 — PL 103-394), specified that tax debts, unlike other charges on credit cards, could not be erased through bankruptcy. *(Bankruptcy rewrite, p. 175)*

Background

The tax simplification legislation dated to 1990, when the Ways and Means Committee launched an effort to simplify the tax code. The initiative stalled in 1992, when President George Bush vetoed two tax bills that contained the bulk of the panel's proposals. *(1992 Almanac, pp. 133, 140)*

Congress typically passed one or two tax correction bills a year to erase inconsistencies in the tax code or to make adjustments for oversights in the bill drafting process. Often, these bills became magnets for broader proposals designed to change tax policy. However, Sponsor Dan Rostenkowski, D-Ill., chairman of the House Ways and Means Committee, insisted that HR 3419 remain clean. "I will stringently oppose any effort to turn the bill into a Christmas tree decorated with special interests and members' amendments," he said.

The Ways and Means Committee approved the bill by voice vote Nov. 3, 1993 (H Rept 103-353). *(1993 Almanac, p. 145)*

During the markup, the committee approved an amendment by Bill Brewster, D-Okla., to preserve an expiring tax provision that allowed football coaches to contribute to a special pension fund designed for coaches who did not work at any single college for more than five years.

Other Provisions

The tax simplification bill also included provisions to:
- Eliminate a tax law that permitted people who received their pensions in one lump sum to average the lump-sum payment over five years.
- Simplify the administration of pension plans by changing rules preventing employers from contributing more to the pension plans of high-salaried employees than to those of lower-paid employees.
- Allow tax-exempt corporations to set up 401(k) accounts for their employees. In 401(k) accounts, employees set aside part of their salaries in tax accounts to be withdrawn after they turned 59 years old.

The Joint Committee on Taxation estimated that, overall, the tax simplification and technical corrections in HR 3419 would cost $467 million over five years. To offset the revenue loss, the bill included provisions to:
- Impose tax withholding on gambling winnings from bingo and keno when the winnings exceeded $10,000, raising $208 million over five years.
- Eliminate (with narrow exceptions) an exemption that permitted owners who rented homes or apartments for less than 15 days to avoid declaring the proceeds as taxable income, raising $97 million over five years.
- Change the rules for tax-exempt entities such as charities or pension trusts to treat certain income from foreign corporations as unrelated business taxable income, raising $98 million over five years.
- Require thrift institutions to take net operating loss carryovers into account when calculating bad debt reserves, raising $64 million over five years.
- Require multi-employer pension plans to follow the same guidelines for vesting enrolled employees as other employer plans. Under existing law, employees were vested — meaning they became eligible for at least part of their pension — in five years. Under multi-employer plans, workers had to wait 10 years to become eligible. ∎

Banking Law Undergoes Revision

In a major and long-sought victory for the nation's large banks, Congress in 1994 completed a significant rewrite of the nation's banking law.

The bill (HR 3841), cleared Sept. 13, allowed banks to set up branch offices nationwide — by consolidating existing subsidiaries, buying existing banks or in some cases, establishing new banks. It also removed the few remaining barriers to interstate bank ownership.

President Clinton signed the bill into law on Sept. 29 (PL 103-328).

The action capped years of lobbying by the nation's largest banking companies, which wanted the freedom to open branch networks across state lines without having to set up separately capitalized subsidiary banks as required under existing law.

Under the new law, super-regional banks such as North Carolina's NationsBank Corp. and California-based Bank America Corp. would be able to expand their operations nationwide. Banking experts said the result would be a more efficient and profitable banking industry and a continued streamlining of the nation's 10,700 banks. Some big banks estimated that they could save up to $50 million per year in reduced overhead costs.

Industry sources predicted that much of the cost savings would be passed on to consumers as banks jockeyed for position in the new nationwide market.

They also said bank service would improve as consumers and business customers were able to make deposits and conduct banking transactions beyond their home states. It was also hoped that geographic diversity would help insulate banks from regional economic slumps.

The changes, to be in place by 1997, were expected to create pressure on middle-tier banks, as the super-regional banks expanded nationwide. Small banks, however, were expected to survive quite well within the niches they had

carved out in particular communities.

Consumer groups and many smaller banks had long expressed concern that interstate branching would lead to too much concentration in the banking industry, but their concerns were far outweighed by a sense, inside Congress and out, that interstate banking and branching was a concept whose time had come. Consumer advocates continued to worry, however, that huge nationwide banks would reduce lending and banking services in the inner cities and poor rural areas that were less profitable for them.

Congress considered the measure in tandem with a bill designed to aid the formation of community development lending institutions (HR 3474 — PL 103-325), which cleared Aug. 9. The linkage between the two bills reflected a political reality in the 103rd Congress: Democrats had made it clear that they would not approve the banks' goal of interstate branching until Congress helped Clinton fulfill his pledge to boost community lending. *(Community development lending, p. 100)*

Key Provisions

Under the bill, the few remaining obstacles to interstate purchases of whole banks were to be lifted one year after enactment. Under existing law, such purchases were allowed in every state but Hawaii, though they were limited along regional lines by about a dozen states, mainly in the Southeast.

The branching provisions allowed multistate bank holding companies to merge their subsidiary banks into branches of a single bank, starting June 1, 1997, provided that banking regulators certified that the consolidation met capital standards and state and nationwide concentration limits. In addition, regulators were to take into account whether the applicant had complied with community lending and service requirements.

States that wanted to permit such mergers before mid-1997 could enact laws to do so; states that wanted to "opt out" of interstate branching had to enact laws to block it.

In a victory for the little banks, so-called de novo branching — allowing banks to branch across state lines without acquiring and converting an existing bank — was allowed only in states that "opted in" by enacting laws to permit such branching. Otherwise, extending branch networks into new states required the purchase of an out-of-state bank. *(Provisions, p. 96)*

Background

Almost every state allowed interstate banking, in which out-of-state holding companies owned separately chartered and capitalized banks within their borders, subject to each state's banking laws. But interstate branching — allowing an out-of-state bank to open a deposit-taking branch without setting up an in-state bank — essentially was prohibited.

The last big congressional debate over interstate branching had taken place in 1991, when Congress took up a bill to

---

BOXSCORE

Interstate Banking and Branching — HR 3841 (S 1963). The bill allowed banks to open branch offices nationwide and allowed interstate bank ownership.

Reports: H Rept 103-448, S Rept 103-240; conference report H Rept 103-651.

KEY ACTION

March 22 — House passed HR 3841 by voice vote.

April 26 — Senate passed HR 3841 by voice vote after substituting text of S 1963.

Aug. 4 — House adopted the conference report by voice vote.

Sept. 13 — Senate cleared the bill, 94-4.

Sept. 29 — President signed HR 3841 — PL 103-328.

---

overhaul deposit insurance. The Bush administration pushed hard for branching, the Senate included it in its version of the deposit-insurance bill, and the House voted 366-4 in favor of an amendment containing an interstate proposal. However, the branching provisions were linked to a controversial proposal, vehemently opposed by banks, to roll back banks' ability to sell insurance. Caught in the congressional crossfire, branching was dropped in conference. *(1991 Almanac, p. 75)*

Getting Started

The bill advanced in fits and starts over the course of the 103rd Congress. Members of the Banking committees were eager to move ahead with the reforms in 1993, but the Clinton administration was slow to embrace them. When the administration did support the idea in October of 1993, it made it clear that it was not willing to invest much political capital toward advancing the effort.

The biggest stumbling block continued to be the powerful insurance agents' lobby, which was willing to see the bill pass only if Congress also agreed to scale back banks' insurance powers. Under existing law, federally chartered banks based in towns with fewer than 5,000 residents were allowed to sell insurance. Bank regulators had interpreted the exemption to allow those banks to sell insurance anywhere nationwide.

The banks were unwilling to pay the insurance agents' price, especially since some of the big banks were already finding ways to use existing law to move toward interstate branching. In one high-profile case, NationsBank Corp. was seeking to merge its Washington, D.C., and Maryland subsidiaries into a single bank by employing a loophole in existing law that allowed a federally chartered bank to move its headquarters 30 miles, even across state lines.

In October 1993, the Clinton administration weighed in, endorsing an interstate banking bill. But in an Oct. 25 speech, Treasury Secretary Lloyd Bentsen urged Congress to move slowly, waiting until it had completed work on bills to finish the savings and loan salvage operation and to establish a system of community development banks.

The administration also indicated that it would not put much energy into the effort, given the likelihood that the insurance powers controversy would doom it once again.

In the House, Stephen L. Neal, D-N.C., who strongly supported interstate branching, agreed to postpone action until 1994. Neal was chairman of the Banking Committee's Financial Institutions Subcommittee.

In the Senate, Banking Committee Chairman Donald W. Riegle Jr., D-Mich., tried to hold a markup Nov. 18, 1993, but was forced to adjourn when Republicans refused to attend. Riegle had promised Christopher J. Dodd, D-Conn., that he would try to move the bill. Dodd, who was both a big booster of the interstate banking bill and the insurance agents' principal advocate in Congress, was planning to attach an amendment rolling back bank insurance powers. He had rounded up enough votes in the committee to add the amendment, as he had done in 1991. *(1993 Almanac, p. 161)*

As the 1993 session ended, prospects for passing an interstate branching bill seemed bleak. But the situation turned around in February 1994, when Dodd announced on the Senate floor that he would no longer seek to pair the insurance rollback with interstate branching.

With the bill enjoying almost unanimous support, sponsors succeeded in keepng the measure clean of unrelated and potentially controversial provisions as it moved through the legislative process.

House Action

The House Banking Subcommittee on Financial Institutions approved a narrow branching bill Feb. 3 by a vote of 29-0.

While the subcommittee vote was impressive, it had been expected. Chairman Neal was the premier advocate for interstate branch banking in the House. His state of North Carolina was home to NationsBank Corp., the fourth-largest bank in the country and perhaps the loudest industry voice for branching.

At the markup, several senior members said it was imperative to keep the narrowly crafted bill free of unrelated provisions, and that is what the subcommittee did. The panel approved a draft bill with the following basic elements:

● **Interstate banking.** The bill effectively repealed the Douglas Amendment to the 1956 Bank Holding Company Act to allow any bank to acquire banks located in any other state, one year after enactment.

● **Interstate branching.** Eighteen months after enactment, bank holding companies that already owned multistate bank networks could consolidate them into branches of a single bank. Three years after enactment, banks could open new interstate branches by purchasing existing banks and converting them into branches.

States were given three years to opt out by enacting laws to prohibit both branching and consolidation. States that chose to opt out of branching could force a rollback of consolidations that had occurred before the three-year period expired.

The subcommittee rejected, 5-25, an amendment by Jim Leach, R-Iowa, to permit branching only by institutions that had equity capital equal to at least 6 percent of total assets. The subcommittee bill permitted only well-capitalized and well-managed banks to branch across state lines, but that standard was lower than what Leach sought.

● **De novo branching.** Banks could branch across state lines without acquiring and converting an existing bank only in states that "opted in" by enacting laws to permit such branching.

● **State laws.** A provision written in consultation with state regulators required interstate branches of federally chartered out-of-state banks to follow state consumer protection, fair lending and community reinvestment laws as if the branches were state-chartered banks.

The provision was strongly backed by consumer groups, which said it was essential in order to avoid rolling back existing state protections. Under existing law, states did not have the authority to regulate federally chartered banks. But under the Bank Holding Company Act, they did have the power to regulate national banks that operated in their states if such banks were owned by out-of-state holding companies. For example, the Texas subsidiary of NationsBank, which was federally chartered, had to follow Texas state banking laws. State regulators had expressed concern that if the bank was converted to a branch, oversight would be left up to federal regulators examining the headquarters bank in Charlotte, N.C.

● **Foreign banks.** The bill allowed foreign banks, which operated so-called "wholesale branches" not subject to

deposit insurance premiums or community reinvestment mandates, to open such branches nationwide. Bankers complained that the language would add to foreign banks' competitive advantage.

● **CRA.** The bill included provisions to ensure that the Community Reinvestment Act (CRA) kept pace with the new universe of national banking being created. The 1977 law required federal regulators to determine that a bank served the credit- and banking-services needs of the communities in which it operated when considering its application to merge with other institutions or to open and close branches. CRA advocates were concerned that without changes to the statute, poor CRA performance by a bank's out-of-state branches might not be reflected in the institution's overall evaluation.

But the CRA provisions — which required state-by-state CRA evaluations of the activities of institutions with multistate branch networks — were not very controversial because they were intended only to update the law, not to make it tougher on banks.

House Full Committee

The House Banking Committee on March 9 approved the bill (HR 3841 — H Rept 103-448) by an overwhelming vote of 50-1. The lone "nay" vote was cast by Independent Bernard Sanders of Vermont.

"Hardly anyone raises objections to this bill on the merits. It's always been some extraneous matter that stood in our way to passage," said Neal. "There are no substantive objections to this legislation that I'm aware of."

The lopsided vote came after the committee rejected two amendments that were backed by consumer advocates but opposed by the banking industry.

The first, offered by Kweisi Mfume, D-Md., would have required banks wishing to branch across state lines to pledge to make loans and offer banking services in poor neighborhoods and underserved banking markets. It also would have blocked banks that had shown a pattern of closing inner-city branches from exercising the new branching powers, and it would have required banks to disclose how much they lent to small and minority-owned businesses. The requirements would have applied to banks with $1 billion or more in assets.

The committee rejected the amendment by a 17-34 vote after bill supporters argued that any controversial add-ons would imperil the bill's passage.

The committee also rejected, 16-34, an amendment by Cleo Fields, D-La., to require banks that opened branches across state lines to provide low-cost basic banking and government check-cashing services.

Consumer advocates were not completely shut out, however. A bipartisan amendment backed by committee leaders and adopted by voice vote included a provision, sought by Maxine Waters, D-Calif., aimed at easing the impact of bank branch closures on communities. It required federal regulators to work with community groups to mitigate the effects of a branch closure and explore the possibility of developing alternative ways to replace the loss of bank services, such as establishing a locally based credit union.

By voice vote, the committee rejected an amendment by Craig Thomas, R-Wyo., to allow the few remaining states that restricted interstate bank acquisitions along regional lines to continue to do so, provided they enacted a law to opt out of such interstate banking.

By a 13-38 vote, the committee rejected an amendment by Thomas to extend the time before consolidation of existing banks from 18 months to three years.

Continued on p. 98

Bank Branching Bill Provisions

The interstate banking and branching bill (HR 3841 — PL 103-328) allowed multistate bank holding companies to merge their subsidiary banks into branches of a single bank, starting June 1, 1997. Three years after enactment, bank holding companies could convert subsidiary out-of-state banks into branches. The bill also lifted the few remaining obstacles to interstate purchases of whole banks one year after enactment.

In a victory for the little banks, so-called de novo branching — allowing banks to branch across state lines without acquiring and converting an existing bank — was allowed only in states that "opted in" by enacting laws to permit such branching. Otherwise, extending branch networks into new states required the purchase of an out-of-state bank.

As enacted, PL 103-328 contained provisions to:

Interstate Banking

● **Bank acquisitions.** Permit adequately capitalized and managed bank holding companies to acquire banks in any state one year after enactment of the legislation (Sept. 29, 1995). State laws that limited holding company acquisitions to banks that had been in existence for a specified period of time, though not to exceed five years, were preserved. Under prior law, acquisitions were allowed when states had enacted reciprocal laws permitting them. Every state but Hawaii permitted interstate purchases of whole banks, though about a dozen states limited such purchases along regional lines.

● **Concentration limits.** Bar interstate acquisitions if they would result in the bank holding company controlling more than 10 percent of U.S. bank and thrift deposits or more than 30 percent of the deposits in the home state of the bank to be acquired. State legislatures or regulators could waive the 30 percent limit. These concentration limits did not apply to the initial entry into a state by a bank holding company. States could stipulate that any bank targeted for acquisition had to have been in existence for a specified period not to exceed five years; this was aimed at preventing the formation of new banks simply for the purpose of selling them to an out-of-state holding company.

● **CRA compliance.** Require the Federal Reserve Board, the primary regulator of bank holding companies, to examine the Community Reinvestment Act (CRA) evaluation of any holding company (and its affiliated institutions) before approving an acquisition. This was a restatement of existing law. The 1977 Community Reinvestment Act required banks and thrifts to demonstrate that they were attempting to meet the credit and bank service needs of the entire community in which they did business. The Fed also was required to take into account an institution's compliance with state community reinvestment laws before approving interstate bank acquisitions; under existing procedures, the Fed considered state CRA evaluations but was not officially required to do so.

● **Affiliated banks.** Permit bank subsidiaries of an interstate bank holding company to act as agents for each other for certain banking activities: receiving deposits, renewing time deposits, closing loans, servicing loans and receiving payments on loans and other obligations for other affiliated institutions. Insured savings and loans that were affiliated with banks as of July 1, 1994, subject to certain conditions, were allowed to act as agents for such banks.

Affiliated banks could act as agents for one another regardless of whether the institutions were in the same or different states.

Interstate Branching

● **Interstate mergers.** Permit adequately capitalized and managed banks to merge with out-of-state subsidiary banks and convert each branch office into a branch of the resulting bank, starting June 1, 1997. The bank could subsequently establish additional branches in the host state.

The law preserved state laws that required out-of-state banks or

bank holding companies to merge with or acquire banks that had been in existence for a specified minimum period of time (not to exceed five years). Banks were allowed to set up branches across state lines via the purchase of individual branches only if permitted by state laws.

● **State opt-out/opt-in.** Give states until June 1, 1997, to enact laws to block out-of-state banks from establishing branches in the state. The process was called "opting out." Banks headquartered in any state that opted out of interstate branching would not be allowed to participate in any interstate merger transaction. States also could enact laws to permit ("opt into") interstate branching before June 1, 1997.

● **De novo branching.** Permit banks to open branches in a state without first acquiring and converting an existing bank only if the state enacted a law to permit such "de novo" branching. Once a bank established a de novo branch in a host state, the bank could freely establish and acquire additional branches at any location in the host state in accordance with federal and state laws.

● **Concentration limits.** Prohibit mergers if the resulting bank would control more than 10 percent of deposits of insured depository institutions in the United States or 30 percent or more of the deposits in any state. The provision, however, contained significant exemptions. States were permitted to waive the 30 percent limit, and the concentration limits did not apply to mergers of existing subsidiary banks, nor did they apply to a bank's initial entry into a state. State concentration caps applied to initial entries.

● **State taxation authority.** Preserve the rights of states to tax banks and bank holding companies. The provision meant that when a bank in a state was converted to a branch of an out-of-state bank, state and local governments retained the right to tax the branch, using their own taxation methods. The bill specifically allowed state and local governments to impose a shares tax on a portion of a bank's stock.

● **State laws.** Apply host-state laws governing community reinvestment, consumer protection and usury, fair lending and intrastate branching to any branch of a federally chartered bank, including branches of banks headquartered out of state. The Office of the Comptroller of the Currency (OCC), which regulated national banks, was made responsible for enforcing such state laws. As under existing law, federal law could pre-empt state laws in certain circumstances. Generally, state law applied to national banks unless it was in direct conflict with or an obstacle to accomplishing the purposes of a federal law, or the federal law was comprehensive enough to demonstrate congressional intent concerning a given subject area.

But some in Congress believed that the OCC had overreached in its use of pre-emption power, particularly in a case in which it ruled that federally chartered banks in New Jersey did not have to comply with New Jersey's basic checking account law. As a result, the bill added procedural requirements onto the federal government's ability to pre-empt state laws. Before pre-empting state law, the comptroller had to publish the proposed ruling with a 30-day comment period; the OCC had to consider the comments it received before making final judgment.

For state-chartered banks, host state banking laws applied to branches of out-of-state banks. State bank regulators were permitted to examine branches of banks chartered in another state; state regulators had the same enforcement authority over such branches as they had for banks chartered by their state.

● **CRA evaluations.** Modify the Community Reinvestment Act (CRA) to adapt it to interstate banks. Generally, under existing law, individual banks were given CRA evaluations during annual examinations. Regulators (the Federal Deposit Insurance Corporation, the Federal Reserve and the OCC) assessed how well the bank was meeting the credit and bank service needs of the community in which it did business, including low- and moderate-income neighborhoods.

Regulators were required to take these CRA evaluations into account when the bank filed any application to the regulator, including applications by the bank or its holding company to establish or

close branches or merge with another bank.

The bill attempted to update the CRA to adapt it to the new rules of interstate banking and branching. It required bank regulators to prepare one overall evaluation of an institution's compliance with the CRA, as well as separate state-by-state evaluations in each state in which it maintained branches. The state-by-state evaluations had to include separate CRA evaluations to measure performance in each city in which the bank had a branch; a separate CRA evaluation was required for each rural area in which the bank had a branch.

Federal banking regulators also were required to take into account banks' CRA performance ratings when considering interstate branching applications from banks desiring to merge and consolidate their out-of-state bank operations. An institution's CRA performance in each state in which it maintained branches had to be considered.

The existing law governing interstate acquisitions of whole banks was the Bank Holding Company Act, enforced by the Federal Reserve Board as the regulator of bank holding companies. Bank mergers were carried out under the Bank Merger Act. The Federal Reserve Board's CRA regulations and practices for interstate bank acquisitions were somewhat more stringent than the CRA rules and practices governing intrastate bank mergers.

When a bank made its initial entry into a state in which it had no banks or affiliates, the bill required that the CRA be applied to such future interstate banking activities in a fashion that paralleled the approach taken by the Federal Reserve. For all other interstate merger applications, existing regulations and practices governing bank mergers were to apply.

● **Thirty-mile rule.** Under a provision in the Civil War-era National Bank Act, a federally chartered bank was permitted to move its headquarters 30 miles, even across state lines. This provision had been used as a means to branch interstate in advance of the new banking and branching law, because banks were permitted to retain branches in the original state after they moved the headquarters across state lines.

In an effort to ensure that banks branched interstate only through the mechanism outlined under the interstate banking law, the bill barred banks from using the 30-mile loophole to branch into states that did not permit interstate branching.

● **Texas home equity loans.** Overturn a recent federal court decision (*First Gibraltar Bank v. Morales*) that held that the Office of Thrift Supervision had the authority to pre-empt a homestead protection provision in the Texas Constitution. Texas was the only state that did not permit lenders to foreclose on borrowers' homes; as a result, it was the only state in which consumers could not borrow against the equity that had built up in their homes. The provision, added by House Banking Committee Chairman Henry B. Gonzalez, D-Texas, as his price for letting the bill pass, reinforced the Texas Constitution and continued to block home equity lending in the Lone Star State.

● **Coordinated examinations.** Permit state banking regulators to examine branches of out-of-state banks for safety and soundness and to ensure compliance with state banking community reinvestment, fair lending and consumer protection laws.

If a host-state examiner discovered that an out-of-state branch was in an unsafe or unsound condition or detected violations of state banking laws, it could take enforcement actions equal to those it could take against a bank chartered in the host state.

State regulators were permitted to enter into cooperative agreements to facilitate supervision of state banks operating interstate. Nothing in this provision affected the authority of federal banking agencies to examine branches of insured depository institutions.

● **Branch closures.** Require that whenever a bank proposed to close a branch in a low- or moderate-income area, the appropriate federal bank regulator upon request by the community consult with community representatives to explore alternative means to meet the community's needs. Such options could include seeking ways to attract or establish a new branch of another bank, chartering a new bank or thrift, or establishing a community development credit union.

Under the 1991 banking law, notices of branch closures had to be mailed to customers; the bill required that such notices include the address of the bank's regulator and inform consumers that they could file comments with the agency. Notwithstanding these consultations, nothing in the provision was to affect the authority of a bank to close a branch, or affect the timing of such closures.

● **Bank fees study.** Require the Federal Reserve to conduct an annual survey of the fees charged by banks for retail banking services. Each report was required to describe national and state trends in the cost and availability of bank services. Reports were required for seven years.

● **Deposit production ban.** Bar banks from using interstate branches to siphon deposits from the community in which the branch was located to other states.

By June 1, 1997, banking regulators were required to draw up regulations to prohibit such so-called deposit production offices. If an out-of-state bank lent less than half as much as the average in-state bank, regulators would be required to examine the bank's loan portfolio to determine whether the bank was reasonably fulfilling the credit needs of the community in the host state. If not, the regulators would be authorized to close the branch and bar the bank from opening new branches in that state.

Foreign Banks

● **Branching.** Enact a delicately negotiated compromise on rules governing establishment of wholesale branches by foreign banks. The Senate-passed bill contained a provision that would have required foreign banks to establish a U.S. subsidiary bank in order to branch across state lines. The House-passed bill would have provided foreign banks with branching powers that mirrored the powers given to U.S. banks (i.e., requiring them to purchase a U.S. bank and convert it to a branch).

The final bill generally accepted the House position, though with several modifications aimed at addressing concerns that foreign banks' wholesale branches might obtain a competitive advantage over U.S. banks. The provision was supported by Democratic Sens. Donald W. Riegle Jr., Mich., and Wendell H. Ford, Ky., who said that uninsured wholesale branch operations of foreign banks — which took large deposits and made loans to big corporate customers — had a competitive advantage over U.S. banks because they were exempt from CRA lending and record-keeping requirements and did not pay deposit insurance premiums.

The bill permitted a foreign bank to establish and operate wholesale bank branches, either de novo or by acquisition and merger, in states other than their home states, to the same extent that a U.S. bank (state- or federally chartered) headquartered in the foreign bank's home state was allowed to establish such branches.

● **CRA requirements.** Continue to subject branches of foreign banks established through the acquisition of existing banks or branches to CRA requirements. Banks that did not accept domestic deposits were not subject to the CRA.

● **Wholesale deposits.** Cap at 1 percent, instead of 5 percent as under existing law, the total amount of so-called retail deposits that could be held by a wholesale branch of a foreign bank.

In addition, bank regulators were directed to revise regulations under the International Banking Act to make sure that they did not favor foreign banks over U.S. banks.

Under existing law, foreign wholesale bank branches were barred from taking retail deposits of less than $100,000 that required deposit insurance. This effectively required foreign banks to establish a U.S. subsidiary bank in order to take deposits of less than $100,000.

Exceptions were made for foreign businesses and governments, foreign citizens not residing in the United States, and U.S.-based foreign employees of foreign banks, businesses, governments and international organizations. The bill directed bank regulators to consider whether to restrict classes of customers who were permitted to make retail deposits of less than $100,000.

● **Capital requirements.** Permit, but not require, the Federal Reserve or the Office of the Comptroller of the Currency (OCC) to require a foreign bank to establish a separate U.S. subsidiary bank in

order to engage in interstate branching if the Fed or the OCC determined that it was the only way to verify that a foreign bank adhered to capital requirements that were equivalent to those applicable to a U.S. bank engaged in interstate branching.

● **Offshore shell branches.** Prohibit foreign banks from using offshore "shell" branches of its U.S. subsidiaries to conduct banking and financial activities that foreign branches of U.S. banks were not permitted to conduct.

● **Consumer protection laws.** Clarify that U.S. consumer protection laws applied to foreign banks, affirming the longtime regulatory interpretation of the Federal Reserve Board, which regulated foreign banks. The provision specified the following laws: Electronic Funds Transfer Act, Equal Credit Opportunity Act, Expedited Funds Availability Act, Fair Credit Billing Act, Fair Credit Reporting Act, Fair Debt Collection Practices Act, Home Mortgage Disclosure Act, Real Estate Settlement Procedures Act, Truth in Leasing Act, Truth in Lending Act and Truth in Savings Act.

● **Foreign bank examination fees.** Provide a three-year moratorium on a provision of the 1991 bank bill that required the Federal Reserve Board and other bank regulators to impose fees to cover the cost of examinations of a branch, agency or representative office of a foreign bank. The moratorium was to begin in July 1995; regulators had delayed implementing the fees because corresponding fees had not been imposed on U.S. banks.

General Provisions

● **Statute of limitations.** Extend the statute of limitations to permit the Federal Deposit Insurance Corporation (FDIC) and the Resolution Trust Corporation (RTC) to "revive" lawsuits that had expired under state statutes of limitation.

The purpose of the provision was to give federal banking regulators additional time to sue officers and directors of failed institutions for actions that contributed to an institution's failure, including fraud, intentional misconduct resulting in unjust enrichment and intentional misconduct resulting in substantial loss to the institution. Examples of such misconduct included self-dealing that resulted in unjust enrichment or a substantial loss to the institution, falsifying financial records to disguise increased financial loss and conspiracy to violate banking rules or regulations.

A proposal to extend the statute of limitations in cases of negligence or gross negligence was dropped in conference.

The FDIC or the RTC, as conservator or receiver of a failed depository institution, could revive such claims within five years of the appointment of the conservator or receiver.

● **Coin bills.** Direct the U.S. Mint to issue several new commemorative coins. Profits derived from sales of the coins were to be used to support the events or institutions to be commemorated. Coins were to be minted to support the following: the 1995 Special Olympics World Games; the National Community Service Trust; the endowment of the Robert F. Kennedy Memorial; the Bicentennial of the United States Military Academy in 2002; and the United States Botanic Garden.

● **Financial Services Commission.** Require a study of the United States financial services system conducted by the Treasury Department in consultation with an Advisory Commission on Financial Services (to be named by the secretary of the Treasury) and other enumerated federal agencies. ∎

Continued from p. 95

House Floor

With an unusual degree of dispatch for an important banking bill, the House easily passed HR 3841 by voice vote March 22 under expedited floor procedures that limited debate and barred amendments. As a result, Banking Committee members Mfume and Joseph P. Kennedy II, D-Mass., were not able to get a floor vote on their amendment to build additional protection for consumers. Although they faced almost certain defeat on the floor, they had wanted a vote.

Senate Action

The bill's prospects in the Senate improved dramatically Feb. 3, when Dodd, a principal force in urging the Senate Banking Committee to take up the interstate bill, announced on the Senate floor that he would no longer attempt to use the bill as a vehicle for the insurance provisions. "While I continue to support legislation to rationalize bank sales of insurance, I do not want to hold up interstate branching," Dodd said.

Senate Banking Committee

With an unusual display of unanimity, the Senate Banking Committee then approved its own draft measure Feb. 23, voting 19-0 to give a green light to interstate branching.

Supporters of the bill (S 1963 — S Rept 103-240) managed to keep the markup free of controversy and unwelcome amendments. "I think the consensus has grown to the point that there's a very good chance of moving this through," said Chairman Riegle. "This bill has a good head of steam."

The Senate bill generally mirrored the House version:

● **Interstate banking.** It effectively repealed the Douglas Amendment to the 1956 Bank Holding Company Act to allow banking companies to own banks in any state, effective one year after enactment.

Like the House bill, it included concentration limits to restrict any one bank's share of deposits in a state, unless the state provided a waiver.

● **Consolidation.** Two years after enactment, bank holding companies could consolidate their existing bank subsidiaries into a single network of branches. They also could purchase out-of-state banks and convert them into branches. States could still enact laws to opt out and prohibit such bank consolidations.

● **De novo branching.** The bill permitted banks to open branches across state lines without acquiring and converting an existing bank only in states that passed laws to allow it.

● **CRA.** Like the House bill, the Senate measure sought to amend the CRA.

The Senate bill did differ from the companion House measure in several significant ways, however:

● **State laws.** Under the Senate bill, federally chartered banks that were converted to branches were no longer to be subject to state laws, which in many states, including California and New York, went beyond federal consumer protections.

● **Foreign banks.** The Senate bill allowed foreign banks to take advantage of the new branching powers only if they set up insured U.S. banks and then branched from those banks. Wendell H. Ford, D-Ky., the chief advocate of the Senate provision, argued that it would level the competitive playing field.

Senate Floor

The Senate passed the bill by voice vote April 26 after substituting the text of S 1963. Byron Dorgan, D-N.D., who feared the measure would produce too much concentration in the banking system, registered the only audible "nay"

vote from a lightly populated Senate floor.

The Senate agreed by voice vote to change the date by which banks could consolidate separate subsidiaries into a single bank to June 1, 1997. The committee bill would have permitted the consolidations two years after enactment, but the nation's governors protested that they needed more time to consider whether to opt out.

Bob Graham, D-Fla., a former member of the Banking Committee, was poised to offer an amendment containing the House language preserving the ability of states to regulate interstate branches of federally chartered out-of-state banks, but he settled for a pledge from Riegle to look at the issue during conference negotiations with the House.

Before passing the bill, the Senate on April 25 adopted a bipartisan amendment offered by Riegle to preserve the authority of states to tax banks. The amendment was sought principally by William V. Roth Jr., R-Del. States feared that they would lose tax revenues as in-state banks that were subject to state taxes were converted into branches of out-of-state banks. The amendment expressly provided that no aspect of the bill affected state taxing authority over banks. But states still faced very complicated questions about how to tax bank branches.

Howard M. Metzenbaum, D-Ohio, came to the floor intending to offer several amendments, including a controversial proposal to require banks to offer low-cost "basic banking" and government check-cashing services. But Metzenbaum declined to offer the amendments — vigorously opposed by the banking lobby as too burdensome — after being rebuffed by bill sponsors.

Metzenbaum did prevail, by voice vote, on another amendment, this one to change federal statute-of-limitations laws to restore $1.6 billion in Federal Deposit Insurance Corporation (FDIC) and Resolution Trust Corporation (RTC) lawsuits against officials of failed banks and thrifts. Recent court rulings had jeopardized the claims by applying state statutes of limitation to federal suits.

Metzenbaum's provision allowed the regulators to bring lawsuits against thrift or bank officials for any negligent or fraudulent behavior that occurred within five years of the time the regulators took over the institution, even if the statute of limitations for the home state of the institution already had run out.

The administration, the RTC and the FDIC avidly sought the change, arguing that, without the authority to pre-empt state statutes of limitations, more than $200 million in future recoveries against bank and thrift executives — or from insurance companies responsible for such losses — would be lost.

Conference

After lengthy behind-the-scenes negotiations, staff aides and administration representatives ironed out almost all the differences between House and Senate versions of the interstate branching bill, including one of the two key issues — how state banking laws would apply to branches of federally chartered banks headquartered in other states. The other chief dispute, over foreign banks, was among the last to be settled. Conferees were negotiating over the community development bank bill at the same time.

● **State laws.** The conferees agreed that state laws regarding community reinvestment, consumer protection, fair lending and in-state branching would apply equally to branches of national banks and to state bank branches.

But the Office of the Comptroller of the Currency, which regulated federally chartered banks, could continue to pre-empt state laws when they conflicted with federal law or when they gave state banks preferential treatment over national banks. However, the comptroller's office had to give prior notice of its intention to pre-empt state laws and had to weigh public comments before taking action.

● **Statute of limitations.** The conferees watered down Metzenbaum's statute-of-limitation provision to apply only in cases of fraud or intentional misconduct that resulted in "unjust enrichment" or losses to the institution — a much more difficult legal standard to prove.

Opponents argued that Metzenbaum's language would effectively revive cases dating back as far as the early 1980s, and that to resurrect such claims would be unfair to outside officers and directors of banks that had only a peripheral role in a bank's failure.

The change was a victory for defenders of the statute of limitations and for a small but powerful group of big insurance companies that wrote liability insurance policies covering actions of bank and thrift executives and directors. While those policies typically did not cover actions such as fraud, they did cover negligence. If the provision had been broadened to cover negligence, they would have stood to assume substantial liability.

● **Foreign banks.** The conferees dropped the provision backed by Riegle and Ford requiring that wholesale branches of foreign banks set up subsidiary banks if they wanted to take advantage of interstate branching powers.

But the final bill contained two other major foreign banking provisions backed by Riegle, though in compromise form. One reduced from 5 percent to 1 percent the statutory limit on the total amount of so-called retail deposits (defined as deposits of less than $100,000) held by a wholesale branch of a foreign bank. In addition, when a foreign bank acquired an existing U.S. bank and converted it to a branch of the foreign bank, the branch was to be subject to Community Reinvestment Act mandates.

The conference committee also added House language that delayed for three years the onset of a requirement that foreign banks be assessed examination fees as required by the 1991 banking bill (PL 102-242). *(1991 Almanac, p. 75)*

Final Action

The House adopted the conference report on the bill (H Rept 103-651) by voice vote on Aug. 4. During the brief and otherwise controversy-free House debate on the measure, Mfume and Kennedy said they were disappointed that the bill had not included their provision barring interstate branching to banks that were shown not to serve poor communities.

The Senate cleared the bill Sept. 13 by a vote of 94-4. *(Vote 298, p. 51-S)*

At least two senators had threatened to delay final action, but both decided to let the bill go forward.

Metzenbaum's anger over the fate of his statute-of-limitations provision was assuaged by a letter from Jonathan Fiechter, acting director of the Office of Thrift Supervision (OTS), who pledged that the agency would more aggressively pursue thrift wrongdoers who were protected from lawsuits by the expiration of state statutes of limitations.

The OTS, whose authority went beyond that of the RTC and FDIC, was not subject to state statutes of limitations. Metzenbaum said the agency could therefore pursue not only fraud cases but also cases of negligence, which were easier to prove and involved far greater potential recoveries by the government.

Sen. Phil Gramm, R-Texas, had threatened to challenge a provision that House Banking Committee Chairman Henry B. Gonzalez, D-Texas, had added in conference effectively preserving Texas as the only state in which lenders could not offer home equity loans. But Gramm was a big supporter of interstate powers, and, in the end, he decided not to carry through with his threat.

Gonzalez's language overturned a recent federal court decision that eroded a "homestead protection" provision in the 1875 Texas Constitution. That provision barred banks and other financial institutions from foreclosing on home loans, effectively leaving Texas as the only state in which homeowners could not obtain home equity loans.

Gramm opposed Gonzalez and supported opening the door to home equity lending in Texas. Gonzalez, who was not an ardent supporter of the underlying bill, insisted on the amendment, which he said would protect Texas citizens from the threat of rapacious home equity lenders. ∎

Alternative Lenders Get Assistance

President Clinton won enactment of a modest initiative to provide federal help to a network of alternative community development lending institutions, but only after Congress included a host of pro-bank "regulatory relief" provisions that greased the bill's way through the legislative process. Congress cleared the measure Aug. 9. Clinton signed the bill into law Sept. 23 (PL 103-325).

The bill (HR 3474) authorized the creation of a wholly owned government corporation, the Community Development Financial Institutions Fund, to provide grants and other aid to community development banks, credit unions and loan funds that made loans in inner cities and poor rural areas generally underserved by traditional banks. The fund was authorized to receive $382 million in appropriations in fiscal 1995-98.

Community development financial institutions could receive up to $5 million in federal aid from the fund over a three-year period. The recipients had to match the federal assistance on a dollar-for-dollar basis, though those with severe financial constraints were eligible for a $2-for-$1 match. The fund also was to provide technical assistance.

One-third of the federal money was directed to mainstream commercial banks as an incentive for making loans or providing banking services in economically marginal neighborhoods.

Clinton had promised during his 1992 presidential campaign to create a network of 100 community development banks patterned after Chicago's South Shore Bank. But the administration and Congress soon gave up on the 100-bank pledge as too ambitious. The final bill offered only a small start at meeting the outstanding credit needs in poor communities, which the Treasury Department estimated in 1993 to be about $15 billion.

Other Banking Law Changes

In addition to the community lending initiative, the bill contained a host of unrelated banking provisions, including the following:

● **Home equity lending.** The bill sought to curb reverse "redlining," in which non-bank lenders targeted low- and moderate-income homeowners, minorities and the elderly for home equity loans on abusive terms. Typically, such second mortgages had large upfront fees and high interest rates. They frequently were obtained to finance home improve-

---

BOXSCORE

Community Development Lending — HR 3474 (S 1275). The bill authorized $382 million over three years to supply financial and technical aid to community development financial institutions.

Reports: S Rept 103-169; conference report H Rept 103-652.

KEY ACTION

March 17 — Senate passed HR 3474 by voice vote, after substituting the text of S 1275.

Aug. 4 — House adopted conference report, 410-12.

Aug. 9 — Senate cleared the bill by voice vote.

Sept. 23 — President signed bill — PL 103-325.

---

ments and were marketed by contractors and finance companies.

The bill required that such high-cost mortgages be subject to additional disclosure requirements to give consumers a clearer picture of the terms of the loans, including a warning that they could lose their homes if they defaulted. Consumers also had to be given the information three days before settlement on the loans, giving them additional time to back away.

The provisions affected loans with interest rates higher than 10 percentage points over comparable Treasury securities (the Federal Reserve could adjust this requirement after two years) or transactions in which upfront points and fees totaled more than 8 percent or $400, whichever was greater.

Several practices were banned outright, including most large end-of-loan balloon payments, abusive prepayment penalties and loans with interest rates so high that they actually increased the amount of principal owed. Lenders were required to consider consumers' ability to repay the loans, and loans could not be disbursed directly to home improvement contractors.

● **Bank regulatory burden.** About 50 separate provisions peeled away layers of paperwork requirements and additional regulatory mandates that had been placed on banks in recent years. A key provision exempted a greater number of small banks from mandatory yearly federal inspections. Another required federal bank regulators to undertake a review of regulations, eliminate outmoded mandates and implement regulations in a uniform manner when enforcing the same statutes.

● **Small-business loans.** The bill included language, principally authored by Sen. Alfonse M. D'Amato, R-N.Y., aimed at easing a "credit crunch" affecting small business. The provisions relaxed capital requirements and other regulations in an effort to encourage the formation of a secondary market for small-business loans. The goal was to encourage banks to make more loans to small businesses by making it possible for them to in turn sell the loans to private firms that would issue securities backed by the loans.

The most important provision made it easier for banks to sell portions of loans by reducing the amount of capital that they had to hold in reserve, provided they had transferred most of the risk to the buyer. The bill required banks to hold capital against these loans in amounts no greater than the

portion of the risk they retained, subject to the approval of regulators and limits on the amount of loans eligible for such preferred treatment.

In addition, the bill applied provisions mirroring the 1984 Secondary Mortgage Market Enhancement Act (PL 98-440), which boosted the private sector secondary market on home mortgages. These provisions removed several impediments to the securitization of small-business loans. Issuers got more time to pool loans and sell securities; paperwork requirements were eased to allow firms to file a single registration form with the Securities and Exchange Commission instead of separate ones with individual states; and banks, thrifts and credit unions were allowed to invest in the securities.

Language added on the Senate floor, which also was sought by key House members, extended the provisions to commercial real estate loans, though the capital rules were not as generous.

● **Flood insurance.** Several provisions aimed at shoring up the National Flood Insurance Program were included in the bill. To more strictly enforce laws that required people living in flood-prone areas to buy flood insurance, the bill required that mortgage lenders place in escrow premium payments for flood insurance. It also authorized lenders to purchase flood insurance for borrowers who refused to do so as required by law.

A mitigation fund, financed by the flood insurance program, was to be established to help protect communities and homeowners against flood risks. The Federal Emergency Management Agency was also to study the problem as it pertained to coastal and river areas.

Background

The community development bank plan largely followed a proposal that Clinton had sent to Congress on July 15, 1993. Clinton called for a $382 billion fund that would be used mainly to assist a fledgling network of alternative institutions, such as credit unions and about 40 community development funds that made loans to nonprofit groups and small businesses that were considered "unbankable" by traditional lenders.

The House passed a bill embodying Clinton's plan by voice vote Nov. 21, 1993.

The House Banking Committee had approved the proposal by voice vote Nov. 10, after sweetening it to win support from the previously indifferent banking industry. Committee Chairman Henry B. Gonzalez, D-Texas, was unenthusiastic about the measure, which he criticized as too limited in scope.

The committee set aside a third of the $382 million in the bill to finance the 1991 Bank Enterprise Act, which authorized rebates on deposit-insurance premiums for banks that made loans in poor and distressed neighborhoods. That decision represented a big win for committee members Floyd H. Flake, D-N.Y., and Tom Ridge, R-Pa. The two had succeeded in including the enterprise act in a larger bill overhauling the deposit-insurance system (PL 102-242). But Congress had never appropriated money to implement the law. *(1991 Almanac, p. 75)*

In another nod to the banks, the committee folded the community development bank provisions into a new bill (HR 3474) designed to provide regulatory relief.

In the Senate, the Banking Committee approved Clinton's plan by a vote of 18-1 on Sept. 21 (S 1275 — S Rept 103-169). In an effort to generate bipartisan support, the committee incorporated provisions to encourage a secondary market in small-business loans, reduce banks' paperwork and regulatory burdens and curb reverse redlining.

The full Senate did not take up the bill in 1993. *(1993 Almanac, p. 158)*

Senate Floor

The Senate passed the community development bank bill by voice vote March 17, 1994, after substituting the text of S 1275.

● **Fair trade.** The most significant change to the bill was the addition of the Fair Trade in Financial Services Act, a widely backed plan to give the Treasury Department new powers to open foreign financial services markets to U.S. firms. The amendment, offered by Banking Committee Chairman Donald W. Riegle Jr., D-Mich., and panel ranking Republican D'Amato, was adopted by voice vote. It was drawn from a bill (S 1527) that had been approved by the Banking Committee on Feb. 10; similar legislation had passed the Senate three times before but had never become law.

The Fair Trade measure authorized the Treasury to block foreign banks and securities firms from expanding existing operations in the United States or starting new ones if their home countries discriminated against U.S. banks and securities firms. *(Fair trade, p. 107; 1993 Almanac, p. 162)*

● **Regulatory changes.** Richard C. Shelby, D-Ala., and Connie Mack, R-Fla., won several additional regulatory changes sought by banks, including one exempting a greater number of small banks from mandated yearly federal examinations.

Under existing law, well-capitalized banks with $100 million or less in assets could be examined every 18 months instead of each year; the amendment raised the threshold to $250 million, thereby exempting hundreds of smaller banks from the annual exams. Banks with assets of $175 million or less that well managed and well capitalized but did not receive top ratings from regulators also were exempted from annual examinations.

The Shelby-Mack language was included in an en bloc amendment crafted by the bill's floor managers, Riegle and D'Amato. The amendment was adopted by voice vote.

In another action popular with banks, the Senate adopted by voice vote an amendment to cut down on the number of currency transaction reports that banks had to file to comply with anti-money-laundering laws. *(Money laundering, p. 116)*

● **Flood insurance.** By voice vote, the Senate adopted an amendment by John Kerry, D-Mass., aimed at shoring up the nation's federal flood insurance program, which had gone deeply into the red in recent years. The amendment required homeowners who lived in flood plains to purchase federal flood insurance and authorized federal grants for communities that mitigated potential flood hazards.

The House had passed a broadly similar companion measure (HR 3191) May 3. *(Flood insurance, p. 411)*

Conference/Final Action

The House easily approved the conference report on the bill (H Rept 103-652) Aug. 4 by a vote of 410-12. The Senate cleared it by voice vote Aug. 9. *(Vote 375, p. 112-H)*

During the nearly five months that had lapsed since the Senate passed its version in March, the fate of the bill had become closely entwined with that of a separate interstate branching measure (HR 3841), aimed at allowing banks to operate branch offices across state lines. Congressional Democrats made it clear they would not finish work on the interstate bill unless the community development bill passed as well. Conferees considered the two bills in tandem, completing work on both measures July 25. They were hurrying to finish before the Banking committees became preoccupied with the politically charged Whitewater hearings, which began July 26. *(Interstate branching, p. 93; Whitewater, p. 108)*

At one point, conferees combined the two bills, but they

separated them at the last minute to avert a possible procedural challenge in the Senate. They were worried that the interstate banking bill might be deemed non-germane (unrelated) to the community lending measure.

● **Financial services.** The chief sticking point in conference was whether to include the Senate's Fair Trade in Financial Services provisions.

The Fair Trade bill was strongly supported by the Senate conferees, as well as by most conferees drawn from the House Banking Committee. But the Ways and Means Committee staunchly opposed the legislation, arguing that it would fracture U.S. trade policy; Ways and Means believed trade policy should rest solely with the Office of the U.S. Trade Representative, over which the committee had jurisdiction.

On July 20, House Energy and Commerce Committee Chairman John D. Dingell, D-Mich., who had been trying to broker a deal, proposed a new version of the Fair Trade pro-

visions that would have vested the sanction authority within the trade representative's office. But Ways and Means rejected the idea, and the final bill dropped the provisions.

On the other major provisions of the community development bank bill, conferees:

● **Small-business loans.** Adopted D'Amato's provisions relaxing certain federal regulations and capital rules to make it easier for the private sector to develop a secondary market in small-business loans. The House Banking Committee had approved a more far-reaching bill (HR 2600), and chief sponsor Paul E. Kanjorski, D-Pa., had hoped to incorporate the measure into the community bank bill but fell short.

● **Reverse redlining.** Retained the bipartisan Senate provision requiring that consumers be given more information about high-cost home-equity loans.

● **Flood insurance.** Agreed to the Senate provision aimed at shoring up the federal flood insurance program. ■

Community Development Banking Provisions

The community development banking bill (HR 3474 — PL 103-325) created the Community Development Financial Institutions Fund to provide matching grants and other aid to community development banks, credit unions and loan funds that made loans in inner cities and poor rural areas generally underserved by traditional banks.

The bill also included a number of "regulatory relief" provisions sought by banks, as well as language to curb abusive home equity lending practices, boost the private sector market in small-business and commercial real estate loans and shore up the federal flood insurance program.

As enacted, PL 103-325 contained provisions to:

Community Development Financial Institutions Fund

● **CDFI Fund.** Establish a Community Development Financial Institutions (CDFI) Fund, a wholly owned government corporation, to provide financial and technical assistance to CDFIs. To be eligible for assistance, CDFIs had to have community development as their primary mission, serve communities in need of economic assistance and provide development services to complement their lending activities. State and local government agencies were not eligible.

The CDFI Fund was authorized to receive up to $382 million in appropriations over fiscal 1995-98. (For fiscal 1995-96, appropriators provided a total of $125 million in the fiscal 1995 VA-HUD appropriations bill.)

The new fund was to be managed by an administrator and overseen by a 15-person board, whose membership was to include several Cabinet secretaries, the administrator of the Small Business Administration and nine private citizens with community development experience.

The fund was to provide several forms of financial assistance, including equity investments, grants, loans, credit union shares and deposits. It also could provide technical assistance and establish a training program.

No CDFI could receive more than $5 million in aid over any three-year period, though an exception could be made for an institution that sought to establish a subsidiary or affiliate in another state.

Institutions receiving federal assistance had to match federal moneys on a $1-to-$1 basis, though the matching requirements could be waived for CDFIs that were particularly cash-strapped. No more than 25 percent of total assistance provided by the fund in any year could be provided on a non-matching basis. To receive assistance,

CDFIs were required to enter into an agreement with the fund that specified terms and conditions of assistance and set performance goals.

To receive assistance, CDFIs were required to prepare a comprehensive strategic plan and detail that plan to secure matching funds. In addition, each CDFI was required to maintain accurate records of its activities, the communities it served, who benefited from its services and how successfully it was carrying out its strategic plan. The fund was to review how well each CDFI implemented its strategic plan and lived up to its assistance agreement.

Each CDFI receiving assistance was required to issue an annual report to the fund.

● **Community partnerships.** Allow community development financial institutions to form "community partnerships" with mainstream banks and bank holding companies, credit unions, nonprofit organizations, state or local government agencies, and investment companies. A community partnership was defined as an agreement between a CDFI and a mainstream institution to provide development services, loans or investments in an underdeveloped area. These combinations were eligible for federal assistance, though any federal funds could be disbursed only to the CDFI.

The idea behind these community partnerships was to bolster collaboration between CDFIs and other institutions and to have the limited federal funds help leverage private money into community development.

● **Bank Enterprise Act.** Provide a financing mechanism for the Bank Enterprise Act (BEA), which was designed to give incentives to mainstream banks and thrifts to make loans and provide banking services in distressed communities.

One-third of the money appropriated to the CDFI fund, up to $127 million, was to finance cash rebates to banks under the Bank Enterprise Act program.

The aim of the BEA program, originally established in a 1991 bill (PL 102-242), was to use federal money to leverage private capital into underdeveloped communities; the administrator of the federal CDFI fund also was to oversee BEA-related activities. But Congress had never appropriated money to implement the law.

To receive a rebate, banks and thrifts had to apply to the fund. The administrator was required to rank the applicants according to several criteria, foremost being the extent to which they made equity investments in CDFIs.

Other criteria included the extent to which a bank made loans in distressed neighborhoods, participated in community development ventures and provided basic banking services. Insured CDFIs were to have an advantage in the competition for the BEA rebates.

The administrator was given broad discretion over BEA program activities and was directed to ensure that, to the maximum extent practicable, BEA rebates supported the activities of CDFIs.

● **Performance report.** Require the General Accounting Office (GAO), the investigative arm of Congress, to issue a progress report on the CDFI program 30 months after the CDFI administrator was named.

● **Credit unions.** Authorize additional appropriations of $10 million over fiscal 1995-98 for the Community Development Credit Union Revolving Loan Fund, an existing fund operated by the National Credit Union Administration.

Home Equity Loan Abuses

● **'Reverse redlining.'** Curb the practice of "reverse redlining," in which non-bank lenders targeted low- and moderate-income homeowners, minorities and the elderly for home equity loans on abusive terms. Typically, such second mortgages had large upfront fees and high interest rates. Repayment terms could be such that homeowners were unable to keep up and ended up losing their homes.

The bill required several new disclosure requirements for such high-cost loans to give consumers a better understanding of their terms, including a warning that people could lose their homes if they defaulted.

The measure amended the Truth in Lending Act (PL 101-73), a 1989 law that required uniform loan terms and disclosures, to provide additional disclosures for high-cost mortgage loans. Such loans were defined as loans with interest rates higher than 10 percentage points over comparable Treasury securities (the Federal Reserve could adjust this requirement after September 1996) or transactions in which upfront points and fees totaled more than 8 percent of the loan, or $400, whichever was greater.

Such loans were not barred, but creditors (such as finance and mortgage companies) were required to provide borrowers with a special, simplified disclosure notice three days before settlement.

The creditor was required to disclose that the consumer could lose his/her home for failure to meet the terms of the loan and that the person still had time to back away from the loan. In addition, the lender had to reveal the annual percentage rate of the loan and what the monthly payments would be.

If a high-cost mortgage (as defined by the law) was made without the required disclosures, the borrower would have three years to rescind the transaction.

● **Prohibited practices.** Ban several high-cost mortgage lending practices. Consumers had the right to rescind any loan (which met the criteria for a high-cost mortgage loan as defined by the bill) that included the following terms or practices:

●**Prepayment penalties.** Such loans could not contain prepayment penalties. However, the prohibition applied only to cases in which consumers were carrying heavy debt burdens (a 50 percent debt-to-income ratio, including the loan in question). Prepayment penalties had been used to trap borrowers in abusive mortgages by making it prohibitively expensive to pay off their loans early.

●**Limitations after default.** Creditors could not charge a higher interest rate after a borrower defaulted than the rate prior to default.

●**Balloon payments.** High end-of-loan balloon payments — which often misled borrowers by making the loan appear less expensive than it really was — generally were barred when the length of the loan was less than five years.

●**Negative amortization.** Negative amortization, which occurred when monthly loan payments did not cover the interest due, was barred. Previously, under such terms, the amount owed grew over the life of the loan.

●**Prepaid payments.** Prepaid payments — periodic loan payments that were consolidated and paid in advance from loan proceeds that otherwise would have gone to the borrower — also were barred.

●**Disregard of ability to pay.** Creditors could not extend high-cost mortgage loans unless they had given consideration to a con-sumer's ability to repay the loans. In determining the ability to pay, creditors were required to evaluate existing or expected income, existing obligations, repayment capacity or employment.

●**Payments to contractors.** Loan proceeds could not be given directly to home improvement contractors, though they could be extended jointly to the borrower and a contractor.

The Federal Reserve retained flexibility to exempt certain mortgage loans from these prohibitions if it determined the exemption to be in the public interest — for example, in the case of certain short-term construction loans that might be covered by the measure. On the other hand, the Federal Reserve was required to prohibit acts and practices that it found unfair, deceptive and aimed at evading the restrictions of the bill.

●**Civil liability.** Borrowers were given the right to sue creditors who failed to provide adequate disclosures or made loans on prohibited terms. Such civil liability was to equal all finance charges and fees paid by the consumer.

State attorneys general had the right to bring actions in federal district courts to enforce the anti-reverse redlining provisions of the bill for up to three years after violations occurred. This provision was designed to strengthen regulation of finance companies, which were only loosely regulated by the federal government under existing law. The state had to notify the appropriate federal agency responsible for enforcement, and the agency had the right to intervene.

●**Purchaser liability.** Purchasers of high-cost mortgage loans were subject to any claims that could be raised against the original lender. This provision sought to curb the secondary market in abusive mortgage loans by making them less desirable to purchase. Any seller of a high-cost mortgage was required to provide a notice of potential liability to the purchaser.

Secondary Market For Small-Business Loans

● **Secondary market.** Relax capital requirements and other regulations to encourage the private sector secondary market for small-business loans. The idea was to encourage banks to make loans to small businesses by making it easier for them to turn around and sell the loans to Wall Street investment firms, which would package them into securities backed by the loans.

The measure removed impediments in existing law that blocked securitization of small-business loans and leases. A new class of "small-business related securities" was created.

The provision was based on the Secondary Mortgage Market Enhancement Act of 1984 (PL 98-440), which had helped pump money into the housing market by removing regulatory impediments to a private sector secondary market in home mortgages.

Securities laws governing margin and securities delivery requirements were eased to permit issuers more time to pool and sell small-business related securities.

Small-business securities were considered acceptable investments for banks, thrifts and credit unions, though regulators were authorized to issue rules to ensure safety and soundness of the institution. State and local governments also were authorized to invest in small-business related securities.

Securities and Exchange Commission (SEC) securities registration rules were relaxed to permit issuers of small-business securities to file a single registration form with the SEC rather than separate ones with each state.

● **Capital requirements.** Change existing regulations that required banks to maintain capital reserves against loans they sold.

(When an institution sold a loan, purchasers usually insisted that the bank retain part of the risk and remain responsible for part of the loan should a borrower default. This was known as selling a loan with "recourse." Under existing rules, banks had to hold 8 percent capital on the total amount of a loan, even if they sold almost all of it.)

The bill changed recourse rules so that banks had to maintain capital reserves only against the portion of loan risk they

retained. Only well-capitalized banks were eligible to take advantage of the new rules. The total amount of recourse retained by an institution was limited to 15 percent of the institution's risk-based capital reserves, though regulators were given flexibility to increase the limit.

● **Commercial real estate loan securitization.** In a provision added during Senate floor consideration of the bill and modified in conference, similar regulatory treatment was given to "commercial mortgage related securities." In essence, the regulatory benefits provided under the Secondary Mortgage Market Enhancement Act to home mortgages (and, under this bill, to small-business related securities) also were accorded to securities derived from commercial real estate loans. This provision was designed to shore up the troubled commercial real estate market.

However, the new capital rules that applied to small-business loans regarding recourse on sold loans did not apply to commercial real estate loans.

● **Impact study.** Direct the Federal Reserve and the SEC to study the impact of small-business and commercial real estate loan securitization on the credit and securities markets. The study was to evaluate the impact of these provisions on business and commercial credit, especially on firms in low- and moderate-income areas, minority- and women-owned businesses, community development programs and community development financial institutions. The study also was to focus on the markets that evolved for securities backed by small business and commercial real estate loans.

● **Capital access program.** Authorize $50 million to provide federal grants to state capital access programs. Such programs encouraged banks to make small-business loans that were somewhat riskier than conventional commercial loans, without posing a threat to the safety and soundness of the bank. In a capital access program, banks, borrowers and states contributed to a loss reserve fund that covered losses from loans made under the program.

The administrator of the new federal Community Development Financial Institutions Fund was to run the program.

Paperwork Reduction and Regulatory Burden Relief

The bill contained more than 50 provisions to reduce bank regulatory burden and paperwork requirements established under recent banking laws. Obtaining this "regulatory relief" was a top priority for bank and thrift lobbyists during the 103rd Congress.

These included provisions to:

● **Regulatory burden evaluation.** Require bank regulators to consider the burdens and benefits of new banking regulations, especially on smaller banks. New regulations were to take effect on the first day of a calendar quarter.

● **Streamlining regulations.** Require each federal banking regulator to review and streamline its regulations within two years and eliminate inconsistent, outmoded or duplicative rules. When different regulatory agencies enforced the same laws, they were required to implement the rules in a uniform fashion.

● **Duplicative filings.** Require bank regulators to work together to curb duplicative reporting requirements.

● **Coordinated examinations.** Require regulators to coordinate their examinations and, within two years, create a system in which one regulator would take the lead in a unified examination of a bank or thrift and its affiliates.

● **18-month examinations.** Raise the asset threshold for eligibility for an 18-month exam cycle from $100 million to $250 million for well-capitalized and well-managed institutions with "outstanding" CAMEL ratings. (CAMEL was an acronym that stood for capital adequacy, asset quality, management, earnings and liquidity; essentially it was a composite rating that signified how strong a bank was.) Existing law required on-site examinations of insured depository institutions every 12 months.

The 18-month exception was broadened to apply to institu-

tions with "good" CAMEL ratings and assets of less than $100 million. After two years, the asset cap could be raised to $175 million for such institutions.

● **Call report simplification.** Direct banking agencies to develop a single report of condition (call report) for the filing of core information to regulators. Banks also were permitted to file call reports electronically, and the public was to have electronic access to the information. Banks no longer were required to publish condition reports in local newspapers.

● **Appeals process.** Require all federal banking agencies and the National Credit Union Administration Board within six months to establish an internal process under which the financial institutions they regulated could appeal regulatory decisions. Each regulator was required to create an ombudsman's office and develop a pilot program to encourage alternative ways such as mediation and arbitration to resolve disputes between institutions and regulators.

● **Currency transaction reports.** Permit banks and thrifts to file currency transaction reports (which detailed cash transactions of $10,000 or more) by electronic means.

● **RESPA exemptions.** Exempt residential real estate loans for business purposes from coverage under the Real Estate Settlement Procedures Act (RESPA), which required extensive paperwork disclosures at settlement. Also, RESPA mortgage disclosure requirements were modified to require that lenders provide a statement indicating whether the bank had sold loans in the past, rather than an analysis of the percentage of loans sold, as required under existing law.

● **Local boards of directors.** Require that a majority, rather than two-thirds, of the board of directors of a federally chartered bank reside in the area in which the bank was located.

● **Audit requirements.** Allow banks and thrifts with total assets of more than $9 billion and CAMEL ratings of 1 or 2 that were subsidiaries of holding companies to meet independent audit requirements at the holding company level.

● **Real estate appraisals.** Encourage states to enter into reciprocity agreements so that appraisers licensed or certified by one state could perform appraisals in other states. States could not impose excessive fees or burdensome requirements on out-of-state appraisers engaged in temporary practice.

● **Bank holding company formation.** Simplify procedures for forming a bank holding company from a stand-alone bank. Instead of a full application, such reorganizations could be approved after filing a 30-day notice. The formation of certain bank holding companies was exempted from securities registration requirements.

● **Bankers' banks.** Modify regulations to make it easier for banks to invest in so-called bankers' banks — insured banks entirely owned by, and dedicated to providing services to, other banks. Federally chartered thrifts also were permitted to invest in bankers' banks.

● **Credit card receivables.** Allow the Federal Deposit Insurance Corporation (FDIC) to waive the right to repudiate, at a later date, an institution's sale of its credit card accounts receivable. (Without such authority, the FDIC could be forced to repudiate such sales by banks that subsequently went into receivership, a situation that had created legal uncertainties for buyers and sellers of such receivables.)

● **Liability on foreign accounts.** Provide that domestic banks were not required to repay deposits made at foreign branches in cases of a sovereign action by that country or in cases of war, insurrection or civil strife.

● **Capital standards study.** Require the Treasury Department to conduct a study of the effect of risk-based capital standards on the safety and soundness of insured depository institutions, economic growth and the availability of credit, particularly for individuals and small businesses.

● **Interest on reserves.** Require the Federal Reserve to study the monetary policy and banking implications of whether financial institutions should receive interest on cash reserves kept at the Fed. The Office of Management and Budget and the Congressional Budget Office were to report on the budgetary impact of such interest payments.

● **Consumer credit study.** Require the Treasury Department to conduct a study of ways to streamline the consumer lending process.

● **Regulatory autonomy.** Clarify the degree of autonomy of the Office of the Comptroller of the Currency (OCC) and the Office of Thrift Supervision (OTS) as bureaus of the Treasury Department. The OCC and the OTS were responsible for supervising and regulating national banks and thrift institutions, which held nearly two-thirds of the total assets in U.S. depository institutions.

Regulations developed by the OCC and the OTS no longer were to be subject to Treasury Department review or clearance. The FDIC, OCC and Federal Reserve were also authorized to conduct litigation through their own attorneys.

● **Check hold study.** Require the Federal Reserve to study whether the existing one-day hold on local checks under the Expedited Funds Availability Act should be extended to two days as a means to combat check fraud.

● **Insider lending.** Permit institutions to make a loan to a bank officer without prior approval of the board of directors, provided the loan was secured by the insider borrower's residence. Such loans remained subject to the individual and aggregate insider lending limits. The Federal Reserve also was permitted to exempt officers and directors of non-bank subsidiaries (who were not involved in bank policy-making) from insider lending limits.

● **Risk-based capital.** Require regulators to ensure that any revisions to risk-based capital standards take into account the size and activities of the institutions and not cause undue reporting burdens.

● **Radio advertising.** Streamline truth-in-lending requirements for radio advertising to permit radio advertisers to reduce the amount of information that had to be disclosed. Additional information would have to be made available through use of a toll-free telephone number.

● **Management interlocks.** Allow individuals who served on boards of directors of more than one bank to apply for a five-year extension of rules barring such "management interlocks." Some individuals had been "grandfathered" repeatedly since laws barring such interlocks took effect in 1978.

● **Fair Credit Reporting Act amendments.** Require credit bureaus to disclose to consumers more specific information (dates, original payees and amounts) of any checks that formed the foundation for a negative characterization of a consumer.

● **Non-federally insured institutions.** Ease rules that required non-federally insured institutions to obtain written customer acknowledgment that they knew the institution was not federally insured. In cases of existing customers of the institution, the requirement could be met through mailed notices to the depositor.

● **Data bank feasibility study.** Require the Federal Financial Institutions Examination Council to study the feasibility of creating a data bank for depository institution reports.

● **Application deadlines.** Require banking regulators to complete action on bank applications within one year of receipt.

● **Right of rescission.** Direct the Federal Reserve Board to study whether waiving or modifying a consumer's right to rescind a loan within three days — only in cases of loan transactions involving a refinancing or consolidation of existing loans — would benefit consumers.

● **Non-banking activities.** Replace the existing application process for bank holding companies to engage in non-banking activities with a 60-day-notice procedure. The provision was aimed at simplifying and speeding up the approval process.

● **State examinations.** Require the Federal Financial Institutions Examination Council to develop standards for state examinations of banks that were also subject to federal exams. Under a provision of the 1991 deposit insurance overhaul law, which required annual bank exams, the federal banking agencies (the FDIC and the Federal Reserve system) could alternate responsibility for such annual examinations. The provision was aimed at spurring federal regulators to allow state authorities to conduct the alternating examinations by establishing federal guidelines for such exams.

● **Revision of recourse rules.** Require all federal bank regulators to review and revise their regulations and policies regarding loans sold with recourse.

(Recourse occurred when the institution that originally made the loan sold the loan but retained a portion of the responsibility should the borrower default. Bank representatives said existing recourse rules were too stringent because they required banks to hold capital against the entire amount of a loan sold with recourse, even if they had sold almost the entire loan.)

The bill required that financial institutions hold capital only to the amount of retained risk of loans sold with recourse. For example, existing rules required banks to hold 8 percent capital on the total amount of a loan. If the bank retained recourse of only 5 percent, it would be required to retain 5 percent in capital reserves.

Bank regulators could permit institutions to hold less capital than the amount at risk in appropriate situations.

Money Laundering

● **Currency transaction reports.** Require the Treasury Department to develop ways to substantially reduce (by 30 percent) the number of currency transaction reports (CTRs) filed by depository institutions under the Bank Secrecy Act. Generally, CTRs had to be filed for every cash transaction of $10,000 or more. This reduction in paperwork was to be accomplished by exempting routine cash transactions between banks and their customers from CTR filing requirements.

● **Exemptions.** Require the Treasury Department to exempt the following from CTR filing requirements:
• Transactions between depository institutions.
• Bank transactions with federal, state and local governments, as well as quasi-governmental entities.
• Transactions between depository institutions and businesses where the CTRs had little or no value for law enforcement purposes.

Treasury also was given discretion to exempt transactions between depository institutions and their qualified business customers, though such customers had to be approved by the department.

● **Civil penalties.** Allow Treasury to delegate authority to assess civil penalties for violations of the Bank Security Act to the appropriate federal bank regulator. (Treasury's Office of Financial Enforcement had such authority, but it had been criticized for failing to process cases in a timely manner.)

● **State exemptions.** Permit the Treasury Department to exempt classes of transactions within a state from Bank Security Act reporting requirements should those transactions fall under state requirements that were substantially similar to federal ones. This could apply, for example, to state-regulated casinos.

● **Money transmitters.** Require check cashing companies, currency exchanges and other so-called money transmitters to register with the Treasury Department as a way to curb money laundering by entities outside the regulated financial services sector. The aim of the provision was to promote Treasury Department enforcement of money laundering laws and to better educate money transmitters about their responsibilities under the law.

The bill expressed the sense of Congress that states should adopt uniform laws to license and regulate money transmitting businesses.

● **Ratzlaf decision.** Respond to a recent Supreme Court decision, *Ratzlaf v. U.S.*, which required that the government prove that a defendant not only tried to evade reporting requirements for large currency transactions but also knew such conduct to be against the law. The provision removed the requirement, established by the court, that the government prove that the defendant knew his or her conduct was illegal.

Flood Insurance

The bill contained several provisions to shore up the National Flood Insurance Program, which was established in 1968 to provide

federal flood insurance (often at subsidized rates) for homes and businesses. The program, which was run by the Federal Emergency Management Agency (FEMA), had faced repeated funding shortfalls resulting from two major problems: Many homeowners who lived in designated flood areas did not regularly buy flood insurance, and those who did tended to live in the most flood-prone areas. The program required a $1.2 billion bailout in the mid-1980s. Only about 17 percent of residents of designated flood hazard areas had flood insurance, which under existing law was supposed to be purchased when financing or refinancing a home.

The bill included provisions to:

● **Compliance.** Ensure that homeowners who should have flood insurance, as required under existing law, obtained and maintained it. The increased compliance and participation in the program was designed to provide additional premiums to the flood insurance fund and shield the federal government from a potential bailout — while protecting possible flood victims.

Under existing law, banks, thrifts and others who issued mortgages were supposed to require the purchase of flood insurance at origination (or at a later date if the loan was extended or renewed) if the property was in an area that had special flood hazards. However, there was no specific sanction for violations of the law.

To increase participation in the program, the bill required lenders and companies that serviced mortgages to escrow flood insurance premiums if they maintained an escrow account for the loan for any other purpose.

To increase compliance with mandatory flood insurance purchase requirements, the bill made it the responsibility of mortgage lenders (and government-sponsored enterprises such as the Federal National Mortgage Association, or Fannie Mae) to ensure obeyance.

Federally regulated lending institutions, including banks, savings and loans, and credit unions, were barred from making or refinancing loans on any structure located in a special flood hazard area unless flood insurance was purchased and maintained for the term of the loan. Exception was made for loans of less than $5,000 with repayment terms of one year or less.

Lenders who demonstrated a "pattern or practice" of non-compliance with flood insurance purchase or notification requirements could be fined by federal regulators up to $350 per loan, to a maximum of $100,000.

Fannie Mae and the Federal Home Loan Mortgage Corporation (Freddie Mac) — government-sponsored enterprises that purchased mortgages — were required to put in place procedures to ensure that any loan they purchased that was required to have flood insurance was indeed covered by a policy.

● **Force placement.** Require lenders and loan servicers to force-place insurance if borrowers who were required by law to purchase it had not done so. If a lender determined that flood insurance had to be purchased, it was required to notify the borrower, who had 45 days to purchase it. If the borrower failed to buy insurance within that time, the lender would have to buy the insurance on the borrower's behalf.

● **Notice requirements.** Require lenders to notify borrowers when property being financed was located in a flood hazard area; such notices had to include the fact that borrowers were required to purchase flood insurance, either through the federal program or through private insurers.

● **Community rating system.** Codify an existing Community Rating System Program administered by FEMA. The program provided incentives, through reduced insurance premiums, to communities that voluntarily adopted and enforced measures to reduce flood risks that exceeded FEMA standards.

● **Flood risk mitigation.** Establish a new National Flood Mitigation Fund, financed by premiums paid to the National Flood Insurance Fund, to provide grants to state and local governments for projects and other programs designed to reduce potential flood damage. All projects had to be technically feasible and cost-beneficial.

Such projects could include minor mitigation efforts such as flood-proofing sewers, installing or improving floodgates, retention ponds, drain pipes and pumping stations. Major flood control projects such as dikes, levees and seawalls were not eligible.

No mitigation grant could be made to a state or community without an approved mitigation plan. FEMA was directed to approve only those plans that were the most cost-effective, meaning that the money drawn from the fund for flood mitigation projects would in effect be paid back because of fewer claims filed.

Total grants from the mitigation fund were capped at $15 million in fiscal 1995 and $20 million thereafter.

● **Task forces.** Establish two flood insurance task forces: the Flood Insurance Interagency Task Force and the task force on the Natural and Beneficial Functions of the Floodplain.

The Flood Insurance Interagency Task Force, with 10 members from federal agencies and private businesses, was directed to recommend standardized procedures to improve enforcement of flood insurance requirements, as well as ways for federal agencies and the secondary market in mortgage loans to improve compliance.

The task force on the Natural and Beneficial Functions of the Floodplain was to be manned by several federal agencies, including FEMA, the under secretary of Commerce for Oceans and Atmosphere, the director of the United States Fish and Wildlife Service, the administrator of the Environmental Protection Agency and the secretary of the Army. The task force was directed to study the natural functions of flood plains that reduced flood losses and make recommendations on how to further reduce flood losses through the protection of flood plains.

● **Flood maps.** Require FEMA to review every five years, and update if necessary, federal maps of flood plains and flood-risk areas. Any changes to federal flood maps (including additions and removals of flood hazard designations that affected flood insurance requirements) had to be published in the Federal Register or some other comparable publication. New flood maps and a compilation of flood map changes were to be made available to bank regulators, state and local governments and the public. The bill established a Technical Mapping Environmental Council of federal, state and private mapping experts to advise FEMA on ways to improve flood mapping and provide an evaluation of FEMA mapping efforts.

● **Erosion hazards study.** Direct FEMA to hire an independent entity to conduct a study on the effect of erosion, particularly of coastlines, on the federal flood insurance program. Critics of the flood insurance program said that in effect it subsidized the building of homes and other structures on coastal lands that eroded easily or on lake shores and flood plains that were subject to repeated flooding. Claims in such cases far exceeded the premiums paid on the policies.

Earlier versions of the bill contained a provision that would have eliminated federal insurance for building on lands that eroded easily. But the provision was blocked by representatives from coastal states.

The study was to determine how much in flood insurance claims was attributable to erosion, as well as the economic impact of denying flood insurance in such communities or making it available at market rates. FEMA also was to study the economic effects of increasing premiums on coastal building that were built prior to the imposition of more stringent building standards in 1975. Insurance claims on such structures exceeded premium income by $668 million over 1978-92.

● **Effective date of policies.** Establish that new contracts for flood insurance would not become effective for 30 days after purchase. This provision came in response to reports that some victims of the 1993 floods in the Midwest bought flood insurance only when flooding was imminent. An exemption was provided when a homeowner was financing or refinancing a loan or if coverage was purchased within one year of a remapping or map revision.

● **Agricultural structures.** Exempt agricultural structures that were substantially damaged by flood from the law's building requirements under the act if they were assessed market (actuarial) rates and were no longer eligible for federal disaster assistance.

● **Prohibited flood disaster assistance.** Establish that any building that was supposed to have flood insurance and received federal disaster assistance after a flood would not be eligible to receive disaster assistance a second time. ■

Financial Services Trade Bill Falters at Session's End

Lawmakers made two attempts — both unsuccessful — to complete legislation aimed at pressuring foreign countries to open their financial markets to U.S. firms. The House Banking Committee approved the Fair Trade in Financial Services Act (HR 3248), but the bill got hung up in a jurisdictional tangle with the Ways and Means and the Energy and Commerce committees. The bill would have covered both the banking and securities industries, and it would have authorized the Treasury Department to impose sanctions on foreign firms from countries that discriminated against U.S. financial firms.

The Senate passed the bill language as part of a community development banking bill (HR 3474), but the provisions were dropped in conference.

In the final days of the session, the House passed a narrower bill (HR 4926) that applied only to banks, but the Senate left town without considering the measure. That bill, titled the National Treatment in Banking Act, would have required the Treasury Department to conduct a study of which foreign countries discriminated against U.S. banks. Banking regulators, principally the Federal Reserve, would have been authorized to take that information into account when deciding whether to approve the applications of foreign banks to expand their U.S. operations or start new ones.

Background

The United States had long followed a policy of national treatment, which meant that it gave foreign banks the same access to the U.S. marketplace that domestic banks enjoyed. But U.S. banks complained that foreign countries, particularly Japan, employed legal and informal barriers that effectively blocked them from gaining a toehold overseas.

Despite widespread support, previous efforts to enact the Fair Trade in Financial Services Act had run into resistance from the State Department, the Federal Reserve and free-traders in Congress, especially on the House Ways and Means Committee. The legislation, aimed at requiring reciprocal national treatment for U.S. banks and securities firms, had passed the Senate on several occasions. The House adopted the measure in 1990 as part of the conference report to an unrelated bill, but that measure then died in the Senate. (1990 Almanac, p. 189)

Members of the House Ways and Means and the Energy and Commerce committees disliked the fair trade bill because they thought it would give the Treasury Department too much power over the domain of the Office of the U.S. Trade Representative (USTR) and the Securities and Exchange Commission (SEC), which fell under their respective jurisdictions. Both committees had to act on the bill before it could advance to the floor.

The Clinton administration avidly supported the Fair Trade measure, seeing it as a way to shore up U.S. leverage in ongoing talks with trading partners, especially Japan, on opening up financial services markets to U.S. companies. Administration officials said the measure was an important tool for U.S. negotiators working on the financial services provisions of the General Agreement on Tariffs and Trade (GATT).

1993 Action

The House Banking Committee's International Finance Subcommittee gave voice vote approval to the Fair Trade bill

(HR 3248) on Nov. 19, 1993. The bill, sponsored by Charles E. Schumer, D-N.Y., authorized the Treasury Department to impose sanctions on foreign banks and securities firms from countries that did not accord national treatment to U.S. firms.

The Senate Banking Committee tried to mark up a virtually identical bill (S 1527) on Nov. 18 but was unable to assemble a quorum. The measure was cosponsored by a bipartisan majority of the Banking Committee, including Chairman Donald W. Riegle Jr., D-Mich., and Ranking Republican Alfonse M. D'Amato of New York. (1993 Almanac, p. 162)

Fair Trade in Financial Services

The Senate Banking Committee altered S 1527 slightly and passed it Feb. 10 by a vote of 17-2. The revised version (S Rept 103-235) added provisions barring sanctions against firms from nations that had promised in the course of the GATT talks to open their financial markets.

Republicans Connie Mack of Florida and Phil Gramm of Texas voted against the measure. A staff member for Mack said the senator was concerned that limiting foreign firms' access to U.S. markets would harm the United States more than any foreign country.

On the House side, a second House Banking Subcommittee, Financial Institutions, amended HR 3248 March 2 and approved it by voice vote. The subcommittee included language stating that if another country exempted U.S. companies from sanctions, that country's firms would be similarly exempted from the Treasury sanctions. Committee Republicans warned that the measure might provoke retaliation from targeted countries.

The full House Banking Committee gave voice vote approval March 9 to a version of HR 3248 that applied only to foreign banks; earlier language covering securities firms was dropped to avoid a jurisdictional problem with the Energy and Commerce Committee. However, the measure stalled after Ways and Means and Energy and Commerce asserted their jurisdiction.

Bill Added to Community Banking Bill

Meanwhile, the Senate agreed March 17 to add the Fair Trade language to a community development banking bill then on the Senate floor (HR 3474). Senators adopted the proposal, made by Riegle and D'Amato, by voice vote. (Community development lending, p. 100)

In preparation for a conference on the community development banking bill, the House and Senate Banking committees agreed on common language outlining a five-step process that could culminate in sanctions against companies from countries that did not apply national treatment to U.S. firms. The secretary of the Treasury would identify those countries and then determine whether any such denial was harming U.S. companies. Thirdly, Treasury, with the concurrence of the USTR or the SEC, would negotiate with the offending country. If those negotiations did not bear fruit, Treasury could direct the appropriate regulator to issue sanctions against foreign companies seeking to expand or start new operations in the United States. Regulators could demur if Treasury's request would have adverse effects on the U.S. financial system and securities markets, and in other limited circumstances.

Sanctions could not be applied if they conflicted with existing bilateral or multilateral financial services agreements such as the North American Free Trade Agreement.

The question of whether to include the Fair Trade provi-

sions was one of the last stumbling blocks when House and Senate conferees negotiated the final text of the community development bank bill. Energy and Commerce Chairman John D. Dingell, D-Mich., attempted to broker a compromise that would satisfy the Banking committees but also win approval from Ways and Means. Three years before, Ways and Means had signed on to a version of the Fair Trade bill that would have provided the new sanction authority, but vested it within the USTR's office. Dingell outlined a proposal generally built along those lines and shopped it to Ways and Means. But the committee said no, and the provisions were dropped from the conference report. *(1992 Almanac, p. 131)*

Scaled-Back Bill

After redrafting the measure to avoid the jurisdictional tangles that had sunk the more ambitious effort, Schumer introduced a scaled-back version of the embattled Fair Trade in Financial Services bill Aug. 9 The new measure (HR 4926) required the Treasury Department to conduct a study of which foreign countries discriminated against U.S. banks and authorized federal regulators to take that information into account when deciding whether to approve a foreign bank's application to start or expand U.S. operations.

The House Banking Committee approved the bill by voice vote Sept. 13 (H Rept 103-727).

To keep the measure from being referred to the Ways and Means and Energy and Commerce committees, bill sponsors dropped language that would have given Treasury the authority to impose sanctions on trading partners that did not provide national treatment to U.S. banks. The bill applied only to banks, not to the securities industry. Also dropped was language that would have required Treasury to negotiate with the offending government.

But acting Ways and Means Trade Subcommittee Chairman Robert T. Matsui, D-Calif., a free-trade advocate who led the earlier fight against the broader bill, said he continued to oppose the legislation. Matsui said he was concerned that trading partners could retaliate against U.S. companies in other sectors, such as insurance and securities.

The House passed the bill Sept. 30 by voice vote without a trace of dissent. But the Senate did not take up the bill, and it died at the end of the 103rd Congress. ∎

Rough 'Whitewater' Ride for Clinton

The controversy that came to be known as "Whitewater" was a distracting, sometimes crippling, sideshow for Congress and for the Clinton administration in 1994.

The year featured lengthy rounds of partisan wrangling between Republicans attacking President Clinton and Democrats supporting him, culminating in congressional hearings that led to the resignations of two senior Treasury Department officials.

Although the Whitewater saga involved a lengthy and complicated sequence of events, there were two basic elements to the controversy: events that occurred in Arkansas in the 1980s and actions by Clinton administration officials after the affair became public.

The Arkansas phase was the subject of investigations first by Justice Department special counsel Robert B. Fiske Jr. and later by independent counsel Kenneth W. Starr. It involved the Clintons' role in the Whitewater Development Co., a failed Arkansas land venture, and their relationship with James B. McDougal, a friend who formed the enterprise with the Clintons and managed it. McDougal also owned a high-flying Arkansas thrift, Madison Guaranty Savings and Loan, which subsequently failed amid allegations of mismanagement and fraud.

The remnants of the Madison thrift were being probed by the Resolution Trust Corporation (RTC), the federal agency responsible for salvaging failed thrifts.

The main subjects under investigation were whether federally guaranteed deposits from Madison were illegally or improperly diverted into Whitewater, whether Madison money went to help pay off a Clinton campaign debt and whether Clinton used his influence as Arkansas governor to assist Madison or the Whitewater venture.

The second, "Washington" phase involved questions about whether members of the White House staff inappropriately learned details of the RTC investigation of Madison and whether they tried to hamstring the RTC probe.

Over loud protests from Republicans, who wanted a much broader investigation, Democrats succeeded in keeping congressional hearings limited to the relatively narrow Washington phase. Democrats argued that this was necessary to avoid interfering with the special counsel's probe; it also enabled them to avoid a host of potentially more embarrassing questions about the Clintons' Whitewater deal and their ties to McDougal.

The controversy peaked during an extraordinary series of Senate Banking Committee hearings the week of Aug. 1 that featured post-midnight sessions, inconsistent testimony by White House and Treasury witnesses, and pleas by the Clinton administration and its congressional supporters to keep the controversy in perspective.

While no evidence was produced to indicate that any Clinton administration official tried to derail the probe by the regulators, the hearings uncovered details of a number of improper contacts, evasive testimony before Congress by administration officials and widespread efforts within the White House to control Whitewater political damage.

The highest-ranking casualty of the affair was Deputy Treasury Secretary Roger C. Altman, who had been acting chief of the RTC. Altman was a longtime friend of the Clintons' and one of the administration's rising stars. His presence at the RTC had created a bridge for the Treasury Department and the White House into the thrift agency, which was supposed to operate independently. Altman resigned Aug. 17. Treasury General Counsel Jean Hanson resigned the following day. The two had given conflicting accounts of the White House-Treasury contacts over the affair.

Congress' interest in Whitewater generally waned as the investigation was transferred in August from Fiske to independent counsel Starr. A partisan Republican, Starr dug into the investigation in earnest and succeeded — in a way Fiske never could — in getting Republicans to delay their efforts to restart the hearings.

On the last full day of the 103rd Congress, Jan. 3, 1995, the Senate Banking Committee issued its final report on the first round of its Whitewater probe. The report, written by the panel's Democratic majority, detailed the conflicts among the accounts of various administration officials but declined to say whose testimony was more accurate. Republicans

issued a stinging minority report that called Altman a liar and blasted the Clinton team on a host of different fronts.

Background

The Whitewater affair had its roots in a tangle of business and political relationships in the 1980s involving then-Arkansas Gov. Bill Clinton and Hillary Rodham Clinton. At the core of the scandal was the friendship between the Clintons and their co-investors in the Whitewater land venture, James McDougal and his then-wife, Susan.

As the owner of the Madison thrift, McDougal allegedly made extensive loans to thrift insiders as well as to other "shell" corporations controlled by him or his associates. Federal regulators ousted McDougal as president of Madison in 1986, citing risky investments in real estate deals, low cash reserves and shoddy record-keeping. The thrift failed in 1989 at a cost to taxpayers of about $60 million.

The RTC investigation began in March 1992, after The New York Times broke the Whitewater story describing the financial ties between the Clintons and McDougal. By September 1992, RTC investigators in Kansas City, Mo., forwarded a criminal referral — a recommendation for additional investigation and possible prosecution — to the FBI and the U.S. attorney in Little Rock. The referral reportedly named the Clintons as potential beneficiaries of wrongdoing at Madison.

RTC investigators looking over Madison's books raised questions about whether money from the Madison thrift had been improperly or illegally diverted to the Whitewater land venture. Questions also arose over whether Madison funds were illegally diverted to help pay Clinton's 1984 gubernatorial campaign debts.

Another aspect of the probe involved allegations by David Hale, a former municipal judge and Arkansas political insider. Hale said that Clinton pressured him in 1986 to make a loan from Capital Management Services Inc., his investment firm, to Susan McDougal. Some $110,000 of the loan ended up in Whitewater accounts.

Information contained in criminal referrals was non-public under RTC regulations — meaning that it could be disclosed only under specific, limited circumstances, generally only to other government agencies involved in the case. However, news of the politically explosive Madison referral quickly reached the Bush White House in the fall of 1992. C. Boyden Gray, White House counsel to President George Bush, asked then-RTC chief Albert Casey about it. Casey was advised by an RTC officer that such information should not be discussed with the White House.

Later, the Clinton White House learned of the referrals through Treasury Department officials with access to RTC information and authority over RTC operations. It was these contacts between White House officials and Treasury officials with knowledge of the probe that were the subject of the congressional hearings.

Spurred on by press accounts that raised questions about the Whitewater affair, Republicans quickly called for the appointment of a special counsel as well as a congressional probe into the matter.

Partisan Sparring

The Clinton administration initially rejected calls for a special counsel, saying that career officials at the Justice Department should handle the probe. But after prominent Democrats led by Daniel Patrick Moynihan, D-N.Y., joined the Republicans calls, Clinton relented in early January 1994, asking Attorney General Janet Reno to appoint a special counsel

to take over the Justice Department probe. Reno chose Fiske, a Wall Street lawyer who had served as a New York-based U.S. attorney from 1976 to 1980.

The option of turning the investigation over to an independent counsel, who would have been separate from the Justice Department, was not available at the time. The law that provided for independent prosecutors to investigate executive branch officials had lapsed. Republicans in particular had opposed renewing it, but with Whitewater erupting, they changed position. Congress cleared the long-stalled reauthorization, and Clinton signed it June 30 (S 24 — PL 103-270). *(Independent counsel law, p. 295)*

Republicans Demand Congressional Probe

The appointment of Fiske did not dampen GOP calls for a congressional inquiry, but Democratic leaders succeeded in holding them off for months.

Fiske cautioned from the outset that a congressional probe might impede his job. "I think the history of these situations is that it is difficult to conduct this kind of investigation at the same time a congressional investigation is going on," he said. In a widely cited case, felony convictions against former Marine Lt. Col. Oliver L. North in the Iran-contra affair had been overturned because they were tainted by a highly publicized congressional inquiry.

Republicans nevertheless renewed their demands for a separate congressional investigation, either by the Banking committees or a select committee. They argued that the legislative branch had critical oversight responsibilities over the executive branch, including actions of a president before he assumed office. They also cited the Banking committees' responsibility to oversee the thrift industry.

"In my view, appointment of a special counsel doesn't take away our responsibility in the Congress," said Senate Minority Leader Bob Dole, R-Kan.

While other Republicans were turning up the heat, ranking House Banking Committee Republican Jim Leach of Iowa — who had spearheaded the congressional call for an independent investigation — urged that the Whitewater matter be kept in perspective. "There may be a little fire with the smoke, but we're talking about a campfire, not a forest fire," Leach said Jan. 11. "I've been trying to stress that this doesn't need to move down a path of dramatic dimensions."

But Leach, too, maintained that a congressional inquiry was appropriate. "I personally think that this is an issue that can be put behind [us] if the executive branch cooperates," Leach said. "Once you have a special counsel, the import of a committee hearing lessens, but it isn't eliminated."

On the Democratic side, however, Senate Majority Leader George J. Mitchell of Maine and House Speaker Thomas S. Foley of Washington made it clear they would quash any effort to create a select committee. Mitchell called the GOP effort "clearly an attempt to politicize this matter" and said that a congressional inquiry would interfere with the special counsel's investigation. The Democratic chairmen of the House and Senate Banking committees immediately rejected calls for investigations and hearings by their panels.

Select committees such as the 1987 Iran-contra panels and the Senate Select Watergate Committee dealt with alleged criminality either by the president or others within the executive branch. The establishment of a select committee to investigate possible actions by Clinton almost 10 years earlier did not appear to equal the standard previously used by Congress when establishing such panels.

"That may be the case. I don't think that makes any difference," Dole said.

Fiske's Letter to Committees

Following is the text of the March 7 letter sent by Whitewater independent counsel Robert B. Fiske Jr. to the Democratic and Republican leaders of the House and Senate Banking committees:

I am writing this letter to express my strong concern about the impact of any hearings that your Committee might hold into the underlying events concerning Madison Guaranty Savings and Loan ("MGS&L"), Whitewater and Capital Management Services ("CMS") on the investigation that this Office is conducting into these matters.

As you know, I was appointed to the position of Independent Counsel pursuant to CFR 603.1 on January 31, 1994. Since that date we have obtained an Order from Chief Judge Stephen M. Reasoner in the Eastern District of Arkansas authorizing the empaneling of a grand jury which will be devoted exclusively to the Whitewater/MGS&L/CMS investigation. In the meantime, we have been using the regular grand jury for this District. We have a team of eight experienced attorneys, six of whom were current or former prosecutors when they joined the staff. We are working in Little Rock with a team of more than twenty FBI agents and financial analysts who are working full time on this matter. We are doing everything possible to conduct and conclude as expeditiously as possible a complete, thorough and impartial investigation.

Inquiry into the underlying events surrounding MGS&L, Whitewater and CMS by a Congressional Committee would pose a severe risk to the integrity of our investigation. Inevitably, any such inquiry would overlap substantially with the grand jury's activities. Among other concerns, the Committee certainly would seek to interview the same witnesses or subjects who are central to the criminal investigation. Such interviews could jeopardize our investigation in several respects, including the dangers of Congressional immunity, the premature disclosures of the contents of documents or of witnesses' testimony to other witnesses on the same subject (creating the risk of tailored testimony) and of premature public disclosure of matters at the core of the criminal investigation. This inherent conflict would be greatly magnified by the fact that the Committee would be covering essentially the same ground as the grand jury.

While we recognize the Committee's oversight responsibilities pursuant to Section 501 of PL 101-73 (FIREAA), we have similar concerns with a Congressional investigation into the recently-disclosed meetings between White House and Treasury Department officials — particularly because we believe these hearings will inevitably lead to the disclosure of the contents of RTC referrals and other information relating to the underlying grand jury investigation.

For these reasons, we request that your Committee not conduct any hearings in the areas covered by the grand jury's ongoing investigation, both in order to avoid compromising that investigation and in order to further the public interest in preserving the fairness, thoroughness, and confidentiality of the grand jury process.

I will be glad to meet with you personally to explain our position further if you feel that would be helpful.

RTC Hearings Serve as Forum

With Democrats quashing their demands to schedule hearings on Whitewater, House and Senate Republicans moved to turn legally required RTC oversight hearings by the Banking committees into forums on the controversy.

It was at a Feb. 24 oversight hearing that Altman acknowledged that Treasury officials had briefed White House officials about RTC procedures for pursuing civil cases against thrift officials and persons who might have benefited from wrongdoing. Altman, who had been acting as interim chief of the RTC, said he participated in the meetings to give White House officials a "heads up" on the RTC procedures. On Feb. 25, Altman recused himself from all aspects of the Whitewater probe and said he would step down as RTC chief.

Altman's testimony set off a furor among Republicans, who, for the first time, could point to potentially improper knowledge within the White House of ongoing federal probes. Then on March 4, subpoenas were served on 10 Treasury and White House officials, bringing the scandal firmly into the White House for the first time.

Altman subsequently disclosed at a March 18 hearing that he had held a second meeting with White House officials in February to discuss disqualifying himself from the case involving Madison.

In the Senate, Mitchell and Dole agreed to hold a vote on a non-binding resolution calling on the leaders to "determine the appropriate timetable, procedures, and forum" for hearings on Whitewater. The hearings were to take place only after Mitchell and Dole agreed that they would not interfere with Fiske's ongoing investigation. The Senate approved the statement March 17 by a vote of 98-0, adding it to an unrelated bill (S 1275) to boost community development lending. *(Vote 62, p. 11-S)*

Meanwhile in the House, Republicans geared up for another stab at the issue at a March 24 Banking Committee oversight hearing on the savings and loan bailout. Among the witnesses scheduled were Altman and Treasury Secretary Lloyd Bentsen. Republicans planned to unveil details from their own investigation at the session. Leach also planned to take advantage of a little-used House rule that would allow Republicans to call their own witnesses during a second day of hearings.

But House Banking Chairman Henry B. Gonzalez, D-Texas, postponed the long-scheduled hearing, saying Republicans had been planning to turn the legally mandated session into a "prosecutorial or judicial adventure." Gonzalez also wrote a March 21 letter to Speaker Foley, calling GOP accusations on Whitewater "half-truths, old rumors, half-baked conspiracy theories and outright lies" and calling for a full set of hearings before a select committee. The outburst prompted criticism from Republicans and dismay from House Democratic leaders, who had been hoping that negotiations with Republicans would lead to a bipartisan agreement to delay the March 24 hearing.

Foley called Leach to apologize; the following day Foley met with House Minority Leader Robert H. Michel, R-Ill., and others, assuring them that the RTC hearing would go forward and that the GOP's right to a second day of hearings would be protected. They then agreed on a sense-of-the-House resolution (H Res 394) that called upon the two leaders to discuss when congressional hearings might be held. The House passed the resolution by a 408-15 vote. The outcome pleased House Democratic leaders, who were eager to erase the appearance of Democratic stonewalling on Whitewater. *(Vote 78, p. 24-H)*

With the hearing for March 24 canceled, Leach took to the House floor that day to present several new allegations. Rising on a "point of personal privilege," he described a host of alleged improprieties surrounding the Clintons' Whitewater land investment and its links to Madison. Most

notably, Leach asserted that:

- Money from the Madison thrift was illegally funneled into the Whitewater Development Co.
- The Clintons made money on their Whitewater investment, contrary to their repeated assertions that they had lost money on the deal.
- Federal officials seeking to protect Clinton interfered with banking regulators probing into Madison and Whitewater.

Leach released a stack of documents that buttressed some, though not all, of his allegations.

The same day, Clinton held a news conference in which he tried to play down the whole affair. "I know that many people around America must believe that Washington is overwhelmingly preoccupied with the Whitewater matter," he said. "But our administration is preoccupied with the business we were sent here to do for the American people."

In rebuttal to Leach, Clinton again said he had "absolutely no knowledge" about the possibility that any money from a failed Arkansas thrift might have flowed into his Whitewater land investment or his 1984 gubernatorial campaign. But he did acknowledge that he and Hillary Clinton lost about $20,000 less on their Whitewater investment than the almost $70,000 they originally had claimed.

Wrangling Over Scope, Timing of Hearings

After two weeks of quiet negotiations in April, Senate Republicans dropped the demand for a "special committee" to look into the Whitewater affair. Mitchell and Dole instead agreed to have the Banking Committee be the venue for hearings. But partisan wrangling over the timing and scope of the hearings was far from over. It would take two more months before the parameters were finally set for the opening round of Whitewater hearings.

Mitchell proposed an initial inquiry limited to the Washington phase of Whitewater, to take place after special counsel Fiske had completed his investigation on these issues. Mitchell proposed that the Senate Banking Committee look into the propriety of contacts between White House aides and Treasury or RTC officials, the investigation of the July 1993 suicide of Deputy White House Counsel Vincent Foster and the handling of Whitewater-related documents in Foster's office. Foster had handled Whitewater-related legal work for the Clintons at one time, and he was in possession of Whitewater papers when he died.

Republicans countered with a plan to create a special subcommittee within the Senate Banking Committee — evenly split along party lines — with a much broader mandate to probe into Whitewater, including aspects of the case that had not been fully investigated by Fiske. Republicans wanted to look into a host of allegations concerning the Whitewater land deal and the Clintons' links to McDougal.

Additionally, they wanted to look into allegations that Hillary Clinton benefited from preferential treatment while turning $1,000 into nearly $100,000 in the cattle futures market during the late 1970s. Mitchell countered that Hillary Clinton's investments were unrelated to the Whitewater probe.

Republicans also pressed for authority to independently issue subpoenas and call hearings, power that Mitchell said would be unprecedented.

Democrats Define Hearings

Finally, in late June, after Senate Republicans called off a weeklong filibuster and House Republicans quietly surrendered, Mitchell's proposal was accepted as the basis for hearings.

On June 21, the Senate adopted Mitchell's plan (S Res 229) on a party-line 54-44 vote. The result came after the Senate rejected, 44-54, a Republican proposal to broaden the hearings to cover any "illegal, improper, unauthorized or unethical" actions by administration officials since Clinton took office. *(Votes 153, 154, p. 27-S)*

Senate Republicans backed off their demand for wide-ranging hearings after losing a string of party-line floor votes June 14-15 during a Whitewater-inspired filibuster that tied up an unrelated airport improvements bill (S 1491). Part of their reason for giving up was their inability to whip up much enthusiasm in the press or the public over the issue. "No one is paying attention" to the filibuster, said William S. Cohen, R-Maine.

On June 15, House Republicans acceded to a Whitewater hearings plan proposed by Foley that mirrored Mitchell's approach. Foley agreed to allow staff aides from other House committees to help the Banking Committee staff prepare for the hearings.

Sensing that the floor show in the Senate had not produced the desired effect, House Republicans decided not to try to bring the issue to the House floor to protest the limited scope of the hearings. "I have a little bit of reservation about the public's image [of Congress] when the really serious legislative business is subordinated to some of the side issues," said House GOP Leader Michel.

Fiske's Initial Findings

On June 30, Fiske announced the initial findings of his probe into the Washington phase of Whitewater. After a four-month investigation, Fiske determined that there was no evidence to warrant charging any White House or Treasury official with obstructing the RTC probe. Fiske also found that there was no evidence of foul play in the circumstances surrounding the suicide of White House aide Foster. Fiske had been unable to complete his investigation of the removal of Whitewater-related documents from Foster's office by White House officials in time for the hearings, and the subject was dropped from the hearing agenda.

"This interim report of the special counsel relates to a very small percentage of the issue called Whitewater," said Leach.

In a statement, Fiske said his investigation of meetings between White House and Treasury Department officials regarding the RTC probe of the Madison thrift found insufficient evidence to establish that any administration official tried to impede the Madison investigation.

Fiske and his staff investigated more than 20 Whitewater-related contacts over a period of six months among administration officials. Because the grand jury's deliberations had to remain secret, Fiske did not provide any additional details on the contacts between White House and Treasury officials. While saying there were no grounds for criminal charges, he did not address whether the contacts were right or wrong. "We express no opinion on the propriety of these meetings or whether anything that occurred at these meetings constitutes a breach of ethical rules or standards," Fiske said.

The bulk of the material released by Fiske documented an extensive investigation into the circumstances surrounding Foster's death. Some had speculated that Foster killed himself because of despair over Whitewater. And some news accounts described a death scene that led some experts to question whether Foster's death was a suicide.

But the inch-thick Fiske report provided a step-by-step rebuttal to a series of questions about Foster's death raised by the media and circulated by Clinton critics. Fiske's findings confirmed the original conclusion reached after a U.S. Park Police investigation. The Park Police originally handled

Troublesome Talks: A Chronology . . .

Congressional hearings focused on one narrow aspect of the Whitewater controversy: whether members of the White House staff inappropriately learned details of a Resolution Trust Corporation (RTC) investigation of the failed Madison Guaranty Savings and Loan.

Madison's owner, James B. McDougal, was a partner of the Clintons in the money-losing Whitewater land development in Arkansas in the late 1970s. Madison failed in 1989, costing taxpayers an estimated $65 million.

The RTC investigation began in March of 1992, after The New York Times broke the Whitewater story describing the financial ties between then-Arkansas Gov. Bill Clinton and his wife and McDougal. By September 1992, RTC investigators in Kansas City, Mo., forwarded a criminal referral — a recommendation for additional investigation and possible prosecution — to the FBI and the U.S. attorney in Little Rock. According to news reports, the referral named the Clintons as "potential beneficiaries" of wrongdoing at Madison. Special counsel Robert B. Fiske Jr. cleared White House and Treasury officials of any criminal wrongdoing, and there was no testimony to indicate that the probe was interfered with by the White House.

What follows is a description, based on sworn testimony, of some of the most significant contacts between Treasury officials and White House aides:

● **March 1993.** Deputy Treasury Secretary Roger C. Altman became interim chief of the RTC. William Roelle, an RTC senior vice president who remained in his RTC position under the new administration, said he briefed Altman on the referral, which named the Clintons as potential beneficiaries of alleged wrongdoing at Madison. Altman said he did not recall being informed of the referral.

Altman faxed White House Counsel Bernard Nussbaum a copy of a New York Times story on Whitewater. The fax was traceable by a paper trail that included the fax cover sheet. Altman later told Congress he did not recollect sending the article. Nussbaum said he did not remember receiving it.

● **Sept. 27, 1993.** Roelle learned that the Kansas City RTC office had prepared nine additional referrals, which named

the Clintons as possible witnesses, and would soon forward them to the Justice Department. Roelle called Altman to inform him of the development; Altman said he did not completely understand what Roelle was talking about and told Roelle to brief Treasury General Counsel Jean E. Hanson about the referrals. Roelle telephoned Hanson, summarized the new referrals and advised her that the information probably would leak to the media. Hanson subsequently briefed Altman and later testified that Altman directed her to advise the White House about the press leaks. Altman said he did not instruct Hanson to brief Nussbaum.

● **Sept. 29, 1993.** Hanson initiated the first Treasury-White House contact. After a White House meeting on an unrelated topic, Hanson told Nussbaum of the referrals and recounted in some detail the information included in them. Also participating was Clifford Sloan, a lawyer on Nussbaum's staff, who became Hanson's designated liaison to the White House. In subsequent days, Hanson and Sloan had further telephone conversations. In a Sept. 30 memo to Altman, Hanson reported that she had briefed Treasury Secretary Lloyd Bentsen about anticipated news stories on Whitewater. Neither Bentsen nor Hanson recollected the briefing, according to their congressional testimony.

● **On or about Oct. 4, 1993.** Senior Clinton aide Bruce Lindsey, who was traveling with the president, informed Clinton of media inquiries about the referrals. He said he "did not suggest, nor did the president ask, that any action be taken" regarding the referrals. Lindsey said he learned of the inquiries from a source outside the government.

● **Oct. 7, 1993.** Hanson learned from Roelle that a Washington Post reporter was working on a Whitewater story. Hanson called Sloan in the White House and briefed him on the development.

● **Oct. 14, 1993.** The first organized meeting between Treasury officials and White House aides occurred. The purpose of the meeting, which took place at the White House, was to discuss intensifying press interest in Whitewater. Treasury spokesman Jack DeVore detailed

the case because Foster's body was found in a national park in the Washington suburbs.

Fiske said investigators found no evidence that matters related to Madison or Whitewater had anything to do with Foster's death.

The Hearings

The House and Senate hearings on Whitewater finally began the week of July 25 and were completed the following week.

During carefully controlled hearings by the House Banking Committee, a dozen current and former White House officials testified under oath. With Chairman Gonzalez strictly enforcing a House rule that limited members to five minutes of questions, Republicans scrambled to develop lines of interrogation before being gaveled down.

Republicans complained that many of the White House

staff aides they were particularly interested in questioning were relegated to a 10-person panel that testified July 28. On the other hand, White House counsel Lloyd N. Cutler and former White House counsel Bernard Nussbaum, both sophisticated attorneys, were solo witnesses.

Cutler gave an account of his own investigation of the White House/Treasury contacts, conducted after the completion of Fiske's probe. While Cutler determined that no ethical lapses had occurred as a result of the contacts — detailed in a sheaf of documents provided to the committee by the White House — he acknowledged that some White House aides behaved inappropriately. "When I reviewed these incidents in their totality, I found that there were too many people having too many discussions about too many sensitive matters," Cutler said.

Nussbaum, who was at the center of the White House-Treasury contacts, said it was entirely appropriate for White

. . . Of White House-Treasury Contacts

inquiries from reporters who were preparing Whitewater stories. Other participants included Hanson, Treasury Chief of Staff Joshua Steiner, Nussbaum and Lindsey.

● **Dec. 30, 1993.** At the Renaissance Weekend in Hilton Head, S.C., Clinton sought Whitewater-related advice from Comptroller of the Currency Eugene Ludwig, a top banking regulator and longtime Clinton friend. Ludwig's recollection was that Clinton asked him to "provide advice and counsel on any of the legal and regulatory issues" surrounding Whitewater. Clinton recalled that he was asking Ludwig if he knew of "other experts in real estate law . . . that might be able to comment publicly" on Whitewater-related issues.

After consulting with White House lawyers, who also consulted among themselves, Ludwig decided it would be inappropriate for him to have any further Whitewater conversations with Clinton. White House Deputy Counsel Joel Klein advised Clinton that any further conversations with Ludwig would be inadvisable, and Clinton agreed.

● **Feb. 2, 1994.** With congressional Republicans calling for an extension of the statute of limitations to give the RTC additional time to pursue civil claims against Madison, Altman briefed White House aides on agency procedures for pursuing such cases. The substance of the case was not discussed, according to those in attendance. Other participants included Hanson, Nussbaum, Deputy Chief of Staff Harold Ickes and Margaret Williams, chief of staff to Hillary Rodham Clinton.

Prior to the White House meeting, Altman decided to recuse himself from consideration of any RTC cases involving the Madison thrift and its Whitewater connection because he was a personal friend of the president. But at the meeting, Nussbaum persuaded Altman to rethink his decision; Nussbaum testified that he did not want Altman to set an undesirable precedent and that the final decision was Altman's. This appeared to conflict with a diary kept by Treasury's Steiner, which said the White House told Altman that his decision to recuse was "unacceptable."

● **Feb. 24, 1994.** During a legally mandated RTC over-

sight hearing before the Senate Banking Committee, Altman revealed the Feb. 2 White House meeting, describing it as the only "substantive contact" he had had with the White House on Whitewater. Despite being pressed by senators, Altman did not volunteer information about previous additional contacts, nor did he mention that one topic discussed at the meeting was whether he should recuse himself from the case.

In the wake of Altman's testimony, White House aides consulted among themselves and were concerned that he did not mention the other meetings and the discussion about recusal.

In congressional testimony the week of Aug. 1, Altman admitted that his testimony was "perhaps incomplete," but he denied any intent "to mislead or not to provide complete and forthright answers."

● **Feb. 25, 1994.** Altman recused. Angered by the news that former U.S. Attorney Jay B. Stephens, a partisan Republican, had been hired by the RTC to pursue civil claims against Madison, senior White House aide George Stephanopoulos called Treasury's Steiner. According to Steiner's diary, Stephanopoulos "suggested to me that we needed to find a way to get rid of [Stephens]" though Steiner was able to convince Stephanopoulos that firing Stephens would be "incredibly stupid and improper."

● **March 1, 1994.** White House Staff Secretary John Podesta telephoned Altman to tell him that the White House believed that his testimony needed to be supplemented to inform the Senate Banking Committee about the Sept. 29 and Oct. 14 meetings and about the issue of recusal. The next day, after Treasury officials learned that The Washington Post was preparing a story on the September and October 1993 meetings, Altman wrote the first of four separate letters to the committee to correct his testimony.

● **March 4, 1994.** In the ensuing political uproar and after Fiske served subpoenas on 10 Treasury and White House officials, the contacts ceased. Because they were under investigation by Fiske, participants were barred from discussing events further.

House staff to be briefed on the matter, in order to respond to press inquiries resulting from leaks out of the RTC. Nussbaum also gave a strong defense of his actions, including a carefully reasoned defense of his request that interim RTC chief Altman reconsider a decision to recuse himself from the RTC's probe into Madison and Whitewater.

Most Democrats characterized the hearings as much ado about nothing and made statements designed to impress upon a nationwide television audience that no one testifying before the committee had been charged with any wrongdoing. They lobbed softball questions to the other White House witnesses, including former Chief of Staff Thomas F. McLarty III and senior advisers Bruce Lindsey and George Stephanopoulos, who smoothly defended their conduct in the Whitewater matter.

Among Democrats, only freshman Eric D. Fingerhut of Ohio developed an aggressive line of questioning with the White House witnesses. Fingerhut expressed concern about

the transmission of information to the White House officials, and he said their justification for obtaining the information — that they needed it to respond to press inquiries — set a questionable precedent.

Generally, the Republicans alternated between serious lines of questioning and open attempts to produce sound bites. Overall, they had little success in jarring the carefully prepared White House witnesses.

The Senate's initial session July 29 was devoted to opening statements and a review of Foster's death. Senators generally accepted the testimony of medical examiners and federal investigators who confirmed that Foster committed suicide.

Second Week of Hearings

The week of Aug. 1 was an extraordinary week of hearings that alternated between political theater and serious inquiry, as a score of Clinton administration officials testified before

increasingly skeptical Senate and House panels. By Aug. 5, members of the Senate Banking Committee — satisfied that they had conducted a serious, senatorial probe — wrapped up their initial inquiry. Their counterparts in the House completed a more partisan, tightly controlled set of sessions.

The administration faced a much more rigorous inquiry in the Senate Banking Committee, which operated under rules that permitted more sustained inquiries than in the House. The Senate probe was led by Committee Chairman Donald W. Riegle Jr., D-Mich., and top Banking Republican Alfonse M. D'Amato of New York.

Before the hearings started, witnesses were required to make lengthy sworn depositions to special committee counsels assigned to the matter; in the House, pre-hearing interviews were briefer and unsworn.

In stark contrast to their Democratic colleagues on the House Banking Committee, who continued to defend the administration, Senate Democrats took a no-nonsense approach. "In my view there were far too many meetings, there were far too many people involved, and the [testimony] gets too cute for my taste, quite frankly," said Christopher J. Dodd, D-Conn.

Senators issued their sternest rebukes to former White House Counsel Nussbaum, and Treasury officials Altman and Hanson, who gave contradictory accounts of various Whitewater-related meetings and contacts between Treasury officials and the White House.

Nussbaum was called on the carpet by senators for pressuring Altman to reconsider his decision to recuse himself from the RTC's probe into Madison and Whitewater.

Clinton, who said he had not watched the televised Whitewater hearings, vowed support for his team, including Altman. "I will say again there was no violation of the law, there was no violation of the ethics rules, the errors which were made have been acknowledged, and questions have been answered at extreme length," Clinton said during an Aug. 3 news conference.

However, the testimony of several administration witnesses wobbled under close scrutiny. At key points, particularly when senators raised questions about sensitive discrepancies, recollections became foggy and officials gave carefully phrased, legalistic answers to direct questions.

A prime example was Treasury Chief of Staff Joshua Steiner, who tried to explain away several controversial passages of his personal diary. The testimony of the 28-year-old Steiner failed to convince most committee members. Paul S. Sarbanes, D-Md., had to rephrase a question three times before Steiner acknowledged that he had heard Altman say that his account of events was at odds with Hanson's version.

While many senators sympathized with Steiner for being a young man in a tough spot, they were less patient with Altman, who they believed misled or lied to the Banking Committee in February and then did not move quickly enough to correct the record. Many committee members came away from Altman's nine-hour Aug. 2 testimony convinced that his account was still inaccurate. "He is good at rephrasing questions and then giving the answer that would fit that question after he restates it," said Richard C. Shelby, D-Ala., who was the first Democrat to call upon Altman to resign. "I think he's been less than candid. He's been very selective in his answers."

The carefully scripted accounts by Steiner and Altman led the usually cautious Riegle to lecture Treasury Secretary Bentsen. The words were polite, but the message was clear. "I would like to have an assurance . . . that any other Treasury official that comes before this committee either now or in the future, when they're asked direct questions, give direct, full, complete answers right then on the spot," said Riegle.

"That certainly is my intention and certainly my direction to anyone representing Treasury," Bentsen responded.

For D'Amato, the pugnacious New Yorker who was the committee's top Republican, the hearings provided a lengthy forum to air a host of charges, some of which stuck and some of which didn't. D'Amato saved his strongest attacks for Altman, at one point calling him "Roger the dodger," and at another point accusing Altman of "throwing the women and children overboard," apparently a reference to conflicts between his testimony and that of Hanson and Steiner.

The Upshot

The hearings failed to produce evidence that raised Whitewater to a level anywhere near that of presidential scandals such as Watergate or Iran-contra.

"Watergate raised separation-of-powers issues involving a president who chose not to recognize the rule of law and chose to put himself above the law," said Sam Dash, former chief counsel of the Senate Watergate Committee. "Whitewater really has nothing to do with the Constitution as such, other than Congress undertaking its constitutional oversight role."

Perhaps more than anything else, the hearings revealed an administration that did not stop to question the propriety of contacts between Treasury officials with knowledge of the RTC probe and White House aides eager to control any political damage resulting from Whitewater. In sworn testimony to the committees, numerous administration officials appeared to give less-than-candid accounts of their roles in the damage control effort.

During the marathon week, several facets of the controversy were explored in considerable depth. New details emerged, including:

● Significant contradictions between the sworn accounts of Treasury Department officials over when and how they learned of the RTC's investigation into Madison and what they did with that knowledge. Hanson's account, buttressed by memos and other documents, was that she notified both Bentsen and Altman of the RTC investigation into Madison when she learned of it in September 1993. Bentsen and Altman denied her account.

● A fuller description of the White House pressure on Altman not to recuse himself from RTC decisions regarding Madison and Whitewater. In July 28 testimony before the House Banking Committee, Nussbaum said he had asked Altman not to recuse to avoid setting a precedent in which officials would recuse only for the sake of appearances, instead of when legally required.

Altman testified that he went to a Feb. 2 meeting at the White House having decided to recuse himself from any Madison decision. After hearing Nussbaum's arguments, Altman said he decided to rethink his decision. Altman told the White House the next day that he had changed his mind and would officially stay in charge, though he would "de facto" recuse and follow the recommendations of his staff.

No testimony emerged to suggest that Altman had been ordered to change his mind, and each participant said the final decision remained in Altman's hands. But other factors were in play, according to other participants in the meeting. White House lawyer Joel Klein testified Aug. 3 that Nussbaum was very concerned about RTC General Counsel Ellen Kulka, whom he had dealt with when he was a lawyer in private practice. Klein said Nussbaum felt Kulka could be "unreasonable," a "difficult person to deal with" and that "she could be unfair."

● Allegations by Leach that Hanson, the Treasury Department's top lawyer, appeared in early October to attempt to impede action on the RTC criminal referrals. Leach alleged that the RTC's legal shop in Washington, which "de facto" reported to Hanson, requested a delay before sending the RTC referral to the U.S. attorney in Little Rock. During the one-week delay, RTC lawyers drafted arguments against the referrals, something they did not do in other cases.

● Increasing evidence that first lady Hillary Rodham Clinton displayed a keen interest in Whitewater. In a March 1 memo, Deputy White House Counsel Harold Ickes kept Hillary Clinton apprised of the results of RTC and Federal Deposit Insurance Corporation (FDIC) investigations into the Rose Law Firm, Hillary Clinton's former law firm. The FDIC concluded that Rose had not engaged in a conflict of interest when it represented Madison and then was hired by the FDIC to sue the thrift's accountants.

White House officials strongly denied that Hillary Clinton sought to limit the scope of Fiske's investigation, as suggested in a diary kept by Altman. Based on conversations with Margaret Williams, the first lady's chief of staff, Altman's diary said that the White House "was trying to negotiate the scope of the independent counsel" with Attorney General Reno and was "having enormous difficulty."

Altman Resigns

Following the hearings, Riegle and Sarbanes told Treasury Secretary Bentsen that Altman's relationship with the committee had been irreparably damaged after members concluded he had misled them. Senate Republicans called for Altman's resignation, as well as those of Hanson and Steiner. In a bow to political reality, Altman resigned Aug. 17. Clinton called the departure "the right move under the circumstances." Hanson also paid with her job for being at the center of many of the contacts with the White House. She resigned Aug. 18.

Starr Takes Over Probe

At the close of the hearings Aug. 5, a federal three-judge panel named former U.S. Solicitor General Starr, a Republican, as the new independent counsel for the investigation, ignoring Reno's recommendation that Fiske carry on the probe.

The legal reasoning behind Fiske's replacement was rooted in the circumstances of his January appointment as a special counsel, which occurred at a time when the independent counsel law had lapsed. The judges determined that because Fiske had been named by Reno, his retention would be inconsistent with the intent of the independent counsel law, which required avoiding even the appearance of being "affiliated with the incumbent administration."

Altman and other administration officials had breathed a sigh of relief when Fiske cleared them of criminal wrongdoing over the White House/Treasury contacts. Starr's appointment threatened to reopen that aspect of the investigation. "It is my intent to build upon Mr. Fiske's investigation and the considerable work he and his team have undertaken," Starr said in a statement Aug. 10. "At the same time, the appointing court's order requires that I make an independent judgment as to the matters involved in this investigation."

The naming of Starr, a solid conservative with ties to Presidents Reagan and Bush, was welcomed by Republicans, who had begun to complain that Fiske's investigation was not thorough enough. It left many Democrats shaking their heads and led to calls for Starr to step down. On the other hand, the change in investigators meant at least some delay in the

probe and eliminated the possibility of additional congressional hearings on Whitewater during the year.

Like Fiske, Starr soon made clear that he did not want Congress to conduct its own probe until he was finished.

Although D'Amato — slated to become Senate Banking Committee chairman in the next, Republican-controlled Congress — initially indicated plans to push forward, he reversed course Dec. 13. Accepting Starr's request, D'Amato announced he would hold off on hearings.

Senate Committee Reports

The Whitewater chapter for 1994 came to a close in the first days of 1995, when, after months of chewing on the same pieces of evidence, Senate Banking Committee Democrats and Republicans on Jan. 3 released reports that, to no one's surprise, reached starkly different conclusions about the extent of wrongdoing by administration officials in the Whitewater affair.

The Democrats, who wrote the official Banking Committee report, found that no laws or ethical standards were breached as a result of contacts between White House aides and Treasury Department officials. The Democrats detailed many conflicts and inconsistencies in the testimony of White House and Treasury officials, but their report did not say whose testimony they believed to be more accurate.

While absolving Clinton officials of criminal and ethical wrongdoing, the Democratic report noted that then-White House Counsel Cutler, as well as the Office of Government Ethics, had found the extensive web of White House/Treasury contacts to be "troubling."

"In my view this report reaffirms . . . that no criminal laws in any way were violated, but that too many people, frankly, were having too many conversations about matters that they shouldn't have had in the first place," said Dodd, a senior Banking Committee Democrat.

Democrats said the episode pointed out the need for new guidelines on contacts between White House aides and agency officials privy to information about criminal referrals and investigations that touch on the administration. They also said the president should issue an executive order reinforcing the existing standard that all administration testimony to Congress be "fully candid and forthcoming" and that standards be in place to correct inaccurate testimony.

Republicans, predictably, were not so charitable in their accompanying report. They countered with a stinging assault on Clinton administration officials, accusing Altman of lying to the committee — both in his initial February testimony about the White House Treasury contacts and while testifying during the summer hearings.

In a section titled "Altman Intentionally Lied to Congress," the Republican report said: "This is an aggravated case of lying before Congress. . . . And he continued his deceptions under oath when he testified before the committee in August."

The GOP report pointed to several areas that Republicans were likely to revisit in any future hearings. It suggested, without offering any proof, that Clinton might have told Arkansas Gov. Jim Guy Tucker, a Democrat, that Tucker was named in an RTC criminal referral. It also raised the possibility that Clinton confidant Webster L. Hubbell, former No. 3 official at the Justice Department, might have been in contact with the White House over Whitewater. Hubbell pleaded guilty in December on unrelated charges involving illegal expense account activity prior to serving in the administration.

Both Democrats and Republicans agreed with Fiske's conclusion that Foster took his own life. ∎

Congress Attempts To Spur Secondary Loan Market

The House Banking Committee approved a bill (HR 2600) to make it easier for private sector companies to sell securities backed by commercial loans. The vote, on March 9, was 46-5. But the measure also fell under the jurisdiction of the Energy and Commerce Committee, which never acted on it.

A competing measure (S 1275), sponsored by Sen. Alfonse M. D'Amato, R-N.Y., was enacted as part of a bill (HR 3474 — PL 103-325) to assist community development banks. The enacted provisions focused specifically on small-business loans, although they also applied to commercial real estate loans. *(Community development lending, p. 100)*

The broader House Banking Committee bill, authored by Paul E. Kanjorski, D-Pa., was designed to ease federal regulations that impeded the formation of a secondary market in commerical loans. Kanjorski argued that banks would make more loans if they knew they could turn around and sell those loans to investment banks and securities firms. Such so-called loan poolers would package the loans into securities for investors. Kanjorski said the bill was aimed at developing securities that would be attractive to big institutional investors, such as pension funds and insurance companies, with money from these big players flowing to businesses.

Before approving the bill, the committee agreed by voice vote to significantly revise the measure, which had been approved by the Economic Growth Subcommittee in 1993. *(1993 Almanac, p. 160)*

Unlike the subcommittee-approved bill, the new version of HR 2600 spelled out what regulations would be changed to boost the market. The most important provision sought to reduce the amount of capital reserves banks had to hold on loans that they had sold. The new version also dropped a requirement that the regulations be relaxed only for securities packages that included loans to poor neighborhoods, minority businesses, community development and areas particularly hard hit by a "credit crunch." The new version authorized, but did not require, the Treasury Department to establish such goals. ∎

Other Banking Legislation Considered in 1994

In other action on the banking front, Congress reduced the paperwork load on banks and considered a bill to authorize funds for international financial institutions. Meanwhile, the administration backed away from a proposal to consolidate bank regulators.

Anti-Money Laundering

Congress cleared legislation aimed at easing the paperwork required of banks under federal anti-money laundering statutes. The revisions were enacted as part of a bill to increase lending by community development financial institutions, which President Clinton signed Sept. 23 (HR 3474 — PL 103-325).

The bill required the Treasury secretary to reduce by 30 percent the number of currency transaction reports that depository institutions filed under the Bank Secrecy Act. Under existing law, banks generally had to file currency transaction reports when amounts of $10,000 or more

changed hands. The reports were intended to help the federal government track money-laundering schemes, but bill sponsors said the requirement was burdensome to banks and did not help regulators spot illegal transactions.

The bill specifically required Treasury to exempt transactions involving other banks and government entities. The measure also included provisions requiring check cashing companies, currency exchange businesses and other so-called money transmitters to register with the Treasury Department as a way to curb money laundering by businesses that were outside the regulated financial services sector.

Action on the legislation began in the House Banking Subcommittee on Financial Institutions, which gave voice vote approval March 2 to a separate bill (HR 3235), sponsored by Banking Chairman Henry B. Gonzalez, D-Texas. The full House Banking Committee gave its approval by voice March 9 (H Rept 103-438). The House passed the bill by voice vote March 21.

On the Senate side, Richard H. Bryan, D-Nev., introduced a similar bill (S 1664). Rather than handling the bill separately, however, the Senate included the provisions as an amendment to the community development bank bill, which it passed March 17. The money-laundering language remained in the final community development bank bill, which the Senate cleared Aug. 9. *(Community development lending, p. 100; money laundering provisions, p. 105)*

Regulatory Consolidation

Concluding that it had too little time and too much opposition, President Clinton's Treasury Department pulled the plug on a plan to streamline regulation of the nation's banks. Treasury officials announced the decision May 27 after almost reaching a deal with the Federal Reserve Board, which had vigorously opposed the initial Treasury plan. The original proposal, announced Nov. 23, 1993, would have merged the banking industry's four regulators into a single super-regulator and sharply curbed the Fed's role in overseeing banks and bank holding companies. *(1993 Almanac, p. 162)*

Opposition from the Fed and a strong lobbying effort by Federal Reserve Board Chairman Alan Greenspan sank that plan. Greenspan argued that a single regulator would be too inflexible and therefore potentially too tough on banks. The Fed also argued that it should keep a hands-on role in bank regulation to efficiently conduct monetary policy and manage markets in times of crisis.

In addition, the super-regulator plan (S 1895) ran into stout opposition from bankers, who feared the possibility of a monolithic banking regulator instead of the existing system of four regulators. State banks, the bulk of which were overseen by the Federal Deposit Insurance Corporation (FDIC), were particularly worried, saying the new federal regulator would rein in the innovative impulses of the state banking system.

After it became clear that the industry and the Fed had enough clout to block Treasury's plan, representatives from both sides discussed a possible compromise. By mid-May, Treasury Under Secretary Frank Newman and Greenspan had almost reached agreement.

Under their tentative deal, the new Federal Banking Commission was to assume the regulatory duties of the Office of the Comptroller of the Currency, chartered banks, the Office of Thrift Supervision and the FDIC. The Federal Reserve was to retain supervisory authority over the largest bank holding companies, as well as the approximately 950 state-chartered banks it oversaw under existing law.

These terms were widely perceived by members of Congress and bankers as a victory for the Fed, which got much of what it wanted. But there were divisions within the administration over how good a deal Treasury had gotten.

A Treasury spokesman said that, given the lateness in the congressional session, it made sense to shelve the initiative and instead concentrate on obtaining final action on the department's two other legislative priorities: the interstate banking and branching bill (HR 3841) and the community development bank bill (HR 3474). *(Community development lending, p. 100; interstate banking and branching, p. 93)*

But political considerations also played a big role. While the tentative compromise would have eased the Fed's reservations, it got a cool reception on Capitol Hill. Both Senate Banking Committee Chairman Donald W. Riegle Jr., D-Mich., and House Banking Committee Chairman Henry B. Gonzalez, D-Texas, supported single-regulator plans. Gonzalez had indicated that there was no way he would act on the proposal.

International Financial Institutions

On June 29, the House Banking Committee gave voice vote approval to a bill (HR 4587) to reauthorize U.S. contributions to several international financial institutions charged with fostering economic development in the Third World. However, the bill, introduced by Barney Frank, D-Mass., went no further.

As approved by the committee, the $900 million measure authorized $400 million for the Global Environmental Facility, a collaborative effort by the United Nations and the World Bank for projects aimed at fighting environmental problems, such as ozone depletion and the pollution of international waters.

The bill also authorized $315 million for the African Development Fund, which made interest-free loans to the poorest African nations. The committee rejected by voice vote an amendment by Doug Bereuter, R-Neb., to cut the authorization by $105 million to pressure the fund to improve its operations.

But the committee halved the administration's $77 million request for the Inter-American Development Bank (IDB), which promoted economic development in Latin America and the Caribbean, though a special fund that made low-cost loans to the region's poorest countries received the full $82 million requested.

The committee also cut the request for the Enhanced Structural Adjustment Facility by 75 percent, to $25 million. The facility, an International Monetary Fund (IMF) agency, helped to ease balance-of-payment problems in the poorest countries, particularly in sub-Saharan Africa.

The cuts were aimed at pressuring the IDB and the IMF to be more open about their operations and to consider the potentially adverse effects that their programs might have on local populations and the poor. ∎

Fair Credit Bill Stumbles in Senate

Legislation to protect consumers from errors in privately compiled credit reports passed both chambers by wide margins but, after running into insurmountable obstacles in the Senate, failed to make it into law.

At issue were questions of whether new federal standards on credit reporting should pre-empt tougher state laws, whether credit bureaus would be required to provide consumers with low-cost copies of their reports, and whether consumers should be allowed to sue creditors who supplied inaccurate information.

The bills (HR 5178, HR 1015, S 783) were intended to update and strengthen the Fair Credit Reporting Act to make it easier for consumers to get access to their credit reports and challenge any erroneous information that might be contained in them. Strengthening the 1970 law that governed the credit reporting industry was a top priority for consumer groups.

The bills sought to restrict the circumstances under which consumer credit histories could be released, requiring credit agencies to notify consumers whenever copies of their histories were requested. Most importantly, the bills required credit reporting agencies to reinvestigate disputed information in a consumer's credit report within 30 days or delete it from the report. They required credit bureaus to set up toll-free telephone numbers for consumers to use in challenging information in their reports.

Banks and other businesses that furnished information to

BOXSCORE

Fair Credit Reporting (HR 5178, HR 1015, S 783). The bills aimed to make it easier for consumers to correct errors in their credit reports.

Reports: H Rept 103-486, S Rept 103-209.

KEY ACTION

May 4 — Senate passed S 783, 87-10.

June 13 — House passed HR 1015 by voice vote.

Sept. 27 — House passed S 783, amended, by voice vote.

Oct. 5 — House passed clean bill, HR 5178, by voice vote.

credit bureaus were to be covered by the law for the first time, which meant they would have to follow procedures ensuring they did not provide erroneous information to credit reporting agencies.

Background

The credit reporting industry had seen large-scale changes over the years, particularly as the result of greater computerization, which made it much easier to collect and disseminate information about people's credit records. But the 1970 Fair Credit Reporting Act had never been significantly revised.

The explosive growth of the industry had been accompanied by significant problems, as mistakes in credit reports resulted in consumers' being wrongfully denied mortgages and other credit. Bill supporters said that despite recent improvements, consumers still faced an uphill battle in getting bureaus to correct these errors.

"Credit bureaus and the companies that supply information to them do wield great power over our lives. Thus, they absolutely must get it right," said House Banking Committee Chairman Henry B. Gonzalez, D-Texas.

The House and Senate Banking committees began work in 1993 on bills to update the credit reporting law. The House Banking Subcommittee approved a version of HR 1015, while the Senate Banking Committee reported its bill (S 783 — S Rept 103-209). But the legislation did not get to the floor in

either chamber. *(1993 Almanac, p.169)*

An earlier effort had failed as the result of a dispute over whether new federal credit reporting standards should pre-empt state laws, which often were tougher on the industry. On March 25, 1992, Gonzalez hastily adjourned a five-hour bill-drafting session in the House Banking Committee after losing a battle to block pre-emption of state laws. Months later, the committee finally sent the bill to the House floor, where Gonzalez lost yet again on the pre-emption issue. At that point he pulled the bill from the floor, and it died. *(1992 Almanac, p. 118)*

Consumer groups considered the pre-emption issue a top priority, arguing that it was unfair to require consumers in the approximately 20 states with tougher credit reporting laws to replace those protections with the weaker federal standard. And they wanted states to retain the ability to enact and enforce tougher laws.

Credit bureaus, banks, credit card companies and retailers, on the other hand, wanted to specify that the new federal standards would take precedence over state laws, arguing that it would be too difficult to comply with a patchwork of state laws.

House Committee

After a short but rancorous markup March 3, the House Banking Committee approved HR 1015 by a party-line vote of 29-20 (H Rept 103-486).

However, a fight between two erstwhile allies gave the markup a decidedly partisan edge. The blowup involved a carefully negotiated deal — which unraveled in full public view — to make changes to a hotly contested section of the bill aimed at allowing affiliates of the same company to more freely share credit information with each other.

On the day before the markup, Joseph P. Kennedy II, D-Mass., chairman of the Consumer Credit Subcommittee and the bill's chief advocate, and senior panel Republican Richard H. Baker of Louisiana, had reached a compromise on an amendment to revise the information-sharing section of the bill.

But when Kennedy's staff delivered the precise legislative language to Republicans the next morning — an hour before the markup was set to reconvene — Baker pulled out of the deal. He appealed to Kennedy and Gonzalez to postpone the markup. But Kennedy insisted on going ahead, and the committee voted 25-24 to table (kill) the Kennedy amendment.

The amendment would have given consumers additional rights when affiliated companies, such as banks and their credit card subsidiaries, shared erroneous information that led to a denial of credit. The death of the amendment infuriated consumer groups, who temporarily withdrew their support for the bill, although it received the committee's approval anyway.

The committee's stamp of approval in March came after a first contentious markup Feb. 9. Then, the committee had lost the quorum necessary to approve the measure, and Gonzalez had gaveled the meeting to a close.

That markup's most vigorous debate had also centered on the question of allowing affiliated companies — banks, other lenders and credit card companies, for example, that were jointly owned — to share credit information about their clients.

Existing law permitted affiliates to share information directly acquired through experiences and transactions with customers. Affiliates could not share credit histories obtained from credit-reporting agencies or application information. Related companies were prohibited from creating a central repository for such information that all affiliates could tap into.

Baker and Cal Dooley, D-Calif., successfully offered an amendment to allow greater information sharing, provided that lenders alerted their customers to the practice and received explicit consent to share the information. Most Democrats, led by Kennedy, opposed the amendment. They argued that the change effectively would permit large companies to function as their own credit reporting agencies without being subject to fair credit laws, and could lead to unjust denial of credit.

The Dooley-Baker amendment was adopted, 30-19, after the committee rejected, 22-27, a Kennedy amendment to allow shared information to be used only to market services, not to make credit decisions. The committee adopted by voice vote an amendment by Doug Bereuter, R-Neb., allowing consumers to prohibit the sharing of information about themselves.

The committee adopted another amendment to pre-empt state credit laws that imposed tougher standards on certain credit bureau activities and affiliate information sharing. Bitter disagreement over pre-empting state laws had derailed a similar bill in 1992.

Consumer advocates did win several victories in the early markup. An amendment by Charles E. Schumer, D-N.Y., to prohibit the use of a consumer's credit history for targeted marketing purposes without prior consent was adopted, 27-23. And one by Bill Orton, D-Utah, to allow credit bureaus to charge consumers up to $8 each for copies of their own credit histories was rejected, 23-26. The Orton amendment would have allowed consumers to receive a free report only after they had suffered an adverse action, such as the denial of credit. The 1992 bill would have allowed credit bureaus to charge the $8 fee.

An amendment by Spencer Bachus, R-Ala., to require the three major nationwide credit bureaus to coordinate corrections of inaccurate information in their files was adopted by voice vote. And, on a party-line vote of 29-19, the committee adopted an amendment by Cleo Fields, D-La., to limit the circumstances under which a credit reporting agency could furnish reports to employers or prospective employers.

House Floor

To the surprise of many supporters, the House on June 13 passed the fair credit bill by voice vote under expedited floor procedures generally reserved for non-controversial bills. Passage came after Republicans and business groups obtained significant concessions that made the measure very similar to S 783, which by then had passed the Senate.

As reported by the Banking Committee, HR 1015 had been seen as too anti-business to pass, forcing Kennedy to negotiate with Republicans to bring a less controversial version to the floor. Among the changes was the elimination of a provision that would have allowed private citizens and consumer groups to sue furnishers of credit information.

Also, the compromise bill required that consumers pay a $3 fee to receive a copy of their credit report; under the committee-approved bill, such reports would have been available free of charge. Free reports still were to be available to the unemployed, people on public assistance or those who believed they were the victims of fraud.

Consumer advocates won a partial victory. Under the compromise bill, the provision allowing the pre-emption of state law was to expire after eight years; after that period, states could enact tougher laws if problems remained.

Senate Action

The Senate passed S 783 on May 4 by a vote of 87-10, after adopting several changes aimed at making the bill more palatable to business interests. *(Vote 100, p. 18-S)*

The bill was propelled to the floor after sponsors Richard H. Bryan, D-Nev., and Christopher S. Bond, R-Mo., threatened to try to attach it to the widely backed interstate banking and branching bill (HR 3841), which passed the Senate on April 26. *(Interstate branching, p. 93)*

A compromise amendment crafted by bill sponsors addressed several issues that were of concern to business. For example, earlier versions of the bill would have subjected banks and others to fines by the Federal Trade Commission (FTC) if they repeatedly and knowingly furnished bad information to credit bureaus. Under the amendment, providers of credit information were largely exempted from the threat of FTC fines, which could be imposed only if credit furnishers violated the commission's cease-and-desist orders.

In addition, the amendment replaced a provision in the committee-reported bill that would have allowed consumers to demand free credit reports every other year with a maximum $3 fee per report.

In a victory for consumer groups, the amendment limited to six years the provision allowing pre-emption of state law.

However, the bill also contained several provisions sought by business interests to relax existing restrictions on the use of credit information, for example, allowing certain information from a consumer's credit report to be included in lists prepared for use by direct marketing companies. The bill also proposed to loosen restrictions on the use of pre-screened lists of creditworthy consumers. Under existing law, when a creditor, such as a credit card company, offered credit based on a pre-screened list prepared by a credit bureau, it had to be a "firm offer" that could not be rescinded except under narrow circumstances. The bill allowed the offer of credit to be taken back based on information provided by the credit applicant.

Final Action

Informal negotiations between the House and Senate — rather than a conference — produced a further compromise. The House passed the newly negotiated version of the bill (S 783) on Sept. 27 by voice vote.

One significant change concerned the use of credit reports for direct marketing. Credit bureaus wanted to be able to compile and sell lists of consumers, but under existing law they generally were barred from doing so. The Senate bill would have allowed limited information from consumers' credit reports to be included in lists prepared for direct marketing companies; the House bill prohibited credit bureaus from compiling and selling such direct marketing lists. Under the compromise, the issue was to be be left to the courts.

Barely a week later, on Oct. 5, the House passed the bill again, after adding several non-germane sweeteners in an effort to improve the bill's prospects in the Senate. The House passed the clean version of the bill (HR 5178) by voice vote.

The most significant of the additions was a provision, sought by Connie Mack, R-Fla., to close a loophole in the Truth in Lending Act that was used by some lawyers to get borrowers out of abusive mortgages. Mack contended that many other attorneys were seeking to use the loophole, opened by a recent federal court decision, to extract many millions of dollars from legitimate mortgage lenders.

Another add-on, sought by two Georgia senators, Democrat Sam Nunn and Republican Paul Coverdell, sought to ease certain bank regulations in parts of Georgia, Alabama and Florida that had been flooded during Tropical Storm Alberto in 1994. The idea was to make sure that compliance with regulations written for normal times did not impede the flow of credit in a disaster area. The provision was similar to a 1992 measure aimed at easing problems caused by the Los Angeles riots and Hurricanes Andrew and Iniki.

But the sweeteners did not save the bill. Republican Sen. Phil Gramm of Texas put a hold on the measure in the final days of the regular session. He opposed the Fair Credit measure, and he had been unsuccessful in attaching to it a provision to lift a state law that made Texas the only state in which residents could not get home equity loans. Gramm had also lost out to Gonzalez during a big fight over the issue in conference negotiations on the interstate banking bill (HR 3841 — PL 103-328). ∎

Insurance Redlining Bill Passes in House

The House passed a bill (HR 1188) aimed at combating insurance "redlining," the practice of refusing to sell policies in certain areas, generally poor or minority neighborhoods. There was no companion bill in the Senate, however, and the legislation died at the end of the year.

The bill's Democratic sponsors argued that public disclosure of such information would pressure companies to avoid engaging in redlining, a problem they insisted was serious and widespread. "I can assure you that insurance redlining is alive, well and thriving," said Cardiss Collins, D-Ill., floor manager for the bill. "Public disclosure of this information would serve as a . . . disincentive to discriminatory behavior."

But many Republicans questioned whether redlining was widespread. Toby Roth, R-Wis., called it "an imaginary national problem" supported by little hard evidence. Many Republicans were interested in gathering data to assess the extent of the problem, rather than to pressure the industry.

The House legislation had been the subject of a bitter fight between the Energy and Commerce Committee and the Banking Committee, both of which had claimed jurisdiction over the legislation. Energy and Commerce won the fight: It was the committee's bill (HR 1188 — H Rept 103-270) that the House approved by voice vote July 20.

The turf battle began in the summer of 1993 at the subcommittee level in both panels. The House parliamentarian had referred the Banking Committee's version of the bill (HR 1257 — H Rept 103-302, Part 1) to Energy and Commerce but not vice versa, giving the Energy committee control of the issue. *(1993 Almanac, p. 166)*

The Banking Committee, which wanted substantially tougher requirements on insurance companies, was twice beaten soundly when it tried to reclaim control over the bill and substitute its own, more aggressive language.

The bill that passed the House required all but the smallest insurance companies that wrote home and automobile policies in the nation's 25 largest metropolitan areas to report a wide range of information on the types and number of policies issued. The information was to be broken down by five-digit ZIP code. The reporting requirements were to begin in 1995 and last for five years, with an optional two-year extension.

The Banking Committee bill would have required insurers to supply data by census tracts, which typically were smaller

than ZIP codes and could yield more precise comparisons with data on family income and other economic measures. Five-digit ZIP codes could include both high-income and low-income neighborhoods. The Banking bill would have required the data for 150 metropolitan areas and 50 rural areas and made the reporting requirement permanent.

Also, the Banking Committee wanted the data collected by the Department of Housing and Urban Development, while the Energy and Commerce bill housed it in the Commerce Department.

An amendment by Joseph P. Kennedy II, D-Mass, that effectively would have reclaimed control of the issue for the Banking Committee failed on an 88-343 vote. *(Vote 337, p. 100-H)*

Kennedy argued that the Energy and Commerce bill was a fatally weak measure that "doesn't do a darn thing" to rein in an "industry that has been racially prejudiced in how it is writing its [insurance] policies." Banking Committee Chairman Henry B. Gonzalez, D-Texas, concurred, calling the bill "a wholesale abasement before this powerful, monstrous [insurance] lobby."

Lucille Roybal-Allard, D-Calif., offered an amendment that would have moved the bill in the Banking Committee's direction. The amendment would have expanded coverage from 25 metropolitan areas to 75 and required companies to divulge claims that they had paid and to report the race, ethnicity and gender of policyholders. It also would have opened the way to requiring that companies submit data by census tract or nine-digit ZIP code areas instead of the broader, five-digit ZIP codes. The amendment failed on a 97-333 vote. *(Vote 338, p. 100-H)* ■

Other Securities-Related Bills Considered in 1994

Congress worked on several additional securities measures in 1994, clearing a short-term extension for the Securities and Exchange Commission (SEC) and a bill to allow regional stock exchanges to trade certain stocks without prior SEC approval. A bill to beef up SEC supervision of financial planners died at the end of the session.

Financial Planners

A long-idled attempt to increase federal oversight of the largely unsupervised financial planning industry came to life at the end of the session, but the measure never became law. The House passed a compromise bill (S 423) Oct. 5 by voice vote, but the Senate did not act on the measure.

The bill would have increased fees on investment advisers, with the proceeds going to hire additional enforcement staff for the Securities and Exchange Commission (SEC). The SEC had only about 50 inspectors to oversee the rapidly growing industry.

The bill would have replaced the existing $150 one-time registration fee for financial planners with annual fees ranging from $300 to $7,000, depending on the amount of assets under the planner's management. This would have raised an additional $16 million for the agency, allowing it to step up the pace of adviser inspections.

Both chambers had passed versions of the legislation in 1993, but the House bill (HR 578 — H Rept 103-75) was more far reaching than the Senate's (S 423 — S Rept 103-177). HR 578 called for financial planners to disclose their fees and their qualifications to give financial advice and to provide periodic reports summarizing all client charges. It also required that financial planners only recommend investments that were "suitable" given a client's financial position. *(1993 Almanac, p. 164)*

Informal negotiations by staff aides, which began in the summer of 1994, finally produced the compromise that passed the House. The measure followed several high-profile cases in which financial planners systematically bilked investors.

The final version dropped the House "suitability" provision. It contained provisions to:

● Authorize the SEC to deputize self-regulatory organizations such as the National Association of Securities Dealers to inspect certain advisers.

● Require the SEC to conduct a survey to detect unregistered financial planners.

● Direct the SEC to investigate potential conflicts of interest arising when financial planners received commissions or other compensation on products they recommended to investors. If a problem was found, the agency would be expected to issue rules requiring that such conflicts of interest be disclosed to investors.

SEC Authorization

After a philosophical rift between the House and Senate killed prospects for a bill reauthorizing the Securities and Exchange Commission (SEC), Congress was forced to pass a stopgap financing measure (HR 5060 — H Rept 103-739, Part 1) to avert a budget crisis at the agency.

What ultimately cleared was a one-year extension that kept SEC securities registration fees at the fiscal 1994 rate of 1/29th of 1 percent of the value of the issue. The House passed HR 5060 by voice vote Sept. 27; the Senate cleared it Oct. 8, also by voice vote. President Clinton signed the short-term bill Oct. 10 (PL 103-352).

The House had passed a bill in 1993 (HR 2239 — H Rept 103-179) to make make the SEC a self-funding agency, while substantially boosting its budget. But the concept of self-funding got chilly reviews in the Senate, which never acted on a funding bill. *(1993 Almanac, p. 170)*

Sen. Phil Gramm, R-Texas, who thought the self-funding measure would give the agency too much autonomy from congressional oversight, led the fight against the idea. He won an important convert in Christopher J. Dodd of Connecticut, top Democrat on the Securities Subcommittee of Senate Banking, who also opposed the House approach.

Key House members, especially Energy and Commerce Committee Chairman John D. Dingell, D-Mich., were frustrated by the impasse, and they tried to force the Senate's hand by slashing the SEC budget. But the Senate refused to budge, creating the need for the end-of-session registration fees bill to fill an almost $200 million budget gap. But the Senate delayed in passing that measure, thus costing the Treasury $19.4 million after several corporations registered securities at the temporarily lowered rate. In an eleventh-hour move before Congress adjourned for midterm elections, the Senate finally cleared the measure.

Regional Exchanges

The Senate on Oct. 6 cleared a bill allowing regional stock exchanges to trade stocks that were already listed on the New York and American stock exchanges without prior approval by the Securities and Exchange Commission (SEC). President Clinton signed the bill into law Oct. 22 (HR 4535 — PL 103-389).

The legislation eliminated a provision of the Securities and Exchange Act of 1934 that required regional exchanges, such as the Boston and Chicago Stock Exchanges, to receive SEC clearance. Previously, regional exchanges had to wait up to 60 days for SEC approval, putting them at a competitive disadvantage with the larger exchanges, particularly in the heavy trading period when stocks were initially offered to the public.

The bill began in the House Energy and Commerce Committee, which approved it by voice vote July 19 (H Rept 103-626). The House passed the bill by voice vote on Aug. 1.

Unclaimed Funds

After a boisterous Aug. 10 markup, the 30-member House Banking Subcommittee on Financial Institutions approved, 22-0, a controversial bill that pitted representatives from 47 states against lawmakers from Massachusetts, New York and Delaware.

The legislation (HR 2443) was designed to overturn court-approved procedures requiring banks and brokerage houses to transfer unclaimed interest and dividends on stocks and bonds to the states where the banks or securities firms were incorporated — most often Massachusetts, New York or Delaware.

Under the bill, the unclaimed funds, known as escheatable funds, were to be distributed instead to the home states of the corporations issuing the stocks or bonds. Subcommittee staff members estimated that $100 million to $150 million per year in unclaimed funds were at stake.

The bill was not taken up by the full Banking committee and died at the end of the session.

Derivatives

Spurred by accounts of some of the nation's biggest corporations taking major losses due to trading in exotic financial instruments called derivatives, Congress began to consider whether it was necessary to rein in the booming market. Also fueling congressional interest was a General Accounting Office (GAO) report that urged lawmakers to enact a law filling the gaps in existing regulatory authority over derivatives.

But with banking and securities regulators taking fresh steps to improve oversight of the multibillion-dollar market and with no consensus as to how or whether Congress should step in, there was no legislative action in 1994.

Derivatives were a class of financial instruments whose value was tied to, or derived from, an underlying asset, such as stocks, foreign currencies or commodities. Because these instruments typically were highly leveraged, small swings in the market could produce big wins or losses for those who invested in them — mostly large institutional investors or corporations.

A key problem, said the GAO, was that the derivatives-related activities undertaken by insurance companies and their affiliates were largely exempt from regulation and capital requirements. ∎

Export Control Update Stalls Again

For the fifth consecutive year, legislation to update U.S. export control laws fell without final action. The effort to overhaul the Export Administration Act (HR 3937, S 1902), which did not reach the floor of either chamber, died for much the same reason it had in previous years: Lawmakers were unable to reconcile the often conflicting goals of developing export markets and curbing the global arms race.

Congress cleared a brief extension while lawmakers tried to reach a compromise on the big bill. The extension, which President Clinton signed July 5 (HR 4635 — PL 103-277), kept the law in force to Aug. 20. An end-of-session attempt to pass a one-year extension of the export control law (HR 5108) succeeded in the House, but the Senate did not act on that bill.

The broader bill aimed to put in place new rules for the way the Defense and Commerce departments controlled the export of "dual-use" goods — goods that had both civilian and military applications. It proposed to ease export restrictions, shorten the time the government had to review export licenses, limit the types of international controls the president could agree to and make it more difficult for U.S. agencies to unilaterally prohibit certain exports.

In response to concerns about the proliferation of weapons of mass destruction, the legislation proposed to increase sanctions against countries that exported technologies that could be used for such weapons.

Background

The Export Administration Act, whose origins dated to the 1940s, regulated the sale of sensitive goods and technologies abroad. The act had been used to keep computers and other sophisticated technology out of the hands of the Soviet Union and other Cold War enemies.

There was almost unanimous agreement in Congress on the need to loosen many of the Cold War export restrictions. High-tech companies clamored for passage of a comprehensive rewrite of the act. But legislators disagreed about what procedures and controls to establish to prevent militarily sensitive goods from falling into the wrong hands. As a result, members had failed in the past several Congresses to pull together the support needed for an overhaul. The law had expired in 1990, and the restrictions had been kept in place by executive order and stopgap legislation. A short-term authorization enacted in 1993 expired June 30. *(1992 Almanac, p. 162; 1993 Almanac, p. 185)*

The sponsors of HR 3937, Sam Gejdenson, D-Conn., and Toby Roth, R-Wis., outlined the reasoning behind the bill in an opinion piece in The New York Times. They argued that Congress owed it to U.S. business to make the export process less burdensome. "Export control policy must be changed to reflect reality, to meet new security threats and competition for world markets," they wrote. "By passing a strong measure this summer, Congress can improve our non-proliferation efforts — and our living standards."

But arms control organizations and defense-minded lawmakers opposed the legislation as too weak to keep sensitive dual-use technologies out of hostile hands.

House Action

Four House committees approved versions of HR 3937 (H Rept 103-531, Parts 1-4). The Foreign Affairs Committee voted May 18. The Armed Services, Intelligence, and Ways and Means committees approved their versions June 15. All acted by voice vote.

The impasse that stalled the House bill was reflected in

the differences between the Foreign Affairs and Armed Services committee versions. Foreign Affairs concentrated on reducing restrictions on exporters. It proposed eliminating controls on most so-called dual-use items and giving the Commerce Department primary responsibility for overseeing exports. Armed Services crafted a version aimed at giving the Defense Department the power to stop exports that could aid the weapons programs of unfriendly nations.

The committees took the following action:

● **Foreign Affairs.** The Foreign Affairs bill gave the Commerce Department 30 days to review export licenses, instead of the existing 120-day period, stipulating that the licenses would be approved automatically if the time limit was not met. The bill called for punitive import sanctions on countries that exported component parts of biological, chemical and nuclear weapons.

● **Ways and Means.** The Ways and Means Committee followed the lead of the Foreign Affairs Committee. It made slight changes to the sanctions language, giving the president discretion over the type of import sanctions that could be applied.

● **Armed Services.** The Armed Services version was somewhat less favorable to U.S. business interests, but committee members hoped it would keep a tighter lid on the proliferation of dangerous weapons and the use of U.S. military technology by countries hostile to the United States.

The committee proposed that the secretary of Defense retain the authority to draft lists of items that should be controlled. Some critics of the existing law contended that the Defense Department was too conservative in granting export approval, resulting in a loss of business to U.S. companies. The committee proposed a 50-day review period for export licenses, giving the agency that had the most expertise in the specific technology to be exported 20 days to review the application.

The Armed Services panel approved several amendments, including one by John R. Kasich, R-Ohio, aimed at deterring other countries from selling goods that were used to produce weapons of mass destruction. It required the president to draw up a list of key technologies used in developing these highly dangerous weapons.

● **Intelligence.** The Intelligence Committee, which had limited jurisdiction, approved its portion of the bill during a closed session. Included was an amendment requiring a study of the impact of export controls on U.S. computer software manufacturers.

Compromise Proves Elusive

Foreign Affairs Chairman Lee H. Hamilton, D-Ind., and Armed Services Chairman Ronald V. Dellums, D-Calif., attempted to broker a compromise that would resolve conflicts that held up the legislation for years. Anticipating an agreement, the leadership scheduled the bill for floor action. But the measure was pulled from the House calendar July 22 and never came to the floor. A single sticking point reportedly remained outstanding — how to deal with some goods that were considered both munitions and dual-use items. Under existing law, dual-use items came under the control of the Export Administration Act, while munitions were regulated by the State Department under the Arms Export Control Act.

HR 3937 required that items be classified as either munitions or dual-use products, not both, to keep exporters from having to undergo two reviews. But lawmakers were not able to agree on where to put some items.

According to sources involved in the negotiations, agreement was reached on the following issues:

● **Pentagon role.** Armed Services members were determined to retain the role of the secretary of Defense in listing exports that either required licenses or could be prohibited. A congressional aide said the "new language clearly provides that the secretary of Defense shall have a seat at the table."

● **Time limits.** Exporters of sensitive technologies frequently complained that export licenses lingered in review for months, giving foreign competition a leg up. An aide said a compromise was reached midway between the 30-day limit proposed by Foreign Affairs and the 50 days allowed under the Armed Services bill.

● **Definitions.** Defense-minded lawmakers also pushed to maintain the existing wording of the standard used to control exports. It prohibited exports that would enable another country to build up its military and could "prove detrimental to the national security of the United States." Gejdenson's bill would have changed this standard to prohibit exports if they "posed a threat to the national security." The negotiators reportedly found a middle ground on that language as well.

Senate Action

The Senate Banking Committee approved its own version of the Export Administration Act reauthorization bill (S 1902) on May 24; the vote was 19-0. The Senate took no further action on S 1902.

As approved by the committee, the bill sought to loosen restrictions on the export of some items to nations that were no longer considered a threat to the United States. At the same time, it tightened controls on the export of weapons and other technologies that could be used against the United States by terrorists or during a war. The bill gave the president authority to impose sanctions on countries that did export such technologies.

Committee Chairman Donald W. Riegle Jr., D-Mich., said the legislation represented a good balance between the concerns of exporters and national security interests. "We must work both unilaterally and with our allies in preventing key technologies . . . from falling into the hands of rogue regimes such as Iran, Iraq, Libya and North Korea," Riegle said.

The committee approved a package of changes to authorize a study of the number of job losses that could result from export controls, and to require that export licenses be processed in 60 days, half the time allotted under existing law.

The committee also approved an amendment, offered by Patty Murray, D-Wash., to require a study on the impact on U.S. companies of unilateral export controls on computer software. The issue was an important one for companies such as Seattle-based Microsoft Corp., which made business software. By law, U.S. software companies could not export software written in so-called Data Encryption Standard (DES) — a security code used in many business software programs to prevent hackers from entering the programs.

Murray and panel members from California, Massachusetts and Utah wanted to see such unilateral restrictions lifted. They argued that because DES software was already available overseas, the "genie is out of the bottle." The National Security Agency, however, opposed decontrolling software.

Short-Term Extension

Unable to reach an agreement on the broad rewrite of the Export Administration Act, the House on Oct. 4 approved a bill (HR 5108) to reauthorize the act for one year. The vote was 407-4. The Foreign Affairs Committee had approved the short-term extension by voice vote Sept. 28. The bill was referred to the Senate Banking Committee, which took no action on it, killing the legislation for the year. *(Vote 477, p. 142-H)* ■

GATT Enacted in Lame-Duck Session

International trade issues were not top priority items in Bill Clinton's 1992 "Putting People First" presidential campaign. Yet the enactment in late 1994 of a bill to implement the new worldwide General Agreement on Tariffs and Trade (GATT) — combined with congressional approval the year before of the North American Free Trade Agreement (NAFTA) with Mexico and Canada — made trade stand out as a success in Clinton's difficult first two years as president.

The bill (HR 5110) made numerous changes in U.S. laws to bring them into agreement with the terms of the GATT agreement; it also provided financing to offset an expected $12 billion in reduced tariff revenues over the first five years of the agreement. By wide margins, the House approved the bill Nov. 30, and the Senate cleared it Dec. 1. Clinton signed the bill Dec. 8 (PL 103-465).

Yet like most of his legislative successes in the 103rd Congress, Clinton's GATT victory was hard won. Opponents of the nation's longstanding free trade policies, though a minority in Congress, used parliamentary procedures to stall action on HR 5110, forcing lawmakers to schedule a lame-duck session after the Nov. 8 election to consider the legislation.

Unlike most previous fights, though, Clinton's main foes were fellow Democrats, led by Commerce Committee Chairman Ernest F. Hollings of South Carolina, who had long criticized U.S. free trade policy as damaging the nation's industrial jobs base. And some of the president's strongest backers were Republicans, whose own support for free trade reflected a consensus in the U.S. business community.

Clinton had placed his international standing on the line for the GATT agreement. Taking up protracted negotiations that were begun in 1986 and carried on by Republican presidents Ronald Reagan and George Bush, Clinton administration trade officials played major roles in hammering out the final draft of the GATT agreement in December 1993. The agreement was signed by the United States and 116 other nations in Marrakesh, Morocco, on April 15, 1994.

Background

The most sweeping change in the world trading system since the original GATT pact was reached in 1947, the agreement promised to slash tariffs worldwide by nearly 40 percent and, for the first time, sharply reduce non-tariff barriers to trade, such as import quotas. The agreement also set up a formal body, known as the World Trade Organization (WTO), to replace the existing informal GATT dispute resolution system and to more strictly enforce trade agreements between nations.

Like all presidents since the end of World War II, Clinton embraced the view that the United States stood to benefit from free trade policies that opened up new markets for U.S.

BOXSCORE

GATT Implementation — HR 5110 (S 2467). The bill brought U.S. law into conformity with the new global trade accord under the General Agreement on Tariffs and Trade (GATT).

KEY ACTION

Aug. 2 — Senate committee approved draft bill.

Aug. 17 — House committee approved draft bill.

Sept. 20 — House-Senate conferees agreed on the draft.

Sept. 27 — President formally submitted HR 5110, S 2467.

Sept. 28 — House committee approved HR 5110, 35-3.

Sept. 29 — Senate committee approved S 2467, 19-0.

Nov. 30 — House passed HR 5110, 288-146.

Dec. 1 — Senate cleared HR 5110, 76-24.

Dec. 8 — President signed HR 5110 — PL 103-465.

exporters. The president's Council of Economic Advisers estimated that annual U.S. national income would increase by $100 billion to $200 billion by the 10th year after the new GATT agreement took effect, an amount equal to 1.5 percent to 3 percent of the existing gross domestic product.

"It is the largest world trade agreement in history," Clinton told a congressional delegation at the White House Sept. 20. "It will provide a global tax cut of $740 billion, reducing tariffs worldwide by more than a third."

One of the biggest projected gains for the U.S. economy was expected to come from the extension of GATT to include intellectual property rights. Companies and individuals in such U.S. industries as computer software, motion pictures, music and publishing hailed this portion of the agreement. They hoped it would force other nations to crack down on the copying or piracy of their products and ideas, which they said cost them hundreds of millions of dollars each year in lost income.

The new agreement also brought trade in such services as business accounting, construction, computer services and tourism under the system of multilateral trade rules. The United States, already the world's leading exporter of such services, stood to benefit from freer international trade in services, supporters said.

A third area being brought under the trade rules for the first time was agriculture. By pushing through reductions in longstanding and politically sacrosanct subsidies and import protections for farmers in European Union states and other nations, administration officials said they had obtained greater market access for U.S. farm producers. Officials said the new agreement would increase U.S. farm exports by $1.6 billion to $4.7 billion a year by 2000. (*Highlights, p. 129*)

Opposition Never Jelled

Opponents of the GATT implementing bill took three main tacks. The first, most strongly voiced by Hollings, was a general assault on U.S. free trade policy. Hollings argued that such a policy had produced a system in which U.S. markets were much more open to foreign goods than vice versa. "In order for this administration to succeed, it has to cut out this nonsense of free trade, free trade. . . . It's time for a sobering up and a reckoning," Hollings said Sept. 29, as he announced plans to keep the GATT bill in the Commerce Committee for 45 days in order to hold hearings, an action which in turn forced the scheduling of the lame-duck session.

Critics also denounced some specific aspects of the agreement, particularly the establishment of the WTO. While the WTO would be empowered to enforce trade rulings against other nations — potentially benefiting the United States — it could also rule that U.S. laws were in violation of the world trade agreement. As such, the opponents argued,

the WTO might violate U.S. sovereignty by forcing, through the threat of trade sanctions, the revocation of U.S. laws.

Finally, opponents went after the financing package that was included in HR 5110, denouncing a number of bookkeeping adjustments and tax compliance changes in the bill as gimmicks.

Leading the campaign against the bill was a patchwork coalition similar to the one that had almost upset NAFTA in 1993: labor unions, environmental organizations, government reform groups, Ross Perot's United We Stand America populist movement, and such "America First" conservatives as Patrick J. Buchanan.

But the GATT debate did not generate nearly as much heat as the NAFTA battle. It was easier to make the case about job losses to Mexico, a single, low-wage neighboring country with a track record of attracting U.S. manufacturing jobs, than about the sweeping, worldwide GATT agreement. And whereas NAFTA, a free-trade agreement that included an economically developing country, was a new concept in U.S. trade policy, the United States had been a member and leader in the GATT system since its establishment nearly 50 years earlier. Clinton's position was helped by the fact that some key Democrats with organized labor constituencies, including Majority Leader Richard A. Gephardt of Missouri, were lined up this time with the president. *(1993 Almanac, p. 171)*

On the Fast Track

Congress considered the GATT implementing bill under "fast track" procedures, developed to expedite consideration of trade agreements, that differed greatly from the normal legislative process.

Under fast-track rules, Congress had 90 days to act on the bill once it was submitted; the bill was unamendable and subject only to up-or-down votes in each chamber. To allow for congressional input, the process began with the president sending a draft bill to the committees of jurisdiction for informal markups, followed by an informal House-Senate conference. The results of this process were sent back to the president, who took them into consideration in shaping the final bill that went to Capitol Hill.

Although Congress could not change the final bill, fast-track rules allowed each committee of jurisdiction up to 45 days to review it. This provision gave Hollings his opportunity to stall action on the bill.

The goal of the expedited process was to prevent Congress from amending trade agreements in ways that might be unacceptable to the other negotiating parties. Like his recent predecessors, Clinton viewed the fast track as an assurance to other nations that the president would be able to uphold the terms of a trade agreement.

Congress had agreed in 1993 to extend fast-track authority through April 15, 1994 (PL 103-49). The extension applied specifically to GATT and did not cover any future bilateral trade deals. An attempt by the Clinton administration to include a more permanent extension of fast track in the GATT implementing bill failed after much negotiation. *(1993 Almanac, p. 182)*

A Time-Consuming Process

Although the terms of the new GATT agreement did not require that it take effect until July 1995, Clinton had said he was determined to have Congress enact a GATT implementing bill before the end of the 1994 session. Clinton wanted both to assert the United States' leadership on world trade issues and to demonstrate, as he had done with NAFTA, that

he was an internationalist who would fight the protectionist impulses on the left within his own Democratic Party and on the Republican far right.

However, in constructing the implementing bill, the administration had to resolve a number of thorny issues with different factions in Congress. The process was time-consuming and at times plodding, as the president and Congress spent much of the year preoccupied with such issues as Clinton's ill-fated proposal to overhaul the U.S. health care system. By the time Clinton sent the final bill to Capitol Hill in late September, only a week and a half remained before Congress' planned adjournment — a situation that Hollings exploited to throw the process into chaos.

Initially, it appeared that the fate of the GATT bill would hinge on the hundreds of technical changes it would require in existing U.S. trade law. For example, executives and workers in industries affected by foreign imports wanted the implementing bill to reinforce provisions of the GATT agreement allowing the United States and other countries to maintain sanctions against the "dumping" of imported goods in their markets at below-market prices.

On the other hand, some members of Congress, mainly Republicans, were concerned about GATT provisions that loosened rules allowing nations, including the United States, to subsidize private sector research and development on new high-technology products, as long as those subsidies would not be used for actual manufacture of those products.

Opponents expressed concern that Clinton, an advocate of such manufacturing research activities, would use subsidies to pursue an "industrial policy" under which the government would use funds to pick "winners and losers" in the U.S. economy. They wanted language in the GATT implementing bill to strictly define and limit the kinds of subsidies that the federal government could provide.

Consensus positions on these issues were eventually drafted into the implementing bill, and they never became the subjects of public debate. However, it took months of behind-the-scenes negotiations between administration officials, members of Congress and their staffs to iron out the specific language. *(Provisions, p. 131)*

Major Issues

Broader and more potentially explosive issues began to come to the fore by the middle of 1994.

● **World Trade Organization.** The most hotly contested of these dealt with whether the United States would be able to pursue independent economic and trade policies as a member of the WTO.

Beginning in the 1950s, the GATT system had operated solely by consensus. Trade disputes were referred to specially appointed panels of trade experts, who examined allegations by one country that another was discriminating against its products. The experts could decide the merits of the case and recommend sanctions. However, all countries, including the alleged perpetrators, had to agree to the panel's ruling for it to take effect. Thus the targeted country could block an adverse trade ruling simply by disagreeing with it.

The WTO was intended to greatly tighten these procedures, making trade rulings enforceable. The agreement turned the concept of consensus on its head. Rather than requiring that all nations agree to a trade ruling, the WTO would put a ruling into force unless all nations disagreed. If the defendant nation refused to change a trade practice that had been ruled GATT-illegal, the WTO would be autho-

History of GATT

U.S. participation in the new GATT agreement marked the culmination of a free trade policy that had been evolving over more than 60 years.

Early in the century, as the United States grew into the world's leading economic power, it relied on trade barriers to protect its manufacturing industries. That policy came to a crashing halt in the Great Depression of the 1930s.

Many economists and historians attributed the severity of the worldwide economic collapse partially to the passage of the hyper-protectionist U.S. Tariff Act of 1930 (better known as the Smoot-Hawley Tariff Act). As the United States raised its tariffs to record highs and U.S. trading partners responded in kind, international trade was severely constricted.

As the United States struggled to recover, it entered into a number of bilateral tariff reduction agreements. Between 1934 and 1945, the United States reached one-on-one trade agreements with 29 countries. However, the agreements lacked enforcement mechanisms and could be summarily canceled.

In the wake of World War II, the United States and other major trading nations embarked on negotiations to establish an organization to oversee international trade. The talks focused on a charter for an International Trade Organization (ITO), which was envisioned as a complement to such institutions as the World Bank and the International Monetary Fund.

Many members of Congress opposed the organization, expressing concerns that U.S. economic interests would be sublimated. The ITO charter never came up for a congressional vote.

However, at a 1947 trade conference in Geneva, the United States and 22 other nations adopted the original General Agreement on Tariffs and Trade, which contained some of the trade rules that were in the draft ITO charter. GATT took force in January 1948.

Over the next 19 years, the United States took part in five "rounds" of negotiations to expand GATT. These talks, held in various locations around the world, focused on continued tariff reductions. A 1955 conference in Geneva led to another attempt to form a worldwide body to oversee trade agreements, known as the Organization for Trade Cooperation. But the proposal again was scuttled by opposition in the U.S. Congress.

The Tokyo Round of negotiations, which lasted from 1973 to 1979, took GATT in a new direction. Although tariff reduction was still a key goal, the participating nations also made a first thrust at reining in non-tariff barriers to trade. An increasing number of nations, seeking creative ways to protect domestic industries without raising tariffs, had turned to such options as subsidies, countervailing duties, import licensing procedures, government procurement, customs valuation and anti-dumping measures.

The Tokyo Round resulted in a series of agreements, or codes of conduct, which set rules for addressing non-tariff barriers to trade. However, the agreements contained many loopholes, and members were not required to adhere to all the negotiated "codes."

Fixing these problems was a major goal of the latest round of GATT talks, which was launched with a 74-nation conference in Punta del Este, Uruguay, in September 1986. With the strong backing of President Ronald Reagan, U.S. negotiators sought to lower tariff barriers, place enforceable sanctions against many non-tariff trade barriers and bring a number of economic sectors not previously covered under the GATT umbrella.

Most major issues were resolved by the time President George Bush took office in 1989. But Bush had to expend much of his GATT effort resolving the major sticking point holding up completion of the agreement: agriculture trade. European Union nations in general, and France in particular, took a hard line against reducing politically popular farm export subsidies.

Finally, in 1992, Bush administration officials helped orchestrate the Blair House Accord, in which the United States and the European Union resolved major agricultural disputes and gave the stalled talks a jump start.

Clinton grabbed the GATT baton when he claimed the presidency in 1993. During the annual economic summit of the Group of Seven leading industrial nations in July 1993, the United States, the European Community, Japan and Canada reached a major agreement on lowering industrial tariffs. The Uruguay Round negotiations were concluded Dec. 15, 1993, and signing ceremonies were held the following April.

While this largest of all GATT agreements was in the works, the United States had negotiated smaller free-trade agreements in its own neighborhood. Congress approved implementing legislation for a trade agreement with Canada in 1988. Those two nations then brought Mexico in as a partner in the North American Free Trade Agreement, which Congress implemented after a heated political battle in 1993. *(1993 Almanac, p. 171)*

rized to permit the complainant nation to retaliate with trade sanctions that would otherwise be barred under GATT.

U.S. Trade Representative Mickey Kantor and other officials hailed the new system. They noted that when the Uruguay Round talks that led to the GATT accord began in 1986, fixing the dispute resolution system was a priority of U.S. negotiators. The United States had frequently brought trade discrimination complaints to GATT panels and won, only to see the defendant country ignore the ruling.

But GATT opponents insisted that U.S. participation in the WTO would lead to a degradation, and perhaps outright violation, of U.S. sovereignty. They said other countries would besiege the WTO with complaints that U.S. laws requiring imported products to meet certain health, safety, consumer protection, environmental or other standards constituted unfair trading practices. They argued that while the existing system allowed other countries to block adverse rulings, it allowed the United States to do the same, thus protecting U.S. laws from attack by trading competitors.

The WTO provisions also raised fears among state officials. Under the GATT agreement, national governments were required to ensure that their political subdivisions abided by its terms. Thus, the federal government could end up pursuing legal action to force states to revoke laws put into place to encourage economic growth within their borders.

Although the issue raised qualms across the political spectrum, the charge against the WTO was led by figures identified with the political right and left.

Hard-line conservatives, who were also attacking the Clinton administration's participation in United Nations peacekeeping operations, portrayed the WTO as more evidence that the president was turning control of U.S. foreign policy-making over to multinational bodies. "I am flat out against world government," declared Sen. Jesse Helms, R-N.C.

Many environmentalists, consumer activists such as Ralph Nader and others opposed the WTO from the left as an assault on U.S. sovereignty. They warned that the WTO would enable other countries to undo laws aimed at protecting health, safety and the environment that had the side effect of limiting imports of certain goods.

Administration officials insisted these concerns were overblown. The WTO, they said, could not overturn any federal or state law. If U.S. officials felt strongly enough, these laws would stay on the books, albeit at the risk of sanctions authorized by the WTO.

● **Fast track.** Ironically, one of the issues that most slowed the GATT implementing bill was the administration's effort to include a long-term extension of fast-track procedures for trade legislation.

Existing fast-track procedures were due to expire at the end of action on the GATT bill. Clinton, who was looking to future steps such as integrating Chile into NAFTA, wanted to use the implementing bill to extend fast-track authority.

Some members of Congress viewed the fast track as an abdication of their responsibility to review and modify legislation. In previous years, much of the opposition had come from Democrats with large constituencies of unionized industrial workers, who generally supported more protectionist trade policies. The Clinton administration, however, sparked opposition from Republicans as well by adding a requirement that the principal negotiating objectives for future trade talks include the protection of workers' rights and the environment.

Many free-trade Republicans, who wanted negotiating objectives limited to trade-specific issues, objected. They argued that requiring that other countries adhere to an international standard for worker rights or the environment would restrain trade.

Pressure to include the worker rights and environmental provisions came largely from House Democrats, including Gephardt. Organized labor agreed to go along with the fast-track extension only if such language was included.

● **Financing.** One of the stickiest issues facing lawmakers was how to pay for the agreement. The administration estimated that tariff cuts required under the new GATT accord would reduce federal revenues by about $12 billion in the first five years after implementation. The budget law required that these funds be offset by program cuts or revenue increases, and Republicans made it clear that they would not support a bill with tax increases.

Under House rules, costs were to be offset for the first five years. Senate rules required revenue-losing bills to be financed for 10 years, which would have required Congress to come up with an additional $30 billion. No attempt was made to meet that goal, which meant that GATT supporters would have to muster 60 votes to overcome a point of order in the Senate that the bill violated budget rules.

Warned by Democratic leaders that the financing issue could thwart election-year efforts to pass a GATT bill, administration officials initially considered putting it off until 1995. But during the week of May 2, Clinton wrote to House

Speaker Thomas S. Foley, D-Wash., and other lawmakers stating his intention to press for a vote in 1994. The position became final in July during a meeting of the Group of Seven leading industrial nations, when Clinton and other leaders informally agreed to have the GATT agreement in effect by Jan. 1, 1995, instead of July 1.

Some Democratic and many Republican GATT supporters contended that the financing crisis was unnecessary. They said the pact would generate a huge upswing in domestic economic activity, which would result in an increase in federal revenues that would dwarf the size of the tariff shortfall. Thus, they said, the administration should simply seek a waiver of congressional budget rules requiring the offsets.

The administration rejected this approach for two major reasons. Officials, including Treasury Secretary Lloyd Bentsen, said the financial markets could see such a waiver as a weakening in the commitment to cut the deficit. Also, seeking a waiver would indicate that the administration was accepting the concept of "dynamic scorekeeping." Some Republicans strongly contended that certain actions, such as tax cuts, would stimulate so much economic activity that tax revenues would ultimately increase. Administration officials were concerned that if they adopted that premise for GATT, Republicans would use the same argument to push for a capital gains tax cut.

The administration instead offered a five-year package that combined a handful of real offsets and a roster of bookkeeping procedures.

The administration anticipated $1.7 billion in farm program savings as a result of the GATT pact. The agreement required the U.S. government to reduce funding for its agricultural Export Enhancement Program by $1 billion over five years; increased income to farmers from expanded trade was expected to reduce the need for support payments to farmers by an additional $700 million. The administration wanted to apply the savings to the financing package. Farm state lawmakers insisted it should be recycled into U.S. farm export programs that would still be allowed under GATT.

Among the other financing proposals were $1 billion in savings from an overhaul of the Pension Benefit Guaranty Corporation that was attached to the GATT bill, more than $1 billion to be raised by auctioning parts of the broadcast spectrum to telecommunications companies developing "personal communications systems," and $1.1 billion from changing tax rules governing inventory accounting.

However, much of the financing package was made up of what Kantor himself referred to as "compliance and timing devices," such as advancing the date on which businesses were required to remit their tax payments.

Informal Committee Markups

While several House and Senate committees participated in the preliminary markups, the main action fell to the two panels with primary responsibility for trade and tax policy — Senate Finance and House Ways and Means.

Senate Finance Committee

The Finance Committee gave tentative approval to an implementation bill Aug. 2, but the panel left out several provisions sought by the White House.

In particular, committee Chairman Daniel Patrick Moynihan, D-N.Y., dropped the extension of fast-track negotiating authority. "There are not now the votes for further fast track," he declared. Moynihan said Congress could take up

the extension in 1995 as stand-alone legislation.

The Finance Committee was deeply divided between a faction led by International Trade Subcommittee Chairman Max Baucus, D-Mont., that wanted the labor and environment language included, and another group, led by John C. Danforth, R-Mo., that wanted language specifically excluding these issues from fast track. Unable to find a middle ground, Moynihan opted to leave out the language.

The Finance Committee on July 29 approved, 11-9, a package of revenue-raising proposals that, along with suggestions expected from other committees, was supposed to pay for the trade deal. The committee adopted the assumption that the Senate Agriculture Committee would apply $1.7 billion in savings expected under GATT — including $1 billion from the Export Enhancement Program — to the financing. Among those who voted no for this reason were Minority Leader Bob Dole, R-Kan.; Baucus; David L. Boren, D-Okla.; and Kent Conrad, D-N.D. "I don't think it's fair," said Baucus, adding that the dispute left the financing package "pretty shaky right now."

House Ways and Means

The other key committee, House Ways and Means, wrapped up its work on the legislation Aug. 17 and opened negotiations with members of the Senate Finance Committee on the draft measure.

The move to conference gave a lift to supporters of the GATT accord. "I don't think there's any question that we're going to get GATT [passed] this year," said Robert T. Matsui, D-Calif., the chairman of the Ways and Means Trade Subcommittee. "I think this was a major step forward."

The Ways and Means Committee was able to declare its readiness for conference only by finessing or reaching tenuous compromises on key issues.

The panel created a financing shortfall in the draft bill by removing a provision that would have changed tax rules governing inventory accounting by retail businesses. The provision was opposed by many Republicans and business-oriented Democrats. That left the bill $800 million short of the $12 billion needed to offset lower tariff receipts and other costs resulting from the trade agreement.

On the question of fast-track authority, the committee approved a compromise reached by administration officials and ranking Republican Bill Archer of Texas that eliminated the controversial labor and environmental requirements. As approved by the committee, the draft measure extended fast-track authority for three years, with an option for an additional three years unless Congress voted against it. Clinton had initially requested a seven-year extension.

The compromise angered a number of liberals. "I appreciate that everybody doesn't share our values as a country in regard to the environment," said Rep. Nancy Pelosi, D-Calif. "But we, as the United States of America, must be the leader."

It also set up a major sticking point between the House and Senate versions of the draft bill.

Mock Conference

House and Senate negotiators held a news conference Sept. 20 to announce that they had reached agreement on the draft bill. The major obstacle to a compromise — the fast track language — was removed not by the conferees, but by the Clinton administration.

● **Fast track.** On Sept. 13, U.S. Trade Representative Kantor announced that the administration would drop the fast track extension from the final bill in exchange for a commitment

from Moynihan and Ways and Means Committee acting Chairman Sam M. Gibbons, D-Fla., that Congress would take up a fast-track renewal bill early in 1995.

The administration had little choice. Its attempt to keep the fast-track provision in the bill had met resistance on several fronts. Business lobbyists objected to the attempt to broaden the rules into the controversial realms of environmental protection and worker rights. When the White House tried to back away from that, organized labor charged that the administration was backtracking on support for strengthening worker rights protections in future trade deals.

By the time of conference Moynihan and other Senate negotiators had hardened their position against the provision, and the stalemate threatened to stall the legislation. "They began to say, 'What do we have to do to get GATT passed?' " said Matsui.

● **Financing.** The biggest remaining stumbling block was the completion of a financing package. The budget already was tight after years of being scrubbed for deficit reduction, and politicians were unwilling to put most big-ticket tax increases or spending cuts on the table for the GATT exercise. So Congress and the White House went on a hunt for funds that sometimes seemed like the federal equivalent of rifling through pants pockets for forgotten change.

For example, the financing package included a requirement that infants get Social Security numbers right after birth, rather than at age 1, as under existing law. The point was to clamp down on adult taxpayers who claimed non-existent children as exemptions to lower their own taxes or qualify for the earned-income tax credit. The estimated revenue increase over five years was about $94 million.

GATT opponents derided the financing proposals. Consumer activist Ralph Nader said several of the "accounting gimmicks" in the package "make for satire even more than severe professional criticism." For example, the plan included a proposal to speed up collection of excise taxes on alcohol, tobacco, airline tickets and many other taxable items to make sure the government got the money in late September instead of early October, which would put it into the following fiscal year. The estimated revenue increase was $466 million.

Such gimmicks had been banned from recent deficit-reduction packages because they only worked once. "A date shift is a cheap way of making money," said Rep. Bill Thomas, R-Calif., a member of the Ways and Means Committee's Trade Subcommittee. "You can't have a 13-month year every year. You can do it once and then you've got to pay for it."

Not all the GATT financing was small or gimmicky. Nearly $1 billion was to come from reforms to the Pension Benefit Guaranty Corporation, strengthening requirements that companies fulfill their pension-funding obligations, thereby reducing government losses. And while farm-state legislators continued to fight the proposal, negotiators expected to use $1.7 billion in cuts from agriculture programs to help offset the lost tariff revenue.

(To respond to farm state concerns, the administration on Sept. 30 sent a letter to congressional Agriculture committee leaders promising not to cut discretionary spending for agriculture programs below the fiscal 1995 level for the following two fiscal years and to support the reauthorization of the Conservation Reserve Program, which paid farmers not to use environmentally sensitive land.)

Negotiators also planned to help finance the GATT pact with $1.7 billion from the so-called PAYGO balance, the sur-

plus that had been built up by various bills enacted to raise taxes or cut mandatory spending. Under "pay as you go" budget rules (PAYGO in budget jargon), any attempt to cut taxes or tariffs (as in the GATT pact) or increase mandatory spending had to be deficit neutral. The White House budget office kept a running tally of all such legislation, and the count showed a surplus of more than $3.5 billion.

The financing package left the plan open to a point of order in the Senate that it violated budget rules. Barely able to come up with the money to offset the bill for five years, negotiators did not even try to pay for 10, as required in the Senate.

Some Issues Left for White House

The negotiators failed to resolve four sticky issues and left it to the Clinton administration to decide their disposition in the final GATT bill.

The issues in question were:

● **Super 301.** The Senate included in its draft bill a provision to re-enact so-called Super 301 authority — a version of the Section 301 provision of the Trade Act of 1974 — which authorized the president to publicly name countries that pursued unfair trade practices against U.S. goods and services and to threaten retaliatory sanctions if those practices were not corrected by a certain date.

The provision was backed by members, mainly Democrats, who believed the president should wield a big stick to force open markets that were closed to U.S. products. But many Republicans and free-trade Democrats opposed Super 301 as a protectionist device that exacerbated economic tensions between the United States and its trading partners. With this sentiment prevailing on the House Ways and Means Committee, the House version of the bill contained no Super 301 provision.

Clinton supported Super 301 and had issued an executive order giving himself the authority to pursue it, but he did not ask for legislative renewal of the provision and did not include it in his original draft of the GATT bill. (Clinton included the codification of Super 301 in the final bill.)

● **Rules of origin.** The House had included a provision to require, after a one-year transition period, that apparel items imported into the United States be labeled as having originated in the country in which they were assembled, rather than where they were cut. The requirement was aimed particularly at manufacturers in Hong Kong and several other Asian nations that had their material cut at home and then sent the pieces to be assembled in China, where wages were lower.

Although the Senate Finance Committee originally defeated a similar provision on an 11-11 vote, the Senate sent to the president rules-of-origin language that would have required the labeling change after five years.

The measure was strongly opposed by many clothing retailers, who feared it would reduce imports of inexpensive clothing items from the Far East and raise prices for consumers. It also could require the renegotiation of existing U.S. trade agreements with many countries. (Clinton included language in the final bill requiring the labeling as of July 1, 1996.)

● **Caribbean basin nations.** The House version gave developing nations in the Caribbean region temporary import preferences for apparel items equal to those provided to Mexico under NAFTA. Proponents said this would stem the flow of factory jobs to Mexico from the Caribbean nations, which threatened to undercut the economic development goals of a U.S. program known as the Caribbean

Basin Initiative (CBI).

Gibbons, whose home state of Florida had trade ties to the CBI countries, was the leading advocate of the provision. But the Senate declined to include it in the compromise draft bill. (Clinton excluded this proposal from the final bill.)

● **Tobacco tariffs.** The House bill authorized the president to impose increased tariffs on foreign tobacco to protect domestic growers from a flood of low-cost imports. The tariffs were to replace a domestic content requirement for U.S. tobacco products that was enacted as part of the 1993 budget-reconciliation bill but had been ruled by a GATT administrative panel as a barrier to trade.

The Senate negotiators, however, objected to the provision. Opponents saw it as an unnecessary protectionist measure that could subject other U.S. industries to cross-retaliation by tobacco-exporting countries under the new GATT agreement. (Clinton included the tobacco tariff increase.)

False Start

The collapse of Clinton's health care overhaul plan in September raised the stakes for the GATT bill. The president needed a major legislative success to boost the shaky prospects of Democratic congressional incumbents running in the November elections.

Clinton submitted the final version of the GATT bill to Congress on Sept. 27 (HR 5110, S 2467), and the measure got a quick start. The Ways and Means Committee endorsed HR 5110 on Sept. 28 by a vote of 35-3. The Senate Finance Committee approved S 2467, an identical bill, Sept. 29 by a vote of 19-0. But the slow-paced process of drafting the bill had put it at risk. By the time Clinton sent the bill up, less than two weeks remained before Congress' planned pre-election adjournment date. And although the fast track rules were meant to expedite consideration of the trade bill, they also allowed the chairman of any committee with jurisdiction up to 45 days to review and hold hearings on the bill.

The Commerce Committee had jurisdiction, and Hollings announced Sept. 28 — the day before the Finance Committee vote — that he would indeed hold the bill in his committee for 45 days. He hoped that by delaying the bill until after the adjournment date, he would force the leadership to put off consideration until the new Congress convened in January 1995 — a prospect that GATT proponents warned could lead to an even longer delay and perhaps kill the bill.

Hollings had a parochial interest that fired his opposition to GATT. While many industries would benefit from the agreement, the textile industry — a major employer in Hollings' home state of South Carolina — faced a surge in cheap imports from Third World countries. However, Hollings said his actions were spurred by his longtime opposition to U.S. free trade policies, which he said had badly damaged the nation's industrial economy. "I'm not shilling for a single industry," he said. "I'm shilling for the United States of America."

But Hollings' attempt to scuttle the bill for 1994 was foiled by Senate Majority Leader George J. Mitchell, D-Maine, and Minority Leader Dole, both GATT supporters, who agreed to schedule a rare, two-day lame-duck session, beginning Nov. 30, solely to debate and vote on the GATT bill.

In the House, Speaker Foley, a strong GATT backer, expressed his determination to push the implementing bill through that chamber before adjournment. But anti-GATT activists sensed an opportunity and urged the House to delay as well. Democratic and Republican House members alike began to betray nervousness about dealing with the poten-

Highlights of the GATT Accord

The bill that President Clinton signed Dec. 8 (PL 103-465) adapted U.S. law to conform with the terms of the new world trade accord strengthening the General Agreement on Tariffs and Trade (GATT). The agreement, which had to be approved by Congress and by the governments of the 116 other participants in the negotiations, sharply reduced international trade barriers, including tariffs, import quotas and export subsidies.

The deal was the result of negotiations that began in September 1986 in Punta del Este, Uruguay, and subsequently became known as the Uruguay Round. The negotiations were concluded in Geneva on Dec. 15, 1993, and the document was signed by U.S. Trade Representative Mickey Kantor and other world trade officials in Marrakesh, Morocco, on April 15, 1994.

The pact was the seventh renegotiation of the GATT, which was created at the end of World War II and governed most world trade. The agreement was scheduled to take effect July 1, 1995, but the participating nations agreed informally to put the terms into effect by Jan. 1, 1995. Key elements of the 550-page GATT agreement include changes in the following areas:

● **Tariffs.** Tariffs were to be cut on approximately 85 percent of world trade and eliminated or significantly reduced on a broad range of products, including construction and agricultural equipment, pharmaceuticals, paper and steel. Tariffs on industrial goods were to drop from an average of about 5 percent to an average of 3 percent. Some cuts were to occur immediately, and most were to take full effect over five years, although sensitive industries such as textiles were given 10-year phase-outs.

● **Agriculture.** The agreement brought trade in farm commodities under GATT for the first time. Governments agreed to reduce agriculture subsidies by an average of 36 percent and to cut subsidized exports by 21 percent.

● **Textiles.** The signatories agreed to phase out the Multi-Fiber Arrangement (MFA), under which industrial nations had imposed quotas on textile imports from developing countries for more than 30 years. The MFA was to be phased out over 10 years.

● **Dumping.** The United States and Europe preserved their existing authority to use domestic anti-dumping laws to impose fines or countervailing duties against countries that exported goods at prices below cost.

● **Subsidies.** In a big win for the U.S. aerospace industry, the pact included civil aircraft products, a leading U.S. export, under new rules restricting government industrial subsidies. That paved the way for lower subsidies to the European Airbus consortium, a major competitor of the Boeing Co.

● **Intellectual property.** GATT rules were extended to protect from piracy such intellectual property as computer programs, semiconductor chip designs, books, films and music. Developing countries had 10 years before they would have to honor patents on drugs.

● **Services.** Applying GATT rules to the world market in services, valued at almost $1 trillion annually, was a key goal of U.S. negotiators. However, multilateral agreements to open markets in specific service sectors, such as shipping, banking, securities and insurance, proved elusive.

● **World Trade Organization.** The Geneva-based GATT organization was to be replaced by the World Trade Organization, a permanent body with greater authority to force member nations to comply with Uruguay Round agreements.

tially controversial bill before the election, especially after the Senate had already put its vote off.

Spectrum License Fight

The final straw was an unexpected flare-up over an obscure provision of the bill's financing package. The provision aimed to raise at least $534 million in license fees from three telecommunications companies — innovators in wireless personal communications systems (PCS) technology — that originally had been promised free licenses to use portions of the federally owned broadcast spectrum.

Under the "pioneer preference" program, established in 1991 by the Federal Communications Commission (FCC), a competition had been held to name three pioneer companies that would be guaranteed spectrum licenses. The program was aimed at encouraging telecommunications companies to make speculative investments in new wireless technologies.

In 1992, the pioneer licenses were awarded to American Personal Communications Inc., an affiliate of the Washington Post Co.; Cox Enterprises Inc., a branch of the company that also owned the Atlanta Journal & Constitution newspaper; and the Colorado-based Omnipoint Communications Inc. In December 1993, these companies were designated to provide service in three of the nation's largest markets: Southern California and the New York and Washington, D.C., metropolitan areas.

At the time the pioneers were named, all FCC broadcast spectrum licenses were awarded for free. However, budget legislation enacted in August 1993 required that the licenses be auctioned to the highest bidder. Initially, the three companies were excluded from this requirement. But in August 1994, the FCC ruled that they also should pay fees, at a rate of 90 percent of the average market value of the auctioned licenses in the 10 next-largest markets.

The pioneer companies sued, charging that the FCC had no authority to retroactively charge the fees. Fearing that the federal government would lose the suit and get nothing, House Energy and Commerce Committee Chairman John D. Dingell, D-Mich., proposed legislation to settle the issue by requiring the companies to pay lower fees, at a rate of 85 percent of the average fees in the next 20 largest markets.

The Clinton administration, shopping around for money-raisers to attach to the GATT implementing bill, adopted Dingell's proposal. However, some of the companies' competitors as well as some federal budget watchdogs objected to the provision. They said the formula — which not only reduced the percentage rate for the fees but also factored in smaller and less lucrative markets in calculating average value — actually would result in deep discounts and an unfair competitive advantage for the three pioneer companies.

With the House poised to debate GATT, the Pacific Telesis telecommunications company ran an advertisement in The

Washington Post accusing the administration of slipping in a $1 billion "sweetheart deal" for its competitors, including The Washington Post itself.

The charge set off a brush fire among House members, particularly Republicans, who warned that they would vote to defeat the rule for floor consideration of the GATT bill if the issue was not explained to their satisfaction.

On Oct. 4, House Minority Whip Newt Gingrich, R-Ga., wrote to Foley calling for the House to put off action as the Senate had. "Nothing is lost by taking our time and doing it right," Gingrich wrote.

Foley initially insisted Oct. 5 that the House would go through with the scheduled debate and vote on GATT that day. But a series of party caucuses and leadership meetings indicated that support for quick action was evaporating.

That evening, Foley reached an agreement with Minority Leader Robert H. Michel to put the GATT debate off until a one-day lame duck session Nov. 29. In a letter to Clinton announcing the postponement of the vote, Foley, Michel, Gephardt and Gingrich wrote, "We will be working with you and all those who believe in the importance of this legislation to assure that GATT overwhelmingly passes the House."

The House did pass a rule Oct. 5, by a 298-123 vote, allowing for four hours of debate on the bill when it finally came to the floor. *(Vote 492, p. 144-H)*

Final Action

The delay gave GATT opponents a chance to breathe new life into what had been a low profile campaign against the implementing bill. With all other legislative business done for the year, they hoped to focus public attention on what they saw as the flaws of the GATT agreement and the implementing bill. They highlighted the threat to U.S. sovereignty supposedly presented by the WTO, the failure of the bill to pay for the tariff losses over the full 10 years required by the Senate, and the fact that the bill would be considered by dozens of retired or defeated members of the 103rd Congress in a lame-duck session.

Hollings, as promised, held a series of Commerce Committee hearings dominated by his own severe critique of U.S. free trade policy. The hearings featured a parade of GATT opponents who confirmed Hollings' views, and only a handful of GATT supporters.

But the anti-GATT forces were never able to capture the public's interest, although they did gain support from some conservative radio talk show hosts, who in turn generated some grass-roots activism against the implementing bill.

Citing this flare of opposition, Dole initially withheld his support, creating one last big hurdle for Clinton and congressional GATT supporters. Dole said his major concern was the WTO; he also cited questions about the telecommunications license fee issue. In addition, Dole floated the idea of asking the administration to look favorably on a capital gains tax cut in 1995 in exchange for his support on GATT.

Finally, after weeks of bargaining, Dole and Clinton reached an arrangement Nov. 23 aimed at settling the Republican leader's qualms. The agreement centered on a "three strikes" proposal, which set up a process for the United States to withdraw from the WTO if it chose. A panel of U.S. judges would review all decisions of the new body. If the panel found that the WTO had acted arbitrarily against U.S. interests in three cases, lawmakers could propose a joint resolution instructing the president to withdraw from the WTO. The joint resolution would have to be signed into law or enacted over the president's veto to take effect.

"We've resolved concerns about the WTO," said Dole, announcing his support for GATT at a Rose Garden ceremony attended by Clinton and key administration officials. Dole also agreed to drop his bid to link the capital gains cut to the GATT bill.

House Easily Passes Bill

With strong bipartisan support from the congressional leadership, House approval of the GATT bill was regarded as a sure thing by the time Congress reconvened for the lame duck session. The House passed HR 5110 on Nov. 30 by a lopsided vote of 288-146, a margin of nearly 2-to-1. *(Vote 507, p. 150-H)*

The four-hour House debate was routine and one-sided, most notable for the valedictory speeches of Speaker Foley, who was defeated in the GOP landslide, and Minority Leader Michel, who was retiring after 40 years in the House. "I believe no single measure, public or private, offers such a potential for economic progress," said Foley. "It will enable us to call forth our powers to greatly expand our export trade and development." Michel called upon his colleagues to "have the political courage and the national confidence to proclaim to the world that we are for GATT because we are Americans and we can compete with anyone at any time in every field in free and open competition."

The opponents struck a populist tone. "Working people in America, there is nothing in this GATT for you and your family," said Marcy Kaptur, D-Ohio, a strong supporter of the labor unions that put up a solid front against the agreement. But they had no chance.

Senate Clears Bill

Although administration officials expressed concern until near the very end about securing the 60 votes needed to overcome a budget point of order in the Senate, the bill cleared that barrier easily. The Senate on Dec. 1 voted, 68-32, to waive the Senate budget rule requiring a 10-year offset of revenue losses. Then, on the implementing bill itself, which required a simple majority to pass, the Senate voted 76-24 in favor. *(Votes 328, 329, p. 57-S)*

The Senate debated the implementing bill for 10 hours, spread over the two days beginning Nov. 30.

"What has been going on is that we are in a disastrous decline," argued Hollings, who led the opposition in the Senate GATT debate.

But many members who typically sided with labor, including some who voted against NAFTA, accepted the administration's promises of booming U.S. export and job growth resulting from the new GATT pact.

"For my home state right now, the key to the future is export jobs," said self-described "blue collar senator" Barbara A. Mikulski, D-Md. "The world is changing and a new economy is about to be born. I do not want the United States of America to be left behind."

GATT supporters stated firmly that the United States' leadership role in the world economy hinged on its affirmation of the GATT pact. "This [agreement] will take its place as one of the most important global agreements — both in terms of its size and in terms of its impact — ever fashioned," said Sen. John H. Chafee, R-R.I. "And it is our leadership that has brought it this far."

In both chambers, the bill received solid bipartisan support. Dole hailed the victory as a signal that the new Republican congressional majority would be willing to work with Clinton where there was room for agreement. "This is bipartisanship," said Dole. ∎

GATT Implementing Bill

On Dec. 8, President Clinton signed a bill (HR 5110 — PL 103-465) making a wide range of changes in U.S. law to bring it into conformity with a new global trade accord reached under the General Agreement on Tariffs and Trade (GATT). The following are the bill's major provisions; introductory material on the GATT agreement itself is in italics.

As enacted, the bill contained provisions to:

World Trade Organization

The new GATT agreement replaced the existing informal system for resolving trade disputes between member nations with a new, formal World Trade Organization (WTO). The WTO was to be empowered to oversee member nations' implementation of their multilateral trade commitments and to make and enforce rulings when nations are in violation of those commitments.

Under the existing system, a country could bring allegations of unfair trade practices by another nation before a GATT dispute resolution panel. But even if the panel upheld the complaint, it had no means of forcing the defendant country to revoke the offending practice or otherwise compensate the complaining nation. The WTO, though, was to have a much stronger hand.

Like the existing GATT system, the WTO would require member nations to seek consensus on trade disputes. But under the old GATT, "consensus" was interpreted to mean that all nations — including the one accused of unfair trade practices — had to agree to a GATT ruling. This allowed countries found guilty of unfair trade practices to unilaterally block adverse GATT rulings.

Under the WTO, "consensus" meant that a ruling would go into effect unless all member nations opposed it. The WTO also would set the amount of compensation, either in the form of trade restrictions on the defendant country or trade concessions to the complaining country, to offset the economic effect of the unfair trade practice. If no settlement was possible under the dispute resolution system, WTO members could vote on the issue in a body, similar to the United Nations General Assembly, in which each member nation would have one vote.

● **U.S. sovereignty.** Specify that U.S. law would prevail in instances when there was a conflict between a United States law and a provision of the trade agreement. Unless specifically provided for, nothing in the implementing bill would amend or modify any U.S. law relating to protection of human, animal or plant life or health, environmental protection or worker safety, or limit any authority conferred under any U.S. law, specifically including Section 301 of the 1974 Trade Act, which allowed the president to take retaliatory action against a nation that restricted imports of U.S. goods.

(However, if the United States were to decline to revoke a law that was ruled by the WTO to create an unfair trade practice, it might face economic penalties. Such penalties would be in the form of trade restrictions or concessions, not cash payments from the U.S. Treasury.)

To prevent WTO dispute resolution panels from being stacked against U.S. interests, the bill required the administration to review membership of such panels annually and ensure that the members were qualified. It also required the United States Trade Representative (USTR) to seek establishment of conflict of interest rules for WTO panel members.

● **State sovereignty.** Require the federal government to get a state law overturned, either through consultation or judicial action, if the WTO ruled that the state law violated a GATT commitment.

The bill required the USTR to set up a federal-state consultation process on GATT issues. Whenever another WTO member nation questioned or challenged a state or local law as conflicting with GATT, the USTR was to consult with the state's governor and chief legal officer of the affected jurisdiction in developing a U.S. position in the dispute.

If the WTO ruled against a state law, the USTR would have to consult with state officials to develop a mutually agreeable response. The only way a state law could be declared invalid for violating the GATT agreement is if the federal government were to pursue a successful lawsuit for such purposes. Only the United States would have legal standing to sue states or localities over GATT issues. No individual or foreign government could sue on such grounds.

● **Congressional and public consultation.** Require the USTR to consult with appropriate congressional committees before any WTO vote on an action that could affect U.S. rights or obligations under the WTO agreement or potentially require a change in federal or state law.

Whenever the United States was a party before a WTO dispute settlement panel, the USTR would have to consult with congressional committees and relevant private sector advisory committees concerning the issue at hand.

The USTR would have to make the United States' written statements to WTO panels available to the public, request the other party in the dispute to do the same and make each WTO report available to the public promptly after it was circulated to WTO members. If other parties did not release their confidential submissions, the USTR would request non-confidential summaries of those submissions.

In the event of an adverse WTO ruling, no federal regulation could be changed until congressional committees were informed, the USTR sought advice from private sector advisory committees and public comment was solicited through the Federal Register. No final rule could take effect until 60 days after consultations with congressional committees began; during that period, the House Ways and Means Committee or Senate Finance Committee could hold a non-binding vote on the proposed rule.

The USTR would have to report to the Ways and Means and Finance committees at least 30 days before bringing a legal action to declare invalid a state law that was ruled inconsistent with the GATT and would have to consult with the committees before the action was brought.

By March 1 of each year beginning in 1996, the USTR would have to submit a report to Congress detailing the WTO bureaucratic structure, including how much the United States and other countries contributed to its budget, any WTO dispute settlement action that affected federal or state law and what progress was made in achieving greater openness ("transparency") of WTO proceedings.

Within 90 days of receiving the first USTR report after the fifth anniversary of U.S. entry into the WTO, and every fifth year thereafter, Congress could withdraw the United States from the WTO by enacting a joint resolution. Relevant committees would have up to 45 days to review a proposed joint resolution.

● **Entry into force.** Specify that U.S. commitments under the new GATT would take effect when the president determined that a sufficient number of countries — including the countries of the European Union, Japan, Canada and Mexico — had accepted the obligations of the agreement to ensure adequate benefits to the United States.

The bill authorized appropriations for U.S. payment of its share of WTO expenses.

● **Extended negotiations.** Call for the United States to pursue its market-opening goals in some industry sectors for which agreements could not be concluded during the Uruguay Round of GATT negotiations — specifically including financial services and basic telecommunications services.

U.S. Trade Retaliation (Section 301)

● **Imposition of duties.** Eliminate the requirement under Section 301 of the Trade Act of 1974 that the USTR always give priority to the imposition of import duties as the preferred U.S. action to retaliate against another country's unfair trade practices.

● **'Super 301.'** Amend the "Super 301" provision of the 1988 trade

law (PL 100-418) by requiring the USTR to report to the Ways and Means and Finance committees within 180 days after publication of the 1995 National Trade Estimate report on "priority" foreign country trade barriers, the removal of which were likely to have the greatest potential to increase U.S. trade. Within 21 days of the submission of that report, the USTR was required to initiate Section 301 investigations of any identified priority practices.

● **Congressional consultation.** Require the USTR to consult periodically with appropriate congressional committees concerning foreign trade barriers and how best to address them.

Safeguards

The new GATT established rules under which member nations were permitted to impose import restrictions, or "safeguards," when import surges caused or threatened to cause serious injury to a domestic industry. Few conforming changes to U.S. laws were necessary, as those laws served as the model for the new GATT safeguard rules.

● **Provisional relief.** Allow U.S. industries to continue to apply to the federal government for provisional "critical circumstances" relief from import surges and expedite the process for providing such relief. The International Trade Commission (ITC) would have up to 60 days from the filing of the petition to decide whether to recommend such relief; if it did, the president would have to decide whether to act within 30 days. Deadlines under previous law were 120 days for the ITC and seven days for the president. Provisional relief was limited to 200 days.

● **Regular safeguards.** Allow an initial safeguard period of up to four years if the president determined that an industry required ongoing safeguard protection. Protection could be extended for an additional four years after public proceedings.

● **Quota levels.** Require that any safeguard quota be at least the average quantity or value of such articles imported into the United States in the most recent representative three years unless the president found that importation of different quantity or value was justified. Safeguards would have to be phased down at regular intervals.

Environment, Workers' Rights

● **Environment.** Require the inclusion of non-governmental environmental and conservation organizations on the federal advisory committee that issued opinions on the impact of trade agreements on the environment.

● **Workers' rights.** Require the president to seek the establishment within WTO of a working party on the linkage between trade and internationally recognized workers' rights, and to report to Congress within a year of enactment on progress toward establishing the working party.

Tariffs

The GATT agreement barred member countries from charging tariffs higher than those specified in their schedule of tariff concessions (the United States' commitments were listed in Schedule XX).

The accord eliminated tariffs on pharmaceuticals, furniture, medical equipment, paper and paper products, steel, agricultural equipment, construction equipment, scientific equipment and toys. The message from the president accompanying the GATT implementing bill noted that the U.S. objective of complete duty elimination on wood products, electronics, distilled spirits, non-ferrous metals and oilseeds and oilseed products was not achieved, and that further negotiations on those products would be sought.

● **Presidential authority.** Authorize the president to modify or add import duties as necessary to carry out U.S. obligations under

Schedule XX and to make technical corrections as necessary.

● **Tariffs on non-signatories.** Authorize the president to increase tariffs on a foreign country that was not a member of the WTO and was not providing adequate trade benefits to the United States. The provision was intended to end the problem, common under the existing GATT system, of "free rider" countries that took advantage of U.S. trade benefits provided under most-favored-nation rules while not joining GATT or providing reciprocal benefits to the United States.

Textiles and Clothing

Since 1974, trade in clothing and textile products, including those from low-wage developing countries, had been largely governed by the Multifiber Arrangement (MFA). This multilateral trade regime allowed nations to use quantitative restrictions, such as quotas, on such products without compensating the affected exporting nation.

The new GATT replaced MFA with an integration of apparel and textile products into GATT prohibitions on quantitative restrictions. The new regime was to be phased in over a 10-year transition period. Each participating country was required to declare those textile and clothing products it chose to integrate into the GATT, using three phases (immediately after the new agreement went into effect, after three years and after seven years). All such products were to be covered by the end of the 10-year period. After a product was integrated, the country could not impose import quotas on it.

The agreement contained "safeguard" provisions that allowed member nations to impose temporary quotas to protect domestic industries from being devastated by import surges. Such quotas had to be applied on a country-by-country and product-by-product basis, but could be based on the cumulative impact of imports from all sources. The quotas could not be lower than the actual import level during a recent 12-month period and could remain in effect for up to three years.

● **Publication of U.S. obligations.** Within 120 days of the new agreement's taking effect, the U.S. secretary of Commerce was to publish in the Federal Register a notice of those textile and apparel products to be integrated during each stage. Within 30 days of publication, the secretary was to notify the WTO Textile Monitoring Body of the lists.

● **Country of origin.** Require the U.S. secretary of the Treasury, no later than July 1, 1995, to produce regulations for enforcing country of origin rules aimed at preventing other countries from circumventing U.S. quotas by mislabeling or transshipping goods through other countries, during the quota phaseout period.

Country of origin was defined as that country in which the textile or apparel product was wholly assembled; where the most important assembly or manufacturing process occurred; or the last country in which important assembly or manufacturing process occurred. Exceptions were provided to those products cut in the United States, assembled overseas, then returned to the United States; products covered by the U.S.-Israel Free Trade Agreement; and products knit to shape.

The rules applied to goods that entered or were withdrawn from a warehouse in the United States on or after July 1, 1996, except that the rules would not apply until Jan. 1, 1998, for those goods covered by a contract entered into before July 20, 1994.

The bill also authorized the Treasury secretary to publish in the Federal Register the names of individuals and companies outside the United States that had provided false documentation of country of origin, used counterfeit documents, falsely labeled items, or abetted the transshipment of products in a manner that concealed country of origin or evaded quotas.

The president was authorized to publish in the Federal Register, after consulting with the secretaries of Commerce and Treasury and other relevant officials, the names of countries that had failed to make good faith efforts to stop illegal country of origin or transshipment activities.

Dumping

The new GATT continued the practice of allowing all member countries, including the United States, to maintain laws against "dumping," defined as the export of goods into another country when the export price of those goods was less than their price in the domestic market.

Although much of the dumping agreement followed existing U.S. practice, a number of changes were necessary to make U.S. laws conform to the GATT. Among these changes were new standards for minimum dumping margins, requirements that cost calculations be adjusted appropriately for start-up operations and the establishment of a five-year sunset review for anti-dumping orders.

The new GATT standards for determining whether a domestic industry was being injured by dumping were little different from those under existing U.S. law. Each nation's authorities would have to examine factors other than unfairly traded imports that might be injuring a domestic industry. The agreement incorporated the U.S. practice of "cumulating" imports from several foreign countries, rather than just individual countries, in order to prove injury to a domestic industry because of dumping.

Most of the anti-dumping provisions in the GATT implementing bill amended Title VII of the Tariff Act of 1930.

● **Measuring dumping.** Provide that in determining whether a good was being dumped in the United States below normal value, U.S. investigators would measure sales of the good in the exporter's home market against sales in the United States. Under existing law, home market sales were measured against the quantities of the good sold to countries other than the United States.

If the home market sales of the good were less than 5 percent of the aggregate of sales to the United States, they would instead be compared with sales of that good to a country other than the United States. Third-country sales would have to be based on a single country, rather than multiple countries as under existing law.

In calculating the normal value of a foreign-made good, a deduction would be made for indirect taxes imposed on the product or component that had been rebated or not collected.

● **Start-up costs.** Make allowance for a company's unusually high costs in starting up a new product or product facility; such costs could temporarily inflate the home market price of a good, making it appear that ensuing export sales were being made below cost. The Commerce Department, which oversaw anti-dumping regulations, could make adjustments for start-up costs only if a company was using new production facilities or making a new product requiring substantial additional investment, and production levels were limited by technical factors associated with the initial phase of commercial production. Start-up cost adjustments would not be applied to routine model year changes of existing plants or improvements to basic products.

The start-up period was considered ended when a level of commercial production characteristic of the merchandise, producer or industry was reached.

● **Country of origin.** Allow an exception to the usual practice of treating an intermediary country as the country of origin for purposes of anti-dumping investigations when an item was exported to an intermediate country and then re-exported to the United States. The original exporter would be regarded as the country of origin when the producer knew the merchandise was destined for re-exportation; when the merchandise was simply transshipped; when not enough of the good was sold in the intermediate country to make possible the calculation of normal value; or the product was not produced in the intermediate country.

● **De minimus standards.** The dumping margin (i.e., the ratio of the U.S. price of the imported good against the home market value of that good) of exports from each country to the United States had to reach a minimum *(de minimus)* threshold to fall under the provisions of U.S. anti-dumping law. To conform with the standard set in the new GATT, the bill required that the weighted average dumping

margin of any producer or exporter that was less than 2 percent ad valorem be treated as *de minimus*. (The existing U.S. *de minimus* standard was 0.5 percent.)

● **Assisting third countries to fight dumping.** Allow the Commerce Department or the ITC to take anti-dumping actions on behalf of a third country when the petitioning country could prove that imported goods being sold in the United States were being sold for less than fair value and were doing material damage to an industry in the petitioning country. Existing law allowed the USTR to ask other countries to take action against dumping that damaged U.S. exporters, but not to take action on behalf of other governments.

● **Captive production.** Provide standards for situations in which a U.S. company made a product that was then used by the same producer in the manufacture of a distinct product (e.g., raw steel, which was then incorporated into a consumer product by the same manufacturer). For the purposes of anti-dumping investigations, authorities would compare the imports of the foreign version of the original component product rather than those of the value-added "downstream" product.

● **Measuring "negligible" imports.** Treat imports as negligible for anti-dumping purposes if they accounted for less than 3 percent of all such merchandise imported in the most recent 12-month period for which data were available. Exceptions would be made when imports that otherwise would be classified as negligible were included with other countries for which investigations were filed on the same day, and the cumulative imports were more than 7 percent of the total imports of that good. The ITC would terminate investigations if it determined imports were negligible.

● **Industry support.** Require that, before pursuing an anti-dumping investigation, U.S. authorities determine whether there was sufficient support within the domestic industry for such an action.

Industry support was to be measured as sufficient when a petition supporting an anti-dumping investigation was backed by domestic producers or workers who accounted for at least 25 percent of the total production of the domestic product and who accounted for more than 50 percent of the production of the domestic product by that portion of the industry expressing an opinion for or against the petition.

"Industry support" could be expressed by either management or workers within the affected industry.

If a petition did not establish majority support, Commerce would poll the industry or, if there were many producers, use any statistically valid sampling method.

In cases of an industry defined as a "regional industry," support would be established only in that region, not the United States as a whole.

The bill allowed interested parties to comment on the issue of industry support. It added trade associations of producers, exporters or importers and the government of the exporting country to the existing list of interested parties.

Industrial users of the merchandise and consumer groups would be given the opportunity to provide relevant information but would not automatically gain interested-party status.

● **Provisional measures.** Specify that provisional anti-dumping measures would not apply until 60 days after initiation of an investigation. Provisional measures would be limited to four months, except the Commerce Department could extend them to six months if it was requested by exporters representing a significant percentage of the exported product.

● **Terminating penalties.** Require parties seeking revocation of an anti-dumping order or a countervailing duty to show that such termination would not lead to continuance or recurrence of material injury against a domestic industry.

● **Sunset provision.** Require automatic five-year reviews of anti-dumping duty orders, countervailing duties or injury determinations.

Subsidy Restrictions

The new GATT agreement greatly expanded multilateral disciplines on export subsidies and other trade-distorting government

benefits to domestic industries. Under the existing GATT, only 24 nations participated in the agreement to limit trade-distorting subsidies. Under the new GATT, the Subsidies Agreement applied to all member countries. The administration described this expansion as "one of most significant U.S. achievements" in the Uruguay Round negotiations.

The new Subsidies Agreement prohibited export subsidies based on domestic content; required all developing countries (other than least developed) to phase out export subsidies and import substitution subsidies; and applied the WTO dispute resolution mechanism so that a subsidizing country could not unilaterally block adoption of panel reports.

The WTO could take action against a subsidy only when it was provided to specific enterprises, not when it was generally available to numerous producers and individuals.

The agreement set up three categories of subsidies: prohibited "red light" subsidies; GATT-legal "green light" subsidies; and "yellow light" subsidies, which technically were GATT-legal but which could be challenged in WTO dispute resolution proceedings and be subject to domestic countervailing duties.

Member nations could phase out prohibited subsidies that existed on April 15, 1994, within three years of the agreement's going into effect, although the subsidies still would be actionable if they caused adverse trade effects.

Subsidies for scientific research and development were generally permitted but were available only to the point of production of the first non-commercial prototype. Subsidies by governments to their nations' disadvantaged regions were permitted, but those regions had to be clearly designated and contiguous, and the aid had to be available to all industries.

Governments could provide subsidies to industries to assist them in meeting new environmental standards. Those subsidies had to be one-time and non-recurring; limited to 20 percent of the cost of the industrial adaptation; and not cover manufacturing cost savings.

The agreement allowed the United States and other member nations to continue to apply countervailing duties when it was determined that a nation was providing its exporting industries with trade-distorting subsidies.

● **Injury test.** Repeal a provision of U.S. law that excluded some countries from an "injury test" used to determine whether to apply countervailing duties. Under existing law, countervailing duties could be applied to most members of the Subsidies Agreement only if the ITC first found that a domestic industry had been materially injured by subsidized imports. The new GATT required that this "injury test" be applied to all member nations.

● **De minimus standards.** Require U.S. authorities to ignore *de minimus* subsidies, defined as less than 1 percent ad valorem, 2 percent for developing countries and 3 percent for least-developed countries. The developing-countries standard expired in eight years.

● **U.S. actions against illegal subsidies.** Put the Commerce Department in charge of coordinating subsidies enforcement efforts for the U.S. government. If Commerce determined that a GATT-actionable subsidy was in place, it was to inform the USTR, which then could take action under Section 301. If a U.S. industry believed there had been a violation of the green-light standards, it could request that Commerce investigate.

The USTR would determine appropriate retaliatory action under Section 301 if a foreign country failed to observe a recommendation by the WTO Subsidies Committee within six months of its issuance.

● **Congressional oversight.** Require that the USTR promptly inform the Ways and Means, Finance and other appropriate committees on WTO Subsidies Committee actions. The USTR and the Commerce Department were required to report to Congress by Feb. 1 every year beginning in 1996 on subsidy practices of major U.S. trading partners and USTR monitoring and enforcement activities.

The WTO Subsidies Committee would review provisions of the Subsidies Agreement after five years to determine whether to extend the agreement. Even if this action was taken, the imple-

menting bill contained a five-year sunset provision requiring Congress to pass a law extending U.S. participation under the Subsidies Agreement.

Agriculture

The new agreement brought agricultural production and export subsidies under GATT disciplines for the first time, a leading goal of the United States during the Uruguay Round negotiations. Although the United States had long employed a wide variety of agricultural subsidies and import restrictions of its own, many other countries maintained even higher barriers against the import of U.S. farm products.

Developed countries belonging to the WTO would be required to reduce tariffs on agricultural goods by 36 percent over six years. Developing countries had to cut tariffs by 24 percent over a 10-year period. Least-developed countries would not be required to make reductions.

Developed nations would have to reduce the amount of products subject to export subsidies by 21 percent from average levels in 1986-1990 and to reduce budgetary outlays for export subsidies by 36 percent from those years' average. The figures were 14 percent and 24 percent respectively for developing countries.

The agreement required the conversion of all non-tariff trade barriers, including import quotas, variable duties and minimum import prices, to tariff equivalents, a process known as "tariffication." Those items also would be subject to the overall tariff cuts.

The new GATT allowed an importing country to apply a "special safeguard" during at least the six-year implementing period to any product subject to tariffication in order to protect domestic producers from import surges or price declines.

The bill established a category of "green box" farm subsidies, allowable under the new GATT, most of which were used in the United States. These included government spending for agricultural research, inspection, marketing, promotion, extension and advisory services; public warehousing for food security purposes; domestic food aid; income "safety nets" for farmers; crop insurance/disaster relief; environmental and conservation programs and regional assistance programs.

Clinton administration officials said that as a result of spending reductions and other actions already put in place by the 1985 and 1990 farm bills and various budget measures, the United States would not need to make any additional farm support reductions to meet its GATT commitments.

A second round of multilateral agriculture negotiations was scheduled to ensue five years after the new GATT went into force.

● **Presidential authority.** Provide the president with broad authority to take action as necessary to ensure that imports under tariff-rate quotas did not disrupt orderly marketing of commodities in the United States.

Under certain circumstances, such as natural disaster, disease or major domestic marketing disruption, when a product was not available to U.S. consumers at a reasonable price, the president could temporarily increase the quantity of imports subject to regular import duties rather than raise over-quota rates.

The bill authorized the president to implement special agricultural product safeguard provisions of the GATT by publishing in the Federal Register the list of safeguarded goods and the level of imports that would trigger the safeguards.

● **Export Enhancement Program.** Reauthorize the Export Enhancement Program, which was scheduled to expire in 1995, until 2001, while committing to adjust the program to meet U.S. obligations under GATT. The bill ended the existing requirement that the program be used only to discourage unfair trade practices, because other countries did not impose a similar restriction on their export programs.

● **Market Promotion Program.** Drop the existing requirement that Market Promotion Program funding be directed against unfair practices of U.S. trading partners, because other countries did not

place such limitations on their export programs.

● **Section 22.** Amend Section 22 of the Agriculture Adjustment Act to bar imposition of quantitative import restrictions or fees on WTO members. The change was waived until Sept. 11, 1995, to allow imposition of fees on Canadian wheat exports to the United States under a one-year Memo of Understanding between the two nations. The president could continue to take Section 22 actions against non-WTO members.

● **Dairy.** Extend the Dairy Export Incentive Program, authorized through 1995, to 2001.

It authorized, rather than mandated as under existing law, that the secretary of Agriculture sell for export certain minimum levels of dairy products from government-owned stocks.

● **Tobacco.** Authorize the president to proclaim tariff increases on certain tobacco products of up to 350 percent ad valorem over rates in effect on Jan. 1, 1975. The language effectively replaced a provision of the 1993 budget-reconciliation bill that placed a 75 percent domestic tobacco content requirement on U.S. cigarettes. Should the president proclaim a tariff-rate quota for these products, the domestic content requirement — which had been ruled in violation of world trade rules by a GATT panel — would expire at the end of 1994.

● **Meat imports.** Repeal the Meat Import Act of 1979 and replace quantitative limitations on meat imports with tariff-rate quotas.

● **Food aid.** Reaffirm the U.S. commitment to provide food aid to developing and least-developed nations.

● **Additional funding.** Authorize the federal government to spend additional funds from the Commodity Credit Corporation (CCC) for export promotion and development, credit financing and development of alternative uses for agricultural products. These additional funds would be credited to the CCC in amounts equaling the fiscal 1995 pay-as-you-go savings or the five-year PAYGO savings resulting from the enactment of the Crop Insurance Reform Act of 1994.

● **Sanitary and phytosanitary standards.** Require the standards information center in the Department of Commerce to make information available to the public on federal and subfederal sanitary and phytosanitary standards and methodology and participation in international and regional systems and organizations.

The new GATT agreement explicitly acknowledged that nations and their subgovernments had a legitimate need to maintain sanitary and phytosanitary standards for farm imports. But it sought to ensure that such standards were based on actual risk and were not disguised trade barriers. It suggested that each nation harmonize its laws with international standards but did not bar higher standards as long as they had a scientific basis.

Administration officials insisted that because most U.S. sanitary and phytosanitary standards were science-based, the new GATT would leave them safe from challenge.

The bill also barred federal agencies from certifying that a sanitary measure of an exporting country was equivalent to the U.S. standard unless it provided at least the same sanitary protection as the comparable U.S. measure. It required the president to authorize an agency to issue an annual public report on international sanitary standard-setting activities.

Intellectual Property

The new agreement brought intellectual property rights under the protections of the GATT system for the first time. It required member countries to observe provisions of the Paris Convention for the Protection of Intellectual Property of 1967 and the Berne Convention for the Protection of Literary and Artistic Works of 1971.

The agreement classified all types of computer programs as "literary works" under the Berne convention, and it required copyright protection for compilations of data and other materials that were original by reason of their selection or arrangement.

The agreement also required member nations to provide producers of computer programs with exclusive rental rights to their properties. The same protection was to be provided for cinema works, but only in

instances when rentals had led to widespread copying.

The agreement provided a 50-year term of protection for sound recordings and gave sound recording producers the right to authorize or prohibit reproduction or rental of their works.

It provided a 10-year period of protection for semiconductor integrated circuit layout designs, a period consistent with that provided under the federal Semiconductor Chip Protection Act.

The agreement also required members to provide for seizures of counterfeit and pirated goods at the border and to institute criminal penalties for willful copyright piracy and trademark counterfeiting on a commercial scale.

● **Patents.** Set the term of patent protection at 20 years from the date on which the patent application was filed. Existing law set the period as 17 years from date on which the patent was granted.

The extension from 17 to 20 years could benefit applicants for patents on conventional items that were routinely approved by the U.S. Patent Office. However, the change in the start of the term — from "time of patent approval" as under existing law to "time of filing" — was highly worrisome to patent applicants from cutting-edge, science-based industries such as microbiology. They said their complicated patent applications often took 10 or more years to be approved. With the new provision starting the patent clock at the time of application, these researchers could find their period of effective patent protection greatly truncated.

The bill provided for an extension of patent protection for up to five years when a patent process had been delayed by interventions by competing patent applicants or other parties, or when an adverse patent decision had been overruled on appeal or by a federal court.

The bill sought to aid U.S. inventors in establishing priority on inventions by allowing them to file provisional applications for a $150 fee. Applicants then would have up to 12 months to file formal applications, the period of which would not be included in calculation of the patent term.

● **Copyrights.** Create new federal civil and criminal penalties for bootlegging of sound recordings of live performances "knowingly and for purposes of commercial advantage or private gain."

It provided for the restoration of copyright protection to foreign works that had fallen into public domain in the United States but were not in the public domain in their country of origin. This would apply even to works that, for technical reasons, never obtained copyright protection in the United States. Protection would exist for the remainder of the term that otherwise would have been granted.

The bill revoked the sunset provision of Computer Software Rental Amendments Act of 1990, thus making computer software rental rights permanent.

● **Trademarks.** Declare that a trademark be considered abandoned after non-use of three years; under existing law, the period of non-use was two years.

The bill barred the registration of trademarks for wines or spirits containing misleading geographical indications (such as "champagne" or "burgundy") if they were first used after the new GATT had been in effect for one year. Existing trademarks of this kind would be unaffected.

Generalized System of Preferences

● **Nine-month extension.** Renew the Generalized System of Preferences (GSP), which provided trade benefits and concessions to developing countries, until July 31, 1995, and provide for refunds on duties paid between Sept. 30, 1994, and the date of enactment of the bill. The law authorizing the GSP had expired Sept. 30, 1994.

Customs Fees

● **Merchandise processing fees.** Increase Customs Service merchandise processing fees from 0.17 percent to 0.21 percent ad valorem and increase the maximum filing fee for a formal entry from $400 to $485 and the minimum fee from $21 to $25, effective Jan. 1, 1995.

Financing Provisions

- **Indian casino profits.** Change the rules for Indian tribes, which were allowed under existing law to make taxable distributions to their members of proceeds from tribe-run or tribe-licensed gambling activities. The bill required tribes to deduct and withhold from such payments a tax in an amount equal to such payment's proportionate share of the individual's annualized tax. Effective Dec. 31, 1994. (Projected five-year revenue increase: $71 million.)

- **Withholding on certain federal payments.** Require that recipients of taxable federal payments for Social Security, crop disaster relief, farm program loans and other payments specified by the secretary of the Treasury be given the option of having federal income taxes withheld from the payments. A taxpayer could request withholding rates of 7 percent, 15 percent, 28 percent or 31 percent. Recipients of unemployment benefit recipients were allowed to have federal income taxes withheld at a 15 percent rate. States could, but were not required to, allow recipients to have state and local income taxes withheld. Effective for payments made after Dec. 31, 1996. (Projected five-year revenue increase: $221 million for federal payments withholding; $156 million for unemployment compensation.)

- **Estimated taxes.** Require taxpayers to include subpart F income and Section 936 intangible property income when calculating their quarterly estimated tax payments. The bill provided "safe harbor" protections from penalties for underpayment of estimated tax on subpart F or Section 936 income if those amounts equaled at least 115 percent of such income for the relevant prior year for corporations, and 100 percent of such payments for individual taxpayers. Effective after Dec. 31, 1994. (Projected five-year revenue increase: $1.4 billion.)

- **Federal excise taxes.** Move due dates for August and September semimonthly payments of federal excise taxes from October to Sept. 29, thus enabling such payments to be recorded in the earlier fiscal year. Effective Jan. 1, 1995, except for commercial air passenger and freight excise taxes, for which the provision was effective Jan. 1, 1997. (Projected five-year revenue increase: $1.2 billion.)

- **Interest on corporate tax overpayments.** Reduce the interest rate that the Internal Revenue Service paid to corporations on tax overpayments in excess of $10,000. The new interest formula was the federal short-term rate plus one-half of a percentage point, down from the existing formula of the federal short-term rate plus 2 percentage points. Effective Dec. 31, 1994. (Projected five-year revenue increase: $800 million.)

- **Earned-income tax credit.** Bar non-resident aliens from claiming the earned-income tax credit on their annual tax returns, unless they were married and agreed to subject all of their income to U.S. income tax, regardless of the country in which it was earned. Net revenues from this provision were reduced somewhat by an amendment that made U.S. military personnel stationed overseas eligible for the earned-income tax credit. Effective Dec. 31, 1994. (Projected five-year revenue increase: $299 million.)

   The bill also removed income received for work done while an inmate in a penal institution from definition of earned income. Effective Dec. 31, 1993. (Projected five-year revenue increase: $14 million.)

- **Excess pension assets.** Extend for five years, until Dec. 31, 2000, a provision in existing law that allowed employers to transfer excess taxable pension plan assets to cover non-taxable contributions to a retiree health benefit plan established under section 401(h) rules. The provision reduced the amount of assets eligible to be transferred by a percentage equal to the amount of money previously set aside for future retiree health liabilities divided by the present value of all future retiree health liabilities. (Projected five-year revenue increase: $399 million.)

- **Rounding rules on COLAs.** Establish new rounding rules for cost of living adjustments (COLAs) to the dollar limit for maximum benefits under defined benefit pension plans. For such plans, COLA increases to the benefit ceiling would be made in increments of $5,000; limits on elective deferrals under a qualified cash or deferred arrangement would be rounded to increments of $500; and the minimum compensation limit for simplified employee pension participation would be rounded to increments of $50. Effective Dec. 31, 1994. (Projected five-year revenue increase: $395 million.)

- **Tax on Social Security benefits to non-residents.** Increase to 85 percent from 50 percent the amount of Social Security or railroad retirement benefits that non-resident aliens were required to include as gross income in determining their taxes. Effective Dec. 31, 1994. (Projected five-year revenue increase: $303 million.)

- **Partnership distribution of marketable securities.** Require that when a business partner exchanged appreciated partnership assets for an increased share in the partnership's marketable securities, that those securities be treated as cash for tax purposes. This was aimed at closing a loophole that allowed partners to make such potentially lucrative exchanges tax-free. Generally effective as of date of enactment. (Projected five-year revenue increase: $211 million.)

- **Taxpayer identification number at birth.** Require taxpayers to obtain taxpayer identification numbers (TINs) for any children, including newborns, whom the taxpayers claimed as dependents for tax exemption purposes. Existing law required TINs for all children older than age 1. This was aimed at reducing fraudulent claiming of dependents. To be phased into effect beginning with tax year 1995. (Projected five-year revenue increase: $94 million.)

- **IRS user fees.** Extend for five years, until Sept. 30, 2000, of user fees charged by the IRS for written responses to questions by individuals, corporations and organizations relating to their tax status or the effects of particular transactions on tax liability. (Projected five-year revenue increase: $124 million.)

- **Underpayment penalty for tax shelter participants.** Require individual taxpayers to include tax shelter income in calculating whether their total income tax was substantially understated, even if there was substantial legal authority for the tax shelter item and the taxpayer reasonably believed that the claimed treatment was proper. Effective date of enactment of the implementing bill. (Projected five-year revenue increase: $95 million.)

- **Savings bond interest rates.** Repeal a requirement that Series E savings bonds pay investment yields of at least 4 percent per year, allowing the Treasury secretary to set market-rate yields. (Projected five-year revenue increase: $122 million.)

- **'Pioneer Preferences.'** Require the recipients of "pioneer" licenses to pay the higher of $400 million plus interest or 85 percent of the average per capita bids for comparable PCS licenses. (Expected to raise at least $534 million.) ∎

Congress Lets Renewal Of China MFN Stand

While acknowledging that China had not made progress in all the areas that he had specified were necessary, President Clinton nonetheless renewed China's most-favored-nation (MFN) status, arguing that remaining engaged in the country was a better policy than cutting off billions of dollars in trade. In announcing his decision May 26, Clinton said it would serve to nurture democracy in China, maintain a strategic relationship with Beijing and, over time, achieve more progress in human rights.

Although the action was not universally supported on Capitol Hill, resistance was not strong enough to pose any threat to Clinton's decision.

The president called for delinking China's progress on human rights from the annual question of whether MFN status should be renewed. In addition, he outlined a new strategy to maintain pressure on Chinese authorities, relying on quieter diplomacy and less brinkmanship. As part of that, Clinton announced modest sanctions that would ban imports of Chinese-made guns and ammunition.

A bipartisan group of lawmakers, which included Democratic leaders in both chambers, favored harsher retaliation against Beijing for what they contended was a continuing failure to make adequate human rights improvements. But their views were not widely shared.

Clinton said that evaluating China's MFN status based on human rights criteria — an annual exercise since the 1989 crackdown on pro-democracy demonstrators in Tiananmen Square — had "reached the end of [its] usefulness." It was a frank acknowledgment that his policy of threatening to withdraw MFN had not worked and that he deemed the economic consequences for both countries to be too severe to carry out the threat.

Several influential Senate moderates, including Democrats Sam Nunn of Georgia and Bill Bradley of New Jersey, declared their support for delinking MFN and human rights.

Background

China gained MFN status with the United States in 1980 as part of an overall trade agreement. MFN status allowed a country to export goods to the United States at the low-tariff levels available to nearly all countries. Under the Jackson-Vanik amendment to the 1974 trade law, which governed U.S. trade relations with communist countries, the president was required to review China's MFN status annually. The decision to renew MFN went through automatically unless Congress voted to reject it. *(1974 Almanac, p. 553)*

Although Congress had never rejected a president's decision to renew China's MFN status, legislators had tried to pass bills restricting future extensions. In 1990, the House passed such legislation, but the Senate did not. Twice in 1992, Congress cleared similar bills and sent them to President George Bush, who vetoed them. While the House voted to override the vetoes, the Senate did not. On three separate occasions, the House also narrowly supported a separate bill to revoke China's MFN status; the Senate did not act on those measures, however, and the votes were seen as largely symbolic. *(1992 Almanac, p. 157; 1991 Almanac, p. 121; 1990 Almanac, p. 764)*

The three-year congressional effort to restrict trade with China until that country improved its human rights record had come to a halt in 1993 after Clinton announced that his administration would insist that China make such reforms.

Clinton issued an executive order, saying he would not renew MFN unless China complied with two mandatory conditions and made "overall significant progress" in five human rights areas. *(1993 Almanac, p. 184)*

In reaching his decision in 1994, Clinton said China had achieved the two mandatory conditions. Specifically, he said Beijing had resolved all outstanding emigration cases. And he said China had made progress in allowing U.S. inspections of prison labor factories and in taking steps to implement a bilateral agreement to prevent the export of goods made with prison labor to the United States. But Clinton acknowledged that China had not made the required progress in other human rights areas.

Legislative Action

A small group of Democratic legislators broke with Clinton over China policy June 16, introducing legislation that would have punished Beijing with trade sanctions for failure to improve its treatment of dissidents and for other human rights shortcomings.

The sanctions bill was introduced by Senate Majority Leader George J. Mitchell, D-Maine, House Majority Leader Richard A. Gephardt, D-Mo., House Majority Whip David E. Bonior, D-Mich., and Rep. Nancy Pelosi, D-Calif. This group had been at the forefront of congressional efforts to use trade sanctions as a weapon to force liberalization in China ever since the Tiananmen Square massacre.

In order to punish the Beijing government and spare China's growing free enterprise sector as much as possible, the measure (HR 4590) provided for higher tariffs on products made by the Chinese army and defense trading companies, as well as certain goods made by state-owned enterprises. Mitchell said the bill would affect about $5 billion in Chinese exports to the United States, which totaled $31 billion in 1993. Over the same period, U.S. exports to China totaled $8 billion. "Obviously, China needs our market more than we need theirs," Mitchell said.

On July 28, the House Ways and Means Committee voted by voice to send the bill to the floor with the recommendation that it be rejected (H Rept 103-640, Part 1).

In a series of votes Aug. 9, the House turned aside attempts to punish China and reaffirmed Clinton's decision to renew MFN status. Lawmakers overwhelmingly defeated a measure (H J Res 373) that would have revoked MFN status for all Chinese products. Bill sponsor Gerald B. H. Solomon, R-N.Y., argued that human rights conditions in China had gotten worse over the previous year and that trading with China cost U.S. jobs because of a $23.6 billion trade deficit. But the House rejected the measure, 75-356. *(Vote 381, p. 114-H)*

Lawmakers then considered the Mitchell-Pelosi bill under a so-called king-of-the-hill procedure, according to which the last proposal adopted prevailed. A substitute sponsored by Lee H. Hamilton, D-Ind., chairman of the Foreign Affairs Committee, was taken up first. Essentially, Hamilton's substitute codified Clinton's executive order extending China's normal, low-tariff trade status. It was approved, 280-152. *(Vote 382, p. 114-H)*

Pelosi then offered her original language as a substitute to the Hamilton version. Her effort was rejected, 158-270, which left Hamilton's language intact. The amended bill then passed by voice vote. *(Vote 383, p. 116-H)*

Gephardt asked Congress not only to send a message to China that the United States would not stand for human rights violations but to "send a message to the working people of America as well: that they should not have to compete with prison labor."

Hamilton argued that the United States should avoid a policy of confrontation. "Do we promote our security, economic and human rights interests in China through engagement or through confrontation?" he asked his colleagues.

With the House having rejected the effort to relink trade and human rights policy toward China, Senate sponsors had no reason to take further action on the bill. ∎

Defense Export Measure Clears

Congress cleared a bill authorizing the Export-Import Bank, which made loans to foreign governments and others who purchased U.S. goods, to provide financing for exports of non-lethal defense goods and services. To qualify, the exports had to be intended primarily for civilian use. The measure was designed to increase opportunities for defense manufacturers to change the focus of their production to the commercial marketplace. President Clinton signed the bill into law Oct. 31 (HR 4455 — PL 103-428).

Under existing law, the Ex-Im Bank could finance defense goods or services only if they were to be used solely for civilian purposes or primarily for anti-narcotics activities. Bill sponsor Doug Bereuter, R-Neb., said, for example, that radar for air-traffic control did not qualify for Ex-Im financing if it was to be used for an air-traffic control system that served both civilian and military aircraft.

The bill began in the House Banking Subcommittee on International Development, which approved it 18-0 on June 24. The subcommittee added an amendment by Joseph P. Kennedy II, D-Mass., aimed at encouraging exports of environmentally beneficial goods and services.

The full committee approved the bill by voice vote June 29, after amending it to require that the Ex-Im Bank report transactions allowed by the bill to the House and Senate Banking and Appropriations committees 15 days in advance (H Rept 103-681). The House passed the bill by voice vote under suspension of the rules Aug. 8.

The Senate passed the bill by voice vote Oct. 5 after modifying the environmental provisions. The House agreed Oct. 7 to the Senate amendment, clearing the bill for the president. ∎

Hill Reauthorizes OPIC

Congress agreed to reauthorize the Overseas Private Investment Corporation (OPIC), which provided insurance, loans and loan guarantees to assist U.S. businesses investing abroad. The agency was designed to promote economic progress in developing countries, particularly those changing to market-oriented economies. OPIC was a self-financing agency, which paid for its expenses through fees and insurance premiums. Its previous reauthorization, enacted in 1992, expired Sept. 30. (1992 Almanac, p. 165)

The House cleared the bill Oct. 7, and President Clinton signed it Oct. 22 (HR 4950 — PL 103-392).

The House first passed HR 4950 by voice vote Sept. 19. The Foreign Affairs Committee had approved the measure (H Rept 103-726) by voice vote Sept. 13. The bill provided for a three-year reauthorization and proposed a number of changes to the agency's operations, including an extension of OPIC programs to Northern Ireland and a special emphasis on the promotion of exports based on environmental technologies. The bill included the text of a separate measure (HR 3813), passed by the House on April 19, that was designed to help preserve the U.S. edge in exporting technologies used to protect the environment.

The Senate bill (S 2438), approved by the Foreign Relations Committee on a voice vote Sept. 22, provided for a routine one-year reauthorization. The Senate passed HR 4950 by voice vote Sept. 30 after substituting the text of its own bill.

House and Senate conferees met and agreed on a compromise two-year reauthorization (H Rept 103-834). The final bill included the provisions aimed at promoting exports of environmental technologies and products. It also authorized the Agency for International Development to establish a program of training and technical assistance to countries wishing to improve their protection of intellectual property rights.

The Senate agreed to the conference report Oct. 6 by voice vote, and the House followed suit the next day. ∎

Rivlin, Tigert, Blinder Win Confirmation

The Senate confirmed President Clinton's nominees for three major economic positions in 1994: Alice M. Rivlin as White House budget director, Ricki R. Tigert as head of the Federal Deposit Insurance Corporation, and Alan S. Blinder as a member of the Federal Reserve Board.

Alice M. Rivlin

The Senate on Oct. 7 confirmed Alice M. Rivlin to be President Clinton's budget director, just in time to give Rivlin full title to the job as she waded into the task of preparing the White House's fiscal 1996 budget.

The Senate Governmental Affairs Committee had approved her nomination by voice vote Sept. 30, after an uneventful confirmation hearing Sept. 27 that turned up no opposition to Rivlin's nomination.

Rivlin became Clinton's second budget director, succeeding former Rep. Leon E. Panetta, D-Calif., who had become Clinton's chief of staff in July. Rivlin had served as acting director since then, and her confirmation encountered no opposition except a last-minute Senate "hold," in which she served as a hostage for unrelated concerns over trade legislation. Her confirmation came by voice vote.

With Rivlin in the top job at the Office of Management and Budget (OMB) and Panetta in a key position at the White House, Clinton had two of Washington's most determined "deficit hawks" at his ear as he decided whether to take another major cut at the deficit in fiscal 1996.

Aside from the eight years she spent as Congressional Budget Office (CBO) director in 1975-83, Rivlin's most consistent affiliation had been with the Brookings Institution, the Washington think tank she joined as a research fellow in 1957 and had returned to in various capacities over the years, serving as director of economic studies from 1983 to 1987. She was on leave from Brookings, teaching at Virginia's George Mason University, when she was tapped by Clinton as OMB deputy director in 1992.

Along the way, Rivlin had earned a reputation as a fierce and outspoken deficit hawk. She and Panetta both openly criticized then-candidate Clinton's "Putting People First" campaign document in 1992, insisting it did not go far enough in attacking the deficit. Clinton nonetheless saw in his two critics the credibility he needed to get his economic plans through Congress.

In "Reviving the American Dream," a book published shortly before she was named to the administration, Rivlin

called the deficit "the biggest single impediment to reviving the American economy" and recommended aggressive action to reduce it.

When Clinton huddled with his economic team early in 1993 to put together the deficit-reduction plan they would later take to Congress, Rivlin staked out the most hawkish end of the spectrum, consistently pushing for a bigger package and a lower deficit, according to several administration officials.

In describing her approach to economic matters, Rivlin had written that she was an optimist who believed the nation's economic problems could be solved. She called herself a "fanatical, card-carrying middle-of-the-roader" who preferred pragmatic policies, and a realist who had a bias against "magic wands and painless solutions."

In October, shortly before the watershed midterm elections, a candid, internal memo by Rivlin outlining the administration's options for reducing the deficit touched off a political flap. Republicans got hold of the memo, leaking it to The Washington Post and asserting that it showed that Clinton was considering raising taxes and cutting Social Security. Clinton and congressional Democrats ran from the memo, potentially limiting their own options for cutting the deficit in fiscal 1996.

Ricki R. Tigert

The Senate on Oct. 4 voted overwhelmingly to confirm Washington banking attorney Ricki R. Tigert to head the Federal Deposit Insurance Corporation (FDIC). The vote was 90-7. The Senate Banking Committee had approved the nomination, 16-1, on Feb. 10. *(Vote 317, p. 55-S)*

Lauch Faircloth, R-N.C., was the only senator to vote against Tigert's nomination in committee, citing her acquaintance with President Clinton. He said their relationship posed a potential conflict of interest, noting that the FDIC would be one agency investigating allegations of financial impropriety at the failed Arkansas-based Madison Guaranty Savings and Loan, which was related to the Whitewater controversy. *(Whitewater, p. 108)*

Earlier, Tigert wrote to panel members and promised to recuse herself from any involvement in the FDIC's investigation of Madison.

After the easy committee approval, Republicans held up the nomination for several months. Initially, they sought to pressure Democrats to hold hearings on the Whitewater controversy involving Clinton and his land investments in Arkansas. Later, the delay was attributed to the questions about Tigert's close relationship with the Clintons.

Ultimately, seven Republicans joined with Democrats on a 63-32 vote Oct. 3 to cut off a threatened GOP filibuster on the nomination. The FDIC had been without a permanent chairman since William Taylor died in August 1992. Bankers had voiced concerns that the void at the top had created a big morale problem at the agency, which was the primary federal regulator for about 8,800 state-chartered banks. *(Vote 316, p. 55-S)*

Tigert, a Washington banking lawyer with experience at the Treasury Department and the Federal Reserve, was the first woman to head the FDIC. She took over at a time when the industry Bank Insurance Fund was returning to health after running a $7 billion deficit two years earlier. As of September 1993, the fund had a reserve balance of $10.5 billion.

Alan S. Blinder

The Senate confirmed Alan S. Blinder as a member of the Federal Reserve Board by voice vote June 24. The confirmation followed easy approval by the Senate Banking Committee on May 24 by a 17-0 vote.

Before becoming a Federal Reserve Board member, Blinder was a member of the president's Council of Economic Advisers and had been a Princeton University economics professor. He became the seven-member board's vice chairman, replacing David W. Mullins Jr.

Blinder had been regarded as less concerned about fighting inflation than other Fed members, but he sought to ease such concerns during his confirmation hearing in Senate Banking on May 6. He received a warm reception by the committee.

"Since I have been accused of being 'soft on inflation,' I would like to take a few minutes to clarify my views on the subject," he said in his opening statement to the panel. "First, it is clear that lower inflation is always better than higher inflation — at least until we reach zero 'true' inflation. In a book of mine which has been cited as evidence that I am a 'friend' of inflation, I wrote: Inflation does indeed bring losses of efficiency. It also makes people feel insecure and unhappy. We would no doubt be better off without it."

Blinder, however, did not offer a specific opinion on whether the Fed was correct in raising short-term interest rates several times in the early part of 1994. "The painful truth is that reducing inflation is costly. America paid a very high price — a deep and long recession — to bring inflation down . . . in the early 1980s," Blinder said. "Having paid the price to achieve these gains on the inflation front, it would be sheer folly to squander them now." ∎

Chapter 3

GOVERNMENT/ COMMERCE

Government
'Reinventing' Government 143
Federal Procurement Overhaul. 144
    Provisions. 146
Federal Worker Buyouts 147
Unfunded Federal Mandates. 150
Other Federal Workers Legislation 152
Other Government Operations Bills. 154
Disaster Legislation 155
Federal Land Payments. 156
Other Government-Related Legislation 156

Transportation
Maritime Reuthorization. 158
Fishermen's Protection Act 160
Coast Guard Reauthorization 161
    Omnibus Maritime Bill 162
Maritime Commission. 164
Maritime Heritage Program. 164
National Highway System 165
    Earthquake-Damaged Bridges 167
FAA Reauthorization. 168

Trucking Deregulation 170
Other Transportation Legislation 171
Commerce
Bankruptcy Code Overhaul. 175
    Provisions. 176
Product Liability 178
    Legislative History. 179
Toy Safety 179
Small-Plane Liability. 180
FTC Reauthorization. 181
Baseball Antitrust 182
Insurance Antitrust 183
Patent Bills. 184
Small Business Administration Reauthorization. 185
Other Small-Business Legislation. 186
Aid to Depressed Regions. 187
Other Commerce-Related Legislation 189
Agriculture
Protection for New Plant Varieties. 190
Agriculture Department Reorganization 191
Crop Insurance Overhaul. 194
Other Agriculture-Related Legislation 197

GOVERNMENT REORGANIZATION

'Reinventing' Government Advances in Steps

Congress passes more than 30 bills implementing recommendations included in the plan

In 1993, President Clinton and Vice President Al Gore issued a call to Congress to help "reinvent" the federal government. The goal was to use the recommendations of a 1993 National Performance Review, spearheaded by Gore, to make the government more efficient and more responsive to the public. Roughly half the changes could be achieved by executive order, though Congress had to agree to most of them. *(1993 Almanac, p. 191)*

Rather than trying to win support for an omnibus reinventing-government bill, lawmakers and the administration took a piecemeal approach with a series of bills addressing various elements of the plan. By the end of the 1994 session, Congress had passed more than 30 bills containing recommendations from Gore's report.

The most significant in dollar terms was an administration plan to reduce the federal work force by 252,000 over six years, saving an estimated $32.5 billion. Congress cleared a bill requiring the reductions and providing cash incentives for employees to resign. Congress also cleared bills to overhaul government procurement and streamline the Agriculture Department. Other bills included measures to rework the federal aid programs for elementary and secondary schools, require audited financial reports from federal agencies, modernize the customs service, and end the subsidies for wool, mohair and honey producers. Altogether, Congress put into law more than one-fourth of the 300 Gore recommendations that required legislation. *(Elementary and secondary education, p. 383; customs, 1993 Almanac, p. 137; wool, mohair, honey, 1993 Almanac, p. 546)*

The administration had put forward one sweeping package of government streamlining proposals in 1993, but it died in the Senate for lack of interest; however, several of its elements were revived in other bills. Other bills with reinventing-government elements that foundered late in the session included proposals to allow the National Park Service to raise fees to pay for park maintenance and to revise maritime subsidies and regulations.

The following are the key bills that Congress enacted or considered:

● **Procurement overhaul.** The procurement bill (S 1587 — PL 103-355), cleared Sept. 22, was designed to streamline federal purchasing and encourage agencies to buy more items in routine commercial transactions, rather than conducting elaborate negotiations to secure items designed to meet unique government specifications. Among other things, the measure exempted from several procurement laws any federal contract worth less than $100,000 and made it easier for a stock clerk to buy "off the shelf" goods, such as pens and notepads. *(Procurement overhaul, p. 144)*

● **Federal employee buyouts.** Congress cleared a bill (HR 3345 — PL 103-226) March 24 that allowed federal agencies to offer cash buyouts of up to $25,000 to targeted workers who voluntarily resigned. The aim was to help agencies prune excess layers of middle management through voluntary retirements rather than layoffs. *(Buyouts, p. 147)*

● **Agriculture Department reorganization.** On Oct. 4, Congress cleared a bill (HR 4217 — PL 103-354) that largely followed the outlines of an administration plan to overhaul the Agriculture Department, long criticized as one of Washington's most overgrown bureaucracies. The bill wrote into law the administration's goal of cutting 7,500 Agriculture Department jobs by 1999, and it created a Consolidated Farm Service Agency to provide "one-stop shopping" for farmers who previously had to go to separate offices to participate in farm subsidy, farm loan and crop insurance programs. *(Agriculture reorganization, p. 191)*

● **HR 3400.** What appeared to be the chief piece of reinventing government legislation in the first session (HR 3400) fell by the wayside in 1994. The House had passed the wide-ranging bill by a vote of 429-1 on Nov. 22, 1993. Most of the bill's savings were to be achieved through reducing the work force, although it contained a variety of other proposals to streamline government. *(1993 Almanac, p. 140)*

On March 23, 1994, the Senate Governmental Affairs Committee gave voice vote approval to those sections of HR 3400 that dealt with financial and personnel management. But no other Senate committee took action, and the bill died at the end of the Congress.

However, a number of the provisions of HR 3400, including the work force reduction, were enacted as part of other bills. Provisions rescinding, or cutting, $2.6 billion in previously appropriated funds — which the House had passed as part of HR 3400 — were attached to a supplemental appropriations bill (HR 3759 — PL 103-211) to pay for the California earthquake. *(Emergency supplemental, p. 548)*

When no other Senate panel with jurisdiction over HR 3400 took action, the Governmental Affairs Committee reported its provisions in a scaled-down bill (S 2170 — S Rept 103-281). The Senate passed the bill by voice vote Sept. 28, the House cleared it Oct. 4, and Clinton signed it Oct. 13 (PL 103-356).

The central feature of the bill was a requirement that 24 federal agencies submit audited financial statements every year, beginning in March 1997. Under existing law, 10 agencies were preparing such statements on a pilot basis.

The bill also limited automatic cost of living raises for members of Congress and other top federal officials to the amount given rank-and-file federal workers. It allowed the White House Office of Management and Budget to recommend consolidation or elimination of any other report that federal agencies made to Congress.

To overcome objections from various quarters, Governmental Affairs Committee Chairman John Glenn, D-Ohio, dropped more than half the items in S 2170 before bringing it to the Senate floor. ■

Procurement Bill Simplifies Buying

In a rare display of bipartisanship, the Senate on Sept. 22 cleared legislation to streamline federal purchasing, with the aim of speeding the acquisition process and saving the government money.

The bill, which President Clinton signed Oct. 13 (S 1587 — PL 103-355), was a key element in the administration's "reinventing government" initiative spearheaded by Vice President Al Gore.

The measure encouraged federal agencies to buy more goods off the shelf in routine commercial transactions, rather than conducting elaborate negotiations to secure items designed to meet unique government specifications.

It also exempted commercial purchases and the purchase of most goods and services costing less than $100,000 from many of the complex procedural requirements that typically delayed and boosted the price of federal purchases. Some of those rules had been designed to head off waste, fraud and abuse; others were intended to promote social policies, such as the development of small and minority-owned companies.

The core argument for revising acquisition laws was that the cumulative impact of these requirements made the purchasing process unduly rigid, complex, expensive and slow. But the large number of interests with a stake in the existing system made the effort to simplify it a complex one.

The final version of S 1587 was the upshot of four years of work, with nearly half that time focused on bipartisan negotiations among members and staff of the government operations, Armed Services and Small Business committees of both chambers.

Ultimately, the legislative effort succeeded because some of the most contentious proposals were dropped. For instance, contrary to the recommendations of both a 1990 Pentagon advisory panel and Gore's proposal for streamlining government, the bill did not exempt contracts worth less than $100,000 from legislation that required payment of "locally prevailing wages" on federally funded projects. The Davis-Bacon Act of 1931 applied that rule to construction projects worth at least $2,000. The Service Contract Act of 1965 applied it to contracts for maintenance and other blue-collar services worth at least $2,500.

Republicans had long contended that the practical effect of these laws was to inflate wages. But organized labor defended them zealously, and after besting the unions in late 1993 in the fight for the North American Free Trade Agreement, the administration backed away from challenging Davis-Bacon. (NAFTA, 1993 Almanac, p. 171)

Similarly, liberals opposed to foreign arms sales quashed the Pentagon panel's recommendation to make U.S.-built weapons more attractive to foreign governments by repealing a law that required a surcharge on overseas arms sales to recoup part of the cost of developing the weapons.

BOXSCORE

Federal Procurement Overhaul — S1587 (HR 2238). The bill streamlined federal purchasing and encouraged agencies to buy more items commercially.

Reports: H Rept 103-545, Parts 1 and 2; S Repts 103-258, 103-259; conference report H Rept 103-712.

KEY ACTION

June 8 — Senate passed S 1587 by voice vote.

June 27 — House passed S 1587 by voice vote after substituting revised text of HR 2238.

Aug. 23 — Senate adopted the conference report by voice vote.

Sept. 20 — House adopted conference report, 425-0, with technical changes.

Sept. 22 — Senate cleared bill by voice vote.

Oct. 13 — President signed the bill — PL 103-355.

Background

The drive to streamline government purchasing got rolling in earnest in 1990, when Congress included in the annual defense authorization bill a provision sponsored by Sen. Jeff Bingaman, D-N.M., requiring the Pentagon to set up a blue-ribbon panel to recommend changes in existing procurement laws. Named for the section of legislation that established it, the so-called Section 800 panel issued an 1,800-page report in January 1993 that recommended amending or repealing nearly 300 laws. The report called for greater reliance on commercial products and simplified contracting methods for small and commercial purchases. (1990 Almanac, p. 671)

Those themes were echoed in the report issued in September 1993 by Gore's reinventing government task force. They also became the core elements of the agenda pursued by the House and Senate committees that began working on S 1587 and various counterpart bills in late 1993. (1993 Almanac, p. 191)

In addition to the high visibility that Clinton and Gore gave the issue, Defense Secretary William J. Perry, whose agency accounted for three-quarters of the federal government's $200 billion annual procurement budget, made procurement streamlining one of his top priorities. He maintained that a revamped purchasing system would give the Pentagon easier access to cutting-edge technology being developed in the marketplace. And he warned that projected Pentagon budgets would not cover the significant increase in weapons procurement slated to begin in fiscal 1997 unless the department used more businesslike acquisition methods and financial management systems to stretch its purchasing dollars.

For the most part, the changes embodied in S 1587 did not alter the tightly regulated process by which the Pentagon bought major weapons systems for which there were no commercial counterparts. But the changes were still expected to substantially reduce Pentagon overhead costs. That was because while the commercial purchases affected by the simplified procedures made up only a small fraction of the Pentagon's procurement budget, they accounted for the vast bulk of the contracts that were written.

In a related move, Perry signed a potentially far-reaching order June 29 intended to slash the number of purchases for which the Pentagon required the supplier to meet highly detailed and unique specifications ("mil-specs") regulating not only how an item performed but also how it was manufactured.

"Instead of relying on mil-specs to tell our contractors how to build something," Perry said, "we're going to tell them what we want it to do and then let them build it."

Perry predicted that the shift would save billions of dollars annually. And, as with the streamlined procurement rules, Perry argued that eliminating the unique military specifications would allow the Pentagon to do business with a broader

range of high-tech companies. Many such companies were loath to deal with federal purchasing rules they deemed too rigid, too complicated and too expensive.

Perry conceded that unique specifications made sense when Pentagon-sponsored research was at the cutting edge of technology. "But in the fields of technology most important to the Defense Department today — semiconductors, computers, software, telecommunications — the technical leadership is in industry," Perry said.

1993 Action

Congress got a start on procurement reform legislation in 1993. The House Government Operations Committee gave voice vote approval July 28 to a bill (HR 2238 — H Rept 103-545, Part 1) sponsored by Chairman John Conyers Jr., D-Mich. In the Senate, Governmental Affairs Committee Chairman John Glenn, D-Ohio, introduced a companion bill (S 1587), but the committee did not act on it in 1993. *(1993 Almanac, p. 197)*

Senate Committee

In the Senate, two committees — Governmental Affairs and Armed Services — approved S 1587 (S Rept 103-258; S Rept 103-259) in quick succession April 26.

The Governmental Affairs Committee approved a substitute amendment for S 1587 by voice vote after agreeing — also by voice vote — to drop provisions that would have exempted some contracts from laws requiring federal officials to give preference to goods shipped in U.S.-registered ships. The Armed Services panel approved the amended bill, 22-0.

Both versions of the bill:

● Authorized simplified procedures and waived many procurement-related laws for any contract worth less than $100,000. Under existing law, the threshold for such simplified purchases was $25,000.

● Authorized simplified contracts and waived certain procurement laws for contracts to buy commercial items on commercial terms.

● Expanded the definition of a "commercial" item to include products on the cutting edge of technology that had not yet been widely sold but were intended for the commercial market.

● Allowed federal agencies to make purchases of less than $2,500 virtually without restriction.

● Required federal agencies to participate in a publicly accessible computer network over which contract bids could be solicited and received electronically. Clinton already had ordered all federal purchasing agencies to participate in such a computer network. Nearly 250 Pentagon offices, which accounted for 80 percent of small defense purchases, were slated to be on-line within two years.

● Eliminated in many cases the "flowdown" rule, by which federal legal obligations cascaded down through an entire network of subcontractors, emcompassing even suppliers with only a minuscule share of the federal contract.

In language not contained in the companion bill that was moving through the House, the committee measure authorized the Pentagon to manage six acquisition projects as "pilot programs" to test more far-reaching waivers of procurement laws that otherwise would be left intact by the pending bills.

The Senate bill also included provisions to waive, in some cases, procurement laws intended to steer more federal contracts toward small and minority-owned businesses. Similar provisions were dropped from HR 2238 at the insistence of the House Small Business Committee.

Senate Floor

The Senate passed S 1587 by voice vote June 8.

The bill had emerged from months of bipartisan deliberations among members and staff of the Governmental Affairs, Armed Services and Small Business committees. Stressing the need for greater efficiency in a time of budgetary constraint, Glenn said the bill reflected "a fine balance of the many interests affected by our procurement system."

Although they did not try to alter S 1587 significantly on the Senate floor, advocates of the politically potent small-business community emphasized that they would try to shift that balance as the bill moved through the legislative process. "The laws that took 20 years to refine to help develop small and [minority-owned and women-owned] businesses need to be kept in place," declared Small Business Committee member Carol Moseley-Braun, D-Ill. In assenting to Senate passage of the bill, she said, she was relying on assurances by Gore that "these concerns will be addressed in conference."

The Senate adopted by voice vote an amendment by Paul Wellstone, D-Minn., exempting small businesses from a provision limiting the reimbursement that companies could demand from the government for legal fees in successful challenges to a contract award.

The bill allowed companies to be reimbursed for attorney's fees and fees for expert witnesses up to a maximum of $75 per hour. Noting that many experienced lawyers charged much higher fees, Wellstone and Small Business Committee Chairman Dale Bumpers, D-Ark., insisted that the limit would unduly handicap a small company that felt it had been wronged but that had to hire outside legal talent.

Other amendments adopted by voice vote included the following:

● By Charles E. Grassley, R-Iowa, requiring that payments to contractors under accelerated procedures be allowed only if the payments were specifically matched with obligations.

● By Grassley, requiring the General Accounting Office to review the independence of legal advice being provided to inspectors general.

● By Kent Conrad, D-N.D., barring contractors from being reimbursed by the government for entertainment costs.

● By Moseley-Braun, setting a non-binding goal of awarding 5 percent of the total value of federal contracts and subcontracts to companies owned by women.

House Committee

The House Armed Services Committee approved a substitute version of the bill by voice vote April 21 (HR 2238 — H Rept 103-545, Part 2). The committee language was offered by Chairman Ronald V. Dellums, D-Calif., and ranking Republican Floyd D. Spence, S.C.

As approved by the committee, HR 2238:

● Authorized greatly simplified procedures and waived many procurement-related laws, for any contract costing less than $100,000. Unlike the Senate bill, the measure allowed the new threshold only if the agency participated in a new publicly accessible computer system.

● Authorized similarly simplified contracting procedures for contracts to buy commercial products and expanded the definition of a commercial item to include cutting-edge products that were not yet widely sold but were intended for the commercial market.

● Allowed federal agencies to make purchases of less than $2,500 virtually without restriction.

Federal Procurement Bill Provisions

Following are the major provisions of S 1587 as enacted:

Small and 'Micro' Purchases

The bill authorized greatly simplified contracts for any purchase that cost less than $100,000, waiving the paperwork and recordkeeping requirements of 15 existing laws.

Once an agency plugged into a publicly accessible Federal Acquisition Computer Network (designated FACNET) over which contract bids could be solicited and received electronically, it was exempt from the existing requirement that any bid solicitation for a contract of more than $25,000 be delayed until 15 days after the agency had published a notice of the impending solicitation in the *Commerce Business Daily.*

The bill also increased from $25,000 to $50,000 the value below which contracts could be awarded by so-called simplified procedures, which involved less administrative work. The threshold for these simplified procedures was raised to $100,000 for any agency that plugged into FACNET. But that limit was to revert to $50,000 after five years unless, by then, the agency had implemented an expanded version of FACNET that allowed a broader range of transactions to be conducted electronically.

Agencies had even greater leeway to make so-called micro purchases that cost less than $2,500. Instead of filling out forms, for example, an office manager could send someone to the nearest discount store for office supplies.

Commercial Items

The bill simplified contracting for commercial purchases along the same lines as those for small purchases. It waived more than 30 laws that required companies to provide the government with data they did not routinely collect for their internal purposes and that were not required by commercial customers.

In addition, the conference report expanded the definition of what constituted a "commercial" item that could be bought under the liberalized procedures. Existing law defined commercial items as products that were sold to the public in substantial quantities at established catalog or market prices. The bill expanded the definition to include: items that had evolved from existing commercial items because of advances in technology; items that had been modified in relatively minor ways to meet government requirements; and services that were sold competitively, in the commercial marketplace, at established catalog prices for specific tasks.

In the case of commercial purchases, federal procurement laws generally were to apply only to prime contractors — not to their subcontractors, the subcontractors' subcontractors and so forth.

In an important boost to commercial purchases, the bill strengthened the exemption of all purchases of commercial items from the requirement that contractors provide federal officials with meticulously detailed cost or pricing data, and that they certify the data to be "current, accurate and complete."

Imposed by the 1962 Truth in Negotiations Act, the data requirement was intended to protect the government against price-gouging when market forces could not be relied on to produce a "fair and reasonable" price — for instance, when a weapons contract was negotiated with a specific company without competition. But critics long had complained that overly cautious procurement bureaucrats routinely applied these rules to situations in which market competition clearly was strong enough to protect the government's interest in getting a fair price.

The bill also permanently increased to $500,000 the level above which the data requirement applied to contracts for all federal agencies.

Small-Business, Minority Issues

Contracts worth more than $2,500 but less than $100,000 were reserved for small businesses, provided that at least two qualified companies bid on the job. Under existing law, this "small-business reserve" applied only to contracts worth less than $25,000.

The bill set a non-binding goal for civilian agencies of awarding to minority-owned companies contracts worth 5 percent of the total value of contracts and subcontracts awarded. To achieve that goal, agencies could use several techniques, such as restricting competition for some contracts to minority-owned firms or awarding a contract to such a company provided that its price was no more than 10 percent higher than the lowest bid. In effect, this provision extended the Defense Department's "Section 1207" program to other agencies.

The bill also established a non-binding goal for all agencies of awarding 5 percent of the total value of contracts and subcontracts to companies owned by women. This provision did not authorize the kind of set-asides and price differentials authorized for minority-owned companies.

The bill made no change in the existing requirement that most companies receiving $500,000 or more as federal contractors or subcontractors prepare "subcontracting plans" stating what percentage of work the company intended to farm out to small and minority-owned businesses. That requirement continued to "flow down" to subcontractors.

Contract Award Protests

The bill changed both the process by which losing bidders were given the bad news and the protest process through which they could appeal. The goal was to reduce the number of protests that were filed by contractors simply to force the government to disgorge information about the basis on which the winning firm was selected. Under the conference report:
• Bidders had to be notified of the result of a competition within three days of a contract award.
• Unsuccessful bidders could request a briefing on the selection within three days of that notification.
• That briefing, to occur within five days of the request, was supposed to report, among other things, the purchasing agency's evaluation of significant weaknesses in that contractor's bid. However, the bill specifically prohibited the briefing from including a point-by-point comparison of that contractor's bid with any other bid.

The bill also authorized the government to pay the fees of consultants and expert witnesses engaged by companies that filed contract award protests. It limited their fees to no more than $150 an hour, but that limit did not apply to consultants or experts retained by small businesses.

Other Provisions

The bill authorized several procurements to be managed on an experimental basis as "pilot programs" to test acquisition management changes beyond the scope of those authorized by the bill.

It also included a provision stipulating that the Pentagon's director of operational testing had the right to communicate directly with the secretary of Defense, without securing the approval of any other official. This reflected the view of Sens. William V. Roth Jr., R-Del., and David Pryor, D-Ark., and others who had contended for years that tests to establish whether a weapon would work under realistic conditions had to be conducted by officials who were not under the thumb of procurement bureaucrats with a vested interest in giving each weapon a passing grade.

- Required federal agencies to participate within five years in a publicly accessible computer system through which most federal contracts would be advertised and awarded.
- Eliminated from some procurement laws the flowdown principle that stipulated that certain federal requirements be met not only by a prime contractor but also by subcontractors.

Complaints From Small Business

Early in the committee's deliberations on the bill, Dellums and Spence agreed to exclude any provisions touching the jurisdiction of any committee other than Armed Services, Governmental Affairs and Small Business. For example, the Armed Services bill made no change in the Davis-Bacon Act that set wage rates on federally funded construction programs.

But in an April 14 letter to Dellums, Small Business Committee Chairman John J. LaFalce, D-N.Y., insisted that the bill be referred to his panel because of several provisions relating to small business.

Armed Services member James Bilbray, D-Nev., who also chaired the Small Business subcommittee on procurement, had been deeply involved in crafting the bill, and he said his subcommittee backed the disputed provisions. But LaFalce, a combative advocate for small business, insisted that he had not been kept abreast of the discussions. "Bilbray had no right to waive the jurisdiction of the Small Business Committee," LaFalce said.

LaFalce was particularly critical of a proposed provision to exempt many contracts from the existing requirement that most companies that received $500,000 or more as a federal contractor or subcontractor had to prepare "subcontracting plans." Those plans outlined how the company intended to farm out some of the work from each contract to small and minority-owned businesses.

Steven Kelman, director of the White House's Office of Federal Procurement Policy, told the House Small Business panel April 28 that many commercial companies simply refused to do business with the federal government rather than have their established business relationships with suppliers disrupted. Eliminating the subcontracting plans for commercial subcontractors, Kelman said, would "increase competition, lower the price the government pays and just introduce a modicum of common sense."

But Guale Duran-Owens of the Minority Business Enterprise Legal Defense and Education Fund contended that mandatory subcontracting plans "seem to be the only inlet into the federal marketplace that small and, especially, disadvantaged businesses have." Duran-Owens found a ready listener in LaFalce. "The administration is off on the wrong track on this one," he told Kelman.

Armed Services also dropped from its version of the bill a provision that would have repealed a law requiring that the government add a surcharge to recoup the cost of developing weapons when it sold them abroad.

House Floor

The House passed S 1587 by voice vote on June 27, after substituting a modified version of its own bill, which had been crafted in negotiations between Armed Services and the Government Operations Committee.

Floor action had been delayed partly because of turf conflicts among committees.

Government Operations and Armed Services were at loggerheads over which panel would have more representatives when House conferees met with their Senate counterparts to craft a final version of the bill. They agreed that they would finesse that dispute by appointing several members who sat on both committees.

Also, at the insistence of the Small Business Committee, the House bill included no provisions dealing with federal acquisition laws designed to foster the growth of small businesses.

Final Action

By voice vote, the Senate approved the conference report on the procurement bill (H Rept 103-712) Aug. 23. The House agreed to the report, 425-0, on Sept. 20. After a round of technical changes, the Senate cleared the bill Sept. 22 by voice vote. *(Vote 425, p. 128-H)*

House and Senate conferees had reached a compromise that raised the threshold for the use of simplified procedures on federal contracts to $50,000 — $100,000 if the agency used a computerized network to solicit and receive the contract.

The bill left intact the existing requirement that most companies receiving $500,000 or more as federal contractors or subcontractors prepare subcontracting plans. In their report, the conferees observed that existing law allowed a commercial firm to meet the requirement for a subcontracting plan by filing one plan to cover all of its operations for a year, instead of filing a separate plan for each federal contract. They implied that such an umbrella plan gave commercial firms sufficient flexibility to avoid disrupting their established supplier relationships. ∎

Worker 'Buyout' Plan Becomes Law

The Senate overcame a filibuster March 24 to clear a bill that allowed federal agencies to offer cash "buyouts" of up to $25,000 to workers who voluntarily resigned. President Clinton signed the measure into law March 30 (PL 103-226).

A key component of Vice President Al Gore's plan for "reinventing government," the buyouts were designed to help agencies prune excess layers of middle management through voluntary retirements rather than layoffs.

The bill (HR 3345) required the federal government to cut 252,000 positions over six years. Agencies were ordered to reduce their personnel on a one-for-one basis for every buyout offer that was accepted. An employee who accepted the voluntary retirement and was rehired by the federal government within five years had to repay the full amount of the buyout.

Although the buyouts had overwhelming bipartisan support in Congress, the bill stalled when it got tangled up in the politics of the unrelated omnibus crime bill (HR 3355).

At dispute was a proposal by Sen. William V. Roth Jr., R-Del., aimed at felons, not bureaucrats. To finance the crime bill then moving through Congress, Roth wanted to funnel the savings from the work force cutback to an anti-crime trust fund. Democrat William L. Clay of Missouri, chairman of the Post Office and Civil Service Committee and a chief House sponsor of the bill, strongly objected to including the provision in the buyout measure. *(Crime bill, p. 273)*

The fight delayed action on the buyout bill long enough that federal agencies did not have enough money left in their fiscal 1994 payroll accounts to entice many workers to retire early that year. As a consequence, officials in some departments expected to lay off workers in 1994 — just what the bill was designed to minimize.

Elaine Kamarck, a top aide to Gore, said that the delay was unfortunate but hardly ruinous. She said the buyouts would still be an important tool to help agencies restructure and trim their work forces in fiscal 1995.

Background

The administration's push for buyouts started in earnest in September 1993, when Gore called for a massive cut in the federal bureaucracy's management ranks as part of the effort to reinvent government.

Gore noted in his report, "From Red Tape to Results: Creating a Government That Works Better and Costs Less," that the average federal agency had one manager for every seven workers, compared with one for every 25 or more in many well-managed private companies. The report recommended that the equivalent of 252,000 full-time workers be trimmed from the federal work force by fiscal 1999, a 12 percent cut. The goal was a federal work force of roughly 1.9 million, the smallest since President Lyndon B. Johnson inaugurated the Great Society social welfare programs. *(1993 Almanac, p. 191)*

Trying to achieve such a goal through layoffs posed a number of problems. Senior employees whose positions were eliminated could collect paychecks for a lengthy severance period if they chose to leave the government: one week's salary for each of their first 10 years' experience, two weeks' salary for each year after that and an additional 10 percent if they were over age 40. For a well-entrenched employee, that translated into nearly a full year's pay.

They also could choose to stay, even if their jobs were terminated. Under the "bump rule," an employee whose position was eliminated could claim the spot of a less senior worker and continue to collect his or her previous salary. The less senior worker could either bump another worker further down the ladder or be laid off.

A better approach, said federal officials, was the one used by private industry: offering cash incentives for middle managers to resign or retire early. The incentive provided by HR 3345 was payment of severance benefits in a lump sum, up front, with a maximum payment of $25,000.

There was a dispute over whether buyouts would be cheaper than layoffs, at least in the short run. The Office of Personnel Management (OPM) said that the average buyout would cost $6,200 less per position than the average layoff. But in a report released in 1993, the Congressional Budget Office (CBO) estimated that buyouts would be more expensive in the short term, although they would save almost as much money in the long term.

Unlike OPM, the budget office assumed that buyouts would be taken not only by employees whose positions were slated to be cut but also by employees who would have to be replaced. CBO also factored in the increase in pension costs caused by employees who would retire immediately after tak-

---

BOXSCORE

Federal Worker Buyouts — HR 3345 (S 1535). The bill authorized agencies to offer buyouts of up to $25,000 per worker to trim the federal work force.

Reports: H Rept 103-386, S Rept 103-223; conference report H Rept 103-435.

KEY ACTION

Feb. 10 — House passed HR 3345, 391-17.

Feb. 11 — Senate passed HR 3345, amended, by voice vote.

March 23 — House adopted the conference report by voice vote.

March 24 — Senate cleared the bill, 99-1.

March 30 — President signed bill — PL 103-226.

---

ing the buyout. The long-term savings, according to CBO, would be great no matter what approach was taken — $951,000 per job eliminated through layoffs; $898,000 to $950,000 per job eliminated through buyouts.

Barry Toiv, a spokesman for OMB, said the dollar costs of buyouts might be higher in the short term, but the human and managerial costs would be much lower.

"First of all, workers leave on a voluntary basis rather than being laid off. Secondly, managers are able to target more precisely the people who need to leave," he said. Layoffs, Toiv said, "hit disproportionately newer employees, which is not necessarily who you want leaving, particularly when you're trying to achieve savings as well as streamline the bureaucracy."

The higher short-term pension costs were a problem under the pay-as-you-go rules of the 1990 budget law, which were intended to stop Congress from running up the deficit. Under those rules, any bill that increased the cost of an entitlement program, such as federal pensions, had to pay for that increase through tax increases or cuts in other entitlements. The savings expected from reducing the work force could not be used because they were savings from discretionary accounts, which were governed by separate budget rules. The need to find a way to pay for the pensions contributed to the delay in enacting the bill.

1993 Committee Action

Committee action on the legislation began in the fall of 1993. The House Post Office and Civil Service Committee approved the buyout bill (HR 3345 — H Rept 103-386), sponsored by committee Chairman William L. Clay, D-Mo., on Oct. 27. The Senate Governmental Affairs Committee approved a companion bill (S 1535 — S Rept 103-223), sponsored by committee Chairman John Glenn, D-Ohio, on Nov. 9.

Both bills authorized temporary separation incentive payments up to $25,000 for federal employees who voluntarily retired or resigned; both allowed agencies to train employees for different positions in their own or other federal agencies.

The House bill required federal workers who took the buyout to repay the full amount if they were rehired by the federal government within two years; the Senate committee extended that to five years. Both bills required agencies to deposit into the federal pension fund an amount equal to 9 percent of the final pay of an employee who took early retirement.

The chief difference was an amendment by Roth, added to the Senate bill, requiring that 252,000 positions be eliminated by 1999. *(1993 Almanac, p. 197)*

House, Senate Floor Action

The two chambers acted quickly on their respective versions of the bill in early 1994, but differences over the crime fund and over paying for the upfront costs of the buyout quickly spelled trouble.

House Action

The House passed its version of the bill Feb. 10 on a lopsided vote of 391-17. *(Vote 25, p. 8-H)*

Members first voted 409-1 to adopt a proposal by Timothy J. Penny, D-Minn., to codify the work force reduction target of 252,000 jobs by fiscal 1999 and to extend the restrictions on rehiring from two years to five. *(Vote 24, p. 8-H)*

The House overcame the pay-as-you-go budget problem by adopting a rule for floor debate Feb. 10 that effectively waived the budget law, a move made possible by the strong bipartisan support for the bill in that chamber.

But leaders of the Senate Governmental Affairs Committee — Chairman Glenn and ranking member Roth — balked at trying a similar move, which would have required the approval of 60 senators.

Rep. Steny H. Hoyer, D-Md., whose district was home to 57,329 federal workers, proposed a way around the problem: attaching the contents of HR 3345 to an emergency supplemental appropriations bill (HR 3759) aimed at providing disaster relief for Southern California. The short-term costs of the buyout would be classified as emergency spending, exempt from the pay-as-you-go rule.

Hoyer's proposal ran into a different procedural snare, however. The Senate had approved its version of the supplemental on Feb. 10 and had agreed not to have a roll call vote on the conference report that was expected the next day. With the implicit understanding that no major changes would be made to the bill, most senators left for a 10-day recess.

In the conference committee on the supplemental the next morning, Hoyer tried to attach the buyout bill as an amendment. The proposal won the support of top Senate appropriators from both parties, but Roth, who wanted to preserve the work force savings to pay for the crime bill, sent word from Delaware that he objected.

Citing the Senate's understanding that the supplemental would not be changed, Appropriations Chairman Robert C. Byrd, D-W.Va., said he would not permit the buyout provisions to be added to the spending bill. *(Emergency supplemental, p. 548)*

Senate Action

Later the same day, Feb. 11, the Senate passed by unanimous consent its own version of the buyout bill, which contained a number of changes added by Roth.

The most contentious was a pair of provisions that required the transfer of $22.3 billion over five years — the estimated savings from reducing the federal work force — into a Violent Crime Reduction Trust Fund and reduced existing limits on discretionary spending by the same amount. The idea for the fund had surfaced the previous year, when the Senate voted to finance a number of anti-crime programs with the savings from the administration's promise to cut 252,000 federal workers. *(1993 Almanac, p. 293)*

To cover the increase in pension costs that would result from the buyout, Roth required that agencies pay into the federal pension fund an amount equal to 17 percent of the salary of each employee taking the buyout. The payment was in addition to the 9 percent going to the Treasury for each early retiree.

Another Go-Round

The Senate sent the amended bill back to the House, but Clay objected so strongly to the Senate changes that he declined to call for a House-Senate conference.

In particular, Clay objected to the anti-crime trust fund, which he said would trade the jobs of thousands of federal employees for less than half that number of police officers. Clay also criticized Roth's proposal to charge federal agencies for the increase in pension costs associated with the buyouts. OPM Director James B. King said that change would make it too expensive for agencies to offer the buyouts to all except the highest-paid civil servants in fiscal 1994.

Roth argued that some way had to be found to pay for the increase in pension costs, adding that the administration itself had given him the idea for his proposal. The White House Office of Management and Budget responded that no such provision was necessary because the cut in payroll would more than offset the increase in pension costs.

On March 8, the House agreed by voice vote to accept a number of minor provisions added by the Senate. But the revised House bill did not include Roth's anti-crime trust fund. It did appear to solve the issue of how much agencies would have to contribute to the federal pension fund for employees who were bought out.

Clay's compromise was to have the agencies pay the pension fund an amount equal to 9 percent of the salaries of employees who took early retirement immediately after accepting a buyout in fiscal 1994 and 1995. For fiscal 1995 through 1998, agencies would also have to pay the pension fund $80 for every active employee participating in the pension plan.

Buyout proponents in the Senate hoped to take the new version quickly to conference, an approach that Roth and Glenn advocated. But Phil Gramm, R-Texas, blocked that move, demanding that the Senate first restore the trust fund.

Bill supporters considered filing a cloture petition to block the Gramm amendment, but they eventually agreed to let Gramm offer it. He did so on March 11. "Let me tell you, there is a greater emergency . . . than just passing this bill," Gramm said. "We have a criminal justice system which is the laughingstock of every hoodlum in America."

The Senate adopted the Gramm amendment, offered on a separate bill, by a 90-2 vote. *(Vote 56, p. 11-S)*

Later the same day, the House agreed to go to conference on the bill and voted 231-150 for a non-binding motion to instruct its conferees to accept the Senate trust fund provision. *(Vote 57, p. 18-H)*

Conference/Final Action

Despite the votes in both chambers, House and Senate conferees, who met March 15, dropped the trust fund from the conference report (H Rept 103-435). Three House committee chairmen — Clay; Jack Brooks, D-Texas, of Judiciary; and John Conyers Jr., D-Mich., of Government Operations — had dug in their heels against adding the trust fund to the buyouts bill. Roth said he would accept a compromise offered by Rep. John T. Myers, R-Ind., that would have dropped the trust fund but kept the $22 billion cut in discretionary spending. But conferees rejected that proposal by voice vote.

Meanwhile, a separate provision sought by Mississippi's two Republican senators, Trent Lott and Thad Cochran, was added to the bill in conference. The provision authorized separation payments of $5,000 each to up to 200 workers who were displaced as a result of the termination of the Advanced Solid Rocket Motor project. Congress had voted in 1993 to cancel the Mississippi project, which would have built a new booster rocket for space shuttle flights. *(1993 Almanac, p. 695)*

Senate Filibuster

The House agreed to the conference report by voice vote March 23. The Senate cleared the bill, 99-1, the following day. But first, bill supporters had to put out still more fires driven by the decision to drop the trust fund. *(Vote 77, p. 13-S)*

In the House, Brooks pledged on the floor to support an anti-crime trust fund in negotiations with the Senate over the separate anti-crime bill (HR 4092).

Brooks' pledge helped Clay defeat another motion to send the bill back to conference with non-binding instructions to restore the trust fund. The motion failed March 23 by a vote of 166-261. *(Vote 88, p. 26-H)*

Brooks' statement was not enough to satisfy Gramm, however. The Texas senator had sent a letter to House members warning that he would filibuster the conference report if it came to the Senate without the trust fund, and he kept his word.

The fate of the bill then came down to its supporters' ability to garner the 60 votes needed to end Gramm's filibuster. They fell short on their first attempt March 24 by a vote of 58-41. The Senate immediately held a second vote, however, and the motion to end the filibuster passed 63-36. *(Votes 75, 76, p. 13-S)*

The critical vote switch was made by Thad Cochran, R-Miss. After providing one of the last two votes to sustain the filibuster on the first motion, Cochran provided the 60th vote to end the filibuster on the second motion. Three more

Republicans quickly followed suit. Cochran apparently was concerned about losing the $1 million that Mississippi stood to gain in benefits for laid-off workers. House Republicans had tried to kill the provision, and buyout supporters warned Lott and Cochran that the benefits might not survive if the bill were sent back to conference. Despite the provision, Lott voted twice against ending Gramm's filibuster.

Nancy Landon Kassebaum, R-Kan., also voted in favor of the second motion to end the filibuster after voting against the first. Republicans Pete V. Domenici of New Mexico, William S. Cohen of Maine and Strom Thurmond of South Carolina voted against the first motion and initially cast similar votes the second time around, but they switched after Cochran provided the deciding vote.

Sen. Paul S. Sarbanes, D-Md., said no deals were made regarding the trust fund in order to win votes for the buyouts. On the other hand, he said, the bill's supporters did make sure that senators knew of Brooks' pledge. ∎

No Agreement on Unfunded Mandates

Congress came close to clearing legislation to curb unfunded federal mandates, but last-minute efforts to pass a compromise bill were thwarted when the Senate bill attracted a raft of unrelated floor amendments and leaders lacked the time to shepherd the bill through.

The legislation (S 993, HR 5128) was aimed at making it harder for Congress to impose requirements on state and local governments without providing them with adequate funding to carry out the edicts. State and local officials complained bitterly that costly federal mandates depleted the funds available for much-needed local services.

Keenly aware of the political potency of the issue, the Clinton administration took steps early on to rein in unfunded mandates. President Clinton issued two executive orders in September and October 1993, one calling for federal agencies to consult with state and local government officials when feasible before making regulations, and the other directing federal agencies to avoid whenever possible regulations that involved unfunded mandates.

The president also pledged to work with Congress to draft some form of mandate relief legislation.

But the issue was a delicate one for Clinton. As a former governor, he understood that this was a burning question for state and local governments. Yet any blanket prohibition against unfunded federal mandates could have threatened the broad domestic policy agenda he had vowed to put in place.

If any version of a "no money, no mandates" bill prevailed, Clinton could have found himself in the awkward position of having to reject the relief he said he would provide.

Background

Federal regulations enacted between 1983 and 1990 imposed from $8.9 billion to $12.7 billion in costs on states

BOXSCORE

Limiting Unfunded Federal Mandates — S 993 (HR 5128). The bills sought to make it harder for Congress to impose requirements on state and local governments without providing corresponding funding.

Report: S Rept 103-330.

KEY ACTION

June 16 — Senate Governmental Affairs Committee approved S 993 by voice vote.

Oct. 5 — House Government Operations Committee approved HR 5128, 35-4.

Oct. 6 — Senate voted 88-0 to proceed to S 993, but the bill was set aside after being swamped by unrelated amendments.

and localities, according to the Advisory Commission on Intergovernmental Relations. Such mandates included anything from setting standards for clean drinking water to providing access to public buildings for disabled people.

The call to stem these federal edicts had galvanized influential state and local government groups. "It's our No. 1 issue," said Victor Ashe, mayor of Knoxville, Tenn., and president of the U.S. Conference of Mayors. "The so-called Big Seven are united, Democrat and Republican alike, in pushing the mandate relief act," Ashe added, referring to seven state and local government associations that had actively opposed unfunded mandates for years. The National Conference of State Legislatures, another "Big Seven" organization, had even devoted a publication to the subject: the Mandate Watch List, a newsletter published 10 to 12 times a year.

But many public interest groups feared that any legislation designed to address the issue would undermine laws designed to protect health, safety and civil rights. Some environmentalists complained that the campaign was a smoke screen for an attack on environmental laws.

"The effect of this attack on federal regulations could be something that most state and local officials don't want any part of — a serious weakening of public health protections," Environmental Protection Agency Administrator Carol M. Browner wrote in a May 30 Washington Post opinion piece.

Senate

The Senate Governmental Affairs Committee gave voice vote approval June 16 to a compromise bill drafted by panel Chairman John Glenn, D-Ohio, and freshman Dirk Kempthorne, R-Idaho. The measure (S 993 — S Rept 103-330) essentially allowed lawmakers to raise a parliamentary point

of order against any bill that imposed more than $50 million in unfunded mandates.

Kempthorne — a former mayor of Boise, Idaho, and a foe of unfunded mandates — had originally introduced an aggressive bill to block all unfunded initiatives, but he agreed to work on a compromise with Glenn and the administration.

Under the Glenn-Kempthorne substitute, any congressional committee reporting an authorization bill that mandated a federal program had to request a Congressional Budget Office (CBO) cost estimate. The budget office was to provide a detailed report on any legislation that would impose net costs on local governments of more than $50 million, a reduction from the existing threshold of $200 million.

To clear the way for floor consideration, CBO would have to certify that a mandate would not impose costs of more than $50 million, or the committee would have to authorize additional assistance to affected local governments. Otherwise, the bill would be subject to a point of order allowing senators to block floor consideration.

"Congress should know the extent and the fiscal implications to both the public and the private sector," said Kempthorne. "I just think it makes us better decision-makers to know how far it goes."

Under the bill, authorizations governing emergency disaster assistance, civil rights, fraud prevention, national security and international treaties were exempt. The bill did not apply to annual appropriations.

Over Glenn's objections, the panel adopted a controversial amendment, sponsored by Byron L. Dorgan, D-N.D., to require that CBO also analyze the cost of new unfunded mandates of more than $200 million on the private sector. To fund the CBO studies, the bill authorized $6 million per year for the budget office in fiscal 1995-98.

Glenn argued that the Dorgan amendment would upset a delicate compromise he had reached with local governments on the bill. CBO Director Robert D. Reischauer also opposed the provision in a letter, saying it would impose "expensive and time-consuming" requirements on the budget office "of limited usefulness to Congress."

The panel nevertheless approved the amendment, with support from three Democrats and all the panel's Republicans.

During the markup, Carl Levin, D-Mich., pointed out that when CBO could not provide a specific cost estimate, or could only give a range of costs, a committee would be unable to provide a proper authorization. Using the example of the 1990 amendments to the Clean Air Act, Levin said, "I don't know how CBO can estimate with specificity the cost on 80,000 local governments."

John McCain, R-Ariz., raised a concern about the exemption of Appropriations committees from the legislation. McCain said appropriators claimed they should be exempt because they did not legislate on appropriations bills. "But the fact is, the opposite is the case," he said.

House Subcommittee

The House Government Operations Subcommittee on Human Resources and Intergovernmental Relations gave voice vote approval Aug. 11 to a bill (HR 4771) that was a companion to the Glenn-Kempthorne measure.

The bill, introduced by subcommittee Chairman Edolphus Towns, D-N.Y., required CBO to review any legislation authorizing an unfunded mandate and to provide a detailed analysis of bills imposing costs of more than $50 million. The measure provided for a point of order against legislation unless

CBO certified that it did not reach the $50 million threshold, or unless the committee authorized funding to cover the costs of the mandate.

Even as the subcommittee acted, however, many House members were rallying behind a more far-reaching bill (HR 140) that sought to bar Congress from imposing mandates without providing funding. Sponsor Gary A. Condit, D-Calif., was gathering signatures on a discharge petition to allow his more sweeping bill to bypass the Government Operations Committee and move directly to the House floor.

At the subcommittee markup, John L. Mica, R-Fla., tried to insert the text of Condit's bill into HR 4771, but the panel rebuffed his amendment, 3-6.

The subcommittee also rejected, 3-6, a group of "parity" amendments by Rob Portman, R-Ohio, aimed at strengthening the bill's enforcement measures to reflect House procedures. Portman's amendments were based on some members' complaints that the point of order requirement, modeled after the provisions in the Senate bill, would be ineffective in the House, where the Rules Committee routinely waived points of order.

The measure also encountered opposition from Henry A. Waxman, D-Calif., who argued that Congress needed to be able to impose mandates in order to set standards in such areas as public health and safety. "I think we ought to look at the impact of cost, but I don't think the impact of cost should keep us from doing things that are reasonable," Waxman said.

House Committee

On Oct. 5, the full Government Operations Committee attempted to usher through a last-minute compromise by approving, 35-4, a revised unfunded mandates bill (HR 5128).

At the behest of GOP members, the committee strengthened the point of order provisions to reduce the Rules Committee's ability to override them. For example, HR 5128 required that a bill containing federal mandates be held for seven days before House consideration. Most of those provisions had been defeated during the Aug. 11 subcommittee markup.

The compromise bill had the backing of the so-called Big Seven. But the revisions were rejected by Condit as too weak and by Waxman as too strong. An attempt by Condit to substitute the text of HR 140 was rejected by a vote of 14-27.

Waxman said the bill would chip away at necessary health and safety protections while creating "a bewildering number of procedural roadblocks, the full implications of which no one understands."

He took particular exception to a provision requiring federal agencies to seek the input of state and local governments before establishing regulatory requirements. He offered an amendment aimed at preventing state and local governments from receiving preferential treatment over private enterprise, which was defeated 7-8 by a show of hands.

Another Waxman amendment, defeated 9-30, would have required that the benefits of federal mandates, such as reduced health care costs, be taken into account when totaling the aggregate cost of an unfunded mandate.

After the markup, Waxman claimed his right to hold the bill for three days to file dissenting views to the committee report, a move that effectively froze the bill in place and prevented the House from taking further action.

Floor Action Stalls

In the Senate, supporters revived prospects for the legislation Oct. 6, winning an 88-0 vote to proceed to the Senate

version of the bill (S 993). *(Vote 324, p. 56-S)*

But immediately after the vote, the bill was overcome by add-ons. It had become an all-too-inviting vehicle for unrelated, end-of-session amendments. Among them were amendments by Paul Simon, D-Ill., to establish a National African-American Museum within the Smithsonian Institution and by Phil Gramm, R-Texas, to repeal a 1993 tax increase on Social Security benefits. The bill's attractiveness forced the Senate to set it aside Oct. 6.

In the House, Waxman's hold effectively killed the bill as Congress rushed to adjourn. Even though HR 5128 never reached the floor, however, supporters called it an important bipartisan compromise.

"The major effort was to ensure that the House bill would be at least as enforceable, if not more so, than the Senate version," said panel ranking Republican William F. Clinger of Pennsylvania, a cosponsor of the legislation who helped work to incorporate the GOP provisions. Clinger said the negotiations laid down a marker for action on the issue for the 104th Congress. ■

Other Federal Workers Bills

Lawmakers considered a handful of other measures in 1994 related to federal government employees, including a family leave bill enacted in the fall.

Wider Use of Annual, Sick Leave

Federal employees gained the right to use sick leave to care for family members who were ill or to attend to the death of a relative under a bill sponsored by Delegate Eleanor Holmes Norton, D-D.C. Congress cleared the measure Oct. 8, and President Clinton signed it into law Oct. 22 (HR 4361 — PL 103-388).

The bill also allowed federal workers to transfer annual leave to family members who worked for the federal government. It authorized the changes for a three-year trial period and required the Office of Personnel Management (OPM) to report to Congress on the results at least six months before the the trial period expired.

Under existing law, federal employees earned 13 days of sick leave a year, but they were allowed to use the time only for their own illness, not to care for a sick relative.

The 1993 National Performance Review, a sweeping administration proposal to make the federal government more efficient, noted that employers in both the private and public sectors permitted their workers to use sick leave to care for family members and recommended that the same benefits be extended to federal employees. *(1993 Almanac, p. 191)*

In response, OPM in May proposed regulations permitting federal workers to use up to five days of sick leave per year to care for sick family members or to attend the funerals of relatives. OPM set the limit at five days based on findings that federal employees typically used only eight of their 13 days of sick leave earned per year. Norton's bill did not include any restrictions on the number of sick days that could be used.

Since 1988, government workers had been able to donate annual leave to fellow workers who faced unpaid absences caused by medical emergencies. Norton's bill changed the program to allow family members to share annual leave as they saw fit, provided that a worker's leave balance did not exceed 30 days. A 1992 survey by the

General Accounting Office found that about 30 percent of all federal employees had family members who also worked for the government.

The House Post Office and Civil Service Subcommittee on Compensation and Employee Benefits approved the measure July 26 by a vote of 4-0. The full committee approved the bill, 19-1, on Aug. 10 (H Rept 103-722), and the House passed the measure by voice vote under suspension of the rules Sept. 19. The Senate passed an amended version of the bill by voice vote Oct. 8, and the House agreed, also by voice vote, clearing the bill.

Federal Workers Safety Bill Gets No Floor Action

The House Post Office Committee approved a measure intended to improve workplace health and safety at federal and postal facilities. But the bill (HR 115 — H Rept 103-858), sponsored by committee Chairman William L. Clay, D-Mo., got no further in the 103rd Congress.

The measure, which the committee approved May 11 by a vote of 16-0, required federal agencies to enforce Occupational Safety and Health Administration (OSHA) standards, extending to federal and postal employees the same protections against unsafe and unhealthy working conditions that applied to private sector workers.

Two of the panel's subcommittees had acted on the bill. On April 20, the Civil Service Subcommittee approved, 3-0, part of the bill applying OSHA standards to all federal agencies. The bill contained provisions requiring that federal managers personally pay penalties if they willfully violated safety standards. Subcommittee Chairman Frank McCloskey, D-Ind., said it would "make job safety not only a regional headquarters responsibility but a work site responsibility."

The measure also required the establishment of health and safety committees at all federal facilities with 11 or more employees. These committees, including worker and management representatives, were to be charged with investigating, documenting and correcting on-site safety and health hazards.

On April 21, the Census Statistics and Postal Personnel Subcommittee approved, 4-0, provisions in the bill that applied OSHA standards to the postal service and required the formation of a health and safety committee at postal facilities. The Postal subcommittee gave voice vote approval to an amendment to require OSHA to set governmentwide ergonomic standards. Ergonomics is the study of the effect of certain types of work, such as repetitive motion, on physical well-being.

Convicted Child Abusers' Pensions Subject to Garnishment

Congress cleared a bill sponsored by Patricia Schroeder, D-Colo., that allowed the pensions of federal retirees found guilty of child abuse to be garnisheed for the purpose of paying court-ordered damages. President Clinton signed the bill into law (HR 3694 — PL 103-358) Oct. 14.

The bill started in the House Post Office and Civil Service Subcommittee on Compensation and Employee Benefits, which approved the measure, 4-0, on July 26. The panel approved by voice vote an amendment by Delegate Eleanor Holmes Norton, D-D.C., broadening the bill's definition of child abuse to include sexual and emotional abuse, in addition to physical abuse. The full com-

mittee approved the bill by voice vote Aug. 10 (H Rept 103-721), the House passed it by voice vote under suspension of the rules Sept. 19, and the Senate cleared the bill by voice vote Sept. 30.

Supporters of the measure noted that convicted child abusers often avoided payment by liquidating their assets and relocating. If the abuser was a federal retiree, the federal government protected that worker's pension by refusing to pay court-ordered damage awards.

Advocates for child abuse victims said court-awarded damages often were levied against retired workers because victims frequently waited until reaching adulthood before taking action against parents or relatives who abused them. "One of the most common damaging effects of sex abuse in childhood is the development of psychological blocks which prevent the victim from discovering that she has been injured," said Sally F. Goldfarb, who testified on behalf of the NOW Legal Defense and Education Fund earlier in the year. "Often these psychological coping mechanisms prevent the survivor from being able to sue until she is well into adulthood," Goldfarb said.

Garnisheeing, a legal remedy for taking part of the regular pay or pension of an employee, was typically used by creditors to recoup debts from a financially delinquent individual. Until 1993, however, federal workers were protected by law from having their wages or pensions garnisheed.

The exemption for federal workers ended when Congress revised the 1939 Hatch Act, the law regulating the political activity of government employees. Included in the 1993 rewrite (PL 103-94) were provisions allowing creditors to garnishee wages of federal employees through the same legal process that they followed with private citizens. Child support and alimony judgments also were required to be given precedence over other legal garnishment orders. *(1993 Almanac, p. 201)*

Schroeder's bill added court-ordered damages for child abuse to the list of debts for which federal pensions could be garnisheed.

Federal workers were also included under a separate bill aimed at strengthening the nation's child support enforcement system (HR 4570), but that measure died at the end of the 103rd Congress. *(Child support, p. 375)*

Displaced FBI Workers Get Job Assistance

Congress agreed to give FBI employees who were unwilling to relocate to a new fingerprint center in West Virginia help finding jobs elsewhere in the federal government. The House passed the legislation as a separate bill (HR 4884) by voice vote Aug. 16. House and Senate negotiators subsequently inserted it into the final version of the fiscal 1995 spending bill for the departments of Commerce, Justice and State. President Clinton signed the appropriations bill into law on Aug. 26 (HR 4603 — PL 103-317).

HR 4884 was introduced by Delegate Eleanor Holmes Norton, D-D.C., in response to FBI plans to relocate the Criminal Justice Information Services Division, which was responsible for maintaining the agency's fingerprint files, from Washington to Clarksburg, W.Va., by 1999.

In 1990, Senate Appropriations Committee Chairman Robert C. Byrd, D-W.Va., inserted language in a supplemental appropriations bill that provided $185 million for a state-of-the-art fingerprint center, with the understanding that it would be in Byrd's home state. *(1990 Almanac, p. 844)*

According to the FBI, nearly half the division's 2,600

employees did not wish to make the move from Washington. Many were African-Americans who cited the low number of minorities in West Virginia as one of their concerns. Despite FBI promises to find other jobs for these employees, budget cuts and hiring freezes had limited the number of openings. The workers could not easily transfer to new jobs elsewhere in the federal government, because FBI employees were "excepted service" personnel, not part of the regular competitive civil service.

In 1992, the FBI and Justice Department sought a waiver of competitive status to allow the fingerprint employees to seek jobs at Justice, where their experience would have been most valuable. But the Office of Personnel Management said it lacked authority to grant such a waiver.

"At a time when they cannot move their homes, they literally have no place in the federal government to go, even though many have considerable years of service," Norton said.

Norton's bill, which was cosponsored by most District-area lawmakers, granted competitive status to the fingerprint division employees for up to two years after they left the FBI, allowing them to seek federal jobs in other agencies, including the rest of the Justice Department.

The House Post Office and Civil Service Committee approved the bill Aug. 10. The committee agreed to an amendment by Civil Service Subcommittee Chairman Frank McCloskey, D-Ind., to provide the special status only to permanent employees at the fingerprint center and offer it for up to two years after their separation from the FBI. The original bill would have included temporary employees and would have been in effect until Sept. 30, 1999.

Job Discrimination Bill

Two House committees reported versions of a bill to overhaul the procedures for handling federal workers' discrimination complaints. But the legislation (HR 2721), sponsored by Matthew G. Martinez, D-Calif., got no further in the 103rd Congress.

The bill was a response to sharp criticism of the existing system, under which federal employees who believed they had been discriminated against on the basis of race, color, religion, sex, national origin, disability or age filed their complaint with their own agency. The agency then carried out the investigation. Critics said the system was too complex and guaranteed a conflict of interest. "The fox is not guarding the chicken coop; he is right there in the chicken coop, eating the chickens," said Evan Kemp, a former chairman of the Equal Employment Opportunity Commission (EEOC).

The Education and Labor Committee on April 13 approved a bill that transferred responsibility for processing discrimination claims from the employee's agency to the EEOC. The panel, which had jurisdiction over the EEOC, approved the measure on a party line vote of 28-14 (H Rept 103-599, Part 1). The committee agreed by voice vote to an amendment by Bill Goodling, R-Pa., to extend the bill's coverage to employees of the House of Representatives.

The House Post Office and Civil Service Committee approved its version of the bill by voice vote May 11 (H Rept 103-599, Part 2). The committee's bill offered federal employees several options for getting their complaints handled, including review by the EEOC. The bill also permitted a federal employee to take a workplace discrimination case to court if the issue was not resolved promptly.

The committee by voice vote adopted three amendments offered by Delegate Eleanor Holmes Norton, D-D.C., designed to alleviate a case backlog and expedite resolutions. Norton was a former EEOC chairman. An attempt by Tom Petri, R-Wis., to extend coverage to legislative branch employees was rejected as being outside the committee's jurisdiction.

Whistleblower Protection Law Expanded

Congress cleared a bill reauthorizing the Office of Special Counsel through fiscal 1997 and expanding existing protections for federal employees who blew the whistle on fraud, waste, abuse or criminal activity in the workplace. President Clinton signed the bill (HR 2970 — PL 103-424) on Oct. 29.

Established in 1979, the Office of Special Counsel was an independent agency within the executive branch charged with investigating allegations by federal employees that they had been demoted, reassigned or otherwise wrongly treated as a result of racial discrimination, as a form of political coercion or as a reprisal for exposing corruption or other violations in the workplace.

HR 2970 extended whistleblower protections to employees in the Department of Veterans Affairs, the Federal Deposit Insurance Corporation (FDIC) and the Resolution Trust Corporation (RTC). In response to concerns raised by the Banking Committee, the bill provided that FDIC and RTC employees who had separate whistleblower protection as a result of the savings and loan bailout legislation had to choose to follow those procedures or the ones in HR 2970.

The bill attempted to strengthen the accountability of agency leaders in protecting whistleblowers. It expanded the list of personnel practices that could not be used as retaliation to include requiring psychiatric testing and denying or revoking a security clearance.

And the bill tightened limits on the information the Office of Special Counsel could disclose on an employee's case. During House floor debate, sponsor Frank McCloskey, D-Ind., said that 59 percent of complainants had reported to the General Accounting Office that the special counsel undercut their rights by leaking information about their cases to their employers.

The House Post Office and Civil Service Committee's Subcommittee on Civil Service amended and approved the bill by a vote of 5-0 on Oct. 20, 1993. The full committee approved the bill by voice vote Aug. 10, 1994 (H Rept 103-769).

In its report, the committee stressed the importance of protecting whistleblowers if the administration's goal of "reinventing government" to make it more efficient was to bear fruit.

The report was highly critical of the special counsel's office, stating that "contrary to its rhetoric, the [Office's] empirical track record is one of hostility to its stated mission as the rule, rather than the exception. Despite 400 to 500 cases yearly and the most sympathetic legal standards in history, the Office still has not litigated a single case to restore a whistleblower's job since the [Whistleblower Protection] Act's 1989 passage, or indeed since 1979." *(1993 Almanac, p. 206)*

The House passed the bill Oct. 3 by voice vote under suspension of the rules.

The Senate passed the bill by voice vote Oct. 7, after eliminating House-passed provisions expanding the legal alternatives open to aggrieved federal employees. The House bill had included the option in certain cases of initiating a civil action in the appropriate U.S. district court.

The House accepted the Senate changes by voice vote the same day, clearing the bill. ∎

Other Government Operations Legislative Action

In 1994, Congress considered but did not complete action on several bills aimed at improving federal government operations.

Office of Government Ethics

A bill to reauthorize the Office of Government Ethics passed the Senate and was approved in various forms by two House committees, but it went no further. Authorization for the agency — which oversaw financial disclosure, conflict of interest and employee conduct matters for the executive branch — ran out Sept. 30.

The Senate Governmental Affairs Committee acted first, giving voice vote approval June 16 to an eight-year reauthorization at unspecified amounts (S 1413 — S Rept 103-315). The bill included several technical changes to the office's authorizing statute, the Ethics in Government Act of 1978. The Senate passed the bill by voice vote Oct. 6.

On June 29, the House Judiciary Committee gave voice vote approval to a version (HR 2289 — H Rept 103-785, Part 2) that authorized appropriations of $8.1 million in fiscal 1995, $8.4 million in fiscal 1996, $8.8 million in fiscal 1997, $9.1 million in fiscal 1998 and $9.5 million in fiscal 1999. The panel's Subcommittee on Governmental Relations had limited the authorization to five years to give Congress more oversight of the office.

The House Post Office and Civil Service Committee also considered the bill, voting Aug. 10 by voice to approve an eight-year reauthorization (H Rept 103-785, Part 1). The committee authorized appropriators to provide up to $14 million a year to the ethics office.

Paperwork Reduction

The Senate on Oct. 6 passed a bill aimed at reducing the burden of federal paperwork on the public, but the measure stalled in the House, which took no further action on it.

The bill (S 560), introduced by Sam Nunn, D-Ga., required that each agency review its paperwork requirements to ensure that they imposed the least possible burden on the public. The bill, which amended the Paperwork Reduction Act of 1980 (PL 96-511), also aimed to improve the opportunity for public comment during the agency review process. The measure sought to improve the government's collection, management and dissemination of information, its use of new information technology and its computer security practices.

The Senate Governmental Affairs Committee approved the five-year authorization bill by voice vote Aug. 2 (S Rept 103-392).

In a related action, the committee also approved by voice vote a bill (S 2156 — S Rept 103-375), sponsored by Sander M. Levin, D-Mich., to eliminate 196 reports that federal agencies were required to submit to Congress and to modify others. That bill got no further.

When the paperwork act was enacted, its main purpose was to reduce the paperwork burden that the federal government imposed on businesses and individuals. The act established a special unit within the Office of Management and Budget (OMB) to review requests for information by federal agencies to determine whether the information was necessary, could not be found elsewhere and was being collected efficiently.

Under the Reagan and Bush administrations, the Office of Information and Regulatory Affairs used its power under the law to gain increasing control over the form and the content of regulations issued by federal agencies. Critics charged that it was misusing its authority to review regulations, delaying proposed rules that the White House disagreed with and changing others behind the scenes without giving the public a chance to comment.

As approved by the committee, S 560 authorized $8 million annually for the OMB unit and maintained the law's goal of reducing the paperwork burden by 5 percent each year.

One of the most controversial portions of the bill was a provision to overturn a 1990 Supreme Court decision that had been hailed by unions and consumer groups but denounced by business groups. The court, in *Dole v. United Steelworkers of America*, said the paperwork law allowed OMB to review requests for data intended for government use but did not extend to regulations intended to force businesses to generate information for a third party, such as the public or their employees. The bill included such third-party disclosures in the definition of "collection of information," making them subject to OMB's paperwork review.

Postal Service Inspector General

The House passed a bill (HR 4400) June 27 by voice vote aimed at establishing an independent inspector general at the U.S. Postal Service. But the Senate did not act on the legislation, and it died at the end of the Congress.

The centerpiece of the bill, sponsored by William L. Clay, D-Mo., was a set of provisions creating the position of inspector general to carry out independent audits and review postal programs and operations. The bill gave the Postal Service's board of governors the job of appointing top management. And it barred the Postal Service from paying confidential informants in drug investigations unless they involved the mail.

The latter provision stemmed from a botched sting operation at the Cleveland Post Office during which convicted felons were hired to go undercover in the post office and report back on drug users. Police said the felons used the drugs themselves and fingered innocent employees.

The House Post Office and Civil Service Committee approved the bill by voice vote June 22 (H Rept 103-561, Part 1) after adopting an amendment by Barbara-Rose Collins, D-Mich., to prohibit the inspector general from interfering with union negotiating rights. ∎

Earthquake Study Refunded; Other Disaster Bills Die

Congress cleared a bill reauthorizing federal earthquake research, but broader bills to refocus the mission of the Federal Emergency Management Agency and to create a fed-

eral disaster insurance program died at the end of the 103rd Congress.

Earthquake Preparedness

The House on Oct. 5 cleared a bill extending federal earthquake research and preparedness programs for two years. President Clinton signed the measure into law Oct. 19 (HR 3485 — PL 103-374).

The bill, sponsored by Rick Boucher, D-Va., reauthorized the National Earthquake Hazards Reduction Program at $103.2 million in fiscal 1995 and $106.3 million in fiscal 1996. It required four agencies, including the Federal Emergency Management Agency, to conduct an assessment of the nation's earthquake monitoring facilities and report their findings to Congress within nine months.

According to the U.S. Geological Survey, 39 states were at significant risk of a damaging earthquake. "Their houses and roads are safer because of the work initiated and advanced by this program," said Science Committee Chairman George E. Brown Jr., D-Calif.

The House had passed a three-year reauthorization (H Rept 103-360, Part 1) by voice vote on Nov. 15, 1993. The Senate passed a two-year version (S Rept 103-354) by voice vote Sept. 30, 1994. On Oct. 5, the House agreed by voice vote to the Senate change, clearing the bill.

Shifting FEMA's Focus

The Senate Governmental Affairs Committee gave voice vote approval Aug. 18 to a bill aimed at recasting the central mission of the Federal Emergency Management Agency (FEMA). But the measure did not reach the Senate floor.

The goal of the bill (S 1697 — S Rept 103-400) was to shift FEMA's focus away from the Cold War scenario of nuclear attack-related disasters and better reflect its primary function of providing relief after natural disasters.

The legislation, introduced by Barbara A. Mikulski, D-Md., required both the president and FEMA to submit plans for providing federal assistance and establishing chains of command. Those plans were to specify both federal duties in case of emergency and the relationship between the federal government and state, local and private agencies.

The bill also specified ways in which FEMA itself should be reorganized, including relocating certain regional offices to high-risk areas. It included provisions to create a targeted grant program to allow state and local governments to better prepare for emergencies. The measure authorized $200 million per year through fiscal 1998 for the grant program.

By voice vote, the committee adopted an amendment by Democrat Daniel K. Akaka to establish a new Pacific region FEMA office in his home state of Hawaii.

The committee also agreed by voice vote to an amendment by John McCain, R-Ariz., to require the director of FEMA to encourage agency employees to establish working relationships with the nation's Indian tribes. McCain's amendment also required the appointment of a FEMA liaison to Indian tribes.

Federal Disaster Insurance

Congress considered, but did not complete action on, legislation aimed at reducing the huge bills for disaster that were regularly being paid by the federal government.

In four of the previous five years, natural disasters had

caused at least four times as many losses as the federal government had budgeted for in its main emergency account. The result: Congress passed eight extraordinary spending bills to provide an additional $23.6 billion for disaster relief.

Sen. Daniel K. Inouye, D-Hawaii, and Rep. Norman Y. Mineta, D-Calif., sponsored similar versions of a bill to create a federal disaster insurance program (S 1350, HR 2873) under the Robert T. Stafford Disaster Relief and Emergency Assistance Act (PL 100-707), the main federal law governing disaster policy.

The bills included financial incentives to encourage insurance companies to include broad-ranging disaster insurance in their homeowners' policies. Premiums were to be based on long-range prospects for earthquakes, tidal waves, volcanic eruptions, hurricanes, tornadoes and other natural disasters in each locale.

By collecting premiums from all property owners and spreading the risk, insurance companies could cut the price of earthquake coverage drastically and still amass a sufficient pool of reserves, supporters of the bill said. Existing earthquake coverage was so expensive that only about 25 percent of the property owners in earthquake-prone areas had it.

To help the insurance industry afford the risk of covering disasters, the bill provided for a backup pool of money funded over time by the industry itself. Private companies already provided such a backup, called reinsurance, but recent disasters had raised its cost and threatened its availability. As a consequence, some leading insurance companies had dropped or cut back their coverage.

To help lower the cost of disasters, S 1350 and HR 2873 also included incentives for the states to adopt and enforce better building codes.

The House Public Works and Transportation Committee approved HR 2873 by voice vote Sept. 28 (H Rept 103-848, Part 1). The Senate Commerce, Science and Transportation Committee had held hearings on S 1350 in 1993 but did not act on it. ∎

House Clears Bill To Increase Federal Land Payments

With the support of Western lawmakers, the House on Oct. 7 cleared a Senate bill authorizing an increase in payments to local governments on lands that were under federal control. President Clinton signed the bill (S 455 — PL 103-397) on Oct. 22.

These "payments in lieu of taxes" were intended to compensate local governments for amounts they would have received in property tax revenue if the lands in their jurisdiction had not been under federal control. The bill adjusted the existing formula to increase the payments gradually over five years to about $227 million in 1999, raising the rate from 75 cents to $1.65 per acre of federal land. Payments in subsequent years were to be indexed to inflation. Congress had appropriated $109 million in fiscal 1994.

The bill also raised the limitation on payments to local governments from $50 times the population to $110 times the population.

Western lawmakers argued that the payment formula had not been changed since it was established in 1976 and that dollar amounts had not kept up with inflation.

The bill was cleared over the objection of House Natural Resources Committee Chairman George Miller, D-Calif., who pressed for a temporary increase while the General Accounting Office (GAO) studied the issue. The Clinton administration supported payments to the states but did not back S 455 because the increase in discretionary spending meant cuts in other programs.

Senate Action

The Senate Energy and Natural Resources Committee approved the bill, 17-3, on Feb. 2 (S Rept 103-231).

The full Senate passed the bill April 13 by a vote of 78-20. (Vote 90, p. 16-S)

"It is only fair that we enact changes so that local governments are provided reasonable payments for the mixed blessing of being neighbors to vast tracts of federal ownerships," said Sen. Larry E. Craig, R-Idaho. Craig said 63 percent of Idaho's land was federally owned and that increased public use of that land had added to the burden of local governments to maintain roads and traffic signs and to provide law enforcement.

Bill sponsor Mark O. Hatfield, R-Ore., also argued that local governments suffered a "double whammy" from the federal government, having to increase support for recreational activities on federal lands, while losing revenue-producing opportunities, such as logging.

But Appropriations Committee Chairman Robert C. Byrd, D-W.Va., said he was concerned about the cost imposed by S 455. "When senators come to me asking that this be funded, I am going to say, 'I don't know where we will get the money. What programs do you want to cut?' " said Byrd.

House Action

The House Natural Resources Committee approved the Senate bill, 31-10, on Sept. 28 (H Rept 103-838).

An effort to strip out the Senate language and replace it with the text of a bill (HR 1181) — cosponsored by Bruce F. Vento, D-Minn., and committee Chairman Miller — failed by a vote of 14-28. The amendment would have authorized a two-year increase in payments, to $132 million in fiscal 1995 and $162 million in fiscal 1966, and ordered a GAO study.

Miller tried again when the bill came to the House floor, arguing that the measure was "a massive, uncapped increase" that would cost $484 million in new spending over four years for a program whose soundness was questionable. But his amendment was rejected Oct. 7 by a vote of 160-262. The House also rejected, 195-223, an amendment by Vento to eliminate the provisions that tied future increases to the rate of inflation. (Votes 502, 503, p. 150-H)

The House then passed the bill by voice vote, clearing it for the president. ∎

Other Government Legislation Considered in 1994

In action on a series of small bills, Congress agreed to authorize funds for the Martin Luther King Jr. Federal Holiday Commission, return lands to Guam that the U.S. military had condemned in the 1940s, and extend the life of a commission appointed to review documents related to the assassination of President John F. Kennedy.

Lawmakers did not complete work on a bill to create an African-American museum.

King Holiday

Brushing aside objections from conservatives, Congress agreed to extend federal funding for the Martin Luther King Jr. Federal Holiday Commission for five years. President Clinton signed the bill into law Aug. 23 (HR 1933 — PL 103-304).

Authorization for the commission, which was established in 1984 to promote a national holiday in observance of the slain civil rights leader, expired April 20. Congress had been appropriating $300,000 annually for the commission, which was privately financed before 1990.

The bill authorized a total of $2 million over five years, gradually increasing annual authorizations to $500,000. It also directed the commission to promote community service activities in memory of King.

The House Post Office and Civil Service Committee had approved the bill Nov. 10, 1993 (H Rept 103-418, Part 1). The House passed the measure by voice vote March 15, 1994. On the Senate side, the Judiciary Committee approved the bill by voice vote May 5. The full Senate passed it by a vote of 94-4 on May 24. *(Vote 128, p. 23-S)*

Opponents, led by Jesse Helms, R-N.C., argued that, with a civil rights holiday observed in all 50 states, the commission had served its purpose. But the Senate rejected, 28-70, a Helms amendment to block federal funding for the commission. *(Vote 127, p. 23-S)*

Helms said the Martin Luther King Center for Non-Violent Social Change raised $20 million to $30 million per year and that such private funds should be used for the advancement of King's teachings. Helms said the federal commission never was intended to "be a permanent drain on the American taxpayers."

But bill supporters, led by Carol Moseley-Braun, D-Ill., the Senate's lone African-American, and Harris Wofford, D-Pa., said that under the legislation, the commission would gain new responsibility to promote community service and other volunteer programs related to King's teachings. On Aug. 10, the House agreed to technical changes in the Senate-passed version, clearing the bill.

African-American Museum

A bill (HR 877) to create a new Smithsonian museum devoted to the history, art and culture of African-Americans died at the end of the session. The National African-American Museum was to be housed in the Smithsonian's Arts and Industries Building.

For years, African-American lawmakers and others had advocated establishment of such a museum. On June 29, 1993, the House passed a bill by voice vote that authorized $5 million in fiscal 1994 to design and plan the museum and unspecified sums in future years. The measure (H Rept 103-140, Parts 1 and 2) was sponsored by John Lewis, D-Ga. *(1993 Almanac, p. 211)*

A year later, on June 28, 1994, the Senate Rules and Administration Committee approved an amended version of the bill (S Rept 103-284) by a vote of 10-0. But first the committee agreed to remove specific fiscal years and funding levels, after members had expressed concern that private funds being sought by the Smithsonian would not be enough to cover the new museum.

Guam

Responding to increasingly bitter complaints from Guam, Congress agreed to return land that the U.S. military had condemned in the 1940s.

The House passed the bill (HR 2144 — H Rept 103-391) by voice vote Jan. 26. The Senate Energy and Natural Resources Committee approved it March 2 by a vote of 19-0 (S Rept 103-293). The Senate cleared the measure by voice vote Sept. 21, and President Clinton signed it Oct. 6 (PL 103-339).

The land consisted of 3,219 acres scattered around U.S. Navy and Air Force installations on the island. Congress had debated but not approved a variety of proposals since 1975 to return the property, despite the Defense Department's declaration 15 years before that it did not need the land. Under federal law, any federal land deemed to be excess was put up for sale to the highest bidder. Guam officials opposed that procedure, though, because it would have allowed investors to outbid the original owners for the land.

The bill's sponsor, Delegate Robert A. Underwood, D-Guam, proposed that the land be turned over without charge to the Guam government on the condition that it be reserved for "public benefit use," such as schools, hospitals, housing or economic development.

The House added requirements that the land be offered first to other federal agencies, then appraised. Congress then had 180 days to review the appraisals and a land-use plan submitted by Guam. No structures tall enough to interfere with air navigation could be built within six nautical miles of an airport.

One final provision added by the House required Guam to grant the National Park Service administrative control over the undeveloped lands it owned within the War in the Pacific National Historical Park. The provision barred any use of those lands that was not compatible with the park.

The federal government owned one-third of the land on Guam, much of it condemned by military tribunals before the island had its own government. Guam officials said many residents thought that they were merely leasing their land to the U.S. military, and they resented the failure to return it.

JFK Commission

Congress cleared a bill (HR 4569) to extend the authorization of a five-member commission appointed to review and release to the public information related to the assassination of President John F. Kennedy. The review board was authorized to continue work until Sept. 30, 1996, with an optional one-year extension if it had not completed its work by then.

The House Government Operations Committee approved the bill, sponsored by Chairman John Conyers Jr., D-Mich, by voice vote June 29. The House took up the bill under suspension of the rules July 12 and passed it by voice vote. The Senate Governmental Affairs Committee amended and approved the bill Aug. 2. The Senate then passed it Aug. 10 by voice vote. Conyers proposed that the House accept the minor Senate changes, and the House agreed by voice vote Sept. 27. President Clinton signed the bill Oct. 6 (PL 103-345).

The controversy over who killed Kennedy had raged since the Warren Commission in 1964 investigated the Nov. 22, 1963, assassination and found that Lee Harvey Oswald acted alone in killing the president. Five years later a special House committee finished its investigation of the assassination, with the majority of panel members concluding that the president "was probably assassinated as a result of a conspiracy."

Congress decided to create a special five-member commission in 1992 in the wake of Oliver Stone's movie "JFK," which renewed interest in whether there was a conspiracy surrounding Kennedy's death. The panel was given authority to make public hundreds of thousands of pages of secret government documents, testimony and evidence surrounding Kennedy's death. *(1992 Almanac, p. 77)* ∎

Shipping Bill Dies in Senate Waters

Shipping industry supporters renewed their drive to provide financial and regulatory relief for the nation's flagging maritime industry. But while their efforts advanced in the House, they ran aground in the Senate.

Proponents said the U.S. industry — the shipyards that built the vessels and the lines that owned and operated the ships — could not compete with foreign companies, which had lower domestic costs, faced fewer regulatory burdens and received more generous government support. Lawmakers responded by proposing to subsidize U.S. shipping lines and shipyards, provide incentives to spur passenger-vessel construction, and extend U.S. labor laws to foreign-flagged ships. None of those initiatives were enacted.

The most far-ranging bill (HR 4003), sponsored by Rep. Gerry E. Studds, D-Mass., would have provided $1.35 billion in subsidies to shipyards and shipping lines over 10 years, paid for by a tax increase on cargo and cruise vessels. The House passed the bill in August, but the measure immediately ran into trouble in the Senate when coal and grain shippers protested the duties. The bill finally died in the Senate in the face of late-session delaying tactics.

The House acted on three other bills aimed at revitalizing the maritime industry; the Senate did not act on any of them.

● **Passenger vessel construction.** A bill (HR 3821) sponsored by Jolene Unsoeld, D-Wash., would have helped to promote the construction of passenger cruise vessels in U.S. shipyards. The House twice passed the bill as part of larger maritime measures; the Senate did not take it up.

● **Tax incentives.** A second Unsoeld bill (HR 3822) would have provided tax breaks for building cruise ships in U.S. yards. The measure won approval from a House Ways and Means subcommittee, but the full committee did not take it up.

● **Extending U.S. labor laws.** A bill (HR 1517) sponsored by William L. Clay, D-Mo., would have required foreign-flagged vessels that frequented U.S. ports to comply with U.S. minimum wage and overtime laws if their owners and at least half their crew were not citizens of the country in which the vessels were registered. The House Education and Labor Committee approved the bill, but the measure never reached the House floor.

Background

Once the dominant world shipping power, the United States ranked 16th in the world in oceangoing ships in 1993. Vessels owned and registered in the United States carried only about 4 percent of all U.S. cargo.

Industry advocates warned that U.S. shipping lines were on the brink of shifting their vessels to foreign registries and that the nation's shipyards were being forced to close. The decline of the maritime industry had cost the nation hundreds of thousands of jobs, supporters said.

In 1993, the chairmen of the two leading U.S. lines, American President Lines Ltd. and Sea-Land Service Inc., asked the Transportation Department for permission to move almost one-third of their vessels to foreign registries. They promised to withdraw their requests if Congress and the administration acted quickly on a new maritime program.

The government had ended its direct subsidies for the shipyards in 1981 as a budget-cutting move. Shipyard advocates argued that foreign yards were heavily subsidized by their governments and that U.S. yards needed similar support to compete in the global marketplace. *(1981 Almanac, p. 570)*

U.S. shipping lines were receiving subsidies that averaged more than $3 million a year for each of 80 vessels, but most of those subsidy contracts were to expire by 1997. U.S. shipping companies said the cost of complying with U.S. laws and regulations was so great that they were not going to be able to keep flying the U.S. flag without new subsidies.

Legislative Efforts

In 1992, the Bush administration had proposed a new, less expensive subsidy program for U.S. cargo lines, but the proposal came too late for congressional action. It was revived in 1993 by Transporation Secretary Federico F. Peña, who made maritime revitalization one of his two top priorities.

On Nov. 4, 1993, the House gave overwhelming approval to a bill (HR 2151) that would have authorized $1.2 billion in new subsidies for the shipping lines over 10 years. The vote was 347-65. HR 2151 went nowhere in the Senate, however, because the subsidies had no funding mechanism. Studds and John B. Breaux, D-La., who headed the Senate Commerce Subcommittee on the Merchant Marine, ended 1993 locked in negotiations with the White House over how to pay for the subsidies. *(1993 Almanac, p. 212)*

After several months of negotiations, the Clinton administration came up with a revised proposal that was self-financing. The plan, unveiled by Peña in March 1994, called for increasing the tonnage fees on ships entering U.S. ports by roughly two-thirds, raising $100 million per year for 10 years to pay for subsidies. The administration said the increase amounted to $1.50 per container, 14 cents per ton of loose dry cargo or 1 cent per barrel of liquid, and 38 cents per cruise ship passenger. The increase was to finance annual subsidies of $2 million to $2.5 million each for 52 vessels.

The administration called for no direct subsidies for shipyards, preferring to offer expanded loan guarantees to boost sales and modernize equipment. The case for direct shipyard subsidies was further weakened in July, when international negotiators reached agreement on a new treaty phasing out shipyard aid in most developed countries. The agreement, at the time still to be ratified by most shipbuilding nations, had long been sought by the U.S. government and U.S. yards.

The administration proposal represented an about-face. Just a year earlier the Clinton administration had opposed new subsidies even for shipping lines. The change of heart came after Peña, congressional leaders and AFL-CIO President Lane Kirkland all appealed to President Clinton.

From the outset, the decision not to include direct shipyard subsidies faced opposition from U.S. shipyards, which usually were part of a united maritime industry front. Of even more concern to the shipyards was the fact that the plan allowed shipping-line subsidies for foreign-built ships. The existing subsidy was limited to U.S.-built vessels in exchange for their pledge to aid the military in times of war or national emergency. U.S. shipping lines, on the other hand, had long argued that the subsidy should be extended to foreign-built vessels. They said aging U.S.-built ships were too costly to operate and replacing them with more expensive U.S.-built ships put them at a disadvantage with competitors with foreign-built ships in their fleet.

House Committee

The House Merchant Marine Subcommittee on the Merchant Marine kicked off action on HR 4003, approving a revised version May 24 by voice vote.

The full committee followed suit two days later, approving the bill by voice vote (H Rept 103-544 — Part 1). The committee-approved measure proposed to raise $1.7 billion over 10 years for shipping line and shipyard subsidies, $700 million more than the administration's plan. The bill proposed to more than triple the fees on commercial vessels entering U.S. ports. The fees applied to oceangoing container ships, cruise vessels, tankers and dry bulk cargo ships.

The bulk of the proposed fee increase was to come from tankers and bulk cargo carriers. The loudest protests, though, came from cruise ship companies and their U.S. ports, whose fees were to increase from about 23 cents per passenger to about $2.09 per passenger.

The bill called for authorizing $613 million for the Maritime Administration in fiscal 1995, compared with $595 million proposed by the administration. The committee version authorized an additional $17.5 million for a program to assist in modernizing ship repair yards.

The measure also included a direct subsidy to shipyards, which was to be higher in its early years to allow shipyards to beef up operations, then gradually to taper off.

Ways and Means Committee

The Ways and Means Committee approved a scaled-back version of HR 4003 (H Rept 103-544, Part 2) on July 27 by voice vote. The committee-trimmed version provided subsidies only for the shipping lines, not the shipyards. Through a combination of fuel taxes, ticket taxes and tonnage taxes, Ways and Means proposed to raise $1 billion over 10 years for the lines.

Proposed by acting Chairman Sam M. Gibbons, D-Fla., the committee bill called for:

● Increasing the tonnage tax from 9 cents per ton to 22 cents per ton on vessels arriving from Western Hemisphere ports and dropping it from 27 cents to 22 cents for other vessels. The provision was expected to raise $532 million.

● Imposing a 1-cent tax on each gallon of diesel fuel used in commercial ships leaving the United States for foreign ports, raising $374 million.

● Increasing the excise tax on cruise-ship passengers from $3 to $5 for tickets costing $150 or more, raising $105 million.

In light of the pending international shipbuilding agreement, Gibbons said Congress should not enact new subsidies for shipbuilders. Once ratified, the hard-won international agreement, which took five years to negotiate, was to phase out shipbuilding subsidies in most developed nations by 1999.

But Gerald D. Kleczka, D-Wis., said there was no guarantee that the international accord would be ratified. He proposed to raise the tax on diesel fuel in Gibbons' proposal to 2 cents from 1 cent, generating an estimated $374 million for shipbuilding subsidies. Gibbons objected, saying the agreement called for countries not to adopt new subsidies. The committee rejected Kleczka's proposal by a vote of 11-24.

Ways and Means voted 13-21 against a proposal by William J. Jefferson, D-La., to reduce taxes on the foreign subsidiaries of U.S. shipping lines.

By a vote of 20-16, the committee requested that the tax provisions of HR 4003 go to the floor under a closed rule, with no amendments allowed. Allies of the shipbuilding industry, however, planned to fight for a more open rule before the Rules Committee.

After the Ways and Means Committee acted, leaders of the Merchant Marine Committee, who had sponsored the more expansive version of HR 4003, searched for ways to restore the shipyard subsidies on the House floor. Unless the legislation aided the shipyards, some lawmakers said, HR 4003 stood to lose the broad, bipartisan support that the previous year's maritime revitalization bill had enjoyed. The chief supporters of HR 4003 on the Merchant Marine Committee proposed to cut the duties back to $1 billion, with grain, coal and other dry bulk cargo shippers exempted from the increase.

That proposal ran into trouble from advocates of the shipyards, which would not have received any direct subsidies if the bill's price tag was trimmed, and from farm-state Republicans, who opposed any aid for the maritime industry.

The shipping lines, meanwhile, were elated that the bill had cleared the Ways and Means Committee hurdle. The administration, which opposed subsidies for the shipyards, also was pleased that the Ways and Means Committee's action mirrored its own proposal.

House Floor

The House amended HR 4003 and then passed it by a vote of 294-122 on Aug. 2. The House-passed bill imposed what amounted to a $1.35 billion tax increase on cargo and cruise vessels over 10 years to pay for subsidies to support U.S. shipping lines and shipyards. The bill incorporated the provisions of HR 2151, the bill the House had passed in 1993. (Vote 371, p. 110-H)

The bill struck a middle ground between the $1.7 billion package of subsidies approved by the Merchant Marine and Fisheries Committee and the more modest $1 billion Ways and Means proposal that included no direct shipyard subsidies.

Allies of the U.S. shipyards fought the Ways and Means Committee proposal on the floor, saying Congress should at least provide subsidies until the international agreement took effect in 1996.

Studds acknowledged that the shipyard subsidies might violate the new international agreement. Still, he proposed to raise $350 million over 10 years for the U.S. yards — as loan guarantees if subsidies were outlawed. To generate the money, Studds and the top Republican on Merchant Marine, Jack Fields of Texas, proposed to replace the Ways and Means tax package with a $1.35 billion increase in tonnage duties.

Gibbons objected, saying the duties would be as high as $9.50 a ton on commodities that sold for as low as $20 a ton.

But the House supported the Studds-Fields amendment by a vote of 268-153. (Vote 370, p. 110-H)

Senate Action

Despite its easy passage in the House, HR 4003 ran into trouble almost immediately in the Senate. Coal and grain companies argued that the addition of a few cents per ton in duties could threaten their sales.

The bill's chief patrons in the Senate — Breaux and Trent Lott, R-Miss. — proposed to cut the increase from $1.35 billion over 10 years to $1 billion over the same period and to exempt shipments of grain, coal and other dry bulk cargo from the higher duties. The exemption was not good enough for at least three Republicans: Larry Pressler of South Dakota, Charles E. Grassley of Iowa and Hank Brown of Colorado.

Efforts to produce a Senate bill were blocked Sept. 23, when Pressler stopped the Senate Commerce Committee from marking up HR 4003. Acting on behalf of his Republican colleagues Grassley and Brown, Pressler invoked a Senate rule

against committees' meeting while the Senate was in session.

Supporters of the bill tried to persuade Pressler to drop his opposition, noting that his main complaint about the bill — that it stood to increase the tonnage duties paid by grain shippers — had been addressed. But Pressler said he planned to continue to oppose the bill every way he could through the end of the session.

In addition to Pressler's objection, HR 4003 ran into trouble from some of the shipyards' Senate allies — most notably the Senate majority leader, George J. Mitchell, D-Maine — who pressed for greater shipyard subsidies. Breaux countered that the House's subsidy program violated the pending international agreement and that loan guarantees would deliver more benefits for the money.

Fields said he planned to try to pass a maritime revitalization measure in 1995 but added, "In all likelihood it will be too late." Another sponsor, Herbert H. Bateman, R-Va., said the opportunity to support U.S. shipyards may have passed. The pending international agreement barred most such aid.

Other Bills

Other attempts to revitalize the maritime industry included:

● **Passenger vessel construction.** The House Merchant Marine and Fisheries Subcommittee on Merchant Marine gave voice vote approval June 23 to HR 3821. The bill proposed to allow foreign-built cruise vessels to carry passengers between U.S. ports if their owners agreed to replace the ships eventually with U.S.-built ones. Under existing law, only U.S.-built vessels were allowed to carry passengers between U.S. ports.

The bill required the foreign-built ships to register in the United States and hire U.S. crews. Under an amendment offered by subcommittee Chairman William O. Lipinski, D-Ill., the ship owners had to enter into contracts within two years to buy U.S.-built ships, not three years as the original bill required.

Bateman, Gene Taylor, D-Miss., and Helen Delich Bentley, R-Md., voiced concern about companies putting foreign-built cruise ships into U.S. routes, then reneging on their promise to buy U.S.-built ships. By voice vote, the subcommittee adopted a Taylor amendment to require companies to put 10 percent of the foreign-built ships' gross revenues into an escrow account until they signed contracts to buy ships from U.S. yards. The amendment required foreign-built ships to forfeit the money if they failed to sign such contracts within two years.

The full Merchant Marine Committee approved HR 3821 by voice vote on Aug. 11.

After a heated debate, the committee voted 14-7 to adopt a substitute amendment by bill sponsor Unsoeld that permitted foreign-built cruise ships to register in the United States, hire U.S. crews and operate permanently in this country. In return, the line had to agree to build another vessel in a U.S. shipyard.

As originally approved by the Merchant Marine Subcommittee, the bill allowed a foreign-registered vessel to travel between U.S. ports only until a new cruise ship was built in a U.S. yard.

The so-called Jones Act prohibited foreign-registered vessels from carrying passengers between U.S. ports. As a result, ports such as Seattle were bypassed, forcing passengers to be bused to Vancouver for a cruise to Alaska.

The amendment also dropped the subcommittee provision that required owners of foreign-built ships to place 10 percent of their gross revenues in escrow until they signed contracts to buy ships from U.S. shipyards.

The House passed HR 3821 twice: on Sept. 22 as part of the Coast Guard reauthorization bill (HR 4422) and on Oct. 7 as part of HR 4852, a wide-ranging package of maritime safety and commerce measures. *(Coast Guard, p. 161; omnibus maritime bill, p. 162)*

● **Tax incentives.** The House Merchant Marine and Fisheries Subcommittee on Merchant Marine gave voice vote approval to HR 3822 on June 23. The subcommittee bill called for tax incentives for buying new U.S.-built cruise ships and for holding conventions on cruise ships. The incentives for conventions on U.S.-flagged ships were to equal the tax breaks provided for conventions on land.

The bill stalled and saw no further action.

● **Extending U.S. labor laws.** The House Education and Labor Subcommittee on Labor Standards, Occupational Health and Safety approved HR 1517 by a vote of 6-3 on Oct. 28, 1993.

The full committee approved the measure (H Rept 103-818) by voice vote April 13, 1994. The bill required foreign-flagged vessels that frequented U.S. ports to comply with U.S. minimum wage and overtime laws if their owners and at least half their crew were not citizens of the country in which the vessels were registered.

The bill called for extending coverage of the 1935 National Labor Relations Act and the 1938 Fair Labor Standards Act to the applicable foreign-registered vessels. Proponents said the bill promised to provide basic employment rights to seafarers on foreign vessels when they engaged in trade in the United States, docked in U.S. ports or transported U.S. tourists. Opponents said the bill threatened to force U.S. cruise lines to move their operations overseas. ■

Fishermen's Protection Act
A Late-Session Casualty

The House twice voted to reauthorize a 1967 law under which the government compensated fishing operators for fines they paid to foreign countries that seized their boats and catches. The legislation passed first as a separate bill (HR 3817) and then as part of a catchall House maritime package (HR 4852) assembled at the end of the session. The Senate passed a companion reauthorization bill (S 2243), but the two chambers did not reconcile their differences, and the legislation died at the end of the Congress.

Both HR 3817 and S 2243 reauthorized the 1967 fishermen's act. But they differed in key provisions written in response to a June 9 decision by Canada to impose a $1,100 fee on U.S. fishing vessels that passed through Canadian waters between Washington and Alaska. The House version proposed to impose an equal fee on Canadian fishing vessels and to restrict nighttime clearance of Canadian vessels into U.S. territorial waters.

The Senate bill harshly condemned the Canadian government's action and urged Clinton to voice disapproval "in the strongest terms."

Background

The 1967 Fishermen's Protective Act (PL 90-482) created two funds allowing the secretary of State to compensate commercial fishing operators whose vessels were seized by a foreign country. The Fishermen's Protective Fund, which received money from appropriations, reimbursed commercial fishing operators for any fines or fees paid to foreign countries to release their vessels. The fishing operators did

not have to contribute to participate in the reimbursement program. The Fishermen's Guarantee Fund acted like insurance. By paying a set amount each year, commercial fishing operators were eligible for reimbursement out of this fund, which also received money from appropriations.

Reauthorization was seen as a routine matter until a dispute erupted over the Canadian transit fee. Canada, which announced the fee June 9, said it was trying to jump-start talks to renew a 1985 treaty on salmon fishing in Alaska, British Columbia and the Pacific Northwest. The fee, which the State Department said violated international law, came at what typically was the peak of the Pacific salmon fishing season.

Under pressure from the U.S. government and sensing a backlash from U.S. lawmakers, Canada announced July 2 that it planned to stop collecting the fee. Both countries pledged to conserve salmon species in 1994.

House Action

HR 3817 began in the House Merchant Marine and Fisheries Subcommittee on Fisheries Management, which approved the measure by voice vote June 15.

Expressing disappointment that the State Department had not been more active in trying to get the Canadian fee rescinded, Don Young, R-Alaska, won an amendment to charge Canadian fishing vessels an equal fee. Under existing law, Canadian fishing vessels were not charged any transit fees and received, as a courtesy, U.S. Customs clearance by radio to enter U.S. territorial waters at night. The new fee was not to apply to Pacific halibut or albacore tuna fishing ships in accordance with U.S.-Canadian treaties. The Canadian fee made no such distinction, according to Young's staff.

The subcommittee also approved an amendment by Jolene Unsoeld, D-Wash., to use money already in the Fisherman's Protective Fund to reimburse U.S. fishermen forced to pay the fee. The bill directed the secretary of State to reclaim the money from Canada. Unsoeld said some of the approximately 500 U.S. fishing vessels affected were trying to avoid the fee by taking an alternative but dangerous route. She also reported that Canadian fishing vessels were blocking U.S. ships to force them to pay the fee.

Subcommittee Chairman Thomas J. Manton, D-N.Y., the bill's sponsor, called the amendments an attempt to "beat the Canadian government at this ill-advised game of 'chicken' on fisheries issues."

With the fishing dispute still unresolved, the full House Merchant Marine Committee approved the bill by voice vote June 29 (H Rept 103-585). The House passed the bill July 12, also by voice vote.

Senate Action

The Senate passed the companion bill (S 2243) on July 1 by voice vote. Like the House bill, S 2243 provided for U.S. fishing vessels to be reimbursed for the fees collected by Canada from the two funds created under the 1967 law. Since mid-June, Canada had collected about $330,000 from more than 200 U.S. fishing vessels.

The bill, sponsored by Frank H. Murkowski, R-Alaska, urged the president "to immediately convey to Canada in the strongest terms that the United States will not now, nor at any time in the future, tolerate any action by Canada which would impede or otherwise restrict the right of passage of vessels of the United States in a manner inconsistent with international law." ∎

Coast Guard Bill Stalls in Senate

The House twice passed a bill to reauthorize the Coast Guard for fiscal 1995 at a level that largely mirrored the Clinton administration's budget request. But the measure fell short in the Senate in the final hours of the 103rd Congress.

The House first passed HR 4422 as a stand-alone bill Sept. 22. Lawmakers passed the measure a second time Oct. 7, inserting its provisions into a catch-all package (HR 4852) assembled in an end-of-session attempt to win passage for a host of maritime safety and commerce bills. The Senate failed to act on the package a day later, however, after several senators objected to some House-passed provisions. *(Omnibus bill, p. 162)*

As passed by the House, the Coast Guard legislation authorized $3.7 billion for the agency, including $2.6 billion for operations, $439 million for vessel and equipment purchases and $13 million for bridge alterations. One item included in the bill that was not in Clinton's budget was a $21 million authorization for drug interdiction. The House authorization bill was $68 million more than Congress provided for the Coast Guard in the fiscal 1995 transportation spending bill (HR 4556 — PL 103-331). Coast Guard programs were authorized at $3.6

BOXSCORE

Coast Guard Reauthorization — HR 4422 (S 2373). The $3.7 billion fiscal 1995 authorization bill incorporated a host of other maritime bills.

Report: H Rept 103-706.

KEY ACTION

Sept. 22 — House passed HR 4422, 402-13, after appending five separate bills.

Aug. 11 — Senate committee approved S 2373 by voice vote.

Oct. 7 — House passed an omnibus bill (HR 4852), which included HR 4422, by voice vote.

---

billion in fiscal 1994. *(Appropriations, p. 530; 1993 Almanac, p. 214)*

Sponsored by Rep. W. J. "Billy" Tauzin, D-La., the legislation also contained provisions authorizing the Coast Guard to charge foreign passenger vessels for the full cost of inspections, to provide child care to its employees stationed in areas without such services, and to increase civil penalties for vessel documentation violations from $500 to $25,000.

Before passing the bill the first time, the House attached the contents of five separate bills aimed at imposing new safety requirements on river barges and towing vessels, reducing the regulatory burden on U.S. shipping lines, easing restrictions on the use of foreign-built vessels in U.S. waterways, imposing new safety requirements on recreational boating and ensuring funding for state boating safety grant programs.

Virtually all of these provisions were also included in HR 4852.

Round One

The fiscal 1995 Coast Guard reauthorization bill originated in the House Merchant Marine Committee in the spring.

Senate Sinks Omnibus Maritime Bill

The House on Oct. 7 passed an omnibus maritime bill (HR 4852) in an end-of-session attempt to win enactment of a host of maritime safety and commerce measures; the House acted by voice vote. The Senate did not take up the bill before adjournment, and HR 4852 and all of the bills it contained died.

HR 4852 began as a measure to approve a new fisheries agreement with the government of Lithuania. But leaders of the House Merchant Marine and Fisheries Committee decided to marry those provisions with a dozen separate measures, most of which had already passed the House, in a last-ditch effort to push them all through the Senate.

The omnibus bill contained the following elements:

• **Coast Guard reauthorization.** The fiscal 1995 Coast Guard reauthorization (HR 4422), which the House had passed once on Sept. 22 by a vote of 402-13. The measure, sponsored by W. J. "Billy" Tauzin, D-La., authorized $3.7 billion for the agency, including $21 million for drug interdiction. *(Coast Guard bill, p. 161)*

Before passage, the House had incorporated the following five maritime bills into HR 4422:

• **Barge and towboat safety.** A bill (HR 3282), sponsored by Tauzin, to promote safer operation of river barges by mandating more navigational equipment and more proficient crews.

• **Maritime deregulation.** A measure (HR 4959), also sponsored by Tauzin, to reduce the regulatory burden on the U.S. maritime industry by bringing Coast Guard regulations into line with the international standards that foreign ships were required to meet.

• **Foreign-built vessels.** A bill (HR 3821), sponsored by Jolene Unsoeld, D-Wash., aimed at encouraging the construction of cruise ships in U.S. yards; it temporarily allowed foreign ships to offer cruises along the U.S. coast.

• **Recreational boating safety.** A measure (HR 3786), sponsored by Tauzin and Jack Fields, R-Texas, containing a range of new safety requirements for recreational boat makers and users.

• **State boating safety grants.** A bill (HR 4477), sponsored by Merchant Marine Committee Chairman Gerry E. Studds, D-Mass., to provide a permanent source of funding for state boating safety grants and to authorize funding for boating access facilities.

The package also included the provisions of several other bills, many of which the House had previously passed.

• **Zebra mussels.** A bill (HR 3360) aimed at preventing the introduction of potentially harmful foreign species, such as zebra mussels, into U.S. waters.

The measure authorized $2 million over two years to study and test ballast water management technologies to prevent vessels from transferring aquatic species from port to port when they emptied ballast waters into waterways. Ships held ballast water to balance the weight of their cargo and dumped the water as they unloaded at their destination. Non-indigenous species, such as the zebra mussel, had multiplied in U.S. waterways after being dumped with ballast water.

According to the Office of Technology Assessment, zebra mussels had caused $3.4 billion in damage since a ship from northern Europe dumped its infected ballast into Lake St. Clair near Detroit in 1986.

The bill had won the approval of two House Merchant Marine and Fisheries panels — the Merchant Marine Subcommittee by voice vote Feb. 3 and the Coast Guard and Navigation Subcommittee by voice vote Feb. 8. The full Merchant Marine Committee approved the bill (H Rept 103-440) by voice vote Feb. 23.

The Merchant Marine Subcommittee gave voice vote approval to an amendment by panel Chairman William O. Lipinski, D-Ill., to specify that $150,000 be used for the evaluation program in fiscal 1995 and $1.85 million be used for the demonstration program in fiscal 1996. Under the amendment, the Aquatic Nuisance Species Task Force was to carry out the programs rather than the Transportation secretary.

The full committee approved another amendment by Lipinski, which required the Maritime Administration rather than an interagency task force to be responsible for administering the technology demonstration program authorized by the bill.

The House passed HR 3360 by voice vote March 21 under expedited procedures that barred amendments.

• **Biotechnology.** A bill (HR 1916 — H Rept 103-170) to promote the development of marine biotechnology.

The bill — which the House had passed July 13, 1993 — provided for the establishment of a marine biotechnology program at selected colleges and universities. HR 1916 authorized $90 million in grants over four years to support research into genetically modified marine organisms. Those grants were in addition to the roughly $44 million being spent each year under an existing federal program for biotechnology. *(1993 Almanac, p. 253)*

• **Fishermen's protection.** A bill (HR 3817), passed by the House July 12, to reauthorize the 1967 Fishermen's Protective Act (PL 90-482), which allowed the government to reimburse commercial fishing operators for fines paid to foreign countries when their boats and catches were seized. The reauthorization was expected to be routine, but it got caught up in a dispute over a Canadian transit fee imposed in June on certain U.S. fishing vessels. The bill proposed to set an equal fee for Canadian fishing vessels and to restrict nighttime clearance of Canadian vessels into U.S. territorial waters. *(Fishermen's protection, p. 160)*

• **Fishing restrictions.** A bill (HR 3188), which the House had passed by voice vote Nov. 2, 1993, to expand certain fishing limits. The bill added new fishing restrictions to a law (PL 102-582) enacted in 1992 that penalized both foreign and U.S. ships that harvested fish in the part of the Bering Sea called the Donut Hole. The bill provided similar punishments for U.S.-flag ships in the nearby Peanut Hole in the Sea of Okhotsk, where such fishing had migrated. *(1993 Almanac, p. 215)*

House Committee

The House Merchant Marine Subcommittee on Coast Guard and Navigation approved HR 4422 by voice vote May 25, recommending a $3.7 billion fiscal 1995 authorization for the Coast Guard's operations, vessel and equipment purchases, research, pensions and environmental compliance.

The bill included $11.5 million for drug interdiction activities. Several members of the panel said they wanted to put even more money into drug interdiction, but the budget was too tight. By voice vote, the subcommittee adopted amendments prohibiting the Coast Guard from moving an icebreaking cutter out of Crisfield, Md., or decommissioning an aging icebreaker in the Great Lakes.

The bill directed the Coast Guard to put an additional rescue and patrol vessel into service on the Mississippi River near Baton Rouge, La. That provision drew questions from Gene Taylor, D-Miss., who noted that the Coast Guard was preparing to close at least 11 stations in a budget-cutting move. Tauzin said the vessel was expected to help direct the Coast Guard's response to emergencies on the river.

The full Merchant Marine Committee gave voice vote approval June 29 to a revised version of HR 4422 (H Rept 103-706). But first, ranking Republican Jack Fields of Texas won voice vote approval for an amendment that increased the fiscal 1995 authorization level for the Coast Guard's drug-fighting efforts from $11.5 million to $21 million in an effort to restore spending cuts made to those programs by appropriators in fiscal 1994. The amendment also required that the portion of the Coast Guard's operating expenses used for drug interdiction not fall below 9.5 percent. The threshold was included to ensure that Coast Guard accounts were not drained by any humanitarian rescue missions, such as the Haitian effort. Both amendments were approved by voice vote.

House Floor

The House passed the bill by a vote of 402-13 on Sept. 22. *(Vote 437, p. 130-H)*

During floor action, the House gave voice vote approval to a block of amendments that included the texts of the five separate bills, all of which the House Merchant Marine and Fisheries Committee had previously approved. The bills were:

● **Barge and towboat navigational safety.** A bill (HR 3282), sponsored by Tauzin, requiring navigational equipment on towing vessels, proficiency tests of key crewmen and a model inspection program for towed vessels. The bill was proposed after river barges had been involved in two major mishaps in 1993.

The House Merchant Marine Subcommittee on Coast Guard and Navigation approved HR 3282 by voice vote April 14. The full Merchant Marine and Fisheries Committee followed suit, approving the bill by voice vote Sept. 21. During committee action, members approved a substitute by Merchant Marine Committee Chairman Gerry E. Studds, D-Mass., adding a requirement that all unlicensed crewmen have Coast Guard-issued merchant mariner documents. Tauzin attempted to eliminate that provision from the amendment but failed, 15-30. The Studds substitute was then approved by voice vote.

The bill required that towing vessels have up-to-date navigational and safety equipment and that their operators be licensed by the Coast Guard. Under the bill, failure to immediately report an accident involving a towing vessel could result in a fine of as much as $25,000. The existing penalty was up to $1,000.

The two 1993 accidents that prompted the bill involved

collisions with bridges. In one case, a bridge in Alabama was damaged by a barge, resulting in the derailment of an Amtrak train and the deaths of 47 people.

● **Maritime industry deregulation.** A bill (HR 4959), also sponsored by Tauzin, aimed at reducing the regulatory burden on the maritime industry.

HR 4959 was intended to address a complaint that the Coast Guard imposed more expensive safety regulations on U.S.-flag vessels than on their foreign competitors. It tried to bring Coast Guard regulations, which applied only to vessels registered in the United States, in line with the international standards that foreign ships had to meet. The bill proposed to cut the number of Coast Guard inspections required of U.S. vessels. Instead, the Coast Guard was authorized to audit a vessel owner's safety program, allow self-inspections, or accept inspection reports from recognized safety organizations, such as the American Bureau of Shipping.

The Merchant Marine and Fisheries Subcommittee on Coast Guard and Navigation approved HR 4959 by voice vote Sept. 13. The subcommittee, which Tauzin chaired, first adopted a substitute amendment by voice vote that addressed some concerns raised about the original proposal. The amendment went further to assure that safety would not be compromised by the shift in standards. It also aimed to open foreign markets to U.S. companies that manufactured boating equipment and materials. The amended version allowed vessels to use equipment and materials approved by foreign governments if the Transportation Department approved. No equipment was permitted, however, from countries that did not approve U.S.-made boating safety equipment.

The full Merchant Marine Committee approved the bill by voice vote on Sept. 21.

The bill was the third major piece of the Clinton administration's efforts to revitalize the U.S. maritime industry. The others were an expanded loan guarantee program for shipyards, which was put into effect administratively, and a new subsidy program for shipping lines (HR 4003), which stalled in the Senate Commerce Committee. *(Maritime reauthorization, p. 158)*

● **Foreign-built vessels.** A bill (HR 3821) sponsored by Jolene Unsoeld, D-Wash., to ease restrictions on the use of foreign-built vessels in U.S. waters as an incentive to encourage the construction of passenger vessels in U.S. shipyards. The House Merchant Marine and Fisheries Subcommittee on Merchant Marine approved HR 3821 by voice vote June 23. The full Merchant Marine Committee approved HR 3821 by voice vote Aug. 11.

The bill proposed to allow foreign-built cruise vessels to carry passengers between U.S. ports if their owners agreed to replace the ships eventually with U.S.-built ones. Under existing law, only U.S.-built vessels were allowed to carry passengers between U.S. ports.

● **Recreational boating safety.** A bill (HR 3786 — H Rept 103-445), sponsored by Tauzin and Fields, to set new safety requirements for recreational boat makers and users. HR 3786 was written in the wake of a tragedy in July 1993 on the Fourche LaFave River in Arkansas in which seven members of a family drowned.

The House Merchant Marine Subcommittee on Coast Guard and Navigation gave voice vote approval to HR 3786 on Feb. 8. The full Merchant Marine and Fisheries Committee approved the bill Feb. 23 by voice vote.

HR 3786 required children age 12 and under to wear life jackets or other flotation devices while they were on the deck of recreational vessels 26 feet long or less.

The bill also provided incentives to states to beef up laws against boating while intoxicated and to require individuals

found to have been operating a boat negligently to complete a boating safety course. Alcohol-related boating accidents accounted for at least half of all boating mishaps. States, for example, were to be eligible for grants from a $10 million trust fund in fiscal 1998 if they adopted laws that banned people from operating boats if they had a blood-alcohol level of more than 0.10 percent.

The legislation also provided for a $1,000 fine for failing to file a boating accident report with state authorities.

Full committee action on the bill came as some lawmakers and state officials were questioning the Clinton administration's commitment to boat safety programs. Clinton recommended in his fiscal 1995 budget proposal that the Coast Guard cut about 1,100 positions. His budget did not include about $70 million for Coast Guard programs that provided states with money for law enforcement and safe boating education programs.

But Merchant Marine Committee Chairman Studds said he planned to protect boat safety programs from the budget knife. he said the money for the program came out of a Highway Trust Fund and could not be used to reduce the deficit anyway.

● **Boating safety grant program.** A bill (HR 4477 — H Rept 103-849), sponsored by Studds, authorizing funding for state boating safety grant programs. The bill was intended to assure permanent future funding for the Coast Guard boating safety grant program for the states. The full Merchant Marine Committee discharged two of its subcommittees from action on HR 4477, approving the bill by voice vote on Aug. 11. The bill proposed to transfer funds from a sport fish restoration trust fund to the boating safety grant program in fiscal years 1995-99. The transfer was sought to address concerns that the Clinton administration fiscal 1995 budget proposal reduced funding for boating safety grant programs to the states.

Senate Committee

The Senate Commerce Committee took the next step, approving a companion Coast Guard reauthorization bill (S 2373 — S Rept 103-372) by voice vote Aug. 11.

Chairman Ernest F. Hollings, D-S.C., moved the bill quickly through markup in hopes of winning its final passage before the close of the 103rd Congress. The bill authorized $3.7 billion in fiscal 1995 for the Coast Guard's operations, vessel and equipment purchases, research, pensions and enforcement of environmental regulations.

Omnibus Maritime Bill

Prospects for final action on the Coast Guard reauthorization improved in the final days of the session, as House and Senate negotiators agreed to an omnibus maritime package that included the Coast Guard provisions. When Studds brought the package (HR 4852) to the House floor Oct. 7, however, it drew an objection from Tauzin and temporarily stalled.

Tauzin protested a proposed requirement that all crew members on river barges obtain federal merchant mariner documents — a provision included in the House-passed version of HR 3282. To accommodate Tauzin, Studds offered a new version of the omnibus package that dropped the proposed requirement. Also, to answer an objection by Robert S. Walker, R-Pa., he removed parts of the proposed reauthorization of National Oceanic and Atmospheric Administration programs (HR 4008). (NOAA, p. 219)

This revised package passed the House by voice vote late on Oct. 7, but it was too late to clear the Senate. ■

Senate Takes No Action On Maritime Board

The House passed a bill (HR 4391) to reauthorize the Federal Maritime Commission for fiscal 1995, but the measure died in the Senate, which took no action on it.

The legislation, sponsored by Rep. William O. Lipinski, D-Ill., authorized the same amount for the commission that Congress had appropriated in fiscal 1994: $18.9 million. The Clinton administration had requested $18.7 million, a cut that leaders of the House Merchant Marine and Fisheries Committee did not support.

Despite the demise of the reauthorization effort, appropriators continued to fund the commission, which regulated domestic and international shipping in U.S. waters. The fiscal 1995 spending bill for the departments of Commerce, Justice and State (HR 4603 — PL 103-317) contained less than $18.6 million for the commission. (Appropriations, p. 483)

The Merchant Marine Subcommittee on the Merchant Marine kicked off action on the bill, approving HR 4391 by voice vote May 24. The subcommittee measure authorized $18.9 million, $200,000 more than the administration had requested.

The panel first adopted an amendment by Helen Delich Bentley, R-Md., that incorporated the provisions of a bill (HR 56) that she had authored to extend so-called minimum compensation rules to all freight forwarders. Freight forwarders reserved space on cargo vessels for shippers.

The bill required shipping lines carrying U.S. imports or exports to pay all freight forwarders at least 1.25 percent of the revenue associated with the cargo provided by the forwarders.

Under existing law, that minimum rate, known as the minimum compensation rule, was guaranteed only for freight forwarders who doubled as customs brokers. Congress had adopted the minimum-compensation rule as part of the 1986 tax overhaul law. (1986 Almanac, p. 491)

The full Merchant Marine and Fisheries Committee gave voice vote approval to the bill (H Rept 103-716) Aug. 11. The House followed suit, passing the bill by voice vote Sept. 12 under expedited procedures that barred amendments.

The bill was referred to the Senate Commerce, Science and Transportation Committee, which took no action on it. ■

Lawmakers Authorize Funds To Preserve Maritime Past

The Senate on Oct. 8 cleared a bill (HR 3059) providing federal aid for maritime preservation and education projects. President Clinton signed the measure Nov. 2 (PL 103-451).

The new Maritime Heritage program was financed with proceeds from ships scrapped from the National Defense Reserve Fleet, a collection of government-owned cargo vessels. A quarter of the proceeds from such sales were to be used for the new program, with the rest going to upgrade other vessels in the fleet and assist state maritime academies.

The House passed the bill by voice vote Oct. 5, and the Senate followed suit by voice vote shortly before adjourning Oct. 8. The sponsor was Rep. Thomas H. Andrews, D-Maine. The program was to provide grants to states, local governments and nonprofit agencies for maritime exhibits, vessel-building and sailing programs, underwater archaeological work, historic-vessel repairs and similar projects. ■

Highway Funds Meet Roadblocks

A flurry of late-session negotiations failed to save a bill to designate elements of the new National Highway System (NHS) and authorize hundreds of new transportation projects. The bill (S 1887) foundered because leaders of the House Public Works and the Senate Environment and Public Works committees could not reconcile their differences over the projects, all of which were proposed by the House.

The main purpose of the bill was to name routes for the NHS. Congress established the NHS in the 1991 surface transportation law (PL 102-240) as a way to concentrate federal dollars on the routes most important to interstate commerce, tourism, military bases and intermodal travel. The roads on this network were to have first dibs on about 30 percent of all federal highway dollars through fiscal 1997, and possibly more in later years.

The 1991 law gave Congress until Sept. 30, 1995, to identify the routes for the NHS. The Department of Transportation started the ball rolling with a proposed map of the new system in December 1993. The map included roughly 160,000 miles of roadway, almost all of it already built. *(1991 Almanac, p. 137)*

Much of the department's proposal had already been dictated by Congress in the 1991 law, which required the NHS to include all the interstates (45,000 miles of roadway), the Defense Department's Strategic Highway Network and major connectors (about 17,000 more), and 21 "high-priority corridors" named by Congress (4,506 miles). The Transportation Department, working with state and local transportation agencies, was left to propose about 88,000 additional miles of highways for the new system.

Background

Unlike the Interstate Highway System, the NHS was not designed to blaze new trails for traffic and development. It was designed to maintain or improve the trails already in greatest use. It was not an expansion of the federal system so much as a retrenchment, a way to focus federal dollars on roads that carried the most commercial traffic.

States took divergent views on the significance of the new system. To some, such as Florida and California, it threatened to impose burdensome, expensive federal standards on road projects. Those states tried to put as little of their mileage onto the new system as possible. To others, such as Washington state, the NHS looked like the future of the federal highway program. These states tried to put as many highways as possible onto the system in the belief that the federal government eventually might tie the amount of money states received to the length of their NHS routes.

Under existing law, states received set portions of the NHS pot no matter how many NHS miles they had. But it was possible that the formula for dividing the NHS money could change in 1997, when Congress was due to write a new surface transportation law.

Overall, the NHS proposed by Transportation Secretary

BOXSCORE

NHS Designation — S 1887 (HR 4385). The bills designated elements of the new National Highway System (NHS). The House version also authorized $2 billion for new highway and transit projects.

Reports: H Rept 103-519, S Rept 103-357.

KEY ACTION

May 25 — House passed HR 4385, 412-12.

Sept. 23 — Senate passed S 1887 by voice vote.

Sept. 29 — House passed S 1887 by voice vote after substituting the text of HR 4385.

Federico F. Peña included only 4 percent of the nation's roads. Those roads carried 40 percent of the country's drivers, though, and 75 percent of its commercial traffic. The Transportation Department's four stated goals in choosing routes were to preserve roads that served military bases; support the long multistate corridors that were important to interstate commerce; share some of the highway dollars generated in densely populated states with states that had little traffic; and ensure links from state to state and from highways to seaways, airports, railroads and bus terminals.

Although the goal of the new system was to direct more federal money to the selected routes, what ultimately happened to each highway was up to state and local transportation officials. Some routes might be widened. Some might have high-technology improvements to reduce congestion. Others might just be resurfaced. And some might never climb high enough on their state's priority list to have anything done.

House Committee

The House effort to designate NHS routes was led by the chairman and the ranking member of the House Public Works Committee — Norman Y. Mineta, D-Calif., and Bud Shuster, R-Pa. — and their counterparts on the Surface Transportation Subcommittee — Nick J. Rahall II, D-W.Va., and Tom Petri, R-Wis. The four decided on a three-part bill that would designate NHS routes, make minor, largely technical changes to the 1991 surface transportation law and direct federal dollars to new highway and mass-transit projects.

Assembling the Bill

The NHS portion was the simplest and least controversial. The sponsors proposed to adopt the Transportation Department's map, which the department had updated in May after consulting again with state officials.

The "technical corrections" portion of the bill was noncontroversial, too, at least in the House. Its provisions came from HR 3276 (H Rept 103-337), which the House had passed late in the 1993 session. *(1993 Almanac, p. 225)*

Putting together the list of new projects was a more complicated task. The committee had engaged in a bitter turf battle in 1993 with the House Transportation Appropriations Subcommittee over the power to direct money to highway projects not fully authorized by Congress. Although Public Works prevailed, its leaders agreed to push a new authorization bill in 1994 that the appropriators could use as their guide. *(1993 Almanac, p. 663)*

Late in the 1993 session, Rahall had invited lawmakers to submit requests for projects by Jan. 7, 1994. The requests poured in, totaling more than 900 proposals that together would cost more than $32.4 billion.

The committee's leaders agreed to limit themselves to a "zero sum" bill that spent no more money from the Highway Trust Fund than Congress already had authorized. That

pledge forced them to conduct a scavenger hunt for unused dollars in the three previous surface transportation bills. The hunt rounded up $526 million for road projects and $623 million for mass transit projects. The money was to come largely from programs that were dormant or underused, including high-speed rail and highway safety.

In addition, after consulting with the Transportation Appropriations Subcommittee, the bill's sponsors decided to authorize roughly $900 million more for road projects over three years out of the general Treasury. The figure corresponded on an annual basis to what the appropriators had proposed to spend in fiscal 1994 on highway projects before Public Works protested.

That gave the committee a total of about $2 billion to spend on projects, or $1 for every $16 in requests. To whittle down the pile, the sponsors first rejected requests that came in after the Jan. 7 deadline. Then they weeded out others on the basis of 18 questions Rahall had asked lawmakers who requested money for projects. Modeled after the "investment criteria" that the Transportation Appropriations Subcommittee had inaugurated in 1993, the questions tried to gauge the economic and environmental impacts of each proposal and the possible alternatives.

Next, the committee consulted federal, state and local officials to eliminate requests that did not fit into their priorities. Even after this vetting, though, the committee still had billions of dollars' worth of projects that met its criteria.

At this point, the selection process shifted from objective criteria to political ones. Mineta and Shuster divided the available pot according to the partisan makeup of Congress — Mineta got roughly 60 percent of the pot for Democratic requests, and Shuster had 40 percent for Republican requests.

Working with Rahall, Mineta weeded through the requests from Democrats to try to achieve a geographic balance. The two lawmakers also tried to follow the highway distribution formulas in the 1991 surface transportation law, which tended to shift money from growing Sun Belt states to sparsely populated Western states and the urbanized Northeast. Further consideration was given to members of the Public Works Committee. The final cut was Mineta's, and it boiled down to this: Democrats who had advocated spending cuts were more likely to have deeper cuts in their own requests than those who had not.

As he moved about Capitol Hill in the days surrounding the bill's introduction, Mineta carried a valise stuffed with information about the requests for projects and the positions members had taken. That way, he could explain how the decisions on projects were made. It did not make every member happy, he said, but at least they understood.

Like Mineta and Rahall, Republicans Shuster and Petri tried not to stray from the formulas set in the 1991 law. They also favored requests from members of Public Works, the Republican leadership and committees important to transportation, such as Appropriations. Unlike their Democratic colleagues, though, Shuster and Petri tried to give some money to every Republican with a valid request. Thus, Democrats who called for spending cuts might find themselves with fewer dollars than Republicans who had taken the same position.

When the bill (HR 4385) was introduced May 11, the final tally was $1.4 billion for 270 specific road, bridge, bike and trail projects and almost $600 million for 55 mass transit projects.

The bill also proposed to authorize $10 million to guarantee loans for a toll road project in Orange County, Calif.,

as requested by California Republicans Ron Packard, Jay C. Kim and Robert K. Dornan; $2.5 million to build a visitors center on the New River Parkway in West Virginia, as requested by Rahall; and $2 million for a "coal heritage trail" tour route in West Virginia, as requested by Rahall. The money for road projects was to come from two pots — the general Treasury (almost $886 million over the next three years, subject to the appropriators' approval) and the Highway Trust Fund ($505 million, which did not require an appropriation).

Subcommittee Action

The Surface Transportation Subcommittee approved HR 4385 by voice vote May 12. There was no discussion of the projects during the markup; instead, most of the debate concerned amendments dealing with motorcycle helmets and metric signs.

The 1991 surface transportation law required states to enact laws requiring motorcycle riders to wear helmets and drivers to wear seat belts. States that failed to do so would have a portion of their highway aid transformed into grants for safety programs. Petri led efforts to repeal the penalty against states that did not comply with the mandate. He said the 28 states that did not require motorcyclists to wear helmets could have $157 million in federal highway aid shifted against their wishes into safety programs in 1995 and 1996.

The original version of HR 4385 would have given states an additional year, until the end of 1995, to comply. By a 20-19 vote, however, the subcommittee adopted a Petri amendment simply to delete the penalty for non-compliance.

The committee also agreed by voice vote to an amendment by Leslie L. Byrne, D-Va., against converting to metric signs. Under Byrne's amendment, the Transportation Department could not require states to convert their highway signs to metric measurements.

Full Committee Action

The bill moved to the full Public Works Committee on May 17, where its sponsors added to the load of special highway and transit projects. The bill was approved by voice vote (H Rept 103-519).

The number of road projects increased to 285, the number of transit projects to 65 and the total proposed spending to a little more than $2 billion. Of the road projects, 128 were to receive more than $513 million straight from the Highway Trust Fund, bypassing the appropriators; the rest of the money was to be distributed at the appropriators' discretion.

As was the case in the Surface Transportation Subcommittee, the projects sparked no debate. Instead, the main fights were over two requirements in the 1991 law — that states use scrap tires in a portion of their pavings and that states compel motorcyclists to wear helmets.

● **Rubberized pavement.** The 1991 law required states to use ground-up tires, also known as crumb rubber, in up to 5 percent of the asphalt on federal road projects in fiscal 1994. The required percentage rose to 20 percent for 1997 and later years, although one-fourth of the mandate could be met by using recycled pavement instead of crumb rubber.

In 1993, Congress put a temporary hold on the crumb-rubber mandate as part of the transportation appropriations law (PL 103-122). Opponents of the mandate, led by the road builders and the industries that made traditional paving materials, urged the Public Works Committee to remove the mandate entirely so that more study could be done. They argued that the long-term performance, the cost and the recyclability of rubberized pavement needed to be examined, as well as

the emissions from plants making rubberized asphalt and the fumes that workers breathed as they laid the pavement.

Supporters of the mandate included companies that ground scrap tires and produced rubberized asphalt, environmental groups, mayors, public health officials, two major tire manufacturers and numerous tire dealers. Their main argument was that California, Arizona and Florida — the states with the most experience with crumb rubber — had proven rubberized asphalt to be more durable and less expensive than conventional pavement.

The bill's sponsors agreed to write a compromise on crumb rubber into HR 4385. The mandate for crumb rubber would be turned into a two-year experiment, with states required to use rubberized asphalt in 2.5 percent of their pavings in 1996 and 5 percent in 1997. An equal amount would have to be used either in pavings or in some other highway use, such as stabilizing embankments. The penalty was reduced, too, to give states credit for any amount of rubberized asphalt used below the minimum required.

At the May 17 markup, Mike Parker, D-Miss., proposed to go even further, offering an amendment to give states the flexibility not to use any crumb rubber in their asphalt. Mineta responded that the amendment would make it harder to push the bill through the Senate, where the author of the crumb-rubber provision — John H. Chafee of Rhode Island — was the top Republican on the Environment and Public Works Committee.

Parker replied, "He needs to start putting up with us, instead of us putting up with him." The committee disagreed, defeating the amendment by voice vote.

At the urging of Mineta and transportation safety advocates, the committee reversed the Surface Transportation Subcommittee's narrow decision to remove the penalties for states that did not mandate motorcycle helmets and car safety belts. The committee agreed to Mineta's amendment to restore the penalties by a vote of 40-24. It then defeated, 25-37, a Petri amendment to let states adopt safety education programs for motorcyclists instead of requiring helmets.

House Floor

The House approved the bill May 25 by a vote of 412-12. *(Vote 200, p. 60-H)*

Before the vote, member after member rose to praise the bill's sponsors — mainly for directing money to a project in that member's district. Only two lawmakers criticized the bill: Olympia J. Snowe, R-Maine, who said the committee should have retained the Petri amendment on motorcycle helmets, and Jon Kyl, R-Ariz., who blasted the money for special projects.

In a statement inserted into the Congressional Record, Kyl said, "The problem with earmarking is that funds are allocated, not necessarily according to merit or which projects will help the United States of America most, but rather according to how well connected politically the project sponsors are. Fifty-five percent of the total funding earmarked in HR 4385 goes to 10 states which just happen to be represented by 36 of the 64 Public Works Committee members."

● **More projects.** Kyl's criticism did not deter Rahall from offering an amendment adding yet more projects to the bill. The amendment was adopted by voice vote, bringing the bill's tally to 287 road and bridge projects worth $1.4 billion and 65 transit projects worth $605 million.

Rahall's amendment also included a proposal by Bill

'Seismic Retrofitting' for Quake-Damaged Bridges

Motivated by the Jan. 17 earthquake in Southern California, the House cleared a bill March 2 that allowed states to use bridge repair funds to gird their bridges against future earthquakes. The bill was cleared by voice vote. President Clinton signed the measure into law March 17 (S 1789 — PL 103-220).

House Public Works Committee Chairman Norman Y. Mineta, D-Calif., said Congress had intended to authorize spending on "seismic retrofits" in the 1991 surface transportation law. The Federal Highway Administration, however, ruled that federal funds could be used for such projects only on bridges that were damaged or structurally deficient.

Mineta introduced a bill (HR 1435) on March 23, 1993, to clarify that states could use bridge repair money for seismic retrofits on bridges that were not otherwise eligible for funding. Such spending would count against each state's share of the bridge repair pot the following year.

Sen. Barbara Boxer, D-Calif., introduced S 1789, a similar proposal, in the Senate eight days after the earthquake rocked Los Angeles, collapsing several highway overpasses. The main difference was that, under Boxer's bill, seismic retrofit projects did not reduce a state's share of the future bridge repair dollars.

The Senate Environment and Public Works Committee approved the bill Jan. 27. The Senate gave voice vote approval Feb. 7.

Richardson, D-N.M., and Dan Hamburg, D-Calif., to allow selected tribal governments to deal directly with the Transportation Department on road projects, rather than working through the Interior Department's Bureau of Indian Affairs. The three-year pilot project was proposed as a way to cut administrative overhead.

Another provision in the amendment was a proposal by Anthony C. Beilenson, D-Calif., to allow states to require contractors on federally funded projects to guarantee the quality of their work.

● **East-West Transamerica Corridor.** The House rejected, 64-364, an amendment by Bob Clement, D-Tenn., to remove a provision of the bill dealing with the East-West Transamerica Corridor, a new interstate-grade highway. The provision required the highway to pass through specific communities in Kentucky and West Virginia, a move that Clement said would undercut a multistate study to identify the best route for the highway. Tom Barlow, D-Ky., said the provision would bring the highway through the communities most in need of economic development. *(Vote 199, p. 60-H)*

● **Trucking safety.** James L. Oberstar, D-Minn., had circulated a major truck-safety amendment, but he decided not to offer it in the face of stiff opposition from the trucking industry and its allies on the committee. Endorsed by a coalition of safety groups, Oberstar's amendment was intended to limit the length and weight of trucks on the NHS. It would have barred new truck trailers longer than a standard cargo container (53 feet) and frozen the existing weight limits on routes added to the NHS. It also would have eliminated the states' ability to waive or skirt the weight limits.

The trucking industry had a powerful ally in Shuster, who argued that the bill was not the place to take up truck safety issues. Oberstar ultimately agreed not to offer his amendment in exchange for a promise that the committee would hold hearings on the issue of truck safety.

Rahall included in his amendment one less controversial element of Oberstar's proposal: a requirement that the Transportation Department define what constituted a "nondivisible load." Without such a definition, states had wide latitude to decide which loads to exempt from the weight limit on the grounds that they could not be dismantled or divided easily.

A final amendment by James A. Traficant Jr., D-Ohio, required the Transportation Department to study ways to reduce accidents caused by truck drivers falling asleep at the wheel. That amendment was approved by voice vote.

Senate Action

Leaders of the Senate Environment and Public Works Committee made it clear that they had far less interest in highway legislation than the House did. With the committee's schedule dominated by major environmental bills, Chairman Max Baucus, D-Mont., said early in 1994 that any House bill loaded with special projects would be dead on arrival in his committee.

Instead, Baucus and seven colleagues on the committee introduced a bill March 3 to designate the NHS routes recommended by the Transportation Department. The committee approved the bill Aug. 12 by voice vote (S 1887 — S Rept 103-357).

Unlike the lengthy House bill, the Environment and Public Works Committee's measure had only two substantive provisions. One designated the initial NHS routes, as in the House bill. The other allowed the Transportation Department to add routes at the states' request without congressional approval.

Baucus said before the markup that he would reject any House attempt at a conference committee to add projects. "It's time to say no to pork. . . . There'll be no bill issued if the House insists on amendments." Still, Senate committee members did not completely rebuff the idea of winning funding for special projects. Harry Reid, D-Nev., said he would like to get some money for demonstration projects in his fast-growing home state, though he offered no amendment to do so.

The Senate passed the bill by voice vote Sept. 23 without amendment and virtually without debate. Said Baucus, "A clean bill is our best chance of enacting the NHS this year. Loading up the bill with controversial matters will only delay action, bringing us closer to the deadline and increasing the uncertainty for all states."

Negotiations Collapse

The House took up the Senate bill Sept. 29. After substituting the contents of HR 4385, the House passed S 1887 by voice vote, requested a conference with the Senate and appointed conferees.

Baucus had said that he would not go to conference unless the House agreed to drop the projects and "technical corrections" from the bill. On Oct. 4, however, he said he would accept some of the House projects on one condition: that the money for each state's projects come out of that state's annual allocation of federal highway aid.

Although Mineta said he could accept the compromise, other leading members of his committee balked. They insisted that money for the projects come out of other transportation programs that the House had proposed to cancel, an approach rejected by Baucus' committee.

The Senate negotiators argued that the House funding mechanism would not pass the Senate's budget rules and would force large-scale cuts in the other highway programs in future years. Unable to narrow their differences, Mineta and Baucus decided not to convene a conference, allowing the legislation to die. Both pledged to renew their efforts in 1995. ■

FAA Reauthorized for Three Years

Ending a battle over airport landing fees that had bottled up almost $1.7 billion in airport construction grants, Congress on Aug. 8 cleared a bill reauthorizing the Federal Aviation Administration (FAA) and the Airport Improvement Program. President Clinton signed the measure Aug. 23 (HR 2739 — PL 103-305).

The bill authorized the FAA to make $2.1 billion in grants to airports in fiscal 1994, $2.2 billion in fiscal 1995 and $2.2 billion in fiscal 1996. Airports were likely to receive far less than those levels in the first two years, however, due to spending ceilings placed by the appropriations bills.

The bill also set up an expedited procedure for the Transportation Department to resolve disputes between airlines and airports over proposed increases in landing fees; toughened the rules against local officials diverting airport revenues for purposes other than airport services and improvements; and required air carriers to give 45 days' notice before terminating service to non-hub airports.

Other provisions of the bill barred the use of gambling devices on international flights; required the FAA to study the effectiveness and cost of child restraint systems on aircraft; and required the FAA to consider testing fewer airline employees for illegal drug use.

The bill gave the FAA administrator a five-year term. FAA

administrators had been serving at the president's discretion, and critics said the agency had been harmed by rapid turnover at the top.

The FAA was not permitted to reduce a U.S. airline's access to O'Hare International Airport in Illinois for the sake of a foreign carrier's access. Nor could it make a similar change at Washington National Airport or John F. Kennedy International or LaGuardia International airports in New York if the foreign airline's country did not grant U.S. airlines equivalent access to its airports.

On non-aviation issues, the bill included language added in the Senate to pre-empt state regulations of trucking prices, routes and other economic matters, although the pre-emption was delayed for three years in Hawaii. *(Trucking deregulation, p. 170)*

The measure also included non-binding recommendations that the United States prepare its forces to defend South Korea and that the Equal Employment Opportunity Commission withdraw its proposed guidelines on religious harassment.

The airport grant program had shut down at the end of September 1993 as the bill bogged down in the Senate. The measure was waylaid by a series of disputes unrelated to the federal aviation program, prompting Congress to pass a stopgap bill (S 2024 — PL 103-260) in May 1994 to authorize $800

million in grants on a temporary basis.

The grants program expired again before the House and Senate could resolve the last of the disputes: whether to accept a Senate proposal eliminating state regulation over trucking companies that made frequent use of aircraft to move freight. The conferees ultimately agreed to a House proposal to exempt all trucking companies from state economic regulations.

The bill also authorized $7.1 billion in fiscal 1994, $7.3 billion in fiscal 1995 and $7.5 billion in fiscal 1996 for the FAA's operations, facilities and equipment purchases.

Background

Congress provided $1.69 billion for airport improvement grants in the fiscal 1994 transportation appropriations bill (PL 103-122). But the FAA could not award the money without congressional authorization, which had run out at the end of fiscal 1993.

The House passed a bill (HR 2739 — H Rept 103-240) on Oct. 13, 1993, to reauthorize the FAA and the Airport Improvement Program for three years. The Senate Commerce Committee approved a one-year reauthorization (S 1491 — S Rept 103-181) by voice vote Nov. 9, 1993. But the bill bogged down before it reached the Senate floor, when Nancy Landon Kassebaum, R-Kan., threatened to offer an amendment to shield manufacturers of small aircraft against some product-liability lawsuits. Opposition to Kassebaum's amendment kept S 1491 from advancing. *(1993 Almanac, p. 218)*

That hurdle was removed March 16, 1994, when the Senate passed Kassebaum's proposal as a free-standing bill (S 1458 — S Rept 103-202). *(Small-plane liability, p. 180)*

By then, however, the FAA reauthorization bill had become embroiled in a landing-fee dispute between airports and airlines. The financially strapped airlines wanted any fee increase to reflect the amount of money airports earned on concessions, a potentially lucrative source of revenue. Some airports, however, wanted their fees to cover all costs associated with the runways, navigational equipment and other facilities used by airlines, regardless of how much money was raised by concessions.

The Supreme Court sided with the airports Jan. 24, ruling that airports had wide latitude to set landing fees and rents as long as they were based on a "fair approximation of use of the facilities."

The airlines lobbied the Senate Commerce Subcommittee on Aviation for a more precise definition of what constituted a reasonable fee, to be included in the FAA reauthorization bill.

Temporary Authorization

When negotiations took a turn for the worse in mid-April, Senate Aviation Subcommittee Chairman Wendell H. Ford, D-Ky., offered the stopgap measure (S 2024), authorizing the FAA to distribute as much as $800 million in airport grants through June 30. The Senate passed the bill by voice vote April 19. The House passed an amended version by voice vote May 3, and the aviation panels from both chambers negotiated a final bill that the Senate approved

---

BOXSCORE

FAA Reauthorization — HR 2739 (S 1491). The bill reauthorized the Federal Aviation Administration (FAA) and the Airport Improvement Program for three years and pre-empted many state trucking regulations.

Reports: H Rept 103-240, S Rept 103-181; conference report H Rept 103-677.

KEY ACTION

June 16 — Senate passed HR 2739 by voice vote after substituting the text of S 1491.

Aug. 8 — House, Senate each adopted the conference report by voice vote.

Aug. 23 — President signed the bill — PL 103-305.

---

by voice vote May 12. The House cleared the stopgap bill May 17, also by voice vote, and Clinton signed it May 26.

The short-term bill gave Transportation Secretary Federico F. Peña temporary authority to resolve disputes between airlines and airports over landing fees.

At the insistence of the House, the bill also required Peña to study ways to improve the FAA's air traffic control system without splitting it off into a government-run corporation, an approach proposed by Peña and Vice President Al Gore. The administration was required to complete the study before submitting legislation to create the traffic control corporation. Ford and the leader of the House Public Works Aviation Subcommittee, Democrat James L. Oberstar of Minnesota, were sharply critical of the administration's air traffic control proposal.

The bill increased the minimum grant for small airports from $400,000 to $500,000, as the House proposed. At the Senate's insistence, the bill reserved at least $325 million each year for grants made at the FAA's discretion.

Senate Floor

After a week debating issues unrelated to air travel, the Senate gave voice vote approval June 16 to HR 2739, after inserting the contents of its own reauthorization proposal, S 1491. The bill came to the floor with a provision by Ford to exempt package delivery services from state trucking regulations.

The Senate attached 10 Democrat-penned amendments — all identical — calling for hearings on the Whitewater imbroglio. Senators also voted 93-3 on June 16 to add an amendment by John McCain, R-Ariz., urging the United States to prepare itself to deter and, if necessary, repel an attack on South Korea by North Korea. *(Vote 150, p. 26-S)*

Shortly after that vote, the Senate voted 94-0 to adopt a sense-of-Congress amendment by Hank Brown, R-Colo., urging the Equal Employment Opportunity Commission to withdraw proposed guidelines on religious harassment and draft new ones that did not conflict with the First Amendment. *(Vote 151, p. 26-S)*

The Senate debated only a handful of aviation amendments. By a vote of 29-65, it rejected a proposal by Howard M. Metzenbaum, D-Ohio, to reserve half the air traffic controller jobs for controllers who had gone on strike and been fired by President Ronald Reagan in 1981. *(Vote 152, p. 26-S)*

It also voted 93-6 to table, or kill, a Metzenbaum amendment to require toilets on all new commercial planes built to carry 10 or more passengers. *(Vote 149, p. 26-S)*

Final Action

The House adopted the conference report to HR 2739 (H Rept 103-677) by voice vote Aug. 8, and the Senate cleared the bill by voice vote later the same day.

The final bill expanded the Senate's provision on package delivery services to pre-empt all state economic regulation of trucking companies, with the exception that regulations in Hawaii were to be left in place for three years. ∎

Congress Further Deregulates Trucking Industry

With little warning or fanfare, Congress eliminated much of the remaining federal regulation of the trucking industry as part of a bill reauthorizing safety programs for hazardous shipments (HR 2178). It also pre-empted state regulation of truck rates, routes and other economic matters as part of a bill reauthorizing the Federal Aviation Administration (FAA) (HR 2739).

Further trucking deregulation was not on anyone's agenda at the beginning of the 103rd Congress. The issue moved to the forefront in response to two unrelated developments: a rifle-shot attempt in the Senate to protect a package delivery company and a move in the House to cut funding for the Interstate Commerce Commission (ICC).

Shrinking the ICC's Role

Congress had partially deregulated the trucking industry in the Motor Carrier Act of 1980 (PL 96-296), the third of three major transportation deregulation measures passed under President Jimmy Carter. The act removed much of the ICC's control over companies entering the interstate trucking business, the routes they took and the prices they charged. What remained were requirements, dating to 1935, that trucking companies obtain an operating license from the ICC. The companies also had to notify the ICC of any change in the prices they charged for their services. *(1980 Almanac, p. 242)*

On June 16, the House unexpectedly voted to eliminate funding for the ICC in the fiscal 1995 transportation spending bill (HR 4556). The amendment, by John R. Kasich, R-Ohio, left the ICC's regulations in place with no money to enforce them. Kasich said the amendment would save $25 million in fiscal 1995 and more than $150 million over five years, but the General Accounting Office said that simply eliminating the ICC would not generate "meaningful cost savings" since the duties would have to be performed by other government agencies. The Senate did not go as far in its version of the transportation spending bill, but it did vote July 21 to trim the ICC's funding by one-third. *(Appropriations, p. 530)*

In response, Jim Exon, D-Neb., and Bob Packwood, R-Ore., drafted a compromise bill (S 2275) aimed at shrinking the ICC by removing some of its trucking duties. In particular, the Exon-Packwood bill eliminated the requirement that trucking companies file their rates with the ICC, leaving that requirement on bus companies and household-goods movers. They also eliminated the requirement that such companies demonstrate "public convenience and necessity" to obtain a license for interstate service, requiring only that they proved that they met federal safety and insurance standards.

Packwood said the proposal was aimed at avoiding the "uncertainty, confusion and potential chaos that could ensue if we simply eliminate the ICC without a larger strategy."

On Aug. 11, the Senate agreed by voice vote to add an amendment modeled on the Exon-Packwood bill to the hazardous waste transportation bill (HR 2178) then on the floor. The Senate passed HR 2178 by voice vote the same day, and the House agreed Aug. 16 to accept the Senate version, also by voice vote, clearing the bill for President Clinton, who signed it Aug. 26 (PL 103-311).

Pre-Empting State Regulations

Meanwhile, in early June, Wendell H. Ford, D-Ky., headed to the Senate floor with S 1491, the Senate's version of the FAA reauthorization bill. That bill included a provision by Ford to exempt package delivery services from state trucking regulations.

More than 40 states exerted some regulatory control over trucking services within their borders. In general, these regulations required trucking companies to gain state approval before changing their prices or serving new areas.

Ford was trying to give the United Parcel Service the same regulatory relief that a federal appeals court had ordered in 1991 for its main competitor, Federal Express. Numerous senators sought to expand the provision, prompting Ford to propose deregulating any trucking company that owned an air carrier or used an air carrier at least 15,000 times each year. On June 16, the Senate passed the FAA reauthorization, after inserting its text into the House bill. *(FAA reauthorization, p. 168)*

The Senate's move to pre-empt state trucking regulations got a cool reception from some leaders of the House Public Works Committee. "Some may find it passingly strange that a provision of this scope and magnitude was included in an airport improvement bill without the benefit of a public airing of the issue or committee consideration. I know I did," said Surface Transportation Subcommittee Chairman Nick J. Rahall II, D-W.Va.

Still, when Rahall held a hearing on the issue July 20, he found widespread support for ending state regulation of rates and routes. The main complaint by the trucking companies' trade association was that the Senate's approach did not exempt all trucking companies, putting some at a competitive disadvantage.

Exon, chairman of the Surface Transportation Subcommittee of the Senate Commerce, Science and Transportation Committee, found a similar level of support for trimming the ICC's oversight of interstate trucking at a hearing on July 12.

Robert A. Voltmann of the National Industrial Transportation League, the shippers' trade association, said trucking regulations cost the national economy $6 billion to $8 billion annually. He added that the average U.S. product moved seven times by truck before it was sold, while the average import moved only once or twice by truck.

When Ford's airport-grants bill went to conference on Aug. 3, House Public Works Committee Chairman Norman Y. Mineta, D-Calif., proposed to pre-empt all state economic regulation of trucking companies. The pre-emption did not apply to safety regulations, size and weight limits, insurance requirements, uniform business rules or regulations on the transportation of household goods.

The Senate negotiators accepted the proposal with one caveat: The regulations in Hawaii were to be left in place for three years. The House approved the conference report (HR 2739 — H Rept 103-677) by voice vote Aug. 8; the Senate cleared it by voice vote the same day; and Clinton signed it Aug. 23 (PL 103-305).

A later attempt to preserve state regulatory power over tow truck operators stalled at the end of the session. *(Tow trucks, p. 174)*

Other Legislation Related To Transportation

A law regulating transport of hazardous materials and a bill funding high speed rail were cleared, while several other transportation bills were considered but not enacted during the second session of the 103rd Congress.

Hazardous Materials Transport

Congress on Aug. 16 cleared a bill authorizing $75.3 million for fiscal years 1994-97 for programs established by the Hazardous Materials Transportation Act.

The measure (HR 2178) also required the Transportation Department to study the use of new highway technologies to promote safe transport of hazardous materials. Unrelated provisions, added in the Senate, eliminated much of the remaining federal regulation of the trucking industry. President Clinton signed the bill into law Aug. 26 (PL 103-311).

The House originally passed a four-year authorization by voice vote Nov. 21, 1993. The bill reflected a compromise between two committees — Energy and Commerce and Public Works — that had approved different versions of the legislation (HR 2178 — H Rept 103-336; HR 3460).

In the Senate, the Commerce, Science and Transportation Committee approved a three-year authorization (S 1640 — S Rept 103-217) on Nov. 9, 1993. But the bill, sponsored by Jim Exon, D-Neb., did not reach the floor that year. *(1993 Almanac, p. 221)*

The Senate took up S 1640 on Aug. 11, 1994, agreeing by voice vote to a bipartisan amendment by Wendell H. Ford, D-Ky., to shrink the Interstate Commerce Commission (ICC) by removing some of its trucking duties. The trucking provisions — modeled on a separate bill sponsored by Exon and Bob Packwood, R-Ore. (S 2275) — came in response to a move by the House to cut all funding for the ICC from the fiscal 1995 transportation spending bill (HR 4556). *(Trucking deregulation, p. 170)*

The revised Senate bill authorized $75.3 million for fiscal years 1994-97 for the Hazardous Materials Transportation Act.

The Senate then passed HR 2178 by voice vote, after substituting the text of S 1640 for the House-passed language. The House agreed by voice vote Aug. 16 to accept the Senate version.

Amtrak Reauthorization

House and Senate committees approved separate versions of a two-year reauthorization for the National Railroad Corp., better known as Amtrak. But the bill did not make it to the floor in either chamber.

The House Energy and Commerce Subcommittee on Transportation and Hazardous Materials approved its version of the bill by voice vote May 24 after a brief debate. The full Energy and Commerce Committee approved the Amtrak reauthorization by voice vote July 19 (HR 4111 — H Rept 103-698).

The government-owned passenger rail system had been the subject of regular attacks by congressional budget-cutters in recent years, but subcommittee Chairman Al Swift, D-Wash., praised Amtrak officials for promoting changes within the system. "Amtrak has new leadership. . . . It is headed in a new direction," he said. "And this legislation gets America's railroad on track."

Other lawmakers on the subcommittee praised the changes already under way at Amtrak but said more needed to be done.

As approved by the committee, the bill raised Amtrak's authorization by $88 million, mainly for equipment and facilities. The total authorized was $878 million in fiscal 1995 and $890 million in fiscal 1996 for the corporation's operations, equipment and retirement contributions, and $250 million each year for the Northeast Corridor high-speed rail project.

Amtrak's fiscal 1995 appropriation was $772 million.

The bill proposed to increase the amount states had to pay to bring Amtrak into areas that it would not otherwise serve, effective in fiscal 1996. States would have to cover 45 percent to 55 percent of the routes' long-term losses, not short-term losses as existing law required. An Amtrak spokesman said the change was aimed at bringing the states' payments more in line with the actual costs of serving those routes.

The bill required a report comparing the percentage of Amtrak trips that arrived on time with the performance by other modes of transportation. On request of California lawmakers, it also required Amtrak to plan for new stations at or near two California airports, Ontario and Burbank-Glendale-Pasadena, to be built without Amtrak's financial help.

The Senate Commerce Committee gave voice vote approval Sept. 23 to a separate Amtrak bill (S 2002), which authorized $788 million in fiscal 1995 and $895 million in fiscal 1996 for Amtrak's operations, equipment and retirement benefits.

The committee's bill required states to pay a higher share of the cost of the routes that Amtrak served at their behest, starting in fiscal 1997. It also authorized $7 million for improvements to stations in Amtrak's planned Missouri River Corridor through the northern Midwest.

Another provision authorized $30 million for fiscal 1995-97 for the Local Rail Freight Assistance program, which provided grants to small freight lines.

High-Speed Rail Funding

A year and a half after the Clinton administration proposed a $1.3 billion investment in futuristic ground transportation, the Senate on Oct. 8 cleared a bill authorizing a much smaller foray into high-speed railroads.

The bill (HR 4867) authorized $184 million over three years, with the money to be used to plan high-speed corridors and develop related technology. President Clinton signed the measure into law Nov. 2 (PL 103-440).

The original proposal, by Transportation Secretary Federico F. Peña, called for a major federal effort to boost construction of high-speed corridors. In contrast, HR 4867 did not authorize any federal spending to actually build or equip a high-speed line.

The bill included provisions from House- and Senate-passed measures to promote rail safety (HR 4545, S 2132). In addition to authorizing $316.7 million for federal rail-safety programs through fiscal 1998, the bill allowed freight railroads to experiment with alternatives to the work schedules mandated by federal law.

Other provisions promoted development of new technologies to avert railroad collisions, mandated minimum federal safety standards for passenger rail cars and required locomotives to sound warnings when approaching crossings.

Background

In April 1993, the Clinton administration proposed a five-year, $1.3 billion initiative to build high-speed rail corridors and

develop related technologies. The proposal was embraced by top Democrats on the House Energy and Commerce Committee and the Senate Commerce Committee, as well as by some Republicans.

The bills quickly ran into trouble, however. The freight railroads, whose tracks were to be used by the new high-speed lines, demanded protection from lawsuits in the event of mishaps. The unions demanded compensation for the job losses that the new lines could cause in other modes of transportation and a guarantee that construction projects on the new lines would not undercut local wage rates. The plan, which required about a 25 percent increase in federal spending on railroads, also ran into budget problems.

The House Energy and Commerce Committee approved its version of the bill (HR 1919 — H Rept 103-258) July 27, 1993, by a vote of 28-16, with most Republicans opposed. The split on the committee indicated the bill's less-than-solid support, and the measure never reached the House floor. On Nov. 9, 1993, the Senate Commerce Committee approved a $1 billion high-speed rail bill (S 839 — S Rept 103-208), which also stalled. *(1993 Almanac, p. 217)*

House Action

In July 1994, backers of high-speed rail introduced a sharply scaled-back rail proposal (HR 4867). Instead of attempting to build high-speed rail corridors, the bill proposed to help states and local governments plan them. It authorized less than $190 million over three years in federal aid for planning and technology development.

The House Energy and Commerce Subcommittee on Transportation and Hazardous Materials approved the new bill by voice vote Aug. 4. The full committee approved it the following day, also by voice vote (H Rept 103-692).

As approved by the committee, the bill authorized $184 million over three years, with none of the money to be used for building or equipping a high-speed line. Instead, the money was for planning and technology development.

"It's cut back, regrettably and dramatically," said Chairman John D. Dingell, D-Mich. "But at least it's a first step, and it's probably the best that can be done at this time." Lynn Schenk, D-Calif., who had introduced the bill Aug. 1, said it was less ambitious than the 1993 efforts but still significant. "This is the first commitment in the nation's history to the development of a high-speed rail network," she said.

The bill authorized grants to states for up to half the cost of environmental assessments, preliminary engineering, right-of-way acquisitions and feasibility studies, Schenk said. The money also could be spent to adapt and implement high-speed rail technologies.

Committee Republicans said state planners should not ignore the freight railroads' liability concerns. Unless that problem was addressed, said Michael G. Oxley of Ohio, "we may never see actual operations of high-speed trains."

The Republicans also urged the Transportation Department to address the issue in its ongoing study of the commercial feasibility of high-speed rail, which Congress ordered in 1991.

Critics had questioned the feasibility of high-speed rail, arguing that it would be more costly than the services already provided. At a hearing in April 1993, a top official at Amtrak, the nation's passenger rail corporation, warned that high-speed rail would always require substantial government aid to cover its costs.

After a relatively brief debate, the House passed the bill under suspension of the rules Aug. 16; the vote was 281-103. *(Vote 398, p. 120-H)*

Senate Action

The Senate passed the bill by voice vote Aug. 18, after substituting the text of S 839.

But first, the Senate agreed by voice vote to substantially scale back the version of S 839 that had been approved by the Commerce Committee in 1993. The result was a bill that authorized $169 million for fiscal 1995 through 1997. As in the House-passed bill, the money was to be used exclusively for research and planning — not for construction.

Although there were few differences between the House- and Senate-passed versions, the Senate bill altered the definition of high-speed rail to include trains that used magnetic levitation, or maglev, technology. According to one Senate staff member, the change was made not to endorse maglev trains over other forms of high-speed rail, but to maintain a degree of flexibility.

The House bill, by contrast, was designed strictly for steel-wheel technology. Because a large maglev program was included in the 1991 surface transportation bill, Energy and Commerce had purposely excluded maglev technology from its bill.

Rather than going to conference to negotiate the text of a final bill, the House and Senate passed the measure back and forth until they agreed on a common version, in the process folding in separate rail safety legislation.

The House on Oct. 7 agreed by voice vote to a three-part substitute amendment. The first part represented a compromise on high-speed rail worked out with the Senate that authorized $184 million over three years and focused on steel-wheel technology.

The second part contained provisions from a separate rail safety bill (HR 4545) that the House had passed Aug. 8. These included provisions authorizing $316.7 million for federal rail safety programs through fiscal 1998, allowing freight railroads to experiment with alternative work schedules, promoting the development of technologies to prevent collisions, mandating minimum safety standards for passenger rail cars and requiring locomotives to sound warnings when approaching crossings. *(Rail safety, this page)*

The third part contained provisions on safety at grade crossings, where the greatest number of fatalities occurred.

The Senate agreed to the House changes by voice vote Oct. 8, clearing the bill for the president.

Railroad Safety Provisions

Congress cleared a package of rail safety provisions, after folding the legislation into a bill that authorized money to plan and develop high-speed rail systems. The Senate cleared the broader bill Oct. 8; President Clinton signed it Nov. 2 (HR 4867 — PL 103-440).

The rail safety provisions began as a separate bill in the House Energy and Commerce Subcommittee on Transportation and Hazardous Waste, which approved it July 13. The full Energy and Commerce Committee approved the measure (HR 4545 — H Rept 103-655) by voice vote July 19. The bill authorized $316.7 million over four years. It funded more than 40 regulatory programs run by the Federal Railroad Administration, including the oversight

and regulation of locomotives, signals, brakes, hours of service and the transportation of hazardous materials.

The measure allowed the Transportation Department to approve variable work schedules for some pilot freight railroad projects. Existing law limited railroad employees to working a maximum of 12 consecutive hours and required that they receive at least eight consecutive hours of rest per 24-hour period.

It also required the Transportation Department to report to Congress within 18 months what it had done to improve railroad bridge damage detection devices. In September 1993, a barge struck a bridge near Mobile, Ala., causing an Amtrak train to derail. The crash killed 47 passengers and crew members.

The House passed HR 4545, by a vote of 395-0, on Aug. 8. *(Vote 379, p. 114-H)*

The Senate Commerce Committee gave voice vote approval Sept. 23 to a competing bill (S 2132) that reauthorized federal railroad safety programs for four years, increasing the authorization levels from $68.3 million in fiscal 1995 to $90.7 million in fiscal 1998. The bill also authorized experiments in work schedules that varied from the limits mandated by federal law.

The committee bill contained provisions to promote safety at railroad crossings, including a potential freeze on the number of crossings allowed per state. It required the Transportation Department to set minimum safety standards for rail cars that carried passengers.

Also attached to the bill were the provisions of S 738, a measure to create incentives for states to adopt tougher laws against unsafe driving by youths and the elderly. The Senate passed S 738 by voice vote Nov. 20, 1993, but it had been stalled by opposition from the House Public Works Committee. *(1993 Almanac, p. 222)*

The full Senate took up the rail safety bill late on Oct. 6, agreeing by voice vote to two amendments. One, added at the request of Jim Exon, D-Neb., and Daniel Patrick Moynihan, D-N.Y., authorized $90 million over two years for a new train station in New York City — a project that had drawn protests in the House. The second amendment, offered by John C. Danforth, R-Mo., scaled back the provisions in the bill that had been culled from S 738.

The Senate then inserted the text of its amended bill into HR 4545 and passed it by voice vote.

Measure Included in High-Speed Rail Bill

Later that night, the House folded the text of the House-passed rail safety bill into the high-speed rail bill (HR 4867), which was about to clear. The bill, which passed by voice vote, authorized $316.7 million for rail safety programs over four years. It also contained several provisions from the Senate's rail safety bill, including ones to improve safety at railroad crossings and to set minimum safety standards for passenger rail cars. It did not include the Senate-passed provisions to authorize funds for the New York train station or to establish a new highway safety program.

The Senate agreed to the high-speed rail bill by voice vote Oct. 8.

Gas Station Protections

The Senate on Oct. 5 cleared a bill aimed at protecting independent service station owners from being driven out of business by oil companies. President Clinton signed the bill into law Oct. 19 (HR 1520 — PL 103-371).

The bill barred an oil company from terminating a lease simply because it could not come to an agreement with an independent dealer on converting the station to a company-owned station. It also spelled out the rights and duties of dealers and refiners in third-party situations.

In urging House passage, bill sponsor Ron Wyden, D-Ore., warned that small gas stations were disappearing, causing particular difficulty in rural areas. "Very often," he said, "this is due to the fact that some oil companies . . . have set in place crippling conditions" on small stations seeking to renew their franchises.

Congress had passed the Petroleum Marketing Practices Act in 1978 in an effort to establish a single set of rules for oil companies wishing to terminate franchises. But lawmakers reopened the issue in the late 1980s at the behest of independent gas station operators, after a series of conflicting federal court decisions raised questions about the extent to which state and local regulations could pre-empt the 1978 law. The station operators sought more federal protection from oil companies that they believed had improperly terminated or refused to renew franchise agreements to force independent owners out of business.

Pressed by the House Energy and Commerce Committee to work out a compromise solution, the station operators, the oil companies, the oil distributors and the independent gasoline marketers negotiated for almost two years before striking a deal in February 1992.

The Energy and Commerce Committee gave voice vote approval on June 8, 1993, to a bill (HR 1520 — H Rept 103-737) that reflected the agreement. While all segments of the oil industry backed the compromise, three powerful oil companies — Texaco, Shell Oil Co. and Mobil Corp. — opposed it because they wanted to prevent their franchise operators from buying gasoline from another company. The legislation got no further in the first session. *(1993 Almanac, p. 223)*

Further compromise eluded the parties involved until September 1994, but once an agreement was reached, the bill moved swiftly. The House passed an amended version of HR 1520 by a vote of 413-0 on Oct. 4. The compromise gave states the authority to regulate certain lease provisions, such as whether independent service station dealers could be forced to remain open 24 hours a day. But it also made it clear that state and local officials could not stop an oil company from terminating the lease of an independent dealer who violated basic agreements, such as failing to pay rent or to check fuel tanks for leaks. *(Vote 476, p. 140-H)*

The Senate cleared HR 1520 by voice vote Oct. 5, after the Energy and Resources Committee had approved its own version of the bill (S 338 — S Rept 103-387) by a vote of 17-3 on Sept. 21.

NTSB Reauthorization

The Senate on Oct. 6 cleared a bill by voice vote reauthorizing the National Transportation Safety Board (NSTB) through fiscal 1996. President Clinton signed the bill Oct. 25 (HR 2240 — PL 103-411).

The House had passed the bill (H Rept 103-239, Parts 1 and 2) on Nov. 8, 1993, by a vote of 353-49. The Senate passed an amended version by voice vote May 12, and the House made additional technical changes Oct. 4. *(1993 Almanac, p. 221)*

The five-member NSTB, which investigated transportation mishaps and made non-binding safety recommendations, was authorized to spend $44 million in fiscal 1995 and $45.1 million in fiscal 1996. The bill also gave the board authority to

investigate accidents involving government-owned aircraft, other than military aircraft, and made more government-owned aircraft subject to federal regulation. These changes were sought by Sen. Larry Pressler, R-S.D., in response to a 1993 plane crash that killed the governor of South Dakota, Republican George S. Mickelson.

Smoking Ban on International Flights

The House passed legislation (HR 4495) Oct. 4 by voice vote to ban smoking on all international flights originating or ending in the United States. The Senate did not act on the measure before adjournment.

Sponsored by Rep. James L. Oberstar, D-Minn., the bill would have extended the prohibition against smoking to the first leg of any international flight departing from a U.S. airport or the last leg of any international flight arriving in the United States. The prohibition on international flights included both U.S. and foreign airlines and covered flights to and from Alaska and Hawaii.

In 1987, Congress imposed a ban on smoking on all domestic flights of two hours or less. Two years later, the restriction was expanded (PL 101-64) to ban smoking on all domestic flights of six hours or less, exempting flights to Alaska and Hawaii.

The House Public Works and Transportation Subcommittee on Aviation approved HR 4495 by voice vote Aug. 10. Subcommittee members approved, by voice vote, a substitute amendment by Oberstar designed to put the onus on airlines to carry out the ban and specifically prohibit smoking in passenger cabins and aircraft lavatories. Under the measure, the Department of Transportation was to require airlines to issue smoking regulations.

The full Public Works Committee gave the bill voice vote approval Sept. 28 (H Rept 103-771). At the markup it was agreed that the smoking ban should include the cockpits of U.S. carriers, while pilots of foreign air carriers would still be able to smoke on flights to and from the United States.

By a vote of 20-42, the committee rejected an amendment by Bob Clement, D-Tenn., to make the ban effective July 1, 1996, instead of 120 days after enactment. Clement's date coincided with a goal set by the International Civil Aviation Organization for eliminating smoking on all international flights.

The bill stalled in the Senate, where the panel with jurisdiction, the Commerce Committee's Aviation Subcommittee, was headed by Wendell H. Ford, D-Ky., who opposed the legislation.

Bill on Unsafe Drivers

The Senate passed a bill at the end of the session designed to encourage states to adopt tougher laws against unsafe driving by youths and the elderly. It was the second time the Senate had tried to win enactment for the legislation in the 103rd Congress, but the bill died because of opposition from the House Public Works Committee.

The bill (S 738) sought to reduce highway accidents by prodding states into cracking down on high-risk drivers —

defined in the bill as drivers 16 to 20 years old, elderly drivers over age 75 and repeat offenders. However, the bill focused primarily on teenagers who drank and drove.

The legislation offered states incentive grants, totaling $100 million over five years, if they instituted provisional licenses for drivers under age 18 and met certain other conditions. Provisional licensing required a new driver to maintain a clean record for one year before receiving a full license.

Under the bill, states were to receive federal grants if they took a number of steps aimed at improving the driving records of drivers under 21. To be eligible for grants, states had to meet four of nine safety guidelines in fiscal 1994, increasing to seven guidelines by fiscal 1998. Among the possible requirements were: setting a blood-alcohol content level of 0.02 percent for drivers under 21, banning possession of open alcoholic beverage containers or consumption of alcohol in automobiles, and confiscating the vehicles of drivers convicted two or more times in five years of driving under the influence of drugs or alcohol.

The Senate Commerce Committee began work on the bill, sponsored by John C. Danforth, R-Mo., in 1993, approving it by voice vote Nov. 9 (S Rept 103-199). The Senate passed S 738 by voice vote Nov. 20. But in the House, the Public Works and Transportation Committee, which had jurisdiction, took no action. *(1993 Almanac, p. 222)*

Nearly a year later, on Sept. 23, Senate Commerce Committee Chairman Ernest F. Hollings, D-S.C., attempted to move the measure forward by attaching it to a bill reauthorizing federal rail safety programs (S 2132). The committee agreed by voice vote to add the highway safety provisions to the rail bill. The Senate passed S 2132 late on Oct. 6, but differences between the House and Senate versions of that bill could not be reconciled before the session came to a close. *(Rail safety, p. 172)*

Tow Truck Regulations

An attempt to preserve state regulatory power over tow truck operators stalled at the end of the session when House and Senate sponsors were unable to reconcile their differences. Congress had pre-empted state regulation of truck rates, routes and other economic matters as part of a bill reauthorizing the Federal Aviation Administration (HR 2739 — PL 103-305). *(Trucking deregulation, p. 170)*

The House gave voice vote approval Sept. 29 to a bill (HR 5123), sponsored by Nick J. Rahall II, D-W.Va., that would have allowed state agencies to continue regulating tow truck and wrecker operations until Jan. 1, 1997. Rahall argued that in passing HR 2739, Congress had intended to deregulate freight truckers, not tow truck operations.

The Senate passed Rahall's bill by voice vote Oct. 6, after adding provisions clarifying that garbage haulers and curbside recycling programs were still subject to state and local regulations, and that local governments could join states in regulating tow truck operations.

After several House members balked at those changes, the House sent its version of the bill back to the Senate late Oct. 7. The Senate adjourned the next day without taking any further action on the measure. ■

Congress Revises Bankruptcy Code

A major rewrite of the federal Bankruptcy Code aimed at making the process faster and fairer for all parties was cleared for the president's signature early Oct. 6. President Clinton signed the bill into law Oct. 22 (HR 5116 — PL 103-394).

The House approved the measure on Oct. 5, and the Senate followed in a session that began Oct. 6.

"I don't believe it is an overstatement to say that this legislation may be one of the most significant pieces of economic legislation to be considered by the House in this Congress," said House Judiciary Committee Chairman Jack Brooks, D-Texas, during floor debate Oct. 4.

Howell Heflin, D-Ala., chief sponsor of the Senate version of the bankruptcy bill (S 540), said, "The main purpose of this legislation is to encourage debtors to repay their lawful obligations."

Although it stopped short of a systematic, top-to-bottom overhaul, HR 5116 revised the three main sections of the code — Chapters 7 and 13, which governed individual bankruptcies, and Chapter 11, which controlled business bankruptcies. It expedited various steps of the process to give both creditors and debtors a swifter resolution.

The bill sought to encourage more individual debtors to work out repayment plans under Chapter 13 rather than simply liquidate their assets and erase their debts under Chapter 7, which often left creditors high and dry.

The bill also paved the way for the use of credit cards to pay federal income taxes by specifying that tax debts, unlike other charges on credit cards, could not be erased through bankruptcy. The change was made in response to recommendations in Vice President Al Gore's 1993 "reinventing government" proposal.

The bill also made it harder to use bankruptcy to avoid payment of alimony and child support.

And the measure created a blue-ribbon commission to study the entire Bankruptcy Code and report back to Congress in two years with recommendations for further changes.

Background

Supporters of bankruptcy reform had been trying to revise the code for more than four years. Their efforts almost bore fruit in 1992, when the House and Senate passed bankruptcy bills, only to run out of time before they could act on a compromise version. *(1992 Almanac, p. 227)*

The Bankruptcy Code had not been rewritten since 1978, when Congress created a new system of bankruptcy judges independent of the federal district courts and consolidated laws dealing with business reorganizations. *(1978 Almanac, p. 179)*

Noting the increase in bankruptcy filings since that time, Heflin said the "sheer volume of cases running through a sys-

---

BOXSCORE

Fiscal Bankruptcy Code Overhaul — HR 5116 (S 540). The bill revised all three chapters of the Bankruptcy Code and sought to encourage more debtors to pay off their creditors.

Reports: H Rept 103-835, S Rept 103-168.

KEY ACTION

April 21 — Senate passed S 540, 94-0.

Oct. 5 — House passed HR 5116 by voice vote after negotiations with Senate staff to make it conform generally to S 540.

Oct. 6 — Senate cleared HR 5116 by voice vote.

Oct. 22 — President signed bill — PL 103-394.

---

tem which was designed many decades ago" necessitated an overhaul.

From 1982 to 1992, bankruptcy filings rose 178 percent, peaking at a record 971,517 in 1992. The 1993 total fell slightly, to 918,734, as economic conditions improved. Nonetheless, roughly 75 percent of all cases brought in federal court were bankruptcy cases. It cost about $587 million annually to administer the bankruptcy system.

In 1993, the average number of cases filed per bankruptcy judge was 2,818. In 1985, that number was 1,571.

Experts cited a number of reasons for the rapid rise in bankruptcy filings, including a reduced social stigma; the ready availability of all types of credit, from home equity loans to credit cards and corporate junk bonds; and two major recessions since 1980.

Individual bankruptcies accounted for 93 percent of all filings. In 1981, a total of 62 million Americans carried 116 million MasterCard or Visa cards. By 1993, 97 million Americans carried about 263 million cards.

The overloaded system prompted complaints from all sides: Creditors complained that courtroom logjams meant they seldom learned about hearings or dismissals in time, while small-business owners said the code ignored their special concerns. Debtors' advocates warned that bankruptcy "petition mills" were duping the poor and immigrants into believing they could clear their credit records and get rid of their debts by declaring bankruptcy.

Other, very specialized interest groups had their own complaints. For example, condominium associations said that bankrupt condo owners backed out on fees during drawn-out bankruptcy proceedings, and airport officials said that lucrative landing rights and gate leases languished while airline companies debated their courtroom options.

1993 Senate Committee Action

In crafting the legislation in 1993, Heflin and cosponsor Charles E. Grassley, R-Iowa, sought common ground among the interest groups that were unhappy with the 1978 code.

As a result, S 540 (and ultimately, HR 5116) read more like a disjointed series of revisions than an overhaul with a distinct legislative mission. "Generally the bill does not have a theme," said Samuel Gerdano, executive director of the American Bankruptcy Institute, which supported the legislation. "It's virtually an in-box stapled together, with some provisions that favor debtors and some which favor creditors."

The Senate Judiciary Committee approved S 540 (S Rept 103-168) by voice vote on Sept. 15, 1993, and its basic outline survived all the way through the legislative process.

The most significant new provision added during the markup was the one dealing with use of credit cards for income tax payments. It was inserted by Chairman Joseph R. Biden Jr., D-Del. *(1993 Almanac, p. 232)*

Major Provisions of Bankruptcy Overhaul

Following are the major provisions included in the final version of the bankruptcy bill. As enacted, HR 5116:

● Required courts to rule within 60 days after a debtor filed for bankruptcy on automatic-stay requests, which allowed debtors to avoid foreclosure on cars, property and other assets. These requests often were used by debtors to stave off creditors who were trying to recover money owed to them.

● Allowed creditors to file an immediate appeal of any court order extending the 180-day deadline under Chapter 11 for debtor companies to file reorganization plans acceptable to the creditors. Creditors complained that debtors often used such extensions to delay reorganizing and beginning their debt repayments.

● Clarified that no separate hearing was required for a debtor to reaffirm his debt, provided the debtor was represented by an attorney who had fully explained the options to him and the nature of his obligations.

● Authorized bankruptcy judges to hold status conferences to manage their dockets more efficiently.

● Provided for the establishment, in each judicial circuit, of a bankruptcy appeals panel composed of sitting bankruptcy judges. These panels were to serve in place of the U.S. District Court in reviewing bankruptcy court decisions, unless special circumstances precluded their creation.

● Authorized bankruptcy judges to conduct jury trials with the consent of all parties involved.

● Required service of process on any insured depository institution to be made by certified mail in contested or adversary bankruptcy proceedings.

● Increased fees paid to private trustees, who generally were responsible for supervising Chapter 7 bankruptcy cases and for distributing funds to creditors.

● Prohibited federal and state governments, when acting as creditors in a bankruptcy case, from using sovereign immunity as a shield to disregard automatic stays and other bankruptcy procedures. This was designed to prevent the government from trying to collect back taxes by seizing assets of a bankrupt taxpayer and then asserting immunity to legal actions aimed at recovering the money or property. The provision required governments to obey the same rules as other creditors in bankruptcy proceedings.

● Set up procedures for dealing with present and future asbestos-exposure claims against companies that sought to reorganize under Chapter 11. Based on the 1982 Johns-Mansville bankruptcy case, the provision called for the establishment of a trust fund into which would be placed stock of the emerging debtor company and a portion of future profits. In return, an injunction would bar new asbestos claims against the emerging debtor company. Seventy-five percent of those with existing claims would have to vote for the plan before it could take effect.

● Expedited the process by which small businesses with aggregate secured and unsecured debts of less than $2 million could reorganize under Chapter 11.

● Limited debtors whose only asset was one piece of commercial property to 90 days for submitting a reorganization plan. Under existing law, debtors with "single asset real estate" could use automatic stays to stave off creditors.

● Gave sellers more time (20 days instead of 10) to reclaim goods sold on credit to a company, usually a retailer, that had filed for bankruptcy.

● Allowed a bankruptcy court to permit a buyer to return to the seller goods shipped before the commencement of the bankruptcy proceeding, thereby reducing the overall size of the company's debt. The order would have to be issued within 120 days of the bankruptcy filing.

● Gave independent sales representatives of a bankrupt company the same priority as employees seeking wage and benefit payments, provided the representative earned at least 75 percent of his income from the bankrupt debtor.

● Required airlines that filed for bankruptcy to honor lease and conditional sales contracts while reorganizing.

● Specified that a creditor who was not a corporate insider could be required to return assets or payments to the bankrupt's estate only if they were made within 90 days prior to the bankruptcy filing, not within one year, as some courts had ruled. Preferential payments made to corporate insiders within the year prior to bankruptcy would still be recoverable, as existing law specified.

● Required trustees in Chapter 7 bankruptcy cases to explain in full to a debtor his option to file for a restructuring of debts under Chapter 13 and the consequences, including the effect on his credit history, of declaring bankruptcy and discharging debts under Chapter 7.

● Raised the amount of debt an individual could have and still file under Chapter 13, which allowed debtors to work out repayment schedules with creditors. The threshold was raised from $100,000 to $250,000 in unsecured debt and from $350,000 to $750,000 in secured debt. The provision was intended to encourage more individuals to file under Chapter 13 instead of Chapter 7.

● Prohibited the discharge through bankruptcy of loans used to pay federal taxes. This was designed to allow the use of credit cards to pay taxes, as recommended by Vice President Al Gore's National Performance Review.

● Allowed a debtor who was under Chapter 13 protection to cure a home mortgage default at least through the completion of a foreclosure sale.

● Prohibited individuals who restructured their debts under Chapter 13 from discharging criminal fines.

● Classified alimony and child support payments as priority debt, making it more difficult to use a bankruptcy filing to avoid these obligations.

● Made it difficult for a divorced person who had assumed the couple's marital debts in exchange for the reduction or elimination of alimony or child support to escape the debt through bankruptcy, thereby saddling the other spouse with the debt.

● Barred debtors from escaping, through bankruptcy, their obligation to pay condominium or cooperative fees so long as they were still living in or collecting rent on a unit.

● Prohibited the denial of a student loan to someone who once failed to pay off such a loan because he or she had declared bankruptcy and discharged all debts.

● Added a new section to the Bankruptcy Code spelling out standards for bankruptcy petition preparers (other than attorneys) and set stiff penalties for negligent or fraudulent filings. Bill sponsors said fee-seeking "bankruptcy typing mills" preyed upon immigrants and the poor.

● Set criminal penalties for those who declared bankruptcy with fraudulent intent.

● Allowed a municipality to file for bankruptcy so long as it was eligible to do so under state law.

● Established a nine-member National Bankruptcy Review Commission to recommend additional changes to the Bankruptcy Code within two years. Four members were to be appointed by Congress, three by the president and two by the Chief Justice of the United States.

Senate Action

The Senate passed its version of the bankruptcy bill by 94-0 on April 21, after lawmakers agreed to drop a potentially deal-breaking provision that would have required companies working under Chapter 11 bankruptcy protection to pay retired workers' health and medical benefits before using loans to pay off operating costs or other expenses. *(Vote 96, p. 17-S)*

Although the bill had had bipartisan support when the Senate Judiciary Committee approved it in 1993, two provisions became sticking points when the measure came to the floor the week of April 18.

The first, which would have set up a new bankruptcy chapter for small business filings, was dispensed with early when floor managers Heflin and Grassley offered an amendment to eliminate the chapter.

Lenders and some bankruptcy attorneys had staunchly opposed the new chapter because it would have allowed small businesses to write off many debts and continue to operate. The Clinton administration also registered misgivings about the concept.

The second major sticking point was the bill wording concerning payment to retiree health plans. Under existing law, companies in Chapter 11 could get low-cost financing and use loans from banks to meet their payroll obligations, maintain their inventory and pay other operating expenses.

But the bill, as approved by the Judiciary Committee, required that before paying other expenses, companies would have to meet their obligations to retiree health and medical plans.

Banking groups and their allies in the Senate argued that bank financing during bankruptcies should go toward operating expenses and helping a company successfully emerge from bankruptcy. "[The language] is far too inflexible and will ultimately lead to the liquidation of many viable business interests, rather than to their successful reorganization," said Utah's Orrin G. Hatch, ranking Republican on the Senate Judiciary Committee.

Howard M. Metzenbaum, D-Ohio, sponsor of the provision and author of the part of the 1978 code that it sought to amend, insisted on the language as the Senate began debate on S 540. The bill bogged down on the floor for two days while senators sought a compromise.

In the end, Metzenbaum agreed to strike the language. Staffers close to the negotiations said labor groups weighed in against the provision because of fears that it would pit current employees, who wanted to keep businesses afloat and their jobs secure, against retired workers.

Late on April 21, Hatch offered an amendment to strike the language, and Metzenbaum agreed. The Senate approved it by voice vote.

Other Amendments

In other floor action, the Senate tabled, or killed, 60-34, an amendment by Harry Reid, D-Nev., to allow individuals to file for Chapter 13 reorganization only once every three years. Heflin said the language would deter people from filing Chapter 13 and drive them into liquidation proceedings instead. *(Vote 95, p. 17-S)*

Senators approved, by voice votes, amendments:
● By Hank Brown, R-Colo., to codify previous judicial rulings that trust funds set up to pay plaintiffs in asbestos injury litigation could not be tapped by creditors during bankruptcy proceedings.
● By Reid, to forbid states to tax the pension benefits of individuals who had moved out of state during retirement. That

provision was subsequently stripped out by the House Judiciary Committee. It moved separately as a bill (HR 546) that passed the House but died in the Senate in the closing days of the session. *(Pension taxes, p. 404)*
● By Metzenbaum, to prohibit rent-to-own businesses from collecting inflated merchandise appraisal rates from clients who declared bankruptcy.
● By Metzenbaum, to forbid the government from denying a student-loan application on the basis of a bankruptcy history.

Debate on Unrelated Amendments

While backroom negotiating was under way over the complicated bill, lawmakers spent hours on the floor debating three extraneous amendments.

One, offered by John McCain, R-Ariz., expressed the sense of the Senate that Washington's Dulles and National airports should end their close-in, free parking privileges for members of Congress, Supreme Court justices and members of the diplomatic corps. It was rejected, 44-53. *(Vote 94, p. 17-S)*

Senate Minority Leader Bob Dole, R-Kan., offered, but later withdrew, an amendment that would have required the administration to ignore a U.N. embargo that barred weapons to Bosnia's Muslims. *(Bosnia, p. 446)*

Dole also offered an amendment to codify the administration's announced policy of allowing police sweeps in public housing developments. The Senate approved it by voice vote, but it later was dropped by the House Judiciary Committee.

House Action

After a long hiatus, the House Judiciary Committee resurrected the bankruptcy overhaul in the final days of the session.

The panel on Sept. 29 gave voice vote approval to a compromise bill (HR 5116 — H Rept 103-835) that House and Senate Judiciary staff members had worked out in round-the-clock negotiations. The Economic and Commercial Law Subcommittee had approved the measure the day before.

HR 5116 represented a complete substitute for HR 2326, the original House bankruptcy bill, which had gone nowhere.

Judiciary Committee Chairman Jack Brooks, D-Texas, sponsor of the compromise bill, said he overcame his reluctance to tackle such a complex issue late in the session because "we are close to mutual assent" with the Senate.

Among the changes made was the addition of language classifying child-support payments as a priority debt. That made it harder for non-custodial parents to escape their obligations by declaring bankruptcy.

In general, the bill was designed to track the Senate-passed S 540 as closely as possible to assure speedy approval once the measure had moved through the House. With only days left in the session, a single senator could have blocked the bill.

Among the provisions incorporated in the substitute was language creating a National Bankruptcy Review Commission to review the Bankruptcy Code and report recommended changes to Congress in two years.

The full House took up HR 5116 on Oct. 4 under suspension of the rules but spent only a few minutes discussing the measure. The following day, the House passed the measure by voice vote, sending it to the Senate.

Senators asked a number of questions clarifying specific points in the compromise as they discussed the bill late the night of Oct. 6, then approved the measure by voice vote in the early morning of Oct. 7. ∎

Product Liability Bill Blocked

A bill to limit product liability lawsuits (S 687) died in the Senate after supporters failed on two occasions to halt a filibuster. A similar bill (HR 1910) never got out of the House Energy and Commerce Committee. Although committee Chairman John D. Dingell, D-Mich., supported the bill, he left it to the Senate to take the lead on product liability.

At issue was whether Congress should establish national standards for lawsuits against companies responsible for products that injured or killed their users. The Senate bill sought to reduce the number of product liability lawsuits that went to trial and to limit the amount of punitive and other non-economic damages that could be awarded.

The major forces behind the bill — manufacturers, insurers and other business groups — had been trying to curb product liability lawsuits for 17 years. Four times — in 1984, 1986, 1990 and 1992 — their bills advanced through the Senate Commerce Committee but were not acted on by the full Senate. Supporters had been no more successful in the House. In 1988, the House Energy and Commerce Committee approved a bill, but the measure died in the House Judiciary Committee.

The bill's supporters argued that excessive jury awards had driven the cost of liability insurance to unreasonable levels, inflating prices, discouraging innovation and damaging U.S. competitiveness. To win adherents, they added provisions to the bill to help victims of long-hidden injury or disease, encourage safer workplaces and promote medical advances.

Opponents, led by the Association of Trial Lawyers of America and consumer groups, argued that the limits would protect corporate negligence at the expense of the injured, who they said already recovered too little compensation for their injuries. They also argued that politicians in Washington should not restrict the juries of 50 states. This proved to be an effective argument, as a number of senators balked at the idea of interfering with state courts.

"No matter how far proponents stretch to characterize this bill as pro-consumer," said opponent Howard M. Metzenbaum, D-Ohio, "it is still the most comprehensive anti-consumer piece of legislation that has been or will be considered in this Congress."

A much narrower bill crafted for the sake of a single industry — the manufacturers of small, non-commercial planes — was enacted in August (S 1458 — PL 103-298). In winning approval, supporters stressed that the small-plane bill was not intended as "the camel's nose under the tent" for the broader product liability bill. (Small-plane liability, p. 180)

Bill Highlights

The bill, which the Senate Commerce Committee had approved in November 1993 (S Rept 103-203), contained provisions to:

● Limit the cases in which juries could award punitive damages. Plaintiffs were required to show by "clear and convincing evidence" that their injuries stemmed from a manufacturer's deliberate and flagrant indifference to safety. Provisions in the bill barred punitive damages against makers of drugs, medical devices and light aircraft whose products were approved by federal regulators, but only if they had kept regulators informed about possible problems.

● End joint liability for pain, emotional damage and other non-economic losses. In lawsuits against more than one company, most states held each company liable for all the damages, regardless of how much they contributed to the plaintiff's injuries. Bill provisions limited each company's liability for non-economic damages to the specific percentage assigned by a jury.

● Promote negotiated settlements. If a manufacturer rejected an injured person's offer to settle a suit and a jury later awarded that person more than the settlement offer, the company would have to pay up to $50,000 of the person's legal fees. If the injured person rejected a settlement offer and received less from a jury, part of the court award would go to the manufacturer for its legal fees. The amount to be awarded to manufacturers for legal costs was to equal what an injured person already had received from medical insurance policies and other so-called collateral sources.

The bill included a similar penalty for manufacturers who refused to participate in negotiations with an independent mediator.

● Absolve sellers of products from liability in most cases. The bill barred product liability claims against companies that sold products without altering or mishandling them, unless the manufacturer was bankrupt or impossible to sue. Under existing law, people could sue a seller as if it were the manufacturer, although the seller could try to recover any losses later from the company that actually made the defective product.

● Hold victims responsible for their use of alcohol or drugs. If a jury found that an injured person's use of alcohol or drugs was at least as great a factor in the injury as any product defect, the damages could not be awarded.

● Cut off lawsuits involving old machinery. Once a machine tool, delivery truck or other "capital good" had been in commercial use for 25 years, the maker could not be sued for any injuries it might inflict on workers. The bill stated that the restriction applied only if the injured person was covered by workers' compensation and the injuries were not caused by toxic chemicals.

● Set new time limits for lawsuits. Injured people had two years to file a product liability claim, but the clock would not begin running until they discovered the injury and its cause. Under existing statutes of limitations, the clock began to run as soon as a product caused an injury, even if the victim could not detect it or could not discern its source. (1993 Almanac, p. 234)

Senate Floor Action

The bill got further in the Senate in 1994 than a similar bill had in 1992. That year, opponents kept sponsor John D. Rockefeller IV, D-W.Va., from even bringing the bill up for debate. In 1994, opponents no longer had the votes to stop the Senate from taking up the bill; debate began June 24. Still, opponents twice stopped Rockefeller from collecting the 60 votes needed to invoke cloture and bring the talking to a close.

Rockefeller's first try, on June 28, fell six votes short. The vote was 54-44. (Vote 169, p. 29-S)

Hoping to sway senators, Rockefeller and cosponsor Slade Gorton, R-Wash., promised to remove a controversial

Legislative History

Congress had debated product liability for more than a decade, but proponents of legislation to limit claims on faulty products had made few inroads against the fierce opposition of consumer groups and trial lawyers.

● **1981.** Congress cleared a bill (PL 97-45) designed to make it easier for businesses to buy insurance to cover claims for damages involving their products. With Republicans in control of the Senate, Bob Kasten, R-Wis., chairman of a Commerce, Science and Transportation subcommittee, kicked off a 12-year effort to limit product liability claims; he introduced a bill that sought to require manufacturers of faulty products to pay for injuries only if they were negligent. (*1981 Almanac, p. 573*)

● **1984.** The Commerce, Science and Transportation Committee approved Kasten's bill in May, but the full Senate took no further action. (*1984 Almanac, p. 296*)

● **1985.** The Senate Commerce Committee in May failed on an 8-8 vote to send a new Kasten bill to the Senate floor. The bill would have imposed national standards on personal injury lawsuits that resulted from faulty products. (*1985 Almanac, p. 278*)

● **1986.** Kasten drafted a compromise bill with John C. Danforth, R-Mo., and Slade Gorton, R-Wash., which the Senate Commerce Committee approved in June. Later that month, Majority Leader Bob Dole, R-Kan., pulled the bill off the Senate floor after Ernest F. Hollings, D-S.C., staged a filibuster. The bill would have limited the time for making product liability claims, allowed drug manufacturers to avoid punitive damages if their products had won federal regulatory approval and permitted manufacturers to avoid liability suits if a victim was under the influence of drugs or alcohol at the time of an injury. (*1986 Almanac, p. 287*)

● **1988.** The House Energy and Commerce Committee in June approved its version of Kasten's bill. But Judiciary Committee Chairman Peter W. Rodino Jr., D-N.J., opposed the measure, and no further action was taken. The bill would have made manufacturers immune from liability claims if they were unaware of a design defect. (*1988 Almanac, p. 573*)

● **1990.** The Senate Commerce Committee in May approved a scaled-back Kasten measure setting national standards for product liability suits. Kasten dropped many controversial provisions to gain the support of several influential Democrats, including Sen. John D. Rockefeller IV of West Virginia and House Energy and Commerce Committee Chairman John D. Dingell of Michigan. The bill languished for two months in the Senate Judiciary Committee, which finally discharged it without recommendation.

Late in the session, Kasten tried to attach the bill to a separate measure to reauthorize technology programs and spur U.S. competitiveness, creating an impasse that killed the technology bill and Kasten's product liability language. (*1990 Almanac, p. 400*)

● **1991.** The Senate Commerce Committee in October approved another bill by Kasten to set national standards for filing personal injury lawsuits. (*1991 Almanac, p. 177*)

● **1992.** The tort reform issue gained momentum in July at the Republican National Convention in Houston, where President George Bush and Vice President Dan Quayle blasted the legal profession and the high cost of litigation. The Senate in September came closer than it had in 12 years to passing Kasten's bill. But opponents waged a filibuster, and the vote to limit debate fell two votes short of the 60 needed to invoke cloture. (*1992 Almanac, p. 210*)

section barring punitive damages against companies whose products were approved by the Food and Drug Administration or Federal Aviation Administration.

Although never carried out, their pledge helped persuade three Democrats and two Republicans to switch their votes the next morning in favor of ending the filibuster. But one supporter from 1992, Dennis DeConcini, D-Ariz., missed the vote, and two others switched sides. This time Rockefeller's motion was rejected 57-41. (*Vote 170, p. 29-S*)

Opponents pursued a two-pronged strategy. In addition to fighting to keep the filibuster going, they also threatened to put the Senate through a number of tough votes on issues relating to gun control, smoking and other hotly disputed topics. The effect, said a lobbyist was to make some of the bill's proponents view it as a Pandora's box that they might not want to open. All told, 240 potential amendments to the bill were filed on June 27 and 28 alone. One amendment that actually was offered, by Democrat Herb Kohl of Wisconsin, would have limited a judge's ability to keep the records of a lawsuit confidential when those records had a bearing on public health and safety. The amendment, which also contained provisions barring settlement agreements that kept information secret from federal or state regulators, was tabled, or killed, by a vote of 51-49. (*Vote 168, p. 29-S*) ∎

New Standards Developed For Toy Safety

Legislation intended to reduce choking accidents and deaths of children was enacted after winning final voice vote approval from the Senate on May 25.

The bill (HR 965) required standardized warning labels on certain toys, games, marbles, balls and balloons that might pose a choking hazard to small children. It also required the Consumer Product Safety Commission to develop uniform safety standards for bicycle helmets, and it established a new program of grants to states that required or encouraged helmet use by cyclists under age 16.

Senate sponsor Slade Gorton, R-Wash., applauded the action, saying, "The costs of prevention are small compared to the costs of accidents."

The administration supported the bill, which President Clinton signed June 16 (PL 103-267).

Final congressional action came just two weeks after 102 children journeyed to Capitol Hill to urge lawmakers to support measures that would help prevent injuries to children. All of the children had survived brushes with death from preventable injuries.

Early legislative action on the bill occurred in 1993. The House passed its version of the measure (H Rept 103-29) by a vote of 362-38 on March 16. The Senate approved a slightly different version (S 680) by voice vote Nov. 20. (*1993 Almanac, p. 232*)

In 1994 action, a House-Senate conference committee reported a compromise measure May 11 (H Rept 103-500), and the House approved it May 23 by voice vote.

Among the provisions dropped during conference negotiations was language calling for mandatory warning labels on household buckets notifying parents that buckets posed a drowning risk. The Consumer Product Safety Commission subsequently notified manufacturers that it intended nonetheless to require such warning labels.

The bill required that warning labels specifically state that

a particular toy posed a choking hazard. It banned sales of balls intended for children under age 3 unless the balls had a diameter of at least 1.75 inches, too big to be swallowed. The bill pre-empted state law.

Bicycle helmets had not previously been subject to government safety requirements, although most did meet voluntary industry-set standards. The bill gave those voluntary standards the force of law while the Consumer Product Safety Commission developed minimum safety standards.

The bill authorized $2 million in fiscal 1995, rising to $4 million in fiscal 1997, for matching grants to states to promote bicycle helmet use by children. The federal share could

not exceed 80 percent. States could use some of the money to purchase helmets for children who could not otherwise afford them.

About 3,200 children a year were treated in hospital emergency rooms for toy related ingestion and aspiration injuries, according to the Consumer Product Safety Commission. Between 1980 and 1991, 186 children choked to death on balloons, marbles and small balls.

Many toy manufacturers voluntarily placed age requirement labels on toy packages, but parents often misinterpreted those labels as clues to what was appropriate for the average child's development, not as safety warnings. ∎

Law Limits Small-Plane Liability

In a rare move to limit state liability law, the House cleared a bill Aug. 3 to restrict product liability claims against the manufacturers of small planes.

The bill (S 1458) applied to non-commercial planes built to carry fewer than 20 passengers. If a crash occurred more than 18 years after the plane was delivered, the manufacturer could not be sued for design or manufacturing defects.

President Clinton signed the bill Aug. 17 (PL 103-298).

Sponsor Nancy Landon Kassebaum, R-Kan., had been trying to limit the liability of light-plane manufacturers for eight years. Her state was home to three of the largest manufacturers — Cessna Aircraft Co., Beech Aircraft Corp. and Learjet Inc. — all of which said that liability insurance costs had forced them to cut back production and jobs.

Kassebaum mollified some of her opponents by dropping a few controversial elements from previous years, such as limits on punitive damages and joint liability. In a compromise with Sen. Howard M. Metzenbaum, D-Ohio, she also moved the cutoff on lawsuits from 15 years to 18 and added several exceptions.

Manufacturers of single-engine, piston-powered airplanes had seen a steep decline in sales and employment in the previous 15 years. Nine companies were making piston-powered aircraft in early 1994, compared with 29 companies in 1980. Kassebaum blamed the decline on substantial cost increases, caused largely by insurance premiums.

Opponents of product liability measures argued that Congress should not interfere with states, whose courts handled most lawsuits involving defective products. But supporters of the bill countered that airplanes were not like most consumer products — they were regulated and certified by federal authorities, not by states, and so a federal liability rule was appropriate.

Critics of the measure also argued that the decline in the small-plane industry stemmed more from the durability of its products than from liability lawsuits.

Some lawmakers and industry lobbyists hoped the Kassebaum bill would pave the way for broad legislation to limit liability claims and punitive damages against all manufacturers. But the broad product liability bill (S 687) fell vic-

BOXSCORE

Small Aircraft Liability — S 1458. The bill limited lawsuits against manufacturers of small planes.

Reports: S Rept 103-202, H Rept 103-525, Parts 1 and 2.

KEY ACTION

March 16 — Senate passed, 91-8.

June 27 — House passed amended bill by voice vote.

Aug. 2 — Senate agreed by voice vote, after amending bill.

Aug. 3 — House cleared bill by voice vote.

Aug. 17 — President signed bill — PL 103-298.

tim to a Senate filibuster in June, and supporters were never able to revive it. Linda Lipsen of Consumers Union, an opponent of product liability limits, said the success of the small-plane bill was a sign of Kassebaum's diligence and popularity among her fellow lawmakers rather than of some new Senate interest in changing product liability laws. (*Product liability, p. 178*)

Passage of the Kassebaum bill did remove the biggest hurdle to a bill reauthorizing federal aviation programs (HR 2739 — PL 103-305), which had gotten bogged down in the waning days of the 1993 session when Kassebaum tried to use it as a vehicle for her aviation liability bill. (*FAA reauthorization, p. 168*)

Senate Action

The Senate passed S 1458 March 16 by a vote of 91-8. The measure had been approved by the Commerce Committee on Nov. 20, 1993 (S Rept 103-202). (*Vote 61, p. 11-S; 1993 Almanac, p. 218*)

Kassebaum won the promise of a floor vote on the bill after one hour of debate in return for agreeing March 9 not to offer it as an amendment to the National Competitiveness Act bill (S 4), which was stalled on the Senate floor.

Under a deal brokered by Metzenbaum, she agreed before bringing the bill to the floor to raise the age of protected planes from more than 15 years to more than 18 years. Supporters argued that 18 years of use should be proof enough that a plane had no design defects. When older planes crashed, they said, poor maintenance and weather were more likely to be at fault than flaws in the original design and production.

Kassebaum also added exceptions to allow lawsuits when there was clear and convincing evidence of fraud, when the crash involved patients being transported for emergency medical treatment, or when people in other planes or on the ground were injured. The idea, Metzenbaum said, was to protect people injured by a manufacturer's deception or by planes they did not choose to board. He said the threat of lawsuits was the only real protection passengers had.

Slade Gorton, R-Wash., said the light-plane industry in the United States had been effectively destroyed by unwarranted liability costs. For example, he said, Beech Aircraft was sued 203

times between 1983 and 1986, paying an average settlement of more than $500,000 in each case — even though the National Transportation Safety Board blamed the accidents on factors other than manufacturing or design defects.

House Committee

Bill proponents struck a deal June 16 with their most formidable opponent in the House, Judiciary Committee Chairman Jack Brooks, D-Texas.

The agreement took the form of a substitute amendment to S 1458, offered by Mike Synar, D-Okla., and Rick Boucher, D-Va. The Judiciary Subcommittee on Economic and Commercial Law approved the amendment by voice vote June 16 and then gave voice vote approval to the amended bill.

The substitute cut off product liability claims after 22 years of service for jet-powered small planes, 18 years for turbine-powered propeller planes and 15 years for piston-powered propeller planes.

It also made a technical change sought by Brooks that assured the Judiciary Committee joint jurisdiction over aviation liability law. The original bill would have given the Public Works Committee exclusive jurisdiction over the issue in the House.

After wishing aloud for the bill to disappear, Brooks said he would support the substitute, which offered the most relief to manufacturers of piston-engine planes, the segment of the industry that had the greatest economic problems, Brooks said. Brooks had held a hearing on the bill May 12 — his first ever on a proposal to limit product liability.

Democrat Dan Glickman of Kansas, a leading supporter of the Senate bill, also embraced the substitute. He said his only concern was the possibility that the new version could get bogged down again when sent back to the Senate.

Brooks had been able to kill previous attempts by Glickman to limit lawsuits against small-plane manufacturers simply by not acting on them. In 1994, however, Glickman and James V. Hansen, R- Utah, pressured Brooks to act by collecting more than 300 cosponsors for their version of the measure (HR 3087) and filing a petition to discharge the Senate bill from Brooks' committee if he did not act. Hansen's state was home to several companies that made parts for light aircraft.

Judiciary Committee Approves Bill

As a result of the agreement, the bill won voice vote approval June 21 from the House Judiciary Committee, where product liability bills usually went to die. Before the committee voted on S 1458, it accepted the Synar-Boucher substitute by voice vote (H Rept 103-525, Part 2).

Glickman emphasized how different the airplane liability measure was from the broader product liability bill. He said he told fellow Democrats on the committee, "Don't get too frightened about the camel's nose under the tent. This is an airplane bill. It's not toasters, it's not refrigerators, it's not lawn mowers, it's airplanes."

Kassebaum said she was satisfied with the changes made by the committee and predicted that the Senate would accept them without further amendment.

The House Public Works Committee, which shared jurisdiction over the issue, had already approved S 1458 without amendment, reporting it May 24 (H Rept 103-525, Part 1). Public Works Chairman Norman Y. Mineta, D-Calif., however, said he would support sending the Judiciary Committee's version to the House floor.

House Floor

The small-plane liability bill sailed through the House on June 27 by voice vote.

Brooks brought the bill to the House floor under suspension of the rules, a procedure reserved for non-controversial measures. No member of Brooks' committee spoke against it on the House floor. Instead, several members cited statistics charting the decline of small-plane manufacturing in the United States and its implications for the entire U.S. aviation industry.

"Unless this legislation is enacted and general aviation manufacturing increases, we will have a whole generation of American pilots being trained on foreign aircraft," warned James L. Oberstar, D-Minn. "Aviation schools and universities are buying [foreign] aircraft . . . on which to train a whole new generation of pilots."

Jim Slattery, D-Kan., said that sales had dropped from 17,000 planes in 1979 to fewer than 1,000 in 1993, causing more than 100,000 workers to lose their jobs. He said one factor was the industry's liability costs, which had risen to more than $200 million annually.

Supporters of the bill emphasized that it would put thousands of people back to work immediately. One manufacturer, Cessna Aircraft Co., had pledged to renew production of piston-powered planes if Congress enacted the Senate bill, creating 1,500 to 2,000 jobs in 18 months, Glickman said.

Supporters also argued that the bill would not harm consumers. "Nearly all defects are discovered, we have learned in our hearings, during the early years of an aircraft's life," Oberstar said. "Design and manufacture are regulated by the FAA [Federal Aviation Administration], which will order corrective action where defects are revealed."

Oberstar also noted that four major groups of pilots and air transportation companies had endorsed the bill. The members of those groups were the most likely to be injured when a small plane crashed but also were the ones most affected by excessive liability costs, he said.

The amended bill went back to the Senate, which passed it by voice vote Aug. 2 after changing the cutoff for lawsuits to 18 years for all planes. That move sent the measure back to the House, which cleared it without debate the next day. ∎

FTC Bill Targets Unfair Ads

After settling a longstanding dispute between the House and Senate over unfair advertising, Congress cleared a bill reauthorizing the Federal Trade Commission (FTC) for the first time since 1983. President Clinton signed the measure into law Aug. 26 (HR 2243 — PL 103-312).

The bill restored the FTC's power to set industrywide rules against unfair advertising and marketing practices, but only under certain conditions. Congress gave the commission that power in the mid-1970s, but took it away in 1980 in response to a series of proposed rules that infuriated the business community.

The groups pushing to expand the commission's rulemaking powers included some consumer advocates, the Coalition on Smoking OR Health, the American Association of Retired Persons and the National Association of State Attorneys General. They had a powerful and persistent ally in John D. Dingell, D-Mich., chairman of the House Energy and Commerce Committee.

On the other side were the advertising firms and their clients, a broad-based group of product manufacturers and

distributors. Serving as a middleman in the search for a compromise was Rep. Thomas J. Manton, D-N.Y., whose state was home to a number of major advertising firms.

Despite the lengthy congressional fight over the issue, however, Bonnie L. Jansen, a spokeswoman for the commission, said the new rulemaking power would make little difference in FTC actions. Commission Chairwoman Janet D. Steiger did not even mention the rulemaking authority in her response to the conference report. Instead, she praised the conferees for giving the commission more authority to gather evidence in investigations and to sue offending companies wherever they did business.

The FTC was charged with monitoring domestic and international trade activities and investigating complaints of unfair business practices. The commission also was responsible for protecting consumers from deceptive marketing practices and for promoting competition in the marketplace by enforcing antitrust laws.

Background

The FTC's reauthorization had been blocked by a 12-year impasse over whether the agency should have authority to prohibit unfair advertising on an industrywide basis. The House was in favor; the Senate was opposed.

The Senate had won the battle the last time Congress reauthorized the commission in 1980, gaining language that barred the FTC from regulating advertising on such grounds. Since then, the commission had been kept alive by annual appropriations bills. It could promulgate rules against "deceptive" advertisements, which made exaggerated or misleading claims, but not "unfair" advertisements, which took advantage of vulnerable audiences like children or the elderly. *(1980 Almanac, p. 233)*

Without such rulemaking power, the commission had been left to address unfair advertisements by filing lawsuits against individual companies rather than setting industrywide standards. For example, before Congress authorized a rule on 900-number services, the commission sued individual companies to stop television spots for those services that aired during Saturday morning cartoon programs.

This approach had some advantages, however: It consumed less of the commission's time and resources, and the penalties sought against a handful of companies could influence an entire industry.

On June 21, 1993, the House passed by voice vote a bill sponsored by Al Swift, D-Wash., to give the FTC unrestricted authority to regulate advertising that it deemed unfair (HR 2243 — H Rept 103-138).

The Senate passed a conflicting version of HR 2243 (S Rept 103-130) by voice vote Sept. 22, 1993. The Senate again sided with the arguments of advertising groups, which said that regulating advertising on the grounds that it was "unfair" was a vague standard that might violate the free-speech clause of the First Amendment. *(1993 Almanac, p. 235)*

Conference Compromise

House and Senate conferees reached a compromise on the bill July 20 (H Rept 103-617) that allowed the FTC to issue rules against unfair marketing practices under three conditions: The advertisement caused or was likely to cause substantial injury to consumers; the injury was not avoidable and not outweighed by benefits to consumers or competition; and public policy considerations were not the primary basis for finding the advertisement to be unfair.

The conditions also applied to lawsuits brought against companies accused of unfair practices.

The public-policy restriction was particularly important to the tobacco and alcohol industries. If public-policy considerations were paramount, said Bruce Silverglade, a consumer activist for the Center for Science in the Public Interest, the commission might ban cigarette ads with youthful-looking models or beer promotions with people engaged in vigorous activity.

Swift, the bill's sponsor, said the conferees based the conditions on the commission's own policy statements in the early 1980s. Among the commission's efforts then were proposals to restrict advertising of over-the-counter medicines and advertising directed at children.

The conference report authorized $92.7 million for the commission in fiscal 1994, $99 million in fiscal 1995 and $102 million for fiscal 1996.

Other provisions allowed rules against unfair or deceptive practices only if they were widespread in an industry; limited the commission's jurisdiction over products marketed by farming cooperatives; and required the commission to notify Congress before intervening in any state or federal rulemaking or legislative proceeding.

The House agreed to the conference report by voice vote July 25 under suspension of the rules. The Senate cleared the bill Aug. 11, also by voice vote. ∎

Lawmakers Consider Baseball's Antitrust Exemption

The threat — and later the reality — of the 1994 baseball strike, which left the country without a World Series for the first time since 1904, prompted members of Congress to consider lifting major-league baseball's 72-year-old exemption from antitrust law. Although Congress proved unwilling to take up such a measure in the end-of-session rush of bills, lawmakers from both parties warned that they would return to the issue in January 1995 if the strike had not been settled.

"The assumption that Congress will stay silent on baseball's antitrust exemption, that we will never question baseball's unique legal status, is no longer valid," said Sen. Orrin G. Hatch, R-Utah.

Organized baseball had been exempt from federal antitrust law since 1922, when a unanimous Supreme Court ruled that it was not a form of interstate commerce. In a series of later rulings, the high court concluded that baseball was, in fact, interstate commerce, but that it was up to Congress to lift the exemption. Congress, it seemed, was not interested.

On Aug. 12, major-league baseball players went on strike in an effort to prevent team owners from imposing a new compensation system that would place a ceiling on players' salaries. The players anticipated that a late-season strike that threatened the lucrative post-season league championships and World Series would enhance their bargaining power.

Mike Synar, D-Okla., sponsor of the main House bill, said players in other professional sports had used the courts to generally avoid the protracted labor disputes that had plagued baseball over the previous two decades. No other organized sport had an antitrust exemption.

But other lawmakers said they still opposed a major weakening of the exemption because it could cause major-league franchises to be uprooted and devastate the minor leagues.

Legislative Action

With a midseason work stoppage looming, the Senate Judiciary Committee took up a bill (S 500) that sponsor

Howard M. Metzenbaum, D-Ohio, said was the best hope for staving off a strike.

Metzenbaum, chairman of the panel's Antitrust Subcommittee, originally sought to rescind all exemptions from antitrust laws enjoyed by professional baseball. But he scaled back the bill before the committee voted on it in an effort to win support. The panel nevertheless balked June 23, rejecting the bill by a vote of 7-10.

The revised bill would have lifted the antitrust exemption only with regard to labor-management relations. Disputes between players and owners could have been settled in court or resolved through other federal labor-management mediation procedures. Metzenbaum said his interest in averting a strike was not spurred solely by his hometown Cleveland Indians' first-place standing in the American League Central Division.

Judiciary Committee Chairman Joseph R. Biden Jr., D-Del., who voted against the bill, said that no matter how Congress acted, it was likely to be blamed if a strike or an owners' lockout ensued. The Major League Baseball Players Association supported the bill; baseball owners strenuously opposed it.

Dianne Feinstein, D-Calif., referred to her experience as mayor of San Francisco in explaining her opposition to the bill. "As someone who for three years as a mayor worked with major-league baseball to try and keep a team in my city, I am unalterably opposed to any change," she said. "For us to get in the middle of what is a labor beef — this isn't national steel — and make a change in antitrust, I think is government interference that isn't necessary now. . . . Cities will lose their teams," she said.

Four months later, with no end to the strike in sight, Metzenbaum on Sept. 30 offered and then withdrew an amendment to partially lift the exemption. The intended vehicle was the spending bill for the District of Columbia. Faced with delaying tactics by Phil Gramm, R-Texas, the retiring liberal admitted there was not enough time left in the session to pass such a measure.

On the House side, the Judiciary Committee on Sept. 29 approved a bill (HR 4994) aimed at easing the labor strife by giving players the right to sue owners on antitrust grounds if the owners imposed certain unilateral conditions, such as a salary cap. That way, players could continue to take to the field while the issue was resolved in court. Supporters said the bill merely gave players the same rights as those enjoyed by all other Americans, including athletes in other sports.

To ease owners' concerns, Synar offered a substitute amendment, first adopted by voice vote Sept. 28 by the Economic and Commercial Law Subcommittee, that specifically exempted the minor leagues. It also removed language directing a court to issue an injunction against unilateral action while a case was pending.

Supporters acknowledged that the measure had little chance of clearing the 103rd Congress, which by then was rushing toward an Oct. 7 adjournment date.

But lawmakers served notice on owners and players alike to settle the protracted strike in time for spring training or face swift congressional reprisals.

Los Angeles Dodgers pitching ace Orel Hershiser, who lobbied legislators on behalf of the players, said the substitute was an acceptable compromise, although he preferred Synar's original bill. He said players would try to return to the field if the substitute passed.

Baseball officials, however, continued to raise two principal objections:

● **The minor leagues.** Despite the revised provisions, minor league teams were so inextricably tied to the big leagues that even a partial lifting of the exemption would have damaging consequences on minor league teams, baseball officials said. For example, courts might begin to question the minor league reserve clause, under which a minor league team could safely invest in a young player because the player could not switch organizations for six years.

● **Congressional meddling.** Congress should not involve itself in the middle of a collective bargaining process because it would give an unfair advantage to the players, baseball officials said.

The owners won over ranking Republican member Hamilton Fish Jr. of New York and several other committee Republicans, who said it would be a bad precedent for Congress to involve itself in a strike that did not imperil national security.

Meanwhile, with baseball stars roaming the halls of the Capitol to drum up support for the effort, a House Education and Labor subcommittee stoked the flames by holding a hearing Sept. 29 on an alternative bill (HR 5095) to end the strike. That measure, by Labor-Management Relations Subcommittee Chairman Pat Williams, D-Mont., would have imposed binding arbitration if players and owners failed to resolve their differences by Feb. 1, 1995. ■

Insurance Antitrust Exemption Stalls With Health Care Bill

House Judiciary Committee Chairman Jack Brooks, D-Texas, steered a bill through his committee that would have partially repealed the insurance industry's 49-year-old exemption from antitrust laws. Although Brooks won the backing of a large segment of the industry he was seeking to regulate, the measure (HR 9) stalled in the face of strong opposition from portions of the industry and misgivings from many Republicans. It went no further in the 103rd Congress.

In an effort to push the measure forward, Brooks tried tacking it onto his committee's contribution to the massive health care reform bill (HR 3600). The panel approved the amendment 20-15, on Aug. 2, but the health reform bill never reached the floor.

Committee Action

The House Judiciary Committee's Economic and Commercial Law Subcommittee voted, 9-6, along party lines July 19 to revise the language in the bill that Brooks originally had introduced. The new language was proposed by Brooks and backed by major insurers.

The revised bill, which the subcommittee then approved by voice vote, placed the insurance industry under key provisions of antitrust law, prohibiting price-fixing and actions that monopolized the insurance market.

The bill included provisions to curtail the industry's long-standing practice of sharing "trending" information used to project future costs and calculate prices. Instead, each company was expected to make its own projections or turn to a private forecasting firm to make them. A three-year transition period was provided to give companies time to make new arrangements for generating such information internally.

Insurers could still form liability pools under the bill to cover high-risk situations, such as hurricanes.

To win over the major insurers, Brooks made a number of concessions, such as preserving industry practices of sharing historical loss data and using a uniform policy form. Insurers could still jointly inspect buildings for fire protection purposes. Brooks also added a provision to allow insurers to

continue using manuals that provided agents with common tables for calculating rates.

Brooks fended off further changes, however: "The bill has got more loopholes than a cheese grater," he grumbled at the subcommittee markup.

The full Judiciary Committee endorsed the subcommittee bill on July 22 by a vote of 20-15 (H Rept 103-853). Fourteen Republicans and Democrat David Mann of Ohio lined up against the bill, fearful that it could put some small and medium-sized insurers out of business.

Background

For 20 years, the insurance industry, led by health and property-casualty carriers, had lobbied to dissuade Congress from repealing its antitrust exemption. The 1945 McCarran-Ferguson Act — designed to spur the insurance industry in the wake of World War II — protected insurers from antitrust statutes, allowing them to pool information to calculate rates. State regulators were responsible for making sure that rates were reasonable.

Insurance companies credited the exemption for spawning a stable industry in which thousands of companies offered consumers an array of products. They argued that they still needed to pool data to accurately set their rates. The process, they said, had resulted in the best rates for consumers and insurers alike.

But to Brooks, a veteran populist, the system simply shielded the industry from antitrust protections and served no public purpose. For years, he sought to repeal sections of the act.

His concessions in 1994 won the backing of the influential American Insurance Association. He also reached an agreement with the Independent Insurance Agents of America, which represented 280,000 members, most of them agents of small insurers.

However, other industry groups, such as the Alliance of American Insurers, a national trade association representing 215 property and casualty insurance companies, continued to oppose the bill. They argued that it could lead to higher costs for consumers, as companies spent more to compile pricing information. Small insurers also worried that the bill would make it difficult for them to compete with the biggest companies if they were not permitted to pool trending information. Unlike the industry giants, many small and medium-sized insurers did not have the resources to crunch their own numbers or to contract with a private organization to provide such a service. ∎

Patent Bills Left Unfinished

Lawmakers considered, but did not complete action on, several patent bills, including measures to reauthorize the patent office, simplify patent applications for biotechnology firms and implement an international accord on trademark protection.

Patent Office Reauthorization

The House on Oct. 3 unexpectedly killed a bill (HR 4608) to reauthorize the Commerce Department's Patent and Trademark Office when 178 lawmakers switched from "yea" to "nay." The bill, which was considered under expedited procedures usually reserved for non-controversial measures, was defeated by a vote of 146-251. (Vote 458, p. 136-H)

The bipartisan vote-switching stampede was prompted in part by a provision, opposed by the Clinton administration, that was intended to shield the patent agency for five years from governmentwide personnel cuts mandated by

Congress earlier in the session (HR 3345 — PL 103-226). (Buyouts, p. 147)

The legislation recommended a $107 million authorization in fiscal 1995 for the patent office, which awarded patent protection to qualified inventions and disseminated technological information disclosed in patents. The office received $88.3 million in fiscal 1994. The office was financed entirely by the fees and surcharges it collected from those who applied for or wished to maintain trademarks and patents. The $107 million was to be taken from the pool of fees collected.

The House Judiciary Subcommittee on Intellectual Property and Judicial Administration gave voice vote approval to the measure Aug. 4. But first, the panel approved by voice vote an amendment to exempt the office from the proposed federal workforce reductions. The amendment, offered by subcommittee chairman and bill sponsor William J. Hughes, D-N.J., also would have reclassified patent office fees as offsetting collections in order to bypass the appropriations process. But Hughes modified the language in full committee to omit the reclassification provision and instead elevate the patent office from assistant secretary to undersecretary status. The committee approved the new amendment by voice vote Sept. 29, then approved the bill, also by voice vote (H Rept 103-777).

Biotech Patents

Both chambers passed versions of a bill (HR 4307) designed to make it easier for biotechnology firms to win patents for the unique or skilled processes they used to make their products. But the measure died because House and Senate negotiators could not agree on how broad the bill should be.

Supporters in both chambers contended that conflicting court rulings on patenting a unique "process" — as opposed to a "product" — had led the U.S. Patent and Trademark Office to apply inconsistent criteria when reviewing patent requests. Bill proponents said the inconsistencies threatened to leave U.S. companies vulnerable to overseas competitors whose production processes often were protected by their countries' patent laws.

The bill was designed primarily to help biotech firms that had found it difficult to patent their products because the materials used were too commonplace. Such firms had tried instead to patent the processes by which they made their products, and that is where they encountered regulatory inconsistencies.

On June 16, the House Judiciary Subcommittee on Intellectual Property and Judicial Administration approved the measure including a substitute amendment by Chairman William J. Hughes, D-N.J., that narrowed the bill to ensure that it did not apply to software and computer companies. The amendment specified that the bill applied only to one of the three categories of inventions protected by U.S. patents: compositions of matter. That language limited the legislation primarily to the biotechnology, pharmaceutical and chemical industries.

The full committee gave voice vote approval to the measure June 29 (H Rept 103-728). The House passed it Sept. 20 by voice vote under suspension of the rules.

In the Senate, lawmakers voiced concern that the House-passed version would threaten the chemical industry. To address those concerns, the Senate on Oct. 6 gave voice vote approval to an amendment by Dennis DeConcini, D-Ariz., that narrowed the scope of the bill to apply only to biotechnological processes. The Senate passed the amended bill by voice vote.

Madrid Protocol

The House passed a bill (HR 2129) containing procedural changes in U.S. law that were needed to implement the 1989 Madrid Protocol, a proposed international agreement on the protection of trademarks. The Senate did not act on the bill, however, largely because the administration had not asked it to ratify the protocol.

The Madrid agreement was designed to provide a simpler system of filing for trademark protection abroad. Proponents of the measure said foreign trademark registration could ensure greater protection for U.S. trademark owners whose products were sold worldwide. However, the administration had been wrangling with the European Union over voting rights in the World International Intellectual Property Organization, the body that was to register trademarks internationally.

On June 16, the House Judiciary Subcommittee on Intellectual Property and Judicial Administration gave voice vote approval to the bill, which included an amendment by subcommittee Chairman William J. Hughes, N.J. The amendment added a new section aimed at making it easier for trademark owners with national registrations to merge with international registrations. It also clarified that to file an international application in the United States, a person had to be a national, or be domiciled or have a real and effective industrial or commercial establishment in the United States.

The full Judiciary Committee gave voice vote approval to the amended legislation Sept. 29 (H Rept 103-780). The House passed the bill Oct. 3 by a vote of 387-3. *(Vote 457, p. 136-H)*

Senate Bills

The Senate passed two patent bills by voice vote in the final days of the session, but neither measure was considered by the House. Both bills were sponsored by Dennis DeConcini, D-Ariz.

The first bill (S 2341), which was approved with an amendment Oct. 4, attempted to broaden the scope of re-examination proceedings at the Patent and Trademark Office. It gave third parties (people who were not patent owners) more authority to initiate re-examination proceedings when challenging the validity of patents. It also gave third parties the right to appeal final re-examination decisions. The re-examination system was an administrative alternative to litigation for patent owners and third parties trying to resolve questions about patent validity.

The second bill (S 2272 — S Rept 103-405) passed with an amendment Oct. 8. It clarified the rights of prior users — people who used or were preparing to use a process that later became the subject of a patent filed by another person. The Senate bill allowed prior users, in certain cases, to continue using at least a portion of the process. But it required that they prove they were using the process commercially in the United States or were making serious preparations to use it when the patent was filed.   ■

Congress Renews, Expands SBA

Congress provided a three-year reauthorization for the Small Business Administration (SBA) in a bill that expanded the agency's popular 7(a) loan guarantee program and eased prepayment penalties for small businesses that wanted to refinance loans they had taken out at high interest rates a decade before. The Senate cleared the bill on Oct. 5, and President Clinton signed it into law Oct. 22 (S 2060 — PL 103-403).

Overall, the bill authorized $16 billion in fiscal 1995, $18 billion in fiscal 1996 and $23 billion in fiscal 1997 for business loans, loan guarantees and bond guarantees.

● **Loan guarantees.** The 7(a) program — by far the agency's biggest — was authorized to guarantee $9.2 billion in loans in fiscal 1995, increasing to $10.5 billion in fiscal 1996 and $13.1 billion in fiscal 1997. Under the program, the SBA acted as a partial guarantor of loans made by commercial lenders to small businesses.

● **Defense conversion loans.** The bill authorized $7.5 billion over three years for defense conversion loans aimed at helping businesses in regions hurt by base closings and the slowdown of defense-related industries.

● **Micro-loans.** The bill expanded the so-called micro-loan program, which provided technical assistance and made

---

BOXSCORE

Small Business Administration Reauthorization — S 2060 (HR 4801). The three-year reauthorization expanded the agency's main business loan guarantee program.

Reports: S Rept 103-332, H Rept 103-616; conference report H Rept 103-824.

KEY ACTION

Aug. 18 — Senate passed S 2060 by voice vote.

Sept. 21 — House passed HR 4801, 370-48; it then passed S 2060 by voice vote, after substituting the text of HR 4801.

Oct. 4 — House agreed to conference report by voice vote.

Oct. 5 — Senate adopted the report by voice vote.

Oct. 22 — President signed bill — PL 103-403.

---

direct loans of up to $25,000 available to very small businesses. These small loans were frequently unavailable from traditional lenders. The bill authorized $758 million for the direct loan program over three years; it also included $90 million for a new pilot program of loan guarantees.

● **Women.** To help businesses owned by women, the bill gave statutory authority to the SBA's Office of Women's Business Ownership and created an Interagency Committee on Women's Business Enterprise.

● **Interest rate relief.** The measure authorized $30 million in fiscal 1995 to help small businesses that were locked into SBA-backed loans that were taken out when interest rates were 12 percent to 15 percent, or higher. Some of those businesses had tried to refinance their loans but faced high prepayment penalties. The bill allowed businesses to pay a lower penalty if they wished to refinance.

In other provisions, the final bill reflected reduced authorization levels for small-business venture capital programs, as requested by the House. It also required the SBA's Office of Advocacy to give Congress a comprehensive report on the federal regulations, paperwork and taxes affecting small businesses.

Background

Demand for loan guarantees under the 7(a) program had risen sharply in recent years, outstripping the funds available to the SBA. The SBA guaranteed 70 percent to 90 percent of the loan amount, enabling small businesses to get larger loans at lower rates and longer terms than otherwise. Often the guarantee made the difference in whether banks were willing to make the loan at all.

"Several factors have contributed to the growth of the 7(a) program in the decade of the 1990s." said Senate sponsor Dale Bumpers, D-Ark. "These include increased regulatory pressure on banks following the savings and loan collapse and ensuing reform legislation, an interest rate environment which made purchase of government securities more profitable for banks than small-business lending, and perhaps increased paperwork burdens for banks." As a result, an unprecedented number of borrowers turned to the SBA.

In 1992, Congress provided additional funds for regular SBA programs as part of an emergency supplemental appropriations bill (PL 103-302). *(1992 Almanac, p. 579)*

With demand for loans escalating, the 7(a) program ran out of funds in 1993 and had to shut down for 10 weeks until Congress responded by reprogramming unspent funds (PL 103-50). Lawmakers in 1993 also passed a bill aimed at broadening the availability of loan guarantees without increasing the cost to the government. The bill cut the SBA loan guarantee rate for certain long-term loans (PL 103-81). *(1993 Almanac, pp. 233, 710)*

Senate Action

On Aug. 10, the Senate Small Business Committee gave voice vote approval to S 2060 (S Rept 103-332). The funding levels differed somewhat from those in a companion bill that had already been approved by the House Small Business Committee. For the 7(a) program, the Senate bill authorized $9 billion in fiscal 1995, $10 billion in fiscal 1996 and $12 billion in fiscal 1997. In addition, it authorized $8 billion over three years for defense conversion loans.

The bill included $743 million over three years for the micro-loan program and $55 million for the guaranteed loan pilot program.

The committee gave voice vote approval to amendments:
● By Carol Moseley-Braun, D-Ill., for Frank R. Lautenberg, D-N.J., to prohibit the SBA from assisting anyone who had failed to make required child support payments. The amendment also provided for a 14-member commission to review and coordinate programs designed to promote women's roles in small business.
● By Larry Pressler, R-S.D., to prohibit the SBA from assisting any business engaged in the production and distribution of pornography.

The Senate passed the bill by voice vote Aug. 18.

House, Final Action

The House Small Business Committee voted 34-9 on July 14 to approve a companion bill (HR 4801 — H Rept 103-616). Sponsored by committee Chairman John J. LaFalce, D-N.Y., the bill authorized the SBA to guarantee $9.3 billion in loans under the 7(a) program in fiscal 1995, increasing to $10.9 billion in fiscal 1996 and $14.2 billion in fiscal 1997. Of the total, $1.5 billion was earmarked in fiscal 1995 for defense conversion loans.

The bill authorized $595 million over three years for direct micro-loans and $60 million for the pilot program in loan guarantees. It required the SBA to study the impact of federal regulations, paperwork and taxes on small businesses.

It also directed the SBA to provide relief for businesses that faced high prepayment penalties on certain SBA-backed loans. The committee defeated two amendments by Jay C. Kim, R-Calif., dealing with health care. The first would have prohibited the SBA from using money appropriated for fiscal 1995 salaries and expenses to promote or support employer mandates in health care legislation. The amendment was rejected 19-24. Kim's second amendment would have expressed the sense of Congress that employer mandates would be destructive to small businesses. It failed narrowly, 21-24.

The House passed the bill on Sept. 21 by a vote of 370-48. It then inserted the text into S 2060 and passed the measure by voice vote. *(Vote 428, p. 128-H)*

Before passing the bill, the House gave voice vote approval to a compromise between Democrats and Republicans over venture capital funding for two small business investment company programs, which Republicans felt were overly risky for major government involvement. LaFalce and ranking member Jan Meyers, R-Kan., offered language scaling back the authorized funding for the programs.

The House agreed by voice vote to an amendment by Michael Bilirakis, R-Fla., to require that applicants for SBA financial assistance certify that they were not in violation of any child support order.

On a 176-242 vote, the House rejected an attempt by Kim to recommit the bill to the Small Business Committee. Kim wanted to reduce the penalties that would fall on small businesses that paid off loans early. *(Vote 427, p. 128-H)*

House and Senate conferees reported a compromise bill on Oct. 3 (H Rept 103-824). The House agreed to the report by voice vote Oct. 4; the Senate followed suit the next day, clearing the bill. ∎

Other Small-Business Legislation

Of legislation aimed at assisting the nation's small businesses, Congress cleared a bill to increase the federal loan guarantees available for small-business capital and construction costs. Lawmakers considered, but did not complete action on, three other small-business bills.

Capital and Construction Loans

Congress cleared a bill authorizing additional funding for two small-business loan programs that were expected to run out of money before the end of the fiscal year. The House passed the bill (HR 4322 — H Rept 103-572) by voice vote July 19 under suspension of the rules. The Senate cleared the measure by voice vote the following day. President Clinton signed it July 22 (PL 103-282).

The bill, introduced by Rep. John J. LaFalce, D-N.Y., increased the authorization for loans under Small Business Administration (SBA) programs known as Sections 502 and 504 by $300 million in fiscal 1994. The programs provided guarantees that assisted small businesses in obtaining long-term loans for construction projects and capital equipment purchases.

The bill also extended to one year the amount of time an SBA employee could spend at a disaster site and be reimbursed for expenses. Under existing law, an SBA employee could spend no more than six months at the site of a natural

disaster to process loan applications from businesses. LaFalce and Rep. Jan Meyers, R-Kan., said it could waste money to rotate employees every six months at disaster sites, such as the California earthquake, that required many more months of loan processing.

Small-Business Investment

The House Energy and Commerce Committee gave voice vote approval Aug. 5 to a bill aimed at stimulating small-business development by partially exempting some investments from regulatory oversight. The Senate passed a similar bill (S 479 — S Rept 103-166), sponsored by Christopher J. Dodd, D-Conn., on Nov. 2, 1993, by voice vote. Neither bill went any further in the 103rd Congress. *(1993 Almanac, p. 149)*

As approved by the committee, the House bill (HR 4858), sponsored by Edward J. Markey, D-Mass., increased from $5 million to $10 million the amount of money a company could raise through securities offerings without having to comply with complete registration procedures required by the Securities and Exchange Commission (SEC).

The committee bill gave the SEC the flexibility to allow small-business development companies to use leverage to increase the amount of capital they could invest in small businesses. Business development companies were established in 1980 to promote investments in small businesses, but they had not performed as well as some members of Congress expected.

The measure also exempted from securities regulations pooled investment funds that put at least 50 percent of their money into small businesses. These funds were to be open only to investors with at least $10 million in securities. Committee Chairman John D. Dingell, D-Mich., said he would oppose any attempt to allow investors with less money into the pools because of the lack of SEC oversight.

Minority-Owned Businesses

The Senate by voice vote Oct. 7 passed a bill (S 2478) intended to help minority-owned businesses and cut down on fraud in a troubled Small Business Administration (SBA) minority program. However, the House did not consider the end-of-session measure, and it died at the end of the Congress.

As passed by the Senate, the bill, sponsored by John Kerry, D-Mass., encouraged teaming relationships between veteran and new minority-owned companies. It also granted waivers of surety bond requirements to certain companies bidding on some government contracts.

The bill included provisions to give long-term assistance to companies in the SBA's Minority Small Business and Capital Ownership Development Program, known as the 8(a) program. Graduates of the program would be allowed to sell a non-controlling equity share of their businesses without losing the right to continue work on government contracts they already had won. They could also compete again for certain contracts.

The 8(a) program had been plagued by various abuses, such as "front companies" masquerading as minority-owned. To curb abuses, the bill sought to strengthen an SBA protest program in which participants could challenge a firm's eligibility. It also required the SBA to increase its efforts to bring more companies into the program, rather than giving the same companies a large share of the contracts every year.

Federal Contracts

The House Small Business Committee approved a bill (HR 4263) intended to ensure that the interests of small and minority-owned businesses were protected in a major initiative overhauling government procurement procedures (S 1587 — PL 103-355). But the bill, sponsored by committee Chairman John J. LaFalce, D-N.Y., got no further and died at the end of the Congress. *(Procurement reform, p. 144)*

The committee divided along partisan lines June 29, approving HR 4263 (H Rept 103-606, Part 1) by a vote of 26-19: Republicans unanimously opposed the measure, while James Bilbray of Nevada was the only Democrat to vote against the bill.

As approved by the committee, the bill included several provisions that were also in the Senate-passed version of the procurement bill (S 1587). For example, it raised the ceiling on government contracts reserved for small businesses from $25,000 to $100,000. It also established a goal of giving enterprises owned by women 5 percent of the value of contracts the government awarded each year.

The debate occasionally turned fractious, as Republicans and members of the Congressional Black Caucus squared off on a number of amendments designed to aid minority-owned businesses. On June 23, the panel approved, 27-18, an amendment by Floyd H. Flake, D-N.Y., to eliminate a requirement that minority business owners prove they were economically disadvantaged in order to participate in programs aimed at helping minority-owned concerns win government contracts. The panel rejected several amendments offered by Kweisi Mfume, D-Md., the black caucus' chairman, that were designed to boost the share of government contracts awarded to minority-owned businesses. ∎

Bill To Aid Depressed Regions Stalls in the Senate

The House twice passed bills (HR 2442, HR 5243) to reauthorize the Economic Development Administration (EDA), and the Appalachia Regional Commission. A Senate committee approved a related bill (S 2257), but the full Senate never took up the measure.

The EDA was established in 1965 (PL 89-4) to steer public works grants to economically distressed areas, such as rural Appalachia, where local infrastructure funds were lacking. The agency provided grants for technical assistance and public works projects to eligible state and local governments.

The Appalachian Regional Commission was established in 1965 (PL 89-136) to alleviate poverty in the 399 chronically depressed counties of Appalachia's 13 states.

Both agencies had lacked formal authorization since 1980. Presidents Ronald Reagan and George Bush had repeatedly targeted them for elimination, arguing that the programs amounted to pork barrel handouts to states. The House had passed reauthorization bills in every Congress since 1980, but the Senate had not followed suit. Still, Congress refused to abolish the programs and continued to fund the agencies through annual appropriations, mainly at the insistence of Senate Appropriations Chairman Robert C. Byrd, D-W.Va.

The Clinton administration, through Commerce Secretary Ronald H. Brown, was trying to use the EDA as a funding source to replenish regions hurt by defense spending cutbacks, military base closings and natural disasters such as the California earthquakes, Midwestern floods and Southern hurricanes.

The fiscal 1995 appropriations bill for the departments of Commerce, Justice, State and the judiciary (HR 4603 — PL 103-317) provided $440.2 million for the EDA. President Clinton

vided $340.6 million for the EDA in fiscal 1994. The fiscal 1995 Energy and Water Appropriations bill (HR 4506 — PL 103-316) provided $282 million for the Appalachian Regional Commission, compared with $249 million in fiscal 1994.

House Action

The House first passed HR 2442 in May; in October, it passed a revised measure (HR 5243) that mirrored a bill (S 2257) that had won committee approval in the Senate. At every turn — in committee and on the floor — members of Congress provided different authorization levels for the agencies covered and varying timeframes for the legislation.

House Committees

The House Public Works Committee began work on the bill in 1993, approving a three-year reauthorization (HR 2442 — H Rept 103-423, Part 1) on Nov. 9. The committee bill authorized $312.6 million for the EDA in fiscal 1994 and $325 million annually in both fiscal 1995 and 1996. The bill also reauthorized the Appalachian Regional Development Act and made it clear that the funds were to be used only for investments in severely distressed and underdeveloped Appalachian counties. The measure authorized $249 million for the commission in fiscal 1994 and $239.6 million annually in both fiscal 1995 and 1996.

The House Banking Subcommittee on Economic Growth and Credit Formation approved a two-year version of the bill (HR 2442) April 13, 1994, by voice vote.

The subcommittee version authorized $342.9 million for fiscal 1994 and $411.7 million for fiscal 1995 for the EDA. It also authorized $249 million for fiscal 1994 and $239.6 million annually for fiscal 1995 for the Appalachian Regional Development Administration.

In addition, the subcommittee approved by voice vote an amendment by Eric D. Fingerhut, D-Ohio, to provide an explicit authorization under the EDA for 12 regional technical assistance centers to help businesses that suffered because of implementation of bilateral trade agreements.

A week later, on April 21, the full House Banking Committee approved the bill (H Rept 103-423, Part 2) by voice vote. The full committee endorsed the subcommittee authorization levels for the EDA.

Members agreed by voice vote, however, to an amendment by Bill Orton, D-Utah, to reduce the fiscal 1995 authorization for the Appalachian Regional Commission from $239.6 million to $187 million, the amount the Clinton administration had requested. Like the subcommittee version, the bill proposed to authorize $249 million for the Appalachian Regional Commission in fiscal 1994.

The committee rejected, 22-28, an amendment by Rod Grams, R-Minn., to bar Congress from appropriating funds for the EDA or the Appalachian Regional Commission unless the programs were specifically authorized — a restriction that threatened to preclude funding for the agencies.

The committee bill sought to steer funds to investment programs in areas bracing for military base closures. Such bases were critical to the local economies. The bill also proposed to establish at the Commerce Department an Office of Strategic Economic Development Planning and Policy to act as a clear-

BOXSCORE

EDA Reauthorization — HR 5243, S 2257 (HR 2442). The bills proposed multi-year reauthorizations for the Economic Development Administration and the Appalachian Regional Commission.

Reports: H Rept 103-423, Parts 1, 2; S Rept 103-391.

KEY ACTION

May 12 — House passed HR 2442, revised, 328-89.

Sept. 27 — Senate committee approved S 2257.

Oct. 7 — House passed HR 5243 by voice vote.

inghouse for information on successful investment programs in distressed areas.

House Floor Action

The House on May 12 passed a revised three-year version of HR 2442 by a vote of 328-89. *(Vote 168, p. 50-H)*

The measure made some revisions to the 1965 laws (PL 89-4, PL 89-136) that created the EDA and the Appalachian commission. Under the House-passed version, communities applying for funds, for example, had to submit an investment strategy to ensure that only the neediest areas would receive the money.

The House-passed bill contained yet another set of authorization figures: For the EDA, it authorized $312.6 million for fiscal 1994 and $386 million for each of fiscal years 1995 and 1996, and for the Appalachian Regional Commission, $249 million in fiscal 1994 and $214 million for each of fiscal years 1995 and 1996.

During two days of floor debate, the House voted 270-135 on May 11 to adopt an amendment by Paul E. Kanjorski, D-Pa., to set up a Commerce Department data base of all federal technologies that could be marketed or used by the private sector. It also allowed the executive branch to set up a private sector corporation to help transfer federally developed technologies to small businesses. *(Vote 162, p. 50-H)*

By large majorities, the House rejected several amendments to eliminate funding for the EDA and the Appalachian commission, as well as amendments to trim their funding. *(Votes 164-166, p. 50-H)*

Senate, Final Action

The Senate Environment and Public Works Committee approved a companion reauthorization bill (S 2257 — S Rept 103-391) by voice vote on Sept. 27.

The committee-approved bill was a three-year authorization, but unlike the House measure, it covered fiscal years 1995-1997. It authorized $415 million for fiscal year 1995 and $295 million plus "such sums as may be necessary" for defense conversion activities for each of fiscal years 1996 and 1997.

In an attempt to win final passage, the House by voice vote Oct. 7 passed a revised EDA reauthorization bill (HR 5243) fashioned after the measure approved by the Senate committee.

Sponsored by Bob Wise, D-W.Va., the bill proposed to authorize the same level as provided by the Senate committee version: $415 million for fiscal year 1995, and $295 million plus "such sums as may be necessary" for defense conversion activities for each of fiscal years 1996 and 1997.

It also required the administration to make allocations based on the level of distress, rather than on preference for a geographic area or a type of distress. And it proposed to encourage aid for communities facing military base closures.

It provided for the creation of an Office of Strategic Economic Development Planning and Policy to study economic development financing tools, such as loan guarantees. It also authorized a new competitive communities pilot program, which was to give awards to distressed communities based on a national competition for the best redevelopment proposals. To speed aid to distressed areas, it required the EDA to respond to grant applications within 60 days.

The Senate did not take up the bill.   ■

Other Commerce-Related Action in Congress

Lawmakers confirmed a new head of the Commerce Department's U.S. and Foreign Commercial Service and took action on a variety of other commerce-related matters during the 1994 session.

Fitz-Pegado Confirmed

The Senate on June 16 confirmed Lauri Fitz-Pegado as head of the Commerce Department's U.S. and Foreign Commercial Service. The vote was 69-30. The confirmation came with some difficulty after Sen. Lauch Faircloth, R-N.C., led an effort to recommit the nomination to committee. The Senate turned back his effort on a vote of 37-61. *(Votes 147, 148, p. 26-S)*

The Senate Banking, Housing and Urban Affairs Committee had approved the nomination Oct. 19, 1993.

Fitz-Pegado's nomination was controversial in part because of accusations that she had helped spread false information about supposed Iraqi atrocities on the eve of the Persian Gulf War. Fitz-Pegado had been a senior vice president at the Hill and Knowlton public relations firm, where she was in charge of its lobbying campaign for the Kuwaiti government after the Iraqi invasion in August 1990.

The Kuwaiti government-in-exile hired Hill and Knowlton to mobilize congressional and public support for U.S. military action against Iraq. As part of that campaign, Fitz-Pegado arranged the October 1990 testimony of a 15-year-old Kuwaiti girl, who told lawmakers that she saw Iraqi soldiers remove babies from incubators and "leave them to die on the cold floor." The girl's story was called into question after Harper's magazine identified her as the daughter of Kuwait's ambassador to the United States and a member of the royal family.

Bumper Damage Standards

The Senate Commerce Committee on Aug. 11 approved by voice vote a bill to set new crash standards for vehicle bumpers. In a swift markup session, Chairman Ernest F. Hollings, D-S.C., quickly moved the bill in hopes of winning its final passage before the close of the 103rd Congress. But the bill saw no further action.

The committee-approved bill (S 1848 — S Rept 103-353) required that bumpers on all new vehicles be capable of withstanding a collision of up to 5 miles per hour with minimal damage. The bill also required manufacturers to include on the vehicles a label verifying that the standard had been met.

Boxing Safety

A bill aimed at ending unsafe practices in the professional boxing industry won voice vote approval from the Senate Commerce Committee on Sept. 23. The measure (S 1991) was placed on the Senate calendar but was never taken up on the Senate floor.

As approved by the committee, the bill, sponsored by John McCain, R-Ariz., required state boxing commissions to report match results and the names of suspended fighters to the Association of Boxing Commissioners and the Florida State Athletic Commission, both of which maintained nationwide information networks. Before a fight, state boxing officials would have to consult this information to ensure that no boxer participated in a match while injured or under suspension in another state.

The bill also required professional fighters to register with a boxing commission in the state in which they resided or where a match was to occur. At the time of registration, each boxer was to be issued an identification card to be presented to state boxing officials before he weighed in for an event. States without boxing commissions were to be prohibited from hosting professional boxing matches unless that state made arrangements with a state that had a boxing commission to oversee the event.

'Made in America' Hotline

The House on Aug. 8 passed a bill to establish a "Made in America" hotline, a toll-free number to provide consumers with information about whether products were manufactured in the United States. The Senate did not act on the measure.

The bill (HR 3342), sponsored by James A. Traficant Jr., D-Ohio, was intended to help promote U.S.-made goods and single out products whose made-in-America claims were inaccurate. The hotline was to be administered by the Commerce Department as a three-year pilot program. Manufacturers were to pay to have their products featured on the hotline. To be eligible, products had to have a retail value of at least $250, contain at least 90 percent U.S.-made parts and have been made by at least 90 percent U.S. labor.

The Federal Trade Commission (FTC) required that 100 percent of goods carrying the "made in America" label be made domestically, but lax regulation had led to widespread abuse. Manufacturers often used the term for products assembled largely from foreign parts or for foreign-made products that were packaged in the United States. Some foreign carmakers operating in the United States claimed their vehicles were "American-made" even though they often fell short of the FTC's domestic-content standards.

The Energy and Commerce Subcommittee on Consumer Protection and Competitiveness approved the bill by voice vote July 14. The subcommittee first adopted an amendment by Cardiss Collins, D-Ill., that required the Commerce secretary to survey U.S. companies to determine the level of interest in the pilot program and determine an annual registration fee before committing to any permanent program. The amendment also required manufacturers to absorb the cost of operating and promoting the hotline.

The full Energy and Commerce Committee approved the bill (H Rept 103-660) July 19. The House passed the measure Aug. 8 by voice vote. The bill was referred to the Senate Commerce, Science and Transportation Committee, which took no action on it.

Hazardous Pipelines

In an effort to prevent dangerous underground pipeline ruptures, the House twice passed legislation (HR 4394, HR 5248) to encourage states to dispense information on the location of hazardous pipelines.

As passed by the House, the legislation authorized $4 million in incentive grants for states to consider establishing or improving one-call notification systems that would allow builders to get information on all underground pipelines from a single source. The Transportation Department was to create a model one-call program. States that adopted the federal program, or certified that their existing programs worked as well as the federal model, would be eligible for the grant program.

The bill, sponsored by Frank Pallone Jr., D-N.J., was

spurred by the March 23 rupture of a natural gas pipeline that destroyed an apartment complex in Edison, N.J. The rupture was thought to have been caused by excavation damage. According to bill sponsors, 60 percent of all pipeline accidents stemmed from damage caused during excavation and digging.

The original version of the bill was far tougher than the measure that passed the House. As approved by the House Energy and Commerce Subcommittee on Energy and Power, HR 4394 required each state to establish a statewide, one-call notification system. The bill directed the Transportation Department to develop a model "call-before-you-dig" program for use by the states, and it authorized $12 million over three years for state grants to get the programs started. The panel approved the bill by voice vote Aug. 4.

The full Energy and Commerce Committee approved the bill by voice vote Aug. 5 (H Rept 103-765, Part 1).

The bill went next to the Public Works and Transportation Subcommittee on Surface Transportation, which approved an amended version by voice vote on Sept. 27. But the subcommittee backed away from requiring that states create one-call systems. Instead, the panel gave voice vote approval to a substitute that required states to "consider" establishing one-call notification systems to protect all underground lines from damage due to excavation. The revised bill authorized $4 million in incentive grants for states. The changes, offered by Nick J. Rahall II, D-W.Va., encouraged states to set up the clearinghouses by opening

the door to a lawsuit by anyone harmed in an accident where such a system was not in place.

The full Public Works and Transportation Committee amended the bill and approved it by voice vote Sept. 28 (H Rept 103-765, Part 2).

The bill was referred to the Senate Commerce, Science and Transportation Committee. When the Senate took no action, the House passed the bill again, combining it with an unrelated measure to discourage drunk driving (HR 5248). The House passed HR 5248 by voice vote Oct. 7, but the Senate did not take up the bill.

Hazardous Spill Exemptions

The Senate by voice vote Oct. 8 passed a bill (S 2559) to exempt shippers of vegetable oil and animal fats from certain hazardous spill regulations. The House did not act on the measure. The bill, which was introduced the same day by Tom Harkin, D-Iowa, was intended to clarify the intent of Congress regarding hazardous materials regulations issued under the Oil Pollution Act of 1990 (PL 101-380). That law, a response to the 1989 *Exxon Valdez* spill in Alaska, greatly increased spillers' liability. In 1993, the Department of Transportation sought to classify animal fats and vegetable oils as hazardous materials. "Common sense and scientific evidence prove that animal fats and vegetable oils do not pose the same threat to our environment that petroleum does," Harkin said. ∎

Law Extends Protections For Plant Developers

Congress cleared a bill implementing a 1991 international agreement reinforcing patentlike protection for developers of new plant varieties. The bill — which brought the Plant Variety Protection Act of 1970 (PL 91-577) into agreement with the Convention of the International Union for the Protection of New Varieties — was signed into law on Oct. 6 by President Clinton (S 1406 — PL 103-349). Generally, the bill made only modest changes in U.S. law. For example, it extended the period of patentlike protection for new plant varieties from 18 years to 20 years.

The bill, sponsored by Bob Kerrey, D-Neb., shot through the Senate on May 25, passing by voice vote without debate.

The House version of the bill (HR 2927) won easy, voice vote approval July 27 from the Agriculture Subcommittee on Department Operations and Nutrition.

But the bill included one provision that stirred controversy when the measure reached the full House Agriculture Committee on Aug. 3: It barred farmers from selling to each other leftover seeds from a protected plant variety without compensating the plant breeder who developed the variety.

There was a long tradition in the United States of farmers who traded "saved seeds" — seeds that were left over because of overpurchase or those obtained from their harvested crops. Supporters of such "brown bag" sales argued that they enabled farmers to stretch their incomes and even helped neighbors in financial distress with low-cost seed. But plant breeders said the sale of saved seeds denied them the return on their work that they needed to sustain further research into new varieties of plants. The international convention barred unauthorized saved-seed sales.

The House Agriculture Committee affirmed this provi-

sion, but just barely. The panel defeated, 10-10, an amendment by Larry Combest, R-Texas, that would have allowed farmers to sell saved seed — up to 10 percent of what they normally planted in a given year. Combest received vocal support from Harold L. Volkmer, D-Mo., who said farmers in his district had been selling saved seed "for years and years and years."

But Charles W. Stenholm, D-Texas, chairman of the Department Operations Subcommittee, backed the seed industry. He cautioned that farmers — many of whom were adamant about protecting their property rights against land-use restrictions embodied in environmental and other regulations — would sacrifice consistency if they took a different position on the seed issue. Despite the narrowness of that vote, the losing side did not press the issue on the House floor.

Stenholm and others warned that without strict observance of their marketing rights, seed companies would abandon their research into new plant varieties, at a high, long-term cost to farmers.

Kansas' Pat Roberts, ranking Republican on the full committee, noted that the Pioneer Seed Co., one of the nation's largest such firms, had quit its efforts to develop new varieties of hard red winter wheat because of low returns on its investments. The company attributed its decision in part to farmers' practice of buying saved seed from other farmers rather than purchasing new seed from the original developer.

The issue, an unusually divisive one for a panel noted for its pro-agriculture consensus, was defeated only after committee Chairman E. "Kika" de la Garza, D-Texas, cast the deciding "nay" vote. De la Garza was the chief sponsor of the House bill.

The House Agriculture Committee approved the bill, 33-8, on Aug. 3 (H Rept 103-699). The House passed S 1406 by voice vote Aug. 12, after substituting the text of HR 2927. The Senate agreed by voice vote Sept. 21 to accept the House version, clearing the bill. ∎

Lawmakers 'Reinvent' Agriculture

When the Clinton administration unveiled in September 1993 its plan to reorganize the huge Agriculture Department bureaucracy, it portrayed the overhaul as the leading edge of the administration's drive to "reinvent" the federal government. Ultimately, the House and Senate accepted that premise, voting by wide margins for legislation aimed at streamlining and reducing the size of the Agriculture Department.

However, the plan took more than a year to go from proposal to enactment. Its path was so convoluted that it ended up being cleared Oct. 4 as part of a separate bill (HR 4217) that contained another of the administration's top agriculture policy priorities: an overhaul of the federal crop insurance program. President Clinton signed the omnibus bill into law Oct. 13 (PL 103-354). *(Crop insurance, p. 194)*

The reorganization proposal got off to a fast start early in 1994. A House Agriculture subcommittee ap-proved a version of the bill (HR 3171) in early February. The Senate passed its version (S 1970) in mid-April. But the legislation soon bogged down in the House, slowed by a dispute over the management of soil and water conservation programs within the proposed new Agriculture Department structure.

HR 3171 embodied the administration's proposal to merge nearly all of the department's conservation programs within a Natural Resources Conservation Service. But many farm-state members argued that this plan would give environmentalists too much influence over conservation policy and result in new, burdensome restrictions on farmers' land use.

Not until late September, with time running out on the 1994 session, were the opposing House factions prepared to accept a compromise proposal. The final bill did create a Natural Resources Conservation Service, but it also required the Agriculture Department to set up an agency to perform cost-benefit analyses of all proposed regulations dealing with health, safety or the environment.

Other major provisions in the final bill:

● Required the Agriculture Department to reduce total employment by 7,500 staff positions over the ensuing five years.

● Specifically authorized the Agriculture secretary to close or consolidate more than 1,000 Agriculture Department field offices.

● Required that staff reductions be proportionately higher in the Washington department headquarters than in the field offices.

● Created a Consolidated Farm Service Agency by merging the agencies that had managed the department's major farm subsidy, farm lending and crop insurance programs. The goal was to provide "one stop shopping" for farmers seeking to participate in department programs.

● Separated the department's meat inspection and food

BOXSCORE

Agriculture Department Reorganization — HR 4217
(S 1970, HR 3171). The bill cut 7,500 positions, created a Farm Service Agency, consolidated conservation programs and subjected regulations to cost-benefit analyses.

Reports: S Rept 103-241; H Rept 103-714, Parts 1 and 2.

KEY ACTION

April 13 — Senate passed S 1970, 98-1.

Aug. 25 — Senate passed HR 4217 by voice vote, after attaching the text of S 1970.

Sept. 28 — House passed S 1970 by voice vote after substituting the text of HR 3171.

Oct. 3 — House passed the revised HR 4217 by voice vote.

Oct. 4 — Senate cleared HR 4217 by voice vote.

Oct. 13 — President signed HR 4217 — PL 103-354.

---

safety responsibilities from its food marketing functions, and elevated the prominence of the inspection activities by placing them under the new position of under secretary for food safety.

● Established a National Appeals Division to handle appeals by farm program participants of decisions by Agriculture Department agencies.

Background

From its founding in 1862 until the 1930s, the Agriculture Department was a relatively small Cabinet department that focused its efforts on research and on providing information to farmers on the latest agricultural techniques and technology.

But the 1930s brought the Great Depression and President Franklin D. Roosevelt's New Deal programs to provide farmers with an economic safety net. Over the ensuing 60 years, Agriculture expanded into a huge bureaucracy that not only issued income and price support subsidies to farmers but also managed a variety of soil, water and forest conservation programs; provided food and nutrition support for millions of low-income Americans; and promoted the use of U.S. farm commodities in both domestic and foreign markets.

By the early 1990s, the Agriculture Department had an annual budget of more than $60 billion and well over 111,000 employees, who were located in its hulking headquarters facility that spanned Constitution Avenue in downtown Washington, dozens of other facilities in the Capital region, and thousands of field offices, with at least one located in nearly every county in the United States.

The department also faced a growing phalanx of critics who said it was overgrown, with too many employees, underused facilities and "alphabet soup" agencies with overlapping jurisdictions that created confusion for citizens who participated in the department's farm or food subsidy programs.

In a September 1991 report, the General Accounting Office (GAO), Congress' investigative arm, recommended a complete overhaul of the department's structure. "Although increased responsibilities in nutrition, international trade and environmental issues have greatly diversified USDA's client base over the years," the report said, "the department's structure and management practices have remained largely unchanged since the 1930s." The Kansas City Star won a Pulitzer Prize for a series in December 1991 that detailed instances of waste, fraud, abuse and discrimination in department activities.

The first serious effort to downsize the Agriculture Department bureaucracy began in 1992. In February of that year, Richard G. Lugar of Indiana, the ranking Republican on the Senate Agriculture Committee, called for the immediate closure of 53 department field offices that had spent more on administrative overhead than on the federal benefits they had disbursed to farmers. He later raised that figure to 92 inefficient offices. Dan Glickman, D-Kan., a senior member of the House Agri-

culture Committee, submitted legislation in April 1992 to consolidate hundreds of field offices. *(1992 Almanac, p. 214)*

The Bush administration responded, with Agriculture Secretary Edward Madigan forming a task force to investigate waste in the field offices. Although Bush was defeated for re-election that November, Madigan released a report days before leaving office in January 1993 that recommended the closure of nearly 1,200 field offices.

Clinton's first Agriculture secretary, former Democratic Rep. Mike Espy of Mississippi, put Madigan's list aside pending his own study of the field offices. But he pledged to make reorganization of the department a top priority. On Sept. 7, 1993, the day Vice President Al Gore unveiled the administration's overall plan to "reinvent" the federal government, Espy was the only Cabinet head prepared to roll out a comprehensive reorganization plan for a department.

Espy's Proposal

Espy's plan called for eliminating and merging more than a dozen Agriculture Department agencies, reducing the total from 43 to 30 or fewer. Espy said the overhaul would reduce the number of department employees by at least 7,500 over the first five years after enactment; administrative savings over that period would amount to $2.3 billion.

He called for the creation of a Farm Service Agency, merging the farm subsidy programs of the department's Agricultural Stabilization and Conservation Service, the farm-lending programs of the Farmers Home Administration and the disaster assistance programs of the Federal Crop Insurance Corporation. He said the change would make the department more "farmer-friendly" by providing a single office to handle multiple programs.

Espy also proposed to create a Natural Resources Conservation Service to consolidate environmental conservation programs, which were managed mainly by the Agricultural Stabilization and Conservation Service and the Soil Conservation Service. This agency and the Forest Service were to be overseen by an assistant secretary for natural resources and environment.

Espy also sought to change the structure of the farmer-elected county committees that carried out the federal farm programs at the local level. He wanted to merge the local five-member committees that oversaw farm subsidy programs with the three-member committees that supervised the farm-lending programs.

He proposed that the secretary be allowed to appoint two members to each of the resulting five-member committees, in part to bring people with expertise in areas such as law and science into the farmer-dominated panels, as well as to increase the committees' racial and gender diversity.

Although Espy had made improvement of the department's meat inspection efforts one of his priorities as secretary, his reorganization proposal left the department's food inspection and food marketing programs together under an assistant secretary for marketing and inspection services. This disappointed many consumer advocates, who said the goal of promoting sales of farm commodities conflicted with the responsibility to crack down on unsafe production practices.

The Espy plan was submitted as a bill (HR 3171) by House Agriculture Committee Chairman E. "Kika" de la Garza, D-Texas, on Sept. 29, 1993.

House Subcommittee Action

The Agriculture Subcommittee on Department Operations and Nutrition approved HR 3171 by voice vote Feb. 8, 1994,

substituting a version offered by subcommittee Chairman Charles W. Stenholm, D-Texas. The subcommittee made few significant changes to the administration proposal.

The provision to create a Farm Service Agency by merging major farm programs received broad support from subcommittee members. The bill sought to lock in the staff reductions promised by Espy, requiring the department to meet the goal of trimming 7,500 staff jobs within five years.

The Stenholm substitute tried to assuage the concerns of farm-state members, who worried that the bulk of the staff reductions would be made at the field office level by requiring that the percentage of jobs cut at the headquarters level be twice the percentage of jobs cut at the local level.

The subcommittee's bill also went further than did Espy in elevating the department's food safety and inspection services, separating them from the food marketing programs and placing them under a newly created under secretary for food safety.

Environmental Dispute

While these provisions faced little argument, consensus broke down on the sensitive question of which agencies should manage the department's environment-related programs. The original version of HR 3171 contained Espy's plan to combine nearly all the conservation programs within the new Natural Resources Conservation Service. But some farm organizations, which had been complaining for years about the proliferation of rural conservation laws and regulations, expressed concerns that the office would become a "mini-Environmental Protection Agency" within the Agriculture Department.

Stenholm, a cotton farmer who shared that concern, modified the Espy plan. His substitute put the Soil Conservation Service in the Natural Resources Conservation Service and created an under secretary for natural resources and environment. But it placed the other conservation programs that had been under the Agricultural Stabilization and Conservation Service into the new Farm Service Agency, along with the farm subsidy, lending and insurance programs.

Some farmer advocates on the subcommittee, led by Wayne Allard, R-Colo., and Cal Dooley, D-Calif., wanted to go further by adding the Soil Conservation Service to the roster of programs under the Farm Service Agency, leaving only the Forest Service under the natural resources agency. Noting that the Soil Conservation Service was one of Agriculture's most-used agencies, Allard said his amendment coincided with Espy's professed goal of a "farmer-friendly" department.

But opponents warned that the amendment could spark a backlash among environmentalist House members, some of whom might wish to have the rural conservation programs moved out of the Agriculture Department altogether. With Stenholm calling the proposal "a fundamental mistake," the Allard-Dooley amendment was defeated on a 10-15 vote.

County Committees

Also sparking some debate was the issue of the makeup of the county committees that administered the department's programs. The Stenholm language merged the county committees dealing with farm subsidy and lending programs, as requested in the Espy plan. But it dropped Espy's proposal to allow the secretary to appoint members to the committees, maintaining the tradition of allowing local farmers to elect all the members of the committees.

The subcommittee defeated a proposal aimed at promoting racial and gender diversity on the panels. Jay Inslee, D-Wash., suggested a "cumulative voting" system, which would have

given each participant in a county committee election a number of votes equal to the number of committee positions up for election. This amendment, which would have given voters from underrepresented groups the option of concentrating all of their votes on a single candidate, was rejected by voice vote.

House Committee Action

After an interlude of more than four months — during which time the Senate passed its version of the bill — the full House committee approved HR 3171 on June 16 by a vote of 27-21 (H Rept 103-714). Republican members voted solidly against the bill, forcing the Democrats to muster their own party-line vote.

The dispute over the treatment of the department's conservation programs had put a brake on the bill's progress. The dispute disrupted the usually strong bipartisan consensus concerning farm issues on the Agriculture Committee, whose Democratic and Republican members alike were virtually all from agricultural districts.

Committee Republicans, led by their ranking member, Pat Roberts of Kansas, warned that they would oppose the bill if it maintained the administration's proposal to merge the conservation programs within a single agency. Seeking to avoid a partisan battle, Chairman de la Garza delayed action on the bill.

But when efforts at a compromise failed, de la Garza went ahead with the markup on June 16. The conservation issue spurred the hottest debate.

Bob Smith, R-Ore., was blunt about his concerns that environmentalists would have too much influence over the proposed Natural Resources Conservation Service. "This is war in farm country," Smith said. "The idea of [the Soil Conservation Service] going unchecked will create a disaster in farm country."

The issue played out as it had during the subcommittee markup. Allard of Colorado proposed to place the Soil Conservation Service within the Farm Service Agency with the farm subsidy and lending programs. Stenholm countered that the amendment "would paint the committee not as pro-farmer but as anti-environment." The Allard amendment was defeated on a 19-29 vote.

The committee's Democratic leadership did seek to reach out to Republican members by accepting an amendment, drafted by Gary A. Condit, D-Calif., to require the Agriculture Department to set up an agency to conduct cost-benefit analyses of any proposed regulation affecting health, safety or the environment.

Condit's amendment had significance beyond the Agriculture reorganization bill. Conservative Republicans and Democrats had argued for years that federal agencies failed to measure the expected benefits of a regulation against the costs that the regulation imposed on individuals, businesses and the economy in general. During the 103rd Congress, this coalition fought on several fronts to get legislation enacted that would require federal bureaucrats to do cost-benefit calculation.

The inclusion of Condit's amendment in turn caused a reaction among environmentalist members, mainly Democrats led by Natural Resources Committee Chairman George Miller, D-Calif., who viewed the cost-benefit issue as a scheme by pro-development members to bog down the regulatory process and place a spurious price tag on human life, health and safety. Their opposition again delayed progress on the bill until close to the end of the 103rd Congress.

Before voting on the measure, the Agriculture Committee

also dealt with the composition of the county committees that administered federal farm programs at the local level. The panel stood by the provision to create a single committee in each county, composed of three to five members, all of them farmer-elected.

The committee rejected, on a 21-24 vote, an amendment by Bill Barrett, R-Neb., that would have allowed local farmers to decide in a referendum whether to merge the county committees or leave them separate.

The panel also rejected, on a 9-23 show of hands, an amendment by Jill L. Long, D-Ind., that would have allowed the Agriculture secretary to appoint one of five county committee members. Her proposal was aimed at increasing racial, ethnic and gender diversity on the county committees. The committee did approve by voice vote a Long amendment requiring the Agriculture secretary to encourage nominations for the farmer-elected county committees from organizations representing socially disadvantaged groups.

House Floor Action

Months of additional negotiations on the conservation issue produced a compromise that was largely a victory for those who wanted to require cost-benefit analyses of proposed federal regulations. The agreement allowed the House to pass HR 3171 by voice vote Sept. 28. The House then inserted its text into S 1970, which by then had passed the Senate, and passed the amended bill by voice vote.

With time running out, environmentalist members yielded on their efforts to block the Condit provision requiring cost-benefit analyses. The language was modified somewhat to apply only to regulations that were expected to have a national economic impact of more than $100 million annually.

The only other significant change made to HR 3171 during House floor debate dealt with the department's county committees. The House approved a manager's amendment by de la Garza to bar the Agriculture secretary from merging farmer-elected county committees unless the local farmers voted for such a merger. The amendment was identical to the proposal offered by Barrett in committee and rejected.

In its only recorded vote, the House defeated, 177-247, an effort by Allard to block the creation of a new Agricultural Service Agency (which had been called the Farm Service Agency in the original version of HR 3171). The House thus agreed to create the new agency by consolidating the department's crop subsidy, farm lending and crop insurance programs. *(Vote 445, p. 132-H)*

Senate Committee Action

On the Senate side, the Agriculture Committee gave easy 17-1 approval March 9 to a bill (S 1970 — S Rept 103-241) tailored after Espy's plan. The bill had been introduced by committee Chairman Patrick J. Leahy, D-Vt. Bob Kerrey, D-Neb., cast the sole "nay" vote, not to oppose the bill, but to protest an unrelated Agriculture Department policy that he said limited farmers' options in choosing crops to meet soil conservation requirements.

The bill as marked up by Senate Agriculture was similar to the House subcommittee-approved bill on most major provisions. Both bills contained provisions to create the Farm Service Agency and to require a 7,500-person staff reduction at the Agriculture Department over five years. The Senate bill said simply that proportionate employee reductions must be "substantially higher" in the Washington headquarters than in the field offices.

The Senate committee bill proposed to place all the conservation programs in the new Natural Resources Conservation Service, but it left the local management of the programs to the county committees that would also oversee the farm subsidy programs.

While also rejecting Espy's proposal to allow the secretary to appoint members to the department's county committees, Senate Agriculture took its own tack on the setup for the panels. It upheld the status quo by maintaining separate committees to oversee the farm subsidy and lending programs.

While the Senate committee bill delinked the food safety and food marketing programs, it did not give the food safety programs as lofty a status as did the House subcommittee: a new Food Safety Service was to be placed at the assistant secretary's level.

Senate Floor Action

With the House bill still stuck in committee, the Senate passed S 1970 April 13 by a 98-1 vote. Again Kerrey, whose unrelated policy dispute with the department remained unresolved, was the only vote against the bill. No member spoke against the bill during the brief floor debate, and there were only two technical amendments, both of which were approved by voice vote. (*Vote 91, p. 16-S*)

As the months passed, and the House bill remained stalled in committee, Senate supporters grew increasingly concerned about the legislation's prospects. Seeking to get the attention of their House counterparts, they succeeded in attaching S 1970 to a separate bill (HR 4217) to overhaul the federal crop insurance program. The action was approved by the Senate Aug. 25 on voice vote, as was HR 4217 as a whole.

Final Action

With barely a week left before the planned adjournment date of Oct. 7, leaders of the House and Senate Agriculture committees held an informal conference to resolve differences between their reorganization bills. To expedite action, the conferees agreed to go along with the Senate action folding the reorganization bill into the crop insurance measure.

The House approved the revised HR 4217 by voice vote Oct. 3. The Senate followed suit, also by voice vote, the next day.

The timing of the House action made the passage of HR 4217 an ironic coda to the brief tenure of Mike Espy as Agriculture secretary. Later on Oct. 3, Espy resigned, the result of controversy stemming from revelations that he had accepted gifts from business interests regulated by the Agriculture Department.

Conference Decisions

In key decisions on the bill, House-Senate conferees:
● Placed most land and water conservation programs under a new Natural Resources Conservation Service. But they also accepted the House-passed provision requiring cost-benefit analyses of proposed Agriculture Department regulations with an expected national economic impact of more than $100 million.
● Settled on Consolidated Farm Service Agency as the name for the new superagency created to administer the department's farm subsidy, lending and crop insurance programs.
● Came up with a somewhat different arrangement for how the department's county committees would be constituted. Unlike the Senate bill, the final bill allowed the Agriculture secretary to consolidate the existing county committees. The secretary was given full authority to conduct such mergers; unlike the House bill, the final bill did not make such mergers contingent on approval by affected local farmers.
● Included House language directing the department to encourage ethnic, gender and racial diversity on the county committees, and required the GAO to study whether minority-group members were underrepresented on those committees.
● Accepted the House-passed provision creating a new position of Under Secretary for Food Safety. ■

Crop Insurance Program Revamped

The Senate on Oct. 4 cleared legislation (HR 4217 — PL 103-354) to overhaul the federal crop insurance program, with the aim of increasing farmer participation and reducing the need for ad hoc federal aid whenever a disaster struck.

The final version of the bill, which President Clinton signed Oct. 13, contained not only the crop insurance provisions, but also legislation to reorganize the Agriculture Department. Originally proposed as separate bills, the crop insurance and reorganization measures — the top two agriculture policy priorities for the Clinton administration and Congress in 1994 — were merged to expedite their enactment before the end of the session. (*Agriculture reorganization, p. 191*)

The crop insurance bill attempted to remedy longstanding problems that had saddled the program with persistent financial losses. Farmers generally had eschewed paying what they regarded as high premiums for the federally subsidized insurance, instead relying on the government to come through with ad hoc disaster relief payments when major crop losses occurred. Only about a third of eligible farmers participated in the insurance program.

The revised program eliminated premiums for basic catastrophic-loss coverage, charging each farmer a processing fee of $50 per crop per county, with maximums of $200 per county and $600 overall. The bill increased the subsidies for farmers who wished to "buy up" to higher levels of coverage.

The legislation also gave the government added muscle to get farmers to join the program. Participants in federal price- and income-support programs were required to purchase at least the basic catastrophic coverage. At the same time, the bill revoked Congress' authority to enact disaster aid bills without fully funding them. Non-subsidized crops for which federal insurance was not provided had to be covered by a regularly funded disaster relief program.

The bill closely followed a Clinton administration proposal, which had drawn widespread praise and was expected to win easy enactment. But the bill's progress was slowed by a pair of contentious issues.

The first was how to pay for the increased costs expected to result from eliminating premiums and increasing subsidies. The second, a side issue that stalled the bill temporarily in the Senate, dealt with the Agriculture Department's handling of gay rights. Jesse Helms, R-N.C., held the bill up for three weeks in August as he sought to reverse a department

decision to demote an employee for publicly denouncing the department's gay rights policies.

Highlights

As enacted, the bill included provisions to:

● Make participation in the federal crop insurance program mandatory for farmers who took part in federal price support programs for such major crops as wheat, feed grains, rice, cotton, tobacco, peanuts, oilseed and sugar.

● Bar Congress from designating ad hoc disaster aid bills for crop losses as "emergency spending," thereby requiring lawmakers to offset the spending rather than simply adding it to the deficit.

● Provide premium-free basic catastrophic coverage to farmers of major crops. Farmers were to pay only an administrative fee of $50 per crop per county farmed, with maximums of $200 per producer per county and $600 regardless of how many counties the producer farmed.

● Provide for insurance benefits to be paid on crop losses in excess of 50 percent of normal yield at a rate of 60 percent of the expected market price for the crop. The price coverage rate was scheduled to drop to 55 percent beginning with the 1999 crop year.

● Encourage farmers to purchase additional coverage by increasing subsidies for "buy up" policies.

● Allow farmers to purchase basic catastrophic policies through either private insurers or the Agriculture Department's Federal Crop Insurance Corporation (FCIC). But buy-up policies could be purchased only through private insurers that were reinsured by the FCIC.

● Set up a permanent Agriculture Department disaster aid program for other crops, with an identical benefit formula for the basic catastrophic policy.

● Require a reduction over five years in federal reimbursements to private insurance companies and agents that participated in the crop insurance program. The rate was scheduled to fall from 31 percent in 1995 to 27.5 percent in 1999.

● Provide funding from mandatory spending accounts to cover the crop insurance program's administrative activities in 1995, 1996 and half of 1997, but the bill left uncertain the funding source for activities beyond that point.

Background

The federal crop insurance program was founded in 1938 as a reaction to the devastating "Dust Bowl" drought, which ruined many farmers. Part of President Franklin D. Roosevelt's New Deal agenda, the program was aimed at providing a financial safety net that would allow farmers to keep their land even in the face of massive crop losses.

Despite its good intentions, however, the crop insurance program never lived up to its billing. Over the ensuing decades, most farmers said it provided too few benefits at too high a premium cost. Also, Congress showed a tendency that increased over the years to pass supplemental spending bills that provided special aid to farmers who suffered catastrophic crop losses — whether or not they had participated in the crop insurance program.

BOXSCORE

**Crop Insurance Overhaul —
HR 4217** (S 2095). The bill provided premium-free basic crop-loss insurance for farmers but barred future "emergency" disaster aid bills to pay for crop losses.

Reports: H Rept 103-649; S Rept 103-301.

KEY ACTION

Aug. 5 — House passed HR 4217 by voice vote.

Aug. 25 — Senate passed HR 4217 by voice vote, substituting text of S 2095 and adding S 1970.

Oct. 3 — House passed the revised HR 4217 by voice vote.

Oct. 4 — Senate cleared HR 4217 by voice vote.

Oct. 13 — President signed HR 4217 — PL 103-354.

Congress sought to boost program participation by enacting legislation in 1980 (PL 96-365) that increased crop insurance subsidies to farmers and private insurance companies. But most farmers continued to view the premiums as too high relative to the potential benefits and opted to gamble on Congress providing special assistance when disaster hit. *(1980 Almanac, p. 95)*

As a result, the program turned into a consistent money-loser for the federal government, with benefits paid to insured farmers exceeding the relatively small pool of premiums in most years. On top of those losses, the federal government regularly shelled out large sums in supplemental disaster aid. In August 1993, Congress provided $1.1 billion to pay farmers for crop losses as part of a disaster aid supplement spending bill (HR 2667 — PL 103-75) that added $5.7 billion to the federal deficit. *(1993 Almanac, p. 714)*

Clinton Administration Proposal

Agriculture Secretary Mike Espy on March 3 outlined an administration plan to overhaul the crop insurance program. He said the changes would greatly increase farmer participation, sharply reduce ad hoc disaster aid spending and restore actuarial soundness to the insurance program.

Espy's proposal included provisions to:

● Provide premium-free basic catastrophic insurance coverage to federal farm program participants, who would be charged only a processing fee of $50 per crop per county with a maximum of $100 per farmer per county.

● Make participation virtually mandatory for farm program participants by barring farmers who were eligible for crop insurance from receiving emergency disaster payments.

● Make future disaster aid bills subject to congressional budget caps rather than adding them to the deficit.

● Allow farmers to sign up for the basic coverage either through Agriculture Department field offices or private insurance agents.

● Provide coverage on crop losses above 50 percent of usual yield at a rate of 60 percent of expected market value, a formula comparable to that used for disaster aid payments.

● Subsidize the purchase of higher levels of coverage, available only through private insurers.

● Create an on-budget contingency fund to provide disaster payments to farmers who were not eligible for crop insurance.

Espy said the added costs for subsidies and insurance payments under the expanded program would be more than offset by reductions in emergency disaster aid payments, resulting in a net federal savings of $750 million over the new program's first five years. The funding plan was critical, because Congress' budget rules required increased spending in any program to be fully funded. If lawmakers rejected Espy's speculative projection of disaster aid savings as a spending cut, they would have to find some other way to offset the increased cost of the crop insurance program.

House Committee

A House Agriculture subcommittee on June 30 held the first full-scale debate on the bill, with the issue of finances

dominating the proceedings. The Subcommittee on Environment, Credit and Rural Development gave voice vote approval to the bill, which closely followed the administration's proposal.

The bill as approved gave farmers premium-free basic coverage against catastrophic crop losses, with participants paying an administrative fee of $50 per crop per county and a maximum of $100 per county.

To ensure increased enrollment and limit federal exposure to disaster relief claims, the subcommittee bill required participants in federal farm subsidy programs to purchase at least the basic insurance coverage. The bill also contained "buy-up" provisions to subsidize premiums for farmers who chose to buy crop insurance above the basic amount to be provided by the government.

The subcommittee accepted the administration's logic that the extra costs in the crop insurance program would be offset by savings from decreased emergency disaster payments.

The markup was punctuated by a sharp exchange, however, when Thomas W. Ewing, R-Ill., tried to increase the premium subsidies for farmers who purchased additional insurance coverage.

Ewing's proposal drew a fiery response from Timothy J. Penny, D-Minn., who maintained that Ewing had no credible way to pay for it. Penny had already announced his plans to retire after the 103rd Congress out of frustration with Congress' inability to balance the federal budget.

Smacking the dais for emphasis, Penny said, "This committee as much as any committee includes members who are ranting and raving about the evils of this god-awful deficit, and the least we should do is pay for our own legislation."

Ewing protested that Penny had made a "personal attack" against him. But subcommittee Chairman Tim Johnson, D-S.D., persuaded Ewing to withdraw his amendment pending further discussions.

Full Committee Action

The House Agriculture Committee gave voice vote approval July 20 to a version of HR 4217 that was little changed from the subcommittee bill (H Rept 103-649).

But first, the committee bogged down in a budget fight sparked by a separate decision made by the appropriations committees. Although crop insurance payments came out of mandatory spending accounts, the money for salaries and administrative expenses was discretionary spending.

To meet their own tight requirements for fiscal 1995, the appropriators had slashed that discretionary spending. Since the money was primarily to reimburse the private insurance companies that administered the program, the committee had to come up with funds to cover the shortfall or see the program shut down. The committee bill solved the problem for fiscal 1995 by classifying the spending as mandatory and paying for it with savings from the elimination of emergency disaster aid bills. But the bill left it to appropriators to finance future administrative expenses out of discretionary spending.

Penny wanted to offset the entire cost of administrative expenses, estimated at $586 million over five years, by reducing reimbursements to private insurance agents and lowering the percentage of crop value that would be covered under the basic insurance package. Despite Penny's protests that his colleagues were putting off inevitable hard decisions, the committee rejected his amendment by a 13-35 vote.

House Floor Action

The House passed the crop insurance bill by voice vote Aug. 5, after Agriculture Committee Chairman E. "Kika" de la Garza, D-Texas, the bill's lead sponsor, headed off another attempt by Penny to find permanent funding for the administrative expenses.

During floor debate, Penny argued that a failure to designate a definite funding source for the administrative costs of the program would leave appropriators with two unfavorable choices in future years: not providing the money, thus killing the program, or making deep cuts in other vital programs, such as the Women, Infants and Children food program for low-income people.

Penny offered an amendment to permanently finance crop insurance administration costs as mandatory spending by immediately reducing reimbursements to private insurers by a small amount and cutting insurance coverage from 60 percent to 56 percent of expected market value. Penny was supported by Agriculture Appropriations Subcommittee Chairman Richard J. Durbin, D-Ill., who said failure to fully finance crop insurance out of mandatory accounts would indeed force him to cut popular programs.

However, de la Garza offered a substitute amendment that proposed to pay for crop insurance from mandatory accounts over the first three years after enactment. Although the funding source for the ensuing two years was left uncertain, de la Garza pledged that he would not allow the program to shift back to discretionary accounts. His amendment did include some provisions aimed at achieving budget savings. It raised the maximum crop insurance administrative fee to be paid by a farmer to $200 per county, up from $100 in the original bill. It also set up a phased reduction in the reimbursement rates for private insurers; after remaining at the existing level of 31 percent in 1995 and 1996, the rates were to slip to 29 percent in 1997 and 28 percent in 1998 and 1999.

De La Garza's substitute was adopted by the House on a 253-156 vote. The Penny amendment, as amended, then was adopted, 401-1. (*Votes 377, 378, p. 114-H*)

Senate Action

The Senate Agriculture Committee had given voice vote approval June 22 to its version of the crop insurance bill (S 2095 — S Rept 103-301), after a brief discussion that emphasized the potential economic benefits of the proposed program overhaul.

The committee largely accepted the administration's position that any additional costs under the bill would be offset by savings resulting from the diminished need for ad hoc disaster aid bills. "This bill is designed to end the annual scramble to pass emergency disaster bills," said committee Chairman Patrick J. Leahy, D-Vt. Unlike the House markups, the Senate session barely touched on the financing issue. The bill's strong sendoff by the Agriculture Committee seemed to presage easy floor passage.

Senate Floor Action

The Senate did pass the bill by voice vote with no serious challenge to the crop provisions. (The Senate passed HR 4217 after substituting the text of S 2095.) But the floor action did not take place until Aug. 25. It had been delayed for weeks by North Carolina's Helms, who placed a "hold" on the bill to protest what he said were gay rights policies in the Agriculture Department. In particular, Helms sought to reverse an administrative action against Karl Mertz, a former

regional Agriculture Department equal employment officer who was transferred from his job because of critical remarks about the department's policy toward homosexual employees.

Helms finally relented after being lobbied by Bob Dole, R-Kan., and Jim Exon, D-Neb., and Agriculture Secretary Espy. The three impressed upon Helms that any further delay could result in cancellation of many farmers' crop insurance policies.

Helms did not give up without a concession, though. During floor debate, he won an amendment barring preemptory removal of any Agriculture employee for comments in opposition to the department's policy on homosexuals and effectively returning Mertz to his original job. Helms had added a similar amendment to the pending fiscal 1995 agriculture spending bill July 20.

The Senate made no other major changes to the crop insurance provisions as passed by the Agriculture Committee. However, senators attached the text of a separate bill to reorganize the Agriculture Department, which it had passed April 13 (S 1970) in hopes of spurring House action on the legislation.

The House Agriculture Committee had approved a parallel bill (HR 3171) on June 16, but it had been blocked from floor action by a dispute over a provision requiring cost-benefit analyses of proposed Agriculture Department environmental regulations.

Other Agriculture-Related Legislation

Congress cleared a number of additional agriculture bills, including measures promoting the use of vegetable oil-based ink, allowing an agriculture agency to charge fees for dispute-resolution services, and giving the quasi-federal Farm Credit System greater ability to finance agricultural exports. A number of other bills saw action but did not clear.

Dairy Export Board

A House Agriculture subcommittee approved a bill (HR 2664) aimed at giving dairy farmers greater opportunity to exploit export markets, but the full Agriculture Committee never took up the measure. The bill, which won voice vote approval from the Livestock Subcommittee on June 8, would have changed the way dairy assessments were calculated. It also would have created a private, farmer-run board responsible for increasing the sales of U.S. milk and dairy products overseas.

A key aim of the bill was to give farmers more control over disposing of excess milk on the U.S. market, thereby keeping the domestic price high.

As approved by the subcommittee, the bill provided for the establishment of an 18-member export board that would contract with the government to sell surplus milk overseas, where the price was often lower than in the United States. Farmers would subsidize the exports.

Advocates said the exports would reduce the amount of surplus milk on the domestic market, thereby accomplishing two goals: reducing the cost to the federal government of dairy price supports and lowering the assessments that farmers paid to offset those supports.

Dairy-state lawmakers — concerned about congressional decisions in 1993 to trim federal honey, wool and mohair programs — also hoped the bill would help pre-empt expected efforts by farm-program critics to cut farmer support pay-

Final Action

With time running out at the end of the session, House Agriculture Committee leaders decided to concur with the Senate action to merge the crop insurance and Agriculture reorganization bills into a single measure, HR 4217.

The House and Senate committee leaders met privately in an informal conference to resolve the few differences between the bills, both closely modeled on administration proposals. The negotiators settled on a financing plan for the crop insurance program that closely tracked that in the House version. The House-passed bill provided funding for the program's administrative costs out of mandatory accounts for fiscal years 1995, 1996 and 1997. Conferees were able to scrape together enough money within the mandatory accounts to cover the expenses for fiscal 1995 and 1996 and only half of 1997. After that point, a new means of funding, either mandatory or discretionary, would have to be developed.

As in the House version of the bill, each farmer participating in the insurance program would be charged a processing fee of $50 per crop per county with maximums of $200 per county and $600 overall.

The House approved the final bill by voice vote Oct. 3. The Senate followed suit the next day. ∎

ments when the farm bill came up for reauthorization in 1995. *(1993 Almanac, p. 546)*

Under existing law, dairy farmers paid assessments equal to 11.25 cents per hundred pounds of milk, or hundredweight, to the Commodity Credit Corporation. That money went toward reducing the federal deficit. In return, the government guaranteed to buy any surplus milk at a price of $10.10 per hundredweight.

As approved by the subcommittee, the bill provided for the assessments to decline to the extent that federal price supports fell. Advocates of the legislation predicted that it would cut assessments by about half.

But the bill did not do away with the government price supports. When annual domestic surpluses exceeded 7 billion pounds, the government was obliged to buy the excess. Farmers who overproduced had to pay a penalty. In addition, the Agriculture Department still had to purchase milk for domestic feeding programs, school lunches and the military.

Separately, the bill required the Agriculture secretary to fully fund the existing Dairy Export Incentive Program. Under this program, private milk exporters could ask the government to help them sell milk overseas by paying the difference between the U.S. price and a lower foreign sales price.

Before approving the measure, the Livestock Subcommittee defeated, 5-9, an amendment by Cal Dooley, D-Calif., that would have deleted the language penalizing dairy farmers who increased supply by increasing farm efficiency. Dooley's state tended to have larger-scale dairy operations than Midwestern and Eastern states.

Earlier, on April 14, the subcommittee rejected an amendment by Steve Gunderson, R-Wis., that would have cut assessments on dairy farmers from the existing level of 11.25 cents to 6 cents per 100 pounds of milk. Half the 6 cents would have helped to pay for the new dairy export board, to develop new products and to buy surplus milk in the domestic market so that the price would stay high. The idea, designed to head off any efforts by non-farm lawmakers to cut the program more

deeply, was supported by Republicans and California Democrats with dairy interests. The vote was 8-8.

Dairy Compact

Lawmakers in both chambers considered legislation (HR 4560, S 2069) aimed at empowering a six-state compact in New England to increase the federally mandated milk price in that region. But neither bill made it to the floor.

The price paid dairy farmers for their product was set by a complex formula called the milk marketing system. Under the system, the nation was divided into several regions. Every farmer in a region was paid the same amount for his cows' milk. Prices varied from region to region and had fluctuated from quarter to quarter, influenced by the availability of milk and other economic factors. Many dairy farmers in the Midwest and Northeast complained that the price was set so low and had fluctuated so much that it was driving them out of business.

The problem had led six states — Maine, Vermont, Massachusetts, Connecticut, New Hampshire and Rhode Island — to draw up a compact for their region, with a commission that could increase the price paid to farmers for milk. If, for example, the milk price in New England was set at $12 per 100 pounds of milk, the commission could decide to add $1, paying farmers $13 for every 100 pounds. Anyone who sold milk in that market would receive that price, even if the farmer lived outside the region.

Under existing law, states could increase the federal milk price. But individual New England states had not done so because milk was sold across many borders in that region. The compact, which needed congressional approval to go into effect, was intended to supplant the existing state authority.

Several members objected that the compact would protect dairy farmers at the expense of poor consumers, who would have had to pay higher prices at the store as a consequence of higher prices that milk processors and grocers would have to pay for milk. But compact supporters argued that there was a huge gap between the shelf price of milk and that paid to farmers.

The House Judiciary Subcommittee on Administrative Law and Governmental Relations voted 5-5 on Oct. 4 to send a bill approving the compact (HR 4560) to the full committee without recommendation. The subcommittee first approved, by voice vote, an amendment by Chairman John Bryant, D-Texas, adding eight reservations to the bill. The most important of these limited the life of the compact to five years. The full Judiciary Committee took no action on the measure.

On the Senate side, the Judiciary Committee gave voice vote approval to a companion bill, sponsored by Agriculture Committee Chairman Patrick J. Leahy, D-Vt. (S 2069 — S Rept 103-333). But objections from other farm state senators kept the bill from coming to the floor. Herb Kohl, D-Wis., in particular, strongly opposed the bill, saying it would benefit New England dairy farmers to the exclusion of those elsewhere.

FIFRA Rewrite

A House Agriculture subcommittee approved a bill (HR 1627) in July to overhaul the nation's major pesticide use laws. But the legislation fell victim to the longstanding stalemate between pro-pesticide interests and those who wanted tighter restrictions on the use of potentially hazardous farm chemicals.

Existing law created separate standards for pesticide residues on raw foods and on processed foods. The 1947 Federal Insecticide, Fungicide and Rodenticide Act (FIFRA) permitted raw food products to contain infinitesimal residues of pesticides that had been scientifically determined to be potentially cancer-causing. But processed foods were covered by a separate provision of the 1938 Federal Food, Drug and Cosmetic Act, known as the Delaney Clause, which barred even the most minute traces of carcinogenic pesticides on processed foods — a policy known as "zero tolerance." Nearly all sides on the issue agreed that the "zero tolerance" standard was impractical and needed to be changed.

FIFRA had been reauthorized last in 1988. (1988 Almanac, p. 139)

Three Approaches

HR 1627 was one of three major legislative initiatives on pesticide use in the 103rd Congress. All three proposed to replace the Delaney Clause with a single standard to govern both raw and processed foods. But there were significant differences over how stringent to make the new standard.

● **Stenholm.** HR 1627, sponsored by Rep. Charles W. Stenholm, D-Texas, retained the existing practice of requiring that the Environmental Protection Agency (EPA) use a cost-benefit analysis when setting pesticide tolerances. The bill required the EPA to continue taking into account the health, nutritional and consumer benefits — as well as the health risks — to be derived from the use of a pesticide. The bill was backed by pesticide manufacturers and their farmer clients.

● **Waxman-Kennedy.** Rep. Henry A. Waxman, D-Calif., and Sen. Edward M. Kennedy, D-Mass., sponsored a pair of bills (HR 872 and S 331, respectively) that required a strictly health-based, numerical standard, which in most cases barred pesticides that caused more than one additional cancer death among each 1 million consumers.

● **Clinton.** The Clinton administration produced its own legislative proposal that was eventually embodied in a series of separate bills (HR 4362, HR 4329, S 2050, S 2084). The administration, too, called for an exclusively health-based standard, but it proposed to write no numerical formula into law. Rather, it wanted to mandate regulators to set tolerance levels for each pesticide.

Committee Action

Stenholm's bill was the only one of the three to advance during the 103rd Congress. The farmer-friendly Agriculture Subcommittee on Department Operations and Nutrition approved it by voice vote July 27. HR 1627 was strongly backed by farm chemical producers and users, who liked the weight it gave to the benefits of pesticides. But it was just as strongly opposed by activist groups that wanted greatly to restrict the use of pesticides suspected to cause cancer or other human health problems. HR 1627 also ran counter to major provisions of the Clinton administration proposal.

Stenholm, the subcommittee chairman, emphasized that the main feature of his bill was a goal shared by all parties in the debate: the creation of a single standard for both raw and processed foods that allowed minute residues of potentially cancer-causing pesticides as long as the health risk was "negligible." Stenholm said his bill provided the basis for a compromise. But advocates of stricter pesticide regulation said HR 1627 tilted the balance too much in favor of pesticide use.

With the bill virtually certain to go no further than the full committee, Agriculture Committee Chairman E. "Kika" de la Garza, D-Texas, said there would be no sweeping pesticide legislation enacted in 1994. Instead, de la Garza pushed through a more limited bill (HR 967) that provided incentives to chemical companies to keep marketing less profitable "minor-use" pesticides, which were applied to fruits and veg-

etables. The House passed HR 967, but it died in the Senate. *(Minor-use pesticides, this page)*

The Senate did not act on any of the major FIFRA bills. Tom Daschle, D-S.D., chairman of the Agriculture subcommittee that oversaw pesticide law, had predicted in July that Senate passage was unlikely. He made the comment after a hearing at which he was unable to get representatives of pro- and anti-pesticide use groups even to come up with a common definition of an acceptable health risk — the level of pesticide residue considered safe.

Minor-Use Pesticides

With no sign that Congress was going to enact a sweeping overhaul of the nation's pesticide use laws, the House passed a more limited bill (HR 967) aimed at keeping less profitable "minor use" pesticides on the market. But in the Senate, those eager to address broader pesticide control issues in a single bill were unwilling to act on HR 967.

In general, a minor crop was defined by what it was not: Wheat, corn, soybeans, cotton and rice were major crops whose prices were supported by the federal government. On the other hand, fruits and vegetables were considered minor crops.

When Congress last overhauled pesticide laws in 1988, it set 1997 as the date for all pesticides to be reviewed and "reregistered" by the Environmental Protection Agency (EPA). To be reregistered, a pesticide had to undergo extensive and expensive testing on the crops for which it was intended in order to ensure that residues were not dangerous to consumers. *(1988 Almanac, p. 139)*

Manufacturers of minor-use pesticides complained that the cost of complying with existing regulations outstripped their sales revenues. But with Congress unable to pass broad legislation revising the nation's pesticide laws, pesticide makers had nowhere to go to win concessions. Unable to gain relief, many were opting not to make the minor-use pesticides at all. That brought protests from farmers, who said these chemicals were often the only pesticides that effectively protected a particular crop against a specific pest.

The House Agriculture Committee approved the bill (H Rept 103-784) on Sept. 30. The full House passed it Oct. 4 by a vote of 334-80. *(Vote 475, p. 140-H)*

As it passed the House, HR 967 provided several incentives to encourage chemical companies to continue production. For example, under the law, pesticide makers got exclusive use of testing information for 10 years (similar to a patent). The bill allowed manufacturers who reregistered certain pesticides three more years of exclusive use of the data.

FIFRA Delay

Congress cleared a bill (S 1913) that postponed implementation of certain pesticide safety training and labeling requirements under the 1947 Federal Insecticide, Fungicide and Rodenticide Act.

The bill put off the effective date of select Environmental Protection Agency (EPA) regulations from April 15 until Jan. 1, 1995. However, it did not postpone pesticide safety protections for farm workers. President Clinton signed the bill into law April 6 (PL 103-231).

The bill delayed a package of mostly administrative requirements, including requirements about pesticide safety training, notification, monitoring of workers who handled pesticides and posting information on the use and application of pesticides. The delay was intended to give the EPA more

time to provide necessary training, education and compliance information to farmers and regulators.

Bill sponsors stressed that the bill did not affect specific worker protection requirements printed on the labels of pesticides. Indeed, the bill required that pesticide users comply with all the provisions for worker protection that appeared directly on the label of pesticides. Such requirements instructed farm workers about the kinds of protective gear to wear when handling pesticides, for example.

The Senate acted first, passing the bill March 9. The bill embodied a compromise that was reached after senators unsuccessfully tried to attach similar language to an unrelated bill regarding industrial competitiveness (S 4). That amendment proposed to delay the pesticide safety regulation until Oct. 23, 1995.

When the bill moved to the House, E. "Kika" de la Garza, D-Texas, proposed a package of technical corrections. The House passed the revised bill on March 17 by voice vote, sending it back to the Senate for final action.

The Senate cleared the bill by voice vote March 24 after accepting the argument of bill sponsor Thad Cochran, R-Miss., that more time was needed to educate and train farmers about the regulations. Cochran described the bill as a compromise among EPA officials, state regulators, agricultural producers and farm worker advocates.

Vegetable Oil-Based Ink

President Clinton on Oct. 6 signed a bill that required the federal government to use ink made from vegetable oil for much of its lithographic printing. The bill (S 716 — PL 103-348), designed to help domestic farmers and improve the environment, mandated that the government use soybean and other vegetable oils and materials derived from renewable resources when technologically feasible.

The bill began in the Senate, which passed it by voice vote Nov. 19, 1993. The measure (S Rept 103-178) was sponsored by Christopher S. Bond, R-Mo. The House took up the Senate bill in 1994, passing it with amendments by voice vote Sept. 20. The Senate cleared the House-amended bill by voice vote Sept. 27. *(1993 Almanac, p. 231)*

The legislation set varying thresholds for different types of government printing. Ink used on newsprint, for example, had to contain at least 40 percent vegetable oil, while ink used in heat-set printing had to contain at least 10 percent vegetable oil. The bill required that the government's cost of using vegetable oil-based ink remain competitive with printing costs using the more common petroleum-based inks. Specific printing jobs were exempted from these requirements if the head of the agency determined that vegetable oil ink was unsuitable.

More than 95 percent of government printing used lithographic inks, which were made from various types of oil, including petroleum and vegetable oil.

Rep. Gary A. Condit, D-Calif., described the bill as a "win-win situation for the American people," because it would "provide another market for our farmers' crops, increase reliance on renewable agricultural resources and improve the environment by reducing emissions of volatile organic compounds." And, he said, "there is no increased cost associated with these benefits."

Condit chaired the House Government Operations Subcommittee on Information, Justice, Transportation and Agriculture, which approved S 716 by voice vote on June 29. The panel first amended the bill, by a vote of 6-0, to allow the use of petroleum-based ink if other inks were prohibitively

expensive and to exempt checks and other secure materials from the rules. The full Government Operations Committee considered the measure the same day and approved it as amended, 34-5 (H Rept 103-625, Part 1).

Many government documents already were printed with soy oil-based ink, rather than the more common petroleum-based pigments. The costs of the two types of ink were competitive. Inks based on soybean, sunflower or other vegetable oils were less likely to rub off on a reader's fingers, and they created fewer environmentally harmful byproducts.

Tax Relief on Disaster Aid

The Senate Finance Committee gave voice vote approval March 24 to a bill (S 1814 — S Rept 103-244) to give farmers flexibility in declaring disaster aid payments on their tax return forms. The Senate did not take up the bill.

The measure, sponsored by Tom Daschle, D-S.D., was spurred by the 1993 floods that devastated the Midwest. It would have amended the tax code to allow farmers to declare crop insurance and disaster aid payments either in the year in which the losses occurred or the year in which the payments were received.

Many farmers did not receive their federal disaster aid checks until 1994, which caused some of them to report — and pay taxes on — unusually high incomes for the year. S 1814 would have altered that scenario by allowing farmers to declare their disaster payments on their 1993 returns — thereby allowing many of them to write the payments off against their disaster losses. The bill would have applied to future farm disasters as well.

Dispute Resolution Fees

Congress cleared a bill that allowed the Agricultural Marketing Service to charge a fee to parties filing complaints with a dispute-resolution service administered by the agency. The service was used by farmers, food brokers, wholesalers and retailers who were unable to resolve disputes about produce quality, grading and other contractual matters. The House passed the bill by voice vote June 16; the Senate cleared it June 28, and President Clinton signed it into law July 5 (HR 4581 — PL 103-276).

The bill gave the financially ailing marketing service temporary authority to charge $60 for informal complaints and $300 for formal complaints. The new fees could be charged only during fiscal years 1995 and 1996. A fee could be incorporated into the damage award if the complaint was upheld by the dispute-resolution mediator.

Under the Perishable Agricultural Commodities Act of 1930, the agency was supposed to be fully funded by licensing fees paid by participating businesses. But the program, which served as an alternative to time-consuming and costly court battles, was running into a budget shortfall that threatened its continuation.

The House had included a similar fee provision in its version of the fiscal 1995 agriculture appropriations bill (HR 4554), which passed June 17. But the Senate Appropriations Committee struck that provision before approving its version of HR 4554 on June 23. (*Appropriations, p. 477*)

Farm Credit System

Congress cleared a bill Oct. 5 that gave the quasi-federal Farm Credit System greater ability to finance foreign purchases of U.S. agricultural products. President Clinton signed the bill into law Oct. 19 (HR 4379 - PL 103-376).

The measure lifted restrictions that previously had limited financing by system banks to products (mostly bulk grains) grown by agricultural cooperatives. The bill allowed the banks to participate in financing arrangements with other domestic or foreign-owned businesses to promote the export of U.S agriculture commodities. It also allowed system banks to finance joint ventures and partnerships in which farm cooperatives participated.

Lifting the restrictions was expected to boost exports of hops, tallow, pork and cattle.

The House Agriculture Committee approved the bill by voice vote Sept. 28. The House passed it by voice vote Sept. 29, and the Senate cleared it Oct. 5, also by voice vote.

FmHA-Backed Loans

Congress cleared legislation (S 1930) that gave the Agriculture secretary authority to hire private lawyers to pursue government claims against individuals who were delinquent on Farmers Home Administration (FmHA) loans. The Senate passed the bill by voice vote March 24, and the House cleared it April 21. President Clinton signed the bill into law May 11 (PL 103-248).

The bill, sponsored by Senate Agriculture Committee Chairman Patrick J. Leahy, D-Vt., allowed the Agriculture secretary to employ private lawyers under contract, as well as Justice Department and Agriculture Department litigators, to pursue legal action against loan scofflaws.

Congressional action was spurred by a front-page exposé published in The Washington Post on Jan. 28 that described how a number of wealthy part-time farmers had gone unpunished for reneging on large FmHA loans. Most of these reported cases involved loans obtained in the early 1980s under a temporary disaster assistance program.

Leahy said in a Senate floor speech March 15 that the authority to hire private lawyers was needed because Justice Department lawyers lacked the time and resources to pursue the backlog of more than 4,000 pending foreclosures involving $4.2 billion in bad debts on FmHA loans. ∎

## Chapter 4

SCIENCE & TECHNOLOGY/ COMMUNICATIONS

Communications

Telecommunications Regulation 203
    Bills Compared 209
    Senate Bill Provisions. 213
Wiretapping 215
Satellite Home Viewer Act. 216
Telemarketing Fraud. 217
FCC Reauthorization. 218

Science & Techonology

NASA Reauthorization 218
NOAA Reauthorization 219
Other Science-Related Legislation 220
Competitiveness Programs 221
Energy Research Laboratories 223

Stumped by Bells' Objections, Senate Kills Overhaul

The yearlong effort to update telecommunications law succumbs to a variety of complaints

With revolutionary digital technologies changing the nature of the telecommunications industry, Congress tried in 1994 to rewrite the federal government's 60-year-old ground rules for competition in telephone and cable television services. The yearlong effort came to an abrupt end in the Senate, however, in the face of industry infighting and procedural roadblocks.

On Sept. 23, Senate Commerce Committee Chairman Ernest F. Hollings, D-S.C., pulled the plug on a committee-approved telecommunications bill, saying too little time remained in the session to overcome the bill's problems. In particular, he blamed some of the regional Bell telephone companies — multibillion-dollar corporate powerhouses that dominated the local phone markets — for trying to scuttle the bill.

The legislation would have allowed the Bells to enter lines of business that the courts and Congress had kept off-limits. It also would have imposed numerous regulations to prevent the Bells from using their local telephone monopolies to compete unfairly in long distance, cable television and other markets. The idea was to shift the local telephone and cable markets gradually from an era of regulated monopolies to an era of free and open competition.

The House overwhelmingly approved a pair of bills (HR 3626 and HR 3636) in June to spur telecommunications competition. HR 3626 proposed to allow the Bells into the long-distance market on two conditions: that the Federal Communications Commission (FCC) ruled that it would be in the public interest, and that the Justice Department ruled that it would not impede competition. Bells also would be permitted to manufacture telephone equipment after a one-year waiting period, provided that the Justice Department did not find that it would impede competition. The second bill, HR 3636, proposed to allow the Bells and other local telephone companies into the cable television business, while compelling those companies to open their own networks to competitors.

The easy passage of the House bill reflected the bipartisan support marshaled by the bills' sponsors, which included two influential Democratic committee chairmen. Their victory was misleading, however, because their strongest opponents — the long-distance companies — held their fire for the Senate

Commerce Committee. There they had allies in Hollings, ranking Republican John C. Danforth of Missouri, and Communications Subcommittee Chairman Daniel K. Inouye, D-Hawaii.

Unlike the House bill, the bill sponsored by Hollings, Danforth and Inouye (S 1822) proposed that the Bells be required to face "actual and demonstrable competition" in their local phone markets before they could provide long-distance services. This sequencing was critical to the long-distance companies but unacceptable to the Bells, which backed a competing bill (S 2111) by Sens. John B. Breaux, D-La., and Bob Packwood, R-Ore. Breaux and Packwood wanted to lift the restrictions on the Bells after a one-year waiting period, while simultaneously eliminating the legal barriers to competition in the local telephone exchanges. That was the quickest, easiest route to long-distance service of any of the bills.

After a month and a half of intense negotiations, the bill's sponsors reached a compromise with the Bells and the long-distance companies. The sponsors also made numerous changes to accommodate rural lawmakers and a variety of interest groups, helping them to win the committee's overwhelming approval Aug. 11.

The revisions, however, only seemed to bring more demands for change as the bill moved closer to the Senate floor. Three senators threatened to filibuster, saying the bill was either too regulatory or not regulatory enough. What really stopped Hollings, though, was the opposition of Minority Leader Bob Dole, R-Kan. When Dole asked Hollings to undo portions of the deal that had been struck between the Bells and the long-distance companies, Hollings threw in the towel.

Background

Since Alexander Graham Bell's first telephone patents expired in the 1890s, thousands of companies had vied for pieces of the telephone market. Still, the dominant players had always been the Bell companies and their erstwhile parent, AT&T.

By the time Congress took up the issue in 1934, the AT&T family controlled about two-thirds of the local phone busi-

BOXSCORE

Telecommunications Regulation — HR 3626, S 1822 (HR 3636). Sweeping legislation to set new ground rules for competition among telecommunications companies, including provisions to allow regional Bells into long distance and other markets.

Reports: H Rept 103-559, Parts 1 and 2; H Rept 103-560; S Rept 103-367.

KEY ACTION

June 28 — House passed HR 3626, 423-5; passed HR 3636, 423-4. The two bills were then combined as HR 3626.

Aug. 11 — Senate Commerce Committee approved S 1822, 18-2.

Sept. 23 — Hollings proclaimed S 1822 dead.

ness in the United States and all of the long-distance market. The Communications Act of 1934 gave the new FCC power to regulate long-distance services and prices without making any direct attempt to break up the burgeoning AT&T monopoly. Local phone service was left to state regulators, most of whom struck their own deals with the local phone companies: In exchange for the companies' promises to service every home at low cost, the states would outlaw competition.

The next major milestone in telecommunications regulation came almost 50 years later, after new communications switching and transmission technologies emerged. In 1974, the Justice Department, which had been critical of AT&T's efforts to discourage competition, filed an antitrust lawsuit against AT&T, Western Electric and Bell Laboratories. The lawsuit led to a 1982 consent decree breaking up the Bell family.

The decree confined AT&T to the long-distance and equipment markets while limiting the seven regional Bells to local phone service. U.S. District Judge Harold H. Greene, who oversaw the decree, was empowered to end the restrictions once he found "no substantial possibility" that competition could be impeded. Greene had lifted only one major restriction by the end of 1994 — the one barring the Bells from offering information services — and he did so only after an appeals court overturned his initial ruling against it.

Congress put one final restriction into place in 1984, when it enacted the Cable Communications Policy Act (PL 98-549). That law forbade local telephone companies to double as cable television programmers within their telephone service areas. *(1984 Almanac, p. 286)*

The Bells chafed under these restrictions from the beginning, and over the years the pressure grew from other quarters to bring down the barriers to competition. A major factor was the emergence of new digital technologies that promised a convergence of telephones, televisions and computers. By unleashing full-blown competition in telecommunications, some officials argued, Congress would give companies more incentive to invest in these new technologies and to build the "information superhighway" — a network of high-capacity cables and fiber-optic wires that would allow much more information to be passed through the telephone lines.

The technological changes also gave rise to a new set of political dynamics. No longer was the issue simply a battle among three entrenched industries — the Bell telephone giants, the newspaper industry and cable companies. Rather, all three industries were joining forces to create a new marketplace for the home delivery of all types of electronic information.

The House Responds

On Nov. 22, 1993, House Energy and Commerce Chairman John D. Dingell, D-Mich., and Judiciary Chairman Jack Brooks, D-Texas, unveiled a long awaited bill to allow the Bells into long distance and manufacturing, provided that the Justice Department and FCC approved. The same day, Reps. Edward J. Markey, D-Mass., who chaired the Energy and Commerce Telecommunications and Finance Subcommittee, and Jack Fields, R-Texas, the subcommittee's top Republican, introduced a companion bill to let the local phone companies into cable television and vice versa. The bill included certain safeguards to prevent either industry from exercising monopoly control in those areas.

● **Brooks-Dingell.** The Brooks-Dingell bill (HR 3626) placed a five-year waiting period on the Bells' entry into the interstate long-distance market. At that point, they could gain entry if they convinced the FCC that it would be in the public interest and the Justice Department that it would not impair competition.

The Bells could cut the waiting period to 18 months by leasing their long-distance links wholesale from AT&T or another long-distance company and reselling the service to their own customers. They also could enter the in-state long-distance market immediately, if state regulators approved. The Justice Department could sue to stop the Bells' entry into the resale or in-state markets, however, if it was concerned about monopolistic behavior by the Bells.

The Bells would be allowed immediately to design and manufacture telecommunications equipment, provided that they did so in the United States.

Finally, the bill included restrictions on the Bells' entry into information services, such as electronic publishing. The Bells would have to enter the market through a separate subsidiary or joint venture, although that provision would expire after four years.

● **Markey-Fields.** The Markey-Fields bill (HR 3636) proposed to pre-empt state regulations that barred competition for local telephone customers. The telephone companies would be required to provide their competitors — most likely the cable television companies and long-distance providers — equal access to and connection with their networks and customers.

The bill also proposed to rescind the portion of the 1984 cable deregulation law that barred telephone companies from providing cable television programming in their own service areas. However, telephone companies would have to set up separate subsidiaries and accounting systems to handle the cable business. Rural companies were exempt from the requirement, and the FCC could waive it for all companies after five years.

Telephone companies were barred from buying cable systems within their service areas, except in rural areas with fewer than 10,000 residents.

Finally, the Markey-Fields bill proposed to set up a board of federal and state regulators to examine how to preserve "universal service" — the policy calling for all households to have equal access to low-cost basic telephone service — as the marketplace shifted from regulation to competition. The board would define what "universal service" meant when voice, text and video became available through the same home appliance. The board also would decide how to subsidize such service by requiring all communications companies that took part in the network to pay into a universal service fund.

Unresolved Issues

The two House bills reflected a number of compromises among lawmakers of different philosophical bents, ranging from trust-busting Democrats who worried about the Bells' muscle to deregulatory Republicans who wanted to unleash the Bells as soon as possible. Still, a number of issues remained to be resolved before the bills reached the floor.

Cable operators, for example, held little hope that they could win provisions to slow the Bells' entry into their business. Instead, they wanted a requirement in the Markey-Fields bill that the FCC certify that a local phone company's network was open to competitors before allowing that company to offer cable. The cable and telephone industries also wanted Congress to grant broad FCC authority to waive a ban on phone companies' buying cable systems in their service areas. The original Markey-Fields bill limited such buyouts.

The Bells, meanwhile, wanted relief from a requirement in Markey-Fields that they make video delivery facilities available to competitors in every market in which they offered cable service, even where there was no demand for such facilities.

The Bells also pushed for nationwide "price caps" — ceilings on how much they could charge for local phone service —

rather than limits on their profits, as most states imposed. If prices were capped, the Bells argued, they would have no incentive to hide their profits and cross-subsidize their ventures in competitive markets, such as long distance. Consumer groups and state regulators opposed price caps, arguing that local phone rates should have gone down over the previous decade, just as long-distance rates had, instead of up.

Television and radio stations lobbied for permission to use parts of their radio band, or spectrum, for ancillary services such as stock quotes, messaging services and — critics feared — emerging digital wireless telephone service.

In the Brooks-Dingell bill, the Bells wanted authority to cross their local market boundaries when providing services that were "incidental" to conventional telephone service, such as cable television, voice mail and electronic publishing. Long-distance companies expressed concern, however, that the Bells might abuse the privilege in order to enter the long-distance market through the back door.

Bell advocates also argued that the Brooks-Dingell bill would stifle their entry into new business ventures. The bill required "clear and convincing evidence" that the Bells lacked the ability to abuse competitors or consumers before they could enter new businesses. The "preponderance of the evidence" standard set by the 1982 consent decree was a lower legal threshold.

Finally, the Brooks-Dingell bill provided extensive protection for the newspaper industry against market abuses by the Bells as they entered the electronic publishing business. But electronic information providers such as Prodigy and America Online wanted the protections to cover all information services, not just newspapers.

House Subcommittee Action

The House bills got started in Markey's Telecommunications and Finance Subcommittee on March 1. At Dingell's request, the subcommittee made no changes to the Brooks-Dingell bill, approving it by voice vote. It also gave voice vote approval to a substitute version of the Markey-Fields bill, one that incorporated a number of changes to accommodate industry concerns.

The following day, the Judiciary Subcommittee on Economic and Commercial Law approved the Brooks-Dingell bill by voice vote. Lawmakers honored Brooks' request to withhold any amendments on his bill until full committee action.

Amendments to Markey-Fields Bill

Key changes made to HR 3636 included:

● A new provision won by the cable industry to require telephone companies seeking to offer video programming to certify to the FCC that they allowed competitors equal access and connection to their video networks.

Lawmakers also helped the phone companies by dropping a requirement that telephone companies offering video service make 75 percent of their video capacity available to competitors. Telephone companies successfully argued that many markets lacked the demand for such a requirement.

● A more detailed definition of a rural telephone company, to mean any company in an area of fewer than 10,000 inhabitants that had fewer than 50,000 phone lines. Rural telephone companies generally were exempt from the bill's requirements that they open their networks to competitors.

● A specification that any new rules requiring phone networks to be open to competitors must be "technology neutral" and not favor existing networks of copper-based wiring over new fiber optics.

The change had been sought by Alex McMillan, R-N.C. He objected to a provision in the original Markey-Fields bill that would have required local telephone companies to use "existing facilities to the maximum extent feasible and economically practicable" when upgrading their networks. Corning Inc., a leading manufacturer of fiber-optic cable, employed 1,000 at its plant in Wilmington, N.C.

● Language won by the computer and electronics industries to require the FCC to report on ways to make television set-top boxes accessible to any video programmer or computer network. Access to cable set-top boxes had been controlled by local cable operators.

● A provision allowing telephone subscribers to opt out of any enhanced communications services that local phone companies might someday provide. Sought by Ron Wyden, D-Ore., the provision would enable customers who wanted only basic telephone services to avoid paying for upgrades to the network. Bell officials later argued that the language would amount to a freeze on the cost of basic telephone services at existing rates.

Unfinished Business

The real fireworks came on two amendments that were offered, then withdrawn pending the full committee markup.

Mike Synar, D-Okla., sparked the first fight with an amendment, backed by consumer groups, to require the Bells and the competing telephone companies that leased their networks to share all the "joint and common costs" incurred in building the networks. The idea was to shift the cost of expanding the networks to the industry, rather than allowing the Bells to pass the costs on to local ratepayers.

Faced with opposition by key subcommittee Democrats and silence from Markey, Synar withdrew his amendment until the full committee took up the bill — at which point Markey indicated he would be inclined to support the effort.

W. J. "Billy" Tauzin, D-La., then offered the most contentious amendment of the day: a proposal to allow broadcasters to use any of their extra radio spectrum to offer ancillary services such as stock quotes, messaging services and perhaps even emerging digital wireless telephone service.

Though broadcasters had not gained access to it by 1994, the FCC in 1992 had promised them 6 megahertz of new radio frequency, or spectrum — roughly equal to what was being used by television — to transmit when available the advanced digital television services that promised superior picture and sound quality. The broadcasters hoped that, with the development of new digital compression technologies that squeezed more data into smaller portions of the radio spectrum, they would not need the entire 6 megahertz for advanced digital television. Television station owners wanted freedom to use this extra spectrum for other services — in large part to help finance the move to digital television —

Tauzin proposed that they be allowed to do so as long as they paid fees to the FCC for using the spectrum for such ancillary services. He also proposed to tie those fees to market rates being paid by the private sector for other portions of the radio spectrum that were to be auctioned by the FCC in 1994.

Opponents argued that allowing broadcasters to use radio spectrum for money-making services would give them an unfair advantage over competitors who had to bid for similar rights. They also predicted that broadcasters would drop out of the bidding for the wireless spectrum, resulting in lower bids and less revenue for the Treasury in the spectrum auctions.

Tauzin withdrew his amendment, saving the battle for full committee.

Full Committee Action

The Energy and Commerce Committee took up both telecommunications bills March 16. After modifying them, the committee approved the Brooks-Dingell bill by voice vote (HR 3626 — H Rept 103-559, Part 1), and the Markey-Fields bill by a vote of 44-0 (HR 3636 — H Rept 103-560).

At the same time, in a nearby hearing room, the Judiciary Committee marked up the Brooks-Dingell bill, approving it by voice vote. (H Rept 103-559, Part 2).

In both cases, the bills won easy committee approval, but with changes that would necessitate more negotiations between the two chairmen. In the Energy and Commerce Committee, the votes broke in favor of the seven regional Bell companies, while Judiciary Committee members sided with the rival long-distance companies.

Energy and Commerce Committee

The Energy and Commerce Committee approved two key amendments that pleased the Bell companies and gave long-distance providers pause.

A substitute draft of the Brooks-Dingell bill, offered by Dingell and approved by voice vote, proposed to allow the Bells to use long-distance phone lines immediately to provide "incidental" services such as cable television, mobile telephone and voice messaging without violating the ban on their offering long-distance telephone service. Long-distance companies called the provision a potentially dangerous loophole that could allow the Bells to skirt rules governing their entry into the long-distance market.

Energy and Commerce also pleased the Bells by amending the Markey-Fields bill to require that states regulate local phone prices, rather than phone company profits. The amendment, which was approved by voice vote, was offered by Tauzin.

The Bells said they favored controls on prices rather than limits on profit levels because they would improve cash flow and free money to use for investments in phone networks. Consumer groups opposed price caps because, they said, they would lock in phone rates that were already too high. Markey expressed the concerns of consumer groups that "no evidence exists" showing that price caps led to more rapid network improvements. Bradley Stillman, legislative counsel for the Consumer Federation of America, said that between 1984 and 1994, total cash flow for the Bells increased by $45 billion as states began to adopt price cap regimes, while investment in networks rose only $9 billion.

Tauzin settled for the price-cap language after failing behind the scenes to win support for another proposal that effectively would have allowed the Bells to avoid most regulation if they operated in a competitive marketplace.

The Bells also were able to take the sting out of an amendment by Synar to the Markey-Fields bill that would have required the Bells to cut rates to reflect any savings achieved as a result of the declining cost of providing local phone service, rather than using the savings to invest in network upgrades.

Lacking the votes on the largely pro-Bell committee, Synar instead won voice vote approval of an amendment that effectively restated existing court-ordered rules governing the Bells. Those rules required that ratepayer revenues be used only to maintain and upgrade basic phone service, not to finance future competitive ventures. Under the amendment, the costs of any network upgrades that benefited both ratepayers and the Bells' competitive ventures would be shared between shareholders and consumers.

The panel considered a number of other amendments, including the following (the first two were to the Markey-Fields bill; the rest were to the Brooks-Dingell measure):

● Tauzin to allow broadcasters to use their designated portions of the spectrum to offer ancillary services, provided that the services did not interfere with the broadcasting of advanced digital television. As with the proposal Tauzin floated in subcommittee, the amendment required the FCC to charge broadcasters for the spectrum used for such ancillary services, based on the rates paid by the private sector for other portions of the radio spectrum. It was adopted by voice vote.

● Wyden to allow basic phone rates to increase only if a Bell company could show regulators that the increase would "prevent competitive disadvantages" and advance the public interest. A revision of the amendment Wyden had offered in subcommittee, it was approved by voice vote.

● Bill Richardson, D-N.M., to require Bell companies offering electronic publishing to comply with equal employment opportunity laws that applied to broadcasters and cable operators. The amendment was adopted by voice vote.

● Jim Slattery, D-Kan., to prevent the Bell companies from charging higher network access rates to small newspaper publishers for their electronic news services than they charged to large publishers. The amendment was adopted by voice vote.

● John Bryant, D-Texas, and Thomas J. Bliley Jr., R-Va., to require the Bells to pass the same tests before offering in-state long distance as interstate long distance. The amendment was rejected. Instead, the committee adopted by a vote of 34-10 a substitute amendment by Michael G. Oxley, R-Ohio, to require the Bells to charge their own long-distance affiliates the same access fees they charged long-distance competitors.

● Oxley to remove a provision in the Brooks-Dingell bill demanding that the Bell companies primarily use U.S.-made parts in the manufacture of communications equipment. The amendment was rejected, 18-25.

Judiciary Committee

Around the corner, in the Judiciary Committee, the tables turned in favor of the long-distance industry as the panel marked up the Brooks-Dingell bill.

Long-distance providers wanted the Bells to have to get approval from the federal government before offering any type of long-distance service — in-state, interstate or resale of services bought wholesale. They won that in the Judiciary Committee's version of the bill, although to a lesser extent for some long-distance services than for others.

The committee bill required that to gain entry into the interstate long-distance service, the Bells had to convince the FCC and the Justice Department that there was "no substantial possibility" that their entry would harm competition — a phrase borrowed from the 1982 consent decree that broke up AT&T.

That market entry test would not apply to Bell requests to enter the in-state or resale long-distance businesses. Those markets were considered crucial by the 398 long-distance providers that, apart from giants AT&T, MCI Communications Corp. and Sprint, accounted for $8.6 billion of the industry's $60 billion in 1993 revenues.

To help address the concern of the small long-distance providers, the Judiciary Committee approved by voice vote a Brooks amendment to give the Justice Department a chance to challenge states that let a Bell company offer in-state long-distance services. The amendment gave the department 120 days after the state regulators' decision to file suit against a Bell's entry. The same 120-day Justice Department review

also would apply to requests by the Bells to resell long-distance services.

In exchange, the amendment dropped the proposed five-year waiting period before the Bells could apply to enter the long-distance market, as well as the 18-month waiting period before the Bells could resell long-distance services.

The committee rejected an amendment by Robert W. Goodlatte, R-Va., to weaken the domestic-content requirements that the bill imposed on Bell manufacturing operations. The vote on the amendment was 16-19.

House Floor Action

The two bills reached the House floor June 28. In an unusual move for such major legislation, the sponsors brought up the bills under suspension of the rules — a maneuver that barred amendments but required a two-thirds vote for passage.

The House passed Brooks-Dingell (HR 3626) by 423-5; the vote on Markey-Fields (HR 3636) was 423-4. Afterward, the provisions of the Markey-Fields bill were inserted into the Brooks-Dingell measure, and the expanded version of HR 3626 was sent to the Senate. *(Votes 292, 293, p. 86-H)*

The overwhelming margins testified to Brooks' and Dingell's power, as well as the four sponsors' thoroughness in addressing members' concerns.

Perhaps equally important, however, was a decision by the long-distance companies not to put up a fight on the House floor. Bliley, whose district was home to a large AT&T plant, told the House that the long-distance companies were not satisfied with the bill's provisions regarding the Bells' entry into the long-distance market. In particular, Bliley said, they wanted to require that the Bells face "effective competition" in their own markets before entering long distance.

Rather than pulling out all the stops in the House, the long-distance companies concentrated on the Senate, where leaders of the Commerce Committee had proposed to bar the Bells from the long-distance market until after they faced competition in the local exchange.

Floor Bill Was a Compromise

Before bringing the bills to the floor, Brooks and Dingell had worked out their key differences. They started their talks in May, after about a six-week delay while the Judiciary Committee was tied up on a major anti-crime bill. On June 23 they announced that they had a deal.

● **Interstate long-distance service.** One key disagreement had been whether the Justice Department could stop the Bells from offering long-distance services within a state. Brooks' committee said yes; Dingell's said no. Dingell had argued that the Justice Department should have a say only over interstate services. Brooks, however, had maintained that the antitrust implications of the Bells' moving into intrastate long distance warranted the attention of Justice.

The compromise gave state regulators the first crack at a Bell company's application to offer long-distance service within that state. If the state approved, the Justice Department would have 90 days to file a lawsuit to block the application.

● **'Incidental' services.** The two bills also differed on whether the Bells could freely offer "incidental" services across the boundaries of their local exchanges. Dingell's committee wanted to give the Bells wide latitude, while Brooks' panel wanted more restrictions.

The new version freed the Bells to offer audio and video programming, interactive services, cable television, mobile telephone services and voice mail across the boundaries of

their local exchanges. Under existing law, the Bells could not carry any communications across those boundaries without a federal court waiver.

● **Domestic content.** Both committees had run into trouble with the Clinton administration and numerous Republicans over the issue of domestic content. Backed by labor unions, Brooks and Dingell proposed to require future Bell manufacturing affiliates to operate in the United States and buy much of their components from U.S. companies.

To satisfy the administration's concern, the compromise bill included a paragraph voiding that requirement if it was "determined to be inconsistent with any multilateral or bilateral agreement to which the United States is a party."

● **Other compromises.** A few more last-minute compromises were worked out before Brooks and Dingell took their bill to the floor. They accepted a provision advocated by Rep. Joe Barton, R-Texas, to bar local telephone companies with message services — for example, voice mail or answering services — from charging competing telemessaging companies higher rates for access to their networks than they charged themselves. They also accepted a provision advocated by Rep. John Conyers Jr., D-Mich., calling for the Bells to use separate subsidiaries when providing enhanced calling services, such as call forwarding. The provision required the FCC within 60 days to reconsider its decision, made in December 1993, not to require separate subsidiaries.

Senate Negotiations

While the House was working on its bills, the Senate Commerce Committee was conducting a long series of hearings on a competing measure (S 1822). Introduced Feb. 3 by 13 senators, it was primarily the work of committee Chairman Hollings, top Republican Danforth and Communications Subcommittee Chairman Inouye.

Before bringing the bill to his committee for formal approval, Hollings first held nine hearings, collected more than 1,300 pages of testimony and engaged in extensive negotiations to produce a modified bill that could win committee backing. The negotiations began in earnest once the House finished work on its bills.

The Hollings Bill

The Hollings bill proposed to allow key sectors of the industry — cable operators and telephone companies — to compete in each other's businesses, while also setting the stage for entry by the seven regional Bell telephone companies into the long-distance, equipment manufacturing and information services businesses.

But the conditions that would have to exist before the Bells could enter important long-distance markets were far tougher than in the House bills. S 1822 also differed in other significant ways from the House legislation. The major provisions included:

● **Universal service.** The bill opened by calling for the FCC and the states to ensure that all citizens had access to "high-quality telephone service" — a major tenet of the 1934 Communications Act.

It required all communications carriers, including phone companies and cable operators, to contribute to a fund that would guarantee low-cost communications services to all. A similar fund already existed to ensure that the long-distance industry helped subsidize rural telephone service. The Markey-Fields bill (HR 3636) left such decisions regarding universal service to a future joint federal-state board.

Under the Hollings bill, the legal and regulatory barriers

preventing telephone and cable companies from entering each other's businesses were to be removed only after mechanisms to protect universal service were established.

● **Long-distance service.** Hollings proposed to let the Bells apply immediately for entry into the long-distance market. To provide long distance inside its original market area, however, a Bell would not simply have to open its facilities to competitors; it would also have to face "actual and demonstrable" competition locally. This standard was harder for a Bell to meet than the one proposed by Brooks and Dingell, which required only the conditions for competition — not actual competition — before a Bell could enter long distance.

To provide long distance outside its market area, a Bell would have to prove only that there was "no substantial possibility" that it could use its market power to impede competition — a similar test to the one in the Brooks-Dingell bill.

The Hollings measure gave the FCC most of the authority over the Bells' attempts to enter new markets, with the Justice Department playing a more advisory role. The Brooks-Dingell bill, by contrast, gave the Justice Department and the FCC virtually equal say.

● **Cable/telephone competition.** As with the Markey-Fields bill, telephone companies would be allowed to provide cable service in their own market areas, but they could not buy out existing cable companies. The Markey-Fields bill offered limited exceptions to the buyout provision; the Hollings bill did not, in keeping with the administration's position.

Also unlike the Markey-Fields bill, Hollings proposed to regulate cable television operators as "common carriers," meaning they would be forced to open their cable network lines and facilities to competitors in order to offer telephone service. The administration backed this approach.

● **Broadcaster issues.** Broadcasters were offered some hope of regulatory relief under the Hollings bill, as in the Markey-Fields bill. The FCC would be directed to study local and national broadcast ownership rules, with the power to eliminate them if media diversity was assured.

Breaux-Packwood

While the long-distance companies supported the bill, the Bells lined up behind an alternative introduced May 12 by Breaux and Packwood.

The Breaux-Packwood bill (S 2111) proposed to let the Bell companies offer all manner of long-distance services one year after enactment — no strings attached. At the same time, all state and local barriers would be lifted on companies entering the market for local phone service, in-state toll calls or virtually any other telecommunications services.

Breaux and Packwood proposed to immediately lift the ban on local telephone companies' offering cable television programming in their regions. State and local governments could continue to limit competition in cable television and information services — for example, directory assistance or telephone news lines. As long as a state or local regulation barred a telephone company from offering cable, however, the local cable companies could not offer telephone service.

Only a few pages long, the Breaux-Packwood bill was silent on most of the issues raised by the Hollings bill, including universal service. Its one regulatory requirement was that the FCC issue rules within 18 months to "ensure that all providers of competitive telecommunications services are subject to equivalent regulation."

Bells vs. Long-Distance Companies

As soon as the House passed its telecommunications bills, the Bells and the long-distance companies squared off in the Senate over the terms for the Bells' entry into the long-distance market. The bottom line was simple: The Bells did not want to put up for grabs any of their $71.3 billion in local telephone revenues until they were allowed to offer other services. But the long-distance companies did not want the Bells to compete for long-distance customers until they gave up their local telephone service monopolies.

The battle focused on the "actual and demonstrable competition" test in the Hollings bill, which required that at least one non-Bell company with its own transmission network was providing service to a "significant number" of customers in a Bell's local market before that Bell could offer long distance. Industry analysts expected that competition to come from the companies that already had wires into people's homes and businesses (the cable television industry and the electric utilities) or that did not need wires (the cellular phone companies and other wireless communications carriers).

The Bells argued that it would take more than a decade for competition in the local exchange to reach the extent required in the Hollings bill. In some rural areas, they said, such competition might never emerge.

At the same time, they argued, two other portions of their telephone business already were facing competition: short-distance toll calls and access to long-distance carriers. In the major urban centers, entrepreneurs were putting in networks of high-capacity fiber-optic cables to give businesses an alternative connection to AT&T, MCI and Sprint. Across the country, hundreds of small companies had emerged to compete for the calls carried across the boundaries of the local exchanges.

The major long-distance companies, meanwhile, were positioning themselves to offer some customers a full range of telephone services: local, cellular and long-distance. This kind of one-stop shopping was seen as the key to future telephone competition, and the Bells did not want to be left at the starting gate.

In the long-distance companies' view, however, the key to fair competition was to end the local telephone monopolies before allowing the Bells to enter long distance. Once alternative local phone companies became established, the long-distance companies would not have to use the Bells to reach their customers.

Also, the competition would drive down the price the Bells charged for connecting callers to long-distance services, said Albert McGann, the executive director of the long-distance companies' lobbying coalition. These access charges made up about 40 percent of the cost of a long-distance call. "Our cost would go down, and we believe we could compete with anyone," McGann said.

The smaller long-distance carriers feared that, if the Bells could freely enter the market, they would drive them out of business. The Bells had sophisticated marketing, a direct link to each home and business in their region and a list of each long-distance company's customers, giving them a leg up on their potential competitors.

They also had the largest pot of revenue in the telecommunications industry. Despite the House bill's proposed safeguards against the Bells' subsidizing their long-distance ventures with revenues from their local services, long-distance companies warned that the Bells would find a way to do just that.

Decker Anstrom, president of a cable television trade association, said the long-distance companies were not alone in worrying about the Bells' cross-subsidizing new ventures. "Competition really is the best safeguard here," he said. "The test may be different for what you think competition should

The Bills' Key Differences

The following is a comparison of key provisions in each of three bills aimed at revamping the telecommunications industry. The first is the House-passed version of HR 3626 — sponsored by Judiciary Chairman Jack Brooks, D-Texas, and Energy and Commerce Chairman John D. Dingell, D-Mich. It included the text of a second bill (HR 3636) by Edward J. Markey, D-Mass., chairman of the Energy and Commerce Telecommunications and Finance Subcommittee, and ranking Republican Jack Fields of Texas. HR 3626 was intended to spur competition in the telecommunications industry by eventually allowing the regional Bell telephone companies to offer

long-distance, cable television and electronic publishing services and to make telecommunications equipment.

The second is a companion Senate bill (S 1822) — sponsored by Ernest F. Hollings, D-S.C., and John C. Danforth, R-Mo. It aimed to keep some regulatory reins on the Bells' entry into the long-distance business.

The third (S 2111) — written by John B. Breaux, D-La., and Bob Packwood, R-Ore. — proposed to allow the Bells to offer long distance and cable television after a one-year waiting period, free of additional regulation. The key differences among the bills were:

Issue	House (HR 3626)	Hollings (S 1822)	Breaux-Packwood (S 2111)
Video Services	Local Bell phone companies no longer would be barred from owning and offering cable television services in their own markets. In exchange, telephone companies would be required to establish a "video platform" service giving all video programmers access to television channel capacity at a reasonable cost through phone networks.	Telephone companies would be allowed to provide video programming. But unlike the House measure, the bill would not require them to open their telephone network facilities to all competitors through a "video platform" service.	The bill would allow telephone companies to provide video services and would permit cable television companies to offer local telephone service, as long as both had unrestricted access to each other's markets.
Long Distance	A Bell company would be permitted to offer long-distance service only if the Justice Department found "no substantial possibility" that the company could impede long-distance competition by using its monopoly power over local calls. The Federal Communications Commission (FCC) also would have to find that the Bell company's proposal was "consistent with the public interest, convenience and necessity." State regulators would be allowed the first crack at a Bell company's application to offer long-distance service within that state or to offer interstate long distance over another company's network. If the state approved, the Justice Department would have 90 days to file a lawsuit to block the application.	Before a Bell company could offer long-distance services within its service area, the FCC would have to ascertain through hearings and consultation with the Justice Department that there was "actual and demonstrable competition" to the Bell company's local telephone exchange services. A Bell company could provide long-distance service outside its market area if the FCC, in consultation with the Justice Department, certified that there was no substantial possibility that the Bell company could use its market power to impede competition.	The bill would drop all restrictions to the Bell companies' offering long-distance service one year after enactment. At the same time, it would remove all restrictions to companies entering the local telephone market. There was no provision requiring the Bells to face local competition before offering long-distance service in or outside their markets.
Universal Service	Under the bill, universal service would not be a prerequisite for allowing the Bell telephone companies to enter new lines of business. The bill also would set up a joint federal-state board to recommend guidelines and funding mechanisms designed to guarantee universal service.	A priority under the Hollings bill, universal service would be defined by the states according to guidelines set by the FCC. States then would have the primary responsibility for ensuring that customers continued to receive low-cost, basic telephone service before approving a Bell company's entry into the long-distance arena. All telecommunications providers also would be required to contribute — in cash, service obligations or other payments — to a fund designed to maintain universal service.	The bill made no mention of universal service goals.

be . . . but the idea that competition is the best safeguard is unassailable."

Searching for a Compromise

In mid-July, Republican Sen. Trent Lott of Mississippi met with Breaux and Hollings in an effort to broker a compromise on the long-distance issue. The three sketched the rough outlines of a deal: The actual competition test would be dropped, but provisions would be added requiring the Bell companies to open their local networks to competition before entering the long-distance market. In addition, the Justice Department would have to determine that a Bell could not use its monopoly over the local network to gain an unfair advantage in the long-distance market.

The result would be quicker entry by the Bells into long distance than the original Hollings bill provided, moving his bill closer to the House position. Translating the deal into legislation proved problematic, however, as aides to Hollings, Lott, Breaux, Danforth and Inouye batted proposals back and forth.

The main sticking point was the regulatory demands, or "preconditions," that the Bells would be required to satisfy before even asking for permission to offer long distance. AT&T and other long-distance companies urged that the Bells face a number of tests that would, in effect, bar any move into their turf before the Bells faced competition in the local exchange. The Bells lobbied against any such "backdoor" tactics.

The Bells did not object to proposals that they make their facilities available to competitors at reasonable cost and that they interconnect their competitors' customers with their own. But they took issue with proposals that they provide:

● **Dialing parity.** The Bells' would-be competitors did not want their customers to have to dial more numbers to make a local call than did the Bells' customers. Otherwise, they argued, few of the Bells' customers would be willing to switch.

A simple approach to dialing parity was the one used for cellular phones: assigning a block of numbers to each competitor. One potential problem was that competitors might quickly exhaust the supply of seven-digit numbers. The solution, advocates of dialing parity said, was to require the Bells and their competitors alike to use eight digits or more.

● **Number portability.** The issue here was whether people could keep their phone numbers if they switched to one of the Bells' competitors. If not, a business that had bought a particular number — 555-TAXI, for example — or a homeowner who had kept the same number for 20 years might be reluctant to leave the Bell.

To achieve number portability, the local network would have to undergo some major modifications. Phone numbers were grouped in switching offices geographically by their exchanges — the first three numbers. To allow a competitor to share the Bells' exchanges, the Bells would have to reprogram their switches to bounce selected calls to new switches.

● **Balloting and presubscription.** Under this proposal, local phone companies would be required to notify each customer about the alternative local phone companies in the area and give them the option of signing up with one of them. The 1982 consent decree required the local phone companies to go through a similar process for long-distance carriers, providing an enormous boost to AT&T's emerging competitors.

The Bells said they might accept some of these responsibilities in the long run, but they objected to requiring dialing parity and balloting before they were allowed into long distance and other new businesses. They also proposed to pro-

vide number portability only when it was "economically reasonable."

In early August, the Bells' lobbying group and the long-distance companies' coalition agreed to an amendment that dropped the "actual and demonstrable competition" requirement, replacing it with several preconditions on the Bell's entry into long distance. These included providing dialing parity for local calls and number portability as soon as technically and economically feasible. If state regulators so chose, the local phone companies would also be required to provide dialing parity for the toll calls they handled. Balloting and presubscription would be mandated, but only after competitors had entered the local markets.

State and local barriers to competition would be preempted after one year, not two as in the original bill.

Rural Telephone Companies

The dispute between the Bells and the long-distance companies was only one of several that Hollings tried to resolve before bringing his bill before the Commerce Committee. A second issue was how to treat rural telephone companies.

Some rural-state senators saw competition as a potentially damaging force in sparsely populated areas. By the week of July 18, six had assembled in a group that dubbed itself the Farm Team: Republicans Ted Stevens of Alaska and Larry Pressler of South Dakota, and Democrats Byron L. Dorgan of North Dakota, Jim Exon of Nebraska, John D. Rockefeller IV of West Virginia and Bob Kerrey of Nebraska.

The Farm Team members had two common concerns. They worried that predatory competition could undermine the health of small, rural phone exchanges by skimming off the most profitable customers. At the same time, they feared that the small telephone companies could not afford the investment needed to bring the information superhighway to rural America. At stake, said Stevens, was "whether or not substantial portions of America are going to be left behind as we go into the 21st century."

The team floated a series of amendments aimed at addressing these two issues, including proposals to:

● Require companies that wanted to compete with the local telephone monopoly in a rural area to obtain state approval. State regulators could require would-be competitors in rural areas to offer service to all potential customers, not just a handful of lucrative business customers.

● Allow telephone and cable companies in small towns to merge or engage in joint ventures. Together, the Farm Team members argued, cable and telephone companies would be more likely to make the investments required to bring high-capacity phone and video networks to sparsely populated areas.

● Require larger telephone companies to share their facilities with small, neighboring companies for a reasonable fee. The small companies' trade association argued that such a requirement would help bring advanced telecommunications services to rural America.

● Limit government telephone subsidies to the so-called carrier of last resort, the local phone company obliged to offer service to any customer who wanted it. The subsidies would cover the difference between the rate charged and the cost of providing home phone service in sparsely populated areas. Without this provision, the rural telephone companies argued, the subsidies would encourage their competitors to pick off the lowest-cost, highest-volume customers in rural areas.

One group of potential competitors, the cable television industry, opposed much of the Farm Team's package. "In a lot

of ways, it makes it very difficult for anybody to get in and compete," said Steve Effros, president of one of the cable industry's trade associations.

The protection for small-town telephone companies seemed particularly inappropriate, Effros said, in light of those companies' large profits. He cited a study by his organization, the Cable Telecommunications Association, showing that smaller companies had significantly higher estimated profits and income per telephone line than did the Bells or the large independents.

The cable industry sided with the Farm Team on at least one point, however: It wanted to allow cable and telephone companies in the same market to engage in joint ventures and mergers.

Hollings proved to be sympathetic to the Farm Team's view, and he incorporated at least some version of all the group's amendments into the bill. The revised bill required companies that wanted to compete with the local telephone monopoly in rural areas to obtain state approval. The states could force those competitors to offer service to all potential customers.

The revised bill exempted rural telephone companies and cable companies from the ban on mergers and joint ventures. However, rural telephone companies that won state protection from competition in phone service would be barred from the cable business, either directly or by merger. Large local telephone companies would be required to share their equipment and services with their smaller rural neighbors. And subsidies for universal service would be limited to carriers of last resort, although more than one telephone company in a region could receive that designation.

Domestic Content

As introduced, the Hollings bill allowed for the Bell companies to begin manufacturing telecommunications equipment as soon as the FCC enacted the necessary regulations. But they would have to perform their manufacturing in the United States, and the aggregate cost of foreign-made parts could not exceed 40 percent of the annual sales revenue from equipment.

This domestic content provision had its origins in Hollings' 1990 proposal to let the Bell companies into manufacturing. When similar Hollings legislation reached the Senate floor in 1991, Republican Sen. Phil Gramm of Texas attempted to strike the domestic content requirement. Hollings prevailed that time by a vote of 64-32. *(1991 Almanac, p. 165)*

The provision had the strong support of the Communications Workers of America, which had opposed the Bells' entry into manufacturing until Hollings added the domestic-content requirement. John T. Watson, a lobbyist for the union, said the requirement was necessary to avoid importing "more and more equipment in from such great democratic bastions as Communist China, Singapore, Thailand, Malaysia . . . [and] Mexico."

On the other side stood a number of Republicans and members of the Clinton administration, who said the provision violated the North American Free Trade Agreement (NAFTA) and other major trading pacts. Said Sen. John McCain, R-Ariz., "It's bizarre that some provision such as this, which is clearly protectionist in nature, should be part of a bill which purports to be deregulatory."

Besides, McCain said, the provision was completely unenforceable. What would federal regulators do, he asked, take apart every cellular phone to make sure the parts had not been made in Mexico? McCain's state of Arizona was home to

numerous companies that manufactured goods in Mexico under a special trading arrangement.

The House bill contained a similar domestic-content requirement, with an added paragraph that nullified the requirement if it was found to violate the United States' trade commitments.

No fan of the House approach, McCain said he was ready to try a filibuster if the domestic-content requirement was not excised from the Senate bill. His prospects, though, depended on his ability to round up support from 40 colleagues, something that opponents of the domestic-content provision had not been able to do in 1991.

Enter: Dole

Although he was not a member of the Commerce Committee, Senate Minority Leader Dole threw a long shadow over the committee's deliberations as Hollings tried to round up votes for S 1822.

In a statement inserted into the Congressional Record on July 18, Dole aligned himself philosophically with Breaux and Packwood. The government must take a flexible, hands-off approach to the communications industry to make way for new technologies, Dole said, although it could not let rural areas be left behind.

Two days later, Dole floated a 30-page draft bill that proposed to unleash the Bells after a two-year waiting period. The Dole draft also proposed to end federal regulation of the cable television industry and any telephone market found to be competitive.

Several of the provisions came straight from the Bells' wish list. For example, Dole wanted to allow the Bells into cable immediately. And rather than having to make a set of federally mandated changes in their networks, the Bells could negotiate with each potential competitor the changes needed to allow competition.

Dole proposed to convene a joint board of federal and state officials to determine whether any existing telecommunications regulations, other than antitrust regulations, were no longer necessary.

The draft offered major prizes to the cable and broadcast industries as well. The 1992 law that reimposed federal control over cable subscriber fees would be repealed, along with the rest of the FCC's authority to regulate cable TV. Broadcasters would be allowed to use portions of their spectrum for new services, and a joint federal-state board would review the regulation forbidding companies from owning more than one broadcast station in a single market.

To assure universal service, Dole's proposal required every company entering the local phone market to contribute to a new universal service fund. The fund's subsidies would be available only to carriers of last resort — a provision sought by the local phone companies' trade associations. The subsidies would not be available in competitive local phone markets.

As in the Brooks-Dingell bill, Dole's draft called for a joint federal-state board to hash out the details of the universal service fund and its subsidy. States would be barred from providing their own subsidies for universal service. And rural or sparsely populated areas could not be forced to pay more for long-distance calls than urban areas were charged.

The initial reaction to Dole's proposal was muted, as industry officials and lawmakers puzzled over the senator's goal. Some suggested that Dole was trying to push Hollings to unleash the Bells more quickly, as in the Breaux-Packwood bill. Others wondered whether Dole was trying to scuttle the bill and deny a major legislative victory to the Clinton administration.

Dole had a longstanding interest in telecommunications, having proposed as early as 1986 to lift some of the restrictions on the Bells. His last major foray into telecommunications policy had been in 1992, when he led unsuccessful efforts in the Senate to sustain President George Bush's veto of the cable reregulation bill. *(1992 Almanac, p. 171)*

Senate Committee Action

After months of negotiations, on Aug. 11 Hollings had a revised bill ready for a formal Commerce Committee markup. The work had paid off: The panel approved the bill (S 1822 — S Rept 103-367) by a vote of 18-2, with only McCain and Packwood dissenting.

The compromises that Hollings had made on actual competition and the rural issues helped solidify the support of at least 10 committee members. But his efforts to bring senators on board had not stopped there. By the time it went to markup, the bill had ballooned from 104 to 191 pages as provisions were added to address concerns raised by virtually every telecommunications industry.

Exemptions were added to protect the wireless telephone industry and the cable companies' telephone services from additional state or local regulation. Similar protections were added for direct broadcast satellites — a new wireless technology that competed with cable television.

The pay phone industry was granted some of the protections it sought against unfair competition by the Bells. Universal service issues were put more squarely in the lap of the FCC, rather than being left to state regulators.

Emerging companies that competed for small segments of the Bells' business — for example, connecting businesses' telephones to long-distance lines — were exempted from having to help pay for universal service. The manufacturers of advanced, digital television equipment won some assurance that advanced television transmissions would not be squeezed out of the broadcast spectrum.

Advocates for the disabled won expanded requirements that phone and video services and equipment be made accessible to them.

Public broadcasters and arts organizations won a provision guaranteeing them 5 percent of the capacity of future telecommunications networks at preferential rates. Backed by Inouye, the public broadcasters and other public interest groups had sought a 20 percent set-aside — at no cost — for educational, civic and cultural programming. They were strenuously opposed by the telephone and cable companies, which argued that the set-aside amounted to a confiscation of property.

Barring 'Indecent' Communications

Shortly before the markup, committee member Exon persuaded the bill's sponsors to include language on indecent communications in the revised version of the bill. Cosponsored by committee member Slade Gorton, R-Wash., Exon's amendment expanded on a 26-year prohibition against unwanted interstate telephone calls that were harassing, "obscene, lewd, lascivious, filthy or indecent" by applying it to faxes, electronic mail or any other form of telecommunication that crossed state lines.

It also extended to all manner of telecommunications the "dial-a-porn" restrictions pushed through Congress in 1988 by Sen. Jesse Helms, R-N.C. Commercial services would be forbidden to provide obscene material; they would be allowed to provide indecent material only to adults who requested it. The services would be required to block the material so that it would not be available to minors, although the amendment did not specify how.

To add teeth to these requirements, the amendment doubled the maximum fines to $100,000 and quadrupled the maximum prison term to two years.

Another part of the Exon amendment required cable television companies to scramble or block both the audio and video of programs not suitable for children so that non-subscribers could not receive any portion of them. "Unsuspecting families should not be assaulted with audio of indecent programming or partially scrambled video," Exon told the Senate on July 26.

In addition, Exon sought to close a loophole in a 1992 law that allowed pay-per-call telephone services, such as telephone sex lines, to be reached through toll-free numbers. This loophole allowed callers to maneuver around the automatic blocking mechanisms that parents, churches, colleges and other phone subscribers employed against pay-per-call services.

The amendment also included a Gorton proposal to let cable companies scrub programs from their public access channels that contained obscenity, indecency or nudity. The proposal was inspired, Gorton said, by a nude talk show on a public-access channel in Seattle. Ironically, the program was intended by its creator as a protest against censorship.

Amendments Offered During Markup

At the markup, the committee adopted an amendment by Charles S. Robb, D-Va., to allow Bell companies to enter the cable television market as soon as they won court approval to do so, rather than waiting for the FCC to adopt regulations. Two of the Bells already had won rulings striking down as unconstitutional the 1984 ban on telephone-cable cross-ownership, and the other five had similar cases pending.

The committee also approved an amendment by Stevens requiring any Bell-affiliated company that entered the local telephone business in Alaska to come under the same regulatory burden as the existing local telephone companies.

The committee rejected, 8-12, an amendment by Danforth to remove the proposed requirement that Bell manufacturing operations be located in the United States. Although bitterly opposed by some Republicans, the provision had bipartisan support and the determined advocacy of Inouye and Hollings. Said Inouye, "I think it's about time we stood up and did a little protection on our side. I think it's about time that we played according to [protectionist foreign] rules, because they don't play according to our rules."

Also rejected was an amendment by Burns to lift all economic regulation of local telephone companies that agreed to rewire their networks with high-capacity cables, the backbone of the so-called information superhighway. An informal show of hands revealed little support on the committee for the proposal, which Burns said would spur development of advanced networks.

Many of the changes made to the bill fell short of what the interest groups had sought, and a number of those groups said they would keep lobbying as the bill moved forward. Still, several senators said the bill had gained a balance that had been missing from the original proposal. "I think we have successfully produced a product that nobody likes, and that's probably pretty good," Breaux said. "The winners will be decided in the marketplace, not in the Congress."

Accommodations Bring Complaints

The cumulative effect of the changes, particularly the ones involving the Bells, was to make the committee-passed bill

Senate Bill Provisions

The following are the major provisions of the bipartisan telecommunications bill approved Aug. 11 by the Senate Commerce Committee (S 1822 — S Rept 103-367):

● **Universal service.** The Federal Communications Commission (FCC), advised by a joint federal-state board, would set the rules for and the scope of universal service. At a minimum, carriers of last resort — the companies that provided universal service — would be required to provide the same services that a substantial majority of residential customers received.

More than one company could agree to serve as a region's carrier of last resort. If no company volunteered, the FCC could compel a company to take on that responsibility.

All carriers of last resort in a particular region would be eligible for subsidies. Long-distance companies providing universal service would have to charge rural customers the same rates they charged urban customers, but they also could be eligible for subsidies.

● **Local competition.** Local phone companies would have to meet a detailed list of obligations to make their networks receptive to competitors, such as providing number portability and access to the data bases that helped route calls. However, they could charge competitors more for the use of their networks than they charged their own customers. For example, if a cable operator decided to offer phone service in competition with the local phone company, the cable company could be required to pay more for access to the phone company's network than a residential customer trying to place a call.

Competitors also would be forbidden to buy one type of service from the local phone company and resell it to a different category of customers. Unless a state barred it, local phone companies also could force some competitors to dial access codes in order to reach customers on the local phone company's network.

● **Long distance.** The Bells could offer long distance as soon as the Justice Department determined that they no longer could abuse their monopoly power and the FCC determined that the Bells complied with the competition-spurring conditions set in the bill. The Bells also would be required to comply with a series of specific requirements designed to guard against their subsidizing their long-distance operations with revenues from local customers.

● **Rural areas.** Companies wishing to enter a rural area's local phone market would be required to obtain state approval first. States could insist that new entrants agree to provide universal service, rather than just offer service in the low-cost, high-profit areas. The FCC could exempt rural phone companies from opening their networks to competitors under certain conditions.

Rural telephone and cable companies also would be exempt from the bill's prohibition on joint ventures and mergers.

● **Public interest.** Telecommunications networks would be required to set aside 5 percent of their capacity to carry video and phone services to schools, libraries and other nonprofit civic, cultural, educational or charitable groups. The networks would be required to give those groups and institutions preferential rates, charging only enough to cover their incremental costs. The requirement would not apply to licensed television or radio broadcasters or to cable television systems.

Telecommunications companies also would be required to meet numerous conditions designed to make their services accessible to the disabled.

● **Cable television.** Telephone companies could establish video platforms to carry all programmers' services. Such video platform services, unlike cable services, would not be subject to local franchise fees. Before getting into the cable business, telephone companies would have to meet competition-enhancing preconditions similar to the ones for the Bells' entry into long distance.

Cable companies that entered the telephone business would be required to pay a greater share of the cost of the utility poles that supported their cables.

---

more regulatory. McCain said the FCC would have to issue some 50 new rules under the bill, quoting an assessment by Citizens for a Sound Economy, a conservative public interest group. "This micromanagement," Packwood said in a press release, "will delay job creation and the development of advanced telecommunications services."

Much of the regulation was demanded by the Bells' potential competitors as a way to protect against monopoly abuses. Such regulation "appears to be the only way to get a bill through," said Ronald Stowe, a lobbyist for Pacific Telesis, the regional Bell based in San Francisco.

Anstrom, president of the National Cable Television Association, argued that this sort of regulation was a necessary first step toward replacing the telecommunications monopolies with a competitive environment. Once competition took hold, he said, Congress could ease the regulation.

In contrast to the protests against regulation, one coalition of consumer groups and telecommunications businesses argued that the revised version of S 1822 did not regulate enough. Called the Unity Coalition, the group argued that too many protections against Bell abuses were dropped in the negotiations over the Bells' entry into long distance and the Farm Team amendments.

Sen. Howard M. Metzenbaum shared their concern, as did other members of the Senate Judiciary Committee. Metzenbaum threatened to hold up the bill, saying it needed more consistent, comprehensive protections against Bell abuses and more spurs to local competition.

Metzenbaum was just one of a number of senators and interest groups trying to slow the bill's progress to the floor. Virtually everyone seemed to want something more:

● **The Bells.** High on the list of dissatisfied parties were the Bells.

After striking a deal with the long-distance companies over their entry into long distance, the Bells had focused their lobbying muscle on provisions that would restrict their entry into cable. They complained that the bill would keep them out of the cable business until long after the cable companies had entered the Bells' local telephone markets.

Just as in the long-distance battle, the Bells drummed up support from a variety of consumer and industry groups that argued for more competition in the cable market. They found an ally in Larry Irving, the Commerce Department's top telecommunications official, who called Sept. 20 for immediate, simultaneous entry of the Bells and the cable companies into each other's turf.

A second Bell complaint about S 1822 was that it would impose too many regulations on them that it would not impose on their competitors, such as the requirement that they establish separate subsidiaries to enter the cable, electronic publishing and equipment markets.

● **Long-distance companies.** The long-distance companies, meanwhile, wanted at least two things: a requirement that the Bells form separate subsidiaries to handle toll calls within the local networks and a requirement that all companies competing for those toll calls be given dialing parity.

● **Unions.** The communications unions, which were aligned with the Bells, opposed the idea of separate subsidiaries on the grounds that they created only temporary jobs. They also wanted the Bells to enter the cable business earlier, in part because the Bells were unionized and many cable companies were not.

● **Cable.** The cable companies were pushing for changes in the provision on utility poles, which they said would make it too costly for them to offer local phone service.

● **Software companies.** The software industry lobbied for more protection of copyrighted material. They also were battling with the cable industry for control of set-top boxes, the computerlike devices that would control the future hybrids of telephone and cable television. In particular, the software industry wanted consumers to be able to buy set-top boxes from any manufacturer. The cable companies argued that they should control the supply to assure compatibility and deter the theft of services.

● **Broadcasters.** Broadcasters were involved in the set-top box debate, too, saying the bill should outlaw boxes that discriminated against certain types of programs. In addition, they wanted more assurances that their programming would be carried on the high-tech transmission networks of the future, just as they were guaranteed space on cable systems.

● **State and local government.** State and local governments complained that the revised bill would shift too much of the authority they had over telecommunications to the FCC. They feared the loss of their ability to protect consumers against fraud, to control the public rights-of-way, and to provide civic and local television programming.

State officials were particularly concerned about one paragraph in the bill that would bar them from placing any requirements on telephone, cable or other telecommunications services that were inconsistent with FCC regulations. That paragraph would turn over regulation of the services within state borders to the FCC, they said, and would encourage lawsuits whenever a state proposed a regulation different from those adopted by the FCC.

Lobbyists for U.S. cities said the Senate bill would hurt their ability to collect fees from telecommunications businesses. Because the bill barred discrimination among telecommunications services, cities could be forced to reduce their fees to match the lowest amount charged any company, or even to zero, said Cara Woodson of the National League of Cities.

The Exon amendment drew opposition from the computer industry, civil libertarians and cable companies. A key concern in the computer industry was that companies providing access to the Internet for a fee would be forced to monitor the materials being transmitted and stop anything potentially indecent from reaching minors to avoid being found liable in federal court.

The cable companies objected to Exon's proposal on scrambling because it would make them judge what was and was not suitable for children. Said Tim Boggs of the Time Warner Inc. communications company, "Such a subjective and ill-defined standard will cause enormous mischief in the television market, with little gain for American families."

Final Action

The Hollings bill and telecommunications legislation in general died abruptly Sept. 23, when Hollings declared that there was not enough time left in the 103rd Congress to overcome the array of opponents. Chief among these was Dole, who wanted Hollings to impose far fewer regulations on the

Bells and other local phone companies.

Three senators besides Dole had threatened to filibuster the bill or bury it under an avalanche of floor amendments. McCain and Packwood wanted to kill the bill on the grounds that it was too regulatory, and Metzenbaum was threatening to filibuster on the grounds that it was not regulatory enough.

The Commerce Department's Irving said he was not ready to give up on the bill, a top Clinton administration priority. Bill McCloskey, a spokesman for the Bells' joint lobbying group, said the Bells had not given up completely, either. But Hollings held the keys as chairman of the committee with jurisdiction, and he made it clear that the bill was going nowhere.

"I reluctantly announce today that we will be unable to pass comprehensive telecommunications reform legislation in this Congress," he said in a prepared statement. "We will not be held hostage at the last minute to ultimatums and to the desires of certain parties to substantially rewrite a bill that passed the committee by an overwhelming and bipartisan vote."

Hollings suggested that the Bells were behind Dole's opposition, and he criticized three of the companies in particular: Ameritech of Chicago, BellSouth of Atlanta and US West of Denver. In response, Dole and the Bells said they were hardly the only ones criticizing the bill. Still, the Bells were engaged in the most extensive lobbying campaign against the bill, a campaign that began not long after it was introduced in February. By September, BellSouth Chairman John L. Clendenin was urging shareholders to lobby for the bill's demise.

Dole picked up on the Bells' deregulatory refrain. On Sept. 22, his staff gave Hollings an 11-page amendment that would have eliminated the bill's proposals for promoting competition in the local phone market and rolled back much of the existing state regulation of local phone companies.

The amendment would have undone the deal that Hollings had struck over the Bells' entry into long distance, allowing the Bells to move forward more quickly. McCloskey said that those provisions had been sought not by the Bells, but by an association of unaffiliated local phone companies. Some Bells, however, clearly were dissatisfied with the deal they had struck on the long-distance provisions, which was criticized by the chief executive of Ameritech in a letter to shareholders.

The U.S. Telephone Association, a trade group seen by many as a Bell ally, also complained about provisions stemming from the long-distance deal. A group of business officials recruited by the Bells' lobbying arm chimed in, sending a letter to senators Sept. 19 arguing for quicker Bell entry into long distance — in direct opposition to the deal the Bells themselves had struck.

Hollings said Dole insisted that his amendment be added without change and protected in conference in the House. "You see how intransigent and determined the gentleman was," he said. A Dole aide disagreed, saying Dole was flexible on the section that affected the Bells' entry into long distance. Dole's main goal, the aide said, was to set simple, market-driven guidelines for promoting competition in the local phone market — the same approach the federal government took for cellular phones.

Hollings' decision to drop S 1822 shocked the Bells, which insisted that they did indeed want a bill. They worked to revive the legislation and escape blame for its downfall, but the clock soon ran out on the session with no further action taken. ■

Bill Facilitates Police Wiretapping

Law enforcement officials won a long sought expansion of the federal wiretapping law in the closing days of the 103rd Congress. The Senate cleared a bill (HR 4922) late Oct. 7 that helped police wiretappers keep pace with advancing telephone technology, overriding objections from local telephone companies and some privacy advocates.

The House had passed the bill by voice vote Oct. 5. President Clinton signed the bill into law Oct. 25 (PL 103-414).

For several years, top law enforcement officials had urged Congress to update the wiretap law. They warned that new services such as call forwarding were confounding court-ordered wiretaps, and if the trend continued, agents might lose one of their most powerful crime-fighting tools.

Congress responded with legislation that gave telephone companies four years to make whatever changes in their networks and services were needed to ensure the success of court-ordered wiretaps. In particular, investigators wanted to be able to track and record calls made to and from targeted phone numbers. Law enforcement officials were forbidden, however, to dictate what communications technologies were to be used or introduced.

The taxpayers would contribute up to $500 million to adapt the networks, while the telephone companies would bear much of the cost of adjusting future equipment and services.

Once introduced, the legislation, a priority for FBI Director Louis J. Freeh, moved swiftly through Congress. But it was long in the making, delayed by lengthy negotiations among the telephone companies; the FBI; privacy groups; and lawmakers, led by Sen. Patrick J. Leahy, D-Vt., and Rep. Don Edwards, D-Calif.

The bill drew sustained protests from some privacy advocates, most notably the Electronic Privacy Information Center and the American Civil Liberties Union. Largely ignored in the House, they found an unlikely ally in Sen. Malcolm Wallop, R-Wyo., who seemed ready to block the Senate from considering the House-passed bill in the waning hours of the session. Wallop lifted his hold on the bill late Oct. 7, however, allowing the bill to clear.

To mollify some privacy advocates, the sponsors inserted several new privacy protections into the bill. These included provisions barring law enforcement agencies from dictating what telecommunications technologies could be introduced, stopping them from obtaining electronic-mail addresses by subpoena, and requiring them to obtain a court order to learn the location of a caller using a mobile phone. The bill also prohibited the intentional interception of calls made on cordless telephones.

Background

House bill sponsor, Edwards, and his Senate counterpart, Leahy, introduced identical bills (HR 4922, S 2375) Aug. 9 aimed at ensuring that no matter how sophisticated the telephone networks became, the police always would be able to tap a suspect's phone.

BOXSCORE

Wiretapping Revisions — HR 4922 (S 2375). The bill updated wiretapping law to enable law enforcement agents to trace and record calls made using new technologies.

Reports: H Rept 103-827, Part 1, S Rept 103-402.

KEY ACTION

Oct. 5 — House passed HR 4922 by voice vote.

Oct. 7 — Senate cleared HR 4922 by voice vote.

Oct. 25 — President signed bill — PL 103-414.

The bills did not go as far as FBI Director Freeh had proposed. Still, some privacy advocates objected to what they saw as fundamental changes in the nature of the telephone networks.

Freeh said wiretaps were a critical tool and that advancements in telecommunications threatened to undercut investigators' ability to record and trace calls. At a hearing in March, he proposed that telephone companies be required to be able within three years to intercept targeted phone calls and to record information on the origins and destinations of calls.

The bills gave phone companies four years to meet those requirements. At the companies' request, the bills also extended the requirements to other telecommunications outlets, although the legislation exempted information and phone services that did not have a substantial portion of the local market.

Freeh embraced the proposals at a hearing Aug. 11. The coalition of privacy advocates and phone companies warned, however, that the bills' high cost threatened to result in companies' skimping on privacy safeguards.

Some privacy advocates argued that the legislation was fundamentally flawed. The problem, they said, was that it proposed to make surveillance, not privacy, the design goal for the networks of the future — the so-called information superhighway.

The bill's supporters argued that the privacy advocates missed the point of the legislation. In the past, law enforcement officials worked in secret with phone company officials to discuss wiretapping issues, but the bill made that process public and accountable, they said.

The telephone companies were unhappy about the bill, too, because it required them to bear all reasonable costs of adapting future networks and services to wiretaps.

The companies were outmaneuvered, however, when Edwards and Leahy decided to move ahead without their support, calculating that the complaints about cost would pale in the face of Freeh's dire warnings about the consequences of not passing the bill.

Committee Action

The House bill began to move through the legislative process when a House Judiciary subcommittee approved it Aug. 17. The Subcommittee on Civil and Constitutional Rights, which was chaired by bill sponsor Edwards, approved the bill by voice vote after a brief debate.

The bill required the Justice Department to cover all the reasonable costs associated with the wiretap requirements during the first four years, or longer if the Federal Communications Commission (FCC) extended the deadline for compliance. The bill also authorized $500 million in spending from fiscal 1995 through fiscal 1998. Industry officials said the changes would cost far more than that in the long run. Edwards vowed to address the issue of long-term costs before the bill reached the full committee.

Some privacy advocates also questioned the need for leg-

islation, demanding proof that certain advanced phone services were obstructing wiretaps. Edwards said the FBI had documented 183 instances where wiretaps were obstructed by cellular phones, call forwarding, voice mail, call waiting and other advanced phone services. Although some might not like the idea of wiretapping, he said, "it is the law . . . and law enforcement agencies are entitled to use it."

Full House, Senate Committee Action

The House and Senate versions of the wiretapping bill easily won full committee approval and headed to the House and Senate floors, with sponsors working on one final compromise to clear the road to passage.

The House Judiciary Committee revised and approved HR 4922 (H Rept 103-827, Part 1) by voice vote Sept. 29.

The day before, the Senate Judiciary Committee adopted a nearly identical revision of S 2375 (S Rept 103-402) by voice vote. It then voted 16-0 to report the bill.

In offering revised versions of their bills for the committee markups, Leahy and Edwards tried to answer the phone companies' concerns that complying with the bill's mandates would cost far more than the $500 million authorized. One significant change forbade penalties against any existing network that was not able to obtain federal aid to make the necessary upgrades.

The revisions also required the federal government to cover the cost of any increase in network capacity required to accommodate wiretaps, no matter when that increase was demanded. This was particularly important to cellular phone carriers, whose networks had tight limits on capacity.

House, Senate Floor Action

The House amended and passed HR 4922 by voice vote Oct. 5 under an expedited procedure, known as suspension of the rules.

The amendment incorporated a compromise that Edwards and Leahy had worked out with the House Energy and Commerce Committee, which had claimed jurisdiction over the bill.

The negotiations — which were conducted in advance of floor action to short-circuit the need for a time-consuming House-Senate conference — were prompted by continuing complaints from local telephone companies about the bill's long-term, future costs. The early versions of the bill would have compelled the government to cover the cost of adapting the existing networks to wiretaps but then required the telephone companies to bear the cost of adapting future networks or services.

Under the compromise, the companies or their customers could ask the FCC to review any changes demanded in facilities or services deployed after Jan. 1, 1995. If the FCC ruled that the cost was unreasonable, the compromise required the federal government to foot the bill or to allow the company not to make the change. In making its determination, the FCC would have to consider the effect on public safety, national security, basic phone rates, privacy, technological innovation and competition, among other factors.

Overriding continuing objections from local telephone companies and some privacy advocates, the Senate cleared HR 4922 by voice vote late Oct. 7.

It had been touch and go for Leahy in the final week of the session. He needed unanimous consent to bring up the bill, and a series of senators objected. Leahy warned of dire consequences if the bill did not pass. "If anybody does want to hold it up, I hope that at this time next year, neither they nor their constituents, nor anybody they know, is a kidnap victim or victim of a terrorist, and have somebody ask why nothing can be done," he told the Senate on Oct. 4.

First, Leahy ran into two problems that had nothing to do with wiretapping or even with telephone networks.

Sen Herb Kohl, D-Wis., who had been tussling with Leahy over milk policy, threatened to take the Senate bill hostage. The two senators were battling over an unrelated Leahy bill (S 2069 — S Rept 103-333) to ratify a six-state dairy compact to regulate the supply and price of milk in the Northeast. At Freeh's urging, Kohl agreed Oct. 4 not to embroil the wiretapping bill in the dairy fight. *(Dairy compact, p. 198)*

Later that day, however, an objection by Sen. Howard M. Metzenbaum, D-Ohio, prevented the wiretapping bill from being called up for Senate debate. Although Metzenbaum had some concerns about the bill, his main goal was to delay the wiretapping measure until after the Senate decided the fate of the conference report on another unrelated bill (HR 6) that reauthorized elementary and secondary education programs. The report contained a Metzenbaum provision to bar federally subsidized adoption agencies from discrimination in adoptions that crossed ethnic or racial lines.

Metzenbaum wanted the wiretapping bill to be available as a vehicle for his adoption provision in case the education bill died. That tactic proved unnecessary when the Senate approved the conference report to HR 6, so Metzenbaum dropped his hold on the wiretapping bill. *(Elementary and secondary education, p. 383)*

The last major barrier to enactment was Wallop, who said the bill infringed on the public's right to privacy.

Wallop dropped his objection late in the evening of Oct. 7, after being lobbied by a succession of law enforcement officials and Senate colleagues. Supporters of the bill emphasized to Wallop that the bill did not make it easier for police to obtain a court's permission to wiretap, it simply increased the chances of obtaining a wiretap once a court ordered it. ∎

Lawmakers Compromise, Clear Satellite Home Viewer Bill

After settling a disagreement over retransmission fees, the Senate cleared a bill Oct. 4 to help satellite dish owners continue to tune in to broadcast network programs.

The bill (S 2406), dubbed the Satellite Home Viewer Act of 1994, allowed satellite-based television services to retransmit the programs carried by the networks and the so-called superstations for five more years. Without the bill, that authority would have expired at the end of 1994. There were an estimated 4.5 million houses with satellite dishes, most of them in isolated rural areas out of the reach of broadcast signals.

President Clinton signed the bill into law Oct. 18 (PL 103-369).

The main point of controversy concerned the fees that satellite companies paid to those holding copyrights to the programs they transmitted — mainly the television networks and the Hollywood studios. Under existing law, the fee was set periodically by an arbitration panel that was appointed by the librarian of Congress. The fee — last set in 1992 — was 6 cents per month per subscriber to each network. The panel was slated to set a new fee in 1996.

Senate Action

The Senate passed an early version of the bill (S 1485 — S Rept 103-407) by voice vote May 18. It proposed to renew the

existing system without change for five years. The Judiciary Committee had approved the bill by voice vote May 5.

The television networks were pushing for higher rates to reflect what they believed to be the fair market value of their signals. But bill sponsor Dennis DeConcini, D-Ariz., resisted the fair market value proposal, saying it threatened to hurt satellite dish owners and the satellite companies that competed with cable. The satellite carriers already paid more for network and superstation programs than the cable industry did, he said.

House Action

The House Judiciary Committee took a different approach in a bill that it approved by voice vote June 29 (HR 1103 — H Rept 103-703). The measure had originated in the Subcommittee on Intellectual Property and Judicial Administration, which approved it Aug. 5, 1993. (1993 Almanac, p. 257)

Sponsored by William J. Hughes, D-N.J., HR 1103 proposed that carriers pay broadcasters the fair market value for retransmitted programs. The bill also extended the right of satellite carriers to transmit network programming without permission. An early version of the House bill proposed to extend these rights through 1998, but the subcommittee gave voice vote approval to an amendment offered by Hamilton Fish Jr., R-N.Y., that limited the extension of transmission rights to one year.

The bill stipulated that the arbitration panel determine the new market-based rates, which were to take effect in 1997, unless carriers and broadcasters voluntarily agreed to another payment scheme before that date. The panel was to base its decisions on what cable companies paid the networks for retransmissions, among other factors.

Hughes said the existing fee was so far below the programs' value that it amounted to a government-mandated subsidy for satellite companies.

Rep. Mike Synar, D-Okla., said the bill did not give the arbitration panels enough guidance on what "fair market value" meant. He also said the change threatened to put the satellite companies at a disadvantage when competing with cable television companies, which did not have to pay fair market value for network programs.

On Aug. 16, the full House passed HR 1103 by voice vote. In preparation for conference, it then inserted the provisions into S 1485, which it passed by voice vote.

Compromise Bill

After negotiating with the satellite companies, the broadcasters and the Motion Picture Association of America, House and Senate lawmakers reached a compromise on setting fees. The compromise instructed the arbitration panel to set fees that "most clearly represent fair market value" but also gave the panel guidelines for determining that value. For example, DeConcini noted that the panel would have to consider the fees paid by cable companies for retransmission rights in setting the fee to ensure they were similar. Having parity between cable and satellite companies was "the central feature of the fair market standard articulated in this legislation," DeConcini said.

The compromise also set up a new procedure for resolving complaints by broadcast stations about satellite companies' serving ineligible homes and businesses. By law, satellite companies were allowed to retransmit network signals only to homes in areas too remote to receive the nearest broadcast station's signal. The bill required satellite companies to test how strong a broadcast signal a disputed sub-

scriber received. If it was strong enough to provide a clear picture, the subscriber's service had to be cut off; if not, the station was mandated to pay the cost of the test.

The compromise also extended retransmission authority to wireless, microwave cable systems.

On Sept. 20, the House tacked the compromise onto a separate Senate-passed bill (S 2406) that required cable systems to carry the local Fox Broadcasting Network station, then passed the amended bill by voice vote. The Senate cleared the measure by voice vote Oct. 4, sending it to the president. ■

Clinton Signs Bill To Curb Telemarketing Fraud

On Aug. 16, President Clinton signed a long delayed bill (HR 868 — PL 103-297) designed to crack down on telemarketing fraud.

Sponsored by Rep. Al Swift, D-Wash., the measure required the Federal Trade Commission (FTC) and the Securities and Exchange Commission (SEC) to enact rules prohibiting telemarketing scams, such as offering bogus oil leases and land deals over the phone. The FTC was required to act within a year, and the SEC had to follow suit within six months. The bill also gave state attorneys general and private citizens the power to file lawsuits based on FTC rules.

Lobbyists for consumers and telemarketers said that giving the state attorneys general enforcement power was important because the federal Justice Department did not move quickly enough to catch fly-by-night operators. Federal prosecutors also declined to act on all but the biggest cases of fraud. John F. Barker, a consumer advocate at the National Consumers League, said attorneys general had been frustrated by their inability to bring cases against telemarketing scams based in other states. "These guys would operate for six to eight months and nobody could do anything about them," Barker said.

Swift said the bill did not impose new regulations on the legitimate telemarketing industry. It did, however, call for new rules to rein in telemarketing practices that some consumers considered abusive, even when they came from established companies. These rules would bar telemarketers from repeatedly disturbing individual consumers with unsolicited telephone calls, limit the hours when unsolicited calls could be made, and require telemarketers to "promptly and clearly disclose that the purpose of the call is to sell goods or services."

The bill targeted fraudulent telemarketers for lawsuits, not prosecution. That meant state attorneys general had to show only that the practices had the effect of deceiving customers, not that the telemarketer had a criminal intent to deceive, in order to win restraining orders and damages.

Congress had been considering legislation to protect consumers from telemarketing scams for at least six years. Although there was broad support in both chambers for a crackdown, the legislation had been held up by a separate dispute between the House and Senate over reauthorizing the FTC.

Both chambers had passed versions of the telemarketing bill in 1993. The House passed its bill (HR 868 — H Rept 103-20) on March 2. The Senate passed an amended version (S Rept 103-80) on June 30. But the bill languished while negotiations continued on an FTC bill (HR 2243). Those negotiations were concluded in July 1994. (FTC, p. 181)

The House then amended HR 868 with a compromise that

had been worked out with the Senate and passed it July 25 by voice vote. The revised bill removed all references to "fraud" and "fraudulent practices." Said Swift: "No common-law fraud, criminal fraud or intent to deceive is necessary to prove that an act or practice under this act is 'deceptive.'" The Senate cleared the bill by voice vote Aug 2. ■

House Passes Increase In FCC Funding

The House passed a bill to authorize a hefty increase in spending by the Federal Communications Commission (FCC), but the measure failed to clear the Senate in the final days of the session.

The House amended and passed the bill (HR 4522 — H Rept 103-844) by voice vote Oct. 7. The next day it was referred to the Senate Commerce Committee, but no further action was taken.

The bill would have authorized $186 million for the FCC in fiscal 1995, a 16 percent increase over fiscal 1994. The FCC received much of that increase anyway, courtesy of the fiscal 1995 appropriations bill for the Commerce, Justice and State departments (HR 4603 — PL 103-317). That measure gave the FCC authority to spend $185.2 million, with almost two-thirds of the money coming from fees on FCC licenses. (*Appropriations, p. 483*)

The final House bill was similar to a version that had been approved Aug. 5 by the Energy and Commerce Committee, although it dropped a provision dealing with licensing fees. That provision would have sent the first $40 million in fees collected to the general Treasury and allowed the FCC to keep any fees above that amount.

The House bill had begun in the Energy and Commerce Subcommittee on Telecommunications and Finance, which gave its voice vote approval July 14. The panel added provisions, offered by bill sponsor and Chairman Edward J. Markey, D-Mass., that sought to improve the FCC's ability to collect enough in fees from regulated companies to cover the commission's legal costs. It also allowed the FCC to waive the broadcast license requirements for recreational boaters and aviators, gave the commission more flexibility in inspecting ship radios and clarified the commission's authority to reject proposed tariffs and order refunds.

While the House was working on its bill, the Senate Commerce Committee tried to move a revised version of a bill (S 2336) by Daniel K. Inouye, D-Hawaii, that would have reauthorized the FCC for two years. Objections from several lawmakers kept that measure from being considered by the full Senate, however.

Similarly, when leaders of the Senate committee tried to push the House-passed bill through the Senate on Oct. 8, they could not obtain the unanimous consent needed to do so. ■

No Accord on Reauthorizing NASA

Although both the House- and Senate-passed versions of a bill (HR 4489) to reauthorize the National Aeronautics and Space Administration (NASA), the two chambers were unable to settle their differences in time to clear a final version, and the bill died at the end of the Congress.

House Science Committee Chairman George E. Brown Jr., D-Calif., had introduced the bill at a time when it appeared that NASA would receive less money from Congress than the $14.3 billion requested by President Clinton. Brown said the authorization would ensure that both the space station and other science projects could be preserved.

Once it became clear that appropriators would fund the agency, Brown turned the bill into a broad statement of policy goals for NASA. While the bill was not controversial, it was no longer a priority, and it could not compete for members' attention in the short time remaining in the session.

House Action

The House Science Subcommittee on Space gave voice vote approval July 13 to a $14.1 billion NASA authorization bill (HR 4489) that would enable the agency to launch eight space shuttle flights a year and fund the Mars surveyor program, a robotic probe to map the surface of the red planet.

Under Brown's original bill, both the Mars surveyor and the shuttle programs were to be cut. But a far-ranging amend-

---

BOXSCORE

NASA Reauthorization — HR 4489. The legislation proposed broad policy goals for NASA; specific spending authority was dropped after appropriators funded the agency.

Report: H Rept 103-654.

KEY ACTION

Aug. 8 — House passed HR 4489 by voice vote.

Oct. 5 — Senate passed HR 4489, revised, by voice vote.

---

ment by subcommittee Chairman Ralph M. Hall, D-Texas, restored the funding, partly offset by NASA cuts in other areas. Overall, the two-year authorization bill proposed to trim NASA's budget by $450 million in fiscal 1995. Some of the savings were to be achieved by eliminating planned shuttle upgrades and trimming the Mission to Planet Earth program.

The subcommittee rejected by voice vote an amendment by space station opponent Tim Roemer, D-Ind., to cut $2.1 billion from the space station. Instead, the panel approved a Roemer amendment to require annual reports on space station expenses.

The full Science, Space and Technology Committee approved the bill July 20 by voice vote (H Rept 103-654).

The committee rejected by voice vote an attempt by Roemer to cancel funding for the space station. Committee members instead adopted by voice vote a Roemer amendment to limit annual funding for the space station to $2.1 billion. The panel adopted by voice vote an amendment by subcommittee Chairman Hall to require NASA to catalog and track any major comets or asteroids that might cross the Earth's orbit.

House Floor Action

The House took up the bill Aug. 8, passing it by voice vote. But first, Brown offered an amendment that stripped the measure of any specific funding levels or spending authority for NASA. Brown said the revised bill focused instead on policy

directives, because his original goal of bringing certainty to NASA's funding levels had already been achieved by House and Senate passage of the fiscal 1995 appropriations bill for Veterans Affairs, Housing and Urban Development, and Independent Agencies (HR 4624), which funded the space agency. *(Appropriations, p. 541)*

The revised bill's broad policy guidelines included encouraging partnerships between NASA and private companies for technology development and promoting better accountability in the often criticized space agency.

The bill made a joint space station venture between the United States and Russia conditional on certification that there was minimal Russian troop presence in the Baltic nations. It required the president to certify each year, in order for the joint venture to continue, that actions by Russia "do not violate the sovereignty" of any former Soviet republic.

The bill also required an accounting of the $112 million in fiscal 1995 and any future U.S. funds sent to Russia for space station development. Some members had raised concerns about the solvency of the Russian space program. "Few [Russian] workers are being paid, and other signs of financial trouble are everywhere," said Roemer. "Few details are available about the exact financial straits of the Russian program, but a financial crisis during the space station construction period could be devastating to the U.S. space program as well." *(1993 Almanac, p. 251)*

The Clinton administration had brought the Russians into the space station program in 1993, amid growing unease in Congress over the cost of the multibillion-dollar project.

The House-passed bill also contained provisions to:

● Require NASA to consider cost savings in the space shuttle program — for example, by submitting a report in 1995 showing how much of the shuttle mission could be accomplished over the next five years if the number of flights were reduced from eight a year to six or seven.

● Revise the Commercial Space Transportation Act, allowing the Transportation secretary to license commercial satellite operations to ensure that re-entry plans were safe. Under existing law, the secretary only had the authority to license commercial space launch vehicles.

● Give NASA and the Commerce Department, rather than the Pentagon, broader authority over launching a new satellite under the Land Remote Sensing Policy Act of 1992 (Landsat). Until 1992, the Commerce Department's National Oceanic and Atmospheric Administration had managed the program, which took pictures of the Earth from space for environmental, military and other purposes. *(1992 Almanac, p. 304)*

Senate Action

The Senate Commerce Committee on Sept. 23 gave voice vote approval to a revised version of HR 4489.

The committee removed the House-passed language that conditioned the joint venture on annual certification that Russia was not violating the sovereignty of any former Soviet republic.

The committee incorporated the provisions of a separate bill (S 1881 — S Rept 103-362) setting criteria for awarding NASA technology development grants. That bill, sponsored by John D. Rockefeller IV, D-W.Va., required that the projects contribute to the economic growth and competitiveness of the United States. It included provisions granting authority to license commercial re-entry spacecraft and prohibiting the launch of outer space advertisements. (The Senate passed S 1881 separately by voice vote Oct. 6, but the House did not act on it.)

The Senate committee bill also contained provisions to:

● Make the Commerce Department, instead of the Pentagon, NASA's primary partner in future launches of Landsat satellites.

● Require NASA by February 1995 to submit a report on cost savings in the space shuttle program.

● Allow the Transportation secretary to license commercial re-entry vehicles.

The Senate passed the amended bill by voice vote Oct. 5. ■

NOAA Renewal Dies in Senate

The House on Sept. 26 passed a bill to reauthorize the ocean, coastal and fisheries programs of the National Oceanic and Atmospheric Administration (NOAA) for two years. But the Senate took no action on the measure, and it died at the end of the Congress.

The House-passed bill (HR 4008) authorized $444 million in fiscal 1995 and $463 million in fiscal 1996. It included fiscal 1995 authorizations of $71 million for the ongoing Global Climate Change Research Program and $10 million for ongoing marine prediction research activities, with those amounts increasing somewhat in fiscal 1996.

The bill, sponsored by Solomon P. Ortiz, D-Texas, also authorized $7 million a year in fiscal 1995-96 to carry out a plan by Vice President Al Gore to create a global network of schoolchildren to collect data about their environment, known as Global Learning and Observations to Benefit the Environment (GLOBE). However, because of Republican concerns about the eventual costs of the programs, beginning in fiscal 1996, appropriations were to be contingent on the program's getting matching, non-federal funds.

The bill included a modified version of HR 4236 authorizing the National Undersea Research Program. The program, which began in 1980 but had never been formally authorized by Congress, involved five centers across the United States and one in the Bahamas that conducted research on ocean habitat, undersea resources and diving safety. The bill authorized about $20 million in fiscal 1995 and $107 million over five years for the program. The Clinton administration wanted to terminate the program.

Legislative Action

The bill began in the House Merchant Marine and Fisheries Subcommittee on Oceanography, Gulf of Mexico and the Outer Continental Shelf, which approved it by voice vote April 19. The subcommittee bill authorized $440 million for the NOAA programs in fiscal 1994 and $479 million in fiscal 1995.

The subcommittee approved four non-controversial amendments by voice vote, including one by Lynn Schenk, D-Calif., to increase the fiscal 1995 authorization by $21 million. It also increased the authorization for climate and global change research from $63 million to slightly more than $84 million, the level requested by the Clinton administration.

The full Merchant Marine and Fisheries Committee gave voice vote approval to a revised version of the bill May 11 (H Rept 103-583, Part 1). The committee bill authorized $315.8 million in fiscal 1995 and $328.3 million in fiscal 1996 with an additional $7.1 million each year for several related programs and studies.

Members turned back, 7-10, an effort by Jack Fields, R-Texas, to remove the $7 million slated for Gore's GLOBE program.

The House Science, Space and Technology Committee, which shared jurisdiction over the oceanic and atmospheric

research and administrative support sections of the bill, began its work in July. The Subcommittee on Space approved its own version of the measure by voice vote July 19, and the full committee gave voice vote approval July 20 (H Rept 103-583, Part 2). The committee approved, by voice vote, an amendment by Robert S. Walker, R-Pa., to lower the fiscal 1995 authorization level for climate and global change research from $84 million to $66 million, the amount approved by the House in its fiscal 1995 appropriations bill for the departments of Commerce, Justice and State (HR 4603).

As approved by the committee, the bill authorized $22.1 million for the National Undersea Research Program and $71.8 million for overall program support in fiscal 1995. The measure included $7 million for GLOBE.

The version of the bill that went to the House floor was a compromise worked out by the two committees. It passed by voice vote Sept. 26. ∎

Various Science Bills Die At Session's End

Bills to reauthorize the National Science Foundation, provide for the coordination of federal science policies and authorize high-energy research programs advanced in 1994. But lawmakers did not complete work on them, and they died at the end of the Congress.

National Science Foundation

Both chambers approved bills (HR 3254, S 2344) to reauthorize the National Science Foundation (NSF), but they did not reconcile their differences before the end of the Congress. The NSF was an independent agency that supported basic and applied research and education programs in more than 2,000 colleges, universities and nonprofit organizations.

A key feature of both bills was an increase in spending for construction of academic research facilities. The Clinton administration sought $55 million for that purpose in fiscal 1995. The House bill nearly tripled that request, authorizing $150 million in fiscal 1995. The Senate bill increased it further, to $300 million.

In the House, the Science, Space and Technology Committee gave voice vote approval March 23 to a version of the bill that authorized $3.2 billion for the NSF in fiscal 1995 and $3.4 billion in fiscal 1996 (HR 3254 — H Rept 103-475).

Bill sponsors were hoping to dissuade House and Senate appropriators from steering money toward specific hometown academic institutions for research facilities, a practice called "earmarking" that critics said unfairly bypassed the merit-based peer review process followed by the NSF. The bill barred the NSF from awarding facilities improvement grants to academic institutions that received earmarked construction money in the future. However, some lawmakers defended earmarks as necessary to address a grant system that favored larger, more prestigious universities.

The committee rejected, 13-32, a GOP move led by Sherwood Boehlert of New York to extend the ban to all NSF grants, not just those for upgrading facilities.

The bill included $2.3 billion for research programs in fiscal 1995, including biological, computer, engineering, earth and physical sciences.

The House passed the bill May 4 by a vote of 396-22. But first, lawmakers agreed, 227-197, to adopt an amendment by

Boehlert that trimmed the authorization to $3.15 billion for fiscal 1995 and $3.23 billion for fiscal 1996. *(Votes 153, 151, p. 46-H)*

In the Senate, similar legislation (S 2344) won voice vote approval from the Labor and Human Resources Committee on Aug. 8 (S Rept 103-328) and from the Commerce, Science and Transportation Committee on Sept. 23. The Senate bill authorized $3.5 billion in fiscal 1995, increasing gradually to $5.1 billion in fiscal 1999. The bill did not include the House-passed provision barring future facilities grants to academic institutions that had received construction money under an earmark.

The NSF's authorization expired at the beginning of fiscal 1994. Congress had last authorized the foundation in 1988 for fiscal years 1989 through 1993. Appropriators provided $3 billion for the agency in fiscal 1994; they provided just under $3.4 billion in the fiscal 1995 spending bill for the departments of Veterans Affairs and Housing and Urban Development (HR 4624 — PL 103-327).

Science Policy

On March 23, the House Science, Space and Technology Committee gave voice vote approval to a bill aimed at addressing an issue that had long confounded science advocates: how to set federal priorities for the vast complex of federally backed research, particularly in a tight, post-Cold War budget climate. But the measure (HR 3476 — H Rept 103-473) went no further. Similar, but pared down, provisions were included in the Senate version of a "competitiveness" bill (S 4) that did not clear Congress.

HR 3476 began in the panel's Science Subcommittee, which approved it by voice vote March 15. The bill proposed to give the White House Office of Science and Technology Policy a more direct role in formulating the government's research and development spending priorities. The science office would be required to work with the Office of Management and Budget to review the budget proposals of each agency and to issue budget guidance to federal agencies to ensure that public policy spurred the nation's science and technology efforts.

In addition, the White House science and budget offices were to prepare an annual report to Congress setting specific priorities for science and technology programs, including a consolidated national research and development budget proposal.

The subcommittee gave voice vote approval to a substitute offered by bill sponsor and panel Chairman Rick Boucher, D-Va., that reduced somewhat the proposed budgetary role for the science office. The amendment eliminated a provision requiring the science director to give written concurrence that research and development budgets conformed with national science and technology policies.

The bill also provided for creation of a National Science and Technology Council to replace the Federal Coordinating Council for Science, Engineering and Technology, which had been criticized as ineffective. The new council, recommended in Vice President Al Gore's 1993 National Performance Review, was to parallel the National Economic Council and the National Security Council to ensure that the president's science priorities were reflected in the budget and other federal policies. The council was to consist of the director of the White House science office, Cabinet secretaries and directors of the National Aeronautics and Space Administration, National Science Foundation, National Institutes of Health and other federal agencies.

Energy Research

The House on Aug. 19 passed by voice vote a bill (HR 4908 — H Rept 103-674) to authorize a variety of energy research programs, including fusion and high-energy physics research. The Senate had passed a related measure (S 646 — S Rept 103-62) on June 29, 1993, that authorized only fusion research. The two chambers could not resolve their differences, and the measure died. *(1993 Almanac, p. 253)*

The House bill authorized $1.3 billion for fusion research through 1997 and $4.3 billion through fiscal 1999 for high-energy and nuclear physics programs at the Department of Energy (DOE).

In an attempt to provide direction for the Energy Department's program, the bill called for demonstrating the potential commercial application of fusion by 2010 and commercial production by 2040. Fusion promised to provide an unlimited power source that was economical and environmentally friendly. Unlike a traditional nuclear reactor, which produced energy by splitting atoms, fusion would generate power by fusing hydrogen atoms.

The measure also reinforced the U.S. commitment to participate in a joint project with Japan, Russia and a host of European nations to build an experimental reactor. The goal was for the reactor, known as the International Thermonuclear Experimental Reactor, to be fully operational by 2005.

The House Science, Space and Technology Subcommittee on Energy had given voice vote approval to the measure July 21; the full committee approved it by voice vote Aug. 3.

The full committee incorporated provisions of a bill (HR 4684) to authorize and provide direction for DOE high-energy and physics programs. Research in these areas had helped spur advances in cancer therapy, radioactive isotope production, high-speed data acquisition and computer development. The bill, which had been approved separately July 26 by the panel's Science Subcommittee, authorized $695.4 million in fiscal 1996, $719.7 million in fiscal 1997, $744.9 million in fiscal 1998 and $713.6 million in fiscal 1999 for high-energy physics.

The measure also authorized $337.1 million in fiscal 1996 for nuclear physics, increasing to $373.7 million by fiscal 1999. That money was to provide for the construction of the Relativistic Heavy Ion Collider at Brookhaven National Laboratory outside Chicago. ∎

Competitiveness Measure Stymied

The House and Senate each passed versions of a bill to help small high-tech industries compete in the global marketplace, but the measure (HR 820) stalled in conference. The two-year bill would have authorized grants and loans by the Commerce Department and the National Science Foundation to help small and midsize businesses compete globally. It also would have authorized funding for the Commerce Department's National Institute of Standards and Technology (NIST), the chief federal research laboratory devoted to helping companies and institutions research technologies that had not reached the marketplace.

Republicans, led by John C. Danforth of Missouri, fought the bill, arguing that it was folly to have the government interfere with marketplace decisions on which companies, products or processes should succeed or fail.

Democrats, led by bill sponsor Ernest F. Hollings of South Carolina, argued that the marketplace alone was too imprecise a mechanism to ensure U.S. competitiveness. They cited other governments, such as Japan and Germany, that played closer roles in steering their industries toward prosperous ventures.

Hollings also stressed that the bill was a crucial component of the president's economic agenda. "This is one of the five main programs that President Clinton wants from Congress in this legislative session," added John D. Rockefeller IV, D-W.Va.

Background

For decades, the White House had followed a policy that allowed federal support for basic science but left applied civilian research aimed at developing new products to the marketplace.

That changed in 1993, when Clinton and Vice President Al Gore unveiled a $17 billion, four-year plan to forge a new partnership between government and industry to increase the competitiveness of U.S. business. Clinton called for new tax breaks for joint private sector and government research projects. They proposed to more than triple funding for research to encourage new technology applications and greatly expand manufacturing "extension" centers to help small businesses modernize.

The House endorsed Clinton's initiative in a bill (HR 820 — H Rept 103-77) passed May 19, 1993. The bill authorized $1.5 billion over two years for grants, loans and research assistance to small and medium-size businesses.

The Senate Commerce, Science and Transportation Committee approved a $2.8 billion companion bill (S 4 — S Rept 103-113) on May 25, but that measure did not reach the floor in 1993. Unlike the House bill, S 4 included funding for federal high-performance computing and communications programs. *(1993 Almanac, p. 241)*

Senate Action

After a week of often heated partisan debate and legislative gridlock, the Senate on March 16 passed its version of HR 820 by a vote of 59-40. The revised bill authorized $1.9 billion over two years to help guide the private sector toward new products and manufacturing processes. *(Vote 60, p. 11-S)*

The Senate first agreed by voice vote to lower the bill's authorization level, then inserted the text of the Senate bill (S 4) into the House-passed version (HR 820). The Senate-

---

BOXSCORE

Competitiveness Programs — HR 820 (S 4). The bill proposed to authorize loans and grants to help U.S. high-tech companies compete globally, and to authorize federal research programs.

Reports: H Rept 103-77, S Rept 103-113.

KEY ACTION

March 16 — Senate passed HR 820, 59-40, after substituting the text of S 4.

Sept. 27 — House-Senate conferees met but failed to reach agreement.

---

passed bill did not detail how specific programs would be affected by the cut, leaving those decisions to conference.

The major difference between the Senate version and the $1.5 billion, two-year House bill was the Senate's inclusion of provisions to authorize $359 million for government research into high-performance computing and computer networks.

Republicans Force Cuts

The bill survived only after Republicans, led by Danforth, won a concession from Democrats to trim the $2.8 billion cost of the original Senate version of the bill. Republicans had mounted a weeklong standoff to protest what they said amounted to the government's "picking winners and losers" in industry by targeting federal dollars toward specific industries and companies. They also complained that the bill's grant and loan programs would serve as useful political tools for Commerce Secretary Ronald H. Brown, a former chairman of the Democratic National Committee.

Republicans were emboldened to stall the bill after they mustered 42 votes March 10 for a sweeping substitute amendment by Alan K. Simpson, R-Wyo., that would have replaced the bill with provisions to reduce regulatory burdens on business and citizens. Although the Senate voted 56-42 to table, or kill, Simpson's amendment, Republicans showed they could deny Democrats the 60 votes needed to break a filibuster. *(Vote 52, p. 10-S)*

Minority Leader Bob Dole, R-Kan., said the filibuster was necessary because Hollings, who was chairman of the Commerce Committee, had refused to compromise on several attempts to pare down the bill. "If changes can't be made, we'll do what we think we have to do," Dole said. Practically none of the debate that occurred through the week was related to the underlying bill. Instead, topics ranged from the Whitewater Development Co. scandal to counterespionage to whether Hollings should expunge from the written record a March 10 complaint that leading opponent Danforth was engaging in "monkeyshines" and "hypocrisy" to stall the bill.

Republican opponents lobbed multiple floor amendments, most of which were unrelated to the bill.

The first was an effort by Nancy Landon Kassebaum, R-Kan., to prohibit lawsuits against makers of small aircraft for defects after a plane was at least 15 years old. Kassebaum's home state was headquarters to three leading small-aircraft companies. Kassebaum on March 9 won the promise of a floor vote on her aircraft liability bill (S 1458) in return for not tying up the competitiveness measure. *(Small-plane liability, p. 180)*

Then came an amendment by Thad Cochran, R-Miss., to delay the April 15 effective date of Environmental Protection Agency regulations mandating new protections for farm workers against harmful pesticides. Cochran proposed that the rules, which included labeling and training requirements, go into effect Oct. 23, 1995. A motion to table, or kill, the amendment failed, 35-65, virtually assuring its adoption. *(Vote 50, p. 10-S)*

But Howard M. Metzenbaum, D-Ohio, who opposed the amendment, complained that the vote took him by surprise and left him unprepared to challenge Cochran. The two worked out a compromise with Agriculture Chairman Patrick J. Leahy, D-Vt., to offer a separate bill (S 1913) changing the effective date to Jan. 1, 1995. The Senate passed that measure by voice vote March 9; it was enacted into law April 6 (PL 103-231).

Other less controversial amendments were adopted by voice vote, including one by William S. Cohen, R-Maine, to increase legal penalties for espionage and to tighten the super-

vision of individuals with access to classified documents.

Hollings initially refused to bargain with GOP opponents, but compromise became necessary when Republicans succeeded March 15 in beating back a motion to end the filibuster. The cloture motion fell short of the 60 votes needed to limit debate; it was defeated by a vote of 56-42. *(Vote 58, p. 11-S)*

But the Senate also rejected an amendment by Danforth — one of the few offered that actually pertained to the bill — that would have killed a $100 million program to spur private sector venture capital investments in small high-tech companies. The amendment failed on a 44-55 vote March 16. *(Vote 59, p. 11-S)*

Danforth's amendment cut to the heart of the decades-long debate between the parties over federal industrial policy. The two-year pilot project, modeled after a similar program run by the Small Business Administration, was to provide loans to investors hoping to put money into one of 25 areas declared by a recent government-industry board to be critical to the nation's industrial competitiveness. Those areas included such fields as supercomputing, low-temperature ceramic conductors and fiber optics.

Danforth said, in essence, that if nobody in the marketplace saw fit to invest in a particular high-tech company, that company probably should not receive funding. Bureaucrats, he said, were in no position to make such judgments.

Danforth's amendment drew support from three Democrats. New Jersey Sen. Bill Bradley argued that, despite efforts in the bill to base such loans solely on merit, lobbyists from politically well-connected companies would receive the lion's share of funds. He was joined by Howell Heflin of Alabama and Herb Kohl of Wisconsin. Rockefeller and Joseph I. Lieberman, D-Conn., defended the program, saying investors too often shied away from such high-risk technologies. Lieberman said the program would address "a failure in the marketplace" to spur cutting-edge innovations.

Senators also accepted by voice vote an amendment by Hank Brown, R-Colo., to require grant recipients to pay at least half the total cost of any projects or joint ventures funded by the bill. The government's participation would also be limited to five years under the Brown amendment.

Key Senate Provisions

The core of the Senate bill was a significant increase in spending for several new civilian technology programs under way at NIST. The institute was the centerpiece of the administration's efforts to build a closer relationship between industry and government, on the theory that the nation's 360,000 small and midsize manufacturers lacked the money and expertise to improve production with computer-controlled technologies or to keep producing innovative products.

Sponsors stressed that the industries involved, not government, would pick the technologies to receive government aid, conduct the research and pay half the costs for the joint government projects.

The bill authorized more than $2 billion for cooperative research programs between NIST and private companies, including:

● $170 million through fiscal 1995 and 1996 for the Manufacturing Extension Partnership program. The program, created as part of the 1988 Omnibus Trade and Competitiveness Act (PL 100-418), was to shift from a pilot program to a full-fledged nationwide network of technology extension centers, modeled after the Agriculture Department extension centers that for decades had provided farmers with technical information.

● $475 million for fiscal 1995 and $575 million for fiscal 1996

for a new Advanced Technology Program to assist industry-led efforts to develop and improve computer-controlled manufacturing systems. That was a significant increase over the $68 million appropriated for fiscal 1993 and the $200 million appropriated for fiscal 1994.

- $320 million in fiscal 1995 and $350 million in fiscal 1996 for research on commercial technologies conducted solely by NIST.
- $100 million through fiscal 1995 and 1996 to help private venture capital companies invest in high-technology companies.

The bill also included a section written by Gore to authorize $359 million through fiscal 1995 and 1996 to further develop computer networks and high-performance computing in selected areas. It proposed to focus federal computer networking dollars on manufacturing, health care, education and the federal laboratory system

Senate Energy and Natural Resources Chairman J. Bennett Johnston, D-La., had won changes in the bill before floor debate to include an authorization of $250 million through fiscal 1995 and 1996 for Energy Department computer networking applications. The Energy Department had previously been left out of administration and computer networking proposals.

Conference

The 103rd Congress ended with the bill stalled in conference. House and Senate negotiators met Sept. 27 but failed to bridge their differences over three issues:

- A Senate provision by Malcolm Wallop, R-Wyo., to allow small businesses to challenge in court federal rules and regulations that were difficult or costly to meet. House negotiators agreed to the provision in principle but tried to place conditions on it. On July 19, the House had approved, 380-36, a non-binding resolution instructing its conferees to concur with the Senate position. *(Vote 331, p. 100-H)*
- A Senate provision by Don Nickles, R-Okla., to require the Congressional Budget Office (CBO) to estimate the economic and employment impact of all legislation and federal regulations. Some Senate Democrats backed away from the provision, saying the CBO lacked the resources for such a task, but Republicans in both chambers supported it.
- A House provision by Thomas J. Manton, D-N.Y., to deny U.S. companies with foreign parent companies from benefiting from the legislation unless the parent companies' host nations offered reciprocal programs. Senate negotiators said the language was too broad and could hurt U.S. companies with overseas operations.

House negotiators, however, did accept a Senate provision to authorize $359 million for government research into high-performance computing and computer networks. ∎

Both Chambers Try To Redefine Energy Research Labs' Role

Lawmakers tried during the 103rd Congress to define a new, post-Cold War mission for the Department of Energy's research laboratories. But they could not agree on how far the labs should be required to go in forging new partnerships with private industry, and the legislation died at the end of the year.

The Senate was the first to act, passing its bill Nov. 20, 1993. Three House committees marked up versions of the legislation in 1994. All the measures proposed to retain the labs' role in weapons and energy-related research. But the Senate

and the House Energy and Commerce Committee wanted to make a top priority of "technology transfer" — collaborations between the labs and the private sector to promote commercial applications of Energy Department research — while the other House panels wanted to make it a subordinate activity with several restrictions.

The Senate bill (S 473 — S Rept 103-69), sponsored by J. Bennett Johnston, proposed to expand the mission of the laboratories to include research, development and commercial application of industrial technologies. It called for some labs to set aside 20 percent of their budgets for partnerships with industry. The Senate acted on the separate bill after it had included most of the provisions in its version of the fiscal 1994 defense authorization bill (S 1298), only to see them dropped in conference. *(1993 Almanac, p. 248)*

In the House, two committees — Armed Services and Science — approved similar versions of a separate bill (HR 1432). A third committee, Energy and Commerce, approved a revised version of the Senate bill. The committees were unable to resolve their jurisdictional disputes and produce a single bill for House floor action.

House Science, Armed Services Subcommittees

Two House subcommittees gave voice vote approval April 13 to a compromise bill (HR 1432) that preserved nuclear weapons research and supervision as the first of three missions for the labs. The other missions were research into energy supply and the environmental impacts of producing energy. The compromise, crafted by Marilyn Lloyd, D-Tenn., was aimed at resolving the dispute over the missions of the three defense laboratories — the Sandia and Los Alamos facilities in New Mexico and the Lawrence Livermore lab in California.

As introduced by Science Committee Chairman George E. Brown Jr., D-Calif., HR 1432 had called for the Energy secretary to develop a plan within one year for the phased consolidation of the nuclear research facilities and the conversion of one lab to civilian research. It also made the labs' nuclear weapons role just one of eight specific missions.

Pentagon-oriented members argued that the labs' central role should remain oversight of the nation's nuclear stockpile and research into nuclear non-proliferation and arms control verification.

Lloyd's substitute dropped the consolidation and conversion language. It also reduced technology transfer from a proposed mission to an authorized activity of the labs. No more than 20 percent of the money authorized for weapons research and development could be set aside for technology transfer.

The substitute won approval from the Science Subcommittee on Energy, which Lloyd chaired, and the Armed Services Subcommittee on Military Acquisition, on which she served.

Floyd D. Spence of South Carolina, ranking Republican on the Armed Services subcommittee, said he supported Lloyd's substitute "because it clearly focuses on the importance of preserving the national security mission of the defense laboratories."

Following the Science subcommittee markup, Brown said he agreed with the removal of the consolidation mandate, stating that it might take several years to determine whether such action was desirable. "We're talking about some of the top scientific and technical people in the country, with a mission that is vital to the security of the United States," Brown said. "A year is pretty fast to make a radical change."

The Science subcommittee approved one amendment to Lloyd's substitute, by Bill Baker, R-Calif., to allow Energy lab-

oratory directors to enter into cooperative agreements involving a federal commitment of $1 million or less without getting approval from Energy Department officials in Washington.

House Science, Armed Services Committees

The full Science Committee gave voice vote approval to HR 1432 on April 20, and the Armed Services Committee did the same a day later (H Rept 103-484, Parts 1 and 2).

The two versions differed slightly, owing to amendments adopted by the Science Committee. For example, the committee adopted by voice votes amendments by Rod Grams, R-Minn., and Anna G. Eshoo, D-Calif., to protect private businesses against competition from the department's laboratories.

In addition, three committee Republicans announced plans to offer more significant amendments when the bill reached the floor. All drew opposition from Energy Secretary Hazel R. O'Leary.

Sherwood Boehlert of New York said he would try to place tighter restrictions on how the Energy Department spent $640 million that Congress appropriated for fiscal 1994 to terminate the superconducting super collider project in Texas. Boehlert wanted to bar the money from being funneled into any new projects at the supercollider site or being spent on grants or contracts unless they were awarded on a competitive basis.

Roscoe G. Bartlett of Maryland planned to offer an amendment to establish an independent commission to recommend Energy Department laboratories for closure or reconfiguration.

Robert S. Walker of Pennsylvania wanted to require the laboratories to recoup financial aid they provided to businesses that developed marketable products or processes.

House Energy and Commerce

The House Energy and Commerce Committee was not given jurisdiction over HR 1432, and the leaders of the Armed Services and Science committees had hoped to move the bill to the House floor without it passing through the panel. But Energy and Commerce, which had no intention of being left out, simply took up the Senate bill, S 473, which had been referred to it. It then pushed to have all three committees' bills combined before a single measure went to the House floor.

The panel's Subcommittee on Energy and Power approved its version of S 473 by voice vote May 17. The bill aimed to shift the Energy labs' focus from national security to industrial competitiveness. It proposed to expand efforts to find commercial applications for such laboratory technologies as pollution reduction and waste disposal, as well as research and development.

The full House Energy and Commerce Committee approved the measure by voice vote June 9 (H Rept 103-611, Part 1).

One contentious amendment offered by Mike Kreidler, D-Wash., and Scott L. Klug, R-Wis., pitted would-be budget cutters against those who wanted to maintain funding for the country's 30 major national laboratories. After prolonged debate, the committee voted 18-26 to defeat the amendment, which would have set specific targets for federal spending cuts at Energy labs over the following three fiscal years.

The amendment also would have established a commission to find ways to reduce funding for the labs by focusing on contracting reforms, increasing private investment and eliminating duplication between laboratories. "Real [Energy Department] reform must include mandated reductions in spending," said Kreidler, who referred to several General Accounting Office reports of wasteful spending at Energy labs.

But critics said the amendment would hurt important laboratory projects in such areas as environmental research. "A cut like this would cripple them," said Bill Richardson, D-N.M., whose state was home to both Sandia and Los Alamos national laboratories. Other members argued that because the Energy Department would continue to spend the money, Congress should focus on reforming the agency's entire budget. "This amendment will not save the government any money," said ranking Republican Carlos J. Moorhead of California.

Members instead approved, 23-20, an amendment by Mike Synar, D-Okla., that did not cut funding but called for the Energy Department to implement cost-saving measures at the laboratories over the following four years. ∎

## Chapter 5

ENVIRONMENT/ ENERGY

Environment

California Desert Protection 227
Superfund Reauthorization 231
Mining Law Rewrite 236
Safe Drinking Water................................. 238
Clean Water Law.................................... 241
   Corps Water Projects.......................... 242
EPA Cabinet Status 243
Risk Assessment Initiative.......................... 244
Montana Wilderness................................. 245
Idaho Wilderness................................... 247
National Park Management........................... 247
   Endangered Species Act 248
National Park Concessions 249
Park User Fees 251
'American Heritage Areas'........................... 252

Steamtown National Historic Site 252
Presidio Management................................ 253
Other National Park Legislation...................... 254
Pacific Northwest Timber Feud 256
Marine Mammal Protection........................... 257
   Rhinoceros and Tiger Conservation Fund............. 258
Fishing Law Reauthorization......................... 259
Interstate Transport of Solid Waste 261
   Waste 'Flow-Control' Legislation 262
Radioactive Waste 263
Environmental Technology........................... 263
Radon Disclosure Bill............................... 264
Other Environmental Legislation..................... 265

Energy

Strategic Petroleum Reserve 267
Other Energy-Related Legislation..................... 268

ENVIRONMENT

Fragile California Desert Bill Blooms Late in Session

*Bipartisan consensus reached on desire to preserve wilderness —
and leave town for last-minute campaigning*

An eight-year battle to protect a huge swath of California's fragile desert ended in the final days of the 103rd Congress with passage of the California Desert Protection Act (S 21). With control of the Senate up for grabs, some Republicans tried to deny sponsor Dianne Feinstein, D-Calif., and President Clinton an environmental victory. But the partisan appeal of keeping an area larger than the state of Maryland away from developers, combined with the lawmakers' desire to get out of town for the campaign season helped cut short a threatened Senate filibuster.

The House approved the conference report on the bill by voice vote Oct. 7. In the Senate, where Malcolm Wallop, R-Wyo., threatened a filibuster, Majority Leader George J. Mitchell, D-Maine, and Energy and Natural Resources Committee Chairman J. Bennett Johnston, D-La., pulled out all the stops to protect the win for Feinstein. In a dramatic Oct. 8 session, the Senate agreed to shut off debate on the bill and approved the conference report. Clinton signed the bill into law Oct. 31 (PL 103-433).

The pressure on Republicans and even some conservative Democrats, such as Richard C. Shelby of Alabama, was so fierce that Johnston called S 21 "the most intensely lobbied bill" in his 22 years in the Senate. Johnston said Republicans leaving a GOP caucus meeting before the vote told him: "This is the control of the Senate hanging in the balance."

The measure protected as wilderness about 7.5 million acres, stretching from the Sierra Nevada to the U.S.-Mexico border, and elevated national monument areas in Death Valley and at Joshua Tree to national parks. As a concession to hunters, the centerpiece Mojave area was designated a national preserve — a notch below the coveted national park status.

Early in the legislative session, Feinstein negotiated more than 50 changes to the bill to win over leery special interest groups and senators. She agreed to open up disputed parcels to mining, ranching, military overflights, border control activities and off-road-vehicle use.

The final bill also included a controversial amendment by Rep. W. J. "Billy" Tauzin, D-La., a vocal critic of the 1973 Endangered Species Act (PL 93-205). The amendment required the federal government to appraise private property needed for wilderness and national parks as though it did not contain

---

BOXSCORE

**California Desert Protection —
S 21** (HR 518). The final bill created the largest wilderness area outside Alaska, two new national parks in Death Valley and Joshua Tree and a national preserve in the Mojave Desert.

Reports: S Rept 103-165, H Rept 103-498; conference report H Rept 103-832.

KEY ACTION

April 13 — Senate passed S 21, 69-29.

July 27 — House passed HR 518, 298-128, then passed S 21 by voice vote after substituting the text of HR 518.

Oct. 7 — House adopted the conference report by voice vote.

Oct. 8 — Senate cleared the bill by voice vote, after voting 68-23 to end debate.

Oct. 31— President signed bill — PL 103-433.

---

endangered or threatened species, which he contended would produce higher property values.

The bill was the largest land protection measure enacted since 1980, when President Jimmy Carter signed the Alaska Lands Act, which protected about 103.4 million acres from development. *(1980 Almanac, p. 575)*

The desert measure authorized $300 million for land acquisition and $36 million over five years for park operations. The Congressional Budget Office estimated that it would cost $36 million over five years to operate the parks proposed in the bill and $100 million to $300 million to acquire the land.

Background

Legislation to protect the California desert had been hotly debated since 1986, when then-Sen. Alan Cranston, D-Calif., introduced a measure to include California desert land in the nation's park and wilderness system. Cranston continued to champion the bill, but its path in the Senate was blocked by then-Sens. Pete Wilson and John Seymour, Republicans of California, who prevented the bill from even getting a vote in committee. The House passed a desert protection bill in 1991, but Seymour blocked action in the Senate. *(1991 Almanac, p. 228)*

The legislation's fortunes improved dramatically in 1992 with the election of two Democratic senators from California, Feinstein and Barbara Boxer, effectively ending partisan squabbling between California senators. Clinton's election gave the measure White House backing for the first time.

The bill cleared a major hurdle in 1993, winning the approval of the Senate Energy Committee on Oct. 5 (S Rept 103-165); the vote was 13-7. Although Feinstein was not a member of the committee, she attended all three of its markups. Robert F. Bennett, R-Utah, said she was "willing to solve the problem instead of trumpeting the issue." That, he said, was unlike the approach taken by Cranston. *(1993 Almanac, p. 276)*

Senate Floor

The Senate passed the bill April 13 by a vote of 69-29, breaking a long deadlock and sending a strong message to

the House, which had yet to consider a companion bill (HR 518). *(Vote 89, p. 16-S)*

The bill was endorsed by Interior Secretary Bruce Babbitt and major environmental groups such as the Wilderness Society and Sierra Club.

The Senate bill designated 74 separate wilderness areas, including 3.7 million acres to be overseen by the Bureau of Land Management. It provided for the creation of a 1.2 million-acre Mojave National Park, the centerpiece of the legislation. The Death Valley and Joshua Tree national monuments were to be expanded and upgraded to national park status.

A Victory for Feinstein

The Senate action was heralded as a political victory for Feinstein. A freshman, Feinstein had campaigned in 1992 promising to pass the desert bill; she was up for re-election in November.

To get the measure onto the Senate floor, Feinstein brokered more than 50 specific changes to make it more acceptable to commercial users of the desert.

Once the bill was on the floor, Feinstein and Energy Committee Chairman Johnston were able to show that it had overwhelming support. Controversies over hunting and land acquisition quickly dissipated when Republicans declined to offer amendments that had failed in committee.

Intent on proving to colleagues that the bill would protect more than a vast, parched space void of anything but sand, Feinstein displayed numerous pictures of the area, which included the world's largest forest of cactus-like Joshua trees, 90 mountain ranges, the only known dinosaur tracks in California and more than 760 wildlife species, such as the threatened desert tortoise. "This is a unique and fragile piece of Americana," Feinstein said.

Few senators quibbled with her assertion that the resources needed protection. But Wallop, ranking member of the Energy Committee, led a chorus of senators who charged that the National Park Service could not afford to operate three new parks when it already was cutting back on operations and maintenance of existing facilities.

Wallop was supported on the floor by Appropriations Committee Chairman Robert C. Byrd, D-W.Va. Byrd warned that the National Park Service in the future could be forced to limit construction projects, cut back on land acquisition or hand over long-term responsibility for some park programs to private groups if the federal government continued to have budget constraints. "One does not go out and buy a Cadillac when one cannot keep up the payments on the family Ford," said Byrd, the only Democrat to vote against S 21 on final passage.

Babbitt, however, said the Interior Department had the financial resources and personnel to implement the bill. He said the department could decide to phase in the costs over a longer period.

Senate Floor Amendments

The Senate took up a number of amendments April 12.

Wallop tried to amend the bill to give the Mojave a national monument designation, a less protective and less expensive status. National monuments usually were smaller in scope and had fewer attractions than did national parks. Wallop's amendment was rejected 35-62. *(Vote 87, p. 16-S)*

Johnston won voice vote approval for an amendment to incorporate provisions of an unrelated bill (S 1586) that he sponsored to create a historical park commemorating New Orleans as the birthplace of jazz.

The Senate rejected, 34-64, an amendment by Bennett to

set a 10-year limit for the federal government to pay for the private lands it needed to create the three national parks in the California desert. Bennett's amendment would have prevented the government from designating the Mojave, Death Valley and Joshua Tree areas as national parks if 90 percent of the private lands were not acquired. In opposition, Johnston argued that the amendment would give veto power over land acquisition deals to any single property owner. *(Vote 88, p. 16-S)*

By voice vote, the Senate approved a Wallop amendment to clarify the rights of law enforcement authorities to use parts of the desert to sweep for illegal drugs and immigrants. The Senate also adopted by voice votes two Johnston amendments to allow livestock grazing to continue in some parks and wilderness areas indefinitely.

House Committee

The legislation moved another step forward May 4 when the House Natural Resources Committee voted 28-14 along party lines to approve a companion bill (HR 518 — H Rept 103-498), sponsored by Richard H. Lehman, D-Calif.

Committee Republicans, who voted unanimously against the bill, objected to the costs of creating three new national parks and to the way Democrats pushed the bill through the committee.

Although the House and Senate bills were largely the same, the House measure provided for a slightly larger Mojave National Park. Committee Chairman George Miller, D-Calif., included about 276,000 acres owned by the state of California and a development company controlled by the state employees' pension fund. The Senate Energy and Natural Resources Committee had dropped that land from the park.

Feinstein had urged the committee to add the private land, which was in Lanfair Valley and had long been targeted for acquisition by the federal government. Some tracts were squeezed between federal lands, forming a checkerboard pattern that was difficult for the government to manage.

The Senate Energy Committee had removed Lanfair Valley from its bill because of concerns about how long it would take to acquire the private property. But environmentalists said the land contained some of the area's most precious wildlife and natural resources and should be acquired and protected under the bill.

The House and Senate bills also differed slightly in provisions that would allow livestock grazing in the proposed Mojave and Death Valley national parks and the number of trails and roads that would be available to off-road vehicle riders.

The committee rejected, 17-25, an amendment by Larry LaRocco, D-Idaho, that would have have allowed hunting in the Mojave by designating the area a national preserve instead of a national park. LaRocco was expected to offer it again on the floor.

Throughout the markup, Republicans objected that the bill had not been properly vetted, that it had bypassed the National Parks Subcommittee and that Miller had made last-minute changes without their input. Miller snapped that a member "had to be Rip Van Winkle" not to know the issues covered by the measure.

GOP attempts to rein in the far-reaching bill through amendments were unsuccessful.

The committee rejected, 16-27, an amendment by Republicans James V. Hansen of Utah and John J. "Jimmy" Duncan Jr. of Tennessee to limit the bill's authorization to $36 million for construction and operational costs and $300 mil-

lion for land acquisition costs. Like the Senate bill, HR 518 authorized "such sums as necessary." Duncan echoed arguments made in the Senate that the government could not afford new national parks when it was having trouble keeping up with the maintenance and operations of existing ones.

The committee also rejected, 17-23, a Lehman amendment to allow additional trails and roads to be used by off-road vehicles.

To make HR 518 conform with the Senate bill, Miller said he was negotiating with Armed Services Committee Chairman Ronald V. Dellums, D-Calif., about a floor amendment to remove protection for certain desert lands that the military needed for overflights and training. Miller chose that route to avoid sending HR 518 to the Armed Services panel for its consideration.

House Floor

The House passed HR 518 July 27, after a protracted and bitter floor debate. The 298-128 vote on passage belied the difficulty that Miller had in steering the bill through a crowded legislative calendar and past a barrage of amendments by Republican opponents. *(Vote 357, p. 108-H)*

The House then called up S 21, amended it with the text of HR 518 and passed it by voice vote.

Republicans were able to win concessions on hunting and private property appraisals but failed to dramatically reduce the bill's size and scope. The drawn-out debate was piecemeal: Often the bill was bumped from the floor to make way for appropriations bills and other more pressing matters.

The bill was opposed by five House Republicans who represented parts of the desert: Jerry Lewis, Al McCandless, Duncan Hunter, Bill Thomas and Howard P. "Buck" McKeon. They argued that it was a costly proposal that would block off huge tracts to residents, recreation enthusiasts and commercial users.

When floor action began May 17, the House approved an unusual rule governing debate that required all amendments to be printed in advance in the Congressional Record. The rule allowed for up to 41 amendments.

Because of the Memorial Day recess and other legislative business, the House did not begin debate on the amendments until June 10. As each proposed change came up, the five California Republicans used the amendment as an opportunity to repeat their objections to the bill and drag out debate. Lewis said his strategy was to thoroughly go over issues that Republicans did not get a chance to air during committee markups in May. Democrats said it was a stall tactic aimed at weakening or killing the bill.

Republicans sought to cast the debate as a referendum on Miller's leadership. "In this case, the chairman has been so arbitrary," said Lewis. "He has not bothered to discuss his proposals with people who represent the desert." Democrat Bruce F. Vento of Minnesota, chairman of the Natural Resources Subcommittee on National Parks, defended the chairman, saying Republican actions were "excessive and petulant" during the debate. "Miller's position is you do not start negotiating when you know we are going to win," he said. "What is he supposed to do in the name of comity, give up 2 million acres of wilderness?"

Stop-and-Go Debate

Floor debate got under way June 10, and at the outset, Republicans generally were unsuccessful in pressing their case. For example, the House rejected, 169-191, an amendment by Richard W. Pombo, R-Calif., that would have allowed off-road vehicle riders to continue to use nearly 200 roads in the desert. *(Vote 231, p. 70-H)*

Amid the partisan wrangling, the House did approve an amendment June 10 to allow the Navy to construct a space energy laser facility on the China Lake Naval Air Warfare Center. The amendment by Thomas of California was approved 396-1. The House also approved 389-0 an amendment by Hunter to broaden the authority of law enforcement agencies to use the wilderness and national park areas to control drug trafficking and illegal immigration. *(Votes 229, 230, p. 70-H)*

As debate plodded along June 13, Miller pleaded with the House's presiding officer to object to the Republicans' repeated requests for long discussions. Otherwise, Miller said, "we are just simply never going to get through the list of amendments."

But Lewis believed Republicans were gaining ground with some of their amendments. For example, the House approved, 360-0, an amendment to give the state of California the authority to protect fish and wildlife in federally protected desert areas and allow state agencies to use motorized vehicles to gain access to those public lands. Hunter said his amendment, which was modified by McCandless, was necessary to allow California to maintain watering holes for bighorn sheep and deer. *(Vote 232, p. 70-H)*

Vento argued that the Hunter amendment would set a precedent by not giving a federal agency such as the Bureau of Land Management access to lands that were in federal jurisdiction. Vento offered a substitute amendment to clarify a federal agency's role in protecting fish and wildlife in the California desert, but it was rejected, 183-189. *(Vote 233, p. 70-H)*

During the week of July 11, the House adopted two significant amendments — one sought by hunters and the other pushed by lawmakers seeking to weaken the 1973 Endangered Species Act (PL 93-205).

Hunting in the Mojave

On July 12, the House voted 239-183 in favor of LaRocco's amendment to allow hunting to continue on 1.5 million acres of the Mojave desert. *(Vote 316, p. 94-H)*

The amendment altered the protected status of the Mojave, designating it as a national preserve instead of a national park. The two labels offered virtually the same protections, but the preserve designation explicitly allowed hunting as long as the natural values of an area were not harmed. LaRocco called it a "common sense" compromise that should appeal to environmentalists who wanted to protect the desert and to hunters who wanted to continue hunting the deer, rabbits and other game found in the Mojave. Hunting was forbidden in national parks.

The House had approved a similar hunting proposal in 1991 on a 235-193 vote. LaRocco had the support of the Congressional Sportsmen's Caucus, a bipartisan group that advocated hunting and trapping and had about 180 members in the House.

Opponents argued that the LaRocco amendment would undermine the bill's conservation goals, raise concerns about safety and go against the wishes of California residents. A 1993 Field Poll showed 75 percent of Californians supported creating a Mojave National Park, even after they were told of a hunting ban.

Miller, Lehman and Vento hoped to scale back the hunting amendment during conference.

Endangered Species

On July 14, the House overwhelmingly adopted an amendment by Tauzin aimed at increasing the value of private land

in the desert that contained endangered species. Tauzin's amendment passed 281-148. *(Vote 325, p. 96-H)*

Specifically, the Tauzin amendment called for the federal government to ignore any endangered species or land-use restrictions, such as local zoning laws, when appraising privately owned property for wilderness designation. He said the provision would allow desert landowners to sell their property to the federal government at a higher price.

Tauzin had won a similar battle in 1993 on a separate measure to authorize the National Biological Survey. Tauzin and others feared the survey bill (HR 1845) would become a tool to expand the endangered species law and restrict property rights if the federal government found endangered or threatened species living on privately owned land. *(1993 Almanac, p. 272)*

Miller said Tauzin's amendment was designed to provide hours of debate on the Endangered Species Act. Debate dragged on for so long that Miller was unable to finish the bill and had to scuttle plans to hold a news conference to hail its passage. In the end, Miller said he thought Tauzin's amendment would have little actual impact in the desert. About 700,000 acres covered in the bill were privately owned, but it was unknown how many parcels contained endangered species.

Moving to a Final Vote

In other action, the House on July 12 rejected, 190-207, an amendment by Vento that would have phased out grazing on federal land in the proposed Death Valley National Park. The bill allowed grazing to continue indefinitely. *(Vote 315, p. 94-H)*

Lawmakers also rejected, 145-274, an amendment by Tom DeLay, R-Texas, that would have prohibited the government from acquiring private land for the proposed Mojave National Park by condemnation. *(Vote 317, p. 94-H)*

On July 13, the House approved, 419-0, an amendment by Miller to allow all landowners in the proposed Mojave park area to exchange their private property for surplus or excess federal lands. *(Vote 319, p. 94-H)*

On July 27, lawmakers rejected, 138-288, an amendment by Ken Calvert, R-Calif., to delay the effective date of the bill until the backlog of lands that the National Park Service already was authorized to acquire had been reduced by 50 percent. *(Vote 355, p. 106-H)*

Miller then moved to limit the time allowed for further debate; the House approved the motion, 246-179, as supporters cheered. *(Vote 356, p. 108-H)*

Members rejected, by voice vote, an amendment by Barbara F. Vucanovich, R-Nev., to allow the Bureau of Mines to waive any provision that resulted in the United States' needing to import an amount of a mineral exceeding 90 percent of 1992 consumption.

Lewis withdrew a substitute amendment, based on a bill (HR 2379) he introduced in 1993, that would have designated 2.3 million acres of wilderness in the area. It would have created no new national parks but would have expanded the Death Valley and Joshua Tree national monuments.

Conference/Final Action

If anything, the road to enactment grew rougher as the bill moved toward conference, buffeted by deepening partisanship and election fever.

The standoff underscored the zeal of Republicans in both chambers to deny Feinstein a legislative victory before she headed home to campaign against a surprisingly strong challenge by Rep. Michael Huffington, R-Calif. The stakes were high: Republicans had their eyes on the California seat as a key element in their drive to take control of the Senate.

The bitter feelings and depth of partisan discord were apparent on the House side Oct. 4, when Lewis and other California Republicans used arcane procedural rules to demand 12 roll call votes and tie up five hours of floor time before the House finally sent the measure to a conference committee. *(Votes 463-474, pp. 138-H, 140-H)*

"This is indicative of how far the Republicans are prepared to go to upset this bill, believing it will upset Sen. Feinstein's election," said Miller.

Concerned about media reports that had touted a conference agreement even before negotiators formally met late Oct. 4, Lewis and the other Republicans said their last-ditch floor battle was aimed at making sure Miller would not abandon the provisions on hunting and land appraisals for property owners. But the Republicans conceded that there was no way they could prevent the House from appointing conferees and reconciling differences in the House and Senate versions of the bill.

In the Senate, Wallop slowed the usually pro forma step of sending the bill to conference. He denied his opposition was political. "If you phrased the question differently and asked if people would support a park if it meant cutting Yosemite's budget or reducing the number of park employees, they would say no," he said. "But that is precisely what this bill does."

On Sept. 23, the Senate voted 73-20 to shut off debate on a motion to disagree with House amendments to the bill, the first of three steps to go to conference. *(Vote 305, p. 90-H)*

Majority Leader Mitchell finally reached an agreement with Senate Republicans to send the measure to conference on Oct. 4. That left little time to get the measure back through both chambers before the targeted Oct. 7 adjournment.

A Quick Conference

Producing a compromise version of the bill was the easy part. On the key provisions, Miller and Johnston easily combined the mostly similar House and Senate measures. The committee chairmen and their staffs had been meeting privately for weeks to resolve differences.

The final bill created the largest wilderness area outside Alaska, two new national parks in Death Valley and Joshua Tree and a national preserve in the Mojave Desert.

Overall, the bill designated 69 wilderness areas covering 3.5 million acres, scattered from the Sierra Nevada to the U.S.-Mexico border, and protected about 4 million acres inside the two parks and preserve as wilderness. In a key concession to the bill's opponents, the measure allowed hunting of small game to continue within the 1.4 million-acre Mojave National Preserve.

Conferees agreed to set aside desert lands within the China Lake Naval Weapons Center and Chocolate Mountain Aerial Gunnery Range for 20 years for use by the military for overflights and training. The House bill had recommended 15 years; the Senate, 25 years.

Johnston was able to keep as part of the conference report unrelated Senate-passed provisions to establish a national park in his home state of Louisiana to commemorate New Orleans as the birthplace of jazz and authorize several studies in the Lower Mississippi Delta aimed at sparking economic development in the impoverished region.

Even before the conference began, Feinstein said she was ready to accept the House-passed language on hunting and preserve status for the Mojave. She said the House vote was too

strong to ignore. But in return, Feinstein said she wanted the House to agree to a Senate-passed package of roads for motorized vehicles. The change was accepted by the conferees.

Final Passage

The House adopted the conference report (H Rept 103-832) by voice vote Oct. 7.

About 10 hours after the House had closed up shop until after the November elections, the Senate voted 68-23 on Oct. 8 to shut off debate on the bill and then gave final voice vote approval to the conference report. With the measure cleared for the president's signature, the Senate adjourned later that day, leaving the California desert bill as the only major environmental law of the 103rd Congress. *(Vote 326, p. 57-S)*

The final vote, while providing its own moments of high drama, actually represented a key concession by opponents, who agreed late Oct. 7 to forgo the two-day layover allowed them under Senate rules for a motion to invoke cloture, thereby limiting debate.

After forcing the bill to be read line-by-line and trying to remove visiting Interior Secretary Babbitt from the Senate floor, Wallop and other Republicans consented to let the cloture vote occur first thing Saturday morning, rather than at 12:01 a.m. Sunday, as Majority Leader Mitchell had threatened.

The importance of the vote was underscored by an extra-ordinary effort to get bill supporters to the chamber on Saturday. Mindful of the wishes of some senators to be at home campaigning but needing every Democratic vote possible that Saturday, Mitchell even arranged for a private plane to ferry one senator back to Washington.

The pivotal 60th vote to invoke cloture came from Carol Moseley-Braun, D-Ill., who ran into the Senate chamber with only minutes to spare on the Senate's voting clock, much to the relief of a clearly worried Feinstein. The electronically controlled garage door at Moseley-Braun's Washington home malfunctioned, and she had to catch a cab to Capitol Hill.

Once Moseley-Braun provided Feinstein with enough votes to end the filibuster, some of the bill's GOP supporters, who had been nervously holding back, quickly cast "yea" votes. Among them were Pete V. Domenici of New Mexico and Nancy Landon Kassebaum of Kansas. John W. Warner, R-Va., who had cast a "nay" vote early in the voting period, switched his vote to "yea" for the final tally.

On the Senate floor, Feinstein hugged and personally thanked some of the bill's bipartisan supporters who had changed their own campaign plans to help her, including William V. Roth Jr., R-Del.; Frank R. Lautenberg, D-N.J.; and Jim Sasser, D-Tenn. Sasser landed at Washington National Airport minutes before the vote.

In the end, 54 of the Senate's 56 Democrats and 14 Republicans voted to invoke cloture. ■

No Floor Action on Superfund Bill

A proposal to overhaul the nation's troubled hazardous waste cleanup program died in the final weeks of the 103rd Congress, derailing one of the Clinton administration's top environmental initiatives. Although the legislation (HR 3800, S 1834) won bipartisan approval from five committees, it failed to make it to the floor of either chamber. Instead, it fell victim to a combination of partisan politics, disputes over labor and tax provisions and a final rush to adjournment.

Supporters and opponents alike predicted a major rematch in 1995, when the taxes that supported the so-called superfund program were due to expire.

The Clinton administration's proposal was designed to institute an arbitration process that would put an end to the protracted litigation that had snarled the superfund cleanup effort. In contrast to existing law, under which a single party could be held liable, the proposal also sought to spread cleanup costs among the companies responsible for polluting a site.

An unusual coalition of polluters, insurers and environmentalists, bound together by a mutual concern over skyrocketing litigation costs, backed the legislation.

But supporters threw in the towel Oct. 5 after House sponsor Al Swift, D-Wash., administration officials and lobbyists from business and environmental groups conceded that they had run out of time to push the bill through both chambers and a conference com-

BOXSCORE

Superfund Reauthorization (HR 3800, S 1834). The bills sought to accelerate the cleanup of the nation's worst toxic waste sites by discouraging litigation and spreading cleanup costs among polluters.

Reports: H Rept 103-582, Parts 1-3; S Repts 103-349, 103-389.

KEY ACTION

May 18 — House Energy and Commerce approved HR 3800, 44-0.

July 28 — House Public Works approved HR 3800 by voice vote.

Aug. 19 — House Ways and Means approved HR 3800 by voice vote.

Aug. 3 — Senate Environment and Public Works approved S 1834, 13-4.

Sept. 28 — Senate Finance approved S 1834 by voice vote.

mittee. "We just slammed up against the time clock," said Jamie Wickett, a lobbyist for the National Federation of Independent Business, a small-business group supporting the effort.

The bill had been limping along since August, slowed by disagreements over tax and labor provisions. Senate Minority Leader Bob Dole, R-Kan., a critic of the bill's liability provisions, delivered the death blow Sept. 28 when he threatened to unleash a flurry of amendments on the Senate floor if the bill came up.

Key issues that stalled the measure included:

● **Insurance taxes.** Small and medium-size insurers protested a provision in both the House and Senate versions that would have levied $8.1 billion in new commercial liability insurance taxes. The money was to go into a fund to settle legal disputes between polluters and their insurers over the cleanup of sites that had lingered on the Environmental Protection Agency (EPA) priority list since 1985. The provision was backed by the American Insurance Association, which included many large insurers.

The dispute delayed action on the bill for several critical weeks in August and September while the administration tried to work out a compromise.

● **Wages.** Businesses strongly opposed a House provision requiring superfund contractors who received federal money

to pay their workers the prevailing local wage, often set by union contracts, as called for by the Davis-Bacon Act. They said such a change in the law would be so expensive that it would almost outweigh any savings gained from reducing the amount of superfund litigation.

The Davis-Bacon controversy stalled the bill in the House Rules Committee throughout September, effectively preventing it from reaching the floor. Although House leaders also were at odds over controversial amendments requiring assessments of the costs of meeting environmental regulations, superfund supporters pointed to the labor flap as the final blow to the bill.

● **Cleanup standards.** Some conservative lawmakers also opposed a provision requiring the EPA to set a single cleanup goal for all sites. Further muddying the waters, the Senate version called for more stringent standards than did the House version. The Senate bill required the EPA to ensure that anyone exposed to a treated site would have a "reasonable certainty of no harm" — generally interpreted as a one-in-a-million chance of getting cancer.

Background

Both bills were designed to overhaul the 1980 Comprehensive Environmental Response, Compensation and Liability Act (PL 96-510), known as the superfund law. The law required polluters to pay to clean up the worst hazardous waste sites or reimburse the EPA for the cost of doing the job. To finance such cleanups, the law established the superfund, which was fed primarily by a tax on oil and chemical manufacturers and an environmental tax on companies.

Superfund originally was envisioned as a five-year, $1.6 billion program to clean up Love Canal in New York and about 400 other toxic waste sites.

But the effort quickly became mired in litigation, and relatively few sites were cleaned up. By the beginning of 1994, the federal government, polluters, insurers and the states had spent roughly $13 billion on the superfund program since its inception, but only 256 of 1,345 priority toxic waste sites so far identified by the EPA had been cleaned up; 168 more were in the final stages of cleanup. A study by the Congressional Budget Office released Jan. 31 estimated that it could take $75 billion to clean up a total of about 4,500 sites that were in need of work.

Deciding which companies or individuals were responsible for cleaning up hazardous waste sites was one of the biggest failures of the superfund program. Polluters often went to court to find other polluters — such as municipalities that hauled household garbage to toxic waste sites — to share the cleanup costs. Polluters also often sued their insurance companies when they balked at paying claims filed to recover cleanup costs. EPA Administrator Carol M. Browner said it could take as long as 15 years to traverse a maze of litigation and actually clean up a toxic waste site.

"A lot of lawyers' kids have gone through college on superfund money," said Michael G. Oxley, R-Ohio, who played a key role in crafting the legislation.

Clinton's Proposal

Clinton made passage of a superfund bill one of his top three environmental priorities for the year. Seizing upon widespread dissatisfaction with the 1980 law, the administration brought together key business, environmental, insurance and community groups to draft an overhaul plan.

On Feb. 3, Browner unveiled the administration plan, quickly characterized as a "fragile compromise." The plan retained the backbone of the superfund law: the principle

that polluters should pay to clean up their own waste sites. But the proposal abandoned the existing policy that allowed the EPA to track down a single polluter — regardless of how much waste was disposed of — and force that polluter to pay all the costs. It was that policy that created the incentive for polluters to try to force their insurers or other responsible parties to share in the expense — leading to thousands of lawsuits and little cleanup.

The liability of polluters that had contributed only incidentally to a hazardous waste site was to be limited. All other polluters were to be given incentives to join an arbitration process to determine how to allocate costs. Polluters that refused to submit to such negotiations would be liable for the entire cleanup costs, as they were under existing law, even if they only marginally contributed to the hazardous waste.

The proposal called for setting aside $300 million a year to pay so-called orphan cleanup costs incurred by polluters that either could not be identified by the government or that were defunct or insolvent.

The Clinton proposal also called for a new trust fund to be made up of taxes levied on property and casualty insurers. The goal was to raise $3 billion over five years to settle old insurance claims stemming from toxic waste problems on a superfund site before 1986.

The Clinton plan also attempted to make cleanup standards more flexible. Existing law treated all sites the same, requiring the future home of an urban parking lot to be as free of hazardous wastes as the site of a housing subdivision. Clinton's plan took the future use of the site into consideration, requiring tougher standards for sites that would be used for housing and recreation, less stringent standards for land that would be converted to shopping malls or industrial centers. The issue was a continuing source of conflict throughout the year. Environmentalists wanted uniform standards to be set for all sites across the country, while industry wanted more flexibility.

The plan also allowed citizens who lived near toxic waste sites to have a say in deciding how far to clean up their neighborhoods before such jobs actually began — a provision that many environmental groups welcomed. The EPA estimated that about 73 million people lived near toxic waste sites.

Key Provisions

The House and Senate bills both largely reflected the administration's proposal. Both contained provisions authorizing the appointment of independent, third-party arbiters to determine how much each polluter should pay. A polluter could accept or reject the arbiter's decision. But a polluter who opted to fight the decision would be subject to higher cleanup costs and more lawsuits.

Both bills provided for the creation of an Environmental Insurance Resolution Fund to settle outstanding insurance claims made by polluters before 1986, when insurance companies began writing new hazardous waste policies that more accurately estimated the high cost of cleaning up such sites.

The fund was to be fed by a tax on insurance companies that was expected to raise $3 billion over five years and $8 billion over 10 years. A board consisting of Treasury and EPA officials and members from the private sector was to oversee the distribution of settlements from the fund.

Companies identified as polluters would apply to the fund for money instead of suing their insurers to pay for cleanups. The administrators would offer a company a settlement based on the percentage that had been determined by studying the history of court decisions in polluter-insurer lawsuits related to superfund.

The amount of money a polluter could expect to get from the fund to settle a pre-1986 insurance claim would be less than that granted in legal settlements of similar court cases. Just the same, polluters were expected to favor a chance to avoid prolonged and costly litigation.

A polluter could opt out of the plan if the company or individual decided it could receive a larger settlement from a court, but not without a risk. The Senate bill required that polluters who lost such lawsuits pay up to 40 percent of their insurance companies' legal fees. The House bill also allowed polluters to opt out but did not penalize them if they went to court and lost. Such a provision was dropped from HR 3800 before the Energy and Commerce Committee marked up the bill because of objections from the insurance companies, which wanted to recover up to 50 percent of their legal fees.

Both bills also provided $300 million annually to clean up sites polluted by companies that were defunct or determined insolvent by the federal government.

House Energy and Commerce

The Energy and Commerce Committee was the first of three House panels with jurisdiction to take up the legislation. On May 11, the committee's Transportation and Hazardous Materials Subcommittee approved a bill reflecting the administration's proposal. The vote was 21-0.

The subcommittee approved by voice vote an amendment by Rick Boucher, D-Va., Fred Upton, R-Mich., and Blanche Lambert, D-Ark., to overhaul the way liability for cleaning up hazardous waste sites was determined.

The amendment provided for the appointment of independent third-party arbiters who would determine how much each polluter should pay. Parties that contributed less than 1 percent of waste to the site, including small businesses, would be given expedited settlements by the EPA.

Participants that agreed to pay the share of cleanup costs determined by the arbitration process would be shielded from further legal action and from any further liability for cleanup costs. Any party that rejected the allocation decisions would be subject to the old rules of liability — potentially unlimited liability and future lawsuits.

The bill included the $300 million annual cleanup fund to cover so-called orphan costs. It also required the government to reimburse polluters that already had paid cleanup costs for any amount that an arbitrator determined was in excess of their fair share.

Boucher and Upton also settled a fight between the EPA and potential polluters over how much power the government should have to reject the arbitrator's decision. Industry lobbyists had argued for little or no government intervention. In the end, Boucher, Upton and Lambert won voice vote approval for an amendment to bar the government from altering the determination of an arbiter unless there was proof of bias, fraud, procedural irregularity or unlawful or "irrational" conduct.

The bill included the creation of the Environmental Insurance Resolution Fund to settle insurance claims that dated before 1986, with insurers paying as much as $8.1 billion in taxes into the fund over 10 years.

There was a catch, however, that drew protests from many insurers. The fund was to be dissolved and the fees returned to the insurers unless 85 percent of the eligible parties accepted settlements offered by fund administrators.

The Alliance of American Insurers, which represented about 220 insurers, opposed the idea of a fund and pressed lawmakers to do away with retroactive liability for cleanups all together. But the American Insurance Association, which con-

trolled the lion's share of industry revenues and held most superfund policies, worked with lawmakers to create the fund.

The panel gave voice vote approval to an amendment by Dan Schaefer, R-Colo., to allow states to win EPA permission to begin cleanups at any facility within their borders, as long as they complied with EPA rules. States also could be delegated to carry out EPA rules covering cleanups at federal facilities. Lawmakers approved by voice vote an amendment by Oxley to encourage states to set up voluntary cleanup programs, with technical, financial and other assistance from the EPA.

The bill made the thoroughness of a cleanup contingent on the future use of the site. In a bow to the environmental lobby, the bill required the EPA to set some broad national standards for cleaning up the most commonly found chemical contaminants. But cleanup plans could be adjusted to account for the future use of a site, the cost of cleanup methods and the site's proximity to "residences, sensitive populations or ecosystems, natural resources or areas of unique historic or cultural significance."

Lawmakers dropped a provision backed by environmentalists that could have led to stiffer cleanup standards for industrial use sites adjacent to neighborhoods, possibly making them as contaminant-free as a residential area. But environmentalists did win a provision to codify the existing practice of treating all ground water as drinking water.

Full Committee Action

The House Energy and Commerce Committee gave speedy approval to the superfund overhaul May 18, voting 44-0 to report the bill (H Rept 103-582, Part 1).

Chairman John D. Dingell, D-Mich., asked members to refrain from offering controversial amendments, and they cooperated in part out of deference to Swift, who had made passage of the measure a priority before he retired at the end of the year.

The panel did approve six non-controversial amendments by voice vote with little debate.

One, by W. J. "Billy" Tauzin, D-La., barred the EPA from placing liens on the properties of people who were not being held responsible for the cost of cleaning up a toxic site. It also barred the agency from placing liens on property owned by people who had erroneously been informed, during an audit or inquiry by a federally certified environmental inspector, that their land was free of hazardous substances.

The panel approved amendments by Cardiss Collins, D-Ill., to require the EPA to make it easier for minority-owned companies to win superfund cleanup contracts; and by Thomas J. Manton, D-N.Y., to allow the EPA to accept payment plans, or annuities, from responsible parties in a cleanup settlement.

House Public Works

The House Public Works Subcommittee on Water Resources and Environment gave voice vote approval July 27 to a consensus substitute offered by ranking Republican Sherwood Boehlert of New York.

The subcommittee-approved substitute changed several liability provisions in the bill. For example, it let companies that dumped only minimal amounts of waste at a site off the hook for any cleanup costs. Municipalities that hauled garbage to a superfund site or a small business that contributed minimally to the hazardous wastes could enter into expedited settlements with the EPA, thereby avoiding ongoing litigation and financial uncertainty. Perhaps most important, polluters that rejected EPA's arbitration process could face steeper liability for a site's cleanup costs, including the

burden of cleaning up waste dumped by a defunct company.

On the issue of how to judge when a site was adequately clean, the substitute required the EPA to set two separate goals regarding health risks — one for chemical carcinogens and another for non-carcinogens. Those goals had to be met at all superfund sites except in those cases where it was "technically impracticable" or "unreasonably costly."

The most contentious debate during the subcommittee markup was over an attempt by Bill Zeliff, R-N.H., to exempt companies from retroactive liability. Zeliff said it was "un-American, immoral and unfair" to penalize companies retroactively when they were not required to keep records on such wastes. But after Boehlert and subcommittee Chairman Douglas Applegate, D-Ohio, said taxpayers would be left to pick up the tab if polluters did not pay, the subcommittee voted down the amendment, 13-25.

The subcommittee, though, approved 20-18 an amendment by Glenn Poshard, D-Ill., to restrict the EPA from recovering money from polluters for the cleanup of materials and contaminants that were not listed as hazardous.

Full Committee Action

The full Public Works Committee approved the bill July 28 by voice vote (H Rept 103-582, Part 2), after supporters beat back attempts to weaken key groundwater cleanup requirements and limit the bill's reach.

"I think this is one bill that is going to make its way through the whole process and is going to be signed into law by the president," said a hopeful Public Works Committee Chairman Norman Y. Mineta, D-Calif.

The amendment to weaken the groundwater provisions, offered by ranking member Bud Shuster, R-Pa., was rejected 30-34.

The bill already granted polluters leeway in treating ground water at a superfund site. Under existing law, polluters first had to attempt to clean polluted ground water to meet stringent federal safe drinking water standards. Only if such action appeared to be technically impractical could the effort be halted. In contrast, the committee bill allowed the EPA to determine at the outset whether the technology existed to make ground water clean enough to meet such standards.

The committee approved, 37-26, a highly controversial amendment by Nick J. Rahall II, D-W.Va., to require most superfund contractors to pay workers prevailing wages as required by the Davis-Bacon Act of 1931. The amendment drew opposition from Republicans and Southern Democrats who warned that it would add billions of dollars to the cost of cleaning up hazardous waste.

Supporters also beat back, 20-42, another effort by Zeliff to exempt companies from liability for any hazardous waste delivered to a site before 1987.

In other action, the Public Works Committee rejected, 28-37, a proposal by Mike Parker, R-Miss., to collect a user fee from dry cleaners in exchange for a partial exemption from superfund liability.

The committee also defeated, 26-36, a proposal by Jennifer Dunn, R-Wash., to have states pay half the cost of providing information to local communities about superfund cleanups.

House Ways and Means

After a protracted debate over who should pay how much to clean up hazardous waste sites, the House Ways and Means Committee on Aug. 19 gave voice vote approval to a compromise package that included $8.1 billion in retrospective and prospective insurance taxes (H Rept 103-582, Part 3).

The compromise had been put together by the Treasury Department, breaking a weeklong impasse over the bill as Congress headed toward its August recess. "It's not exactly what every one of us would like," said Barbara B. Kennelly, D-Conn., who initially opposed any retroactive levy. "This is the best attempt to come to some understanding."

Disputes over the tax issue had delayed committee action on the bill for weeks. Clinton proposed to raise $8 billion over 10 years for the Environmental Insurance Resolution Fund. Of that total, 70 percent was to come from a retroactive tax on insurance companies that wrote liability policies for hazardous waste from 1971 to 1985. The remaining 30 percent was to be raised by a tax on insurers who wrote such policies after the bill's enactment.

The insurance industry was divided over the proposal. Large companies that wrote the superfund-related liability policies of the 1970s and early 1980s did not want to be taxed retroactively. But insurers who had had little to do with such policies resisted a prospective tax that would put some of the superfund burden on them.

At a series of meetings during the week of Aug. 15, the Treasury Department struck a deal with a large segment of the insurance industry, agreeing to raise about half the money from taxes retroactive to 1968 and half from taxes that would take effect after the bill's enactment.

But the deal also raised taxes on a group that was not invited to the bargaining table: Reinsurers, who covered various commercial liability policies.

Specifically, the compromise retained the 70-30 split for the first four years of the tax, although reinsurers were made responsible for about 36 percent of the retroactive taxes. For the last six years, the prospective portion was to increase to 65 percent. About 25 percent was to come from taxes on past reinsurance policies, and 10 percent from payments and claims made by the fund to cover past standard policies.

The tax issue sparked two days of debate. Many members, such as Jim McDermott, D-Wash., who had favored a mostly retrospective tax, supported the compromise as a fair solution. Others remained unconvinced. Several members said they were concerned that the tax ultimately could result in higher premiums for insurance products that had nothing to do with superfund, such as homeowners' policies.

Meanwhile, the reinsurers reacted by launching a furious lobbying effort against the proposal. An amendment by Dan Rostenkowski, D-Ill., approved by voice vote, sought to meet the reinsurers part way by placing some of the tax on reinsurance settlements rather than on premiums.

The agreement also failed to appease many members of the National Association of Mutual Insurance Companies, who believed that the tax should be paid by companies entangled in past superfund liability.

Rules Committee

After winning approval from the three committees with jurisdiction over the superfund law, the bill died in the Rules Committee, which failed to issue a rule to govern floor debate on the bill. With the House deeply divided, the Rules Committee was unable to resolve two key issues:

● **Fair wages.** Oxley, the ranking Republican on the Energy and Commerce subcommittee, and Nathan Deal, D-Ga., wanted to offer floor amendments sharply curtailing or even eliminating the provision inserted into the House bill by Rahall requiring that most superfund contractors pay workers prevailing wages. William D. Ford, D-Mich., called for an alternative amendment that would have exempted

sites from the requirement if federal funding for the cleanup amounted to less than $100,000.

- **Risk assessment.** Conservatives, such as John L. Mica, R-Fla., wanted to require the EPA to do a cost-benefit analysis before before setting a cleanup standard. Disputes over the relative benefits and costs of environmental standards had snarled other environmental legislation during the year, including an overhaul of the 1974 Safe Drinking Water Act.

House leaders came close the week of Sept. 26 to brokering a deal stripping the Davis-Bacon language from the bill in the Rules Committee in exchange for barring Mica's risk-assessment amendment. They were so close to a deal that administration officials had a list Sept. 27 of the five floor amendments that the Rules Committee would permit. Rules had been expected to meet that day to vote on the ground rules for an eight-hour floor debate beginning Sept. 28. But liberal Democrats rebelled. "I don't intend to roll over and play dead," said Rahall, who argued that the House should retain the Davis-Bacon provision and prepare to fight for it in conference with the Senate.

Senate Environment Committee

On the Senate side, the administration's plan to overhaul the superfund law cleared its first hurdle June 14 when an Environment and Public Works panel approved its version of the bill (S 1834) on a 6-4 party-line vote. Republicans refrained from offering any amendments, knowing that Superfund Subcommittee Chairman Frank R. Lautenberg, D-N.J., had enough votes to defeat any attempt to alter the bill. But they said the measure would need major changes to receive their support.

Republicans, led by Robert C. Smith of New Hampshire and ranking member Dave Durenberger of Minnesota, said they voted against the measure because it did not go far enough to revamp the way the law allocated cleanup costs among polluters, failed to establish how clean a contaminated site should be and lacked GOP input. "I find myself in a situation where a deal has been cut, my colleagues have not been involved and we have not had a crack at making the policy," Durenberger said, referring to the administration's spade work that resulted in the bill.

Smith wanted to eliminate the superfund's retroactive liability provision. The other key issue raised by Republicans, particularly Durenberger, was the question of how clean a site should be. The bill required the EPA to determine the human health risk, if any, posed by exposure to a cleaned-up toxic waste site. That risk would be used to help determine how clean a site should be made. Durenberger said Congress, not the EPA, should establish a health risk threshold. He wanted the bill to require that regulators be flexible, allowing some sites to be less clean than others, especially if they were not to become the sites of residential developments.

The panel approved by voice vote a handful of non-controversial amendments, including proposals by:

- Barbara Boxer, D-Calif., to allow federal facilities such as military bases to be used as test sites for developing innovative cleanup technologies.
- Bob Graham, D-Fla., to help reduce the EPA's costs of overseeing the superfund program by allowing alternative administrative procedures.

Full Committee Action

The full Environment and Public Works Committee approved the bill Aug. 3 by a vote of 13-4, with three Republicans joining a united Democratic bloc in support of the measure (S Rept 103-349).

The biggest sparks of the day were set off when Smith offered an amendment to weaken a provision intended to encourage polluters to settle disputes over insurance claims out of court. Under the Senate bill, a polluter who refused to accept an arbitration settlement and instead sued its insurance company and lost had to pay 40 percent of the insurer's court costs. The American Insurance Association strongly backed the provision as a way to prevent polluters from continuing to sue their insurance companies to recover more money. The House bill did not include the provision. The amendment failed on an 8-9 vote.

The committee rejected, 5-12, a Smith amendment that would have exempted companies that dumped hazardous waste before 1980, when such action was legal, from any liability. Two Republicans — John H. Chafee of Rhode Island, ranking member on the committee, and Durenberger — joined the panel's 10 Democrats in opposing the amendment. The two also supported the overall bill. A third Republican, John W. Warner of Virginia, voted for the bill even though he wanted to limit its retroactive reach.

The support of moderate Republicans was considered critical to the bill's prospects in the Senate. Durenberger and Warner had been part of a united Republican opposition to the bill in subcommittee. Committee Chairman Max Baucus, D-Mont., won them over by compromising on the bill's groundwater cleanup requirements.

Instead of requiring polluters to spend millions of dollars to ensure that ground water was restored to drinking water standards, Baucus agreed to allow the EPA to ease standards when the cleanup was technically impractical. In such cases, polluters could simply contain the contaminated ground water to prevent it from leaking beyond the site. That provision was similar to the House language, although the House gave polluters more flexibility when containing slightly contaminated ground water.

Another provision included in the Senate bill directed the EPA to ensure that a waste site was cleaned up so that anyone coming into contact with the site would have a "reasonable certainty of no harm" — generally interpreted to mean a one-in-one million chance of getting cancer. The House bill gave the EPA more flexibility in setting cleanup standards.

Senate Finance Committee

The last panel to vote on the superfund overhaul was the Finance Committee, which approved the bill by voice vote Sept. 28 (S Rept 103-389). Chairman Daniel Patrick Moynihan, D-N.Y., had put off action while the committee focused on legislation to implement the General Agreement on Tariffs and Trade. By the time the committee acted, bill supporters conceded that they were unlikely to have enough time to overcome partisan politics in the Senate and resistance from organized labor in the House. Dole, who opposed the law's retroactive liability, flatly pronounced the bill dead because of a lack of time. "It's time to take a reality check," Dole said at the Finance Committee markup. "It's not going to happen."

Still, supporters refused to give up, drawing cheer from the success of a bipartisan group of Senate Finance Committee members in beating back a series of amendments that could have stalled the bill.

The most difficult issue facing the committee was the administration's proposal for new taxes on commercial liability insurers. Just hours before the markup, Treasury officials came up with a last-ditch compromise to exempt from the tax companies that wrote less than $200 million a year

in commercial liability policies — a proposal that smaller insurers still rejected.

Meanwhile, reinsurers, who had said they would support the Senate measure if it imposed the same tax rate on their businesses as on primary insurers, switched over to oppose the bill. The move came after the Joint Committee on Taxation issued a study Sept. 27 that showed the bill would impose more than twice the tax rate on their segment of the insurance industry than it would on primary insurers. Overall, reinsurers would face a tax rate on policies written between 1968 and 1985 of 0.48 percent, the study concluded. Direct insurers, in contrast, would face a tax rate on those policies of 0.22 percent.

Republicans also raised concerns about the scope of the taxes. Treasury officials recently had increased to $40 billion from $8.1 billion their estimates of the eventual cost of cleaning up lingering superfund sites.

"We are only partially funding a new entitlement program that creates a huge new obligation on the federal government in the form of a federal bailout of some of the larger property and casualty insurance companies," said Orrin G. Hatch, R-Utah.

Malcolm Wallop, R-Wyo., proposed to strip the Environmental Insurance Resolution Fund from the bill. The amendment failed, 7-13, with several moderate Republicans joining Democrats in voting against it.

Dole, along with Republicans Charles E. Grassley of Iowa and Bob Packwood of Oregon, offered an unrelated amendment that would have restored a 25 percent tax reduction for insurance costs to self-employed individuals. To fund the deduction, which had expired in 1993, the amendment would have repealed a new vaccine distribution program slated to go into effect Oct. 1.

Moynihan agreed that the deduction should be renewed. But he and other Democrats defended the vaccine program and said the deduction should not be tacked on to the superfund bill. The amendment was defeated, 6-14. A similar amendment by William V. Roth Jr., R-Del., that would have funded the deduction partly with a cigarette tax, was defeated, 4-13.

Finally, the committee defeated, 7-13, an amendment by Dole to grant tax relief to farmers who received disaster assistance. Democrats conceded that some of the amend-

ments were good policy, but they urged their colleagues to avoid bogging down the superfund bill.

Final Action

With just one week left before Congress' targeted Oct. 7 adjournment and a backlog of bills awaiting action, the prospects for getting the superfund bill through both chambers, a conference committee and final passage were nil.

In the Senate, Dole, whose end-of-session delaying tactics had stymied such Democratic initiatives as campaign finance reform, was threatening to unleash a series of floor amendments that could play havoc with the Senate's schedule.

Moreover, many Democrats facing tough re-election campaigns, including House Speaker Thomas S. Foley, D-Wash., were eager to wrap up the session and get back to the campaign trail as soon as possible. "I think there's really a resignation within Congress that . . . this is really a difficult piece of legislation that will fall off the plate," said Francis Bouchard, a lobbyist for the reinsurers.

At an Oct. 5 strategy session, supporters agreed reluctantly that it was time to give up.

Pressure to take action on superfund legislation was expected to be even greater in 1995, when the taxes that paid for the cleanups were slated to expire. Congress failed to renew the taxes on time when they last expired in 1985, ultimately leading to a delay of up to four years in some cleanups. But legislation to overhaul the 14-year-old program was sure to face many of the same hurdles in the 104th Congress. Conservatives said they would take aim at central provisions of the bill, possibly ripping apart the delicate fabric of the compromise between industry and environmentalists that helped advance the bill in 1994. "My guess is that we clear the decks and start over again," said Zeliff, who led the fight in the House against the bill's liability provisions.

"The best chance of getting this done before the funding runs out in '95 and this turns into a crisis," said Swift, "is to pick up where we left off and move ahead. The other scenario that is possible is that the moderates in industry, in the environmental movement, who really brought this together, get shoved aside by folks who want to wage a holy war, winner take all. And if that happens, I think it becomes a draw, blood on the floor, and nothing gets done." ∎

Rewrite of 1872 Mining Law Falls

A two-year effort to impose royalties and new environmental standards on companies that extracted gold, silver and other valuable minerals from public lands in the West came to an end Sept. 29, when environmentalists and the mining industry acknowledged they could not reconcile their differences over the proposed legislation (HR 322, S 775).

J. Bennett Johnston, D-La., chairman of the Senate Energy and Natural Resources Committee, who had worked hard to find a compromise acceptable to all sides, blamed the demise of the mining law overhaul on the mining industry. The industry, in turn, pointed fingers at environmentalists and the House for wanting too much.

Both chambers had passed bills in 1993 aimed at updating the 1872 Mining Law. Environmentalists had long attacked the frontier-era law, which allowed companies to mine public lands without paying a royalty to the federal government, contained few rules for the repair of damaged lands and pre-

sumed that mining was acceptable on virtually any federal parcel. Under the 1872 law, miners could buy federal land believed to contain valuable subsurface minerals by obtaining a "patent" for as little as $2.50 an acre.

Interior Secretary Bruce Babbitt and environmentalists wanted the law changed to provide a greater return to taxpayers for the commercial use of federal lands, impose tough reclamation standards to protect water supplies and give the secretary more authority to declare some parcels off-limits to hard-rock mining.

The mining industry argued that steep royalties and excessive regulations would drive operations to foreign countries or shut them down completely. The industry did not oppose paying a royalty, but it wanted to be able to deduct the costs of production and development first. The industry also argued that existing state laws were sufficient to repair damaged lands and that new federal regulations were unnecessary.

The defeat of the mining law overhaul was a stinging blow to Babbitt. Already chastened by a bitter fight over grazing fees and suffering from a White House more concerned about maintaining its Western support than in land reform, Babbitt had kept a low profile during the mining law debate. Environmentalists and industry privately criticized the secretary for not weighing in earlier or more forcefully in what was deemed by both groups to be an achievable goal for the session.

When negotiations for a compromise bill reached an impasse, Ralph Regula, R-Ohio, ranking member of the House Interior Appropriations Subcommittee, succeeded in winning a temporary change in the mining law as part of the fiscal 1995 Interior appropriations bill (HR 4602 — PL 103-332). The spending bill imposed a one-year moratorium on new mining patent applications, aimed at stopping the inexpensive sale of mineral-rich lands. An estimated 613 patents covering about 250,000 acres of federal land in the Rocky Mountain and Plains states were awaiting approval from the Interior Department. (Appropriations, p. 513)

Background

Lawmakers had tried since 1987 to revamp the 122-year-old mining law, among the last "homesteading" measures enacted to attract settlers to the Western frontier. But as with other natural resource and public lands issues, Western senators had long managed to outmuscle their House colleagues, and the effort to change the law had remained at a virtual standstill.

Prospects for an overhaul seemed to improve in 1993, however. Led by Babbit, the new administration put a priority on preservation of federal land. And concern about the budget deficit prompted a review of what industry was charged for using federal resources.

Clinton initially planned to include a new 12.5 percent royalty on hard-rock mineral sales as part of his proposed 1993 deficit-reduction package. Before submitting his budget, however, he bowed to Western lawmakers and dropped the proposal, though he promised to push the fee as part of separate legislation.

By the end of the first session, Congress seemed close to overhauling the mining law, though the two chambers remained relatively far apart on the actual mining royalties. (1993 Almanac, p. 261)

The House had given a major boost to supporters of an overhaul by passing a tough bill (HR 322 — H Rept 103-338) on Nov. 18, 1993, by a vote of 316-108. The lopsided vote was expected to give House negotiators extra leverage in conference.

HR 322, sponsored by Nick J. Rahall II, D-W.Va., represented an environmentalists' wish list. It called for an 8 percent royalty on the gross value of minerals extracted after deducting some transportation costs, and an end to the inexpensive transfer of public lands. It also mandated new reclamation standards patterned after regulations on the coal mining industry and gave the Interior secretary sweeping authority to close off lands unsuitable for mining and to deny companies operating permits if they violated environmental standards.

The Senate had passed a much leaner bill (S 775 — S Rept 103-45) by voice vote May 25, 1993; the Senate bill had the backing of the mining industry. In preparation for conference, the Senate on Nov. 22 passed HR 322 after substituting the text of its own bill.

Sponsored by Larry E. Craig, R-Idaho, the Senate bill provided for a 2 percent royalty on the net value of the mineral, after expensive development and production costs had been paid. The Senate measure deferred to existing state laws standards for land reclamation and gave no new powers to the Interior secretary.

Fearing that a stronger bill would never get past the Western-dominated Energy Committee, Johnston had swiftly moved S 775 with no amendments as what he called "a ticket to conference." Craig warned early that any deal that caused a loss of Western mining jobs would be blocked by a filibuster.

Although the bill did not clear in the first session, Babbitt imposed what the mining industry said was effectively a patent moratorium. He halted a Bush administration practice that expedited the review of mining patent applications. Barrick Goldstrike Mines Inc., a Canadian company developing a gold mine in Nevada, sued Babbitt over the delay and eventually won the legal battle in the spring of 1994.

On May 16, 1994, Babbitt held a news conference to sign seven deeds to Barrick that allowed the company to buy about 1,950 acres of public land — believed to contain an estimated $10 billion in gold — for less than $10,000. Babbitt used the occasion to underscore the need for mining law reform.

Final Negotiations

House and Senate conferees began formal negotiations to resolve their difference on the mining overhaul June 29. It was a multi-sided affair with Johnston in the middle. A consummate deal-maker who relished the role, Johnston quickly found himself trying to placate the six constituencies: industry, environmentalists, House Natural Resources Committee Chairman George Miller, D-Calif., and the House, Western Republicans on the Energy Committee, Babbitt and the Clinton administration, and, finally, Western Democrats such as Sen. Harry Reid of Nevada, whose votes were needed to block the GOP.

A flurry of proposals, eight by Johnston's count, went back and forth among the key players over a period of five months. None of the negotiating was done in public. Among the numerous Senate proposals were a sliding-scale royalty that would have imposed a higher fee for gold and copper miners, financial breaks for small and marginal mining operations and environmental standards that took into account state and federal concerns.

Johnston's final offer made late Sept. 28 included a 3.5 percent royalty, relatively tame provisions for the Interior secretary to block mining on fragile lands and a crucial concession by environmentalists that the federal government would not impose new water quality standards for mining. The industry and Western lawmakers had worried that environmentalists were trying to put ever-sensitive water issues in the hands of the Interior secretary. The proposal also included expanded authority for citizens to sue for violations of the law, a provision sought by environmentalists and opposed by industry.

The industry balked at the deal, preferring an earlier proposal floated Aug. 2 by Johnston and Reid. And Miller said the last proposal was unacceptable to the House.

During a Senate meeting billed as a conference committee session, Democrat Dale Bumpers of Arkansas, his chamber's leading advocate of mining law changes, said this was only the end of one battle, not the war.

"This is like fighting with my wife," Bumpers said. "Even those fights I win just ain't over." ∎

Safe Drinking Water Overhaul Fails

To the chagrin of the nation's governors and mayors, the two chambers of Congress could not agree on a final version of a measure to overhaul the 1974 Safe Drinking Water Act.

Legislation (S 2019, HR 3392) to make the law more flexible and less costly for states and local governments hit obstacles in the final hours of the 103rd Congress, despite nearly unanimous agreement that the law needed fixing. In a last-minute effort to put the Senate on record favoring action on its bill and perhaps to soften House resistance, Senate Environment Committee Chairman Max Baucus, D-Mont., attempted to bring a "clean" bill to the floor Oct. 7. But two key senators whose pet provisions were to be removed from the bill blocked action.

As a result, state and local government officials who had been clamoring for an overhaul for years had to continue to abide by the existing statute's rigid requirements for monitoring and testing contaminants found in drinking water supplies.

BOXSCORE

Safe Drinking Water Reauthorization — S 2019, HR 3392. The bills included a new revolving fund for states to improve drinking water systems, along with provisions to ease some regulations on state and local governments.

Reports: H Rept 103-745, Part 1; S Rept 103-250.

KEY ACTION

May 19 — Senate passed S 2019, 95-3.

Sept. 27 — House passed HR 3392 by voice vote.

Background

The 1974 Safe Drinking Water Act (PL 93-523), last reauthorized in 1986, set standards for removing contaminants from tap water and required states to protect groundwater supplies. The 1986 revisions to the act (PL 99-339) provided tougher requirements for the testing and monitoring of contaminants and new provisions to protect groundwater supplies. The law's authority to award grants to states and cities for drinking water programs expired in 1991 and had been kept alive with annual appropriations.

Driving the reauthorization effort were governors, mayors and operators of small water systems, who held up the safe drinking water law as a primary example of stringent federal regulations that were unaccompanied by sufficient funds to carry them out.

To address this concern, the Clinton administration on Sept. 8, 1993, called on Congress to make it easier and less costly for state and local officials to comply with major environmental mandates. Key administration proposals included a new five-year, $4.6 billion revolving loan fund for states to help pay for improvements to drinking water systems and an end to a provision in the drinking water act that required the Environmental Protection Agency (EPA) to set standards for 25 new contaminants every three years.

In addition, while the nation's drinking water supply was considered among the world's safest, a 1993 outbreak of water-borne diseases in Milwaukee and a breakdown at the facility that supplied drinking water to Washington, D.C., added to the pressure for changes in the law.

Senate Committee

Senate action on the legislation began March 24 in the Environment and Public Works Committee, which voted 17-0 in favor of a drinking water overhaul bill sponsored by Baucus. The committee bill, reported as S 2019 (S Rept 103-250), autho-

rized $6.6 billion over seven years for a new state revolving loan fund to allow state and local communities to improve drinking water quality.

The Environment Committee's unanimous vote belied the difficulty Baucus had in reaching consensus with committee Republicans, who had been supporting a coalition of governors, mayors and representatives of local water systems that opposed the original version of the bill. But after weeks of late-night negotiations, the committee's seven Republicans said they were able to support the measure after Baucus agreed to some compromises — for example, allowing small and rural water systems to waive more stringent federal requirements that applied to large urban water systems.

The changes did not entirely satisfy the coalition, led by the National Governors' Association, the U.S. Conference of Mayors and the National League of Cities, which made it clear it wanted the final bill to require fewer tests on contaminants and monitoring only of chemicals that posed risks to human health.

Baucus' attempts to placate the governors, mayors and small water suppliers, meanwhile, cost him the support of the Sierra Club and other environmental groups.

The committee-approved bill contained provisions to:

● **Funding.** Create a new state revolving loan fund to make money available to local governments to pay for the construction and repair of water systems. The loan fund was modeled after a similar clean water revolving loan fund authorized under the 1987 amendments to the Federal Water Pollution Control Act (PL 100-4) that paid for sewage treatment plant construction.

Local governments could use money from the proposed new fund to build drinking water treatment plants; states could use it to help prop up financially ailing water systems. The bill authorized $1 billion annually for the fund in fiscal years 1995 through 2000. It also authorized $600 million in fiscal 1994, money that already had been appropriated.

Baucus included a controversial provision to allow states to transfer money from the safe drinking water fund to the clean water fund to pay for drinking water improvements, or vice versa. *(Clean water, p. 241)*

● **Contaminants.** Eliminate the existing requirement that the EPA set standards for at least 25 additional water contaminants every three years. Instead, the bill called for the agency to identify and limit contaminants that posed the greatest health risk to humans.

● **Small water systems.** Temporarily waive requirements for water systems that served 10,000 or fewer people and could not afford to comply with the existing law. This provision covered entities that supplied water to trailer parks, subdivisions and rural towns. The bill still required small water systems to install a water purifier or an affordable alternative that provided adequate water quality and health protections.

● **Monitoring.** Reduce the monitoring of contaminants that had been identified in drinking water but were not regulated by law. The bill required the EPA to review the monitoring schedule for 12 contaminants and determine whether continued tracking was necessary.

● **Health standards.** Ease health standards for drinking water supplies. The provision required the EPA to weigh the costs as well as the health risks when it developed standards to limit cancer-causing agents in drinking water. The bill mandated that any new standard could not expose consumers to more than a 1 in 1 million chance of developing cancer. The bill allowed the EPA to lower that threshold for small water systems that could not afford the best technology. The existing standard required that water supplies be free of any contaminant that posed a cancer risk.

The bill also required the EPA to establish a standard for radon, an odorless and colorless gas, found in drinking water.

The nation's mayors and governors contended that the Baucus bill would not give states and local communities enough flexibility to determine which chemicals they should test for and how often water supplies should be monitored. Environmentalists, on the other hand, said the bill would weaken the existing law and put people at risk.

The committee also accepted by voice vote amendments:
● By John W. Warner, R-Va., to allow the U.S. Army Corps of Engineers to borrow money to pay for improvements at the Washington Aqueduct.
● By Harry Reid, D-Nev., to require the testing and monitoring of lead leaching into water supplies from new plumbing fixtures.
● By Daniel Patrick Moynihan, D-N.Y., to require the EPA to use cost-benefit analysis and risk assessment when determining its priorities.
● By Baucus to authorize grants to colleges to establish technical assistance centers to provide help to small water systems.

The panel rejected, 6-11, an amendment by Lauch Faircloth, R-N.C., to exempt projects funded by the bill from the Davis-Bacon Act, which required contractors on federal construction projects to hire workers at the local prevailing wage.

Senate Floor

The Senate on May 19 passed S 2019 by a vote of 95-3, after Baucus brokered several deals to gain the support of wavering senators concerned about the bill's impact on state and local governments. *(Vote 122, p. 22-S)*

To address concerns raised by Mark O. Hatfield, R-Ore., and Bob Kerrey, D-Neb., Baucus agreed to allow the EPA to lower existing standards for contaminants that were rarely found in drinking water to save money if the changes would not endanger human health. The committee-passed bill had allowed the EPA to lower standards, but only for cancer-causing agents, not all contaminants.

While the compromise gained crucial support from the coalition led by the National Governors' Association, it angered major environmental groups, such as the Natural Resources Defense Council, which charged that the deal would weaken public health safeguards.

The Senate also agreed by voice vote to add to the bill the key provisions of a separate but controversial measure (S 171 — S Repts 103-38, 103-39) to elevate the EPA to Cabinet-level status. The amendment was sponsored by John Glenn, D-Ohio.

The Senate began debating the drinking water bill May 9, but delayed final passage for more than a week while sponsors worked out agreements to dispose of more than 100 amendments, most of which were adopted by voice vote.

During floor debate, senators frequently held up drinking water problems in Milwaukee and Washington, D.C., as symbols of the condition of the nation's drinking water supply. The Senate approved by voice vote May 12 Warner's amendment to allow the Army Corps of Engineers to borrow money needed to refurbish the Washington Aqueduct, which sup-

plied water to the nation's capital and northern Virginia. The next day, senators approved by voice vote an amendment by Herb Kohl, D-Wis., to require the EPA to expedite a regulation for cryptosporidium, the parasite found in Milwaukee's water supply.

But on May 18, the Senate turned the debate over safe drinking water into a forum on the rights of private property owners and the costs of environmental regulations to business and the Treasury.

Minority Leader Bob Dole, R-Kan., won voice vote approval May 18 for a sweeping amendment to require that all federal agencies complete a "taking impact analysis" when issuing any regulation or policy that was likely to affect private property values. A growing number of lawmakers were urging that the government compensate private property owners whose land had been devalued or whose use of their land had been limited by federal regulations.

Energy and Natural Resources Committee Chairman J. Bennett Johnston, D-La., led the Senate into another political quagmire when he offered an amendment to require the EPA and other federal agencies to conduct cost, benefit and risk analyses on environmental regulations that cost businesses or individuals $100 million or more per year to implement. The Senate approved the amendment, 90-8, on May 18. *(Vote 117, p. 21-S)*

John H. Chafee, R-R.I., ranking member of the Environment Committee, argued that Johnston's amendment would lead to "paralysis by analysis" and delay environmental regulations. More importantly, Chafee said, it would threaten the effort to reauthorize the drinking water law because it was opposed by key House members.

On May 17, the Senate gave voice vote approval to an amendment by Barbara Boxer, D-Calif., to require the EPA to pay special attention to children, pregnant women and other "vulnerable" people in setting drinking water standards.

In other action, the Senate:
● Rejected, 39-60, on May 17 an amendment by Faircloth that would have struck the Davis-Bacon provisions in the bill. A similar amendment by Robert C. Smith, R-N.H., was tabled (killed), 52-46, on May 18. On the same day, senators also rejected, 45-53, another Davis-Bacon amendment by Alan K. Simpson, R-Wyo. *(Votes 116, 118, 119; p. 21-S)*
● Tabled, 65-34, on May 18 an amendment by Johnston that would have suspended royalties for companies that drilled new deep-water oil and gas wells in the Gulf of Mexico. The amendment had been approved by the Energy and Natural Resources Committee March 2 as a separate bill (S 318 — S Rept 103-248). *(Vote 120, p. 21-S)*
● Rejected, 28-67, on May 18 an amendment by Malcolm Wallop, R-Wyo., that would have made the federal drinking water law voluntary for states. *(Vote 121, p. 21-S)*
● Tabled, 75-23, on May 17 an amendment by Dennis DeConcini, D-Ariz., that would have authorized more financial assistance to poor communities along the United States-Mexico border. *(Vote 114, p. 21-S)*
● Tabled, 56-43, on May 17 an amendment by Judd Gregg, R-N.H., that would have eliminated any financial penalties for underfunded local governments or water systems that could not comply with the bill. *(Vote 115, p. 21-S)*

Lurking in the background throughout the debate was a competing measure (S 1920), sponsored by Hatfield, Pete V. Domenici, R-N.M., and and David L. Boren, D-Okla., that had the support of mayors, governors and operators of small water systems.

The Baucus bill gave the EPA administrator some flexibility to consider costs and health benefits when establishing the maximum level for chemicals found in drinking water. By con-

trast, the Domenici bill sought to give the EPA administrator sweeping authority to take into account costs, health benefits, and other scientific and social risks when developing drinking water rules. Baucus said Domenici's approach was "a prescription for paralysis in the standard-setting process."

House Action

Accepting a bipartisan compromise that had been negotiated over the preceding six months, the House Energy and Commerce Committee approved its bill Sept. 20 by a 43-1 vote (HR 3392 — H Rept 103-745, Part 1). Earlier the same day, the Health and the Environment Subcommittee had approved the measure, 23-0.

The bill provided for a new revolving loan fund, authorized at $3.6 billion for four years, to provide money to states and local governments to improve drinking water treatment plants.

Key to the bipartisan accord on the bill was a late-night concession by Subcommittee Chairman Henry A. Waxman, D-Calif., who agreed Sept. 16 to drop a provision that would have expanded citizens' authority to sue for past violations of the law. It was the last stumbling block in sometimes tense negotiations that also dealt with how federal standards were established for drinking water, the costs and benefits of EPA regulations and the timetable for new EPA rules.

In the end, the drinking water deal garnered the support of a broad range of interest groups, including the National Governors' Association and the Natural Resources Defense Council. Waxman called the bill "nothing short of a minor miracle" because it balanced the needs of governors, mayors and operators of small water systems with environmentalists' concerns about human health.

The House bill differed from the Senate bill in allowing the EPA to weigh the costs and benefits only for new drinking water regulations. The Senate bill provided for cost-benefit analysis of existing regulations. House drinking water negotiators had settled on their provisions after months of give-and-take with members who had wanted to cover existing regulations as well.

The lawmakers and interest groups that shaped the House deal agreed to resist Senate-passed provisions to protect private property rights and elevate the EPA to Cabinet status. Democrats such as Waxman, Mike Synar of Oklahoma and Gerry E. Studds of Massachusetts, who helped broker the drinking water compromise, argued that the issue of private property rights should be left to the courts. And several House Republicans were opposed to making the EPA the 15th Cabinet agency unless they were allowed to broadly rewrite environmental policy at the same time.

Like the Senate bill, the House measure called for an end to the existing requirement that the EPA regulate 25 contaminants every three years. Instead, both bills required the EPA to develop a list of at least 12 unregulated contaminants every four years and then issue standards for those contaminants that occurred most frequently in water supplies and posed the greatest risk to human health.

Like the Senate bill, HR 3392 required the EPA to establish a standard for radon in drinking water and to expedite a proposed regulation for the parasite cryptosporidium.

Richard H. Lehman, D-Calif., the lone panel member to vote against the House bill, said he opposed it because the radon requirement would be too costly for states and cities and would provide little health benefit. Although radon could enter the home through evaporation from tap water, the source of most indoor radon was soil.

In providing for the new revolving fund, the committee was careful to craft language that would not spark a turf battle with the Public Works and Transportation Committee similar to one that had bogged down a separate effort in 1993 to provide states with new drinking water money. *(1993 Almanac, p. 274)*

The House bill proposed to authorize the fund at $1 billion annually in fiscal years 1995-97, plus $600 million in fiscal 1994. It did not contain the Senate-passed provision allowing states to transfer money between the safe drinking water and clean water funds.

House Floor Action

With bipartisan backing, HR 3392 sailed through the House Sept. 27 on a voice vote under a rule that prohibited amendments — an expedited procedure usually reserved for non-controversial bills.

Energy and Commerce Committee Chairman John D. Dingell, D-Mich., said he wanted to bring the bill up on the House floor without any procedural or substantive road-blocks because the administration and a broad array of interest groups representing environmentalists and local governments supported the measure.

Conservatives led by Minority Whip Newt Gingrich, R-Ga., who had hoped to amend the bill, objected to the floor strategy, though they did not force a recorded vote, which would have required a two-thirds majority. They said the bill's hard-fought provision to require the EPA to weigh the costs and benefits of new drinking water regulations did not go far enough to guarantee the intended results.

Final Action

Despite nearly unanimous agreement on the need to overhaul the safe drinking water act, lawmakers were unable to resolve differences between House and Senate bills in the final days of the Congress.

The bills shared much common ground on issues relating to drinking water standards. But there were differences on some of the highly technical provisions, on the details of how money from the state revolving loan fund should be distributed, and on how to define a "small water system" that would be eligible for relief from compliance with certain expensive regulations. The Senate wanted it to mean any system serving 10,000 people or fewer. But House members, led by Waxman, pushed to restrict the relief to systems that served 3,300 people or fewer.

The biggest sticking points involved three pieces of major, unrelated legislation attached to the Senate version but rejected by House negotiators — the EPA Cabinet bill, Johnston's "risk assessment" provisions and Dole's amendment on private property rights.

Fearing that they would not get a bill, a coalition of state and local government officials pressured Congress to find a way around the impasse. Lawmakers and aides to the House Energy and Commerce Committee and the Senate Environment and Public Works Committee worked feverishly to iron out the differences. A staff negotiation that began late Oct. 5 lasted until 3 a.m. Oct. 6 and resulted in a House compromise proposal to the Senate. The Senate rejected the plan that afternoon. What was described as a final Senate counteroffer was made and rejected by the House the morning of Oct. 7.

Baucus labored Oct. 7 to bring a "clean bill" to the Senate floor that would strip out the EPA, risk assessment and private property provisions.

But Dole and Johnston objected and put holds on the bill, blocking it from reaching the floor. Even if those issues had been resolved, however, floor action would likely have been prevented by a GOP filibuster on the California desert protection bill (S 21), which took up Congress' final hours. ■

No Update on Clean Water Law

Like many of the other environmental bills that came before the 103rd Congress, efforts to overhaul and reauthorize the nation's clean water law fell victim to changing agendas and conflicting goals.

The Senate Environment and Public Works Committee approved a bill (S 1114) aimed at giving states more flexibility to address water pollution problems. The bill, sponsored by Chairman Max Baucus, D-Mont., and ranking member John H. Chafee, R-R.I., also sought to ease regulatory burdens on farmers and developers who wanted to build on wetlands, while strengthening protections on more environmentally sensitive areas. It authorized $2.5 billion annually in fiscal years 1995-2000 for a state revolving loan fund to help local communities build sewage treatment plants.

The bill never made it to the Senate floor, however. Baucus decided to wait for the House to mark up its bill first; meanwhile, an agricultural coalition headed by Sens. Charles E. Grassley, R-Iowa, and Howell Heflin, D-Ala., raised concerns that the committee-approved bill would be too burdensome for farmers. They argued that some of the issues should be put off until 1995, when Congress was expected to write a comprehensive farm bill.

On the House side, the Public Works and Transportation Committee held hearings on a bill (HR 3948), sponsored by Chairman Norman Y. Mineta, D-Calif., but the measure immediately drew a bipartisan challenge and went no further.

The reauthorization of the revolving fund, which was due to expire Sept. 30, was the main force driving the bill forward. Although the bill died, appropriators continued to provide money for the fund.

Background

Almost a quarter-century had passed since Ohio's once heavily polluted Cuyahoga River ignited for a third time, mobilizing Congress to pass the nation's first sweeping clean water law in 1972. Designed to reduce the dumping of raw industrial sewage into rivers and streams by regulating the discharge of pollutants and the overflow from sewers, the Federal Water Pollution Control Act (PL 92-500) was credited with dramatically improving water quality in many of the nation's lakes, rivers and streams.

The original law provided federal grants to help communities build sewage treatment plants and other pollution-control projects. Congress eliminated the grant program in 1987, the last time the law was reauthorized (PL 100-4), and replaced it with a state revolving loan fund. Under the 1987 rewrite, the federal government provided seed money to states, which in turn made low-interest loans to local communities to help build or refurbish sewage treatment plants. *(1987 Almanac, p. 291)*

The pool of funds was divided among the states based on a 1976 formula that took into account the sewage treatment needs of communities in a particular state as well as other factors, including population. Senators from small states or from those whose population had grown considerably since 1976 wanted to ensure that their states would receive a fair share of the funds.

In addition to the funding formula, lawmakers were faced with the problem of coping with a new generation of pollution not addressed under the 1972 statute. Known as "nonpoint source" pollution, it came from water that had drained from farmland, asphalt roads, and treated lawns and golf courses. Because the origins of the pollution could not be linked to a single pipe or source, it was the most difficult water problem to trace or to regulate.

Solving that kind of problem involved a whole new territory of anti-pollution regulation, one with potentially as many political risks as environmental rewards. Such a regime could limit the kinds of chemicals farmers used on their crops, the types of materials cities and states used to build roads, and the kinds of chemicals people used to fertilize lawns and recreational areas.

Another highly controversial issue was the protection of wetlands to control flooding and maintain water quality. The subject typically sparked high-pitched battles between environmentalists, on the one hand, and the farmers and developers who wanted to develop the land on the other.

A further wrinkle in 1994 was a burgeoning interest in private property rights, which played a role in the debate on several environmental issues during the year. Advocates of property rights were watchful for provisions that would limit landowners' use of their land or that would not ensure proper compensation if the government took control of the land or limited its uses.

Senate Committee

On Feb. 2, the Clean Water, Fisheries and Wildlife Subcommittee of the Environment and Public Works Committee debated an early draft of the bill by Chairman Bob Graham, D-Fla. But the panel took no action on the bill, putting off legislative changes for the full committee.

The bill was strongly backed by the the Clinton administration, which had released similar recommendations Feb. 1 to renew the clean water law. Clinton's proposal, however, contained stricter limits on toxic pollutants and tougher requirements to protect wetlands.

While the subcommittee focused on the differences between the draft and the Clinton plan, key senators launched a debate behind closed doors over how to ensure that money from the revolving loan fund was fairly distributed among the states.

Full Committee Action

The full Environment and Public Works Committee approved a revised bill by Baucus and Chafee on Feb. 25; the vote was 14-3.

The Baucus-Chafee bill included a controversial new proposal for allocating money from the revolving fund. The bill updated the formula to take into consideration a 1992 Environmental Protection Agency (EPA) survey of the cities most in need of new sewage treatment facilities and an expanded list of the kinds of water quality projects needed by heavily populated states. The bill proposed to phase in the formula over four years and mandate that, starting in 1997, no state would receive less than 90 percent of the money it had received in any previous year.

Heavily populated states wanted the new formula put in place more quickly. But states with smaller populations said it placed a heavier emphasis on a wider variety of water quality problems and would be unfair to them. The impasse forced Baucus to delay votes on amendments for a day while senators asked questions about the formula and other proposed changes.

Corps Water Projects Bill Dies in Senate

Legislation to authorize $1.3 billion over two years for Army Corps of Engineers water projects was approved by the House on Oct. 3, but it died in the Senate, blocked by a dispute over a related flood control bill.

The House bill — approved Sept. 28 by the Public Works and Transportation Committee (HR 4460 — H Rept 103-770) — authorized funding for dams, levees and locks and other corps projects in 14 states, the District of Columbia and Puerto Rico. The House-passed bill authorized the federal government to spend up to $1.03 billion on the new projects, with the remaining cost picked up by non-federal sources. The bill also authorized $150 million for existing projects on watershed management, environmental infrastructure and environmental dredging.

In addition, the bill, sponsored by Public Works Chairman Norman Y. Mineta, D-Calif., amended the 1986 Water Resources Act (PL 99-662) to require that non-federal beneficiaries pay 25 percent of the cost of the corps' environmental protection and restoration projects.

The most expensive project in the bill was a $490 million inland navigation project for the Kentucky Lock and Dam on the Tennessee River. Although the federal government was to pick up the entire tab, half the money was to come from the Inland Waterways Trust Fund, which was financed through revenues from fuel taxes paid by commercial users of the nation's inland waterways. The second-largest project was a $261 million inland navigation project on the Marmet Lock on the Kanawha River in West Virginia — also financed entirely by the federal government, with half the money coming from the trust fund.

The bill also called for 42 new Corps of Engineers studies on such projects as flood control, shoreline protection and flood bank stabilization.

On the Senate side, Max Baucus, D-Mont., chairman of the Environment and Public Works Committee, blocked a companion measure (S 2233) in committee because of a controversy with Republicans over a separate flood control bill (S 2418).

Baucus wanted to include provisions from S 2418, which recommended that the corps abandon its preference for dams and levees in preventing floods and instead promote the evacuation of risky flood plains and the restoration of natural flood cycles. The recommendations came from a government task force that had been set up in response to the 1993 Midwest floods.

In a Sept. 22 letter to Baucus, Christopher S. Bond, R-Mo., and several GOP colleagues argued that this would radically re-order the priorities of river management without adequate debate. Critics charged that adding the flood control language would devastate transportation of crops on the rivers in the middle of harvest season. Republicans also complained that it would add to the flood risk by making recreation in upstream states a higher priority than flood control in the downstream states.

An amendment by Graham that would have phased in the new state revolving loan fund formula over two years was rejected, 4-10, on Feb. 25.

Other main features of the committee-approved bill included:

● **Funding levels.** In response to complaints from states and local governments that they did not have enough money to comply with federal environmental regulations, the committee bill increased funding for new sewage treatment plants, from about $2 billion annually to $2.5 billion annually in fiscal years 1995 through 2000. The bill authorized an additional $500 million annually after fiscal 1995 if Congress met deficit-reduction goals set in 1993.

The bill expanded the types of water quality projects that could be paid for with federal money to include the construction of facilities that collected the overflow of untreated waste from sewage treatment projects and urban storm drains.

At Chafee's request, the revised bill also set aside a percentage of the state revolving loan fund money each year for watershed planning programs. The set-aside was to begin at 5 percent in fiscal 1996 and increase up to 25 percent in fiscal 2000. In subcommittee, Graham had proposed to eliminate the set-aside because he wanted states to devise watershed planning projects on a voluntary basis.

● **Wetlands.** In a key title, the bill incorporated wetlands protections included in a separate bill (S 1304) by Baucus and Chafee, as well as proposals unveiled in September 1993 by the Clinton administration. The wetlands provisions sought to ease regulatory burdens on farmers and developers who wanted to build on some wetlands areas, while strengthening protections on other, more environmentally sensitive areas.

The bill authorized $20 million each year from fiscal 1995 to 1998 to encourage states to assume control over the wetlands protection program and issue their own development permits. Under existing law, developers had to obtain federal permits to build on wetlands, and the process could be time-consuming.

The committee rejected, 5-10, an amendment by Graham that would have eliminated the $20 million authorization and replaced it with a grant program to provide states with an amount equal to what the federal government spent in their state to protect wetlands.

● **Regional problems.** The bill also authorized or expanded programs that addressed water problems in regions neighboring the Chesapeake Bay, Long Island Sound, Gulf of Mexico and San Francisco Bay Delta.

In other action, the committee:

● Rejected, 7-9, on Feb. 24 an amendment by Lauch Faircloth, R-N.C., that would have repealed the provision allowing additional money for clean water programs if deficit goals were met. Faircloth said the provision "runs counter to common sense" — to lower the public debt only to turn around and spend more money.

● Approved, 11-6, on Feb. 24 an amendment by Harris Wofford, D-Pa., to extend the 1934 Davis-Bacon Act to the new water quality projects authorized under the bill. The 1934 law required federal contractors to pay the local prevailing wage.

● Defeated, 6-11, on Feb. 24 a related amendment by Robert C. Smith, R-N.H., that would have repealed the Davis-Bacon Act as it applied to sewage treatment plant construction.

● Approved, 15-0, on Feb. 24 an amendment by Alan K. Simpson, R-Wyo., to require the federal government to consider regional differences in hydrology, soil and other criteria when implementing the clean water law.

● Rejected, 6-9, on Feb. 25 an amendment by Harry Reid, D-Nev., that would have authorized $6.4 million to defray the

costs of a Clark County water treatment project built in 1984.

● Approved by voice vote Feb. 24-25 a series of amendments to encourage the use of innovative technology, authorize funding for American Indian tribes that needed to build sewage treatment plants, and authorize the EPA to develop regulations to reduce the level of toxic pollutants discharged into waterways.

● Approved amendments to authorize the EPA to issue training and operation standards for wastewater treatment plant workers and facilities, improve the monitoring of coastal water quality and require states to notify swimmers when beaches failed to meet health standards.

House Committee

The House Public Works and Transportation Committee held hearings on HR 3948, but the bill went no further. The bill, which followed White House proposals, fell victim to discord on the

panel and the environmental community's disparate agenda.

Mineta's bill was designed to deal with pollution caused by agricultural runoff, to protect key watersheds and to mandate no net loss of wetlands. It proposed to reauthorize the state revolving loan fund at $3 billion for fiscal 1995 and increase it by $500 million annually through fiscal 2000.

The bill was opposed by a bipartisan group, led by ranking committee member Bud Shuster, R-Pa., and Jimmy Hayes, D-La. They drafted a less restrictive measure that did not address pollution caused by agriculture runoff, made watershed protection plans voluntary and extended deadlines under the existing law. The bill also incorporated provisions of a separate bill (HR 1330) by Hayes to scale back protections for wetlands.

Further dimming the bill's chances was a shift of emphasis in the environmental community. By the time the House panel began hearings in June, environmentalists were concentrating more on such items as the superfund overhaul. *(Superfund, p. 231)* ∎

EPA Remains Outside Cabinet

Supporters of legislation to elevate the Environmental Protection Agency (EPA) and make it the 15th Cabinet agency were unable to extricate the measure from a tangled legislative web, and it died at the end of the 103rd Congress. The House bill (HR 3425) fell prey to a growing movement to curb regulations by requiring the EPA and other agencies to weigh the costs and benefits of new rules. In the Senate, the EPA bill (S 171) got tied up in a separate attempt to rewrite the Safe Drinking Water Act.

President Clinton had made elevation of the EPA a top priority, hoping to give it more clout in the government and in international negotiations on the environment. With the effort to broaden the EPA's powers through legislation dead, the Clinton administration took steps to strengthen a White House-level agency aimed at enforcing key environmental laws.

Background

The creation of the EPA in 1970 marked the beginning of the federal government's increased involvement in writing rules and enforcing laws devoted to protecting the environment. Since 1989, members of Congress had tried to boost that commitment by proposing legislation to elevate the EPA to the Cabinet.

When he came into office, Clinton vowed to add the EPA to his Cabinet, and he had already given EPA Administrator Carol M. Browner an informal seat at the Cabinet table.

But Clinton also angered environmentalists and key lawmakers by proposing to abolish the Council on Environmental Quality, which was charged with making sure other federal agencies conducted environmental impact studies before undertaking actions that could harm the environment. The office was a frequent target of Republicans who wanted to ease regulations. In its place, Clinton wanted a bureau of statistics that would gather and coordinate the scientific data related to the environment that was spread among several agencies. He also created a White House Office of Environmental Policy charged with coordinating the federal government's response to environmental problems.

Clinton reversed his decision to kill the Council on Environmental Quality in the fall of 1993, after intense lobbying from John D. Dingell, D-Mich., the House Energy and Commerce

Committee chairman, and Gerry E. Studds, D-Mass., the House Merchant Marine and Fisheries Committee chairman.

Once the EPA bill was dead, Clinton announced plans to merge the White House Office of Environmental Policy into the Council on Environmental Quality.

1993 Action

Both chambers began work on the EPA legislation in 1993. *(1993 Almanac, p. 266)*

The Senate passed its bill (S 171 — S Repts 103-38, 103-39) on May 4 by a vote of 79-15. The two-year authorization contained $5 million for the new department and added to its duties, including creating a Bureau of Environmental Statistics to compile and publish data on the environment and an Office of Environmental Justice to document environmental problems in poor neighborhoods. The bill also provided for the abolition of the Council on Environmental Quality. It was sponsored by Governmental Affairs Committee Chairman John Glenn, D-Ohio, who had long advocated elevating the EPA.

In the House, the Government Operations Committee voted 31-11 on Nov. 4 to approve a bill (HR 3425 — H Rept 103-355) that did little more than designate the EPA as a Cabinet-level department and correct some management problems. A number of Democrats had hoped to use the bill to overhaul the agency and broadly rewrite environmental policy, but they had to give up on those goals to move the bill forward.

The bill did call for management changes, such as tightening spending allowances for contractors and requiring performance goals for the agency. It provided for the creation of several new subagencies within the department, including a Bureau of Environmental Statistics, an Office of Environmental Justice to focus on ecological issues affecting racial and ethnic minorities, and an advisory committee to deal with human environmental health risks.

House Action

The House bill fell Feb. 2, 1994, when opponents succeeded in preventing it from coming to the floor. By a vote of 191-227, lawmakers rejected a resolution (H Res 312) that would have set the rules for floor debate on the measure. *(Vote 4, p. 2-H)*

Opponents rejected the rule because it did not allow freshmen John L. Mica, R-Fla., and Karen L. Thurman, D-Fla., to offer an amendment requiring the EPA to consider the economic costs associated with carrying out any new regulations to remedy environmental problems. The amendment also would have required the agency to compare the risks posed by environmental threats with other risks posed in life.

The issues of cost-benefit analysis and risk assessment were high on the agendas of lawmakers who believed the EPA wielded too heavy a hand when issuing environmental standards, and mandates on state and local governments and the public. An EPA official said the agency already used both risk assessment and cost-benefit analysis in "literally hundreds of regulations," and that the amendment therefore was unnecessary. *(Risk assessment, this page)*

The Democratic-controlled Rules Committee had voted Nov. 17, 1993, against allowing the amendment on grounds that it was a "policy" issue not germane to the bill, which was concerned solely with the structure of the agency. The Clinton administration and bill sponsors argued that the amendment would amount to a "one size fits all" policy that would put economic concerns above the health of the public and the environment. "It's very disappointing, because the EPA bill was intended to be a very simple piece of legislation," said John D. Echeverria, chief legal counsel for the National Audubon Society.

Even its foes conceded that the Mica-Thurman amendment probably would have passed if brought to a vote on the floor. "That's what the vote [on the rule] indicates," said freshman Dan Hamburg, D-Calif. That would have made it all but certain that the provision would have been part of a final bill, since the Senate-passed version contained the same language. The Senate had voted 95-3 in May 1993 to adopt an identical amendment by J. Bennett Johnston, D-La.

Vice President Al Gore and EPA Administrator Browner met with freshman Democrats to urge them to support the rule. Ultimately, 64 members of the freshman class voted against the rule, including 15 Democrats.

Senate Action

With the House bill stalled, Senate supporters began looking for ways to jump-start the initiative. Glenn included the text of the Senate's EPA Cabinet bill in an unrelated bill (S 2019) to reauthorize the 1974 Safe Drinking Water Act. The House and Senate failed to agree on a final version of the drinking water bill, however, and it, too, died at the end of the Congress. *(Drinking water, p. 238)* ∎

House Committee Approves Risk Assessment Initiative

A bill (HR 4306) to establish a comprehensive risk assessment program at the Environmental Protection Agency (EPA) won committee approval in the House but went no further in the 103rd Congress.

The bill, introduced by Herb Klein, D-N.J., provided for the establishment of an office and a director of risk assessment at the EPA to ensure that state-of-the-art scientific methods were the basis for any agency risk assessment guidelines. The bill also provided for a pilot program to compare and rank the severity of various environmental hazards, and it required the White House Office of Science and Technology Policy to coordinate risk research among federal agencies.

Background

Under existing law, the EPA assessed risks to human health and safety and issued regulations to combat those risks. But critics said the process was alarmist and vulnerable to political manipulation. They cited instances when the public had been warned about a harmful substance only to learn later that it was much less dangerous than originally thought.

By revising the risk assessment process, proponents hoped to force the EPA to conduct more analysis of economic and social factors before issuing regulations that could be costly to industry and local governments.

Risk assessment had become a hot-button issue in the 103rd Congress, derailing several other environmental initiatives. In February, Republicans blocked House consideration of a bill to elevate the EPA to Cabinet status (HR 3425) after they were denied a chance to offer an amendment calling for greater attention to the risk assessment process.

John L. Mica, R-Fla., one of the amendment sponsors, cited EPA water quality rules that he said required arsenic levels of no more than 2 or 3 parts per billion, while the average plate of shrimp contained roughly 30 parts per billion of the toxic chemical. Meeting such a stringent requirement unnecessarily cost local governments millions of dollars, Mica said. "County officials in Harrisburg, Pa., testified that it would be cheaper to deliver bottled water to households than to comply," he said. "EPA regulations are now becoming the single greatest cost to local governments." *(EPA, p. 243)*

The debate over risk assessment also affected other bills, helping to block efforts to reauthorize the Federal Insecticide, Fungicide and Rodenticide Act. *(FIFRA, p. 199)*

House Action

The bill began in a House Science, Space and Technology subcommittee, which approved it by voice vote May 18. The Technology, Environment and Aviation Subcommittee approved by voice vote a handful of amendments, including two by Dick Zimmer, R-N.J. The first Zimmer amendment directed the EPA to submit a report to Congress prioritizing risk assessment research issues. Zimmer's other amendment required that the complete results of any risk assessment be published and distributed to lawmakers, bureaucrats and others who made key decisions about regulations.

Full Committee Action

After lengthy negotiations on technical terms, the full Science, Space and Technology Committee approved the bill by voice vote July 20 (H Rept 103-857).

At the markup, committee Chairman George E. Brown Jr., D-Calif., said the EPA's risk assessment process needed improvement. But he insisted that members make a distinction between "risk assessment," the process by which scientists determined quantitative estimates of risks, and "risk management," the regulatory decision about how to respond to risks. "Most members, I believe, have risk management decisions in mind when they complain about agency actions that appear to be overreactions to minimal risks," he said, adding that the Science Committee did not have jurisdiction over risk management.

But ranking Republican Robert S. Walker of Pennsylvania stressed that the bill should establish legislative guidelines as to what constituted an accurate risk assessment and the way in

which assessments should be communicated and enforced.

Much of the markup debate centered not on the larger principle of risk assessment, but on ironing out specific words and phrases in the bill.

The panel approved by voice vote a Brown substitute amendment to set deadlines for the EPA to develop risk assessment guidelines and to require that the guidelines be developed with public input.

The amendment also included provisions specifying when a final agency action that relied upon a risk assessment would be subject to judicial rule. That language became a sticking point with industry groups that wanted greater opportunity for the courts to review such actions.

Based on negotiations with the industry groups, Brown offered a second amendment, also approved by voice vote, which made the bill silent on judicial review. Under the second amendment, the review process was to follow traditional guidelines under the Administrative Procedures Act.

The panel then approved, 20-16, an amendment by Walker and Zimmer to insert language requiring that the scientific assessments be "unbiased" and "plausible." Brown said he opposed the amendment because he did not have full knowledge of the implications of the language. But he chose not to exercise the option of using the proxy votes of Democrats absent from the markup, and the amendment was approved on a party-line vote. ∎

Montana Wilderness Bill Stalls

After a prolonged debate, the House on May 17 passed legislation designed to protect a huge swath of Montana from development. Montana's lone House member, Democrat Pat Williams, hoped he had finally hammered out compromise legislation that would be acceptable to all sides of the wilderness dispute.

But disagreements between preservationists and development advocates — and between Montana's two senators — doomed any progress the bill might have made in the Senate. As it had many times before, the bill died at the end of the session.

As passed by the House, the bill (HR 2473) aimed to prevent development on 3 million acres in Montana — 1.7 million of it to be designated as wilderness and 1.3 million acres to be set aside under less restrictive classifications. The bill would have opened to development and motorized recreation another 3 million acres of roadless forest that had been considered for wilderness designation.

Background

Williams had been trying for nearly 16 years to pass wilderness legislation for his state. Montana and Idaho were the only states without congressionally approved, statewide wilderness plans. But his efforts had been stymied by partisan politics and clashes between environmental interests that wanted to preserve the pristine wilderness areas and commercial interests that wanted more land available for logging and mining.

The closest he had come was in 1988, when Congress cleared a bill that would have put about 1.4 million acres of national forest system land in Montana off-limits to logging and development. But President Ronald Reagan killed the measure with a pocket veto, saying it could "cost jobs and eliminate vast mineral development opportunities." In 1992, the House and Senate passed significantly different versions of a Montana wilderness bill and were unable to strike a compromise before the end of the session. *(1988 Almanac, p. 157; 1992 Almanac, p. 289)*

Any wilderness bill had to overcome the traditional opposition of House Republicans and some Democrats from natural resource-rich Western states to wilderness legislation

---

BOXSCORE

Montana Wilderness — HR 2473. The bill sought to protect 3 million acres in Montana from development, while opening another 3 million acres to multiple uses.

Report: H Rept 103-487, Parts 1 & 2.

KEY ACTION

May 17 — House passed HR 2473, 308-111.

---

that barred timber, mining and recreational development on millions of acres of land.

The issue of who had rights to water was also a major concern. States did not want the federal government to usurp their rights to water, but federal lawmakers did not want states siphoning off water that was needed to maintain wilderness areas. This particular legislation had also been caught up in dicey political battles in Montana.

Republican Conrad Burns had supported Reagan's veto of the 1988 Montana wilderness bill — a compromise bill that was backed by Williams and by Montana's Democratic Sens. Max Baucus and John Melcher. The issue helped Burns, regarded as a long-shot candidate, to unseat Melcher in the Senate election that November.

Burns was up for re-election in 1994, and Williams pressed him to support the bill. Williams warned that opposing the measure would alienate Montana voters who, Williams said, wanted to put the issue to rest. Burns' office denied that suggestion, accusing Williams of escalating the political rhetoric and hampering the legislative process.

House Committee

HR 2473 was jointly referred to two committees in the House: Natural Resources and Agriculture.

Natural Resources Committee

The National Parks, Forests and Public Lands Subcommittee of the House Natural Resources Committee marked up the bill March 17, giving it quick voice vote approval after adopting a substitute that, among other things, contained somewhat different acreages than the original.

The bill provided that about 1.7 million acres in Montana's 10 national forests be designated as wilderness and added to the national wilderness system. The land was in addition to 3.4 million wilderness acres already protected in Montana. Another 1.3 million acres were to be given less restrictive classifications, known as wilderness study and special management areas. These designations provided essentially the same protection as wilderness, leaving the land mostly undeveloped.

An additional 3 million acres of roadless forest land, which had been considered for possible wilderness designation, were to be "released" and opened to multiple uses such as logging, mining and motorized recreation.

The subcommittee bill prohibited the federal government from making any new claim to water or water rights in the proposed wilderness area. The water language was similar to provisions approved by Congress in August 1993 in a separate bill (HR 631 — PL 103-77) that designated wilderness in Colorado. *(1993 Almanac, p. 278)*

Williams had worked closely with Subcommittee Chairman Bruce F. Vento, D-Minn., for a year before the markup to craft a bill that would meet both environmental and commercial needs.

HR 2473 won routine voice vote approval from the full House Natural Resources Committee on March 23 (H Rept 103-487, Part 1). But the debate exposed the political gulf that remained between strong supporters of development and those who favored wilderness designation.

During opening statements by committee members, ranking Republican Don Young of Alaska, perhaps the fiercest congressional opponent of expanding the wilderness system, described the practice of putting forested land into wilderness as "stupidity." Young said many of the established wilderness areas were filled with decaying or dying trees, which could become tinder for a forest fire "holocaust" that would kill far more trees and wildlife than a carefully managed timber development program.

Williams denounced Young's "holocaust" depiction as "illogical" and "unsubstantiated" and accused Young and his allies of trying to create fear among citizens to score legislative points.

Agriculture Committee

On April 28, the House Agriculture Committee approved the original version of HR 2473 on a party-line vote of 22-19 (H Rept 103-487, Part 2). The Agriculture Committee bill designated 1.6 million acres as wilderness. It set aside 163,000 acres as "wilderness study areas," as opposed to 376,000 acres in the Natural Resources Committee bill; those areas were to remain undeveloped until Congress determined whether the land should be preserved.

Members rejected, 19-22, an amendment by Bob Smith, R-Ore., that would have prohibited judicial review of the language regarding the release of land for logging and other uses. Smith said that environmental groups had used lawsuits to keep released land in Oregon from being used for commercial or recreational purposes.

House Floor

The House passed the bill May 17 by a vote of 308-111. *(Vote 174, p. 54-H)*

The Rules Committee had chosen to send the Natural Resources Committee version to the floor, rather than the Agriculture Committee version. The House began debate May 12 but put off final action until May 17 because of Republican concerns about the water rights language.

Williams appealed to members on both sides of the wilderness debate to accept the compromise he had crafted, saying that any wilderness measure would have to balance both the economic needs of local constituencies and environmental responsibility.

Some other Western members, however, argued that the bill fell short of its goals. Wayne Allard, R-Colo., criticized the language on releasing lands for uses such as logging, saying it was not strong enough to prevent "frivolous" court challenges.

By voice vote, the House agreed to a Williams amendment to restore the bill's water rights language to its original form, stating that the measure would not create or recognize new federal water rights. Williams made the change in response to some Western members who said the language approved by the Natural Resources Committee might open the door for the federal government to assert new water rights.

The House defeated, 182-244, an amendment by Tom DeLay, R-Texas, to remove from the bill a proposed study of the boundaries of and biological diversity within the Northern Rockies ecosystem. *(Vote 172, p. 54-H)*

Deriding the study as "politically correct," DeLay argued that Congress should not fund a new scientific panel for the study and should instead rely on scientists in existing federal agencies such as the National Biological Survey office. Williams defended the study, saying local governments would use it to help project how much of the area's natural resources could be used by existing industries without environmental disruption.

Another amendment by John Bryant, D-Texas, rejected on a 142-283 vote, sought to prohibit road construction and the clear-cutting of timber and vegetation on the lands released for timber harvesting. *(Vote 173, p. 54-H)*

Bryant said he preferred so-called selection management, in which harvesters cut individual trees within an area but left others standing to regenerate the forest naturally.

Vento argued that the controversial amendment would prevent the Montana bill from passing. He said that although the Forest Service's timber management plan needed reform, a bill addressing only Montana was not an appropriate vehicle and would represent micromanagement.

Senate Stalemate

On the House floor, Williams directed a strong plea to senators to consider the bill, saying, "Please do not draw lines in the sand, but draw upon your sense of duty and help me pass this legislation."

But Montana's two senators could not agree on a plan, and Western Democrats in particular were reluctant to act on wilderness bills that did not have the full support of a state's congressional delegation.

Baucus wrote a letter on May 16 urging Burns to join him in reintroducing a compromise bill that they had crafted in the 102nd Congress. That bill would have designated 1.2 million acres in Montana as wilderness restricted from development and released 4 million acres for multiple-use activities. Baucus warned that unless Burns joined with him in reviving the legislation, the Senate would be deadlocked on the issue.

But on May 18, Burns introduced legislation (S 2125) that was more development-oriented. Burns proposed to designate about 800,000 acres in Montana as wilderness and release more than 5 million acres of land for timber, mining and energy jobs. The following day, Baucus introduced a bill (S 2137) that was identical to the measure he had cosponsored with Burns in the 102nd Congress.

The Senate did not act on either bill. ∎

Split in Idaho Delegation Sinks Wilderness Bill

The House Natural Resources Subcommittee on National Parks, Forests and Public Lands gave voice vote approval June 23 to a bill (HR 3732) to classify 1.36 million acres in Idaho as protected wilderness, but the measure never progressed to the full committee.

Although Idaho had the largest amount of roadless national forest lands in the nation outside Alaska, it was one of only two states that did not have a congressionally approved, statewide wilderness plan. Subcommittee approval of the bill was a first, tentative step in 14 years toward resolving a longstanding dispute in that state.

However, the bill addressed only half the state and had virtually no chance of enactment in 1994: Sponsor Larry LaRocco, D-Idaho, acknowledged that he did not have the support of the state's two GOP senators, Larry E. Craig and Dirk Kempthorne. Spokesmen for Craig and Kempthorne said the senators would only support legislation that addressed the entire state. The offices of Craig, Kempthorne and Republican Rep. Michael D. Crapo, whose district covered the other half of the state, said the issue was too complex to move along as quickly as LaRocco wanted.

As approved by the subcommittee, the bill barred timber, mining, and recreational development on 1.36 million acres in five national forests in LaRocco's district. Another 364,000 acres were to receive a less restrictive classification, known as wilderness study and special management areas. That was a slight increase in the wilderness area and a slight decrease in the special management area designated in the original language LaRocco introduced.

The bill also provided for the release of 2.8 million acres of roadless forestland for multiple uses such as logging, mining and motor vehicles.

The panel also dealt with the contentious issue of water rights. Conservationists said that without control over water in the wilderness areas, the land could not be protected. States, however, believed their rights were being usurped.

LaRocco and subcommittee Chairman Bruce F. Vento, D-Minn., decided to take the approach that had been hammered out for Colorado wilderness and adopted in the Montana wilderness bill (HR 2473). Under an agreement approved by the panel, the federal government was to be prohibited from making a new claim to water in the wilderness area. *(Montana, p. 245)*

The House passed a separate bill (S 2100) at the end of the session that would have authorized the Forest Service to continue for one year a pilot project in the Idaho Panhandle National Forest. The project was intended to demonstrate ecosystem management practices. The Senate had passed a broader version of the bill that would have applied to a number of states. The legislation died at the end of the Congress. *(Ecosystem management, p. 257)* ∎

National Parks Bill Runs Out of Time

Like many other bills related to national parks, legislation to reorganize the management of the national park system died in the crush of legislative business at the end of the 103rd Congress. The legislation proposed to change the way parks were added to or removed from the national park system. The House bill (HR 4476) won passage Sept. 28. A companion bill (S 471) was approved by the Senate Energy and Natural Resources Committee on Sept. 21, but it went no further.

Since its creation in 1916, the national park system had grown to 367 units in 49 states, the District of Columbia and the U.S. territories. There were more than 268 million visitors to national parks annually.

Despite the parks' popularity, their operating budgets had not kept pace. The demand for more national parks and the upkeep of the federal lands, especially the recreation areas found in nearly every state and county, was an expensive proposition.

Congress allocated about $1.1 billion for park operations in fiscal 1994. But the National Park Service estimated that it would cost at least $2 billion — almost double the agency's budget — to repair a host of facilities and reduce a long list of maintenance projects.

Interior Secretary Bruce Babbitt underscored the need for more financial resources for national parks during a speech May 23, at Independence Hall in Philadelphia. As an example, Babbitt described the housing conditions of some park

---

BOXSCORE

National Parks Management — HR 4476, S 471 (HR 1508, HR 3709). The legislation aimed to revise the way Congress created new national parks.

Report: H Rept 103-725.

KEY ACTION

Sept. 28 — House passed HR 4476, 421-0.

Sept. 21 — Senate committee approved S 471, 20-0.

---

rangers as "slums" that were waterlogged, rat-infested and crumbling. With that kind of problem, Babbitt urged Congress to increase park funding.

House Action

The House Natural Resources Subcommittee on National Parks, Forests and Public Lands gave voice vote approval May 19 to two bills to establish new procedures for determining when Congress should create new national parks.

The first (HR 1508), sponsored by Joel Hefley, R-Colo., set out a comprehensive program for establishing new park areas. It also required the national park system to develop a strategic plan to direct the agency for 20 years to come. Hefley had criticized Congress for creating parks when the National Park Service could not afford to maintain existing ones.

Lawmakers were supposed to rely on information from the National Park Service about a proposed park's suitability, but Hefley said some parks had been created without sufficient congressional review.

One of the most often-cited examples was the Steamtown National Historic Site in Scranton, Pa., a controversial museum designed to memorialize the age of steam-powered locomotion. Congress first sanctioned the site in 1986 to provide a home for a collection of 19th century locomotives and rail cars as part of an omnibus spending bill (PL 99-591). Since then, Steamtown had been the

Endangered Species

Action to rewrite the controversial Endangered Species Act (PL 93-205) was put on hold in 1994 while Congress focused on other environmental legislation, including the overhauls of the clean water act and the "superfund" toxic waste cleanup law

The law, which Congress had passed in 1973, made it illegal to kill, injure, trap, harass or otherwise "take" any animal or plant that was deemed endangered or threatened. It also established a comprehensive process for designating an endangered or threatened species and required a plan for its recovery. Among its success stories was the American bald eagle, taken off the endangered list July 4 and bumped down to a less restrictive category.

In recent years, however, the law had been criticized for ignoring economic interests and had sparked an intense debate about balancing the needs of landowners with the goals of environmentalists. The law also was criticized for emphasizing the protection of single species, instead of ecosystems where several species might be in danger.

The law expired in 1992, but annual appropriations had kept enforcement alive. Interior Secretary Bruce Babbitt announced changes June 14 to make the law more flexible and easier to understand for landowners. On Aug. 11, Babbitt pledged that the administration would make no further demands on property owners after they obtained approval for a plan to protect endangered species on their land.

The House Merchant Marine and Fisheries Committee conducted a series of hearings on issues tied to reauthorization, such as breeding rare species in captivity and habitat conservation plans. But it did not mark up conflicting bills by Chairman Gerry E. Studds, D-Mass. (HR 2043), and W. J. "Billy" Tauzin, D-La. (HR 1490).

Tauzin wanted to make sure that landowners who lost their livelihoods or whose property values decreased because of regulations were compensated by the federal government. Environmentalists such as Studds feared that Tauzin's proposals would weaken the law.

Setting the stage for what was expected to be a rancorous debate in 1995, Tauzin had used several land and conservation bills as vehicles to attack the law. In 1993, the House restricted access to private property by federal scientists as part of a bill (HR 1845) to formally authorize a new research agency to study the nation's plants and animals. Tauzin also won approval July 14 for an amendment to the House version of the California desert bill (HR 518) to give landowners more money for private property sold to the federal government if endangered species were present on the land. But Tauzin lost Oct. 5 on an amendment to compensate landowners as part of a bill (HR 5044) to designate "American Heritage" areas. *(1993 Almanac, p. 269)*

In the Senate, a key Environment and Public Works subcommittee held hearings on reauthorization issues, but no markup was scheduled. Environmentalists favored a bill (S 921) by full committee Chairman Max Baucus, D-Mont., and ranking member John H. Chafee, R-R.I. Industry, farmers and developers supported a conflicting bill (S 1521) by Richard C. Shelby, D-Ala., and Slade Gorton, R-Wash.

target of much criticism because it was never authorized by Congress but had received nearly $70 million in appropriations.

The second bill (HR 3709), sponsored by Subcommittee Chairman Bruce F. Vento, D-Minn., required the service to submit an annual report to Congress listing the areas it would like to study for possible inclusion in the park system.

It appeared likely at the time that HR 1508 and HR 3709 would be merged into one bill upon full committee consideration.

Full Committee, Floor Action

The full House Natural Resources Committee on May 25 approved a separate bill (HR 4476 — H Rept 103-725) that sought to establish a long-range expansion plan for the park system. The bill, approved by voice vote, incorporated language from the two measures approved in subcommittee (HR 1508 and HR 3709).

The bill, sponsored by Hefley, proposed to amend a 1970 law (PL 91-383), known as the General Authorities Act, that dealt with the administration of the national park system. Hefley's bill required the park service to prioritize and compile a list of areas that should be studied for possible inclusion in the system, keeping in mind factors such as an area's natural and historic significance and the rarity of its resources.

It also required the park service to consult with various agencies, state officials, advisers, scholars and others about which aspects of American heritage were inadequately represented. The final list would help Congress decide which parks to add to the system.

For the first time, the Interior secretary would be required to submit to Congress an agencywide expansion plan for the park system.

The plan, which was to be submitted within three fiscal years, was to include a list of parks that should be removed from the system. If the list was not submitted to Congress within a year of completion of the overall plan, the bill provided for the establishment of a seven-member commission to determine which park facilities, if any, should be closed. The commission was to be patterned after the commission that recommended a list of Defense Department bases for closure and realignment.

Hefley originally had wanted to create a commission outright and have it develop the park service's long-range plan. But Roger G. Kennedy, director of the National Park Service, opposed that, saying it would dilute his agency's authority. Provisions of the bill were then endorsed by Kennedy and the park service; the National Parks and Conservation Association, a Washington-based advocacy group; and the Association of National Park Rangers.

The House approved HR 4476 on Sept. 28 by a vote of 421-0. *(Vote 444, p. 132-H)*

Senate Action

The Senate Energy and Natural Resources Committee on Sept. 21 voted 20-0 to approve a separate bill (S 471) to establish a national commission to review the utility and function of some national parks. The seven-member commission was also to study whether state governments and private companies should become involved in managing and operating selected national parks, monuments and other sites.

The committee bill required the Interior secretary to outline the objectives and goals of the National Park Service and

spell out its operations and priorities in a National Park System Plan that would be submitted to Congress within three years. The secretary would also be responsible for developing and maintaining a list of potential additions and subtractions to the park system.

Bill sponsor Malcolm Wallop, R-Wyo., cited the increasing costs of financing new national parks as a principal reason why an overall review of the system was needed.

Park service officials opposed the creation of an external panel to survey the agency's progress before they had had an opportunity to do so themselves. The House bill (HR 4476) followed that request, providing for the creation of an outside commission only if the Interior department failed to submit within a year a list of parks to be modified or dropped.

Congress took no further action on the bill. S 471 did not reach the Senate floor, largely because senators were focused on clearing the California Desert Protection Act (S 21 — PL 103-433) at the end of the session. ∎

No Consensus on Park Concessions

The House on July 28 passed a bill (S 208) to force businesses that wanted to provide food, lodging and recreation in national parks to compete for that right. Earlier, on March 22, the Senate had passed its version of the park concessions bill. But the Senate never acted again on the House-approved version, and the measure died at the end of the session.

In a key difference with the Senate-passed bill, the House measure required competitive bidding for outfitters and guides. The Senate measure gave the Interior secretary the authority to set fees for those types of concessions.

Background

In the 20 years prior to 1994, national parks had become a prime tourist destination. But critics said that private concessionaires, not the government, had reaped much of the benefits.

The 1965 Concessions Policy Act (PL 89-249) regulated how the Interior Department awarded and managed concession contracts. Private companies that operated hotels, restaurants, tours, ski lifts and other concessions in the national parks were essentially allowed to renew their contracts automatically without regard to their performance. Although each contract stipulated how much money should be paid to the government for the privilege of operating a concession, in practice these franchise fees had been waived or reduced by the Interior Department in exchange for the private company's paying for a capital improvement, such as a new building, at the facility.

As a result, only a fraction of the money made from national park concessions was returned to the Treasury. In 1991, about 660 concessionaires grossed about $618 million and paid the federal government $18.1 million, or roughly 2.9 percent, in franchise fees.

Concessionaires operated lodges, marinas, ski lifts, restaurants, and snack and souvenir shops, ran sightseeing tours and rafting trips, guided fishing and hunting trips, and provided a variety of other services. They varied in size from individually owned operations with gross receipts of less than $500,000 a year to corporate conglomerates with gross receipts of more than $80 million annually, according to the General Accounting Office (GAO) and testimony submitted to a Senate subcommittee in July 1990 by James R. Richards, then the Interior Department's inspector general.

BOXSCORE

Park Concessions — S 208.
The bill provided for a competitive bidding process for concessions contracts in national parks.

Reports: S Rept 103-226, H Rept 103-571.

KEY ACTION

March 22 — Senate passed S 208, 90-9.

July 28 — House passed S 208, amended, 386-30.

Environmentalists applauded the effort to revise the nation's park concession policy, and the Clinton administration endorsed the call to collect more money from concession operators. The recommendations were included in Vice President Al Gore's 1993 proposal to "reinvent" the federal government.

But concessionaires and their supporters in Congress argued that the concessions provided vital services to the public that the government otherwise would have to supply at a substantial cost to taxpayers. They said many concessionaires had made major investments in buildings, equipment and maintenance that benefited the government.

Senate Committee

With Republicans split on the matter, the Senate Energy and Natural Resources Committee on Feb. 2 approved, 16-4, a bill (S 208 — S Rept 103-226) to repeal the 1965 law and replace it with a competitive bidding process for concessions contracts in national parks. Bill supporters said that would result in higher fee collections.

The bill was sponsored by Dale Bumpers, D-Ark., a frequent critic of government policies that allowed natural resources and public lands to be used commercially with little return to taxpayers.

Malcolm Wallop of Wyoming, the committee's ranking Republican, opposed the bill, saying it would diminish the quality of services at national parks and unfairly alter existing agreements between the government and concessioners. But supporters said the existing system was inherently anti-competitive and long due for an overhaul.

To get the votes to report the bill, Bumpers relied heavily on freshman panel member Robert F. Bennett, R-Utah, who had agreed in July 1993 to work with Bumpers on the legislation. Other Republicans who voted for the bill were Mark O. Hatfield, Ore.; Pete V. Domenici, N.M.; and Trent Lott, Miss.

As approved by the committee, the bill required future concession operators to enter a competitive bidding process to win a contract. The Interior secretary would be required to review contracts at least once every 20 years. Wallop tried unsuccessfully to extend the renewal window to 30 years.

To gain Bennett's favor, Bumpers agreed to amend the bill to allow concessionaires who owned "possessory interests" — ownership rights to structures built on federal lands — to continue to hold those and exchange them at fair market value until their contracts expired.

Senate Floor

The Senate passed the bill March 22 on a vote of 90-9. *(Vote 63, p. 12-S)*

The bill's journey was expedited by an agreement to limit amendments to those bearing directly on the issue of park concessions. Energy and Natural Resources Chairman J. Bennett Johnston, D-La., Bumpers and Wallop reached the agreement to ensure that the bill would move by March 22 to give the Senate enough time to consider the fiscal 1995 budget resolution (S Con Res 63) before beginning a two-week recess.

The bill included provisions to:

● **Competitive bidding.** Set up a competitive bidding process for concession operators who grossed more than $500,000 a year. Under certain circumstances, the Interior secretary could accept a bid from a concession operator that did not provide the Treasury the greatest amount of revenues. Such concession operators would have to offer a skill or experience that other bidders could not provide to park visitors to justify the lower revenues.

● **Contract length.** Limit the maximum term of a contract to 10 years, though the Interior secretary would have the authority under special circumstances to sign a 20-year contract. A longer contract could be awarded to companies that were doing well financially or had made major investments in the park concession they operated.

● **Use of franchise fees.** The franchise fees, which were deposited into the Treasury under existing law, were to be set aside for the maintenance of national parks. Half the money was to be divided among all parks based on need, with the remaining half distributed to each park based on the amount of fees collected at that park.

● **Renewal rights for small businesses.** Grant special preference for renewals to contractors who grossed less than $500,000 a year. Such operators would have to meet minimum bid standards and performance requirements. All other operators would be given no such preference.

● **Depreciation of park improvements.** Require that new concessionaires whose contracts expired be reimbursed for improvements, but not at full cost. Concessionaires would be offered a price that discounted the use of the asset from its value. New concessioners could not be reimbursed for the full cost of an improvement, as they were under existing law. The bill allowed for any existing concession operator to be reimbursed for the full value of any improvement made before the bill's enactment.

GOP Objections

Wallop and Minority Whip Alan K. Simpson, R-Wyo., strongly opposed two provisions that they said would eliminate the financial incentive for companies to make capital improvements by lowering the amount a concessionaire could earn. They also said the provisions would make it more difficult for concession operators to get loans to finance such projects.

First, Wallop and Simpson objected to the change in the way concession operators were to be paid for capital improvements — from the existing system under which operators were reimbursed at the end of their contracts for the full value of any capital improvements to a system requiring that the government discount the use of the asset from its value and base the reimbursement price on that lower value. Also, they opposed the decision to no longer allow most concession operators to renew their contracts nearly automatically. Only small operators would have such preferential treatment.

House Committee

A revised version of S 208 won voice vote approval from a House Natural Resources subcommittee April 21. But Republicans remained concerned that the measure would eliminate financial incentives for small operators to invest in capital improvements, eventually driving them out of business. The National Parks, Forests and Public Lands Subcommittee essentially deferred a solution on the capital improvements issue to the full Natural Resources Committee.

Despite the bill's thrust to change the way contracts were awarded and managed, Bruce F. Vento, D-Minn., chairman of the subcommittee, warned that it would be up to the Interior Department to make agreements that would bring in more money. "Congress or this committee cannot negotiate every contract," he said.

The subcommittee approved by voice vote an amendment by Vento to allow all concession operators who made less than $500,000 a year to get preference when renewing contracts. The Senate-passed bill contained a similar provision, but it also gave contract renewal preferences to companies that provided outfitting, guides or river-running within a national park. Vento said some of those companies made more than $500,000 and should not receive special treatment.

Full Committee Action

On May 11 the full Natural Resources Committee approved S 208 (H Rept 103-571) by voice vote. Debate during the markup focused on efforts to retain parts of the 1965 law that some members claimed were vital to the health of the industry.

The panel rejected, 17-23, an amendment offered by Austin J. Murphy, D-Pa., that would have compensated concession owners for their capital investments at a higher rate than allowed under the bill. The amendment would have allowed operators to sell the property at a price closer to its original cost, allowing for some depreciation but also taking into account the appraised value.

Supporters of the amendment claimed that without incentives, the bill would discourage qualified new concessioners, opening the industry to irresponsible operators. "It's going to have a depressing effect on new investment in the parks," said Allen T. Howe, Washington representative of the National Park Hospitality Association.

Vento said the amendment essentially would gut the bill.

The panel turned back, 15-21, an amendment offered by Peter A. DeFazio, D-Ore., that would have allowed outfitters, guides and river-runners to retain preferential treatment when renewing their contracts. Supporters argued that outfitters and guides were engaged in a uniquely competitive and dangerous business that required preferential treatment to attract qualified and safe operators.

House Floor

The House passed the bill July 28 by a vote of 386-30, after rejecting several attempts to move the bill closer to existing law. *(Vote 363, p. 108-H)*

The House rejected by voice vote an amendment by H. Martin Lancaster, D-N.C., that would have allowed companies with gross revenues of up to $3 million to retain preferential renewal rights.

Murphy failed, by voice vote, to amend the bill to require that when contracts expired, operators be reimbursed for the fair market value of any capital improvement they had made.

The House also rejected, 148-274, a Murphy amendment

that would have deleted from the bill a provision stating that new or expanded visitor facilities should not be built within the national parks if adequate facilities existed or could feasibly be developed outside park boundaries. *(Vote 362, p. 108-H)*

In order to comply with congressional budget rules, the Rules Committee amended S 208 to stipulate that the revenues anticipated from park concession fees under existing law ($22.6 million in fiscal 1995) had to go to the Treasury. Only added revenues could be funneled directly to the parks.

Other differences with the Senate bill included:

● The Senate requirement that franchise fees for outfitters and guides be set unilaterally by the Interior secretary instead of through competitive bids.

● A House provision that allowed the Interior secretary to authorize limited low-impact visitor services, such as bus tours or newspaper vending, through less formal fee arrangements than a concession contract.

The Senate never acted on the measure as amended by the House. ■

Park Fee Increase Falls Victim To Year-End Slowdown

Legislation to permit the National Park Service to increase fees for park users died after failing twice to win the two-thirds majority needed to pass in the House under expedited procedures. After the second failure, on Oct. 5, bill sponsor Bruce F. Vento, D-Minn., acknowledged that there was not enough time left in the session to bring the measure (HR 4533) up a third time. The bill fell victim to an end-of-session Republican strategy of slowing the Democratic-controlled House to a halt.

Congress had last approved an increase to park entrance fees in 1987. Since then, lawmakers had been reluctant to raise the fees, choosing instead in the 1993 Omnibus Budget-Reconciliation Act (PL 103-66) to expand the Interior and Agriculture departments' authority to assess and collect fees from other recreational activities and facilities, such as boat ramps and swimming areas. *(1993 Almanac, p. 128)*

Under existing law, the National Park Service charged entrance fees, either by car or per person, at 133 of the 367 units in the park system. Fees charged per vehicle were capped at $5 each, and individual entrance fees were capped at $3 each, with exceptions granted for larger fees at premier parks such as Yellowstone and the Grand Canyon. The cost of the Golden Eagle Passport, which visitors could use at all national parks and wildlife refuges for one year, was capped at $25.

On April 15, Interior Secretary Bruce Babbitt unveiled a legislative proposal to increase national park entrance fees and said he hoped to raise $32 million in fiscal 1995 from the plan.

House Action

Work on the bill began in the House Natural Resources Subcommittee on National Parks, Forests and Public Lands, which gave voice vote approval to HR 4533 on July 21. Rather than embracing the Clinton administration plan, however, the panel approved a substitute by Chairman Vento.

In a key change, the Vento substitute allowed Congress to retain its authority to set national park fees. The administra-

tion bill would have given that right solely to the Interior secretary. The substitute provided for an increase in the cap on entrance fees from $3 to $6 per person, and from $5 to $20 per vehicle. It boosted the cap for the Golden Eagle Passport from $25 to $40.

The Vento substitute provided that 100 percent of new entrance fees collected, starting in fiscal 1996, would remain in the National Park Service for resource protection, interpretation programs, research and maintenance. The Clinton plan called for 50 percent of entrance fees to remain in the parks. In fiscal 1993, entrance fees raised $41.1 million in revenue. Vento said it was unclear how much would be raised from his substitute because it depended on which parks chose to apply the increases and how much was collected from each site.

The full Natural Resources Committee approved the bill by voice vote Sept. 28 (H Rept 103-793). The panel first gave voice vote approval to an amendment by Pat Williams, D-Mont., capping the maximum total fee charged for passengers in a single non-commercial vehicle at $20.

House Floor

The House bill's troubles began Oct. 4, when Republicans called for a series of roll call votes as a delaying tactic to express their general frustration with the Democratic leadership. Vento tried to bring up the parks bill that day under suspension of the rules, an expedited procedure that prohibited amendments. It failed to win the necessary two-thirds by 37 votes, falling on a 238-174 vote. *(Vote 482, p. 142-H)*

Democratic leaders decided to reconsider the measure Oct. 5, according to Vento, because they thought the bill's first failure was simply attributable to the string of GOP procedural ploys. But the bill failed once again by a vote of 242-174. *(Vote 489, p. 144-H)*

"I guess they meant 'no,' " Vento said afterward.

Senate Committee

The Senate Energy and Natural Resources Committee on Sept. 21 approved its own bill (S 2121) to increase fees paid by national park visitors and restructure the park service's fee system. At the time, the House bill had not yet been taken up by the full House Natural Resources Committee.

Like the House subcommittee, the Senate panel rejected the administration plan to give broad discretion to the Interior secretary to increase or reduce park user fees, instead preserving that authority for Congress. Under S 2121, the Interior secretary could set entrance fees, but those fees would be capped at $6 per person. The cost of a Golden Eagle Passport would increase from $25 to $50.

Unlike the House bill, S 2121 retained the administration's proposal to use the part of the revenue raised from the fee increase for building improvements at the parks. With the revenue raised from fees in fiscal 1993 as a baseline, half the fees above that baseline would be used for the improvements.

A portion of the remaining fee increase would be applied to the cost of collection and the balance earmarked for the 1965 Land and Water Conservation Fund, the government's largest source of money for the purchase of public lands. Beginning in fiscal 1996, all the money raised from entrance fees would go to the National Park Service for resource protection, interpretation programs, research and maintenance.

The National Park Service estimated that it would get at least $36 million in additional fees from the Senate bill. ■

House Approves Creation Of 'Heritage Areas'

Over the objections of property rights advocates, the House passed a bill Oct. 5 authorizing the Interior Department to designate 10 "American Heritage areas" that had historical, natural or cultural significance in their communities but did not quite reach national park status. The bill (HR 5044) authorized $14.5 million for the purpose and urged state and local governments and private companies to manage those areas cooperatively.

However, the Senate took no action on a companion bill (S 2509), and the legislation died at the end of the session.

Work on the measure began in the House Natural Resources Subcommittee on National Parks, Forests and Public Lands. On May 19, the panel gave voice vote approval to a bill (HR 3707) by subcommittee Chairman Bruce F. Vento, D-Minn., to authorize the Interior secretary to develop new criteria to allow cultural, historic, natural and recreational resources to be protected as heritage areas. The full Natural Resources Committee approved the bill May 25 by voice vote (H Rept 103-570).

On Oct. 5, the House passed a revised American Heritage areas bill (HR 5044) by a vote of 281-137. The bill incorporated parts of HR 3707. *(Vote 486, p. 144-H)*

Property rights advocates succeeded in blocking the bill when it was first brought up Sept. 27 under suspension of the rules — an expedited procedure that allowed no amendments and required a two-thirds vote for passage. The vote was 273-150, nine votes short. *(Vote 442, p. 132-H)*

The property rights debate surfaced again when the bill was taken up Oct. 5 under procedures that required a simple majority for passage. Although HR 5044 specifically prohibited federal land acquisitions, advocates of property rights argued that it would permit local governments to include private lands within the boundaries of the heritage areas and establish bicycle and hiking trails on the land without an owner's consent.

Landowners "ought to be full partners in deciding whether to participate fully in these heritage corridors," said W. J. "Billy" Tauzin, D-La., who had led the charge to add protections for property owners on numerous bills.

Supporters of HR 5044 said it would provide residents who might be unable to visit such parks as Yellowstone or Grand Canyon with access to other scenic areas — with minimum imposition on landowners.

"They are not going to take anybody's land," Ralph Regula, R-Ohio, said of the local governments that would establish the heritage areas. "They are going to simply clean up the towpath, cut the brush."

Tauzin had hoped to add two amendments to the legislation: The first would have required local governments to obtain a landowner's consent before including land in a heritage area; the second would have required that landowners be compensated if their property values declined as a result of being included without their consent.

Instead, the House voted, 222-202, to approve a Regula amendment adding language to require county governments, rather than individual property owners, to consent to inclusion of land in a heritage area. *(Vote 484, p. 142-H)*

Lawmakers also adopted, 234-187, an amendment by Nick J. Rahall II, D-W.Va., to require that landowners be told how to seek compensation if their property was included in a heritage area. *(Vote 485, p. 144-H)* ■

Steamtown Site Survives Derailment Attempt

The House on July 12 passed a bill (HR 3708) to scale back funding for the Steamtown National Historic site in Scranton, Pa. The Senate Energy and Natural Resources Committee approved a separate version of the bill, but the Senate took no further action on it.

Since its inception in 1986, critics had characterized Steamtown as a quintessential pork barrel project, raising questions about its historical value and objecting that lawmakers had appropriated $81 million for the site despite the fact that it had never been authorized.

Since Yellowstone was designated the first national park by Congress in 1872, the national park system had grown to 367 sites covering 80 million acres. Every state except Rhode Island and each of the U.S. territories boasted a national park facility.

There was a procedure for designating a national park: The Interior secretary, with help from an advisory board, was asked by Congress for recommendations on proposed additions to the system. But lawmakers had bypassed that process, in essence, sanctioning new national parks through appropriations. That happened in 1986 when federal funds were first provided for the Steamtown National Historic Site, a controversial museum designed to memorialize the age of steam-powered locomotion.

Legislative Action

A House Natural Resources subcommittee gave voice vote approval June 16 to a bill (HR 3708), sponsored by Chairman Bruce F. Vento, D-Minn., aimed at changing the rules governing the operation, maintenance and development of Steamtown. The National Parks, Forests and Public Lands Subcommittee bill allowed the park to use only 5 percent of its operating funds to restore locomotives and rolling stock. The park was required to prepare a plan to get rid of items in its collection that lacked significant historical value and that were unnecessary for interpretive activities. Train rides offered by the park had to be completely financed by passenger fees.

Joel Hefley, R-Colo., successfully offered an amendment requiring the park to look into other ways to run the museum, including partnerships with local governments or private sector management.

The full Natural Resources Committee gave voice vote approval to the bill June 22 (H Rept 103-588). The House passed the bill by voice vote July 12.

The Senate Energy and Natural Resources Committee approved an amended version of HR 3708 by a vote of 20-0 on Sept. 21. The Senate committee's bill authorized operation of the existing site but barred future appropriations for construction and development at Steamtown unless they were specifically authorized. The bill also required that only 5 percent of the operating expenditures for the site be used to restore the locomotives and rolling stock.

Before approving the bill, the committee adopted an unrelated amendment, offered by Trent Lott, R-Miss., to authorize unspecified appropriations to buy land for a new Civil War battlefield park in Corinth, Miss. Under Lott's amendment, the Interior secretary was to acquire land — by donation, by purchase with donated or appropriated money, or by exchanging lands owned by the federal government — near the site of the 1862 battle. Up to $6 million could be appropriated for the construction of a visitors' center on the site.

The full Senate did not take action on the Steamtown bill, letting it die at the end of the session. ■

Presidio Management Bill Stalls

With the historic Presidio military post in San Francisco slated to become a national park, the House twice passed legislation to provide for its management and operation. A Senate committee approved an amended version of the bill, but the legislation never made it to the Senate floor.

The House first approved the Presidio management plan (HR 3433) in August; when the companion Senate bill became bogged down, the House tried a second time, passing an identical bill (HR 5231) on Oct. 7.

The Presidio, established as a Spanish colonial military settlement in 1776, was the oldest continually operating military post in the nation. Located at the foot of the Golden Gate Bridge, the 1,480-acre complex with its 870 buildings was a scenic attraction marked by forests, grasslands and coastal bluffs. The complex contained several office buildings, residences and a hospital that the federal government wanted to lease to private companies. Just over half the area was undeveloped.

A law enacted in 1972 (PL 92-589) mandated that if the Defense Department ever decided that it no longer needed the base the Army facility would be shifted to the National Park Service and become part of the Golden Gate National Recreation Area. In 1988, the Presidio was included in the list of unneeded facilities targeted for shutdown by the Base Realignment and Closure Commission. *(1988 Almanac, p. 439)*

The Presidio was thus slated to be converted to Interior Department control on Oct. 1, 1994, becoming part of the Golden Gate National Recreation Area. The General Accounting Office estimated that it would cost $700 million to $1.2 billion over 15 years to complete the transfer.

In 1993, the base closure commission modified its recommendation to allow the continued presence of the 6th U.S. Army Headquarters at the Presidio. About 500 military and civilian personnel were allowed to remain on about one-third of the property after the Presidio changed hands. *(1993 Almanac, p. 465)*

The park service planned to restore and adapt for new uses about 475 historic buildings on the Presidio lands; it planned to tear down most of the others to create additional open space.

House Committee Action

The House Natural Resources Subcommittee on National Parks, Forests and Public Lands approved HR 3433 by voice vote on June 27. The measure, introduced by Nancy Pelosi, D-Calif., was amended by a substitute offered by Bruce F. Vento, D-Minn. The panel then approved the bill by voice vote.

The full Natural Resources Committee took up HR 3433 on June 29, approving the measure, 28-14, after adopting some minor amendments (H Rept 103-615, Part 1).

The bill provided for the creation of the Presidio Trust, a government corporation within the Interior Department, to manage the facility. For the first five years, while the corporation was being set up, the park service was authorized to

---

BOXSCORE

Presidio Management — HR 5231 (HR 3433, S 1639). The bill provided for maintenance and operation of the Presidio, a historic military base in California that had been transferred to the Interior Department.

Report: H Rept 103-615, Parts 1 and 2.

KEY ACTION

Aug. 18 — House passed HR 3433, 245-168.

Sept. 21 — Senate committee reported HR 3433, amended.

Oct. 7 — House passed HR 5231 by voice vote.

---

lease Presidio properties and use the income to maintain the buildings and grounds. Once the Presidio Trust was up and running, it was to take over the leasing and management of Presidio properties and develop visitor programs and activities at the site. The bill authorized up to $25 million annually for the project.

Vento said use of a government corporation to manage the Presidio would lead to 30 percent savings over traditional park service management and annual savings of $30 million to $40 million over the Pentagon's costs.

The committee rejected, 14-28, an amendment by Wayne Allard, R-Colo., to restrict funds to develop facilities at the Presidio to the ceiling established for the entire Golden Gate National Recreation Area. It also would have required California and the city of San Francisco to share costs of visitor programs at the Presidio and would have barred the use of any park service funds for leased facilities there. Allard said that without his amendment, the Presidio would cost the federal government more than all new parks brought into the system since 1980. "I think it's probably inappropriate to even have it as a park," Allard told the committee.

Vento strenuously objected to the amendment, saying that in many cases it would be impossible to separate improvements to leased facilities from improvements to the rest of the Presidio.

HR 3433 went next to the House Ways and Means Committee, which reluctantly gave voice vote approval Aug. 4 to the bill's tax and borrowing provisions (H Rept 103-615, Part 2).

The borrowing provisions were a sticking point for the committee. After heated debate, the panel approved by voice vote a substitute by acting Chairman Sam M. Gibbons, D-Fla., to allow the Presidio Trust to borrow up to $150 million at any one time directly from the Treasury.

The panel also approved, 18-16, an amendment by ranking member Bill Archer, R-Texas, requiring the Appropriations Committee to allocate any of the funds the Treasury would be lending to the trust. Some members contended that Gibbons' plan would skirt appropriations and budget rules.

As reported by the Natural Resources Committee, the bill would have given the trust broad authority to borrow money from public and private sources to repair federal land and refurbish buildings. It would have set no limits.

House Floor Action

The House passed the bill Aug. 18 by a vote of 245-168. The bill included the Ways and Means provisions. *(Vote 411, p. 124-H)*

During the sometimes contentious floor debate, Republicans argued that the financially strapped National Park Service could not afford to take on new duties. But bill sponsor Pelosi, aided by a phalanx of California Democrats, countered that the proposed management structure would save the federal government money in the long run.

Two Republican proposals aimed at limiting the Presidio's costs were rejected. They were:

● An Allard amendment that would have limited the authorization for the Presidio's development to $58 million and required 50 percent of the costs for the construction of visitor facilities and operation of visitor programs to be picked up by private sources. It was rejected, 171-244. *(Vote 409, p. 122-H)*

● An amendment by Rod Grams, R-Minn., that would have established budget caps for the operation and management of the Presidio. It was rejected, 190-227. *(Vote 410, p. 122-H)*

The bill, as passed, was referred to the Senate Committee on Energy and Natural Resources.

Senate Committee Action

The Senate Energy and Natural Resources Committee approved a companion Presidio management bill (S 1639) on Sept. 21 by a vote of 20-0. The committee then inserted the text of its bill into HR 3433 and reported the revised bill to the full Senate.

The measure provided for the establishment of a public benefit corporation, run by the Interior Department, to oversee the leasing and repair of buildings at the Presidio park. The bill was approved along with an amendment to allow the trust managing the Presidio park to incur as public debt the proceeds from the sale of up to $150 million worth of securities.

The House measure, by contrast, made financing for the trust subject to annual appropriation.

Had it progressed further in the Senate, the measure was likely to face stiff opposition from Republicans and some Democrats who were concerned about the Presidio's costs.

House Approves Clean Bill

On Oct. 7, the House gave voice vote approval to a fresh bill (HR 5231) that was identical to the House-passed version of HR 3433. With the initial measure amended and bogged down in the Senate, sponsors hoped to free up the legislation and win quick Senate passage. The Senate, however, did not act on HR 5231. ■

Other National Parks Bills Considered in 1994

Congress acted on a variety of additional bills related to the national parks system, clearing measures to improve water flow through the Everglades and to ease rules for beach and barrier island restoration projects. A number of other bills saw action but died at the end of the Congress.

Everglades Protection

The Senate on Feb. 10 cleared without debate a House-passed bill to improve water flow through the Everglades into Florida Bay. President Clinton signed the measure into law March 9 (HR 3617 — PL 103-219).

The bill, sponsored by E. Clay Shaw Jr., R-Fla., authorized the Interior secretary to spend $17.4 million to purchase land needed for the water flow project. The tracts to be acquired were primarily agricultural lands located east of Everglades National Park. The funds were to be transferred from an Army Corps of Engineers flood control and pump station project. The Florida Bay water flow project was expected to cost federal, state and local governments $100 million.

The bill began moving through Congress in 1993. The

House Natural Resources Committee approved it by unanimous consent Nov. 22; the House passed it by voice vote the following day. The Senate Energy and Natural Resources Committee approved the bill, 17-3, on Feb. 2, 1994 (S Rept 103-224). *(1993 Almanac, p. 284)*

Urban Recreation

The House on March 22 passed a bill to direct more funding toward recreational programs in urban areas as a way of fighting juvenile crime. The Senate never voted on the bill (HR 4034), but portions of it were included in the omnibus crime bill signed into law by President Clinton on Sept. 13 (HR 3355 — PL 103-322).

The Urban Recreation and At-Risk Youth Act, which the House passed by a vote of 361-59, sought to revise the 1978 Urban Park and Recreation Recovery Act (PL 95-625) to authorize matching grants to urban areas for the rehabilitation of recreation facilities and for the support of innovative recreation programs. *(Vote 82, p. 26-H)*

Drafted by George Miller, D-Calif., the bill called for the creation of a new category of "At-Risk Youth Recreation Grants" for programs that would help keep juveniles from crime, with an emphasis on late-night and after-school programs. The bill also encouraged collaboration between recreation agencies and law enforcement and social service organizations.

The House Natural Resources Committee gave voice vote approval to the bill March 16 (H Rept 103-444). In the Senate, the Energy and Natural Resources Subcommittee on Public Lands, National Parks and Forests held hearings on the legislation on May 19 but took no further action.

Six Rivers National Forest

The House passed a bill Sept. 21 to allow the government to acquire a large, privately owned section of redwood forest in Northern California. But the Senate did not act on the bill, and it died at the of the session.

The House's Headwaters Forest Act (HR 2866) provided for the government to add 44,000 acres of redwood forest to the Six Rivers National Forest in Humboldt County. Supporters said the bill would provide a management plan and protection from accelerated logging. They were particularly concerned about 3,000 acres known as the Headwaters Forest — the nation's largest privately owned tract of ancient redwoods — which was to be included as federally protected wilderness. The Headwaters Forest, which had never been logged, was home to some endangered species. Logging was to be banned there and in about 2,000 surrounding acres but could continue under tighter regulation in the rest of the forest.

The bill was referred jointly to the House Agriculture and Natural Resources committees. The Natural Resources Committee approved its version of the bill by voice vote May 11 (H Rept 103-667, Part 1). The Agriculture Committee approved its version by voice vote July 13 (H Rept 103-667, Part 2).

The House took up the bill Sept. 21 and passed it by a vote of 288-133. *(Vote 433, p. 130-H)*

Lawmakers agreed by voice vote to a block of floor amendments offered by Agriculture Committee Chairman E. "Kika" de la Garza, D-Texas. The amendments included a provision by Richard W. Pombo, R-Calif., to require the government to get the consent of the landowner, Pacific Lumber Co., before acquiring the Headwaters Forest land. The amend-

ment also allowed Pacific Lumber to continue to use the land as it chose until the government bought it.

The House also approved, 240-188, an amendment by John T. Doolittle, R-Calif., to authorize only $200 million for the purchase. The Congressional Budget Office estimated that the land could cost as much as $1 billion. The government, however, could arrange a deal that would involve the exchange of federally owned land. *(Vote 431, p. 128-H)*

Opponents said the bill would infringe on the rights of private landowners by allowing the presence of endangered species or old-growth forest to devalue the land. Under the rule governing the floor debate, Pombo was not allowed to offer an amendment that was meant to prevent such devaluing by ensuring that the 44,000 acres would be sold without regard to the presence of endangered species or old-growth forest.

Russian River

The House Merchant Marine and Fisheries Committee on Aug. 11 approved a bill (HR 4408) calling for the restoration of the fisheries and riverbed of Northern California's Russian River, once home to a bounty of steelhead trout. No other action was taken on the bill by either chamber. The measure called on the Agriculture Department's Soil Conservation Service and the Environmental Protection Agency to work with willing landowners on projects that would reduce erosion and restore fish habitat and on other water management projects. The bill would have authorized $7 million.

Wheeling Heritage Area

The House on April 13 rejected a bill (HR 2843) that would have created a national heritage area in Wheeling, W.Va. The vote was 264-154, 15 short of the two-thirds majority necessary to pass under expedited procedures known as suspension of the rules. *(Vote 101, p. 30-H)*

Provisions of HR 2843 were included in a House-passed bill (HR 5044) authorizing $14.5 million for the designation of 10 "American Heritage areas" that had historical significance in their communities but did not quite reach national park status. The list included Wheeling, W.Va. But the Senate did not act on that measure, and it died at the end of the Congress. *(Heritage areas, p. 252)*

The Wheeling bill, sponsored by Alan B. Mollohan, D-W.Va., would have authorized the Interior secretary to provide $6.5 million in grants to local, state and private groups that had been working to commemorate Wheeling's history as a transportation and industrial site.

Wayne Allard, R-Colo., said the federal government could not afford to pay for the proposed Wheeling heritage area when the National Park Service was already having trouble keeping up with maintenance and daily operations. The park service estimated in 1992 that it would cost $28 million to implement the Wheeling National Heritage Area management plan.

The House Natural Resources Committee had reported the bill April 12 (H Rept 130-471).

Conservation at Military Bases

The House passed a bill (HR 3300) Sept. 12 by voice vote aimed at improving the Defense Department's protection of fish and wildlife at its military installations. But the measure, which would have reauthorized a 1960 law known as the Sikes Act through 1997, never got to the Senate floor.

The House Merchant Marine and Fisheries Committee had approved the measure by voice vote Aug. 11 (H Rept 103-718). The Senate Environment and Public Works Committee approved it Sept. 27.

Introduced by Gerry E. Studds, D-Mass., chairman of the House Merchant Marine and Fisheries Committee, the bill proposed that the Defense Department be required to develop a management plan for about 900 military installations covering about 25 million acres. The department's compliance with the law had been lax. The secretary of Defense was to be given the latitude to determine which military installations were appropriate for wildlife preservation programs and which bases would not be covered. Conservation plans were to be implemented two years after enactment.

The bill also would have required the Defense Department to make annual reports to Congress about its fish and wildlife protection programs.

Outer Continental Shelf

In the waning days of the session, both chambers gave quick approval to a bill authorizing the Interior secretary to negotiate agreements for the use of outer continental shelf resources. The House passed the measure Oct. 3 by voice vote under suspension of the rules. The Senate cleared it Oct. 6, also by voice vote. President Clinton signed the bill Oct. 31 (HR 3678 — PL 103-426).

The bill was aimed at making it easier for coastal states to use outer continental shelf resources such as sand or shells for beach and barrier island restoration projects. It allowed the Interior secretary to waive fees for sand and gravel resources used in coastal management programs that were funded with at least 50 percent federal funds. Under existing law, the federal government was required to lease such rights, a process that bill supporters argued had allowed commercial interests to outbid government entities seeking the same rights.

The bill had been referred to two committees in the House — the panels on Merchant Marine and Fisheries, and on Natural Resources. The Oceanography, Gulf of Mexico and the Outer Continental Shelf panel of the Merchant Marine and Fisheries Committee approved the bill by voice vote Aug. 4. The full Merchant Marine Committee approved HR 3678 by voice vote Aug. 11 (H Rept 103-817, Part 1). The Natural Resources Committee approved the bill by voice vote Sept. 28. ∎

Hill Leaves Timber Feud to Courts

Congress mostly sat on the sidelines as a battle that pitted the threatened northern spotted owl against timber jobs in the Pacific Northwest slogged through the federal courts in 1994. At year's end, the court accepted a plan submitted by the Clinton administration intended to allow limited timber harvests while protecting the owl.

Although Pacific Northwest lawmakers were eager to settle the dispute through legislation, they lacked the political support to do so. They also faced significant opposition from the administration and environmentalists who wanted the courts to resolve the matter.

The Senate did clear a bill (HR 4196) on Oct. 6 that provided modest assistance to selected rural Pacific Northwest communities that were expected to be hard hit by the Clinton administration's forest preservation plan for the region.

Two days later, the Senate cleared a separate measure (HR 5161) that clarified how timber receipts from federal lands were to be distributed among counties in Washington, Oregon and Northern California. Another bill (S 2100) to protect the ecosystem of the Pacific region's forests advanced in the House but died in the Senate.

On a separate front, the administration moved ahead with some aspects of its Pacific Northwest forest preservation plan that did not require court approval, such as establishing an office in Portland, Ore., to assist communities with worker retraining programs and to oversee forest management projects, such as watershed planning.

Background

The federal government had been caught up since 1989 in a protracted legal battle over timber harvests in the Pacific Northwest. The issue became more heated in 1990, when the spotted owl, which inhabited old-growth forests in Washington, Oregon and Northern California, was declared threatened under the 1973 Endangered Species Act (PL 93-205).

In 1991, U.S. District Judge William Dwyer of Seattle halted logging on public lands, ruling that the government was violating environmental laws by overharvesting. The Bush administration tried to suspend the Endangered Species Act and allow logging on some of the timberland that was home to the spotted owl, but it was blocked by court injunctions.

President Clinton submitted his own forest management plan to Judge Dwyer in 1993. The proposal called for an annual timber harvest of 1.2 billion board feet, about half the amount cut before the federal court imposed the logging ban. The plan reserved areas for the spotted owl in which logging was to be greatly restricted. To help workers and families in the region, Clinton proposed spending $1.2 billion over five years for a new Northwest Economic Adjustment Fund to support retraining and activities such as cleaning up logging roads. *(1993 Almanac, p. 270)*

Court Action

On June 6, Judge Dwyer lifted the three-year ban on logging on Forest Service lands in the Pacific Northwest, but delayed implementation of the ruling pending a final decision on the legality of Clinton's forest management plan. Judge Dwyer reached that decision on Dec. 21, upholding the Clinton plan, which was known as "Option 9." The court ruled that the plan met the requirements of the Endangered Species Act and forestry management laws.

In doing so, the court dismissed criticism from environmental groups that the plan did not go far enough to protect owl, salmon and other wildlife in old-growth forests. The timber industry also contested the administration's plan, contending that it was too restrictive and was developed in violation of federal open-meetings laws.

To win over environmentalists and strengthen its case in court, the administration had scaled back the logging proposal on Feb. 23. The revised plan called for harvests of 1.1 billion board feet of timber annually over 10 years, one-fifth the amount cut during peak years in the mid-1980s. The Clinton plan's proposed restrictions on timber harvests applied to forests in western Washington, western Oregon and Northern California. The plan called for establishing reserves of old-growth forests to protect the owl's breeding grounds, as well as key watersheds and streams. An estimated 9,500 jobs were expected to be lost under the plan.

Legislative Action

The lengthy legal action left Congress to focus on less sweeping steps, including allocating money to the region — a key element of Clinton's plan to resolve the long-stalled issue. For example, the fiscal 1995 Interior Appropriations bill (HR 4602 — PL 103-332) included about $169 million to allow timber sales proposed in the administration's plan to proceed and to pay for watershed assessment and restoration projects and ongoing economic development projects. *(Appropriations, p. 513)*

● **Aid to logging areas.** The Senate on Oct. 6 cleared a bill (HR 4196) by voice vote authorizing modest assistance to rural communities that were expected to be hard hit by Clinton's forest preservation plan. Clinton signed the bill Oct. 31 (PL 103-427).

The measure authorized the Rural Development Administration to award water and sewer grants to timber-dependent communities of up to 25,000 in population in the areas affected by logging restrictions. Under the bill, larger communities were eligible for the grants for the first time; previously, the grants had been available for towns of 10,000 or fewer.

The bill began in the House Agriculture Subcommittee on Environment, Credit and Rural Development, which approved it Sept. 21 by voice vote. The full Agriculture Committee approved it by voice vote Sept. 28. The House passed the bill by voice vote the following day.

● **Timber receipts.** By voice vote, the Senate on Oct. 8 cleared a bill that clarified how timber receipts from federal lands were to be distributed among counties in Washington, Oregon and Northern California. Clinton signed the measure Nov. 2 (HR 5161 — PL 103-443).

The bill, sponsored by Rep. Norm Dicks, D-Wash., made technical corrections to the 1993 budget-reconciliation act (PL 103-66). That law established a new formula for dividing timber receipts to counties in the Pacific Northwest that were financially strapped because of the ongoing legal dispute over the spotted owl. *(1993 Almanac, p. 139)*

The bill clarified which account the timber receipts were to come from within the Treasury. It was jointly referred to

the House Agriculture and Natural Resources committees, which sent the bill to the floor without changes. The House passed the bill by voice vote Oct. 5.

● **Ecosystem management.** The House amended and passed by voice vote Oct. 7 a pared-down bill (S 2100) to continue an ecosystem management program in Idaho. The Senate, which had passed a more extensive version of S 2100 by voice vote May 10, took no action on the revised bill, and it died.

The bill proposed to extend for one year a national demonstration project created by the fiscal 1993 Interior appropriations bill (PL 102-381). The project was intended to find the best ways to protect forest ecosystems across the country. Under the House-approved amendment to S 2100, which was offered by Larry LaRocco, D-Idaho, the bill's scope was limited to the Idaho Panhandle National Forest. *(1992 Almanac, p. 686)*

The original Senate-passed version, sponsored by Dennis DeConcini, D-Ariz., proposed to extend ecosystem management projects in several national forests, including those in Vermont, New Hampshire, Maine, Arizona and Alabama. The Forest Service was testing ways to improve wildlife habitats, watersheds, fisheries, timber stands and reforestation. The bill allowed the Forest Service to use all or a portion of receipts from the sale of timber and other wood products in forests in Alabama, Arizona, California, Idaho, New Hampshire, Maine and Vermont to continue such activities.

The bill also proposed to extend such projects for other public lands operated by the Agriculture Department's Forest Service. Some of the projects outside Idaho had been reauthorized, and others had been discontinued because they showed no economic benefit. ■

Hill Revamps Marine Mammal Act

Congress reauthorized the 1972 Marine Mammal Protection Act in a bill that lawmakers said would reduce the accidental killing of marine mammals without harming the economic well-being of commercial fishermen. President Clinton signed the bill into law April 30 (S 1636 — PL 103-238).

The measure was hailed as a compromise between environmentalists and the $10 billion-a-year fishing industry, which had been at odds since Congress first voted to protect marine mammals.

The key issue was how to control and eventually reduce the accidental killing of marine mammals that regularly interfered with fishing operations — without causing a virtual shutdown of the fishing industry. Commercial fishing operations in the United States faced stiff international competition, and some, such as the New England fishing industry, were further hampered by dwindling stocks of fish. Fishermen had bristled at burdensome federal regulations that they said placed wildlife protection over the industry's survival.

The six-year reauthorization, cleared April 26, retained the goal of the 1972 act to reduce the accidental killing of porpoises, whales, seals and other marine mammals to "insignificant levels," meaning as close to zero as possible. The bill required the goal to be reached within seven years, and it authorized $20 million annually in fiscal years 1994-99 to carry out conservation measures.

The bill explicitly outlawed the intentional killing of marine mammals by commercial fishermen. However, it allowed the intentional killing of "nuisance" seals and sea lions that had been eating endangered and threatened fish stocks at dams. It included regulations for the public display of marine mammals in zoos, aquariums and theme parks.

The bill also contained a controversial provision lifting a ban on importing trophies, typically skins, of polar bears that were legally hunted in Canada. Animal protection groups argued that the provision would lead to more killings, but

---

BOXSCORE

Marine Mammal Protection Act Reauthorization — S 1636 (HR 2760). The six-year reauthorization sought to reduce accidental killing of marine mammals without harming the fishing industry.

Reports: S Rept 103-220, H Rept 103-439.

KEY ACTION

March 21 — Senate passed S 1636 by voice vote; **House** passed HR 2760 by voice vote.

March 22 — House amended S 1636 and passed it by voice vote.

April 26 — After further amendments, **House** agreed to S 1636 by voice vote; **Senate** cleared the bill.

April 30 — President signed bill — PL 103-238.

---

supporters noted that Canada had a strict quota on the number of bears that could be killed.

The provision split two of the driving forces behind the bill: Sen. John Kerry, D-Mass., and Rep. Gerry E. Studds, D-Mass., both known as strong environmentalists. Studds agreed to include the polar bear provision in the original House bill (HR 2760) only after writing safeguards to ensure that Canada's sport-hunting rules would be upheld. Kerry's original version of S 1636 did not mention polar bear trophies. He relented March 24 by amending the bill on the Senate floor to include language to require a two-year study on Canada's polar bear stock and allow the Interior secretary to revoke permits for importing trophies if the study found negative effects. The House accepted Kerry's amendment.

Kerry said he regretted that he could not persuade Studds and other House negotiators to drop the polar bear language. Still, he said the final bill represented "a strong environmental package that protects marine mammals and treats fairly all those that interact with them."

Background

The 1972 protection act was designed to prevent the extinction of marine mammals and, in some cases, to return them to healthy populations. At the time it was enacted, porpoises regularly became entangled in tuna nets and seals were clubbed to death for their pelts. The law banned the intentional killing or capture of mammals and prohibited the import of mammal skins or products into the United States. It included highly regulated exceptions for accidental takings by commercial fishermen.

But a 1987 court ruling blocked the National Marine Fisheries Service from issuing permits for some fishermen to accidentally harm marine mammals. The fishing industry argued that the ruling had the potential to shut down

New Rhino, Tiger Fund

Congress cleared a bill (HR 4924) aimed at halting the poaching of rhinoceroses and tigers. The measure authorized $10 million annually in fiscal years 1996-2000 for a new Rhinoceros and Tiger Conservation Fund, to be administered by the Interior secretary. The fund was to make grants to foreign governments and nonprofit groups that were trying to conserve the rare animals in their home countries. President Clinton signed the bill into law Oct. 22 (PL 103-391).

Scientists estimated that at the beginning of the 20th century there were about 1 million rhinos and 100,000 tigers worldwide, but poaching and destruction of their habitat had reduced the numbers to fewer than 11,000 rhinos and 6,000 tigers in the wild. The trading of rhino and tiger body parts and exportation of products made from them were lucrative businesses, with ground rhino horns, which were claimed to treat headaches and control fevers, selling for as much as $60,000 per kilogram. A tiger's pelt was worth up to $14,000, and tiger bone could sell for $900 to $1,300 per kilogram.

The fund created under the new law was modeled after a fund established by Congress in 1988 to protect African elephants as part of the Endangered Species Act reauthorization (PL 100-478).

The House Merchant Marine and Fisheries Committee led the charge to protect the rhinos and tigers. Ranking Republican Jack Fields of Texas introduced HR 4924 as an alternative to a tougher measure (HR 3987) that would have imposed a moratorium on importing wildlife products from foreign countries that engaged in activities harmful to rhinos and tigers. The committee approved HR 4924 by voice vote Aug. 11 (H Rept 103-748). The House passed the bill by voice vote Sept. 27.

When the Senate did not act on the measure, House lawmakers on Oct. 7 attached it to an unrelated maritime bill (HR 3664). When that measure stalled, the Senate on Oct. 8 pulled out HR 4924 and passed it by voice vote, thus clearing it for the president's signature.

U.S. commercial fishing operations. In response, Congress in 1988 passed a five-year exemption allowing permits for the commercial fishing industry. That exemption and the underlying law were set to expire Oct. 1, 1993. *(1988 Almanac, p. 168)*

The legislation was extended in September 1993 (HR 3049 — PL 103-86), giving lawmakers until April 1, 1994, to negotiate protections acceptable to conservationists and the fishing industry. Efforts to produce such a plan in 1993 got no further than the Senate Commerce Committee, which approved a five-year reauthorization bill sponsored by Kerry (S 1636 — S Rept 103-220) on Nov. 9. The House Merchant Marine and Fisheries Committee did not act on a companion bill. *(1993 Almanac, p. 280)*

A 1994 Stopgap Extension

When the 1994 session began, lawmakers hoped to clear the long-term reauthorization bill by the April 1 deadline. But when negotiations became snagged in late March, the two chambers quickly moved to provide a new, 30-day extension.

The House passed the stopgap bill (HR 4122) by voice vote March 24. The Senate cleared it by voice vote the next day, in time for the president to sign it March 31 (PL 103-228).

House Committee

A Merchant Marine and Fisheries subcommittee on March 9 gave voice vote approval to the House version of the long-term bill (HR 2760), sponsored by subcommittee Chairman Studds and Don Young, R-Alaska.

As approved by the Environment and Natural Resources Subcommittee, the five-year reauthorization continued the ban on intentional killing of marine mammals that interfered with fishing operations, although it changed the law to make an exception when a fisherman's life was in danger. The bill also changed the old law to step up monitoring of such animals. And it required the government to work to reduce within five years to "levels approaching zero" the number of marine mammals accidentally killed by commercial fishermen.

Studds and Young hailed their bill as a delicate compromise because it allowed limited killing of animals to protect the fishing industry, while strengthening conservation techniques needed to prevent extinctions.

But environmentalists strongly disagreed, charging that the bill would gut the intent of the original act and allow too many marine mammals to be killed. "The whole bill in our view is an unmitigated disaster," said Wayne Pacelle, national director of the Fund for Animals, a conservation group.

Studds drew special fire for a provision that reversed an import ban on marine mammal parts obtained legally outside the United States. The language, which Studds had included at the request of ranking committee Republican Jack Fields of Texas, specifically allowed sport hunters who killed polar bears in Canada to bring back their trophies, usually the animal's hide, to the United States. Studds said the change would not lead to the killing of more polar bears, since Canada had a quota on how many animals could be hunted annually. Permits, which were sold to sport hunters for $15,000 to $20,000 each, were issued based on that quota.

The panel approved by voice vote a Studds amendment to require polar bear hunters to pay a permit fee to bring the skins into the United States, with the money going to develop a conservation plan for polar bears in Alaska and Russia.

The subcommittee also approved by voice vote an amendment by Jolene Unsoeld, D-Wash., to allow the killing of nuisance marine mammals in certain circumstances. For several years, California sea lions had preyed on steelhead trout in Seattle's Ballard Locks, preventing the fish from spawning during their annual winter run. Washington state officials had tried to move the sea lions with firecrackers, arrows and fake sounds of killer whales — to no avail.

The panel approved by voice vote an amendment by Young to streamline the process required to capture and display marine mammals in zoos and aquariums.

Full Committee

The full Merchant Marine and Fisheries Committee approved the bill by voice vote March 16 (H Rept 103-439) after making it a six-year reauthorization.

The stipulation added by Studds to the polar bear provisions persuaded lawmakers to vote 13-30 against an amendment by Peter Deutsch, D-Fla., on environmental grounds. Deutsch's amendment would have stripped all polar bear language from the bill.

322210

Final Action

Hurrying to make the April 1 deadline, the House and Senate passed their respective bills by voice vote March 21. Negotiators came to an agreement the same night, without a formal conference, and the House approved a compromise version of S 1636 by voice vote March 22.

At that point, however, the bill became hung up over two issues unrelated to marine mammals.

The first was the House provision lifting the ban on the import of polar bear skins. Negotiators included that language in the final bill, even though the provision, which animal protection groups vehemently opposed, was not in the original Senate bill.

Kerry went along, but he amended the House version of S 1636 to call for a two-year study tracking the health of a Canadian polar bear sleuth. The amendment allowed the Interior secretary to revoke trophy permits if the study found negative effects on the sleuth.

The Senate also removed a provision from the House version of S 1636 that would have expanded the bill's definition of "takings" of animals to include actions that would "harm" a mammal population. The timber industry was fearful that expanding the definition would disrupt its efforts to narrow environmental laws that restricted the use of private property. Sen. Ted Stevens, R-Alaska, said that Congress had not had enough time to study the issue.

To satisfy environmentalists, the final bill made explicit that the secretaries of Interior and Commerce had the authority to protect marine mammal habitat. In the case of marine mammals, habitat meant feeding grounds, rookeries, nursery grounds and migration paths.

The back and forth between the two chambers, particularly over the definition of takings, stalled the bill long enough that members saw a need to clear the interim measure.

The House passed S 1636 a final time by voice vote April 26. The Senate cleared the bill the same day, also by voice vote. ∎

Lawmakers Abandon Fishing Bill

The 103rd Congress shelved plans to renew the nation's primary fishing law after a key House committee chairman declared the effort dead Sept. 28.

Gerry E. Studds, D-Mass., chairman of the House Merchant Marine and Fisheries Committee, said there was not enough time to reach consensus on a bipartisan bill (HR 780) to reauthorize the 1976 Magnuson Fishery Conservation and Management Act (PL 94-265). Studds pointed to wide disagreement on controversial issues such as privatizing fisheries and imposing fishing fees.

The announcement ran counter to the hopes of Sen. John Kerry, D-Mass., a key player on fishing issues. Kerry had planned to push for speedy passage of his own comprehensive reauthorization bill in 1993, but his effort never advanced in the Senate.

The 1976 law was designed to halt overfishing by foreign fleets and to bolster the domestic fishing industry. It gave the United States sole management authority of all resources within 200 miles of its shores. The law created eight regional management councils charged with developing plans to allocate fishing rights for species within their jurisdictions. But the councils were filled with commercial and recreational fishing experts, sparking charges of conflicts of interest.

While the Magnuson Act was credited with boosting U.S. access to ocean fisheries, it had not been as successful in making sure there were enough fish to keep recreational and commercial fishing operations in business. More than half the nation's 213 most commercially harvested fish species were severely depleted, according to the National Marine Fisheries Service. Ground fish that swam on the ocean bottom in New England, such as cod and haddock, were particularly hard hit. Yellowtail flounder were considered "economically extinct" because there were not enough fish available to make catches profitable.

To try to address the diminished supply, the federal government had been imposing regulations to sharply reduce fishing. The rules caused many boats to sit idle and, in some cases, forced their operators out of business. In an unprecedented move, Commerce Secretary Ronald H. Brown in March offered $30 million in economic aid to New England fishing operations.

Subcommittee Action

A House Merchant Marine panel approved HR 780 by voice vote Aug. 10. The Fisheries Management Subcommittee first accepted a substitute by Chairman Thomas J. Manton, D-N.Y., and ranking Republican Don Young of Alaska.

The legislation addressed many concerns raised by the Clinton administration, the Commerce Department's inspector general, and fishing industry and conservation groups during 11 hearings held in 1993. But the panel deflected decisions on such issues as user fees and fishing quotas for the full committee — which never acted.

Manton had warned that it was going to be difficult to balance the Magnuson Act's often conflicting goals of commerce and conservation. "We must recognize that responsible conservation and management will still impose burdens on fishermen," he said.

The Manton-Young measure emphasized the protection of fish habitat, attempted to reduce overfishing and the catching of young or unwanted fish, and addressed the possible conflicts of interest in the regional management councils.

Specifically, it proposed to add new definitions to existing law for terms such as "overfishing" and "essential fishery habitat" and to require more detail in the fishing management plans developed by the regional councils. The plans were to include steps to ensure that fish stocks be replenished on a continuing basis and that the areas necessary for the spawning, breeding and growth of fish be protected.

The bill also called for extending a ban on foreign boats fishing for Atlantic herring and Atlantic mackerel. The existing moratorium, which expired Sept. 30, 1993, was to be extended through fiscal 1999.

Amendments

During the subcommittee markup, provisions aimed at improving the regional management councils generated the most controversy.

Under the legislation, the Commerce secretary was directed to consider qualifications other than active participation in a fishery when appointing regional council members. The goal was to include academics, conservationists, consumer advocates and other non-users to the

industry-dominated councils.

Although existing law allowed the appointment of such non-users, members outside the recreational and commercial fishing industries were rarely chosen. The council that oversaw the South Atlantic region, for example, had eight members who represented fishing interests, and the council that oversaw the Gulf of Mexico had three non-users among its 11 members. This type of membership led to concerns about conflicts of interest and what Rep. Maria Cantwell, D-Wash., described as "members voting their pocketbooks."

To eliminate potential conflicts, the legislation proposed that members be required to file financial disclosure forms and that they be barred from voting on matters from which they could benefit financially. But Jolene Unsoeld, D-Wash., and Cantwell wanted tougher provisions that required members to take an oath of office and to make decisions based on a "preponderance of evidence."

Regional management councils often recommended measures to the Commerce secretary about the length of fishing seasons and whether to shut down a fishery for economic reasons. Members conducted extensive hearings and received scientific reports about fish stocks, which sometimes were ignored for social or other reasons by council members.

But Young said the Unsoeld-Cantwell amendment, which was withdrawn, would prohibit a fisherman on the council from ever voting on an issue. "The effect of this is to tear up the Magnuson Act and put fishery management in the hands of the secretary," he said.

Unsoeld and Cantwell also withdrew an amendment that would have expanded the eight regional management councils and required two seats for members who were not commercial or recreational fishing experts. They contended that the bill did not go far enough to ensure that academics, conservationists and other non-fishing users were appointed to the regional panels.

The subcommittee approved by voice vote non-controversial amendments requiring the Commerce secretary to develop a comprehensive plan to restore Pacific salmon stocks, conserve the entire ecosystem of a fishery instead of a single species and address problems with depleted fish stocks that were not related to overfishing.

The panel left for the full committee a proposal essentially to charge fishing operations rent for their share of a harvest. The payment was to be tied to how shares of a fishery's harvest quota were divided among specific users, which was known as "individual transferable quotas." These shares were to be sold, traded or transferred.

Under the Magnuson Act, the federal government collected fees from the issuance of six to eight different fishing permits. Clinton proposed new user fees to raise $82 million for fishery management and conservation programs. But appropriators balked at the new fees. The fiscal 1995 spending bill for the departments of Commerce, Justice and State (HR 4603 — PL 103-317) instead allowed the National Oceanic and Atmospheric Administration, which oversaw fishing programs, to expand existing fees to raise $35 million. *(Appropriations, p. 483)*

Congress took up two other bills related to fish and wildlife.

Striped Bass

The House on July 12 passed by voice vote a bill (HR 4504) to reauthorize a law designed to protect striped bass on the Atlantic Coast from overfishing and water pollution. The Senate did not act on the bill.

The measure, introduced by Merchant Marine and Fish-eries Committee Chairman Gerry E. Studds, D-Mass., proposed to extend through fiscal 1996 the Atlantic Striped Bass Conservation Act (PL 98-613). The 1984 law helped manage the population of the popular sports fish in the waters off the East Coast. *(1984 Almanac, p. 333)*

The bill also proposed to reauthorize a related 1979 law (PL 96-118) that required the Interior secretary to cooperate with states and private groups that researched striped bass populations.

The House Merchant Marine Committee approved the bill June 29 by voice vote (H Rept 103-584).

The 1984 law authorized the Commerce secretary to impose a moratorium on striped bass fishing in states that did not comply with a separate fishery management plan adopted by the Atlantic States Marine Fisheries Commission, a research group chartered by Congress.

The striped bass, also known as rockfish, spawned primarily in the freshwater Chesapeake Bay and the Hudson River but spent its adult life in the ocean. The commercial rockfish catch dropped dramatically from 1973 to 1983 because of overfishing and chemical pollutants in its spawning areas. In 1983, the commission limited the size of fish that could be caught and said the federal government could impose a moratorium on striped bass fishing if a state did not reduce its catch by 55 percent. States began complying in 1984 after Congress passed the law that codified the commission's recommendations.

Fish and Wildlife Foundation

The Senate cleared a bill (S 476) March 25 reauthorizing the National Fish and Wildlife Foundation, after agreeing to a House addition honoring the late Merchant Marine Committee Chairman Walter B. Jones (D-N.C.). The Senate had not included the provision in its original version of the bill. President Clinton signed the measure April 11 (PL 103-232).

The National Fish and Wildlife Foundation was a nonprofit organization that funded natural resources conservation and environmental education projects with a combination of donations from private contributors and federal dollars. The bill reauthorized the foundation through fiscal 1998 and authorized $25 million annually to be used for projects administered by the National Oceanic and Atmospheric Administration and the U.S. Fish and Wildlife Service.

The bill also expanded the foundation's board of directors from nine to 15 members, all of whom were to be appointed by the Interior secretary. The bill also authorized the transfer of the federal Senecaville National Fish Hatchery to Ohio for use in the state's fishery management program. The measure incorporated two separate House bills (HR 2604, HR 2961) that created a wetlands policy center in Brownsville, Texas, and a national wildlife refuge in North Carolina.

The legislation began in the House, which approved its own bill (HR 2684 — H Rept 103-249) on Nov. 3, 1993, by a vote of 368-59. The House-passed measure included a provision to authorize the construction and operation of the Walter B. Jones Center for the Sounds to honor the late Merchant Marine Committee chairman, who died in 1992. The center was to serve as the headquarters for the Pocosin Lakes National Wildlife Refuge in eastern North Carolina and to provide educational information about the region's natural history.

The Senate Environment and Public Works Committee approved a separate bill, which did not include the Jones Center, by voice vote Jan. 27 (S 476 — S Rept 103-225). The Senate passed the bill by voice vote March 8 and sent it to the House. The House amended S 476 to include the Jones Center; the Senate accepted the change and cleared the bill March 25. ■

Senate Kills Waste Transport Bill

Despite a last-ditch push by the House, a bill (S 2345) that would have given states the authority to control the receipt of out-of-state garbage died at the end of the session. With it died a separate proposal (HR 4683) to allow local governments to direct waste to publicly operated waste disposal facilities. Local governments wanted such "flow-control" authority to guarantee a revenue stream for the facilities. *(Flow control, p. 262)*

Although the House easily endorsed a compromise that combined the two bills, John H. Chafee, R-R.I., blocked the Senate from taking up the legislation in the final hours of the regular session.

Background

Municipal solid waste — which included everything from household garbage to non-hazardous industrial wastes — was a growing problem that had given rise to bitter interstate battles. According to the National Solid Wastes Management Association, about 15 million tons of such waste was transported across state lines each year. As disposal costs rose and landfills reached their capacity, the issue had pitted major garbage exporters such as New York and New Jersey against states such as Pennsylvania and Indiana that were the destinations of such shipments. At least 37 states had enacted laws to restrict or otherwise treat out-of-state garbage differently than wastes generated within the state.

The issue moved into the congressional arena in 1992 when the Supreme Court ruled that states did not have the right to ban or place restrictions on out-of-state garbage imports. In *Fort Gratiot Sanitary Landfill v. Michigan Department of Natural Resources*, for example, the court struck down a Michigan law that allowed county governments to ban the importation of any waste generated outside their jurisdiction. The court reiterated that the Constitution prohibited states and localities from discriminating against the commerce of another state unless authorized to do so by Congress.

Lawmakers tried to address the problem in 1992 as part of a bill to reauthorize the Resource Conservation and Recovery Act (RCRA), the nation's main solid and hazardous waste law (PL 94-580). When the reauthorization bill stalled, the Senate passed a narrower measure, sponsored by Daniel R. Coats, R-Ind., that focused specifically on controlling out-of-state garbage imports. But the House did not act on Coats' bill, and it died at the end of the Congress. *(1992 Almanac, p. 272)*

In 1994, supporters initially hoped to deal with out-of-state garbage as part of a new RCRA reauthorization bill. But lawmakers held off trying to rewrite RCRA until they completed work on renewing the superfund toxic waste law. So supporters again chose to move separate legislation. *(Superfund, p. 231)*

The bill had strong support from heavy waste-importing states, but it was opposed by lawmakers from states where local authorities exported much of their solid waste.

Senate Action

The Senate Environment and Public Works Committee on June 23 approved a solid waste bill, sponsored by committee

---

BOXSCORE

Interstate Transport of Solid Waste — S 2345 (HR 4779).

Reports: S Rept 103-322; H Rept 103-720.

KEY ACTION

Sept. 28 — House passed HR 4779, 368-55.

Sept. 30 — Senate passed S 2345 by voice vote.

Oct. 7 — House passed S 2345, amended, by voice vote; amendments included provisions from HR 4683.

Chairman Max Baucus, D-Mont., that was similar to the measure the Senate had passed in 1992. The bill — reported to the Senate on Aug. 1 (S 2345 — S Rept 103-322) — allowed governors to freeze unilaterally municipal solid waste imports at 1993 levels for facilities that were receiving the waste in 1993. It also allowed them, at the request of local communities, to ban future imports to facilities that did not receive such waste in 1993. The bill included provisions aimed at reducing the level of exports from large exporting states and ensuring that no single state received large amounts of municipal solid waste from any other state. Coats, who had crusaded on the issue, applauded the measure as a "reasonable approach" to resolving interstate garbage conflicts.

The Senate passed the bill by voice vote Sept. 30.

House Action

The House Energy and Commerce Subcommittee on Transportation and Hazardous Materials approved a companion bill (HR 4779) by voice vote July 22, after accepting modifications by sponsors Rick Boucher, D-Va., and Fred Upton, R-Mich.

The subcommittee-approved bill allowed state and local governments to ban or limit interstate shipments of municipal solid waste. It barred new interstate shipments unless the affected local government authorized the shipments. Landfills that were already receiving out-of-state solid waste could continue doing so at 1993 levels until they were filled.

The subcommittee adopted, 12-9, an amendment by Thomas J. Manton, D-N.Y., aimed at ensuring that states such as New York could continue shipping waste under existing arrangements that were not covered by contracts. The bill already contained a grandfather clause for existing contracts; Manton's amendment extended that to arrangements not covered by contract, allowing them to continue for three years or the term of the contract.

The panel also adopted by voice vote a Manton amendment establishing 1993 as the baseline year to be used in limiting waste shipments. The original Boucher-Upton proposal would have allowed states to freeze such imports at either 1991 or 1993 levels.

The full Energy and Commerce Committee gave voice vote approval to the bill Aug. 18 (H Rept 103-720), after agreeing to drop a provision that would have required newspapers to use recycled newsprint.

The committee approved by voice vote an amendment by James C. Greenwood, R-Pa., to allow major recipient states — Pennsylvania, Ohio, Illinois, Indiana and Virginia — to reduce by 50 percent over five years the amount of waste they received annually.

Faced with complaints from publishers and committee members such as W. J. "Billy" Tauzin, D-La., a clearly irritated Chairman John D. Dingell, D-Mich., agreed to drop the newspaper recycling provision in order to move the bill and improve its chances on the floor.

House Advances 'Flow-Control' Legislation

The House twice voted to allow local governments to specify where their solid waste was to be dumped, thereby guaranteeing a revenue stream for their waste disposal facilities.

The House passed a so-called flow-control bill (HR 4683) on Sept. 29; on Oct. 7, it passed provisions from the measure as part a bill (S 2345) restricting interstate transport of municipal solid waste. But the Senate did not complete work on either bill, leaving the measure to die at the end of the session. *(Solid waste, p. 261)*

According to the Environmental Protection Agency (EPA), at least 35 states had laws authorizing some or all municipalities to adopt flow control ordinances. Under such laws, municipalities could require that solid waste be disposed of at designated sites, usually a landfill or incinerator in which the local government had a financial stake. Municipalities argued that flow control made it easier for them to invest in a landfill because they knew it would handle enough volume to recoup an investment.

But the Supreme Court ruled May 16 that flow control ordinances unlawfully restricted interstate commerce and prevented competition for local waste management contracts. The 6-3 ruling came in the case of *C & A Carbone v. Town of Clarkstown.* That set Congress in action on flow control issues.

Getting the legislation passed was a top priority for local officials, who feared that, without it, municipalities that relied on flow control could have their bond ratings downgraded. A lower rating could mean higher financing costs on future projects.

The Energy and Commerce Subcommittee on Transportation and Hazardous Materials gave voice vote approval July 21 to a bill (HR 4683) allowing states and local governments to retain authority over disposal of their municipal solid waste.

The bill, sponsored by Frank Pallone Jr., D-N.J., allowed state and local authorities to send their waste to designated landfills or other waste facilities. It also allowed state and local authorities to exercise flow control authority over

municipal solid waste from other sources if they could prove that they had been committed by May 15, 1994, to building a facility to receive the waste.

On Aug. 18, the full Energy and Commerce Committee approved the bill by voice vote (H Rept 103-738).

The panel rejected, 13-20, a substitute amendment by Bill Richardson, D-N.M., that would have banned any future flow control, while grandfathering existing facilities that were built on the assumption that they would receive guaranteed waste flows. The amendment was backed by the Public Interest Research Group and the National Federation of Independent Business, which said the bill as written would give cities a virtual monopoly in providing waste management services.

The House passed the bill by voice vote Sept. 29, after turning back, 161-244, a second attempt by Richardson to ban any future flow control authority. *(Vote 452, p. 134-H)*

With the session nearly over, House and Senate negotiators worked out a plan to merge provisions from HR 4683 into a compromise version of a separate bill (S 2345) aimed at allowing states to restrict the receipt of out-of-state garbage. The compromise allowed local officials to guarantee a revenue stream for waste disposal facilities (many of which were incinerators) by requiring that solid waste be dumped in publicly operated facilities. But the authority applied only in localities that already used flow control.

The House passed the compromise bill by voice vote Oct. 7.

But in the Senate, John H. Chafee, R-R.I., objected to the bill, effectively blocking floor consideration. Among other things, Chafee, whose state was a waste exporter, wanted to restrict the flow control provisions to those local governments that were trying to pay off solid waste bonds.

One local government lobbyist said such a narrow bill would have left out those localities that were not in debt, effectively penalizing them. "It didn't make sense to us to say that only bondholders should be protected but taxpayers should not," said Diane S. Shea of the National Association of Counties.

The provision would have required at least 35 percent of the newsprint used by large newspapers to be made of recycled fibers by 1996. Newspaper publishers argued that their use of recycled newsprint had increased in recent years, making a federal mandate unnecessary. According to industry figures, 22 percent of all newsprint used was made from recycled materials, compared with 10 percent five years before. Dingell, however, dismissed as "a lot of hooey" the publishers' claims of improvement and their complaints of potential economic setbacks from a mandate. He vowed to push for a newsprint recycling mandate the following year.

House Floor Action

Over the objections of members from major waste-producing states, the House passed the bill Sept. 28 by a vote of 368-55. Almost every New York and New Jersey representative voted no. *(Vote 443, p. 132-H)*

During the debate, opponents expressed concern that the bill would allow governors to override local governments that might have an economic interest in receiving the waste. "The

legislation has the potential to impose untold economic harm on communities that export some of their municipal solid waste and on other communities that import waste as a means of economic development," said Manton.

Another opponent, Frank Pallone Jr., D-N.J., won voice vote approval for an amendment to allow facilities that received out-of-state waste under existing contracts to continue doing so for the life of the contract or for six years after enactment. The bill had called for existing contracts to last only up to three years after enactment.

Final Action

During the week of Oct. 3, House and Senate negotiators worked frantically to strike a compromise melding the municipal waste bills passed by both chambers and the separate House-passed flow-control bill.

The negotiators engaged in a high-stakes balancing act between states that exported waste and those that imported it. And they faced objections from waste haulers and small-

business owners, who were concerned that Congress could create local monopolies by giving elected officials total authority over solid waste. They also faced fire from environmentalists, who worried that flow control could lead to the building of more incinerators.

The compromise, reached the evening of Oct. 7, went part way toward restoring state and local authority over the movement of solid waste. For example, it allowed governors to curb interstate shipments to new landfills, but not to landfills that accepted such shipments in 1993. It allowed local governments to continue their existing flow control policies, but not to create new ones.

On Oct. 7, the House amended S 2345 to reflect the compromise and approved it by voice vote. The plan was for the Senate to take the bill up by unanimous consent the next day. "I am not aware that anyone objects to this legislation," said Energy and Commerce subcommittee Chairman Al Swift, D-Wash.

But in the final minutes of the session, Chafee objected, criticizing some of the bill's provisions as overly broad. Chafee opposed a requirement that local officials give their approval before interstate waste could be dumped at a new site. Rhode Island was a waste exporter, and Chafee wanted the bill to allow such shipments — unless a local government objected. He also wanted to restrict the flow control provisions to those local governments that were trying to pay off solid waste bonds. His objections blocked Senate action on the bill, and it died. ■

Bill Aims at Limiting Dumping Of Radioactive Waste

The House on May 23 passed a bill (HR 3982) aimed at bringing the United States in line with an expanded international accord that barred the dumping of all radioactive waste in the ocean. The House tried to move the legislation again at the end of the session, attaching it to an unrelated maritime bill. But the Senate did not take up either measure.

The bill was an amendment to an existing ocean dumping law. The 1972 Marine Protection, Research and Sanctuaries Act (PL 92-532) had been enacted to bring U.S. law into conformity with the London Convention, an international agreement that banned ocean dumping of high-level radioactive waste. The 1972 law allowed the U.S. government to dump low-level radioactive waste into the ocean with specific congressional approval of each instance. In practice, however, the United States stopped dumping all radioactive waste in 1970 and had never used the authority granted to it under the 1972 ocean dumping law.

In 1993, the London Convention was expanded to include low-level waste, following the revelation that Russia had dumped and had been storing large amounts of high- and low-level radioactive waste in the ocean. The new treaty took effect Feb. 20, 1994.

Since 1959, Russia had been dumping waste from nuclear submarines and weapons plants into the Arctic Ocean and the Sea of Japan. Russia had also been storing 10 million curies of waste at Murmansk Harbor, headquarters for much of the Soviet Navy fleet. Bill sponsor Curt Weldon, R-Pa., said 10 million curies were equivalent to 700,000 times as much radioactivity as was released in the Three Mile Island, Pa., nuclear power plant accident in 1979. The radioactive waste in Russia had caused fish to die and water to change color near Murmansk Harbor.

The information about Russia became available to U.S. scientists only as a result of the breakup of the Soviet Union.

The U.S. government had resisted signing the expanded London Convention accord. But the Clinton administration reversed policy in November 1993 and supported the ban's expansion under pressure from environmental groups such as the World Wildlife Fund and an international group of legislators headed by Sen. John Kerry, D-Mass.

Legislative Action

On March 9, the Oceanography, Gulf of Mexico and the Outer Continental Shelf panel of the House Merchant Marine and Fisheries Committee gave voice vote approval to Weldon's bill (HR 3982) to officially ban the ocean dumping of all radioactive waste. Weldon, ranking Republican on the Oceanography subcommittee, said he hoped the bill would encourage Russia to follow suit and stop dumping radioactive waste. Russia was the only country that did not intend to sign the expanded agreement.

The full House Merchant Marine Committee gave voice vote approval to the bill May 11 (H Rept 103-522). By voice vote, the committee adopted a Weldon amendment to clarify that the bill did not apply to material dredged out of harbors. Dredge spoils often included some naturally occurring radioactive materials. The House passed the bill May 23, also by voice vote.

At the end of the session, in an attempt to get the bill through the Senate, the House on Oct. 7 rolled the ocean dumping provisions into an unrelated House maritime measure (HR 3664) that became a vehicle for a number of languishing environmental bills, then passed the measure by voice vote. HR 3664 was sent to the Senate, but that chamber did not act on it. ■

Environmental Technology Bills Taken Up in Both Chambers

The House and Senate passed separate bills (HR 3870, S 978) aimed at helping bring to market innovative technologies to prevent, reduce or clean up environmental pollution. But the two chambers did not reconcile their differences on the legislation, which died at the end of the Congress.

The federal government spent about $4 billion annually researching and developing environmental technologies to help reduce pollution and clean up hazardous wastes. The demand for such technologies was increasing, with the global market expected to reach an estimated $300 billion by 2000. The bills sought to codify a Clinton administration plan to develop an interagency strategy to guide the federal government's future spending on research and development of such environmental technologies. The aim was to help ensure that U.S. companies kept pace with foreign competitors.

Provisions promoting U.S. exports of environmental technology were passed in a House bill (HR 3813) and cleared as part of a bill reauthorizing the Overseas Private Investment Corporation (PL 103-392). *('Green' exports, p. 266; OPIC, p. 138)*

House Committee Action

A key House Science, Space and Technology subcommittee gave voice vote approval March 2 to a bill (HR 3870) aimed at coordinating federal research and development of so-called green technologies, those that helped protect the environment and reduce toxic waste.

The bill, introduced by Committee Chairman George E.

Brown Jr., D-Calif., required the White House Office of Science and Technology Policy (OSTP) to coordinate research efforts among the Commerce Department, Environmental Protection Agency (EPA) and other federal agencies. It also sought to improve access to information about environmental technology on federal data networks and authorized the Commerce secretary to clarify a set of performance standards for these programs.

The measure provided for the establishment of a grant program to support private or public-private initiatives to develop such technologies, and it authorized $80 million in fiscal 1995 and $120 million in fiscal 1996 for the program.

The Technology, Environment and Aviation Subcommittee rejected, 12-19, an amendment by John Linder, R-Ga., to transfer the $80 million for environmental technology grants from an existing research and development program.

The full House Science Committee approved the bill by a 19-9 vote April 13 (H Rept 103-536).

The committee gave voice vote approval to an amendment by Brown that moved the proposed authority for coordinating environmental technologies from the OSTP to the president. The panel rejected, 7-16, another attempt by Linder to transfer money to the environmental technology development grants from the Commerce Department's Advanced Technology Program.

The panel also rejected by voice vote an amendment by ranking committee Republican Robert S. Walker of Pennsylvania to allow the president to suspend spending under the program if any provision was found to violate the General Agreement on Tariffs and Trade or other international agreements.

House Floor Action

The House passed the bill by voice vote July 26.

Brown praised the bill's new approach to the often conflicting goals of maintaining a healthy environment and sustaining economic growth. Supporters also maintained that the measure would help U.S. companies keep pace with foreign competition in the expanding global market for environmental technologies. Republican critics of the bill said the grant provisions duplicated an existing Commerce Department program.

Linder sought to reduce funding to $130 million, but Brown watered down that proposal with a substitute amendment to reduce funding by $10 million. Linder's amendment, as modified, was adopted by voice vote.

Walker offered an amendment to establish legislative criteria and guidelines for environmental risk assessments. He argued that, because the bill instructed the administration to develop priorities for environmental technology research according to assessments of risk, the bill should establish guidelines for making such judgments. At the time, risk assessments were conducted by individual agencies without congressional guidelines.

Brown sought to scuttle Walker's amendment with a substitute that would have given the White House science adviser the power to set risk assessment guidelines. The House rejected Brown's language, 202-225, and subsequently approved Walker's amendment, 286-139. *(Votes 352, 353, p. 106-H)*

Senate Action

Action on the Senate bill began in 1993 in the Environment and Public Works Committee, which approved S 978 by voice vote July 30 (S Rept 103-156). The bill was sponsored by committee Chairman Max Baucus, D-Mont. *(1993 Almanac, p. 283)*

The Senate passed the bill May 11, 1994, by a vote of 85-14. *(Vote 108, p. 32-H)*

The bill called for a new EPA office to provide information to small businesses about the development of new environmental technologies and the federal government's needs for such innovations.

The bill authorized $236 million from fiscal 1994 through fiscal 1996 for grants to private companies, particularly small businesses, to allow them to conduct research and development into such technologies. The bill also authorized $68 million over four years beginning in fiscal 1995 to run the EPA office, test new products and manage the program.

It required that 1.25 percent of the money the EPA received each year to clean up the nation's worst toxic waste dumps be set aside to develop innovative ways to clean up such "superfund" sites. The EPA received about $1.5 billion for the superfund program in fiscal 1994.

Federal laboratories were to be required to test environmental technologies to verify their costs and effectiveness.

Clinton had endorsed Baucus' bill, calling it an essential part of the administration's plan to create jobs and protect the environment.

Before Senate passage, Ted Stevens, R-Alaska, withdrew an amendment that would have required the EPA to create a new fund to help Indian reservations and Alaskan native villages develop new sanitation technologies for the disposal of sewage wastes. ∎

Radon Disclosure Legislation Wins House Approval

The House passed a bill (HR 2448) to require real estate agents and home sellers to inform prospective buyers of the risk of radon in a house and to disclose the results of any known radon tests. The Senate did not act on the bill, however, and it died at the end of the session.

According to the surgeon general and other health authorities, exposure to radon, an odorless, colorless radioactive gas, was the second-leading cause of lung cancers in the United States, next to cigarette smoking. Radon became a risk to humans when it seeped from soil into cracks in building and home foundations. According to government figures, radon exceeded safe levels in about 6 million homes. Some states had required home sellers to disclose such information, but there was no federal requirement.

Rep. Henry A. Waxman, D-Calif., floor manager of the legislation, said the bill was a compromise supported not only by public health and consumer organizations but also by the National Association of Realtors, the National Association of Homebuilders and the Mortgage Bankers Association of America, among others.

Legislative Action

The bill originated in the House Energy and Commerce Subcommittee on Health and the Environment, which approved it by voice vote Sept. 29, 1993. *(1993 Almanac, p. 284)*

The full Energy and Commerce Committee approved the bill, sponsored by subcommittee Chairman Edward J. Markey, D-Mass., by voice vote May 18, 1994 (H Rept 103-574). The House passed the bill July 28 by a vote of 255-164, after brushing aside Republican attempts to spare private property owners the burden of disclosure. *(Vote 361, p. 108-H)*

The House rejected, 193-227, an amendment by Michael G. Oxley, R-Ohio, that would have deleted all requirements that homeowners disclose radon information. The amendment, previously rejected 9-11 in committee, would have replaced

the disclosure requirement with language requiring the Environmental Protection Agency (EPA) to develop a program to distribute radon information in high-radon areas. *(Vote 360, p. 108-H)*

As passed by the House, the bill required real estate salespeople and homeowners to provide pamphlets produced by the EPA warning of radon hazards to potential buyers and renters of residential or commercial properties. The bill also gave buyers the option of having the property tested before the final sale. Those who failed to give out pamphlets or disclose radon test results were to be subject to fines of up to $2,000 for property sellers or an amount equal to two months' rent for lessors. The bill authorized unspecified appropriations for radon control activities in fiscal years 1994-97.

The bill also contained provisions to:
● Require the EPA, within nine months of passage, to identify areas and buildings with "exceptionally high" levels of radon and develop a plan to reduce those levels.
● Specify within two years all radon testing, mitigation services and products that would have to meet EPA performance and certification standards.
● Require the EPA, within two years, to promulgate construction standards and techniques to control radon levels in new buildings in high-risk areas.
● Establish a President's Commission on Radon Awareness to examine existing public awareness programs and to help establish a national public education campaign on radon health risks.
● Authorize states to administer their own radon control programs in lieu of the federal one if the state plan was at least as protective of human health and the environment as the EPA standards.
● Require all federal agencies to comply with federal, state and local requirements for radon control. ∎

Other Environmental Measures Considered in 1994

Congress considered a variety of additional environmental bills during the second session, including measures to reauthorize wetlands programs and promote the export of environmental technologies.

Wetlands Protection

The Senate on Oct. 4 cleared a bill (HR 4308) that extended a program to protect and restore wetlands in the United States, Canada and Mexico. The measure, which passed by voice vote, authorized wetlands conservation grants of $20 million annually in fiscal 1995 and fiscal 1996 and $30 million annually in fiscal 1997 and fiscal 1998. President Clinton signed the bill Oct. 19 (PL 103-375).

The North American Wetlands Conservation Act (PL 101-233) had been credited with protecting more than 1.2 million acres of wetlands in the United States and Canada since its inception in 1989. The law used federal money to get matching funds from private sources for wetlands protection, restoration and management projects.

The bill, sponsored by John D. Dingell, D-Mich., began in the House Merchant Marine and Fisheries Committee, which approved it Aug. 11 by voice vote (HR 103-717). The House passed the bill Sept. 13 by a vote of 368-5. *(Vote 423, p. 126-H)*

The Senate Environment and Public Works Committee

approved a similar bill — (S 1857 — S Rept 103-326), sponsored by Majority Leader George J. Mitchell, D-Maine — by voice vote June 23. Rather than taking up the Mitchell bill, the Senate cleared HR 4308 by voice vote Oct. 4.

Water Bank Extension

The Senate on Oct. 7 cleared by voice vote a one-year extension (HR 5053) of water bank agreements that were due to expire at the end of 1994.

The 24-year-old Water Bank Program provided 10-year agreements for farmers to preserve and restore an estimated 60,000 acres of wetlands. The one-year extension was intended to give Congress time to review the program in the context of the 1995 farm bill.

The House passed the bill by voice vote Oct. 4. President Clinton signed it Oct. 22 (PL 103-393).

Small Landfills

A House subcommittee on Aug. 4 approved a bill (HR 2654) to exempt small landfills from certain environmental regulations, but no further action was taken on the measure. The House Energy and Commerce Subcommittee on Transportation and Hazardous Materials gave voice vote approval to the measure, which would have exempted small, isolated landfills from Environmental Protection Agency (EPA) regulations on groundwater monitoring.

The bill, sponsored by Bill Sarpalius, D-Texas, applied to landfills that received less than 20 tons of solid waste a day and had no signs of groundwater contamination. It also applied to landfills serving communities that had no waste disposal alternatives and received less than 25 inches of precipitation annually. At the time, all landfills had to undergo expensive monitoring of groundwater for possible toxic pollutants.

Indoor Air

As the session neared the end, the House passed a bill (S 656) designed to improve the quality of indoor air. The Senate had passed its own version of the bill in 1993, but it did not have time to act on changes proposed by the House. The legislation would have required the Environmental Protection Agency (EPA) to study indoor air pollution and develop voluntary guidelines aimed at reducing potential health hazards.

Bill sponsors Rep. Joseph P. Kennedy II, D-Mass., and Sen. George J. Mitchell, D-Maine, had tried for four years to get an indoor air quality bill through Congress. The Senate had passed similar measures, but House bills had not made it to the floor because of jurisdictional problems.

The EPA considered indoor air pollution a top environmental health threat. Indoor air was believed to be up to 1,000 times more polluted than outdoor air, and medical and scientific studies showed that constant exposure could lead to cancer, respiratory diseases and headaches.

But some lawmakers criticized the bill, saying it would lead to more regulations on businesses and duplicate extensive rules proposed by the Occupational Safety and Health Administration.

S 656 authorized up to $48.5 million per year in fiscal years 1994 through 1998 for research, grants to states and the assessment of "sick" buildings that had a high concentration of indoor air pollutants. The measure passed the Senate on Oct. 29, 1993, by voice vote. *(1993 Almanac, p. 284)*

The House bill (HR 2919), introduced in 1993, had stalled

in the Energy and Commerce Committee until August, when Kennedy and Health and Environment Subcommittee Chairman Henry A. Waxman, D-Calif., agreed to scale back some of the bill's requirements. The subcommittee approved the bill Aug. 3 by a vote of 18-7, after approving a Waxman substitute that replaced some of the proposed mandates with voluntary programs in an attempt to ease industry concerns and win Republican votes.

The original version required the EPA to develop a national strategy for reducing indoor air pollution and mandatory certification for indoor air inspectors. The amended bill required a voluntary program to certify indoor air inspectors.

The full Energy and Commerce Committee approved the bill by voice vote Aug. 9 (H Rept 103-719). The committee adopted by voice vote an amendment by Waxman to expand the authority of the National Institute for Occupational Safety and Health so it could investigate complaints about indoor air from workers and employees. The bill authorized such sums as might be necessary to carry out its provisions.

The House passed HR 2919 by voice vote Oct. 3. It then inserted the text of its bill into S 656 and passed that bill by voice vote. The Senate did not take up the amended bill.

Lead Exposure

For the fourth consecutive year, lawmakers tried without success to reduce the use of lead in consumer products such as toys and gift wrap. The Senate on May 25 passed a bill (S 729), sponsored by Harry Reid, D-Nev., by a vote of 97-1. A companion House measure made it through an Energy and Commerce subcommittee, but advanced no further. (Vote 133, p. 23-S)

Lead poisoning was the most common disease among children, according to the Centers for Disease Control and Prevention. Exposure to high levels of lead — primarily from ingesting or inhaling soil, paint or drinking water — had been linked to problems with a child's intelligence, and with learning disabilities and nervous disorders.

S 729 proposed to restrict the use of lead in paint, toys and game pieces, curtain weights not encased in vinyl or plastic, inks, glass coatings, lead solder used in plumbing systems, plumbing fittings and fixtures, and packaging materials. Exemptions were included for some materials, such as artists' paint. The bill also proposed to ban the importation, manufacture and processing of the lead-containing products within a year and prohibit their sale within two years.

Reid had tried since 1990 to pass sweeping legislation to reduce exposure to lead. Congress passed one element of Reid's earlier proposals in 1992 when federal agencies were ordered to gradually eliminate lead-based paint from public and private housing as part of the affordable housing law (PL 102-550). (1992 Almanac, p. 367)

But Reid's comprehensive lead exposure bills had never been voted on by the Senate because of opposition from manufacturers, who were concerned about a provision that would have required them to get permission from the Environmental Protection Agency (EPA) before they made or modified a new product containing lead. That provision was not included in S 729.

The bill required the EPA to develop an inventory of products that contained lead and establish a list of uses that posed a health risk. Manufacturers would have to notify the EPA when new lead uses were developed. In addition, the bill required labeling for products containing lead, recycling of lead-acid batteries and state inspections for lead hazards at

schools and day-care centers.

The Senate approved by voice vote May 24 an amendment by Robert C. Smith, R-N.H., calling on the EPA to develop an alternative before it followed through with a proposal to ban fishing sinkers that contained lead or zinc. The EPA proposed the ban in March because fishing sinkers were sometimes eaten by cranes and swans.

As passed, the bill authorized $30 million annually from fiscal 1995 through fiscal 1997 to help states carry out school and day-care inspections. It authorized $95 million over four years to implement the rest of the bill.

Action on S 729 began in the Environment and Public Works Committee, which approved it by voice vote July 30, 1993 (S Rept 103-152). A companion measure, (HR 4882), introduced in the House by Al Swift, D-Wash., on Aug. 1, made it through the Energy and Commerce Subcommittee on Transportation and Hazardous Materials and was approved by voice vote Aug. 11. But the full committee never took up the measure. (1993 Almanac, p. 235)

'Green' Exports

The House passed a bill aimed at preserving the United States' edge in exports of environmental technologies. Although the Senate did not act on a companion bill, provisions of the House measure were ultimately included in a separate measure reauthorizing the Overseas Private Investment Corporation; that bill was signed by President Clinton on Oct. 22 (HR 4950 — PL 103-392). (OPIC, p. 138)

Exports of products and services that helped to reduce pollution or clean up existing environmental problems had produced a $4 billion trade surplus for U.S. companies in 1990. Although the United States had been the leader in the $270 billion worldwide environmental technologies market, other countries were catching up, bill sponsors said. U.S. companies held about 40 percent of the market, which was expected to grow to as much as $600 billion by the end of the decade.

The House passed its bill (HR 3813) on April 19 by a vote of 416-0. Sponsor Sam Gejdenson, D-Conn., said 300,000 jobs would be created if U.S. firms were to capture 20 percent of the global market for environment technologies. (Vote 117, p. 36-H)

The measure had won voice vote approval from the House Foreign Affairs Committee on March 16 (H Rept 103-478). It provided for the creation of an Environmental Technologies Trade Advisory Committee to guide federal environmental export promotion. It required the administration to identify each year the five countries most in need of environmental technology and then work to increase U.S. exports to those nations. The Commerce secretary was to offer matching grants to fund regional centers that promoted "green" technology exports. The centers were to be financed by matching Commerce Department grants and run as business-university cooperatives.

The bill also authorized international initiatives to encourage other countries to adopt U.S.-style environmental standards.

Biodiversity Treaty

The Senate Foreign Relations Committee on June 29 recommended ratification of a treaty to preserve diversity among the world's plant and animal species, despite concerns among some senators about the treaty's cost to the United States. The committee voted 16-3 to send the Convention on Biological Diversity (Treaty Doc 103-20) to the full Senate.

Republican Sens. Paul Coverdell of Georgia, Jesse Helms of North Carolina and Larry Pressler of South Dakota cast the dissenting votes.

The measure never went to the Senate floor, however.

The treaty represented a multinational commitment to protecting the Earth's diverse species. President George Bush had opposed the treaty when it was signed by other nations in June 1992 at an international conference in Rio de Janeiro. But President Clinton supported it, and the United States signed it in June 1993.

In addition to approving the treaty's ratification, the Foreign Relations Committee adopted a non-binding resolution, by Hank Brown, R-Colo., that called on Clinton to make an annual report to Congress on the treaty's costs and other effects, which critics said were too open-ended and uncertain. The resolution also urged the president to ensure that the costs of U.S. participation not exceed $100 million a year and that other U.S. interests were protected.

Fishing Vessel Registration

The Senate did not take up an international agreement intended to prevent fishermen from reflagging their vessels to evade prosecution for violating conservation measures while fishing on the high seas.

The Senate Foreign Relations Committee approved the agreement (Treaty Doc. 103-24) on Sept. 22, and the Senate Commerce Committee on Sept. 23 approved by voice vote a bill (S 2455) to implement it.

Under the terms of the agreement, which was adopted at a Rome conference of the United Nations Food and Agriculture Organization in November 1993, each participating nation was obligated to develop a system for licensing fishing boats that carried its flag on the high seas.

Because the world's fish stocks had dwindled, global and regional fisheries management organizations had responded by adopting more stringent conservation measures. But commercial fishing vessels circumvented these restrictions by "re-flagging" — flying the flag of a nation that did not belong to a regional fish management organization.

The bill, introduced by John Kerry, D-Mass., sought to implement the terms of the Rome agreement by requiring all U.S. fishing vessels operating on the high seas to register with the Commerce Department. Any vessel that previously had a license suspended by a foreign nation for violating conservation measures would have been ineligible for a U.S. license.

The bill also would have required the Commerce secretary to provide the U.N. Food and Agriculture Organization with information on all U.S.-licensed fishing vessels and their activities on the high seas. The Commerce secretary would have been obligated to publish a list of international fisheries' conservation measures recognized by the United States. ∎

Narrow Strategic Reserve Bill Clears

Congress on Oct. 7 reauthorized operations of the nation's oil stockpile, the Strategic Petroleum Reserve, after House and Senate negotiators failed to agree on a more far-ranging alternative. The bare-bones bill (S 2466), by Senate Energy and Natural Resources Committee Chairman J. Bennett Johnston, D-La., reauthorized the reserve through 1996 without making any changes to its operations. President Clinton signed the bill Oct. 22 (PL 103-406).

The House and Senate had passed competing versions of the broader reauthorization (HR 4752, S 2251), but as the session neared its end, it became clear that they would not be able to reconcile their differences.

The reserve, which at the time held 600 million barrels, was the nation's main insurance against oil supply and price disruptions. The reserve was held in underground storage areas in Louisiana. By the end of fiscal 1994, it was to hold an estimated 68 days of "import oil protection." The 1992 Energy Policy Act (PL 102-486) required that the reserve be expanded to 1 billion barrels as soon as possible. *(1992 Almanac, p. 231)*

Broader Reauthorization Bill Stalls

The House on Aug. 8 passed a five-year reauthorization bill (HR 4752 — H Rept 103-663) that proposed to soften the requirement for 1 billion barrels. The bill, passed by voice vote, allowed oil to be bought and stored in the Strategic Petroleum Reserve as funds were made available. The House Energy and Commerce Committee had approved the bill by voice vote July 19.

HR 4752 also extended until 1999 U.S. participation in the International Energy Agency, a group of more than 20 nations formed after the 1973 oil embargo to prepare for supply disruptions.

The bill reauthorized two state conservation programs —

the State Energy Conservation Program, which funded state energy offices that developed energy conservation plans, and the Institutional Conservation Program, which provided matching funds for energy conservation programs at hospitals and schools. It also reauthorized $50 million in federal assistance over three years for renewable energy plants, such as biomass energy, photovoltaics, fuel cells, and wind and geothermal power.

The bill authorized about $146 million in fiscal 1995, $262 million in fiscal 1996, $304 million in fiscal 1997, $312 million in fiscal 1998 and $321 million in fiscal 1999.

The Senate version of the bill (S 2251 — S Rept 103-334), which passed by voice vote Sept. 30, reauthorized the Strategic Petroleum Reserve without changing its mandate. It did, however, eliminate a requirement that the Energy Department go before Congress whenever it wanted to lease oil. The Senate Energy and Natural Resources Committee had approved the measure on a 20-0 vote July 20.

During floor debate, Johnston tacked on two amendments that House negotiators subsequently refused to accept. The first, contained in a separate bill passed by the Senate in 1993 (S 473 — S Rept 103-69), would have fostered cooperation between Energy Department laboratories and private companies, and provided the laboratories with specific research missions. *(Research labs, p. 223)*

The second, also contained in a separate Senate-passed bill (S 991 — S Rept 103-187), would have provided education and job opportunities in the seven-state lower Mississippi Delta region, stretching from Southern Illinois to the Gulf of Mexico. It would have directed the Energy Department to provide grants within the Delta region for energy efficiency improvements and to lay the groundwork for increased use of alternative energy from agricultural products, known as biomass.

1994 CQ ALMANAC — 267

Neither of those measures had made it through the House as stand-alone bills. The Mississippi Delta grants seemed to attract the particular ire of some House members, who viewed them as unwarranted, pork barrel spending. In addition to the Johnston amendments, House and Senate negotiators were at odds over the 1 billion barrel requirement and over how often the Energy Department should submit reports to Congress. As a result, they were unable to agree on a final bill. ∎

Other Energy-Related Legislation

Congress took up a variety of other energy-related bills in 1994, including proposals to reauthorize the Nuclear Regulatory Commission, end government sales of helium, write new regulations for multistate utility companies and reauthorize federal weatherization assistance. None of the bills were enacted.

Nuclear Regulatory Commission

The Senate Environment and Public Works Committee approved two bills June 23 related to the Nuclear Regulatory Commission (NRC); neither saw floor action.

The first bill (S 1162), approved by voice vote, would have reauthorized NRC operations at $530.2 million in fiscal 1994 and $541.4 million in fiscal 1995. The money for the NRC, whose reauthorization ran out in 1985, came entirely from fees paid by its licensees. The Subcommittee on Clean Air and Nuclear Regulation had approved the measure, sponsored by Max Baucus, D-Mont., in October, 1993. *(1993 Almanac, p. 287)*

The bill included new penalties for wrongdoing at nuclear facilities. It authorized the NRC to obtain a warrant from a federal judge to search unlicensed facilities, such as parts suppliers, without giving advance notice. And it made sabotaging a nuclear plant or waste storage facility a federal offense not only when the facility was operating but also while it was under construction.

By voice vote the committee adopted an amendment stripping language that would have allowed the NRC to conduct searches without warrants.

Joseph I. Lieberman, D-Conn., announced an agreement with Alan K. Simpson, R-Wyo., and Dave Durenberger, R-Minn., that the bill would not be brought to the Senate floor until the three of them agreed on how much NRC licensees in different states should pay to the commission.

The committee reported the measure to the Senate on July 25 as a clean bill (S 2313 — S Rept 103-319), but the Senate did not take it up.

The second committee bill (S 1165 — S Rept 103-331), approved by a vote of 10-6, would have allowed people to petition the NRC for sanctions against an operating nuclear facility. A federal appeals court could overturn the NRC's refusal to grant such a petition if the court had evidence that the facility was in "significant non-compliance" or presented a "substantial hazard" to public health, safety or security.

The committee adopted by voice vote an amendment to clarify that the NRC could respond to such petitions in ways it saw fit, but that any decision would be subject to court review. Another amendment adopted by voice vote allowed the NRC to collect up to twice its costs if a court found an appeal of an NRC decision to have been frivolous.

Helium Sales

The House Natural Resources Committee gave voice vote approval July 27 to a bill (HR 3967 — H Rept 103-661) to take the federal government out of the business of selling helium. The panel approved the measure in the wake of widespread criticism of the Bureau of Mines' helium program, which had racked up a $1.3 billion debt and drawn bipartisan charges that it was costly and inefficient. The Energy and Mineral Resources Subcommittee had approved the bill by voice vote July 19. The House did not take up the measure.

The committee bill required that the federal government cease refining and producing helium, but allowed it to continue monitoring domestic resources and conducting some associated research. The government would also sell its 32 billion cubic-foot helium stockpile.

"This legislation stops the needless action of the federal government directly competing with the private helium industry, will save the taxpayers millions of dollars, ensures repayment of the debt and puts an end to a wasteful government program that has long ceased its purpose once and for all," said Barbara F. Vucanovich, R-Nev., a bill cosponsor with Subcommittee Chairman Richard H. Lehman, D-Calif.

The subcommittee gave voice vote approval to an amendment by Vucanovich to begin the sale of the helium stockpile by 2004, or 10 years earlier than the bill originally required.

The federal helium program was put under Bureau of Mines control in 1925, when Congress enacted the Helium Act. In 1960, amid concerns that helium supplies were drying up, Congress amended the act and allowed the Bureau of Mines to borrow $225 million to finance helium purchases from private industries to ensure that the government would have enough helium for scientific projects. But when demand failed to meet projections, the government was left with a stockpile of helium and a debt that had grown to $1.3 billion.

Vucanovich's office reported that it cost the government $21 to deliver 1,000 cubic feet of helium. Private companies, in contrast, could do it for $6 per 1,000 cubic feet, she said. Helium was in demand by the government and private companies alike because it is a chemically inert element and it remains gaseous even at very low temperatures. Such traits allowed the National Aeronautics and Space Administration to use it to purge shuttle lines of hydrogen gas, and industrial companies to use it as a protective gas in welding.

As part of his "reinventing government" initiative, Vice President Al Gore in 1993 had called for improving the program by reducing costs, encouraging increased sales to the private sector and requiring private-sector compensation to the government for program costs. *(1993 Almanac, p. 143)*

Multistate Utility Companies

The Senate Energy and Natural Resources Committee approved a bill July 22 aimed at resolving a complex dispute over the regulation of public utility holding companies that operated in a number of states. The committee approved the bill (S 544 — S Rept 103-351), sponsored by Dale Bumpers, D-Ark., by a vote of 14-5. The measure went no further in the 103rd Congress. Some provisions were included in a bill to rewrite the rules of competition in the telecommunications industry (S 1822), but that measure also died.

The committee's bill continued the division of regulatory authority over the holding companies between the Securities and Exchange Commission (SEC) and the Federal Energy Regulatory Commission. But it restored the energy commission's latitude in setting wholesale electricity rates for utili-

ties affiliated with the holding companies. The commission's discretion had been limited by a 1992 court ruling in the case of *Ohio Power Co. v. Federal Energy Regulatory Commission.*

In that case, Ohio Power, a utility affiliated with a multistate utility holding company, had purchased coal from another of the holding company's affiliates. The SEC, acting in its authority under the Public Utility Holding Company Act, approved the transaction between affiliates.

However, in determining Ohio Power's rates for wholesale electricity sales, the Federal Energy Regulatory Commission ruled that the coal was purchased for well above the market price and disallowed part of that cost.

The U.S. Court of Appeals for the District of Columbia Circuit ruled in favor of Ohio Power's lawsuit to overturn the energy commission's decision. The appeals court ruled that the SEC had sole authority to regulate the costs of goods and services provided under such an interaffiliate contract.

Bumpers strongly opposed the ruling, arguing that the SEC had virtually never barred an interaffiliate transaction on consumer protection grounds. His original bill, proposed in March 1993, would have transferred all regulatory authority over the holding companies to the Federal Energy Regulatory Commission.

By the time the legislation came to committee markup, Bumpers had greatly moderated his proposal. Under his substitute amendment that was approved by the Energy Committee, the SEC was to maintain its authority over transactions by the multistate utility holding companies and their affiliates. But the energy regulatory commission would be permitted to disallow some of the utility company's costs stemming from such transactions in calculating electricity rates. It could do so if it found those costs to be "unjust, unreasonable, or unduly preferential or discriminatory."

Weatherization Program

The House voted Aug. 8 to reauthorize the federal weatherization assistance program for two years. The program, a block grant administered through state community action agencies and energy offices, funded insulation and home energy efficiency repairs for schools, hospitals and low-income families. The bill (HR 4751 — H Rept 103-662) passed by voice vote. However, the Senate did not take it up, and it died at the end of the session.

The House Energy and Commerce Committee, which approved the bill July 19, reduced the authorization from five years to two in an effort to pressure the Energy Department into revising the formula that it used to allocate money under the program.

Southern lawmakers had long complained that the formula heavily favored Northern and rural states. "Extreme heat is just as dangerous to a person's health as extreme cold," said Michael Bilirakis, R-Fla.

In 1990, Congress amended the Energy Conservation and Production Act (PL 101-440) to require the Energy Department to change the formula. However, many Northern lawmakers opposed any change that would reduce funds for their states.

Propane Research and Development

The House Energy and Commerce Subcommittee on Energy and Power gave voice vote approval June 30 to legislation (HR 3546) to encourage propane producers and retailers to promote research and development on the uses of propane gas. The bill, sponsored by W. J. "Billy" Tauzin, D-La., went no further.

The bill would have allowed retailers and producers to form a board to coordinate research and development activities, marketing projects and consumer education efforts. The producers and retailers were to pay for the board's activities. To deal with the concerns of some lawmakers that propane prices might go up, the subcommittee approved language authorizing the secretary of Energy to suspend the board's advertising activities if the price of propane rose significantly, compared with the price increases of other fuels.

Alternative Energy

The House Energy and Commerce Committee on Aug. 5 gave voice vote approval to a bill (HR 4866 — H Rept 103-684) aimed at facilitating the development of alternative energy sources. The bill would have extended for two years an existing provision of law that allowed solar, wind, waste and geothermal power plants larger than 80 megawatts to benefit from certain exemptions to regulatory requirements under the Public Utility Regulatory Policies Act of 1978 (PL 101-575). Without the provision, those exemptions were available only to smaller plants.

Congress had voted in 1990 to lift the size limitation as part of the the Solar, Wind and Geothermal Power Production Incentives Act (PL 101-575), but the 1990 law included a four-year "sunset" provision. Because HR 4866 saw no further action, the exemption for plants larger than 80 megawatts expired Dec. 31.

The Energy and Power Subcommittee approved HR 4866 by voice vote Aug. 4. Philip R. Sharp, D-Ind., chairman of the subcommittee and the bill's sponsor, originally sought to lift the size limitation permanently. Several subcommittee members, led by ranking Republican Michael Bilirakis of Florida, argued that the incentives for alternative energy should be studied to determine how they fit in with the goals, set in the Energy Policy Act of 1992, of increasing competition and limiting consumer costs in the power supply industry. Bilirakis' amendment, which restricted the size limitation waiver to a two-year extension and called for a one-year study of federal power-supply policy, was accepted by Sharp and approved by voice vote. ∎

## Chapter 6

LAW & JUDICIARY

Legislation
Omnibus Crime Bill.................................. 273
   Assault Weapons Ban 276
   Evolution of the Crime Bill........................ 281
   Crime Trust Fund 283
   'Brady 2'.. 284
   Provisions...................................... 287
Immigration Law 294
Independent Counsel 295

Provisions...................................... 297
Other Law-Related Legislation 298
Judicial Appointments Confirmed 300
Supreme Court
Breyer Appointment 303
   Vital Statistics 305
   Past Opinions 306
Supreme Court Cases 310
Congressional Term Limits 314

CRIME PREVENTION

Lawmakers Enact $30.2 Billion Anti-Crime Bill

President and Democrats survive tough fight, get big win with some help from GOP

With crime a major concern among voters and crime legislation a top Clinton administration priority, the Senate on Aug. 25 cleared a huge six-year, $30.2 billion crime bill.

The bill (HR 3355), six years in the making, represented an unprecedented federal venture into crime-fighting. Most of the federal aid, however, was in the form of grants to state and local governments, which were to continue to bear the major responsibility for fighting crime. The measure authorized $8.8 billion to hire more police, $7.9 billion in state prison construction grants and $6.9 billion for prevention programs. It created dozens of new federal capital crimes, mandated life in prison for three-time violent offenders and banned 19 types of semiautomatic assault weapons.

The struggle over the bill, which lasted most of the session, was a fierce match between conservatives — who fought for stiffer punishment for criminals and ridiculed prevention programs as pork — and liberals — who condemned what they said was a failed policy of overzealous incarceration, and pushed instead for crime prevention programs.

Supporters conceded that they did not know whether the bill would dramatically reduce crime and violence, and that any impact would be hard to measure. But many lawmakers felt it stood a better chance than past congressional efforts because its focus was on local government, it combined prevention with punishment and it included an innovative trust fund dedicated to paying for programs authorized by the bill.

President Clinton signed the bill into law Sept. 13 (PL 103-322).

The bill began its legislative odyssey in August 1993, when Clinton outlined the core elements of a Democratic anti-crime package. He asked for money to help hire 100,000 new police officers, new federal death penalties and an overhaul of the federal appeals process for death row inmates. Clinton also endorsed a ban on so-called assault weapons and backed the Brady bill, which required a waiting period and background checks for handgun purchases.

BOXSCORE

Crime Bill — HR 3355
(HR 4092, S 1607). The bill authorized $30.2 billion over six years — mainly to hire police officers, build prisons and help communities prevent crime — and created a crime "trust fund" to pay for the programs. It banned 19 assault weapons and expanded the death penalty to dozens of new federal crimes.

Reports: Conference reports H Rept 103-694, H Rept 103-711.

KEY ACTION

April 21 — House passed HR 4092, 285-141; it then passed HR 3355 by voice vote after substituting the text of HR 4092.

July 28 — House-Senate conferees agreed to the first conference report.

Aug. 11 — House defeated the rule on the conference report, 210-225.

Aug. 21 — Conferees agreed to the second conference report; **House** adopted report, 235-195.

Aug. 25 — Senate cleared HR 3355, 61-38.

Sept. 13 — President signed HR 3355 — PL 103-322.

House Judiciary Committee Chairman Jack Brooks, D-Texas, and Senate Judiciary Committee Chairman Joseph R. Biden Jr., D-Del., subsequently introduced bills including most of those items and some new ones.

Action came first in the Senate, where Biden bypassed his committee and took his bill straight to the floor. Senators agreed in November 1993 to a mammoth $22.3 billion bill that embraced police hiring, prison construction, a ban on certain semiautomatic weapons, programs to prevent and prosecute violence against women and tough new sentencing measures. It also created a novel payment scheme for the bill's programs by dedicating the anticipated savings from planned federal work force reductions to a special crime trust fund.

In the House, Brooks could not galvanize support around his omnibus bill and instead moved several of its more popular components, such as police hiring grants and drug treatment for inmates, through committee and to the floor as separate bills in 1993.

When House members returned in 1994, they decided to craft a more comprehensive response to the Senate package. In April, they voted for a $28 billion crime bill that was similar to the Senate measure but included more than twice as much money for social programs to prevent crime. It also contained a controversial provision to allow defendants to use sentencing statistics to challenge their death sentences as racially discriminatory. The bill did not include an assault weapons ban, but the House narrowly passed a ban as separate legislation May 5. (*Assault weapons, p. 276*)

House and Senate negotiators settled on a final $33.5 billion version of the bill July 28 that included the Senate-passed trust fund. Conferees jettisoned the controversial House provision regarding alleged racial bias in death penalty sentencing but agreed to keep the equally volatile assault weapons ban as part of the overall crime bill.

That proved a dangerous strategy in the House, however, where anti-gun control Democrats joined with most Republicans on Aug. 11 to block the conference report from coming to the floor. Ten days later, after a week of politicking

and relatively small revisions, House members adopted a revised conference report.

The delicately crafted compromise hobbled into the Senate the week of Aug. 22. Over three days, Republican opponents, led by Orrin G. Hatch of Utah, launched a vigorous assault. They said the $30.2 billion bill was a monument to freewheeling Democratic spending. Democratic supporters, led by Biden, dismissed such claims and countered that the GOP was leading a National Rifle Association-backed effort to defeat the measure and its ban on 19 assault-style weapons.

On Aug. 25, the Senate turned back the Republican effort to make further changes in the conference report. Final passage came just before 11 p.m.

Major Provisions

As cleared by Congress, the bill:

● **Funding.** Established a $30.2 billion crime trust fund to pay for programs authorized in the bill, drawing on the expected savings from an administration proposal to eliminate more than 250,000 federal jobs. The money could be spent only on crime programs or used to reduce the federal deficit. It was to be fenced off in the special fund from fiscal 1995 through fiscal 2000. Appropriators were given limited authority to transfer money within the fund.

The federal work force reduction had been mandated in a bill authorizing federal agencies to offer buyouts to selected employees. *(Buyouts, p. 147)*

● **Police hiring.** Authorized $8.8 billion over six years to help communities hire 100,000 new police officers. Republicans said the money would add far fewer officers.

● **Prisons.** Authorized $7.9 billion in state construction grants for prisons and boot camps. Of that money, 50 percent was to be distributed to states that adopted tough truth-in-sentencing laws requiring repeat violent offenders to serve at least 85 percent of their sentences. In addition to the construction grants, $1.8 billion was to go toward reimbursing states for the costs of incarcerating illegal aliens who committed crimes.

● **Prevention programs.** Authorized $6.9 billion for programs aimed at preventing crime, including formula grants to needy communities for crime reduction measures. The programs included $1.6 billion for the Violence Against Women Act, a package of new federal penalties and grant programs designed to reduce domestic violence and other crimes against women. Also included was language making a crime motivated by gender a federal civil rights violation. The package included $1 billion for drug courts, which sought to rehabilitate first-time or non-violent drug offenders with intensive treatment and supervision rather than incarceration.

● **Assault weapons ban.** Banned for 10 years the manufacture, sale or possession of 19 assault weapons as well as copycat models and semiautomatic guns with two or more characteristics associated with assault weapons. The measure specifically exempted more than 670 semiautomatic weapons and allowed gun owners to keep guns that they owned legally at the time. The measure also banned ammunition-feeding devices that held more than 10 rounds.

● **Death penalty.** Authorized the death penalty for dozens of existing or new federal crimes, such as treason, kidnapping that resulted in death, and murder of a federal law enforcement official.

● **Three strikes.** Mandated life imprisonment for a third violent felony — the "three strikes and you're out" provision. The bill allowed the release of inmates sentenced under this provision who were over age 70 and had served at least 30 years.

● **Safety valve.** Provided a potential waiver from existing federal mandatory minimum sentences for certain first-time, non-violent drug offenders who exhibited good behavior while in prison.

● **Juveniles.** Allowed juveniles 13 and older to be tried as adults in the federal court system for certain violent crimes and crimes involving a gun.

Background

Congress had been trying to clear a significant crime package for six years. Lawmakers routinely had produced crime bills in response to perceived gaps in federal law or as political ammunition in an election year. But partisan gridlock had blocked their passage.

The sense of urgency seemed to mount in 1992, following the election of a Democratic president. Polls repeatedly showed voters placed crime at or near the top of their concerns and expected help from the federal as well as local government. Even many lawmakers who were skeptical of federal involvement in what was basically a state and local issue began to insist that Congress act.

Mayors and police chiefs helped keep pressure on for a bill. Democrats repeatedly brought out GOP mayors, such as New York's Rudolph Giuliani and Los Angeles' Richard Riordan, to show that the desire for the bill among city officials cut across party lines.

1993: Getting Started

The Senate grabbed the anti-crime spotlight in the waning days of the 1993 session, passing a sweeping overhaul bill Nov. 19 with a five-year price tag of $22.3 billion. *(1993 Almanac, p. 293)*

In a game of anti-crime one-upmanship, the Senate deliberated for two weeks in mid-November 1993 over how to slow the sale of weapons, crack down on criminals, protect women, treat drug addicts, combat prejudice, impose the death penalty and put more police on the streets. The result was a 95-4 vote in support of an omnibus anti-crime bill (HR 3355, formerly S 1607) that touched on all those issues and more.

Crafted by Biden, the bill embraced competing goals from both sides of the political spectrum. For liberals, the legislation included gun control measures and rehabilitation programs; for conservatives, more jails and more jail time. The bill allocated money for new federal prisons, state boot camps, shelters and services for battered women, 100,000 new police officers, prison drug treatment centers and youth crime prevention projects.

The measure also included harsh penalties for perpetrators of hate crimes, juveniles who committed serious federal crimes and criminals who used a weapon. Under the bill, the federal death penalty was to be extended to about 50 additional crimes, and prisoners could not receive Pell grants for education. The legislation also included an amendment by Dianne Feinstein, D-Calif., to ban the sale, manufacture or possession of 19 assault weapons.

The House took a different approach. After months of slow progress and finger-pointing over who was stalling an omnibus anti-crime bill, Judiciary Chairman Brooks moved a series of smaller bills. These included proposals to hire 50,000 additional police officers, expand prison drug treatment programs, help states fight juvenile gangs and drug trafficking, develop alternative sentencing for youthful offenders, bar youths from buying or possessing handguns and target domestic violence. Ten of the bills won House approval; two were cleared before Congress adjourned.

Congress also cleared the Brady bill (PL 103-159) requiring a five-day waiting period for the purchase of a handgun. *(1993 Almanac, p. 300)*

But sharp partisan divisions, as well as differences within the Democratic Caucus, foiled action on other criminal justice issues such as prison construction and sentencing policies. House members wanted to vote on those proposals before going to conference with the Senate.

Over the winter recess, lawmakers watched the crime issue climb in importance in public opinion polls and heard an earful from constituents about their fear of crime. Republicans and Democrats alike returned to Washington in 1994 declaring crime legislation a top priority for the year.

Clinton raised the stakes for congressional action in his Jan. 25 State of the Union address, calling for prompt action on a "strong, smart, tough crime bill." He also endorsed life imprisonment for repeat offenders, co-opting a GOP rallying cry on crime. *(Text, p. 3-D)*

House Committee

With the question of whether the House would take up a single omnibus bill or a series of smaller bills still undecided, three House Judiciary subcommittees resumed work on anti-crime legislation in March. The three panels churned through 14 crime-fighting proposals March 10 and 11.

The panels approved some "get tough" provisions found in the Senate bill — such as new death penalty offenses, billions of dollars for prison construction and life imprisonment for three-time violent offenders. But they stopped short of many of the Senate's directives on punishment, such as new mandatory minimum sentences. They also voted for pieces of the liberals' anti-crime agenda, most notably $6.5 billion worth of community programs designed to prevent crime.

The subcommittees took the following action, often voting along partisan lines:

● On March 10, the Subcommittee on Intellectual Property and Judicial Administration agreed to authorize $3 billion over five years to help lock up repeat violent offenders.

● The Subcommittee on Civil and Constitutional Rights also met March 10 and approved bills to overhaul the process for death row appeals, allow defendants to challenge their death sentences as racially biased and establish procedures to implement the federal death penalty.

● The Subcommittee on Crime and Criminal Justice, chaired by Charles E. Schumer, D-N.Y., tackled 10 proposals March 11. The panel approved bills to authorize the death penalty for several dozen federal offenses, to allow juveniles as young as 13 to be tried as adults for some crimes and to mandate life in prison for three-time violent felons. The subcommittee also approved the $6.5 billion package of crime prevention programs, along with a bill to allow judges to waive mandatory penalties for first-time, non-violent drug offenders.

Full Committee Acts

The full House Judiciary Committee approved 13 of the subcommittee bills in two days of lengthy and sometimes heated debate March 16 and 17. The committee spent more than 20 hours on the bills but made few major changes in the subcommittees' work.

Together with several crime bills the House had passed the previous fall, the 13 bills constituted a thorough, though more contained, reply to the massive $22.3 billion Senate bill. The House committee package did not include a Senate-passed crime trust fund to wall off $22 billion over five years for crime programs. It also did not include a weapons ban,

which Chairman Brooks said he would handle as separate legislation.

Schumer said the result was a good mix of punishment and prevention. Even so, the package was vulnerable to attack from liberals who opposed the death penalty and conservatives who considered it too skimpy on punishment and prison construction.

Liberals, who were well-represented on the committee, said new death penalties and mandatory sentences were especially hollow at the federal level, since virtually all violent crime was prosecuted in state courts.

But a bloc of moderate Democrats joined with committee Republicans to retain and even bolster some of the stringent punishment initiatives. These lawmakers said the get-tough provisions could help keep violent criminals off the street and encourage similar policies at the state level.

There was little debate about the crime prevention proposals, but they drew sparse Republican support.

The Bills

The following are the 14 subcommittee bills, 13 of which were approved by the full committee:

● **Prison construction.** The bill (HR 3968 — H Rept 103-462) to provide state grants to help build new prisons or expand existing ones began in the Judiciary Subcommittee on Intellectual Property and Judicial Administration, which approved it by voice vote March 10. The measure, sponsored by subcommittee Chairman William J. Hughes, D-N.J., authorized $3 billion over five years.

To qualify for the federal grants, states had to show they had sufficiently severe sentencing policies for violent offenders and a comprehensive prison management plan, including prisoner rehabilitation and other measures to ensure adequate prison space for the most dangerous criminals.

However, Hughes' bill did not include controversial truth-in-sentencing provisions that were part of the Senate-passed crime bill. The Senate bill authorized $3 billion to build regional prisons, but it barred states from taking advantage of the federal aid unless their prisoners served at least 85 percent of their sentences.

State and local officials of both parties complained that the truth-in-sentencing requirements amounted to a vast unfunded mandate. Their complaints notwithstanding, Bill McCollum, R-Fla., sought to add similar requirements to Hughes' bill. McCollum offered a substitute amendment to authorize $10 billion over five years in prison grants, but require states to adopt truth-in-sentencing and other restrictive provisions.

Republican colleagues generally agreed. But most Democrats attacked McCollum's proposal as unduly rigid and perhaps unconstitutional. The amendment was rejected 7-8, with Romano L. Mazzoli, D-Ky., joining Republicans in support of McCollum.

The full committee approved the prison construction bill 21-14 on March 17, after rejecting another attempt by McCollum to increase the amount for grants to $10 billion and require that eligible states adopt mandatory penalties, such as "three strikes and you're out," and certify that violent felons served at least 85 percent of their sentences.

Democrats objected strongly, using an argument more typically heard from Republicans: that it would be arrogant and inappropriate to dictate sentencing policy for the states. The amendment was defeated 13-22.

● **Death row appeals.** The bill (HR 4018 — H Rept 103-470) proposed to overhaul the rules for federal appeals, known as habeas corpus petitions, by death row inmates who had

Gun Control Advocates Claim Victory . . .

In a stunning turnaround, the House on May 5 narrowly passed an assault weapons ban that had eluded gun control advocates for years. The ban eventually was enacted as part of the 1994 omnibus anti-crime bill (HR 3355 — PL 103-322).

The weapons bill (HR 4296) provided for a 10-year ban on the manufacture, sale or possession of 19 specific semiautomatic guns as well as copycat models or guns with two or more features associated with assault weapons, such as flash suppressors. It also prohibited ammunition feeders of more than 10 rounds.

The House passed the bill by two votes. Only 2 1/2 years earlier, in 1991, the House had defeated a similar bill by a 70-vote margin, voting 247-177 to strip an assault weapons ban from a crime bill. *(1991 Almanac, p. 262)*

This time, the framework of the debate had changed, and a vote to ban assault weapons was seen as a vote to fight crime. "At a time when there is a very real and palpable fear of violent crime in this country, when law enforcement officials are outgunned by the offenders . . . we must do something significant to protect our families," said Michael A. Andrews, D-Texas, who switched from his 1991 stance to support the ban.

Polls had long indicated that gun control advocates had a majority of the public on their side. But in the past they could not compete with the intense political pressure generated by gun rights advocates and their leading lobbyist, the National Rifle Association (NRA). Even in 1994, lawmakers said, these opponents held the upper hand in campaign contributions and organized phone calls to members.

But this time, lawmakers faced an equally potent political force on the issue of crime. Just as public anger over violence drove lawmakers to approve record amounts for prison construction and other crime control programs, it pushed many toward a weapons ban that voters and police said could reduce violent killings. Lawmakers also encountered an energetic and high profile lobbying campaign by President Clinton and his Cabinet. Clinton helped keep the issue on the nightly news in the days leading up to the vote and called dozens of members seeking their support.

Gun control advocates also picked up some new supporters by modifying the proposed ban, targeting it more narrowly than the 1991 version.

Supporters prevailed on the strength of votes from freshmen — who broke 64 to 51 in favor of the ban — and from the 30 veteran members who reversed their 1991 position and supported the ban.

The vote marked the second major victory for gun control initiatives in less than a year. Congress had passed a national handgun waiting period, known as the Brady bill, in November 1993. *(1993 Almanac, p. 300)*

House Committee

The House Judiciary Subcommittee on Crime and Criminal Justice approved the assault weapons ban April 26 by an 8-5 party-line vote after agreeing to some minor changes. The full committee approved the ban April 28 by a vote of 20-15 (H Rept 103-489).

The House had passed its version of the omnibus crime bill seven days earlier, leaving out the controversial ban, which was opposed by Judiciary Committee Chairman Jack Brooks, D-Texas. It was the last issue the House had to resolve before negotiating a final crime bill with the Senate. The Senate bill, which had passed in November 1993, included a weapons ban that was virtually identical to the House language. Brooks hoped the House would defeat the separate weapons-ban bill, giving him the leverage to defeat the ban in conference. *(Crime bill, p. 273; 1993 Almanac, p. 293)*

As approved by the full committee, the legislation banned certain assault weapons as well as high-capacity ammunition feeding devices. Existing weapons would not be confiscated from owners, but owners would have to fill out a form if they wanted to transfer the guns. The ban was to expire in 10 years.

By specifically exempting more than 670 guns considered to have a legitimate sporting purpose, sponsors said they had focused the bill on the guns designed to produce a rapid spray of bullets that police said were increasingly popular among criminals.

Gun rights advocates argued that there was no difference between assault weapons and other semiautomatic guns. They opposed the ban as ineffectual and as the first step toward more sweeping prohibitions on gun ownership. But ban supporters said the guns in question had features that made them more efficient for killing humans, yet of little use for sportsmen.

Federal records indicated that assault weapons accounted for a small percentage of the nation's guns and were responsible for about 1 percent of homicides. At the same time, they showed up in a disproportionate number of crimes, lending some credence to claims that they were the preferred weapons of criminals.

Amendments Adopted

At the full committee markup, Dan Glickman, D-Kan., added an amendment clarifying that some guns not on the

exhausted the state appeals process.

Republicans insisted that prisoners made a mockery of the death penalty by delaying its imposition with years of legal appeals. Democratic liberals argued that the Supreme Court had unduly tightened the opportunities for such appeals, increasing the risk that innocent prisoners would be executed. The bill's sponsor, Don Edwards, D-Calif., chairman of the Subcommittee on Civil and Constitutional Rights, said his measure addressed both concerns.

HR 4018 required prisoners to file a habeas corpus petition within one year of exhausting state appeals and generally allowed them only one such petition. But it also required states to provide competent lawyers for indigent defendants and reversed the effect of several Supreme Court rulings that made it difficult for prisoners to appeal their sentences on the basis of new evidence or new rules of law.

The Civil and Constitutional Rights Subcommittee approved the bill 5-3 on March 10. The full committee approved it by voice vote March 17. With Republicans complaining that the bill would prolong rather than shorten the lengthy appeals process,

. . . As Assault Weapons Ban Enacted

exempt list might also be permitted depending on their features.

Charles E. Schumer, D-N.Y., the bill's lead sponsor, agreed to soften the penalties on those who transferred a gun that had been "grandfathered" under the legislation but who failed to fill out the necessary form. Originally, the bill prohibited such people from purchasing another gun. Schumer's amendment, approved by voice vote, deleted that penalty. Violators could still face a fine or six-month jail term, however.

Brooks and Rick Boucher of Virginia were the only Democrats to oppose the measure. Henry J. Hyde, Ill., cast the lone Republican "yea" vote. Hyde, who had voted against the 1991 ban, said he decided the night before the markup to support the 1994 version. Hyde said he backed gun ownership, but not of the weapons in question: "I just don't see the utility, and I can see the disutility."

House Floor

Andrew Jacobs Jr., D-Ind., was like many of the 30 swing votes who gave gun control advocates their stunning 216-214 House victory on the assault weapons ban May 5: They voted for the ban not because they thought it would do much to stop crime, but because it suddenly seemed so important to do even a little. *(Vote 156, p. 48-H)*

Jacobs surprised even himself. In the closing moments of the tense House floor vote, he reversed his recorded vote and cast a pivotal — perhaps deciding — "yea" for the ban. Jacobs said he did not think it made sense to outlaw some semiautomatics and not others as the bill proposed to do. But he said he could not pass up the chance to do away with the large ammunition clips — also proscribed by the measure — that allowed a criminal to fire many shots without reloading.

Other switchers said they were alarmed by violent crime. Most opposition came from Republicans, but there were key defections — including Minority Leader Robert H. Michel of Illinois.

Vote Breakdown

The ban won the support of 177 Democrats, 38 Republicans and one independent. Opposition came from 137 Republicans and 77 Democrats. That was nine more Republican votes than the ban received in 1991; Democrats provided 30 more votes for the ban, compared with 1991. As expected, geography was a good indicator of members' votes. Lawmakers from urban areas and the Northeast corridor generally supported the ban, while those from rural

areas and Southern and Western districts typically opposed it.

All told, 33 members switched their votes from 1991: 30 from no to yes, and three in the other direction. Of the 30, eight were retiring from politics and four were seeking a statewide office.

For Sherwood Boehlert, R-N.Y., one of the switchers, it was the pleas of law enforcement groups who said they were being outgunned by criminals that made the difference. Several said it was the fact that the 1994 bill was narrower.

Of the 33 switchers, only five received NRA contributions in the 1993-94 election cycle, as of March. Four of those voted for the ban while one, Martin Frost, D-Texas, opposed it.

Lobbying

The lobbying campaigns around the legislation, already in high gear at the time of the committee markup, reached a fever pitch the week of May 2.

Clinton, who had endorsed a weapons ban during his campaign, telephoned dozens of members, as did Attorney General Janet Reno and Treasury Secretary Lloyd Bentsen. Bentsen went to the Hill as floor debate began, holding last-minute meetings with undecideds in a room off the House floor.

Unlike the 1993 administration campaigns to pass the Clinton budget and the North American Free Trade Agreement (NAFTA), however, these calls seemed to rely primarily on moral persuasion rather than political horse-trading. Bill sponsor Schumer said the appeals did help win votes, although not with the same force as in 1993. "It's not like NAFTA, where you see 40 people breaking all at once," he said.

Administration calls reportedly had less influence on wavering Republicans — who may have been more susceptible to a May 3 letter endorsing the bill from former Presidents Ronald Reagan, Jimmy Carter and Gerald R. Ford. Former President George Bush did not sign it.

Handgun Control Inc., the leading gun control lobby, worked to mobilize support for the ban in pivotal congressional districts. But most members said the pressure at home was fiercest from gun rights advocates, including telephone campaigns and radio ads that lawmakers attributed to the NRA.

The NRA's campaign spending far outstripped contributions by Handgun Control. Since the 1992 election, the NRA had given more than $535,000 directly to House members, including $150,000 in March. Handgun Control gave $12,000.

Henry J. Hyde, R-Ill., offered a substitute that he said would truly expedite the process. The committee rejected Hyde's amendment by voice vote.

● **Death row appeals based on race.** Known as the Racial Justice Act, the bill (HR 4017 — H Rept 103-458) proposed to allow defendants to use sentencing statistics to challenge a death sentence as racially discriminatory.

Liberals and civil rights groups had been seeking such legislation in response to a 1987 Supreme Court decision that undermined the use of such statistics to challenge death

penalty laws. Democrats pointed to figures indicating that prosecutors were far more likely to seek the death penalty when defendants were black and the victims were white. Republicans strongly criticized the bill, saying it could allow death sentences to be reversed on the basis of statistics without any evidence that race was a factor in those particular cases.

The bill, sponsored by Edwards, was approved by the Civil and Constitutional Rights Subcommittee on a 5-3 vote March 10. The full committee agreed, 20-15, on March 17.

● **Death penalty procedures.** A third bill initiated in the Civil and Constitutional Rights Subcommittee (HR 4035 — H Rept 103-467) dealt with federal death penalty procedures. It contained guidelines for determining whether a defendant should receive the death penalty, applicable to defendants 18 and older. Under the bill, the government had to notify a defendant when it planned to seek the death penalty. The subcommittee approved the bill 5-3 on March 10. The full committee approved it by voice vote March 17.

● **Crime prevention.** Sponsored by Schumer, the bill (HR 4033 — H Rept 103-459, Part 1) endorsed 10 prevention programs in a $6.9 billion package that included money for community crime prevention, midnight sports programs and drug courts. The Crime and Criminal Justice Subcommittee approved it by voice vote March 11.

Schumer's initial version had cost $2.5 billion over five years. But he and John Conyers Jr., D-Mich., offered an amendment in the subcommittee that nearly tripled the bill's price tag. F. James Sensenbrenner Jr., R-Wis., objected, saying members were adding $4 billion in spending "very simply because it sounds good." But other members said Congress had to invest in prevention as well as jail cells. The subcommittee voted 9-4 for the additional spending, then approved the bill by voice vote.

The package included $1.5 billion for up to 10 model programs to funnel intensive community services into high-crime areas to see if they could reduce crime. The measure required the attorney general to evaluate the model programs and make recommendations for national action. Schumer said he and Clinton came up with the idea for the demonstration zones.

Another $2 billion was to go for Conyers' Local Partnership Act, a formula grant program to give localities speedy access to flexible federal funds for anti-crime activities. The prevention legislation also authorized funds for midnight sports programs, so-called ounce of prevention grants, and drug courts for substance abusers.

The full committee approved the bill 23-12 with little debate March 17. Members added a new $525 million jobs program to the bill targeted at poor, high-crime neighborhoods.

Republicans did not attempt to amend the bill, but they complained about it. "It's becoming a license to raid the Treasury for anything and everything if you say it is for stopping crime," said Steven H. Schiff, R-N.M. Only two Republicans voted for the bill.

Schumer said it was the first time the committee had considered such a prevention package in the context of crime legislation, and that it would help win support for the overall crime bill from liberals opposed to the death penalty and mandatory sentences.

● **Repeat offenders.** Popularly known as "three strikes and you're out," the bill (HR 3981 — H Rept 103-463) proposed to mandate life in prison for anyone convicted of a third violent felony. There was broad support for the proposal, which sought to immobilize the most violent career criminals, who were believed to commit a high percentage of all crimes. But it also came under harsh attack from lawmakers, judges and others who said it was too rigid and a waste of federal resources.

Schumer offered a new version of the proposal, backed by the White House, which defined "strikes" far more narrowly than did the Senate bill. For example, it did not include nonviolent drug crimes. The subcommittee approved a provision allowing a "serious" drug offense to count as one of the first two strikes, but not as the third. The subcommittee approved the bill, 10-3, on March 11.

The full committee approved the bill, 27-8, on March 17,

after adding an amendment by Jerrold Nadler, D-N.Y., addressing one of the criticisms — that the bill would require the government to warehouse geriatric prisoners who were unlikely to commit more crimes. The amendment, approved 20-14, permitted the release of criminals sentenced under the three-time-loser law, provided they were at least 70 and had served at least 30 years.

The full committee also modified the subcommittee bill to clarify that, to count as one of the first two strikes, a drug felony had to involve a substantial amount of drugs.

Members voted to restrict the bill's application on tribal lands. Mike Synar, D-Okla., said the change was needed because American Indians made up more than half the defendants prosecuted under federal law.

● **Mandatory sentence reform.** The so-called safety valve proposal (HR 3979 — H Rept 103-460) proposed to give judges discretion to waive the mandatory penalties for nonviolent drug offenders with little or no prior record. During markup, Schumer amended the bill to also adjust the federal sentencing guidelines for such offenses, from a minimum of five years to two. Schumer said the measure would strengthen the mandatory minimum sentencing concept by removing select cases in which penalties were widely seen as too harsh.

Lawmakers agreed to make the safety-valve provision retroactive despite some fears that doing so would burden the federal courts with thousands of federal prisoners applying to have their sentences reduced.

The Crime and Criminal Justice Subcommittee approved the bill 8-5 on March 11. The full committee approved it, 26-9, on March 16.

● **Death penalty crimes.** This bill (HR 4032 — H Rept 103-466), also sponsored by Schumer, established dozens of new federal crimes subject to the death penalty, including first-degree murder, kidnapping, taking hostages, drive-by shootings and carjackings resulting in death.

Many of the crimes that were included, such as assassination of the president, already carried the death penalty. But a 1972 Supreme Court ruling precluded executions for these offenses because existing law did not contain required procedural protections. Other crimes, such as hostage-takings resulting in death, were already federal offenses but would be newly eligible for the death penalty. And some, such as killing by drive-by shooting, were not federal crimes but would become so under the bill.

The crime subcommittee approved the bill 10-3 on March 11. The full committee approved it 25-10 on March 17.

Liberals argued against the measure on moral and practical grounds and cited examples of death row inmates who were found to be innocent. Nadler sought in full committee to replace the death penalty provisions with life imprisonment, but his amendment failed 11-24. The committee also rejected an amendment to restrict the number of new offenses punishable by the death penalty.

Members narrowly agreed to authorize capital punishment for high-level drug traffickers, even if they were not tied to a murder. McCollum, who sponsored the amendment, argued that anyone high up in the drug trade must be indirectly responsible for at least one death and thus deserved to risk capital punishment. Some Democrats said the proposal was probably unconstitutional because the Supreme Court in the past had found the death penalty to be unduly harsh punishment for a crime that did not involve murder. But several Democrats joined all GOP committee members in backing the so-called drug kingpin amendment, which squeaked by, 18-17.

● **Juvenile criminals.** The bill (HR 4031 — H Rept 103-465) allowed, but did not mandate, that individuals 13 and older be

tried as adults in federal court for crimes such as murder, assault, robbery and rape.

The Crime and Criminal Justice Subcommittee approved the measure, 7-5, after an emotional debate March 11. The provision was similar to language that Carol Moseley-Braun, D-Ill., had added to the Senate bill. But unlike that version, Schumer's bill made trying juveniles as adults optional. The prosecutor had to seek such a move and a judge had to agree to it. Craig Washington, D-Texas, objected, saying that "certifying 13-year-olds as adults is an oxymoron." But other members said some juveniles had committed such heinous crimes that they were no longer truly children. The full committee approved the bill, 21-13, on March 17.

● **Crime victims.** The bill (HR 4030 — H Rept 103-464, Part 1) permitted victims of crime and sexual abuse to present information or make a statement at the defendant's sentencing. The bill also revised the formula for the allocation of money in the federal crime victims' fund, established in 1984. The fund compensated victims and helped them get counseling. The Crime and Criminal Justice Subcommittee approved the bill by voice vote March 11. The full committee followed suit March 16, also by voice vote.

● **Insurance fraud.** The bill (HR 665 — H Rept 103-468) proposed to make defrauding an insurance company a federal crime, permitting federal prosecution for filing false statements, embezzling or deceiving an insurance company. The Subcommittee on Crime and Criminal Justice approved it by voice vote March 11. The full committee followed suit March 16.

● **Violence against children.** The bill (HR 1120 — H Rept 103-461) sought to strengthen federal penalties against people convicted of assaulting children 16 and younger. Under existing law, a child could suffer abuse, such as broken bones or cigarette burns, that might not qualify the assault as a "serious" federal offense. Penalties under the bill included a fine or imprisonment up to five years. The crime subcommittee approved the bill by voice vote March 11. The full committee approved it 22-12 on March 16.

● **Sexual abuse of children.** The bill (HR 3993 — H Rept 103-469) provided for stronger laws against individuals who abused children sexually, focusing particularly on international trafficking in child pornography. It also called on states to pass tough laws against child pornography. The crime subcommittee approved it by voice vote March 11. The full committee followed suit March 17.

● **Police Corps scholarships.** The draft bill provided for education grants to college students in exchange for four years of service with a state or local law enforcement agency. Grants were capped at $30,000 per person, and each graduating class was limited to 20,000 participants. Existing officers could obtain grants for advanced training and education. The bill authorized $100 million in fiscal 1995, $250 million in fiscal 1996 and unspecified sums through fiscal 1999.

The crime subcommittee approved the measure by voice vote March 11. Although the full committee did not consider the bill, it was later added to the omnibus House bill.

House Floor

The House began floor debate on the crime bill the week of April 11, after Judiciary Committee Chairman Brooks had combined the 13 committee-passed bills with measures the House had passed the previous fall into a single omnibus anti-crime bill (HR 4092).

After two weeks of floor debate that added more than $12 billion in amendments and pushed the total close to $28 billion, lawmakers passed the massive bill April 21 in a bipartisan vote of 285-141. The House then inserted the text into the Senate-passed bill (HR 3355) and passed it by voice vote. *(Vote 144, p. 42-H)*

The House-passed measure was generally more liberal than the $22.3 billion Senate bill — less punitive and more generous toward prevention programs.

It authorized funding to help states and localities hire police officers, build prisons, offer drug treatment and provide community and educational programs designed to steer children away from crime. It also expanded the death penalty to dozens of new federal crimes and required life imprisonment for repeat violent offenders.

Of the $12 billion in additional spending, $10.5 billion was for federal grants for prison construction, on top of the $3 billion already in the bill.

Some lawmakers, such as Timothy J. Penny, D-Minn., were troubled by the unprecedented federal role proposed by the bill, saying Washington had neither the money nor the ability to effectively fight crime. But many lawmakers embraced the bill, saying crime was too important for Congress to sit on the sidelines.

Clinton, who had called for most of the major programs in both bills, emphatically agreed. "Democrats and Republicans joined together to break gridlock and make our nation's streets safer," he said.

Republicans complained that the bill was too soft on criminals and that Democratic leaders were blocking consideration of some get-tough amendments. "This bill satisfies the academics and the sociologists, but God help you if you work the midnight shift and have to walk home," said Hyde. But many of these critics conceded the bill had worthy components, and 65 Republicans voted for it.

Members of the Congressional Black Caucus, who had criticized the bill as too punitive, split over final passage. They provided almost one-half the 34 Democratic votes against it, although most members voted for it.

Discord Over the Rule

In preparation for the floor action, Brooks took the omnibus crime package to the Rules Committee March 22. After allowing an initial hour of floor debate the following day, the panel circulated a draft rule that would have allowed numerous GOP amendments. But Republicans complained that some key initiatives had been left out. They threatened to hold up floor action with procedural delays, forcing House Speaker Thomas S. Foley, D-Wash., to announce that the House would postpone action on the bill until lawmakers returned from a two-week spring recess.

When the Rules Committee reconvened April 12, it was clear that the recess had done little to bridge the partisan rifts. Committee Democrats offered a second proposed rule for floor debate, which ranking Republican Gerald B. H. Solomon, N.Y., blasted as little better than the first.

Over GOP protests, the rule was approved by a party-line 6-4 vote. Republicans were still complaining the following day, when the House took up the rule and approved it, 244-176. *(Vote 103, p. 30-H)*

Speaker Foley helped shore up support for the rule among members of the Congressional Black Caucus by promising to back their effort to retain the controversial provision to allow death row inmates to use sentencing statistics to challenge their sentences as racially discriminatory.

Expanding the Death Penalty

Floor debate began with the bill's provisions to make dozens of new and existing federal crimes eligible for capital

punishment and to lay out legal procedures for deciding when those convicted of such crimes should receive the death penalty. Although a federal death penalty would not reach the vast majority of the nation's violent criminals, who were prosecuted under state laws, it had become a contentious focus of debate.

The House on April 14 rejected three amendments designed to eliminate the death penalty for all or some crimes in the bill.

The first, by Mike Kopetski, D-Ore., would have replaced the death penalties throughout the bill with life imprisonment without parole. It was defeated 111-314. *(Vote 107, p. 32-H)*

Amendment supporters generally stressed practical rather than moral arguments, asserting that death penalty cases were actually more expensive than locking up offenders for life. "Take this burden off the taxpayers," said Kweisi Mfume, D-Md., chairman of the black caucus. But Brooks said the death penalty was an appropriate and necessary way for society to express its outrage at certain heinous crimes.

Melvin Watt, D-N.C., offered an amendment to remove the death penalty for so-called drug kingpins when they were not directly responsible for a murder. He said African-Americans and Hispanics had been disproportionate targets of prosecutions under the existing drug kingpin law, though they were not usually the masterminds of drug operations. And he noted that the Supreme Court had indicated that the death penalty might be too severe a punishment for crimes other than murder.

But supporters said the provision could withstand a legal challenge, noting that the high court had not invalidated the death penalty for espionage and treason. The amendment failed, 108-316. *(Vote 106, p. 32-H)*

The third amendment, by Robert C. Scott, D-Va., would have eliminated the death penalty for murders committed during carjackings, drive-by shootings, and federal drug and gun crimes. It was defeated by voice vote.

Capital Sentencing Rules, Other Amendments

Opponents of the death penalty lost again when the House took up the legal procedures for imposing capital punishment. As reported by the Judiciary Committee, the bill spelled out rules for a separate sentencing trial for defendants convicted of capital crimes, requiring consideration of both aggravating and mitigating factors.

But George W. Gekas, R-Pa., said the proposed procedures would make it too hard to impose the death penalty. He offered an amendment to adjust them, among other things, by eliminating a requirement that juries be told they were never required to impose the death penalty. Brooks argued against changing the bill's language, and others warned that Gekas' amendment could open the federal death penalty to constitutional challenge. But most lawmakers supported the amendment, and it was adopted April 14 by a vote of 226-198. *(Vote 109, p. 34-H)*

With little debate, lawmakers the same day adopted a package of 35 separate amendments offered by Brooks that helped add about $1.5 billion to the bill's price tag. They included $210 million annually for five years for Treasury Department law enforcement programs, $385 million for rural law enforcement and $36 million to establish Boys and Girls Clubs in public housing. The vote was 395-25. *(Vote 104, p. 32-H)*

Republicans then employed a parliamentary maneuver — usually used to try to kill a bill — to temporarily halt consideration of the crime package. GOP members said they simply wanted to send the bill back to the Rules Committee to win a chance to debate an amendment that had been

blocked from floor consideration. The amendment proposed to make it easier to use some illegally obtained evidence in court. Brooks blasted the GOP effort as an attempt to stall or kill the legislation, and the motion was rejected 170-257. *(Vote 110, p. 34-H)*

Final Week of Debate

The last week of floor action focused largely on the controversial issue of death row appeals. Liberals eked out a victory on the use of sentencing statistics to help invalidate a death penalty as racially discriminatory. But they were unable to retain provisions overhauling the process for habeas corpus petitions.

Members of the black and Hispanic caucuses fought hard for these measures, saying they were critical to ensuring that the death penalty was carried out fairly. But Republicans fought back on the House floor, saying both measures would effectively invalidate the death penalty. They had the backing of national prosecutors; the Clinton administration took no formal position.

● **Death row appeals.** On April 19, Republicans won a 270-159 vote to drop the provisions on habeas corpus petitions. *(Vote 119, p. 36-H)*

Ironically, the deleted provisions also contained some restrictions on death row appeals that Republicans had been seeking for years, such as requiring that inmates file a habeas corpus petition within one year of exhausting state appeals. But Hyde said the restrictions were outweighed by provisions to broaden some legal avenues for appeal by reversing the effect of several recent Supreme Court decisions.

● **Racial statistics.** House liberals had better luck the next day, narrowly retaining the bill's language regarding death penalty statistics.

Lawmakers had clashed over the issue before. A similar provision had prevailed in 1990, but it never became law. The next year, lawmakers voted 223-191 for a substitute offered by McCollum to ban the use of such statistics but add language barring racial discrimination in sentencing. That never became law either. The Senate in 1991 voted 55-41 against a racial justice provision. *(1991 Almanac, pp. 263, 269)*

In 1994, both sides prepared furiously for the rematch. Republicans highlighted the issue in public statements and warned that the provisions could force them to oppose the whole bill. But many black caucus members made it clear that they would be just as likely to oppose the bill if the language were dropped.

On April 20, McCollum offered an amendment to strike the provision and replace it with his 1991 language. Gary A. Franks of Connecticut, the House's only black Republican, spoke against the Racial Justice Act. "We do not correct social problems by constantly defining [the] remedy in terms of black and white," he said.

Several Democrats spoke strongly for the provisions. "There is no check on the prosecutor today," said Delegate Eleanor Holmes Norton, D-D.C. "He chooses blacks for death." Supporters stressed that inmates generally would not be able to overturn their sentences on statistics alone; the bill merely would allow such evidence to be considered.

The McCollum amendment was narrowly defeated on a 212-217 vote. Speaker Foley, who rarely voted, did so this time, opposing the amendment. The tally was even closer than it appeared, since it included the votes of five delegates, including Norton, who could have been excluded from voting if their votes had changed the outcome. In this case, the amendment still would have failed under a tie vote. *(Vote 131, p. 40-H)*

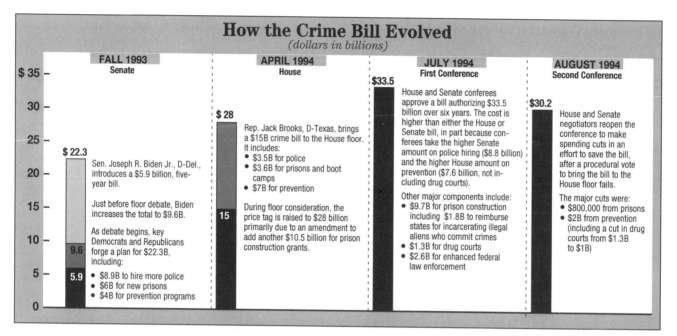

How the Crime Bill Evolved
(dollars in billions)

FALL 1993
Senate

$22.3

Sen. Joseph R. Biden Jr., D-Del., introduces a $5.9 billion, five-year bill.

Just before floor debate, Biden increases the total to $9.6B.

As debate begins, key Democrats and Republicans forge a plan for $22.3B, including:
- $8.9B to hire more police
- $6B for new prisons
- $4B for prevention programs

9.6

5.9

APRIL 1994
House

$28

Rep. Jack Brooks, D-Texas, brings a $15B crime bill to the House floor. It includes:
- $3.5B for police
- $3.6B for prisons and boot camps
- $7B for prevention

During floor consideration, the price tag is raised to $28 billion primarily due to an amendment to add another $10.5 billion for prison construction grants.

15

JULY 1994
First Conference

$33.5

House and Senate conferees approve a bill authorizing $33.5 billion over six years. The cost is higher than either the House or Senate bill, in part because conferees take the higher Senate amount on police hiring ($8.8 billion) and the higher House amount on prevention ($7.6 billion, not including drug courts).

Other major components include:
- $9.7B for prison construction including $1.8B to reimburse states for incarcerating illegal aliens who commit crimes
- $1.3B for drug courts
- $2.6B for enhanced federal law enforcement

AUGUST 1994
Second Conference

$30.2

House and Senate negotiators reopen the conference to make spending cuts in an effort to save the bill, after a procedural vote to bring the bill to the House floor fails.

The major cuts were:
- $800,000 from prisons
- $2B from prevention (including a cut in drug courts from $1.3B to $1B)

The close margin encouraged McCollum to try again the next day, asking members to send the bill back to the Rules Committee with instructions to replace the racial justice language with his own. The House defeated the motion, 192-235. *(Vote 143, p. 42-H)*

● **Prison construction.** Republicans complained that the bill authorized more than $7 billion for social programs aimed at preventing crime, while stinting on constructing prisons to lock up proven criminals. They pressed their point April 19, when the House took up several amendments to give states more than the $3 billion authorized in the subcommittee bill for prison construction.

Jim Chapman, D-Texas, sponsored an amendment to authorize an additional $10.5 billion over five years for prison construction. Most of the money was to be apportioned to states based on the incidence of violent crime, a figure that generally tracked state population. However, 25 percent was to be doled out to states that had the strictest sentencing policies. Chapman said his proposal would offer badly needed resources to states, many of which were under court order to reduce prison overcrowding.

The amendment was an attempt to strike a compromise between demands for more prison construction money and complaints from state and local officials that tying the money to tough sentencing requirements would be too costly for them. It was approved 377-50. *(Vote 124, p. 38-H)*

Republicans supported Chapman's amendment but said it did not go far enough. They urged adoption of a second proposal by McCollum, to authorize $10 billion in prison construction grants for states that adopted specific sentencing provisions, such as life imprisonment for three-time violent felons.

McCollum offered his amendment as a substitute to the $3 billion program in the original bill. But Hughes undercut him by offering a substitute amendment that basically reinstated the $3 billion program already in the bill. Lawmakers narrowly adopted the Hughes substitute, 215-206, then added it to the bill by voice vote. *(Vote 126, p. 38-H)*

● **Three strikes, other amendments.** The House agreed to broaden the "three strikes and you're out" provisions approved by the committee, which said that a drug felony could count as either the first or second strike, but not the third. Members

voted 303-126 to approve an amendment by Solomon to let serious drug offenses count as any or all strikes that could trigger life imprisonment. *(Vote 122, p. 38-H)*

Members added several amendments to the bill on a single vote, including a requirement that the federal government reimburse states for the cost of incarcerating illegal aliens as of October 1998. Another banned weight-training programs or equipment for prisoners. The vote was 402-22. *(Vote 130, p. 40-H)*

Members also voted, 417-12, to authorize 6,000 new Border Patrol agents, more than double the existing number. *(Vote 134, p. 40-H)*

First Conference

After weeks of skirmishing over the Racial Justice Act and other provisions, House and Senate negotiators approved what was supposed to be a final version of the anti-crime measure July 28. But anti-gun control Democrats joined with most Republicans on Aug. 11 to block the conference report from coming to the House floor. Ten days later, after a week of politicking and relatively small revisions, a modestly revised conference agreement won House approval.

The Agreement

House and Senate conferees settled on a $33 billion compromise bill July 28 (H Rept 103-694). Despite vociferous opposition from Brooks and other gun rights advocates, the final bill included the ban on certain semiautomatic assault weapons The conferees, however, did not include the explosive provision in the House bill known as the Racial Justice Act — prompting some members of the black caucus to threaten to vote against a procedural motion to take up the bill.

The legislation included funds to hire 100,000 new police officers, build state prisons and boot camps, expand federal law enforcement and establish an array of community programs aimed at preventing crime — with money to come from the special fund to be created by the bill. It authorized the death penalty for dozens of new and existing federal offenses and required life imprisonment for third-time violent felons — while also loosening existing mandatory penalties for first-time non-violent drug offenders.

Clinton and Democratic leaders hailed the result as a promising blend of crime-fighting strategies and a political breakthrough after years of partisan gridlock. "After nearly six years, congressional leaders and people in both parties have agreed on what will be the toughest, largest and smartest federal attack on crime in the history of the United States of America," Clinton said at a Justice Department rally for the bill held just minutes after the conference finished.

Republicans did not share the enthusiasm. They attacked Democrats for weighing down the bill with billions of dollars for social programs they said had little to do with crime fighting. "This is not a Christmas tree, this is the whole Emerald City of Oz," said Hyde, a House negotiator.

Even some Democrats were lukewarm toward the final product.

Conferees had held a single, ceremonial meeting June 16 before bogging down as Democrats struggled to resolve internal party conflicts, primarily on the death penalty. That logjam broke in mid-July, when the administration and Democratic leaders decided to split with liberals and the black caucus and drop the death penalty statistics measure from the bill.

By that time, Brooks and Biden had narrowed many of the differences between the two bills and had compiled a draft compromise on all but the most contentious issues. The formal conference began in earnest the morning of July 26 and ended about 48 hours later, including a 16-hour marathon session that ran into the early hours of July 28.

House and Senate Republican negotiators initially complained that they had had little advance consultation on the emerging bill and that Brooks was trying to rush it through the conference. They proceeded to offer numerous amendments during the negotiating sessions, several of them aimed at securing more money for prison construction and greatly reducing the $7.6 billion in the bill for crime-prevention programs.

Hatch attacked many of those prevention programs as retreads of abandoned federal programs, such as revenue sharing, and said they had no place in an anti-crime bill. But Democrats defeated efforts to cut such funds, which they said represented an equally if not more promising route toward crime reduction than increased incarceration.

Major issues resolved in conference included the following:
● **Assault weapons ban.** House and Senate negotiators knew that one of the toughest issues to resolve would be the ban on semiautomatic assault weapons. The Senate crime bill included the ban. The House in May narrowly passed a similar ban as separate legislation.

Brooks fought unsuccessfully to weaken the ban in closed-door negotiations leading up to the conference. He scored a smaller victory for gun rights advocates, however, when he attached provisions to limit the 1993 Brady law, which required a waiting period and background check for handgun purchasers.

Pawnshop owners had been seeking relief from the Brady law, saying it was not feasible or necessary for them to conduct the required checks on customers who frequently hocked and redeemed weapons. Brooks had been negotiating with Sen. Howard M. Metzenbaum, D-Ohio, over providing pawnbrokers limited relief from the Brady requirements. When Brooks presented the language, however, it included a total waiver allowing pawnshops to forgo checks on customers trying to reclaim their own guns.

Metzenbaum denounced the proposed waiver, saying many convicted felons caught through the background checks had gone to pawnshops for their guns. Senate confer-

ees voted 5-4 to replace the exemption with a provision allowing a background check at one pawnshop to be good for a year. But House negotiators rejected that approach, and the senators eventually accepted the full waiver.

Brooks also won inclusion of a Senate provision designed to protect hunters from protesters.

Those concessions by gun control advocates helped clear the way for conferees to retain the weapons ban in the final bill. Brooks still offered a motion to remove the ban, but Conyers said the guns posed a particular threat and had to be banned. House negotiators defeated the motion, 4-6, with Hyde joining all the Democratic conferees except Brooks to support the ban.

The conference agreement also strengthened the rules for federal firearms dealers, generally prohibited the sale or transfer of handguns to minors and blocked people subject to a court restraining order from obtaining a gun.

Schumer, a leading gun control advocate, said those provisions and the weapons ban more than outweighed the setback on the Brady requirements. The trade-off had at least tacit support from the Clinton administration. But Handgun Control Inc., the lead lobby for the Brady bill, complained that gun control advocates should not have been forced to soften the Brady law to obtain a weapons ban approved by both chambers.
● **Racial Justice Act.** As expected, negotiators abandoned the controversial House provision that was designed to counter a perceived racial bias in death penalty sentencing.

Democratic lawmakers and the administration had wrestled for weeks over the measure, with most eventually concluding it was too contentious to include in the final crime bill. Senate Republicans threatened to filibuster if the provision remained in the bill and were expected to have backing from numerous Democrats who also opposed the sentencing provision.

The black caucus fought hard to keep the provision, and Conyers, a senior member of the caucus, offered a motion to include it in the final bill. House negotiators voted 6-4, on party lines, to do so.

When Senate conferees took up the matter, however, Biden urged them to put the overall crime bill above the death penalty provision, which he supported. "The question is whether to accept the House provision, racial justice, which will kill the bill." Democratic negotiators rejected the motion 2-3. GOP conferees voted "present," forcing Democratic supporters to kill the provision rather than risk a filibuster.
● **More prisons.** Another key area of dispute was how much to spend on prison construction and what terms to attach to prison building grants.

Republicans wanted to authorize about $13 billion for prison construction but require qualifying states to adopt stringent sentencing laws. Most Democrats supported substantially less prison construction money and greater flexibility for states.

Conference negotiators eventually agreed to provide $8.7 billion for state prisons and boot camps, although only $6.5 billion of that was to be paid for from the crime trust fund.
● **Trust fund.** The Senate had endorsed a $22.3 billion crime trust fund, to be financed by expected savings from the planned federal work force reduction. Although the House bill did not include such a fund in its bill, members supported the idea.

Conferees agreed to $30.2 billion over six years, beginning in fiscal 1995. That money was to be set aside in yearly increments and could be spent only on programs authorized in the bill. Appropriators still would have to approve the spending

through the annual appropriations bills. And negotiators agreed to give appropriators some authority to transfer money between programs within the fund.

Lawmakers already had included the first installment of crime bill funding in the fiscal 1995 appropriations bill for the departments of Commerce, Justice, State and the federal judiciary. *(Appropriations, p. 483)*

But there were considerable doubts that federal work force reductions would produce the full anticipated savings, or that appropriators would approve the full amount of spending authorized. Although most lawmakers involved with the bill insisted it would include only "real money," conferees added about $3 billion in authorizations not backed up by money in the trust fund.

● **Gender-based crime.** One of Biden's top priorities in the bill was a Senate-passed provision to create a new federal civil rights violation for crimes motivated by gender. The measure allowed victims of such crimes to sue for damages or other relief. Advocates said it was an important, practical and symbolic step because many state justice systems did not take attacks on women seriously.

The House bill did not include the provision, and it came under attack as an unwarranted and unwieldy burden to the federal courts. Rep. Synar was among those to speak against it. But aware of the importance Biden and others attached to the provision, Synar ultimately cast the deciding vote to keep it.

● **Other issues.** House conferees held the upper hand on a number of other issues.

Over Republican objections, conferees dropped some of the "get-tough" Senate measures altogether, such as new mandatory minimums for certain gang activity or for carrying or using a gun during a violent crime.

In other areas, such as trying certain juveniles as adults or mandating life imprisonment for a third violent crime, conferees adopted the less stringent versions favored by the House and the administration.

The Rule Rejected

Democrats pulled out all the stops to pass the final version of the $33 billion crime bill Aug. 11, only to crash into a wall of opposition from Republicans and nearly 60 breakaway Democrats opposed to gun control or the death penalty.

Their defeat came over the rule governing floor debate on the bill — a procedural step needed to bring the legislation to the floor. Debate on adopting the rule became a partisan showdown between Democrats, determined to produce a win for Clinton and the party, and Republicans who wanted to defeat or force changes in the bill. In a stunning failure, Democrats lost the key procedural vote, 210-225. *(Vote 394, p. 118-H)*

Republicans prevailed on party discipline, holding all but 11 members on the vote. Democrats had hoped to win over at least four more, but in the final hours several wavering GOP lawmakers decided to vote no.

On the Democrats' side, 58 members defied their leadership to block the bill from coming to the floor. Most were gun rights advocates opposed to the weapons ban. But 10 Democratic "nays" came from black lawmakers who opposed the new death penalties in the bill and the decision to drop the death penalty sentencing language.

Afterward, lawmakers offered dramatically different diagnoses of what brought the bill down and prescriptions to put it back on track.

Democrats fingered tenacious opposition by the National Rifle Association (NRA) and by Republicans intent on denying Clinton a political victory on the crime issue.

Crime Trust Fund

In a highly unusual move, architects of the omnibus anti-crime bill (HR 3355 — PL 103-322) included a special trust fund to provide $30.2 billion over the following six years to pay for the programs authorized in the bill.

It was the dedicated funding from the trust fund that allowed lawmakers to transform what began as a relatively modest crime bill into a behemoth. Senate Judiciary Chairman Joseph R. Biden Jr., D-Del., originally brought a $5.9 billion, five-year bill to the Senate floor in November 1993, and only reluctantly agreed to enlarge it to $9.6 billion, worried that there would be no way to pay for it all. But after Senate Appropriations Committee Chairman Robert C. Byrd, D-W.Va., proposed an amendment to create the trust fund, the measure eventually became a six-year, $30.2 billion bill.

The trust fund was supposed to be fed by the savings from a plan to cut the federal bureaucracy by more than 250,000 employees over the ensuing several years. In fact, Byrd proposed the trust fund idea in large part to block a move to devote the personnel-cut savings to deficit reduction by lowering even further the already tight spending caps on appropriations.

But many budget analysts said that any savings from the personnel cuts already had been "spent," in effect, to shave spending enough to meet the freeze Congress imposed on fiscal 1994 appropriations. They said the savings would not be available for crime programs or any other new spending.

Instead, the effect of the trust fund would be to siphon money out of available funds for other non-crime priorities. "When the whole crime thing started, the caps were already tight," said Ellen Nissenbaum, legislative director of the Center on Budget and Policy Priorities, an advocacy group for low-income programs. "The crime trust fund is essentially going to come out of the hide of domestic programs," she said, arguing that appropriators would be less likely to cut defense and foreign aid to fund crime initiatives than they would be to raid other domestic programs.

Procedurally, the crime trust fund was supposed to work much the same way the budget fire walls worked in 1991-93. The existing cap on appropriations, dictated by the 1990 deficit-reduction bill, was to be reduced (by some $2.4 billion for fiscal 1995) and that amount transferred into the anti-crime category. Appropriators would have only limited ability to move money around among the various anti-crime programs authorized by the bill, and if they elected not to spend any of the money, the unspent remainder could not be used for anything other than deficit reduction.

"Last night the National Rifle Association and the House Republican leadership struck a savage blow for violent criminals and against ordinary American citizens," said Schumer at a news conference the following day. "Their unholy alliance viciously assaulted a sound, tough and balanced crime bill." The vote did mark a major win for the gun rights lobby, which had been on the losing side of several recent critical votes.

Republicans said the bill was brought down by too little in tough punishment, too much in social spending "pork" and an

'Brady 2' Never Makes It Out of Starting Gate

Less than one month after the handgun waiting period required under the 1993 Brady act took effect March 1, gun control advocates pressed for passage of a broad new measure to ban certain firearms and impose licensing and registration requirements on others. The measure was never marked up.

Unofficially dubbed "Brady 2," the bill (S 1882) aimed to keep handguns away from criminals by establishing new requirements for gun purchasers and dealers. The original Brady law (HR 1025 — PL 103-159) mandated a five-day waiting period for handgun purchases to allow police to check the backgrounds of prospective buyers. President Clinton signed it Nov. 30, 1993. (1993 Almanac, p. 300)

At a Senate Judiciary subcommittee hearing on the new bill March 23, sponsor Howard M. Metzenbaum, D-Ohio, argued that stricter controls were needed to reduce the flow of handguns and to stop the "epidemic" of violence resulting from a plentiful supply of firearms.

But Orrin G. Hatch, R-Utah, argued that the bill would do little to reduce violent crime. "Criminals generally obtain firearms in the black market or from other criminals — not gun shops and licensed dealers," he said. "All S 1882 will do is make it harder for law-abiding citizens to purchase firearms for lawful purposes."

The bill as introduced required handgun purchasers to have a valid state handgun license — similar to a driver's license — to be issued to those who passed a background check and a firearms safety course. The measure also contained provisions to tighten regulation and screening of gun dealers and require the sellers of used guns to register the transfer with state police. Retail handgun purchases were to be limited to one per person per month. The bill banned a host of semiautomatic assault weapons and other weapons that supporters said had no apparent sporting purpose. It also required gun manufacturers to install safety devices on handguns to prevent small children from accidentally discharging them.

The Brady bill had taken seven years to enact, and supporters of Brady 2 were digging in for a long fight. The prospects were particularly dim in the House, where Judiciary Crime and Criminal Justice Subcommittee Chairman Charles E. Schumer, D-N.Y., had introduced a companion bill (HR 3932). The measure faced opposition from committee Chairman Jack Brooks, D-Texas, a longtime foe of gun control measures. House Speaker Thomas S. Foley, D-Wash., also opposed gun control legislation.

No Effort To Revise Brady 1

Meanwhile, opponents of the original Brady bill did not pursue earlier claims that they would try to scale back the legislation.

In 1993, to prevent a threatened GOP filibuster on the Brady bill, Democratic leaders had promised Senate Minority Leader Bob Dole, R-Kan., a 1994 vote on a scaled-back version. But Dole did not seek action on his alternative (S 1785).

While the Brady law expired after five years, Dole's bill would have eliminated the waiting period after four years, or even two years if a computer instant check system became available. But the Republican leader said early in the year that he was reformulating the proposal.

Some Senate staff members from both parties said Dole would put off calling up his bill to put some distance between his proposal and the Brady bill. Others said Dole would never offer his alternative and that the 1993 deal was more of a gesture toward gun control opponents.

---

arrogant House leadership that tried to force the final product on GOP members. Senate Minority Leader Bob Dole, R-Kan., said the bill failed because the public recognized it was "an over-hyped, multibillion-dollar boondoggle that emphasized social theory over law enforcement."

Democratic leaders knew they would have trouble putting together a majority to approve the rule, and Speaker Foley had delayed the vote from the week of Aug. 1 in hopes of using the extra time to pick up votes. The delay helped the leadership gather additional support from black caucus members and from moderate Republicans. By Aug. 9, at least 10 Republicans were expected to support the rule with another handful of GOP votes potentially in sight.

But as the week progressed, some supporters fretted they were losing momentum — particularly among moderate Republicans — and said it was time to chance a floor vote. The leadership initially resisted, but on Aug. 10 decided to forge ahead the following day.

Brooks waited until the last minute to file the text of the final bill. He delivered the hefty document to the House desk at 7 p.m. on Aug. 10. One hour later, the Rules Committee convened and approved the procedures for floor consideration on a 6-4 party-line vote.

Though often partisan, rule votes typically were low-key affairs debated before a nearly empty chamber. This vote, by contrast, had all the trappings of the high-stakes showdowns on the North American Free Trade Agreement or the assault weapons ban.

White House Chief of Staff Leon E. Panetta and other administration lobbyists arrived on the Hill to lobby undecided lawmakers. Democratic whips set up a command post in a room off the chamber with an open telephone line for Clinton to speak to wavering lawmakers.

Dozens of lawmakers listened to the debate, applauding and sometimes hissing speakers.

Many Republicans sought to cast the vote as a procedural matter. "How many times have we been had on our side of the aisle by the rules of this House," Minority Leader Robert H. Michel of Illinois thundered to Republican lawmakers. Michel said there were promising elements in the crime bill, but that Democrats had loaded it up until "it looks like Santa Claus with a sheriff's badge." By defeating the rule, Michel said, members could get a chance to pass a leaner, tougher crime bill later.

"There are members in this House who do not want the president to have a crime bill," Hughes responded. Democrats presented the vote as do-or-die for anti-crime legislation in 1994. "The society that cannot protect the physical security of its citizens is a pretty useless society whatever else it can accomplish," said Foley in a rare closing speech.

The contest was closer than the 210-228 tally suggested. As was often the case on close votes, the leaders had several

members prepared to support them if their votes would have made the difference.

Second Conference

There followed an extraordinary week of recrimination, politicking and conciliation, which culminated in the crafting of a new conference report.

Immediately after the House vote, Dole and House Minority Whip Newt Gingrich, R-Ga., faxed Clinton aboard Air Force One, offering to help rework the bill to win GOP votes. Republicans wanted to add more death penalties and mandatory sentences, and more prison construction money, while cutting back on crime prevention activities. Many also opposed the weapons ban.

Democratic leaders emerged after the vote with no clear plan of action. "There is no Plan B," Schumer said. But they shrugged off Republican offers to collaborate on wholesale changes in the bill. "I don't think the conference can meet any more," Brooks said just after the vote. "It's too fragile." Schumer warned that reopening the conference, even on minor issues, could open the whole bill to renegotiation and doom it.

House leaders did not eliminate that possibility, but they explored other options.

The White House and Biden initially urged House leaders to turn around a few votes on the original bill. By midweek, three members of the black caucus announced plans to support the rule if not necessarily the bill itself — Charles B. Rangel of New York, Cleo Fields of Louisiana and John Lewis of Georgia. All three strongly opposed the bill's death penalty provisions but were swayed by calls for party unity, support for the prevention programs and, in Fields' case, assurances from the administration that it would work to combat racial bias in the implementation of the federal death penalty. But those votes were not enough to close the gap.

The White House soon indicated that compromise was possible — as long as the final version contained key elements such as money for 100,000 new police officers, a strong prevention package, life imprisonment for three-time violent felons and the ban on assault weapons. The White House strategy, however, focused on picking up Republicans who supported gun control. The House leadership was leaning toward finding the votes among Democrats, including those who opposed gun control.

Foley and other House leaders spoke publicly of modest changes in the assault weapons ban. Privately, however, they explored forcing a separate vote on the ban or dropping it altogether. Their reasoning stemmed from a reading of the 47 Democrats who opposed the rule solely or in part because of the weapons ban.

House leaders floated proposals to modify the ban, including requiring the Bureau of Alcohol, Tobacco and Firearms to consult with Congress before adding new guns to the banned list. Under the bill, the bureau could ban semiautomatic weapons that had two or more specified features associated with assault weapons.

It eventually became clear, however, that such a formula would yield few if any votes from the gun rights Democrats. Rep. Charles Wilson, D-Texas, for example, said that in his East Texas district, a politician could not support gun control. "It's like asking someone from Brooklyn to vote against Israel," he said.

If the gun rights Democrats were dug in, so was Clinton. As late as the night of Aug. 18, House Democratic leaders reportedly proposed moving the gun ban as a separate bill: Clinton refused. That pushed House leaders toward cutting a deal with Republicans.

GOP support remained a moving target throughout the week, with Republicans split into factions with varied demands. As they recognized their importance to the Democratic leadership, many Republicans were emboldened to ask for provisions that would have been unthinkable the week before.

Gingrich and the four key Republican crime bill conferees on Aug. 18 called for major changes in the bill, including dropping $5.5 billion in spending, generally from the crime prevention programs, and inserting GOP-backed sentencing measures opposed by many Democrats.

While Republicans were elated by the Democratic leadership's defeat on the crime rule, however, many also shared the desire to pass a crime bill and were wary of appearing obstructionist. A group of moderate pro-gun control Republicans conducted their own negotiations with the White House and the House leadership. They helped forge a package of alterations designed to lock in moderate GOP votes with spending cuts and select policy changes. Key Republican negotiators in the final stage included Michael N. Castle of Delaware, Susan Molinari of New York and Scott L. Klug of Wisconsin.

House leaders had scoured the rule books for ways to change the bill without going back to conference. They explored approving modifications through a concurrent resolution or a new rule before concluding that they had to reopen the conference or vote again on the same bill. On Aug. 19, leaders won voice vote approval in the House to go back to conference.

The Second Agreement

A weekend of marathon negotiations produced agreement on a $30.2 billion bill that was approved by conferees shortly after 3 a.m. on Sunday, Aug. 21 (H Rept 103-711).

The revised bill cost $3.3 billion less than the original conference report. That money represented authorizations in the original bill that were not part of the trust fund and would have been subject to annual appropriations in any case. Most of the cuts — $2 billion — came from the prevention programs that Clinton and Democrats had favored. Negotiators cut their funding from $8.9 billion to $6.9 billion. The remaining $1.3 billion was taken from law enforcement and prison construction programs.

To make the prevention cuts, conferees adopted a 10 percent across-the-board reduction in those programs and eliminated $900 million in job training for youths who agreed to avoid crime and drug use. They also consolidated 13 grant programs into a $380 million local crime prevention block grant. Negotiators reduced funding for the Violence Against Women Act from $1.8 billion to $1.6 billion and cut drug court funding from $1.3 billion to $1 billion.

Other key sections in the second crime bill conference report included $8.8 billion for more police officers or "cops on the beat," unchanged from the first version, and $9.7 billion for prison construction funding, down from $10.5 billion.

Clinton succeeded in keeping the controversial ban on 19 assault weapons, although conferees made modest adjustments to it. The measure banned ammunition-feeding devices that held more than 10 rounds, but House negotiators struck a ban on any combination of parts that could be assembled into such a feeding device. Negotiators also changed a provision requiring a defendant charged with possession of a banned ammunition clip to prove that the clip was purchased before the ban was enacted. Instead, the prosecutor was to show that a clip was purchased after the ban.

Final Action

The House adopted the second conference report, 235-195, Aug. 21. Forty-six Republicans supported the anti-crime measure in the unusual Sunday vote, while 64 Democrats deserted their party to vote no. *(Vote 416, p. 124-H)*

The $30.2 billion measure was similar to the one that most Republicans and 58 Democrats had blocked from coming to the floor Aug. 11. But Democrats had made enough concessions to win over 35 more Republicans.

The first hurdle for bill supporters was adoption of the rule governing floor debate. It passed 239-189. *(Vote 414, p. 124-H)*

The second was a motion by McCollum to send the bill back to conference "with instructions" — which would have opened the measure to an amendment, promoted by the NRA, to drop the weapons ban, cut prevention money, add money for prisons and police, and remove some of the new death penalty measures. It was rejected, 197-232, after the White House and Democratic leaders pulled out all the stops to defeat it. *(Vote 415, p. 124-H)*

Senate Clears Bill

Four days later, on Aug. 25, the Senate adopted the conference report, 61-38, clearing the bill for the president. The key vote, however, came earlier that day when Democrats — aided by six Republicans — got the 60 votes needed to waive a GOP procedural motion that would have made the legislation amendable, possibly killing the crime bill. The vote was 61-39. *(Votes 295, 293, p. 50-S)*

The much-heralded spirit of bipartisanship that had prevailed in the House on Aug. 21 had evaporated as soon as the conference report reached the Senate.

Minority Leader Dole rallied GOP members against the legislation, arguing that it contained too much pork barrel spending on social programs and too few tough sentencing provisions. Dole lamented the new $30.2 billion bill as compared with the Senate's original $22.3 billion measure: "We swallowed a little pork last fall," he said Aug. 23. "We can't swallow the whole hog."

Senate Republicans skirmished in advance of the vote to amend the bill to cut spending, add mandatory sentences and drop the weapons ban. But Democratic Party unity and the maneuvering of Majority Leader George J. Mitchell, D-Maine, thwarted all efforts to make further changes.

From the beginning, the measure's fate in the Senate hung with a handful of Republican moderates torn between their inclination to support the bill and their loyalty to Dole and the GOP. Mitchell had the support of all but one of the 56 Democrats and needed only five Republicans to defeat the GOP procedural motion. In the end, Dole's rejection of a compromise offered by Mitchell gave moderate Republicans cover to bolt from their party and join Democrats in supporting the crime bill.

Encouraged by the successful bargaining of their House counterparts, Republicans sought to remove most of the prevention spending from the measure, arguing that Democrats had used the bill as a vehicle for funding social programs that would have little or no impact on reducing crime.

But Biden noted that GOP members had voted to fund most of these same prevention programs when the crime bill had first passed the Senate the previous fall. And some of the programs that Republicans were now calling wasteful originally had been added by GOP members, including Dole, Pete V. Domenici, N.M., and John C. Danforth, Mo.

Republicans also sought to restore what they called

tougher sentencing provisions, including mandatory minimum sentences for gun and drug offenses, which had been part of the original Senate bill, but had been stripped out in the first House-Senate conference in July.

Democrats saw things differently. Many felt that the GOP, at the behest of the NRA, was trying to hold up the bill to remove the weapons ban. "The real reason that many senators are opposing this bill can be summarized in three letters: NRA," said Tom Harkin, D-Iowa.

The NRA lobbied intensely during the week, and some Republicans felt strongly about dropping the gun ban. But GOP leaders said that other issues were fueling their fight. Dole initially had asked for a vote on the weapons ban but later dropped it from his list of demands.

Other Democrats argued that the GOP wanted to embarrass the president by killing the crime bill or at least forcing the White House to make more concessions.

Republicans countered that the administration was attempting to pass any crime bill, regardless of its merits. "They need to win this thing, and they'll take it any way they can get it," said Trent Lott, R-Miss.

Parliamentary Maneuvers

On Aug. 22, Dole threatened to subject the bill to a budgetary point of order, a procedural move seeking to block legislation on the grounds that it violated Senate budget rules. Republicans said the crime bill broke the rules because its funding mechanism — the crime trust fund — had not been reviewed by the Senate Budget Committee. Sixty votes were needed to waive a point of order; 41 were needed to sustain it.

If the point of order had been sustained, the conference report would have been invalidated, and the Senate would have been forced to take up the original House-passed bill, because that was the vehicle that conferees had worked from. Most significantly, that bill contained no weapons ban.

In addition, if the bill had subsequently been amended by the Senate, the measure would have returned to the House, where it also would have been subject to change. Democrats predicted that if amended, the measure would either die in the House or be amended yet again and sent back to the Senate.

On Aug. 23, Dole produced a letter with 40 GOP signatures, not including his own, threatening to offer the point of order unless the administration and Democratic leaders agreed to negotiate changes in the bill. All but three Republicans — Arlen Specter, Pa., James M. Jeffords, Vt., and William V. Roth Jr., Del. — signed the letter. With the expected support of Democrat Richard C. Shelby, Ala., who opposed the crime bill, Dole seemed to have 42 votes — more than enough to back up his threat.

But three other GOP members — Danforth, Nancy Landon Kassebaum, Kan., and John H. Chafee, R.I. — signed the letter only to give Dole a chance to use it to negotiate a deal with Mitchell. "I thought he deserved that chance," Danforth said.

The letter sparked negotiations between Dole and Mitchell, leading to several offers and counteroffers. On Aug. 23, Dole proposed that the conference report be reopened to allow Republicans to offer 13 amendments. These included language to strip $5 billion in prevention spending and impose mandatory minimum sentences for drug and gun crimes. Also included was a motion to strike the weapons ban.

Mitchell rejected this plan and offered to wrap the GOP amendments into a separate bill to be considered after the Senate cleared the conference report. Dole found that unacceptable. The next day, Dole scaled back his demands, asking Mitchell to allow a vote on 10 GOP amendments.

Striking the gun ban was not among them. Mitchell rejected that proposal as well.

On Aug. 25, Mitchell offered to allow a vote on one amendment to cut $5 billion in prevention spending. The vote would have been on a concurrent resolution to make "technical" changes to the report before it was sent to the White House. Dole rejected this offer as inadequate, because it did not allow Republicans to vote on mandatory sentencing provisions. Both sides then abandoned negotiations, leading to the showdown on the floor later that day.

Party Discipline

When Dole rejected Mitchell's offer, Chafee, Kassebaum and Danforth defected. "I am disappointed that a majority of

the Republican Party rejected as inadequate the offer to vote on a $5 billion cut in social spending," Kassebaum said in a written statement.

Senators on both sides said Mitchell's offer was a clever way to attract Republicans who had publicly lined up with Dole out of party loyalty.

After losing on the point of order, Dole demanded a cloture vote to allow those senators — led by Craig — who vehemently opposed the weapons ban to speak and, in essence, vote on the issue once more before the conference report was adopted.

Cloture was invoked to limit debate and allow the Senate to proceed to a vote on the issue at hand. The cloture vote was 61-38. (Vote 294, p. 50-S) ■

Crime Bill Provisions

The omnibus crime bill (HR 3355 — PL 103-322) authorized $30.2 billion over six years — mainly to hire police officers, build prisons and help communities prevent crime. It created a novel crime trust fund to pay for the programs. And it banned 19 assault weapons and expanded the death penalty to dozens of new federal crimes.

As enacted, the law contained provisions to:

Police

● **Community policing.** Authorize $8.8 billion over six years to help communities hire thousands of new police officers. The administration estimated that the money would help hire 100,000 new police officers, but some critics said it would provide substantially fewer new officers. The authorization included $1.3 billion in fiscal 1995, $1.9 billion in fiscal 1996, $1.95 billion in fiscal 1997, $1.7 billion in fiscal 1998, $1.7 billion in fiscal 1999 and $268 million in fiscal 2000.

The money was for a Justice Department grant program to promote community policing, a style of law enforcement that emphasized closer community-police relations. Communities were required to provide matching funds of at least 25 percent, with a preference for those that could pay more. Whenever the Justice Department approved multi-year grants, the federal share was supposed to decline each year. The attorney general had discretion to waive all or part of the match for needy communities.

A portion of the grant money — up to 15 percent — could be used for training or equipment to enhance community policing programs. The bulk of the money — at least 85 percent — had to be used to put more officers on the street, primarily through hiring or rehiring. However, some money could go for non-salary expenditures — such as overtime pay or computers — that had the effect of putting more officers on the street. That pool of money was limited to 20 percent in fiscal 1995 and 1996 and to 10 percent thereafter. The federal share of officer salaries was capped at $75,000 per officer.

The law included a formula guaranteeing that each state that applied for the community policing grants would receive at least one-half of 1 percent of that year's funds. It also reserved half the grants for communities with more than 150,000 people, half for those with smaller populations. Communities with more than 150,000 residents were required to apply directly to the Justice Department for the grants, while smaller communities were to apply through their state governments.

● **Police corps.** Create a police corps program, administered by the Justice Department, to grant college or graduate scholarships for students who agreed to serve as state or local police officers for at least four years. Scholarships for each participant were capped at $10,000 per calendar year, and a total of $30,000. Participants who did not honor their commitments to serve as police officers had to repay the scholarships plus 10 percent interest. Lawmakers intended to authorize $20 million a year from fiscal years 1996 through 2000 for the program, but because of a printing or transcription error, the law specified only $20,000 a year.

The law also authorized $100 million in educational scholarships for police officers with at least two years' experience, as well as summer or part-time jobs for students interested in law enforcement careers. The federal money could provide no more than 60 percent of costs for scholarships and student jobs. The grant program was authorized at $20 million a year from fiscal 1996 through fiscal 2000, with 80 percent going for officer scholarships.

● **Police recruiting.** Authorize $24 million a year from fiscal 1995 through fiscal 2000 for grants to help recruit and train police officers from minority neighborhoods and other areas that were underrepresented on the police force.

● **Family support.** Authorize $25 million over five years for grants to help state and local law enforcement agencies develop "family friendly" policies for their officers. This could include offering family counseling, 24-hour child-care services and stress-reduction programs. Law enforcement agencies were supposed to match the federal funds with money or services from other sources.

● **Police conduct.** Allow the U.S. attorney general to sue for civil relief to prohibit law enforcement officials or government authorities from engaging in a pattern of behavior that denied the civil rights of individuals. The measure required the attorney general to collect annual data on the use of excessive force by law enforcement officers.

Prisons

● **State aid.** Authorize $7.9 billion in grants for states or multistate compacts to build new prison cells or alternative incarceration facilities, such as boot camps, to free up prison beds for violent offenders.

Half the money was for a general prison grant program designed to prod states into developing comprehensive prison management plans and helping pay for new cells. Within this pool of money, 85 percent was to be distributed to states on a formula basis designed to guarantee a minimum amount — one quarter of 1 percent — for every state, including small states. Above the minimum, money was to be allocated in proportion to the state's violent crime rate, a figure that roughly tracked population. The attorney general could award the remaining 15 percent on a discretionary basis for states with the greatest need or the ability to best utilize the money.

The other half of the overall grant money was to be awarded to states with the toughest sentencing laws, an incentive for states to adopt laws to keep prisoners in jail longer. States had to implement specific truth-in-sentencing measures, such as requiring that violent criminals serve at least 85 percent of their sentences. If states did not qualify or apply for all the money in this category, it could be transferred into the more general prison grant fund.

The grants were not supposed to constitute more than 75 percent of the total cost of a prison project. Overall, the law authorized: $175 million in fiscal 1995, $750 million in fiscal 1996, $1 billion in fiscal 1997, $1.9 billion in fiscal 1998, $2 billion in fiscal

1999 and $2.07 billion in fiscal 2000.

● **Young offenders.** Authorize $150 million in grants to help states and localities develop alternatives to traditional incarceration for young offenders. Eligible programs included alternative sanctions, restitution or community service programs, and correctional options such as weekend incarceration and electronic monitoring. Each participating state was guaranteed at least two-fifths of 1 percent of the grant money, with the remaining money to be distributed in proportion to the states' percentage of young offenders. The states in turn were required to distribute that money to local governments in proportion to their share of the state's corrections costs. The grants were limited to 75 percent of program costs.

● **Alien incarceration.** Authorize $1.8 billion to help states pay for incarcerating illegal aliens convicted of felonies. The law directed the attorney general, after receiving a written request from the affected state, to take custody of such criminal aliens — giving priority to incarcerating aggravated felons — or to compensate the state for imprisoning them. The legislation authorized $130 million in fiscal 1995, $300 million in fiscal 1996, $330 million in fiscal 1997, $350 million each in fiscal 1998 and 1999, and $340 million in fiscal 2000.

The first one-third of the money was reserved for seven states with high populations of illegal immigrants: Arizona, California, Florida, Illinois, New Jersey, New York and Texas. All 50 states could apply for the remaining money.

The provisions were initially subject to available appropriations, but the law made the payments mandatory as of October 2004.

● **Scholarships.** Prohibit federal college scholarships — known as Pell grants — for federal or state prison inmates.

● **Tuberculosis.** Authorize $5 million to help develop and implement programs to prevent and treat tuberculosis in federal, state and local prisons.

● **Crowding.** Restrict the ability of federal courts to rule that prison crowding violated the Constitution's prohibition on cruel and unusual punishment by requiring that the prisoner bringing the suit prove that he or she personally was unfairly harmed by the conditions. The law specified that when federal courts did order remedies for prison overcrowding, they had to extend no further than necessary to correct the conditions for the plaintiff bringing the suit. The provisions also allowed states to seek to modify a consent decree or court order related to unfair prison conditions every two years.

● **Prisoner suits.** Make it more difficult for prisoners to sue for civil rights violations by doubling the length of time, from 90 days to 180 days, during which they were blocked from filing suit and had to first exhaust administrative remedies.

● **Job training.** Establish, within the Department of Justice, an office to promote job training and placement for prisoners and ex-offenders. The office would help coordinate such job training and placement within the federal government and provide technical assistance for comparable state and local efforts.

● **Military bases.** Require, within 180 days of enactment, a joint Defense and Justice Department study examining the suitability of creating federal prison facilities at military bases slated to be closed.

● **Post-release drug testing.** Require drug testing for certain federal prisoners who were released on probation or parole. These prisoners had to agree to stay drug-free and would be subject to at least three drug tests, the first within 15 days of their release. A positive result could be grounds for reimprisonment.

● **Release notification.** Require federal prison officials to notify local law enforcement officials when a prisoner convicted of a federal violent crime or drug trafficking offense was released into the community.

Prevention

● **Model intensive grants.** Authorize $625.5 million in fiscal 1996 through 2000 to funnel intensive prevention services to up to 15 poor, high-crime areas.

Communities that applied for grants had to present a comprehensive plan to combat factors that could foster crime — such as inadequate public facilities, poor lighting, unemployment or lack of drug treatment facilities.

The U.S. attorney general had discretion over how to award the grants, but the law directed that the resources be spread among different geographic areas, including rural as well as urban communities. It directed that priority be given to innovative programs and to finance a variety of approaches.

● **Local Partnership Act.** Authorize $1.6 billion in fiscal 1996 through 2000 for direct aid to poor communities. The aid was to be distributed according to a formula that took into account a community's relative poverty and unemployment rates, plus local tax rates — which would reward those that were doing more "self help" through local taxation. The aid was intended for education, substance abuse treatment or jobs programs related to crime prevention. Programs were supposed to be similar to federal efforts such as Head Start and the Job Training Partnership Act. The Department of Housing and Urban Development would distribute the grants.

The law set out fiscal guidelines for local grant expenditures and generally required that at least 10 percent of the contracts go to small businesses run by women or disadvantaged groups, and to colleges that were historically black or whose student bodies were at least 20 percent Hispanic or Native American. Local governments had to hold at least one public hearing on how they planned to spend the money.

● **Ounce of Prevention.** Create an "Ounce of Prevention" council to coordinate prevention programs authorized by the law and to help improve crime prevention policy and assistance to localities.

Nine top administration officials were to sit on the council — the heads of the departments of Justice, Education, Health and Human Services, Housing and Urban Development, Labor, Agriculture, Treasury, and Interior as well as the head of the Office of National Drug Control Policy.

The law also authorized $90 million in fiscal 1995 through 2000 for "Ounce of Prevention" grants for after-school and summer youth programs (such as tutoring or recreation), employment skills and job placement, and substance abuse and prevention programs including outreach to troubled families.

The grants were not to make up more than 75 percent of program costs. The fiscal 1995 authorization to establish the council was $1.5 million, with the grant programs expected to begin in fiscal 1996.

● **School programs.** Support children through several school programs, including:

  ● **In-school.** Grants for school-based programs to provide academic and other support to youth at risk of becoming involved in crime or drugs. The law authorized $243 million for these grants in fiscal 1995 through 2000, to be administered by the Department of Education and aimed at poor and high-crime neighborhoods.

  ● **After-school.** Grants of up to $567 million in fiscal 1995 through 2000 to help community organizations run after-school, weekend and summer programs for youth, including tutoring, crafts and athletics. This was to be a formula grant program to be run by the Department of Health and Human Services. The federal share of these programs would be capped at 75 percent in fiscal 1995 and decline to 60 percent or less in fiscal 1998 and later. The money could not be used for religious activities.

  ● **Youth academies.** Grants of $36 million in fiscal 1996 through 2000 to public agencies and nonprofit organizations to help dropouts and other "at risk" youth, ages 11-19, improve their academic or job skills and enhance their self-esteem.

● **Economic partnerships.** Seek to stimulate business and job opportunities for the unemployed and for low-income people. The law authorized the secretary of Health and Human Services to extend credit to community development corporations, up to $2 million per agency, to help them provide loans for local economic development. These development corporations generally were required to produce local funds equal to or greater than the amount requested from the federal government. The law also authorized annual grants of up to $75,000 per agency to improve management skills within these community agencies and to help them operate or expand.

The program was authorized at $270 million in fiscal 1996 through 1999. Sixty percent of that money was earmarked for creating enhanced loan capability and 40 percent for grants to strengthen the development corporations.

- **Urban parks.** Provide grants to create or expand recreation facilities in urban and high-crime neighborhoods. The law authorized $4.5 million for these grants in fiscal 1996 through 2000.
- **Family unity.** Encourage experimental programs that placed certain non-violent offenders in community corrections facilities where they could continue to live with their children, who would move in. The law authorized $19.8 million in fiscal 1996 through 2000 for such demonstration projects. Of that money, 90 percent was for state grants and 10 percent for use by federal prison officials.
- **Gang resistance.** Expand an existing program to deter juveniles from joining gangs. The law authorized $45.5 million in fiscal 1995 through 2000 for the Gang Resistance Education and Training (GREAT) program, to fund at least 50 new projects.
- **Block grant.** Establish a block grant program to help localities prevent crime, most of it for programs to steer young people away from crime. The law directed the attorney general to distribute grants to local governments under a formula that roughly tracked the violent crime rate but also guaranteed some funds for all states. The law authorized $377 million for the grants in fiscal 1996 through 2000, which could be used for one or more of the following:
  - **Jobs programs.** Programs aimed at steering youth and young adults, ages 16-25, to permanent employment.
  - **Sports programs.** Midnight sports leagues that provided nighttime sports opportunities for youth, in conjunction with mandatory job counseling and education classes; other supervised sports programs outside of school, including Olympic Youth Development Centers to be run in coordination with the United States Olympic Committee.
  - **Boys Clubs and Girls Clubs.** Grants to establish such clubs in public housing.
  - **Visitation centers.** Supervised visitation centers where a parent with a history of child abuse or domestic violence could visit a child.
  - **Youth violence.** Programs to prevent gang and drug involvement and create youth anti-crime councils that would give teenagers a mechanism to work with school and community officials to combat youth violence.
  - **Partnership with Kids.** Partnership programs between police agencies and child and family service organizations, such as round-the-clock consultation services for children who were crime victims, officer training in child psychology and training for children in how to resolve conflicts.
  - **Seniors.** Programs to improve law enforcement and other surveillance in specific areas to create "safety corridors" for the elderly. In particular, the law sought to promote programs based on the "triad" model, involving alliances among local sheriffs, police chiefs and senior citizens' organizations.
  - **Police housing.** Free or subsidized housing for police officers to encourage them to live in high-crime areas.
  - **Family outreach teams.** Teams with experience in youth, parent and school issues to train local volunteers in counseling and mentoring activities.

Violence Against Women

- **Federal crimes.** Create federal penalties for interstate stalking or domestic abuse. The provision applied to cases in which the abuser crossed a state line to harass or injure his or her victim, or forced the victim to cross state lines under duress, and went on to physically harm the victim in the course of a violent crime. Offenders were subject to up to five years in prison for violating the law. Prison terms could run to 10 years, 20 years or life if the offender used a dangerous weapon, caused serious physical harm or killed the victim.

The law strengthened existing federal penalties for repeat sexual offenders and required restitution to victims in federal sex offense cases. It called for pretrial detention in federal sex offense or child pornography felonies and allowed evidence of prior sex offenses to be used in some subsequent trials regarding federal sex crimes.

The law set new rules of evidence specifying that a victim's past sexual behavior generally was not admissible in federal civil or criminal cases regarding sexual misconduct.

- **HIV testing.** Allow rape victims to demand that their alleged assailants be tested for HIV, the virus that caused AIDS. A federal judge could order the testing after determining that the alleged conduct created a risk of HIV transmission. The results would be disclosed to the defendant, the victim and, at the court's discretion, the victim's parents or guardian. The victim would be allowed to share the results only with a doctor, family members, a counselor or any sexual partners since the alleged attack.
- **Civil rights.** Create a civil rights violation for violent crimes motivated by gender, allowing victims of such crimes to sue for damages or court-ordered injunctions. The law applied to violent crimes that were generally classified as felonies provided that the victim could demonstrate, with a preponderance of evidence, that the crime was motivated by gender bias. A victim could bring a suit under this provision regardless of whether the underlying violent act was prosecuted as a criminal case. These civil rights claims could be brought in either state or federal court. The law specified that it did not give federal courts jurisdiction over state legal matters such as divorce settlements or child custody cases.
- **Grants.** Authorize $1.6 billion over six years for programs to fight violence against women.

Of that money, $800 million was authorized in fiscal 1995 through 2000 for state, tribal and local programs to improve law enforcement and victim services for crimes against women. The grants were to be administered by the Justice Department and distributed according to a formula reserving 4 percent for Indian tribes, guaranteeing at least $500,000 to each state, and distributing the rest according to state population. States and tribes were required to use at least 25 percent of the grant money for each of the following types of programs: prosecution, law enforcement and victim services.

To qualify for the grants, these governments had to pay for the medical exams of rape victims and, within two years, stop requiring victims of domestic violence to pay the court costs for filing criminal charges. Grants were limited to 75 percent of program costs.

Other grant programs included $325 million in fiscal 1996 through 2000 for battered women's shelters and $205 million for rape prevention and education programs conducted by rape crisis centers and other nonprofit agencies. The law authorized smaller grant programs to pay for training and other programs to help courts better handle domestic violence and other crimes against women, programs to help homeless or runaway youths who had been sexually abused, programs to help prosecute child abuse cases, safety improvements in parks and on public transportation, and enforcement of domestic violence and child abuse laws in rural areas.

- **Arrest policies.** Seek to encourage states to adopt mandatory arrest policies for domestic abuse or violation of a protection order. The law authorized $120 million in grants from fiscal 1996 through 1998 to help implement such policies. To qualify, states had to show that their policies encouraged or required arrests for domestic violence and did not penalize victims — by forcing them, for instance, to bear the costs of filing criminal charges against their abusers. Grantees would have up to two years to meet the requirements.
- **Hotline.** Establish a toll-free national hotline on family violence, with funding authorized at $1 million in fiscal 1995 and $400,000 per year in fiscal 1996 through 2000.
- **Immigrant women.** Allow battered immigrant spouses or children to petition for legal residency and obtain a work permit. The provision sought to address cases in which immigrants had to stay with an abuser or risk deportation. It set various conditions on who qualified for permission to stay in the United States.

Drug Treatment and Control

- **Prisoners.** Lay out a schedule for all federal inmates addicted to drugs to have access to drug treatment: 50 percent by the end of fiscal 1995, 75 percent by the end of fiscal 1996 and the rest by the end of fiscal 1997. The bill authorized $113 million for this treatment. It authorized the Bureau of Prisons to release non-violent offenders up to one year early once they had successfully completed a drug treatment program.

The law also authorized $270 million for grants to help provide drug treatment for inmates in state prisons. The federal share of such pro-

grams was limited to 75 percent. To qualify for grants, states had to agree to conduct ongoing drug tests of program participants as long as they were in state custody. Each participating state would receive at least two-fifths of 1 percent of the grant money, with the rest allocated in proportion to the number of state prisoners per state.

● **Drug courts.** Authorize $1 billion over six years for grant programs to promote so-called drug courts, aimed at rehabilitating non-violent drug offenders. Typically, a drug court program offered offenders intensive probation, including drug testing, treatment and job training, in place of conventional incarceration. Anyone who violated the program's terms faced alternative punishment such as community service, electronic monitoring or boot camp. If these did not work, the offender eventually could face traditional incarceration.

The law specified that those convicted of violent offenses, including carrying a gun during a crime, could not participate in these programs. The Justice Department was directed to suspend support for a drug court program if this condition was being violated.

The federal share of drug court programs funded under this provision was capped at 75 percent. Annual appropriations were authorized as follows: $100 million in fiscal 1995, $150 million each in fiscal 1996 and 1997, and $200 million annually in fiscal 1998, 1999 and 2000.

● **Drug sentencing.** Direct the U.S. Sentencing Commission to stiffen sentencing guidelines for manufacturing or dealing in areas designated as drug-free zones, usually near schools or playgrounds. The sentencing commission also was instructed to amend its guidelines to enhance sentencing for those possessing, smuggling or distributing illegal narcotics in federal prison. Prisoners convicted of such crimes would not be eligible for parole.

● **Recidivism.** Broaden the legal definition of a "prior felony drug offense" to include any drug offense punishable by more than one year in prison. Defendants with prior drug felonies could draw stiffer sentences for subsequent crimes.

● **Advertising.** Make illegal the placement of any written advertisement in a newspaper, magazine or other publication seeking to sell or offering to buy an illegal narcotic. This prohibition did not apply to ads that advocated a position concerning drugs, as long as they did not seek to facilitate or propose a transaction.

● **Emergency areas.** Allow the president to designate Violent Crime and Drug Emergency Areas in any place with particularly high levels of violence and drug abuse. The president could direct federal agencies to help state and local law enforcement in these areas with manpower, funds and technical and advisory assistance.

● **Drug control strategy.** Codify an executive order requiring the director of the Office of National Drug Control Policy to submit budget directives on July 1 to those agencies involved in drug policy. Agencies were to comply with these instructions, which would address funding priorities.

The director also was to include an evaluation of federal drug control efforts for the previous year in each annual Drug Control Strategy, submitted every Feb. 1. This was to include: an assessment of drug availability, the levels of drug use and availability of drug treatment.

The office was to receive no more than $100 million each year from the Department of Justice's Special Forfeiture Fund, which contained forfeited assets seized by the department from convicted criminals.

The office was reauthorized until Sept. 30, 1997.

Death Penalty Offenses

● **Capital crimes.** Authorize the death penalty for several dozen federal crimes, including treason, genocide and causing a death through a train wreck or mailing explosives. Most, but not all, of the death penalty offenses involved a direct killing. An exception was certain major drug felonies committed by a "drug kingpin." The bill also authorized the federal death penalty for gun murders committed during a federal drug felony or violent felony.

The law effectively reactivated the death penalty for more than a dozen capital crimes already on the books, including assassination of the president or other top government official, espionage and kidnapping resulting in death. These potential death penalties had been unenforceable since 1972, when the U.S. Supreme Court ruled that there were not

sufficient safeguards against arbitrariness in capital punishment litigation. The new anti-crime law sought to correct that legal defect by establishing new procedures for federal death penalty prosecutions, such as laying out aggravating and mitigating factors to be considered when determining if the death penalty should be invoked.

The legislation also extended the federal death penalty to dozens of new and existing federal crimes — including lethal drive-by shootings, a retaliatory murder of an informant or witness, and civil rights murders.

● **Procedures.** Require under the new procedures that federal prosecutors notify the court and the defendant "a reasonable time" before the start of a trial if they planned to seek the death penalty. The law required a two-phase trial, the first to determine guilt and, if there was a conviction, a second to determine whether the death penalty was warranted. Both were to be jury trials unless the defendant requested that a judge determine one or both. The government was required to provide two lawyers for poor defendants, instead of one as required in previous law. Any death penalty sentence was subject to review by a U.S. Court of Appeals and the Supreme Court. The federal government was barred from imposing the death penalty on those under 18 at the time of the crime, or those who were mentally retarded or lacked the mental capacity "to understand the death penalty and why it was imposed on that person." Women could not be executed while they were pregnant.

Jurors had to be told that they should not consider the race, color, religion, national origin or sex of the defendant or victim in determining the proper sentence, and they had to certify that they acted without such bias.

The federal death penalty generally would not apply on tribal lands, which typically were subject to federal jurisdiction, if the location of the crime was the only reason that it fell under federal jurisdiction.

Mandatory Sentences, Other Penalties

● **Three strikes.** Require life imprisonment for someone convicted of a third violent felony, known as the "three strikes and you're out" provision. A "strike" consisted of a serious state or federal violent felony conviction, generally defined as those with a potential sentence of 10 years or more. The first two felonies could be state offenses, while the last had to be a federal violent felony charge. A serious drug offense could constitute one of the first two "strikes," but not the third. At least two of the three felony convictions had to stem from different incidents.

The law included a discretionary release clause for those prisoners sentenced to life under this provision who were at least 70 years old and had served at least 30 years.

The three-strike provisions did not apply to crimes on Indian lands unless the tribe chose to have them apply.

● **Safety valve.** Allow a relaxation of existing mandatory minimum sentences for first-time non-violent drug offenders in select circumstances. Judges were given authority to relax these mandatory sentences after determining that the defendant met certain criteria, among them that the defendant had provided all the information he or she had regarding the crime to law enforcement authorities. The law directed the U.S. Sentencing Commission to re-examine and potentially to adjust the corresponding sentencing guidelines for such offenses, but it also said the commission should retain a minimum penalty of at least two years.

This provision applied to sentences issued 10 days after the law's enactment, and onward.

● **Hate crimes.** Direct the U.S. Sentencing Commission to increase sentences for so-called hate crimes — crimes in which the defendant selected a victim on the basis of race, color, religion, national origin, ethnicity, gender, disability or sexual orientation. The provision generally increased sentences by about one-third.

Guns

● **Assault weapons.** Ban the manufacture, sale or possession of certain semiautomatic guns known as assault weapons. Guns

affected by the ban included a list of about 19 specific guns, copycat models of those guns, or semiautomatic weapons with at least two features associated with assault weapons. Such features, which were specified in the law, included a bayonet mount or grenade launcher, or folding or telescoping stock.

The law specifically exempted about 670 semiautomatic guns that gun control advocates said were used for sporting purposes, as well as guns possessed lawfully before enactment of the ban.

It also banned large-capacity feeding devices that held more than 10 rounds of ammunition. In prosecutions, the burden was to rest with the government to prove that such clips were purchased after the law's enactment. The law required serial numbers for any large capacity ammunition clips manufactured after enactment, presumably for use by law enforcement officials or others still allowed to possess them.

Violators of the weapons ban could be punished with a fine of up to $5,000, a five-year sentence, or both. The restrictions expired after 10 years.

The military and police still could use the banned weapons and feeding devices. The law required the attorney general to complete, within two years of enactment, a study of the impact of the ban on drug trafficking and violent crime.

● **Youth gun ban.** Ban the sale or transfer of a handgun or handgun ammunition to a juvenile without parental consent, and generally prohibit juveniles from possessing a handgun or handgun ammunition except under specific circumstances, such as for ranching work, target practice, hunting or the military. Some of those exceptions required the juvenile to have prior written consent from a parent or guardian.

Violators, juvenile or otherwise, generally were subject to a maximum of one year in jail. But an adult who sold or transferred a handgun or ammunition to a minor knowing that the minor planned to use it in a violent crime could be imprisoned for up to 10 years.

● **Domestic violence.** Prohibit the possession of a firearm by someone subject to a restraining order to prevent him or her from harassing, stalking or interfering with a spouse or intimate partner or that person's child. The court order had to find that the person was a credible threat to the intimate partner or child, and specifically prohibit the use or threat of force against them. Those who knowingly sold, transferred or obtained a gun in violation of the law were subject to up to 10 years in prison.

● **Firearms licenses.** Strengthen federal requirements for obtaining a firearms dealer license, including mandating that applicants submit their photographs and fingerprints and certify that they would be in full compliance with state and local laws. Federal officials had 60 days, instead of 45, to act on applications and also had to notify local law enforcement officials about the application for a dealer license.

Firearms dealers were required to report the theft or loss of a gun within two days and to respond to federal tracing requests within 24 hours. Federal authorities had the right to inspect dealers whenever a gun used during a crime was traced back to them; under prior law, federal officials were limited to one inspection per year without a warrant.

● **Penalties.** Increase penalties for a number of federal gun crimes, including using a semiautomatic weapon in a federal violent or drug trafficking crime, interstate gun trafficking and making a false statement when purchasing a gun from a federally licensed dealer. The law also made it a penalty to smuggle guns into the country for use in a violent crime or drug trafficking.

● **Hunting rights.** Make it a federal crime to physically interfere with a lawful hunt on federal land and provide for court injunctions to block potential interference. Violators were subject to civil penalties of up to $10,000.

● **Pawnbrokers.** Exempt pawnbrokers and their customers from the five-day waiting period required under the Brady bill (PL 103-159) when a customer was redeeming his or her own handgun. The waiting period was to allow for background checks on prospective purchasers.

Terrorism

● **Penalties.** Make it a federal offense to provide material support, such as weapons or lodging, to a terrorist. The offense was punishable by fines and up to 10 years in jail.

The statute extended the legal deadlines for prosecuting certain types of terrorist-related crimes, and directed the U.S. Sentencing Commission to stiffen the recommended punishment for felonies intended to promote terrorism. It sought to extend the reach of U.S. criminal law to cover offenses committed by or against Americans on a ship scheduled to enter or depart from a U.S. port.

● **Informants.** Authorize the U.S. attorney general to admit a limited number of foreigners to the United States if they could provide information about criminal organizations or terrorist activities. These foreigners had to report regularly to the Justice Department and generally could not stay longer than three years.

Immigration

● **Border Patrol.** Authorize $1.2 billion, almost all of it in fiscal 1995 through 1998, to strengthen operations of the Immigration and Naturalization Service.

The money included $675 million in fiscal 1995-98 to improve border enforcement, including adding 4,000 Border Patrol agents and purchasing up-to-date equipment for border agents, as well as strengthening inspection and deportation programs for those who illegally overstayed their visas.

● **Criminal aliens.** Expedite deportation of non-permanent resident aliens convicted of an aggravated felony, eliminating the existing requirement for an administrative deportation hearing. Judicial review of such deportation orders was to be available, but under several restrictions.

The law authorized $160 million in fiscal 1995-98 to expand a program under which federal officials began deportation hearings before criminal aliens finished serving their sentences, allowing for prompt deportation upon release.

It also created a criminal alien tracking center, authorized at $18.4 million in fiscal 1996 through 2000, to help identify and locate aliens who were eligible for deportation because of their criminal records.

● **Asylum claims.** Authorize $338 million in fiscal 1995 through 1998 to speed the processing of asylum claims and the deportation of those whose claims were denied. The money was to be used to hire more asylum officers and judges to hear these cases, which were seriously backlogged. The law generally authorized the U.S. attorney general to institute expedited procedures to hear asylum claims and deport unsuccessful applicants. It specified that asylum applicants were not eligible for work papers except with special Justice Department authorization.

● **Penalties.** Increase penalties for smuggling undocumented aliens into the United States to up to 10 years in prison (and possible fines) for each smuggled alien. Alien smuggling that resulted in a death could bring life imprisonment or the death penalty.

The law also stiffened existing criminal penalties for immigration document fraud, including use of fraudulent work papers. It increased penalties for those who failed to obey a deportation order, or those with criminal records who tried to re-enter the country illegally after deportation.

Youth Violence

● **Adult trials.** Allow for juveniles 13 or older to be tried as adults for certain serious violent crimes and crimes involving a gun. Both the prosecutor and the presiding judge had to opt for an adult trial in these circumstances. However, the law specified that juveniles should not be incarcerated in adult prisons. It authorized sentencing adjustments, including supervised release, for defendants who showed a commitment to avoid further crimes. The provision did not apply on Indian tribal lands unless a tribe opted to implement it.

The law also authorized the federal government to help states develop systems to prosecute more 16- and 17-year-olds as adults for certain violent crimes.

● **Gangs.** Stiffen the sentences for certain federal crimes if they were committed by a repeat offender who was part of a gang. The law added up to 10 years to the sentence for certain federal drug and violent felonies.

Prosecutors were required to show that the defendant had ties to criminal gang activity but did not have to show any connection between those gang ties and the underlying offense.

● **Community prosecutors.** Authorize $50 million over five years for a grant program to help local prosecutors, working with police, school officials and others, to identify and prosecute young violent offenders.

Crimes Against Children

● **Child pornography.** Bar production of child pornography for import into the United States, with fines and up to 10 years in prison for the first offense and up to 20 years for a subsequent conviction. The law added this offense to the list of so-called predicate crimes that could trigger a prosecution under the Racketeer Influenced and Corrupt Organizations (RICO) Act.

The law made it a federal crime to travel overseas to have sex with a minor, even if doing so was legal in the overseas country.

It also clarified congressional intent in the 1984 child pornography law (PL 98-292), specifying that illicit child pornography included the lascivious display of genitals, either nude or covered.

● **Penalties.** Increase penalties for using children younger than 18 to distribute drugs at or near a drug-free zone, such as a school, playground or public swimming pool.

The law also strengthened federal criminal penalties against those who assaulted children 16 or younger, and directed the U.S. Sentencing Commission to stiffen recommended penalties for those who solicited a minor to commit a crime. It established a federal task force to work cooperatively with the National Center for Missing and Exploited Children and to better employ federal resources to help find such children.

Law Enforcement

● **Federal agencies.** Authorize more than $1 billion in fiscal 1995 through 2000 in additional funds to help federal law enforcement agencies handle the increased workload expected to result from the law's enactment. The allocations were as follows: $199 million for the Justice Department; $550 million for law enforcement agencies within the Treasury Department; $245 million for the FBI; $150 million for the Drug Enforcement Administration; and $50 million for U.S. attorneys, the regional federal prosecutors nationwide.

● **Rural crime.** Authorize $245 million from fiscal 1996 through 2000 to enforce anti-drug laws in rural areas, including $5 million for special training programs for rural law enforcement officers. The law also authorized the attorney general to set up interagency task forces to combat drug trafficking in rural areas and increased the penalties for drug trafficking within 1,000 feet of a truck stop or highway rest area.

● **DNA analysis.** Authorize measures to improve DNA analysis to solve crimes, including a total of $40 million from fiscal 1996 through 2000 in grants to states to develop and use genetic tests. The law directed the FBI to establish minimum state and federal standards regarding the quality of such tests and confidentiality of results. The law authorized $25 million to improve DNA analysis programs within the FBI.

● **Training and automation.** Authorize $130 million in fiscal 1996 through 2000 in federal assistance to state, local and tribal criminal justice agencies to improve their training and technological capabilities. Most of the money, $100 million, was for grants for improved computer capabilities and features such as automated fingerprint identification. The rest could go toward training programs, pilot programs for gathering and analyzing information to solve violent serial crimes, and upgrading training facilities at the FBI's center in Quantico, Va.

● **Criminal records.** Authorize $150 million in fiscal 1995 through 2000 to help states upgrade their criminal records to facilitate background checks for handgun purchasers, as required under the Brady law, and for child-care providers.

● **Criminal registry.** Direct the attorney general to create guidelines for state registries of criminals convicted of certain crimes against children, such as kidnapping or sexual misconduct. Such criminals were required to register their addresses with state police

officials for 10 years after their release from prison.

The registry program also applied to those convicted of a sexually violent offense. "Sexually violent predators" — those convicted of a violent sexual offense who a court determined had mental conditions that made them likely to commit such acts — were required to remain registered for life or until a court determined they were no longer likely to make a similar attack.

Law enforcement officials were authorized to release information from the registries to the public if it was considered necessary for public safety. States were supposed to create the registries within three years, with a possible two-year good-faith extension. Those that did not establish such registries would lose 10 percent of their federal crime-fighting funds available under the so-called Byrne program.

● **Byrne grants.** Expand an existing grant program, known as Byrne grants, that helped fund collaborative anti-crime and anti-drug programs by state and local law enforcement agencies. The law authorized $1 billion from the crime trust fund for these grants in fiscal 1995 through 2000. It also expanded the list of eligible programs to include efforts aimed at improving DNA analysis, deterring gang violence, prosecuting drunken driving offenses and prosecuting juveniles as adults for certain violent crimes.

● **Federal judiciary.** Authorize $200 million from fiscal 1996 through 2000 to help pay for increased demands on the federal judiciary resulting from the law, including supervised release, pretrial and probation services.

● **State courts and prosecutors.** Authorize $150 million from fiscal 1996 through 2000 to help state courts, prosecutors and public defenders handle increased workloads resulting from the law's provisions.

Victims' Rights

● **Sentencing hearing.** Expand the right, in federal court, of victims of violent crimes and sexual abuse to be heard at the defendant's sentencing hearing. This right could be exercised by a parent or legal guardian if the victim was younger than 18 or by one or more family members if the victim had died. Existing law gave victims the right to be heard, known as the right of allocution, only in cases where capital punishment was an option.

● **Crime victims' fund.** Mandate that the next $10 million deposited in the Crime Victims' Assistance Fund be made available for grants to states for crime victims' assistance. The fund was established in 1984 to compensate crime victims with money collected from federal offenders. Money on top of the $10 million was to be divided equally between grants for victims' assistance and grants for victims' compensation, with a small portion going for police training and technical assistance.

Protecting the Elderly

● **Alzheimer's program.** Authorize $2.7 million from fiscal 1996 through 1998 to create a Missing Alzheimer's Disease Alert Program to locate missing people with Alzheimer's and related diseases.

● **Crimes against the elderly.** Direct the U.S. Sentencing Commission to review sentencing guidelines for violent crimes against the elderly to determine whether they were tough enough to deter these offenses.

● **Telemarketing fraud.** Allow an additional five-year sentence for anyone convicted of telemarketing fraud. The provision allowed an additional 10-year sentence if the defendant victimized 10 or more people older than 55 or targeted people over 55.

Courts were required to order convicted defendants to pay full restitution to victims. The court was not allowed to consider the defendant's economic circumstances when determining the amount of restitution, but it could consider such circumstances when determining the manner and schedule in which restitution would be paid. The amount paid to a victim would offset any damages subsequently awarded in a civil trial. Payment of restitution was a condition for an offender's parole or supervised release.

● **Sentencing.** Direct the U.S. Sentencing Commission to review sentencing guidelines to ensure that sentences for fraud offenses

against those older than 55 were stiff enough.

- **Rewards.** Allow the U.S. attorney general to pay up to $10,000 for information leading to a possible prosecution for fraud against the elderly. Informers were not eligible for this payment if they knowingly participated in the offense; had been employed by a federal, state or local government agency; gave information already publicly disclosed; or if the award would in some way benefit the person being investigated.
- **Authorization.** Authorize $20 million from fiscal 1996 through 2000 for the Department of Justice and the FBI to hire additional staff to investigate and prosecute telemarketing fraud cases and to coordinate with state agencies to prevent telemarketing fraud against senior citizens.
- **Information network.** Require the U.S. attorney general to establish a toll-free hotline to provide general information on telemarketing fraud and to gather information related to violations.

Summit and Commission

- **Presidential summit.** Request that the president convene a national summit on violence and then establish a Commission on Crime Prevention and Control.
- **Commission on prevention.** Authorize $1 million in fiscal 1996 to establish a 28-member Commission on Crime Prevention and Control. The commission was to develop a comprehensive proposal to prevent crime and violence that included: finding ways for federal, state and local law enforcement agencies to better coordinate their efforts; researching the economic and social factors that led to crime; determining the most efficient use of criminal justice resources such as scarce prison beds; examining the causes of drug use; determining the causes and best solutions for crime in schools and violence against women; and examining the impact of crime on minority groups. The commission was to report its findings to Congress and the president within two years.

Crime Trust Fund

Create a $30.2 billion trust fund to pay for anti-crime programs authorized in the bill, drawing on the expected savings from an administration proposal to eliminate more than 250,000 federal jobs. Those work force reductions were approved by Congress in the Federal Workforce Restructuring Act (HR 3345 — PL 103-226). *(Buyouts, p. 147)*

The trust fund provision acted as a sort of "firewall," establishing a special budget account for the anti-crime programs that was distinct from the general pot of money available for domestic programs. The arrangement effectively protected these crime-related authorizations from the usual competition for discretionary funds, while simultaneously shrinking the pot of money for which other domestic programs had to compete.

The law directed that the $30.2 billion be placed in the special budget account in yearly increments: $2.4 billion in fiscal 1995, $4.3 billion in fiscal 1996, $5 billion in fiscal 1997, $5.5 billion in fiscal 1998, $6.5 billion in fiscal 1999 and $6.5 billion in fiscal 2000.

The law limited outlays — the actual dollars spent in a given fiscal year as opposed to the amount obligated that year in the form of an appropriation — from the trust fund as follows: $703 million in fiscal 1995, $2.3 billion in fiscal 1996, $3.9 billion in fiscal 1997, $4.9 billion in fiscal 1998, $5.6 billion in fiscal 1999 and $6.2 billion in fiscal 2000. It called for sequestration — automatic across-the-board cuts — within the trust fund if spending for programs within the fund exceeded the specified limits. The law also set corresponding reductions in overall discretionary spending caps for those years.

The money was set aside for anti-crime programs, but appropriators still had to approve the spending as part of the annual appropriations process. Unspent trust fund money could not be spent on other programs; it had to go for deficit reduction. Appropriators also had authority to shift up to 10 percent of a program's authorized funding to other anti-crime programs in the law, as long as both programs were within the same one of these three categories: federal law enforcement, state and local law enforcement, and crime prevention.

Other Provisions

- **Motor vehicle records.** Generally ban state motor vehicle departments from disclosing personal information about license holders except to those with a legitimate business interest. The law did not affect access to these records by law enforcement and other government agencies, the courts, insurance agencies and other specific groups. The law established criminal fines for those who knowingly disclosed or obtained this information except as permitted. And it allowed victims of such abuses to sue for civil damages. The provisions were to take effect three years after the law's enactment.
- **Motor vehicle theft.** Give the Justice Department six months to establish a voluntary car theft prevention program. Under the program, car owners could agree to use a decal indicating how they used their car — for instance, only for daytime commuting. The police would be authorized to stop the car if it was being used in a manner inconsistent with the decal, on the presumption that it had been stolen. The law authorized $5 million in fiscal 1996 through 1998 to establish the program.

The law also made it a federal crime to alter or remove motor vehicle identification numbers or the new decals. Offenders were subject to fines and up to five years in jail.
- **Penalties.** Stiffen federal penalties for federal crimes such as assault, manslaughter, civil rights violations, conspiracy to commit murder-for-hire, and drug trafficking near public housing. The law significantly increased federal penalties for arson and extended the statute of limitations for prosecuting such crimes. It also set federal penalties for receiving the proceeds of a kidnapping or extortion, under certain circumstances, or property stolen from the U.S. mail.
- **Insurance fraud.** Establish federal penalties for insurance fraud. The statute made it a federal offense to defraud an insurance company that did interstate business, such as by knowingly filing a false statement with an insurance regulator or by embezzling money from a company. Offenders faced criminal penalties including fines and jail terms of up to 15 years.

The law prohibited anyone convicted of a federal crime involving dishonesty, such as insurance fraud, from working in the insurance business except with the written consent of an insurance regulator. And it authorized the U.S. attorney general to impose civil fines of up to $50,000 for the insurance fraud violations.
- **Financial institutions.** Authorize the Secret Service, through December 2004, to conduct investigations and make arrests in connection with fraud against financial institutions. The law banned those convicted of fraud and similar crimes from working in a federally insured credit union for at least 10 years.
- **Computer crimes.** Establish federal penalties for sending a computer transmission that caused damage or loss of access to another computer that was involved in interstate commerce. Intentional violations were subject to up to five years in jail and fines up to $250,000. Victims of such crimes also could sue for civil damages if the crime was intentional. The law authorized lesser penalties for damage from reckless transmissions.
- **Bail reporting.** Require federal and state court clerks to notify federal law enforcement officials if they received a cash bail payment of more than $10,000 for people charged with certain offenses. The provision applied to crimes such as drug offenses, racketeering or money laundering. The clerks had to provide the names and addresses of the accused and anyone posting the bail, and the amount received.
- **Cocaine study.** Require the U.S. Sentencing Commission to prepare a study by the end of December 1994 on the penalties for the possession or distribution of different forms of cocaine and any recommendations for changes in these penalties. The provision was aimed at addressing the criticism that existing federal penalties, which were stiffer for crack cocaine than for a comparable amount of powder cocaine, discriminated against minorities. Most of those sentenced in federal court on crack cocaine offenses were minorities.
- **Drunken driving.** Add a year to the prison sentence otherwise given to someone convicted of drunken driving if a child under 18 was in the car and the offense was committed on federal property. The sentence could be increased up to five years if the child was seri-

ously injured, and up to 10 years if the child was killed.

● **Wiretaps.** Make it a federal crime to disclose the results of an authorized wiretap with the intention of disrupting a criminal investigation.

● **Art theft.** Make it a federal crime to steal an important artwork or cultural object from a museum, or knowingly receive such a stolen good. The law applied to objects that were at least 100 years old and worth more than $5,000, or those worth at least $100,000. Offenders could be fined and imprisoned for up to 10 years.

● **Travelers.** Authorize the federal government to help state officials investigate violent crimes that appeared aimed at travelers.

● **Domestic violence.** Require that individuals convicted of domestic violence crimes in federal courts participate in a rehabilitation program as a condition of probation or supervised release.

● **Care providers.** Expand an existing law (PL 103-209), which encouraged states to do background checks on child-care providers, to also cover those who provided care to the elderly and disabled. The law also set an $18 cap on the amount states could charge for background checks on volunteers.

● **Lottery tickets.** Expand an existing ban on interstate sale of lottery tickets to close a loophole that had allowed ticket brokers in other states to make such sales.

● **Made in America.** Codify existing penalties, established by the Federal Trade Commission, for fraudulent use of "Made in America" or "Made in U.S.A." labels on products.

● **Residency requirement.** Relax an existing residency requirement for assistant U.S. attorneys, allowing them to live within 25 miles of the jurisdiction in which they worked. Previously these prosecutors generally were required to live in their jurisdiction.

● **Prison capacity.** Require the Justice Department to furnish annual reports on the impact of the preceding year's legislation on federal prison capacity and costs. Any legislation proposed by the executive or judicial branch that could alter the federal prison population had to include a prison impact assessment, and the Justice Department was instructed to prepare assessments for other legislation at the request of Congress. ■

Modest Change to Immigration Law

The 103rd Congress produced much sound and fury on the questions of illegal immigration and recent arrivals, but little action. Amid the intense rhetoric, Congress quietly approved one modest package of revisions to laws governing legal immigration and naturalization (HR 783).

During 1993 and 1994, an uneven economy and some violence tied to foreigners provoked calls for new laws and resources to protect the country's borders. The issue became a major one in many congressional campaigns in states heavily affected by immigration. But key lawmakers and Clinton administration officials opted to move cautiously; what action did occur took place in pieces on several separate bills rather than on a single overarching bill.

A principal vehicle for immigration legislation was the omnibus anti-crime bill (HR 3355 — PL 103-322). The measure included $1.8 billion to reimburse states for the cost of incarcerating criminal aliens, as well as resources for more Border Patrol agents and other immigration controls. The crime bill also included provisions for expedited deportation of criminal aliens and immigrants whose asylum petitions had been denied. *(Crime bill, p. 273)*

The House Judiciary Subcommittee on International Law, Immigration and Refugees took the lead on the problem of immigrants who sought asylum at U.S. airports, endorsing a bill (HR 2602) on Oct. 20, 1993, to tighten the rules for asylum proceedings. The Senate Judiciary Committee on Aug. 11, 1994, gave voice vote approval to a bill (S 1333) by Edward M. Kennedy, D-Mass., that included an expedited hearing process for aliens who arrived after being smuggled on boats. *(1993 Almanac, p. 312)*

But the administration helped undercut the push for such legislation by moving to streamline the asylum review process somewhat, and neither bill progressed beyond the committee level.

Several other bills were discussed but never acted upon in the 103rd Congress, including bills to sharply curtail the number of legal immigrants allowed into the country each year, reimburse local communities for costs associated with large immigrant populations and try to limit services for immigrants. For instance, Sen. Alan K. Simpson, R-Wyo., introduced legislation (S 1884) to restrict legal immigration, expedite deportation procedures for certain aliens who were

criminals and create a border-crossing fee. Several bills that sought to overhaul the nation's welfare system included provisions to restrict federal aid to non-citizens.

Congress generally resisted immigration-related initiatives by Republicans in 1994. Rep. Ron Packard, R-Calif., sought unsuccessfully to amend several appropriations bills in committee to bar the use of the funds on illegal immigrants. The House on March 3 defeated, 78-329, an amendment by Dana Rohrabacher, R-Calif., to an education reauthorization bill (HR 6 — PL 103-382) that would have required local school districts to determine the immigration status of students and parents. And when the House Ways and Means Committee on May 4 considered a measure to make the Social Security Administration an independent agency (HR 4277 — PL 103-296), it rejected, 16-20, an amendment by Rick Santorum, R-Pa., to eliminate Supplemental Security Income benefits to most non-citizens.

The House on July 22 did approve, 220-176, an amendment by Jay C. Kim, R-Calif., to a housing reauthorization bill (HR 3838) to limit illegal aliens to seven days of assistance under the federal emergency food and shelter program for the homeless. The housing bill eventually died. *(Housing, p. 408)*

Visa Waiver Bill

Congress cleared a bill Oct. 7 to continue a popular visa waiver program that allowed tourists and business travelers from 22 countries — mainly in Western Europe — to enter the United States for short-term stays without visas. The program was reauthorized for two years. The bill (HR 783) also created a "probationary" visa waiver program for countries that were close to, but not quite at, the standards needed to qualify under existing law.

In addition, the legislation reauthorized the federal refugee resettlement program through fiscal 1997 and adjusted certain rules regarding naturalization. During final negotiations, lawmakers added provisions making it easier to deport criminal aliens — toughening the language already approved on that issue as part of the crime bill.

President Clinton signed the bill Oct. 25 (PL 103-416).

The waiver program technically expired Sept. 30, but Immigration and Naturalization Service Commissioner Doris

Meissner extended it for 30 days while Congress completed work on the bill. Without the program, millions of tourists and business visitors would have had to obtain visas before entering the United States. The reciprocal arrangements that allowed U.S. citizens to travel to those countries without visas would also have been in jeopardy. Commerce Department officials warned that failure to extend the visa waiver program could wreak havoc on the tourism industry.

The House had passed a more limited version of the bill (HR 783 — H Rept 103-387) on Nov. 20, 1993. The bill was amended by the Senate the same day with "technical corrections" to other immigration laws. *(1993 Almanac, p. 314)*

House Action

The House agreed Sept. 20 to adopt some of the Senate-passed amendments to HR 783. The House made additional changes and sent the bill back to the Senate.

The bill, sponsored by Rep. Romano L. Mazzoli, D-Ky., included an array of alterations to existing immigration and naturalization rules, such as making it easier for the children of U.S. citizens who lived abroad to receive U.S. citizenship.

As passed, the bill relaxed the existing naturalization tests on U.S. history and government for long-term elderly residents as well as testing requirements for those with certain disabilities. For example, it allowed the attorney general to waive the tests for residents over age 65 who had lived in the United States for 20 years.

The new House version extended the existing visa waiver program for two years. Under the experimental program, designed to facilitate tourism and business exchanges, visitors from certain countries could enter the United States without visas.

The legislation also reauthorized for three years at unspecified sums the program under which the federal government provided money to help resettle refugees who had been admitted into the United States.

The House action Sept. 20 came on a procedural motion (H Res 533) that members agreed to by voice vote.

Final Action

The Senate passed a revised version of the bill by voice vote Oct. 7, after adding several new provisions. The House cleared the measure by voice vote late that afternoon.

Among the Senate additions were amendments offered by Simpson to make it easier to deport aliens convicted of serious crimes. The bill authorized judges to issue deportation orders at the time of sentencing, eliminating the need for separate deportation proceedings.

As amended, the bill also expanded the list of crimes that triggered expedited deportation proceedings. Congress had approved such procedures as part of the crime bill.

Hank Brown, R-Colo., offered an amendment to prod the administration to grant visas to high-level officials from Taiwan who sought to enter the United States for talks with state or federal officials concerning trade and other issues. The Senate adopted it by voice vote. ∎

Independent Counsel Law Renewed

Long-stalled legislation to renew the independent counsel law — a statute providing for independent prosecutors to investigate alleged wrongdoing by top government officials — cleared Congress on June 21 with minor revisions to address concerns about costs and accountability. President Clinton signed the bill into law June 30 (S 24 — PL 103-270).

The law had expired in December 1992 amid Republican criticism of independent counsel Lawrence E. Walsh's costly investigation of the Iran-contra affair. Democrats and some Republicans resumed the push for the reauthorization early in the 103rd Congress with the encouragement of Clinton and Attorney General Janet Reno. Clinton's was the first administration to actively support the law.

GOP support for renewing the law grew as Republicans became interested in investigating Clinton's ties to the Whitewater Development Co. *(Whitewater, p. 108)*

Responding to complaints that Walsh and other independent counsels had abused their authority and their budgets, lawmakers included in the five-year reauthorization bill several controls on the expenses and conduct of independent counsels, such as requiring that they comply with Justice Department spending guidelines and mandating regular audits by the General Accounting Office. Some Republicans complained that the changes did not go far enough, but sponsors said they added as many restrictions as possible without jeopardizing the independent counsel's autonomy.

Both chambers rejected GOP calls to require that all investigations involving members of Congress be conducted by an independent counsel, instead clarifying that the attorney general had the option of seeking an outside prosecutor in such cases.

The Senate had passed S 24 (S Rept 103-101) by a vote of 76-21 on Nov. 18, 1993. The House Judiciary Committee had approved a companion bill (HR 811 — H Rept 103-224) in March of 1993 on a 21-14 party-line vote. *(1993 Almanac, p. 309)*

Background

The independent counsel law, first passed in 1978 in response to the Watergate scandal, was designed to avoid the real or perceived conflict of interest presented by having the attorney general investigate other top administration officials. It provided for an independent counsel, operating outside the Justice Department, to investigate cases involving top executive branch officials, including the president, vice president and Cabinet officials — more than 50 positions in all.

The law mandated that the attorney general conduct a preliminary investigation into credible allegations against these administration officials. If there were grounds to proceed, the attorney general had to ask a special three-judge panel to appoint an independent counsel to pursue the investigation and any subsequent prosecution. An attorney general's decision on whether to seek an independent counsel at that stage was final and could not be reviewed by the courts.

In addition, the attorney general could seek an independent counsel for any investigation that posed a conflict of interest for the Justice Department, including cases involving members of Congress. Many House Republicans wanted to make coverage for members of Congress mandatory, eliminating the possibility of investigating lawmakers through traditional Justice Department channels.

Whitewater Investigation

In blocking earlier attempts to extend the law, Republicans complained that Walsh had abused it with his

investigation of how the Reagan administration made secret arms-for-hostages sales to Iran and diverted the funds to aid Nicaraguan contras. Republicans said the statute had allowed Walsh to pursue a costly and destructive vendetta against top officials. The investigation ultimately cost about $37 million. *(1992 Almanac, p. 315)*

But a number of those Republicans had second thoughts in 1994, particularly with GOP leaders calling for an independent counsel to look into allegations of wrongdoing involving Clinton's ties to Whitewater and to the failed Madison Guaranty Savings and Loan. Because the statute had lapsed, Reno had no legislative authority to call for an independent counsel; instead she named a special prosecutor, Robert B. Fiske Jr.

Reno and key congressional Democrats used the debate to reiterate their support for the law, putting political pressure on Republicans to back reauthorization.

Work on the bill began in 1993. The Senate passed S 24 Nov. 18 by a vote of 76-21; the Senate Governmental Affairs Committee had approved the bill June 24 (S Rept 103-101). In the House, a companion bill won approval in the Judiciary Committee on March 24 (HR 811 — H Rept 103-224) but went no further. *(1993 Almanac, p. 310)*

House Action

House lawmakers on Feb. 10 passed HR 811 by a vote of 356-56. Members subsequently passed S 24 by voice vote after inserting the text of HR 811. The overwhelming tally belied lengthy and heated floor debate that touched on the partisan issues of the Iran-contra investigation, the House Post Office scandal and the unfolding Whitewater investigation. *(Vote 23, p. 8-H)*

By far closer votes, House members rejected Republican-sponsored amendments to require that independent counsels conduct all investigations involving members of Congress and to impose greater controls on prosecutors appointed under the law.

The first fight came Feb. 9 on the rule governing floor debate on the bill. Republicans challenged the rule, accusing Democrats of trying to rig the outcome on key GOP-sponsored amendments, but it was adopted 242-174. *(Vote 17, p. 6-H)*

The key debate took place the next day when George W. Gekas, R-Pa., offered an amendment to require the appointment of an independent counsel for all cases involving members of Congress. Several Republicans cited real or perceived conflicts when the attorney general investigated members of Congress, particularly high-ranking lawmakers of the same political party. They said the bill amounted to another example of Congress trying to excuse itself from the laws it passed.

But Democratic sponsors said the bill did treat lawmakers and ordinary citizens the same way; it simply did not treat them as it did a select group of administration officials. They said there was no evidence that attorneys general, past or present, had been reluctant to prosecute lawmakers.

John Bryant, D-Texas, and other Democrats said their position — that the decision about congressional coverage should be left to the attorney general's discretion — should prevail on its merits, as they maintained it had in the Senate.

BOXSCORE

Independent Counsel Reauthorization — S 24 (HR 811). The bill renewed a 1978 law providing for independent prosecutors to investigate alleged wrongdoing by top government officials.

Reports: H Rept 103-224, S Rept 103-101; conference report H Rept 103-511.

KEY ACTION

Feb. 10 — House passed HR 811, 356-56, then passed S 24 by voice vote after inserting the text of HR 811.

May 25 — Senate agreed to conference report by voice vote.

June 21 — House cleared the bill, 317-105.

June 30 — President signed S 24 — PL 103-270.

But Bryant also got permission from the Rules Committee to offer an amendment to Gekas' proposal that restated the bill's original language.

The parliamentary maneuver infuriated Republicans, who said Democrats were trying to prevent a clean vote on the Gekas amendment. Democratic leaders countered that Republicans had made such a move necessary by distorting the issue to capitalize on anti-Congress sentiment.

The Democrats' strategy worked. Members voted 230-188 to substitute Bryant's language for the Gekas proposal. They next adopted the revised Gekas amendment, 339-76, having reshaped it to give the attorney general discretion in cases of members. *(Votes 19, 20, p. 6-H)*

Lawmakers also rejected a comprehensive alternative bill sponsored by Henry J. Hyde, R-Ill., 181-238. Hyde's substitute, which had the backing of many Republicans, included mandatory coverage for lawmakers as well as controls on the tenure and expenses of an independent counsel. Hyde called it an effort to "fine tune" the law. *(Vote 21, p. 8-H)*

Judiciary Committee Chairman Jack Brooks, D-Texas, called it an attempt to "eviscerate every single fiber of the independent counsel statute." Brooks noted that the underlying bill already included new restrictions on an independent counsel, such as requirements to adhere to Justice Department expense and conduct guidelines.

Conference/Final Action

After a brief meeting May 17, House and Senate negotiators approved a final version of the bill (H Rept 103-511). Senate conferees presented a compromise offer, which House conferees adopted on a 4-3 party-line vote.

The Senate agreed to the conference report by voice vote May 25. The House cleared the bill June 21 by a vote of 317-105. *(Vote 258, p. 76-H)*

The conference agreement required the special court to review the progress of an independent counsel two years after the initial appointment, two years after that and every year thereafter. That was a compromise between the House bill, which would have required reviews every three years, and the Senate bill, which called for more frequent reviews.

Negotiators also adjusted an earlier requirement that independent prosecutors file an extensive final report, including reasons for not indicting a person under scrutiny.

The final bill gave the independent counsel discretion to provide such information but did not require it. This was in response to criticism by Senate Minority Leader Bob Dole, R-Kan., and others that Walsh had used his final report to unfairly smear subjects of his investigation who were never indicted. The Senate bill would have circumscribed the final report's scope more dramatically.

The conferees included a special waiver — not originally in either version — to allow Whitewater special prosecutor Fiske to stay on as an independent counsel if his investigation continued under the newly reauthorized law. Ordinarily, the special court would have been barred from considering a federal employee — as Fiske was then — to oversee an independent

counsel investigation. But Reno and key lawmakers wanted to give the courts the option to retain Fiske on Whitewater.

(Later, in a dramatic twist, under the newly renewed law a federal three-judge panel in August ignored Reno's recommendation and named former Republican U.S. Solicitor General Kenneth W. Starr as the new independent counsel for the Whitewater investigation, replacing special prosecutor Fiske.)

After the Fiske provision was added to the conference report, Hyde and other House Republicans questioned whether the move, and the reauthorization generally, would somehow facilitate Clinton or other subjects of the Whitewater investigation in recouping their legal costs at taxpayer expense.

Under the terms of the lapsed law and the reauthorization bill, subjects of an independent counsel investigation who were not indicted could petition the special court to be reimbursed for some or all of their attorney's fees.

Sen. William S. Cohen, R-Maine, a cosponsor of the bill, said it was unlikely that Clinton would qualify for such public funds.

Cohen noted that subjects of an independent counsel investigation were not eligible for attorneys' fees if they would have been investigated anyway — without an independent counsel statute.

However, Carl Levin, D-Mich., the other chief Senate sponsor, would not rule out the possibility that Clinton or other Whitewater targets might qualify for some legal reimbursement under the reauthorization bill.

House Judiciary Chairman Brooks said any such award would apply only to prospective costs, not to legal expenses incurred to date.

Rep. Jim Leach, R-Iowa, who helped lead the push for a Whitewater investigation, was untroubled by the prospect of Clinton's receiving reimbursement for his legal costs, as had Republican targets of previous independent counsel investigations. "Even if there was no precedent," he said, "the only decent thing for a legislative body is to authorize and allow the finest legal representation for the president of the United States." ∎

Independent Counsel Provisions

The following is a description of the main provisions of the bill (S 24 — PL 103-270) reauthorizing the independent counsel law.

Appointing an Independent Counsel

Under the bill, an attorney general who received an allegation of criminal wrongdoing concerning a top official was required to conduct an inquiry to assess whether the charge was credible. A majority in either the House or Senate Judiciary Committee, or a majority of the Democrats or Republicans on those panels, could also trigger such an inquiry with a written request for an independent counsel. This threshold inquiry could last up to 30 days.

An attorney general who determined that the charge was specific and from a credible source was required to begin a preliminary investigation to last up to 90 days. At the end of that time, if there were grounds for further investigation or prosecution, the attorney general was required to petition a special three-judge panel to appoint an independent counsel to continue the case outside the auspices of the Justice Department. The attorney general's decision on whether to seek an independent counsel at that stage was final and could not be reviewed by the courts. The attorney general also had the discretion to apply the law's provisions to investigations regarding members of Congress or any citizen who might pose a conflict of interest for the Justice Department.

The independent counsel operated under the supervision of the three-judge panel, or special court. The independent counsel could be fired only by the attorney general, subject to review by the special court, and only for "good cause" — such as misconduct — or for a physical or mental disability that did not fall within federal protection.

Other Provisions

As enacted the bill also contained provisions to:

● **Threshold inquiry.** Lengthen the time the attorney general had to conduct the initial, threshold inquiry from 15 days to 30 days.

● **Attorney general recusal.** Clarify that attorneys general were required to recuse themselves from any actions under the independent counsel law if they were directly implicated in the case. The conference agreement also retained general provisions from the 1987 bill that last reauthorized the law, directing the attorney general to delegate proceedings under the law to the next-ranking Justice Department official if the attorney general had an existing or recent

financial or personal relationship with the subject of the allegation.

● **Congressional coverage.** Explicitly allow the attorney general to seek an independent counsel to investigate a member of Congress if it would be in "the public interest" to do so.

Under the 1987 law, the attorney general could use the independent counsel process for any person, including a member of Congress, if the attorney general felt it would create a "personal, financial or political conflict of interest" to conduct the investigation through regular Justice Department channels. The conference report retained that discretionary coverage provision for the general public, but made it both easier and more explicit for members of Congress by substituting the simpler "public interest" standard for the "conflict of interest" finding in their case. That change enabled the attorney general to address perceived as well as actual conflicts in investigating members of Congress.

● **Post-employment coverage.** Require that officials covered under the law remain subject to its provisions for one year after leaving office. The 1987 law provided coverage for up to three years in some cases.

● **Independent counsel reports.** Require an independent counsel to file a final and comprehensive report on the investigation, but eliminate a provision in the 1987 law requiring counsels to explain their reasons for not indicting a person under scrutiny. The bill also included a new requirement that independent counsels report annually to Congress on the progress of their investigation or prosecution.

● **Justice Department.** Clarify that independent counsels could request help from the Justice Department, such as a staff member with particular expertise, and that the Justice Department was generally expected to provide such assistance. The bill required that independent counsels follow Justice Department prosecution policies except in cases when doing so would undermine the purpose of the independent counsel law.

● **Expenses.** Include new restrictions on expenses such as salaries, office space and travel costs. The bill required an independent counsel to adhere to Justice Department spending policies except in cases when doing so would undermine the purpose of the independent investigation.

The bill mandated that an independent counsel assign an employee to certify that expenditures were reasonable and generally within specified Justice Department guidelines. And the bill specified that no staff member could be paid more than comparable positions in the U.S. attorney's office for the District of Columbia.

● **Audits.** Increase financial oversight of independent counsel investigations by the General Accounting Office (GAO). The GAO was required to review independent counsel expenses at midyear

and conduct a full audit at year's end and a final audit when the investigation was closed.

- **Attorneys' fees.** Continue to allow subjects of an independent counsel investigation to petition the special court for repayment of their attorneys' fees if they were not indicted, and if they would not have incurred those legal costs if the independent counsel law did not exist. But this provision was tightened. In the past, the special court could ask the attorney general to assess the merits of a fee request. Under the conference agreement, the court would be directed to get such an analysis from the independent counsel who handled the investigation, as well as from the attorney general.
- **Reappointment.** Require the special court to review an independent counsel's activities two years after appointment to determine if the investigation should be terminated. The review was to be conducted again two years later, and annually thereafter. The 1987 law authorized the special court to terminate an investigation if the work was finished or almost finished, without any deadlines for review.
- **Transitions.** Allow special prosecutor Robert B. Fiske Jr. to con-

tinue investigating the failed Whitewater Development Co. — a case involving land purchases by President Clinton and first lady Hillary Rodham Clinton — if that case became an independent counsel investigation under the reauthorized law. Ordinarily, the special court was barred from appointing any federal employee, as Fiske was at the time. The special court was to decide whether to retain him.

The conference agreement also included transition provisions for two ongoing independent counsel investigations that began before the law lapsed — one into improprieties at the Department of Housing and Urban Development and another concerning leaks of Clinton's passport records during the 1992 presidential campaign. For example, the bill specified that the new cost controls on certain travel expenses would apply to existing investigations after one year.

- **White House staff.** Require the White House to file a semiannual report identifying the names and salaries of people employed or detailed to the White House, except for disclosures that would run counter to defense or foreign policy interests. ∎

Busy Year for Legal, Judicial Issues

Congress took up a number of additional law and judiciary bills, clearing measures to renew federal assistance for arson research and prevention, facilitate U.S. government cooperation in international antitrust investigations, reauthorize the Civil Rights Commission and improve the administration of the federal court system.

A variety of other bills saw action but did not clear in the 103rd Congress.

New Law Allows International Sharing Of Antitrust Evidence

The Senate on Oct. 8 cleared legislation that allowed the Justice Department and the Federal Trade Commission (FTC) to negotiate agreements with foreign countries to cooperate on international antitrust investigations. President Clinton signed the bill into law Nov. 2 (HR 4781 — PL 103-438).

Under existing law, both agencies were prohibited from exchanging information on antitrust matters with other countries. The measure allowed the Justice Department and the FTC to work out agreements to share evidence with their foreign counterparts.

At a hearing Aug. 8, Assistant Attorney General Anne K. Bingaman told the House Judiciary Subcommittee on Economic and Commercial Law that difficulty in obtaining evidence abroad was hampering antitrust enforcement, particularly against foreign cartels.

The House passed the bill, sponsored by Judiciary Committee Chairman Jack Brooks, D-Texas, by voice vote on Oct. 3. The House Judiciary Committee had approved it Sept. 29 (H Rept 103-772).

The Senate cleared it by voice vote.

Operating Authority Remains Elusive For Legal Services Corporation

Once again, supporters of the Legal Services Corporation were stymied in their attempts to reauthorize the embattled agency, which had not received formal operating authority since 1980. Draft legislation that aimed to set clear guidelines

on permissible activities for legal services attorneys was approved on a voice vote by a House Judiciary subcommittee on May 26. But the controversial measure, later introduced formally by John Bryant, D-Texas, as HR 4508, stalled in the House as it became apparent that the Senate would not have time to act on it in 1994.

The organization, established in 1974 to provide money to hire lawyers to help poor people in civil court matters, had been kept in operation through annual appropriations while members fought over whether federally supported attorneys should engage in political activities such as lobbying, or take politically charged cases, such as those involving redistricting or abortion. *(1992 Almanac, p. 317)*

The bill approved by the Subcommittee on Administrative Law and Governmental Relations would have reauthorized the corporation for five years.

It would have set strict new accounting requirements for groups that received corporation money and would have authorized a study to determine whether more competition could be injected into a grants process that almost always renewed the funding for legal aid providers that already were receiving money.

It also would have eased some restrictions on when legal services attorneys could engage in lobbying and other controversial activities.

Republicans argued that the corporation should fund only basic legal services such as those needed for landlord-tenant disputes and divorces. Many Democrats said that the poor deserved the same range of legal services that wealthier citizens could obtain. Existing rules allowed some political activities by legal aid lawyers, depending on the source of funding. Legal aid organizations generally received money from private sources and state and local governments as well as the corporation.

Senate Panel Passes Wards Cove Bill

A Senate committee approved legislation Sept. 14 to apply the Civil Rights Act of 1991 to a group of Alaska cannery workers whose unsuccessful discrimination suit against their

employer, Wards Cove Packing Co., led to enactment of the 1991 law (PL 102-166).

The bill (S 1037), approved by the Labor and Human Resources Committee on a 10-7 party-line vote, proposed to reverse a provision in the 1991 law that specifically exempted the Wards Cove workers from the civil rights act that they had helped to spawn. *(1991 Almanac, p. 251)*

Democrats described the 1991 exemption as unfair and ironic. But the bill, sponsored by Patty Murray, D-Wash., did not reach the Senate floor before the end of the 103rd Congress. The committee's ranking Republican, Nancy Landon Kassebaum of Kansas, said limited time and GOP opposition gave bill supporters virtually no chance of passing the measure.

A related House bill (HR 1172) stalled in committee after winning approval in March 1993 from the House Judiciary Subcommittee on Civil and Constitutional Rights. *(1993 Almanac, p. 317)*

The Supreme Court ruled in 1971 in *Griggs v. Duke Power Co.* that employment practices, such as height requirements, that had a disparate impact on the hiring of women and minorities were in violation of the 1964 Civil Rights Act unless an employer could show that the practice was a business necessity. But in 1989 in *Wards Cove Packing Co. v. Atonio*, the high court shifted the burden of proof in disparate-impact cases from employers to workers. After *Wards Cove*, employees could prevail only if they could show that there was no business necessity for the discriminatory practice.

The decision outraged civil rights advocates in Congress, leading to a battle to reverse the ruling legislatively. After two years of partisan wrangling, Democratic leaders forged a compromise in 1991 with Republican members and the Bush administration, and the bill was enacted.

Part of the deal was to let the courts determine whether the law applied to cases that were pending at the time. But members from Alaska succeeded in adding language that specifically barred the plaintiffs in the *Wards Cove* case from reopening their lawsuit.

Lawmakers Authorize Funds for Arson Research, Prevention

The Senate on May 6 cleared legislation that authorized $11 million in federal grants for arson research and prevention.

President Clinton signed it into law May 19.

The measure (HR 1727 — PL 103-254) amended the Fire Prevention and Control Act of 1974, authorizing $2 million in fiscal 1996 to train arson investigators and $4.25 million a year in fiscal 1995 and 1996 to help states combat arson.

The bill also made money available to up to 10 states or groups of states for anti-arson initiatives such as one to reduce arson caused by drug and gang activities. The federal government was authorized to pay as much as 75 percent of the costs of each program.

Slade Gorton, R-Wash., who joined Richard H. Bryan, D-Nev., in introducing the Senate version of the bill (S 798), said the measure would "save lives and prevent countless serious injuries." Arson caused about 700 deaths and $2 billion in property damage a year in the United States.

The House originally passed HR 1727 (H Rept 103-172) by voice vote July 26, 1993. The Senate substituted the text of its bill and passed HR 1727 by voice vote Nov. 22, 1993. The amended version was nearly identical to the original House bill, sponsored by Rick Boucher, D-Va. The House took one

more crack at the legislation, approving an amended version April 26; the Senate cleared it by voice vote.

Senate Backs Expansion Of FOIA Coverage

The Senate on Aug. 25 passed a measure (S 1782) to extend the 1966 Freedom of Information Act (FOIA) to many government records compiled and stored on computers. But the House Government Operations Committee never took up a companion bill (HR 4917), and the legislation died at the end of the session.

The Senate bill, approved by voice vote, proposed to require federal agencies to publish in the Federal Register an index of all information retrievable or stored in electronic form. Public records, such as agency regulations, were to be made accessible by computer telecommunications.

The bill proposed to limit agencies' ability to exempt computerized records from public view and required them to indicate any deletions they made. Government agencies could not delay disclosure of public information even if they faced a backlog of requests.

The measure, sponsored by Patrick J. Leahy, D-Vt., clarified that agencies had to make computerized public records available, just as they did paper records. The bill also required agencies to create computer programs if needed to retrieve requested information.

To encourage quick compliance with FOIA requests, the bill allowed agencies to keep one-half of the fees they collected for providing public records when they released such records in a timely fashion. The other half of the proceeds was to go to the Treasury.

The Senate Judiciary Committee had approved the bill by voice vote Aug. 11 (S Rept 103-365).

Civil Rights Commission Gets Two-Year Reauthorization

The House cleared legislation (S 2372 — PL 103-419) by voice vote Oct. 7 to reauthorize the Civil Rights Commission for two years. The commission, created in 1957, assessed the effectiveness of civil rights policies in areas such as employment and housing. The bill also gave the commission the authority to air public service announcements on civil rights issues. It authorized $9.5 million for the commission in fiscal 1995. Appropriators provided $9 million, up from $7.8 million the previous year.

The Senate passed the bill by voice vote Sept. 30.

The House passed S 2372 by voice vote Oct. 3, after amending it with the contents of companion legislation (HR 4999). The amended measure was then sent to the Senate, which passed it on Oct. 6 and returned it one final time to the House to be cleared for the president's signature. President Clinton signed it Oct. 25.

Torture Lawsuits Bill Dies

Legislation to allow U.S. citizens to sue foreign governments in U.S. federal courts for torture, extra-judicial killings or hostage-taking foundered in the 103rd Congress, after being significantly narrowed by the House.

The House on Oct. 7 passed by voice vote a stripped-down version of HR 934 that would have allowed U.S. citizens to sue the German government in U.S. federal courts for Holocaust-related violence.

The original, broader measure was approved by the

House Judiciary Committee on June 29 on a 21-14 party-line vote (HR 103-702). The panel's International Law, Immigration and Refugees Subcommittee had given voice vote approval to the bill in 1993. *(1993 Almanac, p. 314)*

The Senate Judiciary Subcommittee on Courts and Administrative Practice approved its version (S 825) of the wide-ranging torture lawsuits bill Sept. 22. That bill saw no further action in the Senate, in any form.

The bill would have permitted lawsuits only after plaintiffs had exhausted legal avenues in the country where the torture or wrongful death took place.

The Clinton administration and other critics had warned that such legislation could set a dangerous precedent and potentially open the United States to reciprocal action in foreign courts for less serious crimes. A similar measure failed to pass in the 102nd Congress after the Justice and State departments warned of possible retaliatory action by foreign governments.

New Law Seeks Improvements In Federal Courts System

The House cleared a bill by voice vote Oct. 7 aimed at improving the administration of the federal court system. The Senate had passed the bill by voice vote Aug. 18; President Clinton signed it Oct. 25 (S 2407 — PL 103-420).

The measure extended for three years an existing demonstration project in 20 federal court districts that required courts to provide voluntary or mandatory arbitration for all civil cases as part of an effort to reduce civil caseloads. The bill also reauthorized the Judicial Automation Fund, which aided federal courts in the use of automated products and services.

The House Judiciary Committee considered but did not approve a broader measure (HR 4357) on Sept. 29. That bill, approved Sept. 27 by the panel's Subcommittee on Intellectual Property and Judicial Administration, would have expanded the demonstration program to all federal courts.

House Panel Approves Process For Contractor's Grievance

The House Judiciary Committee on Sept. 29 approved a bill (HR 4862) to give the U.S. Court of Claims jurisdiction to adjudicate longstanding claims by INSLAW Inc., a federal contractor, against the Justice Department. The vote was 20-15. The court was generally charged with deciding contract and other cases against the federal government. The measure never made it to the House floor, and no similar bill was considered in the Senate.

The committee-approved bill prohibited the court from awarding punitive damages. It also prohibited the government from using certain procedural defenses, such as claiming that the statute of limitations had run out.

The case arose from allegations by INSLAW that the Justice Department stole software made by the company after revoking a $10 million contract it had awarded to INSLAW in 1982. Democratic congressional investigators released a report in August 1992 that said the software maker's claims were credible. But a special counsel, appointed in 1991 by Attorney General William Barr, found no wrongdoing on the part of the department. *(1992 Almanac, p. 333)*

Democrats said that INSLAW was a classic case of government mistreating a weaker private entity. House Judiciary Committee Chairman Jack Brooks, D-Texas, said the bill was needed to allow INSLAW to make its claim before an impartial tribunal. But GOP members argued that the special counsel's determination should be final.

The bill had started in the Administrative Law and Governmental Relations Subcommittee, which approved it Sept. 27.

Minimum Wage for Inmates Measure Dies in House Subcommittee

A House Judiciary subcommittee on Sept. 27 tabled (killed) legislation that would have authorized a demonstration project in the federal prison system to pay the minimum wage, $4.25 an hour, to inmates who worked in prison industries. At the time, inmates earned $1 to $1.50 an hour.

The bill (HR 5081) was sponsored by William J. Hughes, D-N.J., chairman of the Intellectual Property and Judicial Administration Subcommittee.

Under the demonstration project, the inmates would have been required to produce products that primarily had been made abroad; they would have been able to sell their products in the private sector. At the time, federal prison industries could sell only to the federal government.

Most subcommittee members opposed the bill, fearing that sales to the private sector would allow prison industries to unfairly compete with U.S. businesses. ∎

Clinton's Judicial Picks Confirmed

Two of Clinton's 19 appeals court nominees, Rosemary Barkett and H. Lee Sarokin, generated considerable controversy — although the Senate ultimately confirmed both by comfortable margins.

The Senate also ended months of controversy over Justice Department slots when it voted March 22 to confirm Jamie S. Gorelick to be deputy attorney general and Deval L. Patrick to head the Civil Rights Division. Neither candidate generated much opposition.

Rosemary Barkett

Following an extended debate on the death penalty and the treatment of violent criminals, the Senate on April 14 confirmed Rosemary Barkett as a federal judge on the 11th U.S. Circuit Court of Appeals, based in Atlanta. The vote was 61-37. *(Vote 92, p. 16-S)*

Republicans generally opposed the nomination, charging that Barkett, 54, who had been serving as the first female chief justice of the Florida Supreme Court, had disregarded established legal precedent in an attempt to advance a liberal agenda.

Utah's Orrin G. Hatch, ranking Republican on the Senate Judiciary Committee, said conservatives were particularly troubled by what they saw as Barkett's judicial hostility to the death penalty. But lacking the votes to sustain a filibuster, Republicans agreed to proceed to a confirmation vote after Democrats agreed to a daylong debate on the nomination.

In Barkett's support, Judiciary Committee Chairman Joseph R. Biden Jr., D-Del., said she met the qualifications for the job and that she maintained an even judicial temperament in her capacity as a judge. But Biden said he might have had reservations about the nomination had it been made for the U.S. Supreme Court instead of an appellate court.

Barkett won a "well-qualified" rating from the American Bar Association panel reviewing her nomination. But conservative groups had geared up to oppose her ever since President Clinton nominated her in 1993.

Committee Hearing

The Senate Judiciary Committee voted 11-7 on March 17 to approve Barkett's nomination, with all but one Republican — William S. Cohen of Maine — voting against her.

In a daylong hearing by the committee Feb. 3, Republican senators grilled Barkett about her judicial philosophy and the death penalty, suggesting that she was a liberal who was soft on crime. But Barkett told lawmakers she was well within the judicial mainstream. And she cautioned them not to focus on isolated cases in her lengthy career.

Sen. Strom Thurmond, R-S.C., recited gruesome details from cases in which Barkett had voted to overturn a lower court's death sentence. But Barkett said she was simply following legal precedents on when to apply the death penalty. She noted that she had voted to uphold the death penalty in scores of cases and said she would have no problem doing so if confirmed to the federal bench.

Hatch pressed Barkett on several cases in which she voted to strike down a state law. Hatch said she appeared too quick to find grounds to invalidate the state Legislature's handiwork, indulging in judicial activism. Barkett said the rulings were grounded in Florida law rather than in her political preferences. She assured the panel she would adhere to federal, not state, precedents if confirmed. "I have no problem following the federal law if and when I'm in the federal system," Barkett said.

Even before the hearing, Barkett's nomination had taken on the markings of a vintage partisan struggle. Activists on both sides had released reports analyzing her lengthy judicial record and responding to the other side's criticisms.

Her prospects got a boost in December 1993 when conservative Florida Republican Sen. Connie Mack announced he would support her. Introducing Barkett to the committee, Mack said, "Even though I disagree with some of the chief justice's conclusions, I respect her judgment and integrity."

After graduating from the University of Florida Law School in 1970, Barkett spent several years in a West Palm Beach law firm before being appointed to a trial court vacancy by then-Gov. Bob Graham. She was later appointed to a Florida appeals court, and in 1985, to the state Supreme Court. In 1992, she won a retention election to the court with about 61 percent of the vote. Her views on the death penalty were fiercely debated in that campaign.

H. Lee Sarokin

U.S. District Judge H. Lee Sarokin won a seat on the 3rd U.S. Circuit Court of Appeals, based in Philadelphia, after surmounting conservatives' apprehensions that he was a judicial renegade unfit for the job. The Senate confirmed Sarokin 63-35 on Oct. 4, after a day of floor debate in which many Republicans derided Sarokin's record, particularly in the area of criminal law. (Vote 319, p. 55-S)

Democratic supporters countered with endorsements from Sarokin's colleagues and other legal professionals and insisted that GOP opponents were unfairly fixating on isolated portions of Sarokin's record. Sarokin won approval with support from 14 Republicans and most Democrats.

When senators could not agree on how long to debate the nomination, Majority Leader George J. Mitchell, D-Maine, filed a cloture petition seeking to cap debate at 30 hours. Orrin G. Hatch, R-Utah, angrily insisted that Republicans had no plans to filibuster, and most joined the 85-12 vote for cloture Oct. 4. (Vote 318, p. 55-S)

But Hatch said Republicans deserved time to air their concerns about Sarokin — and they proceeded to do so.

Sarokin had been attacked for his handling of a major tobacco industry liability case. In 1992, the 3rd Circuit — the same court to which he had been nominated — removed Sarokin from the case because the court said his critical remarks about the industry had jeopardized his appearance of neutrality.

Other criticisms centered on the issue of crime; many Republicans said Sarokin displayed too much sympathy for accused criminals and not enough for their victims. They focused on the particulars of several cases — such as one in which Sarokin ordered a new trial for a man convicted of killing a police officer.

"Judge Sarokin is the poster boy for soft-on-crime judges," said Trent Lott, R-Miss. Some Republicans suggested that in nominating and supporting Sarokin, President Clinton and most Democrats lacked the resolve to hand out tough punishment to criminals.

Judiciary Committee Chairman Joseph R. Biden Jr., D-Del., bristled at such remarks, defending Sarokin's record. Biden and Bill Bradley, D-N.J., spearheaded the floor effort in Sarokin's behalf, arguing that his controversial rulings turned on principled interpretations of complicated legal issues rather than on ideology. Seeking to counter claims that Sarokin's opinions fell out of the judicial mainstream, Bradley noted that only a small fraction of the judge's more than 2,000 judicial opinions had been reversed.

Minority Whip Alan K. Simpson, R-Wyo., was the only Republican to speak in Sarokin's behalf. Simpson said that while the judge had made some "boneheaded" decisions, he was an impressive nominee who deserved confirmation. Sarokin, 65, worked in a private law firm and as a law professor before being named a federal judge by President Jimmy Carter in 1979. As a U.S. District judge in New Jersey, he was twice named chairman of the National Conference of Federal Judges. The American Bar Association, which independently reviewed nominees to the federal bench, rated him "well-qualified."

Committee Hearing

The Senate Judiciary Committee approved Sarokin's nomination in a 12-5 vote Aug. 11.

Hatch, ranking Republican on the panel, voted against the nominee, describing him as a "stridently liberal judicial activist who pursues his own ideological agenda in lieu of applying the law."

Clinton nominated Sarokin in May, and Sarokin appeared before the panel Aug. 3 to answer questions. In introducing him to the committee, Bradley, a longtime friend, called Sarokin "one of the most gifted judges to sit on the bench in New Jersey in many years."

Sarokin's ability to rule fairly in cases in which he might have a bias was the focus of much of the committee's questioning. When Sen. Strom Thurmond, R-S.C., asked Sarokin

several times if he would follow Supreme Court precedent in all cases, Sarokin responded that he had no problem doing so.

Deval L. Patrick

The Senate on March 22 easily confirmed Deval L. Patrick to fill a key vacancy at the Justice Department, ending months of controversy over the slot. Patrick, chosen to head the Civil Rights Division, was confirmed by voice vote on the same day that senators confirmed Jamie S. Gorelick to be deputy attorney general.

Patrick, 37, was nominated after two of President Clinton's earlier choices, including University of Pennsylvania law Professor Lani Guinier, were forced to withdraw from consideration. Unlike Guinier, Patrick was viewed by most lawmakers as a mainstream civil rights attorney. Patrick served at the NAACP's legal defense fund and then spent eight years at Hill and Barlow, a prestigious Boston law firm. His nomination generated almost no opposition.

Accepting the nomination Feb. 1, Patrick, an African-American, paid tribute to the pioneers of the civil rights movement "who had the guts to stand up in some court somewhere and give the Constitution life."

His nomination won ready acclaim from civil rights advocates and several Democratic lawmakers, including members of the Congressional Black Caucus. Moreover, Clinton took a more combative posture on this nominee. "If they attack his record, it means just exactly what we've all suspected all along: They don't give a rip about civil rights," Clinton said.

Clinton came to office pledging to reinvigorate federal enforcement of civil rights laws, which many Democrats said was allowed to languish under 12 years of Republican leadership. But the civil rights post had been a White House headache since the bitter fight over Guinier, which left a rift between Clinton and many black activists.

Clinton had withdrawn the nomination of his first choice, Guinier, in 1993 after a painful period of controversy over her scholarly writings, which many criticized as radical. Clinton's second choice, Washington lawyer John Payton, withdrew after getting tepid reviews from the Congressional Black Caucus, whose members said his failure to vote in recent elections made him ill-qualified to enforce the Voting Rights Act of 1965. *(1993 Almanac, p. 307)*

The nomination of Patrick, followed by the nomination of Gorelick, aimed in part to quiet complaints about disarray at the Justice Department and the administration's nomination process generally.

Patrick emerged from an impoverished childhood on Chicago's South Side to attend Harvard College and Harvard University Law School. He worked with Guinier at the NAACP's Legal Defense and Educational Fund, where he litigated criminal defense and voting rights cases.

Committee Hearing

The Senate Judiciary Committee approved Patrick's nomination by voice vote March 17. The vote followed a cordial hearing March 10.

Committee members praised Patrick for his experience in civil rights litigation and his accomplishments in private practice. And they showed little inclination to challenge his views on issues that might come before the Justice Department. Patrick was the only person to testify at the hearing.

The White House and Patrick clearly had done their homework before the Judiciary Committee hearings began. Senator after senator referred to private meetings they had held with Patrick. And the nominee went to some lengths to portray himself as a mainstream civil rights lawyer. "I come to this challenge, despite some of the things you may have read, as neither a so-called liberal nor a so-called conservative. I come to this as a pragmatist with very high ideals."

Conservative activists had criticized Patrick as a "stealth Guinier," but Republicans on the Senate committee showed little inclination to take up that cudgel.

Like committee Chairman Joseph R. Biden Jr., D-Del., however, they did press Patrick on his views about the death penalty, the Voting Rights Act and appropriate remedies for discrimination.

Patrick acknowledged that he had "serious reservations" about capital punishment but said that he would "enforce the law of the land." The nominee said discrimination remained a fact of life for too many. "We still have Americans who can't get jobs or places to live or bank loans or a decent chance to go to school, or who can't even participate meaningfully in the political process or get to the door of a public building because of some immutable characteristic about them."

He said the Civil Rights Division "must move firmly, fearlessly and unambiguously to enforce the laws you've passed so that it becomes as plain as it can be that the Congress means what it says when it says that discrimination is illegal."

In response to questions, Patrick refused to dismiss outright some voting rights remedies that Guinier had proposed in her writings — including various forms of weighted voting for minorities. But he labeled such remedies "extreme" and said he could envision them only in response to "extreme violations."

Jamie S. Gorelick

The Senate confirmed Jamie S. Gorelick to be deputy attorney general by voice vote March 22, the same day it confirmed Deval L. Patrick to head the Civil Rights Division. That ended months of controversy over both slots, although neither candidate generated much opposition.

Since early 1993, Gorelick, 43, had served as general counsel for the Defense Department. She also served at the Energy Department in 1979-80 and had practiced law in Washington in the public and private sectors since 1975. In moving to Justice, she replaced Philip B. Heymann, who left in February after resigning abruptly, citing irreconcilable management differences with Attorney General Janet Reno. That helped fuel complaints about disarray at the Justice Department and the administration's nomination process generally.

The Senate Judiciary Committee approved Gorelick's nomination by voice vote March 17. At her confirmation hearing March 16, Gorelick said she would serve as the "right arm" for Reno in establishing a "cohesive team" at the department.

As the No. 2 person at Justice, Gorelick was to oversee the day-to-day operations of a department with 89,000 employees. She also was expected to play a key role in formulating the agency's anti-crime policy. ∎

Centrist Justice Easily Confirmed

For the second year in a row, President Clinton went through weeks of agonized indecision over the choice of a nominee to fill a vacancy on the Supreme Court. And once again, he opted for a centrist who could win confirmation without a bruising Senate fight.

This time his choice was federal appeals court Judge Stephen G. Breyer, 55, who succeeded Justice Harry A. Blackmun, 85. Blackmun, who was appointed in 1970 by Republican President Richard M. Nixon, announced his retirement on April 6.

Clinton had indicated repeatedly that he would like to put a politician on the court, but his first choice, retiring Senate Majority Leader George J. Mitchell, D-Maine, took himself out of the running April 12. So Clinton on May 13 turned to Breyer, a low-key pragmatist with solid Capitol Hill credentials, for his second appointment to the Supreme Court.

The Senate confirmed Breyer's nomination July 29 by 87-9. *(Vote 242, p. 42-S)*

In declining to accept an appointment to the court, Mitchell said he was afraid that being a court nominee would hurt his ability to push health care reform through the Senate. "I believe there exists a rare opportunity to achieve comprehensive, meaningful reform of our health care system this year," Mitchell said at a news conference. "I don't think that opportunity is going to come along again any time in the future if we don't seize it this year." Mitchell made clear his interest in serving on the court if another opening should occur during Clinton's presidency. *(Mitchell, p. 57)*

At the time of his appointment, Breyer was chief judge of the 1st U.S. Circuit Court of Appeals, based in Boston. He had been a finalist for the Supreme Court the year before, but Clinton passed him over then in favor of Ruth Bader Ginsburg. *(1993 Almanac, p. 318)*

This time, as in 1993, Clinton vacillated to the end over the selection of a new justice. And, as in 1993, he came within a whisker of choosing Interior Secretary Bruce Babbitt, only to back off in the face of strident opposition from conservatives.

Praised as a brilliant scholar and consensus-builder, Breyer was expected to add heft to the court's growing centrist bloc. "He has earned a reputation as a moderate," said Sen. Orrin G. Hatch of Utah, the ranking Republican on the Judiciary Committee. Hatch and other Judiciary members had known Breyer since he served as the committee's chief counsel in 1979-80.

Breyer's chances in 1993 were hurt by the revelation that he had failed to pay Social Security taxes for a household worker. But that issue was not as politically charged in 1994. By the end of the year, in fact, Congress passed legislation to ease the tax requirement for employers of domestic workers. *(Domestic worker tax, p. 368)*

Blackmun's Legacy

Hailed by Nixon as a judicial conservative when he was nominated in 1970, Blackmun left the court nearly a quarter-century later as one of its liberal anchors. He contended that the court had shifted, not he. But in reality, both had changed.

Blackmun conspicuously changed his position on the death penalty early in 1994, moving from the reluctant support that he had embraced throughout much of his judicial career to outright opposition. "From this day forward," he

wrote in *Callins v. Collins* (February 1994), "I no longer shall tinker with the machinery of death."

But on abortion rights, the court changed more than Blackmun. When Blackmun wrote his famous 1973 decision legalizing abortion in *Roe v. Wade*, he was one of seven justices voting with the majority. When the court curtailed access to abortions in *Webster v. Reproductive Health Services* (1989), Blackmun was one of four justices in dissent.

By then, liberal lions such as William O. Douglas were long gone, and William J. Brennan Jr. and Thurgood Marshall were on the verge of retirement.

When Blackmun joined the court in 1970, it had just completed the Warren era (1954-69), a period of judicial activism that had exerted a strong liberalizing force on American life. Rulings of the Warren Court had initiated and accelerated the civil rights movement, ignited a reapportionment revolution, reformed police procedures and curtailed state powers over controversial matters such as birth control and school prayer.

Many of those decisions were highly controversial. And though Nixon wanted a more conservative court, enough justices remained from the Warren era to prevent a rollback of its landmark decisions. During much of the 1970s and 1980s, Blackmun was part of a "moderate core" on the court that frequently constituted a majority.

But after Presidents Ronald Reagan and George Bush named a total of five justices, the court's balance of power moved to the right. That left Blackmun a liberal by default.

"It's all relative," said David M. O'Brien, a government professor at the University of Virginia. "He's less of an example of a justice growing and maturing on the bench than a conscientious justice remaining consistent on a court that was changing around him."

Blackmun's emphasis on the right of privacy, articulated in *Roe v. Wade*, was a key ingredient of his writings throughout most of his court career. But so was his conservative approach to most areas of criminal justice other than the death penalty.

Blackmun, for example, wrote the majority opinion in *California v. Acevedo* (1991), a decision that allowed police to search a car and all closed containers in it without a warrant, even if the police lacked probable cause to believe that any containers held drugs or other contraband. Blackmun argued that the warrant requirement burdened effective law enforcement.

"He remained as Nixon promised: a law-and-order justice on most issues of criminal procedure," said O'Brien.

Blackmun owed his nomination in large part to his long-time friendship with Warren E. Burger, whom Nixon chose as chief justice in 1969 to succeed Earl Warren. They grew up together in St. Paul, Minn., and Blackmun served as best man at Burger's wedding.

Blackmun, who served 11 years on the 8th U.S. Circuit Court of Appeals, followed Burger onto the Supreme Court by 11 months. In his early years on the bench, he voted with Burger so often that they were called the "Minnesota Twins."

But Blackmun was never the "strict constructionist" that Nixon wanted. In his 1970 confirmation hearings, Blackmun hinted at his future independence by maintaining that while legal precedents were valuable, they were not absolute. And he predicted that he would have no trouble disagreeing with Burger.

The Abortion Ruling

It did not take Blackmun long to work his way out of Burger's shadow. His chance came in 1973 when Burger asked him to write the majority opinion in *Roe v. Wade*. Blackmun agonized over it, even spending several weeks in research at the medical library of the Mayo Clinic in Rochester, Minn., where he had been resident counsel in the 1950s.

In the end, Blackmun placed limits under which abortions could be performed but asserted that the constitutional right of privacy "is broad enough to encompass a woman's decision whether or not to terminate her pregnancy."

Suddenly, the member of the Supreme Court whom radio personality Garrison Keillor dubbed "the shy person's justice" became a lightning rod for controversy.

Over the succeeding two decades, Blackmun received death threats and more than 60,000 pieces of hate mail. The New York Times in 1993 called him "the most vilified member of the Supreme Court in history."

Blackmun never forgot that the cases he was asked to decide involved real people, and his opinions often displayed the human face of sympathy and passion. "Poor Joshua!" he wrote in *DeShaney v. Winnebago County* (1989), dissenting from the majority position that public welfare officials did not have a constitutional obligation to protect a child against abuse from his father.

In the 1972 baseball antitrust case (*Flood v. Kuhn*), Blackmun waxed lyrical about the joys of the sport, even listing dozens of greats from yesteryear who "have sparked the diamond . . . and provided tinder for recaptured thrills."

Blackmun's empathy for average citizens reflected his background. He was the son of a neighborhood grocery-hardware store owner who worked his way through Harvard.

He tended to be more of a loner on the court than a coalition-builder, and he valued his independence. He complained in 1988 that Reagan's appointees (Antonin Scalia, Anthony M. Kennedy and Sandra Day O'Connor) were voting as a conservative bloc. "All of the appointees of the present administration are voting one way," he said. "When I started, we tried to just be good judges."

Clinton's Choice

Clinton announced Breyer's selection on May 13, ending a protracted public deliberation over Breyer, Babbitt and federal Judge Richard S. Arnold of Little Rock, Ark., a longtime friend.

Clinton said Breyer offered "excellence in knowledge, excellence in judgment, excellence in devotion to the Constitution, to the country and to the real people." The president said he had "a wealth of talent" to choose from but once again "could not bear" to lose Babbitt from the Cabinet. Arnold, he said, was undergoing treatment for cancer, a concern that led him to disqualify the judge.

Babbitt Passed Over Again

Breyer and Babbitt were both finalists in 1993 for Clinton's first appointment to the court. Mitchell's decision to remain in the Senate left Babbitt, a former Arizona governor and unsuccessful presidential candidate, as the only contender this time around with a background in electoral politics. But some Republicans opposed Babbitt as too liberal, while others objected to his policies on Western land use. They warned Clinton to expect stiff opposition if Babbitt were the nominee.

Clinton appeared poised to announce his nominee early the week of May 9 but did not do so until late Friday. His delay gave senators and interest groups ample opportunity to lobby for their preferred candidates. All week, White House feelers to key lawmakers focused primarily on Babbitt, feeding perceptions that he was the president's preferred choice.

Despite noisy opposition from some GOP senators, Western Democrats indicated that they could support Babbitt — even if they didn't think much of his conduct as Interior secretary. And even senators who were critical of a Babbitt nomination said he would likely be confirmed.

Sen. John H. Chafee, R-R.I., said Babbitt would be an excellent nominee and added that he was troubled that Clinton might pass him over for fear of Republican opposition. "I think he'd go flying through this place," Chafee said. But as the week dragged on, Babbitt himself predicted that he would not be chosen.

Clinton lingered over the possibility of naming Arnold, the highly regarded chief judge of the 8th U.S. Circuit Court of Appeals, whose record included strong defenses of individual rights. Although Clinton said he was prepared to refute charges of cronyism if he opted for the Little Rock jurist, he conceded that he was concerned about Arnold's long-running battle with lymphoma.

The White House kept quiet about Breyer until late in the game, apparently trying to avoid embarrassing the judge a second time if he was not chosen. In 1993, Breyer left his hospital bed for a face-to-face interview with Clinton, only to see the nomination go to Ginsburg just days later.

In announcing his selection, Clinton asserted that Breyer had the sort of political aptitude he was seeking. "He obviously has a lot of political skills because of his reputation as a consensus builder on a court where most of the appointees were made by Republican presidents," Clinton said.

Liberals Disappointed

The choice of Breyer disappointed many liberals. Justice Byron R. White, whom Ginsburg succeeded, was a moderate-to-conservative jurist, particularly on criminal law issues and privacy rights. Liberals could accept a judicial moderate as a likely improvement, if not as their preferred candidate. And many legal scholars argued for a centrist who could build bridges to the court's frequent swing votes: O'Connor, Kennedy and David H. Souter, who was named to the court by President Bush.

Those considerations were still relevant in 1994, as was the standing political imperative of avoiding a draining confirmation battle. But this time, Clinton was replacing a liberal justice, not a centrist. Some legal scholars argued that the court needed a distinctly liberal voice to serve as an intellectual counterweight to aggressive conservatives such as Scalia and Chief Justice William H. Rehnquist.

In addition to ongoing legal battles over abortion rights and criminal law, the court in the 1990s was expected to make pivotal rulings on issues such as gay rights, voting rights, property rights and church-state relations.

Breyer's Background

By the time Clinton nominated him, Breyer had established a record as a hard-working, non-ideological judge with a keen intellect, pragmatic outlook and a knack for finding common ground. "He is an effective consensus builder," said Kenneth Feinberg, who worked with Breyer when the nominee was chief counsel to the Senate Judiciary Committee.

Feinberg said Breyer developed his considerable political skills during his time on Capitol Hill. "He honed his ability to analyze a problem and work out a political consensus." During that time, Breyer often met with his Republican counterpart for breakfast to anticipate problems and fix them.

As a federal judge, Breyer was known for well-reasoned and

clear opinions, pointing to no particular agenda. He earned a reputation on and off the bench as someone who could find ways to compromise while offending almost no one.

Breyer was born in San Francisco in 1938 and reared in a modest home in an upper-middle-class neighborhood. He excelled as a student. After attending San Francisco's prestigious Lowell High School, he entered Stanford University, where he graduated with honors in 1959. Then he spent two years at Oxford University as a Marshall scholar and three years at Harvard, where he was an editor of the Law Review. In 1967, he married Joanna Hare, a clinical psychologist and daughter of a prominent British politician, Lord John Blakenham. They had three children.

Breyer's rise in the legal world began almost immediately upon graduation from Harvard Law School in 1964, when he clerked for Supreme Court Justice Arthur J. Goldberg. Breyer helped Goldberg draft his concurring opinion in *Griswold v. Connecticut*, a landmark privacy case that struck down a law banning the use of contraceptives. *Griswold* formed the foundation for *Roe v. Wade*.

The next year, Breyer moved to the Justice Department's antitrust division, where he stayed two years, trying both civil and criminal cases. He returned briefly to the department in 1973 to serve on the Watergate Special Prosecution Force.

In 1974-75, Breyer worked for Edward M. Kennedy, D-Mass., as counsel for the Senate Judiciary Subcommittee on Administrative Practices, where he concentrated on regulatory issues. In 1979, he returned as chief counsel for the full committee under then-Chairman Kennedy, helping to draft legislation that led to the deregulation of the airline industry.

Breyer's political acumen earned him respect from senators on both sides of the aisle, and the Senate confirmed his 1980 nomination to the federal bench by outgoing President Jimmy Carter even as Republican Reagan was about to take office. Breyer served 10 years on the 1st U.S. Circuit Court of Appeals in New England before becoming its chief judge in 1990.

In 1985-89 he also served on the Federal Sentencing Commission, which was charged with writing new guidelines to end disparities in sentencing made by different judges for similar crimes. Breyer was credited with helping to steer many commission members away from proposals to create complicated rules and toward a simpler system, ultimately adopted, that was based on existing statistics. The guidelines did not escape criticism, however. Some judges and lawyers contended that they shifted rather than eliminated bias and unduly restrained judges' discretion to determine just punishment.

Breyer never detached himself entirely from the academic world. He taught antitrust law and economic regulation — his area of expertise — at Harvard Law School from 1967 to 1980 and continued to lecture there occasionally after going on the bench. He published numerous articles and wrote or co-authored five books, including a 1982 textbook on business regulation called "Regulation and Its Reform" and the recently published "Breaking the Vicious Circle: Toward Effective Risk Regulation," which proposed new ways to set regulatory priorities.

As a judge, legal analysts said, Breyer was relatively liberal on most civil and individual rights issues, but more conservative on criminal rights and business law.

Breyer did not have an extensive record on the explosive issue of abortion rights. He joined a 1990 opinion striking down a Bush administration ban on abortion counseling at federally funded family planning clinics as a violation of free speech. But abortion rights groups were unhappy with his dissent on a challenge to a Massachusetts parental consent law.

On an issue important to Congress, Breyer strongly

Stephen G. Breyer's Vital Statistics

Born: Aug. 15, 1938, San Francisco.

Home: Cambridge, Mass.

Education: Stanford U., A.B., 1959; Oxford U., B.A., 1961; Harvard Law School, LL.B. magna cum laude, 1964.

Occupation: Federal judge.

Family: Wife, Joanna Breyer; three children.

Religion: Jewish.

Career highlights: Law clerk to Justice Arthur Goldberg, U.S. Supreme Court, 1964-65; assistant special prosecutor, Watergate Special Prosecution Force, 1973; assistant professor, Harvard Law School, 1967-70; professor, Harvard Law School, 1970-80; lecturer, Harvard Law School, 1981-present; chief counsel, Senate Judiciary Committee, 1979-80; judge, 1st U.S. Circuit Court of Appeals, 1980-present; chief judge, 1990-present.

Other distinctions: Marshall scholar at Oxford University; American Bar Association Annual Award for Scholarship in Administrative Law, 1987; Oliver Wendell Holmes Lecturer, Harvard Law School, 1992.

defended the use of legislative history to illuminate what lawmakers intended to accomplish in a given statute. Scalia had fought to keep the high court from examining hearing records, floor statements and other such evidence of intent. *(Breyer's views, p. 306)*

Judiciary Committee Hearings

Breyer maneuvered his way smoothly through lengthy but generally congenial confirmation hearings before the Senate Judiciary Committee on July 12-15, reaffirming his reputation as a thoughtful and soft-spoken pragmatist unlikely to embark on ideological crusades on the high court.

He dampened questions about his ethics, stemming from charges that he may have had a conflict of interest in certain pollution-related cases. And he tried to soften his image as something of a technocrat, speaking often of the human impact of the law and his desire to improve society. "I believe that law must work for people," he said, pledging to search for "the very human goals that underlie the Constitution and the statutes that Congress writes."

He told senators not to mistake his dry prose style or pragmatic reasoning for a lack of caring.

"I always think law requires both a heart and a head," Breyer told the committee. "If you don't have a heart, it becomes a sterile set of rules removed from human problems, and it won't help."

But without a head, he warned, "there's the risk that in trying to decide a particular person's problem . . . you cause trouble for a lot of other people, making their lives yet worse." As on many other issues, Breyer concluded, "it's a question of balance."

Breyer appeared relaxed and confident. He spoke without briefing materials and frequently offered wry commentaries or chuckled at senators' characterizations of his legal opinions and writings. He also displayed the conciliatory tem-

Continued on p. 308

Sampler of Breyer's Past Views . . .

Supreme Court nominee Stephen G. Breyer, chief judge of the 1st U.S. Circuit Court of Appeals, was known as a conservative on economic issues and a liberal on social issues. One of the most contentious issues between Congress and the Supreme Court involved the question of how justices should discern the intent of Congress in passing a particular law. Breyer strongly defended the use of legislative history.

The following excerpts reflect some of his views on regulation, affirmative action, free speech and legislative intent:

Regulation

Breyer was known as a conservative on economic issues and was generally critical of business regulation because he believed it strangled free markets.

From his 1982 textbook, "Regulation and Its Reform":

We already know that classical regulation can cause various sorts of anti-competitive harm. Virtually every form of classical regulation tends to *raise barriers to entry* into the regulated industry. Cost-of-service ratemaking is almost always accompanied by rules or laws that require a commission to allow new firms to enter the industry only if it serves the "public convenience and necessity." Thus, regulation significantly raised entry barriers into the airlines and trucking industries. Standard setting also raises entry barriers. Since standards are written with existing firms in mind, they may exclude or hinder potential competitors.

From testimony Feb. 1 before two House Government Operations subcommittees:

My first proposition is that our regulatory system badly prioritizes the health and environmental risks we face. Tunnel vision, a classic administrative disease, causes agencies to focus so single-mindedly on a given goal for a given substance — say, the "complete" cleanup of a toxic waste dump — that they impose ultra-stringent standards to neutralize the last, tiniest bit of risk posed by the substance. Because of the slightness of the risks involved, the strict standards impose high costs without achieving significant additional safety benefits.

Social Issues

Breyer was regarded as more of a liberal on social issues and was more open to health and safety regulations.

From a 1994 book review in The New York Times Book Review regarding whether economic analyses can guide government policy on AIDS:

There is an important evaluative difference between health and safety policy, in which scientific, medical and practical as well as ethical and emotional factors must play an important role, and more purely economic regulation — say, of transportation and energy — in which public policy traditionally has recognized economic theory as telling at least a very large part of the entire story.

. . . Economics alone cannot prescribe how much a society should spend on health and safety. Even if . . . we make the rather extraordinary assumption that choices about sexual behavior are rational (like mountain climbing), we must still recognize that society does provide massive relief for the California earthquake victims who "chose" to live on a fault line; it does help treat and pay for research for lung cancer, whose victims often "chose" to smoke; it has built a Social Security system around the concern that rational individuals may not properly save for old age and it quite reasonably can and does spend money to rescue mountain climbers in distress. Economics can wisely inform our efforts to attain our goals; but ultimately, if we prefer John Donne to Adam Smith, economists cannot prove us wrong.

From a 1991 decision, *Stuart v. Roache*, upholding an affirmative action plan for the Boston Police Department, including the use of statistics to justify the plan:

The Decree compares the number of black sergeants, not with the Boston population in general, but with those police officers with the minimal qualifications needed to become sergeants. The fact that, of the latter pool, 4.5 percent of the officers are black, as opposed to .45 percent who become sergeant, at least casts doubt on the fairness of the promotion process and requires further explanation.

. . . Plaintiffs, in an effort to discredit these numbers, point out that the Department selects its police sergeants from among those officers who pass the sergeants' examination. They suggest that the pool of qualified applicants (against which the small number of black sergeants are measured) consequently should have been those [who] *passed* the examination, not those who *took* it. However, to treat the former group as the "pool of eligibles" would assume that the examination was a fair non-discriminatory device for screening applicants. And, it is just this assumption that the tiny percentage of black sergeants (measured against the larger percentage of eligible black examination-takers) calls into question.

On First Amendment freedoms, from a 1984 decision, *Ozonoff v. Berzak*, striking down a loyalty oath for employees at the World Health Organization (WHO):

As Dr. Ozonoff points out, the Order lays down certain standards for determining "loyalty" — standards that take account of political associations and speech. As one who has worked for WHO in the past and who has filed an employment application again seeking work, Ozonoff, more than others, may feel constrained to bring his conduct into conformity with the standards that the Order contains. That means he cannot join associations upon which the Order seems to frown or act in ways the Order suggests would show "disloyalty," at least not if he wants to get a job with WHO. The Order is vague enough and general enough to suggest that a serious effort to comply would have an effect — a "chilling effect" — upon what Dr. Ozonoff says or does. . . .

. . . Many Stops Along Opinion Spectrum

. . . If the plaintiff's interest in getting or keeping a job is real, the likely "chilling effect" of an apparent speech-related job qualification constitutes a real injury. . . .

Legislative Intent

On an issue important to Congress, Breyer strongly defended the use of legislative history — congressional floor debates, committee reports and hearing testimony — to illuminate what lawmakers intended to accomplish in a given statute.

From the Justice Lester W. Roth Lecture at the University of Southern California Law Center on Oct. 31, 1991:

Until recently any appellate court trying to interpret unclear statutory language would have thought it natural, and often helpful, to refer to the statute's "legislative history." The judges might have examined congressional floor debates, committee reports, hearing testimony and presidential messages in an effort to determine what Congress really "meant" by particular statutory language.

Should courts refer to legislative history as they try to apply status correctly? Is this practice wise, helpful or proper? Lawyers and judges, teachers and legislators have begun to re-examine this venerable practice, often with a highly critical eye. Some have urged drastically curtailing, or even totally abandoning, its use.

Some argue that courts use legislative history almost arbitrarily. Using legislative history, Judge Leventhal once said, is like "looking over a crowd and picking out your friends." Others maintain that it is constitutionally improper to look beyond a statute's language, or that searching for "congressional intent" is a semi-mystical exercise like hunting the snark.

These and other criticisms are taking their toll. Judge [Patricia] Wald has pointed out that the Supreme Court relied on legislative history in almost every statutory case it decided in 1981. And although Justice [Byron R.] White has recently commented that "the court's practice of utilizing legislative history reaches well into its past, [and we] suspect that the practice will likewise reach well into the future," the Supreme Court's actual use of legislative history is in decline. By 1989, the court decided a significant number of statutory cases (10 out of about 65) without any reference to legislative history at all; and, in the 1990 term, the court decided 19 out of about 55 such statutory cases without its use. Referring to legislative history to resolve even difficult cases may soon be the exception rather than the rule.

Although I recognize the possible "rear guard" nature of my task, I should like to defend the classical practice and convince you that those who attack it ought to claim victory once they have made judges more sensitive to problems of the abuse of legislative history; they ought not to condemn its use altogether. They should confine their attack to the outskirts and leave the citadel at peace.

My defense focuses on the "law-declaring function" of federal appellate courts and considers only cases in which statutory language is unclear (for few other cases raise serious problems on appeal).

First, I demonstrate that we need to use legislative history by providing examples of its usefulness. Second, I address the major arguments against its use in order to show that these arguments call, not for abandonment of the practice, but at most for its careful use. Finally, I offer some institutional reasons for why any significant change in the extent to which courts look to legislative history would likely prove harmful.

I concede at the outset that my arguments are more pragmatic than theoretical. They rest upon two important assumptions. First, I assume that appellate courts are in part administrative institutions that aim to help resolve disputes and, while doing so, interpret, and thereby clarify, the law. Second, I assume that law itself is a human institution, serving basic human or societal needs.

It is therefore properly subject to praise, or to criticism, in terms of certain pragmatic values, including both formal values, such as coherence and workability, and widely shared substantive values, such as helping to achieve justice by interpreting the law in accordance with the "reasonable expectations" of those to whom it applies.

If you do not accept these assumptions, then I am unlikely to convince you of the legitimate role of legislative history in the judicial process.

If you do accept them and if, through example, I can suggest to you that legislative history helps appellate courts reach interpretations that tend to make the law itself more coherent, workable or fair, then I may convince you that courts should not abandon the practice.

Using legislative history to help interpret unclear statutory language seems natural. Legislative history helps a court understand the context and purpose of a statute. Outside the law we often turn to context and purpose to clarify ambiguity. . . .

Is this fact not true of words in statutes as well? Should one not look to the background of a statute, the terms of the debate over its enactment, the factual assumptions the legislators made, the conventions they thought applicable and their expressed objectives in an effort to understand the statute's relevant context, conventions and purposes?

Breyer then spelled out five instances in which courts use legislative history: to avoid "an absurd result," to fix a "drafting error," to recognize the "special meaning" of a particular phrase, to discern a "reasonable purpose" for choosing a particular word or phrase in a law and to choose among possible reasonable interpretations "of a politically controversial statute."

I did not dwell upon the problems of the legislative process . . . because my focus was the judiciary. I have simply argued that, viewed in light of the judiciary's important objective of helping to maintain coherent, workable statutory law, the case for abandoning the use of legislative history has not yet been made. Present practice has proved useful; the alternatives are not promising; radical change is too problematic. The "problem" of legislative history is its "abuse," not its "use." Care, not drastic change, is all that is warranted.

Continued from p. 305

perament that colleagues said characterized his work as a judge and an academic. Breyer laid out his thoughts in a calm voice, deflecting criticism firmly but without defensiveness.

Although Breyer, like previous nominees to the high court, declined to say much on topical issues such as voting rights or the parameters of abortion rights, he was generally responsive on other questions.

On the death penalty, for example, on which both he and Ginsburg had no record, Breyer said the court had clearly established that capital punishment was constitutional in at least some instances. Ginsburg had declined to discuss the matter, irking some committee members.

On abortion rights, Breyer said *Roe v. Wade*, which established a constitutional right to seek abortion, was settled law. However, he would not discuss less established areas of abortion law.

Breyer spoke more freely about issues such as property rights and separation of church and state. Those words struck few sparks, however, calling as they typically did for pragmatic balancing tests between competing rights rather than fixed legal formulas or bold new interpretations of law.

The Lloyd's Connection

On the first morning of hearings, Breyer made a pre-emptive strike against criticisms of his handling of pollution-related cases, saying he had reviewed the cases in question and was comfortable with his actions: "I personally am confident that my sitting in those cases did not represent a conflict of interest," he said. However, Breyer said he was sensitive to concerns on the matter and would move to divest himself of his Lloyd's of London investment and other insurance holdings as soon as possible.

At issue was whether Breyer — given his investment in Lloyd's — acted improperly by ruling on eight pollution cleanup cases involving the 1980 superfund law, which required polluters to pay to clean up certain toxic waste sites. No one suggested that Breyer ruled on any case directly involving Lloyd's. But it was suggested that he could indirectly benefit from his rulings to the extent that they affected general law governing pollution cleanup liabilities.

Some of the questions arose from the unique structure of Lloyd's, in which investors pledged money to cover a "pot" of liabilities on a variety of issues, without knowing exactly which companies they were insuring. Breyer invested in Lloyd's throughout most of the 1980s; he resigned from the syndicate in 1988. He had ongoing liability, however, for a 1985 investment in a Lloyd's syndicate known as Merrett 418. The syndicate wrote insurance policies for companies involved with asbestos and other environmental pollution risks and was hit with substantial claims against those policies.

There was still no final accounting of the syndicate's losses and the investors' personal liability. Breyer was insured for losses of up to about $189,000. Breyer and some analysts believed that that amount would cover his ultimate liability but that it might not. Breyer became concerned about the investment, and beginning in 1988, he recused himself from cases involving asbestos cleanup. He also tried at one point to get out of the syndicate but concluded that it was too expensive to do so.

The Long Island newspaper Newsday raised the investment issue in a June 24 story. It caused little immediate consternation but drew more attention and criticism in the days before the hearing.

The White House moved to counter the criticism July 11, releasing documents and letters from leading legal ethicists that the administration said showed Breyer had done nothing wrong.

In determining whether they had a conflict of interest in ruling on a particular case, federal judges were governed by a federal statute and a related judicial code. The rules required that judges disqualify themselves from cases in which they had a direct financial interest, in which the ruling might have a substantial effect on their finances or when their impartiality might reasonably be questioned.

Breyer stood by his decision on the superfund cases, saying he remained convinced that the cases would not have any significant or predictable impact on his investment.

But Howard M. Metzenbaum, D-Ohio, disagreed. Noting that Breyer eventually did recuse himself from asbestos cases because of Lloyd's heavy liabilities in that area, Metzenbaum faulted Breyer for failing to also stop hearing superfund cases to avoid an appearance of bias.

Geoffrey C. Hazard Jr., a University of Pennsylvania law professor specializing in judicial ethics, likened the Lloyd's syndicate arrangement to a mutual fund in which the investor was a step removed from the companies in which the fund invested. Federal law specifically allowed judges to hold mutual fund investments without automatically recusing themselves from cases affecting companies held by the fund. Likewise, Hazard said, Breyer should not be required to step down from cases touching on all businesses insured by Lloyd's — only those in which Lloyd's itself was a party.

However, Hazard said the insurance business involved so many public policy issues and regulated industries that judges might do better to avoid investing in it — as Breyer said he would do in the future.

Metzenbaum said that once Breyer was on the Supreme Court, he should more readily recuse himself from cases that could indirectly affect his Merrett 418 investment. But Breyer said it was also important that judges not recuse themselves in cases on which they could render fair judgment. And Judiciary Committee Chairman Joseph R. Biden Jr., D-Del., agreed that there was a danger of going too far down the recusal road: "It's a little like saying no judge should rule on a tax case because judges pay taxes," he said.

The federal statute governing judicial recusal was updated after the 1969 Supreme Court nomination of Clement F. Haynsworth Jr., then chief judge of the 4th U.S. Circuit Court of Appeals. Haynsworth's nomination was ultimately rejected, 45-55, after he was attacked for participating in a labor dispute case while he held stock in a company linked to one of the litigants. But some legal ethics experts said Haynsworth had done nothing improper; many observers felt he was undermined by those who opposed him on ideological grounds.

Precedent and Change

Breyer had some words to please virtually everyone on the question of how judges should judge. He assured senators that judges should not try to dictate public policy from the bench, nor readily stray from established precedent. He supported the use of legislative history to help glean the proper application of an unclear statute.

At the same time, Breyer defended the court's right and responsibility to adapt the Constitution to a changing world, as long as the court remained faithful to the document's core values. Breyer said many of those core values were expressed in the preamble to the Constitution and that they encompassed an essential view of human dignity. He praised the landmark 1954 school desegregation case, *Brown v. Board of Education of Topeka*, as putting true meaning into the Constitution's equality guarantees, and he

said it was not an exercise in judicial activism.

Breyer said there were certain constitutionally protected rights beyond those specifically enumerated in the first eight amendments. One of those, Breyer contended, was a right to privacy, which he traced to the guarantee of "liberty" found in the 14th Amendment.

Property Rights

The hearing provided no bombshells, but Breyer did flesh out his views on specific legal issues.

Many questions revolved around economic and regulatory issues, reflecting Breyer's expertise as an academic and the seeming shift of the Supreme Court docket toward such issues. Chairman Biden pressed Breyer on the proper scope of constitutional protection for property rights, expressing alarm that the Supreme Court appeared to be moving toward a more aggressive stance that would restrict government's ability to impose environmental and safety regulations without compensating affected businesses and individuals.

Breyer said government clearly could impose some legitimate regulations without compensation, while other rules could go too far. He said there were no fixed legal rules on where to draw that line. "You always come back to a kind of human judgment — what is too far," he said.

He later said property rights could not be elevated to the same plane as fundamental liberties such as free speech. Conservatives had sought to elevate the status of property rights in that way, and the Supreme Court in its 1993-94 term indicated some willingness to move in that direction.

Biden welcomed Breyer's remarks on that point, but the nominee ran into some trouble over his non-judicial thoughts on regulation, as expressed in his recent book, "Breaking the Vicious Circle." In that book, Breyer suggested that society spent too much money regulating certain risks such as toxic waste, often in response to undue public fear, and not enough on others. He proposed creating an elite corps of regulators to assess risks and apportion resources accordingly. William S. Cohen, R-Maine, wondered whether that would be undemocratic.

Breyer said he was not faulting the public desire for more safety, only pleading for a more rational regime that would save more lives at the same cost. While society invested vast sums in minimizing certain theoretical risks, he said, women died of breast cancer for lack of affordable or readily available mammograms.

Afterward, Biden blasted Breyer's views as "presumptuous and elitist." Biden said public fear and the proper policy response did not always track a cost-benefit analysis. And he told Breyer: "I am delighted as a judge you are not going to be able to take your policy prescriptions into the courthouse."

Antitrust

Metzenbaum criticized Breyer for a series of antitrust rulings that Metzenbaum said favored big business over small entrepreneurs and consumers.

Breyer strongly defended his record as pro-consumer rather than anti-consumer. The judge said the purpose of antitrust law was to spread the benefits of competition to the general public, through greater efficiency, quality and lower prices. "What antitrust is all about is getting low prices for consumers, not high prices," he said.

Metzenbaum was not satisfied but acknowledged that he could do little except hope Breyer would keep such questions in mind when ruling on antitrust questions before the court. If so, "maybe the milk of human kindness will run through you, and you won't be so technical," Metzenbaum said.

Religion and Government

Several senators questioned Breyer about church-state issues in constitutional law, particularly the so-called Establishment Clause of the First Amendment, which prohibits government promotion of religion. Breyer's record on these issues was limited.

Liberals generally favored a relatively strict separation between government and religion; they frowned on activities such as prayer in public schools. But conservatives contended that the court had been too strict, preventing legitimate religious activity in the public arena.

Breyer repeatedly invoked the image of a burning church to show that some government involvement with religion was appropriate. The state did not violate the Constitution by sending firefighters to the scene, he said. But Breyer said it was important that government not get so involved that it favored one religion over another, or religious observance over nonbelief. And he unsettled Hatch somewhat by using the "wall" image when discussing appropriate church-state separation.

Characteristically, he downplayed the schisms on this issue and said the cases usually came down to a practical balance rather than fixed rules.

Death Penalty

Breyer had little to say about the death penalty, except to tell senators that he was not likely to share Blackmun's view that capital punishment was unconstitutional in all cases. Breyer said he had no passionate views on capital punishment that would preclude him from weighing a case on the matter. And he said the Supreme Court had repeatedly upheld death sentences as appropriate in some circumstances, making the issue, in his mind, "settled law."

Breyer would not comment on aspects of death penalty law in which he said the law was not settled, such as how old the defendant had to be or what procedures had to be followed to lawfully sentence someone to death. He sidestepped a question from Strom Thurmond, R-S.C., and others on whether sentencing statistics could be used to establish racial bias in death penalty sentencing. Congress was debating that issue in the pending crime bill (HR 3355), and Breyer called it a question for Congress to decide. *(Crime bill, p. 273)*

On crime generally, Breyer said the Constitution empowered the government to take steps to ensure public safety as long as it did not unduly infringe on individual liberty. He would not speculate on the constitutionality of a pending assault weapons ban beyond observing that the court had done little to spell out the disputed parameters of the Second Amendment's protections for gun ownership.

Objections From the Outside

On July 14, the committee repeated a practice, begun with Ginsburg, of meeting with the nominee in private to discuss any problems raised in FBI background checks.

Biden said nothing arose that would jeopardize Breyer's confirmation. But Biden did raise an issue, later repeated in public session, regarding Breyer's failure to pay Social Security taxes for a part-time domestic worker. Breyer failed to pay required taxes over four years but had since paid them and had been absolved of any penalties by the IRS.

The hearing ended July 15 with an array of public witnesses, most favoring Breyer's nomination. The naysayers included an anti-abortion activist, consumer activist Ralph Nader, and Michael P. Farris, an advocate for home schooling. Farris and others interpreted one of Breyer's church-state decisions as indicating hostility to parents' teaching their children at home, but Breyer assured senators that he respected the practice.

Senate Confirmation

On July 19, the Judiciary Committee voted 18-0 to recommend Breyer's confirmation by the full Senate.

Many senators had indicated support for Breyer before the committee's hearings, but several said Breyer strengthened his position with his oral presentation.

Arlen Specter, R-Pa., who routinely criticized Supreme Court nominees for evading senators' questions, praised Breyer for being relatively forthcoming. And senators cited Breyer's responses to specific questions on such topics as abortion rights, as well as his overall intelligence and legal erudition, as bolstering their inclination to support him.

In some instances, the interpretation of Breyer's remarks seemed to depend on the listener. Hatch, the committee's ranking Republican, said he was comforted by Breyer's comments on the areas for appropriate interaction between government and religious institutions; Hatch said Breyer rejected the idea of an "absolute wall of separation between church and state."

But Specter said he believed the judge understood the importance of a strong separation between government and religious activity — a view Specter supported.

In the end, some Republicans remained concerned that Breyer did not voice stronger support for property rights and that he might be too liberal on social issues such as abortion rights.

On the Democratic side, Metzenbaum reiterated fears that Breyer would not look out for the interests of consumers and small entrepreneurs in antitrust and other business cases. "Judge Breyer seems to be more concerned with the law's impact on business," Metzenbaum said. Yet Metzenbaum voted for Breyer, "with some reservations but also a great deal of hope."

There was bipartisan pleasure at the lack of rancor surrounding Breyer, compared, for example, with the 1991 nomination of Clarence Thomas. "Clinton would have been justified in nominating a judge as liberal as Justices Scalia and Thomas are conservative," said Cohen, who praised Clinton

for choosing a centrist nominee instead. *(Thomas nomination, 1991 Almanac, p. 274)*

Full Senate Votes

Before casting their votes, senators of both parties rose during six hours of floor debate July 29 to note areas of satisfaction and disagreement with the nominee.

Judiciary Committee Chairman Biden expressed dismay that Breyer, in his writings, endorsed the application of cost-benefit analysis to policy dilemmas that Biden said transcended dollars and cents. Still, Biden supported him enthusiastically. "I am convinced he understands the distinction between theories in his book and what is appropriately allowed as a judge," Biden said.

Richard G. Lugar, R-Ind., led the opposition, questioning Breyer's investment in the Lloyd's of London syndicate. Lugar said the decision to enter into an investment with "unlimited liability" showed a lack of prudence and would raise potential conflict of interest problems if various insurance-related issues reached the high court. "This was not simply an unsound investment for two or three years; Judge Breyer signed away everything in a foreign land, subject to a foreign law," Lugar said in floor debate.

But Democrats and Republicans rose to defend Breyer's investment decision, noting that the Judiciary Committee had investigated the matter and subsequently approved him unanimously.

A handful of Republicans observed that Breyer was more liberal than they would like. They said they voted "yes" in deference to Breyer's intellect and Clinton's authority to choose judges. "I would never have nominated Judge Breyer had I been president," said Phil Gramm, a Texas Republican with presidential aspirations. "The person he has chosen is as good as any of us had a right to expect him to be."

In the end, nine Republicans voted against confirmation: Lugar; Robert C. Smith, N.H.; Don Nickles, Okla.; Trent Lott, Miss.; Jesse Helms, N.C.; Paul Coverdell, Ga.; Daniel R. Coats, Ind.; Conrad Burns, Mont.; and Frank H. Murkowski, Alaska. ■

Supreme Court Cautious, Pragmatic

With change its only constant, the Supreme Court continued down a path of moderate-to-conservative jurisprudence in its 1993-94 term. The justices shied away from sweeping declarations of principle, instead deciding most cases on narrow, factual grounds.

For the third time in four years, the court welcomed a new justice — Ruth Bader Ginsburg, President Clinton's first nominee — and bade farewell to a veteran, Harry A. Blackmun, who retired at the end of the term. Clinton nominated Boston jurist Stephen G. Breyer to succeed Blackmun, and the Senate swiftly confirmed him. *(Breyer nomination, p. 303)*

The changing lineup did little to shift the court from its cautious, pragmatic approach to the dwindling number of cases it accepted for review. The justices gave conservatives encouragement in the area of property rights and punitive damages but reassured liberals on issues of church-state separation and sex discrimination. And as usual, they showed an aversion to entering into disputes that appeared political, declining to allow the federal courts to intervene in the politically sensitive process of closing military bases. *(Base closings, p. 435)*

The court decided just 84 cases with signed opinions,

down from 107 in the previous term and a sharp decline from the 140 or so cases that were the norm in the 1980s. The total was the lowest since the 1955-56 term, a reflection in part of the degree to which the lower courts in the federal judiciary appeared to be marching in lockstep with the high court. All were dominated by Reagan-Bush appointees.

The court itself seemed a bit less contentious, issuing just 15 decisions by a 5-4 vote, down from 19 in the preceding term. And Justice Anthony M. Kennedy, a Ronald Reagan appointee who joined the court in 1988, emerged this term as its key swing vote. Blackmun and Justice John Paul Stevens were the court's only liberals, while Chief Justice William H. Rehnquist and Justices Antonin Scalia and Clarence Thomas held sway on the right. Justices Ginsburg, Sandra Day O'Connor and David H. Souter joined Kennedy in the center, although Souter — a George Bush appointee — showed unmistakable signs of moving to the left.

Property Rights

If the court broke new ground anywhere during its 1993-94 term, it was arguably in the realm of property rights. In a 5-4

ruling June 24 cheered by conservative advocacy groups, the justices held that governments must show a "rough proportionality" between conditions imposed on proposed development of private property and the potential impact that development would have; otherwise the conditions would violate the Fifth Amendment's prohibition against the "taking" of property without just compensation.

The case of *Dolan v. City of Tigard* involved the complaint by a hardware store owner in Tigard, Ore., that the city was imposing unfair conditions on permits to enlarge her store, requiring one portion of her lot to be dedicated to the city for a public pedestrian and bicycle path, and another portion for a greenway. In all, the city wanted to take 10 percent of her property for public use, without compensating her.

Writing for the court, Chief Justice Rehnquist declared that there was no reason why the Fifth Amendment's takings clause, "as much a part of the Bill of Rights as the First Amendment or Fourth Amendment, should be relegated to the status of a poor relation." Under *Dolan*, governments must bear the burden of calculating the impact of proposed development and ensuring that any exactions (or conditions) imposed on the property owner are more or less proportional to those impacts.

The ruling sent a chill through environmentalists and other advocates of vigorous government regulation of development; the Clinton administration had argued on the side of the Oregon town, in part out of concern about the impact an adverse ruling could have on federal environmental protection programs.

Abortion Clinic Access

Abortion rights advocates won important victories in two cases during the term. On Jan. 24, the court ruled unanimously that those responsible for violence against abortion clinics could be sued under the federal Racketeer Influenced and Corrupt Organizations Act (RICO), which carried triple damages.

The case, *National Organization for Women Inc. v. Scheidler*, centered on the scope of RICO, a powerful tool in both criminal and civil cases.

A year earlier, the Supreme Court had angered abortion rights advocates when it ruled that they could not use a federal civil rights law to enforce access to abortion clinics. *(1993 Almanac, p. 327)*

The 1994 ruling cut the other way, angering anti-abortion activists who said it threatened their free speech rights. Those groups suffered a second setback at the end of the term, when the court by 6-3 upheld the establishment of a 36-foot buffer zone for protests at abortion clinics. That ruling came in the case of *Madsen v. Women's Health Center*.

Meanwhile, abortion rights groups prevailed in Congress on the issue of clinic access, winning enactment in May of legislation (S 636 — PL 103-259) that made it a federal crime to obstruct access to abortion services. *(Clinic access, p. 355)*

In the *NOW v. Scheidler* case, the national women's organization sued Joseph M. Scheidler of the Pro-Life Action League and other anti-abortion leaders. The suit accused them of orchestrating a nationwide campaign of violence and intimidation against abortion clinics. Scheidler denied any criminal conspiracy and said the suit amounted to harassment.

A federal appeals court dismissed the National Organization for Women's case, saying the RICO law concerned only activities or enterprises motivated by economic gain. But Chief Justice Rehnquist, who wrote the main opinion for

the Supreme Court, rejected that interpretation. Rehnquist said neither the wording of the statute nor its legislative history indicated that Congress wanted to limit RICO to enterprises driven by economic motives. RICO, originally crafted to prosecute organized crime, also had been used against white-collar criminals and pornographers. Under RICO, prosecutors or plaintiffs had to show a "pattern of racketeering," as evidenced by two actions that violated any among several specified state and federal offenses.

The high court's ruling did not settle the case, but rather gave NOW the right to go back to court to try to prove that anti-abortion groups engaged in criminal conspiracy under the RICO law.

Abortion rights groups hailed the ruling, saying it gave clinics an opportunity to take on their attackers and deter violence. It also was a victory for the Clinton Justice Department, which had argued that the narrower interpretation of the RICO statute would hinder its efforts to go after non-economic criminal conspiracies, such as terrorists.

But anti-abortion activists complained of an assault on their First Amendment rights of protest and worried that the ruling would drive away members fearful of being implicated in a RICO lawsuit.

Justice Souter took up these free speech concerns in a concurring opinion, also signed by Justice Kennedy. Souter stressed that the decision "does not bar First Amendment challenges to RICO's application in particular cases." In some cases, Souter wrote, constitutional protections for speech could preclude prosecution under RICO or, in the event of a valid RICO case, limit the potential damages.

In the second clinic access case, *Madsen v. Women's Health Center*, the Supreme Court on June 30 voted 6-3 to uphold a court-ordered, 36-foot buffer zone around a clinic in Melbourne, Fla., citing the government's interest in preserving order and maintaining women's access to pregnancy services. Chief Justice Rehnquist wrote the main opinion, which also upheld certain noise restrictions outside the clinic. Four justices joined the opinion, and Justice Stevens wrote a concurrence.

Rehnquist's ruling struck down as too broad other court-ordered restrictions on abortion protesters — such as banning them from approaching patients within 300 feet of the clinic. Stevens would have upheld that "no approach" zone as well, but the other justices said the restriction went too far in curbing the protesters' speech rights.

Justice Scalia wrote a dissent, joined by Justices Kennedy and Thomas, calling the decision a dangerous departure from past rulings on First Amendment speech protections.

The Florida case did not directly affect the legal status of the new clinic access law, which was challenged in court soon after its enactment as an unconstitutional assault on protesters' religious and free speech rights.

Nevertheless, abortion rights advocates said the *Madsen* decision could bode well for the clinic access law. Eleanor Smeal, president of the Feminist Majority Foundation, said that because state and local officials were not always willing or able to protect abortion clinics, clinic operators could use the federal law to seek injunctions similar to the one used for the Melbourne clinic. And she said the court had endorsed the core principle that government had a strong interest in protecting access to abortion.

Opponents blasted the decision as an assault on free speech rights, noting that it banned even peaceful protest within 36 feet of the clinic. "If pro-lifers can be singled out, so can any other group," said Wanda Franz, president of the National Right to Life Committee.

Voting Rights

In a case involving the Voting Rights Act of 1965 and subsequent court interpretations of it, the justices ruled June 30 that states need not create the maximum possible number of minority-majority legislative districts in order to satisfy the law's requirements.

In deciding *Johnson v. De Grandy*, the court overruled a three-judge federal panel in Florida that had imposed a new map for that state's House. The judges' map had increased the number of Hispanic-majority districts in Dade County from nine to 11, making Hispanic districts more prevalent than Hispanics were in the population.

The court ruled that the lower court ruling had misinterpreted an earlier Supreme Court ruling — the 1986 *Thornburg v. Gingles* decision — that had called for increased use of majority-minority districts.

That decision had been widely seen as a signal to states that they should create majority-minority districts whenever certain criteria were met. In *De Grandy*, the court said that meeting the *Gingles* criteria was not reason enough to force creation of a majority-minority district.

The ruling was the latest in a series as the court struggled to explain when majority-minority districts were required and when they went too far. In a 1993 ruling, *Shaw v. Reno*, the court reinstated a suit by five white North Carolina voters who contended that the state's new congressional district map, which included two oddly shaped majority-black districts, violated their 14th Amendment right to equal protection. That ruling continued to reverberate throughout the South in 1994. *(Redistricting, p. 591; 1993 Almanac, pp. 325, 22-A)*

The voting rights of minorities were also at issue in a second case decided by the court during the term, *Holder v. Hall*. By 5-4, the justices ruled that the Voting Rights Act could not be invoked to challenge the size of a governing body — in this instance, a single-member county commission — as diluting the voting rights of minorities. Justice Blackmun dissented, joined by Justices Stevens, Souter and Ginsburg.

Sex Discrimination

Advocates of gender equity won an important victory April 19 when the court ruled 6-3 that prospective jurors could not be dismissed solely on the basis of their gender. "Gender, like race, is an unconstitutional proxy for juror competence and impartiality," wrote Justice Blackmun in the case of *J.E.B. v. Alabama*. Chief Justice Rehnquist and Justices Scalia and Thomas dissented.

The ruling extended the sweep of the court's 1986 decision in *Batson v. Kentucky*, which prohibited prosecutors from using peremptory strikes based on race. The new case involved a child paternity and support dispute in which the state's lawyer had used peremptory challenges to exclude men from the jury.

Blackmun said: "Since *Batson*, we have reaffirmed repeatedly our commitment to jury selection procedures that are fair and non-discriminatory. We have recognized that whether the trial is criminal or civil, potential jurors, as well as litigants, have an equal protection right to jury selection procedures that are free from state-sponsored group stereotypes rooted in, and reflective of, historical prejudice."

Scalia, writing for the dissenters, warned that the ruling "places *all* peremptory strikes based on *any* group characteristic at risk, since they can all be denominated 'stereotypes.' "

Earlier, in one of the first rulings of its 1993-94 term, the court on Nov. 9, 1993, ruled unanimously that a woman suing her employer for sexual harassment need not show that she suffered severe psychological injury in order to collect damages. Justice O'Connor said that Title VII of the Civil Rights Act of 1964, which prohibited discrimination in employment, was violated "when the workplace is permeated with discriminatory behavior that is sufficiently severe or pervasive to create a discriminatorily hostile or abusive working environment." The test, she said, was how a "reasonable person" would judge the conduct in question.

The decision in *Harris v. Forklift Systems, Inc.* represented only the second Supreme Court decision on sexual harassment in the workplace. The first ruling came in 1986 in *Meritor Savings Bank v. Vinson*.

Copyrights and Parody

In a case that drew friend-of-the-court briefs from giants of the music and entertainment field, the court March 7 unanimously ruled that parody, like other forms of "comment and criticism," can be exempted from copyright laws as a "fair use" of the protected original material.

The case, *Luther R. Campbell v. Acuff-Rose Music Inc.*, pitted Luther R. Campbell, better known as Luke Skyywalker, and the rap group 2 Live Crew against Acuff-Rose Music Inc., which held the copyright to the 1964 Roy Orbison rock song "Oh, Pretty Woman." The rap group had recorded a parody of the song that satirized the original, and the music company sued to protect its copyright.

A long list of songwriters, composers and singers, including Michael Jackson and Dolly Parton, lined up in support of Acuff-Rose Music, while political satirists such as the Capitol Steps and comedian Mark Russell, who both included parodies of copyrighted songs in their acts, sided with the rap group.

Cable TV Reregulation

The 1992 cable television reregulation law remained under constitutional siege after the court on June 27 said federal regulators had to do a better job justifying a key mandate regarding which programs cable operators had to carry.

Faced with a legal challenge to the law's requirement that cable companies reserve a portion of their channel space for local commercial and public broadcast stations, the justices voted 5-4 to send the case back to the lower courts with new guidance on how to weigh the competing interests of the cable industry and government regulators.

The case, *Turner Broadcasting System Inc. v. Federal Communications Commission*, pitted the cable television owners and operators against the Clinton administration and the broadcast television companies.

The 1992 law regulated basic cable rates and services and required cable programmers to deal fairly with competitors such as satellite operators, broadcasters, telephone companies and other cable franchises. But cable interests challenged the law's so-called must-carry provisions. The cable companies said the mandates were an unconstitutional assault on free speech because they forced operators to displace some cable programming to make room for local broadcasters. *(Cable law, 1992 Almanac, p. 171)*

The Clinton administration and the broadcast industry argued that the must-carry rules were an appropriate safeguard against monopolistic tendencies in the cable television industry and were necessary to preserve free television broadcasting. Although broadcast signals reached virtually

every home, more than 60 percent of all homes had their televisions connected to a cable — effectively shutting out the local signals.

The court, while sidestepping a final resolution of the challenge, handed some encouragement to both sides.

The majority opinion, written by Justice Kennedy, for the first time granted cable operators greater protection from government intrusion on First Amendment freedoms than broadcasters received.

The Supreme Court had upheld substantial government regulation of broadcast television because the limited spectrum required some government management for broadcasters to function at all. Because those physical restrictions did not apply to cable, Kennedy wrote, cable companies were entitled to greater freedom from government interference.

But the court stopped short of granting a still stronger level of protection from government regulation sought by the cable industry. And Kennedy said the government might be justified in imposing the must-carry requirements to preserve the public benefits of broadcast television. He remanded the case to the federal District Court for the District of Columbia — which earlier had upheld the provisions of the cable law — to hear more evidence on whether the local broadcasters were truly at risk, and whether the must-carry provisions effectively combated that danger while posing the least possible restriction on cable programming.

The case produced multipart opinions with an array of concurrences and dissents. Chief Justice Rehnquist and Justices Souter and Blackmun joined Kennedy's main opinion.

Justice Stevens signed on to its conclusion. He did so, however, only to prevent a deadlock on the case, and in a separate opinion said he would have preferred to affirm the lower court ruling and the legitimacy of the must-carry rules. Stevens said the cable law was a reasonable legislative response to a threat to the broadcasting industry. "An industry need not be in its death throes before Congress may act to protect it from economic harm threatened by a monopoly," he wrote.

On the other side, four justices were ready to strike down the must-carry provisions as unconstitutional. Justice O'Connor was joined by Scalia, Ginsburg and Thomas. O'Connor's dissent said the must-carry provisions unfairly favored broadcast television "speech" over cable "speech" and should be invalidated.

The court's decision was handed down one day before the House on June 28 passed a major telecommunications bill (HR 3636 — H Rept 103-560) that sought to apply the must-carry requirements to telephone companies that entered the cable television business. A similar requirement was contained in the Senate's telecommunications bill (S 1822). The legislation was not enacted. *(Telecommunications, p. 203)*

Church-State Separation

By 6-3, the court on June 27 ruled that New York violated the constitutionally required separation of church and state when it created a special public school district for a community of Hasidic Jews.

Justice Souter, writing for the majority, said, "We do not deny that the Constitution allows the state to accommodate religious needs by alleviating special burdens." However, he wrote, "accommodation is not a principle without limits."

"It is clear that neutrality as among religions must be honored," he said, adding that the creation of the Kiryas Joel district "fails the test of neutrality" because it "singles out a particular religious sect for special treatment."

The decision in *Board of Education of Kiryas Joel Village School District v. Grumet* affirmed a ruling by New York's highest court, which said the special school district unconstitutionally created a "symbolic union" between the government and the Satmar Hasidic sect.

The Constitution's First Amendment says: "Congress shall make no law respecting an establishment of religion, or prohibiting the free exercise thereof."

Lawyers for the school district argued that state lawmakers, in establishing the district, were simply accommodating the Hasidic Jews' right to religious freedom.

Although many observers had expected the court to use the case to overhaul its landmark 1971 test for interpreting the separation of church and state, it did not do so. That test, spelled out in the case of *Lemon v. Kurtzman*, held that government actions were unconstitutional if they had a religious purpose, primarily advanced or promoted religion or excessively entangled government and religion.

Solid Waste Disposal

The court issued a trio of rulings on solid waste issues that were of concern to many in Congress, although legislation to overturn at least one of the rulings stalled just short of enactment in October.

By 6-3, the court ruled May 16 that municipalities could not dictate that all trash within their borders be sent to designated facilities for disposal. Such "flow control" laws, the justices held, unlawfully interfered with interstate commerce — which Congress alone had the power to regulate.

The ruling, which came in the case of *C & A Carbone v. Town of Clarkstown*, dismayed the many municipalities that had built expensive incinerators and other facilities in recent years in the expectation that they could direct the flow of solid waste to those facilities, thus making them economically viable. The municipal bond market also reacted with jitters, prompting Congress to begin action on legislation authorizing such flow control ordinances. But objections from a single senator, John H. Chafee, R-R.I., blocked final approval of the measure. *(Flow control, p. 262)*

Another ruling during the term touched on a second waste disposal issue considered by Congress — the interstate shipment of garbage. By 7-2 in the case of *Oregon Waste Systems v. Department of Environmental Quality*, the court held April 4 that a state could not charge higher disposal fees for waste generated out-of-state than for that produced in-state. Congress considered but did not complete action on legislation designed to regulate the shipping of trash across state lines. *(Interstate waste shipment, p. 261)*

Finally, lawmakers agreed they might have to address problems created by a third court ruling in which the justices held, 7-2, that incinerator ash from ordinary household waste might have to be treated as hazardous, requiring disposal in expensive special facilities. That ruling came May 2 in the case of *City of Chicago v. Environmental Defense Fund*.

The disposal of solid and hazardous waste was regulated under the Resource Conservation and Recovery Act (RCRA — PL 94-580), which was overdue for reauthorization in 1994. But Congress put off action on the issue until the 104th Congress. *(RCRA background, 1992 Almanac, p. 272)*

Other Issues

● **First Amendment.** By a unanimous vote June 13, the court ruled that communities could not ban virtually all signs on private property in the interest of controlling visual blight.

The case of *City of Ladue v. Gilleo* involved the right of homeowners to put up political placards on their property.
● **Civil rights retroactivity.** By 8-1, the court ruled April 26 that provisions of the Civil Rights Act of 1991 that authorized damage payments and the right to a jury trial in job discrimination cases were not applicable to cases that were pending at the time the law was enacted.

The question of retroactivity had been one of the most hotly fought issues during the two years that Congress spent considering the legislation. Because lawmakers could not agree on the matter, the final bill was silent on the issue, leaving it to the courts to determine. *(1991 Almanac, p. 251)*

Writing for the court in *Landgraf v. USI Film Products*, Justice Stevens said Congress had to state its intentions

clearly when it wished a law to apply retroactively.
● **Punitive Damages.** By 7-2 in the case of *Honda Motor Co. v. Oberg*, the court ruled June 24 that states could not bar judges from reviewing and reducing punitive damages. The case involved a claim by Honda Motor Co. that an Oregon law prohibiting judicial review of punitive damage awards effectively denied it the due process guaranteed under the Constitution. The high court agreed.
● **Forfeitures.** A divided court ruled 5-4 on Dec. 13, 1993, that the federal government could not seize the property of a criminal suspect without providing advance notice and a hearing at which the forfeiture could be contested. The decision came in the case of *United States v. James Daniel Good Real Property*. ■

High Court Hears Term Limits Case

The political battle over term limits for members of Congress took a detour to the Supreme Court in 1994, as the justices agreed to decide the constitutionality of one of several state initiatives purporting to restrict the tenure of federal lawmakers.

By the time the high court heard arguments Nov. 29 in the pivotal Arkansas case, 22 states had sought to restrict the service of their members of Congress, most of them through voter approval of ballot initiatives. *(Ballot initiatives, p. 583)*

If the Supreme Court were to rule against the Arkansas term limits, it likely would invalidate all state-imposed congressional term limits, leaving a constitutional amendment as the only route to impose such restrictions.

"It's probably the single most important issue that this nation faces," Rep. Bill McCollum, R-Fla., said at a news conference Nov. 29 outside the Supreme Court. McCollum and other GOP lawmakers rejected suggestions that Republicans, or the public, might lose interest in the issue given the congressional upheaval of the 1994 elections.

The Arguments

The Supreme Court case concerned a 1992 amendment to the Arkansas Constitution that barred the state's House members from appearing on the ballot after three terms; the limit for senators was two terms. The case combined two lower court cases: *U.S. Term Limits v. Thornton* and *Bryant v. Hill.*

Attorneys for Arkansas and a national term limits group said the Founding Fathers empowered the states to set such restrictions and that the very idea was in keeping with their vision for the nation. "Our Founding Fathers envisioned a Congress of citizen legislators who would serve awhile, return and mix with the people," Arkansas Attorney General J. Winston Bryant said.

But Louis R. Cohen, who represented opponents of the measure, said the constitutional requirements for federal office — regarding age, state residency and U.S. citizenship — were meant to be an exclusive list of qualifications. Cohen said the framers intended for voters to limit terms at the ballot box: "The Constitution gave that choice to the people every second year."

According to Cohen, only a constitutional amendment would suffice to impose congressional term limits. Solicitor General Drew S. Days III also argued against the Arkansas measure, saying that such term limits far overstepped the states' constitutional authority to regulate the "time, place and manner" of elections.

Some justices seemed concerned about the implications of allowing states to limit terms, asking why states would not also be free to restrict the age or other key characteristics of congressional candidates. Yet they also poked holes in arguments against the term limits measure and cited a previous Supreme Court opinion giving states some leeway to limit access to the ballot. Justice Antonin Scalia at one point labeled the case a "very close" call.

That left the lawyers and the justices exploring competing theories of just how the framers meant to distribute control of federal elections among Congress, the states and the voters. Many of the justices' questions concerned whether, and when, Congress could respond to state-imposed restrictions for federal service — or legislate its own.

The Arkansas State Ruling

The Arkansas Supreme Court struck down the federal term limits, saying Article I of the U.S. Constitution set out the only three qualifications for federal office: age, residency and citizenship.

Because those requirements reflected an interest in promoting national uniformity in congressional delegations, the opinion said, states were not free to slap on more restrictions: "The uniformity in qualifications mandated in Article I provides the tenor and the fabric for representation in the Congress. Piecemeal restrictions by [states] would fly in the face of that order."

The majority opinion also rejected the argument, advanced by supporters of the Arkansas law and similarly crafted measures, that the ballot restriction did not really impose new "qualifications" for federal office because incumbents could run as write-in candidates and serve if elected. "These glimmers of opportunity for those disqualified, though, are faint indeed," the justices wrote.

Two justices disagreed, however.

Justice George K. Cracraft accepted the argument that the case did not turn on fundamental qualifications for federal office but on the somewhat different question of access to the state ballot. The courts traditionally had upheld states' rights to impose certain restrictions on ballot access if they served a public interest and did not breach constitutional guarantees of fairness. In this case, Cracraft said, the state's interest in promoting turnover outweighed any constitutional concerns about limiting ballot access.

A second dissenter, Justice Steele Hays, said the qualifications laid out in Article I constituted a minimum of creden-

tials, rather than an exclusive list.

A third justice, Gerald P. Brown, came down against the term limits measure but only after acknowledging certain strong historical factors in favor of Hays' view. Brown said he was pulled away from Hays' conclusion by evidence that the framers had weighed the merits of term limits but had chosen not to include them in the Constitution. He added in a separate opinion that "the specter of the hodge-podge of qualifications which a contrary holding might engender is daunting enough to swing the balance."

In the only other ruling thus far on the constitutionality of congressional term limits, a federal District Court in Washington state also ruled against them in February.

The Founders' Intent

The term limits debate dated back to the nation's founding, when the framers considered but ultimately rejected writing congressional term limits into the U.S. Constitution. Instead, they spelled out the three specific qualifications for senators and three for House members listed in Article I, regarding age, U.S. citizenship and residency in the state in which one was seeking office. These were known as the qualifications clauses.

Alexander Hamilton thought that should settle the matter. "The qualifications of the persons who may . . . be chosen are defined and fixed in the Constitution, and are unalterable by the legislature," he wrote in The Federalist papers.

This was the position the Arkansas Supreme Court and the judge in the Washington state case adopted.

But term limits advocates were undaunted. They said the framers never intended to preclude term limits and that the Constitution did not do so. Instead, they saw the qualifications clause as a floor — setting the minimum requirements for federal legislators. And they found explicit power for the states to impose restrictions on candidates and access to the ballot in a different section of Article I, which authorized states to regulate the "time, place and manner" of elections, as well as in the 10th Amendment's general protection of state powers.

The Supreme Court had never taken up the term limits issue directly, but some legal scholars said the court's response to term limits was contained in its 1969 ruling in *Powell v. McCormack*. That case involved a House vote not to seat Democratic Rep. Adam Clayton Powell Jr. of New York because of alleged financial improprieties. The court ruled 7-1 that the House had acted unconstitutionally, improperly looking beyond the three required qualifications for office stated in Article I.

Former House counsel Steven R. Ross, co-author of a brief in a Florida case arguing that state-imposed congressional term limits violated the Constitution, interpreted the *Powell* decision to mean that the Article I qualifications were an exclusive list. The *Powell* ruling cited statements to that effect from constitutional framers and others. The judges in the Arkansas and Washington cases in turn cited *Powell* to reach their conclusions.

But scholars and activists in the opposing camp rejected the relevance of the *Powell* precedent for the term limits case, instead interpreting the 1969 decision as a narrower ruling on the powers of one chamber of Congress to expel members. And they cited other instances in which the Supreme Court upheld state ballot restrictions that curtailed the field of candidates, such as prohibiting individuals from appearing on the ballot as independents if they recently were affiliated with a particular party.

Paul Jacob, executive director of the national advocacy group U.S. Term Limits, said the fact that the Supreme Court took the case proved that it was not an easy legal call. ∎

## Chapter 7

HEALTH/
HUMAN SERVICES

Health Care Reform

Overview.. 319
    Chronology... 321
    Clinton Plan Highlights............................. 322
Committee Phase.................................... 324
    House Education and Labor....................... 324
        'Single Payer' System.......................... 326
    House Ways and Means 329
        Bill Highlights................................. 332
    House Energy and Commerce 335
    Senate Labor and Human Resources 336
    Senate Finance 338
        Dole Plan Highlights........................... 340
    Other Committees................................ 343
        Clinton, Committee Bills Compared............... 346
Leadership Phase................................... 348
    Gephardt Bill Highlights.......................... 349
    Mitchell Bill Highlights 351
    Clinton, Leadership Bills Compared................. 352
    Compromise Bill Highlights 354

Abortion

Abortion Clinic Access............................. 355
    Other Abortion Legislation 356
Other Health Legislation
Dietary Supplements 357
Minority Health Programs 358
Aid for Disabled 359
Tobacco Industry Controversy 359
Veterinary Drug Use............................... 360
Other Health-Related Legislation 361
Welfare
Welfare Reform.................................... 364
Social Security Independence....................... 366
Domestic Worker Tax.............................. 368
Head Start Reauthorization......................... 369
    Provisions..................................... 371
Child Nutrition 373
Child Support Enforcement......................... 375
Food Stamps..................................... 376
Holocaust Victims' Benefits......................... 377
Indian Independence 377
Other Indian Legislation............................ 378

HEALTH CARE

Clinton's Health Care Plan Laid to Rest

Democrats split over president's approach; most Republicans united in opposing the whole effort

The health care overhaul plan that President Clinton had made the signature of his presidency was officially declared dead Sept. 26. Senate Majority Leader George J. Mitchell, D-Maine, who had passed up a chance to serve on the Supreme Court to see the massive health care bill through, made its demise official at a news conference that day.

The failure of the ambitious plan to restructure the nation's health care system was all but certain in late August when lawmakers left Washington for an abbreviated summer recess without either chamber having passed a health care reform bill. House and Senate leaders maintained that they could complete work when they returned, but by then there was too little time and virtually no momentum left.

Democrats were divided over Clinton's approach, notably his proposals that employers pay for most of their workers' health costs and that the government be given a hands-on role in the health care system. Republicans, for the most part, were united in opposition to the whole effort, which they regarded as relying too heavily on taxes and regulation.

Although big business initially pushed for reform, many of its leaders became convinced that Cinton's proposal would mean new taxes and more detailed prescriptions from the federal government about what kind of health care insurance they could provide. Small-business groups worried that the costs would mean job losses, and they took that message to the public.

"Maybe it was too much to expect that in two years you could have changed so much of the health care system," reflected Sen. John D. Rockefeller IV, D-W.Va., one of the most stalwart supporters of Clinton's plan. "But we didn't know that when we started, and there wasn't any reason for us to know that."

In retrospect, however, it was possible to see at least three basic reasons why the process went awry.

First, Clinton's health care proposal, which sought to remake the entire system, suffered from being too sweeping and too difficult to explain to the public and to lawmakers. The very size of the bill made it vulnerable to criticism by special interests — notably the insurance industry, which used the bill's own language to lampoon the

administration in television advertisements and to raise fears about the legislation.

Second, the congressional committee process broke down, particularly in the House, with multiple committees given jurisdiction and no committee achieving a bipartisan consensus that could serve as a basis for floor action.

Third, there was never any visible effort by the Clinton administration and the Senate leadership to produce a bipartisan measure until the final weeks of the session, when it was too late. Democratic leaders, unwilling to break with Clinton's goal of providing affordable health coverage to all Americans, never made a meaningful compromise offer to Republicans.

GOP leaders, for their part, had the luxury of being in the minority and, therefore, without any ultimate responsibility for the legislation. That freed them to criticize Clinton and the Democrats rather than attempting to craft viable alternatives.

Too Big, Too Complex

From Sept. 22, 1993, the day Clinton unveiled his plan before a joint session of Congress, critics said the bill was too big and too complicated. Even supporters admitted it was an imposing document. In a unique move, the administration held a two-day "health care university" to explain the bill to lawmakers when it was first released on Capitol Hill.

Clinton wanted to provide permanent health care coverage to all Americans by requiring employers to pay 80 percent of the cost of a basic package of benefits for their employees. He proposed to control skyrocketing health care costs by capping the amount that insurance premiums could increase annually. Clinton also proposed that most Americans be required to buy insurance through new, large purchasing groups called alliances.

The proposal was met by an onslaught of negative ads and a barrage of news stories on the subject that left the public bewildered; polls showed public approval peaking with Clinton's speech and then steadily declining.

Conservative Republicans diagrammed the Clinton bill and came up with a mazelike picture that made the new system look like a bureau-

HEALTH CARE REFORM

Introduction .... p. 319
  Chronology .... p. 321
  Clinton plan highlights .... p. 322
Committee Action
  House Education and Labor ...... p. 324
  House Ways and Means .... p. 329
  House Energy and Commerce ..... p. 335
  Senate Labor and Human Resources. . p. 336
  Senate Finance .... p. 338
  Dole plan .... p. 340
  Other committees .... p. 343
  Committee bills compared .... p. 346
Leadership Bills .... p. 348
  Gephardt plan .... p. 349
  Mitchell plan .... p. 351
  Bills compared .... p. 352
  Compromise bill .... p. 354

cratic nightmare. The Health Insurance Association of America began running what became know as its "Harry and Louise" ads. One of the first showed the yuppie couple plowing through the Clinton Health Security Act, whose 1,342 pages rivaled the size of a dictionary. The couple pulled out technical-sounding provisions that, according to the ads, meant that Americans would pay more for less health care.

Lawmakers trying to sell the plan to constituents found they faced the uphill job of simultaneously explaining the new system and combating criticism of it. The administration did little to help, some members said. "They introduced this very complex piece of legislation and then decided all they would say were phrases that had been market-tested, like 'health care security,' " said Rep. Henry A. Waxman, D-Calif., a supporter of the bill. "That led the public to believe the administration was treating them in a superficial way, and they had something to hide. And then when the special interests, the insurers and the drug companies, attacked the bill, the public didn't know what to believe."

But there was no getting around the reality that the bill was immensely complex. Its simple goal was to provide affordable health insurance to all Americans by containing insurance prices and subsidizing care for those who could not afford insurance. But to achieve that end, the bill relied on an entirely new and hard-to-explain financing system.

New quasi-government entities, known as health alliances, were to be set up locally to collect insurance premiums and pay out the money to networks of health providers. The alliances, which were supposed to bolster consumers' purchasing power, quickly came to symbolize what many opponents said was an excessive reliance on government.

In addition, the bill reached to every problem area of the health care system, from workers' compensation to the lack of primary care doctors. "Things went off track with the very inclusiveness of their bill," said Sen. John H. Chafee, R-R.I., who authored a proposal that relied less on government regulation. "Why ever did they reach to things like workman's compensation, not to mention those mammoth alliances?"

Perhaps the final straw in terms of public understanding was the fact that Congress was writing its own complex bills at the same time that committees were working on the Clinton bill. As the Washington press corps scrambled to explain the flotilla of new approaches, the public just stopped reading.

Looking back, experts said it would have been better to start with something smaller that the public could understand. Americans rarely felt comfortable with broad changes made in one fell swoop, said Uwe Reinhardt, a professor of political economy at Princeton University. "In most legislation, America is an incremental country, and we have learned, health care too has to be done incrementally."

Institutional Breakdown

At every point in the congressional process, health care also proved too difficult for the institution to digest. The committee system, designed to resolve both the policy and political problems of legislation, broke down entirely.

During the first half of the year, five major committees and a host of secondary committees struggled to draft versions of the health care overhaul bill. In the end, none of the bills both met Clinton's requirement for universal coverage and had enough support to pass. As a result, on almost every key issue — from employer mandates to cost controls to the basic benefits package — the committee products were at best only building blocks for House and Senate Democratic leaders, who set out at midyear to craft their own bills.

"Typically, the committee process clears out the under-

brush on legislation. That didn't happen on health care," said Rep. David E. Skaggs, D-Colo.

Members and others suggested many reasons for the committees' shortcomings. The complexity of the issue and the number of bills being debated ranked high on everyone's list, but equally serious was the lack of a clear message from constituents.

"People are saying to us, 'Don't change the system, but whatever you do make sure there is coverage for everything but the kitchen sink,' " said Rep. Dan Glickman, D-Kan.

Even the interest groups seemed to lack clear consensus. Small insurance companies and big insurance companies had different priorities; doctors were divided among themselves, and there were many strains of opinions within the business community. Some big businesses supported the Clinton plan, while many small businesses vocally opposed it.

Disarray in the committee process had been foreshadowed the previous fall, when House and Senate leaders declined to resolve the competition for jurisdiction over the bill by rival panels.

In the House, the leadership referred the bill to all three committees that had major jurisdictional claims: Ways and Means, Energy and Commerce, and Education and Labor. Secondary referrals went to seven committees, which were charged with working on specific sections covering issues such as health care for veterans and American Indians, malpractice reform and insurance fraud.

In the Senate, the rules allowed only a single committee to have primary jurisdiction. Neither Finance Committee Chairman Daniel Patrick Moynihan, D-N.Y., nor Labor and Human Resources Committee Chairman Edward M. Kennedy, D-Mass., was willing to let the other have the prime position. Rather than choosing between them, the leadership left the bill on the calendar with plans to bring it directly to the floor in 1994. The Finance and Labor committees were left to draft rival bills that could be offered as floor amendments.

Partisan Approach

The leadership, which was supposed to hammer out compromises, was unable to find a formula that could draw a majority on the floor. Neither the administration nor the Democratic leaders realized until too late, the problem with pursuing a partisan strategy.

Only one committee, Senate Finance, produced a bipartisan bill. In the House, not one Republican voted for a health care bill in a major committee. Even the Democratic majorities were narrow, squeezed out by endless deal-making by Democrats who did not want to be the ones to kill health care early in the year.

Apparently misreading members' sentiment, the House Democratic leadership made the Ways and Means Committee version the basis for the bill they brought to the floor, ignoring the more modest, bipartisan proposals that conservative Democrats had been working on at the same time. The Ways and Means bill involved even more government control than Clinton's plan. As a result, it had no hope of winning Republican votes on the floor, and its Democratic support came almost entirely from the political left of the caucus.

"There were bipartisan bills around," said Burdett Loomis, a political science professor at the University of Kansas, "but they rejected them out of habit and the feeling that they couldn't trust enough Republicans to come on board. They've gotten out of the habit of bipartisanship, and they paid for it."

With the House deeply divided, many members looked to the Senate, led by the usually bipartisan Finance Committee, to show the way to a compromise. Eventually it did — with a

A Health Care Chronology

1993

Jan. 25: President Clinton appoints Hillary Rodham Clinton to head a task force to draft a comprehensive overhaul of the nation's health care system. The goals: to provide universal coverage and cut rising health care costs.

March 3: Rep. Jim McDermott, D-Wash., introduces a bill (HR 1200) to set up a Canadian-style, single-payer system.

May: Task force is disbanded; the Clintons work with Cabinet members and top advisers to flesh out the plan.

Sept. 22: Clinton unveils his long-awaited proposal in a nationally televised speech to a joint session of Congress. His bottom line: universal coverage.

Oct. 6: Reps. Jim Cooper, D-Tenn., and Fred Grandy, R-Iowa, introduce a bill (HR 3222) to increase coverage by reorganizing the health insurance market.

Nov. 20: Clinton's 1,342-page health care bill is introduced (HR 3600, S 1757). House leaders refer entire bill to three committees; two Senate panels compete to take the lead.

Nov. 22: Sen. John H. Chafee, R-R.I., introduces a bill (S 1770) requiring that all Americans have health insurance by 2005.

1994

Jan. 25: In his State of the Union address, Clinton vows to veto any health bill that does not guarantee universal coverage.

June 9: Senate Labor and Human Resources becomes the first full committee to complete work, voting 11-6 along mainly partisan lines to approve a bill modeled on Clinton's plan.

June 23: House Education and Labor Committee votes 26-17 for an expanded version of Clinton's plan. To win the votes of the most liberal members, the committee also sends to the floor without recommendation a single-payer plan (HR 3690).

June 28: House Energy and Commerce Committee Chairman John D. Dingell, D-Mich., notifies leadership that his panel, often seen as a bellwether of congressional opinion, cannot agree on a health care bill.

June 30: House Ways and Means Committee approves a Clinton-style bill, 20-18. "No" votes include all 14 Republicans, joined by three conservative Democrats and one liberal.

July 2: Senate Finance Committee approves the only bipartisan measure to emerge from a committee; the vote is 12-8.

July 21: Democratic leaders tell Clinton his bill will have to be scaled back.

July 29: Majority Leader Richard A. Gephardt, D-Mo., unveils a House leadership bill.

Aug. 2: Majority Leader George J. Mitchell, D-Maine, releases a Senate leadership bill.

Aug. 9: The Senate begins floor debate on the Mitchell bill.

Aug. 19: A rump group of senators — led by Chafee and John B. Breaux, D-La., and known as the Mainstream Group — offers a bipartisan compromise.

Aug. 25: After a bitter debate on the crime bill, the Senate starts its August recess without finishing a health care bill. The next day, Mitchell scraps his bill, conceding that comprehensive health care reform will not come in 1994.

Sept. 26: Mitchell declares health care dead for the year, after a compromise bill that he negotiated with the Mainstream Group fails to attract enough votes.

---

bill that settled for expanding coverage rather than guaranteeing it for all Americans — but it was too late in the game to make a difference in the final outcome.

The committee had proved curiously impotent for months, largely the result of a lack of interest in the issue by Chairman Moynihan. "It was sort of a strange thing the way Sen. Moynihan never got viscerally attached to the health care effort," said Chafee, a Finance Committee member.

The administration, which could have stepped in with a compromise, did not do so because it was loath to give up Clinton's goal of achieving universal coverage. Adherence to that goal drove the administration to stick with a number of other deeply controversial policies, including the requirement that employers pay for most of their employer's health insurance — for which there was never a majority of votes in the Senate — and cost controls, which were even less popular but which would have been necessary to make universal coverage affordable.

"They knew last spring they didn't have the votes, but they kept hoping that something like it would pass, and they kept saying the one thing they couldn't give up was universal coverage," said Sen. Orrin G. Hatch, R-Utah, a member of the Finance Committee who met with administration emissaries on several occasions. "They wanted this big legislative victory, but what they got was a big legislative sinkhole."

Background

Though he offered few details, Clinton had promised repeatedly during his 1992 presidential campaign that he would reform the nation's health care system.

On Jan. 25, 1993, five days after his inauguration, Clinton appointed his wife, Hillary Rodham Clinton, to head a Task Force on National Health Care Reform to draw up plans for a massive health care overhaul. The task force mandate was to draft a proposal that guaranteed health care coverage for all Americans — about 35 million were uninsured — while limiting costs. At the end of January, Clinton optimistically declared that he would send Congress a proposal within 90 days and that he expected lawmakers to complete their work on it by the end of the year. *(1993 Almanac, p. 335)*

Health care reform quickly became the Clinton administration's central focus. The arguments for action seemed compelling to many. Big business was pressing for changes

that would reduce health care costs. Most Americans seemed to feel strongly: a Wall Street Journal/NBC News poll published in March showed 74 percent of those polled believed an overhaul was needed; 66 percent said they would pay higher taxes to fix the health care system.

Clinton argued that controlling the soaring costs of health care was critical to reducing the federal deficit, enabling U.S. business to compete successfully in the world market and maintaining U.S. living standards. The Clintons insisted that a system of universal coverage with cost controls was the only answer: If the government attempted to control costs in a portion of the health care system, such as Medicare, the health care industry would simply make up the difference by increasing costs elsewhere.

Although Hillary Clinton and others consulted intensively with members of Congress, the task force carried out its work behind closed doors. The initial deadline passed without a final proposal. The task force disbanded in May, and over the summer, the Clintons worked with Cabinet members and other key advisers to fill in the plan's details.

Finally, on Sept. 22, Clinton unveiled his long-awaited proposal in a nationally televised speech to a joint session of Congress. The symbolic high point came when he waved a prototype of a "Health Security Card," which he said would guarantee every American health insurance and health care. "Let us agree on this," he said. "Whatever else we disagree on, before this Congress finishes its work next year, you will pass, and I will sign, legislation to guarantee . . . security to every citizen."

Clinton Plan Highlights

Clinton's health care overhaul bill, introduced Nov. 20, 1993 (HR 3600, S 1757), contained provisions to:

• **Universal coverage.** Require all citizens to enroll in a health plan. Employers would pay at least about 80 percent of the average local cost of their employees' health plans; employees would pay the balance. The government would subsidize low-income individuals and families, as well as businesses with fewer than 75 employees.

All health plans would have to offer comprehensive benefits including mental health care, preventive dental care for children and some long-term care. Plans could not charge extra for particular benefits, nor could they limit the use of benefits. However, some benefits would be covered fully only with the consent of the plan.

• **Long-term care.** Create a federal entitlement program for states to pay for home health-care services for eligible individuals. The program would be financed predominantly by the federal government; states would pay a 5 percent to 22 percent match. The administration viewed this as a down payment toward full-fledged long-term care coverage. Eligibility was to be based not on income but on whether an individual met the federal criteria of needing help with at least three activities of daily living, such as eating, going to the bathroom and getting dressed. Nursing home care was not covered, but the grants would cover an extensive list of home health care services and adult day care.

• **Cost sharing.** Limit health insurance premiums to 3.9 percent of an individual's income. Most consumers would choose among three payment formulas: a low-cost plan that was likely to provide care through a health maintenance organization (HMO) with a limited choice of doctors; a mid-price plan that offered care through a loose network of doctors with an option for consumers to go outside the network; and a high-cost plan that allowed consumers to choose their own doctors. Costs would vary by region and by family status, with the amount that each person paid pegged to employment status.

• **Employer and employee responsibilities.** Divide employers into three categories: small, defined as those with fewer than 75 employees; large, defined as those with more than 5,000 employees; and all others. Taxes, subsidies and other financial responsibilities would vary widely among these groups. Self-employed people would be treated as small businesses and would be eligible for the same subsidies on the employer share (80 percent) of the premium as other small businesses.

Employees would be responsible for about 20 percent of the cost. However, the portion of the premium paid by employees would vary depending on employment status (full time, part time, self-employed or retired), income, and family status (single, married or married with children).

• **National Health Board.** Create a new federal entity, known as the National Health Board, to oversee the new system, setting quality standards and reviewing the benefits packages. It would act as a

clearinghouse for information about the new system's problems and would approve state plans. Without National Health Board approval, no state could receive federal subsidies.

• **Other federal responsibilities.** Provide for the Department of Health and Human Services (HHS) and the Department of Labor to oversee the new system jointly. HHS would oversee alliance enrollment policies, premium and cost-sharing discounts and the alliances' overall financial management. HHS would set up a board, called the Advisory Council on Breakthrough Drugs, to review new drug prices. It would publish information about the reasonableness of prices and the cost-effectiveness of new products compared with existing treatments.

The Labor Department would enforce the sections of the bill that dealt with employer premium payments and the creation and operation of corporate alliances. It also would set up an insolvency fund to pay providers and ensure that enrollees continued to have care if a corporate alliance failed.

A new National Quality Management Council would develop national performance measures to be used in assessing every health plan in the country, and would collect and disseminate data on the plans. All health alliances would have to publish clear information for consumers on how local health-care plans were doing in terms of the national quality measures.

• **State role.** Allow states to choose between a Canadian-style single-payer system or a managed-competition system. Once a state chose a system, state flexibility would be limited by federal rules and standards designed to ensure that despite state differences, residents had comparable choices.

States would have an ambiguous role: They would be responsible for making the new system work but would have little latitude to adjust the system's design. States would monitor the local health-care industry, enforce new laws and continue to finance health-care services for poor Americans. However, several state laws would be preempted.

• **Health alliances.** Provide for quasi-governmental entities, to be set up by the states. These health alliances would coordinate the health care system for consumers in a region, replacing the role of insurance companies and employee benefits managers. A regional alliance could be set up as a private nonprofit corporation or as a state agency. Generally, a regional alliance's enrollees would primarily be full-time and part-time employees of businesses of fewer than 5,000 workers, the self-employed, and the working and non-working poor, whose health care would be subsidized by the government. The alliance would be the fiscal heart of the new system, in many states handling hundreds of millions of dollars annually.

All states would permit "corporate alliances" — health care buying groups set up by companies with more than 5,000 employees, by unions or by the Rural Electric and Rural Telephone Cooperatives. The rationale would be to allow large multistate

Clinton's Bill

Clinton's health care bill was not formally introduced until Nov. 20 (HR 3600, S 1757). *(Highlights, 322)*

It offered guaranteed coverage from birth to death for all Americans. Employers were to pay 80 percent of their employee's health insurance costs, with the employees paying the rest. To provide subsidies to small businesses and the poor, the plan called for cuts in Medicare, the federal health insurance program for the elderly, and Medicaid, the federal program for the poor. It also included a 75-cents-a-pack increase in the cigarette tax and a tax on large employers that did not join health alliances.

To make this system work, the bill outlined a new framework for the purchase and regulation of health insurance and the delivery of health care. The federal government would determine a basic package of health benefits to be offered under all plans, set the standards of care and reorganize the market. Once the system was in place, the government would be its watchdog and enforcer.

Consumers would be organized into large purchasing blocs, or health alliances, to bargain for lower prices from medical providers. Health care providers would be organized into "health plans" — groups of doctors, hospitals and other caregivers — who would offer the guaranteed package of benefits to consumers. The alliances would help members choose among plans by supplying them with consumer information. Consumers would pay insurance premiums to the alliance, which would funnel the money to the

---

employers to avoid having to keep track of many different states' health insurance laws.

● **Health plans.** Require most consumers to select a health plan rather than an individual doctor. The plan would be required to offer a package of guaranteed benefits, providing subscribers with access to a group of doctors (primary care physicians and specialists), hospitals, non-physician care providers such as physical therapists, and outpatient clinics that offered services such as mental health treatment. Several plans probably would organize as HMOs or similar networks. Plans could be organized by health-care providers or by an insurance company. Plans could not turn down any subscriber for any reason, nor could they force anyone to pay a surcharge because of an illness or disability.

● **Public health.** Redesign funding of the public health care system to create a block grant program for states. The grants could be used for collecting health data, environmental protection, violence reduction programs and public education about the hazards of tobacco, drugs and behavior that increased the risk of AIDS. The bill called for a total of $325 million for such grants in fiscal 1996, $450 million in fiscal 1997 and up to $750 million in 2000.

The bill also authorized $175 million in fiscal 1996 and $200 million from fiscal 1997 through 2000 for a separate HHS grant program to encourage disease prevention.

● **Medicare.** Retain the existing framework of Medicare, the government's health insurance program for the elderly. In the only major change to Medicare benefits, the bill would provide coverage for prescription drugs for Medicare beneficiaries for the first time.

The price of Medicare coverage would rise sharply for wealthier beneficiaries. The program's rate of growth would be sharply reduced, with most of the cuts borne by doctors and hospitals. The working elderly and their spouses would be required to buy health care through alliances rather than through Medicare.

● **Medicaid.** Subsume Medicaid, the federal-state health insurance program for the poor, into the new health alliance system. Medicaid patients would receive the same benefits package as other Americans. For patients who were receiving such services as transportation or translators, that would mean a reduction in benefits.

● **Malpractice, fraud and antitrust law.** Require each health alliance to adopt an "alternative dispute resolution" system in an effort to avoid going to court over malpractice claims.

The bill also provided for a program to prevent health care fraud and abuse. And it proposed to repeal the McCarran-Ferguson Act of 1945, which effectively exempted the insurance industry from federal antitrust law.

● **Cost controls.** Limit the annual rise in consumers' costs by controlling the percentage that premiums could rise. That would force health plans to limit payments and profits to doctors, hospitals and suppliers of medical equipment and pharmaceuticals. The bill also limited the amount the government could spend annually on subsidies for employers and individuals.

● **Tobacco tax.** Raise the excise tax on cigarettes by 75 cents a pack, effective Oct. 1, 1994, bringing the federal tax on cigarettes to 99 cents. Taxes on other tobacco products would be subject to comparable increases.

● **Corporate alliance tax.** Require corporations of more than 5,000 employees that chose to provide health care through their own alliance to pay a tax equal to 1 percent of their total payroll.

The assessment would begin Jan. 1, 1996, and would help fund academic medical centers, which were being funded through Medicare.

● **Other taxes.** Make a host of other changes in the tax code, including provisions to:

• Require wealthy taxpayers who enrolled in Medicare Part B, which subsidized physician care, to pay more on their individual income taxes. The change would effectively raise Medicare Part B tax payments for these taxpayers from roughly 25 percent of the program's costs to about 75 percent. It would affect individuals with incomes of $90,000 or more (including adjusted gross income and tax-exempt interest income) and joint filers with incomes of $115,000 or more.

• Require all state and local government employees and their employers to pay the hospital insurance portion of the FICA (Social Security) tax, making them eligible for Medicare coverage.

• Impose a 1.5 percent assessment on premiums purchased through regional alliances to help underwrite academic medical centers and medical education.

• Require individuals to report benefits received under cafeteria plans as income for the purpose of calculating taxes owed. Beginning in 2003, employees would be taxed on supplemental health coverage paid by employers.

• Permit self-employed people to deduct the entire cost of premiums paid to a health alliance for the benefits package.

• Require higher-income taxpayers who retired between the ages of 55 and 64 to repay subsidies provided for the employer share of their health insurance premiums. Repayment would be required for individual taxpayers with incomes over $90,000 and couples making above $115,000.

• Prevent employers from receiving a tax break for contributions to so-called retiree medical accounts, used for medical expenses as part of a pension plan.

• Exempt regional health alliances established under the bill from federal income tax.

• Permit individuals to claim a tax deduction on premiums for qualified long-term care insurance. In addition, taxpayers could exclude from their taxable income up to $150 a day for benefits paid through long-term care policies. The $150 cap would rise with inflation. Incapacitated people could claim a deduction for qualified long-term care expenses.

• Allow employers to claim a tax deduction on premiums paid on behalf of employees for long-term care coverage.

• Provide a tax credit of up to $7,500 to help defray the cost of certain services related to daily living purchased by the physically impaired.

• Provide a tax credit of up to $1,000 per month for up to 60 months for qualified physicians who practiced in areas with a shortage of doctors. ■

providers. To control costs, the bill provided for a cap on insurance premiums.

Key to Clinton's plan were checks and balances designed to protect consumers' rights and ensure that all players fulfilled their responsibilities.

In February 1994, the Congressional Budget Office (CBO) issued an analysis of the Clinton plan, spelling out its potential economic consequences for the nation and the federal Treasury. CBO estimated that the plan would increase the federal deficit by $74 billion between 1995 and 2000 and by $126 billion between 1995 and 2004, at which point its effect on the deficit would be less than $500 million. After that, the plan would help reduce the deficit.

CBO also ruled that the premiums that businesses and individuals would pay to the new health alliances should be included in the federal budget because payments were mandatory and integral to financing a new health care entitlement. By 2004, $750 billion a year would flow through the alliances. Clinton argued that the alliances were not federal entities and did not need to be included in the budget.

Alternative Plans

By the time Clinton's bill arrived on Capitol Hill, several alternative proposals were gaining adherents in Congress.

From liberal Democrats came a plan for a Candian-style single-payer system, under which the government would replace private insurance companies, collecting premiums and paying health care providers. The plan promised to cover everyone, control prices, impose massive new taxes and sharply cut health care profits. Rep. Jim McDermott, D-Wash., was its leading proponent. (*Single payer, p. 326*)

From the other end of the ideological spectrum came Republican plans, including one by Sen. Phil Gramm of Texas, to minimize government involvement in health care and instead encourage consumers to put aside savings for their own health care expenses.

The two leading alternatives emerging from centerfield were sponsored by Rep. Jim Cooper D-Tenn., and Sen. Chafee. Neither bill included an employer mandate. Both aimed to reorganize the health care market, rather than controlling it through government regulation. (*1993 Almanac, p. 344*)

The Cooper plan, backed in the Senate by John B. Breaux, D-La., got a boost Feb. 2, 1994, when the Business Roundtable, an influential group of 200 corporate leaders, endorsed it as "the best starting point for reform."

HOUSE EDUCATION AND LABOR

Subsidized Premiums, Generous Benefits

The Education and Labor Committee on June 23 became the first House committee to approve its version of the health care bill (HR 3600 — H Rept 103-601, Part 2). The liberal-leaning panel endorsed an expanded version of Clinton's plan, filled with extra medical benefits and insurance premium subsidies.

As approved by the committee, the bill required employers to pay at least 80 percent of the health insurance premiums for their workers as a means to guarantee health coverage for all Americans. It included significant subsidies to help small businesses pay this cost, and it mandated a large, generous package of benefits that all health insurance policies would

have to offer. It made Clinton's quasi-governmental health care alliances optional for states.

The committee also reported without recommendation a single-payer plan (HR 3960) that required the government to run the insurance system. (*Single payer, p. 326*)

The committee's 1,200-plus page bill represented more than three years of hearings and work. The full committee spent eight days working on the bill, acting on 87 amendments, 46 of which were adopted. The panel's Subcommittee on Labor-Management Relations had worked for five weeks on the bill, from April 21 through May 25.

The amendments that won approval generally dealt with peripheral issues — who was to be a primary care provider, for example. For the most part, the bill's core provisions stayed intact through subcommittee and full committee action.

Republicans took the marathon effort very seriously. Attendance was high, and Republicans offered 49 amendments in full committee, many of which were not intended to embarrass Democrats or to make political points. The committee adopted 10 GOP amendments.

Democrats claimed success with their strategy of producing a bill that was not so costly and bureaucratic as to render their action irrelevant, but that included a wide variety of benefits for members to vote on. Labor-Management Relations Subcommittee Chairman Pat Williams, D-Mont., said it was "obviously more expensive than the final bill will be." But he said he thought the committee had carefully navigated between generous benefits and high costs.

Subcommittee Action

On May 25, the Subcommittee on Labor-Management Relations approved its version of HR 3600 by a party-line vote of 17-10. Subcommittee Chairman Williams described the vote as a major victory for Clinton because the bill held true to the president's broad goals of comprehensive coverage for every American, paid primarily by employers.

The bill included the requirement that employers pay 80 percent of their workers' health insurance premiums. But Williams modified Clinton's mandatory, quasi-governmental health purchasing alliances, allowing states to decide whether to run a single-payer system or set up voluntary or mandatory alliances.

In a series of amendments over five weeks of debate, the panel expanded dental care and mental health benefits, increased subsidies to small businesses and low-income families, and expanded preventive care to include a wide range of cancer screenings, such as mammograms.

The panel defeated repeated Republican attempts to scale back medical benefits, eliminate the employer mandate and prohibit abortion services.

As introduced by Williams, the bill required that businesses with more than 5,000 workers buy their own health insurance and pay a 1 percent payroll tax. During the markup, Williams won approval for an amendment to reduce his threshold to companies with more than 1,000 workers. (Under Clinton's plan, companies of more than 5,000 would be allowed to choose between a health alliance and self-insurance, with those choosing self-insurance paying the 1 percent tax.)

Steve Gunderson, R-Wis., tried repeatedly in subcommittee to allow virtually any firm with a viable self-insurance plan to opt out of the alliances, but those amendments failed.

● **GOP alternative.** One of the first subcommittee actions was to defeat a Republican-sponsored alternative. Unwilling to compromise at such an early stage of the game, Williams spoke passionately against the GOP substitute offered May 3

by ranking Republican Marge Roukema of New Jersey. Members rejected the proposal on a party-line vote of 10-16.

Roukema's amendment called for incremental changes rather than a complete overhaul of health care, and it contained a variety of proposed changes to the health insurance industry. It required employers to offer — but not pay for — health insurance for their workers. Businesses with fewer than 50 employees could band together to voluntarily increase their bargaining power with insurance companies for better policies and prices.

To prohibit exclusion of businesses with very ill workers, these small groups were to define themselves using a touchstone such as geographic area or occupation. Once the group was defined, no business that met the definition could be excluded from the insurance pool.

Roukema also wanted to hold down the cost of insurance policies; premiums could not vary by more than 15 percent for businesses with similar demographics. Finally, under most circumstances, the GOP substitute barred insurers from excluding people with pre-existing conditions from purchasing a policy. Pregnancy could not be defined as a pre-existing condition.

Roukema said her bill would "address the most glaring faults of our system," without tearing apart what was good about health care in the United States.

● **Employer mandate.** Partisan differences surfaced again on May 5, when Republicans, led by John A. Boehner of Ohio, attempted to delete employer mandates from the bill. Again, the GOP proposal was rejected on a straight party-line vote — 10-17.

● **Abortion coverage.** On May 12, the subcommittee beat back attempts to delete abortion services from the basic benefits package that every American would have to purchase. Abortion was not mentioned directly in Clinton's bill, nor in the substitute crafted by Williams. But the administration said it would be covered.

The subcommittee defeated, 11-16, an amendment by Ron Klink, D-Pa., to take abortion out of the benefits package but allow women to purchase it as a supplement to their regular insurance.

Members also rejected, 11-14, an amendment by Dick Armey, R-Texas, to stipulate that nothing in the bill could supersede state abortion laws or the laws in any subdivision of a state.

The three-hour abortion debate turned into a personal, caustic fight. "Americans should not be put in the place of funding abortion when they morally oppose it," said Klink, who called abortion a "land mine beneath the surface" of the health debate. Jolene Unsoeld, D-Wash., replied that denying women full reproductive benefits would be denying them "the coverage that you men have."

But Armey said he was tired of the argument that "abortion is not about anybody but the woman's right to choose" and said he did not want to condone the "self-indulgent conduct" of women who had already demonstrated that they were "damned careless" with their bodies.

In an attempt to deflect the abortion controversy, on May 17, Gunderson offered an amendment to strike from the bill the entire package of guaranteed benefits. Essential decisions about which procedures would be covered by health plans would be left to a National Health Board, a seven-member panel that under the Clinton plan was to be appointed by the president.

But Williams said that taxpayers "deserve to know what benefits they're going to get before the president signs this legislation." The subcommittee rejected the amendment by voice vote.

Subcommittee Amendments Adopted

During the five weeks of subcommittee consideration, the panel approved a variety of other amendments, most by voice vote, including proposals by:

● Armey to increase from one to two the number of fee-for-service options offered by states or alliances. Under fee-for-service plans, doctors were paid for each treatment.

● Eliot L. Engel, D-N.Y., to allow state and local governments with more than 5,000 people in their health care plans to opt to keep their existing insurance programs and not be a part of the regional health care purchasing groups. If they decided to do so, they had to pay a payroll tax of 1 percent.

A second Engel amendment, approved 17-9, lowered the costs to state and local governments that decided to join health care cooperatives.

● Gene Green, D-Texas, to set out grievance procedures for health care providers who had been removed from a regional health care network. The panel also approved a Green amendment to allow people to pay their doctors directly for health care when the doctors were not a part of the person's health care plan.

● Gunderson, to clarify that states could not tax out-of-state companies to help pay for health benefits beyond the basic package.

● Peter Hoekstra, R-Mich., to place a 1 percent payroll tax on employers with health insurance plans negotiated by unions.

● Howard P. "Buck" McKeon, R-Calif., to include community health networks in the definition of a health plan.

● George Miller, D-Calif., to expand dramatically the mental health benefits in the bill. Miller said his proposal could add as much as $224 annually to an individual's insurance premium. The amendment increased from 30 to 90 days the period for which a person's insurance would cover hospital care for mental health reasons. It also allowed unlimited visits for substance abuse counseling, while Williams' plan would have limited this coverage to about 30 sessions.

Miller also won approval for an amendment to make a variety of dental services available to adults as basic benefits from the outset. Williams' bill would have provided such dental benefits beginning in 2001. Williams opposed the amendment, which he said would add an estimated $7.3 billion annually to the bill's cost, without finding some way to pay for it.

● Donald M. Payne, D-N.J., to increase benefits in the bill for poor pregnant women during their pregnancy and for two months after delivery. Although the amendment would increase the bill's cost by as much as $3 billion over five years, Williams said he supported it because he believed the benefits should never have been left out of the original Clinton bill.

● Unsoeld, to require the secretary of Labor to negotiate a fee schedule for benefits not covered in the general package that might be given to certain federal workers as part of their workers' compensation package. The panel adopted a second Unsoeld amendment to cover as basic benefits classes for pregnant women who wanted to stop smoking.

● Williams, to force all companies with more than 1,000 workers to buy their own health insurance and pay a 1 percent payroll tax, offsetting the additional expenses by about $25 billion.

Members rejected, 11-15, an alternative by Gunderson that would have reduced, from 5,000 workers to 50, the size of firms permitted to buy outside the alliance.

Amendments Rejected

The panel rejected a host of other amendments, including proposals by Armey to:

● Eliminate caps on insurance premiums, rejected 10-17.

'Single Payer' Bill to Floor

On June 23, the House Education and Labor Committee narrowly voted to send to the floor a radical health care proposal that was given almost no chance of passage.

The bill (HR 3960 — H Rept 103-618, Part 1) proposed a nationwide "single payer" system, in which the federal government would collect health insurance premiums and pay providers. The most far-reaching plan under consideration by any congressional panel, the bill aimed to eliminate the need for health insurance companies and give control of most of the health care system to the government.

Like the variants on the Clinton health care plan approved by congressional committees, it died at the end of the session without seeing any floor action.

The committee did not approve the bill. Rather, it voted 22-21 to report the measure to the floor without recommendation, pushing it forward but without a stamp of approval. The action was quick, with only one member, sponsor George Miller, D-Calif., speaking in favor of the bill. It came immediately after the committee's lengthy consideration of HR 3600, its version of President Clinton's health care overhaul bill. *(Committee action, p. 324)*

Committee Chairman William D. Ford, D-Mich., allowed the vote on the single-payer bill as a part of a deal that he and Pat Williams, D-Mont., chairman of the Labor-Management Relations Subcommittee, struck with single-payer advocates. In return, all 15 single-payer supporters on the committee voted for HR 3600, providing a margin of support that was broader than that achieved in any other House committee.

Despite the deal, Ford had to work hard to get the single-payer bill out of the committee. Six Democrats joined every Republican in voting against it, even though it was to be sent to the floor without recommendation. Gene Green, a freshman Democrat from Texas, at first voted present. But once it became clear that the motion to report would fail, Green changed his vote to "aye."

About 100 House Democrats backed the single-payer plan. That was far short of the votes needed to win passage for their bill, but the group did represent a significant bloc of votes that could ease passage of — or derail — whatever health care bill the Democratic leadership eventually sent to the floor.

The Labor-Management Relations Subcommittee had approved HR 3960 on June 9 by voice vote. Subcommittee Republicans largely ignored the markup. Marge Roukema of New Jersey was the only Republican to attend the entire one-day session, and she offered no amendments.

The single-payer concept drew on the experience of Canada and some countries in Western Europe, where governments had taken control of the health care system and citizens received care regardless of their ability to pay. The single-payer bill proposed a system under which people would no longer receive health care benefits or insurance through their employers. Instead, every citizen would be issued a health security card; they could chose to go to any doctor or hospital, and the cost would be paid by the government.

The plan was to be financed by a sliding-scale federal payroll tax on employers of up to 8.4 percent. Individuals would pay an additional 2.1 percent in federal income tax. The federal government would distribute the money to the states to administer the plans.

During the markup, Roukema argued that the problems Canada had experienced with its health care system — including rationing of services — would result if a single-payer plan were implemented in the United States. "Everybody knows . . . rationing goes on by waiting lists," she said. Miller responded angrily that rationing in the form of people waiting endlessly in hospital emergency rooms already was a "daily occurrence for millions of Americans."

● Eliminate premium caps during the transition between the plan's enactment and implementation, rejected 10-17.

● Allow patients to pay more for a doctor's service than the established rate, rejected 10-17.

● Eliminate a provision prohibiting people from directly paying for their health care, rejected 10-17.

● Eliminate criminal or civil penalties for people who did not pay their portion of insurance premiums, rejected 8-18.

● Strike requirements that by 2000, more medical graduate students be generalists rather than specialists, rejected 8-18.

● Remove provisions from the bill that he said would force medical schools to use racial and ethnic quotas in admissions, rejected 8-18.

The subcommittee also rejected amendments by:

● Cass Ballenger, R-N.C., to change federal labor law to make union-negotiated health care benefits beyond the mandated federal package a "permissive" subject of collective bargaining. Once a benefit was classified as "permissive," neither workers nor managers had to negotiate it, and it could not become grounds for a strike. Existing law made all health care benefits mandatory. The amendment was rejected by voice vote.

● Harris W. Fawell, R-Ill., to delete a provision in the bill requiring individuals not covered by an employer's insurance to purchase one of the government-defined health care policies; rejected 10-17.

The subcommittee also rejected, 10-17, a Fawell proposal to prohibit states from setting up single-payer systems.

● Green to prohibit states from requiring that a person join an alliance, even if the state set it up; rejected 12-15.

● Gunderson to allow businesses with fewer than 5,000 workers to opt out of health alliances. Clinton's proposal allowed businesses with more than 5,000 employees to opt out. Williams required that those businesses stay out.

Gunderson's amendment would have allowed virtually any business with a viable self-insurance plan to opt out. He said he recognized that if companies with healthier employees opted out, insurance costs could rise for those left in the alliance. To pay for this problem, he proposed to allow an assessment on companies that were outside alliances. The amendment was rejected 10-17.

● Hoekstra to strike the Williams provisions prohibiting employers of 5,000 or more from joining alliances; rejected 10-15.

● Austin J. Murphy, D-Pa., to require all hospitals in a health plan to disclose the compensation for their administrators, physicians, executives and board members; rejected by voice vote.

● Major R. Owens, D-N.Y., to help the poor pay their health

care costs. His amendment was defeated 12-15, with five Democrats joining the Republicans in opposition. However, a revised version of this amendment was approved by the full committee.

Under Williams' bill, people who received cash payments from the government, such as Aid to Families With Dependent Children, would not have had to pay premiums and would have been required to pay minimal co-payments. That did not cover the 40 percent of the users of Medicaid who did not receive any cash assistance. Under Williams' bill, those people were to be treated like everyone else, paying deductibles and annual premiums.

Owens' goal was to reduce co-payment costs for this population. He offered an amendment to set co-payments for people who earned less than 150 percent of the poverty level ($14,800 for a family of four) at no more than $2 per doctor visit or $1 per prescription. To pay for this, he proposed to increase the out-of-pocket costs for catastrophic illnesses from $1,500 to $2,500. After this adjustment, his amendment would have raised premiums by 1.5 percent across the board.

● Payne to require health plans to pay for second opinions from doctors outside the plan for poor people when there was a disagreement over whether a service should be covered. The amendment was rejected by voice vote.

● Roukema to eliminate the states' ability to set reimbursement rates for fee-for-service plans. Williams' bill gave states the power to negotiate payment schedules to ensure that they met national health spending goals. Roukema's amendment also would have dropped a requirement that each state or alliance negotiate with providers on a fee schedule for fee-for-service plans. It was rejected 10-17.

Full Committee Action

The full Education and Labor Committee approved the bill June 23 by a vote of 26-17.

Because of its ideological bent, the panel had been portrayed as a minor player on health care, but its early endorsement of Clinton's goals seemed to give the White House plan a push forward. "I have never been so proud to be associated with this committee," Chairman William D. Ford, D-Mich., told a packed hearing room at the conclusion of the markup. Ford had been on the panel since 1965 and was set to retire at the end of the 103rd Congress.

Every Republican and two Democrats — Robert E. Andrews of New Jersey and Scotty Baesler of Kentucky — voted against the bill, which Republicans dubbed "Clinton chubby." Roukema said she opposed it because it "promises extensive and costly benefits but provides no realistic means of financing them."

Before approving the bill, the committee acted on a variety of amendments:

● **Opting out of alliances.** The lack of cost estimates for the bill played into a weeklong debate on which businesses should be allowed to negotiate on their own for health insurance for their workers. Clinton's proposal gave this option to businesses with 5,000 or more employees; the subcommittee bill reduced the threshold to 1,000, and required those businesses to stay out of the large insurance pools that would cover most workers. Under both proposals, businesses not in the pool would pay a 1 percent payroll tax.

The full committee easily rejected, 19-23, an amendment by Gunderson that would have set the threshold at businesses with 50 or more workers.

But Democrats tried hard to find a way to agree with a move by Tim Roemer, D-Ind., to allow businesses with 500 to 1,000 workers a choice of whether to create their own plans

or get into the larger pool. Under Roemer's amendment, companies with more than 1,000 employees would have been required to find their own coverage.

The amendment was rejected 17-24 on June 23 when committee aides could not estimate what it would cost or what the effect would be on the cost of insurance for companies in the pool. Ford worked to defeat the amendment but promised to work with Roemer before floor action in an effort to reduce the threshold.

● **Limiting benefit costs.** Roemer met with even more opposition on an amendment to give the National Health Board, to be created under the bill, authority to review the standard benefits package for its effects on the federal budget. If the board found that benefits would add to the deficit, it could recommend benefit cuts or additional taxes.

The proposal was modeled on the 1990 law (PL 101-510) that established a procedure for selecting domestic military bases for closure on the basis of military need. As was the case with recommendations of the base-closing commission, once the health board had made its proposals, Congress would have had to vote them up or down, with no amendments allowed.

Supporters of the amendment said it was necessary to inject fiscal reality into the health care debate. Opponents said it would give inordinate decision-making power to an appointed group insulated from voters' objections. The committee rejected the amendment 13-29.

● **Other GOP amendments.** Other Republican attempts to chip away at the bill's structure and its guarantees of benefits met with similar fates.

The full committee June 14 turned back a renewed GOP effort to strip the requirement that employers pay at least 80 percent of the cost of their workers' health insurance premiums. But three Democrats — Roemer, Andrews and Baesler — joined the 15 Republicans in voting for the amendment. The amendment was rejected 18-25.

The committee also rejected Republican amendments that would have:

● Made changes in the insurance industry and in the medical malpractice system, but left much of the health care system alone. The substitute amendment, by ranking committee Republican Bill Goodling of Pennsylvania, was rejected 15-28.

● Allowed people to purchase health insurance plans that did not meet the bill's standards for mandated benefits. The amendment, by Fawell, was rejected 16-27.

● Stripped from the bill a Clinton proposal to provide relatively generous health benefits to people who retired before age 65 and who made less than $90,000. The amendment, by Hoekstra, was rejected 15-28.

● Exempted disabled people who employed someone to help them from the requirement that they provide that worker with health care insurance. The amendment, by Ballenger, was rejected on a voice vote.

● Stripped premium caps from the bill. The amendment, by Armey, was rejected 14-26.

● Removed penalties in the bill for people who did not pay their portion of health care premiums. The amendment, by Armey, was rejected 15-27.

● Deleted the separate health program for seasonal and migrant workers. The amendment, by Hoekstra, was rejected 18-25.

● Eliminated a state's ability to set reimbursement rates for fee-for-service plans. The amendment, offered by Roukema, was rejected on a voice vote.

● Substituted a formula for deciding reimbursement rates for fee-for-service providers instead of the bill's fee schedule.

The amendment, offered by Tom Petri, R-Wis., was rejected 14-28.

● **Abortion.** On June 23, the committee rejected, 17-25, an amendment by Klink that would have stripped abortion from services covered under the package. The committee also rejected, 20-23, a Klink amendment specifying that a national health care law could not bar enforcement of constitutional state abortion regulations.

The Supreme Court had said that states could impose conditions on a woman's right to an abortion — such as a short waiting period — as long as the rules did not constitute an "undue burden" on the underlying right to an abortion.

The committee also rejected by voice vote an amendment by Gunderson offered as a compromise on abortion. Gunderson's amendment would have required each health insurance provider to offer two nearly identical plans — one that included abortion coverage and one that did not.

Other Committee Amendments Adopted

During the eight days of full committee markup, members adopted a variety of other amendments, most by voice vote, including proposals by:

● Ballenger to require coordination of health care plans and school services for special education children, and to require state agencies and health care plans to coordinate federal requirements relating to the disabled.

● Xavier Becerra, D-Calif., to add $6 billion to the bill's cost over five years. The money was to partially reimburse hospitals that provided necessary emergency assistance to people who did not have health insurance or who could not pay for the care. Becerra's language was amended by Randy "Duke" Cunningham, R-Calif., to emphasize that the emergency room providers would get the money straight from the federal government without going through the state government.

The committee also approved an amendment by Bercerra to add the nine regional centers of excellence in cancer research to the definition of an academic health center and eligible teaching hospital.

● William L. Clay, D-Mo., to add $2.5 billion to the bill's cost over five years to provide money to urban and rural areas underserved by medical professionals.

● Fawell to clarify that employers did not need to adopt new education materials on occupational safety and health issues.

● Ford to give businesses with more than 1,000 workers a one-time option to join a health care alliance after 11 years.

● Ford to allow the secretary of Labor to exempt states from the workers' compensation provisions if they had better programs already in place.

● Goodling to strike a program to encourage careers in the health sciences because it was duplicative, and to require state agencies to coordinate differing federal long-term care programs.

● Goodling and Dale E. Kildee, D-Mich., to make increases in the Women, Infants and Children (WIC) program gradual, based on a state's needs and its ability to provide more benefits. The bill called for fully financing the WIC program, which provided food and milk to low-income pregnant women and small children.

● Green to urge the president to consider geographic, racial and gender representation when appointing members of the seven-member National Health Board.

● Hoekstra to specify that no one could be denied treatment based on age, disability, medical need or quality of life. This amendment was in response to reports that some people had been denied treatment through Canada's single-payer system because the government deemed it too expensive, based on

their life expectancy, age or some other factor.

● Kildee to study the impact of health care reform on the dental industry and dental schools, and to give discounts to some employers that provided wellness centers for their employees on the worksite.

● Roemer to include children's hospitals among those places allowed to give specialized treatment.

● Klink to include nurse practitioners in the board overseeing rural health care and to allow them to set up their own clinics in rural areas.

● Miller, D-Calif., to require the appointment of an Advisory Commission on Prescription Drug Prices to issue a yearly report on whether the price of prescription drugs was "reasonable." Williams' bill required the commission to determine the reasonableness of drug prices for new "breakthrough" drugs and publish the findings in the Federal Register. Miller expanded the coverage to all commonly used drugs and required the commission to publish the results in a manner more accessible to the average citizen. The amendment was adopted 26-16.

● Dan Miller, R-Fla., to make the national health care board subject to administrative review by the executive branch and judicial review by federal courts.

● Patsy T. Mink, D-Hawaii, to exempt Hawaii from the bill's regulations as long as the state's health care system met or exceeded the bill's goals for universal coverage, benefits package and cost containment. For 20 years, Hawaii had required employers to pay at least half of their workers' health insurance premiums. Democrats were supportive of Mink's desire to protect Hawaii's health care system from change, but they made it clear that Hawaii was the only state that would get an exemption.

The committee rejected, 16-27, an amendment by Michael N. Castle, R-Del., to extend the waiver to any other state that could meet the requirements. And the committee rejected 14-28 a Hoekstra amendment to require states to hold referendums on whether to join the national health care plan.

● Owens to set up a new system for school-based health education and treatment, authorizing $3.6 billion over six years to build school clinics and education centers.

The committee rejected several Republican attempts to scale back the program, including one by McKeon to strip it from the bill. The attempt was rejected, 13-29.

● Jack Reed, D-R.I., to change the formula for graduate student education to provide more money for people who were training to be primary care physicians as opposed to specialists.

● Reed and Williams, a series of three amendments to clarify the conditions under which states could run purchasing cooperatives to collect insurance premiums, pay providers and monitor the quality of health services. The net effect was to allow states to run such cooperatives if they could prove their fiscal and managerial capacity to do so.

● Roemer, three amendments to ensure that children under the care of the state, including those in foster care, had uninterrupted access to health care; to include podiatry under physician training programs; and to exempt Amish and some Mennonite citizens from the requirements of the bill.

● Roukema to establish rules for insurance companies during the transition period between enactment of the bill and final implementation of its provisions. The amendment in most instances barred companies from denying a person health insurance because of pre-existing health conditions.

● Williams to include gender as a factor the National Health Board should consider when trying to increase the numbers of minority health care providers.

● Lynn Woolsey, D-Calif., to add $3 billion to the bill over five

years to provide scholarships and loan repayments to health care providers who agreed to work in rural or inner-city areas that did not have enough health care providers.

Other Woolsey amendments approved by voice vote added wellness training and alternative therapies to training for primary care physicians and included as beneficiaries of the early retiree program in the bill teachers and other state and local employees who were not usually covered by Medicaid.

Committee Amendments Rejected

During the markup, the committee rejected amendments by:

• Ballenger to strike provisions to ensure that a health care worker at a firm that was taken over or that merged with another firm could not be fired unless the job was eliminated. The amendment was rejected 15-27.

The committee rejected, 14-27, a separate Ballenger amendment to strip provisions requiring that a health care provider who took over another health care company abide by any existing collective bargaining agreement, if a majority of the employees were covered by the agreement. The panel rejected by voice vote a third Ballenger amendment to change federal labor law to make union-negotiated health care benefits that exceeded the mandated federal package a "permissive" subject of collective bargaining.

• Boehner to allow individuals to purchase supplemental health insurance if their primary health plan did not provide some desired service. Rejected 16-24.

• Cunningham to force the federal government to pay for health care provided to an illegal alien because of federal requirements. Rejected 15-27.

• Fawell to preserve pre-emption of states' ability to make laws relating to health care. Rejected 15-27.

The committee rejected, 15-27, another Fawell amendment that would have deleted provisions allowing punitive damages when a health care claim had been unfairly denied. Members rejected, 16-27, a Fawell proposal to remove provisions that directed how workers receiving workers compensation were to get health care.

By voice vote, the panel turned back a Fawell amendment to drop provisions extending the federal Davis-Bacon wage law to certain contracts paid for by government-backed loans. Under Davis-Bacon, a contractor was required to pay what the Labor Department determined was the prevailing wage for that area for that kind of work. The bill applied this law to projects funded by the loans and loan guarantees for school clinic construction.

• Gunderson to delete two new job retraining programs for people in the health care field. Gunderson said the provisions were duplicative because there were 24 programs already in existence to retrain health care workers. The amendment was rejected 14-27.

The committee also rejected by voice vote a Gunderson amendment to eliminate the National Institute for Health Care Workforce Development, which was to be created under the bill to study the industry. Gunderson said that these studies were already being conducted by the Bureau of Health Professionals in the Health and Human Services Department.

• Miller, R-Fla., to allow Medicare recipients who worked for two or more months to be allowed to stay in the Medicare program instead of transferring to a plan paid for by their employer. Rejected 15-27.

The committee rejected, 17-24, a Miller amendment to allow Medicare recipients to stay in Medicare if the state they lived in chose to go to a single-payer system.

• Roukema, to permit an employer to decline to offer the benefits package outlined by the bill if the employer could demonstrate that its health package was equal to or better than those offered under the Federal Employees Health Benefits Program. Rejected 15-27.

The committee also rejected, 17-26, a Roukema proposal that would have denied eligibility for WIC assistance to illegal aliens. She called existing law an "unintended loophole" that prevented benefits from going to U.S. citizens and legal aliens. But Kildee warned that the consequence could be low-birthweight babies born as U.S. citizens and in need of expensive health care.

HOUSE WAYS AND MEANS

Patchwork Measure Pleases No One

Despite deep fissures among committee Democrats, and the loss of veteran dealmaker Dan Rostenkowski, D-Ill., as chairman, the House Ways and Means Committee managed to approve its version of the health care bill June 30.

The measure (HR 3600 — Rept 103-601, Part 1) was shepherded through by Sam M. Gibbons, D-Fla., who became acting chairman May 31 when Rostenkowski was indicted on corruption charges and had to step aside as chairman. The concessions necessary to put together a majority in the committee left Gibbons with a patchwork measure that fully satisfied neither wing of his party. *(Highlights, p. 332)*

The committee's bill aimed to achieve universal coverage by 1998 by requiring most employers to pay at least 80 percent of the costs of health insurance for their workers. It called for the creation of a huge new government insurance program, known as Medicare Part C, to cover the poor, the uninsured and small-business employees. The bill sought to limit the rise in insurance premiums to the increase in the gross domestic product. It proposed to increase the cigarette tax from 24 cents to 69 cents a pack and to impose a 2 percent sales tax on insurance companies' premiums and on employers who self-insured.

Health Subcommittee

The Ways and Means Subcommittee on Health was the first panel in either chamber to approve a version of the health care bill, reporting out its proposal on a narrow 6-5 vote March 23. All four subcommittee Republicans voted against the plan, joined by Michael A. Andrews, D-Texas.

The centerpiece of the bill, crafted by subcommittee Chairman Pete Stark, D-Calif., was a plan to ensure universal coverage by creating a massive, government-run health insurance program. Known as Medicare Part C, it would provide coverage to the poor, small-business employees and others not covered by private insurers. Stark said Part C would cover about 60 million people and cost $80 billion to $100 billion a year. It was to replace Medicaid, the federal-state health insurance program for the poor.

The bill included an employer mandate, under which employers would pay 80 percent of the cost of their workers' health insurance with almost no help from the federal government. Like Clinton, Stark also proposed a tobacco tax increase.

The bill differed from Clinton's in setting up cost controls modeled on Medicare's strictly calibrated reimbursement sys-

tem. Also, while Clinton wanted to organize consumers into large purchasing groups, or health alliances, to buy insurance, Stark made the alliances optional.

Despite the differences with Clinton, the subcommittee's approval handed the president his first congressional victory, giving the administration a much-needed boost. In a news conference March 24, Clinton said that if the Stark bill came across his desk, he would sign it.

Some lawmakers and special interest groups had downplayed Stark's efforts because his subcommittee was dominated by liberal Democrats. But when the panel started work the week of March 8, it was taken seriously. "He's really getting the ball rolling, and that gives him a place at the table at the beginning, and at the end," said Charles N. Kahn, a former Ways and Means staff member and executive vice president of the Health Insurance Association of America, an industry group that represented most health insurance companies.

The block-long line of lobbyists waiting to get into the committee's cavernous hearing room in the Longworth House Office Building was another indication of the seriousness with which Stark's effort was being taken. Representing hospitals and insurance companies, the elderly and intravenous equipment manufacturers, they came to remind lawmakers on the dais that their action would reach far and that every group would be watching.

Adding to Stark's credibility was the tacit approval of Committee Chairman Rostenkowski. "If he hadn't been comfortable, Stark wouldn't be going ahead," said Gibbons.

For the House leadership, which had been worried about getting any bill reported out of committee, content was less important than process. Leaders could use parliamentary mechanisms involving the Rules Committee to reshape the bill before it reached the floor.

Votes Highlight Key Issues

The votes in the Health Subcommittee traversed several of the most difficult issues in the health care debate:

● **Employer mandate.** The panel gave the administration an early win March 15 by defeating, 5-6, a Republican proposal to strip the employer mandate.

● **Medicare Part C.** In an unusual alliance, Nancy L. Johnson, R-Conn., a moderate who preferred to limit change to market reforms, joined Jim McDermott, D-Wash., the leader of the House single-payer faction, in proposing that all consumers be allowed to subscribe to Medicare Part C. Under the Stark bill, only the poor, the self-employed or workers in small firms could subscribe to Part C. Johnson saw the idea as fostering competition. The amendment failed on a tie vote, 5-5.

● **Tobacco tax.** Another cross-party vote came on an amendment by Andrews to increase the cigarette tax from Stark's proposed 99 cents a pack to $2 a pack. The existing tax was 24 cents a pack. Andrews got support from three Democrats — Stark, Sander M. Levin of Michigan and Benjamin L. Cardin of Maryland, as well as from Johnson. But one of his Democratic colleagues, Gerald D. Kleczka, D-Wis., stifled the move with a motion to table it. Kleczka prevailed 6-5 with support from McDermott, John Lewis, D-Ga., and the subcommittee's three other Republicans.

Supporters were looking for revenue to pay for subsidies to help small, low-wage businesses cover the cost of their employees' health insurance. Andrews also wanted a portion of the revenues to pay for the costs of academic medical centers. His Houston district had one of the country's largest complexes of medical schools and teaching hospitals.

Andrews was more successful March 22, winning support from five Democrats and Johnson for an amendment to increase the tax to $1.49 a pack. The amendment, adopted 6-5, stipulated that of about $6 billion to be raised by the additional tax, $4.15 billion would be spent on small-business subsidies; $1 billion would fund academic health centers; $750 million could help inner-city and rural clinics and hospitals, as well as doctors who served the poor. The remainder was to be split among pregnancy prevention programs, lead abatement and job retraining for tobacco farmers.

● **Community rating.** Democrats turned back an amendment offered by Johnson that would have allowed insurance companies to charge consumers different premiums based on age. The proposal was rejected 4-7.

● **Premium deductions.** Another lightning-rod vote came on whether firms should continue to deduct health insurance premiums for employees as a business expense. A vote to limit the deductibility failed 5-6.

● **Prescription drugs.** Tempers flared several times during the markup, but during the discussion on an amendment to strip price limits on prescription drugs, the debate turned unpleasantly personal, drawing gasps from lobbyists, aides and reporters in the committee room.

As McDermott argued with Johnson, the only woman on the subcommittee, Stark, who earlier had accused "the greedy drug companies of wasting taxpayers' money," interrupted Johnson. "The gentle lady got her degree from pillow talk, and the gentleman from Washington got his degree from going to medical school," he said of Johnson and McDermott, a psychiatrist. "You guys can debate it all day long if you choose."

Johnson retorted: "I certainly dissent from that comment. . . . My husband is a physician, but I get my knowledge of the medical system from endless hours as a representative in this Congress, in hospitals and physicians' offices, talking to patients."

The price-limit amendment failed on a voice vote, but drug company representatives said they expected their supporters in Congress to offer it again. "Obviously, we're very disappointed because it will have a tremendously chilling effect on research and development," said Patrick J. Zenner, chief executive officer of Hoffman-La Roche, one of the nation's largest drug companies. He was in Washington to make the industry's case to the media.

● **Financing.** During the final two days of markup, fragile coalitions among the bill's six potential Democratic supporters almost fell apart over the question of financing. Levin could not support a bill financed in part by a 0.8 percent payroll tax. In a last-gasp effort to get Levin's support, Stark rewrote the financing section to remove the payroll tax. But to replace lost revenue, Stark added new taxes on big business, raised the cost of home health care and required states to put more money into the health system. The latter provision angered Kleczka, although he did not jump ship.

● **Cost controls.** In a 5-6 vote, Democrats defeated a GOP-led effort to strip cost-control measures from the bill and replace them with a cap on the tax deductions that businesses could take for their employees' health insurance. The amendment was offered by Jim McCrery, R-La.

Cost controls were a key component of the Clinton plan, and Stark's bill was even more regulatory. Under the bill, cost controls on the private sector were to take effect in 1998 at the earliest. Then any state in which health care spending was rising faster than the annual increase in the gross domestic product would have to institute a system to pay health care providers based on Medicare payment rates.

● **Malpractice damage cap.** A coalition of the four panel Republicans and two Democrats — Andrews and Cardin —

approved, 6-5, an amendment to limit the amount of non-economic damages available in a medical malpractice lawsuit to $350,000. Non-economic damages compensated victims for pain and suffering. The amendment was offered by the panel's ranking Republican, Bill Thomas of California.

Substitutes Fall Short

Five members offered full-fledged substitutes to the Stark bill, all of which failed.

- **Clinton bill.** The Clinton bill failed when the four Republicans voted no, and the seven Democrats voted "present," at the White House's request. The bill included market reforms and caps on national health care spending. It was offered by Thomas in a move that Democrats said was designed to embarrass the president.
- **Chafee bill.** Thomas also offered the bill he had crafted with GOP Sen. John H. Chafee of Rhode Island (HR 3704, S 1770), which aimed to attain universal coverage by 2005 by requiring individuals to have insurance. The bill failed, 5-6, with the support of Andrews. It included voluntary alliances that businesses and individuals could join to buy health insurance, and it proposed cutting Medicare and Medicaid to fund subsidies for the poor.
- **Cooper-Grandy.** Fred Grandy, R-Iowa, offered HR 3222, the bill he co-wrote with Jim Cooper, D-Tenn. It failed 5-6 but won the vote of Andrews, who helped write it. Under the Grandy bill, small businesses that paid for their employees' health insurance would be required to join together to purchase insurance. The bill had no employer mandate, no requirement that individuals purchase health insurance and no guarantee of universal coverage.
- **House GOP bill.** Johnson offered the bill crafted by the House Republican leadership (HR 3080), which took an incremental approach, calling for stricter insurance regulation and making it more difficult for victims of medical malpractice to sue for damages. It failed 4-7 on a party-line vote.
- **McCrery.** McCrery offered a substitute that would have knitted together several strategies, including a cap on the tax deductibility of health insurance and the use of medical savings accounts. The proposal failed 4-7 on a party-line vote.
- **McDermott.** McDermott won three other votes — those of Stark, Kleczka and Lewis — for his single-payer plan to offer guaranteed universal coverage and set a national health care budget. It was to be financed through a payroll tax.

Full Committee

The full committee approved a revised version of the bill June 30 on a narrow vote of 20-18. The climactic vote capped two weeks of grueling negotiations. In the end, four Democrats and all 14 committee Republicans voted against the bill.

Gibbons found the center of gravity on his committee by beginning with a fairly liberal bill and moving rightward to attract a majority. The bill promised to reach Clinton's goal of universal coverage fairly quickly with an employer mandate that would require every company to provide full-time workers with health insurance by 1998 and, in most cases, to pick up 80 percent of the cost.

But the bill took a more centralized approach than Clinton envisioned, adopting Stark's plan for a new Medicare Part C to cover the poor and the uninsured. Stark vigorously defended the plan throughout the committee deliberations, arguing that it could pass because many Americans were familiar and comfortable with the existing Medicare program. Republicans denounced the new entitlement program as an

expense the federal budget could not accommodate.

As a counterweight to such pervasive governmental involvement in health care, the Ways and Means bill attempted to provide a continuing role for private insurers, backtracking on some reforms proposed by Clinton. It also tried to provide flexibility and modest subsidies to businesses to smooth the imposition of the mandate.

Another instrument of governmental control in the bill — cost controls on private insurers to hold down health care costs — was delayed until 2001 at the earliest. And the bill called for a commission to recommend to Congress whether the controls on private sector insurance spending levels should be allowed to take effect. The compromise sewed up the votes of moderate Democrats close to the insurance industry, including Barbara B. Kennelly of Connecticut and Richard E. Neal of Massachusetts.

In addition, committee Democrats added several provisions, many of them conflicting, that helped win votes from particular lawmakers and build support from business interests, doctors and others. For example, Charles B. Rangel, D-N.Y., won language to allow state and local governments to continue to offer so-called cafeteria plans, which permitted employees to choose from a selection of health benefits, through 1998, when New York City's union contracts were due to expire.

A Slow Start

The full committee had begun its deliberations May 18 badly split on basic issues, and it made little progress before the House left May 27 for a weeklong Memorial Day recess. "This is a great sea of Jell-O right now," said McDermott. "It has not set anywhere."

The starting point was the bill approved by Stark's Health Subcommittee.

Rostenkowski began the process despite the fact that he could not, as was his custom, line up votes ahead of time. His 38-member committee was split into three groups: proponents of a single-payer system, a middle-ground group of conservative Democrats and moderate Republicans who wanted to reorganize the market but with less government involvement, and conservative Republicans who wanted only incremental change.

The committee also contained cross tensions between those who wanted to expand the benefits package, and those who were trying to hold down the price tag.

The committee was delayed by the fact that the Congressional Budget Office (CBO) had not yet provided a detailed cost estimate of the bill (an earlier rough CBO estimate showed Stark's plan losing $44 billion by 2000). Without the numbers, lawmakers did not know how much revenue had to be raised to pay for the subcommittee bill and, by extension, how far they could go in changing it.

An architect of some of the most complex pieces of legislation passed in recent years, Rostenkowski conceded that putting together a health care bill "is the most complicated thing I've ever done in my life." With Republicans unanimously opposed to an employer mandate, he needed the support of 20 of the panel's 24 Democrats to move anything. "I will do whatever I need to do to get 20 votes," he said.

Gibbons at the Helm

By the time the markup actually got under way June 6, Rostenkowski had been indicted and Gibbons had taken over as acting chairman. Hoping for a smooth transition, Gibbons introduced a compromise health plan crafted

Highlights of the Ways and Means Bill

The House Ways and Means Committee version of the health care bill (HR 3600 — H Rept 103-601, Part 1) built on an earlier measure drafted by Pete Stark, D-Calif., chairman of the Health Subcommittee. The committee scaled back some of Stark's insurance reforms and made other changes designed to attract moderate Democrats. The committee-approved bill contained provisions to:

● **Employer mandate.** Require employers and individuals to buy health insurance, with companies paying at least 80 percent of the cost of their full-time employees' insurance premiums. The bill specified conditions under which part-time, seasonal and temporary workers would be covered by employers.

Employers with 50 employees or fewer whose average salary was $26,000 or less would be eligible for a tax credit to reduce the cost of premiums. The credit for companies with 25 employees or fewer would be 50 percent of premium costs; for those with 26-50 employees, it would be 37.5 percent.

Companies would be required to pay health care premiums for married workers, even those covered by their spouse's health care plan with another company. To help pay for expanding health care coverage, the federal government through 2001 was to get a portion of the premium payments by employers whose workers were covered under a spouse's plan.

The bill required individuals to pay premium costs not borne by employers. Self-employed individuals could deduct up to 80 percent of the cost of health insurance expenses, beginning in 1998.

● **Benefits.** Require all health plans to offer a set benefits package that included everything covered by Medicare (such as doctor and hospital visits), as well as coverage for prescription drugs, pregnancy related services, chiropractic care, mental health and substance abuse treatment.

Beginning in 2000, the bill provided for the creation of a modest program administered by the states to offer long-term home and community-based care for the severely disabled. Beginning in 2003, out-of-pocket expenses were to be capped at $8,000 per year for individuals and $15,000 for families.

● **Subsidies.** Provide subsidies to the poor to defray premium costs. The subsidies, to be fully phased in 2003, would operate on a sliding scale, becoming more generous for lower income individuals.

● **Medicare Part C.** Establish a new government-run insurance program to provide health coverage for the poor who were on Medicaid, the uninsured and many employees of small businesses. Only companies with 100 workers or fewer could enroll employees in Part C.

● Cost containment. Establish a system of spending controls for private insurance plans that could take effect beginning in 2001 in states that failed to limit growth of health care spending to annual increases in the gross domestic product. The cost controls would limit insurance reimbursements to Medicare payment rates.

The bill provided for the creation of a commission to recommend by 2000 whether Congress should allow the federal cost controls to go into effect. The commission's recommendations were to be introduced as legislation and considered under expedited procedures. Unless Congress overturned the cost controls or chose some other course by Jan. 1, 2001, the system was to go into effect in states not meeting expenditure targets.

● **Insurers.** Require health plans to offer coverage and renewal to all eligible groups or individuals. Exclusions for pre-existing conditions were not allowed. Insurance companies could choose to sell policies in one or more of five market sectors: individuals, employers with two to 100 employees, larger employers, association plans and health alliances.

Community rating, which held down premiums by basing them on average costs for all those covered in a particular area, would apply to policies sold to individuals and employers of 100 or fewer workers. For larger companies, insurers could "experience rate" — meaning they could charge more for policies sold to groups that had proved expensive to insure in the past. Companies with 100 employees or more could self-insure.

Any doctor or health provider could participate and receive reimbursement for services as long as doing so complied with qualifications and cost-control goals set by the plan. Health plans would have to allow enrollees to receive treatment and reimbursement from providers outside the plan, as long as the individuals paid a higher portion of the cost.

● **State option.** Allow states to establish their own health insurance systems. Options open to states included instituting a Canadian-style single-payer system in which the government would replace private insurance companies. Companies with more than 5,000 employees nationally would be exempt from state insurance regulations.

● **Financing.** Increase the federal cigarette tax by 45 cents per pack, phased in over five years. The bill also included a 2 percent excise tax on insurance companies based on their income from premiums, and on employers based on their expenses for self-insured plans. Health benefits provided through a cafeteria plan or flexible spending arrangement would be regarded as income in the hands of the employee. Cafeteria plans and flexible spending arrangements provided for in collective bargaining agreements were grandfathered. The existing Medicare hospital insurance tax would be extended to all state and local employees.

largely by the committee staff. *(Rostenkowski, p. 43)*

Within a few days, CBO issued an estimate showing that the plan would not spend more to expand health care coverage than it would raise in new revenue. Excluding administrative costs, CBO said the bill would reduce the federal deficit every year for the coming decade except in fiscal 1998 and 1999. From 2000 through 2004, estimates showed that the bill would continue to lower the deficit, culminating in a $19.8 billion reduction in 2004.

CBO estimated, however, that the administrative expenses would be on the order of $14 billion, which would significantly increase the deficit from 1998 through 2003 unless a way were found to pay for the added costs. A committee aide said that existing administrative costs borne by the federal government for health care programs would offset some of that and the rest would have to be found every year by the Appropriations committees.

CBO's estimates provided the first clear look at how expensive it would be to help the poor purchase health care coverage. The low-income subsidies for individuals in the Gibbons plan were estimated to cost $102 billion in 1998, rising every year thereafter, reaching $218.4 billion by the year 2004.

Before the committee took its first vote, Gibbons made a number of changes to the bill, many aimed at wooing individual members. To attract business support, Gibbons' draft allowed firms with 250 employees or more to self-insure, compared with firms of 1,000 or more in the Stark bill. (Self-insurance meant the employer, instead of an insurance company, assumed the risk.) Under Gibbons, employers would not have to cover seasonal workers unless they were expected to work for at least four months during the year. Nor would employers have to cover any employee who worked an average of 25 hours a week or less during a three-month period.

To preserve more of the small-business market for private

insurance companies, the bill barred companies with more than 50 employees from participating in Medicare Part C. Stark's bill had exempted companies with more than 100 employees.

To help small businesses defray the cost of paying health premiums, Gibbons proposed a new tax credit for businesses with fewer than 50 employees whose average salary was less than $26,000 a year. The credit would be equal to up to 25 percent of the employer's annual premium cost for Medicare Part C. Spending targets for private insurance plans required by the subcommittee bill were made mandatory in 1999, as opposed to 1998 in Stark's bill.

In an effort to woo L. F. Payne Jr., D-Va., whose district included 5,000 small tobacco farmers, Gibbons reduced the proposed $1.25 increase in the federal tobacco tax to 60 cents a pack and phased it in over six years.

More poor people would qualify for premium subsidies under the Gibbons bill than under the Stark bill. A new federal program to cover long-term care for the disabled was added. Out-of-pocket spending was capped at $5,500, but the cap was not to take effect until 2003.

To help make up for the broader benefits, higher subsidies and reduced tax revenues, Gibbons included a controversial provision requiring that companies pay health care premiums for married workers, even those covered by their spouse's health care plan with another company. Through 2001, a portion of the premium payments for workers covered by a spouse's plan were to go to the federal government to help pay for expanding health care coverage. CBO estimated that the provision would bring in $20 billion to $30 billion a year. After 2001, the revenue was to go to companies paying health premiums for spouses and family members to help defray the cost.

Putting the Bill Together

Most of the bill was written in private caucuses of the committee Democrats, which participants said were chaotic and plodding compared with the autocratic and well-oiled approach that had characterized the committee under Rostenkowski. Gibbons' method for reaching consensus was to work through the bill section by section, discussing objections and, along with Health Subcommittee Chairman Stark, trying to kill amendments that would radically alter the bill's structure for achieving universal health coverage.

Though Gibbons was more willing than Rostenkowski to tolerate debate, lawmakers said Gibbons and Stark stubbornly defended the underlying bill against proposed changes, prolonging the deliberations. "Rostenkowski held his cards close to his vest. With Mr. Gibbons, we have to fight it out, but we come to pretty much the same conclusions," said Cardin.

● **Employer mandate.** Gibbons scored his first strategic victory June 14, narrowly defeating a GOP amendment to eliminate the employer mandate. The amendment, offered by Grandy, was rejected 18-20. Gibbons won over William J. Jefferson, D-La., and Peter Hoagland, D-Neb., both of whom had expressed deep reservations about saddling employers with extra costs. Gibbons said the amendment "would have killed the whole plan."

The Ways and Means endorsement of the employer mandate came just as Clinton, faced with rising opposition to the idea in the Senate, was publicly discussing the possibility of delaying its implementation. Clinton's wavering angered some committee members, who complained that they were being asked to vote for the controversial mandate when its

future was shakier than ever. Some members said events were eerily reminiscent of the previous year's battle over the Btu tax, an energy levy that Clinton proposed then dropped in negotiations with the Senate after House members already had taken the difficult political step of voting for it. *(1993 Almanac, p. 107)*

Hoping to exploit the Democrats' fear, Thomas forced another vote on the mandate the following day, warning that House Democrats were taking a political gamble by sending the bill "into the black hole of the Senate." But the second vote was identical to the first, upholding the mandate.

● **Tobacco, small business, insurance.** On June 16, the committee approved a set of changes aimed at accommodating tobacco, small-business and insurance interests, all of which had their defenders on the committee.

The amendment, offered by Jefferson, cut the proposed cigarette tax increase from 60 cents to 45 cents a pack, phased it in over five years, and reduced a proposed excise tax on insurance premiums from 2 percent to 1 percent.

To build support for the employer mandate, the amendment also offered small businesses with fewer than 50 employees and average wages of less than $26,000 a more generous tax break than the 25 percent credit included in the original bill. Businesses with 25 employees or fewer would receive up to a 50 percent credit on insurance costs. Companies with 26 to 50 workers would get a 37.5 percent credit on premium costs. The more generous subsidies were estimated to cost $53 billion over five years, $20 billion more than Gibbons' original bill.

Hoping to divide the Democrats, Thomas demanded separate votes on each element of the amendment, but the three items were approved on identical, 24-14 party-line votes. Not all the Democrats on the committee supported every provision, but they agreed to vote as a bloc to thwart Thomas' procedural ploy. They also were reacting to calls to Republicans from Minority Whip Newt Gingrich, Ga., to shun bipartisan cooperation. The Georgia Republican told the Washington Post that he had urged Republicans on the committee to remain united and "take every step possible to defeat the Gibbons bill." After reading Gingrich's comments, Andrews said, Democrats decided to vote together "to support the chairman."

To pay for the credit and the other expensive changes, the Democrats opted to delay by three years, until 2000, long-term care benefits for the disabled to be provided under the bill. CBO estimated that would save $36.6 billion over eight years.

Later attempts to revisit individual elements in the amendment met with mixed success. After long and sometimes heated debate, the committee June 29 rejected, 7-31, an amendment by Andrews to restore the proposed $1.25-per-pack increase in the cigarette tax. But the committee did agree, by voice vote, to put the excise tax on health insurance premiums back to 2 percent.

● **Self-insurance.** On June 17, the committee adopted, 36-2, an amendment to allow companies with 100 workers or more to self-insure. Gibbons' draft would have allowed companies with 250 employees or more to self-insure. The vote — the first demonstration of bipartisan cooperation since the markup began — accommodated Neal, whose district was home to Massachusetts Mutual Life Insurance. Only Stark and McDermott, two of the committee's most liberal members, voted against the amendment.

Before adopting Neal's proposal, however, the committee rejected two GOP amendments that would have opened self-insurance to even more companies. Ranking Republican Bill

Archer of Texas, proposed making every business eligible, but that was rejected on a party-line vote. Amo Houghton, R-N.Y., suggested lowering the threshold to 50 employees. That was rejected 16-22.

● **'Experience rating.'** Committee Democrats, who were caucusing daily in an effort to resolve their differences in private, reached a hard-fought compromise on insurance issues June 24 that seemed to help strengthen support for the bill by Democrats Neal, Kennelly and Hoagland. Adopted by voice vote, the amendment offered several concessions to the insurance industry, including the power to charge more for policies sold to a company that had proved expensive to insure in the past, provided that the company had more than 100 employees.

So-called "experience rating" was controversial because it meant that insurers could charge some people more than others for the same coverage. McDermott denounced the concession but did not press for a roll call vote on the compromise, apparently swallowing it to keep the Democrats united. "The reason we are in the problems we are in is because the insurance companies have had free rein in this country," he said. With experience rating, he added, insurers could charge more to small employers with unhealthy employees.

Liberals received several concessions in return for their support. The amendment expanded the number of companies eligible to participate in Medicare Part C by including firms with 100 employees or fewer, rather than those with 50 employees or fewer.

● **Options for consumers.** The committee on June 23 adopted an amendment to require that health insurers allow any doctor or health provider to participate in a plan and receive reimbursement for services as long as he or she complied with the plan's qualifications and terms. The amendment was supported by doctors' groups and opposed by managed-care plans, which contended that their cost-control efforts depended partly on their ability to limit the number of doctors available for patients under their plan.

But the amendment included language intended to alleviate some lawmakers' concerns that it would deny insurers legitimate cost-saving opportunities. It passed with the support of Gibbons and Stark as well as six Republicans.

The committee ignored Gibbons' objections on a subsequent amendment offered by Bill Brewster, D-Okla., to expand consumer choice even further. The amendment, adopted by voice vote, required health plans to allow enrollees to seek treatment outside the plan and to pay a portion of the cost. Gibbons said the amendment "really destroys managed care, as I understand it." But Brewster responded that it "relieves the fears of a lot of people that they won't be able to get care outside of a network" of doctors.

● **Drug companies.** On June 21, the committee approved a Gibbons amendment to give financial breaks to big pharmaceutical manufacturers that did a lot of research and development. The amendment reduced from 17 percent to 15 percent the rebate (or discount) that drug makers had to give Medicare patients for name drugs. The amendment also added a flat 10 percent rebate on generic drugs for Medicare patients.

● **Mammograms.** As part of a deal with Kennelly, the committee adopted by voice vote a $40 million provision to extend annual mammogram screenings to women older than 65. Gibbons' draft had only covered women between 50 and 65. The panel later rejected a GOP amendment to lower the mammogram screening age to 40.

● **Abortion.** On June 22, a combination of party discipline and hard lobbying by abortion rights supporters resulted in a string of lopsided votes that kept coverage for abortion in the standard benefits package that all health plans would have to offer.

Members rejected, 5-33, an amendment by Kleczka to allow each insurance plan to decide whether or not to pay for abortion. The committee rejected, 15-23, an amendment by Jim Bunning, R-Ky., to take abortion out of the standard package in most cases. Johnson said she objected to a national benefits package, but she said that if one was incorporated in a health care bill, it should provide all health services. "It will be a great mistake to take out one benefit. After abortion comes AIDS care," she said. "After AIDS care, sexually transmitted diseases."

The committee also rejected, 16-22, an amendment by Rick Santorum, R-Pa., to bar anything in the bill from precluding constitutional state abortion regulations.

● **Cost controls.** Andrews attempted June 28 to eliminate the private sector cost controls from the bill, but his amendment was rejected, 18-20. Andrews said the proposed controls would give the government too much power and would lead to rationing of health care as providers sought to hold down costs.

● **Self-employed workers.** One of the last amendments adopted reduced from 100 percent to 80 percent a tax deduction available to the self-employed for health insurance costs. That saved $4.4 billion over 10 years, but it also prompted the National Federation of Independent Business to issue a blistering statement denouncing the Ways and Means bill.

Finding the Center

The Ways and Means deliberations showed that there was no elegant way to close the philosophical divide between moderate and conservative Democrats, on the one hand, and liberals, on the other, except to cobble together a compromise at the center. On the final vote, three of the panel's more conservative Democrats — Andrews, Hoagland and Brewster — voted against the bill. But Gibbons also lost the committee's most ardent liberal, McDermott.

Andrews' vote was lost when the committee rejected his cost control amendment. Hoagland, who faced a tough re-election race, was never comfortable with the employer mandate (although he reluctantly voted for it during the markup) or the insurance reforms, which he claimed would undermine private insurers. Brewster had refused to vote for a bill with an employer mandate.

Coming from the other end of the spectrum, McDermott objected to the concessions made to insurers, doctors, pharmaceutical companies and large employers.

According to participants, Rostenkowski attempted to retain some influence over the deliberations, partly by pushing for adoption of a deal he had struck with the Health Insurance Association of America prior to giving up the chairmanship. But he was largely unsuccessful in steering Gibbons and Stark toward a more strategic approach to building support for the bill among outside business groups.

Rostenkowski's frustration at the desultory way the bill had been put together spilled out before the vote when he angrily reminded members that they had "begged to serve on this committee" and that they "have an obligation to take the first bite at the apple." He implicitly criticized Gibbons' approach, saying, "I don't think that I would have been that tolerant."

Panel Finds Consensus Unattainable

Week after week during the spring, John D. Dingell, D-Mich., the powerful chairman of the House Energy and Commerce Committee, could be seen on the House floor, his arm draped round the shoulders of first one, then another committee member whose vote he needed to move a health care bill through his panel. But no matter how long he talked, or what he promised or threatened, the votes never appeared.

On June 28, Dingell notified House leaders that his committee, often seen as a bellwether of congressional opinion, would be unable to act on health care legislation. Energy and Commerce had been paralyzed for months by bipartisan opposition to President Clinton's proposed employer mandate.

Before sending his letter to Speaker Thomas S. Foley, D-Wash., however, Dingell obtained a pledge from House leaders that he and other panel members, notably Health Subcommittee Chairman Henry A. Waxman, D-Calif., would be among those who drafted whatever bill was ultimately brought to the floor.

By the time he gave up, it was clear that two other House committees — Ways and Means and Education and Labor — would be able to complete action on health care bills, apparently giving House leaders a guarantee of floor action whether or not Energy and Commerce approved a bill. "John was at a disadvantage in that there were other routes to the floor," said George Miller, D-Calif.

The Democratic contingent on the Energy and Commerce Committee reflected the caucus as a whole, with members from all regions and from across the ideological spectrum. But in his letter, Dingell specifically blamed the stalemate on two members who "were preoccupied with statewide campaigns" — a swipe at Democrats Jim Cooper, who was running for the Senate in Tennessee, and Jim Slattery, a gubernatorial candidate in Kansas. Both ultimately lost.

At one point during the spring, Dingell appeared to move within a vote or two of winning approval for a Clinton-style bill when he offered an exemption from the employer mandate for businesses with 10 or fewer workers. But the deal and any real hope of committee action fell apart when Slattery said he would not vote for any employer mandate. "The chairman and I have some deep philosophical differences on this," said Slattery, who emphasized that many Midwestern and Southern Democrats shared his view.

Although Democrats enjoyed a 27-17 majority on the committee, Dingell also pointed his finger at Republicans, accusing them of being unwilling to discuss a compromise. Panel Republicans responded that Dingell never approached them seriously, and GOP leaders expressed frustration with his rhetoric. "It's outrageous," said Minority Whip Newt Gingrich, R-Ga. "Dingell knows there's a bipartisan compromise to be found."

But Dingell, whose father served in the House for 23 years and was a New Deal champion of national health insurance, preferred inaction to passage of a bill that fell short of his goals.

Dingell's Plan

For three weeks in March, as the rival Ways and Means Subcommittee on Health moved methodically ahead, Dingell struggled in vain behind the scenes to break the deadlock on his committee and begin marking up a health care bill. Then,

on March 21, Dingell put forward his own alternative, asserting that his committee would not be eclipsed in the legislative effort to produce a health bill.

To win support from other committee Democrats, Dingell altered some of the most controversial provisions of Clinton's bill. He did away with the mandatory government-sponsored health alliances, which under Clinton's plan were to be in charge of purchasing insurance and paying for health care for large groups of consumers. Dingell also softened Clinton's proposal to require all employers to pay for their employees' insurance, and he gave states the lead role in regulating the costs of health care.

But Dingell's draft retained a key tenet of Clinton's plan: the guarantee of universal coverage.

The outline Dingell circulated was drafted to win key votes. It contained provisions to:

● **Universal coverage.** Guarantee a standard package of health benefits, although the benefits were much reduced from those proposed by Clinton. Dingell's bill required consumers to pay higher deductibles and co-payments, allowing out-of-pocket spending of up to $2,500 annually, compared with $1,500 under Clinton's plan.

● **Employer mandate.** Require all employers to pay part of the cost of health insurance for their employees, with the amount tied to the size of the company. Companies with five or fewer employees would pay 1 percent of payroll; businesses with six to 10 employees would pay 2 percent. Companies that had 11 to 75 employees would pay 80 percent of the cost of health insurance for their employees, but subsidies were to be available. Dingell wanted low-wage firms to pay no more than 20 percent of premium costs.

Most employers with 76 to 1,000 employees could expect to pay 80 percent of a standard health insurance package, with subsidies available if they had to spend more than 7.9 percent of payroll on insurance.

● **Health alliances and insurance reforms.** Drop the mandatory health alliances in Clinton's plan but allow consumers and employers to buy insurance through voluntary alliances set up by states. Individuals and employers also could continue to buy insurance directly from private insurance companies or through insurance agents.

Dingell included the insurance reforms in Clinton's plan, which required insurers to accept all applicants; no one could be rejected because of a pre-existing medical condition. Individuals and employers with 1,000 workers or fewer could purchase insurance under a community rating system that based premium rates on the average medical cost for all covered people in a geographic area.

● **Cost containment.** Make states responsible for slowing the rate of growth in national health care costs to the general rate of inflation, adjusted for population. Federal health care spending would be capped; exceeding the caps would prompt automatic spending reductions.

Success Eludes Dingell

In a sharp departure from the committee's bipartisan tradition, Dingell consulted only with Democrats while drafting his proposal. The 44-member panel had 27 Democrats; with Republicans expected to be unanimous in their opposition, Dingell needed 23 Democratic votes to approve a bill. Seventeen panel Democrats were considered firm Dingell votes; four were considered lost; six were on the fence.

The six were Slattery, Rick Boucher of Virginia (concerned about the effect of the employer mandate on small business and the impact of a cigarette tax on tobacco farmers in his district); Richard H. Lehman of California (whose slim

electoral margin kept him cautious), Lynn Schenk of California (worried about the effect of drug restrictions on her district's biotechnology firms); Marjorie Margolies-Mezvinsky of Pennsylvania (whose district was home to powerful insurance and pharmaceutical interests); and Blanche Lambert of Arkansas (whose district was largely rural, poor and resistant to rapid change).

Dingell's difficulties in gathering a majority on health care were at least partly his own doing. During the late 1980s and early 1990s, when his committee faced major battles on clean air and energy legislation, he had handpicked moderate members who shared his home-state interest in protecting the automobile industry from strict environmental controls. *(1990 Almanac, p. 229)*

Three of those former allies were considered certain foes on his health care plan: W. J. "Billy" Tauzin of Louisiana, Ralph M. Hall of Texas and J. Roy Rowland of Georgia. The fourth opponent was Cooper of Tennessee, who was sponsoring an alternative health bill (HR 3222) that had generated business support.

The six undecided members were Dingell's main focus. By the middle of April, he reportedly had whittled the undecided votes to three: Slattery, Boucher and Lehman. During the week of April 19, Dingell floated a proposal to lessen the burden on small business: Those with 10 or fewer workers would be exempt from any employer mandate. Boucher and Lehman both said the chairman was close. But Slattery, who had grown increasingly resolute in his objection to any employer mandate, rejected the bid outright.

Slattery's stance frustrated many Democrats. But given his campaign for the Kansas governorship, he could not afford to focus on the details that were driving committee negotiations. It was the broad political acceptance of any plan that was important to him. Rural Kansas was dominated by small businesses that had led a massive public relations fight against the Clinton plan. In the fast-growing suburban communities, many voters were comfortable with the existing health care system.

Slattery's vote was essential to garner a majority, and once it was lost, several soft votes became elusive, forcing Dingell to back off. An informal bipartisan group of committee members met in an effort to find a consensus, but they, too, gave up.

SENATE LABOR AND HUMAN RESOURCES

Labor Panel's Measure Mirrors Clinton Plan

The Senate Labor and Human Resources Committee became the first full committee to act on health care overhaul voting 11-6 on June 9 to approve a bill modeled on President Clinton's. The committee proposed to provide health insurance for all Americans and require employers to pay the bulk of the costs.

This was the very formula Republicans and many Democrats had dismissed as too bureaucratic and costly for U.S. business, leading critics to spurn the bill, sponsored by Chairman Edward M. Kennedy, D-Mass., and criticize the committee for failing to advance health reform. Indeed, most key decisions were ultimately made on largely party-line votes.

But the bill (S 1757) differed substantially from Clinton's plan, and every Democrat and Vermont Republican James M. Jeffords voted for it. Hardly a bipartisan breakthrough — Jeffords was the lone Republican signed on to Clinton's bill — the bill did incorporate critical compromises crafted with substantive GOP input. Backers said their work would emerge as a benchmark for the other four congressional committees with primary jurisdiction over health care.

"This isn't the end," said Kennedy, as the committee neared the close of its three-week markup. "It's really the beginning."

The committee altered the Clinton plan in three key areas:
● While the committee retained Clinton's requirement that employers provide and pay for the bulk of workers' insurance costs, it included significant new exemptions and subsidies for business that employed 75 or fewer workers.
● The committee bill required states to establish at least one health insurance purchasing cooperative, or alliance, but it did not require participation, as Clinton did, and it cut back on the federal regulatory structure that Clinton proposed.
● The panel approved a standard insurance benefits package for consumers that was more comprehensive than Clinton's. But it included a fail-safe mechanism to trim the package if it would cause unanticipated deficit spending.

For a time, a bipartisan group of panel moderates headed by Democrat Jeff Bingaman of New Mexico hoped to craft compromises that would increase Republican support on these issues. But while the committee accepted substantial changes proposed by Bingaman, they were not enough to win GOP support. Republicans could not swallow any mandate on employers, they rejected requiring states to set up cooperatives and they argued that Congress should not be in the business of writing an insurance benefits package.

"This proposal has reached the end of its trail because it fails to offer a middle ground upon which the public or the majority in the Senate can stand," said ranking committee Republican Nancy Landon Kassebaum of Kansas, whose vote was considered essential to winning passage on the Senate floor.

Jeffords, the only Republican to support Bingaman on every key amendment, said he understood why Republicans were holding back in committee. "The Senate floor is where the action takes place," he said. "This is an incremental process."

Kennedy was able to take the first step in the process in part because he began with a decisive advantage over his fellow chairmen: Democrats on his panel were prepared to pass a sharply partisan bill if necessary. But Kennedy also seemed to understand that tough decisions would only get harder as time wore on.

Bill's Major Components

After three arduous weeks of markup, the Labor Committee did most of the heavy lifting during the final three days the week of June 6.
● **Employer mandates.** Like the Clinton and the initial Kennedy plans, the bill required most employers to offer at least three health insurance options to workers and pay at least 80 percent of the cost.

To ease the burden on small businesses, the panel voted 11-6 on June 8 in favor of a Bingaman amendment to provide companies with 75 or fewer workers with new exemptions and subsidies. Businesses with 10 or fewer workers were to be exempt from these mandates. But the bill included a 1 percent payroll tax for businesses with one to five workers, and a 2 percent tax for those with six to 10 workers.

Low-wage firms with 11 to 75 workers were required to offer health insurance and contribute between 4.2 percent and 12 percent of each worker's wage toward the cost, depending on the size of the firm and the individual's wage.

A Kassebaum amendment to strip the mandate was defeated on a 7-10 vote June 8. Jeffords was the only Republican to oppose her amendment.

● **Insurance purchasing cooperatives.** The bill required each state to establish at least one health insurance purchasing cooperative. Pooling large numbers of consumers, the cooperative was to negotiate insurance rates based on the health needs of entire communities, a practice known as community rating.

Individuals and employers with fewer than 500 workers were not required to purchase insurance from the cooperative. They could purchase it from an agent or directly from an insurer, or they could participate in the Federal Employees Health Benefits Program. Wherever they purchased insurance, their package had to be comparable to the community-rated program offered by the cooperative.

Employers with between 500 and 1,000 workers could choose between offering community-rated insurance or negotiating directly with insurers to establish rates for their own employees, a practice known as experience rating. If they opted for experience rating, they would pay a 1 percent payroll tax. This was included in a Bingaman-Jeffords amendment approved on a 9-8 vote moments before the bill was approved June 9. (The amendment also streamlined the federal regulations that Clinton proposed to place on the cooperatives.)

Employers of 1,000 or more workers were required to negotiate experience-rated plans and pay the 1 percent payroll tax.

Jeffords, Kassebaum and Dave Durenberger, R-Minn., offered an amendment to let states decide whether to establish a cooperative, a structure proposed by John H. Chafee, R-R.I. It was rejected 5-12 on June 8, with Democrats and two conservative Republicans in opposition.

● **Cost controls.** The bill established target ceilings for health insurance premium increases, known as premium caps. By 2000, increases were to be limited to inflation levels in the federal Consumer Price Index. A new national health board was to review insurance premium increases. If average premiums in a state exceeded the caps, high-cost firms would be directed to lower them.

Several Democrats, including Bingaman and Christopher J. Dodd, Conn., expressed skepticism about the caps, but they said they knew of no other way to control costs. Kennedy, too, expressed reservations when he first offered his bill May 18, but in the end, he came to support them. He said he had grown frustrated with critics who first said the caps would lead to rationing of health care and later complained that the same caps would lead to skyrocketing costs.

A Durenberger amendment to strike the premium caps was rejected on an 8-9 vote June 8, with Dodd joining a unanimous Republican faction in support of the amendment.

● **Benefits.** The bill included a detailed outline of benefits that insurers were to offer consumers in a basic health package. It built on the Clinton plan, adding new preventive care for women and adolescents as well as a new program for home and community care for seniors and the disabled, and a long-term nursing care insurance program for everyone.

But, in a bipartisan compromise crafted by Bingaman, the bill also responded to Republican concerns that mandatory benefits, which would be subsidized for low-income people and small businesses, could bankrupt the government. Bingaman's proposal included a national benefits board to review the package before it went into effect and propose changes if it would cause unanticipated deficit spending. The recommendations were to go into effect unless Congress voted them down. Though there was confusion over whether the board's authority extended to changes in premium caps or provider rates, the panel approved this Bingaman proposal May 19 on a bipartisan vote of 17-0.

On June 9, the committee voted 10-7 in favor of a Dodd amendment to restrict the board's authority to make adjustments in the benefits package and co-payments. Dodd, Bingaman and Barbara A. Mikulski, D-Md., joined a unanimous GOP bloc in favor of the amendment. It was the only one adopted over Kennedy's objection in the entire markup.

On a 5-11 party-line vote June 7, the panel rejected a Kassebaum amendment to revamp the benefits package along the lines recommended in the Chafee bill. The amendment would have put most benefit decisions in the hands of a new national board rather than Congress.

The panel rejected, on a 6-11 vote, an amendment by Daniel R. Coats, R-Ind., to strike the entire benefits package June 8.

The panel accepted an amendment by Kennedy and Harris Wofford, D-Pa., that streamlined the benefits package, leaving out detailed immunization schedules and the like. The amendment clipped six pages from the bill.

● **Abortion.** The benefits package required insurers to cover reproductive services. Though it did not explicitly mention abortion, Democrats assumed the procedure would be covered.

On June 7, the panel voted 6-11 against a Coats amendment that would have prohibited abortion coverage in the basic benefits package except in cases of rape, incest or a threat to the woman's life. Jeffords was the only Republican to join a unanimous bloc of Democrats in opposition to the amendment.

The panel then voted 7-10 against an amendment by Judd Gregg, R-N.H., that would have specified that nothing in the bill superseded state regulations on abortion. All Democrats except Wofford opposed Gregg; all Republicans except Jeffords supported him. In arguing against the amendment, Democrats asserted that federal law superseded state law only if the two conflicted. Under the bill, for example, a Pennsylvania law that imposed restrictions on minors seeking abortions and required waiting periods was protected. However, the bill did supersede state regulations that restricted insurance coverage of abortion.

● **Breakthrough drugs.** The bill called for a 38-member advisory committee to review new, old and emerging medical technologies and report on them to the Department of Health and Human Services. The panel was to include experts as well as industry representatives from biotechnology, medical devices and pharmaceutical companies.

On a 16-1 vote June 9, the panel substituted the advisory board for the breakthrough drug council that Clinton had recommended to help control prices. Biotechnology firms strenuously argued that price control recommendations by the council would destroy their fragile industry. They supported the alternative, which was offered by Kennedy and greatly limited the board's power.

● **Tobacco tax.** The bill included an increase in the cigarette tax to $1.49 per pack from the existing level of 24 cents per pack.

Earlier Action

The committee began its work May 18 in a session that opened with partisan squabbling. But the next day, in a surprising show of bipartisanship, the panel adopted, 17-0, Bingaman's compromise proposal on the benefits package.

Kennedy had insisted that Congress define the benefits, and he proposed a broad package, adding new services for women, adolescents and the disabled to the Clinton plan. Democrats who backed the expanded benefits package said that for a bill to succeed, Americans needed to know pre-

cisely what coverage it provided. "It is our responsibility to make those decisions," argued Paul Wellstone of Minnesota.

Republicans countered that the costs of mandatory benefits would overwhelm the government and argued that Congress should not be in the business of outlining insurance plans. "It's hubris to say that we have that kind of expertise," said Coats.

Kassebaum initially offered an amendment to strip out the Kennedy benefits proposal and substitute language from a plan by Chafee that offered a bare-bones benefit outline to be filled in by a national health board. Her amendment would have been defeated on partisan lines, however, so when Bingaman suggested his compromise, Kassebaum embraced it.

Bingaman's idea was to allow Congress to draft a benefits package, in the short run accepting Kennedy's. But the amendment also provided for the creation of a national health board, modeled after the military base closing commission, to review the fiscal impact of the benefits and recommend changes to prevent unanticipated deficit spending. The recommendations were to take effect unless both chambers voted against them within 45 legislative days.

In the next round of markups May 24-26, the committee slogged through a series of tangential amendments, trying to find bipartisan agreement wherever possible. As the panel wrapped up the week's work, Kennedy emphasized that members had accepted 19 of 30 Republican amendments so far. But he acknowledged that winning GOP votes for final passage was "still an uphill battle."

The committee unanimously approved a Kennedy-Kassebaum amendment to fund clinics in public schools.

Kassebaum first offered an amendment May 25 that would have changed the Kennedy bill's authorization of $150 million in 1995 for school-based clinics and its outline of the services they could provide. Kassebaum wanted to reduce both funding and services and give more control to local communities. Her approach caught the attention of panel Democrats who supported Kennedy's intent. "I believe the purpose is to get at the bad rap school clinics have gotten for distributing condoms," said Mikulski.

The next day, the panel voted 17-0 for a compromise that stripped out mention of pregnancy prevention and sexually transmitted disease screening, although such services could be provided under general prevention and screening programs. The amendment sought to expand clinic grants to elementary schools and require parental and community involvement. It authorized up to $100 million in 1995.

On May 25, the panel rejected, 6-11, Kassebaum's effort to strike two Kennedy proposals: an increase in federal funding of academic health centers and a new federal role in allocating physician residencies. Kassebaum agreed that academic centers needed assistance because insurance companies were rejecting the higher rates the centers charged to sustain residencies and research. But she advocated a study of how to best aid them.

On May 24, the panel voted 2-15 against an amendment offered by Gregg to allow states to establish a means test for a new entitlement in the Kennedy bill providing home and community care for seniors and the disabled. Kennedy wanted to impose progressive co-payments for services to people with incomes above 150 percent of the poverty rate. But he argued strenuously against imposing what would have been the nation's first entitlement-program means test on the disabled.

The panel also rejected, 2-15, an amendment by Coats to prohibit cash payments for home care; bill supporters said the cash payments would be monitored and give families more flexibility.

Bipartisan Bill Relies On Market Forces

The Senate Finance Committee was the last of the major committees to complete work on the health care reform bill, approving its proposal (S 2351 — S Rept 103-323) by a vote of 12-8 on July 2. Unlike the other committees, Finance produced a bill with bipartisan support. The measure, which relied far more heavily than the others on market forces, seemed certain to pull the Senate floor debate to the right of President Clinton and to reverberate in the House as well.

Chairman Daniel Patrick Moynihan, D-N.Y., appeared convinced from the outset that he would have to produce a bipartisan measure, a judgment dictated by the committee's makeup and politics: The panel had 11 Democrats, two of whom clearly would not support Clinton's bill, and nine Republicans.

Under pressure from the administration and a good portion of the committee Democrats, the panel considered briefly, and then abandoned, a Clinton-style bill with universal coverage and an employer mandate.

Instead, the bill that was finally approved by the committee set a goal of covering 95 percent of Americans by 2002 through changing insurance market practices and providing subsidies to help low-income people buy insurance.

The subsidies were to be funded by $55 billion in Medicare cuts over five years, cuts in Medicaid and new taxes, including an increase in the cigarette tax to $1 a pack from 24 cents a pack. The bill also included a 1.75 percent tax on insurance premiums to support academic medical centers.

The bill did not require employers to buy insurance for their employees, though it provided for Congress to consider such a mandate if 95 percent of the people were not covered by 2002.

The Finance Committee bill contained no private-sector cost controls, relying instead on a new tax on expensive plans to hold down costs. The bill provided for two standard packages of benefits to be offered by all insurance plans — a comprehensive plan and a plan that would cover major illnesses, requiring consumers to pay for most other medical expenses.

For Clinton, the Finance Committee's movement was a mixed blessing. The bill differed substantially from his proposal. Yet senators and lobbyists on all sides said it was crucial for the committee to report out a bill with bipartisan support. "Can you imagine what would have been said if we couldn't produce a bill?" said Kent Conrad, D-N.D. "It would have been a terrible blow for the president."

The bill's delayed appearance reflected the extreme difficulty the committee had in producing it. The panel's progress was slowed by major disagreements among Democrats about the substance of the bill as well as about how the committee should go about drafting such a measure. Some committee Democrats were unwilling to give up on Clinton's goals of universal coverage and government-run cost containment. Others wanted to work with Republicans on a compromise that would make gradual changes in the existing system and rely on market competition to cut spending.

Majority Leader George J. Mitchell, D-Maine, a member of the committee, hewed to Clinton's plan, as did committee members Tom Daschle, D-S.D., John D. Rockefeller IV, D-W.Va.,

and Donald W. Riegle Jr., D-Mich. All were leading proponents of the Clinton proposal, which their staffs helped prepare.

At the conservative end of the Democratic spectrum were John B. Breaux, La., David L. Boren, Okla., and Conrad, who made up a core group that worked with moderate Republicans in an effort to shape an alternative bill. At the more liberal end were Max Baucus, D-Mont., David Pryor, D-Ark., and Bill Bradley, D-N.J. Chairman Moynihan, a maverick who often held neoconservative views on social issues took a cautious approach, working for weeks to try to find a compromise.

In any other committee, the tensions might have generated less interest, but the Senate Finance Committee occupied a pivotal place in the health care debate. Many lawmakers, especially in the House, were counting on the panel to craft a grand compromise that could attract votes from both parties and pave the way for skittish members to vote for an overhaul bill. The committee's inability to move for many weeks had repercussions throughout Congress, slowing other committees and raising questions about whether any comprehensive bill could emerge in 1994.

A Slow Start

For several weeks during April and May, at 4 p.m. on Tuesdays and Thursdays, committee Democrats and Republicans filed into the Finance Committee's sparsely furnished conference room and talked and talked and talked about health care. The long sessions produced what Daschle called "extremely helpful" discussions and general agreement on many subsidiary issues in the debate, including insurance reforms, subsidy levels for the poor and malpractice reform. But an accord on the core of the health care overhaul plan — its financing and cost containment — continued to elude the lawmakers.

White House officials, meanwhile, were clearly uncomfortable with Moynihan's public talk of bipartisan compromise and his comments that universal coverage was not a realistic goal. They feared that he would compromise at the beginning of the committee process, making it harder for them to cut deals at the end.

Moynihan's Draft

Then, in June, Moynihan did a turnabout — whether from a decision to play the good soldier or a calculation that he needed to put the administration's plan on the table to show the White House how little support it had in his committee.

In any case, Moynihan presented his committee June 9 with the outlines of a bill that bore little resemblance to the bipartisan talk that had preceded it. The reaction of many members of both parties was to back away. "We're a long way," said Orrin G. Hatch, R-Utah. "The chairman is putting . . . this mark out there just to see how well it's received, and I think it's going to have some difficulty."

Moynihan's draft resembled Clinton's proposal in many respects. It called for universal coverage, with a comprehensive package of benefits that included mental health and prescription drug coverage. The benefits were to be paid for through a modified employer mandate, along with new taxes and minimal cuts in Medicare.

Costs were to be held down primarily by competition in the marketplace, though Moynihan proposed a backup mechanism that would give Congress the option of forcing health costs to grow at close to the rate of inflation.

Like many of the previous bills, the draft proposed to bar insurance companies from refusing to insure people because they had a disease or medical condition. The bill proposed to eliminate Medicaid, instead providing subsidies to help low-income people buy insurance.

"It runs counter to everything we know the public wants — it has mandates, price controls and big-government regulation of the health care system," said Pam G. Bailey, executive director of the Healthcare Leadership Council, which represented the country's 50 largest health care companies, including hospital chains, insurers and health maintenance organizations.

But administration officials privately expressed relief. "It is good news if the chairman of the committee comes out with universal coverage," said a White House source. "We didn't know where he was coming from." Moynihan's public statement before presenting his draft to the committee underscored his role as a loyal Democratic chairman. "We are a party; we ran in 1992 saying: Let's get rid of gridlock. We can govern, and we're going to try to do that," he said. "I offered this mark to show the committee what most of us seemed to have agreed to. This is where we begin. You have to begin."

At the same time, by putting forth a controversial draft almost certain to be rejected by his committee, Moynihan was able to send a powerful message to the White House about how little support there was for provisions such as the employer mandate and limits on premium increases. Moynihan, who was running for re-election, got one more benefit: He made sure that two of the local interests he cared about — graduate medical education and the elderly — were well taken care of.

Major elements of Moynihan's bill included provisions to:

● **Employer mandate.** Require employers with more than 20 employees to pay at least 80 percent of their workers' health insurance costs. Employers with fewer than 20 workers would have the option of paying a payroll tax instead. If 98.5 percent of the population was not covered by 2000, an employer mandate would be triggered for small employers as well.

● **Subsidies.** Make working families and individuals eligible for subsidies on the 20 percent of the premiums that they had to pay. Workers in firms that chose not to buy insurance would be eligible for income-based subsidies that capped their payments at 5 percent to 7 percent of their annual incomes. The bill proposed to cap contributions for employers overall at 12 percent of each worker's wage, with lower caps for small firms.

● **Cost containment.** Set a target for the maximum annual increase in premium costs. If the target was exceeded, a new National Health Cost Commission would recommend action to Congress, which would approve or reject the recommendations.

Federal health spending could not increase the budget deficit. If it did, it would trigger automatic reductions in subsidies unless Congress enacted offsetting budget reductions.

● **Financing.** Increase the cigarette tax to $2 a pack; increase the excise tax on handgun ammunition to 50 percent. The bill included a 1 percent employer payroll tax for firms of more than 500 workers (compared with firms with more than 5,000 workers under Clinton's plan), and a payroll tax on small firms that opted out of the mandate.

Moynihan also proposed to increase Medicare Part B premiums for the wealthy, with the money going to academic health centers and medical education.

Medicare spending was to be cut by $33 billion over five years.

● **Health insurance purchase.** Allow, but not require, individuals and employers with fewer than 500 workers to form

Dole Offers GOP Proposal

On June 29, Senate Minority Leader Bob Dole, R-Kan., announced a GOP proposal to boost access to health care, largely by changing insurance practices and providing subsidies to low-income families. It made no claim of achieving universal coverage. The plan avoided any tax increase, relying instead on cuts in Medicare and Medicaid to pay for the subsidies. Dole, who earlier had voiced support for President Clinton's goal of universal coverage, said he now advocated "no employer mandates, no price controls and no taxes."

The plan and the broad support it drew from Republicans amounted to a GOP response to Clinton's repeated threat to veto any bill that did not provide for universal coverage. With 40 of the Senate's 44 Republicans on board, Dole had almost enough votes to sustain a filibuster against Clinton's bill.

The Republican senators who declined to join Dole included John H. Chafee of Rhode Island, Dave Durenberger of Minnesota and John C. Danforth of Missouri, who had been working with Democrats on the Senate Finance Committee to try to craft a bipartisan bill. William V. Roth Jr. of Delaware and James M. Jeffords of Vermont also did not sign on. Some of Dole's cosponsors had also cosponsored a Chafee proposal that was close to the bipartisan proposal being developed by the Finance Committee.

Key elements of the Dole plan included provisions to:

● **Coverage.** Attain universal access, not universal coverage. The bill proposed that individuals and people in businesses with two to 50 workers be allowed to buy into the Federal Employee Health Benefit Plan. It did not require employers or individuals to buy insurance.

● **Subsidies.** Help the poorest, uninsured Americans pay for insurance by providing a full subsidy for people below 100 percent of the poverty level and subsidies on a sliding scale for those between 100 percent and 150 percent of poverty. Senators said that 17.5 million of the estimated 38 million uninsured Americans were below 150 percent of poverty. The subsidies would drop off sharply for people above poverty. The poverty level for a family of four was $14,800 per year.

The bill proposed to gradually increase the existing 25 percent tax deduction for health insurance for self-employed individuals to 100 percent by 2000.

● **Benefits.** Allow insurers to offer any variety of benefits they chose. The only exception would be for families who received subsidies. Their plan would have to include comprehensive coverage, preventive care, mental health and substance abuse services, and take special account of the needs of children and other vulnerable populations.

● **Insurance reform.** Require that insurers take all comers and renew all plans at the enrollees' request. Insurers could require that people with medical conditions wait six months to receive coverage.

Insurers would have to charge people in firms of 50 workers or fewer a "modified community rate," meaning that the insurer would have to charge everyone it insured the same amount. Adjustments would be permitted for age and family status.

The bill also provided for "portability," allowing people to carry insurance plans from one job to the next.

● **Purchasing cooperatives.** Allow, but not require, businesses and individuals to form large pools to purchase health insurance.

purchasing groups to buy insurance. If voluntary cooperatives did not form, then states would have to step in. Employers of fewer than 10 workers could enroll in the Federal Employees Health Benefits Program.

States would have the option of creating a Canadian-style single-payer system.

● **Medicare.** Continue Medicare coverage for the elderly, but require states to give enrollees the option of joining a plan similar to the type offered by HMOs; prescription drugs would not be covered.

Moderates' Alternative

On June 24, a bipartisan group of Senate Finance Committee members unveiled their own proposal, which relied on market-oriented initiatives to create more competition among insurance plans, mainly by forcing insurance firms to offer the same benefit packages to all beneficiaries and charge rates that varied only by age and family class.

The proposal aimed to achieve 95 percent coverage. It provided for a new, seven-member health commission to report to Congress every two years on the demographics of those without health insurance. If, by 2002, more than 5 percent of Americans lacked insurance, the panel would make detailed recommendations to Congress on increasing coverage. Lawmakers would be required to vote on the proposals — but not necessarily to approve them. The mechanism was dubbed a "soft trigger" because it set up a specific date for Congress to

consider the proposals, but it included no enforcement.

The proposal included a tax on high-cost insurance plans to give the insurance industry an incentive to keep prices down. Critics said the tax almost certainly would be passed along to consumers in the form of higher premiums. There were to be full subsidies for the poor up to 100 percent of the poverty line. Partial subsidies would be available on a sliding scale for those with incomes up to 240 percent of the poverty line.

The plan was produced by a group of six moderate lawmakers led by John H. Chafee, R-R.I. The others were Democrats Breaux, Boren and Conrad, and Republicans John C. Danforth of Missouri and Dave Durenberger of Minnesota.

Supporters said that if they could increase coverage to 95 percent, that would reduce the number of uninsured by about 20 million people. Bradley, originally a member of the group, distanced himself from the plan hours before it was released, citing its failure to require that employers and individuals buy insurance. Earlier versions of the plan had included both requirements.

Highlights of the moderates' plan included provisions to:

● **Financing.** Increase the cigarette tax by $1 per pack. The proposal also provided for cuts in Medicare and Medicaid.

● **Cost controls.** Set an annual baseline for federal health care spending. If spending exceeded the baseline in any year, automatic reductions in the subsidies for the poor would go into effect, along with other measures.

● **Health alliances.** Allow businesses with fewer than 100

workers to join together to buy insurance or to enroll in one of the plans offered locally to federal employees through the Federal Employees Health Benefits Program. Large businesses could self-insure or contract directly with insurance plans or with providers.

● **Benefits package.** Provide for a new national health commission to define a standard set of benefits that all plans would have to offer.

● **Insurance requirement.** Require that insurers cover all enrollees, regardless of their medical conditions or demographic factors.

● **Malpractice suits.** Place a $250,000 limit on damages paid to victims of medical malpractice for pain and suffering.

Committee Markup

Finally, on June 29, the Finance Committee began its long awaited markup of the bill. Moynihan had publicly expressed doubts about whether his panel could finish before mid-July, but he sped up his timetable after Mitchell made it clear the week of June 20 that he intended to bring a bill to the floor in July. The Senate Labor and Human Resources Committee had already reported a rival bill June 9 patterned after Clinton's proposal.

The committee completed work Saturday, July 2, approving its draft bill 12-8.

The panel's starting point had been Moynihan's draft, modified to include elements from the moderates' proposal.

In particular, Moynihan had modified the requirement that most employers pay 80 percent of their employee's health insurance costs, by adding a so-called hard trigger. The idea, proposed weeks earlier by Breaux, was to allow market reforms to work for several years to see if they could achieve near universal coverage. Only if they did not would employers be required to pay. Under the plan, businesses with 100 or more workers would have to have 85 percent of their employees covered within three years; businesses of 25-99 would have to have 80 percent covered in four years; and businesses of fewer than 25 would have to have 75 percent covered in five years.

In a key early move June 30, the committee voted 14-6 to strip out the hard trigger, with five Democrats joining all nine committee Republicans in opposition to the delayed form of employer mandate. The vote effectively jettisoned from this version of the bill Clinton's goal of guaranteeing affordable health insurance for all Americans.

The committee subsequently voted 12-8 to replace the hard mandate with the so-called soft trigger: If 95 percent of Americans did not have coverage by 2002, then Congress would have to vote on the recommendations of a nonpartisan commission on how to expand health insurance coverage. The commission could recommend a mandate or any number of other routes, but future Congresses would not have to pass legislation that guaranteed universal coverage.

Finally, to win over the last votes needed to move the bill out of committee, Democrats late on July 1 agreed to an en bloc amendment that largely represented the work of the centrist group led by Chafee and Breaux. The amendment reduced many of the taxes in the bill, such as those on tobacco, ammunition and big business, and it lightened the regulations in the bill, for example by leaving it to a national board to determine a basic benefits package, rather than spelling it out in bill language.

The amendment had the public backing of Mitchell, who repeatedly said that not all the provisions represented his views, but that in the interests of moving the bill to the floor he would nominally support the proposal.

Moderates' Central Role

The Senate Finance bill came together through shifting majorities that revolved around the group of six centrists, much of whose work ended up in the committee bill. The six joined the committee's other Republicans on the key vote to strike the hard-trigger employer mandate. But on the subsequent vote to put in a soft trigger, the six Democrats joined the six centrists against GOP opposition.

Members of the Chafee-Breaux group portrayed themselves as Davids up against the twin Goliaths, Clinton and Senate Minority Leader Bob Dole, R-Kan. In a sharply worded letter released June 28, Durenberger laid out in frank terms the frustration of moderate Republicans who had "labored three years" to find a Republican position on health care. Durenberger criticized Dole for coming up with a new alternative plan that bowed to individual and small-business insurers and proposed charging different prices based on a person's health status. He said it also favored fee-for-service doctors who dominated the medical societies in the South. *(Dole plan, p. 340)*

The centrists also provided the core support for an amendment by Bradley to strip the bill's provisions for controlling the rise of health care costs. The original Moynihan draft required that if the rate of growth in health care costs did not drop to the rate of general inflation over the following six years, then Congress would have to vote on a commission's recommendations for bringing down the growth rate. Five Democrats joined the centrist bloc in an 11-9 vote to eliminate the cost-containment provisions.

Bradley's amendment included a tax on high-cost insurance plans. It required the Internal Revenue Service to set a target price for insurance plans offered in each local area. If a plan's price exceeded the target, there would be a 25 percent tax on the difference between the target price and the plan's price. The target price was to be set so that 40 percent of the plans in each area would be subject to the tax. Administration officials estimated that over 10 years, it would raise about $14 billion to $17 billion.

Danforth, who spoke at length for the amendment, argued that the cost of health care was more worrisome to many Americans than its availability. He pointed out, as had many economists, that the existing system that allowed employers to deduct all the health care costs as a business expense and allowed workers to exclude health benefits from their taxable income was an incentive to buy more expensive plans than were necessary.

Dole retorted: "This is a big tax increase, and we don't know how it is going to work."

The only Democrats who opposed the Bradley amendment were Baucus, Riegle and Moynihan. Labor unions, which represented crucial support for Moynihan in New York, sent a letter shortly before the vote saying they opposed it. The average New York bus driver would pay about $604 more a year in insurance premiums as a result of the amendment, they said.

Mixed Signals on Abortion

Late on July 1, the committee took several close votes on how abortion services would be covered and provided in a reconfigured health care system. The results produced no clear winner and included the approval of at least two provisions that appeared to be in conflict. Finance, which shared jurisdiction over health care reform, had never

before dealt with abortion policy, which had been the domain of the Labor and Human Resources Committee and the Judiciary Committee.

As was true elsewhere in Congress, when it came to abortion, the Finance votes did not track party lines. Two Republicans — Chafee and Packwood — supported the abortion rights position, while two Democrats — Breaux and Conrad — consistently supported the anti-abortion position. Other members crossed back and forth, depending on the wording of the amendment.

While abortion was not mentioned by name, it was implicitly included in bill language that said health care coverage had to include "all medically necessary and appropriate services." Federal courts repeatedly had ruled that such language included abortion. Since abortion would be covered in the standard benefits package, all employers who provided insurance for their employees would be buying a package that included abortion coverage, as would every individual who bought insurance. Similarly, all insurers would have to cover the service.

Anti-abortion advocates tried and failed to explicitly exclude abortion from the list of covered services. An amendment by Hatch that would have permitted abortion coverage only in cases of rape, incest or to save the life of the woman, failed on a 9-11 vote.

But a subsequent vote seemed to contradict that stance. The committee agreed, 12-8, to an amendment offered by Danforth to expand the "conscience clause" in the Finance Committee's draft bill. Like all the committee bills, the Finance version included a provision saying that any health care provider or hospital that had a moral or religious opposition to performing abortion did not have to provide the service. However, a health care plan would have to include coverage for abortion and contract with providers that would be willing to perform the procedure.

Danforth's amendment added a conscience clause for employers, individuals and insurance plans. Under his language, an employer who opposed abortion could refuse to buy a health insurance plan that included it or any other services to which the employer objected on moral or religious grounds. Similarly, no providers would have to perform services to which they objected on moral grounds, and no insurance plan would have to cover services to which the insurer objected on religious or moral grounds.

A third amendment offered by Danforth and adopted, 12-8, raised nearly as controversial an issue: whether every plan would have to contract, or recruit, an abortion provider. Since all plans would have to cover abortion, they also would have to ensure that abortion services were available to all enrollees.

Charles E. Grassley, R-Iowa, won approval, 11-9, for an amendment to allow states to maintain existing restrictions and enact new restrictions on abortion access. Most states had laws requiring that teenagers notify or get consent from a parent or other adult before obtaining an abortion, and several states required that women wait 24 hours between their first visits to abortion clinics and their abortions.

Other Amendments

With most of the major issues addressed or sidestepped, the committee held a rare Saturday markup July 2 to slog through dozens of second- and third-tier amendments.

● **State exemption.** No vote was closer or harder to predict than the fight over an amendment by Durenberger to maintain an exemption from state regulation for self-financed health insurance plans. The draft bill implicitly eliminated the

exemption, which was part of the 1972 Employment Retirement Income Security Act (ERISA).

Durenberger's amendment was backed by large, multistate companies and by national health plans, such as the Kaiser Permanente HMO. They wanted to maintain the ERISA exemption because it allowed large firms that contracted with national insurance plans to make their health insurance plans uniform across state lines, and it ensured that the plans could refer patients to institutions in other states that were part of their network. When Durenberger offered his amendment, the Finance Committee room and the hallway outside were filled with big-business and insurance lobbyists.

The exemption was opposed by the influential National Governors' Association. Companies that financed their own health insurance programs employed about 28.7 percent of the work force, which meant as many as 30 million workers, retirees and their families could be insured through their plans. States contended that they needed to regulate (and tax) these firms to pay for universal coverage.

When the roll was called, the amendment failed on a 10-10 tie. But Durenberger quickly held a whispered conversation with Mitchell, indicating that without the amendment he, and most likely moderate Republicans Chafee and Danforth, would vote against the underlying bill. Mitchell, who had voted no, raised his hand. "It has been brought to my attention that this was very important to some," he said. "I would like to change my no to 'aye.' "

● **Malpractice suit restrictions.** State interests were involved in another close vote when Danforth won approval, 10-9, for an amendment to restrict medical malpractice suits and place a $250,000 cap on the amount of "pain and suffering" damages that could be awarded in malpractice cases.

States had sole jurisdiction over the tort law that governed medical malpractice cases. Although state laws were slowly changing, most states still placed few, if any, limits on pain and suffering damages, which juries could award in addition to compensatory damages for the actual losses incurred by the patients.

Doctors said the fear of malpractice suits — and unlimited pain and suffering awards — forced them to do unnecessary tests that drove up the cost of health care. Consumer groups and trial lawyers who opposed limits on malpractice awards pointed to numerous studies suggesting that it was almost impossible to measure the overall level and cost of such "defensive medicine" practices.

Danforth's amendment required victims to seek arbitration before pursuing a court case and limited attorneys' fees to a third of the first $150,000 recovered and a fourth of additional amounts. It also barred states from maintaining a policy of "joint and several liability" for pain and suffering damages," in which all parties in a suit remained liable for any or all of the damages, regardless of the magnitude of each defendant's participation.

● **Other amendments.** In other action, the Finance Committee:

● Agreed, 15-5, on July 1 to an amendment by Baucus to strip the 50 percent excise tax on gun ammunition, losing about $140 million.

● Approved by voice vote July 1 an amendment by William V. Roth Jr., R-Del., to strip a requirement that the Postal Service pre-fund its health insurance for retirees; the provision would have brought in an estimated $13 billion in revenue over five years.

● Approved, 12-8, on July 1 an amendment by Riegle to

guarantee health insurance subsidies for low-income pregnant women and for children up to 240 percent of the poverty level starting in 1996. Staff estimated that the program would cost $10 billion over five years. The bill would have phased in subsidies for women and children over eight years, along with the rest of the low-income population.

• Approved, 13-7, on July 1 an amendment by Hatch to strip the 1 percent payroll tax on firms of more than 500 workers, which had been estimated to yield $50 billion over five years.

• Approved, 16-4, on July 1 an amendment by Pryor to add a block grant program for community and home health care for the disabled — regardless of age or income. It would be funded by coordinating payments under health insurance and automobile insurance policies to eliminate overlapping payments for the same services. The savings that could be obtained from coordination of payments was estimated by private health care consulting firms to be $16.7 billion over five years.

• Approved, 14-6, on July 2 an amendment by Chafee to cap government spending for all health care programs. It set two baselines: The first included existing health care programs such as Medicare, Medicaid and health-related tax expenditures, such as the employer deduction for providing health benefits. The other baseline included existing health spending costs as modified by the bill and the new health revenues and costs such as subsidies for the poor. If the new costs exceeded the old costs, then spending reductions would go into effect automatically. That would slow the phase-in of subsidies for the poor and the expanded tax deduction for individuals who bought their own health insurance.

• Approved, by voice vote July 2, an amendment by Hatch to require the benefits package to explicitly cover the services of all state-certified health professionals who were authorized to provide those services. Hatch said it was aimed at clarifying that nurse practitioners and chiropractors would be reimbursed for services covered in the standard benefit package as long as they were authorized to perform those services under state law.

• Rejected, 7-13, on July 2 an amendment by Roth to require all health insurance plans to offer the option of a medical savings account combined with an insurance policy that had a high deductible before coverage took effect.

• Rejected, 10-10, on July 2 an amendment by Boren to strip the option in the bill for states to set up a single-payer system.

• Rejected, 6-14, on July 1 an amendment by Rockefeller to institute a community rating system in which all enrollees in a health plan would be charged the same amount if the bill's provisions for a delayed "employer mandate" went into effect. If the requirement that employers provide insurance to all employees did not go into effect, then insurers would be permitted to charge somewhat higher rates to older people. Rockefeller said he was trying to help people 45 to 65 years of age who often were charged high rates. Opponents said it would raise the price of insurance for younger people.

• Rejected, 6-14, on July 2 an amendment by Dole to allow insurance plans to offer a variety of benefit packages instead of just the two standard packages permitted by the bill, with an exception for low-income individuals who would be sold a standard package. Dole said limiting insurance companies to just two plans compromised consumer choice. Critics said the amendment would limit consumers' ability to compare plans on the basis of price and quality.

OTHER COMMITTEES

Five Other Panels Give Input to Leaders

While five committees — three in the House and two in the Senate — had the primary responsibility for drafting health care legislation, a host of secondary committees marked up specific sections of the legislation that dealt with topics over which they had jurisdiction. Their efforts were incorporated, in whole or in part, into the House and Senate leadership bills. The following committees had a role:

• **House, Senate Armed Services.** The House Armed Services Committee focused on how Medicare should reimburse the Defense Department for care provided to eligible military retirees and their families under Medicare. Armed Services approved its section of HR 3600 by voice vote July 26 after just 10 minutes of debate (H Rept 103-601, Part 3). The Subcommittee on Military Forces and Personnel had approved the draft, 7-5, on July 20.

The Armed Services Committee sidestepped a fight over abortion services by declining to act on provisions concerning the benefits package. That effectively deleted language that would have required the Defense Department to offer health care plans with benefits at least as generous as those offered to the rest of the population. Although Clinton's plan did not specifically mention abortion, officials said it would be a covered benefit.

Steve Buyer, R-Ind., said that if the language had remained in the committee's bill, he would have offered an amendment to explicitly eliminate abortion from the services to be covered. Buyer's amendment probably would have succeeded in the conservative Armed Services panel. For that reason, abortion rights supporters such as Patricia Schroeder, D-Colo., said they thought it was better not to open up the issue of benefits at all.

Instead, the lawmakers acted on only a small portion of the changes recommended in Clinton's plan, arguing that such an approach would give the Defense Department greater flexibility in dealing with whatever health care overhaul measure became law.

The language approved by the panel included a provision to require Medicare to reimburse the Defense Department for health care provided to Medicare-eligible retirees or their dependents at military hospitals, a potential $1 billion annual bonus for the Defense Department.

The Senate Armed Services Committee took a somewhat different approach. On July 27, it approved provisions that would require Medicare to reimburse costs for military retirees and their dependents who chose a Defense Department health care plan through a new Pentagon health insurance system called Tricare. The Senate Committee did not require Medicare to pay for services rendered at military hospitals for retirees who did not belong to Tricare.

• **House Government Operations.** On July 27, the House Government Operations Committee gave voice vote approval to legislation designed to beef up the prosecution of fraud and give added privacy protection to patients' medical records (H Rept 103-601, Part 5).

The panel proposed to set up a fund, financed by fines and other financial penalties, that the attorney general could use to boost prosecutions.

It also proposed to designate all health care information that could be traced back to the patient as protected health care information. Unauthorized disclosure of such information could result in federal criminal penalties. The committee also proposed to classify people with access to these records as health information trustees, meaning they would be held liable for any unlawful disclosure.

During the markup, members approved by voice vote an amendment by Edolphus Towns, D-N.Y., to require states to establish programs to house the medical records of doctors and other health care providers that went out of business. Towns said that while some states already had laws to deal with this, many did not.

Earlier the same day, the Subcommittee on Information, Justice, Transportation and Agriculture and the Subcommittee on Human Resources approved their portions of the bill, both by voice vote.

● **House Judiciary.** The House Judiciary Committee approved provisions that aimed to reduce malpractice costs, tighten antitrust rules to promote competition among health insurers and create a program to prevent fraud and abuse in the new health system. Judiciary approved its section of HR 3600 by voice vote Aug. 2.

• **Malpractice suits.** The most contentious battle centered on malpractice suits. Under Clinton's plan, a malpractice claim could not be brought in court until the parties had submitted to some form of alternative dispute resolution — usually mediation or arbitration. A plaintiff dissatisfied with the outcome could then bring suit if a qualified medical specialist determined that he or she had a meritorious claim. An attorney's contingency fee would be limited to one-third of the amount recovered by the plaintiff.

By 21-13, the committee approved an amendment by Chairman Jack Brooks, D-Texas, to make the use of alternative dispute resolution voluntary, not mandatory. Contingency fees still would be capped at one-third of an award, but lawyers could petition the court for an increase if the case were appealed. With court approval, defendants could make periodic payments if damages in a malpractice suit exceeded $250,000.

Republicans said that the possibility of multimillion-dollar damage awards encouraged frivolous suits, driving up the cost of malpractice insurance. Democrats accused panel Republicans of exaggerating the impact of malpractice litigation on health costs, and they expressed concern about protecting the rights of malpractice victims, particularly low-income and minority patients.

The committee rejected, by a near party-line vote of 14-20, an amendment by ranking Republican Hamilton Fish Jr., N.Y., that would have imposed a $350,000 cap on non-economic damages, such as compensation for pain and suffering or emotional distress caused by negligence. The Fish amendment was similar to a $250,000 cap agreed to by the Senate Finance Committee on July 2. But Democrats argued that a cap would disproportionately hurt the poor and minorities, who often could obtain legal counsel only when the prospect of a large damage award offered an attorney a potentially large contingency fee.

The panel also rejected, by a vote of 15-19, a Fish amendment that would have allowed punitive damages only when there was a clear indication that the defendant had committed egregious acts.

• **Antitrust.** Partisan lines blurred somewhat when members took up proposed changes to the McCarran-Ferguson Act of 1945, which exempted the insurance industry from federal antitrust law to allow companies to pool information

needed to calculate rates.

Originally, HR 3600 applied antitrust law to health insurers to stimulate competition. The antitrust exemption was to remain for other types of insurers.

The committee approved, 20-15, an amendment by Brooks to largely eliminate the exemption for all insurers. The Brooks language mirrored separate legislation (HR 9) approved by the committee July 22. Insurers could still share some information, such as data on occupational accidents and illnesses for workers' compensation benefits. But the measure would phase out the sharing of "trending" information, used to project costs and calculate rates. *(Insurance antitrust, p. 183)*

The committee also approved, 20-14, an amendment by Fish to eliminate a provision in HR 3600 requiring pharmaceutical companies to charge the same price to all buyers of a given drug. Fish said that this practice, known as unitary pricing, would lead to higher prices for large health providers, because drug companies could not reward volume buyers without offering the same discount to everyone else.

Mike Synar, D-Okla., argued that drug manufacturers that give big discounts to large-volume buyers made up the difference by charging exorbitant prices to small providers. Synar proposed that unitary pricing be required for Medicare recipients, who accounted for a large segment of the drug-buying market. His amendment was rejected 10-24.

The committee initially approved a Brooks amendment striking a provision in the bill that would have exempted individual doctors from antitrust laws and allowed them to join together to negotiate fees with health providers. But later, the panel partially reversed itself, approving 18-17 an amendment by Charles T. Canady, R-Fla., preserving this antitrust exemption for some doctors, but barring them from joining to negotiate fees.

• **Fraud.** The committee also approved provisions to create a program to coordinate the efforts of federal, state and local agencies to prevent and detect fraud and abuse.

A variety of civil penalties could be imposed on both patients and providers for infractions such as enrolling in a plan under false pretenses or denying enrollment to people on the basis of their medical condition. Criminal fines and jail terms could be levied against those convicted of offenses such as bribery and embezzlement. All fines and penalties collected would be paid into an Anti-Fraud Account to fund the watchdog program.

● **House Natural Resources.** At its markup July 20, the Natural Resources Committee endorsed Clinton's plan to create a new and improved Indian Health Service (IHS) to provide health care to the nation's 1.2 million Indians (H Rept 103-601, Part 6).

Under the provisions, which the panel approved by voice vote, the IHS would expand to eventually offer the same comprehensive set of benefits available to other U.S. citizens under Clinton's plan. Clinton's bill provided for the IHS to continue to offer Indians additional benefits such as adult dental care. The U.S. government was obligated to provide supplemental health benefits under treaties with Indian tribes.

Indians could choose private health plans, but the measure encouraged them to sign up with the IHS by making the coverage free to all Indians. Tribal governments and major employers on reservations, also would be exempt from health payments to the IHS. The measure included an authorization of $220 million in fiscal 1995 to improve IHS services and facilities and to continue supplemental health services. The amount for fiscal 1996 was $380 million; unspecified amounts were authorized thereafter.

At the markup, the committee adopted a broad amendment containing several changes sought by tribal leaders. These included provisions to guarantee the continuation of supplemental health benefits, ensure that all Indians could be covered by the IHS and encourage Indians to join the medical profession. The measure also aimed to increase the number of doctors working in Indian country.

Another amendment, approved by voice vote and sponsored by Karan English, D-Ariz., sought to protect the IHS's 15,000 employees from any staff reductions resulting from the president's plan to streamline and "reinvent" the federal government.

Wayne Allard, R-Colo., offered an amendment to put Clinton's entire health care overhaul plan on budget. His amendment would have defined mandates — such as the proposal to require employers to contribute to employees' health costs — as taxes. All federal spending envisioned by the bill would have been defined as outlays.

Chairman George Miller, D-Calif., refused to consider Allard's amendment, ruling it out of order. Under rules governing committee consideration of the health care bill, committees could consider only provisions directly relevant to their jurisdictions.

● **Senate Indian Affairs.** The Senate Indian Affairs Committee voted 10-8 on June 30 to expand and improve the IHS to serve as the primary health care provider for Indians. The IHS eventually would offer the same comprehensive benefits guaranteed to all Americans under Clinton's plan.

At the markup, the panel adopted by voice vote the package of amendments developed by tribal leaders in conjunction with the Clinton administration and committee members.

The panel turned back an amendment, 3-15, by Harry Reid, D-Nev., that would have required tribal-operated businesses to pay 80 percent of their employees' health insurance premiums. The federal government would have picked up the remaining 20 percent. Under the bill, tribal governments and businesses were to be exempt from contributing to health care premiums. Instead, the federal government would continue to provide health care to all eligible Indians as it was required to do under treaties dating back to the 1700s.

Reid said it was unfair for the government to provide health care to tribal businesses and individual Indians, when other businesses under the Clinton plan would be required to pay 80 percent of their employees' premiums. Chairman Daniel K. Inouye, D-Hawaii, countered that Indians already paid for health care when they gave up their lands under federal treaties.

An effort to put the committee on record in support of turning the IHS into an entitlement program was defeated, 8-10.

● **House Post Office and Civil Service.** The House Post Office and Civil Service Committee on July 28 approved provisions to allow millions of private-sector employees to join the health insurance plan that served Congress and other federal employees (HR 3600 — H Rept 103-601, Part 7). The measure, approved by voice vote, proposed to open the Federal Employees Health Benefits Program to the unemployed, the self-employed, and workers at firms with 100 or fewer employees. Clinton had proposed to eliminate the federal employees' insurance plan.

"Members will be able to tell their constituents that they can receive the same health benefits that members of Congress receive," Chairman William L. Clay, D-Mo., said at the markup. In fact, not all federal health plans were offered at all locations across the country. But the program still offered a wide variety of choices to eligible people. The provision was included in the compromise bill that House Majority Leader Richard A. Gephardt, D-Mo., introduced July 29.

While opening up the plan had widespread appeal among private-sector workers, it was vehemently opposed by the powerful federal employee unions. They contended that adding so many people to the rolls would drive up the cost of insurance premiums for federal employees.

To appease the unions, the Post Office bill proposed to keep federal workers and retirees already on the insurance plan in a separate pool for several years for purposes of calculating insurance premiums. The approach seemed to work. Robert M. Tobias, president of the National Treasury Employees Union said July 29 that his union "supports what the chairman has done."

Moreover, non-federal workers could join the program only after several insurance-industry changes had been put in place, including a ban on the practice of denying coverage to people with existing medical conditions.

● **House Veterans' Affairs.** The House veterans provisions (H Rept 103-601, Part 4) originated in the Veterans' Affairs Subcommittee on Hospitals and Health Care, which approved the measure May 11 by a vote of 18-1.

The provisions largely paralleled Clinton's bill, allowing veterans and their families to choose between the Department of Veterans Affairs (VA) and other private medical providers. The VA would maintain its independent status and would compete with private providers for patients.

But subcommittee Chairman J. Roy Rowland, D-Ga., added provisions, not in the president's plan, aimed at putting the VA on a more secure financial footing. Veterans advocates were concerned that Clinton's plan would not leave the VA strong enough to compete with private providers for patients.

Rowland's draft provided for a new federal entitlement program for veterans who received free care under the existing system, namely, those with service-connected injuries and poor veterans. Under existing law, money to treat these veterans was subject to the annual appropriations process; Rowland proposed that the money be distributed automatically to the VA.

In addition, his draft directed the Treasury to pay the VA more than $4 billion over three years to aid it in gearing up to compete against private providers for patients. This "directed spending" also was not to be subject to annual appropriations.

Before endorsing the legislation, the subcommittee voted 11-8 to adopt an amendment by Christopher H. Smith, R-N.J., to prohibit abortions at any medical facility run by the VA.

The full committee approved the legislation by voice vote July 21 after rejecting an attempt to add abortion to the list of services that were to be available to veterans and their families.

The unsuccessful abortion amendment, offered by Luis V. Gutierrez, D-Ill., would have required the VA to offer all services available under the comprehensive benefits package called for in HR 3600. Although abortion was not specifically mentioned in HR 3600, officials said it would be a covered benefit. Gutierrez argued that the measure as written could "put restrictions on veterans that don't apply to the population as a whole." Joseph P. Kennedy II, D-Mass., agreed, adding that eliminating abortion would make the VA a less attractive option for many veterans and their families.

But Smith said the Gutierrez language would force the VA to perform abortions at taxpayer expense. "Don't turn the VA's 171 hospitals and over 350 outpatient clinics into abortion mills," Smith said. In the end, Smith persuaded all 14 of

Continued on page 348

Clinton Health Care Overhaul ...

Bill	Coverage	Benefits	Alliances
CLINTON PLAN	Guarantee health insurance coverage for all Americans by 1998 by requiring employers to buy insurance for their employees as of Jan. 1 of that year.	Mandate a package of specific benefits covering routine doctor visits, hospitalization and emergency services, preventive care and limited coverage for mental illnesses and substance abuse; prescription drugs; rehabilitation services; hospice, home health and extended nursing care services; and lab and diagnostic services.	Require that states set up large consumer groups called "health alliances" to collect premiums, bargain with health plans and handle payments. All companies with 5,000 or fewer employees would have to buy coverage through an alliance.
SENATE LABOR AND HUMAN RESOURCES	Guarantee universal coverage by Jan. 1, 1998, with a so-called employer mandate, like Clinton's plan, but include exemptions for small businesses.	Build on the Clinton package, adding additional preventive care for women and adolescents, home care for the severely disabled and a new federal program for individuals to purchase long-term nursing-home insurance. A national board would review the package before the bill went into effect for unanticipated deficit spending. The board would propose cost-cutting changes in the package, which would go into effect unless both chambers of Congress rejected them.	Require states to establish at least one insurance purchasing cooperative that would provide access to community rated insurance plans. Individuals would not have to purchase insurance from the cooperative. Instead, insurance could be bought directly from an insurer or independent agent, or individuals could participate in the Federal Employees Health Benefits Plan. Premium rates would be the same regardless of how insurance was obtained.
SENATE FINANCE	Aim to cover 95 percent of Americans by 2002 by reforming the insurance market and by providing subsidies for poor and low-income individuals to buy health insurance.	Provide two standard packages of benefits that all insurance plans would have to offer: a comprehensive plan and a plan that would cover major illness or injuries but require consumers to pay for most other medical services.	Permit the formation of voluntary insurance purchasing pools. If no pools formed by 1996, states would have to create one for underserved areas. Individuals could join the federal plan.
HOUSE EDUCATION AND LABOR	Same as Clinton's plan, though there would be larger subsidies to help small businesses pay for the costs.	Follow outlines of Clinton's package but expand benefits for mental illness, dental coverage and women's and children's care. Include a program to increase the numbers of health care providers in rural areas and a plan for seasonal and migrant workers.	Replace mandatory alliances with consumer purchasing cooperatives established by the states, either on a voluntary or a mandatory basis. Most of the regulatory activities that the alliances would do under the Clinton bill would be given to the states.
HOUSE WAYS AND MEANS	An employer mandate would take effect Jan. 1, 1996, for employers with more than 100 employees. Other employers would have to provide insurance by Jan. 1, 1998. Individuals would be required to have insurance. Establish a new government-run insurance program, called Medicare Part C, to provide health coverage for the uninsured, those on Medicaid, and for many employees of small businesses.	Less generous than the Clinton plan. The standard benefits package offered by all insurers would include everything covered by Medicare (doctor and hospital visits) as well as prescription drugs, pregnancy-related services, chiropractic care, mental health and substance abuse treatment, and other services. A modest long-term care program for the severely disabled would begin in 2000.	Give states the option of creating mandatory alliances. But companies with more than 5,000 employees nationally could opt out of state insurance regulations.

...Compared With Committee Bills

Financing	Taxes	Cost Controls
Require employers to pay 80 percent of the average health insurance plan in their areas for unmarried workers and an average of 55 percent of the family plan, but no more than 7.9 percent of payrolls for companies with fewer than 5,000 workers. Companies with 75 or fewer employees and average wages of $24,000 or less would be eligible for subsidies.	Raise the 24-cents-a-pack cigarette tax by 75 cents, to 99 cents. Impose a 1 percent payroll tax on companies with 5,000 or more workers that did not join health alliances. Allow alliances to levy an additional 2.5 percent assessment to help pay their administrative costs.	Limit the annual increase in the price of health insurance premiums after 2000 to the rate of inflation, adjusted for population and other socioeconomic factors. That was less than half the 10 percent-plus annual rate of growth in health care costs in recent years. Government costs would be controlled by a cap on spending for subsidies.
Require most employers to pay 80 percent of workers' insurance costs, similar to the Clinton plan. Businesses with fewer than 10 workers and a low average wage would be exempt. Firms with one to five workers would pay a 1 percent payroll tax; those with six to 10 workers would pay a 2 percent payroll tax. Low-wage firms with between 10 and 75 workers would be required to pay for a percentage of insurance costs.	Require companies with 1,000 or more employees to pay a 1 percent payroll tax. Increase the cigarette tax to $1.49 per pack.	Establish target ceilings for health insurance premium increases. By 2000, increases would be limited to the general inflation rate. If the average increase in a state exceeded the federal target, a national board would review insurance increases and direct high-cost plans to bring costs down.
No employer mandate. The subsidies would be funded by $55 billion in Medicare cuts over five years, cuts in Medicaid and new taxes.	Increase the cigarette tax to $1.24. Impose a 1.75 percent tax on insurance premiums to support academic medical centers and impose a tax on high-cost insurance plans. Affluent Medicare recipients would face higher premiums and co-payments. The tax deduction for individuals who bought their own insurance would rise from 25 percent to 100 percent.	No private sector cost controls. Use the tax on high-cost insurance to hold down costs. Government health costs would be capped by setting a baseline for all health care spending — Medicare, Medicaid and subsidies under health care reform for the poor. Subsidies would be reduced if government spending exceeded the baseline.
Retain the Clinton provision but provide greater subsidies for the smallest employers with low-wage workers, who were not required to pay more than 2 percent of their payrolls.	Impose a 1 percent assessment on employers of more than 1,000 workers. Retain the tax recommendations in the Clinton package.	Similar to Clinton's plan.
Require most companies to pay at least 80 percent of their full-time employees' insurance premiums. Employers with 50 employers or fewer whose average salary was $26,000 or less would receive a tax credit to reduce the premium cost. For firms with 25 employees or fewer, the maximum credit would reduce the employer premium share to 40 percent. For companies with 26 to 50 employees, it would reduce the employers share by as much as half.	Increase the tobacco tax by 45 cents by 1999. Impose a 2 percent tax on health insurance premiums. Companies would have to pay health care premiums for both married workers; the government through 2001 would claim a portion of payments for those workers already covered under a spouse's plan.	Establish a system of spending controls for private insurance plans that could take effect beginning in 2001 in states that failed to limit the growth of health care spending to annual percentage increases in the gross domestic product. A commission would recommend by 2000 whether Congress should allow the cost controls to take effect; unless Congress overturned the controls or chose some other course, the system would go into effect.

Continued from page 345
the panel's Republicans and five Democrats to join him in killing the amendment, 14-20.

The full committee gave voice vote approval to a substitute amendment, offered by Rowland, that aimed to give the VA the flexibility to function under a number of different health systems being considered by Congress, including plans to sell coverage through a system of voluntary purchasing alliances and plans to establish a taxpayer-financed, single-payer system.

Rowland's changes also aimed to provide the VA with additional financial and purchasing strength to enhance its ability to operate in a new competitive environment. For instance, it allowed the VA to be reimbursed by Medicare for treating Medicare-eligible spouses and dependents of veterans. The original bill language had allowed reimbursement for Medicare-eligible veterans only, not for their families.

In addition, under the amendment, the VA would be allowed to purchase reinsurance coverage. Existing law barred federal agencies from purchasing commercial insurance. But private health insurers regularly reinsured to guard against unforeseen losses that might result from such causes as a natural disaster or an epidemic.

The amendment also waived some federal procurement rules to give the VA additional flexibility in contracting for services. The waiver was aimed at allowing the VA to consider quality and other factors more seriously when contracting out to hospitals, doctors and other medical providers, rather than simply choosing the lowest bidder who could fulfill the contract.

The committee also gave voice vote approval to an amendment by Lane Evans, D-Ill., to authorize the VA to study the impact of "telemedicine" on the delivery and quality of health care. Telemedicine involved the use of the telephone by doctors to advise other doctors and diagnose patients. Evans said the practice could be particularly useful in rural areas, where specialists often were separated from patients by hundreds of miles.

● **Senate Veterans' Affairs.** Like its House counterpart, the Senate Veterans' Affairs Committee sought to integrate veterans health care services into whatever new medical system would ultimately created under health care legislation.

Meeting on July 14, the panel first approved a measure that largely mirrored Clinton's plan for the VA. The 8-4 vote was largely along party lines, with only James M. Jeffords, R-Vt., joining the Democrats.

The committee then approved, 12-0, alternative proposals that would allow the VA to function under a variety of health care systems. "We are trying to be flexible," said committee Chairman John D. Rockefeller IV, D-W.Va., sponsor of the bill.

Rockefeller said the alternatives would be added during Senate floor debate only if needed. For example, if the Senate health care bill did not require employers to contribute to their employees' insurance premiums, the VA would be authorized to collect funds from Medicare or private health insurers when treating veterans who were covered by those providers.

Like Clinton's proposal, Rockefeller's principal bill maintained the independence of the VA's medical system while forcing it to compete with private health care providers. The plan gave most veterans the option of purchasing health care services from the VA or from private medical providers. It also opened the door for spouses and children of veterans to purchase health services from the VA.

The VA still would provide free treatment to poor veterans and those who had been injured as a result of military service.

Party Leaders Attempt To Draft a Viable Bill

Congress' weeklong Independence Day recess marked a turning point in the health care story. With the work of the committees virtually complete, action shifted to Democratic leaders in the House and Senate, who set out to do what five powerful committee chairmen had not managed to accomplish — draft legislation that both met Clinton's demand for universal coverage and could garner enough votes to pass.

The leadership schedule was ambitious, given the task, though time was already running out for the 103rd Congress. Senate Majority Leader George J. Mitchell, D-Maine, hoped to start Senate floor debate the week of July 25; House Majority Leader Richard A. Gephardt, D-Mo., wanted to bring a bill to the House Rules Committee soon thereafter.

For all their work, not one committee had managed to write a health care bill that the leadership was willing to bring to the floor. So Mitchell, Gephardt and others began to stitch together new legislation from pieces of Clinton's plan and from bills passed by various committees. "Even the deal-makers couldn't make deals," said Burdett Loomis, a political scientist at the University of Kansas. "The inability of the committees to come up with some type of working document raises legitimate questions about whether party leaders will be able to do so."

The first decisions that had to be made were what to do about the employer mandate and how universal to make "universal" coverage. These would set the parameters for other decisions, such as how to control costs and what changes to make in insurance practices. The work took place in Democrats-only sessions in the leaders' offices. While congressional leaders had been forced to craft major bills behind closed doors in the past — notably the 1990 Clean Air Act and the 1990 budget agreement — those were two-party operations.

By July 21, Mitchell, Gephardt and House Speaker Thomas S. Foley, D-Wash., were ready to formally tell Clinton that they had to back off from the sweeping overhaul he had envisioned. At a late-night White House meeting, they told the president that the bills they were cobbling together for floor action would contain a long phase-in of the employer mandate and possibly exemptions for small businesses.

Clinton expressed satisfaction with the meeting during a brief exchange with reporters the next day. "I have been saying for four weeks we have agreed to dramatically change this plan," he said. Strategically, the meeting took the heat off Clinton, who had been battered by liberals after he tried to send a similar message July 19 to a meeting of the National Governors' Association. "I am open to any solution to this," he told the governors. "All I ask in these closing weeks of this debate is that we take the political air out of the balloon and ask ourselves what will work for ordinary Americans." Clinton got into trouble, particularly, when he spoke bluntly of "functional universal coverage," which he said meant "around 95 percent" of Americans.

Gephardt Bill

Gephardt went first, unveiling the House Democratic leadership's health care proposal at a July 29 Democratic Caucus

Gephardt Bill: Highlights

The health care bill crafted by House Majority Leader Richard A. Gephardt, D-Mo., aimed to guarantee affordable insurance for all Americans by 1999.

It required employers to pay the bulk of their workers' premiums and provided for a new government program to cover the poor and uninsured. It also proposed that millions of private workers be allowed to join a version of the Federal Employee Health Benefits Plan, which served Congress and the executive branch.

The federal government was to pay about $150 billion annually to subsidize the purchase of premiums for low-income people once it was fully phased in — about the same as was then spent on the government's Medicaid program.

The following are highlights of the bill:

● **Employer mandate.** Employers would have to pay at least 80 percent of their employees' premiums; workers would pay the rest. Employers of more than 100 workers would have to start covering their workers in 1997; smaller employers would start in 1999.

● **Insurance options.** All companies would have to offer workers at least two plans: one with an unlimited choice of doctors and one a managed-care plan, which would limit the choice of doctors and the ability of patients to have tests and consult specialists.

Businesses with fewer than 100 employees could enroll in either a private plan or a new government insurance program known as Medicare Part C. If an employer selected a private plan, its workers could choose to buy a plan offered locally through a version of the federal employee plan.

● **Subsidies.** Low-income families and individuals with incomes of up to 240 percent of the poverty level would receive subsidies on a sliding scale to help them pay for insurance. Full subsidies would be available for those at or below 100 percent of poverty. (The poverty line was about $14,800 for a family of four.)

● **Benefits.** All insurance plans would have to cover doctor visits, hospital care, limited skilled-nursing care, laboratory services, preventive care, family planning including abortion, and limited mental health and substance abuse coverage. Annual deductibles would be set at $500 for individuals and $750 for families. Out-of-pocket costs would be capped, but the level had not been determined. The Ways and Means bill proposed to cap a family's out-of-

pocket spending at $11,000; Clinton wanted to limit it to $3,000.

Prescription drugs would be covered but would be subject to a separate $500 annual deductible, a separate $1,000 out-of-pocket limit and a 20 percent co-insurance payment requirement. Drugs would be subject to a $250 deductible under the Clinton plan.

● **Tax increases.** The cigarette tax would rise by 45 cents a pack, bringing the federal tax to 69 cents a pack. A 2 percent sales tax would be added to all insurance premiums. Workers could no longer exclude from their taxable income the cost of health care bought through so-called cafeteria plans or flexible spending accounts.

● **Tax credits.** Small employers that paid relatively low wages could get tax credits of as much as 50 percent of the cost of their workers' insurance.

● **Cost controls.** Costs of the new Medicare Part C program would be controlled by limiting the amounts that hospitals, doctors and other providers could be reimbursed for services to patients. These limits would be similar to those that applied to Medicare Parts A and B, the government's health insurance program for the elderly and disabled.

For the private sector, cost controls would not occur before 2000, when a commission would determine whether health spending in each state exceeded a national growth target tied to the growth of the gross national product. If spending exceeded the target, reimbursement limits similar to those used in Medicare would be applied to providers in the state.

● **Insurance rules.** Insurance plans could not price insurance based on the health status of enrollees. All plans sold to firms of fewer than 100 workers would have to provide for community rating, meaning that all enrollees would be charged the same price for the same policies.

● **Public health.** All plans would have to contract with the clinics, doctors and hospitals that qualified as essential providers to the local community to ensure that consumers in inner-city and rural areas could continue to get their care from local providers.

● **Single payer.** States could choose to set up a single-payer system. In states that did so, all firms would have to comply with the state single-payer system's rules. In states without single-payer plans, multistate firms could remain exempt from statewide insurance rules.

---

session that at times took on the inspirational tone associated with Pentecostal tent meetings. "This is more than a piece of legislation. It's a piece of the American dream," he told the Democrats. "And if we pass it, if we triumph over the special interests and the party obstructionists, it will be every American's guarantee of security and dignity and decency for as long as they live." *(Highlights, above)*

The bill relied heavily on the version put together by the Ways and Means Committee. It was designed to provide universal coverage by 1999, requiring all employers to pay at least 80 percent of their workers' insurance premiums.

Instead of health care alliances, the bill adopted the Ways and Means plan to create a Medicare Part C, a new government health insurance program to serve the poor, the unemployed and those who worked part-time or in small businesses. Employees of small businesses could also join a version of the Federal Employees Health Benefits Plan — the same insurance plan used by government workers and members of Congress.

Few of the proposed tax increases from Clinton's plan remained in the bill other than a cigarette tax increase of 45 cents a pack and a 2 percent sales tax on all insurance premiums.

In presenting the plan, Gephardt began by solemnly reminding Democrats of their history of support for the country's great social programs — Medicare and Social Security. He outlined his own bill and warned lawmakers that Democratic victory in November would be at risk if health care failed to pass. By the end, as members rose to their feet applauding, the meeting had become an exuberant rally for the cause of universal coverage.

Gephardt and Majority Whip David E. Bonior, D-Mich., had spent the previous two to three weeks meeting almost constantly with House Democrats to ensure that everyone had a hearing before they presented the bill. In Gephardt's first-floor Capitol office he clocked scores of hours with members of the Congressional Black Caucus and the Congressional Hispanic Caucus, with groups of conservative Democrats and with individual members or groups that had concerns specific to their district or region.

In a warm-up session the day before Gephardt's presentation, pollster Mark Mellman told the caucus, "It's quite clear that the Democrats go into this election cycle in some difficulty." He said his data showed two things: "People want the health care system to be reformed, and they want the Clinton plan itself to be reformed." He said the key was to assure the

public that the leadership plan did not include the two things that people hated most about Clinton's proposal — an array of new taxes and health alliances.

Many Democrats argued that the time had come to back the leadership bill, even if it meant compromising. With Democrats in control of both chambers and the White House, they argued, it would be hard to convince voters that Republicans were to blame. "There is growing pressure on moderate Democrats to come home," said Joe Moakley, D-Mass., chairman of the Rules Committee. "We're talking about rallying around the flag; we need to stick together."

Working against that argument, however, was the overwhelming complexity of the legislation, which only a handful of lawmakers understood well. "This is not an issue where the leadership can say to people, 'Trust me,' " said Jim McDermott, D-Wash. "Usually a committee works on a bill, and then committee members say to the rest of us, 'Trust me, this is a good bill,' and we vote for it. But it's very dicey to accept a 'trust me' on this bill. ... This isn't like voting to take some action in Bosnia. It affects every person in every member's district."

But in the end, perhaps the most critical factor in determining the fate of the House bill was the Senate — particularly its disposition of the employer mandate. Many House members did not want to take a vote on the House bill until they saw what the Senate was going to do. But because Senate rules allowed unlimited debate and amendment, Mitchell had limited control over the timing. And, it was to Senate Republicans' advantage to delay action on the employer mandate, thus making it more likely that the Democratic leadership's bill would fail.

A July 28 memo from GOP strategist William Kristol, chairman of the Project for the Republican Future, urged Republicans to defeat any Democratic health care bill and "send them to the voters empty-handed."

Mitchell Plan

Mitchell released his plan Aug. 2. Rather than aiming for universal coverage, he proposed to reach 95 percent coverage by 2000. In response to requests from conservative Democrats, he proposed to give market forces a chance to increase coverage before turning to government enforcement. The bill did not require any employers to contribute to employees' health care costs until 2002. Even if the employer mandate kicked in, firms would never be required to pay more than 50 percent of the cost of their workers' premiums; it would never affect businesses with fewer than 25 workers, and it would be enforced only in states that failed to achieve 95 percent coverage.

Mitchell took weeks to craft the crucial compromise on the mandate and took every political sounding possible. He worked on it until just hours before the outline of the bill was released, to ensure that he had heard out and accommodated every possible senator. *(Highlights, p. 351)*

Mitchell's plan was a political high-wire act designed to push liberals as far to the center as possible without losing them and at the same time appeal to the party's conservatives. But if conservative Democrats still refused to go along, Mitchell could do little to modify the bill without losing liberals. Asked if he and other liberals would vote for a bill that boosted coverage more slowly, or bypassed an employer mandate altogether, John D. Rockefeller IV, D-W.Va., a leading proponent of the Clinton plan, said flatly: "No."

Democrats who supported the Clinton bill or a single-payer system said they had hoped to start with a stronger

mandate since they expected it to be compromised as the debate moved forward. But conservative Democrat John B. Breaux of Louisiana said he was skeptical of the necessity to move ahead with any mandate at all, especially since a July 28 Congressional Budget Office (CBO) report found that 92 percent of Americans could obtain coverage under a plan without a mandate.

But that option would leave about 19 million Americans without insurance and could bring a presidential veto. Liberal Democrats also seemed unlikely to vote for it after speaking so strongly about the need for universal coverage.

The Senate began debate on the bill (S 2351) Aug. 9, with Mitchell insisting that he would keep senators in Washington as long as necessary — giving up part or all of their August recess — to complete action on health care. He brought his bill to the floor as a substitute amendment without the votes to pass it. His only consolation was that his opponents lacked the votes to hand him an outright defeat.

But Mitchell could not break the deadlock. Democrats were divided. Conservative Democrats, many of them Southerners, simply did not see great political gain in supporting the cause of extending insurance coverage to all Americans. The skittishness was heightened by the approach of the November elections, especially for the many members in marginal seats. And Republicans were virtually unanimous in their opposition.

Although the floor debate was historic because of the magnitude of the legislation, it often abandoned the ideological high ground as liberal Democrats and conservative Republicans engaged in rhetorical fistfights. Republicans accused Democrats of being big-government addicts. Democrats countered that Republicans were captives of business interests and willing to leave millions of people without insurance.

As the two sides poked and jabbed in public, Mitchell worked behind the scenes trying to reshape his bill to entice wary Democrats one vote at a time.

Moderates Offer Alternative

Many members of both parties in both chambers continued to believe that the middle ground was where the votes were, but they were unable to draw significant support away from the extreme ends of the spectrum. "We're trying to find the center at the worst possible time: when partisan tempers are flaring," said Will Marshall, president of the Progressive Policy Institute, a think tank allied with the more moderate wing of the Democratic party. "We have to stop holding out for some wholly unrealistic version of health care reform that only liberal Democrats will support."

Unwilling to give up, a bipartisan rump group of moderate senators, led by John H. Chafee, R-R.I., and Breaux, worked daily in Chafee's Capitol hideaway trying to come up with an alternative that could win enough adherents to pass.

On Aug. 19, with the Senate frozen in partisan jockeying, this self-styled Mainstream Group held a news conference to present its plan. The focus was on slowing cost increases for health care and reducing the deficit by $100 billion over 10 years. While the group set a goal of universal coverage, their bill aimed to reach about 93 percent of Americans by 1999. "Health care reform must be achieved one step at a time," said Breaux.

The Chafee-Breaux plan did not require employers to pay for their workers' health care. Rather, it provided for a commission to review the extent of coverage; if coverage were not increased significantly by 2002, Congress would have to vote on the commission's recommendations.

Mitchell Bill: Highlights

The health care bill unveiled Aug. 2 by Senate Majority Leader George J. Mitchell, D-Maine, and offered as an amendment to S 2351, aimed to extend affordable insurance coverage to 95 percent of Americans by 2000. It converted the employer mandate — which Clinton's plan saw as the chief mechanism for attaining universal coverage — into an enforcement tool that would actually take effect only if other measures failed to yield 95 percent coverage. The following are highlights of the bill:

● **Employer mandate.** Employers would not be required to pay worker health care costs before 2002. Then, they would be required to do so only if a series of alternative measures had failed to raise coverage to 95 percent of the population.

The process would begin with a commission report to Congress on the level of coverage nationwide in 2000. If coverage was below 95 percent, the commission would recommend ways to insure additional people. Congress would have to consider the recommendations — which did not have to include an employer mandate — on an expedited schedule and could amend them. If Congress failed to approve any legislation to close the insurance gap, then the employer mandate would go into effect, but only in those states where less than 95 percent of the population was covered and not before 2002.

The mandate would require businesses with 25 or more workers to pay at least 50 percent of the cost of their workers' premiums. It would not apply to companies with fewer than 25 workers.

● **Individual mandate.** A separate requirement that individuals obtain coverage would be triggered if an employer mandate went into effect.

● **Subsidies.** Insurance costs would be subsidized for people with incomes of up to 200 percent of the federal poverty line and for pregnant women and children with incomes of up to 300 percent of the poverty line. People earning up to 100 percent of the poverty level or less would have their coverage fully subsidized.

● **Cost controls.** The measure would control private sector costs primarily through a 25 percent tax on the amount that a plan's premiums exceeded a target rate. This mechanism was a cross between a proposed cap on premium increases in Clinton's health care bill and a proposed tax on high-cost plans approved by the Senate Finance Committee.

In the public sector, the bill would reduce the rate of increase in Medicare costs and cap the amount that could be spent annually on all government health programs, including Medicare and Medicaid.

The bill made two exceptions. Pregnant women and children would continue to receive subsidies, even if that widened the federal budget deficit. The automatic limits would be suspended for everyone if there were a recession.

● **Taxes.** Mitchell picked up an array of taxes from the Senate Finance bill, in contrast to the House bill, which had few tax provisions. The taxes included a 1.75 percent tax on health plan premiums designed to raise $75 billion over 10 years to finance academic health centers and research; an increase of 45 cents per pack in the cigarette tax; a 50 percent excise tax on gun ammunition; and a premium increase for some high-income, elderly individuals and couples receiving Medicare coverage.

● **Savings.** The bill proposed to reduce projected spending for Medicare by $54 billion over 1995-1999 and by an additional $224 billion over the following five years, with $140 billion of the savings paying for prescription drugs and for a program to finance limited, long-term care for the disabled. The bill would eliminate much of the Medicaid program, a strategy designed to save states $232 billion and save the federal government $387 billion over 10 years. That money was to be used to fund the subsidies for the poor.

● **Health alliances.** Businesses and individuals would be allowed, but not required, to form groups to purchase insurance. If no alliance existed in a coverage area, then the Federal Employees Health Benefits Program would be required to establish one. The alliances could bargain with insurers on behalf of their members. Individuals and workers in companies with fewer than 500 workers could buy insurance through the alliance.

● **Insurance reforms.** Require insurance companies to practice community rating, meaning that they would have to charge all subscribers the same amount. Variations would be permitted in order to reflect geography, coverage category (single or family) and age. Companies with fewer than 500 workers and individuals would pay the community rate.

● **State flexibility.** Allow states to choose to put in place single-payer systems. All employers in the state regardless of size would have to participate.

To limit cost increases, the plan relied primarily on required changes in insurance market practices and a controversial cap on the tax deductibility of health insurance costs. All insurance plans would have to offer a standard package of benefits, and no applicant could be denied coverage based on a pre-existing condition.

The so-called tax cap had been left out of most of the other bills under consideration. Liberals feared it would force people with generous plans into ones with less choice and less coverage, while conservatives considered the cap a tax.

The plan proposed drastic cuts in Medicare and Medicaid, in part to cut the deficit and in part to provide health insurance subsidies to people with incomes of up to 200 percent of poverty. Unlike other proposals that included Medicare cuts, the Chafee-Breaux bill did not give the elderly a break on prescription drug coverage or payments for long-term care.

The bill also proposed to increase the tobacco tax from 24 cents to 69 cents per pack of cigarettes.

While the self-styled mainstream group had no formal membership, 15-20 senators took part, including William S. Cohen, R-Maine, John C. Danforth, R-Mo., Dave Durenberger, R-Minn., Nancy Landon Kassebaum, R-Kan., David L. Boren, D-Okla., Dianne Feinstein, D-Calif., and Bob Kerrey, D-Neb.

The "mainstream" plan had problems of its own, however. To get an agreement, the group had scaled back subsidies to help the poor. That pleased Republicans and conservative Democrats such as Kerrey and Boren, who were skeptical of the huge expense and complexity of the subsidies. But the accommodations miffed more liberal members both inside and outside the group who considered expanding coverage for the poor a central goal of the overhaul effort. In a blistering floor speech, Paul Wellstone, D-Minn., said the plan would hurt Americans who needed help most, and benefit insurers.

More damaging to the plan's prospects was the defection of Bill Bradley, D-N.J., an original member of the group. He said the deal would leave too many people uncovered and, therefore, would not restrain health care costs sufficiently. "If you don't cover enough people, your cost-control mechanism will not be as effective as if you had everybody in the pool," Bradley said. He added, "I think the group moved away" from the middle.

Clinton offered encouragement to the Senate at an Aug. 19 news conference. "I would say to them, keep working, keep working at it, because if you delay you may well lose it altogether," he said.

Continued on p. 354

Clinton Health Care Overhaul . . .

Bill	Coverage	Benefits	Alliances
CLINTON PLAN	Guarantee health coverage for all Americans by 1998 by requiring employers to pay at least 80 percent of their employees' premiums as of Jan. 1 of that year.	Mandate a package of specific benefits covering routine doctor visits, hospitalization and emergency services, preventive care and limited coverage for mental illnesses and substance abuse; prescription drugs; rehabilitation services; hospice, home health and extended nursing care services; and lab and diagnostic services.	Require that states set up large consumer groups called "health alliances" to collect premiums, bargain with health plans and handle payments. All companies with 5,000 or fewer employees would have to buy coverage through an alliance.
SENATE LEADERSHIP PLAN	Aim to cover 95 percent of Americans by 2000.	Require plans to provide a comprehensive package from preventive care to home health services and prescription drugs. The bill left the specific scope of coverage to be determined by a commission.	Allow individuals and businesses of fewer than 500 workers to set up groups to purchase insurance. If no alliances were set up in a state, the federal government would set one up through the Federal Employees Health Benefits Program.
DOLE PLAN	Aim to give all Americans access to insurance, although a significant portion of the working poor would likely be uncovered. Provide subsidies to help the poorest, uninsured Americans afford insurance.	No standard package except for the very poor. A plan for families receiving subsidies would have to include comprehensive coverage, preventive care, mental health and substance abuse services and take special account of the needs of children and other vulnerable populations.	Allow but not require businesses and individuals to form large pools to purchase insurance.
HOUSE LEADERSHIP PLAN	Aim to cover all Americans by Jan. 1, 1999, by requiring businesses to help pay for workers' insurance and by setting up a new government insurance program called Medicare Part C.	Require all insurance plans to cover doctor visits, hospital care, limited skilled-nursing care, laboratory services, preventive care, family planning including abortion, and limited mental health and substance abuse coverage.	No requirement for alliances, though they could be formed by groups of businesses and consumers.
SINGLE-PAYER PLAN	Guarantee universal health coverage for all legal U.S. residents within one year of enactment. Replace the insurance industry with a government-run plan that would collect premiums and taxes and pay providers. Most of the program was to be run at the state level.	Establish a comprehensive benefits package with extensive preventive care benefits. Set up a national board to establish the complete package of benefits. There would be co-payments for long-term care, but no co-payments or deductibles for acute or preventive care.	No alliances as there would be no need to buy standard private insurance plans.

...Compared With Other Major Plans

Financing	Taxes	Cost Controls
Require employers to pay at least 80 percent of the average health insurance plan in their areas for unmarried workers and an average of 55 percent of the family plan, but no more than 7.9 percent of payrolls for companies with fewer than 5,000 workers. Companies with 75 or fewer employees and average wages of $24,000 or less would be eligible for subsidies.	Raise the 24-cents-a-pack cigarette tax by 75 cents, to 99 cents. Impose a 1 percent payroll tax on companies with 5,000 or more workers that did not join health alliances. Allow alliances to levy an additional 2.5 percent assessment to help pay their administrative costs.	Limit the annual increase in the price of health insurance premiums after 2000 to the rate of inflation, adjusted for population and other socioeconomic factors. That was less than half the 10 percent-plus annual rate of growth in health care costs in recent years. Government costs would be controlled by a cap on spending for subsidies.
Rely primarily on a combination of cuts in Medicare, a re-targeting of federal and state spending for Medicaid — the government's insurance program for the poor — and taxes to provide subsidies for low-income Americans. In addition, if mandated changes in insurance practices and other measures failed to boost coverage to 95 percent by 2000, employers might have to help pay for workers' insurance in some states.	Impose an array of new taxes, most of them small. Among the larger ones were a 1.75 percent tax on health plan premiums and an excise tax on gun ammunition. Raise premiums for high-income elderly people who received health care through the existing Medicare program.	Control private-sector costs primarily through a 25 percent tax on the amount that a high cost plan's premiums exceeded a target rate. Control public-sector costs by reducing the rate of increase in Medicare costs and capping the amount that could be spent annually on all government health care programs including Medicare and Medicaid. The cost controls on federal programs could be suspended during a recession.
No requirement that employers or individuals buy insurance. Individuals and businesses with two to 50 workers could buy into the Federal Employees Health Benefits Program.	No tax increases. The existing 25 percent deduction for self-employed people would rise to 100 percent by 2000.	No provisions to control prices or costs.
Require employers to pay at least 80 percent of their employees' premiums, starting in 1997 for companies with more than 100 workers and in 1999 for smaller firms. Businesses with fewer than 100 employees could enroll in a private plan or in a new government insurance program called Medicare Part C. If an employer chose a private plan, its workers could buy coverage through a version of the Federal Employees Health Benefits Program.	Increase the cigarette tax by 45 cents to 69 cents a pack and add a sales tax of 2 percent to all insurance premiums.	Control costs of the new Medicare Part C program by limiting the amounts that doctors, hospitals and other providers could be reimbursed for services to patients. Private sector cost controls would not occur before 2000, when a commission would determine whether health spending in each state exceeded a national growth target tied to the gross domestic product. If so, reimbursement limits similar to those used in Medicare would be applied to providers in the state.
Require small employers (defined as fewer than 75 employees with an average salary of $24,000) to pay a 4 percent payroll tax. Larger employers would pay a 8.4 percent pay roll tax. Individuals would pay 2.1 percent of their taxable income.	Raise the tax on cigarettes by $1.76 per pack to a total of $2, make proportional increases in other tobacco taxes and impose a 50-cent excise tax on handguns and ammunition.	Establish a federal budget for health care each year. Require each state to negotiate with health care providers and hospitals to ensure that it met its budget each year. Bill sponsors also argued that eliminating the private insurance system would significantly cut administration costs.

Compromise Bill: Highlights

In a last-ditch attempt to rescue health care reform, Senate Majority Leader George J. Mitchell, D-Maine, and a bipartisan coalition of senators known as the Mainstream Group agreed in September on a market-based health care proposal. Although the plan won wider support than other compromise plans, it failed to attract the 60 votes needed to stop a threatened GOP filibuster.

The bill — the last attempt before Mitchell gave up on health care reform — drew heavily on a plan that the Mainstream Group had drafted in August. The group was led by Sens. John H. Chafee, R-R.I., and John B. Breaux, D-La.

The Mitchell-Mainstream proposal included provisions to:

● **Insurance reform.** Require all insurance plans — whether offered by insurance companies or health maintenance organizations — to accept all comers. They could not refuse people with pre-existing medical conditions or charge them higher rates. Under a modified community rating proposal, insurers would have to offer the same rates to employees of small firms (fewer than 100 workers), individuals and self-employed people, though they could make adjustments for age.

● **Benefits.** Require all insurers to offer a standard benefits plan — comprehensive coverage similar to the standard plans offered by Blue Cross/Blue Shield.

Additionally, insurers could offer a basic plan that had lower premiums but less generous coverage and higher deductibles and/or a catastrophic plan with higher deductibles. The goal was to give consumers a choice in the type of plan they bought and the amount they would pay out-of-pocket.

The benefits for each type of plan would be defined by a nonpartisan benefits commission.

● **Employees and employers.** Allow workers for companies that did not pay for health insurance to buy their coverage through their employers, which would have to provide information on all plans, or through local health insurance purchasing cooperatives. Workers also could opt to buy plans through local branches of the Federal Employees Health Benefits Program, the health plan for

Congress and federal employees.

Employers that paid for their workers' insurance could either self-insure or contract with an insurer; they would have to offer workers a choice of at least two standard plans.

● **Purchasing cooperatives.** Allow individuals and small businesses to form voluntary health insurance cooperatives through which to bargain with insurers. If no voluntary co-ops were formed in a state, the state would be required to form one that was open to all individuals and businesses with fewer than 100 workers.

● **Subsidies.** Provide subsidies, on a sliding scale, to children and pregnant women with family incomes up to 240 percent of the federal poverty line. Subsidies also would be available for individuals and families with incomes up to 200 percent of poverty. The federal poverty line for a family of four was $14,800.

● **Financing and taxes.** Pay for the subsidies largely through drastic cuts in Medicare and Medicaid, the government health insurance programs for the elderly and the poor, respectively.

Medicare would be trimmed about $255 billion over 10 years. Wealthy elderly people would pay more for the portion of their Medicare premiums that went to cover doctor bills (Medicare Part B). Some money also would come from increasing the cigarette tax to 69 cents from 24 cents a pack.

● **Cost containment.** Impose a so-called tax cap that would limit businesses' deductions for health insurance to the average-priced plan in an area. More generous plans would be subject to a 35 percent excise tax.

● **State flexibility.** Allow states to set up single-payer Canadian-style systems under which everyone would receive health care through government-run programs. Also, the federal government was to speed its review of waiver requests from states seeking to pursue health-system restructuring on their own.

● **Malpractice reforms.** Require all health malpractice cases to go through alternative dispute resolution before they could be brought in court. Awards to victims of medical malpractice would be sharply curtailed. Non-economic damages — also known as pain and suffering damages — would be limited to $250,000.

Continued from p. 351

But with each passing day, it became harder to discern what, if any, alternative could attract a majority. "It is becoming increasingly clear to this senator that the window may well have closed on the opportunity for a comprehensive bipartisan reform of our health care system this year," said Mark O. Hatfield, R-Ore., who was working with the rump group.

Crime Bill Dispute Interrupts Debate

The coup de grâce came from a different corner: Two days after the Senate began debating the bill, the House had handed Clinton an unexpected and stunning defeat on another piece of major legislation — the omnibus crime bill (HR 3355). The House rejected the rule for floor debate, thereby blocking the leadership from even bringing the bill to the floor. Reversing the vote quickly became a do-or-die priority for the White House, momentarily eclipsing even health care.

On Aug. 21, House Democrats turned enough votes to pass a slightly revised crime bill. The Senate then interrupted its health care debate to take up the conference report, which provoked a bitter, four-day partisan brawl. The Senate finally cleared the crime bill Aug. 25, but the damage had been done. The rancorous battle had consumed precious floor time and killed any remaining hope for a breakthrough on health care. *(Crime bill, p. 273)*

Exhausted, Congress began its delayed August recess.

The next day, Aug. 26, Mitchell scrapped his own health care plan, conceding that comprehensive action would not come in 1994.

Last Rites

House members left for the August recess without bringing the Gephardt bill to the floor, after Democratic leaders concluded that members would not be willing to vote until the Senate acted. They also cited the lack of an official Congressional Budget Office (CBO) analysis of the budget effects of the bill. Perhaps most important, they had not been able to round up sufficient votes to pass the bill. The leadership was having to add sweeteners just to solidify the support of loyal Democrats, and it was unable to win over the conservatives it needed. The picture grew more complicated Aug. 11, when a bipartisan group of House moderates unveiled a compromise health bill that could provide refuge for members who wanted to support something but could not bring themselves to vote for the Gephardt bill.

The Democratic leadership promised to act in September, but the August recess seemed to sap any remaining energy behind a comprehensive health care bill.

When members returned, all eyes were focused on the November election, and House members were eager to get home to campaign.

Even a "simple" health care bill would still be a complex

piece of legislation, and members worried about passing a hasty bill that could make matters worse. A limited measure, for example, could result in higher insurance premiums for many people. If, for instance, Congress required insurance companies to take all comers regardless of their health status, premium costs would have to rise to generate enough money to pay the claims of less healthy people.

At home during the August break, lawmakers had found that the public, too, had wearied of the debate. "Constituents aren't clamoring for [health care reform]. I think the whole country is exhausted by the debate, and there won't be as much retribution [for failing to act] as I thought," said Bill Richardson, D-N.M.

Republican leaders, meanwhile, saw no point in cooperating even on an incremental bill. "Why should we be enthusiastic about helping Democrats pull their political fat out of the fire with our ideas?" said Dick Armey, R-Texas.

Last Gasp in the Senate

Mitchell continued to hold out hope for a scaled-back bill that would take at least an incremental first step toward health care reform. His colleagues acknowledged that it was up to Mitchell whether the Senate would try again. "If George makes the decision he wants to go, then we go," said Durenberger. Either way, he added, "the optimism level is not high."

Mitchell negotiated through early September with the Mainstream Group, assembling a last-minute compromise bill. The revised Mainstream bill was little changed from its original structure, but it made small accommodations to win the support of most Democrats, including such liberals as Edward M. Kennedy, D-Mass., and about eight to 10 Republicans.

The plan still relied on a reorganized health insurance market rather than government mandates to reduce the numbers of Americans without insurance and to control the growth in health insurance costs. Health insurers and health maintenance organizations would be required to offer the same benefits to all customers so that people could comparison-shop, choosing their health insurance plans based on price and quality. Additionally, no insurer could refuse to cover someone because of a pre-existing medical condition.

While the plan stopped short of achieving universal coverage, CBO analysts estimated that it would result in insurance for 94 percent of Americans by 2002, compared with about 83 percent at the time. Additionally, it would reduce the federal budget deficit by about $56 billion from projected levels over 10 years — considerably more than the Clinton administration's original health proposal. According to CBO analysts, the Clinton plan would not begin to save money until 2004.

But when Mitchell, Chafee and other began counting votes, they could not find 60 senators willing to break a threatened GOP filibuster and bring the negotiated bill to the floor.

Bowing to the inevitable, Mitchell announced Sept. 26 that he would not continue his efforts to pass major health care legislation in 1994. At a news conference to acknowledge the close of the already moribund health debate, Mitchell blamed Republicans and special interests. "Even though Republicans are a minority in Congress, in the Senate they're a minority with a veto. They have the ability to block legislation, and they have chosen to do so."

Moments later, Senate Republican leader Bob Dole of Kansas quickly blamed Democrats. "The bottom line is, the Democrats never had the votes for any reform plan," he said. ∎

Law Protects Abortion Clinic Access

While other abortion rights initiatives remained deadlocked, Congress passed and sent to President Clinton legislation to combat violence at abortion clinics. The bill (S 636) made it a federal crime to use force, or the threat of force, to intimidate abortion clinic workers or women seeking abortions. Violators faced criminal penalties of jail time and fines. The bill also allowed affected individuals to sue for civil remedies, such as compensatory damages or court injunctions to restrain blockaders. The same protections applied to pregnancy counseling centers run by anti-abortion groups and to places of worship. Clinton signed the bill May 26 (PL 103-259).

The legislation was prompted by a rash of violence at abortion clinics nationwide. During the congressional debate, the list of incidents grew to include the shootings of two abortion providers, one of whom died. Supporters said local laws were inadequate to address the problem. And they were successful in framing the issue as a law-and-order question rather than an abortion vote, winning over some strong abortion opponents in both chambers despite complaints from anti-abortion groups that the law would impinge on the free speech rights of abortion foes.

The Supreme Court subsequently affirmed the power of government and the courts to place significant restrictions on anti-abortion protesters to ensure access to abortion clinics. The ruling came June 30 in *Madsen v. Women's Health Center, Inc. (Supreme Court, p. 310)*

Background

Both chambers had passed versions of the bill in the fall of 1993. In addition to the increase in violence outside abortion clinics, bill supporters were eager to act in the wake of a January 1993 Supreme Court ruling, *Bray v. Alexandria Women's Health Clinic*, which struck down one of the federal laws that had been used to bar protesters from harassing women seeking entrance to a clinic. They also were encouraged by the fact that Clinton backed abortion rights.

The House approved its bill (HR 796 — H Rept 103-306) by voice vote Nov. 18, 1993. The Senate passed its bill (S 636 — S Rept 103-117) by a vote of 69-30 on Nov. 16, 1993, but not before making some changes that prevented a quick agreement with the House. One key Senate amendment extended the bill's reach to protect "any person lawfully exercising or seeking to exercise the First Amendment right of religious freedom at a place of worship." A second amendment distinguished between violent and non-violent protest, providing lesser penalties for non-violent actions. *(1993 Almanac, p. 354)*

Action in 1994 centered on the conference report and final passage of the legislation.

House Action

What usually was a routine request to convene a conference with the Senate touched off a passionate debate in

Little Change in Other Abortion Policies

With President Clinton in the White House, abortion rights activists had looked for significant legislative changes in the 103rd Congress, but lawmakers took only limited steps to ensure abortion rights for women. Congress in May cleared a bill to increase federal penalties for blockading abortion clinics, but lawmakers backed away from other initiatives, including efforts to codify abortion rights and to reauthorize and revamp the government's family planning program.

The following is a summary of Congress' handling of abortion-related legislation:

● The clinic access bill (S 636 — PL 103-259) made it a federal crime to use force, or the threat of force, to intimidate abortion clinic workers or women seeking abortions. Clinton signed the bill into law May 26. *(Clinic access, p. 355)*

● The Freedom of Choice bill would have put into statute the right to have an abortion — a right that under existing law was based on Supreme Court rulings interpreting certain clauses of the Constitution to include abortion rights.

The bill was approved in 1993 by the House Judiciary Committee (HR 25) and the Senate Labor and Human Resources Committee (S 25 — S Rept 103-42), but it never reached the floor of either chamber. Congress balked at several of the bill's key provisions, including one that would have barred 24-hour waiting periods before a woman could obtain an abortion. *(1993 Almanac, p. 348)*

● The family planning bill (HR 670 — H Rept 103-14, S Rept 103-84) would have reauthorized the federal Public Health Service program. It would have codified an executive order issued by Clinton lifting a ban that prohibited public health clinics from counseling pregnant women about abortion. The ban had been imposed by President George Bush. The House passed the bill in March 1993. A Senate version was approved by the Labor and Human Resources Committee, but it never reached the Senate floor. *(1993 Almanac, p. 348)*

● The appropriations bill for the departments of Labor, Health and Human Services (HHS), and Education, which for 18 years had been the focus of a fight over whether the government should fund abortions for poor women under Medicaid, was approved on both floors with no discussion of abortion. The fiscal 1995 Labor-HHS bill (HR 4606 — PL 103-333) barred Medicaid-funded abortions except to save the woman's life or in cases of rape or incest. Abortion rights advocates said they avoided the government funding debate to focus their energies on pending legislation to overhaul the nation's health care system. *(Appropriations, p. 519)*

● Neither Clinton's health care bill nor the versions approved by leading committees (HR 3600, S 1757) mentioned abortion by name. But it was implicitly included in bill language that said health care coverage had to include "all medically necessary and appropriate services." Federal courts repeatedly had ruled that such language included abortion. Since abortion would be in the standard benefits package, all employers who provided insurance for their employees would be buying a package that included abortion coverage, as would every individual who bought insurance. Similarly, all insurers would have to cover the service.

Anti-abortion supporters tried and failed in several committees to explicitly exclude abortion from the list of covered services. No version of the bill came up for a vote on either floor. *(Health reform, p. 319)*

---

the House on March 17.

As a prelude to going to conference, both chambers had to act on the same bill. Typically, one chamber simply called up the other's bill, inserted the text of its own version and passed it. In the House, such a procedure usually was handled by unanimous consent or under suspension of the rules.

In this case, however, anti-abortion lawmakers — led by Christopher H. Smith, R-N.J. — insisted on using the process as a forum to air their opposition to the bill, forcing seven separate roll call votes. Along the way, opponents attempted to kill the bill by offering amendments to table it and to recommit it to the Judiciary Committee. In the last vote, the House agreed 398-2 to a non-binding motion instructing its conferees to accept the Senate provisions extending the bill's protections to places of religious worship. *(Votes 66-72, p. 22-H)*

Conference/Final Action

House and Senate negotiators agreed April 26 on the final terms of the clinic access bill (H Rept 103-488). During the conference, Sen. Edward M. Kennedy, D-Mass., offered a compromise proposal to preserve key features of the Senate bill while retaining the House version on several technical issues. Kennedy was chairman of the Senate Labor and Human Resources Committee.

The compromise included the Senate provision, sponsored by Orrin G. Hatch, R-Utah, that applied the rules in the bill to protesters at places of worship. Hatch cited several instances in which churchgoers had been harassed by protesters for various causes. House conferees agreed to the provision after clarifying that it would not create a new legal recourse for those praying while simultaneously demonstrating outside an abortion clinic.

House negotiators also accepted a Senate provision establishing lower maximum criminal penalties for non-violent obstruction, such as lying down in front of a clinic door.

Both bills provided for fines of up to $100,000 and up to one year in prison for a first offense, and up to $250,000 and three years in prison for a subsequent violation. But the Senate set lower penalties for non-violent offenses: up to six months in jail and a $10,000 fine for a first offense, and up to 18 months and $25,000 for a subsequent one.

During conference, negotiators added so-called severability language specifying that if a part of the law was invalidated by the courts as unconstitutional, the rest would remain in effect.

Rep. Henry J. Hyde, R-Ill., a conferee and an abortion foe, argued that the bill unfairly singled out anti-abortion protesters for harsh federal penalties. Hyde asked why the bill did not cover violent demonstrations by union members in labor disputes. Kennedy angrily challenged Hyde to demonstrate the same pattern of labor violence as had occurred at

numerous abortion clinics. "You don't have the case to be made," Kennedy said.

Final Passage

The House adopted the conference report May 5 by a vote of 241-174. *(Vote 159, p. 48-H)*

But first, after nearly two hours of emotional debate, lawmakers rejected a motion by F. James Sensenbrenner Jr., R-Wis., to send the bill back to conferees for further consideration. Sensenbrenner took exception to a provision that allowed only plaintiffs in clinic cases to recoup legal fees. He said a fairer approach would be to allow plaintiffs or defendants to be awarded legal fees, depending on which side won.

His effort to instruct conferees to insert the amendment fell, 193-222. *(Vote 158, p. 48-H)*

Carolyn B. Maloney, D-N.Y., said those who committed violent acts or physically obstructed women's access to clinics had to be deterred by the strongest means possible. "The right to choose is meaningless without the access to choose," she said.

Opponents argued that the measure was so broad that it could be used to prosecute legitimate non-violent protesters and that its penalties were excessive. Smith predicted it would require a ruling by the Supreme Court. "We're just looking for the punishment to be in sync with the crime," he said.

The Senate cleared the bill May 12, by a vote of 69-30. *(Vote 112, p. 20-S)* ∎

Dietary Supplement Rules Get Review

After two years of intense lobbying, manufacturers and consumers of vitamins, minerals and herbal remedies persuaded Congress to limit the federal government's power to regulate dietary supplements. On the final day of the session, the Senate cleared legislation that created a commission to set labeling guidelines for vitamins and other supplements. The legislation allowed the Food and Drug Administration (FDA) to enforce existing regulations for up to four years while the commission completed its work. President Clinton signed the bill Oct. 25 (S 784 — PL 103-417).

The bill seemed likely to result in looser rules for the health claims that dietary supplement manufacturers could make on product labels. But it also preserved the FDA's power to require and review evidence of product safety. And the FDA could halt sales of a supplement if it could show that the product posed a "significant or unreasonable risk" of illness or injury.

The initiative for the legislation came from Sen. Orrin G. Hatch, R-Utah, whose state was home to a number of supplement manufacturers and who was himself an avowed user of the products. Most of the action took place in the Senate.

Background

The legislation had been the centerpiece of an intense national campaign by supplement manufacturers and advocates, who argued that without congressional action, the FDA would cut off access to alternative medical treatments. Health food stores had held petition drives and mail-in campaigns.

Their target was an FDA plan to put in place a new rule prohibiting manufacturers from making health claims unless they were backed up by "significant scientific agreement." That was the standard applied to foods under the 1990 Nutrition Labeling and Education Act (PL 101-535), which also required the FDA to develop labeling requirements for dietary supplements. The FDA began enforcing the new regulations for labeling supplements July 15.

Opponents of the bill welcomed the new rules and said outrageous health claims and a lack of adequate safety standards for dietary supplements were reason enough for more regulation.

As originally introduced by Hatch in 1993, the bill would have blocked the FDA's standards of "significant scientific agreement" to support health claims, instead allowing claims on labels unless the FDA determined through studies and the "totality of scientific evidence" that the claim was invalid. Senate Labor and Human Resources Committee Chairman

Edward M. Kennedy, D-Mass., opposed the Hatch bill, and efforts to work out a compromise in 1993 failed. As a result, the committee put off action on the bill until 1994. *(1993 Almanac, p. 371)*

Senate Action

The Senate Labor and Human Resources Committee approved a revised version of S 784 on May 11 by a vote of 12-5. The panel rejected, 5-12, a substitute proposed by Chairman Kennedy that would have given the FDA more regulatory powers than did Hatch's version.

As approved by the committee, the bill barred the FDA from regulating dietary supplements as drugs or food additives by setting a broad statutory definition of supplements. This addressed manufacturers' complaints that the FDA too often tried to remove products from shelves by claiming that they were food additives or drugs subject to strict pre-market approval and marketing rules.

The legislation also required the FDA to prove that a supplement was unsafe, if used as directed, before pulling it from the shelves. Kennedy's version would have prohibited supplements if they presented a "reasonable possibility of harm."

In a significant concession to critics, Hatch's bill allowed the FDA to enforce the new regulations for two years while a new seven-member independent commission reviewed labeling of dietary supplements and determined what kind of rules were needed. All commissioners would have to have "expertise and experience in dietary supplements and in the manufacture, regulation, distribution and use of such supplements." The bill further stated that "no member of the commission shall be biased against dietary supplements."

The Senate passed the bill by voice vote Aug. 13 after accepting several modifications negotiated by Hatch and Tom Harkin, D-Iowa, in an effort to answer criticisms. For example, they tightened the definition of dietary supplements in response to concerns that the committee-passed language would have allowed many foreign prescription drugs to be sold in the United States without FDA approval. They also provided the FDA with emergency authority to act against dietary supplements that posed an imminent public health hazard.

The bill allowed health food stores and other establishments to display articles, pamphlets and books about supplements from sources other than the manufacturer, provided that the materials were not "false or misleading," did not promote a specific brand of diet supplement and were displayed

in an area physically separate from the products. Health food stores often had sections that included pamphlets and booklets on herbal remedies, and supplement advocates were intent on protecting those publications.

Three other provisions of the bill were more controversial and drew the most intense opposition from House critics. They proposed to:

● Allow supplement manufacturers to seek judicial review of FDA warning letters or similar enforcement threats if an issue had not been resolved within 60 days of the date the warning letter was delivered.

● Allow supplements to be marketed without any safety pre-approval by the FDA.

● Force the FDA to prove that a product was unsafe before removing it from the market.

House/Final Action

In the House, Hatch's bill ran into opposition from Henry A. Waxman, D-Calif., chairman of the Energy and Commerce Subcommittee on Health, and John D. Dingell, D-Mich., chairman of the full committee. They chose not to mark up a companion House bill (HR 1709), sponsored by Bill Richardson, D-N.M. Waxman and Dingell were anxious to preserve the FDA's power to regulate dietary supplements. In particular, they wanted supplement manufacturers to give the FDA data establishing a product's safety before it could be marketed, although under a lesser standard of scrutiny than that required for prescription drugs.

The final bill was hammered out in long negotiations between Hatch, Dingell and Waxman. The House then passed the compromise by voice vote Oct. 7. The Senate cleared S 784 later the same day, also by voice vote.

Major provisions of the final bill:

● Extended to four years the time the FDA was allowed to enforce the existing labeling regulations. During that time, a seven-member, independent commission was to decide what labeling regulations were needed, and the secretary of Health and Human Services was to decide how to adjust the rules. Like the Senate version, the final bill required that commission members "have expertise and experience in dietary supplements and in the manufacture, regulation, distribution and use of such supplements." The original bill said no member could be "biased against dietary supplements." The compromise said commissioners and staff "shall be without bias on the issue of dietary supplements."

● Allowed manufacturers leeway to explain a product's function on its label, with a disclaimer noting that the product did not promise to cure or treat disease. For instance, labels on calcium tablets could say, "Calcium builds strong bones. However, this product does not promise to cure osteoporosis or other related bone diseases."

● Allowed health food stores and other establishments to display articles on supplements from sources other than the manufacturers as long as the information was not "false or misleading."

● Allowed new supplements to be sold without prior FDA approval but required manufacturers to submit evidence of a product's safety to the FDA 75 days before putting it on the market. If the FDA was not satisfied that the information was adequate to assure that the new product was safe, it could block the marketing.

● Allowed the FDA to halt sales of a supplement if it could show that a product caused a significant or unreasonable risk — a lower standard of proof than that required in the original Senate bill.

The measure also established an Office of Dietary Supplements within the National Institutes of Health and directed it to "promote scientific study of the benefits of dietary supplements in maintaining health and preventing chronic disease and other health-related conditions." ■

Senate Republicans Block Action On Minority Health Bill

Despite a two-year push, legislation to reauthorize minority health programs within the Department of Health and Human Services (S 1569), died at the end of the Congress. Both chambers had passed versions of the bill, and conferees produced a House-Senate compromise, but Republicans blocked consideration of the conference report in the Senate.

The bill would have authorized $1.1 billion in fiscal 1995 for several programs, including the Office of Minority Health within the Department of Health and Human Services (HHS), scholarship and loan programs, health centers for migrant workers, health centers for the homeless and state rural health offices. The Office of Minority Health studied disease prevention and promoted research and health delivery for minorities.

First authorized in 1990, the programs sought to increase minority access to primary and preventive health care and to boost federal health scholarships for disadvantaged people, including poor whites.

Provisions of two other measures (S 1224 and S 725) that had been added to the minority health bill also died. S 1224 was aimed at making interracial adoption easier; S 725 provided for studies on the effects of traumatic brain injuries. (Brain injuries, p. 361)

House Action

The House Energy and Commerce Subcommittee on Health and the Environment approved its version of the minority health bill (HR 3804) by voice vote Feb. 9. Sponsored by subcommittee Chairman Henry A. Waxman, D-Calif., the measure reauthorized the HHS minority health office at $21 million a year from fiscal 1995 through 1997. It also reauthorized federal programs that funded migrant health centers, health clinics in public housing developments and scholarships for minority students hoping to enter the health professions.

The subcommittee adopted by voice vote an amendment to authorize $28 million in fiscal 1995, $30 million in fiscal 1996 and $32 million in fiscal 1997 for medical schools in areas with shortages of health care providers.

The full Energy and Commerce Committee approved a clean version of the subcommittee bill (HR 3869 — H Rept 103-501) by voice vote Feb. 23.

The committee approved an amendment by bill sponsor Waxman to establish an Office of Women's Health within HHS. It also approved an amendment by James C. Greenwood, R-Pa., urging the Centers for Disease Control and Prevention and other agencies to study the incidence and prevention of traumatic brain injuries.

The House passed HR 3869 by voice vote May 23. It then took up the Senate-passed version (S 1569) and inserted the provisions of its bill, passed the amended bill and requested a conference.

Senate Action

The Senate had passed its minority health bill (S 1569 — S Rept 103-200) by voice vote March 26.

The measure, sponsored by Edward M. Kennedy, D-Mass., and approved by the Labor and Human Resources Committee in 1993, authorized $20.5 million in fiscal 1994 and unspecified sums through 1998 for the Office of Minority Health. *(1993 Almanac, p. 371)*

The bill was amended to include a measure (S 1224) to prohibit adoption agencies that received federal funding from discriminating against people who wanted to adopt children of another race. The adoption bill, sponsored by Howard M. Metzenbaum, D-Ohio, stipulated that agencies could consider the race, color or national origin of prospective parents but could not use those characteristics as the only criteria in denying adoptions. The Labor and Human Resources Committee had approved S 1224 on Oct. 6. 1993. *(1993 Almanac, p. 381)*

Conference/Final Action

House and Senate conferees reported a compromise version of the minority health bill Oct. 6 (H Rept 103-843).

Among the issues resolved was how much of the $111 million in scholarship money for disadvantaged students to reserve for students who made a commitment to become primary-care physicians rather than specialists. Conferees agreed to channel 70 percent of the scholarship money to students who committed to primary care and 30 percent to students who did not commit to any field when they entered medical school.

The House adopted the conference report Oct. 7 by a vote of 394-5. *(Vote 504, p. 150-H)*

But when the conference report reached the Senate, GOP leader Bob Dole of Kansas objected to it on behalf of several Republicans. Despite efforts by Orrin G. Hatch, R-Utah, who cosponsored the measure with Kennedy, several Republicans refused to lift their holds, and the measure could not come up for a vote. ∎

Help for Disabled Individuals

Congress cleared two bills to authorize federal programs that helped states assist the disabled.

Developmental Disabilities

With broad bipartisan support, Congress cleared a bill March 24 aimed at helping people with developmental disabilities gain more independence. President Clinton signed the bill April 6 (S 1284 — PL 103-230).

The legislation, sponsored by Sen. Tom Harkin, D-Iowa, renewed a 1970 law, authorizing $117 million in fiscal 1994 and unspecified sums in fiscal 1995 and 1996 for states and universities to assist the disabled.

The measure allocated money to four grant programs:
- **State councils.** State developmental disabilities councils provided advice to state agencies that helped the disabled with job training, education, medical assistance, child welfare and other social service programs.
- **Advocacy groups.** The legislation funded nonprofit agencies that published advocacy literature for the disabled and assisted in resolving complaints.
- **University programs.** To help family members and professionals better understand the problems of the disabled, the bill funded university programs that ran early-intervention, aging and community support programs.
- **Discretionary fund.** The legislation authorized a Department of Health and Human Services fund for special projects to promote independence, collect data, issue reports

and assist state councils and university programs.

At the time, more than 3 million Americans suffered from mental or physical disabilities that affected their mobility, learning and ability to take care of themselves.

The Senate had passed its bill (S Rept 103-120) by voice vote Aug. 5, 1993. The House amended the Senate version, substituting its version (HR 3505 — H Rept 103-378) and passing the bill by voice vote Nov. 21. *(1993 Almanac, p. 370)*

Conferees resolved their differences and filed a conference report (H Rept 103-442) on March 21, 1994. The House adopted the conference report by voice vote the same day; the Senate cleared the bill March 24, also by voice vote.

Technology Grants

The Senate cleared a bill by voice vote Feb. 11 that reauthorized for five years federal grants to states to provide technology-related assistance for people with disabilities. The grants could be used for a variety of projects, from increasing public awareness to expanding training. The House passed the bill by voice vote Feb. 8. President Clinton signed it March 9 (HR 2339 — PL 103-218).

The bill also aimed to help states establish low-interest consumer loan programs to aid the disabled in purchasing technology devices and services, such as automated wheelchairs.

Rep. Major R. Owens, D-N.Y., the bill's sponsor, said the 1988 program (PL 100-407) already had gone a long way to help individuals with disabilities to live independently and pursue meaningful careers.

The bill authorized $50 million in fiscal 1994 and unspecified sums through fiscal 1998 to support state efforts to develop technology for the disabled. No state was to receive the federal seed money for more than a total of 10 years.

The House first passed the bill Aug. 2, 1993 (H Rept 103-208). The Senate passed it Aug. 5, substituting its own version (S 1283 — S Rept 103-119). The two chambers worked out a compromise, to which the House agreed Feb. 8, 1994, sending the bill back to the Senate to be cleared. *(1993 Almanac, p. 371)* ∎

Added-Nicotine Controversy Draws Anger, No Action

The tobacco industry came under intense scrutiny in the House through much of the session, after allegations of nicotine manipulation in cigarettes surfaced. But the furor faded as the session came to a close, and a leading Republican ally of the tobacco industry said days after the GOP captured control of Congress that he would halt the investigation immediately.

No legislation was enacted, or even seriously considered, as a result of the probe, which was spearheaded by California Democrat Henry A. Waxman, chairman of the House Energy and Commerce Subcommittee on Health and the Environment.

Waxman's Hearings

The latest onslaught against the tobacco industry began soon after the Environmental Protection Agency (EPA) published a January 1993 report that blamed the lung-cancer deaths of 3,000 non-smokers a year on environmental tobacco smoke, also known as secondhand smoke. This included both the mainstream smoke exhaled by smokers and the sidestream smoke emitted from cigarettes, cigars and pipes.

Tobacco foes, including Waxman, used the EPA report as

ammunition to argue for new smoking restrictions, and the House responded in late 1993 by passing a bill (HR 881) restricting smoking in most federal buildings to separately ventilated rooms. *(1993 Almanac, p. 210)*

In February 1994, Food and Drug Administration (FDA) Commissioner David A. Kessler announced that his agency might consider regulating the nicotine in cigarettes as a drug because of evidence that tobacco manufacturers changed the levels of nicotine, a naturally occurring substance in tobacco, in an attempt to addict smokers.

Waxman began a series of subcommittee hearings soon after that revelation. Testifying before the panel March 25 — the same day that the Labor Department proposed a sweeping ban on smoking in the workplace — Kessler outlined his case against the tobacco companies.

He cited internal tobacco company memos and a series of cigarette patents that both described the effects of nicotine on the body and identified methods of manipulating the amount of nicotine smokers could get from a cigarette, such as adding nicotine to the paper, filter and other parts of the cigarette.

Kessler said the evidence suggested that regulation might be necessary, but he warned Congress that if the FDA regulated the nicotine in cigarettes as a drug under existing law, it would have to ban cigarettes altogether. He asked lawmakers to intervene.

On April 14, the chief executives of the nation's seven largest tobacco companies made an unprecedented joint appearance before the panel, denying all of Kessler's allegations under oath. They also testified that they did not believe nicotine was addictive and that the level of nicotine in cigarettes had actually decreased in recent years.

Waxman and other lawmakers pressed the tobacco executives for access to industry research on the nature of nicotine and requested that some former tobacco company employees be released from their agreements not to discuss such research. The executives reluctantly agreed.

Two weeks later, on April 28, two former scientists with Philip Morris, the largest U.S. tobacco manufacturer, said the company had quashed internal research in the 1980s that suggested the addictive nature of nicotine. A company spokesman denied the allegation.

The probe intensified again in mid-May when Waxman and Ron Wyden, D-Ore., a member of Waxman's subcommittee, along with several news organizations obtained internal documents of the Brown & Williamson Tobacco Corp. Lawyers for Brown & Williamson alleged that the documents were stolen by a former lawyer for the company and thus distributed illegally.

At their request, a Kentucky judge issued subpoenas for the documents possessed by Waxman and Wyden. But U.S. District Judge Harold H. Greene quashed the subpoenas June 6, ruling that they violated the Speech or Debate Clause of the Constitution. The immunity clause gave members of Congress broad protection for actions taken as part of congressional business. The federal court's decision paved the way for the Health subcommittee to continue its investigation.

On June 21, Kessler made his second appearance before the panel. Citing new evidence of nicotine manipulation by Brown & Williamson, he again raised the specter of federal regulation of the tobacco industry and called for congressional "guidance" in that effort. He said the company had developed a high-nicotine tobacco plant in the 1980s and used it in cigarettes as late as 1993 without telling consumers.

Two days later, Brown & Williamson Chairman and Chief Executive Officer Thomas E. Sandefur Jr. testified, disputing Kessler's account of the tobacco plant, known as Y-1, and

accusing Kessler of grandstanding and misleading Congress and the public.

Attempts at Legislative Action Fail

The hearings generated negative publicity for the tobacco industry, but Congress did not heed Kessler's advice to intervene.

Anti-tobacco lawmakers did make one attempt at offering the guidance Kessler sought. Rep. Richard J. Durbin, D-Ill., asked the House Rules Committee for a waiver of the House rule prohibiting legislative language on a spending bill so that he could offer an amendment to the fiscal 1995 agriculture appropriations bill (HR 4554) directing the FDA to regulate tobacco products without banning them.

The committee rejected that request June 15, and Durbin never offered the amendment, which contained some of the language of a broader bill (HR 2147) designed to regulate the manufacturing and marketing of tobacco products. HR 2147 was never considered elsewhere.

The Health subcommittee's investigation waned as the session neared an end, and the Republican sweep of the November elections vaulted one of the tobacco industry's staunchest allies, Virginia Republican Thomas J. Bliley Jr., to the helm of the Energy and Commerce Committee (renamed the Commerce Committee) for the 104th Congress. Days after the election, Bliley announced that the investigation would end under his tenure, arguing, as he had during the hearings, that the probe was unnecessary.

Waxman took one last shot at the tobacco industry Nov. 29 during the lame-duck session. He accused the United States Tobacco Co. of using chemicals to manipulate the amount of nicotine absorbed by users of smokeless tobacco.

The hearing was largely ignored by both the media and the public. In an indication that the tobacco industry no longer felt as threatened by Waxman's investigation, United States Tobacco officials refused to testify, and Bliley did not make an appearance to defend the industry. ∎

Vets Gain Authority To Treat Animals With Human Drugs

Veterinarians, who for years had prescribed insulin for dogs and cats with diabetes, or penicillin to fight common respiratory infections in horses and cattle, finally gained legal authority to do so in 1994.

Although the use of such drugs for animals had been common practice, it was illegal. The Food and Drug Administration (FDA) had approved those medications only for use in humans.

On Oct. 22, President Clinton signed into law a bill (S 340 — PL 103-396) that gave veterinarians the authority to prescribe medication intended for use in other species. The Senate had passed the measure by voice vote Oct. 4, and the House cleared it by voice vote Oct. 7.

Veterinarians said they had long ignored drug use restrictions because the FDA had approved an insufficient number of drugs for all the diseases seen in different animal species. As a result, it was common practice for veterinarians to prescribe drugs approved for sheep, for example, to treat the same conditions in cows.

The American Veterinary Medical Association pushed hard for the bill's passage. "It decriminalizes the ethical practices of veterinary medicine," said Dr. Thomas Vaughan, dean of Auburn University's College of Veterinary Medicine in

Alabama. "The law now makes it possible for us to exercise the professional discretion that we were trained to use."

But the Food Animal Concerns Trust (FACT), a nonprofit organization in Chicago that tracked misuse of veterinary drugs and monitored food-safety issues, strongly opposed the measure. FACT did not oppose broadening a veterinarian's powers to treat household pets, such as dogs and cats. But the group said there were risks in treating food-producing animals such as cattle, chickens, goats and swine with drugs that had not been specifically tested and approved for them.

"This so-called extra-label drug use is hazardous to human health because drug residues may result in meat, milk and eggs," said FACT president Robert Brown. For example, he said, Ivomec, the most widely used medicine to rid animals of worms and other parasites, stayed in a pig's system for 18 days. In beef cattle, the dissipation time was 35 days.

Without studies to test the withdrawal times of medications in different animals, veterinarians had no way of knowing when the drug was out of each animal's system, Brown said. Moreover, dairy cows were not even tested for Ivomec, Brown added. So if a dairy farmer failed to wait for the appropriate dissipation time, a person could drink milk tainted with drug residues.

Ingestion by humans of some drugs used on animals could cause a variety of allergic reactions such as skin rashes and blotches, as well as more serious conditions, such as cardiac arrest and pulmonary edema, doctors said.

Dr. Stephen Sundlof, director of the Center for Veterinary Medicine at the FDA, said he understood Brown's concerns. But the new law required the agency to establish regulations by October 1996 that set safe dosage levels, safe withdrawal times, methods for measuring drug residue in tissue and enforcement procedures. "There's never been an incident in the United States where a person has ingested meat or milk or eggs with harmful drug residues," Sundlof said. "That's due in part to the strict regulations the FDA has already set. And that's before the law was passed." ∎

Lawmakers Consider a Variety Of Other Health-Related Bills

Congress took up a variety of smaller health bills, clearing measures to make technical corrections in federal health programs, give food manufacturers extra time to comply with new labeling standards and set up a United States-Mexico Border Health Commission. Other bills saw some action but died at the end of the session.

Medicare Select

A last-minute deal in the House and Senate preserved a supplemental health insurance program subscribed to by 400,000 older Americans while also making technical corrections in programs such as Medicare, the government's health insurance program for the elderly, and Aid to Families with Dependent Children, the nation's main welfare program. The House passed the bill by voice vote Oct. 7, and the Senate cleared it by voice vote Oct. 8. President Clinton signed it Oct. 31 (HR 5252 — PL 103-432).

The bill, sponsored by Rep. Pete Stark, D-Calif., made minor changes in Medicare, including some adjustments that were important to rural lawmakers. It loosened the rules under which rural hospitals could be reimbursed for serving Medicare patients. It also specified that psychologists as well

as psychiatrists could be reimbursed for treating Medicare patients. That could be crucial for providing mental health care for the elderly in rural areas, where there were few or no psychiatrists.

The supplemental health insurance program, which the bill extended for six months beyond Dec. 31, 1994, originally had been introduced as a free-standing bill (S 2460) by Sen. John H. Chafee, R-R.I. Known as Medicare Select, it was an insurance option that allowed the elderly to subscribe to a less expensive health insurance program run by health maintenance organizations rather than to the traditional fee-for-service option generally used by Medicare recipients.

The Medicare Select program was still experimental and was offered in 15 states. It applied to Medicare Part B, the section of Medicare that covered doctors' visits.

The technical corrections had passed the House as part of the 1993 budget-reconciliation bill (HR 2264 — PL 103-66) but had been dropped in the Senate. *(1993 Almanac, p. 107)*

Organ Transplants

The Senate passed a bill (HR 2659) on March 24 aimed at increasing the number of organs available for transplant operations and expanding federal efforts to help states provide immunizations for children. House lawmakers had passed their version of the bill (HR 2659 — H Rept 103-272) by voice vote Oct. 5, 1993. Both chambers named conferees, but the measure went no further. *(1993 Almanac, p. 371)*

Before passing HR 2659, the Senate struck the House-passed language and substituted that of a Senate measure (S 1597) to reauthorize federal organ transplant programs through fiscal 1996, including an authorization of $8 million for fiscal 1994. The substitute amendment was approved by voice vote.

The Senate version directed the Department of Health and Human Services (HHS) to provide grants to organizations that procured organs for transplant. Procurement groups would be required to assess annually their success in acquiring organs. The bill also required procurement organizations to maintain one waiting list for all transplant candidates within their region for each type of organ.

The Senate Labor and Human Resources Committee had approved S 1597 (S Rept 103-233) by a vote of 17-0 on Feb. 2. The measure was sponsored by committee Chairman Edward M. Kennedy, D-Mass.

A second amendment inserted the provisions of a bill (S 732) to establish national immunization registries to allow doctors to track the immunization histories of particular children. The language authorized $152 million in fiscal 1994 to establish the registries. It also authorized $250 million in fiscal 1994 for states to expand immunization efforts, by extending the hours of clinics that administered immunizations and by educating the public on the importance of immunizing children.

Traumatic Brain Injuries

Debates over federal standards for milk and maple syrup ended up killing a popular bill (S 725 — S Rept 103-243) that would have established Public Health Service programs to prevent and treat traumatic brain injuries. Traumatic brain injury was the leading cause of death and disability for young people and occurred most often from car accidents, sports injuries and falls.

The bill would have authorized state grants to public and nonprofit agencies to study such injuries, and expanded research on the subject at federal agencies such as the

National Institutes of Health and the Centers for Disease Control and Prevention.

The Senate passed the bill, sponsored by Edward M. Kennedy, D-Mass., by voice vote April 21, with an unrelated amendment to waive federal standards for the content of maple syrup.

The House passed the bill by voice vote Aug. 8, but members first added two other non-germane provisions. The first was to allow states to continue to pre-empt weaker, federal standards governing the content of milk in California. Normally, federal law pre-empted state law. California milk historically had contained greater concentrations of whole milk fats than milk produced in other states. Retaining state standards would benefit California farmers and dairies by enabling them to continue their existing pasteurization methods.

The House also added a provision to waive until Dec. 31, 1995, a required federal environmental impact statement for the use of the additive selenium in animal feed.

In an effort to complete action on the bill, the Senate on Oct. 8 passed by voice a clean version of S 725 with the extraneous amendments stripped out. But the House adjourned without considering the revised bill, killing the measure for the year. Provisions similar to S 725 were included in another public health bill on health services for minorities (S 1569), which also died at the end of the Congress. *(Minority health, p. 358)*

Public Health

The Senate Labor and Human Resources Committee gave voice vote approval April 13 to a bill to reauthorize several programs that provided health care to the poor in rural and urban areas. The measure went no further, however.

The bill (S 1995) was sponsored by committee Chairman Edward M. Kennedy, D-Mass. It would have reauthorized programs under the Public Health Service Act (PL 100-386) that funded migrant health centers, community health centers, and homeless and public housing health services.

Orrin G. Hatch, R-Utah, said he objected to "simply ratifying the status quo" and said the committee should instead enhance the community health centers. Kennedy said he agreed with Hatch's sentiment but wanted to wait for a more comprehensive reauthorization effort in 1995, presumably after Congress acted on a health care overhaul bill. That overhaul bill was never enacted. *(Health reform, p. 319)*

Smoking Restrictions

A bill to restrict smoking in most buildings nationwide (HR 3434) was approved by an Energy and Commerce subcommittee May 12 but went no further.

The Smoke-Free Environment Act, which the House Energy and Commerce Subcommittee on Health and the Environment approved by a vote of 14-11, proposed to limit smoking in buildings regularly entered by 10 or more people to separately ventilated rooms. Building managers would have to ban smoking if they chose not to designate such rooms.

Subcommittee Chairman Henry A. Waxman, D-Calif., who sponsored the bill, had difficulty even getting the measure through his subcommittee. He canceled the markup more than once in an effort to secure the votes for approval.

Tobacco state lawmakers, such as Thomas J. Bliley Jr., R-Va., said the legislation would infringe on the rights of smokers and intrude too deeply into people's private lives.

But opposition came from other fronts as well. The "hospitality industry" — restaurants, bars and hotels — argued that the restrictions would cost them the business of smokers, and Republicans objected because the bill would allow non-smokers to file civil suits against building owners.

In an attempt to assuage their concerns, Waxman agreed to narrow the bill's scope. The subcommittee adopted two amendments — one that exempted restaurants, bars, tobacco shops and prisons from the restrictions, and another that exempted private organizations, such as the Elks Lodge and the American Legion.

Those changes won the key support of three Republicans on the subcommittee, and three Democrats who also had expressed reservations about the bill voted for it. Waxman said he would later try to modify the new language to extend the smoking restrictions to "family-oriented" restaurants frequented by children, but he never had that opportunity.

Medical Device Fees

A bill to impose a user fee on manufacturers who sought Food and Drug Administration (FDA) approval for their medical devices died at the end of the 103rd Congress.

The House Energy and Commerce Committee approved the bill Aug. 9 by a vote of 31-13 (HR 4864 — H Rept 103-751). The Subcommittee on Health and the Environment had approved an earlier version by a vote of 16-9 on July 29.

The committee bill allowed the FDA to charge fees to manufacturers who sought the agency's approval to market new or modified medical devices. Manufacturers had complained for years that the agency took too long to test and approve new products. The FDA, which tested medical devices for safety and efficacy, said it needed the fees to hire more employees to do the testing.

The bill, sponsored by Henry A. Waxman, D-Calif., proposed to reduce the approval process to 90 days. The fees could be used to test only medical devices. Application fees would range from $3,200 to $52,000, depending on the device and the level of testing required. The fees were expected to bring the FDA about $115 million through fiscal 1999.

The committee gave voice vote approval to an amendment by Alex McMillan, R-N.C., to allow companies to withhold 50 percent of the fee until an application was approved.

Also approved by voice vote was an amendment by Sherrod Brown, D-Ohio, to allow supply companies to combine applications for approval of modifications on different products, provided that they were modified in similar ways. Edolphus Towns, D-N.Y., won voice vote approval for an amendment to require the secretary of Health and Human Services to submit an annual report to Congress on the types of applications submitted and the number approved.

The panel rejected, 19-25, an amendment by Joe L. Barton, R-Texas, to codify an FDA timetable to reduce the application backlog.

Though Sen. Edward M. Kennedy, D-Mass., introduced a companion bill (S 2276) on July 12, no markup was scheduled, and the measure died without further action.

U.S.-Mexico Border Health

The House cleared a bill Oct. 5 authorizing the president to set up a United States-Mexico Border Health Commission by a vote of 308-103. The Senate had passed the bill by voice vote Sept. 30. President Clinton signed it Oct. 22 (S 1225 — PL 103-400). *(Vote 491, p. 144-H)*

The 26-member commission was to assess health needs in border areas, coordinate public health efforts, educate residents about health problems and recommend ways that one

country could reimburse the other for uncompensated care.

Sponsored by Sen. Jeff Bingaman, D-N.M., the bill had the support of the governors of the four U.S. states bordering on Mexico — California, Arizona, New Mexico and Texas — and of the six Mexican border states — Baja California, Coahila, Chihuahua, Nuevo Leon, Sonora and Tamaulipas. Health problems along the border were among the most severe in the country, in part because several border communities had no public drinking water or sewer systems. Hepatitis and tuberculosis were among the prevalent diseases in those areas.

The House Energy and Commerce Subcommittee on Health and the Environment approved a companion bill July 29. The full committee approved it Aug. 5 (HR 2305 — H Rept 103-710, Part 1).

An initial effort to pass the House bill failed Oct. 4 when members gave the bill less than the two-thirds vote required to pass it under suspension of the rules. The vote was 246-169. (Vote 480, p. 142-H)

Orphan Drugs

House and Senate committees approved separate versions of legislation to reduce the length of time that drug companies had the exclusive right to market drugs developed for rare conditions — also known as orphan drugs. But the bills got no further and died at the end of the Congress.

At the time, companies that developed drugs to treat fewer than 200,000 patients got tax advantages and could market the drugs exclusively for seven years. Competitors were effectively barred even from producing drugs that had the same effect.

The Senate Labor and Human Resources Committee approved its version of the bill (S 1981 — S Rept 103-366) on May 11 by a vote of 13-4. The bill proposed to reduce drug companies' protected marketing rights for most orphan drugs from seven years to four years.

The bill, sponsored by Nancy Landon Kassebaum, R-Kan., left the seven-year protection in place for drugs already on the market or in the approval process.

Panel members rejected an amendment, 4-13, offered by Judd Gregg, R-N.H., to set the exclusivity period at five years. Gregg argued that without the longer protected period, companies would not bother to research new drugs for rare diseases. But backers said that an association of biotechnology firms had endorsed the legislation.

The House Energy and Commerce Committee approved its bill (HR 4865 — H Rept 103-746) on Aug. 5 by a vote of 27-17. The bill, sponsored by Henry A. Waxman, D-Calif., chairman of the Energy and Commerce Subcommittee on Health and the Environment, reduced the period of exclusivity to four years. It allowed a three-year extension for drugs with "limited commercial potential." The definition of limited potential was to be defined by regulations issued by the Department of Health and Human Services. The bill also provided for the withdrawal of exclusive marketing rights if the patient population for the treatment exceeded 200,000.

The panel rejected, 18-26, an amendment by subcommittee ranking Republican Thomas J. Bliley Jr., Va., to leave the seven-year exclusivity intact.

Congress established protection for manufacturers of orphan drugs in 1983 (PL 97-414) to give them financial incentives to research medicines for rare diseases. The law recognized that drug sales for limited markets might be small, requiring a longer time for a company to recoup development costs.

Since then, some patients' rights groups had complained that drug companies, unchecked by competition, could charge excessive prices for the drugs. In addition, some drugs turned out to be useful for more people than expected, and manufacturers reaped huge profits. Efforts to revise the Orphan Drug Act in 1990 and 1992 were blocked by the Bush administration. (1992 Almanac, p. 429)

Food Labels

The House cleared a bill by voice vote May 19 to provide a three-month extension for food manufacturers to comply with the federal nutrition labeling standards set by the 1990 Nutrition Education and Labeling Act (PL 101-535). The Senate passed the bill by voice vote May 17. President Clinton signed it May 26 (S 2087 — PL 103-261).

The strict labeling format required by the 1990 law went into effect May 8. The regulations required labels to include a realistic serving size, the number of calories from fat, and the total grams of carbohydrates, sodium and cholesterol. The new labels were widely praised by consumer groups and nutritionists. (1990 Almanac, p. 575)

Under S 2087, companies had until Aug. 8 to use up old labels that did not meet the format standards. They could not use old labels printed after May 8. An exception was made for milk and perishable food manufacturers, who usually did not have a backlog of packages. They could use labels printed any time up to Aug. 8.

"Nobody's trying to drag their feet," bill sponsor Sen. Dale Bumpers, D-Ark., said May 10. "We just want to make sure that some people are not unnecessarily burdened." Bumpers, chairman of the Small Business Committee, said he had heard from many business owners who said they could not print the new labels on time because of long lines at the printing plant, or who complained about having to throw out unused labels.

Nurses' Training

The Senate passed a bill (S 2433 — S Rept 103-373) by voice vote Oct. 6 to authorize $67 million in fiscal 1995 and unspecified sums in fiscal 1996 and 1997 to aid in the training of nurses, nurse practitioners and certified midwives. But the legislation went no further.

The bill, sponsored by Edward M. Kennedy, D-Mass., was intended to amend Title VIII of the Public Health Service Act to consolidate and reauthorize nursing education programs. Under the bill, funds were to be used by nursing schools and by state and local governments to support training programs and scholarship and loan assistance.

The Labor and Human Resources Committee approved the bill by voice vote Sept. 14.

Office for Rare Diseases

The Senate on Oct. 8 passed a bill (S 1203 — S Rept 103-399), by voice vote to codify the establishment of an Office for Rare Disease Research at the National Institutes of Health. The House did not act on the measure.

The office, which already existed, promoted and coordinated research on rare diseases. Diseases were considered "rare" if they affected fewer than 200,000 Americans. Such ailments included cystic fibrosis, Addison's disease and Marfan syndrome. The Labor and Human Resources Committee approved the measure, sponsored by Mark O. Hatfield, R-Ore., by voice vote Sept. 14.

The House never acted on a related measure, HR 3577. ∎

Welfare Reform Takes a Back Seat

President Clinton's goal of "ending welfare as we know it" — an important element of his 1992 presidential campaign — was postponed during the 103rd Congress, taking a back seat to health care, a crime bill and trade legislation.

Clinton unveiled his welfare reform proposal (S 2224, HR 4605) June 14 and several committees held hearings, but no committee acted or voted on the bill.

The long-advertised centerpiece of Clinton's plan was the requirement that recipients find work within two years of accepting welfare benefits. Those who could not find a job were to be placed in federally subsidized jobs. Because most welfare recipients had little education or job experience, the federal government would ease their transition into the work force by spending more on job training and child care.

"We propose to offer people on welfare a simple contract," Clinton said in a speech at Kansas City, Mo. "We will help you get the skills you need, but after two years, anyone who can go to work must go to work — in the private sector if possible, in a subsidized job if necessary. But work is preferable to welfare. And it must be enforced."

Clinton was forced to phase in his proposal — applying it only to people born after 1971 — because it cost too much to include all welfare recipients immediately, and he had said in April that he would not suggest new taxes to pay for it. He also decided not to follow the lead of House Republicans and some moderate Democrats to cut off most welfare benefits to immigrants, although he did suggest new restrictions.

The administration outlined an array of financing plans worth $9.3 billion over five years to pay for the changes, including some restrictions in aid to immigrants, small cuts in some entitlement programs and fees diverted from unrelated programs.

Congressional Reaction

Reaction in Congress was decidedly mixed. Liberals balked at the two-year limit and objected to allowing states to limit benefit increases when welfare recipients had more children. But the strongest fire came from Republicans, who denounced the plan for encompassing only part of the caseload, providing too much flexibility in the time limits, doing too little to discourage illegitimate births and continuing to give some welfare assistance to immigrants. Senate Minority Leader Bob Dole, R-Kan., quipped that the proposal might only represent "the end of welfare reform as we know it."

A hearing held July 26 by the House Ways and Means Committee's Human Resources Subcommittee highlighted the obstacles to moving the legislation.

Under questioning mainly by Robert T. Matsui, D-Calif., administration spokesmen acknowledged that there was little or no social science research to support Clinton's proposals to impose time limits or permit states to deny additional benefits to recipients of Aid to Families with Dependent Children (AFDC) when they had more children. AFDC was the nation's main welfare program.

The panel's Republicans, by contrast, were more intent on showing that Clinton's plan still would treat welfare recipients more generously than working families. Under questioning by Rick Santorum, R-Pa., and E. Clay Shaw Jr., R-Fla., the officials sought to explain why Clinton proposed to waive work requirements for welfare recipients for a year after the birth of their first child while most Americans were entitled to only 12 weeks of leave under the Family and Medical Leave Act (PL 103-3).

Clinton had been pressured to present his welfare bill by moderate Democrats who were eager to bring a plan before the voters in the fall and by Republicans who taunted him for neglecting his campaign pledge.

In the absence of an administration proposal, a number of welfare bills had been introduced in Congress.

Minority Leader Robert H. Michel, R-Ill., introduced a bill cosponsored by most House Republicans calling for stiff penalties on recipients who refused to work, denying AFDC to most non-citizens and cutting food and nutrition programs.

A group of moderate Democrats, led by Rep. Dave McCurdy of Oklahoma, offered a modified version of Clinton's plan that still cut deeply into aid to non-citizens. The toughest plan was introduced by Sen. Lauch Faircloth, R-N.C., and Rep. James M. Talent, R-Mo., who wanted to deny all AFDC and food stamp benefits to unwed mothers under age 21 and to their children. By contrast, a bill introduced by Matsui disdained time limits while increasing federal aid for educating and training welfare recipients.

By year's end, Republicans were vowing in their "Contract With America" to dismantle the federal welfare system. *(Contract with America, p. 22)*

Details of the Clinton Plan

Clinton's plan to revamp welfare included the following major elements:

● **Time limits.** Clinton proposed that recipients who were capable of working be limited to two years of government cash assistance throughout their lifetime.

Exemptions would be provided to those who were seriously ill or caring for a disabled or seriously ill child. As they entered the welfare system, recipients would receive a 12-month deferral from the time limits for their first child. They would receive a 12-week deferral for another child.

Any time spent on welfare up to age 18 would not be counted toward the two-year time limit.

States could extend the time limit for individuals enrolled in an education or training program and for those who were learning-disabled, illiterate or who faced other "serious obstacles to employment." Extensions also would be given to those who were not given access to the services specified by the state in a written agreement with the applicant. These extensions could not amount to more than 10 percent of the eligible caseload.

● **Work and training.** All welfare recipients born after 1971 would be required to search for a job during their first 12 weeks on the welfare rolls. Those who could not find a job would be required either to attend school or to undergo job training. Those who could not find jobs within two years would be placed in federally subsidized positions.

The requirement was expected to apply to about one-third of the welfare caseload in 1997 and two-thirds of all welfare recipients by 2004. States could include more of the caseload if they wished.

The administration said that focusing on the youngest welfare recipients would encourage teenagers to take more responsibility for their lives. Critics said it would force mothers with the youngest children into the work force first and bypass older recipients who might be more in need of job assistance.

Training was to be provided mainly through expanding the Job Opportunities and Basic Skills (JOBS) program created by the 1988 overhaul (PL 100-485) of federal welfare programs. JOBS gave states funds for education, training and

work for AFDC recipients. Clinton proposed raising the federal contribution to JOBS from $1 billion in fiscal 1994 to $1.5 billion in fiscal 1996 and increasing the federal matching rate to the states. *(1988 Almanac, p. 349)*

In all, the plan envisioned spending an additional $2.8 billion over five years for more education, training and job placement assistance for recipients.

Each state would run a WORK program that made paid work assignments available to recipients who were unable to find private sector jobs within two years. States could choose to subsidize nonprofit or private sector jobs, give employers other financial incentives or hire JOBS graduates for public work.

States were to provide child care, transportation and other services to help individuals participate in the program.

WORK participants generally were to be paid the minimum wage. Each WORK assignment would be for 15 to 35 hours per week, at the state's discretion. Participants who did not work the determined number of hours would have their wages reduced correspondingly.

An individual's WORK assignment could last up to 12 months. Recipients then would be required to search for an unsubsidized job, followed, if necessary, by another WORK assignment. States would have to make a comprehensive assessment of anyone who spent two years in the program.

The plan set aside $1.2 billion over five years for WORK slots. By fiscal 2000, the administration estimated, 394,000 people would be in subsidized jobs under the WORK program.

If a job did not pay as much as AFDC benefits, the worker could receive funds to make up the difference.

Sanctions would be imposed on recipients who did not attend job training programs or refused to work. For example, payment under the WORK program would be by the hour; individuals who skipped work would not get paid for the requisite hours. Those who refused a WORK assignment or an offer for an unsubsidized job would lose their opportunity for pay and any AFDC benefits they might be entitled to for up to six months.

● **Incentives, child care.** The administration argued that forcing poor people off the welfare rolls required making work more financially rewarding.

One incentive, enacted in the 1993 budget-reconciliation bill (PL 103-66), was an expansion of the earned-income tax credit (EITC), which reduced the taxes of the working poor or gave them a check if they owed no taxes. Clinton's plan urged states to bolster the effect of the EITC by trying strategies such as paying the credit in installments throughout the year, rather than at year's end. *(1993 Almanac, p. 107)*

The administration said Clinton's plan to overhaul the health care system would provide another incentive, ensuring that welfare recipients remained eligible for health coverage after they moved into the work force.

The administration called for spending $2.7 billion over five years to pay for child care for those in the mandatory education and training programs, the WORK slots, and for one year after welfare recipients joined the work force. It included another $1.5 billion to expand child care for working poor families.

Clinton also sought to allow welfare recipients to keep more of their income. Under existing law, AFDC recipients generally lost $1 of benefits for each $1 they earned by working. Clinton proposed disregarding at least $120 in earnings per month when calculating an individual's AFDC benefits. States also could let welfare parents keep more than the $50 in child support payments they were allowed to retain under existing law.

● **Illegitimacy, child support.** Saying that illegitimate births made young women more likely to need welfare, Clinton proposed to lead a national campaign, orchestrated by a new nonprofit agency, against teen pregnancy. The plan envisioned a

national information clearinghouse and grants to local programs to combat teen pregnancy, with a five-year cost of $300 million.

Every school-age parent or pregnant teenager who received or applied for welfare would be required to finish school or enroll in a JOBS program.

Parents who were minors would be required to live with a responsible adult, preferably a parent. Under existing law, states had the option of requiring these teenage mothers to reside in their parents' household. Under Clinton's plan, states also would have the option to limit benefit increases when all welfare recipients, including those born before 1972, had more children.

On the principle that parents should be the first source of support for their children, the administration proposed to spend $600 million over five years to improve enforcement of court orders for child support and related programs. Mothers who applied for AFDC would be required to cooperate to establish paternity. Once paternity information was given to the states, officials would have one year to establish paternity or risk losing a portion of their federal matching funds for AFDC benefits.

● **Eligibility changes.** The plan gave states the option of making it easier for two-parent families to be eligible for AFDC payments. Under existing law, AFDC eligibility for two-parent families was limited to those in which the principal wage earner was unemployed but had worked in six of the previous 13 calendar quarters. The administration said this penalized welfare recipients who wanted to get married. However, Republicans said that relaxing the laws would encourage married couples to apply for welfare and thereby expand the rolls significantly.

● **Financing.** The administration proposed to offset the estimated $9.3 billion cost of the bill over five years, through the following changes in federal programs:

• **Aid to non-citizens.** Restricting the eligibility of noncitizens for AFDC, Supplemental Security Income (SSI) and food stamps by requiring an immigrant's sponsor to be financially responsible for the immigrant for five years. Beginning in the sixth year, if the sponsor's income was above the national median family income, the immigrant would have to obtain citizenship before becoming eligible for the benefits. Estimated savings over five years: $3.7 billion.

• **Emergency assistance.** Put a ceiling on each state's spending in the AFDC Emergency Assistance Program. States had wide latitude in using these funds, which were designed for short-term needs to help keep people off welfare. The administration estimated that without changes, the program would rise from $189 million in fiscal 1990 to almost $1 billion by fiscal 1999. Five-year savings: $1.6 billion.

• **Superfund tax.** Extend through 1998 a broad-based corporate tax funding the superfund program to clean up hazardous wastes. The administration said that counting this as revenue for welfare would not affect the superfund. Five-year revenues: $1.6 billion.

• **Benefits to alcoholics, addicts.** Restrict benefits for people who were eligible for SSI benefits because of alcoholism or drug addiction. Five-year savings: approximately $800 million.

• **Farm subsidies.** Limit agricultural subsidies for farmers with more than $100,000 in non-farm income. Five-year savings: $500 million.

• **Meal subsidies.** Restrict certain federal meal subsidies to family day-care homes. Five-year savings: $500 million.

• **Tax credits.** Deny eligibility for the earned-income tax credit to non-resident aliens. Five-year savings: $300 million.

• **Rail safety.** Permanently extend railroad fees that were used to conduct safety inspections. Five-year revenues: $200 million.

• **Food stamp overpayments.** Bar states from keeping a portion of food stamp overpayments that they discovered by pursuing program violations. Five-year savings: $100 million. ■

Social Security Made Independent

After years of serving as a deathbed for legislation to make the Social Security Administration an independent agency, the Senate backed the Social Security Administration Independence Act in 1994, clearing the way for the measure to become law. President Clinton, who had indicated his support in April, signed the bill Aug. 15 (HR 4277 — PL 103-296).

The bill called for Social Security to separate from the Department of Health and Human Services (HHS) by March 31, 1995. The independent Social Security agency was to be governed by a commissioner and deputy commissioner appointed to six-year terms, subject to Senate confirmation. They were to be advised by a seven-member board: three members appointed by the president and two each by the House Speaker and Senate president pro tempore.

The move had long been sought by Senate Finance Committee Chairman Daniel Patrick Moynihan, D-N.Y., and Andrew Jacobs Jr., D-Ind., chairman of the House Ways and Means Subcommittee on Social Security.

"We hope to increase public confidence in Social Security by giving the agency more visibility and accountability, by improving administrative efficiency and by insulating the program from politics," Moynihan said.

The legislation also included provisions to restrict benefits paid to alcoholics and drug addicts under Supplemental Security Income (SSI) and Social Security disability to three years. Recipients of disability payments whose alcoholism or drug use contributed to their disability were to be required to receive their benefits through an intermediary who would be responsible for managing their finances. They also were to be required to participate in substance abuse treatment program. These rules already applied to the SSI program.

Background

Begun in 1935 during the Depression, Social Security initially was administered by a Social Security Board as an independent agency. In 1946, the Social Security Administration replaced the board. It continued as an independent agency until 1953, when it was included in the newly created Department of Health, Education and Welfare, which subsequently became HHS.

The Social Security Administration was the largest agency in HHS and the ninth largest in the federal government, with 65,000 employees and 1,300 field offices. In fiscal 1993, the agency made $298.1 billion in net benefits payments and spent $6.4 billion on administrative and other expenses. It ran the Old Age, Survivors and Disability Insurance program (OASDI) and SSI.

The Old Age and Survivors Insurance program provided monthly cash benefits to retired workers and their dependents and to survivors of insured workers. The Disability Insurance program, added in 1956, provided monthly cash

---

BOXSCORE

Social Security Administration Independence — HR 4277 (S 1560). The bill made the Social Security Agency an independent agency.

Reports: H Rept 103-506, S Rept 103-221; conference report H Rept 103-670.

KEY ACTION

March 2 — Senate passed S 1560 by voice vote.

May 17 — House passed HR 4277, 413-0.

May 23 — Senate passed HR 4277, amended, by voice vote.

Aug. 5 — Senate adopted conference report by voice vote.

Aug. 11 — House cleared HR 4277, 431-0.

Aug. 15 — President signed the bill — PL 103-296.

---

benefits for disabled workers and their dependents. SSI benefits went to poor elderly, blind and otherwise disabled individuals.

Campaigning for Independence

Moynihan had argued for years that the Social Security Administration should be made independent as a way to heighten its visibility and isolate it somewhat from the political party that controlled the White House. Bills that would have granted the agency independence died in the Senate after passing the House in 1986, 1989 and 1992.

The Reagan and Bush administrations had maintained that Social Security was best left under the purview of HHS. Like her predecessors, Clinton's HHS secretary, Donna E. Shalala, also argued against granting the agency independence, saying that its presence within the department made it easier to coordinate services and gave it Cabinet-level leadership.

Moynihan stepped up his appeal in 1993, after assuming the chairmanship of the Finance Committee. His committee approved a bill to create an independent agency (S 1560 — S Rept 103-221) by voice vote on Nov. 19, 1993. Under the Senate measure, the new agency was to be directed by a commissioner appointed to a four-year term by the president, with the consent of the Senate. A seven-member advisory board was to be appointed for six-year terms. The action came shortly before adjournment, and the bill did not make it to the Senate floor. It was the third time in five years that the panel had approved such a bill. *(1993 Almanac, p. 380)*

The Social Security independence bill also became a vehicle for clamping down on drug addicts and alcoholics who received federal payments. A recent General Accounting Office (GAO) study had found that the federal government paid $1.4 billion in fiscal 1993 to 250,000 drug addicts and alcoholics under the SSI and disability insurance programs. Of that group, only the 79,000 SSI recipients were subject to some monitoring of how they used their payments. The Social Security Administration verified that only 10 percent of SSI recipients were in treatment.

Senate/House Action

The Senate passed S 1560 by voice vote March 2.

Moynihan was able to pick up some support from Republicans, who no longer had a GOP White House position to defend, without losing Democratic backing. The bill also benefited from Moynihan's having become chairman of the Finance Committee.

The Senate agreed by voice vote to an amendment by William S. Cohen, R-Maine, to stop unsupervised payments to drug addicts and alcoholics. The amendment was a response to reports of recipients using the money to support their habits.

On May 23, after the House had acted on the legislation, the Senate called up the House-passed version of the bill and approved it by voice vote after substituting the text of S 1560.

After rejecting Republican-led efforts to sharply restrict access to SSI payments, the House Ways and Means Committee on May 4 approved its version of the bill (HR 4277 — H Rept 103-506) by voice vote.

In contrast to the Senate bill, which sought to put the independent Social Security agency under the direction of a single commissioner, advised by a seven-member board, the House bill put it under a three-person board appointed by the president. The board, in turn, was to appoint an executive director to manage Social Security's daily affairs. The board's term was six years.

The bill included a series of amendments restricting payments to those who received SSI or Social Security disability insurance payments because of a drug or alcohol addiction.

The committee adopted an amendment offered by Gerald D. Kleczka, D-Wis., and Bill Brewster, D-Okla., to limit addicts' benefits to 36 months. "After 36 months of payments, I think the taxpayers can say, 'My friend, we've tried to help, and now you have to help yourself,' " Kleczka said.

Wendell E. Primus, HHS deputy assistant secretary for human services policy, said the administration objected to terminating benefits to anyone undergoing required treatment for addiction.

The committee rejected, 15-16, an amendment by Rick Santorum, R-Pa., that would have made SSI beneficiaries whose primary diagnosis was drug addiction subject to random drug tests. Santorum argued that his amendment would send "a very clear signal that we're not going to pay people to do illegal acts." But Charles B. Rangel, D-N.Y., opposed tying benefits to drug tests. "These are political amendments just to see how mean-spirited we can be," he said.

Republicans sought to tighten the restrictions further with amendments to stop paying SSI cash benefits to children under age 18 and to eliminate SSI benefits to most non-citizens. Several of the committee's Democrats, while opposing the amendments, indicated that they shared a desire to further restrict SSI eligibility.

Members expressed concern about reports that some children were being encouraged by their parents or others to act violently or otherwise misbehave in school to qualify as mentally or emotionally disabled, winning eligibility for SSI benefits. Since a 1990 Supreme Court decision that made it easier for children to qualify for SSI, the number of children who received SSI payments had more than doubled, to 770,000.

By voice vote, the committee approved an amendment by Kleczka to require that all disabled children who received SSI benefits be reviewed by Social Security examiners before their 19th birthday. However, the committee rejected, 14-24, an amendment by Jim McCrery, R-La., that would have replaced the SSI cash benefit for children under age 18 with a voucher that could be used for medical expenses not covered by their state's Medicaid program.

The committee also rejected, 16-20, an amendment by Santorum to eliminate SSI benefits to most non-citizens. The amendment would have exempted refugees and certain permanent residents over age 75. Three Democrats voted for the amendment — bill sponsor Jacobs, Michael A. Andrews of Texas and Bill Brewster of Oklahoma. Other Democrats said they wanted to postpone a decision on the issue until Clinton submitted his welfare reform bill.

By voice vote, the panel approved an amendment by J. J. Pickle, D-Texas, to require translators to certify under oath the accuracy of their translations. The requirement was a response to reports that translators were helping immigrants fake mental illness in order to get on the rolls. The amendment authorized civil penalties against translators, physicians and SSI recipients who fraudulently tried to enroll ineligible recipients. And it made SSI fraud a felony rather than a misdemeanor.

The House considered the bill under expedited procedures May 17 and passed it by a vote of 413-0. *(Vote 177, p. 54-H)*

Conference/Final Action

The Senate adopted the conference agreement on the bill (H Rept 103-670) Aug. 5 by voice vote. The House cleared the bill Aug. 11 by a vote of 431-0. *(Vote 392, p. 118-H)*

"Break out the firecrackers, let freedom ring, independence is at hand for the Social Security system," Jacobs said, noting that it had been 10 years since Congress first considered the issue.

House and Senate conferees had completed work on the bill July 20. On the principal issue in dispute — the administrative structure of the independent Social Security agency — they opted for a single commissioner, as approved by the Senate, rather than a bipartisan board, as in the House bill.

In determining who should monitor disability beneficiaries whose disability was affected by alcoholism or drug use, the bill gave preference to nonprofit community-based organizations. Such organizations could receive up to 10 percent of a recipient's benefits — up to $50 a month, instead of $25 a month under previous law — to provide oversight.

For drug addicts and alcoholics receiving disability payments, the 36-month time limit was to exclude months where treatment was not available. For those receiving SSI, the time limit was to run regardless of whether treatment was available. In any case, recipients would continue to be eligible for Medicare or Medicaid after their disability benefits expired.

Additional sanctions were to apply to beneficiaries who did not comply with their treatment programs. For example, those who failed to comply with treatment for 12 successive months would be dropped from the SSI or disability rolls.

The bill required all disabled children who received SSI benefits to be reviewed by Social Security examiners by their 19th birthdays. And it included the requirements and sanctions related to translators for immigrants seeking Social Security benefits.

Conferees also included a number of House additions, some with slight changes, including provisions to:

● Increase the penalties against misusing the names and symbols of the Social Security Administration, Health Care Financing Administration and the Treasury Department. The provision also eliminated the annual $100,000 cap on civil monetary penalties.

● Exclude the pay of election workers who made less than $1,000 annually from Federal Insurance Contributions Act (FICA) taxes. The previous threshold was $100. Taxes on election workers became an issue after the 1990 budget-reconciliation bill required that all state and local workers not covered by state or local retirement systems be covered by Social Security. After hearing from constituents that the $100 exclusion was too low, a measure to raise the threshold to $1,000 was included in the urban aid tax bill (HR 11) that President George Bush vetoed in 1992.

● Require the GAO to assess the Social Security administration's use of voice mail and other technologies to increase public telephone access to local offices, and to report to Congress by Jan. 31, 1996. ∎

Congress Updates 'Nanny Tax'

The Senate on Oct. 6 cleared a bill (HR 4278) updating an often-disregarded law requiring that Social Security taxes be paid for domestic workers.

The law, which had not been changed since 1950, required employers to pay Social Security and Medicare taxes for housekeepers, babysitters, gardeners and other domestic workers if they paid them more than $50 in a calendar quarter. The tax requirement, which also involved the filing of quarterly tax forms, was unknown to many household employers and widely ignored by others.

Lawmakers in both chambers agreed that the $50 wage threshold was outdated and virtually invited non-compliance, but they had difficulty agreeing on a new figure. Finance Committee Chairman Daniel Patrick Moynihan, D-N.Y., and others warned that raising the level too high would jeopardize retirement coverage for many workers. If an employee was no longer covered by payroll taxes, he or she would not receive credit toward Social Security benefits.

The original House-passed version of the bill set the earnings limit at $1,200 per year; the Senate, led by Moynihan, pushed for a lower, $620 annual threshold. The final compromise required employers to pay the tax on domestic workers who were paid more than $1,000 in a year.

The bill did not change the tax rate. Under the Federal Insurance Contributions Act, employers and employees were each required to pay 7.65 percent of the worker's pay (6.2 percent for Social Security and 1.45 percent for Medicare). Many employers of domestic workers paid both halves of the tax.

President Clinton signed the bill into law Oct. 22 (PL 103-387).

Provisions

The final bill indexed the threshold in future years to the national average wage increase and allowed the level to rise in $100 increments. Refunds of the 1994 Social Security tax were to be provided to employees and employers in cases where the tax was paid for workers who earned more than $50 per calendar quarter from an employer but less than $1,000 annually.

The bill also sought to simplify the paperwork involved in paying the taxes.

Employers were required to pay the 7.65 percent tax on domestic workers' pay quarterly for the 1994 taxable year, as under existing law. In subsequent years, they could settle their tax obligations for domestic workers on their annual federal income tax returns.

Beginning in 1998, however, employers had to increase their quarterly estimated tax payments or the amount withheld from their own wages.

The bill generally exempted domestic workers younger than 18 from Social Security taxes, unless their principal occupation was household employment. That excluded occa-

---

BOXSCORE

Domestic Worker Tax — HR 4278 (S 1231). The bill required employers to pay Social Security taxes on domestic workers who were paid more than $1,000 per year.

Reports: H Rept 103-491, S Rept 103-252; conference report H Rept 103-842.

KEY ACTION

March 22 — Senate Finance approved S 1231 by voice vote.

April 28 — House Ways and Means approved HR 4278 by voice vote.

May 12 — House passed HR 4278, 420-0.

May 25 — Senate passed HR 4278, amended, by voice vote.

Oct. 6 — House adopted conference report, 423-0; Senate cleared bill by voice vote.

Oct. 22 — President signed the bill — PL 103-387.

---

sional baby sitters or gardeners but not full-time workers.

To help make up for any loss in federal revenue from increasing the tax threshold, the bill broadened the existing prohibition of Social Security benefits to incarcerated felons. Because the definition of a felony varied by state, the bill extended the prohibition so that it applied to anyone convicted of an offense punishable by imprisonment of more than one year.

In addition, the prohibition applied to similar criminal cases in which the defendant was found not guilty by reason of insanity and confined to an institution by court order.

The bill also responded to concerns by the Social Security Board of Trustees that the disability fund could be depleted by 1995. It reallocated 0.34 percent of both the employer and employee Social Security payroll tax from the Old Age and Survivors Insurance Trust Fund to the disability fund.

Background

Failure to pay the so-called nanny tax had derailed Clinton's first nominee for attorney general, Zoë Baird, and embarrassed a number of other candidates for top government posts. *(1993 Almanac, p. 303)*

In 1993, the House tried to raise the threshold to $1,800 annually as part of the broad-based budget-reconciliation bill (HR 2264 — PL 103-66). But the Social Security provision was dropped in conference after Moynihan balked at the House-passed threshold, which he regarded as too high, and warned that a little-known Senate rule barred consideration of a reconciliation bill that changed Social Security. *(1993 Almanac, p. 378)*

Clinton administration officials never proposed a plan of their own, though they indicated support for a threshold of up to $1,000.

In early 1994, both Moynihan and Rep. Andrew Jacobs Jr., D-Ind., chairman of the Ways and Means Subcommittee on Social Security, expressed frustration that Congress still had not acted to raise the threshold. Moynihan speculated that the Social Security Administration had not proposed a plan of its own because "they're brain-dead." Jacobs said it was an "embarrassment to the government" that the issue "came to light a year ago and still hasn't been rectified."

Since then, other administration appointees had been stung by disclosures that they either failed to pay the taxes for domestic workers or did so late.

In March, reports surfaced that William Kennedy III, a White House attorney, had not paid 1992 Social Security taxes for a part-time nanny until just before he assumed his White House job in 1993; he had not paid the 1991 taxes until 1994. Kennedy's duties included reviewing the background checks of Clinton appointees for matters — such as not paying Social Security taxes for domestic workers — that might embarrass the president. The White House said March 24 that Kennedy was being relieved of those duties.

Senate Committee

The Senate Finance Committee gave voice vote approval March 22 to a plan to raise the threshold to $620 annually for 1994. (That was the same as the amount an employee needed to earn in 1994 to get one quarter of Social Security benefits.) In future years, the threshold was to be indexed to the average national wage increase.

The bill (S 1231 — S Rept 103-252), sponsored by Moynihan, was largely symbolic because it contained revenue-raising provisions and therefore, under the Constitution, had to originate in the House. However, Moynihan wanted to show House leaders that senators were willing to move on the domestic worker problem without adding miscellaneous tax provisions.

The bill provided for employers to pay Social Security taxes along with their annual income tax returns instead of paying quarterly. It also exempted Social Security taxes on wages paid to workers under age 18.

The Congressional Budget Office estimated that increasing the threshold and permitting annual payments would result in $256 million in lost revenues to the Treasury in fiscal 1995 but subsequently would bring net revenue gains of $36 million to $40 million annually over the following four years.

Moynihan's bill partly offset the first-year losses through several initiatives, including a provision to save $51 million over five years by denying Social Security payments to individuals who were found not guilty of a felony offense by reason of insanity.

House Committee

The House Ways and Means Committee on April 28 gave voice vote approval to a version of the bill (HR 4278 — H Rept 103-491) that called for increasing the earnings limit to $1,200 in 1994 and $1,250 in 1995, and indexing it in future years to the national average wage increase. The measure, sponsored by Jacobs, provided for employers to pay Social Security taxes for domestic workers through estimated tax payments or increasing tax withholding from their own wages.

It also denied Social Security benefits to individuals found not guilty by reason of insanity of a criminal offense punishable by imprisonment for more than one year.

It reallocated a small portion of the payroll tax from the Old-Age and Survivors Insurance Trust Fund to the Disability Insurance Trust Fund, to counter concerns about the financial health of the latter.

Floor/Final Action

The House passed the Ways and Means bill without debate on May 12. The vote was 420-0. *(Vote 169, p. 52-H)*

The Senate took up the House-passed measure May 25, amended it to set the earnings threshold at $620 a year in 1994 and approved it by voice vote, setting the stage for a House-Senate conference.

Final passage was delayed over the summer while Moynihan and other key lawmakers turned their attention to health care reform. As a non-controversial tax measure — a rarity in Congress — the bill also was considered a potential vehicle to carry other legislation. In the end, however, it attracted no riders.

Congress completed work on the measure at the end of the session, after Moynihan and Jacobs had agreed to set the threshold at $1,000 a year, to be indexed in future years to the national average wage increase. "We have decriminalized baby sitting," Moynihan declared Oct. 5 as a House-Senate conference approved the compromise (H Rept 103-842).

The House adopted the conference report Oct. 6 by a vote of 423-0; the Senate cleared it by voice vote the same day. *(Vote 494, p. 146-H)*

Law Expands, Improves Head Start

President Clinton, who made Head Start one of his leading domestic initiatives, signed a bill May 18 designed both to expand the program's reach and to improve the quality of the services it provided. The measure (S 2000 — PL 103-252) had cleared Congress on May 12, riding a strong wave of bipartisan support.

Head Start provided preschoolers and their families with education, health care, nutrition and social services. The program served mostly 3- and 4-year-olds who were enrolled in part-day programs during the school year.

The bill authorized the program through fiscal 1998 at unspecified sums. Clinton had requested $4 billion for Head Start in fiscal 1995, a $700 million increase over the fiscal 1994 appropriations and twice as much as appropriated three years before. Congress ultimately provided $3.5 billion as part of the fiscal 1995 appropriations bill for the departments of Labor, Health and Human Services and Education (HR 4606). *(Appropriations, p. 519)*

The Head Start bill included a new program to serve families with infants and toddlers under age 3, setting aside 3 percent of Head Start spending in fiscal 1995 for this initiative. The set-aside was to increase to 5 percent by fiscal 1998.

But the key to the bill's popularity in Congress was the fact that it focused not only on expanding Head Start but also on quality control. It sought to respond to widespread concerns that the quality of Head Start had suffered from rapid expansion, fostering mediocrity while the problems of childhood poverty deepened.

The legislation generally followed the January recommendations of an advisory panel appointed by Health and Human Services (HHS) Secretary Donna E. Shalala that called for new performance standards and quality controls. The legislation required HHS to create a process for identifying poorly run programs and to develop a plan to help them improve. Program operators were required to show that the quality of their day care and social services met these new standards. Programs that fell short would lose their grants within one year.

The measure continued a policy begun in 1990 that set aside 25 percent of each year's increased spending for quality improvements. *(Provisions, p. 371)*

In an extraordinary show of bipartisanship, the leading Democrats and Republicans of the relevant subcommittees and full committees in both chambers were among the bill's cosponsors.

In addition to Head Start funding, the bill also authorized:

● **Community Services Block Grants.** $525 million in fiscal 1995 for the Community Services Block Grants, which primarily funded local community action agencies serving the poor.

● **LIHEAP.** $2 billion annually through fiscal 1999 for the Low Income Home Energy Assistance Program (LIHEAP), which helped low-income families pay heating and cooling bills and insulate their homes. The Clinton administration had recommended that LIHEAP's appropriation be cut from $1.5 billion in fiscal 1994 to $745 million in fiscal 1995. The administration argued that it was better to assist low-income households through more broadly targeted programs.

● **Child abuse prevention.** $50 million in fiscal 1995 for a Community-Based Family Resource Program designed to prevent child abuse.

Background

Head Start, begun during President Lyndon B. Johnson's War on Poverty in 1965, had evolved into one of the federal government's most popular social service programs. The appeal arose largely from its emphasis on providing preventive services to low-income preschoolers and their families, and its record of success — short-term though it was — with participants.

Head Start funds were awarded to about 1,400 grant recipients that ran the programs in cities and counties. Most of the recipients were community action agencies and other nonprofit organizations that could, in turn, contract with local program operators.

Since 1965, nearly 14 million children from low-income families had participated in Head Start. By law, virtually all of them were from families whose incomes were below the federal poverty line, $14,800 a year for a family of four.

Still, the program served fewer than half the eligible children. Despite a 50 percent increase in enrollment since 1989, to nearly 714,000 in 1993, Head Start included only 53 percent of eligible 4-year-olds and 21 percent of eligible 3-year-olds.

Head Start tried to prepare the youngsters for elementary school by teaching them to speak well and get along with others. It also sought to instill good nutrition and hygiene habits, provide medical and dental screenings and immunizations, and conduct home visits to help parents with parenting skills and social service needs.

Recent studies indicated that the program's most lasting benefits were related to health and socialization for school behavior. Improvements in educational achievement tests, on the other hand, generally tended to disappear within one to three years after children started school.

Head Start's advocates maintained that the educational benefits dwindled largely because of the challenges children faced when they left the program. "The best preschool program in the world cannot overcome the effects of poor nutrition and health care, substandard schools, negative role models and family dysfunction," said Edward F. Zigler, a Yale University psychologist who helped found Head Start.

The program had never been trouble-free, even in the heady early days. "The project started off so big and so fast that quality controls were left behind," Zigler said, recalling how program officials were so swamped with applications that they had to file papers in the bathtubs of the hotel where the program initially was headquartered.

BOXSCORE

Head Start Reauthorization — S 2000 (HR 4250). The bill reauthorized and expanded the Head Start program for preschool children.

Reports: S Rept 103-251, H Rept 103-483; conference report H Rept 103-497.

KEY ACTION

April 21 — Senate passed S 2000 by voice vote.

April 28 — House passed S 2000 by voice vote after substituting text of HR 4250.

May 11 — Senate adopted conference report, 98-1.

May 12 — House cleared bill, 393-20.

May 18 — President signed bill — PL 103-252.

"Head Start's most serious problem has always been inconsistent quality," Zigler said.

But Head Start's popularity in Washington was always strong. Among subsequent presidents, only Richard M. Nixon was hostile toward Head Start. Funding rose steadily after he left office, and enrollment increased.

But the program managed to cover more children only by cutting hours of operation, staff training and family visits. From 1980 to 1990, per-pupil expenditures actually declined by 14 percent in inflation-adjusted dollars, even as annual appropriations rose from $735 million to $1.6 billion.

A 1990 law (PL 101-501) required that 10 percent of all appropriations for Head Start in fiscal 1991 and 25 percent of additional funds in subsequent years be set aside for quality improvements. As a result, per-pupil expenditures had begun to rise. *(1990 Almanac, p. 552)*

Observers said the agency's monitoring of the programs had been hindered by a lack of personnel and travel funds, as well as a cumbersome termination process. Only in the most egregious cases were grants terminated.

Head Start continued to reap huge budget increases under President George Bush, who made a big pitch to "fully fund" Head Start so that it could serve every eligible child. But even then, the new policy demand quickly pushed ahead of the money supply; critics said the program's quality continued to suffer.

Most Head Start centers were offering a half-day of preschool four or five days a week during the school year; only about 15 percent of the centers ran a full school day program.

Bipartisan Concern

When Clinton took office, a number of Republicans who had been supportive of Head Start began raising serious questions about its quality. Bill Goodling of Pennsylvania, ranking Republican on the Education and Labor Committee, joined by Susan Molinari of New York and Nancy Landon Kassebaum, Kan., ranking Republican on the Senate Labor and Human Resources Committee, introduced bills (HR 1528, S 670) calling for tough new standards on how Head Start centers should operate.

Molinari said she expected Democrats would accuse Republicans of trying to kill Head Start with the legislation. As it turned out, Democratic supporters of Head Start adopted many elements of the GOP bill in their proposal. "We were coming on a different track but to the same conclusion," she said.

Apparently sensing that questions about Head Start's quality could threaten bipartisan support for the program, HHS Secretary Shalala announced in March 1993 that the Clinton administration's goal of reaching every eligible Head Start child would be slowed down to deal with quality problems.

Shalala later appointed a 47-member bipartisan advisory committee that included Head Start representatives, congressional staff members and child experts, chaired by Mary Jo Bane, assistant secretary for the Administration of Children *Continued on p. 372*

Head Start Provisions

As enacted, the Head Start reauthorization bill (S 2000 — PL 103-252) contained provisions to:

Title I — Head Start Program

- **Authorization.** Reauthorize Head Start through fiscal 1998 at unspecified sums.
- **Quality improvement funds.** Continue a policy begun in 1990 that set aside 25 percent of increased Head Start funding for improvements. The bill specified that these funds could be used to enhance program quality, hire additional staff, evaluate a community's needs for early childhood services and obtain new facilities. The 25 percent set-aside was a minimum level that could be increased by the secretary of Health and Human Services (HHS).
- **Collaboration grants.** Allow HHS to make grants to states to create liaison positions to help coordinate Head Start programs with other social services.
- **Criteria for awarding expansion funds.** Stipulate for the first time that applicants for funds to expand the program be evaluated on the quality of their services and their ability to expand. Other criteria to be used in awarding expansion funds included the number of poor families in the area served by applicants and the number of eligible children in the community who were not served by the program.
- **Flexible hours.** Require HHS to give program operators more flexibility to meet the minimum hours needed to operate a Head Start program. Existing regulations required centers to be open at least three hours a day and four days a week. The bill allowed programs to operate as little as three hours per day but did not permit them to reduce the number of days per week or days per year that they were operating.
- **Migrant grantees.** Require HHS, when funding programs designed specifically to help migrants and their families, to give priority to grant recipients serving families that relocated most frequently. A child from a low-income family was eligible for services under the migrant Head Start program if the family worked in an agricultural enterprise and had moved from one community to another in the past two years.
- **Indian Head Start service area.** Clarify that Indians living near a reservation should be considered to be living in an Indian Head Start service area. Existing statutory language had been interpreted to mean that Indian Head Start programs served only children living within reservation boundaries.
- **New Head Start grantees.** Add to the criteria that HHS considered when designating new Head Start agencies. The prospective grant recipients had to provide, directly or through referral, family literacy services and training in parenting skills. The applicant could also offer training in basic child development, assistance in developing communication skills, opportunities for parents to share their experiences with other parents and counseling against alcohol and drug abuse.
- **Non-English-speaking families.** Require applicants to address how they would meet the needs of non-English-speaking parents and their children. The bill did not specify how the applicants should meet the needs of these families.
- **Quality standards.** Require that within one year of the bill's enactment, HHS develop updated quality standards to guide programs in health, education, parental involvement, social services and helping children make the transition from Head Start to elementary school. The bill directed HHS to develop the standards by consulting with experts in child development, family services, program management, representatives of Head Start agencies and child health experts. The bill also required HHS to develop ways to measure the performance of Head Start grant recipients.
- **Monitoring.** Require each Head Start agency to be evaluated at least once every three years. New agencies had to be evaluated after one year. Program reviews were to be conducted by HHS employees who knew the diverse needs of eligible children and families, including their linguistic and cultural differences. The HHS secretary was required to publish an annual summary of the grant recipient reviews.
- **Corrective action.** Give the HHS secretary the option of either requiring an agency to correct a deficiency immediately or to develop and follow a quality improvement plan. If the deficiency was not eliminated within one year, the agency's funding would be terminated.
- **Coordination with schools.** Require Head Start agencies to coordinate with local education agencies when transferring student records from Head Start programs to schools. Parental consent had to be obtained before transferring the records. In many cases, there was no existing formal system to ensure that the Head Start records were properly transferred. Head Start programs had to work with the schools to help teachers and school officials explain to parents the school registration process, administrative rules and other information. The Head Start programs also had to teach parents about their rights and responsibilities in the public school system and about how they could help their children succeed.
- **Parental involvement.** Require that each Head Start program try to involve parents in their children's education and give parents the opportunity to participate in developing the program. Program operators also had to make family literacy services available to parents, either directly or by referral. In addition, the centers had to formally assess the needs of each participant's family and use the information to determine the type of services offered.
- **Purchasing facilities.** Allow Head Start grant recipients in low-income communities to build facilities if there were no other suitable facilities available, if the lack of facilities would inhibit the program and if construction was cheaper than purchasing an available facility. The bill also allowed grant recipients to finance capital expenditures for constructing and renovating facilities, and to buy cars or vans for the program.
- **Infant and toddler program.** Create a program to serve children from birth to age 3. The intent was to identify participants while the mother was pregnant or while the children were infants. These youngsters and their families were to be provided with education, health care and social services to promote child development and parental self-sufficiency. The services for infants and toddlers had to be coordinated with state and community programs. The bill set aside 3 percent of Head Start funding in fiscal 1995 for the birth-to-3 initiative, 4 percent in fiscal 1996 and 1997, and 5 percent in fiscal 1998.
- **Training and technical assistance.** Give priority in distributing training and technical assistance funds — used to improve staff development and management — to programs that were correcting problems with their management or services, improving staff training, evaluating community needs and improving their facilities. Other uses for the funds included helping programs that were developing full-day and full-year operations, serving the needs of families with very young children, getting parents more involved in the program and working with the children of migrant and seasonal workers.
- **Mentor teachers.** Create a mentor teacher program. Head Start programs were to identify highly qualified and experienced teachers to supervise other teachers in the program by evaluating their performance and observing them in the classroom. The mentor teachers were to assess classroom activities and provide guidance and training to staff and volunteers.
- **Degree requirements.** Extend until Sept. 30, 1996, the requirement that each Head Start classroom contain at least one staff person with a Child Development Associate credential, given to teachers based on their experience and training, or a postsecondary degree.
- **Services to children of Indians, migrants and seasonal workers.** Require HHS to study the availability and delivery of Head Start services to children of Indians, Alaska natives, and migrant and seasonal farm workers.
- **Federal benefits.** Require HHS to study the possibility of providing Head Start employee benefits through the federal retirement system.
- **Ready to Learn program.** Reauthorize the Ready to Learn program through fiscal 1998. The program was designed to develop tele-

vision as a resource for early learning.

- **Dependent care.** Reauthorize State Dependent Care Development Grants for $13 million in fiscal 1995. The grants generally funded information and referral services for child care and after-school programs.
- **Full-day and full-year programs.** Require the HHS secretary to study the need for full-day and full-year Head Start services, releasing the results by January 1997.
- **National and community service.** Require the HHS secretary to consult with the director of the Corporation for National and Community Service to disseminate information to recipients of Head Start funds about the corporation's programs. This could encourage National Service program participants to work with Head Start programs.

Title II — Community Services Block Grant

- **Authorization.** Reauthorize the Community Services Block Grant program at $525 million in fiscal 1995 and unspecified sums through fiscal 1998. The grant primarily provided money to local community action agencies that offered services aimed at helping the poor become self-sufficient.
- **Discretionary programs.** Revise the structure for several programs that were funded at the HHS secretary's discretion but were traditionally earmarked in the Labor-HHS appropriations bill.

One, the Community Initiative Program, consolidated community economic development programs with those that funded rural housing and water assistance into a single community development account. The money was to be used primarily to fund community development corporations, which were non-profit organizations that tried to spur economic development in low-income communities.

A second fund provided money to community development corporations that focused on migrants and seasonal farm workers. A third fund was to be used to help develop interactive computer technology to encourage communication among a network of block grant recipients.

- **Categorical grants.** Reauthorize several categorical grant programs which, unlike block grants, were used to target specific programs. The legislation created a separate authorization for the National Youth Sports Program, which provided low-income youth recreation and counseling opportunities. It also reauthorized Community Food and Nutrition, which funded anti-hunger activities in states, Community Services for the Homeless, and the Demonstration Partnerships Program, which helped community action agencies address certain low-income problems, such as the need for minority youth activities and mentors.
- **Training, technical assistance.** Set aside between 0.5 percent and 1 percent of the block grant appropriation for training and technical assistance. These activities were to address community action

agencies' need to improve their programs, particularly their financial management.

Title III — Low-Income Home Energy Assistance Program

- **Reauthorization.** Reauthorize the Low-Income Home Energy Assistance Program (LIHEAP) for $2 billion annually through fiscal 1999. LIHEAP provided block grants to states to help low-income families pay their home energy bills and improve home insulation. The bill expressed Congress' sense that because of a shortage of funds, LIHEAP's primary purpose should be helping low-income households pay their utility bills.
- **Emergency fund.** Permanently authorize $600 million for a LIHEAP emergency contingency fund. Use of the funds, if appropriated, was contingent on the president submitting a budget request declaring an emergency.
- **Program use.** Allow states to direct funding to households with the highest home energy costs or those with the greatest needs in relation to their income. The bill singled out for special attention households with people who were age 60 or older, disabled people and children under age 6.
- **Leveraging fund.** Authorize $50 million each in fiscal 1996 and 1997 and unspecified sums in fiscal 1998 and 1999 for the leveraging incentive program. States used this money to seek additional LIHEAP funds from non-federal sources. The bill also created a Residential Energy Assistance Challenge to encourage states to conduct more education and counseling on energy usage. The bill set aside up to 25 percent of the leveraging incentive program funds for this purpose.

Title IV — Community-Based Family Resources Programs

- **Authorization.** Authorize $50 million in fiscal 1995 for new Community-Based Family Resources Programs. The bill consolidated three programs — Family Resource and Support Grants, Community-Based Prevention Grants and the Emergency Child Protective Services program. The new initiative funded statewide networks of programs that provided parenting education and support services, linked families with other social services and engaged in child abuse prevention activities.
- **Funding.** Distribute money partly through a formula grant, based on the number of children under age 18 in a state. The rest of the funds were to be distributed based on how much a state raised for the program from other sources, such as other federal, state and private funds.
- **Collaboration.** Encourage states and communities to work together, pooling funds and integrating services, to better serve families. ∎

Continued from p. 370
and Families at HHS. The advisory committee laid the groundwork for legislative reauthorization by calling for improvements in staffing, local management, facilities and federal oversight, as well as continued expansion of services and enrollment.

While leading members of Congress eagerly embraced the resulting legislation, questions remained about the agency's ability to follow through. Zigler, who served on the advisory committee, described the situation as "an understaffed, somewhat demoralized agency that is suddenly given a huge task to do."

Molinari acknowledged that concerns about the agency was something "we should have for just about every piece of authorizing legislation. . . . But it doesn't stop you from trying to achieve that goal. We do owe it to this administration to give them the benefit of the doubt."

Goodling agreed. "We're not just saying, 'Hey, we don't think you're doing well enough, we'd like to see you improve,' " he said. "We're saying, 'There are standards that have to be met, and if you don't meet them, we'll have somebody else attempt to be the grantee.' "

Legislative Action

The Senate Labor and Human Resources Committee approved its version of the Head Start reauthorization bill (S 2000 — S Rept 103-251) on April 13 by a vote of 17-0.

The bill, originally introduced by Christopher J. Dodd, D-Conn., incorporated many provisions from a related bill (S 1852) introduced by committee Chairman Edward M. Kennedy, D-Mass.

The Senate passed the bill April 21 by voice vote.

House Action

The House Education and Labor Committee gave voice vote approval April 21 to a companion bill (HR 4250 — H Rept 103-483).

During the markup, Bill Barrett, R-Neb., sought to strike the provision setting aside funds for an expanded program of Head Start services to families with children under age 3. Barrett said the benefits of the infant and toddler initiative were too uncertain to merit special funding. The amendment prompted little debate, though Matthew G. Martinez, D-Calif., chairman of the Human Resources Subcommittee, said it would be "very damaging to the bill." Barrett's amendment fell on a voice vote.

Patsy T. Mink, D-Hawaii, offered an amendment to set aside 10 percent of any additional funding for Head Start to expand full-day, full-year programs. Mink said such programs were important to enable the parents of preschool children to attend job training classes, which she said was "the only way we're going to really fundamentally change the nature of poverty in America."

Martinez and others countered that local officials ought to decide whether it was better to run full-day programs or to enroll more children in part-time programs. By voice vote, the committee agreed to strip the 10 percent set-aside from Mink's amendment, leaving it with language that merely required HHS to study the benefits of full-day and full-year programs.

By a 10-32 vote, the committee rejected an amendment by Dan Miller, R-Fla., to eliminate categorical grants within the program — as the Clinton administration had suggested — and reduce the authorization to $434.6 million from $525 million.

The full House passed S 2000 by voice vote April 28 after substituting the text of HR 4250.

Conference/Final

House and Senate conferees May 6 worked out what were only minor differences in the two bills, approving a compromise version by voice vote (H Rept 103-497). The Senate agreed to the conference report May 11 by a vote of 98-1. The House followed suit May 12 by a vote of 393-20, clearing the bill for the president. *(Senate vote 109, p. 19-S; House vote 170, p. 52-H)*

Conferees agreed to include a Senate provision allowing Head Start grantees to build new facilities when permitted to do so by HHS. Under existing law, grantees were allowed only to buy existing facilities. The House did not have a similar provision. They struck Senate language that would have made Head Start children automatically eligible for subsidized school lunch and other nutrition programs.

The conferees also agreed with the House to retain separate grant programs within the Community Services Block Grant. The Clinton administration had proposed eliminating the separate grants. The Senate version would have consolidated several programs. Like the House bill, the final measure created a separate authorization within the Community Services Block Grant for the National Youth Sports Program, which provided recreation and counseling for low-income youths. ■

Child Nutrition Program Extended

Congress cleared a bill (S 1614) at the end of the session reauthorizing several child nutrition programs, including the popular Special Supplemental Nutrition Program for Women, Infants and Children (WIC). The bill reauthorized and, in some cases, revised a number of other programs under the National School Lunch Act and the Child Nutrition Act of 1966. President Clinton signed the bill into law Nov. 2 (PL 103-448).

While the main school breakfast and lunch programs governed by the two laws were permanently authorized, related nutrition programs including WIC were set to expire in 1994. Congress often used the reauthorization process as an opportunity to modify the programs.

The bill increased the authorization for programs such as school breakfast and lunches and meals for homeless children under age 6 by about $174 million over five years. Congress appropriated $7.5 billion for child nutrition programs in fiscal 1995.

The measure required schools to meet the Dietary Guidelines for Americans by 1996 or, if they obtained a waiver, by 1998. But the bill also gave school lunch planners flexibility in meeting the guidelines,

BOXSCORE

Child Nutrition — S 1614 (HR 8). The bill reauthorized and refined child nutrition and school lunch programs, including the Women, Infants and Children special nutrition program.

Reports: H Rept 103-535, Parts 1 and 2; S Rept 103-300.

KEY ACTION

July 19 — House passed HR 8, 372-40.

Aug. 25 — Senate passed S 1614 by voice vote.

Oct. 5 — House passed S 1614, revised, by voice vote.

Oct. 7 — Senate cleared S 1614 by voice vote.

Nov. 2 — President signed bill — PL 103-448.

allowing them to continue using a food-based system that analyzed portions of meat, milk, bread, vegetables and fruit, rather than a nutrient analysis.

The bill also contained provisions to:

• Eliminate the existing requirement that schools offer whole milk, requiring instead that varieties of milk be offered based on a survey of the prior year's preference. A type of milk that constituted less than 1 percent of purchases would not have to be served.

• Authorize $9 million to test the feasibility of schools serving all breakfast and lunches free and receiving a flat rate of reimbursement from the federal government.

• Permanently authorize a demonstration project that enabled some schools to receive cash or a commodity letter of credit instead of commodities for their lunch and breakfast programs.

The bill contained a four-year reauthorization of unspecified sums for the WIC program, which provided food vouchers and nutrition education for low-income pregnant women and children up to age 5. It also modified WIC to allow a pregnant woman to participate in the program immediately if she met income eligibility standards, instead of having to wait for the results of a nutri-

tional risk evaluation. Such an evaluation had to be completed within 60 days, however.

It also reauthorized the Summer Food Service program for four years. The program provided food for children in low-income areas during the summer months when school was out of session. In hopes of increasing the program's reach, the bill eliminated a one-year waiting period for private nonprofit organizations that wanted to run summer food service programs. While more than 12 million low-income children received free or subsidized lunches every day during the school year, in 1992 only 1.9 million children ate a meal at a summer food service site.

The bill gave permanent authorization to the homeless preschoolers' nutrition program, the breakfast start-up program and the nutrition education and training program. It made Head Start children automatically eligible to participate in the child- and adult-care food program.

Background

The school lunch program began in 1946 as a federal nutrition initiative after many World War II draftees failed their physical exams. The original focus was on malnutrition; participating schools were required to meet Agriculture Department standards for minimum amounts of specific food items (meat or other high-protein food, bread, vegetables, fruits and dairy products). In the ensuing years, scientific studies raised concerns over excess consumption by Americans — especially of fat, saturated fat and sodium. However, the guidelines for the breakfast and lunch programs had not been updated to reflect those changes.

According to the Agriculture Department, school lunches averaged 38 percent calories from fat even though federal dietary recommendations suggested that people should get only 30 percent of their calories from fat. Most lunch menus also had a high percentage of saturated fat, which could contribute to heart disease and other illnesses.

On June 8, the Agriculture Department's Food and Nutrition Service announced new regulations for nutrition standards for the National School Lunch and School Breakfast programs. School food programs had until July 1, 1998, to comply with the 1990 Dietary Guidelines for Americans, developed by the departments of Agriculture and Health and Human Services. The guidelines restricted fat intake and encouraged the consumption of fruits, vegetables and fiber.

Schools also were required to meet standards based on the nutrient content of meals rather than on whether they included certain food items. The regulations allowed menu planners to balance a week's worth of meals, so that if they served something fried on Monday they could compensate by serving a lower-fat meal on Thursday.

The new guidelines were welcomed by Senate Agriculture Committee Chairman Patrick J. Leahy, D-Vt. "I eat in school lunchrooms often," said Leahy. "Usually you can have warm glop or cold glop . . . . It's easy to see why children don't want to eat it."

However, some lawmakers expressed concern that not all schools could afford to carry out the required nutrient analysis.

House Action

The House Education and Labor Subcommittee on Elementary, Secondary and Vocational Education gave voice

vote approval May 4 to a bill (HR 8) that reauthorized the Child Nutrition Act at unspecified levels through fiscal 1998. The bill was sponsored by the subcommittee's chairman, Dale E. Kildee, D-Mich.

During the brief markup session, members approved by voice vote a group of amendments designed to fine-tune existing programs and discourage fraud by government contractors.

Bill Goodling, R-Pa., who sponsored the amendment on fraudulent activities, said it aimed to deter food suppliers and other companies from engaging in price-fixing, product-switching and other anti-competitive practices. Under the provision, companies that abused the system could be removed from lists of eligible suppliers.

The full Education and Labor Committee approved the bill by voice vote May 18 (H Rept 103-535, Part 1)

The Education and Labor Committee approved several amendments by voice vote, including one by Kildee to make Head Start participants automatically eligible for food programs beginning in fiscal 1996.

The committee also approved an amendment by George Miller, D-Calif., to permit some schools to drop whole milk from their menus if it accounted for less than 1 percent of the total milk consumed at the school in the previous year.

Miller's amendment initially was resisted by Steve Gunderson, R-Wis., whose dairy state long had supported the program's requirement that schools offer whole milk along with other varieties. Gunderson offered a substitute that would have allowed milk purchases to be based on a survey of students' preferences. He withdrew his amendment, saying afterward that he thought Miller's amendment would have little impact in most school districts.

In the only recorded vote during markup, members voted 26-15 along party lines for another Miller amendment to authorize a demonstration program for school breakfasts and lunches. All students could get free breakfast and lunch at a school where at least 30 percent of students qualified for free meals.

Republicans objected that providing free school lunches for all students would be too costly. The amendment authorized $15 million annually through fiscal 1998 for the demonstration program.

On June 16, the House Agriculture Committee approved by voice vote a four-year reauthorization for the Commodity Distribution Program, which fell under its jurisdiction (H Rept 103-535, Part 2).

House Floor Action

The House passed the bill July 19 by a vote of 372-40. "Hungry children cannot learn, and good nutrition is the first defense against disease," Kildee told his colleagues. (Vote 334, p. 100-H)

Senate Action

The Senate Agriculture Committee gave voice vote approval June 22 to a companion bill (S 1614 — S Rept 103-300) sponsored by committee Chairman Leahy.

As approved by the committee, the bill authorized the federal government to increase spending on nutrition programs and school lunches by about $174 million over five years.

Leahy's original bill mandated enough funding for WIC to provide benefits to every eligible family, but he dropped that language before the markup, citing lack of funds. Expanded funding for WIC was included in Clinton's health care bill (HR 3600, S 1757).

The bill also contained many provisions aimed at improving school lunches, including language giving more flexibility to menu planners and lifting requirements that schools offer whole milk, rather than low-fat dairy products. The bill also expanded the number of grants to schools that wanted to start school breakfast programs, increasing annual funding for such projects from $5 million to $7 million by 1999. The legislation also authorized $30 million annually for nutrition education for children, parents and food service employees.

The bill also contained language clarifying that local school boards had the authority to ban the sale of soft drinks and other junk food before and during lunch.

The Senate passed the bill by voice vote Aug. 25.

Final Action

Rather than sending the bill to a House-Senate conference, the House on Oct. 5 gave voice vote approval to a version of S 1614 that had been amended to reconcile differences between the two bills. The amendment had been agreed to beforehand by House and Senate lawmakers. The Senate cleared the bill for the president by voice vote in the early morning hours of Oct. 7.

Elements of Child-Support Bill Pass

Although efforts to enact a comprehensive bill to overhaul the nation's child-support enforcement system fell short, Congress cleared some of the bill's components before leaving for the year.

The comprehensive bill (HR 4570), a priority of the Congressional Caucus for Women's Issues, included a number of enforcement mechanisms aimed at reducing the estimated $34 billion that deadbeat parents, mostly fathers, owed in child support. Some of the bill's key provisions, including plans for a new national child-support payment registry and requirements that hospitals establish paternity at birth, mirrored proposals in the welfare overhaul plan that President Clinton unveiled June 14. *(Welfare reform, p. 364)*

The bill's sponsor, Rep. Patricia Schroeder, D-Colo., and other women members had hoped that even though Congress was not going to act on welfare reform in 1994, it would pass the child-support measure. The Clinton administration, however, argued against separating the provisions. "We believe that our package is a cohesive package. All the parts go together," said Health and Human Services spokeswoman Avis LaVelle.

The comprehensive bill stalled in the House, after only two of seven panels with jurisdiction acted on the measure.

According to the 1990 census, about half of the fathers obligated to make child-support payments failed to do so. The delinquency rate often was cited as a primary reason why many single-parent households ended up on welfare rolls.

Congress took some initial steps in 1993 to force more fathers to support their children. Provisions in the 1993 budget-reconciliation bill (HR 2264 — PL 103-66) required states to establish the paternity of 75 percent of children born out of wedlock who were receiving welfare or child-support services. The provisions set interim improvements that states with lower rates had to meet. States also were required to have laws that promoted voluntary acknowledgment of paternity in hospitals. *(1993 Almanac, p. 374)*

Child-Support Enforcement Bill

The broad child-support bill (HR 4570) had the support of a bipartisan group of congresswomen who argued that the provisions were crucial to welfare reform. "Make no mistake about it: Effective child-support enforcement is welfare prevention," said Marge Roukema, R-N.J.

In addition to requiring that hospitals establish paternity at birth, the bill's enforcement mechanisms included requiring states to withhold driver's licenses from deadbeat parents and modifying the employee federal tax withholding form, known as the W-4 form, to include information about child-support payments. That information was to be compiled in a new national child-support payment registry. The following House committees acted on the bill:

● **House Post Office Committee.** The House Post Office and Civil Service Subcommittee on Compensation and Employee Benefits gave voice vote approval July 26 to those portions of the bill that applied to federal workers. The full Post Office Committee approved the measure by voice vote Aug. 10.

Provisions approved by the panel required federal agencies to withhold court-ordered child-support payments from employees' wages, and they barred federal agencies from paying benefits to workers who were more than three months behind in child-support payments and had not agreed to pay the delinquent amount.

An amendment offered by Frank McCloskey, D-Ind., and approved in the full committee barred individuals who owed more than three months' worth of child-support payments from taking a federal job until they agreed to pay.

The original bill stipulated that a $1,000 delinquent amount in child support would trigger a freeze in employee benefits. The subcommittee gave voice vote approval to an amendment by its chairman, Delegate Eleanor Holmes Norton, D-D.C., that changed the trigger to three months. Norton said the $1,000 was too high a threshold: It would have allowed too many "deadbeat federal employees to escape a substantial portion of their support obligation."

The bill also initially gave federal agencies three days to comply after receiving court child-support payment orders. But in response to concerns raised by the Office of Personnel Management, the subcommittee agreed by voice vote to give agencies five days following a payday to comply. States could levy a $1,000 fine against a federal agency that failed to comply with the order within 10 days of the date wages or benefits were paid to an employee.

● **House Armed Services Subcommittee.** On Sept. 29, a second House panel, the Armed Services Subcommittee on Military Forces and Personnel, approved sections of the bill by voice vote. The full committee did not take up the measure.

The subcommittee-approved provisions required the Department of Defense to establish a centralized personnel locator service, including residential addresses, for every member of the armed forces and to provide the addresses to the Federal Parent Locator Service. Provisions of the bill were included in an end-of-session measure (HR 5140) that the House passed by voice vote Oct. 5.

Other Bills

With time running out late in the session, supporters of the comprehensive bill attempted to pass pieces of the package as separate bills or to attach them to other legislation. It was a strategy that met with mixed success. All told, four measures strengthening child-support enforcement were sent to Clinton for his signature. They barred parents who failed to pay child support from getting small-business loans, designated child-support payments as priority debts when an individual filed for bankruptcy, limited the ability of a state court to modify another state's child-support payment order, and allowed garnishment of federal retirees' pensions to pay damages for child abuse.

Two other bills died.

Bills That Were Enacted

The following child-support bills were enacted:

● **State modification of court orders.** Congress cleared a bill (S 922), introduced by Sen. Carol Moseley-Braun, D-Ill., restricting a state court's ability to modify another state's child-support payment order.

The legislation started in the Senate Judiciary Committee, which approved it by voice vote Aug. 11 (S Rept 103-361). The Senate passed the bill by voice vote Sept. 27, the House cleared it by voice vote Oct. 5, and Clinton signed it into law Oct. 20 (PL 103-383).

The bill barred a state court from modifying a child-support order issued by another state's court unless the child and parent receiving the support payments had moved to the state where the modification was sought or had agreed to the change.

Rep. Barney Frank, D-Mass., filed similar bills in 1992 and 1993 after being contacted by a constituent whose ex-spouse had persuaded an out-of-state court to reduce the monthly support payment. The House passed both bills, but the Senate did not. *(1992 Almanac, p. 474)*

● **Small-business loans.** Parents who failed to pay child support became ineligible for small-business loans under a bill reauthorizing the Small Business Administration (S 2060 — PL 103-403). The Senate Small Business Committee inserted the language into the bill Aug. 10, when it adopted by voice vote an amendment offered by Moseley-Braun for Frank R. Lautenberg, D-N.J. *(SBA reauthorization, p. 185)*

● **Bankruptcy.** A bill overhauling the federal Bankruptcy Code (HR 5116 — PL 103-394) designated child-support payments as priority debts when an individual filed for bankruptcy. The bill made it more difficult for a divorced person who assumed the couple's marital debts in exchange for a reduction or elimination of alimony or child support to escape that obligation through bankruptcy, thereby saddling the other spouse with the debt. *(Bankruptcy overhaul, p. 175)*

● **Child abuse payments.** Congress cleared a separate bill (HR 3694 — PL 103-358), sponsored by Schroeder, that allowed the pensions of federal retirees found guilty of child abuse to be garnisheed for the purpose of paying court-ordered damages. *(Federal workers, p. 152)*

Bills That Fell Short

The House passed two child-support bills in the closing days of the session that did not see Senate action.

● **Federal employee child support.** On Oct. 5, Norton introduced elements of the stalled comprehensive child-support bill as HR 5179. The measure went directly to the House floor, where it won voice vote approval Oct. 7; the Senate did not take up the measure.

As passed by the House, HR 5179 required a federal agency that received a child-support garnishment order to withhold the required sums from a worker's pay and forward the money to the custodial parent within five days of the next payday. Agencies that did not act within 10 days of a payday could be fined $1,000 by the state requesting the child-support payments.

The bill prohibited federal agencies from paying a variety of benefits to government workers who were in arrears on their child-support payments by more than three months or from hiring new employees who were similarly delinquent. The benefits to be denied included many federal grants and loans, as well as professional licenses issued by the federal government. College loans and benefits based upon financial need, such as welfare and food stamps, were exempted. The bill also denied a U.S. passport to parents facing an outstanding arrest warrant for owing more than $10,000 in child support.

● **Armed forces child support.** The House on Oct. 5 gave voice vote approval to a bill (HR 5140) aimed at making it easier to get court-ordered child support from active and retired members of the military. The House-passed measure, sponsored by Ike Skelton, D-Mo., required the secretary of Defense to establish a centralized data bank containing the addresses of all military employees and to make that information available to the Federal Parent Locator Service. ∎

Food Stamp Measure Clears

The House cleared legislation by voice vote March 16 to help convenience stores avoid losing their authorization to accept food stamps. The Senate approved the bill (S 1926) by voice vote March 11, and President Clinton signed it into law March 25 (PL 103-225).

A recent Agriculture Department survey had found that unless Congress acted, about half the 56,000 convenience stores authorized to accept food stamps would be disqualified. The problem was that the existing qualifications, based on the percentage of staple foods sold, had not kept up with changing retail practices or consumer buying habits.

If those stores no longer accepted food stamps, bill supporters said, poor residents of rural areas and inner-city neighborhoods lacking supermarkets would have trouble buying food.

The bill, introduced by Larry Pressler, R-S.D., was based on a measure the House had passed Nov. 10, 1993 (HR 3436 — H Rept 103-352). *(1993 Almanac, p. 376)*

S 1926 required a store to meet one of two conditions in order to accept food stamps.

The first condition was that the store continually offer staples from each of the four basic food groups, such as meat, bread, fruit and dairy products. The store also had to sell perishable foods in at least two of the groups. Alternatively, at least 50 percent of the outlet's total sales — not just food sales — had to consist of staples. The legislation also directed the Agriculture secretary to issue regulations providing for periodic reauthorization of stores.

In addition, the bill modified some food stamp provisions related to Indian reservations contained in the 1990 farm bill (S 2830 — PL 101-624) and set to take effect in 1994. One of those provisions required states to stagger monthly issuing dates of food stamps to Indian reservations. S 1926 allowed states to stagger the dates and required them to do so only if a tribe requested it.

A short-term bill (S 1777 — PL 103-205) that cleared Nov.

23, 1993, had allowed convenience stores to continue accepting food stamps while Congress completed work on the permanent measure. ∎

Law Expands Benefits For Holocaust Victims

The Senate cleared a bill July 19 that made more Holocaust victims living in the United States eligible for federal aid programs such as food stamps and housing subsidies.

The bill (HR 1873), sponsored by Rep. Henry A. Waxman, D-Calif., uniformly exempted reparation payments made by Germany and Austria to World War II Holocaust victims from the income calculations used by federal agencies to determine eligibility for programs such as low-income housing grants or food stamps.

About 30,000 people in the United States received the payments, usually $350 to $600 a month, the Congressional Budget Office (CBO) estimated. A small fraction of those beneficiaries also received federal aid, CBO said. A Waxman staff member said that fewer than 20,000 Americans, mostly elderly, would be affected by the bill.

A Waxman aide said the United States provided similar payments to World War II victims of U.S. policy, including Japanese-Americans, Aleuts and Indians. These payments were uniformly exempt from federal income calculations. But because the Holocaust payments were approved by foreign governments, no uniform rule had been applied.

Under existing law, the reparation payments could be counted as regular income or assets. Some agencies, such as the Internal Revenue Service, did not consider the payments when determining income levels. But other agencies, such as the Department of Housing and Urban Development, included the extra income when determining eligibility for programs based on need, such as low-income housing assistance.

The bill was prompted by the cases of two recipients, one in California and one in Arizona, who faced denial of federal assistance when their monthly payments pushed them over income eligibility levels. "To subject American citizens that receive these payments to additional financial burdens is to interfere with the penitent purpose of the restitution," said Sen. Dennis DeConcini, D-Ariz., who introduced similar legislation (S 827) in 1993.

The bill started in the House Government Operations Committee, which approved it by voice vote June 29. The House passed the bill by voice vote July 12, and the Senate cleared it July 19, also by voice vote. President Clinton signed the measure Aug. 1 (PL 103-286). ∎

Bills Enhance Indians' Status

Congress cleared bills in 1994 aimed at expanding the independence of Indian tribes, including measures to give tribes more authority over federal Indian programs, improve the management of Indian trust funds and bar the government from making distinctions among recognized tribes. A bill to improve the process of granting formal recognition to Indian tribes won approval from the House but died in the Senate.

Tribal Independence

Congress took another step in its 20-year effort to restore the independence of Indian nations, clearing legislation Oct.

7 to streamline and expand programs that granted tribes greater autonomy and authority over federal programs designed for their benefit. President Clinton signed the bill into law Oct. 25 (HR 4842 — PL 103-413).

Through treaties, the United States had recognized Indian tribes as sovereign nations since the 1700s. In these treaties, the government pledged to provide public services, such as education and health care, to the tribes in exchange for land, other resources and peace.

Despite the tribes' independent status, however, the federal government kept a tight grip on the management of public services until 1974, when Congress passed the Indian Self-Determination and Education Assistance Act (PL 93-638) granting tribes greater independence. (1974 Almanac, p. 672)

The law permitted tribes to take over, through self-determination contracts, the administration of individual federal programs that otherwise would have been managed by the Interior Department's Bureau of Indian Affairs (BIA) or by the Indian Health Service, part of the Department of Health and Human Services. But key lawmakers complained that, in practice, tribes were held back in their attempts to take over federal programs by a large federal bureaucracy and excessive regulations.

As enacted, HR 4842 combined two initiatives, both sponsored by Bill Richardson, D-N.M.

The first — the content of the original bill — provided for a model contract that tribes could use to cut through red tape, and it sharply limited the paperwork demands on tribes and exempted many contracts from federal procurement rules.

The second was a bill (HR 3508 — H Rept 103-653), already passed by the House, that expanded and made permanent a demonstration program under which tribes could take over whole blocks of federal programs. The bill permitted up to 20 new tribes to join the self-governance program every year. Under the program, tribes had greater flexibility over how to spend federal funds and could redesign programs to meet unique demands found on their reservations. Indian Health Service programs were to remain a temporary part of the self-governance program while Congress studied their inclusion on a permanent basis.

HR 3508 began in the House Natural Resources Subcommittee on Native American Affairs, which approved it by voice vote April 26. The full committee approved the measure by voice vote May 25, and the House passed it Aug. 16, also by voice vote.

HR 4842 started in the full committee, which approved it Sept. 28 by voice vote. When the bill got to the floor Oct. 6, lawmakers amended it to include HR 3508 and passed the combined measure by voice vote. Skipping committee consideration, the Senate cleared the bill Oct. 7 by voice vote.

Indian Trust Funds

Congress stepped in to clean up a longstanding problem at the Interior Department, whose management of Indian trust funds was widely criticized. The bill, which Clinton signed Oct. 25 (HR 4833 — PL 103-412), allowed tribes to directly manage their funds and to receive periodic statements on accounts that remained with the Interior Department. It established a special trustee within the department to draft and execute a comprehensive plan to clean up and manage the trust funds.

For 150 years, the Interior Department had been entrusted with money that resulted from agreements between the federal government and tribes over land use,

mineral rights and other claims. For years, members of Congress and tribal leaders had blasted the department for its management of the Indian funds, which amounted to $2.1 billion. "The department," said Richardson, "currently is unable to give an accurate balance for these accounts, and tribes have very little say in how their funds are managed."

The bill contained provisions to:

● Create a nine-member advisory board made up of tribal and individual account holder representatives, plus people with experience in investment management to assist the trustee.

● Require the Interior secretary to give all individual and tribal account holders an accurate quarterly statement of their beginning and ending account balances, investment gains and losses, receipts and disbursements.

● Require that funds held in trust for individual Indians be invested in interest-bearing Treasury notes and bonds, just as tribal funds were.

● Authorize Indian tribes to withdraw their accounts from the trust funds and take over the management of those accounts, once they had won approval from the secretary and special trustee.

The House Natural Resources Committee easily approved the measure by voice vote Sept. 28 (H Rept 103-778), and the full House passed the bill, 353-39, on Oct. 3. The Senate took up the House-passed measure Oct. 7, clearing it by voice vote. *(Vote 462, p. 138-H)*

'Historic' Tribes

On May 31, Clinton signed into law a bill (S 1654 — PL 103-263) that prohibited the federal government from making a distinction between "historic" Indian tribes — which included almost all tribes — and "created" tribes.

The Bureau of Indian Affairs considered roughly 20 tribes to be "created" because they could not sufficiently document their tribal history. Historic tribes enjoyed greater autonomy, including the right to levy taxes and handle law enforcement on Indian lands.

Initially, the House Natural Resources Subcommittee on Native American Affairs approved the provisions as a free-standing bill (HR 4231) by voice vote April 26. Instead of sending the bill to the floor, however, supporters attached the language to a Senate bill (S 1654) that made technical changes to Indian land and water claims.

The Senate had passed S 1654 in 1993; the House amended and passed it April 19 by a vote of 414-2. After the Senate made some further changes May 19, the House cleared the final version of the bill by voice vote May 23. *(Vote 116, p. 36-H)*

Tribal Recognition

The House overwhelmingly approved a bill (H Rept 103-782 — HR 4462) designed to improve the process of granting formal recognition to Indian tribes. But the Senate never considered the legislation.

Federally recognized tribes were eligible for government services and other benefits. The bill would have created an independent Commission on Indian Recognition to determine whether specific Indian groups should be recognized as tribes.

The House Natural Resources Committee easily approved the measure by voice vote Sept. 28. The House passed the bill Oct. 3 by a vote of 337-54. *(Vote 461, p. 138-H)* ■

Other Indian Legislation

Congress attempted to address several other problems in the Indian community but managed to clear only two of the bills.

Religious Freedom

In response to increased pressure from Indian groups, the Senate Indian Affairs Committee approved legislation (S 2269 — S Rept 103-411) Aug. 10 that contained broad protections for native religions. But the bill, which the committee approved by voice vote, never made it to the Senate floor.

For years Indian tribes had been demanding federal protection for certain sacred sites so they could worship and gather sacred plants undisturbed. Protection of these areas was a top priority for tribal leaders, who viewed the fight as a struggle to preserve their culture and heritage. But these lands were located off reservations, and loggers, developers, tourists and four-wheel vehicle enthusiasts also demanded the right to use them.

To protect the lands, the committee-approved bill required the federal government to prove a "compelling interest" before it could disturb a sacred Indian site. That standard would have increased the burden on the federal government to show that it needed to take actions that would interfere with Indians' religious practices.

The bill included provisions aimed at establishing ways to facilitate negotiations between tribes and federal land managers to permit multiple use of federal lands.

The bill, introduced by Daniel K. Inouye, D-Hawaii, also addressed several other religious concerns of American Indians. It included provisions to:

● Protect Indians' right to use peyote, an otherwise illegal hallucinogen, in religious ceremonies.

● Permit American Indian prisoners to practice their religions. Prisoners would be allowed to wear traditional headgear and be given access to their religious practitioners.

● Make it easier for Indians to obtain protected eagle feathers and plants from the Fish and Wildlife Service for use in religious ceremonies.

The Senate Indian Affairs Committee approved the religious freedom bill in the face of solid GOP opposition and constitutional concerns raised by the Justice Department. The bill then moved to the Senate Energy and Natural Resources Committee, which had jurisdiction over legislation affecting public lands. There it died for the year.

Peyote

Congress on Sept. 27 cleared a narrower version of the Indian religious freedom bill, which protected the right of Indians to use peyote as a religious sacrament. President Clinton signed the measure into law Oct. 6 (HR 4230 — PL 103-344).

Since 1966, Indians had been exempt from laws banning the use of peyote, a hallucinogenic drug made from spineless cacti found in the Southwest. However, tribal leaders feared that the regulatory exemption did not protect their free exercise of religion under the First Amendment.

Their fears were based, in part, on a 1990 Supreme Court ruling, *Employment Division v. Smith*. The ruling declared that the sacramental use of peyote was not necessarily protected under the Constitution, unless individual states provided exemptions. At the time, 28 states had such laws on the books.

The legislation, introduced by Rep. Bill Richardson, D-N.M., gave the regulatory exemption for peyote use the force of law. It also prohibited states from discriminating against Indians who used the drug.

The House Natural Resources Subcommittee on Native American Affairs moved first on the legislation, approving it by voice vote July 27 (H Rept 103-675). Twelve days later, the House easily passed the bill by voice vote.

In the Senate, the Indian Affairs Committee never marked up the bill, sending it directly to the floor where the Senate cleared it, also by voice vote, on Sept. 27.

Indian Waste Dumps

Congress took steps to clean up potentially toxic waste dumps on Indian reservations Oct. 8, when the Senate cleared legislation that authorized a comprehensive cleanup plan. President Clinton signed the bill on Oct. 22 (S 720 — PL 103-399).

There were roughly 600 potentially hazardous dumps on Indian lands that could pose health risks to livestock and humans. Improperly secured dumps could lead to contamination of groundwater. At the time, only two of the 600 dumps met Environmental Protection Agency regulations governing the disposal of solid waste.

The measure, introduced by John McCain, R-Ariz., moved easily through the Senate in the spring, with the Senate Indian Affairs Committee approving the measure April 13 by voice vote (S Rept 103-253). The Senate passed the bill May 12, also by voice vote.

The House Committee on Natural Resources took up the bill Sept. 28, approving it by voice vote (H Rept 103-783). On Oct. 5 the House also passed the measure by voice vote.

Three days later, the Senate gave voice vote approval to the House version, clearing the measure.

Child Protection

The Senate passed a bill (S 2075) designed to beef up a 1990 law that protected children on Indian reservations, but the bill stalled in the House.

In 1990, Congress cleared legislation (PL 101-630) that authorized new federal programs to treat Indian victims of child abuse and to increase the reporting of abuse cases. Congress passed the bill in response to reports that several teachers employed by the Bureau of Indian Affairs, a division of the Interior Department, had sexually abused Indian stu-

dents. The law also aimed to ensure that workers dealing with Indian children had no criminal record. *(1990 Almanac, p. 421)*

But the two agencies charged with putting the programs in place — the Bureau of Indian Affairs and the Indian Health Service — were unclear about their roles. The bill would have transferred more authority to the health service.

The Senate Indian Affairs Committee approved the bill by voice vote Aug. 1 (S Rept 103-394). At the markup, the panel approved, by voice vote, an amendment by John McCain, R-Ariz., the sponsor of the legislation, to authorize $3 million a year through fiscal 2005 to assist tribes with background checks and investigations of employees on reservations who worked with children. It also authorized $4 million a year through fiscal 2005 for programs to combat family violence.

On Oct. 6 the Senate passed S 2075 by voice vote, completing action on the bill for the year.

Indian Settlements

Members of the House Natural Resources Subcommittee on Native American Affairs gave voice vote approval June 30 to a bill (HR 3437) to give the U.S. government a greater say in negotiations over tribal settlements. But the bill went no further in the 104th Congress.

Tribes, owners of private land and state governments had often clashed over who had the right to certain lands and lucrative water sources mentioned in Indian treaties. Resolutions to these disputes required federal dollars.

The bill, sponsored by Craig Thomas, R-Wyo., would have ensured the Interior Department a place at the bargaining table over settlements that involved federal funds.

Indian Health Service

In an effort to give the director of the Indian Health Service more clout within the Department of Health and Human Services, the Senate passed legislation (S 2067) to elevate the director to an assistant secretary of Indian health. But the measure died in the House.

The Senate Indian Affairs Committee approved the bill, sponsored by John McCain, R-Ariz., by voice vote June 30 (S Rept 103-327).

The Senate passed the bill by voice vote Sept. 21. The measure was then referred to the House committees on Natural Resources and Energy and Commerce, but neither panel took it up. ■

## Chapter 8

EDUCATION/ LABOR/ HOUSING/ VETERANS

Education
Elementary and Secondary Education Act 383
    Provisions 392
Goals 2000: Educate America Act 397
    Provisions 398
'School to Work' Program 400
Other Education-Related Legislation 401
Labor
Striker Replacement Bill 402
OSHA Overhaul 403
Underfunded Pensions 403
Other Pension-Related Legislation 404
Retraining Initiative 405
Other Labor-Related Legislation 406

Housing
Housing Reauthorization 408
    Narrow Housing Bill 410
HUD Property Disposal 411
Homeless Assistance 411
Flood Insurance Program 411
Veterans
Persian Gulf Syndrome 412
    Provisions 413
Women Veterans/Medical Construction 414
VHA Exemptions 416
Other Veterans Legislation 416

ELEMENTARY AND SECONDARY EDUCATION ACT

Lawmakers Renew and Revamp 1965 Education Act

White House proposal to redistribute funds from affluent school districts to poorer ones is rejected

In the closing days of the 103rd Congress, lawmakers cleared a bill that revised and expanded federal programs for the nation's elementary and secondary schools. The five-year reauthorization bill (HR 6) roughly followed President Clinton's proposals for overhauling the 1965 Elementary and Secondary Education Act. However, lawmakers did not go along with a key administration plan that would have dramatically altered the way states received money under Title I, a program created to help educationally disadvantaged students.

The measure authorized $12.7 billion in fiscal 1995 and unspecified sums through fiscal 1999. Clinton signed the bill Oct. 20 (PL 103-382).

Much of the year's debate on HR 6 centered on Clinton's proposal to concentrate more of the money under Title I in the nation's poorest school districts at the expense of more affluent areas. Historically, more than 90 percent of the nation's school districts received Title I money. The administration pushed hard to reshape the formula to target poorer children. But lawmakers proved unwilling to make a change that could jeopardize the flow of federal dollars to their own states or districts.

After months of negotiations and counterproposals, members ultimately agreed to a compromise that left the existing formula largely intact, although it directed slightly more money to low-income children.

As enacted, the bill:

● **Title I funds.** Authorized $7.4 billion for Title I local education grant programs in fiscal 1995.

Beginning in fiscal 1996, Title I funds were to be distributed to states and counties using the existing formula for amounts up to $6.6 billion, the amount appropriated in fiscal 1995. Money appropriated above the $6.6 billion threshold was to be targeted more toward poor children.

The bill authorized a separate state grants program with funding based on a state's willingness to pay taxes for public education and its efforts to equalize spending between poor and rich school districts.

● **Opportunity-to-learn standards.** Struck a compromise on opportunity-to-learn standards aimed at guaranteeing equal access to high-quality teachers, books and other edu-

BOXSCORE

Elementary and Secondary Education Act Reauthorization — HR 6 (S 1513). The five-year bill authorized $12.7 billion in fiscal 1995 and revamped federal school aid programs, the bulk of them aimed at educationally disadvantaged students.

Reports: H Rept 103-425, S Rept 103-292; conference report H Rept 103-761.

KEY ACTION

March 24 — House passed HR 6, 289-128.

Aug. 2 — Senate passed HR 6, 94-6, after substituting the text of S 1513.

Sept. 30 — House adopted the conference report on HR 6, 262-132.

Oct. 5 — Senate cleared HR 6, 77-20.

Oct. 20 — President signed the bill — PL 103-382.

cational resources. The bill required states that did not already have such standards to develop strategies to ensure that all students were held to the same expectations and had equal educational opportunities.

The original House-passed bill included mandatory opportunity-to-learn standards. The Senate had no such provision. Liberal House Democrats argued that the standards were needed to ensure equal access to a high-quality education. But Republicans and conservative Democrats from both chambers argued that such standards could expose school districts to lawsuits from dissatisfied parents, thereby placing the schools under financial strain.

● **Eisenhower grants.** Authorized the Eisenhower program at $800 million in fiscal 1995 and shifted its focus from broad grants to states to promote math and science education, to targeted grants for professional training for teachers, administrators and other school employees.

In other provisions, the bill:

● **Guns in schools.** Required states that received federal funds under the act to adopt a policy that any student who brought a gun to school be expelled for one year. Local school district officials could modify the expulsion requirement on a case-by-case basis.

● **School prayer.** Allowed the withholding of federal funds from any school district that violated a court order to allow "constitutionally protected" voluntary prayer in school.

● **Sex education.** Prohibited the use of federal funds to encourage or support homosexuality as a positive lifestyle; to promote or encourage any sexual activity, either homosexual or heterosexual; or to distribute condoms in schools.

Background

The Elementary and Secondary Education Act was enacted in 1965 as part of President Lyndon B. Johnson's War on Poverty. In addition to Title I grants for remedial education for disadvantaged children, the law included bilingual education, Drug Free Schools grants to prevent and treat alcohol and drug abuse, and Eisenhower grants to improve the teaching of math and science.

Most of the money under the act went to programs under

Title I. Authorized at $6.3 billion in fiscal 1994, it provided 5 million students with extra help in reading, math and other areas in which they had fallen behind. The money went to schools to hire additional teachers, buy computers and pay for field trips, among other things.

The primary intent was to give extra help to poor children to bring them up to par with their classmates. A secondary goal was to help any "educationally disadvantaged" child who was doing poorly in class and on standardized tests, regardless of family income.

But the political reality in 1994 — as it had been in 1965 — was that to gain sufficient congressional support, Title I money had to flow to almost every school district in the country. While that made the program politically popular, it also led to criticism by education experts that it created a system of thinly spread general aid to schools without much regard to need.

In the early 1990s, more than half the students served were not poor, according to a study by the Rand Corp. in Santa Monica, Calif. Schools that received Title I money frequently used it for any child who was not doing well — rather than solely to help poor children.

Originally dubbed Title I, the program was known as Chapter 1 from 1981 to 1994. HR 6 changed the name back to Title I. It had last been reauthorized in 1988. *(1988 Almanac, p. 330)*

Under the existing formula, money was distributed based on census figures of the number of poor children per county, plus average state spending per pupil. On top of that, about 10 percent of the money was aimed directly at high-poverty counties — those in which 15 percent or 6,500 children were poor — through "concentration" grants.

The Clinton Plan

With the Elementary and Secondary Education Act due to expire at the end of fiscal 1994, the Clinton administration presented a draft reauthorization bill Sept. 14, 1993, that included several changes aimed primarily at sending more Title I money to counties and school districts with the highest poverty rates.

The administration proposed to increase the portion of funds devoted to concentration grants to 50 percent from 10 percent, shifting about $500 million from lower-poverty to higher-poverty counties. The wealthiest school districts were to get no money.

The administration offered several reasons to target the money more on areas with high poverty:

● More than half the students in schools with the highest concentrations of poverty were low achievers — scoring below the 35th percentile on standardized tests — compared with only 8 percent of students in schools with the lowest poverty concentrations.

● Test scores declined as the proportion of students eligible for free or reduced-price lunches rose. Such subsidized lunches were a commonly cited indicator of the number of poor students in a school and were frequently used by states to distribute Title I money to school districts.

● In schools with above average enrollment of children eligible for free or reduced-price lunches, the poverty level of the school began to influence test scores of all children, including those from families that were more well off.

● The achievement level of the average student in a high-poverty school was lower than the achievement level of the average Title I student in a low-poverty school.

"We think the argument for targeting is very, very strong," said Marshall S. Smith, under secretary of Education. "There

are lots of examples of schools with 6 and 7 and 4 and 5 percent poverty getting Title I funds. And schools with 50, 55 and 60 percent poverty are not. And we think that is contrary to the intent."

Education Department figures showed that nearly half the country's 3,100 counties would lose money under Clinton's plan, with most of the winners in poor urban areas.

To ensure that children assisted under Title I got high-level instruction, Clinton also proposed that states seeking money be required to submit plans to the Department of Education outlining content and performance standards. Such standards were an integral part of Clinton's Goals 2000 school reform bill (HR 1804 — PL 103-227). But the Goals 2000 program was voluntary, and the administration wanted states to develop standards under the Title I program even if they chose not to participate in Goals 2000. *(Goals 2000, p. 397; 1993 Almanac, p. 407)*

House Subcommittee

After months of closed-door negotiations, a House Education and Labor subcommittee approved HR 6 on Feb. 1 by a nearly party-line vote of 18-8. But the Subcommittee on Elementary, Secondary and Vocational Education rejected Clinton's proposal for reallocating Title I funds.

The administration had insisted on pushing for a vote on the Clinton formula, even though it appeared to be a nonstarter in the subcommittee. Offered as an amendment by Jack Reed, D-R.I., the Clinton funding plan was rejected, 12-14, with six Democrats joining a nearly solid bloc of Republicans opposing it. Most of those voting for Clinton's plan represented poorer districts; most of the votes against it were cast by members from more affluent districts.

The subcommittee gave voice vote approval to an alternative drafted by Chairman Dale E. Kildee, D-Mich., and Tom Petri, R-Wis., that largely retained the existing allocation for most of the Title I money.

Under the Kildee-Petri plan, $6.3 billion — the fiscal 1994 level — was to be distributed under the old formula; the rest was to go out under a new plan slightly more targeted to poor areas. In addition, all the money was to be distributed to the nation's 15,000 school districts, not its 3,100 counties, which also would increase targeting. Poverty counts were to be updated every two years, rather than every 10 years.

Only the very poorest districts stood to get significantly more money under the Kildee-Petri plan than they did under existing law — and they would benefit only if appropriations jumped significantly.

Approved by a minority of Democrats allied with a near-solid bloc of Republicans, the plan left many committee liberals unhappy and angered the Democrats' traditional allies in the anti-poverty lobby. The Leadership Conference on Civil Rights accused the lawmakers of "closing their eyes to the needs of poor children."

Siding with Kildee was full Committee Chairman William D. Ford, D-Mich., who worked the room for votes during the debate and exercised his right to vote even though he was not a regular member of the subcommittee.

Chapter 2 Battle

Although Republicans said going into the markup that they were prepared to support the bill, they bolted after they failed to restore a $400 million block grant program, known as Chapter 2 (Title II in the bill). Republicans preferred the block grants, which allowed states and school districts to spend the money as they saw fit within broad guidelines, over

the more tightly controlled categorical grants favored by many Democrats.

The battle was joined during debate on an amendment offered by Tom Sawyer, D-Ohio, and modified by Tim Roemer, D-Ind., that was adopted by voice vote. Sawyer wanted to specify that the money be used to assist school districts with teacher training and curriculum development. Under Roemer's modification, at least 80 percent of the money was to go for teacher training, with up to 20 percent for curriculum. Based on an administration proposal, the amendments eliminated the Chapter 2 block grant program.

Steve Gunderson, R-Wis., and ranking Republican Bill Goodling, Pa., tried to restore and revamp the block grant program and allow the money to be used for computer equipment, library services and materials, and "promising education reform projects." But their amendment was defeated 10-16. "This side feels intensely on the flexibility of Chapter 2 that has now been eliminated," Gunderson said at the end of the meeting, explaining why every Republican on the panel except Petri voted against the bill.

Other Amendments

Also approved, mostly by voice vote, were amendments by:

● George Miller, D-Calif., requiring all school districts receiving money under the bill to expel for one year any student who brought a gun to school. Rural lawmakers such as Gunderson opposed the measure; he argued that students who went hunting before school could be kicked out just for leaving a shotgun in their pickup truck. Donald M. Payne, D-N.J., a liberal, argued against mandatory punishments of any kind. Miller initially included knives and other weapons in his amendment. After he excluded them, the amendment was approved 11-9.

● Miller, mandating that school districts require each of their educators to be certified to teach in their assigned subject area by 1998 in order for their states to receive certain of the bill's grants.

● Patsy T. Mink, D-Hawaii, to require the Defense Department to cover Pentagon-related "impact aid" payments — education grants to localities with numerous children from families connected to large federal endeavors, such as military bases. Mink said her amendment would "free up $380 million" in education funds by making the Pentagon pay for the grants. Randy "Duke" Cunningham, R-Calif., complained that it would cut defense spending.

● Major R. Owens, D-N.Y., to require school districts to spend 1 percent of their Title I money to promote parent involvement with children and schools.

● Reed, describing actions that states could take against school systems, or that school systems could take against schools, that were deemed lacking under state standards. Corrective actions could include putting the school system in receivership, turning certain schools over to private enterprises, abolishing the local school board or authorizing students to transfer.

The subcommittee defeated, 8-17, an amendment to Reed's proposal by John A. Boehner, R-Ohio, that would have required school districts to allow transfers from schools that failed to improve for long periods.

● Reed, to establish a grant program to improve school libraries. Reed said that in his travels he had come across books referring to President Calvin Coolidge and showing office workers using Smith Corona typewriters.

● Mink, to authorize grants and programs aimed at providing equity for women and girls in school.

● Lynn Woolsey, D-Calif., to allow all schools to offer "coordinated services" programs, in which schools worked with outside agencies to provide health and other social services at school or nearby.

The subcommittee defeated amendments by:
● Goodling, to bar funding for "family planning or reproductive health services." The vote was 10-11.
● Boehner, to allow school districts to use Title I funds for so-called school choice programs. A concept popular mainly with conservatives, such programs aimed to create competitive tension among schools by allowing parents to pick which school their children would attend. Boehner limited his proposal to public schools to attract votes, but still lost, 7-19.

House Committee

After 10 hours of trading barbs over policy in public while cutting deals in private, the full Education and Labor Committee on Feb. 8 approved the bill by a vote of 29-14 (H Rept 103-425).

Most Republicans voted against the bill to protest an amendment aimed at pressuring states to assure students a "high-quality opportunity to learn" — an amendment Republicans argued could lead to federal control of state and local school policy.

The bill's Democratic backers, led by subcommittee Chairman Kildee, said the measure provided flexibility and accountability. Countered Goodling, the committee's top Republican, "We need programs that are less restrictive and more supportive of the genius of our local school programs."

Sponsors said the bill made it easier for states to get federal money — the federal government provided about 5.6 percent of local education budgets nationwide — and gave states and school districts much more spending leeway. For instance, it let more schools use money meant to help disadvantaged children for the benefit of all students. Schools also could create experimental charter schools. The Education Department could waive federal requirements in certain cases. The bill allowed consolidated applications for various grants and provided money to let schools coordinate grant programs.

In return, the bill demanded more results, especially in connection with Title I money. Under the committee bill, states had to adopt challenging, high-quality curriculum content and performance standards for disadvantaged students and show progress toward achieving them. And the bill required states and school districts to take "corrective action" against districts and schools that failed to show enough progress — moves that could include putting the school system in receivership, turning certain schools over to private enterprises, or authorizing students to transfer out.

● **Opportunity-to-learn standards.** Republicans were particularly upset by an Owens amendment to require states seeking Title I money to adopt standards to ensure that educationally disadvantaged students got an "opportunity to learn" by assuring them high-quality learning materials, teachers, school buildings, libraries, laboratories and intangibles, such as gender equity policies. As with the bill's curriculum and performance standards, these standards had to be "as challenging and of the same high quality as they are for all children."

The amendment was approved on a mostly partisan vote of 26-16, with one Democrat, Ron Klink, Pa., voting no. When the markup ended, Goodling blamed the provision for the loss of GOP votes on the bill. "You knew from Day One that we couldn't participate if you had opportunity to learn and no

money to pay for it," he told Chairman Ford. The only Republican to support the bill was Petri.

Owens tried to appease Republicans by barring the Education Department from withholding funds from a state "on the basis of the specific content" of opportunity-to-learn standards — a curb on the department's power that did not apply to the other standards.

But Republicans called the proposal yet another "unfunded mandate" because the department could withhold funds by rejecting state plans, which were to include all the bill's required standards.

"The department is going to set all kinds of minimum requirements," Gunderson said. Not so, Owens said. "To put it crudely, a state could put in one sentence to meet the opportunity-to-learn standards," he said. When Goodling noted that his amendment listed eight items to be addressed by the standards, Owens replied, "You could do it in one long sentence."

Owens argued that the amendment would merely force states to confront the poor conditions in some schools and perhaps persuade them to fix them up because the annual progress reports required by his proposal would prove "very embarrassing."

● **Title I funds.** The fight over how to allocate Title I money had raged for months, mostly behind closed doors. Internal Education Department documents detailing how Clinton's proposed formula would affect committee members' counties illustrated why it was so unpopular. About half the members could have been losers under the Clinton plan, with some losing up to 15 percent of their grants a year. "I can't get the votes to do anything that does that much to that many people," Ford said.

By Feb. 8, Kildee and Petri had devised a new formula that was somewhat more targeted toward poor areas than the subcommittee version.

Administration officials, realizing the liberal and urban-dominated subcommittee had been their best shot, came up with their own compromise, and Education Secretary Richard W. Riley worked the phones for it. But by markup day, members were coalescing around "Kildee-Petri II."

Democrats persuaded Republicans whose districts would lose under the more targeted formula to go along by agreeing to a GOP amendment to restore the $435 million in Chapter 2 block grants.

The committee approved the grant program by voice vote and the funding formula, 41-1, with Reed dissenting. He called the committee's decision one of "pork over policy."

Other Amendments

The committee also approved amendments by:
● Dan Miller, R-Fla., to replace the subcommittee provision on guns in schools. Approved 24-13, the new provision required districts to adopt gun policies but did not mandate expulsion.
● Various Democrats to authorize $200 million for a library materials program, crafted by Reed; $200 million for a school facilities loan program by Miller, D-Calif.; and $125 million each for two demonstration grant programs for rural and urban schools, by Pat Williams, D-Mont., and New Jersey's Payne respectively. Republicans scoffed at some of the new programs but did not actively fight them.
● Dick Armey, R-Texas, amending the Miller, D-Calif., teacher certification mandate to clarify that states could use "alternative" certification methods. Miller's amendment later caused an uproar when home-schooling parents became convinced that it would require certification for

home-school teachers.

The committee rejected amendments by:
● Armey, to prohibit adjusting test scores on the basis of race, by 15-26.
● Armey, who offered two school choice amendments for an absent Boehner. The amendments were defeated, as they had been in subcommittee. The first was rejected by 17-25, the second by voice vote.
● Armey, for Boehner, to kill four programs proposed for elimination in Clinton's budget, by 14-27.
● Goodling, to bar funds from being used for "family planning or reproductive health services," by 14-27.
● By Miller, D-Calif., to authorize "character education" grants for teaching ethics and values, by 6-23.

House Floor

Four weeks after it first took up the bill, the House on March 24 approved HR 6 on a 289-128 vote. The main tenets of the $12.7 billion bill had been largely resolved several weeks earlier, but House members had continued to battle over volatile issues such as school prayer and homosexual lifestyles. *(Vote 95, p. 28-H)*

The House did not alter the compromise adopted by the committee for distributing up to $7.4 billion in Title I money to nearly every school district in the nation. No one offered Clinton's plan as an amendment on the floor.

The only challenge to the committee's plan came when Puerto Rico Resident Commissioner Carlos Romero-Barceló, D/NPP, twice attempted to lift a cap that the bill imposed on Title I money for the commonwealth. His amendments were rejected, 70-358 and 76-340, on March 2 and March 3 after members were told that more for Puerto Rico meant less for their districts. *(Votes 35, 39, p. 12-H)*

During its lengthy debate on the bill, the House also took the following actions:
● **Home schooling.** As the floor debate began the week of Feb. 21, thousands of angry religious conservatives, convinced that the House was about to require that home-schooling parents be certified by the government, besieged members with phone calls, letters and faxes, pressuring them into killing a mandate actually aimed only at public school teachers.

Miller, D-Calif., who had attached the teacher-certification mandate in subcommittee, affirmed that the provision was aimed at public school teachers to make sure they were qualified to teach their subjects.

But attorneys for the Home School Legal Defense Association concluded that the provision could be interpreted as requiring home-schoolers to be certified. "This is the equivalent of a nuclear attack upon the home schooling community," Michael Farris, the group's leader, wrote in a letter to House members.

Democratic bill sponsors proposed to make a simple amendment asserting that nothing in the bill would affect home-schoolers. But Armey, who was defending the home-schoolers' cause, refused to go along.

Ford and other Democrats then decided to kill the Miller amendment altogether and add language stating that the bill did not affect home-schoolers. Armey, still not satisfied, introduced a broader amendment stating that the bill did not "permit, allow, encourage or authorize any federal control over any aspect of any private, religious or home school."

In the end, the House approved both amendments, as home-schooling advocates crowded the galleries, even though Catholic schools and some Democrats expressed concern that Armey's amendment might inadvertently invite law-

suits from groups opposed to religious schools benefiting from federal education programs, as some did at the time.

The House approved the Democrats' amendment, 424-1, with Miller, D-Calif., the lone dissenter. Lawmakers then adopted Armey's amendment, 374-53. *(Votes 31, 32, p. 10-H)*

After spending most of five hours of floor time on the certification provision — one paragraph in the 901-page bill — the House adjourned for the weekend.

● **Opportunity-to-learn standards.** Democrats on Feb. 24 agreed to water down the bill's opportunity-to-learn provisions, approving a bipartisan compromise as part of a package of technical amendments, 422-1. *(Vote 33, p. 10-H)*

Goodling had lined up Democrats Charles W. Stenholm of Texas and Gary A. Condit of California to back an amendment to kill the standards. Goodling said he was promised 70 Democratic votes, more than enough to win with a presumably solid Republican bloc. But Owens and the Democrats agreed to a compromise that narrowed the list of specific standards from seven to two, barred lawsuits over them, asserted that implementing them was strictly voluntary and limited the reporting requirements.

● **Illegal aliens.** After hours of emotionally charged debate, the House on March 3 rejected a proposal to require schools to identify and count illegal aliens. The amendment, by Dana Rohrabacher, R-Calif., would have required school districts to determine the immigration status of students and their parents. Rohrabacher said the data would help the federal government more accurately account for the money spent on illegal immigrants.

Pat Roberts, R-Kan., offered a modification that would have reimbursed schools for the cost of carrying out the provision. Roberts' proposal was defeated by voice vote, and debate on Rohrabacher's amendment continued for nearly three hours.

Democrats and many moderate Republicans criticized the amendment as ill-advised and mean-spirited. Conservative Republicans such as Dan Burton of Indiana, however, said illegal aliens were costing U.S. taxpayers billions of dollars in education, health and other social services. Majority Leader Richard A. Gephardt, D-Mo, conceded that immigration policy needed improvement, but he chastised conservatives for attempting to attach the amendment to the education bill. Rohrabacher's amendment was defeated, 78-329. *(Vote 41, p. 12-H)*

● **School choice.** The House approved an amendment by Boehner to allow school districts to use Title I funds for programs that allowed parents to choose which public school their children would attend. Opposed by the bill's Democratic sponsors, similar language had been rejected on party-line votes in both the committee and subcommittee. Subcommittee Chairman Kildee at first told members he opposed the amendment but then allowed it to be approved by voice vote. In an interview, he said he was not sure he could have won a roll call to defeat it.

● **Other amendments.** In other action, the House rejected, 128-287, a Boehner amendment to eliminate $10 million in transition programs for students moving from preschool to elementary school. Lawmakers approved by voice vote a Gunderson amendment to establish a presidential awards program for outstanding schools. *(Vote 40, p. 12-H)*

● **Anti-tobacco programs.** On March 9, the House approved an amendment requiring that elementary and secondary school students be taught that tobacco was a dangerous substance, not unlike alcohol and drugs. The vote was 353-70. *(Vote 49, p. 14-H)*

The amendment was offered by Richard J. Durbin, D-Ill.,

who said that although tobacco was legal, it represented a danger to the country's youths. "Tobacco in fact is the nation's No. 1 addiction," Durbin said. The amendment was to the part of the bill that authorized $655 million for the Drug Free Schools Program.

Boehner and Cass Ballenger, R-N.C., opposed the amendment, arguing that tobacco was a legal agricultural product. They said the amendment represented government intrusion into citizens' lives. (Durbin's amendment eventually died in conference.)

The House later passed by voice vote a Durbin amendment to require all schools receiving federal funding to prohibit smoking, except in separately ventilated areas where children were not present. The provision eventually was dropped in conference but survived as part of the Goals 2000 bill.

In related action, Bill Barrett, R-Neb., and Roemer proposed an amendment to reserve 20 percent of a state's Drug Free Schools money for discretionary use by the governor. The amendment also required that 10 percent of a state's Title IV money be spent on Drug Abuse Resistance Education (DARE) programs.

The bill, as written, proposed to eliminate what historically had been a 30 percent set-aside for governors and target the money directly toward schools and local districts. Barrett contended that giving money to governors would provide greater flexibility. Opponents said the money could be used for unintended purposes if not adequately targeted. After a lengthy debate, Barrett's proposal was approved 418-1. *(Vote 47, p. 14-H)*

Conservatives Protest

The final week of debate was dominated by conservative attacks on social and spending issues.

Among amendments offered March 24 was one by Mel Hancock, R-Mo., to prohibit school districts from using funds received under the act for programs that encouraged or supported homosexuality as a positive lifestyle.

Jolene Unsoeld, D-Wash., calling Hancock's amendment broad and intrusive, offered an amendment to his language stating that school districts, not the federal government, would determine the acceptability of educational programs. Some moderate Republicans, such as Gunderson, argued that Hancock's language was so far reaching that it might prevent schools from carrying out AIDS-prevention programs. The House approved Unsoeld's modifying amendment, 224-194, before adopting the amended Hancock language, 301-120. *(Votes 91, 92, p. 28-H)*

John T. Doolittle, R-Calif., proposed March 22 to require all public elementary and secondary schools to teach abstinence as the only guarantee against sexually transmitted diseases and unintended pregnancies.

Democrats, again led by Unsoeld, argued that Doolittle's amendment would usurp the authority of school districts. Unsoeld proposed to amend Doolittle's language to encourage schools to include abstinence in sex education classes, but to allow local officials control over the curriculum content. Unsoeld's amendment was approved, 262-166, and Doolittle's modified amendment then passed, 407-20. *(Votes 76, 77, p. 24-H)*

Rohrabacher sparked extended debate March 22 with yet another amendment to prohibit any funds under the act from being used to assist in the education of students whose parents were illegal aliens. Rohrabacher acknowledged that the amendment could be construed as harsh, but he said the economic times warranted drastic moves. "We can't take care of everyone in the world," he said.

Democrats pointed out that Rohrabacher's amendment, similar to one overwhelmingly rejected on March 3, would force school officials into the intrusive position of determining the immigration status of students and their parents. The amendment fell on a voice vote.

School prayer also entered the debate March 21, as Republican Sam Johnson of Texas proposed to withdraw all federal funds from schools that denied students the right to "constitutionally protected" school prayer. Several Democrats objected, arguing that the provision would divide schools and put school officials in the position of trying to make constitutional judgments.

Democrat Williams of Montana sought to amend Johnson's proposal with language to support voluntary school prayer but remove the threat of losing federal funds. Williams' amendment tracked language inserted by House-Senate conferees in the related Goals 2000 education bill. The House rejected Williams' language, 171-239, before adopting Johnson's proposal, 345-64. (Votes 74, 75, p. 24-H)

Throughout debate on the bill, conservatives attacked the measure for what they called its lack of flexibility for school districts. Republicans also said it was loaded with redundant programs that would benefit only small groups of students.

Before passing the bill March 24, the House rejected, 173-245, a broad substitute amendment by Minority Leader Robert H. Michel, R-Ill., to cut funding in the bill, cancel all new programs and eliminate the authorization of funds for family planning and abortion counseling. (Vote 94, p. 28-H)

Senate Subcommittee

A Senate Labor and Human Resources subcommittee approved a $12.7 billion companion bill (S 1513) on May 17. The vote in the Education, Arts and Humanities Subcommittee was 17-0. The bill reauthorized federal contributions to elementary and secondary schools through fiscal 1999.

The main point of contention in the subcommittee was the Title I program. Hoping to avoid a funding fight, Labor and Human Resources Committee Chairman Edward M. Kennedy, D-Mass., and subcommittee Chairman Claiborne Pell, D-R.I., crafted a formula designed to aim money at needier students while also ensuring that states did not lose large portions of their federal aid. Needy students were targeted more than under the House-passed version but less than in Clinton's plan.

The Kennedy-Pell proposal did away with the concentration grants that went to counties with high poverty rates under existing law. Instead, all the money was to be distributed according to a formula that assigned various "weights," or valuations to students, depending on whether they lived in low-poverty areas or high-poverty areas. Proponents said this would be more effective than concentration grants in sending money to poorer children.

Grants still would be distributed using the number of poor children in a county as a factor, but the number could be derived either from the U.S. census or from the county — whichever yielded more money. Average state spending per pupil would continue to be a factor.

The Kennedy-Pell formula also provided for bonuses for states that demonstrated high levels of "effort" and "equity" in educating students. Effort referred to willingness to pay taxes for education. Equity referred to efforts to equalize school spending between rich and poor areas.

During the subcommittee markup, Jeff Bingaman, D-N.M., offered an amendment with a formula virtually identical to the administration's plan. Bingaman said the Kennedy-Pell

formula might be more politically palatable, but that it had serious inequities.

Citing Education Department statistics, Bingaman said that more than 26 percent of New Mexico's school-age children lived in poverty. Only Mississippi, Louisiana and Puerto Rico had higher percentages of poor children. Under the Clinton plan, New Mexico was to receive $12.4 million more in Title I funding in fiscal 1995 than it received in fiscal 1994; under the Kennedy-Pell plan, New Mexico would receive $4.9 million more.

Bingaman was not alone in his criticism. Paul Simon, D-Ill., said that although Illinois was to fare better under the Kennedy-Pell proposal, he agreed that the money should reach the neediest students.

Kennedy said he would work with Bingaman before the full committee markup to achieve better targeting of needy students but warned that it would not be easy to change the formula.

Senate Committee

After nearly three hours of debate, the full Senate Labor and Human Resources Committee approved S 1513 on June 15 by a vote of 16-1 (S Rept 103-292). The bill got a relatively easy ride, but several thorny issues — including the distribution formula for the Title I program — remained unresolved.

Members opted to stick with the Kennedy-Pell formula for allocating Title I money. While Kennedy-Pell targeted significant resources to poorer states, it also tended to reward certain wealthier areas represented by senators on the Labor panel.

For example, Vermont, represented on the committee by Republican James M. Jeffords, had a relatively low child poverty rate of 11.6 percent. Yet the state stood to get a relatively high 17.7 percent increase in Title I funding under the Kennedy-Pell plan — from $11.8 million in fiscal 1994 to $13.9 million in fiscal 1995. Republican Orrin G. Hatch's state, Utah, stood to get a 16.8 percent increase, to $34.7 million, although its child poverty rate was 10.9 percent.

California and Texas senators complained, however, saying Kennedy-Pell was inadequate to meet growing demands on their education systems caused largely by an influx of immigrants. Although the child poverty rate in California was 18.1 percent, close to 1 million children, the state would get a 7.4 percent increase in funding, to $744.3 million in fiscal 1995. Under the Clinton proposal, California stood to get $826.7 million, a 19.3 percent increase.

At the committee markup, Bingaman offered a new proposal, which he said would achieve slightly more targeting than the Kennedy-Pell formula, but substantially less than Clinton's. A state-by-state breakdown of the Bingaman plan showed that certain states with high percentages of poor children — such as Alabama, Mississippi and Louisiana — would benefit. But the plan also benefited affluent states such as Connecticut, while taking money away from poorer states such as West Virginia and New Mexico.

Several senators, weary of an issue that had been discussed for months, said they could not support Bingaman. Tom Harkin, D-Iowa, noted that several states, including Iowa, Massachusetts, Kansas and Ohio, would lose federal funds if Bingaman's plan were adopted instead of the Kennedy-Pell plan. The panel included members from those states.

The amendment failed on a voice vote. Several lawmakers expressed support for Bingaman, including Hatch, Daniel R. Coats, R-Ind., and Christopher J. Dodd, D-Conn. Their states would have benefited under the proposal.

Opportunity-to-Learn Standards Rejected

Members also rejected efforts to insert opportunity-to-learn standards in the Senate bill. Paul Wellstone, D-Minn., proposed an amendment to require school districts to incorporate into their Title I grant applications "opportunity to learn strategies" to ensure that all students had equal access to high-quality teachers, school materials and other educational resources.

But several members argued that the standards amounted to an unfunded federal mandate that potentially could expose school districts to lawsuits from disgruntled parents. "It's a Trojan horse for the nationalizing of education," said Judd Gregg, R-N.H.

To defuse the issue, Kennedy offered a weaker substitute amendment to encourage states to help school districts develop the capacity to meet high standards, instead of requiring them to do so. The panel approved Kennedy's substitute by voice vote and rejected the Wellstone amendment, 3-14.

Other Amendments

The committee approved by voice vote a proposal by Harris Wofford, D-Pa., to promote the incorporation of computers and other advanced technologies into U.S. businesses. The measure authorized federal grants to employers who wanted to involve workers in decisions regarding advanced technologies. The Labor panel had approved the provision as a separate bill (S 1020) on Feb. 23. *(Workplace technology, p. 407)*

The committee rejected, by voice vote, an amendment by Wellstone to authorize $1.5 billion in fiscal 1995 for school repair and restoration. Conservative estimates indicated that one in every four schools in the country was in serious disrepair.

The panel also rejected, by voice vote, an amendment by Gregg, to give school districts flexibility to use Title I money to fund educational services to certain developmentally disabled students.

Senate Floor

The Senate passed the $12.7 billion bill, 94-6, on Aug. 2, after debating the funding formula for more than a week. Before passing HR 6, the Senate substituted its own text from S 1513. *(Vote 252, p. 43-S)*

After two hours of sometimes emotional debate July 28, senators defeated an alternative formula proposed by Dale Bumpers, D-Ark., by a vote of 46-54. *(Vote 241, p. 41-S)*

Under Bumpers' amendment, the nation's 10 poorest states — including Alabama, Arkansas, Louisiana and New Mexico — would have received large increases in Title I funding. The increased targeting would have been achieved by replacing the "effort" and "equity" factors in the Kennedy-Pell plan with a formula to allot money at least in part based on per capita income in a county and income per school-age child.

Bumpers called the Kennedy-Pell plan a gimmick aimed at gaining votes for the bill, not at helping low-income children. Shouting at times, Bumpers said the formula would allow rich states with few poor children to receive relatively large amounts of federal money at the expense of poorer states. "It is one of the most perverse formulas I have ever seen," Bumpers said. "It is discriminatory in the extreme."

But Kennedy argued that the committee formula was "a comprehensive political compromise" that should not be discarded at the expense of other states, which also had poor children.

Although Kennedy prevailed that week, senators dramatically altered the proposed formula Aug. 1, adopting by voice vote a Hatch amendment that promised most states more money than they stood to receive under the Kennedy-Pell plan.

Like other senators, Hatch took exception to the "equity" factor in the committee formula, which provided bonuses to states that equalized spending, with a carefully crafted minimum and maximum bonus that any one state could receive. This tended to favor small and more affluent states with relatively high marks for equity.

During floor action, several senators, including Kay Bailey Hutchison, R-Texas, and Dianne Feinstein, D-Calif., said the minimum and maximum elements were unfair to children in states that found themselves increasingly strapped for resources because of an influx of immigrant children. "States spend what they can," Feinstein said, but "a poor child is a poor child."

Hatch's amendment removed the maximum and minimum constraints from the Kennedy-Pell formula. With this change, 38 states stood to receive more Title I money than under Kennedy-Pell, drawing the money primarily from eight others: Georgia, Illinois, Massachusetts, Michigan, Missouri, New York, Ohio and Pennsylvania. Four states would receive the same amount as they did in fiscal 1994.

To blunt the effect, Hatch's amendment phased in the change over three years. In fiscal 1995, no state was to have its allocation changed by more than 2 percent. That was to rise to 4 percent in fiscal 1996 and 6 percent in fiscal 1997. In fiscal 1998, the Hatch plan would take full effect.

Kennedy opposed any modification to the funding formula. But recognizing the political reality of at least 38 senators ready to vote against his plan, he reluctantly accepted the Hatch amendment.

Before the Senate passed the overall bill Aug. 2, Kennedy offered an amendment, which he described as "technical," to slightly alter the funding for Title I and school construction programs. It was adopted by voice vote, with no debate.

The amendment contained a formula adjustment to guarantee minimum funding for the nation's five least populous states: Alaska, Delaware, New Hampshire, Vermont and Wyoming. Under the amendment, each of these states would get at least one-quarter of 1 percent of the total Title I allocation.

Also in the Kennedy package was an adjustment to a $400 million federal construction grant program aimed at poorer school districts with physically deteriorating buildings. The program authorized grants to states that could demonstrate a need for renovation or construction of schools, libraries or other education facilities. Before the Kennedy amendment, the grants were targeted primarily at urban areas such as Chicago and Detroit. The adjustment aimed to spread the money to rural areas as well. To qualify for grants, school districts had to have a child poverty rate of 15 percent or more.

School Prayer

The school prayer issue returned to the Senate floor July 27, when the Labor panel's ranking Republican, Nancy Landon Kassebaum of Kansas, successfully offered an amendment to withhold federal money from any local school district found guilty of willfully violating a court order to allow constitutionally protected prayer. The proposal was designed to appease conservative Republicans while holding the support of moderates and liberal Democrats. Senators adopted it 93-7. *(Vote 237, p. 40-S)*

Prayer in public schools had been prohibited as a regular devotional exercise since 1962, when the U.S. Supreme Court ruled that government-sponsored prayer was unconstitu-

tional. Students could continue to pray voluntarily as long as prayer was not sponsored by local school officials. Exactly what type of school prayer was "constitutionally protected" remained unclear.

Kassebaum's proposal withstood a challenge from Jesse Helms, R-N.C., who called it "do-nothing language." Helms offered an amendment to cut off federal funds to districts that denied students their right to "constitutionally protected" prayer. The amendment did not explicitly state at what point a school district would lose its money or who would determine what type of prayer was protected. Helms argued that his amendment would not mandate school prayer but would encourage administrators to allow students to pray voluntarily. It was rejected, 47-53. (Vote 236, p. 40-S)

Sex Education

Disagreements over sex education flared again July 27, when Robert C. Smith, R-N.H., offered an amendment to prohibit schools from using instructional materials or other resources to encourage or promote homosexuality. The Smith amendment was adopted, 91-9, on Aug. 2. (Vote 250, p. 43-S)

In a parliamentary move designed to protect Smith's proposal from substitute amendments, Helms offered a substitute containing essentially the same language as Smith's. It was approved, 63-36, on Aug. 1. The House bill had similar language. (Vote 244, p. 42-S)

Kennedy and Jeffords subsequently added an amendment to the Helms-Smith provision to prohibit the use of federal funds to encourage or promote any sexual activity, either homosexual or heterosexual. It was adopted 99-0. (Vote 246, p. 42-S)

Kennedy said he offered the amendment to give members "an opportunity to express their view on this particular policy issue." By modifying the Smith proposal and making it different from the House bill, the issue became one that could be discussed — and possibly dropped — in conference.

Other Amendments

In other action the weeks of July 25 and Aug. 1, the Senate:

● Adopted, 60-40, an amendment by Slade Gorton, R-Wash., to allow local schools to set disciplinary policy for all students, including those with developmental disabilities, who brought weapons to school or demonstrated life-threatening behavior. (Vote 239, p. 41-S)

Existing federal law prohibited the removal of disabled students from classrooms for more than 10 days, regardless of their actions. Under the Gorton amendment, local schools could place disabled students in an alternative educational setting for up to 90 days for violent or disruptive behavior.

Later, senators approved, 100-0, an amendment by Jeffords that was similar to Gorton's but applied only to students who brought weapons to school. Unarmed disabled students who threatened to bodily harm themselves or others were to be placed in alternative settings until it could be determined whether the violent behavior was related to their disability. If it was, they could return to the classroom. (Vote 240, p. 41-S)

● Rejected, 45-53, an amendment cosponsored by Coats and Minority Leader Bob Dole, R-Kan., that would have targeted $30 million for a school choice demonstration project to allow parents of low-income students in 20 violence-prone schools to use vouchers to move their children to safer schools. (Vote 238, p. 40-S)

● Approved by voice vote an amendment by Pete V. Domenici, R-N.M., to create a $6 million grant program to develop 10 pilot "character education" programs nationwide.

The local programs were to teach such concepts as respect, honesty and responsibility.

● Approved, 100-0, an amendment by Larry Pressler, R-S.D., to require that teachers hired to teach bilingual programs in the nation's public schools demonstrate written and verbal proficiency in English. (Vote 249, p. 42-S)

● Adopted, 63-37, an amendment by Kassebaum to prohibit the Education Department from issuing new regulations to carry out the Vocational Education Act of 1990 (PL 101-392) until the bill was reauthorized in 1995. (Vote 247, p. 42-S)

● Adopted, 66-33, an amendment by John C. Danforth, R-Mo., to create 10 demonstration projects in school districts approved by the Department of Education to allow experimentation with single-sex classes for low-income, educationally disadvantaged students. (Vote 245, p. 42-S)

Conference

House-Senate conferees began negotiations Sept. 20 and settled their differences Sept. 27 after reaching an uneasy compromise on a funding formula for the Title I program (H Rept 103-761).

Arguments over the formula centered on economic winners and losers. House members argued that their formula was superior because it spread the money widely. "Practically speaking, we're going to lose a lot of support" for the program if it is dramatically altered, Kildee said. "We wrote the formula with a cross section of America in mind."

Senate formula supporters argued that their chamber did a better job of targeting limited federal resources to the educationally deprived.

Conferees exchanged several formula proposals before striking a deal that ultimately directed slightly more money at low-income children than under existing law or under the House bill. But the compromise targeted poor children far less than the Senate or Clinton had proposed.

The existing funding formula was to stay in effect for fiscal 1995, with states distributing the money to local school districts based on census data on the number of low-income children in a county, the number of students whose families received Aid to Families with Dependent Children, and average state spending per pupil.

Beginning in fiscal 1996, money was to be distributed to counties using the existing formula for amounts appropriated up to the Title I fiscal 1995 funding level of $6.6 billion. For appropriations above the $6.6 billion threshold, a "targeted" grant formula was to take effect. Under targeted grants, students were to be assigned weights, or valuations, depending on their level of poverty.

In fiscal 1996, the federal government could begin eliminating federal funding for any school district in which low-income students made up 2 percent or less of the student population. However, no district could receive less in fiscal 1996 than it received in fiscal 1995. The hold-harmless provision dropped to 85 percent of the previous year's grant for fiscal years 1997 through 1999.

The compromise also guaranteed that the five least populous states — Alaska, Delaware, New Hampshire, Vermont and Wyoming — would each receive no less than one-quarter of 1 percent of annual Title I appropriations.

Conferees also agreed to use updated county census data beginning in fiscal 1997 and updated school district census data beginning in fiscal 1999. Critics said the 10-year data used under the existing formula was often out of date, failing to take population shifts into account; the money, therefore, failed to reach poor children.

Members also included the Senate's controversial "effort" and "equity" bonuses as a separate program. Effort and equity grants were authorized at $200 million in fiscal 1995.

Several members, including Petri, called the compromise haphazard and proposed that conferees either negotiate a better deal or put off the reauthorization until 1995. "No bill would be preferable to a bad bill," he said.

But Ford said that according to appropriations rules, education programs could be lost if the authorization bill was not signed into law by Sept. 30. Further negotiations, he said, would effectively kill the bill's new programs for fiscal 1995.

Other Issues Resolved

On other issues, conferees agreed to:

● **School prayer.** Retain Senate language requiring the Education Department to withhold federal funds from any school that was found by a court to have willfully violated a court order to allow constitutionally protected voluntary prayer.

Kassebaum's language won out over the more stringent House-passed provision to cut off federal money if a school denied students the right to engage in voluntary prayer. The House voted 369-55 on Sept. 20 to instruct its conferees to insist on the House provision. Such instructions were not binding. *(Vote 426, p. 128-H)*

Conservatives considered Kassebaum's language ineffective because sanctions could only be imposed after a court order had been issued and violated. Moderates and liberals in both chambers opposed the stronger Johnson language because it could put school officials in the position of making decisions about what represented constitutionally protected prayer.

● **Sex education.** Bar the use of federal funds to promote any heterosexual or homosexual activity, to distribute condoms at school or to develop or distribute obscene materials.

● **Migrant students.** Continue federal aid to school districts for migrant students for up to three years after they moved to another district. The House had proposed reducing the existing six-year provision to two years. The Senate had suggested four years.

● **Single-gender classes.** Rejected a Senate provision to allow 10 schools nationwide to experiment with single-gender classes for five years. The provision's sponsor, Danforth, tried to persuade conferees that the demonstration projects would provide data on the effectiveness of single-gender education. "Indications are that it works," Danforth said. "Not for all children and not for all circumstances. But it is a very limited amendment. It does give researchers something to study."

But Ford argued against the amendment, saying it would require the Education Department to waive civil rights laws on equal treatment of women. "You can't fool around with women's civil rights in this country," Ford said. "It would be an interesting and devastating signal to send."

● **Unfunded mandates.** Accepted Senate language stipulating that no programs under the bill could impose unfunded federal mandates on states and localities. Gregg, sponsor of the provision, cautioned conferees that they were inviting trouble from fiscal conservatives in both chambers if they failed to include the provision. Miller, R-Fla., countered that states that did not want to follow federal rules did not have to take federal money.

In other action, conferees agreed to:

● Authorize $370 million for the Title II teacher training and professional development program.

● Authorize $200 million in fiscal 1995 in state grants to upgrade school facilities.

● Require local school districts to adopt a policy of expelling for one year any student who brought a gun to school. Local school officials could waive the policy on a case-by-case basis. Students with disabilities who brought a gun to school or otherwise acted in a threatening manner could be removed from classrooms and placed in an alternative settings for up to 45 days.

Final Action

The House adopted the conference report to the $12.7 billion education bill Sept. 30, after rejecting a motion to renegotiate language on public school prayer. The vote was 262-132. *(Vote 456, p. 136-H)*

A move by conservative Republicans to send the bill back to conference with instructions to insist on the House-passed school prayer language was rejected, 184-215. *(Vote 455, p. 136-H)*

The funding formula also drew criticism on the House floor. Several Republicans suggested delaying a vote and sending the bill back to conference for fine tuning. Goodling criticized the formula compromise because members were being asked to vote on it without estimates of its long-term effects. Gunderson said the formula would benefit inner-city schools to the detriment of equally poor rural school districts.

But Democrats, led by Ford, said the compromise formula was fair. They pointed out that it closely resembled the House version that had received bipartisan support earlier in the year. Ford charged Republicans with playing politics with a bill that should enjoy bipartisan support. Because the formula would reflect demographic shifts, Ford said predicting the amount of money that school districts would receive in the future would be nearly impossible.

After Delays, Senate Clears Bill

A Republican filibuster over prayer in public schools delayed final passage of the bill for two days until Oct. 5, when senators cleared the bill, 77-20. *(Vote 321, p. 55-S)*

Helms, angry because conferees had dropped the stronger House school prayer provision, began the filibuster Oct. 3. Majority Leader George J. Mitchell, D-Maine, filed a motion to shut off debate the same day.

Helms and other conservatives said Kassebaum's school prayer provision would substantially lengthen the process of adjudicating such cases. Sanctions could be imposed only after a court order had been issued and violated. Moderate Republicans and Democrats, however, opposed the more stringent prayer language, arguing that it would place local school officials in the position of deciding what represented constitutionally protected prayer. They also said it would be unwieldy. "We don't need the federal government telling us how to pray, what to pray and when to pray," said Barbara Boxer, D-Calif.

After waiting two days as required under Senate rules regarding cloture petitions, members voted 75-24 on Oct. 5 to limit debate and proceed to a vote on the reauthorization. *(Vote 320, p. 55-S)*

Bill supporters also had to overcome complaints from several senators about the compromise reached on the funding distribution mechanism for the bill's massive Title I state grants program.

The state grants portion of the program was authorized at $7.5 billion in fiscal 1995. Appropriators provided $6.6 billion in grants for fiscal 1995, which funded programs for the 1995-96 academic year. *(Appropriations, p. 519)*

Because appropriations levels were unknown beyond fis-

cal 1995, the formula's long-term effects were difficult to calculate, several members said.

Senate Labor Committee Chairman Kennedy described the bill as far from perfect but said it represented a step in the right direction. He asked, "Are we going to do business as usual or would Congress provide what he called "a very modest" effort to send more money to poor children?

Coats criticized the compromise formula, saying its implications were uncertain. "It's hard to buy the argument this money is better targeted," Coats said. He said the formula would pit poor children in one part of the country against their counterparts elsewhere.

Gorton criticized the final provisions on guns in schools for not allowing developmentally disabled students who exhibited threatening behavior to be removed from the classroom for 90 days, and for allowing local school officials to waive expulsion of students who brought guns to school.

But Kennedy said new initiatives in the bill, such as $100 million for school construction grants and $80 million for safe and drug-free school programs, would be lost if the Senate failed to clear the measure. ∎

Elementary, Secondary Education Provisions

The five-year Elementary and Secondary Education Act reauthorization (HR 6) authorized $12.7 billion in fiscal 1995 and revamped federal school aid programs. Following are provisions of the bill, as enacted:

Title I — Educationally Disadvantaged Students

Title I's main element was a $7.4 billion grants program to states to serve educationally disadvantaged children. Under a House-Senate compromise, the funding formula for state grants remained unchanged in fiscal 1995.

Beginning in fiscal 1996, money was to be distributed to counties using key elements of the formula originally included in the House-passed version of HR 6. Money up to Title I's fiscal 1995 appropriation of $6.6 billion was to be sent to counties using the old formula. For amounts appropriated above that level, a targeted grant formula was to take effect.

Under targeted grants, students were to be assigned "weights," or valuations, depending on their level of poverty. Using the weights was expected to mean that schools serving children in high-poverty areas would receive slightly more money, benefiting school districts in such high-growth states as California and Texas, which were grappling with large influxes of immigrants.

In fiscal 1996, no school district was to receive less money than it received in fiscal 1995. This hold-harmless provision was to then drop to 85 percent of the previous year's grant for fiscal 1997 through fiscal 1999. The formula guaranteed that the five least populous states — Alaska, Delaware, New Hampshire, Vermont and Wyoming — would receive no less than one-quarter of 1 percent of annual Title I appropriations.

The formula also called for the use of updated county census data beginning in fiscal 1997 and updated school district census data beginning in fiscal 1999. The updates were in response to criticism of the existing formula, which used traditional 10-year census data.

The compromise formula also incorporated "effort" and "equity" elements of the Senate-passed bill as a separately authorized state grants program. Effort referred to a state's willingness to pay taxes for public education. Equity reflected a state's attempts to equalize spending between poor and rich school districts. Grants were to be allocated based on states' performances in these areas, beginning in fiscal 1996.

Title I also included the Even Start family literacy program, authorized at $118 million in fiscal 1995, and programs for migrant students, authorized at $310 million in fiscal 1995.

Title I also contained provisions to:

● **Academic standards.** Require state educational agencies that received Title I grants to develop state educational plans in cooperation with school district officials, teachers, school administrators, parents and other school personnel.

Such plans were supposed to contain challenging content and student performance standards in subjects such as English, math and reading. States that already had such standards could be required to modify them to ensure that all children were held to the same high standards, regardless of their socioeconomic status. School districts also were required to submit similarly comprehensive plans to state educational agencies.

Any state or local school district whose students failed to make progress in academic performance could be subject to corrective action. Such actions eventually could include withholding federal funds or authorizing the transfer of students to other schools.

● **Assessments.** Require that each state plan include a description of the standardized tests conducted annually in such subjects as math, reading and English. Tests administered to Title I students were to be the same as those given to other students, and the results of all tests were to be used as the primary means for measuring local school districts' performance in meeting state-mandated content and performance standards. School districts were required to use state-approved tests.

● **Language assessments.** Require state plans to identify all foreign languages spoken by students. If a state had students who spoke English as a second language and had no means to test such students' English language skills, the Education Department's Office of Bilingual Education and Minority Languages could provide the information necessary to develop appropriate tests.

● **Transitional tests.** Allow states that had no statewide tests to use temporary "transitional" tests for up to four years, with approval from the Education Department. During that time, those states had to make progress toward establishing permanent tests. If they did not, they could be forced to adopt tests and standards contained in other state plans previously approved by the Education Department.

● **Local plans.** Require that any local school district receiving Title I funds have an approved educational plan on file with the state educational agency; districts were to consult with parents, teachers and other school employees in devising their plans. The plans had to detail the progress being made toward meeting state student performance standards and describe revisions to instructional programs undertaken to enable all children to meet such standards.

The bill required that plans also describe strategies that local educational agencies would use to provide ongoing professional development, or training, for parents, teachers and other school employees.

● **Local assistance.** Require local school districts to provide schools with the information and assistance needed to improve schools and to meet the state content and student performance standards.

● **Eligible school attendance areas.** Require local school districts to use Title I money only in areas where the percentage of poor children was equal to or greater than the percentage of poor children in the entire school district. In general, schools in which at least 35 percent of students came from low-income families were eligible for Title I money. However, in school districts where the amount of Title I money was insufficient to serve all eligible schools, districts were required to provide money first to schools with low-income populations of 75 percent or more. Money was to be provided to schools in rank order, from those with the highest poverty rates to those with the lowest.

● **Waiver for desegregation plans.** Authorize the Education

Department to provide Title I money to schools in which at least 25 percent of the students were from low-income families if such schools were part of a state- or court-ordered desegregation plan. In non-eligible areas where desegregation plans were in effect, schools could receive federal assistance if the percentage of students from low-income families was equal to or greater than ratios found in eligible schools in the district.

● **Schoolwide programs.** Beginning in the 1995-96 school year, allow schools to use Title I money for compensatory efforts for an entire school — rather than just for Title I children — if at least 60 percent of students in the school were from low-income families. In the 1996-97 school year, the percentage was to decrease to 50 percent.

● **Alternative schools.** Permit Title I money to be sent to alternative public schools that served students who were failing or at risk of failing a state's performance standards. Such students could include those from low-income families, children with disabilities, migrants or students with limited proficiency in English.

● **School choice.** Allow school districts to use Title I money in combination with funds from other public or private sources to develop school choice plans for students eligible for Title I funds. Parents of such students were permitted to send their children to another public school within that system.

● **School improvement.** Require school districts to identify schools in need of improvement if they had failed to make adequate progress as defined by the state's education plan for two consecutive school years. Such schools could be identified for mandatory school improvement activities such as professional training for teachers, administrators and other school employees.

States were required to support school improvement efforts. Such assistance could include establishing school support teams made up of teachers, educational experts and consultants, who periodically analyzed the performance of school districts and made recommendations.

● **Corrective action.** Authorize school districts to take punitive actions against schools that failed to make adequate yearly progress. Such corrective actions could include withholding Title I money, revoking a school's authority to operate a schoolwide Title I program and allowing students to transfer to other public schools within the district.

State educational agencies were required to review the progress of school districts annually and to disseminate results to teachers, other school employees, parents, students and the local community.

States also were required to provide technical assistance or other help needed by local districts to improve schools. Such assistance could include information and support teams of teachers that had been particularly successful in helping children make significant progress toward meeting the state's student performance standards.

● **Distinguished schools.** Permit states annually to designate distinguished schools that exceeded a state's definition of adequate yearly progress for three consecutive years. Such designations could include monetary awards to schools, which could be used for further improvements. School districts also could reward distinguished schools by granting them more authority to make decisions at the school level.

● **Distinguished educators.** Require states to establish a corps of distinguished teachers and educational experts to help assist school districts in making school improvements.

● **Parental involvement.** Require schools, in collaboration with parents, to develop written plans detailing the organized involvement of parents in the planning and review of school programs.

● **Professional development.** Require school districts to provide teachers and other school professionals with opportunities to develop their skills. Special attention was to be given to activities such as elimination of gender and racial biases, integration of academic and vocational curricula, instruction about effective use of student tests and instruction in the use of technology.

● **Private school participation.** Consistent with previous law, allow educationally disadvantaged students who attended private elementary and secondary schools to receive secular, neutral and non-ideological educational services. For example, private school students could be given access to such services as educational radio

and television programs, computer equipment and materials, and other technologies.

● **Fiscal requirements.** Mandate that local school districts receiving Title I money use the funds to supplement — not replace — educational funding received from other sources.

● **Even Start.** Authorize $118 million in fiscal 1995 for the Even Start program, which aimed to promote literacy among adults and provide them with the skills necessary to become their children's first teachers. These services also were to be made available to teenage parents.

● **Effort and equity grants.** Authorize $200 million in fiscal 1996 and unspecified sums in subsequent years for state grants based on states' performance in the areas of equity and effort. Effort referred to a state's willingness to pay taxes for the education of its children. Equity referred to a state's attempts to equalize education spending between richer and poorer areas.

● **Migrant education.** Authorize $310 million in fiscal 1995 to help the children of migrant workers overcome educational disadvantages caused by their mobility. States and school districts were allowed to develop customized programs to assist migrant children.

● **At-risk youths.** Authorize $40 million in fiscal 1995 for programs for juvenile delinquents and pregnant teens. Services were to be provided at juvenile corrections facilities to help students make the transition back to school.

● **Implementation manual.** Require the Education Department to prepare and distribute a program assistance manual aimed at helping state educational agencies, local school districts, parents and others to better understand how to implement Title I programs.

● **Prohibition on federal control.** Prohibit the federal government from exercising direct control or influence over the Title I activities of a state agency, school or local school district.

Title II — Dwight D. Eisenhower Professional Development Program

This title authorized the Eisenhower program at $800 million in fiscal 1995 and shifted its focus from math and science education to professional training for teachers, administrators and other school employees. Under the revamped program, the federal government provided grants to states to ensure that employees of state educational agencies and local school districts had access to professional training and development to enhance their skills. The law also authorized national teaching networks and demonstration projects. The title contained provisions to:

● **Eisenhower Professional Development Program.** Authorize $800 million in fiscal 1995 for professional development for teachers, administrators and other school employees. Special emphasis was placed on improvement of teaching in the following core subjects: math, science, English, civics and government, foreign languages, arts, geography, history and economics. States were to apply to the Education Department for the grants, and local school districts were to apply to state agencies for money after submitting detailed training plans.

The bill required that if Title II appropriations fell below $250 million any year, all the money would be used for professional development in math and science.

● **National Teacher Training Project.** Organize national teacher training programs, particularly in core subjects and early childhood development, for those who taught kindergarten through college.

● **State activities.** Authorize states to use grant money for such purposes as reforming teacher and administrator certification requirements, providing technical assistance to local school districts and developing teacher performance tests and peer review systems.

● **Local improvement plans.** Require school districts applying for Title II grants to submit plans to the state, including an assessment of training needs and specific descriptions of how teaching and learning in core academic subjects would be improved. The school district had to supply at least one-third of the cost of the training.

● **Higher education activities.** Encourage state education agencies to develop partnerships and cooperative agreements with insti-

tutions of higher education to provide training opportunities to the state's teachers.

● **Training demonstration projects.** Authorize the Education Department to establish an unspecified number of demonstration projects across the country aimed at improving teachers' knowledge and performance. Projects were to include teachers, administrators and other school employees.

Title III — Technology for Education

Title III authorized $350 million in fiscal 1995 and unspecified sums through fiscal 1999 for the nation's elementary and secondary schools to acquire advanced technology.

Another $200 million was authorized to purchase advanced technology for school libraries. State grants were to be used to encourage student access to educational tools such as computers, videos and telecommunications systems. Federal money was to be used to purchase equipment and develop networks of organizations and partnerships to provide technical assistance to participating schools. The bill contained provisions to:

● **National long-range plan.** Require the Education Department to publish by October 1995 a national long-range plan describing the effective use of technology in education.

● **Federal leadership.** Authorize the Education Department to work with other federal agencies, such as the National Science Foundation, the Commerce Department and the U.S. National Commission on Libraries and Information Sciences, to provide technical assistance to state educational agencies or local school districts. The assistance was to be provided through competitive grants or federal contracts to public or private for-profit or nonprofit organizations.

● **Funding alternatives.** Require the Education Department to submit a study to Congress by October 1995 on the feasibility of providing a steady flow of public or private money to schools to acquire and maintain advanced educational technology.

● **Technology grant applications.** Require states seeking grants to outline long-term strategies for financing technology education and describe how the equipment they wanted to purchase would improve teaching and learning. The plans had to be approved by the Education Department. School districts also had to provide similar plans to states to receive grant money.

● **National challenge grants.** Authorize the Education Department, through competitive grants, to encourage local partnerships among school districts, institutions of higher education, businesses and software designers. Consortiums made up of such entities could receive five-year grants to provide technological education to students as well as training to teachers and other school employees.

● **Regional technical support.** Authorize $10 million in grants in fiscal 1995 to establish technical support groups known as regional educational technology consortiums. Such consortiums were to work with state educational agencies and local school districts to develop programs to improve teaching and learning through the use of advanced technology. The regional groups were to be made up of state educational agencies, institutions of higher education and nonprofit organizations.

● **Educational product development.** Authorize $50 million in fiscal 1995 to develop educational hardware and software aimed at improving teaching and learning. Money was to be directed toward groups made up of state educational agencies, local school districts, postsecondary institutions and public or private nonprofit organizations.

● **Star Schools program.** Authorize $35 million in fiscal 1995 to improve teaching through the use of audio and video telecommunications services. The emphasis was on student access to telecommunications services for instruction in such subjects as mathematics, science, foreign languages and vocational education. Students who could not read and those with limited proficiency in English also were targeted for assistance.

● **Ready-to-learn television.** Authorize $30 million in fiscal 1995 to develop educational television programs for preschool and elementary schoolchildren.

● **Telecommunications math demonstration project.** Authorize

$5 million in grants in fiscal 1995 to establish a national project aimed at improving math instruction through the use of telecommunications devices such as cable and broadcast television. Money was to be awarded to nonprofit telecommunications firms or partnerships.

● **Math and science equipment.** Authorize $30 million in fiscal 1995 to purchase equipment and materials needed to improve teaching and learning in math and science.

● **School libraries.** Authorize $200 million in fiscal 1995 to buy school library educational materials, including equipment and software.

Title IV — Safer Schools

Title IV authorized $655 million in fiscal 1995 for programs to prevent violence and the use of illegal drugs in and around the nation's schools. The measure also aimed to prevent the use of alcohol and tobacco. It authorized general early intervention programs and counseling services. Originally introduced as HR 3453, this title reauthorized the Drug Free Schools and Communities Act (PL 100-297) enacted in 1988 and addressed the national goal of making schools safe and free of drugs. The title included provisons to:

● **Governors' programs.** Give governors a discretionary set-aside equal to 20 percent of their state's allotment under this section. Money could be used for drug and violence prevention and public awareness campaigns; drug prevention and intervention training for parents, law enforcement officers, social service providers and others who regularly interacted with students; and extra-curricular student activities that promoted drug-free and non-violent lifestyles. A mandatory minimum of 10 percent of a state's 20 percent set-aside had to be used to establish partnerships with local law enforcement officials for Drug Abuse Resistance Education (DARE) programs.

● **Local drug and violence prevention.** Require local districts to develop programs to prevent students and school employees from engaging in violent acts or using illegal drugs, alcohol or tobacco.

● **Evaluation and reporting.** Require the Education Department, in conjunction with the Department of Health and Human Services and other federal agencies, to evaluate the effect of prevention and intervention programs every two years. The Education Department was required to collect data and file a report to Congress by Jan. 1, 1998, on the frequency of violence in the nation's schools. States were required to submit similar reports to the department, and local school districts to file such reports with the state.

● **Grants to institutions of higher education.** Permit the Education Department to contract with institutions of higher education to develop drug and violence prevention programs on campus.

● **Hate-crime prevention.** Authorize a grants program to local school districts and community-based organizations to assist areas directly affected by hate crimes — generally acts in which the defendant selected a victim on the basis of race, color, religion, national origin, ethnicity, gender, disability or sexual orientation.

Title V — Promoting Equity

● **Magnet schools assistance.** Authorize $120 million in fiscal 1995 for competitive grants to prevent minority students at magnet schools from becoming isolated from the rest of the student body. Magnet schools attempted to desegregate schools by offering special programs — in such subjects as the arts, computers and science — to attract white students to majority-black schools or black students to majority-white schools. Grant money was to be used to expand existing magnet programs while also ensuring ethnic and gender diversity within them.

● **Equity for women.** Authorize $5 million in fiscal 1995 in state grants to promote equity for women and girls and to combat discrimination against girls based on gender, race, ethnicity, limited English proficiency, disability or age. The money was to be used for model programs.

● **School dropout prevention.** Authorize $50 million in state grants for programs to identify troubled students and to prevent them from dropping out of school. Such programs also were to address the needs of dropouts, pregnant students and teen-age parents.

Title VI — State Discretionary Grants

The law authorized $370 million in state grants for fiscal 1995 to be used by school districts at their discretion. The money could be used to reduce administrative burdens, provide services for private school students and encourage local flexibility and innovation.

The title allowed local districts and schools to use money to buy advanced technology, such as computer hardware and software, for educational purposes. Money also could be used to train teachers and other school officials in the effective use of advanced technology in education reform efforts.

Title VII — Bilingual Education

The law authorized $215 million in fiscal 1995 for bilingual education programs for students with limited proficiency in English, including American Indians and native Alaskans. The title also authorized teacher training programs in schools that served students who spoke limited English. The law included provisions to:

● **Education grants.** Authorize grants to schools to establish bilingual educational programs. Money also could be used for innovative projects, such as family education, outreach to parents and training programs to encourage parents to become more involved in the education of their children.

● **Schoolwide grants.** Permit schools that served a majority of students with limited proficiency in English to use federal money to develop schoolwide bilingual education programs.

● **Systemwide improvement grants.** Allow school districts to use federal money to develop bilingual education instruction programs.

● **National clearinghouse.** Allow the Education Department to establish a national clearinghouse for bilingual education to analyze the nation's bilingual programs.

● **Training grants.** Provide unspecified amounts in grants for bilingual education teachers, school administrators and appropriate school employees to receive training at colleges, universities or other institutions that offered professional development courses in bilingual education.

● **Career ladder program.** Establish a program aimed at improving the qualifications and skills of non-certified school employees such as teachers' aides who assisted in the education of bilingual students. Federal money could be used to provide such employees with training courses — offered by colleges, universities or the local school district — that would allow them to become teachers. The program also aimed to recruit and train secondary school students for careers in bilingual education.

● **Graduate fellowships.** Authorize the Education Department to award bilingual education fellowships for graduate and postgraduate studies in such areas as teacher training, administration and research. Those receiving such fellowships were required to work in bilingual education for a period equivalent to the length of the fellowship. Fellowship recipients had to repay the money if they did not complete the work requirement.

● **Foreign language assistance.** Authorize $35 million in fiscal 1995 for state grants to improve foreign language instruction.

● **Emergency immigrant education.** Authorize $100 million in fiscal 1995 to aid local school districts, such as those in Texas, California and other Southwestern border states, that experienced large and unexpected student population increases because of immigration.

Title VIII — Impact Aid

The law authorized $866 million in fiscal 1995 in assistance for local school districts financially affected by the presence of children whose parents were connected to large federal endeavors, such as military bases.

The money was to be used to educate children who lived on federal property, students whose parents worked on federal property, and local school districts that experienced sudden enrollment increases because of military realignments.

Because many of the nation's public schools relied on property taxes as a primary source of education money, federal funds also could be used to aid school districts affected by the federal government's acquisition of taxable land.

Title IX — Indian Education

The law authorized $114 million in fiscal 1995 for ongoing education programs for American Indians, native Alaskans and native Hawaiians.

Title X — Programs of National Significance

The law authorized $422 million in fiscal 1995 for more than a dozen small state grant programs, including such initiatives as arts education, assistance to U.S. territories and money for gifted and talented students. The title included provisions to:

● **Fund for the improvement of education.** Authorize unspecified amounts in state grants for fiscal 1995 to promote education reforms or provide support for any "nationally significant" program. Money could be used to develop new curricula in math, English, science and social studies. It also could be used to train teachers, counselors and other school employees.

● **Elementary counseling demonstration.** Authorize the Education Department to award grants to school districts to expand guidance counseling services at schools.

● **Character education pilot project.** Authorize the Education Department to award up to 10 grants annually to develop character education programs. The money was to be awarded to partnerships of state educational agencies and local school districts. Character programs were to focus on such issues as caring, respect, responsibility and trustworthiness. States and localities were to consult with parents and teachers while developing such projects.

● **Scholar-athlete competition.** Authorize the Education Department to award grant money to a nonprofit organization to produce a scholar-athlete event in 1995 as a way to foster understanding and friendships among people of different backgrounds.

● **Small learning communities.** With approval from the Education Department, authorize local school districts to create small learning communities of students to improve teaching and learning opportunities.

● **National student and parent mock election.** Authorize unspecified sums in fiscal 1995 to establish voter participation and education programs for students and their parents, to be administered by nonprofit, nonpartisan organizations.

● **Gifted and talented children.** Authorize $10 million in fiscal 1995 for research programs on the education of gifted and talented children. This included demonstration projects and professional training for educators who taught gifted and talented students from economically disadvantaged backgrounds.

● **Public charter schools.** Authorize $15 million in fiscal 1995 in public charter school grants, which could be used to provide financial assistance for the design and establishment of such schools. Charter schools could be either public or private enterprises operating within public school systems. Often they were based on a contract between a school board and a private business seeking to run a certain school or group of schools. These schools often were released from most regulatory requirements and allowed to develop innovative teaching and learning techniques. Money also was to be used to evaluate student achievement in such schools.

● **Arts in education.** Authorize $45 million in grants in fiscal 1995 for arts education research, development of arts curricula and model arts education programs. Money also could be used to provide at-risk youths with cultural activities designed to develop an appreciation for the arts.

● **Book distribution program.** Authorize $10.3 million in fiscal 1995 to promote reading by supplying educationally disadvantaged students with inexpensive books.

● **Civic education.** Authorize $15 million in fiscal 1995 to support programs that educated students about the Constitution, the Bill of

Rights and the roles of civics, law and government in U.S. society.

● **Allen J. Ellender fellowship program.** Authorize $4.4 million in fiscal 1995 for fellowships through the Close-Up Foundation of Washington, D.C. The foundation was a nonpartisan, nonprofit organization that promoted knowledge about the federal government. Fellowships were to go to teachers and low-income students, recent immigrants, students of migrant parents and older Americans to improve teaching and learning about government issues. Ellender, D-La., was a U.S. senator from 1937 to 1972.

● **De Lugo Territorial education improvement.** Reauthorize $3 million a year from fiscal 1994 through 1999 for education improvement grants to the Virgin Islands, Guam, American Samoa, the Northern Mariana Islands and Palau. The program was named for Ron de Lugo, D-Virgin Islands, a delegate to the U.S. House of Representatives first elected in 1972. He served, with one break, through 1994.

● **21st century community learning centers.** Authorize $20 million in fiscal 1995 to encourage collaboration between schools and other public and private nonprofit groups. Under these partnerships, schools could become local community centers for such activities as vocational and adult education, or school-to-work programs aimed at helping high school students who were not going to college make a smooth transition to the workplace.

● **Urban and rural education assistance.** Authorize $125 million in fiscal 1995 for state grants to assist poor urban and rural school districts. Money could be used for such purposes as tutoring, dropout prevention programs and teacher training. Another $25 million in grants to institutions of higher education was authorized in fiscal 1995 for the training and recruitment of teachers in rural school districts.

● **National writing project.** Reauthorize programs offered by the National Writing Project, a nonprofit organization that trained teachers to teach writing skills more effectively. The law authorized $4 million in fiscal 1995.

● **Longer school year.** Authorize $90 million in fiscal 1995 for grants to promote flexibility in school scheduling and increase the amount of time students spent in academic programs.

● **Territorial assistance.** Authorize $5 million a year from fiscal 1994 through 1999 for education assistance to the Virgin Islands.

Title XI — Coordinated Services

The law authorized unspecified sums to encourage local school districts to provide elementary and secondary school students and their families with better access to social, health and educational services. Such coordinated services could be provided in or near the school through a communitywide partnership with local public and private service agencies.

Title XII — School Facilities Improvement

This title authorized $200 million in state grants for fiscal 1995 for the repair, renovation and construction of public schools, libraries and other structures used for academic or vocational instruction. About 25 percent of U.S. schools were in serious physical decline.

Grants were to be based on such factors as a school district's financial capacity and its percentage of low-income children. Money was to be competitively allocated to districts in six categories based on student population. The smallest category included districts with up to 2,500 students; the largest included those with more than 50,000.

Title XIII — Support and Assistance Programs

● **Comprehensive regional centers.** Authorize $70 million in fiscal 1995 to establish 15 regional educational centers to assist states and school districts that received federal money under the act. Staff members were expected to have expertise in such areas as instruction, curriculum improvement, bilingual education and school reform.

● **National network.** Authorize $25 million in fiscal 1995 to establish a national network of educational professionals to identify effective programs and disseminate information about them statewide or nationwide.

● **Eisenhower regional math and science consortia.** Authorize $23 million in fiscal 1995 to establish regional consortia made up of public and private organizations to provide training to math and science teachers and to disseminate information about exemplary math and science instructional materials.

● **Technology-based assistance.** Authorize the Education Department to provide computer-based technical assistance to states and local school districts to support programs under the act. Such assistance could include legal and regulatory information and technical guidance for administrators.

Title XIV — General Provisions

● **School prayer.** Require the Education Department to withhold federal money under the act from any school district found guilty of violating a federal court order to allow students to engage in constitutionally protected voluntary school prayer.

● **Discouraging sexual activity.** Prohibit the use of federal money received under the act to distribute materials or sex education programs that promoted or encouraged heterosexual or homosexual activity.

● **Prohibition on federal mandates.** Prohibit anything in the act from being construed to authorize the federal government to mandate, direct, or control any aspect of state, school district or school activities.

● **Gun possession.** Require any state receiving federal funds under the act to have a policy requiring that any student who brought a gun to school be expelled for at least one year. Local school district officials could modify the expulsion requirement on a case-by-case basis. School districts also had to refer such students to local law enforcement officials.

Developmentally disabled children also were subject to expulsion for one year if they brought a gun to school. But if school officials established that the behavior of such students was related to their disability, the student could be placed in an alternative educational setting for up to 45 days, instead of being expelled.

● **Disclosure of athletic program financial data.** Require institutions of higher education that participated in intercollegiate athletics to submit annual reports to the Education Department disclosing expenses and revenues from men's and women's sports programs. This provision aimed to show whether there were inequities between men's and women's athletic programs.

● **Albert Einstein distinguished educator fellowship.** Authorize $700,000 in fiscal 1995 to establish a national fellowship program within the Department of Energy for up to 12 elementary and secondary school math and science teachers to increase their knowledge and enhance their teaching skills.

● **Community-school partnerships.** Authorize $10 million in fiscal 1995 grants to local community-based centers to provide educational support to students from low-income families. Money could be used for counseling, tutoring and scholarships for postsecondary education.

● **Workers technology skill development.** Authorize unspecified grants in fiscal 1995 to local nonprofit organizations to improve workers' ability to incorporate advanced technologies into the workplace.

● **Multiethnic adoptions.** Prohibit any organization that received federal assistance and was involved in adoption or foster care from discriminating on the basis of race, color or national origin. The provision aimed to ease the process of adoptions across racial lines.

National Education Goals Set

It took an early morning Saturday vote to complete the task, but Congress on March 26 cleared a bill that for the first time established national education goals for the country's schools. State participation was voluntary.

Under the new law, dubbed the "Goals 2000: Educate America Act" (HR 1804), states could apply for grants to improve their schools regardless of whether they participated in the goals program. The grants were to be awarded competitively. States that opted to take part in the program were expected to work toward such goals as ensuring that schools were safe and free of drugs, achieving a 90 percent graduation rate and increasing parental involvement.

Congress cleared the bill in time to use $105 million that had been appropriated in fiscal 1994 for the program. Congress had specified that the money would be available only if the bill were signed by April 1. President Clinton signed the measure into law March 31 (PL 103-227).

Supporters said the bill — which closely tracked a proposal that Clinton had sent to Congress in April 1993 — would provide a framework for what was expected of schools, teachers and students. The measure wrote into law a set of eight national education goals — six proposed by Clinton and the last two added by the House. The goals proscribed that by 2000:

- All children would start school ready to learn.
- At least 90 percent of students would finish high school.
- Students would leave grades four, eight and 12 with demonstrated competence in English, math, science, foreign languages, civics and government, economics, arts, history and geography.
- Teachers would have access to programs for the continued improvement of their skills.
- The United States would be first in the world in math and science achievement.
- Every adult would be literate and possess the skills to compete in a global economy.
- Every school would be free of drugs and violence.
- Every school would promote involvement of parents in their children's education.

Most of the money in the bill — $400 million — was to be competitively awarded in grants to states, which could use the funds at their discretion to reform their local education systems.

The chief dispute concerned controversial opportunity-to-learn standards, a concept revered by liberal House Democrats and reviled by Republicans from both chambers.

Opportunity-to-learn standards, dubbed OTL by some lawmakers, prescribed what schools should provide — such as qualified teachers and up-to-date textbooks — in order for children to attain the national standards. Supporters argued that such requirements were essential to ensure that all students, especially those from educationally or economically disadvantaged backgrounds, be given equal chances to learn and to meet the national standards.

BOXSCORE

Goals 2000: Educate America Act — HR 1804 (S 1150). The bill established a set of eight national education goals for elementary and secondary schools; state participation was voluntary.

Reports: H Rept 103-168, S Rept 103-85; conference report H Rept 103-446.

KEY ACTION

Feb. 8 — Senate passed HR 1804, 71-25, after substituting the text of S 1150.

March 23 — House adopted conference report, 306-121.

March 26 — Senate cleared the bill, 63-22.

March 31 — President signed the bill — PL 103-227.

Republicans from both chambers expressed fear that such standards could easily become unfunded federal mandates on the nation's school districts, many of which were already financially strapped. They also argued that the standards would encourage parents to sue schools that did not meet them.

The compromise referred to "standards or strategies" and stated explicitly that implementation by the states was voluntary.

Background

Efforts to pass a bill to improve public schools died in the 102nd Congress after President George Bush and congressional Democrats locked horns over the basic elements of the legislation. The biggest dispute was over "school choice" — Bush's proposal to use federal funds to give parents more choice over whether to send their children to public or private schools.

In April 1993, Clinton's Education Secretary Richard W. Riley brought a new school reform proposal to Capitol Hill. Clinton sought $420 million in fiscal 1994 to institute a system of voluntary national goals, standards and tests. The initial draft of the bill did not include opportunity-to-learn standards, but House Democrats insisted they be added to the bill.

1993 Action

Despite partisan fights in committee, the House easily passed the bill Oct. 13, 1993, by a vote of 307-118. The measure (HR 1804 — H Rept 103-168) wrote the eight standards into law and included provisions requiring states that received money under the program to develop opportunity-to-learn standards. To win GOP support, Democrats agreed to a floor amendment specifying that nothing in the bill should be interpreted to give the federal government control over local prerogatives.

The Senate Labor and Human Resources Committee approved its version of the bill (S 1150 — S Rept 103-85) on May 19. *(1993 Almanac, p. 404)*

Senate Action

The Senate passed the Goals 2000 bill Feb. 8 on a 71-25 vote, after substituting the text of S 1150. The bill contained Clinton's six original goals. *(Vote 34, p. 12-H)*

Like the House version, the Senate bill required that states applying for Goals 2000 aid try to reach the national goals.

Each state plan was to include a way to create standards of content — what children should know in English, math and other subjects at certain grades, how to assess what students had learned, and ideas for teacher training. The bill encouraged states to develop strategies, rather than standards, for providing all students with an opportunity to learn — a somewhat less prescriptive approach than that in the House bill.

Goals 2000 Provisions

As enacted, the Goals 2000: Educate America Act (HR 1804) contained provisions to:

- **National goals.** Establish eight national education goals for all students and schools:
  - All children would start school ready to learn.
  - At least 90 percent of students would finish high school.
  - Students would leave grades four, eight and 12 with demonstrated competence in English, math, science, foreign languages, civics and government, economics, arts, history and geography.
  - Teachers would have access to programs for the continued improvement of their skills.
  - The United States would be first in the world in math and science achievement.
  - Every adult would be literate and possess the skills to compete in a global economy.
  - Every school would be free of drugs and violence.
  - Every school would promote involvement of parents in their children's education.
- **Standards of content.** Establish a 19-member National Education Standards and Improvement Council to develop national curriculum content and student performance standards identifying what students should know and be able to do. The standards were voluntary.

  Standards were to be created in such subjects as math, science, English, history, geography, foreign languages and the arts. The aim was to better prepare students for high-wage jobs in a competitive marketplace, increase opportunities for minorities and women, and improve national productivity.

  States opting to participate in the Goals 2000 program had to adopt all or part of the national standards, or develop their own standards of equal or higher quality than those established by the national council. No school or local educational agency stood to lose any federal funding if it did not participate in the program.
- **Opportunity-to-learn standards.** Provide that the council also establish national opportunity-to-learn standards, outlining what schools needed to provide in order for students to meet the curriculum and performance standards. These standards, too, were voluntary.

  In setting such standards, the council was to consider curriculum quality, materials and supplies, teacher qualifications, student assessment methods and physical surroundings.

  States could either adopt the national standards or use them as a guide to set their own standards, which had to be at least as rigorous as the council standards.
- **Aid to states and local districts.** Authorize $400 million over five years beginning in fiscal 1994 to improve local schools. Money was to be distributed to states using the funding formula that was used at the time to calculate local education agencies' participation in Titles I and II of the Elementary and Secondary Education Act of 1965.

  Under existing law, Title I funds were targeted toward educationally disadvantaged students, who tended to be poor. Based on census data, money under Title I was being distributed to about 90 percent of the nation's schools. Title II provided grants to increase local flexibility and encourage innovation.

  States were required to apply to the secretary of Education for grants by submitting a state improvement plan that detailed how education reforms would be carried out locally.
- **Oversight boards.** Create an 18-member National Education Goals Panel to oversee and report on the nation's progress toward the eight goals. The panel was to include two presidential appointees, eight governors, four members of Congress and four state legislators.

  The bill also created a National Skill Standards Board, made up of 28 representatives from business, labor, government and community organizations, to develop a national system of standards and testing to ensure that students had the skills necessary to compete in the work force.
- **Safe schools.** Authorize up to $3 million over two years for local educational agencies that had schools in urban and rural areas with high rates of violent crime. Local districts would determine how to spend the money to combat their problems. The law authorized $50 million in fiscal 1994.
- **Research institutes.** Establish five new research institutes within the Office of Educational Research and Improvement, which was authorized at $68 million in fiscal 1995. Modeled after the National Science Foundation, the five research arms were expected to support basic and applied research, apply research to schools and serve as a national data base on model programs.

  They were the National Institutes on: Student Achievement, Curriculum and Assessment; Education of At-Risk Students; Educational Governance, Finance, Policy-Making and Management; Early Childhood Development and Education; and Postsecondary Education, Libraries, and Lifelong Education.

Before passing the bill, the Senate took up a variety of amendments. Senators:

- **Contraceptives.** Rejected, 34-59, an amendment by Jesse Helms, R-N.C., that would have prohibited the departments of Education and Health and Human Services from promoting or distributing contraceptives — not only at schools — without parental consent. Opponents said the amendment was too broad. *(Vote 28, p. 6-S)*

  The Senate then voted 91-2 in favor of an amendment by Labor and Human Resources Committee Chairman Edward M. Kennedy, D-Mass., to encourage family participation in all federally funded contraceptive distribution programs. *(Vote 29, p. 6-S)*
- **School choice.** Rejected, 41-52, an amendment by Daniel R. Coats, R-Ind., that would have set aside $30 million for a demonstration project to allow some low-income children to attend private schools at public expense. Supporters said the opportunity to leave the public school system ought to extend to poor children. Opponents warned that the proposal could drain public schools of money and students. *(Vote 25, p. 6-S)*
- **Opportunity-to-learn standards.** Rejected, 42-52, an amendment by Judd Gregg, R-N.H., to strip the bill of references to opportunity-to-learn standards, which he described as "basically a grand scheme to design a national curriculum." *(Vote 20, p. 5-S)*
- **National education standards.** Voted 32-61 against an amendment by Connie Mack, R-Fla., that would have provided the money in the bill directly to local school boards without requiring them to address the Goals 2000 standards. *(Vote 27, p. 6-S)*
- **Parental consent.** Voted 93-0 for an amendment by Charles E. Grassley, R-Iowa, to require parental consent for surveys or evaluations related to political affiliations, psychological problems, sexual behavior or other private matters. *(Vote 26, p. 6-S)*
- **School prayer.** Approved, 75-22, a Helms amendment to deny federal school funds to state or local agencies that barred constitutionally protected prayer in public schools.

  Senators subsequently approved by voice vote an amend-

ment by Carl Levin, D-Mich., to ensure that no federal funds would be denied to a state or local agency because it had adopted a constitutionally permissible policy related to school prayer.

Senators also voted 78-8 for an amendment by John C. Danforth, R-Mo., expressing "the sense of the Senate" that schools be encouraged to offer a daily moment of silence. *(Vote 24, p. 6-S)*

● **Crime.** Agreed by voice vote to an amendment by Christopher J. Dodd, D-Conn., to authorize grants of $75 million in fiscal 1994 and $100 million in fiscal 1995 to the school districts most troubled by crime and violence. Similar provisions had been passed in the House as a free-standing bill (HR 2455), sponsored by Major R. Owens, D-N.Y. The House bill, passed by voice vote Feb. 22, provided for a one-year, $50 million authorization.

Conference/Final Action

The House adopted the conference report on the bill (H Rept 103-446) by a vote of 306-121 on March 23, but only after overcoming Republican objections to the weakening of the school prayer provision. *(Vote 86, p. 26-H)*

Senate Democrats faced similar objections from Helms, who threatened a filibuster against the bill. However, with the April 1 deadline for using the fiscal 1994 money looming, the Senate closed off debate and cleared the bill 63-22 on March 26. *(Vote 86, p. 15-S)*

● **Opportunity-to-learn standards.** The most contentious issue during the three-day House-Senate conference on the bill, which began March 15, was the opportunity-to-learn standards.

Led by Owens and George Miller, D-Calif., House liberals insisted that the word "standards" be included in the bill's final language.

"If ever you want to doom a piece of legislation, make OTL the centerpiece," responded Pennsylvania Republican Bill Goodling, ranking minority member on the House Education and Labor Committee. "You micromanage everything, and you don't provide them one single dime."

House Education and Labor Committee Chairman William D. Ford, D-Mich., disagreed, saying the bill would provide flexibility by allowing decisions to be made at the state and local levels. "We don't tell them from Washington how to do one single thing," he said.

After several failed attempts to compromise, Sen. Paul Simon, D-Ill., suggested including the word "standards" but making clear that they would be voluntary for states; each state would establish its own standards. The alternative term, "strategies," used in the Senate bill, was also included.

Goodling and Rep. Steve Gunderson, R-Wis., said they opposed Simon's compromise, arguing that school districts would still be open to lawsuits despite the softened language. But Senate Republicans, led by James M. Jeffords of Vermont and Nancy Landon Kassebaum of Kansas, joined Democrats from both chambers in adopting the compromise.

● **School privatization.** Sen. Arlen Specter, R-Pa., argued for a Senate amendment to allow public education agencies to use Goals 2000 money for privatization of local schools, in

which companies contracted with local school districts to run public schools. House members insisted that all the planning and start-up costs be borne by the private firms, not school districts. The Senate agreed, and the House accepted the Senate provision.

● **Tobacco ban.** An amendment to ban tobacco use from schools and "any place children might be present" ran into difficulty. Members ultimately agreed to include language banning smoking from places such as elementary and secondary school libraries, pediatric wings of hospitals, school gymnasiums and commercial day-care centers.

● **School prayer.** Conferees modified the language on school prayer that had been offered by Helms and approved overwhelmingly by the Senate. Helms' provision would have withdrawn all federal education funds from any school that denied students a chance to engage in "constitutionally protected" school prayer. Conferees softened the language to merely prohibit schools from using federal money to deny students the right to pray voluntarily.

● **Crime.** Conferees authorized $50 million in fiscal 1994 for grants to local school systems to combat violence and enhance school safety.

Final Fights Over School Prayer

When the conference report came up in the House on March 22, Democrats believed the bipartisan bill would pass easily. But House Republicans were emboldened by a strong vote the previous day in favor of adding Helms' school prayer language to a separate education bill (HR 6). *(Elementary and secondary education, p. 383)*

John J. "Jimmy" Duncan Jr., R-Tenn., tried to send the goals bill back to conference to rewrite the provision, but moderate Republicans as well as Democrats warned that that would essentially kill the bill. "This is it," said Gunderson. "Either today you vote for education reform, or you go back home and admit you're not really in support of it."

Majority Leader Richard A. Gephardt, D-Mo., argued that the school prayer issue had been settled on March 21 when the language was attached to HR 6. "There is not a need to reiterate that policy in this bill," Gephardt said.

Duncan's motion failed, 195-232, and the House subsequently adopted the conference report. *(Vote 85, p. 26-H)*

In the Senate, backed by many of his Republican colleagues, Helms employed arcane parliamentary procedures to delay the bill's passage until well after many senators had hoped to begin a scheduled two-week recess March 25. Senate Majority Leader George J. Mitchell, D-Maine, countered with several parliamentary tactics of his own to force a vote. Despite the absence of 15 senators, Mitchell persuaded the other 85 members to remain in town for a vote to limit debate on the bill, followed by a vote to clear the measure, scheduled for Saturday, March 26.

Shortly after midnight March 26, the Senate voted 62-23 to invoke cloture, thus limiting debate and moving to final consideration of the bill. Nine Republicans joined 53 Democrats in voting for cloture; 60 votes were required. *(Vote 85, p. 15-S)*

The Senate voted on final passage of the goals bill at 12:30 a.m. Ten Republicans supported it. But Helms was not there. He had left the Capitol for North Carolina during the afternoon to attend a birthday party for his wife. ■

Clinton Signs School-to-Work Bill

In April, Congress cleared a school-to-work bill (HR 2884) aimed at helping students who did not plan to attend college to move smoothly from high school into skilled jobs. The measure was a priority for the Clinton administration, which promoted it as a way to raise education standards and improve the nation's competitiveness.

The new program, which was authorized at $300 million in fiscal 1995 and unspecified sums through fiscal 1999, was to be administered jointly by the Education and Labor departments. It had the backing of business and labor groups and enjoyed bipartisan support in Congress. President Clinton signed the bill into law May 4 (PL 103-239).

Patterned after apprenticeship programs in Europe, the measure aimed to offer students on-site, work-based career training. By contrast, traditional vocational programs tended to focus on in-school learning that often had little relationship to the type of job the student eventually chose. The School-to-Work Opportunities program also included career planning and academic training — typically with a year or two at a postsecondary school.

The bill authorized planning grants of up to $1 million a year for states to develop school-to-work programs and unspecified sums for up to five years for states to implement them. After five years states were to pay for their own programs.

Bill supporters, led by Senate sponsor Paul Simon, D-Ill., said the government historically had focused on college-bound students while giving short shrift to the 75 percent of U.S. high school graduates who did not get a college degree. The measure had few critics, although the Senate Labor and Human Resources Committee's ranking Republican, Nancy Landon Kassebaum of Kansas, questioned the need for the legislation when the government already ran more than 150 job training programs at a cost of about $25 billion a year.

Background

Clinton sent his school-to-work initiative to Capitol Hill on Aug. 5, 1993, as part of an effort to raise education standards and the quality of the nation's work force.

The House passed HR 2884 (H Rept 103-345) by voice vote Nov. 15, 1993. The Senate Labor and Human Resources Committee approved a similar bill (S 1361 — S Rept 103-179) on Nov. 3, but the full Senate did not consider it before the end of the 1993 session. *(1993 Almanac, p. 408)*

The two bills authorized grants for educators, employers and labor representatives to develop partnerships to allow high school juniors and seniors to go to school part time and to work part time. Students who finished the program were to receive a high school diploma, a certificate or diploma from a postsecondary school, and an occupational skill certificate.

The legislation gave the states flexibility to design programs the way they thought best. The federal government

---

BOXSCORE

School-to-Work Program — HR 2884 (S 1361). A five-year authorization for a new program of grants to states to help students not bound for college to move smoothly into the work force.

Reports: H Rept 103-345, S Rept 103-179; conference report H Rept 103-480.

KEY ACTION

Feb. 8 — Senate passed HR 2884, 62-31, after substituting the text of S 1361.

April 20 — House adopted conference report, 339-79.

April 21 — Senate cleared HR 2884 by voice vote.

May 4 — President signed HR 2884 — PL 103-239.

---

was to provide a one-year planning grant and one five-year grant to inaugurate the partnerships. Programs could vary, but each had to provide job training, paid work experience and workplace mentoring, along with academic training.

Senate Floor

The Senate passed HR 2884 by a vote of 62-31 on Feb. 8, the same day it passed the broad Goals 2000 school improvement bill (HR 1804). Before passing the school-to-work measure, the Senate inserted the text of S 1361. Under the Senate bill, students were to work as apprentices in local industries while attending school part time, eventually receiving high school diplomas and certificates of competency in their chosen fields. The bill authorized $300 million in fiscal 1995. *(Vote 32, p. 7-S; Goals 2000 bill, p. 397)*

Bill supporters argued that government had focused too long on college students. "We invest a disproportionate amount of our resources in the 25 percent" who earn bachelor's degrees, Simon said during debate Feb. 7.

While allowing that "overall . . . the present system does not work very well," Kassebaum responded that better coordination of existing programs would be more appropriate. She called creating new programs "because we are disappointed with the ineffectiveness of the old ones . . . a time-honored tradition in Congress."

Senators approved an amendment by Larry Pressler, R-S.D., to allow several congressional districts with low populations to form consortia to apply for grants. The amendment, approved by voice vote Feb. 7, was intended to ensure that rural areas would not be underfunded.

The Senate also gave voice vote approval to the following amendments:

● By Kassebaum to reduce the program's authorization from eight years to five years.

● By Don Nickles, R-Okla., to set the annual authorization for the program at $400 million in fiscal years 1996 and 1997, $330 million in fiscal 1998 and $220 million in fiscal 1999. (These were unspecified sums in the final bill.)

● By Strom Thurmond, R-S.C., to give a preference, in approving grants, to states that placed students in paying jobs.

The Senate rejected an amendment by Slade Gorton, R-Wash., that would have required administrators for the Summer Youth Employment and Training Program to give priority to placing students in private-sector jobs. The program provided work for disadvantaged young people. A motion by Simon to table (kill) Gorton's amendment was adopted, 50-43. *(Vote 31, p. 6-S)*

Conference and Final Action

Few differences separated the House and Senate bills. Nevertheless, Democratic and Republican staff members

from both sides of the Capitol worked for several weeks to resolve snags.

One problem arose over whether states should be required to make sure that students in the program worked at paying jobs. Democrats argued that students would derive greater benefit from their experiences if they were paid. Republicans said such a mandate might make it economically impossible for some employers to participate in school-to-work programs.

The final language provided for the secretaries of Labor and Education to give preference to applications from programs that included paid work.

Conferees also resolved differences over which state officials were to have authority over school-to-work programs. The House version gave the most power to chief state school officers; the Senate bill gave it to governors.

Under the agreement, governors were required to submit their states' plans to the Education and Labor departments, which were given joint responsibility for the program. Other state officials, such as chief school officers, could submit dissenting views with the application.

The House adopted the conference report (H Rept 103-480) April 20 by a vote of 339-79. The Senate cleared the bill by voice vote April 21. *(Vote 128, p. 38-H)*

Anticipating congressional approval, more than 20 states already had grant applications pending. ■

Other Bills Related To Education

Congress took up three other education bills in 1994:

Student Loan Defaults

Lawmakers agreed to extend by four years a deadline for historically black colleges and tribally controlled Indian community colleges to reduce their student loan default rates. The measure allowed such schools to have a loan default rate of 25 percent or more until July 1, 1998. President Clinton signed the bill April 28 (S 2004 — PL 103-235).

The Senate had passed the measure, sponsored by Dale Bumpers, D-Ark., by voice vote March 25. The House cleared the bill April 13 by a vote of 283-136. *(Vote 102, p. 30-H)*

Under the budget-reconciliation law of 1990 (PL 101-508) and the Higher Education Act of 1992 (PL 102-325), schools with high default rates generally lost the ability to participate in federal guaranteed student loan programs. *(1992 Almanac, p. 441)*

However, existing law exempted historically black and tribally controlled Indian schools until July 1, 1994. Democratic sponsors said the deadline extension would give such schools more time to develop the institutional reforms to achieve long-term success in reducing high default rates.

Historically Black Colleges

The Senate passed a bill (HR 2921) to authorize $65 million in matching grants over four years for the restoration and preservation of significant buildings at the nation's historically black colleges and universities. The House had passed a separate version of the bill in 1993. The two chambers did not reconcile their differences over the legislation, however, and it died at the end of the Congress.

The Senate Committee on Energy and Natural Resources

amended and approved HR 2921 (S Rept 103-279) on May 11 by a vote of 20-0. The bill authorized the Interior secretary to make grants from the Historic Preservation Fund to restore and preserve buildings and architecture at qualifying institutions. The Senate passed the bill by voice vote Aug. 10, breaking a deadlock that had lasted for weeks between Senate Minority Leader Bob Dole, R-Kan., and the bill's chief Senate sponsor, Carol Moseley-Braun, D-Ill.

Dole had sought $3.6 million in funding over three years for Sterling College, a small liberal arts institution in Sterling, Kan., with a student enrollment that was 3 percent black. Dole said the college had historical significance because it admitted blacks at the turn of the century. Using a similar argument, Charles E. Grassley, R-Iowa, sought to add Simpson College in Indianola, Iowa, to the schools eligible for federal money. Most students at Simpson were white.

In a compromise, lawmakers adopted by voice vote an amendment, offered for Dole by Robert F. Bennett, R-Utah, to include Sterling and Simpson colleges in a separate section of the bill. That meant they would not compete directly against historically black schools for money. The amendment authorized $3.6 million for Sterling and $1.5 million for Simpson.

Of the nation's 104 historically black colleges and universities, 46 had expressed interest in restoring their historic buildings. Among those with pending applications at the Interior Department were Fisk University in Nashville, Tenn.; Howard University in Washington, D.C.; and Savannah State College in Savannah, Ga.

The amended Senate measure was to go back to the House for consideration, but the House never took it up. Several House members were expected to oppose funding for Sterling and Simpson colleges.

The House had passed its version of the bill (HR 2921 — H Rept 103-398) by voice vote Nov. 22, 1993. The House Natural Resources Subcommittee on National Parks, Forests and Public Lands had approved the bill by voice vote Nov. 4, 1993, and the full committee approved it by voice vote Nov. 10. Introduced by Bob Clement, D-Tenn., the bill authorized a grant program to preserve and restore historic buildings at historically black colleges and universities. It authorized $20 million in the first year, fiscal 1995, and no more than $15 million a year in fiscal 1996-98. Of the $20 million in fiscal 1995, it authorized $5 million for Fisk University and $10 million for the 11 structures at historically black colleges that had already been identified by the Interior Department as in need of the most help.

School Technology

With the aim of increasing competitiveness, helping schools with their cash crisis and giving industry a nudge, the Senate Labor and Human Resources Committee on Feb. 23 approved by voice vote a bill to authorize $352.5 million in fiscal 1995 to help equip the nation's classrooms with the latest technologies, such as interactive educational software and computer networks. The bill (S 1040 — S Rept 103-234) went no further.

Some of its provisions, however, were incorporated in the Goals 2000 education bill and the Elementary and Secondary Education reauthorization act. For example, the Goals 2000 bill (HR 1804 — PL 103-227) provided for the creation of an Office of Educational Technology to carry out such goals as using technology to help ensure that all students could meet state performance standards. The elementary-secondary reauthorization act (HR 6 — PL 103-382) included millions of dollars to help schools acquire advanced

technology. *(Goals 2000, p. 397; elementary and secondary education, p. 383)*

Sens. Jeff Bingaman, D-N.M., and Thad Cochran, R-Miss., sponsors of the school technology bill, feared that poor and remote schools might be the last to take part in the rapid changes under way in education and communications. Their bill targeted the poorest school districts, authorizing $200 million in grants to help them acquire new equipment and software and to train educators.

Among other programs authorized, $50 million was to go toward regional centers run by industry and schools to provide technical support; $50 million more was to support development of software to help students learn and teachers teach.

"Without a work force that is prepared to use new technology effectively, the promise of greater productivity and higher wages will be more difficult to achieve," said Labor Committee Chairman Edward M. Kennedy, D-Mass.

Before the Education Department was created in 1979, the former U.S. Office of Education had played a lead role in fostering educational television and computing in schools. But in 1981, Congress consolidated spending on such programs into the broader pool of the Chapter 2 block-grant program to states. As a result, the direction provided by the federal government to help schools keep pace with technology was lost. The Education Department's Star Schools program, an experiment in distance learning, was created in 1988 and in 1994 reached roughly 200,000 students. Apart from that, the federal role in coordinating school technology efforts remained minimal.

S 1040 proposed to create a new Office of Educational Technology within the Education Department to oversee efforts to upgrade schools.

The federal government was to grant states money using existing Education Department formulas that favored poorer school districts. Schools would then apply to the states for the funds, showing how they would use the money to improve their classroom communications technology. The grant program would be in addition to other federal efforts under way to help schools adapt to new technologies. ∎

Striker Replacement Bill Blocked

Legislation to prohibit companies from permanently replacing striking workers died for the year after the Senate twice failed to shut off a Republican-led filibuster.

Efforts to get the 60 votes needed to invoke cloture, limit debate and proceed to a vote on the bill (S 55) failed July 12 and July 13, despite attempts by bill supporters to compromise with a small bipartisan group of senators who opposed the bill but supported the general idea of expanding protection of striking workers.

The House had passed a similar bill (HR 5) by a comfortable 239-190 margin June 15, 1993. *(1993 Almanac, p. 396)*

Both bills aimed to nullify a 1938 Supreme Court ruling that allowed employers to replace workers who were striking for economic reasons, such as higher pay. Organized labor had long argued that overturning the 1938 decision was necessary to ensure a worker's right to strike. But business groups and others argued that passage of such a bill would encourage employees to walk out rather than negotiate with employers.

The National Labor Relations Act of 1935 gave workers the right to strike and employers the option to hire replacements during a walkout. The act allowed temporary replacements; the question of permanent replacements remained in dispute. In 1938, the Supreme Court ruled in *National Labor Relations Board v. Mackay Radio and Telegraph* that employees could be replaced permanently if they were striking for economic benefits, such as higher pay, but not if they had walked out over unfair labor practices.

Bill supporters wanted to overturn that decision, and ban the use of permanent replacements. They noted that in the previous decade, tens of thousands of workers at companies including Greyhound Lines, Eastern Air Lines and Diamond Walnut Growers had been replaced permanently. "Hundreds of thousands more have refrained from exercising their right to engage in collective action because of the threat of permanent replacement," Senate bill sponsor Howard M. Metzenbaum, D-Ohio, said during debate July 11.

But opponents argued that the bill would disrupt the delicate balance that gave workers and management roughly equal leverage in a dispute. "Current law is based on the tried and true concept that, by making a strike risky . . . both sides will have a vested interest in finding a reasonable solution to their labor disputes," Orrin G. Hatch, R-Utah, said July 11.

Hatch and others also said the issue had been blown out of proportion. They pointed to a General Accounting Office study showing that between 1985 and 1989, only 3 percent to 4 percent of workers striking for benefits were replaced permanently.

Cloture Votes Fall Short

The first cloture vote, on July 12, was 53-47 — seven votes short of the 60 that supporters needed to limit debate. The second vote was 53-46, with Paul Coverdell, R-Ga., who voted against cloture July 12, absent. *(Votes 188, 189, p. 33-S)*

The core of the opposition came from 40 Republicans. But six Democrats — David L. Boren of Oklahoma, Dale Bumpers and David Pryor of Arkansas, Ernest F. Hollings of South Carolina, Harlan Mathews of Tennessee and Sam Nunn of Georgia — crossed party lines to give opponents a comfortable margin of victory. All but Mathews, who was appointed in 1993, and Nunn had voted against cloture in 1992, when attempts to break a GOP filibuster over a similar bill failed 57-42. *(1992 Almanac, p. 361)*

The three GOP votes for cloture in 1994 came from Alfonse M. D'Amato of New York, Arlen Specter of Pennsylvania and Mark O. Hatfield of Oregon.

In the weeks preceding the cloture votes, bill supporters tried to find common ground with a small group of Senate moderates — including Democrats Bumpers and Pryor, and Republicans James M. Jeffords of Vermont and John H. Chafee of Rhode Island — who opposed the measure as written but favored additional protection for workers involved in economic strikes.

One proposed amendment would have applied the law only to large employers. Another would have limited the number of years that the legislation would remain in effect.

By the evening of July 12, hope of compromise had vanished. "It was just too late in the game," said Jeffords, who had proposed limiting the bill's protections to workers who struck to retain benefits that employers wanted to reduce or eliminate.

President Clinton supported the bill, but with less enthusiasm than advocates had hoped for. Union officials said they were angry that the administration had not made the bill a greater priority. Ron Carey, president of the International Brotherhood of Teamsters, expressed disappointment that Clinton had not made the same effort on striker replacement that he made in 1993 on the North American Free Trade Agreement, which the unions opposed. *(1993 Almanac, p. 171)* ∎

OSHA Overhaul Legislation Hangs Up in the House

Legislation aimed at substantially overhauling the law governing the Occupational Safety and Health Administration (OSHA) — the federal agency that set safety standards in the workplace — stalled in the House after winning the approval of the Education and Labor Committee early in the year. A similar bill (S 575) was introduced in the Senate, but supporters waited for the House to go first, and the Senate never acted on its bill.

The cornerstone of the House bill (HR 1280) was a requirement that employers with 11 or more workers use OSHA recommendations to establish a written health and safety plan to reduce hazardous working conditions. The committee-approved bill also required OSHA to investigate potential safety violations within 24 hours of an accident in which unsafe conditions might have been a cause.

The bill sought to streamline the process for setting health and safety standards, requiring the federal government to respond within 90 days whenever employers, workers or others requested new health or safety rules. If a new standard was deemed necessary, the agency would have one year to issue a proposed rule.

The 1970 Occupational Safety and Health Act (PL 91-596) — which applied to the private sector and the federal government — would be extended to state and local governments.

The bill also contained tougher criminal sanctions for employers whose neglect of safety standards led to the death or injury of a worker. A deliberate violation of OSHA standards that resulted in death could get a manager up to 10 years in prison. Under existing law, supervisors were not personally liable for such OSHA violations.

The House Education and Labor Committee had approved a similar bill in 1992, but the legislation stalled under a veto threat from President George Bush. The election of President Clinton boosted supporters' hopes that OSHA reform could become law. *(1992 Almanac, p. 364)*

But the bill was staunchly opposed by House Republicans, who argued that it would lead to excessive regulation. In addition, moderate and conservative Democrats were concerned that the measure as written would impose more burdensome mandates on state and local governments.

House Committee

On March 10, the House Education and Labor Committee approved HR 1280 (H Rept 103-825, Part 1) on a largely party line vote of 26-17.

At the markup, bill sponsor and Chairman William D. Ford, D-Mich., and other Democratic supporters maintained that an overhaul of OSHA was long overdue. They pointed to National Safety Council statistics showing that 8,500 people were killed in work-related accidents in 1992. The safety council was a clearinghouse on occupational safety issues based in Itasca, Ill.

But Republicans countered that the bill would lead to excessive regulation, hampering businesses and slowing economic growth. John A. Boehner, R-Ohio, complained that people in "the real world" would not comply with many of the bill's requirements. "They don't pay any attention to what we do because they can't afford to," he said.

GOP members also pointed to a long-term decrease in the number of on-the-job fatalities as indicating that the law generally worked well and did not need significant changes. The National Safety Council reported 14,200 work-related deaths in 1970, the year the law was enacted. That figure had dropped to 13,000 in 1980 and 8,500 in 1992.

The committee approved several amendments, including one offered by Ron Klink, D-Pa., to apply OSHA standards to congressional offices. Under Klink's language, the U.S. comptroller general was to hire a safety expert to look for health and safety hazards on Capitol Hill. It was approved by voice vote.

The committee also approved, 25-16, an amendment offered by Austin J. Murphy, D-Pa., to create an Office of Construction Safety, Health and Education within the Labor Department. The office was to suggest health and safety standards and train OSHA and other inspectors concerning safe procedures at construction sites.

Among the amendments rejected by the committee was language offered by ranking Republican Bill Goodling of Pennsylvania that would have allowed states and localities to refuse to comply with any requirement in the bill if the cost was not covered by the federal government. Goodling said that states were already overburdened by unfunded federal mandates. His amendment was defeated, 15-26.

The committee also rejected, 16-27, an amendment by Cass Ballenger, R-N.C., that would have allowed business owners to reimburse managers who were personally fined for OSHA violations. ∎

Law Enacted To Crack Down On Underfunded Pensions

Congress tightened federal requirements on businesses that underfunded their employee pension plans. The provisions cleared Dec. 1 as part of the implementing legislation for the General Agreement on Tariffs and Trade (GATT). President Clinton signed the GATT bill Dec. 8 (HR 5110 — PL 103-465). *(GATT, p. 123)*

The language, which began as a separate bill (HR 3396), was approved by two House committees in July and August. But action on HR 3396 stopped after the provisions were included in the GATT bill, introduced Sept. 27. The pension reform provisions were added to help offset the $12 billion in tariff income that was expected to be lost over the first five years of the GATT accord. It was estimated that these provisions would reduce federal liability for pension failures, saving the government nearly $1 billion. A related Senate measure (S 1780) was never taken up.

Government officials and others had long feared that a large number of privately funded pension plans might be underfunded. On July 19, Labor Secretary Robert B. Reich warned members of the House Education and Labor Committee that unless action was taken to shore up private pension plans, the government might get stuck with the tab for a massive bailout. "This is not yet a crisis, but it could be . . . if we let it go," Reich said.

Under the 1974 Employee Retirement Income Security Act (ERISA), which governed employee benefit plans, employers

were supposed to set aside enough money to meet future pension commitments. Most private pensions were fully funded, Reich said, but some companies had failed to contribute all the money needed to pay future retiree benefits. Concern about these underfunded pensions focused in particular on steel and automobile companies and other Rust Belt industries that had faltered during the 1980s.

From 1987 to 1992, underfunded pensions doubled in size, from a $27 billion shortfall to $53 billion, according to the Pension Benefit Guaranty Corporation (PBGC). The PBGC, a federal nonprofit corporation, guaranteed private, single-employer pensions up to a maximum of $30,682 per worker per year, even if a company went out of business or its retirement plan did not have enough money to meet its obligations. In 1994, the agency guaranteed the benefits of about 41 million workers and retirees in 65,000 pension plans.

To cover the cost of those guarantees, the PBGC collected an annual fee of $19 per participant from companies with pension plans. Companies with underfunded plans could be required to pay up to an additional $53 per participant, depending on the degree of the funding deficit.

Legislative Action

The final bill gradually raised the $53 cap on premiums, phasing it out entirely after three years. This was intended to allow the PBGC to collect more from employers who were more likely to default on future benefits payments.

The bill also required companies to maintain enough money in their pension accounts to pay at least three years' worth of benefits. Any new benefits given to workers had to be fully paid for within five to 14 years. Underfunded companies were required to notify workers of the pension plan's status.

In addition, employers were required to use uniform mortality and interest rate tables when determining future liability. PBGC officials said that many employers used high interest rate and mortality estimates to lower their future liability. That allowed them to pay less into the plan.

The bill was first taken up on July 22 by the House Ways and Means Committee, which approved it by voice vote (H Rept 103-632, Part 1).

The committee gave voice vote approval to an amendment offered by acting Chairman Sam Gibbons, D-Fla., that lengthened to 14 years the deadline for a company to fully fund new employee benefits. In addition, the amendment waived the worker notification requirement if an underfunded plan was at least 90 percent funded.

The House Education and Labor Committee acted next, approving HR 3396 by voice vote Aug. 11 (H Rept 103-632, Part 2). Pat Williams, D-Mont., decided against offering an amendment to require that the PBGC guarantee annuities; the amendment was opposed by the administration.

Companies often paid insurers to convert individual pensions into annuities, or long-term periodic payments. Williams and others said that workers should not lose PBGC protection as a result. Labor Secretary Reich said the administration was sympathetic to this concern, but he opposed adding annuities to the PBGC's responsibilities until traditional pension plans were better funded.

Williams did offer two less controversial amendments, both of which were approved by voice vote. The first required companies that added new pension benefits before 1995 to take 12 years to fully fund those benefits, down from the 14 years approved by the Ways and Means Committee. The second allowed companies to "double count" 5 percent of all reductions in their pension plan liability. Double counting allowed an employer to pay less into the plan. ∎

Congress Considers Pension Bills

On other pension-related legislation, Congress cleared a bill to help retirees whose pension benefits were threatened by the insolvency of one insurance company. But two broader bills — to give states greater flexibility in regulating certain employee benefits, and to restrict states' ability to tax pension benefits of former residents — died at the end of the Congress.

Executive Life Benefits

Congress cleared a bill aimed at helping 84,000 retirees and employees whose pension benefits were threatened by the insolvency of the Executive Life Insurance Company. The Senate had passed the measure Oct. 28, 1993. The House cleared it by voice vote Oct. 3, 1994; President Clinton signed it Oct. 22 (S 1312 — PL 103-401). *(1993 Almanac, p. 398)*

During the 1980s, many employers had terminated their defined-benefit pension plans and replaced them with annuities offered by insurance companies. Under this arrangement, the employer paid the insurance company to assume responsibility for providing fixed monthly payments to the retirees.

Bill sponsor Sen. Howard M. Metzenbaum, D-Ohio, argued that most of the employers who turned to Executive Life did so with an eye toward saving money and with little regard for the future stability of their employees' pensions. In some cases, the employers spent less to purchase the annuities than they had set aside to cover future pension obligations, thus capturing the excess funds for other corporate purposes.

Metzenbaum also accused some employers of purchasing Executive Life annuities with the knowledge that the company was not on sound financial footing.

In 1991, Executive Life became insolvent and was seized by state regulators. As a result, annuity payments to retirees were reduced for one year.

While benefits from standard company pension plans were largely guaranteed by the federal government through the Pension Benefit Guaranty Corporation, annuities carried no such protection under the basic federal pension law, the 1974 Employee Retirement Income Security Act (ERISA). Attempts by retirees to recover their lost benefits through lawsuits against their former employers had proved unsuccessful.

In 1993, the Supreme Court ruled 5-4 in an unrelated case, *Mertens v. Hewitt Associates*, that retirees could not sue their employers for compensation in cases where benefits had been lost due to violations of ERISA. Metzenbaum contended that the court had construed ERISA too narrowly.

S 1312 gave retirees and workers who were or would be receiving benefits through an Executive Life annuity the authority to sue their former employers and any other responsible parties to recover their lost benefits plus interest. Specifically, it clarified that workers could sue employers who purchased the Executive Life annuities for breaching their fiduciary duty to act in their employees' best interest when managing their pension plans.

In early 1993, Metzenbaum had hoped to expand the language in the bill to cover all those wrongfully denied pension benefits paid through annuities, regardless of whether Executive Life was involved. At one point, such a provision was included in the Senate version of the 1993 budget-reconciliation bill. *(1993 Almanac, p. 107)*

But Nancy Landon Kassebaum, R-Kan., and other Republicans argued that broadening the protection to so

many employees might prompt many employers to stop offering pension plans altogether. Faced with strong GOP opposition, Metzenbaum agreed to remove the provision from the budget-reconciliation bill and settle for the narrow language covering only those affected by Executive Life.

ERISA Pre-emption

The Senate Labor and Human Resources Committee on April 13 approved a bill (HR 1036 — S Rept 103-299) on a 10-7 party-line vote that would have given states more latitude in regulating certain employee benefits. But the Senate bill stalled over Republican concerns that it would hurt businesses and unfairly favor union workers. The House had passed the measure Nov. 9, 1993. *(1993 Almanac, p. 397)*

Pension plans and other worker benefits were governed by the 1974 Employee Retirement Income Security Act (ERISA). The act sought to eliminate contradictory federal and state regulations by spelling out that federal law preempted state law.

Supporters of the bill, which was sponsored by Rep. Howard L. Berman, D-Calif., said that recent court decisions had expanded the scope of ERISA's pre-emption clause beyond the intent of Congress, interfering with the legitimate regulatory rights of states.

They cited three particular areas. HR 1036 sought to bar the pre-emption of state law under ERISA in all three:

● **Prevailing wages.** In 1994, 31 states had laws that required employers to pay workers the prevailing local wage, in money and benefits, for work on state contracts. But some state courts had struck down these laws as a violation of the ERISA pre-emption clause.

● **Apprenticeship programs.** All 50 states had passed laws establishing minimum standards for apprenticeship or other job training programs. But some of these laws were overturned because of the pre-emption clause. Bill supporters said Congress intended ERISA to govern only disclosure and reporting requirements for apprenticeship programs, not training standards.

● **Liens for unpaid pensions.** Some states allowed workers to acquire liens on the properties of those employers who had not fully paid into pension plans that were administered by more than one company. Two state court decisions struck down these laws, again on ERISA pre-emption grounds.

Orrin G. Hatch of Utah and other Republican committee members expressed concern at the markup that HR 1036 would erode the uniform regulation in worker benefits law that ERISA provided. "You're going to cause a furor all over this country," he said. Hatch also argued that without ERISA pre-emption, some states would set apprenticeship standards that would allow only union workers to receive job training. "We need greater flexibility, not less, in apprenticeship programs," he said, noting that this was especially true for women and minorities.

Taxes on Pension Benefits

The House on Oct. 3 passed by voice vote a bill (HR 546) to restrict a state's right to tax the pension benefits of former residents, but the measure stalled in the Senate during the final days of the 103rd Congress. Sen. Malcolm Wallop, R-Wyo., put a hold on the bill, arguing that it did not go enough in relieving the burden of "double taxation" on senior citizens. Wallop said that Congress should prohibit all state taxation of non-resident income.

The House-passed bill barred states from taxing non-resi-

dents whose annual pension payments totaled $30,000 or less. Any pension income in excess of $30,000 remained taxable. The $30,000 threshold was to increase annually to reflect inflation. The tax limitation applied to all pension payments received after Dec. 31, 1994.

Much of the debate on HR 546 centered on California, which aggressively pursued retirees who had moved, usually to nearby states such as Washington and Nevada that imposed no personal income taxes. Nine other states — Connecticut, Idaho, Iowa, Kansas, Massachusetts, New Hampshire, New York, Oregon and Tennessee — also imposed some sort of "source tax" on the pension benefits of former residents.

Like California, these states pointed out that while individuals were still working, the state deferred taxation of the interest earned in their pension accounts in an effort to encourage them to participate in a pension plan. Because that buildup was never taxed, these states argued, they had a right to collect once the workers retired and began drawing their pensions — regardless of where the retirees lived.

Retirees, on the other hand, said it was unjust for a state to tax the income of non-residents who could not vote in that state or benefit from any of the services financed by their taxes. "The American Revolution was fought some 200 years ago in large part to end the injustice of taxation without representation," said sponsor Jolene Unsoeld, D-Wash.

The House Judiciary Committee approved the bill by voice vote Sept. 29 (H Rept 103-776); the Economic and Commercial Law Subcommittee had approved it the previous day. ■

Retraining Initiative Stalls

A House Ways and Means subcommittee in July initiated action on one of President Clinton's human investment initiatives — a plan to consolidate six federal programs for laid-off workers into a single program to provide access to career counseling, training, unemployment insurance and other services. But the bill advanced no further because the Ways and Means Committee spent much of the remainder of the year grappling with health care reform.

The Subcommittee on Human Resources approved the financial components of the Re-employment Act of 1994 (HR 4040), which proposed to consolidate six federal retraining programs and create a network of one-stop career centers.

The six programs to be reorganized served dislocated workers, including people who lost their jobs because of defense cuts and military base closures, clean air legislation and the North American Free Trade Agreement. The initiative aimed to give access to retraining services and benefits to workers who were permanently laid off and had been unemployed at least six months.

At the markup, both Democrats and Republicans said uncertain economic conditions had made the issue a timely one. "The needs are very deep," said Sander M. Levin, D-Mich., noting that chronic unemployment was beginning to outpace cyclic worker displacement. Fred Grandy, R-Iowa, agreed. "I think this is a small, good first step."

But some Republicans expressed doubts about how to pay for the new program. Other members said the bill did not go far enough to consolidate the 150 job training programs already operated by the Labor Department.

Members offered no amendments, and Ways and Means Democrats said they hoped their portion of the bill could

be approved by the full committee and ready for the House floor by mid-August.

The programmatic, or non-tax, aspects of the bill were under the jurisdiction of the Education and Labor Committee. Chairman William D. Ford, D-Mich., held hearings on his version of the bill (HR 4050) but did not mark it up.

Under the retraining program outlined in both bills, dislocated workers who were at their last jobs for at least one year but less than three could receive up to six months of retraining benefits while retooling their skills in a government-approved job training program. Workers who had worked for the same employer for three years or more would be eligible for up to a year of retraining.

The retraining benefits, estimated to cost $2 billion a year for five years, were to be paid as an entitlement to all qualified applicants.

Money to pay for the program was to come from several sources: repeal of the Trade Adjustment Assistance training program for workers displaced by U.S. foreign trade policies; tax revenues resulting from the permanent extension of the 0.2 percent federal employer payroll tax that paid for unemployment benefits under existing law; and a federal income tax on unemployment benefits. The bill also proposed to authorize $250 million annually for fiscal years 1995 to 1999 for states to establish one-stop career centers, where temporarily displaced workers could file claims for unemployment compensation and permanently dislocated workers could file for retraining benefits.

Rick Santorum of Pennsylvania, the subcommittee's ranking Republican, said he feared the program could become what he called a budget-busting entitlement similar to Medicare, the government's health insurance program for the elderly and disabled. ∎

Other Labor-Related Legislation

Lawmakers took up a variety of additional labor bills, including proposals to raise the threshold for government contracts subject to the Davis-Bacon Act and to facilitate disability payments to sufferers of black lung disease.

Davis-Bacon Revision

On a strict 28-14 party-line vote, the House Education and Labor Committee on April 13 approved revisions to a Depression-era labor law that set standards for wages on federal contracts. However, the measure went no further in the 103rd Congress.

The bill (HR 1231 — H Rept 103-856), sponsored by Austin J. Murphy, D-Pa., proposed to raise the threshold for projects covered by the 1931 Davis-Bacon Act from $2,000 to $100,000 — $15,000 for repairs or changes to existing structures. Under Davis-Bacon, contractors on federally financed public works projects were required to pay workers the prevailing local wage rate, usually a union rate. The bill included provisions to expand the law to cover independent contractors, off-site suppliers and manufacturers.

The Davis-Bacon Act was intended to prevent big construction companies from hiring low-wage, itinerant workers and underbidding local companies for coveted government contracts during the Depression.

Republicans had long argued that the law should be rescinded. They said it was the product of another era when there were few federal labor standards. Now, they said, it

unnecessarily drove up construction costs because the prevailing local wage rate was usually a union rate that was higher than non-union private sector pay rates.

Democrats who backed Davis-Bacon had tried repeatedly but unsuccessfully to update the law by offering higher thresholds. Murphy argued that raising the threshold to $100,000 would ease paperwork and other requirements for small public works projects.

At the committee markup, several GOP amendments failed, 14-28, including proposals by:
● Cass Ballenger, R-N.C., to raise the threshold to $1 million.
● John A. Boehner, R-Ohio, to exclude from coverage projects in areas with high unemployment rates.
● Harris W. Fawell, R-Ill., to limit coverage to laborers and mechanics on the site of the work. Fawell said Murphy's proposal would create new difficulties for small businesses because the prevailing wage rate requirement would be expanded to cover off-site contractors and suppliers as well as on-site workers.

The Education and Labor Subcommittee on Labor Standards had approved the bill, 6-3, on Nov. 16, 1993. (1993 Almanac, p. 399)

Black Lung Disease

The House passed a bill May 19 aimed at making it easier for coal miners suffering from black lung disease to receive federally mandated disability benefits. The vote was 252-166. The bill (HR 2108) went no further. (Vote 186, p. 56-H)

The measure, sponsored by Austin J. Murphy, D-Pa., would have amended the Black Lung Act of 1969, which required coal companies to compensate former employees who suffered from the illness.

Under existing law, if a dispute arose, the burden of proof was on workers to establish that they had acquired black lung while working in a coal mine. Companies and miners were both allowed to present unlimited evidence to support their positions.

Bill supporters contended that the system inherently favored coal companies, which had more resources to devote to building cases against black lung claimants.

The House-passed bill allowed miners to present three medical exams as evidence at claims hearings. Opponents, however, were to be allowed to present only one exam.

During a five-hour debate, Harris W. Fawell, R-Ill., tried to eliminate the provision on medical evidence, calling it unconstitutional and saying it would bias cases in favor of claimants. His amendment was rejected, 181-238. (Vote 182, p. 56-H)

John A. Boehner, R-Ohio, offered an amendment to require the Black Lung Disability Trust Fund, the account from which benefits were paid, to bring its indebtedness down to $600 million before new benefits could be disbursed. Estimates at the time placed the trust fund somewhere between $3.4 billion and $4 billion in debt. The amendment failed, 189-234. (Vote 181, p. 56-H)

The House also rejected an amendment by Dick Armey, R-Texas, to eliminate a provision to award attorney's fees to claimants at each stage in the process. The vote was 176-250. (Vote 183, p. 56-H)

The House Education and Labor Committee had approved the bill April 13 over Republican objections (H Rept 103-507). The party-line vote was 28-14. The panel's Labor Standards Subcommittee had approved it Sept. 21, 1993. At the time, the Congressional Budget Office estimated that the bill would cost the federal government $185.5 million over five years.

Republicans said the coal industry and taxpayers would bear the cost of paying for new benefits. *(1993 Almanac, p. 399)*

Boxing Commission

Professional boxing was to be subject to federal regulation under the terms of two bills approved July 26 by a House Education and Labor panel. The Subcommittee on Labor Standards, Occupational Health and Safety approved both measures (HR 2607, HR 3311) on a single 6-0 vote after little discussion. The bills went no further.

"What is needed in the boxing world . . . is some board to monitor the health conditions of the boxers," said subcommittee Chairman Austin J. Murphy, D-Pa.

Professional boxing was regulated at the time on a state-by-state basis. Critics said the state regulations varied widely, and boxing officials avoided scheduling matches in states such as New York that had stringent rules on issues such as how soon a boxer could fight again after being knocked out.

Most state regulations did little to protect the health of boxers, said Major R. Owens, D-N.Y., sponsor of HR 3311. Bill Richardson, D-N.M., sponsored HR 2607. Owens said that few who participated in the sport were provided with health insurance benefits, pensions or compensation for injuries. "Professional boxing is a great opportunity industry for young, black males," he said, "and they get exploited terribly."

The two bills approved by the Labor Standards Subcommittee sought to establish a Professional Boxing Corporation to curtail what critics called the exploitation of boxers and favoritism in the judging of matches.

The bills were virtually identical, and Owens said he expected minor differences to be resolved easily before full committee consideration.

Both measures required boxers, judges and referees to obtain licenses annually from the new boxing corporation. Boxers were to be required to show that they were physically and mentally fit to get a license. Promoters, matchmakers, trainers and others associated with the sport would have to register with the panel.

Under Richardson's bill, the president was to nominate a "boxing czar" to head the corporation, subject to Senate confirmation. The czar was to name a seven-member boxing advisory board to advise the corporation on how to enforce minimum health and safety standards for boxers.

Owens' bill went further, granting the corporation authority to regulate the telecasting of boxing matches as well as matters related to boxers' safety.

Workplace Technology

The Senate Labor and Human Resources Committee approved two measures Feb. 23 designed to promote the use of technology in schools and businesses. The bills went no further, although parts of them were included in other measures.

The school measure (S 1040 — S Rept 103-234), introduced by Jeff Bingaman, D-N.M., authorized $352.5 million in fiscal 1995 to help upgrade the nation's classrooms with new technologies such as computer networks. It was approved by voice vote. *(School technology, p. 401)*

The business measure (S 1020 — S Rept 103-401), approved 17-0, authorized the Labor Department to award grants, at unspecified sums, to nonprofit groups that aided discussions between workers and managers about the development of advanced workplace technologies. Such groups included labor unions, educational institutions and industrial resource centers.

Nancy Landon Kassebaum, R-Kan., offered an amendment to allow employers to discuss workplace issues with employees apart from collective bargaining agreements. Committee Chairman Edward M. Kennedy, D-Mass., and bill sponsor Harris Wofford, D-Pa., opposed the amendment, which was defeated 7-10.

Provisions of S 1020 later were included in the Senate's version of the National Competitiveness Act (HR 820), which stalled in conference. *(Competitiveness, p. 221)*

Some provisions were also included in the elementary and secondary school reauthorization bill (HR 6 — PL 103-382). As cleared, that bill authorized unspecified grants in fiscal 1995 to local nonprofit organizations to improve workers' ability to incorporate advanced technologies into the workplace. *(Elementary and secondary education, p. 383)*

Worker Monitoring

A House Education and Labor subcommittee approved a bill (HR 1900) on Feb. 23 that aimed to protect workers from technology that could infringe on their rights. The vote in the Labor-Management Relations Subcommittee was 17-8. The measure went no further.

The bill, sponsored by Subcommittee Chairman Pat Williams, D-Mont., sought to prevent employer abuse of electronic monitoring by computer, telephone, radio or other means. Some Republicans who opposed the bill said it would cut too broadly into employers' rights to manage their businesses.

Under the bill, employers were to be required to notify workers before electronically monitoring their workplace activities. Workers would have the right to know how the monitoring would be conducted. Monitoring included such practices as intercepting an employee's non-work-related communications and checking what was on an employee's computer screen to determine the type of work being done.

The subcommittee rejected, 9-15, an amendment by Harris W. Fawell, R-Ill, to eliminate an employee's right to sue for compensatory and punitive damages if an employer violated restrictions on electronic monitoring.

The panel also rejected, by voice vote, an amendment by Peter Hoekstra, R-Mich., to eliminate the requirement that employers tell prospective employees at their initial job interview of electronic monitoring.

Railroad Workers

The House on Aug. 16 passed by voice vote a bill to modify the unemployment insurance system for railroad workers. The measure, sponsored by Al Swift, D-Wash., went no further.

The bill (HR 4868) aimed to reduce from two weeks to seven days the time a temporarily disabled or displaced rail worker had to wait before receiving unemployment benefits.

Under existing law, such workers received maximum daily benefits of $36. Under the proposed change, the rate was to rise to $40 a day, and the limit on extended benefits was to be reduced from 130 days to 65 days.

The measure was endorsed by rail management and labor organizations. Proponents said it would bring the railroad unemployment system in line with the unemployment system of most states.

The House Energy and Commerce Subcommittee on Transportation and Hazardous Materials approved the bill Aug. 4, and the full committee approved it by voice vote Aug. 5 (H Rept 103-693). ∎

Progress Halts on Housing Bill

The House passed a comprehensive reauthorization of federal housing programs (HR 3838) on July 22, but the legislation died in the Senate in the crush of end-of-session business. The companion Senate bill (S 2281) won approval from the Banking Committee but never made it to the floor.

The House gave last-minute approval to a leaner housing bill (HR 5245) that would have reauthorized a limited number of housing programs through fiscal 1995, but the Senate did not act on that bill either. While authorization for most housing programs expired at the end of fiscal 1994, all but a few continued to operate based on their fiscal 1995 appropriations. *(Box, p. 410)*

The two chambers took similar approaches to the broader, two-year reauthorization bill, which covered most housing programs under the Department of Housing and Urban Development (HUD) and the Farmers Home Administration. Both bills sought to give local authorities more say over how to spend money to assist the homeless and more flexibility when replacing public housing units in line to be demolished or sold. The bills also contained provisions to lower rents for working families in public housing and to combat crime in and around public housing developments.

But the two chambers broke ranks over relaxing restrictions on Federal Housing Administration (FHA) insurance for single-family home loans.

The FHA program was designed to encourage private sector lenders to make loans to first-time buyers and others who did not have the money for conventional down payments. It did so by insuring the lenders against the risk of mortgage default.

The House appeared more willing than the Senate to embrace a Clinton administration plan to allow the FHA to insure higher mortgages on single-family homes. Under existing law, the basic limit was $67,500 — $151,725 in high-cost areas. The administration suggested raising the limits to reflect existing home prices and to stimulate more home ownership. Opponents said that would plunge the FHA too deeply into the middle-income housing market, pulling resources from lower-end buyers and diminishing business for private mortgage insurance companies.

In the absence of action on the housing bill, the fiscal 1995 VA-HUD appropriations bill (HR 4624 — PL 103-327) raised the basic limit to $152,363. Both limits were to be indexed in future years to changes in the confirming loan limit for government-sponsored enterprises. *(Appropriations, p. 541)*

Associations representing builders, mortgage bankers and real estate agents supported the higher FHA limits, anticipating that they would stimulate housing activity. But the effort was opposed by private mortgage insurance companies, which viewed it as government intrusion into their business, and by some advocates of low-income families, who feared that it would pull resources from lower-end buyers. Both sides lobbied Congress hard.

Bill Provisions

Although some differences in detail remained, the House and Senate bills had similar thrusts.

> ## BOXSCORE
>
> **Housing Reauthorization — HR 3838, S 2281** (S 2049). The bills contained a two-year extension for housing programs, more flexibility for local housing authorities and new anti-crime provisions.
>
> **Report:** H Rept 103-607, S Rept 103-307.
>
> ### KEY ACTION
>
> **June 21 — Senate** committee approved S 2281 (S 2049), 15-3.
>
> **July 22 — House** passed HR 3838, 345-36.

● **Rent ceilings.** Under existing law, public housing authorities were required to charge most residents rent equal to 30 percent of their adjusted incomes. Thus the rents of working families increased as their incomes rose — with the result that in many public housing projects, few families with stable jobs remained. Both the House and Senate bills excluded part of tenants' earned incomes from rent calculations, phased in rent increases and gave local authorities more flexibility to set ceiling rents.

● **Modernization funds.** The bills gave localities more flexibility in using federal public housing funds. For example, modernization funds, which under existing law could be used only to renovate public housing, could be used to build or replace old units.

● **One-for-one replacement.** A provision in the Housing and Community Development Act of 1987 (PL 100-242) essentially required authorities to replace, one for one, any housing unit that was demolished. The bills allowed local authorities to replace obsolete units with different forms of subsidized private housing, instead of building new public housing units.

● **Direct loans.** The Senate bill contained a provision to allow local authorities to finance the replacement of obsolete housing by borrowing against future years' federal modernization grants.

● **Regulatory relief.** Both bills sought to ease the regulatory burden on some of the best-performing public housing authorities, giving them added flexibility.

● **Crime prevention.** The Drug Elimination Grant Program, which provided money to public housing agencies to fight drug-related crime, was to be broadened into a new effort, called Community Partnerships Against Crime.

● **Homeless assistance.** Six homeless programs authorized by the Stewart B. McKinney Homeless Assistance Act of 1987 (PL 100-77) were to be combined into a block grant.

● **Section 8.** The two forms of subsidized private housing under the Section 8 program, certificates and vouchers, were to be merged into a single rental assistance program.

Background

Created in 1937 by the U.S. Housing Act, public housing was a joint venture by federal and local governments to provide affordable housing to low-income families.

For a dozen years, federal housing policy was an ideological battleground between congressional Democrats who wanted the government to provide more low-income housing and Republicans who wanted to get government out of the housing business. Democrats concentrated on enacting legislation that tied the hands of federal bureaucrats who, under President Ronald Reagan, had been permitting housing authorities to tear down public housing without any plans for replacing it. But the restrictions, coupled with a lack of funds, often meant that dilapidated projects were kept in place.

The political dynamics changed dramatically in 1994, with both parties embracing legislation to give state and local officials more control over housing initiatives.

Democrats said they were willing to loosen the federal requirements because they were no longer battling a Republican administration to preserve the programs. They also attributed some of the shortcomings of their previous efforts to a lack of funding. But implicit in the housing bill was a recognition that the quality of public housing had fallen short.

The Clinton administration opened the debate on federal housing programs April 20, when HUD Secretary Henry G. Cisneros unveiled a series of initiatives to direct more money into assistance for the homeless, subsidized private housing and fair housing, while decreasing funds for public housing. Cisneros recommended cuts in public housing operating subsidies and modernization accounts; the HOME program, which provided matching grants to states and localities for affordable housing; and the Section 202 program, which provided grants to groups that developed housing for the elderly.

Cisneros also proposed giving public housing authorities the flexibility to use modernization funds to demolish and replace blighted public housing.

House Committee

Members of the House Banking, Finance and Urban Affairs Subcommittee on Housing and Community Development approved their version of the reauthorization bill (HR 3838) by voice vote May 26.

The subcommittee-approved bill, sponsored by Henry B. Gonzalez, D-Texas, authorized $31.3 billion for HUD and Farmers Home Administration (FmHA) programs in fiscal 1995 and $33.7 billion in fiscal 1996. The bill relaxed the rent ceilings on working families who lived in public housing and gave local housing authorities more flexibility in using federal funds. It also merged the two forms of Section 8 subsidized private housing.

The most heated exchanges during the markup, however, concerned not housing but crime. The panel approved, 18-13, an amendment offered by Charles E. Schumer, D-N.Y., to pre-empt state and local laws and allow local housing authorities to obtain information about an applicant's or tenant's criminal convictions. Amendment supporters argued that law-abiding citizens in crime-ridden public housing buildings deserved more protection. Opponents said the amendment was too broad and objected to creating separate rules for low-income residents of public housing.

A second significant amendment was offered by Thomas M. Barrett, D-Wis., to pre-empt state and local law and allow public housing residents to ban guns on the premises. Opponents again argued that the amendment amounted to a double standard. But supporters stressed the need to pay special attention to crime in public housing developments.

Barrett's amendment initially lost on a 15-15 vote. But shortly before the subcommittee approved the bill, Albert R. Wynn, D-Md., requested that the amendment be reconsidered and switched his vote from opposition to support. The amendment then passed, 16-14. Wynn said he had been on the House floor during the initial vote and had erroneously been recorded as giving a no vote by proxy.

Members also debated how to apportion anti-crime funds among local housing authorities. The Clinton administration had requested $265 million in fiscal 1995 for a new program called Community Partnerships Against Crime (COMPAC). The bill provided for 85 percent of the funds to be distributed to public housing authorities that had 250 units or more.

Luis V. Gutierrez, D-Ill., offered an amendment to require that 75 percent of the funds be distributed to local authorities with 1,250 units or more. Gutierrez said his formula reflected the fact that more crimes occurred in developments in larger

cities. However, Bruce F. Vento, D-Minn., said that the crime statistics were not necessarily accurate and that the formula should reflect the dispersal of public housing units. Most members who did not represent big cities opposed the amendment, and it failed, 13-18.

Full Committee

After 12 hours of debate, most of it again devoted to how the government should attack crime in public housing, weary members of the full Banking Committee approved the bill by voice vote June 16. The committee's bill (H Rept 103-607) authorized $31.2 billion in fiscal 1995 and $33.6 billion in fiscal 1996.

The committee retained Schumer's amendment, adopted in subcommittee, to help local authorities obtain information about an applicant's or tenant's criminal convictions.

The provision continued to anger most black and Hispanic members, however, who complained that it singled out public housing residents for special treatment. "I think we ought to go ahead to just order that public housing tenants be branded," said Gonzalez sarcastically. Schumer tried to dampen the opposition by offering an amendment to limit records searches to 10 years and provide penalties for unauthorized disclosure of the information. But opponents called the provision offensive and forced a roll call vote; the panel then voted 33-15 to adopt Schumer's modified proposal. Most Democrats, including all seven black members of the committee, voted to strike the provision, but they were defeated, 21-29.

The committee voted 28-21 to strike the subcommittee provision allowing tenants to ban guns in their developments. Craig Thomas, R-Wyo., who joined with four other members in offering the change, called the gun ban "a very poor solution to a very real problem" because criminals would continue to get guns. Supporters countered that public housing residents ought to have the same right as those who lived in condominiums, apartments and nursing homes and were able to ban guns from their buildings. But because the proposal contained elements of gun control, a majority of Republicans joined with some liberals to overturn it.

With little discussion and by voice vote, the committee also approved an amendment to provide waivers to the so-called one-for-one replacement rule. The amendment responded to a situation in which many decrepit public housing buildings remained standing because authorities could not afford replacements or were unable to find locations for new units. *(1987 Almanac, p. 682)*

Seeking flexibility in another area, the committee voted to consolidate several housing programs under the 1987 Stewart B. McKinney Homeless Assistance Act into a new grant program. The amendment, offered by Vento, was aimed at giving states, localities and nonprofit agencies more latitude in combating homelessness, beginning in fiscal 1996. *(1987 Almanac, p. 506)*

The committee bill authorized $635 million in fiscal 1995 for homeless grants under the existing system and $786.6 million in fiscal 1996 for the consolidated program. The McKinney programs were also included in a free-standing bill (HR 4578), which was approved June 15 by the House Banking Committee but went no further.

The committee also approved a series of amendments designed to boost FHA activity, raising the amounts that could be insured under the FHA's single-family loan program. The committee voted 37-13 in favor of an amendment by Vento to raise the FHA's basic limit on mortgages to $101,575. That change came after the panel agreed by voice vote to an amendment by Herb Klein, D-N.J., to raise the high-cost limit to $172,675, a figure he said better reflected the costs of mod-

Leaner Housing Bill Dies

When it seemed unlikely that Congress would clear a comprehensive reauthorization of federal housing programs, supporters tried but failed to pass a leaner bill that would have reauthorized some federal housing programs. The House passed the stripped-down version, but it died in the Senate.

The measure (HR 5245), sponsored by House Banking Committee Chairman Henry B. Gonzalez, D-Texas, would have authorized the Farmers Home Administration (FmHA) to issue loans to individuals, companies or Indian tribes to build or renovate rural rental housing. It also would have authorized the Department of Housing and Urban Development to extend certain low-income subsidized housing contracts with apartment owners.

The bill included some provisions that originally were in the comprehensive bill (HR 3838) to revise and reauthorize the nation's housing laws through fiscal 1996. That bill died in the Senate. *(Housing, p. 408)*

The bill was introduced Oct. 7, and the Banking Committee sent it directly to the House floor without considering it. The House passed the bill Oct. 7 by voice vote.

est houses in relatively expensive areas such as northern New Jersey.

In addition, the bill permitted the FHA to form partnerships with state housing finance agencies to insure mortgages of up to $203,150 in high-cost areas. Barrett warned that this could be risky for government agencies at both the federal and state level. The committee adopted, 27-21, a Barrett amendment to restrict the portion of the mortgage that FHA could insure in this arrangement to 35 percent of the principal.

Maxine Waters, D-Calif., proposed a requirement that a majority of each housing board be composed of residents of public housing. After a flurry of objections, she accepted a compromise that reduced the requirement to a quarter of the board; the amendment was approved by voice vote.

The committee also gave voice vote approval to an amendment by Rod Grams, R-Minn., to allow housing authorities to speed up the process of removing tenants whose activities threatened other tenants or employees. Existing law allowed such procedures only for criminal activity.

House Floor

The House passed the wide-ranging housing reauthorization bill July 22 by a vote of 345-36. *(Vote 349, p. 106-H)*

The main controversy came over an amendment by Jay C. Kim, R-Calif., to prohibit illegal aliens from receiving aid under the McKinney Act for more than seven days. The proposal was part of an ongoing effort to restrict federal aid to illegal aliens. Kim argued that it was important "to put Americans' needs first."

Democrats sharply criticized Kim, saying it was hardhearted as well as overly bureaucratic to insist that people made homeless by the January earthquake in the Los Angeles areas produce proof of citizenship to get help.

Marge Roukema, R-N.J., ranking Republican on the Housing Subcommittee, amended Kim's proposal so that it did not apply to any presidentially declared disaster. Her modification was adopted by a standing vote of 235-0 before Kim's amend-

ment was approved 220-176. *(Vote 348, p. 106-H)*

Near the end of the debate, Jose E. Serrano, D-N.Y., offered an amendment that would have blocked Kim's provision unless federal funds were provided to enable states, localities and other agencies to determine who would be entitled to the aid. Roukema countered by amending Serrano's proposal to authorize whatever funds were necessary to carry out the provisions. Both members' proposals were approved by voice vote.

Members adopted by voice vote another amendment, offered by Peter I. Blute, R-Mass., to generally prohibit non-elderly people with a history of drug or alcohol abuse from living in subsidized housing designated primarily for the elderly. In addition, non-elderly applicants for such housing were to be required to sign a statement that no one would live in the unit who "uses (or has a history of use of) alcohol" or drugs.

Senate Action

The Senate Banking Committee approved a companion housing reauthorization bill (S 2049) with little debate June 21; the vote was 15-3. The votes against the bill came from Republicans Lauch Faircloth of North Carolina, Phil Gramm of Texas and Connie Mack of Florida. The committee reported the measure as a clean bill (S 2281 — S Rept 103-307).

The committee took a similar approach to that of the House in reauthorizing federal housing programs, although it disagreed over how big a loan the FHA should be able to insure for a single-family house. As approved by the committee, the Senate bill raised the FHA's basic limit on mortgages from $67,500 to $77,500 and left unchanged the $151,725 limit in high-cost areas. However, the bill indexed the high-cost limit to annual percentage changes in the conforming loan limit for government-sponsored enterprises.

The committee bill authorized $28.1 billion for federal housing programs in fiscal 1995 and $39.1 billion in fiscal 1996. Like the House bill, S 2049 sought to give federal and local officials more flexibility in using federal funds.

Like HR 3838, the bill consolidated several programs under the Stewart B. McKinney Act into a new grant program, and it merged the Section 8 certificate and voucher programs into a single rental assistance program.

The only significant amendment considered by the Senate panel was one by Faircloth to require most public housing residents to perform public service tasks in and around their buildings for 10 hours a month. It was defeated on an 8-10 party-line vote.

The Senate bill allowed local housing authorities to obtain a record of an applicant's or tenant's criminal conviction. Without discussion, however, the Senate committee struck a provision that would have ensured that tenants could ban guns in their developments.

Unlike HR 3838, the Senate bill permitted public housing authorities to finance the replacement of obsolete public housing developments.

Although there was unusually widespread agreement among Democrats and Republicans (as well as between the chambers) on the legislation, Senate proponents were unable to schedule floor time to consider S 2281. Part of the problem was the fact that senators were threatening to raise a number of contentious issues, including the FHA mortgage limits; a dispute involving the First Amendment rights of critics who opposed subsidized housing developments; a House amendment prohibiting non-elderly alcoholics and drug abusers in subsidized elderly housing; and a possible Senate amendment requiring public housing residents to perform public service tasks. ∎

HUD Gains Greater Leeway On Property Disposals

A bill cleared in March (S 1299) gave the Department of Housing and Urban Development (HUD) greater flexibility in disposing of apartment buildings that had fallen into government possession through foreclosure. President Clinton signed the bill into law April 11 (PL 103-233).

HUD had inherited the buildings when private developers defaulted on mortgages that had been insured by the Federal Housing Administration (FHA) as part of a program to expand the supply of rental housing for low- and moderate-income families.

To ensure that low-income housing stock was preserved and even enlarged, existing law required HUD to provide costly federal housing subsidies when it sold the properties. But HUD had received much less from Congress than it needed to offer those subsidies. As a result, the department had been unable to sell many of the properties, and its inventory was growing rapidly.

S 1299 grandfathered all tenants who had been receiving subsidies when the owner of the building defaulted, but HUD was no longer required to provide subsidies to tenants who had not previously received them. To protect low-income families in units that were not receiving federal subsidies, the bill stipulated that rents could be frozen for two years as a condition of the building sale.

The bill permitted the use of federal housing subsidies to help build replacement units. It also encouraged states and localities to make more use of the HOME Investments Partnerships Act, a block grant for housing needs. The bill removed a restriction that had made the program available only to first-time home buyers. It also reduced from 30 percent to 25 percent the amount that states and localities had to contribute to new housing construction activities under the HOME program.

The bill also expanded the use of a low-interest loan guarantee program designed to help communities spur economic development.

Legislative Action

The Senate first passed S 1299 (S Rept 103-174) by voice vote Nov. 19, 1993. The House included a different version of the measure in a bill (HR 3400) to cut federal spending and streamline government operations; while HR 3400 passed the House on Nov. 22, it never reached the Senate floor. *(1993 Almanac, p. 424)*

The House took up a modified version of the 1993 provisions, passing a new bill (HR 4067) March 22 by a vote of 413-9. The House then inserted the text of its bill into S 1299 and passed the Senate measure by voice vote. The House version did not contain several provisions unrelated to the disposal of FHA buildings, including rent reforms for public housing and a crime prevention initiative. *(Vote 81, p. 26-H)*

The Senate agreed to the House-passed version March 25, clearing the bill by voice vote. ∎

Bill for Homeless Dies in House

The Senate approved a bill (S 2218) reauthorizing a program that provided emergency food and shelter to the homeless, but the legislation died in the House. The Senate bill, sponsored by John Glenn, D-Ohio, authorized $187.6 million in each of fiscal years 1995 and 1996.

The Senate Governmental Affairs Committee approved the legislation by voice vote Aug. 2. The full Senate passed the measure by voice vote Aug. 10. The program was created in 1987 as part of the Stewart B. McKinney Homeless Assistance Act (PL 100-77).

The House tried to extend the program as part of a comprehensive reauthorization of federal housing programs (HR 3838), but that legislation never made it to the Senate floor. *(Housing, p. 408)*

The fiscal 1995 appropriations bill for Veterans Affairs, HUD and independent agencies (HR 4624 — PL 103-327) kept the program running through fiscal 1995. President Clinton had asked that the program, which was administered by the Federal Emergency Management Agency (FEMA), be transferred to the Department of Housing and Urban Development, but the appropriations bill kept it in FEMA. ∎

'93 Floods Prompt Revamping Of Insurance Program

Congress cleared legislation to shore up the nation's federal flood insurance program. The measure was enacted as part of an unrelated bill aimed at encouraging community development banks, which President Clinton signed into law Sept. 23 (HR 3474 — PL 103-325).

Part of the push to reform the program stemmed from the record floods that devastated the Midwest in 1993. Although all owners of homes in a flood plain were legally required to buy flood insurance, many allowed their policies — underwritten by the federal flood insurance fund — to lapse. As a result, only about 10 percent of those affected had flood insurance. Most residents whose homes were destroyed by the rains and rivers had to rely on federal disaster aid to help rebuild.

The federal program was established in 1968, largely because private insurers found it too risky to provide flood insurance. Although the fund was set up to be self-sustaining, shortfalls had arisen since the beginning; in each case, the Treasury had made good on all claims.

The program suffered from two major problems: Many homeowners did not regularly buy flood insurance policies, and those who did tended to live in the most flood-prone areas.

The bill required that mortgage lenders place in escrow flood-insurance premium payments for people living in flood-prone areas. It also authorized lenders to purchase flood insurance for borrowers who refused to do so as required by law. The bill established a mitigation fund, financed by the flood insurance program, to help protect communities and homeowners against flood risks. The Federal Emergency Management Agency was also directed to study the problem as it pertained to coastal and river areas.

Legislative Action

The House Banking Committee approved its version of the flood insurance bill (HR 3191 — H Rept 103-414) on Nov. 4, 1993, but the measure did not reach the floor. A similar bill (S 1405) stalled in the Senate Banking Committee, where Alfonse M. D'Amato of New York and other Republicans raised objections. *(1993 Almanac, p. 425)*

On March 17, 1994, the Senate adopted an amendment, offered by John Kerry, D-Mass., that attached the bulk of S 1405 to the community development bank bill. The Senate approved the amendment by voice vote and passed the bill by voice vote later the same day.

The House passed HR 3191 on May 3 by a vote of 335-60.

The House version was considered somewhat tougher than the Senate's. Among other things, it contained a surcharge on policy buyers to create the mitigation fund; the Senate bill authorized $45 million in spending from the insurance program for mitigation efforts through fiscal 1996. *(Vote 149, p. 46-H)*

Before the floor debate, bill sponsor Joseph P. Kennedy II, D-Mass., stripped out the most controversial provision — language that would have eliminated federally subsidized flood insurance for buildings located on land that eroded easily. The compromise mollified coastal lawmakers, who had argued that the insurance cutoff would hurt economic development in their areas. But the new version prompted criticism from members who argued that subsidizing insurance in those regions encouraged people to build in unwise locations.

Senate sponsors also removed language that would have eliminated flood insurance in areas in which a major flood or major erosion was expected every 30 or 60 years.

Conferees on the community banking bill agreed to incorporate the flood insurance reform in that legislation after working out differences between the House and Senate versions. The House adopted the conference report to HR 3474 on Aug. 4 by a vote of 410-12. The Senate cleared the bill by voice vote Aug. 9. *(Vote 375, p.112-H)* ∎

Bill Targets Persian Gulf Syndrome

Mindful of criticism that Congress did not move fast enough to help Vietnam veterans exposed to the herbicide Agent Orange, the Senate Oct. 8 cleared a bill authorizing the Department of Veterans Affairs (VA) to make disability payments to veterans suffering from so-called Persian Gulf syndrome. The House had passed the bill the previous day. It was signed by President Clinton on Nov. 2 (HR 5244 — PL 103-446).

Persian Gulf syndrome referred to a variety of unexplained ailments that affected more than 3,000 veterans of the 1991 war against Iraq.

VA Secretary Jesse Brown had insisted that he needed the legislation because existing law prohibited him from compensating veterans disabled by undiagnosed conditions such as Persian Gulf syndrome. Brown's position had strong support in the House, which moved quickly to authorize the compensation.

But the legislation was held up for a time in the Senate, where Veterans' Affairs Committee Chairman John D. Rockefeller IV, D-W.Va., and others said it was unnecessary. Rockefeller argued that Brown already had the authority to grant benefits and should do so. In the end though, the Senate largely acceded to the position held by Brown and the House.

HR 5244 gave the VA the authority to pay compensation to veterans who were at least 10 percent disabled. The Secretary of Veterans Affairs was given the power to decide how long the agency would pay compensation and by what date the first symptoms would have to appear for a veteran to be eligible.

It also authorized the VA to study the impact of Persian Gulf syndrome on the spouses and children of veterans who served in the 1991 war. In addition, the bill included a number of other, unrelated veterans provisions. *(Provisions, p. 413)*

Background

First noticed shortly after soldiers returned from the war against Iraq in 1991, Persian Gulf syndrome became a catchword for unexplained maladies afflicting thousands of veterans. Symptoms included nausea, hair loss, fatigue, rashes, and heart and respiratory problems.

BOXSCORE

Persian Gulf Syndrome Compensation — HR 5244 (HR 4386, S 2330). The bill authorized disability payments to veterans with Persian Gulf syndrome.

Reports: H Rept 103-669, S Rept 103-386.

KEY ACTION

Aug. 8 — House passed HR 4386 by voice vote.

Oct. 7 — House passed HR 5244 by voice vote.

Oct. 8 — Senate cleared HR 5244 by voice vote.

Nov. 2 — President signed HR 5244 — PL 103-446.

Researchers were unable to isolate a cause for the syndrome. But their work suggested a variety of sources that alone or in combination could have been responsible. The most frequently cited were exposure to oil fires in Kuwait, indigenous parasites, military vehicle paint and depleted uranium used to reinforce tank and artillery shells.

Some reports suggested that U.S. and other soldiers might have been exposed to Iraqi chemical and biological weapons. A Department of Defense study released June 23, 1994, found no such evidence of exposure for U.S. soldiers.

During the 1980s, Congress and the Reagan administration had declined to provide assistance to veterans exposed to Agent Orange until researchers concluded that it had, indeed, caused cancer and other diseases. Benefits were finally authorized in 1991 (PL 102-4). *(1991 Almanac, p. 320)*

Not waiting for researchers to pinpoint the causes of Persian Gulf syndrome, veterans' advocates on Capitol Hill won enactment in 1993 of legislation requiring the VA to provide medical treatment to veterans suffering from the syndrome (HR 2535 — PL 103-210). *(1993 Almanac, p. 416)*

The total number of soldiers and veterans suffering from Persian Gulf syndrome was not known. About 700,000 men and women served in the Persian Gulf region during the conflict. Of those, more than 300,000 had been discharged and were veterans by the summer of 1994.

In 1992, the VA created a registry to collect data and identify patterns among veterans who had been examined by the VA for medical conditions related to their service in the gulf war. Of 24,000 veterans examined by the summer of 1994, roughly 2,500 had unexplained illnesses that could have corresponded to Persian Gulf syndrome.

The Congressional Budget Office (CBO) estimated that about 4,000 gulf war veterans had or would have undiagnosed conditions that could be classified as Persian Gulf syndrome. But veterans' advocates in Congress argued that the CBO estimate was probably too low.

Compensation Rules

Existing law governing compensation stated that the United States would pay benefits to veterans for "a disability

Gulf Syndrome Bill Provisions

The following are the major provisions of HR 5244 — PL 103-446, a bill authorizing the Department of Veterans Affairs (VA) to provide disability benefits to veterans suffering from Persian Gulf syndrome. The bill contained a variety of other VA provisions unrelated to the ailment. As enacted, the measure:

● Gave the VA the authority to pay compensation to veterans who were at least 10 percent disabled. The Secretary of Veterans Affairs was given the power to decide how long the agency would pay compensation and by what date the first symptoms would have to appear for a veteran to be eligible.

● Authorized the VA to study the impact of Persian Gulf syndrome on the spouses and children of veterans who served in the 1991 war.

● Effectively exempted the Veterans Health Administration from all but 4,676 of the 21,000 job cuts that it otherwise would have had to make under Clinton's plan to "reinvent" the federal government. *(VHA exemption, p. 416)*

● Gradually raised the salaries of the 65 members of the Board of Veterans Appeals to match the level of pay received by administrative law judges.

In 1994, board members made an average of $20,000 a year less than administrative judges, who could earn a maximum of $108,000 annually. Yet the two jobs entailed similar duties. Provision supporters argued that board members would leave to become administrative judges unless their pay prospects improved.

The language had been part of S 2325, a bill to aid homeless veterans, which the Senate Veterans' Affairs Committee had approved Sept. 23. It also had been part of S 1927 (formerly HR 4088 — H Rept 103-668), which authorized a cost of living adjustment (COLA) for veterans benefits. *(Homeless vets, p. 417; COLA, p. 416)*

● Clarified that all veterans who participated in the atmospheric testing of a nuclear weapon by a foreign country were eligible to receive the same medical treatment and compensation from the VA that was offered to those who had been present at a nuclear test conducted by the United States.

● Granted eligibility for burial in a VA cemetery to veterans' spouses who died before the veteran. Eligibility was also given to spouses of deceased veterans who remarried. Previously, only spouses who survived the veteran and did not remarry could be buried in a veterans cemetery.

The House passed part of this provision as a separate bill (HR 3456) in November 1993. It died in the Senate. *(1993 Almanac, p. 420)*

● Established a Center for Women Veterans to coordinate women's programs at the VA and to inform women about available services and benefits. Women were expected to make up 11 percent of the veterans population by 2004.

This provision had passed the House June 13 as HR 3013 — H Rept 103-538.

● Expanded eligibility for VA-guaranteed home loans, allowing veterans to obtain mortgages without a down payment. The provision waived a requirement that reservists discharged for service-connected injuries serve at least six years to qualify for a loan. Spouses of reservists killed on active duty also qualified for these loans. This language had been part of HR 4724 — H Rept 103-629, which the House passed Aug. 1.

● Authorized the VA to establish up to eight facilities to provide comprehensive services to homeless veterans and to submit an annual report to Congress on services provided to homeless veterans.

● Expanded educational benefits by permanently reauthorizing a vocational flight training program available to all veterans. The language also increased, from $5 million to $6 million, the authorization for vocational counseling services that were contracted out by the VA.

These provisions had been part of a separate bill (HR 4768 — H Rept 103-631, Part 1) that the House passed Aug. 1.

● Required private companies with a federal contract valued at more than $10,000 to give hiring preference to any veteran who served in combat. The provision also required these contractors to inform veterans through local employment offices of job openings before announcing them to the general public.

resulting from personal injury suffered or disease contracted in the line of duty."

Brown argued that the law generally required the VA "to find evidence an illness was incurred or aggravated during service before . . . providing a monthly compensation check." The problem with Persian Gulf syndrome, he maintained, was that the government had not established a direct cause for it. He argued that the VA could not provide the disability benefits without special authority, such as that contained in the House bill.

House Action

On June 30, the House Veterans' Affairs Subcommittee on Compensation, Pension and Insurance approved HR 4386 by a vote of 10-0.

"We are committed to giving Persian Gulf veterans the benefit of the doubt as long as the search for answers continues," said subcommittee Chairman Jim Slattery, D-Kan.

The benefits in the bill, sponsored by Veterans' Affairs Committee Chairman G. V. "Sonny" Montgomery, D-Miss., were expanded after the subcommittee approved a substitute that incorporated provisions from a rival measure (HR 4540) introduced by committee member Lane Evans, D-Ill.

Evans and Montgomery had sparred publicly over the mer-

its of their respective bills at a June 9 hearing on Persian Gulf syndrome. Evans had criticized Montgomery's bill as inadequate, comparing the chairman's efforts to the past congressional foot-dragging over Agent Orange. An angry Montgomery responded that Evans had never consulted with him on the legislation. "He should have come to me and talked to me," Montgomery said.

Evans and Montgomery had been rivals ever since Evans came within four votes of defeating Montgomery for the committee chairmanship in 1992. But the two men agreed to patch up their differences over the issue, and the amended bill reflected their compromise.

For example, Montgomery's original bill would have allowed veterans to qualify for benefits only if their symptoms appeared within one year of leaving the Persian Gulf. Evans favored three years after a veteran's discharge from the military. They compromised on 1996.

Montgomery's bill had specified that benefits would end Oct. 1, 1997. Evans wanted benefits to continue — potentially indefinitely — until the VA proved that a veteran's symptoms were not a result of service in the gulf. They settled on the three-year extension after 1997 subject to the approval of the VA secretary.

The bill also authorized $5 million a year for three years, beginning in fiscal 1995, for medical research into the syn-

drome's causes and treatment.

The full committee approved the bill by voice vote July 21 (H Rept 103-669).

The committee first agreed by voice vote to an amendment offered by Joseph P. Kennedy II, D-Mass., to extend VA marriage and family counseling services to Persian Gulf veterans through 1998. These services had been provided to gulf war veterans, but they were set to expire Sept. 30, 1994.

On Aug. 8, with little fanfare or discussion, the House passed the measure by voice vote.

Senate Action

While veterans' advocates in the House moved quickly to push through a Persian Gulf compensation bill, their counterparts in the Senate were not eager to follow suit.

Throughout the debate, Rockefeller had maintained that the VA had the authority to compensate veterans with undiagnosed conditions — such as Persian Gulf syndrome — that occurred directly after military service. He said that the link between the illness and the time and place of military service was sufficient to warrant compensation.

But Brown and his House allies succeeded in pressuring Rockefeller and others on the Senate Veterans' Affairs Committee to accept the need for compensation legislation.

On July 27, Rockefeller took a step away from his original position, introducing a bill (S 2330) to codify his contention that the VA already had the authority to compensate veterans with undiagnosed conditions, such as Persian Gulf syndrome.

But prospects for a settlement looked dim as late as Sept.

14, when an angry Rockefeller told Brown at a hearing that he was "astonished and frankly disappointed that the VA has taken the position that it cannot compensate these veterans." Others, including Frank H. Murkowski of Alaska, the committee's ranking Republican, said Brown was hiding behind legal technicalities instead of fulfilling an obligation.

The feud ended shortly after that exchange when, at the urging of Tom Daschle, D-S.D., Rockefeller agreed to add language to his bill that specifically gave the VA the option to write regulations to compensate veterans disabled by Persian Gulf syndrome. He also added a provision to allow the VA secretary to propose that Congress compensate affected veterans if a similar situation arose in the future. The new language was much closer to that in the House-passed bill.

Compromise Bill Approved

On Sept. 23 the Senate Veterans' Affairs Committee approved the new version of S 2330 by voice vote (S Rept 103-386). The committee included an amendment by Daschle that required the VA to include in its research and data collection the family members of Persian Gulf veterans who exhibited symptoms associated with the syndrome.

In agreeing to the new bill, Rockefeller opened the door for staff negotiators to quickly forge the deal that allowed the compensation legislation to clear Congress. By early October, the negotiators had agreed to language that largely mirrored the House bill.

A clean bill was introduced (HR 5244) with the agreed upon provisions. The House passed it by voice vote Oct. 7. The Senate followed suit the next day. ∎

Women Lose in Fight Over Benefits

What began in 1993 as a legislative effort to expand medical services for women veterans ended in the last weeks of the 103rd Congress as little more than a routine construction authorization measure, after a fight over abortion led lawmakers to drop key women's health provisions.

The bill (HR 3313 — PL 103-452), which cleared Congress on Oct. 8 and was signed by President Clinton on Nov. 2, authorized $379.3 million for construction of VA medical facilities. It also slightly expanded medical treatment for women at the Department of Veterans Affairs (VA).

Both chambers had passed bills that authorized an array of new services for women veterans. But after months of negotiation, some members who opposed abortion remained concerned that the bill could be interpreted by the courts to allow a women veteran to terminate her pregnancy at a VA facility.

The fight over abortion finally led the bill's Senate sponsors to strip most of its provisions in the hope of moving a new, comprehensive bill in the 104th Congress. The scaled-back measure was then used largely as a vehicle for language authorizing the construction of major VA medical projects.

Women's Health Bill

The movement to expand women's health services began in 1993 in recognition of a new demographic reality: Steady increases in the number of women in the armed forces were certain to lead to steady increases in the number of women veterans.

On Nov. 16, 1993, the House passed a bill (HR 3313 — H Rept 103-349) to expand the number of services offered by the VA to the growing number of women veterans. *(1993 Almanac, p. 415)*

In the Senate, a related measure (S 1030 — S Rept 103-136) was approved by the Veterans' Affairs Committee on July 15, 1993. The Senate passed the bill by voice vote May 25, 1994. It passed HR 3313, amended, on June 8.

Both HR 3313 and S 1030 contained provisions to:
● Require the VA to offer pap smears, breast exams and mammography, and treatment for osteoporosis, sexually transmitted diseases, and conditions arising from menopause.
● Require counseling and other treatment for sexual trauma.
● Prohibit the VA from offering mammograms unless the test met federal quality standards.
● Ensure that the VA conducted medical research related to the health care needs of women veterans.

But there was one important difference: S 1030 authorized pre- and postnatal care and delivery services for women veterans. J. Roy Rowland, D-Ga., who had sponsored the House bill, had left maternity services out of his measure, arguing that adding them would be too costly.

The Senate bill also extended to 2003 the requirement that the VA provide priority treatment to veterans with illnesses related to exposure to Agent Orange or other herbicides used during the Vietnam War. The same extension for priority treatment applied to veterans suffering from Persian Gulf syndrome, ailments linked to service in the 1990-91 gulf war. *(Gulf syndrome, p. 412)*

Bill Scaled Back

Staff negotiators from the House and Senate Veterans' Affairs committees had been trying on and off since late 1993 to produce a bill satisfactory to both anti-abortion lawmakers and abortion rights supporters. As the 103rd Congress entered its final months, negotiations became more focused, driven by the realization that little time remained.

From the outset, the major problem had been the Senate language requiring the VA to provide pre- and postnatal care as well as delivery services.

Rep. Christopher H. Smith, R-N.J., an abortion opponent, argued that "pregnancy services" could be interpreted to allow abortions to be performed at VA facilities. Smith demanded that language be added prohibiting VA abortions. In the final days of the negotiations, he threatened to block the bill procedurally if the provision remained unchanged. But Democratic negotiators refused. They offered instead to remove any references in the bill they thought could be construed to allow abortions. Smith rejected this. The impasse finally led negotiators to remove pregnancy services from the bill.

A similar fate befell language that would have allowed the VA to participate in up to five state health care reform plans, restructuring its health system in each state to fit the local plan. This provision had passed the House by voice vote as a separate bill (HR 4013) on April 28; the Senate had passed its version of HR 4013, also by voice vote, on June 8. Bill supporters had planned to add this language to the women's health bill. Smith said this, too, could open the door to VA-provided abortions, and he requested that a prohibition be included in the bill. Again negotiators refused, and the language was removed.

This led Senate Democratic staff members to move to strip most of the other provisions in the bill even though no one had objected to them.

House Democratic members and staff favored retaining these non-controversial provisions, such as the language requiring the VA to offer pap smears, mammograms and treatment for osteoporosis. But Senate Democrats decided that removing the pregnancy care and state pilot project provisions had irrevocably damaged the legislation for the year. They agreed only to leave in language pertaining to sexual trauma and a number of other small provisions, with an eye toward reintroducing a comprehensive women's health bill early in 1995.

In the interest of time and convenience, the House bill (HR 3313) containing the few remaining provisions on women's health agreed to by negotiators was then used as a legislative vehicle for language from the non-controversial construction authorization bills (HR 4425, S 2277).

The House passed HR 3313 by voice vote Oct. 7, and the Senate cleared it the same day, also by voice vote.

VA Construction Projects

The hospital construction provisions had originated in the House Veterans' Affairs Subcommittee on Hospitals and Health Care, which gave voice vote approval to HR 4425 on May 12. The full committee approved HR 4425 (H Rept 103-

518) by voice vote on May 17. Six days later, on May 23, the House passed the bill by voice vote.

Sponsored by Rowland, the bill authorized $343.8 million in fiscal 1995 for nine major construction projects, roughly triple the $115 million requested by the administration. The bill also required the VA to establish missions for each of its health care facilities to encourage better allocation of construction money in the future.

On the Senate side, the Veterans' Affairs Committee gave voice vote approval June 9 to a companion bill (S 2277) that authorized $325.2 million in fiscal 1995 to build and repair major VA medical facilities. The full Senate passed the bill by voice vote Aug. 19.

The Senate bill, sponsored by John D. Rockefeller IV, D-W.Va., authorized 11 new construction projects. It included the same construction projects as the House-passed bill, with two exceptions. The House bill included $9.6 million for an outpatient clinic in Fort Myers, Fla., that was not in Rockefeller's bill. That project was dropped in the final bill. And Rockefeller's bill included $16.1 million for a research facility in Portland, Ore., that the House subcommittee had dropped from its bill. The final bill included that provision.

Final Provisions

The final bill authorized the VA to provide counseling and treatment for sexual trauma. It also required the VA, when possible, to include women and minorities in clinical research and testing.

The measure extended until June 30, 1995, the requirement that the VA give priority medical treatment to veterans suffering from exposure to dioxin or radiation. Priority treatment, which virtually guaranteed admission to a VA medical facility, normally was given to veterans who were poor or who had conditions related to their service.

The bill included funding for the following medical construction projects:

● $17.2 million in design funds for a medical center with ambulatory care facilities and a nursing home in Brevard County, Fla.
● $14 million for an outpatient clinic and nursing home in Brevard County.
● $16.1 million for a research addition at a VA hospital in Portland, Ore.
● $9.6 million to buy and renovate an outpatient clinic in Bay Pines, Fla.
● $48 million for an ambulatory care addition to a VA medical center in Boston.
● $22.9 million for an ambulatory care unit in Columbia, Mo.
● $29.2 million for an ambulatory care unit in Hampton, Va.
● $48.6 million for an ambulatory care unit in West Haven, Conn.
● $50 million for an outpatient care facility in Phoenix.
● $12.8 million for a nursing home in Fort Myers, Fla.
● $7.3 million for a nursing home in Charleston, S.C.
● $103.7 million for an ambulatory care facility and other projects in Sepulveda, Calif.

Congress Grants Exemptions To VHA Personnel

Congress agreed to exempt the Veterans Health Administration (VHA) from government-wide personnel cuts required under President Clinton's plan to "reinvent government."

The exemption language, originally a separate bill (HR 4013), was cleared Oct. 8 as part of an end-of-session catch-all veterans measure that President Clinton signed into law Nov. 2 (HR 5244 — PL 103-446). *(Gulf syndrome, p. 412)*

Congress mandated the government-wide staff cuts in a bill authorizing federal agencies to offer buyouts to selected employees (HR 3345 — PL 103-226). The aim was to reduce the federal work force by 10 percent, or 252,000, over six years. As part of the plan, the Department of Veterans Affairs (VA) was supposed to reduce the VHA staff by 21,000 over five years beginning in 1995, when the health care facilities were to lose almost 4,000 positions. The VHA ran 171 hospitals and more than 350 outpatient clinics nationwide with a staff of 205,000. *(Buyouts, p. 147)*

Veterans' advocates argued that the personnel reductions conflicted with the new health care mission envisioned for the VA under Clinton's health care plan, which called on the VA to compete with private medical providers for patients.

Legislative Action

The House Veterans' Affairs Subcommittee on Hospitals and Health Care gave voice vote approval to HR 4013 on March 16. That version of the bill fully exempted the VHA from all personnel cuts. In addition, it authorized the VA to establish pilot projects in up to five states that were overhauling their health care systems.

At the markup, bill sponsor J. Roy Rowland, D-Ga., chairman of the Hospitals and Health Care Subcommittee, said "ill-advised cutbacks" would result in "bed closures, program cuts and longer waiting times." But Joseph P. Kennedy II, D-Mass., questioned whether preserving staff levels at the VHA would force other sections of the VA to make disproportionately large cuts. Still, the bill moved ahead, with the House Veterans' Affairs Committee giving the measure voice vote approval on March 23 (H Rept 103-447).

Roughly one month later, on April 28, the House passed the bill, 282-118. *(Vote 148, p. 44-H)*

On the House floor, opponents expanded on Kennedy's earlier arguments, warning that the bill would invite a flood of exemptions and eventually render the work force reduction plan meaningless. "One exemption leads to another exemption and another and another," said Timothy J. Penny, D-Minn. Penny forced a roll call vote on the bill, saying he hoped to hold members accountable for supporting government-wide reductions on one hand while opposing VA cutbacks at the same time.

The White House also weighed in against HR 4013. In an April 26 letter to House Speaker Thomas S. Foley, D-Wash., Office of Management and Budget Director Leon E. Panetta argued that it would hamstring administration efforts to downsize government. "This is a zero sum game. If one agency is exempted, others will suffer the consequences," Panetta said in a separate statement issued after the April 28 vote.

Those arguments resonated in the Senate, which stripped the staff exemption from the bill before passing HR 4013 by voice vote June 8. All that remained was the pilot project language, which had been introduced as S 1974 in the Senate.

Veterans' Affairs Committee Chairman John D. Rockefeller IV, D-W.Va., said he was concerned that the bill would open other agencies to deeper personnel cuts to make up for the VHA exemption.

That left the House and Senate poised for a confrontation over the issue. But the matter was not taken up again until the final weeks of the session, when the VHA exemption and a number of other bills were added to the bill providing for compensation to veterans suffering from Persian Gulf syndrome (HR 5244).

During negotiations over HR 5244, House and Senate Veterans' Affairs committee staff ultimately agreed to require the VHA to cut a total of 10,051 full-time positions. But the VHA was allowed to count as part of the personnel cuts all those federal employees whose salaries were not paid out of appropriated funds. This group of 5,375 workers included employees of the veterans canteen service, who were paid from the income generated though sales at each canteen. As a result, the VHA had to eliminate only 4,676 positions. ∎

Other Veterans Legislation Considered in 1994

Bills were enacted to adjust cost of living payments to disabled veterans, clarify veterans' reemployment rights, reduce a case backlog at the Board of Veterans' Appeals, and permit longtime reservists to be buried in national veterans cemeteries. Lawmakers considered, but did not complete work on, a number of other veterans bills.

Vets' COLA

Congress on Oct. 7 agreed to set the annual cost of living adjustment (COLA) for disabled veterans and their survivors at 3 percent. The adjustment, which covered benefits for 2.2 million veterans and 345,000 survivors and dependents, took effect Dec. 1., 1994. President Clinton signed the bill into law Oct. 25 (S 1927 — PL 103-418).

The bill had begun in the Senate Veterans' Affairs Committee, which approved it by voice vote April 26 (S Rept 103-254). The Senate passed it by voice vote May 4.

The House worked on its own COLA bill (HR 4088 — H Rept 103-668), with the Veterans' Affairs Committee approving the measure by voice vote July 21. The House passed S 1927 by voice vote Aug. 8, after amending it to include language to phase in a raise for Veterans Board of Appeals members. This provision had been part of HR 4088.

The Senate stripped this provision from the bill Oct. 6, to ensure that it would not obstruct passage of the COLA provisions. The House accepted the Senate change, clearing the bill by voice vote Oct. 7.

Veterans Re-Employment

The Senate cleared legislation by voice vote Sept. 28 that clarified and expanded re-employment rights for veterans after they returned from active duty. The bill (HR 995 — PL 103-353) was signed by President Clinton on Oct. 13.

Sponsored by House Veterans' Affairs Committee Chairman G. V. "Sonny" Montgomery, D-Miss., the bill was a response to longtime complaints from veterans that the 1940 Soldiers' and Sailors' Civil Relief Act, which governed re-employment, was confusing and difficult to interpret.

The bill reaffirmed the obligation of employers, regardless

of size, to rehire any veteran who returned from military service within five years of his or her last employment. Under the measure, returning veterans were entitled to the same or a comparable job as well as any promotions that would have accrued had they not served in the military.

The bill made few substantive changes to existing law, but it did extend from four years to five years the length of time a person could serve and still retain the right to a job. It also required service personnel to give reasonable notice to employers before leaving.

The House had originally passed the bill (H Rept 103-65, Part 1) on May 4, 1993. The Senate approved a slightly different version (S 843 — S Rept 103-158) in November 1993, amending its measure to include unrelated language from a bill (S 1510) that increased from $184,000 to $203,000 the maximum amount that could be borrowed under the veterans' guaranteed home loan program. The House accepted the home loan provision Sept. 13, 1994, passing an amended version of the bill by voice vote. *(1993 Almanac, p. 418)*

The language was added because larger loans generated larger loan fees to the government, offsetting the estimated $2 million cost of the re-employment bill. Pay-as-you-go budget rules required that newly authorized mandatory spending be offset with corresponding savings.

Vet Centers

The Senate passed a bill (S 1226 — S Rept 103-236) by voice vote March 24 to expand the mandate of Vet Centers to provide services to all combat veterans, including those who fought in World War II and Korea. But the measure, which had been approved by the Senate Veterans' Affairs Committee in November 1993, was never taken up in the House. *(1993 Almanac, p. 420)*

The Department of Veterans Affairs' 202 centers provided counseling and other services to Vietnam War and post-Vietnam War combat veterans. The bill, sponsored by Daniel K. Akaka, D-Hawaii, also included a two-year pilot program to provide limited health care services at 10 or more centers. The centers were to offer blood pressure screening and other routine medical tests.

Board of Veterans Appeals

The Senate cleared legislation by voice vote June 15 that aimed to reduce the backlog of veterans' claims pending before the Board of Veterans Appeals. The bill was signed by President Clinton on July 1 (S 1904 — PL 103-271) .

The 65-member board heard benefits claims filed against the Department of Veterans Affairs (VA). In 1994 there were 40,000 appeals pending. "A veteran filing today would have to wait over two years for a decision," House Veterans' Affairs Committee Chairman G. V. "Sonny" Montgomery, D-Miss., said during House floor debate on June 13.

The bill, sponsored by Sen. John D. Rockefeller IV, D-W.Va., attempted to speed up the claims process by reducing from three to one the number of board members needed to adjudicate a claim. The measure also removed the 65-member cap on the number of board members to allow the panel to expand.

The Senate first passed S 1904 on April 21 after winning the approval of the Veterans' Affairs Committee on April 14. The House passed the bill with minor modifications by voice vote on June 13 and sent it back to the Senate, which adopted the House version.

Radiation Lawsuits

The Senate passed by voice vote a bill (S 1908 — S Rept 103-280) to ease the rules governing lawsuits by veterans who claimed to have been exposed to radiation during military service and to be suffering its effects. While the measure, sponsored by John D. Rockefeller IV, D-W.Va., was never taken up by the House, part of it was included in the Persian Gulf syndrome compensation bill enacted in 1994.

Under existing rules, veterans were entitled to receive benefits only if they had a specific disease within a certain time frame. On a case-by-case basis, the bill would have relaxed the time requirements and allowed benefits for unlisted diseases caused by exposure to radiation.

The measure, which won the voice vote approval of the Senate Veterans' Affairs Committee on April 14, also called for an 18-month study on the effectiveness of the VA's adjudication and appeals system.

In addition, the bill clarified that any veteran who had participated in the testing of a nuclear weapon by a foreign country was still eligible for VA treatment and compensation. This last provision was included in the Persian Gulf syndrome compensation bill (HR 5244 — PL 103-446) that cleared Congress Oct. 8. *(Gulf syndrome, p. 412)*

Cemetery Benefits

The Senate cleared legislation by voice vote April 20 that extended the right to be buried in national veterans cemeteries to people who served 20 years or more in the military reserves or the National Guard. President Clinton signed the bill May 4 (HR 821 — PL 103-240).

Under existing law, only active-duty military personnel and reservists who had been called up for active duty were eligible for burial in the cemeteries. The Department of Veterans Affairs, while not actively opposing the bill, had expressed concern that expanding eligibility would greatly increase cemetery maintenance costs.

The House had originally passed the bill Aug. 2, 1993. The Senate passed it Nov. 11, after expanding it to include spouses and dependent children. The House added some technical changes to the bill on April 18, 1994, and sent it back to the Senate for final action. *(1993 Almanac, p. 418)*

Homeless Veterans

On Sept. 23, the Senate Veterans' Affairs Committee gave voice vote approval to a bill (S 2325 — S Rept 103-385) that would have authorized a total of $48 million over three years, beginning in fiscal 1995, to provide homeless veterans with halfway houses and services such as psychiatric and therapeutic treatment. The bill moved no further in the 103rd Congress.

The measure also would have created an Advisory Committee on Minority Veterans at the Department of Veterans Affairs (VA) and required that a representative be designated at each VA facility to assess the special needs of minority veterans. It also called for a study on whether there were health consequences for spouses and children of veterans who were exposed to radiation while in the military.

The panel gave voice vote approval to an amendment, offered by Daniel K. Akaka, D-Hawaii, to gradually raise the salaries of the 65 members of the Board of Veterans Appeals to match the pay of administrative law judges. Board members made an average of $20,000 a year less than administrative judges, who earned up to $108,000 annually in 1994.

Akaka and others said board members were leaving to become administrative judges because the work was similar but the pay was higher.

The Akaka amendment was ultimately included in the Persian Gulf syndrome compensation bill (HR 5244 — PL 103-446) that cleared Congress Oct. 8. *(Gulf syndrome, p. 412)*

Mental Health

The Senate passed a bill by voice vote March 24 that would have established up to five centers at existing Department of Veterans Affairs (VA) facilities to study and treat veterans suffering from mental illness. But the measure was not taken up by the House and died at the end of the session.

The bill (S 1512 — S Rept 103-237), sponsored by John D. Rockefeller IV, D-W.Va., had received voice vote approval from the Senate Veterans' Affairs Committee on Nov. 3, 1993. It would have authorized $3.1 million in fiscal 1994 and $6.3 million each year from fiscal 1995 through 1997.

Job Training

On Sept. 23, the Senate Veterans' Affairs Committee gave voice vote approval to a bill (S 2094 — S Rept 103-384) to make permanent a Department of Veterans Affairs (VA) program subsidizing vocational assistance for veterans who wanted to train to be civilian pilots. While S 2094 was never taken up by the full Senate, the vocational assistance language was included in the Persian Gulf syndrome compensation bill (HR 5244 — PL 103-446) that cleared Congress Oct. 8. *(Gulf syndrome, p. 412)*

The bill also would have eased restrictions for veterans who qualified for VA subsidized on-the-job training, which lasted a maximum of 18 months. The measure would have allowed veterans and employers to continue the training after the subsidy ran out. This provision was not added to HR 5244.

Home Loans

Congress made a change in the rules governing Department of Veterans Affairs (VA) home loans, with the aim of helping veterans who, through divorce or job transfer, had to buy a new house before selling their existing residence.

The change, which was approved April 14 by the Senate Veterans Affairs Committee (S 1626 — S Rept 103-267), allowed a veteran to apply for a second VA guaranteed home loan before disposing of a home purchased with a first VA loan. The bill was approved 12-0. While S 1626 never reached the Senate floor, language from the bill was included in legislation (HR 5244 — PL 103-446) that compensated veterans disabled by Persian Gulf syndrome; S 5244 was signed Oct. 8. *(Gulf syndrome, p. 412)* ■

Chapter 9

DEFENSE

Defense Legislation
Defense Authorization 421
    Provisions. 428
B-2 Bomber Production. 432
C-17 Cargo Plane Construction 433
Women in the Military 435
Base Closings 435

Chemical Weapons Treaty. 437
Arms Cuts 438
Nominations, Promotions
Perry Confirmation 438
Halperin Withdrawal 439
Military Promotions. 439

Congress Backs Clinton's Plans To Hold the Line on Defense

Lawmakers agree to spending levels sought by the White House and defer tough decisions through artful compromises

President Clinton's $263.8 billion defense budget request for fiscal 1995 proved remarkably resistant to attacks from both the left and the right. The president's program was enacted essentially intact in the voluminous provisions of the defense authorization measure (S 2182) that the Senate cleared Sept. 13. Clinton signed the bill Oct. 5 (PL 103-337).

The administration's request amounted to an inflation-adjusted reduction of less than 1 percent from the previous year's spending level. Liberals wanted bigger cuts in Pentagon spending, and conservatives wanted less retrenchment.

On the festering question of whether the United States should break the U.N.-sponsored arms embargo against Bosnia, the bill urged — but did not require — the president to seek a U.N. decision to lift the embargo if Serbian forces in Bosnia had not accepted by mid-October an internationally sponsored settlement to the ethnic civil war. *(Bosnia policy, p. 446)*

On a major weapons procurement matter, the measure ordered a high-level Pentagon review of whether the Air Force needed more long-range bombers than projected budgets would allow. The bill earmarked up to $125 million to study options for acquiring additional bombers and to keep intact for one year critical parts of the network of companies that built and equipped such planes. This formulation sidestepped the long-running dispute over whether to keep building a particular aircraft: the B-2 stealth bomber. *(B-2 bomber, p. 432)*

The Bosnia embargo and B-2 production were among the most contentious issues confronting the defense authorization conferees. On most big-ticket items in the bill, the Senate and House were in substantial agreement. For instance, both chambers backed Clinton's request for an aircraft carrier, approving $2.4 billion in new budget authority plus $1.2 billion transferred from the fiscal 1994 budget. And both voted to authorize a 2.6 percent pay raise for military personnel, instead of the 1.6 percent raise proposed by Clinton.

The compromise bill did resolve disagreements over several issues. For example, both chambers had approved Clinton's request for six C-17 long-range transport planes, but only the Senate had approved a contract modification that

---

BOXSCORE

Fiscal 1995 Defense Authorization — S 2182 (HR 4301). The $263.8 billion bill closely followed President Clinton's request.

Reports: H Rept 103-499, S Rept 103-282; conference report H Rept 103-701.

KEY ACTION

June 9 — House passed HR 4301, 260-158.

July 1 — Senate passed S 2182 by voice vote.

July 25 — House passed S 2182 by voice vote, after substituting text of HR 4301.

Aug. 17 — House adopted conference report on S 2182, 280-137.

Sept. 13 — Senate cleared bill, 80-18.

Oct. 5 — President signed S 2182 — PL 103-337.

---

was negotiated to settle several legal issues in dispute between the Pentagon and C-17 builder McDonnell Douglas Corp. The conference report approved the contract settlement. *(C-17, p. 433)*

And following the lead of the House, the conferees rejected Clinton's request that the Pentagon pay $300 million of the U.S. government's assessment to cover the cost of U.N. peacekeeping operations. In the past, such costs had been funded from the State Department budget.

Background

By the second year of his administration, Clinton had put his stamp on the Pentagon — setting its funding, choosing its key personnel and approving its new strategy. He built his defense policy around the conclusions of the Defense Department's 1993 "bottom-up review," which sought to determine how large, combat-ready and modern the military needed to be for the post-Cold War world. The plan called for the United States to be capable of fighting two nearly simultaneous "major regional conflicts." *(1993 Almanac, p. 452)*

Daunted in part by concern about the federal deficit, moderates and conservatives shied away from trying to force Clinton to restore any significant portion of the $123 billion he had pledged to cut over five years from the long-term Pentagon spending plan he inherited from President George Bush.

On the other hand, Clinton pledged in his State of the Union speech on Jan. 25, 1994, to hold the line against liberals who might cut deeper: "The budget I send to Congress draws the line against further defense cuts. . . . We must not cut defense further."

Clinton's Gamble

The budget request that Clinton presented on Feb. 7 was the first installment of a five-year, $1.3 trillion defense program that rested on a complex budgetary gamble: It assumed that inflation would boost future Pentagon expenses more slowly than forecast, thus cutting budgetary requirements by at least $20 billion. And it assumed that the Pentagon would be able to trim its annual costs significantly by revamping the way it bought weapons and man-

aged its financial affairs and by disposing of unneeded facilities. *(Clinton budget, p. 68)*

Some combination of lower inflation and cost-cutting reforms had to yield tens of billions of dollars in net savings for the Pentagon over the next five years. Otherwise, Clinton's projected budgets would be too small to cover an upturn in weapons procurement funding slated to come in fiscal 1998. That resurgence in procurement spending was a key element of Clinton's plan to maintain a force of 1.4 million active-duty military personnel, all combat-ready and equipped with high-tech weaponry.

For a few years, the administration argued, procurement funding could be held down to keep the total defense budget within limits. Meanwhile, the services would have to live off the large inventories of modern weaponry amassed during the flush years of the 1980s.

Reflecting that assumption, Clinton's procurement request for fiscal 1995 was $43 billion — $1 billion less than the fiscal 1994 procurement budget and only one-third the inflation-adjusted size of the procurement budget in fiscal 1985.

Because this would be the 10th consecutive year in which procurement funding declined, most of the major programs in the Reagan administration's weapons buildup already had been killed. The fiscal 1995 budget sought to terminate only a handful of major programs, including production of the Air Force's F-16 fighter and several models of a helicopter used by the Navy to hunt submarines and rescue downed pilots.

But Defense Secretary William J. Perry told the Senate Armed Services Committee on Feb. 8, "There will come a time when we have used up that excess inventory, and then we will have to start building at higher rates than we now are building." Testifying together, Perry and Gen. John M. Shalikashvili, chairman of the Joint Chiefs of Staff, defended the budget as the minimum needed to deliver on Clinton's defense strategy.

The president's plan faced criticism from liberals, who found his goal of a 1.4 million-person force unduly ambitious. House Armed Services Committee Chairman Ronald V. Dellums, D-Calif., called it "an enormous commitment of scarce economic resources that may not be justified by our national security needs."

At least initially, however, the more vocal criticism came from conservatives who accepted Clinton's defense goals but faulted his budget as inadequate to the purpose. "Our forces are going hollow," warned Senate Armed Services Committee Republican John McCain, Ariz. "If we are not ready, the men and women we send into combat will pay for our negligence with their lives."

House Committee

The House Armed Services Committee approved its version of the fiscal 1995 defense authorization bill (HR 4301 — H Rept 103-499), 55-1, on May 5. The lone dissenter was Arizona Republican Bob Stump.

Most members of the House panel regarded Clinton's long-term plans for defense spending as too stingy. Its $263.3 billion authorization bill underscored that view with provisions such as non-binding language urging a larger Army than the administration planned.

But the concern over cuts did not play out in the bottom line. Committee Democrats blocked Republican efforts to repudiate the Clinton budget by adding funds. To make the measure match the House-passed version of the congressional budget resolution, the committee even made a slight reduction in Clinton's $263.7 billion defense funding request

for fiscal 1995. *(Budget resolution, p. 81)*

The key test came on an amendment by Duncan Hunter, R-Calif., that would have increased the total authorization by $6.8 billion. The move was purely symbolic because the budget resolution would have blocked appropriation of the additional funds. But Hunter insisted that the Armed Services panel had an obligation to give the House its collective judgment that Clinton's defense budgets were too low. "If not us, who? If not now, when?" he demanded.

Liberal Chairman Dellums linked arms with much more conservative Democrats to blast Hunter's amendment. If Armed Services authorized more spending than the budget resolution allowed, they warned, the Appropriations Committee would make the choices about defense priorities. "What you're doing is giving the Appropriations Committee a blank check," said Military Forces and Personnel Subcommittee Chairman Ike Skelton, D-Mo.

Dellums reacted in more pungent terms, calling Hunter's amendment a "burlesque" that would vitiate the hard work Armed Services had put into crafting its bill. "Why in hell are we sitting here?" he asked.

The Hunter amendment was rejected on a party-line vote of 22-34.

Major Issues

On most issues, the committee bill adhered to the administration's budget request, approving, for example:

● $3.7 billion for a nuclear-powered aircraft carrier.
● $2.5 billion to develop the Air Force's F-22 fighter.
● $2.9 billion for three Navy destroyers.
● $525 million to develop the Army's Comanche missile-armed scout helicopter.
● A reduction of nearly 86,000 in the number of active-duty military personnel, setting a new ceiling of 1.53 million.

But the committee whacked some of the administration's funding requests. The panel:

● Cut $513 million from the Ballistic Missile Defense program — formerly known as the Strategic Defense Initiative — authorizing $2.74 billion.
● Denied the entire $606 million requested to develop and begin production of a short-range stealth missile designated TSSAM, ordering the program's cancellation.
● Approved four C-17 cargo jets ($1.85 billion) rather than the six planes requested ($2.77 billion). But the committee also ordered the Air Force to begin buying off-the-shelf additional cargo jets of some other type to supplement the C-17 fleet. The plane had a history of cost increases and technical problems.

The committee proposed increased funding for some purposes. It approved a 2.6 percent pay raise for military personnel rather than the 1.6 percent increase proposed in the budget, a change with a price tag of about $550 million.

And it authorized purchase of six additional Apache missile-armed helicopters. The purpose was to prevent a temporary shutdown of that production line that would boost the cost of a planned program to upgrade Apaches already in service.

The committee approved, 26-23, an amendment urging an Army of 520,000 active-duty members, rather than the 495,000-member force envisioned by Clinton. The symbolic swipe at the administration's defense plans was sponsored by Joel Hefley, R-Colo. The vote was by show of hands, rather than a roll call. But it appeared that eight conservative Democrats voted for Hefley's amendment, then voted against Hunter's budget increase proposal.

The committee also approved report language drafted by

Skelton challenging Clinton's plan to organize the Army's combat units into 10 divisions staffed entirely by active-duty personnel, with National Guard combat forces relegated to a backup role. The Skelton language recommended instead that the Army retain 12 active-duty divisions, four of which would be composed partly of National Guard units.

Besides blasting Clinton's budget as too small, committee Republicans hammered at the theme that core defense programs were being cut even more deeply than it appeared because Pentagon funds were being earmarked for new missions, such as cleaning up toxic waste on abandoned military bases and helping former republics of the Soviet Union dismantle the nuclear weapons they inherited. "The defense budget is being cannibalized from within by non-traditional missions," complained ranking committee Republican Floyd D. Spence, S.C.

One such mission — opposed by committee Republicans as well as conservative Democrats — was Clinton's proposal to earmark $300 million in defense funds to pay the U.S. share of certain United Nations peacekeeping costs previously paid from the State Department's budget.

The committee scotched that plan, earmarking the funds instead to pay for unanticipated deployments involving peacekeeping, humanitarian assistance or disaster relief. But Republicans, led by James V. Hansen of Utah, objected that leaving the $300 million in funds would tempt an amendment on the House floor that would redirect the money to pay U.N. assessments.

To reduce that risk, Hansen offered an amendment cutting the fund to $50 million and earmarking the remaining $250 million to beef up combat readiness. That amendment was rejected on a party line vote of 22-34. But the committee subsequently approved 43-11 a proposal by Jon Kyl, R-Ariz., to include in its report a statement strongly opposing the use of Pentagon funds to pay U.N. assessments.

House Floor

The House passed the fiscal 1995 defense authorization bill (HR 4301), 260-158, on June 9. Subsequently, in preparation for conference, the House agreed July 25 by voice vote to pass the Senate bill (S 2182) after substituting the text of HR 4301. *(Vote 226, p. 68-H)*

Before endorsing the bill, lawmakers defied the administration on foreign policy by voting, 244-178, to adopt an amendment that sought to force the United States to break a United Nations arms embargo in order to provide weapons to the outgunned Muslim forces in Bosnia. *(Vote 222, p. 68-H)*

The House then rejected a more moderate, administration-backed amendment that urged the president to seek the backing of NATO allies and the United Nations for the lifting of the ban. The substitute, crafted by House Foreign Affairs Committee Chairman Lee H. Hamilton, D-Ind., was rejected 181-242. *(Vote 223, p. 68-H)*

The House also scuttled the administration's plans to tap defense funds to pay assessed contributions for U.N. peacekeeping operations. The ban on financing peacekeeping through the Pentagon was one of 27 largely non-controversial proposals incorporated en bloc into a single amendment, which the House adopted by voice vote.

But the House rejected, 185-237, a Republican-led move to impose stiff conditions on the deployment of U.S. forces under foreign command in such multilaterial missions. *(Vote 225, p. 68-H)*

On the nuts and bolts of defense spending, the House rejected efforts to cut funding for the Trident II missile and

for anti-ballistic missile research. And it voted decisively, 330-100, to stand by Clinton's full request for six C-17 planes, spurning a plan by the Armed Services Committee to limit the purchases to four of the controversial transport planes. *(Vote 195, p. 60-H)*

● **Burden sharing.** Only on the politically neuralgic issue of "burden-sharing" — pressuring U.S. allies to pay more of the cost of stationing U.S. forces overseas — did the proponents of deeper defense cuts draw blood from the bill drafted by the House Armed Services Committee. By a hefty margin, the House adopted, 268-144, an amendment to reduce the number of U.S. personnel stationed in Europe by up to 75,000 if European allies were not paying 75 percent of the non-salary costs of their deployment by the end of fiscal 1998. *(Vote 187, p. 58-H)*

The amendment was strongly opposed by the administration. But cosponsors Barney Frank, D-Mass., and Christopher Shays, R-Conn., prevailed, tapping into the deeply rooted belief on Capitol Hill that many wealthy allies — who were also commercial competitors — underspent on their own military. "Since they do not have to pay their fair share for their own defense," argued Thomas H. Andrews, D-Maine, "they invest their dollars in taking our jobs."

Opponents such as Armed Services member Norman Sisisky, D-Va., argued that U.S. interests were furthered by stationing forces overseas, closer to potential trouble spots.

But Frank and Shays leveraged their position with adroit tactics. They offered their amendment after Texas Democrat John Bryant advanced a more radical proposal, which the House rejected 163-260. Bryant's amendment would have required a pullout of all troops by 2000 if the allies did not begin paying all costs of overseas U.S. forces. To make their amendment more tolerable to Republicans, Frank and Shays wrote into it a loophole: Even if the allies did not increase their payments for U.S. troop costs, the president could waive the requirement for a withdrawal if he declared an emergency. *(Vote 180, p. 56-H)*

● **Russian arsenal.** The House also voted to earmark $400 million of the funds in the bill for a program to assist former Soviet states in disposing of the nuclear and chemical weapons they inherited. This provision was one of several non-controversial proposals presented by Armed Services Chairman Dellums as an en bloc amendment and passed by voice vote.

Clinton had included the $400 million in his defense budget request, and Armed Services had approved it when it marked up HR 4301. But Dellums temporarily struck the demilitarization funds to avoid a turf fight over the bill: The House Foreign Affairs Committee claimed jurisdiction over those provisions and demanded that it be permitted a formal review of the bill.

Dellums' en bloc amendment also restored funding for two other projects that Armed Services had approved but then dropped at Foreign Affairs' insistence. It authorized $60 million for overseas humanitarian and disaster relief and $25 million to help clear deadly land mines that remained from past wars in a number of countries.

● **Anti-missile defenses.** By a comfortable margin, the House rejected, 155-271, an amendment by Martin T. Meehan, D-Mass., that would have sliced an additional $200 million from the $2.72 billion approved by the Armed Services panel for ballistic missile defenses. Clinton requested $3.25 billion for the program. *(Vote 179, p. 56-H)*

President Ronald Reagan launched the anti-missile effort in 1983. Officially named the Strategic Defense Initiative — and derisively called "star wars" by critics — the program

was intended chiefly to shield U.S. territory against attacks by long-range Soviet missiles. The Clinton administration substantially trimmed the size of the anti-missile effort and it focused the program on developing defenses against relatively short-range ballistic missiles. *(1993 Almanac, p. 448)*

Meehan's amendment would have reduced the committee's proposal by $200 million, cut from 42 specific research projects that he contended involved futuristic technologies that could not be fielded for more than a decade.

But Meehan's opponents argued that the proposed cuts would hit projects that might pay off against short-range missiles and also provide a starting point for any future decision to deploy nationwide defenses against long-range missiles.

● **Trident II missile.** The House rejected, 166-229, an amendment by Timothy J. Penny, D-Minn., that would have eliminated from the bill $696 million earmarked to continue production of the Trident II long-range, submarine-launched nuclear missile. *(Vote 189, p. 58-H)*

Of the 18 Trident submarines that were in service or under construction, the eight oldest carried the Trident I multiple-warhead missile. The 10 newer subs were built to carry the Trident II, which had a longer range and could lob eight warheads accurately enough to destroy armored underground missile silos. A high-level Pentagon review of U.S. nuclear forces was analyzing whether the eight older subs should be "retrofitted" with the more powerful missile.

Penny called the Trident II "a Cold War system designed to destroy hardened missile targets found only in the former Soviet Union." Dellums and Wisconsin Republican Scott L. Klug urged "deficit hawks" to support Penny. "If we can't adopt this amendment, where can we cut?" Dellums asked. "No one in this room believes we are going to fight a nuclear war."

But opponents of Penny's amendment contended that additional Trident IIs would be needed for test launches over the next 23 years. They also argued that it was important to keep the Trident II's production line running because it was the only long-range U.S. ballistic missile being built.

The House adopted, 226-169, an amendment to give the Pentagon discretion to install Trident IIs in the eight oldest subs, a move expected to cost about $3 billion. The amendment, sponsored by Norm Dicks, D-Wash., allowed the secretary of Defense to waive a provision added to the bill by the Armed Services Committee to prohibit such a move. *(Vote 188, p. 58-H)*

● **Latin American school.** By a vote of 175-217, the House rejected an amendment by Joseph P. Kennedy II, D-Mass., that would have barred further funding of the Pentagon's School of the Americas. *(Vote 190, p. 58-H)*

According to its proponents, the school at Fort Benning, Ga., trained Latin American military officers in standards of professional conduct in a democracy. But human rights activists cited many notorious anti-democrats among the school's alumni, including Panamanian strongmen Omar Torrijos and Manuel Antonio Noriega and 19 of the 26 Salvadoran officers accused of murdering six Jesuit priests in 1989.

The vote came shortly after opponents of the school, led by the Rev. Roy Bourgeois, a Maryknoll priest, ended a 40-day hunger strike intended to dramatize their opposition to continued funding. Arguing that the School of the Americas had trained "a 'Who's Who' of the hemisphere's dictators," Georgia Democrat Cynthia A. McKinney said the school was ineffective at best and, at worst, gave its graduates the know-how to overthrow duly elected governments.

But supporters countered that the critics were singling out relatively few bad apples from the nearly 60,000 military officers who had attended the school. Minority Whip Newt Gingrich, R-Ga., insisted that the school had a mostly positive influence on Latin American officers who were "learning what we're trying to teach the Russians: how to be a soldier in a democracy."

● **Haiti.** The House first opposed U.S. intervention in Haiti, but later, in a symbolic victory for Clinton, lawmakers reversed themselves. *(Haiti, p. 449)*

The first vote came May 24, when the House adopted, 223-201, a sense-of-Congress amendment offered by Porter J. Goss, R-Fla., urging the president not to invade Haiti unless he first certified that there was a "clear and present danger" to U.S. citizens in that country. The amendment also urged the administration to use an island off the Haitian coast as a "safe haven" for Haitian refugees. *(Vote 197, p. 60-H)*

On June 9, the House voted again, rejecting the amendment 195-226. *(Vote 224, p. 68-H)*

Other Amendments

In other action, the House:

● Rejected, 68-362, an amendment by Hansen to delay until 1997 the round of expedited military base closings that was slated for 1995. *(Vote 194, p. 58-H; base closings, p. 435)*

● Rejected an amendment by Dellums to end Selective Service registration. It was rejected 125-273. *(Vote 192, p. 58-H)*

● Adopted, 271-126, an amendment sponsored by Gerald B. H. Solomon, R-N.Y., to prohibit awarding funds in the bill to any college that barred military recruiters from its campuses. The amendment was a response to schools that had kept recruiters off campus on the rationale that the military's ban on homosexuals was discriminatory. *(Vote 191, p. 58-H)*

● Approved, 415-1, an amendment sponsored by Solomon calling for international sanctions against North Korea if that country did not allow inspection of its nuclear facilities. The United States was concerned about signs that the North Koreans might already have one or two nuclear weapons. At the time, a crisis was building because the North Koreans had removed the core of their reactor, potentially giving them enough plutonium for five or six additional bombs. *(Vote 217, p. 66-H)*

An amendment calling on Clinton to urge South Korea to upgrade its military readiness, proposed by Ohio Republican John R. Kasich, was adopted 414-3. *(Vote 221, p. 66-H)*

● Rejected, 68-349, a non-binding amendment by Edward J. Markey, D-Mass., urging the president to suspend Japan's continued use of U.S.-supplied plutonium until international agencies could verify the status of 150 pounds of the material that was alleged to be unaccounted for at a Japanese plant. *(Vote 220, p. 66-H)*

● Approved an amendment by Jane Harman, D-Calif., intended to water down a provision that required the services to discharge personnel who could not be assigned to certain areas because of their medical conditions. The provision, sponsored in the Armed Services Committee by Robert K. Dornan, R-Calif., applied to service members with diabetes, cancer and certain other medical conditions. But Harman and other opponents contended that it was intended chiefly to expel from the services members who were HIV-positive. Harman's amendment was adopted 227-192. *(Vote 219, p. 66-H)*

● Approved an amendment by Mike Kopetski, D-Ore., commending the president for extending the moratorium on underground nuclear weapons tests and urging completion

by the end of 1994 of a multilateral treaty banning all nuclear tests. The amendment was adopted, 263-156. *(Vote 218, p. 66-H)*

Senate Committee

The Senate Armed Services Committee approved its $263.3 billion defense authorization bill by a vote of 19-3 on June 9 (S Rept 103-282), essentially embracing all the major weapons programs that Clinton requested.

The most hotly contested issue was something Clinton did not request: $150 million added by the committee to preserve the option of buying additional B-2 stealth bombers. The money was intended to keep the B-2 production network alive for one more year.

Chairman Sam Nunn, D-Ga., said half the added money would be used to accelerate the acquisition of spare parts that were slated for later purchase even if no additional bombers were bought. He called the remaining $75 million "an insurance policy."

The House-passed version of the bill limited the B-2 force to the 20 planes previously authorized.

Endorsing other initiatives to beef up the bomber force, the committee:

● Ordered the Air Force to keep in active service the 95 B-1s and 95 B-52s that were in its inventory. It also ordered the service to budget funds to modify the entire B-1 fleet to carry conventional weapons.

● Added $90 million to develop a stopgap, ultra-accurate bombing system that could be used until a new "smart bomb" — designated JDAM — was ready for service.

● Approved $488 million of the $604 million requested for a stealth missile called TSSAM, which the House-passed version of the bill sought to cancel. The missile, several of which could be fired from one bomber, was designed to scatter dozens of anti-tank warheads over an enemy column up to 100 miles away.

Other Highlights

The Senate committee's bill sliced $300 million from Clinton's defense request. But Nunn said the committee was concerned that optimistic assumptions in Clinton's long-range budget plans would force de facto reductions in Pentagon programs, "eroding the overall future capability of our military forces."

The committee's bill authorized the amounts requested for most major programs, including:

● $2.7 billion for three Navy destroyers.
● $2.5 billion to develop the Air Force's F-22 fighter.
● $1.4 billion to develop enlarged "E" and "F" versions of the Navy's F/A-18 fighter-bomber.
● $525 million to develop the Army's Comanche missile-armed helicopter.

The bill approved production of six more C-17 wide-body cargo planes, as requested. But it authorized only $2.2 billion of the $2.5 billion requested. It increased by $46 million, to $150 million, the amount earmarked to resume production of an existing wide-body jet that might be bought to supplement the C-17 fleet.

The committee cut $251 million from Clinton's $3.25 billion request for anti-missile defenses.

It sliced $1.1 billion from the amount requested for Pentagon civilian pay on the rationale that more employees than anticipated were retiring.

On the other hand, the bill made several additions to Clinton's budget request, including:

● $450 million to provide a 2.6 percent military pay raise, rather than the 1.6 percent raise requested.
● $601 million toward the $1.4 billion cost of a large helicopter carrier to land 2,000 Marines in hostile territory.
● $600 million for equipment for National Guard and reserve units.
● $100 million to restore to limited service some retired SR-71 high-speed reconnaissance jets.

Senate Floor

As members began slipping away for the Fourth of July recess, the Senate debated its $263.1 billion version of the defense authorization bill into the night of July 1. After disposing of the last in a long list of amendments — 90 on that day alone — the Senate passed the bill by voice vote.

Members handed Clinton a narrow but tactical victory by stopping one vote short of approving an amendment that would have ordered the president to permit arms to flow to Bosnia's Muslim forces. The Senate rejected, on a 50-50 tie, an amendment sponsored by Minority Leader Bob Dole, R-Kan., and Joseph I. Lieberman, D-Conn., that would have mandated the weapons shipments in defiance of a U.N. embargo against arming the combatants in the former Yugoslavia. *(Vote 181, p. 31-S)*

Before that vote, the Senate approved, 52-48, an administration-backed amendment sponsored by Armed Services Chairman Nunn and Virginia Republican John W. Warner. Their non-binding amendment urged Clinton to seek a multilateral end to the embargo if the Serbian forces battling the Bosnian government derailed efforts to negotiate a peace settlement. *(Vote 180, p. 31-S)*

Senators handed Nunn a victory by rejecting, 45-55, an effort to delete the $150 million he wanted to set aside to preserve the option of building more B-2 bombers. *(Vote 179, p. 31-S)*

Armed Services member Carl Levin, D-Mich., offered the amendment to cancel the committee's B-2 initiative and use the money instead to beef up the Pentagon's fund for closing unneeded military bases. Levin said the amendment had the support of senior Pentagon officials. Suggesting that the military was bowing to pressure from civilian leaders in opposing more B-2s, Nunn predicted that Senate rejection of Levin's anti-B-2 amendment would produce "a little more courageous position from the Department of Defense."

In defeating other amendments, senators reaffirmed the Pentagon's plans to build an aircraft carrier, revise the contract requirements for the C-17 cargo jet and earmark some Pentagon funds to pay for U.N. peacekeeping operations in which U.S. forces took part.

● **Base closings.** By a vote of 71-27, the Senate tabled (killed) an amendment by Arlen Specter, R-Pa., that would have given federal courts limited power to intervene in the process that Congress had created to permit the closing of excess military bases. *(Vote 163, p. 28-S)*

The expedited closure process was designed expressly to circumvent congressional and legal obstacles that had blocked efforts to close bases in the past. The new process was built around an independent commission charged with drawing up a list of bases to be closed. The president and Congress could only accept the list or reject it, in toto.

Specter's amendment would have allowed supporters of a base to go to court if they had clear evidence that the process had been tainted by "fraudulent concealment" of relevant information. Specter had been fighting closure of the Philadelphia Naval Shipyard, arguing that information had been

concealed in that case. Opponents of the amendment warned that it would kill the base closure process as champions of endangered bases filed litigation.

● **Peacekeeping costs.** By a vote of 35-61, the Senate rejected an amendment by Dirk Kempthorne, R-Idaho, that would have nullified a provision earmarking $300 million to pay the U.S. share of U.N. peacekeeping operations. The amendment would have used that money instead to beef up the training and maintenance of U.S. forces. *(Vote 165, p. 28-S)*

The administration had requested that the $300 be available to pay the U.S. share of any U.N. peacekeeping assessment. But the Armed Services Committee specified that such funds could be used only for operations in which U.S. troops were involved. Arguing that the Pentagon's "readiness" funding was stretched too thin, Kempthorne warned that the $300 million fiscal 1995 assessment would be an opening wedge for much larger raids on the defense budget in future years.

The vote on the amendment broke largely on partisan lines. But eight centrist Republicans joined all the voting Democrats except Charles S. Robb, D-Va., to vote no.

The Senate also adopted by voice vote several other amendments, including one by Ted Stevens, R-Alaska, to limit the maximum compensation for officials of federally funded research institutions.

● **Aircraft carrier.** By a vote of 72-24, the Senate tabled (killed) an amendment by Russell D. Feingold, D-Wis., that would have barred work on a new nuclear-powered aircraft carrier, for which the bill authorized $3.65 billion. As requested in Clinton's budget, the bill earmarked $2.45 billion in new budget authority for the project and transferred $1.2 billion appropriated to a different Pentagon project in fiscal 1994. The Navy also could use $830 million worth of components Congress approved as part of the fiscal 1993 budget. *(Vote 164, p. 28-S)*

● **C-17 cargo jet.** By a vote of 32-66, the Senate rejected an amendment intended to scrap a deal between the Pentagon and McDonnell Douglas Corp., builder of the C-17 cargo jet. The amendment by Charles E. Grassley, R-Iowa, would have eliminated a provision of the bill authorizing the deal, which was negotiated in response to a raft of troubles bedeviling the wide-body jet. *(Vote 162, p. 28-S)*

The House version of the defense bill was silent on the Pentagon's deal with the contractor.

In addition to authorizing the C-17 settlement, the Senate bill approved $2.19 billion for six additional C-17s, a reduction of $284 million from the administration's request. It also authorized $150 million — $46 million more than was requested — to study whether an off-the-shelf wide-body jet could be used to supplement the C-17 fleet.

● **Retirees' cost of living.** By a vote of 88-12, the Senate accepted a Warner amendment to accelerate the 1995 cost of living increase for military pensions by six months so that it would occur April 1. That was the date that civil service retirees were slated to receive their cost of living adjustment. *(Vote 182, p. 31-S)*

Warner's amendment was vigorously supported by organizations of military retirees. But Appropriations Committee Chairman Robert C. Byrd, D-W.Va., insisted that they did not grasp the consequences. "The proponents want to cut defense, a move most military retirees would oppose if they understood what was going on," he said.

The amendment was expected to cost $376 million in outlays, which had to be offset by reductions to other parts of the defense budget. If funds for the cost of living shift were drawn from the military personnel account, Byrd said, 21,000 service

members would have to be dropped from the rolls. The cut would be even more severe if funds were drawn from other parts of the defense budget, Nunn warned, because only a fraction of the budget authority appropriated for some accounts in a given fiscal year was spent as outlays in the same year.

To yield the $376 million in outlays required by Warner's amendment, the operations and maintenance budget would have to be cut by $500 million, the research and development budget by $800 million or the procurement budget by billions, Nunn said.

Proponents insisted the fundamental issue was one of fairness to the military retirees. "The first obligation is not to the tanks and the planes and the ships," Warner said, "but to the men and women who operate them."

Other Provisions

The Senate rejected an amendment by Malcolm Wallop, R-Wyo., that would have barred the deployment of U.S. forces on the Golan Heights as part of a Middle East peace settlement until the president reported to Congress on the potential risks, costs, duration and impact on overall combat readiness of U.S. forces. Secretary of State Warren Christopher strongly opposed the amendment, warning in a letter to Nunn that it could derail peace talks between Israel and Syria. It was rejected 3-67. *(Vote 187, p. 32-S)*

Dennis DeConcini, D-Ariz., offered an amendment designed to force the Defense Department to more vigorously investigate allegations of sexual impropriety and to keep data on the status of such investigations. The amendment would have made it a criminal offense for any member of the Defense Department not to report any such allegation to a new investigative office.

By a vote of 93-3, the Senate gutted DeConcini's amendment by approving a substitute offered by Nunn with the support of Democrats Patty Murray of Washington and Carol Moseley-Braun of Illinois. The substitute required the other services to adopt procedures that had been established by the Army to investigate and prosecute cases of sexual harassment. *(Vote 184, p. 32-S)*

By a vote of 68-14, the Senate tabled (killed) an amendment by David Pryor, D-Ark., that would have barred the government from sponsoring the overseas sale of the ASPJ radar-jamming system. It also tabled, 50-30, an amendment by Bill Bradley, D-N.J., to eliminate the Selective Service System. *(Votes 185, 186, p. 32-S)*

By voice vote, the Senate adopted amendments:

● By J. Bennett Johnston, D-La., shifting $601 million from construction of a helicopter carrier to construction of two high-speed cargo ships. This restored an administration request that the committee had overturned in order to partially fund the helicopter ship.

● By Trent Lott, R-Miss., a non-binding provision urging the Navy to budget for construction of the Mississippi-built helicopter carrier.

● By Pete V. Domenici, R-N.M., providing that when a service member was dishonorably discharged for spouse abuse, the abused spouse would retain access to certain military benefits.

● By Warner, providing that if the president negotiated an international agreement that would "substantially change" the 1972 treaty limiting anti-ballistic missiles, the agreement would take effect only with the advice and consent of the Senate.

● By Don Nickles, R-Okla., barring the award of Defense Department research funds to any university that refused to allow military recruiters access to its campus.

• By McCain, imposing a cap on the cost of two *Seawolf*-class submarines that were under construction. But before approving McCain's provision, the Senate adopted an amendment to it sponsored by Connecticut Democrats Lieberman and Christopher J. Dodd to increase the proposed cost cap for the subs, which were being built in their state, to $4.76 billion.

• By Hank Brown, R-Colo., urging the president to engage in various types of defense cooperation — including turning over surplus military equipment — with "countries like Poland, Hungary and the Czech Republic, who are making significant progress in working with NATO." It was a substitute for a previous Brown amendment that would have specifically authorized such cooperation with Poland, Hungary and the Czech Republic.

• By John Kerry, D-Mass., exempting the U.S. government from liability if another government accidentally destroyed an innocent aircraft when trying to interdict drug-smuggling planes on the basis of radar information from U.S. military sources. Fearing U.S. liability, the Pentagon on May 1 had stopped providing radar information to Peru and Columbia.

• By Johnston eliminating a provision that would have shifted from the Energy Department to the Defense Department responsibility for manufacturing tritium, a radioactive form of hydrogen used to boost the explosive power of nuclear weapons.

Final Action

The Senate on Sept. 13 cleared for the White House a $263.8 billion defense authorization bill for fiscal 1995 that largely tracked Clinton's budget request.

Final action came when the Senate adopted the conference report on the bill (H Rept 103-701) by a vote of 80-18. All but two of the "nay" votes were cast by Republicans protesting Clinton's cuts in military spending. "The fact is, our military is going hollow," Minority Leader Dole said. "While this bill is probably the best under the circumstances, it represents another step down a disastrous road to unpreparedness." Two Senate Democrats voted against the conference report, Paul Wellstone, Minn., and Feingold. (*Vote 297, p. 51-S*)

The House had approved the conference report, 280-137, on Aug. 17. Republicans accounted for virtually all of the "nays." (*Vote 404, 122-H*)

Although Congress generally followed Clinton's requests, the final bill boosted funding in certain areas: It approved a 2.6 percent military pay raise instead of the 1.6 percent proposed by the president, and it authorized $125 million to study the options for acquiring additional long-range bombers.

On most big-ticket items, the Senate and House were in substantial agreement. For instance, both chambers backed Clinton's request for an aircraft carrier, approving $2.4 billion in new budget authority plus $1.2 billion transferred from the fiscal 1994 budget.

Key Compromises

Artful compromises that deferred final decisions on two contentious issues allowed Senate-House conferees to knit together a compromise version of the annual defense authorization bill on Aug. 10.

• **Bosnia.** On the question of whether the United States should break the U.N.-sponsored arms embargo against Bosnia, the bill urged — but did not require — the president to seek a U.N. decision to lift the embargo if Serbian forces in Bosnia had not accepted by mid-October an internationally sponsored settlement to the ethnic civil war.

• **Bomber program.** On another issue, the measure ordered

a high-level Pentagon review of whether the Air Force needed more long-range bombers than projected budgets would allow. It earmarked the $125 million to study options for acquiring additional bombers and to keep intact for one year critical parts of the network of companies that built and equipped such planes.

Senate Armed Services Chairman Nunn had earmarked $150 million in the Senate version of the bill expressly to preserve the option of buying more B-2 stealth bombers.

Deferring to the adamant stance of House Armed Services Chairman Dellums, the compromise bill prohibited using any of the $125 million in bomber industrial base funds for components in anticipation that future budgets would buy additional B-2s, beyond the 20 planes previously approved.

Even so, Nunn insisted that some of the funds could go to B-2 subcontractors, which would make it easier and cheaper to build additional copies.

Aside from the B-2 production issue, conferees earmarked $136 million for various other projects to beef up the bomber force. The bill:

• Blocked administration plans to save money by temporarily taking some existing bombers out of regular service.

• Accelerated the deployment of the JDAM smart bomb.

• Earmarked $78 million for various "interim" smart bombs that bombers could carry pending JDAM deployment.

The conference also approved $305 million to wring the bugs out of the TSSAM, a stealthy cruise missile with a range of more than 100 miles intended to be launched from bombers or ships to scatter small warheads over enemy columns. The budget requested $606 million for TSSAM, including funds to begin production. Subsequently, however, the Pentagon acknowledged that production would be premature and revised the funding plan along lines that were accepted by the conferees. And in December, Defense Secretary Perry ordered cancellation of the TSSAM program.

Other Provisions

The compromise bill also resolved the disagreements over the following issues:

• **C-17 cargo jet.** Both chambers had approved the request for six planes, but only the Senate had approved a contract modification that was negotiated to settle several legal issues in dispute between the Pentagon and C-17 builder McDonnell Douglas Corp. The conference report approved the contract settlement.

• **Peacekeeping costs.** Following the lead of the House, the conferees rejected Clinton's request that the Pentagon pay $300 million of the U.S. government's assessment to cover the cost of U.N. peacekeeping operations. In the past, such costs had been funded from the State Department budget.

Floor Debate

Floor debate on the conference report underscored the unresolved dispute over whether Clinton was spending too much on defense — or failing to provide the resources to back up his purported defense strategy.

In the House, Armed Services Chairman Dellums said Clinton's effort to maintain a force capable of fighting two major regional wars was too rich a goal. But, acknowledging the uncertainties of the post-Cold War world, Dellums told the House, "It is understandable that most of my colleagues . . . have chosen to proceed cautiously."

On the other hand, many Republicans and conservative Democrats decried both the bill and Clinton's request as dangerously lean. These critics argued that Clinton's planned force was too small to begin with and that his bud-

get was inadequate to fund it.

They also warned that shortages of money and manpower were exacerbated when Clinton spent Pentagon money on non-defense projects at the same time that he deployed U.S. forces for a wide array of humanitarian missions. "He is giving us an internationalist foreign policy with an isolationist defense budget," Curt Weldon, R-Pa., told the House. Clinton "cut our budget by dramatic means . . . but [committed] our young men and women to Haiti, to Bosnia, to Somalia, to wherever they are needed for U.N. operations," he said.

In the Senate, Nunn warned that Clinton's projected funding levels "will not be adequate to maintain the current readiness of our forces, provide for their needed modernization and still support the force structure necessary."

The concerns about a coming crunch were underscored by an Aug. 18 memo written by Deputy Secretary John M. Deutch. He directed the armed services to prepare alternative budget plans that would fund the higher military pay raises on which Congress had insisted — and which Defense Secretary Perry had come to embrace. Deutch's memo instructed the services to consider budget alternatives that would cancel, postpone or slow production of nine major weapons, including the F-22 fighter and the Comanche helicopter. Deutch insisted that the administration likely would propose only a handful of the potential cutbacks.

Postscript

In the months that followed, the administration made several significant adjustments to its long-range defense plans. On Dec. 1, Clinton added $25 billion to his projected defense requests over six years to improve the readiness of troops and their quality of life. And on Dec. 9, the Pentagon announced plans to save $7.7 billion in fiscal 1996 through fiscal 2001 by slowing production of several major weapons, canceling the TSSAM stealth missile and indefinitely delaying production of the Comanche helicopter. ∎

Defense Authorization Provisions

S 2182 (PL 103-337) authorized $263.8 billion in defense spending for fiscal 1995. Following are the major provisions of the final bill, including comparisons with President Clinton's budget requests and with the versions originally passed by the House and Senate:

Ground Combat

Both chambers had approved the $525 million requested to continue developing the Army's Comanche scout helicopter, one of nine major weapons programs that Deputy Defense Secretary John M. Deutch placed under review in August for possible cutbacks in order to fund higher military pay raises.

Two helicopter programs that were candidates for expansion if the Comanche were canceled also fared well at the authorizers' hands. The report of the conference committee that crafted the final version of the defense bill recommended:

● $309 million, as requested, to gear up for equipping larger Apache attack helicopters with the Longbow target-finding radar and other upgrades.

● $72 million, not requested, to buy six additional Apaches, so that the production line would be intact when the time came to begin the Longbow modifications.

● $150 million, not requested, to upgrade 24 small Kiowas with anti-tank missiles and target-finding electronics.

The conferees reasoned that if the Army's plan to replace Kiowas with Comanches were spiked, the gap could be filled by putting the Longbow upgrade on more Apaches or by upgrading more Kiowas. But neither of the existing aircraft had the Comanche's "stealth" design, which was intended to protect against the shoulder-fired anti-aircraft missiles that were in global circulation.

Another consideration was that the Comanche and the Longbow Apache — but not the Kiowa — would be equipped with digital communications links, a key part of the Army's plan to make its forces more agile on battlefields. This "digitization" plan sought to provide all major combat vehicles and helicopters with radio links so that all the elements of a combat force could share information about their locations and those of enemy units.

To accelerate the digitization program, the conferees approved $96 million — $20 million more than requested. They also insisted that the Army include Marine Corps ground units in the program.

The administration requested $175 million to upgrade M-1 tanks, partly to keep the tank production line intact, but also to equip the tanks with digital links and other improvements. The conferees boosted funding for M-1 upgrades to $318 million, including an addition of $108 million to modify 24 extra tanks that were to be trans-

ferred to the Marine Corps Reserve.

Both chambers had approved the $145 million requested to modify Bradley armored troop carriers. As with the M-1 modification, this program served the dual purposes of preserving an industrial base for armored vehicles and equipping vehicles already in service with digital communications and other improvements.

The conferees recommended $239 million, $12 million more than requested, to continue developing a new mobile cannon that would use liquid fuel instead of gunpowder to fire shells. But they added $18 million to continue developing more conventional alternatives.

The new cannon, designated AFAS, was another potential target of Deutch's memo. One alternative to it was for the Army to expand a plan to upgrade some of its artillery with digital communications and other equipment to allow more mobile operations. The conferees approved $218 million of the $238 million requested for this program, called Paladin.

The final bill authorized slightly more than requested to develop two kinds of "smart" munitions intended to destroy enemy tanks at ranges of 10 miles or more. The conference report recommended:

● $72 million for a coffee can-sized warhead designated SADARM, designed to be scattered from cannon shells over an enemy column. The budget request initially earmarked the entire amount to continue developing the weapon. But by April, successful weapons tests had persuaded the Army to ask that $30 million of the funds be earmarked instead to start production.

● $119 million, $10 million more than requested, to continue developing BAT, a yard-long glider designed to be scattered from missiles to home in on the noise and heat of enemy vehicles.

The budget request included $56 million to continue developing a longer-range version of the MLRS artillery rocket, which already had a range of 20 miles. The conferees approved that request but added $26 million to keep the production line running and to speed up, if possible, the start of production of the longer-range missile.

The bill also authorized more anti-tank missiles and small arms than the administration requested. Conferees cited similar "industrial base" concerns as the reason. They approved:

● $127 million to buy more than 1,200 helicopter-launched Hellfires, compared with the budget request of $121 million for 830 missiles.

● $28 million to continue buying smaller TOW missiles (the administration requested that amount to shut down the TOW production line).

● $214 million for nearly 900 shoulder-fired Javelins, compared with the administration request of $131 million for fewer than 400 Javelins.

● $94 million, nearly four times the amount requested, to buy machine guns, rifles, mortars and other small arms.

Long-Range Bombers

Deadlocked over a Senate provision that would have earmarked $150 million to preserve the option of buying additional B-2 "stealth" bombers in future budgets, the conferees finessed the issue. They ordered the Pentagon to review whether the Air Force needed more long-range bombers than projected budgets would pay for. And they added to the bill $125 million that could be used to study options for buying additional bombers and to keep intact the critical nodes in the network of companies that built such aircraft.

The Pentagon planned to rely heavily on long-range bombers carrying non-nuclear weapons, especially precision-guided bombs and missiles, for rapid intervention in distant conflicts. However, the House and Senate Armed Services panels both faulted the Clinton team for shortchanging the bomber force.

The Air Force had recommended a force of 184 planes, including B-1s and B-52s as well as the 20 B-2s previously authorized. But to stay within projected budgets, the service would have had to cut back to about 100 bombers in the succeeding years, keeping about half the 95 B-52s mothballed and 26 of 95 B-1s maintained in operational condition but not routinely flown.

Senate Armed Services Committee Chairman Sam Nunn, D-Ga., who contended that the B-2's stealthiness could revolutionize combat, wanted to set the stage for lifting the cap of 20 planes that Congress had set on that program in 1993. But House Armed Services Committee Chairman Ronald V. Dellums, D-Calif., a leading B-2 critic, vigorously resisted any reprieve for the program.

Some of the $125 million authorized by the conference report could go to B-2 subcontractors, thus serving Nunn's aim. But none of it could be used to buy components in anticipation that they would be used to build additional B-2s. In practical terms, the outcome underscored the political reality that Nunn had conceded all along: Additional B-2s were unlikely unless the Clinton administration fought hard for them. But Defense Secretary William J. Perry, an early sponsor of stealth technology and of the B-2, was adamant in 1994 that the budgets in prospect could not pay for more of the big planes.

The conference report also included a provision prohibiting the retirement of any bomber in service, and it added $23 million to keep operating 24 B-52s that the budget had slated for retirement.

It included $305 million of the $604 million requested for the TSSAM stealth missile, another potential victim of Deutch's budget review. A bomber could fire several of these missiles, each of which was designed to scatter anti-tank warheads over an enemy column up to 100 miles away. More than half the budget request was earmarked to begin TSSAM production. By summer, however, the Air Force conceded that more bugs had to be wrung out of the new missile. The conference report funded the Air Force's revised TSSAM program.

Besides the option of canceling TSSAM, Deutch told the Air Force to prepare a budget plan that would keep that program and spend an additional $100 million annually for other precision-guided "smart" munitions. The conferees also boosted smart-bomb funding, adding more than $120 million to accelerate the deployment of various weapons. The bill authorized:

● $26 million, added to the request, to buy 36 Israeli-designed Have Nap missiles to be carried by some B-52s.

● $128 million, an increase of $17 million over the request, to accelerate development of a one-ton bomb designated JDAM.

● $78 million, added to the bill, to develop various kinds of "interim" smart bombs that could be used until JDAM was ready for service.

● $160 million, as requested, to develop a glider bomb designated JSOW, so planes could attack targets from beyond the reach of their anti-aircraft missiles.

Tactical Air Combat

Both chambers had approved Clinton's request for $2.46 billion to continue development of the Air Force's F-22 fighter, slated for production beginning in 1998. In addition, the conferees approved $10

million to begin developing a version of the plane that could operate off Navy carriers.

The F-22 was the most expensive of the programs that Deutch's memo called into question. Army officials, facing a particularly tight procurement squeeze, publicly challenged the need for the new plane, which was designed in the late 1980s to outfight high-tech planes the Soviet Union was expected to produce.

However, proponents insisted that the stealthy F-22 was needed to give U.S. pilots an edge over the latest Soviet-designed planes — which were still being built by Russia and sold abroad to earn hard currency. The Russian aircraft nearly matched the technology of U.S. fighters that were designed more than 20 years previously but were still in service. The conferees also approved:

● $1.02 billion for 24 F/A-18s, used by the Navy and Marines as both fighters and bombers. This was $98 million less than the budget requested.

● $1.35 billion, as requested, to develop larger "E" and "F" models of the F/A-18.

● $130 million, as requested, to rebuild four Harrier vertical takeoff jets used by the Marines as bombers.

● $158 million, as requested, to modernize some of the Navy's F-14 fighters. But the conferees rejected a House proposal that would have earmarked $142 million to equip some late-model F-14s to carry large payloads of smart bombs and electronics capable of finding ground targets at night or in bad weather.

The budget included $201 million for a joint Navy-Air Force project to develop prototypes of a combat plane that could enter service toward the end of the next decade. And it requested an additional $29 million to develop a prototype of a new vertical takeoff jet with hotter performance than the Harrier. The conferees folded the two projects together and approved the total requested — $230 million.

The bill included $108 million of the $123 million requested to buy the first three of a new type of basic training plane, designated JPATS, intended for use by both the Navy and Air Force. Several aircraft manufacturers were vigorously competing for this contract, most of them proposing to build domestically a trainer designed and used abroad.

Deutch directed the Navy and Air Force to game out the alternatives of either delaying JPATS production for seven years or buying the planes at a slower annual rate than was planned.

The conferees approved $26 million to modify the midair refueling equipment on Air Force tankers so they could refuel Navy planes.

They also added to the bill $100 million to return to service three aircraft from the Air Force's fleet of SR-71 high-speed reconnaissance planes, which were retired in 1990 because of their high operating cost.

The conference report authorized $445 million, as requested, for two additional JSTARS radar planes, intended to locate ground targets far behind enemy lines. Following the Senate's lead, it also added to the bill $100 million to buy used Boeing jetliners for future conversion into JSTARS planes.

Naval Forces

Both chambers had approved the administration plan to provide nearly $3.7 billion for construction of a nuclear-powered aircraft carrier. The conferees, like the Senate, agreed to fund the ship the way the administration requested: $2.46 billion in new budget authority plus $1.2 billion previously appropriated as part of the fiscal 1994 budget.

Both chambers had approved the $2.7 billion request for three additional *Arleigh Burke*-class destroyers equipped with the Aegis system of powerful, computer-controlled radars and anti-aircraft missiles. Even as the Navy shrank by more than one-third, it needed new ships to replace the glut of 1960s-vintage cruisers and destroyers that had been retired in recent years.

However, Deutch ordered the Navy to consider buying the new destroyers at a slower rate. That might quash the practice of soliciting competitive bids for the destroyers from two shipyards: Bath Iron

Works in Maine and Litton Industries' Ingalls Shipbuilding division in Pascagoula, Miss.

Both chambers had approved the amounts requested for shipborne anti-aircraft missiles: $258 million for 202 long-range Standards and $64 million for 240 short-range RAM missiles.

The conferees approved $398 million — $24 million more than requested — for a set of programs intended to develop better anti-aircraft defenses for ships not equipped with the Aegis system. And they added $7 million to test a blimp as a radar picket for a fleet.

The $507 million requested to continue developing a new class of nuclear-powered submarine was approved by both chambers.

The conference report endorsed a Senate proposal earmarking $5 million to speed the process of modifying Navy ships to provide separate quarters for women. And it approved the $54 million requested to modernize two supply ships. The latter were to get new machinery and more spacious quarters so they could be operated by largely civilian crews that would be much smaller — and thus less expensive — than all-Navy crews.

The conferees approved a total of $352 million, as requested, to buy nuclear reactor components and modify the power plants on nuclear-powered ships. The House had recommended a $52 million reduction in that request. However, the conferees accused Navy officials of "attempts to scare members of Congress about the effects of potential reductions." Moreover, the conferees contended, some of the Navy's warnings seemed to be false. "Claimed economic impacts on various geographic areas greatly exceed the total potential reductions being considered," they said. "The [Pentagon] inspector general is directed to investigate the accuracy of the Navy information papers prepared for Congress on this matter."

Air and Sea Transport

The conferees trimmed $304 million from the budget request for six C-17 wide-body cargo jets, approving $2.17 billion, plus $190 million, as requested, for components that would be used in eight additional planes slated for funding in the fiscal 1996 budget.

The bill also authorized a package deal under which the government and C-17 contractor McDonnell Douglas Corp. were to abandon legal claims against each other and the Pentagon was to slightly relax the plane's contract schedule and performance specifications.

Conferees also approved the $104 million requested to test off-the-shelf wide-body cargo planes as supplements to the C-17.

The bill added $50 million to the budget request in hopes of accelerating construction of a large helicopter carrier intended to deploy 2,000 Marines and the aircraft to haul them ashore. The Navy planned to fund the Pascagoula-built ship in its fiscal 2000 budget.

Deutch's memo cited as potential targets for budget cuts two Marine Corps programs to develop vehicles to carry combat units ashore from amphibious transport ships:

● The V-22 Osprey, a hybrid airplane/helicopter that Congress kept alive during the Bush administration despite efforts by then-Defense Secretary Dick Cheney to kill it on grounds that it was too expensive. Both chambers approved the request for $497 million to continue developing the V-22.

● A high-speed amphibious tractor, designated AAAV, designed to carry nearly 20 Marines toward shore at triple the 10 mph pace of the personnel carriers already in service. The conference committee approved $30 million, $4 million more than requested, to continue AAAV development. In the report on its version of the bill, Senate Armed Services had urged the Marines to consider cutting the cost of the project by putting into production a test-bed AAAV that was only seven-eighths the size of the planned vehicle.

Both chambers had approved the request for $601 million to buy two so-called RO/RO cargo ships. These vessels were to have large ramps over which an Army division's tanks and other vehicles could quickly "roll on" at a U.S. port and "roll off" at a distant trouble spot.

The conferees also approved a Senate initiative adding to the bill $220 million to buy two additional ships for conversion to floating depots that would carry tanks and other equipment for a Marine brigade.

Strategic Systems

Both chambers approved the $641 million requested for 18 additional Trident II submarine-launched ballistic missiles. Of the 18 Trident submarines in service or under construction, 10 were slated to each carry 24 of the 4,000-mile range Trident IIs, which carried eight nuclear warheads apiece. The conferees added a House provision barring conversion of the eight oldest of the subs to carry Trident IIs instead of the less powerful Trident Is on board. The Defense secretary could waive the prohibition on grounds of "a significant national security risk."

The conferees approved $2.80 billion of the $3.25 billion requested for anti-missile defenses. That included:

● $400 million of the $587 million requested for work on components of a "national" defense of U.S. territory against missile attack. The conferees' reduction included $120 million that had been earmarked to develop the Brilliant Eyes missile detection satellite. That project was not killed but was made independent of the anti-missile defense program.

● $273 million, as requested, to begin buying defenses against "theater-range" missiles, such as the Soviet-designed Scuds used by Iraq in the Persian Gulf War. The bulk of this money was to buy a new version of the Patriot missile.

● $1.69 billion of the $1.73 billion earmarked to develop anti-theater missile defenses. This included $285 million to develop a replacement for the Patriot, designated ERINT; $496 million to develop a longer-range interceptor, designated THAAD; and $140 million to modify the Aegis anti-aircraft system on some Navy ships to intercept theater-range missiles.

● $433 million of the $624 million requested for support activities and program management.

Including the $120 million for Brilliant Eyes, the conference report included a total of $365 million for three projects intended to develop more effective satellites to detect missile launches, which was $19 million more than was requested.

Military Personnel Issues

The conferees approved an active-duty personnel ceiling of 1,525,692 as requested — a reduction of more than 85,000 from fiscal 1994. They dropped a House provision that would have required the Pentagon to substitute civilian employees for military personnel in 30,000 administrative jobs over the next three years, thus freeing the troops for combat-related assignments.

The bill included the 2.6 percent military pay increase that both chambers had approved rather than the 1.6 percent Clinton proposed.

The conference report provided $418 million for active-duty recruiting and advertising, a 20 percent increase over the budget request. And it repealed a 1992 law requiring a cut in the number of recruiters.

The bill also included a routine provision extending authority to pay enlistment and re-enlistment bonuses and various other kinds of extra payments to pilots, medical professionals and others in critical specialties.

The conferees also recommended a personnel ceiling for National Guard and reserve units of 989,247 — a level more than 3,000 above the budget request, but still a reduction of more than 45,000 compared with the fiscal 1994 Guard and reserve manpower.

The customary add-on to the budget request for equipment earmarked for Guard and reserve units amounted to $640 million. That total included $300 million for 10 Hercules cargo planes and $130 million — located in the Army's budget — to buy MLRS rocket launchers for a National Guard battalion.

Clinton had requested two changes of law to make it easier for the president to mobilize Guard and reserve units. One would have doubled to 12 months the period for which he could call up as many as

200,000 personnel; the other would have allowed the president to delegate to the secretary of Defense authority to mobilize up to 25,000 reservists for up to 90 days.

But the Senate balked at these proposals. Armed Services Chairman Nunn pointed out repeatedly that the president had unlimited authority to mobilize Guard and reserve members if he declared a national emergency. The conferees agreed only to increase to nine months the period for which the president could call up large numbers of reservists without a declaration of war or national emergency.

The conference report also included provisions:
- Requiring the Pentagon to adopt a policy for processing complaints of sexual harassment or discrimination.
- Extending the period after a service member's death during which his or her survivors remained eligible for housing and medical benefits.
- Mandating that military retirees receive cost of living increases in their pensions at the same time that civilian federal retirees received their annual pay increases. Raises for military retirees had been delayed by the previous year's budget-reconciliation process.

Operations and Maintenance

The conference report authorized $91.5 billion for operations and maintenance costs, a net reduction of $1.38 billion from the budget request. The conferees approved several major additions, including:
- $305 million more than requested for major overhauls of ships, planes and vehicles.
- $100 million more than requested for maintenance of facilities.
- $20 million for training to reduce the risk of "friendly fire" incidents.

But those initiatives were more than offset by several hefty reductions to the budget request, including:
- $725 million cut to reflect the fact that the Pentagon was reducing its civilian payroll during fiscal 1994 more quickly than the budget assumed.
- $140 million cut to force the services to draw down their large Cold War-era inventories by replacing only 65 percent of the parts and supplies used up during the year.
- $140 million cut to reduce the "unobligated balances" of funds appropriated in prior years but not yet committed by contract.

The bill included a provision blocking the administration's proposal to close the armed services' medical school in Bethesda, Md. And it earmarked funds for several high-profile medical projects, including:
- $40 million for work on health care issues affecting women in the military.
- $20 million for research into the so-called Persian Gulf syndrome afflicting veterans of the 1990-91 deployment to the Persian Gulf region.

The conferees also approved provisions establishing policies intended to improve medical treatment of Persian Gulf War veterans.

The bill earmarked $10 million for Pentagon support of the 1996 Olympic Games in Atlanta and $3 million for support of the 1995 Special Olympics.

'Burden Sharing'

The conferees authorized $8.2 billion of the $8.6 billion requested to operate U.S. bases overseas, shifting $400 million to the budget for domestic base operations. However, the secretary of Defense could waive the reduction if the overseas cuts mandated by the conferees could not be made.

Another provision required the president to attempt to revise the bilateral agreements under which U.S. forces were stationed in the territory of other NATO members so that those countries would pay 37.5 percent of the non-payroll costs of U.S. installations in Europe. By the Pentagon's calculation, the allies were covering 36 percent of such costs.

Bipartisan resentment over the much lower defense budgets of most U.S. allies made "burden sharing" a politically explosive issue. But in their report, the conferees argued that some allies bore heavy shares of the burden of collective security in ways that were not reflected by the size of their military budgets. They cited NATO troop deployments as part of the U.N. peacekeeping force in the former Yugoslavia and Germany's expenditures to reconstruct the states of Eastern Europe and the former Soviet Union.

In the portion of the bill authorizing military construction, the conferees approved $119 million of the $219 million requested for the annual U.S. contribution to NATO's infrastructure fund, the alliance's kitty for building facilities for common use. One reason they cited for that cut was to offset $35 million they added to the budget request to improve the living quarters for U.S. troops stationed in South Korea.

Public vs. Private Jobs

The conference report reaffirmed previous law requiring that at least 60 percent by dollar value of major overhauls be performed by government depots rather than by private contractors, thus blocking the administration's plan to shift more overhaul work to the private sector.

But the conferees dropped or diluted several House-passed provisions intended to steer more work toward the 31 government depots, which had a combined payroll of 130,000 civilian and military personnel. For instance, the final bill did not include a House provision that would have required that 60 percent of all maintenance for any new weapon be performed by government depots within five years of the weapon's initial delivery.

On the other hand, the conference report:
- Required the Pentagon to review the extent of alleged cost overruns on overhauls that had been contracted out.
- Authorized government depots to boost their income by leasing excess space or equipment, by competing for contracts to perform work for other federal agencies and by producing non-defense-related commercial products, provided they did not compete with the private sector.

Post-Cold War Initiatives

The conferees approved a total of $3.09 billion for a panoply of programs intended to help displaced military personnel, defense contractors and their communities adjust to the decline in defense spending. This total included:
- $2.19 billion to help small and mid-size companies develop new technologies and "dual use" products having both military and commercial application.
- $188 million for community assistance programs.
- $715 million for severance bonuses, job retraining and other personnel transition programs.

An additional $392 million in the fiscal 1995 budget, which did not require authorization by this bill, was to go to fund early pensions. Some military personnel were being allowed to retire on a reduced pension after 15 years of service instead of the usual 20 years.

Both chambers approved the $400 million requested to help former Soviet republics dispose of the nuclear weapons they inherited.

The conferees approved a total of $86 million to cover the cost of humanitarian and disaster relief operations. Of this amount, $20 million was earmarked for clearing land mines, which claimed a large and gruesome toll of civilian victims long after the end of the wars during which the mines were laid.

The bill also authorized supplemental appropriations for fiscal 1994 to cover the cost of humanitarian operations: $1.2 billion to cover Somalia, Bosnia, Southwest Asia and Haiti, and $270 million to cover Rwanda.

But the conferees could not agree on rules governing the use of $300 million the administration requested as a contingency fund to cover U.N. peacekeeping operations. The House was adamant that such payments should continue to come out of the State Department's budget, so the funds were dropped.

Other Provisions

The conferees approved with minor changes a Senate provision intended to further strengthen the hand of the chairman of the Joint Chiefs of Staff in dealing with the separate armed services. Previously, the secretary of Defense recommended to the president the commanders in chief of the major combat forces, choosing from among three nominees, one offered by each of the armed services. The new provision authorized the Joint Chiefs chairman to nominate a fourth candidate if he was dissatisfied with the other three.

Other provisions:

● Increased from 10 to 11 the number of assistant secretaries of Defense. The 11th slot was considered likely to be filled by the Pentagon's public affairs chief. That office was filled by an official of assistant secretary rank before 1993.

● Allowed defense contractors, under some circumstances, to charge against their contracts some of the costs associated with reorganization following a merger. Administration officials insisted that mergers frequently benefited the government by allowing contractors to cut overhead and thus reduce prices. The provision required the secretary of Defense to report on whether such anticipated savings were being realized. It also authorized the General Accounting Office to analyze each case.

● Urged the president to begin a diplomatic process aimed at securing multilateral agreement to end the embargo on arms shipments to Bosnia.

● Barred the award of any grant or contract to a college that had a policy of barring military recruiters from its campus. The provision was aimed at schools that barred representatives of the armed services on grounds that the services' ban on gay and lesbian conduct was a form of discrimination. ■

B-2 Bomber Production Revisited

Opponents of the B-2 stealth bomber had mixed success in a last-ditch effort to preserve the option of buying additional copies of the bomber in future years.

Since 1990, the radar-evading B-2 had been the focus of vigorous debate. The bomber's price tag of several hundred million dollars per plane made such battles inevitable. But the B-2 also took on a symbolic aspect. Designed for nuclear strikes against the Soviet Union, the plane seemed a perfect target for those who insisted that the demise of the Soviet state permitted dramatic cuts in Pentagon spending. But B-2 supporters contended that, equipped with super-accurate "smart" bombs, it would be an invaluable example of the high-tech weaponry that would give U.S. forces the edge over enemy forces in non-nuclear combat.

In 1993, Congress gave final approval to building the last five of the 20 authorized B-2s in the fiscal 1994 defense authorization bill (HR 2401 — PL 103-160.) The measure also reaffirmed earlier legislation limiting the B-2 force to those 20 planes. *(1993 Almanac, p. 433)*

In 1994, Northrop-Grumman Corp., the prime contractor, and some Air Force personnel began lobbying to add $150 million to the fiscal 1995 budget to keep intact some parts of the B-2 production network that otherwise would begin to wind down during work on the final five planes.

The conference report on the fiscal 1995 defense authorization bill (S 2182 — PL 103-337) reaffirmed the 20-plane limit on the B-2 force, but it also directed the Defense secretary to review the need for additional bombers and authorized $125 million to support that review. The fiscal 1995 defense appropriations bill (HR 4650 — PL 103-335) provided $125 million specifically to preserve the B-2 industrial base. *(Authorization, p. 421; appropriations, p. 488)*

Senate Action

The notion of building more B-2s was vehemently opposed by House Armed Services Committee Chairman Ronald V. Dellums, D-Calif., and committee member John R. Kasich, R-Ohio. So B-2 proponents made no effort to add funds for future B-2 production to the House version of the defense authorization bill.

Instead, the initiative was launched on the Senate side, where the B-2 had a powerful advocate in Armed Services Committee Chairman Sam Nunn, D-Ga. Although President Clinton had not requested the money, the committee bill approved June 9 added $150 million to preserve the option of buying additional B-2 stealth bombers.

At a June 10 news conference, Nunn noted that the administration's "bottom-up review" of U.S. defenses had concluded that at least 185 long-range bombers, equipped to carry non-nuclear "smart" bombs, would be needed to meet the goal of a force that could fend off two virtually simultaneous attacks — for example, on Persian Gulf oil fields and on South Korea.

Because of budgetary limitations, however, the administration planned to mothball some existing B-52 and B-1 bombers, reducing the active force to about 100 planes.

Of the $150 million the committee added to Clinton's request to keep the B-2 production network alive for one more year, Nunn said half would be used to accelerate the purchase of spare parts that were slated for later purchase even if no additional bombers were ordered. He called the remaining $75 million "an insurance policy," adding, "We're taking some temporary steps as hedges against what we think is a serious problem that the administration has not yet been able to come to grips with."

Northrop-Grumman, the B-2's prime contractor, estimated that it could produce 20 additional B-2s — two or three annually — for $12 billion.

Nunn failed in efforts to solicit support for the B-2 funding from top administration officials. He circulated a June 22 letter from Deputy Defense Secretary John M. Deutch disclaiming any interest in the committee initiative: "Absent an unlikely budget windfall . . . or a radical shift in our budget priorities, we simply can't afford additional B-2 aircraft," Deutch wrote.

When the bill came to the floor, Armed Services member Carl Levin, D-Mich., the key Senate opponent of the B-2 initiative, tried to delete the $150 million. The Senate rejected Levin's amendment by a vote of 45-55 on July 1. *(Vote 179, p. 31-S)*

Levin cited the support of senior Pentagon officials for both facets of the amendment he offered: to cancel the committee's $150 million B-2 initiative and to use the money instead to beef up the Pentagon's fund for closing unneeded military bases. *(Base closings, p. 435)*

Levin argued that the 20 B-2s previously authorized were

adequate for U.S. needs, considering the hundreds of other bombers and the thousands of smaller planes and cruise missiles that could also be used to strike overseas targets. "At some point, you terminate a system when you balance it with all the other capabilities you've got," he said.

But Nunn maintained that the B-2 was a uniquely valuable weapon because of its long range and stealthiness, which would allow it to strike key targets with precision-guided "smart" bombs. Nunn insisted that the bomber force that the Clinton budgets would keep in the field fell short of what would be required to carry out the administration's own strategy. He discounted the Pentagon leadership's vocal opposition to the committee's B-2 initiative. "If they see the Senate . . . stand up for the B-2, I think we'll see a little more courageous position from the Department of Defense," he said.

But Nunn acknowledged that winning the B-2 funding in conference with the House would be a tough challenge.

The Senate passed the defense bill (HR 4301, formerly S 2182) by voice vote July 1.

Final Action

The House-Senate conferees who negotiated the final version of the defense authorization bill (S 2182 — H Rept 103-701) ordered a high-level Pentagon review of whether the Air Force needed more long-range bombers than projected budgets allowed.

In a watered-down version of Nunn's initiative, the bill earmarked up to $125 million to study options for acquiring additional bombers and to keep intact for one year critical parts of the network of companies that built and equipped such planes. Deferring to Dellums, the compromise bill prohibited using any of the $125 million for components in anticipation that future budgets would buy additional B-2s, beyond the 20 planes previously approved.

Even so, Nunn insisted that some of the funds could go to B-2 subcontractors, which would make it easier and less expensive to build additional copies later.

While Nunn intended the so-called "bomber industrial base" fund as a foot in the door for additional B-2 production, such production appeared to be highly unlikely as long as the administration opposed building more planes.

Aside from the B-2 production base issue, conferees earmarked $136 million for various other projects to beef up the bomber force. The bill:

● Blocked administration plans to save money by temporarily taking some existing bombers out of regular service.

● Accelerated the deployment of the JDAM smart bomb.

● Earmarked $78 million for various "interim" smart bombs that bombers could carry pending JDAM deployment.

Conferees also approved $305 million to wring the bugs out of the TSSAM — a stealthy cruise missile with a range of more than 100 miles intended to be launched from bombers or ships to scatter small warheads over enemy columns. Clinton requested $606 million for TSSAM, including funds to begin production, but the Pentagon later acknowledged that production would be premature. On Dec. 9, the Pentagon announced plans to cancel the TSSAM.

The House adopted the conference report on the defense authorization bill, 280-137, on Aug. 17. The Senate cleared the bill, 80-18, on Sept. 13. (House vote 404, 122-H; Senate vote 297, p. 51-S)

President Clinton signed the bill Oct. 5. ■

C-17 Construction To Continue

Despite continuing problems in the effort to build a fleet of new wide-body cargo planes, Congress approved President Clinton's request to continue production of the huge C-17, authorizing and appropriating $2.4 billion of the $2.7 billion requested for fiscal 1995. Lawmakers also approved a deal negotiated between the Pentagon and McDonnell Douglas Corp., the plane's manufacturer, to settle several contract disputes. (Authorization, p. 421; appropriations, p. 488)

The C-17 was designed to carry objects as heavy as a tank into primitive airstrips close to a combat zone. It enjoyed strong support from Army and Air Force leaders but came under scrutiny on Capitol Hill because of cost increases and schedule slips, many of which were related to technical shortcomings discovered during prototype testing. In addition, Pentagon officials sharply criticized McDonnell Douglas' management of the program.

In December 1993, John M. Deutch — then the Pentagon's acquisition chief and later the deputy Defense secretary — announced that the Air Force would buy no more than 40 of the big planes, the number it planned to fund through fiscal 1996, unless McDonnell Douglas solved within two years the problems besetting the program. Deutch also said the Pentagon would consider buying off-the-shelf cargo planes to make up for the loss of C-17s. (1993 Almanac, p. 450)

Background

Like the huge C-5 cargo jet that was its predecessor, the C-17 had a cavernous belly that could haul "outsize" items too bulky for other cargo planes — such as M-1 tanks, Patriot anti-missile batteries and Bradley armored troop carriers. Unlike commercial wide-body jets, the C-17 and C-5 had a low-slung fuselage from which vehicles could quickly be driven on and off the aircraft.

The C-17 was smaller than the C-5 — about the size of the narrow-body C-141 cargo hauler — and more agile on the ground. Thus, a fleet of C-17s was supposed to be able to deliver more cargo faster and to make use of runways too short to accommodate the C-5.

By fall of 1993, the program's problems were compounded by a welter of contending legal claims by the government and McDonnell Douglas. Senior administration officials spoke openly of terminating the program.

In December, the Pentagon and the company struck a tentative agreement. Under the package deal:

● The government and the contractor would abandon certain pending and prospective legal claims.

● Each would invest several hundred million additional dollars in the C-17 program.

● The Pentagon would slightly reduce the plane's specifications for range and payload weight.

● The Pentagon would buy a total of 14 additional C-17s in fiscal 1995-96. That would bring the total number of operational planes to 40, the smallest fleet that would be militarily useful, according to the Pentagon.

● Depending on how well McDonnell Douglas met its budget, schedule and performance specifications through fiscal

1996, the Defense Department would decide how many additional C-17s to budget for.

Pentagon plans had called for a total of 120 C-17s. But, depending on the company's performance, as many as 80 of the McDonnell Douglas planes could be replaced by other widebody jets, such as the C-5s built by Lockheed or Boeing 747s.

Clinton asked Congress for legislation to waive any provisions of law that would obstruct the proposed deal with McDonnell Douglas.

House Action

At the behest of Chairman Ronald V. Dellums, D-Calif., the Armed Services Committee sliced from the House defense authorization bill (HR 4301) $1.1 billion of the $2.7 billion that the administration requested for C-17 procurement. The committee also authorized $550 million to explore the "off the shelf" option, rather than the $104 million requested.

The House approach reflected a critique of Clinton's plan by the General Accounting Office (GAO). Dellums later insisted that his panel responded the way it did because the Pentagon had not made a compelling response to the GAO arguments at the time the panel marked up the bill.

Dellums argued that the experience of the Persian Gulf War indicated that only a small portion of the cargo needed in a regional war was outsize and required the unique capacity of the C-5 or C-17. A more critical problem, he said, would be the decline in total capacity for air cargo as C-141s that dated back to the Vietnam War were retired over the following decade. And as the defense budget continued to shrink, he argued, the total amount that could be spent on airlift procurement would be about $2.5 billion annually.

"The issue is not the C-17," Dellums later insisted when the bill was on the House floor. "The issue is airlift . . . how to provide enough overall airlift capability and [specialized] C-17 capabilities within a realistic spending level."

If the limited budgets Dellums projected were spent solely on C-17s, he maintained, total cargo capacity would shrink and not be restored to existing levels for 14 years. To avoid such a trough in total cargo capacity, the committee's proposed alternative was to buy only four C-17s annually, spending the money saved to buy some other, less expensive wide-body cargo jets.

Dellums also refused to back House action on the legislative waiver required by the government's proposed settlement with McDonnell Douglas. The Judiciary and Government Operations committees claimed jurisdiction over that issue.

Armed Services' rejection of the administration's six-plane C-17 request galvanized supporters of the plane. In the House, they were led by two Californians, Republican Steve Horn, whose Long Beach district was home to the C-17 assembly plant, and Democrat Jane Harman, an Armed Services Committee member whose district adjoined Horn's.

The turning point in their efforts came at a May 17 Armed Services hearing — nearly two weeks after the committee finished drafting HR 4301 — when Deputy Defense Secretary Deutch forcefully argued the case for the administration's request.

Deutch rejected Dellums' emphasis on maximizing the overall carrying capacity of the Air Force's long-range cargo fleet. The critical requirement, he insisted, was the one that was the C-17's forte: quickly delivering a lot of bulky equipment such as attack helicopters, troop carriers and anti-missile batteries to primitive airstrips.

"Getting that equipment in the early stages of a conflict is the most important way to minimize casualties, to reduce the length of a conflict and to have military success," Deutch

said. "We are not here discussing the transport of cargo . . . from Dulles Airport to Frankfurt."

So important was that specialized capacity, Deutch insisted, that Clinton's projected airlift budgets were much higher than Dellums postulated.

Deutch also warned that the lower C-17 production rate proposed by the committee would not give the Pentagon a reliable indication of how well McDonnell Douglas could meet its price and schedule commitments if the Pentagon decided to buy more than 40 planes.

After Deutch's appearance, 33 of the 56 Armed Services members signed a letter endorsing the administration's request for six planes.

On May 24, Harman offered an amendment to that effect. The House voted to overturn Dellums' air transport initiative by a vote of 330-100, approving the C-17 funds requested by the administration. The House bill was silent on the proposed contract settlement with McDonnell Douglas. *(Vote 195, p. 60-H)*

Senate Action

In its version of the defense authorization bill (S 2182), the Senate Armed Services Committee trimmed funding for C-17 procurement from $2.7 billion to $2.4 billion. However, it authorized the six planes requested, and it added to the bill language endorsing the proposed settlement with McDonnell Douglas.

The committee also approved $150 million — $46 million more than requested — to study whether an off-the-shelf wide-body jet could be used to supplement the C-17 fleet.

A floor amendment to the defense bill that would have eliminated the language approving the contract settlement was rejected June 22 by a vote of 32-66. *(Vote 162, p. 28-S)*

Amendment sponsor Charles E. Grassley, R-Iowa, blasted the agreement as "a lousy deal for taxpayers." He objected particularly to the reduction in C-17 performance requirements: "The plane doesn't meet the specs. . . . The specs meet the plane," he said. "We pay more and get less."

But Edward M. Kennedy, D-Mass., and other Armed Services members insisted that the package deal was essential to get the C-17 program back on track. "The claims and recriminations between the government and the contractor are the single largest obstacle to a successful C-17 program," Kennedy said. "If you do not authorize the settlement, you might as well not bother with the program."

Final Action

The House-Senate conferees who negotiated the final version of the fiscal 1995 defense authorization bill (S 2182 — H Rept 103-701) trimmed $304 million from the budget request for six C-17 wide-body cargo jets. They approved $2.17 billion, plus $190 million, as requested, for components that would be used in eight additional planes slated for funding in the fiscal 1996 budget.

The bill also authorized the package deal with McDonnell Douglas. And the conferees approved the $104 million requested to test off-the-shelf wide-body cargo planes as supplements to the C-17.

The House approved the conference report, 280-137, on Aug. 17. The Senate cleared the bill by a vote of 80-18 on Sept. 13. Clinton signed the bill (PL 103-337) on Oct. 5. *(House vote 404, p. 122-H; Senate vote 297, p. 51-S)*

The final defense appropriations bill (HR 4650 — PL 103-335) contained the $2.17 billion for six C-17s and the $190 million for additional planes. But it dropped the $104 million authorized to test the feasibility of buying existing wide-body jets off the shelf. ■

Advances for Military Women Come at High Cost for Some

The Pentagon opened more military positions to women in the armed services in 1994, but a hearing before the House Armed Services Committee indicated that at least some women were paying a price for their advancement.

Combat Openings

In one of his last acts before leaving office, Defense Secretary Les Aspin on Jan. 13 ordered a policy change that allowed women to apply for combat support positions in the Army and Marine Corps. Nine months earlier, he had ordered the armed services to allow women to serve on combat air crews and on warships. *(1993 Almanac, p. 463)*

Aspin scrapped the Pentagon's so-called risk rule under which the services had barred women from certain types of non-combat units solely on the basis that personnel in such units routinely incurred a significant risk of being killed, wounded or captured by enemy forces.

Under the new policy, women could only be excluded outright from units that were primarily intended to engage in "direct combat," which was defined as "engaging an enemy on the ground with . . . weapons, while being exposed to hostile fire and to a high probability of direct physical contact with" enemy troops.

The services could request permission from the Defense secretary to exclude women from units under certain other conditions, such as when those units routinely were located alongside ground combat units.

The new policy was expected to open about 18,000 Army positions to women.

Harassment in the Military

Members of the House Armed Services Committee expressed revulsion at the military's treatment of four women who appeared before them March 9 with vivid tales of sexual harassment.

The witnesses, one from each of the four services, said the retribution exacted upon them for complaining of sexual harassment was worse than the original offense.

Chairman Ronald V. Dellums, D-Calif., called the testimony "very powerful, very compelling and very painful." And a subdued Floyd D. Spence of South Carolina, the committee's ranking Republican, said, "I guess I have to be reminded how indecent people can be to other people."

Members of both parties hinted that Congress might force changes through legislation if the Pentagon failed to act. And members included provisions strengthening protections against sexual harassment in the fiscal 1995 defense authorization (PL 103-337). *(Defense authorization, p. 421)*

Navy Lt. Darlene S. Simmons, a lawyer in the Naval Reserve, testified that one of her supervisors aboard the submarine tender USS *Canopus* made repeated sexual advances toward her, including sliding a sexually explicit letter under her cabin door one evening.

She reported the harassment to her commanding officer and gave him the letter as evidence, but she said no investigation had been conducted. Her commanding officer burned the letter, Simmons said. When she complained to Sen. John B. Breaux, D-La., her superiors sent her to a mental institution for psychiatric evaluation. Although the exam took only one day, Simmons said she was kept in a locked ward for three more days because her commander did not ask for her release.

Sgt. Zenaida Martinez said that when she filed a sexual harassment complaint with her Air Force superiors, her car tires were slashed and the wheels' lug nuts were loosened.

Marine Corps Sgt. Carol L. Fuehrmann cried as she told of her case: While members of a court-martial believed she had been harassed, they found the defendant not guilty because they thought the punishment, automatic separation from the Corps, was too harsh.

James V. Hansen, R-Utah, said the military's system to address complaints "isn't working . . . and if the military won't [fix] it, it falls to this committee" to see that things change.

All four witnesses told the committee that the best solution would be to take the complaint system outside the armed services' chain of command. ■

Hill Addresses Base Closing Issues

With the next scheduled round of base closings a year away, Congress was not required to approve any shutdowns in 1994. However, several base closing matters did attract attention.

● The Supreme Court ruled that the 1990 law that established the process for closing unneeded military facilities was not subject to judicial review.

● The House overwhelming rejected an attempt to postpone the next round of base closings, set for 1995, until 1997.

● Congress cleared a bill (S 2534) to make it easier for local communities to get land from bases that were being closed.

● The Senate set the 1995 round of base closings in motion by approving the nomination of former Sen. Alan J. Dixon, D-Ill., to be chairman of the Defense Base Closure and Realignment Commission.

Background

The 1990 base closings law (PL 101-510) represented one of the most successful deals Congress and the president ever made. In return for strict controls on the process, Congress agreed to give the president wide latitude in closing unneeded domestic military bases.

Under the 1990 law, the president (with bipartisan input from House and Senate leaders) appointed an eight-member commission to handle each round of base closings, subject to confirmation by the Senate. The commission weighed base closings recommended by the Defense Department.

The commission conducted public hearings to elicit the views of affected communities, members of Congress and other interested parties. It then sent a revised list to the president, who had to accept or reject it unchanged. If the president rejected the revised list, the process for that year stopped. If he approved it, the decisions took effect automatically. Congress could stop the closings by acting within 45 legislative days to pass a bill blocking the entire list.

In two rounds of decisions in 1991 and 1993, Congress agreed to close a total of 60 major and 104 minor bases. The law required another round of base closures in 1995. *(1993 Almanac, p. 465)*

Supreme Court Decision

On May 23, the Supreme Court unanimously cleared the way for the president to continue shutting down unwanted bases without second-guessing by the courts. The court ruled in *Dalton v. Specter* that President George Bush had acted within his powers in 1991 when he accepted the recommendation of the commission to close the Philadelphia Naval Shipyard.

Sen. Arlen Specter, R-Pa., argued the case before the high court March 2, the first sitting member of Congress to appear before the court since 1972.

Specter had been fighting the case for the Philadelphia Naval Shipyard since its closure was approved. The base was slated to close in mid-1995, and several thousand workers already had been let go in preparation. Specter and other elected officials from New Jersey, Pennsylvania and Delaware sued the government in July 1991, claiming that the Navy and the base closure commission had violated the law's detailed procedures for closure decisions. *(1991 Almanac, p. 427)*

A U.S. District Court threw out the case, saying that the base closure law prohibited judicial review. The 3rd U.S. Circuit Court of Appeals reversed that decision, ruling that the law prohibited judicial review only of certain aspects of the process. Courts, it said, could assess whether the commission and the Defense Department followed statutory guidelines.

The government appealed to the Supreme Court. Had Specter prevailed, it could have opened the gates for lawsuits by cities and states fighting to keep their bases open.

In oral arguments, the Clinton administration urged the high court to stay out of the complicated process for closing domestic military bases.

Solicitor General Drew S. Days III told the justices that the statute did not provide for judicial review and that Congress did not intend to allow it. Moreover, he said, the Administrative Procedures Act, which allowed judicial review of final agency actions, did not apply in this case because the final action was taken by the president, who was not subject to that law.

Specter countered that "the courts must always be able to review the delegation of authority by Congress." He further argued that the base-closure commission made the final decision, since the president could not add or subtract a base from the closure list.

Chief Justice William H. Rehnquist wrote the main opinion, saying Specter and other plaintiffs could not challenge the commission's recommendation under the Administrative Procedures Act because the president, not the commission, made the actual determination to close the bases.

Rehnquist said Congress gave the president ample discretion to accept or reject the commission's recommendations. "How the President chooses to exercise the discretion Congress has granted him is not a matter for our review," he wrote.

In a concurring opinion joined by Justices Harry A. Blackmun, Ruth Bader Ginsburg and John Paul Stevens, Justice David H. Souter said that Congress did not want to provide judicial review for provisions of the base closing law.

"The very reasons that led Congress by this enactment to bind its hands from untying a package, once assembled, go far to persuade me that Congress did not mean the courts to have any such power through judicial review," Souter wrote.

1995 Round Confirmed

On May 24, the day after the Supreme Court ruling, the House rejected, 68-362, an amendment to its version of the defense authorization bill (HR 4301) that would have delayed until 1997 the round of base closings scheduled for 1995. *(Vote 194, p. 58-H; defense authorization, p. 421)*

Under existing law, the 1995 round was to be the last one conducted under the 1990 procedures. Pentagon officials predicted that the 1995 closures would eliminate as many jobs as the three previous base-closing rounds combined. But the administration had also broached the idea of adding a round of closures in 1997 to delay some of the pain until after the 1996 elections.

Armed Services Committee member James V. Hansen, R-Utah, the amendment's sponsor, called for "a two-year pause so the defense budget can catch up with the enormous, upfront cost of base closures and realignments and communities can catch up with the needed economic adjustment."

But even some of the most ardent GOP critics of Clinton's defense cutbacks argued that additional bases had to be closed. "Although I do not like where we are, we are here," said Curt Weldon, R-Pa. "We are cutting defense dramatically. To do that we have to continue to downsize . . . our installations."

Dixon Nomination

Clinton launched the 1995 round of base closings Oct. 4, nominating Dixon to chair the Defense Base Closure and Realignment Commission that was to decide the fate of dozens of domestic military bases in 1995.

The Senate Armed Services Committee easily approved the nomination of their former colleague Oct. 5, and the full Senate ratified the decision by voice vote on Oct. 7.

Dixon, who had been defeated by Carol Moseley-Braun in the 1992 Democratic primary, succeeded former Rep. James A. Courter, R-N.J., who chaired the commission for the two previous rounds of closings.

At the confirmation hearing, senators raised concerns ranging from the estimated costs of environmental restoration at bases that were being shut down to the Pentagon's methodology for calculating the military worth of a base. But overall, the session was reminiscent of a family reunion as senators warmly greeted their former colleague.

As a senator, Dixon had had a reputation as a dogged dealmaker in securing benefits for his Illinois constituents. In 1989, during debate on the Senate floor, he expressed outrage at "an American tragedy" after the Pentagon decided to close Chanute Air Force Base in Rantoul, Ill. But Dixon also said he recognized the Pentagon's need to downsize, telling a reporter at the time, "You've got to understand. This process was designed to *stop* a guy like me."

Dixon, who pledged to be fair and objective as commission chairman, told reporters after the hearing that he would recuse himself from any decisions regarding Scott Air Force Base, a sprawling multipurpose facility just outside Belleville, Ill. "You know where my heart is on that," he said.

Dixon told senators he disagreed with the policy of the base closure commission in 1993, when the panel added dozens of bases to the original list prepared by the Pentagon. The commission had argued that it could not make a fair judgment about which of several similar bases to close without examining all similar bases in the country, most of which never made the Pentagon's original closure list.

Dixon also said that the tremendous cleanup costs should not affect decisions on whether to close a base. "It's an open secret that there isn't enough money to clean up the bases they want to close," he said.

Use of Closed Bases

Advocates for the homeless no longer could claim first rights to use closed military bases under a bill that the Senate and House passed by voice vote Oct. 6 and Oct. 7, respectively. The bill added an exemption for military bases to the 1987 McKinney act, which required that underutilized federal facilities be used to assist the homeless. Clinton signed the measure Oct. 25 (S 2534 — PL 103-421).

Many communities had tried to ease the economic impact of base closings by promoting commercial redevelopment of the sites. In several cases, homeless assistance advocates and local officials eager to promote commercial uses locked horns, delaying decisions on how to reuse closing bases.

The bill exempted from the McKinney act any military bases targeted for closure in 1995. It also applied to bases already being closed if local communities opted in.

But it also created a strong incentive for homeless advocates and local officials to negotiate reuse plans taking into account both economic factors and needs of the homeless. ■

Chemical Weapons Treaty Not Ratified in 1994

The Senate Foreign Relations Committee held a series of seven hearings on the Chemical Weapons Convention, but due to objections from several members of the committee, it did not vote on the huge treaty in 1994.

The far reaching treaty had a bold aim: to rid the world of chemical weapons.

It required all signatory nations to destroy their chemical weapons within 10 years, although extensions were possible. It provided for the creation of an international monitoring agency to conduct both scheduled and surprise inspections of chemical plants and other companies that used chemicals covered by the treaty.

Although the Clinton administration called the accord one of its top foreign policy priorities, events in Haiti, Cuba and Bosnia kept the president's team focused elsewhere.

Background

Appalled by the large-scale use of chemical agents in World War I, the leading nations of the world in 1925 agreed to the Geneva Protocol outlawing the use of chemical weapons. It soon became apparent that the protocol was of little value, however, because it did not ban production or storage of the weapons. Many signatory nations reserved the right to retaliate in kind if attacked by a foe using chemical weapons. The U.S. Senate did not ratify the treaty until 1975, and then only with such a reservation.

In 1968, negotiations began in Geneva for the total elimination of chemical weapons. The same year, a chemical weapons test at the Dugway Proving Ground in Utah accidentally killed several thousand sheep 20 miles from the site. The resulting congressional investigation and public outcry eventually forced the Nixon administration to unilaterally cease production of chemical weapons.

The 1991 Persian Gulf War and Iraqi President Saddam Hussein's threat to use chemical weapons was the galvanizing force needed to conclude the negotiations. On Jan. 13, 1993, the 450-page Chemical Weapons Convention was complete. The United States and the Russian Federation were among the original signatories, though both nations already had agreed in 1990 to destroy most of their chemical weapons stockpiles. *(1993 Almanac, p. 474)*

Reporting Requirements

CIA Director R. James Woolsey told the Senate Foreign Relations Committee on June 23 that because chemical weapons were so easy to make, verification procedures of the Chemical Weapons Convention were "the most comprehensive and intrusive of any arms control agreement yet negotiated."

The treaty provided for the creation of an Organization for the Prohibition of Chemical Weapons, an international body designed to enforce the convention's requirements and monitor the results.

The chemical weapons treaty was to come into force after 65 nations had ratified it. At that point, each signatory country would have to report to the new international organization:

● The location and inventory of all chemical weapons storage sites.
● The location and capacities of all chemical weapons production and research facilities.
● Details of all chemical weapons and chemical weapons equipment transfers since 1946.
● Plans for the destruction of the chemical weapons.
● The location and activities of any facility using or producing controlled chemicals.

The convention separated all chemicals that could be involved in weapons production into three "schedules," or categories. Chemicals on any of the three schedules were to be considered controlled and their use in any sizable quantity monitored.

Schedule 1 chemicals were military agents with little or no commercial value, such as mustard gas, alkyl phosphonofluorides and other nerve agents.

Schedule 2 chemicals were those that could easily be transformed into chemical weapons and toxic chemicals with moderate commercial use.

Schedule 3 consisted of dual-use chemicals — ones with major commercial uses that also could be used in creating chemical weapons. For example, some plastics were made with the Schedule 3 chemical phosgene, the deadly gas used in World War I.

Once the treaty went into effect, signatory nations could not export any Schedule 1 chemicals to countries that had not signed the treaty. Within three years, the same restrictions were to apply to Schedule 2 chemicals. Schedule 3 chemicals could be freely traded as long as the recipient specified how it would use the chemicals.

While these reporting requirements represented incremental changes for the U.S. chemical industry, already one of the nation's most regulated businesses, they were a potential burden for companies that used controlled chemicals.

Surprise Inspections

In addition, companies that used or produced chemicals on Schedules 1 or 2 were to be subject to regular, scheduled inspections.

But the most controversial item during negotiations of the Chemical Weapons Convention also was likely to be the most problematic for U.S. businesses — the challenge, or "surprise," inspection. It was "the central element of the verification regime," said Don Mahley, acting assistant director for multilateral affairs at the Arms Control and Disarmament Agency (ACDA).

Any business in any signatory country would be subject to a surprise inspection if they were challenged by another member of the compact. "Challenge inspections can be on

any site anywhere," said Michael Moodie, president of a non-profit organization called the Chemical and Biological Arms Control Institute.

The request would go to the Executive Council of the Organization for the Prohibition of Chemical Weapons. Unless 31 of the 41 country representatives on the council believed that the inspection request was frivolous, the inspection would be conducted.

Within 48 hours, an international inspection team of 15 to 18 members would arrive. For three days, the company could negotiate the terms of the inspection with the international team, but after that the inspectors would have to be allowed into the plant.

Supporters of the treaty argued that the international organization would hire relatively few inspectors, thus keeping the number of inspections low. Most inspections would be scheduled reviews of chemical weapons plants and chemical companies, not surprise inspections, they said.

ACDA's Mahley said the agency would have about 232 inspectors who would conduct 300 to 400 inspections a year. There were about 100 declared military sites, 100 Schedule 1 sites, and about 700 Schedule 2 and 3 sites worldwide that would require periodic scheduled inspections.

The Office of Technology Assessment had estimated that a one-time inspection of a large, complex facility that used many chemicals in its products could cost as much as $500,000. The U.S. government had no plans to reimburse businesses for these expenses.

Even more troubling to companies than the costs were fears that business secrets might be revealed during an inspection.

The convention included some protections against bad faith inspectors — those who would give away or sell crucial business information — including waiving an inspector's diplomatic immunity from prosecution. If the monetary incentives to steal the information were big enough, however, such a threat could be relatively meaningless.

Even if all the inspectors were honest, there was still tremendous potential for leaks from the central data banks that would store reports from businesses. ∎

Arms Cuts Announced

Defense Secretary William J. Perry announced Sept. 22 that the Clinton administration planned to reduce the number of nuclear-armed bombers and submarines in service, but that it would not cut the number of nuclear warheads that U.S. forces could deliver below levels previously agreed upon.

Under the new policy, the U.S. arsenal was to decline to 3,500 weapons by 2003. That was the ceiling set by the second Strategic Arms Reduction Treaty (START II), which was signed in 1993 but had not yet been approved by the Senate.

Critics warned that unless the nuclear powers demonstrated that they were moving toward eventual nuclear disarmament, non-nuclear states might balk in 1995 at renewing a 1968 non-proliferation treaty. But Perry contended that the force being planned by the Pentagon was needed in case an authoritarian regime returned to power in Russia and tried to brandish the country's 25,000 remaining nuclear weapons. "We do not believe that reversal is likely, and we are working with Russia to minimize the risk of it occurring," Perry said. "Nevertheless, we still feel that it is prudent to provide some hedge against that happening."

Under the new policy, the result of a 10-month Pentagon study, the administration planned to:

● Reduce from 94 to 66 the number of B-52 bombers in service. All 90-plus B-1 bombers were to be equipped for non-nuclear missions.

● Retire the four oldest Trident missile submarines, leaving in service 14 ships, each carrying 24 missiles.

● Equip all Trident subs with Trident II missiles. This required retrofitting four subs that were carrying the Trident I missile with the larger Trident II.

● Keep in service 450 to 500 Minuteman III land-based missiles, each carrying a single warhead. A proposal to reduce the number of missiles to 300 was dropped at the last minute.

● Eliminate the option of carrying nuclear weapons on aircraft carriers and nuclear-armed cruise missiles on surface ships. Submarines were to retain the capability of launching nuclear cruise missiles, though they did not routinely carry such weapons.

● Upgrade the electronic locks on nuclear weapons intended to prevent their unauthorized use and install such locks for the first time on missile-launching submarines. ∎

Perry Wins Swift, Unanimous Defense Confirmation

The Senate on Feb. 3 unanimously confirmed the nomination of William J. Perry to become President Clinton's second secretary of Defense.

Perry succeeded Les Aspin, who had been forced to resign in part because of White House dissatisfaction with his loose management at the Pentagon. Aspin had also frequently gotten bogged down in controversies that ranged from gays in the military to peacekeeping in Somalia. He announced his plans to resign on Dec. 15, 1993. Clinton first tapped retired Adm. Bobby Ray Inman to replace Aspin, but Inman abruptly withdrew Jan. 18. *(1993 Almanac, p. 474)*

The Senate's swift action on Perry — it confirmed him just 10 days after he was selected — and the 97-0 vote underscored the extraordinarily high regard that Democrats and Republicans alike had for Perry, a 66-year-old defense technologist who had served as Aspin's deputy. *(Vote 23, p. 5-S)*

That regard was demonstrated by the effusion of praise during the Senate Armed Services Committee's Feb. 2 hearing on the nomination. "One of the bright spots at the Department of Defense of this past year," ranking Republican Strom Thurmond, S.C., said of Perry. "I am confident he will not disappoint us."

Armed Services Chairman Sam Nunn, D-Ga., underscored his enthusiasm by departing from his practice of keeping confidential his advice to presidents. Nunn said that since the 1992 election, he had talked with Clinton three times to recommend potential defense secretaries: "Each time, I put Bill Perry's name at the top of the list."

Notwithstanding all that bipartisan support, Perry's nomination was grazed by Republican fire aimed at Clinton administration policies. Repeatedly during the three-hour Armed Services hearing, committee Republicans linked kudos for Perry with broadsides at Clinton. They accused the president of seeking budgets too small to fund his announced defense strategy and of taking too soft a line toward North Korea, which was widely believed to be developing nuclear weapons.

"There's no question . . . in this panel or even in the Congress about your experience or competence or commitment to this job," Daniel R. Coats, R-Ind., told Perry in one such

remark. "The question is . . . why would anybody want this job at this particular time?"

The committee approved Perry's nomination Feb. 3 by a vote of 22-0.

'Daunting Challenge'

During the Feb. 2 hearing, Perry acknowledged that he would face "a daunting challenge" in trying to manage the contraction of the U.S. defense establishment in the post-Soviet world. "Historically, we have not managed well such budget declines and attendant downsizing," he said. "This time, we must get it right, or we will pay the cost later either in blood or treasure or both."

Perry emphasized his support for Aspin's major initiatives to guide the retrenchment, including the fiscal 1995 defense budget request and the "bottom-up review" concluded in September 1993, which set out the Clinton team's long-term defense objectives. *(1993 Almanac, p. 452)*

"We worked hand in hand," Perry said of his relationship with Aspin. "You should reasonably expect continuity." At the same time, Perry acknowledged that his leadership style would differ from that of Aspin. And he distanced himself from his predecessor on at least two points.

He said the oversight of war plans would be his priority as secretary, adding: "I pledge to provide the required support to [combat commanders] as they direct our forces in the field." This recalled Aspin's refusal to send to Somalia tanks requested by the U.S. commander there, a decision that became a lightning rod for Aspin's critics.

And Perry said he would reorganize the "ineffective" network of assistant secretaries that Aspin had set up under Frank Wisner, the under secretary of Defense for policy, to deal with strategic planning, future nuclear threats and other issues.

Several Republicans contended that Clinton's projected budgets were too stingy to pay for the goal set in the bottom-up review of fielding a U.S. force large enough to fight two major wars breaking out "nearly simultaneously" in widely separated regions such as the Persian Gulf and the Korean Peninsula. By the administration's own estimates, projected defense requests through fiscal 1999 would amount to $20 billion less than needed.

"I see an erosion in readiness," Arizona Republican John McCain warned. "I see us unable to recruit and retain the quality men and women that we have been able to attract and keep in the past. I see us on a slippery slope."

Perry contended that the administration did not have to begin dealing with the $20 billion shortfall until the following year. By then, he said, the Pentagon would have a better idea of how quickly inflation would boost prices and how much money might be saved by reforming the way the Pentagon acquired weapons.

Whether by cutting costs or increasing the budget, Perry pledged, the administration would pay for the force that was recommended by the bottom-up review: "I've committed to [it]. The president has committed to it. All that remains is filling in the details."

Perry defended his policy of continuing production of some weapons that were not required — such as the $2.5 billion *Seawolf* submarine — for the sake of preserving a critical sector of the defense industry that would be needed in the future. "It costs us some front-end money," Perry said, "but it actually saves us over the long term."

Addressing concerns about his image as a technocrat, Perry vowed to be "fully engaged on all issues of national security significance" as a member of Clinton's national security team. ■

Halperin Withdraws His Name From Pentagon Consideration

Controversial Pentagon nominee Morton H. Halperin formally asked President Clinton on Jan. 10 not to renominate him to oversee U.S. participation in international peacekeeping activities. Clinton complied.

A prolific defense analyst and a civil liberties activist who forcefully criticized U.S. covert operations in the 1970s and 1980s, Halperin had been tapped by Defense Secretary Les Aspin to fill a new job as assistant secretary of Defense for democracy and peacekeeping. *(1993 Almanac, p. 476)*

But even before Clinton formally sent Halperin's name to the Senate Aug. 6, 1993, conservatives mounted a strenuous campaign to block the nomination. The critics contended that Halperin's public statements and writings revealed a dangerous aversion to the use of military force or covert operations to further U.S. interests abroad.

As Clinton's peacekeeping initiatives went awry in Somalia and Haiti, Halperin's nomination also became a focal point for critics of the administration's penchant for military interventions in risky circumstances under multilateral auspices.

Neither the Armed Services panel nor the Senate acted on the nomination, which thus lapsed at the end of the first session of the 103rd Congress. The administration insisted Clinton would resubmit the nomination in 1994. But on Dec. 15, 1993, Halperin's sponsor, Aspin, announced he would step down as Pentagon chief early in 1994.

In a Jan. 10 exchange of letters, Halperin wrote, "I believe that Cabinet officers should have the freedom to select their subordinates." Clinton responded that he appreciated Halperin's "understanding of the circumstances involved in a new secretary of Defense coming on board."

Halperin subsequently went to the National Security Council, where he was given the title of Senior Director for Democracy. The White House job was not subject to Senate confirmation. ■

Congress Challenges, Confirms Clinton's Military Promotions

Three times in 1994, the Senate became embroiled in debates over the rank of a retiring military officer. In all three cases, the Senate ratified the Clinton administration's recommendations, but not without controversy.

By law, officers holding the two highest military ranks (admiral and vice admiral in the Navy, and general and lieutenant general in the other services) reverted to the third-highest rank (rear admiral in the Navy and major general in the other services) upon retirement. However, presidents routinely nominated these officers to retire at the higher rank, a step that required Senate confirmation, and the Senate routinely concurred.

Narrowly defined, the question was one of dollars and cents. Rank was a critical component in calculating a retiring officer's pension, which was a percentage of the annual salary for the rank at which he or she retired.

In 1994, however, senators used retirement nominations to highlight concerns with the military — from the 1991 Tailhook scandal, where Navy and Marine Corps aviators sexually assaulted women at their annual convention, to how well the C-17 cargo program was proceeding.

Kelso and Tailhook

Perhaps the most controversial of the nominations was that of Adm. Frank B. Kelso II. As chief of naval operations since June 1990, Kelso had headed the Navy during the rowdy 1991 convention of the Tailhook Association, where numerous women and a few men were sexually assaulted by naval officers. *(1992 Almanac, p. 520)*

The Navy investigation into the incident was widely criticized as incomplete and incompetent. It was followed in 1993 by a scathing Defense Department inspector general's report, which found that 117 officers were implicated in assaults on 83 women and seven men.

The Clinton administration pulled out all the stops in a campaign to let Kelso retire with all his stars. For four hours April 12, the Senate Armed Services Committee heard praise of Kelso from Defense Secretary William J. Perry, Navy Secretary John H. Dalton and Gen. John M. Shalikashvili, chairman of the Joint Chiefs of Staff. Each argued that Kelso should not be penalized upon retirement even though the Tailhook sexual assault case happened on his watch.

It was an easy sell in the committee; on April 14, the panel voted 20-2 to recommend that Kelso be permitted to retire in grade with full benefits. But the extraordinary show of support was aimed not so much at the committee as at potential opposition on the Senate floor.

Perry told the panel that the admiral might have displayed poor leadership in handling the investigation but that the lapse was "not sufficient enough to offset" his 38 years of military service. Dalton added, "We cannot go back and change the past, and I would caution against reaction to the frustration with the results [of the investigation] by singling out Adm. Kelso." Armed Services Chairman Sam Nunn, D-Ga., agreed. "There's no doubt [Kelso] could have done better" in dealing with Tailhook, he said, but "a two-grade reduction in rank would not be appropriate."

Kay Bailey Hutchison, R-Texas, the lone woman on the committee, disagreed. "I don't think the investigation conducted by the Navy was adequate, and he must be held accountable," she said. Hutchison and Senate Appropriations Committee Chairman Robert C. Byrd, D-W.Va., were the two committee members who voted against giving Kelso top retirement benefits.

For Kelso, the difference in pension was between the $84,340 per year for a four-star admiral's pension level and the $67,422 per year that a two-star rank would receive. But far more sensitive issues were at stake. Shalikashvili said April 12 that his testimony was "likely to fuel charges that we in the services are operating an old-boy network by trying to shield Adm. Kelso from blame. Nothing could be further from the truth."

Nunn spoke at length about conflicting reports on Kelso's conduct. Kelso said he was not at the Las Vegas convention of the Tailhook Association the day most of the assaults took place, and he said he saw no misbehavior during his brief visit the previous day. The report by the Defense Department's inspector general backed Kelso's assertions. But in February, a military judge, who threw out charges against lower-ranking personnel, alleged on the basis of trial testimony that Kelso not only witnessed misbehavior but also manipulated the Navy's investigation.

Perry, Dalton and Shalikashvili said the judge's conclusions were erroneous and were skewed because Kelso was not a party to the proceedings and could not offer a defense.

Kelso Wins Four Stars

On April 19, the Senate voted 54-43 to permit Kelso to retire with four stars. *(Vote 93, p. 17-S)*

Although they lost, the seven women in the Senate had pulled together across party lines to force a protracted, emotional and sometimes bitter six-hour floor debate over the Navy's handling of its female work force, particularly in cases of sexual abuse and harassment.

In addition to the women — five of them Democrats and two Republicans — the opposition to Kelso came from a variety of corners. It included Bob Packwood, R-Ore., who was under investigation by the Senate Ethics Committee for allegedly sexually harassing numerous women, and Arlen Specter, R-Pa., who was criticized by women's groups for his prosecutorial questioning of Anita Hill during her sexual harassment testimony in Clarence Thomas' Supreme Court confirmation.

"If the Senate does act today to hold Adm. Kelso accountable," Byrd argued, "it will do more than any sexual harassment training session to bring home the responsibility and accountability of all uniformed personnel to conduct themselves professionally."

Armed Services member Jim Exon, D-Neb., said Kelso had been a champion of women in the Navy, having supported their advancement and "legislation that opens combat ships and aircraft to women."

But Kelso's Senate supporters were clearly uncomfortable. Alan K. Simpson, R-Wyo., wryly told The Associated Press that news coverage of the debate would conclude that the "bozo, baldheaded old" senators "still don't get it."

Mauz Retirement Causes Concern

Despite concerns among female senators, the Senate on Sept. 20 approved the retirement at the rank of admiral a man whose diligence in handling sexual harassment complaints had been questioned. By 92-6, the Senate agreed to retire Adm. Henry H. Mauz Jr., commander of the Atlantic Fleet, at an admiral's rank. *(Vote 300, p. 52-S)*

In Mauz's case, the higher rank was worth about $17,000 annually in additional retirement benefits.

Patty Murray, Wash., and the Senate's four other Democratic women contended that Mauz had not acted quickly enough to protect Lt. Darlene Simmons, an officer aboard the submarine tender USS *Canopus*, against retribution by other officers after she successfully brought a sexual harassment complaint against a superior officer in 1992.

Murray and others also noted an unrelated incident in which a petty officer complained that, after he had exposed a junket by Mauz to Bermuda that drew highly critical television coverage, the admiral manipulated the Navy's legal system to retaliate.

Nunn, whose Armed Services panel had twice deferred action on the nomination to probe new allegations, insisted that inquiries by the Navy and the Pentagon's inspector general had satisfied the committee that Mauz was innocent of any wrongdoing. The Armed Services Committee favorably reported Mauz's nomination Aug. 12 by a unanimous vote of 22-0.

When the Senate took up the matter Sept. 14, Murray offered a motion to recommit the nomination to the Armed Services Committee with instructions that the panel hold a hearing on the allegations against Mauz. Nunn and other Armed Services members vehemently opposed the motion.

The matter never came to a head because Republicans seized on Murray's motion as a vehicle for trying to force a vote on President Clinton's plan to send U.S. troops to remove Haiti's military junta from power. Rather than allow a vote that would have been embarrassing to Clinton, Majority

Leader George J. Mitchell, D-Maine, stalled until the Senate quit for the weekend.

By the time the Senate resumed debate on the nomination Sept. 19, eleventh-hour negotiations had allowed U.S. forces to enter Haiti peacefully, and GOP critics of the Clinton policy no longer sought to force a floor vote. *(Haiti, p. 449)*

Murray withdrew her recommittal motion, although she and two other women, Barbara Boxer, D-Calif., and Carol Moseley-Braun, D-Ill., voted against Mauz. All five Democratic women in the Senate demanded in a letter to Defense Secretary Perry that the Pentagon establish procedures to ensure that serious allegations against nominees received a thorough review in the future.

Glosson Nomination Prevails

In the final hours before the Oct. 8 recess, the Senate confirmed promotions for three senior Air Force officers whose nominations had been contested by Iowa Republican Charles E. Grassley, a frequent Pentagon critic.

The most contentious of the three cases was the nomination of Lt. Gen. Buster C. Glosson to retire at the lieutenant general rank.

Glosson, a former fighter pilot and Vietnam veteran who was the chief planner of the 1991 air war against Iraq, had been a rising star in the Air Force. But his career stalled in 1993,

when the Air Force and Defense Department inspectors general concluded that Glosson had attempted to prejudice a promotion board against a more junior officer and subsequently lied about his actions to cover his tracks. Glosson received a letter of admonishment from the Air Force, which in effect barred him from future advancement. He opted to resign.

Clinton nominated Glosson to retire as a lieutenant general, for an annual pension about $6,700, higher than the one he would have gotten if he retired at the lower rank. Ultimately, a specially convened panel concluded that although Glosson broke the rules by trying to influence the promotion board, he did not deliberately lie.

The Senate Armed Services Committee approved the nomination 14-7. The Senate confirmed it, 59-30. *(Vote 327, p. 57-S)*

Grassley also tried to derail Senate action on the nominations of Lt. Gen. Edward P. Barry Jr. to retire at the lieutenant general rank and Col. Claude M. Bolton Jr. to be promoted to brigadier general. Bolton was not retiring.

Barry was in charge of several aircraft procurement programs, including the C-17 cargo jet, and Bolton was the program manager for a long-range, bomber-launched cruise missile. Citing reports by the Pentagon's inspector general, Grassley said both programs had been improperly managed. But the committee unanimously approved the two nominations, and the Senate confirmed them by voice vote. ∎

Chapter 10

FOREIGN
POLICY

Foreign Policy
Changing World Order 445
War in Bosnia 446
Haiti Occupation 449
Foreign Aid Reform 452
State Department Authorization 454
Intelligence
Intelligence Authorization 458
NRO Undercover Office Complex 461

Ames Spy Case 463
Ames Interview Excerpts 464
Bilateral, Other Issues
Russian Aid 466
Vietnam Trade Embargo Ends 467
Iran-Contra Probe Concluded 468
Other Foreign Policy Legislation 469
Foreign Policy Appointments 471

Changing World Order

Clinton, Congress Struggle To Define U.S. Interests

*With framework imposed by the Cold War gone,
focus shifts from one crisis to the next*

True to post-Cold War predictions, the challenge for the world's remaining superpower was to forge a foreign policy tailored not to one easily identifiable threat but to multiple, murky trouble spots around the globe.

After the fall of communism, it became increasingly difficult for U.S. presidents to articulate bona fide threats to U.S. interests and to propose acceptable solutions. President Clinton, in the second year of his term, continued a policy as unfocused as the new world order, while Congress looked for ways to curb the administration's impulse to respond to global brush fires where U.S. interests seemed peripheral.

From week to week, the focus of Washington's foreign policy establishment seemed to swing from one region to another. A marketplace massacre in the Bosnian capital of Sarajevo was quickly overshadowed by renewed tensions over North Korea's putative nuclear weapons program. Russia's growing assertiveness sparked fears of a new rivalry with Moscow, then just as rapidly faded from discussion.

As they confronted high-stakes policy issues, the White House and Congress were traveling without a compass.

For more than four decades, the Soviet threat had served as the lodestar for U.S. foreign policy. The United States had had the dubious luxury of concentrating its attention on the single, apocalyptic peril posed by a nuclear-armed Soviet Union. "Presidents Bush and Clinton have both spoken about the 'new world order' as if it's close by," said House Foreign Affairs Committee Chairman Lee H. Hamilton, D-Ind. "But I don't think we're going to see our way too clearly on these matters for some years to come."

U.S. policy-makers were unable to define national security interests except through a messy process of trial and error, a process that alarmed many lawmakers with its uncertainty and inconsistency.

The reasons were manifest. Clinton, determined to champion his domestic agenda, devoted limited time and attention to national security matters. In Congress, the partisan and ideological alliances that endured for much of the Cold War had largely disappeared, and nothing emerged to replace them in providing overarching principles of foreign policy.

Debating Intervention

Of the three major conflicts where U.S. intervention was at issue in 1994 — Bosnia, Haiti and Iraq — only Iraq presented a virtually uncontested case for action. The civil war in Bosnia and the refusal of the oppressive military regime in Haiti to give up power posed more difficult problems for an ill-defined U.S. foreign policy.

● **Iraq.** U.S. interests in the region had been debated and decided during the buildup to the 1991 Persian Gulf War. When, in October 1994, Iraqi President Saddam Hussein began amassing a large military force near the southern bor-

der with Kuwait, Clinton responded with a breakneck display of U.S. military power. Within a week, the Pentagon set in motion the deployment of 36,000 Army and Marine troops to Kuwait and Saudi Arabia. Saddam backed down and moved his military units away from the border with Kuwait, the small, oil-rich sheikdom that the United States had stepped into to protect three years earlier after it was invaded by Iraq.

● **Bosnia.** Clinton's approach to Bosnia vacillated between bold calls for airstrikes and conciliatory nods to European allies who favored diplomatic efforts. Congress was no more decisive. Some lawmakers worried that without bold action by the United States and its allies, regional wars would proliferate. Others feared getting trapped in a Vietnam-style military escalation in a conflict that they believed did not threaten U.S. interests.

By the end of the year, the Clinton administration had bowed to the wishes of its allies and ceased its saber-rattling over Bosnia. Serbian forces, viewed by many in the United States as aggressors in the conflict, continued to wage war on poorly armed Bosnian Muslims. But, under pressure from Senate Minority Leader Bob Dole, R-Kan., and others in Congress, the administration agreed to stop using the U.S. military to enforce an arms embargo against the Muslims. *(Bosnia, p. 446)*

● **Haiti.** In the case of Haiti, a vocal but small group of liberal and African-American members of Congress pressured Clinton to use force if necessary to restore to power democratically elected President Jean-Bertrand Aristide, who had been ousted in 1991 in a military coup. Clinton first attempted to dislodge the junta through harsh economic sanctions approved by the United Nations. When those measures only emboldened the regime, the administration moved decisively and laid plans to invade the tiny, poverty-ridden island nation.

Although there was no question that U.S. forces easily could have overrun the country's ragtag military, opposition to an invasion was widespread in Congress. Many lawmakers believed the United States would get tied down in Haiti as it attempted to bring about political stability in a country that had known mostly upheaval and violence. In the end, the invasion was averted by the last-minute diplomatic efforts of a U.S. team led by former President Jimmy Carter. The Haitian military leaders agreed to relinquish power to Aristide, and U.S. forces landed peacefully in Haiti Sept. 19 to maintain civil order during the transition. *(Haiti, p. 449)*

Cautious Approach to Peacekeeping

Despite sporadic success in peacekeeping, Congress wanted to limit the U.S. role overseas. On Capitol Hill, the image of peacekeeping missions remained inextricably linked, not to the restoration of democracy in Haiti, but to the

1993 debacle in Somalia, where 18 U.S. soldiers were killed in a street battle with a local warlord. The tragedy came to symbolize the price of indiscriminate U.S. participation in the peculiar local problems of countries with violent histories.

The Clinton administration imposed new conditions on direct participation by U.S. troops in U.N. peacekeeping missions. The president would no longer relinquish command authority over U.S. forces participating in any U.N. mission. And the administration would thoroughly review any new missions — even those that did not involve U.S. forces — to determine whether there was a clear "exit strategy" to conclude the operation. U.N. Ambassador Madeleine K. Albright told congressional appropriators March 22, "We can't afford peacekeeping without being more judicious. . . . We are learning from Somalia."

When the White House requested $1.2 billion for peacekeeping missions in fiscal 1994 and 1995, lawmakers approved the request but attached a long list of conditions, most of them mirroring the administration's revamped policy. Congress approved the funds as part of the annual appropri-

ations bill for the departments of Commerce, Justice and State and the federal judiciary. Clinton signed the bill into law Aug. 26 (HR 4603 — PL 103-317). *(Appropriations, p. 483)*

Part of the money was withheld until the United Nations established a separate office of inspector general, a position the administration had sought to oversee the world body's finances. Lawmakers also prohibited the United States from paying for more than 25 percent of U.N. peacekeeping operations beginning in fiscal 1996, a reduction from the 31 percent share the United States had been paying.

After the November elections, Republicans, who were poised to take control of both chambers for the first time in 40 years, increased the pressure on the White House to restrict peacekeeping ventures. House Republicans drafted a bill based on their campaign manifesto, the "Contract With America." The bill barred the placement of U.S. troops under foreign command and ordered the executive branch to deduct from its payments to the United Nations the costs the Pentagon incurred to support U.N.-sponsored peacekeeping. *('Contract With America,' p. 22)*   ■

Bosnian War Remains Intractable

The war in the Balkan republic of Bosnia continued for a third year with the United States and its NATO allies no closer to imposing peace than they were when the war broke out.

The Clinton administration's policy in the region vacillated between assertiveness and restraint. The White House first advocated air strikes against Serb-held positions, arguing that the United States had a stake in stopping the war from spreading. Later, the administration acquiesced in the more conciliatory approach taken by NATO allies, which opposed military measures.

Congress, with its constitutionally assigned second-string role in foreign affairs, was no more decisive on Bosnia than the president. Some lawmakers favored U.N.-sponsored bombing raids against the Serbs and lifting the arms embargo against the outgunned Bosnian Muslims. But many others had reservations about ensnaring the United States in a civil war where no clear U.S. interests were at stake.

Some members of Congress worried that without bold action by the United Nations and NATO, the West would look impotent in the face of regionally spawned threats to peace, fostering a cycle of instability in the post-Cold War era. But other members feared the United States would get trapped in a Vietnam-style spiral of military escalation in the Balkans.

Throughout the year, the debate repeatedly returned to two issues, whether air strikes would work to deter Serbian aggression and whether the United States should act unilaterally to lift an arms embargo that prevented Bosnian Muslims from adequately defending themselves against the heavily armed Serbs.

In the end, Congress never went on record with a vote explicitly supporting or opposing the administration on the issue of air strikes. Over the course of several months, the White House authorized sporadic and limited air strikes against Serbian positions, which were considered largely unsuccessful in deterring further aggression by the Serbs.

Although Congress stepped back from ordering the unilateral lifting of the arms embargo, it did set a deadline for the United States to cease enforcing the restraints. The United States stopped helping NATO countries enforce the embargo

in November, but it continued to observe the U.N.-mandated restriction and sold no arms to the Bosnian Muslims.

Background

The war in the former Yugoslavia was touched off by the fall of communism in Eastern Europe. The formerly communist-run country splintered into smaller republics, including Croatia, Slovenia and Bosnia-Herzegovina. What remained of the erstwhile federation was controlled by Serbia. Led by President Slobodan Milosevic, Serbia attempted to assert territorial and political dominance over the newly formed neighboring republics, especially Bosnia-Herzegovina and its capital city, Sarajevo. Open warfare erupted in 1992 after Bosnia-Herzegovina declared its independence from the Serbian-run Yugoslavian federation.

The initial U.S. response was to shy away from involvement in the conflict. The warring factions had no constituencies in the United States to speak of, and the jumble of small republics and their ethnic affiliations were little understood by most Americans. But over time, calls for action in Congress intensified with the rising death toll and with revelations of Serbian-sponsored atrocities, including Nazi-style detention camps where prisoners starved to death and the "ethnic cleansing" — systematic rape and murder — of Muslim populations.

Both President Clinton and his predecessor, President George Bush, struggled in vain to forge an effective policy toward Bosnia. As a presidential candidate in 1992, Clinton urged Republican incumbent Bush to use multilateral air strikes to ensure the delivery of humanitarian aid to the Bosnian Muslims. Once Clinton took office however, he was less sure-footed on the question of intervention and instead stressed diplomatic solutions, none of which did much to advance the cause of peace. *(1993 Almanac, p. 493)*

The West's record of failure in resolving the conflict haunted its leaders, including Clinton. Though the United States and NATO had threatened and warned the Serbs they would act militarily to stop the aggression, little was done to stop the siege of the Bosnian capital of Sarajevo. Likewise,

Secretary of State Warren Christopher had been unable to forge a diplomatic solution despite earnest attempts to do so.

Clinton Wins Praise

The year 1994 opened with an air of nagging ambivalence about the war, which had claimed an estimated 200,000 lives.

But the violence in Bosnia once again proved difficult to ignore. In late January, a Serbian mortar killed six children in Sarajevo, prompting an international outcry. Then in February, 68 people died during a Saturday morning mortar attack on a crowded marketplace — the worst single massacre of the then 22-month war.

Many lawmakers had long felt that allowing the Muslims to arm themselves was the best way of stopping Serbian aggression without involving U.S. troops in the war. On Jan. 27, the Senate voted overwhelmingly to urge the administration to provide arms to Bosnia's Muslim-led government forces in their battle against Serbian troops. The Senate backed, 87-9, a non-binding amendment to its version of the State Department authorization bill (S 1281) calling on Clinton to unilaterally lift the embargo. The amendment was sponsored by Minority Leader Bob Dole, R-Kan., who had become one of the few outspoken advocates in Congress for the Muslims after having personally witnessed the struggle of the lightly armed defenders during visits to the Bosnian capital. *(Vote 8, p. 3-S; State Department authorization, p. 454)*

Though Clinton liked the idea of arming the Muslims, whom he viewed as the principal victims of the factional fighting, he strongly opposed unilateral action. He feared it would jeopardize other important U.S. goals, such as international economic sanctions against Iraq, which had been defeated by the United States in the Persian Gulf War.

The non-binding Senate vote was mostly symbolic. Joseph R. Biden, Jr., D-Del., an advocate of tough allied action to counter Serb aggression in Bosnia, expressed regret that the United States lacked the political will to act decisively. "We're not going to have the courage to really do anything in the end, probably," said Biden.

Clinton Threatens Airstrikes

The administration had other worries in Bosnia. With the Serbs showing no signs of slowing their march into Muslim-held territory or their attacks on civilian neighborhoods, the United States and its NATO allies in February issued an ultimatum to the Serb forces to stop the shelling of Sarajevo. NATO warned the Serbs to withdraw their tanks, mortars and other heavy weapons about 12 miles from the center of Sarajevo by Feb. 21 or face allied airstrikes. "No one should doubt NATO's resolve. NATO is now set to act," Clinton said in a televised address to the nation Feb. 9.

In pledging U.S. air power to help stop Serbian attacks, the president risked yet another unwanted confrontation with Congress over deploying military forces abroad. Few lawmakers were willing to support costly, dangerous military missions in situations where no clear U.S. interests were at stake. Not yet forgotten was an episode of the previous October, when a botched raid in Somalia cost the lives of 18 U.S. servicemen and touched off an open congressional revolt that forced Clinton to wind down the U.S. peacekeeping operation there. *(1993 Almanac, p. 486)*

But most lawmakers initially rallied around the president and welcomed a rare unified stance by NATO. Congress was willing to forget the failure of earlier attempts to sway the Serbs with ultimatums and diplomacy. No one had a better

idea or a politically palatable solution. Lawmakers were willing to put their faith in what John P. Murtha, D-Pa., chairman of the House Appropriations Defense Subcommittee, acknowledged was "a glimmer of hope" that the president's plan would work.

For a time, it seemed that it would. The heavy artillery of Bosnia's Serbs that had rained terror on Sarajevo for months fell silent. The Serbs responded to the NATO mandate by moving most of their guns away from the Bosnian capital or placing them under U.N. control.

The diplomatic momentum picked up. The administration announced new talks in Washington aimed at establishing a Muslim-Croat union within Bosnia. A rapprochement between the Muslims and Croats was considered a way of getting to an overall settlement. Bosnian Prime Minister Haris Silajdzic met with administration officials and lawmakers during the week of Feb. 21, and backed the proposed Muslim-Croat confederation. It also won tentative support from Croatian President Franjo Tudjman.

For the first time in his presidency, Clinton won praise for his Bosnia policy from even his harshest congressional critics.

Congress Grows Skeptical

The climate of success created an opening for discussion about the possible commitment of U.S. ground troops to enforce a Bosnian peace accord — something that had been politically unthinkable just a few weeks earlier. Testifying before Congress on Feb. 23 and Feb. 24, Secretary of State Christopher said Bosnian officials believed that without a commitment of U.S. forces to enforce an accord, the fragile peace process would founder.

The administration promised to seek congressional approval before deploying forces to Bosnia and to subject the operation to tough conditions in line with the administration's new, scaled-back approach to multilateral peacekeeping. The United States, alone, would command its forces abroad, correcting what many felt was the fatal error of Somalia, where U.S. forces operated under a U.N. mandate. And the president would lay out an "exit strategy" for concluding the operation.

Clinton, who in the past had been reluctant to speak publicly about Bosnia, launched an effort to justify the widening U.S. involvement there and attempted to lay out a rationale for a U.S. interest in resolving the war. Clinton said that the United States could not afford to ignore problems in Europe and that it had a stake in preventing the conflict from spreading on the continent.

But most members of Congress remained skeptical. Despite efforts by Democratic allies of the White House, Congress declined to go on record with a resolution backing the NATO strategy of threatening air strikes against the Serbs.

Rep. Frank McCloskey, D-Ind., was one of the few lawmakers who called for even stronger NATO intervention, including the bombing of Serbian supply routes. If the Serbs were to overrun the Muslim enclave of Gorazde, he said, "the damage to our credibility is going to be beyond belief." McCloskey had traveled to the former Yugoslavia several times, where he developed close ties with Bosnian leaders.

On April 20, the president proposed NATO airstrikes to counter continued Serbian attacks on Gorazde and the other towns in Bosnia designated by the United Nations as "safe havens." The Serbs, he said, must be made to pay a higher price for their continued attacks as a way of pushing them back to the negotiating table. Two days later, NATO ministers

warned Serbian forces to stop shelling Gorazde or face air attacks, and ordered them to withdraw heavy weapons from the area. The Serbs responded by pledging a cease-fire.

Senators Express Concerns

This time, Clinton's strategy was criticized in Congress. Lawmakers predicted that airstrikes would lead the United States into a murky, ill-defined war. And some suggested that the Serbs would simply shift weapons to areas not covered by the protective zones.

Among the leading voices in the debate were some of the 18 lawmakers who had fought in the Vietnam War two decades earlier. Republican veterans of Vietnam were the most outspoken critics of Clinton's policy. They believed that threatening NATO airstrikes to quell Serbian aggression would ultimately enmesh the United States in a land war in the Balkans.

Sen. John McCain, R-Ariz., a former naval aviator who spent nearly six years as a prisoner of war in Vietnam, said the United States could become trapped in a Vietnam-style cycle of military escalation. "My fear is that the Serbs' reaction will beget new NATO strikes, which will beget stronger Serb reactions, which will beget stronger strikes, which ultimately will amount to failure reinforcing failure," he said.

Sen. John Kerry, D-Mass., defended Clinton's strategy, saying it was aimed not at rolling back the Serbs or altering the balance of power, but simply at forcing the Serbs to the negotiating table. "The alternative is to admit failure," he said. "The alternative is to accept that the United Nations and NATO are impotent in the face of any kind of threat."

The one point of agreement was the non-binding language that Dole had added to the State Department authorization bill urging arms sales to the Muslims. Over the objections of the White House, which continued to oppose unilateral abandonment of the arms ban, House and Senate conferees agreed April 19 to include the language in the final bill. Both chambers approved the measure, and it was signed into law April 30 (HR 2333 — PL 103-236).

Dole and other advocates of arming the Muslims wanted to go further, however. They pushed for legislation that would force the president to end U.S. participation in the embargo. But the Senate was not ready to take that step.

Votes on Arming Muslims

Though the Senate heaped blame on the administration for an unfocused policy in the war, its vision was no clearer, a condition evidenced in two votes on May 12.

The upper chamber adopted, 50-49, a tough amendment to a Bosnia bill (S 2042) requiring the president to act alone to reject the U.N. embargo. But the Senate also endorsed, by an identical margin, a much weaker, competing amendment. That language instructed the president to try to reach an agreement with NATO allies and the United Nations on lifting the embargo, but, failing that, he was required only to consult with Congress on the prospects of ending the arms ban unilaterally. *(Votes 110, 111, p. 20-S)*

The outcome confused even senators. "We give clear guidance except when we change our minds," said John Glenn, D-Ohio.

The weaker counterproposal was sponsored by Senate Majority Leader George J. Mitchell of Maine, a Clinton ally. The amendment split the Senate along party lines. It failed to garner a single Republican vote. Five Democrats, including Bill Bradley, N.J., and Carl Levin, Mich., bucked the president and voted against it.

Thirteen Democrats voted for the tougher amendment, which was offered by Dole. Eight Democrats, including Daniel Patrick Moynihan, N.Y., Carol Moseley-Braun, Ill. and Charles S. Robb, Va., voted for both amendments. Moynihan, who said he saw no contradiction in supporting both proposals, indicated that he was most interested in reaffirming the rights of Bosnians to defend themselves.

The debate centered on whether the United States should cleave to its allies or be prepared to go it alone as it dealt with overseas crises in the post-Cold War era. Many senators were also concerned about possible fallout from U.S. allies at a time the United States was seeking international support for economic sanctions against North Korea, whose unstable communist regime was thought to be developing nuclear weapons in violation of nonproliferation treaties.

House Takes the Lead

Most of the congressional debate over Bosnia was concentrated in the Senate, which traditionally placed greater emphasis on foreign policy matters. But it was the House that took the first decisive action toward arming the Muslims.

On June 9, the House voted to force Clinton to unilaterally abandon the U.N. embargo on weapons shipments to Bosnia's outgunned government forces. The 244-178 vote came on an amendment to the House version of the 1995 defense authorization bill (HR 4301). The amendment, sponsored by Frank McCloskey, D-Ind., and House Democratic Whip David E. Bonior of Michigan, drew support from 117 Democrats while 132 opposed it. Republicans overwhelmingly endorsed it, 127-45. *(Vote 222, p. 68-H; defense authorization, p. 421)*

"If we don't lift this embargo and at least let the people of Bosnia defend themselves," Bonior pleaded, "then the blood of Bosnia isn't just on the hands of the Serbs, it's on all of us."

Foreign Affairs Committee Committee Chairman Lee H. Hamilton, D-Ind., and other opponents of the amendment said it would "Americanize the war" because it would also authorize up to $200 million in military equipment and training for the government's forces.

Senate Retreats

In July, it was the Senate's turn to take up the defense authorization bill. Vigorous lobbying by Clinton and top administration officials paid off in a narrow but important tactical victory July 1, as the Senate stopped one vote short of ordering the president to ship arms to Bosnia's Muslims. The Senate rejected, on a 50-50 tie, an amendment sponsored by Dole and Connecticut Democrat Joseph I. Lieberman that would have required the weapons shipments in defiance of the U.N. embargo. *(Vote 181, p. 31-S)*

Before that vote, the Senate approved, 52-48, an administration-backed amendment sponsored by Armed Services Committee Chairman Sam Nunn, D-Ga., and Virginia Republican John W. Warner. Their non-binding amendment urged the president to seek a multilateral end to the embargo if the Serbian forces battling the Bosnian government derailed efforts to negotiate a peace settlement. *(Vote 180, p. 31-S)*

In August, House and Senate conferees worked out a final version of the defense authorization bill (S 2182 — H Rept 103-701). Nunn engineered a compromise meant to satisify Clinton's goals and also to quiet the Dole forces, which had been growing steadily. His proposal prodded Clinton toward a more active approach without imposing a deadline for unilateral action.

But it also forced the administration to make significant concessions. If the United Nations failed to lift the embargo by Nov. 15 — and the Serbs continued to reject an interna-

tionally brokered peace agreement — the administration would have to stop militarily enforcing the arms ban. While Nunn's compromise did not eliminate the prohibition on shipments of U.S. weapons to the Muslims, but it would stop U.S. ships and planes in the region from blocking arms shipments by other countries.

Senior officials warned that terminating funding for U.S. participation in an ongoing NATO mission would severely strain ties with the alliance.

Both chambers approved a conference report with the provision setting a Nov. 15 deadline for ending U.S. participation in the embargo. The president signed the bill into law on Oct. 5 (PL 103-337).

No End in Sight

In November, the Bosnian government changed the terms of the embargo debate when it backed off its long-standing demand for an immediate termination of the U.N. ban on arms sales. Instead, the government declared it would accept a firm, six-month deadline for ending the embargo. The concession was designed in part to thaw opposition to lifting the arms ban from Britain, France and Russia. But those countries remained dead-set against arming the Bosnians. Britain and France worried that lifting the embargo would widen the war and jeopardize their peacekeepers in Bosnia. Russia was leery of tilting the military balance away from the Serbs, its traditional allies.

When the congressionally mandated Nov. 15 deadline arrived, the United States officially ceased to participate in enforcing the embargo though its NATO allies continued to do so. But the debate about whether to go the extra step — lifting the embargo and selling arms to the Muslims — remained unresolved.

In the closing days of November, U.S. policy veered in a new direction when the administration abruptly abandoned its protracted effort to convince its European allies to take strong military steps to counter Serbian aggression in Bosnia.

The administration reversed course and indicated it would acquiesce in the more conciliatory approach favored by the Europeans.

The administration wanted to heal divisions with its allies that had widened in the wake of NATO's reluctance to take military steps against the Serbs after their brutal assault on the Bosnian Muslim enclave of Bihac. But the move also created an opening for congressional Republicans who, emboldened by the Nov. 8 elections that toppled the Democratic majority in both chambers, were eager to expand their influence over policy toward Bosnia.

Incoming Republican House Speaker Newt Gingrich of Georgia, who as a member of the minority had been leery of U.S. involvement in the Balkans, advocated a U.S. bombing mission to counter future aggression by the Serbs. Gingrich said that to "have NATO . . . looking pathetic and helpless before Serbians strikes me as a signal to the world that is unbelievably dangerous."

Dole, now the incoming Senate majority leader, embarked a post-election tour of European capitals, where he bluntly criticized the Clinton administration, NATO and the United Nations for a collective failure to stop the Serbs' territorial march. Dole's high-profile trip was unusual for a member of Congress, but less so for a senator contemplating a race for president in 1996. "NATO has been helpless, hopeless, or however, maybe irrelevant in this whole process," Dole said.

By year's end, the Serbs' relentless and seemingly unstoppable territorial drive in Bosnia rendered the political bickering moot. The Serbs occupied 70 percent of the country, and the Muslims had no prospects of winning that territory back, Defense Secretary William J. Perry told Congress. In December, the administration announced that it was considering committing U.S. ground troops to Bosnia, not to stop the Serbs, but to try to rescue the widely dispersed U.N. peacekeeping force.

There was a growing sense that nothing, neither force nor diplomatic concessions, could stop the Serbs. "It may be a lost cause," said Dole. ∎

Clinton's Haiti Gamble Pays Off

The Clinton administration enjoyed a rare foreign policy success with the peaceful occupation of the island nation of Haiti and the restoration of its democratically elected government.

But it was not accomplished without a lively dialogue with Congress, which second-guessed Clinton's policy at every step. The president had to employ as much diplomacy on Capitol Hill as he did in Port-au-Prince. When Clinton's policy achieved many of its goals, his congressional critics fell silent, failing to muster support for even a mild resolution setting a timetable for the mission.

Haiti forced its way onto the U.S. foreign policy agenda in 1991, when a military coup drove democratically elected President Jean-Bertrand Aristide from power. Aristide, elected with 70 percent of the vote, was popular with Haiti's vast underclass. His ouster by military leaders, who were backed by an elite upper class, brought a period of instability to the tiny island nation.

The Clinton administration for months had attempted without success to dislodge Haiti's military junta through an international embargo on arms and oil. The administration's policy had been frustrated by events the year before, when

the United States was humiliated by armed Haitian demonstrators who prevented a U.S. Navy ship from landing and delivering a group of military engineers. *(1993 Almanac, p. 499)*

Political unrest in Haiti set waves of "boat people" on a course for U.S. shores in makeshift craft, fueling a growing anti-immigrant sentiment among Americans and in Congress.

Clinton came under increasing pressure from a small but vocal band of liberal lawmakers who advocated tougher measures. The embargo of oil and arms, they said, was only enriching the Haitian military and its supporters, who acquired gasoline from the Dominican Republic and resold it for a profit. Rep. Joseph P. Kennedy II, D-Mass., and others called on the administration to support a near-total commercial embargo. Other Democrats, particularly the 40-member Congressional Black Caucus, urged Clinton to end the policy of summarily returning refugees to Haiti.

On April 21, Kennedy and five members of the Black Caucus were arrested as they protested Clinton's Haiti policy in front of the White House.

Also in April, six senators — Democrats Christopher J. Dodd of Connecticut, Tom Harkin of Iowa, Russell D.

Feingold of Wisconsin, John Kerry of Massachusetts, Carol Moseley-Braun of Illinois and Paul Wellstone of Minnesota — sponsored the Haitian Restoration of Democracy Act of 1994. It called for a complete commercial embargo (except for humanitarian aid), a ban on air traffic between Haiti and the United States and a freeze on the financial assets of the Haitian military and their financial backers in the United States.

Rep. Barney Frank, D-Mass., introduced a bill (HR 4249) on April 19 that would have given Haitians lawful permanent residency after one year in the United States, an opportunity already provided to those who fled Fidel Castro's Cuba.

The issue brought together an unusual coalition of congressional liberals, members of the black caucus and Florida lawmakers concerned about the influx of boat people. They were among the first to urge Clinton to consider the use of force to remove the military from power, but they were small in number. Support for Aristide and dramatic action in Haiti was not widespread in Congress. GOP critics contended that tighter economic sanctions would have no impact except to increase the misery of Haiti's poor and drive more of them to flee by boat to Florida.

Although lawmakers abhorred the takeover by the Haitian military, many were not terribly fond of Aristide, a leftist Catholic priest. Claims that Aristide urged his supporters to torture political opponents had gained currency in Congress. In 1993, Sen. Jesse Helms of North Carolina, the ranking Republican on the Foreign Relations Committee, had called Aristide a mentally unstable "psychopath."

Congress Frets Over Possible Invasion

On May 8, Clinton announced new procedures for processing the political asylum claims of Haitian boat people. Fleeing Haitians would be allowed to seek asylum aboard U.S. ships or in third-country processing centers rather than being returned immediately to Haiti.

The Florida delegation warned that the revised policy would prompt a new wave of boat people, perhaps as many as 10,000 a month.

Clinton also sought to reinvigorate diplomatic efforts to resolve the crisis by appointing former Rep. William H. Gray III, D-Pa., once a leading member of the Congressional Black Caucus, as his special envoy to Haiti.

But the regime signaled it had no intention of giving up power. On May 11, Haiti's military leaders installed a judge in his 80s as the country's provisional president. The inauguration of Judge Emile Jonassaint as a figurehead president underscored their determination to remain in control.

Meanwhile, concern in Congress about a U.S. military invasion intensified. On May 24, moderate and conservative lawmakers from both parties supported a nonbinding amendment to the House fiscal 1995 defense authorization bill (HR 4301) opposing the use of force in Haiti. The amendment, sponsored by Rep. Porter J. Goss, R-Fla., passed 223-201. But the statement was nullified when the House voted on the question a second time June 9. That time the vote was 195-226. *(Votes 197, p. 60 H; vote 224, p. 68-H)*

The United Nations in May announced an almost complete economic embargo against Haiti. The Clinton administration the next month imposed additional restrictions, including limits on financial transactions and a ban on commercial air service between Haiti and the United States. Special envoy Gray did not rule out other actions, including military intervention. "Democracy in Haiti will prevail," Gray said.

A growing number of lawmakers believed that an invasion by U.S. forces had become inevitable. They harbored doubts

that sanctions alone would pry the junta from power. The sanctions, in fact, seemed to exacerbate the Haitian refugee problem, increasing the likelihood that more flotillas of poor Haitians would head for Florida.

Republicans were almost unanimously opposed to an invasion, and they were joined by centrist Democrats. Few lawmakers, however, doubted that the United States could make short work of Haiti's ragtag military. The broader question was whether the United States was prepared to take on a long-term commitment to bring about political stability. "We could prevail militarily, but then what do you do?" said Sen. John Glenn, D-Ohio. "How do you establish order? How do you maintain order? And how do you get out?"

Haiti's defiant military leaders fueled the crisis July 11 when they ordered the expulsion of about 100 international human rights monitors from the island, a move that outraged both U.S. and U.N. officials.

Congressional debate was centered in the Senate, customarily more vocal than the House on foreign policy matters. Senate Minority Leader Bob Dole, R-Kan., led the charge against the administration's policy with a proposal to create a bipartisan commission of senior lawmakers to assess diplomatic and political conditions in Haiti. The real objective of the measure, which Dole introduced as an amendment to the fiscal 1995 foreign operations spending bill (HR 4426), was to slow momentum toward an invasion. As Mitch McConnell, R-Ky., put it, "I think we are saying in a rather unified chorus, 'Don't invade, Mr. President.' "

But the tables turned on Dole when Haiti's military chief, Lt. Gen. Raoul Cédras, enthusiastically endorsed his measure, calling it "an excellent initiative." Democrats wasted no time trying to link Dole with Cédras, whose regime was known for brutality and oppression. The Senate voted 57-42 to table (kill) Dole's amendment after opponents argued it would undercut international pressure on the military rulers. *(Vote 194, p. 34-S)*

On Aug. 6, however, the Senate unanimously approved a non-binding sense of the Senate resolution by Dole stating that Clinton needed congressional approval before dispatching troops overseas. *(Vote 254, p. 43-S)*

Preparations Unfold

By early fall, the administration had plans to invade. A grim-faced Clinton went on national television Sept. 15 to issue a blunt, final warning to Cédras and his allies. "Your time is up," he said. "Leave now, or we'll force you from power." *(Text, p. 27-D)*

Clinton also responded to congressional critics who contended that the United States had no interests in Haiti that justified placing troops in harm's way. The president listed several justifications for the mission: to stop human rights abuses by Haiti's military, to restore Aristide to power, to prevent a new wave of refugees and to uphold the international credibility of the United States.

The following day, in an eleventh-hour attempt to resolve the Haiti problem without bloodshed, Clinton dispatched a high-level delegation to persuade Cédras to step down. The group consisted of former President Jimmy Carter, former Joint Chiefs of Staff Chairman Gen. Colin L. Powell Jr. and Senate Armed Services Committee Chairman Sam Nunn, D-Ga.

Meanwhile, an armada of warships steamed toward the Caribbean, 1,600 reservists were activated and the Pentagon finalized its battle plans. It was estimated that 15,000 U.S. troops ultimately would be part of the mission, called Operation Uphold Democracy.

Although the vast majority of lawmakers opposed an inva-

sion, they did nothing to block it. Still, by ignoring demands that he seek authorization from Congress before moving against the military regime in Haiti, Clinton took a gamble.

"If things go well, fine, he'll get the credit," said Sen. William S. Cohen, R-Maine. "If things go awry, it could do mortal damage to his presidency."

Several times during the previous few decades, presidents had dispatched troops into combat with barely a nod in the direction of Capitol Hill. President Ronald Reagan launched a surprise invasion of the Caribbean island of Grenada in 1983, and President George Bush sent troops to Panama in 1989. *(1983 Almanac, p. 135; 1989 Almanac, p. 595)*

In this case, unlike the actions in Panama and Grenada, the Senate had gone on record demanding the president seek its authorization before sending troops to Haiti. The administration's GOP critics insisted that the defining precedent for Haiti was the 1991 war with Iraq, which was one of six cases in history when Congress authorized military action in advance. *(1991 Almanac, p. 437)*

Like his predecessors, Clinton felt it was more important to preserve presidential prerogatives in matters of war and peace than it was to win congressional support. Said Secretary of State Warren Christopher, "It's more important to establish and maintain the principle of presidential authority and power."

Congress possessed limited means to end the deployment of troops abroad. It theoretically could have invoked the 1973 War Powers Resolution, which, enacted over the veto of a Watergate-weakened President Richard M. Nixon, required the president to consult with Congress "in every possible instance" before committing U.S. forces abroad. The resolution also required the termination of a troop commitment within 60 days unless Congress specifically authorized its continuation.

However, Nixon and every subsequent U.S. president considered the resolution unconstitutional. Chief executives had accorded it no more than cursory compliance, generally observing its after-the-fact reporting requirements but otherwise ignoring it.

Congress also had the option of cutting off funds for a military operation in Haiti, but many lawmakers viewed that as too blunt an instrument of policy-making.

In the 1970s, Congress eliminated funding for military operations at the end of the Vietnam War. And in 1993, lawmakers forced Clinton to accept a six-month deadline for withdrawing U.S. troops from Somalia — backed up by a funding restriction — after 18 U.S. Army Rangers were killed in a firefight with supporters of a Somalian warlord. But both of those operations were winding down when Congress intervened. To impose a funding cutoff in the early stages of the Haiti mission would have constituted an extraordinary assertion of Congress' power of the purse. *(1993 Almanac, p. 486)*

Some of the harshest criticism of the administration came from Democrats who faced re-election contests in the fall, such as Sens. Jim Sasser of Tennessee, Paul S. Sarbanes of Maryland and Jeff Bingaman of New Mexico. Virtually the only support for an invasion came from a handful of members of the Congressional Black Caucus, a few liberals and a few members of the Florida delegation.

Invasion Averted

The use of force to oust the military junta was averted by a dramatic agreement forged by the Carter delegation and Haitian military leaders. The coup leaders agreed to relinquish power in return for guarantees they could leave the country safely, taking their financial windfalls with them.

U.S. troops began arriving peacefully in the Haitian capital

of Port-au-Prince on Sept 19. They easily neutralized Haitian military forces and were greeted by cheering throngs of Haitian citizens. Exiled President Aristide was assured of returning to power on Oct. 15, and the United States and the international community moved to drop harsh sanctions that had been strangling the Haitian economy.

In Congress, Republicans accused the administration of seeking to occupy Haiti for an indefinite period. And while Democratic leaders chalked up much of the criticism to election-year politics, many rank-and-file Democrats also expressed serious reservations.

For all the criticism, however, lawmakers were reluctant to interfere. Congress debated whether to set a deadline for withdrawing the troops, backed up by a cutoff in funding if the deadline was not met. But support for a hard-and-fast deadline quickly dissipated.

After an exhaustive, sometimes rancorous debate, the House and Senate on Oct. 6 passed identical resolutions that did little more than require the president to provide detailed reports on the mission. Congress sent the president the Senate version of the measure after the House adopted it by voice vote Oct. 7. President Clinton signed it into law Oct. 25 (S J Res 229 — PL 103-423).

The resolution did not authorize the mission, nor did it limit its duration. It simply required the administration to make several reports on the cost, scope and projected timetable of the operation and called for a "prompt and orderly withdrawal" of U.S. forces from Haiti. Reflecting lawmakers' frustration over being bypassed when the operation was launched, the measure stated that "the president should have sought and welcomed" congressional support before deploying troops to Haiti.

The bipartisan measure, which received at least tacit administration approval, sailed through the Senate, 91-8. *(Vote 323, p. 56-S)*

The lowest-common-denominator approach to the crisis attracted broad, if not enthusiastic, support. Only five Democrats and three Republicans voted against the measure. No one really believed that it would have much effect on U.S. policy toward Haiti, however. Christopher J. Dodd, D-Conn., said the resolution's extensive reporting requirements "read more like an OSHA regulation than a resolution on Haiti."

In the House, members chose among three sharply divergent, though largely symbolic, statements on the military operation. The three proposals were substitute amendments to a resolution (H J Res 416) providing limited authorization for the deployment of troops until March 1, 1995, which had been approved by the Foreign Affairs Committee on Sept. 28 (H Rept 103-819, Part 1).

The House first rejected a GOP alternative by Minority Leader Robert H. Michel of Illinois and Benjamin A. Gilman of New York that would not have placed binding restraints on the administration, but seemed intended instead to embarrass the White House by criticizing the mission. The amendment was rejected 205-225, a vote largely divided along partisan lines. *(Vote 497, p. 146-H)*

The House then handily approved, 258-167, an amendment that mirrored the resolution the Senate had adopted a few hours earlier. The House passed the amended resolution, 236-182. *(Votes 498, 500, p. 148-H)*

The inconclusive result — the product of an unlikely group of pro-Pentagon lawmakers and liberal members of the Congressional Black Caucus — outraged many longtime defenders of Congress' foreign policy prerogatives. "We have not approved of the policy, we have not disapproved of the policy," said House Foreign Affairs Committee Chairman Lee H. Hamilton, D-Ind. "We simply default."

In mid-October, Aristide returned to power in Haiti. ∎

Foreign Aid Reform Plans Scrapped

In a busy legislative session preoccupied with domestic issues, a proposal to revamp the way lawmakers funded about $20 billion a year in foreign aid and international programs was edged out.

The legislation — a cornerstone of the administration's foreign policy — would have scrapped the 1961 law (PL 87-195) governing foreign aid, which had become encrusted with scores of outdated provisions and numerous congressionally mandated objectives and accounts.

In its place, Secretary of State Warren Christopher and Agency for International Development (AID) administrator J. Brian Atwood, proposed to link foreign assistance more closely to clearly identifiable goals such as promoting peace and democracy that mirrored President Clinton's overall foreign policy objectives.

But the administration encountered a host of procedural and political difficulties in trying to move the legislation through Congress, which had not enacted a foreign aid authorization bill since 1985. Since that time, all foreign aid had been provided through the companion foreign operations appropriations bills.

Virtually no one on Capitol Hill disputed Atwood's basic argument that the 33-year-old foreign assistance law was hopelessly out of date and that the aid program had been adrift for years without a compelling rationale. But lawmakers could not agree on a new approach, and they strongly resisted proposals that would reduce their own power to target foreign aid.

"Everyone in the Congress wants reform of foreign aid," said House Foreign Affairs Committee Chairman Lee H. Hamilton, D-Ind., a chief proponent of the legislation. "The problem is that everyone wants to reform it in a different way."

The bill's chances were also weakened by election year pressures. Most members of Congress customarily took a dim view of anything associated with foreign aid, even legislation that purported to improve the program's efficiency. And few Democrats were eager to take up legislation that would give Republicans another chance to bash Clinton's handling of overseas crises.

After an initial buildup, the administration's lobbying campaign flagged. Clinton did not weigh in, and Christopher and other members of Clinton's foreign policy team became preoccupied with high-stakes international crises, such as the nuclear crisis in North Korea. Consequently, the lobbying effort fell largely on the shoulders of AID, an agency with scant congressional support or loyalty.

A Senate Foreign Relations subcommittee was the only panel to take action on the bill. In the end, foreign aid once again was provided solely through the foreign operations appropriations bill (HR 4426 — PL 103-306). (Appropriations, p. 505)

Background

For decades, U.S. aid had been apportioned largely to advance U.S. interests in ideological, economic and military competition against the Soviet Union, a goal that had been overtaken by events. The 1961 foreign aid law had also become loaded with aid accounts and programs and with scores of congressional mandates and policy recommendations.

The Clinton administration was not the first, however, to find it virtually impossible to translate a broad, bipartisan desire to reform foreign aid into legislation.

In 1991, the Bush administration offered a plan to overhaul the aid program by sweeping away congressional restrictions. The House Foreign Affairs Committee incorporated portions of the Bush plan in a foreign aid authorization bill along with more of the restrictions that the administration sought to eliminate, but the authorization bill died in the House vote on final passage. A similar effort in 1989, led by House Foreign Affairs Committee Chairman Hamilton also failed. (1991 Almanac, p. 470; 1989 Almanac, p. 609)

Aside from the persistent unpopularity of sending any aid abroad, one stumbling block had been the lack of consensus over how to revamp the program.

Much of the congressional interest in rewriting the foreign aid law came from Hamilton and other members of the authorizing committees, who had seen their relevance slip. In theory, they had an opportunity to set overall policy though the annual foreign aid authorization bill. But no such measure had become law since 1985. As a result, the Appropriations committees effectively had assumed sole jurisdiction over the program.

Some lawmakers outside the authorizing committees insisted that the existing law, while flawed, was not an insurmountable obstacle to improving the foreign aid program. David R. Obey, D-Wis., said the formula for real reform was simple: Hire good people to manage the program. Obey chaired the House Appropriations Foreign Operations Subcommittee and in March became chairman of the full committee.

Administration Proposal

The administration presented its blueprint for revamping the foreign aid law Feb. 2, more than a year after Christopher had promised to submit a plan for change. Hamilton and ranking Foreign Affairs Committee Republican Benjamin A. Gilman of New York formally introduced the measure (HR 3765), which was similar to a "discussion draft" that the administration had sent to Congress in November 1993. (1993 Almanac, p. 502)

The bill proposed to de-emphasize traditional country-to-country, or bilateral, aid programs in favor of funding to advance six broad goals: promoting democracy, promoting peace, providing humanitarian aid, promoting growth through trade and investment, advancing diplomacy and promoting sustainable development.

The lofty, if amorphous, quality of the categories was illustrated by "sustainable development," which the administration defined as "broad-based economic growth which protects the environment, enhances human capabilities, upholds democratic values, and improves the quality of life for current generations while preserving that opportunity for future generations."

Atwood told reporters that the administration crafted its initiative in part to maintain U.S. leadership in the world in spite of a steady decline in foreign aid funding in recent years. He called the proposal "a new and more relevant framework for American foreign policy and foreign assistance programs."

Administration officials asserted that far more was at stake than organizational charts or congressional turf. They argued that the voluminous 1961 law had spawned an inefficient system in which AID mission directors had to take into account more than 100 statutory priorities and criteria before committing resources.

For instance, there were 28 sections in the law dealing

with development assistance, aid targeted at the poorest countries, covering everything from the importance of protecting endangered species to the need to integrate women into national economies. There also was language promoting the use of vaccines for immunization and salts for oral rehydration as the best means to improve the health of poor children. The chapter even distinguished between "least developed countries" and "relatively least developed countries."

None of those detailed, congressionally mandated provisions, taken alone, presented a problem, said AID officials, but when multiplied many times over, they created management headaches.

Protecting Turf, Priorities

But where the administration saw reform, many lawmakers saw a potential raid on their authority in foreign policy and on their power of the purse. "We will not give to an unelected bureaucracy federal authority to spend dollars any way they want, so long as they call it 'pursuit of democracy' or 'expanding economic development,'" Obey warned. "There will be no blank checks."

Like the Bush administration's proposal, the Clinton plan proposed to eliminate all congressional spending mandates, known as earmarks. As in the past, that drew fire from a variety of corners.

The earmarks for Israel and Egypt — which had received $3 billion and $2.1 billion, respectively, in recent years — were regarded as symbols of U.S. support for Israel and for its chief Arab partner in the Middle East Peace process and thus had become politically sacrosanct. Supporters of Israel asserted that the aid earmarked for that country was the "engine" that had pulled the foreign operations appropriations bill through Congress in recent years. The earmark ensured the backing of politically influential Jewish-American organizations for the legislation.

The administration indicated it would accept an earmark for Israel, but that threatened to open the door for lawmakers to establish minimum spending levels for other countries and programs. "If that happens, the new bill could start looking like the old bill," said one AID official.

The legislation also proposed to eliminate the Development Fund for Africa, a popular program established by Congress to support economic reform in Africa. That drew the ire of members of the Congressional Black Caucus. "We feel that the administration is turning its back on an area that should get more consideration," said Donald M. Payne, D-N.J., a member of the caucus.

Many of the restrictions and conditions on aid for individual countries in existing law also had strong backing in Congress. Clinton proposed to replace such country-specific provisions with generic prohibitions on aid to countries that engaged in such activities as promoting terrorism and fueling nuclear proliferation.

The administration's initial draft had eliminated the so-called Pressler amendment named for its sponsor, Sen. Larry Pressler, R-S.D., barring aid for Pakistan because of the country's nuclear weapons program. But the bill that was submitted restored that 1985 provision. "We heard the Congress loudly and clearly on that, not simply through the press but in our consultations," Atwood said Feb. 3. "And we've decided to retain the Pressler amendment as well as the Glenn-Symington amendment," another longstanding restriction on nuclear proliferation.

Under Secretary of State Richard M. Moose said the administration had also agreed to allow Congress to set a specific authorization level for military assistance. The lack of such a provision in the draft had triggered complaints that lawmakers would not be able to exert effective oversight for the program.

A Low Priority for Congress

For all of the substantive objections that were raised, however, a more important factor was the unwillingness of House and Senate Democratic leaders to make room in the crowded congressional calendar — or expend the political capital necessary — to pass a foreign aid reform bill.

Mindful that several previous foreign aid authorization bills had died in the Senate, House Democrats wanted to delay action on the bill until they received assurances that any reform measure voted out of the Senate Foreign Relations Committee would be considered by the full Senate.

But with the summer's legislative calendar dominated by health care and other important domestic issues, Senate Democrats were never able to provide such a commitment. The task was more complicated in the Senate, which, unlike the House, had no Rules Committee to control debate and limit the number of amendments. As a result, any bill had the potential to trigger an extended debate or a filibuster. A measure to revamp the foreign aid program was almost certain to stir controversy and perhaps to tie the Senate into knots.

Senate Committee

The only congressional action taken on the proposal came in the Senate Foreign Relations Subcommittee on International Economic Policy, which approved the draft bill by voice vote June 15.

Like the administration proposal, the subcommittee bill sought to replace scores of outdated provisions and conflicting objectives in existing law with a handful of goals tailored for the post-Cold War era. The bill emphasized "sustainable development," assistance programs aimed at fostering environmentally sound economic growth in poor countries, a strategy strongly favored by the administration.

The subcommittee bill authorized $10.9 billion in fiscal 1995 foreign assistance spending, closely tracking the $13.6 billion foreign operations appropriations bill approved by the House in May (HR 4426). The price tags differed because the subcommittee's bill did not include some programs that were funded by the spending measure.

Subcommittee Chairman Paul S. Sarbanes, D-Md., called the draft bill a "good, responsible proposal." He said it balanced the administration's desire for broad flexibility in allocating assistance with Congress' traditional oversight role.

While the bill scrapped most of the provisions from the 1961 law, it retained some restrictions and conditions on foreign assistance that had strong support in Congress. For instance, it included the 1985 amendment barring aid to Pakistan because of that nation's nuclear program.

The bill also proposed to impose a new annual cap of $250 million on the transfer of excess defense equipment to foreign governments.

Before approving the measure, the panel approved a host of amendments by voice vote. Although the amendments were relatively minor, many included the sort of detailed policy recommendations that the administration had sought to eliminate when it proposed its foreign aid bill. One amendment, offered by Hank Brown, R-Colo., called for establishing high-level diplomatic contacts between the United States and Taiwan, a move that seemed sure to trigger China's ire.

The bill went no further and died at the end of the Congress. ∎

State Bill Reflects Changing Climate

On April 28, nearly a year after Congress began work on the measure, the House cleared a bill authorizing $13.5 billion for the State Department, the United States Information Agency (USIA) and related agencies for fiscal 1994 and 1995.

In addition to the funding, the bill (HR 2333) revamped the foreign policy bureaucracy and served as an important barometer of congressional sentiment on Bosnia-Herzegovina, U.S. relations with Vietnam and other controversial issues.

President Clinton signed the measure into law April 30 (PL 103-236), although he raised constitutional concerns over several of the bill's provisions. The measure was enacted just in time to meet a deadline set the previous year, when Congress temporarily allowed programs covered by the bill to receive fiscal 1994 appropriations even though they had not been reauthorized. That waiver expired April 30.

Policy Barometer

Over the years, the State Department authorization bill had become nearly as important for signaling Congress' mood on foreign policy as for the funding it provided. The fiscal 1994-95 authorization included several major statements on policy:

● **Bosnia.** Over the strong objections of the administration, the bill urged Clinton to provide weapons to the forces of Bosnia's beleaguered Muslim-led government despite the United Nations embargo on arms to the region.

● **Vietnam.** The bill also contained a non-binding provision approved by the Senate in January calling on Clinton to end economic sanctions against Vietnam. Buttressed by the Senate provision, Clinton on Feb. 3 ended the embargo, which had been in place since the Vietnam War.

● **China.** Another important non-binding provision asserted that a 1982 law providing for unlimited transfers of defensive arms to Taiwan took precedence over a U.S.-China communiqué of the same year, in which the United States agreed to gradually reduce arms sales to Taiwan. As a result of negotiations on the provision, the administration signaled it would approve new sales of advanced military electronics to Taiwan.

The legislation also:

● Authorized the administration's long-sought $670 million supplemental request for fiscal 1994 U.N. peacekeeping contributions. But the bill also set new restrictions on U.S. support for peacekeeping and withheld half the $670 million unless the United Nations established an independent inspector general. Congress appropriated the money separately as part of the annual spending bill for the departments of Commerce, Justice and State (HR 4603). *(Appropriations, p. 483)*

● Imposed stiff sanctions on nations that engaged in the trade of nuclear weapons parts or weapons-related design information and on private companies that sold nuclear mate-

BOXSCORE

State Department Authorization — HR 2333, (S 1281). The $13.5 billion bill authorized funds for the State Department, United States Information Agency and related agencies for fiscal years 1994 and 1995.

Reports: H Rept 103-126, S Rept 103-107; conference report H Rept 103-482.

KEY ACTION

Feb. 2 — Senate passed HR 2333, 92-8, after substituting the text of S 1281.

April 19 — Conferees complete work.

April 26 — Senate agreed by voice vote to deem the conference report cleared when the House adopted it.

April 28 — House adopted conference report by voice vote.

April 30 — President signed HR 2333— PL 103-236.

rial that could be used in making weapons.

● Prohibited U.S. arms sales to countries that upheld the Arab economic boycott of companies that did business with Israel. The provision was to go into effect one year after enactment of the bill. The president could waive the restriction if he determined that to be in the national interest.

Reorganizing State

The bill included most elements of a plan put forward by the administration for reorganizing the State Department. It provided for the establishment of a new under secretary of global affairs, a job set to be filled by former Sen. Timothy E. Wirth, D-Colo. Wirth effectively had been carrying out the duties for nearly a year, while holding the title of counselor.

The bill, however, did not go along with an administration plan to merge the State Department's office of counterterrorism with its new global affairs section, opting instead to preserve a separate post of coordinator for counterterrorism for a year after enactment.

The legislation consolidated all U.S.-funded international broadcasting — the Voice of America, Radio Free Europe, Radio Liberty, and Radio and TV Marti — under a single broadcasting board of governors. It also authorized creation of a new Radio Free Asia — a "surrogate" broadcasting service to provide uncensored news to China and other totalitarian states in Asia. The service was the brainchild of Sen. Joseph R. Biden Jr., D-Del., who acknowledged that it would ruffle China's feathers. "To be sure, China will be unhappy," Biden said. "But Beijing's petulance ought not to guide American policy."

Clinton Signs but Objects

In a signing statement reminiscent of those issued by Clinton's Republican predecessors, Clinton objected to several sections of the law that he said "could be construed so as to interfere with the discharge of my constitutional responsibilities."

Those provisions included: a requirement that the United States vote against loans by multilateral development banks to countries that had expropriated the property of U.S. citizens; similar restrictions on development bank loans that facilitated the spread of nuclear weapons-related materials; and new standards for refugee aid that gave greater priority to the needs of women and children.

Clinton said his role under the Constitution "necessarily entails discretion" over these matters. He added that he would regard those sections of the law as "precatory" — in essence, congressional entreaties — rather than as requirements.

Clinton was particularly troubled by the bill's comprehensive sanctions on companies engaging in nuclear proliferation. He called the sanctions "essentially unworkable," adding, "I have been assured that this provision will be corrected."

Background

The House had passed its original version of the bill June 22, 1993, by a vote of 273-144. The House measure (HR 2333 — H Rept 103-126) generally stuck to the so-called core issues — the organizational structure of the State Department, U.S.-backed broadcasting services and international scholarship programs. It was the Senate — acting in committee in 1993 and on the floor in 1994 — that added scores of policy-related amendments. *(1993 Almanac, p. 505)*

The Senate Foreign Relations Committee weighed in July 15, 1993, approving its version of the legislation (S 1281 — S Rept 103-107) by a vote of 19-0.

The most heated debate during the markup concerned an administration proposal to overhaul government-sponsored broadcasting programs, placing them under the USIA. Biden objected strongly but failed to add an amendment to maintain the independent status of two Cold-War-era networks, Radio Free Europe and Radio Liberty.

The committee eliminated a $175 million contingency fund proposed by the administration for U.N. peacekeeping operations. But the panel strongly backed another administration request — for $50 million for the National Endowment for Democracy, a nonprofit corporation that supported pro-democracy activities in scores of countries. The House had adopted an amendment by Paul E. Kanjorski, D-Pa., to strike all funding for the organization.

The committee bill languished for months, largely because of the dispute over international broadcasting. Just before the end of the 1993 session, the administration reached a compromise with Biden, acquiescing in his demand that Radio Free Europe and Radio Liberty retain their status as independent, government-funded contractors. That freed the bill for floor action in 1994.

To allow State Department and other programs covered under the bill to continue operating in the interim, Congress included a temporary waiver of authorization in the fiscal 1994 Commerce, Justice, State and Judiciary appropriations bill (HR 2519 — PL 103-121). *(1993 Almanac, p. 555)*

Senate Floor

The Senate passed the State Department authorization bill, by a vote of 92-8, on Feb. 2, after substituting its own version, S 1281. *(Vote 18, p. 4-S)*

Senate consideration of the bill, which in the past had provided a forum for highly charged debates over administration policy, turned out to be relatively tame this time. "I don't think it has quite the same zip now that the Cold War is over," said Christopher J. Dodd, D-Conn. The administration may have benefited from fortuitous timing. In 1993, the Senate took up the defense appropriations bill (HR 3116 — PL 103-139) shortly after well-publicized military and foreign policy disasters in Somalia and Haiti, and the measure became a vehicle for days of debate over intervention in such regional conflicts. *(1993 Almanac, p. 483)*

During six days of debate on the State Department bill, senators did adopt amendments urging administration action on issues ranging from nuclear proliferation in North Korea to preferential trade status for China. But few posed any real threat to the administration's policies.

● **Vietnam.** Most significant, perhaps, the Senate went on record Jan. 27 in favor of lifting the U.S. economic embargo against Vietnam. The 62-38 vote provided Clinton with the political equivalent of a flak jacket. Just a week later, he for-

mally ended 18 years of trade sanctions that were imposed at the conclusion of the U.S. war in Southeast Asia. The historic action overshadowed the scores of other foreign policy issues addressed in the bill. *(Vote 5, p. 2-S)*

The vote followed a poignant debate that stirred memories of the bitter Vietnam conflict. Consideration of the issue was tinged with irony as some of the Senate's Vietnam veterans emerged as the strongest advocates for lifting the restrictions. The amendment was sponsored by a pair of highly decorated veterans — John Kerry, D-Mass., and John McCain, R-Ariz. *(Vietnam, p. 467)*

● **Bosnia.** The Senate addressed the brutal conflict in Bosnia-Herzegovina by overwhelmingly supporting nonbinding language urging the president to unilaterally lift the international arms embargo that barred weapons shipments to the Bosnian government and to provide arms for the Muslim-led government forces. But the 87-9 vote belied deep reservations over direct U.S. military intervention in Bosnia and divisions over how the United States should proceed. *(Vote 8, p. 3-S)*

While the administration long had favored arming the outgunned Muslims, it had stopped well short of taking action on its own, which would have violated the U.N.-imposed arms embargo. *(Bosnia, p. 446)*

● **North Korea.** On North Korea, as on many significant matters, Republicans seemed to have little appetite for all-out political combat. McCain substantially modified a sense of the Congress amendment on North Korea's nuclear weapons program, though he accompanied it with a scathing denunciation of the administration's policy as insufficiently forceful.

The amendment, adopted by voice vote, called on Clinton to seek an international consensus to isolate North Korea economically until it had halted its nuclear program. It also backed continuation of joint U.S. military exercises with South Korea, a response to reports that the administration was using the prospect of suspending the troop training as a bargaining chip in its negotiations with Pyongyang.

Virginia Democrat Charles S. Robb appeared to go further than McCain by offering an amendment urging Clinton to consider reintroducing tactical nuclear weapons in South Korea to pressure the North to live up to its nuclear treaty obligations. That amendment also was adopted by voice vote.

● **Peacekeeping.** Minority Leader Bob Dole, R-Kan., seemed headed for confrontation with the administration with a sweeping proposal on international peacekeeping. As originally drafted, the amendment would have barred the president from committing U.S. troops to peacekeeping operations unless Congress approved the operation or the president declared it to be in the interest of national security. But Dole watered down the amendment significantly, dropping the section containing those limits.

Kerry whittled the amendment further, cosponsoring a substitute amendment with Majority Leader George J. Mitchell, D-Maine, that replaced some of the statutory provisions in Dole's proposal with language expressing the sense of the Congress. That was adopted by voice vote.

Then, the Senate separately approved several aspects of Dole's original proposal, including a requirement that the administration tighten its budgeting procedures for peacekeeping contributions.

● **China MFN.** Kerry adopted a similar strategy toward another potentially troublesome amendment for the administration — a non-binding proposal by Jesse Helms, R-N.C., explicitly linking the renewal of China's non-discriminatory most-favored-nation trade status to its performance on

human rights and proliferation issues. *(China MFN, p. 137)*

Kerry proposed a far milder substitute amendment, which declared, among other things, that the "president's efforts have led to some recent progress on some issues of concern to the United States." The Senate approved Kerry's substitute, 61-39. *(Vote 16, p. 4-S)*

● **Russia.** Senators barely mentioned the continuing political turmoil in Russia — though there was broad agreement that the country's evolution was the leading national security issue confronting the United States. "There is not an obvious solution," said McCain. With the stakes so high, most senators preferred not to weigh in.

The Senate, however, did chide Clinton for failing to spell out the criteria that Eastern European governments would have to meet to qualify for admission to NATO. The Senate endorsed, 94-3, a non-binding amendment by Mitch McConnell, R-Ky., urging "prompt" admission to NATO for European nations after they had met several conditions, including establishment of civilian control over the military and support for NATO's goals. *(Vote 9, p. 3-S)*

Echoing his previous criticisms of U.S. policy toward Russia, McConnell accused the administration of "Moscow myopia." He said that by refusing to admit Hungary, Poland and the Czech Republic to NATO, the United States had "capitulated to Russian interests and Russian pressure." But several senators, including Carl Levin, D-Mich., persuaded McConnell to tone down the amendment, which originally had called for the immediate admission into NATO of qualified countries.

Other Amendments

On a few occasions, the Senate rejected Republican amendments on straight up-and-down votes. An amendment by Helms to freeze the number of assistant secretary slots at the State Department was tabled (killed), 51-49. *(Vote 15, p. 4-S)*

And the Senate defeated an amendment by Helms and Trent Lott, R-Miss., that would have required the administration to cut off security-related assistance to countries that voted with the United States less than 25 percent of the time in the U.N. General Assembly. That amendment also was tabled, 66-34. *(Vote 17, p. 4-S)*

Perhaps the most surprising challenge to the administration came from Foreign Relations Committee Chairman Claiborne Pell, D-R.I. In an unusual move three years before, Pell, who had been widely criticized for weak leadership, ceded responsibility for managing such bills to the Foreign Relations subcommittee chairmen.

He generally stayed on the sidelines as Kerry shepherded the State Department bill through the Senate. But Pell proposed an amendment calling for tough mandatory economic sanctions against Croatia that appeared to catch everyone off guard. One of Pell's former committee staff aides, Peter Galbraith, was the ambassador to Croatia, which reportedly had deployed thousands of troops in Bosnia.

But Pell eventually agreed to water down the amendment at the urging of the administration. His modified amendment, which replaced the mandatory provision with sense-of-the-Senate language urging Clinton to consider imposing sanctions, was approved by voice vote.

The Senate also approved an amendment by Maine Republican William S. Cohen encouraging Germany to take a more active role in peacekeeping. The amendment was approved 96-1. *(Vote 13, p. 4-S)*

In other action, the Senate:

● Adopted by voice vote an amendment by John Glenn, D-Ohio, requiring the United States to impose sanctions on

nations engaging in the trade of nuclear weapons parts or weapons-related design information and to punish private companies that sold nuclear material that could be used in making weapons. The amendment set out circumstances under which the president could waive the sanctions against countries or companies.

● Voted 93-0 to prohibit U.S. arms sales to Arab countries that upheld their longstanding economic boycott of companies that dealt with Israel. The arms ban, which was to begin a year after the legislation took effect, reflected the enduring congressional support for Israel. The amendment, sponsored by Hank Brown, R-Colo., allowed the president to waive the restrictions for one year if he determined sales would be in the national interest. *(Vote 12, p. 4-S)*

● Rejected an attempt by Helms to strip language from the bill supporting establishment of an international criminal court. The Senate voted 55-45 to table (kill) the amendment. *(Vote 3, p. 2-S)*

It later approved, 91-3, Helms' amendment to prevent the United States from participating in any criminal court that did not protect constitutional rights of U.S. citizens. *(Vote 10, p. 3-S)*

● Approved an amendment by Frank R. Lautenberg, D-N.J., extending a statutory provision that made it easier for certain ethnic and religious groups — including Jews and evangelical Christians in the former Soviet Union — to be accorded refugee status by the United States. The amendment was adopted, 85-15. *(Vote 14, p. 4-S)*

● Approved by voice vote a pair of amendments offered by Helms to cut off U.S. assistance and backing for international loans to foreign governments that had expropriated the property of U.S. citizens. The president could waive the restrictions if he determined it was in the national interest.

● **International broadcasting.** By voice vote, adopted a compromise Biden amendment under which Radio Free Europe and other "surrogate" radio services could maintain their status as independent government contractors.

The debate over revamping the government's broadcasting services had raged for months, pitting Biden — one of the Senate's best-known figures — against freshman Russell D. Feingold, D-Wis.

Biden succeeded in maintaining the independence of the government-funded operations, which he argued was essential to ensure their journalistic integrity. The amendment also fulfilled another of Biden's longstanding goals by authorizing for five years a new U.S.-backed broadcasting service for Asia, called Radio Free Asia.

But the compromise incorporated a proposal by Feingold to tighten financial management of the radio services, saving an estimated $250 million over four years. Feingold bitterly attacked what he alleged was a long history of fiscal abuses by the services, particularly Radio Free Europe.

● **National Endowment for Democracy.** The Senate also renewed a longstanding battle over funding for the National Endowment for Democracy. Dale Bumpers, D-Ark., a fierce critic of the endowment, successfully trimmed $15 million from the $50 million originally approved in the bill. That brought the authorized funding in line with the $35 million provided in the fiscal 1994 Commerce, Justice, State appropriations bill (PL 103-121). An effort to table (kill) Bumpers' amendment failed by 41-59. The amendment was then adopted by voice vote. *(Vote 7, p. 2-S)*

Agency supporters had been lobbying intensely to restore funds for the endowment, after the House voted in 1993 to eliminate them from its version of the bill.

● Approved, 93-6, an amendment by South Dakota Republican

Larry Pressler requiring the administration to withhold 10 percent of U.S. contributions to the United Nations in fiscal 1994 unless the world body establishes an independent inspector general. *(Vote 4, p. 2-S)*

● Approved, 99-0, Helms' amendment to withhold any funds for U.N. agencies that granted recognition to organizations that condoned pedophilia. Helms said a U.N. agency had recognized a gay and lesbian association that had, in turn, recognized the North American Man-Boy Love Association. *(Vote 2, p. 2-S)*

● Quietly eliminated a provision in the bill — originally sponsored by Helms — restricting the State Department's inspector general to a six-year term. By voice vote, the Senate agreed to strip the provision, which would have forced out Inspector General Sherman M. Funk, with whom Helms has feuded.

● Approved an amendment by Pell aimed at expanding the non-proliferation activities of the Arms Control and Disarmament Agency. The House bill included a similar provision.

Conference/Final

House and Senate conferees completed work on the long-stalled bill April 19, after hammering out agreements on Bosnia, international broadcasting, U.N. peacekeeping missions and other thorny foreign policy issues during a daylong conference. In all, they had to resolve 235 differences between the House and Senate versions of the bill.

The House approved the conference report (H Rept 103-482) by voice vote April 28. A Republican-led effort in the House to return the legislation to conference to remove the Vietnam provision fell short, 195-209. *(Vote 147, p. 44-H)*

The House vote cleared the bill for the president. The Senate had agreed two days earlier to deem the legislation cleared as soon as it was approved by the House, a step that ensured that the funeral of former President Richard M. Nixon, which interrupted the Senate schedule, would not delay enactment of the bill past the April 30 deadline.

Conference

Key decisions by the conference committee include the following:

● **Bosnia.** Despite strong administration objections, the conferees endorsed the Senate-backed provision calling on Clinton to provide weapons to the besieged Muslims despite a U.N. embargo barring weapons to combatants in the former Yugoslavia.

Dole's language did not require action, but Rep. Henry J. Hyde, R-Ill., argued that it had strong symbolic significance. "This is a statement we have to make, or we disqualify ourselves from being moral players in the world," he said. House Foreign Affairs Committee chairman Lee H. Hamilton, D-Ind., led opposition to the proposal, warning that it could "Americanize the war." But Hamilton, who chaired the conference, acknowledged that sentiment was running against him. House conferees agreed to accept Dole's amendment.

● **Peacekeeping funds.** After an appeal from the president, the conference committee authorized the administration's request for $670 million in new peacekeeping funds for fiscal 1994. The panel also approved $510 million for fiscal 1995.

Clinton sent the conferees a letter urging them to support payment "of our projected U.N. peacekeeping payment arrearages." The administration had warned for months that the United States could fall as much as $1 billion behind in assessed peacekeeping contributions by the fiscal year's end.

The conferees attached a long list of conditions to their approval of the funds, although most appeared to be in line with the administration's revamped policy toward peacekeeping.

Only half of the $670 million was to be provided immediately, with the rest becoming available only when the United Nations established a separate office of inspector general, a position the administration had sought to oversee the world body's finances.

The conference report also prohibited the United States from paying for more than 25 percent of U.N. peacekeeping operations beginning in fiscal 1996. The administration had been working to reduce the 31 percent U.S. share of such missions.

● **International broadcasting.** The conferees also appeared to resolve the long-running dispute over international broadcasting by authorizing the establishment of a new radio service to provide uncensored news to totalitarian countries in Asia.

The only challenge to the new Asian radio service came from Howard L. Berman, D-Calif., who said the administration had requested $10 million for Radio Free Asia in fiscal 1995. He expressed concern that that would not be enough to get the operation running. Biden conceded that the initiative had been underfunded, but vowed to press members of the Appropriations Committee to raise the budget. House conferees accepted that assurance.

● **Cuba.** Berman engaged in an intense behind-the-scenes debate over policy toward Cuba with Cuban-American lawmakers and with officials of the Cuban-American National Foundation, the pre-eminent Cuban-American exile lobbying group.

Berman wanted to attach language to the bill expanding the range of cultural and educational materials available for export to Cuba and other countries that were subject to U.S. economic sanctions. But the proposal faced opposition from the foundation and from Cuban-American lawmakers, who objected to any expansion of commerce with Fidel Castro's regime.

After hours of wrangling, the two sides reached a complicated compromise: The conferees adopted Berman's provision. They added non-binding language — sought by the anti-Castro lawmakers and groups — urging the president to seek a U.N. trade embargo against Cuba. Berman also dropped various challenges to U.S. radio and television broadcasting to Cuba, although an aide insisted there was no linkage between that issue and the compromise over trade in cultural materials.

● **Vietnam.** Some of the most passionate debate occurred on the issue of U.S. trade with Vietnam. Benjamin A. Gilman, R-N.Y., said signing on to the Senate's amendment after Clinton already had lifted the embargo "is like rubbing salt into the wound." Gilman and another Republican — Olympia J. Snowe of Maine — said Vietnam still had not cooperated enough on cases of missing U.S. servicemen to warrant lifting the trade ban.

House conferees split along party lines, voting 7-5 to accept the Senate provision.

● **Nuclear proliferation.** House and Senate conferees waged a spirited turf battle over Glenn's amendment imposing stiff economic sanctions on companies and countries that assisted in the spread of nuclear arms and weapons-related materials.

House conferees backed the substance of Glenn's amendment, but Rep. Sam Gejdenson, D-Conn., argued that it should be included in a proposed reauthorization of the Export Administration Act. Gejdenson chaired the House

Foreign Affairs Subcommittee on Economic Policy, which had jurisdiction over that bill. But the Senate, which had approved Glenn's amendment on several occasions only to see it die, seemed in no mood to compromise. The Senate conferees rejected, 13-0, Gejdenson's offer to include a sunset clause phasing out Glenn's amendment in June 1995. The House members had backed that proposal, 9-4.

The two sides eventually agreed that Glenn's amendment would remain in place until the next State Department authorization bill was enacted. John Kerry, D-Mass., who led the Senate's conferees, promised that the Foreign Relations Committee would not try to strip the provision from legislation reauthorizing the Export Administration Act.

In other action, the conference committee:

● **China.** Agreed to modify a Senate-approved amendment intended to ensure that the United States did not reduce arms sales to Taiwan. Republican Frank H. Murkowski of Alaska offered the amendment, which originally declared that a 1982 law providing for unlimited weapons transfers to Taiwan took precedence over a U.S.-China communique that year in which the United States pledged to reduce arms sales to Taiwan. After the administration raised objections, the con-

ferees made Murkowski's proposal non-binding.

● **Terrorism.** Agreed to maintain a separate Office of Counter-Terrorism at the State Department until a year after the bill's enactment. The administration had proposed to move the office into a new bureau with responsibility over crime, narcotics and terrorism. Gilman bitterly opposed that plan, arguing that the move would diminish the importance of anti-terrorist activities. He won strong support from his colleagues April 18, when the House voted 357-2 to instruct its conferees to support a separate Office of Counter-Terrorism. *(Vote 113, p. 36-H)*

● **Korea.** Rejected a Senate-approved amendment calling on Clinton to reintroduce U.S. tactical nuclear weapons to the Korean peninsula unless North Korea complied with the terms of the nuclear non-proliferation treaty. The Senate agreed to give way to the House on that issue.

● **PLO.** Extended a waiver of various statutory restrictions on the Palestine Liberation Organization (PLO) until one year after the enactment of the bill. The Senate bill had included a provision allowing the president to waive the restrictions indefinitely if he certified every six months that the PLO had been abiding by its peace agreement with Israel. ■

Intelligence Agencies Face Review

Congress cleared an intelligence authorization bill Sept. 30 that kept overall funding for the nation's intelligence agencies relatively constant. But the fiscal 1995 bill (HR 4299) contained changes with potentially sweeping consequences for the nation's intelligence community. Over the objections of the Clinton administration, the bill effectively put the FBI in charge of counterintelligence and established a 17-member blue-ribbon panel to carry out a wholesale review of the mission and conduct of the CIA and the other intelligence agencies. President Clinton signed the bill into law Oct. 14 (PL 103-359).

The aggregate funding level in the authorization bill was classified, as were the figures for the CIA, Defense Intelligence Agency, National Security Agency and other government bureaus with intelligence-gathering functions. But the total for fiscal 1995 was reportedly about $28 billion, similar to the level approved for fiscal 1994.

The policy changes came in the wake of revelations of perhaps the worst case ever of espionage against the United States. On Feb. 21, longtime CIA official Aldrich H. Ames and his wife, Maria Del Rosario Casas Ames, were arrested for having sold top-secret information to the Soviet Union and, subsequently, to Russia from 1985 until their arrest. Ames' revelations to Soviet officials led to the execution of at least 10 Soviet sources of the CIA and FBI and the imprisonment of others.

The intelligence bill also reflected a general concern in Congress that predated the Ames scandal over the size, management and focus of the nation's intelligence establishment

BOXSCORE

Fiscal 1995 Intelligence Authorization — HR 4299 (S 2082). The bill effectively put the FBI in charge of counterintelligence and set in motion a re-examination of the nation's intelligence agencies.

Reports: H Rept 103-541, Part 1, S Repts 103-256, 103-295; conference report H Rept 103-753.

KEY ACTION

July 20 — House passed HR 4299, 410-16.

Aug. 12 — Senate passed HR 4299, 97-2, after substituting the text of S 2082.

Sept. 30 — House, Senate adopted the conference report, each by voice vote.

Oct. 14 — President signed the bill — PL 103-359.

in the aftermath of the Cold War.

The provisions strengthening the role of the FBI in counterintelligence were inserted by the Senate. The bill required all intelligence agencies to report immediately to the FBI any suspected leaks of classified information and to give the FBI access to relevant agency and employee files. The bill also gave spy-catchers greater access to the financial and travel records of espionage suspects.

The Clinton administration argued that while changes clearly were required, they should be accomplished through executive orders, which would give the president more flexibility, rather than by statute. But leaders of the Senate Intelligence Committee said many prior executive branch efforts to coordinate and strengthen counterintelligence activities had failed, and they insisted on giving primary responsibility to one agency, the FBI.

The bill also established new restrictions on the size and scope of buildings contracted for the intelligence agencies. The provision resulted from a flap over an expensive new office complex being built to house the National Reconnaissance Office (NRO).

Background

Debate on the fiscal 1995 intelligence authorization bill took place in the shadow of the Ames spy case. Ames, a 31-year CIA employee, and his wife were were apprehended by FBI counterintelligence agents and charged with having received $1.5 million over nine years for selling secrets to the

Soviets and later to the Russians. Ames formally accepted a plea bargain April 28 under which he received a life sentence in federal prison and revealed his espionage activities to government investigators. In exchange, Ames' wife received a five-year sentence. *(Ames case, p. 463)*

Ames' ability to escape detection for nearly nine years led both the Clinton administration and key members of Congress to conclude that the government's spy-catching structure was badly in need of redesign. In particular, action was needed to end turf fights and lack of communication between the CIA, which conducted foreign intelligence and counterintelligence activities, and the FBI, which handled counterespionage investigations within the United States. FBI officials told Congress that the CIA's failure to share its early suspicions might have delayed Ames' detection and capture.

But the administration was a reluctant player in legislative efforts to reshape procedures for spy-catching. Taking the traditional position that intelligence policy-making was an executive branch function, the administration opposed locking new arrangements into law.

Clinton laid down his marker May 3, signing a presidential directive that set up a policy board to coordinate the government's counterespionage efforts and improve information-sharing arrangements between the CIA and FBI.

The directive created a new National Counterintelligence Policy Board, made up of representatives of the CIA, FBI, National Security Council and the departments of State, Defense and Justice. A National Counterintelligence Operations Board and a National Counterintelligence Center were established under the board. The directive gave the FBI greater prominence and access to CIA information. An FBI official was to head the Counterintelligence Center for its first four years and was always to serve either as chief or deputy chief. Also, a senior executive from the FBI was to be put in charge of the CIA's counterespionage group; in turn, CIA officials were to be placed in the FBI's national security division.

"Our administration feels very strongly that the standards setting in the counterintelligence area is most properly [done] in the executive branch," Deputy Attorney General Jamie S. Gorelick told the Senate Intelligence Committee at a hearing May 3.

But committee Chairman Dennis DeConcini, D-Ariz., cited a series of failed attempts over the years to coordinate the counterintelligence bureaucracy through executive action and said legislation was needed to correct the problem.

Clinton's directive, which reportedly was signed only minutes before the Senate Intelligence hearing, was aimed at preempting a bill (S 1948) introduced in March by DeConcini and John W. Warner of Virginia, the Intelligence Committee's ranking Republican. That bill would have put the FBI director directly in charge of all counterespionage activities. S 1948 also contained provisions to give government investigators expanded access to the financial and travel records of individuals who had national security clearances.

Revising Classification Standards

The government's system for classifying documents also received new attention as a result of the Ames case.

Since World War II, when government secrecy practices were established, classification standards for most material had been set by presidential executive order.

Intelligence officials were under increasing pressure to end what critics called the unnecessary classification of millions of less critical documents and records. In March,

DeConcini and Dan Glickman, D-Kan., chairman of the House Intelligence Committee, introduced parallel bills to create statutory standards for classifying government documents. At a press conference March 2, the two lawmakers said that millions of classified documents had little bearing on national security while draining money and resources from more crucial efforts, such as improving supervision of intelligence personnel. "All the classifications in the world didn't stop the Ames situation," said Glickman.

The lawmakers said 7.1 million documents were classified in fiscal 1991 and 6.3 million in fiscal 1992.

Glickman said the bills would create a strong presumption in favor of disclosing government information, placing the burden of proof on those who would restrict access. Both bills sought to reduce the classification categories from three — top secret, secret and confidential — to two.

DeConcini wanted to allow information to be designated as secret for up to 10 years or top secret for up to 15 years. Glickman's bill provided for classification for up to six years for documents likely to cause "serious damage" to the national security and up to 10 years for those that could cause "exceptionally grave damage."

The bills also required the president to issue a uniform set of classification procedures to be administered by a single federal official. Under the existing system, each of the seven federal departments and agencies that had classification authority maintained its own procedures. Advocates of revamping the system argued that this led to weak controls over who was authorized to classify documents and who got access to them. "Almost anybody can classify and can stamp a document top secret or secret," Glickman said.

The intelligence community agreed in principle, but opposed efforts to write new classification standards into the law.

In a report delivered to CIA Director R. James Woolsey and Defense Secretary William J. Perry on March 1, a panel made up of former defense and intelligence officials, described the existing classification system as "overkill."

The report, which commission Chairman Jeffrey H. Smith described to the Senate Intelligence Committee on March 3, called for the administration to create a single subcommittee of the National Security Council to oversee clearance procedures. "Current security policy formulation and execution is fragmented throughout the government," Smith said. "This fragmentation is probably the greatest single cause of the confusion, waste and inefficiency in the system."

But executive branch representatives told lawmakers that the standards should be revamped through a new executive order that the Clinton administration was drafting rather than through legislation. They said an executive order would allow for greater flexibility in overhauling the secrecy rules.

In the end, lawmakers decided to allow the president to complete work on the executive order, rather than writing the standards into the bill. But they required that Clinton issue the order within 90 days.

House Subcommittee

Two House Intelligence subcommittees marked up the House version of the intelligence authorization bill (HR 4299) in May.

The Subcommittee on Program and Budget Authorization had jurisdiction over the programs of the CIA, the National Security Agency and the NRO, and it produced much of the content of the authorization bill.

The subcommittee approved its portion of the bill May 5 in

a session that was closed to the public.

The Ames case did not appear to have affected support for the intelligence budget. "It would be a fair statement that every time the Intelligence Committee meets, the Ames case is discussed," Glickman said. However, he added, "it was not necessarily a material factor in our budget considerations."

The House Intelligence Subcommittee on Legislation approved its portion of the bill by voice vote May 11 at an open markup session that lasted just 10 minutes. The panel had jurisdiction mainly over employee pay and benefits and management procedures at the CIA, the Defense Intelligence Agency, the National Security Agency and the government's other bureaus involved in foreign intelligence gathering.

Some issues under its jurisdiction were among the few in the intelligence authorization bill that were not classified secret.

The panel approved several new provisions as an amendment in the form of a substitute by subcommittee Chairman Ronald D. Coleman, D-Texas. One provision, championed by David E. Skaggs, D-Colo., required intelligence agencies that received more than $1 million for security, countermeasures and related activities to allocate 2 percent of those funds to develop a phased plan for the declassification of secret government documents.

The amended authorization bill made permanent the inspector general positions at the Defense Intelligence Agency and the National Security Agency. Those agencies already had hired inspectors general on their own initiative, but the provision required those positions to be maintained, as was the inspector general's post at the CIA. Inspectors general at federal agencies were responsible for auditing the agencies' financial records and investigating allegations of employee misconduct.

The bill also contained a provision aimed at making it easier for Defense Department intelligence agents to recruit U.S. citizens living abroad as foreign intelligence sources. The measure clarified that privacy laws did not bar Defense officers from making initial contact with U.S. nationals overseas without first announcing their affiliation with the U.S. government.

House Full Committee

The House Intelligence Committee approved the bill in closed session May 17 (H Rept 103-541, Part 1).

The bill contained provisions to increase federal investigators' access to the financial records of potential espionage suspects by waiving privacy law protections for many intelligence community employees.

Although funding levels in the bill were classified, the total for fiscal 1995 reportedly was about $28 billion. Following the markup, Glickman said the amounts provided were "pretty close to a freeze" and were somewhat less than Clinton had requested. Agencies would have enough resources to conduct vital intelligence programs, Glickman said, but he added, "You will find the signal was sent" that many in Congress were unhappy with management practices at the CIA.

The effort to expand investigators' access to the financial records of intelligence employees was offered as an amendment by Glickman. Anyone who had access to classified information was required to give prior consent for government investigators to probe their financial, consumer and foreign travel records. Those records were to be obtained when an investigative agency determined that an individual might be disclosing classified information to a foreign entity or was showing signs of unexplained affluence or excessive debt.

The bill also provided for forfeiture to the government of any proceeds from espionage against the United States and any personal property used in committing such crimes. It also authorized financial and job-finding assistance for intelligence employees with access to sensitive information who were laid off — an effort to prevent them from succumbing to the lure of selling secrets.

Another Glickman amendment gave Clinton 90 days to issue his executive order revising procedures for classifying documents. The bill also included Skaggs' requirement that intelligence agencies set aside 2 percent of the money they received for security-related activities to plan for the phased declassification of government documents.

The previous day, Skaggs had released a study based on reports required from federal agencies that showed that 20 of the agencies devoted an estimated $2.3 billion and 32,400 employees to classification-related activities in fiscal 1994. The figures did not include the CIA, whose report Glickman and Skaggs called inadequate and "disappointing."

House Floor

The House passed the fiscal 1995 intelligence authorization bill July 20 by a vote of 410-16, spurning efforts to make public its ostensibly secret $28 billion bottom line. (Vote 336, p. 100-H)

Because most major provisions were classified as top secret, the public debate had an oblique quality.

No voices were raised in rebuke when several opponents of the bill quoted the $28 billion figure from news reports. But the House rejected, 194-221, an amendment by Glickman to declassify the aggregate intelligence budget total as of fiscal 1996. (Vote 332, p. 100-H)

Glickman contended that secret budgeting violated the Constitution. With the Soviet Union no longer looming as a superpower opponent, Glickman said, "continuing to classify the aggregate budget figure in the absence of a justifiable reason to do so only deepens the suspicion that secrecy is necessary to protect a budget which cannot otherwise be defended."

The CIA strongly opposed releasing the information on the basis that adversarial nations could deduce major U.S. intelligence policy shifts from the year-to-year changes in the overall budget figure. Woolsey had also warned lawmakers that publication of the aggregate figure would put Congress on a "slippery slope" that would inexorably lead to demands for public disclosure of more detailed spending figures.

Constrained from openly discussing the dollars and cents of the bill he was managing, Glickman described its spending total as essentially a freeze at the level of the fiscal 1994 authorization, 1.7 percent less than the fiscal 1994 appropriation and 2.1 percent less than Clinton's budget request.

A coalition of liberal Intelligence members staged an unsuccessful effort to cut the overall spending for fiscal 1995 by 10 percent. They argued that the intelligence price tag was still too high, given the end of the Cold War. The budget-cut amendment was rejected, 106-315. (Vote 333, p. 100-H)

Republicans on the Intelligence Committee cited previous reductions in intelligence spending and said they strongly opposed the cuts that were incorporated in the bill. But they called the measure the best deal they could get.

Senate Committee

The Senate Intelligence Committee approved a separate version of the legislation in a closed session April 26 (S 2082 — S Rept 103-256).

The NRO Undercover Office Complex

It could have been called "The Hunt for the 1 Million-Square-Foot, $302 Million Intelligence Agency Office Project."

But the case of the headquarters complex under construction in Chantilly, Va., for the super-secretive National Reconnaissance Office (NRO), which developed and operated the nation's spy satellites, was less a story for novelist Tom Clancy than for illusionist David Copperfield, who had been known to make buildings disappear as part of his act.

The mystery was how senators with responsibility for overseeing the nation's intelligence agencies could have failed to notice that the NRO was building a four-office-tower headquarters complex, with nearly a fifth of the space of the Pentagon, in plain sight in the suburban Washington countryside near Dulles International Airport.

Senators accused the NRO of having kept them in the dark about the size and cost of the building project. "The minimal — and I emphasize minimal — notification to this committee [about the project] by the NRO has outraged this member," said Senate Intelligence Committee Chairman Dennis DeConcini, D-Ariz., at an Aug. 10 hearing at which national security officials, including CIA Director R. James Woolsey and Deputy Defense Secretary John M. Deutch, were grilled about the project.

But members of the House Intelligence Committee, in a hearing Aug. 11, came to the defense of the intelligence officials, stating that they had sufficiently informed the House of their building plans. "Based on a review of documents . . . I have concluded that there was no effort by the NRO to hide the existence of the project from Congress," said committee Chairman Dan Glickman, D-Kan.

Other House committee members accused their Senate counterparts of trumping up charges of subterfuge to cover their own failure to keep up with the project. "I am at a loss why members of the other body would try to deceive the American people that a part of this government was trying to deceive them," said Greg Laughlin, D-Texas.

Even as he excoriated the intelligence officials, DeConcini conceded that his panel had not asked the right questions about the project. "This committee came up short on its oversight responsibility in regard to the NRO headquarters," DeConcini said.

The idea of consolidating the NRO's widely scattered office facilities in a single complex originally emanated from Congress in 1989. The agency notified Congress in September 1990 of its intention to purchase land and begin site planning. But DeConcini and other senators said they did not know that the NRO was nearing completion of the immense and costly compound until the Senate committee staff turned it up in an audit begun in April.

Rather than breaking out the building project as a line item in its annual budget requests, NRO officials had included the cost in an unitemized "base" budget that was supposed to cover expenses that sustained the agency's base level of services.

Woolsey and other officials explained that the procedure was a legacy of the deeply covert nature of the NRO, the very existence of which was classified until 1992. Even the land deal for the project was conducted as a cover operation, with a division of Rockwell International, a major defense contractor, making the purchase.

Intelligence officials handed lawmakers and reporters loose-leaf binders containing excerpts from 22 documents and briefings on the project that they said had been provided over the years to members and their staffs.

In response, several senators complained that the information was provided in jigsaw puzzle-type fashion rather than in a single, easily digestible document. They said congressional committees lacked the personnel to pull together such disparate clues and relied on the good faith of the agency officials to spell out where the money was going. "We simply do not have, nor should we have, the institutional infrastructure in the Congress to go over every single item in the detail that is necessary," said John W. Warner, Va., ranking Republican on Senate Intelligence. "That detail must be forthcoming from the executive branch."

But House members, working from the same briefing book at their hearing, pointed to passages that indicated efforts by NRO officials to inform Congress and that implied a tacit, if not express, congressional authorization for the project.

The Senate reacted quickly on the issue. On Aug. 10, it amended the fiscal 1995 defense spending bill, requiring a specific line item for any intelligence agency building project costing more than $300,000 and barring new contracts for the NRO project until it had been fully investigated by Congress. The final version of the bill (HR 4650 — PL 103-335) deleted the prohibition on the NRO project but included the language requiring a specific line item for each building request. (*Appropriations, p. 488*)

And on Aug. 12, members voted 99-0 to cap the project's cost at $310 million. The provision, an amendment to the fiscal 1995 intelligence authorization (S 2082) offered by Chairman DeConcini, also required that the CIA and the Defense Department review the project and report back to Congress. The final version of the intelligence authorization (HR 4299 — PL 103-359) included that provision, along with language requiring all intelligence agencies to get specific authorization from Congress for any building that would cost $750,000 or more. (*Intelligence authorization, p. 458*)

The measure was said to authorize about the same amount as the fiscal 1994 bill, which reportedly totaled $28 billion. "It's a no-growth budget; I think that's fair to say," said Chairman DeConcini. DeConcini said the committee had reduced the Clinton administration's request by about 1 percent and defeated two amendments to increase the intelligence budget. But despite the Ames case, there were no amendments in committee to slice deeply into intelligence spending.

An unclassified provision of the bill lifted a 1986 ban on U.S. intelligence relations with South Africa. The committee acted as South Africa held its first multiracial elections, ending the apartheid system of white dominance over the nation's black majority.

Although the committee did not act on warnings by some lawmakers that the intelligence budget might be chopped to force changes at the agency, DeConcini said committee mem-

bers voiced "a great deal of frustration over lack of policy, lack of procedures, lack of reorganization" at the CIA.

In an initiative inspired by the Ames case, the committee-approved bill gave the FBI greater access to individuals' consumer credit records during counterintelligence investigations.

Separate Counterespionage Bill

On May 24, the Senate Intelligence Committee approved a separate measure aimed at better coordinating efforts by federal agencies to detect and prevent espionage against the United States. The bill (S 2056 — S Rept 103-296), approved by a vote of 16-0, was subsequently appended to the intelligence authorization bill on the Senate floor.

S 2056 included provisions putting into statute the requirement that the president create a National Counterintelligence Policy Board made up of the heads of various agencies with counterintelligence responsibilities, including the FBI, CIA, Defense Department, State Department and National Security Council.

The bill did not include a proposal, contained in the original DeConcini-Warner bill (S 1948), to put the FBI director in charge of all counterintelligence activities. In negotiations with the White House, Warner worked out compromise language to put the new policy board in charge of counterintelligence, but the bill still made the FBI the lead agency. All federal agencies were required to refer to the FBI all allegations and leads about possible espionage.

Just hours before the markup session, the committee received a revised proposal from Anthony Lake, Clinton's national security adviser, to allow the president to waive that requirement at his discretion. Citing a lack of time to fully study Lake's submission, DeConcini prevailed upon the committee to report the bill without the administration's suggested revision.

The committee also set up another point of potential disagreement with the White House, approving by voice vote an amendment by Slade Gorton, R-Wash., to designate the attorney general as the permanent chairman of the counterintelligence policy board. The administration wanted to rotate the chairmanship among the CIA, FBI and Defense Department.

The bill also required all those who worked with classified information to provide prior consent for federal investigators to gain access to their financial, credit and travel records. The investigative agencies could obtain such records in response to allegations that a person was disclosing classified information to a foreign entity or when a person working with classified information showed signs of unexplained affluence or excessive debt; the latter could become a motive to sell secrets.

Investigators could obtain such records during the employee's period of access to classified information and for five years afterward. Counterintelligence officials said that such access might have led to a more timely apprehension of Ames.

The bill also required:

● All employees working with "particularly sensitive" classified information, as determined by the president, to file reports on their finances and foreign travel with their employing agency.

● Federal agencies to develop uniform standards for background investigations and reinvestigations of employees with access to classified information.

● Agencies to give any employee who was denied access to classified information the reasons for such action and to provide the employee with an opportunity to respond.

Other provisions allowed the attorney general to provide financial rewards to individuals who provided information leading to the arrest and conviction of people spying against the United States and required the forfeiture of property used in the commission of espionage.

The committee agreed by voice vote to an amendment by Bob Kerrey, D-Neb., to make it a misdemeanor to take classified documents outside the workplace without authorization.

Senate Floor

Defying the Clinton administration, the Senate on Aug. 12 passed its version of the fiscal 1995 intelligence authorization bill, after adding provisions tacitly placing the FBI in charge of counterespionage investigations. The Senate passed HR 4299, by a vote of 97-2, after substituting the text of its own amended bill (S 2082). *(Vote 285, p. 48-S)*

DeConcini and others argued that past executive branch attempts to improve counterintelligence coordination had failed. "We cannot depend on personalities or good intentions," added Warner. "It must be based on bedrock sound law."

The Senate adopted a DeConcini amendment appending S 2056 to the bill by voice vote. The amendment, which required that the FBI take the lead on all counterespionage probes, also contained provisions requiring the FBI to keep relevant agencies informed of its own counterintelligence investigations and allowing the president to waive the requirement that the FBI be informed immediately of suspected spying if it was determined that withholding the information was in the interest of national security.

DeConcini's amendment included provisions from S 2056 aimed at giving spycatchers greater access to the financial records of espionage suspects.

In addition, the Senate adopted, by a 99-0 vote, an amendment by Warner and Bob Graham, D-Fla., to establish a presidential commission to examine the roles and missions of the intelligence agencies in the post-Cold War era.

Responding to a flap over the cost of the new headquarters complex for the NRO in Chantilly, Va., the Senate adopted, 99-0, a DeConcini amendment capping the project's cost at $310 million and requiring the CIA and Defense Department to review the project and report back to Congress. *(Box, p. 461)*

Conference/Final Action

House and Senate conferees completed work on the bill Sept. 22 (H Rept 103-753). They agreed to accept the Senate amendments effectively placing the FBI in charge of all counterespionage investigations and setting up a commission to look into the operations of the intelligence community.

The House adopted the conference report by voice vote Sept. 30; the Senate concurred shortly thereafter, also by voice vote, clearing the bill for the president.

Glickman said the final bill authorized 2 percent less in overall spending than Clinton had requested and than was appropriated in fiscal 1994.

Like the Senate-passed bill, the conference report required all intelligence agencies to report immediately to the FBI any suspected leaks of classified information and to give the FBI access to relevant agency and employee files.

The final intelligence bill also included provisions from both earlier versions requiring executive branch employees who had access to classified information to consent to the disclosure of their financial and credit records. It required the president to issue an executive order within 90 days of enactment establishing uniform standards for classifying

government documents.

In return for the House's agreement to the FBI provision, Senate conferees dropped their objections to a satellite project that was backed by House members. Senators had argued that the intelligence budget was not big enough to pay for the satellite project. The conference agreement required the CIA director to provide a detailed explanation of project costs to the intelligence committees before proceeding.

The new Commission on the Roles and Capabilities of the United States Intelligence Community was expected to be chaired by former Defense Secretary Les Aspin, who had become the head of the President's Foreign Intelligence Advisory Board, co-chaired by former Sen. Warren B. Rudman, R-N.H.

At least nine of the 17 members were not to have held leadership positions in the intelligence community, although this definition did not exclude current and past members of Congress who had had oversight responsibility for intelligence. The president was to appoint nine commission members, with the other eight appointments divided between the Senate and House. Of the eight appointed by Congress, four were to be members and four were to be private citizens.

The commission was required to report its recommendations to Congress by March 1, 1996. The panel was to explore everything from the roles and missions of the intelligence agencies to which operations were run best and what man-

agement structure was most effective. "The commission has an opportunity to have quite a bit of influence if it does what it's supposed to do and is objective. If it doesn't get co-opted by the intelligence community" it can be of tremendous help, DeConcini said.

To maintain independence from the intelligence community, all but three of the commission's staff members were to be private citizens with no links to the community.

The conference report included the provision capping spending for the NRO office complex at $310 million. It also required all intelligence agencies to get specific authorization from Congress for any building that would cost $750,000 or more.

The final bill also:
● Omitted the House provisions that would have made permanent the positions of inspector general at the Defense Intelligence Agency and National Security Agency.
● Provided for a $1,000 fine or imprisonment for not more than one year, or both, for people who knowingly removed classified documents with the intent to keep them in an unauthorized place.
● Included Skaggs' provision requiring intelligence agencies that received more than $1 million for security to allocate 2 percent to develop a phased plan for declassifying documents.
● Lifted the ban on intelligence relations with South Africa. ■

Spy Case Shines Harsh Light on CIA

Lawmakers reacted with growing outrage to revelations that CIA employee Aldrich H. Ames had gone undetected for nine years while he acted as a double agent, selling critical U.S. secrets to the Soviet Union and later to the Russians.

Ames, a 31-year CIA employee, and his wife, Rosario, were arrested Feb. 21 and charged with taking $1.5 million from the Soviets in exchange for classified information. Ames pleaded guilty to espionage and was sentenced to life in prison. His wife was sentenced to 63 months on Oct. 21. Their treachery resulted in the execution of 10 CIA and FBI sources in the Soviet Union and the imprisonment of untold others.

Congressional criticism — which grew increasingly harsh as details of the scandal emerged — focused on three issues: the CIA's failure to detect and stop the massive security breach, despite obvious signs of trouble and Ames' own clumsiness; the lack of an aggressive response to the scandal by CIA Director R. James Woolsey; and the discovery that the CIA had failed repeatedly to notify lawmakers of intelligence compromises in the mid-1980s, which were later linked to Ames.

The Senate and House Intelligence Committees each produced public reports on the case.

"Like all government agencies, the CIA ultimately depends upon the support of the American people and the Congress to carry out its unique functions and maintain its unique capabilities," the Senate committee said in its report. "To restore that confidence, the CIA must deal effectively with the serious deficiencies highlighted by the Ames case."

The reports came in a congressional climate increasingly critical of the intelligence agency, with some lawmakers pushing to reduce the CIA's budget and others suggesting that the agency be folded into the Defense Department. A special 17-member commission was slated to begin work in 1995 on a broad review of the CIA's role in the post-Cold War era.

The blue-ribbon panel was expected to be headed by former Defense Secretary Les Aspin, who was serving as the head of President Clinton's Foreign Intelligence Advisory Board. The panel was expected to make recommendations to Congress by March 1, 1996. Lawmakers authorized the commission's creation as part of the fiscal 1995 intelligence authorization bill (HR 4299 — PL 103-359) in the wake of the Ames scandal. In the same bill, they required the CIA to begin coordinating with the FBI on counterintelligence cases. *(Intelligence authorization, p. 458)*

Senate Report

The Senate Select Committee on Intelligence issued a scalding appraisal of the CIA on Nov. 1. The report, the first formal response by Congress to the Ames debacle, was a 116-page indictment of an institution slack in its security, seemingly oblivious to serious personal problems among its employees and unwilling to come to grips with the possibility of a "mole" in its midst.

The intelligence panel called Ames' betrayal "the most egregious in American history" and identified seven major agency failures that were exploited by a bungling spy with a drinking problem. The CIA, the panel said, was guilty of "gross negligence — both individually and institutionally — in creating and perpetuating the environment in which Ames was able to carry out his espionage activities for nine years without detection."

The report listed 23 steps to rectify problems, including random polygraph tests and listing personal problems on official employee records. The committee stressed that it regarded the agency's response to be of "special oversight interest" and requested a progress report by Sept. 1, 1995.

Senators also expressed deep dissatisfaction with the dis-

Aldrich Ames: On the Record

The following are edited excerpts from an Aug. 5 interview that Sen. Dennis DeConcini, D-Ariz., conducted with Aldrich H. Ames at the city jail in Alexandria, Va.:

On becoming a spy for the Soviets in early 1985:

Ames: I felt a great deal of financial pressure, which I, in retrospect, was clearly overreacting to. The previous two years I had incurred a certain amount of personal debt. . . . It was not a truly desperate situation, but it was one that somehow really placed a great deal of pressure on me. We did not live extravagantly by any means. But through my inability to manage things on my salary, I let things slip. . . .

I had no house, and we had strong plans to have a family, and so I was thinking also in the longer term.

DeConcini: They were going to give you money and you were going to give them useless information?

Ames: That's exactly right. And I saw it as a one-time thing. To get $50,000 to get me out of the hole and to provide a nest egg for the future. At that time, in May, when I had got the money, I figured I was finished. . . .

I'm still puzzled as to what took me to the next steps. It came home to me, after the middle of May, the enormity of what I had done, the fear that I had crossed a line, which I had not clearly considered before, that I crossed a line I could never step back. It was as if I were sleepwalking. I can't really reconstruct my thinking. It was as if I were in almost a state of shock.

But certainly underlying it was the conviction that there was as much money as I could ever use. . . . And I think I sort of just threw myself at the KGB — lock, stock and barrel.

DeConcini: So in June you made another contact?

Ames: So in June I gathered up from my desk documents, cables, traffic — reflecting virtually all of the most important cases we had and gave it to them. Gave it to them with no preconditions. I said nothing about, you know, give me more money. I just said, "Here." In a sense, I was delivering myself along with them.

DeConcini: Did you have to ask for the payments?

Ames: No. I had lunch with [a Soviet Embassy official] and he passed me a note, a package with money and a note from the KGB. And we never spoke of what was going on beneath the surface. We would exchange shopping bags, and we never so much as winked at each other. And, in the note, the KGB said that they had set aside $2 million for me.

On divulging the names of U.S. spies in the KGB:

DeConcini: When you gave these names, Mr. Ames, did you have any realization of the significance of what you were doing, as to the danger that these people would be in?

Ames: Yes I did.

DeConcini: Did you just rationalize that this was not —

Ames: I did not. I did not agonize over it.

On the CIA's failure to catch him for nine years:

Ames: I think it reflects a couple of things. The fact that the agency has not had, like the British or like the KGB, a long history of disasters, of penetrations, recruitment or traitors within its own ranks makes it very difficult to deal with.

DeConcini: You were surprised when they arrested you?

Ames: I was completely shocked and surprised.

---

ciplinary steps taken by CIA Director Woolsey in response to the Ames case. They noted that the agency's own inspector general recommended that 23 current and former CIA employees be held accountable for the Ames fiasco. Woolsey instead issued letters of reprimand to four current and seven retired agency employees.

"All committee members believe that the director's disciplinary actions in this case are seriously inadequate and disproportionate to the magnitude of the problems identified in the inspector general's report," the intelligence panel said.

The committee withheld judgment on Woolsey's attempts to fix the agency's problems, including measures to shore up the counterintelligence unit, a review of the polygraph system, the initiation of random package searches and the creation of evaluation boards for promotions. "While the committee believes in general that stronger measures are needed, it is too early to pass judgment on the director's recent action," the panel said.

Lawmakers acknowledged the difficulty of imposing change on the intelligence community. "The culture is that they come to feel they are different, that they do not have to be responsible and follow procedures of reporting a fellow colleague in the service who is drunk, or is not suitable for the job, or gets a promotion or fails a polygraph test," said committee Chairman Dennis DeConcini, D-Ariz. "You change

that with new leadership and new people and new procedures and enforcement of the procedures." John W. Warner of Virginia, ranking Republican on the committee, said real change would come only as the next generation of agents moved into senior management positions.

New Details of Ames Case

The Senate panel's richly detailed report offered new revelations about the case.

More than 100 intelligence operations of allied nations, the CIA, the FBI and the U.S. military were compromised, as were countless other operations that Ames said he did not specifically recall. The compromises during the 1985-86 period "resulted in a virtual collapse of CIA's Soviet operations at the height of the Cold War," the report said. Ames also gave thousands of classified documents to the KGB, removing some of them in shopping bags from CIA offices.

The report painted a portrait of a mediocre CIA employee who rose through the ranks despite a chronic drinking problem, security lapses and several evaluations that categorized his work as poor. It described an agency that responded tentatively to a significant number of deaths of Soviet agents and failed to launch a full-blown investigation.

Perhaps the CIA's most serious failing was an inability to

fathom the possibility of a traitor in its ranks. Institutional myopia allowed even a clumsy spy like Ames to operate unchallenged for years, the Senate panel concluded.

Employee appraisals of Ames described him as a procrastinator and a poor administrator inattentive to detail, according to the report.

While en route to a meeting with a Soviet agent, Ames left his briefcase, containing classified documents that could have undermined his contact, on a New York City subway train. In an interview with DeConcini on Aug. 5 at the city jail in Alexandria, Va., Ames said that he and CIA officials had planned to post an advertisement for the briefcase on the bottom of the front page of The New York Times, where brief ads were sometimes carried. But the problem was solved when the FBI called to say that a schoolteacher from Queens, N.Y., found the case. *(Interview excerpts, p. 464)*

Ames' official file failed to note his drinking problem. While assigned to Mexico in the early 1980s, an inebriated Ames got into an argument with a Cuban official at a U.S. Embassy reception. Colleagues told investigators that Ames would go out for long lunches and would be too drunk to work when he returned. One supervisor said Ames was drunk about three times a week from 1986 to 1988.

Ames sometimes became confused and missed meetings with his Soviet contacts. He failed to show for an October 1990 meeting with the KGB because he mistakenly went to Zurich instead of Vienna. Another meeting in Vienna never took place because Ames again got the location wrong.

Luckily for Ames, it was not difficult to remove sensitive documents from CIA headquarters in Langley, Va. He exploited the agency's decision to stop examining hand-carried packages of employees and one day stuffed five to seven pounds of message traffic in plastic bags and walked out of the building.

On June 13, 1985, Ames met with a Soviet officer named Sergey Chuvakhin and delivered the contents of his plastic bags. The information identified more than 10 top-level CIA and FBI sources who were reporting on Soviet actions. The committee report quoted CIA officials as saying Ames' action that day represented "the largest amount of sensitive documents and critical information, that we know anyway, that have ever been passed to the KGB in one particular meeting."

Ames' marriage was a source of concern within the agency, but nothing was done to resolve the security questions it raised for some officials. When Ames informed the CIA that he planned to marry Maria del Rosario Casas, a Colombian, the staff of the Directorate of Operations recommended that Ames be assigned to a less sensitive job because his wife-to-be was a foreign national. But although the deputy director of operations accepted the recommendation, the CIA inspector general found that no steps were taken to implement it.

In September 1983, Ames was named counterintelligence branch chief for Soviet operations, a job that gave him access to CIA operations that involved Soviet intelligence officers. Eventually, he was promoted to a highly sensitive post in the Soviet-East European Division of the Directorate of Operations.

Ames told DeConcini that the pressure from personal debts of roughly $13,000 led him to sell information to the KGB.

Eventually, Ames had income of $1,326,310 that "could not be accounted for through salary and other known sources," the Senate report said. He used the money to buy two Jaguars in three years; a $540,000 house in northern Virginia, purchased in cash; furniture; home improvements; and his wife's

tuition at Georgetown University.

Ames' lifestyle, which was lavish beyond his salary of roughly $70,000 a year, proved to be his downfall. A colleague tipped off the CIA in November 1989, but it was not until June 1992 that the CIA found out that the Ameses had charged almost $20,000 to $30,000 per month on their credit cards.

The Senate report was based on committee hearings, briefings, interviews and the CIA inspector general's review, which totaled more than 450 pages.

The report faulted the CIA leadership from 1986 to 1991, which included Directors William J. Casey and William H. Webster and former Deputy Directors Robert M. Gates and Richard J. Kerr. "Whatever they may have personally understood the situation to be, they were in charge," the committee said. "It was their responsibility to find out what was being done to resolve the 1985 [security] compromises. Based upon the information available to the committee, they failed to do so."

House Report

In a report issued Nov. 30, the House Intelligence Committee ordered the CIA to explain why it failed to tell the panel about an unusually high number of deaths and disappearances of agents spying for the United States in the Soviet Union. Angry members of the House Intelligence Committee accused the agency of remaining silent although it had several opportunities to notify Congress of intelligence compromises in the mid-1980s, which had since been linked to Ames.

The 79-page committee report was highly critical of both the CIA and the FBI. The panel said that despite repeated and pointed questions to the agency from its members about rumors of lost intelligence agents, the CIA was mum. It also found that the FBI was "inexplicably passive" in the Ames' espionage case despite access to CIA files.

Committee members said they were determined to find out whether the CIA's failure to notify oversight committees as required by law was a blatant disregard of the 1947 National Security Act or plain incompetence on the part of senior intelligence officials. They instructed Woolsey to submit a written report on the issue by Dec. 31, which was to include all corrective steps under consideration.

Larry Combest of Texas, the panel's ranking Republican, said the committee planned to hold hearings in 1995 and to call several intelligence officials as witnesses. Combest was slated to become committee chairman in the Republican-controlled 104th Congress.

The National Security Act required the CIA to keep congressional committees informed of all intelligence activities, including "any significant intelligence failures." The House committee's report said, "While there is rarely a reluctance to provide information when there is an intelligence success, the committee's experience when there is bad news has been uneven at best. Notification, however, is not discretionary."

In a last-minute addition to the report reflecting the committee's determination to shore up the disclosure process, the panel recommended that the CIA and FBI directors provide a written report to the intelligence committees twice a year on all counterintelligence and counterespionage investigations.

The House report also pointed to weaknesses in the CIA system, including a breakdown in communications in which investigators failed to apprise senior officials of information that could have led to Ames' arrest several years earlier.

It was less harsh than the Senate report in its assessment of Woolsey's directorship, faulting him for giving senior offi-

cials the benefit of the doubt.

The committee's main complaint with the agency was the lack of notification, especially troubling for a panel that in 1985 alone held more than 25 hours of hearings and interviewed scores of witnesses in a review of counterintelligence activities.

In 1988, members of the committee questioned agency officials about the slow pace of counterintelligence reforms, which were unrelated to the Ames case. At the time, the CIA's assistant deputy director of operations for counterintelligence knew of the deaths of the agents and failed to give that information to the committee.

In 1990 and 1992, two committee members, whom the report did not identify, received a general description of losses in the Soviet program. They met separately with senior CIA counterintelligence officials but still received no information.

Another member met with then-CIA Director Webster and then-Deputy Director Richard J. Kerr about a newspaper story describing a KGB general who allegedly reported on the execution of suspected Soviet spies. "It does not appear that the director was even fully informed about the losses at the time," the report said.

The committee was particularly offended by the discovery that CIA officials had briefed a retired deputy director about the losses and sought his advice during the summer of 1993. ∎

Congress OKs More Aid for Russia

Despite lawmakers' anger over the Aldrich H. Ames spy scandal and rising concern over Russia's new assertiveness in foreign affairs, Congress agreed to appropriate $850 million in fiscal 1995 economic assistance to Russia and the other former Soviet republics and to provide another $400 million to dismantle nuclear weapons. Ames had pleaded guilty in May to selling top-secret information to the Soviet Union and subsequently to Russia from 1995 until his arrest in February. *(Ames case, p. 463)*

Meanwhile, President Clinton took a step toward fully normalizing trade relations by certifying that Russia was in compliance with the Jackson-Vanik amendment to the 1974 Trade Act. That law barred trade with countries that had so-called non-market economies and that did not allow free emigration. In September, Clinton hosted Russian President Boris N. Yeltsin in Washington in a meeting that was notable for its matter-of-fact tenor. Clinton and Yeltsin also announced an agreement to accelerate nuclear arms reductions.

House Votes for Economic Aid

The fiscal 1995 foreign aid appropriations bill, signed Aug. 23, included $850 million for Russia and the other former Soviet republics (HR 4426 — PL 103-306). That was just $50 million less than Clinton had requested but a significant reduction from the $2.5 billion in aid Congress had provided in fiscal 1994. Congress also added conditions to the aid, requiring that Russia abide by agreements to remove its forces from the Baltic nations to get the money. The president could waive the provision if he determined it was in the national security interest.

House appropriators recommended fully funding the administration's request for $900 million, and on the floor, leaders from both parties joined to support the aid package. Members rejected an attempt by Sonny Callahan, R-Ala., to cut $348 million from the portion specifically targeted for Russia.

Callahan argued that Russia had made little progress in moving toward free markets, but that brought a heated rejoinder from his fellow Republican, Robert L. Livingston of Louisiana. "The Cold War ended three years ago," said Livingston. "We can't expect miracles, but if this amendment passes we won't get one." Foreign Affairs Committee Chairman Lee H. Hamilton, D-Ind., and other lawmakers who previously had expressed concern over the aid program voiced similar sentiments.

The House rejected Callahan's amendment, 144-286. He had offered a similar amendment to the fiscal 1994 foreign operations bill and was defeated by almost the same margin, 140-289. *(Vote 205, p. 62-H; 1993 Almanac, p. 603)*

With some last-minute maneuvering, Callahan did manage to trim about $25 million in aid for Russia and the other former republics, bringing the total to $875 million.

Senate Cuts Aid; Lawmakers Reach Compromise

In the Senate, the Appropriations Committee approved a version of the bill by voice vote June 16 that trimmed the aid to Russia and the other republics and specified where the money would go. Reflecting growing frustration over the administration's handling of the assistance program for the ex-Soviet republics, the Senate bill provided $839 million, $61 million less than the administration requested. "The management of this program has been uncoordinated and short on vision," said subcommittee Chairman Patrick J. Leahy, D-N.H., "and the implementation has been no better."

Mitch McConnell of Kentucky, the ranking Republican on the Foreign Operations Appropriations Subcommittee, offered a series of amendments to mandate minimum levels of assistance for several of the ex-Soviet republics. McConnell frequently had accused the administration of what he called "Moscow myopia," favoring Russia with aid and attention at the expense of Ukraine, Armenia and other former republics. His amendments earmarked $150 million for Ukraine, $75 million for Armenia and $50 million for Georgia. Other McConnell amendments earmarked $80 million for Jewish refugees resettling in Israel and $270 million for international children's programs. All were adopted by a single voice vote.

On the Senate floor, lawmakers backed several Republican-sponsored amendments aimed at establishing new conditions on the aid. McConnell attached a provision to link the aid to Moscow's fulfillment of a longstanding pledge to withdraw Russian forces from the Baltic nations by Aug. 31. The amendment came in response to a July 10 statement by Yeltsin that he did not intend to withdraw about 2,000 troops still stationed in Estonia by the deadline. The Senate adopted the amendment, 89-8. But the provision allowed the president to waive the restriction if he found it to be in the national security interest. *(Vote 190, p. 33-S)*

Senators adopted by voice vote an amendment by Jesse Helms, R-N.C., to prohibit aid to Russia unless the president certified that Moscow had "demonstrated a commitment" to complying with treaties barring the export of chemical and biological weapons.

The Senate also backed an amendment offered by Pete V. Domenici, R-N.M., authorizing the president to tap the aid to Moscow provided in the foreign operations bill to dismantle nuclear weapons in the former Soviet Union. Funds for the program had come from the Pentagon's budget, but Domenici

protested that the Pentagon had become a "cash cow" for funding non-defense programs. The Senate approved Domenici's amendment, 56-38. *(Vote 201, p. 35-S)*

The Senate adopted by votes of 100-0 a pair of amendments to boost the portion of the aid to the former Soviet Union that was devoted to law enforcement activities. An amendment by Alfonse M. D'Amato, R-N.Y., provided $15 million for the FBI to combat organized crime in the former Soviet bloc. An amendment by McConnell earmarked $15 million to help train Russian police officers. *(Votes 192, 193, p. 33-S)*

When the bill went to conference, House and Senate appropriators roughly split the difference, approving $850 million in aid for the former Soviet republics.

House Appropriations Committee Chairman David R. Obey, D-Wis., was sharply critical of all the spending mandates in the Senate bill, arguing that they would hamstring the administration in allocating aid. The showdown came on McConnell's $150 million earmark for Ukraine. Obey kept his Democratic troops in line, and House conferees rejected that proposal, 4-8. At Obey's urging, conferees agreed to urge, but not require, the administration to provide $150 million for Ukraine, $75 million for Armenia and $50 million for the republic of Georgia.

The conference committee also rejected McConnell's amendment barring aid to Russia unless it pulled its remaining troops out of the three Baltic states by Aug. 31. Opponents argued that the provision had been made moot by a recent agreement by Moscow to withdraw the 2,000 remaining Russian troops from Estonia. The House delegation voted against that amendment, 3-8. The conferees then accepted Obey's milder substitute, which set no specific deadline for troop withdrawals.

Nunn-Lugar Program Funded

The fiscal 1995 defense spending bill (HR 4650 — PL 103-335), signed Sept. 30, provided $400 million requested by Clinton for the so-called Nunn-Lugar program to assist former Soviet republics in dismantling nuclear and chemical weapons arsenals. The program was named after its sponsors, Sens. Sam Nunn, D-Ga., and Richard G. Lugar, R-Ind. House appropriators cut the funds, but they were restored in the Senate. *(Defense appropriations, p. 488)*

Russia Found in Compliance With Jackson-Vanik

In preparation for a Sept. 27-28 meeting with Yeltsin, Clinton submitted a letter to Congress stating that Russia was in compliance with the Jackson-Vanik amendment to the 1974 Trade Act. Jackson-Vanik barred most-favored-nation (MFN) status for countries with non-market economies that did not permit free emigration. The provision was named after its sponsors, Sen. Henry M. "Scoop" Jackson, D-Wash., and Rep. Charles A. Vanik, D-Ohio. Despite its name, MFN status was the norm rather than the exception for U.S. trading partners; nearly all nations were accorded such treatment. *(1974 Almanac, p. 553, 514)*

Goods from Russia had received MFN treatment since 1992, but only because Presidents George Bush and Clinton had provided annual waivers from the Jackson-Vanik requirement.

Clinton's announcement met with the approval of the Jewish-American community, which had been the main force behind the Jackson-Vanik amendment. "We feel that it is very important to recognize ongoing progress," said Mark B. Levin, executive director of the National Conference on Soviet Jewry, an umbrella organization for 50 national Jewish

agencies and 300 community groups.

However, Yeltsin renewed his request to lawmakers during his visit to go further by passing legislation to remove Russia from the roster of countries subject to Jackson-Vanik. Yeltsin, who had made the 20-year-old trade law a focal point at every meeting with Clinton, joked, "I've already said that every single kid in Russia knows who these people are — Jackson and this guy, Vanik." Congress, however, was not ready to take that step.

A Low-Key Summit

After riding a roller coaster for two years, U.S.-Russian relations appeared to be on a more solid footing as Yeltsin arrived Sept. 27 for a two-day summit with Clinton. While the meeting produced significant new agreements on a range of arms control and national security issues, the absence of a crisis mentality might have been its most salient feature. "What strikes me most," said Hamilton, "is that this is really a routine visit, a bilateral meeting between two presidents. No crisis, no confrontation, as so often marked the meetings in the past."

Clinton and Yeltsin announced a new deal to speed up the timetable for deactivating nuclear warheads established by the 1993 Strategic Arms Reduction Treaty (START II). The agreement was not to take effect until START II was ratified. Both countries had been slow to act because other former Soviet republics were delaying the implementation of the original START treaty, which laid the groundwork for the subsequent pact. Still, Clinton asserted that by shaving several years off the START II timetable, "we will make the world safer for all of us."

At the end of the meeting, the administration said it would transfer $100 million in previously appropriated funds to underwrite trade and investment programs for Russia at the Commerce Department and Overseas Private Investment Corporation. Another $30 million would pay for anti-crime programs and support the establishment of new legal systems in Russia. ∎

Clinton Lifts Trade Embargo Against Vietnam

In a simple executive action that followed years of difficult and often emotionally charged congressional investigations into the fate of missing servicemen from the Vietnam War, President Clinton on Feb. 3 lifted what had been an 18-year U.S. trade embargo against Vietnam.

Clinton's executive order came a week after the Senate voted 62-38 to urge the president to lift the embargo. The Jan. 27 Senate vote was on a nonbinding amendment to a bill (S 1281) authorizing fiscal 1994-95 appropriations for the State Department. *(Vote 5, p. 2-S)*

The embargo, which had been in place since the end of the Vietnam War, had been maintained under Presidents Jimmy Carter, Ronald Reagan, George Bush and Clinton largely to pressure the Vietnamese government to turn over all available information about U.S. servicemen listed as missing in action during the war. A sensitive political and social subject, the POW-MIA issue resonated in the public and on radio talk shows. It had been fanned by charges from some Vietnam veterans groups that U.S. soldiers were detained well into the late 1980s and that the Defense Department was covering up information about POW-MIA cases.

"Today I am lifting the trade embargo against Vietnam

because I am absolutely convinced it offers the best way to resolve the fate of those who remain missing and about whom we are not sure," Clinton said in a televised address Feb. 3. (Text, p. 12-D)

Clinton's decision was influenced by Hanoi's cooperation in 1993 in helping to resolve some of the more than 2,200 cases of Americans missing in action from the conflict.

A report issued in January 1993 by the Senate Select Committee on POW-MIA Affairs had concluded that there was "no compelling evidence" that any U.S. soldiers were held against their will in Vietnam at the time of the committee's investigation. It did, however, hold open the possibility that some soldiers had languished in captivity after the hostilities ended and after Hanoi said it had returned all POWs. (1993 Almanac, p. 527)

But it was the Senate vote that provided Clinton with the political cover to end the embargo. The Senate amendment was written by John Kerry, D-Mass., a decorated Vietnam veteran who was the chairman of the Senate Select Committee on POW-MIA Affairs, and John McCain, R-Ariz., a committee member who had spent nearly six years as a POW in Vietnam.

The Senate the same day rejected, 42-58, an amendment by Robert C. Smith, R-N.H., and Minority Leader Bob Dole, R-Kan., that would have conditioned the lifting of the embargo on the president's certification that the U.S. intelligence community was satisfied that Vietnam was providing the fullest accounting possible. Smith, the vice chairman of the select committee, contended that the intelligence community was convinced that Vietnam was not fully forthcoming on the POW issue.

Representatives of the American Legion and the Veterans of Foreign Wars lobbied against the Kerry amendment. Behind the scenes, however, lawmakers had been lobbied by Mobil, Amoco, the U.S. Chamber of Commerce and other interests that saw rich potential in Vietnam's oil reserves and economic development.

Bob Kerrey, D-Neb., who lost a leg in the war, urged in the Jan. 27 debate that while lifting the embargo the United States also press Vietnam heavily for better performance on human rights and for democratic reforms. "It is not time for us to stop fighting for the Vietnamese," Kerrey said.

Some members were deeply critical of the decision to end the embargo, saying it removed the last best lever to force more information from the Vietnamese government. Smith said in floor debate Jan. 27 that lifting the embargo was the equivalent of "getting down on your hands and knees and hoping and praying that the Vietnamese will give us all this information." ∎

Walsh Completes Iran-Contra Probe

Independent Counsel Lawrence E. Walsh concluded his seven-year investigation into the Iran-contra affair on a note of ambiguity that was in keeping with one of the murkiest political scandals in history.

In his long anticipated final report, released Jan. 18, Walsh exonerated former President Ronald Reagan of criminal culpability in the affair even as he bluntly accused the former president of creating a climate in which his senior aides felt free to violate the law. "They skirted the law, some of them broke the law, and almost all of them tried to cover up the president's willful activities," the report said.

Walsh, a retired federal judge, sharply disputed former President George Bush's repeated assertions that, as Reagan's vice president, he was "out of the loop" during the arms-for-hostages dealings with Iran. But Walsh also said he found no evidence of criminal wrongdoing by Bush.

The 566-page final report on Iran-contra painted a damning portrait of the Reagan administration, which Walsh said was bent on covering up its secret policies of selling arms to Iran and supporting Nicaragua's anti-communist contra rebels.

The report's main conclusion differed significantly from the one reached by the select congressional committees that investigated Iran-contra, which alleged that the scheme had been carried out largely by a "cabal of zealots" in the middle reaches of the Reagan administration.

By contrast, Walsh said Reagan and his entire foreign policy team knowingly pursued secret programs that directly contravened the U.S. embargo on arms sales to Iran and the congressional restrictions on aid to the contras.

The report said, "Congress was defrauded. Its appropriations restrictions having been circumvented, Congress was led to believe that the administration was following the law." Moreover, Walsh alleged there had been a deliberate attempt by Cabinet-level officials to make "scapegoats" of a handful of staff members of the National Security Council.

Despite the gravity of the charges against Reagan and his top lieutenants, Walsh achieved negligible prosecutorial success after an investigation that cost about $38 million. None of the high-level officials alleged to have been responsible for the scandal was brought to trial.

Walsh's investigation was stymied by several factors, including the controversial decision by Congress' Iran-contra committees to grant immunity to key players in the scandal and Bush's post-election pardon in 1992 of six Iran-contra defendants. (1992 Almanac, p. 571)

Just as the high-profile congressional probe of Iran-contra eventually triggered a powerful backlash, Walsh wrapped up his inquiry with his reputation tarnished. Walsh's longstanding Republican credentials did not protect him from the charge, made repeatedly by many congressional Republicans, that the investigation amounted to little more than a high-priced fishing expedition intended to sully the reputations of a pair of GOP presidents.

That line of attack resurfaced with a vengeance in the scorching written responses to Walsh's findings. The responses ran 1,150 pages and were included as part of the three-volume final report.

Reagan and Bush denied wrongdoing and denounced the investigation, as did most of the other former officials named by Walsh. "His final report is not a chronicle of facts," said the response prepared by Reagan's attorneys, "but a prolonged justification of his own excessive investigation and a defamation of the individuals he was empowered to investigate."

The Final Word

Walsh's report represented the last official word on a scandal that erupted with the stunning disclosure Nov. 25, 1986, that some of the proceeds from secret arms sales to Iran had been diverted to the Nicaraguan contras.

Walsh was appointed independent counsel Dec. 19, 1986, by a panel of three federal judges under terms of a law requiring appointment of such prosecutors to pursue allegations of

wrongdoing by high-ranking officials. The law, enacted in 1978 after the Watergate scandal and reauthorized in 1987 after the Iran-contra affair, expired in 1992. It was renewed in 1994 (S 24 — PL 103-270). *(Independent counsel, p. 295)*

Much had changed since Walsh's probe began.

Oliver L. North, the retired Marine lieutenant colonel and former National Security Council staff aide who engineered the so-called diversion, ran and narrowly lost a campaign to represent Virginia in the U.S. Senate. North's 1989 conviction on charges of obstruction and shredding documents, probably the high-water mark of Walsh's investigation to that point, was overturned by an appeals court in 1990.

Walsh retraced much of the ground covered by the select committees, which lost a battle for public opinion when North became a media sensation, delivering his defiant testimony in full-dress uniform.

But the uproar caused by the diversion of funds for the contras largely had been overtaken by allegations that senior administration officials took concerted steps to hide Reagan's knowledge of an initial arms shipment made to Iran in 1985. As details of the Iran initiative began leaking to the press in November 1986, former Attorney General Edwin Meese III scrambled to investigate the weapons transfers. But Walsh's report asserted that Meese's inquiry "was more of a damage-control exercise than an effort to find the facts."

Some of the harshest passages in the report concerned Meese's efforts to, as Walsh put it, persuade other officials to follow the "party line" — the assertion that Reagan was not aware of the apparently illegal shipment of Hawk missiles to Iran a year earlier. Walsh concluded that Meese "was not so much searching for the truth . . . as he was building a case of deniability for his client-in-fact, President Reagan."

Meese fired back at the stinging criticism with both barrels. In denying the charge of a cover-up, he accused Walsh of resorting to Soviet-style tactics: "You're guilty because I say you're guilty, and damn the truth."

In his report, Walsh took to task even some of the most respected public figures from the Reagan era, such as former Secretary of State George P. Shultz.

Walsh said he uncovered documentary evidence during the later stages of his investigation casting doubt on Shultz's assertion that he was unaware of the 1985 arms transfers to Iran. The evidence suggested that Shultz, who long had been viewed as an opponent of the Iran arms sales within the Reagan administration, "painted a misleading and incorrect picture" of his knowledge of the sales, the report said.

As for Reagan, Walsh was unsparing in his assessment that the former president should bear most of the blame for the scandal. But the prosecutor indicated that Reagan's behavior could at least be rationalized by the fact that he was pursuing deeply felt convictions, such as the need to free the U.S. hostages in Lebanon.

"The simple fact is that President Reagan seems not to have been ashamed of what he had done," Walsh's report said. "He had convinced himself that he was not trading arms for hostages, that he was selling the arms to develop a new opening with Iran, and that the recovery of the hostages was incidental to a broader purpose."

After the report was released, Walsh added, "The fact that [Reagan] disregarded certain laws and statutes in the course of it was not because of any possibly self-centered purpose."

Walsh said he found no such rationale for Bush's decision to grant pardons to former Secretary of Defense Caspar W. Weinberger and five other officials. "I think that was the most unjustifiable act," he said. "There was no public purpose served by that."

Lessons for Congress

Walsh offered some parting advice to Congress, urging lawmakers to think carefully before granting immunity to secure the testimony of any witness. Appellate courts threw out Walsh's most important convictions, those of North and former Reagan national security adviser John M. Poindexter, on grounds that trial witnesses had been tainted by their exposure to the immunized congressional testimony of the two men.

Walsh said he accepted Congress' need to investigate high-profile cases quickly and thoroughly. But he warned that "if it wants to compel testimony by granting immunity, it has to realize that the odds are very strong that it's going to kill any resulting criminal prosecution."

He also expressed frustration with the section of the independent counsel law that essentially gave the attorney general the final say over the release of classified material in cases brought by independent counsels. "That gives [the attorney general] the power to kill the prosecution of an independent counsel," Walsh said. ∎

Other Foreign Policy Issues Addressed in 1994

Lawmakers considered a number of additional foreign policy issues in 1994, including the following:

Iraqi Claims

The House easily passed legislation April 28 (HR 3221) to set up a system to distribute approximately $1.2 billion in Iraqi assets that the United States froze when Iraq invaded Kuwait in August 1990. But the measure, sought by the administration, stalled in the Senate, where key senators objected that the House-passed bill gave insufficient priority to the claims of U.S. businesses and private citizens. Without legislative action, the funds remained frozen.

The House bill authorized the U.S. Foreign Claims Settlement Commission to use the frozen assets to pay longstanding private and government claims brought against the government of Iraq. But the $1.2 billion was expected to resolve only a fraction of the estimated $5 billion in claims. Iraq owed the U.S. government about $2 billion; private claims accounted for about $3 billion. *(1991 Almanac, p. 437)*

Among those vying for the blocked Iraqi funds were major corporations whose contracts with Iraq were placed in limbo after the United States imposed economic sanctions on Baghdad in 1990. Relatives of servicemen killed in the Persian Gulf War and those killed or injured in the 1987 Iraqi missile attack on the *USS Stark* also sought funds.

The House passed the Iraqi Claims Act (HR 3221) by a vote of 398-5, after a brief but intense debate over allowing former Iraqi soldiers to immigrate to the United States. *(Vote 146, p. 44-H)*

The House bill gave priority to the claims of soldiers injured in the Persian Gulf War, to relatives of those killed and to the soldiers and relatives of those injured on the *USS Stark*. Once all claimants were paid $10,000 each, members of these preferred groups would get an additional $90,000. Without such a provision, supporters of the bill argued, well-heeled corporations would capture most of the funds through litigation.

The House bill gave the president the right to claim about 40 percent of the $1.2 billion for the government.

The substance of the legislation was not controversial in

the House. But some lawmakers wanted to toughen non-binding language in the bill stating that former Iraqi soldiers should not be admitted into the United States as refugees except in extraordinary circumstances.

Pennsylvania Democrats Paul E. Kanjorski and Paul McHale were outraged by reports that about 500 former Iraqi soldiers were admitted to the United States as refugees in 1993. Their anger was not assuaged by the fact that the vast majority of the Iraqi defectors apparently never fought against the United States.

McHale, a veteran of the war, called the non-binding provision "a bone in the throat of every gulf war veteran." He and Kanjorski pressed for a statutory ban on admitting the soldiers. They tried to return the measure to the Foreign Affairs Committee with instructions to add the prohibition. But Foreign Affairs Chairman Lee H. Hamilton, D-Ind., blocked the effort by raising procedural objections.

Before approving the Iraqi claims bill, the House approved a pair of non-binding amendments calling for humanitarian aid for Iraqi citizens and the establishment of a U.N. tribunal to prosecute Iraqi President Saddam Hussein for war crimes.

After passing the House, the bill ran into trouble in the Senate. At a Senate Foreign Relations subcommittee hearing Sept. 21, members told Clinton administration officials that private citizens and businesses with claims against Iraq should get first shot at the $1.2 billion in assets.

Sen. Paul S. Sarbanes, D-Md., chairman of the Foreign Relations Subcommittee on International Economic Policy, Trade, Oceans and Environment, repeatedly asked the representatives of the Treasury and State departments at the hearing why the U.S. government should be ahead of private citizens and businesses for repayment. He noted that the government could continue to go after Iraq for the debts, while private parties would not have the resources to do so.

Michael J. Matheson, principal deputy legal adviser for the State Department, said the administration wanted the authority to get some of the money back for the government, "since we represent the taxpayers."

Missing in Cyprus

Congress cleared a bill Oct. 5 providing for the State Department to hunt for five Americans who had vanished 20 years before during ethnic conflict on the Mediterranean island of Cyprus. President Clinton signed the measure Oct. 19 (HR 2826 — PL 103-372).

The bill directed the president to report results of the inquiry to both Congress and the families of the missing people. It said the president "shall do everything possible to return to their families, as soon as is [practical], the United States citizens who have been missing since 1974." That year, five Americans vanished during a bloody conflict between Greeks and Turks in Cyprus. Four of the missing Americans were elderly people who had retired to the island. The fifth was Andrew Kassapis, who at the time was a 17-year-old visiting Cyprus with his family.

The war began when the Greek-controlled military overthrew the elected government of Cyprus. Five days later, armed forces from Turkey invaded on behalf of the Turkish minority on the island. The interim military-led government fell and the elected government was restored, except in the northern third of the country, which was controlled by Turkey. Over the years, U.N. efforts to look for missing people on Cyprus bogged down, and little was accomplished.

"By passing this legislation, we take an important step toward ending the pain still suffered by families of the miss-

ing," said bill sponsor Eliot L. Engel, D-N.Y. "After 20 years, we must finally expose this dark chapter in the history of Cyprus and bring to light the fate of the missing Americans."

The House first passed the bill by voice vote Aug. 1, calling for a much broader investigation into the disappearances of 1,600 Greeks who remained unaccounted for, as well as 800 Turks who disappeared during Greek control of the island from 1963 to 1974. The State Department objected to the broader bill, saying that it would require three years and an additional 12 employees to conduct such an investigation.

The Senate passed the scaled-down version of the bill by voice vote Oct. 3. The House agreed to the Senate changes by voice vote Oct. 5, clearing the bill for the president.

South Africa

South African President Nelson Mandela addressed a joint meeting of Congress on Oct. 6, saying that raising living standards for South Africa's vast underclass should be considered essential to the national interest of prosperous democracies like the United States.

Mandela, who had been inaugurated May 10 as South Africa's first black president, threaded his speech with phrases from the Rev. Martin Luther King Jr. and poets T. S. Eliot and Walt Whitman. But his message focused on the theme of shared responsibility. He asked, "If what we say is true, that manifestly the world is one stage and the actions of all its inhabitants part of the same drama, does it not then follow that each one of us nations, including yourselves, should begin to define the national interest to include the genuine happiness of others, however distant in time and space their domicile might be?"

The previous day, President Clinton announced $100 million in new economic aid for southern Africa, about half to go to South Africa.

Earlier in the year, responding to South Africa's historic multiracial elections, the Clinton administration moved quickly to increase aid to that country's first black-led government. At a White House ceremony May 5, Clinton promised $600 million in assistance to South Africa over the following three years, including a doubling of aid in fiscal 1994 to $206 million.

Clinton called Mandela's landslide election a "miracle" that occurred in part because of steadfast U.S. support for majority rule. "Now we must not turn our backs," Clinton said.

Administration officials said the expanded aid package would primarily support U.S. trade and investment opportunities and promote the black private sector in South Africa.

Some members of the Congressional Black Caucus expressed irritation that the increased aid for South Africa would be provided at the expense of other African countries. The administration tried to address those concerns by shifting funds from African countries such as Togo and Cameroon where the United States had already announced it was shutting down its aid missions. "This is a relatively painless exercise in FY '94," said one official.

Mostly, lawmakers exulted as the final vestiges of apartheid were dismantled. "Who would have imagined only a few years ago that such a transformation would be possible?" asked Sen. Nancy Landon Kassebaum, R-Kan. Kassebaum supported the 1986 law (HR 4868 — PL 99-440) that imposed stiff economic sanctions on South Africa. It was enacted over then-President Ronald Reagan's veto. Mandela said the sanctions were crucial in forcing the white-led government to abandon apartheid. (1986 Almanac, p. 359)

Treaty on Women

Fourteen years after President Jimmy Carter pledged U.S. support for a treaty designed to eliminate discrimination against women, the Senate Foreign Relations Committee on Sept. 29 approved the pact, 13-4. However the Senate did not take up the treaty before adjourning.

Paul S. Sarbanes, D-Md., applauded the committee vote. "We've waited a long time for this day to come," he said.

Lack of support from both the Reagan and Bush administrations was the primary reason the treaty, known as the Convention on the Elimination of All Forms of Discrimination Against Women, languished so long. Neither administration asked Congress to ratify the treaty, so it remained in diplomatic limbo. But in September, Secretary of State Warren Christopher sent a letter to Congress asking that the Senate ratify it.

The four votes against the treaty came from panel Republicans. Nancy Landon Kassebaum, R-Kan., for example, said she voted no because the treaty would be "too intrusive."

The accord, which had been ratified by 136 nations, set out a long list of goals for the women of the world, such as making sure that they had equal opportunities to work, draw benefits and earn the same pay as men. It also required signatories to set national minimum ages for marriage.

Because of the potentially broad interpretation of some of these provisions, the State Department drew up a set of "reservations" to U.S. ratification that, among other things, explicitly said the treaty did not include a right to an abortion. ∎

Senate Draws Battle Lines Over Foreign Policy Picks

Several of President Clinton's choices to fill foreign policy positions that were subject to Senate confirmation sparked controversy in 1994.

Strobe Talbott

The Senate confirmed Strobe Talbott on Feb. 22 as deputy secretary of State, but not before leading Republicans sharpened their attacks on his past writings and his prospects for a future promotion. Dividing along partisan lines, the Senate voted 66-31 to confirm Talbott as the State Department's second-ranking official. Republicans cast all 31 nay votes, while 12 GOP senators joined with 54 Democrats to provide the margin of victory. *(Vote 46, p. 9-S)*

The Senate Foreign Relations Committee had voted 17-2 on Feb. 9 to confirm the 47-year-old Russia scholar and former journalist, who was serving at the time as ambassador-at-large to the former Soviet Union.

Talbott had been expected to waltz into the deputy secretary's slot without significant opposition. But many Republicans appeared in no mood for a coronation as they skewered the former Time magazine columnist and the administration's posture on international affairs.

At times, the debate evoked the bitter ideological battles of the Cold War. Conservatives were particularly incensed by a column Talbott wrote in 1990 in which he asserted that Cold War "doves" had been vindicated by the demise of the Soviet Union. Trent Lott, R-Miss., accused Talbott of being "soft on the former Soviet Union, touting its legitimacy while denigrating this nation's legitimacy."

Republicans also sought to pre-empt a widely anticipated move by Clinton to tap Talbott, a former Oxford roommate and close friend of the president's, as the heir apparent to Secretary of State Warren Christopher. "Maybe it's time to say, 'Enough promotions for Strobe Talbott,'" said Senate Minority Leader Bob Dole, R-Kan., adding that he wanted to send a "strong signal."

A central complaint lodged by Dole and other Republicans was that Talbott had linked U.S. policy toward Russia too closely to the fate of Russian President Boris N. Yeltsin. John McCain, Ariz., said that Talbott could jeopardize U.S. national interests "in a much larger area of the globe" in his new role. "Frankly, I find it alarming that Ambassador Talbott could possess the same ability to influence our policy in Korea that he has had with regard to our policies in Europe and the former Soviet Union," he said.

With the nomination never in real doubt, few Democrats felt compelled to man the barricades on Talbott's behalf. Some shared concerns with Republicans that Talbott's past writings on Israel had been unduly harsh. Those columns were the focal point of Talbott's confirmation hearing before the Foreign Relations Committee.

During his testimony to the committee Feb. 8, Talbott tried to defuse the controversy by affirming his unqualified support for Israel. "I have always believed that the U.S.-Israel relationship is unshakable," he said.

The uproar had erupted after a pair of conservative U.S. Jewish organizations, the National Jewish Coalition and the Zionist Organization of America, circulated some of Talbott's old columns from Time, including one written in 1981 that questioned Israel's strategic importance to the United States. Talbott wrote that Israel "is well on its way to becoming not just a dubious asset but an outright liability to American security interests, both in the Middle East and worldwide."

Talbott told the committee that he no longer had any doubts about Israel's strategic value to the United States. "On that I have simply changed my opinion," he said. He also reminded senators that part of his role as a columnist was to stimulate debate. "It was my job — and I carried it out with relish — to go in with my dukes up, into fights on various subjects," he said.

Despite the controversy, Talbott went into his confirmation hearing with the support of Israel's ambassador to the United States and that of Howard M. Metzenbaum, D-Ohio, a longtime champion of Israel.

Robert Pastor

Over the passionate objections of ranking Republican Jesse Helms of North Carolina, the Senate Foreign Relations Committee approved the nomination of Robert Pastor to be U.S. ambassador to Panama. But, given the near certainty of a Helms filibuster on the floor, Senate Democratic leaders declined to bring up the nomination, effectively killing it for the year.

The Foreign Relations Committee agreed to recommend Pastor's nomination Oct. 4 by a vote of 14-3. Helms persuaded only two committee Republicans, Hank Brown of Colorado and Judd Gregg of New Hampshire, to join him in opposition. Earlier, on Sept. 29, Helms had effectively filibustered the nomination in committee and prevented the panel from voting. Helms described Pastor as a "man whose career has been punctuated by troubling decisions." He railed against Pastor for accompanying former President Jimmy Carter on his recent mission to Haiti while waiting for Senate confirmation. Pastor had maintained a close working relationship with

Carter, serving most recently as a Latin America specialist at the Carter Center in Atlanta.

But Helms reserved most of his ire for Pastor's role in negotiating the 1978 treaty to turn over the Panama Canal to Panama by 2000. Helms called Pastor, who served as a Latin America specialist on the National Security Council during the Carter administration, the architect of the "policy that gave away our most valuable strategic asset outside the continental United States."

Helms spoke against the nomination for almost an hour and a half. Then he invoked a Senate rule that prohibited committees from meeting for more than two hours while the Senate was in session. The committee was forced to quit for that day without acting on Pastor's nomination.

Sam Brown

Conservative Senate Republicans blocked President Clinton's nomination of Sam Brown, who had once led nationwide protests against the Vietnam War, as ambassador to head the U.S. delegation to the Conference on Security and Cooperation in Europe (CSCE). Based in Vienna, the multilateral organization monitored arms control agreements and served as a forum for European security. Brown had organized a national moratorium against the Vietnam War in 1969.

Brown eventually went to represent the United States at the CSCE but without ambassadorial rank.

After a debate that touched on old divisions over Vietnam and sharp criticism of Clinton's foreign policy, the Senate twice rejected Democratic attempts to break a GOP-led filibuster against Brown's nomination.

The first bid to end the filibuster, on May 24, attracted only 54 votes. Five Democrats, including Armed Services Committee Chairman Sam Nunn of Georgia and Vietnam veteran Bob Kerrey of Nebraska, joined 39 Republicans in voting against blocking a filibuster. Five Republicans supported the cloture petition. Democrats tried again the next day and failed, 56-42. *(Votes 131, 132, p. 23-S)*

Hank Brown, R-Colo., a Vietnam veteran who led opposition to the nomination (he was no relation to the nominee),

had some of Sam Brown's more controversial quotes from the 1970s blown up and displayed on placards on the Senate floor. Among the highlighted statements was a 1977 comment in an interview with Penthouse magazine in which Brown reportedly said: "I take second place to no one in my hatred of the intelligence agencies."

Sen. Brown generally steered away from personal attacks on the nominee, citing the litany of old quotes instead. He argued that Sam Brown's lack of national security experience as well his rocky tenure as head of the ACTION volunteer service agency during the Carter administration should disqualify him from the ambassadorial post.

Many other Republicans were less restrained, labeling Brown an unreconstructed 1960s radical.

But John Kerry, D-Mass., another veteran of the war in Southeast Asia, vigorously denounced the Republican allegations that Brown had espoused radical views. "It is worse than wrong," he said. "It is a verbal political lynching on the floor of the Senate." He told reporters after the second failed cloture vote that Republicans were more interested in cutting down Clinton than in revisiting the Vietnam War. "This was not as much about Vietnam as it was a target of opportunity for the president's agenda," he said.

Derek Shearer

The Senate handed Clinton a victory May 24, confirming his embattled nominee, Derek Shearer, as ambassador to Finland. But Democrats had to block a threatened filibuster before approving the nomination 67-31. *(Vote 130, p. 23-S)*

Conservative Republicans seized on the nomination to paint Clinton as outside the political mainstream. Phil Gramm, R-Texas, said that past writings by Shearer, a college professor and the brother-in-law of Deputy Secretary of State Strobe Talbott, showed him to be a "socialist."

Robert C. Smith, R-N.H., said, "The president continues to surround himself with the type of people he protested with in the golden years of the anti-war movement, and it is having a devastating effect on the quality and effectiveness of our national security policy." ■

Chapter 11

APPROPRIATIONS

Fiscal 1995 Appropriations

Appropriations Overview 475
    Mileposts 476
Agriculture 477
    Chart 478
    The Fight Over Food Stamps 480
Commerce, Justice, State 483
    Chart 484
Defense... 488
    Chart 489
    Provisions... 495
District of Columbia 498
    Chart 499
    Fiscal 1996 D.C. Authorization 500
Energy and Water.................................. 502
Foreign Operations................................. 505
    Chart 506
Interior 513
    Chart... 514
    The Art Debate 516

    Grazing Fees 518
Labor, HHS, Education 519
    Chart... 520
Legislative Branch.................................. 524
    Chart... 525
Military Construction 527
    Chart... 528
Transportation..................................... 530
    Chart... 531
Treasury, Postal Service 536
    Chart... 537
VA, HUD, Independent Agencies 541
    Chart... 542
    Revamped Space Station 545
Supplemental Appropriations
Emergency Supplemental 548
    Chart... 549
    Provisions... 551
Spring Supplemental 557

OVERVIEW

Congress Clears All 13 Bills In Near-Record Time

For only the third time in almost 50 years, appropriators completed work before the start of the new fiscal year

Congress repeated one of its rarest accomplishments Sept. 30 by clearing all 13 of its annual spending bills before the 12:01 a.m. beginning of the new fiscal year Oct. 1. It was only the third time lawmakers had done that since 1948. Congress had cleared 12 of the 13 fiscal 1995 bills by Sept. 29. But as the clock ticked toward the midnight deadline Sept. 30, the Senate remained stubbornly hung up on the last one, the District of Columbia bill.

The D.C. bill became a target because it was the last must-pass bill of the session, and several senators wanted to hitch a ride for unrelated legislation. But late on the last day of the old fiscal year, leaders persuaded them to back off, and the bill cleared before the deadline.

Whether out of habit, lack of urgency or trouble on one or more of the bills, Congress almost never cleared all 13 appropriations measures on time. Usually, the House and Senate had to buy themselves a few additional days or weeks with a continuing resolution, or CR, which provided stopgap funding for unfinished bills.

But appropriators were determined that 1994 would be different. House appropriators, who by tradition initiated all spending measures, played eleventh-hour hardball with Senate procrastinators by sending them no CR, hoping to force action.

Since 1948, Congress had cleared all its spending bills on time twice — in 1976 and 1988. It did so in 1988 only because angry and embarrassed Democrats were determined to show that President Ronald Reagan was wrong when he ridiculed Congress for being unable to perform its most fundamental job.

Congress had to work literally until the last minute to meet the deadline that year. The Senate cleared the last three conference reports between 11 p.m. and midnight Sept. 30 and had to approve one measure sight unseen at 11:57 p.m., before the papers had even arrived from the House. A panting House clerk then burst through the doors of the Senate chamber with the bill, and the work was officially done. *(1988 Almanac, p. 649)*

Appropriators had no such presidential goad in 1994. Instead, they attributed the unusually quick finish to other factors:

● Appropriators knew early on how much they could spend. Spending limits set in the 1990 budget-reconciliation bill and extended in 1993 enabled them to do preliminary work quickly, without waiting for the budget resolution.

● There was an early push to get the spending bills out of the way to clear floor debate time in the fall for health care reform.

● New House Appropriations Chairman David R. Obey, D-Wis., cracked the whip, determined to finish on time in his first year. Senate Appropriations Chairman Robert C. Byrd, D-W.Va., did likewise.

● Individual problems that had slowed bills in the past, such

as public lands disputes on the Interior bill, melted away.

● Finally, said one aide, "everybody wants to get out of here."

Tight Budget Constraints

The fact that the spending bills were passed with dispatch did not mean it was a painless process for Congress. Five years of increasingly tight spending caps dictated by the 1990 budget deal produced a phenomenon lawmakers had not seen in nearly three decades: the first year-to-year drop in actual discretionary spending (outlays) since 1969.

Not counting "emergency spending" outside the budget caps, discretionary outlays were projected to fall from $543.3 billion in fiscal 1994 to $540.1 billion in 1995, according to the Senate Appropriations Committee.

In addition to tight spending caps, appropriators had to cope with an activist president with an aggressive "investment" agenda. President Clinton's budget called for widespread cutbacks and program eliminations to make way for his own spending priorities, which did not always match those long favored by Congress. The result was the sort of zero-sum game that deficit hawks had long advocated, in which most moves to spend money on new programs required scaling back or killing old ones.

House Chairman Obey, who succeeded the late William H. Natcher, D-Ky., in the spring, said appropriators killed 40 programs altogether and cut another 408 below their 1994 spending levels. That allowed them to remain under their spending limits while still giving Clinton about 65 percent of the priority spending he asked for.

Swift Action

The House adopted the conference reports on the 13 bills by Sept. 29, when it approved the defense appropriations bill. The House originally passed 12 of its 13 bills by the July Fourth congressional recess, the traditional (but rarely met) deadline for initial House action. The House passed the District of Columbia bill July 13 after working out a dispute over the local government's budget.

The Senate cleared 12 of the 13 bills by Sept. 29, and the 13th (D.C.) on Sept. 30. The Senate originally passed the last of its versions of the 13 regular 1995 spending bills Aug. 11, when it approved the defense appropriations bill.

Lawmakers also passed two fiscal 1994 supplemental appropriations bills. An $11 billion bill, signed Feb. 12, provided assistance for victims of the January earthquake in California and for other natural disasters, as well as funds for U.S. peacekeeping operations and for a variety of other federal programs. A second supplemental, enacted July 5, provided just $18.1 million in new spending authority, but it lifted loan ceilings by $93 billion for the Federal Housing Administration and the Government National Mortgage Association. *(Appropriations mileposts, p. 476)* ■

Appropriations Mileposts
103rd Congress – 2nd Session

Bill	House Passed	Senate Passed	Bill Cleared	Bill Signed	Story
Agriculture (HR 4554 — PL 103-330)	6/17/94	7/20/94	9/27/94	9/30/94	477
Commerce, Justice, State, Judiciary (HR 4603 — PL 103-317)	6/28/94	7/22/94	8/19/94	8/26/94	483
Defense (HR 4650 — PL 103-335)	6/29/94	8/11/94	9/29/94	9/30/94	488
District of Columbia (HR 4649 — PL 103-334)	7/13/94	7/21/94	9/30/94	9/30/94	498
Energy and Water Development (HR 4506 — PL 103-316)	6/14/94	6/30/94	8/11/94	8/26/94	502
Foreign Operations (HR 4426 — PL 103-306)	5/25/94	7/15/94	8/10/94	8/23/94	505
Interior (HR 4602 — PL 103-332)	6/23/94	7/26/94	9/28/94	9/30/94	513
Labor, Health and Human Services, Education (HR 4606 — PL 103-333)	6/29/94	8/10/94	9/28/94	9/30/94	519
Legislative Branch (HR 4454 — PL 103-283)	5/26/94	6/16/94	7/1/94	7/22/94	524
Military Construction (HR 4453 — PL 103-307)	5/24/94	7/15/94	8/10/94	8/23/94	527
Transportation (HR 4556 — PL 103-331)	6/16/94	7/21/94	9/29/94	9/30/94	530
Treasury, Postal Service, General Government (HR 4539 — PL 103-329)	6/15/94	6/22/94	9/28/94	9/30/94	536
Veterans Affairs, Housing and Urban Development, Independent Agencies (HR 4624 — PL 103-327)	6/29/94	8/4/94	9/27/94	9/28/94	541
Emergency Fiscal 1994 Supplemental (HR 3759 — PL 103-211)	2/3/94	2/10/94	2/11/94	2/12/94	548
Fiscal 1994 Supplemental (Housing Loans) (HR 4568 — PL 103-275)	6/21/94	6/22/94	6/22/94	7/5/94	557

Agriculture Funds Drop $3 Billion

Congress on Sept. 27 cleared a $69.1 billion spending bill for federal agriculture and nutrition programs. The bill (HR 4554), which funded most activities of the Agriculture Department and the Food and Drug Administration (FDA), represented a drop of nearly $3 billion in new budget authority compared with the fiscal 1994 agriculture spending bill. President Clinton signed the bill into law Sept. 30 (PL 103-330)

House Agriculture Appropriations Subcommittee Chairman Richard J. Durbin, D-Ill., called the spending measure "Exhibit One of the new regime we face in deficit reduction." Though describing the reductions as necessary, Durbin lamented as shortsighted cuts in programs such as watershed improvement and flood prevention. He said the nation ultimately would pay more to correct problems left unattended than would be saved by cutting programs aimed at dealing with those problems.

A discretionary nutrition program was among the bill's biggest winners. The Women, Infants and Children (WIC) program, a supplemental feeding program for women with children under age 5, received $3.5 billion, $260 million more than in fiscal 1994.

Farm subsidies proved to be less expensive than in previous years, but only by force of nature. Because the massive flooding that struck the Midwest in 1993 reduced crop yields and raised market prices, the Commodity Credit Corporation (CCC) paid out less in subsidies than it otherwise would have. As a result, the 1995 bill provided the agency with a $15.5 billion reimbursement, $2.5 billion less than in fiscal 1994.

Most of the funding in the bill, 80 percent, was tied up in mandatory spending programs such as food stamps — which alone was slated to receive $28.8 billion — and farm subsidies. As a result, most of the remaining cuts had to come out of the relatively small pool of discretionary funds. The bill contained about $13 billion in budget authority for discretionary programs, down $1.3 billion from fiscal 1994 levels.

House Committee

The bill began in the House Agriculture Appropriations Subcommittee, which approved it by voice vote May 26. The full Appropriations Committee followed suit June 9, approving the $68 billion bill by voice vote with only minor changes (H Rept 103-542). While entitlement spending in the bill was down 3 percent from fiscal 1994 levels, discretionary spending was to decline 9 percent.

During the full committee markup, Durbin took a poke at deficit hawks, such as supporters of the "A to Z" proposal to let spending critics target individual federal programs for elimination. He noted that his subcommittee had listed alphabetically by members' names the 1,119 requests it had received to earmark funds for specific agricultural projects. "They ran from A to Z, if you catch my drift," he said.

BOXSCORE

Fiscal 1995 Agriculture Appropriations — HR 4554. The $69.1 billion bill funded programs at the Agriculture Department and the Food and Drug Administration.

Reports: H Rept 103-542, S Rept 103-290; conference report H Rept 103-734.

KEY ACTION

June 17 — House passed HR 4554, 278-127.

July 20 — Senate passed HR 4554, amended, 92-8.

Sept. 23 — House adopted the conference report, 287-107.

Sept. 27 — Senate cleared HR 4554 by voice vote.

Sept. 30 — President signed HR 4554 — PL 103-330.

Nicking Programs

The appropriators achieved their savings by nicking nearly all of the programs funded by the bill. In the process, they had to juggle their own spending priorities with those of the Clinton administration.

They salvaged funding for some programs that the administration proposed to slash. For example, watershed and flood prevention operations got $65 million — a steep $155.8 million decline from the fiscal 1994 appropriation, but $40 million more than Clinton requested.

The Emergency Food Assistance Program, which provided administrative assistance and food commodities to food banks, was slated to receive $80 million, $40 million less than in the previous year but $40 million more than requested by Clinton. The Market Promotion Program was to receive $90 million, $10 million less than in fiscal 1994 but $15 million more than the president wanted. The much debated program provided subsidies to U.S. commodity trade organizations and food processors to advertise their products in foreign markets.

The appropriators also sought to rescue a program that partially funded agriculture research facilities at colleges and universities under the Cooperative State Research Service. The administration wanted to end the program, which received $54 million in fiscal 1994; the committee bill provided $34.1 million.

However, the bill cut deeply into several of Clinton's spending requests. It sliced the request for Section 515 rural rental housing loan subsidies by nearly $100 million, from $115.5 million to $15.8 million. Durbin attributed the reduction to a recent Appropriations Committee investigation that reported financial abuse by housing developers and mismanagement of the program in some Farmers Home Administration state offices.

The committee also tempered administration efforts to increase spending for a handful of programs. Funding for the wetlands reserve program, which paid landowners to remove ecologically sensitive wetlands from agricultural production, was to increase from $66.7 million in fiscal 1994 to $93.2 million in fiscal 1995. That was far less than the $240.9 million sought by Clinton.

The WIC low-income food and nutrition assistance program was to get a hefty $260 million increase, rising from $3.21 billion in fiscal 1994 to $3.47 billion. But that was $93.6 million less than the administration's request.

Durbin's strongest personal mark on the spending bill was the elimination of research programs on tobacco and tobacco products, which cost $3.7 million in fiscal 1994. Durbin was one of Congress' leading anti-smoking activists.

The appropriators' job was made more difficult by the Clinton administration's inclusion in its budget request of controversial user fees to offset some of the spending.

The panel rejected a request for $252 million in new FDA user fees. Durbin, an advocate of the consumer-oriented FDA, supported Clinton's effort to increase the funds avail-

Agriculture Spending

(in thousands of dollars)

	Fiscal 1994 Appropriations	Fiscal 1995 Clinton Request	House Bill	Senate Bill	Final Bill
Agriculture Programs					
Agricultural Research Service	$ 727,712	$ 743,239	$ 717,377	$ 742,505	$ 740,100
Cooperative State Research	495,250	418,517	448,108	485,827	496,182
Extension Service	435,982	432,386	429,200	439,244	438,744
Animal and plant inspection	449,709	442,552	457,624	445,874	450,624
Food safety and inspection	516,738	533,929	430,929	533,929	516,738
Crop insurance	525,910	504,688	281,903	291,903	287,991
Commodity Credit Corporation	18,900,000	15,500,000	15,500,000	16,500,000	16,500,000
Other	1,287,238	1,360,988	1,256,823	1,262,240	1,259,778
Subtotal	**$ 23,338,539**	**$ 19,936,299**	**$ 19,521,964**	**$ 20,701,522**	**$ 20,690,157**
Conservation Programs					
Soil Conservation Service	1,235,362	718,439	709,595	741,082	697,595
Conservation Reserve Program	1,743,274	1,752,216	1,743,274	1,743,274	1,743,274
Wetlands Reserve Program	66,675	240,900	93,200	93,200	93,200
Other conservation	254,828	126,717	112,302	100,677	111,802
Subtotal	**$ 3,300,139**	**$ 2,838,272**	**$ 2,658,371**	**$ 2,678,233**	**$ 2,645,871**
Rural Development Programs					
Farmers Home Administration (FmHA)					
Rural Housing	1,526,489	1,268,900	1,316,032	1,330,567	1,292,647
Loan authorization	*(3,275,007)*	*(3,547,890)*	*(2,594,886)*	*(2,671,547)*	*(2,471,547)*
Agricultural Credit	466,350	420,910	396,771	396,590	396,590
Loan authorization	*(3,618,319)*	*(3,815,444)*	*(3,189,067)*	*(3,184,755)*	*(3,184,755)*
Rural Development	201,825	237,026	203,281	223,613	213,649
Loan authorization	*(1,418,824)*	*(2,468,197)*	*(1,634,193)*	*(1,776,853)*	*(1,705,523)*
Rural water and waste disposal	487,500	525,000	500,000	500,000	500,000
Other FmHA accounts	214,852	293,867	221,547	221,233	219,647
Rural Electrification Administration	134,428	65,562	117,711	111,460	111,853
Total loan authorization	*(1,922,729)*	*(1,354,430)*	*(1,368,250)*	*(1,467,250)*	*(1,467,250)*
Other rural development	580	586	568	568	568
Subtotal	**$ 3,032,024**	**$ 2,811,851**	**$ 2,755,910**	**$ 2,784,031**	**$ 2,734,954**
Domestic Food Programs					
Food stamps program	28,136,655	28,830,710	28,817,457	28,830,710	28,830,710
Child nutrition programs	7,497,131	7,451,351	7,451,351	7,452,210	7,451,351
Transfer from Customs receipts	(4,770,109)	(5,212,818)	(5,249,077)	(5,249,077)	(5,249,077)
Women, Infants and Children	3,210,000	3,563,588	3,470,000	3,470,000	3,470,000
Other food programs	601,736	489,208	522,748	487,998	498,248
Subtotal	**$ 39,445,522**	**$ 40,334,857**	**$ 40,261,556**	**$ 40,240,918**	**$ 40,250,309**
International Programs					
PL 480 (Food for Peace)	1,444,505	1,245,440	1,246,165	1,246,165	1,246,165
Program level	*(1,538,690)*	*(1,307,258)*	*(1,298,884)*	*(1,298,884)*	*(1,298,884)*
CCC export loan subsidy	403,238	394,393	394,393	394,393	394,393
Loan authorization	*(5,700,000)*	*(5,700,000)*	*(5,700,000)*	*(5,700,000)*	*(5,700,000)*
Other	121,408	117,137	112,261	112,261	112,261
Subtotal	**$ 1,969,151**	**$ 1,756,970**	**$ 1,752,819**	**$ 1,752,819**	**$ 1,752,819**
Related Agencies					
Food and Drug Administration	870,264	641,177	899,415	729,808	884,415
New user fees	—	(252,000)	—	—	—
Other	110,181	108,765	109,506	107,835	106,670
GRAND TOTAL					
New budget authority	**$ 72,065,820**	**$ 68,428,191**	**$ 67,954,541**	**$ 69,027,866**	**$ 69,097,365**
Loan authorizations	*(16,042,300)*	*(17,032,163)*	*(14,575,037)*	*(14,894,645)*	*(14,617,716)*

SOURCE: House Appropriations Committee

able to the agency but opposed the user fees. He opted instead to provide $899.4 million in appropriated funds for the FDA — $258.2 million more than Clinton requested.

Appropriators did accept some of the proposed user fees, adopting the administration's unlikely assumption that the House Agriculture Committee would authorize $103 million in new fees from meatpacking companies to pay the salaries of federal inspectors who worked the second and third daily shifts in meat factories. That enabled them to reduce appropriations for the service by $103 million, shifting the money to other programs.

The bill also assumed $217 million in reduced spending for the Federal Crop Insurance Corporation resulting from passage of pending legislation (HR 4217, S 2095) to revise payment of commissions to reinsured companies. *(Crop insurance, p. 194)*

Amendments

One member lost out in an attempt to get a favored cause into the bill. Longtime food safety advocate Neal Smith, D-Iowa, described the standard practice by poultry processors of washing fecal matter and other contaminants off carcasses as an imperfect means of protecting public health. He offered an amendment in subcommittee to require tainted parts to be cut away and not sold for human consumption.

But Democrat Ray Thornton, from the major chicken-raising state of Arkansas, argued there was no sound scientific basis for such a requirement. The subcommittee agreed, defeating Smith's amendment, 3-6, before approving report language by Thornton and Smith requiring the Agriculture Department to study the issue.

Ron Packard, R-Calif., sparked one of the committee markup's few debates as he pursued his continuing effort to bar federal funds for illegal immigrants by amending appropriations bills. The committee accepted one Packard amendment that called for the Agriculture Department to enforce existing statutes that barred 16 programs from providing funds to illegal aliens.

But Packard withdrew a second amendment, which would have created new prohibitions for 34 additional programs, in the face of objections by Durbin and Appropriations Committee Chairman David R. Obey, D-Wis. They said such legislation first should be considered by the relevant authorizing committees and as part of immigration reform.

In its only roll call vote, the full committee rejected, 21 to 27, an amendment by Tom DeLay, R-Texas, to strike a provision in the bill that allowed the Agricultural Marketing Service to increase user fees to cover the full cost of its arbitration services. Under the Perishable Agricultural Commodities Act, the marketing service mediated disputes over commodity quality among growers, shippers, wholesalers and retailers. DeLay said grocery retailers and wholesalers objected to the fee increase and had concerns about how the program was run. Durbin countered that, by eliminating the user fee increase, the amendment would force the government to use taxpayer funds to subsidize the mediation process.

House Floor

The House easily passed the $67.95 billion agriculture appropriations measure June 17, despite complaints by some Republicans that farmers' interests were getting short shrift. The vote was 278-127. *(Vote 256, p. 76-H)*

Pat Roberts of Kansas, the ranking Republican on the House Agriculture Committee, urged members to defeat the annual spending measure. Roberts complained of a continu-

ing shift in spending priorities from farmer-oriented programs, such as flood prevention, farm-commodity export promotion and rural housing, to other programs funded by the bill, such as food stamps and the FDA. Roberts said, "Every farmer and rancher knows there are no sacred cows, and they have practiced self-sacrifice. . . . But when these cuts are used not to reduce the deficit but to increase other programs, I must object."

Responding that only a handful of programs in the bill received more money, Durbin blamed the cuts on the clamor in Congress to cut federal spending. "Unless and until members realize that yes, in fact we can cut too much in spending when it comes to important programs, we will continue down this path," Durbin said.

The bill and its spending priorities received a strong endorsement from Joe Skeen of New Mexico, ranking Republican on the Agriculture Appropriations Subcommittee, who had worked closely with Durbin in crafting the measure.

The brief floor debate included no serious effort to slash additional spending or eliminate programs covered by the bill. That contrasted with the 1993 House floor debate on the fiscal 1994 agriculture spending bill. Then, sponsors had to fend off amendments that would have killed the Agriculture Department's Market Promotion Program, deeply reduced spending for agricultural research and rural development programs and sliced spending 5 percent across the board. *(1993 Almanac, p. 540)*

Only one additional spending cut was accepted during floor debate. By voice vote, the House approved an amendment by Mike Kreidler, D-Wash., to strike a $25 million contingency fund for expenses in reorganizing the Agriculture Department. Durbin accepted the amendment, saying that the Agriculture Committee's approval of an Agriculture Department reorganization bill (HR 3171) June 16 rendered the contingency money unnecessary. *(Agriculture reorganization, p. 191)*

The House defeated, 139-264, an amendment by Dan Burton, R-Ind., to kill a $3 million program to provide technical assistance to socially disadvantaged farmers. *(Vote 254, p. 76-H)*

It also rejected, by voice vote, an amendment by Lamar Smith, R-Texas, to cut FDA funding by $467,000, a proposal Smith said was aimed at reducing spending on a uniformed division of the Public Health Service.

Even potentially controversial issues were easily dismissed. Despite criticisms from some Republicans that producers and consumers would have to absorb added costs, the House retained the provision for $103 million in new user fees to be collected from meat processors.

What might have been a furious policy debate over tobacco was pre-empted by the House Rules Committee on June 15. Democrats Durbin, Mike Synar of Oklahoma and Ron Wyden of Oregon wanted to propose an amendment to direct the FDA to regulate tobacco products as health hazards. But the Rules panel declined to provide a waiver from the prohibition against writing new laws on appropriations bills.

Senate Committee

The Senate Appropriations Committee approved a $68 billion version of the agriculture spending bill June 23 by a vote of 26-0 (S Rept 103-290). One day earlier, the bill had received voice vote approval from the Agriculture Appropriations Subcommittee.

The need to reduce spending required cuts in a number of programs and forced Agriculture Subcommittee Chairman Dale Bumpers, D-Ark., to turn down requests for additional

The Fight Over Food Stamps

A single sentence in the agriculture appropriations bill sparked the year's first legislative skirmish over how to overhaul the nation's welfare laws — an issue that would take on added momentum after Republicans won the Nov. 8 election.

The narrow provision pertained to experiments in administering the food stamp program, funded under the agriculture bill. Nine states had received federal waivers either to provide low-income food stamp recipients with cash instead of food stamps or to use the grants to subsidize jobs for the recipients. The most recent was Oregon, which planned to provide minimum-wage jobs for about 1,200 welfare recipients in six counties by converting food stamp and other welfare benefits to wages.

The House quietly inserted a provision in its version of the fiscal 1995 agriculture appropriations bill (HR 4554 — H Rept 103-542) to bar further waivers for such experiments. The little-noticed sentence was suggested by Neal Smith, D-Iowa, the chairman of the Labor/HHS Appropriations Subcommittee, who said the cash-out concept could deprive children of enough nutritional food.

His provision touched off an emotional debate in the Senate on July 19, when John McCain, R-Ariz., and Bob Kerrey, D-Neb., successfully offered an amendment to strike the prohibition and let the federal government approve more cash-out experiments.

The Program's History

The food stamp program began in the Kennedy administration as a pilot project to dispose of surplus food. In 1964, President Lyndon B. Johnson turned what had been a modest demonstration program into a pillar of his "Great Society" domestic policy.

Most Republicans derided it as a welfare program being charged to farmers. But Democrats hailed food stamps as a way to end a humiliating experience for the needy, who previously had lined up monthly with sacks in hand to cart away foods from a central depot.

The measure (PL 88-525) passed as part of an arrangement under which Southern Democrats backed the food stamp bill in exchange for Northern Democrats' support of a wheat-cotton bill. The few Republicans who supported food stamps were mainly from farm districts or urban areas with needy constituents. *(1964 Almanac, p. 110)*

The food stamp program eventually became a permanent part of the social welfare landscape, defended by a similar coalition of representatives of the urban poor and farm states (including many Republicans). Their mutual self-interest also boosted congressional support for the overall agriculture appropriations bill.

Food stamp benefits normally were distributed to recipients as coupons that could be redeemed by retailers. In fiscal 1993, the federal government provided $23 billion in food stamp benefits to 27 million recipients. The average monthly benefit per person was $68.

Some states, most notably Maryland, were experimenting with a credit card-like system called electronic benefits transfer in which recipients used plastic cards similar to credit cards that kept track of their welfare and food stamp benefits. It was designed both to reduce the stigma of presenting coupons to a retailer and to limit fraud.

Nine states had gotten federal waivers to experiment further, giving some food stamp recipients cash instead, either as a benefit check or indirectly as a wage subsidy. Their experiments generally were restricted to certain counties. Demonstration programs that had been approved adopted one of the following approaches:

● Giving all food stamp recipients the choice of receiving the benefits in cash instead of coupons.

● Giving only working families who received food stamps the opportunity to receive the benefits in cash.

● Providing a wage subsidy through employers, giving working recipients benefits as part of a paycheck.

The effect of the demonstrations on the poor had been mixed, according to an overview provided by the Agriculture Department's Food and Nutrition Service. They appeared to reduce household food expenditures, but the size of the reduction was uncertain. Recipients tended to reduce their nutritional intake, but it was unclear whether that meant they were not eating well enough.

---

spending from a number of his colleagues. Bumpers quipped during the subcommittee markup that one senator had told him, "I could do better with a dead man chairing that committee than I can with you."

In a move that was expected to complicate efforts to craft a final version of the bill, the Senate accepted some of the user fees proposed by Clinton — but not the same batch as the House.

The bill contained $150.8 million of the $252 million in new FDA user fees that were rejected by the House. Bumpers freely conceded that these anticipated revenues might prove illusory, saying that the Labor and Human Resources Committee, which had authorizing jurisdiction over such fees, would not approve them. He nonetheless agreed to include the fees, allowing appropriators to cut direct federal spending for FDA programs by an equivalent amount and freeing that money at least temporarily for other programs in the bill.

Bumpers' original draft included a lower figure of $123.2 million in new FDA user fees. But the Agriculture Sub-

committee approved by voice vote an amendment by Thad Cochran, R-Miss., to add $27.6 million in fees to free up more money for a watershed and flood prevention program, which provided funds for dams and other flood control projects.

Senate appropriators, however, rejected House-passed user fees to pay for meat inspectors, stating in their report accompanying HR 4554 that "meat and poultry inspection activities are too important to be left to assumed funding." Instead, the Senate version appropriated $103 million to the Food Safety and Inspection Service to pay for the late-shift meat inspection.

The Senate did include $212.8 million in speculative savings to be realized if Congress endorsed the administration's proposal to overhaul federal crop insurance.

The Senate bill contained several other significant differences from the House-passed measure. For example, it included $40 million for the Emergency Food Assistance Program, half as much as the House bill. Senate appropriators limited the spending to administrative expenses and

technical assistance provided to local food banks, soup kitchens and similar nonprofit food distribution centers. Since its establishment in the early 1980s, the program also had provided commodities to the food banks. These donations originally were intended to reduce federal commodity surpluses, but in recent years they had required off-the-shelf federal purchases of foodstuffs, a practice that had been criticized by some in Congress.

The subcommittee approved, 8-3, an amendment by Slade Gorton, R-Wash., to provide up to $90 million for the Market Promotion Program. Bumpers sought to eliminate spending for the program, which he had blasted as a boondoggle for corporate interests. But he was trumped by Gorton and Dianne Feinstein, D-Calif., who asserted that the program had spurred exports of their states' farm products. Gorton's amendment proposed to offset the market promotion funds by applying an across-the-board 1.5 percent reduction in the salaries and expense accounts of 27 Agriculture Department programs, creating numerous conflicts with the House version of the bill.

In another difference with the House, the Senate appropriators excluded Durbin's House-passed language barring federal spending for research on tobacco and tobacco products. The Senate bill also included $28.83 billion for the food stamp program, $13.3 million more than the House.

But the two versions of HR 4554 were identical on most major provisions. For example, both included $3.47 billion for WIC, $260 million more than in fiscal 1994 but $93.6 million less than requested by Clinton. Both versions also sought to rein in Clinton's requested expansion of the wetlands reserve program, providing $93.2 million, $26.5 million more than in fiscal 1994, but $147.7 million less than Clinton's request.

Senate Floor

The Senate passed a $69 billion version of the bill July 20 by a vote of 92-8 after adding emergency supplemental aid in "such sums as may be necessary" for disaster relief to victims of recent heavy flooding in the Southeast and other 1994 natural disasters. (Vote 216, p. 37-S)

The Senate voted 62-38 to uphold an Appropriations Committee amendment authorizing up to $90 million for the Market Promotion Program. (Vote 206, p. 35-S)

Richard H. Bryan, D-Nev., forced the vote and urged his colleagues to kill the program. Bumpers argued in floor debate that many of the subsidies simply replaced money that companies otherwise would spend on their own to advertise their products. "Do you think if Gallo wines saw a market someplace that they thought they could develop, they would say, 'No, we are not going to try to develop that market unless the U.S. government gives us some money?' " Bumpers asked. "How silly can you get?"

But supporters responded that certain exports had grown substantially after advertising campaigns funded by the Market Promotion Program. "It is a vitally important program for literally thousands of agricultural entrepreneurs across the United States," said Gorton.

The Senate also rejected, 46-54, an amendment by Bill Bradley, D-N.J., to cut $13 million from a $38.7 million allocation for construction and repair of Agriculture Research Service buildings and facilities. (Vote 211, p. 36-S)

However, it accepted, 76-23, an amendment by Patrick J. Leahy, D-Vt., to allow the Agriculture Department to close 19 Agriculture Research Service facilities it deemed unnecessary. The House had included language in its bill report seeking to block the closures of several of these facilities. (Vote 209, p. 36-S)

Emotional Debate Over Food Stamps

A provision that had been quietly tucked into the House bill sparked an emotional Senate debate that foreshadowed coming conflicts over welfare. It involved widespread interest among states in obtaining federal waivers to provide food stamp benefits in cash. Nine states had received federal waivers along those lines. (Food stamps, p. 480)

However, at the urging of Smith of Iowa, the House bill included a provision to prohibit any more such experiments. Smith said the cash-out concept could deprive children of enough nutritional food.

During Senate floor action July 19, John McCain, R-Ariz., and Bob Kerrey, D-Neb., successfully offered an amendment to strike the prohibition and let the federal government approve more cash-out experiments. Bumpers tried to kill the McCain-Kerrey amendment, but he failed, 37-62. The amendment was then adopted 63-34. Every Republican except James M. Jeffords, R-Vt., supported the amendment, while Democrats opposed it by a 20-33 margin. (Votes 207, 208, p. 36-S)

Debate on Gay Rights

The floor debate also included an extended discussion of a topic not usually associated with the Agriculture spending bill: homosexuality. Jesse Helms, R-N.C., raised the issue, asserting that the Agriculture Department's leadership helped department employees active in the gay rights movement to promote their cause. Helms spoke at length to protest the recent job transfer of a regional Agriculture Department equal employment program manager for making a televised remark that was regarded as insulting to homosexuals.

"Every American is entitled to know where his or her senators stand at the crossroads of twisted values," Helms said July 19 before the Senate adopted the first of his two amendments on the issue.

Helms said the employee, Karl Mertz, had a First Amendment right to criticize Agriculture Department policy and portrayed him as a victim of political correctness. The senator also denounced the department's certification of the Gay, Lesbian and Bisexual Employees Organization as an officially sanctioned employees' organization.

On July 19, Helms won approval, on a 92-8 vote, of an amendment barring the use of funds for any Agriculture Department seminar or program aimed at recruiting homosexuals for employment on the basis of their sexual orientation or condoning homosexuality as a normal or legitimate lifestyle. (Vote 212, p. 36-S)

The following day, Helms won a 59-41 vote for an amendment requiring the department to provide a public hearing for any employee facing removal from a job for making critical remarks on personal time about department policy regarding homosexuals. It also contained a clause aimed at restoring Mertz to the job from which he had been transferred. (Vote 214, p. 36-S)

Questioning the effort to provide new protection solely for those who criticized gay rights policies, Bumpers pushed through his own, broader amendment, which was approved 100-0. It required a hearing for any employee facing job removal for personal comments criticizing any departmental policy. It also dropped the provision aimed at restoring Mertz to his job. (Vote 215, p. 37-S)

Defending Tobacco

Helms also got to reprise another of his career-long roles, as a defender of his state's tobacco interests. Helms assisted

Wendell H. Ford, D-Ky., and other tobacco state senators in defeating an attack by Hank Brown, R-Colo., on the federal tobacco price support program. Brown, a critic of many farm subsidy programs, proposed an amendment requiring that any trade protections provided for tobacco result in no net cost to U.S. taxpayers.

Under the General Agreement on Tariffs and Trade, the chief international trade agreement, countries could invoke tariffs on imported products, but foreign producers unfairly affected by those tariffs were allowed to seek financial compensation. Brown contended that proposed tariffs to protect the domestic tobacco industry would result in compensation claims that might have to be paid by the U.S. Treasury, a situation he described as a de facto subsidy to tobacco growers.

Tobacco's defenders argued that Brown had distorted the issue. Ford said a tariff was necessary to protect domestic growers from being deluged with a flood of imported tobacco from countries that maintained high barriers against tobacco exported from the United States.

Ford also countered with an unsubtle threat to go after one of Brown's parochial interests. "If it gets into a position at some point that this amendment passes, the Senate will vote on increased grazing fees," Ford warned. Brown and other senators from Western states had blocked an administration proposal to raise fees paid by ranchers to graze their cattle on federal lands.

The Senate killed Brown's amendment, 63-37, on a tabling motion. *(Vote 213, p. 36-S)*

Conference/Final Action

House and Senate conferees reached agreement Sept. 20 on a $69.1 billion fiscal 1995 agriculture spending bill, approving cuts in a wide variety of programs and limiting the number of places where states could experiment with "cashing out" the food stamp program (H Rept 103-734).

The House adopted the conference report Sept. 23 by a vote of 287-107. The Senate cleared the bill Sept. 27 by voice vote. *(Vote 438, p. 132-H)*

Durbin and Bumpers said reconciling the two versions was particularly tough because both chambers had assumed more than $100 million in new user fees that ultimately were stripped from the bill because they had not been authorized. Without those revenues to fall back on, conferees had to find program cuts to stay within their spending allocation.

Before the conference began, the House passed a resolution (H Res 518) on Aug. 12 by voice vote insisting that the

Senate remove $150.8 million in new, unauthorized FDA user fees from its version of the bill. The House's "blue-slipping" of HR 4554 over the user fees was based on its constitutional prerogative to originate revenue-raising measures. That only accelerated the process of finding cuts to replace the fees.

Whenever conferees suggested increasing funding for their favorite programs or adding an earmarked project, Durbin challenged them to find offsetting revenues. "It was a pretty gloomy mood in there," Durbin said after the first of two days of meetings.

One of the more contentious items in conference was not a spending issue but the question of how much latitude to give states on the food stamp program. Kerrey argued that states ought to be allowed to experiment, particularly in conjunction with plans to overhaul state welfare programs. "We should let these waivers go forward when there's such broad-based support," he said, noting that the approach was backed in Nebraska by the governor, Legislature and public welfare administrators.

But proponents of the existing system insisted that food stamps were important to ensure that recipients got the proper nutrition. "Why do you want a hodgepodge of programs in 50 different states?" asked Rosa DeLauro, D-Conn.

Conferees finally agreed, despite Kerrey's objections, to limit such experiments to 25 locations nationwide. States typically applied for demonstrations in a small number of counties. The bill further limited experiments to no more than 3 percent of food stamp households nationwide. There were 27 million food stamp participants in fiscal 1993.

Other Compromises

Conferees accepted the assumption that Congress would pass a crop insurance overhaul bill, allowing them to cut appropriated spending for administrative and operating expenses for the Federal Crop Insurance Corporation to $68.9 million, down from $290 million in fiscal 1994.

The negotiators agreed to provide $70 million for watershed and flood prevention operations, down from $220.8 million. The Agriculture Market Promotion Program got $85.5 million, down from $100 million.

Also cut was the Emergency Food Assistance Program, which received $65 million, compared with $120 million in fiscal 1994. Conferees rejected Helms' provision to bar the use of funds for Agriculture Department programs aimed at recruiting homosexuals for employment. They accepted Bumper's language requiring a hearing for any employee facing job removal for personal comments criticizing departmental policy. ∎

$2.3 Billion Appropriated for Crime Fund

Congress gave final approval the week of Aug. 15 to legislation appropriating $27.7 billion in fiscal 1995 for the departments of Commerce, Justice and State, related agencies and the federal judiciary. President Clinton signed the bill into law Aug. 26 (PL 103-317).

The bill (HR 4603) funded a diverse collection of programs — from high-tech initiatives and public television broadcasting to federal magistrates and the U.S. share of U.N. peacekeeping missions. But the centerpiece of the fiscal 1995 bill was funding for anti-crime initiatives.

The measure provided $2.3 billion for a new anti-crime trust fund to be created under the omnibus anti-crime bill (HR 3355 — PL 103-322). Of that money, $1.3 billion was to be used for police hiring grants, in keeping with Clinton's pledge to put more officers on the street. Clinton had originally sought $1.7 billion for that program. *(Crime bill, p. 273)*

The anti-crime money accounted for most of the bill's $4 billion funding increase over fiscal 1994. The administration had requested $767 million more for the bill.

The bill was placed on a fast track because it also contained emergency aid for victims of natural disasters, including the January earthquake in the Los Angeles area, summer floods in several Southern states and wildfires in the West. The measure provided $470 million in Small Business Administration (SBA) disaster loans and $55 million in grants from the Commerce Department's Economic Development Administration. The $525 million package was included as an emergency supplemental appropriation for fiscal 1994.

The legislation included $1.2 billion, the full administration request, for U.N. peacekeeping operations. Of that amount, $670 million was a supplemental appropriation of fiscal 1994 funds.

The measure provided a significant increase in funding for border control activities, including $284 million for Clinton's immigration initiatives. The money was to be used to hire 700 new border control agents and redirect an additional 250 agents to enforcement activities. Altogether, the bill provided $1.5 billion for the Immigration and Naturalization Service (INS).

The bill also appropriated $855 million for the Commerce Department's National Institute of Standards and Technology (NIST), a federal research laboratory that was a key component of the administration's technology policy. That was a reduction of about $80 million from Clinton's request, but it represented a $334 million increase over fiscal 1994.

The legislation provided about $2 billion for the National Oceanic and Atmospheric Administration (NOAA) — $148 million more than Clinton requested and $34 million over fiscal 1994.

By contrast, the State Department received about $4.2 billion, $105 million below Clinton's request. That figure was a modest $161 million increase over the fiscal 1994 level.

The bill also:
● Included the text of a bill (HR 4884) aimed at helping FBI

BOXSCORE

Fiscal 1995 Commerce-Justice-State and Federal Judiciary Appropriations — HR 4603. The $27.7 billion bill included $2.3 billion for anti-crime initiatives and $1.2 billion for U.N. peacekeeping operations.

Reports: H Rept 103-552, S Rept 103-309; conference report H Rept 103-708.

KEY ACTION

June 28 — House passed HR 4603, 286-112.

July 22 — Senate passed HR 4603, amended, by voice vote.

Aug. 18 — House adopted the conference report, 322-98.

Aug. 19 — Senate cleared the bill, 88-10.

Aug. 26 — President signed HR 4603— PL 103-317.

employees who did not want to move from Washington, D.C., to the bureau's new fingerprinting facility in Clarksburg, W.Va. The legislation assisted those employees who did not wish to move in finding other jobs in the federal government. *(FBI workers, p. 153)*
● Provided $10 million for Radio Free Asia, a new government-backed radio service aimed primarily at China.
● Provided about $25 million for government-backed radio and television broadcasting to Cuba.

Background

While appropriators struggled to find money for crime fighting, they also faced the controversial issue of how to pay for a far less popular program — U.N. peacekeeping activities.

The United States expected to owe the United Nations close to $1 billion for peacekeeping activities by the end of the fiscal year, and the administration had been pressing Congress to find money to pay the bill.

The previous year, Clinton had asked for $642 million for international peacekeeping efforts, but Congress allowed only $402 million — and even that was provided grudgingly. Lawmakers complained that U.S. taxpayers were being asked to pay too much for programs that were ill-advised or ill-managed. *(1993 Almanac, p. 555)*

In February, Clinton requested an additional $670 million in peacekeeping money for fiscal 1994 as part of a supplemental appropriations bill intended for disaster relief, but Congress rejected that idea. *(Supplemental, p. 548)*

Congress agreed to authorize the $670 million as part of the fiscal 1994-95 State Department authorization bill (HR 2333 — PL 103-236). But lawmakers specified that only half of that money would be available until the United Nations established a separate office of inspector general to oversee expenses. *(State Department authorization, p. 454)*

Harold Rogers of Kentucky, the ranking Republican on the House Commerce-Justice-State Appropriations Subcommittee had been fighting for years to reduce the U.S. assessment for U.N. peacekeeping missions. Rogers wanted to cut the U.S. portion of total mission costs from 30.4 percent to 25 percent, which was the U.S. share for general U.N. dues.

"Peacekeeping is a runaway fiscal train that's on a direct collision course headed for our domestic programs," Rogers argued during House consideration of the fiscal 1995 bill. But David R. Obey, D-Wis., and Robert C. Byrd, D-W.Va. — chairmen of the House and Senate Appropriations committee respectively — said the United States had to honor its commitments.

House Committee

The Commerce, Justice, State Appropriations Subcommittee approved a fiscal 1995 spending bill in a closed session June 8. Chairman Alan B. Mollohan, D-W.Va., embargoed information on

Commerce-Justice-State Spending

(in thousands of dollars)

	Fiscal 1995 Clinton Request	House Bill	Senate Bill	Final Bill
Department of Justice				
Office of Justice programs	$ 1,147,292	$ 2,486,347	$ 1,272,067	$ 1,106,067
Legal activities	2,277,570	2,200,604	2,271,354	2,237,705
Community policing (trust fund)	1,720,000	(1,332,000)	1,300,000	1,300,000
Organized-crime drug enforcement	369,943	383,250	369,943	374,943
Federal Bureau of Investigation	2,131,067	2,178,218	2,230,511	2,206,871
Drug Enforcement Administration	720,342	742,497	760,801	757,204
Immigration and Naturalization Service	1,146,930	1,349,759	1,537,556	1,482,871
Other crime trust fund	(1,053,000)	(1,091,000)	(1,214,000)	(1,045,000)
Federal prison system	2,607,669	2,604,842	2,653,572	2,647,242
Other	465,252	197,729	199,629	191,647
TOTAL, Justice Department	**$ 12,586,065**	**$ 12,143,246**	**$ 12,595,433**	**$ 12,304,550**
Related Agencies				
EEOC	244,804	238,000	240,000	233,000
Federal Communications Commission	−568	50,432	81,832	68,832
Federal Trade Commission	61,968	59,968	65,468	54,788
Securities and Exchange Commission	—	900	57,856	74,856
Other related agencies	43,715	41,619	40,532	41,119
The Judiciary				
Supreme Court	27,403	27,157	27,368	27,240
Courts of Appeals, District Courts, judicial services	2,940,829	2,735,397	2,815,100	2,748,723
Administrative Office of the U.S. Courts	48,804	46,500	47,734	47,500
Other	90,717	80,894	82,541	81,226
TOTAL, Judiciary	**$ 3,107,753**	**$ 2,889,948**	**$ 2,972,743**	**$ 2,904,689**
Department of Commerce				
National Institute of Standards and Technology	934,966	840,066	878,686	854,686
National Oceanic and Atmospheric Administration	1,811,938	1,837,149	1,982,712	1,959,562
Bureau of the Census	305,404	283,848	280,000	278,576
International Trade Administration	261,790	268,723	262,000	266,450
Patent and Trademark Office	107,000	88,329	75,000	83,000
Economic Development Administration	411,539	370,729	448,198	440,229
Other	375,073	341,416	314,160	335,635
TOTAL, Commerce Department	**$ 4,207,710**	**$ 4,030,260**	**$ 4,240,756**	**$ 4,218,138**
Related Agencies				
Maritime Administration	380,969	255,515	85,000	95,100
Small Business Administration	815,682	829,489	760,854	814,448
Legal Services Corporation	500,000	415,000	400,000	415,000
Other related agencies	26,357	26,153	26,617	26,617
Department of State				
Administration of Foreign Affairs	2,783,491	2,672,171	2,784,543	2,729,147
International organizations and conferences	1,453,245	1,453,245	1,379,222 [1]	1,416,526
Other	64,054	56,060	56,060	49,971
TOTAL, State Department	**$ 4,300,790**	**$ 4,181,476**	**$ 4,219,825**	**$ 4,195,644**
Related Agencies				
Arms Control and Disarmament Agency	61,195	54,500	54,500	54,500
International Broadcasting (USIA)	1,428,467	1,350,506	1,401,199	1,373,557
Other related agencies	46,110	45,653	44,706	43,953
Fiscal 1994 supplemental appropriation				
Small Business Administration	400,000	400,000	470,000	470,000
Economic Development Administration	—	—	55,000	55,000
International peacekeeping	670,000	670,000	670,000	670,000
Federal aid highways (rescission)	−400,000	−400,000	−400,000	−400,000
GRAND TOTAL	**$ 28,434,837** [1]	**$ 27,236,485** [1]	**$ 28,036,141** [1]	**$ 27,667,611** [1]

[1] *Grand totals include estimated savings of $46,180,000 under procurement reform and other scorekeeping adjustments.*

SOURCE: House Appropriations Committee

the bill until the full committee acted.

The markup lasted several hours. Neal Smith, D-Iowa, made the motion to close the session, citing the presence of classified information in the bill. Charles H. Taylor, R-N.C., was the only member to oppose the move. Smith had chaired the subcommittee until 1994, when he took charge of the Appropriations subcommittee on the departments of Labor, Health and Human Services, and Education.

Full Committee Action

The full Appropriations Committee approved the $27.2 billion spending bill by voice vote June 15 (H Rept 103-552). The measure contained $26.5 billion for fiscal 1995, plus extra fiscal 1994 funds for peacekeeping.

The bill provided the full $2.4 billion requested by Clinton for crimefighting programs.

● **Peacekeeping.** Appropriators argued for some time over the $1.2 billion for international peacekeeping efforts. Rogers offered an amendment to prohibit the United States from paying any more than 25 percent of the mission cost for past or future peacekeeping. He said negotiations between administration and U.N. officials on the issue had proved fruitless and there was no other way to get action on the matter than for Congress to cut off funds: "Say 25 percent and no more — take it or leave it," Rogers urged.

Appropriations Chairman Obey said he backed Rogers' goal but not the amendment. Obey said the amendment would force the United States to renege on a past commitment and prompt Clinton to veto the appropriations bill. Rogers eventually withdrew the amendment without a vote, but he said he planned to pursue the matter.

The appropriations bill did specify that half the supplemental fiscal 1994 money for peacekeeping expenses would be withheld until the United Nations appointed an inspector general to oversee expenses.

● **Haiti.** Robert L. Livingston, La., offered an amendment for GOP colleague Jim Ross Lightfoot of Iowa, to require congressional approval before Clinton could send troops to Haiti as part of a future peacekeeping mission there. The Clinton administration had been pressing sanctions — and threatening possible military intervention — against Haiti's military rulers in an effort to restore ousted President Jean-Bertrand Aristide. *(Haiti, p. 449)*

Subcommittee Chairman Mollohan urged lawmakers not to include such a policy statement in the spending bill, and the amendment failed, 17-32.

● **Crime initiatives.** Appropriators gave Clinton most of what he wanted on new crime initiatives. The amount approved for police hiring grants — $1.3 billion — was almost $390 million below the administration request, but it still was a healthy endorsement of the program.

But lawmakers asserted their own preferences on some other crime-related allocations.

To free money for new crime initiatives, the administration had proposed cuts in federal law enforcement personnel and in a popular formula grant program — known as Byrne grants — that helped states fight crime.

Instead, the committee bill provided almost $70 million more than Clinton's $2.9 billion request for the FBI and Drug Enforcement Administration (DEA) to retain personnel and hire new agents. It restored and expanded the Byrne grant program, allocating $804 million, compared with $358 million in fiscal 1994. Mollohan said that besides using the money for traditional Byrne programs, such as coordinated drug task forces, states could use the money to offset the costs of incarcerating illegal aliens or to carry out the Brady law, which

required background checks for handgun purchases. *(1993 Almanac, p. 300)*

But with a subcommittee allocation for fiscal 1995 that was $1.2 billion below the president's request, appropriators cut other programs.

● **TV Marti.** In a move that was bound to draw controversy, the panel dropped funding for pro-democracy television broadcasts to Cuba, known as TV Marti. Members did include $8.6 million to continue the radio counterpart, Radio Marti. The decision to include no money for TV Marti was reportedly made in the subcommittee, setting the stage for a repeat of a 1993 battle over whether to continue funding for the broadcasts. *(1993 Almanac, p. 559)*

Supporters, led by Cuban émigrés, argued that TV Marti and Radio Marti aided the free flow of information into a closed society. Opponents called the television programming a waste of money because Cuban President Fidel Castro had effectively jammed the broadcast signal, preventing most Cubans from seeing it.

For fiscal 1994, Congress eventually appropriated $7 million for TV Marti (and another $14 million for Radio Marti) but required a study on the quality and efficacy of the television and radio broadcasts. That report critiqued certain aspects of the programming, recommending, for instance, that broadcasters try to avoid jamming by the Cuban government by transmitting on the UHF band.

● **Other.** The bill appropriated $300 million above fiscal 1994 levels for the INS, including money to hire 700 new Border Patrol agents. It also contained almost $500 million, an increase of $263 million, for technology research and development programs at NIST.

The bill provided $33 million for the National Endowment for Democracy, which aimed to promote democracy around the world; Clinton had requested $45 million.

House Floor

The House passed the $27.2 billion spending bill June 28 by a vote of 286-112. *(Vote 291, p. 86-H)*

The House-passed bill increased the Justice Department's budget 26.5 percent to $12.1 billion in fiscal 1995. It provided $2.4 billion as the first installment on the new anti-crime trust fund. It contained $4 billion for the Commerce Department and $4.2 billion for State. The total also included fiscal 1994 supplemental appropriations of $400 million for the SBA and $670 million for international peacekeeping.

The House defeated an attempt by Rogers to add $207 million to crime-fighting efforts by limiting payments for the U.S. share of U.N. peacekeeping operations to 25 percent. The House rejected the amendment, 178-228, in a largely party-line vote. *(Vote 288, p. 84-H)*

● **State Department.** The House made a handful of small cuts in State Department funding, adopting amendments:

• By Cliff Stearns, R-Fla., to cut $2.8 million out of $1.7 billion in administrative costs. Stearns said that was the annual cost of an administration program, which he strongly opposed, that allowed some Iraqi refugees to resettle in the United States. The amendment was adopted, 284-122. *(Vote 284, p. 84-H)*

• By Jay Inslee, D-Wash., to reduce by 3.6 percent the $422 million allocated to the State Department to acquire and maintain buildings abroad. It was approved, 268-139. *(Vote 285, p. 84-H)*

• By John Edward Porter, R-Ill., to transfer $10 million in United States Information Agency radio construction money to start Radio Free Asia. The amendment was adopted, 318-

89. *(Vote 286, p. 84-H)*

• By Taylor to prohibit funding that would allow the Equal Employment Opportunity Commission to implement controversial proposed guidelines intended to stem religious harassment in the workplace. The vote was 366-37. *(Vote 289, p. 84-H)*

● **Anti-crime initiatives.** The House did not follow the administration's requests for all programs.

For example, lawmakers followed the Appropriations Committee's lead and added nearly $70 million to Clinton's $2.9 billion request for the FBI and the DEA to retain personnel and hire new agents. The House also agreed with the appropriators' decision to retain and expand the Byrne law enforcement grant program for states.

Gary A. Condit, D-Calif., and Karen L. Thurman, D-Fla., said they were concerned that states with large numbers of illegal aliens in prison would be forced to use their Byrne money for incarceration. They offered an amendment to authorize $600 million to reimburse states and local governments for incarceration costs. To offset that, Condit and Thurman proposed a 2.5 percent across-the-board cut in the bill's other programs. Opponents argued that the $600 million would benefit only a handful of states, while the cuts would harm many programs. The amendment was defeated, 148-256. *(Vote 287, p. 84-H)*

● **NOAA.** Members voted to retain funding for 20 marine and weather programs, worth $47 million, slated for termination under the administration's budget request. Many of the programs were under NOAA.

Timothy J. Penny, D-Minn., proposed cutting $39 million from NOAA by eliminating controversial programs such as the National Undersea Research Project, which funded deep sea diving and other oceanic research; federal and state grants used to modernize weather service stations; and grants for research on the zebra mussel, a prolific mollusk known to clog water pipes. The House rejected Penny's amendment by voice vote.

Similarly, the House rejected, 128-272, an amendment by Robert W. Goodlatte, R-Va., to trim $26 million from NOAA's $1.8 billion budget by eliminating three marine programs. *(Vote 282, p. 82-H)*

● **Other.** The House rejected, 110-282, a Penny amendment to cut almost $68 million from the $371 million budget for the Economic Development Administration, which was charged with stimulating job creation through public works and technical assistance grants. *(Vote 281, p. 82-H)*

In contrast to prior years, the House indicated overwhelming support for the National Endowment for Democracy. A proposal by Joel Hefley, R-Colo., to eliminate the $33 million program prompted members of both parties to defend it on the floor. Lawmakers rejected Hefley's amendment 89-317. *(Vote 283, p. 84-H)*

The House also accepted by voice vote amendments offered by Mollohan to reduce funding for two programs that had been at the center of turf battles.

As the result of a procedural move, the House bill slashed fiscal 1995 funding for the Securities and Exchange Commission (SEC) to $59.6 million from $297 million. The action was set in motion when a provision to allow the SEC to raise its fees to offset expenses was stricken on a point of order for violating a House rule against legislating on an appropriations bill. Mollohan then said his bill exceeded budget caps, and he proposed to cut SEC funds by the amount of the fees. The action was intended to serve notice to the Senate that some House members wanted action on legislation (HR 2239) to overhaul the commission's financing. *(SEC, p. 120)*

Members also accepted an amendment by Mollohan to reduce the U.S. Travel and Tourism Administration's $17.9 million budget by $3 million. The measure was intended to keep the agency from exceeding its budget allocation after authorizers struck a provision to allow the agency to collect $3 million in user fees from distribution of such products as travel brochures. Authorizers argued that members were breaking the rules by legislating on an appropriations bill.

During initial debate on the bill, the House rejected amendments intended to cut spending in various agencies. These included proposals:

• By Lamar Smith, R-Texas, to cut salaries and expenses at the Bureau of Prisons by $1 million out of $2.4 billion. The aim was to kill funding for special personnel who were assigned to the bureau at a higher salary than the agency's regular employees. It failed by voice vote.

• By Smith to cut $925,000 from Attorney General Janet Reno's office, to protest Reno's policies. Smith described her as too liberal. It was rejected, 171-212. *(Vote 275, p. 82-H)*

• By Steven H. Schiff, R-N.M., to cut $5.5 million from the Justice antitrust division and add those funds to the U.S. Attorney's Office, increasing funding for that division to $832.5 million. The amendment failed, 160-241. *(Vote 276, p. 82-H)*

• By Jack Fields, R-Texas, to kill a $7 million NOAA program aimed at fostering international appreciation of the environment. It was rejected, 184-184. *(Vote 278, p. 82-H)*

Senate Committee

The Senate Appropriations Committee approved a $27.3 billion version of the bill (S Rept 103-309) by a vote of 27-2 on July 14. The appropriators sharply increased spending for the Justice Department, going from $9.6 billion in fiscal 1994 to $12.5 billion in fiscal 1995.

Senators lost no time touting the bill's popular message. Pete V. Domenici, R-N.M., ranking Republican on the Commerce, Justice, State Appropriations Subcommittee, called the measure a "home run" against crime. "Our whole anti-crime effort was pretty hollow until this bill," said Phil Gramm, R-Texas.

● **Anti-crime programs.** The bulk of the $2.4 billion in the bill for anti-crime programs was for the community police program, including $1.3 billion for police-hiring grants. The money for police grants was about $30 million less than the House provided and about $420 million below the president's request.

The Senate panel transferred $423 million from the program to the popular Byrne grant program for state anti-crime efforts; the House bill contained $804 million for the program.

Senate appropriators provided money for three programs not specifically financed in the House-passed version of the bill. They provided $86 million for the Violence Against Women Act, which was part of the big crime bill, and $175 million for boot camps for youthful offenders and state correctional grants. They also included $100 million to help states implement the Brady handgun waiting period law. The money was to help states automate their criminal record systems to allow them to check instantly to see if a would-be handgun purchaser had a criminal record.

The Senate committee bill included a $171 million increase for the FBI, the DEA and federal prosecutors. Subcommittee Chairman Ernest F. Hollings, D-S.C., said the money would permit the FBI to hire 436 agents, the DEA to hire 311 agents and would allow the hiring of 123 additional assistant U.S. attorneys and support staff.

The Senate bill allowed about $100 million more than the House.

● **INS.** Programs to help states deal with illegal immigrants got a significant increase under the Senate bill. The measure appropriated $2.2 billion for INS programs — $483 million more than appropriated in fiscal 1994, $188 million more than in the House-passed bill and $126 million more than the administration requested.

As did the House, the committee provided a $54.5 million increase to hire 700 additional Border Patrol agents and 110 support personnel.

The committee agreed to provide $100 million for construction and/or renovation of INS Border Patrol offices. Of that amount, the committee earmarked $46 million for two new detention centers for illegal aliens caught entering the country. The INS had tentatively picked San Diego, Calif., and Del Rio, Texas, as sites for the facilities.

● **International programs.** Senators were unusually quiet about international programs that usually drew their ire. The bill included nearly $1.2 billion for past and present U.S. contributions to U.N. peacekeeping programs.

The committee restored spending for TV Marti, providing $24.8 million to the TV and radio broadcast outlets, $2.8 million less than the president requested.

Senate Floor

After two days of debate, the Senate late on July 22 passed its version of the spending bill by voice vote.

The $28 billion measure included fiscal 1994 supplemental appropriations of $670 million for international peacekeeping operations and $525 million for disaster relief. Overall, the Senate bill provided about $800 million more than the House version.

● **U.N. peacekeeping.** As in past years, lawmakers sought to reduce spending on international programs. The Senate on July 22 voted to take $350 million from the peacekeeping account to help reimburse states for the costs of incarcerating illegal aliens. The amendment was approved by voice vote after a tabling motion failed, 44-52. *(Vote 226, p. 39-S)*

The administration had proposed spending $350 million for alien incarceration, drawing the money from cuts in the federal judiciary and a proposed increase in Federal Communications Commission user fees. But House and Senate appropriators rejected that idea.

Kay Bailey Hutchison, R-Texas, joined with Minority Leader Bob Dole, R-Kan., to offer the amendment to siphon $350 million from the peacekeeping account to pay for alien incarceration.

Appropriations Committee Chairman Byrd argued that the United States had to make good on its peacekeeping debts and could not afford transferring money to another program. But senators from states with large immigrant populations, notably California and Florida, enthusiastically supported the amendment, saying the federal government had shirked its responsibilities in paying the price of lax border enforcement.

● **National Endowment for Democracy.** Lawmakers continued to squabble over whether the National Endowment for Democracy was a lifeline to democratic activists or a slush fund for U.S. political consultants. After substantial debate July 22, senators defeated, 39-57, an amendment to cut the endowment's recommended funding from $35 million to $25 million. *(Vote 224, p. 39-S)*

● **Other.** The Senate agreed by voice vote to give the president discretion to use up to $100 million in the bill's funds to aid Rwandan refugees. This was in addition to $41 million Clinton already had earmarked for the Rwanda crisis.

Senators rejected by voice vote a Dole amendment to block the Justice Department from implementing any policies regarding the death penalty that would let racial sentencing statistics be taken into account. It was aimed at ambushing a rumored compromise between the administration and the Congressional Black Caucus on disputed death penalty sentencing language in the House crime bill.

Gramm offered an amendment to bar the Legal Services Corporation, which provided legal aid to the poor, from challenging any state or federal welfare reform legislation. But other senators, mostly liberal Democrats, said the amendment would restrict the legal rights of the poor and set a dangerous precedent by dictating policy for Legal Services lawyers. Senators tabled, or killed, the amendment 56-44. *(Vote 223, p. 38-S)*

In other action, senators approved by voice votes a pair of amendments by Georgia Sens. Sam Nunn, D, and Paul Coverdell, R, to provide emergency fiscal 1994 funds to help victims of recent flooding in Georgia, Alabama and Florida: $70 million for emergency SBA loans and $55 million for loan assistance under the Economic Development Administration.

Final Action

House and Senate negotiators completed work on the final version of the bill Aug. 16. The conferees hammered out an agreement in closed-door meetings, then approved the conference report (H Rept 103-708) by voice vote in open session.

The House adopted the conference report Aug. 18 by a vote of 322-98. The Senate followed suit the next day, voting 88-10 to clear the measure for the president. *(House vote 408, p. 122-H; Senate vote 292, p. 50-S)*

Conferees agreed to provide $1.2 billion, the full administration request, for U.N. peacekeeping operations, dropping the Senate amendment to shift $350 million to reimburse states for the costs of incarcerating illegal aliens.

They agreed on $25 million for government-backed radio and television broadcasting to Cuba. Although the House had not funded the administration's $12 million request for TV Marti, Hollings persuaded conferees to go along with the Senate level.

The measure provided $125 million for the SEC. The funding was intended as a stopgap to keep the SEC operating while Congress tried to resolve a dispute over how the agency should be financed. ■

Defense Bill Mirrors Request

President Clinton's defense spending request for fiscal 1995 proved remarkably resistant to attacks from both the left and the right. Liberals wanted bigger cuts in Pentagon spending, and conservatives wanted less retrenchment. But Congress on Sept. 29 cleared a $243.7 billion defense appropriations bill (HR 4650) that represented a reduction of less than 1 percent in the president's request of $244.7 billion.

Clinton signed the bill into law Sept. 30, just in time for the start of the new fiscal year (PL 103-335).

The bill generally supported the force size, tempo of operations and weapons procurement plans in Clinton's budget. It funded a new aircraft carrier, continued production of the controversial C-17 cargo jet and continued development of new generations of combat helicopters for the Army and jet fighters for the Navy and Air Force.

HR 4650 also provided $299 million in supplemental funding for fiscal 1994 to reimburse the Defense Department for some of the costs of humanitarian relief operations in Rwanda and for the care of refugees from Cuba and Haiti.

Defense appropriators, many of them pro-military conservatives, did what they could within tight spending limits to reverse what they said were signs of decline in the military's combat readiness and morale. Clinton himself signaled that he was aware that congressional tolerance of defense cuts had reached its outer limit. He received a standing ovation during his Jan. 25 State of the Union address when he said that his budget would protect defense spending and vowed, "We must not cut defense further." *(Text, p. 3-D)*

But defense appropriators continued to argue that the dollars being invested in defense were not sufficient to support the administration policy of maintaining a defense establishment capable of fighting two major regional wars simultaneously. And lawmakers increasingly questioned the president's use of scarce defense dollars for non-traditional military missions like humanitarian relief to Rwanda and the pro-democracy mission in Haiti.

House appropriators contemplated cutting a major weapons program such as the Air Force's F-22 fighter to illustrate the point that something had to give, but they decided against it. In a symbolic move, however, they lopped off $900 million in politically popular university research grants. Most of the research money was later restored in the Senate.

Concern over the preparedness of the military continued to shape the spending debate as the year wore on. Congress did shift funds within the budget to put more emphasis on combat readiness. For instance, the bill added nearly $550 million to Clinton's $11 billion request to overhaul ships, planes and vehicles and maintain facilities. And Senate appropriators, angry that the Army had used training funds for other expenses, ordered the service to seek congressional approval before rechanneling training moneys to other uses.

Both chambers disagreed with Clinton's proposal for a

BOXSCORE

Fiscal 1995 Defense Appropriations — HR 4650. The Pentagon funding bill provided $243.7 billion, a reduction of less than 1 percent from President Clinton's request.

Reports: H Rept 103-562, S Rept 103-321; conference report H Rept 103-747.

KEY ACTION

June 29 — House passed HR 4650, 330-91.

Aug. 11 — Senate passed HR 4650, amended, 86-14.

Sept. 29 — House adopted conference report, 327-86; **Senate** cleared bill by voice vote.

Sept. 30 — President signed HR 4650 — PL 103-335.

---

modest 1.6 percent increase in military pay. The final bill called for a 2.6 percent raise for military personnel, though it did not fully fund the increase. Lawmakers also provided for an increase for civilians that included "locality" pay to partially offset the high cost of living in certain areas, and they appropriated $85 million for child care and other family support services aimed at boosting troop morale.

Despite the tight budget, lawmakers also found room for several initiatives beneficial to the constituencies of House and Senate defense appropriators. For instance, $50 million was earmarked for clearing unexploded munitions from Kahoolawe, a small island in the home state of Senate Defense Appropriations Subcommittee Chairman Daniel K. Inouye, D-Hawaii, that had been used as a Navy bombing range for nearly 50 years. Funds were also earmarked to beef up National Guard squadrons in the home states of Senate Appropriations Committee Chairman Robert C. Byrd, D-W.Va., Majority Whip Wendell H. Ford, D-Ky., and Military Construction Appropriations Subcommittee Chairman Jim Sasser, D-Tenn. And $6 million was set aside for the maintenance of Navy facilities in New Orleans. Louisiana was the home state of appropriators Sen. J. Bennett Johnston, D, and Rep. Robert L. Livingston, R.

Weapons Programs

Congress agreed with the president on most major weapons programs, providing:

● **Aircraft carrier.** $2.45 billion for the purchase of a new $5 billion nuclear-powered aircraft carrier. The carrier, which was to house as many as 80 combat planes and 6,000 sailors, would boost the nation's carrier fleet to 12. It survived opposition from Ronald V. Dellums, D-Calif., the liberal chairman of the House Armed Services Committee.

● **B-2 bomber.** $125 million to keep the B-2 stealth bomber production network alive and thus preserve the option of future B-2 purchases. The plane was designed for nuclear strikes against the Soviet Union and so seemed a perfect target to those who believed that the demise of the Soviet state should allow dramatic cuts in Pentagon spending. But B-2 supporters contended that, once the plane was equipped with super-accurate "smart" bombs, it would be an example of the kind of high-tech weaponry that would give U.S. forces the edge over enemy forces in non-nuclear combat.

● **C-17 cargo jet.** $2.4 billion for continued development of the C-17 long-range cargo jet and for the purchase of six C-17s.

● **New submarine.** $500 million for continued development of a new type of nuclear-powered submarine that would be smaller and cheaper than the *Seawolf*-class submarine. While the *Seawolf* sub was designed to hunt Soviet subs in the North Atlantic depths, the new submarine was designed to operate more easily in coastal waters. It also was modular, enabling it to be adapted for alternative purposes — to hunt enemy subs, to haul commando landing parties or to deluge

Defense Spending

(in thousands of dollars)

	Fiscal 1994 Appropriations	Fiscal 1995 Clinton Request	House Bill	Senate Bill	Final Bill
Personnel					
Army	$ 21,296,177	$ 20,601,170	$ 20,737,470	$ 20,629,770	$ 20,609,770
Navy	18,330,950	17,580,983	17,692,537	17,638,483	17,569,137
Marines	5,772,317	5,778,571	5,816,671	5,806,471	5,774,871
Air Force	15,823,030	17,218,579	17,311,379	17,031,179	17,181,479
National Guard, reserves	9,401,570	9,296,094	9,335,445	9,339,609	9,253,945
Subtotal	**$ 70,624,044**	**$ 70,475,397**	**$ 70,893,502**	**$ 70,445,512**	**$ 70,389,202**
Operations and maintenance					
Army	15,802,057	17,766,814	17,836,504	17,475,806	17,507,088
Navy	19,860,309	21,176,570	21,316,555	21,275,770	21,054,470
Marines	1,857,699	1,918,395	2,097,395	1,968,965	1,988,215
Air Force	19,093,805	19,026,623	18,913,050	18,786,243	18,763,427
Defense agencies	9,456,801	10,208,413	8,945,266	9,986,654	10,500,104
National Guard, reserves	8,119,478	8,869,306	8,941,421	8,840,275	8,841,011
Environmental restoration	1,962,300	2,180,200	1,880,200	2,034,075	1,780,200
Humanitarian assistance	48,000	71,900	60,000	71,900	65,000
International peacekeeping contribution	—	300,000	—	—	—
Former Soviet Union threat reduction	400,000	400,000	—	400,000	400,000
Other	16,338	8,670	16,570	521,670	26,070
Subtotal	**$ 76,616,787**	**$ 81,926,891**	**$ 80,006,961**	**$ 81,361,358**	**$ 80,925,585**
Procurement					
Army	6,932,223	6,090,239	6,617,616	6,423,799	6,883,242
Navy *	15,957,001	16,223,561	16,026,045	15,661,476	15,946,139
(By transfer)	(761,101)	—	(1,200,000)	(1,200,000)	(1,200,000)
Marines	364,461	422,178	452,178	403,410	422,410
Air Force	18,199,354	18,218,025	16,105,778	17,372,448	17,283,826
National Guard, reserves	1,200,000	—	796,200	952,000	800,000
Defense agencies	1,810,039	1,744,916	3,020,616	1,894,916	2,088,230
Defense Production Act	200,000	—	—	—	—
Subtotal	**$ 44,663,078**	**$ 42,698,919**	**$ 43,018,433**	**$ 42,708,049**	**$ 43,423,847**
Research, development and testing					
Army	5,427,546	5,260,082	5,456,498	5,304,329	5,521,413
Navy	8,365,786	8,934,718	8,598,958	8,790,331	8,796,168
Air Force	12,314,362	12,349,362	10,728,533	12,151,011	12,202,572
Other	9,083,797	9,680,851	9,683,951	9,159,503	9,349,891
Subtotal	**$ 35,191,491**	**$ 36,225,013**	**$ 34,467,940**	**$ 35,405,174**	**$ 35,870,044**
Intelligence programs					
CIA retirement and disability	182,300	198,000	198,000	198,000	198,000
Community Management	151,288	93,084	83,084	105,084	92,684
National Security education	10,000	14,300	—	8,500	8,500
Other	60,000	—	—	50,000	50,000
Subtotal	**$ 403,588**	**$ 305,384**	**$ 281,084**	**$ 361,584**	**$ 349,184**
Other programs					
Defense conversion	—	—	1,401,944	—	—
General provisions	−618,958	−297,769	−17,869	104,992	−570,958
Revolving and management funds	2,643,095	1,777,638	1,949,038	1,618,000	1,669,638
Chemical agents destruction	389,947	575,349	562,949	590,149	575,449
Drug interdiction	868,200	704,200	713,053	700,100	721,266
Inspector general	137,601	128,098	142,098	140,872	140,872
Defense Health Program	9,626,072	9,922,059	9,895,159	9,808,239	9,930,759
Korean Readiness Account	—	—	250,000	—	—
Fiscal 1994 emergency supplemental	—	270,000	—	170,000	299,300
GRAND TOTAL	**$ 240,544,945**	**$ 244,711,179**	**$ 243,564,292**	**$ 243,414,029**	**$ 243,724,188**

Includes Marine as well as Navy ammunition.

SOURCE: House Appropriations Committee

ground targets with cruise missiles.

● **Comanche helicopter.** $495 million for continued development of the Army's Comanche helicopter, a small, armed scout craft designed to locate targets for larger Apache attack helicopters.

Background

The fiscal 1995 defense spending bill continued the gradual, post-Cold War retrenchment of the defense establishment begun under Clinton's predecessor, George Bush. It raised defense spending over the previous year's level by just $3.2 billion. *(1993 Almanac, p. 569)*

As in past years, the bill reflected the close collaboration between appropriators and the Armed Services committees, both traditionally dominated by pro-defense lawmakers. *(Defense authorization, p. 421)*

Clinton launched the funding debate in his Jan. 25 State of the Union address, declaring that defense cuts had gone about as far as they could go. His position was reinforced by the reluctance of most members to impose deeper cuts on an already shrinking defense industrial base and by their unease over the sporadic turmoil around the globe that had supplanted the relative stability of the Cold War superpower standoff. At the same time, alarm over the deficit and lawmakers' aversion to tax increases deterred conservatives from pushing very hard to increase defense spending.

The overall defense spending level was set, for all practical purposes, by the fiscal 1995 congressional budget resolution (H Con Res 218). A vigorous counterattack by the White House and the House Democratic leadership killed an amendment to the budget resolution that called for a $2.4 billion cut in defense. The House rejected the proposal, by Barney Frank, D-Mass., by a vote of 105-313 on March 10. Even among non-Southern Democrats it lost, 82-85. *(Vote 51, p. 16-H; budget resolution, p. 81)*

The Senate had no free-standing votes specifically on the fiscal 1995 defense spending level. But it rejected several amendments to both the authorization and appropriations bills that would have sliced funding for various big-ticket weapons programs.

Funding provided in other bills, mainly for military construction and defense-related nuclear programs conducted by the Energy Department, brought the total amount appropriated for national defense in fiscal 1995 to nearly $263 billion.

House Committee

The House Defense Appropriations Subcommittee approved its version of the fiscal 1995 bill June 16. Defense hawks, including subcommittee Chairman John P. Murtha, D-Pa., had repeatedly argued that Clinton's projected defense budgets were not sufficient to pay for the administration's long-term defense plan.

When the subcommittee's initial draft exceeded by roughly $700 million the limit on outlays imposed by the full Appropriations Committee, Murtha pressed the Pentagon to sacrifice a major weapons program. His suggested menu included the Air Force's F-22 fighter, the enlarged "E" and "F" versions of the Navy's F/A-18 attack plane, the Army's Comanche armed helicopter and the Marine Corps' Osprey, a hybrid airplane and helicopter to be used as a troop carrier.

Slowing or axing a program like the F-22 to save money, Murtha argued, was one of the few options the government had for averting a $20 billion to $40 billion shortfall over five years. But the Pentagon in the end persuaded the subcom-

mittee to cut the $700 million elsewhere in the budget, mostly in personnel.

Full Committee Action

The full Appropriations Committee approved the Defense Subcommittee's draft bill by voice vote June 27 (H Rept 103-562).

The $243.6 billion spending measure gave Clinton most of what he sought for major weapons, including $2.45 billion for a new nuclear-powered aircraft carrier for the Navy, $525 million to continue development of the Army's Comanche helicopter, and $2.3 billion for the purchase of six wide-body C-17 cargo jets.

But appropriators added nearly $3.2 billion to redress what they called early signs of a decline in combat readiness. And they added $995 million to pay for a 2.6 percent raise for military personnel and a 2 percent raise for civilians. Clinton had proposed a 1.6 percent raise.

Partly to offset the funds added for readiness and partly to dramatize the budget squeeze, appropriators cut $900 million from university research. It was the kind of draconian move Murtha had used successfully in the past to establish a bargaining position with the executive branch. "We'll work it out in conference," Murtha said.

Overall, the House bill cut $1.75 billion from Clinton's request for research, development and testing.

Bill Highlights

The committee bill included the following major provisions:

● **Readiness initiatives.** The largest single piece of the committee's readiness package was $607 million added to the amount requested for overhaul of ships, planes and land vehicles. Panel members said they wanted to reduce a backlog of deferred maintenance that approached $2 billion under the administration's budget. House appropriators also added:

• $517 million to reduce a $12 billion backlog of deferred maintenance of buildings and facilities.

• $310 million to increase the number of training exercises.

• $90 million to expand the stockpile of parts and equipment stored for use in war.

• $250 million to beef up the supply, communications and intelligence networks of U.S. forces in South Korea in recognition of the tense standoff over North Korea's apparent efforts to develop nuclear weapons.

● **Personnel costs.** As requested by the administration, the bill provided funding for an active-duty force of 1.53 million, a reduction of 85,000 personnel from fiscal 1994. The measure slightly increased the administration's request for 978,997 National Guard and reserve personnel.

Appropriators added funding for 65 Air Force reservists detailed to a Mississippi-based squadron of "hurricane hunters," weather reconnaissance planes famed for their efforts to hunt down and probe powerful storms in the Gulf of Mexico and off the southern Atlantic Coast. As in previous years, the Air Force sought to hand the job off to some other agency, but Gulf Coast state lawmakers on the appropriations panels insisted that the Air Force keep the weather planes flying.

The largest single item added to personnel spending was the $995 million to facilitate a bigger raise — $465 to fund a 2.6 percent raise for military personnel and $530 million to give civilians a 2 percent raise plus locality pay in high cost of living areas.

The bill did not include $376 million to accelerate cost of living (COLA) increases for military retirees as outlined in the companion defense authorization bill. House autho-

rizers wanted to undo a provision of the 1993 budget-reconciliation bill that gave retirees their pay adjustment six months later than civilian federal retirees. House appropriators said they endorsed the idea of redressing the inequity, but they believed that the military retirement fund could cover the COLA acceleration. Moreover, they objected as a matter of policy to the use of discretionary appropriations to pay mandatory obligations like pensions. *(1993 Almanac, p. 107)*

Appropriators also were able to shave $720 million from various accounts because the budget request had overestimated the number of reservists and civilians on the payroll in fiscal 1995.

● **Industrial base.** The bill endorsed several administration funding requests aimed at trying to keep intact a network of experienced defense contractors in a time of shrinking Pentagon budgets. For instance, although the bill did not allocate money for new tanks, it tried to keep tank companies busy by providing funding for upgrades of existing tanks.

The House panel went further than Clinton, however, and added $450 million for other defense industrial base initiatives. These included:

● $310 million to buy ammunition, ranging from bullets for M-16 rifles to 155 mm artillery shells. These were to be used for training and to bolster war reserves.

● $15 million, on top of $95 million requested by Clinton, to dismantle obsolete ammunition.

● $59 million, on top of the $27 million requested, to dismantle some unused munitions factories and to mothball others, keeping them available for future use.

● $16 million, in addition to the $44 million requested, to adapt ammunition assembly lines for "agile" manufacturing, a system that enabled one production line to turn out several types of products.

● $46 million to keep several Army missile production lines ticking at a slow rate.

● **Ground combat.** The bill provided $389 million to buy 60 additional Blackhawk troop-carrying helicopters.

In their report accompanying the bill, House appropriators complained that the Army had ignored the $15 million Congress set aside in fiscal 1994 to rebuild Vietnam War-era Huey helicopters for reserve and National Guard units not slated to receive the larger Blackhawks. The committee ordered the Army to use the money as Congress had intended, and then added $3 million to the 1995 bill for the Huey upgrades.

Other ground combat appropriations included:

● $525 million, as requested, for the Army's Comanche scout helicopter. The committee added to the president's request $225 million to upgrade 36 existing scout helicopters with missiles and target-finding electronics.

● $191 million, as requested, for development of Longbow modifications to existing Apache attack helicopters. These included radar-guided missiles designed to find ground targets in rainstorms.

● $217 million to buy 18 smaller Cobra attack helicopters for the Marine Corps, rather than the $142 million Clinton had requested to buy 12 helicopters. The additional Cobras were slated for reserve units.

● $175 million, as requested, to upgrade existing M-1 tanks with new target-finding electronics and with digital communications to link similarly equipped tanks, artillery, troop carriers and helicopters. This "digitization" — intended to give all elements of a combat force a shared view of their locations and those of the enemy — was central to the Army's modernization plan.

● $109 million, as requested, to develop the BAT warhead, a warhead the size of a baseball bat designed to be carried by several types of missiles and to home in on ground vehicles. The committee added to Clinton's request $3 million to develop a less expensive anti-tank warhead for the Army's MLRS artillery rocket.

● **Air combat.** The bill made only minor changes in Clinton's request to continue developing a new generation of combat planes for Air Force and Navy squadrons in the next century. It provided:

● $2.44 billion of the $2.46 billion requested for the Air Force's F-22.

● $1.42 billion, $12 million more than requested, to develop enlarged "E" and "F" models of the F/A-18.

● $201 million, $29 million less than requested, for two projects that the House bill ordered the Pentagon to meld: a joint Navy-Air Force project to develop prototypes of a combat jet slated to enter service at the end of the decade, and a vertical takeoff jet more advanced than the Marine Corps' Harrier. The bill also included $130 million to rebuild four of the Harrier vertical takeoff jets, which were used as bombers.

The committee also approved:

● $934 million for 24 F/A-18 fighters rather than the $1.03 billion Clinton requested.

● $172 million to equip some of the Navy's F-14 fighters to drop precision-guided "smart" bombs, but not the $131 million requested to outfit other F-14s with a less extensive upgrade.

● $128 million for new basic training planes for the Air Force and Navy.

For the B-2 stealth bomber, the committee approved the $793 million Clinton had requested to continue building 20 previously authorized planes. However, although the appropriators urged the administration to keep open the option of building additional B-2s, they included no funds in the bill for that purpose. Murtha, a strong B-2 proponent, said if he had included funds to keep the manufacturing complex warm, "we'd probably have lost it on the floor."

The appropriators did take steps, however, to stop the administration from mothballing 10 older B-52s in 1995, adding $70 million to the bill to fund continued operation of the planes.

Mirroring the position of the House Armed Services Committee, the Appropriations panel ordered the Pentagon to cancel development of a stealthy missile designated TSSAM. A centerpiece of Pentagon plans for blunting large-scale ground attacks on U.S. allies, TSSAM was designed to be launched from several types of bombers and warships, with each missile able to scatter several BAT homing warheads over targets more than 100 miles away.

Noting the project's long history of test failures and delays, the committee rejected the president's request for $604 million for development and early production of the TSSAM.

But it added to the bill funds for other bomber-launched weapons, including $9 million for additional copies of the Israeli-designed Popeye missile, which had a one-ton warhead and was carried by some B-52s; $29 million to convert nuclear-armed, bomber-launched cruise missiles to non-nuclear weapons; and $8 million to develop a version of those converted cruise missiles that would carry anti-armor weapons such as BAT.

● **Naval forces.** The bill included the $2.45 billion in new budget authority requested for a nuclear-powered carrier. The administration was to combine that money with $1.2 billion in fiscal 1994 funds that Congress had parked in another Pentagon account in expectation that the funds would be shifted to the carrier program.

The bill provided $2.61 billion for the purchase of three Aegis destroyers, slightly less than the $2.7 billion Clinton requested for the three ships. Appropriators also slightly reduced funding for 202 Standard anti-aircraft missiles, providing $249 million rather than $258 million.

They added $92 million to the $374 million requested for two projects intended to beef up the anti-aircraft defenses of ships not equipped with the Aegis system's powerful computer-driven radars and missiles.

The bill also included:

• $256 million, rather than the $286 million requested, for four Hawkeye radar planes, which were smaller, carrier-based counterparts of the Air Force's AWACS intended to detect aerial threats at a distance.

• $64 million the administration requested for sonobuoys, which were small, throw-away sonars dropped from aircraft to locate submarines.

• $408 million of the $508 million requested for development of the Navy's new nuclear-powered submarine. The Navy estimated it could build the new subs for $1.5 billion apiece, but House appropriators warned that it would lose support if the cost per sub exceeded $1.2 billion.

Appropriators also added:

• $32 million for 40 missiles designed to throw anti-sub homing torpedoes up to 15 miles.

• $214 million for seven Seahawk helicopters, which were Blackhawks modified to fly off warships and to hunt subs.

• $10 million to adapt for shallow-water work a new sonar being developed for sub-hunting helicopters.

• **Air and sea transport.** In their report, the appropriators endorsed administration plans to buy six big C-17 cargo jets in fiscal 1995 and eight in fiscal 1996, but they withheld endorsement of a complicated agreement negotiated in 1993 by the Pentagon and McDonnell Douglas Corp. to revise the C-17 contract with the aim of settling the many disputes that had ensnarled the program. The bill provided $2.3 billion for C-17 production; the administration had requested $2.88 billion. The cut included $318 million that had been intended to fund the proposed settlement.

The committee provided $104 million, as requested, to study the possible purchase of existing wide-body cargo jets to take up the slack in case the Pentagon decided to buy fewer C-17s than the 120 it had planned.

Also approved were:

• $859 million to buy cargo ships, $250 million more than requested.

• $497 million to continue developing the V-22 Osprey, a hybrid airplane and helicopter to serve as a Marine Corps troop carrier.

• **Strategic weapons.** The bill included $2.75 billion for anti-missile defenses, the same amount authorized in the House-passed defense authorization bill. Clinton had requested $3.25 billion. The bill channeled most of the anti-missile funds to systems designed to protect U.S. forces from relatively short-range "theater" missile attacks rather than to more ambitious "national" defense systems intended to shield U.S. territory.

But the appropriations measure provided only $444 million of the $770 million requested for national missile defense, compared with $584 million authorized by the House. The appropriations panel said the cut reflected budget constraints and the low priority it gave to national defense systems.

The bill also allocated $641 million to buy 18 additional Trident II submarine-launched nuclear missiles, as proposed by Clinton.

• **Space launchers and satellites.** The appropriators approved $13.5 billion for Pentagon space operations, noting that the allocation was likely to account for more than half of all federal spending on space activities in fiscal 1995. NASA's $14.3 billion budget request included many non-space programs.

Complaining that the Pentagon's many space programs were insufficiently coordinated, the panel combined all funding for space-related procurement in one part of the defense bill and funding for space-related development programs in another section. And it ordered the Pentagon to appoint a single official to oversee all space-related procurement.

The panel also zeroed in on the high cost of the Titan IV launcher, used to put large satellites into orbit. It ordered the Defense Department to begin developing a smaller, less expensive launcher that could carry most military payloads once the inventory of Titan IVs was exhausted. The relatively few large payloads should be put into orbit using the space shuttle, the committee said.

• **Other provisions.** The committee provided $3.49 billion for economic conversion programs designed to aid military employees and communities as the defense establishment shrank. The allocation was an increase of $152 million over the president's request for this top administration priority.

But the panel denied funding for several other administration initiatives, including $400 million to continue the so-called Nunn-Lugar program to help Soviet states dismantle nuclear weapons and $300 million to pay the U.S. share of U.N.-sponsored peacekeeping operations.

The bill provided $9.9 billion for Pentagon medical programs, a reduction of $27 million from the president's request. But the committee increased spending related to high-profile medical problems, adding money for research in these areas: $159 million for breast cancer and mammography; $40 million for other women's health problems; $34 million for bone marrow transplant research; $20 million for AIDS; and $10 million for prostate cancer.

To enforce an administration decision to close the Pentagon's medical school, the bill barred the recruitment or enrollment of new students.

House Floor Action

The House quickly passed the $243.6 billion defense appropriations bill June 29 with little change. The vote was 330-91. *(Vote 313, p. 92-H)*

Most battles over defense spending in the House were fought during the writing of the authorization bill. Liberals had failed in attempts to block the Navy's nuclear carrier project, to scale back spending on so-called Star Wars ballistic missile defenses and to discontinue the Trident II missile.

By contrast, Murtha whisked his appropriations bill through the House. Just 15 minutes elapsed between the time the House took up the measure and the time it started the roll call vote on passage. In that interval, the House dealt with only two amendments.

Lawmakers rejected a proposal by Carolyn B. Maloney, D-N.Y., to eliminate a $2.5 million program that distributed rifle ammunition to private organizations. The marksmanship program, founded after the Spanish-American War of 1898, was backed by the National Rifle Association.

"The Army doesn't want it. The Department of Defense doesn't want it. [The Office of Management and Budget] doesn't want it," Maloney said. "If we can't cut here, where can we cut?" The amendment was rejected on a standing vote of 20-69. Maloney's request for a roll call vote was rejected because too few members supported it.

The House accepted by voice vote an amendment by Elizabeth Furse, D-Ore., that cut $30 million from funds for research and development management.

Senate Committee

The Senate Defense Appropriations Subcommittee approved its version of the spending bill by voice vote July 25. The full Appropriations Committee approved the $243.6 billion bill 30-0 on July 29 (S Rept 103-321).

In subcommittee, senators restored $821 million of the $900 million that the House had cut from Pentagon-sponsored research programs. Panicked universities had lobbied furiously to restore the lucrative grants.

The Senate bill endorsed much of Clinton's budget, but it included several significant departures. Appropriators:

● Added $150 million to preserve the option of buying additional B-2 bombers.

● Added $380 million to move up by six months the annual COLA for military retirees.

● Eliminated $300 million that Clinton requested to pay the U.S. share of U.N. peacekeeping operations.

Senators also used the opportunity to express unhappiness with aspects of the president's foreign policy. Though the committee granted a last-minute Clinton request to fund immediate aid to Rwandan refugees, it restricted U.S. forces in Rwanda to humanitarian relief missions, barring them from participating in military operations without congressional approval.

Clinton requested $270 million for Rwandan aid, but Appropriations Chairman Byrd agreed to only $170 million, saying the president could come back at a later date to ask for more if he needed it. Byrd also crafted the limitations on the relief money, saying U.S. forces had to be prevented from becoming entangled in a sticky security mission in a country wracked by a tribal war. "We had enough of that in Somalia," Byrd said.

In their report accompanying the bill, the appropriators also ordered the administration to try to secure commitments of funding and military forces from other countries to reduce the burden on the United States. The administration was instructed to credit U.S. Rwandan relief expenditures against the U.S. backlog of unpaid U.N. assessments.

Bill Highlights

● **Readiness.** As in the House, Senate appropriators emphasized combat-readiness, endorsing everything the president requested for "operating tempo" — routine activities measured in the number of hours per month that pilots flew, the number of days per quarter that ships were under way and the number of miles per year that tanks were driven.

Distressed that the Army had cut back on such training activities in order to use the money for base housekeeping, Senate appropriators ordered the service to obtain approval from Congress before reallocating training money.

They also added $16 million to expand the number of trained Air Force crew members for the AWACS radar plane. A Pentagon investigation cited overworked AWACS crew members as a factor in the accidental destruction by U.S. fighters of two U.S. Army helicopters over Iraq in April 1994.

The bill included $236 million more than was requested for overhauling ships, planes and tanks. And it added $86 million to the Air Force's budget request for rebuilding jet engines and other major components. It also added $500 million to the amount requested for maintenance and repair of facilities.

Noting the importance of high morale and family welfare, the appropriators added $142 million for child care and other family support services.

● **Personnel.** The Senate panel backed the House's 2.6 percent pay raise for the military in fiscal 1995. And like the House bill, the Senate version paid for a force of nearly 1.53 million active-duty personnel and more than 979,000 National Guard and reserve members — essentially the number requested by Clinton.

The Senate committee modified the bill to:

● Slice $230 million from the personnel funding request, reasoning that the administration's budget assumed that an excessive number of officers would remain on duty and that the average rank of officers would increase.

● Cut $223 million from the amount the Air Force requested for incentive programs intended to encourage enlisted personnel to leave the service voluntarily. The committee said the administration underestimated the number of members who would leave the Air Force in any case.

● Cut $521 million from the amount requested for civilian pay, noting that the Pentagon's civilian payroll was shrinking faster than the president's budget assumed. To encourage that rapid retrenchment, the bill included $177.5 million more than was requested for "early-out" incentive programs for civilian employees.

● Instructed the services to stop paying flight pay to generals and to personnel with more than 25 years of service. The change saved just $500,000, and was an example of the hundreds of small adjustments that appropriators made in the Pentagon's budget request each year.

● Added $19 million for two reservist-manned amphibious transport ships to shuttle troops from Pearl Harbor to training grounds on the island of Hawaii in the home state of subcommittee Chairman Inouye.

● Added $21.5 million to beef up National Guard squadrons of C-130 cargo planes in the home states of Byrd, Ford and Sasser.

● **Operations and maintenance.** The committee made several reductions that it said reflected the ongoing reduction in the size of the active-duty force. It cut $25 million from the funding for Army and Air Force training; $15 million from the budget for war colleges attended by the most promising mid-rank officers of each service; and $65 million from the amount earmarked for communications networks on bases.

As they had in the past, appropriators also made several cuts aimed at forcing agencies to operate more efficiently. Among these were reductions of $85 million from the Defense Finance and Accounting Service, the Pentagon's bookkeeping agency; $141 million from the Defense Logistics Agency, which purchased small items and consumables such as fuel; $113.5 million from computer services; and $49.5 million from travel budgets.

The appropriators approved $2.03 billion to clean up toxic and hazardous waste on military bases, $146 million less than the president requested. But they provided all of the $1.78 billion requested to ensure that the services complied with environmental laws.

● **Ground combat.** The Senate panel ordered the Army to select a single contractor to manage both of its new combat helicopter programs — the Comanche armed scout, run by a Boeing-Sikorsky consortium, and modernization of the larger Apache attack helicopter to carry the Longbow target-finding radar, a McDonnell Douglas project. The committee said the Army's long-range budget plans could not pay for two programs run by competing companies. Citing the overhead expense of awarding such projects to different contractors,

the appropriators ordered the Army to cancel the existing contracts and hold a new competition that would award both projects to one company.

The committee added to the bill $77.6 million to buy six additional Apaches, an increase that was offset by a $72 million cut in Longbow production.

The Senate bill also included:

- $99 million of the $112 million Clinton requested to equip some older scout helicopters with missiles, but it eliminated $225 million that the House added to the bill to upgrade additional older scout craft.
- $219 million, $100 million more than requested, to buy a dozen used jetliners for modification into JSTARS planes, Boeing jetliners equipped to locate ground targets far behind enemy lines.
- $28 million to buy 1,000 smaller TOWs. The administration requested that amount, but for the purpose of closing down the TOW production line.
- $214 million for nearly 900 shoulder-fired Javelins, an increase of $83 million and nearly 500 missiles.
- $119 million, $10 million more than requested, to continue development of BAT homing warheads.

Appropriators also added:

- $108 million (and 24 tanks) more than Clinton requested and the House approved to upgrade 58 M-1 tanks to "A2" models.
- $12 million to the $134 million requested for Hellfire anti-tank missiles.
- $70 million for small-arms production, which quadrupled the Pentagon's budget request. But the committee dropped $285 million added by the House to keep several ammunition production lines humming.

● **Air combat.** Appropriators ordered the Pentagon to contract with an outside think tank to compare the effectiveness of alternative long-range bomber forces in meeting the goal of fighting two major regional wars simultaneously. Citing the effectiveness of the F-117 stealth fighter in striking Iraqi targets in 1991, the committee speculated that "a cost-effectiveness analysis of all the alternatives could demonstrate that the overall capability of the stealthy B-2 overrides its high acquisition costs."

The panel agreed to the $793 million requested to continue flight tests of the B-2 bomber. And it added $150 million to preserve the option of buying additional B-2s in future years.

The committee provided $356 million to continue developing the stealthy TSSAM missile. The administration had requested $606 million for TSSAM; the House bill provided nothing.

Other changes in the bill included:

- $876 million to buy 17 additional F/A-18 jets, a reduction of $58 million and seven planes from Clinton's request.
- $189 million to upgrade existing F-14 jets, $141 million less than requested. Like the Senate Armed Services Committee, the appropriations panel denied the funds that had been earmarked to modify these fighter planes to drop "smart" bombs on ground targets.
- $241 million, $40 million more than the administration proposed, for a joint Navy-Air Force program intended to develop prototypes of future combat planes.
- An increase of $100 million to put back in service three ultra-high-speed SR-71 photo-reconnaissance planes, which the Air Force retired in 1990 for budgetary reasons. The panel noted that the SR-71 would have provided invaluable intelligence during the Persian Gulf War.

● **Naval forces.** The committee approved:

- $2.28 billion of the $2.45 billion requested for a nuclear-powered aircraft carrier, the same amount approved by the House.
- $2.66 billion, $37 million less than requested, for three destroyers equipped with the Aegis missile defense system.
- Funding for two types of cruise missiles to enable destroyers to strike distant targets that previously could be attacked only by a carrier's airplanes — $302 million for 217 Tomahawks, with a range of several hundred miles, and $69 million for 58 smaller Harpoons.
- Funding for shipborne anti-aircraft missiles: $258 million for 202 long-range Standard missiles, and $64 million for 240 short-range missiles.
- $403 million, $29 million more than requested, to develop improved anti-missile defenses for amphibious landing transports and other less heavily armed ships.
- $500 million to develop a new nuclear submarine smaller than the *Seawolf*-class ships.
- $229 million, $61 million less than requested, for four Hawkeye radar planes. (Noting a 22 percent cost increase for the planes, the committee barred the Navy from spending the money until the price came down by 20 percent.)

● **Air and sea transport.** The Senate panel approved $2.47 billion, a little less than the House, for six additional C-17 long-range cargo jets. In its report accompanying the bill, Senate appropriators expressly endorsed the Pentagon-McDonnell Douglas Corp. agreement aimed at settling many contractual disputes.

The Senate bill included none of the $104 million requested by Clinton, and approved by the House, to test the feasibility of buying existing wide-body jets off the shelf to complement the C-17 force. The Senate panel noted that $98 million appropriated for the project in fiscal 1994 had not been spent.

The Senate committee concurred with the House in approving $497 million to develop the V-22 Osprey.

● **Other provisions.** The panel restored the $400 million cut by the House for the Nunn-Lugar program to assist former Soviet republics in dismantling nuclear arsenals. But it concurred with the House in eliminating the $300 million Clinton requested to pay the U.S. share of U.N. peacekeeping operations. It added to the bill $30 million for initiatives to foster working relationships between NATO and Eastern Europe and the former Soviet Union.

Senate Floor Action

After four days of debate, the Senate on Aug. 11 passed the spending bill by a vote of 86-14. The $243.4 billion measure appropriated $1.3 billion less than Clinton had sought and $2.9 billion more than fiscal 1994 spending. *(Vote 282, p. 47-S)*

The bill retained the committee mandates instructing Clinton to limit U.S. participation in Rwanda to humanitarian aid. Floor debate on the bill provided a chance for the Senate to weigh in on another foreign policy matter — whether Congress should force Clinton to break the U.N.-mandated arms embargo against outgunned Muslim forces in Bosnia. As it often had done in the past in the foreign policy realm, where presidential prerogatives traditionally dominated, the Senate equivocated.

On a vote of 58-42, the Senate adopted an amendment by Minority Leader Bob Dole, R-Kan., and Joseph I. Lieberman, D-Conn., to require Clinton to end the embargo by Nov. 15. But it also approved, 56-44, an amendment by Armed Services Committee Chairman Sam Nunn, D-Ga., and Majority Leader George J. Mitchell, D-Maine, to urge, but not require, Clinton

Continued on p. 497

Defense Appropriations Provisions

In a year when lawmakers fought the president on social issues from health care to welfare reform, they for the most part gave him the defense program that he wanted. Clinton submitted a Pentagon budget request of $244.7 billion. Congress approved $243.7 billion — a reduction of less than 1 percent (HR 4650 — PL 103-335).

The bill generally supported the force size, tempo of operations and weapons procurement plans in Clinton's budget. In crafting the final bill, House and Senate conferees made the following decisions:

Personnel

● **Force size.** The bill endorsed the 1.53 million-member force requested by Clinton, a reduction of more than 85,000 personnel from the size of the fiscal 1994 force. The bill also funded a National Guard and reserve force slightly larger than the roster of 978,997 members requested by the president. Compared with Clinton's budget request, this had the effect of adding:

● 192 members to the Naval Reserve to crew two amphibious transport ships to shuttle troops from Pearl Harbor to training grounds on the nearby island of Hawaii. A Senate initiative, the troop shuttle project cost $17 million.

● 65 members to the Air Force Reserve, to continue operating a Mississippi-based squadron of "hurricane hunters" — weather reconnaissance planes famed for tracking storms at sea. The cost was $2.7 million in operating and personnel funds.

● **Pay increase.** Both chambers endorsed a 2.6 percent military pay raise in fiscal 1995. However, the bill provided only $186 million of the $465 million needed for the increase. The conferees directed the Defense Department to find the remaining funds elsewhere in its fiscal 1995 appropriation.

The bill also provided $129 million to cover part of the cost of a raise for civilian Pentagon employees, including "locality" pay to partly offset the high cost of living in certain parts of the country.

More than offsetting the pay raises was a total of $800 million cut from various personnel accounts. Lawmakers said that the administration overestimated the number of reservists and civilians who would be on the Pentagon payroll in fiscal 1995.

● **Senate cuts.** Conferees agreed, with modifications, to two Senate cuts that shaved:

● $50 million from an Air Force request for incentive programs to encourage enlisted personnel to leave the service voluntarily. The Senate had called for a more dramatic, $223 million cut, maintaining that the administration underestimated the number of personnel who would leave the Air Force regardless of incentives.

● $70 million in payroll reductions to discourage a planned increase in the average rank of officers. However, the conferees rejected another Senate cut of $91 million intended to reduce the planned number of officers.

● **Retiree COLAs.** The bill accelerated by six months a cost of living (COLA) increase for military retirees in fiscal 1995, nullifying a provision of the 1993 budget-reconciliation bill that required military retirees to get their pay increase six months later than civilian federal retirees. The cost of the change was $376 million.

Readiness and Operations

● **Overhaul and repair.** The measure added to the president's budget request over $350 million for the overhaul of ships, planes and vehicles. It also added $200 million for the maintenance and repair of facilities.

An additional $6 million was earmarked for the maintenance of Navy facilities in New Orleans, a venue that had powerful backing from two Louisiana defense appropriators — Senate Democrat J. Bennett Johnston and House Republican Robert L. Livingston.

● **Korea.** Conferees dropped a House provision that would have added $250 million to the budget request to reinforce U.S. forces in South Korea. However, they did add $67 million to the bill to pay

for specific actions already taken, including the deployment of a Patriot missile battalion and a battalion of missile-armed helicopters.

● **AWACS.** The bill incorporated a Senate initiative adding $16 million to fund Defense Secretary William J. Perry's order to expand the Air Force's pool of trained crew members for AWACS radar planes. A Pentagon investigation cited overworked AWACS crew members as a factor in the accidental downing of two U.S. Army helicopters by U.S. jets over Iraq in April 1994.

● **Family services.** The bill contained $85 million of the $142 million the Senate had added to buttress service members' morale by providing additional child care and other family support services.

● **Miscellaneous cuts.** The bill supported several of the broad cuts typically favored by the appropriations panels to force agencies to tighten their operations. Among them were proposed reductions of $116 million for supply operations, $107 million for travel, $175 million to reduce the use of consultants and $200 million to trim spending on computer services.

Ground Combat Forces

● **Helicopter programs.** The conferees spiked a Senate provision that would have required the Army to choose one contractor to develop both of the combat helicopter projects in its pipeline — the Comanche armed scout, run by a Boeing-Sikorsky consortium, and modernization of the larger Apache attack helicopter to carry the Longbow target-finding radar, a McDonnell Douglas project.

Senate appropriators had said the Army could not pay for two programs run by competing companies. The conferees said they shared the Senate committee's concern, but they deferred to the Army, which said it could find ways to cover the costs of the two-contractor system.

The bill granted $495 million of the $525 million requested to develop the Comanche. And it provided $251 million to continue developing the Longbow modification for the Apache. (In a cost-saving move, Defense Secretary Perry announced in December that no Comanches beyond the two planned protoypes would be built.)

The bill also contained a $78 million Senate provision to buy six additional Apaches that were not requested. The Senate argued that the new orders would keep the Apache production line running until it was time to begin the Longbow radar retrofit, reducing costs over the long run.

The bill included $99 million of the $112 million requested by the administration to arm some older scout helicopters that had been upgraded with new target-finding electronics, and $120 million — about half the amount the House had added to the bill — to outfit additional old helicopters with the new electronics.

● **M-1 tank.** The bill provided $175 million to upgrade M-1 tanks with new target-finding electronics and digital communications that could link similarly equipped tanks, troop carriers and helicopters. The conferees added $108 million to upgrade 24 additional M-1s.

● **'Digitization.'** Conferees included $84 million for "digitization," intended to give all elements of a U.S. force a view of their own locations and those of the enemy. That was far less than the $116 million that the House had approved, but $8 million more than the president requested.

● **Rockets.** The bill contained $144 million for mobile launchers for long-range artillery rockets — $84 million more than requested — and $26 million to keep the production line for 20 mile-range MLRS rockets moving slowly. The president's budget included no MLRS funds, but the House bill did.

● **Ammunition.** The bill contained $1.18 billion rather than the $845 million requested for Army ammunition. Most of the increase reflected the conferees' support of all or part of several House provisions intended to modernize stocks of some types of ammunition and to accelerate the mothballing of some ammunition plants and the retooling of others.

Air Combat

● **Bomber force.** The bill added to the president's request $125 million to preserve the option of buying additional B-2 stealth bombers in future years. It also added $60 million to keep in service 10 B-52 bombers the administration had planned to retire. And it contained a provision barring the Pentagon from retiring any long-range bombers during fiscal 1995. Conferees ordered the Pentagon to do an elaborate analysis of the fleet of F-111 long-range ground attack planes, which many Air Force officers wanted to retire to cut costs.

● **Smart bombs.** The bill provided $95 million of $110 million requested to continue developing a new smart bomb called JDAM, which was designed to hit within 10 feet of its target. And it allocated $172 million — $12 million more than requested — to continue development of a super-accurate glide-bomb designated JSOW, which a plane could drop 20 miles from its target, beyond the reach of enemy defenses.

Because of technical glitches in the development of the TSSAM, a stealthy plane-launched missile designed to have a range of more than 100 miles, the conference committee approved only $222 million of the $604 million requested. (In December, the Pentagon canceled the TSSAM program altogether in a cost-saving move.)

The conferees also added to the bill $80 million to buy or develop other types of smart bombs intended for interim service until the more accurate TSSAM and JDAM could be deployed.

● **SR-71 spy planes.** Conferees included $100 million to put back in service three ultra high-speed SR-71 reconnaissance jets, which the Air Force had retired in 1990 to save money.

● **Navy aircraft.** The bill provided funds to modernize the Navy's carrier-based air squadrons, including:

• $934 million of the $1.03 billion requested for F/A-18 fighters, to buy about 24 planes.

• $42 million of the $172 million requested to develop modifications for the F-14 fighter. The reduction ruled out efforts to equip the planes to hunt ground targets at night and to attack them with large payloads of precision-guided bombs. Funds remained, however, to modify F-14s to carry a small number of JDAMs.

• $123 million of the $130 million requested to continue the rebuilding of the fleet of Harrier vertical-takeoff jets used by the Marine Corps as bombers.

● **Combat planes.** In general, the bill endorsed Clinton's plan to develop a new generation of combat planes for the Air Force and Navy, providing:

• $2.35 billion of the $2.46 billion requested to continue developing the Air Force's F-22 fighter.

• $1.34 billion of the $1.41 billion requested to continue work on an enlarged version of the F/A-18.

• $186 million of the $201 million requested for a project to develop prototypes of combat jets slated to be in service at the end of the next decade.

Naval Forces

● **Aircraft carrier.** The bill provided $2.28 billion for construction of a new nuclear-powered aircraft carrier, a reduction of just $162 million from the administration's request.

● **Submarine.** The bill also granted the president's request for $500 million to continue development of a new nuclear-powered submarine, which was to be smaller and cheaper than the *Seawolf*-class sub. But conferees also said the estimated $1.5 billion cost for each ship was too high and insisted that the Navy bring it down to $1.2 billion apiece.

● **Anti-missile defenses.** It made a small reduction in the request for three destroyers equipped with the Aegis system of powerful computer-driven radars and anti-aircraft missiles — $2.66 billion of the $2.70 billion requested.

To develop a more effective defense against high-speed cruise missiles for ships not equipped with the Aegis system, the conferees approved $458 million, more than the $374 million requested. They

also ordered the Navy to install the new anti-cruise missile defenses in a new class of amphibious landing transport ships, slated for construction late in the decade.

Air and Sea Transport

● **C-17 cargo jets.** Conferees approved the purchase of six additional C-17 long-range cargo jets and approved $2.17 billion of the $2.47 billion requested, the same amount that had been authorized. They also approved $190 million of the $221 million requested to continue flight-testing the plane.

The bill contained $190 million requested for components to be used in eight additional planes slated for funding in fiscal 1996. But it dropped $104 million requested to test the feasibility of buying existing wide-body jets off the shelf, possibly including commercial aircraft, to complement the C-17 force.

● **Osprey.** Without explanation, the conferees trimmed $30 million from $497 million that both chambers had approved for development of the V-22 Osprey, a hybrid airplane-helicopter designed for the Marines as a troop carrier.

● **Cargo ships.** The bill included $546 million to buy two new cargo ships. These so-called RO/RO (roll on/roll off) ships were to have ramps so that Army vehicles could quickly roll on at a U.S. port and roll off near a distant trouble spot. The bill boosted the president's request by $110 million to add another vessel to the flotilla of 13 large cargo ships used by the Marines as floating depots near potential trouble spots.

Strategic Weapons

● **Anti-missile systems.** Conferees approved $2.8 billion of the $3.25 billion requested to develop and buy anti-ballistic missile defenses. They also approved $120 million to develop missile detection satellites dubbed "Brilliant Eyes."

● **Trident II.** The bill contained funds for the purchase of 18 Trident II submarine-launched missiles, but earmarked $616 million instead of the $641 million requested.

Space Launchers and Satellites

● **Titan IV.** Congress gave Clinton the $382 million he requested to continue buying the big Titan IV used to launch the largest military satellites. However, the conferees included a slightly modified version of a House provision barring the purchase of more than 47 Titan IV's. They also earmarked $40 million for the development of new, less expensive satellite launchers.

Other Provisions

● **Medical care.** The conference approved $9.9 billion for medical care of active-duty personnel, their dependents and retirees. As had become customary, it earmarked sums for research projects that had active constituencies, giving $155 million for breast cancer, $40 million to women's health problems, $34 million to bone marrow research and registration, and $10 million for prostate cancer.

● **Defense conversion.** The bill provided $3.3 billion for so-called defense conversion efforts aimed at helping military personnel, contractors, and their employees and communities adjust to big drops in defense spending.

● **Research.** The conferees cut $200 million from Pentagon-sponsored university research, a much smaller cut than the $900 million the House had voted for. Clinton's total request for research earmarks was estimated to be between $1.5 billion and $1.8 billion.

● **Nunn-Lugar program.** They approved the $400 million Clinton requested for the so-called Nunn-Lugar program to assist former Soviet republics in dismantling nuclear and chemical weapons arsenals.

● **NATO.** Conferees also approved the Senate's addition of $30 million to the bill to support NATO initiatives designed to foster working relationships between NATO members and countries in Eastern Europe and the former Soviet Union. ■

Continued from p. 494

to seek international agreement to end the embargo if Serbian forces refused to accept an internationally sponsored settlement of the Bosnian civil war. *(Votes 280, 279, p. 47-S; Bosnia, p. 446)*

Weapons Amendments

The Senate rejected three amendments that would have significantly altered the Appropriations Committee's funding recommendations for major weapons programs.

By 38-62, it rejected a proposal by longtime Pentagon critic Dale Bumpers, D-Ark., to stop deployment of the Milstar communications satellite and force the Pentagon to find a less expensive replacement. Bumpers called Milstar a "Cold War relic" designed in the early 1980s to survive a prolonged U.S.-Soviet nuclear war. But supporters successfully argued that the satellite had been stripped of some of its nuclear war-oriented features and given capacity to transmit military communications in conventional warfare. *(Vote 273, p. 46-S)*

Another Bumpers amendment, rejected 40-60, would have eliminated funds for the Trident II submarine-launched missile. *(Vote 274, p. 46-S)*

By a vote of 38-60, the Senate rejected an amendment by Malcolm Wallop, R-Wyo., that would have boosted from $18 million to $120 million funds to equip Navy warships to intercept short-range, theater ballistic missiles at a great distance. *(Vote 277, p. 46-S)*

Following the recommendation of the Senate Appropriations Committee, the bill provided $2.83 billion of the $3.25 billion requested for anti-missile defense projects. It also provided an additional $120 million, the amount the president requested to develop the so-called "Brilliant Eyes" missile attack warning satellite.

Other Foreign Policy Issues

In addition to the Bosnia provisions, the Senate tacked several other foreign policy amendments onto the defense bill. Among these was an amendment by Dirk Kempthorne, R-Idaho, adopted 54-44, to require the withdrawal by Oct. 1 of the small U.S. security force stationed in Somalia. *(Vote 278, p. 46-S)*

The Senate tabled (killed) by a vote of 53-47 an amendment by Jesse Helms, R-N.C., that would have limited military assistance to Colombia until the president certified that the Colombian government was fully cooperating in the war on drugs. *(Vote 275, p. 46-S)*

By voice vote, the Senate adopted amendments by:

• Hank Brown, R-Colo., to guarantee that high-ranking officials of the government of Taiwan could enter the United States for official purposes.

• Brown, to make Poland, Hungary, the Czech Republic and Slovakia eligible for certain kinds of allied defense cooperation with NATO.

• Brown, expressing the sense of Congress in support of progress toward democracy in Bulgaria.

• Mitch McConnell, R-Ky., requiring the president to report to Congress on specific political, military and economic standards that countries of Eastern Europe would have to meet to become members of NATO.

Other Amendments

The Senate also adopted a few dozen relatively minor amendments, many of which earmarked money for specific project funds.

It rejected, 21-77, an amendment by John McCain, R-Ariz., that would have required profitable civilian sporting events such as the Olympic Games to reimburse the Pentagon for the cost of military support services. The bill included $10 million for Pentagon support of the 1996 Olympiad in Atlanta. McCain's amendment was vigorously opposed by Georgia Sens. Nunn and Paul Coverdell. *(Vote 276, p. 46-S)*

The Senate approved by voice votes two amendments relating to an office complex being built for the National Reconnaissance Office (NRO) in the Virginia suburbs of Washington. The first, by David L. Boren, D-Okla., required that any intelligence agency construction project slated to cost more than $300,000 be clearly identified in administration budget requests. The second, by Richard H. Bryan, D-Nev., called for the NRO to halt work on the facility pending further congressional review. *(NRO, p. 461)*

Final Action

The House and Senate each agreed Sept. 29 to a final, $243.7 billion fiscal 1995 defense bill. The House adopted the conference report on the bill (H Rept 103-747) by a vote of 327-86, and the Senate cleared the bill by voice vote. *(Vote 446, p. 134-H; provisions, p. 495)*

While the bill generally supported both the thrust and the specifics of Clinton's proposal, it also incorporated significant congressional initiatives, including:

• The 2.6 percent pay raise for military personnel.

• $100 million to put back in service three ultra-high-speed SR-71 reconnaissance jets.

• $125 million to preserve the option of buying additional B-2 stealth bombers.

• More than $500 million requested to continue building a new type of nuclear-powered sub. At the same time, the bill called on the Navy to try to ratchet down the price to $1.2 billion from $1.5 billion.

• $382 million requested by Clinton to continue buying Titan IV rockets used to launch big military satellites. At the same time, the bill included a slightly modified version of a House provision barring the Pentagon from buying more than 47 of the Titan IVs. Conferees also earmarked $40 million to develop new, less expensive satellite launchers. ∎

D.C. Funding Clears at 11th Hour

Congress cleared the spending bill for the District of Columbia on Sept. 30, just hours before the start of the new fiscal year, after senators had stalled the bill with a host of unrelated amendments. It was the last of the 13 regular fiscal 1995 appropriations bills to clear. President Clinton signed it on Sept. 30 (HR 4649 — PL 103-334).

The bill appropriated $712 million in federal funds for the city for fiscal 1995. The original House version would have provided $720 million; the Senate figure was $700 million.

The measure also placed strong restrictions on the city. It required $140 million in cuts from the D.C. budget in fiscal 1995 and provided stiff penalties if the city failed to make the cuts. It also required the city to eliminate 2,000 full-time jobs, or their equivalent, in fiscal 1995.

The measure barred the District from using federal funds for abortions and from implementing the city's domestic partners ordinance. But unlike in previous years, the bill did not spark debate on social policy issues. Instead, the debate was dominated by concern over the city's growing financial crisis.

District supporters pleaded for quick action on the measure to free up much-needed funds for the financially strapped city. But the bill was one of the last moving legislative vehicles of the year, which made it an inviting target for end-of-session amendments. Several senators tried to use the bill to carry amendments on issues ranging from crime to health care to congressional reform to major-league baseball's antitrust exemption. All of them were eventually stripped.

Background

When Congress granted the city home rule in 1973, residents were allowed to elect a mayor and city council to run city affairs. But lawmakers retained control over the city's finances through the annual appropriations bill. Congress not only provided federal funds to the city; it also had to approve the D.C. budget before the city could spend its own money. That gave lawmakers an annual opportunity to tell D.C. officials what they liked or disliked about the way the city was being run.

Lawmakers had used the D.C. bill to complain about the city's crime rate, to try to protect firefighter jobs slated to be cut by the D.C. government, to criticize the salaries of D.C. council members, to condemn D.C. statehood protests being held outside House office buildings, to direct money to local universities and even to deplore the conditions of bridges leading into the city.

Since 1979, the city had been prevented from using federal funds for abortions, and that ban was broadened to include local funds in 1988. City advocates regarded it as a significant victory when Congress voted in 1993 to allow D.C. to use fed-

---

BOXSCORE

Fiscal 1995 District of Columbia Appropriations— HR 4649. The spending bill provided $712 million to the District, including a $660 million federal payment, and required the city to cut $140 million from its budget.

Reports: H Rept 103-558; S Rept 103-313; conference report H Rept 103-671.

KEY ACTION

July 13 — House passed HR 4649, 213-210.

July 21 — Senate passed HR 4649, amended, 68-32.

Aug. 8 — House agreed to conference report by voice vote.

Sept. 21 — Senate agreed to conference report, 71-27.

Sept. 30 — Senate cleared conference report by voice vote.

Sept. 30 — President signed the bill — PL 103-334.

---

eral funds for abortion in cases of rape or incest or when the pregnancy endangered the life of the woman. *(1993 Almanac, p. 584)*

Congress also voted in 1993 to continue prohibiting the city from implementing a domestic partners law, which allowed unmarried partners and homosexual couples to register with the local government. If implemented, the law would have made registered partners of D.C. city employees eligible for coverage under the city's group health insurance, as long as they paid for the additional coverage.

But in 1994, reports that the city was in dire financial straits kept Congress from addressing social policy or other city matters. Instead, lawmakers looked almost exclusively at the city's financial management practices.

At a May 11 hearing on the city's fiscal 1994 budget, D.C. Appropriations Subcommittee Chairman Julian C. Dixon, D-Calif., said he would rather the District solve its own problems than have Congress intercede. But he did call the city's budget problem "as serious as it's ever been," suggesting that the city might eventually need a federal bailout. Dixon said he was concerned in particular about the city's plan to defer a portion of its pension payments for fiscal 1994 and 1995. In addition, Dixon said that the city's pattern of short-term borrowing could be problematic.

House Committee

The House District of Columbia Appropriations Subcommittee approved a draft fiscal 1995 spending bill by voice vote June 17. As approved by the subcommittee, the measure provided $720 million to the city, $2 million less than Clinton had requested, but $20 million more than was appropriated in fiscal 1994.

Included in that amount was $667.9 million for the federal payment, an annual allotment provided to the District to compensate the city for tax revenues lost because it was home to federal agencies that could not be taxed. Also included was $52.1 million for the annual contribution to the city's pension fund for District retirees.

The panel defeated by a show of hands an amendment by ranking Republican James T. Walsh of New York that would have set aside $295 million from the federal payment to be used to aid the city's underfunded pension program.

The subcommittee also turned back by a show of hands a Walsh amendment that would have implemented a freeze in salary increases for District employees. Dixon said such spending decisions should be made by the city government.

The panel also defeated by a show of hands an amendment by Ernest Jim Istook Jr., R-Okla., that would have barred unmarried partners of District government employees from being covered by the city's group health insurance.

District of Columbia Spending

(in thousands of dollars)

	Fiscal 1994 Appropriations	Fiscal 1995 Clinton Request	House Bill	Senate Bill	Final Bill
Appropriations to D.C.					
Federal payment	$ 630,603	$ 669,930	$ 667,930	$ 647,930	$ 660,000
Contributions to retirement fund	52,070	52,070	52,070	52,070	52,070
Federal contribution to crime and youth initiative	17,327	—	—	—	—
Subtotal, federal funds	**$ 700,000**	**$ 722,000**	**$ 720,000**	**$ 700,000**	**$ 712,070**
Total D.C. budget	$ 3,740,382	$ 3,690,439	$ 3,534,737	$ 3,589,737	$ 3,536,807

SOURCE: House Appropriations Committee

After the markup, D.C. government representatives expressed relief that the panel had considered the bill without fierce debates or burdensome amendments.

Full Committee

The House Appropriations Committee gave voice vote approval to the bill June 24 (H Rept 103-558). At the markup, members focused almost exclusively on the city's growing fiscal problems.

A General Accounting Office (GAO) report released the previous day indicated that unless the city compensated for potential cash shortfalls, it could be forced to borrow from the U.S. Treasury in 1995. Walsh argued that Congress should be more involved in the city's financial management. "The GAO report is dramatic evidence that the District is out of control and headed for bankruptcy," he said.

The committee defeated, 18-25, a second attempt by Walsh to set aside $295 million from the federal payment for the city's underfunded pension program. It defeated by voice vote another Walsh amendment to institute a single annual cost of living adjustment for District retirees, rather than the existing semiannual adjustment. Dixon reiterated that he felt Congress should not attempt to run the city's finances. "Let's let them make the hard decisions," he said.

But the panel, with Dixon's support, gave voice vote approval to a Walsh amendment requiring the city to provide Congress with quarterly financial reports.

Missing from the markup were any further debates about the city's policies on funding abortions and benefits for so-called domestic partners.

House Floor

On July 13, the House approved the D.C. spending measure by a vote of 213-210, after amending it to require that the city cut its fiscal 1995 budget by $150 million. The House bill kept the federal contribution at $720 million, as recommended by the appropriators. *(Vote 322, p. 96-H)*

House action began June 27 with a barrage of questions about the soundness of the city's budget. Thomas J. Bliley Jr., R-Va., who led the assault, said the city's proposed budget was rife with inaccuracies. He threatened to send the spending bill back to the Appropriations Committee until the District made further revisions in its budget.

Responding to concerns that the bill could not pass without significant changes, Dixon and Walsh worked with Bliley to draft a compromise amendment aimed at reining in the District's spending. The compromise, approved by voice vote, required the city to submit a report to Congress within 30 days of enactment showing how it planned to make the $150 million in cuts.

Under the House-approved compromise, the city also could incur no deficit in fiscal 1995. To put teeth into the requirement, the amendment provided that the federal government would reduce the city's fiscal 1996 federal payment by an amount equal to any deficit.

"The District government is in a precarious financial situation and has lost its credibility with this Congress, so I feel it necessary, in order to get sufficient support for this bill, to enter into an agreement," said Dixon, who had consistently resisted attempts by members to cut the city's spending. Democrat Eleanor Holmes Norton, the delegate for the District, praised Dixon for fighting to allow the city to make its own budget decisions. "He has given up more on the battlefield than he should have had to give, but he has saved the federal payment," she said.

In other action on the bill, the House approved, 251-176, an amendment by Joe L. Barton, R-Texas, to prohibit the city from using any funds to implement the so-called domestic partners law. Members defeated by voice vote a Dixon amendment that would have allowed the city to carry out the domestic partners law using only its own funds. *(Vote 321, p. 94-H)*

Senate Action

The Senate Appropriations Committee on July 14 approved its version of the spending bill (S Rept 103-313) by a vote of 27-2. The measure directed the city to cut $75 million from its budget, compared with $150 million in the House bill. But the Senate bill included no enforcement mechanism.

The committee bill provided $700 million in federal funds, $20 million less than the House bill and the same as the District got in fiscal 1994. Of the total, $52.1 million was to go toward Congress' annual contribution to the city's pension fund for District retirees.

Herb Kohl, D-Wis., chairman of the Senate District of Columbia Appropriations Subcommittee, said freezing the

funds at the fiscal 1994 level was not as severe as it appeared. He said the city could eliminate 652 full-time District employees to account for the difference in funding.

The bill recommended eliminating the D.C. School of Law, leaving money in the budget to allow District students attending the school to receive support to study at other law schools. The Senate bill retained the House-passed language prohibiting the District from implementing its domestic partners policy.

The Senate D.C. Appropriations Subcommittee did not hold a separate markup of the bill.

Senate Floor

The Senate on July 21 approved the D.C. spending bill by a vote of 68-32. *(Vote 217, p. 37-S)*

The Senate gave voice vote approval to an amendment offered by Kohl for Phil Gramm, R-Texas, aimed at reducing the number of city employees by an amount proportional to the 252,000 federal jobs Vice President Al Gore called for eliminating in his "reinventing government" initiative. The amendment, which set ceilings on full-time jobs or their equivalents, was expected to eliminate 3,559 such jobs over five years.

Kohl said the budget cuts were not meant as an attack on the law that gave the city's government some autonomy. He said they paralleled other cuts made throughout the federal budget. In addition, Kohl said that the bill recommended that public safety, health, education and revenue-raising agencies be exempt from the reductions.

Conrad Burns of Montana, ranking Republican on the D.C. Appropriations Subcommittee, said he was not convinced that the Senate's action to reduce the federal payment would rein in the city's spending. But he added that he was more optimistic about efforts to direct the city to cut its own budget.

During the debate, senators wrangled over the same points that were at issue in the House: how much the federal government should intervene in the affairs of the city in the face of its serious financial problems.

Conference/Final Action

After two weeks of negotiations, House and Senate conferees agreed Aug. 4 to appropriate $712 million in federal funds for the District in fiscal 1995, down from the $720 million requested by the House and up from the Senate bill's recommendation of $700 million (H Rept 103-671). The total comprised a $660 million payment to compensate the city for the costs of hosting the federal government and a $52 million contribution to the city's retirement fund.

The final bill also approved an overall city budget of $3.5 billion for fiscal 1995.

Conferees came close to the House position on spending cuts, requiring the District to slice $140 million from its fiscal 1995 budget. In addition, they required that 20 percent of the fiscal 1996 federal payment to the District be escrowed until two separate independent audits certified that the city had reduced its fiscal 1995 budget by $140 million and that it had not incurred a deficit. If the District failed to meet those criteria, it had to pay the Treasury the difference — the amount by which the $140 million cut was not made plus the overspending — with the money to be taken from the escrowed amount and from other funds.

The conferees agreed to require the city to cut 2,000 full-time positions, or their equivalent, in fiscal 1995. Senate negotiators expressed some concern that Gramm, who had

proposed the five-year cut of 3,559 positions, would disapprove of the compromise, but they voted 5-0 to accept it. Kohl said the agreement should achieve Gramm's goals in the near term.

Senate Slows Final Action

The House adopted the conference report by voice vote Aug. 8, despite an earlier vote instructing negotiators to keep the House's cuts intact. Walsh offered that motion July 28, and House members approved it, 316-101. Walsh said after the conference that he thought the House would accept the compromise because there was not much of a net loss from the House bill. *(Vote 358, p. 108-H)*

The Senate, however, did not clear the measure until Sept. 30.

Senators did agree to the conference report Sept. 21 by a vote of 71-27. *(Vote 302, p. 52-S)*

But Gramm immediately seized on the next step in the path to final approval — taking up conflicting provisions from the House and Senate bills that conferees had been

unable to resolve. Gramm made it clear he planned to use that step to force votes on a series of amendments that Republicans had been blocked from offering when the Senate considered the conference report on the omnibus crime bill in August. The amendments included proposals to cut social spending and impose mandatory minimum sentences for crimes involving the use of a firearm. *(Crime bill, p. 273)*

When the Senate picked up the spending bill again Sept. 28, Kohl pleaded with members not to hold up much-needed funds for the District. But by then, other senators had lined up to join in the amendment fest.

Pete V. Domenici, R-N.M., and David L. Boren, D-Okla., tried to add a congressional reform amendment to the spending bill Sept. 28. The amendment would have put in place the recommendations of the Joint Committee on the Organization of Congress. Boren had served as chairman of the committee, and Domenici was the vice chairman. The amendment proposed a series of major institutional changes in Congress, including a 50 percent reduction in the number of Senate subcommittees, a two-year budget cycle and a 12 percent cut in congressional staff. *(Congressional reform, p. 27)*

But Appropriations Committee Chairman Robert C. Byrd, D-W.Va., said the amendment faced a procedural point of order because it had not been considered by the Budget Committee. On Sept. 29, by a vote of 58-41, supporters fell two votes short of the 60 needed to waive the point of order. *(Vote 313, p. 54-S)*

William S. Cohen, R-Maine, offered an amendment to combat unnecessary health care costs by expanding prosecutors' ability to crack down on abuse and fraud in health care programs. Cohen defended his move to add the amendment, even if it meant slowing passage of the District bill. "We can stand here and wait and raise points of order and say [the amendment] does not belong here," he said. "In the meantime, the losers are the American taxpayers." The Senate agreed by voice vote Sept. 30 to remove Cohen's amendment from the bill.

Dave Durenberger, R-Minn., offered an amendment to extend a demonstration program that provided supplemental benefits to Medicare recipients in 15 states. It was removed by voice vote Sept. 30.

Howard M. Metzenbaum, D-Ohio, then introduced an amendment to partially lift the special antitrust exemption enjoyed by owners of baseball franchises to allow players to sue if baseball owners unilaterally imposed a salary cap. But after three hours of debate, Metzenbaum withdrew the amendment, saying he realized that even if it could get through the Senate, there was no chance of getting it through the House before the end of the session. *(Baseball, p. 182)*

Gramm's amendment finally fell Sept. 30, when congressional leaders worked out a deal to strip all unrelated amendments from the bill and accept en bloc the provisions that remained in disagreement with the House. The move was agreed to by voice vote, clearing the bill. ∎

No Sparks Over Energy, Water Funds

The Senate on Aug. 11 cleared a $20.5 billion energy and water development spending bill (HR 4506) that reduced funding for civilian and military nuclear research and provided no additional funds to shut down the superconducting super collider.

Roughly three-quarters of the money in the bill — $15.9 billion — went to the Energy Department for research and development programs, and for the massive task of cleaning up mothballed nuclear weapons production facilities. The bill also contained money for the Army Corps of Engineers, which administered more than 1,000 water projects, touching nearly every congressional district.

Action on the bill ignited none of the fireworks that had characterized past debates, such as the 1993 fight over killing the superconducting super collider. *(1993 Almanac, p. 589)*

President Clinton signed the bill Aug. 26 (PL 103-316).

The fiscal 1995 energy and water bill provided about $1.3 billion less than the amount appropriated for fiscal 1994. Most of the difference was the result of a decision to provide no new funds to close down the superconducting super collider, the elaborate $11 billion physics experiment that Congress had terminated the previous October.

The Clinton administration had requested $180 million in fiscal 1995 to continue the shutdown. That would have been in addition to $640 million provided the previous year. But appropriators decided to put off allocating any additional funds until the Energy Department, which administered the atom-smasher program, and the state of Texas completed negotiations to determine ownership and the ultimate fate of the site.

The bill provided for the termination of the Advanced Liquid Metal Reactor, a controversial nuclear power reactor designed to use weapons-grade plutonium as fuel.

House and Senate lawmakers had been split over the fate of the liquid metal reactor for the preceding two years. In 1993, Senate conferees prevailed upon their House counterparts to continue funding the research project, which had a powerful backer in Senate Energy and Water Development Appropriations Subcommittee Chairman J. Bennett Johnston, D-La. Supporters said the project presented the best long-term solution to the disposal of the hundreds of tons of plutonium contained in nuclear warheads. They also argued that it would cost as much to terminate the project as it would to complete the research. Opponents argued that the reactor would undercut U.S. non-proliferation efforts by using weapons-grade plutonium as a civilian energy source.

The bill included funds to design a new experimental fusion reactor, known as Tokamak, in Princeton, N.J. But, bowing to Bennett's concern that Congress not pour money into the project until it had firm backing, appropriators agreed not to allocate funds for construction until Congress had authorized the project.

BOXSCORE

Fiscal 1995 Energy and Water Appropriations — HR 4506. The $20.5 billion bill funded most Energy Department programs and the Army Corps of Engineers.

Reports: H Rept 103-533, S Rept 103-291; conference report, H Rept 103-672.

KEY ACTION

June 14 — House passed HR 4506, 393-29.

June 30 — Senate passed HR 4506, amended, 91-8.

Aug. 10 — House adopted conference report, 393-34.

Aug. 11 — Senate cleared bill by voice vote.

Aug. 26 — President signed HR 4506 — PL 103-316.

Highlights of the Bill

● **Energy Department.** The $15.9 billion in the bill for Energy Department programs was roughly $1 billion less than the fiscal 1994 funding level.

Of that amount, $3.3 billion was for energy research and development programs — including solar energy ($289 million), fusion energy ($373 million), and basic energy sciences ($747 million). Funding for nuclear power was reduced to $293 million from $341 million in fiscal 1994.

Roughly a third of the Energy Department funds — $5.1 billion — went for the environmental cleanup work that was under way at virtually every Energy Department facility once involved in nuclear weapons production. Funding for this program had grown rapidly in recent years, but budget constraints slowed the climb in fiscal 1995; appropriators provided $89 million less than in the previous year.

The bill provided $1.5 billion for research, development and testing of nuclear weapons, programs that were the responsibility of the Energy Department. Of that amount, $203 million was appropriated for weapons testing, compared with $403 million the previous year. The amount was considered sufficient to preserve the option of conducting underground nuclear tests; Clinton had instituted a moratorium on actual testing.

The bill also provided $152.4 million to fund a program to ensure the performance and reliability of U.S. nuclear weapons in the absence of tests.

● **Corps of Engineers.** The Army Corps of Engineers received $3.4 billion, $568 million less than in fiscal 1994.

The corps was charged with ensuring the navigability of the nation's water ways, as well as enhancing flood control and environmental restoration through water construction and maintenance projects. The bill funded the planning or construction of 528 water resource projects and maintenance work at hundreds of completed sites. It included $328 million for dredging and levee construction in Midwestern states that were regularly hit by flooding from the Mississippi River and its tributaries.

● **Land reclamation.** The bill contained $881 million for the Interior Department's Bureau of Reclamation, which was charged with managing water resources in the Western states.

● **Independent agencies.** Finally, the bill contained $470 million for nine independent agencies, including the Tennessee Valley Authority ($143 million), the Nuclear Regulatory Commission ($22 million) and the Appalachian Regional Commission ($282 million).

House Committee

The House Appropriations Committee approved a $20.4 billion version of the bill by voice vote May 26 (H Rept 103-533). The Energy and Water Development Subcommittee had

approved the measure in closed session May 23.

During the full committee markup, Energy and Water Subcommittee Chairman Tom Bevill, D-Ala., complained about the $1.3 billion reduction his subcommittee had been ordered to make. The amount available to each subcommittee was set by the subcommittee chairmen, known collectively as the cardinals. Bevill said that he was forced to work with the "biggest cuts in the history of this bill." Ranking member John T. Myers, R-Ind., used stronger language: "Between the White House, OMB [the Office of Management and Budget] and the cardinals, they just whacked the hell out of us."

The bill allocated no money for the supercollider shutdown, pending an agreement between the Energy Department and the state of Texas.

Related high-energy physics research under way at the nation's three major particle accelerators was to receive $647 million.

The bill contained $70.5 million to shut down the Advanced Liquid Metal Reactor. Myers expressed dismay over the project's termination, arguing that the nation would now be developing only one new type of nuclear reactor — the light water reactor.

The bill also included close to $3.5 billion for the Army Corps of Engineers, almost $140 million more than Clinton requested, but about $500 million less than the fiscal 1994 spending levels. The bill funded 19 new projects that the administration did not request.

House Floor

The House took the measure up June 14 and passed it overwhelmingly, 393-29, after rejecting efforts to cut money from fusion and nuclear energy research. *(Vote 235, p. 70-H)*

● **Tokamak reactor.** Most of the large science projects in the bill did not come under serious attack. But critics challenged funding for the $67 million Tokamak reactor.

The project was intended to provide scientists with a research tool as a step toward development of a commercially successful fusion plant by the middle of the next century. Some scientists contended that fusion would offer an energy source that was more economical and environmentally sound than that provided by traditional nuclear fission reactors.

Dick Swett, D-N.H., who offered an amendment to delete all funding for the project, argued that Tokamak was not the path to an efficient commercial fusion reactor. "It would cost more to operate than a fission plant and create more radioactive waste," he said.

But Dean A. Gallo, R-N.J., countered that fusion represented the greatest potential for a long-term energy source for the world and that Tokamak would be the cornerstone of U.S. efforts to develop a fusion reactor. House members agreed, rejecting Swett's amendment by voice vote.

● **Helium reactor.** The House also rejected an attempt by Leslie L. Byrne, D-Va., to eliminate $12 million for development of the Gas Turbine-Modular Helium Reactor.

Project advocates said that once the reactor was built early in the next century, it would provide a safe, economical and efficient source of nuclear energy. George J. Hochbrueckner, D-N.Y., told the House on June 14 that the project, which would run on weapons grade plutonium, promised to be the best way to dispose of an estimated 50 tons of plutonium that would be accumulated as the United States and Russia shrank their nuclear arsenals.

But the project had serious opposition both in and out of Congress. Clinton had included no money for it in his fiscal 1995 budget request, and Energy Secretary Hazel R. O'Leary

wrote to Congress June 13 urging lawmakers not to finance the reactor.

The National Academy of Sciences had recommended terminating the reactor. In 1993, the Senate voted to kill the project but bowed to House pressure in conference and agreed to allocate $12 million to continue research.

Byrne said the government would have to spend an estimated $5.3 billion to build a prototype helium reactor "that might — might — produce an economically competitive plant sometime in the 21st century."

Much of the work on the reactor was being done by General Atomics, a government contractor in California Democrat Lynn Schenk's San Diego district. During the House debate, four San Diego area members — Schenk and Republicans Randy "Duke" Cunningham, Ron Packard and Duncan Hunter — rose to defend the reactor. Later, Schenk said that termination of the project would cost her district more than 100 jobs.

Vic Fazio, D-Calif., said Byrne's criticisms were based on an earlier design. "The gas reactor we are dealing with today produces 70 percent more power . . . [and] is 25 percent more efficient than the earlier system," Fazio said.

These arguments won the day; Byrne's amendment to delete money for the reactor was rejected, 188-241. *(Vote 234, p. 70-H)*

Senate Committee

The Senate Appropriations Committee approved a $20.5 billion version of the spending bill (S Rept 103-291) June 23 by a vote of 26-0. The Energy and Water Development Subcommittee had approved it by voice vote earlier that day.

Senate appropriators included $35.7 million to continue the Advanced Liquid Metal Reactor. Johnston and other advocates argued that the project was an integral part of the nation's nuclear future and that it would cost almost as much to terminate it as to continue development. The administration argued that the reactor could pose a proliferation threat because the reprocessed plutonium used as fuel could also be used to make nuclear weapons.

While they allocated $363 million for fusion research, Senate appropriators provided none of the $45 million that the House-passed bill had earmarked for construction of the Tokamak reactor.

At the markup, Johnston said he would support fusion in general and the Tokamak project in particular if he was assured of long-term administration support. Johnston said the termination of the supercollider made him wary of spending on big-science projects that did not have the total backing of Congress and the White House.

The Senate bill provided $130 million more for Energy Department programs than its House counterpart. The bill contained $44.5 million less than the House bill to clean up nuclear waste sites, but it proposed to increase the civilian nuclear waste disposal program by $98 million to $402.8 million.

Water projects were slightly reduced under the Senate bill. The measure contained $3.4 billion for the Army Corps of Engineers, $62 million less than the House bill. The bill provided for 11 new construction starts, fewer than the 19 new starts in the House version.

Senate Floor

The Senate passed the bill June 30 by a vote of 91-8, after narrowly agreeing to preserve the Advanced Liquid Metal Reactor. *(Vote 178, p. 30-S)*

Senators tabled, or killed, an amendment to terminate the

reactor; the vote was 52-46. That left $35.7 million for the project in the bill and set up a conference confrontation with the House. *(Vote 175, p. 30-S)*

John Kerry, D-Mass., led the fight to kill the reactor, as he had the previous year. Voicing many of the same arguments made by House opponents, Kerry argued that plutonium would be too dangerous as a civilian energy source and that the project would undercut U.S. nonproliferation efforts. But Johnston prevailed.

By 53-45, the Senate tabled an amendment offered by Tom Harkin, D-Iowa, that would have provided an additional $33 million for solar and other renewable energy research. Harkin proposed to offset the increase by cutting the same amount from nuclear weapons testing and stockpile maintenance.

Harkin said that solar energy, wind and other renewables were the most promising future energy sources because they were environmentally clean. But opponents, including Johnston and Armed Services Committee Chairman Sam Nunn, D-Ga., argued that further cuts in nuclear weapons spending would endanger the safety of the nuclear stockpile. *(Vote 176, p. 30-S)*

A compromise amendment, offered by Paul Wellstone, D-Minn., adding $14 million for solar energy and wind research later was approved by voice vote. Wellstone's language did not specify what spending would be cut to provide the money. "We'll have to find it, and we'll do so," Johnston said.

The Senate agreed, 69-30, to an amendment by Frank R. Lautenberg, D-N.J., to restore the $45 million in construction money for the Tokamak fusion project but made the spending contingent on a separate congressional authorization. *(Vote 177, p. 30-S)*

Conference/Final Action

House and Senate negotiators agreed to a compromise $20.5 billion energy and water spending bill Aug. 4 (H Rept 103-672), after Senate conferees reluctantly agreed to terminate the Advanced Liquid Metal Reactor and struck a compromise on the Tokamak project.

That paved the way for both chambers to approve the conference report without much fanfare. The House agreed to the report, 393-34 on Aug. 10. The Senate cleared the bill by voice vote the next day. *(Vote 385, p. 116-H)*

Decisions made by the conferees included:

● **Liquid reactor.** Johnston searched in vain for some way to save the liquid metal reactor project. "Does anyone think there's a chance the House will support this?" he asked House negotiators. Johnston's question met with silence.

"All we're going to do is kill our bill," said House Subcommittee Chairman Bevill earlier. "It's time to move on to something else, because the House is not going to change its mind."

In the end, Johnston agreed to a House proposal to provide $84 million to terminate the project with instructions to maximize the research that already had been done. "This is not the last word on this matter," Johnston said, vowing to resurrect the issue in the next Congress.

● **Super collider.** Conferees had far less difficulty finding common ground on a plan to turn over $65 million in previously appropriated funds to transform a linear accelerator, built as part of the super collider, into a cancer treatment center to be administered by Southwest Texas State University.

In July, the Energy Department had agreed to allot Texas $145 million to compensate the state for the loss of the super collider project. The bill endorsed the additional $65 million payment to Texas to convert the accelerator.

While congressional ratification of the settlement was not necessary, the Senate had added the language to its version of the bill, and House conferees agreed to the earmark, although Myers proposed delaying the funding until the project could be authorized.

● **Tokamak reactor.** The negotiators also resolved differences over funding for the Tokamak fusion project. The House had voted to provide $21 million for design and $45 million for construction of the reactor. The Senate bill called for construction money to be withheld until the project was authorized by Congress.

In conference, Johnston repeated his concern that Tokamak eventually would be killed by budget cutters unless both Congress and the Clinton administration were firmly committed to the project. As a result, he would not allow funding for construction of the project until it was formally authorized.

Gallo, who had led the fight in the House to save the reactor, agreed to delay the construction funding. But the New Jersey Republican asked that some of the construction money allocated in the House bill be redirected to increase the funding to design Tokamak. Johnston agreed, and conferees voted to double, to $42 million, the funds provided to design, but not build, the Tokamak project. ■

Foreign Aid Bill Clears Easily

For the third year in a row, the foreign aid appropriations bill — long considered one of the least popular measures lawmakers had to tackle each year — encountered minimal opposition. The $13.8 billion fiscal 1995 bill (HR 4426) endorsed the status quo in most programs, which enabled skittish lawmakers to justify a vote for sending aid abroad in an election year. The House passed the measure, 341-85, on Aug. 4, and the Senate cleared it Aug. 10, by a vote of 88-12. President Clinton signed the measure into law Aug. 23 (PL 103-306).

The measure included two supplemental appropriations of fiscal 1994 funds in response to a last-minute administration request to provide up to $220 million in debt relief for Jordan, which had just agreed to cease hostilities with Israel, and $50 million in emergency aid for refugees from a bloody tribal conflict in Rwanda.

As in previous years, much of the fiscal 1995 funding was reserved for two countries: The bill earmarked $3 billion for Israel and $2.1 billion for Egypt.

The measure provided $850 million for the former Soviet republics — just $50 million less than than Clinton had requested but a significant reduction from the $2.5 billion in aid Congress voted in fiscal 1994. It required that Russia abide by agreements to remove its forces from the Baltic nations in order to get the U.S. aid. The president could waive the provision if he determined it was in the national security interest.

The bill barred aid to countries that violated U.N. Security Council sanctions against Serbia and Montenegro. The provision was identical to statutory prohibitions on aid to countries that evaded U.N. sanctions against Iraq.

It explicitly barred the administration from using aid appropriated under the bill for North Korea, though existing provisions already barred such assistance. And the legislation tightened conditions on aid to the Palestine Liberation Organization (PLO).

The legislation included $365 million in loans to Turkey and $255 million to Greece — continuing a longstanding practice of providing $7 in military aid to Greece for each $10 provided to Turkey. But it also imposed new restrictions on the loans to the two NATO allies.

The bill included a provision barring sales of light arms to Indonesia until the secretary of State reported that the Indonesian government had made "significant progress" in eliminating human rights abuses by security forces in East Timor. But sales of major weapons were not affected. And while the bill prohibited the use of U.S. aid to underwrite Pentagon training for Indonesian officers, Jakarta could still pay for the training itself.

The bill repealed several longstanding restrictions on U.S. aid to Vietnam, though it stopped short of removing all statutory obstacles to providing such aid.

Multilateral Aid Is Big Winner

International financial institutions, such as the World Bank and International Monetary Fund (IMF), were the big winners

---

BOXSCORE

Fiscal 1995 Foreign Operations Appropriations — HR 4426. The bill provided $13.8 billion for bilateral and multilateral foreign aid programs.

Reports: H Rept 103-524, S Rept 103-287; conference report H Rept 103-633.

KEY ACTION

May 25 — House passed HR 4426, 337-87.

July 15 — Senate passed HR 4426, amended, 84-9.

Aug. 4 — House adopted the conference report, 341-85.

Aug. 10 — Senate cleared the bill, 88-12.

Aug. 23 — President signed the bill — PL 103-306.

---

in the bill. The previous year, Congress had slashed the administration's $2 billion request for those institutions by about $450 million. But the fiscal 1995 bill restored most of the reduction, providing $1.9 billion for the international banks; the administration had requested $2.1 billion.

The final bill included $25 million — the Senate-approved level — for the IMF's Enhanced Structural Adjustment Facility, a program of debt relief for poor countries. The administration had requested $100 million, but the House had not included money for the program in its bill.

The bill continued existing conditions on funding for the United Nations Population Fund, which had been criticized for operating in China, where the government carried out a coercive population control policy. The legislation reduced the administration's $60 million request for the fund by $10 million. But it did not include a House-passed provision that would have cut another $10 million from the request unless the U.N. agency shut down its China operations.

Obey Blasts Lobbying

While the measure had a smooth path in both chambers, the process was not entirely free of controversy. House Appropriations Committee Chairman David R. Obey, D-Wis., complained about the hardball lobbying tactics employed by advocates for foreign governments — and the tendency of some lawmakers to accede to their demands. "There is no party entitled to money under this bill," Obey said.

Obey did not specifically criticize any countries or their U.S. supporters, but the conference committee had skirmished for hours over Republican-backed earmarks for several former Soviet republics.

In the Senate, Mark O. Hatfield, Ore., the ranking Republican on the Appropriations Committee, declined to sign the conference report. Hatfield apparently wanted to signal his dissatisfaction with the administration's failure to consult Republicans before requesting the supplemental appropriations. Republicans on the Foreign Operations Subcommittee followed Hatfield's lead and did not sign the report.

Background

The congressional debate on foreign aid had taken place mostly on the margins in recent years because the bulk of the funding in the bill had been reserved for the same handful of programs: aid to the Middle East and former Soviet republics, support for international financial institutions and operating expenses for agencies such as the Peace Corps.

The bill's overall spending level had fallen significantly over 10 years, and it was difficult to reduce spending further without cutting politically sacrosanct programs such as aid to Israel and Egypt. The report accompanying the fiscal 1995 legislation noted that funding had declined by 24 percent

Foreign Aid Spending

(in thousands of dollars)

	Fiscal 1995 Clinton Request	House Bill	Senate Bill	Final Bill
Multilateral Aid				
World Bank				
Paid-in capital	$ 23,289	$ 23,009	$ 23,009	$ 23,009
Global Environment Facility	100,000	88,800	98,800	90,000
Limitation on callable capital	*(752,959)*	*(743,924)*	*(743,924)*	*(743,924)*
International Development Association	1,250,000	1,235,000	1,207,750	1,235,000
International Finance Corporation	88,743	68,743	68,743	68,743
Inter-American Development Bank	50,240	49,640	49,640	49,640
Limitation on callable capital	*(1,614,586)*	*(1,594,568)*	*(1,594,568)*	*(1,594,568)*
Enterprise for the Americas	100,000	75,000	75,000	75,000
Asian Development Fund	170,000	167,960	167,960	167,960
African Development Fund/Bank	125,871	124,362	124,362	124,362
European Development Bank	70,021	69,180	69,180	69,180
International Monetary Fund	100,000	—	25,000	25,000
Other multilateral banks	23,813	—	—	—
State Department international programs	403,000	366,000	382,000	374,000
TOTAL, multilateral aid	**$ 2,504,977**	**$ 2,267,695**	**$ 2,291,445**	**$ 2,301,895**
Bilateral Aid				
Agency for International Development (AID)				
Development assistance	811,000	811,000	882,000	853,000
Sub-Saharan Africa development aid	782,700	790,000	802,000	802,000
International disaster aid	169,998	169,998	169,998	169,998
AID operating expenses	566,065	556,618	556,918	556,618
Debt restructuring	7,000	7,000	7,000	7,000
Economic Support Fund	2,414,502	2,339,000	2,359,200	2,349,000
Assistance for Eastern Europe	380,000	360,000	359,000	359,000
Assistance for ex-Soviets	900,000	875,500	839,000	850,000
Other	542,820	542,420	537,820	542,420
Subtotal, AID	**$ 6,574,085**	**$ 6,451,536**	**$ 6,512,936**	**$ 6,489,036**
State Department				
International narcotics control	152,400	115,000	100,000	105,000
Migration and refugee aid	632,888	670,688	671,000	671,000
Anti-terrorism assistance	15,244	15,244	15,244	15,244
Other	60,000	72,000	60,000	66,000
Subtotal, State Department	**$ 860,532**	**$ 872,932**	**$ 846,244**	**$ 857,244**
Peace Corps	225,411	219,745	221,745	219,745
Other	47,865	42,199	44,199	42,199
TOTAL, bilateral aid	**$ 7,707,893**	**$ 7,592,078**	**$ 7,628,790**	**$ 7,613,890**
Bilateral Military Aid (appropriated to the president)				
Foreign military financing (grants)	3,162,458	3,149,279	3,151,279	3,151,279
Foreign military (loans)	*(770,000)*	*(619,650)*	*(619,650)*	*(619,650)*
Loan subsidy	59,598	47,917	47,917	47,917
International military education and training	25,500	25,500	25,500	25,500
Special defense acquisition fund *(offsetting collections)*	−282,000	−282,000	−282,000	−282,000
Other	121,300	87,000	87,000	87,000
TOTAL, military aid	**$ 3,086,856**	**$ 3,027,696**	**$ 3,029,696**	**$ 3,029,696**
Export Assistance				
Export-Import Bank	795,445	787,547	782,123	782,123
Export assistance *(loan limitation)*	*(17,637,000)*	*(19,000,000)*	*(—)*	*(—)*
Trade and development	44,986	44,986	44,986	44,986
Overseas Private Investment Corp. *(loan levels)*	*(501,808)*	*(501,808)*	*(505,385)*	*(501,808)*
Subsidy/offsets	−115,200	−104,002	−92,354	−93,354
GRAND TOTAL	**$ 14,074,957**	**$ 13,616,000**	**$ 13,684,686**	**$ 13,828,236**

NOTE: *Numbers may not add due to rounding.*

SOURCE: House Appropriations Committee

since 1985 — the year Obey took over the subcommittee.

Aid to NATO allies in Europe had been a prominent target. A decade before, the bill had included $1.7 billion in military assistance for the NATO base rights countries: Spain, Portugal, Greece and Turkey. In fiscal 1995, only Greece and Turkey were to receive any aid. The $620 million in military loans for the two countries required a direct appropriation of just $48 million.

The fiscal 1994 foreign aid bill (PL 103-87) provided a total of $14.6 billion. But $1.6 billion of that amount was aid to the former Soviet republics that was drawn from unspent fiscal 1993 funds for foreign assistance and defense programs. The original overall appropriation was later reduced to $14.3 billion by recissions. *(1993 Almanac, p. 603)*

House Subcommittee Action

The House Appropriations Subcommittee on Foreign Operations on May 18 easily approved a $13.6 billion fiscal 1995 foreign aid bill. The panel acted by voice vote.

Obey, who also chaired the subcommittee, had crafted a bill with bipartisan backing that funded most of the president's foreign policy initiatives.

For the most part, the subcommittee approved the big-ticket items in the bill with minimal debate.

The measure fully funded the administration's request for $900 million for Russia and the other former Soviet republics and assumed that $3 billion in aid would be provided to Israel and $2.1 billion to Egypt.

● **Greece, Turkey.** The subcommittee spent much of the markup sparring over aid to Turkey and Greece. Obey proposed treating the bitter adversaries equivalently. With criticism of Turkey's human rights record mounting, he recommended withholding 25 percent of U.S. military loans to Turkey until the president reported to Congress on allegations of abuses by that country's military forces. He proposed withholding 25 percent of the military loans for Greece until the president reported on allegations that that country had repeatedly contravened the U.N. embargo against Serbia.

But the formula drew opposition from John Edward Porter, R-Ill., who sharply denounced the tactics adopted by Turkey in its counter-insurgency campaign against Kurdish separatists. Contending that 11,000 people had been killed since 1984 in southeast Turkey, Porter asked, "Who killed them? They were killed by the Turkish government."

Porter, a longtime supporter of Greece, demanded that the entire military aid package for Turkey be subject to conditions. But he faced staunch opposition from Charles W. Wilson, D-Texas, an advocate for Turkey who had squared off against Porter on similar issues in the past. With Obey strongly defending his carefully calibrated compromise, Porter refrained from offering the amendment.

In addition to the reporting requirement, the subcommittee retained the option of cutting off one-quarter of the military aid to either country. Equally significant, the bill continued the recent trend of reducing military assistance to both NATO allies. It cut $88 million from the administration's request for Turkey and $62 million from the request for Greece.

● **International financial institutions.** The subcommittee recommended $1.9 billion for the World Bank, the IMF and other international financial institutions — $190 million less than the administration had requested. More than half the reduction came by eliminating a proposed $100 million

contribution to the IMF's Enhanced Structural Adjustment Facility.

The measure included $69 million for the European Bank for Reconstruction and Development (EBRD), created in 1990 to aid emerging democracies in Central and Eastern Europe. Outraged over reports of lavish spending by EBRD officials, Congress had refused to provide funding for the bank in fiscal 1994. But Obey said that under pressure from Congress, the bank had cleaned up its act and replaced the officials responsible for the abuses. "This is an instance when pulling somebody's chain worked," he said.

The bill allocated $99 million for the Global Environment Facility, a World Bank program designed to reduce global warming and promote biological diversity. That amount was three times the $30 million appropriated in fiscal 1994.

The subcommittee also funded the administration's $450 million request for family planning programs, another account repeatedly identified as a priority by senior officials. That represented a $58 million increase over the appropriated level in fiscal 1994.

The panel approved the administration's $60 million request for the U.N. Population Fund in fiscal 1995. But, under a complicated formula, it fenced off $20 million pending a decision by the agency to pull out of China. The remaining $40 million was to be reduced by any amount the population fund budgeted for its China operation in 1995 in excess of $7 million. And the bill prohibited the agency from spending any U.S. funds in China.

Porter, a supporter of abortion rights, argued that the restrictions were too arduous. He offered an amendment to eliminate the provision linking $20 million of the funds to the agency's withdrawal from China. But the subcommittee backed Obey's original recommendation. In its only roll call vote, the panel defeated Porter's amendment 3-8.

● **Other.** The bill included $78 million for the administration's request to support a host of assistance programs on the West Bank and Gaza Strip. That was part of a five-year, $500 million package of U.S. aid and loans intended to support infrastructure development and private enterprise in those areas.

The subcommittee bill provided $360 million for countries in Eastern Europe, a reduction from the $390 million appropriated in fiscal 1994.

Sub-Saharan countries were slated to receive a modest $6 million increase over the $784 million provided in fiscal 1994.

As in past years, the bill bore Obey's strong imprint. The legislation cut $52 million from the administration's $152 million request for international anti-narcotics activities — a program that the Wisconsin Democrat disparaged. "Virtually every dime in this account is wasted," Obey said. "I'm embarrassed to be providing any money to this program."

And for the second consecutive year, the panel's bill was free of earmarks — requirements that the administration provide a minimum level of funding for a program.

As approved by the subcommittee, the bill also expanded the conditions under which the administration could provide weapons to the Muslim-led government forces in Bosnia-Herzegovina. The panel, by voice vote, accepted an amendment by Robert L. Livingston of Louisiana, the subcommittee's ranking Republican, authorizing the president to provide military equipment to Bosnia even if the United Nations did not lift its arms embargo against the country.

It provided about $20 million in aid for the International Fund for Ireland. News reports painted the program as a boondoggle, but it had strong support from influential Irish-American lawmakers.

The bill also retained a longstanding provision requiring the administration to transfer Israel's $3 billion in military and economic aid by Oct. 31, or within 30 days after enactment of the bill. The provision enabled Israel to reap interest income by investing the money in securities. No other country was accorded that benefit.

House Committee

The full Appropriations Committee approved the bill by voice vote May 23 (H Rept 103-524). Debate in the committee was dominated by concerns over U.S. policy toward the two-year-old war in Bosnia-Herzegovina. *(Bosnia, p. 446)*

Steny H. Hoyer, D-Md., roiled the otherwise uneventful markup by offering an amendment to bar the use of funds in the bill to enforce the international arms embargo against Bosnia's Muslim-led government forces. Hoyer expressed the widely shared view that the embargo had only worked to the benefit of the better-armed Bosnian Serbs. "We have a moral responsibility to allow those people to defend themselves and their homes and their families and their children," he said.

But Obey and Defense Appropriations Subcommittee Chairman John P. Murtha, D-Pa., joined forces to oppose the amendment. Murtha, who recently had visited Bosnia, urged the committee not to "interfere with words that may encourage one side or the other."

Obey argued that there was no money in the bill to enforce the embargo and that the defense authorization bill was a more appropriate vehicle for such amendments. Hoyer's amendment was narrowly defeated, 18-22.

The panel also rejected by voice vote an amendment by Sonny Callahan, R-Ala., to strip most aid for Russia from the bill.

Many of the amendments proposed in committee involved relatively small sums or sought mostly symbolic changes in the report accompanying the bill.

The committee report on the bill touched only lightly on Clinton's foreign policy and on issues relating to specific countries. But it harshly criticized the administration for continuing to provide U.S. training for Indonesia's military officers. Congress had terminated military training assistance to Indonesia in 1992 because of a massacre by Indonesian security forces a year earlier on the island of East Timor. But the administration had allowed Indonesia to continue receiving the training by paying for it, itself. *(1992 Almanac, p. 622)*

"The committee is outraged therefore that the new administration, despite its vocal embrace of human rights, decided to provide the same training to the Indonesian military for a fee," the report said. "It was and is the intent of Congress to prohibit United States military training for Indonesia."

House Floor

The House passed the $13.8 billion foreign aid bill May 25 by a vote of 337-87. Democrats voted for the legislation 225-25, while Republicans backed it 112-61. *(Vote 208, p. 62-H)*

Despite anger over the Aldrich Ames spy scandal, the House declined to punish Russia by cutting U.S. aid. Ames had pleaded guilty in May to selling top-secret information to the Soviet Union and subsequently to Russia from 1995 until his arrest in February. However, the House rejected an amendment offered by Sonny Callahan, R-Ala., to cut $348 million from the administration's $390 million aid proposal for Russia. Only $42 million in humanitarian aid would have been exempted under the amendment. *(Ames case, p. 463; Russian aid, p. 466)*

The House rejected Callahan's amendment, 144-286. A similar amendment by Callahan in 1993 had been defeated by almost the same margin, 140-289. *(Vote 205, p. 62-H)*

With some last-minute maneuvering, Callahan did manage to trim about $25 million in aid for Russia and the other former republics, bringing the total to $875 billion. In a complicated shift of funds, the action — approved by voice vote — restored about $15 million that had been cut from the State Department's anti-narcotics program. That brought funding for the drug-fighting program to $115 million, which still was $37 million less than the administration's request.

The generally amicable floor debate on the bill turned bitter when Dan Burton, R-Ind., offered an amendment to freeze fiscal 1995 aid to the new government of South Africa at fiscal 1994 levels — about $80 million. Although the bill contained no spending mandates, known as earmarks, for South Africa aid, the administration was planning to provide $206 million in aid and credits in fiscal 1995.

Burton protested that several members of President Nelson Mandela's Cabinet were communists. He urged the administration to expand trade and investment in South Africa rather than increase direct assistance.

Members of the Congressional Black Caucus and other lawmakers from both parties denounced the proposal, which was defeated 103-321. Only four Democrats joined 99 Republicans in supporting Burton's amendment. *(Vote 206, p. 62-H)*

The House also rejected a bid by Anthony C. Beilenson, D-Calif., to add $100 million for population programs to the $450 million already provided in the bill. Beilenson proposed to finance the increase with a 0.75 percent across-the-board reduction from other accounts in the bill.

Several members said they sympathized with Beilenson's goals but insisted that the amendment would force cuts in important programs. Because the bill included no earmarks, even politically popular items such as aid to Israel and Egypt would have been subject to the across-the-board cut. The House defeated Beilenson's amendment 54-371. *(Vote 207, p. 62-H)*

The House approved by voice vote an amendment by Obey to trim $10 million from the $99 million provided in the bill for the World Bank's Global Environment Facility. That was a substitute for an amendment by Texas Republican Tom DeLay that would have reduced funding for the World Bank program to $30 million, the level provided in fiscal 1994.

Senate Subcommittee

The Senate Appropriations Subcommittee on Foreign Operations gave voice vote approval June 16 to a $13.7 billion version of the bill.

The subcommittee generally endorsed the funding blueprint contained in the House-passed version. However, the Senate panel loaded the measure with earmarks. It trimmed the Clinton administration's request for aid to the former Soviet republics and specified where the money would go.

● **Russian aid.** Reflecting growing frustration over the administration's handling of the assistance program for the ex-Soviet republics, the Senate bill provided $839 million for those nations, compared with $875 million in the House bill. "The management of this program has been uncoordinated and short on vision," said Foreign Operations Subcommittee Chairman Patrick J. Leahy, D-Vt., "and the implementation has been no better."

Mitch McConnell of Kentucky, the ranking Republican on

the subcommittee, offered a series of amendments to mandate minimum levels of assistance for several ex-Soviet republics. McConnell had frequently accused the administration of "Moscow myopia" — favoring Russia with aid and attention at the expense of Ukraine, Armenia and other former republics. His amendments earmarked $150 million for Ukraine, $75 million for Armenia and $50 million for Georgia. Other McConnell amendments earmarked $80 million for Jewish refugees resettling in Israel and $270 million for international children's programs. All were adopted by a single voice vote.

The bill also retained the longstanding earmarks for $3 billion in aid for Israel and $2.1 billion for Egypt. The House bill supported the same funding, but without the spending mandates. The earmarks were viewed as an important symbol of U.S. support for Israel and received strong backing from U.S. Jewish organizations.

The subcommittee also earmarked $15 million in aid for Cyprus and $7 million for the Middle East Regional Cooperation Program, which underwrote cooperative projects involving Israelis and Arabs.

At the subcommittee markup, members sparred over aid to Azerbaijan, which had been locked in a bitter conflict with neighboring Armenia for more than five years. Phil Gramm, R-Texas, offered an amendment aimed at cutting off U.S. humanitarian aid to Azerbaijan unless it lifted its blockade of international relief assistance to Armenia. Leahy protested that the amendment ultimately could cause aid from private humanitarian groups to Azerbaijan to dry up. But the panel, which had strongly supported Armenia in the past, approved Gramm's amendment by voice vote. Gramm agreed to work with Leahy to add language stating that the amendment did not seek to restrict non-governmental assistance to Azerbaijan.

Senate Committee

The full Appropriations Committee approved the bill (S Rept 103-287) by voice vote June 16, just hours after the subcommittee had acted.

The markup was largely uncontroversial, except for a debate over U.S. military ties with the government of Indonesia. The Senate bill struck the House-passed restrictions but added new conditions on arms sales to Indonesia. The measure barred Indonesia from using in East Timor any military equipment purchased from the United States.

The provision drew the ire of some supporters of Indonesia, who argued that it would insult an important U.S. trading partner. "This is the largest Muslim country in the world, and we're poking them in the eye? Over what?" asked J. Bennett Johnston, D-La. Hatfield countered that Indonesia still had not allowed independent human rights organizations to visit East Timor.

The committee-approved bill made only modest changes in the funding levels contained in the House legislation. The bill:
● Provided $25 million for the IMF's Enhanced Structural Adjustment Facility; the House had provided no funding for the program.
● Included $359 million for nations in Eastern Europe, $1 million less than the House provided and $21 million less than the administration's request. Sub-Saharan African nations were to receive $802 million, a $12 million increase over the House and $19 million more than the requested level.
● Provided $80 million to support programs in the West Bank and Gaza Strip, an increase of about $2 million over the House bill and the Clinton request.

● Provided $365 million in military loans to Turkey and $255 million to Greece, the House-approved levels for both nations. But the Senate's bill softened several House-passed restrictions on aid to the two NATO allies. It made military aid to Turkey contingent upon an agreement that Turkey not use new U.S. military equipment "for internal security and police purposes." Similarly, Greece was required to agree not to use U.S. military equipment to violate economic sanctions against Serbia.
● Dropped the House provision to withhold $20 million out of $60 million appropriated for the U.N. Population Fund until it shut down its operation in China. The Senate bill retained other conditions on U.S. support for the U.N. agency.
● Provided $787 million as a subsidy to support direct loans and grants from the Export-Import Bank. That was about $6 million less than the House bill and approximately $13 million less than the administration's request.
● Provided $100 million for the State Department's anti-narcotics program, $52 million less than the administration request and $15 million less than the House level. Both chambers had criticized the program as ineffective.
● Provided $15 million, $5 million less than the administration's request, for the International Fund for Ireland. The House bill included $19.6 million.
● Recommended $80 million for programs aiding Palestinians on the West Bank and Gaza Strip. That was a modest increase of $1.7 million over the administration's request and the House appropriation. The Senate bill also provided for the establishment a $20 million fund to promote private sector activities on the West Bank and Gaza.
● Removed Mongolia from the list of communist nations that were prohibited from receiving U.S. assistance. North Korea, China, Tibet, Cuba and Vietnam remained on the list.
● Expanded or continued several programs that benefited Israel, though they required no appropriation of funds. Both bills expanded existing authority allowing Israel to receive up to $775 million in military equipment drawn down from U.S. stocks. The program was previously capped at $700 million.

Senate Floor

The Senate passed the $13.7 billion foreign operations bill July 15 by a vote of 84-9. Senators began debate on the measure June 29, but a crowded pre-recess calendar prompted the leadership to delay most of the action until after the July 4 recess. *(Vote 203, p. 35-S)*

The bill afforded Republicans an opportunity to criticize the administration's policy on Haiti and other issues, but only a handful of the scores of amendments adopted by the Senate appeared to create significant problems for the administration. The big-ticket items in the bill were left untouched.
● **Haiti.** Freshman Republican Judd Gregg of New Hampshire ignited the Haiti debate June 29, offering an amendment to require that the president seek congressional authorization before ordering military action against Haiti. The president could waive the requirement by submitting a written report to Congress on the objectives of such a mission.

After sparring over the administration's policy toward Haiti and over whether Gregg's amendment went too far in tying the president's hands, the Senate rejected Gregg's amendment by a vote of 34-65. It then voted 93-4 in favor of a milder, non-binding amendment urging the president to seek congressional approval before committing troops to Haiti. *(Votes 172, 173 p. 29-S)*

With concern rising over a potential U.S. invasion of Haiti,

Minority Leader Bob Dole, R-Kan., offered an amendment that lawmakers on both sides of the aisle said was intended to slow the momentum. The amendment would have established a bipartisan commission of senior lawmakers to assess diplomatic and political conditions in Haiti and report on its findings within 45 days. The Senate voted 57-42 to table (kill) the amendment July 14, after opponents argued it would undercut international pressure on Haiti's military rulers. (*Vote 194, p. 34-S; Haiti, p. 449*)

● **Indonesia.** A sizable majority of senators agreed June 29 to strike the restrictions on aid to Indonesia that had been inserted by the Senate Appropriations Committee. The motion to table (kill) the Indonesia language was approved 59-35. (*Vote 174, p. 30-S*)

The committee provision had drawn strong opposition from the Pentagon, the State Department and some large U.S. corporations with operations in Indonesia. Secretary of State Warren Christopher weighed in with a letter stating that the conditions on arms sales were "unnecessary and inconsistent with our policy objectives in Indonesia."

Several senators hammered away at the economic argument, asserting that the restriction on arms sales would insult an important U.S. trading partner. "The effect of the amendment would be damaging to our trade, political and security relationship with a country of over 190 million people," said McConnell.

● **Turkey, Greece.** The Senate also modified the restrictions on arms sales to Turkey and Greece. An amendment by Leahy, adopted by voice vote June 29, significantly weakened the restrictions on aid to Greece.

The subcommittee's provision would have barred sales to Greece unless Athens agreed that the equipment would not be used in violation of the U.N. economic embargo against Serbia. Instead, the amendment required that the State Department report on how U.S. aid to Greece "is promoting respect for principles and obligations" under the U.N. sanctions against Serbia.

Leahy apparently wanted to block an amendment proposed by Thad Cochran, R-Miss., to strike all restrictions on arms sales to Turkey and Greece. Cochran eventually dropped that amendment.

● **North Korea.** The Senate on July 15 adopted, 95-0, an amendment by Frank H. Murkowski, R-Alaska, to bar any U.S. aid for North Korea unless the president certified that Pyongyang did not possess nuclear weapons and had not exported weapons-grade plutonium. (*Vote 200, p. 35-S*)

The United States had long barred aid to North Korea, denouncing its staunch communism and support for international terrorism. But the administration had suggested it might join with other countries in providing North Korea with light-water nuclear reactors if the government abandoned its existing reactors; those reactors generated plutonium that could be extracted for use in nuclear weapons. The light-water reactors were the centerpiece of a package of economic, diplomatic and security incentives that the administration hoped would entice North Korea to give up its nuclear weapons development program.

● **Eastern Europe.** The Senate also put more pressure on the administration to support NATO membership for several Eastern European countries.

Senators on July 14 voted 76-22 to adopt an amendment offered by Hank Brown, R-Colo., to expand defense cooperation with Poland, Hungary and the Czech Republic. The proposal, which the administration opposed, broadened the terms of a similar amendment that Brown had attached to the defense authorization bill. (*Vote 196, p. 34-S*)

The Senate voted 53-44 to table a McConnell amendment that would have required the administration to spell out criteria for admitting several Eastern European nations to NATO. But the substantial vote in favor of the proposal meant the issue almost certainly would resurface. The amendment also would have required a report on steps needed to guarantee the "interoperability" of the armed forces of such countries as Poland and Hungary with NATO. (*Vote 195, p. 34-S*)

McConnell long had been frustrated with the administration's Partnership for Peace, a program that invited Eastern European nations to participate in military exercises with NATO but stopped short of offering them full-fledged membership in the alliance.

● **Russian aid.** The Senate backed several Republican-sponsored amendments aimed at establishing new conditions on U.S. economic assistance to Russia.

McConnell attached a provision to link the aid to Moscow's fulfillment of a longstanding pledge to withdraw Russian forces from the Baltic nations by Aug. 31. The amendment came in response to a statement July 10 by Russian President Boris N. Yeltsin that he did not intend to withdraw about 2,000 troops still stationed in Estonia by the deadline. But the provision allowed the president to waive the restriction if he found it to be in the national security interest. The Senate adopted the amendment, 89-8. (*Vote 190, p. 33-S*)

Senators adopted by voice vote an amendment by Helms to prohibit aid to Russia unless the president certified that Moscow had "demonstrated a commitment" to comply with treaties barring the export of chemical and biological weapons.

The Senate also backed an amendment offered by Pete V. Domenici, R-N.M., authorizing the president to tap the aid to Moscow provided in the foreign operations bill to dismantle nuclear weapons in the former Soviet Union. Funds for the Nunn-Lugar program — named for its original sponsors, Sam Nunn, D-Ga., and Richard G. Lugar, R-Ind. — had come from the Pentagon's budget. But Domenici protested that the Pentagon had become a "cash cow" for funding non-defense programs. The Senate approved Domenici's amendment, 56-38. (*Vote 201, p. 35-S*)

The Senate adopted by votes of 100-0 a pair of amendments to boost the portion of the aid to the former Soviet Union that was devoted to law enforcement activities. An amendment by Alfonse M. D'Amato, R-N.Y., provided $15 million for the FBI to combat organized crime in the former Soviet bloc. An amendment by McConnell earmarked $15 million to help train Russian police officers. (*Votes 192, 193, p. 33-S*)

● **Other amendments.** The Senate on June 29 also approved by voice vote an amendment by Frank R. Lautenberg, D-N.J., to withhold economic aid from countries that refused to accept the return of their nationals who were in prison in the United States. The amendment, part of an effort to reduce the costs states faced from illegal immigration, required the president to report to congress on negotiations with such countries. If the president indicated that the talks had not made progress, those nations could lose up to 10 percent of their bilateral assistance.

The Senate rejected, 34-66, an amendment by Jesse Helms, R-N.C., to eliminate $1.2 billion in the bill for the International Development Association, an agency of the World Bank. (*Vote 171, p. 29-S*)

As had become customary, the foreign aid bill also attracted amendments on a wide range of less publicized for-

eign policy matters. The Senate:

• Approved, 94-0, a Helms amendment prohibiting aid to Colombia unless the president certified that its government was eliminating corruption of government officials by drug cartels. *(Vote 202, p. 35-S)*

• Approved, 60-38, an amendment by Dale Bumpers, D-Ark., cutting $600,000 from the bill that had been earmarked to support democracy training programs in China. *(Vote 197, p. 34-S)*

• Rejected, 39-59, an amendment by Helms to cut off aid to the United Nations Development Program. Helms argued that the U.N. agency funded activities in nations identified by the State Department as supporters of terrorism. *(Vote 198, p. 34-S)*

• Rejected, 42-58, a Helms amendment to prohibit any funds to underwrite lobbying activities targeting the laws of foreign governments that concerned abortion. Helms disputed an assertion by opponents of the amendment that it could limit U.S. participation in an international population conference in Cairo, Egypt, later in the year. *(Vote 191, p. 33-S)*

• Rejected, 38-57, an amendment by Don Nickles, R-Okla., to boost aid for the State Department's international narcotics control programs. Nickles proposed to trim funding for affiliates of the World Bank to finance a $52 million increase over the $100 million provided by the bill for the anti-drug effort. *(Vote 199, p. 35-S)*

Conference/Final Action

After scuttling many of the GOP-backed amendments that challenged the Clinton administration's foreign policy, House and Senate conferees completed a marathon negotiating session at about 3 a.m. July 29, approving a compromise $13.8 billion foreign operations bill for fiscal 1995 (H Rept 103-633).

The House adopted the conference report Aug. 4 by a vote of 341-85. The Senate cleared the measure for the president Aug. 10 on a 88-12 vote. *(House vote 376, p. 112-H; Senate vote 271, p. 46-S)*

Supplemental Appropriations

At the administration's request, conferees agreed to include in the bill supplemental fiscal 1994 funds for Jordan and Rwanda. Although the requests came too late for appropriators in either chamber to consider them in committee or on the floor, conferees approved them without much dissent.

Conferees backed a hastily crafted administration proposal to provide up to $220 million in debt relief for Jordan. The approval came on the heels of Jordan's July 25 agreement with Israel to end their 46-year state of war. The conference committee backed a supplemental appropriation for fiscal 1994 of $99 million to cover these loan losses. The conference report made clear, however, that Jordan would have to conclude a formal peace agreement with Israel before Congress provided the funds to forgive the remainder of the kingdom's $700 million U.S. debt.

In addition, the conference committee authorized the president to tap the Pentagon's stocks of excess military equipment to provide light weaponry to Jordan.

Conferees also approved $50 million in fiscal 1994 funds to aid Rwanda, which had been devastated by tribal bloodletting that had cost an estimated 500,000 lives.

Conference Sparring

The 12-hour conference saw a long tug of war over the Senate earmarks. There also was a good measure of partisan sparring over the administration's handling of foreign policy.

Obey waged a largely successful campaign against Republican-backed policy amendments and a pile of senators' earmarks for individual countries. Conferees dropped or weakened Senate provisions targeting the administration's policies toward the former Soviet Union, Eastern Europe and North Korea.

• **Russian aid.** The conferees approved $850 million in aid for the former Soviet republics, a compromise between the House-approved level of $876 million and the $839 million in the Senate bill.

Obey sharply criticized the spending mandates in the Senate bill, arguing that they would hamstring the administration in allocating aid. The showdown came on McConnell's $150 million earmark for Ukraine, which he said had been badly shortchanged in the administration's obligation of aid. Obey kept his Democratic troops in line, and House conferees rejected that proposal 4-8.

House members seemed more inclined to support McConnell's $75 million spending mandate for war-torn Armenia, which had an influential domestic constituency. But just as momentum appeared to be building in favor of that proposal, Charles W. Wilson, D-Texas, Wilson moved that the House adopt a substitute crafted by Obey. The House conferees went along, sealing the fate of McConnell's package of earmarks. Under Obey's alternative, the bill urged — but did not require — the administration to provide $150 million for Ukraine, $75 million for Armenia and $50 million for the republic of Georgia.

The conference committee also rejected McConnell's amendment in the Senate bill barring aid to Russia unless it pulled its remaining troops out of the three Baltic states by Aug. 31. Opponents argued that the provision had been made moot by a recent agreement by Moscow to withdraw some 2,000 remaining Russian troops from Estonia.

The House delegation voted against that amendment, 3-8. The conferees then accepted Obey's milder substitute, which set no specific deadline for troop withdrawals.

A Senate amendment aimed at expanding NATO military contacts with Eastern European nations also fell. In addition, the conferees modified an amendment by Helms linking aid for Moscow to its commitment to comply with chemical and biological weapons treaties. The conferees included language requiring the administration to submit a report on Russia's commitment to such treaties.

Reacting to the series of Senate defeats, McConnell complained bitterly that "essentially what has happened here is that the House of Representatives has insisted upon the Russia-first policy of the administration."

• **North Korea.** The conference then moved on to North Korea. Conferees agreed to strip the Senate amendment prohibiting the United States from providing any aid to Pyongyang, but they included North Korea on the list of countries specifically barred from receiving aid appropriated under the fiscal 1995 foreign operations bill.

Secretary of State Christopher had sent a letter opposing the Senate language, saying it "could block activities that are crucial" in bringing Pyongyang into compliance with its international treaty obligations.

• **PLO restrictions.** Although the administration got most of what it wanted from the conference, not everything went according to plan.

A Senate amendment to tighten existing restrictions on aid to the PLO — a provision that caught many lawmakers unaware — was adopted by the conference committee. The restrictions were intended to ensure that the PLO lived up to its peace agreement with Israel.

Obey and Leahy led opposition to the amendment, which

eliminated language in existing law that allowed the president to waive the conditions if he determined it to be in the national interest. Obey said the provision — sponsored by Sens. Arlen Specter, R-Pa., and Richard C. Shelby, D-Ala. — could result in an aid cutoff even if the PLO engaged in only "marginally dubious" violations of the accord.

But the amendment was strongly supported by some Jewish groups, including the Zionist Organization of America. Nita M. Lowey, D-N.Y., and other House Democrats made a rare break with the House chairman. Lowey said the national-interest waiver was not needed because the president would retain the option of determining whether the PLO was in compliance with its agreement.

By a show of hands, House conferees appeared to support the amendment 6-4, though no tally was announced. After quickly caucusing, Obey and Leahy said they would support language in the conference report's statement of managers reaffirming the president's option to use other statutory authority to waive the restriction.

● **Indonesia.** Conferees agreed to a compromise on restricting U.S. military training for Indonesia: Indonesia was allowed to pay for such training, though it was barred from receiving U.S. aid for that purpose. The conference report

also backed the administration's policy of denying small arms sales to Jakarta.

● **Greece, Turkey.** The negotiations produced a similar agreement on military aid to Turkey and Greece. The bill withheld 10 percent of the $365 million in military loans for Turkey until the administration reported on alleged abuses by Turkish military forces against Kurdish civilians. It withheld 10 percent of $255 million in military loans for Greece until the administration submitted a report on alleged Greek violations of international sanctions against Serbia.

● **Other.** Conferees also dropped Helms' harshly worded amendment to bar aid to Colombia unless its government investigated internal corruption and stepped up its anti-narcotics activities. The provision had triggered complaints from Colombia's government and Hispanic members of Congress. The conferees endorsed milder language in the report accompanying the bill.

They earmarked $80 million in refugee aid for Israel — on top of the $3 billion in economic and military assistance — and $15 million in funding for Cyprus. But conferees stripped numerous other Senate-backed spending mandates.

They adopted Dole's amendment barring aid for countries that violated U.N. sanctions against Serbia and Montenegro. ∎

Interior Bill Wins Easy Passage

Although efforts to revamp key public lands policies sputtered in 1994, the fiscal 1995 spending bill to pay for the upkeep of the nation's vast natural resources quietly cleared. The $13.7 billion bill for the Interior Department and related agencies (HR 4602) largely followed President Clinton's request to cut back on construction and land acquisition and to direct limited financial resources to such priorities as ecosystem management plans for the Pacific Northwest and South Florida.

Clinton signed the bill into law Sept. 30 (PL 103-332).

The spending bill included the only major public lands policy change in the 103rd Congress: a one-year moratorium on processing new mining patent applications. The ban was aimed at stopping mining companies from buying mineral-rich land for as little as $2.50 an acre, although more than two-thirds of the pending applications would move forward.

A separate House-Senate conference on Sept. 29 abandoned its efforts to overhaul the 1872 Mining Law. *(Mining, p. 236)*

To help fight wildfires that continued to rage in the West, the bill provided $450 million in emergency money that Clinton requested to replenish a depleted firefighting fund. The money did not count against the Interior subcommittee's discretionary spending allocation for fiscal 1995.

After subtracting the firefighting funds and making other scorekeeping adjustments, the bill appropriated about $197 million less than Clinton's fiscal 1995 budget request and about $211 million less than Congress provided in fiscal 1994.

The bulk of the funds, $6.6 billion, went to the Interior Department, including $1.4 billion for the National Park Service. Another $2.8 billion went to the Forest Service. Indian health and education programs received $2.1 billion. The bill also contained funding for a number of cultural programs, including the Smithsonian Institution, the National Endowment for the Arts (NEA) and the National Endowment for the Humanities.

As usual, Interior appropriators were deluged with requests from the administration and lawmakers, but there were fewer dollars to spend. Most of the bill's individual accounts were cut by 0.191 percent, a total of $25 million, to meet the Interior measure's $13.7 billion discretionary spending target.

"Discretionary funding is being squeezed like a lemon," said Senate Appropriations Committee Chairman Robert C. Byrd, D-W.Va., who also led the Interior subcommittee. "This is just a drop in the bucket compared with the pain that is going to come next year."

Despite the pain, Interior appropriators managed to increase fiscal 1995 spending for three major accounts:
● The Bureau of Land Management, the steward for much of the West's public land, received an increase of $34 million to slightly more than $1.1 billion.
● The Smithsonian Institution, which operated 16 museums and the National Zoo, was provided $371.8 million, up by $29.7 million from the fiscal 1994 level of $342.1 million.

BOXSCORE

Fiscal 1995 Interior Appropriations — HR 4602. The $13.7 billion bill funded the Interior Department and related agencies.

Reports: H Rept 103-551, S Rept 103-294; conference report H Rept 103-740.

KEY ACTION

June 23 — House passed HR 4602, 338-85.

July 26 — Senate passed HR 4602, amended, by voice vote.

Sept. 27 — House adopted conference report by voice vote.

Sept. 28 — Senate cleared the bill, 92-7.

Sept. 30 — President signed the bill — PL 103-332.

● The Indian Health Service, which built and maintained hospitals and clinics on Indian lands, was boosted by $24 million to $1.97 billion, an increase from $1.94 billion in fiscal 1994.

Congress trimmed Clinton's request for the NEA, a frequent target of conservative lawmakers, by 2 percent, to $167.7 million.

Background

The one-year moratorium on new mining applications was enacted as part of the Interior bill when it became clear that congressional efforts to agree on a broader rewrite of the 1872 Mining Law would not succeed.

Under the law, miners could obtain a patent or title to federal land believed to contain valuable hard-rock minerals for as little as $2.50 an acre. The moratorium stopped the Interior Department from transferring federal land in fiscal 1995 to miners eager to extract at least $34 billion in gold, copper and other hard-rock minerals.

The move came in the wake of a federal court order that forced Interior Secretary Bruce Babbitt to sign over 1,950 acres of federal land in Nevada to a Canadian mining company for $10,000. The company planned to extract the lands' estimated $10 billion in gold deposits.

The Clinton administration actively pursued a comprehensive rewrite of the law, along the lines of a House-passed bill (HR 322 — H Rept 103-338), which proposed to eliminate the patenting process and impose an 8 percent royalty on the gross value of hard-rock minerals, allowing for the deduction of some transportation costs.

A Senate-passed bill (S 775 — S Rept 103-45) proposed a 2 percent royalty on the net value of hard-rock minerals extracted, allowing all exploration and development costs to be deducted. It would have limited, though not eliminated, the patenting process. After repeated efforts to forge a compromise, Senate Energy and Natural Resources Committee Chairman J. Bennett Johnston, D-La., announced Sept. 29 that the legislation was dead.

House Committee

The House Interior Appropriations Subcommittee on June 9 gave voice vote approval to a draft $13.5 billion spending bill that called for a one-year moratorium on the processing of any new mining patents.

Chairman Sidney R. Yates, D-Ill., had tried to steer clear of major policy disputes that could spark a fight with authorizing committees. He persuaded the panel, for example, to exclude proposals to boost entrance fees at national parks and to impose royalties on hard-rock miners. Clinton included both policy proposals in his fiscal 1995 budget request.

But ranking Republican Ralph Regula of Ohio said he pushed and won the mining moratorium during the closed-door markup session in an attempt to "end the giveaway" of

Interior Spending

(in thousands of dollars)

	Fiscal 1994 Appropriations	Fiscal 1995 Clinton Request	House Bill	Senate Bill	Final Bill
Interior Department					
Bureau of Land Management					
Management of lands	$ 599,860	$ 605,099	$ 596,349	$ 598,480	$ 598,449
Fire protection, firefighting	233,817	236,144	236,144	236,144	236,144
Payments in lieu of taxes	104,108	104,108	104,108	104,108	104,108
Other	131,603	171,874	162,046	161,914	164,716
Subtotal	**$ 1,069,388**	**$ 1,117,225**	**$ 1,098,647**	**$ 1,100,646**	**$ 1,103,417**
Fish and Wildlife Service					
Resource management	481,623	539,083	514,650	502,936	513,815
Construction	73,565	35,095	25,264	49,848	53,914
Land acquisition	82,655	86,162	62,300	63,700	67,410
Other	41,869	48,192	29,869	41,869	38,869
Subtotal	**$ 679,712**	**$ 708,532**	**$ 632,083**	**$ 658,353**	**$ 674,008**
National Park Service					
Operations	1,061,823	1,124,715	1,083,973	1,061,276	1,079,963
Construction	201,724	148,568	171,417	170,503	184,941
Land acquisition, state aid	95,250	82,696	88,596	80,759	87,936
Other	57,835	57,479	57,946	61,128	62,023
Subtotal	**$ 1,416,632**	**$ 1,413,458**	**$ 1,401,932**	**$ 1,373,666**	**$ 1,414,863**
Bureau of Indian Affairs					
Indian programs	1,490,805	1,498,430	1,527,786	1,525,399	1,526,778
Claim settlements, payments	103,259	174,045	82,896	77,096	77,096
Other	183,589	94,633	145,174	139,840	146,414
Subtotal	**$ 1,777,653**	**$ 1,767,108**	**$ 1,755,856**	**$ 1,742,335**	**$ 1,750,288**
National Biological Survey	167,209	176,450	167,209	166,358	167,209
Geological Survey	584,685	580,680	576,775	565,316	572,556
Minerals Management Service	198,528	200,358	196,658	195,486	195,508
Bureau of Mines	169,436	148,919	152,269	152,389	152,719
Surface Mining Reclamation	301,849	277,900	283,800	304,794	293,968
Territorial affairs	127,847	107,697	118,697	117,779	124,679
Department offices	132,147	125,572	124,958	122,132	124,258
TOTAL, Interior	**$ 6,625,086**	**$ 6,623,899**	**$ 6,508,884**	**$ 6,499,254**	**$ 6,573,473**
Forest Service (Agriculture Department)					
National forest system	1,308,823	1,355,312	1,336,162	1,322,857	1,333,112
Forest research	193,083	203,280	201,780	198,076	200,130
Fire protection, firefighting	375,390	382,790	386,790	383,108	385,790
Construction	252,802	221,791	191,740	219,234	203,186
Timber receipts (to Treasury)	(−48,289)	(−51,828)	(−51,828)	(−51,828)	(−51,828)
Other	257,672	238,533	249,930	252,187	706,835
TOTAL, Forest Service	**$ 2,387,770**	**$ 2,401,706**	**$ 2,366,402**	**$ 2,375,462**	**$ 2,829,053**
Energy Department					
Clean-coal technology	−175,000	−337,879	−337,879	−337,879	−337,879
Fossil energy research	430,674	451,130	428,544	419,451	425,614
Naval Petroleum Reserve	214,772	199,456	193,956	187,406	187,406
Energy conservation	690,375	976,856	824,585	743,741	793,194
Strategic Petroleum Reserve	206,810	153,247	153,247	153,247	153,247
Other	103,650	101,164	101,164	100,943	101,164
TOTAL, Energy Department	**$ 1,471,281**	**$ 1,543,974**	**$ 1,363,617**	**$ 1,266,909**	**$ 1,322,746**
Other Related Agencies					
Indian health	1,942,859	1,818,968	1,959,994	1,968,819	1,966,819
Indian education	83,500	86,000	83,500	83,500	83,500
Smithsonian Institution	342,149	398,879	373,454	369,105	371,804
National Endowment for the Arts	170,228	170,100	167,678	161,596	167,678
National Endowment for the Humanities	177,491	177,383	177,383	177,383	177,383
Other agencies	203,076	203,390	202,822	194,806	177,084
GRAND TOTAL	**$ 13,403,440**	**$ 13,424,299**	**$ 13,203,734**	**$ 13,096,834**	**$ 13,669,540**

SOURCE: House Appropriations Committee

public lands. Regula, a moderate who supported higher grazing fees and similar changes to public land policy, had included the same mining language in the fiscal 1994 Interior spending bill. That language was dropped in conference because negotiations on the House and Senate mining bills were imminent. *(1993 Almanac, p. 618)*

The subcommittee spending bill generally followed the contours of Clinton's fiscal 1995 budget request. To meet tight budget caps, however, members cut $200 million by trimming virtually every agency covered under the bill. For example, the bill supported Clinton's call to invest in special ecosystem restoration projects such as a Pacific Northwest plan to protect the threatened northern spotted owl and preserve timber jobs. But it provided only partial funding of $103 million.

The subcommittee also called for significant cuts in four key construction budgets, providing:

- $26 million for the Fish and Wildlife Service's building account for fish hatcheries and bird sanctuaries, compared with nearly $74 million provided in fiscal 1994.
- $171 million for the National Park Service's construction account for park facilities, down from $202 million in fiscal 1994.
- $201 million for the Forest Service's construction fund for forest roads and trails, compared with $249 million in fiscal 1994.
- $129 million for the Bureau of Indian Affairs' fund to build schools and irrigation systems, down from nearly $167 million in fiscal 1994.

Yates said the one agency that appropriators tried to spare from the budget ax was the Indian Health Service, which provided medical care to roughly 1 million American Indians and Alaskans. The subcommittee provided nearly $2 billion for Indian health programs for fiscal 1995.

Conservation programs designed to improve energy efficiency got a 20 percent increase, receiving $825 million for fiscal 1995, compared with $690 million allocated in fiscal 1994. The panel also proposed extending for another year a moratorium on new oil and natural gas leases along the East and West coasts, the eastern Gulf of Mexico and Alaska's Bristol Bay.

Full Committee Action

The full Appropriations Committee gave voice vote approval June 17 to a $13.2 billion version of the bill (H Rept 103-551).

The bill provided about $194.5 million less than fiscal 1994 spending and $230 million less than Clinton sought in his budget plan. Before approving the bill, the Appropriations Committee adopted by voice vote an amendment by Yates to require the Interior Department to obtain written permission from landowners before conducting any new surveys on their property. The restriction was similar to language in the fiscal 1994 Interior spending bill.

The bill also cut the Fish and Wildlife Service's budget to $632.1 million for fiscal 1995 from $679.7 million in fiscal 1994. The service managed wildlife refuges and bird sanctuaries. The Forest Service was to receive $2.35 billion in fiscal 1995, about $22 million less than it received in fiscal 1994.

House Floor

The House passed the $13.2 billion bill June 23 by a vote of 338-85, after turning back repeated attempts to reduce funding for the arts and the protection of endangered species. *(Vote 272, p. 80-H)*

"We must concentrate our scarce resources on what is absolutely necessary, not on what is simply desirable," said Cliff Stearns, R-Fla., who lost a bid to cut arts spending by 5 percent.

Opponents focused their attacks on the National Biological Survey, a new Interior agency program to inventory plants and animals, and on the NEA, a perennial target of conservatives eager to limit the agency's scope.

- **National Biological Survey.** Lawmakers opened debate June 22 with their eyes trained on the National Biological Survey, a Clinton administration initiative aimed at preventing the kind of controversies that had arisen over the 1973 Endangered Species Act (PL 93-205) — such as the dispute in the Pacific Northwest that pitted timber jobs against protection of the northern spotted owl.

The survey was designed to help regulators prevent species from becoming threatened or endangered under the law by keeping tabs on their population levels. It was created as a separate agency in the Interior Department in 1993 after research activities of eight different federal agencies were combined. Opponents of the survey feared it would be used to expand the reach of the endangered species law and restrict property rights if scientists determined endangered or threatened species lived on privately owned land. *(1993 Almanac, p. 269)*

Although Interior Secretary Babbitt had the authority to shuffle scientists and programs throughout his department, the House in 1993 passed separate legislation (HR 1845) to make the survey permanent. The Senate took no action on the measure.

Opponents, including Wayne Allard, R-Colo., tried to use the survey's fiscal 1995 funding to jump-start efforts to weaken the endangered species law, which expired in 1994. Merchant Marine and Fisheries Committee Chairman Gerry E. Studds, D-Mass., argued that the survey provided "good science" that was critical to protecting species and could prevent them from requiring federal protection under the 1973 law. The House rejected an amendment by Allard to essentially abolish the new agency and kill the $167.2 million in funding for fiscal 1995, voting 169-259 on June 22. *(Vote 260, p. 76-H)*

Lawmakers also tried, and failed, to reduce spending for several proposed additions to the national park system, saying the National Park Service could not afford upkeep on the parks in its inventory and should not add any parcels.

- **NEA funds.** For two days, June 22 and 23, House conservatives led by Philip M. Crane, R-Ill., sought to reduce or eliminate the $171.1 million in the bill for the arts endowment. The NEA had incurred the wrath of Crane and other members of Congress earlier in the year when members learned that NEA money had helped pay for a controversial show by an HIV-positive performance artist in Minneapolis.

The artist cut himself and a fellow performer; paper towels used to blot blood from the second performer were suspended above the audience. The performance was intended to depict the plight of those with the AIDS virus. The Walker Art Center spent less than $150 in federal funds on the show but received $104,500 from the endowment in fiscal 1994.

Crane said the performance was objectionable and should not have received federal funds. Joined by other conservatives, he said the federal government should leave arts funding to the private sector.

But Jerrold Nadler, D-N.Y., called attempts by Crane and other Republicans to cut the endowment's budget a thinly veiled effort at censorship. Nadler and Yates, an avid arts supporter, said decisions about what art was worthy of federal funding should be left to the endowment. The endowment extended about 4,000 grants a year culled from some 17,000

Debate Over the Definition of Art Continues

The National Endowment for the Arts (NEA) generally tried to stay out of the limelight. But every so often an NEA grant created such a stir that it reverberated in Congress. During the 1970s and early '80s, for example, federal funding for pornographic poetry, a sexually explicit book and a children's stage show that used profanity angered some lawmakers. Their rage, however, did not translate into much of a threat to the endowment's funding.

Those earlier disputes were minor compared with the outrage sparked by the funding of works by artists Andres Serrano and the late Robert Mapplethorpe in 1989. NEA grants had partly paid for a display of a Serrano photograph of a crucifix submerged in a jar of urine and a Mapplethorpe exhibit featuring graphic displays of unusual gay sex practices.

The 1989 dispute forced Congress into an intense and uncomfortable debate about sex, religion and morality. In response, Congress passed the first ban on federal funding for works that could be considered obscene and that did not have "serious literary, artistic, political or scientific value." *(1989 Almanac, p. 731)*

A year later, after much back and forth, Congress dropped the ban. In its place, lawmakers empowered the NEA chairman to ensure that grants were made on "general standards of decency and respect for the diverse beliefs and values of the American public." The issue of obscenity was left to the courts. *(1990 Almanac, p. 430)*

All was quiet at the NEA until June 1994, when a Minneapolis show by performance artist Ron Athey prompted attempts in both chambers to slash NEA funding in the Interior appropriations bill (HR 4602). Congress ultimately agreed to cut the agency's funds by a modest 2 percent. *(Appropriations, p. 513)*

During the performance, Athey, who was infected with the AIDS virus, cut himself and a fellow performer; paper towels used to blot blood from the second performer were suspended above the audience. The performance, intended to depict the plight of those with AIDS, was sponsored by the Walker Art Center, which used less than $150 from a $104,500 all-purpose NEA grant to stage the controversial show.

History of the NEA

Congress created the NEA in 1965 as part of the Great Society, which President Lyndon B. Johnson said should include the "pursuit of artistic achievement."

Since then, it had awarded more than 110,000 grants worth $2.5 billion that had been used as leverage to obtain private funding for the arts. Every federal dollar brought in an estimated $6 in private money.

Grants were awarded for artistic disciplines, such as dance, theater or music, and to the institutions that presented these works. There also were "partnership program" grants for states and for arts education.

The law that established the arts endowment (PL 89-209) specified that money be distributed for work that had "substantial artistic and cultural significance," but it did not define excellence or merit.

The endowment received about 18,000 grant applications each year and approved about 4,000. Obtaining a grant was a four-step process:

- NEA staff reviewed the application to make sure it was prepared properly.
- The document then went to an independent review panel that determined whether the request met NEA guidelines for artistic excellence, merit and decency. This panel recommended who should receive funding and how much money to allocate. The review panel, whose size varied, consisted mostly of experts in a chosen artistic field. Congress in 1990 required that at least one member be a lay person with no background in that field.
- The National Council on the Arts met in open session to accept or reject the review panel's recommendations. The council's 26 members were appointed by the president and confirmed by the Senate.
- The council's recommendations were then submitted to the NEA chairman, whose decisions were final.

requests. "The arts are blossoming. That is the story of the NEA in action . . . not the cesspool of pornography or the cesspool of horrible activities that [opponents] have portrayed," Yates said.

On June 22, the House essentially agreed with Yates and Nadler, rejecting, 113-313, an amendment by Crane to eliminate the $171.1 million for the endowment. It was the third year in a row that the House mustered a 2-1 margin to defeat an attempt by Crane to eliminate arts funding. *(Vote 263, p. 78-H)*

The following day, the House turned back another run on the endowment, rejecting an attempt by Spencer Bachus, R-Ala., to strip the bulk of its funding by eliminating grants to individual artists and cultural programs — funds that typically generated controversy. Bachus' amendment to cut $92.7 million from the endowment was defeated, 132-297. *(Vote 265, p. 78-H)*

Before approving the bill, however, the House bowed to calls from deficit hawks to trim funding for the endowment. The decision came after a raucous series of five votes in which NEA supporters Yates and Norm Dicks, D-Wash., alter-

nately tried to weaken amendments offered by arts spending opponents Stearns and Bachus. The two Republicans called for trimming endowment funding by 5 percent and 4.99 percent respectively, triggering attempts by Dicks and Yates to limit the cuts to 1.5 percent and 1 percent, respectively. *(Votes 266-270, pp. 78-H, 80-H)*

The House ultimately adopted, 222-204, language offered by Dicks to cut the endowment's spending by 2 percent to $167.7 million in fiscal 1995. *(Vote 269, p. 80-H)*

- **Mining moratorium.** The one-year moratorium on the processing of new mining patents drew little debate in the House. Regula said he wanted to include the moratorium in the spending bill just in case negotiators meeting on separate legislation to overhaul the mining law hit an impasse.
- **Other amendments.** The House on June 22 rejected by voice vote an amendment by Richard W. Pombo, R-Calif., that would have cut $20 million from the Fish and Wildlife Service's budget for the implementation of the Endangered Species Act. Studds said debate about the 1973 law should be held in 1995 when Congress was slated to reauthorize the act.

In other action, the House also defeated several attempts

to cut funding for specific national parks and energy research projects. They included:

• An amendment by John J. "Jimmy" Duncan Jr., R-Tenn., on June 22 that would have cut $14 million from National Park Service operations. The amendment, rejected 171-257, was aimed at reducing the $25 million provided in the bill to convert San Francisco's Presidio Army Base into a national park. *(Vote 261, p. 78-H; Presidio, p. 253)*

• An amendment by Joel Hefley, R-Colo., to cut the National Park Service's $171 million construction budget by $6.3 million. The amendment was rejected, 146-282, on June 22. Hefley was trying to eliminate $5 million earmarked for the Fisher Peak Mountain Center on the Blue Ridge Parkway in Virginia and about $1.3 million to refurbish the Allegheny Portage Railroad in Pennsylvania. *(Vote 262, p. 78-H)*

• An amendment by Scott L. Klug, R-Wis., to cut $27 million from the $428.5 million in new budget authority for the Energy Department's fossil energy research programs was defeated, 182-242, on June 23. *(Vote 271, p. 80-H)*

Senate Committee

Saving the contentious issues for the floor, Senate appropriators June 28 easily approved a $13.1 billion version of the Interior bill. The full Appropriations Committee approved the bill, 29-0, just hours after the Interior Subcommittee endorsed the measure by voice vote (S Rept 103-294).

The bill provided about $360 million less than Clinton had requested and $123 million less than the House-passed version. Appropriators delayed until after the July 4 recess expected fights over federal funding for the arts and mining patents on federal lands.

The bill provided $161.6 million for the NEA, a 5 percent cut. "It is expected that only the most meritorious examples of artistic excellence . . . will be funded," the committee report noted, in an effort to appease those who wanted to cut the funding altogether.

The Senate committee bill did not contain the one-year mining patent moratorium added in the House.

As part of the plan to implement logging in the Pacific Northwest, the bill included $146 million. It also included $42.5 million to begin work on South Florida's ecosystem restoration, including the Everglades.

Subcommittee Chairman Byrd reordered some of the bill's priorities, cutting $263.5 million from Energy Department programs on alternative energy sources and conservation, for example, to be able to increase by nearly $150 million funding for the Indian Health Service.

Byrd said tight budget caps made it impossible to fund all the 1,600 projects members had sought. That did not mean, however, that special projects got no funding. Byrd said the bill included about $221.1 million for federal land acquisition and state outdoor recreation grants, and it appropriated $443.4 million for construction by the land management agencies, such as the National Park Service.

As in previous years, Senate appropriators made additions to the House's wish list of construction and acquisition projects, including:

• $3.2 million for work on Harper's Ferry National Historical Park and $26 million as an installment on a National Education and Training Center, both in Byrd's home state of West Virginia.

• $2 million to add to the land in Pinelands National Reserve in New Jersey, home of Democratic appropriator Frank R. Lautenberg, who was in a tight re-election race.

• $3.5 million for work at the Jean Lafitte National Historical Park and Preserve in Louisiana, home of Democratic appropriator J. Bennett Johnston.

Senate Floor

Carefully sidestepping most of the controversies that threatened to bog down the measure, the Senate passed the $13.1 billion Interior spending bill by voice vote July 26.

Floor managers persuaded senators to withdraw or water down potentially threatening amendments and succeeded in either delaying most contentious issues or shifting them to other venues. For example, the Senate put off until the House-Senate conference the decision on how much to cut arts funding.

In the end, the Senate took just one close vote on a broadly controversial issue, agreeing 49-42 to table (kill) an amendment by Jesse Helms, R-N.C., that would have barred federal funding of certain art that Helms argued was offensive. By focusing on Helms' proposed art content restriction, the Senate avoided taking a direct vote on how much to cut NEA funding, letting stand the 5 percent cut approved by the committee and leaving the matter for conference. *(Vote 230, p. 39-S)*

Byrd argued that the cut was an appropriate way to push NEA officials to try to avoid creating controversies with its grants. Quoting from William Shakespeare, Byrd said the cut was intended to "root away the noisome weeds which, without profit, suck the soil's fertility from wholesome flowers." Byrd promised he would go to conference with the House with "an open mind" in hopes of preserving the NEA's "wholesome flowers." And he persuaded James M. Jeffords, R-Vt., to withdraw an amendment that would have restored most of the NEA funding by instead cutting the entire bill by the amount of the NEA cut.

Helms' amendment on content restriction would have prohibited the use of NEA funds for "human mutilation or invasive bodily procedures on human beings dead or alive; or the drawing or letting of blood." In addition to the Minneapolis performance, Helms was protesting the work of an NEA-supported photographer who had mutilated and photographed the heads from two cadavers (a project that was not part of any NEA grant, the agency said).

Christopher J. Dodd, D-Conn., argued against Helms' amendment on the grounds that a strict interpretation of it would bar NEA support of much of the artwork in the Capitol — some of which showed battle scenes with wounded and bleeding victims — or even of the crucifixion of Christ. "This goes too far in trying to deal with the problem," Dodd said before the Senate agreed to kill Helms' proposal.

Other issues the Senate dealt with during consideration of the measure included:

• **Mining law.** Dale Bumpers, D-Ark., argued again, as he had since 1990, that the "patenting," or sale, of federal land containing gold, silver, copper or other hard-rock minerals to mining companies for as little as $2.50 an acre was "easily the greatest scandal in America." Bumpers said he wanted to offer an amendment for a one-year moratorium on patents — such as one the House had included in its version of the bill — but decided to defer the matter to the ongoing conference revising the 1872 Mining Law.

• **Tongass National Forest.** Alaskan Republicans Ted Stevens and Frank H. Murkowski said they would have preferred stronger language to bar what they said were unilateral moves by the Forest Service to protect goshawk nests and wolf habitats in the Tongass National Forest by restricting

Grazing Fees Abandoned

The Clinton administration decided Dec. 21 to throw in the towel over its controversial proposal to raise grazing fees on federal lands, removing a major source of friction with powerful Western congressmen, such as incoming Senate Budget Chairman Pete V. Domenici, R-N.M. But the decision, one of a series of steps President Clinton took following Election Day to move to the political center, left environmentalists unhappy. It also removed a potential source of increased federal revenue.

Interior Secretary Bruce Babbitt, who had made the grazing reform one of his top priorities in 1993, said in a printed statement that he would defer to Congress on the issue. He also agreed to give Congress six months to review the environmental portions of his proposed grazing plan before issuing a final rule.

His announcement came after Sens. Domenici and Larry E. Craig, R-Idaho, sent him a letter Dec. 6 warning that Congress might use "all possible means" to stop the regulations unless there was more congressional and public input. The Westerners praised Babbitt's change of heart on the issue. Craig said Babbit "has wisely recognized the new political reality following the recent election."

Critics had long contended that federal grazing fees were so low that they amounted to a subsidy for 27,000 ranchers and were allowing once-verdant range and grasslands to be damaged. Clinton initially tried to pursue the issue in Congress in 1993, but pulled back after protests by Western senators. Babbitt then considered raising the fees through an executive order, but ran into more strong protests.

The Senate considered a compromise amendment by Harry Reid, D-Nev., attached to the fiscal 1994 Interior appropriations bill, that would have increased the fees from a $1.86 unit price per month to $3.45 over three years, and codified most of Babbitt's land management proposals. But Domenici and his allies balked at the end of the 1993 session, saying the proposal was too sweeping, and the amendment was ultimately dropped from the bill. *(1993 Almanac, p. 273)*

timber harvesting. They said the practice violated a law that required the Forest Service to make available a certain amount of timber each year.

But faced with strong opposition from Environment Committee Chairman Max Baucus, D-Mont., Murkowski settled for a sense of the Senate amendment that the Forest Service should not restrict logging unless it had complied with public participation requirements in the National Forest Management Act. Baucus said this and similar problems would be taken up in his committee's upcoming rewrite of the Endangered Species Act. The Murkowski amendment passed by voice vote.

● **Cutting national parks.** Arguing that funding cuts had left the National Park and Fish and Wildlife services without enough money to maintain the parks and wildlife refuges they already had, Malcolm Wallop, R-Wyo., said the agencies should each pick out five parks, refuges or other holdings to deauthorize to save money.

The Senate approved by voice vote an amendment that required the Park Service and Fish and Wildlife Service to

submit five candidates each for deletion by the end of 1995. Congress was to make any final decision.

Conference/Final Action

Both chambers easily approved a final $13.7 billion version of the bill (H Rept 103-740). The House adopted the conference report by voice vote Sept. 27, and the Senate followed suit the next day by a 92-7 vote. *(Vote 311, p. 53-S)*

On the issues that stirred controversy as the bill moved along, conferees:

● **NEA.** Cut Clinton's request for $170.1 million for the NEA by 2 percent, providing $167.7 million. Conferees agreed to the House-passed level at the request of Yates.

● **Biological Survey.** Provided $167.2 million for the National Biological Survey — the same amount as in fiscal 1994; Clinton had requested $176.5 million.

In other decisions, the conferees allocated $235.6 million for the Land and Water Conservation Fund, the primary source of money to buy property for national parks, forests and refuges managed by the federal government.

The fund received money from the sale of oil and gas leases in the Outer Continental Shelf. Although nearly $900 million was authorized for the fund every year, actual spending was only a fraction of that amount. The National Park Service estimated that it would take $1.1 billion to buy more than 355,000 acres in its acquisition backlog.

The bill called for spending about $169 million through the Interior Department and Forest Service in the Pacific Northwest, mostly for the administration's forest management plan. That plan, formulated in 1993, aimed to revive and diversify the region's timber-dependent economy, which had been hurt by a legal dispute over protection of the northern spotted owl. The money was to allow timber sales proposed in the plan to proceed and to pay for watershed assessment and restoration projects, and such ongoing economic development as a "jobs in the woods" program.

Although it was not as much money as she would have preferred, Sen. Patty Murray, D-Wash., said the bill's allocation for the Pacific Northwest would ensure that Clinton's forest plan would be implemented. "There is still a lot of hurt in the region," she said. "But we have made tremendous progress in the last couple of years."

For another highly touted ecosystem management plan, the bill provided $9.5 million to the National Park Service to buy land in South Florida to help restore the ailing Everglades. An additional $4.5 million was allocated to help water flow through the area more naturally.

One provision of the conference report drew particular concern from House Natural Resources Committee Chairman George Miller, D-Calif. Miller was a chief architect of a 1990 law (PL 101-626) that required environmental protections for the Tongass National Forest and specified that a certain amount of timber be made available for harvest each year. *(1990 Almanac, p. 294)*

The conference report directed the Forest Service to "explore the possibility of a 10-year contract" for the Alaska Pulp Corp., a company that the Forest Service found to have violated its 50-year contract to supply Tongass timber.

In a colloquy with Yates, Miller said he wanted to make sure that the conference report did not require a 10-year contract with Alaska Pulp and that the company's financial practices, antitrust violations and non-compliance with environmental laws would be examined before the federal government decided to do business again with the company. Yates confirmed that this was the conferees' intent. ■

Labor-HHS Bill Requires Trade-Offs

The Senate on Sept. 28 cleared the largest of the 13 regular appropriations bills — a $250.6 billion measure that funded more than 500 programs in the departments of Labor, Health and Human Services (HHS), and Education. President Clinton signed the bill Sept. 30 (HR 4606 — PL 103-333).

More than two-thirds of the money went to mandatory spending programs such as Medicare, Medicaid and Aid to Families with Dependent Children (AFDC). Slightly more than $70 billion paid for discretionary programs, over which the appropriators had annual control, such as AIDS research, college financial aid, elementary and secondary education, and worker retraining.

The major struggles were over how much to allocate for Clinton's request for "human investment" in areas such as education and job training. Funding those initiatives meant cutting other established programs, and lawmakers were somewhat reluctant to do that.

For example, Clinton wanted to increase funding for Head Start, the popular preschool program for children from low-income families, from $3.3 billion in fiscal 1994 to $4 billion in fiscal 1995. The final bill provided $3.5 billion.

The administration wanted to get money for other programs by cutting spending on the $1.5 billion Low Income Home Energy Assistance Program (LIHEAP), which helped low-income families pay heating and cooling bills and weatherize their homes. Clinton requested a $745 million cut for LIHEAP. Unwilling to cut that much, lawmakers provided $1.3 billion.

Tom Harkin, D-Iowa, chairman of the Senate Appropriations Labor-HHS-Education Subcommittee, said strict budget caps adopted by Congress in 1993, along with increased demands from Clinton and other lawmakers, left appropriators with little leeway in 1994. "The president sent us a size 12 foot that we had to fit into a size 9 shoe," he said.

Sidestepping Abortion Fight

One perennial feature of congressional debate on the Labor-HHS bill — a battle over abortion — did not occur in 1994. For many years, the bill had engendered heated debate over whether the government should pay for abortions for low-income women under Medicaid, the federal-state health insurance program for the poor. Abortion funding had been banned since 1978 under the so-called Hyde amendment, named after its original sponsor, Henry J. Hyde, R-Ill.

As part of the fiscal 1994 bill, Congress agreed to slightly relax the law, which traditionally allowed an exception to the ban to save the life of the woman. Lawmakers added exceptions for cases of rape and incest, while also soundly rejecting efforts to overturn the overall Hyde amendment. (*1993 Almanac, p. 632*)

In 1994, abortion rights supporters and opponents in both chambers averted a confrontation by agreeing early on

---

BOXSCORE

Fiscal 1995 Labor-HHS-Education Appropriations — HR 4606. The $250.6 billion bill funded programs in the departments of Labor, Health and Human Services (HHS), and Education.

Reports: H Rept 103-553, S Rept 103-318; conference report H Rept 103-733.

KEY ACTION

June 29 — House passed HR 4606, 339-89.

Aug. 10 — Senate passed HR 4606, amended, 87-13.

Sept. 22 — House agreed to the conference report, 331-89.

Sept. 27 — Senate agreed to the report, 83-16.

Sept. 28 — Senate cleared the bill by voice vote.

Sept. 30 — President signed HR 4606 — PL 103-333.

---

to retain language from the fiscal 1993 bill. Abortion opponents said abortion rights supporters backed off because they knew any attempt to block or weaken the Hyde amendment would fail. "It was total capitulation on their part; they realized they wouldn't win," said an aide to Hyde. But abortion rights advocates said they abandoned the Labor-HHS fight to focus on efforts to include abortion benefits in the health care overhaul bill then making its way through Congress. (*Abortion, p. 355*)

House Committee

The bill began in the House Labor-HHS Appropriations Subcommittee, which approved it by voice vote June 14. To meet the budget caps and create room for some of Clinton's initiatives, Subcommittee Chairman Neal Smith, D-Iowa, chose to spread the pain broadly instead of slashing a particular program. He called the $249.7 billion bill "the best we can do."

The allocations approved by the panel reflected Smith's stated preference for funding existing and proven programs over some of Clinton's proposals. Among Clinton's initiatives, job training and employment were favored over education. The subcommittee included $3.5 billion for Head Start, compared with Clinton's request of $4 billion. Clinton proposed $7 billion in Title I education money for disadvantaged students; the House appropriators recommended $6.7 billion.

Among Clinton's priorities, job training fared well. Clinton requested $1.5 billion in assistance for dislocated workers; House appropriators recommended $1.3 billion. The newly enacted School-to-Work plan (HR 2884 — PL 103-239), which aimed to help high school graduates who were not going to college make a smooth transition to the workplace, received nearly full funding of $280 million. (*School-to-Work, p. 400*)

But the new Goals 2000 education program enacted in March (HR 1804 — PL 103-227) received only $388 million of the $708 million Clinton requested. The program aimed to establish national education goals for the first time in the nation's history. (*Goals 2000, p. 397*)

The appropriators settled on a $250 million reduction for LIHEAP, providing $1.2 billion. Established in the early 1980s, the program originally had aimed to ease temporarily the financial pinch caused by soaring energy costs. Over the years, however, LIHEAP had expanded and become a favorite of lawmakers, particularly those from the Northeast, South and Southwest.

Full Committee

The full House Appropriations Committee easily passed the $249.7 billion bill by voice vote June 21, while avoiding a fight over abortion funding (H Rept 103-553).

Members approved by voice vote an amendment by Henry Bonilla, R-Texas, to delay the implementation of new regulations on trade and proprietary schools. Under the 1992 higher

Labor-HHS-Education Spending

(in thousands of dollars)

	Fiscal 1994 Appropriations	Fiscal 1995 Clinton Request	House Bill	Senate Bill	Final Bill
Labor Department					
Training and employment services	$ 5,013,510	$ 5,833,580	$ 5,524,991	$ 5,418,217	$ 5,455,885
Trade adjustment, allowances	190,000	274,400	274,400	274,400	274,400
Unemployment insurance (advance)	2,961,300	686,000	686,000	686,000	686,000
Trust fund	*(3,376,617)*	*(3,283,592)*	*(3,269,013)*	*(3,274,155)*	*(3,269,097)*
Black lung disability	1,002,625	995,620	995,620	995,620	995,620
Occupational Safety & Health	296,428	320,007	312,500	312,500	312,500
Other	5,563,483	5,736,201	5,513,299	5,535,965	5,528,834
Total, Labor Department	**$ 15,027,346**	**$ 13,845,808**	**$ 13,306,810**	**$ 13,222,702**	**$ 13,253,239**
Health and Human Services					
Public Health					
AIDS programs	602,800	695,406	649,189	657,189	656,189
Health resources and services	2,926,170	2,974,509	3,008,225	3,066,254	3,056,203
Centers for Disease Control	2,051,132	1,954,188	2,086,850	2,050,931	2,089,443
National Institutes of Health	10,937,653	11,471,887	11,322,023	11,333,181	11,334,098
Substance abuse/mental health	2,125,178	2,365,877	2,166,148	2,164,179	2,181,407
Health Care Financing/Social Security					
Medicaid grants to states	91,077,413	89,685,492	89,685,492	89,688,492	89,688,492
Medicare and other Medicaid	45,731,440	37,546,758	37,546,758	37,546,758	37,546,758
Supplemental Security Income	26,942,866	28,148,601	28,297,101	28,252,101	28,285,101
Public Welfare					
Family support payments (AFDC)	16,373,281	17,161,788	17,161,788	17,161,788	17,161,788
Workfare programs	1,100,000	1,300,000	1,300,000	1,300,000	1,300,000
Low-Income Home Energy Assistance	1,475,000	745,000	1,225,000	1,475,000	1,319,204
Refugee assistance	399,779	413,786	399,779	399,779	399,779
Community Services Block Grants	464,219	434,622	465,714	476,219	472,920
Child-care grants	892,641	1,090,662	934,656	934,656	934,656
Social Services Block Grants	3,800,000	2,800,000	2,800,000	2,800,000	2,800,000
Head Start, misc. family assistance	4,234,273	4,911,037	4,408,775	4,415,514	4,419,888
Programs for the aging	871,687	875,603	869,823	873,662	877,223
Foster care, adoption assistance	2,992,900	3,597,371	3,440,871	3,597,371	3,597,371
Other	1,024,106	140,626	717,683	856,002	732,680
Total, HHS	**$ 216,022,538**	**$ 208,313,213**	**$ 208,485,875**	**$ 209,049,076**	**$ 208,853,200**
Education Department					
Elementary and Secondary Education					
Compensatory education (Title 1)	6,911,689	7,578,514	7,245,655	7,233,411	7,232,722
Impact aid	798,208	750,000	728,000	666,880	728,000
Education improvement (Chapter 2)	620,498	752,000	667,548	667,548	667,548
Bilingual, immigrant education	227,431	253,920	247,572	238,082	245,200
Special education	3,108,702	3,294,959	3,106,634	3,299,459	3,252,846
Higher Education					
Pell grants, student financial aid	8,020,160	7,863,935	7,825,417	7,685,524	7,702,970
Guaranteed student loan administration	69,966 [1]	64,191 [1]	62,191 [1]	62,191 [1]	62,191 [1]
Higher education grants	893,688	889,489	954,686	946,703	962,842
Vocational, adult education	1,481,183	1,447,265	1,456,383	1,475,736	1,473,175
Rehabilitation services	2,296,936	2,361,458	2,355,600	2,413,675	2,393,352
Libraries	146,309	102,976	115,996	147,558	144,161
Education research	290,755	368,199	318,775	371,586	354,892
Other	1,694,013	2,597,822	2,064,823	2,191,395	2,208,413
Total, Education Department	**$ 26,559,538**	**$ 28,324,728**	**$ 27,149,280**	**$ 27,399,748**	**$ 27,428,312**
Domestic Volunteer Service Programs	204,153	238,830	205,771	217,688	214,710
Corporation for Public Broadcasting	312,000	292,640	—	330,000	315,000
Other related agencies	553,499	539,873	520,852	542,935	538,516
GRAND TOTAL	**$ 258,454,074** [2]	**$ 251,555,092**	**$ 249,668,588**	**$ 250,762,149**	**$ 250,610,477** [3]

[1] *Appropriation for guaranteed student loan account does not include $693,630,000 in fiscal 1995 for new direct student loan program or $2,600,031,000 in fiscal 1995 for Federal Family Education Loans provided under permanent authority.*
[2] *Fiscal 1994 grand total includes $225,000 rescission in the Weed and Seed program.*
[3] *Final bill total includes $7,500 for crime reduction programs.*

SOURCE: House Appropriations Committee

education law (PL 102-325), the nation's 4,000 for-profit trade schools were required as of July 1 to derive at least 15 percent of their annual revenues from sources other than federally backed student loans.

Previously, such schools had been allowed to receive 100 percent of their money from federal loan programs. The regulation aimed to eliminate schools that provided dubious job training to students who often defaulted on their loans. *(1992 Almanac, p. 438)*

Bonilla proposed delaying the July 1 starting date by one year. He said many schools relied almost exclusively on students who received federally backed loans and contended that the new regulation would put many schools out of business. Richard J. Durbin, D-Ill., argued against the extension, saying many of the schools were "rip-offs, milking the federal government for money."

Committee members also:

● Rejected by voice vote an amendment by Tom DeLay, R-Texas, to strike a section of a Depression era labor law, the Davis-Bacon Act, requiring that workers on federal construction projects be paid the local prevailing wage, usually union wages. Conservative House Republicans contended yearly that such wages inflated construction costs at the expense of taxpayers. Many Democrats supported Davis-Bacon because it boosted workers' wages.

● Rejected, 20-20, an amendment by Ron Packard, R-Calif., to deny illegal aliens benefits under the bill. Packard estimated that as much as $10 billion in services, such as food stamps or medical care, was provided to undocumented immigrants every year. He agreed that existing law already prohibited such aliens from receiving benefits but said the point needed reiteration. "It's time to start enforcing what is in law," Packard said. "I think that's an important message to send to agency heads."

Packard's comment drew a spirited response from several lawmakers. Carrie P. Meek, D-Fla., reminded members that they or their ancestors had probably immigrated to the United States. "I feel this committee is sending a very wrong message," she said.

● Rejected, in a 15-28 party-line vote, an amendment by ranking Labor-HHS Subcommittee Republican John Edward Porter of Illinois to establish 125 community health centers nationwide, primarily in urban centers and rural communities. Porter argued that such facilities would go a long way toward easing the health care crisis for low-income Americans. But Smith called the amendment little more than partisan gamesmanship by conservative Republicans. "This is an amendment to convince people we don't need a new health bill," he said.

● Persuaded Porter to withdraw an amendment to increase funding for the National Institutes of Health by $105 million to keep up with inflation. NIH, which conducted biomedical research, was to receive $11.3 billion in fiscal 1995 under the House committee bill. "If we underfund NIH, we will lose a whole generation of researchers," said Porter, who proposed to offset the increase with cuts in drug and alcohol abuse treatment programs and administrative costs. Durbin countered that while NIH programs were worthy, "you can't talk deficit reduction without facing exactly these kinds of choices."

House Floor

After two days of floor action, the House on June 29 passed the $249.7 billion bill by a vote of 339-89. *(Vote 304, p. 88-H)*

Jose E. Serrano, D-N.Y., a member of the Labor-HHS Ap-

propriations Subcommittee, echoed the sentiments of many lawmakers when he said hundreds of worthy programs would be forced to do with less than they deserved. "We simply weren't allocated enough money to do it all," Serrano said.

In a surprise victory for Republicans on June 28, members voted to adopt Porter's proposal to establish 125 new community health centers across the nation. The vote was 224-205. *(Vote 294, p. 86-H)*

But the upset proved short-lived. The next day, committee leaders demanded a revote as allowed under the rules, and the House rejected the Porter amendment, 211-217. Democratic leaders had leaned on some of the 53 members who had crossed party lines to vote for the clinics. *(Vote 302, p. 88-H)*

The amendment would have shifted $87 million in administrative costs at the three Cabinet agencies to pay for 125 clinics. Porter and other Republicans said that increasing the number of clinics would improve access to health care for more than 800,000 low-income citizens in rural and urban areas. HHS already operated about 1,500 community health centers nationwide.

Democrats again denounced the proposal as an effort to undermine any health care reform package that Congress might produce in 1994. "What we have here is a political fig leaf," said Appropriations Committee Chairman David R. Obey, D-Wis. "They want to be on the record, somewhere, somehow, on the cheap, in voting for health care. I don't think that's the way to do business."

House Minority Leader Robert H. Michel, Ill., disagreed. "Regardless of what health care reform we eventually undertake, we still need expansion of the community health center network," he said.

The House also rejected, 63-365, an amendment by Maxine Waters, D-Calif., to strike the provision added in committee to delay until July 1, 1995, the implementation of new regulations on trade and proprietary schools. *(Vote 301, p. 88-H)*

Waters cited reports showing that "up to one-fifth of the $20 billion in federal student loan funds is hemorrhaging from the system each year because of abuse and fraud." But Bonilla, who sponsored the committee amendment, said implementing such a rule would put many trade schools out of business.

Members also rejected, 188-233, an amendment to eliminate an $8.2 million Native Hawaiian Education program. The amendment was offered by John A. Boehner, R-Ohio, who led conservatives in arguing that funding for such narrow, special interests was an inefficient use of money. But Patsy T. Mink, D-Hawaii, defended the program by likening it to similar ones provided for American Indians. Mink said the money helped perpetuate Native Hawaiian culture among the island nation's children, many of whom were from low-income families. *(Vote 295, p. 86-H)*

House members also:

● Approved by voice vote an amendment by Rick Santorum, R-Pa., to shift $32 million from the Social Security Administration's administrative costs to the agency's disability claims area to reduce a backlog in processing applications.

● Adopted, 319-109, an amendment by Bill Baker, R-Calif., to increase funding for public libraries by $1 million to $115.9 million. *(Vote 299, p. 86-H)*

● Rejected, 35-393, an amendment by John L. Mica, R-Fla., to increase immigrant education programs by $25 million to $272.6 million and to use the money to reimburse states for the costs of educating the children of illegal aliens. *(Vote 298, p. 86-H)*

● Rejected, 42-384, an amendment by Philip M. Crane, R-Ill.,

to eliminate the $293 million appropriation in the bill for the Corporation for Public Broadcasting (CPB). Crane argued that with the advent of cable television, CPB no longer needed federal subsidies as an alternative broadcasting outlet. Opponents said funding was still necessary because many people could not afford cable television. The House did adopt, by voice vote, an amendment by Joel Hefley, R-Colo., to cut the corporation's funding by $1 million. *(Vote 300, p. 88-H)*

● Rejected, 194-232, an amendment by Rod Grams, R-Minn., to eliminate a $15 million education program that funded legal clinics for low-income people. Grants were provided to law schools, which operated the centers to give law students a chance to perform legal services. *(Vote 297, p. 86-H)*

Senate Committee

The Senate Appropriations Committee approved its version of the bill July 20 (S Rept 103-318) that closely tracked the House-passed measure. The vote was 28-0. The spending plan had been approved by voice vote earlier in the day by the Labor-HHS Appropriations Subcommittee.

As in the House, Senate appropriators came up significantly shy of Clinton's request for "human investment" initiatives in education, job training and health. For example, they:

● Recommended $428 million for the Goals 2000 program, compared with $388 million in the House bill and $708 million in Clinton's budget.

● Approved $200 million for the School-to-Work vocational education training program, compared with $280 million in the House bill and $300 million in Clinton's budget.

● Approved $634 million for Ryan White AIDS prevention and intervention programs. The House recommended $626 million; Clinton requested $672 million.

● Approved just over $3.5 billion for Head Start, nearly the same as the House. Clinton wanted a $700 million increase, to $4 billion.

Senate appropriators also rejected many of the program cuts that Clinton requested to offset his initiatives. For instance, they recommended $1.4 billion for LIHEAP. The House approved $1.2 billion; Clinton wanted $745 million. Clinton wanted to kill the $8.1 million Education for Native Hawaiians program. But the House approved $8.2 million, and Senate appropriators approved $15 million.

Like the House, Senate appropriators avoided a confrontation over abortion.

Appropriators' Amendments

At the subcommittee markup, members adopted by voice vote an amendment by ranking Republican Arlen Specter of Pennsylvania, to shift $20 million from the federal Perkins college loan program to an education technology program. The technology initiative, part of the elementary and secondary education reauthorization bill (S 1513) awaiting Senate consideration, was intended to finance the purchase of computers and software for schools in poor regions.

At the full committee markup, members adopted by voice vote a proposal by Dale Bumpers, D-Ark., that had the potential to delay indefinitely the implementation of a vaccine distribution program set to take effect Oct. 1. Under the existing system, vaccines were shipped directly from manufacturers to 60 private sites nationwide for storage and eventual use in doctors' offices or health clinics.

The new plan involved opening a government warehouse for vaccine storage and creating a program under the Centers for Disease Control and Prevention to distribute vaccines to 64,000 physicians. Advocates said government distribution would save time and money. Opponents said the government had no experience handling vaccines.

Bumpers' amendment, similar to one adopted by the House, required the HHS secretary to certify to Congress when the new system was ready to go. Meanwhile, vaccines were to be delivered under the existing system.

Senate Floor

The Senate passed the $250.8 billion bill Aug. 10 by a vote of 87-13, after it rejected an effort by senators from Florida, California and Texas to add $100 million in fiscal 1995 funding for the education of immigrant children. *(Vote 270, p. 45-S)*

In other action before final passage, the Senate tabled (killed), 100-0, an amendment by Jesse Helms, R-N.C. seeking to postpone debate until 1995 on health care overhaul. Helms voted to table his own amendment because he preferred a similar one that he offered on the appropriations bill for the Department of Defense (HR 4650). That amendment also failed. *(Vote 267, p. 45-S)*

Helms did win unanimous approval for an amendment to make it a felony for anyone knowingly infected with the AIDS virus to donate blood, tissues, organs or any bodily fluids. The penalty for violators could be a $20,000 fine and up to 10 years in prison. Several states, including California, Ohio and South Carolina, already had similar laws. *(Vote 266, p. 45-S)*

Senators voted 66-34 to table (kill) an amendment by Bob Graham, D-Fla., to increase fiscal 1995 spending for immigrant education programs from $50 million to $150 million. Congress appropriated $38.9 million in fiscal 1994 in so-called emergency immigrant education aid to help schools deal with immigrant children, and Clinton requested the same amount for fiscal 1995. *(Vote 269, p. 45-S)*

Graham, who cosponsored the amendment with Kay Bailey Hutchison, R-Texas, and Dianne Feinstein, D-Calif., said the influx of illegal immigrants in recent years had overwhelmed school systems in many states, particularly those along the nation's southern border. He blamed part of the problem on lax border enforcement by the federal government. "Our states are facing an emergency situation," he said. Under Graham's amendment, the additional money would have come from cutting salaries and expenses at the departments of Labor, Health and Human Services, and Education.

Chairman Harkin said his subcommittee recognized the difficulty that many states were experiencing and noted that House and Senate appropriators had recommended an $11 million increase in funding for immigrant education over fiscal 1994 levels. But he described as "draconian" the prospect of cutting $100 million from the three Cabinet agencies. He said it could result in agency layoffs as well as processing backlogs at the Social Security Administration.

In earlier action, the Senate on Aug. 5 turned back an attempt to limit CPB funding. On a 68-26 tabling motion, senators killed an amendment by John McCain, R-Ariz., to shift $37.4 million from the corporation to HHS for AIDS research and prevention in fiscal 1997. *(Vote 264, p. 45-S)*

Senate appropriators recommended $330 million for the CPB in fiscal 1995. Clinton proposed $292.6 million; the House approved $271.5 million.

McCain said he appreciated the importance of public broadcasting but that the proliferation of cable TV in recent years had provided the public with alternatives to for-profit broadcasting outlets. Ted Stevens, R-Alaska, argued that the

additional money was necessary to continue reaching people who could not afford cable television, especially those living in isolated and rural areas. "These people are already underserved and unserved," he said.

Senators voted 63-31 to table (kill) an amendment by Specter to prohibit Clinton from deploying U.S. armed forces in Haiti without the consent of Congress. McCain opposed the Specter amendment, saying that approval of such a measure could set a dangerous precedent that might effectively tie the hands of presidents during crisis situations. *(Vote 263, p. 45-S)*

Conference/Final Action

House and Senate negotiators breezed through a 12-minute conference session on the bill Sept. 20, agreeing to appropriate $250.6 billion in fiscal 1995 (H Rept 103-733).

As expected, Clinton's initiatives for education, health and job training received significantly less than requested.

For example, the bill provided $403 million for the Goals 2000 education reform bill; Clinton asked for $708 million in fiscal 1995. Carnie Hayes, a lobbyist for the Council of Chief State School Officers, a Washington, D.C., group that represented top school administrators, said the money was inadequate. "Overall, the year is a big disappointment" for education funding, said Hayes, who added that if programs such as Goals 2000 were going to have an impact, full funding would be critical in coming years. "These are not isolated programs without a framework," Hayes said. "That's very important money."

Conferees agreed to split the difference between the two chambers on LIHEAP, providing $1.3 billion for the program, compared with the $745 million requested by Clinton.

Over the objections of House Appropriations Chairman Obey, the conferees allocated $100 million in fiscal 1995 to help rehabilitate dilapidated schools. A bill to reauthorize elementary and secondary school programs that cleared at the end of the regular session (HR 6 — PL 103-382) included a new title authorizing funds to upgrade school facilities. *(Elementary and secondary education, p. 383)*

Obey questioned whether Congress would have the political will or adequate resources to address the problem year after year. "I really believe this is a long-term mistake," he said. Obey said that instead of funding school repairs, the government should encourage states to avoid infrastructure problems by equalizing education spending between rich and poor school districts. He added that Congress should not attempt to cure problems that were primarily the responsibility of local governments. Obey did not try to remove the program's funding from the bill, but said he would resist such appropriations in the future.

Harkin said he was committed to providing poorer schools with federal funding. "We do it with bridges and roads," he said. "Why can't we do it with education?"

In other action, House conferees readily accepted the Senate amendment making it a felony for anyone knowingly infected with the AIDS virus to donate blood, tissues, organs or any bodily fluids.

Final Action

The House adopted the conference report in a 331-89 vote Sept. 22. *(Vote 434, p. 130-H)*

Senators voted 83-16 on Sept. 27 to adopt the conference report, but formal clearance was delayed until the next day while senators debated two proposed amendments that remained subject to individual consideration. *(Vote 310, p. 53-S)*

William S. Cohen, R-Maine, proposed an amendment to establish a data base to allow the federal government to track people who had benefited from health care fraud at taxpayers' expense. He said millions of dollars were lost each year when unscrupulous doctors and other providers took government money for nonexistent patients or charged for services not performed.

Senators had approved provisions of the amendment as part of the Senate-passed crime bill (HR 3355, formerly S 1607), but the health fraud provisions were dropped in a House-Senate conference committee before the crime bill became law (PL 103-322). *(Crime bill, p. 273)*

With few pieces of legislation remaining before adjournment, Cohen said the Labor-HHS bill provided an opportunity to enact the fraud provisions. But after pleas from colleagues, Cohen withdrew the amendment, saying he would offer it again on the conference report for the fiscal 1995 District of Columbia appropriations bill (HR 4649).

Howard M. Metzenbaum, D-Ohio, then said he would offer an amendment to partially lift major-league baseball's 72-year-old exemption from antitrust laws. Harkin said that if Metzenbaum persisted, other senators would be encouraged to offer amendments that could further delay the spending plan. "It's open season, and this whole bill would become bogged down," Harkin said.

The next day, Metzenbaum abandoned the amendment after learning that a House subcommittee was expected to act on a similar bill; that bill never advanced. *(Baseball, p. 182)* ■

Slight Increase for Legislative Branch

Without controversy, Congress more than offset two years of modest cuts in spending for legislative operations with a $2.37 billion fiscal 1995 bill for the legislative branch. The measure, which cleared July 1, gave the House, Senate and congressional agencies an average spending increase of 4 percent over the previous year. President Clinton signed the bill into law July 22 (HR 4454 — PL 103-283)

The bill included $96.7 million more in funding than the fiscal 1994 version. Excluding an accounting adjustment (which subtracted $23 million from the fiscal 1995 total to reflect a rescission of excess funds previously appropriated to the Senate), the bill rose $119.7 million over fiscal 1994 — a 5 percent increase. Congress had approved cuts of less than 2 percent in both fiscal 1993 and 1994 — a total of about $60 million. *(1993 Almanac, p. 646)*

Among other things, the increase financed raises of at least 2 percent for most legislative branch employees. Some salary accounts included increases of 5 percent or more.

However, Rep. Vic Fazio, D-Calif., chairman of the House Appropriations Legislative Branch Subcommittee, said the bill's total was actually 12.3 percent below the fiscal 1992 level when inflation was taken into account.

House Committee

After initiating spending cuts for two consecutive years, the House Legislative Branch Appropriations Subcommittee proposed increasing the appropriation for congressional operations by $102 million over fiscal 1994 — a 5.7 percent hike. That recommendation came May 12 as the subpanel gave voice vote approval to a bill to provide $1.9 billion for the House and other congressional agencies. The measure went to the full Appropriations Committee May 19, where it was accepted by voice vote (H Rept 103-517). The House bill did not include money for Senate operations, which was to be added later by that chamber.

The bill contained $35 million for House members' mailing expenses — down from $40 million from fiscal 1994, which had been an election year.

Among the increases approved in the bill were $6.6 million for six new elevators for the Longworth House Office Building and $1.3 million for modernizing existing elevators and escalators. The bill also provided $7 million to begin renovation of the dilapidated conservatory at the Botanic Garden. The $28 million project had been delayed for years to save money. The committee also approved 26 new employees for the Congressional Research Service to ward off threats of reduced services for members.

The full committee rejected two Republican amendments by voice vote. The first, by Ron Packard of California, would have restricted the use of money in the bill to benefit illegal aliens. Packard offered similar amendments to other bills in

1994. The second amendment, by Robert L. Livingston of Louisiana, would have saved $108,234 by eliminating the House's special deputy to the Federal Election Commission, an official whose status as a non-voting member of the Federal Election Commission was ruled unconstitutional in 1993.

House Floor

After sailing through committee, the legislative branch spending bill was only narrowly approved by the full House May 26. With rank and file members apprehensive about increasing Congress' budget at a time when funds were tight and the institution was low in opinion polls, the measure escaped by a vote of 210-205. Though the House clipped $23 million from the committee-approved bill, a total of 35 Democrats joined the 170 Republicans in opposition. Only two Republicans voted for the measure. The bill provided nearly $1.86 billion for congressional operations. *(Vote 216, p. 64-H)*

Republicans objected vociferously to the rule governing floor debate, which allowed votes on only 12 amendments, but debate on the bill itself lacked the fireworks of years past. The only spirited exchange came on an amendment to eliminate the $6.6 million set aside for construction of new elevators for the Longworth building; lawmakers quickly rejected that amendment by voice vote.

Although the bill increased legislative branch spending by about $78.8 million, or 4.2 percent, Democratic leaders said members had proven their austerity by putting the congressional budget on a downward slope the previous two years. In a presentation rife with charts, subcommittee Chairman Fazio said the 15-year record was even more telling: Adjusted for inflation, judicial branch spending more than doubled during that time period, and executive branch spending increased by almost 30 percent. Over the same time, Fazio said, legislative branch spending decreased by 1.4 percent.

Republicans generally agreed that lawmakers had made some progress in controlling their own expenditures but said that more could be done without impinging on the ability of Congress and other agencies covered under the measure to do their work.

Amendments

During floor debate, the House adopted amendments to:
● Trim the House mail account by $4 million, to $31 million from $35 million in the committee-approved bill. The 375-48 vote to cut the spending continued a recent trend. The House franking privilege, used by members to send out newsletters and other mailings, had become a politically popular target for cuts, particularly for younger members. *(Vote 212, p. 64-H)*

Freshman Earl Pomeroy, D-N.D., sponsored the amendment. Noting that he depended more heavily than many members on mail to communicate with his constituents because of the size of his district, he said he still was able to return 25

Legislative Spending

(in millions of dollars)

	Fiscal 1994 Appropriations	House Bill	Senate Bill	Final Bill
Congressional Operations				
Senate	$444.4	—	$437.6	$437.6
House of Representatives	686.5	728.6	728.6	728.6
Joint Items	78.8	82.8	86.2	88.2
Office of Technology Assessment	21.3	21.9	22.0	22.0
Congressional Budget Office	22.3	23.1	23.2	23.2
Architect of the Capitol	150.2	111.3	159.7	159.7
Congressional Research Service	56.7	58.9	60.5	60.1
Government Printing Office (congressional printing)	88.4	87.7	89.7	89.7
Subtotal	**$ 1,548.5**	**$ 1,114.4**	**$ 1,607.4**	**$ 1,607.0**
Related Agencies				
Botanic Garden	3.0	3.2	3.2	3.2
Library of Congress	249.8	260.2	263.1	263.1
Architect of the Capitol (library buildings)	10.0	9.9	13.5	12.5
Copyright Royalty Tribunal	0.1	—	—	—
Government Printing Office (non-congressional)	29.1	30.6	32.2	32.2
General Accounting Office	430.2	439.5	449.4	449.4
Subtotal	**$ 722.2**	**$ 743.4**	**$ 761.4**	**$ 760.4**
Grand Total	**$ 2,270.7**	**$ 1,857.8**	**$ 2,368.8**	**$ 2,367.4**

SOURCE: House Appropriations Committee

percent of his franking allocation. Several Republicans wanted to offer amendments to cut franking more deeply but were barred from doing so by the rule.

● Cut funds for the Government Printing Office (GPO), the federal government's main printer, by a total of $8.9 million and eliminate 300 jobs at the agency, which employed nearly 5,000 people. The House adopted, by voice vote, four separate amendments dealing with the GPO account. Republicans criticized the agency for losing money. Pat Roberts, R-Kan., who sponsored one of the amendments, said the GPO estimated that it would lose $27 million in fiscal 1994 and another $29 million in fiscal 1995.

● Decrease funding for the Botanic Garden to $3.2 million.

● Trim the amounts for salaries and expenses for House support offices, including those of the clerk and doorkeeper.

● Increase the mandatory retirement age for Capitol Police officers from 55 to 57.

In addition to the amendment on elevators, the House rejected 193-232 an amendment that would have cut funding for the General Accounting Office (GAO) by $31 million from the $439.5 million in the bill. Many Republicans said the agency was too large and that it generally investigated issues favorable to the liberal agenda of congressional Democratic leaders. *(Vote 213, p. 64-H)*

Republicans Protest Rule

The biggest floor fight came over the rule that restricted Republicans to a dozen amendments.

As in the past, Democrats argued that the legislative branch bill attracted amendments that were intended to embarrass Congress, and their leadership used its power to set the rules governing debate to quash those amendments before they got to the floor. In a session that stretched over 15 hours and ended in the early morning hours of May 26, the Rules Committee adopted, on a 5-4 party-line vote with one member voting "present," a rule that made in order only 12 of the 43 proposed amendments, most of them backed by Republicans.

Even C. W. Bill Young of Florida, who as ranking Republican on the Legislative Branch Subcommittee cautioned members of his party against proposing amendments that merely looked good back home, opposed the rule. He voted against the bill as well.

Democrats argued that the total spending in the bill, as drafted by the Appropriations Committee, was low enough and that the amendments made in order would trim away any excess fat. The rule was adopted on a virtual party-line vote of 249-177. Only three Democrats voted against it. Robert S. Walker, R-Pa., declared: "I will guarantee one thing: If you put Republicans in charge of this body next January, one of the first bills that we will revisit is this legislative appropriations bill." *(Vote 210, p. 64-H)*

Senate Committee

The Senate Appropriations Committee approved its version of the legislative branch bill June 14 on a 29-0 vote (S Rept 103-283). Its $2.37 billion bottom line included $500 million added to the House bill to cover Senate expenses. For the first time, the committee accepted a ban on unsolicited mass mailings.

According to Appropriations Committee figures, the Senate's overall budget would decrease slightly, but that was only because the bill rescinded $23 million in unspent funds from prior years. Not counting the rescission, the Senate's total was set to increase by nearly 4 percent, and the size of the entire bill would increase by 5 percent.

In its report, the committee said the fiscal 1995 bill was $330 million smaller than the fiscal 1992 measure in inflation-adjusted dollars. The report depicted service-reducing personnel cuts in congressional support agencies, including the Capitol Police, the Library of Congress and the GAO. The report also said that Senate committee staff had been reduced by 10 percent since fiscal 1992 to 1,005 employees. The bill report warned that further reductions would "put the analytical capabilities and independence of the legislative branch at serious risk."

In explaining the bill to committee colleagues, subcommittee Chairman Harry Reid, D-Nev., said he had been asked repeatedly about rumors that it included a pay raise for members, which he denied. Members' pay, he explained, increased automatically with inflation each year unless Congress passed a bill to the contrary.

The bill, however, included some good news for members: The committee approved a $20,000 increase for each member's annual office budget.

Other major provisions of the committee bill provided raises of at least 2 percent and in many cases more for congressional employees; revamped the twice-yearly reports that disclosed members' expenditures to make them easier to understand; and appropriated $1 million for a new account to pay employment discrimination settlements arising from complaints to the Senate's recently created Office of Fair Employment Practices. The bill also gave the employment office's staff an extra aide, for a total of six.

The bill provided $7 million in funds left over from previous years to begin renovating the dilapidated conservatory at the Botanic Garden — money that was cut from the House bill on the floor. Also included was $3.5 million for improvements to the Library of Congress complex. The bill required the secretary of the Senate to draft a report on how to improve the "educational experience" of visitors to the Senate. And it provided an increase for the Office of Technology Assessment (3 percent) that was smaller than most other entities funded in the bill. The committee criticized the 22-year-old agency for issuing reports that had little direct bearing on its original mission — to advise Congress on emerging technologies.

The committee report showed that various congressional agencies were meeting or exceeding staffing cuts of 4 percent over two years that were mandated by the fiscal 1994 bill. But the report did not say whether staffing levels in members' offices, which totaled more than 4,000 aides in all, had declined. According to a top GOP aide, they had not come down significantly.

Senate Floor

The full Senate approved the legislative branch appropriations bill June 16, after defeating a motion by Robert C. Smith, R-N.H., to send the bill back to the committee with instructions to reduce its funding by $93 million to the fiscal 1994 level. Both decisions came on voice votes.

The increased spending approved by the Senate largely offset a 2.5 percent cut imposed in the fiscal 1994 bill on members' budgets, which ranged from about $1.4 million to $2.4 million, depending on state size and distance from Washington. The increase also represented a retreat from a warning in the Appropriations Committee's report on the 1994 measure, which predicted that "a comparable reduction will be necessary in fiscal 1995."

Rural senators, led by Alaska Republican Ted Stevens, successfully fought the committee-approved ban on unsolicited mass mailings. They maintained that they had few other effective ways to communicate with rural constituents. In 1993, the Senate had voted 48-47 to kill a similar amendment by Connie Mack, R-Fla.

The compromise that emerged on the floor, which was approved by voice vote, cut the official mail budget by $4 million to $11 million and barred senators from using the funds for mass mail. But $3 million was added to the office expense account ($30,000 per senator), and language was added authorizing senators to spend up to $50,000 from the account on mass mailings. In effect, this allowed senators from small states to do mass mailings but was not enough to blanket states such as California. Senators who chose not to do mass mailings were permitted to spend the funds on other office expenses.

The cost of the frank in both chambers had decreased gradually as a result of reforms limiting lawmakers' mailing budget and making such expenditures public. The fiscal 1994 appropriation included $20 for official Senate mail, down from $32 million two years earlier. By backing off the full ban, the Senate effectively let the House off the hook. Though House mail costs also had dropped, members there historically were more resistant to franking limits, arguing that they lacked senators' access to news media attention.

The Senate bill included language to permit locality pay increases for all workers paid with funds appropriated by the bill, except those who worked for the House, Senate, CBO and the Office of Technology Assessment. The Senate approved an amendment to release those funds only if a locality pay increase was included in the Treasury-Postal Service appropriations bill. The exception was the Capitol Police, who were to be guaranteed the pay increase. Locality pay allowed salary increases for white-collar workers in high-cost areas where federal pay lagged behind that found in the private sector. The Treasury-Postal appropriations bill (HR 4539 — PL 103-329) did include a locality pay increase. (Treasury-Postal appropriations, p. 536)

Other Floor Amendments

The Senate by voice vote approved amendments by:
● Conrad Burns, R-Mont., to require large printing jobs to be sent to the 21 regional Government Printing Offices, where they would be open to competitive bids by the private sector.
● Reid, modifying a proposal by Barbara A. Mikulski, D-Md., to pressure the Architect of the Capitol, George M. White, to improve job opportunities for minorities and women. A GAO audit had found that women and minorities in the architect's office, which employed more than 2,000 people to take care of Capitol Hill buildings and grounds, were concentrated in low-pay, low-skill jobs. The amendment required the office to establish a new personnel management system and a grievance process for job discrimination complaints.
● James M. Jeffords, R-Vt., to eliminate the Capitol Police force's mandatory retirement age of 55 for its officers.

Conference/Final Action

With no items in serious dispute, the House-Senate conference meeting on the bill was perfunctory. Negotiators agreed June 28 to a $2.4 billion compromise based on the bills passed by the two chambers (H Rept 103-567).

Each chamber passed the $2.4 billion conference agreement without formal debate. The House approved it by voice vote June 29. The Senate cleared the measure for the president's signature July 1 by a vote of 73-27. (Vote 183, p. 31-S)

The most significant difference involved Conrad's amendment limiting the ability of federal agencies to go around the GPO to procure printing services. The private printing industry, to which the GPO subcontracted most government printing work, backed the amendment. The final bill included an altered version of the provision that was not as strict as the Senate amendment, but conferees said they hoped to revisit the issue in 1995.

The final bill included a slightly altered version of Mikulski's amendment to revamp the Architect of the Capitol's personnel management system in response to numerous discrimination complaints. Also in the bill was $7 million from previously appropriated funds to begin renovating the conservatory at the U.S. Botanic Garden near the Capitol.

Jeffords' amendment to eliminate the Capitol Police force's mandatory retirement age of 55, was dropped from the bill. The measure instead raised the age to 57, the same as for other federal law enforcement agencies. ■

Military Construction Pared Down

Congress appropriated $8.84 billion for military construction in fiscal 1995, rejecting sharp cutbacks requested by President Clinton but still providing $628 million less than was available for fiscal 1994. The bill (HR 4453) funded road, building and housing projects on military bases; environmental cleanup at defense facilities; and the expensive process of cleaning up and closing unneeded bases so that they could be sold or converted to other uses. The Senate cleared the measure Aug. 10. Clinton, who had requested a total of $8.35 billion for military construction, signed the bill into law Aug. 23 (PL 103-307). *(1993 Almanac, p. 657)*

National Guard and reserve unit facilities fared well under the bill, receiving $574 million for construction projects. Senate lawmakers, in particular, said these military services had received short shrift in the Clinton budget, which had recommended $171 million for facility construction.

The final bill included:

● **Base closures.** $2.68 billion, as requested, to close down, clean up and convert bases for alternative uses.

● **Family housing.** $3.52 billion for family housing on bases. Of that, $2.81 billion was for operations and maintenance of existing housing, with only $714 million allocated for new construction.

● **Military construction.** $2.65 billion for military construction and renovation projects. Two of the largest projects requested by the Clinton administration, but rejected by conferees, were Army ammunition demilitarization facilities in Pine Bluff, Ark., and Umatilla, Ore.

● **NATO.** $119 million for NATO infrastructure costs. Clinton had requested $219 million.

House Action

After a 10-minute, closed-door session, the House Appropriations Military Construction Subcommittee on May 12 approved a draft fiscal 1995 bill that provided about $8.84 billion. "We're happy with it, because it's the best we could do," Subcommittee Chairman W. G. "Bill" Hefner, D-N.C., said, referring to the tight fiscal 1995 federal budget.

The panel approved $119 million, $100 million less than Clinton requested, for NATO's infrastructure fund, the pooled contributions that paid for improvements to bases used by NATO. This line item had been controversial in the past, with Congress asking "host nations" to pay a greater share.

Full Committee Action

The full House Appropriations Committee gave voice vote approval May 19 to an $8.82 billion fiscal 1995 military construction spending bill (H Rept 103-516).

Introducing the bill to colleagues, Subcommittee Chairman Hefner emphasized that it would provide about $3.5 billion for family housing for military personnel. "I can't emphasize enough how important housing is to the quality

---

BOXSCORE

Fiscal 1995 Military Construction Appropriations — HR 4453. The $8.84 billion bill paid for building U.S. and overseas military bases, housing military personnel and closing unneeded bases.

Reports: H Rept 103-516, S Rept 103-312; conference report H Rept 103-624.

KEY ACTION

May 24 — House passed HR 4453, 380-42.

July 15 — Senate passed HR 4453, amended, 84-2.

Aug. 1 — House adopted the conference report by voice vote.

Aug. 10 — Senate cleared the bill, 95-5.

Aug. 23 — President signed bill — PL 103-307.

---

of life of our military men and women," Hefner said.

The measure included $2.68 billion to continue the process of closing unneeded military bases, a program that had become a thorn in the military construction budget, absorbing more funds each year. The amount for base closings exceeded the $2.52 billion provided for construction and repair projects at military facilities. *(Base closings, p. 435)*

New construction took the largest hit. The portion of the bill that funded barracks, weapons facilities and other base construction was 31 percent less than in fiscal 1994.

In their report, panel members complained that meeting environmental regulations and dismantling chemical arms were eating up funding that should go to construction and improvements. "Many readiness, revitalization and quality-of-life projects have been deferred," the report said.

As was usually the case with the military construction bill, the markup went quickly and prompted little debate. Two amendments to the committee report were approved by voice vote.

The first, offered by Robert L. Livingston, R-La., prohibited funds from going to the Defense Information Systems Agency until the agency issued a report explaining a $108 million discrepancy in its cost estimates for the recent consolidation of a defense data center.

The second amendment, offered by Frank R. Wolf, R-Va., barred the military from removing items such as office furniture, vehicles or other property from bases slated for closure. There had been complaints that the services were stripping the bases, making them less useful to the neighboring communities.

The bill also included $40.8 million to build new or improved barracks at three Army stations on the Korean peninsula, where tensions were running high over North Korea's reported nuclear weapons program. According to the committee report, U.S. soldiers were being housed in overcrowded, deteriorating Quonset huts.

Members rejected two amendments by voice vote.

One, by Livingston, would have cut about $12 million in improvements for Homestead Air Force Base in Florida. Homestead had been badly damaged by Hurricane Andrew in 1992 and was slated for for conversion to reserve status.

The other amendment, by Ron Packard, R-Calif., would have barred any funding in the bill from going to undocumented aliens. Hefner opposed the amendment as inappropriate for the military construction budget.

Members' Projects

Because the sole function of the military construction bill was to fund improvements to military bases, it had long been considered an opportunity for lawmakers to lobby for hometown projects. The House bill contained 132 domestic construction projects that had not been requested by the presi-

Military Construction

(in thousands of dollars)

	Fiscal 1995 Clinton Request	House Bill	Senate Bill	Final Bill
Military construction				
Army	$ 690,576	$ 623,511	$ 489,076	$ 550,476
Navy	320,470	462,701	340,455	385,110
Air Force	357,313	514,977	525,863	516,813
Defense agencies	481,729	467,169	561,039	504,118
NATO infrastructure	219,000	119,000	219,000	119,000
National Guard and reserves	171,154	451,925	533,369	574,302
Subtotal	**$ 2,240,242**	**$ 2,639,283**	**$ 2,668,802**	**$ 2,649,819**
Family housing				
Army	1,273,610	1,281,810	1,239,210	1,183,710
Navy	1,082,894	1,122,634	1,166,894	1,205,064
Air Force	1,054,338	1,077,827	1,098,200	1,102,289
Defense agencies	29,381	29,381	29,381	29,381
Subtotal	**$ 3,440,223**	**$ 3,511,652**	**$ 3,533,685**	**$ 3,520,444**
Base realignment and closure				
Part I	87,600	87,600	87,600	87,600
Part II	265,700	265,700	265,700	265,700
Part III	2,322,858	2,322,858	2,322,858	2,322,858
Procurement reform	−10,421	−10,421	−41,921	−10,421
GRAND TOTAL	**$ 8,346,202**	**$ 8,816,672**	**$ 8,836,724**	**$ 8,836,000**

SOURCE: House Appropriations Committee

House Floor Action

The House passed the bill May 24 by an overwhelming majority. The vote was 380-42. *(Vote 193, p. 58-H)*

There was little floor debate on the bill, which sponsors worked hard each year to keep free of controversy. An amendment that could have been germane — to postpone the 1995 round of base closures — was instead offered as new language on the defense authorization bill and rejected. *(Authorization, p. 421)*

The extra spending in the bill — $470 million more than the Defense Department's fiscal 1995 request — prompted Dan Burton, R-Ind., to question whether all additional projects in the bill were vital for military preparedness. Hefner responded, "There was not one project in this bill that is not authorized. There was some $1.5 billion requested [by lawmakers] for add-ons, and we did not have money to even come close to doing those."

Senate Action

The Senate passed an $8.84 billion version of the bill July 15 by a vote of 84-2. The Senate Appropriations Committee had approved the measure, 27-2, the previous day (S Rept 103-312). *(Vote 205, p. 35-S)*

The Senate-passed bill totaled $20.1 million more than the House version and $490.5 million more than Clinton had requested.

Military Construction Appropriations Subcommittee Chairman Jim Sasser, D-Tenn., emphasized that the bill was $362 million more generous to the National Guard and reserves than was the Clinton administration's request. "The administration's request for military construction for fiscal year 1995 was unrealistic as submitted and was unbalanced in defining its priorities," Sasser said.

Like the House bill, the Senate version routed more money toward closing bases than to new construction. The Senate-passed bill contained $2.7 billion for base closures, an increase of $501 million over fiscal 1994. The bulk of that — $2.3 billion — was to be used to implement the round of base closures announced in 1993.

Lawmakers made their biggest cuts in the section of the bill that funded new construction and renovations on military bases. In particular, legislators recommended $64.9 million for base construction in Texas, $71.7 million less than their House counterparts set aside for that state. The Senate also cut the House allocation for California bases by $50.7 million to $124 million.

Sasser added $3.2 million for bases in his home state, including new funding for armories in Oneida and Rogersville, and Air National Guard facilities in Nashville and Memphis. Washington, the home of ranking Republican Slade Gorton, was slated to receive $4.3 million less under the Senate version than under the House-approved bill.

The Senate bill omitted the $40.8 million that House law-

dent but were squeezed in by appropriators. Several Pentagon recommendations, including improvements to the Pine Bluff arsenal in Arkansas, were not fully funded.

Among the biggest winners was Texas, with funding for 24 construction projects at 10 bases and five Army National Guard sites. Fort Bliss, which was partially in the El Paso district of subcommittee member Ronald D. Coleman, D, was targeted to receive $20.8 million for a child development center, a sergeants major academy and a tactical equipment shop.

Pennsylvania bases also did well, with appropriators recommending $41 million over the Clinton administration request for eight projects. The biggest, a $17 million industrial operations facility at the Tobyhanna Army Depot, was in the district of Joseph M. McDade, the Appropriations Committee's ranking Republican.

Maryland, which had two members on the subcommittee, was slated to get $57 million for new construction, $38.7 million of which was not requested by the Pentagon. Two of the president's proposals — a $14.8 million airport annex purchase and a $12.7 million supercomputer facility — were left unfunded.

In family housing construction, the bill included six projects that the Defense Department had not requested. The largest was an order to build 100 units of family housing, at an estimated cost of $17.6 million, on Navy-owned land in Hawaii called Moanalua Terrace.

makers had approved for new or improved barracks at three Army stations on the Korean peninsula.

Senators chose to fully fund the president's $219 million request for NATO's infrastructure fund, the alliance's military construction account.

An amendment approved by voice vote on the Senate floor took aim at the military construction bill's reputation as a repository of pork barrel projects for members' districts. The language, sponsored by John McCain, R-Ariz., expressed the sense of the Senate that any military construction projects that had not been authorized by the Senate had to meet specific criteria of need and national security importance before they could be included in the appropriations bill.

Conference/Final Action

House and Senate conferees agreed July 27 on an $8.84 billion military construction bill (H Rept 103-624), boosting spending for domestic construction projects by as much as one-third above the amount Clinton requested. The House adopted the conference report by voice vote Aug. 1. The Senate cleared the bill Aug. 10 by a vote of 95-5. *(Senate vote 272, p. 46-S)*

The compromise moderated, but did not offset entirely, the sharp spending cut that Clinton proposed for defense installations and military family housing. The bill provided a total of $628 million less than Congress appropriated for military construction in fiscal 1994 but $490 million more than Clinton requested.

That increase, combined with reductions in various Clinton requests, paid for a rise of nearly $700 million in funding for domestic construction.

Apart from spending associated with base closings, Clinton requested $2.2 billion for domestic construction projects; the final bill provided $2.9 billion.

More than 40 percent of the increase for domestic construction was accounted for by six states, each of which received increases of more than $40 million: Texas ($59 million), California ($53 million), Georgia ($50 million), Pennsylvania ($47 million), South Carolina ($47 million) and Virginia ($48 million).

More than half the increase for domestic construction projects — nearly $400 million — was earmarked for dozens of National Guard and reserve facilities, most of which were relatively minor projects costing less than $10 million apiece. Sasser's home state of Tennessee fared particularly well, receiving money for Guard and reserve projects at 13 sites.

Conferees also approved $34.6 million to build barracks at three sites in Korea.

Conferees went with the House in slicing $100 million from the president's $219 million request for the annual U.S. contribution to NATO's Infrastructure Fund.

They also ordered the Pentagon to find $137 million in reductions within its total fiscal 1995 construction program. Such reductions should be made, the conferees said in their report, to take account of "project savings from favorable bids, reduced overhead costs, cancellations due to force structure changes and cancellations due to the 1995 base . . . closure decisions."

The largest cuts the conferees made in Clinton's requests for specific projects affected two plants intended to dismantle chemical weapons and neutralize their toxic ingredients. Clinton requested $97 million for a so-called "demilitarization" facility at Pine Bluff, Ark., and $179 million for a similar installation at Umatilla, Ore.

Instead, conferees approved only small amounts for each plant — $3 million for Pine Bluff and $12 million for Umatilla, conforming with the Senate's version of the fiscal 1995 defense authorization bill (S 2182). ∎

Pet Projects Threaten Transport Bill

For the second year in a row, the annual transportation spending bill ran into trouble in the House over lawmakers' pet highway projects.

The dispute emerged when the fiscal 1995 Transportation Department appropriations bill (HR 4556) went to a House-Senate conference committee. There, the ranking Republican on the House Transportation Appropriations Subcommittee, Frank R. Wolf of Virginia, protested a proposed $90 million grant to a single highway project in West Virginia. When the dispute threatened to bubble over to the House floor, Sen. Robert C. Byrd, D-W.Va., agreed to cut his request to $35 million. The remainder of the $90 million was redistributed among a number of House and Senate projects.

Both chambers gave swift approval to the modified conference report, and President Clinton signed the $14.3 billion measure into law Sept. 30 (PL 103-331).

The year before, the fiscal 1994 transportation spending bill (HR 2750 — PL 103-122) became embroiled in a protracted turf battle between the House Public Works Committee, which authorized spending on transportation programs, and the Transportation Appropriations Subcommittee, which distributed money to those programs. Public Works won that battle, reclaiming sole power to initiate or increase funding for projects. (*1993 Almanac, p. 663*)

The Budget Tightens

The main challenge for the Transportation Appropriations subcommittees in 1994 was the shrinking purse. In 1993, the conferees had almost $38.6 billion to spend from the general Treasury and the transportation trust funds. In 1994, that amount dropped to $38.3 billion.

The appropriators made their biggest cuts in grants for highways. They cut $430 million from the $17.6 billion federal-aid highway program, the main, formula-driven grant program for state highway departments. The cut left the program $1.1 billion below the level authorized by the 1991 surface transportation law (PL 102-240). To offset this cut somewhat, they directed $352 million to lawmakers' special highway projects — an increase of almost $200 million over fiscal 1994. Still, total spending on highway construction, maintenance and safety programs fell about $100 million, from $20.2 billion to $20.1 billion.

The appropriators also cut $240 million from the $1.7 billion Airport Improvement Program, a grant program that helped airport authorities pay for upgrades to terminals, runways and other facilities. And they trimmed $92 million from the $802 million in operating assistance that had been given to local bus and commuter rail lines.

The remaining transportation programs escaped major cuts, although most were nicked. Even those programs receiving increases did not gain as much as their supporters had hoped.

Amtrak, the national passenger rail corporation, received $812 million, up $118 million from fiscal 1994. But the administration had sought $878 million, and late in 1994 Amtrak

BOXSCORE

Fiscal 1995 Transportation Appropriations — HR 4556. The bill for highway and mass transit programs appropriated $14.3 billion and provided $24 billion in trust-fund spending.

Reports: H Rept 103-543, S Rept 103-310; conference report H 103-752.

KEY ACTION

June 16 — House passed HR 4556, 363-59.

July 21 — Senate passed HR 4556, amended, 91-9.

Sept. 28 — House adopted conference report by voice vote.

Sept. 29 — Senate cleared bill, 89-11.

Sept. 30 — President signed HR 4556 — PL 103-331.

announced a significant reduction in services.

For mass transit, the bill provided $4.6 billion, up $32 million from fiscal 1994. The appropriators provided a 32 percent boost to the formula grant program, which aided state and local transit programs, raising it from $483 million to $640 million. At the same time, however, they cut $60 million from the discretionary grant program, another aid program for state and local transit agencies, and operating subsidies. The final tally was almost $150 million less than the administration requested.

Finally, the Coast Guard saw its funding increase by less than 1 percent, to roughly $3.7 billion. The amount was $85 million less than the administration had requested, with most of the shortfall coming in the accounts for vessel and equipment purchases.

The administration proposed more for virtually every program than the appropriators provided. It could do so because it assumed that Congress would rescind more than $800 million from the special highway projects that lawmakers had inserted into the 1991 surface transportation law. That assumption proved so fanciful, however, that the administration did not even make a formal request that the projects be rescinded.

Old Turf Fights

Although the transportation spending bill typically involved close to $40 billion in total spending, much of the focus had been on the roughly $1 billion in grants for lawmakers' favorite bus, rail and highway projects. Shortly after becoming chairman of the House Transportation Appropriations Subcommittee in 1993, Bob Carr, D-Mich., launched a more objective system for evaluating the economic value of the projects that lawmakers requested.

Carr's subcommittee ran into trouble, however, when it tried to funnel more than $300 million to 61 highway projects and studies. House Public Works Committee Chairman Norman Y. Mineta, D-Calif., protested that the money went beyond previously authorized levels and so violated a House rule against funding unauthorized projects.

Mineta prevailed in that fight, but he agreed to push a new authorization bill through the House in time for the fiscal 1995 transportation spending bill. His committee even adopted Carr's criteria for selecting projects. (*1993 Almanac, p. 666*)

The fiscal 1995 authorization bill (HR 4385 — H Rept 103-519) passed the House May 25, 1994.

House Committee

The House Transportation Appropriations Subcommittee approved its $14.2 billion version of the fiscal 1995 spending bill in closed session May 25, the same day the House passed the authorization bill.

Transportation

(in thousands of dollars)

	Fiscal 1994 Appropriations	Fiscal 1995 Clinton Request	House Bill	Senate Bill	Final Bill
Transportation Department					
Office of the secretary	$ 222,031	$ 224,336	$ 231,166	$ 223,161	$ 218,766
Rural airline subsidies (trust fund)	*(33,423)*	*(25,600)*	*(25,600)*	*(33,423)*	*(33,423)*
Coast Guard					
Operating expenses	2,570,000	2,630,505	2,580,000	2,600,000	2,598,000
Acquisition, construction	327,500	439,200	385,200	370,400	362,950
Other	703,064	672,927	695,895	696,876	696,376
Subtotal, Coast Guard	**$ 3,600,564**	**$ 3,742,632**	**$ 3,661,095**	**$ 3,667,276**	**$ 3,657,326**
Federal Aviation Administration					
Operations	4,580,518	4,580,900	4,585,000	4,591,440	4,595,394
Facilities and equipment	2,120,104	2,269,100	2,176,700	2,086,941	2,087,489
Research, engineering, development	254,000	266,800	254,000	264,440	259,192
Other	150	148	—	148	148
Subtotal, FAA	**$ 6,954,772**	**$ 7,116,948**	**$ 7,015,700**	**$ 6,942,969**	**$ 6,942,223**
Airport Trust Fund limit	*(1,690,000)*	*(1,690,000)*	*(1,500,000)*	*(1,450,000)*	*(1,450,000)*
Federal Highway Administration					
Special road and bridge projects	143,562	—	299,862	352,055	352,055
Baltimore-Washington Parkway	12,800	—	—	—	—
Subtotal, FHwA	**$ 156,362**	**—**	**$ 299,862**	**$ 352,055**	**$ 352,055**
Highway Trust Fund limit	*(17,665,000)*	*(20,061,872)*	*(17,244,000)*	*(17,629,650)*	*(17,244,800)*
Obligations exempt from limit	*(2,117,009)*	*(100,000)*	*(2,267,701)*	*(2,267,701)*	*(2,267,701)*
National Highway Traffic Safety Administration	124,145	125,835	121,349	128,887	126,553
Highway Trust Fund limit	*(174,000)*	*(151,400)*	*(151,400)*	*(151,400)*	*(151,400)*
Federal Railroad Administration					
Local rail freight assistance	17,000	—	17,000	17,000	17,000
Amtrak	693,700	878,000	771,700	812,000	812,000
Northeast Corridor improvement	225,000	199,600	165,000	230,000	200,000
Other	94,294	114,270	97,862	105,485	106,319
Subtotal, railroads	**$ 1,029,994**	**$ 1,191,870**	**$ 1,051,562**	**$ 1,164,485**	**$ 1,135,319**
Federal Transit Administration					
Formula grants	1,284,916	1,731,050	1,356,050	1,350,000	1,350,000
Highway Trust Fund	*(1,129,951)*	*(1,150,000)*	*(1,150,000)*	*(1,150,000)*	*(1,150,000)*
Discretionary grants					
Highway Trust Fund	*(1,785,000)*	*(1,501,000)*	*(1,725,000)*	*(1,725,000)*	*(1,725,000)*
Washington Metro	200,000	200,000	200,000	200,000	200,000
Other	117,658	179,840	189,340	179,840	189,340
Subtotal, Transit	**$ 1,602,574**	**$ 2,110,890**	**$ 1,745,390**	**$ 1,729,840**	**$ 1,739,340**
Highway Trust Fund limit	*(2,980,000)*	*(2,651,000)*	*(2,875,000)*	*(2,875,000)*	*(2,875,000)*
Other Transportation Department *	−26,081	−577,354	207,141	250,706	243,415
TOTAL					
Transportation Department *	**$ 13,442,330**	**$ 13,710,821**	**$ 14,102,099**	**$ 14,236,218**	**$ 14,196,231**
Related Agencies					
Architectural and Transportation Barriers Compliance Board	3,348	3,232	3,350	3,350	3,350
National Transportation Safety Board	37,105	37,046	37,392	37,046	37,392
Interstate Commerce Commission	44,960	43,827	—	30,302	30,302
Panama Canal Commission					
(limitation on expenses)	*(540,000)*	*(540,000)*	*(540,000)*	*(540,000)*	*(540,000)*
St. Lawrence Seaway Toll Rebate	9,707	9,319	9,319	—	—
Other	51,663	9,193	9,193	9,193	9,193
Additional special highway projects	—	—	8,000	14,000	14,000
GRAND TOTAL *	**$ 13,589,113**	**$ 13,813,438**	**$ 14,169,353**	**$ 14,330,109**	**$ 14,290,468**
(Trust fund limit)	*($ 24,678,859)*	*($ 24,696,697)*	*($ 24,079,726)*	*($ 24,423,849)*	*($ 24,038,599)*

* Totals for the Transportation Department and the bill account for rescissions of $341.7 million in fiscal 1994, $850 million in the 1995 budget request, $68.6 million in the House bill, $24 million in the Senate bill and $24.5 million in the final bill.

SOURCE: House Appropriations Committee

Honoring Carr's deal with Mineta, the subcommittee proposed $285 million for highway projects, all of them authorized or included in HR 4385.

Symbolizing the new comity between the two sides, Carr's bill also proposed $35 million for two commuter rail projects near Mineta's Bay Area district for which Carr had tried to bar funding during the 1993 turf battle.

The subcommittee proposed three deep cuts: $465 million in the federal-aid highway program, $190 million in the Airport Improvement Program, and $102 million in the operating subsidies for local mass transit systems. It also proposed to trim $60 million from Amtrak's Northeast Corridor, a high-speed rail development project, and it offered no funding for Amtrak's new train station in New York City — a project for which the administration had sought $90 million. Finally, it proposed to cut $60 million from discretionary grants to modernize old transit systems and build new ones.

On the other hand, the subcommittee called for a $78 million increase in Amtrak's operations and equipment purchases. Offsetting the cuts in transit operating subsidies and discretionary grants, the subcommittee proposed to raise other forms of aid to local transit systems by $293 million, or 18 percent. It also proposed small increases for Coast Guard vessels and equipment and Federal Aviation Administration (FAA) facilities.

Full Committee

The full Appropriations Committee approved the bill by voice vote June 9 (H Rept 103-543).

During the markup, the bill drew protests from ranking subcommittee Republican Wolf and Tom DeLay, R-Texas. The two objected to changes that Carr proposed in the list of road and rail projects approved by the subcommittee. Those changes, they suggested, were politically motivated.

The Carr amendment, which the committee adopted by voice vote, increased the proposed funding for four rail and 15 road projects, while cutting funding for one rail and five road projects. The proposed total for special highway projects rose to $300 million, and for new rail and bus projects to $647 million. The amendment also added $35 million to the proposed amount for the federal-aid highway program, while cutting $100 million from the aid to rail and bus systems.

DeLay and Wolf seemed most concerned about proposals to more than double the funding for the South Boston Piers Transitway project — the subcommittee proposed $20 million, Carr's amendment $48 million — and to raise the grant for the Chicago Circulator trolley project from $38.3 million to $50 million. Said DeLay, "We're pouring money down a couple of black holes here."

The $348 million South Boston project — championed by a top House Democrat, Rules Committee Chairman Joe Moakley of Massachusetts — had received $56.25 million from the appropriators in the past. The $750 million Chicago Circulator project — backed by a member of the Transportation Appropriation Subcommittee, Democrat Richard J. Durbin of Illinois — had received almost $92 million in previous years.

In drawing up their version of the bill, DeLay said, the subcommittee members lived by the economic criteria Carr had established in 1993. The proposed changes, on the other hand, would "stick a bunch of losers in there," he said, adding, "We are subjecting ourselves to some real shots on the [House] floor."

Carr said some changes had to be made to the subcommittee-approved list to match last-minute changes in the Public Works Committee's bill authorizing road and transit projects. The biggest change was in the proposed grant to the

Pittsburgh Busway, linking downtown Pittsburgh with the city's airport. It was cut from $40 million to $10 million. All the projects added to the list met the subcommittee's investment criteria, Carr said, adding that they would have been funded earlier had the money been available.

DeLay and Wolf emphasized that they had no quarrel with Carr, but they condemned the process. The changes, they said, stemmed from influential members pressuring Carr for more money than the subcommittee had provided. "It's not fair to the chairman of this subcommittee to be treated like this. It's an outrage," DeLay said. "I think we all know how they [the new projects] got funded."

Wolf's dissatisfaction led him to suggest that the committee try going a year or two without earmarking money for specific projects. For a transportation appropriator, that remark came close to apostasy.

Aside from the increases for Boston and Chicago, the largest add-ons were a new $10 million grant to the Salt Lake City light rail system, an increase of $5.3 million for the two transit projects near Mineta's Bay Area district, and a new $2 million grant for an expressway in Fairfax County, Va., represented by Democrat James P. Moran Jr.

All told, the committee-approved bill proposed grants to 108 highway construction projects in 30 states — with 20 percent of the money going to Carr's home state of Michigan — and an $8 million subsidy for a new toll road being built in Orange County, California.

The appropriators also proposed $53.1 million for nine high-technology traffic-management programs. More than 70 percent of the money was for projects in states represented by members of Carr's subcommittee, including $20 million for one in suburban Detroit. Those earmarks were in the report accompanying HR 4556, and so acted more as recommendations than orders.

For mass transit, the bill proposed $966 million to 80 specified bus and commuter rail systems. California topped the list with just under $240 million, including $165 million for a segment of the new Los Angeles subway.

The appropriators also proposed more than $31 million for eight railroad projects. These included $12 million for repairs at three maintenance yards run by Amtrak, $15 million for freight tracks and sidings in Connecticut and Rhode Island, and $3.5 million for railroad upgrades near the western Illinois district represented by Durbin.

Finally, the appropriators recommended that the FAA award $41.5 million to airport runway projects in Orlando, Philadelphia, Detroit and San Juan, Puerto Rico. The recommendation was not binding, though, and the FAA had not followed a similar set of recommendations in the fiscal 1994 bill.

One other change approved by the committee had Carr grumbling about timeliness and Wolf again complaining about political influence.

Steny H. Hoyer, D-Md., who held top spots both on the Appropriations Committee and in the Democratic Caucus, won voice vote approval for an amendment exempting his state from new dump truck axle-weight limits. The amendment proposed to leave the limits at 70,000 pounds for four axles, instead of 65,000 pounds for three axles. Carr said the amendment came in at the last minute, after the subcommittee had finished its work on the bill, and that it violated the House rule against legislating on an appropriations bill, something he had promised Mineta that he would not do. Hoyer, however, said Mineta had approved the proposal.

Wolf said Public Works' Democratic leadership seemed to have a double standard about such proposals: Democrats such as Hoyer got the green light from Mineta, but Republicans could not even get their calls returned.

Wolf had been trying without success to get Mineta to sign off on a provision to allow Republican Virginia Gov. George Allen to let cars with two occupants use the lanes on Interstate 66 reserved for cars with three or more occupants. Like Hoyer's provision, Wolf's proposal violated the House rule against legislating on an appropriations bill and faced being knocked out on the House floor.

Carr's quest to avoid turf battles led him to drop a provision approved by the subcommittee that would have temporarily waived a section of the Clean Air Act. The section made it harder for states to build highway projects that would increase ozone smog, unless the projects were part of a clean air plan approved by the Environmental Protection Agency (EPA).

The waiver had been sought by Republican Ralph Regula of Ohio, who said the section could block $2 billion worth of highway projects in his state alone.

Carr said the House Energy and Commerce Committee had jurisdiction over the Clean Air Act, and Chairman John D. Dingell, D-Mich., objected to Regula's proposal. In its place, the committee adopted by voice vote a non-binding Regula amendment urging the EPA and the Transportation Department to find an administrative solution to the problem.

Environmental groups had asked committee members to reject the original Regula proposal, saying it would have allowed states to ignore the major contribution that highway programs made to air pollution.

House Floor

The House approved the $14.2 billion bill by a vote of 363-59 on June 16. *(Vote 252, p. 74-H)*

The bill reached the floor after a brief, partisan fight over the rule proposed by the Democrat-controlled Rules Committee. Republicans complained that the rule shielded Hoyer's axle-weight provision against procedural challenges but did not protect Wolf's. Mineta and Rules Committee Chairman Moakley said the difference stemmed from local politics, not partisan politics. The entire Maryland delegation, as well as state and local officials, supported Hoyer's proposal, but a number of local transportation officials in Northern Virginia opposed Wolf's proposal, they said.

The House voted largely along party lines to approve the rule, 239-180. Later, Wolf's provision was knocked out of the bill on a procedural challenge by Moran. *(Vote 249, p. 74-H)*

Republicans soon turned the tide, knocking out funding for a program they long had sought to eliminate. Aided by a sizable block of Democrats, John R. Kasich, R-Ohio, successfully moved to strike all $43.5 million in the bill for the Interstate Commerce Commission (ICC). The vote was 234-192. *(Vote 250, p. 74-H)*

Kasich's amendment did not eliminate the ICC's statutory authority, however, or its duties. Although Congress had eliminated most of the ICC's power to regulate railroads, trucking, bus lines and other forms of surface transportation in the preceding 15 years, those companies still were required to obtain licenses from and file their rates with the commission. Kasich said his amendment would save $25 million in fiscal 1995 and more than $150 million over five years. But Carr said the amendment would not save any money because the Transportation Department would have to perform all of the commission's duties.

Carr was joined by two influential House chairmen in opposing the amendment: Dingell of Energy and Commerce, and Mineta of Public Works. Mineta argued that the commission had quasi-legislative and quasi-judicial duties that were best left to an independent agency, not the Transportation Department.

Stopping short of the House vote on the ICC, the Senate on Aug. 11 added language to a separate bill on hazardous waste transportation to shrink the ICC by removing some of its trucking duties; that bill (HR 2178 — PL 103-311) cleared Aug. 16. *(Trucking deregulation, p. 170)*

Lawmakers had tried in vain to eliminate the ICC several times since Congress started deregulating the transportation industries in the late 1970s. The House narrowly defeated a similar amendment by Joel Hefley, R-Colo., during the debate over the fiscal 1994 transportation spending bill. *(1993 Almanac, pp. 110-H, 148-H)*

The Kasich amendment succeeded because it was supported by almost all Republicans and 66 Democrats, including such liberal Democrats as Barney Frank and Joseph P. Kennedy II of Massachusetts, Kweisi Mfume of Maryland and George Miller of California.

By contrast, a Hefley amendment to cut $77 million from Amtrak attracted a bare majority of Republicans and only nine Democrats. It fell by a vote of 103-326. *(Vote 251, p. 74-H)*

A proposal to cut grants to new mass transit systems by $247 million drew protests from both sides of the aisle. The amendment by Timothy J. Penny, D-Minn., was defeated by voice vote, as were Penny proposals to eliminate $17 million in aid to private rail freight lines and $25 million in boating safety grants.

Senate Committee

Carr's counterpart at the Senate Transportation Appropriations Subcommittee, Democrat Frank R. Lautenberg of New Jersey, had also tried in 1993 to change his subcommittee's approach to lawmakers' pet projects. Overriding objections from his fellow appropriators, he insisted that no money go to any unauthorized highway projects, and he refused to direct any money to specific bus projects.

In 1994, Lautenberg took a friendlier approach to lawmakers' pet projects, allowing earmarks for unauthorized projects and for bus systems. The version of the bill that Lautenberg's subcommittee approved by voice vote July 13 included $1.1 billion for highway, commuter rail and bus projects requested by lawmakers — a 40 percent increase over the previous year's Senate bill.

"I don't want this to be read as too much of a policy change at this juncture," Lautenberg said in an interview July 13. ""We are trying seriously to establish rules by which the process moves efficiently."

In total, the bill proposed $14.3 billion in budget authority and $24.4 billion in trust-fund spending. Other major features of the bill included:

- $17.5 billion for the federal-aid highway program and $20.3 billion total for highways, which was almost a half-billion dollars more than the House proposed. Of that amount, $352 million was reserved for lawmakers' pet highway projects.
- $3.7 billion for the Coast Guard, $48.5 million more than in fiscal 1994 and $14 million more than the House bill, but almost $68 million less than the administration requested.
- $8.4 billion for the FAA, $186 million below fiscal 1994, $414 million less than the administration requested and $123 million less than the House bill proposed. The biggest hit was on grants for airport improvements, which the Senate proposed to cut by $240 million.
- $4.6 billion for mass transit, a slight increase over fiscal 1994 but $157 million less than the administration requested. The bill proposed an $87 million increase in grants to purchase equipment and build facilities, but a $72 million cut in operating subsidies.
- $1.2 billion for railroads, a 15 percent increase over fiscal

1994. The total included $772 million for Amtrak, $230 million for the Northeast Corridor high-speed rail project and $40 million to develop a new Amtrak station in New York City.

Unlike the House, Lautenberg's subcommittee did not propose to eliminate funding for the ICC. Instead, it called for cutting the ICC's budget by 33 percent, in keeping with a proposal by Jim Exon, D-Neb., to trim its trucking oversight duties.

Nor did the subcommittee agree with the House proposal to waive a requirement that states use recycled tires in at least 5 percent of their repaving work in 1994 — a requirement that the American Association of State Highway and Transportation Officials vigorously opposed.

Full Committee

The bill moved to the full Appropriations Committee on July 14, where it was approved by a vote of 27-2 (S Rept 103-310). The committee made only a handful of changes to the bill, cutting $10 million from the federal-aid highway program, directing $446,000 in unspent funds to a rail relocation project in Indiana and proposing to block any federal regulations that would restrict overflights or landings on federal lands in Alaska.

The bulk of the discussion centered on the decision by Lautenberg and the subcommittee's top Republican, Alfonse M. D'Amato of New York, to eliminate funding for virtually all of the special projects that the House had proposed to fund. D'Amato said they took that position for tactical reasons, not because they did not support the projects. "To put in matching funds does not give us any leverage when we go to conference."

Not that the bill was short on projects — on the contrary, it proposed funding for 27 road projects and 50 bus and commuter rail systems. The largest Senate-initiated proposals were $146 million for commuter rail in Lautenberg's home state of New Jersey; $140 million for the Appalachian Regional Corridor H highway project in West Virginia, home of Appropriations Committee Chairman Byrd; and $112 million for commuter rail in Oregon, home of the top Republican appropriator, Mark Hatfield.

D'Amato tried to reassure his fellow appropriators that the projects left out of the Senate bill would not suffer in conference. But Phil Gramm, R-Texas, a vocal foe of federal spending, was not satisfied. "I have to protest just a little bit this game we engaged in with the House," Gramm said. The appropriators eventually would fund all the projects named in each version of the bill, Gramm said, so why put the projects' supporters through "six weeks of misery" by shutting them out of the Senate bill? Despite the criticism, Lautenberg and D'Amato did not budge. The bill went to the floor with funding for few projects from the House bill — two highway projects, one bus project and five commuter rail projects.

Senate Floor

The Senate passed its $14.3 billion bill July 21 by a vote of 91-9. (Vote 221, p. 38-S)

The lawmakers' projects came under symbolic attack when John McCain, R-Ariz., offered a non-binding sense-of-the-Senate resolution declaring that Congress should not direct money to specific highway and mass transit projects. The resolution was swatted down with a tabling motion by a vote of 63-37. The appropriators voted 21-7 to kill the McCain amendment; the rest of the Senate membership voted 42-30 against it. (Vote 219, p. 37-S)

The amendment declared that states and the Federal Transit Administration should be allowed to pick projects based on their own criteria. "The process of earmarking," McCain said, "is

an abuse whose correction is long overdue." Robert C. Smith, R-N.H., threw his support behind McCain, saying that federal spending should be based on national priorities, not a senator's seniority or membership on the Appropriations Committee.

Indeed, more than 92 percent of the highway dollars earmarked in the bill were targeted for 16 states represented by appropriators. More than 92 percent of the commuter rail earmarks were targeted to eight states represented by appropriators. And more than 84 percent of the money earmarked for buses was for 17 states represented by appropriators.

Lautenberg and D'Amato rose to the defense of earmarking. "I'd rather see, as relates to some of these projects, that there be some congressional input," D'Amato said, adding, "the House isn't going to give up their prerogatives."

Lautenberg noted that the highway aid to states came out of the Highway Trust Fund, while the earmarks came out of the general Treasury. For that reason, he said, the earmarks competed for funding with the Coast Guard, the FAA and other transportation programs funded out of the Treasury, not the state highway aid program.

The Transportation Department, state highway officials and Carr all disagreed with Lautenberg. In their view, the appropriators made room for highway earmarks by trimming the highway aid to states. And because the appropriators' earmarks tended to be spent more quickly than other appropriations, every $3 in earmarks had to be offset with a $4 cut in the state aid program.

The Senate debated only two proposed cuts in the bill. The first, by McCain, would have eliminated the $40 million grant to develop the new Amtrak station in New York City. McCain argued that the House was right to provide no money for the $315 million project, which had not been authorized. The Senate disagreed, rejecting McCain's motion by a vote of 23-77. (Vote 218, p. 37-S)

The second cut was proposed by Smith, who offered a motion to send the bill back to the Appropriations Committee with instructions to reduce it to the 1994 level. The fiscal 1995 bill had $741 million more in appropriations from the Treasury, but $255 million less in spending from the highway and aviation trust funds. Smith's proposal was killed on a tabling motion by a vote of 72-28. (Vote 220, p. 38-S)

Final Action

The bill went to conference Sept. 22, where House and Senate appropriators quickly settled on the outlines of a bill with $14.3 billion in new budget authority and $24 billion in trust-fund spending (H Rept 103-752).

They agreed to the House's proposal, $17.2 billion, for the federal-aid highway program, but took the Senate's proposal, $352 million, for lawmakers' special highway projects. Total highway spending was $19.9 billion, plus $278 million for the National Highway Traffic Safety Administration.

The conferees accepted the Senate's proposal for total spending on aviation, $8.4 billion. They split their differences on mass transit operating subsidies and formula grants, proposing a total of $4.6 billion in transit spending.

For railroads, the conferees accepted the Senate's proposal on Amtrak, then split the difference between the House and Senate on railroad safety and research. They dropped the Coast Guard to $3.7 billion, $4 million below what either chamber had proposed.

The conferees also agreed to the Senate's position on the ICC, cutting its funding by one-third rather than eliminating it as the House proposed.

The thorniest issue for conferees was the special projects. Carr and Lautenberg agreed to spend 52 percent of the $352

million highway pot on Senate projects, 48 percent on House projects. The House controlled 58 percent of the $353 million pot for bus grants, and the two sides split the $647 million for new transit systems 50-50, Carr said.

Several House conferees grumbled about the split for highway dollars, particularly in light of the $90 million that the Senate conferees proposed for Byrd's Corridor H project. The proposal came on top of the $75 million that Byrd had steered to Corridor H in the energy and water appropriations act (HR 4506 — PL 103-316).

The House had spread its highway earmarks among 30 states, the Senate among 20, with almost half of the Senate's money proposed for Byrd's home state. Wolf was particularly irked by the fact that West Virginia was planning to tuck away most of the $90 million for use in fiscal 1996. Noting that the next largest highway grant was $15 million, Wolf tried to slash the $90 million in conference. But he was blocked by Lautenberg, who said he would not permit House conferees to vote on the projects chosen by Senate conferees.

While Wolf called the proposed grant "greedy" and "obscene," Byrd said the money needed to be put in context: "We don't have transit systems in West Virginia. We don't have big airports. We have to depend upon highways. That's our lifeblood." Byrd said the $90 million paled in comparison with the money Congress had spent on transit projects such as the Washington Metro system, which he said would cost the taxpayers an estimated $9 billion by the time it was completed.

The conferees did accept two amendments by Wolf. One was his proposal to let Virginia's governor allow cars with two occupants to use the high-occupancy vehicle lanes on 1-66 on a trial basis for one year. The second barred the Transportation Department from supporting the construction of a sixth runway at the troubled Denver International Airport.

Another provision added by the conferees provided $5 million to help Rhode Island build a third railroad track to accommodate tall freight cars. Freight railroads had complained that the track upgrades done for the high-speed Northeast Corridor passenger route were cutting off their ability to haul double-stacked containers.

For the second year in a row, the conferees agreed to suspend the requirement that states use recycled tires in some of their paving projects. The conferees further agreed to provide a $40 million grant for a new train station in New York City if Congress authorized the project. The House had voted Sept. 20 against funding the station, but the vote was not binding on the conferees.

The conferees accepted House-passed provisions to bar federal highway money for metric highway signs and to deny any federal transportation aid to state or local governments that diverted revenues from public airports for non-airport uses. They also left in place a Senate provision waiving tolls for commercial vessels on the Saint Lawrence Seaway, rather than rebating the tolls as in existing law.

The conferees ultimately approved the conference report by voice vote.

Final Passage

The dispute between Wolf and Byrd related in part to the opposition in Wolf's district to the Corridor H project, which threatened to bring more traffic into the neighboring Virginia communities. But it also reflected their chambers' different pork barrel philosophies.

House transportation appropriators favored projects in states that were ready to spend the money. They also had more colleagues to accommodate, which led them to propose smaller grants to more projects than the Senate appropriators did.

Byrd argued that Congress often appropriated money for expensive projects before it could be used because that spread the cost more evenly. But Carr said the idea of tying up large chunks of money before it could be spent made more sense in the Senate, where most members were not up for re-election each Congress, than it did in the House.

On Sept. 26, Wolf held a news conference to amplify his criticism of the proposed grant for Corridor H. If the conference report reached the House floor with Byrd's $90 million, Wolf said, he would force a symbolic vote on Corridor H — a vote that any pork barrel project would probably lose.

Meanwhile, Byrd and House Appropriations Committee Chairman David R. Obey, D-Wis., were negotiating changes to the conference report that would soon mollify Wolf. When the report was filed at the end of the day, Corridor H's grant had been cut to $35 million. A provision also had been inserted calling for larger grants to Corridor H in future years. Roughly $7 million of the money taken from Corridor H was distributed to House highway projects, with the rest going to Senate projects. The implication of the shift in dollars was that House conferees were able to second-guess Senate conferees' choice of projects.

Lautenberg said the Senate might have been more willing to fight if more time had remained before the start of fiscal 1995. Under the circumstances, however, any delay in HR 4556 would have forced Congress to adopt a stopgap spending bill for the Transportation Department — something Byrd was eager to avoid.

With Wolf off the warpath, the conference report went to the House on Sept. 28. The House approved it by voice vote with little debate. The Senate cleared the conference report the next day by a vote of 89-11. (Vote 312, p. 54-S)

The $352 million in the conference report for special road and bridge projects was divided among 36 states, with the largest portions going to states represented by top appropriators. Carr's home state of Michigan received $46.5 million for eight projects, West Virginia received $44 million for three projects, and Lautenberg's home state of New Jersey received $24 million for three projects. Together the three states consumed one-third of the pot for special highway projects.

Conferees also targeted $76 million to specific high-technology traffic-management projects, with more than 93 percent going to their own states. Unlike the other highway earmarks, the money for these projects came out of the Highway Trust Fund.

The conference report directed $646.7 million to 32 new transit systems in 18 states and Puerto Rico. The top recipients: California, with $190.2 million for three projects; New Jersey, with $112.5 million for three projects; and Oregon, with $98 million for one project.

An additional $323.3 million in the conference report went to 85 bus systems in 37 states. Pennsylvania — home of two conferees, Republican Sen. Arlen Specter and Democratic Rep. Thomas M. Foglietta — collected $26.5 million for five projects; Michigan collected $24 million for five projects; Ohio — home of one conferee, Republican Regula — collected $20.5 million for four projects; and California collected $19.5 million for seven projects.

The conferees also directed $31 million of the $1.45 billion for airport improvement projects to five cities: $10 million for runway repairs in Orlando, Fla.; $10 million for a new runway in Philadelphia; $7 million for a taxiway in San Juan, Puerto Rico; and $2 million each for a new heliport in Manhattan and a runway extension in Detroit. ■

Hill Passes Trim Treasury-Postal Bill

Although it was one of the least controversial of the fiscal 1995 appropriations bills, the spending bill for the Treasury, Postal Service and General Government did not have an entirely smooth path into law.

The bill (HR 4539) appropriated $23.5 billion, nearly $1 billion more than its fiscal 1994 predecessor, with most of the increase devoted to mandatory entitlement programs for retired federal employees.

The retiree programs, over which appropriators had no control, accounted for $11.7 billion — more than half the spending in the bill. Most of the remaining funds, $10.5 billion, went to the Treasury Department and its agencies, including the Internal Revenue Service (IRS), the Secret Service and the Customs Service. The bill also funded the budgets for the Executive Office of the President, the Office of Personnel Management and the General Services Administration (GSA).

With Democratic leaders trying to clear their floor schedules for an anticipated debate on the Clinton administration's ambitious health care overhaul, the measure passed both chambers by the July 4th recess. But final action did not come until the end of September. House Treasury-Postal Service Appropriations Subcommittee Chairman Steny H. Hoyer, D-Md., and his Senate counterpart Dennis DeConcini, D-Ariz., held off convening the conference on the bill while they awaited $40 million in additional spending that became available through the omnibus anti-crime bill (HR 3355 — PL 103-322).

By the time the conference report on the bill was ready, it ran into a House eager to demonstrate it was tough on spending. Shaken by the unexpected primary defeat of Democratic loyalist Mike Synar of Oklahoma, a wave of Democrats voted with Republicans to send the bill back to conference with instructions to cut $368 million. After conferees made $157 million of the cuts, principally from federal courthouse projects located in the districts of members who voted to trim the bill, the House Sept. 27 easily adopted the conference report. The Senate cleared it Sept. 28, and President Clinton signed the bill into law Sept. 30 (PL 103-329).

The Clinton administration was forced to absorb two major losses during deliberations on the bill.

Members refused to pay for a $1 billion administration proposal to buy out federal government leases of privately owned office buildings. Because of budget rules, the proposal would have been counted as new spending, even though it could have saved billions of dollars over the long run. Congress also cut back a White House request for $989 million to modernize IRS computers, earmarking $650 million for the job.

An attempt by Hoyer to provide a hefty pay raise for federal workers was scaled back considerably. The final bill provided $1.8 billion, half of what Hoyer had proposed but $700 million more than Clinton requested.

BOXSCORE

Fiscal 1995 Treasury-Postal Service Appropriations — HR 4539. The $23.5 billion bill included funds for Treasury, the IRS, the GSA, the Executive Office of the President, and federal retiree benefits.

Reports: H Rept 103-534, S Rept 103-286; conference reports H Rept 103-729, H Rept 103-741.

KEY ACTION

June 15 — House passed HR 4539, 276-139.

June 22 — Senate passed HR 4539, revised, 72-27.

Sept. 22 — House sent conference report back for additional cuts, 234-192.

Sept. 27 — House adopted revised conference report, 360-53.

Sept. 28 — Senate cleared HR 4539 by voice vote.

Sept. 30 — President signed HR 4539 — PL 103-329.

One of the most controversial aspects of the bill — whether women who worked for the federal government could undergo abortions paid by their health care plans — was not debated at all throughout deliberations on the bill.

The previous year, a Clinton administration effort to lift a decade-long ban on such taxpayer-subsidized abortions succeeded, but only by the barest of margins in both the House and Senate. Abortion opponents in the House failed by one vote to defeat the fiscal 1994 Treasury-Postal appropriations conference report. (*1993 Almanac, p. 679*)

Anti-abortion Republicans wanted to restore the restrictions, which had barred abortions paid for by federal health care plans, except in cases of rape, incest or when the life of the woman was in danger. The restrictions had been included in the Treasury-Postal bill every year from fiscal 1984 to fiscal 1993. But abortion opponents did not try — as they had the year before — to restore the language in subcommittee. Hoyer had enough allies on the panel to prevail there, and adding the restrictions in full committee or on the floor would have been tricky, because House rules would have subjected the language to a point of order against legislating on an appropriations bill. Abortion opponents instead focused their lobbying muscle on the health care overhaul debate.

House Committee

Deliberations on the bill kicked off May 18, when the House Treasury-Postal Appropriations Subcommittee approved a $23.3 billion version by voice vote.

In its first public markup in recent memory, the subcommittee spent about three hours fine-tuning a draft prepared by Hoyer. Working under a tight $11.6 billion allocation for the discretionary accounts in the bill, the subcommittee provided an amount in new budget authority just under that ceiling. Hoyer said that to provide all of the budget authority available under the cap would have put too much pressure on outlays (actual spending) in future years. Outlays were also tightly capped by existing budget rules.

The bill contained $11.7 billion for entitlements and other mandatory spending — most of it to pay part of the health and pension benefits for retired federal workers. That was an increase of about $700 million over fiscal 1994.

The Treasury Department was to receive $10.5 billion, $124 million less than Clinton requested. Hoyer took the nearly unprecedented step of cutting the president's request for the White House staff. Other related executive offices, such as the Office of Management and Budget, were frozen at or below fiscal 1994 levels.

The $1 billion proposal to buy out federal government leases of privately owned office buildings was caught in the spending crunch. Though the proposal could have saved the

Treasury-Postal Spending

(in thousands of dollars)

	Fiscal 1994 Appropriations	Fiscal 1995 Clinton Request	House Bill	Senate Bill	Final Bill
Treasury Department					
U.S. Customs Service					
Salaries and expenses	$ 1,350,668	$ 1,392,490	$ 1,391,700	$ 1,378,914	$ 1,394,793
Operations, air interdiction	96,956	83,091	78,991	91,891	89,041
Air facilities construction	5,000	—	—	1,000	1,000
Customs services/small airports	1,406	1,406	1,406	1,406	1,406
Subtotal, Customs	**$ 1,454,030**	**$ 1,476,987**	**$ 1,472,097**	**$ 1,473,211**	**$ 1,486,240**
Internal Revenue Service					
Administration and management	167,822	233,318	225,632	163,431	225,632
Processing tax returns, assistance	1,696,853	1,616,295	1,616,295	1,586,028	1,511,266
Tax law enforcement	4,007,962	3,986,280	4,412,580	4,358,180	4,358,459
Information systems	1,471,448	1,757,614	1,240,357	1,388,000	1,388,000
Subtotal, IRS	**$ 7,344,085**	**$ 7,593,507**	**$ 7,494,864**	**$ 7,495,639**	**$ 7,510,357**
Bureau of Alcohol, Tobacco and Firearms	366,446	378,915	376,181	385,315	385,315
U.S. Secret Service	461,931	470,117	476,931	474,988	476,931
Bureau of the Public Debt	187,209	183,458	183,458	183,458	183,458
Financial Management Service	209,877	185,389	185,389	183,697	183,889
Other	300,254	248,981	245,688	257,319	255,333
TOTAL, Treasury Department	**$ 10,323,832**	**$ 10,537,354**	**$ 10,434,608**	**$ 10,453,627**	**$ 10,481,523**
Postal Service					
Postal subsidies	91,434	92,317	85,717	102,317	92,317
Non-funded liabilities	38,803	37,776	37,776	37,776	37,776
TOTAL, Postal Service	**$ 130,237**	**$ 130,093**	**$ 123,493**	**$ 140,093**	**$ 130,093**
Executive Office of the President					
President's compensation	250	250	250	250	250
White House Office	38,754	41,632	38,754	40,193	40,193
Vice President's residence	324	327	324	324	324
National Security Council	6,648	6,832	6,648	8,222	6,648
Office of Management and Budget	56,539	56,272	56,272	55,081	57,754
Office of National Drug Control Policy	11,687	9,942	9,942	9,942	9,942
Federal drug control programs	138,500	150,500	112,800	162,500	148,900
Other	45,587	48,100	45,308	46,704	46,704
TOTAL, Executive Office	**$ 298,289**	**$ 313,855**	**$ 270,298**	**$ 323,216**	**$ 310,715**
Independent Agencies					
General Services Administration					
Federal Buildings Fund	288,486	−69,931	361,616	500,000	310,197
Limitation on use of revenues	*(5,251,117)*	*(4,468,074)*	*(4,973,826)*	*(5,055,641)*	*(4,932,322)*
Construction and acquisition	—	1,478,690	—	—	—
Other	186,428	160,241	149,366	156,382	156,382
Subtotal, GSA	**$ 474,914**	**$ 1,569,000**	**$ 510,982**	**$ 656,382**	**$ 466,579**
Office of Personnel Management					
Annuitants, health benefits	3,805,480	4,210,560	4,210,560	4,210,560	4,210,560
Annuitants, life insurance	1,607	19,159	19,159	19,159	19,159
Civil Service retirement and disability	7,065,819	7,339,638	7,339,638	7,339,638	7,339,638
Salaries and expenses	118,533	112,139	115,139	111,778	115,139
Other OPM	4,253	2,753	2,753	2,753	2,753
Subtotal, OPM	**$ 10,995,692**	**$ 11,684,249**	**$ 11,687,249**	**$ 11,683,888**	**$ 11,687,249**
Federal Election Commission	23,564	27,106	23,564	27,106	27,106
National Archives	190,232	194,638	194,638	200,238	195,238
U.S. Tax Court	33,650	35,313	33,650	34,427	34,039
Other agencies	68,412	80,209	69,032	72,613	83,564
GRAND TOTAL	**$ 22,538,822**	**$ 24,571,817 ***	**$ 23,347,514 ***	**$ 23,591,590 ***	**$ 23,454,806 * †**

Included $44,094,000 in projected savings from procurement reform.
† *Included $38,700,000 for violent crime control and law enforcement funding.*

SOURCE: House Appropriations Committee

government billions of dollars over the long term, it would have been scored as new spending under budget rules, and appropriators would have had to cut into agency overhead and operating expenses to pay for the buyouts.

● **IRS.** The Clinton administration's $1.8 billion request for the IRS' Tax Systems Modernization Program also took a hit. With no other large pots of money in the bill to tap for other programs, the subcommittee cut the president's request for new computers by $517 million. "I do not believe it is good policy" to scrimp on the IRS computers, said Hoyer. "I wish we had the money to do it."

● **GSA.** One of the spending accounts in the bill that was of perennial interest to members was the GSA's Federal Buildings Fund, which was the major source in the bill for construction projects — often courthouses — that members brought home to their districts.

The administration requested $479 million in new construction projects, much less than the $925 million appropriated for fiscal 1994. The subcommittee found room in the bill for $508 million worth.

● **Federal pay increase.** The subcommittee also approved an ambitious federal pay raise. Hoyer, a longtime advocate for federal employees, inserted a provision in the bill to mandate $3.5 billion in raises called for under existing federal pay raise formulas. The cost was to be spread, by agency, across all the appropriations bills. The bill also removed the broad discretion that the president had under existing law to curb such raises. Hoyer said at the markup that he was unsure whether he would be able to keep the entire pay raise in the bill as it went through subsequent legislative stages.

Clinton had proposed a 1.6 percent raise that would have cost $1.1 billion, though he did not say how much of that should be in the form of locality pay.

● **Smoking ban.** The subcommittee also approved an amendment by Peter J. Visclosky, D-Ind., to ban smoking in federal buildings, except in designated, specially ventilated areas. Visclosky's language went further than an existing, but limited, GSA edict that limited smoking to designated areas that did not have to be specially ventilated. The GSA estimated that it would cost up to $98 million to establish ventilated smoking areas.

The House had passed a similarly strict smoking ban bill (HR 881) in 1993, but the Senate did not act on it. *(1993 Almanac, p. 210)*

Full Committee Action

The full Appropriations Committee approved the bill May 26 by voice vote (H Rept 103-534). The session was dominated by debate over Hoyer's federal pay raise provision and Visclosky's smoking ban amendment.

● **Pay increase.** The committee agreed by voice vote to an amendment, crafted by Hoyer, that cut the subcommittee-approved pay raise in half — from $3.5 billion to $1.8 billion. The new language gave non-defense federal workers a 2 percent across-the-board raise and additional "locality pay" raises, with amounts that were to be determined later but that were expected to average 0.6 percent nationwide. Locality pay was intended to close the gap between federal and private sector white-collar workers. One of the aims was to stem the departures of federal workers for higher paying non-government jobs.

Some appropriators feared that the additional raises, though small, would force cash-strapped agencies to lay off workers or curb new initiatives. But the committee rejected on a party-line vote of 20-28 an amendment by top committee Republican Joseph M. McDade of Pennsylvania to finance the

pay raise from money that had been appropriated for fiscal 1994 but remained unspent. Hoyer and Budget Committee Chairman Martin Olav Sabo, D-Minn., said that financing the fiscal 1995 pay raise through such a one-time mechanism would only make it harder for agencies to find the money in future years.

● **Smoking ban.** The only other significant amendment adopted during the three-hour committee markup represented a victory for smokers and the tobacco lobby. By 24-14, the committee approved an amendment by Carrie Meek, D-Fla., to strip from the bill Visclosky's provisions to ban smoking in federal buildings except in specially ventilated areas.

House Floor

The House passed the $23.3 billion bill June 15 by a vote of 276-139. *(Vote 247, p. 74-H)*

The bill came to the floor under a rule that left members free to offer spending-cut amendments, and the 13-hour debate featured much partisan bickering. But in the end, the debate yielded only $18.5 million in mostly symbolic nicks in the bill's price tag — an amount that was quickly exceeded when Ways and Means Committee member Robert T. Matsui, D-Calif., stripped an additional $33 million from the bill on parliamentary points of order.

Appropriators had sought to spend money from a Treasury Department forfeiture fund that collected cash and other assets seized by the department during drug busts and other criminal prosecutions. Money from the fund was supposed to be used specifically for anti-crime efforts, but appropriators wanted to tap the $33 million to help finance other programs.

The floor debate turned partisan when Republicans offered four amendments — each defeated — to cut the White House budget by anywhere from 20 percent to $13,139.66, the estimated cost of an unauthorized golf outing by a White House aide who traveled on the president's helicopter. Calling the GOP-proposed cuts a "petty, partisan attack," Hoyer noted that the Democratic-controlled Congress had not gone after the White House budgets of Republican Presidents Ronald Reagan and George Bush.

The House bill froze the White House budget at $38.8 million, the amount appropriated for fiscal 1994. The administration had requested $41.6 million.

The House adopted amendments offered by:

● Sam Coppersmith, D-Ariz., to cut $6.6 million from the Postal Service's account that provided free mailings for the blind. Coppersmith was protesting the Postal Service's decision to spend that amount to install its new logo on buildings, uniforms and trucks. The amendment was adopted by voice vote.

● Earl Pomeroy, D-N.D., to cut 6 percent of the money for 13 new courthouse projects, to produce a savings of $5.6 million, adopted 302-120. *(Vote 242, p. 72-H)*

● Ernest Jim Istook Jr., R-Okla., who won approval of two amendments to eliminate small agencies. One, approved by voice vote, zeroed out $1.8 million for the Administrative Conference of the United States, which was responsible for helping federal agencies improve administrative procedures. The other, approved 223-210, axed the Advisory Council on Intergovernmental Relations, which was intended to boost cooperation among federal, state and local governments. *(Vote 240, p. 72-H)*

● Robert L. Livingston, R-La., to cut $3.5 million from the $27.1 million budget for the Federal Election Commission, bringing the agency's budget to fiscal 1994 levels. Livingston said the agency's budget had been growing much too quickly

in recent years. The House adopted the amendment, 231-197. *(Vote 241, p. 72-H)*

Tempers flared during debate on an amendment by self-described "porkbuster" Harris W. Fawell, R-Ill., who tried to strip three Democratic-sponsored projects out of the bill. Appropriations Committee Chairman David R. Obey, D-Wis., noted that there were GOP projects in the bill that had not been fully authorized, and he said maybe those should be stripped out as well.

When Obey alluded to a $25.2 million appropriation to finish a courthouse near the district of former Navy pilot Randy "Duke" Cunningham, R-Calif., things got nasty. "If the gentleman wants to do something, he can come over here," Cunningham said, as if he was ready for a fistfight. The House rejected Fawell's amendment on a 145-271 vote. *(Vote 244, p. 72-H)*

Senate Action

Only hours after the House passed the bill, the Senate Appropriations Treasury-Postal Subcommittee met June 16 and approved its version of HR 4539 by a vote of 5-0. The full committee approved the measure by voice vote that same afternoon (S Rept 103-286).

● **Pay increase.** The subcommittee version of the bill deleted the House-passed pay raise for federal workers, leaving the decision to Clinton. The Senate bill made no allowance for locality pay increases. Subcommittee Chairman DeConcini said in opposing the raise that cash-strapped agencies would have to lay off workers or curb new initiatives to cover the cost.

● **IRS.** Other than the pay raise dispute, the Senate bill generally mirrored the House measure on major issues. However, it did restore $132 million of the House cut in the IRS computer upgrade project.

● **Projects.** As expected, the Senate committee set different priorities for federal courthouse construction projects; it added $218 million to the total for projects — including a $99 million courthouse for Tucson, in Arizona, DeConcini's home state. The administration had requested $12 million for site acquisition and design for the courthouse, but DeConcini added construction money, although it was not to be spent in fiscal 1995. The project came on the heels of a $120 million courthouse in Phoenix, financed by the fiscal 1994 Treasury-Postal bill (PL 103-123).

The Senate committee also added a $30 million down payment on a $200 million courthouse project in Islip, N.Y., at the request of Alfonse M. D'Amato, R-N.Y. Another winner was Pete V. Domenici, R-N.M., who obtained $49 million for a new federal courthouse in Albuquerque.

Senate Floor Action

After a debate that ranged from taxes to White House drug testing policy, the Senate passed a $23.6 billion version of the bill June 22 by a vote of 72-27, rejecting two attempts to reduce the price tag. *(Vote 161, p. 28-S)*

Charles E. Grassley, R-Iowa, tried to eliminate $405 million in the bill that was being provided to finance a $2.2 billion IRS initiative to beef up tax collection efforts. The money was to be used to hire new IRS agents and tax collectors; it was expected to generate $9 billion to $10 billion in revenues over the following five years. Grassley objected to hiring additional agents without providing a "taxpayer bill of rights" that would give taxpayers additional protections from possible abuses by IRS agents. The Senate tabled, or killed, Grassley's amendment on a 54-43 vote. *(Vote 155, p. 27-S)*

A motion by Robert C. Smith, R-N.H., to freeze the total amount of spending in the bill at the fiscal 1994 level was tabled on a 56-38 vote. Bill drafters argued that to freeze overall spending would require across-the-board cuts of 10 percent in the discretionary programs in the bill. *(Vote 156, p. 27-S)*

The debate became heated June 21 when Lauch Faircloth, R-N.C., began a personal attack on Patsy Thomasson, the head of the White House Office of Administration and a friend of Clinton's, who oversaw the drug testing program at the White House.

Faircloth, a staunch administration opponent, noted that Thomasson had worked for Arkansas businessman Dan Lasater, who had been convicted on federal charges of dealing cocaine. While not accusing Thomasson outright of having used drugs, Faircloth offered an amendment that, in effect, required that officials responsible for the White House drug testing program not be found by the FBI to have a history of drug use. "It is wrong to have a business partner and confidant of a drug dealer in charge of the White House drug testing program," Faircloth said.

That was too much for Democrats, who lashed out at Faircloth. "It is absolutely enough to make you regurgitate," said DeConcini. By the next morning, tempers had cooled, and Faircloth's amendment was adopted on a 98-0 vote. *(Vote 157, p. 27-S)*

The Senate also voted, 79-20, to allow an amendment by Slade Gorton, R-Wash., to permit recreational boaters to purchase diesel fuel that had been specially dyed for commercial customers as a way to enforce a new diesel fuel tax. Fuel for commercial boats was taxed at a lower rate than fuel for recreational boats. Because many marinas had only one fuel tank, they were choosing to sell only to their big commercial customers. Gorton wanted to allow recreational boaters to buy the dyed fuel provided they paid taxes at the rate for recreational boaters. Senators approved the tax change by voice vote despite warnings by Finance Committee Chairman Daniel Patrick Moynihan, D-N.Y., that the House would "blue slip" the bill, or send it back. *(Vote 159, p. 27-S)*

The Senate quickly reversed itself July 15, however, after the House sent the bill back to the Senate with a demand that it strip out Gorton's tax provision. The House, which agreed to the move by voice vote July 14, was acting to protect its right to generate all tax bills.

Conference/Final Action

The House-Senate conference on the bill convened Sept. 20, and conferees promptly accepted Hoyer's provision to raise federal employees' pay by an average of 2.6 percent nationwide, including higher locality pay raises for those who worked in high-cost areas.

Although Clinton had originally proposed a 1.6 percent raise, he agreed in August to embrace Hoyer's proposal, using his presidential powers. As a result, the provision was no longer needed, and conferees had planned to drop it. But the provision also included language to block a cost of living increase (COLA) for members of Congress, negotiated under a 1989 congressional pay increase law. *(1989 Almanac, p. 51)*

Jim Ross Lightfoot of Iowa, ranking Republican among House conferees, insisted that deleting the federal pay provision would amount to voting for a congressional raise of about $3,500. Lightfoot insisted that the entire provision — including the COLA — be retained, and the conferees reluctantly went along.

An attempt to preserve $94 million in Senate-passed Customs Service fees that would have been directed to the IRS computer upgrade had to be abandoned after objections were raised by the House Ways and Means Committee, which had jurisdiction over revenue-raising bills.

Final conference action had been delayed for three months while appropriators waited for enactment of the big anti-crime bill (HR 3355 — PL 103-322), which provided an additional $40 million through a new trust fund. Of the total, conferees designated $7 million for the Bureau of Alcohol, Tobacco and Firearms (ATF) to help implement the Brady handgun control law (PL 103-159). Another $5 million was earmarked to fight counterfeiting, and $9 million was set aside for ATF anti-gang programs. *(Crime bill, p. 273)*

Conferees filed their report (H Rept 103-729) on Sept. 20, and final passage was expected to be routine.

But when the conference report reached the House floor Sept. 22, skittish lawmakers voted to cut $368 million from the bill, including $218 million from new construction projects eagerly sought by members. The 234-192 vote came on a procedural motion that sent the bill back to the conference committee with instructions to cut its price tag. *(Vote 436, p. 130-H)*

The floor vote was forced by Istook, who was unhappy that conferees had sent the bill to the House with $736 million for new construction, $234 million more than the House had initially approved. Istook also opposed a provision to levy $149.7 million in new IRS user fees.

As the vote began, appropriators were confident they would prevail. But Republicans actively whipped the vote, and a wave of Democrats uneasy with the threat of being depicted as soft on spending cuts deserted the appropriators. Playing a role in the vote, several members said, was the surprising primary loss of Democratic loyalist Synar of Oklahoma, which worried many members.

Most of the 65 Democrats and 169 Republicans who voted to recommit the bill could rest easy. But those with projects in it were nervous, and rightly so.

Exacting a Little Revenge

After the vote, Hoyer huddled with aides to identify projects in the districts of members who deserted the bill. Initially, he drafted a plan that would have stripped out all of the IRS user fees. Another $53 million in repair projects, con-

centrated in districts of members who voted to trim the bill, also were slated to be cut. Republicans, led by Istook and Frank R. Wolf of Virginia, cried foul. Since most of the votes for Istook's motion came from Republicans, they would have borne the brunt of the cuts.

"This isn't about punishment. This is about making members put their districts where their mouths are," said Obey. As worried representatives from the IRS watched, desperately hoping to retain the user fees crucial to their budget, Obey asked for a recess to discuss the bill further.

Hours later, conferees met and approved $157 million in cuts ($135 million from new construction). The conference committee filed a new report (H Rept 103-741) late that night.

"Those people who believe we could cut $200 million, we're taking them at their word," said Hoyer. Except for J. J. Pickle, D-Texas, who voted against the cuts but had a $1.4 million project in Austin deleted by mistake, the cuts were taken solely from the districts of members who voted for them. Each of the excised projects had been requested by the GSA. Though the cuts were likely to delay work, most projects were expected to resurface the following year.

Left untouched were three new projects in Maryland and Arizona slipped into the bill in conference by Hoyer and DeConcini.

Conferees restored $119 million of the IRS user fees along with most of the proposed cuts in repair projects.

The final, revised version of the bill appropriated $602 million for new projects, almost $100 million more than the original House bill. Additional minor cuts were made in projects to repair existing facilities.

Final Passage

The House and Senate quickly finished action on the bill, getting the measure to Clinton's desk in time for the Oct. 1 start of the fiscal year.

The House adopted the conference report on a 360-53 vote Sept. 27. The wide margin probably was attributable to the inclusion of the unpopular — but politically necessary — provision to freeze congressional pay by denying members the COLA increase. Members apparently did not want to be recorded as having voted against what some had dubbed the "un-COLA." *(Vote 441, p. 132-H)*

The Senate cleared the measure the next day by voice vote. ∎

Battles Flare Over VA-HUD Bill

As in past years, the fate of the space station dominated early consideration of the fiscal 1995 appropriations bill for the departments of Veterans Affairs (VA), Housing and Urban Development (HUD) and related agencies (HR 4624). But there was no shortage of controversies as Congress considered the bill, a catchall measure that also included funding for the Environmental Protection Agency (EPA) and the National Aeronautics and Space Administration (NASA). Battles flared over issues ranging from members' special projects, to new EPA rules for ethanol, to a proposal to expand the federal home loan program.

Overall, the bill provided $90.1 billion in spending authority — $1.8 billion more than the fiscal 1994 VA-HUD bill, but $200 million less than President Clinton had requested. Clinton signed the bill into law Sept. 28 (PL 103-327).

The House and Senate resolved funding differences for the major agencies by agreeing to increases over fiscal 1994 for the VA and EPA, and reductions for HUD and NASA. Even at HUD and NASA, however, Congress managed to find money for certain programs, appropriating more than Clinton recommended for public and elderly housing, and funding a new wind tunnel project for NASA.

Some of the biggest battles were not reserved for big ticket items. These included:
- **Special projects.** Congress added hundreds of millions of dollars' worth of site-specific special projects one year after it had passed a relatively "clean" VA-HUD appropriations bill. Opponents derided the projects — most of which were under HUD and the EPA — as pork barrel spending that would mainly benefit the states and districts of powerful members, but the projects survived.
- **Ethanol.** Senators battled over a proposal to block a new EPA rule requiring that corn-based ethanol be used in reformulated, or cleaner-burning, gasoline. This was essentially a fight between farm states, which supported the EPA rule as a boon to corn products, and oil-producing states, which opposed the rule. The farm states eventually got the upper hand.
- **Foreign refiners.** The House had its own scrap over reformulated gasoline. It involved a proposed EPA rule that would have given foreign refiners more flexibility to certify that their gasoline was reformulated. In this case, Congress decided to block the proposed EPA rule.
- **Home loans.** A dispute over how active the Federal Housing Administration (FHA) ought to be in the single-family home loan market arose during conference negotiations on the final bill. Conferees opted for only modest increases in existing limits, resisting House appeals for higher thresholds.

Background

Most of the key issues that dogged the bill during the year had long histories:
- **Space station.** Congress had demonstrated in 1993 that

BOXSCORE

Fiscal 1995 VA-HUD Appropriations — HR 4624. The $90.1 billion bill included funds for the departments of Veterans Affairs and Housing and Urban Development, as well as the Environmental Protection Agency and NASA.

Reports: H Rept 103-555, S Rept 103-311; conference report H Rept 103-715.

KEY ACTION

June 29 — House passed HR 4624, 344-84.

Aug. 4 — Senate passed HR 4624, amended, 86-9.

Sept. 12 — House agreed to the conference report, 313-61.

Sept. 27 — Senate cleared the bill, 90-9.

Sept. 28 — President signed HR 4624 — PL 103-327.

---

big-science projects were not immune to budget cutting fervor when it killed the superconducting super collider. The House had served notice that the space station could be next to go when members failed by just one vote to end its authorization and by 24 votes to ax its fiscal 1994 appropriation. *(1993 Almanac, pp. 691, 249)*

The space station's prospects were further clouded in the spring of 1994 when two key lawmakers said they were noncommital about continuing the project. House Science Committee Chairman George E. Brown Jr., D-Calif., was concerned that the space station would siphon funds from other NASA science programs. And Louis Stokes, D-Ohio, warned that the space station might suffer if there was a shortage of funds in the VA-HUD Appropriations Subcommittee, which he chaired.

The space station, originally known as *Freedom*, was conceived in 1984 as an $8 billion orbiting manned laboratory. But the federal government had already spent $11.2 billion on the space station, and the renamed *Alpha* project now carried a total price tag of about $30 billion. *(Space station, p. 545)*

By June, both Brown and Stokes had decided to support spending $2.1 billion in fiscal 1995 for the project. Stokes said he decided to endorse the space station "because the president wanted it and felt that it was a vital part of his foreign policy." He was alluding to a cooperative agreement on the space station with the Russians.

Besides touting the station's scientific merit and foreign policy implications, supporters asserted that a series of redesign efforts had made the project more efficient. "I think it's going to be very hard to argue that NASA hasn't done its part for deficit reduction," said Rep. Tom DeLay, R-Texas, a VA-HUD Subcommittee member.

Opponents argued that the Russian agreement was unreliable and that the space station was drawing funds from more worthy NASA projects. "The space station will cost far more than its sticker price and will continue to displace more cost-effective space research," said Rep. Dick Zimmer, R-N.J.
- **Ethanol.** The ethanol controversy stemmed from the 1990 rewrite of the Clean Air Act (PL 101-549), which required that in 1995 nine cities with poor air quality begin selling gasoline reformulated to increase oxygen content — and thereby decrease carbon monoxide pollution. The act left it up to the marketplace to determine how to reformulate the gasoline. *(1990 Almanac, p. 229)*

In a rule proposed in December 1993 and issued June 30, the EPA required that at least 30 percent of the gasoline sold in those markets contain a "renewable" oxygenate. That meant ethanol or its derivative, and it effectively required about one-tenth of all gasoline sold in the United States to contain ethanol.

The EPA concluded that the use of ethanol would cut dependence on foreign oil and that it would reduce emissions

VA-HUD-Independent Agencies Spending

(in thousands of dollars)

	Fiscal 1994 Appropriations	Fiscal 1995 Clinton Request	House Bill	Senate Bill	Final Bill
Veterans Affairs					
Compensation and pensions	$ 17,526,446	$ 17,626,892	$ 17,626,892	$ 17,626,892	$ 17,626,892
Readjustment benefits	1,050,600	1,286,600	1,286,600	1,286,600	1,286,600
Loan funds and expenses	620,792	513,832	508,432	508,432	508,432
Medical care	15,622,452	16,121,756	16,232,756	16,232,756	16,232,756
Medical research	252,000	211,000	252,000	252,000	252,000
Construction projects	568,862	311,780	298,280	414,315	561,927
Other	1,026,314	1,034,060	1,078,903	1,098,779	1,096,094
TOTAL, Veterans Affairs	**$ 36,667,466**	**$ 37,105,920**	**$ 37,283,863**	**$ 37,419,774**	**$ 37,564,701**
Housing and Urban Development					
HOPE grants	109,190	100,000	100,000	50,000	50,000
HOME program	1,275,000	1,100,000	1,275,000	1,500,000	1,400,000
Assisted housing	9,312,900	10,283,918	11,473,019	10,600,000	11,083,000
Renewal of Section 8 subsidies	5,358,106	5,092,000	4,505,000	2,992,000	2,536,000
Public housing subsidies	2,620,808	2,496,000	2,900,000	2,900,000	2,900,000
Severely distressed public housing	778,240	500,000	500,000	500,000	500,000
Drug elimination grants	265,000	—[1]	265,000	315,000	290,000
Federal Housing Administration	231,990	145,636	109,241	145,636	145,636
Ginnie Mae (receipts)	−269,300	−262,700	−262,700	−262,700	−262,700
Homeless assistance	822,747	1,250,000	1,120,000	1,120,000	1,120,000
Community development grants	4,420,000	4,400,000	4,600,000	4,600,000	4,600,000
Other HUD accounts	571,953	1,084,224	519,224	573,582	579,582
Rescissions	−609,953	−288,000	−288,000	−288,000	−288,000
TOTAL, HUD	**$ 24,886,681**	**$ 25,901,078**	**$ 26,815,784**	**$ 24,745,518**	**$ 24,653,518**
NASA					
Human space flight	6,069,700	5,719,900	5,592,900	5,573,900	5,573,900
Space station	(1,946,000)	(2,120,900)	(2,120,900)	(2,120,900)	(2,120,900)
Science, aeronautics, technology	5,847,300	5,901,200	5,901,200	5,901,200	5,901,200
Aeronautical facilities (wind tunnels)	—	—	—	400,000	400,000
Mission support, other	2,610,399	2,619,584	2,506,584	2,566,387	2,501,584
TOTAL, NASA	**$ 14,527,399**	**$ 14,240,684**	**$ 14,000,684**	**$ 14,441,487**	**$ 14,376,684**
Environmental Protection Agency					
Research, anti-pollution programs	1,691,236	1,886,146	1,600,300	1,777,000	1,767,000
Superfund	1,464,575	1,482,819	1,419,616	1,184,616	1,419,616
Leaking underground storage tanks	74,710	76,015	69,331	69,331	69,331
Water infrastructure/state funds	2,477,000	2,650,000	2,732,000	3,400,000	2,962,000
Personnel, other	912,459	1,063,115	1,166,770	1,022,940	1,022,940
TOTAL, EPA	**$ 6,619,980**	**$ 7,158,095**	**$ 6,988,017**	**$ 7,453,887**	**$ 7,240,887**
Selected Independent Agencies					
FEMA	786,289	702,000	831,322	498,907	821,907
Disaster relief	(292,000)	(320,000)	(320,000)	—	(320,000)
Emergency funding	(4,709,000)	—	—	—	—
National Science Foundation	3,017,797	3,198,909	3,106,063	3,454,520	3,360,520
National Service	365,000	611,388	491,388	612,000	577,000
Selective Service System	25,000	22,930	22,930	22,930	22,930
FSLIC resolution, RTC funds	1,212,314	874,000	874,000	859,000	874,000
GRAND TOTAL	**$ 88,313,838**	**$ 90,318,793**	**$ 90,547,927**	**$ 90,116,109**	**$ 90,118,186**

[1] *The administration suggested replacing Drug Elimination Grants with a wider anti-crime effort called Community Partnerships Against Crime (COMPAC).*

SOURCE: House Appropriations Committee

that could cause global warming. Ethanol's emissions resulted in less ozone-producing hydrocarbons than gasoline's.

The National Corn Growers Association welcomed the proposal, saying it could generate sales of an additional 250 million to 500 million bushels of corn, reduce farm subsidies and stimulate economic growth in rural America.

But the petroleum industry objected strongly, saying that fuels such as methanol, propane or compressed natural gas were superior alternatives to the corn-based products. The American Petroleum Institute said ethanol could actually increase pollution largely because so much energy was needed to harvest the corn and operate ethanol distilleries.

Some leading environmental groups joined in opposing both the EPA rule and congressional efforts to block it, largely because they preferred that the battle be fought in the courts.

● **Foreign refiners.** A separate dispute grew out of a provision of the Clean Air Act amendments that required reformulated gasoline to burn 15 percent more cleanly than conventional 1990 fuels. To determine the 1990 baseline, an EPA rule issued in December 1993 required each U.S. refiner to be guided by its 1990 average of pollutants. However, because of the difficulty of tracking and verifying data from foreign sources, the baseline for foreign refiners was set at the 1990 average for all U.S. refiners.

Venezuela, one of the largest suppliers of foreign oil to the United States, objected, saying the rule treated foreign suppliers differently from domestic refineries, violating the General Agreement on Tariffs and Trade. At Venezuela's behest, the EPA proposed to amend the rule to allow foreign refiners to be guided by their individual 1990 baseline for pollutants if their baseline could be verified.

Lawmakers who opposed the revised rule predicted that it would result in job losses in the U.S. oil and gas industry because of the increased foreign competition. They said the original rule would keep Venezuela and other foreign refiners from exporting "dirtier" gasoline than domestic refiners would have to manufacture. Efforts to stop the revision were supported by big domestic oil and gasoline companies, as well as some environmental groups.

Those who defended the revision said it would treat foreign refiners the same as domestic. To do otherwise, they said, would risk gasoline shortages, higher gasoline prices and retaliatory trade practices. They also denied that the reformulated gasoline from foreign refineries such as those in Venezuela would be any dirtier than that from U.S. refineries.

● **Special projects.** The fiscal 1994 VA-HUD bill restored the practice of funding site-specific projects that had not been authorized but were inserted at the request of individual members.

In the past, the HUD account in particular had served as a prime location for member projects. The House typically had refrained from including such earmarks until the Senate did so. Then the House would match the Senate amount. These special projects ballooned from $73 million in fiscal 1991 to $260 million in fiscal 1993.

When then-HUD Secretary Jack F. Kemp vehemently objected to the earmarks in the fiscal 1991 bill, the Senate VA-HUD Subcommittee responded by restricting his travel privileges and zeroing out his public affairs staff. Although the money was restored in the final bill, Kemp toned down his objections in subsequent years.

In 1993, Stokes and Senate VA-HUD Subcommittee Chairwoman Barbara A. Mikulsi, D-Md., agreed not to include money for unauthorized site-specific projects in the fiscal 1994 bill, citing criticism of the earmarks from autho-

rizing committees and federal agencies. *(1993 Almanac, p. 691)*

Some members were clearly frustrated by this no-pork policy, however, perhaps none more so than Senate Appropriations Committee Chairman Robert C. Byrd, D-W.Va., who was renowned for bringing federal largess to his state. During the markup of the fiscal 1994 VA-HUD spending bill, Byrd had complained that appropriators needed the flexibility to fund worthy, small-scale projects that authorizers ignored. "That's what we're here for," he said.

The final fiscal 1995 bill contained $290 billion in HUD "special purpose" grants for a wide variety of projects. It also included $1.28 billion in EPA grants to "cities with special needs."

The controversy over the EPA grants related to Congress' difficulty in reauthorizing the Clean Water Act. The act, which was set to expire Sept. 30, established a revolving loan fund for states, which then lent money to cities and towns to build and repair sewage treatment plants and implement other water quality programs.

A bill reauthorizing the clean water law (S 1114, HR 3948) was stalled in Congress over disputes about protecting wetlands, controlling agricultural runoff and how the clean water funds ought to be reallocated to the states. *(Clean water, p. 241)*

"We can't wait for the authorizers," said Mikulski. "We gave them a year; we're ready to go."

● **FHA loans.** The Clinton administration had recommended that the FHA be allowed to insure higher-priced mortgages to more realistically reflect home prices and to stimulate more home ownership.

FHA's single-family loan guarantee program was designed to encourage lenders to make loans to first-time buyers and others who did not have the money for a conventional down payment. It did so by insuring the private sector lenders against the risk of mortgage default. Under existing law, the basic limit for FHA guarantees was $67,500, increasing to $151,725 in high-cost areas.

The proposal to increase the limit, thereby allowing the FHA to become more active in the single-family housing market, was backed by associations representing real estate agents, mortgage bankers and home builders, all of whom stood to benefit from the increased housing activity.

But private mortgage insurance companies resisted the effort, viewing it as government intrusion into their business. They were joined by advocates of low-income families, who said it would pull resources from lower-end buyers.

The issue also arose in debate over a separate housing authorization bill (HR 3838).

House Committee

The annual battle over whether to build a space station began June 9 when the House VA-HUD Appropriations Subcommittee agreed to spend $2.1 billion for the project as part of the fiscal 1995 spending bill. The bill, approved by voice vote, contained a total of $70.4 billion in discretionary spending and $20.1 billion in mandatory spending.

At Stokes' behest, the subcommittee also offered more than the Clinton administration had requested for public housing and for veterans' medical care.

To do so, the panel recommended smaller increases than the administration sought for the EPA, the National Science Foundation, and the Corporation for National and Community Service. It also opted to cut the overall NASA budget further than the administration recommended and

declined to fund several new housing initiatives.

"I think we made it clear to the administration that we didn't have the money to do all these things," Stokes said. "We had to make some very painful choices."

Full Committee Approval

The full Appropriations Committee approved HR 4624 by voice vote June 22, leaving the subcommittee-approved measure largely intact (H Rept 103-555).

Both Stokes and the subcommittee's ranking Republican, Jerry Lewis, Calif., spoke of the difficulty of keeping within the overall limits allocated to the subcommittee, particularly because of the administration's funding initiatives. "For the next year and for the foreseeable future," Lewis said, "it's a matter of making expectations more realistic."

Stokes also pointed out that the committee bill did not include funding for projects that were unauthorized or specific to one location.

Shortly after the Appropriations Committee vote, space station opponents, led by Zimmer and Tim Roemer, D-Ind., held a news conference to portray the space station as a pork barrel project that was drawing funds from more worthy scientific undertakings. They said they would try to amend the bill on the House floor so that the $2.1 billion for the space station would be distributed to other NASA endeavors. Appropriators had provided $14 billion for NASA, $240 million less than the administration requested and $526.7 million less than had been appropriated for the space agency in fiscal 1994.

Zimmer said the project "does not have a definitive design, does not have a believable cost estimate and does not have significant scientific value." Carolyn B. Maloney, D-N.Y., derided the space station as "a Motel 6 in space," and Fred Upton, R-Mich., said the project resembled Spam because it was "pork in a can."

Stokes said that the 25th anniversary of the first moon landing and the increased involvement of Russia in the project should help the program's standing. The committee report indicated that $111.9 million would be available for cooperation with the Russians, enabling the United States to tap into the Russians' experience with the *Mir* space station and their superior rocket liftoff capability. Opponents said the Russian agreement was unreliable.

In an attempt to tie up loose ends from a 1993 controversy, the report supported NASA's decision to build and refurbish space shuttle nozzles at Yellow Creek, Miss. The project was to be located on a site that had been prepared to build the advanced solid rocket motor (ASRM). Congress, at the House's insistence, had killed the ASRM project in the fiscal 1994 bill. Thiokol Corp., which made the redesigned motor used by the shuttle, had favored shifting the nozzle operations from the company's Utah plant to the Mississippi facility. *(1993 Almanac, p. 695)*

On another issue, Stokes successfully resisted an attempt by Dean A. Gallo, R-N.J., to prohibit the EPA from requiring that corn-based ethanol account for at least 30 percent of cleaner-burning reformulated gasoline.

Gallo warned that the EPA mandate would cause gasoline price increases, as well as a loss of federal highway trust funds because of ethanol's tax exemptions. Opponents objected that Gallo was trying to legislate on an appropriations bill, and he withdrew his amendment when it appeared to face defeat.

The bill also contained a provision to raise the limit on single-family loans insured by the FHA in high-cost areas to $172,675 from $151,725.

House Floor

After rejecting all major attempts to amend the bill crafted by the subcommittee, the House passed the $90.5 billion VA-HUD spending bill June 29 by a vote of 344-84. *(Vote 312, p. 92-H)*

By a surprisingly comfortable margin of 155-278, members first rejected an attempt by Zimmer and Roemer to kill the space station. *(Vote 309, p. 90-H)*

Clinton, Vice President Al Gore and NASA Administrator Daniel S. Goldin personally lobbied members to support the station. They argued that the 1993 agreement with Russia to cooperate on the project — and international agreements with other countries — were essential to the administration's foreign policy goals, and that the project's redesign would keep costs under control.

Opponents blasted the project as being too expensive, unfocused in its mission, dependent on unreliable agreements with Russia and too reliant on job creation for its political support.

Although their amendment would not have reduced the fiscal 1995 deficit, Zimmer and Roemer argued that it would cut the deficit in the future. "It's time for the Congress to do what it should have done years ago — cut our losses . . . and put an end to this budgetary black hole in space," Zimmer said.

But momentum had shifted in favor of funding the space station. After the vote, Roemer said the close call on the NASA authorization bill in 1993 actually helped the station. "The 216-215 vote last year woke up a sleeping giant," he said of the lobbying blitz that preceded the 1994 vote. Zimmer said the agreement with Russia "created considerably more support for the program on the Democratic side of the aisle and, to my surprise, on the Republican side."

Station supporters expressed hope that the vote would end the annual tussles. "One of the reasons I waffled was to put the fear of God in the administration, the contractors, the labor groups and other interest groups; I thought they were coasting," Brown said. As the vote drew near, he said, "they put on a full-court press."

In other action, the House defeated 162-269 an amendment by Nick Smith, R-Mich., to cut $448 million in public housing funds and to increase funding for HUD's rent voucher program by $179.7 million. *(Vote 307, p. 90-H)*

Senate Committee

The Senate VA-HUD Appropriations Subcommittee on July 14 gave voice vote approval to its version of the spending bill, which contained $70.4 billion for discretionary programs and $20.1 billion in mandatory spending. That afternoon, the full Appropriations Committee approved the bill 27-2 (S Rept 103-311).

During the markup, a dustup over an amendment to block the new federal rule requiring ethanol in some gasoline set off enough sparks to show that a conflagration awaited on the Senate floor.

The gasoline dispute began in the subcommittee, where Democrat J. Bennett Johnston, from oil-rich Louisiana, succeeded in amending the bill to block the EPA rule. Johnston's amendment was adopted, 9-3. Johnston called the rule a giveaway to special interests. "It just happens that ethanol is produced 70 percent by Archer-Daniels-Midland," he said, referring to an agricultural conglomerate based in Decatur, Ill., whose heavy political contributions to Clinton and other Democrats were detailed in a July 6 article in The Wall Street Journal.

Other senators joined the refrain. "This is the biggest pork project — pig, pig, pig thing — I've ever seen," said Alfonse M. D'Amato, R-N.Y.

But farm-state senators warned Johnston to back off. Natural gas — a big industry in Louisiana — could lose support when it needed help in the future, they said.

By the afternoon, two Democratic senators from corn-growing states — Bob Kerrey of Nebraska and Tom Harkin of Iowa — had become adamant. When the full Appropriations Committee convened, they protested vociferously, threatening to block action on all five appropriations bills scheduled for consideration that day. "There are lives at stake with this," Kerrey said. "There's an awful lot of jobs."

Faced with the prospect of slowing the committee's work, not to mention a budget estimate that his amendment would cost $20 million by increasing subsidies to corn growers, Johnston allowed the amendment to be removed, saying he would wait for floor action.

Other Changes

Although Subcommittee Chairwoman Mikulski described the fiscal 1995 VA-HUD bill as particularly tight, she succeeded in freeing up enough dollars to override administration cuts and to permit hundreds of millions of dollars to be set aside for special projects dear to individual members. To do so, the bill accepted several changes in subsidized private housing that had been advocated by the administration, deferred new disaster aid and changed the schedule for grants under the National Service program.

"I like to call my chairman 'Deep Pockets,' because she always manages to find a way to do it," said Dianne Feinstein, D-Calif.

The changes enabled the Senate committee to double to $208 million the House's figure for construction of major VA projects, specifying where the new projects should be built. Like the House version, the Senate bill included substantially more than the administration requested for housing subsidies for the elderly, as well as additional money for public housing development, modernization and subsidy accounts.

Senate appropriators also added $400 million to NASA's budget to build two wind tunnels to test future commercial jet transports. The Appropriations Committee report on the bill said the tunnels would cost $2.5 billion, with some of the costs paid by private industry, and be operating by 2002.

Appropriators also set aside $610 million for the Corporation for National and Community Service, approximately what the administration requested, and $119.6 million more than the House approved.

Special Projects

After joining their House counterparts in disdaining members' site-specific projects in the fiscal 1994 bill, Senate appropriators reversed course and embraced such projects with gusto in the fiscal 1995 bill.

The most prominent example was $135 million worth of HUD special purpose grants. The committee report on the bill listed 102 HUD projects benefiting 37 states, the District of Columbia and Puerto Rico. The projects entailed diverse endeavors such as building homeless shelters, renovating downtown buildings, expanding hospitals and providing social services to poor youngsters.

A Senate aide said member requests for HUD special projects totaled $500 million. "There is a tremendous amount of need in cities and rural areas and suburban counties for funding that is flexible, that can go for bricks and mortar in many instances, and that can address many of the pressing needs that some of the federal programs don't go for," the aide said.

The states that stood to gain the most were West Virginia, Byrd's home, with four projects totaling $19 million; New York,

The Revamped Space Station

The space station, redesigned in 1993 to save U.S. taxpayers money and to broaden the participation of other nations, was a massive undertaking whose eventual price tag was far from firm.

The station was intended to be a floating platform for microgravity research in biotechnology, chemistry and physics. It was proposed in 1984 by President Ronald Reagan as the space station *Freedom*, an $8 billion orbiting laboratory. But the project was continually dogged by questions about its cost and feasibility. President Clinton's 1993 redesign reduced the projected cost for its construction and first 10 years of operation from $100 billion to $70.8 billion, brought in other nations and renamed the space station *Alpha*. (*1993 Almanac, p. 251*)

The key partner was to be Russia, because the former Soviet Union had 20 years' experience in keeping astronauts in space for months on stations such as *Mir*. Japan and European countries were to participate beginning in 2000.

The redesigned station, the size of two football fields when completed, was expected to use approximately 75 percent of the hardware designed for *Freedom*.

NASA estimated that the United States had spent $11.4 billion on the project from fiscal 1985 through 1993. The agency estimated the future U.S. cost of construction (not including putting the equipment into space) at $17.4 billion. Those costs included paying Russia $400 million for the use of *Mir* and Russian launches.

The station was to be managed from the ground by NASA's control center in Houston, with the Russian Kaliningrad Control Center as backup. Construction was expected to take from 1997 to 2002. Once the station became operational, crews were expected to work in six-month shifts, with crews and supplies being replaced through U.S. and Russian launches.

The station was being designed to house six crew members on a permanent basis. The Russian carrier Soyuz and U.S. space shuttles were to continue to replace crews and supplies.

with seven projects totaling $15 million; and Oregon, home of the committee's ranking Republican, Mark O. Hatfield, with four projects totaling $10.4 million — including $5 million for the Mark O. Hatfield Marine Science Center in Newport.

After the Senate appropriators acted, Stokes began to sift through similar requests from House members. He said he told Mikulski that "if she put them in her bill, I would then do so." He indicated that he would match the $135 million in Senate projects, and had no shortage of member requests to choose from.

But the HUD account was not the only place where Senate appropriators made room for site-specific projects that had not been authorized in other legislation.

Under an EPA account, they set aside $369.7 million in clean water grants "to cities with special needs," and named 16 recipients. They also sought to release $327.5 million in fiscal 1994 funds for "needy cities," again with specific instructions about which cities should get the money.

Boston was the biggest winner, with $125 million in fiscal 1995 funds and $100 million in fiscal 1994 funds for a new sewage treatment facility. While the Clinton administration

supported earmarking funds to the Boston project, it opposed the other EPA earmarks.

The House version of the bill had set aside $500 million for communities with "unique circumstances or difficulties" in meeting water quality standards. But the House had expressed "serious reservations" about funding projects before they were authorized. "I have meticulously avoided conflicts with authorizing committee chairmen," Stokes said in an interview.

Senate Floor

The Senate passed a $90.1 billion version of the spending bill, 86-9, on Aug. 4. *(Vote 262, p. 44-S)*

But first, with Gore casting the deciding vote, the Senate on Aug. 3 rejected an effort by Johnston and Bill Bradley, D-N.J., to block the new EPA rule requiring the use of ethanol in reformulated gasoline. Senators voted 51-50 to kill their amendment, which would have denied the EPA the funding to carry out the ruling. It was only the third time Gore had cast a deciding vote in the Senate since becoming vice president. *(Vote 255, p. 43-S)*

The rule's opponents criticized it as a costly and unfair subsidy to agricultural interests that would offer no assurances of providing cleaner air. Johnston called it "a gigantic flim-flam to the American public." He said it would cost consumers more at the gasoline pump, deplete funds from the highway trust fund, increase oil imports and fail to improve the environment. Opponents also said the EPA's action amounted to a political payoff from Clinton to farm states and agricultural interests who had supported him.

Proponents, led by Harkin, insisted that the rule simply assured that ethanol could compete with the oil industry, which they said benefited from heavy federal subsidies of its own. They said that the rule would create U.S. jobs, ensure competition with oil in producing the new gasoline, boost agricultural industries and help clean the air.

"The oil industry does not like competition," said Charles E. Grassley, R-Iowa, noting federal protections given to the domestic oil market. "They may not like an ethanol mandate, but they like mandates."

The final outcome seemed determined less by party affiliation or ideology than home state interests. In only eight states did the pair of senators split their votes; those from 42 states voted the same way. Support centered on states along the Gulf of Mexico and in the Northeast. Senators from the nation's midsection provided unanimous opposition to the amendment.

Afterward, Harkin noted that the rule was being challenged by the oil industry in the U.S. Court of Appeals. "This will signal to the court that although the margin is slim, it's Congress' intention to uphold the rule," he said.

He attributed the amendment's defeat to a bipartisan effort and to phone calls to a handful of undecided senators from Clinton.

Space Station, Other Action

The intensity of the ethanol debate and the uncertainty of its outcome overshadowed Senate consideration of the space station. Funding for the space station seemed assured after the House overwhelmingly defeated the attempt to kill the orbiting laboratory. The Senate, normally more supportive of the space station, defeated an attempt to kill the project with similar dispatch Aug. 3, 36-64. *(Vote 253, p. 43-S)*

During the space station debate, Dale Bumpers, D-Ark., argued that the project would eventually cost more than $70 billion to build and operate, was essentially a jobs creation project, with most of the benefits going to three states, and provided little commercial or scientific value.

But the space station's recent reorganization effort, strong support from the Clinton administration and foreign policy implications through international agreements made the Senate's support of the project something of a foregone conclusion.

In other action, the Senate:

● Killed, 62-36, an amendment by Frank H. Murkowski, R-Alaska, to restrict the use of funds to build or modernize inpatient facilities at Veterans Affairs hospitals. Murkowski tried to halt funding for three construction projects worth $87.7 million, at Memphis, Tenn., Honolulu and Travis, Calif., saying there was excess hospital bed capacity in those areas. *(Vote 256, p. 44-S)*

● Killed, 55-43, an amendment by William S. Cohen, R-Maine, to eliminate funding for a housing initiative that would use $350 million in federal funds to entice additional investment from pension funds. Cohen argued that it would be too risky an investment. *(Vote 257, p. 44-S)*

● Rejected, 27-71, an amendment by Robert C. Smith, R-N.H., to eliminate $135 million from the HUD special projects account and distribute the money instead through the Community Development Block Grant program. Smith said the bill had unfairly awarded the money to states with well-connected senators and members on the Appropriations Committee. *(Vote 260, p. 44-S)*

● Rejected, 37-60, an amendment by Smith to eliminate $697.2 million in clean water grants for unauthorized projects and direct the money instead through the Clean Water Act's state revolving fund. Smith maintained again that the grants had been unfairly distributed. *(Vote 261, p. 44-S)*

● Approved, 100-0, an amendment by Minority Leader Bob Dole, R-Kan., that expressed the non-binding sense of the Senate that Clinton was not authorized to send troops to Haiti on the basis of a U.N. Security Council resolution. Republicans argued that under the Constitution and the War Powers Resolution, Clinton needed congressional approval before sending troops overseas. *(Vote 254, p. 43-S)*

Conference

House and Senate conferees wrapped up a compromise VA-HUD appropriations spending bill Aug. 18 after agreeing to include $290 million worth of HUD special purpose grants and approving a small increase in the limit on FHA home loans (H Rept 103-715).

Most other issues covered by the $90.1 billion bill were resolved without controversy in conference.

Decisions made by the conferees included the following:

● **FHA loan limits.** The dispute over how active the FHA should be in the single-family home loan market was the most contentious issue. House conferees finally acceded to Senate demands for only a small increase in FHA loan limits, raising the basic cap from $67,500 to $77,197, and the cap in high-cost areas from $151,725 to $152,363. Both limits were to be indexed in future years to changes in the conforming loan limit for government-sponsored enterprises.

The conflict had stalled the conference Aug. 17, with House members insisting on raising the ceiling as high as $172,675. But senators warned that if the House did not back down, Senate opponents could wind up filibustering the bill.

Stokes finally agreed to the Senate's demand, though some of his House colleagues were disappointed that he had not continued to push for a compromise. Jim Chapman, D-Texas, and Feinstein both said afterward that they thought the Senate had been willing to compromise on higher limits.

Stokes said later that he had no choice. "Any compromise would have encroached upon the rights of the authorizing committee," he said.

Supporters of a higher FHA loan limit looked to a housing reauthorization bill (HR 3838) as an alternative vehicle for their proposals. In the end, the House passed the bill, but it died in the Senate. *(Housing bill, p. 408)*

● **Special projects.** Members agreed to appropriate $290 million for 266 HUD special purpose grants in 45 states, the District of Columbia and Puerto Rico. Projects included sewer and water lines; science, health and educational facilities; restoration of railroad stations, municipal plazas and civic coliseums; clinical labs; industrial developments; social services; housing; and unspecified economic development activities.

The bill also included $1.3 billion in special EPA projects. These site-specific "grants to cities with special needs" consisted of 45 wastewater treatment grants worth $782 million in fiscal 1995 funds, plus eight grants carrying $500 million in fiscal 1994 funds. Boston was the biggest winner of the wastewater grants, receiving $100 million in fiscal 1995 funds and $150 million in fiscal 1994 funds for a new sewage treatment facility.

● **Foreign refiners.** One issue that the conferees could not resolve concerned the EPA rule giving foreign refiners more flexibility to meet 1990 Clean Air Act requirements for reformulated gasoline.

Senate conferees insisted on their provision that barred the EPA from carrying out the propsed rule; House conferees resisted the provision, sending the matter back to the two chambers for a vote.

● **Other provisions.** The bill also appropriated:

● $1.2 billion for the state wastewater revolving loan fund, to be available Nov. 1, 1994, or sooner if a Clean Water Act reauthorization was enacted. Another $700,000 would be available for the state drinking water revolving loan fund when the program was authorized.

● $225 million in community development grants to finance housing repairs in areas affected by the January earthquake in Southern California. Another $180 million in community development grants was approved for areas damaged during the summer by Tropical Storm Alberto, which primarily hit Georgia.

● $355.6 million in major VA construction projects, tripling the Clinton administration's request.

● $1.1 billion for a new block grant that consolidated housing assistance for the homeless. This item was not authorized and died.

● $400 million for NASA to build two wind tunnels to test future commercial jet transports. However, the funds were to be released only if the administration met planning criteria.

Final Action

The House approved the conference report Sept. 12 by a vote of 313-61, after narrowly rebuffing an attempt to strip the $290 million in HUD special purpose grants from the bill. The Senate cleared the bill Sept. 27 on a 90-9 vote. *(House vote 417, p. 126-H; Senate vote 306, p. 53-S)*

Special Projects Criticized in House

Most issues covered by the wide-ranging bill — including the $2.1 billion for the NASA space station — prompted little discussion during House consideration of the conference report.

But the inclusion of the unauthorized HUD special purpose grants stirred a sharp debate. Opponents characterized them as pork barrel projects for a few powerful members,

while proponents argued that the grants responded to unique needs in their districts. A motion to accept the special projects was approved on a 189-180 vote. *(Vote 418, p. 126-H)*

Stokes tried to deflect criticism of the grants by noting their popularity. "Seldom could I walk on the floor of this House without members asking me to sit down so they could tell me about a special project in their district," he said. He added that he had received more than 300 requests for HUD special purpose grants, and more than 1,000 requests for grants in the bill overall.

Opponents, led by Harris W. Fawell, R-Ill., argued that the unauthorized projects, regardless of their merit, did not belong in the appropriations bill. He said only $7 million of the HUD special projects had been properly authorized.

Several members denounced the conference report for taking the House version of the bill, which had no funding for special projects, and the Senate version, which had $135 million worth, and compromising at $290 million. "That is the kind of mathematics that puzzles the people of this country," Brown said.

Brown was among the most vehement opponents of the grants. He said that nearly $130 million, almost half of the special purpose grants, went to seven states represented by 12 members of the conference committee. "This will destroy the sense of the members of the authorizing committee that they are co-equal members," Brown said, noting that $68.2 million of the funds were academic earmarks that should have been under his committee's jurisdiction.

But several members said they had special needs in their districts and were unwilling to let an agency or formula determine whether they deserved federal funds.

Carrie Meek, Fla., the only Democratic freshman appropriator, urged members not to apologize for determining their districts' needs. "That is why they elected you," she said of constituents, "so you can come up here and every once in a while give them a little something to take back to them."

Although Brown said the projects had been proportionately distributed to Republicans, Democrats voted 153-59 for the projects, while Republicans opposed them, 36-120.

There was no discussion in the House of $1.3 billion in unauthorized EPA projects included in the bill.

Members did resolve the one issue that the conferees could not, agreeing to the Senate provision blocking the proposed EPA rule on foreign refiners. Stokes had balked in conference, saying it was not an appropriations matter. But the House voted 222-148 to agree to the provision and block the proposed EPA rule. House Republicans provided the margin of support in favor of the Senate amendment, 124-31. Democrats voted 97-117. *(Vote 419, p. 126-H)*

Senate Action

The Senate cleared the bill Sept. 27 after resisting attempts to either remove members' special earmarks from the bill or require future appropriations bills to highlight such projects.

The main controversy in the Senate was over the HUD and EPA special projects.

Opponents attacked the site-specific grants as pork barrel politics that mainly benefited Appropriations Committee members. But senators rejected, 28-72, an amendment by John McCain, R-Ariz., to prohibit expenditures on any unauthorized project added in conference. *(Vote 307, p. 53-S)*

They also rejected, 45-55, an amendment by Smith that would have required conference reports on appropriations bills to identify any earmarks and to note whether they were included by the House, by the Senate or by conferees. *(Vote 308, p. 53-S)*   ■

Early Vote for Emergency Funds

Rushing to aid the victims of a major earthquake that struck the Los Angeles area Jan. 17, Congress pushed through a package of emergency transportation, housing, education and health benefits in the first two weeks of February. The $11 billion fiscal 1994 supplemental appropriations bill (HR 3759) went well beyond disaster relief for California, however, to include funds for Midwestern farmers who had been inundated by floods in 1993 and for U.S. peacekeeping operations abroad. It also included $1 billion in routine supplemental appropriations for 17 federal programs.

The bill paused long enough in the Senate to allow lawmakers to test the waters for new deficit reduction before heading for President Clinton's desk. Clinton signed the measure into law Feb. 12 (PL 103-211).

While appropriators, led by Senate Appropriations Committee Chairman Robert C. Byrd, D-W.Va., succeeded in fending off attempts to use the bill as a vehicle for unrelated moves to cut the deficit, the measure did include $3.25 billion in rescissions — cuts in already appropriated spending — to offset part of its cost.

That marked a significant shift in congressional attitude. In July 1993, the House had rejected a proposal to offset the cost of a disaster relief bill for the flooded Midwest. In the space of seven months, the issue had changed from whether emergency aid should be paid for, to the size of the offsetting cuts. Even those who argued against offsets in principle were proposing increasingly large cuts as a matter of political reality.

The final bill contained $10 billion in fiscal 1994 emergency spending not subject to budget constraints, with more than $7.8 billion of it targeted at Southern California. More than $4.7 billion of the earthquake relief was to go through the Federal Emergency Management Agency (FEMA).

In addition to the aid for California, the emergency spending included:

● $1.2 billion for peacekeeping operations in Iraq, Somalia, Bosnia and Haiti.

● $315 million to rebuild a highway in Oakland, Calif., damaged by the Loma Prieta earthquake in 1989.

● $685.5 million for flood control and repairs related to the 1993 Midwest flood and miscellaneous other disasters.

● $550 million for disaster relief at the president's discretion. *(Chart, p. 549)*

The bill also contained $1 billion in non-emergency budget authority for routine supplemental items. Most of those funds were for veterans' training, disability and pension benefits, which were mandated by federal law, and unemployment benefits. Also included were $10 million to design a new Amtrak station in New York City; $25.5 million to replenish Interior Department construction accounts that were tapped for disaster relief funds; $10.1 million for a new employment survey by the Bureau of Labor Statistics; and $6.4 million to produce copies of White House electronic-mail messages as the result of a lawsuit under the Freedom of Information Act.

The bill's rapid passage stemmed in part from the warn-

BOXSCORE

Emergency Supplemental Appropriations — HR 3759. The bill made supplemental appropriations for fiscal 1994.

Reports: H Rept 103-415; conference report H Rept 103-424.

KEY ACTION

Feb. 3 — House approved, 337-74.

Feb. 10 — Senate approved, 85-10.

Feb. 11 — House adopted the conference report, 245-65; **Senate** deemed the bill cleared by voice vote.

Feb. 12 — President signed the bill — PL 103-211.

---

ings sounded by California's two Democratic senators — Dianne Feinstein and Barbara Boxer — who noted repeatedly during the debate that FEMA was running out of money. FEMA officials said that by the time the measure passed, they had no money left to rebuild public facilities.

Background

A number of disaster-aid bills had sailed through Congress in recent years as emergency spending, which meant the money was not subject to the budget caps that limited regular appropriations. Such emergency disaster relief was not paid for with taxes or cuts in other spending; it was simply borrowed and added to the deficit.

In 1993, however, Congress was embroiled in controversy over a massive deficit-reduction package when it took up a bill to aid victims of widespread flooding in the Midwest. A bipartisan group of "deficit hawks" stalled the Midwest flood bill briefly in July, arguing that the disaster aid should be offset with cuts in other programs. The Democratic leadership eventually pushed through a restrictive rule that blocked such amendments, and the $5.7 billion supplemental appropriation was enacted (PL 103-75).

However, on Aug. 5, House Speaker Thomas S. Foley, D-Wash., and Majority Leader Richard A. Gephardt, D-Mo., released a joint statement pledging that "an opportunity will be made available for a vote on a pay-as-you-go amendment on any future emergency disaster relief legislation." *(1993 Almanac, p. 714)*

In separate action in 1994, the House overwhelmingly approved a bill (HR 4906) aimed at barring Congress from mixing emergency spending with non-emergency add-ons in the future. However, the Senate did not act on the bill, and it died at the end of the Congress. *(Budget process, p. 87)*

Earthquake Relief

The 1994 earthquake supplemental began its quick trip through Congress in late January, when Clinton requested $6.2 billion in spending and $559 million in loans to aid the relief efforts around Los Angeles. The president asked that all the appropriations be treated as emergency spending not subject to the budget caps that limited overall spending for fiscal 1994.

The scope of the bill broadened Feb. 1 when Clinton asked for another $3.5 billion in spending and $550 million in loans to aid California. The add-ons consisted of $1.6 billion more for Southern California, $1.2 billion for peacekeeping operations, $435.5 million for miscellaneous disaster-relief efforts and $315 million to repair the Oakland highway.

Like supporters of the 1993 flood relief bill, backers of the measure argued that Congress should not delay the aid with a fight over spending cuts. A few California lawmakers found themselves on the other side of the fence this time. Said Jerry Lewis, R-Calif., a pay-as-you-go advocate in 1993, "Consistency

Supplemental Spending

This chart does not include $1.04 billion in non-emergency spending that was part of the package *(in thousands of dollars):*

Department/Agency	Clinton Request	House Bill	Senate Bill	Final Bill
Small Business Administration				
Disaster loans, subsidy	$ 254,750	$ 254,750	$ 254,750	$ 254,750
(Limitation on direct loans)	*(1,109,000)*	*(1,109,000)*	*(1,109,000)*	*(1,109,000)*
Administrative expenses	55,000	55,000	55,000	55,000
Agriculture				
Soil Conservation Service	340,500	340,500	340,500	340,500
Agricultural Stabilization and Conservation Service	25,000	25,000	25,000	25,000
Defense				
Humanitarian assistance, peacekeeping	1,198,300	1,198,300	1,198,300	1,198,300
Corps of Engineers				
Flood control, coastal emergencies	70,000	70,000	70,000	70,000
Low-Income Home Energy Assistance	—*	—*	—*	—*
Education				
Impact aid	165,000	165,000	165,000	165,000
Student financial assistance	80,000	80,000	80,000	80,000
Federal Highway Administration				
Emergency relief	1,265,000	1,265,000	1,265,000	1,265,000
Contingency funds	400,000	400,000	400,000	400,000
Veterans Affairs				
Medical care	21,000	21,000	21,000	21,000
Construction	45,600	45,600	45,600	45,600
Housing & Urban Development				
Assisted housing	225,000	225,000	225,000	225,000
Flexible subsidy fund	100,000	100,000	100,000	100,000
Community Development Block Grants	500,000	250,000	500,000	500,000
Federal Emergency Management Agency				
Disaster relief	4,709,000	4,709,000	4,709,000	4,709,000
Emergency management planning and assistance	15,000	15,000	15,000	15,000
Funds Appropriated to the President				
Unanticipated needs (contingency appropriation)	550,000	500,000	550,000	550,000
TOTAL				
New budget authority	$ 10,019,150	$ 9,719,150	$ 10,019,150	$ 10,019,150
(Limitation on direct loans)	*($ 1,109,000)*	*($ 1,109,000)*	*($ 1,109,000)*	*($ 1,109,000)*

* Language was included to allow the secretary of Health and Human Services to target $200 million in previously appropriated contingency funds. The Senate bill increased that to $300 million.

SOURCE: Senate Appropriations Committee

is not required in this process. . . . A crisis gets more real as it gets closer to your door."

House Committee

House Appropriations Committee Chairman William H. Natcher, D-Ky., introduced the combined request Feb. 1 in the form of a $9.7 billion supplemental bill; his committee approved the measure by voice vote later that afternoon (H

Rept 103-415). At the administration's request, all of the money in the bill was designated as emergency spending.

Before approving the bill, however, the committee added an amendment to bar federal relief agencies from providing anything but short-term aid to illegal aliens. Illegal aliens usually were eligible for only two types of benefits — public school education for their children and Medicaid payments for emergency medical care. In a disaster, however, federal law prohibited FEMA from withholding benefits on the basis of a person's nationality.

Illegal immigration was a hot issue in California, where Gov. Pete Wilson, R, had blamed the immigrants for much of the state's budget shortfall.

Ron Packard, R-Calif., originally offered an amendment that would have prevented federal relief agencies from providing anything but emergency medical assistance to known illegal aliens.

To lessen the impact of the Packard amendment, Esteban E. Torres, D-Calif., offered a modified version to allow illegal immigrants to remain eligible for emergency food, shelter, medical services, hazard-removal and safety programs. The appropriators adopted the Torres amendment by a 38-12 show of hands.

Democratic leaders backed the Torres amendment in hopes of pre-empting one of Packard's main allies, Dana Rohrabacher, R-Calif., from offering a more restrictive amendment on the House floor.

In other action, the committee left out a provision requested by the administration to help federal departments reduce their work forces by 252,000 without layoffs by offering cash to employees who resigned voluntarily. Republicans and Democrats could not agree on how to count the 252,000 positions. Steny H. Hoyer, D-Md., said that Democrats wanted to subtract 31,000 positions that had been cut since Clinton took office, but House Republican leaders would not concur. Congress later cleared a separate bill (HR 3345 – PL 103-226) allowing cash buyouts of up to $25,000 per worker. *(Buyouts, p. 147)*

House Floor

The House approved the $9.7 billion measure Feb. 3 by a vote of 337-74, after agreeing to pay for some of the spending with roughly $2.6 billion in cuts from other programs. Like the provision on illegal immigrants, the spending cuts were backed by the Democratic leadership in an effort to fend off more stringent proposals. *(Vote 13, p. 4-H)*

Protecting Defense

The first question taken up by the House concerned the scope of the bill. In an odd alliance, liberal Barney Frank, D-

Mass., and conservative Dan Burton, R-Ind., joined forces behind an amendment to knock out the $1.2 billion in emergency appropriations for Defense Department peacekeeping operations. Frank argued that those operations should be paid for through the regular defense budget, in part because they were under way when the budget was adopted.

Democrat John P. Murtha of Pennsylvania, chairman of the Defense Appropriations Subcommittee, responded that the Defense Department's $241 billion fiscal 1994 budget was so tight, any humanitarian missions should be financed through supplemental appropriations.

Burton, who described himself as one of the House's strongest advocates of defense, nevertheless argued that HR 3759 was the wrong bill for defense funding. "The fact of the matter is, this is a disaster relief bill for the people of California who are hurting," Burton said.

The House sided with Murtha, rejecting the Frank-Burton amendment by a vote of 158-260. *(Vote 8, p. 4-H)*

Deciding on Offsets

The House then took up a series of amendments aimed at determining how much of the bill's spending to offset.

The drive to find ways to pay for the aid was led by Timothy J. Penny, D-Minn., and Jim Nussle, R-Iowa, the same pair who had pushed unsuccessfully for offsets in the 1993 emergency spending bill. Also on board were John R. Kasich, R-Ohio, and Gary A. Condit, D-Calif. The four sponsored an amendment to cut more than $9.7 billion from more than 80 federal programs.

The cuts were a replay of a proposal that Penny and Kasich had offered the previous November, when the House was considering an end-of-session spending-cut bill (HR 3400). The 1993 Penny-Kasich amendment would have cut $90 billion in spending over five years, largely by limiting the growth of entitlements and shrinking the federal work force. The House narrowly defeated that proposal, instead adopting an administration-backed plan to save $37 billion, most of it through personnel cuts. *(1993 Almanac, p. 140)*

The new Nussle-Penny amendment dropped the restraints on entitlements but added cuts in foreign aid and federal land purchases. When the amendment came to the floor, it was sandwiched between two other amendments — a package of cuts offered by John T. Myers of Indiana, a senior Republican appropriator, and a milder proposal that the Democratic leadership had unexpectedly thrown into the mix. Foley said the leadership amendment was offered because some Democrats were reluctant to vote against the Nussle-Penny proposal unless they had the chance to vote for some kind of spending cuts.

The order in which the amendments were considered was specified by the leadership in the rule that governed debate on the bill. Under a legislative tactic known as king-of-the-hill, the last amendment to receive a majority was the one that would be added to the bill; that way, the deficit hawks could pass stiff cuts and still be overridden by the leadership proposal.

● **Myers.** Myers' amendment, which came first, would have offset the disaster aid with $7.5 billion in spending cuts. More than half of Myers' savings were from administrative cuts ($3.2 billion) and layoffs ($750 million) from all federal departments and agencies other than the Pentagon.

Myers also included $2.6 billion in rescissions that the House had passed in 1993 as part of HR 3400, and he proposed cuts of $2 million to $400 million in 13 programs, ranging from the legal aid program for the poor to economic-development grants for cities.

The proposal drew a string of dire-sounding warnings

from senior appropriators. Natcher, for example, said that law enforcement, air-traffic control, drug enforcement, tax collection, education, human service and food inspection programs all would suffer if Myers' cuts were approved.

Myers argued that the 4 percent cut he was advocating for federal departments was less of a sacrifice than many taxpayers were asked to make in Clinton's economic plan. The House rejected the Myers amendment, 207-211. *(Vote 9, p. 4-H)*

● **Nussle-Penny.** The $9.7 billion in cuts proposed by Nussle and Penny drew similar protests from appropriators, who said they would lead to cuts in the Border Patrol and veterans' hospitals and for federal drug and crime investigators and tax advisers. Others protested the proposed cuts in food shipments to starving countries and development aid for Africa.

"For once," Penny responded, "we challenge ourselves to do what all of America must do when faced with a crisis . . . and that is to pay as we go." He added, "Borrowing money is never a tough choice. We found that out in the 1980s."

Kasich accused his opponents of exaggerating the potential impact of the amendment, which he said would cut only 2 percent of all discretionary spending. Referring to a proposed constitutional amendment, he said, "We're going to vote on a balanced-budget amendment, and you're telling me we can't cut 2 percent."

The House rejected the Nussle-Penny amendment, 178-240. *(Vote 10, p. 4-H)*

● **Fazio.** Then, with no debate, the House adopted the leadership amendment, offered by Vic Fazio, D-Calif., by a vote of 415-2. The $2.6 billion amendment used most of the rescissions included in HR 3400, which had passed the House in November but had been largely ignored by the Senate. *(Vote 11, p. 4-H)*

Senate Committee

The Senate Appropriations Committee approved its version of the bill by voice vote Feb. 8. The measure provided $10 billion in emergency budget authority and contained more than $3.4 billion in rescissions.

The administration had proposed $3.2 billion in rescissions (a combination of proposals made in November 1993 and in the fiscal 1995 budget released Feb. 7), many of which targeted pet projects earmarked by lawmakers. The appropriators substituted their own list, sparing many of their favored programs.

The committee also added close to $1 billion in non-emergency supplemental appropriations that had been requested by the administration.

Senate Floor

On Feb. 9, Byrd took the bill to the Senate floor. After defeating a series of attempts to add spending cuts — some of them sweeping, others more targeted — the Senate on Feb. 10 approved an $11 billion version of the bill with $3.4 billion in rescissions. The vote was 85-10. *(Vote 45, p. 8-S)*

Bob Kerrey, D-Neb., and Hank Brown, R-Colo., proposed the most dramatic budget cuts — $94 billion over five years. Kerrey, Brown and four colleagues had been working on the proposal since the previous November. The main elements of the amendment, which had 11 cosponsors, were to cut spending on Medicare by $30.5 billion through higher charges on selected participants; reduce the federal work force by 252,000, saving $26.7 billion; and limit government adminis-

Continued on page 556

Emergency Supplemental Provisions

The fiscal 1994 supplemental appropriations bill, passed to aid Southern California in the wake of an earthquake Jan. 17, provided a total of $11 billion in budget authority and made $3.25 billion in rescissions. As enacted, the bill (HR 3759 — PL 103-211):

Emergency Spending

Agriculture Department

● **Soil Conservation Service:** Provided $340.5 million for watershed repairs and flood-relief efforts related to the Midwest floods, California fires and other disasters, with no deadline on the spending. Up to $50 million could be spent to rebuild about 200 levees that protected areas ordinarily considered too small for federal aid. The provision also allowed the department to buy farmland for the Wetlands Reserve program if the property owner was willing, and if the cost of repairs exceeded fair market value of the land.

● **Agricultural Stabilization and Conservation Service:** Provided $25 million for emergency conservation efforts related to the Midwest floods, California fires and other natural disasters. The money was to remain available until Sept. 30, 1995.

● **Previous appropriations for flood relief:** Allowed the Commodity Credit Corporation to use money from the 1993 flood relief bill (PL 103-75) to help the owners of commercial trees and seedlings reseed and replant their land. The money also could be used to pay those owners for the loss of trees that would have been sold in 1993, 1994 or 1995.

In addition, the flood-relief money could be tapped to pay Hawaiian papaya growers who lost trees in Hurricanes Andrew or Iniki or Typhoon Omar. This provision was sought by Sen. Daniel K. Inouye, D-Hawaii.

Defense Department

● **Peacekeeping:** Limited the supplemental defense spending to ongoing U.S. operations in Somalia, Bosnia, Iraq and Haiti, with no money available for any new missions or changes in existing missions. This was done at the request of Rep. John P. Murtha, D-Pa.

The law also allowed the Defense Department to obligate up to $250 million for post-Desert Storm operations in Kuwait in advance of the Kuwaiti government paying for those operations.

● **Procurement:** Provided $20.5 million for the Army and $26.8 million for the Air Force, available until Sept. 30, 1996.

● **Personnel costs:** Provided $6.6 million for the Army, $19.4 million for the Navy and $18.4 million for the Air Force to cover combat pay and other benefits stemming from peacekeeping and humanitarian operations.

● **Operations and maintenance:** Provided $420.1 million for the Army, $104.8 million for the Navy, $560.1 million for the Air Force and $21.6 million for unspecified defense expenses.

● **Army Corps of Engineers:** Provided $70 million to repair eligible non-federal levees damaged by the Midwest floods.

Interior Department

● **Bureau of Reclamation:** Authorized the bureau to obligate money immediately for repairing Ochoco Dam in central Oregon, rather than reporting to Congress and waiting 60 days as required by the 1978 Reclamation Safety of Dams Act. The provision was sought by Sen. Mark O. Hatfield, R-Ore., after the bureau declared the dam unsafe and ordered thousands of acres behind it to be evacuated.

Health and Human Services Department

● **Low-Income Home Energy Assistance:** Authorized the president to extend up to $300 million in grants to the states hit hardest by the January cold wave, rather than distributing the money by formula to all states. The money came out of a $600 million contingency fund that Congress established for the low-income home energy assistance program in fiscal 1994.

Education Department

● **School districts:** Provided $165 million for school districts that incurred higher operating costs as a result of the Jan. 17 Northridge, Calif., earthquake.

● **College grants:** Provided $80 million for college grants to students from earthquake-damaged areas, with the money remaining available until Sept. 30, 1995. The law also authorized the use of leftover student-loan and work-study money in the 1994-95 school year to benefit students affected by natural disasters.

Transportation Department

● **Federal highways:** Provided $950 million to cover disaster-related repairs, which was to remain available until spent. The federal government would pay 100 percent of the costs incurred within 180 days after the earthquake.

● **Cypress Freeway:** Allotted an additional $315 million in emergency funding for repairs to the Cypress Freeway in Oakland, Calif., damaged by the Loma Prieta earthquake in 1989.

● **Hawaii:** Made Kauai County eligible for $337,000 of the transportation planning funds that the state received in fiscal 1992.

Housing and Urban Development Department

● **Housing programs:** Provided $200 million for rent vouchers and $125 million for various improvements to housing projects, available until Sept. 30, 1995, and Dec. 31, 1995, respectively. The law allowed the department to waive any law or regulation, other than environmental, fair housing and labor regulations, to speed the flow of money.

● **Federal Housing Administration loans:** Allowed the Federal Housing Administration to provide higher amounts of insurance for mortgages and home-repair loans in the Los Angeles area for 18 months. The insurance was available only to homeowners whose principal residences were damaged or destroyed by the earthquake.

● **Community Development Block Grants:** Provided $500 million, half for the Los Angeles area hit by the earthquake and half for Midwest communities flooded in 1993, available until Sept. 30, 1996. The money could be used for a range of improvements to public facilities and services, except for those covered by federal disaster-relief programs. HUD could transfer up to $75 million into block grants for affordable housing.

● **Reuse of flooded property:** Required state and local governments that bought flooded property with Community Development Block Grants to promise that the property would be preserved as open space, wetlands or a public recreation area, as required by a federal law passed in the wake of the Midwest floods.

Veterans Affairs Department

● **Veterans health programs:** Provided $66.6 million for the department's medical center in Sepulveda, Calif., which was so damaged by the Northridge earthquake that it had to be closed. The money, which was to remain available until spent, included $45.6 million for repairs and $21 million to treat the center's patients at other veterans hospitals.

Independent Agencies

● **Federal Emergency Management Agency:** Provided $4.7 billion to relieve any disaster declared by the president. The money was to remain available until spent. The total included $1.43 billion to repair public buildings; $1.34 billion for human services and individual assistance; $315 million for such emergency measures as police, firefighting and shelter; $315 million for mass transit; $200 million for local road repairs; and $100 million for debris removal.

The law also provided the agency $15 million, to be available until spent, for a post-earthquake investigation to be coordinated by the U.S. Geological Survey.

● **Small Business Administration (SBA):** Provided $309.8 million

to support $1.1 billion in disaster loans. On the request of Rep. Neal Smith, D-Iowa, this provision also instructed the SBA to give priority to areas that had been hit by major disasters when distributing grants for tree-planting. The $18 million provided for tree-planting in fiscal 1994 was made available for an additional year, until Sept. 30, 1995.

Contingency Funds

● **Funds appropriated to the president:** Provided $550 million, to remain available until spent, for additional, unforeseen needs stemming from the Los Angeles earthquake and the Midwest floods. The money was to become available 15 days after the administration submitted an official budget request for a specific dollar amount to Congress.

● **Federal highways:** Provided $400 million, to remain available until spent, for repairs to highways damaged by natural disasters. The money was to become available 15 days after the administration submitted an official budget request for a specific dollar amount to Congress.

Non-Emergency Spending

Agriculture Department

● **Extension Service:** Provided $1.4 million to help battle the outbreak of Late Blight potato fungus in Maine, home state of Senate Majority Leader George J. Mitchell, D.

● **Departmental consolidations:** Transferred all funds from the Human Nutrition Information Service to the Agricultural Research Service. Congress merged the nutrition program into the Agriculture Research Service in 1993, but Agriculture Secretary Mike Espy separated them again Sept. 30.

Similarly, the law transferred all funds from the Agricultural Cooperative Service to the Rural Development Administration. Congress had merged the cooperative service into the Rural Development Administration in 1993, but Espy separated them as well. The law also transferred $435,000 to the Rural Development Administration that Espy had shifted into the cooperative service from a third program.

The law did not contain a provision proposed by the House that would have cut $1.1 million from the $15.2 million being transferred. The House appropriators called for the cut late in 1993, based on the savings they expected to come from merging the four programs into two.

Health and Human Services Department

● **Food and Drug Administration:** Provided $2.3 million to cover the agency's pay increases. The provision authorized an increase in the amount of fees collected from the manufacturers of prescription drugs, vaccines and some blood products.

Justice Department

● **Federal Bureau of Investigation:** Provided $20 million to hire 500 employees for the fingerprint laboratory in Clarksburg, W.Va., a provision sought by Sen. Robert C. Byrd, D-W.Va. These positions could be filled regardless of the limit on total FBI hiring.

● **Local drug enforcement programs:** Allowed states to give disaster-stricken communities one additional year of funding from their Edward Byrne Memorial Program grants. States used the grants to pay 75 percent of the cost of local drug-enforcement programs. Under normal circumstances, communities could not receive funding for more than four years.

U.S. Information Agency (USIA)

● **Salaries and expenses:** Allowed $2 million of the money appropriated in fiscal 1994 to be used for "certain security construction projects." The projects, not specified in the law or accompanying report, were at USIA facilities overseas that were not located on the same sites as State Department facilities. The money was to remain available until spent.

Interior Department

● **Fish and Wildlife Service:** Provided $2.1 million to promulgate a special rule to allow more timber harvesting on non-federal

lands in the Pacific Northwest.

The administration had pledged to ease restrictions on timber harvesting, which a federal court imposed to protect the threatened northern spotted owl.

To pay for the spending, $1.7 million in unused funds was to be transferred from an account for the Territory of Palau; $400,000 was to be transferred from the department's Oilspill Emergency Fund.

● **Land acquisition:** Transferred $4 million within the Fish and Wildlife Service's budget from construction to land acquisition. The money was to be used to buy flooded property in the Midwest in lieu of repairing dikes or levees.

● **National Park Service:** Provided $13.1 million for construction, replenishing an account that the administration dipped into in 1993 to fund various disaster relief efforts. At the same time, the law authorized the Park Service to give Florida up to $5 million in leftover construction funds to buy land or easements in the watershed of the Everglades and Florida Bay.

The law also provided $1.3 million, to be available until spent, for another account that was tapped to fund disaster-relief efforts: land acquisition and state assistance.

● **Bureau of Indian Affairs:** Provided $12.4 million for construction, replenishing an account that the administration dipped into in 1993 to fund various emergency construction and cleanup projects. The money was to remain available until spent.

Energy Department

● **Staffing:** Repealed the minimum staffing levels enacted for various department programs since 1982.

Labor Department

● **Employment and Training Administration:** Provided $61.4 million to cover anticipated unemployment and job-training claims. The money was to be available until Sept. 30, 1995.

● **Bureau of Labor Statistics:** Provided $10.1 million to continue testing a new method of measuring unemployment.

Congress

● **Senate:** Provided more than $1 million to cover the cost of the fledgling Office of Senate Legal Counsel for Employee-Management Relations, including $600,000 to retain private lawyers and other experts. The office was established in May 1993 to provide advice on employment problems such as sexual harassment and job discrimination.

● **House:** Provided $133,600 for Karen A. Henry, the widow of the late Rep. Paul B. Henry, R-Mich., who died July 31, 1993. Congress historically provided a gratuity to the surviving spouse of a member who died in office.

Transportation Department

● **Maritime Administration:** Allowed the department to spend up to $1.5 million to relocate and repair the *Savannah*, the first nuclear-powered merchant ship. While serving as a museum in Charleston, S.C., the *Savannah* developed leaks in its hull that required it to be drydocked. The money for the work was to come from the sale of National Defense Reserve Fleet vessels.

● **Coast Guard:** Transferred $4 million from operating expenses and $7 million in unspent funds from fiscal 1993 to provide new facilities for Coast Guard bases that were damaged in the Midwest floods. The money was to remain available until spent.

● **New York train station:** Provided $10 million for preliminary efforts to adapt the James A. Farley Post Office in New York City to be used as a train station for Amtrak, the national passenger rail corporation. The money was to remain available until spent, but none could be spent until the department reported to Congress on the project's impact on Pennsylvania Station, New York's main Amtrak station.

● **High-speed rail:** Provided an additional $4.5 million from the Highway Trust Fund for developing high-speed rail technology. The money originally was appropriated in fiscal 1993, but it reverted to the Treasury when the Federal Railroad Administration failed to spend it in time.

● **Highway research programs:** Required that federal highway

programs dealing with applied and seismic research be subject to the congressionally imposed limit on spending from the Highway Trust Fund.

Executive Office of the President

● **Office of the U.S. Trade Representative:** Provided $550,000 to cover travel and other expenses associated with trade negotiations.

● **Armstrong lawsuit resolution:** Provided $13.1 million to convert, copy and maintain electronic records in response to a federal judge's order. The order came in a Freedom of Information Act lawsuit by Scott Armstrong, then of the National Security Archives, and several public-interest groups. The money was to remain available until spent.

● **Office of Science and Technology Policy:** Deleted a requirement that the office reimburse other agencies for at least half the cost of the staff they provided. The requirement was adopted in 1993.

● **Council on Environmental Quality:** Provided $300,000 for additional employees at the council to oversee compliance with the National Environmental Policy Act. The administration had sought $425,000 for 10 additional employees, despite its stated plans to eliminate the council.

Veterans Affairs Department

● **Benefits administration:** Provided $698 million for increased disability payments and pension benefits and $103.2 million for higher readjustment benefits. The money was to remain available until spent.

● **Health programs:** Transferred $2.5 million from medical care to medical administration, most of which was to be used to avoid layoffs at the Veterans Health Administration headquarters in Washington. The money also was to cover the cost of a $500,000 contract awarded to help the department plan for health care reform.

Housing and Urban Development Department

● **Housing programs:** Raised by $22 billion the limit on loan guarantees provided by the Federal Housing Administration. The increase, which was to aid homebuyers and homeowners seeking to refinance their loans, was expected pay for itself by generating more fees and premiums.

● **Hawaiian sugar mills:** Made $1.3 million in previously appropriated funds available to community-based, employee-support organizations along the Hamakua coast of Hawaii. One of dozens of special projects inserted into a fiscal 1993 appropriations bill, the money originally was intended for "continued assistance" to two sugar cane mills on the Hilo-Hamakua coast. The provision was sought by Sen. Daniel K. Inouye, D-Hawaii.

● **Louisiana community development grant:** Gave the city of Slidell, La., until Feb. 22, 1994, to submit two planning and financial documents required to qualify for a Community Development Block Grant in fiscal 1994. The city had submitted the documents Sept. 21, 1993, apparently unaware that the deadline had been changed from Sept. 30 to Sept. 1.

Independent Agencies

● **Environmental Protection Agency:** Delayed until Sept. 30, 1994, the $500 million in water treatment grants that Congress reserved for as-yet unspecified projects. The money would have been available May 31, 1994.

● **National Aeronautics and Space Administration:** Provided $20 million immediately and an additional $20 million Oct. 1, 1994, to continue paying for the "spacehab" module on the space shuttle developed by NASA and private contractors. The provision was sought by Sen. Christopher S. Bond, R-Mo.

The law also provided $56 million for increases in payroll that were higher than anticipated.

● **Space station:** Removed the ceiling on spending on the redesigned space station, which had been set at $1.9 billion. The change, sought by the administration and the project's prime contractor, ensured that NASA would be able to cover $160 million in termination costs if the space station were to be canceled late in the fiscal year.

The law also allowed NASA to spend up to $117.2 million of previously appropriated funds on cooperative space ventures with Russia. The fiscal 1994 appropriations act that funded NASA limited that amount to $100 million.

General Provisions

● **Discrimination complaints:** Allowed the Architect of the Capitol to use money from the Senate Office Building account to settle discrimination and harassment complaints brought by employees of the Senate. The provision was made retroactive to Oct. 1, 1992.

● **Disaster relief task force:** Recommended that the Senate establish a "Bipartisan Task Force on Funding Disaster Relief" to evaluate federal disaster programs, recommend ways to fund them and report by the beginning of the next Congress.

● **New Treasury Department post:** Created the office of Under Secretary for Enforcement at the Treasury Department. The office was in addition to the two under secretaries provided by previous law.

Rescissions

Agriculture Department

● **Cooperative State Research Service:** Rescinded $15.4 million, including $4.4 million in contracts and grants for research, $6.7 million for competitive research grants, $2.9 million for construction grants and $1.4 million for expenses. The administration had recommended rescinding $64 million, mainly from lawmakers' special building and research projects.

● **Soil Conservation Service:** Rescinded $21.2 million for emergency watershed repairs and flood prevention operations. The administration had recommended rescinding $12.2 million from conservation operations.

● **Farmers Home Administration:** Rescinded $102.7 million, including $35 million in loan subsidies for low-income housing, rental housing, home repairs and farm-labor housing; $8 million in subsidies for credit sales of acquired property; $10 million in subsidies for rural development loans; all $25 million for a new rural housing voucher program; $12.5 million for rural water and waste disposal grants; and $12.2 million for salaries and expenses. The administration had recommended rescinding $20.7 million in excess subsidies and $12.2 million in salaries and expenses.

● **Rural Electrification Administration:** Rescinded $3.3 million in subsidies for low-cost rural electrification and telephone loans. The administration had recommended rescinding $12.1 million in subsidies that were expected to be unneeded.

● **Food and Nutrition Service:** Rescinded $10 million from the program that bought surplus food and distributed it to poor families. The administration recommended a rescission of $12.6 million based on an inventory of the program's commodities.

● **Food programs for foreign countries:** Rescinded $25 million in food grants and $22.9 million in loan subsidies for developing nations, as well as $4.6 million for shipping payments to U.S. cargo vessels. The administration had suggested rescinding $84.6 million from these programs.

Commerce Department

● **National Oceanic and Atmospheric Administration:** Rescinded $3 million for the maintenance of real property. The administration had recommended rescinding $10 million from the agency's construction and operations accounts.

● **International Trade Administration:** Rescinded $2 million in funds left over from previous years, rather than cutting lawmakers' special projects as the administration had requested. The agency had planned to use the money for computer software, trade initiatives and trade information studies.

● **Minority Business Development Agency:** Rescinded $500,000 from a grant for the Catawba Indian Tribe in South Carolina.

● **Economic Development Administration:** Rescinded $29 million in leftover revolving funds. The money was not expected to be needed to meet the fund's obligations.

State Department

● **Administration of Foreign Affairs:** Rescinded $8.8 million from a fund that covered increases in expenses caused by currency fluctuations, as the administration requested. With the dollar expected to remain strong against foreign currencies, this money was not expected to be needed.

● **New diplomatic posts:** Rescinded $1 million from the $5 million appropriated for the USIA to set up shop in republics of the former Soviet Union. The administration had proposed instead to trim $600,000 by reducing the number of Marine Corps detachments at overseas State Department missions.

The Judiciary

● **Defender services:** Rescinded $3 million from the program to provide lawyers for people accused of federal crimes who could not afford to hire their own. The program had $21 million left over from fiscal 1993, which was $3 million more than anticipated.

Defense Department

● **Procurement:** Rescinded $89.8 million, including $10 million for modifications to the Navy's A-6 attack planes; $12.8 million for the Air Force's Advanced Tactical Airborne Reconnaissance System; $27.5 million for Air Force mobility command and control, and $15 million for other unspecified Air Force purchases; $10 million for the defense reconnaissance support program; and $14.5 million for the Landsat-7 satellite program. The administration had recommended $255.3 million in cuts, largely from four areas that the appropriators rejected: the TOW II missile, the SH-60 helicopters, the LHD-7 amphibious assault ship and modifications to the Air Force's C-135 aircraft.

● **Research and development:** Rescinded $160.5 million, including $34.5 million from the Landsat-7 high-resolution multispectral imager project; $50 million for the Milstar satellite communications system; $6 million for the East-West Space Launch Facilities; $50 million for foreign material acquisition and exploitation; $10 million for the theater missile defense program; and $10 million for the Advanced Research Projects Agency's space program. The administration had recommended a $50 million cut from the Advanced Research Projects Agency's space programs.

● **Military construction:** Rescinded $93.5 million, to be applied to savings from favorable bids, lower overhead and other "cost reduction initiatives." The report accompanying the law directed that none of the special projects specified by Congress for fiscal 1994 could be reduced in scope as a consequence of the rescissions. The administration had called for $601.2 million in rescissions in military construction.

● **Base closure and realignment:** Rescinded $507.7 million, or 44 percent of the money appropriated for the third phase of base closures. The amount included a cut of up to $100 million in environmental restoration and compliance.

● **Army Corps of Engineers:** Rescinded $122.3 million for various flood control, navigation and related projects, the amount requested by the administration. The report accompanying the law, however, instructed the Corps not to stop work on the special projects funded by Congress in the fiscal 1994 Energy and Water Appropriations Act (PL 103-126).

Energy Department

● **Energy supply research:** Rescinded $10 million for the superconducting magnetic energy storage project, and ordered an across-the-board cut of $97.3 million in the rest of the department's energy supply research and development program. The administration had recommended achieving the same amount of rescissions by shutting down experimental nuclear reactors, such as the high-temperature gas-cooled reactor.

● **Uranium enrichment:** Rescinded $42 million from unobligated balances in the department's account for uranium supply and enrichment programs. The administration had proposed to save the same amount from the canceled Atomic Vapor Laser Isotope Separation project.

Foreign Aid

● **International Financial Institutions:** Rescinded $27.9 million carried over in the account for payments to the International Bank for Reconstruction and Development.

● **Agency for International Development:** Rescinded $220.4 million, including $165.4 million in development assistance and other foreign aid carried over from 1987 through 1993, and $55 million in aid to the newly independent states of the former Soviet Union. The administration had recommended a $250 million cut in foreign aid, although no reduction for the former Soviet Union.

● **Military aid:** Rescinded $91.7 million, including $91.3 million in unspent grants to help foreign countries purchase arms and $438,000 from the foreign military assistance program. The administration had recommended cutting $66 million in unspent grants and military assistance.

Interior Department

● **Bureau of Reclamation:** Rescinded $30 million in funds carried over from fiscal 1993, or $14 million more than the administration requested. The report accompanying the law instructed the bureau not to stop work on the special projects funded by Congress in the fiscal 1994 Energy and Water Appropriations Act.

● **Fish and Wildlife Service:** Rescinded $3.9 million from the Umbarger Dam modifications at Buffalo Lake National Wildlife Refuge in Texas. The project was completed at a lower cost than Congress anticipated when it was funded.

Labor Department

● **Salaries, expenses and administrative costs:** Rescinded $4 million, reducing by roughly 25 percent the increase in these accounts over fiscal 1993. The law also allowed the department to spend up to $1.75 million from its fiscal 1994 appropriation on obligations incurred in the North American Free Trade Agreement Labor Supplement Agreement, as requested by the administration.

Health and Human Services Department

● **Salaries, expenses and administrative costs:** Rescinded $27.5 million, reducing by roughly 18 percent the increase in these accounts over fiscal 1993. The cut was to be made proportionately from each agency except the Social Security Administration, which was exempt.

● **Social Security Administration:** Rescinded $80 million in trust fund spending for the automation project, a 27 percent cut. Of that amount, $10.9 million was derived from the Supplemental Security Income account.

Education Department

● **Salaries, expenses and administrative costs:** Rescinded $8.5 million, reducing by roughly 25 percent the increase in these accounts over fiscal 1993.

Congress

● **Senate:** Rescinded $1.5 million from the account for contingent expenses, reflecting savings from projects in fiscal 1993 that were completed under budget.

● **House:** Rescinded $3 million in various salary and expense accounts, including $633,000 left over from fiscal 1991 and $2.4 million from fiscal 1992. The largest cuts were $876,000 from members' official expenses, $595,000 from House Appropriations Committee investigations and studies, $378,000 from special and select committees, $364,000 from the purchase, lease and maintenance of office equipment and $253,000 from House leadership offices.

● **Library of Congress:** Rescinded $1 million in salaries and expenses, which represented the anticipated savings from staff reductions through voluntary retirements and resignations.

● **General Accounting Office:** Rescinded $650,000 in salaries and expenses, reflecting savings from staff reductions.

Transportation Department

● **Rural airport subsidies:** Rescinded $10 million in leftover funds, as requested by the administration.

● **Rental payments:** Rescinded $1.8 million in rental payments for

departmental office space, as requested by the administration.

- **Vocational programs for aircraft maintenance:** Rescinded all $750,000 appropriated for grants to technical colleges with aircraft maintenance programs.
- **Aviation facilities and equipment:** Rescinded $65.4 million from the unobligated balances in a variety of accounts, some dating back to fiscal 1985. The cuts included $7.9 million in unspent grants to university aviation programs.
- **Airport improvements:** Rescinded $488.2 million in unused contract authority from fiscal 1993 and previous years, as recommended by the administration. Congressionally imposed limits on airport spending had prevented the Federal Aviation Administration from distributing the money.
- **Highway projects:** Rescinded $32.3 million in funds for 20 special highway projects funded by Congress that were not yet under construction. The House and Senate appropriators had separately proposed $100 million in cuts from 42 projects, but 22 of them were rescued in conference. The administration had proposed to rescind $175 million for highway "demonstration" projects funded by Congress. The law also rescinded $9.5 million in unobligated balances in the account for building bridges on federal dams and $20 million from the revolving fund for advance purchases of highway rights of way.
- **Advanced driving simulator:** The law did not rescind $7.1 million for the National Advanced Driving Simulator program to study driving behavior at the University of Iowa, a project sponsored by a senior Senate appropriator, Democrat Tom Harkin of Iowa. The accompanying report did pledge, however, that the appropriators would rescind $3.1 million from the program in fiscal 1995 unless the university raised $7.8 million of the $11 million in required matching funds in fiscal 1994.
- **Highway Traffic Safety Grants:** Rescinded $220 million in unused funds for four safety programs. Congressionally imposed limits on spending from the Highway Trust Fund prevented the government from distributing the grants.
- **Magnetic levitation train research:** Rescinded all $17 million in unspent appropriations for this program in fiscal 1994, as requested by the administration.
- **Mass transit projects:** Rescinded $3.3 million in unspent grants to two bus programs favored by Congress, including $809,000 for Buffalo, N.Y., and $2.5 million for Clark County, Nev. The administration had proposed cutting $52 million, or all the unspent money for special bus and rail projects chosen by Congress before fiscal 1992.

Treasury Department

- **Biomass energy development:** Rescinded $16.3 million from a program to administer loan guarantees for and assets from alcohol-fuel plants, as requested by the administration. The program's revenues and previous appropriations were expected to exceed its needs by at least this amount.
- **Internal Revenue Service:** Rescinded $6.4 million in unobligated balances in an Internal Revenue Service equipment modernization program.

Veterans Affairs Department

- **Homeownership and Opportunity for People Everywhere (HOPE) grants:** Rescinded $66 million in funds unspent at the end of fiscal 1993, as requested by the administration. The program, the brainchild of former President George Bush's administration, was being phased out.
- **Assisted housing programs:** Rescinded $176 million in funds left unspent at the end of fiscal 1993, including $75 million for housing preservation and $101 million for low-income housing. The administration had proposed to rescind $180 million from programs to modernize public housing and remove lead-based paint hazards.

Independent Agencies

- **Board for International Broadcasting:** Rescinded $1.7 million from a defunct program to build a transmitter in Israel for the board

and the Voice of America, as recommended by the administration. The project was canceled in the fiscal 1993 supplemental appropriations act (PL 103-50), but more than $10 million in termination costs were left in the account. Because negotiations with contractors had bogged down, the administration asked that some of the termination costs be rescinded.

- **Small Business Administration:** Rescinded $4.1 million in subsidies for the Small Business Investment Company Participating Securities program, which provided a source of equity capital for emerging small businesses and guaranteed the performance of securities issued by such companies. A delay in adopted program regulations made it unlikely that this money would have been spent. The administration had recommended cutting $13.1 million from the special projects funded by lawmakers.
- **United States Information Agency:** Rescinded $5.85 million, including $2 million in salaries and expenses, $850,000 in education and cultural exchange programs, $2 million in radio construction and $1 million from the North-South Center at the University of Miami. More than $5 million of these funds were carried over from previous years, and the rest reflected anticipated savings from restructuring. The administration had recommended rescinding $11.7 million, including all $8.7 million granted to the North-South Center and $3 million in estimated savings from the restructuring proposed by Vice President Al Gore's "reinventing government" plan.
- **Nuclear Regulatory Commission:** Rescinded $12.7 million for salaries and expenses, as proposed by the administration. The cut reflected the savings achieved through streamlining the agency.
- **General Services Administration (GSA):** Rescinded $127.7 million carried over from fiscal 1990 and 1991 for buildings at the planned Southeast Federal Center in Washington, including the new headquarters for the GSA and the Army Corps of Engineers. The law also rescinded $6 million in rental payments for federal offices in fiscal 1994. The administration had proposed cutting $115.1 million in construction projects and $10.4 million in repair work that had been added by Congress.
- **Chemical Safety and Hazard Investigation Board:** Rescinded $770,000 for salaries and expenses at the board, which investigated accidental releases of hazardous substances into the air.
- **Environmental Protection Agency:** Rescinded $22 million in revolving funds for water treatment plants, a 1 percent cut.
- **Federal Emergency Management Agency:** Rescinded $2 million for emergency management planning and assistance, a 1 percent cut.
- **National Aeronautics and Space Administration:** Rescinded $63 million for research, $32 million for space flight and communications, and $25 million for new facilities. None of the cuts were to be made in high-priority areas identified by Congress in 1993. The administration had recommended $145 million in cuts.
- **National Science Foundation:** Rescinded $5 million for research and $5 million in grants to universities for equipment and facilities. The administration had proposed to rescind $10 million from the grants to universities.
- **National Service initiative:** Rescinded $5 million — a 1 percent cut — from the Corporation for National and Community Service.

General Provisions

- **Availability of funds:** Made the appropriations in the law available only until Sept. 30, 1994, unless otherwise specified.
- **Energy efficiency at the Capitol:** Gave the Architect of the Capitol authority to enter into contracts with energy-service companies. These companies installed energy-efficient lighting at no cost, then received a portion of the savings in electricity bills.
- **Disaster aid for illegal aliens:** Restricted the aid provided in the law to U.S. citizens and legal residents, except for emergency food, water, shelter, medicine and other essential needs, search and rescue services and hazard warnings. The provision, authored by Rep. Ron Packard, R-Calif., Rep. Julian C. Dixon, D-Calif., and Sen. Harry Reid, D-Nev., required federal officials to take "reasonable steps" to determine the residency status of those seeking aid. That

requirement did not apply to temporary housing benefits until 90 days after the aid was provided.

- **Unfunded mandates study:** Directed the Comptroller General to determine whether unfunded mandates or other federal regulatory requirements were hindering efforts to rebuild earthquake damaged areas quickly. The findings and any recommended improvements had to be reported within 30 days of the law's enactment.
- **Buy American:** Recommended that the money provided in the law be used by recipients to buy U.S.-made products and equipment. The provision was sought by Rep. James A. Traficant Jr., D-Ohio.
- **Savings and loan lawsuits:** Extended the statute of limitations for the Resolution Trust Corporation (RTC) to bring lawsuits for fraud or gross negligence by failed savings and loan associations. The law extended the limit until Dec. 31, 1995, or the termination of the RTC, whichever came later. The provision was sought by Sens. Alfonse M. D'Amato, R-N.Y., Frank H. Murkowski, R-Alaska, and Howard M. Metzenbaum, D-Ohio.
- **Indian lands transfer:** Repealed a portion of a law enacted in 1992 that would have sold land around two North Dakota dam projects back to the Indian tribes that owned the land originally. Federal officials estimated that the administrative costs of such a sale would far exceed the revenues. The law included language making it possible for the land to be transferred to the tribes without charge. The provision was sponsored by Sen. Kent Conrad, D-N.D.
- **New Army medical research institute:** Recommended that the Defense Department proceed with plans to build a new facility for the Walter Reed Army Institute of Research at Forest Glen, Md., within 45 days of the law's enactment. Congress appropriated $13.3 million for the work in fiscal 1993, but the Pentagon declined to spend it. The provision was sought by Maryland's two Democratic senators, Paul S. Sarbanes and Barbara A. Mikulski.
- **New flight service station:** Ordered the Federal Aviation Administration to establish an auxiliary flight service station in Marquette, Mich., by Sept. 1, 1994. The agency had planned since 1991 to open such a station to help pilots cope with the volatile local weather conditions, but the station had been delayed. The provision was sought by Sen. Carl Levin, D-Mich.
- **Transfers for LANDSAT-7:** Allowed the Defense Department to transfer up to $90 million from procurement accounts in fiscal 1994 through 1996 to the National Aeronautics and Space Administration (NASA) for the LANDSAT-7 satellite project. The transfer could not take place until the NASA administrator submitted a plan to Congress for fully funding LANDSAT-7 in the NASA budget from 1995 forward. ∎

Continued from page 550

trative expenses, saving $21 billion. Other provisions would have stopped the government from buying any more buildings, saving $2 billion; denied unemployment benefits to those who left the military voluntarily, saving $1.2 billion; limited cost of living increases for retired government employees, saving $1.2 billion; and cut the salaries of congressmen and senior government executives, saving $297 million.

Byrd called the savings largely fictitious. He said any Medicare savings were likely to be spent on overhauling the health-care system, the Senate had already dedicated the payroll savings to hiring police officers as part of a separate crime bill, and the administration had placed a lower limit on government expenses than the amendment would impose.

Mark O. Hatfield, R-Ore., offered a substitute to the Kerrey-Brown proposal that would have cut $18.6 billion in weapons programs. Both amendments were killed when the Senate voted 65-31 on Feb. 9 in favor of a motion by Byrd to table the Kerrey-Brown amendment. *(Vote 35, p. 7-S)*

More proposals to cut spending followed on Feb. 9 and 10. These included:

- An amendment by John Kerry, D-Mass., and six other Democrats to cut $43 billion over five years. Saying it was time for the Senate to choose between what the federal government wanted to do and what it needed to do, Kerry proposed to terminate the space station, cut $22.8 billion in defense projects, end an advanced nuclear reactor research program and put a moratorium on the purchase of federal buildings.

Opponents said that the amendment would gut the U.S. defense and science programs. The Senate defeated the amendment Feb. 10 by a vote of 20-75. *(Vote 39, p. 8-S)*

- An amendment by Minority Leader Bob Dole, R-Kan., and five other Republicans to lower the bill's cost by $6.6 billion. In addition to eliminating the proposed $315 million in emergency funds for the Oakland highway, the amendment would have cut government administrative expenses by $6 billion, reduced foreign aid and peacekeeping costs by $270 million and cut the Economic Development Administration by $40 million.

Byrd raised a point of order against the Dole amendment, saying it violated a provision of the Budget Act. A motion to waive the Budget Act to allow consideration of the Dole amendment fell Feb. 10 by a vote of 43-52, far short of the 60 required for passage. *(Vote 43, p. 8-S)*

- An amendment by John McCain, R-Ariz., to rescind $2.2 billion in appropriations and contract authority for highway projects specified by Congress in previous laws. It was defeated the same day by a vote of 23-72. *(Vote 42, p. 8-S)*
- An amendment by Russell D. Feingold, D-Wis., to eliminate the $1.2 billion in the bill for military peacekeeping missions. The amendment was defeated Feb. 10 by a vote of 19-76. *(Vote 40, p. 8-S)*
- An amendment by Brown to eliminate all provisions of the bill other than the $8.5 billion for earthquake, flood and other disaster relief. The amendment was rejected by voice vote.

The Senate also rejected two proposals to create or endorse disaster relief trust funds. Instead, the final bill endorsed a Senate task force to examine how Congress should prepare for and respond to disasters, not unlike a task force that the House already had created.

As the debate stretched into its second day, California's senators, Feinstein and Boxer, repeatedly urged their colleagues to stop delaying the bill with amendments not directly related to the disaster aid.

Nevertheless, senators tried to attach a wide variety of provisions to the fast-moving bill. One proposed by Alfonse M. D'Amato, R-N.Y., Frank H. Murkowski, R-Alaska, and Howard M. Metzenbaum, D-Ohio, touched on the controversy over the Whitewater Development Co. Their amendment, which the Senate adopted 95-0, gave the Resolution Trust Corporation until Dec. 31, 1995, to bring lawsuits against savings and loan associations accused of committing fraud and gross negligence. *(Vote 36, p. 7-S)*

The Senate also adopted by voice vote an amendment by Harry Reid, D-Nev., requiring federal officials to ensure that no disaster benefits went to illegal aliens after 90 days.

Conference/Final Action

After an amicable conference the next morning — chaired by Rep. Neal Smith, D-Iowa, in place of the ailing Natcher, — the House on Feb. 11 adopted the conference report (H Rept 103-424) by a vote of 245-65. The Senate had

already deemed the final version cleared by voice vote. *(Vote 27, 8-H)*

The final $11 billion bill included $3.25 billion in rescissions — more than the $2.56 billion in the House bill, but somewhat less than the Senate's $3.4 billion. Among the rescissions added by the Senate was a cut of $305 million from the Pentagon's budget for procurement and for research and development. The conferees reduced that to $250 million.

The other main cuts in the final bill were in military construction and base closures ($601 million); unused money for airports ($488 million); energy and water projects ($314 million); foreign aid ($340 million); and unused highway traffic safety grants ($220 million).

The conference report included a provision allowing only short-term disaster assistance to illegal immigrants. However, the conferees added an amendment by Rep. Julian C. Dixon, D-Calif., to ensure that federal agencies did not discriminate in carrying out the provision. ∎

Second Supplemental Keeps Mortgage Programs Alive

Congress cleared a second fiscal 1994 supplemental appropriations bill (HR 4568) in June to keep key federal home mortgage programs funded through the end of the fiscal year. President Clinton signed the bill into law July 5 (PL 103-275).

The measure included just $18.1 million in new spending authority, but it lifted loan ceilings by $93 billion for the Federal Housing Authority (FHA) and the Government National Mortgage Association (Ginnie Mae). Without that action, the FHA would have been forced to stop providing mortgage insurance in late June, and Ginnie Mae would have had to stop guaranteeing mortgage-backed securities by mid-

July. Demand for federal mortgage insurance had been higher than anticipated in 1994 because unusually low interest rates had sparked heavy mortgage refinancing.

The additional loan authority did not have to be offset under budget rules because the money came from revolving funds that were continually replenished as earlier loans were repaid.

The House Appropriations Committee approved the bill (H Rept 103-550) by voice vote June 17, and the House passed it June 21 by a vote of 410-9. *(Vote 259, p. 76-H)*

In an unusual step, the bill went to the Senate floor without stopping in the Senate Appropriations Committee. The Senate cleared the measure by voice vote June 22.

Key items in the bill included:

● **Ginnie Mae.** A $55 billion increase in the limit on guarantees of mortgage-backed securities.

● **FHA.** A $35 billion increase in loan authority for the agency's Mutual Mortgage Insurance program.

● **FHA.** A $3 billion increase in loan authority for the agency's General and Special Risk Insurance program for condominium and other housing insurance programs.

● **FHA.** An additional $18.1 million in new budget authority to subsidize mortgages to buy or build rental housing.

The bill that Clinton signed contained only a fraction of the $418 million in supplemental budget authority that he originally requested in June. Much of that request was to provide more loans to victims of the January 1994 Los Angeles earthquake. The White House proposal also called for an increase in Federal Emergency Management Agency (FEMA) loan authority to help the state of California pay for earthquake recovery.

But appropriators opted to put that money in regular fiscal 1995 spending bills, which were moving more quickly than usual to clear the way for the debate on health care reform. Left over was the money to keep the housing programs going. ∎

## Chapter 12

POLITICAL REPORT

Election 1994
Election Overview 561
  Midterm Ballot-Box Revolutions..................... 562
  Election Highlights............................... 563
  Republican Surge 564
Senate Races.................................... 565
  Senate Membership — 104th Congress.............. 567
  Newcomers List.................................. 568
House Races 570
  House Membership — 104th Congress 572

  Defeated Incumbents 574
Governors' Races 578
  Governors List..................................... 581
Changing South.................................... 582
Ballot Initiatives.................................... 583
1994 Election Results............................... 584
Other
Redistricting....................................... 591
House Special Elections............................. 592

ELECTION 1994

Rare Combination of Forces Makes '94 Vote Historic

Democratic apathy and Republican strength suggest landslide may have ushered in a lasting change

Great partisan shifts in Congress had different origins. Sometimes they were caused by great surges in voter support for one party or by widespread apathy that debilitated the other.

The powerful Republican tide of 1994 combined elements of both. Voters flocked to GOP congressional candidates in record numbers in the election that marked the middle of the term that President Clinton had won in 1992. At the same time, the president's own party had difficulty motivating its core constituents.

That extraordinary combination had the potential to give the 1994 election, which turned over the House and Senate to GOP control, a long-term significance well beyond that of other recent landslides in Congress.

At a minimum, the 1994 election provided an abrupt change from the electoral arithmetic to which both parties had long since become accustomed.

Up and Down

Republicans, whose nationwide vote for House seats had never totaled more than 28 million in a midterm election, won 36.6 million votes in 1994. That was nearly 9 million more than the GOP had won in 1990 and represented the largest midterm-to-midterm increase in one party's vote total in the nation's history.

Democratic House candidates, on the other hand, drew almost 1 million fewer votes than in 1990, continuing a general downward slide in their congressional voting strength that had begun in the mid-1980s. In 1982, when recession politics were putting a brake on the popularity of Republican President Ronald Reagan, Democratic candidates for House seats collected more than 35 million votes. In 1994, they drew fewer than 32 million. "I think it was a realigning election," said Republican demographer John Morgan. "The Democrats have not stopped hemorrhaging."

Although it would take another election or two to see the full ramifications of the 1994 vote, it was clear on Election Day that something big had happened. The combination of shrinking vote totals for the Democrats with an exploding GOP vote (nearly one-third larger than in 1990) was unparalleled since the Democrats' own growth spurt during the Depression and early days of the New Deal. Then, the number of votes won by Democratic House candi-

dates grew by one-third from 1926 to 1930 and increased again by more than 50 percent from 1930 to 1934. In the process, the Democrats went from being a hopeless minority to unassailable status as the nation's majority party for the next generation. Indeed, after 1934, the Democrats dominated in the House for all but four of the next 60 years.

While Republicans were potentially poised for a run of their own, their standing after the November election more closely resembled the Democrats' on the eve of their hegemony (1930) rather than at the party's height. By 1930, the Democrats had the momentum, but the GOP still held the White House. It took the election of Franklin D. Roosevelt in 1932 and a pro-Democratic vote in the midterm election of 1934 to cement the Democratic majority.

Positive Landslides

Elections like those of 1930, 1934 and 1994 could be considered "positive" landslides because of the large surge in votes for one party. They did not happen very often.

The decisive Democratic midterm victories of 1958 and 1974 were basically "negative" landslides, driven by apathy and a corresponding lack of votes on the Republican side.

The big Republican midterm victories of 1946 and 1966 featured vote increases for both parties. It just so happened that the GOP vote total showed a greater increase each time.

Midterm elections, even one-sided ones, were not always a reliable harbinger of the next presidential election, however. The legendary example was the midterm of 1946. Large GOP congressional gains that year were overturned by a Democratic comeback two years later, which allowed the party to regain control of Congress and returned embattled President Harry S Truman to office.

Elephant Romp

Ever since Clinton's election, the GOP had been on a sustained elephant romp. Before 1992 had ended, Republicans had picked up a Senate seat (Paul Coverdell) in a runoff election in Georgia. In 1993, they added another (Kay Bailey Hutchison) in a special election in Texas. The same year, they swept to victory in the gubernatorial contests in New Jersey and Virginia.

In 1994, Republicans took away Democratic House seats in districts

Voter Turnout: Upswing in the '90s

(Turnout Rate as Percentage of Voting-Age Population)

SOURCE: Census Bureau, 1960-92; Congressional Quarterly, 1994, using voting-age population projections from the Census Bureau. Midterm House turnout rate since 1972 includes vote cast for delegate in the District of Columbia.

Midterm Ballot-Box Revolutions

The dramatic Democratic losses in the 1994 elections were a throwback to the way midterm elections had once been, when the congressional strength of the president's party ebbed and flowed on a regular basis.

Eight times between the end of the Civil War and the end of World War II, the party occupying the White House lost more than 50 House seats in midterm elections. But since then, such ballot-box revolutions had been rare. The last time the president's party lost more than 50 seats was in the postwar midterm of 1946. On just three occasions since then had the midterm losses of the president's party surpassed 40 House seats — in 1958, 1966 and 1974.

● **1946.** Voters were ready for a change after World War II and 14 years of Democratic control of both ends of Pennsylvania Avenue. Republicans won both houses of Congress, as Democrats lost 55 seats in the House and 12 in the Senate. But GOP domination did not last long. Spearheaded by President Harry S Truman's feisty campaign against the "Do-Nothing 80th Congress" and a passive Republican response, Democrats not only retained the White House but also regained control of both chambers in 1948.

● **1958.** Recession and the right to work were two stumbling blocks for Republicans, even though President Dwight D. Eisenhower remained personally popular. Buffeted by the economic downdraft, farmers were particularly angry, while organized labor mobilized to fight right-to-work ballot measures in several key states. The result: substantial Democratic gains across the Midwestern Farm Belt and in heavily blue-collar districts. Altogether, Republicans lost 48 House and 13 Senate seats. Two years later, they lost the White House.

● **1966.** Democrats suffered their worst midterm election in 20 years, as voters went to the polls for the first time since the unveiling of President Lyndon B. Johnson's "Great Society." Not only did that produce a voter backlash, but Democrats were increasingly at odds with each other over the deepening involvement in Vietnam. LBJ's role diminished as the campaign progressed, and he campaigned rarely after Labor Day. The Democrats lost 47 seats in the House and four in the Senate, but they maintained control. Republicans won the White House two years later.

● **1974.** President Richard M. Nixon resigned in August 1974, but the pall of Watergate hung over Republican candidates all year. In addition, concern about the economy subsumed issues such as race, law-and-order, school busing and student rioting that had helped fuel a nationwide GOP comeback in the late 1960s and the early 1970s. Republicans lost 48 House and five Senate seats in 1974 as the Democrats made big gains in the suburbs and the South. Democrats regained the White House two years later, while the large Democratic class of 1974 assumed a major role in redefining the House.

in Oklahoma and Kentucky, the latter of which had never before sent a Republican to the House. And in the fall, Republicans outpolled Democrats by more than 7 million votes in gubernatorial races, by nearly 5 million votes in House elections and by almost 4 million votes in Senate races. *(Special elections, p. 592)*

The 1994 election was historic, said former Republican National Committee Chairman Frank J. Fahrenkopf Jr., for the "depth and reach" of the Republican success. *(1994 Vote count, p. 584)*

The Democratic debacle was truly national in scope. In 1992, the Democrats had won more House votes than the Republicans in every region of the country. But in 1994, the Democrats were outpolled in every region except the East and in every state with at least 10 congressional districts except Massachusetts.

In a number of megastates, the GOP edge was substantial. Republicans took 59 percent of the congressional ballots cast in Florida, 58 percent in Ohio, 57 percent in North Carolina, 56 percent in Texas, 54 percent in New Jersey and Pennsylvania, and a plurality 49 percent share in California and New York (even though Democrats wound up with more seats in California, New York, Texas and Pennsylvania).

The Democrats won more House votes than the Republicans in only a dozen small to medium-sized states. In terms of electoral votes, the states where the Democrats won more votes totaled just 73 electoral votes. The states where Republicans had the edge totaled 450 electoral votes. (The District of Columbia and Louisiana, which elected their members of Congress in October primaries, were not included in the tally.)

Nothing Cheap

GOP success was not accomplished in the milieu of a low turnout election. For a midterm contest, the turnout was relatively high. In spite of media talk of an electorate turned off by negative campaigning, the number of ballots cast for the House jumped from 61 million in 1990 (which represented 33 percent of the nation's voting-age population) to nearly 70 million in 1994 (36 percent).

Republicans were the almost exclusive beneficiaries of the increased vote. The total number of votes won by GOP congressional candidates was up dramatically from 1990 in every region of the country — by nearly 4 million votes in the South, by more than 2 million in the Midwest, by almost 1.7 million in the West and by 1.3 million in the East. Meanwhile, the number of ballots cast for Democratic House candidates was up marginally from 1990 on the East Coast and West Coast but down elsewhere. Democrats won nearly 600,000 more House votes in the East and 400,000 more in the West. But the Democratic House vote collapsed in the nation's heartland. It was down by nearly 1 million from four years earlier in the Midwest and by 800,000 in the South. *(GOP's historic growth spurt, box, p. 564)*

The number of votes won by Republican House candidates was higher than in 1990 in all but four isolated states — Connecticut, Rhode Island, North Carolina and Montana. Meanwhile, the Democratic vote total was down from 1990 in most states. Where the Democrats did show an increase in their vote total, it was usually dwarfed by the rise in the Republican vote.

In California, for instance, the Democrats won nearly 400,000 more House votes than in 1990, but the Republicans

were up more than 700,000. In New York, the Democratic total was also nearly 400,000 votes higher than it was four years earlier, but the GOP total jumped almost 600,000. And in Washington, where the Democrats suffered more carnage per district than in any other state — losing former House Speaker Thomas S. Foley, four other incumbents and a formerly Democratic open seat — the Democrats actually drew 130,000 more House votes than in 1990. But it was just half the size of the increase in the Republican vote.

Heartland Collapse

More typical of 1994, though, was the vote in the bellwether state of Ohio, which had supported the winning candidate in the previous eight presidential elections. There, the number of House votes for Republicans was up more than 300,000 from the previous midterm, while the Democratic vote was off by nearly 500,000.

Republicans not only picked up four House seats in Ohio, they easily won the Senate seat vacated by Democrat Howard M. Metzenbaum. And they re-elected Gov. George V. Voinovich with 72 percent of the vote, the highest share for any Ohio gubernatorial candidate since 1826.

Ohio, though, was not a unique problem area for the Democrats. Republicans picked up 15 House seats in the region, won all four open Senate races and swept eight of the nine governorships, six of them with more than 60 percent of the vote. In the process, the GOP re-established its hegemony in the region where it was born.

Dixie Debacle

For unrelieved misery for Democrats, though, no region could touch the South. The party historically rooted in Dixie won only one Senate race and three gubernatorial contests there (with two of the winners, Florida's Lawton Chiles and Georgia's Zell Miller, taking only 51 percent of the vote).

Democrats were outpolled by Republican House candidates in every Southern state except Mississippi, where most of the Democratic members were so conservative they could just as readily have been Republicans. *(Dixie, p. 582)*

In a number of districts, the Democrats went down without a fight. They conceded 21 seats across the region, including nine in Florida, five in Texas and three in Virginia.

By contrast, Democrats were offered free rides by the GOP in only four Southern districts — two minority-oriented constituencies in South Florida, represented by Carrie P. Meek and Alcee L. Hastings, plus the districts of veterans Tom Bevill in northern Alabama and W. J. "Billy" Tauzin in the Cajun country of Louisiana.

Altogether, the Democrats lost 19 House seats across the South, more than in any other region. Republicans won most of them by comfortable margins in politically congenial terrain. "I think the changes in the South are permanent," said University of California at San Diego political scientist Gary C. Jacobson.

In Senate races, six GOP candidates easily won seats that not long before had been held by Democrats. The region's lone Democratic winner was Sen. Charles S. Robb of Virginia, who needed a split in GOP ranks to eke out a plurality victory over Republican Oliver L. North with 46 percent of the vote.

Coastal Comfort

Compared with the decisive Republican trends in the South and Midwest, the voting on the two coasts was not quite so severe for the Democrats.

They lost 15 House seats in the West, including six in

1994 Election Highlights

- Nearly 70 million ballots were cast in the 1994 House elections, the highest number in any midterm election.
- Republican House candidates won 36.6 million votes, the most for one party in any midterm.
- Republican House candidates drew nearly 9 million more votes than in 1990, the largest increase ever in one party's vote total from one midterm to another.
- The vote for Democratic House candidates fell nearly 1 million from 1990 to a level more than 3 million votes below the party's total in 1982.
- The GOP's 52.4 percent share of the House vote was the party's largest since 1946. It was also the first time since 1946 that GOP House candidates received a majority of the total House vote.
- In another historic reversal, Republican House candidates received more free rides than the Democrats. In the South alone, 21 GOP winners had no Democratic opposition.
- Voter turnout was up for the second straight election: Fifty-five percent of the voting-age population cast ballots for president in 1992, the highest turnout rate in 20 years; 36 percent cast ballots in 1994 House elections, the highest turnout rate for a midterm since 1982.
- In spite of the GOP success, Democrat Daniel K. Akaka of Hawaii paced the senators, winning re-election with 72 percent of the vote. Democrat Ben Nelson of Nebraska led the governors, winning re-election with 73 percent of the vote.

Profile of the Defeated

Of the 34 House incumbents who were defeated for re-election in November:

- All were Democrats.
- 29 had voted for the 1994 Clinton crime bill.
- 28 had voted for the 1993 Clinton budget-reconciliation bill.
- 21 had won in 1992 with less than 55 percent of the vote.
- 16 were freshmen.
- 16 had voted for NAFTA.
- 15 represented districts that voted for President George Bush in 1992.
- 13 had at least one overdraft at the House bank.
- 9 were outspent by their Republican challengers.
- 5 were from the state of Washington, including House Speaker Thomas S. Foley, the first Speaker to be defeated for re-election since 1862.

Washington alone. But Democrats also scored some high-profile victories across the region, from Sen. Dianne Feinstein's triumph over the $30 million candidacy of GOP Rep. Michael Huffington in California, to Democratic gubernatorial wins in Alaska, Colorado, Hawaii, Nevada and Oregon.

There was a potentially ominous sign for the GOP in Oregon, where former Republican Rep. Denny Smith could

Republican Share of House, Senate, Governorships by Region

(as of April 14, 1995)

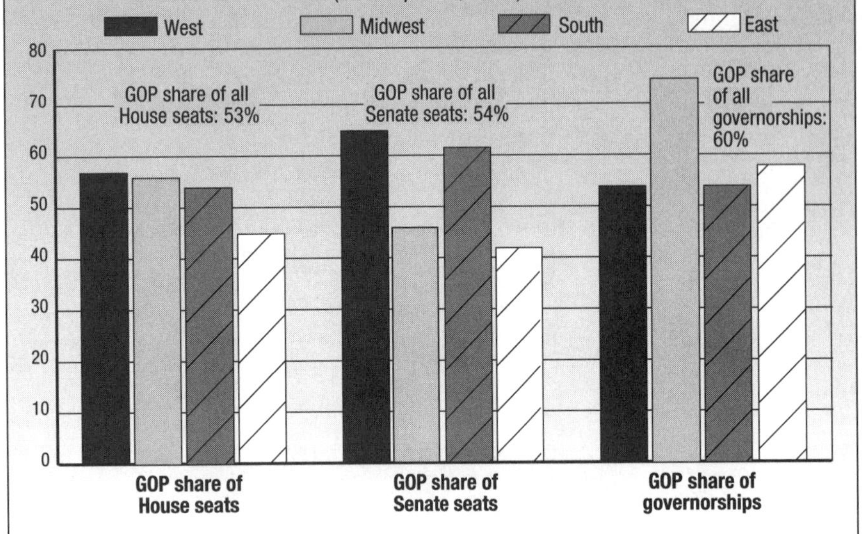

West
Midwest
South
East
80
70
60
50
40
30
20
10
0
GOP share of all House seats: 53%
GOP share of all Senate seats: 54%
GOP share of all governorships: 60%
GOP share of House seats
GOP share of Senate seats
GOP share of governorships

not come close to beating former Democratic state Sen. John Kitzhaber in the governor's race, in spite of the favorable Republican mood. Smith was backed by the conservative wing that increasingly dominated Oregon GOP primaries, but he was unable to substantially expand his base in the fall.

Meanwhile, the Democrats' base in the Northeast was penetrated but not demolished by the 1994 vote. Democrats lost only three House seats in the East, retaining a regional majority. Most of the incumbents in both parties won re-election to the Senate. And though the GOP picked up governorships in New York, Pennsylvania, Connecticut and Rhode Island, none of those seats were won with a majority of the vote.

The independent movement, which elected Lowell P. Weicker Jr. to the governorship of Connecticut in 1990, remained strong across the Northeast. Independent Angus King won the governorship in Maine, a pair of independent candidates garnered 30 percent of the gubernatorial vote in Connecticut, and an independent right-to-life candidate drew 13 percent of the vote for governor of Pennsylvania.

Poster Child Lost

The only incumbent senator in the East to lose his re-election bid was Democrat Harris Wofford of Pennsylvania, whose brief Senate career closely reflected the ups and downs of the Democratic Party in the 1990s. Wofford's upset victory in a 1991 special election proved a harbinger of the party's success nationally the following year; his loss in 1994 typified the Democrats' collapse.

Wofford won in 1991 by running as a champion of the "forgotten middle class" against former GOP Gov. and U.S. Attorney General Dick Thornburgh, who allowed himself to be painted as a Washington insider. Democratic strategists were impressed by Wofford's campaign, which included an emphasis on the health care issue, and he emerged as a finalist for the Democratic vice presidential nomination in 1992.

But in 1994, Wofford was thrown on the defensive by his aggressive young GOP foe, then-Rep. Rick Santorum, who pounded away at Wofford as a friend of Clinton's and of big government. Santorum easily won the Republican countryside, reclaimed the Philadelphia suburbs and made deep inroads among socially conservative Democrats in his home base of western Pennsylvania."There was palpable fear in 1991," said Wofford, and people were apt to vote their economic interests. In 1994, he added, "there was a lot of itchiness but not fear," and issues such as guns and abortion swung votes to the Republicans' advantage. ■

The GOP's Historic Surge

Republican House candidates in 1994 drew nearly 9 million more votes than in 1990. That gain easily eclipsed the largest previous increase ever recorded by one party from one midterm House election to another.

Prior to 1994, the largest increase was 6.3 million votes, registered by the Democrats from 1930 to 1934.

Much of the GOP vote increase in November 1994 was in the South, although the party scored dramatic gains in every region.

Vote totals shown below are in thousands.

	1994 House Vote		Votes Gained or Lost, 1990-94	
	Republicans	**Democrats**	**Republicans**	**Democrats**
South	10,322	7,861	+ 3,798	- 798
Midwest	10,147	8,414	+ 2,176	- 956
West	8,237	7,424	+ 1,692	+ 403
East	7,885	7,999	+ 1,319	+ 583
NATIONAL TOTAL	**36,590**	**31,698**	**+ 8,985**	**- 769**

SOURCE: Congressional Quarterly calculations based on official state-by-state election results. Some totals do not add due to rounding.

Republicans Capture Senate

After eight years as the Senate minority, Republicans reversed their fortunes in dramatic fashion Nov. 8, capturing 52-48 control of the Senate by sweeping all nine open-seat races and ousting two Democratic incumbents.

The day after the election added insult to the Democrats' injury, as one of their number, Alabama Sen. Richard C. Shelby, announced on Capitol Hill that he was switching parties, giving the GOP a 53-seat majority to start the 104th Congress. "I thought there was room in the Democratic Party for a conservative Southern Democrat such as myself," Shelby said. "But I can tell you there's not." A roomful of GOP partisans cheered lustily, and Senate Republican leader Bob Dole of Kansas quipped, "We'll be happy to accept other applications."

Dole, who was slated to become Senate majority leader in January 1995, would be the first Republican in that job with a Democratic president since Wallace H. White Jr. of Maine (who led the Senate from 1947 to 1949, when Harry S Truman was president).

In the final weeks of the 1994 campaign, national Republican strategists became increasingly hopeful that their party could erase its 44-56 deficit in the Senate. Democrats were defending 22 of the 35 seats at stake Nov. 8, and in a dozen of those races, GOP candidates were leading or very competitive. Democrats were making a serious run at a half-dozen seats held by Republicans, and GOP gains were expected to be at least partially offset by Democratic take-aways.

But 1994 was a historic election that shattered convention. The GOP did not lose a single Senate seat. The party re-elected all 10 of its incumbents, retained the three open seats it was defending, captured six seats of retiring Democratic incumbents and defeated Democrats Jim Sasser of Tennessee and Harris Wofford of Pennsylvania.

The incoming Senate freshman class had 11 Republicans and no Democrats. Since 1914, when the popular election of senators began, there had never been an all-GOP Senate freshman class.

Republican Senate candidates thrived in every region of the country, taking Democratic seats in the East (Maine and Pennsylvania), the Midwest (Ohio and Michigan), the West (Arizona) and the South (Oklahoma and Tennessee).

Although a Republican takeover of the Senate was hardly common — the party had led the chamber for only 10 of the previous 62 years — the 1994 Senate outcome was over-shadowed by the far more rare occurrence of Republicans' winning control of the House of Representatives. Still, even on an Election Day that offered broad disappointment for Democrats, some of the Senate contests stood out as notable voter indictments of the party's ruling class in Washington.

In Tennessee, home state of Vice President Al Gore, Democrats lost two Senate races. The Senate seat that Gore held through 1992 went by a runaway tally of 61 percent to Republican Fred Thompson. In the other contest, voters dumped three-term veteran Sasser, who had been a leading

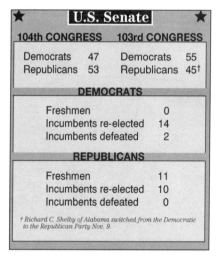

★	U.S. Senate	★
104th CONGRESS		**103rd CONGRESS**
Democrats	47	Democrats	55
Republicans	53	Republicans	45†
DEMOCRATS		
Freshmen		0
Incumbents re-elected		14
Incumbents defeated		2
REPUBLICANS		
Freshmen		11
Incumbents re-elected		10
Incumbents defeated		0

† Richard C. Shelby of Alabama switched from the Democratic to the Republican Party Nov. 9.

candidate to be the Senate's Democratic leader in the 104th Congress. Republican challenger Bill Frist held Sasser to 42 percent of the vote, the worst-ever general-election showing by a Tennessee senator.

In Pennsylvania, GOP Rep. Rick Santorum ousted Wofford, who had become a national Democratic celebrity with a 1991 special-election victory that made health care a marquee issue for the party. Bill Clinton borrowed from Wofford's campaign strategies in his 1992 presidential campaign. To win his first Senate race, Wofford had defeated Bush Attorney General and former Pennsylvania Gov. Richard L. Thornburgh, but this time he could not hold off the dogged conservative challenge of Santorum, who at age 36 would be the Senate's youngest member.

In Maine, the GOP prevailed in the race to pick a successor to Senate Majority Leader George J. Mitchell, who was retiring. Republican Rep. Olympia J. Snowe won with 60 percent of the vote. She was the only woman newly elected to the Senate; the chamber would have eight women members in 1995.

In addition to the defeats of Sasser and Wofford, the more pronounced cases of voters' ideological shift in 1994 came in Ohio (where Republican Lt. Gov. Mike DeWine succeeded Democratic Sen. Howard M. Metzenbaum, who was retiring), Michigan (where Republican Spencer Abraham succeeded retiring Democratic Sen. Donald W. Riegle Jr.) and in two Midwestern states where newly elected Republicans replaced more moderate party colleagues (Rep. Rod Grams for retiring Sen. Dave Durenberger in Minnesota and former Gov. John Ashcroft for retiring Sen. John C. Danforth in Missouri).

In three states where moderate House Democrats were running for seats occupied by retiring Democratic moderates, none got more than 40 percent of the vote. Thompson won in Tennessee over Democratic Rep. Jim Cooper, GOP Rep. James M. Inhofe won in Oklahoma over Democratic Rep. Dave McCurdy, and GOP Rep. Jon Kyl won in Arizona over Democratic Rep. Sam Coppersmith. The new senators succeeded Democrats Harlan Mathews, David L. Boren and Dennis DeConcini, respectively.

Similarly, Wyoming voters had a choice between the state's centrist Democratic Gov. Mike Sullivan and its conservative House member, Craig Thomas. It was no contest, with Thomas winning by 19 points to succeed retiring GOP Sen. Malcolm Wallop, a conservative soul mate who shared Thomas' view that the Clinton administration was waging a "War on the West" with its proposals to change mining, grazing and other land-use regulations.

Still, election night was not without Senate Democratic victory celebrations.

In Virginia, voter turnout was strong for a midterm, and that helped embattled Democratic Sen. Charles S. Robb fend off the fiercely loyal followers of Republican challenger Oliver L. North. In Massachusetts, liberal Democratic icon Sen. Edward M. Kennedy won re-election comfortably over GOP challenger Mitt Romney. And in California, Democratic Sen. Dianne Feinstein defeated her heavy-spending chal-

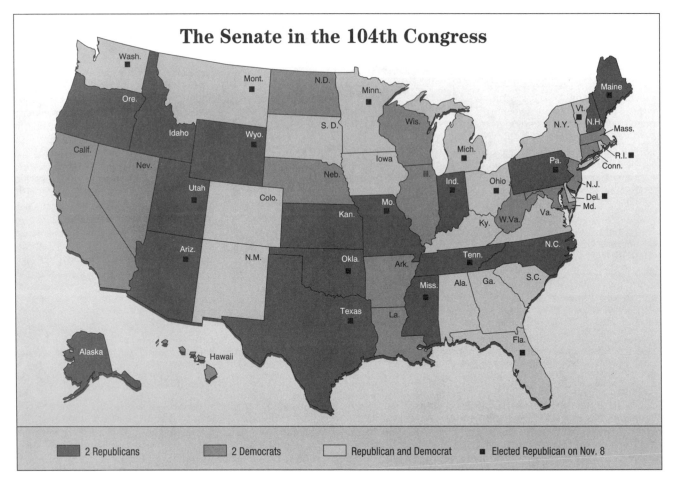

The Senate in the 104th Congress

■ 2 Republicans   ■ 2 Democrats   □ Republican and Democrat   ■ Elected Republican on Nov. 8

lenger, GOP Rep. Michael Huffington.

Following are reports on the Senate races:

Republicans Win Eight New Seats

● **Tennessee.** In a state where Democrats had long dominated turnout, self-identified Republicans were a plurality of voters at 39 percent. Exit polls indicated that Democrats made up 35 percent, followed by 26 percent self-identified independents. Clinton's approval rating was only 39 percent among all voters.

Democrat Sasser did not appear to be in trouble until late in the year, when polls showed the damage caused by dissatisfaction with Clinton and by Frist's attack ads.

From the start, Cooper matched Thompson's conservative, anti-Congress line, but Thompson was the better salesman. After correcting his early organizational and fundraising problems, Thompson got into the role of populist candidate, stumping from the back of his red pickup truck. Cooper's attacks on Thompson's work as a Washington lobbyist never connected.

● **Pennsylvania.** Wofford's defeat typified voter frustration with Democratic incumbents. Santorum ousted him with an energetic, grass-roots campaign that focused on the need for less government.

A disciple of Rep. Newt Gingrich, R-Ga., Santorum was not in the mold of moderate GOP senators who had represented Pennsylvania over the past 30 years. But he won comfortably in the suburbs of Philadelphia, where statewide races were often decided. Wofford ran even there in 1991. Santorum carried them by more than 75,000 votes this time, which repre-

sented almost his entire statewide margin of victory.

● **Ohio.** Republican DeWine handily defeated Democrat Joel Hyatt, winning 53 percent of the vote to Hyatt's 39 percent, with a third-party candidate in the race. The unfocused, stiff Hyatt — the son-in-law of retiring Sen. Metzenbaum — consistently failed to provide voters with a reason to back him. Democrats had declared this race a top priority early in the year, only to watch their standard-bearer fizzle by July.

The Hyatt campaign made a series of tactical errors, chief of which was its failure after a divisive May primary to respond to DeWine's inroads (mostly in the form of television spots) into what should have been Hyatt's base. In the end, this allowed DeWine to nearly match Hyatt in vote-rich and usually Democratic Cuyahoga County.

● **Michigan.** Abraham was the first Republican elected to the Senate from Michigan since 1978. Both Democrats and Republicans viewed this race as competitive, and polls consistently showed the race as tight until the last days of the campaign, when Abraham, a former state party chairman and aide to former Vice President Dan Quayle, appeared to take a lead. He went on to defeat Democratic Rep. Bob Carr 52 percent to 43 percent.

While touting traditional GOP themes such as less taxation and government, Abraham was able to define Carr early in the race as a liberal Washington insider and captive of special interests with attacks that went unanswered for weeks. Despite his reputation as a moderate Democratic member, Carr had trouble shaking the liberal insider label Abraham had pasted on him.

● **Oklahoma.** In one of the nation's most hotly contested races, Republican Inhofe cruised to a surprisingly easy vic-

Senate Membership — 104th Congress

(As of Dec. 31, 1994)

Republicans   53   Democrats   47
(Freshmen   11)

Freshmen are designated with a #, seats that switched parties with a †, and 1994 winners are in italic.

Alabama
Howell Heflin (D)
Richard C. Shelby (R) †[1]

Alaska
Ted Stevens (R)
Frank H. Murkowski (R)

Arizona
John McCain (R)
Jon Kyl (R) # †

Arkansas
Dale Bumpers (D)
David Pryor (D)

California
Dianne Feinstein (D)
Barbara Boxer (D)

Colorado
Hank Brown (R)
Ben Nighthorse
    Campbell (D) [2]

Connecticut
Christopher J. Dodd (D)
Joseph I. Lieberman (D)

Delaware
William V. Roth Jr. (R)
Joseph R. Biden Jr. (D)

Florida
Bob Graham (D)
Connie Mack (R)

Georgia
Sam Nunn (D)
Paul Coverdell (R)

Hawaii
Daniel K. Inouye (D)
Daniel K. Akaka (D)

Idaho
Larry E. Craig (R)
Dirk Kempthorne (R)

Illinois
Paul Simon (D)
Carol Moseley-Braun (D)

Indiana
Richard G. Lugar (R)
Daniel R. Coats (R)

Iowa
Charles E. Grassley (R)
Tom Harkin (D)

Kansas
Bob Dole (R)
Nancy Landon
    Kassebaum (R)

Kentucky
Wendell H. Ford (D)
Mitch McConnell (R)

Louisiana
J. Bennett Johnston (D)
John B. Breaux (D)

Maine
William S. Cohen (R)
Olympia J. Snowe (R) # †

Maryland
Paul S. Sarbanes (D)
Barbara A. Mikulski (D)

Massachusetts
Edward M. Kennedy (D)
John Kerry (D)

Michigan
Carl Levin (D)
Spencer Abraham (R) # †

Minnesota
Paul Wellstone (D)
Rod Grams (R) #

Mississippi
Thad Cochran (R)
Trent Lott (R)

Missouri
Christopher S. Bond (R)
John Ashcroft (R) #

Montana
Max Baucus (D)
Conrad Burns (R)

Nebraska
Jim Exon (D)
Bob Kerrey (D)

Nevada
Harry Reid (D)
Richard H. Bryan (D)

New Hampshire
Robert C. Smith (R)
Judd Gregg (R)

New Jersey
Bill Bradley (D)
Frank R. Lautenberg (D)

New Mexico
Pete V. Domenici (R)
Jeff Bingaman (D)

New York
Daniel Patrick Moynihan (D)
Alfonse M. D'Amato (R)

North Carolina
Jesse Helms (R)
Lauch Faircloth (R)

North Dakota
Kent Conrad (D)
Byron L. Dorgan (D)

Ohio
John Glenn (D)
Mike DeWine (R) # †

Oklahoma
Don Nickles (R)
James M. Inhofe (R) # †

Oregon
Mark O. Hatfield (R)
Bob Packwood (R)

Pennsylvania
Arlen Specter (R)
Rick Santorum (R) # †

Rhode Island
Claiborne Pell (D)
John H. Chafee (R)

South Carolina
Strom Thurmond (R)
Ernest F. Hollings (D)

South Dakota
Larry Pressler (R)
Tom Daschle (D)

Tennessee
Fred Thompson (R) # †
Bill Frist (R) # †

Texas
Phil Gramm (R)
Kay Bailey Hutchison (R)

Utah
Orrin G. Hatch (R)
Robert F. Bennett (R)

Vermont
Patrick J. Leahy (D)
James M. Jeffords (R)

Virginia
John W. Warner (R)
Charles S. Robb (D)

Washington
Slade Gorton (R)
Patty Murray (D)

West Virginia
Robert C. Byrd (D)
John D. Rockefeller IV (D)

Wisconsin
Herb Kohl (D)
Russell D. Feingold (D)

Wyoming
Alan K. Simpson (R)
Craig Thomas (R) #

[1] Shelby switched to the Republican Party on Nov. 9.
[2] Campbell switched to the Republican Party on March 3, 1995, making the party ratio 54-to-46.

Newcomers to the Senate

State	103rd	104th	Winner	Loser	Incumbent
Arizona	D	R	Jon Kyl	Sam Coppersmith	Dennis DeConcini *
Maine	D	R	Olympia J. Snowe	Thomas H. Andrews	George J. Mitchell *
Michigan	D	R	Spencer Abraham	Bob Carr	Donald W. Riegle Jr. *
Minnesota	R	R	Rod Grams	Ann Wynia	Dave Durenberger *
Missouri	R	R	John Ashcroft	Alan Wheat	John C. Danforth *
Ohio	D	R	Mike DeWine	Joel Hyatt	Howard M. Metzenbaum *
Oklahoma	D	R	James M. Inhofe	Dave McCurdy	David L. Boren *
Pennsylvania	D	R	Rick Santorum	Harris Wofford	Wofford
Tennessee	D	R	Bill Frist	Jim Sasser	Sasser
Tennessee	D	R	Fred Thompson	Jim Cooper	Harlan Mathews *
Wyoming	R	R	Craig Thomas	Mike Sullivan	Malcolm Wallop *

* Retired

tory over McCurdy. Inhofe, who had represented the Tulsa-based 1st District, took 55 percent of the vote to fill the last two years of Boren's term. Boren had left to become president of the University of Oklahoma.

McCurdy, who had represented the southwestern 4th District for seven terms, emphasized beliefs that often put him to the right of others in his party and promised to be a "Democrat in the Boren tradition." Inhofe highlighted his conservative credentials and reminded voters at every turn of McCurdy's party affiliation and ties to the decidedly unpopular Clinton.

● **Arizona.** After struggling to win a four-candidate primary in September, only to wait until a recount certified his 59-vote victory, Democrat Coppersmith never gained his footing in the general election against Kyl. The Republican, with no primary opposition, had already amassed a huge fundraising advantage and won by 14 percentage points.

According to statewide exit polls, 55 percent of voters disapproved of Clinton's performance, compared with 40 percent who approved. Of those disapproving, Kyl beat Coppersmith 78 percent to 14 percent. Voters who had backed independent presidential candidate Ross Perot in 1992 supported Kyl over Coppersmith, 60 percent to 26 percent.

● **Maine.** Snowe moved to an early lead over Democratic Rep. Thomas H. Andrews to replace the retiring Mitchell, and she never looked back. She took 60 percent of the vote to Andrews' 37 percent. An independent candidate took 3 percent.

GOP Holds Its Three Open Seats

● **Minnesota.** Widely regarded as offering the best chance for a Democratic pickup, Durenberger's seat ended up remaining in GOP hands, despite several campaign appearances by Clinton.

Freshman Republican Rep. Grams' margin of victory over former Democratic state Rep. Ann Wynia was 5 percentage points. Democrats sought to dismiss Grams as a conservative ideologue beholden to the religious right, but Grams' call for lower taxes and smaller government resonated well. In a state where independent candidate Ross Perot won nearly one-fourth of the presidential vote in 1992, Grams' 2-1 advantage among Perot voters made the difference.

● **Wyoming.** For a time, Democrats had hoped they could win the seat of retiring Republican Sen. Wallop. Their

chances looked good on paper, especially when popular Gov. Sullivan agreed to take on GOP Rep. Thomas. But with Clinton's unpopularity fueling the Republicans' "War on the West" campaign, Sullivan never could get in the race. He lost to Thomas by nearly 40,000 votes out of the 202,000 cast.

● **Missouri.** After a two-year hiatus from political life following eight years as Missouri governor, Ashcroft crushed Democratic Rep. Alan Wheat 60 percent to 36 percent to win the Senate seat being vacated by Danforth. Wheat, a liberal six-term member from Kansas City, was seeking to become the first African-American to win a statewide election in Missouri. Ashcroft's good-natured, easygoing style had made him a difficult target throughout his political career, as Wheat found out when he sought to paint the Republican as a conservative extremist. Exit polls showed Ashcroft even received 36 percent from self-described "liberals."

Four Endangered Democrats Survive

● **California.** Many analysts outside the state wrote off Republican Huffington after he admitted that he had employed an immigrant as a nanny for years despite knowing she was illegal. The news broke shortly after Huffington had made illegal immigration the central issue of his campaign. The disclosure might have sapped Huffington's late momentum, but it did not cause a major shift in the polls. One reason was that Feinstein was also shown to have employed a housekeeper with an expired work permit in the early 1980s.

The campaign was likely to be remembered for its cost. Feinstein spent close to $10 million; Huffington shattered all records with an outlay of about $30 million, nearly all of it his own.

● **Virginia.** The battle among incumbent Robb, Republican North and a well-known independent, former Republican state Attorney General J. Marshall Coleman, lured more than 2 million voters to the polls, a record for a Virginia Senate race in a non-presidential election year.

North, a central figure in the Iran-contra scandal, waged an insurgent, anti-Washington campaign backed by the Christian conservative wing of the state GOP but not by all state Republicans. The state's senior senator, Republican John W. Warner, called him unfit to serve in the Senate and backed Coleman.

Robb, whose career had stalled partly because of a running public spat with former Democratic Gov. L. Douglas Wilder, may have owed his re-election to Wilder, who

dropped out of the race as an independent candidate and campaigned for Robb among black voters. Exit polls showed that 91 percent of black voters backed Robb; 5 percent supported North. White voters backed North 51 percent to 37 percent. Among Republicans, North received 75 percent of the vote, Coleman took 13 percent, and Robb won 12 percent.

● **New Jersey.** Democrat Frank R. Lautenberg won a third term with 50 percent of the vote to the 47 percent garnered by Republican Garabed "Chuck" Haytaian, Speaker of the state Assembly. Although the sometimes unfocused Lautenberg did not seem to light a fire under voters, many more still did not know who Haytaian was come Election Day. The anti-Democratic, anti-Washington anger present in many other regions failed to rear its head in New Jersey — in part because voters blew off some of this steam by voting for Republican Christine Todd Whitman for governor over Democrat James J. Florio in 1993.

While many undecided voters broke for Haytaian in the campaign's final days, Lautenberg undercut these gains with victories in some of the state's most Republican areas — including Bergen County. African-American voters also came out in solid numbers for Lautenberg.

● **Massachusetts.** The Republican wave did not reach Massachusetts, one of the few states where Clinton's popularity was still high and where the electorate favored clout in Congress. Kennedy's victory over his aggressive challenger Romney showed how strong the Kennedy brand remained — even though half the electorate was registered independent.

At one point Romney led Kennedy in the polls, but the incumbent, slow over the summer to respond to the challenger's attacks, awakened to the fight. He aired a series of hard-hitting television ads, including one with workers who blamed Romney's venture capital firm for their loss of jobs. Kennedy then cemented his comeback with strong showings in two televised debates against Romney in late October.

All GOP Incumbents Re-Elected

● **Vermont.** Liberal GOP Sen. James M. Jeffords struck down one of the most serious challenges in his congressional career with a 50 percent win — the lowest winning percentage of his career — over Democratic state Sen. Jan Backus.

Backus managed to reduce a 20-point Jeffords lead to 9 points by arguing that Jeffords had lost touch with ordinary Vermonters. She attacked Jeffords for his heavy reliance on political action committee funds, acceptance of trips paid for by special interests and use of campaign money to buy clothing and airline tickets for his family. She also benefited from widespread disenchantment with Jeffords among conservatives and opponents of gun control. But Jeffords lashed back with negative ads criticizing Backus' record on crime and votes against "three strikes and you're out" sentencing legislation.

● **Washington.** Democrats' hope of defeating GOP Sen. Slade Gorton faded when Gorton pulled out his strongest showing ever. Gorton won 56 percent against King County Councilman Ron Sims, one of two African-Americans nominated for the Senate in 1994. That was tantamount to a landslide for Gorton, who was defeated in his 1986 re-election bid before coming back two years later and winning the other Senate seat with just 51 percent. Gorton benefited not just from the GOP tide, but from his own strong organization, fence mending and good fundraising.

● **Delaware.** Democrats pointed to Delaware as one of their best opportunities to defeat an incumbent Republican senator, William V. Roth Jr. But the Democratic nominee, three-term state Attorney General Charles M. Oberly III, never

demonstrated why state voters should replace Roth, the longest-serving politician in Delaware history. Roth was elected to a record fifth term.

● **Montana.** Sen. Conrad Burns became the first Montana Republican voters had returned to Washington in the 20th century. He took 62 percent of the vote against Democrat Jack Mudd, former dean of the University of Montana law school. Setting a statewide precedent for Montana Republicans, Burns captured 53 out of the state's 56 counties. In Democratic strongholds like Butte and Missoula, Mudd's hometown, Burns nearly matched his opponent.

● **Texas.** After beating back a criminal indictment, Republican Kay Bailey Hutchison easily won re-election to her first full term by defeating Dallas businessman Richard Fisher 61 percent to 38 percent. In a 1993 special election, Hutchison won the right to finish the term of Lloyd Bentsen, who resigned to become Treasury secretary.

● **Indiana.** Republican Richard G. Lugar became the first Indiana senator to be re-elected to a fourth term. At 67 percent, Lugar nearly matched his 68 percent blowout in 1988. While Lugar initially was expected to face a tougher challenge against former Democratic Rep. Jim Jontz, the race never developed.

● **Utah.** Republican Orrin G. Hatch sailed to a fourth term with 69 percent of the vote against Democrat Pat Shea, a former party chairman. Shea could not match the Utah veteran's fundraising firepower and get-out-the-vote operation.

● **Mississippi.** Republican Trent Lott won a second term, capturing 69 percent of the vote against former state Sen. Ken Harper.

● **Florida.** Hugh Rodham, brother of first lady Hillary Rodham Clinton, could not break 30 percent against popular Republican freshman Connie Mack.

● **Rhode Island.** Republican John H. Chafee easily won a fourth term over state Rep. Linda Kushner.

Most Democratic Incumbents Survive

● **Nevada.** Republicans viewed Democratic Sen. Richard H. Bryan as vulnerable but failed to recruit a top-drawer candidate. Bryan, who had distanced himself from Clinton by opposing the 1993 deficit-reduction bill that raised taxes, won with 53 percent to Republican Hal Furman's 42 percent.

● **Nebraska.** After holding a hefty lead in the last few weeks of the campaign, Democrat Bob Kerrey was limited to 55 percent by his GOP challenger, Jan Stoney. Stoney received strong support from the national party, and a parade of Republican figures, such as Senate Minority Leader Dole and Sen. Phil Gramm of Texas, campaigned for her.

The National Rifle Association spent $125,000 in Stoney's behalf; a television spot criticizing Kerrey's vote for the assault weapons ban featured actor Charlton Heston. Heston, however, put his foot in his mouth while trying to defend his criticism of Kerrey, saying "he's a hero" and predicting his re-election.

● **New Mexico.** Democrat Jeff Bingaman was re-elected to a third term with 54 percent after holding on in a race that had become much more competitive than initially expected. Bingaman turned aside a well-funded campaign by Colin R. McMillan, a rancher and former Pentagon official. McMillan used some of his own $1.3 million contribution to place ads attacking Bingaman's stance on grazing fees and his support for Clinton's 1993 budget. The ads brought Bingaman down in the polls.

● **Wisconsin.** With the help of his hefty bankroll, Democrat Herb Kohl easily won re-election, defeating conservative GOP challenger Robert T. Welch, a state representative. Kohl, a multimillionaire, outspent Welch 6-to-1. Welch attacked the

incumbent for voting for the president's 1993 budget plan. Kohl, who garnered 58 percent of the vote, painted Welch, who vowed to resign if he ever voted to raise taxes, as a conservative extremist.

● **Maryland.** Despite a strong GOP showing in other Maryland races, Democrat Paul S. Sarbanes cruised to a fourth term. He took 59 percent over Bill Brock, former Republican senator from Tennessee. In addition to suffering from the carpetbagger label, Brock never developed a focused message. After saying in August that Clinton was not an issue, Brock picked up on that theme — and hired his third campaign manager — in September.

● **New York.** With all attention riveted on Democratic Gov. Mario M. Cuomo's re-election bid, virtually none was allotted to the Senate race. Democrat Daniel Patrick Moynihan staved off a GOP statewide sweep, winning a fourth term against former sofa bed company executive Bernadette Castro, 55 percent to 42 percent. Exit polls showed Moynihan got one-

fourth of the vote from self-described Republicans.

● **North Dakota.** Democrat Kent Conrad did not have a difficult time winning a second full term. He defeated Ben Clayburgh, a 70-year-old orthopedic surgeon and former GOP National Committee member, 58 percent to 42 percent. Conrad took no chances: As a buffer against Clinton's unpopularity, he aired a TV ad saying that he had voted with Republican leader Dole "a majority of the time."

● **Connecticut.** Democratic incumbent Joseph I. Lieberman coasted to an easy victory over former state Sen. Gerald Labriola, 67 percent to 31 percent.

● **West Virginia.** Robert C. Byrd, the senior Democrat in the Senate, earned a seventh term by quietly dispatching token challenger Stan Klos with 69 percent of the vote.

● **Hawaii.** Despite the GOP tide, the highest margin of victory in 1994 went to a Democratic incumbent, Daniel K. Akaka of Hawaii, who captured 72 percent in this heavily Democratic state.   ■

After 40 Years, GOP Wins House

The watchword from both parties the night of Nov. 8 was "history." After 40 years of one-party rule in the House of Representatives, Republicans were set to become the majority.

"This was, and is, history — big time," said a beaming Bill Paxon of New York, chairman of the National Republican Congressional Committee (NRCC). "We made history last night," acknowledged departing Democratic National Committee Chairman David Wilhelm. "We got our butts kicked."

Fittingly, it was a history professor who claimed the spoils of the GOP's earthshaking election of 1994: Georgia Rep. Newt Gingrich was in line to become the first Republican Speaker of the House from the South.

Gingrich's ascendancy accompanied the long anticipated realignment of the South. For the first time since the end of Reconstruction in the 1870s, Republicans won a majority of the congressional districts in the South. Democrats' 83-54 majority vanished with a GOP pickup of 19 seats, giving Republicans a 73-64 majority. *(Dixie, p. 582))*

And another record intact since the Civil War also was shattered: Thomas S. Foley of Washington became the first sitting House Speaker to lose re-election since Galusha A. Grow of Pennsylvania lost in 1862.

Republicans gained 52 House seats, increasing their numbers in the House from 178 to 230.

A Democratic president held in disfavor and a Democratic-controlled Congress held in disrepute gave Republican candidates a target they could not miss. In district after district, Republicans shackled their Democratic opponents to President Clinton.

But Republicans offered more than simple opposition. Gingrich and Dick Armey of Texas, chairman of the House Republican Conference, designed the "Contract With America," a list of 10 items that Republicans promised to bring to the floor for a vote within the first 100 days of taking over the House.

★ U.S. House ★	
104th CONGRESS	**103rd CONGRESS**
Democrats 204	Democrats 256
Republicans 230	Republicans 177
Independents 1	Independents 1
	Vacancy 1
DEMOCRATS	
Net Loss	52
Freshmen	13
Incumbents re-elected	191
Incumbents defeated	34
REPUBLICANS	
Net Gain	52
Freshmen	73
Incumbents re-elected	157
Incumbents defeated	0

Republicans also reaped the gains they had anticipated from redistricting after the 1990 census. The strong Democratic showing in 1992 delayed the effect of a round of remapping largely favorable to the GOP. In states such as California and Washington, the redistricting "lag effect" flushed out Democrats who won GOP-leaning districts in 1992.

Money made the difference for some Republican challengers. According to the Federal Election Commission, Republican challengers had an easier time raising money from political action committees and other committees than in previous years. Much of that increase reflected heavy investment from the NRCC, the Republican National Committee and a substantial number of GOP incumbents who made contributions of their own. Conservative interest groups, from the National Rifle Association (NRA) to term limits advocates, played active roles in several congressional races, including Foley's narrow defeat. And several Republican freshmen were elected with the prominent support of conservative Christian activists.

Hard To Match

The GOP posted a near-perfect record: No Republican incumbent was defeated, and Republicans retained control of 17 of the 21 GOP-held open seats. Freshmen accounted for nearly half of all Democratic incumbent defeats. Of the 34 Democratic incumbents who lost, 16 were in their first term.

Foley was not the only venerable House Democrat to fall in the Nov. 8 balloting. Other veterans who lost included:

● 18-term Rep. Dan Rostenkowski of Illinois, the former chairman of the Ways and Means Committee.

● 21-term Rep. Jack Brooks of Texas, chairman of the Judiciary Committee.

● 18-term Rep. Neal Smith of Iowa, chairman of the Appropriations Subcommittee on Labor, Health and Human Services, and Education.

• Nine-term Rep. Dan Glickman of Kansas, chairman of the Intelligence Committee.

Republicans enjoyed big gains among the 52 seats in which no incumbent was running. Democrats had many more open seats to defend: 31 of the 52 open seats had been held by Democrats. Republicans won 22 Democratic-held open seats; Democrats were able to win only four GOP-held open seats.

Overall, Republicans made their biggest gains in the South (19 seats), followed by the West (15 seats) and the Midwest (15 seats). Democrats fared best in the East, holding their losses to three.

Following is a state-by-state report on the House elections by region.

The South

The GOP took over the House delegations in six Southern states where Democrats either had the majority of seats or where the parties were tied before the elections: Georgia, Kentucky, North Carolina, Oklahoma, South Carolina and Tennessee. Neither Georgia nor North Carolina had had Republican majorities since Reconstruction.

• **Georgia.** In Georgia, Republicans defeated two incumbent Democrats seen as being too closely aligned with Clinton and picked up one open seat previously held by a Democrat.

Former U.S. Attorney Bob Barr, who had the support of conservative Christians, knocked off 11-year incumbent George "Buddy" Darden, while freshman Rep. Don Johnson was easily defeated by retired dentist Charlie Norwood. Both incumbents had a tough time defending their votes for Clinton's 1993 tax-raising deficit-reduction budget plan and fending off well-funded attacks by the NRA for voting for the crime bill with the assault weapons ban.

In the open 8th, Republican lawyer Saxby Chambliss easily defeated Craig Mathis, the son of former Democratic Rep. Dawson Mathis (1971-81).

• **North Carolina.** In the 3rd District, Republican Walter B. Jones Jr., the son of the popular former Democratic representative of the same name, relied heavily on the Clinton factor to defeat Democratic Rep. H. Martin Lancaster, setting a national trend with a TV ad featuring a picture of Clinton and the incumbent jogging together.

Republican Fred Heineman, a former police chief, was not viewed as a threat to 4th District Democratic Rep. David Price, but he nonetheless narrowly defeated the four-term incumbent.

Republicans captured two Democratic-held open seats. In the 2nd, Republican David Funderburk, a former ambassador to Romania, was aided by the district's conservative nature and his close ties to GOP Sen. Jesse Helms in his defeat of Democratic state Rep. Richard H. Moore. In the 5th, GOP businessman Richard M. Burr used state Sen. A. P. "Sandy" Sands' vote for a 3-cent tobacco tax increase to paint him as a potential tax-and-spend ally of Clinton's. In the open 9th, Republican Sue Myrick held on to the seat for the GOP.

• **Florida.** No House incumbent lost a re-election bid in Florida. Republicans, however, prevailed in three open seats, two of them Democratic-held.

Republicans captured two conservative districts long held by Democrats: the Panhandle-based 1st, won by attorney Joe Scarborough, and the "Space Coast" 15th, which elected physician Dave Weldon. Both Republicans enjoyed backing from conservative Christian activists. In the 16th District, retiring Republican Rep. Tom Lewis was replaced by GOP state Sen. Mark Foley.

In the 11th District, acting Ways and Means Chairman Sam

M. Gibbons withstood a rematch with Republican Mark Sharpe, prevailing with just 52 percent of the vote.

• **Kentucky.** Republicans gained a majority in Kentucky's House delegation for the first time since 1928. The 1st District gained its first-ever GOP representative in Edward Whitfield, a former Democratic legislator who defeated Democratic Rep. Tom Barlow.

In the 3rd District race to replace retiring Democratic incumbent Romano L. Mazzoli, Democrat Mike Ward was declared the winner over Republican Susan B. Stokes, who was also the GOP's 1992 nominee. Results were delayed by a power surge that forced election officials to count the ballots by hand. Ward came away with a 427-vote margin Nov. 8, which prompted the Stokes campaign to request a recanvass.

• **Mississippi.** The GOP picked up one seat with Republican state Sen. Roger Wicker's capture of the northeastern 1st District — a seat that had not been held by the GOP since Reconstruction. Wicker, who succeeded former Appropriations Committee Chairman Jamie L. Whitten, trounced Democratic state Rep. Bill Wheeler with 63 percent of the vote.

• **Oklahoma.** Republicans swept the three open seats in Oklahoma to gain control of the House delegation for the first time since 1920. All three winners stressed their conservative values and lambasted the Democrats as potential pawns for the White House.

In the Tulsa-based 1st District vacated by Republican James M. Inhofe (who won the Senate race), Republican Steve Largent, a former Seattle Seahawks superstar, easily outdistanced Democratic neophyte Stuart Price with 63 percent of the vote.

In the 2nd, physician Tom Coburn defeated Democrat Virgil R. Cooper to replace eight-term Democratic incumbent Mike Synar. Cooper, who became something of a folk hero after his runoff upset of Synar, had neither the money nor the operation to compete with Coburn.

Republican J. C. Watts, a former star quarterback at the University of Oklahoma, got 52 percent of the vote against Democratic lawyer David Perryman in a vituperative contest for the 4th District seat vacated by Democratic Rep. Dave McCurdy, who lost his bid for the Senate. Watts joined Connecticut's Gary A. Franks as the only black Republicans in the House.

• **South Carolina.** Republicans picked up one open seat and held the other, to give the GOP a 4-2 majority of House seats. Political newcomer Mark Sanford, who donned camouflage gear in the campaign to declare a "war on career politicians," easily won the coastal 1st District, which previously had been held by a Republican.

The 3rd District, which retiring Democratic Rep. Butler Derrick held for 20 years, revealed its true GOP colors. Freshman GOP state Rep. Lindsey Graham took 60 percent against state Sen. James E. Bryan Jr.

• **Tennessee.** Tennessee Republicans picked up two Democratic-held open seats, to give them a 5-4 lead in the delegation.

Republicans had expected little trouble winning the 3rd District seat of retiring Democratic Rep. Marilyn Lloyd, who had had several close races. But Republican Zach Wamp's personal problems, which included admitted past cocaine use, helped make his victory a close 52 percent over Roane County Property Assessor Randy Button.

The GOP easily snared the rural 4th District, vacated by Democratic Rep. Jim Cooper, who lost a Senate bid. Republican Van Hilleary won 57 percent over Jeff Whorley, a former aide to Democratic Rep. Bart Gordon who tried to match Hilleary's conservatism.

Continued on p. 574

House Membership in 104th Congress

Alabama

1 Sonny Callahan (R)
2 Terry Everett (R)
3 Glen Browder (D)
4 Tom Bevill (D)
5 Robert E. "Bud" Cramer (D)
6 Spencer Bachus (R)
7 Earl F. Hilliard (D)

Alaska

AL Don Young (R)

Arizona

1 Matt Salmon (R) #
2 Ed Pastor (D)
3 Bob Stump (R)
4 John Shadegg (R) #
5 Jim Kolbe (R)
6 J. D. Hayworth (R) #

Arkansas

1 Blanche Lambert Lincoln (D)
2 Ray Thornton (D)
3 Tim Hutchinson (R)
4 Jay Dickey (R)

California

1 Frank Riggs (R)
2 Wally Herger (R)
3 Vic Fazio (D)
4 John T. Doolittle (R)
5 Robert T. Matsui (D)
6 Lynn Woolsey (D)
7 George Miller (D)
8 Nancy Pelosi (D)
9 Ronald V. Dellums (D)
10 Bill Baker (R)
11 Richard W. Pombo (R)
12 Tom Lantos (D)
13 Pete Stark (D)
14 Anna G. Eshoo (D)
15 Norman Y. Mineta (D)
16 Zoe Lofgren (D) #
17 Sam Farr (D)
18 Gary A. Condit (D)
19 George P. Radanovich (R) #
20 Cal Dooley (D)
21 Bill Thomas (R)
22 Andrea Seastrand (R) #
23 Elton Gallegly (R)
24 Anthony C. Beilenson (D)
25 Howard P. "Buck" McKeon (R)
26 Howard L. Berman (D)
27 Carlos J. Moorhead (R)
28 David Dreier (R)
29 Henry A. Waxman (D)
30 Xavier Becerra (D)
31 Matthew G. Martinez (D)
32 Julian C. Dixon (D)
33 Lucille Roybal-Allard (D)
34 Esteban E. Torres (D)
35 Maxine Waters (D)
36 Jane Harman (D)
37 Walter R. Tucker III (D)
38 Steve Horn (R)
39 Ed Royce (R)
40 Jerry Lewis (R)
41 Jay C. Kim (R)
42 George E. Brown Jr. (D)

43 Ken Calvert (R)
44 Sonny Bono (R) #
45 Dana Rohrabacher (R)
46 Robert K. Dornan (R)
47 Christopher Cox (R)
48 Ron Packard (R)
49 Brian P. Bilbray (R) #
50 Bob Filner (D)
51 Randy "Duke" Cunningham (R)
52 Duncan Hunter (R)

Colorado

1 Patricia Schroeder (D)
2 David E. Skaggs (D)
3 Scott McInnis (R)
4 Wayne Allard (R)
5 Joel Hefley (R)
6 Dan Schaefer (R)

Connecticut

1 Barbara B. Kennelly (D)
2 Sam Gejdenson (D)
3 Rosa DeLauro (D)
4 Christopher Shays (R)
5 Gary A. Franks (R)
6 Nancy L. Johnson (R)

Delaware

AL Michael N. Castle (R)

Florida

1 Joe Scarborough (R) #
2 Pete Peterson (D)
3 Corrine Brown (D)
4 Tillie Fowler (R)
5 Karen L. Thurman (D)
6 Cliff Stearns (R)
7 John L. Mica (R)
8 Bill McCollum (R)
9 Michael Bilirakis (R)
10 C. W. Bill Young (R)
11 Sam M. Gibbons (D)
12 Charles T. Canady (R)
13 Dan Miller (R)
14 Porter J. Goss (R)
15 Dave Weldon (R) #
16 Mark Foley (R) #
17 Carrie P. Meek (D)
18 Ileana Ros-Lehtinen (R)
19 Harry A. Johnston (D)
20 Peter Deutsch (D)
21 Lincoln Diaz-Balart (R)
22 E. Clay Shaw Jr. (R)
23 Alcee L. Hastings (D)

Lineup

(as of Dec. 31, 1994)

Republicans	230	Freshmen	73
Democrats	204	Freshmen	13
Independent	1		

 # Denotes freshman representative.

Georgia

1 Jack Kingston (R)
2 Sanford D. Bishop Jr. (D)
3 Mac Collins (R)
4 John Linder (R)
5 John Lewis (D)
6 Newt Gingrich (R)
7 Bob Barr (R) #
8 Saxby Chambliss (R) #
9 Nathan Deal (D)
10 Charlie Norwood (R) #
11 Cynthia A. McKinney (D)

Hawaii

1 Neil Abercrombie (D)
2 Patsy T. Mink (D)

Idaho

1 Helen Chenoweth (R) #
2 Michael D. Crapo (R)

Illinois

1 Bobby L. Rush (D)
2 Mel Reynolds (D)
3 William O. Lipinski (D)
4 Luis V. Gutierrez (D)
5 Michael Patrick Flanagan (R) #
6 Henry J. Hyde (R)
7 Cardiss Collins (D)
8 Philip M. Crane (R)
9 Sidney R. Yates (D)
10 John Edward Porter (R)
11 Jerry Weller (R) #
12 Jerry F. Costello (D)
13 Harris W. Fawell (R)
14 Dennis Hastert (R)
15 Thomas W. Ewing (R)
16 Donald Manzullo (R)
17 Lane Evans (D)
18 Ray LaHood (R) #
19 Glenn Poshard (D)
20 Richard J. Durbin (D)

Indiana

1 Peter J. Visclosky (D)
2 David M. McIntosh (R) #
3 Tim Roemer (D)
4 Mark E. Souder (R) #
5 Steve Buyer (R)
6 Dan Burton (R)
7 John T. Myers (R)
8 John Hostettler (R) #
9 Lee H. Hamilton (D)

10 Andrew Jacobs Jr. (D)

Iowa

1 Jim Leach (R)
2 Jim Nussle (R)
3 Jim Ross Lightfoot (R)
4 Greg Ganske (R) #
5 Tom Latham (R) #

Kansas

1 Pat Roberts (R)
2 Sam Brownback (R) #
3 Jan Meyers (R)
4 Todd Tiahrt (R) #

Kentucky

1 Edward Whitfield (R) #
2 Ron Lewis (R)
3 Mike Ward (D) #
4 Jim Bunning (R)
5 Harold Rogers (R)
6 Scotty Baesler (D)

Louisiana

1 Robert L. Livingston (R)
2 William J. Jefferson (D)
3 W. J. "Billy" Tauzin (D)
4 Cleo Fields (D)
5 Jim McCrery (R)
6 Richard H. Baker (R)
7 Jimmy Hayes (D)

Maine

1 James B. Longley Jr. (R) #
2 John Baldacci (D) #

Maryland

1 Wayne T. Gilchrest (R)
2 Robert L. Ehrlich Jr. (R) #
3 Benjamin L. Cardin (D)
4 Albert R. Wynn (D)
5 Steny H. Hoyer (D)
6 Roscoe G. Bartlett (R)
7 Kweisi Mfume (D)
8 Constance A. Morella (R)

Massachusetts

1 John W. Olver (D)
2 Richard E. Neal (D)
3 Peter I. Blute (R)
4 Barney Frank (D)
5 Martin T. Meehan (D)
6 Peter G. Torkildsen (R)
7 Edward J. Markey (D)
8 Joseph P. Kennedy II (D)
9 Joe Moakley (D)
10 Gerry E. Studds (D)

Michigan

1 Bart Stupak (D)
2 Peter Hoekstra (R)
3 Vernon J. Ehlers (R)
4 Dave Camp (R)
5 James A. Barcia (D)
6 Fred Upton (R)
7 Nick Smith (R)

8 Dick Chrysler (R) #
9 Dale E. Kildee (D)
10 David E. Bonior (D)
11 Joe Knollenberg (R)
12 Sander M. Levin (D)
13 Lynn Rivers (D) #
14 John Conyers Jr. (D)
15 Barbara-Rose Collins (D)
16 John D. Dingell (D)

Minnesota

1 Gil Gutknecht (R) #
2 David Minge (D)
3 Jim Ramstad (R)
4 Bruce F. Vento (D)
5 Martin Olav Sabo (D)
6 William P. "Bill" Luther (D) #
7 Collin C. Peterson (D)
8 James L. Oberstar (D)

Mississippi

1 Roger Wicker (R) #
2 Bennie Thompson (D)
3 G. V. "Sonny" Montgomery (D)
4 Mike Parker (D)
5 Gene Taylor (D)

Missouri

1 William L. Clay (D)
2 James M. Talent (R)
3 Richard A. Gephardt (D)
4 Ike Skelton (D)
5 Karen McCarthy (D) #
6 Pat Danner (D)
7 Mel Hancock (R)
8 Bill Emerson (R)
9 Harold L. Volkmer (D)

Montana

AL Pat Williams (D)

Nebraska

1 Doug Bereuter (R)
2 Jon Christensen (R) #
3 Bill Barrett (R)

Nevada

1 John Ensign (R) #
2 Barbara F. Vucanovich (R)

New Hampshire

1 Bill Zeliff (R)
2 Charles Bass (R) #

New Jersey

1 Robert E. Andrews (D)
2 Frank A. LoBiondo (R) #
3 H. James Saxton (R)
4 Christopher H. Smith (R)
5 Marge Roukema (R)
6 Frank Pallone Jr. (D)
7 Bob Franks (R)
8 Bill Martini (R) #
9 Robert G. Torricelli (D)
10 Donald M. Payne (D)
11 Rodney Frelinghuysen (R) #
12 Dick Zimmer (R)
13 Robert Menendez (D)

New Mexico

1 Steven H. Schiff (R)

2 Joe Skeen (R)
3 Bill Richardson (D)

New York

1 Michael P. Forbes (R) #
2 Rick A. Lazio (R)
3 Peter T. King (R)
4 Daniel Frisa (R) #
5 Gary L. Ackerman (D)
6 Floyd H. Flake (D)
7 Thomas J. Manton (D)
8 Jerrold Nadler (D)
9 Charles E. Schumer (D)
10 Edolphus Towns (D)
11 Major R. Owens (D)
12 Nydia M. Velázquez (D)
13 Susan Molinari (R)
14 Carolyn B. Maloney (D)
15 Charles B. Rangel (D)
16 Jose E. Serrano (D)
17 Eliot L. Engel (D)
18 Nita M. Lowey (D)
19 Sue W. Kelly (R) #
20 Benjamin A. Gilman (R)
21 Michael R. McNulty (D)
22 Gerald B. H. Solomon (R)
23 Sherwood Boehlert (R)
24 John M. McHugh (R)
25 James T. Walsh (R)
26 Maurice D. Hinchey (D)
27 Bill Paxon (R)
28 Louise M. Slaughter (D)
29 John J. LaFalce (D)
30 Jack Quinn (R)
31 Amo Houghton (R)

North Carolina

1 Eva Clayton (D)
2 David Funderburk (R) #
3 Walter B. Jones Jr. (R) #
4 Fred Heineman (R) #
5 Richard M. Burr (R) #
6 Howard Coble (R)
7 Charlie Rose (D)
8 W. G. "Bill" Hefner (D)
9 Sue Myrick (R) #
10 Cass Ballenger (R)
11 Charles H. Taylor (R)
12 Melvin Watt (D)

North Dakota

AL Earl Pomeroy (D)

Ohio

1 Steve Chabot (R) #
2 Rob Portman (R)
3 Tony P. Hall (D)
4 Michael G. Oxley (R)
5 Paul E. Gillmor (R)
6 Frank A. Cremeans (R) #
7 David L. Hobson (R)
8 John A. Boehner (R)
9 Marcy Kaptur (D)
10 Martin R. Hoke (R)
11 Louis Stokes (D)
12 John R. Kasich (R)
13 Sherrod Brown (D)
14 Tom Sawyer (D)
15 Deborah Pryce (R)
16 Ralph Regula (R)
17 James A. Traficant Jr. (D)
18 Bob Ney (R) #
19 Steven C. LaTourette (R) #

Oklahoma

1 Steve Largent (R) #

2 Tom Coburn (R) #
3 Bill Brewster (D)
4 J.C. Watts (R) #
5 Ernest Jim Istook Jr. (R)
6 Frank D. Lucas (R)

Oregon

1 Elizabeth Furse (D)
2 Wes Cooley (R) #
3 Ron Wyden (D)
4 Peter A. DeFazio (D)
5 Jim Bunn (R) #

Pennsylvania

1 Thomas M. Foglietta (D)
2 Chaka Fattah (D) #
3 Robert A. Borski (D)
4 Ron Klink (D)
5 William F. Clinger (R)
6 Tim Holden (D)
7 Curt Weldon (R)
8 James C. Greenwood (R)
9 Bud Shuster (R)
10 Joseph M. McDade (R)
11 Paul E. Kanjorski (D)
12 John P. Murtha (D)
13 Jon D. Fox (R) #
14 William J. Coyne (D)
15 Paul McHale (D)
16 Robert S. Walker (R)
17 George W. Gekas (R)
18 Mike Doyle (D)
19 Bill Goodling (R)
20 Frank R. Mascara (D) #
21 Phil English (R) #

Rhode Island

1 Patrick J. Kennedy (D) #
2 Jack Reed (D)

South Carolina

1 Mark Sanford (R) #
2 Floyd D. Spence (R)
3 Lindsey Graham (R) #
4 Bob Inglis (R)
5 John M. Spratt Jr. (D)
6 James E. Clyburn (D)

South Dakota

AL Tim Johnson (D)

Tennessee

1 James H. Quillen (R)
2 John J. "Jimmy" Duncan Jr. (R)
3 Zach Wamp (R) #
4 Van Hilleary (R) #
5 Bob Clement (D)
6 Bart Gordon (D)
7 Ed Bryant (R) #
8 John Tanner (D)
9 Harold E. Ford (D)

Texas

1 Jim Chapman (D)
2 Charles Wilson (D)
3 Sam Johnson (R)
4 Ralph M. Hall (D)
5 John Bryant (D)
6 Joe L. Barton (R)
7 Bill Archer (R)
8 Jack Fields (R)
9 Steve Stockman (R) #
10 Lloyd Doggett (D) #

11 Chet Edwards (D)
12 Pete Geren (D)
13 William M. "Mac" Thornberry (R) #
14 Greg Laughlin (D)
15 E. "Kika" de la Garza (D)
16 Ronald D. Coleman (D)
17 Charles W. Stenholm (D)
18 Sheila Jackson-Lee (D) #
19 Larry Combest (R)
20 Henry B. Gonzalez (D)
21 Lamar Smith (R)
22 Tom DeLay (R)
23 Henry Bonilla (R)
24 Martin Frost (D)
25 Ken Bentsen (D) #
26 Dick Armey (R)
27 Solomon P. Ortiz (D)
28 Frank Tejeda (D)
29 Gene Green (D)
30 Eddie Bernice Johnson (D)

Utah

1 James V. Hansen (R)
2 Enid Greene Waldholtz (R) #
3 Bill Orton (D)

Vermont

AL Bernard Sanders (I)

Virginia

1 Herbert H. Bateman (R)
2 Owen B. Pickett (D)
3 Robert C. Scott (D)
4 Norman Sisisky (D)
5 L. F. Payne Jr. (D)
6 Robert W. Goodlatte (R)
7 Thomas J. Bliley Jr. (R)
8 James P. Moran (D)
9 Rick Boucher (D)
10 Frank R. Wolf (R)
11 Thomas M. Davis III (R) #

Washington

1 Rick White (R) #
2 Jack Metcalf (R) #
3 Linda Smith (R) #
4 Richard "Doc" Hastings (R) #
5 George Nethercutt (R) #
6 Norm Dicks (D)
7 Jim McDermott (D)
8 Jennifer Dunn (R)
9 Randy Tate (R) #

West Virginia

1 Alan B. Mollohan (D)
2 Bob Wise (D)
3 Nick J. Rahall II (D)

Wisconsin

1 Mark W. Neumann (R) #
2 Scott L. Klug (R)
3 Steve Gunderson (R)
4 Gerald D. Kleczka (D)
5 Thomas M. Barrett (D)
6 Tom Petri (R)
7 David R. Obey (D)
8 Toby Roth (R)
9 F. James Sensenbrenner Jr. (R)

Wyoming

AL Barbara Cubin (R) #

Defeated Incumbents

Following is a list of the House members defeated Nov. 8. An asterisk indicates a freshman.

* Karan English, D-Ariz.
* Dan Hamburg, D-Calif.
  Richard H. Lehman, D-Calif.
* Lynn Schenk, D-Calif.
  George "Buddy" Darden, D-Ga.
* Don Johnson, D-Ga.
  Larry LaRocco, D-Idaho
  Dan Rostenkowski, D-Ill.
  Jill L. Long, D-Ind.
  Frank McCloskey, D-Ind.
  Neal Smith, D-Iowa
  Dan Glickman, D-Kan.
* Tom Barlow, D-Ky.
  Peter Hoagland, D-Neb.
  James Bilbray, D-Nev.
  Dick Swett, D-N.H.
* Herbert C. Klein, D-N.J.

George J. Hochbrueckner, D-N.Y.
H. Martin Lancaster, D-N.C.
David Price, D-N.C.
* David Mann, D-Ohio
* Ted Strickland, D-Ohio
* Eric D. Fingerhut, D-Ohio
* Marjorie Margolies-Mezvinsky, D-Pa.
Jack Brooks, D-Texas
Bill Sarpalius, D-Texas
* Karen Shepherd, D-Utah
* Leslie L. Byrne, D-Va.
* Maria Cantwell, D-Wash.
Jolene Unsoeld, D-Wash.
Thomas S. Foley, D-Wash.
* Jay Inslee, D-Wash.
* Mike Kreidler, D-Wash.
* Peter W. Barca, D-Wis.

Continued from p. 571

Republican Ed Bryant kept the open 7th in GOP hands.

● **Texas.** Republicans picked up only two House seats in Texas, but the Democrats' losses were significant: Judiciary Chairman Brooks in the 9th District and Bill Sarpalius, chairman of an Agriculture subcommittee, in the 13th. Three Democrats — Lloyd Doggett, Sheila Jackson-Lee and Ken Bentsen — held on to seats vacated by members of their own party.

A longtime opponent of gun control, Brooks was targeted for defeat by the 125,000-member Gun Owners of America for his support of the 1994 crime bill, which banned certain types of assault weapons. Republican accountant Steve Stockman, who had kept Brooks to 54 percent in 1992, won this time, 52 percent to 46 percent, after being outspent by Brooks by a nearly 8-1 ratio.

In the Eastern Panhandle's 13th, Republican William M. "Mac" Thornberry capitalized on Sarpalius' vote for Clinton's budget plan and the president's unpopularity to defeat the three-term incumbent.

● **Virginia.** Three Democratic incumbents in conservative districts, L. F. Payne Jr., Norman Sisisky and Owen B. Pickett, won their races by surprisingly comfortable margins. Republicans had to content themselves with the defeat of freshman Democratic Rep. Leslie L. Byrne by the state party's leading moderate, Fairfax County Board of Supervisors Chairman Thomas M. Davis III.

● **Alabama.** The GOP made no gains in Alabama. Democratic incumbent Robert E. "Bud" Cramer had the only close call, holding off a challenge from Republican Wayne Parker by fewer than 2,000 votes.

● **Arkansas.** The state's four incumbents won re-election, including Republican Rep. Jay Dickey, one of the Democrats' top targets for defeat. Dickey, who represented the heavily Democratic 4th, won re-election with 52 percent.

● **Louisiana.** All seven incumbents were re-elected in the Oct. 1 all-party primary, when each received 50 percent or more of the vote.

The Midwest

The biggest turnovers came in Ohio and Indiana, where the GOP gained a majority of the seats in both states' House delegations.

● **Indiana.** Republicans defeated Jill L. Long and Frank McCloskey and took the open 2nd District left by retiring Democratic Rep. Philip R. Sharp. The 1994 election gave the GOP a majority of the delegation for the first time in 22 years.

In the 4th District, Long was ousted by Mark E. Souder, a former aide to GOP Sen. Daniel R. Coats. Souder was late in getting support from the national party but went early on the attack, winning with 55 percent of the vote.

McCloskey had always had a tough time hanging on to his conservative 8th District, and the GOP rallied around engineer John Hostettler, who had the support of Christian activists. Hostettler pulled out 52 percent. In the 2nd, Republican David M. McIntosh, a former aide to Vice President Dan Quayle, beat Democratic Secretary of State Joseph H. Hogsett.

● **Ohio.** Republicans went from a 9-10 minority in the House delegation to a 13-6 majority. Three of Ohio's Democratic freshmen fell, and Republicans also gained an open Democratic seat with state Sen. Bob Ney's defeat of Democrat Greg DiDonato in the 18th District.

Democratic incumbent David Mann of Cincinnati's 1st District lost to Republican Steve Chabot, who garnered 56 percent of the vote. Mann did not survive despite going to extraordinary lengths to distance himself from Clinton, including airing a TV ad detailing his opposition to a series of the president's priorities.

In the 6th District, Republican Frank A. Cremeans overcame incumbent Ted Strickland, 51 percent to 49 percent, with the help of the area's churches and religious groups. In the suburban Cleveland 19th, popular GOP Lake County Prosecutor Steven C. LaTourette defeated Rep. Eric D. Fingerhut in part by hammering away at the incumbent's vote for Clinton's budget plan.

● **Illinois.** Republicans picked up two seats to claim half the 20 seats in the delegation. Rostenkowski fell to a virtually unknown political newcomer, Michael Patrick Flanagan. The powerful former chairman of the Ways and Means Committee, facing a 17-count federal indictment, managed only 46 percent. In contrast to the heavy media attention and high-profile display of Rostenkowski's clout in the competitive primary campaign, few paid much attention to the race until GOP polls the week before Election Day showed that the 18-term incumbent was in trouble. Help promised by Chicago Mayor Richard M. Daley, who rallied the troops for Rostenkowski in the primary, never materialized.

GOP state Rep. Jerry Weller picked up the 11th District seat of retiring Democratic Rep. George E. Sangmeister. Retiring GOP Minority Leader Robert H. Michel's chief of staff, Ray LaHood, held his boss' 18th District seat for the GOP.

● **Iowa.** Republicans swept all five 11th District seats by ousting Neal Smith and holding on to another vacated by GOP Rep. Fred Grandy. Smith lost to a political newcomer, plastic surgeon Greg Ganske. Smith tried to ward off Ganske's challenge with charges that the Republican supported deep cuts in Social Security. But Ganske used the two things that the incumbent tried to run on — his seniority and ability to bring home earmarked projects to Iowa — as reasons that Smith should not be returned to Washington.

● **Kansas.** Kansas provided one of the surprise knockouts when Glickman fell to freshman Republican state Sen. Todd Tiahrt, 53 percent to 47 percent. Glickman was not on an

endangered list, because he was the most successful vote-getter among the state's major Democratic officeholders. His 1992 challenger was considered more formidable than Tiahrt. But Tiahrt had the support of Christian activists and appealed to economic conservatives with his central theme of lower taxes and less government.

By also capturing the Topeka-based 2nd, which Democratic Rep. Jim Slattery gave up for an unsuccessful gubernatorial bid, the GOP completed its lock on the four-member delegation. Republican Sam Brownback, a former state agriculture secretary, took 66 percent against former Democratic Gov. John Carlin.

● **Michigan.** Democrats held on to four of the five seats targeted by the GOP for takeover despite well-funded challenges by Republican opponents. The one GOP pickup came in the 8th District, which Democratic Rep. Bob Carr gave up for his unsuccessful bid for the Senate. Manufacturer Dick Chrysler defeated Democrat Bob Mitchell, even though the Democrat tried to highlight old allegations lodged against the Republican of unemployment fraud and sexual harassment. Democrat Lynn Rivers managed to retain the open 13th District, defeating Republican John A. Schall.

● **Minnesota.** Democrats and Republicans traded open House seats in Minnesota, leaving the Democrats with the same 6-2 advantage they had in the state delegation in the 103rd Congress.

State Rep. Gil Gutknecht reclaimed the historically Republican southeast Minnesota 1st District for the GOP, held for the previous 12 years by Democratic Rep. Timothy J. Penny, who retired. Meanwhile, Democratic state Sen. William P. "Bill" Luther narrowly captured the 6th District seat in the Twin Cities' suburbs being vacated by successful GOP Senate candidate Rod Grams.

● **Nebraska.** Republicans won all three House seats, as Jon Christensen pulled off a narrow victory — 50 percent to 49 percent — over three-term Democratic Rep. Peter Hoagland. Hoagland, who had had a tough time holding on to his district in past elections, moved from the start to label Christensen as a conservative religious extremist. Christensen, who was aided by Christian activists, countered by tying Hoagland to Clinton.

● **Wisconsin.** Republicans gained one seat in Wisconsin. After two unsuccessful tries, Republican Mark W. Neumann succeeded in capturing the 1st District. Neumann lost to Democratic Rep. Peter W. Barca in a 1993 special election by 675 votes. He eked out a 1,120-vote win this time around (he also ran in 1992). Neumann focused on Barca's vote for the 1993 tax-raising deficit-reduction bill, saying that the incumbent broke his promise not to vote for a plan that included a Social Security tax increase or an energy tax.

● **Missouri.** Only one incumbent had a serious race, but conservative Democratic Rep. Harold L. Volkmer, aided by the NRA, scored an unexpectedly large 50 percent to 45 percent victory over state prosecutor Kenny Hulshof in the northeastern 9th District. The state's only open seat stayed in Democratic hands. State Rep. Karen McCarthy easily won her bid to succeed unsuccessful Senate candidate Alan Wheat in the Kansas City-based 5th District.

● **Dakotas.** Incumbents in North Dakota and South Dakota managed to hold on to their seats.

The West

Seats that Democrats had gained in Washington, California and Arizona returned to the GOP, while Democrats whose districts became more Republican in redistricting were washed out in the GOP tide. Clinton's unpopular policies on mining rights and endangered species proved problematic for Democrats in some states. Republicans gained 15 seats in the 13-state region, turning the Democrats' 55-38 seat majority into a 53-40 GOP advantage.

● **California.** California presented the biggest target of all in 1994, with one-third of its 30 Democrats defending seats in swing districts. The national tide proved strong enough for a three-seat GOP gain.

Two of the defeated Democrats were freshmen: Dan Hamburg in the northern coastal 1st District and Lynn Schenk in the 49th, which included parts of San Diego and its suburbs.

Hamburg's district was the more Democratic of the two (52 percent) but had shown itself willing to vote Republican before. In fact, Hamburg's successor was former Rep. Frank Riggs, whom Hamburg had defeated in 1992. Riggs won with 53 percent after successfully portraying Hamburg as too liberal for the district, which stretched from the outer suburbs of San Francisco to the Oregon line.

Schenk lost by about 4,700 votes to Brian P. Bilbray, a popular San Diego County supervisor who managed to downplay the abortion issue and neutralize Schenk's million-dollar campaign with effective door-to-door efforts.

The third incumbent to lose was Richard H. Lehman of the 19th District, who had won his sixth term in 1992 by 1 percentage point after the district had become less Democratic through redistricting. This time, Lehman lost by 17 percentage points to George P. Radanovich, a young winery owner from the highlands northeast of Fresno who campaigned hard on the Contract With America as well as on his penurious record as a Mariposa County supervisor.

California's other three freshmen were elected to open seats. Democrat Zoe Lofgren cruised to victory in the San Jose 16th District to succeed retiring Democrat Don Edwards, the delegation's dean. Former singer-songwriter Sonny Bono, a Republican, had no trouble claiming the 44th District seat of retiring Republican Al McCandless in Riverside County.

The third open seat was in the 22nd District (Santa Barbara, San Luis Obispo) previously held by GOP Senate candidate Michael Huffington. Despite deep divisions within the Santa Barbara County GOP, State Rep. Andrea Seastrand won by 1,563 votes, aided by the support of the Christian Coalition and the Eagle Forum.

Three senior Democrats had close calls. Vic Fazio, chairman of the Democratic Congressional Campaign Committee, managed only 50 percent against 33-year-old Tim Lefever in the 3rd District, despite a big fundraising advantage. George E. Brown Jr., chairman of the House Science Committee, had a near-death experience, getting by Republican Rob Guzman by 2 percentage points in the 42nd. And Anthony C. Beilenson defied the odds once again by turning back the well-funded challenge of Richard Sybert with just 49 percent of the vote in the 24th District (San Fernando Valley).

Republican freshman Ken Calvert, once thought highly vulnerable after damaging stories surfaced about his personal life and finances, won the 43rd District with 55 percent. The only Republican in the delegation to receive less was its new dean, Carlos J. Moorhead, who was re-elected with 53 percent in the Pasadena-based 27th District.

● **Washington.** The state's delegation had the biggest shakeout in the nation. In addition to knocking out Speaker Foley, Republicans defeated four other incumbents and picked up a Democratic-held open seat, leaving the GOP with a 7-2 majority in the delegation, virtually reversing the Democrats' previous 8-1 majority. Freshmen Maria Cantwell, Jay Inslee and

House Delegations in the 104th Congress

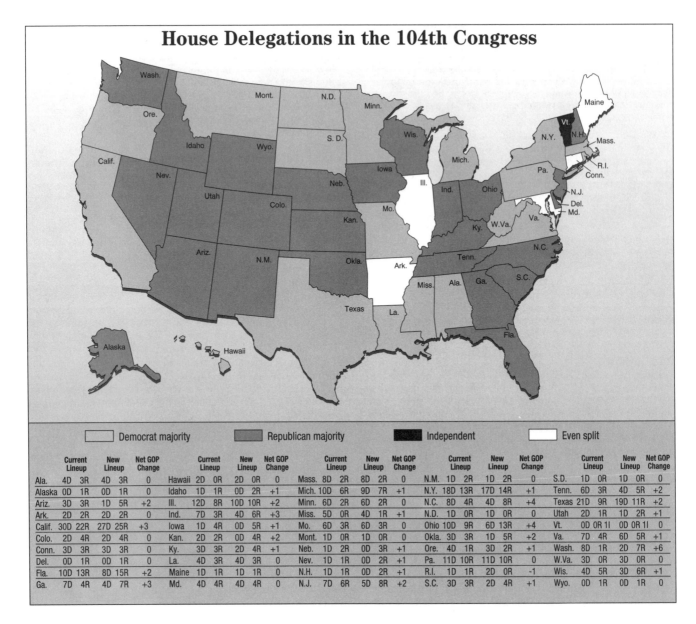

	Current Lineup		New Lineup		Net GOP Change
Democrat majority					
Republican majority					
Independent					
Even split					

	Current Lineup		New Lineup		Net GOP Change		Current Lineup		New Lineup		Net GOP Change		Current Lineup		New Lineup		Net GOP Change		Current Lineup		New Lineup		Net GOP Change		Current Lineup		New Lineup		Net GOP Change
Ala.	4D	3R	4D	3R	0	Hawaii	2D	0R	2D	0R	0	Mass.	8D	2R	8D	2R	0	N.M.	1D	2R	1D	2R	0	S.D.	1D	0R	1D	0R	0
Alaska	0D	1R	0D	1R	0	Idaho	1D	1R	0D	2R	+1	Mich.	10D	6R	9D	7R	+1	N.Y.	18D	13R	17D	14R	+1	Tenn.	6D	3R	4D	5R	+2
Ariz.	3D	3R	1D	5R	+2	Ill.	12D	8R	10D	10R	+2	Minn.	6D	2R	6D	2R	0	N.C.	8D	4R	4D	8R	+4	Texas	21D	9R	19D	11R	+2
Ark.	2D	2R	2D	2R	0	Ind.	7D	3R	4D	6R	+3	Miss.	5D	0R	4D	1R	+1	N.D.	1D	0R	1D	0R	0	Utah	2D	1R	1D	2R	+1
Calif.	30D	22R	27D	25R	+3	Iowa	1D	4R	0D	5R	+1	Mo.	6D	3R	6D	3R	0	Ohio	10D	9R	6D	13R	+4	Vt.	0D	0R 1I	0D	0R 1I	0
Colo.	2D	4R	2D	4R	0	Kan.	2D	2R	0D	4R	+2	Mont.	1D	0R	1D	0R	0	Okla.	3D	3R	1D	5R	+2	Va.	7D	4R	6D	5R	+1
Conn.	3D	3R	3D	3R	0	Ky.	3D	3R	2D	4R	+1	Neb.	1D	2R	0D	3R	+1	Ore.	4D	1R	3D	2R	+1	Wash.	8D	1R	2D	7R	+6
Del.	0D	1R	0D	1R	0	La.	4D	3R	4D	3R	0	Nev.	1D	1R	0D	2R	+1	Pa.	11D	10R	11D	10R	0	W.Va.	3D	0R	3D	0R	0
Fla.	10D	13R	8D	15R	+2	Maine	1D	1R	1D	1R	0	N.H.	1D	1R	0D	2R	+1	R.I.	1D	1R	2D	0R	-1	Wis.	4D	5R	3D	6R	+1
Ga.	7D	4R	4D	7R	+3	Md.	4D	4R	4D	4R	0	N.J.	7D	6R	5D	8R	+2	S.C.	3D	3R	2D	4R	+1	Wyo.	0D	1R	0D	1R	0

Mike Kreidler, who came in on the equally strong Democratic surge in 1992, lost their bids for re-election, as did three-term incumbent Jolene Unsoeld. Republicans also picked up the 2nd District seat of retiring Rep. Al Swift.

Foley's race, the nation's most high-profile House contest, was closer than the September primary had led some to expect. Possibly due to Foley's personal appeal and argument that the Spokane-based 5th District could not afford to lose his influence, Foley lost by only 2 percentage points to GOP lawyer George Nethercutt.

Making his first bid at elective office, Nethercutt had argued that the district needed a listener, not a Speaker, and echoed many voters' stated desire for less government. Foley was also the target of heavy spending from outside groups including the NRA, Americans for Limited Terms and a group opposing D.C. statehood. In addition, 1992 independent presidential candidate Ross Perot stumped for Nethercutt.

Cantwell, who had been the first Democrat in 40 years to represent the 1st District's North Seattle suburban area, lost by 6,444 votes and 4 percentage points to GOP lawyer Rick White, who accused her of voting more liberal than she talked.

Inslee lost a rematch with his 1992 opponent, former state Rep. Richard "Doc" Hastings, who took back the Republican 4th District with 53 percent. Two of Hastings' radio commercials featured a Clinton-sounding actor leaving a message on Inslee's answering machine, thanking Inslee for voting for his "tax increase" and for "every serious domestic spending" measure. Hastings also benefited from strong NRA support.

Kreidler lost to Randy Tate, another NRA-backed candidate who also had assistance from a conservative talk radio station that helped mobilize volunteers. Kreidler focused on Tate's conservative views but was on the defensive for his support of Clinton's budget and the crime bill.

Unsoeld, who had always had close races in her southwestern 3rd District, lost to state Sen. Linda Smith, who benefited from her grass-roots ties among Christian and anti-tax activists to become the state's first successful write-in nominee for Congress. Smith won with 52 percent.

In the 2nd, former state Sen. Jack Metcalf, who unsuccessfully challenged Swift in 1992, won with 55 percent against state Sen. Harriet Spanel. While Metcalf expressed some unconventional views, including calling for a return to

the gold standard, Spanel's liberal voting record was a major liability.

● **Arizona.** Democrats lost two of their three House seats in Arizona, as Republicans picked up the open 1st District vacated by unsuccessful Senate candidate Sam Coppersmith and defeated freshman Karan English.

In the 1st, Republican state Sen. Matt Salmon won a bitter, tightly fought contest with Democratic state Sen. Chuck Blanchard. The tension was not reflected in the result, however: Salmon won convincingly, 56 percent to 39 percent.

Waging his first political campaign, J. D. Hayworth, a popular former TV sports anchor, dealt English a resounding defeat, 55 percent to 41 percent, to capture the vast northeastern 6th District. Hayworth attacked English for voting with the House Democratic leadership and for Clinton's tax-raising deficit-reduction bill. He embraced the Contract With America as well as his own "Action Plan for Arizona."

● **Idaho.** Democratic incumbent Larry LaRocco began denouncing his GOP opponent, Helen Chenoweth, as a "mouthpiece for the radical right" only days after her surprise victory in the Republican primary — a strategy that appeared to be working for much of the campaign. But last-minute revelations that LaRocco had lied about the existence of a sexual discrimination dispute involving a former female assistant scuttled any chance the Democrat had of winning a third term. Chenoweth won by 10 percentage points.

● **Nevada.** Democratic incumbent James Bilbray helped make his 1st District a Democratic fortress in redistricting following the 1990 census. That almost enabled him to withstand a late-breaking scandal and gun control foes' anger over his vote for the crime bill. He fell fewer than 1,500 votes short of veterinarian and former casino executive John Ensign. Ironically, Bilbray lost just as his first cousin, Republican Brian P. Bilbray, was winning a seat in California, defeating freshman Democrat Schenk.

● **Utah.** After pumping at least $1.5 million of her own funds into Utah's 2nd District three-way brawl, Republican Enid Greene Waldholtz walked away with a victory over freshman Democrat Karen Shepherd and conservative independent Merrill Cook. Waldholtz, who narrowly lost to Shepherd in 1992, captured 46 percent of the vote to Shepherd's 36 percent, while Cook grabbed 18 percent.

Waldholtz, who may have been aided by GOP Sen. Orrin G. Hatch's renowned get-out-the-vote effort, highlighted her support for the GOP's Contract With America in some of her TV spots. Waldholtz also used targeted radio spots and direct mail to attack Shepherd as a liberal supporter of Clinton and to paint support for Cook as a wasted vote.

● **Montana.** Democratic incumbent Pat Williams, a staunch New Deal liberal viewed as vulnerable to an anti-Clinton tide, blunted a challenge by Republican Cy Jamison. Williams won his ninth term with 49 percent; Jamison received 42 percent. Jamison, the former head of the Bureau of Land Management, assailed Williams as "Bill Clinton's Pat" (mocking Williams' self-styled moniker, "Montana's Pat"). But Montana voters were far more familiar with Williams than with Jamison, a first-time candidate.

● **Oregon.** Freshman Democrat Elizabeth Furse survived an aggressive Republican challenger in the largely suburban 1st District. Absentee ballots put GOP state Sen. Jim Bunn on top in the 5th District, which was vacated by Democrat Mike Kopetski. The GOP retained its hold on eastern Oregon's 2nd District, where state Sen. Wes Cooley won the seat of retiring GOP Rep. Bob Smith.

● **Wyoming.** Republicans retained the open House seat of successful Senate candidate Craig Thomas. Republican state

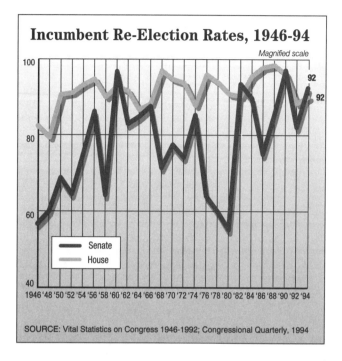

Incumbent Re-Election Rates, 1946-94

Magnified scale

Senate
House

1946 '48 '50 '52 '54 '56 '58 '60 '62 '64 '66 '68 '70 '72 '74 '76 '78 '80 '82 '84 '86 '88 '90 '92 '94

SOURCE: Vital Statistics on Congress 1946-1992; Congressional Quarterly, 1994

Sen. Barbara Cubin won it by 12 percentage points.

● Incumbents in Alaska, Colorado, Hawaii and New Mexico all won re-election without significant difficulty.

The East

Republicans realized their fewest gains in the 12 Eastern states. Indeed, three of the four Republican-held seats won by Democrats were in the East: Maine's 2nd District, Rhode Island's 1st and Pennsylvania's 18th.

● **Connecticut.** The closest race of 1994 was the rematch in Connecticut's 2nd between Sam Gejdenson and Republican former state Sen. Edward Munster. Unofficial returns gave Gejdenson a two-vote edge Nov. 8. The Connecticut Supreme Court declared Gejdenson the winner Dec. 16 by 21 votes.

During the campaign, Democrats including Clinton and Vice President Al Gore came to the state to boost Gejdenson's candidacy. But Munster told voters that Gejdenson had not done what he could have to preserve defense and insurance jobs in the district.

Gary A. Franks, named on almost every list of endangered House Republicans, managed to stay on the crest of the GOP tidal wave to win a third term in the 5th District. No longer the only black Republican in the House, Franks was to be joined by Oklahoma's Watts.

● **New York.** Despite Democratic Gov. Mario M. Cuomo's loss, the GOP gained virtually nothing in House races. Only one Democratic incumbent was defeated — George J. Hochbrueckner, who had never had an easy time holding on to his Republican-leaning Long Island 1st District. He lost to Michael P. Forbes, a former aide to GOP Sens. Alfonse M. D'Amato of New York and Connie Mack of Florida.

Freshman Democrat Maurice D. Hinchey was another top GOP target. Hinchey won his first term by 8,819 votes against Republican Bob Moppert, a conservative Broome County (Binghamton) legislator. Moppert returned for a second try, and while he came closer, he fell short once again.

Republicans managed to retain two GOP-leaning districts despite intraparty dissension that could have cost them the

race in less favorable years.

In the Hudson Valley 19th, moderate Republican Sue W. Kelly, a first-time candidate, won her race with 52 percent, a remarkable showing considering her opposition: Democrat Hamilton Fish Jr., the son of the 13-term Republican incumbent, Hamilton Fish Sr., and former Republican Rep. Joseph J. DioGuardi, who was running to her right on the Conservative and Right to Life ballot lines. Kelly likely was boosted by a heavy turnout for successful GOP gubernatorial candidate George E. Pataki, whose hometown, Peekskill, was in the 19th.

The only Republican House member to lose in a primary in 1994 was 4th District freshman David A. Levy. Former state Rep. Daniel Frisa narrowly defeated Levy, the candidate of the Nassau County GOP organization, in a stunning upset. Levy remained on the ballot, however, as the Conservative Party nominee and tried to overturn Frisa's primary win in court. But all the distractions did not hinder Frisa; he beat Democrat Philip M. Schiliro, who was also the 1992 nominee, 50 percent to 37 percent.

● **Pennsylvania.** The cliffhanger was in the 15th District, where freshman Paul McHale squeaked by challenger Jim Yeager.

In the 13th District, another freshman Democrat, Marjorie Margolies-Mezvinsky, was unable to overcome the residue from her pivotal 1993 vote for Clinton's controversial budget-reconciliation bill. She lost the suburban district to the candidate she defeated in 1992, Montgomery County Commissioner Jon D. Fox. Democrats offset her loss by capturing the seat in western Pennsylvania being vacated by Republican Senate winner Rick Santorum. It was won by Mike Doyle, an insurance company owner.

● **Maine.** In the 1st District, vacated when Democrat Thomas H. Andrews decided to try for the Senate seat, political newcomer James B. Longley Jr., a Republican, defeated Democrat Dennis L. Dutremble, the state Senate president and member of a prominent York County political family. In the 2nd District, which Republican Olympia J. Snowe gave up to run for the Senate, state Sen. John Baldacci outpaced GOP state Rep. Richard A. Bennett and two independents.

● **New Hampshire.** Republican Bill Zeliff swept to re-election in the 1st District with nearly two-thirds of the vote.

Democrat Dick Swett lost in the 2nd to Republican challenger Charles Bass, a son of the district's one-time congressman, Perkins Bass. Bass' victory returned to Republican hands a seat that had not been held by a Democrat in 76 years before Swett's election in 1990.

● **New Jersey.** Only one incumbent came to grief in 1994: freshman Democrat Herb Klein, who lost a tight race to Republican Bill Martini in the northern New Jersey 8th. Advertising himself as a fresh, fiscally responsible, socially moderate Republican, Martini, a Passaic County freeholder, cut into Klein's support among conservative Democrats and women voters in the politically competitive district.

Republican state Rep. Frank A. LoBiondo had little trouble winning the 2nd District vacated by retiring Democratic Rep. William J. Hughes. And GOP state Rep. Rodney Frelinghuysen, scion of a political family whose tradition in public service dated to the Revolutionary War, won the 11th District seat of the late GOP Rep. Dean A. Gallo.

● **Rhode Island.** Rhode Island was the only state where the GOP suffered a net loss (one) in House seats.

Bucking the national trend, Democratic state Rep. Patrick J. Kennedy, the younger son of Massachusetts Sen. Edward M. Kennedy, succeeded in handing the traditionally Democratic 1st District back to his party. Kennedy handily defeated Republican physician Kevin C. Vigilante, making him the youngest member in the 104th Congress. The seat was vacated when Republican Ronald K. Machtley ran for governor. (He lost in the GOP primary.)

● **Maryland.** No House incumbent in Maryland had a close call. But Republican state Rep. Robert L. Ehrlich Jr. scored a resounding victory in the open 2nd District, a Baltimore-area seat with a 2-1 Democratic registration edge.

● Incumbents in Vermont, Delaware, Massachusetts and West Virginia all won re-election. The closest calls were in Vermont and Massachusetts.

Vermont Rep. Bernard Sanders, the House's only independent member, narrowly hung on for a third term.

Although Sanders escaped a Democratic challenger, Republican state Senate Majority Leader John Carroll held Sanders to 50 percent, taking 47 percent himself. Massachusetts freshman Republican Rep. Peter G. Torkildsen beat Salem lawyer John F. Tierney by 4 percentage points. ∎

GOP Surge Extends to Statehouses

Elections for governor and state legislative seats Nov. 8 were not as dramatic as the congressional elections, but they were close. No incumbent Republican governor lost, and no legislative chamber changed hands in favor of the Democrats. Republicans increased their share of governorships to 30, their first majority since 1970. They also reached near parity in state legislatures, a status they had not enjoyed since 1968.

Independent Angus King was elected governor in Maine, while two previously independent governorships reverted to party control in Connecticut and Alaska.

Maine was the only governorship the GOP lost. One Republican governor, South Dakota's Walter D. Miller, had been defeated in the primary by William J. Janklow, who subsequently won. By contrast, the Democrats lost 10 governorships. One incumbent, Rhode Island's Bruce Sundlun, was defeated in his September primary by state Sen. Myrth York, who then lost the general election. Four other incumbents lost Nov. 8 (Mario M. Cuomo in New York, Bruce King in New Mexico, Ann W.

Richards in Texas and James E. Folsom Jr. in Alabama). Six open seats that had been Democratic went Republican.

Seven Democratic incumbents were re-elected, but only three got 60 percent of the vote or more, a mark surpassed by seven of the 10 Republicans re-elected.

As a result of the Nov. 8 elections, Republicans controlled the governor's mansion in four of the five most populous states and eight of the most populous nine. They also had a majority of governorships in each geographic region.

For Indiana Gov. Evan Bayh, chairman of the Democratic Governors' Association, the results represented voters' disillusionment with government.

"It's apparent that there was a tidal wave running across the country, and it hit the statehouse just as it hit the U.S. House," he said. "The American people are disenchanted with government. They don't want big government, bureaucracy or higher taxes, and they want to see progress toward solving the problems they encounter in their daily lives."

The Midwest

The GOP's best region in recent years had been the Midwest, and it remained so, proving that voters' disenchantment was with Democrats, not incumbents. Touting their records of fiscal responsibility, Republican incumbents in Illinois, Michigan, Ohio and Wisconsin cruised to victories.

Iowa's GOP Gov. Terry E. Branstad barely survived a primary challenge, yet he was easily re-elected to a fourth term with 57 percent against Democratic Attorney General Bonnie Campbell. Branstad, who criticized Campbell for her opposition to the death penalty, was helped by the strong backing from conservative Christians.

Although Christian activists opposed Gov. Arne Carlson in the Minnesota Republican convention, Carlson followed up on his primary victory with a 62 percent win over Democratic state Sen. John Marty. Carlson's total was the highest for any Minnesota GOP gubernatorial candidate ever.

The only Midwestern Democrat facing voters in 1994, Nebraska's Ben Nelson, garnered the highest vote of any gubernatorial candidate. His 73 percent win in a conservative state where Republicans outnumbered Democrats was attributed to the weaknesses of GOP challenger Gene Spence and Nelson's fiscal conservatism.

The one governorship to change hands in the Midwest was in Kansas, where GOP Secretary of State Bill Graves won 64 percent over Democratic Rep. Jim Slattery to succeed retiring Democratic Gov. Joan Finney. Initially perceived to be the front-runner, Slattery was dragged down in the heavily Republican-leaning state by his association with an unpopular Congress, president and governor.

The East

Republicans won four seats in the usually Democratic East: New York, Pennsylvania, Connecticut and Rhode Island.

The tax cut platform that gained national attention in 1993 when New Jersey Gov. Christine Todd Whitman upset incumbent Democrat James J. Florio also worked to unseat New York's Cuomo, who was arguably the nation's most prominent liberal Democratic governor. After 12 years in office, Cuomo had absorbed most of New York voters' dissatisfaction with the state's economic and social ailments. They turned to George E. Pataki, a little-known legislator whose party nomination was engineered by GOP Sen. Alfonse M. D'Amato.

With the election of Republican Tom Ridge, Pennsylvania voters continued their 40-year pattern of changing party control of the governorship at eight-year intervals. Ridge defeated a field that included Democratic Lt. Gov. Mark Singel and independent anti-abortion candidate Peg Luksik. A telegenic Vietnam veteran, Ridge ran a tight campaign and made the most of revelations that Singel, as head of the Board of Pardons, recommended parole for a man later charged with rape and murder in New York. Ridge was one of three GOP former congressmen elected to governorships in 1994.

Republican John G. Rowland, also a former congressman, pulled ahead to win the Connecticut slot, garnering 36 percent to Democrat William Curry's 33 percent. Rowland emphasized his promise to repeal the state income tax instituted by his predecessor, retiring independent Gov. Lowell P. Weicker.

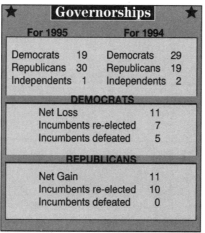

Governorships

For 1995		For 1994	
Democrats	19	Democrats	29
Republicans	30	Republicans	19
Independents	1	Independents	2

DEMOCRATS
Net Loss	11
Incumbents re-elected	7
Incumbents defeated	5

REPUBLICANS
Net Gain	11
Incumbents re-elected	10
Incumbents defeated	0

In Rhode Island, one of the nation's most decidedly Democratic states, state Sen. York was unable to fend off the challenge of Republican Lincoln C. Almond, a former U.S. attorney. With crime a top priority of Rhode Islanders, Almond's take-charge, tell-it-like-it-is style scored points.

In Maryland, where Democrats had a 2-1 registration advantage and Republicans had not elected a governor since Spiro T. Agnew in 1966, conservative state Rep. Ellen Sauerbrey came within 6,000 votes of a shocking upset. Despite being outspent, Sauerbrey and her promise of a 24 percent tax cut stayed on the heels of Prince George's County Executive Parris N. Glendening.

In Maine, where independent presidential candidate Ross Perot made his best showing nationwide in 1992, voters again showed their fondness for outsiders, electing King. A millionaire talk show host who promised to bring a new approach to government, King took 35 percent in the four-candidate field that included former Democratic Gov. Joseph E. Brennan.

For a handful of Eastern incumbents, the question was not whether they would win re-election, but by how much. Democratic Gov. Howard Dean in Vermont captured 69 percent. GOP Gov. William F. Weld in Massachusetts and GOP Gov. Stephen Merrill in New Hampshire won with 70 percent or more.

The South

Republican gains penetrated the heart of the South, capturing the majority of governorships for the first time since Reconstruction. Republicans laid claim to four previously Democratic-held slots: Alabama, Texas, Oklahoma and Tennessee. The GOP also captured two Southern legislative chambers — North Carolina's House and Florida's Senate — for the first time in the 20th century.

Party switching was popular in Alabama. Not only did Sen. Richard C. Shelby bolt to the GOP one day after the elections, but former Democratic Gov. Fob James Jr. (1979-83) was swept back into office as a Republican. His narrow victory over the unelected Democratic incumbent James E. Folsom Jr. was the GOP's third straight gubernatorial victory in Alabama. Folsom was sworn in as governor after his Republican predecessor was removed from office in April 1993 upon conviction on charges of misusing campaign funds.

In Texas, Republican George W. Bush, eldest son of former President George Bush, beat colorful Democrat Richards by running an aggressive, gaffe-free campaign in which he portrayed her as soft on crime and unable to deliver on her 1990 promise of a "new Texas." Bush became only the second Republican governor of Texas in more than a century by touting plans to curb state regulation of schools, cut welfare spending and impose tougher penalties on criminals.

Former U.S. Attorney Frank Keating rode the GOP wave in Oklahoma to become the state's fourth Republican governor in the postwar era. Keating took 47 percent of the vote against Democratic Lt. Gov. Jack Mildren, who got 30 percent, and independent Wes Watkins, a former Democratic House member who took 23 percent.

Nashville Mayor Phil Bredesen's personal wealth was no match for the GOP tide in Tennessee. Despite spending more

Governors After 1994 Election

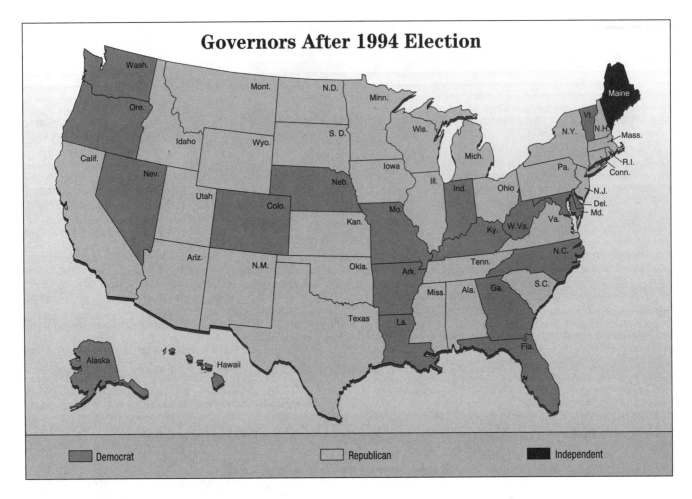

Democrat   Republican   Independent

than $6 million of his own money, Democrat Bredesen took only 45 percent against GOP Rep. Don Sundquist. Sundquist emphasized his opposition to a state income tax and his promise to make government, including the state's new health care system, more responsive.

In South Carolina, former state Rep. David Beasley narrowly retained the slot of retiring GOP Gov. Carroll A. Campbell, with help from Christian activists and Campbell's campaign organization. A convert to the GOP in 1992, Beasley managed to bridge the gap in the state Republican Party, which had been wracked by divisions between Christian conservatives and more moderate old guard Republicans. While Beasley's religious ties were used against him, Democratic Lt. Gov. Nick Theodore's campaign stumbled after his narrow runoff win.

The sole exception to the large-state trend toward the GOP, Florida Democratic Gov. Lawton Chiles narrowly headed off a stiff challenge by Republican Jeb Bush, another son of the former president, to win a second term. Chiles, who riled some with a tax increase proposal early in his term, largely relied on his folksy charm and personal popularity. Bush had difficulty convincing voters that his conservative mantle of change would make up for his lack of governing experience.

In addition to Chiles, two Southern Democrats — both of whom had close ties to Clinton — held on to their posts. In Georgia, Democrat Zell Miller squeaked by with 51 percent over wealthy GOP businessman Guy Millner, who made Clinton a major theme of his campaign. And Clinton's successor in Arkansas, Jim Guy Tucker, scored a Democratic

landslide victory over GOP businessman Sheffield Nelson, taking every county in the state but one.

The West

Opposition to Clinton's environmental policies contributed to the GOP's pickup of three seats in the West — Wyoming, Idaho and New Mexico — giving Republicans control of seven of the region's 13 gubernatorial seats.

Democrats normally held little in Wyoming except the governorship, but they lost even that. State Sen. Jim Geringer, a farmer, was the first Republican since 1970 to win the office, taking 59 percent over Democratic Secretary of State Kathy Karpan, one of the first state officeholders to endorse Clinton in 1992.

In Idaho, Democrat Larry EchoHawk hoped to make history as the nation's first American Indian governor. But voter anger aimed at the Democratic candidates helped erase what had been a double-digit lead. Phil Batt became the first GOP governor in Idaho in 24 years.

In Arizona, Republican Gov. Fife Symington had been considered the nation's most endangered GOP incumbent because of a federal grand jury investigation into his role in the failure of a savings and loan. But after trailing in statewide polls for much of the year, Symington surged past Democrat Eddie Basha, owner of a chain of supermarkets, to a 53 percent victory.

In California, Republican Pete Wilson staged a model political comeback to win re-election as governor of the nation's largest state. After his approval rating tumbled as low as the teens, Wilson rebuilt his standing with conservative

Governors and Governors-Elect

Listed below are the governors and governors-elect of the 50 states and the year in which the their terms expired. The names of governors elected in November are in boldface.

Alabama - Fob James Jr. (R) 1998
Alaska - Tony Knowles (D) 1998
Arizona - Fife Symington (R) 1998 *
Arkansas - Jim Guy Tucker (D) 1998 *
California - Pete Wilson (R) 1998 *
Colorado - Roy Romer (D) 1998 *
Connecticut - John G. Rowland (R) 1998
Delaware - Thomas R. Carper (D) 1996
Florida - Lawton Chiles (D) 1998 *
Georgia - Zell Miller (D) 1998 *
Hawaii - Benjamin J. Cayetano (D) 1998
Idaho - Phil Batt (R) 1998
Illinois - Jim Edgar (R) 1998 *
Indiana - Evan Bayh (D) 1996
Iowa - Terry E. Branstad (R) 1998 *
Kansas - Bill Graves (R) 1998
Kentucky - Brereton Jones (D) 1995
Louisiana - Edwin W. Edwards (D) 1995
Maine - Angus King (I) 1998
Maryland - Parris N. Glendening (D) 1998
Massachusetts - William F. Weld (R) 1998 *
Michigan - John Engler (R) 1998 *
Minnesota - Arne Carlson (R) 1998 *
Mississippi - Kirk Fordice (R) 1995
Missouri - Mel Carnahan (D) 1996

Montana - Marc Racicot (R) 1996
Nebraska - Ben Nelson (D) 1998 *
Nevada - Bob Miller (D) 1998 *
New Hampshire - Stephen Merrill (R) 1996 *
New Jersey - Christine Todd Whitman (R) 1997
New Mexico - Gary E. Johnson (R) 1998
New York - George E. Pataki (R) 1998
North Carolina - James B. Hunt Jr. (D) 1996
North Dakota - Edward T. Schafer (R) 1996
Ohio - George V. Voinovich (R) 1998 *
Oklahoma - Frank Keating (R) 1998
Oregon - John Kitzhaber (D) 1998
Pennsylvania - Tom Ridge (R) 1998
Rhode Island - Lincoln C. Almond (R) 1998
South Carolina - David Beasley (R) 1998
South Dakota - William J. Janklow (R) 1998
Tennessee - Don Sundquist (R) 1998
Texas - George W. Bush (R) 1998
Utah - Michael O. Leavitt (R) 1996
Vermont - Howard Dean (D) 1996 *
Virginia - George F. Allen (R) 1997
Washington - Mike Lowry (D) 1996
West Virginia - Gaston Caperton (D) 1996
Wisconsin - Tommy G. Thompson (R) 1998 *
Wyoming - Jim Geringer (R) 1998

* Incumbent

Note: New Hampshire and Vermont elected governors every two years.

---

positions on crime, welfare, school choice and immigration. Wilson embraced Proposition 187, aimed at denying nearly all public services to undocumented immigrants, which was overwhelmingly approved Nov. 8.

The Democratic nominee, state Treasurer Kathleen Brown, opposed the ballot measure. The daughter and sister of the state's last two Democratic governors, Brown showed virtually no appeal beyond the party's base and wound up with 41 percent of the vote.

In Alaska, GOP businessman Jim Campbell's anti-Clinton campaign went so far as to compare Democrat Tony Knowles' hair with Clinton's. Campbell charged that the physical similarities between Knowles and Clinton mirrored their willingness to increase taxes and environmental restrictions. Knowles was certified as the winner Nov. 30 with a 583-vote advantage.

Bucking the trend, Democratic incumbents prevailed in Nevada and Colorado.

Nevada Gov. Bob Miller's re-election ended a turbulent year in which his prospects were widely downplayed. But Miller, a centrist in the tradition of Democratic Sens. Richard H. Bryan and Harry Reid, emphatically rebuffed a challenge by Las Vegas Mayor Jan Laverty Jones in the Sept. 6 Democratic primary and went on to defeat GOP state Rep. Jim Gibbons, a conservative running on an anti-tax platform.

Trying for a third term, Colorado's Roy Romer had been blasted for being "too liberal for too long" by wealthy GOP oilman Bruce Benson. But Benson's momentum was stopped by a series of negative personal disclosures that emerged midway through the campaign. Romer took 55 percent.

Despite the unpopularity of Oregon's retiring Gov. Barbara Roberts, Democrats held on. Former Rep. Denny Smith never recovered from a bruising GOP primary fight and ended up losing to former state Sen. John Kitzhaber by 9 percentage points.

Kitzhaber, an emergency room physician, was best known as the author of a 1991 state health plan that rationed coverage for a range of illnesses under Medicaid.

In Hawaii, Lt. Gov. Benjamin J. Cayetano retained the governorship of the nation's most Democratic state. Cayetano was the nation's first governor of Filipino ancestry. Former GOP Rep. Patricia F. Saiki (1987-1991), who had been the GOP's best chance of capturing the governor's mansion in 35 years, finished third.

In New Mexico, Green Party candidate Roberto Mondragon captured 10 percent of the vote, most of which otherwise probably would have gone to incumbent Gov. Bruce King. Hampered by the perception that he had been in office too long, Democrat King was denied a fourth term by GOP newcomer Gary E. Johnson, who took 50 percent of the vote. ∎

Democrats Lose Stronghold in South

While the Republican tide of 1994 was boosted by major GOP gains in the West and Midwest, the flood's most dramatic source was the long delayed bursting of the dam that had restrained Southern conservatives from voting Republican. It had been more than a quarter century since the Republicans peeled away the presidential level of the once Democratic South. On Nov. 8, they peeled away the congressional and gubernatorial levels in such convincing fashion that if the "Solid South" rose again, it would do so for the Republicans.

Never since Reconstruction had the GOP held a majority of the governorships in the South. Nor had it held a majority of the region's seats in the House or in the Senate. But after Nov. 8, they held majorities in all three categories. (Congressional Quarterly's definition of the South included the 11 states of the Confederacy plus Kentucky and Oklahoma.)

The party of Abraham Lincoln picked up 19 House seats across Dixie, to turn a 54-83 deficit into a 73-64 advantage.

Republicans gained three Southern Senate seats at the polls and with the Nov. 9 party switch of Alabama Sen. Richard C. Shelby transformed a 12-14 deficit into a 16-10 edge.

They won four governorships in the South, to jump from three to seven of the region's 13.

The election changed the whole political map. Before the Nov. 8 vote, the lone Southern state in which the GOP held a majority of U.S. House seats was Florida. In the 104th Congress, Republicans would hold a majority in seven states — Florida, Georgia, Kentucky, North Carolina, Oklahoma, South Carolina and Tennessee. In Oklahoma and Tennessee, Republican dominance was almost complete: The GOP controlled the governorship, both Senate seats and a majority of House seats.

A population influx in the past few decades had reshaped the political landscape to the Republicans' advantage. Long-time Democratic voters had been overwhelmed in many parts of the South by more independent or GOP-oriented newcomers. Younger voters had found the region's historical Democratic roots irrelevant to their concerns.

And the GOP assumed a more aggressive role, fielding candidates where it once gave the Democrats a free ride. The Republican candidates emphasized traditional values that resonated among the region's white voters, who constituted a majority of the electorate in every Southern state.

No Help From Clinton

Although President Clinton was a Southerner, the growing gulf between the Democratic Party and Southern whites had widened during his presidency. He was viewed with some suspicion by them during the 1992 campaign, ending up with less than one-third of the region's electoral votes.

Clinton got his presidency off on the wrong foot with many Southern whites by siding with a group that was not widely popular in Dixie, homosexuals, over an institution that was, the military. On issues from personal character to gun control, he continued to rub many Southerners the wrong way.

And what was already difficult terrain for many Democratic congressional candidates had been made worse by the latest round of redistricting. That remapping created more minority districts across the South, in turn leaving a number of moderate Democrats to run in increasingly conservative districts.

Most of the Democrats' Southern losses came in districts that voted for George Bush for president in 1988 and 1992. Of the 19 seats that Democrats lost in the region in 1994, 14 were in districts that Bush carried in 1992. That included all nine seats that were open as a result of Democrats who were leaving office.

Five of the Bush-district Democrats won

The Last Republican House: 83rd Congress 1953-54

House-83rd Congress
- Republican majority
- Democratic majority
- Even split

Forty Years of Change in Dixie

House

	1955	1965	1975	1985	1994	1995
Ala.	9D-0R	3D-5R	4D-3R	5D-2R	4D-3R	4D-3R
Ark.	6-0	4-0	3-1	3-1	2-2	2-2
Fla.	7-1	10-2	10-5	12-7	10-13	8-15
Ga.	10-0	9-1	10-0	8-2	7-4	4-7
Ky.	6-2	6-1	5-2	4-3	3-3	2-4
La.	8-0	8-0	6-2	6-2	4-3	4-3
Miss.	6-0	4-1	3-2	3-2	5-0	4-1
N.C.	11-1	9-2	9-2	6-5	8-4	4-8
Okla.	5-1	5-1	6-0	5-1	3-3	1-5
S.C.	6-0	6-0	5-1	3-3	3-3	2-4
Tenn.	7-2	6-3	5-3	6-3	6-3	4-5
Texas	21-1	23-0	21-3	17-10	21-9	19-11
Va.	8-2	8-2	5-5	4-6	7-4	6-5
Total	110-10	101-18	92-29	83-47	83-54	64-73

Senate

	1955	1965	1975	1985	1994	1995
Total	26-0	22-4	17-8-1	14-12	14-12	10-16

re-election with less than 55 percent of the vote, including Robert E. "Bud" Cramer of Alabama, W. G. "Bill" Hefner of North Carolina, John M. Spratt Jr. of South Carolina, Charles W. Stenholm of Texas and L. F. Payne Jr. of Virginia.

One Southern Democratic officeholder decided not to wait for the voters' judgment but to defect to the GOP on his own. Shelby made the jump the day after the election.

Shelby had been a prospective party switcher for some time: He was the only Senate Democrat to vote with Clinton and with his party less than half the time in 1993.

Democratic Presidents Aid GOP

It had not been under conservative GOP presidents such as Richard M. Nixon or Ronald Reagan that the GOP had made its most dramatic gains in the South, but rather under recent Democratic presidents, ironically all of them Southerners.

It was out of the racial friction that exploded during the Lyndon B. Johnson administration in the 1960s that Republicans crafted a presidential campaign strategy keyed to attracting Southern whites. Under LBJ, the number of Southern GOP House seats rose from 14 to 31, GOP Senate seats from three to seven and Republican governorships from one to four.

Republicans did not move forward again in the South until Jimmy Carter took office. But under Carter, the number of GOP House members in the South jumped from 30 to 43, Republican senators from seven to 11 and governors from two to five.

After a dozen years of Republican ups and downs in the South, an even more dramatic upsurge was under way under Clinton. Within weeks of Clinton's election, Democrats lost a Senate seat in Georgia. Within months of his inauguration, Democrats lost another Senate seat in Texas. And earlier in 1994, historically Democratic House seats in Kentucky and Oklahoma fell to the Republicans. ∎

Voters Favor Term Limits, Reject Tax Restrictions

Voters across the country considered more than 70 citizen initiatives Nov. 8, rejecting about half of them overall. Initiatives were on the ballot in 22 states. Among the most successful were calls for term limits, campaign finance reform and victims' rights. Several states confounded conventional wisdom by rejecting proposals that would have restricted lawmakers' ability to impose new taxes. "It shows that the voters really have thought out the initiatives before voting on them," said Elizabeth Bender with Americans for Tax Reform. "If everything had passed, we'd have been a little worried."

California passed one of the more controversial measures in the country, Proposition 187, to bar illegal immigrants from receiving any public benefits other than emergency medical care. Parts of the proposition were to take effect immediately but were delayed by court order.

To even appear on the ballot, voter initiatives first had to garner a requisite number of voter signatures; 24 states allowed such "direct democracy" procedures.

● **Term limits.** Congressional term limits were on the ballot in eight states and were approved in seven. Voters in Utah departed from the trend slightly by rejecting a measure to restrict House members to four terms. Utah previously had adopted limits of six terms for House members and two terms for senators.

Alaska, Idaho, Maine, Massachusetts, Nebraska and Nevada all passed limits for their members of Congress, while Colorado tightened the limits it had imposed in 1990 (the first

for Congress in the nation).

Overall, 22 states had congressional term limits. Mississippi, the only state that accepted citizen initiatives yet had not passed congressional term limits, scheduled a vote on such a measure for 1995.

House Republicans had vowed to bring a federal constitutional amendment on congressional term limits to the floor during their first 100 days in office in 1995 as part of their "Contract With America." *(Term limits, p. 314)*

● **Taxes.** While voters passed restrictions on congressional service, they overwhelmingly opposed calls to limit the taxing power of their elected officials. Of the four states with measures requiring either legislative supermajorities or voter approval of new taxes, only one, Nevada, passed its initiative. Voters in Missouri, Montana and Oregon all rejected such requirements.

● **Campaign reform.** Voters across the country largely voted in favor of moves to reform financing of state campaigns. Missouri, Montana, Oregon and Nevada passed various restrictions on campaign contributions, while Colorado and Massachusetts defeated restrictive measures.

● **Crime.** Calls to impose tougher punishments on criminals and protect victims' rights also proved popular among voters. Oregon set mandatory sentences for felons 15 and older, while California enacted its "three-strikes-you're-out" measure, toughening sentences for repeat offenders.

● **Other.** In other initiative action Nov. 8:
● Oregon banned hunting black bears with bait or cougars with dogs.
● Oregon decided to allow terminally ill adults to obtain prescriptions for lethal drugs.
● Washington state decided to allow people other than dentists to make and sell false teeth.
● Massachusetts banned rent control.
● Alaska decided not to move its capital from Juneau to Wasilla.
● Idaho and Oregon voted down measures directed against expanded rights for homosexuals.
● Wyoming rejected a measure that would have subjected doctors who performed abortions to felony prosecution except in the case of rape, incest or threat to a woman's life. ∎

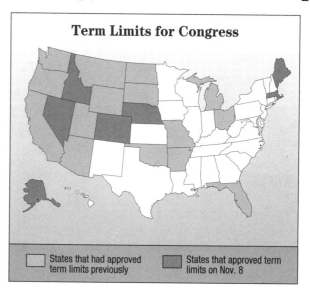

Term Limits for Congress

☐ States that had approved term limits previously   ▨ States that approved term limits on Nov. 8

Utah had previously limited House members to six terms and senators to two. A ballot measure limiting House members to four terms was rejected in that state Nov. 8.

1994 Election Results

Here are the official 1994 vote returns for House, Senate and gubernatorial races from the 50 state election boards. Vote totals are included for all candidates who were listed on the ballot and for write-ins whose votes equaled at least 0.1 percent of the total, either individually or as a group. The vote percentages for each race do not always add to 100 due to rounding and the exclusion of scattered write-ins, as well as the "None of these candidates" line in Nevada.

The box below is a key to party designation.
Other symbols:
- • incumbent
- x candidate without opposition; no vote was tallied
- AL at-large district

	Vote Total	%

ALABAMA

Governor
Fob James Jr. (R)	604,926	50.3
• James E. Folsom Jr. (D)	594,169	49.4
Write-ins	2,874	.2

House
1 • Sonny Callahan (R)	103,431	67.3
Don Womack (D)	50,227	32.7
Write-ins	109	.1
2 • Terry Everett (R)	124,465	73.6
Brian Dowling (D)	44,694	26.4
3 • Glen Browder (D)	93,924	63.6
Ben Hand (R)	53,757	36.4
4 • Tom Bevill (D)	119,436	98.5
Write-ins	1,826	1.5
5 • Robert E. "Bud" Cramer (D)	88,693	50.5
Wayne Parker (R)	86,923	49.5
6 • Spencer Bachus (R)	155,047	79.0
Larry Fortenberry (D)	41,030	20.9
Write-ins	145	.1
7 • Earl F. Hilliard (D)	116,150	76.9
Alfred J. Middleton Sr. (R)	34,814	23.0
Write-ins	153	.1

ALASKA

Governor
Tony Knowles (D)	87,693	41.1
James O. "Jim" Campbell (R)	87,157	40.8
John B. "Jack" Coghill (AKI)	27,838	13.0
Jim Sykes (GREEN)	8,727	4.1
Ralph K. Winterrowd II (PP)	1,743	.8
Write-ins	277	.1

House
AL • Don Young (R)	118,537	56.9
Tony Smith (D)	68,172	32.7
Jonni Whitmore (GREEN)	21,277	10.2
Write-ins	254	.1

ARIZONA

Governor
• Fife Symington (R)	593,492	52.5
Eddie Basha (D)	500,702	44.3
John Buttrick (LIBERT)	35,222	3.1

Senate
Jon Kyl (R)	600,999	53.7
Sam Coppersmith (D)	442,510	39.5
Scott Grainger (LIBERT)	75,493	6.7

House
1 Matt Salmon (R)	101,350	56.0
Chuck Blanchard (D)	70,627	39.0
Bob Howarth (LIBERT)	8,890	4.9
2 • Ed Pastor (D)	62,589	62.3
Robert MacDonald (R)	32,797	32.7
James Bertrand (LIBERT)	5,060	5.0
3 • Bob Stump (R)	145,396	70.1
Howard Lee Sprague (D)	61,939	29.9
4 John Shadegg (R)	116,714	60.2
Carol Cure (D)	69,760	36.0
Mark J. Yannone (LIBERT)	7,428	3.8
5 • Jim Kolbe (R)	149,514	67.7
Gary Auerbach (D)	63,436	28.7
Phillip W. Murphy (LIBERT)	7,821	3.5
6 J.D. Hayworth (R)	107,060	54.6
• Karan English (D)	81,321	41.5
Sequoia R. Fuller (LIBERT)	7,687	3.9

ARKANSAS

Governor
• Jim Guy Tucker (D)	428,936	59.8
Sheffield Nelson (R)	287,904	40.2

House
1 • Blanche Lambert (D)	95,290	53.4
Warren Dupwe (R)	83,147	46.6
2 • Ray Thornton (D)	97,580	57.4
Bill Powell (R)	72,473	42.6
3 • Tim Hutchinson (R)	129,800	67.7
Berta L. Seitz (D)	61,883	32.3

4 • Jay Dickey (R)	87,469	51.8
Jay Bradford (D)	81,370	48.2

CALIFORNIA

Governor
• Pete Wilson (R)	4,777,674	55.2
Kathleen Brown (D)	3,517,777	40.6
Richard Rider (LIBERT)	149,123	1.7
Jerome "Jerry" McCready (AMI)	133,734	1.5
Gloria Estela La Riva (PFP)	80,354	.9

Senate
• Diane Feinstein (D)	3,977,063	46.8
Michael Huffington (R)	3,811,501	44.8
Elizabeth Cervantes Barron (PFP)	255,036	3.0
Richard Benjamin Boddie (LIBERT)	178,951	2.1
Paul Meeuwenberg (AMI)	142,630	1.7
Barbara Blong (GREEN)	137,710	1.6

House
1 Frank Riggs (R)	106,870	53.3
• Dan Hamburg (D)	93,717	46.7
2 • Wally Herger (R)	137,863	64.2
Mary Jacobs (D)	55,958	26.1
Devvy Kidd (AMI)	15,569	7.2
Harry H. "Doc" Pendery (LIBERT)	5,417	2.5
3 • Vic Fazio (D)	97,093	49.8
Tim Lefever (R)	89,964	46.1
Ross Crain (LIBERT)	8,100	4.2
4 • John T. Doolittle (R)	144,936	61.3
Katie Hirning (D)	82,505	34.9
Damon C. Falconi (LIBERT)	8,882	3.8
5 • Robert T. Matsui (D)	125,042	68.5
Robert S. Dinsmore (R)	52,905	29.0
Gordon Mors (AMI)	4,649	2.5
6 • Lynn Woolsey (D)	137,642	58.1
Michael J. Nugent (R)	88,940	37.6
Louis Beary (LIBERT)	6,203	2.6
Ernest K. Jones Jr. (PFP)	4,055	1.7
7 • George Miller (D)	116,105	69.7
Charles V. Hughes (R)	45,698	27.4
William A. "Bill" Callison (PFP)	4,798	2.9
8 • Nancy Pelosi (D)	137,642	81.8

Abbreviations for Party Designations

ACP	— A Connecticut Party	DFL	— Democratic Farmer-Labor	KTAX	— Taxpayers Party of Kentucky	PHA	— Perot Hispano American
ADEP	— A Delaware Party			L	— Liberal	PP	— People's Party
AKI	— Alaskan Independence	DIA	— Democracy In Action	LAWR	— LaRouche Was Right	PV	— People of Vermont
AM	— American	FAS	— Fascist	LIBERT	— Libertarian	R	— Republican
AMI	— American Independent	FUP	— Fed Up Party	LIF	— Long Island First	RTL	— Right to Life
ATP	— Ax Taxes Party	GC	— Gun Control Party	LU	— Liberty Union	SW	— Socialist Worker
BP	— Best Party	GR	— Grassroots	MSTAX	— Mississippi Taxpayers	TAX	— Taxpayers
C	— Conservative	GREEN	— Green	NA	— New Alliance	TBAGRN	— T.B.A. Green
CAP	— Capitalist	I	— Independent	NJC	— N.J. Conservative Party	TCN	— Tax Cut Now
CC	— Concerned Citizens	IA	— Independent American	NL	— Natural Law	UNI	— United Independents
CONSTL	— Constitutional	IF	— Independence Fusion	NR	— Nutritional Rights Alliance	USTAX	— U.S. Taxpayers
COP	— Colorado Prohibition	IFH	— Inflation Fighting Housewife			UWS	— United We Serve
COPP	— Concerns of People			PAC	— Politicians Are Crooks	VG	— Vermont Grassroots
D	— Democratic	IR	— Independent Republican	PAT	— Patriot Party	WL	— Workers League
DCSTATE	— DC Statehood	JPR	— Jobs, Property Rights	PFP	— Peace and Freedom	WTP	— We The People
DDD	— Damn Drug Dealers	KAF	— Keep America First			WW	— Workers World

	Vote Total	%
Elsa C. Cheung (R)	30,528	18.2
9 • Ronald V. Dellums (D)	129,233	72.2
Deborah Wright (R)	40,448	22.6
Emma Wong Mar (PFP)	9,194	5.1
10 • Bill Baker (R)	138,916	59.3
Ellen Schwartz (D)	90,523	38.6
Craig W. Cooper (PFP)	4,802	2.1
11 • Richard W. Pombo (R)	99,302	62.1
Randy A. Perry (D)	55,794	34.9
Joseph B. Miller (LIBERT)	4,718	3.0
12 • Tom Lantos (D)	118,408	67.4
Deborah Wilder (R)	57,228	32.6
13 • Pete Stark (D)	97,344	64.6
Larry Molton (R)	45,555	30.2
Robert "Bob" Gough (LIBERT)	7,743	5.1
14 • Anna G. Eshoo (D)	120,713	60.6
Ben Brink (R)	78,475	39.4
15 • Norman Y. Mineta (D)	119,921	59.9
Robert Wick (R)	80,266	40.1
16 Zoe Lofgren (D)	74,935	65.0
Lyle J. Smith (R)	40,409	35.0
17 • Sam Farr (D)	87,222	52.2
Bill McCampbell (R)	74,380	44.5
E. Craig Coffin (GREEN)	5,591	3.3
18 • Gary A. Condit (D)	91,105	65.5
Tom Carter (R)	44,046	31.7
James B. Morzella (LIBERT)	3,901	2.8
19 George P. Radanovich (R)	104,435	56.8
• Richard H. Lehman (D)	72,912	39.6
Dolores Comstock (LIBERT)	6,579	3.6
20 • Cal Dooley (D)	57,394	56.7
Paul Young (R)	43,836	43.3
21 • Bill Thomas (R)	116,874	68.1
John L. Evans (D)	47,517	27.7
Mike Hodges (LIBERT)	6,899	4.0
Deborah A. Vollmer (write-in)	339	.2
22 Andrea Seastrand (R)	102,987	49.3
Walter Holden Capps (D)	101,424	48.5
David L. Bersohn (LIBERT)	4,597	2.2
23 • Elton Gallegly (R)	114,043	66.2
Kevin Ready (D)	47,345	27.5
Bill Brown (LIBERT)	6,481	3.8
Robert T. Marston (GREEN)	4,457	2.6
24 • Anthony C. Beilenson (D)	95,342	49.4
Rich Sybert (R)	91,806	47.5
John C. Koehler (LIBERT)	6,031	3.1
25 • Howard P. "Buck" McKeon (R)	110,301	64.9
James H. Gilmartin (D)	53,445	31.4
Devin Cutler (LIBERT)	6,205	3.7
26 • Howard L. Berman (D)	55,145	62.6
Gary E. Forsch (R)	28,423	32.2
Erich D. Miller (LIBERT)	4,570	5.2
27 • Carlos J. Moorhead (R)	88,341	53.0
Doug Kahn (D)	70,267	42.1
Bill Gibbs (AMI)	4,328	2.6
Dennis Decherd (LIBERT)	3,838	2.3
28 • David Dreier (R)	110,179	67.1
Tommy Randle (D)	50,022	30.4
Jorj Clayton Baker (LIBERT)	4,069	2.5
29 • Henry A. Waxman (D)	129,413	68.0
Paul Stepanek (R)	53,801	28.3
Michael J. Binkley (LIBERT)	7,162	3.8
30 • Xavier Becerra (D)	43,943	66.2
David A. Ramirez (R)	18,741	28.2
R. William Weilburg (LIBERT)	3,741	5.6
31 • Matthew G. Martinez (D)	50,541	59.1
John V. Flores (R)	34,926	40.9
32 • Julian C. Dixon (D)	98,017	77.6
Ernie A. Farhat (R)	22,190	17.6
John Honigsfeld (PFP)	6,099	4.8
33 • Lucille Roybal-Allard (D)	33,814	81.5
Kermit Booker (PFP)	7,694	18.5
34 • Esteban E. Torres (D)	72,439	61.7
Albert J. Nunez (R)	40,068	34.1
Carl M. "Marty" Swinney (LIBERT)	4,921	4.2
35 • Maxine Waters (D)	65,688	78.1
Nate Truman (R)	18,390	21.9
36 • Jane Harman (D)	93,939	48.0
Susan M. Brooks (R)	93,127	47.6
Jack Tyler (LIBERT)	4,932	2.5
Joseph G. "Joe" Fields (AMI)	3,810	1.9
37 • Walter R. Tucker III (D)	64,166	77.4
Guy Wilson (R)	18,502	22.3
Lewis B. Prulitsky (write-in)	263	.3
38 • Steve Horn (R)	85,225	58.5

	Vote Total	%
Peter Mathews (D)	53,681	36.8
Lester W. Mueller (LIBERT)	3,795	2.6
Richard K. Green (PFP)	2,995	2.1
John Duke (write-in)	73	.1
39 • Ed Royce (R)	113,037	66.4
R.O. "Bob" Davis (D)	49,459	29.0
Jack Dean (LIBERT)	7,862	4.6
40 • Jerry Lewis (R)	115,728	70.7
Donald M. "Don" Rusk (D)	48,003	29.3
41 • Jay C. Kim (R)	81,854	62.1
Ed Tessier (D)	49,924	37.9
42 • George E. Brown Jr. (D)	58,888	51.1
Rob Guzman (R)	56,259	48.8
Write-ins	58	.1
43 • Ken Calvert (R)	84,500	54.7
Mark A. Takano (D)	59,342	38.4
Gene L. Berkman (LIBERT)	9,636	6.2
John Schwab (write-in)	767	.5
Velma Hickey (write-in)	141	.1
44 Sonny Bono (R)	95,521	55.6
Steve Clute (D)	65,370	38.1
Donald Cochran (AMI)	10,885	6.3
45 • Dana Rohrabacher (R)	124,006	69.1
Brett Williamson (D)	55,489	30.9
46 • Robert K. Dornan (R)	50,126	57.1
Michael Farber (D)	32,577	37.1
Richard G. Newhouse (LIBERT)	5,018	5.7
47 • Christopher Cox (R)	152,413	71.7
Gary Kingsbury (D)	53,035	24.9
Victor A. Wagner Jr. (LIBERT)	7,175	3.4
48 • Ron Packard (R)	143,275	73.4
Andrei Leschick (D)	43,446	22.3
Donna White (PFP)	8,520	4.4
49 Brian P. Bilbray (R)	90,283	48.5
• Lynn Schenk (D)	85,597	46.0
Chris Hoogenboom (LIBERT)	5,288	2.8
Renate M. Kline (PFP)	4,948	2.7
50 • Bob Filner (D)	59,214	56.7
Mary Alice Acevedo (R)	36,955	35.4
Ricardo Duenez (LIBERT)	3,326	3.2
Guillermo Ramirez (PFP)	3,002	2.9
Kip Krueger (GREEN)	1,954	1.9
51 • Randy "Duke" Cunningham (R)	138,547	66.9
Rita K. Tamerius (D)	57,374	27.7
Bill Holmes (LIBERT)	6,968	3.4
Miriam E. Clark (PFP)	4,099	2.0
52 • Duncan Hunter (R)	109,201	64.0
Janet M. Gastil (D)	53,024	31.1
Joe Shea (LIBERT)	5,240	3.1
Art Edelman (PFP)	3,221	1.9

COLORADO

Governor

	Vote Total	%
• Roy Romer (D)	619,205	55.5
Bruce Benson (R)	432,042	38.7
Kevin Swanson (TAX)	40,397	3.6
Phillip Hufford (GREEN)	16,956	1.5
Earl F. Dodge (COP)	7,584	.7

House

	Vote Total	%
1 • Patricia Schroeder (D)	93,123	60.0
William Eggert (R)	61,978	39.9
Gary Cooper (write-in)	154	.1
2 • David E. Skaggs (D)	105,938	56.7
Patricia "Pat" Miller (R)	80,723	43.2
3 • Scott McInnis (R)	145,365	69.6
Linda Powers (D)	63,427	30.4
4 • Wayne Allard (R)	136,251	72.3
Cathy Kipp (D)	52,202	27.7
5 • Joel Hefley (R)	138,674	100.0
6 • Dan Schaefer (R)	124,079	69.8
John Hallen (D)	49,701	28.0
John Heckman (COPP)	2,536	1.4
Stephen D. Dawson (NL)	1,393	.8

CONNECTICUT

Governor

	Vote Total	%
John G. Rowland (R)	415,201	36.2
Bill Curry (D)	375,133	32.7
Eunice Strong Groark (ACP)	216,585	18.9
Tom Scott (I)	130,128	11.3
Joseph A. Zdonczyk (CC)	10,007	.9

Senate

	Vote Total	%
• Joseph I. Lieberman (D,ACP)	723,842	67.0
Jerry Labriola (R)	334,833	31.0
Gary R. Garneau (CC)	20,989	1.9

House

	Vote Total	%
1 • Barbara B. Kennelly (D,ACP)	138,637	73.4
Douglas T. Putnam (R)	46,865	24.8
John F. Forry III (CC)	3,405	1.8
2 • Sam Gejdenson (D)	79,188	42.6
Edward W. Munster (R)	79,167	42.5
David Bingham (ACP)	27,716	14.9
3 • Rosa L. DeLauro (D)	111,261	63.4
Susan H. Johnson (R,ACP)	64,094	36.6
4 • Christopher Shays (R)	109,436	74.4
Jonathan D. Kantrowitz (D)	34,962	23.8
Irving Sussman (LIBERT)	1,976	1.3
Terry M. Nevas (NL)	688	.5
5 • Gary A. Franks (R)	93,471	52.2
James H. Maloney (D,ACP)	81,523	45.5
Rosita Rodriguez (CC)	4,059	2.3
6 • Nancy L. Johnson (R)	123,101	63.9
Charlotte Koskoff (D,ACP)	60,701	31.5
Patrick J. Danford (CC)	8,915	4.6

DELAWARE

Senate

	Vote Total	%
• William V. Roth Jr. (R)	111,088	55.8
Charles M. Oberly (D)	84,554	42.5
John C. Dierickx (LIBERT)	3,387	1.7

House

	Vote Total	%
AL • Michael N. Castle (R)	137,960	70.7
Carol Ann DeSantis (D)	51,803	26.6
Danny Ray Beaver (LIBERT)	3,869	2.0
Donald M. Hockmuth (ADEP)	1,405	.7

FLORIDA

Governor

	Vote Total	%
• Lawton Chiles (D)	2,135,008	50.8
Jeb Bush (R)	2,071,068	49.2

Senate

	Vote Total	%
• Connie Mack (R)	2,894,726	70.5
Hugh E. Rodham (D)	1,210,412	29.5

House

	Vote Total	%
1 Joe Scarborough (R)	112,901	61.6
Vince Whibbs Jr. (D)	70,389	38.4
Ralph Boone Jr. (write-in)	106	.1
2 • Pete Peterson (D)	117,404	61.3
Carole Griffin (R)	74,011	38.7
3 • Corrine Brown (D)	63,845	57.7
Marc Little (R)	46,895	42.3
4 • Tillie Fowler (R)	x	x
5 • Karen L. Thurman (D)	125,780	57.2
"Big Daddy" Don Garlits (R)	94,093	42.8
6 • Cliff Stearns (R)	148,698	99.1
Phil Denton (write-in)	1,332	.9
7 • John L. Mica (R)	131,711	73.4
Edward D. Goddard (D)	47,747	26.6
8 • Bill McCollum (R)	131,376	99.7
Ron Bedell (write-in)	439	.3
9 • Michael Bilirakis (R)	177,253	99.9
Richard Grayson (write-in)	152	.1
10 • C.W. Bill Young (R)	x	x
11 • Sam M. Gibbons (D)	76,814	51.6
Mark Sharpe (R)	72,119	48.4
12 • Charles T. Canady (R)	106,123	65.0
Robert Connors (D)	57,203	35.0
13 • Dan Miller (R)	x	x
14 • Porter J. Goss (R)	x	x
15 • Dave Weldon (R)	117,027	53.7
Sue Munsey (D)	100,513	46.1
Jim Owen (write-in)	246	.1
16 • Mark Foley (R)	122,734	58.1
John Comerford (D)	88,646	41.9
17 • Carrie P. Meek (D)	75,741	100.0
18 • Ileana Ros-Lehtinen (R)	x	x
19 • Harry A. Johnston (D)	147,591	66.1
Peter J. Tsakanikas (R)	75,779	33.9
20 • Peter Deutsch (D)	114,615	61.2
Beverly "Bev" Kennedy (R)	72,516	38.8
21 • Lincoln Diaz-Balart (R)	90,948	100.0

	Vote Total	%
22 • E. Clay Shaw Jr. (R)	119,690	63.4
Hermine L. Wiener (D)	69,215	36.6
23 • Alcee L. Hastings (D)	x	x

GEORGIA

Governor

	Vote Total	%
• Zell Miller (D)	788,926	51.1
Guy Millner (R)	756,371	48.9

House

	Vote Total	%
1 • Jack Kingston (R)	88,788	76.6
Raymond Beckworth (D)	27,197	23.4
2 • Sanford D. Bishop Jr. (D)	65,383	66.2
John Clayton (R)	33,429	33.8
3 • Mac Collins (R)	94,717	65.5
Fred Overby (D)	49,828	34.5
4 • John Linder (R)	90,063	57.9
Comer Yates (D)	65,566	42.1
5 • John Lewis (D)	85,094	69.1
Dale Dixon (R)	37,999	30.9
6 • Newt Gingrich (R)	119,432	64.2
Ben Jones (D)	66,700	35.8
7 Bob Barr (R)	71,265	51.9
• George "Buddy" Darden (D)	65,978	48.1
8 Saxby Chambliss (R)	89,591	62.7
Craig Mathis (D)	53,408	37.3
9 • Nathan Deal (D)	79,145	57.9
Robert L. Castello (R)	57,568	42.1
10 Charlie Norwood (R)	96,099	65.2
• Don Johnson (D)	51,192	34.8
11 • Cynthia A. McKinney (D)	71,560	65.6
Woodrow Lovett (R)	37,533	34.4

HAWAII

Governor

	Vote Total	%
Benjamin J. Cayetano (D)	134,978	36.6
Frank F. Fasi (BP)	113,158	30.7
Patricia F. Saiki (R)	107,908	29.2
Michael Kioni Dudley (GREEN)	12,969	3.5

Senate

	Vote Total	%
• Daniel K. Akaka (D)	256,189	71.8
Maria M. Hustace (R)	86,320	24.2
Richard O. Rowland (LIBERT)	14,393	4.0

House

	Vote Total	%
1 • Neil Abercrombie (D)	94,754	53.6
Orson Swindle (R)	76,623	43.4
Alexandra Kaan (BP)	2,815	1.6
Roger L. Taylor (LIBERT)	2,514	1.4
2 • Patsy T. Mink (D)	124,431	70.1
Robert H. Garner (R)	42,891	24.2
Lawrence R. Bartley (LIBERT)	10,074	5.7

IDAHO

Governor

	Vote Total	%
Phil Batt (R)	216,123	52.3
Larry EchoHawk (D)	181,363	43.9
Ronald B. Rankin (I)	15,793	3.8

House

	Vote Total	%
1 Helen Chenoweth (R)	111,728	55.4
• Larry LaRocco (D)	89,826	44.6
2 • Michael D. Crapo (R)	143,593	75.0
Penny Fletcher (D)	47,936	25.0

ILLINOIS

Governor

	Vote Total	%
• Jim Edgar (R)	1,984,318	63.9
Dawn Clark Netsch (D)	1,069,850	34.4
David L. Kelley (LIBERT)	52,388	1.7

House

	Vote Total	%
1 • Bobby L. Rush (D)	112,474	75.7
William J. Kelly (R)	36,038	24.3
2 • Mel Reynolds (D)	93,998	98.1
Carl Lanier Bibbs (write-in)	1,565	1.6
Lionel O. Pittman (write-in)	139	.1
John P. Grey (write-in)	83	.1
Other write-ins	70	.1
3 • William O. Lipinski (D)	92,353	54.2
Jim Nalepa (R)	78,163	45.8

	Vote Total	%
4 • Luis V. Gutierrez (D)	46,695	75.2
Steven Valtierra (R)	15,384	24.8
5 Michael Patrick Flanagan (R)	75,328	54.4
• Dan Rostenkowski (D)	63,065	45.6
6 • Henry J. Hyde (R)	115,664	73.5
Tom Berry (D)	37,163	23.6
Robert L. Hogan (LIBERT)	2,633	1.7
Robert L. Wheat (UNI)	1,918	1.2
7 • Cardiss Collins (D)	93,457	79.6
Charles "Chuck" Mobley (R)	24,011	20.4
8 • Philip M. Crane (R)	88,225	64.9
Robert C. Walberg (D)	47,654	35.1
9 • Sidney R. Yates (D)	94,404	66.1
George Edward Larney (R)	48,419	33.9
10 • John Edward Porter (R)	114,884	75.1
Andrew M. Krupp (D)	38,191	24.9
11 • Gerald C. "Jerry" Weller (R)	97,241	60.6
Frank Giglio (D)	63,150	39.4
12 • Jerry F. Costello (D)	101,391	65.9
Jan Morris (R)	52,419	34.1
13 • Harris W. Fawell (R)	124,312	73.1
William A. Riley (D)	45,709	26.9
14 • Dennis Hastert (R)	110,204	76.5
Steve Denari (D)	33,891	23.5
15 • Thomas W. Ewing (R)	108,857	68.2
Paul Alexander (D)	50,874	31.8
16 • Donald Manzullo (R)	117,238	70.6
Pete Sullivan (D)	48,736	29.4
17 • Lane Evans (D)	95,312	54.5
Jim Anderson (R)	79,471	45.5
18 Ray LaHood (R)	119,838	60.2
G. Douglas Stephens (D)	78,332	39.3
Joyce Harant (write-in)	955	.5
19 • Glenn Poshard (D)	115,045	58.4
Brent Winters (R)	81,995	41.6
20 • Richard J. Durbin (D)	108,034	54.8
Bill Owens (R)	88,964	45.2

INDIANA

Senate

	Vote Total	%
• Richard G. Lugar (R)	1,039,625	67.4
Jim Jontz (D)	470,799	30.5
Barbara Bourland (LIBERT)	17,343	1.1
Mary Catherine Barton (NA)	15,801	1.0

House

	Vote Total	%
1 • Peter J. Visclosky (D)	68,612	56.5
John Larson (R)	52,920	43.5
2 David M. McIntosh (R)	93,592	54.5
Joseph H. Hogsett (D)	78,241	45.5
3 • Tim Roemer (D)	72,497	55.2
Richard Burkett (R)	58,878	44.8
4 Mark Edward Souder (R)	88,584	55.4
• Jill L. Long (D)	71,235	44.6
5 • Steve Buyer (R)	111,031	69.5
J.D. Beatty (D)	45,224	28.3
Clayton L. Alfred (I)	3,403	2.1
6 • Dan Burton (R)	136,876	77.0
Natalie M. Bruner (D)	40,815	23.0
7 • John T. Myers (R)	104,359	65.1
Michael M. Harmless (D)	55,941	34.9
8 John Hostettler (R)	93,529	52.4
• Frank McCloskey (D)	84,857	47.6
9 • Lee H. Hamilton (D)	91,459	52.0
Jean Leising (R)	84,315	48.0
10 • Andrew Jacobs Jr. (D)	58,573	53.5
Marvin Bailey Scott (R)	50,998	46.5

IOWA

Governor

	Vote Total	%
• Terry E. Branstad (R)	566,395	56.8
Bonnie J. Campbell (D)	414,453	41.6
Richard O'Dell Hughes (I)	5,505	.6
Veronica Wells Butler (NL)	3,737	.4
Write-ins	3,616	.4
Carl E. Olson (LIBERT)	2,772	.3
Michael Galati (SW)	770	.1

House

	Vote Total	%
1 • Jim Leach (R)	110,448	60.2
Glen Winekauf (D)	69,461	37.9
Jan J. Zonneveld (I)	2,264	1.2

	Vote Total	%
Michael Cuddehe (NL)	1,213	.7
2 • Jim Nussle (R)	111,076	56.0
Dave Nagle (D)	86,087	43.4
Albert W. Schoeman (LIBERT)	1,281	.6
3 • Jim Ross Lightfoot (R)	111,862	57.8
Elaine Baxter (D)	79,310	41.0
Derrick P. Grimmer (GR)	2,282	1.2
4 Greg Ganske (R)	111,935	52.5
• Neal Smith (D)	98,824	46.4
Joshua A. Roberts (NL)	898	.4
William C. Oviatt (GR)	803	.4
Angela Lariscy (SW)	606	.3
Write-ins	140	.1
5 Tom Latham (R)	114,796	60.8
Sheila McGuire (D)	73,627	39.0
Write-ins	298	.2

KANSAS

Governor

	Vote Total	%
Bill Graves (R)	526,113	64.1
Jim Slattery (D)	294,733	35.9

House

	Vote Total	%
1 • Pat Roberts (R)	169,531	77.4
Terry L. Nichols (D)	49,477	22.6
2 Sam Brownback (R)	135,725	65.6
John Carlin (D)	71,025	34.4
3 • Jan Meyers (R)	102,218	56.6
Judy Hancock (D)	78,401	43.4
4 Todd Tiahrt (R)	111,653	52.9
• Dan Glickman (D)	99,366	47.1

KENTUCKY

House

	Vote Total	%
1 Edward Whitfield (R)	64,849	51.0
• Tom Barlow (D)	62,387	49.0
2 • Ron Lewis (R)	90,535	59.8
David Adkisson (D)	60,867	40.2
3 Mike Ward (D)	67,663	44.4
Susan B. Stokes (R)	67,238	44.1
Richard Lewis (KTAX)	17,591	11.5
4 • Jim Bunning (R)	96,695	74.1
Sally Harris Skaggs (D)	33,717	25.9
5 • Harold Rogers (R)	82,291	79.4
Walter "Doc" Blevins (D)	21,318	20.6
6 • Scotty Baesler (D)	70,085	58.8
Matthew Eric Wills (R)	49,032	41.2

LOUISIANA

House

1 • Robert L. Livingston (R)	Won in primary
2 • William J. Jefferson (D)	Won in primary
3 • W.J. "Billy" Tauzin (D)	Won in primary
4 • Cleo Fields (D)	Won in primary
5 • Jim McCrery (R)	Won in primary
6 • Richard H. Baker (R)	Won in primary
7 • Jimmy Hayes (D)	Won in primary

MAINE

Governor

	Vote Total	%
Angus King (I)	180,829	35.4
Joseph E. Brennan (D)	172,951	33.8
Susan M. Collins (R)	117,990	23.1
Jonathan K. Carter (I)	32,695	6.4
Mark S. Finks (write-in)	6,576	1.3
Write-ins	267	.1

Senate

	Vote Total	%
Olympia J. Snowe (R)	308,244	60.2
Thomas H. Andrews (D)	186,042	36.4
Plato Truman (I)	17,205	3.4

House

	Vote Total	%
1 James B. Longley Jr. (R)	136,316	51.9
Dennis L. Dutremble (D)	126,373	48.1
2 John Baldacci (D)	109,615	45.7
Richard A. Bennett (R)	97,754	40.7
John M. Michael (I)	21,117	8.8
Charles FitzGerald (I)	11,353	4.7

	Vote Total	%

MARYLAND

Governor
Parris N. Glendening (D)	708,094	50.2
Ellen R. Sauerbrey (R)	702,101	49.8

Senate
• Paul S. Sarbanes (D)	809,125	59.1
William Brock (R)	559,908	40.9

House
1 • Wayne T. Gilchrest (R)	120,975	67.7
Ralph T. Gies (D)	57,712	32.3
Wayne Boyle (write-in)	127	.1
2 Robert L. Ehrlich Jr. (R)	125,162	62.7
Gerry L. Brewster (D)	74,275	37.2
3 • Benjamin L. Cardin (D)	117,269	71.0
Robert Ryan Tousey (R)	47,966	29.0
4 • Albert R. Wynn (D)	93,148	75.0
Michele Dyson (R)	30,999	25.0
5 • Steny H. Hoyer (D)	98,821	58.8
Donald Devine (R)	69,211	41.2
6 • Roscoe G. Bartlett (R)	122,809	65.9
Paul Muldowney (D)	63,411	34.1
7 • Kweisi Mfume (D)	97,016	81.5
Kenneth Kondner (R)	22,007	18.5
8 • Constance A. Morella (R)	143,449	70.3
Steven Van Grack (D)	60,660	29.7

MASSACHUSETTS

Governor
• William F. Weld (R)	1,533,380	70.9
Mark Roosevelt (D)	611,641	28.3
Dean Cook (LIBERT)	14,698	.7
Jeffrey Rebello (LAWR)	3,907	.2

Senate
• Edward M. Kennedy (D)	1,265,997	58.1
W. Mitt Romney (R)	894,000	41.0
Lauraleigh Dozier (LIBERT)	14,484	.7
William Ferguson Jr. (LAWR)	4,776	.2

House
1 • John W. Olver (D)	150,047	99.4
Write-ins	971	.6
2 • Richard E. Neal (D)	117,178	58.6
John M. Briare (R)	72,732	36.3
Kate Ross (NL)	10,167	5.1
3 • Peter I. Blute (R)	115,810	54.6
Kevin O'Sullivan (D)	93,689	44.2
Dale E. Friedgen (NL)	2,375	1.1
Write-ins	161	.1
4 • Barney Frank (D)	168,942	99.5
Write-ins	853	.5
5 • Martin T. Meehan (D)	140,725	69.8
David E. Coleman (R)	60,734	30.1
6 • Peter G. Torkildsen (R)	120,952	50.5
John F. Tierney (D)	113,481	47.4
Benjamin A. Gatchell (I)	4,960	2.1
7 • Edward J. Markey (D)	146,246	64.4
Brad Bailey (R)	80,674	35.5
8 • Joseph P. Kennedy II (D)	113,224	99.0
Write-ins	1,199	1.0
9 • Joe Moakley (D)	146,287	69.8
Michael M. Murphy (R)	63,369	30.2
10 • Gerry E. Studds (D)	172,753	68.7
Keith Jason Hemeon (R)	78,487	31.2

MICHIGAN

Governor
• John Engler (R)	1,899,101	61.5
Howard Wolpe (D)	1,188,438	38.5

Senate
Spencer Abraham (R)	1,578,770	51.9
Bob Carr (D)	1,300,960	42.7
Jon Coon (LIBERT)	128,393	4.2
William Roundtree (WW)	20,010	.7
Chris Wege (NL)	14,746	.5

House
1 • Bart Stupak (D)	121,433	56.9
Gil Ziegler (R)	89,660	42.0
Michael McPeak (NL)	2,399	1.1
2 • Peter Hoekstra (R)	146,164	75.3
Marcus Pete Hoover (D)	46,097	23.7

	Vote Total	%
Lu Wiggins (NL)	1,892	1.0
3 • Vernon J. Ehlers (R)	136,711	73.9
Betsy J. Flory (D)	43,580	23.5
Barrie Leslie Konicov (LIBERT)	2,960	1.6
Susan H. Normandin (NL)	1,815	1.0
4 • Dave Camp (R)	145,176	73.1
Damion Frasier (D)	50,544	25.5
Michael Lee (NL)	2,797	1.4
5 • James A. Barcia (D)	126,456	65.5
William T. Anderson (R)	61,342	31.8
Larry L. Fairchild (I)	3,022	1.6
Susan I. Arnold (NL)	2,323	1.2
6 • Fred Upton (R)	121,923	73.5
David Taylor (D)	42,348	25.5
E.A. Berker (NL)	1,667	1.0
7 • Nick Smith (R)	115,621	65.1
Kim McCaughtry (D)	57,326	32.3
Kenneth L. Proctor (LIBERT)	3,311	1.9
Scott K. Williamson (NL)	1,223	.7
8 • Dick Chrysler (R)	109,663	51.6
Bob Mitchell (D)	95,383	44.9
Gerald Ralph Turcotte, Jr. (LIBERT)	4,348	2.0
Susan Ilene McPeak (NL)	3,076	1.4
9 • Dale E. Kildee (D)	97,096	51.2
Megan O'Neill (R)	89,148	47.0
Karen Blasdell (NL)	3,240	1.7
10 • David E. Bonior (D)	121,876	62.2
Donald J. Lobsinger (R)	73,862	37.7
11 • Joe Knollenberg (R)	154,696	68.2
Mike Breshgold (D)	69,168	30.5
John R. Hocking (NL)	2,928	1.3
12 • Sander M. Levin (D)	103,508	52.0
John Pappageorge (R)	92,762	46.6
Jerome White (I)	1,386	.7
Eric R. Anderson (NL)	1,340	.7
13 Lynn Nancy Rivers (D)	89,573	51.9
John A. Schall (R)	77,908	45.1
Craig L. Seymour (LIBERT)	3,186	1.8
Helen Halyard (I)	1,388	.8
Gail Anne Petrosoff (NL)	606	.4
14 • John Conyers Jr. (D)	128,463	81.5
Richard Charles Fornier (R)	26,215	16.6
Richard R. Miller (NL)	2,953	1.9
15 • Barbara-Rose Collins (D)	119,442	84.1
John W. Savage II (R)	20,074	14.1
Cynthia M. Jaquith (I)	987	.7
Henry Ogden Clark (NL)	848	.6
Larry Roberts (I)	654	.5
16 • John D. Dingell (D)	105,849	59.1
Ken Larkin (R)	71,159	39.8
Noha F. Hamze (NL)	1,968	1.1

MINNESOTA

Governor
• Arne H. Carlson (R)	1,094,165	62.0
John Marty (D)	589,344	33.4
Write-ins	38,196	2.2
Will Shetterly (GR)	20,785	1.2
Eric Arthur Olson (LIBERT)	15,467	.9
Leslie Davis (NR)	4,611	.3
Jon Hillson (SW)	3,022	.2

Senate
Rod Grams (R)	869,653	49.1
Ann Wynia (D)	781,860	44.1
Dean M. Barkley (I)	95,400	5.4
Candice E. Sjostrom (GR)	15,920	.9
Stephen Johnson (NL)	5,054	.3
Write-ins	2,614	.1
Marea Himelgrin (SW)	2,428	.1

House
1 Gil Gutknecht (R)	117,613	55.2
John C. Hottinger (D)	95,328	44.7
Write-ins	277	.1
2 • David Minge (D)	114,289	52.0
Gary B. Revier (R)	98,881	45.0
Stan Bentz (I)	6,535	3.0
3 • Jim Ramstad (R)	173,223	73.2
Bob Olson (D)	62,211	26.3
Write-ins	1,097	.5
4 • Bruce F. Vento (D)	115,638	54.9
Dennis Newinski (R)	88,344	41.9
Dan R. Vacek (GR)	6,211	2.9
Write-ins	437	.2

	Vote Total	%
5 • Martin Olav Sabo (D)	121,515	61.9
Dorothy LeGrand (R)	73,258	37.3
Write-ins	1,399	.7
6 William P. "Bill" Luther (D)	113,740	49.9
Tad Jude (R)	113,190	49.7
Write-ins	845	.4
7 • Collin C. Peterson (D)	108,023	51.2
Bernie Omann (R)	102,623	48.6
Write-ins	357	.2
8 • James L. Oberstar (D)	153,161	65.7
Phil Herwig (R)	79,818	34.2
Write-ins	292	.1

MISSISSIPPI

Senate
• Trent Lott (R)	418,333	68.8
Ken Harper (D)	189,752	31.2

House
1 Roger Wicker (R)	80,553	63.1
Bill Wheeler (D)	47,192	36.9
2 • Bennie Thompson (D)	68,014	53.7
Bill Jordan (R)	49,270	38.9
Vince Thornton (MSTAX)	9,408	7.4
3 • G.V. "Sonny" Montgomery (D)	83,163	67.6
Dutch Dabbs (R)	39,826	32.4
4 • Mike Parker (D)	82,939	68.5
Mike Wood (R)	38,200	31.5
5 • Gene Taylor (D)	73,179	60.1
George Barlos (R)	48,575	39.9

MISSOURI

Senate
John Ashcroft (R)	1,060,149	59.7
Alan Wheat (D)	633,697	35.7
Bill Johnson (LIBERT)	81,264	4.6

House
1 • William L. Clay (D)	97,061	63.4
Donald R. Counts (R)	50,303	32.9
Craig W. Williamson (LIBERT)	5,654	3.7
2 • James M. Talent (R)	154,882	67.3
Pat Kelly (D)	70,480	30.6
Jim Higgins (LIBERT)	4,925	2.1
3 • Richard A. Gephardt (D)	117,601	57.7
Gary Gill (R)	80,977	39.7
Bradley Ems (LIBERT)	5,362	2.6
4 • Ike Skelton (D)	137,876	67.8
James A. Noland Jr. (R)	65,616	32.2
5 Karen McCarthy (D)	100,391	56.6
Ron Freeman (R)	77,120	43.4
6 • Pat Danner (D)	140,108	66.1
Tina Tucker (R)	71,709	33.9
7 • Mel Hancock (R)	112,228	57.3
James R. Fossard (D)	77,836	39.7
Doug Burlison (LIBERT)	5,852	3.0
8 • Bill Emerson (R)	129,320	70.1
James L. "Jay" Thompson (D)	48,987	26.5
Greg Tlapek	6,279	3.4
9 • Harold L. Volkmer (D)	103,443	50.5
Kenny Hulshof (R)	92,301	45.0
Mitchell Moore	9,198	4.5

MONTANA

Senate
• Conrad Burns (R)	218,542	62.4
Jack Mudd (D)	131,845	37.6

House
AL • Pat Williams (D)	171,372	48.7
Cy Jamison (R)	148,715	42.2
Steve Kelly (I)	32,046	9.1

NEBRASKA

Governor
• Ben Nelson (D)	423,270	73.0
Gene Spence (R)	148,230	25.6
Ernie Chambers (write-in)	5,085	.9
Write-ins	2,976	.5

	Vote Total	%
Senate		
• Bob Kerrey (D)	317,297	54.8
Jan Stoney (R)	260,668	45.0
Write-ins	1,240	.2
House		
1 • Doug Bereuter (R)	117,967	62.6
Patrick Combs (D)	70,369	37.3
Write-ins	214	.1
2 Jon Christensen (R)	92,516	49.9
• Peter Hoagland (D)	90,750	49.0
Write-ins	2,044	1.1
3 • Bill Barrett (R)	154,919	78.7
Gil Chapin (D)	41,943	21.3

NEVADA

	Vote Total	%
Governor		
• Bob Miller (D)	200,026	52.7
Jim Gibbons (R)	156,875	41.3
Daniel Hansen (IA)	10,012	2.6
Denis Sholty (LIBERT)	3,978	1.0
Senate		
• Richard H. Bryan (D)	193,804	50.9
Hal Furman (R)	156,020	41.0
Anna Nevenich (I)	6,666	1.8
Bob Days (LIBERT)	5,964	1.6
Neal A. Grasteit (IA)	5,450	1.4
House		
1 John Ensign (R)	73,769	48.5
• James Bilbray (D)	72,333	47.5
Gary Wood (LIBERT)	6,065	4.0
2 • Barbara F. Vucanovich (R)	142,202	63.5
Janet Greeson (D)	65,390	29.2
Thomas F. Jefferson (IA)	9,615	4.3
Lois Avery (NL)	6,725	3.0

NEW HAMPSHIRE

	Vote Total	%
Governor		
• Stephen Merrill (R)	218,134	69.9
Wayne D. King (D)	79,686	25.6
Steve Winter (LIBERT)	13,709	4.4
Write-ins	353	.1
House		
1 • Bill Zeliff (R)	97,017	65.6
Bill Verge (D)	42,481	28.7
Scott Tosti (I)	4,203	2.8
Paul Lannon (LIBERT)	3,548	2.4
Merle Braley (NL)	573	.4
2 Charles Bass (R)	83,121	51.4
• Dick Swett (D)	74,243	46.0
John Lewicke (LIBERT)	2,986	1.8
Linda Spitzfaden (NL)	1,223	.8

NEW JERSEY

	Vote Total	%
Senate		
• Frank R. Lautenberg (D)	1,033,487	50.3
Garabed "Chuck" Haytaian (R)	966,244	47.0
Michael P. Kelly (KAF)	14,343	.7
Ben Grindlinger (LIBERT)	14,042	.7
Richard J. Pezzullo (NJC)	9,387	.5
Andrea Lippi (JPR)	6,303	.3
George Patrick Predham (DDD)	4,226	.2
Joanne Kuniansky (SW)	3,606	.2
Arlene Gold (NL)	3,249	.2
House		
1 • Robert E. Andrews (D)	108,155	72.3
James N. Hogan (R)	41,505	27.7
2 Frank A. LoBiondo (R)	102,566	64.6
Louis N. Magazzu (D)	56,151	35.4
3 • H. James Saxton (R)	115,750	66.4
James Smith (D)	54,441	31.2
D. James Hill (UWS)	3,015	1.7
Arthur Fulvio Croce (DIA)	1,122	.6
4 Christopher H. Smith (R)	109,818	67.9
Ralph Walsh (D)	49,537	30.6
Leonard P. Marshall (NJC)	1,579	1.0
Arnold Kokans (NL)	833	.5
5 • Marge Roukema (R)	139,964	74.2
Bill Auer (D)	41,275	21.9

	Vote Total	%
William J. Leonard (I)	3,746	2.0
Roger Bacon (LIBERT)	2,882	1.5
Helen Hamilton (NL)	638	.3
6 • Frank Pallone Jr. (D)	88,922	60.4
Mike Herson (R)	55,287	37.5
Charles H. Dickson (CAP)	1,774	1.2
Gary J. Rich (NJC)	800	.5
Richard Quinn (NL)	548	.4
7 • Bob Franks (R)	98,814	59.6
Karen Carroll (D)	64,231	38.7
James J. Cleary (LAWR)	2,331	1.4
Claire Greene (NL)	481	.3
8 Bill Martini (R)	70,494	49.9
• Herb Klein (D)	68,661	48.6
Bernard George (C)	2,213	1.6
9 • Robert G. Torricelli (D)	99,984	62.5
Peter J. Russo (R)	57,651	36.1
Gregory Pason (I)	1,490	.9
Kenneth Ebel (NL)	763	.5
10 • Donald M. Payne (D)	74,622	75.9
Jim Ford (R)	21,524	21.9
Rose Monyek (IFH)	1,598	1.6
Maurice Williams (SW)	624	.6
11 Rodney Frelinghuysen (R)	127,868	71.2
Frank Herbert (D)	50,211	28.0
Mary Frueholz (LAWR)	1,065	.6
Stuart Bacha (FAS)	436	.2
12 • Dick Zimmer (R)	125,939	68.3
Joseph D. Youssouf (D)	55,977	30.4
Anthony M. Provenzano (NJC)	2,364	1.3
13 • Robert Menendez (D)	67,688	70.9
Fernando A. Alonso (R)	24,071	25.2
Frank J. Rubino Jr. (WTP)	1,494	1.6
Herbert H. Shaw (PAC)	1,319	1.4
Steven Marshall (SW)	895	.9

NEW MEXICO

	Vote Total	%
Governor		
Gary E. Johnson (R)	232,945	49.8
• Bruce King (D)	186,686	39.9
Roberto Mondragon (GREEN)	47,990	10.3
Senate		
• Jeff Bingaman (D)	249,989	54.0
Colin R. McMillan (R)	213,025	46.0
House		
1 • Steven H. Schiff (R)	119,996	73.9
Peter L. Zollinger (D)	42,316	26.1
2 • Joe Skeen (R)	89,966	63.3
Benjamin Anthony Chavez (D)	45,316	31.9
Rex Johnson (GREEN)	6,898	4.9
3 • Bill Richardson (D)	99,900	63.6
F. Gregg Bemis Jr. (R)	53,515	34.1
Ed Nagel (LIBERT)	3,697	2.4

NEW YORK

	Vote Total	%
Governor		
George E. Pataki (R,C,TCN)	2,538,702	48.8
• Mario M. Cuomo (D,L)	2,364,904	45.4
Blase T. Golisano (IF)	217,490	4.2
Robert T. Walsh Sr. (RTL)	67,750	1.3
Bob Schulz (LIBERT)	9,506	.2
Lawrence A. Lane (SW)	5,410	.1
Senate		
• Daniel Patrick Moynihan (D,L)	2,646,541	55.2
Bernadette Castro (R,C,TCN)	1,988,308	41.5
Henry F. Hewes (RTL)	95,954	2.0
Ismael Betancourt Jr. (IF)	26,650	.6
Norma Segal (LIBERT)	17,991	.4
Naomi L. Craine (SW)	14,892	.3
House		
1 • Michael P. Forbes (R,C,RTL,WTP)	90,491	52.5
• George J. Hochbrueckner (D,LIF)	80,146	46.5
Michael Strong (FUP)	1,603	.9
2 • Rick A. Lazio (R,C,WTP)	100,107	68.2
James Manfre (D,LIF)	41,102	28.0
Alice Cort Ross (RTL)	5,567	3.8
3 • Peter T. King (R,C)	115,236	59.2
Norma Grill (D)	77,774	40.0
John A. DePrima (L)	1,522	.8
4 Daniel Frisa (R)	87,815	50.2
Philip M. Schiliro (D)	65,286	37.3

	Vote Total	%
• David A. Levy (C)	15,173	8.7
Vincent P. Garbitelli (RTL)	5,280	3.0
Robert S. Berkowitz (L)	1,409	.8
5 • Gary L. Ackerman (D,L)	93,896	55.0
Grant M. Lally (R,C)	73,884	43.3
Edward Elkowitz (RTL)	2,862	1.7
6 • Floyd H. Flake (D)	68,596	80.4
Denny D. Bhagwandin (R,C)	16,675	19.6
7 • Thomas J. Manton (D)	58,935	87.1
Robert E. Hurley (C)	8,698	12.9
8 • Jerrold Nadler (D,L)	109,946	82.0
David L. Askren (R)	21,132	15.8
Margaret V. Byrnes (C)	3,008	2.2
9 • Charles E. Schumer (D,L)	95,139	72.6
James McCall (R,C)	35,880	27.4
10 • Edolphus Towns (D,L)	77,026	89.0
Amelia Smith Parker (R)	7,995	9.2
Mildred K. Mahoney (C)	1,489	1.7
11 • Major R. Owens (D,L)	61,945	88.9
Gary S. Popkin (R,LIBERT)	6,605	9.5
Michael Gaffney (C)	1,150	1.6
12 • Nydia M. Velázquez (D,L)	39,929	92.3
Genevieve R. Brennan (C)	2,747	6.3
Eric Ruano-Melendez (PHA)	589	1.4
13 • Susan Molinari (R,C)	96,491	71.4
Tyrone G. Butler (D,L)	33,937	25.1
Elisa Disimone (RTL)	4,655	3.4
14 • Carolyn B. Maloney (D,IN)	98,479	64.2
Charles Millard (R,L)	54,277	35.4
Thomas K. Leighton (TBAGRN)	566	.4
15 • Charles B. Rangel (D,L)	77,830	96.5
Jose Suero (RTL,IF)	2,812	3.5
16 • Jose E. Serrano (D,L)	58,572	96.3
Michael Walters (C)	2,257	3.7
17 • Eliot L. Engel (D,L)	73,321	77.6
Edward T. Marshall (R)	16,896	17.9
Kevin Brawley (C)	2,187	2.3
Ann M. Noonan (RTL)	2,075	2.2
18 • Nita M. Lowey (D)	91,663	57.3
Andrew C. Hartzell Jr. (R,C)	65,517	40.9
Florence T. O'Grady (RTL)	2,873	1.8
19 Sue W. Kelly (R)	100,173	52.1
Hamilton Fish Jr. (D)	70,696	36.8
Joseph J. DioGuardi (C,RTL)	19,761	10.3
Catherine Portman-Laux (ATP)	1,679	.9
20 • Benjamin A. Gilman (R)	120,334	67.5
Gregory B. Julian (D)	52,345	29.4
Lois M. Colandrea (RTL)	5,612	3.1
21 • Michael R. McNulty (D,C)	147,804	67.0
Joseph A. Gomez (R)	68,745	31.2
Timothy J. Wood (RTL)	4,125	1.9
22 • Gerald B.H. Solomon (R,C,RTL)	157,717	73.4
L. Robert Lawrence (D)	57,064	26.6
23 • Sherwood Boehlert (R)	124,486	70.5
Charles W. Skeele Jr. (D)	40,786	23.1
Donald J. Thomas (RTL)	11,216	6.4
24 • John M. McHugh (R,C)	124,645	78.6
Danny M. Francis (D)	34,032	21.4
25 • James T. Walsh (R,C)	113,949	57.6
Rhea Jezer (D,CHGC)	83,853	42.4
26 • Maurice D. Hinchey (D,L)	95,492	49.1
Bob Moppert (R,C)	94,244	48.5
Thomas F. Kovach (RTL)	4,772	2.5
27 • Bill Paxon (R,C,RTL)	152,610	74.5
William A. Long Jr. (D)	52,160	25.5
28 • Louise M. Slaughter (D)	110,987	56.6
Renee Forgensi Davison (R,C)	78,516	40.1
John A. Clendenin (IF)	6,464	3.3
29 • John J. LaFalce (D,L)	103,053	55.2
William E. Miller (R,C)	80,355	43.0
Patrick Murty (RTL)	3,296	1.7
30 • Jack Quinn (R,C)	124,738	67.0
David A. Franczyk (D,L)	61,392	33.0
31 • Amo Houghton (R,C)	121,178	84.8
Gretchen S. McManus (RTL)	21,747	15.2

NORTH CAROLINA

	Vote Total	%
House		
1 • Eva Clayton (D)	66,827	61.1
Ted Tyler (R)	42,602	38.9
2 David Funderburk (R)	79,207	56.0
Richard Moore (D)	62,122	44.0

	Vote Total	%
3 Walter B. Jones Jr. (R)	72,464	52.7
• H. Martin Lancaster (D)	65,013	47.3
4 Frederick Kenneth Heineman (R)	77,773	50.4
• David Price (D)	76,558	49.6
5 Richard Burr (R)	84,741	57.3
A.P. "Sandy" Sands (D)	63,194	42.7
6 • Howard Coble (R)	98,355	100.0
7 • Charlie Rose (D)	62,670	51.6
Robert C. Anderson (R)	58,849	48.4
8 • W.G. "Bill" Hefner (D)	62,845	52.4
Sherrill Morgan (R)	57,140	47.6
9 Sue Myrick (R)	82,374	65.0
Rory Blake (D)	44,379	35.0
10 • Cass Ballenger (R)	107,829	71.5
Robert Wayne Avery (D)	42,939	28.5
11 • Charles H. Taylor (R)	115,826	60.1
Maggie Palmer Lauterer (D)	76,862	39.9
12 • Melvin Watt (D)	57,655	65.8
Joseph A. "Joe" Martino (R)	29,933	34.2

NORTH DAKOTA

Senate

	Vote Total	%
• Kent Conrad (D)	137,157	58.0
Ben Clayburgh (R)	99,390	42.0

House

	Vote Total	%
AL • Earl Pomeroy (D)	123,134	52.3
Gary Porter (R)	105,988	45.0
James Germalic (I)	6,267	2.7

OHIO

Governor

	Vote Total	%
• George V. Voinovich (R)	2,401,572	71.8
Robert L. Burch Jr. (D)	835,849	25.0
Billy R. Inmon (I)	108,745	3.2

Senate

	Vote Total	%
Mike DeWine (R)	1,836,556	53.4
Joel Hyatt (D)	1,348,213	39.2
Joseph J. Slovenec (I)	252,031	7.3

House

	Vote Total	%
1 Steve Chabot (R)	92,997	56.1
• David Mann (D)	72,822	43.9
2 • Rob Portman (R)	150,128	77.4
Les Mann (D)	43,730	22.6
3 • Tony P. Hall (D)	105,342	59.3
David A. Westbrock (R)	72,314	40.7
4 • Michael G. Oxley (R)	139,841	100.0
5 • Paul E. Gillmor (R)	135,879	73.4
Jarrod Tudor (D)	49,335	26.6
6 Frank A. Cremeans (R)	91,263	50.9
• Ted Strickland (D)	87,861	49.1
7 • David L. Hobson (R)	140,124	100.0
8 • John A. Boehner (R)	148,338	99.9
Rogers H. Campbell (write-in)	87	.1
9 • Marcy Kaptur (D)	118,120	75.3
R. Randy Whitman (R)	38,665	24.7
10 • Martin R. Hoke (R)	95,226	51.9
Francis E. Gaul (D)	70,918	38.6
Joseph J. Jacobs Jr. (I)	17,495	9.5
11 • Louis Stokes (D)	114,220	77.7
James J. Sykora (R)	33,705	22.8
12 • John R. Kasich (R)	114,608	66.5
Cynthia L. Ruccia (D)	57,294	33.2
John Yiamouyianni (write-in)	244	.1
John B. Hurd (write-in)	117	.1
13 • Sherrod Brown (D)	93,147	49.1
Gregory A. White (R)	86,422	45.5
Howard Mason (I)	7,777	4.1
John Michael Ryan (I)	2,430	1.3
14 • Tom Sawyer (D)	96,274	51.9
Lynn Slaby (R)	89,106	48.1
15 • Deborah Pryce (R)	112,912	70.7
Bill Buckel (D)	46,480	29.1
Ronald D. Dempsey (write-in)	274	.2
16 • Ralph Regula (R)	137,322	75.0
J. Michael Finn (D)	45,781	25.0
17 • James A. Traficant Jr. (D)	149,004	77.4
Mike G. Meister (R)	43,490	22.6
18 Bob Ney (R)	103,115	54.0
Greg A. DiDonato (D)	87,926	46.0

	Vote Total	%
19 Steven C. LaTourette (R)	99,997	48.5
• Eric D. Fingerhut (D)	89,701	43.5
Ronald E. Young (I)	11,364	5.5
Jerome A. Bruntar (I)	5,180	2.5

OKLAHOMA

Governor

	Vote Total	%
Frank Keating (R)	466,740	46.9
Jack Mildren (D)	294,936	29.6
Wes Watkins (I)	233,336	23.5

Senate

	Vote Total	%
James M. Inhofe (R)	542,390	55.2
Dave McCurdy (D)	392,488	40.0
Danny Corn (I)	47,552	4.8

House

	Vote Total	%
1 Steve Largent (R)	107,085	62.7
Stuart Price (D)	63,753	37.3
2 Tom Coburn (R)	82,479	52.1
Virgil R. Cooper (D)	75,943	47.9
3 • Bill Brewster (D)	115,731	73.8
Darrel Dewayne Tallant (R)	41,147	26.2
4 J.C. Watts (R)	80,251	51.6
David Perryman (D)	67,237	43.3
Bill Tiffee (I)	7,913	5.1
5 • Ernest Jim Istook, Jr. (R)	136,877	78.1
Tom Keith (I)	38,270	21.9
6 • Frank D. Lucas (R)	106,961	70.2
Jeffrey S. Tollett (D)	45,399	29.8

OREGON

Governor

	Vote Total	%
John Kitzhaber (D)	622,083	50.9
Denny Smith (R)	517,874	42.4
Ed Hickam (AM)	58,449	4.8
Danford P. Vander Ploeg (LIBERT)	20,183	1.7
Write-ins	2,421	.2

House

	Vote Total	%
1 • Elizabeth Furse (D)	121,147	47.7
Bill Witt (R)	120,846	47.6
Brewster Gillett (AM)	6,695	2.6
Daniel E. Wilson (LIBERT)	5,161	2.0
Write-ins	140	.1
2 Wes Cooley (R)	134,255	57.3
Sue C. Kupillas (D)	90,822	38.7
Gary L. Sublett (LIBERT)	9,063	3.9
Write-ins	241	.1
3 • Ron Wyden (D)	161,624	72.5
Everett Hall (R)	43,211	19.4
Mark Brunelle (I)	13,550	6.1
Gene Nanni (LIBERT)	4,164	1.9
Write-ins	273	.1
4 • Peter A. DeFazio (D)	158,981	66.8
John D. Newkirk (R)	78,947	33.2
Write-ins	221	.1
5 Jim Bunn (R)	121,369	49.8
Catherine Webber (D)	114,015	46.8
Jon E. Zimmer (LIBERT)	7,929	3.3
Write-ins	303	.1

PENNSYLVANIA

Governor

	Vote Total	%
Tom Ridge (R)	1,627,976	45.4
Mark S. Singel (D)	1,430,099	39.9
Peg Luksik (CONSTL)	460,269	12.8
Patrick Fallon (LIBERT)	33,602	.9
Timothy E. Holloway (PAT)	33,235	.9

Senate

	Vote Total	%
Rick Santorum (R)	1,735,691	49.4
• Harris Wofford (D)	1,648,481	46.9
Diane Blough (PAT)	69,825	2.0
Donald C. Ernsberger (LIBERT)	59,115	1.7

House

	Vote Total	%
1 • Thomas M. Foglietta (D)	99,669	81.5
Roger F. Gordon (R)	22,595	18.5
2 Chaka Fattah (D)	120,553	85.9
Lawrence R. Watson (R)	19,824	14.1
3 • Robert A. Borski (D)	92,702	62.7
James C. Hasher (R)	55,209	37.3
4 • Ron Klink (D)	119,115	64.2
Ed Peglow (R)	66,509	35.8

	Vote Total	%
5 • William F. Clinger (R)	145,335	99.9
Write-ins	96	.1
6 • Tim Holden (D)	90,023	56.7
Fred Levering (R)	68,610	43.3
7 • Curt Weldon (R)	137,480	69.7
Sara Nichols (D)	59,845	30.3
8 • James C. Greenwood (R)	110,499	66.1
John P. Murray (D)	44,559	26.7
Jay Russell (LIBERT)	7,925	4.7
Robert J. Cash (I)	4,191	2.5
9 • Bud Shuster (R)	146,688	99.7
Write-ins	515	.3
10 • Joseph M. McDade (R)	106,992	65.7
Daniel J. Schreffler (D)	50,635	31.1
Albert A. Smith (LIBERT)	5,196	3.2
11 • Paul E. Kanjorski (D)	101,966	66.5
J. Andrew Podolak (R)	51,295	33.5
12 • John P. Murtha (D)	117,825	68.9
Bill Choby (R)	53,147	31.1
13 Jon D. Fox (R)	96,254	49.4
• Marjorie Margolies-Mezvinsky (D)	88,073	45.2
Lee D. Hustead (LIBERT)	7,183	3.7
Frank W. Szabo (I)	3,278	1.7
14 • William J. Coyne (D)	105,310	64.1
John Robert Clark (R)	53,221	32.4
Edward L. Stewart (PAT)	3,826	2.3
Paul Scherrer (WL)	1,819	1.1
15 • Paul McHale (D)	72,073	47.8
Jim Yeager (R)	71,602	47.4
Victor Mazziotti (PAT)	7,227	4.8
16 • Robert S. Walker (R)	109,759	69.7
Bill Chertok (D)	47,680	30.3
17 • George W. Gekas (R)	133,788	99.9
Write-ins	187	.1
18 Mike Doyle (D)	101,784	54.8
John McCarty (R)	83,881	45.2
19 • Bill Goodling (R)	124,496	99.5
Write-ins	621	.5
20 Frank R. Mascara (D)	95,251	53.1
Mike McCormick (R)	84,156	46.9
21 Phil English (R)	89,439	49.5
Bill Leavens (D)	84,796	46.9
Arthur E. Drew (I)	6,588	3.6

RHODE ISLAND

Governor

	Vote Total	%
Lincoln C. Almond (R)	171,194	47.4
Myrth York (D)	157,361	43.5
Robert J. Healey (I)	32,822	9.1

Senate

	Vote Total	%
• John H. Chafee (R)	222,856	64.5
Linda J. Kushner (D)	122,532	35.5

House

	Vote Total	%
1 Patrick J. Kennedy (D)	89,832	54.1
Kevin Vigilante (R)	76,069	45.9
2 • Jack Reed (D)	119,659	68.0
A. John Elliot (R)	56,348	32.0

SOUTH CAROLINA

Governor

	Vote Total	%
David Beasley (R)	470,756	50.4
Nick A. Theodore (D)	447,002	47.9
John Peeples (USTAX)	8,003	.9
Wayne B. Griffin (NA)	5,875	.6
Write-ins	1,537	.2
Joe Riley (write-in)	557	.1

House

	Vote Total	%
1 Marshall "Mark" Sanford (R)	97,803	66.3
Robert Barber (D)	47,769	32.4
Robert Paine (LIBERT)	1,836	1.2
2 • Floyd D. Spence (R)	133,307	99.8
Write-ins	285	.2
3 Lindsey Graham (R)	90,123	60.1
James Bryan (D)	59,932	39.9
4 • Bob Inglis (R)	109,626	73.5
Jerry Fowler (D)	39,396	26.4
Write-ins	154	.1
5 • John M. Spratt Jr. (D)	77,311	52.1
Larry Bigham (R)	70,967	47.8
Write-ins	85	.1

	Vote Total	%

6 • James E. Clyburn (D)	88,635	63.8
Gary McLeod (R)	50,259	36.2

SOUTH DAKOTA

Governor

William J. Janklow (R)	172,515	55.4
Jim Beddow (D)	126,273	40.5
Nathan A. Barton (LIBERT)	12,825	4.1

House

AL • Tim Johnson (D)	183,036	59.8
Jan Berkhout (R)	112,054	36.6
Ronald Wieczorek (I)	10,832	3.5

TENNESSEE

Governor

Don Sundquist (R)	807,104	54.3
Phil Bredesen (D)	664,252	44.7
Stephanie Holt (I)	9,981	.7
Will Smith (I)	3,365	.2
Charlie Moffet (I)	2,347	.2

Senate (Full Term)

Bill Frist (R)	834,226	56.4
• Jim Sasser (D)	623,164	42.1
John Jay Hooker (I)	13,244	.9
Charles F. Johnson (I)	6,631	.4
Philip L. Kienlen (I)	3,087	.2

Senate (Short Term)

Fred Thompson (R)	885,998	60.4
Jim Cooper (D)	565,930	38.6
Charles N. Hancock (I)	4,169	.3
Charles M. Moore (I)	2,219	.2
Terry L. Lytle (I)	1,934	.1
Kerry Martin (I)	1,719	.1
Jon Walls (I)	1,532	.1
Hobart Lumpkin (I)	1,184	.1
Don Schneller (I)	1,150	.1

House

1 • James H. Quillen (R)	102,947	72.9
J. Carr "Jack" Christian (D)	34,691	24.6
George "Doc" Mauer (I)	3,576	2.5
2 • John J. "Jimmy" Duncan Jr. (R)	128,937	90.5
Randon J. Krieg (I)	6,854	4.8
Greg Samples (I)	6,682	4.7
3 Zach Wamp (R)	84,583	52.3
Randy Button (D)	73,839	45.6
Thomas Ed Morrell (I)	1,929	1.2
Richard M. Sims (I)	1,498	.9
4 Van Hilleary (R)	81,539	56.6
Jeff Whorley (D)	60,489	42.0
J. Patrick Lyons (I)	1,944	1.4
5 • Bob Clement (D)	95,953	60.2
John Osborne (R)	61,692	38.7
Lloyd Botway (I)	978	.6
Chuck Lokey (I)	664	.4
6 • Bart Gordon (D)	90,933	50.6
Steve Gill (R)	88,759	49.4
7 Ed Bryant (R)	102,587	60.2
Harold Byrd (D)	65,851	38.6
Tom Jeanette (I)	1,944	1.1
8 • John Tanner (D)	97,951	63.8
Neal R. Morris (R)	55,573	36.2
9 • Harold E. Ford (D)	94,805	57.8
Rod DeBerry (R)	69,226	42.2

TEXAS

Governor

George W. Bush (R)	2,350,994	53.5
• Ann Richards (D)	2,016,928	45.9
Keary Ehlers (LIBERT)	28,320	.6

Senate

• Kay Bailey Hutchison (R)	2,604,218	60.8
Richard Fisher (D)	1,639,615	38.3
Pierre Blondeau (LIBERT)	36,107	.8

House

1 • Jim Chapman (D)	86,480	55.3
Mike Blankenship (R)	63,911	40.9
Thomas "Jefferson" Mosser (I)	6,001	3.8
2 • Charles Wilson (D)	87,709	57.0
Donna Peterson (R)	66,071	43.0

3 • Sam Johnson (R)	157,011	91.0
Tom Donahue (LIBERT)	15,611	9.0
4 • Ralph M. Hall (D)	99,303	58.8
David L. Bridges (R)	67,267	39.8
Steven Rothacker (LIBERT)	2,377	1.4
5 • John Bryant (D)	61,877	50.1
Pete Sessions (R)	58,521	47.3
Barbara Morgan (I)	1,715	1.4
Noel Kopala (LIBERT)	876	.7
Regina Arashvand (I)	627	.5
6 • Joe L. Barton (R)	152,038	75.6
Terry Jesmore (D)	44,286	22.0
Bill Baird (LIBERT)	4,688	2.3
7 • Bill Archer (R)	116,873	100.0
8 • Jack Fields (R)	148,473	92.0
Russ Klecka (I)	12,831	8.0
9 Steve Stockman (R)	81,353	51.9
• Jack Brooks (D)	71,643	45.7
Bill Felton (I)	2,145	1.4
Darla K. Beenau (LIBERT)	1,656	1.1
10 Lloyd Doggett (D)	113,738	56.3
A. Jo Baylor (R)	80,382	39.8
Jeff Hill (LIBERT)	2,953	1.5
Michael L. Brandes (I)	2,579	1.3
Jeff Davis (I)	2,334	1.2
11 • Chet Edwards (D)	76,667	59.2
Jim Broyles (R)	52,876	40.8
12 • Pete Geren (D)	96,372	68.7
Ernest J. Anderson Jr. (R)	43,959	31.3
13 William M. "Mac" Thornberry (R)	79,466	55.4
• Bill Sarpalius (D)	63,923	44.6
14 • Greg Laughlin (D)	86,175	55.6
Jim Deats (R)	68,793	44.4
15 • E. "Kika" de la Garza (D)	61,527	59.0
Tom Haughey (R)	41,119	39.4
John c.c. Hamilton (I)	1,720	1.6
16 • Ronald D. Coleman (D)	49,815	57.1
Bobby Ortiz (R)	37,409	42.9
17 • Charles W. Stenholm (D)	83,497	53.7
Phil Boone (R)	72,108	46.3
18 Sheila Jackson-Lee (D)	84,790	73.5
Jerry Burley (R)	28,153	24.4
J. Larry Snellings (I)	1,278	1.1
George M. Hollenbeck (LIBERT)	1,169	1.0
19 • Larry Combest (R)	120,641	100.0
20 • Henry B. Gonzalez (D)	60,114	62.5
Carl Bill Colyer (R)	36,035	37.5
21 • Lamar Smith (R)	165,595	90.0
Kerry Lowry (I)	18,480	10.0
22 • Tom DeLay (R)	120,302	73.7
Scott Douglas Cunningham (D)	38,826	23.8
Gregory D. Pepper (I)	4,016	2.5
23 • Henry Bonilla (R)	73,815	62.6
Rolando L. Rios (D)	44,101	37.4
24 • Martin Frost (D)	65,019	52.8
Ed Harrison (R)	58,062	47.2
25 Ken Bentsen (D)	61,959	52.3
Gene Fontenot (R)	53,321	45.0
Sarah Klein-Tower (I)	2,060	1.7
Robert F. Lockhart (LIBERT)	1,189	1.0
26 • Dick Armey (R)	135,398	76.4
LeEarl Ann Bryant (D)	39,763	22.4
Alfred Adask (LIBERT)	2,030	1.1
27 • Solomon P. Ortiz (D)	65,325	59.4
Erol A. Stone (R)	44,693	40.6
28 • Frank Tejeda (D)	73,986	70.9
David C. Slatter (R)	28,777	27.6
Stephen "Steve" Rothstein (LIBERT)	1,612	1.5
29 • Gene Green (D)	44,102	73.4
Harold "Oilman" Eide (R)	15,952	26.6
30 • Eddie Bernice Johnson (D)	73,166	72.6
Lucy Cain (R)	25,848	25.7
Ken Ashby (LIBERT)	1,728	1.7

UTAH

Senate

• Orrin G. Hatch (R)	357,297	68.8
Patrick A. Shea (D)	146,938	28.3
Craig Oliver (I)	9,550	1.8
Gary R. Van Horn (AM)	2,543	.5
Nelson Gonzalez (SW)	1,514	.3
Lawrence Rey Topham (IA)	1,462	.3

House

1 • James V. Hansen (R)	104,954	64.5
Bobbie Coray (D)	57,644	35.5
2 Enid Greene Waldholtz (R)	85,507	45.8
• Karen Shepherd (D)	66,911	35.9
Merrill Cook (I)	34,167	18.3
3 • Bill Orton (D)	91,505	59.0
Dixie Thompson (R)	61,839	39.9
Barbara Greenway (SW)	1,802	1.2

VERMONT

Governor

• Howard Dean (D)	145,661	68.7
David Kelley (R)	40,292	19.0
Thomas J. Morse (I)	15,000	7.1
Dennis Lane (VG)	2,118	1.0
William "Turkeybill" Brueckner (I)	2,071	1.0
August "Gus" Jaccaci (PV)	2,043	1.0
Richard Gottlieb (LU)	1,733	.8
Bill Brunelle (NL)	1,668	.8
Write-ins	1,460	.7

Senate

• James M. Jeffords (R)	106,505	50.3
Jan Backus (D)	85,868	40.6
Gavin T. Mills (I)	12,465	5.9
Matthew S. Mulligan (I)	3,141	1.5
Bob Melamede (VG)	1,416	.7
Jerry Levy (LU)	1,376	.7
Joseph Victor Pardo (NL)	709	.3
Write-ins	192	.1

House

AL • Bernard Sanders (I)	105,502	49.9
John Carroll (R)	98,523	46.6
Carole Banus (NL)	2,963	1.4
Jack "Buck" Rogers (VG)	2,664	1.3
Annette Larson (LU)	1,493	.7
Write-ins	304	.1

VIRGINIA

Senate

• Charles S. Robb (D)	938,376	45.6
Oliver L. North (R)	882,213	42.9
J. Marshall Coleman (I)	235,324	11.4
Write-ins	1,437	.1

House

1 • Herbert H. Bateman (R)	142,930	74.3
Mary Sinclair (D)	45,173	23.5
Matt B. Voorhees (I)	4,365	2.3
2 • Owen Pickett (D)	81,372	59.0
Jim Chapman (R)	56,375	40.9
3 • Robert C. Scott (D)	108,532	79.4
Tom Ward (R)	28,080	20.6
4 • Norman Sisisky (D)	115,055	61.6
George Sweet (R)	71,678	38.4
5 • Lewis F. Payne Jr. (D)	95,308	53.3
George C. Landrith III (R)	83,555	46.7
6 • Robert W. Goodlatte (R)	126,455	99.9
Write-ins	189	.1
7 • Thomas J. Bliley Jr. (R)	176,941	84.0
Gerald E. "Jerry" Berg (I)	33,220	15.8
Write-ins	471	.2
8 • James P. Moran (D)	120,281	59.3
Kyle E. McSlarrow (R)	79,568	39.3
R. Ward Edmonds (I)	1,858	.9
William C. Jones (I)	868	.4
9 • Rick Boucher (D)	102,876	58.8
Steve Fast (R)	72,133	41.2
10 • Frank R. Wolf (R)	153,311	87.3
Alan R. Ogden (I)	13,687	7.8
Robert L. "Bob" Rilee (I)	8,267	4.7
Write-ins	266	.2
11 Thomas M. Davis III (R)	98,216	52.9
• Leslie L. Byrne (D)	84,104	45.3
Gordon S. Cruickshank (I)	3,246	1.7
Write-ins	114	.1

WASHINGTON

Senate

• Slade Gorton (R)	947,821	55.7
Ron Sims (D)	752,352	44.3

		Vote Total	%
House			
1	Rick White (R)	100,554	51.7
	• Maria Cantwell (D)	94,110	48.3
2	Jack Metcalf (R)	107,430	54.7
	Harriet A. Spanel (D)	89,096	45.3
3	Linda Smith (R)	100,188	52.0
	• Jolene Unsoeld (D)	85,826	44.6
	Caitlin Davis Carlson (GC)	6,620	3.4
4	Doc Hastings (R)	92,828	53.3
	• Jay Inslee (D)	81,198	46.7
5	George Nethercutt (R)	110,057	50.9
	• Thomas S. Foley (D)	106,074	49.1
6	• Norm Dicks (D)	105,480	58.3
	Benjamin Gregg (R)	75,322	41.7
7	• Jim McDermott (D)	148,353	75.1
	Keith Harris (R)	49,091	24.9
8	• Jennifer Dunn (R)	140,409	76.1
	Jim Wyrick (D)	44,165	23.9
9	Randy Tate (R)	77,833	51.8
	• Mike Kreidler (D)	72,451	48.2

WEST VIRGINIA

		Vote Total	%
Senate			
	• Robert C. Byrd (D)	290,495	69.0
	Stan Klos (R)	130,441	31.0
House			
1	• Alan B. Mollohan (D)	103,177	70.3
	Sally Rossy Riley (R)	43,590	29.7
2	• Bob Wise (D)	90,757	63.7
	Sam Cravotta (R)	51,691	36.3

		Vote Total	%
3	• Nick J. Rahall II (D)	74,967	63.9
	Ben Waldman (R)	42,382	36.1

WISCONSIN

		Vote Total	%
Governor			
	• Tommy G. Thompson (R)	1,051,326	67.2
	Chuck Chvala (D)	482,850	30.9
	David S. Harmon (LIBERT)	11,639	.7
	Edward J. Frami (TAX)	9,188	.6
	Michael J. Mangan (I)	8,150	.5
Senate			
	• Herb Kohl (D)	912,662	58.3
	Robert T. Welch (R)	636,989	40.7
	James Dean (LIBERT)	15,439	1.0
House			
1	Mark W. Neumann (R)	83,937	49.4
	• Peter W. Barca (D)	82,817	48.8
	Edward J. Kozak (LIBERT)	3,085	1.8
2	• Scott L. Klug (R)	133,734	69.2
	Thomas C. Hecht (D)	55,406	28.7
	John J. Stumpf (TAX)	2,676	1.4
	Joseph E. Schumacher (I)	1,327	.7
	Write-ins	106	.1
3	• Steve Gunderson (R)	89,338	55.7
	Harvey Stower (D)	65,758	41.0
	Chuck Lee (TAX)	2,837	1.8
	Mark Weinhold (I)	2,279	1.4
	Write-ins	101	.1

		Vote Total	%
4	• Gerald D. Kleczka (D)	93,789	53.7
	Tom Reynolds (R)	78,225	44.8
	James Harold Hause (TAX)	2,611	1.5
5	• Thomas M. Barrett (D)	87,806	62.4
	Stephen B. Hollingshead (R)	51,145	36.4
	David J. Schall (I)	1,576	1.1
	Write-ins	113	.1
6	• Tom Petri (R)	119,384	99.5
	Write-ins	603	.5
7	• David R. Obey (D)	97,184	54.3
	Scott West (R)	81,706	45.7
8	• Toby Roth (R)	114,319	63.7
	Stan Gruszynski (D)	65,065	36.3
9	• F. James Sensenbrenner (R)	141,617	99.8
	Write-ins	336	.2

WYOMING

		Vote Total	%
Governor			
	Jim Geringer (R)	118,016	58.7
	Kathy Karpan (D)	80,747	40.2
	Seaghan Uibreaslain (LIBERT)	2,227	1.1
Senate			
	Craig Thomas (R)	118,754	58.9
	Mike Sullivan (D)	79,287	39.3
	Craig Alan McCune (LIBERT)	3,669	1.8
House			
AL	Barbara Cubin (R)	104,426	53.2
	Bob Schuster (D)	81,022	41.3
	Dave Dawson (LIBERT)	10,749	5.5

Redistricting Still Troubles Several States

Most states redrew their congressional district maps in 1991 or 1992 to adapt to 1990 census data and the subsequent shuffling of House seats between states. But for a handful of states, redistricting had been a persistent legal and political puzzle, and several disputes remained unresolved at the end of 1994.

In Louisiana, for example, the shape of the seven districts on the map changed four times between December 1993 and August 1994. In the fall of 1994, the state wound up using the same lines it had in 1992. But a legal challenge to that map was still pending before the Supreme Court at year's end, and it was by no means certain where the lines would be drawn for the 1996 elections.

The Supreme Court was also considering appeals of lower court rulings regarding the district lines in Georgia, North Carolina and Texas. Another suit pending with regard to Florida's congressional district map was a candidate for eventual consideration by the Supreme Court, as was a lawsuit revived in September by a federal court in California. The latter case maintained that the House districts in California violated the Voting Rights Act by diluting the Latino population in southern Santa Clara and Monterey counties and in parts of Southern California.

Most observers were watching the Louisiana case, however, as the likeliest to be heard and decided by the high court. The case stemmed from the map the Legislature had drawn prior to the 1992 elections. It created two black-majority districts, including one based in New Orleans and one that wandered across the state, picking up pockets of African-American voters in communities widely separated geographically.

The Louisiana plaintiffs claimed the seven districts were "so skewed by race that blacks who live in the five mostly white congressional districts have no say in their government, and whites in the two black-majority districts have no say in theirs."

In prior decades, redistricting plans written by Southern state legislatures were more often challenged by advocates for minority groups, who argued that the maps violated the Voting Rights Act by diluting the minority vote. But in the 1990s, the reverse had been the rule: Whites were filing suit against redistricting plans that created majority-minority districts.

The district maps to which these plantiffs objected were drawn at the insistence of the Justice Department under Republican President George Bush as well as under President Clinton. And many strategists observed that the creation of majority-minority districts tended to help the GOP. While such districts almost invariably elected black or Hispanic Democrats, the concentration of minority voters in these districts tended to help white Republican candidates win in surrounding districts.

After Georgia created three black-majority districts in 1992, white Republican candidates proceeded to win four seats in 1992 and seven in 1994.

Nevertheless, Democrats generally and racial-minority Democrats in particular defended the creation of majority-minority districts. The plaintiffs who filed challenges to these districts tended to be white Republicans.

The Supreme Court's 1993 ruling in *Shaw v. Reno* encouraged such challenges. In that ruling, the court allowed five white North Carolinians to challenge the state's congressional district map, which contained two black-majority districts, on the grounds that their 14th Amendment right to "equal protection of the laws" may have been violated. In its 5-4 decision, the court called into question the constitutionality of drawing congressional districts with "bizarre" shapes to ensure minority representation. In so doing, it appeared to be establishing a new standard for scrutiny — the appearance of the majority-minority district — by which race-based district-drawing would be judged. (*1993 Almanac, p. 25-A*)

The principal byproduct of the *Shaw* decision was a skein

of lawsuits challenging maps drawn to satisfy the dictates of the Voting Rights Act as enforced by the Bush administration's Justice Department. Of the nine Southern states that were required by the Voting Rights Act to submit any election-law changes to the Justice Department for approval, five — Florida, Georgia, Louisiana, North Carolina and Texas — had had their plans challenged in federal court as products of "racial gerrymandering." As of early 1995, all but Florida's case had been appealed to the Supreme Court.

Using the *Shaw* decision as a guidepost, special federal-court three-judge panels in Louisiana, Georgia and Texas ruled that the plans used for the 1992 election were unconstitutional. ∎

House Special Elections

Two special elections held in May to fill vacant House seats in Oklahoma and Kentucky replaced a pair of veteran Democrats with younger Republicans, offering a harbinger of the historic election to come in November.

Oklahoma's western 6th District became vacant when 10-term veteran Glenn English retired in the middle of the 103rd Congress to become head of the National Rural Electric Cooperative Association. Despite the Democrats' 2-1 advantage in 6th District registration, the May 10 special election was won by Republican Frank D. Lucas, 34, a farmer-rancher and state legislator.

Even more stunning was the May 24 capture of Kentucky's 2nd District by Ron Lewis, 48, the first Republican ever to represent the area in Congress. Lewis succeeded William H. Natcher, chairman of the House Appropriations Committee, who died March 29 at the age of 84. *(Natcher, p. 58)*

Lucas Prevails in Oklahoma's Western 6th

The Texans who settled Oklahoma's southwestern counties helped put a Democratic stamp on this district long ago. But as the state grew and diversified, its westernmost 6th District saw its boundaries move east to encompass much of Oklahoma City and its suburbs. That trend, combined with the unpopularity of the Clinton administration in the rural Southwest, made 1994 a tough year for Democrats to hold English's district.

Lucas (R)	71,354	54%
Webber (D)	60,411	46%

The task fell to Dan Webber Jr., a former staff member for Oklahoma's Democratic Sen. David L. Boren. Webber, 28, benefited from Boren's help in the March 8 primary, but the popular senator's backing was not enough to counter the Republican tide on May 10.

Lucas, meanwhile, had finished a close second in the GOP balloting March 8, forcing a runoff with state Sen. Brooks Douglass on April 5. Heavy snows had limited turnout to about 11.5 percent of the district's registered Republicans in March. But in April, nearly twice as many voters appeared, and they gave Lucas 56 percent of their votes.

Lucas, a former president of the Young Republicans at Oklahoma State University, kept his momentum rolling into May, emphasizing his rural roots in Roger Mills County. He berated Webber for the latter's years in Washington.

On Election Day, a big turnout (43 percent of all registered voters) was prompted in part by religious activists opposing a gambling referendum. Their efforts, along with heavy support from members of United We Stand Inc., propelled Lucas, who carried 19 of the district's 24 counties.

Lewis Shocks in Kentucky's 2nd

In winning 20 terms in this district, the legendary Natcher refused political contributions and paid for his bare-bones campaigns out of his own pocket. It was rare for him to face much competition. But his would-be Democratic successor, former state Sen. Joseph W. Prather, soon learned that the Natcher style would not suffice for him.

Lewis (R)	40,126	55%
Prather (D)	32,625	45%

Lewis, a Baptist minister and religious bookstore owner, spoke for those who felt alienated from the Democratic Party on social and cultural issues. Both he and Prather were chosen to run by party committees, rather than by party primaries, so as to expedite a replacement for Natcher.

Lewis benefited from a textbook campaign of the 1990s, replete with appeals to Perot voters and conservative Christian activists. He was aided by the National Republican Congressional Committee with ads equating a vote for Prather with a vote for Clinton. The tactic worked well in a district that had preferred President George Bush in 1992 as well as in 1988. Lewis also got a boost on the stump from such big GOP names as Senate Minority Leader Bob Dole of Kansas.

Prather, meanwhile, kept his campaign in low gear until the final days and refused help from the national party. He felt sure he would prevail on the district's 2-1 registration edge for Democrats and on the longstanding local affection for Natcher. But Lewis' combination of message, money, organization and timely campaign glamour proved to be more than the Democrats had bargained for. ∎

GLOSSARY

Glossary of Congressional Terms

Act — The term for legislation once it has passed both houses of Congress and has been signed by the president or passed over his veto, thus becoming law. *(See also Pocket Veto, Veto.)*

Also used in parliamentary terminology for a bill that has been passed by one house and engrossed. *(See also Engrossed Bill.)*

Adjournment Sine Die — Adjournment without definitely fixing a day for reconvening; literally, "adjournment without a day." Usually used to connote the final adjournment of a session of Congress. A session can continue until noon Jan. 3 of the following year, when, under the 20th Amendment to the Constitution, it automatically terminates. Both houses must agree to a concurrent resolution for either house to adjourn for more than three days.

Adjournment to a Day Certain — Adjournment under a motion or resolution that fixes the next time of meeting. Under the Constitution, neither house can adjourn for more than three days without the concurrence of the other. A session of Congress is not ended by adjournment to a day certain.

Amendment — A proposal of a member of Congress to alter the language, provisions or stipulations in a bill or in another amendment. An amendment usually is printed, debated and voted upon in the same manner as a bill.

Amendment in the Nature of a Substitute — Usually an amendment that seeks to replace the entire text of a bill. Passage of this type of amendment strikes out everything after the enacting clause and inserts a new version of the bill. An amendment in the nature of a substitute also can refer to an amendment that replaces a large portion of the text of a bill.

Appeal — A member's challenge of a ruling or decision made by the presiding officer of the chamber. In the Senate, the senator appeals to members of the chamber to override the decision. If carried by a majority vote, the appeal nullifies the chair's ruling. In the House, the decision of the Speaker traditionally has been final; seldom are there appeals to the members to reverse the Speaker's stand. To appeal a ruling is considered an attack on the Speaker.

Appropriations Bill — A bill that gives legal authority to spend or obligate money from the Treasury. The Constitution disallows money to be drawn from the Treasury "but in Consequence of Appropriations made by Law."

By congressional custom, an appropriations bill originates in the House, and it is not supposed to be considered by the full House or Senate until a related measure authorizing the funding is enacted. An appropriations bill grants the actual budget authority approved by authorization bills, but not necessarily the full amount permissible under the authorization. For decades, appropriations often have not been final until well after the fiscal year begins, requiring a succession of stopgap bills to continue the government's functions. About half of all budget authority, notably that for Social Security and interest on the federal debt, does not require annual appropriations; those programs exist under permanent appropriations. *(See also Authorization Bill, Backdoor Spending Authority, Budget Authority, Budget Process, Continuing Resolution, Entitlement Program, Supplemental Appropriations Bill.)*

Authorization Bill — Basic, substantive legislation that establishes or continues the legal operation of a federal program or agency, either indefinitely or for a specific period of time, or which sanctions a particular type of obligation or expenditure. An authorization normally is a prerequisite for an appropriation or other kind of budget authority. Under the rules of both chambers, the appropriation for a program or agency may not be considered until its authorization has been considered (although this requirement is often waived). An authorization sets the maximum amount of funds that can be given to a program or agency, but sometimes it merely authorizes "such sums as may be necessary." *(See also Backdoor Spending Authority.)*

Backdoor Spending Authority — Budget authority provided in legislation outside the normal appropriations process. The most common forms of backdoor spending are borrowing authority, contract authority, entitlements and loan guarantees that commit the government to payments of principal and interest on loans — such as guaranteed student loans — made by banks or other private lenders. Loan guarantees result in actual outlays only when there is a default by the borrower.

In some cases, such as interest on the public debt, a permanent appropriation is provided that becomes available without further action by Congress.

Bills — Most legislative proposals before Congress are in the form of bills and are designated by HR in the House of Representatives or S in the Senate, according to the house in which they originate, and by a number assigned in the order in which they are introduced during the two-year period of a congressional term. "Public bills" deal with general questions and become public laws if approved by Congress and signed by the president. "Private bills" deal with individual matters, such as claims against the government, immigration and naturalization cases or land titles, and become private laws if approved and signed. *(See also Concurrent Resolution, Joint Resolution, Resolution.)*

Bills Introduced — In both the House and Senate, any number of members may join in introducing a single bill or resolution. The first member listed is the sponsor of the bill, and all subsequent members listed are the bill's cosponsors.

Many bills are committee bills and are introduced under the name of the chairman of the committee or subcommittee. All appropriations bills fall into this category. A committee frequently holds hearings on a number of related bills and may agree to one of them or to an entirely new bill. *(See also By Request, Clean Bill, Report.)*

Bills Referred — When introduced, a bill is referred to the committee or committees that have jurisdiction over the subject with which the bill is concerned. Under the standing rules of the House and Senate, bills are referred by the Speaker in the House and by the presiding officer in the Senate. In practice, the House and Senate parliamentarians act for these officials and refer the vast majority of bills.

Borrowing Authority — Statutory authority that permits a federal agency to incur obligations and make payments for specified purposes with borrowed money.

Budget — The document sent to Congress by the president early each year estimating government revenue and expenditures for the ensuing fiscal year.

Budget Act — The common name for the Congressional Budget and Impoundment Control Act of 1974, which established the current budget process and created the Congressional Budget Office. The act also put limits on presidential authority to spend appropriated money. It has undergone several major revisions since 1974. *(See also Budget Process, Impoundments.)*

Budget Authority — Authority for federal agencies to enter into obligations that will result in immediate or future outlays. The basic forms of budget authority are appropriations, contract authority and borrowing authority. Budget authority may be classified by (1) the period of availability (one-year, multiple-year or without a time limitation), (2) the timing of congressional action (current or permanent) or (3) the manner of determining the amount available (definite

or indefinite). *(See also Appropriations, Outlays)*

Budget Process — The annual budget process was created by the Congressional Budget and Impoundment Control Act of 1974, with a timetable that was modified in 1990. Under the law, the president must submit his proposed budget by the first Monday in February. Congress is supposed to complete an annual budget resolution by April 15, setting guidelines for congressional action on spending and tax measures.

The budget resolution sets a strict ceiling on discretionary budget authority, and it also may contain "reconciliation instructions" directing authorizing and tax-writing committees to meet specified deficit-reduction goals. The committees' proposals are then bundled into a reconciliation bill.

Budget rules enacted in the 1990 Budget Enforcement Act and extended in 1993 freeze discretionary outlays at the 1993 level or below through 1998. The caps can be adjusted annually to account for changes in the economy and other limited factors. In addition, pay-as-you-go rules require that any tax cut, new entitlement program or expansion of existing entitlement benefits be offset by an increase in taxes or a cut in entitlement spending. The rules hold Congress harmless for budget-deficit increases that lawmakers do not explicitly cause — for example, increases due to a recession or to an expansion in the number of beneficiaries qualifying for existing entitlement programs, such as Medicare or food stamps.

If Congress exceeds the discretionary spending caps in its appropriations bills, the law requires an across-the-board cut — known as sequestration — in non-exempt discretionary spending accounts. If Congress violates the pay-as-you-go rules, entitlement programs are subject to a sequester. Supplemental appropriations are subject to similar controls, with the proviso that if both Congress and the president agree, spending designated as an emergency can exceed the caps. *(See also Budget Resolution, Reconciliation, Sequester Order.)*

Budget Resolution — A concurrent resolution that is passed by both chambers of Congress but does not require the president's signature. The measure sets a strict ceiling on the budget authority available for discretionary spending, along with non-binding recommendations about how the spending should be allocated. It may also contain "reconciliation instructions" requiring authorizing and tax-writing committees to propose changes in existing law to meet deficit-reduction goals. The Budget committees then bundle those proposals into a reconciliation bill. *(See also Budget Process, Reconciliation.)*

By Request — A phrase used when a senator or representative introduces a bill at the request of an executive agency or private organization but does not necessarily endorse the legislation.

Calendar — An agenda or list of business awaiting possible action by each chamber. The House uses five legislative calendars. *(See also Consent, Discharge, House, Private, Union Calendars.)*

In the Senate, all legislative matters reported from committee go on one calendar. They are listed there in the order in which committees report them or the Senate places them on the calendar, but they may be called up out of order by the majority leader, either by obtaining unanimous consent of the Senate or by a motion to call up a bill. The Senate also uses one non-legislative calendar; this is used for treaties and nominations. *(See also Executive Calendar.)*

Calendar Wednesday — A procedure in the House, now rarely used, whereby committees on Wednesdays may be called in the order in which they appear in Rule X of the House, for the purpose of bringing up any of their bills from either the House or the Union Calendar, except bills that are privileged. General debate is limited to two hours. Bills called up from the Union Calendar are considered in the Committee of the Whole. Calendar Wednesday is not observed during the last two weeks of a session

and may be dispensed with at other times by a two-thirds vote. This procedure now routinely is dispensed with by unanimous consent.

Call of the Calendar — Senate bills that are not brought up for debate by a motion, unanimous consent or a unanimous consent agreement are brought before the Senate for action when the calendar listing them is "called." Bills must be called in the order listed. Measures considered by this method usually are noncontroversial, and debate on the bill and any proposed amendments is limited to five minutes for each senator.

Chamber — The meeting place for the membership of either the House or the Senate; also the membership of the House or Senate meeting as such.

Clean Bill — Frequently after a committee has finished a major revision of a bill, one of the committee members, usually the chairman, will assemble the changes and what is left of the original bill into a new measure and introduce it as a "clean bill." The revised measure, which is given a new number, then is referred back to the committee, which reports it to the floor for consideration. This often is a timesaver, as committee-recommended changes in a clean bill do not have to be considered and voted on by the chamber. Reporting a clean bill also protects committee amendments that could be subject to points of order concerning germaneness.

Clerk of the House — An officer of the House of Representatives who supervises its records and legislative business. Many former administrative duties were transferred in 1992 to a new position, the director of non-legislative and financial services. *(See also Secretary of the Senate.)*

Cloture — The process by which a filibuster can be ended in the Senate other than by unanimous consent. A motion for cloture can apply to any measure before the Senate, including a proposal to change the chamber's rules. A cloture motion requires the signatures of 16 senators to be introduced. To end a filibuster, the cloture motion must obtain the votes of three-fifths of the entire Senate membership (60 if there are no vacancies), except when the filibuster is against a proposal to amend the standing rules of the Senate and a two-thirds vote of senators present and voting is required. The cloture request is put to a roll call vote one hour after the Senate meets on the second day following introduction of the motion. If approved, cloture limits each senator to one hour of debate. The bill or amendment in question comes to a final vote after 30 hours of consideration (including debate time and the time it takes to conduct roll calls, quorum calls and other procedural motions). *(See also Filibuster.)*

Committee — A division of the House or Senate that prepares legislation for action by the parent chamber or makes investigations as directed by the parent chamber.

There are several types of committees. Most standing committees are divided into subcommittees, which study legislation, hold hearings and report bills, with or without amendments, to the full committee. Only the full committee can report legislation for action by the House or Senate. *(See also Standing, Oversight, Select or Special Committees.)*

Committee of the Whole — The working title of what is formally "The Committee of the Whole House [of Representatives] on the State of the Union." The membership is composed of all House members sitting as a committee. Any 100 members who are present on the floor of the chamber to consider legislation comprise a quorum of the committee. Any legislation, however, must first have passed through the regular legislative or Appropriations committee and have been placed on the calendar.

Technically, the Committee of the Whole considers only bills directly or indirectly appropriating money, authorizing appropriations or involving taxes or charges on the public. Because the Committee of the Whole need number only 100 representatives, a

quorum is more readily attained, and legislative business is expedited. Before 1971, members' positions were not individually recorded on votes taken in the Committee of the Whole. *(See also Teller Vote.)*

When the full House resolves itself into the Committee of the Whole, it replaces the Speaker with a "chairman." A measure is debated and amendments may be proposed, with votes on amendments as needed. *(See also Five-Minute Rule.)*

When the committee completes its work on the measure, it dissolves itself by "rising." The Speaker returns, and the chairman of the Committee of the Whole reports to the House that the committee's work has been completed. At this time, members may demand a roll call vote on any amendment adopted in the Committee of the Whole. The final vote is on passage of the legislation.

Since 1993, the four delegates from the territories and the resident commissioner of Puerto Rico have been allowed to vote on questions before the Committee of the Whole. If their votes are decisive in the outcome, however, the matter is automatically revoted, with the delegates and resident commissioner ineligible. They cannot vote on final passage of bills or on separate votes demanded after the Committee of the Whole rises. This limited voting right was rescinded in 1995.

Committee Veto — A requirement added to a few statutes directing that certain policy directives by an executive department or agency be reviewed by certain congressional committees before they are implemented. Under common practice, the government department or agency and the committees involved are expected to reach a consensus before the directives are carried out. *(See also Legislative Veto.)*

Concurrent Resolution — A concurrent resolution, designated H Con Res or S Con Res, must be adopted by both houses, but it is not sent to the president for approval and, therefore, does not have the force of law. A concurrent resolution, for example, is used to fix the time for adjournment of a Congress. It also is used to express the sense of Congress on a foreign policy or domestic issue. The annual budget resolution is a concurrent resolution. *(See also Bills, Joint Resolution, Resolution.)*

Conference — A meeting between representatives of the House and the Senate to reconcile differences between the two chambers on provisions of a bill. Members of the conference committee are appointed by the Speaker and the presiding officer of the Senate and are called "managers" for their respective chambers. In 1993, the Speaker was given the power to remove members from a conference committee and appoint new conferees.

A majority of the conferees for each house must reach agreement on the provisions of the bill (often a compromise between the versions of the two chambers) before it can be considered by either chamber in the form of a "conference report." When the conference report goes to the floor, it is difficult to amend, and, if it is not approved by both chambers, the bill may go back to conference under certain situations, or a new conference must be convened. Many rules and informal practices govern the conduct of conference committees.

Bills that are passed by both houses with only minor differences need not be sent to conference. Either chamber may "concur" in the other's amendments, completing action on the legislation. Sometimes leaders of the committees of jurisdiction work out an informal compromise instead of having a formal conference. *(See also Custody of the Papers.)*

Confirmations — *(See Nominations.)*

Congressional Record — The daily, printed account of proceedings in both the House and Senate chambers, showing substantially verbatim debate, statements and a record of floor action. Highlights of legislative and committee action are embodied in a Daily Digest section of the Record, and members are entitled to have their extraneous remarks printed in an appendix known as "Extension of Remarks." Members may edit and revise remarks made on the floor during debate, and quotations from debate reported by the press are not always found in the Record.

The Congressional Record provides a way to distinguish remarks spoken on the floor of the House and Senate from undelivered speeches. In the Senate, all speeches, articles and other matter that members insert in the Record without actually reading them on the floor are set off by large black dots, or bullets. However, a loophole allows a member to avoid the bulleting if he or she delivers any portion of the speech in person. In the House, undelivered speeches and other material are printed in a distinctive typeface. The record is also available in electronic form. *(See also Journal.)*

Congressional Terms of Office — Normally begin on Jan. 3 of the year following a general election and are two years for representatives and six years for senators. Representatives elected in special elections are sworn in for the remainder of a term. A person may be appointed to fill a Senate vacancy and serve until a successor is elected; the successor serves until the end of the term applying to the vacant seat.

Consent Calendar — Members of the House may place on this calendar most bills on the Union or House Calendar that are considered non-controversial. Bills on the Consent Calendar normally are called on the first and third Mondays of each month. On the first occasion that a bill is called in this manner, consideration may be blocked by the objection of any member. The second time, if there are three objections, the bill is stricken from the Consent Calendar. If fewer than three members object, the bill is given immediate consideration.

A bill on the Consent Calendar may be postponed in another way. A member may ask that the measure be passed over "without prejudice." In that case, no objection is recorded against the bill, and its status on the Consent Calendar remains unchanged. A bill stricken from the Consent Calendar remains on the Union or House Calendar. The consent calendar has seldom been used in recent years. *(See also Calendar and House, Private, Union Calendars.)*

Continuing Resolution — A joint resolution, cleared by Congress and signed by the president (when the new fiscal year is about to begin or has begun), to provide new budget authority for federal agencies and programs to continue operating until the regular appropriations bills have been enacted. The continuing resolution usually specifies a maximum rate at which an agency may incur obligations, based on the rate of the prior year, the president's budget request or an appropriations bill passed by either or both chambers of Congress but not yet enacted. Continuing resolutions also are called "CRs" or continuing appropriations.

Contract Authority — Budget authority contained in an authorization bill that permits the federal government to enter into contracts or other obligations for future payments from funds not yet appropriated by Congress. The assumption is that funds will be available for payment in a subsequent appropriation act.

Correcting Recorded Votes — Rules prohibit members from changing their votes after the result has been announced. But, occasionally, hours, days or months after a vote has been taken, a member may announce he or she was "incorrectly recorded." In the Senate, a request to change one's vote almost always receives unanimous consent, so long as it does not change the outcome. In the House, members are prohibited from changing their votes if tallied by the electronic voting system.

Cosponsor — *(See Bills Introduced.)*

Current Services Estimates — Estimated budget authority and outlays for federal programs and operations for the forthcoming fiscal year based on continuation of existing levels of service without policy changes but with adjustments for inflation and for demographic changes that affect programs. These estimates, accompanied by the underlying economic and policy assumptions upon which they are based, are transmitted by the president to Congress when the budget is submitted.

Custody of the Papers — To reconcile differences between the House and Senate versions of a bill, a conference may be arranged. The chamber with "custody of the papers" — the engrossed bill, engrossed amendments, messages of transmittal — is the only body empowered to request the conference. By custom, the chamber that asks for a conference is the last to act on the conference report once agreement has been reached on the bill by the conferees.

Custody of the papers sometimes is manipulated to ensure that a particular chamber acts either first or last on the conference report.

Deferral — Executive branch action to defer, or delay, the spending of appropriated money. The 1974 Congressional Budget and Impoundment Control Act requires a special message from the president to Congress reporting a proposed deferral of spending. Deferrals may not extend beyond the end of the fiscal year in which the message is transmitted. A federal district court in 1986 struck down the president's authority to defer spending for policy reasons; the ruling was upheld by a federal appeals court in 1987. Congress can prohibit proposed deferrals by enacting a law doing so; most often, cancellations of proposed deferrals are included in appropriations bills. *(See also Rescission.)*

Dilatory Motion — A motion made for the purpose of killing time and preventing action on a bill or amendment. House rules outlaw dilatory motions, but enforcement is largely within the discretion of the Speaker or chairman of the Committee of the Whole. The Senate does not have a rule banning dilatory motions, except under cloture.

Discharge a Committee — Occasionally, attempts are made to relieve a committee from jurisdiction over a measure before it. This is attempted more often in the House than in the Senate, and the procedure rarely is successful.

In the House, if a committee does not report a bill within 30 days after the measure is referred to it, any member may file a discharge motion. Once offered, the motion is treated as a petition needing the signatures of a majority of members (218 if there are no vacancies). After the required signatures have been obtained, there is a delay of seven days. Thereafter, on the second and fourth Mondays of each month, except during the last six days of a session, any member who has signed the petition must be recognized, if he or she so desires, to move that the committee be discharged. Debate on the motion to discharge is limited to 20 minutes, and, if the motion is carried, consideration of the bill becomes a matter of high privilege.

If a resolution to consider a bill is held up in the Rules Committee for more than seven legislative days, any member may enter a motion to discharge the committee. The motion is handled like any other discharge petition in the House. Occasionally, to expedite non-controversial legislative business, a committee is discharged by unanimous consent of the House, and a petition is not required. In 1993, the signatures on pending discharge petitions — previously kept secret — were made a matter of public record. *(For Senate procedure, see Discharge Resolution.)*

Discharge Calendar — The House calendar to which motions to discharge committees are referred when they have the required number of signatures (218) and are awaiting floor action.

Discharge Petition — *(See Discharge a Committee.)*

Discharge Resolution — In the Senate, a special motion that any senator may introduce to relieve a committee from consideration of a bill before it. The resolution can be called up for Senate approval or disapproval in the same manner as any other Senate business. *(For House procedure, see Discharge a Committee.)*

Division of a Question for Voting — A practice that is more common in the Senate but also used in the House whereby a member may demand a division of an amendment or a motion for purposes of voting. Where an amendment or motion can be divided, the individual parts are voted on separately when a member demands a division. This procedure occurs most often during the consideration of conference reports.

Division Vote — *(See Standing Vote.)*

Enacting Clause — Key phrase in bills beginning, "Be it enacted by the Senate and House of Representatives . . ." A successful motion to strike it from legislation kills the measure.

Engrossed Bill — The final copy of a bill as passed by one chamber, with the text as amended by floor action and certified by the clerk of the House or the secretary of the Senate.

Enrolled Bill — The final copy of a bill that has been passed in identical form by both chambers. It is certified by an officer of the house of origin (clerk of the House or secretary of the Senate) and then sent on for the signatures of the House Speaker, the Senate president pro tempore and the president of the United States. An enrolled bill is printed on parchment.

Entitlement Program — A federal program that guarantees a certain level of benefits to people or other entities who meet requirements set by law, such as Social Security, farm price supports or unemployment benefits. It thus gives Congress no discretion over how much money to appropriate, and some entitlements carry permanent appropriations.

Executive Calendar — This is a non-legislative calendar in the Senate on which presidential documents such as treaties and nominations are listed. *(See also Calendar.)*

Executive Document — A document, usually a treaty, sent to the Senate by the president for consideration or approval. Executive documents are referred to committee in the same manner as other measures. Unlike legislative documents, however, treaties do not die at the end of a Congress but remain "live" proposals until acted on by the Senate or withdrawn by the president.

Executive Session — A meeting of a Senate or House committee (or occasionally of either chamber) that only its members may attend. Witnesses regularly appear at committee meetings in executive session — for example, Defense Department officials during presentations of classified defense information. Other members of Congress may be invited, but the public and news media are not allowed to attend.

Filibuster — A time-delaying tactic associated with the Senate and used by a minority in an effort to prevent a vote on a bill or amendment that probably would pass if voted upon directly. The most common method is to take advantage of the Senate's rules permitting unlimited debate, but other forms of parliamentary maneuvering may be used.

The stricter rules of the House make filibusters more difficult, but delaying tactics are employed occasionally through various procedural devices allowed by House rules. *(For Senate filibusters, see Cloture.)*

Fiscal Year — Financial operations of the government are carried out in a 12-month fiscal year, beginning on Oct. 1 and ending on Sept. 30. The fiscal year carries the date of the calendar year in which it ends. (From fiscal year 1844 to fiscal year 1976, the fiscal year began July 1 and ended the following June 30.)

Five-Minute Rule — A debate-limiting rule of the House that is invoked when the House sits as the Committee of the Whole. Under the rule, a member offering an amendment is allowed to speak five minutes in its favor, and an opponent of the amendment is allowed to speak five minutes in opposition. Debate is then closed. In practice, amendments regularly are debated more than 10 minutes, with members gaining the floor by offering

pro forma amendments or obtaining unanimous consent to speak longer than five minutes. *(See also Committee of the Whole, Hour Rule, Strike Out the Last Word.)*

Floor Manager — A member who has the task of steering legislation through floor debate and the amendment process to a final vote in the House or the Senate. Floor managers usually are chairmen or ranking members of the committee that reported the bill. Managers are responsible for apportioning the debate time granted to supporters of the bill. The ranking minority member of the committee normally apportions time for the minority party's participation in the debate.

Frank — A member's facsimile signature, which is used on envelopes in lieu of stamps for the member's official outgoing mail. The "franking privilege" is the right to send mail postage-free.

Germane — Pertaining to the subject matter of the measure at hand. All House amendments must be germane to the bill being considered. The Senate requires that amendments be germane when they are proposed to general appropriations bills or to bills being considered once cloture has been adopted or, frequently, when the Senate is proceeding under a unanimous consent agreement placing a time limit on consideration of a bill. The 1974 budget act also requires that amendments to concurrent budget resolutions be germane. In the House, floor debate must be germane, and the first three hours of debate each day in the Senate must be germane to the pending business.

Gramm-Rudman-Hollings Deficit Reduction Act — *(See Budget Process, Sequestration.)*

Grandfather Clause — A provision that exempts people or other entities already engaged in an activity from rules or legislation affecting that activity.

Hearings — Committee sessions for taking testimony from witnesses. At hearings on legislation, witnesses usually include specialists, government officials and spokesmen for individuals or entities affected by the bill or bills under study. Hearings related to special investigations bring forth a variety of witnesses. Committees sometimes use their subpoena power to summon reluctant witnesses. The public and news media may attend open hearings but are barred from closed, or "executive," hearings. The vast majority of hearings are open to the public. *(See also Executive Session.)*

Hold-Harmless Clause — A provision added to legislation to ensure that recipients of federal funds do not receive less in a future year than they did in the current year if a new formula for allocating funds authorized in the legislation would result in a reduction to the recipients. This clause has been used most often to soften the impact of sudden reductions in federal grants.

Hopper — Box on House clerk's desk where members deposit bills and resolutions to introduce them. *(See also Bills Introduced.)*

Hour Rule — A provision in the rules of the House that permits one hour of debate time for each member on amendments debated in the House of Representatives sitting as the House. Therefore, the House normally amends bills while sitting as the Committee of the Whole, where the five-minute rule on amendments operates. *(See also Committee of the Whole, Five-Minute Rule.)*

House as in the Committee of the Whole — A procedure that can be used to expedite consideration of certain measures such as continuing resolutions and, when there is debate, private bills. The procedure only can be invoked with the unanimous consent of the House or a rule from the Rules Committee and has procedural elements of both the House sitting as the House of Representatives, such as the Speaker presiding and the previous question motion being in order, and the House sitting as the Committee of the Whole, with the five-minute rule being in order.

House Calendar — A listing for action by the House of public bills that do not directly or indirectly appropriate money or raise revenue. *(See also Calendar and Consent, Discharge, Private, Union Calendars.)*

Immunity — The constitutional privilege of members of Congress to make verbal statements on the floor and in committee for which they cannot be sued or arrested for slander or libel. Also, freedom from arrest while traveling to or from sessions of Congress or on official business. Members in this status may be arrested only for treason, felonies or a breach of the peace, as defined by congressional manuals.

Joint Committee — A committee composed of a specified number of members of both the House and Senate. A joint committee may be investigative or research-oriented, an example of the latter being the Joint Economic Committee. Others have housekeeping duties such as the joint committees on Printing and on the Library of Congress. For 1992-93, a Joint Committee on the Organziation of Congress was established to make recommendations for congressional reforms. *(See also Committee, Oversight, Select or Special Committee, Standing Committees.)*

Joint Resolution — A joint resolution, designated H J Res or S J Res, requires the approval of both houses and the signature of the president, just as a bill does, and has the force of law if approved. There is no practical difference between a bill and a joint resolution. A joint resolution generally is used to deal with a limited matter such as a single appropriation.

Joint resolutions also are used to propose amendments to the Constitution. They do not require a presidential signature but become a part of the Constitution when three-fourths of the states have ratified them. *(See also Concurrent Resolution, Resolution.)*

Journal — The official record of the proceedings of the House and Senate. The Journal records the actions taken in each chamber, but, unlike the Congressional Record, it does not include the substantially verbatim report of speeches, debates, statements and the like. *(See also Congressional Record.)*

Law — An act of Congress that has been signed by the president or passed over his veto by Congress. Public bills, when signed, become public laws and are cited by the letters PL and a hyphenated number. The number before the hyphen corresponds to the Congress, and the one or more digits after the hyphen refer to the numerical sequence in which the president signed the bills during that Congress. Private bills, when signed, become private laws. *(See also Pocket Veto, Slip Laws, Statutes at Large, U.S. Code.)*

Legislative Day — The "day" extending from the time either chamber meets after an adjournment until the time it next adjourns. Because the House normally adjourns from day to day, legislative days and calendar days usually coincide. But in the Senate, a legislative day may, and frequently does, extend over several calendar days. *(See also Recess.)*

Legislative Veto — A procedure, held unconstitutional by the Supreme Court, permitting either the House or Senate, or both chambers, to review proposed executive branch regulations or actions and to block or modify those with which they disagreed.

The Supreme Court in 1983 struck down the legislative veto as an unconstitutional violation of the lawmaking procedure provided in the Constitution.

Loan Guarantees — Loans to third parties for which the federal government in the event of default guarantees, in whole or in part, the repayment of principal or interest to a lender or holder of a security.

Lobby — A group seeking to influence the passage or defeat of

legislation. Originally the term referred to people frequenting the lobbies or corridors of legislative chambers to speak to lawmakers.

The definition of a lobby and the activity of lobbying is a matter of differing interpretation. By some definitions, lobbying is limited to direct attempts to influence lawmakers through personal interviews and persuasion. Under other definitions, lobbying includes attempts at indirect, or "grass-roots," influence, such as persuading members of a group to write or visit their district's representative and state's senators or attempting to create a climate of opinion favorable to a desired legislative goal.

The right to attempt to influence legislation is based on the First Amendment to the Constitution, which says Congress shall make no law abridging the right of the people "to petition the government for a redress of grievances."

Majority Leader — Floor leader for the majority party in each chamber. In the Senate, in consultation with the minority leader and his colleagues, the majority leader directs the legislative schedule for the chamber. He also is his party's spokesperson and chief strategist. In the House, the majority leader is second to the Speaker in the majority party's leadership and serves as his party's legislative strategist.

Majority Whip — In effect, the assistant majority leader, in either the House or Senate. His job is to help marshal majority forces in support of party strategy and legislation.

Manual — The official handbook in each chamber prescribing in detail its organization, procedures and operations.

Marking Up a Bill — Going through the contents of a piece of legislation in committee or subcommittee to, for example, consider its provisions, act on amendments to provisions and proposed revisions to the language, and insert new sections and phraseology. If the bill is extensively amended, the committee's version may be introduced as a separate bill, with a new number, before being considered by the full House or Senate. *(See also Clean Bill.)*

Minority Leader — Floor leader for the minority party in each chamber. *(See also Majority Leader.)*

Minority Whip — Performs duties of whip for the minority party. *(See also Majority Whip.)*

Morning Hour — The time set aside at the beginning of each legislative day for the consideration of regular, routine business. The "hour" is of indefinite duration in the House, where it is rarely used.

In the Senate, it is the first two hours of a session following an adjournment, as distinguished from a recess. The morning hour can be terminated earlier if the morning business has been completed. Business includes such matters as messages from the president, communications from the heads of departments, messages from the House, the presentation of petitions, reports of standing and select committees and the introduction of bills and resolutions. During the first hour of the morning hour in the Senate, no motion to proceed to the consideration of any bill on the calendar is in order except by unanimous consent. During the second hour, motions can be made but must be decided without debate. Senate committees may meet while the Senate conducts the morning hour.

Motion — In the House or Senate chamber, a request by a member to institute any one of a wide array of parliamentary actions. He or she "moves" for a certain procedure, such as the consideration of a measure. The precedence of motions, and whether they are debatable, is set forth in the House and Senate manuals.

Nominations — Presidential appointments to office subject to Senate confirmation. Although most nominations win quick Senate approval, some are controversial and become the topic of hearings and debate. Sometimes senators object to appointees for

patronage reasons — for example, when a nomination to a local federal job is made without consulting the senators of the state concerned. In some situations a senator may object that the nominee is "personally obnoxious" to him. Usually other senators join in blocking such appointments out of courtesy to their colleagues. *(See also Senatorial Courtesy.)*

One-Minute Speeches — Addresses by House members at the beginning of a legislative day. The speeches may cover any subject but are limited to one minute's duration.

Outlays — Actual spending that flows from the liquidation of budget authority. Appropriations bills provide budget authority — the authority to spend money. The outlays associated with appropriations bills are just estimates of future spending made by the Congressional Budget Office (CBO). The White House's Office of Management and Budget (OMB) also estimates outlays, but CBO's estimates govern bills for the purpose of congressional floor debate. OMB's numbers govern when it comes to determining whether legislation exceeds spending caps. While budget authority is analagous to putting money in a checking account, outlays are when the check actually is written. Outlays in a given fiscal year may result from budget authority provided in the current year or in previous years. *(See also Budget Authority, Budget Process)*

Override a Veto — If the president disapproves a bill and sends it back to Congress with his objections, Congress may try to override his veto and enact the bill into law. Neither house is required to attempt to override a veto. The override of a veto requires a recorded vote with a two-thirds majority of those present and voting in each chamber. The question put to each house is: "Shall the bill pass, the objections of the president to the contrary notwithstanding?" *(See also Pocket Veto, Veto.)*

Oversight Committee — A congressional committee, or designated subcommittee, that is charged with general oversight of one or more federal agencies' programs and activities. Usually, the oversight panel for a particular agency also is the authorizing committee for that agency's programs and operations.

Pair — A voluntary, informal arrangement that two lawmakers, usually on opposite sides of an issue, make on recorded votes. In many cases the result is to subtract a vote from each side, with no effect on the outcome. Pairs are not authorized in the rules of either house, are not counted in tabulating the final result and have no official standing. However, members pairing are identified in the Congressional Record, along with their positions on such votes, if known. A member who expects to be absent for a vote can pair with a member who plans to vote, with the latter agreeing to withhold his or her vote.

There are three types of pairs: 1) A live pair involves a member who is present for a vote and another who is absent. The member in attendance votes and then withdraws the vote, announcing that he or she has a live pair with colleague "X" and stating how the two members would have voted, one in favor, the other opposed. A live pair may affect the outcome of a closely contested vote, since it subtracts one "yea" or one "nay" from the final tally. A live pair may cover one or several specific issues. 2) A general pair, widely used in the House, does not entail any arrangement between two members and does not affect the vote. Members who expect to be absent notify the clerk that they wish to make a general pair. Each member then is paired with another desiring a pair, and their names are listed in the Congressional Record. The member may or may not be paired with another taking the opposite position, and no indication of how the members would have voted is given. 3) A specific pair is similar to a general pair, except that the opposing stands of the two members are identified and printed in the Record.

Petition — A request or plea sent to one or both chambers from an organization or private citizens group seeking support for particular legislation or favorable consideration of a matter not yet receiving congressional attention. Petitions are referred to appro-

priate committees. In the House, a petition signed by a majority of members (218) can discharge a bill from a committee. *(See also Discharge a Committee.)*

Pocket Veto — The act of the president in withholding his approval of a bill after Congress has adjourned. When Congress is in session, a bill becomes law without the president's signature if he does not act upon it within 10 days, excluding Sundays, from the time he gets it. But if Congress adjourns sine die within that 10-day period, the bill will die even if the president does not formally veto it.

The Supreme Court in 1986 agreed to decide whether the president can pocket veto a bill during recesses and between sessions of the same Congress or only between Congresses. The justices in 1987 declared the case moot, however, because the bill in question was invalid once the case reached the court. *(See also Adjournment Sine Die, Veto.)*

Point of Order — An objection raised by a member that the chamber is departing from rules governing its conduct of business. The objector cites the rule violated, with the chair sustaining his or her objection if correctly made. Order is restored by the chair's suspending proceedings of the chamber until it conforms to the prescribed "order of business."

President of the Senate — Under the Constitution, the vice president of the United States presides over the Senate. In his absence, the president pro tempore, or a senator designated by the president pro tempore, presides over the chamber.

President Pro Tempore — The chief officer of the Senate in the absence of the vice president; literally, but loosely, the president for a time. The president pro tempore is elected by his fellow senators, and the recent practice has been to elect the senator of the majority party with the longest period of continuous service.

Previous Question — A motion for the previous question, when carried, has the effect of cutting off all debate, preventing the offering of further amendments and forcing a vote on the pending matter. In the House, a motion for the previous question is not permitted in the Committee of the Whole, unless a rule governing debate provides otherwise. The motion for the previous question is a debate-limiting device and is not in order in the Senate.

Printed Amendment — A House rule guarantees five minutes of floor debate in support and five minutes in opposition, and no other debate time, on amendments printed in the Congressional Record at least one day prior to the amendment's consideration in the Committee of the Whole. In the Senate, while amendments may be submitted for printing, they have no parliamentary standing or status. An amendment submitted for printing in the Senate, however, may be called up by any senator.

Private Calendar — In the House, private bills dealing with individual matters such as claims against the government, immigration or land titles are put on this calendar. The Private Calendar must be called on the first Tuesday of each month, and the Speaker may call it on the third Tuesday of each month as well.

When a private bill is before the chamber, two members may block its consideration, which recommits the bill to committee. Backers of a recommitted private bill have recourse. The measure can be put into an "omnibus claims bill" — several private bills rolled into one. As with any bill, no part of an omnibus claims bill may be deleted without a vote. When the private bill goes back to the House floor in this form, it can be deleted from the omnibus bill only by majority vote. *(See also Calendar and Consent, Discharge, House, Union Calendars.)*

Privileged Questions — The order in which bills, motions and other legislative measures are considered on the floor of the Senate and House is governed by strict priorities. A motion to table, for instance, is more privileged than a motion to recommit. Thus, if a member moves to recommit a bill to committee for

further consideration, another member could supersede the first action by moving to table it, and a vote would occur first on the motion to table (or kill) the motion to recommit. A motion to adjourn is considered "of the highest privilege" and would have to be considered before virtually any other motion. *(See also Questions of Privilege.)*

Pro Forma Amendment — *(See Strike Out the Last Word.)*

Public Laws — *(See Law.)*

Questions of Privilege — These are matters affecting members of Congress individually or collectively. Matters affecting the rights, safety, dignity and integrity of proceedings of the House or Senate as a whole are questions of privilege in both chambers.

Questions involving individual members are called questions of "personal privilege." A member rising to ask a question of personal privilege is given precedence over almost all other proceedings. For instance, if a member feels that he or she has been improperly impugned in comments by another member, he or she can immediately demand to be heard on the floor on a question of personal privilege. An annotation in the House rules points out that the privilege rests primarily on the Constitution, which gives members a conditional immunity from arrest and an unconditional freedom to speak in the House.

In 1993, the House changed its rules to allow the Speaker to delay for two legislative days the floor consideration of a question of the privileges of the House unless it is offered by the majority leader or minority leader. *(See also Privileged Questions.)*

Quorum — The number of members whose presence is necessary for the transaction of business. In the Senate and House, it is a majority of the membership. A quorum is 100 in the Committee of the Whole House. If a point of order is made that a quorum is not present, the only business that is in order is either a motion to adjourn or a motion to direct the sergeant-at-arms to request the attendance of absentees. In practice, however, both chambers conduct much of their business without a quorum present.

Readings of Bills — Traditional parliamentary procedure required bills to be read three times before they were passed. This custom is of little modern significance. Normally a bill is considered to have its first reading when it is introduced and printed, by title, in the Congressional Record. In the House, its second reading comes when floor consideration begins. (This is the most likely point at which there is an actual reading of the bill, if there is any.) The second reading in the Senate is supposed to occur on the legislative day after the measure is introduced, but before it is referred to committee. The third reading (again, usually by title) takes place when floor action has been completed on amendments.

Recess — Distinguished from adjournment in that a recess does not end a legislative day and therefore does not interrupt unfinished business. The rules in each house set forth certain matters to be taken up and disposed of at the beginning of each legislative day. The House usually adjourns from day to day. The Senate often recesses, thus meeting on the same legislative day for several calendar days or even weeks at a time.

Recognition — The power of recognition of a member is lodged in the Speaker of the House and the presiding officer of the Senate. The presiding officer names the member to speak first when two or more members simultaneously request recognition. The order of recognition is governed by precedents and tradition for many situations. In the Senate, for instance, the majority leader has the right to be recognized first.

Recommit to Committee — A motion, made on the floor after a bill has been debated, to return it to the committee that reported it. If approved, recommittal usually is considered a death blow to the bill. In the House, a motion to recommit can be made only by a member opposed to the bill, and, in recognizing a member to make the motion, the Speaker gives preference to

members of the minority party over majority-party members.

A motion to recommit may include instructions to the committee to report the bill again with specific amendments or by a certain date. Or the instructions may direct that a particular study be made, with no definite deadline for further action. If the recommittal motion includes instructions to "report the bill back forthwith" and the motion is adopted, floor action on the bill continues with the changes directed by the instructions automatically incorporated into the bill; the committee does not actually reconsider the legislation.

Reconciliation — The 1974 budget act provided for a "reconciliation" procedure for bringing existing tax and spending laws into conformity with ceilings set in the congressional budget resolution. Under the procedure, the budget resolution sets specific deficit-reduction targets and instructs tax-writing and authorizing committees to propose changes in existing law to meet those targets. Those recommendations are consolidated without change by the Budget committees into an omnibus reconciliation bill, which then must be considered and approved by both chambers of Congress.

Special rules in the Senate limit debate on a reconciliation bill to 20 hours and bar extraneous or non-germane amendments. *(See also Budget Resolution, Sequestration.)*

Reconsider a Vote — A motion to reconsider the vote by which an action was taken has, until it is disposed of, the effect of putting the action in abeyance. In the Senate, the motion can be made only by a member who voted on the prevailing side of the original question or by a member who did not vote at all. In the House, it can be made only by a member on the prevailing side.

A common practice in the Senate after close votes on an issue is a motion to reconsider, followed by a motion to table the motion to reconsider. On this motion to table, senators vote as they voted on the original question, which allows the motion to table to prevail, assuming there are no switches. The matter then is finally closed, and further motions to reconsider are not entertained. In the House, as a routine precaution, a motion to reconsider usually is made every time a measure is passed. Such a motion almost always is tabled immediately, thus shutting off the possibility of future reconsideration, except by unanimous consent.

Motions to reconsider must be entered in the Senate within the next two days the Senate is in session after the original vote has been taken. In the House, they must be entered either on the same day or on the next succeeding day the House is in session. Sometimes on a close vote, a member will switch his or her vote to be eligible to offer a motion to reconsider.

Recorded Vote — A vote upon which each member's stand is individually made known. In the Senate, this is accomplished through a roll call of the entire membership, to which each senator on the floor must answer "yea," "nay" or "present." Since January 1973, the House has used an electronic voting system for recorded votes, including yea-and-nay votes formerly taken by roll call.

When not required by the Constitution, a recorded vote can be obtained on questions in the House on the demand of one-fifth (44 members) of a quorum or one-fourth (25) of a quorum in the Committee of the Whole. *(See also Yeas and Nays.)*

Report — Both a verb and a noun as a congressional term. A committee that has been examining a bill referred to it by the parent chamber "reports" its findings and recommendations to the chamber when it completes consideration and returns the measure. The process is called "reporting" a bill.

A "report" is the document setting forth the committee's explanation of its action. Senate and House reports are numbered separately and are designated S Rept or H Rept. When a committee report is not unanimous, the dissenting committee members may file a statement of their views, called minority or dissenting views and referred to as a minority report. Members in disagreement with some provisions of a bill may file additional or supplementary views. Sometimes a bill is reported without a committee recommendation.

Legislative committees occasionally submit adverse reports. However, when a committee is opposed to a bill, it usually fails to report the bill at all. Some laws require that committee reports — favorable or adverse — be made.

Rescission — What happens when Congress acts to rescind, or cancel, budget authority that was previously appropriated but has not yet been spent. Under the 1974 budget act, the president may recommend a rescission, but unless Congress approves the cut within 45 days of continuous session after receiving the proposal, the funds must be made available for obligation. *(See also Deferral.)*

Resolution — A "simple" resolution, designated H Res or S Res, deals with matters entirely within the prerogatives of one house or the other. It requires neither passage by the other chamber nor approval by the president, and it does not have the force of law. Most resolutions deal with the rules or procedures of one house. They also are used to express the sentiments of a single house such as condolences to the family of a deceased member or to comment on foreign policy or executive business. A simple resolution is the vehicle for a "rule" from the House Rules Committee. *(See also Concurrent and Joint Resolutions, Rules.)*

Rider — An amendment, usually not germane, that its sponsor hopes to get through more easily by including it in other legislation. A rider becomes law if the bill to which it is attached is enacted. Amendments providing legislative directives in appropriations bills are examples of riders, though technically legislation is banned from appropriations bills.

The House, unlike the Senate, has a strict germaneness rule; thus, riders usually are Senate devices to get legislation enacted quickly or to bypass lengthy House consideration and, possibly, opposition.

Rules — A rule is a standing order governing the conduct of House or Senate business and is listed among the permanent rules of either chamber. The rules deal with issues such as duties of officers, the order of business, admission to the floor, parliamentary procedures on handling amendments and voting and jurisdictions of committees.

In the House, a rule also may be a resolution reported by its Rules Committee to govern the handling of a particular bill on the floor. The committee may report a rule, also called a special order, in the form of a simple resolution. If the House adopts the resolution, the temporary rule becomes as valid as any standing rule and lapses only after action has been completed on the measure to which it pertains. A rule sets the time limit on general debate. It also may waive points of order against provisions of the bill in question such as non-germane language or against certain amendments intended to be proposed to the bill from the floor. It may even forbid all amendments or all amendments except those proposed by the legislative committee that handled the bill. In this instance, it is known as a "closed" rule as opposed to an "open" rule, which puts no limitation on floor amendments, thus leaving the bill completely open to alteration by the adoption of germane amendments.

Secretary of the Senate — Chief administrative officer of the Senate, responsible for overseeing the duties of Senate employees, educating Senate pages, administering oaths, overseeing the registration of lobbyists and handling other tasks necessary for the continuing operation of the Senate. *(See also Clerk of the House.)*

Select or Special Committee — A committee set up for a special purpose and, usually, for a limited time by resolution of either the House or Senate. Most special committees are investigative and lack legislative authority: Legislation is not referred to them, and they cannot report bills to their parent chamber. The House in 1993 terminated its four select committees. *(See also Committee and Joint, Oversight, Standing Committees.)*

Senatorial Courtesy — Sometimes referred to as "the cour-

tesy of the Senate," it is a general practice — with no written rule — applied to consideration of executive nominations. Generally, it means that nominations from a state are not to be confirmed unless they have been approved by the senators of the president's party of that state, with other senators following their colleagues' lead in the attitude they take toward consideration of such nominations. *(See also Nominations.)*

Sequester — An automatic, across-the-board spending cut. Under the 1985 Gramm-Rudman anti-deficit law, modified in 1987, a year-end, across-the-board spending cut known as a sequester would be triggered if the deficit exceeded a pre-set maximum. However, the Budget Enforcement Act of 1990, updated in 1993, effectively replaced that procedure through fiscal 1998.

Instead, if Congress exceeds an annual cap on discretionary spending, a sequester is triggered for all eligible discretionary spending to make up the difference. If Congress violates pay-as-you-go rules — which require that new or expanded mandatory spending (for entitlement programs such as Medicare and food stamps) and tax cuts be deficit-neutral — a sequester is triggered for all non-exempt entitlement programs. Similar procedures apply to supplemental appropriations bills. *(See also Budget Process.)*

Sine Die — *(See Adjournment Sine Die.)*

Speaker — The presiding officer of the House of Representatives, selected by the caucus of the party to which he belongs and formally elected by the whole House.

Special Session — A session of Congress after it has adjourned sine die, completing its regular session. Special sessions are convened by the president.

Spending Authority — The 1974 budget act defines spending authority as borrowing authority, contract authority and entitlement authority for which budget authority is not provided in advance by appropriation acts.

Sponsor — *(See Bills Introduced.)*

Standing Committees — Committees that are permanently established by House and Senate rules. The standing committees of the House were last reorganized by the committee reorganization of 1974. The last major realignment of Senate committees was in the committee system reorganization of 1977. The standing committees are legislative committees: Legislation may be referred to them and they may report bills and resolutions to their parent chambers. *(See also Committee, Joint, Oversight and Select or Special Committees.)*

Standing Vote — A non-recorded vote used in both the House and Senate. (A standing vote also is called a division vote.) Members in favor of a proposal stand and are counted by the presiding officer. Then members opposed stand and are counted. There is no record of how individual members voted.

Statutes at Large — A chronological arrangement of the laws enacted in each session of Congress. Though indexed, the laws are not arranged by subject matter, and there is no indication of how they changed previously enacted laws. *(See also Law, Slip Laws, U.S. Code.)*

Strike From the Record — Remarks made on the House floor may offend some member, who moves that the offending words be "taken down" for the Speaker's cognizance and then expunged from the debate as published in the Congressional Record.

Strike Out the Last Word — A motion whereby a House member is entitled to speak for five minutes on an amendment then being debated by the chamber. A member gains recognition from the chair by moving to "strike out the last word" of the

amendment or section of the bill under consideration. The motion is pro forma, requires no vote and does not change the amendment being debated. *(See also Five-Minute Rule.)*

Substitute — A motion, amendment or entire bill introduced in place of the pending legislative business. Passage of a substitute measure kills the original measure by supplanting it. The substitute also may be amended. *(See also Amendment in the Nature of a Substitute.)*

Supplemental Appropriations Bill — Legislation appropriating funds after the regular annual appropriations bill for a federal department or agency has been enacted. A supplemental appropriation provides additional budget authority beyond original estimates for programs or activities, including new programs authorized after the enactment of the regular appropriation act for which the need for funds is too urgent to be postponed until enactment of the next year's regular appropriations bill.

Suspend the Rules — Often a time-saving procedure for passing bills in the House. The wording of the motion, which may be made by any member recognized by the Speaker, is: "I move to suspend the rules and pass the bill . . ." A favorable vote by two-thirds of those present is required for passage. Debate is limited to 40 minutes and no amendments from the floor are permitted. If a two-thirds favorable vote is not attained, the bill may be considered later under regular procedures. The suspension procedure is in order every Monday and Tuesday and is intended to be reserved for non-controversial bills.

Table a Bill — Motions to table, or to "lay on the table," are used to block or kill amendments or other parliamentary questions. When approved, a tabling motion is considered the final disposition of that issue. One of the most widely used parliamentary procedures, the motion to table is not debatable, and adoption requires a simple majority vote.

In the Senate, however, different language sometimes is used. The motion may be worded to let a bill "lie on the table," perhaps for subsequent "picking up." This motion is more flexible, keeping the bill pending for later action, if desired. Tabling motions on amendments are effective debate-ending devices in the Senate.

Treaties — Executive proposals — in the form of resolutions of ratification — which must be submitted to the Senate for approval by two-thirds of the senators present. Treaties are normally sent to the Foreign Relations Committee for scrutiny before the Senate takes action. Foreign Relations has jurisdiction over all treaties, regardless of the subject matter. Treaties are read three times and debated on the floor in much the same manner as legislative proposals. After approval by the Senate, treaties are formally ratified by the president.

Trust Funds — Funds collected and used by the federal government for carrying out specific purposes and programs according to terms of a trust agreement or statute such as the Social Security and unemployment compensation trust funds. Such funds are administered by the government in a fiduciary capacity and are not available for the general purposes of the government.

Unanimous Consent — Proceedings of the House or Senate and action on legislation often take place upon the unanimous consent of the chamber, whether or not a rule of the chamber is being violated. Unanimous consent is used to expedite floor action and frequently is used in a routine fashion such as by a senator requesting the unanimous consent of the Senate to have specified members of his or her staff present on the floor during debate on a specific amendment. A single member's objection blocks a unanimous consent request.

Unanimous Consent Agreement — A device used in the Senate to expedite legislation. Much of the Senate's legislative business, dealing with both minor and controversial issues, is conducted through unanimous consent or unanimous consent agreements. On major legislation, such agreements usually are printed and

transmitted to all senators in advance of floor debate. Once agreed to, they are binding on all members unless the Senate, by unanimous consent, agrees to modify them. An agreement may list the order in which various bills are to be considered, specify the length of time bills and contested amendments are to be debated and when they are to be voted upon and, frequently, require that all amendments introduced be germane to the bill under consideration.

In this regard, unanimous consent agreements are similar to the "rules" issued by the House Rules Committee for bills pending in the House.

Union Calendar — Bills that directly or indirectly appropriate money or raise revenue are placed on this House calendar according to the date they are reported from committee. *(See also Calendar and Consent, Discharge, House, Private Calendars.)*

U.S. Code — A consolidation and codification of the general and permanent laws of the United States arranged by subject under 50 titles, the first six dealing with general or political subjects, and the other 44 alphabetically arranged from agriculture to war. The U.S. Code is updated annually, and a new set of bound volumes is published every six years. *(See also Law, Statutes at Large.)*

Veto — Disapproval by the president of a bill or joint resolution (other than one proposing an amendment to the Constitution). When Congress is in session, the president must veto a bill within 10 days, excluding Sundays, after he has received it; otherwise, it becomes law without his signature. When the president vetoes a bill, he returns it to the house of origin along with a message stating his objections. *(See also Pocket Veto, Override a Veto.)*

Voice Vote — In either the House or Senate, members answer "aye" or "no" in chorus, and the presiding officer decides the result. The term also is used loosely to indicate action by unanimous consent or without objection.

Whip — *(See Majority and Minority Whip.)*

Without Objection — Used in lieu of a vote on non-controversial motions, amendments or bills that may be passed in either the House or Senate if no member voices an objection.

Yeas and Nays — The Constitution requires that yea-and-nay votes be taken and recorded when requested by one-fifth of the members present. In the House, the Speaker determines whether one-fifth of the members present requested a vote. In the Senate, practice requires only 11 members. The Constitution requires the yeas and nays on a veto override attempt. *(See also Recorded Vote.)*

Yielding — When a member has been recognized to speak, no other member may speak unless he or she obtains permission from the member recognized. This permission is called yielding and usually is requested in the form, "Will the gentleman (or gentlelady) yield to me?" While this activity occasionally is seen in the Senate, the Senate has no rule or practice to parcel out time.

In the House, the floor manager of a bill usually apportions debate time by yielding specific amounts of time to members who have requested it. ■

CONGRESS
AND
ITS MEMBERS

The Legislative Process in Brief........................ 3-B

List of Members — 103rd Congress, 2nd Session 6-B

Senators' Committee Assignments 8-B

Representatives' Committee Assignments 10-B

Pronunciation Guide.................................. 15-B

Capitol Hill Map 16-B

The Legislative Process in Brief

(Parliamentary terms used below are defined in the glossary, p. 3-A.)

Introduction of Bills

A House member (including the resident commissioner of Puerto Rico and non-voting delegates of the District of Columbia, Guam, the Virgin Islands and American Samoa) may introduce any one of several types of bills and resolutions by handing it to the clerk of the House or placing it in a box called the hopper.

A senator first gains recognition of the presiding officer to announce the introduction of a bill. If objection is offered by any senator, the introduction of the bill is postponed until the following day.

As the next step in either the House or Senate, the bill is numbered, referred to committee, labeled with the sponsor's name and sent to the Government Printing Office so that copies can be made for subsequent study and action. Senate bills may be sponsored jointly and carry several senators' names.

Until 1978, the House limited the number of members who could cosponsor any one bill; the ceiling was eliminated at the beginning of the 96th Congress.

A bill written in the executive branch and proposed as an administration measure usually is introduced by the chairman of the congressional committee that has jurisdiction over the subject.

Bills. Prefixed with HR in the House, S in the Senate, followed by a number. Used as the form for most legislation, whether general or special, public or private.

Joint Resolutions. Designated H J Res or S J Res. Subject to the same procedure as bills, with the exception of a joint resolution proposing an amendment to the Constitution. The latter must be approved by two-thirds of both houses and is thereupon sent directly to the administrator of general services for submission to the states for ratification instead of being presented to the president for approval.

Concurrent Resolutions. Designated H Con Res or S Con Res. Used for matters affecting the operations of both houses. These resolutions do not become law.

Resolutions. Designated H Res or S Res. Used for a matter concerning the operation of either house alone and adopted only by the chamber in which they originate.

Committee Action

With few exceptions, bills are referred to the appropriate standing committees. The job of referral formally is the responsibility of the Speaker of the House and the presiding officer of the Senate, but this task usually is carried out on their behalf by the parliamentarians of the House and Senate.

Precedent, statute and the jurisdictional mandates of the committees as set forth in the rules of the House and Senate determine which committees receive what kinds of bills. An exception is the referral of private bills, which are sent to whatever committee is designated by their sponsors. Bills are technically considered "read for the first time" when referred to House committees.

When a bill reaches a committee, it is placed on the committee's calendar. At that time the bill comes under the sharpest congressional focus. Its chances for passage are quickly determined; the great majority of bills fall by the legislative roadside.

Failure of a committee to act on a bill is equivalent to killing it; the measure can be withdrawn from the committee's purview only by a discharge petition signed by a majority of the House membership on House bills or by adoption of a special resolution in the Senate. Discharge attempts rarely succeed.

The first committee action taken on a bill usually is a request for comment on it by interested government agencies. The committee chairman may assign the bill to a subcommittee for study and hearings, or it may be considered by the full committee. Hearings may be public, closed (executive session) or both. After considering a bill, a subcommittee reports to the full committee its recommendations for action and any proposed amendments.

The full committee then votes on its recommendation to the House or Senate. This procedure is called "ordering a bill reported."

Occasionally a committee may order a bill reported unfavorably; most of the time a report, submitted by the committee chairman to the House or Senate, calls for favorable action on the measure since the committee can effectively "kill" a bill by simply not taking any action.

After the bill is reported, the committee chairman instructs the staff to prepare a written report. The report describes the bill's purposes and scope, explains the committee revisions, notes proposed changes in existing law and, usually, includes the views of the executive branch agencies consulted. Often committee members opposing a bill include dissenting views in the report.

Usually, the committee "marks up" or proposes amendments to the bill. If they are substantial and the measure is complicated, the committee may order a "clean bill" introduced, which will embody the proposed amendments. The original bill then is put aside and the clean bill, with a new number, is reported to the floor.

The chamber must approve, alter or reject the committee amendments before the bill itself can be put to a vote.

Floor Action

After a bill is reported back to the house where it originated, it is placed on the calendar.

Debate. A bill is brought to debate by varying procedures. If it is a routine measure, it may await the call of the calendar. If it is urgent or important, it can be taken up in

the Senate either by unanimous consent or by a majority vote. The majority leader, in consultation with the minority leader and others, schedules the bills that will be taken up for debate.

In the House, precedence is granted if a special rule is obtained from the Rules Committee. A request for a special rule usually is made by the chairman of the committee that favorably reported the bill, supported by the bill's sponsor and other committee members. The request, considered by the Rules Committee in the same way that other committees consider legislative measures, is in the form of a resolution providing for immediate consideration of the bill.

The Rules Committee reports the resolution to the House, where it is debated and voted upon in the same fashion as regular bills. If the Rules Committee should fail to report a rule requested by a committee, there are several ways to bring the bill to the House floor — under suspension of the rules, on Calendar Wednesday or by a discharge motion.

The resolutions providing special rules are important because they specify how long the bill may be debated and whether it may be amended from the floor. If floor amendments are banned, the bill is considered under a "closed rule," which usually allows only changes proposed by the committee that first reported the measure to the House, subject to chamber acceptance.

When a bill is debated under an "open rule," amendments may be offered from the floor. Committee amendments always are taken up first but may be changed, like all amendments up to the second degree; that is, an amendment to an amendment to an amendment is not in order.

Duration of debate in the House depends on whether the bill is under discussion by the House proper or before the House when it is sitting as the Committee of the Whole House on the State of the Union.

In the House, the amount of time for debate either is determined by special rule or, if the measure is under consideration without a rule, is allocated with an hour for each member.

In the Committee of the Whole, the amount of time agreed on for general debate is equally divided between proponents and opponents. At the end of general discussion, the bill is read section by section for amendment. Debate on an amendment is limited to five minutes for each side; this is called the "five-minute rule." In practice, amendments regularly are debated more than 10 minutes, with members gaining the floor by offering pro forma amendments or obtaining unanimous consent to speak longer than five minutes.

Senate debate usually is unlimited. It can be halted only by unanimous consent or by "cloture," which requires a three-fifths majority of the entire Senate or, in the case of a proposed change in the Senate rules, a two-thirds vote.

The House considers almost all important bills within a parliamentary framework known as the Committee of the Whole. It is not a committee as the word usually is understood; it is the full House meeting under another name for the purpose of speeding action on legislation.

Technically, the House sits as the Committee of the Whole when it considers any tax measure or bill dealing with public appropriations. It also can resolve itself into the Committee of the Whole if a member moves to do so and the motion is carried. The Speaker appoints a member to serve as the chairman.

The rules of the House permit the Committee of the Whole to meet when a quorum of 100 members is present on the floor and to amend and act on bills, within certain time limitations. When the Committee of the Whole has acted, it "rises," the Speaker returns as the presiding officer of the House and the member appointed chairman of the Committee of the Whole reports the action of the committee and its recommendations.

The Committee of the Whole cannot pass a bill; it reports the measure to the full House with whatever changes it has approved. The full House then may pass or reject the bill — or, on occasion, recommit the bill to committee. Amendments adopted in the Committee of the Whole may be put to a second vote in the full House.

In the 103rd Congress only, the delegates from the territories, the District of Columbia and the resident commissioner of Puerto Rico were allowed to vote in the Committee of the Whole. But any question decided by their votes had to be re-voted by the House, without their participation.

Votes. Voting on bills may occur repeatedly before they are finally approved or rejected. The House votes on the rule for a bill and on various amendments to the bill. Voting on amendments often is a more illuminating test of a bill's support than is the final tally. Sometimes members approve final passage of bills after vigorously supporting amendments that, if adopted, would scuttle the legislation.

The Senate has three different methods of voting: an untabulated voice vote, a standing vote (called a division) and a recorded roll call, to which members answer "yea" or "nay" when their names are called.

The House also employs voice and standing votes, but since January 1973, yeas and nays have been recorded by an electronic voting device, eliminating the need for time-consuming roll calls.

Since 1971, one-fifth of a quorum can demand that the votes of individual members be recorded, thereby forcing them to take a public position on amendments to key bills.

After amendments to a bill have been voted upon, a vote may be taken on a motion to recommit the bill to committee. If carried, this vote removes the bill from the chamber's calendar and is usually a death blow to the bill — unless the motion carries specific instructions on how to change the bill; in that case, the bill is usually re-reported immediately with the instructed changes. If the motion is unsuccessful, the bill then is "read for the third time." An actual reading usually is dispensed with. Until 1965, an opponent of a bill could delay this move by objecting and asking for a full reading of an engrossed (certified in final form) copy of the bill. After the "third reading," the vote on final passage is taken.

The final vote may be followed by a motion to reconsider, and this motion may be followed by a move to lay the motion on the table. Usually, those voting for the bill's passage vote for the tabling motion, thus safeguarding the final passage action. With that, the bill is formally passed by the chamber. While a motion to reconsider a Senate vote is pending on a bill, the measure cannot be sent to the House.

Action in Second House

After a bill is passed, it is sent to the other chamber. This body may then take one of several steps. It may pass

the bill as is — accepting the other chamber's language. It may send the bill to committee for scrutiny or alteration, or reject the entire bill, advising the other house of its actions. Or it simply may ignore the bill submitted while it continues work on its own version of the proposed legislation. Frequently, one chamber may approve a version of a bill that is greatly at variance with the version passed by the other house, and then substitute its contents for the language of the other, retaining only the latter's bill number.

A provision of the Legislative Reorganization Act of 1970 permits a separate House vote on any non-germane amendment added by the Senate to a House-passed bill and requires a majority vote to retain the amendment. Previously, the House was forced to act on the bill as a whole; the only way to defeat the non-germane amendment was to reject the entire bill.

Often, the second chamber makes only minor changes. If these are readily agreed to by the other house, the bill then is sent to the president.

If the opposite chamber significantly alters the bill submitted to it, however, the measure usually is "sent to conference." The chamber that has possession of the "papers" (engrossed bill, engrossed amendments, messages of transmittal) requests a conference, and the other chamber must agree to it. If the second house does not agree, the bill dies.

Conference, Final Action

Conference. A conference reconciles the differences between House and Senate versions of a legislative bill. The conferees usually are senior members appointed by the presiding officers of the two houses, from the committees that managed the bills. Under this arrangement the conferees of one house have the duty of trying to maintain their chamber's position in the face of amending actions by the conferees (also referred to as "managers") of the other house.

The number of conferees from each chamber varies, depending upon the length or complexity of the bill involved. A majority vote controls the action of each group; a large representation does not give one chamber a voting advantage over the other.

Theoretically, conferees are not allowed to write new legislation in reconciling the two versions before them, but this curb sometimes is bypassed. Many bills have been put into acceptable compromise form only after new language was provided by the conferees.

The 1970 Reorganization Act attempted to tighten restrictions on conferees by forbidding them to introduce any language on a topic that neither chamber sent to conference or to modify any topic beyond the scope of the differing versions of the bill.

Frequently, the ironing out of difficulties takes days or even weeks. As a conference proceeds, conferees reconcile differences between the versions. Generally, they grant concessions only insofar as they are sure that the chamber they represent will accept the compromises.

Occasionally, uncertainty over how either house will react, or the refusal of a chamber to back down on a disputed amendment, results in an impasse, and the bills die in conference even though each was approved by its sponsoring chamber.

Conferees may go back to their respective chambers for further instructions, when they report certain portions in disagreement. Then the chamber concerned can either "recede and concur" in the amendment of the other house or "insist on its amendment."

When the conferees have reached agreement, they prepare a conference report embodying their recommendations. The report, in document form, must be submitted to each house.

The conference report must be adopted by each house; adoption of the report is approval of the compromise bill. The chamber that asked for a conference yields to the other chamber the opportunity to vote first.

Final Steps. After a bill has been passed by both the House and Senate in identical form, all of the original papers are sent to the enrolling clerk of the chamber in which the bill originated. He then prepares an enrolled bill, which is printed on parchment paper.

When this bill has been certified as correct by the secretary of the Senate or the clerk of the House, depending on which chamber originated the bill, it is signed first (no matter whether it originated in the Senate or House) by the Speaker of the House and then by the presiding officer of the Senate. It is next sent to the White House to await action.

If the president approves the bill, he signs it, dates it and usually writes the word "approved" on the document. If he does not sign it within 10 days (Sundays excepted) and Congress is in session, the bill becomes law without his signature. Should Congress adjourn before the 10 days expire, and the president fails to sign the measure, it does not become law. This procedure is called the pocket veto.

A president vetoes a bill by refusing to sign it and, before the 10-day period expires, returning it to Congress with a message stating his reasons. The message is sent to the chamber that originated the bill. If no action is taken on the message, the bill dies.

Congress, however, can attempt to override the veto and enact the bill, "the objections of the president to the contrary notwithstanding." Overriding a veto requires a two-thirds vote of those present, who must number a quorum and vote by roll call.

Debate can precede this vote, with motions permitted to lay the message on the table, postpone action on it or refer it to committee. If the president's veto is overridden in both houses, the bill becomes law. Otherwise, it is dead.

When bills are passed finally and signed, or passed over a veto, they are given law numbers in numerical order as they become law. There are two series of numbers, one for public and one for private laws, starting with the number "1" for each two-year term of Congress. They then are identified by law number and by Congress — for example, Private Law 21, 97th Congress; Public Law 250, 97th Congress (or PL 97-250). ∎

Members of the 103rd Congress, 2nd Session . . .

(As of Dec. 31, 1994)

Representatives
D 256; R 177; I 1; Vacancy 1

— A —

Abercrombie, Neil, D-Hawaii (1)
Ackerman, Gary L., D-N.Y. (5)
Allard, Wayne, R-Colo. (4)
Andrews, Michael A., D-Texas (25)
Andrews, Robert E., D-N.J. (1)
Andrews, Thomas H., D-Maine (1)
Applegate, Douglas, D-Ohio (18)
Archer, Bill, R-Texas (7)
Armey, Dick, R-Texas (26)

— B —

Bacchus, Jim, D-Fla. (15)
Bachus, Spencer, R-Ala. (6)
Baesler, Scotty, D-Ky. (6)
Baker, Bill, R-Calif. (10)
Baker, Richard H., R-La. (6)
Ballenger, Cass, R-N.C. (10)
Barca, Peter W., D-Wis. (1)
Barcia, James A., D-Mich. (5)
Barlow, Tom, D-Ky. (1)
Barrett, Bill, R-Neb. (3)
Barrett, Thomas M., D-Wis. (5)
Bartlett, Roscoe G., R-Md. (6)
Barton, Joe L., R-Texas (6)
Bateman, Herbert H., R-Va. (1)
Becerra, Xavier, D-Calif. (30)
Beilenson, Anthony C., D-Calif. (24)
Bentley, Helen Delich, R-Md. (2)
Bereuter, Doug, R-Neb. (1)
Berman, Howard L., D-Calif. (26)
Bevill, Tom, D-Ala. (4)
Bilbray, James, D-Nev. (1)
Bilirakis, Michael, R-Fla. (9)
Bishop, Sanford D. Jr., D-Ga. (2)
Blackwell, Lucien E., D-Pa. (2)
Bliley, Thomas J. Jr., R-Va. (7)
Blute, Peter I., R-Mass. (3)
Boehlert, Sherwood, R-N.Y. (23)
Boehner, John A., R-Ohio (8)
Bonilla, Henry, R-Texas (23)
Bonior, David E., D-Mich. (10)
Borski, Robert A., D-Pa. (3)
Boucher, Rick, D-Va. (9)
Brewster, Bill, D-Okla. (3)
Brooks, Jack, D-Texas (9)
Browder, Glen, D-Ala. (3)
Brown, Corrine, D-Fla. (3)
Brown, George E. Jr., D-Calif. (42)
Brown, Sherrod, D-Ohio (13)
Bryant, John, D-Texas (5)
Bunning, Jim, R-Ky. (4)
Burton, Dan, R-Ind. (6)
Buyer, Steve, R-Ind. (5)
Byrne, Leslie L., D-Va. (11)

— C —

Callahan, Sonny, R-Ala. (1)
Calvert, Ken, R-Calif. (43)
Camp, Dave, R-Mich. (4)
Canady, Charles T., R-Fla. (12)
Cantwell, Maria, D-Wash. (1)
Cardin, Benjamin L., D-Md. (3)
Carr, Bob, D-Mich. (8)
Castle, Michael N., R-Del. (AL)
Chapman, Jim, D-Texas (1)
Clay, William L., D-Mo. (1)
Clayton, Eva, D-N.C. (1)
Clement, Bob, D-Tenn. (5)
Clinger, William F., R-Pa. (5)
Clyburn, James E., D-S.C. (6)
Coble, Howard, R-N.C. (6)
Coleman, Ronald D., D-Texas (16)
Collins, Barbara-Rose, D-Mich. (15)
Collins, Cardiss, D-Ill. (7)
Collins, Mac, R-Ga. (3)
Combest, Larry, R-Texas (19)
Condit, Gary A., D-Calif. (18)
Conyers, John Jr., D-Mich. (14)
Cooper, Jim, D-Tenn. (4)
Coppersmith, Sam, D-Ariz. (1)

Costello, Jerry F., D-Ill. (12)
Cox, Christopher, R-Calif. (47)
Coyne, William J., D-Pa. (14)
Cramer, Robert E. "Bud," D-Ala. (5)
Crane, Philip M., R-Ill. (8)
Crapo, Michael D., R-Idaho (2)
Cunningham, Randy "Duke," R-Calif. (51)

— D —

Danner, Pat, D-Mo. (6)
Darden, George "Buddy," D-Ga. (7)
de la Garza, E. "Kika," D-Texas (15)
Deal, Nathan, D-Ga. (9)
DeFazio, Peter A., D-Ore. (4)
DeLauro, Rosa, D-Conn. (3)
DeLay, Tom, R-Texas (22)
Dellums, Ronald V., D-Calif. (9)
Derrick, Butler, D-S.C. (3)
Deutsch, Peter, D-Fla. (20)
Diaz-Balart, Lincoln, R-Fla. (21)
Dickey, Jay, R-Ark. (4)
Dicks, Norm, D-Wash. (6)
Dingell, John D., D-Mich. (16)
Dixon, Julian C., D-Calif. (32)
Dooley, Cal, D-Calif. (20)
Doolittle, John T., R-Calif. (4)
Dornan, Robert K., R-Calif. (46)
Dreier, David, R-Calif. (28)
Duncan, John J. "Jimmy" Jr., R-Tenn. (2)
Dunn, Jennifer, R-Wash. (8)
Durbin, Richard J., D-Ill. (20)

— E —

Edwards, Chet, D-Texas (11)
Edwards, Don, D-Calif. (16)
Ehlers, Vernon J., R-Mich. (3)
Emerson, Bill, R-Mo. (8)
Engel, Eliot L., D-N.Y. (17)
English, Karan, D-Ariz. (6)
Eshoo, Anna G., D-Calif. (14)
Evans, Lane, D-Ill. (17)
Everett, Terry, R-Ala. (2)
Ewing, Thomas W., R-Ill. (15)

— F —

Farr, Sam, D-Calif. (17)
Fawell, Harris W., R-Ill. (13)
Fazio, Vic, D-Calif. (3)
Fields, Cleo, D-La. (4)
Fields, Jack, R-Texas (8)
Filner, Bob, D-Calif. (50)
Fingerhut, Eric D., D-Ohio (19)
Fish, Hamilton Jr., R-N.Y. (19)
Flake, Floyd H., D-N.Y. (6)
Foglietta, Thomas M., D-Pa. (1)
Foley, Thomas S., D-Wash. (5)
Ford, Harold E., D-Tenn. (9)
Ford, William D., D-Mich. (13)
Fowler, Tillie, R-Fla. (4)
Frank, Barney, D-Mass. (4)
Franks, Bob, R-N.J. (7)
Franks, Gary A., R-Conn. (5)
Frost, Martin, D-Texas (24)
Furse, Elizabeth, D-Ore. (1)

— G —

Gallegly, Elton, R-Calif. (23)
Gejdenson, Sam, D-Conn. (2)
Gekas, George W., R-Pa. (17)
Gephardt, Richard A., D-Mo. (3)
Geren, Pete, D-Texas (12)
Gibbons, Sam M., D-Fla. (11)
Gilchrest, Wayne T., R-Md. (1)
Gillmor, Paul E., R-Ohio (5)
Gilman, Benjamin A., R-N.Y. (20)
Gingrich, Newt, R-Ga. (6)
Glickman, Dan, D-Kan. (4)
Gonzalez, Henry B., D-Texas (20)
Goodlatte, Robert W., R-Va. (6)
Goodling, Bill, R-Pa. (19)
Gordon, Bart, D-Tenn. (6)
Goss, Porter J., R-Fla. (14)
Grams, Rod, R-Minn. (6)
Grandy, Fred, R-Iowa (5)
Green, Gene, D-Texas (29)
Greenwood, James C., R-Pa. (8)
Gunderson, Steve, R-Wis. (3)
Gutierrez, Luis V., D-Ill. (4)

— H —

Hall, Ralph M., D-Texas (4)
Hall, Tony P., D-Ohio (3)
Hamburg, Dan, D-Calif. (1)
Hamilton, Lee H., D-Ind. (9)
Hancock, Mel, R-Mo. (7)
Hansen, James V., R-Utah (1)
Harman, Jane, D-Calif. (36)
Hastert, Dennis, R-Ill. (14)
Hastings, Alcee L., D-Fla. (23)
Hayes, Jimmy, D-La. (7)
Hefley, Joel, R-Colo. (5)
Hefner, W. G. "Bill," D-N.C. (8)
Herger, Wally, R-Calif. (2)
Hilliard, Earl F., D-Ala. (7)
Hinchey, Maurice D., D-N.Y. (26)
Hoagland, Peter, D-Neb. (2)
Hobson, David L., R-Ohio (7)
Hochbrueckner, George J., D-N.Y. (1)
Hoekstra, Peter, R-Mich. (2)
Hoke, Martin R., R-Ohio (10)
Holden, Tim, D-Pa. (6)
Horn, Steve, R-Calif. (38)
Houghton, Amo, R-N.Y. (31)
Hoyer, Steny H., D-Md. (5)
Huffington, Michael, R-Calif. (22)
Hughes, William J., D-N.J. (2)
Hunter, Duncan, R-Calif. (52)
Hutchinson, Tim, R-Ark. (3)
Hutto, Earl, D-Fla. (1)
Hyde, Henry J., R-Ill. (6)

— I —

Inglis, Bob, R-S.C. (4)
Inslee, Jay, D-Wash. (4)
Istook, Ernest Jim Jr., R-Okla. (5)

— J —

Jacobs, Andrew Jr., D-Ind. (10)
Jefferson, William J., D-La. (2)
Johnson, Don, D-Ga. (10)
Johnson, Eddie Bernice, D-Texas (30)
Johnson, Nancy L., R-Conn. (6)
Johnson, Sam, R-Texas (3)
Johnson, Tim, D-S.D. (AL)
Johnston, Harry A., D-Fla. (19)

— K —

Kanjorski, Paul E., D-Pa. (11)
Kaptur, Marcy, D-Ohio (9)
Kasich, John R., R-Ohio (12)
Kennedy, Joseph P. II, D-Mass. (8)
Kennelly, Barbara B., D-Conn. (1)
Kildee, Dale E., D-Mich. (9)
Kim, Jay C., R-Calif. (41)
King, Peter T., R-N.Y. (3)
Kingston, Jack, R-Ga. (1)
Kleczka, Gerald D., D-Wis. (4)
Klein, Herb, D-N.J. (8)
Klink, Ron, D-Pa. (4)
Klug, Scott L., R-Wis. (2)
Knollenberg, Joe, R-Mich. (11)
Kolbe, Jim, R-Ariz. (5)
Kopetski, Mike, D-Ore. (5)
Kreidler, Mike, D-Wash. (9)
Kyl, Jon, R-Ariz. (4)

— L —

LaFalce, John J., D-N.Y. (29)
Lambert, Blanche, D-Ark. (1)
Lancaster, H. Martin, D-N.C. (3)
Lantos, Tom, D-Calif. (12)
Largent, Steve, R-Okla. (1)
LaRocco, Larry, D-Idaho (1)
Laughlin, Greg, D-Texas (14)
Lazio, Rick A., R-N.Y. (2)
Leach, Jim, R-Iowa (1)
Lehman, Richard H., D-Calif. (19)
Levin, Sander M., D-Mich. (12)
Levy, David A., R-N.Y. (4)
Lewis, Jerry, R-Calif. (40)
Lewis, John, D-Ga. (5)
Lewis, Ron, R-Ky. (2)
Lewis, Tom, R-Fla. (16)
Lightfoot, Jim Ross, R-Iowa (3)
Linder, John, R-Ga. (4)
Lipinski, William O., D-Ill. (3)
Livingston, Robert L., R-La. (1)
Lloyd, Marilyn, D-Tenn. (3)

Long, Jill L., D-Ind. (4)
Lowey, Nita M., D-N.Y. (18)
Lucas, Frank D., R-Okla. (6)

— M —

Machtley, Ronald K., R-R.I. (1)
Maloney, Carolyn B., D-N.Y. (14)
Mann, David, D-Ohio (1)
Manton, Thomas J., D-N.Y. (7)
Manzullo, Donald, R-Ill. (16)
Margolies-Mezvinsky, Marjorie, D-Pa. (13)
Markey, Edward J., D-Mass. (7)
Martinez, Matthew G., D-Calif. (31)
Matsui, Robert T., D-Calif. (5)
Mazzoli, Romano L., D-Ky. (3)
McCandless, Al, R-Calif. (44)
McCloskey, Frank, D-Ind. (8)
McCollum, Bill, R-Fla. (8)
McCrery, Jim, R-La. (5)
McCurdy, Dave, D-Okla. (4)
McDade, Joseph M., R-Pa. (10)
McDermott, Jim, D-Wash. (7)
McHale, Paul, D-Pa. (15)
McHugh, John M., R-N.Y. (24)
McInnis, Scott, R-Colo. (3)
McKeon, Howard P. "Buck," R-Calif. (25)
McKinney, Cynthia A., D-Ga. (11)
McMillan, Alex, R-N.C. (9)
McNulty, Michael R., D-N.Y. (21)
Meehan, Martin T., D-Mass. (5)
Meek, Carrie P., D-Fla. (17)
Menendez, Robert, D-N.J. (13)
Meyers, Jan, R-Kan. (3)
Mfume, Kweisi, D-Md. (7)
Mica, John L., R-Fla. (7)
Michel, Robert H., R-Ill. (18)
Miller, Dan, R-Fla. (13)
Miller, George, D-Calif. (7)
Mineta, Norman Y., D-Calif. (15)
Minge, David, D-Minn. (2)
Mink, Patsy T., D-Hawaii (2)
Moakley, Joe, D-Mass. (9)
Molinari, Susan, R-N.Y. (13)
Mollohan, Alan B., D-W.Va. (1)
Montgomery, G. V. "Sonny," D-Miss. (3)
Moorhead, Carlos J., R-Calif. (27)
Moran, James P., D-Va. (8)
Morella, Constance A., R-Md. (8)
Murphy, Austin J., D-Pa. (20)
Murtha, John P., D-Pa. (12)
Myers, John T., R-Ind. (7)

— N —

Nadler, Jerrold, D-N.Y. (8)
Neal, Richard E., D-Mass. (2)
Neal, Stephen L., D-N.C. (5)
Nussle, Jim, R-Iowa (2)

— O —

Oberstar, James L., D-Minn. (8)
Obey, David R., D-Wis. (7)
Olver, John W., D-Mass. (1)
Ortiz, Solomon P., D-Texas (27)
Orton, Bill, D-Utah (3)
Owens, Major R., D-N.Y. (11)
Oxley, Michael G., R-Ohio (4)

— P —

Packard, Ron, R-Calif. (48)
Pallone, Frank Jr., D-N.J. (6)
Parker, Mike, D-Miss. (4)
Pastor, Ed, D-Ariz. (2)
Paxon, Bill, R-N.Y. (27)
Payne, Donald M., D-N.J. (10)
Payne, L. F. Jr., D-Va. (5)
Pelosi, Nancy, D-Calif. (8)
Penny, Timothy J., D-Minn. (1)
Peterson, Collin C., D-Minn. (7)
Peterson, Pete, D-Fla. (2)
Petri, Tom, R-Wis. (6)
Pickett, Owen B., D-Va. (2)
Pickle, J. J., D-Texas (10)
Pombo, Richard W., R-Calif. (11)
Pomeroy, Earl, D-N.D. (AL)
Porter, John Edward, R-Ill. (10)
Portman, Rob, R-Ohio (2)
Poshard, Glenn, D-Ill. (19)
Price, David, D-N.C. (4)
Pryce, Deborah, R-Ohio (15)

... Governors, Justices, Cabinet-Rank Officers

—Q—

Quillen, James H., R-Tenn. (1)
Quinn, Jack, R-N.Y. (30)

—R—

Rahall, Nick J. II, D-W.Va. (3)
Ramstad, Jim, R-Minn. (3)
Rangel, Charles B., D-N.Y. (15)
Ravenel, Arthur Jr., R-S.C. (1)
Reed, Jack, D-R.I. (2)
Regula, Ralph, R-Ohio (16)
Reynolds, Mel, D-Ill. (2)
Richardson, Bill, D-N.M. (3)
Ridge, Tom, R-Pa. (21)
Roberts, Pat, R-Kan. (1)
Roemer, Tim, D-Ind. (3)
Rogers, Harold, R-Ky. (5)
Rohrabacher, Dana, R-Calif. (45)
Rose, Charlie, D-N.C. (7)
Ros-Lehtinen, Ileana, R-Fla. (18)
Rostenkowski, Dan, D-Ill. (5)
Roth, Toby, R-Wis. (8)
Roukema, Marge, R-N.J. (5)
Rowland, J. Roy, D-Ga. (8)
Roybal-Allard, Lucille, D-Calif. (33)
Royce, Ed, R-Calif. (39)
Rush, Bobby L., D-Ill. (1)

—S—

Sabo, Martin Olav, D-Minn. (5)
Sanders, Bernard, I-Vt. (AL)
Sangmeister, George E., D-Ill. (11)
Santorum, Rick, R-Pa. (18)
Sarpalius, Bill, D-Texas (13)
Sawyer, Tom, D-Ohio (14)
Saxton, H. James, R-N.J. (3)
Schaefer, Dan, R-Colo. (6)
Schenk, Lynn, D-Calif. (49)
Schiff, Steven H., R-N.M. (1)
Schroeder, Patricia, D-Colo. (1)
Schumer, Charles E., D-N.Y. (9)
Scott, Robert C., D-Va. (3)
Sensenbrenner, F. James Jr., R-Wis. (9)
Serrano, José E., D-N.Y. (16)
Sharp, Philip R., D-Ind. (2)
Shaw, E. Clay Jr., R-Fla. (22)
Shays, Christopher, R-Conn. (4)
Shepherd, Karen, D-Utah (2)
Shuster, Bud, R-Pa. (9)
Sisisky, Norman, D-Va. (4)
Skaggs, David E., D-Colo. (2)
Skeen, Joe, R-N.M. (2)
Skelton, Ike, D-Mo. (4)
Slattery, Jim, D-Kan. (2)
Slaughter, Louise M., D-N.Y. (28)
Smith, Bob, R-Ore. (2)
Smith, Christopher H., R-N.J. (4)
Smith, Lamar, R-Texas (21)
Smith, Neal, D-Iowa (4)
Smith, Nick, R-Mich. (7)
Snowe, Olympia J., R-Maine (2)
Solomon, Gerald B. H., R-N.Y. (22)
Spence, Floyd D., R-S.C. (2)
Spratt, John M. Jr., D-S.C. (5)
Stark, Pete, D-Calif. (13)
Stearns, Cliff, R-Fla. (6)
Stenholm, Charles W., D-Texas (17)
Stokes, Louis, D-Ohio (11)
Strickland, Ted, D-Ohio (6)
Studds, Gerry E., D-Mass. (10)
Stump, Bob, R-Ariz. (3)
Stupak, Bart, D-Mich. (1)
Sundquist, Don, R-Tenn. (7)
Swett, Dick, D-N.H. (2)
Swift, Al, D-Wash. (2)
Synar, Mike, D-Okla. (2)

—T—

Talent, James M., R-Mo. (2)
Tanner, John, D-Tenn. (8)
Tauzin, W. J. "Billy," D-La. (3)
Taylor, Charles H., R-N.C. (11)
Taylor, Gene, D-Miss. (5)
Tejeda, Frank, D-Texas (28)
Thomas, Bill, R-Calif. (21)
Thomas, Craig, R-Wyo. (AL)
Thompson, Bennie, D-Miss. (2)
Thornton, Ray, D-Ark. (2)

Thurman, Karen L., D-Fla. (5)
Torkildsen, Peter G., R-Mass. (6)
Torres, Esteban E., D-Calif. (34)
Torricelli, Robert G., D-N.J. (9)
Towns, Edolphus, D-N.Y. (10)
Traficant, James A. Jr., D-Ohio (17)
Tucker, Walter R. III, D-Calif. (37)

—U—

Unsoeld, Jolene, D-Wash. (3)
Upton, Fred, R-Mich. (6)

—V—

Valentine, Tim, D-N.C. (2)
Velázquez, Nydia M., D-N.Y. (12)
Vento, Bruce F., D-Minn. (4)
Visclosky, Peter J., D-Ind. (1)
Volkmer, Harold L., D-Mo. (9)
Vucanovich, Barbara F., R-Nev. (2)

—W—

Walker, Robert S., R-Pa. (16)
Walsh, James T., R-N.Y. (25)
Washington, Craig, D-Texas (18)
Waters, Maxine, D-Calif. (35)
Watt, Melvin, D-N.C. (12)
Waxman, Henry A., D-Calif. (29)
Weldon, Curt, R-Pa. (7)
Wheat, Alan, D-Mo. (5)
Whitten, Jamie L., D-Miss. (1)
Williams, Pat, D-Mont. (AL)
Wilson, Charles, D-Texas (2)
Wise, Bob, D-W.Va. (2)
Wolf, Frank R., R-Va. (10)
Woolsey, Lynn, D-Calif. (6)
Wyden, Ron, D-Ore. (3)
Wynn, Albert R., D-Md. (4)

—Y—

Yates, Sidney R., D-Ill. (9)
Young, C. W. Bill, R-Fla. (10)
Young, Don, R-Alaska (AL)

—Z—

Zeliff, Bill, R-N.H. (1)
Zimmer, Dick, R-N.J. (12)

Delegates

de Lugo, Ron, D-Virgin Islands
Faleomavaega, Eni F. H., D-Am. Samoa
Norton, Eleanor Holmes, D-D.C.
Underwood, Robert A., D-Guam

Resident Commissioner

Romero-Barceló, Carlos, D-Puerto Rico

Senators
D 54; R 46

Akaka, Daniel K., D-Hawaii
Baucus, Max, D-Mont.
Bennett, Robert F., R-Utah
Biden, Joseph R. Jr., D-Del.
Bingaman, Jeff, D-N.M.
Bond, Christopher S., R-Mo.
Boxer, Barbara, D-Calif.
Bradley, Bill, D-N.J.
Breaux, John B., D-La.
Brown, Hank, R-Colo.
Bryan, Richard H., D-Nev.
Bumpers, Dale, D-Ark.
Burns, Conrad, R-Mont.
Byrd, Robert C., D-W.Va.
Campbell, Ben Nighthorse, D-Colo.
Chafee, John H., R-R.I.
Coats, Daniel R., R-Ind.
Cochran, Thad, R-Miss.
Cohen, William S., R-Maine
Conrad, Kent, D-N.D.
Coverdell, Paul, R-Ga.
Craig, Larry E., R-Idaho
D'Amato, Alfonse M., R-N.Y.
Danforth, John C., R-Mo.
Daschle, Tom, D-S.D.
DeConcini, Dennis, D-Ariz.
Dodd, Christopher J., D-Conn.
Dole, Bob, R-Kan.
Domenici, Pete V., R-N.M.

Dorgan, Byron L., D-N.D.
Durenberger, Dave, R-Minn.
Exon, Jim, D-Neb.
Faircloth, Lauch, R-N.C.
Feingold, Russell D., D-Wis.
Feinstein, Dianne, D-Calif.
Ford, Wendell H., D-Ky.
Glenn, John, D-Ohio
Gorton, Slade, R-Wash.
Graham, Bob, D-Fla.
Gramm, Phil, R-Texas
Grassley, Charles E., R-Iowa
Gregg, Judd, R-N.H.
Harkin, Tom, D-Iowa
Hatch, Orrin G., R-Utah
Hatfield, Mark O., R-Ore.
Heflin, Howell, D-Ala.
Helms, Jesse, R-N.C.
Hollings, Ernest F., D-S.C.
Hutchison, Kay Bailey, R-Texas
Inhofe, James M., R-Okla.
Inouye, Daniel K., D-Hawaii
Jeffords, James M., R-Vt.
Johnston, J. Bennett, D-La.
Kassebaum, Nancy Landon, R-Kan.
Kempthorne, Dirk, R-Idaho
Kennedy, Edward M., D-Mass.
Kerrey, Bob, D-Neb.
Kerry, John, D-Mass.
Kohl, Herb, D-Wis.
Lautenberg, Frank R., D-N.J.
Leahy, Patrick J., D-Vt.
Levin, Carl, D-Mich.
Lieberman, Joseph I., D-Conn.
Lott, Trent, R-Miss.
Lugar, Richard G., R-Ind.
Mack, Connie, R-Fla.
Mathews, Harlan, D-Tenn.
McCain, John, R-Ariz.
McConnell, Mitch, R-Ky.
Metzenbaum, Howard M., D-Ohio
Mikulski, Barbara A., D-Md.
Mitchell, George J., D-Maine
Moseley-Braun, Carol, D-Ill.
Moynihan, Daniel Patrick, D-N.Y.
Murkowski, Frank H., R-Alaska
Murray, Patty, D-Wash.
Nickles, Don, R-Okla.
Nunn, Sam, D-Ga.
Packwood, Bob, R-Ore.
Pell, Claiborne, D-R.I.
Pressler, Larry, R-S.D.
Pryor, David, D-Ark.
Reid, Harry, D-Nev.
Riegle, Donald W. Jr., D-Mich.
Robb, Charles S., D-Va.
Rockefeller, John D. IV, D-W.Va.
Roth, William V. Jr., R-Del.
Sarbanes, Paul S., D-Md.
Sasser, Jim, D-Tenn.
Shelby, Richard C., R-Ala.
Simon, Paul, D-Ill.
Simpson, Alan K., R-Wyo.
Smith, Robert C., R-N.H.
Specter, Arlen, R-Pa.
Stevens, Ted, R-Alaska
Thurmond, Strom, R-S.C.
Wallop, Malcolm, R-Wyo.
Warner, John W., R-Va.
Wellstone, Paul, D-Minn.
Wofford, Harris, D-Pa.

Governors
D 29; R 19; I 2

Ala. — James E. Folsom Jr., D
Alaska — Walter J. Hickel, I
Ariz. — Fife Symington, R
Ark. — Jim Guy Tucker, D
Calif. — Pete Wilson, R
Colo. — Roy Romer, D
Conn. — Lowell P. Weicker Jr., I
Del. — Thomas R. Carper, D
Fla. — Lawton Chiles, D
Ga. — Zell Miller, D
Hawaii — John Waihee III, D
Idaho — Cecil D. Andrus, D
Ill. — Jim Edgar, R

Ind. — Evan Bayh, D
Iowa — Terry E. Branstad, R
Kan. — Joan Finney, D
Ky. — Brereton Jones, D
La. — Edwin W. Edwards, D
Maine — John R. McKernan Jr., R
Md. — William Donald Schaefer, D
Mass. — William F. Weld, R
Mich. — John Engler, R
Minn. — Arne Carlson, R
Miss. — Kirk Fordice, R
Mo. — Mel Carnahan, D
Mont. — Marc Racicot, R
Neb. — Ben Nelson, D
Nev. — Bob Miller, D
N.H. — Stephen Merrill, R
N.J. — Christine Todd Whitman, R
N.M. — Bruce King, D
N.Y. — Mario M. Cuomo, D
N.C. — James B. Hunt Jr., D
N.D. — Edward T. Schafer, R
Ohio — George V. Voinovich, R
Okla. — David Walters, D
Ore. — Barbara Roberts, D
Pa. — Robert P. Casey, D
R.I. — Bruce Sundlun, D
S.C. — Carroll A. Campbell Jr., R
S.D. — Walter D. Miller, R
Tenn. — Ned McWherter, D
Texas — Ann W. Richards, D
Utah — Michael O. Leavitt, R
Vt. — Howard Dean, D
Va. — George F. Allen, R
Wash. — Mike Lowry, D
W.Va. — Gaston Caperton, D
Wis. — Tommy G. Thompson, R
Wyo. — Mike Sullivan, D

Supreme Court

Rehnquist, William H. — Va.,
  Chief Justice
Breyer, Stephen G. — Mass.
Ginsburg, Ruth Bader — N.Y.
Kennedy, Anthony M. — Calif.
O'Connor, Sandra Day — Ariz.
Scalia, Antonin — Va.
Souter, David H. — N.H.
Stevens, John Paul — Ill.
Thomas, Clarence — Ga.

Cabinet

Albright, Madeleine K. — U.N.
  Representative
Babbitt, Bruce — Interior
Bentsen, Lloyd — Treasury
Brown, Jesse — Veterans Affairs
Brown, Ronald H. — Commerce
Christopher, Warren — State
Cisneros, Henry G. — HUD
Espy, Mike — Agriculture
O'Leary, Hazel R. — Energy
Peña, Federico F. — Transportation
Perry, William J. — Defense
Reich, Robert B. — Labor
Reno, Janet — Attorney General
Riley, Richard W. — Education
Shalala, Donna E. — HHS

Other Executive Branch Officers

Gore, Al — Vice President
Kantor, Mickey — U.S. Trade
  Representative
Panetta, Leon E. — Chief of Staff
Rivlin, Alice M. — OMB Director
Browner, Carol M. — EPA Administrator
Lake, Anthony — National Security
  Adviser
Rubin, Robert E. — Chairman, National
  Economic Council
Tyson, Laura D'Andrea — Chairwoman,
  Council of Economic Advisers
Woolsey, R. James — Director of Central
  Intelligence

Senators' Committee Assignments

Akaka: Energy & Natural Resources; Governmental Affairs; Select Indian Affairs; Veterans' Affairs

Baucus: Agriculture, Nutrition & Forestry; Environment & Public Works (chairman); Finance; Joint Taxation; Select Intelligence

Bennett: Banking, Housing & Urban Affairs; Energy & Natural Resources; Governmental Affairs; Joint Economic; Small Business

Biden: Foreign Relations; Judiciary (chairman)

Bingaman: Armed Services; Energy & Natural Resources; Joint Economic; Labor & Human Resources

Bond: Appropriations; Banking, Housing & Urban Affairs; Budget; Small Business

Boren [1]: Agriculture, Nutrition & Forestry; Finance; Joint Taxation

Boxer: Banking, Housing & Urban Affairs; Budget; Environment & Public Works; Joint Economic

Bradley: Energy & Natural Resources; Finance; Special Aging

Breaux: Commerce, Science & Transportation; Finance; Special Aging

Brown: Budget; Foreign Relations; Judiciary

Bryan: Banking, Housing & Urban Affairs; Commerce, Science & Transportation; Select Ethics (chairman); Select Intelligence; Armed Services

Bumpers: Appropriations; Energy & Natural Resources; Small Business (chairman)

Burns: Appropriations; Commerce, Science & Transportation; Small Business; Special Aging

Byrd: Appropriations (chairman); Armed Services; Rules & Administration

Campbell: Banking, Housing & Urban Affairs; Energy & Natural Resources; Select Indian Affairs; Veterans' Affairs

Chafee: Environment & Public Works (ranking member); Finance; Select Intelligence; Small Business

Coats: Armed Services; Labor & Human Resources

Cochran: Agriculture, Nutrition & Forestry; Appropriations; Governmental Affairs; Select Indian Affairs; Rules & Administration

Cohen: Armed Services; Governmental Affairs; Judiciary; Special Aging (ranking member)

Conrad: Agriculture, Nutrition & Forestry; Budget; Finance; Select Indian Affairs

Coverdell: Agriculture, Nutrition & Forestry; Foreign Relations; Small Business

Craig: Agriculture, Nutrition & Forestry; Energy & Natural Resources; Joint Economic; Special Aging; Select Ethics

D'Amato: Appropriations; Banking, Housing & Urban Affairs (ranking member); Select Intelligence

Danforth: Commerce, Science & Transportation (ranking member); Finance; Select Intelligence

Daschle: Agriculture, Nutrition & Forestry; Finance; Select Indian Affairs; Select Ethics; Veterans' Affairs

DeConcini: Appropriations; Select Indian Affairs; Joint Library; Joint Printing; Judiciary; Rules & Administration; Select Intelligence (chairman); Veterans' Affairs

Dodd: Banking, Housing & Urban Affairs; Budget; Foreign Relations; Labor & Human Resources; Rules & Administration

Dole: Agriculture, Nutrition & Forestry; Finance; Joint Taxation; Rules & Administration

Domenici: Appropriations; Banking, Housing & Urban Affairs; Budget (ranking member); Energy & Natural Resources; Select Indian Affairs

Dorgan: Commerce, Science & Transportation; Energy and Natural Resources; Governmental Affairs; Select Indian Affairs; Joint Economic

Durenberger: Environment & Public Works; Finance; Labor & Human Resources; Special Aging

Exon: Armed Services; Budget; Commerce, Science & Transportation

Faircloth: Armed Services; Banking, Housing & Urban Affairs; Environment & Public Works

Feingold: Agriculture, Nutrition & Forestry; Foreign Relations; Special Aging

Feinstein: Appropriations; Judiciary; Rules & Administration

Ford: Commerce, Science & Transportation; Energy & Natural Resources; Joint Printing (chairman); Rules & Administration (chairman)

Glenn: Armed Services; Governmental Affairs (chairman); Select Intelligence; Special Aging

Gorton: Appropriations; Budget; Commerce, Science & Transportation; Select Indian Affairs; Select Intelligence

Graham: Armed Services; Environment & Public Works; Select Intelligence; Special Aging; Veterans' Affairs

Gramm: Appropriations; Banking, Housing & Urban Affairs; Budget

Grassley: Agriculture, Nutrition & Forestry; Budget; Finance; Judiciary; Special Aging

Gregg: Budget; Foreign Relations; Labor & Human Resources

Harkin: Agriculture, Nutrition & Forestry; Appropriations; Labor & Human Resources; Small Business

Hatch: Finance; Judiciary (ranking member); Labor & Human Resources

Hatfield: Appropriations (ranking member); Energy & Natural Resources; Select Indian Affairs; Joint Library (ranking member); Joint Printing; Rules & Administration

Heflin: Agriculture, Nutrition & Forestry; Judiciary; Small Business

Helms: Agriculture, Nutrition & Forestry; Foreign Relations (ranking member); Rules & Administration

Hollings: Appropriations; Budget; Commerce, Science & Transportation (chairman)

Hutchison: Armed Services; Small Business

Inouye: Appropriations; Commerce, Science & Transportation; Select Indian Affairs (chairman); Rules & Administration

Jeffords: Foreign Relations; Labor & Human Resources; Special Aging; Veterans' Affairs

Johnston: Appropriations; Budget; Energy & Natural Resources (chairman); Select Intelligence; Special Aging

[1] Boren resigned Nov. 15, 1994, and was replaced by Republican James M. Inhofe, who was sworn in Nov. 17.

Kassebaum: Foreign Relations; Select Indian Affairs; Labor & Human Resources (ranking member)

Kempthorne: Armed Services; Environment & Public Works; Small Business

Kennedy: Armed Services; Joint Economic; Judiciary; Labor & Human Resources (chairman)

Kerrey: Agriculture, Nutrition & Forestry; Appropriations; Select Intelligence

Kerry: Banking, Housing & Urban Affairs; Commerce, Science & Transportation; Foreign Relations; Select Intelligence; Small Business

Kohl: Appropriations; Judiciary; Small Business; Special Aging

Lautenberg: Appropriations; Budget; Environment & Public Works; Small Business

Leahy: Agriculture, Nutrition & Forestry (chairman); Appropriations; Judiciary

Levin: Armed Services; Governmental Affairs; Small Business

Lieberman: Armed Services; Environment & Public Works; Governmental Affairs; Small Business

Lott: Armed Services; Budget; Commerce, Science & Transportation; Energy & Natural Resources

Lugar: Agriculture, Nutrition & Forestry (ranking member); Foreign Relations; Select Intelligence

Mack: Appropriations; Banking, Housing & Urban Affairs; Joint Economic; Small Business

Mathews[2]: Commerce, Science & Transportation; Energy & Natural Resources; Foreign Relations; Joint Printing; Rules & Administration

McCain: Armed Services; Commerce, Science & Transportation; Governmental Affairs; Select Indian Affairs (vice chairman); Special Aging

McConnell: Agriculture, Nutrition & Forestry; Appropriations; Rules & Administration; Select Ethics (vice chairman)

Metzenbaum: Environment & Public Works; Judiciary; Labor & Human Resources; Select Intelligence

Mikulski: Appropriations; Labor & Human Resources; Select Ethics

Mitchell: Environment & Public Works; Finance; Veterans' Affairs

Moseley-Braun: Banking, Housing & Urban Affairs; Judiciary; Small Business

Moynihan: Environment & Public Works; Finance (chairman); Foreign Relations; Joint Library; Joint Taxation (chairman); Rules & Administration

Murkowski: Energy & Natural Resources; Foreign Relations; Select Indian Affairs; Veterans' Affairs (ranking member)

Murray: Appropriations; Banking, Housing & Urban Affairs; Budget

Nickles: Appropriations; Budget; Energy & Natural Resources; Select Indian Affairs

Nunn: Armed Services (chairman); Governmental Affairs; Small Business

Packwood: Commerce, Science & Transportation; Finance (ranking member); Joint Taxation

Pell: Foreign Relations (chairman); Joint Library (vice chairman); Labor & Human Resources; Rules & Administration

Pressler: Commerce, Science & Transportation; Foreign Relations; Judiciary; Small Business (ranking member); Special Aging

Pryor: Agriculture, Nutrition & Forestry; Finance; Governmental Affairs; Special Aging (chairman)

Reid: Appropriations; Environment & Public Works; Select Indian Affairs; Special Aging

Riegle: Banking, Housing & Urban Affairs (chairman); Budget; Finance; Special Aging

Robb: Armed Services; Commerce, Science & Transportation; Foreign Relations; Joint Economic

Rockefeller: Commerce, Science & Transportation; Finance; Veterans' Affairs (chairman)

Roth: Banking, Housing & Urban Affairs; Finance; Governmental Affairs (ranking member); Joint Economic

Sarbanes: Banking, Housing & Urban Affairs; Budget; Foreign Relations; Joint Economic (vice chairman)

Sasser: Appropriations; Banking, Housing & Urban Affairs; Budget (chairman); Governmental Affairs

Shelby: Armed Services; Banking, Housing & Urban Affairs; Energy & Natural Resources; Special Aging

Simon: Budget; Foreign Relations; Select Indian Affairs; Judiciary; Labor & Human Resources

Simpson: Environment & Public Works; Judiciary; Special Aging; Veterans' Affairs

Smith: Armed Services; Environment & Public Works; Select Ethics

Specter: Appropriations; Energy & Natural Resources; Judiciary; Special Aging; Veterans' Affairs

Stevens: Appropriations; Commerce, Science & Transportation; Governmental Affairs; Joint Library; Joint Printing (ranking member); Rules & Administration (ranking member); Select Intelligence

Thurmond: Armed Services (ranking member); Judiciary; Labor & Human Resources; Veterans' Affairs

Wallop: Energy & Natural Resources (ranking member); Finance; Select Intelligence; Small Business

Warner: Armed Services; Environment & Public Works; Rules & Administration; Select Intelligence (vice chairman)

Wellstone: Energy & Natural Resources; Select Indian Affairs; Labor & Human Resources; Small Business

Wofford: Environment & Public Works; Foreign Relations; Labor & Human Resources; Small Business

[2] Mathews resigned Dec. 2, 1994, and was replaced by Fred Thompson, who was sworn in Dec. 9.

Representatives' Committee Assignments

Abercrombie: Armed Services; Natural Resources

Ackerman: Foreign Affairs; Merchant Marine & Fisheries; Post Office & Civil Service

Allard: Agriculture; Budget; Natural Resources

Andrews (Texas): Budget; Joint Economic; Ways & Means

Andrews (N.J.): Education & Labor; Foreign Affairs

Andrews (Maine): Armed Services; Merchant Marine & Fisheries; Small Business

Applegate: Public Works & Transportation; Veterans' Affairs

Archer: Joint Taxation; Ways & Means (ranking member)

Armey: Education & Labor; Joint Economic

Bacchus: Banking, Finance & Urban Affairs; Science, Space & Technology

Bachus: Banking, Finance & Urban Affairs; Veterans' Affairs

Baesler: Agriculture; Education & Labor; Veterans' Affairs

Baker (Calif.): Public Works & Transportation; Science, Space & Technology

Baker (La.): Banking, Finance & Urban Affairs; Natural Resources; Small Business

Ballenger: District of Columbia; Education & Labor; Foreign Affairs

Barca: Public Works & Transportation; Science, Space & Technology

Barcia: Public Works & Transportation; Science, Space & Technology

Barlow: Agriculture; Merchant Marine & Fisheries; Natural Resources

Barrett (Neb.): Agriculture; Education & Labor; House Administration

Barrett (Wis.): Banking, Finance & Urban Affairs; Government Operations; Natural Resources

Bartlett: Armed Services; Science, Space & Technology

Barton: Energy & Commerce; Science, Space & Technology

Bateman: Armed Services; Merchant Marine & Fisheries

Becerra: Education & Labor; Judiciary; Science, Space & Technology

Beilenson: Budget; Rules

Bentley: Appropriations; Merchant Marine & Fisheries

Bereuter: Banking, Finance & Urban Affairs; Foreign Affairs; Select Intelligence

Berman: Budget; Foreign Affairs; Judiciary; Natural Resources

Bevill: Appropriations

Bilbray: Armed Services; Select Intelligence; Small Business

Bilirakis: Energy & Commerce; Veterans' Affairs

Bishop: Agriculture; Post Office & Civil Service; Veterans' Affairs

Blackwell: Budget; Public Works & Transportation

Bliley: District of Columbia (ranking member); Energy & Commerce

Blute: Public Works & Transportation; Science, Space & Technology

Boehlert: Post Office & Civil Service; Public Works & Transportation; Science, Space & Technology

Boehner: Agriculture; Education & Labor; House Administration

Bonilla: Appropriations

Bonior: Rules

Borski: Foreign Affairs; Public Works & Transportation; Standards of Official Conduct

Boucher: Energy & Commerce; Judiciary; Science, Space & Technology

Brewster: Ways & Means

Brooks: Judiciary (chairman)

Browder: Armed Services; Budget

Brown (Fla.): Government Operations; Public Works & Transportation; Veterans' Affairs

Brown (Calif.): Agriculture; Science, Space & Technology (chairman)

Brown (Ohio): Energy & Commerce; Foreign Affairs; Post Office & Civil Service

Bryant: Budget; Energy & Commerce; Judiciary

Bunning: Budget; Standards of Official Conduct; Ways & Means

Burton: Foreign Affairs; Post Office & Civil Service; Veterans' Affairs

Buyer: Armed Services; Veterans' Affairs

Byrne: Post Office & Civil Service; Public Works & Transportation

Callahan: Appropriations

Calvert: Natural Resources; Science, Space & Technology

Camp: Ways & Means

Canady: Agriculture; Judiciary

Cantwell: Foreign Affairs; Merchant Marine & Fisheries; Public Works & Transportation

Cardin: House Administration; Standards of Official Conduct; Ways & Means

Carr: Appropriations

Castle: Banking, Finance & Urban Affairs; Education & Labor; Merchant Marine & Fisheries

Chapman: Appropriations

Clay: Education & Labor; House Administration; Post Office & Civil Service (chairman)

Clayton: Agriculture; Small Business

Clement: Public Works & Transportation; Veterans' Affairs

Clinger: Government Operations (ranking member); Public Works & Transportation

Clyburn: Public Works & Transportation; Veterans' Affairs

Coble: Judiciary; Merchant Marine & Fisheries

Coleman: Appropriations; Select Intelligence

Collins (Mich.): Government Operations; Post Office & Civil Service; Public Works & Transportation

Collins (Ill.): Energy & Commerce; Government Operations

Collins (Ga.): Public Works & Transportation; Small Business

Combest: Agriculture; Select Intelligence (ranking member); Small Business

Condit: Agriculture; Government Operations

Conyers: Government Operations (chairman); Judiciary; Small Business

Cooper: Budget; Energy & Commerce

Coppersmith: Public Works & Transportation; Science, Space & Technology

Costello: Budget; Public Works & Transportation

Cox: Budget; Government Operations; Joint Economic

Coyne: Budget; Ways & Means

Cramer: Public Works & Transportation; Science, Space & Technology; Select Intelligence

Crane: Joint Taxation; Ways & Means

Crapo: Energy & Commerce

Cunningham: Armed Services; Education & Labor; Merchant Marine & Fisheries

Danner: Public Works & Transportation; Small Business

Darden: Appropriations; Standards of Official Conduct

de la Garza: Agriculture (chairman)

de Lugo: Education & Labor; Natural Resources; Public Works & Transportation

Deal: Natural Resources; Public Works & Transportation; Science, Space & Technology

DeFazio: Natural Resources; Public Works & Transportation

DeLauro: Appropriations

DeLay: Appropriations

Dellums: Armed Services (chairman); District of Columbia

Derrick: House Administration; Rules

Deutsch: Banking, Finance & Urban Affairs; Foreign Affairs; Merchant Marine & Fisheries

Diaz-Balart: Foreign Affairs; Merchant Marine & Fisheries

Dickey: Agriculture; Natural Resources; Small Business

Dicks: Appropriations; Select Intelligence

Dingell: Energy & Commerce (chairman)

Dixon: Appropriations; Select Intelligence

Dooley: Agriculture; Banking, Finance & Urban Affairs; Natural Resources

Doolittle: Agriculture; Natural Resources

Dornan: Armed Services; Select Intelligence

Dreier: Rules

Duncan: Natural Resources; Public Works & Transportation

Dunn: House Administration; Public Works & Transportation; Science, Space & Technology

Durbin: Appropriations

Edwards: (Calif.): Foreign Affairs; Judiciary; Veterans' Affairs

Edwards: (Texas): Armed Services; Veterans' Affairs

Ehlers: Public Works & Transportation; Science, Space & Technology

Emerson: Agriculture; Public Works & Transportation

Engel: Education & Labor; Foreign Affairs

Eshoo: Merchant Marine & Fisheries; Science, Space & Technology

Evans: Armed Services; Natural Resources; Veterans' Affairs

Everett: Agriculture; Armed Services; Veterans' Affairs

Ewing: Agriculture; Public Works & Transportation

Faleomavaega: Education & Labor; Foreign Affairs; Natural Resources

Farr: Agriculture; Armed Services; Natural Resources

Fawell: Education & Labor; Science, Space & Technology

Fazio: Appropriations

Fields (Texas): Energy & Commerce; Merchant Marine & Fisheries (ranking member)

Fields (La.): Banking, Finance & Urban Affairs; Small Business

Filner: Public Works & Transportation; Veterans' Affairs

Fingerhut: Banking, Finance & Urban Affairs; Foreign Affairs; Science, Space & Technology

Fish: Judiciary (ranking member)

Flake: Banking, Finance & Urban Affairs; Government Operations; Small Business

Foglietta: Appropriations

Foley: Speaker of the House

Ford (Mich.): Education & Labor (chairman)

Ford (Tenn.): Ways & Means

Fowler: Armed Services; Merchant Marine & Fisheries

Frank: Banking, Finance & Urban Affairs; Budget; Judiciary

Franks (N.J.): Budget; Public Works & Transportation

Franks (Conn.): Energy & Commerce

Frost: House Administration; Rules

Furse: Armed Services; Banking, Finance & Urban Affairs; Merchant Marine & Fisheries

Gallegly: Foreign Affairs; Judiciary; Natural Resources

Gallo[1]: Appropriations

Gejdenson: Foreign Affairs; House Administration; Joint Printing; Natural Resources

Gekas: Judiciary; Select Intelligence

Gephardt: Budget (majority leader)

Geren: Armed Services; Public Works & Transportation; Science, Space & Technology

Gibbons: Joint Taxation; Ways & Means

Gilchrest: Merchant Marine & Fisheries; Public Works & Transportation

Gillmor: Energy & Commerce

Gilman: Foreign Affairs (ranking member); Post Office & Civil Service

Gingrich: House Administration; Joint Printing

Glickman: Agriculture; Judiciary; Science, Space & Technology; Select Intelligence (chairman)

Gonzalez: Banking, Finance & Urban Affairs (chairman)

Goodlatte: Agriculture; Judiciary

Goodling: Education & Labor (ranking member); Foreign Affairs

Gordon: Budget; Rules

Goss: Rules; Standards of Official Conduct

Grams: Banking, Finance & Urban Affairs; Science, Space & Technology

Grandy: Standards of Official Conduct (ranking member); Ways & Means

Green: Education & Labor; Government Operations; Merchant Marine & Fisheries

[1] *Dean A. Gallo died Nov. 6, 1994.*

Greenwood: Energy & Commerce

Gunderson: Agriculture; Education & Labor

Gutierrez: Banking, Finance & Urban Affairs; Foreign Affairs; Veterans' Affairs

Hall (Ohio): Rules

Hall (Texas): Energy & Commerce; Science, Space & Technology

Hamburg: Merchant Marine & Fisheries; Public Works & Transportation

Hamilton: Foreign Affairs (chairman); Joint Economic

Hancock: Ways & Means

Hansen: Armed Services; Natural Resources; Select Intelligence

Harman: Armed Services; Science, Space & Technology

Hastert: Energy & Commerce; Government Operations

Hastings: Foreign Affairs; Merchant Marine & Fisheries; Post Office & Civil Service

Hayes: Government Operations; Public Works & Transportation; Science, Space & Technology

Hefley: Armed Services; Natural Resources; Small Business

Hefner: Appropriations

Herger: Budget; Ways & Means

Hilliard: Agriculture; Small Business

Hinchey: Banking, Finance & Urban Affairs; Natural Resources

Hoagland: Ways & Means

Hobson: Appropriations; Budget; Standards of Official Conduct

Hochbrueckner: Armed Services; Merchant Marine & Fisheries

Hoekstra: Education & Labor; Public Works & Transportation

Hoke: Budget; Science, Space & Technology

Holden: Agriculture; Armed Services

Horn: Government Operations; Public Works & Transportation

Houghton: Ways & Means

Hoyer: Appropriations; House Administration

Huffington: Banking, Finance & Urban Affairs; Small Business

Hughes: Judiciary; Merchant Marine & Fisheries

Hunter: Armed Services

Hutchinson: Public Works & Transportation; Veterans' Affairs

Hutto: Armed Services; Merchant Marine & Fisheries

Hyde: Foreign Affairs; Judiciary

Inglis: Budget; Judiciary

Inhofe [2]: Armed Services; Merchant Marine & Fisheries; Public Works & Transportation

Inslee: Agriculture; Science, Space & Technology

Istook: Appropriations

Jacobs: Ways & Means

Jefferson: District of Columbia; Ways & Means

Johnson, Sam: Banking, Finance & Urban Affairs; Science, Space & Technology; Small Business

Johnson, Eddie Bernice: Public Works & Transportation; Science, Space & Technology

Johnson (Ga.): Armed Services; Science, Space & Technology

Johnson (S.D.): Agriculture; Natural Resources

Johnson (Conn.): Standards of Official Conduct; Ways & Means

Johnston: Budget; Foreign Affairs

Kanjorski: Banking, Finance & Urban Affairs; Post Office & Civil Service

Kaptur: Appropriations

Kasich: Armed Services; Budget (ranking member)

Kennedy: Banking, Finance & Urban Affairs; Veterans' Affairs

Kennelly: Budget; House Administration; Ways & Means

Kildee: Budget; Education & Labor; House Administration

Kim: Public Works & Transportation; Small Business

King: Banking, Finance & Urban Affairs; Merchant Marine & Fisheries; Veterans' Affairs;

Kingston: Agriculture; Merchant Marine & Fisheries

Kleczka: House Administration; Joint Printing; Ways & Means

Klein: Banking, Finance & Urban Affairs; Science, Space & Technology

Klink: Banking, Finance & Urban Affairs; Education & Labor; Small Business

Klug: Energy & Commerce

Knollenberg: Banking, Finance & Urban Affairs; Small Business

Kolbe: Appropriations; Budget

Kopetski: Ways & Means

Kreidler: Energy & Commerce; Veterans' Affairs

Kyl: Armed Services; Government Operations; Standards of Official Conduct

LaFalce: Banking, Finance & Urban Affairs; Small Business (chairman)

Lambert: Agriculture; Energy & Commerce; Merchant Marine & Fisheries

Lancaster: Armed Services; Merchant Marine & Fisheries; Small Business

Lantos: Foreign Affairs; Government Operations

LaRocco: Banking, Finance & Urban Affairs; Natural Resources

Laughlin: Merchant Marine & Fisheries; Post Office & Civil Service; Public Works & Transportation; Select Intelligence

Lazio: Banking, Finance & Urban Affairs; Budget

Leach: Banking, Finance & Urban Affairs (ranking member); Foreign Affairs

Lehman: Energy & Commerce; Natural Resources

Levin: Ways & Means

Levy: Foreign Affairs; Public Works & Transportation

Lewis (Calif.): Appropriations; Select Intelligence

Lewis (Fla.): Agriculture; Science, Space & Technology

Lewis (Ga.): District of Columbia; Ways & Means

Lewis [3] (Ky.): Agriculture; Veterans' Affairs

Lightfoot: Appropriations

Linder: Banking, Finance & Urban Affairs; Science, Space & Technology; Veterans' Affairs

---

[2] James M. Inhofe resigned Nov. 15, 1994; Steve Largent was sworn in Nov. 29 to replace him.

[3] Ron Lewis was sworn in May 26, 1994, to replace William H. Natcher, who died March 29.

Lipinski: Merchant Marine & Fisheries; Public Works & Transportation

Livingston: Appropriations; House Administration

Lloyd: Armed Services; Science, Space & Technology

Long: Agriculture; Veterans' Affairs

Lowey: Appropriations

Lucas [4]**:** Agriculture; Government Operations

Machtley: Armed Services; Small Business

Maloney: Banking, Finance & Urban Affairs; Government Operations

Mann: Armed Services; Judiciary

Manton: Energy & Commerce; House Administration; Merchant Marine & Fisheries

Manzullo: Foreign Affairs; Small Business

Margolies-Mezvinsky: Energy & Commerce; Government Operations; Small Business

Markey: Energy & Commerce; Natural Resources

Martinez: Education & Labor; Foreign Affairs

Matsui: Ways & Means

Mazzoli: Judiciary; Small Business

McCandless: Banking, Finance & Urban Affairs; Government Operations

McCloskey: Armed Services; Foreign Affairs; Post Office & Civil Service

McCollum: Banking, Finance & Urban Affairs; Judiciary

McCrery: Ways & Means

McCurdy: Armed Services; Science, Space & Technology

McDade: Appropriations (ranking member)

McDermott: District of Columbia; Standards of Official Conduct (chairman); Ways & Means

McHale: Armed Services; Science, Space & Technology

McHugh: Armed Services; Government Operations

McInnis: Natural Resources; Small Business

McKeon: Education & Labor; Public Works & Transportation

McKinney: Agriculture; Foreign Affairs

McMillan: Budget; Energy & Commerce

McNulty: Ways & Means

Meehan: Armed Services; Small Business

Meek: Appropriations

Menendez: Foreign Affairs; Public Works & Transportation

Meyers: Foreign Affairs; Small Business (ranking member)

Mfume: Banking, Finance & Urban Affairs; Joint Economic; Small Business; Standards of Official Conduct

Mica: Government Operations; Public Works & Transportation

Michel: (minority leader)

Miller (Calif.): Education & Labor; Natural Resources (chairman)

Miller (Fla.): Budget; Education & Labor

Mineta: Public Works & Transportation (chairman)

Minge: Agriculture; Science, Space & Technology

Mink: Budget; Education & Labor; Natural Resources

Moakley: Rules (chairman)

Molinari: Education & Labor; Public Works & Transportation

Mollohan: Appropriations; Budget

Montgomery: Armed Services; Veterans' Affairs (chairman)

Moorhead: Energy & Commerce (ranking member); Judiciary

Moran: Appropriations

Morella: Post Office & Civil Service; Science, Space & Technology

Murphy: Education & Labor; Natural Resources

Murtha: Appropriations

Myers: Appropriations; Post Office & Civil Service (ranking member)

Nadler: Judiciary; Public Works & Transportation

Natcher [5]**:** Appropriations (chairman)

Neal (N.C.): Banking, Finance & Urban Affairs; Government Operations

Neal (Mass.): Ways & Means

Norton: District of Columbia; Post Office & Civil Service; Public Works & Transportation

Nussle: Agriculture; Banking, Finance & Urban Affairs

Oberstar: Foreign Affairs; Public Works & Transportation

Obey: Appropriations; Joint Economic (chairman)

Olver: Appropriations

Ortiz: Armed Services; Merchant Marine & Fisheries

Orton: Banking, Finance & Urban Affairs; Budget

Owens: Education & Labor; Government Operations

Oxley: Energy & Commerce

Packard: Appropriations

Pallone: Energy & Commerce; Merchant Marine & Fisheries

Parker: Budget; Public Works & Transportation

Pastor: Appropriations

Paxon: Energy & Commerce

Payne (Va.): Ways & Means

Payne (N.J.): Education & Labor; Foreign Affairs; Government Operations

Pelosi: Appropriations; Select Intelligence; Standards of Official Conduct

Penny: Agriculture; Veterans' Affairs

Peterson (Fla.): Appropriations

Peterson (Minn.): Agriculture; Government Operations

Petri: Education & Labor; Post Office & Civil Service; Public Works & Transportation

Pickett: Armed Services; Merchant Marine & Fisheries

Pickle: Joint Taxation; Ways & Means

Pombo: Agriculture; Merchant Marine & Fisheries; Natural Resources

Pomeroy: Agriculture; Budget

Porter: Appropriations

Portman: Government Operations; Small Business

Poshard: Public Works & Transportation; Small Business

Price: Appropriations; Budget

Pryce: Banking, Finance & Urban Affairs; Government Operations

Quillen: Rules

Quinn: Public Works & Transportation; Veterans' Affairs

Rahall: Natural Resources; Public Works & Transportation

Ramstad: Joint Economic; Judiciary; Small Business

---

[4] *Frank Lucas was sworn in May 17, 1994, to replace Glenn English, who resigned Jan. 7.*

[5] *William H. Natcher died Mar. 29, 1994; Ron Lewis was sworn in May 26 to replace him.*

Rangel: Ways & Means

Ravenel: Armed Services; Merchant Marine & Fisheries

Reed: Education & Labor; Judiciary; Merchant Marine & Fisheries; Select Intelligence

Regula: Appropriations

Reynolds: Ways & Means

Richardson: Energy & Commerce; Natural Resources; Select Intelligence

Ridge: Banking, Finance & Urban Affairs; Post Office & Civil Service; Veterans' Affairs

Roberts: Agriculture (ranking member); House Administration; Joint Printing

Roemer: Education & Labor; Science, Space & Technology

Rogers: Appropriations

Rohrabacher: District of Columbia; Foreign Affairs; Science, Space & Technology

Romero-Barcelo: Education & Labor; Natural Resources

Rose: Agriculture; House Administration (chairman); Joint Library (chairman); Joint Printing (vice chairman)

Ros-Lehtinen: Foreign Affairs; Government Operations

Rostenkowski: Joint Taxation (vice chairman); Ways & Means (chairman)

Roth: Banking, Finance & Urban Affairs; Foreign Affairs

Roukema: Banking, Finance & Urban Affairs; Education & Labor

Rowland: Energy & Commerce; Veterans' Affairs

Roybal-Allard: Banking, Finance & Urban Affairs; Small Business

Royce: Foreign Affairs; Science, Space & Technology

Rush: Banking, Finance & Urban Affairs; Government Operations; Science, Space & Technology

Sabo: Appropriations; Budget (chairman)

Sanders: Banking, Finance & Urban Affairs; Government Operations

Sangmeister: Judiciary; Public Works & Transportation; Veterans' Affairs

Santorum: Ways & Means

Sarpalius: Agriculture; Small Business

Saxton: Armed Services; District of Columbia; Joint Economic; Merchant Marine & Fisheries

Schaefer: Energy & Commerce

Schenk: Energy & Commerce; Merchant Marine & Fisheries

Schiff: Government Operations; Judiciary; Science, Space & Technology; Standards of Official Conduct

Schroeder: Armed Services; Judiciary; Post Office & Civil Service

Schumer: Banking, Finance & Urban Affairs; Foreign Affairs; Judiciary

Scott: Education & Labor; Judiciary; Science, Space & Technology

Sensenbrenner: Judiciary; Science, Space & Technology

Serrano: Appropriations

Sharp: Energy & Commerce; Natural Resources

Shaw: Ways & Means

Shays: Budget; Government Operations

Shepherd: Natural Resources; Public Works & Transportation

Shuster: Public Works & Transportation (ranking member)

Sisisky: Armed Services; Small Business

Skaggs: Appropriations; Select Intelligence

Skeen: Appropriations

Skelton: Armed Services; Small Business

Slattery: Energy & Commerce; Veterans' Affairs

Slaughter: Budget; Rules

Smith (Iowa): Appropriations; Small Business

Smith (Ore.): Agriculture; Natural Resources

Smith (Texas): Budget; Judiciary

Smith (N.J.): Foreign Affairs; Veterans' Affairs

Smith (Mich.): Agriculture; Budget; Science, Space & Technology

Snowe: Budget; Foreign Affairs

Solomon: Rules (ranking member)

Spence: Armed Services (ranking member); Veterans' Affairs

Spratt: Armed Services; Government Operations

Stark: District of Columbia (chairman); Joint Economic; Ways & Means

Stearns: Energy & Commerce; Veterans' Affairs

Stenholm: Agriculture; Budget

Stokes: Appropriations

Strickland: Education & Labor; Small Business

Studds: Energy & Commerce; Merchant Marine & Fisheries (chairman)

Stump: Armed Services; Veterans' Affairs (ranking member)

Stupak: Armed Services; Government Operations; Merchant Marine & Fisheries

Sundquist: Ways & Means

Swett: Public Works & Transportation; Science, Space & Technology

Swift: Energy & Commerce; House Administration

Synar: Energy & Commerce; Government Operations; Judiciary

Talent: Armed Services; Small Business

Tanner: Armed Services; Science, Space & Technology

Tauzin: Energy & Commerce; Merchant Marine & Fisheries

Taylor (N.C.): Appropriations; Merchant Marine & Fisheries

Taylor (Miss.): Armed Services; Merchant Marine & Fisheries

Tejeda: Armed Services; Veterans' Affairs

Thomas (Calif.): House Administration (ranking member); Ways & Means

Thomas (Wyo.): Banking, Finance & Urban Affairs; Government Operations; Natural Resources

Thompson: Agriculture; Small Business; Merchant Marine & Fisheries

Thornton: Appropriations

Thurman: Agriculture; Government Operations

Torkildsen: Armed Services; Merchant Marine & Fisheries; Small Business

Torres: Appropriations

Torricelli: Foreign Affairs; Science, Space & Technology; Select Intelligence

Towns: Energy & Commerce; Government Operations

Traficant: Public Works & Transportation; Science, Space & Technology

Tucker: Public Works & Transportation; Small Business

Underwood: Armed Services; Natural Resources; Education & Labor

Unsoeld: Education & Labor; Merchant Marine & Fisheries

Upton: Energy & Commerce

Valentine: Public Works & Transportation; Science, Space & Technology

Velázquez: Banking, Finance & Urban Affairs; Small Business

Vento: Banking, Finance & Urban Affairs; Natural Resources

Visclosky: Appropriations

Volkmer: Agriculture; Science, Space & Technology

Vucanovich: Appropriations; Natural Resources

Walker: Science, Space & Technology (ranking member)

Walsh: Appropriations

Washington: Energy & Commerce; Government Operations; Judiciary

Waters: Banking, Finance & Urban Affairs; Small Business; Veterans' Affairs

Watt: Banking, Finance & Urban Affairs; Judiciary; Post Office & Civil Service

Waxman: Energy & Commerce; Government Operations

Weldon: Armed Services; Merchant Marine & Fisheries

Wheat: District of Columbia; Rules

Whitten: Appropriations

Williams: Agriculture; Education & Labor; Natural Resources

Wilson: Appropriations

Wise: Budget; Public Works & Transportation

Wolf: Appropriations

Woolsey: Budget; Education & Labor; Government Operations

Wyden: Energy & Commerce; Joint Economic; Small Business

Wynn: Banking, Finance & Urban Affairs; Foreign Affairs; Post Office & Civil Service

Yates: Appropriations

Young (Fla.): Appropriations; Select Intelligence

Young (Alaska): Merchant Marine & Fisheries; Natural Resources (ranking member); Post Office & Civil Service

Zeliff: Government Operations; Public Works & Transportation; Small Business

Zimmer: Government Operations; Science, Space & Technology

Pronunciation Guide

The following are some of the most often mispronounced names of members of Congress.

Senators

John B. Breaux, D-La. — BRO
Alfonse M. D'Amato, R-N.Y. — da-MAH-toe
Tom Daschle, D-S.D. — DASH-el
Dennis DeConcini, D-Ariz. — dee-con-SEE-nee
Pete V. Domenici, R-N.M. — da-MEN-ih-chee
Lauch Faircloth, R-N.C. — LOCK
Dianne Feinstein, D-Calif. — FINE-stine
Daniel K. Inouye, D-Hawaii — in-NO-ay

Representatives/Delegates

Jim Bacchus, D-Fla. — BACK-us
Spencer Bachus, R-Ala. — BACK-us
Scotty Baesler, D-Ky. — BAA-zler
James A. Barcia, D-Mich. — BAR-sha
Xavier Becerra, D-Calif. — HAH-vee-air beh-SEH-ra
Anthony C. Beilenson, D-Calif. — BEE-lin-son
Doug Bereuter, R-Neb. — BEE-right-er
Michael Bilirakis, R-Fla. — bil-li-RACK-us
John A. Boehner, R-Ohio — BAY-ner
Henry Bonilla, R-Texas — bo-NEE-uh
David E. Bonior, D-Mich. — BON-yer
Rick Boucher, D-Va. — BOUGH-cher
Steve Buyer, R-Ind. — BOO-yer
Charles T. Canady, R-Fla. — CAN-uh-dee
Michael D. Crapo, R-Idaho — CRAY-poe
Peter A. DeFazio, D-Ore. — da-FAH-zee-o
Peter Deutsch, D-Fla. — DOYCH
Lincoln Diaz-Balart, R-Fla. — DEE-az BAA-lart
Vernon J. Ehlers, R-Mich. — AY-lurz
Eni F. H. Faleomavaega, D-Am. Samoa — EN-ee FOL-ee-oh-mav-ah-ENG-uh
Harris W. Fawell, R-Ill. — FAY-well
Vic Fazio, D-Calif. — FAY-zee-o
Thomas M. Foglietta, D-Pa. — fo-lee-ET-uh
Elton Gallegly, R-Calif. — GAL-uh-glee
Sam Gejdenson, D-Conn. — GAY-den-son
Robert W. Goodlatte, R-Va. — GOOD-lat

Luis V. Gutierrez, D-Ill. — loo-EES goo-tee-AIR-ez
George J. Hochbrueckner, D-N.Y. — HOCK-brewk-ner
Peter Hoekstra, R-Mich. — HOKE-struh
Amo Houghton, R-N.Y. — HO-tun
John R. Kasich, R-Ohio — KAY-sick
Gerald D. Kleczka, D-Wis. — KLETCH-kuh
Scott L. Klug, R-Wis. — KLOOG
Jim Kolbe, R-Ariz. — COLE-bee
Mike Kopetski, D-Ore. — ka-PET-skee
Greg Laughlin, D-Texas — LAWF-lin
Rick A. Lazio, R-N.Y. — LAZZ-ee-o
Richard H. Lehman, D-Calif. — LEE-mun
Nita M. Lowey, D-N.Y. — LOW-ee
Ronald K. Machtley, R-R.I. — MAKE-lee
Donald Manzullo, R-Ill. — man-ZOO-low
Marjorie Margolies-Mezvinsky, D-Pa. — mar-GO-lees mez-VIN-skee
Kweisi Mfume, D-Md. — kwy-EE-say mm-FU-may
David Minge, D-Minn. — MIN-gee
David R. Obey, D-Wis. — O-bee
Frank Pallone Jr., D-N.J. — pa-LOAN
Ed Pastor, D-Ariz.— pas-TORE
Nancy Pelosi, D-Calif. — pa-LOH-see
Tom Petri, R-Wis. — PEE-try
Glenn Poshard, D-Ill. — pa-SHARD
Arthur Ravenel Jr., R-S.C. — RAV-nel
Ralph Regula, R-Ohio — REG-you-luh
Dana Rohrabacher, R-Calif. — ROAR-ah-BAH-ker
Ileana Ros-Lehtinen, R-Fla. — il-ee-AH-na ross-LAY-tin-nen
Marge Roukema, R-N.J. — ROCK-ah-muh
Bill Sarpalius, D-Texas — sar-POHL-us
José E. Serrano, D-N.Y. — ho-ZAY sa-RAH-no (rolled 'R')
Bart Stupak, D-Mich. — STEW-pack
W. J. "Billy" Tauzin, D-La. — TOE-zan
Frank Tejeda, D-Texas — tuh-HAY-duh
Robert G. Torricelli, D-N.J. — tor-uh-SELL-ee
Jolene Unsoeld, D-Wash. — UN-sold
Nydia M. Velázquez, D-N.Y. — NID-ee-uh veh-LASS-kez
Barbara F. Vucanovich, R-Nev. — voo-CAN-oh-vitch
Bill Zeliff, R-N.H. — ZELL-iff

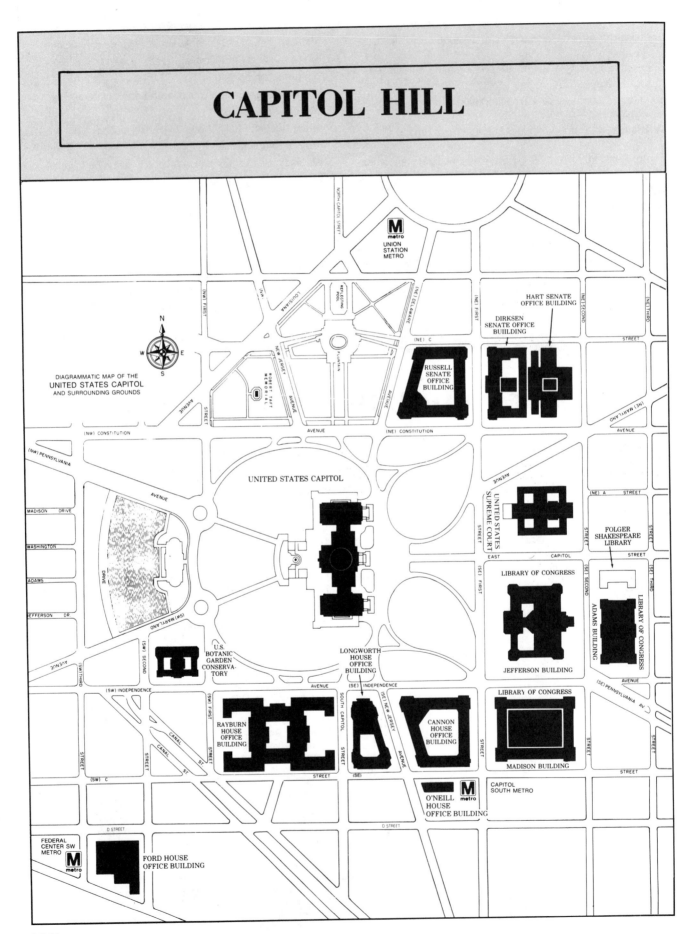

CAPITOL HILL

DIAGRAMMATIC MAP OF THE
UNITED STATES CAPITOL
AND SURROUNDING GROUNDS

VOTE STUDIES

Presidential Support................................... 3-C
    Leading Scorers 5-C
Party Unity.. 6-C
    Leading Scorers 8-C
Conservative Coalition............................... 9-C
    Leading Scorers 10-C
Voting Participation 11-C
Key Votes... 13-C
    House 13-C
    Senate... 21-C
Background Material
Presidential Support
    Definitions and Data............................ 29-C
    List of Votes.................................... 30-C

Individual Members' Scores 32-C
Party Unity
    Definitions and Data............................. 35-C
    List of Votes.................................... 36-C
    Individual Members' Scores 37-C
Conservative Coalition
    Definitions and Data............................. 40-C
    List of Votes.................................... 41-C
    Individual Members' Scores 42-C
Voting Participation
    Individual Members' Scores 45-C
Key Votes
    Individual House Members' Scores 48-C
    Individual Senators' Scores....................... 54-C

PRESIDENTIAL SUPPORT

Clinton's High Victory Rate Conceals Disappointments

President lost on few votes, but some big issues never made it to the floor of either chamber

When Congress voted in 1994, it backed President Clinton a very high percentage of the time. Unfortunately for him, Congress did not vote on a large chunk of his agenda — health care legislation above all else.

That helps explain the paradox of how Clinton could win on a remarkable 86.4 percent of the votes on which he took a position in 1994 — yet by most accounts have a mediocre year legislatively on Capitol Hill and a disastrous year politically.

On the legislative front, "I have to come to the conclusion that he was moderately successful," said Jon R. Bond, a professor of political science at Texas A&M University. But, he added, "If you go down the list of major legislation, there does seem to be a falloff from the first year."

In Clinton's first year in office, he tallied the same score of 86.4 percent, and even Republicans conceded that he was remarkably effective. He had victories on major legislation to back up his score in 1993, including most of his economic package and a trade agreement. *(1993 Almanac, p. 3-C)*

In 1994, he put most of his legislative chips on one issue, health care, and lost. The ambitious plan crafted by his administration did not even make it to the floor of either chamber, except for a few warm-up votes in the Senate. Clinton had posed the issue as the proof of his leadership, and he and Democratic congressional leaders shoved aside other priorities, such as welfare reform, to concentrate on health care.

The collapse of the health care effort overshadowed the rest of the year. "This was a disaster," said David R. Mayhew, author of "Divided We Govern" (1991) and a political science professor at Yale University. "I can't think of something a president has put so much into and gotten so little out of since [Woodrow] Wilson and the Versailles treaty in 1919."

Clinton's High Score

Clinton won 121 of 140 votes in both chambers, doing slightly better in the House, for an overall success rate of 86.4 percent.

That high score made him unmatched as a second-year president since Lyndon B. Johnson, who in 1965 racked up a 93 percent record. The year paled, however, in comparison with the extraordinary session of 1965, which saw the enactment of Medicare, Medicaid, the Voting Rights Act, federal aid to elementary and secondary schools, the student loan program and the establishment of the Department of Housing and Urban Development.

Health care was not Clinton's only problem area in 1994. As Congress wrapped up for the year, legislation on clean water, telecommunications, the superfund, campaign finance and lobbyist registration expired, often without a vote. "It was like a Shakespearean play; there was blood all over the floor," said Mayhew.

In terms of votes that did occur, none reverberated more strongly than the Aug. 11 defeat of a rule to allow debate on the crime bill. Clinton suffered a stunning setback when 58 Democrats broke ranks to help the GOP kill, at least temporarily, one of Clinton's legislative priorities. Republicans then forced concessions that made it difficult for Clinton to claim full credit for the final bill.

Even the implementing legislation for the General Agreement on Tariffs and Trade (GATT), a business-oriented deal engineered by two Republican presidents that should have been an easy win, got caught up in the grinder. Congress had to return for a brief lame-duck session to approve it, giving Clinton a crucial victory only after the November elections.

What Went Wrong?

There were several explanations for the multiple legislative deaths that tarnished Clinton's high success score. "It reflected the partisanship of the Democratic leaders," said Charles O. Jones, a visiting fellow at the Brookings Institution, a think tank in Washington. Democratic leaders in Congress, he said, mistakenly advised Clinton that they could deliver his legislative agenda without the help of Republicans. James A. Thurber, director of the Center for Congressional and Presidential Studies at American University, also in Washington, agreed, saying that congressional Democratic leaders were uniform in their counsel: " 'Let's cut the Republicans out.' The advice was coming from the Hill to do that."

In 1993, Clinton was able to squeak by on issue after issue without GOP support — sometimes by a single vote. In 1994, his troops were less loyal, as exemplified by the crime bill rule vote and disunity on health care, and overall support scores among Democrats dipped by a percentage point in the Senate and two points in the House. That meant he needed more support from the GOP. Republican support scores rose significantly in both chambers: from a 29 percent average in 1993 to 42 percent in the Senate; from 39 percent in 1993 to 47 percent in the House. And party unity scores went down for both parties. But these changes probably reflected only the fact that partisanship kept the most divisive measures from the floor.

One of Clinton's biggest boosters, Senate Majority Leader George J. Mitchell, D-Maine — who forswore a potential appointment to the Supreme Court to push health care legislation — blamed Republicans for the less productive year. "Unfortunately, the public perception is that it was not a successful year legislatively, in part because the Republicans very successfully and cynically followed a policy of total obstructionism," he said.

Jones said that Republicans were emboldened by Clinton's plummeting approval ratings and by the increasingly tough treatment the administration was getting in newspaper editorials. "Republicans concluded, 'We can knock all this stuff off and there's not much cost to us,' " he said.

Presidential Success History

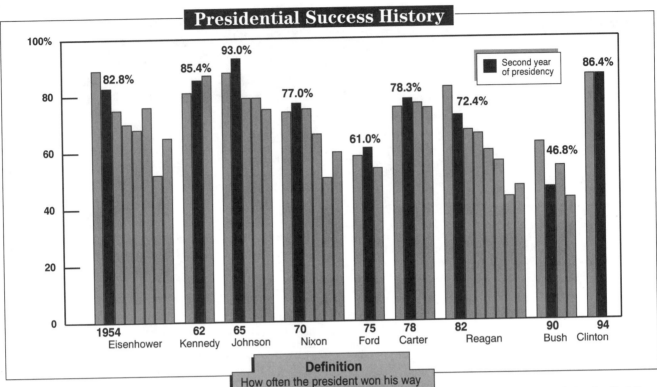

Definition

How often the president won his way on roll call votes on which he took a clear position.

1994 Data

Senate	53 victories
	9 defeats
House	68 victories
	10 defeats

Total Clinton success rate **86.4%**

Data, votes, pp. 29-C – 34-C

Republicans said the problems lay with the administration. "Had they had legislation they could have brought to the floor in good standing with the public, I'm sure they would have seized the opportunity to bring it out," said Texas Republican Dick Armey, the incoming House majority leader.

Republicans asserted that Democrats had only themselves to blame for the legislative train wreck of the closing days. "We spent too much time on health care. A lot of things died at the end that would have been saved if we'd have started earlier," said Mississippi Republican Trent Lott, the incoming Senate majority whip.

Jones agreed that this was a strategic blunder by Democrats: "Why did they pile all of this stuff in the last period?"

Victories

Mitchell said so much attention was paid to health care that Clinton's successes got lost. "The agenda was so large, even passing several important bills doesn't get the attention the president deserved," he said. In defense of Clinton, Mitchell listed several areas of legislative accomplishment:

● **Crime.** Many Democrats thought the crime bill was going to be an easy victory after Clinton made it clear that he would accept tough provisions on the death penalty, sentencing and prison construction. So it was a shock when House Republicans forced changes and Senate Republicans almost killed it anyway on grounds of pork barrel spending. The White House hailed the enacted bill as a triumph, but some of the things Clinton wanted, such as a ban on military-style assault weapons, hurt Democrats in some areas of the country.

● **Education.** Congress embraced one of Clinton's key "human investment" initiatives in clearing the $400 million

"Goals 2000" bill, which for the first time established national education standards. Some of the groundwork for the bill had been laid under Presidents Ronald Reagan and George Bush.

● **GATT.** The passage of implementing legislation for the worldwide trade agreement was another instance where a Democratic president finished the work of his GOP predecessors. In scope, GATT was much larger than the North American Free Trade Agreement, which Clinton pushed through Congress in 1993.

Congress also passed measures implementing Clinton's "reinventing government" effort, including procurement reform, buyouts for federal workers who retired early and a reorganization of the Agriculture Department. "There are a lot of bills directly related to making government work better that we feel good about," said Tom Daschle, D-S.D. But Clinton's diffuse and deliberative effort — which several academics said was potentially significant — did not have the pizazz of the government-busting promises of the House Republicans' "Contract With America," and Clinton seemed to get little credit for it.

Defeats

In addition to health care, Clinton fell short on several other priorities:

● **Telecommunications.** Congress failed to act on a telecommunications bill promoting competition in the telephone and cable markets.

● **Superfund.** The administration failed to overcome GOP opposition to legislation that would have overhauled laws providing for cleanups of hazardous waste sites.

● **Political reform.** Several "reform" measures, including an overhaul of campaign finance and lobbying disclosure

Leading Scorers: Clinton's Support, Opposition

Support indicates those who in 1994 voted most often for President Clinton's position; opposition shows how often members voted against the president's position.

Scores are based on actual votes cast, and members are listed alphabetically when their scores are tied. Members who missed half the votes are not listed.

Support

Senate

Pell **Chafee**

House

Matsui **Morella**

Democrats		Republicans		Democrats		Republicans	
Pell, R.I.	98%	Chafee, R.I.	80%	Matsui, Calif.	93%	Morella, Md.	78%
Akaka, Hawaii	97	Jeffords, Vt.	79	Torres, Calif.	93	Torkildsen, Mass.	73
Mitchell, Maine	97	Hatfield, Ore.	77	Sawyer, Ohio	92	Houghton, N.Y.	72
Riegle, Mich.	97	Kassebaum, Kan.	74	Dicks, Wash.	91	Lazio, N.Y.	72
Rockefeller, W.Va.	97	Cohen, Maine	63	Dixon, Calif.	91	Machtley, R.I.	72
Bumpers, Ark.	95	Danforth, Mo.	63	Gephardt, Mo.	91	Boehlert, N.Y.	71
Dodd, Conn.	95	Durenberger, Minn.	60	Reed, R.I.	91	Castle, Del.	71
Glenn, Ohio	95	Warner, Va.	60	Visclosky, Ind.	91	Franks, Conn.	71
Inouye, Hawaii	95	Roth, Del.	56			Gilman, N.Y.	71
Kennedy, Mass.	95	Specter, Pa.	56			Meyers, Kan.	70
Pryor, Ark.	95	Packwood, Ore.	55			Walsh, N.Y.	70

Opposition

Senate

Feingold **Helms**

House

Stenholm **Sensenbrenner**

Democrats		Republicans		Democrats		Republicans	
Feingold, Wis.	35%	Helms, N.C.	81%	Stenholm, Texas	47%	Sensenbrenner, Wis.	79%
Shelby, Ala.	33	Smith, N.H.	80	Hall, Texas	46	Duncan, Tenn.	75
Byrd, W.Va.	26	Brown, Colo.	79	Penny, Minn.	46	Stump, Ariz.	73
Bradley, N.J.	20	Wallop, Wyo.	78	Tauzin, La.	44	Coble, N.C.	72
Dorgan, N.D.	19	Faircloth, N.C.	76	Peterson, Minn.	42	Burton, Ind.	71
Kohl, Wis.	19	Nickles, Okla.	75	Hayes, La.	40	Crane, Ill.	71
Lautenberg, N.J.	18	Craig, Idaho	70	Taylor, Miss.	40	Hancock, Mo.	71
Wellstone, Minn.	18	Kempthorne, Idaho	69	Orton, Utah	39	Rohrabacher, Calif.	71
		D'Amato, N.Y.	66	DeFazio, Ore.	38	Bunning, Ky.	69
		Grassley, Iowa	66	Poshard, Ill.	37	DeLay, Texas	69
		Murkowski, Alaska	66			Walker, Pa.	69
		Pressler, S.D.	66				

laws, died — along with congressional initiatives on internal reorganization, ending Congress' exemptions from workplace laws, and a ban on lobbyists' gifts to members.

Some Caveats

In conducting the presidential support study, CQ reporters and editors examined each roll call vote to determine if Clinton took a position on it. Of the 497 recorded votes in the House (other than quorum calls), CQ identified 78 on which the president took a position. In the Senate, Clinton took an unambiguous position on 62 of the 329 votes.

Those votes were the raw material for the two indicators used to measure presidential support:

● The first was presidential success. This measured how often Clinton won on votes on which he took a position.

● The second was members' support — how often a member voted the same way as the president's position. A 100 percent score for a senator, for instance, meant that a member voted to back the president's position every time he or she voted on one of the 62 presidential position questions.

The CQ study, first conducted in 1953, has several limitations and should be regarded as only one of several tools for measuring a president's effectiveness.

One limitation is that the study does not include voice votes, even though some important issues were decided without a recorded vote, particularly in the Senate. In addition, the study does not include presidential initiatives, such as health care, that never reached the floor.

The study also tends to conceal those instances when Clinton settled for less than he sought, as with the crime bill.

Also, it is important to note that the CQ study gave equal standing to all floor votes, regardless of their importance. The president's win on GATT was weighed equally in the CQ study with comparatively insignificant votes, such as a 419-9 vote to give the government greater flexibility in disposing of apartment buildings.

Individual Scores

Of the 56 Democratic senators, 26 had presidential support scores of 90 percent or higher when they voted, 10 fewer than in 1993. The 56 included Richard C. Shelby of Alabama, who switched parties Nov. 9. Shelby, with 67 percent, was one of three Democratic senators who had scores lower than 80 percent. The other two were Robert C. Byrd, W.Va. (74 percent), and Russell D. Feingold, Wis. (65 percent). *(1993 Almanac, p. 3-C)*

Feingold's score was 20 points lower than in 1993, but he said, "I didn't consciously change my support." The vote study included several votes on Bosnia policy and spending that he said skewed his rating.

Four Republican senators supported Clinton more often than the bottom three Democrats: John H. Chafee, R.I. (80 percent); James M. Jeffords, Vt. (79 percent); Mark O. Hatfield, Ore. (77 percent); and Nancy Landon Kassebaum, Kan. (74 percent). The average Republican score in the Senate (including absences) was 42 percent, up from 29 percent in 1993. The average Senate Democrat's score was 86 percent, compared with 87 percent in 1993.

The most supportive senator was Claiborne Pell, D-R.I., with a 98 percent tally. The least supportive was Jesse Helms, R-N.C., who backed Clinton only 19 percent of the time.

In the House, Robert T. Matsui, D-Calif., was the president's most loyal backer, with a support score of 93 percent. The least loyal Democrat was Charles W. Stenholm, Texas, who backed Clinton on 53 percent of the votes.

Most supportive on the Republican side of the aisle was Constance A. Morella, Md., who voted with Clinton 78 percent of the time. Least supportive was F. James Sensenbrenner Jr., Wis., with a 21 percent score.

The average House Democrat (including absences) had a score of 75 percent, compared with 77 percent in 1993. For Republicans, the average was 47 percent, compared with 39 percent in 1993. ∎

Political Heat Puts a Chill On Partisan Vote Rate

Congress cast fewer partisan votes than in the previous several years, but it was not for lack of partisan rancor. Rather, the political heat was turned up so high that it deterred votes on important issues such as health care and welfare reform, leaving the 103rd Congress colored by a partisanship not reflected in actual voting patterns.

Although Democrats controlled both ends of Pennsylvania Avenue, their agenda was undermined by infighting, a Republican Party emboldened by the prospects of election gains and a public underwhelmed by Democratic proposals.

"The biggest issue was health care, and they didn't vote on it," said David R. Mayhew, political science professor at Yale University and author of the 1991 book "Divided We Govern." Some of the most contentious legislation, he said, never made it out of committee.

A dip in party-line votes in 1994 followed the record set for partisanship in 1993, when the first Democratic White House in a dozen years maneuvered a controversial agenda that included topics such as tax increases, family leave and gays in the military through a Democrat-controlled Congress.

In the Senate this time, 51.7 percent of votes were party-line votes, a substantial drop from the record high of 67 percent in 1993. The decrease put the Senate closer to the 53 percent level of 1992, the last year of the Bush administration, and more in line with recent years.

The drop-off was not as steep in the House, where minority Republicans often challenged Democrats on procedural votes and where partisan behavior had been for a decade more prevalent than in the Senate. House Democrats and Republicans voted against each other on 61.8 percent of House roll call votes, down from an all-time high of 65.5 percent in 1993.

The trend toward greater partisanship began in President Ronald Reagan's second term and continued into the Clinton administration. Since Congressional Quarterly began measuring party unity in 1945, the House had exceeded 60 percent partisanship five times — in 1985 and 1987, during the Reagan administration; in the final year of the Bush administration; and in the first two years of President Clinton's term. In the Senate, the proportion of partisan voting surpassed the 60 percent mark twice — in 1993 and in 1961, the first year of President John F. Kennedy's administration.

Democrats in both chambers strayed from their party a bit more often than in 1993. The average Senate Democrat voted with the party majority 84 percent of the time compared with 85 percent of the time in 1993. House Democrats were party followers on 83 percent of party-line votes, a decrease of two percentage points. *(1993 Almanac, p. 14-C)*

The average Senate Republican voted with the party majority 79 percent of the time, and the average House Republican followed the party line 84 percent of the time.

Senate Moderates Buck the Party

The lower level of party unity among Senate Republicans was attributable to the GOP moderates who were up for re-election in Democratic-leaning states and some mavericks who bucked the party. The ascension of many of these Republicans to committee chairmanships in the 104th Congress held the potential for fireworks in the party.

Mark O. Hatfield of Oregon, incoming chairman of the Appropriations Committee, had chafed during the Reagan years as the GOP moved further right, going so far as to assail Democrats for ineffective criticism of the defense buildup. He voted with his Republican colleagues 59 percent of the time in 1993 and 34 percent of the time in 1994.

Joining Hatfield in buck-the-party voting were John H. Chafee of Rhode Island, the next chairman of the Environment and Public Works Committee; James M. Jeffords of Vermont, who was set to chair the Veterans' Affairs Committee; Arlen Specter of Pennsylvania, the likely head of the Intelligence panel; and Nancy Landon Kassebaum of Kansas, who was taking over Labor and Human Resources.

All voted with their party less frequently in 1994 than in 1993. Chafee backed the GOP on 58 percent of partisan votes in 1993 and 46 percent in 1994. Jeffords, who, like Chafee, won his re-election bid in a strongly Democratic state, had scores of 46 percent in 1993 and 32 percent in 1994.

Kassebaum, like Chafee, broke with the Republicans on one of the most contentious issues of the year, the crime bill. Her unity score dropped from 77 percent to 61 percent. Specter, who won re-election in 1992, continued to stake out his own positions with a score that dropped from 64 percent in 1993 to 56 percent in 1994. Bob Packwood of Oregon, the incoming chairman of the Finance Committee, voted with Republicans on party-line votes 72 percent of the time in 1993 and 63 percent of the time in 1994.

When many of the GOP moderates were first elected, there were a lot more of them in Congress. But as they climbed the seniority ladder, moderates became atypical of their party, said David W. Rohde, political science professor at Michigan State University. The Republican situation, he said, was analogous to

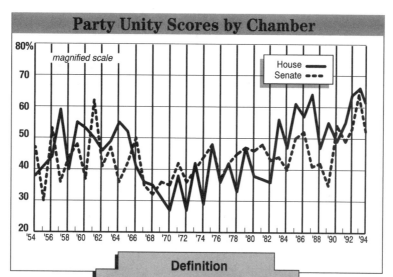

Party Unity Scores by Chamber

80%

magnified scale

House ——
Senate - - -

70

60

50

40

30

20

'54 '56 '58 '60 '62 '64 '66 '68 '70 '72 '74 '76 '78 '80 '82 '84 '86 '88 '90 '92 '94

Definition

The percentage of recorded floor votes in each chamber on which a majority of one party voted against a majority of the other party.

1994 Data

	Partisan Votes	Total Votes	Percent
Senate	170	329	51.7
House	307	497	61.8

Data, votes, pp. 35-C – 39-C

that of previous years when liberals swelled the ranks of the Democratic majority but senior Southern conservative Democrats ruled the committees.

One issue prompted Republicans across the ideological spectrum to band together — Whitewater. GOP senators cast 12 party-line votes in June on the format and timing of the Whitewater hearings, but ultimately lost their campaign for wide-ranging hearings into the Clintons' financial dealings with a failed Arkansas thrift.

One Senate Democrat who built a reputation for opposing his party, Richard C. Shelby of Alabama, switched to the GOP ranks Nov. 9. Shelby voted with the Democrats 50 percent of the time and opposed them by the same percentage.

Incoming House Chairmen Stand by GOP

Three-fourths of the 33 incoming House committee and Appropriations subcommittee chairmen solidly backed the GOP in 1993. But eight lawmakers displayed independence.

Benjamin A. Gilman of New York, the next chairman of the International Relations Committee, challenged Clinton's policies on Haiti and Bosnia but was a non-conformist on other issues. He joined Republicans on party-lines votes only 45 percent of the time in 1994. Jim Leach of Iowa, who was likely to oversee Whitewater hearings as chairman of the Banking and Financial Services Committee, maintained his party unity score of 69 percent from 1993.

Six other incoming Republican chairmen voted with their party about 75 percent of the time: William F. Clinger, Pa., who was set to head the Government Reform and Oversight Committee; Jan Meyers, Kan., tapped to lead the Small Business Committee; and four incoming chairmen of Appropriations subcommittees: John T. Myers, Ind., (Energy and Water Development); Ralph Regula, Ohio, (Interior); James T. Walsh, N.Y., (District of Columbia); and John Edward Porter, Ill., (Labor, Health and Human Services, and Education).

Striving To Impress the Voters

The lower partisanship scores reflected the election-year trend in which lawmakers running for re-election often sought to present themselves to voters as independent thinkers unbeholden to party leaders in Washington.

Rep. Jim Cooper, D-Tenn., was a high-profile opponent of Clinton's health plan and staked out a position far from the Democrats'. His support score on party-line votes dropped to 55 percent from 73 percent in 1993. But if Cooper hoped his approach would boost his bid for an open Senate seat, it did not work; he lost to Fred Thompson, 61 percent to 39 percent.

Leading Scorers: Party Unity

Support indicates those who in 1994 most consistently voted with their party's majority against the majority of the other party; opposition shows how often members voted against their party's majority. Scores are based on actual votes cast; members are listed alphabetically when scores are tied. Members who missed half the votes are not listed.

Support

Senate

Murray   Craig

Democrats

Murray, Wash.	98%	Simon, Ill.	96%	Biden, Del.	92%
Sarbanes, Md.	98	Riegle, Mich.	95	Boxer, Calif.	92
Harkin, Iowa	97	Akaka, Hawaii	94	Inouye, Hawaii	92
Leahy, Vt.	96	Kennedy, Mass.	94	Levin, Mich.	92
Metzenbaum, Ohio	96	Kerry, Mass.	94	Moynihan, N.Y.	92
Mitchell, Maine	96	Wellstone, Minn.	94	Pell, R.I.	92

Republicans

Craig, Idaho	98	Coverdell, Ga.	95	Nickles, Okla.	94
Faircloth, N.C.	98	Hatch, Utah	95	Brown, Colo.	93
Kempthorne, Idaho	98	Helms, N.C.	95	Thurmond, S.C.	93
Lott, Miss.	97	Wallop, Wyo.	95	McConnell, Ky.	92
Dole, Kan.	96	Gramm, Texas	94	Murkowski, Alaska	92
Smith, N.H.	96	Hutchison, Texas	94		

House

Blackwell   Archer

Democrats

Blackwell, Pa.	99%	Foglietta, Pa.	99%	Olver, Mass.	99%
Bonior, Mich.	99	Gejdenson, Conn.	99	Pelosi, Calif.	99
Collins, Mich.	99	Gephardt, Mo.	99	Reynolds, Ill.	99
Coyne, Pa.	99	Hamburg, Calif.	99	Roybal-Allard, Calif.	99
Dellums, Calif.	99	Hinchey, N.Y.	99	Sabo, Minn.	99
Dixon, Calif.	99	Markey, Mass.	99	Slaughter, N.Y.	99
Evans, Ill.	99	McKinney, Ga.	99	Studds, Mass.	99
Farr, Calif.	99	Mink, Hawaii	99	Wheat, Mo.	99
Flake, N.Y.	99	Moakley, Mass.	99	Woolsey, Calif.	99

Republicans

Archer, Texas	99	Doolittle, Calif.	99	Stearns, Fla.	99
Armey, Texas	99	Dreier, Calif.	99	Stump, Ariz.	99
Bartlett, Md.	99	Grams, Minn.	99		
Burton, Ind.	99	Inhofe, Okla.	99		

Opposition

Senate

Shelby   Jeffords

Democrats

Shelby, Ala.	50%	Lieberman, Conn.	24%	Exon, Neb.	22%
Heflin, Ala.	34	Johnston, La.	23	Mathews, Tenn.	21
Nunn, Ga.	34	Sasser, Tenn.	23	Hollings, S.C.	20
Byrd, W.Va.	27	Breaux, La.	22		
Kohl, Wis.	25	Campbell, Colo.	22		

Republicans

Jeffords, Vt.	68	Durenberger, Minn.	40	Packwood, Ore.	37
Hatfield, Ore.	66	Cohen, Maine	39	Stevens, Alaska	27
Chafee, R.I.	54	Danforth, Mo.	39		
Specter, Pa.	44	Kassebaum, Kan.	39		

House

Hall   Gilman

Democrats

Hall, Texas	63%	Hayes, La.	43%	Jacobs, Ind.	38%
Taylor, Miss.	63	Geren, Texas	42	Parker, Miss.	38
Stenholm, Texas	58	Orton, Utah	42	Deal, Ga.	37
Tauzin, La.	49	Penny, Minn.	42	Poshard, Ill.	35
Cooper, Tenn.	45	Condit, Calif.	41	Sarpalius, Texas	34
Hutto, Fla.	44	Peterson, Minn.	41		

Republicans

Gilman, N.Y.	55	Houghton, N.Y.	39	Snowe, Maine	33
Morella, Md.	54	Johnson, Conn.	38	Gillmor, Ohio	32
Boehlert, N.Y.	42	Smith, N.J.	34		
Fish, N.Y.	42	Shays, Conn.	33		

"Politicians probably have a tendency to think people are looking at their record more closely than they are," said Christoper J. Deering, a political scientist at George Washington University. "Opponents don't have a problem going back a year."

In his Senate re-election bid, Democrat Frank R. Lautenberg of New Jersey was up against a Republican surge that nearly claimed fellow New Jersey Democratic Sen. Bill Bradley in 1990 and elected Republican Christine Todd Whitman governor in 1993. Lautenberg's party unity numbers barely changed, from 86 percent in 1993 to 84 percent in 1994. But in 1993, he broke with the Democrats on two of the biggest votes of the year — the votes on Clinton's economic package. Lautenberg defeated his Republican opponent, Garabed "Chuck" Haytaian, 50 percent to 47 percent.

"People remember the headlines," Deering said. ∎

Last Hurrah for Southern Democrats And Their Longtime Voting Bloc?

The so-called conservative coalition of white Southern Democrats and Republicans, which once dominated Capitol Hill, continued to fade. In 1994, this informal voting bloc came together on just 68 votes out of a possible 826, a record low appearance rate of 8.23 percent. That showing, slightly less than the 8.26 percent of 1987, followed years of waning influence for the coalition.

Some political scientists predicted that the bloc's influence would be all but eclipsed in the 104th Congress, which would contain far fewer Southern Democrats and be controlled by Republicans who might not need much Democratic support to pass their legislative agenda. "This may be the end of the conservative coalition," said Burdett Loomis, a political scientist at the University of Kansas. "It's been this long-term anomaly in American politics."

The coalition was not going out quietly, however. When it appeared in 1994, it usually won, amassing an impressive 82.4 percent victory rate and deciding several significant votes.

For example, the coalition supported President Clinton in a critical House vote by rejecting an attempt to terminate production of the Trident II missile program. The coalition was crucial to passage of an amendment to the House-passed crime bill aimed at restricting the number of appeals permitted by inmates on death row.

And it helped reject an attempt to weaken language on an education bill that would have withheld federal money from any school district that had a policy of denying students the right to engage in voluntary prayer. The provision was

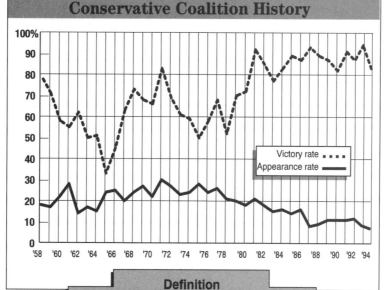

Conservative Coalition History

Victory rate ····
Appearance rate ▬▬

'58 '60 '62 '64 '66 '68 '70 '72 '74 '76 '78 '80 '82 '84 '86 '88 '90 '92 '94

Definition

A voting bloc in the House and Senate consisting of a majority of Republicans and a majority of Southern Democrats, combined against a majority of Northern Democrats.

1994 Data

Senate	23 victories	
	9 defeats	
	32 appearances in 329 votes	
House	33 victories	
	3 defeats	
	36 appearances in 497 votes	

Total Congress appearance rate **8.2%**
Total Congress victory rate **82.4%**

Data, votes, pp. 40-C – 44-C

approved by the House but later dropped in conference with the Senate.

The coalition also lost on a few high-profile votes in both chambers. For example, most conservative Southern Democrats in the House joined Republicans in unsuccessfully opposing a bill banning 19 specific assault weapons. The measure was backed by Clinton and most House Democrats.

The bloc also failed to win approval of a constitutional amendment requiring a balanced budget.

Coalition History

Congressional Quarterly had tracked the voting patterns of the conservative coalition for more than 40 years.

Historically, the coalition typically formed on such issues as crime, national security, economics and social policy. For example, a group of so-called Boll Weevil Democrats frequently joined Republicans in 1981 to give President Ronald Reagan a series of crucial victories on the economic and defense initiatives that became the hallmarks of his first term. More recently, the coalition had had significant influence on social issues such as school prayer, gay rights and sex education.

As defined by Congressional Quarterly, the South consisted of 13 states: Alabama, Arkansas, Florida, Georgia, Kentucky, Louisiana, Mississippi, North Carolina, Oklahoma, South Carolina, Tennessee, Texas and Virginia.

For many years, the coalition's considerable influence could be traced directly to the large number of Southern Democratic members, from whom the conservative coalition

Leading Scorers: Conservative Coalition

High scorers in support are those who in 1994 voted most often with the conservative coalition. Opposition figures are for those who voted most often against the coalition. Scores are based on actual votes cast, and members are listed alphabetically when their scores were tied. Members who missed half the votes are not listed.

Support

Senate

Shelby   **Faircloth**   **Byrd**

Southern Democrats

Shelby, Ala.	96%	Breaux, La.	78%
Nunn, Ga.	91	Johnston, La.	74
Heflin, Ala.	88		

Hollings, S.C.	71%
Sasser, Tenn.	71

Republicans

Faircloth, N.C.	100	Bennett, Utah	94	Hatch, Utah	94
Lott, Miss.	100	Burns, Mont.	94	Hutchison, Texas	94
Simpson, Wyo.	100	Cochran, Miss.	94	Kempthorne, Idaho	94
Dole, Kan.	97	Craig, Idaho	94	Mack, Fla.	94
Thurmond, S.C.	97	Domenici, N.M.	94		

Northern Democrats

Byrd, W.Va.	69	Baucus, Mont.	50	Lieberman, Conn.	45
Exon, Neb.	63	Bryan, Nev.	48	DeConcini, Ariz.	44
Bingaman, N.M.	53	Campbell, Colo.	48	Dorgan, N.D.	44
Conrad, N.D.	53	Kerrey, Neb.	47	Feinstein, Calif.	44

House

Parker   **Baker**   **Skelton**

Southern Democrats

Parker, Miss.	100%	Hall, Texas	97%	Stenholm, Texas	97%
Cramer, Ala.	97	Montgomery, Miss.	97	Taylor, Miss.	97
Geren, Texas	97	Sarpalius, Texas	97		

Republicans

Baker, La.	100	Emerson, Mo.	100	Lucas, Okla.	100
Bartlett, Md.	100	Fields, Texas	100	McKeon, Calif.	100
Bentley, Md.	100	Gallegly, Calif.	100	Pombo, Calif.	100
Bonilla, Texas	100	Gingrich, Ga.	100	Skeen, N.M.	100
Callahan, Ala.	100	Hansen, Utah	100	Smith, Ore.	100
Calvert, Calif.	100	Kim, Calif.	100	Sundquist, Tenn.	100
Canady, Fla.	100	Lewis, Fla.	100	Vucanovich, Nev.	100
Dreier, Calif.	100	Linder, Ga.	100		

Northern Democrats

Skelton, Mo.	100	Volkmer, Mo.	83	Murtha, Pa.	78
Orton, Utah	86	LaRocco, Idaho	78	Danner, Mo.	77

Opposition

Senate

Robb   **Jeffords**   **Metzenbaum**

Southern Democrats

Robb, Va.	55%	Mathews, Tenn.	44%	Bumpers, Ark.	38%
Graham, Fla.	47	Ford, Ky.	39	Pryor, Ark.	38
Boren, Okla.	45				

Republicans

Jeffords, Vt.	75	Packwood, Ore.	53	Kassebaum, Kan.	38
Hatfield, Ore.	66	Durenberger, Minn.	41	Cohen, Maine	35
Chafee, R.I.	58	Specter, Pa.	39	Roth, Del.	34

Northern Democrats

Metzenbaum, Ohio	97	Harkin, Iowa	90	Levin, Mich.	84
Wellstone, Minn.	97	Murray, Wash.	88	Mitchell, Maine	84
Leahy, Vt.	94	Sarbanes, Md.	88	Moynihan, N.Y.	84
Bradley, N.J.	93	Moseley-Braun, Ill.	87		
Feingold, Wis.	91	Kerry, Mass.	84		

House

McKinney   **Shays**   **Dellums**

Southern Democrats

McKinney, Ga.	97%	Lewis, Ga.	94%	Johnston, Fla.	86%
Watt, N.C.	97	Synar, Okla.	94	Hastings, Fla.	79

Republicans

Shays, Conn.	58	Porter, Ill.	39	Johnson, Conn.	34
Morella, Md.	49	Boehlert, N.Y.	37		
Klug, Wis.	39	Upton, Mich.	36		

Northern Democrats

Dellums, Calif.	100	Collins, Ill.	97	Mink, Hawaii	97
Frank, Mass.	100	Collins, Mich.	97	Olver, Mass.	97
Pelosi, Calif.	100	Coyne, Pa.	97	Payne, N.J.	97
Stark, Calif.	100	Edwards, Calif.	97	Waxman, Calif.	97
Studds, Mass.	100	Markey, Mass.	97		
Yates, Ill.	100	Miller, Calif.	97		

typically drew its strongest support. But the defeats, retirements and deaths of such members in recent years had sharply reduced their ranks. The number of Southern Democrats would fall to 74 in the 104th Congress from 97 in the 103rd.

The number of House seats held by non-Hispanic white Southern Democrats would fall to 43 in the 104th from 62 in the 103rd. The number of Southern black and Hispanic Democrats, who typically voted more frequently with the party's liberal wing, would be unchanged, with 17 seats held by black members and four held by Hispanic members.

One notable exception was Georgia's Sanford D. Bishop Jr., an African-American who represented a rural district with a constituency fairly evenly split between blacks and whites. In 1994, Bishop voted with the coalition 70 percent of the time, making him a better-than-average supporter among all Southern Democrats. Bishop's 1994 conservative coalition support, in fact, was up modestly from a score of 59 percent in 1993.

In the Senate, the number of white Southern Democrats in the 104th Congress would fall to 10 from 14. The Democrats lost three seats in the election, and Richard C. Shelby of Alabama switched to the GOP Nov. 9. There were no non-white Southern senators.

Whether the loss of so many conservative Southern Democrats actually meant the end of the coalition was likely to depend on how cohesive the GOP itself was as a voting bloc in 1995. Loomis said, "The numbers are so small, and you've got a Republican majority — Southern Democrats are not crucial. The question is: Is there going to be anything left to measure?"

If fissures developed in the Republican ranks, however, the GOP could have to turn to Democrats, probably those from the conservative South. The Republican takeover in the 104th Congress seemed almost certain to mean that Congress would revisit controversial issues such as the balanced-budget amendment and school prayer, issues on which the coalition had been influential in the past.

Appearances in House, Senate

Despite the conservative coalition's infrequent appearances and waning clout in the 103rd, the bloc was nonetheless a potent force in the House when it did appear.

On the 36 occasions that the coalition formed in the House in 1994, it won 33 times, with a success rate of 91.7 percent. Furthermore, on 13 key House votes on which Clinton had a

known position, the coalition supported him nine times and opposed him four times.

The coalition lost twice against Clinton in the House. One setback came on the assault weapons ban, and the other on the balanced-budget amendment. The latter vote, however, was only a qualified loss for the coalition. The bloc helped supply a simple majority of members in favor of the balanced-budget resolution, but a supermajority vote of two-thirds was required for adopting a constitutional amendment. The resolution failed narrowly, 13 votes shy.

The coalition successfully opposed Clinton when it voted to toughen the House-passed version of the crime bill by allowing serious drug offenses to count as one of the "three strikes" in the measure, which was aimed at imprisoning criminals for life without parole after three violent acts.

The voting bloc also turned back an attempt by Clinton to cut further development of a $12 million nuclear reactor program in the fiscal 1995 Energy and Water Development appropriations bill.

True to its history, the House coalition also emerged on several controversial social issues. In addition to the school prayer amendment to the education bill, it marshaled its forces to push through an amendment to the bill prohibiting school districts from using federal money to support or promote homosexuality as a positive lifestyle.

In the Senate, the coalition appeared 32 times in 1994, winning 23 times for a success rate of 71.9 percent. On six coalition votes upon which Clinton had a known position, the bloc voted against him four times, winning twice. Notably, the two votes on which Clinton received the coalition's support were retirement confirmations for two career military officers.

On a key national security vote, the Senate coalition formed to reject an amendment to the fiscal 1995 Defense authorization bill that would have taken $150 million appropriated for the B-2 stealth bomber to pay for environmental cleanups at former military bases.

Also against Clinton's wishes, the coalition successfully turned back an effort to terminate a liquid metal reactor program in the Senate's fiscal 1995 Energy and Water Development appropriations bill.

Just as in the House, however, Senate centrists suffered a narrow, but high-profile loss against Clinton in 1994 on the balanced-budget amendment. A two-thirds majority of 67 votes was required for passage, but the measure fell short by four votes, at 63. ∎

Despite Campaign Pressures, Participation Remains High

The year 1994 featured two poles of congressional voting behavior. William H. Natcher, the courtly Kentucky Democrat, was rolled into the House chamber on a gurney March 2 to cast the last of his 18,401 consecutive votes. His fatal illness broke his 40-year voting streak the next day. At the other end of the spectrum, Craig Washington, D-Texas, closed out his two-term House career by missing 403 of 497 votes in 1994, for a 19 percent participation score.

With few exceptions, members of Congress imitated Natcher rather than Washington. In 1994, despite an election year that made many Democrats desperate to stay home to

campaign, members voted 95 percent of the time. That matched the election-year record of 1990.

The all-time high since Congressional Quarterly began tracking votes in 1953 came in 1993, when members voted 96.2 percent of the time. *(1993 Almanac, p. 31-C)*

In 1994, senators voted 97 percent of the time, compared with a 95 percent rate in the House. The overall number was closer to House levels because of the larger size of its membership. Republicans outscored Democrats 96.0 percent to 94.4 percent.

Eric M. Uslaner, professor of government and politics at

the University of Maryland, saw two reasons for the high participation rate of those years. First, he said, "in an era of strong partisanship, particularly when the relative balance of power between the parties is fairly close, every vote counts."

His second reason was a crescendo of voter cynicism. "The last thing incumbents want to do is give challengers ammunition to paint a picture of them eating $100 lunches with a lobbyist while the rest of Congress votes," he said. "Members are scared to death that something as small as a missed vote can mean a political career."

Indeed, Washington's relatively low participation rate (74 percent in 1993) helped Sheila Jackson Lee, D-Texas, unseat him in the Texas Democratic primary March 8. Washington maintained that he could best serve his constituents by doing things other than attending insignificant votes. After he lost, however, he rarely voted at all. The National Taxpayers Union filed an ethics complaint against House Speaker Thomas S. Foley, D-Wash., for not enforcing a rarely used law that called for docking a member's pay for unexcused absences.

Washington did return Nov. 29 for the lame-duck session to vote for the General Agreement on Tariffs and Trade — although he skipped a procedural vote that day.

In the Public Eye

The high vote scores of the early 90s contrasted with 1970, when participation hit a low of 79 percent.

"Before this became a big attack issue, incumbents could largely conduct business out of the public eye with most incumbents sticking up for each other," Uslaner said. "Now you have the 'Gingrichization' of American politics, meaning basically there is nothing that is immune from attack."

Roger H. Davidson, professor of government and politics at the University of Maryland, cautioned against using voting participation numbers out of context. "The number itself is not as an important as what the votes were on," he said. "Were they votes on the Journal or were they actually on matters of substance?"

He said that judging a member's diligence should take into account a member's attendance in committee. Other duties such as constituent service and raising campaign funds also impinged on members' abilities to make floor votes.

One reason for the high numbers was that leaders scheduled votes to protect members.

"The leadership has tried to make it easier for members

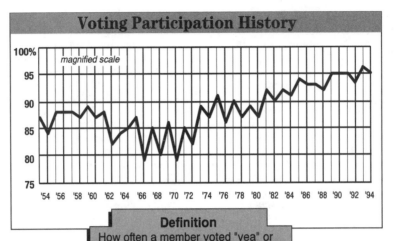

Voting Participation History

magnified scale

Definition
How often a member voted "yea" or "nay" on roll call votes on the floor of the House or Senate.

1994 Data

	Recorded Votes	Participation Rate
Senate	329	97%
House	497	95%
Total Congress	826	95%

Votes, pp. 45-C – 47-C

by clustering the votes at particular hours and giving warning to members that votes are going to be taken," Davidson said.

The man in charge of the Senate's schedule, George J. Mitchell, D-Maine, never missed a vote while majority leader from 1989 through 1994.

Record a Burden

Natcher often advised freshmen to miss a vote early in their careers because the pressure of maintaining an unblemished streak could become a burden.

However, some House members did not follow that advice. Dale E. Kildee, D-Mich., had a flawless record going back to October 1985 (although he voted "present" three times in 1986), and Christopher Shays, R-Conn., had not missed a vote since his special election in 1987. "I don't play golf; I don't play tennis; I vote," Kildee said. They said they did not feel shackled by their voting streaks.

Altogether, 17 people had perfect records in the House in 1994. Two House freshmen made it to every vote: Californians Jay C. Kim and Bob Filner, who said he once jumped out of a car stuck in traffic and ran up Capitol Hill to preserve his record. Kim, a Republican, and Filner, a Democrat, jested that they had a perfect record of canceling out each other.

In the Senate, 12 members had perfect scores in 1994. Daniel K. Akaka, D-Hawaii, had not missed a vote since 1991, despite the long distance from his home state. Freshman Russell D. Feingold, D-Wis., did not miss a roll call during his first two years in Congress.

"I try real hard to be there for the votes," Feingold said. "It is our first obligation."

Those with low scores usually had reasons. Illness was a major factor, as was the case with Reps. Natcher (39 percent); Dean A. Gallo, R-N.J. (48 percent), who died Nov. 6; and Hamilton Fish Jr., R-N.Y. (73 percent).

Senators at the bottom were Richard C. Shelby, D-Ala. (83 percent), who missed votes between April 5 and June 8 due to an operation, and Malcolm Wallop, R-Wyo. (87 percent), who was retiring. Phil Gramm, R-Texas, had the third-lowest Senate score (90 percent), missing 33 votes — 10 of them on one day.

The year brought a caveat to retirees considering a return to office: Voting scores had a shelf life. In the Maryland Senate race, Democratic incumbent Paul S. Sarbanes unearthed the 1963-77 record of his challenger, former Tennessee Republican Sen. Bill Brock, and criticized him for missing 20 percent of votes during that period. ∎

Second Session Fails To Meet Accomplishments of First

The second session of the 103rd Congress produced fewer legislative accomplishments and more partisan bickering than the first — plus the usual amount of election-year maneuvering.

As in 1993, President Clinton had a high success score on floor votes in 1994, but only because some of his biggest initiatives — health care, in particular — died without even making it to a vote. On other issues, Clinton was forced to alter his proposals to win congressional support — from Democrats as well as Republicans.

The crime bill (HR 3355 — PL 103-322) was a case in point. A key vote came Aug. 11 when 58 House Democrats joined all but 11 Republicans in defeating the rule governing floor debate. Clinton launched a huge comeback effort that narrowly succeeded two weeks later, but only after he agreed to alter the bill to meet GOP demands.

Following is a rundown of the key votes of 1994:

KEY HOUSE VOTES

How CQ Picks Key Votes

Since 1945, Congressional Quarterly has selected a series of key votes on major issues of the year.

An issue is judged by the extent to which it represents:
- A matter of major controversy.
- A matter of presidential or political power.
- A matter of potentially great impact on the nation and lives of Americans.

For each group of related votes on an issue, one key vote usually is chosen — one that, in the opinion of CQ editors, was most important in determining the outcome.

Charts showing how each member of Congress voted on these issues start on page 48-C.

1. EPA Cabinet

A House vote Feb. 2 on a routine procedural motion sparked a politically explosive backlash against federal regulations that also proved disastrous to elements of President Clinton's environmental agenda in 1994. The issue would later form the basis for an anti-regulatory proposal in the Republicans' "Contract With America."

At issue was whether the proposed Department of Environmental Protection should be required to study the costs and benefits of regulations before implementing new rules.

These types of studies were just a small part of a scientific process, known as risk assessment, that tried to estimate the type and magnitude of risks to human health posed by the exposure to chemical substances.

The Rules Committee did not allow first-term Florida Reps. John L. Mica, R, and Karen L. Thurman, D, to offer an amendment requiring cost-benefit studies to a bill (HR 3425) to elevate the Environmental Protection Agency (EPA) to Cabinet status. That made the rule for floor debate the key vote.

At stake was more than Clinton's promise to quickly give the EPA a formal seat at the Cabinet table.

Environmentalists contended that the Mica-Thurman amendment would have paralyzed the federal government through costly studies, whose results could then be used to weaken existing health and safety laws.

But Mica and Thurman, with the help of the GOP leadership, argued that environmental regulations had become a financial burden on states and local governments. They said some regulations also provided little health benefit.

The goal of the amendment, Mica and Thurman said, was to provide some common-sense and sound scientific reasoning to environmental rule-making.

Vice President Al Gore heavily lobbied the large Democratic freshman class to vote for the rule (H Res 312), which banned all amendments except those pertaining to the structure of the proposed Department of Environmental Protection. Gore, a key environmental ally, and other supporters of the bill argued that it was the wrong measure through which to try to broadly rewrite environmental policy.

The rule was rejected 191-227: R 5-167; D 185-60 (ND 140-28; SD 45-32); I 1-0. It was one of the rare occasions in the 103rd Congress in which a rule was defeated.

Only five Republicans — Christopher Shays of Connecticut, Constance A. Morella of Maryland, John Edward Porter of Illinois and New York members Sherwood Boehlert and Benjamin A. Gilman — voted to adopt the rule. All five members had voting records that favored environmental policies.

Gore's tactic of targeting freshmen also proved futile. Sixty-four freshmen, many of whom campaigned on a plank of less government and a new way of doing federal business, voted to reject the procedural motion.

The vote was seen as a sign that the House favored cost-benefit studies and less government regulation. With no rule, the EPA Cabinet bill was never brought up again on the House floor, and Clinton was unable to fulfill his promise for speedy action on the measure.

The subject of risk assessment also would scuttle an attempt to make the Safe Drinking Water Act more flexible for states, local governments and small water system operators and bog down an effort to reorganize the Agriculture Department. *(Related Senate vote, p. 23-C)*

House Republicans promised a vote on an anti-regulatory proposal, which included a cost-benefit provision similar to the Mica-Thurman amendment, as part of their "Contract With America" in the first 100 days of the 104th Congress.

2. Defense Spending

Early in the year, the House beat back an effort by liberals to make relatively minor cuts in defense spending to pay for new social programs, demonstrating that Congress would not tolerate raids on defense beyond reductions contained in President Clinton's budget.

In his fiscal 1995 budget, Clinton requested $263.7 billion to fund national defense programs. He said in his State of the Union address that his request "draws the line against further defense cuts. . . . We must not cut defense further."

Nevertheless, liberal activists in Congress believed that Clinton would not fight hard to fend off cuts in the defense request. That assumption was driven, in part, by the fact that

cuts in the defense budget were virtually the only source from which Congress could squeeze funds to pay for new domestic initiatives.

The liberals made their move on the budget resolution (H Con Res 218), with an amendment sponsored by Rep. Barney Frank, D-Mass., to reduce defense budget authority in fiscal 1995 by $2.4 billion.

However, Clinton, his top aides and the House Democratic leadership lobbied vigorously against the Frank amendment. It was defeated March 10 by a vote of 105-313: R 12-160; D 92-153 (ND 82-85, SD 10-68).

After that, no other effort to significantly reduce the defense budget request came close to adoption in either the House or the Senate.

During the 1992 presidential campaign, Clinton had vowed to cut $60 billion from the $1.4 trillion that President George Bush projected in total defense budgets for fiscal 1994-97. But the defense program Clinton unveiled early in 1993 cut Bush's projected total by $123 billion — more than twice the promised amount.

Administration officials insisted that changing economic circumstances accounted for the deeper cut and that Clinton's program would meet his goal of paying for a modernized and combat-ready force large enough to win two simultaneous regional wars. But Republican defense specialists and some centrist Democrats warned that Clinton's budgets were shortchanging the "two-war" force.

The funding squeeze was exacerbated when Congress rejected out of hand Clinton's plan to restrain the annual cost of living raises for military personnel. The fiscal 1994 defense authorization and appropriations bills included a 2.2 percent military pay raise, rather than the freeze that Clinton proposed.

To cover the future costs of only the fiscal 1994 congressionally mandated military raise, the administration agreed to boost Clinton's multi-year defense funding plan by $11.4 billion. Clinton's request for fiscal 1995 included $2.4 billion of that pay-raise add-on, the amount the liberals targeted for elimination with the Frank amendment.

3. Balanced-Budget Amendment

With the Senate having rejected the proposal only two weeks before, members of the House could have taken a free ride and cast a politically popular vote to adopt a proposed constitutional amendment to require a balanced federal budget.

But House Democratic leaders opposed to the balanced-budget amendment worked the issue hard, and after they used subtle but effective procedural tactics and demanded discipline from the large class of Democratic freshmen, the proposed amendment fell 12 votes short of the two-thirds majority required to pass.

The measure (H J Res 103) came to the floor only after chief sponsor Charles W. Stenholm, D-Texas, gathered more than the necessary 218 signatures from colleagues on a so-called discharge petition to force a floor vote without committee action.

The fact that Stenholm was able to get the signatures in a single afternoon attested to the frustration many lawmakers felt over the inability of Congress to reduce the deficit. And the constitutional amendment was a popular refuge for members to prove they were deficit hawks while not having to vote for the specific spending cuts or taxes needed to make a balanced budget a reality.

Stenholm's amendment was identical to the version previously rejected by the Senate. It would have required a balanced budget by fiscal 2001 or the second year after ratifica-

tion by the states, whichever came later. A three-fifths vote would have been required to approve deficit spending. (Related Senate vote, p. 22-C)

Having won the right to get a vote on his proposal, Stenholm faced a difficult battle as House leaders opposed to the measure structured debate on several alternatives to siphon sufficient votes to derail Stenholm's version. The measure ultimately failed March 17, 271-153: R 171-1; D 99-151 (ND 47-122, SD 59-29); I 0-1. It needed 283 "yeas" to pass.

During the debate, the House considered four alternative balanced-budget amendments. A significantly less stringent version, drafted by Bob Wise, D-W.Va., with the blessing of Democratic leaders, was soundly defeated on a 111-318 vote. Sixty-four Democrats who voted for Wise's alternative did not vote for Stenholm's.

Another alternative, pushed by Reps. Joe L. Barton, R-Texas, and W. J. "Billy" Tauzin, D-La., was more stringent. Their version — which paralleled one outlined later in the House GOP's "Contract With America" — would have required Congress to muster a three-fifths supermajority for any tax increase.

Needing only a simple majority for preliminary approval, the Barton-Tauzin version was adopted 211-204. But Stenholm's version was sent on for final consideration — and eventual defeat — after it was adopted later by voice vote under a so-called king of the hill rule.

The constitutional amendment had returned to the House floor two years after the House defeated a similar measure on a 280-153 vote, after a late lobbying blitz by organized labor and senior citizens. (1992 Almanac, p. 108)

Seniors, led by the American Association of Retired Persons (AARP), again pulled out all stops, blasting the proposal for threatening Social Security. Phones in the Capitol started ringing off the hook after the AARP sent out a huge overnight mailing to its members asking them to lobby against the amendment. But Wise's version, which would have protected Social Security, gave members political cover, allowing them to vote in favor of the politically popular constitutional limitation while not alienating seniors.

In light of the preceeding action by the Senate, Democratic leaders urged rank-and-file members, especially freshmen, to avoid the temptation to consider support of the Stenholm version a free vote. To go on record supporting Stenholm would have given the proposal a better chance of passing in the future. In the end, the critical voting bloc of 64 Democratic freshmen stayed with the leadership by a 2-1 ratio; only 20 Democratic freshmen voted for the Stenholm amendment, and 43 were opposed.

4. Budget Resolution

In contrast to the battle Congress went through in 1993, the budget resolution debate was almost a non-event, in large part because President Clinton asked that Congress hold the line on further spending cuts. The request came as a relief to the Democratic Congress, which already had a full agenda wrestling with the mammoth task of trying to reshape the nation's health care system.

Still, it took a barrage of last-minute lobbying by the administration to turn the tide April 14 when deficit hawks demanded a vote on a motion to instruct conferees (H Con Res 218) to increase the budget cuts in the fiscal 1995 budget resolution. Offered by Rep. John R. Kasich, R-Ohio, it was rejected on a largely party line vote of 202-216: R 159-6; D 43-209 (ND 29-141, SD 14-68); I 0-1. (Related Senate vote, p. 23-C)

The motion would have required conferees to accept the Senate's proposal to cut an additional $26.1 billion in appro-

priations outlays over five years. The cuts would have gone beyond the $433 billion already in the five-year package Congress passed in 1993, which Clinton and Democratic leaders said provided sufficient deficit reduction for the next few years. *(1993 Almanac, p. 107)*

The main argument that administration officials advanced against the Senate proposal was that it could result in cuts in defense which, Clinton said during his State of the Union speech, should not be cut any further. The administration made its case with the help of the Joint Chiefs of Staff, who led the lobbying effort against the motion saying the cuts posed a serious threat to defense and had to be stopped.

Kasich and Democratic budget cutters who joined him in support of the reductions rejected that argument, pointing out that the Senate's proposed cuts represented the only chance lawmakers would have to pursue serious deficit reduction. They said the administration's contention that the cuts were a threat to defense was a scare tactic.

The House and Senate Appropriations committees had the authority to allocate the cuts in any way they saw fit when they divided up the discretionary budget among the 13 appropriations subcommittees — something they did once the budget resolution set their overall spending limit. The House's pattern had been to allocate about half the cuts to defense because defense made up half the budget's discretionary spending.

The effort to make deeper cuts and its rejection was a familiar theme for House deficit hawks, who had tried before to promote spending cuts.

In 1993, Kasich tried unsuccessfully to make an additional $90 billion in cuts in the budget resolution beyond the $433 billion already in it. *(1993 Almanac, p. 102)*

5. Assault Weapons Ban

Gun control advocates won their second major victory in less than a year when Congress, in late August 1994, passed a ban on certain semiautomatic assault weapons as part of its omnibus anti-crime bill (HR 3355 — PL 103-322). The pivotal vote came in the House, which approved the gun ban 216-214 on May 5. The Senate already had approved a similar proposal in 1993 as part of its sweeping crime bill, and the House action made it all but certain that the gun control measure would become law.

Gun control groups knew their fortunes had changed when President Clinton took office in 1993. Clinton was the first president in recent years to actively support gun control. By the end of the year, gun control supporters had passed the Brady bill (HR 1025 — PL 103-159), a nationwide waiting period and background check for handgun purchasers. *(1993 Almanac, p. 300)*

Prospects for the assault weapons ban (HR 4296), however, were considered far slimmer. When the House voted on the issue in 1991, lawmakers defeated the ban by 70 votes. The National Rifle Association (NRA) had been a powerful lobby in the House, and Rep. Jack Brooks, D-Texas, chairman of the Judiciary Committee, which oversaw crime legislation, had long fought off gun control proposals. Even when the Senate passed the assault weapons ban in November 1993 as part of its crime bill, many observers predicted it would die in the House. *(1993 Almanac, p. 293; 1991 Almanac, p. 262)*

But gun control advocates had new leverage: With crime at the top of voter concerns, lawmakers were eager to embrace anything seen as a tool for fighting violence. Moreover, many law enforcement groups lobbied for the ban and helped transform the issue from a "gun control" cause into a "tough on crime" issue.

The proposed ban explicitly outlawed 19 assault-style weapons, as well as copycat models and other semiautomatic guns with two or more features identified with assault weapons. It also banned large-capacity ammunition clips. But the proposal specifically exempted more than 650 guns that presumably were used by hunters and other sportsmen, as well as any gun legally owned at the time of the law's passage.

Gun control advocates and law enforcement groups pushed for the ban, saying assault weapons were the preferred weapons of criminals and were designed to kill humans rather than for sporting use. The NRA and its allies said the guns were no more lethal than other semiautomatic firearms and that banning them would do nothing to stop criminals from killing.

As the floor vote approached, both sides mounted furious publicity and lobbying campaigns. The Clinton administration added its weight to the battle, with the president and several Cabinet members making phone calls to undecided lawmakers leading up to the vote May 5.

House members began an emotional floor debate on the legislation with the outcome too close to call. Marge Roukema, R-N.J., a leading Republican supporter of the ban, invoked images of the gruesome carnage caused by the weapons. "Today our cities are war zones and our hospital emergency rooms are MASH units," she said. Other supporters cited polls showing strong popular support for the ban.

But opponents ridiculed the ban as ineffective and perhaps unconstitutional. They said the guns to be banned under the legislation were no more powerful than hundreds of others that would be exempt — just uglier.

Once the roll call began, the two sides stayed closely matched. In the final minutes the tally hovered at 213-214, giving opponents the edge. But Rep. Andrew Jacobs Jr., D-Ind., shocked his colleagues by reversing his vote — drawing cheers from the bill's supporters as the vote total flipped to 214-213 in favor of passage. Three holdouts divided 2-1 in casting the final votes, bringing the final tally to 216-214: R 38-137; D 177-77 (ND 137-34, SD 40-43); I 1-0.

The vote was a stunning setback for the NRA and its allies. They went on to fight the ban during House-Senate negotiations on the final crime bill. But with both chambers on record in favor of the ban, the stage was set for final passage. It was approved as part of the crime bill conference report in late August and signed into law by Clinton in September. *(Related House votes, pp. 18-C, 19-C; related Senate vote, p. 26-C)*

6. Abortion Clinic Access

Abortion rights supporters expected to make big gains in the 103rd Congress — even in the recalcitrant House — with the arrival of President Clinton, who supported their cause. But abortion remained a deeply controversial and complicated issue, and most initiatives to secure abortion rights stalled. The only significant legislation that emerged was one focused on safeguarding access to abortion clinics (S 636 — PL 103-259), and even that had to overcome persistent opposition in both chambers.

The bill's advocates were prodded by a January 1993 Supreme Court decision blocking clinic operators from using a 19th century civil rights law to obtain injunctions and other relief against blockaders. A rash of violence at abortion clinics nationwide, including shootings, arson and massive blockades, further fueled the quest for a federal solution. Supporters framed the measure not as a vote on abortion rights but as a law-and-order issue.

Even so, abortion rights advocates were on the defensive from the time the House first considered the legislation in

1993. Many members — including several who opposed legal abortion — condemned the behavior of radical anti-abortion activists, but they also expressed concern about approving a bill that might limit the First Amendment right to freedom of expression. From subcommittee action to House approval Nov. 18, 1993, the bill's opponents tried to limit its scope and leave the issue in the hands of local authorities. *(1993 Almanac, p. 354)*

The legislation made it a federal crime to intimidate abortion clinic workers or women seeking abortions, by force or threat of force. Violators faced criminal penalties of jail time and fines. The law also allowed affected individuals to sue for civil remedies, such as compensatory damages or court injunctions to restrain blockaders. *(Related Senate vote, p. 22-C)*

During House floor debate, much of the criticism centered on questions about the measure's constitutionality. Opponents charged that it singled out one point of view for censure. But the bill ultimately gained the support of several members who were ambivalent or even opposed to abortion rights but were disturbed enough by the violence to support legislation focused on that aspect of the problem.

Both chambers had passed similar measures in 1993, and a conference committee met in 1994 to work out minor differences. Even getting to a conference took some doing, however, given the emotional nature of the issue. Opponents, led by Christopher H. Smith, R-N.J., forced a series of procedural votes March 17, using them to pound away at the bill.

After conferees ironed out their differences, the House on May 5 considered adopting the conference report, setting off another wave of emotional debate.

F. James Sensenbrenner Jr., R-Wis., objected to a provision to allow plaintiffs but not defendants in clinic cases to recoup legal fees, and he tried to return the bill to conference. When that failed, opponents complained that the measure was too broad and its penalties excessive. "We're just looking for the punishment to be in sync with the crime," Smith said.

Supporters noted the increased violence at abortion clinics and maintained that local trespassing laws were insufficient or unenforced. "The right to choose is meaningless without the access to choose," said Carolyn B. Maloney, D-N.Y. The vote to approve the conference report was 241-174: R 40-131; D 200-43 (ND 139-26, SD 61-17); I 1-0.

7. Bosnia Arms Embargo

For two years, lawmakers had expressed increasing frustration with the inability of successive administrations to halt Serbian aggression in Bosnia. But they always stopped short of actually trying to dictate policy toward the former Yugoslavian republic.

That changed June 9, when the House voted overwhelmingly to require President Clinton to end compliance with the international arms embargo against the Bosnian Muslims. The House approved the measure, which was an amendment to the fiscal 1995 defense authorization bill, 244-178: R 127-45; D 117-132; I 0-1; (ND 84-87, SD 33-45). The Senate rejected a similar proposal July 1 on a 50-50 tie and approved a non-binding amendment urging the president to look for a peaceful solution to the Bosnian conflict. *(Related Senate vote, p. 25-C)*

Debate on the amendment highlighted the sharply conflicting views among House members over how to end the brutal conflict.

Supporters of the amendment argued that the U.N. arms embargo, which was imposed on all the former Yugoslavia republics in 1991, had worked to the disadvantage of Bosnia's Muslim-led government forces. The Serbs, widely viewed as

the aggressors in the conflict, had inherited heavy weaponry from the Yugoslavian army. The Muslims were relatively lightly armed.

House Democratic Whip David E. Bonior, D-Mich., cast the issue in stark terms. "If we don't lift this embargo and at least let the people of Bosnia defend themselves," he said, "then the blood of Bosnia isn't just on the hands of the Serbs — it's on all of us."

But Foreign Affairs Committee Chairman Lee H. Hamilton, D-Ind., argued that the amendment would eliminate chances for a peaceful resolution of the conflict. "If we lift this embargo, we are going to intensify the war, and by intensifying the war, that is another way of saying we are going to be killing a lot more people," he said.

The Clinton administration also worked to defeat the amendment, as senior officials warned lawmakers that ending the embargo would undermine the fragile multilateral peace negotiations.

The administration labored under a tactical disadvantage. The vote on the amendment originally was scheduled to coincide with the president's trip to Europe. The White House, concerned that Clinton might be dealt a high-profile setback as he met with allied leaders, successfully won a delay of the vote.

But in return, administration officials promised not to personally lobby lawmakers on the embargo issue. In the end, the administration lost many of its Democratic allies, including Bonior and Democratic Caucus Chairman Steny H. Hoyer of Maryland.

8. Telecommunications

Thanks largely to the work of two powerhouse committee chairmen, the House on June 28 overwhelmingly approved a major and contentious bill to rewrite the nation's 60-year-old communications law. The victory proved hollow, however, when lingering disagreements within the telecommunications industry scuttled the legislation in the Senate.

Still, the House vote on the bill (HR 3626) demonstrated that it was possible to unite trust-busting Democrats and deregulatory Republicans in support of a move toward unfettered competition in telecommunications products and services. The tally was 423-5: R 173-1; D 249-4 (ND 168-3, SD 81-1); I 1-0.

The bill would have superceded the 1982 court order that limited the regional Bell telephone monopolies mainly to the local telephone market and AT&T mainly to long distance and equipment manufacturing. Instead of having a federal judge decide when to remove those restrictions, the bill would have put the issue in the hands of the Federal Communications Commission, the Justice Department and state regulators.

The Bells were eager to lift those restrictions, and they had a key ally in Energy and Commerce Committee Chairman John D. Dingell, D-Mich. But another House titan, Judiciary Committee Chairman Jack Brooks, D-Texas, argued for maintaining tough limits on what the Bells could do as long as they dominated the local phone markets.

Through a series of compromises, Dingell and Brooks came up with a proposal for lifting the restrictions that had the unanimous support of their committees and the endorsement of almost every segment of the telecommunications industry. They whisked their bill to the House floor under a fast-track, no-amendment procedure usually reserved for minor bills — a stunning achievement for such a complex piece of legislation on a topic involving diverse, competing interests.

A companion bill by Reps. Edward J. Markey, D-Mass., and Jack Fields, R-Texas, that would have enabled competition in the local telephone and cable-television markets (HR 3636)

passed the same day by a similar margin, 423-4. The House then folded HR 3636 into HR 3626. So broad was the support for the two bills that both Minority Whip Newt Gingrich, R-Ga., and Majority Whip David E. Bonior, D-Mich., took the floor to urge "yes" votes.

The easy passage of the Brooks-Dingell bill disguised a major weakness in its legislative foundation, however: The $60 billion long-distance industry did not support it. Rather than trying to fight it out in the House, the long-distance carriers focused their attention on the Senate, where leaders of the Senate Commerce Committee had introduced a companion bill (S 1822) far more favorable to their interests.

Thus, an important legislative battle was postponed until the Senate Commerce Committee tried to move S 1822 in July. And even though the leaders of the committee were able to broker a deal between the Bells and the long-distance carriers over the Bells' entry into the long-distance market, they could not unite the telecommunications industry behind the legislation. After several senators threatened end-of-session filibusters, Commerce Committee Chairman Ernest F. Hollings, D-S.C., pulled the plug on the bill.

9. Space Station

The year dawned ominously for NASA's space station. Congress had demonstrated in 1993 that big-science projects were not immune to budget-cutting fervor when it killed the superconducting super collider. The House served notice that the space station could be the next to go when members came within one vote of ending its authorization and within 24 votes of axing its fiscal 1994 appropriation. *(1993 Almanac, pp. 249, 592, 691)*

Then, in the spring, two key lawmakers said they were noncommittal about continuing the project in fiscal 1995. House Science Committee Chairman George E. Brown Jr., D-Calif., was concerned that the space station would siphon funds from other National Aeronautics and Space Administration science programs. And House VA-HUD Appropriations Subcommittee Chairman Louis Stokes, D-Ohio, warned that the space station might suffer if there was a shortage of money in the VA-HUD appropriations bill, which funded the departments of Veterans Affairs (VA), Housing and Urban Development (HUD) and independent agencies such as NASA.

But by June, Brown and Stokes had decided to support spending $2.1 billion in fiscal 1995 for the station, intended to be an orbiting space laboratory for research in biotechnology, chemistry and physics. After a closed-door subcommittee markup June 9, Stokes said he endorsed the project "because the president wanted it and felt that it was a vital part of his foreign policy."

Nevertheless, the space station's future was uncertain — as it had been for several years when it was the most controversial element of the VA-HUD spending bill. The federal government already had spent more than $11 billion on the space station, once known as *Freedom*, which it had envisioned in 1984 as an $8 billion project. The renamed *Alpha* project, a scaled-back version of the original, now carried a total price tag of about $30 billion.

Leading the anti-station fight again were Tim Roemer, D-Ind., and Dick Zimmer, R-N.J. On June 29, they offered an amendment to the VA-HUD bill (HR 4624 — PL 103-327) to bar using money to continue the project and redistributing the $2.1 billion to other NASA programs.

Opponents blasted the project for being too expensive, unfocused in its mission, dependent on unreliable agreements with Russia and too reliant on job creation for its polit-

ical support. "It's time for the Congress to do what it should have done years ago — cut our losses . . . and put an end to this budgetary black hole in space," Zimmer said.

But momentum had shifted in favor of funding the space station. The project's redesign, strong support from the Clinton administration and foreign policy implications through international agreements with Russia and other countries helped strengthen its support. "The 216-215 vote last year woke up a sleeping giant," Roemer said of the lobbying blitz that preceded the 1994 vote. Roemer's amendment was defeated 155-278: R 40-136; D 114-142 (ND 101-72, SD 13-70); I 1-0.

Afterward, Brown said one reason he had waffled earlier in the year was to prod the station's supporters to step up their efforts. And Vice President Al Gore — who along with President Clinton and NASA Administrator Daniel S. Goldin had personally lobbied members to support the project — expressed hope that the outcome would end the annual funding battle. "The strength of the House vote signals the end of doubt about America's commitment to space exploration," Gore said in a statement.

The Senate, traditionally a stronger supporter of the project, on Aug. 3 rejected an amendment to kill the space station, 36-64.

10. California Desert

The political muscle of environmentalists in the House proved to be no match for gun control opponents in a key vote July 12 on whether to permit hunting in an ecologically sensitive part of California's desert.

Due largely to the support of the bipartisan Congressional Sportsmen's Caucus, one of the largest membership-driven organizations on Capitol Hill, the gun control opponents won by a vote of 239-183: R 146-26; D 92-157 (ND 39-131, SD 53-26); I 1-0.

The strength of the vote later persuaded Sen. Dianne Feinstein, D-Calif., and House Natural Resources Committee Chairman George Miller, D-Calif., to compromise on a crucial provision of a bill (S 21 — PL 103-433) aimed at keeping a huge swath of California desert out of the hands of developers. *(Related Senate vote, p. 27-C)*

The vote came on an amendment by Larry LaRocco, D-Idaho, to designate the East Mojave Scenic Area as a national preserve instead of the more coveted national park status preferred by Feinstein, Miller, the Clinton administration and a host of environmental groups.

"Preserve" was a label rarely used by the National Park Service that allowed hunting, fishing and trapping to continue on protected federal land.

The House easily approved a similar amendment in 1991. But environmentalists considered the California desert protection bill one of their legislative priorities for 1993-94 and pressured lawmakers to give maximum protection to the land.

The LaRocco amendment eventually became a crucial element in the floor strategy of Rep. Jerry Lewis and four other California Republicans to try to weaken the desert bill before it moved to a House-Senate conference committee. Lewis signed on as the amendment's chief cosponsor.

LaRocco, a member of the sportsmen's caucus, initially lost to Miller when the Natural Resources Committee voted 17-25 on May 4 to reject the amendment. But LaRocco lobbied hard among the caucus' 182 House members and was supported on the floor by such groups as the National Rifle Association and the Safari Club.

Although the sportsmen's caucus took no formal position on gun control, its members generally opposed such legislation. The caucus worked to preserve the interests of hunters,

fishermen and people who shot for sport. A comparison of the votes for LaRocco's hunting amendment and the assault weapons ban in the 1994 crime bill showed that only 11 of the caucus's 182 House members voted against both measures.

Several senior committee Democrats — LaRocco, Nick J. Rahall II of West Virginia, Austin J. Murphy of Pennsylvania and Pat Williams of Montana — voted for the hunting amendment. Miller downplayed the vote, saying Democrats were voting the wishes of their districts.

11. Budget Process

Deficit hawks generally pointed to entitlements such as Social Security, Medicare and food stamps, which made up roughly half the federal budget, as the place to look for serious deficit reduction.

But when a bill (HR 4604) to rein in entitlement spending came to the floor in July, there was more agreement on what *not* to cut than on anything else.

The bill would have set limits on entitlement spending and required spending cuts or tax increases or both if the entitlement caps were breached.

In a vote that stood as testament that Social Security remained the untouchable "third rail" of American politics, the House overwhelmingly rejected a substitute plan put forward by Charles W. Stenholm, D-Texas, that would have kept Social Security on the chopping block along with entitlements such as Medicare, Medicaid, unemployment insurance and others.

Stenholm's plan would have forced real cuts. It would have set entitlement caps from 1996 through 2000 low enough to force as much as $150 billion in cuts from projected entitlement spending. His proposal would have capped entitlements at fiscal 1995 levels, with adjustments for the Consumer Price Index and demographic changes. If the Office of Management and Budget determined that the limits would be breached, the president would have had to propose legislation to close the gap or raise the caps. If Congress failed to agree on how to meet the targets, sequestration procedures would have kicked in.

With Social Security making up 44 percent of all entitlements, members were loath to vote with Stenholm, especially since the underlying bill gave them a more politically palatable alternative. Stenholm's entitlement cutting plan was overwhelmingly defeated July 21, 37-392: R 9-165; D 28-226 (ND 15-157, SD 13-69); I 0-1.

Instead, the House passed, 316-107, a plan that would have required the White House to set the entitlement targets. The final bill was virtually identical to the plan passed by the House (but not the Senate) during the 1993 debate over President Clinton's five-year deficit-reduction package and later implemented by executive order.

But with entitlement spending remaining below the targets set in 1993, neither the existing rules nor the House-passed bill would have caused cuts in the near future. Along the way, the House rejected, 194-233, an alternative offered by John R. Kasich, R-Ohio, that would have required Congress and the White House each year to set caps on individual entitlement programs except Social Security.

The action on entitlements came amid a growing sense that spiraling growth in such programs needed to be addressed if Congress was going to seriously attempt to cut the deficit. The 1993 budget deal put a major squeeze on money available to appropriators for discretionary spending but largely left entitlements alone.

While the lopsidedness of the vote on Stenholm's amendment was attributable in part to the fact that members had politically palatable alternatives to vote for, the fact that it attracted so few votes highlighted one enduring truth: Congress might want to attack the deficit by curbing growth in entitlement spending, but not if it meant cutting Social Security, the biggest entitlement of them all.

12. Crime Bill/Rule

President Clinton and House Democratic leaders suffered one of their most embarrassing moments of the 103rd Congress on Aug. 11, when lawmakers blocked action on a major anti-crime bill. Democratic leaders had pulled out all the stops to pass a procedural motion allowing the crime bill (HR 3355) to come to the House floor.

But nearly 60 Democrats joined with almost all Republicans to defeat the rule (H Res 517). The vote highlighted divisions within the Democratic Caucus and severely imperiled passage of one of the president's key legislative priorities.

Democrats had struggled from the beginning to write a crime bill that could win House approval. When the House passed its version of the crime bill in April, they thought they had succeeded. That bill cost about $28 billion. It included dozens of new death penalties and other criminal punishments, as well as billions of dollars for police hiring, prison construction and social programs designed to prevent crime. It was a balance that satisfied a majority of Democrats and some Republicans, and the bill passed by a comfortable 285-141 margin.

The final, $33 billion crime bill that emerged from House-Senate negotiations generally followed the House bill with a notable exception — it added a ban on certain semiautomatic assault-style weapons. House lawmakers had approved a ban as separate legislation (HR 4296) in May, but without the votes of some of the lawmakers who had supported the crime bill. *(Related House vote, p. 15-C)*

That presented House leaders with a difficult equation as they rounded up votes to bring the conference report to the floor. While numerous Republicans were expected to vote for the bill on final passage, GOP lawmakers routinely voted against proposed rules for floor debate because they saw such rules as a tool used by Democrats to suppress Republican views. Democratic leaders usually could count on solid party support for such votes.

In this case, however, a large group of Democrats who opposed gun control insisted they could not cast a vote that would facilitate bringing the assault weapons ban to the House floor. Several members of the Congressional Black Caucus also withheld their support because of objections to the death penalty provisions in the measure.

Clinton and the House leadership mounted a furious campaign to round up the necessary 218 votes. With little movement among the gun-rights Democrats, these leaders pinned their hopes on a group of Republican lawmakers who had voted for the House crime bill and also supported the assault weapons ban. But these Republicans also felt pressure from their own party leadership, which insisted that GOP lawmakers hold together on the procedural vote.

Republican leaders made procedural complaints about the crime legislation, saying Democratic leaders had ridden roughshod over GOP attempts to amend or influence the bill. And they attacked the substance of the final product as weak on punishment and fiscally bloated, particularly with respect to crime prevention programs.

Democrats defended the final bill as worthy and essential, and many charged that Republicans were simply trying to

deny Clinton and his party a legislative success on an issue of great concern to voters.

In the test of party allegiances, the Republicans prevailed. All but 11 GOP lawmakers voted against the rule while 58 Democrats broke with their party leadership on the issue. Most of those Democratic votes came from opponents of the gun ban, but 10 were from black lawmakers upset about the death penalty language and the decision to omit a provision aimed at combating alleged racial bias in death penalty sentencing.

The final vote was 210-225: R 11-167; D 198-58 (ND 148-25, SD 50-33); I 1-0. In the aftermath, Republicans were jubilant about their show of power. Democratic leaders, badly shaken, began scrambling for ways to salvage the crime bill, which eventually cleared in late August (PL 103-322). *(Related House vote, below; related Senate vote, p. 26-C)*

13. Crime Bill/Conference

Public distress over violent crime proved stronger than congressional infighting Aug. 21, when House lawmakers overcame bitter disagreements to adopt the conference report on a massive, $30.2 billion anti-crime bill (HR 3355). Just 10 days earlier, House Republicans and renegade Democrats had blocked action on the legislation. That vote was a stunning setback for President Clinton and the Democratic leadership, and it set up the possibility of lawmakers heading home empty-handed on an issue that many voters had identified as their top concern. *(Related House vote, 18-C)*

Ultimately, that scenario was too threatening to numerous lawmakers in both parties. After a week of frantic and wearying negotiations, Democratic leaders agreed to revise the final bill to attract additional Republican votes. The new version trimmed $3.3 billion from the original bill and adjusted certain policy provisions.

When the crime measure emerged from House-Senate negotiations in late July, most lawmakers and political analysts considered it unstoppable. Lawmakers in both parties were eager to take action on the issue of violent crime, and Democratic leaders appeared to have crafted an acceptable compromise: The final legislation included billions for prison construction sought by conservatives, social programs advocated by liberals and police hiring supported by almost everyone. To make sure the programs actually received promised funding, the legislation included a novel trust fund designed to devote the expected savings from federal layoffs to the anti-crime programs.

Even so, the measure foundered on two highly contentious issues: gun control and the death penalty. Almost 60 House Democrats opposed to either the assault weapons ban or the death penalty provisions in the bill joined forces with all but 11 Republicans to keep the legislation from the House floor Aug. 11. As the legislation lay wounded, lawmakers became more vocal about other complaints — some longstanding, some newly articulated. Republicans had complained that the bill was larded with wasteful social programs that they said would do little to reduce crime, while stinting on some of the penalties advocated by GOP lawmakers. They pressed these and other complaints in the days following the Aug. 11 vote.

Democratic leaders defended the bill and complained that Republicans were simply seeking to deny Clinton and his party an important legislative success. Still, they had little choice but to negotiate. Although some House Democratic leaders advocated dropping the assault weapons ban to pick up support from Democrats opposed to gun control, Clinton insisted that the ban remain in the bill. That left key

Democrats struggling to craft a package of modifications that could attract moderate Republican votes without jeopardizing any existing support within their own party.

Some Republicans also had ample incentive to find a solution. Several dozen GOP lawmakers had supported the crime bill and assault weapons ban in earlier House votes and did not want to be seen as killing the legislation. Some Republican leaders also were skittish about appearing obstructionist on an issue of such concern to voters.

After several days of tense, marathon negotiations, Democrats came up with a package that could pick up the needed extra votes from pro-gun control Republicans: cut $3.3 billion, most of it from crime prevention programs, and adjust certain penalties — agreeing, for example, to track convicted sex offenders after they were released from prison. House and Senate conferees convened shortly after 3 a.m. on Aug. 21 to adopt the changes. The new conference report went to the House floor later that day, where lawmakers voted 239-189 to take up the legislation. Forty-two Republicans were among those supporting the parliamentary motion. Shortly thereafter, the House approved the conference report, 235-195: R 46-131; D 188-64 (ND 141-31, SD 47-33); I 1-0.

Although the legislation went on to face last-minute difficulties in the Senate, the House vote was a major victory for its supporters and one that renewed momentum toward final passage. It was a flawed but vital victory for Clinton and his party as they headed into the fall elections, particularly with the Democrats' goal of health care reform all but abandoned for the year. *(Related Senate vote, p. 26-C)*

The vote also represented a watershed in Congress' crime-fighting efforts; the legislation (PL 103-322) marked an unprecedented federal commitment on the issue of violent crime, which had been primarily a state and local responsibility, and some lawmakers predicted that Congress would find the responsibility hard to abandon in the future.

14. Lobbying

Considered a certainty earlier in the year, passage of a bill (S 349) to overhaul lobbying disclosure requirements and ban lobbyist gifts to members was nearly derailed in the House on a procedural vote Sept. 29. But House Democratic leaders saved the measure — a key element of their agenda of political reform — by leaving the vote open for several minutes while they twisted arms and persuaded several pliable Democrats to switch their votes.

The closeness of the vote, however, presaged the bill's death at the hands of the Senate a week later. *(Related Senate vote, p. 27-C)*

The vote was on whether to adopt the rule (H Res 550) accompanying the conference report on the lobbying disclosure bill — in effect, a vote on whether to bring the bill up for a final vote. Sponsors knew that few members would have the temerity to vote down the lobbying bill, and risk being tagged as anti-reform, on the final vote. So the rule vote was the opponents' last chance to stop the bill in the House.

Ninety-three members who eventually voted for the bill tried to kill it by voting against the rule. Finally, the rule was approved 216-205 (R 5-170; D 210-35; ND 156-13, SD 54-22, I 1-0). Shortly afterward the conference report itself was approved 306-112.

The vote was close for several reasons.

House Republican leaders, emboldened by their success at frustrating President Clinton and the Democrats on many fronts, tried to kill the bill on the procedural vote, even

though many of them had voted for it when the House passed its first version of the bill 315-110 on March 24.

Some lawmakers from both parties privately disliked a provision in the bill that barred members from accepting most meals, gifts and entertainment from lobbyists. But the public debate centered on last-minute objections raised by GOP Whip Newt Gingrich of Georgia. He contended that the disclosure requirement on grass-roots organizations would force them to disclose contributors to grass-roots efforts. He predicted that the Clinton administration would fill the directorship of the new office handling lobby registrations with a "secular, anti-religious liberal" who could use his powers to squelch religious viewpoints.

The bill's House sponsor, John Bryant, D-Texas, countered that the bill would specifically exempt religious groups from disclosure requirements unless they hired lobbyists to conduct the campaign. Gingrich's arguments failed in the House, but they bore fruit in the Senate.

Democratic leaders not only had to contend with Republicans who wanted to deny them a legislative victory and with Democrats wanting to preserve privileges, they also had to woo normally loyal allies in the Congressional Black Caucus. Several members of the caucus decided to vote against the rule merely to remind Democratic leaders not to take their votes for granted. Caucus Chairman Kweisi Mfume, D-Md., switched his vote from no to yes in the waning moments of the vote. That helped save the bill from going down.

15. Haiti

Almost as soon as President Clinton dispatched thousands of troops to Haiti on Sept. 19, some lawmakers began discussing plans to bring them home. By the time the House took up a resolution (H J Res 16) providing limited authorization for the deployment of troops until March 1, 1995, however, any momentum for setting a hard and fast deadline was gone. The administration, with the strong backing of senior military officers, had convinced Congress that setting a date certain for withdrawal could endanger American forces.

But Republicans, who had been itching for an opportunity to debate Haiti policy, were determined to voice their objections. Minority Leader Robert H. Michel, R-Ill., and Benjamin A. Gilman, R-N.Y., offered a GOP alternative that blasted Clinton for dispatching troops to Haiti in the first place.

The amendment called for a pullout of U.S. forces from the Caribbean island "as soon as possible in a manner consistent with the safety of those forces." And it provided expedited procedures for a vote to shut down the mission after the 104th Congress convened in January.

During the hours of debate on the amendment, Republicans went to the well to warn their colleagues that the administration was on the way toward becoming trapped in a "quagmire" in Haiti.

While the proposal would not have placed any binding restraints on the administration, it clearly had the potential to embarrass Clinton. Democrats, overcoming their own uneasiness with the operation, rallied behind the president. The Michel-Gilman amendment was rejected 205-225 in a vote that divided largely along partisan lines: R 173-1; D 32-223 (ND 21-153, S 11-70); I 0-1.

After the House defeated the Michel-Gilman amendment, it adopted a far milder substitute that did little more than require detailed reports from the president on the Haiti oper-

ation. It chided the president for failing to seek congressional assent before dispatching U.S. forces, but it included no withdrawal deadline. *(Related Senate vote, p. 24-C)*

The vote on that amendment, which was offered by an unlikely alliance of pro-Pentagon lawmakers and liberal members of the Congressional Black Caucus, was 258-167.

16. GATT

Acting in a rare lame-duck session, the House on Nov. 29 and the Senate on Dec. 1 gave President Clinton a big legislative victory by passing the bill (HR 5110 — PL 103-465) to implement the Uruguay Round pact strengthening the General Agreement on Tariffs and Trade (GATT).

The GATT victory reaffirmed trade policy as the strong suit of Clinton's agenda in the 103rd Congress.

It came almost exactly one year after the enactment of the North American Free Trade Agreement (NAFTA) linking the United States, Canada and Mexico. *(1993 Almanac, p. 171)*

However, the GATT victory came nearly a month too late to give the election-year political boost that Clinton had hoped the bill could provide for himself and his beleaguered fellow Democrats, who lost control of both chambers of Congress with the Nov. 8 elections.

The trade pact sharply reduced tariffs and trade barriers around the world and brought such key industries as intellectual property, agriculture and services under worldwide trade disciplines.

The administration promised it would result in billions of dollars in economic growth and thousands of new jobs for the United States.

The same coalition of organized labor, environmentalists, political populists and "America First" conservatives who spearheaded the emotional fight against NAFTA tried again on GATT. They failed to arouse much interest. But the administration and congressional GATT supporters took several months to fine-tune the implementing bill, giving opponents an opportunity to delay action.

The president finally submitted the bill to Congress on Sept. 27, under rules that gave each committee chairman with jurisdiction up to 45 days to review the bill. Sen. Ernest F. Hollings, D-S.C., who insisted that free-trade policies had damaged the U.S. economy, demanded his 45 days, forcing the Senate leadership to schedule a two-day lame-duck session beginning Nov. 30.

Clinton asked for the House to press on and approve the bill before its October adjournment. But many members of both parties expressed anxiety about taking a stand on the complex legislation before the election, and Minority Whip Newt Gingrich, R-Ga., warned that he could not promise sufficient Republican votes to guarantee passage of the bill.

The Democratic House leadership therefore delayed consideration of the legislation until the one-day session Nov. 29. The House returned on that date for a debate that was tepid compared with the previous one on NAFTA. Even the opponents recognized that supporters had more than enough votes to pass HR 5110 and reserved their stronger efforts for the Senate, where the bill first had to clear a key procedural hurdle.

Voting under fast-track procedures for trade legislation, which allowed only for an up-or-down vote with no amendments, the House passed the GATT bill 288-146: R 121-56; D 167-89 (ND 107-66, SD 60-23); I 0-1.

GATT supporters hailed the outcome as a sign that Clinton would find room for bipartisan cooperation with the incoming Republican majority. *(Related Senate vote, p. 28-C)*

1. Vietnam Trade Embargo

For nearly two decades, the U.S. trade embargo against Vietnam served as an enduring reminder of the decade-long Vietnam War. But the Senate opened a new chapter in relations between the United States and Vietnam on Jan. 27 when it voted overwhelmingly in favor of lifting the trade ban against Hanoi.

Over the strong objections of some veterans groups and their congressional allies, the Senate voted to adopt an amendment to the biennial State Department authorization bill (S 1281) calling on President Clinton to scrap the long-standing economic embargo. The amendment had significant bipartisan support; it was adopted 62-38: R 20-24; D 42-14 (ND 31-11; SD 11-3).

While the amendment was non-binding, the vote proved to be one of the most important foreign policy votes of the year. Just one week after the Senate adopted the amendment, Clinton ordered an end to the 19-year-old trade embargo.

The president did not need Congress' go-ahead to lift the Vietnam sanctions. He could have accomplished that with the stroke of a pen. But Clinton, who evaded the draft during the Vietnam War, clearly was uncomfortable with the prospect of acting without the cover of a congressional vote. Equally important was the involvement of a pair of senators who served with distinction in Vietnam, John McCain, R-Ariz., and John Kerry, D-Mass. They led the movement to end the embargo.

For years, the trade embargo had been linked to painful questions surrounding the fate of more than 2,000 American servicemen listed as missing in action (MIA) from the war. Many veterans groups argued that the embargo provided the United States with its only effective leverage in its talks with Hanoi over the MIAs.

McCain and Kerry argued that ending the embargo would actually spur Vietnam to greater cooperation. "This is not a reward to Vietnam," Kerry said. "It's not a question of taking away leverage, but of giving leverage to us."

Sen. Robert C. Smith, R-N.H., another Vietnam veteran who had devoted much of his career to investigating the fate of MIAs, led opposition to the amendment. Smith charged that lifting the embargo would be the equivalent of "getting down on your knees and hoping and praying that the Vietnamese will give us all this information."

But after nearly 20 years of a U.S. policy designed to isolate Vietnam economically, most senators wanted to put trade relations on more normal footing. In addition, some U.S. oil companies and other business interests, which had been frozen out of a potentially lucrative market, conducted an effective lobbying campaign against the trade ban.

2. 'Goals 2000'

In 1989, President George Bush, concerned about poor schools and the potential inability of U.S. workers to compete in a global economy, convened a two-day summit in Virginia with the nation's governors to produce an education reform plan. They reached an unprecedented agreement to set national performance goals by 1990.

In 1991, Bush proposed "America 2000" legislation to establish voluntary national testing, create non-traditional schools and send limited federal aid to states and localities to fund model programs. The measure also included a controversial "school choice" voucher program that would have

sent public funds to some private schools. Democrats fought school choice, and in the end, neither Democrats nor Republicans could muster much enthusiasm for the measure, which died in the Senate in a Republican filibuster. *(1992 Almanac, p. 455)*

The political dynamic changed in 1993 after Bill Clinton was elected president. Democrats renewed the education reform debate, hoping to capitalize on control of the White House and both chambers of Congress for the first time since 1980.

The Clinton administration introduced a $420 million "Goals 2000" bill (HR 1804 — PL 103-227), using the Bush proposal as a basis. But Clinton removed the school choice provisions and added national standards and goals. These standards, although voluntary, opened the door for federal involvement in public schools and set markers that many local school districts would have difficulty ignoring. School districts seeking grants were required to strive for the national goals; they were given the flexibility to either adopt national content and performance standards, or to develop their own standards to reach the goals. The House easily passed the measure in 1993. *(1993 Almanac, p. 404)*

The bill included such goals as improving high school graduation rates and making schools safer. It also included controversial "opportunity to learn" standards prescribing what a school needed — such as competent teachers and up-to-date textbooks — to give children the opportunity to meet the goals and standards.

Liberal Democrats argued such standards were necessary to ensure that all students had access to high quality educational programs. Conservatives said they could leave school districts open to lawsuits from parents displeased about their child's school.

In the end, a majority of members decided that the opportunity to learn standards were acceptable because they were voluntary and states would be able to develop them locally.

With major sticking points such as school choice and opportunity to learn out of the way, Senate Democrats and moderate Republicans found common ground on the school reform measure. Before passing the bill Feb. 8, senators waded through a series of amendments, including an unsuccessful last-ditch effort by conservatives to include a school choice demonstration project. The Senate subsequently passed the bill, 71-25: R 17-25; D 54-0; (ND 41-0, SD 13-0).

After House-Senate conferees ironed out their differences, the House adopted the conference report March 23 and the Senate cleared the bill March 26.

3. Budget Deficit

Using an earthquake relief bill for Southern California as their vehicle, a bipartisan group of senators moved early in the 1994 session to test Congress' will to cut the budget deficit more deeply than it had in 1993.

The bill (HR 3759 — PL 103-211) combined $10 billion in emergency spending on disaster relief and military missions with $1 billion in routine supplemental appropriations and $3.26 billion in rescissions. On Feb. 9, the bipartisan group — led by Bob Kerrey, D-Neb., and Hank Brown, R-Colo. — offered an amendment to slash spending by $94 billion over five years.

Their proposal was killed on a key tabling motion by Appropriations Committee Chairman Robert C. Byrd, D-W.Va. The vote was 65-31: R 23-19; D 42-12 (ND 31-9, SD 11-3).

The defeat foreshadowed the difficulties that deficit hawks would have all year: Unlike in 1993, Congress rejected all the major spending cuts proposed in 1994.

The Kerrey-Brown amendment also epitomized the changed politics of disaster relief. After years of routinely handing out millions to communities hit by natural disasters, Congress could not help victims of the devastating California earthquake without at least a nod in the direction of offsetting spending cuts.

The first sign of this political shift had come the previous year, when Republicans and conservative Democrats in the House temporarily derailed an emergency flood-relief bill (HR 2667 — PL 103-75) to protest its impact on the deficit. The bill passed only after the Democratic leadership promised to create a task force examining how Congress responds to disasters. *(1993 Almanac, p. 714)*

Kerrey, Brown and four colleagues began work on their plan for spending cuts in November 1993. Their original target had been HR 3400, a bill containing numerous elements from Vice President Al Gore's "reinventing government" plan. That bill passed the House at the end of the 1993 session but never made it to the Senate floor. *(1993 Almanac, p. 140)*

When the bipartisan group offered its amendment on the disaster-relief bill, it attracted 11 cosponsors. The amendment's main elements were cuts in spending on Medicare of $30.5 billion over five years through higher charges on selected participants; reductions of 252,000 in the federal work force, saving $26.7 billion; and limits on government administrative expenses, saving $21 billion.

Other provisions of the amendment would have stopped the government from buying any more buildings, saving $2 billion; denied unemployment benefits to those who left the military voluntarily, saving $1.2 billion; limited cost of living increases for retired government employees, saving $1.2 billion; and cut the salaries of congressmen and senior government executives, saving $297 million.

Byrd cast the savings as largely fictitious. Any Medicare savings would be consumed by health care reform, he said, and the personnel savings would be channeled to crime-fighting programs. The Clinton administration, meanwhile, already had placed a lower limit on government expenses than the Kerrey-Brown amendment would have imposed.

Byrd's hand was strengthened by the Senate Appropriations Committee, which increased the amount of rescissions to $3.41 billion from the House-passed level of $2.56 billion. This amount was enough to offset not only the routine supplemental spending proposals, but also the additional defense spending and some of the disaster aid.

The Senate went on to clear the $11 billion package by voice vote Feb. 11.

4. Balanced-Budget Amendment

It took a furious lobbying effort by the administration and key Senate leaders, but in the end their efforts secured enough votes to defeat a constitutional amendment requiring a balanced budget (S J Res 41).

With Democratic opponents uncertain of their ability to muster the 34 votes needed to kill the proposed amendment outright, Senate leaders put forward a less stringent alternative in a successful effort to siphon enough votes away from a bipartisan effort led by Sens. Paul Simon, D-Ill., and Orrin G. Hatch, R-Utah.

The original measure would have banned deficit spending unless three-fifths of the full House and Senate approved it. A

separate three-fifths vote would have been required to raise the limit on the total public debt, and a majority vote would have been needed to raise taxes.

In the end, the tactics of amendment opponents paid off, and supporters fell four votes shy of the two-thirds required as the Senate rejected the amendment March 1 by a 63-37 vote: R 41-3; D 22-34 (ND 12-30, SD 10-4).

After the painful debate in 1993 over the budget, congressional leaders and the administration wanted 1994 to be relatively calm on the budget front as the health care overhaul debate took precedence. Adoption of the amendment could have pressured Congress to deliberate over painful spending cuts in politically sensitive areas.

But after failing to win approval in either the House or Senate in 1992 and failing even to get the proposal to the floor of either chamber in 1993, advocates won a pledge from Senate Majority Leader George J. Mitchell, D-Maine, to bring it to a vote early in 1994.

Supporters of the amendment hoped that election year pressure would be enough to reverse earlier defeats. In 1986, the amendment fell just one vote short. *(1986 Almanac, p. 578)*

The lobbying in the weeks leading up to the vote was intense. Mitchell and Appropriations Committee Chairman Robert C. Byrd, D-W.Va., led the opponents' charge. Only five of the 15 Democrats who served under Byrd on the committee defied the chairman and voted for the amendment.

President Clinton also weighed in, saying that a provision in the Simon-Hatch amendment that would have required a three-fifths majority to approve an increase in the national debt limit provided too much power to a minority and amounted to "a recipe for total paralysis."

But supporters countered that Congress repeatedly had demonstrated that it lacked the political courage to make the painful budget cuts or politically risky tax increases to balance the budget and that a constitutional requirement was the only way to make it happen.

Many of the opponents of the amendment said the 1993 deficit-reduction bill had brought the deficit under sufficient control and that further cuts might undermine the economy.

At the same time, concern over Social Security played into the hands of opponents. The American Association of Retired Persons conducted an all-out drive against the amendment, saying it eventually would lead to cuts in Social Security.

Only three Republicans, Nancy Landon Kassebaum, Kan., Mark O. Hatfield, Ore., and Ted Stevens, Alaska, voted against the amendment. Twenty-two Democrats voted for it; 34 were opposed. In 1986, 10 Republicans voted against the amendment.

Twenty-two senators voted for the milder alternative, offered by Harry Reid, D-Nev.; but seven of them, having gone on record as supporting Reid's effort, then voted against the tougher version.

Supporters of the amendment said Reid's alternative was critical in providing political cover for opponents. Reid's version contained several provisions that would have made it more likely that Congress could continue to run a deficit, and it would have protected Social Security by keeping surplus Social Security receipts off-limits to deficit cutters. *(Related House vote, p. 14-C)*

5. Abortion Clinic Access

Legislation designed to safeguard access to abortion clinics found a receptive audience in the Senate, which traditionally had been more supportive of abortion rights than

the House. But even in the Senate, supporters had to frame the issue narrowly — as a law-and-order matter rather than as a question of abortion rights — to gain passage. The bill's advocates fended off criticism that the legislation (S 636 — PL 103-259) would infringe on the free speech rights of abortion opponents, but in the end, they had to make some concessions.

The quest for legislation was prodded by a January 1993 Supreme Court decision barring clinic operators from using a 19th century civil rights law to obtain relief from blockaders. Advocates also pointed to a rash of violence at abortion clinics nationwide, including shootings, arson and massive blockades. They won support for the legislation from the new Democratic president, Bill Clinton, and from Attorney General Janet Reno, who gave the measure the administration's official endorsement at a hearing before the Senate Labor and Human Resources Committee on May 12, 1993.

The legislation made it a federal crime to intimidate abortion clinic workers or women seeking abortions, by force or threat of force. Violators faced criminal penalties of jail time and fines. The law also allowed affected individuals to sue for civil remedies, such as compensatory damages or court injunctions to restrain blockaders. *(Related House vote, p. 15-C; 1993 Almanac, p. 354)*

Most Democratic senators and some Republicans supported the measure, condemning the violent behavior of radical anti-abortion activists. But others thought the legislation would impinge on the free speech rights of protesters and sought to further narrow the bill's scope.

These objections led the Senate to make some changes that ultimately prevented a quick agreement with the House in 1993. One provision, suggested by Orrin G. Hatch, R-Utah, extended the bill's protections to places of worship. Another, offered by Labor Committee Chairman Edward M. Kennedy, D-Mass., set lower maximum criminal penalties for non-violent obstruction, such as lying down in front of a clinic door. House and Senate negotiators adopted these provisions when they reached a final accord April 26.

Still, Senate opponents, unconvinced by assurances that the bill was modeled on civil rights laws to discourage violent conduct, warned that the legislation would have a chilling effect on those seeking to oppose abortion through non-violent means. "To inflict harsher punishment on one group is discrimination against a particular political viewpoint," said Don Nickles, R-Okla., during Senate consideration of the conference report.

But supporters argued that local trespassing laws were inadequate and that national resources were needed to combat a national effort to disrupt clinic operations. They again concentrated on the law-and-order aspect of the bill. "We're reacting to violence, not words," said Barbara Boxer, D-Calif. The final vote on May 12 to adopt the conference report, clearing the bill, was 69-30: R 17-27; D 52-3 (ND 41-1, SD 11-2).

6. Budget Resolution

Although it took weeks of bickering to reach an agreement, the Senate's final approval of the conference report on the 1995 budget resolution largely endorsed President Clinton's request that Congress take a year off from deep budget cuts, frustrating those lawmakers who had hoped to make additional reductions.

On May 12, a largely Democratic majority approved the conference report of the 1995 budget resolution (H Con Res 218) 53-46: R 2-42; D 51-4 (ND 39-3, SD 12-1).

The vote and debate were striking primarily for their low profile in contrast to the previous year's budget vote, which was Clinton's first major legislative victory, setting the course for some $433 billion in deficit reduction over five years. *(1993 Almanac, p. 107)*

The fiscal 1995 budget resolution, an internal congressional document that did not need to be signed by the president, required just $13 billion in additional spending cuts over five years, all of it from appropriations outlays. That differed from the previous year's resolution, which was accompanied by controversial reconciliation instructions that required tax increases and spending cuts in both appropriated and entitlement programs in order to meet specific deficit reduction targets.

The conference report to H Con Res 218 highlighted the intense frustration of Appropriations Committee members, who felt that their domestic spending budgets already were tight. The opposition to additional spending cuts came from a new coalition of liberals and conservatives who opposed deeper budget cuts — liberals because they did not want to make deeper cuts in social programs and conservatives because they wanted to avoid further cuts in defense spending.

When the budget resolution was under consideration in the Senate, deficit hawks succeeded in cutting the appropriations budget by an additional $26.1 billion over five years. But they ran into trouble in conference, when, in a reversal of his previous stance, Senate Budget Committee ranking Republican Pete V. Domenici, N.M., surprised his colleagues by opposing the cuts because he was worried that they would fall mainly on defense spending.

His turnaround put him on the same side as Clinton and Democratic leaders, who eschewed the cuts because of the potential impact on defense and other programs. The House budget did not contain the additional $26.1 billion in cuts. After a tortuous debate, conferees agreed to limit cuts to $13 billion. *(Related House vote, p. 14-C)*

The extra cuts were phased in gradually, with just $500 million taking effect in 1995. That accelerated to an additional $5.4 billion in 1996 and the balance of $7.1 billion in 1997-99.

7. Safe Drinking Water

A key Senate vote to require the Environmental Protection Agency (EPA) to study the costs and benefits of new, major regulations underscored the Clinton administration's difficulty in trying to appease states that felt burdened by costly federal mandates without jeopardizing public health and safety.

Known as risk assessment, the issue was a major element of a larger and potent backlash against federal regulations that became a recurrent theme during environmental debates in the 103rd Congress.

The backlash eventually would derail key elements of President Clinton's ambitious environmental agenda, including an overhaul of the 1974 Safe Drinking Water Act and an ongoing effort to make the EPA the 15th Cabinet-level department.

The key vote came May 18 on an amendment by J. Bennett Johnston, D-La., to a bill (S 2019) designed to make the Safe Drinking Water Act more flexible for states, local governments and small water system operators.

A conservative Democrat, Johnston said he was concerned that federal environmental regulations were sometimes based on public opinion rather than on scientific facts. A commonly cited example was the rush to evacuate Times Beach, Mo., in the 1980s because of the presence of dioxin,

believed to cause cancer.

The Johnston amendment was considered one of the stumbling blocks for the drinking water bill, which eventually passed the Senate and House but died at the end of the legislative session.

The Senate passed the cost-benefit amendment 90-8: R 41-3; D 49-5 (ND 36-5, SD 13-0). But the overwhelming margin belied the behind-the-scenes struggle of Johnston, Senate Environment and Public Works Committee Chairman Max Baucus, D-Mont., and the White House Office of Management and Budget (OMB).

Under existing law, the EPA conducted some cost-benefit studies for regulations, but not on a widespread basis.

A chief concern of Baucus' and such environmental groups as the Natural Resources Defense Council was that an amendment requiring more studies would lead to "paralysis by analysis." They also argued that the results of these studies could be used to weaken existing health or safety rules if it was determined that the regulation actually posed little benefit for its costs.

Johnston sparked this politically explosive debate in 1993 with a much broader but little-noticed amendment to a bill to elevate the EPA to Cabinet-level status (S 171). That earlier amendment would have required cost-benefit studies of all federal agencies. It also would have required these studies to include comparisons to health risks more commonly understood by people, such as being hit by a car or struck by lightning. *(1993 Almanac, p. 266)*

Eventually, the negotiators were able to persuade Johnston to limit the amendment on the drinking water bill to new EPA regulations that would have an economic impact of $100 million or more. He also agreed to restrict any risk studies to six comparisons: three regulated by the EPA or other federal agencies and three not regulated by the federal government.

Sally Katzen, who oversaw regulatory affairs for OMB, said the compromise would affect about 20 to 25 EPA regulations — a fraction of the 600 to 900 reviewed annually by the EPA. The compromise was able to sway such environmentally minded Democrats as Baucus, Senate Majority Leader George J. Mitchell, D-Maine, and Daniel Patrick Moynihan, D-N.Y. Moynihan had long argued that the EPA should prioritize regulations.

But the deal did little to satisfy the concerns of eight senators, most of whom were close allies of the environmental movement, including John H. Chafee, R-R.I. It also eventually became a sticking point with the House. *(Related House vote, p. 13-C)*

8. Product Liability

After 17 years of lobbying and deal-making, advocates of limiting product liability thought that 1994 would be the year they finally pushed a bill through Congress. Instead, trial lawyers and consumer groups who opposed the effort demonstrated how adept they were at turning supporters into opponents.

The fate of the bill (S 687) was decided June 29. That day, the Senate rejected a motion to limit debate, falling three votes short of the 60 necessary to end the opponents' filibuster. The motion to invoke cloture failed 57-41: R 38-6; D 19-35 (ND 13-27, SD 6-8).

Senate Majority Leader George J. Mitchell, D-Maine, pulled the bill off the floor, and its supporters vowed to try again in 1995.

Business groups and insurance companies had been trying to limit product liability suits since the mid-1970s, arguing that the suits stifled innovation and forced companies to devote significant resources to combating plaintiffs, many of whom had dubious claims. But their allies in Congress had never been able to bring any legislation to the House or Senate floors.

Their primary goal had been to set tough new standards for awarding punitive damages — which were designed to punish a defendant for particularly gross and malicious negligence. Among the most important provisions in S 687 was language that would have required plaintiffs in personal injury cases to present "clear and convincing" evidence that their injuries stemmed from a defendant's flagrant disregard for safety. Also included was language that would have ended joint liability for non-economic damages. With joint liability, one defendant was responsible for paying the share of a damage award owed by other defendants if they were unable to pay.

To broaden the bill's appeal, a bipartisan group of sponsors, led by John D. Rockefeller IV, D-W.Va., added provisions aimed at benefiting victims of faulty products. For instance, they included language that would have extended the traditional two-year statute of limitations in cases where the nature or cause of an injury had not been discovered. They also removed the proposed penalties for victims who rejected out-of-court settlements, while proposing less protection from punitive damages for the manufacturers of drugs and medical devices.

The changes seemed to bring a number of lawmakers into the supporters' camp. A narrower bill to protect light-plane manufacturers from liability lawsuits (S 1458 — PL 103-298) easily passed the Senate on March 16, further encouraging Rockefeller's allies. As S 687 neared the floor, Rockefeller said he was confident he had the 60 votes needed to overcome the expected filibuster.

Opponents of the measure, meanwhile, made an emotional pitch that focused on people maimed by faulty medicines and medical devices. They said the bill, which would have banned punitive damages against companies whose products had been approved by the Food and Drug Administration or the Federal Aviation Administration, would remove incentives for greedy corporations to act responsibly and not hurt people with their products.

The opponents' Senate allies also threatened to bring up a number of amendments designed to force their colleagues to vote on tough, unrelated issues such as gun control and smoking.

Rockefeller fell six votes short of breaking the filibuster June 28. In order to attract more support, he and cosponsor Slade Gorton, R-Wash., promised to remove the section prohibiting punitive damages against companies with federally approved products. These changes brought three more Democrats and two Republicans into the supporters' column. But the following day, supporters could only muster 57 votes, still three short of the needed 60. This was due to two defections among the supporters — Larry Pressler, R-S.D., and Donald W. Riegle Jr., D-Mich., — and the absence of Dennis DeConcini, D-Ariz., a bill supporter who missed the vote.

9. Haiti

As President Clinton moved inexorably toward ordering a military invasion of Haiti, the Senate rejected several Republican-led proposals to halt an intervention.

But the defeat of those amendments hardly represented a sweeping endorsement of military action to oust Haiti's ruling

dictators. Rather, it demonstrated the Senate's traditional reluctance to tie the president's hands on crucial national security issues.

Sen. Judd Gregg, R-N.H., tried to tap into the anti-invasion mood June 29 by offering an amendment to the fiscal 1995 foreign operations appropriations bill (HR 4426) that would have barred U.S. military intervention in Haiti unless the president first sought congressional approval or determined that intervention was necessary to protect U.S. citizens or security interests.

The Senate rejected the amendment 34-65, with Democrats voting unanimously against it. Republicans supported the amendment 34-10, but some critics of an invasion were uneasy with an imposition of restraints on a president's ability to commit troops abroad.

Gregg and other Republicans insisted that Clinton had an obligation to come to Congress before committing thousands of troops to an operation that was widely viewed as risky. Jesse Helms, R-N.C., bluntly warned the president against intervening in Haiti.

"Surely they have not gone out of their minds entirely down there on Pennsylvania Avenue, because if the president does, in fact, do that, I suspect it will be a decision he will long regret," Helms said.

But Democrats countered that the Republicans were trying to embarrass the president for partisan reasons.

Some conservatives, such as John McCain, R-Ariz., were concerned that the amendment would set a dangerous precedent. "I cannot support any resolution which prospectively limits the powers of the president as commander in chief," he said.

In the House, Clinton avoided a rebuke when members defeated an amendment harshly criticizing the deployment in Haiti. The House adopted a milder substitute requiring reports from the president on the operation. *(Related House vote, p. 20-C)*

Congress' ambivalence over policy toward Haiti continued well after Clinton launched the military occupation of the Caribbean island nation Sept. 19. But as the mission proceeded with virtually no U.S. casualties, lawmakers adjourned without imposing significant restrictions.

10. Bosnia Arms Embargo

For more than two years, Congress had been torn by the question of whether the United States should level the military balance in the Bosnian war by providing weapons to the outgunned Muslims.

Those deep divisions were on display July 1 when the Senate cast a key vote on an amendment that would have forced President Clinton to cease complying with the international arms embargo against the former Yugoslavia and begin arming the Muslims. The House had approved similar language June 9. *(Related House vote, p. 16-C)*

The Senate was split down the middle as it rejected the proposal on a 50-50 tie. The vote came on an amendment offered by Senate Minority Leader Bob Dole, R-Kan., and Joseph I. Lieberman, D-Conn., to the fiscal 1995 defense authorization bill (S 2182).

Republicans supported the amendment 37-7, while Democrats opposed it 13-43 (ND 11-31; SD 2-12).

The Senate's action proved crucial in the back-and-forth congressional battle over the embargo.

In June, the House had approved an amendment for a mandatory end to the embargo, but House and Senate negotiators on the defense authorization bill rejected that provision. The conference committee eventually agreed on a compromise that cut off U.S. funding for enforcement of the embargo Nov. 15.

Senate proponents of the Dole-Lieberman amendment argued that the embargo favored the heavily armed Serbs, who were widely seen as the aggressors in the Bosnian conflict, by preserving their military advantage over the Muslims.

But Clinton and his top aides weighed in with a strong lobbying campaign against the amendment. The president said taking unilateral action to break the U.N.-mandated arms ban would encourage other nations to violate international sanctions that the United States supports, such as the trade sanctions against Iraq. The president's personal touch may have been decisive. Several Democrats hailed the effectiveness of the president's lobbying effort.

Democrats by and large supported an alternative nonbinding amendment, offered by Armed Services Committee Chairman Sam Nunn, D-Ga., which urged the president to seek a peaceful solution to the Bosnian conflict. That proposal was approved 52-48 on July 1.

11. Ethanol Use

A federal rule promoting the use of ethanol in reformulated gasoline engulfed the Senate in such a conflagration that it took Vice President Al Gore's tie-breaking vote to beat back a drive to kill the regulation. The vote came on an amendment to the fiscal 1995 appropriations bill for the departments of Veterans Affairs and Housing and Urban Development (HR 4624).

The vote posed a classic conflict between two industry titans — agriculture and oil — each vying for a lucrative share of the domestic energy market. The skirmish breached party lines, and instead broke along regional ones. Each side boasted powerful Senate backers: Farm-state senators who favored ethanol, a derivative of agricultural products such as corn, lined up against oil-state senators who favored methanol, a derivative of natural gas.

The issue stemmed from the 1990 rewrite of the Clean Air Act. The law required nine cities with poor air quality to begin in 1995 selling gasoline reformulated to increase its oxygen content, thereby decreasing its carbon monoxide pollution. The act had left it up to the marketplace to determine how to reformulate the gasoline.

The Environmental Protection Agency (EPA), however, proposed a rule in December 1993 requiring that at least 30 percent of the gasoline sold in certain markets contain a "renewable" oxygenate. The rule effectively required one-tenth of all gasoline sold in the United States to contain ethanol or its derivative. The EPA had concluded that the use of ethanol would cut dependence on foreign oil and lower vehicle emissions that could cause global warming.

Agriculture groups such as the National Corn Growers Association hailed the decision and rallied corn-state senators to their side. But with billions of dollars of the U.S. gasoline market at stake, the oil industry decried the rule as a political ploy by the Clinton administration to win favor in the farm belt. Oil industry lobbyists solicited the help of senators with ties to their industry.

Enter Senate Energy and Natural Resources Chairman J. Bennett Johnston, a Democrat from oil-rich Louisiana. Johnston led the charge against the regulation in committee, proposing an amendment to the VA-HUD bill to block its implementation. After fellow Democrats Bob Kerrey of Nebraska and Tom Harkin of Iowa, both corn-state senators, objected, Johnston allowed the amendment to be withdrawn at a full Appropriations Committee markup July 14.

Johnston did not give up, though. He returned to the fray Aug. 3 as the full Senate considered the VA-HUD appropriations bill. He cosponsored another amendment with Democrat Bill Bradley, whose state of New Jersey was home to many oil refineries, to deny EPA funding to carry out the rule. Johnston assailed the administration's position as "a gigantic flim-flam to the American public."

Midwestern farm-state senators mounted an impressive counterattack, saying the rule would create jobs and help clean the air. They were backed by powerful agriculture companies, most notably the Archer-Daniels-Midland Corp.

The vote broke down so strongly along regional lines that senators from just eight states split their votes, with those from the other 42 states voting the same way. Northeastern and Gulf Coast senators with petroleum interests supported Johnston's move, while senators from the nation's heartland opposed it unanimously. The division was so close that Gore had to cast his third deciding vote in the Senate since becoming vice president, killing the Johnston amendment on a tabling motion 51-50; R 19-25; D 31-25 (ND 26-16, SD 5-9).

12. Crime Bill

Given the crime bill's tortured six-year journey through Congress, it was not surprising that the last crucial votes clearing the measure Aug. 25 came after four days of partisan maneuvering and acrimonious debate.

The action came on the heels of a GOP triumph in the House, where Republican leaders forced Democrats to trim more than $3 billion from the measure before agreeing Aug. 21 to support adoption of the conference report. *(Related House votes, pp. 18-C, 19-C)*

The omnibus bill (HR 3355 — PL 103-322) represented an unprecedented federal venture into crime fighting designed to appeal to liberals, conservatives and voters fed up with crime. It included billions of dollars to hire more police officers, build more prisons and support crime-prevention programs. It also created dozens of new federal capital crimes and banned 19 types of semiautomatic assault weapons.

Surprised and emboldened by the success of their upstart House counterparts, Minority Leader Bob Dole, R-Kan., and Senate Judiciary Committee ranking Republican Orrin G. Hatch, Utah, complained that their concerns had not been considered seriously during House negotiations on the bill. Dole threatened to use Senate procedure to stall the $30.2 billion measure unless Democrats agreed to vote on several amendments to further cut spending on prevention programs and stiffen sentencing provisions.

But Democrats were in no mood to compromise. President Clinton insisted on the weapons ban, and Majority Leader George J. Mitchell, D-Maine, argued that House Democrats already had addressed GOP concerns. Other Senate Democrats accused Republicans of trying to deny Clinton a legislative victory before the November elections. "This has an awful lot to do with presidential politics," said David Pryor, D-Ark.

For the four days after the House adopted the conference report, both sides scrambled for votes to deal with a Republican plan to raise a point of order that would have blocked the bill on the grounds that it violated budget rules. Republicans said the bill's funding mechanism — a crime trust fund — had not been reviewed by the Senate Budget Committee. The GOP needed 41 votes to sustain the point of order.

The vote to waive the budget rules determined the crime bill's fate. If the point of order had been sustained, the conference report would have been invalidated and the Senate would have been forced to take up the original House-passed bill because that was the vehicle that conferees worked from. The bill, which contained no assault weapons ban, would have been open for amendment. The legislative process effectively would have reverted to a much earlier stage, which most lawmakers agreed would have killed the crime bill for the year.

Dole and Mitchell met several times in an effort to hammer out an agreement. Dole wanted up or down votes on 10 amendments, including provisions to impose mandatory minimum sentences for drug and gun offenses and to cut $5 billion in crime prevention programs. Mitchell offered to allow one vote on an amendment to cut spending on crime prevention. This amendment, which almost certainly would have been rejected, would have saved Senate Democrats from having to vote against tougher new sentences. GOP leaders rejected the offer.

With no deal in sight, the measure's fate hung with a handful of Republican moderates torn between party loyalty and their inclination to support the bill. Mitchell had support from 55 of 56 Democrats. He needed five Republicans to cross party lines to waive the budget point of order.

Dole had received 40 Republican signatures, not including his own, on a letter demanding changes in the bill. But GOP solidarity was never strong. Several of the 40 Republicans who signed the letter did so only to let Dole use it as a negotiating tool. When Mitchell offered to allow a vote on the spending-cut amendment, three moderate Republican letter-signers — John C. Danforth, Mo.; Nancy Landon Kassebaum, Kan.; and John H. Chafee, R.I. — decided that Mitchell had made a good faith effort and joined bill supporters.

In the end, the point of order was defeated 61-39: R 6-38; D 55-1 (ND 42-0, SD 13-1), with support from six Republicans: Kassebaum; Danforth; Chafee; Arlen Specter, Pa.; James M. Jeffords, Vt.; and William V. Roth Jr., Del.

Later that day, Democrats invoked cloture, 61-38, leading to final adoption of the conference report, 61-38. William S. Cohen, R-Maine, who had voted to sustain the point of order, voted for final passage. Russell D. Feingold, D-Wis., who had supported Mitchell on the point of order, voted against the bill, saying he opposed its death penalty provisions. Malcolm Wallop, R-Wyo., who had voted to sustain the point of order, missed the final vote.

13. Campaign Finance

Reformers fighting to change the way congressional campaigns were financed thought they saw the light at the end of the tunnel after seven years.

Efforts to change campaign finance laws in 1987 and 1989 died at the hands of a Senate Republican filibuster. A bill finally made it through the Senate in 1992, only to be vetoed by President George Bush.

But the new occupant of the White House, Bill Clinton, had pledged to sign a bill. And when the Senate passed an overhaul bill (S 3) on June 17, 1993, and the House followed suit on Nov. 22 of that same year, the long battle appeared to be ending. *(1993 Almanac, p. 37)*

It was not to be. Clinton turned his attention to other issues. Democrats in the House and Senate were badly divided. Democratic leaders spent almost 10 months trying to find a compromise. When they were ready to stitch one together at the last minute, it could not attract GOP votes and became one of several bills filibustered to death by Senate

Republicans in the closing days of the regular session.

Actually, the bill itself never got to the floor of the Senate in 1994. The GOP waged its war over an ordinarily routine motion to request a conference with the House on the legislation. Republican senators forced several cloture votes on procedural motions, each requiring 60 votes, and the Democrats never had a chance against a near-unanimous GOP. On the fourth such vote, on Sept. 30, only two Republicans joined with the Democratic majority to shut off debate, while six Democrats defected to the other side. That left campaign finance supporters eight votes short, 52-46: R 2-40; D 50-6 (ND 40-2, SD 10-4). Senate Majority Leader George J. Mitchell, D-Maine, said it was the first-ever cloture vote on a motion to go to conference.

Following the vote, Democratic congressional leaders proclaimed the campaign finance effort dead. "The worst case of obstruction by filibuster by any party that I've ever seen in my 30 years in Congress," declared House Speaker Thomas S. Foley, D-Wash.

But the Democrats paved the way for the bill's defeat by taking so long to come up with a final bill. Most Republicans said the Democratic plan would hurt their party, and a small group of Senate Republicans who had voted for that chamber's bill had warned in 1993 that they would not support a bill that did not meet criteria such as tight limits on political action committees (PACs) and a single system for both chambers' campaigns.

Nevertheless, the House and Senate remained deadlocked until September 1994, largely because House Democrats would not hear of PAC limits. Finally, as Congress prepared to adjourn for the fall elections, Foley agreed to restrict PAC contributions to $6,000 per election cycle instead of the existing $10,000 limit. Mitchell signed off on the compromise. But that was not enough for Senate Republicans, particularly since the bill would have set up separate rules for House and Senate campaigns. Republicans seized on the time crunch to prevent a conference from convening, and that scuttled the campaign finance effort for the fourth consecutive Congress.

14. Lobbying

The Democrats were seeing bill after bill on their agenda blocked when the Senate turned to consideration of the conference report on the lobbying disclosure and gift ban bill (S 349) in the last days of the regular session. They did not expect the same fate to befall the lobbying bill, but they were not prepared for an onslaught of opposition that stripped the already tenuous support for the bill.

The measure never even came to a final vote in the Senate. It died Oct. 6 when the Senate failed to limit debate on the measure, permitting a GOP-led filibuster to continue. The cloture motion failed 52-46 (R 7-36; D 45-10; ND 38-4, SD 7-6), and Democratic leaders pulled the bill the next day after a last-ditch effort yielded only three additional votes for cloture, which required a two-thirds vote because it would change Senate rules.

Defeat of the cloture motion ended an extraordinary odyssey for the bill. Efforts to stiffen lobbying disclosure laws had gone on for decades; restrictions on gifts to members were tagged to the bill in the Senate in 1993. Initially passed overwhelmingly by both chambers, the lobbying disclosure and gift bans were stalled for months during 1994 while House-Senate negotiators tried to work out a final bill.

The conference agreement was completed in late September, and it seemed headed for easy passage until it ran into problems in the House and was turned back in the

Senate. *(Related House vote, p. 19-C)*

Opposition to the bill emerged in the days before the vote as trade organizations and lobbying groups, many of which would have had to disclose their contributors for the first time, voiced objections about the bill's scope.

Expanding on a theme first heard in the House, Republicans seized on language that called for disclosure of the name, address and place of business of "any person or entity" who provided contributions to fund a lobbying campaign. They said that provision could be used to require grass-roots lobbying organizations to disclose information about their contributors that could chill citizen involvement in politics.

Groups as diverse as the American Civil Liberties Union and the National Right to Life Committee came out against the bill. "They know that under this legislation, their members' names will be reported," said Sen. Don Nickles, R-Okla.

In a blistering floor speech before the vote, Senate Majority Leader George J. Mitchell, D-Maine, called that assertion "a fictional objection" that senators were using "to change their position." Backing up Mitchell's assertion, several grass-roots organizations, including Public Citizen, Common Cause and United We Stand America, endorsed the bill, saying it would not infringe on their members' activities.

The chief Senate sponsor, Carl Levin, D-Mich., said that the sudden opposition to the bill was part of a GOP strategy "to stop us from doing anything significant in the way of reform, trying to persuade the public that Congress can't reform itself." *(1993 Almanac, p. 50)*

15. California Desert

After eight years of trying to protect a huge swath of California's fragile desert from developers, the Senate was faced with a crucial vote that carried serious implications for which political party would control the upper chamber after the 1994 elections.

It also paved the way for passage of the only environmental bill in 1994.

The vote came Oct. 8 on a motion to shut off debate on the conference report to a bill (S 21 — PL 103-433) that kept about 7.5 million acres of California desert away from developers and designated it as wilderness. It passed, 68-23: R 14-23; D 54-0 (ND 41-0, SD 13-0).

Republicans, led by Malcolm Wallop of Wyoming, argued that the bill would block access to the desert and that the federal government could not afford the bill's centerpiece of creating two national parks and a hunting preserve.

But the debate over substance was overshadowed by political maneuverings.

Bill sponsor Dianne Feinstein, D-Calif., who was facing a tough re-election challenge from GOP Rep. Michael Huffington, portrayed the issue as though her political future was at stake. With Republicans poised to wrest control of the Senate from the Democrats, members of both political parties agreed that the outcome of the California election could be a decisive factor in determining which political party would be in power.

A last-minute deal between Senate Majority Leader George J. Mitchell, D-Maine, and Minority Leader Bob Dole, R-Kan., meant that the vote to invoke cloture would come on a Saturday morning — about 10 hours after the House had closed up shop for the regular legislative year.

The Senate had passed the bill in April by a decisive 69-29 margin, breaking an eight-year deadlock by California Republicans on the measure. But Mitchell and Feinstein could afford to lose only nine votes to still have the necessary

60 votes to shut off debate.

Mitchell, for instance, arranged for a private plane to carry back one Democratic senator from the campaign trail and cajoled others to change their schedules.

"He made sure the fat lady never got to sing," said Barbara Boxer, D-Calif.

Feinstein persuaded colleagues such as William V. Roth Jr., R-Del.; Frank R. Lautenberg, D-N.J.; and James Sasser, D-Tenn., to suspend for a few hours their own re-election campaigning and come back to Washington for the vote. Joseph I. Lieberman, D-Conn., an Orthodox Jew, spent Friday night in a hotel near Capitol Hill so that he could observe the religious practice of not driving on Saturday, the Sabbath.

Republicans, meanwhile, furiously lobbied their own with the notion of denying Feinstein a victory and damaging her re-election bid.

Sources said a GOP caucus meeting Oct. 8 during the final hour of debate was tense with the idea that control of the Senate was hanging in the balance. But in the end, it was the balky garage door of Carol Moseley-Braun, D-Ill., that nearly thwarted the Democrats. With the voting clock ticking away and Feinstein just one vote short of the required 60, Moseley-Braun came running onto the Senate floor to cast an "aye" vote for her clearly worried friend.

Moseley-Braun's vote provided political cover for several Republicans, such as Pete V. Domenici of New Mexico and Nancy Landon Kassebaum of Kansas, who were holding back as the votes were being tallied.

Fourteen Republicans eventually voted for the bill, many of them either with moderate views on the environment or mindful of the Senate tradition of not opposing conservation measures pertaining to only one state that have the support of both senators from that state. *(Related House vote, p. 17-C)*

16. GATT

Following a 20-hour debate, the Senate on Dec. 1 gave overwhelming approval to a bill (HR 5110 — PL 103-465) to implement the Uruguay Round pact strengthening the General Agreement on Tariffs and Trade (GATT). The United States signed the agreement April 15.

The House had passed the GATT bill 288-146 on Nov. 29.

At the heart of the GATT debate was a sharp philosophical difference on U.S. trade policy. The Clinton administration insisted that the continued reduction of trade barriers would greatly benefit U.S. businesses, spurring billions of dollars in economic growth and thousands of new jobs. But opponents, led by Sen. Ernest F. Hollings, D-S.C., insisted that free-trade policies had over the years left U.S. industries vulnerable to foreign competition, destroying millions of jobs.

Congress had a longstanding pattern of supporting the free-trade viewpoint. That gave supporters of HR 5110 confidence to predict passage before the planned early October congressional adjournment.

However, it took the administration and lawmakers several months to fine-tune the GATT implementing bill, providing Hollings with an opportunity to delay action.

The bill was submitted Sept. 27 under fast-track rules for trade legislation, which allowed each chamber only an up-or-down vote on the bill without amendments. But the rules also allowed every committee chairman with jurisdiction to take up to 45 days to review the bill. Hollings, chairman of the Commerce Committee, demanded this prerogative, forcing the Democratic Senate leadership to delay the debate and vote until a two-day post-election session that began Nov. 30.

Hollings held eight Commerce Committee hearings to lay

out his case against U.S. free-trade policy. He also raised other arguments against the agreement, including the claim that the new World Trade Organization (WTO) — created under the deal to arbitrate and strictly enforce multilateral trade agreements — would impinge on U.S. legal sovereignty.

Hollings brought his critique to the Senate floor, leading the opposition during the lame-duck debate. He was parried by the GATT bill's managers, Finance Committee Chairman Daniel Patrick Moynihan, D-N.Y., and ranking Republican Bob Packwood of Oregon.

The supporters argued that the agreement would be a boon to U.S. exporters who had been hindered by other countries' trade barriers in such areas as agriculture, services and intellectual property. They rebutted the sovereignty issue, noting that the bill would require express congressional action to change any law even if the WTO had found it in violation of U.S. trade commitments.

With the numbers running against them on the merits of the bill, the opponents hung their hopes on blocking a procedural motion that required 60 votes to pass.

The Senate's pay-as-you-go budget rules required that new legislation fully offset any federal spending increases or revenue reductions over the first 10 years after enactment, an obligation that the GATT bill fell about $30 billion short of meeting.

Contending that U.S. voters had made a strong call for fiscal responsibility when they elected Republican majorities in the House and Senate on Nov. 8, the GATT opponents rallied around a point of order raised by Sen. Robert C. Byrd, D-W.Va., that HR 5110 violated the Senate budget rules. GATT supporters trumped that claim by arguing that increased economic activity spurred by the new trade deal ultimately would result in increased revenues to the federal Treasury.

A motion by Moynihan to waive the budget rules carried, 68-32: R 31-15; D 37-17 (ND 29-13, SD 8-4). The Senate then immediately voted to clear the implementing bill itself by a vote of 76-24. *(Related House vote, p. 20-C)* ■

Methodology

House scores include the votes of delegates, with the number of votes for which they were eligible under rules adopted in 1993 noted on the chart of House votes.

In most charts of individual members' scores that follow, a member's score is calculated two ways: once based on all votes, regardless of whether the member voted or not; another time based only on the votes he or she actually cast. For consistency with previous years, graphs and breakdowns of chambers, parties and regions are based on the first set of scores. Lists of individual leaders are based on votes cast, not counting absences. *(Methodology, 1987 CQ Almanac, p. 22-C)*

Scores are rounded off to the nearest percentage point, except that no score is rounded up to 100 percent.

Congressional Quarterly defines regions of the United States as follows: **East:** Conn., Del., Maine, Md., Mass., N.H., N.J., N.Y., Pa., R.I., Vt., W.Va. **West:** Alaska, Ariz., Calif., Colo., Hawaii, Idaho, Mont., Nev., N.M., Ore., Utah, Wash., Wyo. **South:** Ala., Ark., Fla., Ga., Ky., La., Miss., N.C., Okla., S.C., Tenn., Texas, Va. **Midwest:** Ill., Ind., Iowa, Kan., Mich., Minn., Mo., Neb., N.D., Ohio, S.D., Wis.

Presidential Support Definitions

Congressional Quarterly determines presidential positions on congressional votes by examining the statements made by President Clinton or his authorized spokesmen. *Support* measures the percentage of the time members voted in accord with the position of the president. *Opposition* measures the percentage of the time members voted against the president's position. *Success* measures the percentage of the contested votes on which the president prevailed. Absences lowered parties' scores.

National Security vs. Domestic Issues

Following are 1994 presidential success scores broken down into domestic and national security issues, with national security including foreign policy and defense. Scores for 1993 are in parentheses:

	National Security		Domestic		Average	
Senate	78%	(93)	90%	(84)	86%	(85)
House	86%	(80)	88%	(90)	87%	(87)
Average	82%	(85)	89%	(87)	86%	(86)

Average Scores

Scores for 1993 are in parentheses:

	Support					**Opposition**			
	Democrats		**Republicans**			**Democrats**		**Republicans**	
Senate	86%	(87)	42%	(29)	Senate	11%	(11)	54%	(68)
House	75%	(77)	47%	(39)	House	20%	(20)	50%	(59)

Regional Averages

Scores for 1993 are in parentheses:

	Support								**Opposition**							
	East		**West**		**South**		**Midwest**			**East**		**West**		**South**		**Midwest**	
Democrats									**Democrats**							
Senate	87%	(92)	88%	(86)	84%	(82)	85%	(87)	Senate	10%	(7)	10%	(11)	11%	(16)	14%	(11)
House	74	(76)	77	(78)	75	(78)	73	(74)	House	21	(20)	19	(19)	20	(19)	22	(23)
Republicans									**Republicans**							
Senate	52	(37)	40	(27)	35	(23)	47	(34)	Senate	45	(60)	56	(70)	61	(76)	51	(64)
House	56	(49)	43	(34)	43	(35)	46	(38)	House	40	(49)	54	(63)	54	(63)	51	(60)

Success Rate History

Average scores for both chambers of Congress:

Eisenhower		Johnson		Ford		Reagan		Bush	
1953	89.0%	1964	88.0%	1974	58.2%	1981	82.4%	1989	62.6%
1954	82.8	1965	93.0	1975	61.0	1982	72.4	1990	46.8
1955	75.0	1966	79.0	1976	53.8	1983	67.1	1991	54.2
1956	70.0	1967	79.0			1984	65.8	1992	43.0
1957	68.0	1968	75.0			1985	59.9		
1958	76.0	**Nixon**				1986	56.1	**Clinton**	
1959	52.0			**Carter**		1987	43.5		
1960	65.0	1969	74.0	1977	75.4%	1988	47.4	1993	86.4%
Kennedy		1970	77.0	1978	78.3			1994	86.4
		1971	75.0	1979	76.8				
1961	81.0%	1972	66.0	1980	75.1				
1962	85.4	1973	50.6						
1963	87.1	1974	59.6						

1994 Senate Presidential Position Votes

The following is a list of Senate votes in 1994 on which there was a clear presidential position, listed by roll call number with a brief description and categorized by topic. *(Definition, p. 29-C)*

Vote Number	Description

Domestic Policy

19 Victories

Vote Number	Description
32	Education
34	Education
60	Competitiveness
76	Federal employees (cloture)
77	Federal employees
86	Education
89	California desert
108	Environmental technology
109	Head Start
112	Abortion clinic access
122	Safe drinking water
252	Education
253	Space station
255	Ethanol
293	Crime
294	Crime (cloture)
295	Crime
321	Education
326	California desert

4 Defeats

Vote Number	Description
75	Federal employees (cloture)
175	Liquid metal reactor
314	Campaign finance (cloture)
325	Lobbying disclosure (cloture)

Nominations

15 Victories

Vote Number	Description
23	William J. Perry confirmation
33	M. Larry Lawrence confirmation
46	Strobe Talbott confirmation
49	William B. Gould IV confirmation
92	Rosemary Barkett confirmation
93	Adm. Frank B. Kelso II retirement
130	Derek Shearer confirmation
147	Lori Fitz-Pegado confirmation (recommit)
148	Lori Fitz-Pegado confirmation
242	Stephen G. Breyer nomination
281	Janet L. Yellen confirmation
300	Adm. Henry H. Mauz confirmation
317	Ricki R. Tigert confirmation
319	H. Lee Sorokin confirmation
327	Lt. Gen. Buster C. Glosson retirement

1 Defeat

Vote Number	Description
132	Sam W. Brown Jr. confirmation (cloture)

Defense and Foreign Policy

11 Victories

Vote Number	Description
40	Peacekeeping funds
110	Bosnia arms embargo
162	Transport planes
165	Peacekeeping funds
172	Haiti operations
181	Bosnia arms embargo
187	Israel peacekeeping
194	Haiti operations
263	Haiti operations
279	Bosnia arms embargo
297	Defense spending

4 Defeats

Vote Number	Description
111	Bosnia arms embargo
179	Stealth bombers
226	U.N. peacekeeping
280	Bosnia arms embargo

Economic Affairs and Trade

8 Victories

Vote Number	Description
35	Supplemental funds
45	Supplemental funds
48	Balanced-budget amendment
66	Budget
82	Budget
298	Banking
328	General Agreement on Tariffs and Trade
329	General Agreement on Tariffs and Trade

0 Defeats

Senate Success Rate

Victories	53
Defeats	9
Total	62
Success Rate	85.5%

1994 House Presidential Position Votes

The following is a list of House votes in 1994 on which there was a clear presidential position, listed by roll call number with a brief description and categorized by topic. *(Definition, p. 29-C)*

Vote Number	Description	Vote Number	Description
	Domestic Policy		**Defense and Foreign Policy**
	39 Victories		**15 Victories**
19	Independent counsel	8	Peacekeeping funds
23	Independent counsel	51	Defense spending
25	Federal employees	146	Iraqi claims
81	Housing	147	Vietnam embargo
86	Education	179	Missile defense
90	Lobbying disclosure	180	Burdensharing
94	Education	188	Trident II missiles
95	Education	189	Trident II missiles
107	Crime	192	Selective Service System
124	Crime	194	Base closures
128	Education	195	Transport planes
138	Crime	198	U.N. peacekeeping
144	Crime	332	Intelligence disclosure
153	National Science Foundation	404	Defense spending
156	Assault weapons	497	Haiti operations
159	Abortion clinic access		
170	Head Start		**3 Defeats**
174	Montana wilderness		
251	Amtrak	187	Burdensharing
258	Independent counsel	222	Bosnia arms embargo
259	Housing funds	223	Bosnia arms embargo
260	Biological survey		
263	National Endowment for the Arts		**Economic Affairs and Trade**
265	National Endowment for the Arts		
292	Telecommunications		**14 Victories**
293	Telecommunications		
309	Space station	9	Supplemental funds
349	Housing	10	Supplemental funds
357	California desert	13	Supplemental funds
363	National parks	27	Supplemental funds
371	Maritime Administration	55	Budget
411	Presidio management	56	Budget
414	Crime	65	Balanced-budget amendment
415	Crime	112	Budget
416	Crime	168	Economic Development Administration
425	Procurement overhaul	346	Entitlement spending
428	Small Business Administration	381	China MFN
451	Lobbying disclosure	382	China MFN
456	Education	383	China MFN
		507	General Agreement on Tariffs and Trade
	7 Defeats		
			0 Defeats
122	Crime		
136	Crime		
148	Federal employees		
234	Helium reactor		
250	Interstate Commerce Commission		
270	National Endowment for the Arts		
394	Crime		

House Success Rate

Victories	68
Defeats	10
Total	78
Success Rate	87.2%

Presidential Support and Opposition: House

1. Clinton Support Score, 1994. Percentage of 78 recorded votes in 1994 on which President Clinton took a position and on which a representative voted "yea" or "nay" *in agreement* with the president's position. Failures to vote lowered both support and opposition scores.

2. Clinton Opposition Score, 1994. Percentage of 78 recorded votes in 1994 on which President Clinton took a position and on which a representative voted "yea" or "nay" *in disagreement* with the president's position. Failures to vote lowered both support and opposition scores.

3. Clinton Support Score, 1994. Percentage of 78 recorded votes in 1994 on which President Clinton took a position and on which a representative was present and voted "yea" or "nay" *in agreement* with the president's position. In this version of the study, absences were not counted; therefore, failures to vote did not lower support or opposition scores. Opposition scores, not listed here, are the inverse of the support score; i.e., the opposition score is equal to 100 percent minus the individual's support score.

NOTE: Delegates were eligible for 35 of the 78 presidential support votes in 1994.

[1] *Ron Lewis, R-Ky., was sworn in May 26, 1994, to succeed William H. Natcher, D-Ky., who died March 29. Natcher was eligible for 17 presidential support votes in 1994. His presidential support score was 47 percent; opposition score, 0 percent; support score, adjusted for absences, 100 percent. Lewis was eligible for 35 presidential support votes in 1994.*

[2] *Dean A. Gallo, R-N.J., died Nov. 6, 1994. He was eligible for 77 presidential support votes in 1994.*

[3] *James M. Inhofe, R-Okla., resigned Nov. 15, 1994, to replace Sen. David L. Boren, D-Okla. Inhofe was eligible for 77 presidential support votes in 1994. Steve Largent, R-Okla., was sworn in Nov. 29, 1994, to replace Inhofe. Largent was eligible for one presidential support vote in 1994. His presidential support score was 0 percent; opposition score, 100 percent; support score, adjusted for absences, 0 percent.*

[4] *Frank D. Lucas, R-Okla., was sworn in May 17, 1994, to succeed Glenn English, D-Okla., who resigned effective Jan. 7, 1994. Lucas was eligible for 45 presidential support votes in 1994. English was eligible for no presidential support votes in 1994.*

[5] *Rep. Thomas S. Foley, D-Wash., as Speaker of the House, voted at his discretion on 14 presidential support votes in 1994.*

KEY

† Not eligible for all recorded votes in 1994 or voted "present" to avoid possible conflict of interest.

Democrats | *Republicans* | *Independent*

	1	2	3
Alabama			
1 *Callahan*	38	55	41
2 *Everett*	44	55	44
3 Browder	77	23	77
4 Bevill	87	12	88
5 Cramer	85	14	86
6 *Bachus*	44	56	44
7 Hilliard	69	23	75
Alaska			
AL *Young*	44	54	45
Arizona			
1 Coppersmith	78	22	78
2 Pastor	83	15	84
3 *Stump*	27	73	27
4 *Kyl*	41	53	44
5 *Kolbe*	50	47	51
6 English†	69	27	72
Arkansas			
1 Lambert	72	27	73
2 Thornton	88	10	90
3 *Hutchinson*	38	62	38
4 *Dickey*	42	58	42
California			
1 Hamburg	76	24	76
2 *Herger*	36	56	39
3 Fazio	87	13	87
4 *Doolittle*	35	60	36
5 Matsui	86	6	93
6 Woolsey	77	23	77
7 Miller	72	19	79
8 Pelosi	74	19	79
9 Dellums	74	26	74
10 *Baker*	40	56	41
11 *Pombo*	38	58	40
12 Lantos	79	15	84
13 Stark	72	21	78
14 Eshoo	81	19	81
15 Mineta	85	9	90
16 Edwards	77	21	79
17 Farr	81	15	84
18 Condit	63	32	66
19 Lehman	72	19	79
20 Dooley	69	24	74
21 *Thomas*	47	46	51
22 *Huffington*	60	28	68
23 *Gallegly*	49	42	54
24 Beilenson	85	15	85
25 *McKeon*	47	51	48
26 Berman	83	15	84
27 *Moorhead*	41	59	41
28 *Dreier*	38	62	38
29 Waxman	76	23	77
30 Becerra	73	21	78
31 Martinez	83	14	86
32 Dixon	87	9	91
33 Roybal-Allard	87	13	87
34 Torres	90	6	93
35 Waters	72	24	75
36 Harman	86	12	88
37 Tucker	63	19	77
38 *Horn*	65	29	69
39 *Royce*	32	63	34
40 *Lewis*	50	41	55
41 *Kim*	44	56	44

	1	2	3
42 Brown	82	10	89
43 *Calvert*	55	40	58
44 *McCandless*	45	54	45
45 *Rohrabacher*	28	71	29
46 *Dornan*	35	60	36
47 *Cox*	36	60	37
48 *Packard*	45	55	45
49 Schenk	77	22	78
50 Filner	79	21	79
51 *Cunningham*	55	45	55
52 *Hunter*	33	67	33
Colorado			
1 Schroeder	74	26	74
2 Skaggs	90	10	90
3 *McInnis*	42	56	43
4 *Allard*	40	60	40
5 *Hefley*	32	65	33
6 *Schaefer*	35	65	35
Connecticut			
1 Kennelly	90	10	90
2 Gejdenson	87	13	87
3 DeLauro	82	13	86
4 *Shays*	56	44	56
5 *Franks*	71	28	71
6 *Johnson*	67	31	68
Delaware			
AL *Castle*	71	29	71
Florida			
1 Hutto	68	26	73
2 Peterson	82	15	84
3 Brown	88	10	90
4 *Fowler*	62	37	62
5 Thurman	73	27	73
6 *Stearns*	35	64	35
7 *Mica*	41	58	42
8 *McCollum*	40	51	44
9 *Bilirakis*	47	47	50
10 *Young*	54	44	55
11 Gibbons	83	9	90
12 *Canady*	54	46	54
13 *Miller*	41	58	42
14 *Goss*	51	49	51
15 *Bacchus*	83	13	87
16 *Lewis*	32	51	38
17 Meek	83	14	86
18 *Ros-Lehtinen*	58	37	61
19 Johnston	81	17	83
20 Deutsch	83	15	84
21 *Diaz-Balart*	60	38	61
22 *Shaw*	60	35	64
23 Hastings	64	18	78
Georgia			
1 *Kingston*	42	56	43
2 Bishop	88	10	90
3 *Collins*	36	63	36
4 *Linder*	46	54	46
5 Lewis	71	26	73
6 *Gingrich*	44	54	45
7 Darden	87	12	88
8 Rowland	78	17	82
9 Deal	63	36	64
10 Johnson	86	14	86
11 McKinney	77	23	77
Hawaii			
1 Abercrombie	71	27	72
2 Mink	74	26	74
Idaho			
1 LaRocco	78	22	78
2 *Crapo*	40	60	40
Illinois			
1 Rush	68	24	74
2 Reynolds	69	12	86
3 Lipinski	72	26	74
4 Gutierrez	63	28	69
5 Rostenkowski	78	15	84
6 *Hyde*	54	46	54
7 Collins	58	24	70
8 *Crane*	24	60	29
9 Yates	72	28	72
10 *Porter*	54	45	55
11 Sangmeister	79	18	82
12 Costello	73	27	73
13 *Fawell*	51	49	51
14 *Hastert*	45	50	47
15 *Ewing*	41	54	43
16 *Manzullo*	46	54	46
17 Evans	77	23	77

ND Northern Democrats   SD Southern Democrats

	1	2	3
18 *Michel*	46	36	56
19 Poshard	63	37	63
20 Durbin	78	22	78

Indiana
	1	2	3
1 Visclosky	91	9	91
2 Sharp	73	17	81
3 Roemer	83	17	83
4 Long	73	23	76
5 *Buyer*	50	50	50
6 *Burton*	28	71	29
7 *Myers*	42	58	42
8 McCloskey	85	15	85
9 Hamilton	82	18	82
10 Jacobs	69	28	71

Iowa
	1	2	3
1 *Leach*	63	35	64
2 *Nussle*	42	56	43
3 *Lightfoot*	50	47	51
4 Smith	81	14	85
5 *Grandy*	35	22	61

Kansas
	1	2	3
1 *Roberts*	38	58	40
2 Slattery	56	6	90
3 *Meyers*	69	29	70
4 Glickman	82	17	83

Kentucky
	1	2	3
1 Barlow	67	17	80
2 *Lewis* [1]†	40	60	40
3 Mazzoli	83	15	84
4 *Bunning*	31	69	31
5 *Rogers*	47	49	49
6 Baesler	85	15	85

Louisiana
	1	2	3
1 *Livingston*	41	54	43
2 Jefferson	85	10	89
3 Tauzin	54	42	56
4 Fields	74	23	76
5 *McCrery*	53	41	56
6 *Baker*	46	51	47
7 Hayes	55	37	60

Maine
	1	2	3
1 Andrews	77	23	77
2 *Snowe*	59	40	60

Maryland
	1	2	3
1 *Gilchrest*	64	36	64
2 *Bentley*	50	42	54
3 Cardin	74	19	79
4 Wynn	82	18	82
5 Hoyer	86	14	84
6 *Bartlett*	40	60	40
7 Mfume	69	26	73
8 *Morella*	76	22	78

Massachusetts
	1	2	3
1 Olver	78	22	78
2 Neal	77	21	79
3 *Blute*	68	32	68
4 Frank	69	31	69
5 Meehan	68	29	70
6 *Torkildsen*	73	27	73
7 Markey	71	22	76
8 Kennedy	76	22	78
9 Moakley	78	22	78
10 Studds	82	18	82

Michigan
	1	2	3
1 Stupak	72	28	72
2 *Hoekstra*	40	60	40
3 *Ehlers*	47	53	47
4 *Camp*	51	49	51
5 Barcia	64	36	64
6 *Upton*	49	51	49
7 *Smith*	45	51	47
8 Carr	73	17	81
9 Kildee	77	23	77
10 Bonior	79	21	79
11 *Knollenberg*	44	56	44
12 Levin	83	15	84
13 Ford	63	21	75
14 Conyers	71	24	74
15 Collins	65	29	69
16 Dingell	76	17	82

Minnesota
	1	2	3
1 Penny	54	46	54
2 Minge	68	32	68
3 *Ramstad*	55	45	55
4 Vento	76	22	78
5 Sabo	83	17	83
6 *Grams*	36	56	39
7 Peterson	58	42	58
8 Oberstar	72	26	74

Mississippi
	1	2	3
1 Whitten	62	13	83
2 Thompson	86	12	88
3 Montgomery	78	21	79
4 Parker	64	31	68
5 Taylor	60	40	60

Missouri
	1	2	3
1 Clay	60	24	71
2 *Talent*	50	49	51
3 Gephardt	86	9	91
4 Skelton	78	22	78
5 Wheat	68	18	79
6 Danner	69	29	70
7 *Hancock*	29	71	29
8 *Emerson*	44	49	47
9 Volkmer	72	26	74

Montana
	1	2	3
AL Williams	72	26	74

Nebraska
	1	2	3
1 *Bereuter*	55	45	55
2 Hoagland	83	14	86
3 *Barrett*	46	51	47

Nevada
	1	2	3
1 Bilbray	77	23	77
2 *Vucanovich*	50	45	53

New Hampshire
	1	2	3
1 *Zeliff*	49	49	50
2 Swett	71	28	71

New Jersey
	1	2	3
1 Andrews	68	28	71
2 Hughes	86	13	87
3 *Saxton*	63	37	63
4 *Smith*	53	45	54
5 *Roukema*	62	31	67
6 Pallone	71	29	71
7 *Franks*	54	45	55
8 Klein	81	17	83
9 Torricelli	72	21	78
10 Payne	73	26	74
11 *Gallo* [2]†	38	19	66
12 *Zimmer*	44	56	44
13 Menendez	79	21	79

New Mexico
	1	2	3
1 *Schiff*	53	47	53
2 *Skeen*	53	47	53
3 Richardson	86	10	89

New York
	1	2	3
1 Hochbrueckner	87	13	87
2 *Lazio*	72	28	72
3 *King*	45	54	45
4 *Levy*	56	44	56
5 Ackerman	74	14	81
6 Flake	74	14	84
7 Manton	83	14	86
8 Nadler	72	26	74
9 Schumer	79	17	83
10 Towns	67	15	81
11 Owens	63	23	73
12 Velazquez	71	28	71
13 *Molinari*	60	40	60
14 Maloney	74	23	76
15 Rangel	72	18	80
16 Serrano	71	26	73
17 Engel	78	19	80
18 Lowey	82	18	82
19 *Fish*	50	33	60
20 *Gilman*	71	28	71
21 McNulty	69	23	75
22 *Solomon*	32	60	35
23 *Boehlert*	71	28	71
24 *McHugh*	51	49	51
25 *Walsh*	69	29	70
26 Hinchey	78	21	79
27 *Paxon*	35	65	35
28 Slaughter	82	18	82
29 LaFalce	82	12	88
30 *Quinn*	60	35	64
31 Houghton	68	27	72

North Carolina
	1	2	3
1 Clayton	81	18	82
2 Valentine	69	22	76
3 Lancaster	77	23	77
4 Price	83	15	84
5 Neal	69	15	82
6 *Coble*	28	72	28
7 Rose	77	18	81
8 Hefner	79	21	79
9 *McMillan*	55	35	61
10 *Ballenger*	35	62	36
11 *Taylor*	36	63	36
12 Watt	73	27	73

North Dakota
	1	2	3
AL Pomeroy	76	21	79

Ohio
	1	2	3
1 Mann	82	18	82
2 *Portman*	44	54	45
3 Hall	77	18	81
4 *Oxley*	47	51	48
5 *Gillmor*	63	36	64
6 Strickland	72	27	73
7 *Hobson*	58	42	58
8 *Boehner*	37	60	38
9 Kaptur	76	19	80
10 *Hoke*	44	53	45
11 Stokes	71	27	72
12 *Kasich*	46	53	47
13 Brown	64	36	64
14 Sawyer	90	8	92
15 *Pryce*	55	45	55
16 *Regula*	59	41	59
17 Traficant	68	32	68
18 Applegate	72	22	77
19 Fingerhut	73	24	75

Oklahoma
	1	2	3
1 *Inhofe* [3]†	40	49	45
2 Synar	72	21	78
3 Brewster	73	24	75
4 McCurdy	71	18	80
5 *Istook*	36	59	38
6 *Lucas* [4]†	49	51	49

Oregon
	1	2	3
1 Furse	79	19	81
2 *Smith*	47	44	52
3 Wyden	79	19	81
4 DeFazio	56	35	62
5 Kopetski	74	17	82

Pennsylvania
	1	2	3
1 Foglietta	78	18	81
2 Blackwell	72	15	82
3 Borski	86	14	86
4 Klink	72	28	72
5 *Clinger*	58	40	59
6 Holden	68	32	68
7 *Weldon*	63	33	65
8 *Greenwood*	65	29	69
9 *Shuster*	45	54	45
10 *McDade*	62	28	69
11 Kanjorski	82	18	82
12 Murtha	81	14	85
13 Margolies-Mezv.	64	33	66
14 Coyne	74	24	75
15 McHale	78	22	78
16 *Walker*	31	69	31
17 *Gekas*	41	59	41
18 *Santorum*	51	41	56
19 *Goodling*	46	54	46
20 Murphy	64	21	76
21 *Ridge*	45	35	56

Rhode Island
	1	2	3
1 *Machtley*	63	24	72
2 Reed	90	9	91

South Carolina
	1	2	3
1 *Ravenel*	49	46	51
2 *Spence*	53	46	53
3 Derrick	78	12	87
4 *Inglis*	38	62	38
5 Spratt	81	18	82
6 Clyburn	85	10	89

South Dakota
	1	2	3
AL Johnson	81	18	82

Tennessee
	1	2	3
1 *Quillen*	46	49	49
2 *Duncan*	24	74	25
3 Lloyd	72	9	89
4 Cooper	69	28	71
5 Clement	81	17	83
6 Gordon	73	23	76
7 *Sundquist*	42	40	52
8 Tanner	74	26	74
9 Ford	67	14	83

Texas
	1	2	3
1 Chapman	67	24	73
2 Wilson	68	23	75
3 *Johnson, Sam*	37	63	37
4 Hall	54	46	54
5 Bryant	76	17	82
6 *Barton*	33	55	38
7 *Archer*	33	67	33
8 *Fields*	36	56	39
9 Brooks	74	13	85
10 Pickle	77	13	86
11 Edwards	82	18	82
12 Geren	68	31	69
13 Sarpalius	69	31	69
14 Laughlin	68	21	77
15 de la Garza	73	21	78
16 Coleman	83	12	88
17 Stenholm	53	47	53
18 Washington	21	9	70
19 *Combest*	40	59	40
20 Gonzalez	78	19	80
21 *Smith*	41	54	43
22 *DeLay*	31	68	31
23 *Bonilla*	44	56	44
24 Frost	76	13	86
25 Andrews	73	13	85
26 *Armey*	37	62	38
27 Ortiz	73	19	79
28 Tejeda	78	22	78
29 Green	68	19	78
30 Johnson, E. B.	85	14	86

Utah
	1	2	3
1 *Hansen*	36	60	37
2 Shepherd	74	21	78
3 Orton	59	37	61

Vermont
	1	2	3
AL *Sanders*	73	27	73

Virginia
	1	2	3
1 *Bateman*	60	40	60
2 Pickett	76	22	78
3 Scott	82	18	82
4 Sisisky	79	19	81
5 Payne	76	23	77
6 *Goodlatte*	37	59	39
7 *Bliley*	44	55	44
8 Moran	86	12	88
9 Boucher	76	19	80
10 *Wolf*	53	46	53
11 Byrne	81	17	83

Washington
	1	2	3
1 Cantwell	86	14	86
2 Swift	86	12	88
3 Unsoeld	74	26	74
4 Inslee	78	22	78
5 Foley [5]			
6 Dicks	90	9	91
7 McDermott	78	21	79
8 *Dunn*	54	45	55
9 Kreidler	81	19	81

West Virginia
	1	2	3
1 Mollohan	74	24	75
2 Wise	81	18	82
3 Rahall	64	35	65

Wisconsin
	1	2	3
1 Barca	67	33	67
2 *Klug*	51	49	51
3 *Gunderson*	53	47	53
4 Kleczka	86	13	87
5 Barrett	74	22	77
6 *Petri*	41	59	41
7 Obey	71	27	72
8 *Roth*	33	63	35
9 *Sensenbrenner*	21	79	21

Wyoming
	1	2	3
AL *Thomas*	40	55	42

Delegates
	1	2	3
de Lugo, V.I.	69	29	71
Faleomavaega, Am.S.	51	3	95
Norton, D.C.	54	46	54
Romero-B., P.R.	60	17	78
Underwood, Guam	49	29	63

Southern states - Ala., Ark., Fla., Ga., Ky., La., Miss., N.C., Okla., S.C., Tenn., Texas, Va.
Omitted votes are quorum calls, which CQ does not include in its vote charts.

KEY

† Not eligible for all recorded votes in 1994 or voted "present" to avoid possible conflict of interest.

	1	2	3
Alabama			
Heflin	82	15	85
Shelby [1]	53	26	67
Alaska			
Murkowski	32	61	34
Stevens	45	42	52
Arizona			
DeConcini	82	16	84
McCain	42	53	44
Arkansas			
Bumpers	95	5	95
Pryor	90	5	95
California			
Boxer	85	13	87
Feinstein	92	8	92
Colorado			
Campbell	81	16	83
Brown	21	77	21
Connecticut			
Dodd	90	5	95
Lieberman	85	11	88
Delaware			
Biden	82	10	89
Roth	56	44	56
Florida			
Graham	90	8	92
Mack	40	60	40
Georgia			
Nunn	89	11	89
Coverdell	35	65	35
Hawaii			
Akaka	97	3	97
Inouye	92	5	95
Idaho			
Craig	29	69	30
Kempthorne	31	69	31
Illinois			
Moseley-Braun	82	13	86
Simon	84	15	85
Indiana			
Coats	42	58	42
Lugar	45	55	45

	1	2	3
Iowa			
Harkin	90	8	92
Grassley	34	66	34
Kansas			
Dole	35	65	35
Kassebaum	74	26	74
Kentucky			
Ford	90	8	92
McConnell	35	61	37
Louisiana			
Breaux	81	15	85
Johnston	85	8	91
Maine			
Mitchell	97	3	97
Cohen	60	35	63
Maryland			
Mikulski	89	6	93
Sarbanes	95	5	95
Massachusetts			
Kennedy	90	5	95
Kerry	89	10	90
Michigan			
Levin	90	10	90
Riegle	94	3	97
Minnesota			
Wellstone	81	18	82
Durenberger	55	37	60
Mississippi			
Cochran	45	55	45
Lott	39	58	40
Missouri			
Bond	47	48	49
Danforth	61	35	63
Montana			
Baucus	89	11	89
Burns	42	55	43
Nebraska			
Exon	84	16	84
Kerrey	89	10	90
Nevada			
Bryan	82	15	85
Reid	90	10	90

	1	2	3
New Hampshire			
Gregg	40	56	42
Smith	19	79	20
New Jersey			
Bradley	73	18	80
Lautenberg	81	18	82
New Mexico			
Bingaman	89	11	89
Domenici	53	47	53
New York			
Moynihan	84	16	84
D'Amato	34	65	34
North Carolina			
Faircloth	23	73	24
Helms	18	76	19
North Dakota			
Conrad	89	11	89
Dorgan	81	19	81
Ohio			
Glenn	92	5	95
Metzenbaum	81	16	83
Oklahoma			
Boren [2]†	82	13	86
Nickles	24	73	25
Oregon			
Hatfield	74	23	77
Packwood	52	42	55
Pennsylvania			
Wofford	87	13	87
Specter	55	44	56
Rhode Island			
Pell	94	2	98
Chafee	76	19	80
South Carolina			
Hollings	81	13	86
Thurmond	39	60	39
South Dakota			
Daschle	94	6	94
Pressler	34	66	34
Tennessee			
Mathews	89	10	90
Sasser	89	10	90

Democrats   *Republicans*

■■■

	1	2	3
Texas			
Gramm	32	56	36
Hutchison	34	56	38
Utah			
Bennett	35	58	38
Hatch	37	63	37
Vermont			
Leahy	89	11	89
Jeffords	77	21	79
Virginia			
Robb	85	15	85
Warner	58	39	60
Washington			
Murray	94	6	94
Gorton	48	52	48
West Virginia			
Byrd	74	26	74
Rockefeller	92	3	97
Wisconsin			
Feingold	65	35	65
Kohl	81	19	81
Wyoming			
Simpson	39	58	40
Wallop	19	68	22

Presidential Support and Opposition: Senate

1. Clinton Support Score, 1994. Percentage of 62 recorded votes in 1994 on which President Clinton took a position and on which a senator voted "yea" or "nay" *in agreement* with the president's position. Failures to vote lowered both support and opposition scores.

2. Clinton Opposition Score, 1994. Percentage of 62 recorded votes in 1994 on which President Clinton took a position and on which a senator voted "yea" or "nay" *in disagreement* with the president's position. Failures to vote lowered both support and opposition scores.

3. Clinton Support Score, 1994. Percentage of 62 recorded votes in 1994 on which President Clinton took a position and on which a senator was present and voted "yea" or "nay" *in agreement* with the president's position. In this version of the study, absences were not counted; therefore, failures to vote did not lower support or opposition scores. Opposition scores, not listed here, are the inverse of the support score; i.e., the opposition score is equal to 100 percent minus the individual's support score.

[1] *Richard C. Shelby, Ala., switched to the Republican Party on Nov. 9, 1994. As a Democrat, he was eligible for 60 presidential support votes in 1994; as a Republican, he was eligible for two presidential support votes in 1994. His presidential support score includes votes he cast both as a Democrat and a Republican.*

[2] *David L. Boren, D-Okla., resigned Nov. 15, 1994. He was eligible for 60 presidential support votes in 1994. James M. Inhofe, R-Okla., was sworn in Nov. 17, 1994, replacing Boren. Inhofe was eligible for two presidential support votes in 1994. His presidential support score was 0 percent; opposition score, 100 percent; support score, adjusted for absences, 0 percent.*

Party Unity Definitions

Party unity votes. Recorded votes in the Senate or the House that split the parties, with a majority of voting Democrats opposing a majority of voting Republicans.

Party unity support. Percentage of party unity votes on which members voted "yea" or "nay" *in agreement* with a majority of their party. Failures to vote lowered scores for chambers and parties.

Opposition to party. Percentage of party unity votes on which members voted "yea" or "nay" *in disagreement* with a majority of their party. Failures to vote lowered scores for chambers and parties.

Average Scores by Chamber

	1994		1993			1994		1993	
	Dem.	Rep.	Dem.	Rep.		Dem.	Rep.	Dem.	Rep.
Party Unity	83%	83%	85%	84%	**Opposition**	11%	13%	11%	13%
Senate	84	79	85	84	Senate	14	18	13	14
House	83	84	85	84	House	11	12	11	12

Sectional Support, Opposition

SENATE	Support	Opposition	HOUSE	Support	Opposition
Northern Democrats	87%	11%	Northern Democrats	86%	8%
Southern Democrats	74	22	Southern Democrats	77	16
Northern Republicans	76	22	Northern Republicans	82	14
Southern Republicans	89	8	Southern Republicans	87	9

1994 Victories, Defeats

	Senate	House	Total
Democrats won, Republicans lost	129	257	386
Republicans won, Democrats lost	41	50	91

Unanimous Voting by Parties

The number of times each party voted unanimously on 1994 party unity votes. Scores for 1993 in parentheses:

	Senate		House		Total	
Democrats voted unanimously	37	(29)	7	(13)	44	(42)
Republicans voted unanimously	19	(57)	38	(65)	57	(122)

Party Unity Average Scores

Average scores for each party in both chambers of Congress:

Year	Democrats	Republicans	Year	Democrats	Republicans
1961	71%	72%	1978	64%	67%
1962	69	68	1979		69 72
1963	71	72	1980	68	70
1964	67	69	1981	69	76
1965	69	70	1982	72	71
1966	61	67	1983	76	74
1967	66	71	1984	74	72
1968	57	63	1985	79	75
1969	62	62	1986	78	71
1970	57	59	1987	81	74
1971	62	66	1988	79	73
1972	57	64	1989	81	73
1973	68	68	1990	81	74
1974	63	62	1991	81	78
1975	69	70	1992	79	79
1976	65	66	1993	85	84
1977	67	70	1994	83	83

1994 Party Unity Votes

Following are the votes, by roll call number, on which a majority of Democrats voted against a majority of Republicans.

House

(307 of 497 "yea/nay" votes)

2	40	76	110	154	182	214	245	269	303	346	384	414	450	484
3	42	79	112	155	183	215	246	271	305	348	386	415	451	485
4	43	80	115	156	184	216	247	273	306	352	389	416	452	486
5	44	83	119	157	185	218	248	274	307	353	391	418	453	488
6	50	84	120	158	186	219	249	275	308	355	393	419	454	489
9	53	85	121	159	187	222	250	276	310	356	394	420	455	490
10	55	86	123	160	188	223	251	277	311	357	395	427	456	491
12	56	87	125	161	189	224	253	278	315	360	396	429	463	495
14	57	88	126	162	190	225	254	279	316	361	398	430	464	497
15	58	89	127	163	191	226	255	280	317	362	399	431	465	498
16	60	91	131	164	196	227	256	281	318	364	400	432	466	500
17	62	93	132	165	197	231	257	282	320	365	401	433	467	501
18	63	94	137	166	198	233	258	285	321	366	404	435	468	506
19	65	95	138	171	201	236	260	287	322	367	405	436	469	
21	66	98	140	172	202	237	261	288	325	368	406	438	470	
22	67	100	143	174	203	238	262	290	326	370	407	439	471	
28	68	101	144	175	205	239	263	291	327	371	409	440	473	
34	69	102	145	176	206	240	265	294	332	372	410	442	474	
36	70	103	147	179	209	241	266	295	341	373	411	445	480	
37	71	105	150	180	210	242	267	297	342	374	412	447	481	
38	74	109	151	181	213	244	268	302	343	380	413	449	482	

Senate

(170 of 329 "yea/nay" votes)

3	32	52	73	88	113	132	148	172	194	220	245	268	294	325
5	34	53	74	89	115	137	152	174	195	223	247	269	295	326
6	37	55	75	92	116	138	153	175	197	226	248	273	302	
11	38	58	76	93	118	139	154	176	198	227	251	274	305	
15	41	59	78	101	119	140	155	177	199	230	253	275	308	
16	43	60	79	103	120	141	156	179	201	233	255	277	309	
17	44	64	80	104	121	142	160	180	207	236	256	278	313	
20	46	66	81	105	126	143	165	181	208	238	257	279	314	
25	48	69	82	106	127	144	168	186	210	239	260	280	316	
27	49	70	85	110	129	145	169	188	213	241	261	286	319	
28	50	71	86	111	130	146	170	189	214	243	263	288	320	
31	51	72	87	112	131	147	171	191	217	244	264	293	322	

Proportion of Partisan Roll Calls

How often a majority of Democrats voted against a majority of Republicans:

Year	House	Senate	Year	House	Senate	Year	House	Senate	Year	House	Senate
1954	38%	47%	1965	52%	42%	1976	36%	37%	1987	64%	41%
1955	41	30	1966	41	50	1977	42	42	1988	47	42
1956	44	53	1967	36	35	1978	33	45	1989	55	35
1957	59	36	1968	35	32	1979	47	47	1990	49	54
1958	40	44	1969	31	36	1980	38	46	1991	55	49
1959	55	48	1970	27	35	1981	37	48	1992	64	53
1960	53	37	1971	38	42	1982	36	43	1993	65	67
1961	50	62	1972	27	36	1983	56	44	1994	62	52
1962	46	41	1973	42	40	1984	47	40			
1963	49	47	1974	29	44	1985	61	50			
1964	55	36	1975	48	48	1986	57	52			

	1	2	3		1	2	3		1	2	3		1	2	3
Alabama				**Iowa**				**New Hampshire**				**Texas**			
Heflin	64	32	66	Harkin	95	3	97	*Gregg*	83	16	84	*Gramm*	87	5	94
Shelby [1]	41	41	50	*Grassley*	87	13	87	*Smith*	95	4	96	*Hutchison*	88	6	94
Alaska				**Kansas**				**New Jersey**				**Utah**			
Murkowski	89	8	92	*Dole*	95	4	96	Bradley	79	15	84	*Bennett*	88	9	91
Stevens	69	25	73	*Kassebaum*	59	38	61	Lautenberg	84	16	84	*Hatch*	94	5	95
Arizona				**Kentucky**				**New Mexico**				**Vermont**			
DeConcini	79	17	82	Ford	81	18	82	Bingaman	84	16	84	Leahy	96	4	96
McCain	88	8	91	*McConnell*	91	8	92	*Domenici*	78	22	78	*Jeffords*	31	68	32
Arkansas				**Louisiana**				**New York**				**Virginia**			
Bumpers	85	14	86	Breaux	74	21	78	Moynihan	92	8	92	Robb	81	18	82
Pryor	75	15	84	Johnston	73	21	78	*D'Amato*	79	18	82	*Warner*	76	23	77
California				**Maine**				**North Carolina**				**Washington**			
Boxer	91	8	92	Mitchell	96	4	96	*Faircloth*	96	2	98	Murray	97	2	98
Feinstein	89	11	89	*Cohen*	59	37	61	*Helms*	91	5	95	*Gorton*	76	24	76
Colorado				**Maryland**				**North Dakota**				**West Virginia**			
Campbell	74	21	78	Mikulski	89	9	90	Conrad	84	15	85	Byrd	73	27	73
Brown	93	6	93	Sarbanes	98	2	98	Dorgan	86	14	86	Rockefeller	86	9	90
Connecticut				**Massachusetts**				**Ohio**				**Wisconsin**			
Dodd	84	9	90	Kennedy	92	6	94	Glenn	89	9	90	Feingold	84	16	84
Lieberman	75	24	76	Kerry	94	6	94	Metzenbaum	91	4	96	Kohl	75	25	75
Delaware				**Michigan**				**Oklahoma**				**Wyoming**			
Biden	86	8	92	Levin	92	8	92	Boren [2]†	73	18	81	*Simpson*	84	14	86
Roth	76	22	77	Riegle	90	5	95	*Nickles*	92	6	94	*Wallop*	84	4	95
Florida				**Minnesota**				**Oregon**							
Graham	85	15	85	Wellstone	94	6	94	*Hatfield*	33	65	34				
Mack	89	11	89	*Durenberger*	55	37	60	*Packwood*	59	35	63				
Georgia				**Mississippi**				**Pennsylvania**							
Nunn	65	34	66	*Cochran*	81	18	82	Wofford	89	11	89				
Coverdell	92	5	95	*Lott*	92	3	97	*Specter*	55	43	56				
Hawaii				**Missouri**				**Rhode Island**							
Akaka	94	6	94	*Bond*	75	21	78	Pell	92	8	92				
Inouye	89	8	92	*Danforth*	59	38	61	*Chafee*	44	51	46				
Idaho				**Montana**				**South Carolina**							
Craig	96	2	98	Baucus	86	14	86	Hollings	78	19	80				
Kempthorne	98	2	98	*Burns*	82	15	84	*Thurmond*	93	6	93				
Illinois				**Nebraska**				**South Dakota**							
Moseley-Braun	86	9	91	Exon	78	22	78	Daschle	91	9	91				
Simon	94	4	96	Kerrey	83	17	83	*Pressler*	89	11	89				
Indiana				**Nevada**				**Tennessee**							
Coats	88	11	89	Bryan	83	14	85	Mathews	78	21	79				
Lugar	78	22	78	Reid	85	12	88	Sasser	76	23	77				

KEY

† Not eligible for all recorded votes in 1994 or voted "present" to avoid possible conflict of interest.

Democrats   *Republicans*

Party Unity and Opposition: Senate

1. Party Unity, 1994. Percentage of 170 party unity recorded votes in 1994 on which a senator voted "yea" or "nay" *in agreement* with a majority of his or her party. (Party unity roll calls are those on which a majority of voting Democrats opposed a majority of voting Republicans.) Failures to vote lowered both party unity and party opposition scores.

2. Party Opposition, 1994. Percentage of 170 party unity recorded votes in 1994 on which a senator voted "yea" or "nay" *in disagreement* with a majority of his or her party. Failures to vote lowered both party unity and party opposition scores.

3. Party Unity, 1994. Percentage of 170 party unity recorded votes in 1994 on which a senator was present and voted "yea" or "nay" *in agreement* with a majority of his or her party. In this version of the study, absences were not counted; therefore, failures to vote did not lower unity or opposition scores. Opposition scores, not listed here, are the inverse of the unity score; i.e., the opposition score is equal to 100 percent minus the individual's unity score.

[1] *Richard C. Shelby, Ala., switched to the Republican Party on Nov. 9, 1994. As a Democrat, he was eligible for all 170 party unity votes in 1994; as a Republican, he was eligible for no party unity votes in 1994. His party unity score includes only votes he cast as a Democrat.*

[2] *David L. Boren, D-Okla., resigned Nov. 15, 1994. He was eligible for all 170 party unity votes in 1994. James M. Inhofe, R-Okla., was sworn in Nov. 17, 1994, replacing Boren. Inhofe was eligible for no party unity votes in 1994.*

Party Unity and Opposition: House

1. Party Unity, 1994. Percentage of 307 party unity recorded votes in 1994 on which a representative voted "yea" or "nay" *in agreement* with a majority of his or her party. (Party unity roll calls are those on which a majority of voting Democrats opposed a majority of voting Republicans.) Failures to vote lowered both party unity and party opposition scores.

2. Party Opposition, 1994. Percentage of 307 party unity recorded votes in 1994 on which a representative voted "yea" or "nay" *in disagreement* with a majority of his or her party. Failures to vote lowered both party unity and party opposition scores.

3. Party Unity, 1994. Percentage of 307 party unity recorded votes in 1994 on which a representative was present and voted "yea" or "nay" *in agreement* with a majority of his or her party. In this version of the study, absences were not counted; therefore, failures to vote did not lower unity or opposition scores. Opposition scores, not listed here, are the inverse of the unity score; i.e., the opposition score is equal to 100 percent minus the individual's unity score.

NOTE: Delegates were eligible for 133 of the 307 party unity votes in 1994.

[1] *Ron Lewis, R-Ky., was sworn in May 26, 1994, to succeed William H. Natcher, D-Ky., who died March 29. Natcher was eligible for 56 party unity votes in 1994. His party unity support score was 36 percent; opposition score, 0 percent; support score, adjusted for absences, 100 percent. Lewis was eligible for 183 party unity votes in 1994.*

[2] *Dean A. Gallo, R-N.J., died Nov. 6, 1994. He was eligible for 306 party unity votes in 1994.*

[3] *James M. Inhofe, R-Okla., resigned Nov. 15, 1994, to replace Sen. David L. Boren, D-Okla. Inhofe was eligible for 306 party unity votes in 1994. Steve Largent, R-Okla., was sworn in Nov. 29, 1994, to replace Inhofe. Largent was eligible for no party unity votes in 1994.*

[4] *Frank D. Lucas, R-Okla., was sworn in May 17, 1994, to succeed Glenn English, D-Okla., who resigned effective Jan. 7, 1994. Lucas was eligible for 209 party unity votes in 1994. English was eligible for no party unity votes in 1994.*

[5] *Rep. Bernard Sanders, I-Vt., voted as an independent. Had he voted as a Democrat, his party unity score would have been 92 percent; opposition score would have been 4 percent; unity score, adjusted for absences, would have been 96 percent.*

[6] *Rep. Thomas S. Foley, D-Wash., as Speaker of the House, voted at his discretion on 16 party unity votes in 1994.*

KEY

† Not eligible for all recorded votes in 1994 or voted "present" to avoid possible conflict of interest.

Democrats *Republicans*
Independent

	1	2	3
Alabama			
1 *Callahan*	82	11	88
2 *Everett*	79	20	80
3 Browder	73	23	76
4 Bevill	79	14	85
5 Cramer	78	19	81
6 *Bachus*	91	6	94
7 Hilliard	81	6	94
Alaska			
AL *Young*	80	17	83
Arizona			
1 Coppersmith	83	15	84
2 Pastor	95	5	95
3 *Stump*	99	1	99
4 *Kyl*	93	4	96
5 *Kolbe*	81	17	83
6 *English*†	89	8	92
Arkansas			
1 Lambert	78	20	79
2 Thornton	91	7	93
3 *Hutchinson*	93	5	95
4 *Dickey*	90	7	93
California			
1 Hamburg	97	1	99
2 *Herger*	90	3	97
3 Fazio	93	5	95
4 *Doolittle*	96	1	99
5 Matsui	92	2	98
6 Woolsey	98	1	99
7 Miller	92	2	98
8 Pelosi	93	1	99
9 Dellums	92	1	99
10 *Baker*	96	2	98
11 *Pombo*	82	13	87
12 Lantos	85	5	95
13 Stark	92	2	98
14 Eshoo	98	2	98
15 Mineta	96	2	98
16 Edwards	93	2	98
17 Farr	94	1	99
18 Condit	58	39	59
19 Lehman	76	18	81
20 Dooley	78	18	82
21 *Thomas*	84	10	90
22 *Huffington*	74	12	86
23 *Gallegly*	86	6	94
24 Beilenson	96	3	97
25 *McKeon*	94	4	96
26 Berman	91	2	98
27 *Moorhead*	96	3	97
28 *Dreier*	96	1	99
29 Waxman	93	2	98
30 Becerra	88	2	98
31 Martinez	90	6	94
32 Dixon	93	1	99
33 Roybal-Allard	99	1	99
34 Torres	90	2	98
35 Waters	92	3	97
36 Harman	79	17	83
37 Tucker	72	3	97
38 *Horn*	65	30	69
39 *Royce*	93	3	97
40 *Lewis*	77	18	81
41 *Kim*	96	4	96

	1	2	3
42 Brown	79	3	96
43 *Calvert*	86	8	91
44 *McCandless*	85	9	91
45 *Rohrabacher*	96	3	97
46 *Dornan*	88	3	97
47 *Cox*	92	2	98
48 *Packard*	90	9	91
49 Schenk	87	13	87
50 Filner	98	2	98
51 *Cunningham*	90	9	91
52 *Hunter*	88	6	93
Colorado			
1 Schroeder	81	17	83
2 Skaggs	96	3	97
3 *McInnis*	85	14	86
4 *Allard*	96	3	97
5 *Hefley*	95	4	96
6 *Schaefer*	92	4	96
Connecticut			
1 Kennelly	94	4	96
2 Gejdenson	95	1	99
3 DeLauro	96	3	97
4 *Shays*	67	33	67
5 *Franks*	72	25	74
6 *Johnson*	60	37	62
Delaware			
AL *Castle*	81	18	82
Florida			
1 Hutto	53	41	56
2 Peterson	84	13	87
3 Brown	89	4	95
4 *Fowler*	86	11	89
5 Thurman	80	19	81
6 *Stearns*	98	1	99
7 *Mica*	92	6	94
8 *McCollum*	83	8	91
9 *Bilirakis*	84	11	89
10 *Young*	84	12	87
11 Gibbons	87	6	94
12 *Canady*	94	6	94
13 *Miller*	94	4	96
14 *Goss*	94	6	94
15 Bacchus	83	8	91
16 *Lewis*	86	2	97
17 Meek	92	3	97
18 *Ros-Lehtinen*	74	21	78
19 Johnston	91	3	97
20 Deutsch	91	8	92
21 *Diaz-Balart*	71	29	71
22 *Shaw*	85	11	89
23 Hastings	77	2	97
Georgia			
1 *Kingston*	88	11	89
2 Bishop	87	7	92
3 *Collins*	90	8	92
4 *Linder*	95	4	96
5 Lewis	93	3	97
6 *Gingrich*	90	5	95
7 Darden	86	13	87
8 Rowland	70	25	74
9 Deal	61	36	63
10 Johnson	82	16	84
11 McKinney	98	1	99
Hawaii			
1 Abercrombie	95	2	98
2 Mink	97	1	99
Idaho			
1 LaRocco	88	12	88
2 *Crapo*	95	4	96
Illinois			
1 Rush	87	2	97
2 Reynolds	72	1	99
3 Lipinski	73	22	77
4 Gutierrez	91	4	96
5 Rostenkowski	82	2	98
6 *Hyde*†	85	13	87
7 Collins	81	3	96
8 *Crane*	90	2	98
9 Yates	94	2	98
10 *Porter*	71	27	73
11 Sangmeister	87	10	89
12 Costello	75	23	76
13 *Fawell*	85	15	85
14 *Hastert*	92	5	95
15 *Ewing*	92	6	94
16 *Manzullo*	94	6	94
17 Evans	99	0	99

ND Northern Democrats   SD Southern Democrats

	1	2	3
18 *Michel*	76	9	89
19 Poshard	65	35	65
20 Durbin	97	2	98
Indiana			
1 Visclosky	93	4	96
2 Sharp	85	3	97
3 Roemer	85	14	86
4 Long	84	12	87
5 *Buyer*	92	6	94
6 *Burton*	97	1	99
7 *Myers*	74	25	75
8 McCloskey	88	6	94
9 Hamilton	78	22	78
10 Jacobs	61	37	62
Iowa			
1 *Leach*	68	31	69
2 *Nussle*	93	6	94
3 *Lightfoot*	86	11	89
4 Smith	83	12	88
5 *Grandy*	55	10	84
Kansas			
1 *Roberts*	93	4	96
2 Slattery	48	7	86
3 *Meyers*	74	25	75
4 Glickman	80	16	83
Kentucky			
1 Barlow	87	7	92
2 *Lewis* [1]†	96	4	96
3 Mazzoli	84	14	86
4 *Bunning*	95	4	96
5 *Rogers*	79	19	81
6 Baesler	82	17	83
Louisiana			
1 *Livingston*	77	15	84
2 Jefferson	86	3	97
3 Tauzin	50	47	51
4 Fields	93	3	97
5 *McCrery*	80	13	86
6 *Baker*	89	5	94
7 Hayes	51	38	57
Maine			
1 Andrews	92	5	95
2 *Snowe*	66	33	67
Maryland			
1 *Gilchrest*	72	28	72
2 *Bentley*	79	14	85
3 Cardin	93	4	96
4 Wynn	95	3	97
5 Hoyer	91	5	95
6 *Bartlett*	98	1	99
7 Mfume	90	4	96
8 *Morella*	45	52	46
Massachusetts			
1 Olver	98	1	99
2 Neal	95	2	98
3 *Blute*	71	28	72
4 Frank	94	2	98
5 Meehan	85	8	91
6 *Torkildsen*	67	30	69
7 Markey	95	1	99
8 Kennedy	94	2	98
9 Moakley	97	0	99
10 Studds	97	1	99
Michigan			
1 Stupak	84	15	85
2 *Hoekstra*	94	6	94
3 *Ehlers*	76	23	77
4 *Camp*	90	8	92
5 Barcia	68	30	70
6 *Upton*	83	17	83
7 *Smith*	91	7	93
8 Carr	79	6	94
9 Kildee	93	7	93
10 Bonior	97	1	99
11 *Knollenberg*	95	4	96
12 Levin	95	5	95
13 Ford	72	3	97
14 Conyers	92	2	98
15 Collins	87	1	99
16 Dingell	87	6	94
Minnesota			
1 Penny	57	41	58
2 Minge	72	28	72
3 *Ramstad*	82	18	82
4 Vento	95	2	98

	1	2	3
5 Sabo	97	1	99
6 *Grams*	88	1	99
7 Peterson	58	41	59
8 Oberstar	93	4	96
Mississippi			
1 Whitten	62	5	92
2 Thompson	88	3	96
3 Montgomery	74	23	76
4 Parker	59	36	62
5 Taylor	36	62	37
Missouri			
1 Clay	74	12	86
2 *Talent*	94	5	95
3 Gephardt	93	0	99
4 Skelton	67	29	70
5 Wheat	81	1	99
6 Danner	80	19	81
7 *Hancock*	97	2	98
8 *Emerson*	84	11	88
9 Volkmer	77	22	78
Montana			
AL Williams	78	11	88
Nebraska			
1 *Bereuter*	77	22	78
2 Hoagland	85	13	87
3 *Barrett*	94	5	95
Nevada			
1 Bilbray	83	15	84
2 *Vucanovich*	86	12	88
New Hampshire			
1 *Zeliff*	89	7	93
2 Swett	66	29	70
New Jersey			
1 Andrews	64	29	69
2 Hughes	93	6	94
3 *Saxton*	81	17	83
4 *Smith*	64	34	66
5 *Roukema*	64	29	69
6 Pallone	89	11	89
7 *Franks*	76	23	77
8 Klein	87	10	90
9 Torricelli	83	9	90
10 Payne	94	2	98
11 *Gallo* [2]†	40	11	79
12 *Zimmer*	81	19	81
13 Menendez	95	4	96
New Mexico			
1 *Schiff*	79	19	81
2 *Skeen*	82	17	83
3 Richardson	92	6	94
New York			
1 Hochbrueckner	92	6	94
2 *Lazio*	77	23	77
3 *King*	91	8	92
4 *Levy*	92	8	92
5 Ackerman	90	4	96
6 Flake	86	1	99
7 Manton	86	6	94
8 Nadler	88	4	96
9 Schumer	86	5	94
10 Towns	79	2	98
11 Owens	79	2	97
12 Velazquez	94	2	98
13 *Molinari*	83	16	84
14 Maloney	91	6	94
15 Rangel	82	2	98
16 Serrano	94	2	98
17 Engel	89	3	97
18 Lowey	97	2	98
19 *Fish*	43	32	58
20 *Gilman*	45	54	45
21 McNulty	78	15	84
22 *Solomon*	91	3	97
23 *Boehlert*	57	41	58
24 *McHugh*	94	6	94
25 *Walsh*	73	26	74
26 Hinchey	97	1	99
27 *Paxon*	98	2	98
28 Slaughter	97	1	99
29 LaFalce	86	10	89
30 *Quinn*	78	17	82
31 *Houghton*	57	36	61
North Carolina			
1 Clayton	93	2	98
2 Valentine	69	23	75

	1	2	3
3 Lancaster	77	22	78
4 Price	93	5	95
5 Neal	72	7	91
6 *Coble*	97	3	97
7 Rose	87	5	94
8 Hefner	90	7	93
9 *McMillan*	69	11	86
10 *Ballenger*	95	2	98
11 *Taylor*	92	6	94
12 Watt	95	2	98
North Dakota			
AL Pomeroy	84	14	86
Ohio			
1 Mann	83	15	84
2 *Portman*	90	6	94
3 Hall	85	9	91
4 *Oxley*	88	8	92
5 *Gillmor*	67	32	68
6 Strickland	91	8	92
7 *Hobson*	82	18	82
8 *Boehner*	95	2	98
9 Kaptur	83	10	89
10 *Hoke*	85	11	88
11 Stokes	91	2	98
12 *Kasich*	81	19	81
13 Brown	91	8	92
14 Sawyer	97	2	98
15 *Pryce*	85	9	90
16 Regula	76	24	76
17 Traficant	80	20	80
18 Applegate	75	15	84
19 Fingerhut	81	17	83
Oklahoma			
1 *Inhofe* [3]†	88	1	99
2 Synar	92	3	97
3 Brewster	69	25	73
4 McCurdy	54	23	70
5 *Istook*	92	4	96
6 *Lucas* [4]†	93	7	93
Oregon			
1 Furse	94	4	96
2 *Smith*	79	4	95
3 Wyden	94	4	96
4 DeFazio	83	9	90
5 Kopetski	91	3	97
Pennsylvania			
1 Foglietta	92	1	99
2 Blackwell	73	0	99
3 Borski	93	5	95
4 Klink	81	17	83
5 *Clinger*	71	26	73
6 Holden	75	25	75
7 *Weldon*	77	19	81
8 *Greenwood*	69	28	71
9 *Shuster*	92	7	93
10 *McDade*	61	23	73
11 Kanjorski	87	12	88
12 Murtha	83	11	88
13 Margolies-Mezv.	78	20	80
14 Coyne	98	1	99
15 McHale	84	16	84
16 *Walker*	98	2	98
17 *Gekas*	93	7	93
18 *Santorum*	76	16	83
19 *Goodling*	89	9	90
20 Murphy	65	23	74
21 *Ridge*	54	20	73
Rhode Island			
1 *Machtley*	59	24	71
2 Reed	96	3	97
South Carolina			
1 *Ravenel*	73	23	76
2 *Spence*	87	11	89
3 Derrick	90	2	98
4 *Inglis*	85	14	86
5 Spratt	89	9	91
6 Clyburn	93	4	96
South Dakota			
AL Johnson	89	10	90
Tennessee			
1 *Quillen*	72	21	77
2 *Duncan*	95	5	95
3 Lloyd	64	20	76
4 Cooper	50	40	55
5 Clement	79	15	84

	1	2	3
6 Gordon	83	15	85
7 *Sundquist*	60	12	84
8 Tanner	68	31	69
9 Ford	74	3	96
Texas			
1 Chapman	65	23	74
2 Wilson	72	16	82
3 *Johnson, Sam*	95	2	98
4 Hall	36	62	37
5 Bryant	91	5	95
6 *Barton*	89	5	95
7 *Archer*	97	1	99
8 *Fields*	88	3	97
9 Brooks	85	6	93
10 Pickle	80	11	88
11 Edwards	74	23	76
12 Geren	57	41	58
13 Sarpalius	66	33	66
14 Laughlin	64	22	74
15 de la Garza	73	17	81
16 Coleman	91	4	96
17 Stenholm	41	58	42
18 Washington	20	1	95
19 *Combest*	86	14	86
20 Gonzalez	96	4	96
21 *Smith*	93	4	96
22 *DeLay*	95	2	98
23 *Bonilla*	93	7	93
24 Frost	81	10	89
25 Andrews	73	14	84
26 *Armey*	98	1	99
27 Ortiz	77	20	79
28 Tejeda	80	19	81
29 Green	83	9	90
30 Johnson, E. B.	94	4	96
Utah			
1 *Hansen*	93	5	95
2 Shepherd	87	11	89
3 Orton	57	42	58
Vermont			
AL *Sanders* [5]	--	--	--
Virginia			
1 *Bateman*	67	30	69
2 Pickett	68	29	70
3 Scott	94	4	96
4 Sisisky	70	27	72
5 Payne	75	24	76
6 *Goodlatte*	95	4	96
7 *Bliley*	91	7	92
8 Moran	84	8	91
9 Boucher	86	8	91
10 *Wolf*	86	13	87
11 Byrne	89	8	91
Washington			
1 Cantwell	92	8	92
2 Swift	93	4	96
3 Unsoeld	97	2	98
4 Inslee	82	17	83
5 Foley [6]			
6 Dicks	92	6	94
7 McDermott	95	2	98
8 *Dunn*	91	9	91
9 Kreidler	88	12	88
West Virginia			
1 Mollohan	86	11	89
2 Wise	91	6	94
3 Rahall	86	13	87
Wisconsin			
1 Barca	77	22	77
2 *Klug*	79	20	80
3 *Gunderson*	84	14	86
4 Kleczka	92	6	94
5 Barrett	89	9	90
6 *Petri*	93	7	93
7 Obey	92	3	97
8 *Roth*	91	7	93
9 *Sensenbrenner*	96	4	96
Wyoming			
AL *Thomas*	86	7	92
Delegates			
de Lugo, V.I.	92	5	95
Faleomavaega, Am.S.	52	1	99
Norton, D.C.	95	2	98
Romero-B., P.R.	74	7	92
Underwood, Guam	74	4	95

Southern states - Ala., Ark., Fla., Ga., Ky., La., Miss., N.C., Okla., S.C., Tenn., Texas, Va.
Omitted votes are quorum calls, which CQ does not include in its vote charts.

Conservative Coalition Definitions

Conservative coalition. As used in this study, "conservative coalition" means a voting alliance of Republicans and Southern Democrats against the Northern Democrats in Congress. This meaning, rather than any philosophic definition of the "conservative coalition" position, provides the basis for CQ's selection of coalition votes.

Conservative coalition vote. Any vote in the Senate or the House on which a majority of voting Southern Democrats and a majority of voting Republicans opposed the stand taken by a majority of voting Northern Democrats. Votes on which there was an even division

within the ranks of voting Northern Democrats, Southern Democrats or Republicans are not included.

Conservative coalition support score. Percentage of conservative coalition votes on which a member voted "yea" or "nay" *in agreement* with the position of the conservative coalition. Failures to vote, even if a member announced a stand, lower the score.

Conservative coalition opposition score. Percentage of conservative coalition votes on which a member voted "yea" or "nay" *in disagreement* with the position of the conservative coalition. Failures to vote, even if a member announced a stand, lower the score.

Average Scores

Scores for 1993 are in parentheses:

	Coalition Support					Coalition Opposition		
	Southern Democrats	Republicans	Northern Democrats			Southern Democrats	Republicans	Northern Democrats
Senate	66% (68)	79% (82)	29% (30)	Senate		30% (29)	19% (15)	69% (67)
House	62 (61)	85 (85)	33 (30)	House		31 (36)	11 (13)	61 (67)

Regional Averages

Scores for 1993 are in parentheses:

	Support					Opposition			
	East	West	South	Midwest		East	West	South	Midwest
Democrats					**Democrats**				
Senate	25% (26)	38% (38)	66% (68)	26% (29)	Senate	73% (72)	59% (59)	30% (29)	72% (68)
House	29 (27)	31 (25)	62 (61)	40 (37)	House	64 (68)	64 (72)	31 (36)	54 (60)
Republicans					**Republicans**				
Senate	63 (63)	81 (83)	90 (93)	76 (80)	Senate	36 (34)	16 (13)	8 (4)	23 (18)
House	78 (80)	91 (88)	88 (91)	82 (82)	House	17 (18)	5 (9)	8 (8)	14 (16)

Conservative Coalition History

Following is the percentage of the recorded votes for both chambers of Congress on which the coalition appeared and its percentage of victories:

Year	Appearances	Victories	Year	Appearances	Victories
1969	27%	68%	1982	18%	85%
1970	22	66	1983	15	77
1971	30	83	1984	16	83
1972	27	69	1985	14	89
1973	23	61	1986	16	87
1974	24	59	1987	8	93
1975	28	50	1988	9	89
1976	24	58	1989	11	87
1977	26	68	1990	11	82
1978	21	52	1991	11	91
1979	20	70	1992	12	87
1980	18	72	1993	9	94
1981	21	92	1994	8	82

1994 Conservative Coalition Votes

The following is a list of votes, by roll call number, cast in 1994 on which a majority of Southern Democrats and a majority of Republicans voted against a majority of all other Democrats.

House	Senate

House

33 Victories

Vote No.	Description
46	Education
57	Crime
74	School prayer
92	Education
107	Crime
111	Crime
119	Crime
122	Crime
179	Missile defense
180	Burden sharing
188	Trident II missiles
189	Trident II missiles
190	Defense
191	Military recruiters
192	Selective Service system
234	Helium reactor
253	Crime
284	Iraqi POWs
285	Overseas buildings
309	Space station
316	California desert
321	District of Columbia domestic partners
324	Crime
325	California desert
328	Expedited rescissions
332	Intelligence disclosure
339	Insurance disclosure
353	Environmental risks
368	Orchard Street historic site
377	Crop insurance
383	China MFN
419	Reformulated gasoline
503	Local government payments

3 Defeats

Vote No.	Description
65	Balanced-budget amendment
156	Assault weapons
484	Landowner consent

Senate

23 Victories

Vote No.	Description
50	Pesticide safety
53	Regulatory flexibility
93	Adm. Frank B. Kelso II retirement
106	Crime
124	Crime
152	Air-traffic controllers
158	Border crossing fees
174	Indonesia military aid
175	Liquid metal reactor
176	Nuclear weapons research
179	Stealth bombers
186	Selective Service system
201	Russian aid
206	Agriculture promotion
211	Agricultural Research Service
214	Federal employees
239	Education
244	Education
245	Education
247	Education
274	Trident II missiles
278	Somalia operations
327	Lt. Gen. Buster C. Glosson retirement

9 Defeats

Vote No.	Description
48	Balanced-budget amendment
101	Congressional gift limits
118	Federal wage requirements
210	Agricultural Research Service
223	Legal Services Corporation
236	School prayer
241	Education
255	Ethanol
313	Congressional reform

House Victory Rate

Victories	33
Defeats	3
Total	36
Victory Rate	91.7%

Senate Victory Rate

Victories	23
Defeats	9
Total	32
Victory Rate	71.9%

Conservative Coalition Support and Opposition: House

1. Conservative Coalition Support, 1994. Percentage of 36 recorded votes in 1994 on which the conservative coalition appeared and on which a representative voted "yea" or "nay" *in agreement* with the position of the conservative coalition. Failures to vote lowered both support and opposition scores.

2. Conservative Coalition Opposition, 1994. Percentage of 36 recorded votes in 1994 on which the conservative coalition appeared and on which a representative voted "yea" or "nay" *in disagreement* with the position of the conservative coalition. Failures to vote lowered both support and opposition scores.

3. Conservative Coalition Support, 1994. Percentage of 36 recorded votes in 1994 on which the conservative coalition appeared and on which a representative was present and voted "yea" or "nay" *in agreement* with the position of the conservative coalition. In this version of the study, absences were not counted; therefore, failures to vote did not lower support or opposition scores. Opposition scores, not listed here, are the inverse of the support score; i.e., the opposition score is equal to 100 percent minus the individual's support score.

NOTE: Delegates were eligible for 29 of the 36 conservative coalition votes in 1993.

[1] Ron Lewis, R-Ky., was sworn in May 26, 1994, to succeed William H. Natcher, D-Ky., who died March 29. Natcher was eligible for five conservative coalition votes in 1994, and did not vote. His conservative coalition support score was 0 percent; opposition score, 0 percent; support score, adjusted for absences, 0 percent. Lewis was eligible for 19 conservative coalition votes in 1994.

[2] Dean A. Gallo, R-N.J., died Nov. 6, 1994. He was eligible for all 36 conservative coalition votes in 1994.

[3] James M. Inhofe, R-Okla., resigned Nov. 15, 1994, to replace Sen. David L. Boren, D-Okla. Inhofe was eligible for all 36 conservative coalition votes in 1994. Steve Largent, R-Okla., was sworn in Nov. 29, 1994, to replace Inhofe. Largent was eligible for no conservative coalition votes in 1994.

[4] Frank D. Lucas, R-Okla., was sworn in May 17, 1994, to succeed Glenn English, D-Okla., who resigned effective Jan. 7, 1994. Lucas was eligible for 26 conservative coalition votes in 1994. English was eligible for no conservative coalition votes in 1994.

[5] Rep. Thomas S. Foley, D-Wash., as Speaker of the House, voted at his discretion on one conservative coalition vote in 1994.

	1	2	3
Alabama			
1 Callahan	94	0	100
2 Everett	97	3	97
3 Browder	92	6	94
4 Bevill	86	6	94
5 Cramer	94	3	97
6 Bachus	94	3	97
7 Hilliard	33	53	39
Alaska			
AL Young	97	3	97
Arizona			
1 Coppersmith	47	50	49
2 Pastor	42	58	42
3 Stump	94	6	94
4 Kyl	94	6	94
5 Kolbe	75	17	82
6 English	44	56	44
Arkansas			
1 Lambert	67	33	67
2 Thornton	69	28	71
3 Hutchinson	86	14	86
4 Dickey	89	8	91
California			
1 Hamburg	8	89	9
2 Herger	86	6	94
3 Fazio	50	50	50
4 Doolittle	94	3	97
5 Matsui	28	58	32
6 Woolsey	8	92	8
7 Miller	3	83	3
8 Pelosi	0	97	0
9 Dellums	0	100	0
10 Baker	92	3	97
11 Pombo	94	0	100
12 Lantos	44	53	46
13 Stark	0	94	0
14 Eshoo	11	89	11
15 Mineta	14	81	15
16 Edwards	3	89	3
17 Farr	11	78	13
18 Condit	64	33	66
19 Lehman	67	25	73
20 Dooley	69	28	71
21 Thomas	86	6	94
22 Huffington	83	3	97
23 Gallegly	94	0	100
24 Beilenson	19	81	19
25 McKeon	100	0	100
26 Berman	14	78	15
27 Moorhead	97	3	97
28 Dreier	97	0	100
29 Waxman	3	94	3
30 Becerra	11	72	13
31 Martinez	61	36	63
32 Dixon	14	78	15
33 Roybal-Allard	14	86	14
34 Torres	25	67	27
35 Waters	6	92	6
36 Harman	72	25	74
37 Tucker	22	67	25
38 Horn	81	14	85
39 Royce	78	17	82
40 Lewis	81	8	91
41 Kim	100	0	100

	1	2	3
42 Brown	22	61	27
43 Calvert	92	0	100
44 McCandless	89	3	97
45 Rohrabacher	69	31	69
46 Dornan	94	3	97
47 Cox	86	11	89
48 Packard	97	3	97
49 Schenk	53	44	54
50 Filner	17	83	17
51 Cunningham	94	6	94
52 Hunter	92	6	94
Colorado			
1 Schroeder	14	83	14
2 Skaggs	19	78	20
3 McInnis	83	11	88
4 Allard	94	6	94
5 Hefley	89	11	89
6 Schaefer	92	8	92
Connecticut			
1 Kennelly	42	58	42
2 Gejdenson	17	83	17
3 DeLauro	31	69	31
4 Shays	42	58	42
5 Franks	86	14	86
6 Johnson	64	33	66
Delaware			
AL Castle	92	8	92
Florida			
1 Hutto	94	6	94
2 Peterson	81	14	85
3 Brown	44	50	47
4 Fowler	94	6	94
5 Thurman	69	31	69
6 Stearns	89	11	89
7 Mica	97	3	97
8 McCollum	78	6	93
9 Bilirakis	89	6	94
10 Young	78	14	85
11 Gibbons	50	47	51
12 Canady	100	0	100
13 Miller	78	17	82
14 Goss	89	11	89
15 Bacchus	44	44	50
16 Lewis	83	0	100
17 Meek	31	64	32
18 Ros-Lehtinen	64	25	72
19 Johnston	14	83	14
20 Deutsch	47	50	49
21 Diaz-Balart	78	19	80
22 Shaw	89	6	94
23 Hastings	17	64	21
Georgia			
1 Kingston	94	3	97
2 Bishop	58	25	70
3 Collins	86	14	86
4 Linder	100	0	100
5 Lewis	6	94	6
6 Gingrich	97	0	100
7 Darden	89	8	91
8 Rowland	86	6	94
9 Deal	86	8	91
10 Johnson	83	14	86
11 McKinney	3	97	3
Hawaii			
1 Abercrombie	17	81	17
2 Mink	3	94	3
Idaho			
1 LaRocco	78	22	78
2 Crapo	97	3	97
Illinois			
1 Rush	6	86	6
2 Reynolds	17	61	21
3 Lipinski	67	28	71
4 Gutierrez	6	92	6
5 Rostenkowski	22	56	29
6 Hyde	83	14	86
7 Collins	3	78	3
8 Crane	69	17	81
9 Yates	0	94	0
10 Porter	61	39	61
11 Sangmeister	61	33	65
12 Costello	72	28	72
13 Fawell	78	22	78
14 Hastert	94	6	94
15 Ewing	94	6	94
16 Manzullo	94	6	94
17 Evans	6	94	6

ND Northern Democrats SD Southern Democrats

	1	2	3
18 *Michel*	72	11	87
19 Poshard	69	31	69
20 Durbin	22	78	22
Indiana			
1 Visclosky	36	64	36
2 Sharp	22	75	23
3 Roemer	69	31	69
4 Long	61	36	63
5 *Buyer*	94	3	97
6 *Burton*	94	3	97
7 *Myers*	92	8	92
8 McCloskey	44	47	48
9 Hamilton	69	31	69
10 Jacobs	39	58	40
Iowa			
1 *Leach*	69	31	69
2 *Nussle*	81	19	81
3 *Lightfoot*	92	6	94
4 Smith	50	42	55
5 *Grandy*	50	6	90
Kansas			
1 *Roberts*	89	3	97
2 Slattery	36	11	76
3 *Meyers*	78	22	78
4 Glickman	72	25	74
Kentucky			
1 Barlow	58	28	68
2 *Lewis* [1]†	89	11	89
3 Mazzoli	72	28	72
4 *Bunning*	83	17	83
5 *Rogers*	83	14	86
6 Baesler	83	17	83
Louisiana			
1 *Livingston*	83	6	94
2 Jefferson	28	67	29
3 Tauzin	92	8	92
4 Fields	25	75	25
5 *McCrery*	92	8	92
6 *Baker*	92	0	100
7 Hayes	89	6	94
Maine			
1 Andrews	11	89	11
2 *Snowe*	75	19	79
Maryland			
1 *Gilchrest*	78	22	78
2 *Bentley*	97	0	100
3 Cardin	31	67	31
4 Wynn	25	72	26
5 Hoyer	56	42	57
6 *Bartlett*	100	0	100
7 Mfume	8	89	9
8 Morella	50	47	51
Massachusetts			
1 Olver	3	97	3
2 Neal	25	72	26
3 *Blute*	78	22	78
4 Frank	0	97	0
5 Meehan	11	81	12
6 *Torkildsen*	78	22	78
7 Markey	3	97	3
8 Kennedy	19	78	20
9 Moakley	25	75	25
10 Studds	0	97	0
Michigan			
1 Stupak	67	33	67
2 *Hoekstra*	81	19	81
3 *Ehlers*	81	19	81
4 *Camp*	86	11	89
5 Barcia	75	25	75
6 *Upton*	64	36	64
7 *Smith*	89	8	91
8 Carr	36	44	45
9 Kildee	25	75	25
10 Bonior	11	86	11
11 *Knollenberg*	92	6	94
12 Levin	28	72	28
13 Ford	17	53	24
14 Conyers	11	75	13
15 Collins	3	94	3
16 Dingell	36	53	41
Minnesota			
1 Penny	53	47	53
2 Minge	61	39	61
3 *Ramstad*	72	28	72
4 Vento	6	94	6

	1	2	3
5 Sabo	6	94	6
6 *Grams*	81	3	97
7 Peterson	72	25	74
8 Oberstar	14	86	14
Mississippi			
1 Whitten	44	17	73
2 Thompson	36	61	37
3 Montgomery	97	3	97
4 Parker	100	0	100
5 Taylor	97	3	97
Missouri			
1 Clay	8	83	9
2 *Talent*	97	3	97
3 Gephardt	17	64	21
4 Skelton	97	0	100
5 Wheat	14	67	17
6 Danner	75	22	77
7 *Hancock*	89	11	89
8 *Emerson*	86	0	100
9 Volkmer	83	17	83
Montana			
AL Williams	53	44	54
Nebraska			
1 *Bereuter*	81	17	83
2 Hoagland	64	36	64
3 *Barrett*	97	3	97
Nevada			
1 Bilbray	75	25	75
2 *Vucanovich*	100	0	100
New Hampshire			
1 *Zeliff*	92	6	94
2 Swett	56	42	57
New Jersey			
1 *Andrews*	72	28	72
2 Hughes	47	53	47
3 *Saxton*	89	11	89
4 *Smith*	72	25	74
5 Roukema	61	31	67
6 Pallone	39	61	39
7 *Franks*	67	31	69
8 Klein	47	47	50
9 Torricelli	42	42	50
10 Payne	3	94	3
11 *Gallo* [2]†	39	3	93
12 *Zimmer*	67	33	67
13 Menendez	31	69	31
New Mexico			
1 *Schiff*	89	11	89
2 *Skeen*	100	0	100
3 Richardson	56	42	57
New York			
1 Hochbrueckner	67	33	67
2 *Lazio*	83	17	83
3 *King*	83	17	83
4 *Levy*	89	8	91
5 Ackerman	25	64	28
6 Flake	14	72	16
7 Manton	47	50	49
8 Nadler	6	83	6
9 Schumer	31	69	31
10 Towns	11	58	16
11 Owens	3	72	4
12 Velazquez	6	92	6
13 *Molinari*	83	17	83
14 Maloney	22	78	22
15 Rangel	8	64	12
16 Serrano	8	89	9
17 Engel	11	86	11
18 Lowey	11	89	11
19 Fish	50	14	78
20 Gilman	69	31	69
21 McNulty	58	39	60
22 *Solomon*	83	11	88
23 Boehlert	61	36	63
24 *McHugh*	89	11	89
25 *Walsh*	86	14	86
26 Hinchey	14	86	14
27 *Paxon*	92	8	92
28 Slaughter	14	86	14
29 LaFalce	47	42	53
30 *Quinn*	83	17	83
31 *Houghton*	75	17	82
North Carolina			
1 Clayton	22	78	22
2 Valentine	61	33	65

	1	2	3
3 Lancaster	81	19	81
4 Price	50	50	50
5 Neal	53	28	66
6 *Coble*	83	17	83
7 Rose	44	33	57
8 Hefner	67	28	71
9 *McMillan*	75	8	90
10 *Ballenger*	86	8	91
11 *Taylor*	92	6	94
12 Watt	3	94	3
North Dakota			
AL Pomeroy	72	28	72
Ohio			
1 Mann	42	56	43
2 *Portman*	81	11	88
3 Hall	44	53	46
4 *Oxley*	86	8	91
5 *Gillmor*	86	11	89
6 Strickland	44	56	44
7 *Hobson*	83	17	83
8 *Boehner*	92	3	97
9 Kaptur	58	42	58
10 *Hoke*	83	11	88
11 Stokes	8	89	9
12 *Kasich*	86	14	86
13 Brown	36	64	36
14 Sawyer	28	64	30
15 *Pryce*	83	11	88
16 *Regula*	89	11	89
17 Traficant	67	33	67
18 Applegate	58	36	62
19 Fingerhut	56	42	57
Oklahoma			
1 *Inhofe* [3]†	89	3	97
2 Synar	6	86	6
3 Brewster	83	8	91
4 McCurdy	69	6	93
5 *Istook*	81	8	91
6 *Lucas* [4]†	100	0	100
Oregon			
1 Furse	22	78	22
2 *Smith*	89	0	100
3 Wyden	33	67	33
4 DeFazio	31	58	34
5 Kopetski	22	72	24
Pennsylvania			
1 Foglietta	8	86	9
2 Blackwell	6	72	7
3 Borski	44	53	46
4 Klink	53	47	53
5 *Clinger*	92	3	97
6 Holden	72	28	72
7 *Weldon*	81	19	81
8 *Greenwood*	78	22	78
9 *Shuster*	92	6	94
10 *McDade*	86	6	94
11 Kanjorski	47	53	47
12 Murtha	69	19	78
13 Margolies-Mezv.	36	58	38
14 Coyne	3	92	3
15 McHale	69	31	69
16 *Walker*	94	6	94
17 *Gekas*	94	3	97
18 Santorum	81	6	94
19 *Goodling*	81	14	85
20 Murphy	42	33	56
21 *Ridge*	67	8	89
Rhode Island			
1 *Machtley*	72	8	90
2 Reed	28	72	28
South Carolina			
1 Ravenel	75	17	82
2 *Spence*	92	8	92
3 Derrick	33	56	38
4 *Inglis*	92	8	92
5 Spratt	78	22	78
6 Clyburn	36	61	37
South Dakota			
AL Johnson	58	36	62
Tennessee			
1 *Quillen*	86	6	94
2 *Duncan*	67	33	67
3 Lloyd	86	11	89
4 Cooper	92	6	94
5 Clement	78	17	82

	1	2	3
6 Gordon	75	19	79
7 *Sundquist*	72	0	100
8 Tanner	94	6	94
9 Ford	17	53	24
Texas			
1 Chapman	94	6	94
2 Wilson	69	11	86
3 *Johnson, Sam*	97	3	97
4 Hall	97	3	97
5 Bryant	47	47	50
6 *Barton*	92	3	97
7 *Archer*	94	6	94
8 *Fields*	83	0	100
9 Brooks	47	36	57
10 Pickle	56	31	65
11 Edwards	94	6	94
12 Geren	97	3	97
13 Sarpalius	97	3	97
14 Laughlin	72	11	87
15 de la Garza	86	14	86
16 Coleman	58	36	62
17 Stenholm	92	3	97
18 Washington	3	19	13
19 *Combest*	97	3	97
20 Gonzalez	22	78	22
21 *Smith*	81	6	94
22 *DeLay*	86	6	94
23 *Bonilla*	100	0	100
24 Frost	78	17	82
25 Andrews	67	25	73
26 *Armey*	92	6	94
27 Ortiz	78	17	82
28 Tejeda	86	14	86
29 Green	50	39	56
30 Johnson, E. B.	28	69	29
Utah			
1 *Hansen*	100	0	100
2 Shepherd	53	47	53
3 Orton	83	14	86
Vermont			
AL *Sanders*	11	89	11
Virginia			
1 *Bateman*	86	14	86
2 Pickett	89	8	91
3 Scott	28	72	28
4 Sisisky	89	8	91
5 Payne	89	11	89
6 *Goodlatte*	86	14	86
7 *Bliley*	92	3	97
8 Moran	53	47	53
9 Boucher	61	33	65
10 *Wolf*	89	11	89
11 Byrne	50	47	51
Washington			
1 Cantwell	56	44	56
2 Swift	36	64	36
3 Unsoeld	14	86	14
4 Inslee	67	33	67
5 Foley [5]			
6 Dicks	58	42	58
7 McDermott	14	78	15
8 *Dunn*	97	3	97
9 Kreidler	42	58	42
West Virginia			
1 Mollohan	58	42	58
2 Wise	69	28	71
3 Rahall	47	53	47
Wisconsin			
1 Barca	61	36	63
2 *Klug*	61	39	61
3 *Gunderson*	86	14	86
4 Kleczka	33	61	35
5 Barrett	22	78	22
6 *Petri*	81	19	81
7 Obey	14	72	16
8 *Roth*	75	22	77
9 Sensenbrenner	69	31	69
Wyoming			
AL *Thomas*	78	3	97
Delegates			
de Lugo, V.I.	31	66	32
Faleomavaega, Am.S.	14	24	36
Norton, D.C.	7	90	7
Romero-B., P.R.	24	34	41
Underwood, Guam	14	72	16

Southern states - Ala., Ark., Fla., Ga., Ky., La., Miss., N.C., Okla., S.C., Tenn., Texas, Va.
Omitted votes are quorum calls, which CQ does not include in its vote charts.

	1	2	3
Alabama			
Heflin	88	13	88
Shelby [1]	78	3	96
Alaska			
Murkowski	84	9	90
Stevens	84	13	87
Arizona			
DeConcini	44	56	44
McCain	69	25	73
Arkansas			
Bumpers	63	38	63
Pryor	56	34	62
California			
Boxer	19	78	19
Feinstein	44	56	44
Colorado			
Campbell	44	47	48
Brown	75	22	77
Connecticut			
Dodd	22	69	24
Lieberman	44	53	45
Delaware			
Biden	31	69	31
Roth	66	34	66
Florida			
Graham	53	47	53
Mack	94	6	94
Georgia			
Nunn	91	9	91
Coverdell	88	9	90
Hawaii			
Akaka	31	69	31
Inouye	41	56	42
Idaho			
Craig	94	6	94
Kempthorne	94	6	94
Illinois			
Moseley-Braun	13	84	13
Simon	16	78	17
Indiana			
Coats	78	19	81
Lugar	78	22	78

	1	2	3
Iowa			
Harkin	9	88	10
Grassley	69	31	69
Kansas			
Dole	97	3	97
Kassebaum	63	38	63
Kentucky			
Ford	59	38	61
McConnell	84	13	87
Louisiana			
Breaux	78	22	78
Johnston	72	25	74
Maine			
Mitchell	16	84	16
Cohen	63	34	65
Maryland			
Mikulski	28	69	29
Sarbanes	13	88	13
Massachusetts			
Kennedy	19	78	19
Kerry	16	84	16
Michigan			
Levin	16	84	16
Riegle	16	72	18
Minnesota			
Wellstone	3	97	3
Durenberger	59	41	59
Mississippi			
Cochran	91	6	94
Lott	97	0	100
Missouri			
Bond	88	9	90
Danforth	69	31	69
Montana			
Baucus	50	50	50
Burns	91	6	94
Nebraska			
Exon	63	38	63
Kerrey	47	53	47
Nevada			
Bryan	44	47	48
Reid	41	59	41

	1	2	3
New Hampshire			
Gregg	78	22	78
Smith	88	13	88
New Jersey			
Bradley	6	88	7
Lautenberg	19	78	19
New Mexico			
Bingaman	53	47	53
Domenici	94	6	94
New York			
Moynihan	16	84	16
D'Amato	81	16	84
North Carolina			
Faircloth	100	0	100
Helms	81	13	87
North Dakota			
Conrad	53	47	53
Dorgan	44	56	44
Ohio			
Glenn	22	75	23
Metzenbaum	3	94	3
Oklahoma			
Boren [2]†	53	44	55
Nickles	88	13	88
Oregon			
Hatfield	34	66	34
Packwood	44	50	47
Pennsylvania			
Wofford	34	66	34
Specter	59	38	61
Rhode Island			
Pell	28	72	28
Chafee	41	56	42
South Carolina			
Hollings	69	28	71
Thurmond	97	3	97
South Dakota			
Daschle	38	63	38
Pressler	84	16	84
Tennessee			
Mathews	56	44	56
Sasser	69	28	71

	1	2	3
Texas			
Gramm	88	6	93
Hutchison	94	6	94
Utah			
Bennett	91	6	94
Hatch	94	6	94
Vermont			
Leahy	6	94	6
Jeffords	25	75	25
Virginia			
Robb	44	53	45
Warner	84	16	84
Washington			
Murray	13	88	13
Gorton	84	16	84
West Virginia			
Byrd	69	31	69
Rockefeller	34	66	34
Wisconsin			
Feingold	9	91	9
Kohl	41	59	41
Wyoming			
Simpson	97	0	100
Wallop	81	6	93

Conservative Coalition Support and Opposition: Senate

1. Conservative Coalition Support, 1994. Percentage of 32 recorded votes in 1994 on which the conservative coalition appeared and on which a senator voted "yea" or "nay" *in agreement* with the position of the conservative coalition. Failures to vote lowered both support and opposition scores.

2. Conservative Coalition Opposition, 1994. Percentage of 32 recorded votes in 1994 on which the conservative coalition appeared and on which a senator voted "yea" or "nay" *in disagreement* with the position of the conservative coalition. Failures to vote lowered both support and opposition scores.

3. Conservative Coalition Support, 1994. Percentage of 32 recorded votes in 1994 on which the conservative coalition appeared and on which a senator was present and voted "yea" or "nay" *in agreement* with the position of the conservative coalition. In this version of the study, absences were not counted; therefore, failures to vote did not lower support or opposition scores. Opposition scores, not listed here, are the inverse of the support score; i.e., the opposition score is equal to 100 percent minus the individual's support score.

[1] *Richard C. Shelby, Ala., switched to the Republican Party on Nov. 9, 1994. As a Democrat, he was eligible for all 32 conservative coalition votes in 1994; as a Republican, he was eligible for no conservative coalition votes in 1994. His conservative coalition score includes only votes he cast as a Democrat.*

[2] *David L. Boren, D-Okla., resigned Nov. 15, 1994. He was eligible for all 32 conservative coalition votes in 1994. James M. Inhofe, R-Okla., was sworn in Nov. 17, 1994, replacing Boren. Inhofe was eligible for no conservative coalition votes in 1994.*

	1	2
Alabama		
Heflin	96	96
Shelby ¹#	83	83
Alaska		
Murkowski	96	97
Stevens	93	93
Arizona		
DeConcini	97	98
McCain	94	94
Arkansas		
Bumpers	99	99
Pryor	93	92
California		
Boxer	97	98
Feinstein	99	99
Colorado		
Campbell	94	94
Brown	99	99
Connecticut		
Dodd#	92	92
Lieberman	97	97
Delaware		
Biden#	94	95
Roth	98	99
Florida		
Graham	99	99
Mack	99	99
Georgia		
Nunn	98	98
Coverdell	97	97
Hawaii		
Akaka	100	100
Inouye	94	95
Idaho		
Craig	98	99
Kempthorne	99	99
Illinois		
Moseley-Braun	95	95
Simon	98	98
Indiana		
Coats	99	99
Lugar	100	100

	1	2
Iowa		
Harkin	95	96
Grassley	100	100
Kansas		
Dole	99	99
Kassebaum	97	97
Kentucky		
Ford	99	99
McConnell	99	99
Louisiana		
Breaux	95	95
Johnston	95	95
Maine		
Mitchell	100	100
Cohen	95	95
Maryland		
Mikulski#	96	96
Sarbanes	100	100
Massachusetts		
Kennedy	95	95
Kerry	99	99
Michigan		
Levin	100	100
Riegle#	95	95
Minnesota		
Wellstone	98	99
Durenberger	91	91
Mississippi		
Cochran	98	98
Lott	95	95
Missouri		
Bond	95	96
Danforth	97	97
Montana		
Baucus	99	99
Burns	98	98
Nebraska		
Exon	99	99
Kerrey	99	99
Nevada		
Bryan	98	98
Reid	97	97

	1	2
New Hampshire		
Gregg	98	98
Smith	99	99
New Jersey		
Bradley	95	94
Lautenberg	99	99
New Mexico		
Bingaman	99	99
Domenici	99	99
New York		
Moynihan	99	99
D'Amato	96	97
North Carolina		
Faircloth	98	99
Helms	95	95
North Dakota		
Conrad	99	99
Dorgan	99	99
Ohio		
Glenn	98	99
Metzenbaum	94	94
Oklahoma		
Boren ²†	91	91
Nickles	96	97
Oregon		
Hatfield	97	97
Packwood	95	95
Pennsylvania		
Wofford	99	99
Specter	97	98
Rhode Island		
Pell	98	98
Chafee	94	94
South Carolina		
Hollings	97	97
Thurmond	98	98
South Dakota		
Daschle	100	100
Pressler	98	98
Tennessee		
Mathews	99	99
Sasser	98	98

KEY

† Not eligible for all recorded votes in 1994 or voted "present" to avoid possible conflict of interest.

Member absent a day or more in 1994 due to illness or to a relative's death or illness.

Democrats   *Republicans*

	1	2
Texas		
Gramm	90	91
Hutchison	93	93
Utah		
Bennett	96	97
Hatch	98	98
Vermont		
Leahy	100	100
Jeffords	98	98
Virginia		
Robb	99	99
Warner	99	99
Washington		
Murray	98	98
Gorton	100	100
West Virginia		
Byrd	100	100
Rockefeller	97	97
Wisconsin		
Feingold	100	100
Kohl	100	100
Wyoming		
Simpson	96	97
Wallop	87	88

Voting Participation: Senate

1. Voting Participation, 1994. Percentage of 329 recorded votes in 1994 on which a senator voted "yea" or "nay."

2. Voting Participation, 1994. Percentage of 317 recorded votes in 1994 on which a senator voted "yea" or "nay." In this version of the study, votes to instruct the sergeant at arms to request the attendance of absent senators are not included.

NOTE: Scores are rounded to nearest percentage, except that no scores are rounded up to 100 percent. Members with 100 percent scores participated in all recorded votes for which they were eligible.

¹ *Richard C. Shelby, Ala., switched to the Republican Party on Nov. 9, 1994. As a Democrat, he was eligible for 327 votes in 1994, 317 not including sergeant at arms votes. As a Republican, he was eligible for two votes, neither of which was a sergeant at arms vote. His voting participation score includes votes he cast both as a Democrat and a Republican.*

² *David L. Boren, D-Okla., resigned Nov. 15, 1994. He was eligible for 327 votes in 1994, 315 not including sergeant at arms votes. James M. Inhofe, R-Okla., was sworn in Nov. 17, 1994, replacing Boren. Inhofe was eligible for two votes in 1994, neither of which was a sergeant at arms vote. His voting participation score for 1994 was 100 percent for two votes.*

Voting Participation: House

1. Voting Participation, 1994. Percentage of 497 recorded votes in 1994 on which a representative voted "yea" or "nay."

2. Voting Participation, 1994. Percentage of 464 recorded votes in 1994 on which a representative voted "yea" or "nay." In this version of the study, votes on approval of the House Journal were not included.

NOTES: Scores are rounded to nearest percentage, except that no scores are rounded up to 100 percent. Members with a 100 percent score participated in all recorded votes for which they were eligible.

Delegates were eligible for 215 of the 497 votes in 1994 and for 215 of the 464 votes excluding the approval of the House Journal.

[1] *Ron Lewis, R-Ky., was sworn in May 26, 1994, to succeed William H. Natcher, D-Ky., who died March 29. Natcher was eligible for 92 votes in 1994, 80 not including votes to approve the Journal. His voting participation scores were 39 percent and 36 percent, respectively. Lewis was eligible for 291 votes in 1994, 279 not including votes to approve the Journal.*

[2] *Dean A. Gallo, R-N.J., died Nov. 6, 1994. He was eligible for 495 votes in 1994, 463 not including votes to approve the Journal.*

[3] *James M. Inhofe, R-Okla., resigned Nov. 15, 1994, to replace Sen. David L. Boren, D-Okla. Inhofe was eligible for 495 votes in 1994, 463 not including votes to approve the Journal. Steve Largent, R-Okla., was sworn in Nov. 29, 1994, to replace Inhofe. Largent was eligible for one vote in 1994, which was not a vote to approve the Journal. His voting participation score was 100 percent for one vote.*

[4] *Frank D. Lucas, R-Okla., was sworn in May 17, 1994, to succeed Glenn English, D-Okla., who resigned effective Jan. 7, 1994. Lucas was eligible for 329 votes in 1994, 316 not including votes to approve the Journal. English was eligible for no votes in 1994.*

[5] *Rep. Thomas S. Foley, D-Wash., as Speaker of the House, voted at his discretion.*

KEY

† Not eligible for all recorded votes in 1994 or voted "present" to avoid possible conflict of interest.

\# Member absent a day or more in 1994 due to illness or to a relative's death or illness.

Democrats *Republicans*
Independent

		1	2
Alabama			
1	Callahan#	94	94
2	Everett	99	99
3	Browder	97	97
4	Bevill	95	95
5	Cramer	97	98
6	*Bachus*	96	96
7	Hilliard	86	86
Alaska			
AL	*Young*	97	98
Arizona			
1	Coppersmith	98	98
2	Pastor	98	98
3	*Stump*	99	99
4	*Kyl*	96	96
5	*Kolbe*	99	99
6	English†#	97	97
Arkansas			
1	Lambert	99	98
2	Thornton	97	97
3	*Hutchinson*	98	98
4	*Dickey*	97	97
California			
1	Hamburg	98	98
2	*Herger*	94	95
3	Fazio	98	98
4	*Doolittle*	97	97
5	Matsui	95	95
6	Woolsey	99	99
7	Miller	93	93
8	Pelosi	94	95
9	Dellums	94	96
10	*Baker*	98	98
11	*Pombo*#	95	95
12	Lantos	91	91
13	Stark	93	94
14	Eshoo	100	100
15	Mineta#	98	98
16	Edwards	93	94
17	Farr	96	96
18	Condit	97	97
19	Lehman#	94	94
20	Dooley	96	97
21	*Thomas*	96	96
22	*Huffington*	87	88
23	*Gallegly*	92	92
24	Beilenson	99	99
25	*McKeon*	98	98
26	Berman	92	92
27	*Moorhead*	99	99
28	*Dreier*	98	98
29	Waxman	95	96
30	Becerra	89	90
31	Martinez	96	96
32	Dixon	96	97
33	Roybal-Allard	99	99
34	Torres	94	94
35	Waters#	95	96
36	Harman	96	96
37	Tucker	76	77
38	*Horn*	95	95
39	*Royce*#	96	95
40	*Lewis*	95	95
41	*Kim*	100	100

		1	2
42	Brown	87	92
43	*Calvert*	93	93
44	*McCandless*	94	94
45	*Rohrabacher*	99	99
46	*Dornan*	92	95
47	*Cox*	94	94
48	*Packard*	99	98
49	Schenk	99	99
50	Filner	100	100
51	*Cunningham*	98	98
52	*Hunter*	96	97
Colorado			
1	Schroeder	99	99
2	Skaggs	99	99
3	*McInnis*	99	99
4	*Allard*	99	99
5	*Hefley*	99	99
6	*Schaefer*	96	97
Connecticut			
1	Kennelly	98	99
2	Gejdenson	96	97
3	DeLauro	99	99
4	*Shays*	100	100
5	*Franks*	98	98
6	*Johnson*	97	97
Delaware			
AL	*Castle*	99	100
Florida			
1	Hutto	95	96
2	Peterson#	96	96
3	Brown	94	95
4	*Fowler*	97	97
5	Thurman	99	100
6	*Stearns*	99	99
7	*Mica*	98	98
8	*McCollum*	91	91
9	*Bilirakis*#	95	95
10	*Young*#	97	97
11	Gibbons	93	94
12	*Canady*	99	100
13	*Miller*	98	98
14	*Goss*	100	100
15	Bacchus	92	93
16	Lewis	87	87
17	Meek#	95	95
18	*Ros-Lehtinen*#	94	94
19	Johnston	92	92
20	Deutsch	99	99
21	*Diaz-Balart*	99	99
22	*Shaw*	96	97
23	Hastings#	78	79
Georgia			
1	*Kingston*	99	99
2	Bishop	95	95
3	*Collins*#	98	98
4	*Linder*	99	99
5	Lewis	96	96
6	*Gingrich*	95	95
7	Darden	97	97
8	Rowland	96	97
9	Deal	98	98
10	Johnson	98	99
11	McKinney	99	99
Hawaii			
1	Abercrombie	97	98
2	Mink	98	98
Idaho			
1	LaRocco	99	99
2	*Crapo*	99	99
Illinois			
1	Rush	90	91
2	Reynolds	77	77
3	Lipinski	95	96
4	Gutierrez	93	93
5	Rostenkowski	85	84
6	*Hyde*†	98	98
7	Collins#	85	86
8	*Crane*	91	92
9	Yates#	95	96
10	*Porter*	97	98
11	Sangmeister	97	97
12	Costello	98	98
13	*Fawell*	99	99
14	*Hastert*#	97	97
15	*Ewing*	96	97
16	*Manzullo*	99	99
17	Evans	99	99

ND Northern Democrats   SD Southern Democrats

	1	2
18 *Michel*	86	86
19 Poshard	100	100
20 Durbin	99	99
Indiana		
1 Visclosky	98	99
2 Sharp	87	88
3 Roemer	99	99
4 Long#	97	98
5 *Buyer#*	98	98
6 *Burton*	97	97
7 *Myers*	99	99
8 McCloskey	94	95
9 Hamilton	99	100
10 *Jacobs#*	98	98
Iowa		
1 *Leach*	99	99
2 *Nussle*	99	99
3 *Lightfoot*	98	98
4 Smith	96	97
5 *Grandy*	62	62
Kansas		
1 *Roberts*	98	98
2 Slattery	57	56
3 *Meyers*	99	99
4 Glickman	97	97
Kentucky		
1 Barlow	94	94
2 *Lewis ¹†*	100	100
3 Mazzoli	99	99
4 *Bunning*	99	99
5 *Rogers*	98	98
6 Baesler	99	99
Louisiana		
1 *Livingston*	93	94
2 Jefferson	92	93
3 Tauzin	97	97
4 Fields	97	97
5 *McCrery*	95	96
6 *Baker*	93	93
7 Hayes	90	90
Maine		
1 Andrews	97	97
2 *Snowe*	99	99
Maryland		
1 *Gilchrest*	99	99
2 *Bentley#*	92	93
3 Cardin	97	97
4 Wynn	97	98
5 Hoyer	97	98
6 *Bartlett*	99	99
7 Mfume	94	94
8 *Morella*	98	99
Massachusetts		
1 Olver	99	99
2 Neal	96	96
3 *Blute*	99	99
4 Frank	97	97
5 Meehan	93	94
6 *Torkildsen*	98	98
7 Markey	97	97
8 Kennedy	96	97
9 Moakley	98	98
10 Studds	97	97
Michigan		
1 Stupak	99	99
2 *Hoekstra*	99	100
3 *Ehlers*	99	99
4 *Camp*	98	98
5 Barcia	98	99
6 *Upton*	100	100
7 *Smith*	97	97
8 Carr	85	85
9 Kildee	100	100
10 Bonior	97	98
11 *Knollenberg*	99	99
12 Levin	99	99
13 Ford	76	78
14 Conyers	95	95
15 Collins#	91	92
16 Dingell	93	93
Minnesota		
1 Penny	98	98
2 Minge	99	99
3 *Ramstad*	99	99
4 Vento	98	98

	1	2
5 Sabo	98	99
6 *Grams*	91	91
7 Peterson	99	99
8 Oberstar	98	98
Mississippi		
1 Whitten	64	67
2 Thompson	94	94
3 Montgomery	98	98
4 Parker	96	96
5 Taylor	98	99
Missouri		
1 Clay	86	85
2 *Talent*	99	99
3 Gephardt	95	96
4 Skelton	96	96
5 Wheat	82	83
6 Danner	98	98
7 *Hancock*	99	99
8 *Emerson*	96	96
9 Volkmer	98	98
Montana		
AL Williams	91	94
Nebraska		
1 *Bereuter*	99	99
2 Hoagland	98	98
3 *Barrett*	99	99
Nevada		
1 Bilbray	99	99
2 *Vucanovich*	98	98
New Hampshire		
1 *Zeliff*	95	95
2 Swett	95	96
New Jersey		
1 Andrews	95	95
2 Hughes	99	99
3 *Saxton*	98	98
4 *Smith*	98	99
5 Roukema	92	93
6 Pallone	100	100
7 *Franks*	99	99
8 Klein	97	97
9 Torricelli	91	91
10 Payne#	96	97
11 *Gallo ²†*	48	48
12 *Zimmer*	99	100
13 Menendez	99	99
New Mexico		
1 *Schiff#*	97	98
2 *Skeen*	99	99
3 Richardson	96	96
New York		
1 Hochbrueckner	98	98
2 *Lazio*	100	100
3 *King*	99	99
4 *Levy*	99	99
5 Ackerman	93	93
6 Flake	88	89
7 Manton	94	95
8 Nadler	93	93
9 Schumer	93	93
10 Towns#	83	84
11 Owens	81	81
12 Velazquez	96	96
13 *Molinari*	99	99
14 Maloney	95	95
15 Rangel#	82	83
16 Serrano	96	96
17 Engel	93	95
18 Lowey	97	97
19 *Fish#*	73	74
20 Gilman	99	99
21 McNulty	93	93
22 *Solomon*	95	95
23 *Boehlert*	98	98
24 *McHugh*	99	99
25 Walsh	98	98
26 Hinchey	98	99
27 *Paxon*	99	100
28 Slaughter#	98	98
29 LaFalce	97	97
30 *Quinn*	95	96
31 *Houghton#*	93	93
North Carolina		
1 Clayton	97	97
2 Valentine	93	94

	1	2
3 Lancaster	99	99
4 Price	98	99
5 Neal	84	86
6 *Coble*	100	100
7 Rose	91	91
8 Hefner	97	98
9 *McMillan#*	81	83
10 *Ballenger*	97	97
11 *Taylor*	97	98
12 Watt	98	98
North Dakota		
AL Pomeroy	98	99
Ohio		
1 Mann	98	98
2 *Portman#*	96	96
3 Hall	94	95
4 *Oxley*	96	96
5 *Gillmor*	98	98
6 Strickland	98	99
7 *Hobson*	99	100
8 *Boehner*	96	97
9 Kaptur	94	95
10 *Hoke*	95	96
11 Stokes	93	94
12 *Kasich*	99	99
13 Brown	99	99
14 Sawyer	99	99
15 *Pryce*	94	94
16 *Regula*	100	100
17 Traficant	99	99
18 Applegate	89	89
19 Fingerhut	97	97
Oklahoma		
1 *Inhofe ³†*	87	86
2 Synar	93	93
3 Brewster	95	95
4 McCurdy	76	76
5 *Istook*	95	95
6 *Lucas ⁴†*	99	99
Oregon		
1 Furse	98	98
2 *Smith*	83	84
3 Wyden	99	99
4 DeFazio#	91	92
5 Kopetski	94	94
Pennsylvania		
1 Foglietta	92	92
2 Blackwell	74	76
3 Borski	96	97
4 Klink	99	99
5 *Clinger#*	96	96
6 Holden	100	100
7 *Weldon*	96	96
8 *Greenwood*	97	98
9 *Shuster*	98	99
10 *McDade#*	83	84
11 Kanjorski	99	99
12 Murtha	92	92
13 Margolies-Mezv.	98	98
14 Coyne	98	99
15 McHale	100	100
16 *Walker*	100	100
17 Gekas	99	99
18 Santorum	93	93
19 *Goodling*	97	97
20 Murphy	87	86
21 *Ridge*	73	74
Rhode Island		
1 *Machtley*	84	84
2 Reed	99	99
South Carolina		
1 Ravenel	95	95
2 *Spence*	98	98
3 Derrick#	93	93
4 *Inglis*	99	99
5 Spratt	98	98
6 Clyburn	96	97
South Dakota		
AL Johnson	99	99
Tennessee		
1 *Quillen*	93	93
2 *Duncan*	99	99
3 Lloyd	87	89
4 Cooper	91	91
5 Clement	94	93

	1	2
6 Gordon	98	98
7 *Sundquist*	69	68
8 Tanner	99	99
9 Ford	77	78
Texas		
1 Chapman	89	91
2 Wilson	89	90
3 *Johnson, Sam*	98	98
4 Hall	98	99
5 Bryant	96	97
6 *Barton*	94	94
7 *Archer*	99	99
8 *Fields*	90	91
9 Brooks	92	92
10 Pickle#	92	92
11 Edwards	98	99
12 Geren	98	99
13 Sarpalius	99	99
14 Laughlin	84	84
15 de la Garza	91	93
16 Coleman	95	96
17 Stenholm	99	98
18 Washington	19	20
19 *Combest*	99	99
20 Gonzalez	99	99
21 *Smith*	97	97
22 *DeLay*	95	96
23 *Bonilla*	99	99
24 Frost#	93	93
25 Andrews	84	86
26 *Armey*	98	98
27 Ortiz#	96	96
28 Tejeda	99	100
29 Green	90	90
30 Johnson, E. B.	98	98
Utah		
1 *Hansen*	98	98
2 Shepherd	98	98
3 Orton	97	97
Vermont		
AL *Sanders*	97	97
Virginia		
1 *Bateman*	97	97
2 Pickett	97	97
3 Scott	98	98
4 Sisisky	97	98
5 Payne#	98	98
6 *Goodlatte*	99	99
7 *Bliley*	98	98
8 Moran#	93	95
9 Boucher	95	96
10 *Wolf*	99	99
11 Byrne	98	98
Washington		
1 Cantwell	99	99
2 Swift	96	97
3 Unsoeld	99	100
4 Inslee	99	99
5 Foley ⁵		
6 Dicks	97	97
7 McDermott	96	96
8 *Dunn*	99	99
9 Kreidler	99	100
West Virginia		
1 Mollohan	97	98
2 Wise	97	98
3 Rahall	99	99
Wisconsin		
1 Barca	99	99
2 *Klug*	99	99
3 *Gunderson#*	98	98
4 Kleczka	97	97
5 Barrett	98	98
6 *Petri*	99	99
7 Obey#	95	95
8 *Roth*	96	96
9 *Sensenbrenner*	100	100
Wyoming		
AL *Thomas*	92	92
Delegates		
de Lugo, V.I.	95	95
Faleomavaega, Am. S.	56	56
Norton, D.C.	97	97
Romero-B., P.R.	81	81
Underwood, Guam	77	77

Southern states - Ala., Ark., Fla., Ga., Ky., La., Miss., N.C., Okla., S.C., Tenn., Texas, Va.
Omitted votes are quorum calls, which CQ does not include in its vote charts.

HOUSE KEY VOTES 1, 2, 3, 4, 5, 6

Following are votes from 1994 selected by Congressional Quarterly as key votes (Explanations of key votes, p. 28-C). Original vote number is provided in parentheses.

1. HR 3425. Department of Environmental Protection/ Rule. Adoption of the rule (H Res 312) to provide for House floor consideration of the bill to elevate the Environmental Protection Agency to Cabinet-level status. Rejected 191-227: R 5-167; D 185-60 (ND 140-28, SD 45-32); I 1-0, Feb. 2, 1994. (House vote 4)

2. H Con Res 218. Fiscal 1995 Budget Resolution/Defense Cuts. Frank, D-Mass., substitute amendment to reduce the $263.3 billion in defense budget authority in the resolution by $2.4 billion. Rejected in the Committee of the Whole 105-313: R 12-160; D 92-153 (ND 82-85, SD 10-68); I 1-0, March 10, 1994. A "nay" was a vote in support of the president's position. (House vote 51)

3. H J Res 103. Balanced-Budget Constitutional Amendment/Passage. Passage of the joint resolution to propose a constitutional amendment to require a balanced budget by 2001 or the second fiscal year after ratification by three-fourths of the states, whichever is later. Congress could waive the balanced-budget requirement if three-fifths of the House and Senate approve, or when a declaration of war was in effect or when there was a declared military threat to national security. Rejected 271-153: R 172-1; D 99-151 (ND 47-122, SD 52-29); I 0-1, March 17, 1994. A two-thirds majority vote of those present and voting (283 in this case) is required to pass a joint resolution proposing an amendment to the Constitution. A "nay" was a vote in support of the president's position. (House vote 65)

4. H Con Res 218. Fiscal 1995 Budget Resolution/ Instruct Conferees. Kasich, R-Ohio, motion to instruct the House conferees to agree to the Senate amendment to provide an additional $26.1 billion in deficit reduction over the following five years and to protect defense spending from further cuts. Motion rejected 202-216: R 159-6; D 43-209 (ND 29-141, SD 14-68); I 0-1, April 14, 1994. A "nay" was a vote in support of the president's position. (House vote 112)

5. HR 4296. Assault Weapons Ban/Passage. Passage of the bill to ban the manufacture and possession of 19 types of semiautomatic weapons and high-capacity ammunition clips but exempt existing guns and about 670 guns that are deemed to have a legitimate sporting purpose. Passed 216-214: R 38-137; D 177-77 (ND 137-34, SD 40-43); I 1-0, May 5, 1994. A "yea" was a vote in support of the president's position. (House vote 156)

6. S 636. Abortion Clinic Access/Conference Report. Adoption of the conference report to establish federal criminal and civil penalties for persons who use force, the threat of force or physical obstruction to block access to abortion clinics. Adopted 241-174: R 40-131; D 200-43 (ND 139-26, SD 61-17); I 1-0, May 5, 1994. A "yea" was a vote in support of the president's position. (House vote 159)

[1] *William H. Natcher, D-Ky., died March 29. The last vote for which he was eligible was key vote 3. Ron Lewis, R-Ky., was sworn in May 26, 1994. The first key vote for which he was eligible was key vote 7.*

[2] *Glenn English, D-Okla., resigned effective Jan. 7, 1994. Frank D. Lucas, R-Okla., was sworn in May 17, 1994. The first vote for which he was eligible was key vote 7.*

[3] *Rep. Thomas S. Foley, D-Wash., as Speaker of the House, voted at his discretion.*

KEY

Y   Voted for (yea).
Paired for.
+   Announced for.
N   Voted against (nay).
X   Paired against.
—   Announced against.
P   Voted "present."
C   Voted "present" to avoid possible conflict of interest.
?   Did not vote or otherwise make a position known.
D   Delegates ineligible to vote.

Democrats   *Republicans*
Independent

	1	2	3	4	5	6
ALABAMA						
1 *Callahan*	N	N	Y	Y	N	N
2 *Everett*	N	N	Y	Y	N	N
3 Browder	N	N	Y	Y	N	N
4 Bevill	Y	N	Y	N	N	?
5 Cramer	N	N	Y	N	N	Y
6 *Bachus*	N	N	Y	Y	N	N
7 Hilliard	Y	N	N	N	N	Y
ALASKA						
AL *Young*	N	N	Y	Y	N	N
ARIZONA						
1 Coppersmith	Y	N	Y	Y	Y	Y
2 Pastor	Y	N	N	N	Y	Y
3 *Stump*	N	N	Y	Y	N	N
4 *Kyl*	N	N	Y	Y	N	N
5 *Kolbe*	N	N	Y	Y	N	Y
6 English	Y	Y	Y	Y	Y	Y
ARKANSAS						
1 Lambert	Y	Y	Y	Y	Y	Y
2 Thornton	Y	N	N	N	N	Y
3 *Hutchinson*	N	N	Y	Y	N	N
4 *Dickey*	N	N	Y	Y	N	N
CALIFORNIA						
1 Hamburg	Y	Y	N	N	Y	Y
2 *Herger*	N	N	Y	Y	N	?
3 Fazio	Y	N	N	N	Y	Y
4 *Doolittle*	N	N	Y	?	N	X
5 Matsui	Y	N	N	N	Y	Y
6 Woolsey	Y	Y	N	Y	Y	Y
7 Miller	Y	?	N	N	Y	Y
8 Pelosi	Y	?	N	N	Y	Y
9 Dellums	Y	Y	N	N	Y	Y
10 *Baker*	N	N	Y	Y	N	N
11 *Pombo*	N	N	Y	Y	N	N
12 Lantos	Y	N	N	Y	Y	Y
13 Stark	Y	Y	N	N	Y	#
14 Eshoo	Y	Y	N	Y	Y	Y
15 Mineta	Y	N	N	N	Y	Y
16 Edwards	Y	?	N	N	Y	Y
17 Farr	Y	Y	?	N	Y	Y
18 Condit	N	N	Y	Y	Y	Y
19 Lehman	X	N	N	Y	Y	Y
20 Dooley	N	?	Y	Y	Y	Y
21 *Thomas*	N	N	Y	?	N	Y
22 *Huffington*	N	N	Y	Y	Y	Y
23 *Gallegly*	N	N	Y	Y	N	N
24 Beilenson	Y	Y	N	N	Y	Y
25 *McKeon*	N	N	Y	Y	N	N
26 Berman	Y	Y	N	Y	Y	Y
27 *Moorhead*	N	N	Y	Y	N	N
28 *Dreier*	N	N	Y	Y	N	N
29 Waxman	Y	Y	N	N	Y	Y
30 Becerra	Y	Y	N	N	Y	Y
31 Martinez	Y	N	Y	N	Y	Y
32 Dixon	Y	N	N	N	Y	Y
33 Roybal-Allard	Y	Y	N	N	Y	Y
34 Torres	Y	N	N	N	Y	Y
35 Waters	Y	Y	N	N	Y	Y
36 Harman	N	N	Y	N	Y	Y
37 Tucker	Y	N	N	N	Y	Y
38 *Horn*	N	N	Y	Y	Y	Y
39 *Royce*	N	N	Y	Y	N	N
40 *Lewis*	N	?	Y	#	N	N
41 *Kim*	N	N	Y	Y	N	N

	1	2	3	4	5	6
42 Brown	Y	N	N	N	Y	Y
43 *Calvert*	N	N	Y	Y	N	N
44 *McCandless*	N	N	Y	Y	N	Y
45 *Rohrabacher*	N	N	Y	Y	N	N
46 *Dornan*	X	N	Y	Y	N	N
47 *Cox*	N	N	Y	Y	N	N
48 *Packard*	N	N	Y	Y	N	N
49 Schenk	Y	N	Y	Y	Y	Y
50 Filner	Y	Y	N	N	Y	Y
51 *Cunningham*	N	N	Y	Y	N	N
52 *Hunter*	N	N	Y	Y	N	N
COLORADO						
1 Schroeder	Y	Y	N	N	Y	Y
2 Skaggs	Y	N	N	N	Y	Y
3 *McInnis*	N	N	Y	Y	N	Y
4 *Allard*	N	N	Y	Y	N	N
5 *Hefley*	N	N	Y	N	N	N
6 *Schaefer*	N	N	Y	Y	N	N
CONNECTICUT						
1 Kennelly	Y	N	N	N	Y	Y
2 Gejdenson	Y	N	N	Y	Y	Y
3 DeLauro	Y	N	N	N	Y	Y
4 *Shays*	Y	Y	Y	Y	Y	Y
5 *Franks*	N	N	Y	?	N	Y
6 *Johnson*	N	N	Y	Y	Y	Y
DELAWARE						
AL *Castle*	N	N	Y	Y	Y	Y
FLORIDA						
1 Hutto	N	N	Y	N	N	N
2 Peterson	N	N	Y	N	N	Y
3 Brown	Y	N	N	N	Y	Y
4 *Fowler*	N	N	Y	Y	N	Y
5 Thurman	N	N	N	N	N	Y
6 *Stearns*	N	N	Y	Y	N	N
7 *Mica*	N	N	Y	N	N	N
8 *McCollum*	N	N	Y	N	N	X
9 *Bilirakis*	N	N	Y	N	N	N
10 *Young*	N	N	Y	N	N	N
11 Gibbons	Y	N	N	N	Y	Y
12 *Canady*	N	N	Y	Y	N	N
13 *Miller*	N	N	Y	Y	N	N
14 *Goss*	N	N	Y	N	N	N
15 Bacchus	Y	N	Y	N	Y	Y
16 *Lewis*	X	N	Y	N	N	N
17 Meek	?	N	N	N	Y	Y
18 *Ros-Lehtinen*	N	N	Y	Y	N	N
19 Johnston	Y	Y	N	Y	Y	Y
20 Deutsch	Y	N	Y	N	Y	Y
21 *Diaz-Balart*	N	N	Y	Y	N	N
22 *Shaw*	N	N	Y	Y	N	N
23 Hastings	?	?	?	N	Y	Y
GEORGIA						
1 *Kingston*	N	N	Y	Y	N	N
2 Bishop	N	N	Y	N	Y	N
3 *Collins*	N	N	Y	Y	N	N
4 *Linder*	N	N	Y	Y	N	N
5 Lewis	Y	Y	N	N	Y	Y
6 *Gingrich*	N	N	Y	Y	N	N
7 Darden	N	N	Y	N	N	Y
8 Rowland	N	N	Y	N	N	Y
9 Deal	N	N	Y	N	N	N
10 Johnson	N	N	Y	Y	Y	Y
11 McKinney	Y	Y	N	N	Y	Y
HAWAII						
1 Abercrombie	Y	Y	N	N	Y	Y
2 Mink	Y	Y	N	N	Y	Y
IDAHO						
1 LaRocco	N	N	Y	Y	N	Y
2 *Crapo*	N	N	Y	Y	N	N
ILLINOIS						
1 Rush	Y	Y	N	N	Y	Y
2 Reynolds	?	?	N	N	Y	Y
3 Lipinski	Y	N	Y	N	N	N
4 Gutierrez	Y	?	N	N	Y	Y
5 Rostenkowski	Y	N	N	N	Y	Y
6 *Hyde*	N	N	Y	Y	N	N
7 Collins	Y	?	N	N	Y	Y
8 *Crane*	N	?	Y	Y	N	N
9 Yates	Y	Y	N	N	Y	Y
10 *Porter*	Y	N	Y	Y	Y	Y
11 Sangmeister	Y	Y	Y	N	Y	Y
12 Costello	Y	N	Y	N	N	N
13 *Fawell*	N	N	Y	Y	Y	Y
14 *Hastert*	N	N	Y	N	N	N
15 *Ewing*	N	N	Y	Y	N	N
16 *Manzullo*	N	N	Y	Y	N	N
17 Evans	Y	Y	N	N	Y	Y

ND   Northern Democrats   SD   Southern Democrats

	1	2	3	4	5	6
18 ***Michel***	N	N	#	Y	Y	N
19 Poshard	N	Y	Y	Y	N	N
20 Durbin	Y	Y	N	N	Y	Y
INDIANA						
1 Visclosky	Y	N	N	N	Y	Y
2 Sharp	N	N	Y	N	Y	Y
3 Roemer	N	N	Y	Y	Y	Y
4 Long	Y	N	Y	N	—	#
5 ***Buyer***	N	N	Y	Y	N	N
6 ***Burton***	N	N	Y	Y	N	N
7 ***Myers***	N	N	Y	Y	N	N
8 McCloskey	Y	N	Y	N	N	Y
9 Hamilton	N	N	N	Y	N	Y
10 Jacobs	Y	Y	Y	N	Y	Y
IOWA						
1 ***Leach***	N	Y	Y	Y	Y	Y
2 ***Nussle***	N	Y	Y	Y	N	N
3 ***Lightfoot***	N	N	Y	Y	N	N
4 Smith	N	N	N	N	N	Y
5 ***Grandy***	N	N	#	?	N	N
KANSAS						
1 ***Roberts***	N	N	Y	Y	N	N
2 Slattery	N	N	N	N	Y	Y
3 ***Meyers***	N	N	Y	Y	Y	Y
4 Glickman	N	N	Y	N	Y	Y
KENTUCKY						
1 Barlow	Y	N	N	N	N	N
2 Natcher[1]	Y	?	?			
3 Mazzoli	Y	N	Y	N	Y	N
4 ***Bunning***	N	N	Y	Y	N	N
5 ***Rogers***	N	N	Y	Y	?	X
6 Baesler	N	N	Y	N	Y	Y
LOUISIANA						
1 ***Livingston***	N	N	Y	Y	N	N
2 Jefferson	Y	N	N	N	Y	Y
3 Tauzin	N	N	Y	Y	N	N
4 Fields	Y	Y	N	N	Y	Y
5 ***McCrery***	N	N	Y	Y	N	N
6 ***Baker***	N	N	Y	Y	N	N
7 Hayes	N	N	Y	Y	N	N
MAINE						
1 Andrews	Y	Y	N	N	Y	Y
2 ***Snowe***	N	N	Y	Y	N	Y
MARYLAND						
1 ***Gilchrest***	N	N	Y	Y	Y	N
2 ***Bentley***	N	N	Y	Y	N	N
3 Cardin	Y	Y	N	N	Y	Y
4 Wynn	Y	Y	N	N	Y	Y
5 Hoyer	Y	N	Y	N	Y	Y
6 ***Bartlett***	N	N	Y	Y	N	N
7 Mfume	Y	Y	N	N	Y	Y
8 ***Morella***	Y	Y	Y	N	Y	Y
MASSACHUSETTS						
1 Olver	Y	Y	N	N	Y	Y
2 Neal	Y	Y	N	N	Y	Y
3 ***Blute***	N	N	Y	Y	Y	N
4 Frank	Y	Y	N	N	Y	Y
5 Meehan	Y	Y	Y	Y	Y	Y
6 ***Torkildsen***	N	N	Y	Y	N	Y
7 Markey	Y	Y	N	N	Y	Y
8 Kennedy	Y	Y	Y	N	Y	Y
9 Moakley	Y	Y	N	N	Y	Y
10 Studds	Y	Y	N	N	Y	Y
MICHIGAN						
1 Stupak	N	N	N	N	N	N
2 ***Hoekstra***	N	N	Y	Y	N	N
3 ***Ehlers***	N	N	Y	Y	N	N
4 ***Camp***	N	N	Y	Y	N	N
5 Barcia	Y	N	Y	N	N	N
6 ***Upton***	N	Y	Y	Y	N	N
7 ***Smith***	N	N	Y	Y	N	N
8 Carr	Y	N	Y	N	Y	Y
9 Kildee	Y	Y	N	N	Y	N
10 Bonior	Y	N	N	N	Y	Y
11 ***Knollenberg***	N	N	Y	Y	N	N
12 Levin	Y	N	N	N	Y	Y
13 Ford	Y	Y	N	N	Y	Y
14 Conyers	Y	Y	N	N	Y	Y
15 Collins	Y	Y	N	N	Y	Y
16 Dingell	Y	N	N	N	N	Y
MINNESOTA						
1 Penny	N	Y	Y	Y	Y	N
2 Minge	N	Y	Y	Y	Y	Y
3 ***Ramstad***	N	N	Y	Y	N	Y
4 Vento	Y	Y	N	N	Y	Y

	1	2	3	4	5	6
5 Sabo	Y	N	N	N	Y	Y
6 ***Grams***	N	N	Y	Y	N	N
7 Peterson	N	Y	Y	Y	N	N
8 Oberstar	Y	Y	N	N	N	N
MISSISSIPPI						
1 Whitten	N	N	Y	N	N	N
2 Thompson	Y	N	N	N	Y	Y
3 Montgomery	Y	N	Y	N	N	N
4 Parker	N	N	Y	N	N	N
5 Taylor	N	N	Y	N	N	N
MISSOURI						
1 Clay	Y	N	N	N	Y	Y
2 ***Talent***	N	N	Y	Y	N	N
3 Gephardt	Y	N	N	N	Y	Y
4 Skelton	N	N	Y	N	N	N
5 Wheat	Y	N	N	N	Y	Y
6 Danner	N	Y	Y	N	N	Y
7 ***Hancock***	N	N	Y	Y	N	N
8 ***Emerson***	N	N	Y	Y	N	N
9 Volkmer	Y	N	Y	N	N	N
MONTANA						
AL Williams	N	N	N	N	N	Y
NEBRASKA						
1 ***Bereuter***	N	N	Y	Y	Y	Y
2 Hoagland	Y	N	Y	Y	Y	Y
3 ***Barrett***	N	N	Y	Y	N	N
NEVADA						
1 Bilbray	N	N	Y	N	N	Y
2 ***Vucanovich***	N	N	Y	Y	N	N
NEW HAMPSHIRE						
1 ***Zeliff***	N	N	Y	Y	N	Y
2 Swett	Y	N	Y	Y	Y	#
NEW JERSEY						
1 Andrews	Y	?	Y	Y	Y	Y
2 Hughes	Y	N	N	N	Y	Y
3 ***Saxton***	N	N	Y	Y	Y	N
4 ***Smith***	N	N	Y	Y	Y	N
5 ***Roukema***	N	Y	Y	+	Y	Y
6 Pallone	Y	N	Y	Y	Y	Y
7 ***Franks***	N	N	Y	Y	Y	Y
8 Klein	Y	Y	N	N	Y	Y
9 Torricelli	Y	?	Y	N	Y	Y
10 Payne	Y	Y	—	N	Y	Y
11 ***Gallo***	N	?	?	?	N	Y
12 ***Zimmer***	N	Y	Y	Y	N	Y
13 Menendez	Y	N	N	N	Y	Y
NEW MEXICO						
1 ***Schiff***	N	N	Y	Y	N	Y
2 ***Skeen***	N	N	Y	Y	N	N
3 Richardson	Y	N	Y	N	N	?
NEW YORK						
1 Hochbrueckner	Y	N	N	N	Y	Y
2 ***Lazio***	N	N	Y	Y	Y	Y
3 ***King***	N	N	Y	Y	Y	N
4 ***Levy***	N	N	Y	Y	Y	N
5 Ackerman	Y	Y	N	N	Y	Y
6 Flake	Y	Y	N	N	Y	Y
7 Manton	Y	N	?	N	Y	N
8 Nadler	Y	Y	N	N	Y	Y
9 Schumer	Y	Y	N	N	Y	Y
10 Towns	Y	Y	N	N	Y	Y
11 Owens	Y	Y	N	N	Y	Y
12 Velazquez	Y	Y	N	N	Y	Y
13 ***Molinari***	N	N	Y	Y	Y	Y
14 Maloney	Y	Y	N	N	Y	Y
15 Rangel	Y	Y	N	N	Y	Y
16 Serrano	Y	Y	N	N	Y	?
17 Engel	Y	Y	N	N	Y	Y
18 Lowey	Y	N	N	N	Y	Y
19 ***Fish***	N	N	Y	?	N	?
20 ***Gilman***	Y	N	N	N	N	Y
21 McNulty	Y	N	Y	N	Y	N
22 ***Solomon***	N	N	Y	Y	N	N
23 ***Boehlert***	Y	N	Y	N	Y	Y
24 ***McHugh***	N	N	Y	Y	N	Y
25 ***Walsh***	N	N	Y	Y	N	N
26 Hinchey	Y	Y	N	N	N	Y
27 ***Paxon***	N	N	Y	Y	N	N
28 Slaughter	Y	Y	N	N	Y	Y
29 LaFalce	Y	Y	N	N	Y	N
30 ***Quinn***	N	N	Y	Y	Y	N
31 ***Houghton***	N	N	Y	Y	Y	Y
NORTH CAROLINA						
1 Clayton	Y	Y	N	N	Y	Y
2 Valentine	Y	N	Y	N	Y	Y

	1	2	3	4	5	6
3 Lancaster	N	N	Y	N	N	Y
4 Price	Y	N	N	N	Y	?
5 Neal	Y	N	Y	N	Y	?
6 ***Coble***	N	N	Y	Y	N	N
7 Rose	Y	N	N	N	N	Y
8 Hefner	Y	N	Y	N	N	Y
9 ***McMillan***	N	?	Y	Y	N	Y
10 ***Ballenger***	N	N	Y	Y	N	N
11 ***Taylor***	N	N	Y	Y	N	N
12 Watt	Y	Y	N	N	Y	Y
NORTH DAKOTA						
AL Pomeroy	N	N	N	Y	Y	Y
OHIO						
1 Mann	Y	N	Y	Y	Y	Y
2 ***Portman***	N	N	Y	Y	N	N
3 Hall	Y	N	N	N	Y	N
4 ***Oxley***	N	N	Y	Y	N	N
5 ***Gillmor***	N	N	Y	Y	N	N
6 Strickland	N	N	N	N	N	Y
7 ***Hobson***	N	N	Y	Y	N	N
8 ***Boehner***	N	N	Y	Y	N	N
9 Kaptur	Y	N	N	?	Y	N
10 ***Hoke***	N	Y	Y	Y	N	N
11 Stokes	Y	Y	N	N	Y	Y
12 ***Kasich***	N	N	Y	Y	Y	N
13 Brown	Y	Y	Y	Y	Y	Y
14 Sawyer	Y	N	N	N	Y	Y
15 ***Pryce***	N	N	Y	Y	Y	Y
16 ***Regula***	N	N	Y	Y	N	N
17 Traficant	Y	N	N	N	Y	Y
18 Applegate	N	N	N	N	Y	N
19 Fingerhut	N	N	Y	Y	Y	Y
OKLAHOMA						
1 ***Inhofe***	N	N	Y	Y	N	N
2 Synar	Y	Y	N	N	Y	Y
3 Brewster	N	N	Y	Y	N	Y
4 McCurdy	N	N	Y	N	Y	Y
5 ***Istook***	N	N	Y	Y	N	N
6 Vacancy[2]						
OREGON						
1 Furse	Y	Y	N	N	Y	Y
2 ***Smith***	?	N	Y	Y	N	N
3 Wyden	Y	Y	N	N	Y	Y
4 DeFazio	Y	Y	Y	Y	N	Y
5 Kopetski	Y	?	N	N	N	Y
PENNSYLVANIA						
1 Foglietta	Y	Y	N	N	Y	?
2 Blackwell	Y	Y	N	?	Y	?
3 Borski	#	N	N	N	Y	N
4 Klink	N	N	N	N	N	N
5 ***Clinger***	N	N	Y	Y	N	N
6 Holden	Y	N	N	N	N	N
7 ***Weldon***	N	N	Y	Y	N	N
8 ***Greenwood***	N	N	Y	Y	Y	Y
9 ***Shuster***	N	N	Y	Y	N	N
10 ***McDade***	N	N	Y	Y	Y	N
11 Kanjorski	Y	N	N	N	N	N
12 Murtha	Y	N	N	N	N	N
13 Margolies-Mezv.	Y	Y	N	Y	Y	Y
14 Coyne	Y	Y	N	N	Y	Y
15 McHale	Y	N	Y	Y	Y	Y
16 ***Walker***	N	N	Y	Y	N	N
17 ***Gekas***	N	N	Y	Y	N	N
18 ***Santorum***	N	N	Y	Y	N	N
19 ***Goodling***	N	N	Y	Y	N	N
20 Murphy	N	N	N	?	N	N
21 ***Ridge***	?	N	Y	?	Y	Y
RHODE ISLAND						
1 ***Machtley***	N	N	Y	Y	Y	Y
2 Reed	Y	N	N	N	Y	Y
SOUTH CAROLINA						
1 ***Ravenel***	N	N	Y	Y	N	N
2 ***Spence***	N	N	Y	Y	N	N
3 Derrick	Y	N	Y	N	Y	Y
4 ***Inglis***	N	N	Y	Y	N	N
5 Spratt	Y	N	Y	N	Y	Y
6 Clyburn	Y	N	N	N	Y	Y
SOUTH DAKOTA						
AL Johnson	N	Y	Y	N	N	Y
TENNESSEE						
1 ***Quillen***	N	N	Y	?	N	N
2 ***Duncan***	N	Y	Y	Y	N	N
3 Lloyd	N	N	Y	N	Y	Y
4 Cooper	Y	N	Y	Y	N	Y
5 Clement	Y	N	Y	Y	N	?

	1	2	3	4	5	6
6 Gordon	Y	Y	Y	Y	N	Y
7 ***Sundquist***	N	N	Y	Y	N	N
8 Tanner	N	N	Y	N	N	Y
9 Ford	?	?	N	N	Y	Y
TEXAS						
1 Chapman	?	N	Y	N	N	Y
2 Wilson	?	N	Y	N	N	Y
3 ***Johnson, Sam***	N	N	Y	Y	N	N
4 Hall	N	N	Y	Y	N	N
5 Bryant	Y	Y	Y	N	Y	Y
6 ***Barton***	N	N	Y	?	N	N
7 ***Archer***	N	N	Y	Y	N	N
8 ***Fields***	N	N	Y	Y	N	N
9 Brooks	Y	?	N	N	N	Y
10 Pickle	Y	N	Y	N	Y	Y
11 Edwards	N	N	Y	N	Y	Y
12 Geren	N	N	Y	N	N	Y
13 Sarpalius	N	N	Y	N	N	N
14 Laughlin	Y	N	Y	N	N	?
15 de la Garza	?	N	Y	N	N	N
16 Coleman	Y	N	N	N	Y	Y
17 Stenholm	N	N	Y	Y	N	N
18 Washington	Y	?	N	X	Y	Y
19 ***Combest***	N	N	Y	Y	N	N
20 Gonzalez	Y	N	N	N	Y	Y
21 ***Smith***	N	N	Y	Y	N	N
22 ***DeLay***	N	N	Y	Y	N	N
23 ***Bonilla***	N	N	Y	Y	N	N
24 Frost	Y	N	Y	N	N	Y
25 Andrews	#	?	Y	Y	Y	Y
26 ***Armey***	N	N	Y	Y	N	N
27 Ortiz	N	N	Y	N	N	N
28 Tejeda	N	N	N	N	N	N
29 Green	Y	N	X	N	N	Y
30 Johnson, E.B.	Y	N	N	N	Y	Y
UTAH						
1 ***Hansen***	N	N	Y	Y	N	N
2 Shepherd	#	Y	Y	N	Y	Y
3 Orton	N	N	Y	Y	N	Y
VERMONT						
AL *Sanders*	Y	Y	N	N	Y	Y
VIRGINIA						
1 ***Bateman***	N	N	Y	Y	Y	N
2 Pickett	N	N	N	N	N	Y
3 Scott	Y	N	N	N	Y	Y
4 Sisisky	N	N	Y	N	N	Y
5 Payne	N	N	Y	Y	N	Y
6 ***Goodlatte***	N	N	Y	Y	N	N
7 ***Bliley***	N	N	Y	Y	N	N
8 Moran	N	N	Y	N	Y	Y
9 Boucher	Y	N	N	N	N	Y
10 ***Wolf***	N	N	Y	Y	N	N
11 Byrne	Y	N	N	N	Y	Y
WASHINGTON						
1 Cantwell	Y	N	N	Y	Y	Y
2 Swift	Y	N	N	N	Y	Y
3 Unsoeld	Y	Y	N	N	N	Y
4 Inslee	Y	Y	Y	Y	Y	Y
5 Foley[3]				N		
6 Dicks	Y	N	N	N	Y	Y
7 McDermott	Y	Y	N	N	Y	Y
8 ***Dunn***	N	N	Y	Y	N	Y
9 Kreidler	Y	N	N	N	Y	Y
WEST VIRGINIA						
1 Mollohan	Y	N	N	N	N	N
2 Wise	Y	N	N	N	N	Y
3 Rahall	Y	Y	N	N	N	N
WISCONSIN						
1 Barca	N	Y	N	Y	N	Y
2 ***Klug***	N	Y	Y	Y	Y	Y
3 ***Gunderson***	N	N	Y	Y	N	N
4 Kleczka	Y	Y	N	N	Y	Y
5 Barrett	Y	Y	N	N	Y	Y
6 ***Petri***	N	Y	Y	Y	N	N
7 Obey	Y	N	N	N	N	Y
8 ***Roth***	N	N	Y	Y	N	N
9 ***Sensenbrenner***	N	Y	Y	Y	N	N
WYOMING						
AL ***Thomas***	N	N	Y	Y	N	N
DELEGATES						
de Lugo, V.I.	D	Y	D	D	D	D
Faleomavaega, Am.S.	D	N	D	D	D	D
Norton, D.C.	D	Y	D	D	D	D
Romero-B., P.R.	D	N	D	D	D	D
Underwood, Guam	D	N	D	D	D	D

Southern states - Ala., Ark., Fla., Ga., Ky., La., Miss., N.C., Okla., S.C., Tenn., Texas, Va.
Omitted votes are quorum calls, which CQ does not include in its vote charts.

7. HR 4301. Fiscal 1995 Defense Authorization/Bosnia Arms Embargo Unilateral Termination. McCloskey, D-Ind., amendment to require the president to terminate unilaterally the arms embargo of Bosnia-Herzegovina upon receipt from that government of a request for assistance in its right of self-defense, authorizing the president to provide up to $200 million in defense articles and services. Adopted in the Committee of the Whole 244-178: R 127-45; D 117-132 (ND 84-87, SD 33-45); I 0-1, June 9, 1994. A "nay" was a vote in support of the president's position. (House vote 222)

8. HR 3626. Revising Restrictions on the Regional Bell Companies/Passage. Brooks, D-Texas, motion to suspend the rules and pass the bill to set conditions for the regional Bell telephone companies to enter the long-distance, telecommunications manufacturing, alarm service and electronic publishing markets. Motion agreed to 423-5: R 173-1; D 249-4 (ND 168-3, SD 81-1); I 1-0, June 28, 1994. A two-thirds majority of those present and voting (286 in this case) is required for passage under suspension of the rules. A "yea" was a vote in support of the president's position. (House vote 292)

9. HR 4624. Fiscal 1995 VA, HUD Appropriations/ Space Station. Roemer, D-Ind., amendment to terminate the space station and reallocate the $2.1 billion to other NASA programs. Rejected in the Committee of the Whole 155-278: R 40-136; D 114-142 (ND 101-72, SD 13-70); I 1-0, June 29, 1994. A "nay" was a vote in support of the president's position. (House vote 309)

10. HR 518. California Desert Protection/Hunting Exception. LaRocco, D-Idaho, en bloc amendment to designate the East Mojave Scenic Area a national preserve rather than a national park, thus permitting hunting, fishing and trapping to continue in the area. Adopted in the Committee of the Whole 239-183: R 146-26; D 92-157 (ND 39-131, SD 53-26); I 1-0, July 12, 1994. (House vote 316)

11. HR 4604. Entitlement Spending Control/Stenholm Substitute. Stenholm, D-Texas, substitute amendment to set caps on all entitlement spending (including Social Security) for fiscal 1996-2000 that would result in some $150 billion in cuts below projections; require automatic cuts in all programs (including Social Security) if Congress failed to pass reconciliation legislation to prevent spending from exceeding the caps; and prohibit the use of tax increases or cuts in discretionary spending to offset excess entitlement spending. Rejected in the Committee of the Whole 37-392: R 9-165; D 28-226 (ND 15-157, SD 13-69); I 0-1, July 21, 1994. (House vote 344)

[1] *William H. Natcher, D-Ky., died March 29. The last vote for which he was eligible was key vote 3. Ron Lewis, R-Ky., was sworn in May 26, 1994. The first vote for which he was eligible was key vote 7.*

[2] *Glenn English, D-Okla., resigned effective Jan. 7, 1994. Frank D. Lucas, R-Okla., was sworn in May 17, 1994. The first vote for which he was eligible was key vote 7.*

[3] *Rep. Thomas S. Foley, D-Wash., as Speaker of the House, voted at his discretion.*

KEY

Y	Voted for (yea).
#	Paired for.
+	Announced for.
N	Voted against (nay).
X	Paired against.
−	Announced against.
P	Voted "present."
C	Voted "present" to avoid possible conflict of interest.
?	Did not vote or otherwise make a position known.
D	Delegates ineligible to vote.

Democrats *Republicans*
Independent

	7	8	9	10	11
ALABAMA					
1 *Callahan*	Y	Y	N	Y	N
2 *Everett*	Y	Y	N	Y	N
3 Browder	N	Y	N	Y	Y
4 Bevill	N	Y	N	Y	N
5 Cramer	N	Y	N	Y	N
6 *Bachus*	N	Y	N	Y	N
7 Hilliard	N	?	N	Y	N
ALASKA					
AL *Young*	Y	Y	N	Y	N
ARIZONA					
1 Coppersmith	Y	Y	Y	N	N
2 Pastor	Y	Y	N	N	N
3 *Stump*	Y	Y	N	Y	N
4 *Kyl*	Y	Y	N	Y	N
5 *Kolbe*	Y	Y	Y	Y	N
6 English	Y	Y	Y	N	N
ARKANSAS					
1 Lambert	Y	Y	Y	Y	Y
2 Thornton	N	Y	N	Y	N
3 *Hutchinson*	Y	Y	Y	Y	N
4 Dickey	Y	Y	N	Y	N
CALIFORNIA					
1 Hamburg	N	Y	Y	N	N
2 *Herger*	N	Y	N	?	N
3 Fazio	Y	Y	N	N	N
4 *Doolittle*	Y	Y	N	Y	N
5 Matsui	N	Y	N	N	N
6 Woolsey	N	Y	Y	N	N
7 Miller	N	Y	Y	N	N
8 Pelosi	N	Y	N	N	N
9 Dellums	N	Y	Y	N	N
10 *Baker*	N	Y	N	Y	N
11 *Pombo*	Y	?	N	Y	N
12 Lantos	Y	Y	N	N	N
13 Stark	N	Y	Y	N	N
14 Eshoo	N	Y	N	N	N
15 Mineta	N	Y	N	N	N
16 Edwards	N	Y	N	N	N
17 Farr	N	Y	N	N	N
18 Condit	N	Y	Y	Y	N
19 Lehman	N	Y	Y	N	N
20 Dooley	Y	Y	N	Y	N
21 *Thomas*	Y	Y	N	Y	?
22 *Huffington*	?	Y	N	?	?
23 *Gallegly*	Y	Y	N	Y	N
24 Beilenson	Y	Y	N	N	N
25 *McKeon*	Y	Y	N	Y	N
26 Berman	Y	Y	N	N	N
27 *Moorhead*	Y	Y	N	Y	N
28 *Dreier*	Y	Y	N	Y	N
29 Waxman	N	Y	Y	N	N
30 Becerra	Y	Y	N	N	N
31 Martinez	Y	Y	N	N	N
32 Dixon	Y	Y	N	N	N
33 Roybal-Allard	N	Y	N	N	N
34 Torres	N	Y	N	N	N
35 Waters	Y	Y	N	N	N
36 Harman	N	Y	N	N	N
37 Tucker	X	Y	N	N	?
38 *Horn*	Y	Y	N	Y	N
39 *Royce*	?	Y	N	Y	N
40 *Lewis*	Y	Y	N	Y	N
41 *Kim*	Y	Y	N	Y	N
42 Brown	N	Y	N	?	N
43 *Calvert*	Y	Y	N	Y	N
44 *McCandless*	Y	Y	N	Y	N
45 *Rohrabacher*	Y	Y	N	Y	N
46 Dornan	Y	?	N	Y	N
47 *Cox*	Y	Y	N	Y	N
48 *Packard*	Y	Y	N	Y	N
49 Schenk	Y	Y	Y	N	N
50 Filner	N	Y	N	N	N
51 *Cunningham*	N	Y	N	Y	N
52 *Hunter*	Y	Y	N	Y	N
COLORADO					
1 Schroeder	N	Y	Y	N	N
2 Skaggs	N	Y	Y	N	Y
3 *McInnis*	Y	Y	N	Y	N
4 *Allard*	Y	Y	N	Y	N
5 *Hefley*	N	Y	N	Y	N
6 *Schaefer*	Y	Y	Y	Y	Y
CONNECTICUT					
1 Kennelly	Y	Y	N	N	N
2 Gejdenson	N	Y	N	N	N
3 DeLauro	Y	Y	N	N	N
4 *Shays*	Y	Y	Y	Y	N
5 *Franks*	Y	Y	N	N	N
6 *Johnson*	N	Y	N	Y	Y
DELAWARE					
AL *Castle*	Y	Y	N	Y	N
FLORIDA					
1 Hutto	N	Y	N	Y	Y
2 Peterson	N	Y	N	Y	N
3 Brown	N	Y	N	N	N
4 Fowler	N	Y	N	Y	N
5 Thurman	Y	Y	N	Y	N
6 *Stearns*	Y	Y	Y	Y	N
7 *Mica*	Y	Y	N	Y	N
8 *McCollum*	N	Y	N	Y	N
9 *Bilirakis*	N	Y	N	Y	N
10 *Young*	Y	Y	N	Y	N
11 Gibbons	N	Y	N	N	N
12 *Canady*	N	Y	N	Y	N
13 *Miller*	Y	Y	N	Y	N
14 *Goss*	Y	Y	N	N	N
15 Bacchus	N	Y	N	N	Y
16 *Lewis*	Y	Y	N	Y	N
17 Meek	N	Y	N	N	N
18 *Ros-Lehtinen*	Y	Y	N	N	?
19 Johnston	N	Y	N	N	N
20 Deutsch	N	Y	N	N	N
21 *Diaz-Balart*	Y	Y	N	N	N
22 *Shaw*	Y	Y	N	Y	N
23 Hastings	Y	Y	N	N	N
GEORGIA					
1 *Kingston*	Y	Y	N	Y	N
2 Bishop	N	Y	N	Y	N
3 *Collins*	Y	Y	Y	Y	N
4 *Linder*	Y	Y	N	Y	N
5 Lewis	Y	Y	N	N	N
6 *Gingrich*	Y	Y	N	Y	N
7 Darden	N	Y	N	Y	N
8 Rowland	N	Y	N	Y	N
9 Deal	N	Y	N	Y	Y
10 Johnson	N	Y	Y	Y	Y
11 McKinney	N	Y	Y	N	N
HAWAII					
1 Abercrombie	Y	Y	N	N	N
2 Mink	Y	Y	Y	N	N
IDAHO					
1 LaRocco	N	Y	N	Y	Y
2 *Crapo*	Y	Y	N	Y	N
ILLINOIS					
1 Rush	Y	Y	Y	N	N
2 Reynolds	N	Y	N	N	N
3 Lipinski	Y	Y	Y	Y	N
4 Gutierrez	Y	Y	N	N	N
5 Rostenkowski	N	Y	N	N	N
6 *Hyde*	Y	Y	N	N	N
7 Collins	N	Y	Y	N	N
8 *Crane*	N	Y	N	Y	N
9 Yates	Y	N	Y	N	N
10 *Porter*	Y	Y	Y	N	N
11 Sangmeister	N	Y	Y	Y	Y
12 Costello	Y	Y	Y	N	N
13 *Fawell*	Y	Y	N	N	N
14 *Hastert*	N	Y	Y	N	N
15 *Ewing*	Y	Y	N	Y	N
16 *Manzullo*	N	Y	N	Y	N
17 Evans	N	Y	Y	N	N

ND Northern Democrats   SD Southern Democrats

	7	8	9	10	11
18 *Michel*	N	Y	N	Y	N
19 Poshard	N	Y	Y	Y	N
20 Durbin	N	Y	Y	N	N
INDIANA					
1 Visclosky	N	Y	Y	Y	Y
2 Sharp	Y	Y	N	N	N
3 Roemer	N	Y	Y	N	N
4 Long	Y	Y	Y	N	Y
5 *Buyer*	N	Y	N	Y	N
6 *Burton*	Y	Y	N	Y	N
7 *Myers*	Y	Y	N	Y	N
8 McCloskey	Y	Y	N	N	N
9 Hamilton	N	Y	N	N	N
10 Jacobs	N	Y	Y	N	N
IOWA					
1 *Leach*	Y	Y	Y	Y	N
2 *Nussle*	N	Y	Y	Y	N
3 *Lightfoot*	N	Y	N	Y	N
4 Smith	N	Y	N	Y	N
5 *Grandy*	?	Y	?	Y	Y
KANSAS					
1 *Roberts*	Y	Y	N	Y	N
2 Slattery	Y	Y	N	?	N
3 *Meyers*	Y	Y	N	N	N
4 Glickman	Y	Y	N	N	N
KENTUCKY					
1 Barlow	–	Y	Y	Y	N
2 *Lewis* [1]	Y	Y	N	Y	N
3 Mazzoli	N	Y	Y	N	N
4 *Bunning*	Y	Y	Y	Y	N
5 *Rogers*	Y	Y	N	Y	N
6 Baesler	N	Y	Y	N	N
LOUISIANA					
1 *Livingston*	Y	Y	N	Y	N
2 Jefferson	?	Y	N	N	N
3 Tauzin	?	Y	Y	Y	N
4 Fields	Y	Y	N	N	N
5 *McCrery*	N	Y	N	Y	N
6 *Baker*	Y	Y	N	Y	N
7 Hayes	Y	Y	N	Y	N
MAINE					
1 Andrews	N	Y	Y	N	N
2 *Snowe*	Y	Y	Y	Y	N
MARYLAND					
1 *Gilchrest*	Y	Y	N	N	N
2 *Bentley*	N	Y	N	Y	N
3 Cardin	Y	Y	N	N	Y
4 Wynn	Y	Y	N	N	N
5 Hoyer	Y	Y	Y	N	N
6 *Bartlett*	Y	Y	N	Y	N
7 Mfume	Y	Y	N	N	N
8 *Morella*	?	Y	N	N	N
MASSACHUSETTS					
1 Olver	Y	Y	N	N	N
2 Neal	Y	Y	N	N	N
3 *Blute*	Y	Y	Y	Y	N
4 Frank	Y	Y	N	N	N
5 Meehan	Y	Y	Y	N	Y
6 *Torkildsen*	N	Y	Y	Y	N
7 Markey	Y	Y	N	N	N
8 Kennedy	N	Y	Y	N	N
9 Moakley	N	Y	Y	N	N
10 Studds	N	Y	Y	N	N
MICHIGAN					
1 Stupak	N	Y	Y	N	N
2 *Hoekstra*	Y	Y	Y	Y	N
3 *Ehlers*	N	Y	N	N	N
4 *Camp*	Y	Y	Y	Y	N
5 Barcia	Y	Y	N	Y	N
6 *Upton*	Y	Y	Y	N	N
7 *Smith*	N	Y	Y	Y	N
8 Carr	Y	Y	N	?	?
9 Kildee	N	Y	Y	N	N
10 Bonior	Y	Y	N	N	N
11 *Knollenberg*	N	Y	Y	Y	N
12 Levin	Y	Y	Y	N	N
13 Ford	Y	Y	?	Y	?
14 Conyers	N	Y	Y	N	N
15 Collins	#	Y	Y	N	N
16 Dingell	Y	Y	N	N	N
MINNESOTA					
1 Penny	N	Y	Y	N	Y
2 Minge	N	Y	Y	Y	Y
3 *Ramstad*	Y	Y	Y	Y	N
4 Vento	Y	Y	Y	N	N

	7	8	9	10	11
5 Sabo	N	Y	Y	N	N
6 *Grams*	Y	Y	N	Y	N
7 Peterson	Y	Y	Y	Y	N
8 Oberstar	N	Y	Y	Y	N
MISSISSIPPI					
1 Whitten	?	Y	N	?	N
2 Thompson	Y	Y	N	N	N
3 Montgomery	N	Y	N	Y	Y
4 Parker	N	Y	N	Y	Y
5 Taylor	N	Y	N	Y	N
MISSOURI					
1 Clay	N	Y	N	N	N
2 *Talent*	Y	Y	N	Y	N
3 Gephardt	N	Y	N	N	N
4 Skelton	N	Y	N	Y	N
5 Wheat	Y	Y	Y	?	N
6 Danner	Y	Y	Y	Y	N
7 *Hancock*	N	Y	Y	Y	N
8 *Emerson*	N	Y	N	Y	N
9 Volkmer	Y	Y	N	Y	N
MONTANA					
AL Williams	N	Y	Y	Y	N
NEBRASKA					
1 *Bereuter*	Y	Y	Y	Y	N
2 Hoagland	N	Y	Y	N	N
3 *Barrett*	Y	Y	Y	N	N
NEVADA					
1 Bilbray	Y	Y	Y	N	N
2 *Vucanovich*	N	Y	N	Y	N
NEW HAMPSHIRE					
1 *Zeliff*	Y	Y	N	Y	N
2 Swett	Y	Y	Y	Y	N
NEW JERSEY					
1 Andrews	Y	Y	N	N	Y
2 Hughes	N	Y	N	N	N
3 *Saxton*	Y	Y	N	Y	N
4 *Smith*	Y	Y	N	Y	N
5 *Roukema*	N	Y	N	Y	N
6 Pallone	Y	Y	Y	N	N
7 *Franks*	Y	Y	N	Y	N
8 Klein	Y	Y	Y	N	N
9 Torricelli	Y	Y	N	Y	Y
10 Payne	Y	Y	Y	N	N
11 *Gallo*	Y	Y	N	?	?
12 *Zimmer*	Y	Y	Y	N	N
13 Menendez	Y	Y	Y	N	N
NEW MEXICO					
1 *Schiff*	Y	Y	N	Y	N
2 *Skeen*	Y	Y	Y	N	N
3 Richardson	N	Y	N	N	N
NEW YORK					
1 Hochbrueckner	N	Y	N	N	N
2 *Lazio*	Y	Y	Y	N	N
3 *King*	Y	Y	Y	Y	N
4 *Levy*	Y	Y	N	Y	N
5 Ackerman	Y	Y	Y	N	N
6 Flake	N	+	N	?	N
7 Manton	Y	Y	N	N	N
8 Nadler	Y	Y	Y	N	N
9 Schumer	Y	Y	Y	N	N
10 Towns	?	Y	Y	N	N
11 Owens	Y	Y	Y	N	N
12 Velazquez	N	Y	Y	N	N
13 *Molinari*	Y	Y	N	Y	N
14 Maloney	Y	Y	Y	N	N
15 Rangel	N	Y	?	N	N
16 Serrano	Y	Y	Y	N	N
17 Engel	Y	Y	N	N	N
18 Lowey	Y	Y	N	N	N
19 *Fish*	Y	Y	N	N	N
20 *Gilman*	Y	Y	N	N	N
21 McNulty	Y	Y	Y	N	N
22 *Solomon*	Y	Y	Y	Y	N
23 *Boehlert*	Y	Y	N	N	N
24 *McHugh*	Y	Y	N	Y	N
25 *Walsh*	Y	Y	N	Y	N
26 Hinchey	Y	Y	N	N	N
27 *Paxon*	Y	Y	Y	Y	N
28 Slaughter	Y	Y	N	N	N
29 LaFalce	Y	Y	Y	N	N
30 *Quinn*	Y	Y	N	Y	N
31 *Houghton*	N	Y	N	Y	N
NORTH CAROLINA					
1 Clayton	Y	Y	N	N	N
2 Valentine	N	Y	N	N	Y

	7	8	9	10	11
3 Lancaster	Y	Y	Y	Y	N
4 Price	Y	Y	N	N	N
5 Neal	Y	Y	Y	N	N
6 *Coble*	Y	Y	N	Y	N
7 Rose	N	Y	N	N	N
8 Hefner	N	Y	N	N	N
9 *McMillan*	Y	Y	N	Y	Y
10 *Ballenger*	N	Y	N	Y	N
11 *Taylor*	Y	Y	N	Y	N
12 Watt	N	Y	N	N	N
NORTH DAKOTA					
AL Pomeroy	N	Y	Y	Y	N
OHIO					
1 Mann	N	Y	Y	N	N
2 *Portman*	+	Y	Y	Y	N
3 Hall	Y	Y	N	Y	N
4 *Oxley*	Y	Y	N	Y	N
5 *Gillmor*	Y	Y	N	N	N
6 Strickland	N	Y	N	Y	N
7 *Hobson*	Y	Y	Y	N	N
8 *Boehner*	Y	Y	N	N	N
9 Kaptur	Y	Y	Y	N	N
10 *Hoke*	Y	?	N	Y	N
11 Stokes	N	Y	N	N	N
12 *Kasich*	Y	Y	N	N	N
13 Brown	Y	Y	N	N	N
14 Sawyer	Y	Y	Y	N	N
15 *Pryce*	Y	Y	N	Y	N
16 *Regula*	Y	Y	N	Y	N
17 Traficant	Y	Y	N	Y	N
18 Applegate	N	Y	N	Y	N
19 Fingerhut	Y	Y	N	N	N
OKLAHOMA					
1 *Inhofe*	Y	Y	N	Y	N
2 Synar	N	Y	Y	N	N
3 Brewster	N	Y	N	Y	N
4 McCurdy	Y	Y	N	?	N
5 *Istook*	Y	Y	Y	?	N
6 Lucas [2]	Y	Y	N	Y	N
OREGON					
1 Furse	N	Y	Y	Y	N
2 *Smith*	N	Y	N	Y	N
3 Wyden	N	Y	N	N	N
4 DeFazio	N	Y	?	Y	N
5 Kopetski	+	Y	N	Y	N
PENNSYLVANIA					
1 Foglietta	?	Y	Y	N	N
2 Blackwell	N	Y	N	N	N
3 Borski	N	Y	N	N	N
4 Klink	Y	Y	N	N	N
5 *Clinger*	Y	Y	Y	Y	N
6 Holden	Y	N	N	Y	N
7 *Weldon*	Y	Y	N	N	N
8 *Greenwood*	Y	Y	Y	N	N
9 *Shuster*	N	Y	Y	N	N
10 *McDade*	N	Y	N	?	N
11 Kanjorski	N	Y	Y	N	N
12 Murtha	N	Y	Y	N	N
13 Margolies-Mezv.	Y	Y	Y	N	Y
14 Coyne	Y	Y	N	N	N
15 McHale	Y	Y	N	N	Y
16 *Walker*	Y	Y	Y	Y	N
17 Gekas	Y	Y	N	Y	N
18 Santorum	Y	Y	N	Y	N
19 *Goodling*	N	Y	Y	Y	N
20 Murphy	N	Y	N	Y	N
21 *Ridge*	Y	?	N	?	N
RHODE ISLAND					
1 *Machtley*	Y	Y	?	Y	N
2 Reed	N	Y	Y	N	N
SOUTH CAROLINA					
1 *Ravenel*	Y	Y	N	Y	N
2 *Spence*	N	Y	N	Y	N
3 Derrick	N	Y	N	N	N
4 *Inglis*	N	Y	Y	Y	Y
5 Spratt	Y	Y	Y	N	N
6 Clyburn	Y	Y	N	Y	N
SOUTH DAKOTA					
AL Johnson	N	Y	Y	Y	N
TENNESSEE					
1 *Quillen*	Y	Y	N	Y	N
2 *Duncan*	N	Y	Y	Y	N
3 Lloyd	N	Y	N	Y	Y
4 Cooper	N	Y	N	Y	N
5 Clement	N	Y	N	Y	N

	7	8	9	10	11
6 Gordon	N	Y	Y	Y	N
7 *Sundquist*	?	Y	N	Y	N
8 Tanner	Y	Y	N	Y	N
9 Ford	Y	Y	N	Y	N
TEXAS					
1 Chapman	N	Y	N	Y	N
2 Wilson	N	Y	N	Y	N
3 *Johnson, Sam*	N	Y	N	Y	N
4 Hall	N	Y	N	Y	N
5 Bryant	Y	Y	N	N	N
6 *Barton*	Y	Y	Y	Y	N
7 *Archer*	N	Y	N	Y	N
8 *Fields*	N	Y	N	Y	N
9 Brooks	N	Y	N	Y	N
10 Pickle	Y	Y	N	Y	Y
11 Edwards	N	Y	Y	N	N
12 Geren	Y	Y	Y	Y	Y
13 Sarpalius	N	Y	N	Y	N
14 Laughlin	N	Y	N	?	N
15 de la Garza	Y	Y	N	Y	N
16 Coleman	Y	Y	Y	N	N
17 Stenholm	Y	Y	Y	Y	Y
18 Washington	?	Y	N	?	?
19 *Combest*	N	Y	N	Y	N
20 Gonzalez	N	N	N	N	N
21 *Smith*	Y	Y	N	Y	N
22 *DeLay*	N	Y	N	Y	N
23 *Bonilla*	Y	Y	N	Y	N
24 Frost	Y	Y	N	N	N
25 Andrews	N	Y	N	N	N
26 *Armey*	N	Y	N	Y	N
27 Ortiz	Y	Y	N	Y	N
28 Tejeda	Y	Y	N	Y	N
29 Green	Y	Y	N	N	N
30 Johnson, E.B.	Y	Y	N	N	N
UTAH					
1 *Hansen*	Y	Y	N	Y	Y
2 Shepherd	N	Y	Y	N	N
3 Orton	N	Y	Y	Y	Y
VERMONT					
AL *Sanders*	N	Y	Y	Y	N
VIRGINIA					
1 *Bateman*	N	Y	N	Y	Y
2 Pickett	Y	Y	N	Y	N
3 Scott	N	Y	N	N	N
4 Sisisky	N	Y	N	N	N
5 Payne	N	Y	Y	N	N
6 *Goodlatte*	Y	Y	N	Y	N
7 *Bliley*	Y	Y	N	Y	N
8 Moran	Y	Y	N	N	N
9 Boucher	Y	Y	N	Y	N
10 *Wolf*	Y	Y	N	Y	N
11 Byrne	Y	Y	N	N	N
WASHINGTON					
1 Cantwell	N	Y	Y	N	N
2 Swift	Y	Y	N	N	N
3 Unsoeld	N	Y	Y	N	N
4 Inslee	N	Y	Y	N	N
5 Foley [3]					
6 Dicks	N	Y	N	N	N
7 McDermott	Y	Y	N	N	N
8 *Dunn*	Y	Y	N	Y	N
9 Kreidler	N	Y	Y	N	N
WEST VIRGINIA					
1 Mollohan	N	Y	N	N	N
2 Wise	N	Y	N	Y	N
3 Rahall	Y	Y	N	Y	N
WISCONSIN					
1 Barca	N	Y	Y	N	N
2 *Klug*	Y	Y	Y	N	N
3 *Gunderson*	Y	Y	N	N	N
4 Kleczka	N	Y	Y	N	N
5 Barrett	N	Y	Y	N	N
6 *Petri*	N	N	N	Y	N
7 Obey	Y	N	Y	?	N
8 *Roth*	N	Y	N	Y	N
9 *Sensenbrenner*	Y	Y	N	Y	N
WYOMING					
AL *Thomas*	Y	Y	Y	Y	N
DELEGATES					
de Lugo, V.I.	Y	D	Y	N	N
Faleomavaega, Am.S.	?	D	?	N	?
Norton, D.C.	N	D	Y	N	N
Romero-B., P.R.	Y	D	Y	N	N
Underwood, Guam	N	D	Y	N	?

Southern states – Ala., Ark., Fla., Ga., Ky., La., Miss., N.C., Okla., S.C., Tenn., Texas, Va.
Omitted votes are quorum calls, which CQ does not include in its vote charts.

12. HR 3355. Omnibus Crime Bill/Rule. Adoption of the rule (H Res 517) to waive points of order against and provide for House floor consideration of the $33 billion crime conference report to help hire 100,000 new police officers through an $8.8 billion community policing program, build state and local prisons through an $8.7 billion state grant program, provide $7.6 billion for crime prevention programs such as after-school sports leagues and job training programs, create a crime trust fund directing $30.2 billion over six years to combat crime, ban 19 specific assault weapons and expand the death penalty to dozens of federal crimes. Rejected 210-225: R 11-167; D 198-58 (ND 148-25, SD 50-33); I 1-0, Aug. 11, 1994. A "yea" was a vote in support of the president's position. (House vote 394)

13. HR 3355. Omnibus Crime Bill/Conference Report. Adoption of the conference report to authorize $30.2 billion over six years and to require that all spending authorized by the bill come from a six-year, $30.2 billion crime trust fund realized from eliminating 270,000 federal jobs. The bill would authorize $6.9 billion for crime prevention programs, such as after-school sports leagues and job training programs, $8.8 billion for community policing programs and the hiring of 100,000 new police officers, and a $7.9 billion grant program to build state and local prisons. The bill also would ban 19 specific assault weapons, expand the death penalty to dozens of new federal crimes, mandate life imprisonment without parole for three-time violent felons, provide for community notification of violent sex offenders, allow prior sex offenses to be considered at federal trials and require HIV testing when requested in federal rape trials. Adopted (thus sent to the Senate) 235-195: R 46-131; D 188-64 (ND 141-31, SD 47-33); I 1-0, Aug. 21, 1994. A "yea" was a vote in support of the president's position. (House vote 416)

14. S 349. Lobbying Disclosure/Rule. Adoption of the rule (H Res 550) to provide for House floor consideration of the conference report to expand the disclosure of lobbying activities and impose new restrictions on gifts to members of Congress and their staffs. Adopted 216-205: R 5-170; D 210-35 (ND 156-13, SD 54-22); I 1-0, Sept. 29, 1994. (House vote 449)

15. H J Res 416. U.S. Troops in Haiti/Immediate Withdrawal. Gilman, R-N.Y., substitute amendment to express the sense of Congress that the president should not have ordered U.S. troops to occupy Haiti and that the president should immediately commence "the safe and orderly withdrawal" of all U.S. forces from Haiti. The substitute also would provide for consideration of a joint resolution to be introduced Jan. 3, 1995, that if enacted would prohibit the continued use of U.S troops in Haiti within 30 days. Rejected in the Committee of the Whole 205-225: R 173-1; D 32-223 (ND 21-153, SD 11-70); I 0-1, Oct. 6, 1994. A "nay" was a vote in support of the president's position. (House vote 497)

16. HR 5110. General Agreement on Tariffs and Trade/Passage. Passage of the bill to make statutory changes to implement the new world trade agreement negotiated under the Uruguay Round of the General Agreement on Tariffs and Trade (GATT). The agreement would reduce tariffs and trade barriers, ensure stricter enforcement of world trade rules through the newly established World Trade Organization (WTO), and expand GATT rules to cover such economic sectors as agriculture, services and intellectual property. The bill also would accelerate tax payment schedules, change eligibility standards for certain federal programs, and make other changes to offset lost revenues from tariff reductions in order to comply with pay-as-you-go budget rules. Passed 288-146: R 121-56; D 167-89 (ND 107-66, SD 60-23); I 0-1, Nov. 29, 1994. A "yea" was a vote in support of the president's position. (House vote 507)

[1] *Dean A. Gallo, R-N.J., died Nov. 6, 1994. Key vote 15 was the last vote for which he was eligible.*

[2] *Rep. James M. Inhofe, R-Okla., resigned Nov. 15, 1994, to replace Sen. David L. Boren, D-Okla. The last vote for which Inhofe was eligible was key vote 15. Steve Largent, R-Okla., was sworn in Nov. 29, 1994, to replace Inhofe. The first vote for which he was eligible was key vote 16.*

[3] *Rep. Thomas S. Foley, D-Wash., as Speaker of the House, voted at his discretion.*

KEY

Y	Voted for (yea).
#	Paired for.
+	Announced for.
N	Voted against (nay).
X	Paired against.
−	Announced against.
P	Voted "present."
C	Voted "present" to avoid possible conflict of interest.
?	Did not vote or otherwise make a position known.
D	Delegates ineligible to vote.

Democrats **Republicans**
Independent

	12	13	14	15	16
ALABAMA					
1 Callahan	N	?	N	Y	Y
2 Everett	N	N	N	Y	N
3 Browder	N	Y	Y	N	N
4 Bevill	Y	N	Y	N	Y
5 Cramer	Y	Y	Y	N	N
6 Bachus	N	N	N	Y	N
7 Hilliard	N	N	Y	N	N
ALASKA					
AL Young	N	N	N	Y	N
ARIZONA					
1 Coppersmith	Y	Y	Y	Y	Y
2 Pastor	Y	Y	Y	N	Y
3 Stump	N	N	N	Y	N
4 Kyl	N	Y	N	Y	Y
5 Kolbe	N	Y	N	Y	Y
6 English	Y	Y	Y	N	Y
ARKANSAS					
1 Lambert	Y	Y	Y	Y	Y
2 Thornton	Y	Y	Y	N	Y
3 Hutchinson	N	N	N	Y	N
4 Dickey	N	N	N	N	N
CALIFORNIA					
1 Hamburg	Y	Y	Y	N	N
2 Herger	N	N	N	Y	N
3 Fazio	Y	Y	Y	N	Y
4 Doolittle	N	N	N	Y	N
5 Matsui	Y	Y	Y	N	Y
6 Woolsey	Y	Y	Y	N	N
7 Miller	Y	Y	Y	N	N
8 Pelosi	Y	Y	Y	N	Y
9 Dellums	Y	N	Y	N	N
10 Baker	N	N	N	Y	Y
11 Pombo	N	N	N	Y	N
12 Lantos	Y	Y	Y	N	N
13 Stark	Y	Y	Y	N	N
14 Eshoo	Y	Y	Y	N	Y
15 Mineta	Y	Y	Y	N	Y
16 Edwards	Y	Y	Y	N	N
17 Farr	Y	Y	Y	N	Y
18 Condit	Y	Y	N	Y	N
19 Lehman	Y	Y	N	N	Y
20 Dooley	Y	Y	N	N	Y
21 Thomas	N	N	N	Y	Y
22 Huffington	N	Y	N	?	Y
23 Gallegly	N	Y	N	N	N
24 Beilenson	Y	Y	Y	N	Y
25 McKeon	N	N	N	Y	Y
26 Berman	Y	Y	Y	N	Y
27 Moorhead	N	N	N	Y	Y
28 Dreier	N	N	N	Y	Y
29 Waxman	Y	Y	Y	N	N
30 Becerra	Y	Y	Y	N	Y
31 Martinez	Y	Y	Y	N	Y
32 Dixon	Y	Y	Y	N	N
33 Roybal-Allard	Y	Y	Y	N	Y
34 Torres	Y	Y	Y	N	Y
35 Waters	N	N	Y	N	N
36 Harman	Y	Y	Y	Y	Y
37 Tucker	Y	?	Y	?	N
38 Horn	N	Y	N	Y	Y
39 Royce	N	N	N	Y	Y
40 Lewis	N	N	N	Y	Y
41 Kim	N	N	N	Y	Y
42 Brown	Y	Y	Y	N	Y
43 Calvert	N	N	N	Y	N
44 McCandless	N	N	N	Y	N
45 Rohrabacher	N	N	N	Y	N
46 Dornan	N	N	N	Y	N
47 Cox	N	N	N	Y	Y
48 Packard	N	N	N	Y	Y
49 Schenk	Y	Y	Y	Y	Y
50 Filner	Y	Y	Y	Y	Y
51 Cunningham	N	N	N	Y	N
52 Hunter	N	N	N	Y	N
COLORADO					
1 Schroeder	Y	Y	Y	N	Y
2 Skaggs	Y	Y	Y	N	Y
3 McInnis	N	N	N	Y	N
4 Allard	N	N	N	Y	N
5 Hefley	N	N	N	Y	N
6 Schaefer	N	N	N	Y	N
CONNECTICUT					
1 Kennelly	Y	Y	Y	N	Y
2 Gejdenson	Y	Y	Y	N	Y
3 DeLauro	Y	Y	Y	N	Y
4 Shays	Y	Y	Y	N	Y
5 Franks	N	Y	Y	Y	Y
6 Johnson	Y	Y	N	Y	Y
DELAWARE					
AL Castle	N	Y	N	Y	Y
FLORIDA					
1 Hutto	Y	N	?	N	Y
2 Peterson	N	N	Y	N	Y
3 Brown	Y	Y	Y	N	Y
4 Fowler	N	N	N	Y	Y
5 Thurman	N	N	Y	N	N
6 Stearns	N	N	N	Y	N
7 Mica	N	N	N	Y	Y
8 McCollum	N	N	N	Y	Y
9 Bilirakis	N	N	N	Y	Y
10 Young	N	N	N	Y	Y
11 Gibbons	Y	Y	Y	N	Y
12 Canady	N	Y	Y	Y	Y
13 Miller	N	N	N	Y	Y
14 Goss	N	N	N	Y	Y
15 Bacchus	Y	Y	Y	N	Y
16 Lewis	N	N	N	Y	Y
17 Meek	Y	Y	N	N	Y
18 Ros-Lehtinen	N	Y	N	Y	Y
19 Johnston	Y	Y	Y	N	Y
20 Deutsch	Y	Y	Y	N	Y
21 Diaz-Balart	N	Y	N	Y	Y
22 Shaw	N	Y	N	Y	Y
23 Hastings	Y	Y	Y	N	N
GEORGIA					
1 Kingston	N	N	N	Y	N
2 Bishop	Y	Y	Y	N	Y
3 Collins	N	N	N	Y	N
4 Linder	N	N	N	Y	Y
5 Lewis	N	N	Y	N	N
6 Gingrich	N	N	N	Y	Y
7 Darden	Y	Y	Y	N	Y
8 Rowland	Y	—	N	N	Y
9 Deal	N	N	N	N	N
10 Johnson	Y	Y	Y	N	Y
11 McKinney	Y	Y	Y	N	N
HAWAII					
1 Abercrombie	Y	Y	Y	N	Y
2 Mink	Y	Y	Y	N	Y
IDAHO					
1 LaRocco	N	N	Y	N	Y
2 Crapo	N	N	N	Y	N
ILLINOIS					
1 Rush	Y	Y	Y	N	N
2 Reynolds	Y	Y	Y	N	Y
3 Lipinski	Y	Y	Y	N	N
4 Gutierrez	Y	Y	Y	N	N
5 Rostenkowski	Y	Y	Y	N	Y
6 Hyde	N	N	N	Y	Y
7 Collins	Y	Y	N	N	N
8 Crane	N	N	N	Y	Y
9 Yates	Y	Y	Y	N	Y
10 Porter	N	Y	N	Y	Y
11 Sangmeister	Y	Y	Y	N	Y
12 Costello	Y	Y	Y	N	N
13 Fawell	N	N	N	Y	Y
14 Hastert	N	N	N	Y	Y
15 Ewing	N	N	N	Y	Y
16 Manzullo	N	N	N	Y	N
17 Evans	Y	Y	Y	N	N

ND Northern Democrats   SD Southern Democrats

Member	12	13	14	15	16
18 *Michel*	N	N	N	Y	Y
19 Poshard	N	Y	Y	N	Y
20 Durbin	Y	Y	Y	N	Y
INDIANA					
1 Visclosky	Y	Y	Y	N	Y
2 Sharp	Y	Y	Y	N	Y
3 Roemer	Y	Y	Y	N	Y
4 Long	Y	Y	Y	N	Y
5 *Buyer*	N	N	N	Y	Y
6 *Burton*	N	N	N	Y	N
7 *Myers*	N	N	N	Y	N
8 McCloskey	Y	Y	Y	N	Y
9 Hamilton	N	Y	Y	N	Y
10 Jacobs	Y	Y	Y	N	Y
IOWA					
1 *Leach*	N	Y	N	Y	Y
2 *Nussle*	N	N	N	Y	Y
3 *Lightfoot*	N	N	N	Y	Y
4 Smith	N	Y	Y	N	Y
5 *Grandy*	Y	Y	N	N	Y
KANSAS					
1 *Roberts*	N	N	N	Y	Y
2 Slattery	Y	Y	?	?	Y
3 *Meyers*	Y	Y	Y	N	Y
4 Glickman	Y	Y	Y	N	N
KENTUCKY					
1 Barlow	Y	N	Y	N	N
2 *Lewis*	N	N	N	Y	N
3 Mazzoli	Y	Y	Y	Y	Y
4 *Bunning*	N	N	N	Y	N
5 *Rogers*	N	N	N	Y	N
6 Baesler	Y	Y	N	Y	Y
LOUISIANA					
1 *Livingston*	N	N	N	Y	N
2 Jefferson	Y	Y	Y	N	Y
3 Tauzin	N	N	N	N	Y
4 Fields	N	N	?	N	Y
5 *McCrery*	N	N	?	Y	Y
6 *Baker*	N	N	N	Y	Y
7 Hayes	N	N	?	N	N
MAINE					
1 Andrews	Y	Y	Y	N	N
2 *Snowe*	N	Y	Y	N	N
MARYLAND					
1 *Gilchrest*	N	Y	N	Y	Y
2 *Bentley*	N	N	N	Y	N
3 Cardin	Y	Y	Y	N	Y
4 Wynn	Y	Y	Y	N	Y
5 Hoyer	Y	Y	Y	N	Y
6 *Bartlett*	N	N	N	Y	Y
7 Mfume	Y	Y	Y	–	N
8 *Morella*	Y	Y	Y	Y	Y
MASSACHUSETTS					
1 Olver	Y	Y	Y	N	Y
2 Neal	Y	Y	Y	N	Y
3 *Blute*	Y	Y	Y	N	Y
4 Frank	Y	Y	Y	N	Y
5 Meehan	Y	Y	Y	N	Y
6 *Torkildsen*	N	Y	Y	N	Y
7 Markey	Y	Y	Y	N	Y
8 Kennedy	Y	Y	Y	N	Y
9 Moakley	Y	Y	Y	N	N
10 Studds	Y	Y	Y	N	Y
MICHIGAN					
1 Stupak	N	N	N	Y	N
2 *Hoekstra*	N	N	N	Y	N
3 *Ehlers*	N	N	N	Y	Y
4 *Camp*	N	N	N	Y	Y
5 Barcia	N	Y	Y	N	Y
6 *Upton*	N	Y	N	Y	Y
7 *Smith*	N	N	N	Y	Y
8 Carr	Y	Y	Y	Y	Y
9 Kildee	Y	Y	Y	N	Y
10 Bonior	Y	Y	Y	N	N
11 *Knollenberg*	N	N	N	Y	Y
12 Levin	Y	Y	Y	N	Y
13 Ford	Y	Y	Y	N	Y
14 Conyers	Y	N	Y	N	N
15 Collins	Y	N	Y	N	N
16 Dingell	Y	Y	Y	N	Y
MINNESOTA					
1 Penny	Y	N	Y	N	Y
2 Minge	Y	Y	Y	N	Y
3 *Ramstad*	Y	Y	N	Y	N
4 Vento	Y	Y	Y	N	Y
5 Sabo	Y	N	Y	N	N
6 *Grams*	N	N	N	Y	Y
7 Peterson	N	N	Y	Y	N
8 Oberstar	Y	N	Y	N	N
MISSISSIPPI					
1 Whitten	Y	Y	Y	?	Y
2 Thompson	Y	Y	?	N	N
3 Montgomery	Y	N	Y	Y	N
4 Parker	N	N	N	Y	Y
5 Taylor	N	N	Y	Y	N
MISSOURI					
1 Clay	N	N	N	N	N
2 *Talent*	N	Y	N	Y	Y
3 Gephardt	Y	Y	Y	N	Y
4 Skelton	N	N	Y	N	Y
5 Wheat	Y	Y	?	N	Y
6 Danner	N	N	Y	Y	N
7 *Hancock*	N	N	N	Y	N
8 *Emerson*	N	N	N	Y	Y
9 Volkmer	N	N	Y	N	N
MONTANA					
AL Williams	N	N	N	N	
NEBRASKA					
1 *Bereuter*	N	N	N	Y	Y
2 Hoagland	Y	Y	Y	N	Y
3 *Barrett*	N	N	N	P	Y
NEVADA					
1 Bilbray	Y	Y	Y	N	N
2 *Vucanovich*	N	N	N	Y	Y
NEW HAMPSHIRE					
1 *Zeliff*	N	N	N	Y	Y
2 Swett	Y	Y	N	Y	N
NEW JERSEY					
1 Andrews	Y	Y	Y	Y	Y
2 Hughes	Y	Y	Y	Y	N
3 *Saxton*	Y	Y	Y	N	Y
4 *Smith*	N	Y	Y	N	N
5 Roukema	Y	Y	N	Y	Y
6 Pallone	Y	Y	Y	N	N
7 *Franks*	N	Y	Y	N	Y
8 Klein	Y	Y	Y	N	Y
9 Torricelli	Y	Y	Y	N	Y
10 Payne	Y	N	Y	N	N
11 *Gallo*[1]	N	N	?	?	
12 *Zimmer*	N	Y	N	Y	Y
13 Menendez	Y	Y	Y	N	Y
NEW MEXICO					
1 *Schiff*	N	N	N	Y	N
2 *Skeen*	N	N	N	Y	N
3 Richardson	Y	Y	Y	N	Y
NEW YORK					
1 Hochbrueckner	Y	Y	Y	N	N
2 *Lazio*	N	Y	N	Y	Y
3 *King*	N	Y	N	Y	Y
4 *Levy*	N	Y	N	Y	Y
5 Ackerman	Y	Y	Y	N	Y
6 Flake	Y	Y	Y	N	Y
7 Manton	Y	Y	Y	N	Y
8 Nadler	Y	N	Y	N	Y
9 Schumer	Y	Y	Y	N	Y
10 Towns	Y	Y	Y	N	Y
11 Owens	Y	Y	Y	N	N
12 Velazquez	Y	Y	Y	N	N
13 *Molinari*	N	Y	N	Y	Y
14 Maloney	Y	Y	Y	N	Y
15 Rangel	N	N	Y	N	N
16 Serrano	Y	Y	Y	N	Y
17 Engel	Y	Y	Y	N	Y
18 Lowey	Y	Y	Y	N	Y
19 *Fish*	N	N	N	Y	Y
20 *Gilman*	N	N	N	Y	Y
21 McNulty	Y	Y	?	Y	Y
22 *Solomon*	N	N	N	Y	N
23 *Boehlert*	Y	Y	N	Y	Y
24 *McHugh*	N	N	N	Y	Y
25 *Walsh*	N	Y	N	Y	Y
26 Hinchey	Y	Y	Y	N	N
27 *Paxon*	N	N	N	Y	Y
28 Slaughter	Y	Y	Y	N	Y
29 LaFalce	Y	Y	Y	N	Y
30 Quinn	Y	Y	Y	N	N
31 *Houghton*	Y	N	Y	N	Y
NORTH CAROLINA					
1 Clayton	Y	Y	Y	N	Y
2 Valentine	Y	?	N	N	Y
3 Lancaster	N	Y	Y	N	Y
4 Price	Y	Y	Y	N	Y
5 Neal	Y	Y	Y	N	Y
6 *Coble*	N	N	N	Y	N
7 Rose	Y	Y	Y	N	N
8 Hefner	Y	Y	Y	N	N
9 *McMillan*	N	N	N	Y	Y
10 *Ballenger*	N	N	N	Y	Y
11 *Taylor*	N	N	N	Y	N
12 Watt	N	N	Y	N	N
NORTH DAKOTA					
AL Pomeroy	Y	Y	Y	Y	Y
OHIO					
1 Mann	Y	Y	Y	N	Y
2 *Portman*	N	N	N	Y	Y
3 Hall	Y	Y	Y	N	Y
4 *Oxley*	N	N	N	Y	Y
5 *Gillmor*	N	N	N	Y	Y
6 Strickland	N	Y	N	Y	Y
7 *Hobson*	N	Y	N	Y	Y
8 *Boehner*	N	N	N	Y	Y
9 Kaptur	Y	Y	Y	N	N
10 *Hoke*	N	N	N	Y	Y
11 Stokes	N	N	Y	N	N
12 *Kasich*	N	Y	N	Y	N
13 Brown	Y	Y	Y	N	N
14 Sawyer	Y	Y	Y	N	Y
15 *Pryce*	N	N	N	Y	Y
16 *Regula*	N	N	N	Y	Y
17 Traficant	Y	N	Y	N	N
18 Applegate	Y	Y	?	?	N
19 Fingerhut	Y	Y	Y	N	Y
OKLAHOMA					
1 *Inhofe/Largent*[2]	N	N	N	N	N
2 Synar	Y	N	Y	N	Y
3 Brewster	N	N	N	Y	N
4 McCurdy	N	Y	?	Y	Y
5 *Istook*	N	N	N	Y	N
6 *Lucas*	N	N	N	Y	N
OREGON					
1 Furse	Y	Y	Y	N	Y
2 *Smith*	N	N	N	Y	Y
3 Wyden	Y	Y	Y	N	Y
4 DeFazio	N	N	Y	N	N
5 Kopetski	Y	N	Y	N	Y
PENNSYLVANIA					
1 Foglietta	Y	Y	Y	N	Y
2 Blackwell	Y	Y	Y	N	Y
3 Borski	Y	Y	Y	N	Y
4 Klink	N	Y	N	Y	N
5 *Clinger*	N	N	N	Y	Y
6 Holden	N	Y	N	Y	N
7 *Weldon*	N	Y	N	Y	N
8 *Greenwood*	Y	Y	Y	N	Y
9 *Shuster*	N	N	N	Y	Y
10 McDade	N	N	?	Y	Y
11 Kanjorski	Y	N	Y	N	N
12 Murtha	N	N	N	Y	N
13 Margolies-Mezv.	Y	Y	Y	N	Y
14 Coyne	Y	Y	Y	N	Y
15 McHale	Y	Y	Y	N	Y
16 *Walker*	N	N	N	Y	Y
17 *Gekas*	N	N	N	Y	Y
18 *Santorum*	N	N	N	Y	Y
19 *Goodling*	N	N	N	Y	Y
20 Murphy	Y	N	Y	N	N
21 *Ridge*	N	Y	Y	Y	Y
RHODE ISLAND					
1 *Machtley*	N	Y	N	Y	Y
2 Reed	Y	Y	Y	N	Y
SOUTH CAROLINA					
1 *Ravenel*	N	N	N	Y	N
2 *Spence*	N	N	N	Y	N
3 Derrick	Y	Y	Y	N	Y
4 *Inglis*	N	N	N	Y	N
5 Spratt	Y	Y	Y	N	N
6 Clyburn	Y	Y	Y	N	Y
SOUTH DAKOTA					
AL Johnson	Y	Y	Y	Y	Y
TENNESSEE					
1 *Quillen*	N	N	N	Y	Y
2 *Duncan*	N	N	N	Y	N
3 Lloyd	Y	Y	?	N	Y
4 Cooper	N	N	Y	N	Y
5 Clement	Y	Y	Y	N	N
6 Gordon	Y	Y	Y	N	Y
7 *Sundquist*	N	N	N	?	Y
8 Tanner	N	N	N	N	Y
9 Ford	Y	Y	Y	N	Y
TEXAS					
1 Chapman	N	N	N	N	N
2 Wilson	N	N	N	N	N
3 *Johnson, Sam*	N	N	N	Y	N
4 Hall	N	N	N	Y	N
5 Bryant	Y	Y	Y	N	Y
6 *Barton*	N	N	N	Y	Y
7 *Archer*	N	N	N	Y	Y
8 *Fields*	N	N	N	Y	Y
9 Brooks	Y	Y	Y	N	Y
10 Pickle	Y	Y	Y	N	Y
11 Edwards	Y	Y	Y	N	Y
12 Geren	N	N	N	Y	Y
13 Sarpalius	N	N	N	Y	Y
14 Laughlin	N	N	N	Y	Y
15 de la Garza	N	N	Y	N	Y
16 Coleman	Y	Y	Y	N	Y
17 Stenholm	N	N	N	Y	Y
18 Washington	N	?	?	?	Y
19 *Combest*	N	N	N	Y	N
20 Gonzalez	Y	Y	Y	N	N
21 *Smith*	N	N	N	Y	N
22 *DeLay*	N	N	N	Y	N
23 *Bonilla*	N	N	N	Y	N
24 Frost	Y	Y	Y	N	Y
25 Andrews	Y	Y	Y	N	Y
26 *Armey*	N	N	N	Y	N
27 Ortiz	N	N	Y	N	Y
28 Tejeda	N	N	N	Y	N
29 Green	Y	Y	Y	N	Y
30 Johnson, E.B.	Y	Y	Y	N	Y
UTAH					
1 *Hansen*	N	N	N	Y	Y
2 Shepherd	Y	Y	Y	N	Y
3 Orton	N	N	N	Y	Y
VERMONT					
AL *Sanders*	Y	Y	Y	N	N
VIRGINIA					
1 *Bateman*	N	N	N	Y	Y
2 Pickett	N	N	N	N	Y
3 Scott	N	N	Y	N	Y
4 Sisisky	N	N	N	N	N
5 Payne	N	N	N	N	N
6 *Goodlatte*	N	N	N	Y	Y
7 *Bliley*	N	N	N	Y	Y
8 Moran	Y	Y	Y	N	Y
9 Boucher	N	N	Y	N	Y
10 *Wolf*	N	N	N	Y	Y
11 Byrne	Y	Y	Y	N	Y
WASHINGTON					
1 Cantwell	Y	Y	Y	N	Y
2 Swift	Y	Y	Y	N	Y
3 Unsoeld	N	N	Y	N	Y
4 Inslee	Y	Y	Y	N	Y
5 Foley[3]	Y	Y	Y	N	Y
6 Dicks	Y	Y	Y	N	Y
7 McDermott	Y	Y	Y	N	Y
8 *Dunn*	N	N	N	Y	Y
9 Kreidler	Y	Y	Y	N	Y
WEST VIRGINIA					
1 Mollohan	N	N	Y	N	N
2 Wise	N	N	Y	N	N
3 Rahall	N	N	Y	N	N
WISCONSIN					
1 Barca	Y	Y	Y	Y	N
2 *Klug*	N	Y	N	Y	N
3 *Gunderson*	N	N	N	Y	N
4 Kleczka	Y	Y	Y	N	Y
5 Barrett	Y	Y	Y	N	Y
6 *Petri*	N	N	N	Y	Y
7 Obey	Y	Y	Y	N	N
8 *Roth*	N	N	N	Y	N
9 *Sensenbrenner*	N	N	N	Y	N
WYOMING					
AL *Thomas*	N	N	N	Y	Y
DELEGATES					
de Lugo, V.I.	D	D	D	N	D
Faleomavaega, Am.S.	D	D	D	N	D
Norton, D.C.	D	D	D	N	D
Romero-B., P.R.	D	D	D	N	D
Underwood, Guam	D	D	D	N	D

Southern states - Ala., Ark., Fla., Ga., Ky., La., Miss., N.C., Okla., S.C., Tenn., Texas, Va.
Omitted votes are quorum calls, which CQ does not include in its vote charts.

ALABAMA	1	2	3	4	5	6
Heflin	N	Y	Y	Y	Y	Y
Shelby	N	Y	Y	Y	?	?
ALASKA						
Murkowski	Y	N	Y	Y	N	N
Stevens	Y	Y	Y	N	Y	N
ARIZONA						
DeConcini	N	Y	N	Y	Y	Y
McCain	Y	N	N	Y	N	N
ARKANSAS						
Bumpers	Y	Y	Y	N	Y	Y
Pryor	Y	Y	Y	N	Y	Y
CALIFORNIA						
Boxer	Y	Y	Y	N	Y	Y
Feinstein	Y	Y	Y	Y	Y	Y
COLORADO						
Campbell	N	Y	Y	Y	Y	Y
Brown	N	N	N	Y	Y	N
CONNECTICUT						
Dodd	Y	Y	Y	N	Y	Y
Lieberman	Y	Y	N	N	Y	Y
DELAWARE						
Biden	Y	Y	Y	N	Y	Y
Roth	N	Y	Y	Y	Y	Y
FLORIDA						
Graham	Y	Y	N	Y	Y	Y
Mack	N	N	N	Y	N	N
GEORGIA						
Nunn	Y	Y	Y	Y	Y	N
Coverdell	N	N	N	Y	N	N
HAWAII						
Akaka	Y	Y	Y	N	Y	Y
Inouye	Y	Y	Y	N	Y	Y
IDAHO						
Craig	N	N	N	Y	N	N
Kempthorne	N	N	N	Y	N	N
ILLINOIS						
Moseley-Braun	N	+	Y	Y	Y	Y
Simon	Y	Y	N	Y	Y	Y
INDIANA						
Coats	N	N	Y	N	N	N
Lugar	N	N	Y	N	N	N

IOWA	1	2	3	4	5	6
Harkin	Y	Y	Y	N	Y	Y
Grassley	N	N	N	Y	N	N
KANSAS						
Dole	N	N	Y	Y	N	N
Kassebaum	Y	Y	N	N	Y	N
KENTUCKY						
Ford	Y	Y	Y	Y	Y	Y
McConnell	Y	N	Y	Y	Y	N
LOUISIANA						
Breaux	Y	Y	Y	Y	N	Y
Johnston	Y	?	Y	N	N	Y
MAINE						
Mitchell	Y	Y	Y	N	Y	Y
Cohen	Y	Y	N	Y	Y	N
MARYLAND						
Mikulski	Y	Y	+	N	Y	Y
Sarbanes	Y	Y	Y	N	Y	Y
MASSACHUSETTS						
Kennedy	Y	Y	Y	N	Y	Y
Kerry	Y	Y	Y	N	Y	Y
MICHIGAN						
Levin	Y	Y	Y	N	Y	Y
Riegle	N	Y	Y	N	Y	Y
MINNESOTA						
Wellstone	N	Y	Y	N	Y	Y
Durenberger	N	Y	N	Y	Y	Y
MISSISSIPPI						
Cochran	Y	Y	Y	Y	N	N
Lott	N	N	Y	Y	N	N
MISSOURI						
Bond	Y	Y	Y	Y	N	N
Danforth	Y	Y	N	Y	Y	N
MONTANA						
Baucus	Y	Y	N	N	Y	Y
Burns	N	N	Y	Y	N	N
NEBRASKA						
Exon	Y	Y	N	Y	N	Y
Kerrey	Y	Y	N	N	Y	Y
NEVADA						
Bryan	Y	Y	Y	Y	Y	Y
Reid	Y	Y	Y	N	Y	Y

NEW HAMPSHIRE	1	2	3	4	5	6
Gregg	N	N	N	Y	N	N
Smith	N	N	N	Y	N	N
NEW JERSEY						
Bradley	Y	Y	?	N	Y	N
Lautenberg	N	Y	N	N	Y	Y
NEW MEXICO						
Bingaman	Y	Y	Y	Y	Y	Y
Domenici	N	Y	Y	Y	Y	N
NEW YORK						
Moynihan	Y	Y	Y	N	Y	Y
D'Amato	N	N	Y	Y	N	N
NORTH CAROLINA						
Faircloth	N	N	N	Y	N	N
Helms	N	N	Y	Y	N	N
NORTH DAKOTA						
Conrad	N	Y	Y	N	Y	Y
Dorgan	N	Y	Y	N	Y	Y
OHIO						
Glenn	Y	Y	Y	N	Y	Y
Metzenbaum	Y	Y	Y	N	Y	Y
OKLAHOMA						
Boren	Y	Y	N	Y	Y	Y
Nickles	Y	N	N	Y	N	N
OREGON						
Hatfield	Y	Y	Y	N	Y	Y
Packwood	Y	Y	N	Y	Y	N
PENNSYLVANIA						
Wofford	N	Y	Y	N	Y	Y
Specter	N	Y	N	Y	Y	Y
RHODE ISLAND						
Pell	Y	Y	Y	N	Y	Y
Chafee	Y	Y	N	Y	Y	N
SOUTH CAROLINA						
Hollings	Y	Y	Y	Y	Y	Y
Thurmond	N	Y	Y	Y	N	N
SOUTH DAKOTA						
Daschle	Y	Y	Y	Y	Y	Y
Pressler	Y	N	Y	N	N	N
TENNESSEE						
Mathews	Y	Y	Y	N	Y	Y
Sasser	N	Y	Y	Y	Y	Y

KEY

Y   Voted for (yea).
Paired for.
+   Announced for.
N   Voted against (nay).
X   Paired against.
−   Announced against.
P   Voted "present."
C   Voted "present" to avoid possible conflict of interest.
?   Did not vote or otherwise make a position known.

Democrats   *Republicans*

TEXAS	1	2	3	4	5	6
Gramm	N	−	?	Y	N	N
Hutchison	N	?	?	Y	Y	N
UTAH						
Bennett	Y	N	Y	Y	N	N
Hatch	N	N	Y	Y	N	N
VERMONT						
Leahy	Y	Y	Y	N	Y	Y
Jeffords	Y	Y	Y	Y	Y	Y
VIRGINIA						
Robb	Y	Y	N	Y	Y	Y
Warner	Y	N	Y	N	Y	N
WASHINGTON						
Murray	Y	Y	Y	N	Y	Y
Gorton	Y	Y	Y	N	Y	Y
WEST VIRGINIA						
Byrd	N	Y	Y	N	Y	Y
Rockefeller	Y	Y	N	Y	N	Y
WISCONSIN						
Feingold	N	Y	N	N	Y	Y
Kohl	Y	Y	N	Y	Y	Y
WYOMING						
Simpson	Y	Y	N	Y	Y	N
Wallop	Y	N	Y	Y	N	N

ND   Northern Democrats   SD   Southern Democrats   Southern states - Ala., Ark., Fla., Ga., Ky., La., Miss., N.C., Okla., S.C., Tenn., Texas, Va.

Following are votes from 1994 selected by Congressional Quarterly as key votes (Explanations of key votes, p. 28-C). Original vote number is provided in parentheses.

1. S 1281. Fiscal 1994-95 State Department Authorization/Relations With Vietnam. Kerry, D-Mass., amendment to express the sense of the Senate that in order to expand and maintain Vietnamese cooperation in resolving POW/MIA cases, the president should lift the U.S. trade embargo against Vietnam. Adopted 62-38: R 20-24; D 42-14 (ND 31-11, SD 11-3), Jan. 27, 1994. (Senate vote 5)

2. HR 1804. Goals 2000: Educate America/Passage. Passage of the bill to authorize $422 million for competitive grants for schools seeking to improve their performance, write into law six national education goals and establish tests and standards for elementary and secondary students. Passed 71-25: R 17-25; D 54-0 (ND 41-0, SD 13-0), Feb. 8, 1994. (Before passage the Senate struck all after the enacting clause and inserted the text of S 1150 as amended.) A "yea" was a vote in support of the president's position. (Senate vote 34)

3. HR 3759. Fiscal 1994 Disaster Supplemental Appropriations/Rescissions. Byrd, D-W.Va., motion to table (kill) the Kerrey, D-Neb., amendment to rescind $94 billion over five years from 54 programs. Motion agreed to 65-31: R 23-19; D 42-12 (ND 31-9, SD 11-3), Feb. 9, 1994. (The motion also killed a Hatfield, R-Ore., substitute amendment to the Kerrey amendment, with $18.6 billion in defense rescissions.) A "yea" was a vote in support of the president's position. (Senate vote 35)

4. S J Res 41. Balanced-Budget Amendment/Passage. Passage of the joint resolution to propose a constitutional amendment to require a balanced budget by 2001 or the second fiscal year after ratification by three-fourths of the states, whichever is later. Congress could waive the balanced-budget requirement if three-fifths of the House and Senate approved deficit spending, or by a simple majority when a declaration of war was in effect or when there was a threat to national security. The amendment would prohibit the courts from ordering tax increases or spending cuts unless specifically authorized by Congress. Rejected 63-37: R 41-3; D 22-34 (ND 12-30, SD 10-4), March 1, 1994. A two-thirds majority vote (67 in this case) is required to pass a joint resolution proposing an amendment to the Constitution. A "nay" was a vote in support of the president's position. (Senate vote 48)

5. S 636. Abortion Clinic Access/Conference Report. Adoption of the conference report to establish federal criminal and civil penalties for people who use force, the threat of force or physical obstruction to block access to abortion clinics. Adopted (thus cleared for the president) 69-30: R 17-27; D 52-3 (ND 41-1, SD 11-2), May 12, 1994. A "yea" was a vote in support of the president's position. (Senate vote 112)

6. H Con Res 218. Fiscal 1995 Budget Resolution/Conference Report. Adoption of the conference report to set budget levels for the fiscal year ending Sept. 30, 1995: budget authority, $1.541 trillion; outlays, $1.514 trillion; revenues, $1.338 trillion; and a deficit of $175.4 billion. The resolution calls for an additional $13 billion in cuts over five years below the spending caps established in 1993. Adopted (thus cleared) 53-46: R 2-42; D 51-4 (ND 39-3, SD 12-1), May 12, 1994. (Senate vote 113)

SENATE KEY VOTES 7, 8, 9, 10, 11

	7	8	9	10	11
ALABAMA					
Heflin	Y	N	N	N	N
Shelby	?	N	N	Y	N
ALASKA					
Murkowski	Y	Y	Y	Y	N
Stevens	Y	Y	Y	Y	N
ARIZONA					
DeConcini	Y	#	N	Y	Y
McCain	Y	Y	N	Y	N
ARKANSAS					
Bumpers	Y	N	N	N	Y
Pryor	Y	Y	N	N	Y
CALIFORNIA					
Boxer	N	N	N	Y	N
Feinstein	Y	Y	N	N	N
COLORADO					
Campbell	Y	N	N	N	Y
Brown	Y	Y	Y	Y	N
CONNECTICUT					
Dodd	Y	Y	N	N	Y
Lieberman	Y	Y	N	Y	Y
DELAWARE					
Biden	Y	N	N	Y	N
Roth	N	N	Y	Y	N
FLORIDA					
Graham	Y	N	N	N	N
Mack	Y	Y	N	Y	N
GEORGIA					
Nunn	Y	Y	N	N	N
Coverdell	Y	Y	Y	Y	N
HAWAII					
Akaka	Y	N	N	N	Y
Inouye	Y	N	N	N	Y
IDAHO					
Craig	Y	Y	Y	Y	Y
Kempthorne	Y	Y	Y	Y	Y
ILLINOIS					
Moseley-Braun	Y	N	N	Y	Y
Simon	Y	N	N	Y	Y
INDIANA					
Coats	Y	Y	Y	Y	Y
Lugar	Y	Y	Y	Y	Y
IOWA					
Harkin	Y	N	N	N	Y
Grassley	Y	Y	Y	Y	Y
KANSAS					
Dole	Y	Y	Y	Y	Y
Kassebaum	Y	Y	N	N	Y
KENTUCKY					
Ford	Y	N	N	N	Y
McConnell	Y	Y	Y	Y	Y
LOUISIANA					
Breaux	Y	N	N	N	N
Johnston	Y	N	N	N	N
MAINE					
Mitchell	Y	N	N	N	N
Cohen	Y	N	N	Y	N
MARYLAND					
Mikulski	Y	Y	N	N	Y
Sarbanes	Y	N	N	N	Y
MASSACHUSETTS					
Kennedy	Y	N	N	N	N
Kerry	Y	N	N	N	N
MICHIGAN					
Levin	Y	N	N	Y	Y
Riegle	?	N	N	N	Y
MINNESOTA					
Wellstone	N	N	N	N	Y
Durenberger	Y	Y	N	Y	Y
MISSISSIPPI					
Cochran	Y	N	Y	N	Y
Lott	Y	Y	Y	Y	N
MISSOURI					
Bond	Y	Y	Y	Y	Y
Danforth	Y	Y	Y	N	Y
MONTANA					
Baucus	Y	N	N	N	Y
Burns	Y	Y	N	N	Y
NEBRASKA					
Exon	Y	Y	N	N	Y
Kerrey	Y	N	N	N	Y
NEVADA					
Bryan	N	N	?	N	Y
Reid	Y	N	N	N	Y
NEW HAMPSHIRE					
Gregg	Y	Y	Y	N	N
Smith	Y	Y	Y	Y	N
NEW JERSEY					
Bradley	Y	N	N	Y	N
Lautenberg	Y	N	N	Y	N
NEW MEXICO					
Bingaman	Y	N	N	N	N
Domenici	Y	Y	Y	Y	N
NEW YORK					
Moynihan	Y	N	N	Y	N
D'Amato	Y	N	Y	Y	N
NORTH CAROLINA					
Faircloth	Y	Y	Y	Y	N
Helms	Y	Y	Y	Y	Y
NORTH DAKOTA					
Conrad	Y	Y	N	N	Y
Dorgan	Y	Y	N	N	Y
OHIO					
Glenn	Y	Y	N	N	Y
Metzenbaum	N	X	N	N	Y
OKLAHOMA					
Boren	Y	Y	N	N	Y
Nickles	Y	Y	Y	Y	N
OREGON					
Hatfield	Y	Y	Y	N	N
Packwood	Y	Y	Y	Y	Y
PENNSYLVANIA					
Wofford	Y	N	N	N	N
Specter	Y	Y	Y	Y	N
RHODE ISLAND					
Pell	Y	Y	N	N	Y
Chafee	N	Y	N	N	Y
SOUTH CAROLINA					
Hollings	Y	N	N	N	N
Thurmond	Y	Y	Y	Y	N
SOUTH DAKOTA					
Daschle	Y	Y	N	N	Y
Pressler	Y	N	Y	Y	N
TENNESSEE					
Mathews	Y	Y	N	N	Y
Sasser	Y	Y	N	N	Y
TEXAS					
Gramm	Y	Y	N	Y	N
Hutchison	Y	Y	Y	Y	N
UTAH					
Bennett	Y	Y	Y	Y	N
Hatch	Y	Y	Y	Y	N
VERMONT					
Leahy	Y	N	N	N	Y
Jeffords	N	Y	N	Y	Y
VIRGINIA					
Robb	Y	Y	N	Y	N
Warner	Y	Y	N	N	N
WASHINGTON					
Murray	Y	N	N	N	N
Gorton	Y	Y	Y	Y	Y
WEST VIRGINIA					
Byrd	Y	Y	N	N	N
Rockefeller	Y	Y	N	N	N
WISCONSIN					
Feingold	N	N	N	Y	Y
Kohl	Y	Y	N	Y	Y
WYOMING					
Simpson	Y	N	Y	Y	N
Wallop	Y	Y	Y	Y	N

ND   Northern Democrats   SD   Southern Democrats

Southern states - Ala., Ark., Fla., Ga., Ky., La., Miss., N.C., Okla., S.C., Tenn., Texas, Va.

7. S 2019. Safe Drinking Water Act Reauthorization/Risk Assessment. Johnston, D-La., amendment to require an analysis of risk, costs and benefits for regulations issued by the Environmental Protection Agency to enforce the bill that would have an impact of $100 million or more. Adopted 90-8: R 41-3; D 49-5 (ND 36-5, SD 13-0), May 18, 1994. (Senate vote 117)

8. S 687. Product Liability/Cloture. Motion to invoke cloture (thus limiting debate) on the bill to set standards for awarding punitive damages, encourage out-of-court settlements, bar product liability claims against most product sellers, set new time limits for such lawsuits, end joint liability for non-economic damages and hold injured parties responsible for their own use of alcohol or drugs. Motion rejected 57-41: R 38-6; D 19-35 (ND 13-27, SD 6-8), June 29, 1994. Three-fifths of the total Senate (60) is required to invoke cloture. (Senate vote 170)

9. HR 4426. Fiscal 1995 Foreign Operations Appropriations/Congressional Approval for Action in Haiti. Gregg, R-N.H., amendment to prohibit military action in Haiti unless the operations are authorized in advance by Congress or the action is necessary to protect U.S. citizens or national security interests. Re-jected 34-65: R 34-10; D 0-55 (ND 0-41, SD 0-14), June 29, 1994. A "nay" was a vote in support of the president's position. (Senate vote 172)

10. S 2182. Fiscal 1995 Defense Authorization/Unilateral Termination. Dole, R-Kan., amendment to require the president to terminate the U.S. arms embargo of Bosnia-Herzegovina upon receipt from that government of a request for assistance in its right of self-defense. Rejected 50-50: R 37-7; D 13-43 (ND 11-31, SD 2-12), July 1, 1994. A "nay" was a vote in support of the president's position. (Senate vote 181)

11. HR 4624. Fiscal 1995 VA-HUD Appropriations/Ethanol Mandate. Mikulski, D-Md., motion to table (kill) the Johnston, D-La., amendment to prohibit the Environmental Protection Agency from implementing its renewable oxygenates rule for reformulated gasoline, which would require a minimum of 15 percent and eventually 30 percent of the oxygenates used in reformulated gasoline to come from renewable sources, such as ethanol. The amendment also would have cut NASA's procurement budget by $39.3 million. Motion agreed to 51-50: R 19-25; D 31-25 (ND 26-16, SD 5-9), with Vice President Gore casting a "yea" vote, Aug. 3, 1994. A "yea" was a vote in support of the president's position. (Senate vote 255)

KEY

Y	Voted for (yea).
#	Paired for.
+	Announced for.
N	Voted against (nay).
X	Paired against.
−	Announced against.
P	Voted "present."
C	Voted "present" to avoid possible conflict of interest.
?	Did not vote or otherwise make a position known.

Democrats *Republicans*

	12	13	14	15	16
ALABAMA					
Heflin	Y	N	N	Y	N
Shelby [1]	N	N	N	Y	N
ALASKA					
Murkowski	N	N	N	?	N
Stevens	N	N	?	?	N
ARIZONA					
DeConcini	Y	Y	Y	Y	Y
McCain	N	N	N	N	Y
ARKANSAS					
Bumpers	Y	Y	Y	Y	Y
Pryor	Y	Y	Y	Y	Y
CALIFORNIA					
Boxer	Y	Y	Y	Y	Y
Feinstein	Y	Y	Y	Y	Y
COLORADO					
Campbell	Y	N	N	Y	N
Brown	N	N	Y	N	N
CONNECTICUT					
Dodd	Y	Y	Y	Y	Y
Lieberman	Y	Y	Y	Y	Y
DELAWARE					
Biden	Y	Y	Y	Y	Y
Roth	Y	N	Y	Y	Y
FLORIDA					
Graham	Y	Y	Y	Y	Y
Mack	N	N	N	N	Y
GEORGIA					
Nunn	Y	Y	N	Y	Y
Coverdell	N	N	N	N	Y
HAWAII					
Akaka	Y	Y	Y	Y	Y
Inouye	Y	Y	Y	Y	N
IDAHO					
Craig	N	N	N	N	N
Kempthorne	N	N	N	N	N
ILLINOIS					
Moseley-Braun	Y	Y	Y	Y	Y
Simon	Y	Y	Y	Y	Y
INDIANA					
Coats	N	N	N	N	Y
Lugar	N	N	N	Y	Y

	12	13	14	15	16
IOWA					
Harkin	Y	Y	Y	Y	N
Grassley	N	N	N	Y	Y
KANSAS					
Dole	N	N	N	N	Y
Kassebaum	Y	N	N	Y	Y
KENTUCKY					
Ford	Y	Y	Y	Y	N
McConnell	N	N	N	?	Y
LOUISIANA					
Breaux	Y	Y	N	Y	Y
Johnston	Y	N	Y	Y	Y
MAINE					
Mitchell	Y	Y	Y	Y	Y
Cohen	N	N	Y	Y	Y
MARYLAND					
Mikulski	Y	Y	Y	Y	Y
Sarbanes	Y	Y	Y	Y	Y
MASSACHUSETTS					
Kennedy	Y	Y	Y	Y	Y
Kerry	Y	Y	Y	Y	Y
MICHIGAN					
Levin	Y	Y	Y	Y	Y
Riegle	Y	Y	Y	Y	Y
MINNESOTA					
Wellstone	Y	Y	Y	Y	N
Durenberger	N	N	N	Y	Y
MISSISSIPPI					
Cochran	N	N	N	N	Y
Lott	N	N	N	N	Y
MISSOURI					
Bond	N	N	N	?	Y
Danforth	Y	N	N	Y	Y
MONTANA					
Baucus	Y	Y	Y	Y	N
Burns	N	N	N	?	N
NEBRASKA					
Exon	Y	Y	Y	Y	N
Kerrey	Y	N	Y	Y	Y
NEVADA					
Bryan	Y	Y	Y	Y	N
Reid	Y	Y	Y	Y	N

	12	13	14	15	16
NEW HAMPSHIRE					
Gregg	N	N	N	Y	Y
Smith	N	N	N	N	N
NEW JERSEY					
Bradley	Y	Y	Y	?	Y
Lautenberg	Y	Y	Y	Y	Y
NEW MEXICO					
Bingaman	Y	Y	N	Y	Y
Domenici	N	N	N	Y	Y
NEW YORK					
Moynihan	Y	Y	Y	Y	Y
D'Amato	N	N	N	N	Y
NORTH CAROLINA					
Faircloth	N	N	N	N	N
Helms	N	N	N	−	N
NORTH DAKOTA					
Conrad	Y	Y	N	Y	Y
Dorgan	Y	Y	Y	Y	N
OHIO					
Glenn	Y	Y	Y	Y	Y
Metzenbaum	Y	Y	Y	Y	N
OKLAHOMA					
Boren/*Inhofe* [2]	Y	Y	Y	Y	N
Nickles	N	?	N	N	Y
OREGON					
Hatfield	N	N	Y	Y	Y
Packwood	N	N	N	?	Y
PENNSYLVANIA					
Wofford	Y	Y	Y	Y	Y
Specter	Y	N	Y	Y	Y
RHODE ISLAND					
Pell	Y	Y	Y	Y	Y
Chafee	Y	Y	Y	Y	Y
SOUTH CAROLINA					
Hollings	Y	Y	N	?	N
Thurmond	N	N	N	N	N
SOUTH DAKOTA					
Daschle	Y	Y	Y	Y	Y
Pressler	N	N	N	N	Y
TENNESSEE					
Mathews	Y	N	N	Y	N
Sasser	Y	Y	?	Y	Y

	12	13	14	15	16
TEXAS					
Gramm	N	N	N	N	Y
Hutchison	N	N	N	N	Y
UTAH					
Bennett	N	?	N	N	Y
Hatch	N	N	N	N	Y
VERMONT					
Leahy	Y	Y	Y	Y	N
Jeffords	Y	Y	Y	Y	N
VIRGINIA					
Robb	Y	Y	Y	Y	Y
Warner	N	N	N	Y	Y
WASHINGTON					
Murray	Y	Y	Y	Y	Y
Gorton	N	N	N	N	Y
WEST VIRGINIA					
Byrd	Y	Y	N	Y	N
Rockefeller	Y	Y	Y	Y	Y
WISCONSIN					
Feingold	Y	Y	Y	Y	N
Kohl	Y	Y	Y	Y	Y
WYOMING					
Simpson	N	N	N	N	Y
Wallop	N	N	N	N	N

ND Northern Democrats SD Southern Democrats Southern states - Ala., Ark., Fla., Ga., Ky., La., Miss., N.C., Okla., S.C., Tenn., Texas, Va.

12. HR 3355. Omnibus Crime Bill/Budget Act Waiver. Mitchell, D-Maine, motion to waive the budget act with respect to the Domenici, R-N.M., point of order against the crime conference report for violating Section 306 of the 1974 Congressional Budget Act and encroaching on the Budget Committee's jurisdiction by establishing a trust fund not considered by the committee. The conference report would authorize $30.2 billion over six years and require that all spending authorized by the bill come from a crime trust fund realized from eliminating 270,000 federal jobs. The bill would authorize $6.9 billion for crime prevention programs, $8.8 billion for community policing programs and the hiring of 100,000 new police officers, and a $7.9 billion grant program to build state and local prisons. The bill also would ban 19 specific assault weapons, expand the death penalty to dozens of new federal crimes, mandate life imprisonment without parole for three-time violent felons, provide for community notification of violent sex offenders, and allow prior sex offenses to be admitted in federal trials. Motion agreed to 61-39: R 6-38; D 55-1 (ND 42-0, SD 13-1), Aug. 25, 1994. A three-fifths majority vote (60) of the total Senate is required to waive the budget act. (Subsequently, the point of order fell.) A "yea" was a vote in support of the president's position. (Senate vote 293)

13. S 3. Campaign Finance/Cloture. Motion to invoke cloture (thus limiting debate) on the motion to request a conference with the House on the bill to establish a system for voluntary spending caps on congressional campaigns. Motion rejected 52-46: R 2-40; D 50-6 (ND 40-2, SD 10-4), Sept. 30, 1994. Three-fifths of the total Senate (60) is required to invoke cloture. A "yea" was a vote in support of the president's position. (Senate vote 314)

14. S 349. Lobbying Disclosure/Cloture. Motion to invoke cloture (thus limiting debate) on the conference report to expand the disclosure of lobbying activities and impose new restrictions on gifts to members of Congress and their staffs. Motion rejected 52-46: R 7-36; D 45-10 (ND 38-4, SD 7-6), Oct. 6, 1994. Because the bill would change Senate rules, two-thirds of those present and voting (66 in this case) is required to invoke cloture. (Senate vote 322)

15. S 21. California Desert Protection/Cloture. Motion to invoke cloture (thus limiting debate) on the conference report to designate about 7.5 million acres of California desert as wilderness and to establish the Death Valley and Joshua Tree national parks and the Mojave National Preserve. Motion agreed to 68-23: R 14-23; D 54-0 (ND 41-0, SD 13-0), Oct. 8, 1994. Three-fifths of the total Senate (60) is required to invoke cloture. A "yea" was a vote in support of the president's position. (Senate vote 326)

16. HR 5110. General Agreement on Tariffs and Trade/Budget Waiver. Moynihan, D-N.Y., motion to waive the budget act with respect to the Byrd, D-W.Va., point of order against the bill to implement the General Agreement on Tariffs and Trade (GATT) for violating the budget act. The bill would make statutory changes to implement the new world trade agreement negotiated under the Uruguay Round of GATT. Motion agreed to 68-32: R 31-15; D 37-17 (ND 29-13, SD 8-4), Dec. 1, 1994. A three-fifths majority vote (60) of the total Senate is required to waive the budget act. (Subsequently, the budget act was waived and the point of order fell.) A "yea" was a vote in support of the president's position. (Senate vote 328)

[1] *Richard C. Shelby, Ala., switched to the Republican Party on Nov. 9, 1994. He voted as a Republican on key vote 16*

[2] *David L. Boren, D-Okla., resigned Nov. 15, 1994. He voted on all key votes through vote 15. James M. Inhofe, R-Okla., was sworn in on Nov. 17, 1994, replacing Boren. He voted on key vote 16.*

TEXT

State of the Union Address 3-D
   Republican Response 8-D
Packwood Diaries Court Decision 10-D
Delegate Voting Court Decision 11-D
Lifting of Vietnam Embargo 12-D
Rostenkowski Repayment 13-D
Mitchell Supreme Court Withdrawal 14-D
Nixon Funeral 16-D
Breyer Hearings 17-D
Clinton on Crime Bill 26-D

Haiti Invasion Plan 27-D
Haiti Agreement 29-D
Clinton's Election Response 33-D
Gingrich's Election Response 35-D
Dole's Election Response 38-D
GOP 'Contract With America' 39-D
Dole, White House on GATT 53-D
Gingrich Acceptance Speech 57-D
Presidential Agenda 60-D
   Republican Response 61-D

THE STATE OF THE UNION

Clinton Stresses Welfare, Health Care Reform

Following is a transcript from U.S. Newswire of President Clinton's State of the Union address as delivered Jan. 25 before a joint session of Congress.

PRESIDENT CLINTON: Thank you very much. Mr. Speaker, Mr. President, members of the 103rd Congress, my fellow Americans:

I'm not at all sure what speech is in the TelePrompTer tonight, but I hope we can talk about the state of the union.

I ask you to begin by recalling the memory of the giant who presided over this chamber with such force and grace. Tip O'Neill liked to call himself "a man of the House." And he surely was that. But, even more, he was a man of the people, a bricklayer's son who helped to build the great American middle class. Tip O'Neill never forgot who he was, where he came from or who sent him here. Tonight he's smiling down on us for the first time from the Lord's gallery. But in his honor, may we, too, always remember who we are, where we come from and who sent us here.

If we do that we will return over and over again to the principle that if we simply give ordinary people equal opportunity, quality education and a fair shot at the American dream, they will do extraordinary things.

We gather tonight in a world of changes so profound and rapid that all nations are tested. Our American heritage has always been to master such change, to use it to expand opportunity at home and our leadership abroad. But for too long, and in too many ways, that heritage was abandoned, and our country drifted.

For 30 years, family life in America has been breaking down. For 20 years, the wages of working people have been stagnant or declining. For the 12 years of trickle-down economics, we built a false prosperity on a hollow base as our national debt quadrupled. From 1989 to 1992, we experienced the slowest growth in a half-century. For too many families, even when both parents were working, the American dream has been slipping away.

In 1992, the American people demanded that we change. A year ago I asked all of you to join me in accepting responsibility for the future of our country. Well, we did. We replaced drift and deadlock with renewal and reform. And I want to thank every one of you here who heard the American people, who broke gridlock, who gave them the most successful teamwork between a president and a Congress in 30 years.

This Congress produced a budget that cut the deficit by half a trillion dollars, cut spending and raised income taxes on only the wealthiest Americans. This Congress produced tax relief for millions of low-income workers to reward work over welfare. It produced NAFTA [the North American Free Trade Agreement]. It produced the Brady bill, now the Brady law. And thank you, Jim Brady, for being here, and God bless you, sir.

This Congress produced tax cuts to reduce the taxes of nine out of 10 small businesses who use the money to invest more and create jobs.

It produced more research and treatment for AIDS, more childhood immunizations, more support for women's health research, more affordable college loans for the middle class; a new National Service program for those who want to give something back to their country and their communities for higher education; a dramatic increase in high-tech investments to move us from a defense to a domestic high-tech economy. This Congress produced a new law, the "motor voter" bill, to help millions of people register to vote. It produced family and medical leave.

All passed. All signed into law with not one single veto. These accomplishments were all commitments I made when I sought this office. And, in fairness, they all had to be passed by you in this Congress. But I am persuaded that the real credit belongs to the people who sent us here, who pay our salaries, who hold our feet to the fire.

But what we do here is really beginning to change lives. Let me just give you one example. I will never forget what the family and medical leave law meant to just one father I met early one Sunday morning in the White House.

It was unusual to see a family there touring early Sunday morning, but he had his wife and his three children there, one of them in a wheelchair. I came up, and after we had our picture taken and had a little visit, I was walking off, and that man grabbed me by the arm and he said, "Mr. President, let me tell you something. My little girl here is desperately ill. She's probably not going to make it. But because of the family leave law, I was able to take time off to spend with her — the most important time I ever spent in my life — without losing my job and hurting the rest of my family. It means more to me than I will ever be able to say. Don't you people up here ever think what you do doesn't make a difference. It does."

Though we are making a difference, our work has just begun. Many Americans still haven't felt the impact of what we've done. The recovery still hasn't touched every community or created enough jobs. Incomes are still stagnant; there's still too much violence and not enough hope in too many places. Abroad, the young democracies we are strongly supporting still face very difficult times and look to us for leadership. And so tonight, let us resolve to continue the journey of renewal, to create more and better jobs, to guarantee health security for all, to reward work over welfare, to promote democracy abroad, and to begin to reclaim our streets from violent crime and drugs and gangs, to renew our own American community.

Last year we began to put our house in order by tackling the budget deficit that was driving us toward bankruptcy. We cut $255 billion in spending, including entitlements, and over 340 separate budget items. We froze domestic spending and used honest budget numbers.

Led by the vice president, we launched a campaign to reinvent government. We cut staff, cut perks, even trimmed the fleet of federal limousines. After years of leaders whose rhetoric attacked bureaucracy but whose actions expanded it, we will actually reduce it by 252,000 people over the next five years. By the time we have finished, the federal bureaucracy will be at its lowest point in 30 years.

Because the deficit was so large and because they benefited from tax cuts in the 1980s, we did ask the wealthiest Americans to pay more to reduce the deficit. So on April 15, the American people will discover the truth about what we did last year on taxes. Only the top 1 — yes, listen — the top 1.2 percent of Americans, as I said all along, will pay higher income tax rates. Let me repeat — only the wealthiest 1.2 percent of Americans will face higher income tax rates, and no one else will. And that is the truth.

Of course, there were, as there always are in politics, naysayers who said this plan wouldn't work. But they were wrong. When I became president, the experts predicted that next year's deficit would be $300 billion. But because we acted, those same people now say the deficit is going to be under $180 billion — 40 percent lower than was previously predicted.

Our economic program has helped to produce the lowest core inflation rate and the lowest interest rates in 20 years. And because those interest rates are down, business investment and equipment [are] growing at seven times the rate of the previous four

years; auto sales are way up; home sales are at a record high. Millions of Americans have refinanced their homes, and our economy has produced 1.6 million private sector jobs in 1993 — more than were created in the previous four years combined.

The people who supported this economic plan should be proud of its early results. Proud. But everyone in this chamber should know and acknowledge that there is more to do.

Next month I will send you one of the toughest budgets ever presented to Congress. It will cut spending in more than 300 programs, eliminate 100 domestic programs, and reform the ways in which governments buy goods and services. This year we must again make the hard choices to live within the hard spending ceilings we have set. We must do it. We have proved we can bring the deficit down without choking off recovery, without punishing seniors or the middle class and without putting our national security at risk. If you will stick with this plan, we will post three consecutive years of declining deficits for the first time since Harry Truman lived in the White House. And once again, the buck stops here.

Our economic plan also bolsters our strength and our credibility around the world. Once we reduced the deficit and put the steel back into our competitive edge, the world echoed with the sound of falling trade barriers. In one year, with NAFTA, with GATT [the General Agreement on Tariffs and Trade], with our efforts in Asia and the National Export Strategy, we did more to open world markets to American products than at any time in the last two generations.

That means more jobs and rising living standards for the American people, low deficits, low inflation, low interest rates, low trade barriers and high investments. These are the building blocks of our recovery. But if we want to take full advantage of the opportunities before us in the global economy, you all know we must do more.

As we reduce defense spending, I ask Congress to invest more in the technologies of tomorrow. Defense conversion will keep us strong militarily and create jobs for our people here at home.

As we protect our environment, we must invest in the environmental technologies of the future which will create jobs. This year we will fight for a revitalized clean water act and a Safe Drinking Water Act and a reformed superfund program. And the vice president is right — we must also work with the private sector to connect every classroom, every clinic, every library, every hospital in America into a national information superhighway by the year 2000.

Think of it — instant access to information will increase productivity, will help to educate our children. It will provide better medical care. It will create jobs. And I call on the Congress to pass legislation to establish that information superhighway this year.

As we expand opportunity and create jobs, no one can be left out. We must continue to enforce fair lending and fair housing and all civil rights laws, because America will never be complete in its renewal until everyone shares in its bounty.

But we all know, too, we can do all these things — put our economic house in order, expand world trade, target the jobs of the future, guarantee equal opportunity — but if we're honest, we'll all admit that this strategy still cannot work unless we also give our people the education, training and skills they need to seize the opportunities of tomorrow.

We must set tough, world-class academic and occupational standards for all our children and give our teachers and students the tools they need to meet them. Our Goals 2000 proposal will empower individual school districts to experiment with ideas like chartering their schools to be run by private corporations, or having more public school choice — to do whatever they wish to do as long as we measure every school by one high standard: Are our children learning what they need to know to compete and win in the global economy?

Goals 2000 links world-class standards to grass-roots reforms. And I hope Congress will pass it without delay.

Our School to Work Initiative will for the first time link school to the world of work, providing at least one year of apprenticeship beyond high school. After all, most of the people we're counting on to build our economic future won't graduate from college. It's time to stop ignoring them and start empowering them.

We must literally transform our outdated unemployment system into a new reemployment system. The old unemployment system just sort of kept you going while you waited for your old job to come back. We've got to have a new system to move people into new and better jobs because most of those old jobs just don't come back. And we know that the only way to have real job security in the future, to get a good job with a growing income, is to have real skills and the ability to learn new ones. So we've got to streamline today's patchwork of training programs and make them a source of new skills for our people who lose their jobs.

Re-employment, not unemployment, must become the centerpiece of our economic renewal. I urge you to pass it in this session of Congress.

And just as we must transform our unemployment system, so must we also revolutionize our welfare system. It doesn't work. It defies our values as a nation. If we value work, we can't justify a system that makes welfare more attractive than work if people are worried about losing their health care. If we value responsibility, we can't ignore the $34 billion in child support absent parents ought to be paying to millions of parents who are taking care of their children. If we value strong families, we can't perpetuate a system that actually penalizes those who stay together.

Can you believe that a child who has a child gets more money from the government for leaving home than for staying home with a parent or a grandparent? That's not just bad policy, it's wrong. And we ought to change it.

I worked on this problem for years before I became president, with other governors and with members of Congress of both parties and with the previous administration of another party. I worked on it with people who were on welfare — lots of them. And I want to say something to everybody here who cares about this issue. The people who most want to change this system are the people who are dependent on it. They want to get off welfare. They want to go back to work. They want to do right by their kids.

I once had a hearing when I was a governor, and I brought in people on welfare from all over America who had found their way to work. The woman from my state who testified was asked this question: What's the best thing about being off welfare and in a job? And, without blinking an eye, she looked at 40 governors and she said, "When my boy goes to school and they say, 'What does your mother do for a living?' he can give an answer." These people want a better system, and we ought to give it to them.

Last year we began this. We gave the states more power to innovate because we know that a lot of great ideas come from outside Washington, and many states are already using it. Then this Congress took a dramatic step. Instead of taxing people with modest incomes into poverty, we helped them to work their way out of poverty by dramatically increasing the earned-income tax credit. It will lift 15 million working families out of poverty, rewarding work over welfare, making it possible for people to be successful workers and successful parents.

Now that's real welfare reform.

But there is more to be done. This spring I will send you a comprehensive welfare reform bill that builds on the Family Support Act of 1988 and restores the basic values of responsibility. We'll say to teenagers, "If you have a child out of wedlock, we will no longer give you a check to set up a separate household. We want families to stay together." Say to absent parents who aren't paying their child support, "If you're not providing for your children, we'll [garnishee] your wages, suspend your license, track you across state lines, and if necessary, make some of you work off what you owe."

People who bring children into this world cannot and must not walk away from them. But to all those who depend on welfare, we should offer ultimately a simple compact. We'll provide the support, the job training, the child care you need for up to two years. But after that, anyone who can work must — in the private sector, wherever possible; in community services, if necessary. That's the only way we'll ever make welfare what it ought to be — a second chance, not a way of life.

I know it will be difficult to tackle welfare reform in 1994 at the same time we

tackle health care. But let me point out, I think it is inevitable and imperative. It is estimated that 1 million people are on welfare today because it's the only way they can get health care coverage for their children. Those who choose to leave welfare for jobs without health benefits — and many entry jobs don't have health benefits — find themselves in the incredible position of paying taxes that help to pay for health care coverage for those who made the other choice to stay on welfare. No wonder people leave work and go back to welfare to get health care coverage. We have got to solve the health care problem to have real welfare reform.

So this year, we will make history by reforming the health care system. And I would say to you, all of you, my fellow public servants, this is another issue where the people are way ahead of the politicians. That may not be popular with either party, but it happens to be the truth.

You know, the first lady has received now almost a million letters from people all across America and from all walks of life. I'd like to share just one of them with you. Richard Anderson of Reno, Nev., lost his job and, with it, his health insurance. Two weeks later, his wife, Judy, suffered a cerebral aneurysm. He rushed her to the hospital, where she stayed in intensive care for 21 days.

The Andersons' bills were over $120,000. Although Judy recovered and Richard went back to work, at $8 an hour, the bills were too much for them, and they were literally forced into bankruptcy.

"Mrs. Clinton," he wrote to Hillary, "no one in the United States of America should have to lose everything they've worked for all their lives because they were unfortunate enough to become ill."

It was to help the Richard and Judy Andersons of America that the first lady and so many others have worked so hard and so long on this health care reform issue. We owe them our thanks and our action.

I know there are people here who say there's no health care crisis. Tell it to Richard and Judy Anderson. Tell it to the 58 million Americans who have no coverage at all for some time each year. Tell it to the 81 million Americans with those pre-existing conditions — those folks are paying more or they can't get insurance at all, or they can't ever change their jobs because they or someone in their family has one of those pre-existing conditions. Tell it to the small businesses burdened by the skyrocketing cost of insurance. Most small businesses cover their employees, and they pay on average 35 percent more in premiums than big businesses or government. Or tell it to the 76 percent of insured Americans, three out of four whose policies have lifetime limits. And that means they can find themselves without any coverage at all just when they need it the most.

So if any of you believe there's no crisis, you tell it to those people — because I can't.

There are some people who literally do not understand the impact of this problem on people's lives. And all you have to do is go out and listen to them. Just go talk to them anywhere in any congressional district in this country. They're Republicans and Democrats and independents — it doesn't have a lick to do with party. They think we don't get it. And it's time we show them that we do get it.

From the day we began, our health care initiative has been designed to strengthen what is good about our health care system: the world's best health care professionals, cutting-edge research and wonderful research institutions, Medicare for older Americans. None of this, none of it should be put at risk.

But we're paying more and more money for less and less care. Every year fewer and fewer Americans even get to choose their doctors. Every year doctors and nurses spend more time on paperwork and less time with patients because of the absolute bureaucratic nightmare the present system has become. This system is riddled with inefficiency, with abuse, with fraud, and everybody knows it.

In today's health care system, insurance companies call the shots. They pick whom they cover and how they cover them. They can cut off your benefits when you need your coverage the most. They are in charge.

What does it mean? It means every night millions of well-insured Americans go to bed just an illness, an accident or a pink slip away from having no coverage or financial ruin. It means every morning millions of Americans go to work without any health insurance at all — something the workers in no other advanced country in the world do. It means that every year, more and more hard-working people are told to pick a new doctor because their boss has had to pick a new plan. And countless others turn down better jobs because they know if they take the better job, they will lose their health insurance.

If we just let the health care system continue to drift, our country will have people with less care, fewer choices and higher bills.

Now, our approach protects the quality of care and people's choices. It builds on what works today in the private sector — to expand employer-based coverage, to guarantee private insurance for every American. And I might say, employer-based private insurance for every American was proposed 20 years ago by President Richard Nixon to the United States Congress. It was a good idea then, and it's a better idea today.

Why do we want guaranteed private insurance? Because right now nine out of 10 people who have insurance get it through their employers. And that should continue. And if your employer is providing good benefits at reasonable prices, that should continue, too. That ought to make the Congress and the president feel better.

Our goal is health insurance everybody can depend on — comprehensive benefits that cover preventive care and prescription drugs; health premiums that don't just explode when you get sick or you get older; the power no matter how small your business is to choose dependable insurance at the same competitive rates governments and big business get today; one simple form for people who are sick; and, most of all, the freedom to choose a plan and the right to choose your own doctor.

Our approach protects older Americans. Every plan before the Congress proposes to slow the growth of Medicare. The difference is this: We believe those savings should be used to improve health care for senior citizens. Medicare must be protected, and it should cover prescription drugs, and we should take the first steps in covering long-term care.

To those who would cut Medicare without protecting seniors, I say the solution to today's squeeze on middle-class working people's health care is not to put the squeeze on middle-class retired people's health care. We can do better than that.

When it's all said and done, it's pretty simple to me. Insurance ought to mean what it used to mean — you pay a fair price for security, and when you get sick, health care's always there, no matter what.

Along with the guarantee of health security, we all have to admit, too, there must be more responsibility on the part of all of us in how we use this system. People have to take their kids to get immunized. We should all take advantage of preventive care. We must all work together to stop the violence that explodes our emergency rooms. We have to practice better health habits, and we can't abuse the system. And those who don't have insurance under our approach will get coverage, but they'll have to pay something for it, too. The minority of businesses that provide no insurance at all, and in so doing, shift the cost of the care of their employees to others, should contribute something. People who smoke should pay more for a pack of cigarettes. Everybody can contribute something if we want to solve the health care crisis. There can't be any more something for nothing. It will not be easy, but it can be done.

Now, in the coming months I hope very much to work with both Democrats and Republicans to reform a health care system by using the market to bring down costs and to achieve lasting health security. But if you look at history, we see that for 60 years this country has tried to reform health care. President [Franklin D.] Roosevelt tried. President Truman tried. President Nixon tried. President [Jimmy] Carter tried. Every time, the special interests were powerful enough to defeat them. But not this time.

I know that facing up to these interests will require courage. It will raise critical questions about the way we finance our campaigns and how lobbyists wield their influence. The work of change, frankly, will never get any easier until we limit the influence of well-financed interests who profit from this current system. So I also must now to call on you to finish the job both houses began last year by passing tough and meaningful campaign finance reform and lobby reform legislation this year.

You know, my fellow Americans, this is really a test for all of us. The American people provide those of us in government service with terrific health care benefits at reasonable costs. We have health care that's always there. I think we need to give every hard-working, tax-paying American the same health care security they have already given to us.

I want to make this very clear. I am open, as I have said repeatedly, to the best ideas of concerned members of both parties. I have no special brief for any specific approach, even in our own bill, except this: If you send me legislation that does not guarantee every American private health insurance that can never be taken away, you will force me to take this pen, veto the legislation, and we'll come right back here and start all over again.

But I don't think that's going to happen. I think we're ready to act now. I believe that you're ready to act now. And if you're ready to guarantee every American the same health care that you have, health care that can never be taken away, now —not next year or the year after — now is the time to stand with the people who sent us here. Now.

As we take these steps together to renew our strength at home, we cannot turn away from our obligation to renew our leadership abroad. This is a promising moment. Because of the agreements we have reached this year, last year, Russia's strategic nuclear missiles soon will no longer be pointed at the United States, nor will we point ours at them. Instead of building weapons in space, Russian scientists will help us to build the international space station.

Of course, there are still dangers in the world — rampant arms proliferation, bitter regional conflicts, ethnic and nationalist tensions in many new democracies, severe environmental degradation the world over, and fanatics who seek to cripple the world's cities with terror. As the world's greatest power, we must, therefore, maintain our defenses and our responsibilities.

This year, we secured indictments against terrorists and sanctions against those who harbor them. We worked to promote environmentally sustainable economic growth. We achieved agreements with Ukraine, with Belarus, with Kazakhstan to eliminate completely their nuclear arsenal. We are working to achieve a Korean Peninsula free of nuclear weapons. We will seek early ratification of a treaty to ban chemical weapons worldwide. And earlier today, we joined with over 30 nations to begin negotiations on a comprehensive ban to stop all nuclear testing.

But nothing, nothing is more important to our security than our nation's armed forces. We honor their contributions, including those who are carrying out the longest humanitarian airlift in history in Bosnia; those who will complete their mission in Somalia this year and their brave comrades who gave their lives there.

Our forces are the finest military our nation has ever had. And I have pledged that as long as I am president, they will remain the best-equipped, the best-trained and the best-prepared fighting force on the face of the Earth.

Last year I proposed a defense plan that maintains our post-Cold War security at a lower cost. This year many people urged me to cut our defense spending further to pay for other government programs. I said no. The budget I send to Congress draws the line against further defense cuts. It protects the readiness and quality of our forces.

Ultimately, the best strategy is to do that. We must not cut defense further. I hope the Congress without regard to party will support that position.

Ultimately, the best strategy to ensure our security and to build a durable peace is to support the advance of democracy elsewhere. Democracies don't attack each other, they make better trading partners and partners in diplomacy. That is why we have supported, you and I, the democratic reformers in Russia and in the other states of the former Soviet bloc. I applaud the bipartisan support this Congress provided last year for our initiatives to help Russia, Ukraine and the other states through their epic transformations.

Our support of reform must combine patience for the enormity of the task and vigilance for our fundamental interest and values. We will continue to urge Russia and the other states to press ahead with economic reforms. And we will seek to cooperate with Russia to solve regional problems, while insisting that if Russian troops operate in neighboring states, they do so only when those states agree to their presence and in strict accord with international standards.

But we must also remember as these nations chart their own futures — and they must chart their own futures — how much more secure and more prosperous our own people will be if democratic and market reform succeed all across the former communist bloc. Our policy has been to support that move and that has been the policy of the Congress. We should continue it.

That is why I went to Europe earlier this month — to work with our European partners, to help to integrate all the former communist countries into a Europe that has a possibility of becoming unified for the first time in its entire history — its entire history — based on the simple commitments of all nations in Europe to democracy, to free markets and to respect for existing borders.

With our allies we have created a Partnership for Peace that invites states from the former Soviet bloc and other non-NATO members to work with NATO in military cooperation. When I met with Central Europe's leaders, including [President of Poland] Lech Walesa and [President of the Czech Republic] Vaclav Havel, men who put their lives on the line for freedom, I told them that the security of their region is important to our country's security.

This year we must also do more to support democratic renewal and human rights and sustainable development all around the world. We will ask Congress to ratify the new

GATT accord. We will continue standing by South Africa as it works its way through its bold and hopeful and difficult transition to democracy. We will convene a summit of the Western Hemisphere's leaders from Canada to the tip of South America. And we will continue to press for the restoration of true democracy in Haiti.

And as we build a more constructive relationship with China, we must continue to insist on clear signs of improvement in that nation's human rights record.

We will also work for new progress toward the Middle East peace. Last year the world watched Yitzhak Rabin [the prime minister of Israel] and Yasir Arafat [the leader of the Palestine Liberation Organization] at the White House when they had their historic handshake of reconciliation. But there is a long, hard road ahead. And on that road I am determined that I and our administration will do all we can to achieve a comprehensive and lasting peace for all the peoples of the region.

Now, there are some in our country who argue that with the Cold War over, America should turn its back on the rest of the world. Many around the world were afraid we would do just that. But I took this office on a pledge that had no partisan tinge to keep our nation secure by remaining engaged in the rest of the world. And this year, because of our work together — enacting NAFTA, keeping our military strong and prepared, supporting democracy abroad — we have reaffirmed America's leadership, America's engagement. And as a result, the American people are more secure than they were before.

But while Americans are more secure from threats abroad, I think we all know that in many ways we are less secure from threats here at home. Every day the national peace is shattered by crime. In Petaluma, Calif., an innocent slumber party gives way to agonizing tragedy for the family of Polly Klaas. An ordinary train ride on Long Island [N.Y.] ends in a hail of 9mm rounds. A tourist in Florida is nearly burned alive by bigots simply because he is black. Right here in our nation's capital, a brave young man named Jason White, a policeman, the son and grandson of policemen, is ruthlessly gunned down. Violent crime and the fear it provokes are crippling our society, limiting personal freedom and fraying the ties that bind us.

The crime bill before Congress gives you a chance to do something about it — a chance to be tough and smart. What does that mean? Let me begin by saying I care a lot about this issue. Many years ago, when I started out in public life, I was the attorney general of my state. I served as a governor for a dozen years; I know what it's like to sign laws increasing penalties, to build more prison cells, to carry out the death penalty. I understand this issue. And it is not a simple thing.

First, we must recognize that most violent crimes are committed by a small percentage of criminals who too often break the laws even when they are on parole. Now those who commit crimes should be

punished. And those who commit repeated, violent crimes should be told, when you commit a third violent crime, you will be put away, and put away for good. Three strikes, and you are out.

Second, we must take serious steps to reduce violence and prevent crime, beginning with more police officers and more community policing. We know right now that police who work the streets, know the folks, have the respect of the neighborhood kids, focus on high crime areas — we know that they are more likely to prevent crime as well as catch criminals. Look at the experience of Houston, where the crime rate dropped 17 percent in one year when that approach was taken.

Here tonight is one of those community policemen — a brave young detective, Kevin Jett, whose beat is eight square blocks in one of the toughest neighborhoods in New York. Every day he restores some sanity and safety and a sense of values and connections to the people whose lives he protects. I'd like to ask him to stand up and be recognized tonight.

Thank you, sir.

You will be given a chance to give the children of this country, the law-abiding, working people of this country — and don't forget, in the toughest neighborhoods in this country, in the highest crime neighborhoods in this country, the vast majority of people get up every day and obey the law, pay their taxes, do their best to raise their kids; they deserve people like Kevin Jett — and you're going to be given a chance to give the American people another 100,000 of them, well-trained. And I urge you to do it.

You have before you crime legislation which also establishes a police corps to encourage young people to get an education and pay it off by serving as police officers; which encourages retiring military personnel to move into police forces, an inordinate resource for our country — one which has a safe schools provision which will give our young people the chance to walk to school in safety and to be in school in safety instead of dodging bullets. These are important things.

The third thing we have to do is to build on the Brady bill — the Brady law. To take further steps to keep guns out of the hands of criminals.

I want to say something about this issue. Hunters must always be free to hunt. Law-abiding adults should always be free to own guns to protect their homes. I respect that part of our culture; I grew up in it. But I want to ask the sportsmen and others who lawfully own guns to join us in this campaign to reduce gun violence. I say to you, I know you didn't create this problem, but we need your help to solve it. There is no sporting purpose on Earth that should stop the United States Congress from banishing assault weapons that outgun police and cut down children.

Fourth, we must remember that drugs are a factor in an enormous percentage of crimes. Recent studies indicate, sadly, that drug use is on the rise again among our young people. The crime bill contains — all

the crime bills contain — more money for drug treatment for criminal addicts, and boot camps for youthful offenders that include incentives to get off drugs and to stay off drugs.

Our administration's budget with all its cuts contains a large increase in funding for drug treatment and drug education. You must pass them both. We need them desperately.

My fellow Americans, the problem of violence is an American problem. It has no partisan or philosophical element. Therefore, I urge you to find ways as quickly as possible to set aside partisan differences and pass a strong, smart, tough crime bill. But further, I urge you to consider this: As you demand tougher penalties for those who choose violence, let us also remember how we came to this sad point.

In our toughest neighborhoods, on our meanest streets, in our poorest rural areas, we have seen a stunning and simultaneous breakdown of community, family and work — the heart and soul of civilized society. This has created a vast vacuum, which has been filled by violence and drugs and gangs. So I ask you to remember that even as we say no to crime, we must give people — especially our young people — something to say yes to.

Many of our initiatives — from job training to welfare reform to health care to national service — will help to rebuild distressed communities, to strengthen families, to provide work. But more needs to be done. That's what our community empowerment agenda is all about — challenging businesses to provide more investment through empowerment zones; ensuring banks will make loans in the same communities their deposits come from; passing legislation to unleash the power of capital through community development banks to create jobs — opportunity and hope where they're needed most.

I think you know that to really solve this problem, we'll all have to put our heads together, leave our ideological armor aside and find some new ideas to do even more. And let's be honest; we all know something else too: Our problems go way beyond the reach of government. They're rooted in the loss of values, in the disappearance of work and the breakdown of our families and our communities.

My fellow Americans, we can cut the deficit, create jobs, promote democracy around the world, pass welfare reform and health care, pass the toughest crime bill in history, but still leave too many of our people behind.

The American people have got to want to change from within if we're going to bring back work and family and community. We cannot renew our country when within a decade, more than half of the children will be born into families where there has been no marriage. We cannot renew this country when 13-year-old boys get semiautomatic weapons to shoot 9-year-olds for kicks. We can't renew our country when children are having children and the fathers walk away as if the kids don't

amount to anything. We can't renew the country when our businesses eagerly look for new investments and new customers abroad but ignore those people right here at home who would give anything to have their jobs and would gladly buy their products if they had the money to do it.

We can't renew our country unless more of us — I mean all of us — are willing to join the churches and the other good citizens — people like all the black ministers I've worked with over the years, or the priests and the nuns I met at Our Lady of Help in East Los Angeles, or my good friend, Tony Campollo in Philadelphia — unless we're willing to work with people like that, people who are saving kids, adopting schools, making streets safer — all of us can do that. We can't renew our country until we realize that governments don't raise children, parents do.

Parents who know their children's teachers and turn off the television and help with the homework and teach their kids right from wrong — those kinds of parents can make all the difference. I know, I had one.

I'm telling you, we have got to stop pointing our fingers at these kids who have no future and reach our hands out to them. Our country needs it, we need it, and they deserve it.

So I say to you tonight, let's give our children a future. Let us take away their guns and give them books. Let us overcome their despair and replace it with hope. Let us, by our example, teach them to obey the law, respect our neighbors and cherish our values. Let us weave these sturdy threads into a new American community that can once more stand strong against the forces of despair and evil because everybody has a chance to walk into a better tomorrow.

Oh, there will be naysayers who fear that we won't be equal to the challenges of this time. But they misread our history, our heritage. Even today's headlines — all those things tell us we can and we will overcome any challenge.

When the earth shook and fires raged in California, when I saw the Mississippi deluge the farmlands of the Midwest in a 500-year flood, when the century's bitterest cold swept from North Dakota to Newport News, it seemed as though the world itself was coming apart at the seams. But the American people — they just came together. They rose to the occasion, neighbor helping neighbor, strangers risking life and limb to save total strangers — showing the better angels of our nature.

Let us not reserve the better angels only for natural disasters, leaving our deepest and most profound problems to petty political fighting. Let us instead be true to our spirit — facing facts, coming together, bringing hope and moving forward.

Tonight, my fellow Americans, we are summoned to answer a question as old as the Republic itself: What is the state of our Union? It is growing stronger, but it must be stronger still. With your help, and God's help, it will be.

Thank you and God bless America. ∎

REPUBLICAN RESPONSE

Dole: No Health Care Crisis, Clinton on Wrong Road

Following is a Federal News Service transcript of the Republican response, as delivered Jan. 25 by Senate Minority Leader Bob Dole, R-Kan., to President Clinton's State of the Union address.

SEN. DOLE: Good evening. I'm Bob Dole, the Senate Republican leader. Tonight, I'm speaking for congressional Republicans, for Republican governors, state legislators, mayors and other elected officials, and I hope for you, if you believe as we do, that America's taxes should be lower, that the government should spend less, that the people — not the government — should control more, and that our armed forces must be strong.

Now, here in Congress we're the minority party. The Democrats have many more votes than we do in both the House and the Senate. So, when the president spoke tonight, and he did a good job, he knew that whatever he really wants he stands a good chance of getting because most Democrats will vote with him. And when Republicans believe President Clinton is moving America in the right direction, as he did with the North American Free Trade Agreement, then he can count on our votes and our cooperation, too.

But far more often than not, the president and his Democrat majority have taken what we believe is the wrong fork in the road, not just on one or two matters of policy, but on their entire approach to government. And health care is a good example.

The president and Mrs. Clinton deserve credit for starting the debate. It has been very helpful. Now, nearly a year later, we really better understand this most important issue. We know that America has the best health-care system in the world, that people from every corner of the globe come here when they need the very best treatment, and that our goal should be to ensure that every American has access to this system.

Of course, there are many Americans with a sick child or sick parent in real need, both in rural and urban America. Our country has health-care problems, but not a health-care crisis. But we will have a crisis if we take the president's medicine — a massive overdose of government control. How massive? My colleague, Sen. Arlen Specter [R] of Pennsylvania, has prepared a chart of what the health-care bureaucracy would look like under the president's plan, and I'd like to show you this chart. It's a great big chart. It contains 207 boxes. It would take a long time to fully explain it, and frankly, I have difficulty understanding it myself.

Let me point out some of the new

bureaucracies that the president's plan will create. Way up here is the National Health Board. Over here is the Advisory Commission on Regional Variations of Health Expenditures. And here's the National Institute for Health Care Workforce Development.

Now, you and I are way down here, way at the bottom. I don't know why we're not at the top, but we're at the bottom.

Now, the president's idea is to put a mountain of bureaucrats between you and your doctor. For example, if you are a family member and want to receive care from a specialist or a clinic outside your own state — let's say you live in Kansas and you want to go to Minnesota — then you probably can't do it without asking for approval. And under his plan, information about your health and your treatment can be sent to a national data bank without your approval. And that's a compromise of privacy none of us should accept.

Now, these just are two examples, but there are many, many more. Clearly, the president is asking you to trust the government more than you trust your doctor and yourselves with your lives and the lives of your loved ones. More cost, less choice, more taxes, less quality, more government control and less control for you and your family — that's what the president's government-run plan is likely to give you.

Now, we can fix our most pressing problems without performing a triple bypass operation on our health care system. We can do it without the estimated $1 trillion gap — yes, $1 trillion gap — between the administration's own projections, their projections, of spending under the plan and the funds available to pay for it, and we can do it now. Republicans, and I believe many, many Democrats, are ready to vote for legislation containing some common-sense solutions — solutions like guaranteeing uninterrupted coverage to everyone who is insured, even if you leave or lose your job, and guaranteeing that your coverage cannot be denied because of a serious illness or pre-existing condition; giving relief to small businesses by allowing them to join together to buy insurance— that lowers the rates, that saves them money — giving individuals like yourselves who buy their own insurance 100 percent tax deduction; changing the law to allow you to open your own medical savings account or to buy what we refer to or call medical IRAs; and helping uninsured low-income Americans pay for coverage through tax credits or vouchers; and finally cutting government red tape and reforming medical malpractice laws that make our health care system so expensive.

A debate on the president's massive and complex program will continue for most of the year, but the changes I just mentioned can be made now, so why wait? Why not act to put you and your family in control of your health care right now?

This evening the president also spoke at length about crime, and he's right. We all must take responsibility as individuals. And after years of debate, many Democrats are now joining Republicans behind this view.

Criminals are not the victims of society, society is the victim of criminals; and the best way to make America's streets and schools and homes safer is to put violent criminals in jail and to keep them there. And most provisions of this bill do just that. It passed the Senate last November by a vote of 94-4.

Now let me give you just a few examples. Life imprisonment for those convicted of three violent felonies, call it three strikes and you're in, you're in for life; tough mandatory sentences for those who use a gun in the commission of a crime; violent juveniles will be treated as adults when they use a gun in a crime. But as you know very well, just putting criminals behind bars is not enough. There is a big, big second step, and that's padlocking the revolving door, keeping violent criminals in jail for their entire sentence. A 20-year sentence should mean just that, 20 years or darned close to it, not five, not 10, not even 15.

So this bill would authorize 10 new regional prisons, federal prisons. But before states can send their violent criminals to those prisons, they must adopt truth-in-sentencing laws. In other words, if you do the crime, you are really going to do the time.

Now, the Senate has passed tough crime bills before, but every time we do, liberal congressional Democrats remove the toughest provisions, and that must not happen again. Republicans want President Clinton to sign the toughest bill possible, and I've got the toughest bill around this town in my hands right now. Here it is, here it is. We hope the House passes it; we hope the Senate . . . the president will sign it.

Now, the president used some tough, tough language tonight, and that's good, but will he follow through, and will he act on it? Will he insist on the tough provisions — like 10 new regional federal prisons, like truth-in-sentencing laws, like [a] tough, mandatory sentence for using a gun, and the death penalty for drug kingpins?

Unfortunately, the administration has damaged its credibility on the crime issue by cutting the federal prison construction budget by 20 percent, and by the 94 percent cut in the drug czar's office. And yes, the talk in the administration of legalizing drugs doesn't help much either.

Now, many people are confused when the president's actions appear different than his words. For example, the president talks about education, but he opposes school choice, which could give parents

more control over the education of their children. He promised to end welfare as we know it, yet everyone waits for his proposal.

In the meantime, Republicans here in Congress and Republican governors across the nation are fighting for changes that make work and self-sufficiency, and reducing illegitimacy, top priorities.

The president promised a middle-class tax cut, yet he and his party imposed the largest tax increase in American history. This $255 billion tax increase was opposed by every Republican in the House and in the Senate. We hope his higher taxes will not cut short the economic recovery and declining interest rates that he inherited.

The two-year mark, coming at the end of this year, is when the economy usually starts to feel the results of a new administration's policies. Now instead of stifling growth and expansion through higher taxes and increased government regulations, Republicans would take America in a different direction, and we can do that through alternatives that reward risk-taking, and the creation of new jobs, and they give our small-business men and women relief from the heavy hand of government.

Now, the president told you tonight that the deficit is projected to decrease next year, and that's true. After all, the largest tax increase in American history would decrease any deficit — temporarily.

But in the words of [radio commentator] Paul Harvey, I want to tell you "the rest of the story." Under [Clinton's] budget, government spending will increase by at least $343 billion in the next five years, and in the same time period, the nonpartisan — let me repeat, the nonpartisan — Congressional Budget Office projects that $1 trillion will be added to our national debt.

Now, the one place the president has cut drastically is precisely the wrong place — national security. Slashed to the lowest level since before Pearl Harbor. History tells us, and many of us know firsthand, that America cannot afford to have a hollow military, nor can we afford to let the United Nations dictate what is in America's national interest.

But I want to close tonight by talking about America, the greatest country on the face of the Earth. I believe America has an enduring mission, a mission of leadership. Fifty years ago, when Hitler's tyranny was on the march, it was only because of strong American leadership that freedom was preserved. In the Cold War, for millions behind the Iron Curtain and in the many nations that depended on us to protect them, it was again only because of strong American leadership that freedom prevailed. And now, as countries that were tyrannies learn democracy, as people learn about free markets where a short time ago buying and selling without the state's per-

mission was illegal, the world again waits and wants strong — and needs strong — American leadership so that freedom will endure.

You know, many times over the past few years, right here in this office in the Capitol, I've met with representatives from the new emerging democracies. Some were leaders of their countries. Some were ordinary citizens. Some had been in jail for many years for just speaking out in public. And they all told me about the same thing — some with tears in their eyes, some could hardly speak — and they all said, "We want to be like America." That's what they said. "We want to be like America." In this great, good and generous nation, the American mission endures here at home and around the world. We are its stewards, and it's up to us to ensure that, wherever the road divides, that America takes the right path, remains true to our mission of leadership and remains the light and the hope of humanity.

Thank you. And to the people of Southern California, please know that all of us in Washington will be working with [Republican] Gov. [Pete] Wilson and your congressional delegation to provide the help you need.

And if you'd like a copy of this chart, just write Sen. Arlen Specter, care of the Capitol, Washington, D.C.

Thank you and good night. ∎

COURT DECISION

Judge Upholds Subpoena Of Packwood Diaries

On Jan. 24, U.S. District Judge Thomas Penfield Jackson upheld a subpoena from the Senate Ethics Committee for the diaries of Sen. Bob Packwood, R-Ore. Packwood had argued that the subpoena violated his rights. Following is the judge's order, not including his summary of the facts of the case:

Senator Packwood contends that the reach of the Ethics Committee's subpoena exceeds its legitimate grasp, in that it calls for him to divulge portions of the diaries which are not relevant to the Committee's investigation into allegations of sexual misconduct, witness intimidation and misuse of staff. In essence, Senator Packwood asserts that each diary entry should be considered as a separate document, and contends that the Ethics Committee may only require that he produce those entries which relate directly to its original investigation as defined on February 4, 1993.

This Court, however, has no authority to restrict the scope of the Ethics Committee's investigation. The cases upon which Senator Packwood relies provide no support for such a proposition. [8] In determining the proper scope of a legislative subpoena, this Court may only inquire as to whether the documents sought by the subpoena are ' "not plainly incompetent or irrelevant to any lawful purpose [of the Subcommittee] in the discharge of [its] duties.' " *McPhaul v. United States*, 364 U.S. 372, 381 (1960) (quoting *Endicott Johnson Corp. v. Perkins*, 317 U.S. 501, 509 (1943)).

The Constitution itself confers upon the Senate the power to discipline its Members for "disorderly [b]ehaviour," U.S. Const. art. I, § 5, cl. 2, and to that end the Senate has established its Ethics Committee to receive complaints and investigate allegations of improper conduct, including violations of law, Senate rules, and the Senate Code of Official Conduct. The Senate has authorized the Ethics Committee to issue subpoenas for such documentary material "as it deems advisable," and Congress has by legislation made such subpoenas judicially enforceable in this federal district court. [9]

Senator Packwood correctly observes that the records sought must at least be "pertinent" to the congressional inquiry. See *Rumely v. United States*, 197 F.2d 166, 177 (D.C. Cir. 1952). Yet it is undisputed — indeed, acknowledged by respondent himself — that his diaries contain at least some information which is relevant to the Ethics Committee's investigation, and it is manifestly impracticable to leave to the subject of the investigation alone the determination of what information may or may not be probative of the matters being investigated. Senator Packwood has rejected any suggestion that this Court, or some other neutral arbiter, do so.

Senator Packwood's principal apprehension appears to be that somewhere within the diaries will be found evidence of other conduct presently not within anyone's contemplation (other than perhaps his own) that the Ethics Committee will deem to be senatorial misbehavior. Yet where, as here, an investigative subpoena is challenged on relevancy grounds, the Supreme Court has stated that the subpoena is to be enforced "unless the district court determines that there is no reasonable possibility that the category of materials the Government seeks will produce information relevant to the general subject of the ... investigation." *United States v. R. Enterprises, Inc.*, 498 U.S. 292, 301 (1991). Because the Ethics Committee possesses the power to investigate allegations of misconduct, and the diaries contain entries pertinent to this inquiry, the subpoena is not impermissibly broad, even though the diaries might prove compromising to Senator Packwood in respects the Committee has not yet foreseen.

At this stage of its proceedings the Ethics Committee is performing the office of a legislative branch equivalent of a grand jury, in furtherance of an express constitutional grant of authority to Congress to keep its own house in order. It is well-established that such investigative bodies enjoy wide latitude in pursuing possible claims of wrongdoing, and the authority of the courts to confine their investigations is extremely limited. "The function of the grand jury is to inquire about all information that might possibly bear on its investigation until it has identified an offense or has satisfied itself that none has occurred." *R. Enterprises, Inc.*, 498 U.S. at 297.

III.

Senator Packwood next argues that the subpoena violates his right to privacy under the Fourth Amendment to the U.S. Constitution, [10] complaining that the subpoena authorizes the Ethics Committee to "rummage" through his most private thoughts and reflections and intimate details of his personal life.

The Fourth Amendment serves primarily to protect the right of privacy. *Warden v. Hayden*, 387 U.S. 294, 304 (1967); *O'Connor v. Ortega*, 480 U.S. 709, 730 (1987) (Scalia, J., concurring). And, as Senator Packwood notes, numerous courts have recognized the special nature of personal papers such as diaries to which they have accorded the greatest respect, and hence the broadest of constitutional protections. See, e.g., *Nixon v. Administrator of General Services*, 433 U.S. 425 (1977); *Nixon v. Freeman*, 670 F.2d 346 (D.C. Cir. 1982); *United States v. Bennett*, 409 F.2d 888 (2d Cir. 1969); *United States v. Poindexter*, 727 F. Supp. 1470 (D.D.C. 1989).

Recognition of the peculiarly sensitive nature of personal diaries, and the Court's duty to protect them from unreasonable government intrusion, however, does not end the inquiry into whether the proposed "search" of them that will ensue if the Committee's subpoena is enforced in this action violates the Constitution. "A determination of the standard of reasonableness applicable to a particular class of searches requires 'balanc[ing] the nature and quality of the intrusion on the individual's Fourth Amendment interests against the importance of the governmental interests alleged to justify the intrusion.' " *O'Connor*, 480 U.S. at 719 (citations omitted). This Court must thus balance Senator Packwood's expectations of privacy in his personal diaries against the Ethics Committee's interest in examining them for evidence of misconduct, and the nature of the scrutiny it proposes to give them.

The interest of the Ethics Committee and the manner in which it has examined and will continue to examine Senator Packwood's diaries satisfy this Court that the Fourth Amendment's standard of "reasonableness" has been met. As previously noted, the Ethics Committee is the Senate's tribunal of first resort responsible for enforcing the Senate's express constitutional power to discipline its members for misconduct. [11] As such it endeavors to ensure the integrity of the Members of the Senate, and in doing so to maintain public confidence in the Senate as an institution, the importance of which the Supreme Court has expressly recognized in measuring the reasonableness of a search under the Fourth Amendment. *In re Chapman*, 166 U.S. 661, 668-69 (1897).

The protocol to be followed in the examination of Senator Packwood's diaries appears to be far more solicitous of respondent's sensitivities than were those procedures approved in *Nixon v. Administrator of General Services*, 433 U.S. 425 (1977) and *Nixon v. Freeman*, 670 F.2d 346 (D.C. Cir. 1982). The Ethics Committee proposes to conduct a focused, temporally limited review of a fraction of the diaries of most recent origin with many passages masked to protect the most vital of Senator Packwood's interests in privacy. The examination will occur in the presence of Senator Packwood's counsel, and the original diaries will be returned immediately to Senator Packwood, marked only to identify the entries perceived as relevant by the Committee for Senator Packwood to copy for it.

It would be presumptuous for this Court to find the Ethics Committee's procedure to represent an "unreasonable" search when the Supreme Court and its own Circuit Court of Appeals have sus-

tained a more extensive and intrusive examination of similar private papers and recordings of a former President in the vindication of a governmental interest in the "historical" legacy of the nation, surely no more compelling than that of preserving the probity of the United States Senate in the public's perception and in fact.

IV.

Finally, Senator Packwood maintains that enforcement of the subpoena will violate his right against self-incrimination guaranteed by the Fifth Amendment. [12] Relying principally on the case of *Boyd v. United States*, 116 U.S. 616 (1886), he contends that the Constitution prohibits the compelled disclosure of private papers such as his diaries which contain potentially incriminating entries or statements. In *Boyd*, the Supreme Court reversed a criminal conviction procured in part with business records seized by government agents, stating "[W]e have been unable to perceive that the seizure of a man's private books and papers to be used in evidence against him is substantially different from compelling him to be a witness against himself." *Id.* at 633.

Senator Packwood concedes that much of *Boyd's* vitality with respect to business records such as were at issue in that case has evaporated with decisions in subsequent cases, but nonetheless maintains that the Supreme Court has never expressly overruled the case with regard to personal papers such as diaries. In more recent cases, however, the Supreme Court has largely repudiated the expansive language of *Boyd* importing an absolute Fifth Amendment protection for incriminating documentary evidence sought by compulsion. In *Fisher v. United States*, 425 U.S. 391 (1976) and *United States v. Doe*, 465 U.S. 605 (1984), the Supreme Court held that the privilege obtains only if the act of producing papers or records, by itself, would have communicative or testimonial aspects which could incriminate the individual compelled to produce them, but it does not protect against their incriminating *contents* voluntarily committed to paper before the government makes demand for them. [13]

V.

In summary, the Ethics Committee subpoena commands the production of personal diaries of Senator Packwood which are unquestionably relevant in some part to a constitutionally authorized and properly focused inquiry by a committee of the U.S. Senate having jurisdiction to investigate allegations of misconduct of a Member of that body. While the material sought to be examined is acknowledged to be extremely personal and private in nature, and merits an appropriately exalted degree of constitutional protection, the manner in which the Ethics Committee will review these diaries respects Senator Packwood's legitimate expectations of privacy and is, therefore, "reasonable" under the Fourth Amendment. Finally, Senator Packwood

enjoys no Fifth Amendment privilege to avoid surrendering his personal diaries to the Ethics Committee, the act itself presenting no risk of incrimination beyond that he has already reduced to written or recorded form.

Therefore, it is, this 24th day of January, 1994,

ORDERED, that the application of the Senate Select Committee on Ethics to enforce the subpoena *duces tecum* served on Senator Bob Packwood on October 21, 1993, is granted; and it is

FURTHER ORDERED, that the parties shall appear for a status conference on January 27, 1994, at 9:30 a.m. to settle upon procedures for the production of Senator Packwood's diaries for inspection by the Ethics Committee that will accommodate the several interests concerned.

[8] *Watkins v. United States*, 354 U.S. 178 (1957), and *Gibson v. Florida Legislative Investigation Committee*, 372 U.S. 539 (1963), hold only that legislative investigative bodies must have a proper legislative purpose, and must inform subjects of the inquiry of the nature of that purpose to justify the compulsory production of evidence. Neither the legitimacy of the Committee's purpose nor Senator Packwood's awareness of it are in dispute here.

[9] S. Res. 338, 88th Cong. § 3(a) (1964) (as amended), S. Prt. No. 32, 103d Cong., 1st Sess. (1993).

[10] The Fourth Amendment states, "The right of the people to be secure in their persons, houses, papers, and effects, against unreasonable searches and seizures, shall not be violated...." U.S. Const. amend. IV.

[11] It is also significant that the Senate may, with respect to certain kinds of senatorial misbehavior, be the only tribunal with the power to punish. The "Speech and Debate" clause declares, "[F]or any Speech or Debate in either House, [Senators or Representatives] shall not be questioned in any other Place." U.S. Const. art. I, § 6, cl. 1, which has been held to confer immunity from prosecution on Senators for any "legislative acts," including those corruptly performed. See *United States v. Brewster*, 408 U.S. 501 (1972).

[12] The Fifth Amendment declares, "No person ... shall be compelled in any criminal case to be a witness against himself...." U.S. Const. amend. V.

[13] The Supreme Court recognized that compelled production of documents could constitute an admission of the existence of and defendant's control over such papers, as well as provide a means to authenticate them. See *Fisher*, 425 U.S. at 410; *Doe*, 465 U.S. at 612.

Senator Packwood has conceded both the existence and his possession of the diaries, and their authenticity as well. ∎

Judges' Ruling OKs Delegate Voting

On Jan. 25, the U.S. Court of Appeals for the District of Columbia Circuit ruled that the voting privileges given to delegates by the House in 1993 were constitutional. In a 3-0 decision written by Judge Laurence H. Silberman, it rejected an appeal from a lower court decision by House Minority Leader Robert H. Michel, R-Ill., and other members. Following are excerpts:

... As House counsel concedes, were the House to create members not "chosen every second year by the People of the several states," and bestow upon them full voting privileges, such an action, whether or not pursuant to House rules, would be blatantly unconstitutional....

The appellants do not challenge the constitutionality of the practice of permitting delegates to vote on standing committees, although, recognizing the difficulty in drawing a constitutional line between the Committee of the Whole and the standing committees, they do not concede the constitutionality of the prior House rule permitting delegates to vote in the latter. The appellees, for their part, forthrightly concede that the House could not permit persons other than the traditional territorial delegates to perform the role currently played by the delegates. It would, thus, not be open to the House to authorize by rule, say, the mayors of the 100 largest cities to serve and vote on House committees. Nor could the House, appellees agree, deprive any *member* of the right to vote in the Committee of the Whole (or in a standing committee)....

Nevertheless, it would blink reality to deny the close operational connection between the Committee of the Whole and the full House. The House itself recognized how perilously close the rule change came to granting delegates a vote in the House. That is why the House sought to ameliorate the impact of the change through the revote provision.... Appellees are put in the awkward position of claiming that the revote provision causes the grant of voting authority to the delegates to be only symbolic. It is not necessary to explore and analyze all the scenarios about which the parties conjecture. Suffice it to say that we think that insofar as the rule change bestowed additional authority on the delegates, that additional authority is largely symbolic and is not significantly greater than that which they enjoyed serving and voting on the standing committees. Since we do not believe that the ancient practice of delegates serving on standing committees of the House can be successfully challenged as bestowing "membership" on the delegates, we do not think this minor addition to the office of delegates has constitutional significance. ∎

PRESIDENTIAL ANNOUNCEMENT

Clinton Explains Lifting Of Vietnam Embargo

Following are excerpts from the Federal News Service transcript of President Clinton's Feb. 3 announcement that he was lifting the longstanding U.S. economic embargo against Vietnam:

PRESIDENT CLINTON: From the beginning of my administration, I have said that any decisions about our relationships with Vietnam should be guided by one factor and one factor only — gaining the fullest possible accounting for our prisoners of war and our missing in action. We owe that to all who served in Vietnam and to the families of those whose fate remains unknown.

Today I am lifting the trade embargo against Vietnam because I am absolutely convinced it offers the best way to resolve the fate of those who remain missing and about whom we are not sure.

We've worked hard over the last year to achieve progress. On Memorial Day, I pledged to declassify and make available virtually all government documents related to our POWs and MIA. On Veterans Day, I announced that we had fulfilled that pledge.

Last April, and again in July, I sent two presidential delegations to Vietnam to expand our search for remains and documents. We intensified our diplomatic efforts. We have devoted more resources to this effort than any previous administration. Today more than 500 dedicated military and civilian personnel are involved in this effort under the leadership of [Joint Chiefs of Staff Chairman] Gen. [John M.] Shalikashvili, [Defense] Secretary [Les] Aspin, and our commander in the Pacific, Adm. [Charles R.] Larson. Many worked daily in the fields, the jungles, the mountains of Vietnam, Cambodia and Laos, often braving very dangerous conditions, trying to find the truth about those about whom we are not sure.

Last July, I said any improvement in our relations with Vietnam would depend on tangible progress in four specific areas: First, the recovery and return of remains of our POWs and MIA; second, the continued resolution of discrepancy cases, cases in which there is reason to believe individuals could have survived the incident in which they were lost; third, further assistance from Vietnam and Laos on investigations along their common border, an area where many U.S. servicemen were lost and pilots downed; and fourth, accelerated efforts to provide all relevant POW/MIA-related documents. Today I can report that significant tangible progress has been made in all these four areas.

Let me describe it. First, on remains. Since the beginning of this administration, we have recovered the remains of 67 American servicemen. In the seven months since July, we've recovered 39 sets of remains,

more than during all of 1992.

Second, on the discrepancy cases. Since the beginning of the administration, we've reduced the number of these cases from 135 to 73. Since last July, we've confirmed the deaths of 19 servicemen who were on the list. A special United States team in Vietnam continues to investigate the remaining cases.

Third, on cooperation with Laos. As a direct result of the conditions set out in July, the governments of Vietnam and Laos agreed to work with us to investigate their common border. The first such investigation took place in December and located new remains as well as crash sites that will soon be excavated.

Fourth, on the documents. Since July we have received important wartime documents from Vietnam's military archives that provide leads on unresolved POW/MIA cases.

The progress achieved on unresolved questions is encouraging, but it must not end here. I remain personally committed to continuing the search for the answers and the peace of mind that the families of the missing deserve. There's been a substantial increase in Vietnamese cooperation on these matters over the past year. Everyone involved in the issue has affirmed that.

I have carefully considered the question of how best to sustain that cooperation in securing the fullest possible accounting. I've consulted with my national security and veterans' affairs advisers, with several outside experts such as Gen. John W. Vessey, the former chairman of the Joint Chiefs of Staff, who has been an emissary to Vietnam for three presidents now. It was their view that the key to continued progress lies in expanding our contacts with Vietnam. This was also the view of many distinguished Vietnam veterans and former POWs who now serve in the Congress, such as Sen. Bob Kerrey [D-Neb.] and Congressman Pete Peterson [D-Fla.], who are here.

And I want to say a special word of thanks to Sen. John Kerry [D-Mass.] — is he here? There he is, he just came in — and Sen. John McCain [R-Ariz.], who had to go home on a family matter and could not be here, but I thank the two of you so much for your leadership and your steadfastness; and all the rest of you — Sen. [Charles S.] Robb [D-Va.] and so many others, especially those who served in Vietnam — for being counted on this issue and by, for taking all the care you have for such a long time.

I have made the judgment that the best way to ensure cooperation from Vietnam and to continue getting the information Americans want on POWs and MIAs is to end the trade embargo. I've also decided to establish a liaison office in Vietnam to provide services

for Americans there and help us to pursue a human rights dialogue with the Vietnamese government. I want to be clear: These actions do not constitute a normalization of our relationships. Before that happens, we must have more progress, more cooperation, and more answers. Toward that end, this spring I will send another high-level U.S. delegation to Vietnam to continue the search for remains and for documents.

Earlier today, I met with the leaders of our nation's veterans organizations. I deeply respect their views. Many of the families they represent have [endured] enormous suffering and uncertainty, and their opinions also deserve special consideration. I talked with them about my decision, and I explained the reasons for that decision. Some of them, in all candor, do not agree with the action I am taking today, but I believe we all agree on the ultimate goal: to secure the fullest possible accounting of those who remain missing. And I was pleased that they committed to continue working with us toward that goal....

Q: Mr. President, aren't you giving up some leverage, sir?.... And what do you anticipate in terms of American trade? What's the size of the market? What do you think the opportunities are?

P: I have no idea, because I can — I wanted to make sure that the trade questions did not enter into this decision. So, we never — I never had a briefing on it and we never had a discussion about it. I thought it was very important that that not be a part of this decision. I don't think we're giving up anything. It was the consensus of all those who had been there, who had worked there, that we have gotten so much more cooperation that we needed to keep moving the process forward, and that we would lose leverage if there were no forward movement.... Nothing we're doing today is irreversible, if the cooperation ceases. So I'm convinced we're moving in the right direction, for the right reasons.

Q: Mr. President, you named some people who had been to Vietnam and had served; you did not. Did this have any role in your decision, and was it essentially more difficult for you to reach this decision?

P: I do think, however, everybody my age, whether they were in Vietnam or not, knew someone who died there, knew someone who was wounded there. And I think people in our generation are perhaps more insistent on trying to get a full accounting, more obsessed with it.... I think that was the only thing. We — I have spent an enormous amount of time on this issue. I got a personal briefing when I was in Hawaii last summer. I talked to some of the young people who were there, digging in the jungles for the remains. I have really thought about this, and I've tried to listen hard. When Sen. Kerrey and Sen. McCain and their delegation came back, we had a long meeting here about it.

I think the people, all the people my age just want to know we've done everything we can. And I think this is consistent with doing that. ∎

INVESTIGATIONS

Rostenkowski Explains Why He Repaid Government

Following is a Jan. 6 letter sent by Rep. Dan Rostenkowski, D-Ill., to House Administration Committee Chairman Charlie Rose, D-N.C., explaining why he sent two checks totaling $64,728.62 to reimburse the U.S. Treasury for purchases in 1990-93 from the House stationery store. This letter was followed on Feb. 1 with another letter and a check for $17,366.54 to cover purchases in 1988-89.

As you know, I have been the subject of an investigation for more than two years, as part of a probe initiated by former United States Attorney Jay [B.] Stephens. Recently, the investigation started to focus on a new area, that being my purchases from the House Office Supply Service, or stationery store. As a result of this inquiry, I have for the first time reviewed records of purchases made by myself and others at the stationery store over the past few years, as well as the House rules and procedures regarding such purchases. I was not aware of some of these purchases. As to many others, I was surprised to learn during this review that a number which I considered to be ordinary and necessary expenses in the course of performing my public duties, arguably may not have conformed to House rules.

It was never my intention or the intention of my staff to have the House pay for non-official items. Therefore, in order to remove any doubt about that, today I am sending two checks, one from me personally and one from my campaign committee, for the purpose of reimbursing the House for items purchased on my account since 1990 about which doubt or question may be raised.

Many of the purchases for which I am making reimbursement today — including various bowls, mugs, plates, china, clocks, paperweights and decorative items such as those bearing the Congressional seal — were used as gifts to officials both abroad and in this country, or in some cases, as gifts to those who had counseled, assisted or supported my activities in public service, including my representational or legislative duties. A few of these items also were donated to charities in my district to use as items at fundraising auctions. Others, including mugs and crystal statues in the shape of the Capitol, were given to individuals who assisted and supported me in my public duties.

I now understand that the House Administration Committee's regulations prohibit the use of official funds for gifts or donations — even gifts that are related to an official purpose — except on overseas trips. I was unaware of the applicable rules, and this was not a matter I focused on, given my legislative duties. Although many of these purchases were in fact presented as gifts to foreign dignitaries during my official overseas trips, it is difficult at this late date to determine definitively which items were used for this purpose. Therefore, rather than "split hairs," the House is being reimbursed for all these items. In particular, my campaign committee will pay for the crystal Capitols and certain of the mugs, and I will pay for the rest.

Similarly, my office acquired more than 800 books entitled "We The People" from the stationery store, as well as other items of nominal value such as key chains. These small items, individually or as part of "visitor packets," were given to constituents and others who visited my House office. Although I believe this practice is common on Capitol Hill, I am personally making reimbursement for these items in order to avoid any question regarding this practice under the Committee's gift rule.

Other of the purchases now being questioned include chairs bearing a picture of the Capitol. Some of these were used in conference areas in my old district office in Chicago, and several were given as gifts to individuals who have been a source of assistance, support and counsel to me in the performance of my public duties. In 1993, because of redistricting, I moved my operations to two, smaller offices in my new Congressional district. As a result, chairs were no longer needed in large numbers, so many of the remaining "Capitol chairs" were placed in storage. These chairs can be used for campaign purposes, however. Therefore, and in order to remove any question concerning these chairs, my campaign committee is acquiring all of them and is making reimbursement for these as well as any chairs that previously were given as gifts.

My review also revealed that there are a number of items purchased by my office that might appear to others to be personal in nature, but actually were used for official purposes or in the course of performing official duties, and hence, were, I believed, appropriately chargeable to my official account. These include, for example, some clocks, magnifying glasses, picture frames, cameras, albums and some luggage. These are expenses that I would not have incurred but for the fact that I am a Member of Congress. Nonetheless, so that there can be no question about these items, I have decided that I personally will reimburse the House for them.

Finally, it appears that there were some purchases by myself or others of items for personal use. I fully intended to pay for these items. However, I relied, unjustifiably as it turns out, on office procedures that proved to be inadequate to insure that such expenditures would be identified and brought to my attention. Had this been done at the time, I most certainly would have taken steps to insure that reimbursement was made, and do so now.

Although I believe most of the purchases discussed above were appropriate, or were made in the good faith belief that they were appropriate at the time they were made, it is difficult at this point to specifically identify these, due to the passage of time, the incompleteness of some records and the changed use of some of these items over time. Therefore, out of an abundance of caution, I have decided to resolve any doubt in favor of the House, and have determined that the House should be reimbursed for any item about which a question conceivably might be raised. Although this will result in the House being reimbursed for many legitimate purchases, I believe that I, and not the House, should bear the cost of any inability to "unscramble the egg" at this point.

Accordingly, enclosed you will find checks totaling $64,728.62. For the reasons set forth above, I have decided to absorb $19,695.74 of these costs myself, and my campaign committee will pay $45,032.88 of these costs, to cover the crystal Capitols, the chairs and certain of the mugs. In addition, I recently learned that items purchased for non-official purposes at the stationery store are subject to a ten percent surcharge. Therefore, the checks tendered today include that surcharge. I further understand that because the purchases involved were made in prior years, checks for reimbursement must be made to the U.S. Treasury, and that your Committee, in appropriate circumstances, will assist in effecting reimbursement. I hereby request your assistance in this regard.

I intend to continue the inquiry into my office's stationery store account for years prior to 1990. As you may be aware, however, it can be difficult to reconstruct records and events from the past. If as a result of this inquiry we are able to confirm that there were similar questionable purchases in prior years, I intend to arrange for reimbursement, as appropriate.

As Chairman of the House Administration Committee, you know better than anyone that the line between "official" and "non-official" expenses is hard to draw and has been the source of much confusion among Members over the years. I regret that I was unaware of your Committee's regulations, and that I did not focus on this matter earlier. With warm personal regards, I am

Sincerely,
Dan Rostenkowski

■

Senate Duty Swayed Decision About Court, Mitchell Says

Senate Majority Leader George J. Mitchell, D-Maine, held a news conference at the Capitol on April 12 to announce he had withdrawn from consideration for Supreme Court justice. Following are excerpts from the news conference, as provided by the Federal News Service:

MITCHELL: Good afternoon, ladies and gentlemen. Thanks for joining me again today. I have a brief statement to make, and then I'll be pleased to respond to your questions on any subject about which you may inquire.

I've asked President Clinton not to consider me for nomination to the vacancy on the Supreme Court to be created by Justice [Harry A.] Blackmun's retirement. Although it would be an honor to be considered for the court, I believe I can best serve by concentrating this year on health care reform and the rest of the president's agenda for change, including crime control legislation, welfare reform, campaign finance reform, the Clean Water Act and the Safe Drinking Water Act, and other measures. It is an agenda which I strongly support.

I believe there exists a rare opportunity to achieve comprehensive, meaningful reform of our health care system this year, and I don't want to do anything that might detract from that effort.

I look forward to working with the president and with my colleagues in the Congress, Democrats and Republicans, to enact health care reform and other important legislation this year.

I'm deeply grateful for the support I've received from senators of both parties and the many kind comments that have been made about me by others. And I'll be pleased now to take [questions].

Q: Senator, I wonder whether you could tell us your position on whether to lift the antitrust exemption on major-league baseball?

MITCHELL: I have always been and continue to be opposed to lifting the antitrust exemption.

Q: Have you accepted the job as baseball commissioner?

MITCHELL: No, it has not been offered to me.

Q: Do you want it?

MITCHELL: If it's offered, I will consider it.

Q: When, sir, did you begin this process of deciding in your own mind you would not be — willing to be considered as a candidate for the court?

MITCHELL: I had no — yes, I had no prior notice of the timing of Justice

Blackmun's retirement announcement.

I learned of it through press reports and shortly thereafter received a number of telephone calls from reporters telling me that I was at the top of the list for replacement. I began to consider the matter then. In the days since then, I've thought about it a good deal, and then yesterday I wrote out the statement which I've just read and requested a meeting with the president.

I went to the White House at about 6 last evening, met with the president for about an hour. He asked me what I thought should happen with respect to the court, and I told him in essentially the words I've used here today. In fact, I had a copy of the statement, and I showed it to him. He told me that he wanted to appoint me to the court, that he intended to appoint me to the court, but that he was concerned, as I was, about the prospect [that] the nomination would affect my ability to serve as majority leader for the remainder of this session. And he asked me not to release the statement last evening, which was my original intention, but rather to wait until today to give both of us a chance to reflect on it overnight.

This morning, he telephoned me to tell me that he had thought about it and that, while he repeated that it was his wish to appoint me to the court, that he was concerned about health care and other matters, and he accepted my assessment of the situation with respect to the effect it might have this year and therefore reluctantly agreed.

Q: So it was his decision to go forward with — were you actually withdrawing unequivocally, without any reservations?

MITCHELL: I have — yes.

Q: Would you have reconsidered if he had said, "I really need you on the court?" Would you have reconsidered?

MITCHELL: I would have thought about it further, but that didn't happen.

Q: There are rumors that [another justice will leave the court] at some point. If there was indeed another opening on the Supreme Court, would you be interested?

MITCHELL: That's a double hypothetical, one or two less than I usually get in these questions. My answer is simply that, if another vacancy occurs and if the president tells me that he wants to nominate me, I will consider it at that time. There's really not more to that. I've not heard of this rumor to which we referred, but — and I know nothing about it.

Q: But did you just decide, Senator, that it would — you couldn't stay on as majority leader and try to lead this effort to pass health care and be a nominee? Was

that what it was?

MITCHELL: It was the latter. I believe it could have been done and I believe I could have done it, but I recognize that enactment of this major agenda, including, but not limited to, health care reform, welfare reform and many other subjects to which I've referred, will be difficult enough under the best of circumstances and will require a great deal of my time and effort. And I told the president that I felt that a nomination to the Supreme Court at this time could affect my ability to serve as majority leader in ways which neither he nor I could now foresee. This is not a situation through which I've been, and therefore, I have no personal experience on which to judge it, but you folks cover the Senate and you know that it's tough enough to get anything done here, and it would add a major — at best, it would add a major complicating factor, the outcome of which I could not foresee, and that I feel strongly about the importance of completing the president's agenda for change to the extent possible this year. And therefore, I concluded that it would be best for the president, for his agenda and, I believe, for the effective functioning of the Senate if he did not consider me for this vacancy.

Q: Senator, how much did the constitutional issue that had been raised have to do with your decision? . . .

MITCHELL: That was not a factor. . . .

Q: Senator, as important as all these issues are that you speak of — health care and welfare reform — a Supreme Court justice gets to tackle issues over a period. . . . You could do this for maybe 20, 30 years, you know, and tackle many issues instead of just dealing with these specific issues over a six-month period.

MITCHELL: . . . You make a very good point, and it is something which I thought about a great deal over the past several days, and I acknowledge that it was a difficult decision in that respect. But I believe that the agenda for change that the president has set forth, including health care, is extremely important to the future not just for this coming year but for a very long time to come, and that it is something on which I have worked since I entered the Senate.

I remind you that I have served on the Senate Health Subcommittee since entering the Senate, and I was chairman of that Health Subcommittee before I became majority leader. I don't think that opportunity is going to come along again at any time in the future if we don't seize it this year. I think it's a rare opportunity.

Secondly, while I'm very flattered at

the suggestions about my ability to serve effectively on the court, I am keenly aware that there are many other persons well-qualified to serve on the court, many others who have more experience than I in judicial matters, and I think the president will make a superb selection, and I expect his nominee to be confirmed, whoever he or she is, and serve very well on the court. In the meantime, I made the judgment that I can best serve what I perceive to be the national interest overall by continuing in my current position and doing the best job I can during the time that remains.

Q: Senator, since your announcement about your plans to retire, what's been the extent of your discussions with the powers that be about the baseball commissioner's job, and did that in any way factor in? I take it that this — the major reason was your desire to put forward the agenda, but did you also think about the prospects of that job being open?

MITCHELL: That was not a factor in my decision. I have talked only with one person in baseball over the last couple of months, and no position has been offered to me. I've read a lot about the so-called secret deals and other things. There was a column in the paper yesterday, which I will just, in a digression, note as completely false and untrue, but if the position is offered to me, I will consider it at that time. I know a few people in the baseball business, not — most of the owners of baseball I've never met. But as I said earlier, if it's offered to me, I will consider it. If other positions are offered to me, I'll consider them.

Q: Could you be a little more explicit about what the problems would have been? Was it simply a matter of time, or was it the awkwardness of going through confirmation hearings for another branch of government at the same time [as you were running] the Senate? What were the problems?

MITCHELL: I believe you've identified two of them.... First, it obviously would have been demanding of my time in a circumstance in which I'm going to try very hard to complete other matters. I don't know if I would characterize it as awkwardness. It would simply be a new situation, one with which I've not dealt and I think most of my colleagues have not dealt.

And, therefore, I felt that it could pose complications and difficulties in a situation which will be difficult enough. I expect that we will pass health care legislation this year, but I think it's going to be tough. I think it's going to require every bit of energy and effort and concentration that I have to pass that and the other important measures which I've described.

So I think you've identified some of the factors. And I think, since it is a situation through which neither I nor any of my colleagues have been, it is likely to be complicated in ways that no one can now foresee or predict.

Q: Did you offer the president any suggestions as to who should serve on the high court? Do you have any personal preferences?

MITCHELL: No. The answer to both questions is no. I do not have a personal preference, and I did not offer any advice to the president.

Q: Sen. Mitchell, since you said the president [was going] to appoint you, is this now a setback [for him] to have to go back to the drawing board?

MITCHELL: No, no. No, no, no. The president has been considering a number of other people, and they've got a whole lot of people involved. He indicated that he wanted to appoint me, but he also was concerned about the ability to enact health care and other important reform legislation. That was a subject which he and his aides apparently had discussed during the day yesterday. He described to me some of their conversation about it. And, of course, there have been published reports to that effect, that there was some apprehension in that regard. And so he did have that concern and has, in effect, accepted my assessment of that situation that it would pose a difficulty. I think his view is that I being the person involved and probably the person best able to judge that, and even I can't judge it for sure because it's nothing through which I've ever been. That is, I have no personal basis on which to make an assessment. But he accepted my judgment in that....

Q: Excuse me, Senator, having served so long in sort of the hurly-burly political combat for so long, did you have some reservations about sort of retiring to the court?

MITCHELL: No. I had served previously as a judge in what I guess would be the non-hurly-burly of the non-combat, and I enjoyed it. I enjoyed it.

Q: But it does have to deal with the everyday events, rather than these lofty concepts.

MITCHELL: Well, let me repeat, I do not regard the law as lofty concepts. I think it's an important part of our society. In fact, I think it's one of the things that makes the United States a unique society, one that is a nation of laws, not men and women, and I'd just repeat what I said on Bob Schieffer's show, "Face the Nation," this Sunday....

I have enjoyed every job I have ever had. I have enjoyed being Senate majority leader, but I enjoyed very much being a federal district judge. I enjoyed being United States attorney. And so, the notion, and I have worked since I was a very small boy at a large number of jobs, so the notion that, "Gosh, you can't leave this position because you might not enjoy another job," is really foreign to me.

I think if a person works hard at what he or she does, and takes pride at what he or she does, there is fulfillment in life, and it doesn't have to be in an elected office, or a high public position, or one which achieves a great deal of public attention....

Q: Were you disappointed that it didn't work out?

MITCHELL: In some respects. As I said earlier, I believe I would have enjoyed serving on the court. I believe I would enjoy serving as commissioner of baseball if that opportunity arises. I believe I would be — enjoy serving as host of "Face the Nation," and lest there not be equal time, as host of "Meet the Press," as well, or "This Week with George Mitchell," if that — opportu-

nity arises, so — but of course, in some respects, that is the case.

And I must say, I feel the same with respect to leaving my current position. I am convinced I have made the right decision in not seeking re-election to the Senate because my concept of public service, which is personal to me, is one that indicates it's an appropriate time to leave. But that does not mean that I don't have regrets. I obviously do. I'll miss a great deal of it....

Q: Can I ask you a Whitewater question?

MITCHELL: Sure.

Q: Whitewater hearings?

MITCHELL: Yes.

Q: Are you still negotiating, and what is the status?

MITCHELL: The status is that late yesterday afternoon, Sen. [Bob] Dole [R-Kan.] delivered to my office a letter setting forth a proposed structure, and I will respond to that in the near future. As I've said on many occasions, we have an important oversight responsibility in the Congress, we will meet that responsibility, but we will do so in a manner and at a time and under circumstances that do not undermine or interfere with the investigation of the special counsel. And I emphasize, as I have from the beginning, that such oversight will include hearings. I've always said we'll have hearings.

I think it is significant that the Republicans have abandoned their request for immediate hearings. I think that reflects their reading of the sentiment of the American people that the manner in which this has been discussed in the public has been excessive and serving no useful purpose, and I think now what we should do is to concentrate on doing our job, which consists, in the context of this question, in two respects — first, meeting our oversight responsibilities in Whitewater in a responsible manner which will not interfere with the special counsel's investigation; and secondly, getting on with the important legislative matters that the American people want and expect us to act on — health care reform, welfare reform, crime control, the many other measures to which I referred.

Q: Do the Republicans still want a special committee or a select committee?

MITCHELL: Yes. And I've indicated that I will, of course, review the matter, and I mean this seriously and not facetiously at all. I take very carefully any suggestion made to me by Sen. Dole. He is a friend, and we work together, and I respect his view. But so far, I've not been persuaded that there's any reason to remove this from the Banking Committee. The Banking Committee has jurisdiction. It is the committee which had the previous hearings that were requested by the Republicans, and now this, a request which comes at a somewhat later time, that all of a sudden it be removed from the Banking Committee, is one for which at least to me at this point there's been no persuasive rationale for. Now, I will consider it. I'll listen to any argument with an open mind and have not made a final decision, but that's my view at this time.... ∎

NIXON FUNERAL

Nation Says Its Goodbyes To a 'Seminal President'

Funeral services for former President Richard M. Nixon took place April 27 at the Richard Nixon Library in Yorba Linda, Calif. Following are the eulogies delivered by former Secretary of State Henry A. Kissinger and President Clinton:

KISSINGER: During the final week of Richard Nixon's life, I often imagined how he would have reacted to the tide of concern, respect, admiration and affection evoked by his last great battle. His gruff pose of never paying attention to media comment would have been contradicted by a warm glow and the ever-so-subtle hint that another recital of the commentary would not be unwelcome. And without quite saying so, he would have conveyed that it would mean a lot to him if Julie and Tricia, David and Ed were told of his friends' pride in this culmination to an astonishing life.

When I learned the final news, by then so expected yet so hard to accept, I felt a profound void. In the words of Shakespeare, "He was a man. Take him for all in all, I shall not look upon his like again."

In the conduct of foreign policy, Richard Nixon was one of the seminal presidents. He came into office when the forces of history were moving America from a position of dominance to one of leadership. Dominance reflects strength; leadership must be earned. And Richard Nixon earned that leadership role for his country with courage, dedication and skill.

When Richard Nixon took his oath of office, 550,000 Americans were engaged in combat in a place as far away from the United States as it was possible to be. America had no contact with China, the world's most populous nation, no negotiations with the Soviet Union, the other nuclear superpower. Most Muslim countries had broken diplomatic relations with the United States, and Middle East diplomacy was stalemated. All of this in the midst of the most anguishing domestic crisis since the Civil War.

When Richard Nixon left office, an agreement to end the war in Vietnam had been concluded, and the main lines of all subsequent policy were established — permanent dialogue with China; readiness without illusion to ease tension with the Soviet Union; a peace process in the Middle East; the beginning, via the European Security Conference, of establishing human rights as an international issue, weakening Soviet hold on Eastern Europe.

Richard Nixon's foreign policy goals were long range, and he pursued them without regard to domestic political consequences.

When he considered our nation's interest at stake, he dared confrontations despite the imminence of elections and also in the midst of the worst crisis of his life. And he bore, if with some pain, the disapproval of longtime friends and allies over relaxing tensions with China and the Soviet Union.

He drew strength from a conviction he often expressed to me: "The price for doing things halfway is no less than for doing them completely, so we might as well do them properly." Thus Richard Nixon's greatest accomplishment was as much moral as it was political: to lead from strength at a moment of apparent weakness, to husband a nation's resilience and thus to lay the basis for victory in the Cold War.

Shy and withdrawn, Richard Nixon made himself succeed in the most gregarious of professions and steeled himself to conspicuous acts of extraordinary courage. In the face of wrenching domestic controversy, he held fast to his basic theme, that the greatest free nation in the world had a duty to lead and no right to abdicate.

Richard Nixon would be so proud that President Clinton and all living former presidents of the United States are here, symbolizing that his long and sometimes bitter journey had concluded in reconciliation. . . .

So let us now say goodbye to our gallant friend. He stood on pinnacles that dissolved in the precipice. He achieved greatly, and he suffered deeply, but he never gave up. In his solitude, he envisaged a new international order that would reduce lingering enmities, strengthen historic friendships and give new hope to mankind — a vision where dreams and possibilities conjoined.

Richard Nixon ended a war, and he advanced the vision of peace of his Quaker youth. He was devoted to his family. He loved his country. And he considered service his honor. It was a privilege to have been allowed to help him.

PRESIDENT CLINTON: President Nixon opened his memoirs with a simple sentence: I was born in a house my father built. Today we can look back at this little house and still imagine a young boy sitting by the window of the attic he shared with his three brothers, looking out to a world he could then, himself, only imagine.

From those humble roots, as from so many humble beginnings in this country, grew the force of a driving dream, a dream that led to the remarkable journey that ends here today where it all began — beside the same tiny home mail-ordered from back East, near this towering oak tree which back then was a mere seedling.

President Nixon's journey across the American landscape mirrored that of his entire nation in this remarkable century. His life was bound up with the striving of our whole people, with our crises and our triumphs. When he became president, he took on challenges here at home on matters from cancer research to environmental protection, putting the power of the federal government where Republicans and Democrats had neglected to put it in the past, in foreign policy.

He came to the presidency at a time in our history when Americans were tempted to say we had had enough of the world. Instead, he knew we had to reach out to old friends and old enemies alike. He would not allow America to quit the world.

Remarkably, he wrote nine of his 10 books after he left the presidency, working his way back into the arena he so loved by writing and thinking and engaging us in his dialogue. For the past year, even in the final weeks of his life, he gave me his wise counsel, especially with regard to Russia. One thing in particular left a profound impression on me. Though this man was in his ninth decade, he had an incredibly sharp and vigorous and rigorous mind.

As a public man, he always seemed to believe the greatest sin was remaining passive in the face of challenges, and he never stopped living by that creed. He gave of himself with intelligence and energy and devotion to duty, and his entire country owes him a debt of gratitude for that service.

Oh, yes, he knew great controversy amid defeat as well as victory. He made mistakes, and they, like his accomplishments, are part of his life and record. But the enduring lesson of Richard Nixon is that he never gave up being part of the action and passion of his times. He said many times that unless a person has a goal, a new mountain to climb, his spirit will die. Well, based on our last phone conversation and the letter he wrote me just a month ago, I can say that his spirit was very much alive to the very end. That is a great tribute to him, to his wonderful wife, Pat, to his children and to his grandchildren, whose love he so depended on and whose love he returned in full measure.

Today is a day for his family, his friends and his nation to remember President Nixon's life in totality. To them let us say, may the day of judging President Nixon on anything less than his entire life and career come to a close. May we heed his call to maintain the will and the wisdom to build on America's greatest gift, its freedom, to lead a world full of difficulty to the just and lasting peace he dreamed of.

As it is written in the words of a hymn I heard in my church last Sunday, "Grant that I may realize that the trifling of life creates differences, but that in the higher things, we are all one."

In the twilight of his life, President Nixon knew that lesson well. It is, I feel certain, a faith he would want us all to keep. And so, on behalf of all four former presidents who are here — President Ford, President Carter, President Reagan, President Bush — and on behalf of a grateful nation, we bid farewell to Richard Milhous Nixon. ∎

CONFIRMATION HEARINGS

Breyer Gets Warm Reception From Senate Judiciary

Supreme Court nominee Judge Stephen G. Breyer appeared July 12-14 before the Senate Judiciary Committee, chaired by Joseph R. Biden Jr., D-Del. Following are excerpts from the hearings, transcribed by Federal News Service and beginning with Breyer's opening remarks:

JUDGE BREYER: I'd like to begin by telling you a little bit about myself, though you've heard quite a lot, and maybe, though, a few of the experiences that I think have had an important effect on my life — how I think and what I am.

I was born, as you heard, and I grew up in San Francisco. I attended public schools — Grant Grammar School, Lowell High School. My mother was from St. Paul, Minnesota. Her parents were immigrants from East Prussia, which is now part of Poland.

My mother was a very intelligent, very practical, public-spirited kind of person, and she, like many mothers, had an enormous influence on me.

She was the one who made absolutely clear to me in no uncertain terms that whatever intellectual ability I might have means nothing and won't mean anything unless I can work with other people and use whatever talents I have to help them. So I joined the Boy Scouts, I did work as a delivery boy, I did dig ditches for the Pacific Gas & Electric Co., and I mixed salads up in the city's summer camp. It was nice, Camp Mather, because at that time you had policemen and firemen and lawyers and doctors and businessmen and their families, and they were all there together at the city camp for two weeks in the summer. It was great, great.

My mother really didn't want me to spend too much time with my books, and she was right. I mean, my ideas about people do not come from libraries.

My father was born in San Francisco. He worked as a lawyer and an administrator in the San Francisco public school system for 40 years. I have his watch, as you said, Senator. He was a very kind, very astute and very considerate man. He and San Francisco helped me develop something I would call a trust in, almost a love for the possibilities of a democracy. My father always took me — as a child, he'd take me with him into the voting booth. I'd pull down the lever, and he'd say, "We're exercising our prerogative." He'd take me to candidates' nights. Our school used to go up to Sacramento to see the Legislature in session. There was Youth in Government Day. There was Boys' State.

All this led me to believe not just that

Breyer: "Law must work for people. That vast array of Constitution, statutes, rules, regulations, practices, procedures ... has a single basic purpose."

government can help people, but that government is the people, it is created through their active participation. And that's really why, despite the increased cynicism about basic government — and we have really seen vast improvements in the fairness of government — I still believe that with trust and cooperation and participation, people can work through their government to improve their lives.

Love for Teaching

In 1957, as you said, I was — I served in the Army for a little while. I studied in England. I returned to Harvard Law School. And then I clerked for Justice Arthur [J.] Goldberg, who became a wonderful, lifelong friend. After two years in the Antitrust Division in the Justice Department, I went back to Harvard to teach, and to Massachusetts to live, and for the last 27 years I have been privileged to live in Cambridge and work in Boston. I love teaching. I love my students. But if I were to pick out one feature of the academic side of my life that really influ-

enced me especially, I think it would be this: The opportunity to study law as a whole helped me understand that everything in the law is related to every other thing, and always, as [Justice Oliver Wendell] Holmes [Jr.] pointed out, that whole law reflects not so much logic as history and experience.

Academic lawyers, practicing lawyers, government lawyers, judges, in my opinion, have a special responsibility to try to understand how different parts of that seamless web of the law interact with each other and how legal decisions will actually work in practice to affect people and to help them.

Working here on this committee in the 1970s, I learned a great deal about Congress, about government and about political life. There were disagreements to resolve, but everyone shared the same basic ground rules, basic assumptions about democracy, freedom, fairness and the need to help others. These vast areas of widely shared belief are what has shaped the law of America and the lives of all Americans.

Since 1980, I've been a judge on the U.S. Court of Appeals for the 1st Circuit. That's Maine, Massachusetts, New Hampshire, Puerto Rico and Rhode Island. Because of my colleagues and the work itself, this job is a great honor, a great privilege, and it's been a great pleasure to have.

I've tried to minimize what I think of as some of the less desirable aspects of the job, one that Justice Goldberg really felt strongly about, that judges can become isolated from the people whose lives their decisions affect. I've continued to teach and to participate in the community and in other activities which are important in connecting me to the world outside the courtroom. I have been helped in this task by my wife and her work at Dana-Farber [Cancer Institute] and at Cambridge Hospital, which shows me and others some of the sadness in this world as well as its hopes and its joys.

The Law's Purpose

I believe that law must work for people. That vast array of Constitution, statutes, rules, regulations, practices, procedures — that huge, vast web — has a single basic purpose. That purpose is to help the many different individuals who make up America from so many different backgrounds and circumstances, with so many different needs and hopes. Its purpose is to help them live together productively, harmoniously, and in freedom. Keeping that ultimate purpose in mind helps guide a judge through the labyrinth of rules and regulations that the law too often becomes, to reach what is there at bottom — the very

human goals that underlie the Constitution and the statutes that Congress writes.

I believe, too, in the importance of listening to other points of view. As a teacher, I discovered I could learn as much from students as from books. On the staff of this committee, it was easy to see how much senators and staff alike learn from each other, from constituents, from hearings. I think the system works that way. It works better than any other system. And our task is to keep trying to improve it.

My law school diploma refers to law simply as those wise restraints that make men free. Women, too. All of us. I believe that, too.

I really felt the particular importance of all this when, two years ago, I had the good fortune to attend a meeting of 600 judges in the new Russia. Those judges wanted to know what words ... might they write in a constitution, what words would guarantee democracy and freedom. That's what they were asking over a two-day meeting. They asked me. I mean, they were interesting discussions, very interesting. My own reply was that words alone are not sufficient; that the words of our Constitution work because of the traditions of our people, because the vast majority of Americans believe in democracy. They try to be tolerant and fair to others and to respect the liberty of each other, even those who are unpopular, because their protection is our protection, too.

You are now considering my appointment to the Supreme Court of the United States. That court works within a grand tradition that has made meaningful in practice the guarantees of fairness and of freedom that the Constitution provides. Justice [Harry A.] Blackmun certainly served that tradition well. Indeed, so have those who — all of those who have served in the recent past — Justice [Byron R.] White, Justice [William J.] Brennan, and Justice [Thurgood] Marshall. They leave an inspiring legacy that I have correctly called humbling to consider. I promise you and I promise the American people that if I am confirmed to be a member of the Supreme Court, I will try to be worthy of that great tradition. I will work hard. I will listen. I will try to interpret the law carefully in accordance with its basic purposes.

Above all, I will remember that the decisions I help to make will have an effect upon the lives of many, many Americans.

And that fact means that I must do my absolute utmost to see that those decisions reflect both the letter and the spirit of a law that is meant to help them.

Thank you, Mr. Chairman.

Conflict of Interest

I might add one thing, if I might, on a slightly different subject. I want to add this, if I may, and that is recently I know that — and this is important to me — that in recent weeks there have been questions raised about the ethical standard that I applied in sitting on certain environmental cases in the 1st Circuit at a time when I

had an investment, an insurance investment in Lloyd's [of London].

I recognize that this question has been raised by people of good faith, and there is nothing more important to me than my integrity and my reputation for impartiality. It is obviously a most important thing to preserve total public confidence in the integrity of the judicial branch of government. I have reviewed those cases again, and the judicial recusal statute, and I personally am confident that my sitting in those cases did not present any conflict of interest. Of course my investment was disclosed to the public. There has been absolutely no suggestion that Lloyd's was involved as a name party in any of the cases on which I sat. I know of no such involvement.

The judicial recusal statute does require recusal as well if you have one case that has some kind of direct and predictable financial impact on some investment; that is to say if it's not a speculative or remote or contingent impact. The cases on which I sat did not violate this standard either. That issue has been carefully looked into by independent ethics experts, who share my view.

But, Mr. Chairman, as I said, I recognize the importance of avoiding conflicts of interest or even the appearance of such conflicts, and that standard is essential for all judges, and especially essential for judges of the nation's highest court. So I certainly promise I will do all I can to meet it, including what I shall immediately do is ask the people who handle my investments to divest any holdings in insurance companies as soon as possible. And with respect to Lloyd's itself, I resigned in 1988, though because of one syndicate that remains open I have been advised that I — I can leave altogether by the end of 1995, but I intend to ask the people involved to expedite my complete termination of any Lloyd's relationship. I'll be out of that as soon as I possibly can be. And finally, as I go forward, I certainly will keep in mind the discussion that has arisen over the last few days, and I will take it into account in reviewing any possible conflict whatsoever.

Property Rights

SEN. BIDEN: In recent years we have seen new challenges to the efforts of government at all levels to adopt regulations that government believes are designed to protect the environment and promote a public goal. These challenges have taken the form of asking the court to change how it has interpreted the takings clause of the Fifth Amendment.

Less than three weeks ago, the Supreme Court of the United States decided a case called *Dolan v. Tigard* ... where, using the takings clause, the court rejected a local town measure intended to reduce flooding and traffic congestion caused by a business' development along a river.

This decision follows a case decided two years earlier, *Lucas v. South Carolina Coastal Council.* And in these two cases, the court adopted a new standard for re-

viewing the takings clause. ...

Now, my question is this: Is there any doubt in your mind that after *Dolan* and after *Lucas* that it is at least incrementally more difficult for the government to regulate zoning and environmental laws than it was prior? Not impossible, not — but just incrementally at least more difficult, or am I off on that?

JUDGE BREYER: No, no, you're not off. ... The dissent you see in that absolutely thought that that was so.

And the reason that I hesitate a little bit is there is something special about that case, and what is I think a little special about the case is that it did at last arguably involve a physical occupation of a piece of property. And at the same time, they didn't make all that much out of it, and then, as you just point out, as you just pointed out, they used this test "rough proportionality," and what exactly is that? It looks as if it's a lot — a little tougher.

And so where I end up in my mind is that this is an area that's not determined forever, that there are likely to be quite a few cases coming up, that this problem of how you work out when it goes too far is something [that] undoubtedly will come up again in the future. ...

SEN. BIDEN: In these cases, which affect economic rights and affect public health and welfare, whomever has the burden makes a big difference. Now, this, as you know, Judge Breyer, this is not the first time the Supreme Court has of late elevated — elevated — I don't want to be pejorative here — has moved the bar on economic rights.

In the early part of this century ... the so-called *Lochner* era, named after the leading case of the time, the Supreme Court routinely struck down health and safety measures as unconstitutional. The court struck down the types of regulation that everyone in this room now considers normal and appropriate. It struck down minimum wage laws, which we now take for granted. It struck down child labor laws. It struck down workplace safety laws. And the court finally changed course and put an end to this so-called Lochnerizing in the end of the '30s.

Now, would our society look different today if the Supreme Court had not gone back on Lochner and still gave economic rights the same level of protection that it did during the *Lochner* era? What effect would there have been on labor laws, for example, and environmental laws had *West Coast Hotel Co. v. Parrish* not come along and overruled *Lochner*? Talk to us about that. Be a professor for a minute here. Tell us what the effect would be as you would see [it].

JUDGE BREYER: I think, Senator, that you'd have very, very wide agreement with you across a very, very wide spectrum with what Holmes [said], that the Constitution does not enact into law Herbert Spencer's social status, and what he meant by that is there is no particular theory of the economy that the Constitution enacts into law.

That doesn't mean property has no

protection; there is a takings clause in the Constitution. It doesn't mean that people's clothes and toothbrushes are somehow at stake and could be swept away randomly. What it means is that the Constitution, which is a document that basically wants to guarantee people rights that will enable them to lead lives of dignity, foresees over the course of history that a person's right to speak freely and to practice his religion is something that is of value, is not going to change.

But one particular economic theory or some other economic theory is a function of the circumstances of the moment, and if the world changes so that it becomes crucially important to all of us that we protect the environment, that we protect health, that we protect safety, the Constitution is not a bar to that, because its basic object is to permit people to lead lives of dignity.

SEN. BIDEN: . . . Now, can you articulate or think of any principal standard to stop the movement announced in *Dolan* or *Lucas*? Where — how does that stop? How does this shifting of the burden not automatically take you into the area that I worry most about, which is the one I've just articulated? Is there a principled way in which to say: OK, shifting the burden and requiring this relationship enunciated in *Dolan* does not automatically lead you to the concern I've stated in a case I've just made up?

JUDGE BREYER: I think the principal concern as I listen to you, Mr. Chairman, is the Justice Holmes concern. As I listen to you, what you're saying is: Think back to those columns in the coal mine.

SEN. BIDEN: Exactly.

JUDGE BREYER: Are you really serious that it should impose, that the law should prevent people in a practical way, through their government, requiring columns that protect coal miners? And you are saying of course not.

And as I hear that, I think you're saying a law or an interpretation of the Constitution that would seriously impede the coal columns that protect the miners and protect the cities, that would be going too far. And I agree with you, but that is what Justice Holmes would have had in mind, and that's what I think what the court is trying to work out, is in my own mind, I can't read other people's minds. But it's what's called a practical accommodation.

Of course there is a compensation clause in the Constitution. Of course property is given some protection. At the same time, one must not go too far, and what too far means is imposing significant practical obstacles, it sounds to me.

Legislative Intent

SEN. BIDEN: Another way to affect the basic rights of individuals who do not have economic power is the way in which the court interprets statutes, passed by the legislature and signed by the president. And it is my view, I'll say up front, that whether courts grudgingly interpret the wishes of elected representatives, or in a

generous way interpret them, obviously has significant impact. . . .

Now several years ago the Environmental Protection Agency [EPA] decided to phase out the use of asbestos because it posed many health risks, including the risk of cancer. A federal appeals court reversed the EPA's ban on asbestos in a case you discussed in your most recent book.

The court decided that the statute under which the EPA acted could not possibly have been intended to allow EPA's asbestos ban because the ban cost so much money for every human life it might save.

Now, my question, Judge, is, is it reasonable for a judge to infer what Congress intended by looking at how much it cost to implement what Congress intended?

JUDGE BREYER: You can't answer the question "never." It would depend very much on what you had in mind in the statute. I wrote about that case in my book. . . . And I wrote really two opposite things about [it], absolutely opposite. The first thing I wrote about it is I thought what was in the mind of the court. And I thought what was in the mind of the court is they found an example where they thought that EPA was imposing a ban that cost about a quarter of a billion dollars and it would save hardly anybody. . . .

SEN. BIDEN: But it would save somebody.

JUDGE BREYER: Yes, it was a — it was like the number of people — they used a kind of absurd example about the number of people who die of toothpicks or eating toothpicks, or something like that. But that's the first way I used it in the book was to show that there are some EPA regulations which indeed seem to be very expensive ways of going about saving lives.

The second way is the opposite way I used that case in the book, because that case also provided an example of what you're suggesting, that it isn't a very good idea for courts to get involved in making that decision; that's more a decision for Congress to make.

And what I said when I discussed the case for the second time is: Look how the judges, even if they have an example of what they think is absolutely wrong, look what they have to do; they have to say that there is a rule of law that prevents that. And the rule of law that they enunciated in that case was a rule of law that said agencies have to look at all the alternatives, or many of them, before they do anything. But if you take that rule of law seriously, how can agencies have the time to do all that kind of thing? . . .

SEN. BIDEN: Let me make sure I understand your — for lack of a better phrase — rules of construction. If Congress delegates to the EPA the authority to make a judgment [about] what is necessary or reasonable to protect against the risk, and not delegate that to the court, then doesn't the court basically have to show that the agency acted in a capricious manner or a manner that is —

JUDGE BREYER: Yes, absolutely.

SEN. BIDEN: Now, if Congress delegates authority to an agency to consider cost and benefits in implementing the statute, your view is then that the court should, unless there is a clear disregard of that requirement, yield to the agency.

JUDGE BREYER: Absolutely. Absolutely. . . .

Church-State Separation

SEN. ORRIN G. HATCH, R-UTAH: The Establishment Clause of the First Amendment provides that Congress shall make no law respecting an establishment of religion. Under the test devised by the Supreme Court in 1971, the *Lemon v. Kurtzman* case, the practice satisfies the Establishment Clause only if it, No. 1, reflects a clearly secular purpose; No. 2, has a primary effect that neither advances nor inhibits religion; and No. 3, effectively avoids an excessive entanglement with religion.

Now I'm very concerned that this abstract, arid and ahistorical test is often applied in a manner that is insensitive to the practices that are part and parcel of our political and cultural heritage. In particular, narrow reliance on the *Lemon* test ignores a richer strain of Supreme Court precedent that recognizes the interpretation of the Establishment Clause, that it should comport with what history reveals was the contemporaneous understanding of its guarantees. In Justice Brennan's words, "The existence from the beginning of the nation's life of a practice is a fact of considerable import in the interpretation of the Establishment Clause."

Now do you agree or disagree that the historical pedigree of a practice should be given considerable weight in the determination of whether a practice amounts to an establishment of religion? You mentioned that historical precedent is important to you. Do you feel it is important in this instance?

JUDGE BREYER: It is important. There is no question. The Establishment Clause has tremendous foresight — tremendous foresight, I think. The simple model — there's always in my mind, like, you know, two or three fairly simple things, and I think of the Establishment Clause, I think of Jefferson, and I think of a wall. And the reason that there was that wall, the reason, which has become so much more important, perhaps even [more] now than it was then, is that we are a country of so many different people, of so many different religions, and it's so terribly important to members of each religion to be able to practice that religion freely, to be able to pass that religion on to their children. And each religion in a country of many, many different religions would not want the state to decide with some other religion, so each must be concerned that the state remain neutral.

Then also cases arise. And when cases arise with secular institutions, the question becomes: Have you injected too much religion into them? You can inject some. I

mean, you have chaplains in Congress. Schools? What about schools? You see, teaching your own children . . . it becomes very important not to, in a secular school, inject much religion into a school.

Look at the other side of the wall. Can the state aid religion? The answer is: Certainly, sometimes. Nobody thinks — nobody thinks that you're not going to send the fire brigade if the church catches fire. Nobody thinks that the church doesn't have the advantage of public services. The question becomes: When is it too much? And again, schools are critically important because of the importance of schools to religious people.

So that's the framework that I use. And in trying to decide whether and when, what is too much, of course you look at history and you look at tradition and you look at the current world as we live [in] it in the United States.

SEN. HATCH: At one time you stated that, quote, "Of course the wall between church and state is not absolute," unquote.

JUDGE BREYER: No. No one is going to say — to use an extreme example, no one would say that if the church is on fire, don't send the fire department. No one would say that the public services of a city are not available to a church. The question becomes: When have you gone too far in terms of trying to preserve a country of many different religions where government is basically neutral as among them? Those are very difficult questions.

SEN. HATCH: Well, I think, as we've seen up here on Capitol Hill, the word "wall" of separation is a . . . metaphor.

JUDGE BREYER: That's true.

SEN. HATCH: And it leads to a lot of hostility. And there has to be some reason brought into the system, and *Lee v. Weisman* back in 1992, the Supreme Court, relying on the Warren Court ruling, or on Warren Court rulings, held by a 5-4 vote that a school district violated the Establishment Clause when it invited a rabbi to lead a prayer at a school graduation. Now, in my view we've reached new depths when a non-sectarian prayer by a rabbi at a school graduation ceremony is censored by the Establishment Clause. Notwithstanding the fact-specific language of the court's opinion in *Lee*, some have since tried to portray *Lee* as having invalidated all prayer at school graduation ceremonies, including, for example, non-sectarian student-led prayer.

Now, would you consider it a relevant factor for purposes of the Establishment Clause whether it is a member of the clergy or a student who leads the prayer?

JUDGE BREYER: That's very specific, and I'm not sure I've thought that through. . . . It sounds as if it's relevant. As you say it, it sounds as if it's a relevant factor. And I understand the point and agree that it isn't absolute, these things. They're not — and I do think it's — it sounds as if it would be a relevant factor.

SEN. HATCH: Would you consider it

relevant whether the decision to have prayer at a graduation was made by school officials or students?

JUDGE BREYER: You bring up matters, Senator, which sound as if they're relevant. . . .

Government Regulation

SEN. EDWARD M. KENNEDY, D-MASS.: You've been one of the leading scholarly commentators on administrative law and regulations, and why — obviously these subjects seem dry and arcane — they can be of enormous importance to every American.

Americans have a right to expect that the food they eat, and the water they drink, and the medications they take, and the air they breathe, and the place where they work will be safe and free from dangerous substances or machinery. Congress passes the law that set the broad standards in these and other areas, but it's up to the administrative agencies like the EPA and the Occupational Safety and Health Administration and then the FDA [Food and Drug Administration] to adopt the regulations that spell out the standards, to apply them in particular situations to protect the health and safety.

This is the important work of administrative agencies, and a great deal has been written about your views on these subjects. Most of them — of what has been written has been complimentary, but I'd like to give you the opportunity to respond to some of the rest. My question is: How do you respond to the suggestion that some have made that you are hostile to health and safety regulation?

JUDGE BREYER: I've said in my book that I think regulation is necessary in those areas. I guess that, if you wanted a simple statement, a simple statement, I wrote a book review not too long ago in which I tried, because it was written about the economics of AIDS, and I wanted to explain in that book what I saw as an important difference, as you have said, actually, an important difference between what you might call classical economic regulation, like airlines or trucks, and the regulation involving health, safety and the environment.

And I said, "As to the first, trucking, airlines, it isn't really surprising that economics may help; it isn't the whole story, but it tells a significant amount of the story because our object there is to get low prices for consumers, and maybe economics can help us."

When you start talking about health, safety and the environment, the role is much more limited, because there no one would think that economics is going to tell you how much you want to spend helping the life of another person. If in fact people want to spend a lot of money to help save earthquake victims in California, who could say that was wrong?

And what I ended up there saying is that in this kind of area it's probably John Donne, the poet, who has more to tell us

about what to do than Adam Smith, the economist. That's a decision for Congress to make reflecting the values of people.

So I tried to draw that distinction, and that doesn't mean all those areas work perfectly either. Everyone can have a lot of criticisms about every area. But, nonetheless, there's a difference in the way economics feeds into the enterprise. And that's what I've tried to spell out in that review.

Death Penalty

SEN. STROM THURMOND, R-S.C.: Judge Breyer, if confirmed, you will succeed Justice Blackmun, who recently stated his belief that capital punishment is inherently flawed under the Constitution. While I disagree with his pronouncement, I want to know if you find his position reasonable in light of Supreme Court decisions in this area and your own personal reflections on whether capital punishment is constitutional under appropriate circumstances.

JUDGE BREYER: Senator, if a judge has strong personal views on a matter as important as the death penalty, views that he believes might affect his decision in such a case, he should perhaps, if they are very strong — and this happens sometimes in lower courts, I've seen it happen where you feel you have a personal view that doesn't necessarily reflect the law, and you might take yourself out of the case. I have no such personal view in respect to the death penalty, so I would sit on such a case in respect to the constitutionality of the death penalty.

It seems to me that the Supreme Court has considered that matter for quite a long time in a large number of cases. And indeed, if you look at those cases, you will see that the fact that there are some circumstances in which the death penalty is consistent with the Cruel and Unusual Punishment Clause of the Constitution is, in my opinion, settled law. At this point it is settled.

Abortion

SEN. THURMOND: Judge Breyer, it is likely that Justice Blackmun is most widely known to the public as the author of *Roe v. Wade*. What was your impression of his majority opinion in that landmark decision?

In particular, give us your thought˜ on where he draws the line at different points during pregnancy as it relates to the state's interest in the regulation of abortion-related services. For instance, do you agree that the first trimester of pregnancy is distinctive and that the state should not be able to prohibit abortion during that period?

JUDGE BREYER: You're asking questions, Senator, that I know are matters of enormous controversy. . . . The case of *Roe v. Wade* has been the law for 21 years, or more, and it was recently affirmed by the Supreme Court of the United States, in the case of *Casey [v. Planned Parenthood*

of Southeastern Pennsylvania]. That is the law. The questions that you're putting to me are matters of how that basic right applies, where it applies, under what circumstances. And I don't think I should go into those, for the reason that those are likely to be the subject of litigation in front of the court.

Taxation

SEN. THURMOND: Judge Breyer, Article One of the Constitution gives specific legislative powers to the Congress. One particular power granted to the Congress is the power to tax. Members of Congress are elected by the people and are accountable through the ballot box for their support or opposition on tax matters. Do you believe that federal judges who serve for life and are unaccountable to the American electorate should have the power to order tax increases or new taxes as part of a judicial remedy?

JUDGE BREYER: Again, Senator, I think there it's not possible to be categorical. I think much depends on the circumstance. I know that the Supreme Court has held that there are circumstances in which such tax orders are permissible, and therefore I start with the assumption that that is the holding of the court, and since the court has held that there could be such circumstances. Exactly what they are, I can't tell you at this moment.

SEN. THURMOND: Then Congress, of course, then would have to change it if we think it's improper.

JUDGE BREYER: That's correct. That's correct.

Judicial Activism

SEN. THURMOND: Judge Breyer, we frequently hear the argument that courts act in response to various social problems because the legislature has failed to act on its own. How would you respond to this defense of an activist judiciary?...

JUDGE BREYER: The judge can't act unless there is more than a simple belief that there is a social problem. Rather, it must be the case that there is a statute or the Constitution itself that creates a law that perhaps another branch of government would be better off implementing with sub-laws or statutes or regulations, that basically the judge's decision must be tied back to a law, just as the greatest law, which has led to the greatest change, is the 14th Amendment to the Constitution, and judges who implemented that great law, which promised fairness to all Americans, were not following their own point of view. They were, rather, carrying out the basic promise of fairness that was written into the Constitution, and it's that grounding of law that I think made those decisions lawful, justified and effective....

Antitrust Issues

SEN. THURMOND: As a judge who has written extensively on antitrust laws, could you please summarize your views

very briefly on purposes and goals of the antitrust laws and their importance to the competitiveness to U.S. business both here and abroad?

JUDGE BREYER: Senator, I was quite lucky about I guess a year and a half, two years ago now, and was at this conference I spoke of earlier with 500 Russian judges, and they are very interested there — I get into a lot of private conversations — and they're very interested in not only basic constitutional protections but also economic organizations. And the point that I would frequently make in those conversations is that if you are going to have a free-enterprise economy, if you're not going to have the government running everything, then you must have a strong and effective antitrust law.

If you are not going to regulate airlines, you must have a strong antitrust law for airlines. The reason is that antitrust law is the policeman. Antitrust law aims through the competitive process at bringing about low prices for consumers, better products and more efficient methods of production.

Those three things, in my mind, are the key to antitrust law and really a strong justification for an economy in which there are winners and losers, and some people get rich and others don't. The justification lies in the fact that that kind of economy is better for almost everyone, and it won't be better for almost everyone unless the gains of productivity are spread, and the gains of productivity are spread through competition that brings about low prices, better products and more efficient methods of production. And that's what I think antitrust law is about, and that's what I think that policeman of the free enterprise system has to do. It's called protect the consumer....

SEN. HOWARD M. METZEN-BAUM, D-OHIO: There isn't much question about the fact that you have exceptional legal credentials. I must say, however, that I am concerned about your position and your views on the fair competition laws which affect the day-to-day lives of all Americans.

I am talking about the antitrust laws that Sen. Thurmond just raised with you, the antitrust laws that are in place in order to keep prices low and products safe for consumers, to make the competitive market work. Those same laws protect small businesses against abusive corporate giants and prevent price gouging, monopolies and cartels from harming consumers.

You've been outspoken with respect to the consumer protection laws known as antitrust, but your record suggests, unfortunately to my mind, that you almost always vote against the very people the antitrust laws are in place to protect. A 1991 study in the Fordham Law Review reported that in all 16 of your antitrust decisions, Judge Breyer voted against the alleged victim of antitrust abuse.

You seem — you seem to see antitrust laws in terms of abstract economics. And it

seems that theories of economic efficiency, displayed in complicated charts, one of which I will use at a later point in the hearing, and graphs, replace individual justice for small businesses and consumers. As you well know, that's not my view of antitrust. I see it as the protector of mom-and-pop businesses and the guardian of consumer rights....

JUDGE BREYER: I think, Senator, I should start with a general point, a negative general point, then a positive general point and then something rather specific. The negative general point is, of course, I don't count up how many victories are for plaintiffs or defendants and do statistics. Sometimes plaintiffs did win in antitrust cases I've had, and as you point out, defendants often won. The plaintiff sometimes is a big business and sometimes isn't. The defendant sometimes is and sometimes isn't.

What I'm interested in is: Is the case correct as a matter of law? And I consider the cases one at a time, and I consider the merits, the legal merits of the arguments in front of me.

My general positive point is this, where I hope and expect very much that you will agree because, frankly, I've read what you say often on antitrust, and you're going to think that this comes from things that you have said to businesspeople, because I've read them, and I think it does. But there is a keystone to antitrust, and you've said it before, and you say it again. And the keystone to antitrust, what antitrust is all about, is getting low prices for consumers, not high prices; and getting better products for consumers, not worse products; and getting more efficient methods of production. And that simple three-part key, which I carry around, I think, engraved in my brain....

It's a difficult area, and I can't be certain as I sit here now that we've come to the exactly correct result. What I can be certain of is what our court tried to do. We tried to focus on where the ball really is, which is the low price for the consumer, and we tried to work our way through a very complicated area to see if antitrust law, which has that as its objective, technically would come to that result. I don't guarantee I was right; I don't guarantee that others don't have good arguments the other way. What I do guarantee is what we were trying to do, how we were trying to interpret the law.

Televised Court Proceedings

SEN. PATRICK J. LEAHY, D-VT.: What do you think about having television in the Supreme Court for arguments? Would you be in favor of that?

JUDGE BREYER: I'd say this, Senator. The issue came up in the Judicial Conference of the United States, of which I was a member. That's the — they have representatives of all the circuits and also the district courts. And I voted in favor of that. We voted to have a television in the — the question was the [U.S. Circuit] Court of

Appeals and the district courts, and we would run an experimental program. And it's been going on now in the district courts, but also in the courts of appeals. I volunteered our 1st Circuit with the concurrence of the other judges for the program, but we were not accepted as an experimental circuit. So, I have expressed a view that that is appropriate in that way in the Judicial Conference.

Now, I should add that before making any decision about [television] in the Supreme Court of the United States, if that issue arose, obviously I would listen to other members of the court and try to understand their points of view and what they were thinking, too....

Freedom of Speech

SEN. LEAHY: Judge, I grew up in a family where the idea of the First Amendment was greatly respected — both parts of it. My parents had a printing business and a weekly newspaper and also held religion very deeply. So I'm going to go first to the power of the First Amendment dealing with speech.

Do you think there is a core of political speech that's entitled to greater constitutional protection than other forms of speech?

JUDGE BREYER: There is a core of political speech, but it's not the only thing at the core. It seems to me that there are a cluster of things that are at the core of the First Amendment, including expression of a person as he talks, as he creates and also including what I think of as a dialogue in a civilized society. What do I mean by that?

Actually, it's Michael, my son, who really gave me a good compliment once that set me thinking about this. What he said — and I don't always get compliments from him — but what he said was, well, we did use to argue a lot at the dinner table — I mean discuss — and he said, "You know," he said, "I always felt you were listening to me."

Now that of course doesn't mean we always agreed. But you see, there is something in that idea of listening that promotes the dignity of the person who is listened to, and I've noticed in court sometimes, if there are two people arguing and I'll listen, and then I try to repeat the argument in my own words to the other side, and as you go back and forth, it promotes a good feeling because people feel they've been listened to even if you disagreed with them, you took in what they were saying.

Now that kind of conversation — I was thinking that kind of conversation that has to do with dignity and the way that the democracy functions, the expressive value of speech, the political value of free speech — all of those things are a cluster of things. And then as you move out sort of from that center in different ways, you can discover that some of those things are mixed with more conduct, or some of those things are mixed with activity that could cause a lot

of harm....

SEN. LEAHY: But you would protect non-political speech like, say, a scientific debate?... And art?... Literature?

JUDGE BREYER: Of course.

Free Press vs. Fair Trial

SEN. LEAHY: Let me go into another area, then, as we sort of follow this a little bit. I've been both a prosecutor and a defense attorney — and brought up to believe you try your cases in the courtroom. But it seems to me — and we've had of recent days even more of an example of this — where you have witnesses in a high-profile criminal case that are going to be out selling their story to tabloids or television or whatever else before they even go in to testify.

They are obviously telling their story not under oath, but they've sold it for a great deal of money, and then they have to come in under oath, and certainly it's going to be awkward for them to contradict what they've just sold it for; and sometimes, as we have discovered, that those buying it want to make sure that it is as spectacular as possible. The suggestion has been made sometimes the stories are changed to accommodate that.

I wonder if this kind of checkbook journalism undercuts the pursuit of justice or witnesses' credibility, what it does to the tension between the First Amendment rights and the rights of the public and the defendant to a fair trial. What would you think of the constitutionality of a statute that would prohibit persons identified as witnesses at a preliminary hearing on a trial from selling their stories prior to the time they testify? Could you write such a statute?

JUDGE BREYER: I'm not going to be, or am I, in Congress, and I understand the difficulty that your ... question is getting at. And I have two observations.

Obviously, I can't discuss the legality of that particular thing because that could come up, but underlying your question it seems to me that there are two important points. The first is what you hone in on specifically is likely to be a problem over the next 20 years, 30 years, maybe indefinitely, where you have two important sets of rights that all Americans value. All Americans value free speech. All Americans value the important right to a trial that is fair so that an innocent person is not convicted. And sometimes those rights can clash, and then you're in a difficult area of how you're going to reconcile.

Now, that's fairly well-known, I suppose, but the other point that I'd like to emphasize, and this is a little self-serving as a judge, but also, as you recognize, not every, not every clash of this sort need be resolved in a court.

That is, I've always thought that the press, too, is sensitive to the problems of fair trial. I've always thought that lawyers, too, are sensitive to the problems of a free

press. And sometimes that kind of communication — this is things I've said in speeches, I'm not saying anything new, that I haven't said before — but sometime that communication among groups outside of courts, before creating a legal issue out of everything, can help. Those are the only two general comments, which may be fairly obvious....

Censorship

SEN. LEAHY: If the government is giving out federal funds or whatever — art, libraries, so on — can they require recipients of federal funds to express only those views that the government finds acceptable?

JUDGE BREYER: As you put it like that, it doesn't sound likely ... that they could.

SEN. LEAHY: Well, let me give a couple of examples. Could the government — and I've asked this of other nominees — could the government further a policy of protecting the public from sexually explicit material? Could they prohibit libraries receiving federal funds from making books like Alice Walker's "The Color Purple" or J.D. Salinger's "Catcher in the Rye" available?

JUDGE BREYER: In principle, in principle, censorship is undesirable. It's undesirable, and when actual cases of censorship come up, typically it's going to be some issue which is a borderline issue. And on this borderline issue, you typically decide it in reading the briefs, reading the arguments, thinking about the particular case and what the particular thing is. And the reason that I answered in this way is I think the cases will come up like this, and I will have to think about it, and I mean I —

SEN. LEAHY: Could I suggest that you may want to think — just the view of one Vermonter — that the further you move away from the First Amendment being an absolute, the more of those cases you're going to have?

JUDGE BREYER: Well, that's right.... I mean — you see, I mean what's at the bottom of it, it does seem to me, and people forget that, that it's there to protect speech and writing that we don't agree with. And how often people say, "Oh, it's not there to protect that." That's too bad. But that's what it's there for, and that principle I think is exhibited in lots and lots of different ways, and I think that's a fairly absolute principle.

Sex Discrimination

SEN. DENNIS DECONCINI, D-ARIZ.: Judge Breyer, turning to the Equal Protection Clause ... although the 14th Amendment states that no state shall, quote, "deny to any person within its jurisdiction the equal protection of the laws," it is generally believed that the authors of the 14th Amendment were concerned with racial discrimination and did not specifically have women or gender discrimination in mind.

In regard to cases based upon gender, the standard of review is one of intermediate or heightened scrutiny. Under this standard, a classification must serve an important governmental objective and be substantially related to that objective. This standard was developed over time and has been effective in protecting against gender discrimination.

Judge, do you believe that this standard is the proper one for reviewing gender-related cases, and do you have any expansion that you think is necessary at this time?

JUDGE BREYER: I'm hesitating because of the fact that this is likely to be before the court, but I would like to say something, which is this: It seems to me that it's absolutely established that gender discrimination falls within the scope of the 14th Amendment. That's clear and totally accepted, I think, across the spectrum.

As I think of the 14th Amendment, to speak generally, the 14th Amendment perfected a Constitution that before it, lacked something very important, and that something was a promise of basic fairness. That promise of basic fairness was not carried out, even though it was in the Constitution, for many, many years. And ever since *Brown* [*v. Board of Education*] the country in all of its branches of government has been trying to make real that promise of fairness. It applies to women, too, and to many others.

The tests that you're talking about have in a sense a substantive part, and they have a communications part. The substantive part I might describe as this. Imagine saying to a minority person there is a rule of law here that harms you through a discrimination. Wouldn't you, as soon as you say that, think, but what possible justification could there be? And that, I think, is what the substance is when the Supreme Court makes its tough tests.

Now think of Chloe or Nell or their equivalents all over the country going into the workplace and think of some kind of rule that makes their life worse because they're women. Wouldn't you say, but what kind of justification for that could there be? Now that, it seems to me, to be the kind of substance that's pretty widely accepted and going on.

Now, the exact way in which that's communicated through the vast administrative network which is called the court system, through judges, to lawyers, to employers, to others — that I think is a matter of words, and those words may be the subject of litigation. So it seems to me I have to stop with the statement of general principle.

SEN. DECONCINI: Well, let me ask you this. The recent case of *J. E. B. v. Alabama*, the Supreme Court used the Equal Protection Clause to find that gender-based peremptory challenges were unconstitutional. Now, I realize you can't comment on that case, and I'm not suggesting that you should. But it appears to me very clearly that the court seems to be moving closer to applying a strict scrutiny in cases of gender discrimination.... Do you believe in the general sense that the intermediate scrutiny for gender discrimination, do you believe it will always be sufficient to meet potentially hypothetical cases regarding gender discrimination?

JUDGE BREYER: It may not be, and that will be up for litigation and I'll read the briefs with care, and I'll listen to the arguments and I'll —

SEN. DECONCINI: You're not stuck on the intermediate by any means. You will —

JUDGE BREYER: No, I'm certainly not....

Day Two of the Hearings

Following are excerpts from Judge Breyer's testimony July 13, his second day before the Judiciary Committee:

Judicial Philosophy

SEN. WILLIAM S. COHEN, R-MAINE: On my first day of law school, at the conclusion of the day, my law professor said that any connection between law and justice is purely coincidental. And I thought he was engaging in some sort of professional cleverness at the time until I went out to practice law, and I found — I started to lose all my cases. I had justice on my side, and my opponent had the law on their side.

But I raise this in connection [to U.S. 2nd Circuit Court] Judge [Learned] Hand, whom you are a great fan of, and I was looking through his book, "The Spirit of Liberty," and he was talking about his relationship with [Justice Oliver Wendell Holmes Jr.], whom you are also a great devotee of in terms of his writings and decisions.

And Holmes used to frequently say, "I hate justice," and of course Hand would go on to say he really didn't mean that, but he tried to make the point that on one occasion when they were driving and an automobile passed the Supreme Court when Holmes was going to a weekly conference, he tried to pique him a little bit, and he said, "Well, sir, goodbye. Do justice." And Holmes turned around and snapped at him and said, "That's not my job. My job is to play the game according to the rules."

And the question I have as I listened to your opening statement about the need for the justices, the court system to strike some sort of a harmonious balance in the lives of such a diverse population to preserve liberty for as many as possible, all if possible.

At no time did you say that you intended to do justice. I take it that your reluctance to do that was the same for Holmes as well, of not seeking to do justice in the sense of intervening into an area that was properly before that of the Congress or the state legislatures. Is that how you would interpret Holmes' statement? I don't — "My job is not to do justice, but to play the game according to the rules?"

JUDGE BREYER: In part, yes. But I think that Holmes means more than that. I think Holmes — and it's another reason I do admire him.... I think he sees all this vast set of rules as interrelated. And I suspect, though I'm not positive, that he sees ultimately the vast object of this vast interrelated sets of rules, including rules that say whose job is what, as working out for society in a way that's better for people rather than worse.

I suppose when you say, "Do justice," or you say, "No, no, I'm just following the rules," what you worry about is someone trying to decide an individual case without thinking out the effect of that decision on a lot of other cases. That's why I always think law requires both a heart and a head. If you don't have a heart, it becomes a sterile set of rules removed from human problems, and it won't help. If you don't have a head, there's the risk that in trying to decide a particular person's problem in a case that may look fine for that person, you cause trouble for a lot of other people, making their lives yet worse. So it's a question of balance, and I'd say both.

SEN. COHEN: Judge, yesterday, you indicated that the black robe had great symbolic significance, that when you place the robe around your shoulders, that you're no longer speaking as an individual and that you would convey to the litigants that the decisions that were reached or rendered were done so irrespective of personality, the personality of the judge.

And then I think you quoted Hand's speech about [Justice Benjamin N.] Cardozo in describing a judge as someone — a runner who is stripped for the race. I was interested in that, because Hand himself has written in this wonderful biography of Gerald Gunther's — he says a man doesn't get to be a justice of the Supreme Court chiefly because he can detach himself from the convictions and prejudices of his class or his time.

Furthermore, Judge — Justice Cardozo, in that wonderful book, "The Nature of the Judicial Process," also said in the long run, there's no guarantee of justice except for the personality of the judge. So both Hand and Cardozo would seem to contradict the notion that, once you put the black robe on, you in fact are one of these blind oracles that simply, dispassionately rule upon the law as such.

And I mention this in connection with who you are as a person. I think that's one of the features of this type of hearing, is to try and gauge you as a person. And in that connection, again I would turn to Hand because you have turned to him so many times during the course of these proceedings.

And Hand said, "I venture to believe that it's as important to a judge called upon to pass upon a question of constitutional law to have at least a bowing acquaintance with Acton and Maitland, with Thucydides and Gibbon and Carlyle and Homer and Dante, Shakespeare, Milton,

Machiavelli, Montaigne, Rabelais, Plato, Bacon, Hume, Kant, as with the books that have been so specifically written on the subject, for" — in the key words — "in such matters, everything turns upon the spirit in which he approaches the questions before him. The words he must construe are empty vessels into which he can pour nearly anything he will."

And I think that's a terribly important statement that Hand made. And I've listened to the introductions that were given yesterday on your behalf, and I know that you're a learned individual who has studied Spanish and is fluent in French and apparently reads architecture in his spare time and quotes from John Donne vs. Adam Smith.

But if I had to ask you today if you could just — if I went into your library and I asked you to point at the 10 most important books that you have there, what would you point to? . . .

JUDGE BREYER: My goodness. I mean, my reading, people may exaggerate this a little bit and expect me — my reading is not like the list you just read. . . .

Where do people start? They start with Shakespeare. Say why Shakespeare, and you say why — this I tell students, you know, a lot of them that come from some different school, and they'll come from some place, they say, "What's in Shakespeare for me?" You say, "Well, if you're willing to put in the time, he's a little bit archaic, you know, the language, but if you put in the time, what you see there is, you see every different person, you see every different kind of person, you see every situation there is in the world; you see people saying things that they would say if only they had that ability to say them, and you see the whole thing in poetry."

I mean, that's why people turn to that, and they turn to that a little bit in literature to get some of the things that Sen. [Paul] Simon [D-Ill.] was talking about, I think, which is: What's in the heart of that person who is leading that different kind of life?

And sometimes you can find some of that in literature. I like Conrad very much. Why? I think because I'm moved often by the way in which he talks about the need for people — all of us — to learn from the past and then to give something to the future. Whether that's through our families or whether that's through our careers, we do learn from our parents, we do learn from the past, we do try to transmit things of value, and I think he finds value in human communities. I think he finds human communities to be ultimately the sources of obligations and values towards each other. . . . And so sometimes I've found literature very helpful as a way out of the tower.

Judicial Precedent

SEN. HATCH: Let me just ask a few questions about the principle of stare decisis, the common law prudential doctrine of

adherence to precedents. Now, some have argued that a vastly different rule of stare decisis should operate for precedent that creates a new constitutional right. That's on the one hand. And they also argue for precedent that declines to create a new constitutional right on the other.

Specifically, some have expressed the view that precedent, no matter how incorrect, that creates a new right should rarely if ever be overturned, while precedent that declines to create a new right should be freely overturned. Some have argued for this.

Now under this view, for example, many liberals will argue that cases like *Roe v. Wade* and *Miranda [v. Arizona]* are sacrosanct precedent, but precedents like *Bowers v. Hardwick*, which held that there is no constitutional right to engage in homosexual sodomy, and cases upholding the death penalty, should be overturned. Now, what is your view of the theory of stare decisis?

JUDGE BREYER: My view is there are — stare decisis is very important to the law, obviously. You can't have a legal system that doesn't operate with a lot of weight given to stare decisis because people build their lives, they build their lives on what they believe to be the law. And insofar as you begin to start overturning things, you upset the lives of men, women, children, people all over the country. So, be careful, because people can adjust, and even when something is wrong they can adjust it. And once they've adjusted, be careful of fooling with their expectations. Now, that's the most general.

When I become a little bit more specific, it seems to me that there are identifiable factors that are pretty well established. If you're, as a judge, thinking of overturning or voting to overturn a pre-existing case, what you do is ask a number of fairly specific questions: How wrong do you think that prior precedent really was as a matter of law? That is, how badly reasoned was it? You ask yourself how the law has changed since — all the adjacent laws, all the adjacent rules and regulations. Does it no longer fit?

You ask yourself how have the facts changed. Has the world changed in very important ways? You ask yourself, insofar — irrespective of how wrong that prior decision was — as a matter of reasoning, how as it worked out in practice? Has it proved impossible or very difficult to administer? Has it really confused matters? And finally you look to the degree of reliance that people have had in their ordinary lives on that previous precedent. Those are the kinds of questions you ask.

I think you ask questions in relation to statutes. I think you ask those questions in relation to the Constitution. The real difference between the two areas is that Congress can correct a constitutional court if it's a statutory question, but it can't make a correction if it's a constitutional matter. So be pretty careful.

SEN. HATCH: Unless they pass a

constitutional amendment to do so.

JUDGE BREYER: Yes, that's true. Very hard to do.

Day Three of the Hearings

Following are excerpts from Judge Breyer's testimony July 14, his third day before the Judiciary Committee:

Economic Cost-Benefit Analysis

SEN. COHEN: I wanted to go back to that book you wrote, that Sen. Biden had on his desk yesterday, called "Breaking The Vicious Circle." . . . You talked about the vicious cycle of public demand and the excessive retaliatory — regulatory response — is the product of several factors that work in tandem. At the root is an ill-informed public, with skewed perceptions of the risk, fed by unsystematic media reports, a distrust of experts and low levels of mathematical understanding. I believe I've summarized your basic analysis of this vicious cycle you've talked about.

You pointed out that Congress is susceptible to public concerns; it contributes to the distortions of priorities. The public fears are picked up and translated into policy by a Congress that does not have the institutional resources to resist draconian legislation establishing rigid objectives with little room for adjusting priorities, within limited budgets or balancing costs against benefits. And then you go from Congress to the regulators who compound the problem as bureaucrats respond with overly conservative assumptions in order to forestall charges of inattention and neglect. And the regulators also aim their rules narrowly to deal with one problem by worsening another.

For example, proposed rules concerning disposal of sewage sludge designed to save one statistical life every five years would encourage waste incineration 'likely to cause two statistical cancer deaths annually. And what you recommend, as I recall in this particular book, is to create a small, centralized administrative unit within the executive branch, with a mandate to rationalize risk policies across agencies. And critics have pointed to that and suggested that it's unrealistic, in the United States of America, to establish a sort of platonic administrative group of wise men — circle of wise men — who would in fact be a, quote, "elite top down policy coordination group" — would be unthinkable in a society that prizes open debate, delivery — diversity of opinion and easy access to government. In other words, they suggest this is a proposal that might work well in Singapore, but not in Seattle or indeed, Washington, D.C. How do you respond to that?

JUDGE BREYER: Thank you, Senator. . . . The problem that the book is aimed at is spending a lot of money over here to save a statistical life that may not even exist, at the same time that there are women with breast cancer who would live but who don't because they can't afford or find a place to go for the mammograms. And there are children who don't have the

vaccines that will save them from death or a lot of diseases, and there are two pages, I think, in that book, that summarize one sentence after another — all those things that might be done but aren't done.

And so the book is a plea — though it's put in technical terms — it's put in a plea, not to cut back by one penny this nation's commitment to health, safety and the environment; but please, let's think about the possibility of reorganizing that commitment so that there are fewer women and children who are dying of things they really will die of because the money wasn't there, when there are moneys being spent on the statistical life that might not exist. That's the first point.

The second point is, there is a plan there for reorganization. The point about the reorganization is not really to create a new bureaucracy that will take power from the people. Rather, the people have delegated already to the bureaucracy, power to do particular things. And there, it seems to me wise, or at least I suggested, that the people who already are there, in, let's say, parts of the Office of Management and Budget, not be trained solely as cost-cutters, not be trained solely as people who do policy analysis, but perhaps take on a career where they learn what really goes on at EPA for part of their career, where they come over to Congress and work for a while and learn something like that — about that, where they go out into the field and maybe learn what people are really thinking and then come back and have with that experience more ability to transfer resources from one program to another that a pure cost-cutter might lack....

I absolutely think that people want more safety, and that's the basic power that should be delegated. I think it becomes very, very, very difficult to expect people to become experts on risk analysis or how many molecules there ought to be in what kind of substance. And that's the kind of concern that I'm worried about, that leads me to think there are ways of organizing the bureaucracy better to save more human lives with the same commitment of resources that we now have.

SEN. COHEN: But you say the root of it is an ill-informed public with skewed perceptions of risk . . . fed by unsystematic media reports and a distrust of the experts. How do you propose to break — compounded by Congress, which is also contributing — the distortions of priorities. How do you break that cycle by having this small . . . group of experts in the field or in OMB or some of the other agencies who will then do what? Better inform the public? Better inform Congress?

JUDGE BREYER: And this you might say is Utopian, I know. But you realize what it is I think the public is informed about. I don't think they're not informed about what they want. I don't think they're not informed about there being a problem. I think they are — they do know what they want. And I think the public does know that there's a problem. And I think they're right. What it's very hard to get public consensus

about is the right number of molecules or the right chemical substance exactly where. That's the problem of information.

And what is perhaps a little Utopian, I would call the biggest problem that I find from a policy point of view, the problem of building trust in the government. And my suggestion there has been a little bit like this: Suppose the president of the United States had — this is what I've said before — had somewhat broader authority to take money or resources from one program and to move it to another and that he was under a mandate to meet the following condition: Come back and prove to us that in doing so you have saved more human lives. And suppose that began to be done. Then you might gradually build public trust in that kind of circulating career path where people come to Congress and EPA and OMB and create this institution and people in the country begin to understand more life is being saved.

A little at a time, you might gradually build some confidence in that institution, hard though it is to break into a mode of public trust. And if you could do that, you would end up saving more life. And that's the thrust of the book.

SEN. COHEN: Well, I think that sort of outcomes analysis is probably unrealistic in view of the life cycle of any president of this country, that by the time one were able to demonstrate that, that he or she would certainly long be out of office. So I'm not sure that's going to be a practical solution. But I see my time is up, and I appreciate your answer, Judge.

SEN. BIDEN: Judge, I hope that was spoken as a political scientist . . . and not as a judge.

JUDGE BREYER: Absolutely.

SEN. BIDEN: Because we make those judgments every day. The American people have no doubt that more people die from coal dust than from nuclear reactors, but they fear the prospect of a nuclear reactor more than they do the empirical data that would suggest that more people die from coal dust and having coal-fired burners. They also know that more lives would be saved — if we took that 25 percent we spend in the intensive care units in the last three months of the elderly's lives, more children would be saved. But part of our culture is that we've concluded that as a culture that we are going to, rightly or wrongly, we are going to spend the money, costing more lives, on the elderly. We made that judgment.

I think it's incredibly presumptuous and elitist for political scientists to conclude that the American people's cultural values in fact are not ones that lend themselves to a cost-benefit analysis and presume that they would change their cultural values if, in fact, they were aware of the cost-benefit analysis. I have no doubt that more people know that more people die of cigarettes than they do of other substances, but they've concluded they'd rather have the money spent on research and other areas. We make those decisions every day, and I am delighted [that] as a judge you are

not going to be able to take your policy prescriptions into the court.

Lloyd's of London

SEN. METZENBAUM: Judge Breyer, I'd like to ask you a few questions about your decision in the *[U.S. v. Ottati & Goss Inc.]* case. As I understand the *Ottati* case, you upheld a ruling that allowed a company responsible for polluting 34 acres in Kingston, N.H., to clean up that site about one-tenth as much as EPA determined was necessary to protect Kingston's residents from 439 cases of cancer over their lifetime.

I don't want to question you about the merits of your decision in that case. What concerns me, however, Judge, is that you decided a case that reduces polluters' and their insurance companies' liability for cleaning up hazardous waste at a time when your investment at Lloyd's of London included environmental liability insurance policies. In retrospect, Judge, do you feel that possibly you should have recused yourself from hearing that case?

JUDGE BREYER: Senator, I've looked at this very carefully. There was no party that I had invested in the case. It had been fully disclosed. The issue, to me, and I think the issue under the canons is whether there would flow from that investment a substantial effect on my investment from that decision in that case. That's not a speculative effect, it's not a remote effect, it's not a contingent effect; it is a real, substantial effect. And having looked at that case before and looked at it again, it seems to me that it was correct under the canons that I could sit in that case. I do think that, though I understand, in fact, the various problems you've raised.

SEN. METZENBAUM: Well, I know that there are some who think that it was proper under the canons; there are some who disagree. Justice [Antonin] Scalia, whom I didn't think I would ever be courting in connection with the law, but he says . . . "Quite simply and quite universally, recusal was required whenever impartiality might reasonably be questioned. . . ."

Now . . . you acknowledged that as [Yale University] Professor [Gregory] Hazard said, it was possibly imprudent for you as a federal judge to invest in Lloyd's. Isn't the corollary of that reasoning that it was possibly imprudent for you to decide the *Ottati* case, since your Lloyd's syndicates included environmental pollution liability?

JUDGE BREYER: What he said was "imprudent," Senator, is — he believes that it's ethical, that no ethical canon was violated, and he is concerned — and I've since read this — whether or not it is prudent for a judge to have an investment in an insurance company.

And having listened to your concerns, which I realize were in very good faith and were very, very important to address thoroughly, I've come to the conclusion that it would be best not to have such an investment. And that's a matter of prudence, it is not a matter of ethics. But having listened to that, that is how I feel about it. ■

Clinton Says Vote on Crime Bill 'Failed the American People'

After the House defeated efforts to bring the crime bill conference report (H Rept 103-324) to the floor Aug. 11, President Clinton appeared in the White House pressroom to denounce the vote. Following are excerpts from the official transcript:

PRESIDENT CLINTON: Ladies and gentlemen, under any circumstances I would be disappointed if the House of Representatives turned its back on the toughest and largest attack on crime in the history of our country, at a time when the American people say it is the most important issue to them.

But it is especially disheartening to see 225 members of the House participate in a procedural trick orchestrated by the National Rifle Association (NRA), then heavily, heavily pushed by the Republican leadership in the House, and designed with only one thing in mind — to put the protection of particular interests over the protection of ordinary Americans.

I don't know how many people in the run up to this vote — of both parties, unfortunately — told me, "I'll vote for that bill, but I just have to vote against this procedural bill." "Oh, I'll vote for it if it ever gets to the floor, but I just have to vote against this rule" — because of the assault weapons ban or because they had decided, many of them after the fact, that there was too much money in here for preventing crime and to give our children something to say yes to instead of something just to say no to, even though two-thirds of this money is for police and prisons and punishment.

Well, tonight a majority of the House attempted to take the easy way out. But they have failed the American people. And now I say to them, the easy way out is not an option. Fear and violence, especially among our children, will still be there tonight when they go home to bed. So I want them to come back tomorrow and the day after that and the day after that, and to keep coming back until we give the American people the essential elements of this crime bill — until we put 100,000 police on the street, and take our children and the guns off the street with the assault weapons ban and with the ban on ownership of handguns by juveniles; until we make 'three strikes and you're out' the law of the land.

We have got to do these things. And, yes, we have to both build more prisons and give our kids something to say yes to, not just something to say no to. The amazing thing is that this prevention money was supported by every major law enforcement organization in the United States, representing over a half a million police officers who know something about fighting crime and putting their lives on the line.

Today's vote is a vote against all of them — those people in law enforcement who stand out day in and day out and try to make our streets safer. It's a vote against their organizations who pleaded for this bill, the sheriffs, the police chiefs, the prosecutors, the attorneys general; a vote against the teachers and the others who work to keep our kids safe and secure....

Now, we can do better than this. And I want the Congress and the House to go back to work tomorrow and figure out how to save the elements of this crime bill. This is about the American people. It is their No. 1 concern. And the American people are not foolish enough to be conned into believing that people are really for doing something about crime, but they had to pull a political trick to keep the bill from being voted on.

Q: Mr. President, where do you go from here? Some of the main supporters of the bill say it's dead.

P: Oh, I don't think so. But, of course, that's what we were all worried about. We were afraid that this would be like Humpty Dumpty, you know. And, of course, that's what they want — the people that are fighting against it. But they're going to be given a chance.

You know, for the last few days, all they heard from were the special interests and people that had been stirred up by a lot of the disinformation that had been put out. But tonight I think they've got a lot of explaining to do, because we know — you all know — that there were a majority of votes in the House for this, and the bill still went down on the rule because they thought they could pull a political trick and satisfy particular pressures on them without aggravating the rank-and-file citizens of this country. I think they're wrong; I think the people will figure it out.

Q: Mr. President, are you saying that you will keep the Congress in session until this is done? Are you going to keep the Congress in session?

P: I don't think they ought to go home. You know, the people who are committing these crimes are not going to take a vacation; they're going to be out there working overtime.

Q: There were 58 Democrats, including 10 members of the [Congressional] Black Caucus, one Republican member of the black caucus. What do you say to them? They went against you on this issue.

P: Well, I say, first of all, let's look at the whole thing. There were 20 fewer Democrats voting against the rule than those who voted against the assault weapons ban. So there were 20 Democrats — probably 30

— who said, "OK, I lost that fight. But the safety of the people in my district is more important than my view on this particular issue, and certainly more important than my killing this bill on a procedural vote." They were very brave. They stood up and took a lot of heat.

Now, there were 10 [Democratic] members of the black caucus whose opposition to the death penalty was so strong that they could not overcome their personal opposition. At least they had a principled position. But almost three times that many, including many who were disappointed because they didn't get what they wanted in that bill, still voted for it.

There were 11 brave Republicans who weathered enormous pressure. But there were 38 who voted against the assault weapons ban, and there were 65 — 65 — who voted for the crime bill with about the same amount of prevention money in it when it passed as it has today. Now I hear them say, "Well, there's just too much prevention money here. We're doing too much in these programs to help these kids who are in trouble." Well, all I know is when it passed the first time at about this same dollar amount, there were 65 Republican votes for it. But I can tell you, they were put under a lot of pressure.

Now, they can figure out how to do this. I'm not in the Congress; I'm not a part of it. But they can figure out how to get this done. They know what the elements are. There is a majority now in both Houses for all of the elements of this crime bill; to let special interests use parliamentary maneuvers to undermine what is clearly the will of the majority of the American people and a majority of the Congress on each discrete element is a bad mistake, and I don't think the people will forget about it....

Q: What's your response to those who will say that this is an enormous personal defeat for you?

P: I can say that I worked my heart out on it, and I did everything I could. And on this day, the NRA and the Republican leadership had their way. The American people have to decide whether they think this is about which politicians are winning and losing in Washington, or about kids like [crime victims] James Darby and Polly Klaas who are still alive.

I believe the American people will not like viewing this as some sort of political circus up here. I'm on their side, and I think we better see who's on what side. That is the only thing that matters, what happens to the American people.

Did I lose tonight? You bet I did in the sense that I wanted it to pass. But what happens to me is not important. If everybody in America had the security I had, we wouldn't need a crime bill.

Look at — what happens to me is not — what matters is all these kids that are going to be out on the street tonight that could just get shot. That's what's important. And I think that, in the end, if that is felt in the heart of the members of the House, we'll still get this crime bill. ■

Clinton Offers Justification For Invasion of Haiti

President says, 'We must act' to restore democracy, but he stops short of setting firm deadline

Following is the text of President Clinton's Sept. 15 address to the nation on the situation in Haiti:

My fellow Americans, tonight I want to speak with you about why the United States is leading the international effort to restore democratic government in Haiti. Haiti's dictators, led by [Lt.] Gen. Raoul Cédras, control the most violent regime in our hemisphere. For three years, they have rejected every peaceful solution that the international community has proposed. They have broken an agreement that they made to give up power. They have brutalized their people and destroyed their economy, and for three years we and other nations have worked exhaustively to find a diplomatic solution, only to have the dictators reject each one.

Now the United States must protect our interests — to stop the brutal atrocities that threaten tens of thousands of Haitians, to secure our borders and to preserve stability and promote democracy in our hemisphere and to uphold the reliability of the commitments we make, and the commitments others make to us.

Earlier today, I ordered Secretary of Defense [William J.] Perry to call up the military reserve personnel necessary to support United States troops in any action we might undertake in Haiti. I have also ordered two aircraft carriers, USS *[Dwight D.] Eisenhower* and the USS *America* into the region.

I issued these orders after giving full consideration to what is at stake. The message of the United States to the Haitian dictators is clear: Your time is up. Leave now, or we will force you from power.

I want the American people to understand the background of the situation in Haiti, how what has happened there affects our national security interests, and why I believe we must act now. Nearly 200 years ago, the Haitian people rose up out of slavery and declared their independence. Unfortunately, the promise of liberty was quickly snuffed out. And ever since, Haiti has known more suffering and repression than freedom. In our time, as democracy has spread throughout our hemisphere, Haiti has been left behind.

Then, just four years ago, the Haitian people held the first free and fair elections since their independence. They elected a parliament and a new president, Father Jean-Bertrand Aristide, a Catholic priest who received almost 70 percent of the vote. But eight months later, Haitian dreams of democracy became a nightmare of bloodshed.

Gen. Raoul Cédras led a military coup that overthrew President Aristide, the man who had appointed Cédras to lead the army. Resisters were beaten and murdered. The dictators launched a horrible intimidation campaign of rape, torture and mutilation. People starved; children died; thousands of Haitians fled their country, heading to the United States across dan-

---

> **"In the face of this continued defiance and with atrocities rising, the United States has agreed to lead a multinational force to carry out the will of the United Nations."**

---

gerous seas. At that time, President [George] Bush declared the situation posed, and I quote, an unusual and extraordinary threat to the national security, foreign policy and economy of the United States.

Cédras and his armed thugs have conducted a reign of terror. Executing children. Raping women. Killing priests. As the dictators have grown more desperate, the atrocities have grown ever more brutal. Recent news reports have documented the slaying of Haitian orphans by the nation's deadly police thugs. The dictators are said to suspect the children of harboring sympathy toward President Aristide for no other reason than he ran an orphanage in his days as a parish priest. The children fled the orphanages for the streets. Now they can't even sleep there because they're so afraid. As one young boy told a visitor, "I do not care if the police kill me because it only brings an end to my suffering."

International observers uncovered a terrifying pattern of soldiers and policemen raping the wives and daughters of suspected political dissidents. Young girls, 13 years old, 16 years old. People slain and mutilated with

body parts left as warnings to terrify others. Children forced to watch as their mothers' faces are slashed with machetes.

A year ago, the dictators assassinated the minister of justice. Just last month, they gunned down Father Jean-Marie Vincent, a peasant leader and close friend of Father Aristide. Vincent was executed on the doorstep of his home, a monastery. He refused to give up his ministry. And for that, he was murdered.

Let me be clear: Gen. Cédras and his accomplices alone are responsible for this suffering and terrible human tragedy. It is their actions that have isolated Haiti.

Neither the international community nor the United States has sought a confrontation. For nearly three years we've worked hard on diplomatic efforts. The United Nations, the Organization of American States, the Caribbean Community, the six Central American presidents all have sought a peaceful end to this crisis. We have tried everything — persuasion and negotiation, mediation and condemnation. Emissaries were dispatched to Port-au-Prince and were turned away.

The United Nations labored for months to reach an agreement acceptable to all parties. Then last year, Gen. Cédras himself came here to the United States and signed an agreement on Governors Island in New York in which he pledged to give up power, along with the other dictators.

But when the day came for the plan to take effect, the dictators refused to leave, and instead increased the brutality they are using to cling to power. Even then, the nations of the world continued to seek a peaceful solution while strengthening the embargo we had imposed. We sent massive amounts of humanitarian aid — food for a million Haitians and medicine to try to help the ordinary Haitian people as the dictators continued to loot the economy. Then this summer, they threw out the international observers who had blown the whistle on the regime's human rights atrocities.

In response to that action, in July the United Nations Security Council approved a resolution that authorizes the use of all necessary means, including force, to remove the Haitian dictators from power and restore democratic government. Still, we continue to seek a peaceful solution, but the dictators would not even meet with the United Nations special envoy. In the face

of this continued defiance and with atrocities rising, the United States has agreed to lead a multinational force to carry out the will of the United Nations.

More than 20 countries from around the globe — including almost all the Caribbean Community and nations from as far away as Poland, which has so recently won its own freedom; Israel and Jordan, which have been struggling for decades to preserve their own security; and Bangladesh, a country working for its own economic problems — have joined nations like Belgium and Great Britain. They have all agreed to join us because they think this problem in our neighborhood is important to their future interests and their security.

I know that the United States cannot — indeed, we should not — be the world's policeman. And I know that this is a time with the Cold War over that so many Americans are reluctant to commit military resources and our personnel beyond our borders. But when brutality occurs close to our shore, it affects our national interests. And we have a responsibility to act.

Thousands of Haitians have already fled toward the United States, risking their lives to escape the reign of terror. As long as Cédras rules, Haitians will continue to seek sanctuary in our nation. This year, in less than two months, more than 21,000 Haitians were rescued at sea by our Coast Guard and Navy. Today, more than 14,000 refugees are living at our naval base in Guantánamo. The American people have already expended almost $200 million to support them, to maintain the economic embargo, and the prospect of millions and millions more being spent every month for an indefinite period of time looms ahead unless we act.

Three hundred thousand more Haitians, 5 percent of their entire population, are in hiding in their own country. If we don't act, they could be the next wave of refugees at our door. We will continue to face the threat of a mass exodus of refugees and its constant threat to stability in our region and control of our borders.

No American should be surprised that the recent tide of migrants seeking refuge on our shores comes from Haiti and from Cuba. After all, they're the only nations left in the Western Hemisphere where democratic government is denied, the only countries where dictators have managed to hold back the wave of democracy and progress that has swept over our entire region, and that our own government has so actively promoted and supported for years.

Today, 33 of the 35 countries in the Americas have democratically elected leaders. And Haiti is the only nation in our hemisphere where the people actually elected their own government and chose democracy, only to have tyrants steal it away.

There's no question that the Haitian people want to embrace democracy; we know it because they went to the ballot box and told the world. History has taught us that preserving democracy in our own hemisphere strengthens America's security and prosperity. Democracies here are more

likely to keep the peace and to stabilize our region. They're more likely to create free markets and economic opportunity, and to become strong, reliable trading partners. And they're more likely to provide their own people with the opportunities that will encourage them to stay in their nation and to build their own futures.

Restoring Haiti's democratic government will help lead to more stability and prosperity in our region, just as our actions in Panama and Grenada did. Beyond the human rights violations, the immigration problems, the importance of democracy,

---

"The Haitian people should know that we come in peace. And you, the American people, should know that our soldiers will not be involved in rebuilding Haiti or its economy."

---

the United States also has strong interest in not letting dictators — especially in our own region — break their word to the United States and the United Nations.

In the post-Cold War world, we will assure the security and prosperity of the United States with our military strength, our economic power, our constant efforts to promote peace and growth. But when our national security interests are threatened, we will use diplomacy when possible and force when necessary.

In Haiti, we have a case in which the right is clear, in which the country in question is nearby, in which our own interests are plain, in which the mission is achievable and limited, and in which the nations of the world stand with us. We must act.

Our mission in Haiti, as it was in Panama and Grenada, will be limited and specific. Our plan to remove the dictators will follow two phases. First, it will remove dictators from power and restore Haiti's legitimate, democratically elected government. We will train a civilian-controlled Haitian security force that will protect the people rather than repress them. During this period, police monitors from all around the world will work with the authorities to maximize basic security and civil order and minimize retribution.

The Haitian people should know that we come in peace. And you, the American people, should know that our soldiers will not be involved in rebuilding Haiti or its economy. The international community, working together, must provide that economic, humanitarian and technical assistance necessary to help the Haitians rebuild.

When this first phase is completed, the vast majority of our troops will come home — in months, not years. I want our troops

and their families to know that we'll bring them home just as soon as we possibly can.

Then, in the second phase, a much smaller U.S. force will join forces from other members of the United Nations. And their mission will leave Haiti after elections are held next year and a new Haitian [government] takes office in early 1996.

Tonight, I can announce that President Aristide has pledged to step down when his term ends, in accordance with the constitution he has sworn to uphold. He has committed himself to promote reconciliation among all Haitians, and to set an historic example by peacefully transferring power to a duly elected successor. He knows, as we know, that when you start a democracy, the most important election is the second election.

President Aristide has told me that he will consider his mission fulfilled not when he regains office, but when he leaves office to the next democratically elected president of Haiti. He has pledged to honor the Haitian voters who put their faith in the ballot box.

In closing, let me say that I know the American people are rightfully concerned whenever our soldiers are put at risk. Our volunteer military is the world's finest, and its leaders have worked hard to minimize risks to all our forces. But the risks are there, and we must be prepared for that.

I assure you that no president makes decisions like this one without deep thought and prayer. But it's my job as president and commander in chief to take those actions that I believe will best protect our national security interests.

Let me say again, the nations of the world have tried every possible way to restore Haiti's democratic government peacefully. The dictators have rejected every possible solution. The terror, the desperation, and the instability will not end until they leave. Once again, I urge them to do so. They can still move now and reduce the chaos and disorder, increase the security, stability and the safety in which this transfer back to democracy can occur.

But if they do not leave now, the international community will act to honor our commitments; to give democracy a chance, not to guarantee it; to remove stubborn and cruel dictators, not to impose a future.

I know many people believe that we shouldn't help the Haitian people recover their democracy and find their hard-won freedoms, that the Haitians should accept the violence and repression as their fate. But remember: The same was said of a people who, more than 200 years ago, took up arms against a tyrant whose forces occupied their land. But they were a stubborn bunch, a people who fought for their freedoms and appealed to all those who believed in democracy to help their cause. And their cries were answered, and a new nation was born — a nation that, ever since, has believed that the rights of life, liberty and the pursuit of happiness should be denied to none.

May God bless the people of the United States and the cause of freedom. Good night. ■

PRESIDENTIAL NEWS CONFERENCE

Haiti Deal To Restore Democracy, Minimize Risk, Clinton Says

President Clinton announced the agreement with Haitian rulers in an address to the nation Sept. 18. Following is the official White House transcript of his remarks:

My fellow Americans, I want to announce that the military leaders of Haiti have agreed to step down from power. The dictators have recognized that it is in their best interest and in the best interest of the Haitian people to relinquish power peacefully, rather than to face imminent action by the forces of the multinational coalition we are leading.

Our objective over the last three years has been to make sure that the military dictators leave power and that the democratically elected government is returned. This agreement guarantees both those objectives. It minimizes the risks for American forces and the forces of the 24 nations of the international coalition. And the agreement maximizes the orderly transfer of power to Haiti's democratically elected government.

This is a good agreement for the United States and for Haiti. The military leaders will leave. The United States and coalition forces will arrive beginning tomorrow. And they'll do so in conditions that are less dangerous, although still not without risk. It will be much easier to preserve human rights. And there is a real chance of a more orderly and less violent transfer of power.

And to the supporters of President [Jean-Bertrand] Aristide, he will be returned. I ask that all Haitians remember what President Aristide said just a couple of days ago: no vengeance, no violence, no retribution. This is a time for peace. That is what the United States is going, along with our coalition partners, to work for.

As all of you know, at my request, President [Jimmy] Carter, Gen. Colin [L.] Powell [Jr.] and Sen. Sam Nunn [D-Ga.], went to Haiti to facilitate the dictators' departure just yesterday. I have been in constant contact with them for the last two days. They have worked tirelessly, almost around the clock. And I want to thank them for undertaking this crucial mission on behalf of all of Americans.

Just as important, I want also to thank the men and women of the United States armed forces. It was their presence and their preparations that played a pivotal part in this agreement.

Under the agreement, the dictators have agreed to leave power as soon as the Haitian Parliament passes an amnesty law, as called for by the Governors Island Agreement, but in any event, no later than Oct. 15. They've agreed to immediate in-troduction of troops from the international coalition, beginning, as I said, as early as tomorrow. They have also pledged to cooperate fully with the coalition troops during the peaceful transition of power — something we have wanted very much.

I have directed United States forces to begin deployment into Haiti as a part of the U.N. coalition. And [Lt.] Gen. [Henry H.] Shelton, our commander, will be there tomorrow. The presence of the 15,000-member multinational force will guarantee that the dictators carry out the terms of the agreement. It is clear from our discussions with the delegation that this agreement only came because of the credible and imminent threat of the multinational force. In fact, it was signed after Haiti received evidence that paratroopers from our 82nd Airborne Division, based at Fort Bragg, N.C., had begun to load up to begin the invasion, which I had ordered to start this evening. Indeed, at the time the agreement was reached, 61 American planes were already in the air.

Because of this agreement, the United States and other coalition troops going to Haiti will now be able to go under much more favorable conditions than they would have faced had the generals not decided to leave power.

But let me emphasize that this mission still has its risks, and we must be prepared for them. Haiti is still a troubled country, and there remain possibilities of violence directed at American troops. But this agreement minimizes those risks and maximizes our chance to protect the human rights of all Haitians, both those who support President Aristide and those who oppose him; and to create an environment in which President Aristide can return, as he said, without violence, without vengeance, without retribution.

Under the terms of United Nations Security [Council] Resolution 940, an international coalition from 25 nations will soon go into Haiti to begin the task of restoring democratic government. President Aristide will return to Haiti when the dictators depart.

On Thursday night I told you that the United States must act here to protect our interest, to stop the brutal atrocities that threaten tens of thousands of Haitians, to secure our borders and preserve stability and promote democracy in our hemisphere, to uphold the reliability of commitments we make to others and the commitments others make to us. This agreement furthers all these goals.

From the beginning I have said that the Haitian dictators must go; tonight I can tell you that they will go. And to our troops tonight who are headed to Haiti under less risky conditions, I am confident you will carry out your mission as you already have, effectively and professionally. We depend upon you to do well tomorrow as you have done so very well today; and in the weeks and days before, when you planned this exercise, prepared for it and then began to carry it out.

To all of you I say, thank you, your nation is proud of you. Good night, and God bless America.

Joint News Conference

On Sept. 19, Clinton, Carter, Powell and Nunn held a news conference at the White House. Following is the official transcript:

PRESIDENT CLINTON: Good morning. I'd like to begin by thanking President Carter, Gen. Powell and Sen. Nunn for their extraordinary work in Haiti. They got in very early this morning; they have had hardly any sleep for the last two nights, as they have worked virtually around the clock.

The peaceful solution they helped to work out is another major contribution in all their careers, which have been devoted to the pursuit of peace and democracy. They have done a great service to our country, as well as to the people of Haiti, the people in our hemisphere and the efforts of the United Nations, and we owe them a great deal of gratitude.

I also want to thank the men and women of our United States armed services, who are beginning their operations in Haiti even as we meet here today. Their preparation and presence made a crucial difference in convincing the Haitian leaders to leave power.

In the end, two things led to the agreement to leave. The first was this delegation's appeal to the Haitians to do the right and honorable thing for their own people in accordance with the United Nations Security Council resolutions. The second was the clear imminence of military action by the United States.

This is a good agreement. It will further our goals in Haiti. [Lt.] Gen. [Raoul] Cédras and the other leaders will leave power no later than Oct. 15. After three years and a series of broken promises, American steadfastness has given us the opportunity to restore Haiti's democratically elected government and President Aristide.

American troops are beginning to take up their positions in Haiti today, and they will be there to make sure that the leaders keep their word. The agreement means

that our troops do not have to invade. They have entered Haiti peacefully today. It minimizes the risks to American forces and to our coalition partners.

But I want to emphasize that the situation in Haiti remains difficult, it remains uncertain, the mission still has risks. But, clearly, we are in a better position to work for peace in a peaceable way today than we were yesterday.

My first concern, and the most important one, obviously, is for the safety and security of our troops. Gen. [John M.] Shalikashvili, the chairman of the Joint Chiefs, and Lt. Gen. Shelton, our commander in Haiti, have made it clear to all involved that the protection of American lives is our first order of business.

Let me repeat what I said last night and what I said on Thursday night: This mission will be limited in time and scope. It is clearly designed to provide a secure environment for the restoration of President Aristide and democracy, to begin the work of retraining the police and the military in a professional manner and to facilitate a quick handoff to the United Nations mission so that the work of restoring democracy can be continued, the developmental aid can begin to flow, Haiti can be rebuilt and, in 1995, another free and fair election for president can be held.

I also have to say again that we remain ready to pursue our interests and our obligations in whatever way we have to. But we hope that good faith and reasonableness will prevail today and tomorrow and in the days ahead so that this will not be another violated agreement that the United States has to impose and enforce. We believe that, because of the work of this delegation, we have a chance to achieve that kind of good faith and cooperation.

And I want to thank, again, President Carter, Gen. Powell and Sen. Nunn, and ask them each in turn to come and make an opening statement, and then we will be available for your questions.

PRESIDENT CARTER: Thank you, Mr. President. First of all, I want to comment on a superb balancing of the use of American military power conjunctively with a proper use of diplomacy that has defused a potential crisis that could have cost many lives.

We went to Haiti with the full support of President Clinton and with a limited objective: to carry out the mandates of the United Nations resolution, including the inexorable return of President Aristide to his office and the resignation from the offices of the three officials listed in U.N. Resolution 917.

This was a very difficult mission, but we had constant support, constant consultation with President Clinton, for which we are very grateful.

We believe that the overriding result has been the avoidance of massive bloodshed, and perhaps an extended period of occupation that could have been very troubling to our country and to the world. Instead, there is a peaceful, cooperative entry of international forces into Haiti with a mutual respect between American com-

manders and the Haitian military commanders.

I had a telephone conversation within the last five minutes from Dr. Robert Pastor, who is in the office with the military leaders of both nations. He said everything is going perfectly. I think the mutual respect with which this has been done is a notable achievement.

The final point I want to make is that we have accomplished our goals as assigned to us by our president. The international agreement that has been worked out was done over a period of not much more than 24 hours total when a lot of us hadn't had much sleep. I don't want it to be examined in the most minute detail by lawyers who can spend weeks seeing what we did in just a few minutes.

But the overwhelming point is that all of our objectives were accomplished, and all of the U.N. resolutions are being honored, and it could not have been possible without the superb respect that the Haitian military leaders have for Gen. Colin Powell. They see him as a fellow officer whose global reputation is unexcelled. And Sen. Sam Nunn brought the parliamentary approach to the discussions in their crucial stages, when a lot depended on the return of one man to Haiti — President Aristide — but Sen. Nunn made it plain that one man does not mean democracy. There has to be a national commitment to the sharing of power, and I think this was the crucial element contributed. . . .

GEN. POWELL: Thank you, Mr. President, for your kind words. It was a great honor for me to be a member of this delegation. And, Mr. President, my congratulations to you for your enormous achievement; and thank you, Mr. President, for the confidence you placed in me.

The image that we were all afraid we would see sometime this week has been avoided. And that image was of American youngsters killing Haitian youngsters, and Haitian youngsters killing American youngsters. Instead, what we see on our television screens this morning are tentative beginnings in the new relationship, where these armed forces are talking to one another. Gen. Shelton is now talking to Gen. Cédras. We have not had to do something which may have contaminated the relationship between these two countries for years, decades to come.

We were able to achieve this over the weekend by, first, having solid support from President Clinton and the members of his administration in giving us the guidance we needed; by conveying to the Haitian leaders the inevitability of the arrival of U.S. forces, and encouraging them to cooperate so that arrival would take place in a peaceful way. And I think the role that I may have played with some effect is to appeal to their sense of honor and to appeal to their sense of what is right and what is wrong at this particular point in their history.

And we had long and painful conversations, and there was a lot of emotion in the room. But we kept coming back to that point: What is best for the people of Haiti, what is best for the future of Haiti and how

can you be a part of that? And at the end of the day, that worked.

There will be many questions asked at a fairly low level, in my judgment, about details and when do they leave and who leaves and do they leave or don't they leave. All that will be worked out in due course. It was not part of our full mandate, and those questions will be resolved in due course.

But as those questions are resolved, let's not lose sight of the overall achievement. The U.N. resolutions will be executed. President Aristide will return. And we have the opportunity for a future of peace and democracy in Haiti and a superb relationship between our two countries.

But this is only Day One — not even the completion of Day One. There will be difficult times ahead. There may well be injuries and casualties; we can't guarantee anything. But we're off to an exceptionally good start. And, Mr. President, I thank you for giving me the opportunity to be a part of that.

SEN. NUNN: First, to President Clinton: Thank you, Mr. President, for your strong leadership. To President Carter and to Gen. Powell, this was a unique team. I was a very small part of it. Without President Carter's initiative, without President Carter's persistent, dogged determination to bring about peace, this could not have happened.

Without Gen. Powell's great respect with the Haitian military and the Haitian people, this could not have happened. He was able to talk straight with the military, and he was able to talk with President Carter to carry on a very sensitive and very important discussion with Mrs. [Yannick] Cédras on Sunday morning, which was an important meeting.

So, President Clinton, thank you for your strong leadership. Thank you for giving us a couple more hours to conclude this under some very difficult circumstances. I will repeat the point that I made over and over again to the Haitian leadership, and that is that returning one man, even though elected and even though he certainly should and will be returned, is not democracy.

Democracy involves institutions; democracy involves an elected parliament. I hope that the focal point of our foreign policy can be, in addition to returning President Aristide, free and fair elections of a parliament. Democracies don't work unless minorities are protected. In Haiti today, when you lose an election, there is a fear of the minority that they may lose their lives. That fear has to be dealt with through a parliamentary election and protections under the constitution with an independent judicial system.

So this is going to be the challenge ahead for the Haitian people, and I know that we will help facilitate that, President Clinton, in every way possible. Thank you.

Questions From the Media

Q: Mr. President, you accused the military leaders in Haiti of maintaining a reign of terror; you said that they were responsible for 3,000 deaths. Why did you accept an agreement that allows them to stay in Haiti and perhaps run for elected office there?

And can you tell us, is President Aristide satisfied with this agreement?

CLINTON: Well, first of all, I'm not entirely sure that they will stay in Haiti, but that was not the charge of this mission. [The U.S. delegation] only had about a day and a half to stay down there, and they worked for probably 21 or 22 hours during that time they were there. Their charge was to assure that [the military leaders] would leave power.

Secondly, I don't take back anything I say about what has happened there in the last three years, and the absence of any effort by the authorities to stop it and sometimes some direct responsibility for it. But with regard to the amnesty provision, that was a part of the Governors Island Agreement. And we had always felt that we should follow through on the agreements to which we had all been a part and that we had to demonstrate a willingness to do that.

I cannot answer all the questions that you have asked about what will happen in the future and what decisions people will make in the future and where they'll wind up living; I don't know the answers to all that. But I do believe that this agreement substantially furthers our objectives there and dramatically increases the chances of a peaceful transition of power, a peaceful restoration of democracy, a peaceful restoration of President Aristide. He will have to determine for himself what he thinks about it; but it won't be very long before he'll have the opportunity to be back in Haiti, governing as president. And it won't be very long before we'll have new parliamentary elections, which I think everyone, on all sides in Haiti, believes is a very important thing.

Lack of Congressional Approval

Q: Mr. President, granted that victory has 1,000 fathers and defeat is an orphan, but do you intend to make as a pattern using military action without the consent of Congress or the approval of the American people?

CLINTON: Well, those are two different things. And with regard to the consent of Congress, I think that every president and all my predecessors in both parties have clearly maintained that they did not require, by Constitution, did not have to have congressional approval for every kind of military action.

I obviously think the bigger and more prolonged the action, the better it is to have congressional approval. If you look at the pattern of my two immediate predecessors, there was congressional approval sought in the Desert Storm operation where there was a 5½-month buildup and a half a million troops facing hundreds of thousands of troops on the other side. There was not congressional approval in advance of the actions in Panama and Grenada. So I think that we will have to take that on a case-by-case basis.

In terms of popular approval, the American people — probably wisely — are almost always against any kind of military action when they first hear about it, unless our people have been directly attacked. And they have historically felt that way. And obviously at the end of the Cold War,

they may be more inclined to feel that way.

The job of the president is to try to do what is right, particularly in matters affecting our long-term security interests. And unfortunately not all of the decisions that are right can be popular. So I don't believe that the president, that I or any other president, could conduct foreign policy by a public opinion poll, and I would hope the American people would not wish me to.

Q: You would grant that you would have to have the support of the people in the long run for any engagement....

CLINTON: Any sustained endeavor involving our military forces requires the support of the people over the long run. We have learned that, mostly in good ways and sometimes in sad ways, in our country's history.

Expanded Negotiations

Q: Mr. President, you and your aides said repeatedly last week there was only one thing about which you would be willing to discuss anything with the leaders in Haiti, and that was the modalities, as it was repeatedly called, of their departure. As President Carter has made clear today, it became necessary for him to conduct a somewhat more extensive negotiation. And I just wanted to ask you, sir, what prompted you, what made you decide to change your mind and go along with that?

CLINTON: Well, I think if you look at this agreement, the details of the agreement are consistent with the modalities of their leaving power. What I told President Carter and Gen. Powell and Sen. Nunn was — and I think we talked three times each before they went — was that I basically did not care what was discussed as long as there was no attempt to change the timetable of the administration for action or to derail the ultimate possibility of action.

And if the objective of their departure from power was achieved, then, if other things had to be discussed, I did not object to that. In fact, it was obvious to me that one — let me just back off and say, one of the things that will determine whether this United Nations-sanctioned mission, that is, to restore democracy, is successful and one of the things that will determine whether we can do it with a minimum of risk to our people, is whether there can be an orderly transfer of power and an orderly retraining of police and military forces, rather than a total collapse of the structures of Haitian society which could cause a much more violent set of activities, perhaps involving us only peripherally. They have avoided that, I think, by the terms of this agreement if it can be implemented, which, of course, is what I hope will happen.

Q: Did President Carter say something to you that made you decide that it would be well to allow him to conduct a broader discussion? Was that his suggestion, sir?

CLINTON: No, we never — what we discussed, what I said to him was — and I said to each of the three gentlemen — was, I want you to pledge to me, No. 1, that the objective is removing them from power; No. 2, that there will be no attempt to change the

timetable on which, that I will set unilaterally for doing so forcibly if we have to; and No. 3, that there'll be no attempt to derail the possibility of taking that kind of action if it becomes necessary. Beyond that, whatever you feel you should discuss, feel free to discuss it within those three criteria.

Differences With Carter

Q: President Clinton, there have been a lot of reports that you and President Carter have had some tension in the past, and I wondered if you might comment on that. And, in particular, was there a point at which President Carter wanted to go to Haiti and the administration was not ready for him to go at that time? And was there a point when you wanted him to come home and he wasn't ready to come home? And if President Carter would comment on that as well, I'd appreciate it.

CLINTON: The answer to the first question is, no, there was not a point where he wanted to go and I didn't want him to go. The answer to the second question is, maybe, but not for the reason you think. And let me try to answer what I mean by that.

President Carter and I have discussed Haiti, I think, beginning before I became president on a regular and repeated basis. And he has a deep interest there because, among other things, he's not only been there many times, but he and his group monitored the election which resulted in President Aristide's election.

I have also discussed Haiti repeatedly with Gen. Powell, both when he was the chairman of the Joint Chiefs of Staff in my tenure and after he left office. I have called him at least two and maybe more occasions and said, "I'm tearing my hair out about this problem; what do you think? What about this, that or the other thing?" And Sen. Nunn and I have discussed it before.

When President Carter called me and told me that he had heard from Gen. Cédras, we began to talk about this and about the prospect of a mission. We talked about Gen. Powell, Sen. Nunn. I picked up the phone, and I called Gen. Powell and Sen. Nunn to find out if they would be willing to go there. It wasn't the first item on the list of what they had planned to do last weekend, but they were open.

A number of other calls ensued. We had to determine, A, that they would be received, and B, that there was a serious chance of at least affecting this agreement, because there was no agreement in advance by them — by the Haitians — to leave.

Once all that was worked out, we decided it was quite a good thing and certainly worth the risk for them to go. Any kind of mission like this is full of risk.

In answer to your second question, there was never a point when I wanted him to leave in the sense that I wanted him to stop talking. There was a point last evening, as you know, when I became worried that we needed to get them out of there because of the timetable of the mission. In other words, I was just beginning — I was concerned about — I wanted them to be

safe, I wanted them to be secure, I wanted them to be out of Haiti in a timely fashion. That is the only issue about their leaving.

And the last time we talked, he said, "Well, we're almost there. We've about got this nailed. We're going over to the presidential palace." And I said, "OK, you have 30 more minutes, and then I will have to order you to leave," because I was worried about their personal security. There was no political debate at all. They were making progress. But the time was running out on the hourglass.

Q: Mr. President, President Carter was quoted today as saying that the launching of the first wave came while they were still negotiating peace. And he said that that was very disturbing to us and to them — to the Haitian leaders with whom he was negotiating.

Could I ask both of you to comment on that and whether you felt that the launching of the 82nd Airborne was, in fact, interfering with their attempts to negotiate? . . .

CARTER: The key to our success, to the extent it is successful, was the inexorability of the entry of the forces into Haiti. And we spent the first hours of discussion with the military leaders to convince them that this was going to happen, it would be with an overwhelming capability, and that the schedule was set, and that we had no intention or authority to change the schedule. And it was that inevitability that was a major factor in that decision.

Another one, I should hasten to say, was their quandary about what to do that was right and honorable. Haiti is one of the — I think is perhaps one of the proudest nations I have ever seen because of their long history and because of the turmoil in which they have often lived. And it was very difficult for Haitian military commanders to accept the proposition that foreign forces could come on their soil without their fighting. But we all worked to convince them that this was the best thing to do for their country and for their people.

Now, we recognized the difficulty of this. And we were down to the last stages of negotiating, which involved the last date that the military leaders could stay in office. At that time, [Brig.] Gen. [Philippe] Biamby received a report from Fort Bragg, he told us, that the initial operation had already commenced. And they were on the verge of saying, "We will not negotiate anymore; this may be a trick just to keep us occupied, all of us military commanders in the same room while the invasion takes place."

We obviously assured them this was not the case. And the thing was about to break down. They finally decided, let's go over to the president's house, the presidential palace. President [Emil] Jonassaint, we have been led to believe — . . . and I believed it ahead of time, was a figurehead. This proved to be absolutely incorrect. When we got to President Jonassaint's office with his ministers sitting in front of him and the commanders of the military in front of him and I sitting next to him and Sen. Nunn and Gen. Powell there, he said — very quickly to summarize my answer — we will take peace instead of war; I will sign this agreement.

All of his people in the room disagreed. One of his ministers, a minister of defense, said, "I resign tomorrow." The others belabored the point. But there was no doubt that his decision was what brought about the consummation of the agreement.

All the time through this, we were consulting fervently and constantly with President Clinton.

So the inextricability of the force coming in made it possible. There was a setback when we found, to my surprise, that the initial stages had begun as soon as President Clinton knew that President Jonassaint and I had reached an agreement. So as far as I know, the planes reversed their course.

Q: Did he ask you why they had taken off and asked you to turn them back?

CLINTON: No. No, when they went, I told them that we needed to conclude the negotiations by 12 p.m. Sunday. Then I said that they could clearly stay until 3 p.m. And then the thing kept getting put back. They were very dogged; they didn't want to give up.

I frankly had come to the conclusion that we were not going to reach an agreement. What I — and let me say, there had never been a plan to have them talking while American planes were flying. That was never a plan. The inference — because I wanted them out of there, I wanted them safe. And I think President Carter has made it clear what — to the extent that it was disrupted, it was because they thought the whole thing maybe had been pointless, a ruse.

To the extent it was helpful, it was the final evidence that President Jonassaint needed to push the agreements. But it was one of those things that happened. It was not a thing that we calculated, because I would never have put the lives of these three men in any kind of jeopardy. They were just determined to stay until the last moment. And they had — literally, when they reached that agreement — they had 30 more minutes before I — I told President Carter, I said, this is uncomfortable for me; we've been friends a long time; I'm going to have to order you out of there in 30 more minutes. You have got to get out. They had to get out before dark. So they worked it out.

Departure of Cédras

Q: Mr. President, there still is this very sensitive issue, as you well know, involving the so-called status of exile for Gens. Biamby and Cédras. They maintain that there is no commitment, no need and that they don't want to leave their country forever.

Now, a senior administration official last night suggested that while there is no formal commitment, the U.S. anticipates that they will leave once President Aristide returns and they do receive amnesty. What exactly do you believe will happen?

CLINTON: First, let me say that our objective is twofold as a part of restoring democracy and President Aristide. The first was to have the step-down. The second is to retrain and to help professionalize the army and the police forces so that they can never be either a participant in or a bystander while gross human rights violations occur and so that they can help to secure the country and preserve order.

It has been our feeling that that was the most important thing. And, therefore, that was not an issue that I was ready to let this mission founder on, as long as they could achieve that. I think they should leave, and I think they probably will leave at some point. But that is something that still has to be worked out, and something that subsequent actions by all the actors in the Haitian drama will have to be heavily relied upon.

Gen. Powell made a comment to me — he might want to comment about this — because I think it's very important that we not let this issue cloud the enormity of what has occurred and the practicality of what is likely to occur.

POWELL: I'd just like to add to that, that I am very pleased this morning — the thing I was looking for — would Gen. Cédras be cooperating with Gen. Shelton for real? Signing an agreement last night was one thing, but what would happen today? He is cooperating. And so the transition of power has begun. And sometime over the next month or so, either as a result of parliamentary action or the Oct. 15 date arriving, Gen. Cédras will step down, having done what I believe is the right and honorable thing in these circumstances.

It will remain an issue for President Aristide and Gen. Cédras and others to consider where he should go or what he should do. But I don't think we need to spend a lot of time on that at this point. Let that flow out, and we will see what happens. He is stepping down from power, which I think is the important point.

Q: Last week you told America that these people treated their own people shamefully, that they've massacred them and raped them and tortured them, and did all these frightful things. And now, all of a sudden, we've appealed to their military honor. I wonder how you detected that, and they're our partners and presumably our friends. It's a little. . . .

CLINTON: No, that's not accurate. But we did say, I did say last week that they had one last chance to effect a peaceful transfer of power. And, you know, when you've got a country deeply divided, I mean, think of the things which have happened in South Africa when reconciliation was possible.

Remember what President Aristide himself said when he came here — after I spoke — the next day — he said we have to say no to violence, no to vengeance, yes to reconciliation. What this delegation did, and all this delegation did, was to give these people the chance to do something that is — to use their words — was right and honorable; and to do it in a peaceful way and to have a peaceful transfer of power. And I think that was an appropriate thing to do. In terms of the amnesty issue, I would remind you that was an issue raised and agreed to by all the parties in Governors Island. So that is something that has been on the board for quite a long while now. Thank you very much. ∎

PRESIDENTIAL NEWS CONFERENCE

Clinton Reaches Out to GOP, Assesses Voters' Message

President Clinton discussed the results of the elections at a White House news conference Nov. 9. Following are excerpts from the official transcript:

PRESIDENT CLINTON: Ladies and gentlemen, last night and again this morning I spoke with both Republicans and Democrats to congratulate those who won and console those who lost their elections. I also called the leaders of the next Congress, Senator [Bob] Dole [R-Kan.] and Congressman [Newt] Gingrich [R-Ga.], to tell them after this hard-fought campaign that we are ready to work together to serve all the American people in a nonpartisan manner.

The American people sent us here to rebuild the American Dream, to change the way Washington does business to make our country work for ordinary citizens again. We've made a good start by cutting the deficit, by reducing the size of the federal government, by reinventing much of our government to do more with less. We have increased our investment in education and expanded trade, and our economy has created more than 5 million jobs.

We've also made a serious start in the fight against the terrible plague of crime and violence in this country. I remain committed to completing the work we have done. Still, in the course of this work, there has been too much politics, as usual, in Washington; too much partisan conflicts; too little reform of Congress and the political process. And though we have made progress, not enough people have felt more prosperous and more secure, or believe we were meeting their desires for fundamental change in the role of government in their lives.

With the Democrats in control of both the White House and the Congress, we were held accountable yesterday. And I accept my share of the responsibility in the result of the elections.

When the Republican Party assumes leadership in the House and in the Senate, they will also have a larger responsibility for acting in the best interest of the American people. I reach out to them today, and I ask them to join me in this center of the public debate where the best ideas for the next generation of American progress must come.

Democrats and Republicans have often joined together when it was clearly in the national interest. For example, they have often chosen to put international affairs above politics. I urge them to do so again by passing the GATT [General Agreement on Tariffs and Trade] agreement this year. Our prosperity depends

upon it, and there can be no compromise when the national interest and the livelihood of American households are at stake.

Last night the voters not only voted for sweeping changes, they demanded that a more equally divided Congress work more closely together with the president for the interest of all the American people. So I hope that we can do that on GATT, and that by doing so, we will pave the way for further cooperation on welfare reform and on health care reform, on a continued investment in our people's educational opportunities, and the continued strength of our economy.

We must also take more steps to restore the people's faith in our political institutions, and agree that, further, in the best tradition of our own foreign policy, that politics will continue to stop at the water's edge.

To those who believe we must keep moving forward, I want to say again, I will do everything in my power to reach out to the leaders and the members of this new Congress. It must be possible to make it a more effective, more functioning institution. It must be possible for us to give our people a government that is smaller, that is more effective, that reflects both our interests and our values.

But to those who would use this election to turn us back, let me say this: I will do all in my power to keep anyone from jeopardizing this economic recovery by taking us back to the policies that failed us before. I will still work for those things that make America strong — strong families, better education, safer streets, more high-paying jobs, a more prosperous and peaceful world.

There is too much at stake for our children and our future to do anything else. Well, a lot has changed since yesterday. But what hasn't changed is the reason I was sent here and the reason the members of the Congress will be sent here — to restore the American Dream and to make this country work, this government work, this city work for the interest of ordinary Americans again. That is what the American people expect of us.

Last night, they said they were not satisfied with the progress we had made. They said the Democrats had been in control of the White House and the Congress. They said they were going to make a change, and they did make a change. But they still want the same goal. I pledge today to work with all the members of the Congress, and especially the new Republican leadership, to achieve that goal. If they will work with me, and they have pledged to do so today, then we can make great progress for this country. We should be

optimistic, and we should work to make that optimism real.

Questions

Q: Yesterday not a single Republican incumbent lost in any race for governor, House or Senate, while the Democratic Party, your party, suffered its worst losses for decades. Do you view this as a repudiation of you, or is there another common denominator in this election that we're missing?

P: Well, I think that I have some responsibility for it. I'm the president. I am the leader of the efforts that we have made in the last two years. And to whatever extent that we didn't do what the people wanted us to do, or they were not aware of what we had done, I must certainly bear my share of responsibility, and I accept that. . . . [W]hat I think they said is, they still don't like what they see when they watch us working here. They still haven't felt the positive results of things that have been done here that they agree with when they hear about them, but they don't feel them. They're still not sure that we understand what they expect the role of government to be.

I think they want a smaller government that gives them better value for their dollar, that reflects both their interest and their values, that is not a burden to them, but empowers them. That's what I have tried to do, but I don't think they believe we're there yet — by a long shot. They want us to do more.

I went back today and read my announcement speech for president, and I said in that speech that the job of government was to create opportunity and then to expect citizens to assume the responsibility to make the most of that opportunity. I think that's about where the American people are. They don't think we've done that yet.

And the only thing I think they knew to do yesterday was to try to make a change in the people who were in control and who had been. I regret that some of the people who lost are people who made this a lot better country and who will always, when the history books are written, get the credit they deserve, with hindsight, for helping to make the American people more secure.

I don't believe the American people were saying we're sorry the deficit has been reduced; we're sorry the size of government has been reduced; and we're sorry you've taken the tough stand on crime; we're sorry you're expanding trade. I don't believe that. I don't think they were disagreeing with a lot of the specifics. I do think they still just don't like it when they watch what we do up here, and they haven't felt the positive impact of what

has been done. And since I'm the president, I have to take some responsibility for that.

Clinton's Standing

Q: Would you have survived if you had been on the ballot yesterday?

P: Well, some Democrats did. I like to think I would have because I believe that I would have been a ferocious defender of what we have done, and I hope that I could have characterized what the choices were. But I don't know that, and neither does anybody else.

I think it's important to say that yesterday's election, like every election, was fundamentally about the American people. And they looked at us and they said, we want some more changes, and we're going to try this and see if this works. There is a lot of evidence — I've read it in a lot of your reporting — that the American people believe, a majority of them, and have believed for decades now that divided government may work better than united government. As you know, I disagree with that — why I did my best to make it work the other way.

But they didn't agree, and they're in charge. We all work for them, every one of us. And their will, their voice was heard. We got the message. And now we have to think about it, analyze it, rest up and move on. But this country is facing its problems. And what I think they told us was, look, two years ago we made one change; now we made another change. We want you to keep on moving this country forward, and we want you to accelerate the pace of change in the areas that I mentioned.

I do not believe they voted for reversals of economic policy or the positions on crime. I don't think they voted for a reversal of the Brady bill or the military assault weapons ban. I don't believe that. So — but I do think they sent us a message, and I tried to hear it. And we're going to work together and do the best we can.

Q: What do you think this does for your expected bid for re-election, and how will you deal with [the "Contract With America"] if there are proposed cuts to Social Security, Medicare, veterans' benefits, the whole nine yards?

P: Well, first of all, we've got plenty of time to worry about the next election. . . . I think we should think about the people, their interests. I think we should say, what message were they sending us and what are we going to do about it and how can we pull this country together. How can the Democrats and the Republicans in the Congress and the White House and the Republican leadership work together in a nonpartisan way to push this country forward.

Now, on the contract, as I said specifically in Cleveland and elsewhere, there are some things in that contract that I like. I hope the Congress will give me the line-item veto and do it quickly. If they do, we'll bring this deficit down even more quickly. I hope that we will have aggressive efforts to work together on welfare reform. I hope we will be able to still reduce several areas of federal spending and continue this whole reinventing

government effort to do more with less.

The issue in the contract is what it has always been. I do not believe that we can afford to go back to the days of exploding deficits, which I believe would lead to a weaker economy, to lost jobs and to a more difficult future for ourselves and for our children. So the question there is, how will all of this be paid for?

I do not believe — now many Republicans in the campaign said they do not believe — that we should cut Social Security or Medicare. So if we can't cut Social Security or Medicare, if we must maintain the world's strongest defense — which I think the Republican leadership and I are strongly in agreement on — then what else are we going to do? And that will be a challenge. But, you know, give them a chance. They've got to enjoy their victory today. Give them a day or so to enjoy their victory, and don't push them too far in the future — they will come to grips with that I'm sure.

Republican Agenda

Q: Are you going to be able to compromise with them on that?

P: Well, I'm not going to compromise on my convictions. . . . We are stronger today, but we have more strength to get. . . . I'll say again what I think makes our country strong — strong families, better education, safer streets, more high paying jobs, a government that reflects their values and the interest of the American people, and work to make a world that's more prosperous and more peaceful. Those are the principles on which I do not intend to compromise.

But I want to work with them. Look, let me give you one example. I have always wanted to make the tax code more fair. The tax code is more fair today than it was when I took office. We did cut income tax rates for families with incomes of up to $27,000. They want to go further than that. I would like to go further than that. The question is, how far can we go? Can we focus on working families with children? How are we going to pay for it? We have to answer now the details. And in large measure, that is a question that can only be answered by some sort of partnership and by getting their views. . . .

Smaller Government

Q: Mr. President, if one of the signal messages of yesterday is that Americans want smaller government, how much smaller do they want it, and what can you do to shrink it?

P: Well, we're shrinking it already. One thing we can do —

Q: What can you do that you haven't done already to shrink it?

P: Well, I think it's important, though — let me put the record out. All we have to do is to stay with the present six-year plan, and we will reduce the size of government by 272,000. We have already passed major laws to deregulate banking and interstate trucking. We have already given 20 states total freedom from federal regulations to pursue their welfare reform experiments, and about nine states freedom to pursue their health care experiments. And the

education bill cuts a lot of federal strings that are tied to the states to improve the performance of children in the schools.

So what I think we have to do is to look at every single government department, every single government program and especially the nature of government regulation and ask ourselves: Is there a better way to do this? Is this something where the American people will think we're more of a burden than a help? Is there a way to give more flexibility to people at the state and local level and in private life to achieve the same goal?

We're going to have to continue, in other words, to review everything that this government does. And I think that there are more things that can be done. I'm going to propose them. I encourage the Republicans in Congress to propose them and the Democrats in Congress to propose them. I think that this is — we're in the middle of a revolution here in the way organizations work in America and the world, and the government is still behind the eight ball, and we're going to have to keep pushing until people believe that they have a government that works for them, that they have confidence in and that they think gives them good value for their dollar, and it doesn't overreach where they think it shouldn't overreach. . . .

Q: Even before you ran for president, you had an idea of where the Democratic Party had to go to reclaim the center and become a majority again. Now that your party is a minority in Congress and in the statehouses, what do Democrats have to do to avoid becoming a permanent minority party?

P: . . . Sometimes in life, you have to be in the minority, because you just cannot, in good conscience, go along with what's popular. Sometimes that happens. I really regret the loss of some of these fine young progressive members of Congress who clearly are in the mainstream of their views to the people back home, because they could not defend themselves against either the efforts of certain groups on votes like the crime bill, or because they couldn't find a way to convince the majority of their constituents that when they voted for that economic plan it would bring the deficit down; it was a sacrifice worth making; it will make the country stronger. I regret that.

But I think we have to analyze the results of the elections, hear what the voters were saying, and go back to them and say: We believe that the government is not inherently bad. We agree that the government needs to be smaller and more efficient. We believe it needs to reflect our values as well as our interests. And we believe that we have more to offer in that regard, and here is what it is, and here is what the distinctions are.

That, I think, was the work that we have been trying to do for 10 years. I believe that a lot of these things that we saw yesterday were the culmination of many years of trends, as well as a dissatisfaction with the last two years. And I think that we have an opportunity now to go back and capture the imagination of the American people with good ideas consistent with democratic values. ■

GOP ELECTION VICTORY

New House Speaker Envisions Cooperation, Cuts, Hard Work

House Republican Whip Newt Gingrich of Georgia, who became Speaker in January 1995, outlined his view of the GOP election mandate in a speech to the Washington Research Symposium on Nov. 11. Following are excerpts from the speech, provided by the Federal News Service:

GINGRICH: ... Let me say first of all that in a way that is peculiarly fitting, 76 years today the armistice was declared at the 11th hour of the 11th day of the 11th month in what was then called the Great War. In an indirect way, that had an enormous impact on my life, because it was while my dad was stationed with the Army in Europe and I was a 14-year-old freshman in high school that we went to the battlefield in Verdun, which was the largest battlefield in the Western front of that war, and spent a weekend with a friend of his who had been on a death march in the Philippines and served three years in a Japanese prison camp. The Great War was both an example of what happens when leadership fails and societies collide, and it was an example in its aftermath of what happens when people lie to themselves about the objective realities of the human condition, because instead of leading to world peace as [President] Woodrow Wilson had so devoutly hoped, it, in fact, ultimately led to the second world war. And instead of leading to greater freedom for all human beings, as Woodrow Wilson's 14 Points had hoped, it led to Nazism and the Soviet empire, the gulag and Auschwitz.

And so it is both good for us today to remember the cost paid by those who believe[d] enough in freedom to have died for it and useful to remind ourselves that that price has to be paid every year and every week, and that it is better by far to pay that price in peacetime by being vigilant and by trying to do that which is right than it is to allow your society to decay or to have inadequate leadership and drift into a cataclysm comparable to the first and second world wars.

And that's not just a foreign policy or national defense battle cry. I think it's important to recognize that what is ultimately at stake in our current environment is literally the future of American civilization as it has existed for the last several hundred years. I'm a history teacher by background, and I would assert and defend on any campus in this country that it is impossible to maintain civilization with 12-year-olds having babies, with 15-year-olds killing each other, with 17-year-olds dying of AIDS and with 18-year-olds ending up with diplomas they can't even read. And that what is at issue is literally not

Republican or Democrat or liberal or conservative, but the question of whether or not our civilization will survive.

News Coverage

Now, I've been sort of intrigued by the press coverage since the election on a couple of levels. First of all, I think the article which has most accurately captured the essence of what just happened is Charles Krauthammer's column this morning in The Washington Post, which makes the correct point that you have the most explicitly ideologically committed House Republican Party in modern history. That we held an event [the Sept. 27 unveiling of the Republican "Contract With America"] on the Capitol steps that 330 members signed or candidates signed up for. That we told the country in a full-page ad in TV Guide where we were going and the direction we would take. That the president and [former Democratic Rep.] Tony Coelho took up the challenge. That the Democratic National Committee ran $2 million [worth] of ads attacking the contract. That the president personally attacked the contract virtually everywhere he went. And that in the end, there was the most shatteringly one-sided Republican victory since 1946.

Now, there's been an enormous effort in the Washington elite to avoid the reality that this lesson was actually about some fairly big ideas — Which direction do you want to go in? — and that those who argued for counterculture values, bigger government, redistributionist economics and bureaucracies deciding how you should spend your money were on the losing end in virtually every part of the country.

When in Georgia we elect five statewide officials, we have a majority 7-to-4 in the House delegation, there may be something that's a message. And you can either say, well, but that's those Southern Christian religious groups. Fine. In Washington state we went from 7-to-1 Democrat to 6-to-1 Republican. You can hardly argue that it's that Southern fundamentalism that swept Washington state. And yet I've seen talk shows where learned experts who were totally wrong a week ago are equally wrong now.

I was reminded of [Newsweek columnist] Meg Greenfield's wonderful essay about a year ago: that it's amazing how often we can watch experts who had no idea what was about to happen explain to us afterwards what it meant. And part of the problem is stereotyping.

Let me discuss several stereotypes that I think are very important — or several things that break out of the stereotype.

And let me suggest to all of you that part of our problem is the level at which we think. And those of you who were here when I last spoke here will recognize part of this.

I use a planning model and a leadership model that [are] very explicit. The planning model is derived from how [Gen.] George [C.] Marshall and Dwight [D.] Eisenhower and Franklin [D.] Roosevelt managed World War II, which is the most complex, large human activity ever undertaken. And essentially they had a four-layer model, and it's a hierarchy. The top of it was vision, and after you understood your vision of what you're doing you design strategies, and once you have your vision and strategies clear, you design projects which were the building blocks of your strategies. And inside the context of those projects, you delegated dramatically an entrepreneurial model in which a project was a definable, delegatable achievement. Eisenhower's job was to invade the continent of Europe, defeat the German army and occupy the German heartland. His actual order from the combined chiefs is two paragraphs, all the rest was detail. That's delegation on a fairly grand scale.

At the bottom of the model is tactics, what do you do every day.

This is a city so consumed in its own tactical self-amusement that it's very hard for the city to have any sense of projects, and the concept of vision and strategies is almost beyond its comprehension. So I want to bring you back to that model in just a moment.

The second model I follow fairly rigorously is a leadership model that is four words that are a process. That is they're not a hierarchy, all the words are equally important, but there's a sequence that matters. It's a very direct sequence: Listen, learn, help and lead. You listen to the American people, you learn from the American people, you help the American people; and in a rational society, if people know you'll listen to them, learn from them and help them, they want you to lead them.

So the job of a leader is first of all to think about things, develop a vision and strategies and projects and tactics, and then go back out and listen to the people and find out whether or not in fact they're on the same wavelength. And if not, to assume that there's at least a better than even chance that it is the people and not [the] elite who are right.

That's a very specific model. You may disagree with it or not like it, but it's a very specific motto; and if you want to understand what the next Speaker of the House is going to function like, it's a model that will in fact be fairly predictive.

Now, I find just a couple of examples —

I want to cite three of them. First of all, it's very hard for the Washington elite to come to grips with the reality that there's now a national Republican Party, and that's the biggest single message of this election. That for the first time in history, the Civil War, in effect, is over, and Republicans were able to run everywhere simultaneously. And, standing on [former President] Ronald Reagan's shoulders, the Republican Party now has enough recruits and enough resources and enough leaders to actually be capable of running everywhere. And it was literally the first election in history where there were fewer Democrats without opposition than Republicans. We had more Republicans running unopposed for the House this year than there were Democrats. That has never, ever, in the history of the two parties, for 140 years, been true. And, we won, which would make it even more historic.

So the first point I would argue is this was clearly a historic election, which clearly had a mandate. And that's outside the Washington elite's view, and they don't want to believe that, because it's not the mandate they wanted.

Second, I want to draw a distinction between two words, because we're going to get into a lot of confusion at the vision level about these two words. I am very prepared to co-operate with the Clinton administration. I am not prepared to compromise. The two words are very different. On everything on which we can find agreement, I will cooperate.

On those things that are at the core of our contract, those things which are at the core of our philosophy, and on those things where we believe we represent the vast majority of Americans, there will be no compromise. So let me draw the distinction: Cooperation, yes; compromise, no.

Third, . . . [p]eople have been trying to figure out how to put me in a box, and it's very hard because I don't fit boxes very well. Probably — and therefore, I must either be a hypocrite or I must be doing — you know, if you watch the Washington press coverage, some of it just verges on bizarre. The best description of me is that I'm a conservative futurist. [My wife] Marianne and I have for a long time been friends with Alvin and Heidi Toffler, the authors of "Future Shock" and "The Third Wave." We really believe it's useful to think about the 21st century. On the other hand, I believe the most powerful single doctrine for the leadership of human beings and for their opportunity to pursue happiness is The Federalist papers, [Alexis] de Tocqueville's travels in — "Democracy in America," the Declaration of Independence and the Constitution.

So on the one hand, I recommend to all the congressional staffs, buy [Peter F.] Drucker's "The Effective Executive," study [William Edwards] Deming's concepts of quality, look at [The New Perspective, a fortnightly from Carroll College in Waukesha, Wis.] and [International] Freedom Foundation's report on Alvin Toffler's works, and that will help you in one direction. On the other direction, I suggest to them: Immerse yourself in the Founding Fathers. These peo-

ple thought a long time about the nature of being human, about the problems of power, about how to organize a free society so it could sustain freedom. And if you can combine the two, you can begin to create an opportunity for every American to participate in ways that will prove to be quite remarkable.

Now, that obviously doesn't fit anybody's current word processor. I mean, there's no, you know, "Newt Gingrich, conservative futurist." It doesn't exist yet. Therefore, it has to be something else, and so they keep trying to say, "Well, are you going back to the '80s?" Or "Are you doing this," or "Are you doing" — no. I mean, we're in fact trying to get to the 21st century, and we want to do so in a way that's very effective.

The Five Large Changes

There are five large changes we have to go through. I will be teaching a course called "Renewing American Civilization" at Reinhardt College [in Waleska, Ga.] in January which is designed to outline these changes in some detail.

It takes about 20 hours. I obviously am not going to give them to you today. But I want to just describe the five changes very briefly to give you a taste of what they are because I think they're central to everything that will be organizing our activities over the next two years.

First, we have to accelerate the transition from a second-wave mechanical, bureaucratic society to a third-wave information society, to use Alvin Toffler's model. Two simple examples: One, imagine the speed and ease with which you use a bank teller card anywhere on the planet and electronically verify your account and get money and then call the federal government about a case. There's no objective reason that institutions of government have to be two or three generations behind the curve in information systems and management, but they are. And that means, for example, if we're really serious about distance medicine and about distance learning and about distance work, we could revolutionize the quality of life in rural America and create the greatest explosion of new opportunity for rural America ever in history. And yet, we're currently moving in the opposite direction, so that at a time when the IRS should be making it easier to have a home office, they make it harder. Now that's foolish. It's exactly the wrong direction.

Second, the second example I'll give you is, we will change the rules of the House to require that all documents and all conference reports and all committee reports be filed electronically as well as in writing and that they cannot be filed until they are available to any citizen who wants to pull them up simultaneously so that information is available to every citizen in the country at the same moment that it is available to the highest paid Washington lobbyist. That will change over time the entire flow of information and the entire quality of knowledge in the country, and it will change the way people will try to play games in the legislative process.

The second big change is to recognize

the objective reality of the world market, to realize that we create American jobs through world sales and to make a conscious national decision that we want to have the highest value-added jobs on the planet with greatest productivity so we can have the highest take-home pay and the greatest range of choices in lifestyles. In order to do that we have to literally rethink the assumptions that grew up in a self-indulgent national economy, and they have to recognize that litigation, taxation, regulation, welfare, education, the very structure of government, the structure of health — all those things have to be re-examined from the standpoint of what will make us the most competitive society on the planet, the most desirable place to invest to create jobs and the place with the best-trained and most entrepreneurial work force, most committed to Deming's concepts of quality.

Now that's a big challenge. One step, frankly, has to be that every child in America should be required to do at least two hours of homework a night, or they're being cheated for the rest of their lives in their ability to compete with the Germans and the Japanese and the Chinese. Now, one of the differences I would suggest between where we are going and where our friends on the left would go, is I do not derive from that a belief that we need a federal department of homework checkers. I believe that we should say to every parent in the country, "Your child ought to be doing two hours of homework. If they're not, go see the teacher. If you can't convince the teacher, get a better teacher, and in the interim assign it yourself." I was taught to read by my grandmother. Gen. George Marshall was taught to read by his aunt. I mean the objective fact is, historically, this was a country that got the job done, not a country that found scapegoats for the failure. And so we've simply got to reassert — and it's a topic I'll come back to — a level of civic responsibility we're not used to.

Third, we have to replace the welfare state with an opportunity society. Let me be very explicit. It is impossible to take the Great Society structure of bureaucracy, the redistributionist model of how wealth is acquired and the counterculture value system that now permeates the way we deal with the poor, and have any hope of fixing them. They are a disaster. They ruin the poor; they create a culture of poverty and a culture of violence which is destructive of this civilization; and they have to be replaced thoroughly from the ground up.

Now, that should be done in cooperation with the poor. The people who have the most to gain from eliminating the culture of poverty and replacing it with a culture of productivity are the people currently trapped in a nightmare, living in public housing projects with no one going to work, living in neighborhoods with no physical safety, their children forced to walk into buildings where there will be no learning, and living in a community where taxes and red tape and regulation destroy their hope of creating new entrepreneurial small businesses and doing what ev-

ery other generation of poor Americans have done, which is to leave poverty behind by acquiring productivity.

Now we simply need to reach out and erase the slate and start over, and we need to start with the premise that every American is endowed by their Creator with certain inalienable rights, among which are life, liberty and the pursuit of happiness, and that extends to the poorest child in Washington, D.C., and the poorest child in West Virginia, and the poorest child [on] American Indian reservations. And we have been failing all of them because we have lacked the courage to be mentally tough enough to get the job done, and I think it can be done, but I think it's very deep and very bold change.

Fourth, we have to recognize that American exceptionalism — to use [political science educator and author] Everett Carll Ladd's phrase — is real; that this has been the most successful civilization in the history of the human race at liberating people to pursue happiness. I think that's an objective fact. There is no other society in history where as many people from as many cultures speaking as many languages could come together and become a nation, and where they could then be liberated to go off and be who they wanted to be. This is a country where [retired Gen.] Colin [L.] Powell [Jr.] and [Gen.] John [M.] Shalikashvili can both be chairman of the Joint Chiefs and nobody even thinks about the remarkable difference in ethnicity because they're Americans, and that's the way it should be.

And that means we have to say to the counterculture: Nice try, you failed, you're wrong. And we have to simply, calmly, methodically reassert American civilization and re-establish the conditions, which I believe starts with the work ethic. You cannot study 300 years of American civilization without coming to the conclusion that working and being expected to work and being involved — and work may be for money or it may be at home, it may be a hobby that you pursue, but the sense of energy, the pursuit of happiness, which is not — it's an active verb — not happiness stamps, not a department of happiness, not therapy for happiness. Pursuit. This is also a muscular society, and we've been kidding ourselves about it. The New Hampshire slogan is, "Live free or die." It is not "Live free or whine." And so we have to think through what are the deeper underlying cultural meanings of being American and how do we reassert them.

Lastly, and this is one where I, frankly, became more radical all fall. . . . [L]et me tell all of you flatly, the long experiment in professional politicians and professional government is over, and it failed. You cannot hire a teacher to teach your child and walk off and then blame the teacher. You cannot hire a policeman to protect your neighborhood and then walk off and blame the police. You cannot hire a public health service to protect your health and then walk off and blame the public health service. . . .

Now, this means that my challenge to the American people is real simple. You really want to dramatically reduce power in

Washington? You have to be willing to take more responsibility back home. You really want to reduce the bureaucracy of the welfare state? You have to accept greater responsibility back home. We are going to have to be partners. . . .

[The GOP House candidates and members who signed the "Contract With America"] basically said, "Look, we are a team; we are going to go in a dramatically different direction; we're going to give you eight reforms on the opening day, starting with the Shays Act, which will apply to the Congress every law it applies to the rest of the country so congressmen will learn all the problems they've imposed on everybody else."

Cuts and the 'Contract' Ahead

We are going to cut the number of congressional committee staffs by a third, and we sent a letter to that effect to Speaker [Thomas S.] Foley [D-Wash.] on Wednesday, frankly in order to allow the Democratic staff to know that a substantial number of them ought to be looking for jobs, because we thought that was the most decent and most correct way to deal with it. We are going to cut the number of congressional committees. We are going to eliminate the current services budget and replace it with a straight line budget, where if you have a dollar increase it counts as a dollar increase. This is the only place in the world where you can increase spending massively, and it counts as a cut. And it has been a major source of the problem of dealing with the deficit because you create a linguistic barrier to honesty. And so we're simply going to eliminate it. You're not going to get a current services budget in this Congress — not on the House side.

Now, at the end of the opening day, we will introduce the 10 bills we described in the contract. It was printed in TV Guide. We will read the contract as the opening item of business every day for the first 100 days, and at the end of the first 100 days, the American people, at Easter, will be able to say they saw a group of people who actually said what they were going to do and then kept their word. Now, we don't guarantee we'll pass all 10, and it's very clear in the contract that what — some of these are very controversial — litigation reform, including malpractice, product liability and strike law firms is one item; a balanced-budget amendment to the Constitution; a vote on term limits; an effective, enforceable death penalty with a one-time unified appeal; beginning to phase out the marriage penalty in the tax code; allowing senior citizens to earn up to $39,000 a year without penalty from Social Security; a capital gains cut and indexing. These are not small things, but they are the right direction. Welfare reform, emphasizing work and family. A line-item veto, including frankly, a line-item veto for this president, so that we as Republican conservatives are prepared to give to President Clinton a line-item veto because we think it's right for America. Now, they're real changes; it's going to be real hard to do, and it's going to take a lot of people helping.

Let me say one last thing. If this just degenerates after an historic election back

into the usual baloney of politics in Washington and pettiness in Washington, then the American people I believe will move towards a third party in a massive way. I think they are fed up with this city; they are fed up with its games; they are fed up with petty partisanship. I don't think they mind grand partisanship, and there's a big difference. To have a profound disagreement over the direction of your country or over the principles by which your economy works or over the manner in which your government should structure resources, that is legitimate, and the American people believe in that level of debate and relish it.

And the question will be over the next six months: Can we reach out to the American people, can we recruit enough of them — notice I didn't say "Republicans" — the American people. Can we reach out to enough Democrats? And I just talked to [Bush administration Housing and Urban Development Secretary] Jack [F.] Kemp a little while ago. He had a very encouraging talk with a leading member of the [Congressional] Black Caucus about working together and developing a program that is very bold and very dramatic in terms of helping the poor create jobs and helping those who want to rise have a real opportunity to acquire wealth and to create a better future for themselves.

Now, if we can reach out and truly try to do this — and remember what I quoted on the Capitol steps, which was [President] Franklin Delano Roosevelt, on March 4, 1933, standing in his braces in a time when it was inconceivable that somebody who had polio could be elected to major office, and standing there and saying on a wintry, overcast day in the middle of the Great Depression that we have nothing to fear but fear itself.

When you hear gunshots in your nation's capital at night, and you know that young Americans have died needlessly, then I would suggest to you that we have every reason to have the moral courage to confront every weakness of the current structure and to replace it. And if the first wave of experiments fail, to have the courage to say, "Well, that one didn't work," and have a second one and a third one and a fourth one. And the Monday morning we wake up and we can look on the morning news and no young American was killed anywhere in America, and we can know that every one of them is going to a school where they're actually learning how to read, and we know that they live under a tax code where, if they want to, it's easy to start creating jobs and to have your own business, and it's easy to start accumulating a little money to create a better future, that morning I think we can say, "OK, this journey has been worth it." But until that day, it just stays politics.

And so we have an enormous amount of work to do. All I can promise you on the side of the House Republicans is that we're going to be open to working with everyone, that we will cooperate with anyone, and we will compromise with no one, and that's the base of where we're going and that's what we believe this election is all about. ■

NEWS CONFERENCE

Dole Signals Cooperation, Says GOP Must Produce

Bob Dole, R-Kan., who is expected to be the new majority leader of the Senate, met with reporters Nov. 9. Following are excerpts from the news conference, as provided by the Federal News Service.

DOLE: I want to underscore again that it's been an historic 24 hours. Congress is under new management for the first time in 42 years. I've been talking to governors and — some who lost and many who won — House members, senators, and there's no doubt in my mind that we sent a very powerful message yesterday, and it was a vote of confidence in Republicans.

And of course, the amazing thing is not a single incumbent Republican governor, House member, or senator lost. So it can't be dismissed as anti-incumbency, because we didn't lose any. It was an anti-Clinton-agenda or anti-Clinton-vote, and the pro-Clinton supporters, those who supported [the] president 85, 90 percent of the time, were in trouble. And it was a result of the big-tax and big-spending agenda, and I think the American people gave us a message loud and clear.

I've also talked with the president briefly this morning, as I indicated I would, and I told him I thought there were areas where we could work together, that we had a responsibility to him and to the American people. He said he was headed for the Asian conference, and he'd like to sit down and meet with me and I guess also Congressman [Newt] Gingrich [R-Ga.] when he comes back.

I've talked briefly with Speaker-elect, I guess, Newt Gingrich, and he's obviously excited about all of this, as I am. But he's been waiting — well, he hasn't been waiting — but Republicans have been waiting 40 years for this to happen on the House side — 42 years — and we haven't waited quite that long.

So I would just say that we're going to be working on a number of areas, whether it's welfare reform or health care, tax fairness, whatever — we'll start working with Congressman Gingrich, and we can coordinate our efforts and also work with the governors.

I've talked to state legislators today. We've picked up state Senates in certain areas, a state House in Ohio, and all of them suggest that if we're going to make this work and make it last, we have to work together, because if we say we've gotten the message and we don't produce, we'll get kicked out for a long time again. We don't want that to happen, so it's up to us. We know we have a responsibility. We know we have responsibility, as I said, to the American people, to the president, to ourselves, to each other, and we're prepared to go to work....

Balanced Budget

Q: [Will a balanced-budget amendment be a priority?]

DOLE: Well, I don't know whether I can say the priority items. We've talked in general terms about a balanced-budget amendment. I've talked to Sen. [Bob] Packwood [R-Ore., expected to become chairman of the Finance Committee] briefly about some of the ideas he has. He thinks a balanced-budget amendment. Welfare reform. Maybe a vote on term limits. Maybe a vote on ethics reform. Congressional reform, which was blocked by Democrats, not Republicans, in the last session, Sen. [Robert C.] Byrd [D-W.Va.]. Go back and look at lobbying reform.

I think many of the things we're going to do early on is to address what some people are convinced are problems with the institution, with Congress — reduction in staff. So we'll be looking at all these areas. And we're going to have to do it. I mean, we can't let somebody say, 'Well, we won the election, and we don't have to worry about that for a couple of years.' We won the election because I think the American people want to give us the opportunity. If we don't do some of these things, they're going to cancel our lease....

GATT

Q: Senator, are you committed to the GATT [General Agreement on Tariffs and Trade] vote on Dec. 1? And do you envision other issues being brought up in the lame-duck session?

DOLE: I told the president this morning that I'd never — I'm a strong supporter of trade and a strong supporter of the North American Free Trade Agreement, have been in the past. We've had more concern expressed in Kansas over GATT than we had — much more than we had over NAFTA, over the World Trade Organization [WTO]. And I said to the president, "There's got to be some way we can explain to the American people what WTO is and isn't," and he said he'd be happy to work on that. Mickey Kantor [the U.S. trade representative] has been trying to — has been very helpful. But it causes me some concern. In fact, we put language in the implementing legislation that at least the committees of jurisdiction, the Ways and Means Committee and Finance Committee, could vote on decisions made in Geneva, so at least you'd send a signal to the administration. But we haven't explained that fully. I think the president needs to get out front and tell people across the country, what is the World Trade Organization and what it isn't, and the fact that we review every five years. And he said he'd be happy to have [White House Chief of Staff] Leon [E.] Panetta visit

about that while he was gone, and we'd talk about it when he came back....

Ties With Gingrich

Q: How would you describe your relationship [with GOP whip Gingrich]?

DOLE: Well, I think in years past I think he once referred to me as the tax collector for the welfare state — that's been years ago, but I notice in Newsweek it said I was maturing, so ... so I'm a mature tax collector for the — but in any event ... No, I think we have a good understanding, good relationship. I've always felt it was much different when you were in the leadership than when you were not. I mean, I remember not being in the leadership, I haven't been in the leadership that long, and you always had much more flexibility. You could be a free spirit on most anything.

But Newt understands — in fact, he's asked me if I would meet with and sit down and talk to him about being in the majority, and I'm certainly happy to do that. We may do it as early as Friday of this week.

Q: Senator, if I could follow on the philosophical splits, though, within the party between moderates and conservatives, this morning Sen. Phil Gramm [R-Texas] said he sees this election as a strong endorsement of the right wing of the party. Would you go along with that? Do you see any problems in that split?

DOLE: Well, I didn't hear the statement, I don't know, right wing — we are the conservative party in America, there's no question about that. I've never considered it to be right wing. Whether he meant the more conservative elements of the party, I'm not prepared to say. I think there are a lot of people who consider themselves conservative who still understand the government has some responsibility and the government does a lot of good things — it's not that the government does everything bad. But at the same time, there is this feeling that too much this, too much this, too much that.

I don't dispute what Sen. Gramm said, I just maybe have a little different view....

Working With Clinton

Q: Senator, if you and Congressman Gingrich work with the president the way that [Senate Majority Leader] Lyndon B. Johnson and [House Speaker] Sam Rayburn did with [President Dwight D.] Eisenhower, don't you run the danger of making the president look more effective and therefore more electable in '96?

DOLE: I think that's probably true, but I'm not certain that's maybe relevant. But if in fact we work out some of the legislative problems and agree on it, I'm not certain, I think everybody gets credit for it. With a Republican Congress, I'd assume we'd get some credit. But if we agree on it, I guess we can't worry about whether it helps the president or helps the Congress.

I indicated to the president this morning there'll probably be some things we couldn't agree on. And he's going to have a press conference in about three minutes, so I'll stop here so you can ... ∎

'CONTRACT WITH AMERICA'

House GOP Offers Descriptions Of Bills To Enact 'Contract'

The House Republican leadership on Nov. 15 released the text and descriptions of draft bills designed to incorporate the 10 elements of their "Contract With America." Following are the GOP-drafted descriptions of the 10 bills:

Balanced Budget/ Line-Item Veto

The bill contains two budgetary reforms: a constitutional balanced-budget amendment and a permanent line-item veto.

Supporters of a balanced-budget amendment (BBA) argue that Congress has shown itself both unwilling and incapable of balancing the federal budget. A constitutional amendment is necessary to force lawmakers to do what, on their own, they cannot: Get a handle on out-of-control spending. Opponents of the idea argue it will transfer budget decision-making to the courts, will result in massive cuts in Social Security and usurp Congress' constitutional authority to control government purse strings.

Proponents of the line-item veto maintain that given our current deficit situation, the president should have the authority to single out unnecessary and wasteful spending provisions in bills passed by Congress. Many critics assert, however, that the line-item veto will give too much power to the executive branch to control federal spending — a responsibility clearly given to the legislative branch in the U.S. Constitution.

Background

The impetus. Perpetual annual deficits, compounded by the fact that the federal government has not ended a fiscal year in surplus since 1969, has led many economists, former presidents, members of Congress and the public-at-large to call for more stringent and binding budget mechanisms — mechanisms that Congress will not be able to routinely waive or ignore. Many Americans have become disillusioned with a Congress that has consistently found ways to circumvent the few budgetary restraints it has set for itself:

In 1985, Congress passed the Balanced Budget and Emergency Deficit Control Act (PL 99-177; popularly known as Gramm-Rudman-Hollings) to establish steadily declining deficit targets, supposedly bringing

a balanced budget in FY 1991. In September 1987, faced with a projected budget deficit of $183 billion for FY 1988 (far exceeding the $108 billion target), Congress revised the law (PL 100-119) and adopted higher deficit levels supposedly bringing a balanced budget in FY 1993. In 1990, and again in 1993, Congress revised and extended these targets — postponing a balanced budget indefinitely.

Congressional budget rules allow the House to automatically raise the ceiling on the federal debt without a separate vote — protecting members from the difficult decision of increasing the federal debt.

These and other actions demonstrate to many that Congress has neither the will nor the desire to cut wasteful government spending and enact a balanced budget.

The BBA's recent history. In addition to the line-item veto, one of the more rigorous proposals that has garnered significant popular and congressional support is the balanced-budget amendment. A June 11, 1992, Investors' Business Daily article cited a Washington Post/ABC News poll finding that 75 percent of Americans favor a balanced-budget amendment. However, Congress has been considering balanced-budget amendments since 1936 with little success. The closest Congress ever came to passing one was in 1986 when the Senate defeated a balanced-budget resolution by one vote.

The House last considered a balanced-budget amendment in March 1994. At that time, four different versions of the amendment were debated. The first, a Stenholm/Smith (Ore.) resolution, would have amended the U.S. Constitution to require that total outlays for any fiscal year not exceed total receipts for that year unless three-fifths of the House and three-fifths of the Senate vote to incur a deficit. The authors made an exception for any fiscal year in which a declaration of war is in effect or the United States is engaged in a military conflict that poses a threat to national security. Their proposal also required (1) a three-fifths roll call vote in each chamber to increase the public debt limit and (2) that a majority of the membership of each chamber approve a tax increase. On final passage, it failed 271-153 — 12 votes shy of the two-thirds margin.

The House also rejected a Kyl substitute giving the president the line-item veto, limiting outlays to 19 percent of GDP for a given fiscal year, and requiring a three-fifths vote in both chambers to waive the requirement, and a Wise/Pomeroy/Price substitute allowing a majority of the House

and Senate to waive the balanced-budget requirement in times of war, military conflict or economic recession and exempting Social Security. Although the House adopted a Barton/Tauzin amendment requiring three-fifths roll call votes of the total membership of the House and Senate or a declaration of war to waive the balanced-budget amendment, and a three-fifths vote to increase the debt limit or raise taxes, it was not considered to be finally adopted since the substitutes were considered under king-of-the-hill procedures (i.e., the last amendment adopted in Committee of the Whole is reported back to the House for a vote on final passage). Because the Stenholm/Smith amendment was considered and passed after passage of the Barton/Tauzin amendment, only the former was considered to have been adopted in the Committee of the Whole. Only the Stenholm/Smith version was reported back to the House, where it failed to receive the necessary two-thirds vote.

A few weeks prior to House consideration of the BBA, the Senate debated a similar resolution, rejecting it on March 1, 1994, by a vote of 63-37 — four votes short of the required two-thirds margin. That measure (SJ Res 41), sponsored by Sen. [Paul] Simon [D-Ill.], would have made the balanced-budget requirement effective two years after its ratification or in 2002, whichever came later. During consideration, the Senate also rejected an alternative resolution offered by Sen. [Harry] Reid [D-Nev.,] (1) ensuring that courts cannot impose tax hikes if Congress fails to balance the budget, (2) exempting Social Security, (3) allowing Congress to waive the balanced-budget requirement in times of economic recession, and (4) permitting the government to borrow for infrastructure needs. It was defeated 22-78.

Amendments to the Constitution. As stipulated in the U.S. Constitution, amendments to our founding document must be approved by two-thirds of those present and voting in both the House and Senate and three-fourths (38) of the 50 state legislatures. The Constitution has been amended 27 times, including amendments protecting the free exercise of religion; protecting the right to keep and bear arms; protecting against unreasonable searches and seizures; guaranteeing the right to a speedy and public trial; protecting against cruel and unusual punishment; abolishing slavery; guaranteeing equal protection under the law to all; giving Congress the power to tax; prohibiting the manufacture, sale or transportation of alco-

hol and then later repealing this prohibition; and giving women the right to vote. The most recent constitutional amendment — prohibiting a congressional pay raise from taking effect during the Congress in which it was adopted — was ratified on May 7, 1992.

Line-item veto. A rescission bill rescinds or cancels, in whole or part, budget authority previously granted by Congress to reduce spending or because budget authority is no longer needed. Under current law, rescissions proposed by the president must be transmitted in a special message to Congress. Under the 1974 Impoundment Control Act (ICA, PL 93-344), Congress must complete action on a rescission bill within 45 days of continuous session after receipt of the proposal or else the budget authority must be made available for obligation.

Budget rules governing rescissions stipulate that if the Appropriations Committee does not act on rescissions submitted by the president within 25 days of continuous session, one-fifth of the members of the House can call for discharge of the bill from committee. (House rules for other bills require a waiting period of 30 days and that a majority of members sign a discharge petition.)

The Impoundment Control Act of 1974 was the congressional response to the Nixon administration's fondness for rescinding or deferring budget authority previously approved by Congress. This confrontation intensified in the 92nd and 93rd Congresses as President Nixon used the impoundment tool to reorder national priorities and alter programs supported by lawmakers. In the ICA, Congress required the president to inform it of all proposed rescissions and deferrals and submit specific information regarding each proposal. The original provisions of the ICA allowed a deferral to take effect unless either the House or the Senate took action to disapprove it — effectively providing for a one-house veto. This procedure was invalidated by the 1983 Supreme Court decision in *INS v. Chadha*. In 1986, a federal district court ruled that the president's deferral authority under ICA was no longer available, since it was inextricably linked to the one-house veto provision in the law. The lower court decision was upheld by the appeals court in 1987. Congress responded to these rulings with the Balanced Budget Affirmation Act (PL 100-119), which did away with policy-based deferrals and amended the ICA to comply with the court's decision.

The current debate on presidential authority arises out of the fact that presidents can veto appropriations bills in their entirety but not in part. Supporters of the line-item veto argue that the president should be able to selectively weed out wasteful pork barrel spending in an otherwise good bill. This Congress, over 20 line-item veto bills have been introduced. The House also has twice passed so-called "expedited rescissions" legislation (HR 1578 and HR 4600), which require presidential rescissions to be approved by Congress under accelerated committee and floor procedures. Another version of the line-item veto, considered as an amendment to these bills, is the "enhanced rescission" proposal, which forces Congress to pass a disapproval bill to block proposed presidential cuts. A constitutional line-item veto or a stand-alone legislative line-item veto has never been considered by the House — all line-item veto proposals have been considered as amendments to other bills, and have either failed or been dropped from the final version of the legislation. Forty-three of the nation's governors have a line-item veto authority of some sort.

Provisions

Balanced-budget amendment. The bill amends the U.S. Constitution to require that total outlays for any fiscal year do not exceed total receipts for that year. The resolution defines "receipts" as all receipts except those derived from borrowing, and "outlays" as all outlays except principal payments on the debt. It requires that the president submit, and Congress pass, a balanced budget each fiscal year unless three-fifths of the whole House and three-fifths of the whole Senate vote to incur a deficit. The resolution waives the balanced-budget requirement for any fiscal year in which a declaration of war is in effect or the United States is engaged in an "imminent and serious threat to national security." A joint resolution indicating this situation must be adopted by a majority of the total membership of each house and must be signed by the president.

The bill stipulates that the federal public debt will be limited to its level on the first day of the second fiscal year beginning after ratification of the BBA. The limit may only be increased by a three-fifths roll call vote in each chamber. Tax increases must also be approved by a three-fifths majority of the membership of each house.

Finally, the bill mandates that all associated votes must be roll call votes, and that the balanced-budget requirement will take effect in FY 2002 or the second fiscal year after it is ratified, whichever is later.

Line-item veto. The bill gives the president a permanent legislative line-item veto. Under this procedure, the president could strike any appropriation or targeted tax provision (a provision that provides special treatment to a particular taxpayer or limited class of taxpayers) in any bill. The president is required to submit his rescission proposal within 20 calendar days (not including weekends or holidays) after Congress finally passes a bill or resolution and must submit a separate rescission proposal for each piece of legislation. The president's proposed rescissions are to take effect unless Congress disapproves them in an up-or-down vote within 20 days after receipt of the proposal. If the president vetoes the disapproval bill, Congress would have to override it by a two-thirds vote.

The bill also sets forth the procedures for Senate consideration of a proposed rescission, including limiting debate time on a disapproval bill to 10 hours.

Finally, the bill limits a disapproval bill to only those matters relating to the proposed rescissions transmitted by the president and stipulates that a disapproval bill is unamendable. These provisions, however, are made in accordance with House rules and may be waived by the Rules Committee at any point.

This bill is identical to the Michel-Solomon amendment offered during House consideration of HR 4600, the Expedited Rescissions Act of 1994. The amendment was rejected 205-218 on July 14, 1994 (Roll Call No. 327).

Crime

The bill embodies the Republican approach to fighting crime: making punishments severe enough to deter criminals from committing crimes, making sure that the criminal justice system is fair and impartial for all, and making sure that local law enforcement officials (who are on the streets every day), and not Washington bureaucrats, direct the distribution of federal law enforcement funds.

The bill sets mandatory sentences for crimes involving the use of firearms, authorizes $10.5 billion for state prison construction grants, establishes truth-in-sentencing guidelines, reforms the habeas corpus appeals process, allows police officers who in good faith seized incriminating evidence in violation of the "exclusionary rule" to use the evidence in court, requires that convicted criminals make restitution to their victims and authorizes $10 billion for local law enforcement spending. Finally, in addressing one of the most pressing problems in our country today, the bill streamlines the current alien deportation system, while still allowing convicted aliens the right to judicial review and appeal.

Bill sponsors argue that this legislation strikes at the heart of our violent crime problem by deterring criminals from committing crimes in the first place, and making sure that if they do commit a crime, they serve the sentence they are given and are not able to abuse the appeals process. Supporters contend that this bill fixes a number of problems created by the recently enacted omnibus crime bill, as well as serious problems left unaddressed by that legislation. Critics maintain that the measure concentrates too much on punishment and not enough on prevention; the way to stop crime, they argue, is not to keep filling our jails, but to keep at-risk youth from going there in the first place.

Background

Crime in America: putting the debate in context. Statistics paint a grim picture, illustrating clearly that the United

States has failed to get a handle on its growing crime problem. One expert has estimated that a 20-year-old black male has a greater chance of being murdered on the streets than a soldier in World War II stood of dying in combat. According to the FBI, the rate of violent crime in the United States is worse than in any other Western-developed country, with a murder occurring every 21 minutes, a rape every five minutes, a robbery every 46 seconds and an aggravated assault every 29 seconds. Violent crime or property crime victimizes one in four U.S. households. Every year, nearly 5 million people are victims of violent crime such as murder, rape, robbery or assault, and 19 million Americans are victims of property crimes such as arson or burglary. Juvenile crime has increased by 60 percent between 1981 and 1990 (compared to an increase of 5 percent among adults) and the number of inmates convicted of drug offenses rose 14 percent from 1983 to 1989. On all fronts, the problem has reached epidemic proportions.

This crime crisis is particularly severe among minorities and the poor. The U.S. homicide rate for black males between the ages of 15 and 24 is 283 times that of male homicide rates in 17 other nations. And homicide is now the leading cause of death for blacks aged 15 to 34. Poor households are victimized more often than upper-income households. In 1992, households with incomes of less than $7,500 experienced crime at a rate of 136.7 per 1,000, compared to the rate of 83.3 per 1,000 for households with incomes between $30,000 and $49,000.

While the problem is severe, statistics illustrate that a small percentage of criminals commit the vast majority of violent crimes. Just 7 percent of criminals commit two-thirds of all violent crime, including three-fourths of rapes and robberies, and virtually all murders. A 1991 study done by the Bureau of Alcohol, Tobacco and Firearms indicated that 471 armed criminals had a total of 3,088 felony convictions — an average of 6.55 felonies each. To make matters worse, many of these criminals either are never caught, or, if found guilty, do not serve their entire prison sentence. Every year, over 60,000 criminals convicted of a violent crime never go to prison — for every 100 crimes reported only three criminals go to prison. The Bureau of Justice Statistics has found that only 45.4 percent of court-ordered confinement is served on average, and 51 percent of violent offenders sent to prison are released in two years or less. These numbers are even more telling in light of the fact that at least 30 percent of the murders in this country are committed by people on probation, parole or bail. Faced with prison overcrowding, 17 states have begun emergency release programs. Overall, the risk of punishment has declined in the past 40 years while the annual number of serious crimes committed has skyrocketed.

All this has led to public calls for "truth-in-sentencing" laws (requiring criminals to serve a significant percentage of

their sentences without a chance of parole) and "three strikes, you're out" laws (requiring life in prison for recidivists convicted of their third violent felony). Opponents of strict sentencing laws like these argue that "locking people up" does not address the problem of why crimes are committed in the first place. Evidence suggests, however, that there is a strong correlation between increased incarceration and decreased crime rates: From 1990 to 1991, states with the greatest increases in criminal incarceration rates experienced, on average, a 12.7 percent decrease in crime, while the 10 states with the weakest incarceration rates experienced an average 6.9 percent increase in crime.

Recent legislation. Just a few weeks ago, President Clinton signed PL 103-322, the Omnibus Crime Control Act of 1994, after nearly one year of congressional hearings, mark-ups, floor votes, conference wranglings, a delayed recess and weekend votes. Many members spoke out against the legislation, arguing that it did little to address the fundamental crime problem in our country. Relying on expensive "Great Society-esque" programs, the bill attempted to do what all other big government social programs have failed to do: make individuals responsible for their actions and instill a sense of right and wrong in those with a propensity to commit a crime. Criticism focused not only on what the bill contained, but what it lacked. Republicans argued that it should have included reform of the habeas corpus process (the process by which inmates challenge the constitutionality of their sentences), a good faith exemption for the exclusionary rule, tough language against sexual predators, more money for state prison construction and stronger requirements that states enact truth-in-sentencing laws to be eligible for grant assistance.

After a crazy weekend session at the end of August, the conference agreement was finally approved by the House 235-195 (Roll Call No. 416). When all was said and done, the compromise authorized a total of $30 billion over six years, including $5.4 billion for prevention programs, $7.9 billion for new prison construction and $8.8 billion for new police officers. It also included the so-called "three strikes, you're out" provision, applied the death penalty to over 50 new crimes, increased penalties for repeat federal sex offenders and banned at least 150 semiautomatic weapons. The final version did not include the controversial Racial Justice Act (which allows defendants to introduce in their defense statistical evidence that blacks receive death sentences more often than whites) or any reform of the habeas corpus process.

In addition to passing the first omnibus crime bill in four years, the 103rd Congress also passed the Brady Bill, which established a five-day waiting period for the purchase of a handgun. The House approved that measure (HR 1025) on Nov. 10, 1993, by a vote of 238-189. President Clinton signed it into law on Nov. 30, 1993, as

PL 103-159. Other smaller crime-related bills passed during this Congress include the National Child Protection Act of 1993 (PL 103-209), which established criminal background checks for child-care providers, and the International Parental Kidnapping Crime Act (PL 103-173), which made it a federal crime for a parent to kidnap a child under the age of 16 years from his custodial parent and remove him from the United States.

Provisions

Death Penalty Provisions (Title I): General habeas corpus reform. The bill makes a number of revisions to federal and state habeas corpus processes (the process by which prisoners who have exhausted all direct appeals challenge the constitutionality of their sentences). Specifically, it places a one-year limitation on the filing of general federal habeas corpus appeals after all state remedies have been exhausted. State capital cases must be filed in a federal court within six months, and state capital prisoners who file a second or successive federal habeas appeal must receive a certificate of probable cause stating that their case has merit. Non-capital federal prisoners must file within two years. The bill also forces federal courts to consider federal habeas petitions within a certain time frame.

In addition to placing a time limit on when appeals may be made, the bill limits prisoners to one appeal unless the defendant can show by "clear and convincing evidence, that but for constitutional error, no reasonable fact finder would have found [him] guilty of the underlying offense or eligible for the death penalty."

Under current law, there are virtually no limits or restrictions on when prisoners can file habeas corpus appeals. For example, under current law, defendants can appeal any time there is a change in the law or a new Supreme Court ruling. Bill sponsors argue that delays of up to 14 years are not uncommon, making abuse of the habeas corpus system the most significant factor in states' inability to implement credible death penalties. They also contend that current law favors the convicted criminal. For example, the recently enacted crime legislation included a requirement that at least two lawyers be appointed to represent the defendant at every stage of the process.

Latin for "you have the body," a habeas corpus writ is used to determine whether a person is lawfully imprisoned. Originally designed as a remedy for imprisonment without trial, it is now a tool of federal and state defendants who have been convicted and exhausted all direct appeals (prisoners currently have three successive procedures to challenge a conviction or sentence: appeal, state habeas corpus and federal habeas corpus). Critics of the current habeas corpus process argue that (1) most petitions are totally lacking in merit, (2) thousands upon thousands of frivolous petitions clog the federal district

court dockets each year, and (3) it allows prisoners on death row to almost indefinitely delay their punishment.

Authorization of funds for states to prosecute capital cases. Congress already provides funds for death penalty resource centers to litigate federal habeas corpus petitions for death row inmates. The bill authorizes equal funding for states to prosecute these cases. Bill sponsors argue that equal funds should be provided to both the defense and the prosecution in these cases.

Reform of death penalty procedures. The bill mandates that juries be instructed to recommend a death sentence if aggravating factors (circumstances of the crime that increase the level of guilt) outweigh "mitigating factors" (circumstances that reduce the degree of moral culpability). Juries must also be instructed to avoid any "influence of sympathy, sentiment, passion, prejudice or other arbitrary factors" in their decisions.

Under the recent Omnibus Crime Control Act [PL 103-322], the Justice Department is required to notify the court and the defendant that it intends to seek the death penalty, and it must indicate the "aggravating" factors it intends to prove as the basis for imposition of a capital sentence. The law specifically states that a jury is never required to impose a death sentence (even if it finds that aggravating factors outweigh mitigating factors), and that death penalties can never be imposed on individuals who are mentally retarded, incompetent or under 18 years of age at the time of their crime. Critics of current law argue that it (1) establishes an elaborate system of aggravating and mitigating factors, but then allows juries to ignore the evidence and make an arbitrary sentencing recommendation; (2) gives too much discretion to a judge and jury; (3) weakens current law; and (4) greatly complicates the use of any new federal death penalty.

Mandatory Minimum Sentencing for Drug Crimes (Title II). The Comprehensive Crime Control Act of 1984 (PL 98-473) created the U.S. Sentencing Commission to develop and monitor sentencing guidelines to be used by federal judges when sentencing criminal defendants. Despite the commission's suggestions that mandatory minimum sentences tend to warp the guidelines system, Congress has enacted about 100 mandatory minimum sentences for a variety of federal crimes. Many federal judges have complained that these restrictions are foolish, wasteful and cruel (sometimes requiring them to impose a sentence without regard to the nature of the offense or the character and background of the offender), and that they have no deterrent effect on crime.

Supporters of mandatory sentences counter that they complement the sentencing guidelines, prevent disparity in sentencing and ensure certainty of punishment. Mandatory minimums send a strong and unmistakable message to criminals that they will serve a set minimum sentence if they commit certain violent crimes. Mandatory minimums are also used by prosecutors to extract confessions from low-level offenders in exchange for reduced sentences. The information is then used to build cases against criminal crime bosses. Although judges object to mandatory minimums because they take away their sentencing discretion, prosecutors see them as important law enforcement tools.

The bill establishes a mandatory minimum sentence of 10 years for state or federal drug or violent crimes that involve possession of a gun. Penalties increase to 20 years for a second conviction and life in prison for a third. For those who discharge a firearm with intent to injure another person, the first offense is punishable by a minimum of 20 years in prison, second offenses are punishable by a minimum of 30 years, and third violations get life in prison.

Finally, possession or use of a machine gun or other destructive device during the commission of these crimes is punishable by no less than 30 years. Second-time offenses are punishable by life in prison.

Mandatory Victim Restitution (Title III). The bill mandates that criminals pay full restitution to their victims for damages caused as a result of the crime. (Current law allows the court to order that such restitution be made, but it does not require it.) In addition, the bill allows (but does not require) the court to order restitution of any person who, as shown by a preponderance of the evidence, was harmed physically, emotionally or financially by the unlawful conduct of the defendant.

Court responsibility. Under the bill, restitution is to reimburse the victim for necessary child care, transportation and other expenses incurred while participating in the investigation or court proceedings. The court is to determine the amount of restitution based on the victim's situation and not on the economic resources of the offender or the fact that the victim is entitled to insurance or other compensation. The court is also to set the payment schedule (e.g., a single, lump-sum payment or a partial payment at specified intervals) and method of payment (e.g., cash, return of property, or replacement of property).

Limitations on restitution awards. Court-ordered compensation is not to affect the victim's eligibility to receive insurance awards or other compensation until such time that the court-ordered compensation fully compensates the victim for his losses. In addition, the bill stipulates that if the claimant seeks additional awards in a civil case, any new award is to be reduced by the amount of the criminal court restitution order (bill supporters argue that claimants may seek additional awards but should not be able to receive a second, full compensation).

Defendant compliance. Compliance with the schedule of payment and other terms of the restitution order is a condition for probation, parole or any other form of release. If the defendant fails to comply

with the restitution order, the court may revoke probation or parole, modify the conditions of probation or parole, hold the defendant in contempt of court, enter a restraining order or injunction against the defendant, order the sale of the defendant's property, or take any other action necessary to insure compliance with the restitution order. The victim or offender may, at any time, petition the court to modify a restitution order if the offender's economic circumstances change.

Law Enforcement Block Grants (Title IV). The bill authorizes a total of $10 million over five years ($2 million in each of FY 1996-2000) for local governments to fund law enforcement programs. These block grants replace the police, prevention and drug courts titles of the recently enacted crime bill. Under the bill, money may be used to (1) hire, train or employ law enforcement officers; (2) pay overtime to police officers; (3) purchase equipment and technology directly related to basic law enforcement purposes; (4) enhance school security measures (e.g., police patrols around school grounds, metal detectors, fences, closed circuit cameras, gun hotlines, etc.); (5) establish citizen neighborhood watch programs; and/or (6) fund programs that advance moral standards and the values of citizenship and involve local law enforcement officials.

To qualify for these grants, a unit of local government must show that it will (1) establish a trust fund in which block grant money is to be deposited; (2) use the money within two years; (3) spend the money in accordance with the guidelines in this section; (4) use approved accounting, audit and fiscal procedures; (5) make any requested records available to the Bureau of Justice Assistance and the comptroller of the United States for review; and (6) submit the required progress reports. Each state that applies is to automatically receive 0.25 percent of the funds as well as additional funds based on its number of reported violent crimes in 1993 compared to the rest of the country. States are to distribute the funds among local units of government based on their population and the number of reported violent crimes in 1993 compared to the rest of the local governmental units in the state.

If a unit of local government does not spend all of its grant money within two years of receipt, it must repay the unused portion to the Bureau of Justice Assistance within three months. The bill also stipulates that (1) this grant money is intended to supplement, not supplant, state funds; (2) grantees may not use more than 2.5 percent of their grant for administrative costs; and (3) grantees must hold one public hearing on the proposed use of their grant. The bill also sets out procedures to be used if a local government violates any portion of this title.

As noted above, the bill repeals sections of the recently enacted crime control act that provide specific funds for drug courts, recreational programs, community

justice programs and other social prevention spending. Bill sponsors argue that providing money directly to local law enforcers and letting them decide how to spend the funds (as the Taking Back Our Streets Act does) is preferable to the current law approach of authorizing specific amounts of money for programs approved by Washington bureaucrats.

Grants for Prison Construction Based on Truth-in-Sentencing (Title V). The bill authorizes $10.5 billion over six years ($232 million in FY 1995, $997.5 million in FY 1996, $1.3 billion in FY 1997, $2.5 billion in FY 1998, $2.7 billion in FY 1999 and $2.8 billion in FY 2000) for the attorney general to make grants to states so they can build, expand and operate prisons for serious violent felons. This title replaces the prison section in the recently enacted crime bill. The bill also authorizes the attorney general to make grants for states to move non-violent offenders and criminal aliens to other correctional facilities (including old military bases) to make room for violent criminals at existing prisons. Grants are to be awarded based on two formulas: a percentage that applies to all states (0.4 percent) and a percentage based on population.

Fifty percent of the funds authorized under this section are designated as "general grants." To receive these funds, states must show that since 1993 (1) an increased percentage of convicted violent offenders have been sentenced to prison, (2) the state has increased the average prison time actually served in prison, and (3) the state has increased the percentage of sentences to be actually served. The other 50 percent is reserved for truth-in-sentencing incentive grants. To be eligible for these funds, states must show that they require serious violent felons to serve at least 85 percent of the sentence imposed, and require sentencing or releasing authorities to allow the defendant's victim (or the victim's family) to testify on the issue of sentencing and any post-conviction release.

The bill includes an exception for prisoners over the age of 70 years after a public hearing in which representatives of the public and the prisoner's victims have an opportunity to testify on the issue of release. It also stipulates that (1) grant money is to supplement, not supplant, state funds; (2) no more than 3 percent of the grant is to be used by states for administrative costs; (3) the federal share of a grant is not to exceed 75 percent of the total cost of a state proposal; and (4) any funds not spent in one year will carry over and remain available until spent.

Reform of the Exclusionary Rule (Title VI). The Supreme Court enforces the Constitution's Fourth Amendment (which protects Americans against unreasonable searches and seizures) through the so-called exclusionary rule. The rule holds that any evidence discovered as a result of improper police action cannot be introduced in a federal or state criminal trial — i.e., "the criminal is to go free because the constable has blundered." Critics of the rule's rigidity argue that it suppresses evidence of unquestionable reliability and leads to the acquittal of many who are obviously guilty. In 1984, the Supreme Court modified the exclusionary rule to permit the introduction of evidence that was obtained in good faith reliance on a search warrant that was later found to be invalid. However, many have called for a "good faith exemption" in cases where the police officer, acting in good faith, conducted a search or seizure without a warrant.

The bill amends current law to allow introduction of evidence obtained during a search or seizure that was conducted with the objectively reasonable belief that it was in accordance with the Fourth Amendment, regardless of whether a search warrant had been granted.

Prisoner Lawsuits (Title VII). The bill directs federal courts to dismiss any frivolous or malicious action brought by an adult convicted of a crime and confined in any jail, prison or other correctional facility. The bill also requires that prisoners filing a suit include a statement of all assets in their possession so the court can require a full or partial payment of filing fees based on the prisoner's ability to pay.

Bill sponsors argue that states are forced to spend millions of dollars defending prisoner lawsuits to improve prison conditions — many of which are frivolous. Critics of the proposal argue that it will restrict prisoners' rights to seek legitimate redress of grievances.

Deportation of Criminal Aliens (Title VIII). This title of the bill provides for the prompt deportation of any alien without a green card who has been convicted of an aggravated felony and who is deportable. According to bill sponsors, it addresses the current problem of releasing these felons into the general population prior to finalization of deportation proceedings, since few of those released ever show up for their deportation hearings.

Definition of an aggravated felony. For purposes of alien felon deportation, the bill expands the definition of an aggravated felony to include any state or federal offense involving (1) firearms violations; (2) failure to appear in court for a felony carrying a sentence of two or more years; (3) demanding or receiving ransom money; (4) a Racketeer Influenced and Corrupt Organizations Act violation; (5) owning, controlling, managing or supervising a prostitution business; (6) treason; (7) tax evasion exceeding $200,000; and (8) certain immigration-related offenses including alien smuggling and sale of fraudulent documents. Sponsors of the bill argue that these crimes are serious enough to put a convicted alien on the fast track for deportation.

The current law definition of an aggravated felony includes murder, drug trafficking, trafficking in firearms or explosives, money laundering, terrorism and any crime of violence carrying a prison sentence of at least five years.

Criminal alien deportation proceedings. The bill allows the attorney general to issue a final order of deportation against any alien determined to be deportable for conviction of an aggravated felony (without requiring a deportation hearing). An alien is defined as anyone who (1) was not lawfully admitted for permanent residence in the United States at the time that proceedings for the commission of an aggravated crime began or (2) had permanent resident status on a conditional basis at the time that proceedings for the commission of an aggravated crime began. An alien against whom a deportation order is issued may appeal for judicial review in federal court; however, the court action is limited to challenging only the defendant's identification (whether the person is who the Immigration and Naturalization Service says he is and whether he committed the aggravated felony).

Judicial deportations. When an alien whose conviction causes him to be deemed deportable is sentenced, a federal court may issue a judicial order of deportation if the U.S. attorney requested one prior to sentencing and the INS commissioner is in agreement. A judicial order of deportation or a denial of such order may be appealed by either party to the circuit court of appeals. A court action, however, is limited to challenging only the defendant's identification (whether the person is who the Immigration and Naturalization Service [INS] says he is and whether he committed the aggravated felony).

If a judicial order is denied, the attorney general may still pursue a deportation order through administrative channels.

Defenses based on permanent residence. Under current law, when an alien is in deportation proceedings, he can use certain defenses to get out. One such defense is showing that he has been a permanent resident of the United States for the past seven years. The bill does not change the underlying defense, but changes the time frame in which INS can begin deportation proceedings against an alien convicted of an aggravated offense. Under current law, deportation proceedings are to begin after the alien has served five years. The bill allows INS to begin deportation proceedings when an alien is sentenced to a term of at least five years. Bill sponsors argue that this standard is more relevant for judging the seriousness of a crime since dangerous criminals may be released prematurely due to prison overcrowding, or other reasons not related to the seriousness of the crime.

Defenses based on withholding of deportation. Aliens may also reverse deportation proceedings by showing that they will suffer physical harm if returned to their native country. As defined by international law, "withholding of deportation" is a higher standard of protection than asylum: If an alien can prove such a situation exists, he must be retained in the United States unless he poses a danger to the public. The bill clarifies current law to stipu-

late that aggravated felons pose a serious danger to the public and are not allowed to request or be granted this protection.

Enhanced penalties for failing to deport or re-entering. Under current law, aliens who are deportable for criminal offenses, for document fraud or because they are a security risk to the United States face up to 10 years in prison for failure to depart. Bill sponsors argue that there are no penalties for aliens who are deportable for other reasons but refuse to leave. The bill retains the current law penalty and establishes a penalty of up to four years in prison for all other deportable aliens who refuse to leave.

The bill also establishes civil penalties for those who refuse to leave. Under current law, an alien who is convicted of a felony (other than an aggravated offense), is deported and then re-enters the country is subject to five years in prison and a criminal fine. The bill extends such penalties to aliens convicted of three or more misdemeanors and increases the maximum sentence to 10 years. Deported aggravated felons who re-enter the United States are currently subject to criminal fines and up to 15 years in prison. The bill increases the maximum prison sentence to 20 years.

Finally, under the bill, a deported alien who re-enters the United States cannot challenge his original deportation unless he can show that (1) all available administrative remedies were exhausted, (2) an opportunity for judicial review was denied, and (3) the deportation order was fundamentally unfair.

Criminal alien tracking center. The bill directs the INS commissioner and the director of the FBI, with the heads of other agencies, to operate a criminal tracking center. The measure authorizes $14 million over four years ($5 million in FY 1994 and $2 million in each of FY 1995-98) for the center, which is to [help] federal, state and local law enforcement agencies identify and locate aliens who may be subject to deportation due to conviction of an aggravated felony.

Welfare

The Personal Responsibility Act overhauls the American welfare system to reduce government dependency, attack illegitimacy, require welfare recipients to enter work programs and cap total welfare spending. The bill's main thrust is to give states greater control over the benefits programs, work programs and Aid to Families with Dependent Children (AFDC) payments and requirements.

Under the bill, the structure for AFDC payments will drastically change. Mothers under the age of 18 may no longer receive AFDC payments for children born out of wedlock, and mothers who are ages 18, 19 and 20 can be prohibited by the states from

receiving AFDC payments and housing benefits. Mothers must also establish paternity as a condition for receiving AFDC payments, except in cases of rape [or] incest. Also, in order to reduce the amount of time families are on welfare, states must begin moving welfare recipients into work programs if they have received welfare for two years. States are given the option to drop families from receiving AFDC benefits after they have received welfare for two years if at least one year has been spent in a work program. To further limit the length of time on AFDC, states must drop families from the program after they have received a total of five years of AFDC benefits.

The bill allows states to design their own work programs and determine who will be required to participate. Welfare recipients must work an average of 35 hours a week or enroll in work training programs. By the year 2001, 1.5 million AFDC recipients will be required to work.

The bill caps the spending growth of several major welfare programs, AFDC, Supplemental Security Income (SSI) and public housing, and consolidates 10 nutrition programs, including food stamps, the Women, Infants and Children (WIC) and the school lunch program, into one discretionary block grant to states.

Finally, the bill grants greater flexibility to states, allowing them to design their own work programs and determine who participates in them and [allowing them] to opt out of the current AFDC program by converting their share of AFDC payments into fixed annual block grants.

Background

In the mid-1960s President Lyndon B. Johnson launched a war on poverty with the hope of creating a "Great Society." The federal government was mobilized to fight poverty by creating a slew of new federal programs and expanding existing ones, such as AFDC. Established in 1935 under the Social Security Act, AFDC was created to help widows care for their children. It now serves divorced, deserted and never-married individuals and their children. AFDC continues to be the major cash welfare program for families. Federal funds pay at least 50 percent of each state's benefits and administrative costs. In June 1994, enrollment reached 5,028,000 families, just below the record of 5,083,000 set in March 1994. Individual recipients numbered 14.2 million, and unemployed two-parent families totaled 362,000. Also, food stamp enrollment in June 1994 was 27.4 million persons — a record high. Although almost half of the mothers who enter AFDC can be expected to leave within two years, most return. Long-term users often are young, never-married and high school dropouts; and most AFDC families begin with a birth to a teenager.

In the past few years, the federal governments and state governments have tried to change and improve the welfare system. The Clinton administration campaigned to

"end welfare as we know it;" though, to date, Congress has not held a vote on its proposal. The administration proposal limits AFDC benefits to two years, during which employment services would be provided to recipients. Nearly 20 welfare reform bills were introduced in the 103rd Congress, including three major proposals offered by Republican members:

● The GOP Leadership Welfare Reform Bill (HR 3500). After two years on AFDC (or less at a state's option), welfare recipients must work 35 hours per week in a private or public sector job. It also requires mothers to establish paternity before receiving AFDC benefits, denies AFDC benefits to parents under age 18 and denies increased AFDC benefits for having additional children while on welfare — unless a state enacts laws to exempt itself from any of these requirements.

● The Real Welfare Reform Act (HR 4566). This measure prohibits AFDC, food stamps and public housing to unmarried mothers under age 21 (the age limit is raised to 25 in 1998); requires paternity to be established as a condition for receiving AFDC, food stamps and public housing; provides a $1,000 pro-marriage tax credit, requires 50 percent of AFDC recipients to work by 1996; requires single able-bodied food stamp recipients to work for benefits; and freezes the rate of growth in several welfare programs at 3.5 percent per year.

● The Welfare and Teenage Pregnancy Reduction Act (HR 1293). This measure freezes AFDC at current funding levels and returns the program to the states in the form of block grants, giving states maximum discretion to design their own welfare-to-work programs. The bill also prohibits AFDC benefits to parents under age 18 and requires that paternity be established in order to receive AFDC benefits.

Provisions

Reducing illegitimacy. The bill is designed to diminish the number of teenage pregnancies and illegitimate births. It prohibits AFDC payments and housing benefits to mothers under age 18 who give birth to out-of-wedlock children. The state has the option of extending this prohibition to mothers ages 18, 19, and 20. The savings generated from this provision to deny AFDC to minor mothers (and to mothers age 18 to 20 if the state elects that option) is returned to the states in the form of block grants to provide services — but not cash payments — to help these young mothers with illegitimate children. The state will use the funds for programs to reduce out-of-wedlock pregnancies, to promote adoption, to establish and operate orphanages, to establish and operate residential group homes for unwed mothers, or for any purpose the state deems appropriate. None of the funds may be used for abortion services or abortion counseling.

The bill also includes a number of other provisions to reduce illegitimacy. While AFDC is prohibited to mothers ages 17 and younger who have children out of

wedlock, mothers age 18 [to 20] who give birth to illegitimate children must live at home in order to receive aid — unless the mother marries the biological father or marries an individual who legally adopts the child. Mothers already receiving AFDC will not receive an increase in benefits if additional children are born out of wedlock.

Finally, the bill requires mothers to establish paternity as a condition for receiving AFDC. Exceptions are provided for cases of rape [or] incest and if the state determines that efforts to establish paternity would result in physical danger to the mother. The bill requires states to establish paternity in 90 percent of their cases. Also, states are encouraged to develop procedures in public hospitals and clinics to determine paternity and establish legal procedures that help pinpoint paternity in a reasonable time period.

Requiring work. States are allowed to establish their own work training and education programs to help recipients move from the welfare program to paid employment as soon as possible. The training programs require recipients to work for an average of 35 hours a week or 30 hours per week plus five hours engaged in job search activities. One parent in a two-parent family is required to work 32 hours a week plus eight hours of job searching. States may not provide the work programs for more than two years to any individual or family which receives welfare benefits. States have the option of ending AFDC to families that have been on the welfare rolls for two years if at least one year was spent in a work program. All states must terminate AFDC payments to families who have received a total of five years of welfare benefits — regardless of whether or not the AFDC recipient has participated in a jobs program.

As long as states meet the participation requirements, the federal government will not [revise] other parts of the program. States will design their own work programs and determine who will be required to participate in them. Part of the participation requirement is requiring a certain number of recipients to participate in the job program. Starting in 1996, 100,000 AFDC recipients will be required to work; in 1997, 200,000 recipients will be required; in 1998, 400,000 will be required; in 1999, 600,000 recipients will be required; in 2000, 900,000 will be required; and by 2001, 1.5 million recipients will be required to work.

Identified non-parents, usually men, who receive food stamp benefits are required to work — eight hours per week for those benefits.

Capping the growth of welfare spending. The bill caps the spending growth of AFDC, SSI and numerous public housing programs, and the mandatory work program established under the bill. The cap equals the amount spent the preceding year for these programs with an adjustment for inflation plus growth in poverty population. The entitlement status of these programs is ended.

The bill also consolidates a number of nutrition programs into a block grant to states, funded in the first year at 95 percent of the aggregate amount of the individual programs. Programs consolidated into the block grant include food stamps, the supplemental feeding program for women, infants and children (WIC), and the school lunch and breakfast programs, among others. Under the block grant, states will distribute food assistance to economically disadvantaged individuals more freely.

To further reduce welfare spending, welfare assistance (AFDC, SSI, food stamps, housing and a host of other public assistance) is denied to non-citizens, except refugees over 75 years of age, those lawfully admitted to the United States, or those who have resided in the United States for at least five years. Emergency medical assistance will continue to be provided to non-citizens.

State flexibility. The bill allows states to create their own work programs and determine who participates in them. States can also opt out of the AFDC program and convert their AFDC payments into a fixed annual block grant and have the option to provide new residents AFDC benefits comparable to the level provided in the state in which they previously resided. To help combat illiteracy, states may reduce AFDC payments by up to $75 per month to mothers under the age of 21 who have not completed high school or earned their high school "equivalency" [diploma]. Payments may also be reduced if a dependent child does not maintain minimum school attendance.

Other Provisions

State adoption agencies are encouraged to decrease the amount of time a child must wait to be adopted (today, the average child waits approximately 2.8 years). Specifically, the bill prohibits states from discriminating on the basis of race, color or national origin when placing children for adoption.

Also, AFDC beneficiaries who the state identifies as addicted to drugs or alcohol must enroll in an addiction treatment program and participate in random drug testing in order to continue receiving welfare benefits.

Estimated savings. The bill is estimated to result in net savings of approximately $40 billion over five years. The denial of welfare to non-citizens saves about $22 billion, the cap on welfare spending saves about $18 billion, the nutrition block grant saves about $11 billion, and the requirement for paternity establishment saves about $2 billion. The costs included in the bill are $9.9 billion for the work program and approximately $2 billion for miscellaneous state options.

Children

The Family Reinforcement Act (1) protects parents' rights to supervise their children's participation in any federally funded program and shield them from federally sponsored surveys that involve intrusive questioning; (2) requires states to give "full faith and credit" to child support orders issued by the courts or [to] the administrative procedures of other states; (3) provides a refundable tax credit of up to $5,000 for families adopting a child; (4) strengthens penalties for child pornography and criminal sexual conduct involving minors; and (5) provides a $500 tax credit for families caring for a dependent elderly parent or grandparent.

Provisions

Family privacy protection. The bill requires parental consent for the participation of a minor in any federally funded survey or analysis regarding (1) parental political affiliations; (2) any mental or psychological problems in the family; (3) family or individual sexual behavior and attitudes; (4) any illegal or self-incriminating behavior; (5) privileged relationships with lawyers, physicians or clergymen; (6) any household income information other than that required by law for federal program participation; (7) religious beliefs; and (8) appraisals of other individuals with whom the minor has had a familial relationship.

Child support enforcement. The bill requires states to give "full faith and credit" to child support orders from other states. It provides federal assistance in developing a uniform child support/visitation order in order to streamline interstate enforcement. Finally, the bill requires non-custodial parents who receive state aid to participate in a state job-search program if they have child support arrearages.

Adoption assistance. The bill establishes a refundable tax credit of up to $5,000 for adoption expenses such as adoption fees, court costs and attorney fees. The tax credit is phased out for incomes beginning at $60,000.

Elder care assistance. The bill provides a $500 refundable tax credit for individuals who care for a parent or grandparent at home.

Child Protection. The bill increases sentences for sexual offenses against children and closes certain loopholes in federal laws protecting children. Today, computers with their enhanced graphics and rapid communication are increasingly used by pornographers. To address this, the bill increases federal sentencing guidelines by two levels for the use of a computer in the shipment of pornography.

Current law provides a maximum sentence of 10 years for the prostitution of children. The bill establishes a three-year minimum sentence for anyone who forces children into prostitution. It also assures that an increase in the age of the victimized child will not result in lighter punishment.

Finally, the bill creates mandatory three-year minimum sentences for sexual abuse of a minor or a minor who is a ward in federal custody. Currently, federal laws are much weaker than most state laws in these

areas and are therefore seldom used. Creating mandatory minimum sentences will reactivate prosecutions under these federal laws.

Middle-Class Tax Cut

The American Dream Restoration Act (ADRA) provides a tax credit for families, reforms the so-called "marriage penalty" and establishes a new and improved individual retirement account. Today, the average family spends more on taxes than it spends on food, clothing and shelter combined. Many families now need a second earner not to support the household, but to support the government. Middle-income families are forced to buy their first homes later in life and must scramble to send their children to college. ADRA is designed to deliver relief from the heavy burden of government and let families keep more of their hard-earned dollars to pursue their version of the American Dream.

$500 family tax credit. Effective in 1996, the bill provides a $500 per child tax credit for families with annual incomes up to $200,000. (A child is defined as an individual under 18 years of age.) The tax credit will benefit approximately 50 million families, 90 percent of which earn less than $75,000 per year.

Reform of the marriage penalty. The 1993 tax increases and expanded Earned Income Tax Credit resulted in many married couples across the income spectrum paying higher taxes than they would by filing as two singles. The bill provides up to $2 billion annually of marriage penalty relief. Each family currently subject to the marriage penalty would be entitled to a credit to an amount determined by the Secretary of Treasury.

Tax deductible individual retirement accounts (IRAs). The bill allows individuals to contribute up to $2,000 a year into an American Dream Savings Account (ADSA). Non-employed spouses may also participate. The ADSA is "back-ended," meaning the individual pays income taxes on the amount deposited, but not on the amount withdrawn if used for (1) retirement income; (2) purchase of a first-owner occupied home; (3) education expenses at a post-secondary institution (college or training institution) for self, spouse or dependent child; or (4) medical costs, including purchase of insurance for long-term care.

Within two years of enactment of ADRA, current IRA participants can cash out their current IRA and pay the tax due on it without having to pay any penalty, provided that the money is transferred to an ADSA.

National Security

The National Security Restoration Act reforms the Department of Defense (DOD)

to ensure that U.S. troops are only deployed to support missions in the United States' national security interests, to reinvigorate a national missile defense and to accelerate the expansion of NATO. Other provisions in the bill are designed to address concerns that readiness has suffered because defense spending has been cut too far and too quickly in order to pay for expensive social programs.

U.S. defense spending (as a percentage of gross domestic product) is at its lowest level since World War II and many assert that any more military reductions could leave the United States unprepared to respond to unforeseen global threats. Despite severe personnel reductions and shortfalls in funding over the last 10 years, U.S. troops have been deployed more often and have taken part in more operations per year than ever before. Presently, over 48,000 U.S. personnel serve in unstable regions such as Haiti, Iraq, Bosnia, Macedonia, the Adriatic Sea, Rwanda and the Caribbean.

The National Security Restoration Act addresses this problem by:

● Restricting DOD from taking part in military operations that would place U.S. troops under foreign command.

● Requiring an accurate and comprehensive review of U.S. defense needs by authorizing a blue-ribbon panel of independent defense experts to assess military readiness, maintenance practices and general operational needs.

● Restoring defense spending "firewalls" that prohibit the transfer of DOD funds to other departments and agencies in order to fund social spending programs unrelated to military readiness. Future defense spending cuts are to be used only for deficit reduction.

● Renewing the United States' commitment to an effective national missile defense by requiring DOD to deploy anti-ballistic missile systems capable of defending the United States against ballistic missile attacks.

● Renewing the United States' commitment to a strong North Atlantic Treaty Organization (NATO) by urging the Clinton administration to proceed with full NATO partnership discussions with nations that are striving to embrace democracy, enact free market economic reforms and place their armies under civilian control.

Provisions

Prohibition of foreign command of U.S. armed forces. DOD is prohibited from taking part in military operations which place U.S. troops under foreign command. The president may waive this provision if he certifies to Congress that operational control of our troops under foreign command is vital to U.S. national security interests.

No later than 10 days after this certification, the president must report to Congress with (1) a description of the vital national security interest that requires the

placement of U.S. troops under foreign command; (2) the size, composition, mission and objectives of the U.S. troops involved and the estimated time the troops will serve under foreign command; (3) the United States' cost for the mission; (4) the precise command and control relationship between the United States and the foreign command structure; and (5) the extent to which the U.S. troops will rely on non-U.S. military forces for security and self defense and an assessment of those forces' ability to carry out these duties.

Placing U.S. troops under foreign command for U.N. peacekeeping activities. The bill stipulates that any special peacekeeping agreement negotiated between the president and the U.N. Security Council which places U.S. troops under foreign command must be approved by Congress.

The president may not place U.S. troops under foreign command unless he (1) reports to Congress with the size, composition, mission and command structure of U.S. troops involved; (2) certifies that placing U.S. troops under foreign command is vital to national security; (3) retains the option to remove U.S. troops from peacekeeping activities at any time; and (4) guarantees that all U.S. troops placed under foreign leadership will remain under U.S. administrative command for discipline and evaluation. The above stipulations must be met no less than 15 days before U.S. troops are placed under foreign command.

Notice to Congress of proposed U.N. peacekeeping activities. The president must report to Congress at least 15 days prior to any U.N. Security Council vote authorizing U.N. peacekeeping activities which involve the use of U.S. troops and funds. The report is to include a description of U.S. force involvement, the mission of the U.S. troops, the cost and source of funding for the United States's share of the mission, and an estimated termination date for troop involvement.

Transmittal to Congress of U.N. resolutions and reports. Within 24 hours after the U.N. Security Council adopts a resolution authorizing peacekeeping activities involving U.S. troops, the president must submit the text and supporting documentation of the resolution to Congress.

Reports to Congress on U.S. contributions for U.N. peacekeeping activities. The president must (1) notify Congress within 15 days after the United Nations submits a billing statement to the United States for its share of peacekeeping activities and (2) notify Congress at least 15 days prior to disbursing funds for peacekeeping.

Budgeting for annual U.S. contributions for U.N. peacekeeping activities. The president is directed to submit to Congress, along with his annual budget, a report with estimates of the United States' fiscal year funding requirements for U.N. peacekeeping. Beginning

with the FY 1996 budget, the president is to submit to Congress an estimate of all U.S. costs associated with U.N. peacekeeping for each of FY 1996, 1997 and 1998.

Annual reports to Congress on peacekeeping. No later than 90 days after enactment, and each year thereafter at the time of the president's annual budget submission, the president is to report to Congress on U.S. contributions to U.N. peacekeeping. The report is to include (1) the number and nature of ongoing peacekeeping activities, (2) the priority and anticipated duration of each ongoing activity, (3) an assessment of each ongoing peacekeeping operation and its effect on U.S. national security, (4) the total costs of each U.N. peacekeeping mission and the U.S. contribution to each of these missions, and (5) an assessment of U.N. management of peacekeeping activities. The initial report is to include the costs for all U.N. peacekeeping activities since October 1945. Subsequent reports are to include the same information for the preceding and current fiscal year.

U.S. reimbursement for in-kind contributions to U.N. peacekeeping operations. Beginning in FY 1995, appropriated peacekeeping funds may not be used to pay the U.S. share of U.N. operations unless DOD certifies to Congress that the United Nations has reimbursed DOD for all goods and services that have been provided to the United Nations on a reimbursable basis.

Limitation on the use of DOD funds for U.N. peacekeeping. Beginning Oct. 1, 1995, DOD Operations and Maintenance funds for U.S. contributions to U.N. peacekeeping missions are subject to congressional authorization.

Assessed contributions for U.N. peacekeeping activities. The bill expresses the sense of Congress that (1) the United States should not fund more than 25 percent of the total cost of any U.N. peacekeeping mission and (2) the United Nations should review each nation's assessed contributions for U.N. peacekeeping activities.

Buy America requirement. No U.S. funds may be contributed to the United Nations for peacekeeping activities unless the secretary of State determines that U.S. manufacturers and suppliers are being given the opportunity to provide equipment, services and material for peacekeeping mission activities equivalent to those being given to foreign manufacturers and suppliers.

U.S. personnel taken prisoner while serving in multilateral peacekeeping missions. The bill expresses the sense of Congress that the president should take all necessary steps to (1) ensure that any U.S. military personnel captured during U.N. peacekeeping activities are to be treated as prisoners of war and (2) bring to justice all individuals responsible for the mistreatment, torture and death of American prisoners.

Provision of intelligence to the United Nations. The United States is authorized to provide intelligence assets to the United Nations only if the president and the secretary general of the United Nations agree to the types of intelligence to be provided, the circumstances under which the intelligence assistance is to be provided and the procedures to be observed by the United Nations to ensure the secrecy of the intelligence. The president must report to Congress at least 30 days prior to entering into such an agreement.

U.N. peacekeeping budgetary and management reform. The bill contains numerous budgetary reforms to ensure efficiency when the United States contributes funds to the United Nations. At the beginning of each fiscal year (beginning in FY 1995), 50 percent of all U.S. funds made available for U.N. peacekeeping must be withheld until the president certifies to Congress that (1) the United Nations has established an independent and objective Office of Inspector General to audit, inspect and investigate peacekeeping activities; and (2) the secretary general of the United Nations has appointed an inspector general who is proficient in accounting, financial analysis, law and public administration.

Independent blue-ribbon panel. The bill establishes a blue-ribbon panel to conduct an accurate and comprehensive review of the United States' national security needs, force readiness requirements and modernization plans. This provision comes in response to critics of President Clinton's "bottom-up review" who assert that it contained unrealistic financing for the established goals.

Restoring budget firewalls for defense spending. The bill stipulates that DOD funds may not be transferred to any other department or agency unless the secretary of Defense reports to Congress, at least 30 days before these funds are to be made available, with proof that it is vital to U.S. national security interests. DOD may waive this provision during periods of national emergency declared by the president or Congress, however the waiver may not take effect until Congress has been notified.

Renewed commitment to a national missile defense. DOD is directed to (1) develop for deployment at the earliest possible date a cost-effective, operational anti-ballistic missile defense system to protect the United States against ballistic missile threats (e.g., accidental or unauthorized launches or Third World attacks); (2) implement as quickly as possible advanced theater missile defense systems; and (3) report to Congress within 60 days of enactment with a plan for both missile defense systems.

Renewed commitment to a strong North Atlantic Treaty Organization (NATO). On Jan. 10, 1994, leaders of the NATO member nations meeting in Brussels, Belgium, issued an invitation to European countries that do not belong to

NATO to participate in the Partnership for Peace program. In that invitation, NATO reaffirmed its commitment to expand the organization to increase the security of the North Atlantic area. NATO pointed out that many European countries that in the past had been adversaries, had rejected ideological hostility to the West and, in varying degrees, had begun to implement policies aimed at achieving democracy, protecting human rights and building free market economies.

The bill expresses the sense of Congress that (1) the United States should continue its commitment to an active leadership in NATO; (2) the United States should join with its NATO allies to redefine the alliance's role in the post-Cold War world (taking into account the changes in central and eastern Europe and the emerging security threats posed by nuclear, chemical and biological weapons of mass destruction); (3) the United States should reaffirm that NATO military planning includes joint military operations outside of NATO jurisdiction; (4) that Poland, Hungary, the Czech Republic and Slovakia should be in a position to further the principles of the North Atlantic Treaty and contribute to the security of the North Atlantic area no later than Jan. 10, 1999 (the bill also states that these countries should continue working toward democracy, free market economics and civilian control of their militaries); (5) the United States should assist these nations as they work towards inclusion in NATO; and (6) other European nations should be invited to join NATO in the future if they agree to contribute to the security of the North Atlantic.

The president is given authority to establish a program to assist Poland, Hungary, the Czech Republic, Slovakia and other European countries that are working toward full membership in NATO. The program is to assist the new nations with joint planning and military exercises with NATO forces and encourage greater interoperability of military equipment to achieve a uniform military doctrine. The president may also provide assistance to other European countries emerging from communist domination if he certifies that they have made significant progress in embracing democracy and establishing free-market economies.

President's report to Congress. Within one year after enactment, and at least once every year thereafter, the president is to report to Congress on the progress made by Poland, Hungary, the Czech Republic, Slovakia and other emerging European countries in their efforts to achieve full NATO membership.

Background

The present landscape of the DOD review process [Bottom Up Review]. In 1990-91, the Bush administration studied how U.S. military forces should be restructured after the end of the Cold War and produced a blueprint for a base force

20-25 percent smaller in budget and forces than the current structure.

In spite of this review, the Clinton administration decided to undertake its own bottom-up review — making its own assessment of the United States' post-Cold War defense needs and making its own proposals to restructure the military to meet them. In September 1993, the bottom-up review (BUR) was released with its recommendation to cut an additional 10 percent on top of the Bush administration's proposals. BUR's FY 1995-99 defense spending recommendation was $91 billion below the Bush administration's adjusted baseline of $1.325 trillion and $13 billion more than the Clinton administration's own defense spending target of $1.221 trillion. Former Defense Secretary Aspin expressed the administration's intent to trim down spending to meet the target. The FY 1995 defense authorization bill was the first defense authorization measure drafted in accordance with BUR.

BUR's proposals are based on maintaining a force structure sufficient to win two major regional conflicts simultaneously (a strategy called win-win). BUR claims savings of (1) $24 billion from cutting 160,000 more active duty personnel than the Bush administration, (2) $19 billion from infrastructure changes, including base closings, and cutting 115,000 more civilian personnel than the Bush administration, (3) $21 billion from realigning ballistic missile defense programs, and (4) $32 billion from reduced development and procurement of many systems. Savings were also achieved in weapons modernization programs.

The Clinton administration argues the BUR force structure reflects a cautious strategy to maintain U.S. freedom of action in a still dangerous world. The U.S. military will have greater strategic mobility, more firepower and be armed with "smart" and "brilliant" weapons. Moreover, additional savings will be possible from changes in strategic nuclear programs and minor procurement programs, acquisition reform, and Vice President Al Gore's national performance review.

Critics have charged that (1) the win-win strategy is purely military — that is, the Clinton administration has yet to develop a national security strategy encompassing all its concerns and priorities; (2) the proposed force is inadequate; it is the same force that previous DOD analyses considered appropriate for less-demanding strategies; (3) the strategy overestimates the savings to be achieved from base closures; (4) the BUR force cannot be maintained within the Clinton administration's own budget guidelines; (5) the Army, with only 10 active divisions, will be hard pressed to support the win-win strategy while fulfilling peacekeeping missions around the globe; (6) cutting the aircraft carrier fleet from 13 to 11 will create gaps in global coverage; and (7) the Air Force may have too few long range attack aircraft, too few aerial tankers and an insuffi-

cient airlift capacity to support two major regional conflicts.

The current outlook for defense spending. On Feb. 7, 1994, President Clinton presented his FY 1995 defense budget to Congress. Recommending $263.7 billion in new BA [budget authority] and $270.7 billion in outlays, the plan continues the decline in military spending that began in the late 1980s. Under the president's proposal, by FY 1997, BA for national defense will fall to about 40 percent of the FY 1985 spending peak (in constant, inflation-adjusted dollars), with spending beginning to level off after that.

Late in 1993, discussion of the defense budget focused on a five-year $50 billion gap between the projected cost of planned military programs and the amount available under budget plans formulated last year.

The projected gap was mainly due to higher estimates of inflation and a congressionally mandated military pay raise. Subsequently, revised inflation estimates reduced the projected gap, and the president approved an increase of $11.4 billion over five years in defense funding to cover costs of the pay raise. These changes narrowed the gap to about $20 billion, but the administration decided to postpone dealing with the shortfall until this year.

Following debate on the defense funding shortfall, the president reaffirmed support for his long-term defense spending plan by arguing in his State of the Union address against further cuts. Perhaps partly because of the president's endorsement of the defense plan, debate over defense spending levels was relatively muted once the House and Senate considered the annual congressional budget resolution in March 1994.

In the House, a proposal to reduce FY 1995 defense budget authority by $2.4 billion was defeated by a substantial margin. But both chambers also rejected proposals to increase five-year defense spending levels by at least the $20 billion shortfall. The Senate approved a measure to reduce caps on overall discretionary spending by $46 billion in BA and $26 billion in outlays. Although many supporters of the measure argued that the cuts should not come from defense, critics warned that DOD would likely bear a large share of the reductions. The House, which had no comparable provision, narrowly rejected a motion to instruct conferees to include these Senate-passed cuts, and the final conference agreement split the difference between the House and the Senate, cutting $13 billion in outlays over five years. The allocation of the reductions is left to the appropriations committees.

Debate over the FY 1995 defense budget was heated, with a number of longer-term defense spending and policy issues emerging to the forefront. Major issues included whether the administration budget is sufficient to maintain high levels of military readiness, whether the planned military force is large enough to support the

military strategy articulated in BUR, and whether the necessary pace of weapons modernization will outrun likely weapons budgets after the turn of the century.

Spending trends. Over the past several years, debate has focused not on whether defense spending should be cut, but rather by how much. Proponents of greater and accelerated reductions have argued that with the end of the Cold War, funds previously allocated for defense are now free to be spent on urgent domestic needs.

With defense spending currently at its lowest level (as a percentage of gross domestic product) since World War II, others have argued that downsizing must be done methodically and carefully, warning that quick and deep reductions in the past have left the United States unprepared to respond to unforeseen global threats.

A key issue in the current defense policy debate is whether the defense budget projected by the Clinton administration for the next several years is sufficient to support a well-equipped, well-trained, high-quality military force. Defense analysts have generally assumed that if the size of the military force remains stable, then defense spending will and probably should grow moderately over time in order to purchase and operate more modern equipment and to improve the quality of life in the military.

Some observers see current defense budgets as comparable (in inflation-adjusted prices) to average Cold War-era budgets, and conclude that a continuing "Cold War level of funding" should suffice to support a substantially smaller, post-Cold War force. Because defense spending normally has grown over time relative to the size of the force, however, such a comparison may not be very meaningful.

When the normal growth in defense funding per troop is taken into account, it appears that currently planned budgets will begin to fall below the historical trend over the next few years. How well or how poorly the budget fits the force will depend on the impact of a slowdown in weapons modernization and on how well efforts to protect readiness are managed. Senior administration officials acknowledge that procurement funding has declined substantially in recent years, but, they say this is acceptable in the short run. Judging by historical standards, however, significant increases in defense funding may be necessary in the future to maintain a capable force of the planned size unless there are significant changes in patterns of acquisition and operations.

International peacekeeping operations. The United States participates in a number of peacekeeping operations worldwide, most of which are organized, carried out and paid for by the United States in association with U.N. efforts. Currently, the incremental costs associated with the mission — costs above and beyond normal peacetime operating expenses — are funded through (1) supplemental appropri-

ations, (2) DOD reprogramming, (3) absorption by DOD accounts, and (4) earmarkings in annual defense funding bills. The United States has 13 ongoing missions. Last year, President Clinton requested $597 million for peacekeeping and Congress appropriated $401.6 million.

Because of the rapid increase in both the number and cost of peacekeeping operations since the end of the Cold War, some members of Congress have expressed concern about the existing funding procedures. One solution is to create a new account to hold advanced funding of U.S. peacekeeping missions. The Clinton administration tried to do this in the FY 1994 defense budget, calling the account the Global Cooperative Initiative, but it was rejected by Congress.

The United States also funds peacekeeping operations through mandatory contributions to the United Nations. The United States is responsible for 25 percent of the United Nations' normal operating budget and 31.7 percent of the cost of each U.N.-sponsored peacekeeping activity. The peacekeeping assessment was raised from 30.4 percent to 31.7 percent last year to compensate for reduced contributions by the now-dissolved Soviet Union. This increase added fire to existing concerns about the United Nations' management practices, causing the administration to demand that the U.S. share be reduced to 25 percent.

At the end of the Cold War, partially fueled by the success of Operation Desert Storm, enthusiasm for peacekeeping operations peaked. But the mood quickly changed as Americans monitored an inconclusive U.S. mission in Somalia and considered the possibility of many American deaths in a ground war in Bosnia.

On May 8, 1994, the Clinton administration unveiled criteria the president will use to decide which peacekeeping efforts to support with money, troops or both. Under these criteria, in order for the United States to vote in favor of a mission it must advance U.S. interests; result from a threat to international peace and security; and have clear, realistic objectives. The criteria for deciding whether to commit troops to the mission, especially if combat is expected, are more stringent. The directive also makes clear that American forces can never be placed under foreign command unless doing so would serve American security interests. White House National Security Adviser Anthony Lake describes these guidelines as an attempt to reform and limit U.S. participation for such activities.

Senior Citizens

The Senior Citizens' Equity Act removes financial burdens on American senior citizens to (1) allow them to earn more income without losing Social Security

benefits and (2) reduce the percentage of Social Security benefits on which they must pay taxes to the level before they were increased by the Clinton administration in 1993. The bill provides tax incentives to encourage individuals to buy private long-term care insurance and makes it easier for seniors to reserve retirement communities for adults only without facing lawsuits.

Increase of the Social Security earnings limit threshold. Under current law, senior citizens between the ages of 65 and 69 lose $1 in Social Security benefits for every $3 they earn above $11,160. This earnings test amounts to an additional 33 percent marginal tax rate, on top of existing income taxes, and punishes seniors who choose to remain productive beyond age 64. Over five years, the bill raises to $30,000 the amount which seniors can earn before losing Social Security benefits. The limit will be raised according to the following schedule. By Jan. 1, 1996, seniors can earn $15,000 without losing Social Security benefits; by Jan. 1, 1997, $19,000; by Jan. 1, 1998, $23,000; by Jan. 1, 1999, $27,000; by Jan. 1, 2000, $30,000.

Repeal of Clinton's Social Security benefits tax. The 1993 Omnibus Budget Reconciliation Act (OBRA 1993) requires senior citizens who earn more than $34,000 (singles) or $44,000 (couples) to pay income taxes on 85 percent of their Social Security benefits. Over five years this bill restores the amount of Social Security benefits subject to income tax to 50 percent, the level of benefits taxable before OBRA. The percentage of Social Security benefits subject to income taxes will drop from 85 percent to: 75 percent for tax year 1996, 65 percent for tax year 1997, 60 percent for tax year 1998, 55 percent for tax year 1999, and 50 percent for tax year 2000.

Tax incentives for private long-term care insurance. The bill includes several provisions pertaining to the tax treatment of long-term health care included in the Affordable Health Care Now Act (HR 3080), the House Republican health reform package: allows tax-free withdrawals from IRAs, 401(k) plans and other qualified pension plans in order to purchase long-term care insurance; allows accelerated death benefits to be paid from life insurance policies for individuals who are terminally ill or permanently confined to a nursing home; and treats long-term care insurance as a tax-free fringe benefit and the same as accident and health insurance for taxation purposes. The bill also allows deductions for long-term care premiums, limited to the following amounts (indexed for inflation annually): age 40 and under, $200; age 40 to 50, $375; age 50 to 60, $750; age 60 to 70, $1,600; age 70 and older, $2,000.

Senior citizen retirement communities. Current law is vague on what constitutes senior housing. Consequently, lawsuits have been brought against real estate agents and retirement community board members. The bill allows housing commu-

nities to meet the Fair Housing Amendment Act's "adults-only housing test" if those communities can prove that at least 80 percent of their units have occupants age 55 or older.

The Fair Housing Amendments Act of 1988 prohibits discrimination based on familial status, although it does include a vague definition of adults-only housing. Under current law, senior communities are exempt from the 1988 law's anti-discrimination provisions if at least 80 percent of the units in a senior community are occupied by those 55 and over, and the community has "significant facilities" such as support rails and transportation vans. The law, however, does not specifically state what must be present to merit exemption.

This current vague definition has posed problems for many retirement communities and has resulted in lawsuits against real estate agents and retirement community board members. This provision of the bill repeals the significant facilities test and exempts real estate agents and community board members from liability for monetary damages in lawsuits if they acted on a good-faith belief that the community was exempt. Thus, senior communities must only meet the 80 percent test to be awarded an exemption.

Background

Americans over the age of 65 number more than 30 million and constitute more than 12 percent of the population. Two important areas of concern for them are Social Security and the cost of long-term care.

Social Security earnings test. Congress passed the Social Security Act in 1935 as part of President Franklin D. Roosevelt's New Deal, establishing a program to provide income to older Americans. The program has always included an earnings test. There have been many proposals to alter or end the earnings test, but none has been enacted. Social Security benefits are intended to compensate for income lost because of retirement, but many seniors have complained that it is unfair to punish those who keep working by not allowing them to collect Social Security benefits when they have paid into the system all their working lives.

Social Security benefits tax. The other provision of the bill affecting Social Security deals with a relatively new phenomenon. Social Security benefits were not taxed at all until 1984. It was then that a system was established whereby individuals with total income of $25,000 or more and couples with a total income of $32,000 or more would have to pay taxes on up to 50 percent of their Social Security benefits.

In 1993 President Clinton sought to tax up to 85 percent of Social Security benefits. Although the House approved this provision as part of the 1993 Omnibus Budget Reconciliation bill (OBRA 1993), the provision was modified in conference. The final version of the bill increased the maximum percentage of benefits that could

be taxed to 85 percent but also created a second set of thresholds at $34,000 for individuals and $44,000 for couples. OBRA 1993 created a complicated system whereby recipients who had to pay taxes on 50 percent of benefits continue to do so, and those whose income exceeds the new threshold have to pay taxes on up to 85 percent of benefits.

Long-term care. The cost of long-term care concerns senior citizens and others. About 7.1 million of the elderly need long-term care, and estimates indicate 13.8 million may need it by 2030. Most long-term care is paid for by private individuals and Medicaid. Many elderly do not need constant medical attention but do need assistance with daily activities. Medicare and most other health insurance plans do not cover most services associated with long-term care. In order to qualify for Medicaid assistance for long-term care, individuals must first "spend down" a significant portion of their own savings and other assets.

Capital Gains Taxes/ Regulatory Changes

The Job Creation and Wage Enhancement Act includes a variety of tax-law changes and federal bureaucratic reforms designed to enhance private property rights and economic liberty and make government more accountable for the burdens it imposes on American workers.

Specifically, the bill:

● Provides a 50 percent capital gains rate cut and prospectively indexes capital gains to account for inflation.

● Increases the value of investment depreciation to equal the full value of original investment.

● Allows small businesses to deduct the first $25,000 worth of investment each year.

● Clarifies the home office deduction.

● Empowers taxpayers to designate a portion of their tax liability to a public debt reduction fund.

● Requires federal agencies to assess the risk and cost of each imposed regulation.

● Forces federal agencies to publicly announce the cost of their policies.

● Requires Congress to report the cost of mandates it imposes on state and local governments.

● Reduces the paperwork burden imposed on American business 5 percent.

● Limits the government's ability to impose undue burdens on private property owners.

● Requires federal agencies to complete regulatory impact analyses.

Government-imposed mandates and regulations suppress wages, and excessive taxation of capital and investment stifles economic growth and job creation. Current federal policies threaten the competitiveness of American business, stifle entrepreneurial activity and suppress economic

growth and job creation. Regulations can also have a direct impact on the lives of all Americans — raising the prices they pay for goods and services, restricting the use of their private property and limiting the availability of credit. The bill lowers taxes on investment and reins in regulation to create additional jobs, enhance wages and recognize private property rights.

The Job Creation and Wage Enhancement Act, its sponsors assert, is consistent with the maintenance of a competitive marketplace. It is committed to breaking down unnecessary barriers to entry created by regulations, statutes and judicial decisions, and calls for open, simultaneous and immediate competition within all industries in the United States.

Provisions

Capital gains reform. The Job Creation Act allows individuals to exclude from taxes 50 percent of capital gains income, effectively halving the rate. Under the bill, individuals in the 15 percent income tax bracket would pay an effective capital gains tax rate of 7.5 percent, those in the 28 percent bracket would effectively pay 14 percent, and those in the top bracket of 39.6 percent would pay 19.8 percent on capital gains. Corporations would pay a 17.5 percent capital gains rate. In addition, individuals may deduct any capital loss with respect to the sale or exchange of a principal residence. The bill indexes the basis of capital assets for inflation (prospectively) so taxes are not paid on illusory earnings.

Neutral cost recovery. The bill increases the value of investment depreciation to equal the full value of the original investment. The current value of investment depreciation is less than the original investment because the amounts deducted in later years are eroded by inflation. The bill adjusts the amounts written off after the first year by a discount rate. The neutral cost recovery provision makes taxpayers pay interest on the delayed portions of the write-off. The bill is expected to (1) add approximately a percentage point to the economic growth rate, (2) increase the [Gross Domestic Product] by $4 trillion between 1995 and 2000, and (3) create almost 2.7 million jobs.

Small-business appreciation. The bill recognizes the important contribution small businesses make in our economy by encouraging investment and alleviating the cumbersome paperwork of depreciation schedules. Its provisions include:

● Raising the expensing level from $17,500 to $25,000, allowing small businesses to deduct the first $25,000 they invest in equipment and inventory each year.

● Clarifying the home office deduction allowing taxpayers to qualify if the home office is (1) used exclusively for business purposes, (2) used on a regular basis, (3) used to perform tasks that could not easily be performed elsewhere, and (4) is essential to the taxpayer's business.

● Increasing the estate tax exemption

from $600,000 to $750,000, thus restoring the value eroded by inflation and making it easier for small business owners and family farmers to keep their shops and farms in the family.

Taxpayer debt buy-down. The bill allows taxpayers to designate up to 10 percent of their tax liability to be used to help reduce the public debt. The designated funds would be transferred to the Public Debt Reduction trust fund to be established by the Department of Treasury. Congress is required to reduce spending equivalent to the amount designated by the taxpayer. If for some reason the spending cuts do not occur, an across-the-board sequester will be imposed on all government accounts except the Federal Deposit Insurance Corporation, the National Credit Union Administration and the Resolution Trust Corporation.

Risk assessment/cost benefit analysis. The Job Creation and Wage Enhancement Act requires each federal agency to assess the risks to human health and safety and the environment for each new regulation. Agencies must also provide the cost associated with the regulation and an analysis comparing the economic and compliance costs of the regulation to the public. Each agency must form an independent peer review panel to certify the assessment and incorporate the best available scientific data. The review panel members must either possess professional experience conducting risk assessment or in the given field of study.

Regulatory budget. The bill requires federal agencies to issue an annual report projecting the cost to the private sector of compliance with all federal regulations. The cost of the regulations will then be capped below its current level, forcing agencies to (1) find more cost-effective ways to reach goals and (2) identify regulatory policies whose benefits exceed their costs to the private sector.

Unfunded mandate reform. The Congressional Budget Office (CBO) is required to issue an analysis of each piece of legislation containing a federal mandate (a program that burdens state and local governments with [undue] costs resulting in over $50 million annually). The analysis must include a description of the mandate, the expected cost to state and local governments, and if the mandates are to be partly or entirely unfunded. CBO budgetary impact reports are to be printed in the committee reports accompanying legislation. The bill caps the mandate's cost below its level for the proceeding year.

Strengthen the Paperwork Reduction Act and the Regulatory Flexibility Act. Compliance with federal regulations consumes tens of thousands of man-hours annually. Employers must hire lawyers and other experts to fill out the government paperwork. Consequently, they hire fewer workers to produce goods and services. To address this problem, the bill requires the government to reduce the paperwork burden by 5 percent annually.

Also, the bill subjects the Regulatory Flexibility Act to judicial review, so small businesses can sue to enforce the law. The Regulatory Flexibility Act determines whether or not a regulation has a substantial impact on a significant number of small businesses.

Protection against federal regulatory abuse. The bill provides individuals a Citizens' Bill of Rights when being inspected or investigated by a federal agency. The bill of rights affirms individuals' rights to (1) remain silent, (2) refuse a warrantless search, (3) be warned that statements can be used against them, (4) have an attorney or accountant present, (5) be present at an inspection or investigation, and (6) be reimbursed for unreasonable damages. Also, the bill allows individuals who are threatened by a prohibited regulatory practice to take legal action against the responsible agency. A prohibited regulatory practice is defined as an inconsistent application of any law, rule or regulation causing mismanagement of agency resources by any agency or employee of the agency.

Private property. The bill allows private property owners to receive compensation (up to 10 percent of fair market value) from the federal government for any reduction in the value of their property. If a question arises over the value of the property, the private property owner may use an arbitrator to decide the outcome.

Regulatory impact analysis. The bill requires federal agencies to complete a regulatory impact analysis when drafting a major rule (affecting more than 100 people and costing more than $1 million). The bill lists 23 specific criteria the agencies must follow, including: (1) explaining the necessity and appropriateness of the rule, (2) a statement of whether the rule is in accord with or in conflict with any legal precedent, (3) a demonstration that the rule is cost-effective, (4) an estimate of the number of persons affected by the rule, and (5) an estimate of the costs to the agency for implementation of the rule.

Legal Reforms/ Product Liability

The bill makes a number of legal reforms to, among other things, make sure that expert witness testimony is based on scientifically sound evidence, that product liability laws are uniformly applied, that abusive securities lawsuits are limited, and that opportunities for alternative dispute resolution are expanded.

Background

Almost everyone agrees that America has become a litigious society: We sue each other too often and too easily. In the federal courts alone, the number of lawsuits filed each year has almost tripled in the last 30 years — from approximately 90,000 in 1960 to more than 250,000 in 1990.

As President Bush's Council on Competitiveness found, this dramatic growth in litigation carries high costs for the U.S. economy: manufacturers withdraw products from the market, discontinue product research, reduce their work forces and raise their prices.

In addition to the sheer volume of lawsuits that filter through the legal system each year are the problems associated with frivolous suits. In many cases, defendants know that the suit would not stand on its own merits, but agree to settle out of court just to avoid the endless and expensive claim and appeal processes. Such responses merely perpetuate our propensity to sue.

Legal experts point to a few straightforward reforms that can help stem abuse of the system. Promoting voluntary settlements instead of court trials, and encouraging meritorious claims while discouraging baseless suits and devious trial tactics are just some of these proposals.

Provisions

Loser pays rule. The bill applies the so-called "loser pays rule" (in which the unsuccessful party in a suit pays the attorneys' fees of the prevailing party) to diversity cases filed in federal court. A diversity case involves citizens from different states. However, the bill limits the size of the coverage to the loser's own attorneys' fees costs (e.g., if the prevailing party spent $100 defending himself and the unsuccessful party spent $50, then the unsuccessful party is only responsible for $50 of the prevailing party's court costs). Courts may also impose other limits on the award of attorneys' fees.

Bill sponsors argue that the "loser pays rule" strongly discourages the filing of weak cases as well as encourages the pursuit of strong cases, since claimants can get their court costs reimbursed if they win.

Honesty in evidence. The bill amends Rule 702 of the Federal Rules of Evidence regarding expert witness testimony to state that expert testimony is not admissible in a federal court (1) unless it is based on "scientifically valid reasoning" and (2) if the expert is paid a contingency fee (however, the bill allows the judge to waive this second prohibition). Bill sponsors argue that so-called experts too often base their opinions on "junk science" in order to justify absurd claims.

Product liability. The legislation creates a uniform product liability law (covering state and federal actions) in three areas: punitive damages, joint and several liability, and fault-based liability for product sellers. For punitive damages, the bill requires that claimants establish by "clear and convincing evidence" that the harm they suffered was the direct result of malicious conduct. Under the measure, punitive damages are limited to three times the actual harm (i.e., the economic damages awarded). For claimants with little actual harm, awards of up to $250,000 could be awarded.

The bill also abolishes joint liability for non-economic losses (mental distress, pain and suffering, etc.) and holds defendants liable only for their proportion of the harm. Under current law, a defendant can be held responsible for the entire award, even if he is not completely responsible for all the harm done. For example, if a consumer sues the manufacturer, the buyer, the shipper and the merchant, and only the merchant is solvent, the merchant becomes responsible for the total amount of damages awarded by the court — including the portions owed by the other parties. The solvent individual is then forced to recover the others' portions on his own. This legislation would make an individual party responsible only for the portion of damages directly attributable to it.

Finally, the bill makes product sellers liable only for harms caused by their own negligence (e.g., altering or assembling a product or making false claims about the product). Product sellers would only be responsible for manufacturer errors when the manufacturer cannot be brought to court or lacks the funds to pay a settlement.

Attorney accountability. The bill expresses the sense of Congress that states should enact laws requiring attorneys practicing within their borders to disclose certain information to clients. Specifically, in contingency fee cases, states should make attorneys disclose (1) the actual duties performed for each client and (2) the precise number of hours actually spent performing these duties.

The bill also amends Rule 11 of the Federal Rules of Civil Procedure to restore the mandatory requirement that courts sanction attorneys for improper actions and frivolous arguments intended to harass, unnecessarily delay and needlessly increase the cost of litigation. Sanctions are to be determined by the judge and may involve financial penalties, contempt orders, limits on discovery and other procedural penalties. Prior to Dec. 1, 1993, federal courts were required to impose sanctions for violations of Rule 11. However, on that date the Federal Judicial Conference's recommendations to amend Rule 11 (making sanctions optional rather than mandatory) took effect since Congress did not act on the proposed rule change.

In addition to reinstating the mandatory sanction, the bill requires, for the first time, that sanctioned attorneys compensate injured parties.

Prior notice. At least 30 days before a plaintiff can bring a suit, he must transmit written notice to the defendant of the specific claims involved and the actual amount of damages sought. Proponents of the legislation argue that prior notice of a grievance provides an opportunity for both parties to resolve the dispute without going to court.

Legislative checklist. This section of the bill is designed to limit needless and costly litigation resulting from poorly drafted legislation. Frequently Congress fails to directly address basic issues that later result in court challenges. For exam-

ple, during consideration of the most recent amendments to the Civil Rights Act, Congress failed to resolve the issue of retroactivity. Litigation dragged on for two years until the Supreme Court ruled that the law was not retroactive. Bill sponsors argue that this could have been avoided if Congress had been forced to take a decisive stand on the issue.

The bill seeks to limit such situations by requiring that committee reports address the following issues: pre-emptive effect, retroactive effect, authorization for private suits and applicability to the federal government.

Strike lawsuits. The bill reforms federal securities law to limit so-called strike lawsuits — lawsuits filed by class action attorneys on behalf of shareholders whose once-attractive stock purchases have failed to live up to their expectations. Although these suits claim that the holding company misrepresented the healthiness of their stocks, many times the downturn can only be blamed on market violatility.

Bill sponsors argue that these cases usually involve highly speculative investments in the securities field (less than 1 percent involve truly fraudulent companies), and it is the attorney, not the shareholder, that benefits from the suit. Since class action lawyers can make decisions that are not in the best interest of the clients without fear of reprisal and take a big chunk of the settlement off the top, shareholders are often exploited. Strike suits are money-makers for the lawyers, but such frivolous claims destroy jobs and hurt the economy. Instead of spending money on research and development, or hiring more employees, or reducing the cost of their products, companies end up spending big bucks on strike suit insurance and legal fees.

High-technology, biotechnology and other growth companies are hardest hit because their stocks are naturally volatile. Small and medium-sized companies alone have paid out nearly $500 million during the last two years (settling a case is oftentimes cheaper and quicker than defending in court). The problem is rapidly getting worse: in the last five years, the number of strike suits has tripled.

To address these abuses, the bill (1) provides a court-appointed trustee for plaintiffs (to make sure that lawyers act in the best interests of their clients), (2) guarantees plaintiffs full disclosure of key settlement terms (including a breakdown of how much is to go to them and how much to their lawyers to pay legal fees), (3) limits "professional plaintiffs" to five class-action lawsuits every three years (these individuals typically purchase one share of every stock on the New York Stock Exchange and wait for the stock to drop. They then work with the class action lawyer to initiate the class action and receive bonus payments for their cooperation), (4) makes losing litigants responsible for the winner's costs, (5) prohibits application of the Racketeer Influence and Corrupt Organizations (RICO) Act to securities cases, and (6) prohibits vague and open-ended complaints. In a key reform, the bill requires that claimants show they relied on intentionally misrepresented information or omissions of information in deciding to purchase their stock, and that their losses were not caused by bad luck in the stock market.

Congressional Term Limits

This resolution provides for consideration of two joint resolutions which propose amendments to the Constitution limiting the number of terms members of the Senate and the House of Representatives can serve. The first joint resolution (identical to H J Res 38 as introduced in the 103rd Congress) limits the number of Senate terms to two and the number of House terms to six. The second joint resolution (identical to H J Res 160 as introduced in the 103rd Congress) also limits senators to two terms, but it limits members of the House to three terms.

Under the terms of this resolution, the joint resolution with the text of H J Res 38 will be debated first and the first amendment in order will be a substitute consisting of H J Res 160.

Background

The idea of limiting the tenure of elected officials has recurred through our history, but it has become more popular in the last few years.

As of 1992, 14 states passed initiatives limiting the tenure of federal legislators. Two of these laws, however, have been challenged and found unconstitutional in court. The U.S. Supreme Court will review the ruling by the Arkansas Supreme Court. Since there is a chance the high court will uphold the state court's ruling, a constitutional amendment may be necessary to limit congressional tenure. ∎

TRADE

Dole-Administration Exchange on GATT

Following is a Nov. 23 statement on the General Agreement on Tariffs and Trade (GATT) by Senate Minority Leader Bob Dole, R-Kan., followed by letters he received from Clinton administration officials:

There are many good provisions in the GATT agreement, but it has never been perfect. While it is still not perfect, I am pleased that we have been able to fix so much of it with significant changes.

I had especially deep concerns about giving up U.S. sovereignty to the World Trade Organization [WTO]. I have also been concerned about the legislation to implement the GATT agreement, which contains many inappropriate provisions that should have been removed, or that should at least be remedied.

Over the past few months, I have been working with the administration to remedy as many of these problems as possible now, before Congress considers the GATT bill in the special session next week. I am pleased to say we were able to address many of the issues that were of concern to me, and to the thousands of Americans from Kansas and across the country who have called me or written to me about GATT.

WTO concerns. My major concern was that the GATT agreement establishes a new dispute settlement process that could seriously harm U.S. interests. I was concerned that WTO dispute settlement panels in Geneva could rule against the U.S., and even if that ruling was clearly wrong, we could have been required to accept that bad ruling, and maybe even pay penalties to other countries.

The Dole proposal: 3 strikes and we're out. That's why I proposed that we establish a procedure here in the U.S. to ensure that U.S. interests are protected. I am pleased that the administration agreed with me, and we have worked out the details. A permanent commission of sitting appellate court judges will review dispute settlement decisions by the WTO. If the WTO dispute settlement panel decides arbitrarily or improperly against the [United States], Congress will vote to re-negotiate the rules in the WTO. After the third bad WTO decision, Congress will vote on whether to withdraw from the WTO. We call it "three strikes and we're out."

This process is unprecedented in the history of U.S. trade agreements. It is not a fig-leaf; it is not just another layer of complexity. It provides a clear, quick exit if our rights are being trampled in the WTO. It provides Congress with a decisive role in determining whether the interests of the U.S. are being served by continued mem-

bership in the WTO. If not, we will withdraw.

Real and effective protection for U.S. interests. This process is vastly different from the six-month withdrawal provision in the WTO agreement itself. That provision does nothing more than state every country's right to withdraw. Unlike my proposal, it does not provide for careful scrutiny of individual cases, it does not provide for any congressional role, and in fact, it is unlikely that such a provision would ever be used. My new proposal provides real and effective protection against abuses of U.S. sovereignty in the World Trade Organization.

Agricultural issues. We also reached agreement on agriculture issues. The administration agreed not to single out agriculture for spending cuts. The Export Enhancement Program [EEP] will be reformed, and used to the maximum extent permissible. The Conservation Reserve Program will be extended on a multiple-year basis. The approval process for EEP sales will be speeded up — this will significantly help our wheat sales abroad. Oilseed products will receive the benefit of "greenbox" export promotion funds. The U.S. will push hard for meaningful access to the Chinese market for oilseeds and other products.

Pioneer preferences. We agreed to work together to determine whether the pioneer preference licenses bring a fair return to the government. I hope we will act next year to clean up this particularly egregious special deal.

Patent provisions. The administration will not oppose our efforts to change the length of time patents are protected. Therefore, we will seek a change next year in the patent provision in the implementing bill. I believe this is important for all the inventors and creative people in America, to give maximum protection to their intellectual property.

Capital gains rate reduction. On the issue of capital gains rate reduction, my objective all along has been to ensure that the issue gets a fair hearing from this administration. We have certainly gotten the administration's attention on this idea to create jobs and economic growth, and to take advantage of the new opportunities that GATT may provide. While he has not made any commitments, I am pleased that Secretary [of the Treasury Lloyd] Bentsen has indicated his openness to fairly examining this issue when it comes up in the 104th Congress.

With these agreements, I am prepared to lend my support to the effort to pass the GATT agreement next week. International trade has always been a bipartisan issue,

and I look forward to working with the president to keep it that way.

White House Letter No. 1
November 23, 1994

The Honorable Robert Dole
United States Senate
Washington, D.C. 20510

Dear Senator Dole:

I appreciate the opportunity to respond to your concerns about the so-called pioneers' preference provision, which is found in Title VIII of the GATT implementing legislation.

As you know, this provision serves two basic purposes. First, it prevents the pioneers from obtaining the use of radio spectrum for free. Absent the GATT provision, there is, in our judgment, an unacceptable risk that the pioneers will succeed in overturning the current FCC [Federal Communication Commission] order which, reversing an earlier order, now requires payment from the pioneers. Second, it rewards the innovation produced by the pioneers who, in the judgment of the FCC, have helped to spur the current interest in the provision of Personal Communications Services [PCS]. Indeed, we are only days away from the beginning of the broadband PCS auction. The PCS auctions, which were proposed by President Clinton and established in the budget reconciliation act of 1993, are expected by OMB [Office of Management and Budget] to raise $12.6 billion for the federal government.

Under the GATT provision, the three pioneers will contribute a significant percentage of the total proceeds to be gained from the PCS spectrum. OMB estimates that, over a five-year period, the three pioneers will pay about $1.5 billion to the federal Treasury.

We are aware, of course, of competing estimates that have been made by opponents of the GATT agreement and potential competitors of the pioneers. In general, those assertions attempt to compare mature, small markets for established wireless services that possess a significant customer base with the incipient, multistate, demographically diverse markets for new PCS services. In our judgment, no known alternative estimate establishes a credible basis for analysis.

Of course, as the administration has consistently noted, no one can predict with certainty the outcome of the coming PCS auctions and, therefore, it is impossible to be absolutely sure how much the pioneers will pay under the GATT provision or how much that payment might differ from the alternative formulae contained in the current FCC Order.

I can commit to you, therefore, that the administration will work with Congress next year to do the following:

1. Compare the price paid by the pioneers to the payments paid by the PCS auction winners;

2. Determine whether the government received a fair return for the licenses obtained by the pioneers;

3. If the determination in (2) above is negative, pass legislation that would adequately compensate the United States in accordance with the determination on fair return.

Congress, of course, could still act on its own. We are sending under separate cover a letter expressing our views with regard to the constitutionality of future legislation on this issue.

Sincerely,
Leon E. Panetta
Chief of Staff

White House Letter No.2
[Undated]

The Honorable Robert Dole
United States Senate
Washington, D.C. 20510

Dear Senator Dole:

It was good to meet with you on Saturday regarding a number of your concerns about the GATT legislation. Lloyd Bentsen, Mickey Kantor and I felt that we had a constructive discussion and are hopeful that you will be joining all of us on both sides of the aisle who are supporting the GATT legislation.

You had raised some specific concerns related to agriculture, which I wanted to follow-up with this brief note. Overall, as you know, U.S. agriculture is projected to benefit substantially from the GATT agreement. The coalition of some 265 agricultural organizations who are supporting GATT cite the projections that GATT will lead to increases in U.S. agricultural exports by $5 [billion] to $14 billion over the next five years, which will help to create over 110,000 new jobs in the agriculture sector and help to generate $10 [billion to] $30 billion in related economic activity throughout the U.S. economy.

One of your concerns was whether the administration was singling out agriculture programs for spending cuts. I can reassure you that this is not the case. The administration will honor the commitments in this area made by [OMB] Director [Alice M.] Rivlin and Secretary [of Agriculture Mike] Espy in their Sept. 30, 1994, joint letters to the leadership of the Senate and House Agriculture committees. Those letters committed the administration to maintaining discretionary spending on USDA agricultural programs at or above the FY 1995 level in the FY 1996 and 1997 budget requests to Congress. Regarding mandatory programs, the administration will consider potential spending changes only in the context of its overall reviews of entitlement programs and in the farm bill process.

You asked specifically about the Export Enhancement Program (EEP) and the Conservation Reserve Program (CRP). With respect to the EEP program, we are

following through on our commitment to use it to the maximum extent allowed, as demonstrated by our recent EEP actions on wheat, barley and pork. In fact, for the FY 1995 budget just enacted, the administration requested full funding for EEP and it was the Congress that reduced the funding by 20 percent. We have also decided, as part of the implementation of GATT to reform EEP to focus on market expansion and promotion, not just for combating unfair trade practices.

Regarding the CRP, the administration strongly supports this program and will propose reauthorization and extension of the CRP in 1995. In addition, we will take further administrative actions as needed to support a continuation of the CRP at the fullest possible level. That will be reflected in the FY 1996 Budget baseline for FY96 and future years.

In the context of concerns held by wheat growers, you asked if the administration is willing to streamline the approval process for EEP decisions. I am happy to report that we are already moving forward on our commitment in the Rivlin/Espy letters to do exactly that. As a result, the most recent EEP decisions were cleared in periods ranging from one to four weeks, in contrast to earlier actions which sometimes took six months.

Finally, you raised questions about how the administration could aid the oilseed industry. Unfortunately, the funds that you identified to pay for purchases of vegetable oil for food assistance programs have already been included in the GATT legislation to help cover the overall costs of the package. However, oilseed products are specifically included in the additional $600 million of "greenbox" export promotion program levels that the administration proposed to carry forward if the GATT passes. Decisions on greenbox spending will be based on criteria such as the importance of programs in promoting value-added products, additionally, and other criteria to be developed in consultation with the Congress.

Oilseeds would benefit from further reductions in trade barriers. The U.S. industry took the lead on the oilseeds zero-for-zero initiative in the Uruguay Round, and the administration, as stated in the Statement of Administrative Action accompanying the GATT legislation, intends to pursue negotiations to achieve duty reduction and elimination for oilseeds. Our negotiations with China are directed in part toward achieving meaningful access for U.S. agricultural products, including oilseeds, to the Chinese market.

We appreciate the strong support for GATT that the overall U.S. agriculture community has given over the past weeks. I hope that the information I've provided here will reinforce that support and demonstrate the seriousness of our commitments to the industry.

I hope we will have your support in passing the GATT legislation for the good of agriculture and the whole U.S. economy.

Sincerely,
Leon E. Panetta
Chief of Staff

Treasury Department Letter
[Undated]

The Honorable Robert Dole
United State Senate
Washington, D.C., 20510

Dear Bob:

I appreciate the work you have done to address the concerns of your constituents and other senators before making a final decision about the GATT agreement. I am encouraged that the sovereignty issue has been resolved. I believe your announcement today in support of GATT will certainly bring us closer to the 60 votes needed for the budget waiver.

As the president stated in his press conference Tuesday [Nov. 22], the administration is unwilling to link any conversation regarding capital gains to GATT. But members of the Congress will no doubt set forth ideas for capital formation. I can assure you that these proposals will be carefully reviewed.

It would of course be our hope that the work of the 103rd Congress be completed next week with a bipartisan victory, not by a narrow margin, but by a resounding vote of confidence. You and I have lead important fights in the past to expand economic growth in our country. Few are as important as this one. If we can achieve this, I believe the American people will hold both our political parties in greater esteem. With my best wishes for a Happy Thanksgiving.

Sincerely,
Lloyd Bentsen
[Secretary]

U.S. Trade Representative Letter
Nov. 23, 1994

The Honorable Bob Dole
Senate Minority Leader
United States Senate
Washington, D.C.

Dear Senator Dole:

Secretary Bentsen, Leon Panetta, and I appreciated the chance to discuss the remaining issues of concern to you in the Uruguay Round implementing legislation. We believe that your concerns can be addressed in a way that enables you to join us in providing the leadership to bring the Uruguay Round effort to a successful conclusion.

You have expressed concern about (1) the World Trade Organization (WTO), dispute settlement, and sovereignty; and (2) the change proposed in the term of patent protection. Let me respond on each issue.

WTO, dispute settlement, and sovereignty. Critics of the Uruguay Round

have charged that proposed WTO and the Dispute Settlement Understanding (DSU) would unacceptably infringe U.S. and state sovereignty. I agree that no trade agreement, whatever its economic benefits, should be approved if it infringes U.S. or state sovereignty. But it is clear, as I have testified many times, that the critics' fears concerning sovereignty are without foundation.

Three administrations — two Republican and one Democratic — steadfastly safeguarded our sovereignty throughout the negotiations. This year, working together on a bipartisan basis, the administration and Congress established further protections for sovereignty through the implementing legislation.

A broad range of individuals and groups of diverse views across the political spectrum support the view that the Uruguay Round agreements do not affect U.S. sovereignty. These include Consumers Union, the Heritage Foundation, the American Enterprise Institute, Judge Robert [H.] Bork, the National Governors Association, the National Conference of State Legislatures, Citizens for a Sound Economy, the American Bar Association, just to name a few.

Section 102(a)(1) of the implementing legislation unequivocally reaffirms that U.S. law prevails in every situation over any conflicting provision of the Uruguay Round agreements. Further, Articles IX and X of the WTO agreement make it clear that no substantive right or obligation of the [United States] can be altered or changed unless we agree. Article IX establishes that the WTO will operate by consensus — just as the GATT has. The charge that the United States will be outvoted on important issues in a system where each country has one vote is a "scarecrow" in the view of Judge Bork. In its recent report on the WTO, the Heritage Foundation posed the question: "Does the WTO have any power over the United States that could undermine U.S. sovereignty?" The foundation's unequivocal answer was "none whatsoever."

Neither the WTO nor WTO dispute settlement panels will have the power to change, or order any change, in federal, state, or local laws or regulations. Only we in the United States can change our laws. Longstanding practice of the GATT, continued in the WTO, assures that in disputes, we will only be in front of panelists approved by the United States.

Moreover, while the dispute settlement process is not yet as open as the litigation process in the United States, it is far removed from being the "secret tribunal" that critics allege. U.S. briefs in panel cases will take into account congressional advice and the views of the public. In addition we will provide prompt access to our submissions, and access to at least nonconfidential summaries of other WTO member submissions. Panel reports will be made public as soon as we receive them, and our response to any panel report will be developed with Congress. Also, section 123(g)(3) of the implementing legislation permits the appropriate committees of Congress to vote on whether the United States should comply with a panel report.

We have fully safeguarded the right of federal, state, and local governments to protect human, plant, and animal health and safety at whatever level of protection we see fit. Furthermore, state governments may impose more stringent standards than the federal government and we will be free to exceed international standards when necessary to achieve the level of protection we believe appropriate.

Thanks to extensive consultation with groups of state officials, led by the National Association of Attorneys General and the Multistate Tax Commissioners, state sovereignty is fully protected. This includes the right of the states to participate at every stage of the dispute settlement process if a state law is challenged.

Finally, while the administration believes that U.S. interests are fully protected, the WTO agreement permits the United States to withdraw on six months' notice at any time and for any reason. Additionally, section 125 of the implementing legislation provides an expedited process by which Congress can review U.S. participation in the WTO every five years, and revoke approval of the WTO agreement if it so chooses.

Sovereignty has been the central issue in the debate on the WTO throughout this year. When members of Congress or other individuals or groups have come forward with concerns, we have worked hard, and effectively, to address them. Nevertheless, we recognize that concerns remain, in Congress and around the country, about our sovereignty under the WTO, and particularly the impact of a dispute settlement system where "blocking" of panel reports is no longer permitted. We believe that it is important to approve the Uruguay Round agreements with the broadest possible bipartisan support and public confidence. Consequently, the administration wants to ensure that WTO dispute settlement decisions are fully consistent with the Uruguay Round agreements by providing additional guarantees that WTO dispute settlement decisions will be vigorously monitored to ensure that U.S. sovereignty is not adversely affected.

To that end, the administration will support legislation next year to establish a WTO Dispute Settlement Review Commission. The commission would consist of five federal appellate judges, appointed by the president in consultation with the leadership of both Houses and the chairmen and ranking members of the Ways and Means and Finance committees. Each commissioner would have a four-year term with possible renewals. Provision would be made for appropriate staggering of the terms of the commissioners.

The commission will review all final (i.e., adopted) WTO dispute settlement reports (by a panel if the panel report is not appealed or by the appellate body) where the final report is adverse to the United States. In each such case, the commission would determine whether the panel or appellate body:

1. Demonstrably exceeded its authority or terms of reference or, where the matter concerned the Uruguay Round Antidumping Agreement, failed to apply Article 17.6 concerning standard of review;

2. Added to the obligations or diminished the rights the United States assumed under the pertinent Uruguay Round agreement;

3. Acted arbitrarily or capriciously, engaged in misconduct, or demonstrably departed from the procedures specified for panels or the appellate body in the agreements; and whether

4. The action in 1, 2, or 3 materially affects the outcome of the report.

The commission would issue its determination within 120 days after the report is adopted. Three votes would be required for an affirmative determination. The U.S. government and interested parties would have the right to be heard by the commission.

Following issuance of any affirmative determination by the commission, any member of each House would be able to introduce a joint resolution calling on the president to negotiate new dispute settlement rules that would address and correct the problem identified by the commission. The resolution would be privileged. The resolution would be discharged from the Ways and Means and Finance committees under the same procedures provided in section 125 of the implementing legislation; floor action would be expedited under the same procedures.

If there are three affirmative determinations in any five-year period, any member of each House would be able to introduce a joint resolution to disapprove U.S. participation in the Uruguay Round agreements under the same procedures set forth in section 125 of the implementing legislation. If the resolution is enacted by the Congress and signed by the president, the United States will commence withdrawal from the WTO agreement.

Term of patent protection. You have expressed concern about the provision of the implementing legislation which would change the terms of patents in the United States. Specifically, you have asked the administration to support legislation next year which would change the patent term to grant patents for a term beginning on the date on which the patent issues, and ending on the later of 20 years from the date on which the patent application was filed in the United States or 17 years after the date of the grant.

Under present law, patent rights exist for a term of 17 years measured from the date the patent is granted. The legislation would change our current system to provide for a patent term of 20 years measured from the earliest effective filing date of the application that leads to the patent.

This change, which has the strong, bipartisan support of the House and Senate Judiciary committees, has been recommended numerous times by expert study groups starting as far back as 1967. One reason the committees support both the change and the approach taken in the implementing bill is that it will address the problem of "submarine patents."

A "submarine patent" can exist when a patent applicant delays grant of the patent, sometimes for years, even after the Patent and Trademark Office has determined that a patent can be granted. In the meantime, an entire industry has built up around the technology, since patent applications are held secret until after the patent is issued. When the patent issues, the inventor often demands high royalties as the price of not suing companies for patent infringement. The proposal of providing a term of the longer of 20 years from filing or 17 from grant of the patent would not address this problem, since there still will be no incentive for the patent applicant to stop delaying patent grant.

Under the implementing bill, almost all U.S. patent owners will have a longer term of protection than they now have. There are several reasons for this, but the key point is that we included provisions that would add up to five years to the 20 year term provided under the implementing bill if there is delay in getting the patent and that delay is not the fault of the patent owner.

For all these reasons, we believe that the case for the change is compelling, and it will bring great benefits to our patent holders and innovators. The proposed change has extraordinarily broad support in the business and intellectual property communities, ranging from manufacturing and chemical companies, such as 3M, Dow Chemical, Westinghouse, MARS, Exxon Research and Engineering Company, Deere & Company, Bridgestone/Firestone, Du-Pont, Cincinnati Milacron, Pioneer Hybred, and Fisher-Rosemount to the Intellectual Property Law Section of the ABA, the American Intellectual Property Owners' Association (AIPLA), and the Intellectual Property Owners' Association (IPO).

We believe that if Congress reconsiders the issue next year it will reach the same conclusion reached by the administration and the Judiciary committees over the nine months that we work on the implementing bill. Nevertheless, if the Congress does revisit the issue and reaches the conclusion that a change in accordance with your proposal should be made, the administration would not oppose legislation to achieve that change.

Once again, thank you for discussing this matter with us. I look forward to working with you to secure approval of this historic agreement.

Sincerely,
Michael Kantor
[U.S. Trade Representative]

Department of Commerce Letter

November 23, 1994

Honorable Robert Dole
Minority Leader
United States Senate
Washington, D.C. 20510

Dear Senator Dole:

One of the revenue measures included in the GATT implementing legislation would require the Federal Communications Commission [FCC] to recover for the public a portion of the value of the public spectrum that has been awarded by the commission to licenses granted under the "pioneers preference" program. The legislation requires the pioneers to pay not less than 85 percent, on a per population basis, of the highest bids for licenses in the 20 largest markets in which no applicant has obtained preferential treatment (the 3 pioneer markets).

Assuming enactment of the GATT legislation, we understand that a question has been raised whether Congress could pass subsequent legislation free from constitutional infirmities that re-calculates the fees to be paid by the pioneers. This subsequent legislation would likely occur after the FCC proceeds to issue the licenses to the pioneers and would raise a constitutional question whether such subsequent legislation could be effective on a retroactive basis. We believe that the Congress retains wide discretion to enact retroactive economic legislation to support legitimate legislative purposes and such legislation would be permissible from a legal perspective.

In a case decided June 13, 1994, the Supreme Court held in *United States v. Carlton*, 114 S.Ct. 2018 (1994), that due process was not violated by retroactive application of an amendment to a federal estate tax statute limiting availability of a deduction despite evidence that a taxpayer detrimentally relied on the previous provision and had no notice that the provision would be retroactively amended. In the case, the court noted that the due process standard to be applied to tax statutes with retroactive effect "is the same as that generally applicable to retroactive economic legislation." 114 S.Ct., at 2022. In quoting from its decision in *Pension Benefit Guaranty Corp. v. R.A. Gray & Co.*, 104 S.Ct. 2709 (1984), the court stated:

"Provided that the retroactive application of a statute is supported by a legitimate legislative purpose furthered by rational means, judgments about the wisdom of such legislation remain within the exclusive province of the legislative and executive branches."

We believe that the Supreme Court's holding in the *Carlton* case would be controlling if the Congress enacted subsequent legislation with retroactive effect regarding the price paid by the pioneers. There, as here, the subsequent congressional action would be intended as a "curative" measure to correct previous legislation with "significant and unanticipated" revenue consequences (Congress had estimated the revenue loss from the deduction in the *Carlton* case at $300 million over 5 years but subsequently discovered the loss could be as much as $7 billion). There, as here, the "corrective" legislation would be enacted promptly with only a "modest period of retroactivity." Just as a taxpayer "has no vested right in the Internal Revenue Code," no party has a vested right in conveyance of government spectrum . . . at a discount. See 114 S.Ct., at 2023. In addition, two factors which the appellate court found troubling in that, a lack of notice and detrimental reliance, would not be present provided the Congress included floor statements in the Congressional Record noting the possibility of subsequent legislation relating to the fee question.

For these reasons, we believe that Congress could, if it wished, enact subsequent legislation with retroactive effect regarding the assessment of fees to be paid by the pioneers.

Sincerely,
Ginger Lew
[General Counsel]

REPUBLICAN CONFERENCE

Taking Speaker's Mantle, Gingrich Vows 'Profound Transformation'

The House Republican Conference voted Dec. 5 to make Rep. Newt Gingrich, R-Ga., the next Speaker of the House. Following are excerpts from Gingrich's acceptance speech, as provided by the Federal News Service:

REP. GINGRICH: . . . I think as the country will rapidly learn once again as we get beyond the shadows of Vietnam and Watergate and the cynicism of the last quarter-century, this process of public life is at its best a very human process, and as all of the members here know, it's a process that inevitably involves families, and the truth is, even most of the reporters know that. And I think you're going to see over time a more decent and a more open and a more idealistic and a more romantic vision of what self-government's about.

And that's part of what we have to be called to do. There have to be large changes for this country to succeed and work in the 21st century, but those changes can be brought about together by a people with a big enough heart to have the courage to lower its defenses and to truly talk.

I was incredibly excited on Friday to pick up USA Today — I don't know how many of you have seen this — and read the very front page: "Public backs GOP agenda." In this particular survey, 64 percent agree with Republican views on what the role of government should be. Then if you turn to the inside — and I commend this to all of you if you haven't done it — "GOP contract support strong."

Tougher anti-crime legislation, 88 percent; 63 percent wanted it passed in the first hundred days. Balanced-budget amendment, 85 percent; 50 percent want it passed in the first hundred days. Tax cut, 83 percent; 53 percent want it passed in the first hundred days.

Limiting welfare payments, 79 percent. Presidential line-item veto, 77 percent. Congressional term limits, 73 percent. Cutting capital gains tax, 58 percent. Tort reform, 58 percent. . . .

I carry a copy of the TV Guide contract ad. This will be read the opening day — the opening speech of every day, starting on Jan. 4, until it's finished. And as I've already warned the freshmen — and this is my first chance to meet with the senior members — the opening day will be the longest opening day in history. We will pass nine reforms that day, and we are going to get it done. And at the end of that day — I want to invite every American who can tune in that day. I'd like to invite every high school class and every elementary school class to tune in that day, to make it a day of watching democracy in action on C-SPAN, to understand that we in fact are different.

We were elected to keep our word; we will keep our word. We've already begun. There will be fewer committees. That vote will be tomorrow. There'll be one-third fewer committee staff, as we've pledged. That vote will be tomorrow. I am told last night that the freshmen will make a motion to reduce personal staff some. I support that and hope it passes. I am told that the freshmen tomorrow will make a motion to sell at least one office building. I support that, and I believe we can reduce the staff enough as a goal to sell one of the buildings owned by the House as our gift to the American people for Christmas, to paraphrase [Rep.] John [R.] Kasich's [R-Ohio] idea. Now, Kasich wants to go down and put a large red ribbon over it. If he will provide the ribbon and if the current leadership will allow us to do it, we might do that. But I think the deeper point for the American people is, the changes are going to be real. They're going to be substantive. You're going to be able to see them, and they're going to make a difference in the government and a difference in your lives.

So, for the first hundred days, we have a lot to do. But the truth is that this Congress and this movement is about a lot more than a hundred days. Remember, it was 25 years ago that [Ronald] Reagan first spoke on a time for choosing. And the truth is in the legislative branch, we are only now for the first time getting to that time for choosing. While the executive branch under the president was moving in that direction, at no point in the last 25 years have people who shared our values been in control of the House.

Now, we're going to work very hard for the first hundred days. Our tentative plan, frankly, is going to be to take three weeks off. One week I'm going to urge you to take with your family. . . . That would give you a week with your family and two weeks to be with your constituents, to take stock and to make sure that we're doing the right thing and that we are with the American people having a dialogue that allows us to move in the right direction. Then we would come back, to what I believe are the two great challenges of the second quarter.

The budget, which John Kasich will have a tremendous role, but only a role, in passing, because every one of us and every American is going to be involved — and the appropriations bills. Because remember, we don't have to de-authorize, we simply have to not pay for them. And under our — and under our Constitution all we have — if the spending doesn't originate in the House and Senate, it cannot be spent. Now I want to really drive this home for a second so that every American can understand the potential and the importance of the legislative branch. We have the opportunity this spring and summer to begin decisively changing the shape of the government. . . .

We are going to model on the successful Republican governors the profound transformation of this system, and the appropriations bills, in that sense, are going to be very, very important. We will also pass other reforms as quickly as they can be coordinated with the Republican Senate — and I believe Sen. [Bob] Dole [R-Kan.] will be here tomorrow morning. Let me say on behalf of Sen. Dole, no member campaigned in more places, worked harder, did more things than Bob Dole. He is truly an extraordinary leader — and tomorrow he'll be reporting on where the Senate's going — and all of us owe him a great debt of gratitude for his leadership.

And let me say that when we met with President Clinton on Friday, Sen. Dole and I had a very good meeting with the president. I think that the concept of cooperation but not compromise is beginning to get clearer, and I think that — for example, the president indicated a willingness to sign the Shays Act to apply to the Congress every law that applies to the rest of the country, to sign an unfunded mandates bill and to sign a line-item veto bill. And it's possible — if we can work it out with the administration and with the Senate Democrats, who have the leverage to block things if they work at it — but if we could work out those three, it is conceivable all three will be signed well before the end of January as proof that the American system works and that the voters have been heard, and how, far from gridlock, we can have a remarkably productive 1995. . . .

The only way that we can get through this is to be able to genuinely reach out and genuinely have a chance to have a dialogue with the American people. And I think it has to occur in two steps, and I hope every member is going to be determined, and I hope, frankly, the Democrats decide to join us. One is to have a discussion about definitions. When you see a person without money, are they victims or are they opportunities for a better future? Are they people to have care-taking or are they people who, in fact, if you care for them, you can give them a helping hand and change their lives? Which are we looking at? When you see a large government bureaucracy, is it an inevitable relic of the past that can't be changed or is it an opportunity for an extraordinary transformation to provide bet-

ter services and better opportunities at lower cost — exactly what every major corporation is going through?

And so again and again, first we have to have a discussion about definitions — what world are we trying to create and what language are we trying to use?

And second, we have to have a dialogue about the budget because the budget is the transformational document for this system. When you change the budget, you've really changed government, and until you change the budget, you've just talked about changing government. And we can't do that in Washington. We can't have a secret Republican budget task force after two years of watching the failure of a secret Democrat health task force. So our 500 experts aren't any smarter than theirs, they're just more conservative. What we have to do is reach out to every family in every community and every neighborhood — and I've already told the governors and the mayors and the county commissioners we hope they're going to join us in town hall meetings and in dialogues across the whole country learning how we can truly change things....

Now, because I am a college teacher, let me say to you that in addition to your two handouts there are eight documents I want to refer you to during the Christmas break, four of them are historic and four of them are current....

The four historic documents I want to recommend are, first of all, the Declaration of Independence. We don't read it enough; we don't pay attention to it. It was written quite deliberately by the wisest group of secular leaders in human history, and it is very powerful. And I commend to you in particular to think a long time about its central sentence: "We are endowed by our Creator with certain unalienable rights, among which are life, liberty and the pursuit of happiness." The three big powerful messages in one sentence: First of all, it's the *pursuit* of happiness. There are no happiness stamps, there is no federal department of happiness. Each individual has to be engaged in the pursuit — not guaranteed the finding.

Second, rights are unalienable. Let me make that very clear. The American people, unlike any people in history, loan power to the government. [Rep.] Dick Armey [R-Texas] said it brilliantly when he was asked at a press conference, "How does it feel to have the American people give you this power?" And he said, "No, the American people have given us responsibility. We are their servants, they retain the power." And those of you who are freshmen who beat incumbents can report cheerfully later on what it's like to be in a campaign with somebody who forgot where power comes from. Power does not come from Washington, power comes from God to the people, and from the people to their government as they see fit to loan it.

And third — and a comment that got me in a trouble a few weeks ago, and occasionally — I appreciate your forbearance — for some reason I will say or do something

controversial that people will get all excited about. I know, I know it's hard to believe. But the word "creator" matters. You cannot explain America without recognizing that every one of the Founding Fathers believed deeply in a creator. And by the way, for our liberal friends who treasure Jefferson and their particular interpretation of him, I encourage them to go down in this city to the Jefferson Memorial and look at the quotation around the top of it: "I have pledged upon the altar of God Almighty eternal hostility towards all forms of tyranny over the minds of man." One might even think Jefferson had used "the altar of God Almighty" because he thought there was a God Almighty, but that's a radical and academic question for another day.

In addition, look at the Constitution again. What does the 10th Amendment mean? And our friends out West will tell you it means a lot different things than some other people think. But it's a debate we have to have. What does the 2nd Amendment mean? What is the energy — or what does the commerce clause mean, and does it really mean what the Supreme Court said in 1935, which is radically different than what it said before 1935? And I'm not suggesting that we're going to in one day change it, but I do think it's helpful occasionally to have a generation stop and look at the governing documents from the Founding Fathers and ask why America became America and what it's all about.

Get a copy of the Federalist Papers, if you don't already have one. They say, by the way, that the legislative branch in peacetime is pre-eminent. There's a very interesting argument about where — how freedom operates.

And finally, get a copy of [Alexis] de Toqueville's "Democracy in America," because in 1831 and '32 when he traveled we begin to become America, and it's the most voluntaristic, most open society in which everybody is expected to be a citizen, and he talks about it at length.

If you want to see the two what I think is the best modern interpretations, I would commend to you Gordon Wood's magnificent works, "The Meaning of the American Revolution" and "The Radicalism of the American Revolution," and [James T.] Flexner's one-volume condensation of his four-volume work on Washington....

First, in order to understand the scale of change we're living through, let me suggest to you Alvin and Heidi Toffler's "Creating a New Civilization: The Politics of the Third Wave." It just came out — from the Progress and Freedom Foundation. Here in a hundred pages is 25 years of work by the couple who wrote "Future Shock" and coined the phrase in 1970; who wrote "The Third Wave" in 1980; and who wrote "War and Anti-War" a little over a year ago. Three books that encompass the scale of change we're living through. In this 100 pages, you'll begin to sense what the 21st century America, the 21st century government and the 21st century Congress need to be.

Second, because every American in the

information age will be making decisions that in the 1950s we would have thought of as an executive. Every American will have a cellular phone, which will probably be a fax, which will probably be a modem, which will probably in some way tie them into a world — whether they want to or not, frankly — every American will be competing in the world market with Germany and China and Japan. I want to suggest to everybody that you buy a copy, in paperback, of Peter Drucker's "The Effective Executive," which remains, I think, the definitive work for the modern world on how to be effective.

This little book ought to be taught to every freshman in high school. It is the essence of how to think about problems, how to think about your schedule, how to lead a team, and every American — if you're going to be effective in your neighborhood, in your family, in your community — every American is an executive.

Third, at a lot lower level of intensity but a book I found useful that Verne Ayles is working on to help us with, a book by Mary Boone called "Leadership and the Computer." I recommend it particularly for members just from this standpoint....

Finally, and again I cite this not so you'll think I'm doing anything fancy, but because I want you to understand the model that I think is unavoidable for the 21st century. I spent six hours on Saturday in a class, and I wasn't teaching, I was studying. We had Morris and Leah Shechtman come in. They are both psychotherapists — despite what some people may think, no, it was not personal counseling — their specialty is, How do institutions change? They've looked at places like Wal-Mart and major insurance companies. Morris Shechtman travels worldwide. He has a brand new book coming out called "Working Without a Net" that I commend to you.

I thought — the thing that actually got to me — Morris Shechtman has a model which distinguishes between care-taking and caring. He says — and think about supplemental security insurance. Care-taking is when you pretend you care about somebody and you do something so you feel good, but it may ruin them. And I thought it was the most perfect description of what's happened in the welfare state and how we've lost the argument over language in the last 35 years....

Let me close with these thoughts. And I say it in part because I've already had a number of you point out to me ways that I could have done the last three weeks better. And it's true. I mean, let's not kid each other. We're drowning. We're doing the best we can. We're making as many judgments as we can as rapidly as we can. We're including everybody as fast as we can figure out how to do it. The truth is we're drowning. We're doing everything we can to keep us moving in the right direction, and every time we make a mistake, we try to go back and fix it as fast as the cybernetic feedback loop of people talking to each other gets it to us.

But I want to close with two quotes

that help us better understand the notion of making mistakes, listening to each other and recovering, and what's really at stake on a change of this scale, because I really want to make sure that you members, your staffs and the American people understand that this is all going to require your help, your prayers and your courage — your help as members and your prayers and your courage as members, the same of your staffs because without our staffs we can't get this done. It's too big a job. But also to every American, I would say that we in the Congress will need your help and your prayers and your courage. The courage to tell us when we're wrong. The courage to give us a new idea. The courage sometimes to take us by the hand and together to walk into a different future doing different things that were never done before.

I want to close with two people, both of whom love freedom and both of whom I think had a message for us. I want to go back again to that day in March 1933 be-cause I think you can — just as you can never study Washington too much, if you truly love democracy and you truly believe in representative self-government, you can never study Franklin Delano Roosevelt too much. He did bring us out of the Depression. He did lead the Allied movement in World War II. In many ways he created the modern world. He was clearly, I think, as a political leader the greatest figure of the 20th century. And I think his concept that we have nothing to fear but fear itself, that we'll take an experiment, and if it fails, we'll do another one — and if you go back and read the New Deal, they tried again and again. They didn't always get it right and we would have voted against much of it, but the truth is we would have voted for much of it.

And second, Winston Churchill, who in 1940 in the darkest and grimmest days said, "I have nothing to offer but blood, sweat, toil and tears."

This is not a guaranteed performance. This is not a guaranteed success. But if each of us every day will wake up committed to helping America, and if we will remember that the real success isn't a Republican re-election; the real success isn't even a balanced budget; the real success is no law. The real success is the morning we wake up on a Monday and no child has been killed anywhere in America that weekend, and every child is going to a school their parents think is worth attending, and across the country there is a smaller, more customer-friendly government doing effectively what government should do, and every American has a chance to create a job or find a job, and across the planet freedom is winning and civility and decency are driving barbarism out of our lives, then we will truly succeed. And if each of us will on behalf of the American people offer the best version we have of blood, sweat, toil and tears, then together I believe the American people will in fact renew American civilization.

Thank you, and I look forward to working with you. ■

<u>PRESIDENTIAL ADDRESS</u>

Clinton Proposes Tax Cuts To Help Middle Class

Following is the official White House transcript of President Clinton's address from the Oval Office on Dec. 15.

Good evening. My fellow Americans, ours is a great country with a lot to be proud of. But at this holiday season, everybody knows that all is not well with America; that millions of Americans are hurting, frustrated, disappointed, even angry.

In this time of enormous change, our challenge is both political and personal. It involves government, all right, but it goes way beyond government, to the very core of what matters most to us.

The question is, what are we going to do about it?

Let's start with the economic situation. I ran for president to restore the American Dream and to prepare the American people to compete and win in the new American economy. For too long, too many Americans have worked longer for stagnant wages and less security. For two years, we pursued an economic strategy that has helped to produce over 5 million new jobs. But even though the economic statistics are moving up, most of our living standards aren't. It's almost as if some Americans are being punished for their productivity in this new economy. We've got to change that. More jobs aren't enough. We have to raise incomes.

Fifty years ago, an American president proposed the G.I. Bill of Rights, to help returning veterans from World War II go to college, buy a home and raise their children. That built this country. Tonight, I propose a "Middle Class Bill of Rights."

There are four central ideas in this Bill of Rights: First, college tuition should be tax deductible. Just as we make mortgage interest tax deductible because we want people to own their own homes, we should make college tuition deductible because we want people to go to college.

Specifically, I propose that all tuition for college, community college, graduate school, professional school, vocational education or worker retraining after high school be fully deductible, phased up to $10,000 a year for families making up to $120,000 a year. Education, after all, has a bigger impact on earnings and job security than ever before. So let's invest the fruits of today's recovery into tomorrow's opportunity.

Second, bringing up a child is a tough job in this economy. So we should help middle-class families raise their children. We made a good start last year by passing the Family Leave Law, making college loans more affordable and by giving 15 million American families with incomes of $25,000 a year or less an average tax cut of more than $1,000 a year.

Now, I want to cut taxes for each child under 13, phased up to $500 per child. This tax cut would be available to any family whose income is less than $75,000.

Third, we should help middle-income people save money by allowing every American family earning under $100,000 to put $2,000 a year tax-free in an IRA, an Individual Retirement Account. But I want you to be able to use the money to live on, not just retire on. You'll be able to withdraw from this fund, tax-free — money for education, medical expenses, the purchase of a first home, the care of an elderly parent.

Fourth, since every American needs the skills necessary to prosper in the new economy — and most of you will change jobs from time to time — we should take the billions of dollars the government now spends on dozens of different training programs and give it directly to you, to pay for training if you lose your job or want a better one.

We can pay for this Middle Class Bill of Rights by continuing to reduce government spending, including subsidies to powerful interests based more on influence than need. We can sell off entire operations the government no longer needs to run, and turn dozens of programs over to states and communities that know best how to solve their own problems.

My plan will save billions of dollars from the Energy Department, cut down the Transportation Department and shrink 60 programs into four at the Department of Housing and Urban Development. Our re-inventing government initiative, led by Vice President [Al] Gore, already has helped to shrink bureaucracy and free up money to pay down the deficit and invest in our people. Already, we've passed budgets to reduce the federal government to its smallest size in 30 years, and to cut the deficit by $700 billion. That's over $10,000 for every American family.

In the next few days, we'll unveil more of our proposals. And I've instructed the vice president to review every single government department program for further reductions.

We've worked hard to get control of this deficit after the government debt increased four times over in the 12 years before I took office. That's a big burden on you. About 5 percent of your income tax goes to pay for welfare and foreign aid, but 28 percent of it goes to pay for interest on the debt run up between 1981 and the day I was inaugurated president. I challenge the new Congress to work with me to enact a Middle Class Bill of Rights without adding to the deficit and without any new cuts in Social Security or Medicare.

I know some people just want to cut the government blindly, and I know that's popular now. But I won't do it. I want a leaner, not a meaner government, that's back on the side of hard-working Americans; a new government for the new economy — creative, flexible, high quality, low cost, service oriented — just like our most innovative private companies.

I'll work with the new Republican majority and my fellow Democrats in Congress to build a new American economy and to restore the American Dream. It won't be easy. Believe you me, the special interests have not gone into hiding just because there was an election in November. As a matter of fact, they're up here stronger than ever. And that's why, more than ever, we need lobby reform, campaign finance reform and reform to make Congress live by the laws it puts on other people.

Together, we can pass welfare reform and health care reform that work. I'll say more about what I'll do to work with the new Congress in the State of the Union address in January.

But here's what I won't do. I won't support ideas that sound good, but aren't paid for — ideas that weaken the progress we've made in the previous two years for working families; ideas that hurt poor people who are doing their dead-level best to raise their kids and work their way into the middle class; ideas that undermine our fight against crime, or for a clean environment, or for better schools, or for the strength and well-being of our armed forces in foreign policy. In other words, we must be straight with the American people about the real consequences of all budgetary decisions.

My test will be: Does an idea expand middle-class incomes and opportunities? Does it promote values like family, work responsibility and community? Does it contribute to strengthening the new economy? If it does, I'll be for it, no matter who proposes it. And I hope Congress will treat my ideas the same way. Let's worry about making progress, not taking credit.

But our work in Washington won't be enough. And that's where you come in. This all starts with you. Oh, we can cut taxes and expand opportunities, but governments can't raise your children, go to school for you, give your employees who have earned it a raise or solve problems in your neighborhood that require your per-

sonal commitment. In short, government can't exercise your citizenship. It works the other way around.

The problems of this new world are complicated, and we've all got a lot to learn. That means citizens have to listen as well as talk. We need less hot rhetoric and more open conversation; less malice, and more charity. We need to put aside the politics of personal destruction and demonization that have dominated too much of our debate. Most of us are good people trying to do better. And if we all treated each other that way, we would do better. We have got to be a community again.

Yes, some people do take advantage of the rest of us — by breaking the law, abusing the welfare system, and flaunting our immigration laws. That's wrong, and I'm working to stop it. But the truth is that most people in this country, without regard to their race, their religion, their income, their position on divisive issues, most Americans get up every day, go to work, obey the law, pay their taxes and raise their kids the best they can. And most of us share the same real challenges in this new economy. We'll do a lot better job of meeting those challenges if we work together and find unity and strength in our diversity.

We do have more in common, more uniting us than dividing us. And if we start acting like it, we can face the future with confidence. I still believe deeply that there is nothing wrong with America that can't be fixed by what's right with America. This is not about politics as usual. As I've said for years, it's not about moving left or right, but moving forward; not about government being bad or good, but about what kind of government will best enable us to fulfill our God-given potential. And it's not about the next election, either. That's in your hands.

Meanwhile, I'm going to do what I think is right. My rule for the next two years will be: Country first and politics as usual dead last. I hope the new Congress will follow the same rule. And I hope you will, too.

This country works best when it works together. For decades after World War II, we gave more and more Americans a chance to live out their dreams. I know — I'm blessed to be one of them. I was born to a widowed mother at a time when my state's income was barely half the national average; the first person in my family to finish college, thanks to money my parents couldn't really afford — scholarships, loans, and a half a dozen jobs. It breaks my heart to see people with their own dreams for themselves and their children shattered. And I'm going to do all I can to turn it around. But I need your help. We can do it.

With all of our problems, this is still the greatest country in the world — standing not at the twilight, but at the dawn of our greatest days. We still have a lot to be thankful for. Let's all remember that.

Happy holidays, and God bless America. ■

Sen. Thompson Outlines GOP Plans for Change

The Republican response to President Clinton's Dec. 15 address was delivered by Sen. Fred Thompson of Tennessee. Following is a transcript of his remarks, as provided by the Federal News Service:

Hello, I am Fred Thompson.

On Nov. 8, the voters of Tennessee elected me to represent them in the United States Senate, and tonight I have been asked to speak to you on behalf of the new Republican majority in Congress and Republican elected officials in your state and community.

The first thing I want to do is thank you for the support and confidence you placed in Republicans on Election Day. You elected a record number of Republican governors, state legislators and mayors all around the country.

And for the first time in 40 years Republicans will be in the majority in both the House and the Senate. Our government, especially in Washington, needed that big change.

Those of us who just came to town don't claim to have all the answers. I am still just unpacking my boxes. But one thing we do know, we know why you sent us here, to cut big government down to size, to turn Congress around, and to set our country in a new direction.

We campaigned on these principles and now we're going to do something that has become all too unusual in American politics. We're going to do exactly what we said. In fact, the change is already taking place.

First, Congress is getting its own house in order. Republicans are cutting the number of committees and we're cutting staff.

One of the first bills we pass in January says that Congress has to live under the same laws that Congress imposes on everybody else. Maybe Congress won't pass so many laws when it actually starts having to live under a few of them.

We are also working with Republican governors.

We're going to stop the Washington-knows-best crowd from mandating that your state and local governments do all kinds of things that end up costing you higher taxes. And we're going to pass a balanced-budget amendment to the Constitution to control government spending. That's what we'll do in January.

Other changes will take more time, but we will continue to move straight ahead, to term limits, and to reducing the tax burden on families and working people. And we're going to tackle a welfare system that pays people more not to work than to work.

One of our most important efforts will be to cut back the executive branch of government and the faceless bureaucracies which more and more run our lives. This week, the Republican congressional leadership asked the president to immediately stop federal agencies from issuing new regulations until we've had a chance to cut some of the old ones.

On some of these issues we need the support of the president and the Democrats in Congress, and we want to work together with them.

But over the past two years the president and the Democrat-controlled Congress have opposed the balanced-budget amendment, proposed more big government spending and tried to put a bunch of new government bureaucrats in charge of your health care.

Until a few weeks ago they were even saying we didn't even need a tax cut.

Yet, from what we heard tonight, the president's vision for the future now looks a lot like what Republicans just campaigned for, at least until we start looking at the details.

Your vote this election apparently got the president's attention.

If the president's new position tonight represents a real change of heart we say, "Welcome aboard."

If we can actually cut Washington down to size and put the savings back into the pockets of the people who earned it, we won't need to argue over who gets the credit, or who thought of the idea first.

If, however, the president's words are based more upon public opinion polls than real conviction, if we're just talking about politics here instead of fundamental change in direction, then we're going to be very much at cross-purposes.

We must do more than reshuffle agencies and take money from one place just to add it somewhere else.

We welcome the president to help us lead America in a new direction. But if he will not, we will welcome the president to follow because we're moving ahead. We know it's time to change a system where Americans who work hard, raise their families and obey the law are taxed, regulated and ignored while their government becomes bigger and more arrogant every day.

Republicans have come together to reverse that trend and set America back on the right road.

That's what you hired us for. It's your government and your continued support can change it because whatever Americans can dream, we can do.

Thanks for listening and may you and your family have a happy and healthy holiday season. ■

PUBLIC LAWS

PUBLIC LAWS

Public laws 103-162 to 103-210 were cleared in the first session of the 103rd Congress. (For public laws signed earlier in 1993, see 1993 Almanac, Appendix E.)

PL 103-162 (HR 2650) Designate portions of the Maurice River and its tributaries in the state of New Jersey as components of the National Wild and Scenic Rivers System. Introduced by HUGHES, D-N.J., July 15, 1993. House Natural Resources reported, amended, Oct. 12 (H Rept 103-282). House passed, amended, under suspension of the rules, Oct. 12. Senate Energy and Natural Resources reported, Nov. 17. Senate passed Nov. 19. President signed Dec. 1, 1993.

PL 103-163 (HR 898) Authorize the Air Force Memorial Foundation to establish a memorial in the District of Columbia or its environs. Introduced by HUTTO, D-Fla., Feb. 16, 1993. House passed, under suspension of the rules, Nov. 16. Senate passed Nov. 20. President signed Dec. 2, 1993.

PL 103-164 (H J Res 75) Designate Jan. 16, 1994, as National Good Teen Day. Introduced by TRAFICANT, D-Ohio, Jan. 26, 1993. House Post Office and Civil Service discharged. House passed Nov. 8. Senate Judiciary discharged. Senate passed Nov. 20. President signed Dec. 2, 1993.

PL 103-165 (H J Res 294) Express appreciation to W. Graham Claytor Jr., retiring chairman and president of the National Railroad Passenger Corp., for a lifetime of dedicated and inspired service to the nation. Introduced by DINGELL, D-Mich., Nov. 18, 1993. House Energy and Commerce discharged. House passed Nov. 19. Senate passed Nov. 20. President signed Dec. 2, 1993.

PL 103-166 (S 1667) Extend authorities under the Middle East Peace Facilitation Act of 1993 by six months. Introduced by PELL, D-R.I., Nov. 17, 1993. Senate passed Nov. 17. House passed Nov. 18. President signed Dec. 2, 1993.

PL 103-167 (S J Res 75) Designate Jan. 2, 1994, through Jan. 8, 1994, as National Law Enforcement Training Week. Introduced by ROTH, R-Del., March 30, 1993. Senate Judiciary reported Oct. 28. Senate passed Oct. 28. House Post Office and Civil Service discharged. House passed Nov. 18. President signed Dec. 2, 1993.

PL 103-168 (S J Res 122) Designate December 1993 as National Drunk and Drugged Driving Prevention Month. Introduced by LAUTENBERG, D-N.J., Aug. 5, 1993. Senate Judiciary reported Oct. 28. Senate passed Oct. 28. House Post Office and Civil Service discharged. House passed Nov. 18. President signed Dec. 2, 1993.

PL 103-169 (HR 698) Protect Lechuguilla Cave and other resources and values in and adjacent to Carlsbad Caverns National Park in New Mexico. Introduced by VENTO, D-Minn., Jan. 27, 1993. House Natural Resources reported, amended, May 11 (H Rept 103-86). House passed, amended, under suspension of the rules, May 11. Senate Energy and Natural Resources reported, amended, Nov. 17. Senate passed, amended, Nov. 19. House agreed to Senate amendment Nov. 21. President signed Dec. 2, 1993.

PL 103-170 (HR 914) Amend the Wild and Scenic Rivers Act to designate certain segments of the Red River in Kentucky as components of the National Wild and Scenic Rivers System. Introduced by ROGERS, R-Ky., Feb. 16, 1993. House Natural Resources reported, amended, Oct. 12 (H Rept 103-281). House passed, amended, under suspension of the rules, Oct. 18. Senate Energy and Natural Resources reported Nov. 17 (S Rept 103-206). Senate passed Nov. 19. President signed Dec. 2, 1993.

PL 103-171 (HR 3161) Make technical amendments necessitated by the enactment of the Older Americans Act Amendments of 1992. Introduced by MARTINEZ, D-Calif., Sept. 28, 1993. House Education and Labor discharged. House Banking, Finance and Urban Affairs discharged. House Education and Labor reported, amended, Nov. 8 (H Rept 103-330). House passed, amended, Nov. 8. Senate passed Nov. 16. President signed Dec. 2, 1993.

PL 103-172 (HR 3318) Amend Title 5, U.S. Code, to provide for the establishment of programs to encourage federal employees to commute by means other than single-occupancy motor vehicles. Introduced by NORTON, D-D.C., Oct. 20, 1993. House Post Office and Civil Service reported Nov. 10 (H Rept 103-356, Part I). House passed, under suspension of the rules, Nov. 15. Senate passed Nov. 20. President signed Dec. 2, 1993.

PL 103-173 (HR 3378) Amend Title 18, U.S. Code, with respect to parental kidnapping. Introduced by GEKAS, R-Pa., Oct. 27, 1993. House Judiciary reported Nov. 20 (H Rept 103-390). House passed, under suspension of the rules, Nov. 20. Senate passed Nov. 20. President signed Dec. 2, 1993.

PL 103-174 (HR 3471) Authorize the leasing of naval vessels to certain foreign countries. Introduced by HAMILTON, D-Ind., Nov. 9, 1993. House Foreign Affairs discharged. House passed Nov. 18. Senate passed Nov. 20. President signed Dec. 2, 1993.

PL 103-175 (S 433) Authorize and direct the secretary of the Interior to convey certain lands in Cameron Parish, La. Introduced by JOHNSTON, D-La., Feb. 24, 1993. Senate Energy and Natural Resources reported March 11 (S Rept 103-18). Senate passed, amended, March 25. House Natural Resources reported, amended, Nov. 15 (H Rept 103-365). House passed, amended, under suspension of the rules, Nov. 15. Senate agreed to House amendment Nov. 17. President signed Dec. 2, 1993.

PL 103-176 (HR 1268) Assist the development of tribal judicial systems. Introduced by RICHARDSON, D-N.M., March 9, 1993. House Natural Resources reported, amended, Aug. 2 (H Rept 103-205). House passed, amended, under suspension of the rules, Aug. 2. Senate Indian Affairs discharged. Senate passed, amended, Aug. 6. Conference report filed in the House on Nov. 19 (H Rept 103-383). House agreed to conference report Nov. 19. Senate agreed to conference report Nov. 20. President signed Dec. 3, 1993.

PL 103-177 (HR 1425) Improve the management, productivity and use of Indian agricultural lands and resources. Introduced by RICHARDSON, D-N.M., March 18, 1993. House Natural Resources reported, amended, Nov. 16 (H Rept 103-367). House passed, amended, under suspension of the rules, Nov 16. Senate Indian Affairs reported Nov. 18 (S Rept 103-186). Senate passed Nov. 20. President signed Dec. 3, 1993.

PL 103-178 (HR 2330) Authorize appropriations for fiscal 1994 for intelligence and intelligence-related activities of the U.S. government and Central Intelligence Agency Retirement and Disability System. Introduced by GLICKMAN, D-Kan., June 8, 1993. House Intelligence reported, amended, June 29 (H Rept 103-162, Part I). House Armed Services reported July 21 (H Rept 103-162, Part II). House passed, amended, Aug. 4. Senate Intelligence discharged. Senate passed, amended, Nov. 10. Conference report filed in the House on Nov. 18 (H Rept 103-377). House agreed to conference report Nov. 20. Senate agreed to conference report Nov. 20. President signed Dec. 3, 1993.

PL 103-179 (HR 2632) Authorize appropriations for the Patent and Trademark Office in the Department of Commerce for fiscal 1994. Introduced by HUGHES, D-N.J., July 14, 1993. House Judiciary reported, amended, Oct. 12 (H Rept 103-285). House passed, amended, under suspension of the rules, Oct. 12. Senate

passed, amended, Nov. 11. House agreed to Senate amendment with amendments Nov. 19. Senate agreed to House amendments to Senate amendment Nov. 20. President signed Dec. 3, 1993.

PL 103-180 (S 412) Amend Title 49, U.S. Code, regarding the collection of certain payments for shipments via motor common carriers of property and non-household goods freight forwarders. Introduced by EXON, D-Neb., Feb. 18, 1993. Senate Commerce, Science and Transportation reported, amended, June 29 (H Rept 103-79). Senate passed, amended, July 1. House Public Works and Transportation discharged. House passed, amended, Nov. 15. Senate agreed to House amendments Nov. 19. President signed Dec. 3, 1993.

PL 103-181 (S 1670) Improve hazard mitigation and relocation assistance in connection with flooding, and for other purposes. Introduced by HARKIN, D-Iowa, Nov. 18, 1993. Senate Environment and Public Works discharged. Senate passed Nov. 20. House passed Nov. 20. President signed Dec. 3, 1993.

PL 103-182 (HR 3450) Implement the North American Free Trade Agreement. Introduced by ROSTENKOWSKI, D-Ill., Nov. 4, 1993. House Ways and Means reported Nov. 15 (H Rept 103-361, Part I). House Banking, Finance and Urban Affairs adversely reported Nov. 15 (H Rept 103-361, Part II). House Energy and Commerce reported Nov. 15 (H Rept 103-361, Part III). House Agriculture, House Foreign Affairs, House Government Operations, House Judiciary and House Public Works and Transportation discharged. House passed Nov. 17. Senate considered Nov. 19. Senate passed Nov. 20. President signed Dec. 8, 1993.

PL 103-183 (HR 2202) Amend the Public Health Service Act to revise and extend the program of grants relating to preventive health measures with respect to breast and cervical cancer. Introduced by WAXMAN, D-Calif., May 20, 1993. House Energy and Commerce reported, amended, June 10 (H Rept 103-120). House passed, amended, under suspension of the rules, June 14. Senate passed, amended, Nov. 2. Conference report filed in the House on Nov. 20 (H Rept 103-397). House agreed to conference report, under suspension of the rules, Nov. 21. Senate agreed to the conference report Nov. 22. President signed Dec. 14, 1993.

PL 103-184 (HR 486) Provide for the addition of the Truman Farm Home to the Harry S Truman National Historic Site in the state of Missouri. Introduced by WHEAT, D-Mo., Jan. 6, 1993. House Natural Resources reported, amended, Nov. 20 (H Rept 103-399). House passed, amended, Nov. 23. Senate passed Nov. 24. President signed Dec. 14, 1993.

PL 103-185 (HR 3321) Provide increased flexibility to states in carrying out the Low-Income Home Energy Assistance Program. Introduced by FRANK, D-Mass., Oct. 20, 1993. House passed, amended, under suspension of the rules, Nov. 15. Senate passed Nov. 22. President signed Dec. 14, 1993.

PL 103-186 (HR 3616) Require the secretary of the Treasury to mint coins in commemoration of the 250th anniversary of the birth of Thomas Jefferson, Americans who have been prisoners of war, the Vietnam Veterans Memorial on the occasion of the 10th anniversary of the memorial, and the Women in Military Service for America Memorial. Introduced by KENNEDY, D-Mass., Nov. 22, 1993. House Banking, Finance and Urban Affairs discharged. House passed Nov. 23. Senate passed Nov. 24. President signed Dec. 14, 1993.

PL 103-187 (H J Res 272) Designate Oct. 29, 1993, as National Firefighters Day. Introduced by HOYER, D-Md., Sept. 30, 1993. House Post Office and Civil Service discharged. House passed, amended, Nov. 21. Senate passed Nov. 22. President signed Dec. 14, 1993.

PL 103-188 (S 717) Amend the Egg Research and Consumer Information Act to modify the provisions governing the rate of assessment and to expand the exemption of egg producers from such act. Introduced by PRYOR, D-Ark., April 1, 1993. Senate Agriculture, Nutrition and Forestry reported, amended, Nov. 19. Senate passed, amended, Nov. 20. House passed Nov. 21. President signed Dec. 14, 1993.

PL 103-189 (S 778) Amend the Watermelon Research and Promotion Act to expand operation of the act to the United States, to authorize the revocation of the refund provision of the act, and to modify the referendum procedures of the act. Introduced by BOREN, D-Okla., April 7, 1993. Senate Agriculture, Nutrition and Forestry discharged. Senate passed, amended, Nov. 20. House passed Nov. 21. President signed Dec. 14, 1993.

PL 103-190 (S 994) Authorize the establishment of a fresh cut flowers and fresh cut greens promotion and consumer information program for the benefit of the floricultural industry and other persons. Introduced by PRYOR, D-Ark., May 20, 1993. Senate Agriculture, Nutrition and Forestry reported, amended, Nov. 19. Senate passed, amended, Nov. 20. House passed Nov. 21. President signed Dec. 14, 1993.

PL 103-191 (S 1716) Amend the Thomas Jefferson Commemoration Commission Act to extend the deadlines for reports. Introduced by ROBB, D-Va., Nov. 19, 1993. Senate Judiciary discharged. Senate passed Nov. 20. House passed, under suspension of the rules, Nov. 21. President signed Dec. 14, 1993.

PL 103-192 (S 1732) Extend arbitration under the provisions of Chapter 44 of Title 28, U.S. Code. Introduced by HEFLIN, D-Ala., Nov. 19, 1993. Senate passed Nov. 20. Senate requested the return of papers Nov. 22. Senate Judiciary discharged. House passed, amended, Nov. 23. Senate agreed to House amendment Nov. 24. President signed Dec. 14, 1993.

PL 103-193 (S 1764) Provide for the extension of certain authority for the marshal of the Supreme Court and the Supreme Court Police. Introduced by BIDEN, D-Del., Nov. 20, 1993. Senate passed Nov. 20. House Public Works and Transportation discharged. House Judiciary discharged. House passed Nov. 23. President signed Dec. 14, 1993.

PL 103-194 (S 1766) Amend the Lime Research, Promotion and Consumer Information Act of 1990 to cover seedless and not seeded limes, to increase the exemption level, to delay the initial referendum date, and to alter the composition of the Lime Board. Introduced by GORTON, R-Wash., Nov. 20, 1993. Senate passed Nov. 20. House passed Nov. 21. President signed Dec. 14, 1993.

PL 103-195 (S 1769) Relating to a statement of community development objectives for the city of Slidell, La. Introduced by JOHNSTON, D-La., Nov. 22, 1993. Senate passed, amended, Nov. 22. House passed, amended, Nov. 23. Senate agreed to House amendment Nov. 24. President signed Dec. 14, 1993.

PL 103-196 (S J Res 154) Designate Jan. 16, 1994, as Religious Freedom Day. Introduced by ROBB, D-Va., Nov. 19, 1993. Senate Judiciary discharged. Senate passed Nov. 20. House Post Office and Civil Service discharged. House passed Nov. 21. President signed Dec. 14, 1993.

PL 103-197 (HR 1944) Provide for additional development at War in the Pacific National Historical Park. Introduced by UNDERWOOD, D-Guam, April 29, 1993. House Natural Resources reported, amended, June 21 (H Rept 103-145). House passed, amended, under suspension of the rules, June 21. Senate Energy and Natural Resources reported, amended, July 16 (S Rept 103-98). Senate passed, amended, July 21. House agreed to Senate amendment with amendment Nov. 21. Senate agreed to House amendment to Senate amendment Nov. 22. President signed Dec. 17, 1993.

PL 103-198 (HR 2840) Amend Title 17, U.S. Code, to estab-

lish copyright arbitration royalty panels to replace the Copyright Royalty Tribunal. Introduced by HUGHES, D-N.J., Aug. 3, 1993. House Judiciary reported, amended, Oct. 12 (S Rept 103-286). House passed, amended, under suspension of the rules, Oct. 12. Senate passed, amended, Oct. 20. House agreed to Senate amendment Nov. 23. President signed Dec. 17, 1993.

PL 103-199 (HR 3000) For reform in emerging new democracies and support and help for improved partnership with Russia, Ukraine and other new independent states of the former Soviet Union. Introduced by GEPHARDT, D-Mo., Aug. 6, 1993. House Foreign Affairs reported, amended, Oct. 15 (H Rept 103-297, Part I). House passed, amended, under suspension of the rules, Nov. 15. Senate passed, amended, Nov. 22. House agreed to Senate amendment Nov. 23. President signed Dec. 17, 1993.

PL 103-200 (HR 3216) Amend the Comprehensive Drug Abuse Prevention and Control Act of 1970 to control illicit production of controlled substances such as methcathinine and methamphetamine. Introduced by STUPAK, D-Mich., Oct. 5, 1993. House Energy and Commerce reported, amended, Nov. 18 (H Rept 103-379, Part I). House passed, under suspension of the rules, Nov. 21. Senate passed Nov. 24. President signed Dec. 17, 1993.

PL 103-201 (HR 3514) Clarify the regulatory oversight exercised by the Rural Electrification Administration with respect to certain electric borrowers. Introduced by de la GARZA, D-Texas, Nov. 16, 1993. House Agriculture reported Nov. 19 (H Rept 103-381). House passed Nov. 19. Senate passed Nov. 22. President signed Dec. 17, 1993.

PL 103-202 (S 422) Amend the Securities Exchange Act of 1934 to ensure the efficient and fair operation of the government securities market, in order to protect investors and facilitate government borrowing at the lowest possible cost to taxpayers, and to prevent false and misleading statements in connection with offerings of government securities. Introduced by DODD, D-Conn., Feb. 24, 1993. Senate Banking, Housing and Urban Affairs reported, amended, July 27 (S Rept 103-109). Senate passed, amended, July 29. House passed, amended, Oct. 5. Senate agreed to House amendments with amendment Nov. 22. House agreed to Senate amendment to House amendments Nov. 23. President signed Dec. 17, 1993.

PL 103-203 (S 664) Make a technical amendment to the Clayton Act. Introduced by METZENBAUM, D-Ohio, March 26, 1993. Senate passed Nov. 22. House passed Nov. 23. President signed Dec. 17, 1993.

PL 103-204 (S 714) Provide funding for the resolution of failed savings associations. Introduced by RIEGLE, D-Mich., April 1, 1993. Senate Banking, Housing and Urban Affairs reported April 1 (S Rept 103-36). Senate considered May 12. Senate passed, amended, May 13. House passed, amended, Sept. 14. Conference report filed in the House on Nov. 19 (H Rept 103-380). Senate agreed to conference report Nov. 20. House agreed to conference report Nov. 23. President signed Dec. 17, 1993.

PL 103-205 (S 1777) Extend the suspended implementation of certain requirements of the food stamp program on Indian reservations, and suspend certain eligibility requirements for the participation of retail food stores in the food stamp program. Introduced by PRESSLER, R-S.D., Nov. 22, 1993. Senate passed Nov. 22. House passed Nov. 23. President signed Dec. 17, 1993.

PL 103-206 (HR 2150) Authorize appropriations for fiscal 1994 for the U.S. Coast Guard. Introduced by TAUZIN, D-La., May 19, 1993. House Merchant Marine and Fisheries reported, amended, June 21 (H Rept 103-146). House passed, amended, July 30. Senate Commerce, Science and Transportation discharged. Senate passed, amended, Nov. 22. House agreed to Senate amendment Nov. 23. President signed Dec. 20, 1993.

PL 103-207 (H J Res 300) Provide for the convening of the

second session of the 103rd Congress. Introduced by GEPHARDT, D-Mo., Nov. 22, 1993. House passed Nov. 23. Senate passed Nov. 24. President signed Dec. 20, 1993.

PL 103-208 (S 1507) Make technical amendments to the Higher Education Amendments of 1992 and the Higher Education Act of 1965. Introduced by PELL, D-R.I., Sept. 30, 1993. Senate passed Oct. 7. House passed, amended, Nov. 2. Senate agreed to House amendments with amendment Nov. 20. House agreed to Senate amendment to House amendments Nov. 20. President signed Dec. 20, 1993.

PL 103-209 (HR 1237) Establish procedures for national criminal background checks for child-care providers. Introduced by SCHROEDER, D-Colo., March 4, 1993. House Judiciary reported, amended, Nov. 20 (H Rept 103-393). House passed, amended, under suspension of the rules, Nov. 20. Senate passed Nov. 20. President signed Dec. 20, 1993.

PL 103-210 (HR 2535) Amend Title 38, U.S. Code, to provide additional authority for the secretary of Veterans Affairs to provide health care for veterans of the Persian Gulf War. Introduced by ROWLAND, D-Ga., June 28, 1993. House Veterans' Affairs reported, amended, July 29 (H Rept 103-198). House passed, amended, under suspension of the rules, Aug. 2. Senate Veterans' Affairs discharged. Senate passed, amended, Nov. 20. House agreed to Senate amendment Nov. 22. President signed Dec. 20, 1993.

PL 103-211 (HR 3759) Make emergency supplemental appropriations for the fiscal year ending Sept. 30, 1994. Introduced by NATCHER, D-Ky., Feb. 1, 1994. House Appropriations reported Feb. 1 (H Rept 103-415). House passed, amended, Feb. 3. Senate Appropriations reported, amended, Feb. 8. Senate considered Feb. 9. Senate passed, amended, Feb. 10. Conference report filed in the House on Feb. 11 (H Rept 103-424). House agreed to conference report Feb. 11. Senate agreed to conference report Feb. 11. President signed Feb. 12, 1994.

PL 103-212 (HR 1303) Designate the federal building and U.S. courthouse located at 402 E. State St. in Trenton, N.J., as the Clarkson S. Fisher Federal Building and United States Courthouse. Introduced by SMITH, R-N.J., March 10, 1993. House Public Works and Transportation reported April 29 (H Rept 103-72). House passed, under suspension of the rules, May 4. Senate Environment and Public Works reported Jan. 28, 1994. Senate passed Feb. 1. President signed Feb. 16, 1994.

PL 103-213 (HR 2223) Designate the federal building located at 525 Griffin St. in Dallas as the A. Maceo Smith Federal Building. Introduced by JOHNSON, D-Texas, May 20, 1993. House Public Works and Transportation reported Sept. 9 (H Rept 103-226). House passed, under suspension of the rules, Sept. 13. Senate Environment and Public Works reported Jan. 28, 1994. Senate passed Feb. 1. President signed Feb. 16, 1994.

PL 103-214 (HR 2555) Designate the federal building located at 100 E. Fifth St. in Cincinnati as the Potter Stewart United States Courthouse. Introduced by PORTMAN, R-Ohio, June 29, 1993. House Public Works and Transportation reported Sept. 9 (H Rept 103-229). House passed, under suspension of the rules, Sept. 13. Senate Environment and Public Works reported Jan. 28, 1994. Senate passed Feb. 1. President signed Feb. 16, 1994.

PL 103-215 (HR 3186) Designate the U.S. courthouse located in Houma, La., as the George Arceneaux Jr. United States Courthouse. Introduced by TAUZIN, D-La., Sept. 29, 1993. House Public Works and Transportation reported Nov. 10 (H Rept 103-347). House passed, under suspension of the rules, Nov. 15. Senate Environment and Public Works reported Jan. 28, 1994. Senate passed Feb. 1. President signed Feb. 16, 1994.

PL 103-216 (HR 3356) Designate the U.S. courthouse under

construction at 611 Broad St., in Lake Charles, La., as the Edwin Ford Hunter Jr. United States Courthouse. Introduced by HAYES, D-La., Oct. 26, 1993. House Public Works and Transportation reported Nov. 10 (H Rept 103-348). House passed, under suspension of the rules, Nov. 15. Senate Environment and Public Works reported Jan. 28, 1994. Senate passed Feb. 1. President signed Feb. 16, 1994.

PL 103-217 (S J Res 119) Designate the month of March 1994 as Irish-American Heritage Month. Introduced by KENNEDY, D-Mass., Aug. 3, 1993. Senate Judiciary reported Oct. 28. Senate passed Oct. 28. House Post Office and Civil Service discharged. House passed Feb. 8, 1994. President signed Feb. 22, 1994.

PL 103-218 (HR 2339) Amend the Technology-Related Assistance for Individuals With Disabilities Act of 1988 to authorize appropriations for each of the fiscal years 1994 through 1998. Introduced by OWENS, D-N.Y., June 8, 1993. House Education and Labor reported, amended, Aug. 2 (H Rept 103-208). House passed, amended, under suspension of the rules, Aug. 2. Senate passed, amended, Aug. 5. House agreed to Senate amendment with an amendment Feb. 8, 1994. Senate agreed to the House amendment to the Senate amendment Feb. 11. President signed March 9, 1994.

PL 103-219 (HR 3617) Amend the Everglades National Park Protection and Expansion Act of 1989. Introduced by SHAW, R-Fla., Nov. 22, 1993. House Natural Resources discharged. House passed Nov. 23. Senate Energy and Natural Resources reported Feb. 7, 1994 (S Rept 103-224). Senate passed Feb. 10. President signed March 9, 1994.

PL 103-220 (S 1789) Amend Title 23, U.S. Code, to permit the use of funds under the highway bridge replacement and rehabilitation program for seismic retrofit of bridges. Introduced by BOXER, D-Calif., Jan. 25, 1994. Senate Environment and Public Works reported Feb. 4. Senate passed Feb. 7. House passed March 2. President signed March 17, 1994.

PL 103-221 (S J Res 56) Designate the week beginning April 12, 1993, as National Public Safety Telecommunicators Week. Introduced by BIDEN, D-Del., March 3, 1993. Senate Judiciary discharged. Senate passed March 29. House Post Office and Civil Service discharged. House passed, amended, March 11, 1994. Senate agreed to House amendments March 17. President signed March 24, 1994.

PL 103-222 (S J Res 162) Designate March 25, 1994, as Greek Independence Day: A Celebration of Greek and American Democracy. Introduced by SPECTER, R-Pa., Feb. 9, 1994. Senate Judiciary reported March 9. Senate passed March 10. House Post Office and Civil Service discharged. House passed March 11. President signed March 24, 1994.

PL 103-223 (S J Res 163) Proclaim March 20, 1994, as National Agricultural Day. Introduced by LEAHY, D-Vt., Feb. 10, 1994. Senate Judiciary reported March 9. Senate passed March 10. House Post Office and Civil Service discharged. House passed March 11. President signed March 24, 1994.

PL 103-224 (S J Res 171) Designate March 20 through March 26, 1994, as Small Family Farm Week. Introduced by HELMS, R-N.C., March 15, 1994. Senate Judiciary discharged. Senate passed March 17. House Post Office and Civil Service discharged. House passed March 21. President signed March 24, 1994.

PL 103-225 (S 1926) Amend the Food Stamp Act of 1977 to modify the requirements relating to monthly reporting and staggered issuance of coupons for households residing on Indian reservations, to ensure adequate access to retail food stores by food stamp households and to maintain the integrity of the food stamp program. Introduced by PRESSLER, R-S.D. March 11, 1994. Senate passed March 11. House passed March 16. President signed March 25, 1994.

PL 103-226 (HR 3345) Amend Title 5, U.S. Code, to eliminate certain restrictions on employee training; to provide temporary authority to agencies relating to voluntary separation incentive payments. Introduced by CLAY, D-Mo., Oct. 22, 1993. House Post Office and Civil Service reported, Nov. 19 (H Rept 103-386). House passed, amended, Feb. 10, 1994. Senate passed, amended, Feb. 11. House agreed to Senate amendment with an amendment March 8. Senate agreed to House amendment to Senate amendment with amendments March 11. Conference report filed in the House on March 16 (H Rept 103-435). House adopted conference report March 23. Senate adopted conference report March 24. President signed March 30, 1994.

PL 103-227 (HR 1804) Improve learning and teaching by providing a national framework for education reform; to promote the research, consensus-building and systemic changes needed to ensure equitable educational achievement for all American students; to provide a framework for reauthorization of all federal education programs; to promote the development and adoption of a voluntary national system of skill standards and certifications. Introduced by KILDEE, D-Mich., April 22, 1993. House Education and Labor Committee reported, amended, July 1 (H Rept 103-168). House passed, amended, Oct. 13. Senate passed, amended, Feb. 8, 1994. Conference report filed in the House on March 21 (H Rept 103-446). House adopted conference report March 23. Senate considered conference report March 25. Senate adopted conference report March 26 (in the session that began and the Congressional Record dated March 25). President signed March 31, 1994.

PL 103-228 (HR 4122) Temporarily extend certain provisions of the Marine Mammal Protection Act. Introduced by YOUNG, R-Alaska, March 23, 1994. House Committee on Merchant Marine and Fisheries discharged. House passed March 24. Senate passed March 25. President signed March 31, 1994.

PL 103-229 (H J Res 329) Designate March 23, 1994, as Education and Sharing Day, U.S.A. Introduced by GEPHARDT, D-Mo., March 3, 1994. House Post Office and Civil Service discharged. House passed March 21. Senate passed March 24. President signed April 6, 1994.

PL 103-230 (S 1284) Amend the Developmental Disabilities Assistance Bill of Rights Act to expand or modify certain provisions relating to programs for certain individuals with disabilities, federal assistance for priority area activities for individuals with developmental disabilities, protection and advocacy of individual rights, university affiliated programs, and projects of national significance. Introduced by HARKIN, D-Iowa, July 23, 1993. Senate Labor and Human Resources reported Aug. 3 (S Rept 103-120). Senate passed Aug. 5. House passed, amended, Nov. 21. Conference report filed in the House on March 21, 1994 (H Rept 103-442). House adopted conference report, under suspension of the rules, March 21. Senate adopted conference report March 24. President signed April 6, 1994.

PL 103-231 (S 1913) Extend certain compliance dates for pesticide safety training and labeling requirements. Introduced by COCHRAN, R-Miss., March 9, 1994. Senate passed March 9. House Agriculture Committee discharged. House passed, amended, March 17. Senate agreed to House amendments March 24. President signed April 6, 1994.

PL 103-232 (S 476) Reauthorize and amend the National Fish and Wildlife Foundation Establishment Act. Introduced by CHAFEE, R-R.I., March 2, 1993. Senate Environment and Public Works reported, amended, Feb. 10, 1994 (S Rept 103-225). Senate passed, amended, March 8. House passed, amended, under suspension of the rules, March 21. Senate agreed to House amendments March 25. President signed April 11, 1994.

PL 103-233 (S 1299) Reform requirements for the disposition of multifamily property owned by the Department of Hous-

ing and Urban Development, enhance program flexibility, authorize a program to combat crime and for other purposes. Introduced by RIEGLE, D-Mich., July 28, 1993. Senate Banking, Housing and Urban Affairs reported, amended, Nov. 9 (S Rept 103-174). Senate passed, amended, Nov. 19. House passed, amended, March 22, 1994. Senate agreed to House amendments March 25. President signed April 11, 1994.

PL 103-234 (S 1206) Redesignate the federal building located at 380 Trapelo Road in Waltham, Mass., as the Frederick C. Murphy Federal Center. Introduced by KERRY, D-Mass., July 1, 1993. Senate Environment and Public Works reported Jan. 28, 1994. Senate passed Feb. 1. House Public Works and Transportation reported March 24 (H Rept 103-455). House passed, under suspension of the rules, April 12. President signed April 14, 1994.

PL 103-235 (S 2004) Extend until July 1, 1998, the exemption from ineligibility based on a high default rate for certain institutions of higher education. Introduced by BUMPERS, D-Ark., March 25, 1994. Senate passed March 25. House considered April 12. House passed, under suspension of the rules, April 13. President signed April 28, 1994.

PL 103-236 (HR 2333) Authorize appropriations for the Department of State, the U.S. Information Agency and related agencies, to authorize appropriations for foreign assistance programs, and for other purposes. Introduced by HAMILTON, D-Ind., June 8, 1993. House Foreign Affairs reported, amended, June 11 (H Rept 103-126). House considered June 15 and 16. House passed, amended, June 22. Senate Foreign Relations discharged. Senate passed, amended, Feb. 2, 1994. Conference report filed in the House April 25 (H Rept 103-482). House agreed to conference report April 28. Senate agreed to conference report April 28. President signed April 30, 1994.

PL 103-237 (HR 4066) Suspend temporarily the duty on the personal effects of participants in, and certain other individuals associated with, the 1994 World Cup Soccer Games, the 1994 World Rowing Championships, the 1995 Special Olympics World Games, the 1996 Summer Olympics, and the 1996 Paralympics. Introduced by ROSTENKOWSKI, D-Ill., March 17, 1994. House Ways and Means reported March 24 (H Rept 103-454). House passed, amended, under suspension of the rules, April 12. Senate passed April 14. President signed April 30, 1994.

PL 103-238 (S 1636) Authorize appropriations for the Marine Mammal Protection Act of 1972 and to improve the program to reduce the incidental taking of marine mammals during the course of commercial fishing operations, and for other purposes. Introduced by KERRY, D-Mass., Nov. 8, 1993. Senate Commerce, Science and Transportation reported, amended, Jan. 25, 1994 (S Rept 103-220). Senate passed, amended, March 21. House passed, amended, under suspension of the rules, March 22. Senate agreed to House amendment with amendment March 24. House agreed to Senate amendment to House amendment with an amendment April 26. Senate agreed to the House amendment to the Senate amendment to the House amendment April 26. President signed April 30, 1994.

PL 103-239 (HR 2884) Establish a national framework for the development of school-to-work opportunities systems in all states, and for other purposes. Introduced by FORD, D-Mich., Aug. 5, 1993. House Education and Labor reported, amended, Nov. 10 (H Rept 103-345). House passed, amended, under suspension of the rules, Nov. 15. Senate passed, amended, Feb. 8, 1994. Conference report filed in the House on April 19 (H Rept 103-480). House agreed to conference report April 20. Senate agreed to conference report April 21. President signed May 4, 1994.

PL 103-240 (HR 821) Amend Title 38, U.S. Code, to extend eligibility for burial in national cemeteries to persons who have 20 years of service creditable for retired pay as members of a reserve component of the armed forces. Introduced by BONILLA, R-

Texas, Feb. 4, 1993. House Veterans' Affairs reported July 29 (H Rept 103-197). House passed, under suspension of the rules, Aug. 2. Senate Veterans' Affairs discharged. Senate passed, amended, Nov. 11. House agreed to Senate amendment with amendments April 18, 1994. Senate agreed to the House amendments to Senate amendment April 20. President signed May 4, 1994.

PL 103-241 (HR 3693) Designate the U.S. courthouse under construction in Denver as the Byron White United States Courthouse. Introduced by SCHAEFER, R-Colo., Nov. 22, 1993. House Public Works and Transportation reported March 24, 1994 (H Rept 103-456). House passed, under suspension of the rules, April 12. Senate passed April 20. President signed May 4, 1994.

PL 103-242 (S 375) Amend the Wild and Scenic Rivers Act by designating a segment of the Rio Grande in New Mexico as a component of the National Wild and Scenic Rivers System, and for other purposes. Introduced by BINGAMAN, D-N.M., Feb. 16, 1993. Senate Energy and Natural Resources reported March 11 (S Rept 103-17). Senate passed March 17. House Natural Resources reported, amended, March 10, 1994 (H Rept 103-431). House passed, amended, under suspension of the rules, March 15. Senate agreed to House amendment April 19. President signed May 4, 1994.

PL 103-243 (S 1574) Authorize appropriations for the Coast Heritage Trail Route in the state of New Jersey, and for other purposes. Introduced by BRADLEY, D-N.J., Oct. 20, 1993. Senate Energy and Natural Resources reported Nov. 17 (S Rept 103-212). Senate passed Nov. 20. House Natural Resources reported, amended, March 21, 1994 (H Rept 103-443). House passed, amended, under suspension of the rules, March 21. Senate agreed to the House amendment April 19. President signed May 4, 1994.

PL 103-244 (S J Res 143) Provide for the appointment of Frank Anderson Shrontz as a citizen regent of the Board of Regents of the Smithsonian Institution. Introduced by SASSER, D-Tenn., Oct. 14, 1993. Senate Rules and Administration reported Nov. 4 (S Rept 103-170). Senate passed Nov. 11. House passed April 26, 1994. President signed May 4, 1994.

PL 103-245 (S J Res 144) Provide for the appointment of Manuel Luis Ibanez as a citizen regent of the Board of Regents of the Smithsonian Institution. Introduced by SASSER, D-Tenn., Oct. 14, 1993. Senate Rules and Administration reported Nov. 4 (S Rept 103-171). Senate passed Nov. 11. House passed April 26, 1994. President signed May 4, 1994.

PL 103-246 (S J Res 150) Designate the week of May 2 through May 8, 1994, as Public Service Recognition Week. Introduced by SARBANES, D-Md., Oct. 29, 1993. Senate Judiciary reported March 9, 1994. Senate passed March 10. House Post Office and Civil Service discharged. House passed April 21. President signed May 4, 1994.

PL 103-247 (S 2005) Make certain technical corrections [to Agriculture Act], and for other purposes. Introduced by LEAHY, D-Vt., March 25, 1994. Senate Agriculture, Nutrition and Forestry discharged. Senate passed March 25. House passed April 21. President signed May 6, 1994.

PL 103-248 (S 1930) Amend the Consolidated Farm and Rural Development Act to improve the administration of claims and obligations of the Farmers Home Administration, and for other purposes. Introduced by LEAHY, D-Vt., Mar. 15, 1994. Senate Agriculture, Nutrition and Forestry discharged. Senate passed March 24. House Agriculture discharged. House passed April 21. President signed May 11, 1994.

PL 103-249 (HR 4204) Designate the federal building located at 711 Washington St. in Boston as the Jean Mayer Human Nutrition Research Center on Aging. Introduced by MOAKLEY, D-Mass. April 13, 1994. House passed, under suspension of the rules, April 26. Senate passed May 3. President signed May 16, 1994.

PL 103-250 (H J Res 239) Authorize the president to proclaim September 1994 as Classical Music Month. Introduced by YATES, D-Ill., July 26, 1993. House Post Office and Civil Service discharged. House passed March 11, 1994. Senate Judiciary discharged. Senate passed May 2. President signed May 16, 1994.

PL 103-251 (S J Res 146) Designate May 1 through May 7, 1994, as National Walking Week. Introduced by WOFFORD, D-Pa., Oct. 20, 1993. Senate Judiciary discharged. Senate passed May 2, 1994. House Post Office and Civil Service discharged. House passed May 3. President signed May 16, 1994.

PL 103-252 (S 2000) Authorize appropriations for fiscal 1995-98 to carry out the Head Start Act and the Community Services Block Grant Act, and for other purposes. Introduced by DODD, D-Conn., March 25, 1994. Senate Labor and Human Resources reported, amended, April 19 (S Rept 103-251). Senate passed, amended, April 21. House passed, amended, April 28. Conference report filed in the House on May 9 (H Rept 103-497). Senate agreed to conference report May 11. House agreed to conference report May 12. President signed May 18, 1994.

PL 103-253 (HR 1134) Provide for the transfer of certain public lands in Clear Creek County, Colo., to the U.S. Forest Service, the state of Colorado and certain local governments in the state of Colorado, and for other purposes. Introduced by SKAGGS, D-Colo., Feb. 24, 1993. House Natural Resources reported, amended, June 21 (H Rept 103-141). House passed, amended, under suspension of the rules, June 21. Senate Energy and Natural Resources reported, amended, Feb. 23, 1994 (S Rept 103-228). Senate passed, amended, April 12. House agreed to the Senate amendments, under suspension of the rules, May 10. President signed May 19, 1994.

PL 103-254 (HR 1727) Establish a program of grants to states for arson research, prevention and control, and for other purposes. Introduced by BOUCHER, D-Va., April 20, 1993. House Science, Space and Technology reported, amended, July 13 (H Rept 103-172). House passed, amended, under suspension of the rules, July 26. Senate passed, amended, Nov. 22. House agreed to Senate amendment with an amendment April 26, 1994. Senate agreed to the House amendment to the Senate amendment May 6. President signed May 19, 1994.

PL 103-255 (S 341) Provide for a land exchange between the secretary of Agriculture and Eagle and Pitkin counties in Colorado, and for other purposes. Introduced by CAMPBELL, D-Colo., Feb. 4, 1993. Senate Energy and Natural Resources reported, amended, June 22 (S Rept 103-61). Senate passed, amended, June 29. House Natural Resources reported March 10, 1994 (H Rept 103-432, Part I). House passed, under suspension of the rules, May 10. President signed May 19, 1994.

PL 103-256 (HR 2868) Designate the federal building at 600 Camp St. in New Orleans, La., as the John Minor Wisdom U. S. Courthouse. Introduced by JEFFERSON, D-La., Aug. 4, 1993. House Public Works and Transportation reported Nov. 10 (H Rept 103-346). House passed, under suspension of the rules Nov. 15. Senate Environment and Public Works reported Jan. 28, 1994. Senate passed, amended, Feb. 1. House agreed to Senate amendments, under suspension of the rules, May 10. President signed May 25, 1994.

PL 103-257 (H J Res 303) Designate June 6, 1994, as D-Day National Remembrance Day. Introduced by LANTOS, D-Calif., Nov. 22, 1993. House Post Office and Civil Service discharged. House passed May 3, 1994. Senate Judiciary discharged. Senate passed May 11. President signed May 25, 1994.

PL 103-258 (S J Res 168) Designate May 11, 1994, as Vietnam Human Rights Day. Introduced by ROBB, D-Va., March 11, 1994. Senate Judiciary discharged. Senate passed May 4. House Post Office and Civil Service discharged. House passed, amended, May 11. Senate agreed to House amendments May 17. President signed May 25, 1994.

PL 103-259 (S 636) Amend the Public Health Service Act to permit individuals to have freedom of access to certain medical clinics and facilities, and for other purposes. Introduced by KENNEDY, D-Mass., March 23, 1993. Senate Labor and Human Resources reported, amended, July 29 (S Rept 103-117). Senate passed, amended, Nov. 16. House passed, amended, March 17, 1994. Conference report filed in the House on May 2 (H Rept 103-488). House agreed to the conference report May 5. Senate agreed to the conference report May 12. President signed May 26, 1994.

PL 103-260 (S 2024) Provide temporary obligational authority for the airport improvement program and to provide for certain airport fees to be maintained at existing levels for up to 60 days, and for other purposes. Introduced by FORD, D-Ky., April 19, 1994. Senate passed April 19. House passed, amended, under suspension of the rules, May 3. Senate agreed to the House amendment with an amendment May 12. House agreed to the Senate amendment to the House amendment, under suspension of the rules, May 17. President signed May 26, 1994.

PL 103-261 (S 2087) Extend the time period for compliance with the Nutrition Labeling and Education Act of 1990 for certain food products packaged prior to Aug. 8, 1994. Introduced by BUMPERS, D-Ark., May 6, 1994. Senate Labor and Human Resources discharged. Senate passed, amended, May 17. House passed May 19. President signed May 26, 1994.

PL 103-262 (HR 2139) Amend Title 44, U.S. Code, to authorize appropriations for the National Historical Publications and Records Commission. Introduced by CONDIT, D-Calif., May 18, 1993. House Government Operations reported Aug. 4 (H Rept 103-215). House passed, under suspension of the rules, Sept. 13. Senate Governmental Affairs discharged. Senate passed, amended, March 17, 1994. House agreed to Senate amendments May 18. President signed May 31, 1994.

PL 103-263 (S 1654) Make certain technical corrections. Introduced by INOUYE, D-Hawaii, Nov. 10, 1993. Senate Indian Affairs reported, amended, Nov. 19 (S Rept 103-191). Senate passed, amended, Nov. 24. House Natural Resources reported, amended, April 19, 1994 (H Rept 103-479, Part I). House passed, amended, under suspension of the rules, April 19. Senate agreed to House amendment with amendments May 19. House agreed to Senate amendments to the House amendment, under suspension of the rules, May 23. President signed May 31, 1994.

PL 103-264 (S J Res 179) Designate the week of June 12 through June 19, 1994, as National Men's Health Week. Introduced by DOLE, R-Kan., March 26, 1994. Senate passed March 26. House Post Office and Civil Service discharged. House passed May 24. President signed May 31, 1994.

PL 103-265 (HR 3863) Designate the Post Office building at 401 E. South St., Jackson, Miss., as the Medgar Wiley Evers Post Office. Introduced by THOMPSON, D-Miss., Feb. 10, 1994. House passed, under suspension of the rules, May 23. Senate passed May 25. President signed June 10, 1994.

PL 103-266 (HR 1632) Amend Title 11, District of Columbia Code, and Part C of Title IV of the District of Columbia Self-Government and Governmental Reorganization Act to remove gender-specific references. Introduced by NORTON, D-D.C., April 1, 1993. House District of Columbia reported, amended, July 13 (H Rept 103-175). House passed, under suspension of the rules, July 19. Senate Governmental Affairs reported May 18, 1994 (S Rept 103-262). Senate passed May 25. President signed June 13, 1994.

PL 103-267 (HR 965) Provide for toy safety and for other purposes. Introduced by COLLINS, D-Ill., Feb. 18, 1993. House Energy and Commerce reported, amended, March 10, 1993 (H

Rept 103-29). House passed, amended, under suspension of the rules, March 16, 1993. Senate Commerce, Science and Transportation discharged. Senate passed, amended, Nov. 20. House agreed to the Senate amendment with an amendment March 9, 1994. Conference report filed in the House May 11 (H Rept 103-500). House agreed to the conference report, under suspension of the rules, May 23. Senate agreed to the conference report May 25. President signed June 16, 1994.

PL 103-268 (HR 3637) Amend the District of Columbia Spouse Equity Act of 1988 to provide for coverage of the former spouses of judges of the District of Columbia courts. Introduced by NORTON, D-D.C., Nov. 22, 1993. House District of Columbia Committee discharged. House passed May 25, 1994. Senate passed June 14. President signed June 28, 1994.

PL 103-269 (HR 4205) Amend Title 11, D.C. Code, to clarify that blind individuals are eligible to serve as jurors in the Superior Court of the District of Columbia. Introduced by NORTON, D-D.C., April 13, 1994. House District of Columbia Committee discharged. House passed May 25. Senate passed June 14. President signed June 28, 1994.

PL 103-270 (S 24) Reauthorize the independent counsel law for an additional five years, and for other purposes. Introduced by LEVIN, D-Mich., Jan. 21, 1993. Senate Governmental Affairs reported, amended, July 20 (S Rept 103-101). Senate passed, amended, Nov. 18. House passed, amended, Feb. 10, 1994. Conference report filed in the House May 19 (H Rept 103-511). Senate agreed to the conference report May 25. House agreed to the conference report June 21. President signed June 30, 1994.

PL 103-271 (S 1904) Amend Title 38, U.S. Code, to improve the organization and procedures of the Board of Veterans' Appeals. Introduced by ROCKEFELLER, D-W.Va., March 8, 1994. Senate Veterans' Affairs reported, amended, April 14. Senate passed, amended, April 21. House passed, amended, under suspension of the rules, June 13. Senate agreed to the House amendment June 15. President signed July 1, 1994.

PL 103-272 (HR 1758) Revise, codify and enact without substantive change certain general and permanent laws, related to transportation, as Subtitles II, and V-X of Title 49, U. S. Code, "Transportation," and to make other technical improvements in the code. Introduced by BROOKS, D-Texas, April 21, 1993. House Judiciary reported, amended, July 15 (H Rept 103-180). House passed, amended, July 27. Senate Judiciary reported May 19, 1994 (S Rept 103-265). Senate passed June 10. President signed July 5, 1994.

PL 103-273 (HR 2559) Designate the federal building at 601 E. 12th St., Kansas City, Mo., as the Richard Bolling Federal Building. Introduced by WHEAT, D-Mo., June 29, 1993. House Public Works and Transportation reported Sept. 9 (H Rept 103-230). House passed, under suspension of the rules, Nov. 15. Senate Environment and Public Works reported, amended, Jan. 28, 1994. Senate passed, amended, March 24. House agreed to the Senate amendments, under suspension of the rules, June 27. President signed July 5, 1994.

PL 103-274 (HR 3724) Designate the U.S. courthouse in Bridgeport, Conn., as the Brien McMahon Federal Building. Introduced by KENNELLY, D-Conn., Jan. 25, 1994. House Public Works and Transportation reported May 19 (H Rept 103-513). House passed, under suspension of the rules, May 23. Senate passed June 22. President signed July 5, 1994.

PL 103-275 (HR 4568) Make supplemental appropriations for the Department of Housing and Urban Development for the fiscal year ending Sept. 30, 1994, and for other purposes. Introduced by OBEY, D-Wis., June 13, 1994. House Appropriations reported June 17 (H Rept 103-550). House passed June 21. Senate passed June 22. President signed July 5, 1994.

PL 103-276 (HR 4581) Provide for the imposition of temporary fees in connection with the handling of complaints of violations of the Perishable Agriculture Commodities Act of 1930. Introduced by de la GARZA, D-Texas, June 15, 1994. House Agriculture discharged. House passed June 16. Senate Agriculture, Nutrition and Forestry discharged. Senate passed June 28. President signed July 5, 1994.

PL 103-277 (HR 4635) Extend the Export Administration Act of 1979. Introduced by HAMILTON, D-Ind., June 23, 1994. House passed, under suspension of the rules, June 27. Senate passed June 30. President signed July 5, 1994.

PL 103-278 (S J Res 187) Designate July 16 through July 24, 1994, as National Apollo Anniversary Observance. Introduced by HOLLINGS, D-S.C., May 11, 1994. Senate Judiciary reported June 23. Senate passed June 24. House Post Office and Civil Service discharged. House passed July 12, 1994. President signed July 20, 1994.

PL 103-279 (HR 3567) Amend the John F. Kennedy Center Act to transfer operating responsibilities to the board of trustees of the John F. Kennedy Center for the Performing Arts, and for other purposes. Introduced by MINETA, D-Calif., Nov. 19, 1993. House Public Works and Transportation reported, amended, March 24, 1994 (H Rept 103-453, Part 1). House Natural Resources reported, amended, May 6 (H Rept 103-453, Part 2). House passed, amended, under suspension of the rules, May 10. Senate Environment and Public Works reported, amended, June 23. Senate passed, amended, June 27. House agreed to the Senate amendment, under suspension of the rules, June 28. President signed July 21, 1994.

PL 103-280 (S 273) Remove certain restrictions from a parcel of land owned by the city of North Charleston, S.C., in order to permit a land exchange, and for other purposes. Introduced by HOLLINGS, D-S.C., Feb. 2, 1993. Senate Energy and Natural Resources reported, amended, July 16 (S Rept 103-89). Senate passed, amended, July 21. House Natural Resources reported July 12, 1994 (H Rept 103-591). House passed, under suspension of the rules, July 12. President signed July 22, 1994.

PL 103-281 (S 1402) Convey a certain parcel of public land to the county of Twin Falls, Idaho, for use as a landfill, and for other purposes. Introduced by CRAIG, R-Idaho, Aug. 6, 1993. Senate Energy and Natural Resources discharged. Senate passed, amended, March 25, 1994. House Natural Resources reported July 12 (H Rept 103-589). House passed, under suspension of the rules, July 12. President signed July 22, 1994.

PL 103-282 (HR 4322) Amend the Small Business Act to increase the authorization for the development company program, and for other purposes. Introduced by LaFALCE, D-N.Y., May 2, 1994. House Small Business reported, amended, June 30 (H Rept 103-572). House passed, amended, under suspension of the rules, July 19. Senate passed July 20. President signed July 22, 1994.

PL 103-283 (HR 4454) Make appropriations for the legislative branch for the fiscal year ending Sept. 30, 1995, and for other purposes. Introduced by FAZIO, D-Calif., May 19, 1994. House Appropriations reported May 19, 1994 (H Rept 103-517). House passed, amended, May 26. Senate Appropriations reported, amended, June 14 (S Rept 103-283). Senate passed, amended, June 16. Conference report filed in the House June 28 (H Rept 103-567). House agreed to conference report June 29. Senate agreed to conference report July 1. President signed July 22, 1994.

PL 103-284 (S 832) Designate the plaza to be constructed on the Federal Triangle property in Washington, D.C., as the Woodrow Wilson Plaza. Introduced by MOYNIHAN, D-N.Y., April 27, 1993. Senate Environment and Public Works reported Sept. 30. Senate passed Oct. 7. House Natural Resources Committee and House Public Works and Transportation Committee discharged. House passed July 19, 1994. President signed Aug. 1, 1994.

PL 103-285 (HR 1346) Designate the federal building located on St. Croix, Virgin Islands, as the Almeric L. Christian Federal Building. Introduced by de LUGO, D-Virgin Islands, March 16, 1993. House Public Works and Transportation reported April 28 (H Rept 103-73). House passed, amended, under suspension of the rules, May 4. Senate Environment and Public Works reported June 23, 1994. Senate passed July 15. President signed Aug. 1, 1994.

PL 103-286 (HR 1873) Require certain payments made to victims of Nazi persecution to be disregarded in determining eligibility for and the amount of benefits or services based on need. Introduced by WAXMAN, D-Calif., April 27, 1993. House passed, under suspension of the rules, July, 12, 1994. Senate passed July 19. President signed Aug. 1, 1994.

PL 103-287 (HR 2532) Designate the federal building and U.S. courthouse in Lubbock, Texas, as the George H. Mahon Federal Building and U.S. Courthouse. Introduced by COMBEST, R-Texas, June 28, 1993. House Public Works and Transportation reported, Sept. 9 (H Rept 103-228). House passed, under suspension of the rules, Sept. 13. Senate Environment and Public Works reported June 23, 1994. Senate passed July 15, 1994. President signed Aug. 1, 1994.

PL 103-288 (HR 3770) Designate the U.S. courthouse located at 940 Front St. in San Diego and the federal building attached to the courthouse as the Edward J. Schwartz Courthouse and Federal Building. Introduced by SCHENK, D-Calif., Feb. 2, 1994. House Public Works and Transportation reported March 24 (H Rept 103-457). House considered April 12. House passed, under suspension of the rules, April 13. Senate Environment and Public Works reported June 23. Senate passed July 15. President signed Aug. 1, 1994.

PL 103-289 (HR 3840) Designate the federal building and U.S. courthouse located at 100 E. Houston St., Marshall, Texas, as the Sam B. Hall Jr. Federal Building and United States Courthouse. Introduced by CHAPMAN, D-Texas, Feb. 10, 1994. House Public Works and Transportation reported May 19 (H Rept 103-514). House passed, under suspension of the rules, May 23. Senate Governmental Affairs discharged June 21. Senate Environment and Public Works reported June 23. Senate passed July 15. President signed Aug. 1, 1994.

PL 103-290 (S 1880) Provide that the National Education Commission on Time and Learning shall terminate Sept. 30, 1994. Introduced by BINGAMAN, D-N.M., March 1, 1994. Senate Labor and Human Resources discharged. Senate passed July 15. House passed July 19. President signed Aug. 1, 1994.

PL 103-291 (S J Res 172) Designate May 29, 1995, through June 6, 1995, as a Time for the National Observance of the Fiftieth Anniversary of World War II. Introduced by DOLE, R-Kan., March 15, 1994. Senate Judiciary reported June 23. Senate passed June 24. House passed, amended, July 12. Senate agreed to the House amendments July 20. President signed Aug. 1, 1994.

PL 103-292 (HR 2457) Direct the secretary of the Interior to conduct a salmon captive broodstock program. Introduced by PELOSI, D-Calif., June 17, 1993. House passed, amended, under suspension of the rules, Nov. 20. Senate Environment and Public Works reported July 1, 1994 (S Rept 103-298). Senate passed Aug. 2. President signed Aug. 11, 1994.

PL 103-293 (H J Res 374) Designate Aug. 2, 1994, as National Neighborhood Crime Watch Day. Introduced by STUPAK, D-Mich., June 9, 1994. House Post Office and Civil Service discharged. House passed, amended, July 25. Senate Judiciary discharged. Senate passed Aug. 2. President signed Aug. 11, 1994.

PL 103-294 (S J Res 195) Designate Aug. 1, 1994, as Helsinki Human Rights Day. Introduced by DeCONCINI, D-Ariz.,

May 19, 1994. Senate Judiciary discharged. Senate passed July 25. House passed, under suspension of the rules, Aug. 1. President signed Aug. 11, 1994.

PL 103-295 (HR 4429) Authorize the transfer of naval vessels to certain foreign countries. Introduced by HAMILTON, D-Ind., May 17, 1994. House passed, amended, under suspension of the rules, May 23. Senate Armed Services reported, amended, July 13. Senate passed, amended, July 15. House agreed to Senate amendments with amendments Aug. 1. Senate agreed to the House amendments to the Senate amendments Aug. 5. President signed Aug. 12.

PL 103-296 (HR 4277) Establish the Social Security Administration as an independent agency and make other improvements in the old-age, survivors and disability insurance program. Introduced by JACOBS, D-Ind., April 21, 1994. House Ways and Means reported, amended, May 12 (H Rept 103-506). House passed, amended, under suspension of the rules, May 17. Senate passed, amended, May 23. Conference report filed in the House on Aug. 4 (H Rept 103-670). House agreed to conference report Aug. 5. Senate agreed to the conference report Aug. 11. President signed Aug. 15, 1994.

PL 103-297 (HR 868) Strengthen the authority of the Federal Trade Commission to protect consumers in connection with sales made with a telephone, and for other purposes. Introduced by SWIFT, D-Wash., Feb. 4, 1993. House Energy and Commerce reported Feb. 24 (H Rept 103-20). House passed, under suspension of the rules, March 2. Senate Commerce, Science and Transportation discharged. Senate passed, amended, June 30. House agreed to the Senate amendment with an amendment July 25, 1994. Senate agreed to the House amendment to the Senate amendment Aug. 2. President signed Aug. 16, 1994.

PL 103-298 (S 1458) Amend the Federal Aviation Act of 1958 to establish time limitations on certain civil actions against aircraft manufacturers, and for other purposes. Introduced by KASSEBAUM, R-Kan., Sept. 14, 1993. Senate Commerce, Science and Transportation reported, amended, Nov. 20 (S Rept 103-202). Senate Judiciary discharged March 9, 1994. Senate passed, amended, March 16. House Public Works and Transportation reported May 24 (H Rept 103-525, Part 1). House Judiciary reported, amended, June 24 (H Rept 103-525, Part 2). House passed, amended, under suspension of the rules, June 27. Senate agreed to the House amendment with an amendment Aug. 2. House agreed to the Senate amendment to the House amendment Aug. 3. President signed Aug. 17, 1994.

PL 103-299 (S J Res 204) Recognize the American Academy in Rome, an American overseas center for independent study and advanced research, on the occasion of the 100th anniversary of its founding. Introduced by MOYNIHAN, D-N.Y., June 24, 1994. Senate Judiciary discharged. Senate Foreign Relations reported June 29. Senate passed July 15. House passed, under suspension of the rules, Aug. 8. President signed Aug. 18, 1994.

PL 103-300 (HR 4790) Designate the U.S. courthouse under construction in St. Louis as the Thomas F. Eagleton United States Courthouse. Introduced by GEPHARDT, D-Mo., July 19, 1994. House Public Works and Transportation reported Aug. 1 (H Rept 103-637). House passed, under suspension of the rules, Aug. 8. Senate Environment and Public Works reported Aug. 12. Senate passed Aug. 17. President signed Aug. 19.

PL 103-301 (S J Res 178) Proclaim the week of Oct. 16 through Oct. 22, 1994, as National Character Counts Week. Introduced by DOMENICI, R-N.M., March 24, 1994. Senate Judiciary reported June 23. Senate passed June 24. House Post Office and Civil Service discharged. House passed Aug. 5. President signed Aug. 19, 1994.

PL 103-302 (HR 1426) Provide for the maintenance of dams on Indian lands by the Bureau of Indian Affairs or through con-

tracts with Indian tribes. Introduced by RICHARDSON, D-N.M., March 18, 1993. House Natural Resources reported, amended, July 14, 1994 (H Rept 103-600). House passed, under suspension of the rules, July 25. Senate Indian Affairs discharged. Senate passed Aug. 11. President signed Aug. 23, 1994.

PL 103-303 (HR 1631) Amend Title 11, District of Columbia Code, to increase the maximum amount in controversy permitted for cases under the jurisdiction of the Small Claims and Conciliation Branch of the Superior Court of the District of Columbia. Introduced by NORTON, D-D.C. April 1, 1993. House District of Columbia reported July 13 (H Rept 103-174). House passed, under suspension of the rules, July 19. Senate Governmental Affairs reported, amended, May 18, 1994 (S Rept 103-261). Senate passed, amended, May 25. House agreed to the Senate amendment Aug. 8. President signed Aug. 23, 1994.

PL 103-304 (HR 1933) Authorize appropriations for the Martin Luther King Jr. Federal Holiday Commission, extend such commission, establish a National Service Day to promote community service, and for other purposes. Introduced by LEWIS, D-Ga., April 29, 1993. House Post Office and Civil Service reported, amended, Feb. 3, 1994 (H Rept 103-418, Part 1). House passed, amended, under suspension of the rules, March 15. Senate Judiciary reported May 5. Senate considered May 23. Senate passed, amended, May 24. House agreed to the Senate amendments Aug. 10. President signed Aug. 23, 1994.

PL 103-305 (HR 2739) Amend the Airport and Airway Improvement Act of 1982 to authorize appropriations for fiscal 1994, 1995 and 1996, and for other purposes. Introduced by OBERSTAR, D-Minn., July 26, 1993. House Public Works and Transportation reported, amended, Sept. 14 (H Rept 103-240). House considered Oct. 7. House passed, amended, Oct. 13. Senate passed, amended, June 16, 1994. Conference report filed in the House Aug. 5 (H Rept 103-677). House agreed to the conference report, under suspension of the rules, Aug. 8. Senate agreed to the conference report Aug. 8. President signed Aug. 23, 1994.

PL 103-306 (HR 4426) Make appropriations for foreign operations, export financing and related programs for the fiscal year ending Sept. 30, 1995. Introduced by OBEY, D-Wis., May 16, 1994. House Appropriations reported, amended, May 23 (H Rept 103-524). House passed, amended, May 25. Senate Appropriations reported, amended, June 16 (S Rept 103-287). Senate considered June 29, July 13, 14. Senate passed, amended, July 15. Conference report filed in the House on Aug. 1 (H Rept 103-633). House agreed to the conference report Aug. 4. Senate considered the conference report Aug. 9. Senate agreed to the conference report Aug. 10. President signed Aug. 23, 1994.

PL 103-307 (HR 4453) Make appropriations for military construction for the Department of Defense for the fiscal year ending Sept. 30, 1995, and for other purposes. Introduced by HEFNER, D-N.C., May 19, 1994. House Appropriations reported May 19 (H Rept 103-516). House passed May 24. Senate Appropriations reported, amended, July 14 (S Rept 103-312). Senate passed, amended, July 15. Conference report filed in the House July 27 (H Rept 103-624). House agreed to the conference report Aug. 1. Senate agreed to the conference report Aug. 10. President signed Aug. 23, 1994.

PL 103-308 (H J Res 131) Designate Dec. 7 of each year as National Pearl Harbor Remembrance Day. Introduced by SANGMEISTER, D-Ill., March 3, 1993. House Post Office and Civil Service reported July 12, 1994 (H Rept 103-595). House passed Aug. 5. Senate passed Aug. 10. President signed Aug. 23, 1994.

PL 103-309 (H J Res 175) Designate October 1993 and October 1994 as Italian-American Heritage and Culture Month. Introduced by ENGEL, D-N.Y., April 1, 1993. House Post Office and Civil Service discharged. House passed, amended, Aug. 5, 1994. Senate passed Aug. 10. President signed Aug. 23, 1994.

PL 103-310 (HR 4812) Direct the administrator of the General Services Administration to acquire by transfer the Old U.S. Mint in San Francisco and for other purposes. Introduced by MINETA, D-Calif., July 21, 1994. House Public Works and Transportation reported Aug. 1 (H Rept 103-634). House passed, under suspension of the rules, Aug. 8. Senate passed, amended, Aug. 11. House agreed to the Senate amendment, under suspension of the rules, Aug. 16. President signed Aug. 25, 1994.

PL 103-311 (HR 2178) Amend the Hazardous Materials Transportation Act to authorize appropriations for fiscal 1994, 1995, 1996 and 1997, and for other purposes. Introduced by RAHALL, D-W.Va., May 19, 1993. House Energy and Commerce reported, amended, Nov. 8 (H Rept 103-336, Part 1). House passed, amended, under suspension of the rules, Nov. 21. Senate Commerce, Science and Transportation discharged. Senate passed, amended, Aug. 11, 1994. House agreed to the Senate amendment, under suspension of the rules, Aug. 16. President signed Aug. 26, 1994.

PL 103-312 (HR 2243) Amend the Federal Trade Commission Act to extend the authorization of appropriations, and for other purposes. Introduced by SWIFT, D-Wash., May 24, 1993. House Energy and Commerce reported June 17 (H Rept 103-138). House passed, under suspension of the rules, June 21. Senate Commerce, Science and Transportation discharged. Senate passed, amended, Sept. 22. Conference report filed in the House on July 21, 1994 (H Rept 103-617). House agreed to the conference report, under suspension of the rules, July 25. Senate agreed to the conference report Aug. 11. President signed Aug. 26, 1994.

PL 103-313 (HR 2815) Designate a portion of the Farmington River in Connecticut as a component of the National Wild and Scenic Rivers System. Introduced by JOHNSON, R-Conn., July 30, 1993. House Natural Resources reported, amended, March 10, 1994. (H Rept 103-430). House passed, amended, under suspension of the rules, March 15. Senate Energy and Natural Resources reported, amended, May 25 (H Sept 103-278). Senate passed, amended, June 16. House agreed to the Senate amendments under suspension of the rules Aug. 16. President signed Aug. 26, 1994.

PL 103-314 (HR 2942) Designate certain lands in the Commonwealth of Virginia as the George Washington National Forest Mount Pleasant Scenic Area. Introduced by GOODLATTE, R-Va., Aug. 6, 1993. House Agriculture reported, amended, Aug. 8, 1994 (H Rept 103-686). House passed, amended, under suspension of the rules, Aug. 8. Senate passed Aug. 19. President signed Aug. 26, 1994.

PL 103-315 (HR 3197) Redesignate the Post Office building at 13th and Rockland streets in Reading, Pa., as the Gus Yatron Federal Postal Facility. Introduced by HOLDEN, D-Pa., Sept. 30, 1993. House passed, amended, under suspension of the rules, Nov. 8. Senate Governmental Affairs reported Aug. 12, 1994. Senate passed Aug. 19. President signed Aug. 26, 1994.

PL 103-316 (HR 4506) Make appropriations for energy and water development for the fiscal year ending Sept. 30, 1995, and for other purposes. Introduced by BEVILL, D-Ala., May 26, 1994. House Appropriations reported May 26 (H Rept 103-533). House passed, amended, June 14. Senate Appropriations reported, amended, June 23 (H Sept 103-291). Senate passed, amended, June 30. Conference report filed in the House Aug. 4 (H Rept 103-672). House agreed to the conference report Aug. 10. Senate agreed to the conference report Aug. 11. President signed Aug. 26, 1994.

PL 103-317 (HR 4603) Make appropriations for the departments of Commerce, Justice, State, the judiciary, and related agencies' programs for the fiscal year ending Sept. 30, 1995, and making supplemental appropriations for these departments and agencies for the fiscal year ending Sept. 30, 1994, and for other purposes. Introduced by MOLLOHAN, D-W.Va., June 21, 1994. House Appropriations reported June 21 (H Rept 103-552). House considered June 23, 24. House passed, amended, June 27. Senate

Appropriations reported, amended, July 17 (H Sept 103-309). Senate considered July 21. Senate passed, amended, July 22. Conference report filed in the House Aug. 16 (H Rept 103-708). House agreed to the conference report Aug. 18. Senate agreed to the conference report Aug. 19. President signed Aug. 26, 1994.

PL 103-318 (S 2099) Establish the Northern Great Plains Rural Development Commission, and for other purposes. Introduced by DASCHLE, D-S.D., May 10, 1994. Senate Agriculture, Nutrition and Forestry discharged. Senate passed, amended, June 22. House Agriculture reported Aug. 12 (H Rept 103-700). House passed Aug. 12. President signed Aug. 26, 1994.

PL 103-319 (S J Res 153) Designate the week of Nov. 21, 1993, through Nov. 27, 1993, and the week of Nov. 20, 1994, through Nov. 26, 1994, as National Family Caregivers Week. Introduced by MURKOWSKI, R-Alaska, Nov. 18, 1993. Senate Judiciary reported June 23, 1994. Senate passed June 24. House Post Office and Civil Service discharged. House passed, amended, Aug. 5. Senate agreed to the House amendments Aug. 12. President signed Aug. 26, 1994.

PL 103-320 (S J Res 196) Designate Sept. 16, 1994, as National POW/MIA Recognition Day and authorize the display of the National League of Families POW/MIA flag. Introduced by SMITH, R-N.H., May 25, 1994. Senate Judiciary discharged. Senate passed Aug. 2. House Post Office and Civil Service discharged. House passed Aug. 12. President signed Aug. 26, 1994.

PL 103-321 (HR 2947) Amend the Commemorative Works Act, and for other purposes. Introduced by JOHNSON, R-Conn., Aug. 6, 1993. House Natural Resources reported, amended, Nov. 20 (H Rept 103-400). House passed, amended, Nov. 22. Senate Energy and Natural Resources reported, amended, April 5, 1994 (H Sept 103-247). Senate passed, amended, April 12. House agreed to the Senate amendments, under suspension of the rules, Aug. 16. President signed Aug. 26, 1994.

PL 103-322 (HR 3355) Amend the Omnibus Crime Control and Safe Streets Act of 1968 to allow grants to increase police presence, to expand and improve cooperative efforts between law enforcement agencies and members of the community to address crime and disorder problems, and otherwise to enhance public safety. Introduced by BROOKS, D-Texas, Oct. 26, 1993. House Judiciary reported, amended, Nov. 3 (H Rept 103-324). House passed, amended, under suspension of the rules, Nov. 3. Senate passed Nov. 19. Conference report filed in the House Aug. 10, 1994 (H Rept 103-694). House recommitted the conference report Aug. 19. Conference report filed in the House Aug. 21 (H Rept 103-711). House agreed to the conference report Aug. 21. Senate considered the conference report Aug. 22, 23, 24. Senate agreed to the conference report Aug. 25. President signed Sept. 13, 1994.

PL 103-323 (S 1066) Restore federal services to the Pokagon Band of Potawatomi Indians. Introduced by RIEGLE, D-Mich., May 28, 1993. Senate Indian Affairs reported May 23, 1994 (S Rept 103-266). Senate passed, amended, June 10. House Natural Resources reported July 25 (H Rept 103-620). House passed Aug. 3. President signed Sept. 21, 1994.

PL 103-324 (S 1357) Reaffirm and clarify the federal relationship of the Little Traverse Bay Bands of Odawa Indians and the Little River Band of Ottawa Indians as distinct federally recognized Indian tribes, and for other purposes. Introduced by LEVIN, D-Mich., Aug. 4, 1993. Senate Indian Affairs reported May 16, 1994 (S Rept 103-260). Senate passed, amended, May 25. House Natural Resources reported July 25 (H Rept 103-621). House passed Aug. 3. President signed Sept. 21, 1994.

PL 103-325 (HR 3474) Reduce administrative requirements for insured depository institutions to the extent consistent with safe and sound banking practices, to facilitate the establishment of community development financial institutions, and for other pur-

poses. Introduced by GONZALEZ, D-Texas, Nov. 9, 1993. House Banking, Finance and Urban Affairs reported, amended, Nov. 10. House passed, amended, under suspension of the rules, Nov. 21. Senate Banking, Housing and Urban Affairs discharged. Senate passed, amended, March 17, 1994. Conference report filed in the House on Aug. 2 (H Rept 103-652). House agreed to the conference report Aug. 4. Senate agreed to the conference report Aug. 9. President signed Sept. 23, 1994.

PL 103-326 (S 859) Reduce the restrictions on lands conveyed by deed under the Act of June 8, 1926. Introduced by HATCH, R-Utah, April 30, 1993. Senate Energy and Natural Resources reported, amended, April 5, 1994 (S Rept 103-245). Senate passed, amended, April 12. House Natural Resources reported, amended, July 12 (H Rept 103-590). House passed, amended, under suspension of the rules, July 12. Senate agreed to House amendment Aug. 25. President signed Sept. 23, 1994.

PL 103-327 (HR 4624) Make appropriations for the departments of Veterans Affairs and Housing and Urban Development, and for sundry independent agencies, boards, commissions, corporations and offices for fiscal year ending Sept. 30, 1995, and for other purposes. Introduced by STOKES, D-Ohio, June 22, 1994. House Appropriations reported June 22 (H Rept 103-555). House passed, amended, June 29. Senate Appropriations reported, amended, July 14 (S Rept 103-311). Senate considered Aug. 2 and 3. Senate passed, amended, Aug. 4. Conference report filed in the House on Aug. 26 (H Rept 103-715). House agreed to conference report Sept. 12. Senate considered conference report Sept. 22 and 26. Senate agreed to conference report Sept. 27. President signed Sept. 28, 1994.

PL 103-328 (HR 3841) Amend the Bank Holding Company Act of 1956, the Revised Statutes of the United States and the Federal Deposit Insurance Act to provide for interstate banking and branching. Introduced by NEAL, D-N.C., Feb. 10, 1994. House Banking, Finance and Urban Affairs reported, amended, March 22 (H Rept 103-448). House passed, amended, under suspension of the rules, March 22. Senate Banking, Housing and Urban Affairs discharged. Senate passed, amended, April 26. Conference report filed in the House on Aug. 2 (H Rept 103-651). House agreed to conference report Aug. 4. Senate agreed to conference report Sept. 13. President signed Sept. 29, 1994.

PL 103-329 (HR 4539) Make appropriations for the Treasury Department, the U.S. Postal Service, the Executive Office of the President, and certain independent agencies, for the fiscal year ending Sept. 30, 1995, and for other purposes. Introduced by HOYER, D-Md., May 26, 1994. House Appropriations reported May 26 (H Rept 103-534). House Appropriations reported June 9 (H Rept 103-534, Part 2). House passed, amended, June 15. Senate Appropriations reported, amended, June 16 (S Rept 103-286). Senate considered June 20 and 21. Senate passed, amended, June 22. Conference report filed in the House on Sept. 20 (H Rept 103-729). House recommitted conference report Sept. 22. Conference report filed in the House Sept. 22 (H Rept 103-741). House agreed to conference report Sept. 27. Senate agreed to conference report Sept. 28. President signed Sept. 30, 1994.

PL 103-330 (HR 4554) Make appropriations for the Department of Agriculture, Rural Development, Food and Drug Administration, and related agencies programs for the fiscal year ending Sept. 30, 1995, and for other purposes. Introduced by DURBIN, D-Ill., June 9, 1994. House Appropriations reported June 9 (H Rept 103-542). House considered June 16. House passed, amended, June 17. Senate Appropriations reported, amended, June 23 (S Rept 103-290). Senate considered July 18 and 19. Senate passed, amended, July 20. Conference report filed in the House Sept. 20 (H Rept 103-734). House agreed to conference report Sept. 23. Senate agreed to conference report Sept. 27. President signed Sept. 30, 1994.

PL 103-331 (HR 4556) Make appropriations for the Department of Transportation and related agencies for the fiscal year ending Sept. 30, 1995, and for other purposes. Introduced by

CARR, D-Mich., June 9, 1994. House Appropriations reported June 9 (H Rept 103-543). House Appropriations filed supplemental report June 13 (H Rept 103-543, Part 2). House passed, amended, June 16. Senate Appropriations reported, amended, July 14 (S Rept 103-310). Senate passed, amended, July 21. Conference report filed in the House on Sept. 26 (H Rept 103-752). House agreed to conference report Sept. 28. Senate agreed to conference report Sept. 29. President signed Sept. 30, 1994.

PL 103-332 (HR 4602) Make appropriations for the Department of the Interior and related agencies for the fiscal year ending Sept. 30, 1995, and for other purposes. Introduced by YATES, D-Ill., June 17, 1994. House Appropriations reported June 17 (H Rept 103-551). House considered June 22. House passed, amended, June 23. Senate Appropriations reported, amended, June 28 (S Rept 103-294). Senate considered July 25. Senate passed, amended, July 26. Conference report filed in the House Sept. 22 (H Rept 103-740). House agreed to conference report Sept. 27. Senate agreed to conference report Sept. 28. President signed Sept. 30, 1994.

PL 103-333 (HR 4606) Make appropriations for the Departments of Labor, Health and Human Services, and Education, and related agencies, for the fiscal year ending Sept. 30, 1995, and for other purposes. Introduced by SMITH, D-Iowa, June 21, 1994. House Appropriations reported June 21 (H Rept 103-553). House considered June 28. House passed, amended, June 29. Senate Appropriations reported, amended, July 20 (S Rept 103-318). Senate considered Aug. 5 and 8. Senate passed, amended, Aug. 10. Conference report filed in the House on Sept. 20 (H Rept 103-733). House agreed to conference report Sept. 22. Senate agreed to conference report Sept. 27. Senate agreed to amendments in disagreement Sept. 28. President signed Sept. 30, 1994.

PL 103-334 (HR 4649) Make appropriations for the government of the District of Columbia and other activities chargeable in whole or in part against the revenues of said District for the fiscal year ending Sept. 30, 1995, and for other purposes. Introduced by DIXON, D-Calif., June 24, 1994. House Appropriations reported June 24 (H Rept 103-558). House passed, amended, July 13. Senate Appropriations reported, amended, July 14 (S Rept 103-313). Senate considered July 20. Senate passed, amended, July 21. Conference report filed in the House on Aug. 4 (H Rept 103-671). House agreed to conference report Aug. 8. Senate agreed to conference report Sept. 21. Senate agreed to amendments in disagreement Sept. 28, 29 and 30. President signed Sept. 30, 1994.

PL 103-335 (HR 4650) Make appropriations for the Department of Defense for the fiscal year ending Sept. 30, 1995, and for other purposes. Introduced by MURTHA, D-Pa., June 27, 1994. House Appropriations reported June 27 (H Rept 103-562). House passed, amended, June 29. Senate Appropriations reported, amended, July 29 (S Rept 103-321). Senate considered Aug. 5, 8, 9 and 10. Senate passed, amended, Aug. 11. Conference report filed in the House on Sept. 26 (H Rept 103-747). House agreed to conference report Sept. 29. Senate agreed to conference report Sept. 29. President signed Sept. 30, 1994.

PL 103-336 (HR 4190) Designate the building located at 41-42 Norre Gade in St. Thomas, Virgin Islands, for the period of time during which it houses operations of the U.S. Postal Service, as the Alvaro de Lugo United States Post Office. Introduced by de LUGO, D-Virgin Islands, on April 13, 1994. House passed, amended, under suspension of the rules, May 23. Senate Governmental Affairs reported, amended, Aug. 12. Senate passed, amended, Aug. 25. House agreed to Senate amendments Sept. 19. President signed Oct. 3, 1994.

PL 103-337 (S 2182) Authorize appropriations for fiscal 1995 for military activities of the Department of Defense, for military construction, and for defense activities of the Department of Energy, to prescribe personnel strengths for such fiscal year for the armed forces, and for other purposes. Introduced by NUNN,

D-Ga., June 14, 1994. Senate Armed Services reported June 14 (S Rept 103-282). Senate considered June 22, 23, 24 and 30. Senate passed, amended, July 1. House passed, amended, July 25. Conference report filed in the House on Aug. 12 (H Rept 103-701). House agreed to conference report Aug. 17. Senate considered conference report Sept. 12. Senate agreed to conference report Sept. 13. President signed Oct. 5, 1994.

PL 103-338 (HR 1779) Designate the facility of the U.S. Postal Service located at 401 S. Washington St. in Chilicothe, Mo., as the Jerry L. Litton United States Post Office Building. Introduced by DANNER, D-Mo., April 21, 1993. House passed, under suspension of the rules, May 24. Senate Governmental Affairs reported, amended, Aug. 12. Senate passed, amended, Aug. 19. House agreed to the Senate amendments with amendments Sept. 19. Senate agreed to the House amendments to the Senate amendments Sept. 21. President signed Oct. 6, 1994.

PL 103-339 (HR 2144) Provide for the transfer of excess land to the government of Guam, and for other purposes. Introduced by UNDERWOOD, D-Guam, May 18, 1993. House Natural Resources reported Nov. 20 (H Rept 103-391, Part 1). House passed, amended, under suspension of the rules, Jan. 26, 1994. Senate Energy and Natural Resources reported June 24 (S Rept 103-293). Senate passed Sept. 21. President signed Oct. 6, 1994.

PL 103-340 (HR 3679) Authorize appropriations to expand implementation of the Junior Duck Stamp Conservation Program conducted by the U.S. Fish and Wildlife Service. Introduced by ORTIZ, D-Texas, Nov. 22, 1993. House Merchant Marine and Fisheries reported, amended, May 23, 1994 (H Rept 103-521). House passed, amended, under suspension of the rules, May 23. Senate Environment and Public Works reported Sept. 12 (S Rept 103-363). Senate passed Sept. 21. President signed Oct. 6, 1994.

PL 103-341 (HR 3839) Designate the U.S. Post Office located at 220 S. 40th Ave. in Hattiesburg, Miss., as the Roy M. Wheat Post Office. Introduced by TAYLOR, D-Miss., Feb. 10, 1994. House passed, amended, under suspension of the rules, May 23. Senate Governmental Affairs reported Sept. 26. Senate passed Sept. 27. President signed Oct. 6, 1994.

PL 103-342 (HR 4177) Designate the Post Office building located at 1601 Highway 35 in Middletown, N.J., as the Candace White United States Post Office. Introduced by PALLONE, D-N.J. April 12, 1994. House passed, amended, under suspension of the rules, May 23. Senate Governmental Affairs discharged. Senate passed Sept. 27. President signed Oct. 6, 1994.

PL 103-343 (HR 4191) Designate the U.S. Post Office located at 9630 Estate Thomas in St. Thomas, Virgin Islands, as the Aubrey C. Ottley United States Post Office. Introduced by de LUGO, D-Virgin Islands, April 13, 1994. House passed, amended, under suspension of the rules, May 23. Senate Governmental Affairs reported Sept. 26. Senate passed Sept. 27. President signed Oct. 6, 1994.

PL 103-344 (HR 4230) Amend the American Indian Religious Freedom Act to provide for the traditional use of peyote by Indians for religious purposes, and for other purposes. Introduced by RICHARDSON, D-N.M., April 14, 1994. House Natural Resources reported, amended, Aug. 5 (H Rept 103-675). House passed, amended, under suspension of the rules, Aug. 8. Senate Indian Affairs discharged. Senate passed Sept. 27. President signed Oct. 6, 1994.

PL 103-345 (HR 4569) Extend and make amendments to the President John F. Kennedy Assassination Records Collection Act of 1992. Introduced by CONYERS, D-Mich., June 13, 1994. House passed, amended, under suspension of the rules, July 12. Senate Governmental Affairs reported, amended, Aug. 2. Senate passed, amended, Aug. 10. House agreed to Senate amendments, under suspension of the rules, Sept. 27. President signed Oct. 6, 1994.

PL 103-346 (HR 4637) Direct the secretary of the Interior to convey to the city of Imperial Beach, Calif., approximately 1 acre of land in the Tijuana Slough National Wildlife Refuge. Introduced by SCHENK, D-Calif., June 24, 1994. House passed, under suspension of the rules, July 12. Senate Environment and Public Works reported Aug. 24 (S Rept 103-360). Senate passed Sept. 21. President signed Oct. 6, 1994.

PL 103-347 (H J Res 363) Designate October 1994 as Crime Prevention Month. Introduced by BARRETT, D-Wis., May 4, 1994. House Post Office and Civil Service discharged. House passed July 25. Senate Judiciary discharged. Senate passed Sept. 21. President signed Oct. 6, 1994.

PL 103-348 (S 716) Require that all federal lithographic printing be performed using ink made from vegetable oil, and for other purposes. Introduced by BOND, R-Mo., April 1, 1993. Senate Rules and Administration reported, amended, Nov. 10 (S Rept 103-178). Senate passed, amended, Nov. 18. House Government Operations reported, amended, July 28, 1994 (H Rept 103-625, Part 1). House passed, amended, under suspension of the rules, Sept. 20. Senate agreed to the House amendment Sept. 27. President signed Oct. 6, 1994.

PL 103-349 (S 1406) Amend the Plant Variety Protection Act to make such act consistent with the International Convention for the Protection of New Varieties of Plants of March 19, 1991, to which the United States is a signatory, and for other purposes. Introduced by KERREY, D-Neb., Aug. 6, 1993. Senate Agriculture, Nutrition and Forestry discharged. Senate passed, amended, May 25, 1994. House passed, amended, Aug. 12. Senate agreed to House amendment Sept. 21. President signed Oct. 6, 1994.

PL 103-350 (S 1703) Expand the boundaries of Piscataway National Park, and for other purposes. Introduced by SARBANES, D-Md., Nov. 19, 1993. Senate Energy and Natural Resources reported, amended, May 25, 1994 (S Rept 103-275). Senate passed, amended, June 16. House Natural Resources reported, amended, Aug. 8 (H Rept 103-682). House passed, amended, under suspension of the rules, Aug. 8. Senate agreed to the House amendments Sept. 21. President signed Oct. 6, 1994.

PL 103-351 (S J Res 221) Express the sense of the Congress in commemoration of the 75th anniversary of Grand Canyon National Park. Introduced by McCAIN, R-Ariz., Sept. 22, 1994. Senate passed Sept. 22. House passed Oct. 6. President signed Oct. 8, 1994.

PL 103-352 (HR 5060) Provide for the continuation of certain fee collections for the expenses of the Securities and Exchange Commission for fiscal 1995. Introduced by GIBBONS, D-Fla., Sept. 20, 1994. House Ways and Means reported Sept. 22 (H Rept 103-739, Part 1). House passed, under suspension of the rules, Sept. 27. Senate passed Oct. 8. President signed Oct. 10, 1994.

PL 103-353 (HR 995) Amend Title 38, U.S. Code, to improve re-employment rights and benefits of veterans and other benefits of employment of certain members of the uniformed services, and for other purposes. Introduced by MONTGOMERY, D-Miss., Feb. 18, 1993. House Veterans' Affairs reported, amended, April 28 (H Rept 103-65, Part 1). House passed, amended, under suspension of the rules, May 4. Senate Veterans' Affairs discharged. Senate passed, amended, Nov. 8. House agreed to the Senate amendment with an amendment Sept. 13, 1994. Senate agreed to the House amendment to the Senate amendment Sept. 28. President signed Oct. 13, 1994.

PL 103-354 (HR 4217) Reform the federal crop insurance program, and for other purposes. Introduced by de la GARZA, D-Texas, April 14, 1994. House Agriculture reported, amended, Aug. 1 (H Rept 103-649). House passed, amended, Aug. 5. Senate passed, amended, Aug. 25. House agreed to the Senate amendment with an amendment, under suspension of the rules, Oct. 3. Senate agreed to the House amendment to the Senate amendment Oct. 4. President signed Oct. 13, 1994.

PL 103-355 (S 1587) Revise and streamline the acquisition laws of the federal government, and for other purposes. Introduced by GLENN, D-Ohio, Oct. 26, 1993. Senate Governmental Affairs reported, amended, May 11, 1994 (S Rept 103-258). Senate Armed Services reported May 12 (S Rept 103-259). Senate Small Business discharged. Senate considered June 7. Senate passed, amended, June 8. House passed, amended, June 27. Conference report filed in the House on Aug. 21 (H Rept 103-712). Senate agreed to conference report Aug. 23. House agreed to conference report Sept. 20. President signed Oct. 13, 1994.

PL 103-356 (S 2170) Provide a more effective, efficient, and responsive government. Introduced by GLENN, D-Ohio, June 9, 1994. Senate Governmental Affairs reported June 9 (S Rept 103-281). Senate passed, amended, Sept. 28. House considered Oct. 3. House passed, under suspension of the rules, Oct. 4. President signed Oct. 13, 1994.

PL 103-357 (HR 734) Amend the act entitled "An act to provide for the extension of certain federal benefits, services, and assistance to the Pascua Yaqui Indians of Arizona, and for other purposes." Introduced by PASTOR, D-Ariz., Feb. 2, 1993. House Natural Resources reported Aug. 2 (H Rept 103-204). House passed, under suspension of the rules, Aug. 2. Senate Indian Affairs reported, amended, Aug. 16, 1994 (S Rept 103-338). Senate passed, amended, Aug. 19. House agreed to the Senate amendment, under suspension of the rules, Oct. 3. President signed Oct. 14, 1994.

PL 103-358 (HR 3694) Amend Title 5, U.S. Code, to permit the garnishment of an annuity under the Civil Service Retirement System or the Federal Employees' Retirement System, if necessary to satisfy a judgment against an annuitant for physically, sexually, or emotionally abusing a child. Introduced by SCHROEDER, D-Colo., Nov. 22, 1993. House passed, amended, under suspension of the rules, Sept. 19, 1994. Senate passed Sept. 30. President signed Oct. 14, 1994.

PL 103-359 (HR 4299) Authorize appropriations for fiscal 1995 for intelligence and intelligence-related activities of the U.S. government, the community management account, and the Central Intelligence Agency Retirement and Disability System, and for other purposes. Introduced by GLICKMAN, D-Kan., April 26, 1994. House Intelligence reported, amended, June 9 (H Rept 103-541, Part 1). House Armed Services and House Judiciary discharged. House considered July 19. House passed, amended, July 20. Senate passed, amended, Aug. 12. Conference report filed in the House Sept. 27 (H Rept 103-753). House agreed to conference report Sept. 30. Senate agreed to conference report Sept. 30. President signed Oct. 14, 1994.

PL 103-360 (HR 4543) Designate the U.S. courthouse to be constructed at 907 Richland St., Columbia, S.C., as the Matthew J. Perry Jr. United States Courthouse. Introduced by CLYBURN, D-S.C., June 8, 1994. House Public Works and Transportation reported Aug. 1 (H Rept 103-636). House passed, under suspension of the rules Aug. 8. Senate Energy and Natural Resources reported Sept. 27. Senate passed Sept. 30. President signed Oct. 14, 1994.

PL 103-361 (H J Res 389) Designate the second Sunday in October 1994 as National Children's Day. Introduced by KENNEDY, D-Mass., July 14, 1994. House Post Office and Civil Service discharged. House passed Sept. 30. Senate passed Oct. 4. President signed Oct. 14, 1994.

PL 103-362 (H J Res 398) Establish the fourth Sunday of July as Parents' Day. Introduced by BURTON, R-Ind., Aug. 5, 1994. House Post Office and Civil Service discharged. House passed Sept. 30. Senate passed Oct. 4. President signed Oct. 14, 1994.

PL 103-363 (H J Res 415) Designate the week beginning Oct. 16, 1994, as National Penny Charity Week. Introduced by PORTER, R-Ill., Sept. 27, 1994. House Post Office and Civil Service discharged. House passed Sept. 30. Senate passed Oct. 4. President signed Oct. 14, 1994.

PL 103-364 (S 316) Establish the Saguaro National Park in the state of Arizona, and for other purposes. Introduced by De-CONCINI, D-Ariz., Feb. 4, 1993. Senate Energy and Natural Resources reported, amended, May 25, 1994 (S Rept 103-270). Senate passed, amended, June 16. House Natural Resources reported Oct. 3 (H Rept 103-815). House passed, under suspension of the rules, Oct. 3, 1994. President signed Oct. 14, 1994.

PL 103-365 (S 1233) Resolve the status of certain lands in Arizona that are subject to a claim as a grant of public lands for railroad purposes, and for other purposes. Introduced by DeCON-CINI, D-Ariz., July 15, 1993. Senate Energy and Natural Resources reported, amended, May 25, 1994 (S Rept 103-274). Senate passed, amended, June 24. House Judiciary reported Oct. 3 (H Rept 103-773, Part 1). House Natural Resources reported Oct. 3 (H Rept 103-773, Part 2). House passed, under suspension of the rules, Oct. 3. President signed Oct. 14, 1994.

PL 103-366 (S J Res 157) Designate 1994 as The Year of Gospel Music. Introduced by SASSER, D-Tenn., Nov. 19, 1993. Senate Judiciary discharged. Senate passed Aug. 2, 1994. House Post Office and Civil Service discharged. House passed Sept. 30. President signed Oct. 14, 1994.

PL 103-367 (S J Res 185) Designate October 1994 as National Breast Cancer Awareness Month. Introduced by PELL, D-R.I., May 5, 1994. Senate Judiciary reported Aug. 11. Senate passed Aug. 12. House Post Office and Civil Service discharged. House passed Sept. 30. President signed Oct. 14, 1994.

PL 103-368 (S J Res 198) Designate 1995 as the Year of the Grandparent. Introduced by PRYOR, D-Ark., June 9, 1994. Senate Judiciary reported Aug. 11. Senate passed Aug. 12. House Post Office and Civil Service discharged. House passed Sept. 30. President signed Oct. 14.

PL 103-369 (S 2406) Amend Title 17, U.S. Code, relating to the definition of a local service area of a primary transmitter, and for other purposes. Introduced by HUTCHISON, R-Texas, Aug. 18, 1994. Senate passed Aug. 18. House passed, amended, under suspension of the rules, Sept. 20. Senate agreed to House amendments Oct. 4. President signed Oct. 18, 1994.

PL 103-370 (S J Res 220) Designate Oct. 19, 1994, as National Mammography Day. Introduced by BIDEN, D-Del., Sept. 21, 1994. Senate Judiciary discharged. Senate passed Oct. 6. House passed Oct. 7. President signed Oct. 18, 1994.

PL 103-371 (HR 1520) Amend the Petroleum Marketing Practices Act. Introduced by WYDEN, D-Ore., March 30, 1993. House Energy and Commerce reported, amended, Sept. 22, 1994 (H Rept 103-737). House considered Oct. 3. House passed, amended, under suspension of the rules, Oct. 4. Senate passed Oct. 5. President signed Oct. 19, 1994.

PL 103-372 (HR 2826) Provide for an investigation of the whereabouts of the U.S. citizens and others who have been missing from Cyprus since 1974. Introduced by ENGEL, D-N.Y., Aug. 2, 1993. House passed, under suspension of the rules, Aug. 1, 1994. Senate Foreign Relations discharged. Senate passed, amended, Oct. 3. House considered Oct. 4. House agreed to Senate amendment, under suspension of the rules, Oct. 5. President signed Oct. 19, 1994.

PL 103-373 (HR 2902) Amend the District of Columbia Self-Government and Governmental Reorganization Act to revise and make permanent the use of a formula based on adjusted

District General Fund revenues as the basis for determining the amount of the annual federal payment to the District of Columbia, and for other purposes. Introduced by STARK, D-Calif., Aug. 5, 1993. House District of Columbia reported, amended, Sept. 27, 1994 (H Rept 103-754). House passed, amended, Oct. 3. Senate passed Oct. 4. President signed Oct. 19, 1994.

PL 103-374 (HR 3485) Authorize appropriations for carrying out the Earthquake Hazards Reduction Act of 1977 for fiscal 1994, 1995 and 1996. Introduced by BOUCHER, D-Va., Nov. 10, 1993. House Science, Space and Technology reported Nov. 15 (H Rept 103-360, Part 1). House passed, under suspension of the rules, Nov. 15. Senate Commerce, Science and Transportation reported, amended, Aug. 22, 1994 (S Rept 103-354). Senate passed, amended, Sept. 30. House considered Oct. 4. House agreed to Senate amendments, under suspension of the rules, Oct. 5. President signed Oct. 19, 1994.

PL 103-375 (HR 4308) Authorize appropriations to assist in carrying out the North American Wetlands Conservation Act for fiscal 1995 through 1998, and for other purposes. Introduced by DINGELL, D-Mich., April 28, 1994. House Merchant Marine and Fisheries reported, amended, Sept. 12 (H Rept 103-717). House considered Sept. 12. House passed, amended, under suspension of the rules, Sept. 13. Senate passed Oct. 4. President signed Oct. 19, 1994.

PL 103-376 (HR 4379) Amend the Farm Credit Act of 1971 to enhance the ability of the banks for cooperatives to finance agriculture exports, and for other purposes. Introduced by de la GARZA, D-Texas, May 10, 1994. House Agriculture discharged. House passed, amended, Sept. 29. Senate passed Oct. 5. President signed Oct. 19, 1994.

PL 103-377 (HR 4653) Settle Indian land claims within the state of Connecticut, and for other purposes. Introduced by GEJDENSON, D-Conn., June 27, 1994. House Natural Resources reported, amended, Aug. 5 (H Rept 103-676). House passed, amended, under suspension of the rules, Aug. 8. Senate passed, amended, Oct. 3. House considered Oct. 4. House agreed to Senate amendment, under suspension of the rules, Oct. 5. President signed Oct. 19, 1994.

PL 103-378 (HR 5155) Authorize the transfer of naval vessels to certain foreign countries. Introduced by HAMILTON, D-Ind., Oct. 3, 1994. House considered Oct. 4. House passed, amended, under suspension of the rules, Oct. 5. Senate passed Oct. 7. President signed Oct. 19, 1994.

PL 103-379 (H J Res 401) Designate the months of March 1995 and March 1996 as Irish-American Heritage Month. Introduced by MANTON, D-N.Y., Aug. 11, 1994. House Post Office and Civil Service discharged. House passed Sept. 30. Senate passed Oct. 4. President signed Oct. 19, 1994.

PL 103-380 (H J Res 417) Provide for temporary extension of the application of the final paragraph of Section 10 of the Railway Labor Act with respect to the dispute between the Soo Line Railroad Co. and certain of its employees. Introduced by DINGELL, D-Mich., Sept. 28, 1994. House passed, under suspension of the rules, Oct. 3. Senate passed Oct. 5. President signed Oct. 19, 1994.

PL 103-381 (S 2475) Authorize assistance to promote the peaceful resolution of conflicts in Africa. Introduced by PELL, D-R.I., Sept. 29, 1994. Senate Foreign Relations reported Sept. 29. Senate passed Oct. 4. House passed Oct. 5. Senate Foreign Relations filed a report Oct. 7 (S Rept 103-404). President signed Oct. 19, 1994.

PL 103-382 (HR 6) Extend for six years the authorizations of appropriations for the programs under the Elementary and Secondary Education Act of 1965 and for other purposes. Introduced

by KILDEE, D-Mich., Jan. 1, 1993. House Education and Labor reported, amended, Feb. 16, 1994 (H Rept 103-425). House considered Feb. 24, March 2, 3, 9, 21 and 22. House passed, amended, March 24. Senate Labor and Human Resources discharged. Senate passed, amended, Aug. 2. Conference report filed in the House on Sept. 28 (H Rept 103-761). House agreed to conference report Sept. 30. Senate considered conference report Sept. 30, Oct. 3 and 4. Senate agreed to conference report Oct. 5. President signed Oct. 20, 1994.

PL 103-383 (S 922) Provide that a state court may not modify an order of another state court requiring the payment of child support unless the recipient of child support payments resides in the state in which the modification is sought or consents to the seeking of the modification in that court. Introduced by MOSELEY-BRAUN, D-Ill., May 6, 1993. Senate Judiciary reported, amended, Aug. 25, 1994 (S Rept 103-361). Senate passed, amended, Sept. 27. House considered Oct. 4. House passed, under suspension of the rules, Oct. 5. President signed Oct. 20, 1994.

PL 103-384 (HR 2135) Provide for a National Native American Veterans' Memorial. Introduced by THOMAS, R-Wyo., May 17, 1993. House considered Oct. 4, 1994. House passed, amended, under suspension of the rules, Oct. 5. Senate passed Oct. 8. President signed Oct. 22, 1994.

PL 103-385 (HR 2294) Redesignate the Post Office building at 1000 Lamar St., Wichita Falls, Texas, as the Graham B. Purcell Jr. Post Office Building. Introduced by SARPALIUS, D-Texas, May 26, 1993. House passed, under suspension of the rules, Sept. 21. Senate Governmental Affairs discharged. Senate passed Oct. 7, 1994. President signed Oct. 22, 1994.

PL 103-386 (HR 4192) Designate the U.S. Post Office building located at 3000 Veterans Drive in Saint Thomas, Virgin Islands, as the Arturo R. Watlington Sr. Post Office. Introduced by de LUGO, D-Virgin Islands, April 13, 1994. House passed, amended, under suspension of the rules, Sept. 19. Senate Governmental Affairs discharged. Senate passed Oct. 7. President signed Oct. 22, 1994.

PL 103-387 (HR 4278) Make improvements in the old-age, survivors, and disability insurance program under Title II of the Social Security Act. Introduced by JACOBS, D-Ind., April 21, 1994. House Ways and Means reported May 4 (H Rept 103-491). House considered May 10. House passed, amended, under suspension of the rules, May 12. Senate passed, amended, May 25. Conference report filed in the House Oct. 6 (H Rept 103-842). House agreed to conference report Oct. 6. Senate agreed to conference report Oct. 6. President signed Oct. 22, 1994.

PL 103-388 (HR 4361) Amend Title 5, U.S. Code, to provide that an employee of the federal government may use sick leave to attend to the medical needs of a family member, to modify the voluntary leave transfer program with respect to employees who are members of the same family, and for other purposes. Introduced by NORTON, D-D.C., May 5, 1994. House Post Office and Civil Service reported, amended, Sept. 19 (H Rept 103-722). House passed, amended, under suspension of the rules, Sept. 19. Senate Governmental Affairs discharged. Senate passed, amended, Oct. 7. House agreed to Senate amendments Oct. 7. President signed Oct. 22, 1994.

PL 103-389 (HR 4535) Amend the Securities Exchange Act of 1934 with respect to the extension of unlisted trading privileges for corporate securities, and for other purposes. Introduced by WYDEN, D-Ore., May 26, 1994. House Energy and Commerce reported July 28 (H Rept 103-626). House passed, under suspension of the rules, Aug. 1. Senate Banking, Housing and Urban Affairs discharged. Senate passed Oct. 6. President signed Oct. 22, 1994.

PL 103-390 (HR 4896) Grant the consent of the Congress to the Kansas and Missouri Metropolitan Culture District Compact. Introduced by WHEAT, D-Mo., Aug. 3, 1994. House Judiciary reported Oct. 3 (H Rept 103-774). House passed, under suspension of the rules, Oct. 3. Senate passed Oct. 8. President signed Oct. 22, 1994.

PL 103-391 (HR 4924) Assist in the conservation of rhinoceroses and tigers by supporting and providing financial resources for the conservation programs of nations whose activities directly or indirectly affect rhinoceros and tiger populations, and of the CITES [Convention on International Trade in Endangered Species of Wild Fauna and Flora] Secretariat. Introduced by FIELDS, D-Texas, Aug. 9, 1994. House Merchant Marine and Fisheries reported Sept. 26 (H Rept 103-748). House passed, amended, Sept. 27. Senate passed Oct. 7. President signed Oct. 22, 1994.

PL 103-392 (HR 4950) Extend the authorities of the Overseas Private Investment Corporation, and for other purposes. Introduced by GEJDENSON, D-Conn., Aug. 12, 1994. House Foreign Affairs reported, amended, Sept. 19 (H Rept 103-726). House passed, under suspension of the rules, amended, Sept. 19. Senate Foreign Relations discharged. Senate passed, amended, Sept. 30. Conference report filed in the House Oct. 4 (H Rept 103-834). Senate agreed to conference report Oct. 6. House agreed to conference report Oct. 7. President signed Oct. 22, 1994.

PL 103-393 (HR 5053) Authorize the secretary of Agriculture to extend for one year Water Bank Act agreements that are due to expire on Dec. 31, 1994. Introduced by POMEROY, D-N.D., Sept. 19, 1994. House Agriculture discharged. House passed, amended, Oct. 4. Senate passed Oct. 7. President signed Oct. 22, 1994.

PL 103-394 (HR 5116) Amend Title 11, U.S. Code. Introduced by BROOKS, D-Texas, Sept. 28, 1994. House Judiciary reported, amended, Oct. 4 (H Rept 103-835). House considered Oct. 4. House passed, under suspension of the rules, Oct. 5. Senate passed Oct. 6. President signed Oct. 22, 1994.

PL 103-395 (H J Res 425) Provide for the convening of the first session of the 104th Congress. Introduced by HOYER, D-Md., Oct. 7, 1994. House passed Oct. 7. Senate passed Oct. 8. President signed Oct. 22, 1994.

PL 103-396 (S 340) Amend the Federal Food, Drug and Cosmetic Act to clarify the application of the act with respect to alternate uses of new animal drugs and new drugs intended for human use, and for other purposes. Introduced by HEFLIN, D-Ala., Feb. 4, 1993. Senate Labor and Human Resources discharged. Senate passed, amended, Oct. 4, 1994. House Energy and Commerce discharged. House passed Oct. 6. President signed Oct. 22, 1994.

PL 103-397 (S 455) Amend Title 31, U.S. Code, to increase federal payments to units of general local government for entitlement lands, and for other purposes. Introduced by HATFIELD, R-Ore., Feb. 25, 1993. Senate Energy and Natural Resources reported, amended, Feb. 25, 1994 (S Rept 103-231). Senate passed, amended, April 13. House Natural Resources reported Oct. 5 (H Rept 103-838). House considered Oct. 5 and 6. House passed Oct. 7. President signed Oct. 22, 1994.

PL 103-398 (S 528) Provide for the transfer of certain U.S. Forest Service lands in Lincoln County, Mont., to Lincoln County in the state of Montana. Introduced by BURNS, R-Mont., March 9, 1993. Senate Energy and Natural Resources reported, amended, Aug. 23, 1994 (S Rept 103-355). Senate passed, amended, Aug. 25. House Natural Resources discharged. House passed Oct. 7. President signed Oct. 22, 1994.

PL 103-399 (S 720) Clean up open dumps on Indian lands, and for other purposes. Introduced by McCAIN, R-Ariz., April 1, 1993. Senate Indian Affairs reported, amended, April 25, 1994

(S Rept 103-253). Senate passed, amended, May 12. House Natural Resources reported, amended, Oct. 3 (H Rept 103-783). House considered Oct. 4. House passed, amended, under suspension of the rules, Oct. 5. Senate agreed to House amendment Oct. 8. President signed Oct. 22, 1994.

PL 103-400 (S 1225) Authorize and encourage the president to conclude an agreement with Mexico to establish a United States-Mexico Border Health Commission. Introduced by BINGAMAN, D-N.M., July 14, 1993. Senate Foreign Relations reported Sept. 22. Senate passed, amended, Sept. 30. House considered Oct. 3 and 4. House passed, under suspension of the rules, Oct. 5. President signed Oct. 22, 1994.

PL 103-401 (S 1312) Amend the Employee Retirement Income Security Act of 1974 in order to provide for the availability of remedies for certain former pension plan participants and beneficiaries. Introduced by METZENBAUM, D-Ohio, July 29, 1993. Senate Labor and Human Resources discharged. Senate passed, amended, Oct. 28. House passed, under suspension of the rules, Oct. 3, 1994. President signed Oct. 22, 1994.

PL 103-402 (S 1457) Amend the Aleutian and Pribilof Restitution Act to include authorization for appropriation to compensate Aleut villages for church property lost, damaged, or destroyed during World War II. Introduced by STEVENS, R-Alaska, Sept. 14, 1993. Senate Governmental Affairs discharged. Senate passed Nov. 20. House Judiciary reported Oct. 4, 1994 (H Rept 103-833). House considered Oct. 4. House passed, amended, under suspension of the rules, Oct. 5. Senate agreed to House amendment Oct. 8. President signed Oct. 22, 1994.

PL 103-403 (S 2060) Amend the Small Business Act. Introduced by BUMPERS, D-Ark., May 3, 1994. Senate Small Business reported, amended, Aug. 11 (S Rept 103-332). Senate passed, amended, Aug. 18. House passed, amended, Sept. 21. Conference report filed in the House Oct. 3 (H Rept 103-824). House agreed to conference report Oct. 4. Senate agreed to conference report Oct. 5. President signed Oct. 22, 1994.

PL 103-404 (S 2073) Designate the U.S. courthouse that is scheduled to be constructed in Concord, N.H., as the Warren B. Rudman United States Courthouse, and for other purposes. Introduced by SMITH, R-N.H., May 4, 1994. Senate Environment and Public Works reported Aug. 12. Senate passed Aug. 17. House Public Works and Transportation discharged. House passed, amended, Oct. 7. Senate agreed to House amendments Oct. 7. President signed Oct. 22, 1994.

PL 103-405 (S 2395) Designate the U.S. Federal Building and Courthouse in Detroit, Mich., as the Theodore Levin Federal Building and Courthouse, and for other purposes. Introduced by RIEGLE, D-Mich., Aug. 16, 1994. Senate Energy and Natural Resources reported, amended, Sept. 27. Senate passed, amended, Sept. 30. House passed Oct. 7. President signed Oct. 22, 1994.

PL 103-406 (S 2466) Amend the Energy Policy and Conservation Act to manage the Strategic Petroleum Reserve more effectively and for other purposes. Introduced by JOHNSTON, D-La., Sept. 27, 1994. Senate Energy and Natural Resources discharged. Senate passed Sept. 30. House passed Oct. 7. President signed Oct. 22, 1994.

PL 103-407 (S 2500) Enable producers and feeders of sheep and importers of sheep and sheep products to develop, finance and carry out a nationally coordinated program for sheep and sheep product promotion, research and information, and for other purposes. Introduced by LEAHY, D-Vt., Oct. 4, 1994. Senate passed Oct. 4. House passed Oct. 5. President signed Oct. 22, 1994.

PL 103-408 (S J Res 90) Recognize the achievements of radio amateurs, and to establish support for such amateurs as national policy. Introduced by ROBB, D-Va., May 7, 1993. Senate

Commerce, Science and Transportation reported Sept. 14, 1994 (S Rept 103-368). Senate passed Oct. 6. House passed Oct. 6. President signed Oct. 22, 1994.

PL 103-409 (HR 512) Amend Chapter 87 of Title 5, U.S. Code, to provide that group life insurance benefits under such chapter may, upon application, be paid out to an insured individual who is terminally ill, and for other purposes. Introduced by GILMAN, R-N.Y., Jan. 21, 1993. House Post Office and Civil Service reported, amended, July 18, 1994 (H Rept 103-608). House passed amended, under suspension of the rules, July 19. Senate Governmental Affairs reported Oct. 3 (S Rept 103-395). Senate passed, amended, Oct. 7. House agreed to Senate amendments Oct. 7. President signed Oct. 25, 1994.

PL 103-410 (HR 2056) Redesignate the post office building located at 600 Princess Anne St., Fredericksburg, Va., as the Samuel E. Perry Post Office Building. Introduced by BATEMAN, R-Va., May 11, 1993. House passed, amended, under suspension of the rules, Sept. 21. Senate Governmental Affairs discharged. Senate passed Oct. 7, 1994. President signed Oct. 25, 1994.

PL 103-411 (HR 2440) Amend the Independent Safety Board Act of 1974 to authorize appropriations for fiscal 1994, 1995 and 1996, and for other purposes. Introduced by OBERSTAR, D-Minn., June 16, 1993. House Public Works and Transportation reported Sept. 14 (H Rept 103-239, Part 1). House Energy and Commerce reported Nov. 3 (H Rept 103-239, Part 2). House passed, under suspension of the rules, Nov. 8. Senate Commerce, Science, and Transportation discharged. Senate passed, amended, May 12, 1994. House agreed to Senate amendment with an amendment Oct. 4. Senate agreed to House amendment to Senate amendment Oct. 6. President signed Oct. 25, 1994.

PL 103-412 (HR 4833) Reform the management of Indian trust funds, and for other purposes. Introduced by RICHARDSON, D-N.M., July 26, 1994. House Natural Resources reported, amended, Oct. 3 (H Rept 103-778). House passed, amended, under suspension of the rules, Oct. 3. Senate passed Oct. 7. President signed Oct. 25, 1994.

PL 103-413 (HR 4842) Specify the terms of contracts entered into by the United States and Indian tribal organizations under the Indian Self-Determination and Education Assistance Act, and for other purposes. Introduced by RICHARDSON, D-N.M., July 27, 1994. House passed, amended, Oct. 6. Senate passed Oct. 7. President signed Oct. 25, 1994.

PL 103-414 (HR 4922) Amend Title 18, U.S. Code, to make clear a telecommunications carrier's duty to cooperate in the interception of communications for law enforcement purposes, and for other purposes. Introduced by EDWARDS, D-Calif., Aug. 9, 1994. House Judiciary reported, amended, Oct. 4 (H Rept 103-827, Part 1). House considered Oct. 4. House passed, amended, under suspension of the rules, Oct. 5. Senate passed Oct. 7. President signed Oct. 25, 1994.

PL 103-415 (HR 5034) Make certain technical amendments relating to the State Department Basic Authorities Act of 1956, the United States Information and Educational Exchange Act of 1948, and other provisions of law. Introduced by BERMAN, D-Calif., Sept. 13, 1994. House passed, under suspension of the rules, Sept. 19. Senate passed Oct. 7, 1994. President signed Oct. 25, 1994.

PL 103-416 (HR 783) Amend Title III of the Immigration and Nationality Act to make changes in the laws relating to nationality and naturalization. Introduced by MAZZOLI, D-Ky., Feb. 3, 1993. House Judiciary reported, amended, Nov. 20 (H Rept 103-387). House passed, amended, under suspension of the rules, Nov. 20. Senate passed, amended, Nov. 20. House agreed to Senate amendment with an amendment Sept. 20, 1994. Senate agreed to House amendment to the Senate amendment with an amendment Oct. 6. House agreed to Senate amendment to House amendment

to the Senate amendment Oct. 7. President signed Oct. 25, 1994.

PL 103-417 (S 784) Amend the Federal Food, Drug and Cosmetic Act to establish standards with respect to dietary supplements, and for other purposes. Introduced by HATCH, R-Utah, April 7, 1993. Senate Labor and Human Resources discharged. Senate passed, amended, Aug. 13, 1994. House Energy and Commerce discharged. House passed, amended, Oct. 6. Senate agreed to House amendment Oct. 7. Senate Labor and Human Resources filed report Oct. 8 (S Rept 103-410). President signed Oct. 25, 1994.

PL 103-418 (S 1927) Increase the rates of compensation for veterans with service-connected disabilities and the rates of dependency and indemnity compensation for the survivors of certain disabled veterans. Introduced by ROCKEFELLER, D-W.Va., March 11, 1994. Senate Veterans' Affairs reported, amended, April 26. Senate passed, amended, May 4, 1994. House Veterans' Affairs discharged. House passed, amended, Aug. 8. Senate agreed to House amendment with an amendment Oct. 6. House agreed to Senate amendment to House amendment Oct. 7. President signed Oct. 25, 1994.

PL 103-419 (S 2372) Reauthorize for three years the Commission on Civil Rights, and for other purposes. Introduced by SIMON, D-Ill., Aug. 9, 1994. Senate Judiciary reported Sept. 28. Senate passed, amended, Sept. 30. House passed, amended, Oct. 3. Senate agreed to House amendments with an amendment Oct. 6. House agreed to Senate amendment to House amendments Oct. 7. President signed Oct. 25, 1994.

PL 103-420 (S 2407) Make improvements in the operation and administration of the federal courts, and for other purposes. Introduced by HEFLIN, D-Ala., Aug. 18, 1994. Senate passed Aug. 18. House Judiciary discharged. House passed Oct. 7. President signed Oct. 25, 1994.

PL 103-421 (S 2534) Revise and improve the process for disposing of buildings and property at military installations under the base-closure laws. Introduced by MITCHELL, D-Maine, Oct. 6, 1994. Senate passed Oct. 6. House passed Oct. 6. President signed Oct. 25, 1994.

PL 103-422 (S J Res 227) Approve the location of a Thomas Paine Memorial. Introduced by FORD, D-Ky., Sept. 30, 1994. Senate passed Sept. 30. House passed, amended, Oct. 6. Senate agreed to House amendment Oct. 7. President signed Oct. 25, 1994.

PL 103-423 (S J Res 229) Regarding U.S. policy toward Haiti. Introduced by MITCHELL, D-Maine, Oct. 6, 1994. Senate passed Oct. 6. House passed Oct. 7. President signed Oct. 25, 1994.

PL 103-424 (HR 2970) Reauthorize the Office of Special Counsel, and for other purposes. Introduced by McCLOSKEY, D-Ind., Aug. 6, 1993. House Post Office and Civil Service reported, amended, Sept. 30, 1994 (H Rept 103-769). House passed, amended, under suspension of the rules, Oct. 3. Senate passed, amended, Oct. 7. House agreed to Senate amendment Oct. 7. President signed Oct. 29, 1994.

PL 103-425 (HR 3499) Amend the Defense Department Overseas Teachers Pay and Personnel Practices Act. Introduced by McCLOSKEY, D-Ind., Nov. 10, 1993. House Post Office and Civil Service reported, amended, July 13, 1994 (H Rept 103-598, Part 1). House passed, amended, under suspension of the rules, July 19. Senate Governmental Affairs reported Oct. 3 (S Rept 103-396). Senate passed, amended, Oct. 7. House agreed to Senate amendment Oct. 7. President signed Oct. 31, 1994.

PL 103-426 (HR 3678) Authorize the secretary of the Interior to negotiate agreements for the use of Outer Continental Shelf sand, gravel and shell resources. Introduced by ORTIZ, D-Texas, Nov. 22, 1993. House Natural Resources reported, amended, Oct. 3, 1994 (H Rept 103-817, Part 1). House passed, amended, under

suspension of the rules, Oct. 3. Senate passed Oct. 6. President signed Oct. 31, 1994.

PL 103-427 (HR 4196) Ensure that timber-dependent communities adversely affected by the Forest Plan for a Sustainable Economy and a Sustainable Environment qualify for loans and grants from the Rural Development Administration. Introduced by DICKS, D-Wash., April 13, 1994. House Agriculture discharged. House passed, amended, Sept. 29. Senate passed Oct. 6. President signed Oct. 31, 1994.

PL 103-428 (HR 4455) Authorize the Export-Import Bank of the United States to provide financing for export of non-lethal defense articles and defense services, of which the primary end use will be for civilian purposes. Introduced by BEREUTER, R-Neb., May 19, 1994. House Banking, Finance and Urban Affairs reported, amended, Aug. 8 (H Rept 103-681). House passed, amended, under suspension of the rules, Aug. 8. Senate passed, amended, Oct. 5. House agreed to Senate amendment Oct. 6. President signed Oct. 31, 1994.

PL 103-429 (HR 4778) Codify without substantive change recent laws related to transportation and to improve the U.S. Code. Introduced by BROOKS, D-Texas, July 18, 1994. House Judiciary reported, amended, Oct. 4 (H Rept 103-831). House passed, amended, under suspension of the rules, Oct. 4. Senate passed Oct. 7. President signed Oct. 31, 1994.

PL 103-430 (HR 5084) Amend Title 13, U.S. Code, to improve the accuracy of census address lists, and for other purposes. Introduced by SAWYER, D-Ohio, Sept. 23, 1994. House passed, amended, under suspension of the rules, Oct. 3. Senate passed Oct. 6. President signed Oct. 31, 1994.

PL 103-431 (HR 5176) Amend the Federal Water Pollution Control Act relating to San Diego ocean discharge and wastewater reclamation. Introduced by FILNER, D-Calif., Oct. 5, 1994. House passed Oct. 5. Senate passed Oct. 8. President signed Oct. 31, 1994.

PL 103-432 (HR 5252) Amend the Social Security Act and related acts to make miscellaneous and technical amendments, and for other purposes. Introduced by STARK, D-Calif., Oct. 7, 1994. House Ways and Means and House Energy and Commerce discharged. House passed Oct. 7, 1994. Senate passed Oct. 8. President signed Oct. 31, 1994.

PL 103-433 (S 21) Designate certain lands in the California desert as wilderness, to establish Death Valley, Joshua Tree and Mojave national parks, and for other purposes. Introduced by FEINSTEIN, D-Calif., Jan. 21, 1993. Senate Energy and Natural Resources reported, amended, Oct. 26 (S Rept 103-165). Senate considered April 12, 1994. Senate passed, amended, April 13. House passed, amended, July 27. Conference report filed in the House Oct. 4 (H Rept 103-832). House agreed to conference report Oct. 7. Senate agreed to conference report Oct. 8. President signed Oct. 31, 1994.

PL 103-434 (S 1146) Provide for the settlement of the water rights claims of the Yavapai-Prescott Indian Tribe in Yavapai County, Ariz., and for other purposes. Introduced by McCAIN, R-Ariz., June 23, 1993. Senate Indian Affairs reported, amended, March 22, 1994 (S Rept 103-239). Senate passed, amended, July 26. House Natural Resources reported, amended, Oct. 3 (H Rept 103-812). House passed, amended, under suspension of the rules, Oct. 3. Senate agreed to House amendment Oct. 4. President signed Oct. 31, 1994.

PL 103-435 (HR 4709) Make certain technical corrections, and for other purposes. Introduced by RICHARDSON, D-N.M., June 30, 1994. House Natural Resources reported, amended, Aug. 16 (H Rept 103-704). House passed, amended, under suspension of the rules, Aug. 16. Senate Indian Affairs reported, amended, Oct. 4. Senate passed, amended, Oct. 4. House agreed to Senate amend-

ment Oct. 6. President signed Nov. 2, 1994.

PL 103-436 (HR 4757) Provide for the settlement of the claims of the confederated tribes of the Colville Reservation concerning their contribution to the production of hydropower by the Grand Coulee Dam, and for other purposes. Introduced by MILLER, D-Calif., July 14, 1994. House Natural Resources reported Aug. 8 (H Rept 103-685). House passed, amended, under suspension of the rules, Oct. 3. Senate passed Oct. 7. President signed Nov. 2, 1994.

PL 103-437 (HR 4777) Make technical improvements in the U.S. Code by amending provisions to reflect the current names of congressional committees. Introduced by BROOKS, D-Texas, July 18, 1994. House Judiciary reported, amended, Oct. 3 (H Rept 103-779). House passed, amended, under suspension of the rules, Oct. 3. Senate passed Oct. 6. President signed Nov. 2, 1994.

PL 103-438 (HR 4781) Facilitate obtaining foreign-located antitrust evidence by authorizing the attorney general of the United States and the Federal Trade Commission to provide, in accordance with antitrust mutual assistance agreements, antitrust evidence to foreign antitrust authorities on a reciprocal basis, and for other purposes. Introduced by BROOKS, D-Texas, July 19, 1994. House Judiciary reported, amended, Oct. 3 (H Rept 103-772). House passed, amended, under suspension of the rules, Oct. 3. Senate passed Oct. 8. President signed Nov. 2, 1994.

PL 103-439 (HR 4814) Grant the consent of the Congress to amendments to the Central Midwest Interstate Low-Level Radioactive Waste Compact. Introduced by DURBIN, D-Ill., July 22, 1994. House Natural Resources reported, amended, Oct. 3 (H Rept 103-816, Part 1). House passed, amended, under suspension of the rules, Oct. 3. Senate passed Oct. 8. President signed Nov. 2, 1994.

PL 103-440 (HR 4867) Authorize appropriations for high-speed rail transportation, and for other purposes. Introduced by SCHENK, D-Calif., Aug. 1, 1994. House Energy and Commerce reported, amended, Aug. 10 (H Rept 103-692). House passed, amended, under suspension of the rules, Aug. 16. Senate passed, amended, Aug. 18. House agreed to Senate amendment with an amendment Oct. 6. Senate agreed to House amendment to Senate amendments Oct. 8. President signed Nov. 2, 1994.

PL 103-441 (HR 4967) Designate the U.S. courthouse located at 231 W. Lafayette St., Detroit, Mich., as the Theodore Levin United States Courthouse, and to designate the postal facility located at 1401 W. Fort St., Detroit, Mich., as the George W. Young Post Office. Introduced by COLLINS, D-Mich., Aug. 16, 1994. House Public Works and Transportation reported, amended, Sept. 29 (H Rept 103-762). House considered Oct. 3. House passed, amended, under suspension of the rules, Oct. 4. Senate passed Oct. 7. President signed Nov. 2, 1994.

PL 103-442 (HR 5102) Amend Title 18, U.S. Code, with respect to certain crimes relating to Congressional Medals of Honor. Introduced by McCANDLESS, R-Calif., Sept. 26, 1994. House Judiciary reported Oct. 3 (H Rept 103-786). House passed, amended, under suspension of the rules, Oct. 3. Senate passed Oct. 7. President signed Nov. 2, 1994.

PL 103-443 (HR 5161) Amend the Omnibus Budget Reconciliation Act of 1993 to permit the prompt sharing of timber sale receipts of the Forest Service and the Bureau of Land Management. Introduced by DICKS, D-Wash., Oct. 4, 1994. House passed Oct. 5. Senate passed Oct. 8. President signed Nov. 2, 1994.

PL 103-444 (HR 5200) Resolve the 107th Meridian boundary dispute between the Crow Indian Tribe and the United States. Introduced by WILLIAMS, D-Mont., Oct. 6, 1994. House passed Oct. 6. Senate passed Oct. 7. President signed Nov. 2, 1994.

PL 103-445 (HR 5220) Provide for the acceptance by the

secretary of Education of applications submitted by the local educational agency serving the Window Rock Unified School District, Window Rock, Ariz., under Section 3 of the act of Sept. 30, 1950 (PL 81-874) for fiscal 1994 and 1995. Introduced by ENGLISH, D-Ariz., Oct. 6, 1994. House Education and Labor discharged. House passed Oct. 7. Senate passed Oct. 8. President signed Nov. 2, 1994.

PL 103-446 (HR 5244) Amend Title 38, U.S. Code, to revise and improve veterans benefits programs, and for other purposes. Introduced by MONTGOMERY, D-Miss., Oct. 7, 1994. House Veterans' Affairs discharged. House passed, amended, Oct. 7. Senate passed Oct. 8. President signed Nov. 2, 1994.

PL 103-447 (HR 5246) Amend the Foreign Assistance Act of 1961 to make certain corrections relating to international narcotics control activities, and for other purposes. Introduced by GEJDENSON, D-Conn., Oct. 7, 1994. House passed Oct. 7. Senate passed Oct. 8. President signed Nov. 2, 1994.

PL 103-448 (S 1614) Amend the Child Nutrition Act of 1966 and the National Lunch Act to promote healthy eating habits for children and to extend certain authorities contained in such acts through fiscal 1998, and for other purposes. Introduced by LEAHY, D-Vt., Nov. 2, 1993. Senate Agriculture, Nutrition and Forestry reported, amended, July 1, 1994 (S Rept 103-300). Senate considered Aug. 12. Senate passed, amended, Aug. 25. House considered Oct. 4. House passed, amended, under suspension of the rules, Oct. 5. Senate agreed to House amendment Oct. 6. President signed Nov. 2, 1994.

PL 103-449 (HR 1348) Establish the Quinebaug and Shetucket Rivers Valley National Heritage Corridor in the state of Connecticut, and for other purposes. Introduced by GEJDENSON, D-Conn., March 16, 1993. House Natural Resources reported, amended, Sept. 9 (H Rept 103-233). House passed, under suspension of the rules, Sept. 13. Senate Energy and Natural Resources reported, amended, July 7, 1994 (S Rept 103-305). Senate passed, amended, Oct. 6. House agreed to Senate amendment Oct. 7. President signed Nov. 2, 1994.

PL 103-450 (HR 3050) Expand the boundaries of the Red Rock Canyon National Conservation Area. Introduced by BILBRAY, D-Nev., Sept. 13, 1993. House Natural Resources reported, amended, Aug. 8, 1994 (H Rept 103-679). House passed, amended, under suspension of the rules, Aug. 8. Senate Energy and Natural Resources reported Sept. 27. Senate passed Oct. 6. President signed Nov. 2, 1994.

PL 103-451 (HR 3059) Establish a National Maritime Heritage Program to make grants available for educational programs and the restoration of America's cultural resources for the purpose of preserving America's endangered maritime heritage. Introduced by ANDREWS, D-Maine, Sept. 14, 1993. House considered Oct. 4, 1994. House passed, amended, under suspension of the rules, Oct. 5. Senate passed Oct. 8. President signed Nov. 2, 1994.

PL 103-452 (HR 3313) Amend Title 38, U.S. Code, to improve health care services of the Department of Veterans Affairs relating to women veterans, to extend and expand authority for the secretary of Veterans Affairs to provide priority health care to veterans who were exposed to ionizing radiation or to Agent Orange, to expand the scope of services that may be provided to veterans through Vet Centers, and for other purposes. Introduced by ROWLAND, D-Ga., Oct. 19, 1993. House Veterans' Affairs reported, amended, Nov. 10 (H Rept 103-349). House passed amended, under suspension of the rules, Nov. 16. Senate passed, amended, June 8, 1994. House agreed to Senate amendments with amendments Oct. 7. Senate agreed to House amendments to Senate amendments Oct. 7. President signed Nov. 2, 1994.

PL 103-453 (HR 3984) Designate the building at 216 Coleman Ave., Waveland, Miss., for the period of time during which it houses operations of the U.S. Postal Service, as the John Longo Jr.

Post Office. Introduced by TAYLOR, D-Miss., March 9, 1994. House passed, amended, under suspension of the rules, May 23. Senate Governmental Affairs discharged. Senate passed Oct. 7. President signed Nov. 2, 1994.

PL 103-454 (HR 4180) Prohibit the withdrawal of acknowledgment or recognition of an Indian tribe or Alaska native group or of the leaders of an Indian tribe or Alaska native group, without an act of Congress. Introduced by THOMAS, R-Wyo., April 12, 1994. House Natural Resources reported, amended, Oct. 3. House passed, amended, under suspension of the rules, Oct. 3. Senate passed, amended, Oct. 7. Senate vitiated action of Oct. 7 and passed unamended Oct. 8. President signed Nov. 2, 1994.

PL 103-455 (HR 4193) Designate the building at 100 Vester Gade, Cruz Bay, Saint Thomas, Virgin Islands, for the period of time during which it houses operations of the U.S. Postal Service, as the Ubaldina Simmons Post Office. Introduced by de LUGO, D-Virgin Islands, April 13, 1994. House passed, amended, under suspension of the rules, Sept. 19. Senate Governmental Affairs discharged. Senate passed Oct. 7. President signed Nov. 2, 1994.

PL 103-456 (HR 4452) Designate the U.S. Post Office building located at 115 N. Chester in Ruleville, Miss., as the Fannie Lou Hamer Post Office. Introduced by THOMPSON, D-Miss., May 18, 1994. House passed, amended, under suspension of the rules, Sept. 19. Senate Governmental Affairs discharged. Senate passed Oct. 7. President signed Nov. 2, 1994.

PL 103-457 (HR 4497) Award a congressional gold medal to Rabbi Menachem Mendel Schneerson. Introduced by SCHUMER, D-N.Y., May 25, 1994. House Banking, Finance and Urban Affairs discharged. House passed Oct. 7. Senate passed Oct. 8. President signed Nov. 2, 1994.

PL 103-458 (HR 4551) Designate the U.S. Post Office building located at 301 W. Lexington Ave., Independence, Mo., as the William J. Randall Post Office. Introduced by WHEAT, D-Mo., June 8, 1994. House passed, amended, under suspension of the rules, Sept. 19. Senate Governmental Affairs discharged. Senate passed Oct. 7. President signed Nov. 2, 1994.

PL 103-459 (HR 4571) Designate the U.S. Post Office located at 103-104 Estate Richmond, Saint Croix, Virgin Islands, as the Wilbert Armstrong Post Office. Introduced by de LUGO, D-Virgin Islands, June 13, 1994. House passed, amended, under suspension of the rules, Sept. 19. Senate Governmental Affairs discharged. Senate passed Oct. 7. President signed Nov. 2, 1994.

PL 103-460 (HR 4595) Designate the building located at 4021 Laclede Ave., St. Louis, Mo., for the period of time during which it houses operations of the U.S. Postal Service, as the Marian Oldham Post Office. Introduced by CLAY, D-Mo., June 17, 1994. House passed, under suspension of the rules, June 27. Senate Governmental Affairs discharged. Senate passed Oct. 7. President signed Nov. 2, 1994.

PL 103-461 (HR 4598) Direct the secretary of the Interior to make technical corrections to maps relating to the Coastal Barrier Resources System, and to authorize appropriations to carry out the Coastal Barrier Resources Act. Introduced by FOWLER, R-Fla., June 17, 1994. House passed, amended, under suspension of the rules, July 12. Senate Commerce, Science and Transportation discharged. Senate Environment and Public Works reported, amended, Oct. 4 (S Rept 103-398). Senate passed, amended, Oct. 7. House agreed to Senate amendment Oct. 7. President signed Nov. 2, 1994.

PL 103-462 (H J Res 271) Designate November of each year as National American Indian Heritage Month. Introduced by FALEOMAVAEGA, D-American Samoa, Sept. 30, 1993. House Post Office and Civil Service discharged. House passed, amended, Nov. 2. Senate Judiciary discharged. Senate passed Oct. 6, 1994. President signed Nov. 2, 1994.

PL 103-463 (H J Res 326) Designate Jan. 16, 1995, as National Good Teen Day. Introduced by TRAFICANT, D-Ohio, Feb. 22, 1994. House Post Office and Civil Service discharged. House passed Sept. 30. Senate passed Oct. 7. President signed Nov. 2, 1994.

PL 103-464 (H J Res 390) Designate Sept. 17, 1994, as Constitution Day. Introduced by BORSKI, D-Pa., July 19, 1994. House Post Office and Civil Service discharged. House passed Aug. 5. Senate Judiciary discharged. Senate passed Oct. 7. President signed Nov. 9, 1994.

PL 103-465 (HR 5110) Approve and implement the trade agreements concluded in the Uruguay Round of multilateral trade negotiations. Introduced by GEPHARDT, D-Mo., Sept. 27, 1994. House Ways and Means reported Oct. 3 (H Rept 103-826, Part 1). House Energy and Commerce reported Oct. 3 (H Rept 103-826, Part 2). House passed Nov. 29. Senate considered Nov. 30. Senate passed Dec. 1. President signed Dec. 8, 1994.

C_Q

HOUSE
ROLL CALL
VOTES

KEY

Y Voted for (yea).
\# Paired for.
\+ Announced for.
N Voted against (nay).
X Paired against.
− Announced against.
P Voted "present."
C Voted "present" to avoid possible conflict of interest.
? Did not vote or otherwise make a position known.
D Delegates ineligible to vote.

Democrats   **Republicans**
Independent

* 2. Procedural Motion. Approval of the House Journal of Tuesday, Jan. 25. Approved 247-140: R 24-136; D 222-4 (ND 150-3, SD 72-1); I 1-0, Jan. 26, 1994.

3. Procedural Motion. Approval of the House Journal of Tuesday, Feb. 1. Approved 237-154: R 19-148; D 218-6 (ND 149-5, SD 69-1); I 0-0, Feb. 2, 1994.

4. HR 3425. Department of Environmental Protection/ Rule. Adoption of the rule (H Res 312) to provide for House floor consideration of the bill to elevate the Environmental Protection Agency to Cabinet-level status. Rejected 191-227: R 5-167; D 185-60 (ND 140-28, SD 45-32); I 1-0, Feb. 2, 1994.

5. Procedural Motion. Approval of the House Journal of Wednesday, Feb. 2. Approved 245-144: R 19-140; D 225-4 (ND 152-3, SD 73-1); I 1-0, Feb. 3, 1994.

6. HR 3759. Fiscal 1994 Disaster Supplemental Appropriations/Previous Question. Beilenson, D-Calif., motion to order the previous question (thus limiting debate and the possibility of amendment) on adoption of the rule (H Res 336) to provide for House floor consideration of the bill to provide $9,719,150,000 in appropriations for the emergency expenses of the Los Angeles-area earthquake; humanitarian assistance and peacekeeping activities; Midwest flood assistance; and highway reconstruction in San Francisco. Motion agreed to 244-168: R 5-166; D 238-2 (ND 160-2, SD 78-0); I 1-0, Feb. 3, 1994.

7. HR 3759. Fiscal 1994 Disaster Supplemental Appropriations/Rule. Adoption of the rule (H Res 336) to provide for House floor consideration of the bill to provide $9,719,150,000 in appropriations for the emergency expenses of the Los Angeles-area earthquake; humanitarian assistance and peacekeeping activities; Midwest flood assistance; and highway reconstruction in San Francisco. Adopted 342-65: R 107-64; D 234-1 (ND 160-0, SD 74-1); I 1-0, Feb. 3, 1994.

* Omitted votes are quorum calls, which CQ does not include in its vote charts.

[1] *Vernon J. Ehlers, R-Mich., was sworn in Jan. 25, 1994. The first vote for which he was eligible was vote 2.*

[2] *Glenn English, D-Okla., resigned effective Jan. 7, 1994.*

	2	3	4	5	6	7
ALABAMA						
1 Callahan	N	N	N	N	N	N
2 *Everett*	N	Y	N	?	N	Y
3 Browder	?	Y	N	Y	?	Y
4 Bevill	Y	Y	Y	Y	Y	Y
5 Cramer	Y	Y	N	Y	Y	Y
6 *Bachus*	N	N	N	N	Y	Y
7 Hilliard	Y	Y	Y	Y	Y	Y
ALASKA						
AL *Young*	?	P	N	?	N	N
ARIZONA						
1 Coppersmith	Y	Y	Y	Y	Y	Y
2 Pastor	Y	Y	Y	Y	Y	Y
3 *Stump*	N	N	N	N	N	N
4 *Kyl*	?	N	N	N	N	Y
5 *Kolbe*	N	N	N	N	N	Y
6 English	Y	Y	Y	Y	Y	Y
ARKANSAS						
1 Lambert	Y	Y	Y	Y	Y	Y
2 Thornton	Y	Y	Y	Y	Y	Y
3 *Hutchinson*	Y	N	N	N	N	Y
4 *Dickey*	N	N	N	N	N	Y
CALIFORNIA						
1 Hamburg	Y	Y	Y	Y	Y	Y
2 *Herger*	N	N	N	N	N	N
3 Fazio	Y	Y	Y	Y	Y	Y
4 *Doolittle*	N	N	N	N	N	N
5 Matsui	N	?	Y	Y	Y	Y
6 Woolsey	Y	Y	Y	Y	Y	Y
7 Miller	Y	?	Y	Y	Y	Y
8 Pelosi	?	Y	Y	Y	Y	Y
9 Dellums	?	?	Y	Y	Y	Y
10 *Baker*	N	N	N	N	N	N
11 *Pombo*	Y	Y	N	?	N	N
12 Lantos	Y	Y	Y	Y	Y	Y
13 Stark	Y	Y	Y	Y	Y	Y
14 Eshoo	Y	Y	Y	Y	Y	Y
15 Mineta	Y	?	Y	Y	Y	Y
16 Edwards	?	Y	Y	Y	Y	Y
17 Farr	Y	Y	Y	Y	Y	Y
18 Condit	Y	Y	N	Y	Y	Y
19 Lehman	?	?	X	?	?	?
20 Dooley	Y	Y	N	Y	Y	Y
21 *Thomas*	?	?	N	N	N	Y
22 *Huffington*	N	N	N	N	N	N
23 *Gallegly*	?	N	N	N	N	Y
24 Beilenson	Y	Y	Y	Y	Y	Y
25 *McKeon*	N	N	N	?	N	Y
26 Berman	Y	Y	Y	Y	Y	Y
27 *Moorhead*	N	N	N	N	N	Y
28 *Dreier*	N	N	N	N	N	Y
29 Waxman	?	Y	Y	Y	Y	Y
30 Becerra	Y	Y	Y	Y	Y	Y
31 Martinez	Y	Y	Y	Y	Y	Y
32 Dixon	Y	Y	Y	Y	Y	Y
33 Roybal-Allard	Y	Y	Y	Y	Y	Y
34 Torres	?	Y	Y	Y	Y	Y
35 Waters	Y	Y	Y	Y	Y	Y
36 Harman	Y	Y	N	Y	Y	Y
37 Tucker	Y	Y	Y	Y	Y	Y
38 *Horn*	N	N	N	N	N	N
39 *Royce*	N	N	N	N	N	N
40 *Lewis*	N	N	N	N	N	Y
41 *Kim*	N	N	N	N	N	Y
42 Brown	?	?	Y	Y	Y	Y
43 *Calvert*	N	N	N	N	N	Y
44 *McCandless*	?	N	N	N	N	Y
45 *Rohrabacher*	N	N	N	N	N	N
46 *Dornan*	?	?	X	?	N	N
47 *Cox*	N	N	N	N	N	N
48 *Packard*	N	Y	N	N	N	Y
49 Schenk	Y	Y	Y	Y	Y	Y
50 Filner	Y	Y	Y	Y	Y	Y
51 *Cunningham*	N	N	N	N	N	Y
52 *Hunter*	N	N	N	N	N	Y
COLORADO						
1 Schroeder	N	N	Y	N	Y	Y
2 Skaggs	Y	Y	Y	Y	Y	Y
3 *McInnis*	Y	Y	N	Y	N	Y
4 *Allard*	N	N	N	N	N	N
5 *Hefley*	N	N	N	N	N	N
6 *Schaefer*	N	N	N	N	N	?
CONNECTICUT						
1 Kennelly	?	Y	Y	Y	Y	Y
2 Gejdenson	Y	?	Y	Y	Y	Y
3 DeLauro	Y	Y	Y	Y	Y	Y
4 *Shays*	N	N	Y	N	Y	Y
5 *Franks*	N	N	N	N	N	N
6 *Johnson*	N	N	N	N	N	Y
DELAWARE						
AL *Castle*	N	N	N	N	N	N
FLORIDA						
1 Hutto	?	Y	N	Y	Y	?
2 Peterson	Y	Y	N	Y	Y	Y
3 Brown	Y	?	Y	Y	Y	Y
4 *Fowler*	N	N	N	N	N	Y
5 Thurman	Y	Y	N	Y	Y	Y
6 *Stearns*	N	N	N	N	N	N
7 *Mica*	N	N	Y	N	N	N
8 *McCollum*	?	N	N	Y	N	N
9 *Bilirakis*	N	N	N	N	Y	Y
10 *Young*	Y	N	N	Y	N	N
11 Gibbons	Y	?	Y	Y	Y	Y
12 *Canady*	N	N	N	N	N	Y
13 *Miller*	N	Y	N	N	N	Y
14 *Goss*	N	N	N	N	N	Y
15 Bacchus	Y	Y	Y	Y	Y	Y
16 *Lewis*	N	?	X	?	?	?
17 Meek	Y	Y	?	?	?	?
18 *Ros-Lehtinen*	?	N	N	N	N	N
19 Johnston	Y	Y	Y	Y	Y	Y
20 Deutsch	Y	Y	Y	Y	Y	Y
21 *Diaz-Balart*	N	N	N	N	N	N
22 *Shaw*	N	N	N	N	N	N
23 Hastings	?	?	?	?	?	?
GEORGIA						
1 *Kingston*	?	N	N	N	N	Y
2 Bishop	Y	Y	N	Y	Y	Y
3 *Collins*	N	N	N	N	N	N
4 *Linder*	N	N	N	N	N	N
5 Lewis	Y	Y	Y	Y	Y	Y
6 *Gingrich*	N	?	N	N	N	Y
7 Darden	Y	Y	N	Y	Y	Y
8 Rowland	Y	Y	N	Y	Y	Y
9 Deal	Y	Y	N	Y	Y	Y
10 Johnson	?	Y	N	Y	Y	Y
11 McKinney	Y	Y	Y	Y	Y	Y
HAWAII						
1 Abercrombie	Y	Y	Y	Y	Y	Y
2 Mink	Y	Y	Y	Y	Y	Y
IDAHO						
1 LaRocco	Y	Y	N	Y	Y	Y
2 *Crapo*	Y	N	N	N	N	N
ILLINOIS						
1 Rush	Y	Y	Y	Y	Y	Y
2 Reynolds	Y	?	?	?	?	?
3 Lipinski	Y	Y	Y	Y	Y	Y
4 Gutierrez	Y	Y	Y	Y	Y	Y
5 Rostenkowski	Y	Y	Y	Y	Y	Y
6 *Hyde*	N	Y	N	N	N	Y
7 Collins	?	Y	Y	?	?	?
8 *Crane*	N	N	N	?	?	?
9 Yates	Y	Y	Y	Y	Y	Y
10 *Porter*	N	N	Y	N	N	Y
11 Sangmeister	Y	Y	Y	Y	Y	Y
12 Costello	Y	Y	Y	Y	Y	Y
13 *Fawell*	N	N	N	N	N	N
14 *Hastert*	N	N	N	?	N	Y
15 *Ewing*	N	N	N	N	N	N
16 *Manzullo*	Y	N	N	N	N	Y
17 Evans	Y	Y	Y	Y	Y	Y

ND Northern Democrats   SD Southern Democrats

	2	3	4	5	6	7
18 ***Michel***	Y	N	N	N	N	Y
19 Poshard	Y	Y	N	Y	Y	Y
20 Durbin	Y	Y	Y	Y	Y	Y
INDIANA						
1 Visclosky	Y	Y	Y	Y	Y	Y
2 Sharp	Y	Y	N	Y	Y	?
3 Roemer	Y	Y	N	Y	Y	Y
4 Long	Y	Y	Y	Y	Y	Y
5 ***Buyer***	N	N	N	N	N	N
6 ***Burton***	N	N	N	N	N	Y
7 ***Myers***	N	Y	N	Y	Y	Y
8 McCloskey	Y	Y	Y	Y	Y	Y
9 Hamilton	Y	Y	N	Y	Y	Y
10 Jacobs	N	N	Y	N	N	Y
IOWA						
1 ***Leach***	N	N	N	N	N	Y
2 ***Nussle***	N	N	N	N	N	Y
3 ***Lightfoot***	?	N	N	N	N	Y
4 Smith	Y	Y	N	Y	Y	Y
5 ***Grandy***	N	N	N	N	N	Y
KANSAS						
1 ***Roberts***	N	N	N	N	N	N
2 Slattery	?	?	N	Y	Y	Y
3 ***Meyers***	N	N	N	N	N	Y
4 Glickman	Y	Y	N	Y	Y	Y
KENTUCKY						
1 Barlow	Y	Y	Y	Y	Y	Y
2 Natcher	Y	Y	Y	Y	Y	Y
3 Mazzoli	Y	Y	Y	Y	Y	Y
4 ***Bunning***	N	N	N	N	N	Y
5 ***Rogers***	N	N	N	N	N	Y
6 Baesler	Y	Y	N	Y	Y	Y
LOUISIANA						
1 ***Livingston***	Y	?	N	N	N	Y
2 Jefferson	Y	?	Y	Y	Y	Y
3 Tauzin	Y	Y	N	Y	Y	?
4 Fields	Y	Y	Y	Y	Y	Y
5 ***McCrery***	N	N	N	?	N	Y
6 ***Baker***	?	N	N	N	N	Y
7 Hayes	Y	Y	N	Y	Y	Y
MAINE						
1 Andrews	Y	Y	Y	Y	Y	Y
2 ***Snowe***	N	N	N	N	N	Y
MARYLAND						
1 ***Gilchrest***	N	N	N	N	N	N
2 ***Bentley***	N	N	N	?	?	?
3 Cardin	Y	Y	Y	Y	Y	Y
4 Wynn	Y	Y	Y	Y	Y	Y
5 Hoyer	Y	Y	Y	Y	Y	Y
6 ***Bartlett***	N	N	N	N	N	N
7 Mfume	Y	?	Y	Y	+	+
8 ***Morella***	N	N	Y	?	N	Y
MASSACHUSETTS						
1 Olver	Y	Y	Y	?	Y	Y
2 Neal	Y	Y	Y	Y	Y	Y
3 ***Blute***	N	N	N	N	N	Y
4 Frank	Y	Y	Y	Y	Y	Y
5 Meehan	Y	Y	Y	Y	Y	Y
6 ***Torkildsen***	N	N	N	N	N	N
7 Markey	Y	Y	Y	Y	Y	Y
8 Kennedy	Y	Y	Y	?	?	?
9 Moakley	Y	Y	Y	Y	Y	Y
10 Studds	Y	Y	Y	Y	Y	Y
MICHIGAN						
1 Stupak	Y	Y	N	Y	Y	Y
2 ***Hoekstra***	N	N	N	N	N	Y
3 ***Ehlers*** [1]	N	N	N	N	N	Y
4 ***Camp***	N	N	N	N	N	Y
5 Barcia	Y	Y	Y	Y	Y	Y
6 ***Upton***	N	N	N	N	N	N
7 ***Smith***	N	N	N	N	N	N
8 Carr	Y	Y	Y	Y	Y	Y
9 Kildee	Y	Y	Y	Y	Y	Y
10 Bonior	Y	Y	Y	Y	Y	Y
11 ***Knollenberg***	N	N	N	N	N	Y
12 Levin	Y	Y	Y	Y	Y	Y
13 Ford	Y	?	Y	?	?	Y
14 Conyers	Y	Y	Y	Y	Y	Y
15 Collins	Y	Y	Y	Y	Y	Y
16 Dingell	Y	Y	Y	Y	Y	Y
MINNESOTA						
1 Penny	Y	Y	N	Y	Y	Y
2 Minge	Y	Y	N	Y	Y	Y
3 ***Ramstad***	N	N	N	N	N	N
4 Vento	Y	Y	Y	Y	Y	Y
5 Sabo	Y	Y	Y	Y	Y	Y
6 ***Grams***	N	N	N	N	N	N
7 Peterson	Y	Y	N	Y	Y	Y
8 Oberstar	Y	Y	Y	Y	Y	Y
MISSISSIPPI						
1 Whitten	?	Y	N	?	Y	Y
2 Thompson	Y	Y	Y	Y	Y	Y
3 Montgomery	Y	Y	Y	Y	Y	Y
4 Parker	Y	Y	N	Y	Y	Y
5 Taylor	N	N	N	N	Y	Y
MISSOURI						
1 Clay	?	N	Y	N	Y	Y
2 ***Talent***	N	N	N	N	N	Y
3 Gephardt	Y	Y	Y	Y	Y	Y
4 Skelton	Y	Y	N	Y	Y	Y
5 Wheat	?	Y	Y	Y	Y	Y
6 Danner	?	Y	N	Y	Y	Y
7 ***Hancock***	N	N	N	N	N	N
8 ***Emerson***	Y	N	N	N	N	Y
9 Volkmer	Y	Y	Y	Y	Y	Y
MONTANA						
AL Williams	?	?	N	?	Y	Y
NEBRASKA						
1 ***Bereuter***	N	N	N	N	N	Y
2 Hoagland	Y	Y	Y	Y	Y	Y
3 ***Barrett***	N	N	N	N	N	Y
NEVADA						
1 Bilbray	Y	Y	N	Y	Y	Y
2 ***Vucanovich***	N	N	N	N	N	N
NEW HAMPSHIRE						
1 ***Zeliff***	N	N	N	N	N	Y
2 Swett	Y	Y	Y	Y	Y	Y
NEW JERSEY						
1 Andrews	Y	Y	Y	Y	Y	Y
2 Hughes	Y	Y	Y	Y	Y	Y
3 ***Saxton***	N	N	N	N	N	Y
4 ***Smith***	Y	?	N	Y	N	Y
5 ***Roukema***	N	N	N	?	N	Y
6 Pallone	Y	Y	Y	Y	Y	Y
7 ***Franks***	N	N	N	N	N	Y
8 Klein	Y	Y	Y	Y	Y	Y
9 Torricelli	Y	?	Y	?	Y	Y
10 Payne	?	Y	Y	Y	Y	Y
11 ***Gallo***	?	N	N	N	N	Y
12 ***Zimmer***	N	N	N	N	N	N
13 Menendez	Y	Y	Y	Y	Y	Y
NEW MEXICO						
1 ***Schiff***	N	N	N	N	N	Y
2 ***Skeen***	N	N	N	N	N	Y
3 Richardson	Y	Y	Y	Y	Y	Y
NEW YORK						
1 Hochbrueckner	Y	Y	Y	Y	Y	Y
2 ***Lazio***	N	N	N	N	N	Y
3 ***King***	N	N	N	N	N	Y
4 ***Levy***	N	N	N	N	N	Y
5 Ackerman	Y	Y	Y	?	Y	Y
6 Flake	?	Y	Y	Y	Y	Y
7 Manton	Y	Y	Y	Y	Y	Y
8 Nadler	Y	Y	Y	Y	Y	Y
9 Schumer	Y	Y	Y	Y	Y	Y
10 Towns	?	Y	Y	Y	Y	Y
11 Owens	Y	Y	Y	?	Y	?
12 Velazquez	Y	Y	Y	Y	Y	Y
13 ***Molinari***	N	N	N	N	N	Y
14 Maloney	Y	Y	Y	Y	Y	Y
15 Rangel	Y	?	Y	Y	Y	Y
16 Serrano	Y	Y	Y	Y	Y	Y
17 Engel	Y	Y	Y	Y	Y	Y
18 Lowey	Y	Y	Y	Y	Y	Y
19 ***Fish***	Y	Y	N	Y	N	Y
20 ***Gilman***	Y	Y	Y	Y	N	Y
21 McNulty	Y	Y	Y	Y	Y	Y
22 ***Solomon***	N	N	N	?	N	Y
23 ***Boehlert***	N	N	Y	N	N	Y
24 ***McHugh***	N	N	N	N	N	N
25 ***Walsh***	N	N	N	N	N	Y
26 Hinchey	Y	Y	Y	?	Y	Y
27 ***Paxon***	N	N	N	N	N	N
28 Slaughter	Y	Y	Y	Y	Y	Y
29 LaFalce	Y	Y	Y	Y	Y	Y
30 ***Quinn***	N	N	N	N	N	Y
31 ***Houghton***	Y	Y	N	Y	N	N
NORTH CAROLINA						
1 Clayton	Y	?	Y	Y	Y	Y
2 Valentine	Y	Y	Y	Y	Y	Y
3 Lancaster	Y	Y	N	Y	Y	Y
4 Price	Y	Y	Y	Y	Y	Y
5 Neal	Y	Y	Y	Y	Y	Y
6 ***Coble***	N	N	N	N	N	N
7 Rose	Y	Y	Y	Y	Y	?
8 Hefner	?	Y	Y	Y	Y	Y
9 ***McMillan***	Y	N	N	N	N	Y
10 ***Ballenger***	Y	Y	N	N	N	N
11 ***Taylor***	N	N	N	N	N	Y
12 Watt	Y	?	Y	Y	Y	Y
NORTH DAKOTA						
AL Pomeroy	Y	Y	N	?	Y	Y
OHIO						
1 Mann	Y	Y	Y	Y	Y	Y
2 ***Portman***	N	N	N	N	N	N
3 Hall	Y	?	Y	?	?	?
4 ***Oxley***	N	N	N	N	N	Y
5 ***Gillmor***	Y	Y	N	Y	N	Y
6 Strickland	Y	Y	N	Y	Y	Y
7 ***Hobson***	N	N	N	Y	N	N
8 ***Boehner***	N	N	N	N	N	N
9 Kaptur	Y	Y	Y	Y	Y	Y
10 ***Hoke***	N	N	N	N	N	Y
11 Stokes	Y	Y	Y	Y	Y	Y
12 ***Kasich***	Y	Y	N	Y	N	Y
13 Brown	Y	Y	Y	Y	Y	Y
14 Sawyer	Y	Y	Y	Y	Y	Y
15 ***Pryce***	?	N	N	N	N	N
16 ***Regula***	N	N	N	N	N	Y
17 Traficant	Y	Y	Y	Y	Y	Y
18 Applegate	Y	Y	N	Y	Y	Y
19 Fingerhut	Y	Y	N	Y	Y	Y
OKLAHOMA						
1 ***Inhofe***	N	N	N	N	N	N
2 Synar	Y	Y	Y	Y	Y	Y
3 Brewster	?	Y	N	Y	Y	Y
4 McCurdy	Y	Y	N	Y	Y	?
5 ***Istook***	N	N	N	N	N	N
6 Vacancy[2]						
OREGON						
1 Furse	Y	Y	Y	Y	Y	Y
2 ***Smith***	?	?	?	?	?	X
3 Wyden	Y	Y	Y	Y	Y	Y
4 DeFazio	Y	Y	Y	Y	Y	Y
5 Kopetski	Y	?	Y	Y	Y	?
PENNSYLVANIA						
1 Foglietta	Y	Y	Y	Y	Y	Y
2 Blackwell	Y	?	Y	Y	Y	Y
3 Borski	Y	Y	#	?	Y	Y
4 Klink	Y	Y	N	Y	Y	Y
5 ***Clinger***	N	N	N	Y	Y	Y
6 Holden	Y	Y	Y	Y	Y	Y
7 ***Weldon***	N	N	N	N	N	Y
8 ***Greenwood***	Y	Y	N	Y	N	N
9 ***Shuster***	N	N	N	N	N	N
10 ***McDade***	?	N	N	N	Y	Y
11 Kanjorski	Y	Y	Y	Y	Y	Y
12 Murtha	?	Y	Y	Y	Y	Y
13 Margolies-Mezv.	Y	Y	Y	Y	Y	Y
14 Coyne	?	Y	Y	Y	Y	Y
15 McHale	Y	Y	Y	Y	Y	Y
16 ***Walker***	N	N	N	N	N	Y
17 ***Gekas***	N	N	N	N	N	Y
18 ***Santorum***	Y	Y	N	Y	N	N
19 ***Goodling***	N	N	N	?	N	Y
20 Murphy	N	N	N	?	?	?
21 ***Ridge***	N	?	?	N	N	Y
RHODE ISLAND						
1 ***Machtley***	N	N	N	?	N	Y
2 Reed	Y	Y	Y	Y	Y	Y
SOUTH CAROLINA						
1 ***Ravenel***	Y	N	N	N	N	Y
2 ***Spence***	Y	N	N	N	?	Y
3 Derrick	Y	Y	Y	Y	Y	Y
4 ***Inglis***	Y	Y	N	Y	N	Y
5 Spratt	Y	Y	Y	Y	Y	Y
6 Clyburn	Y	Y	Y	Y	Y	Y
SOUTH DAKOTA						
AL Johnson	Y	Y	N	Y	Y	Y
TENNESSEE						
1 ***Quillen***	N	N	N	N	N	Y
2 ***Duncan***	N	N	N	N	N	N
3 Lloyd	Y	?	N	?	Y	Y
4 Cooper	Y	Y	Y	Y	Y	Y
5 Clement	Y	Y	Y	Y	Y	Y
6 Gordon	Y	Y	Y	Y	Y	Y
7 ***Sundquist***	N	N	N	N	N	Y
8 Tanner	Y	Y	N	Y	Y	Y
9 Ford	Y	?	?	Y	Y	Y
TEXAS						
1 Chapman	Y	?	?	?	?	?
2 Wilson	Y	?	?	?	Y	Y
3 ***Johnson, Sam***	N	N	N	N	N	N
4 Hall	Y	Y	N	?	Y	Y
5 Bryant	?	Y	Y	Y	Y	Y
6 ***Barton***	N	N	N	N	N	N
7 ***Archer***	N	N	N	N	N	N
8 ***Fields***	N	N	N	N	N	N
9 Brooks	Y	Y	Y	Y	Y	Y
10 Pickle	Y	?	Y	Y	Y	Y
11 Edwards	Y	Y	N	Y	Y	Y
12 Geren	Y	Y	N	Y	Y	Y
13 Sarpalius	Y	Y	N	Y	Y	Y
14 Laughlin	Y	Y	Y	Y	Y	Y
15 de la Garza	?	?	?	Y	Y	Y
16 Coleman	Y	Y	Y	Y	Y	N
17 Stenholm	Y	Y	N	Y	Y	Y
18 Washington	Y	Y	Y	Y	Y	Y
19 ***Combest***	Y	Y	N	Y	N	N
20 Gonzalez	Y	Y	Y	Y	Y	Y
21 ***Smith***	N	N	N	N	N	Y
22 ***DeLay***	N	N	N	N	N	N
23 ***Bonilla***	N	N	N	N	N	N
24 Frost	Y	Y	Y	Y	Y	Y
25 Andrews	?	?	#	?	?	#
26 ***Armey***	?	N	N	N	N	N
27 Ortiz	?	Y	N	Y	Y	Y
28 Tejeda	Y	Y	N	Y	Y	Y
29 Green	Y	Y	Y	Y	Y	Y
30 Johnson, E.B.	Y	Y	Y	Y	Y	Y
UTAH						
1 ***Hansen***	N	N	N	Y	N	N
2 Shepherd	Y	Y	#	+	+	+
3 Orton	Y	Y	N	Y	Y	Y
VERMONT						
AL *Sanders*	Y	?	Y	Y	Y	Y
VIRGINIA						
1 ***Bateman***	Y	Y	N	Y	N	Y
2 Pickett	Y	Y	N	Y	Y	Y
3 Scott	Y	Y	Y	?	Y	Y
4 Sisisky	Y	?	N	Y	Y	Y
5 Payne	Y	Y	N	?	?	?
6 ***Goodlatte***	N	N	N	N	N	Y
7 ***Bliley***	N	N	N	N	N	Y
8 Moran	Y	Y	N	Y	Y	Y
9 Boucher	Y	Y	Y	Y	Y	Y
10 ***Wolf***	N	N	N	N	N	Y
11 Byrne	Y	Y	Y	Y	Y	Y
WASHINGTON						
1 Cantwell	Y	Y	Y	Y	Y	Y
2 Swift	Y	Y	Y	Y	Y	?
3 Unsoeld	Y	Y	Y	Y	Y	Y
4 Inslee	Y	Y	Y	Y	Y	Y
5 Foley						
6 Dicks	Y	Y	Y	Y	Y	Y
7 McDermott	Y	Y	Y	Y	Y	Y
8 ***Dunn***	N	N	N	N	N	Y
9 Kreidler	Y	N	Y	Y	Y	Y
WEST VIRGINIA						
1 Mollohan	Y	Y	Y	Y	Y	Y
2 Wise	Y	?	Y	Y	Y	Y
3 Rahall	Y	Y	Y	Y	Y	Y
WISCONSIN						
1 Barca	Y	Y	N	Y	Y	Y
2 ***Klug***	N	N	N	N	N	Y
3 ***Gunderson***	N	N	N	?	N	Y
4 Kleczka	Y	Y	Y	Y	?	Y
5 Barrett	Y	Y	Y	Y	Y	Y
6 ***Petri***	N	N	N	N	N	Y
7 Obey	Y	Y	Y	Y	Y	Y
8 ***Roth***	N	N	N	N	N	N
9 ***Sensenbrenner***	N	N	N	N	N	N
WYOMING						
AL ***Thomas***	N	N	N	N	N	N
DELEGATES						
de Lugo, V.I.	D	D	D	D	D	D
Faleomavaega, Am.S.	D	D	D	D	D	D
Norton, D.C.	D	D	D	D	D	D
Romero-B., P.R.	D	D	D	D	D	D
Underwood, Guam	D	D	D	D	D	D

Southern states - Ala., Ark., Fla., Ga., Ky., La., Miss., N.C., Okla., S.C., Tenn., Texas, Va.
Omitted votes are quorum calls, which CQ does not include in its vote charts.

8. HR 3759. Fiscal 1994 Disaster Supplemental Appropriations/Defense Department Peacekeeping. Frank, D-Mass., amendment to delete the $1.2 billion provided by the bill for peacekeeping and humanitarian assistance in Bosnia, Somalia, the Iraqi "no-fly zone" and Haiti. Rejected in the Committee of the Whole 158-260: R 66-106; D 91-154 (ND 72-94, SD 19-60); I 1-0, Feb. 3, 1994. A "nay" was a vote in support of the president's position.

9. HR 3759. Fiscal 1994 Distaster Supplemental Appropriations/$7.5 Billion Offset. Myers, R-Ind., amendment to offset $7.5 billion of the $9.7 billion in the bill by rescinding funding for executive full-time equivalent positions; the Strategic Petroleum Reserve; the Tennessee Valley Authority; the Legal Services Corporation; the Bureau of Alcohol, Tobacco and Firearms; Community Development Block Grants; the World Bank; certain defense programs; the legislative branch; and other programs. Rejected in the Committee of the Whole 207-211: R 161-10; D 46-200 (ND 25-142, SD 21-58); I 0-1, Feb. 3, 1994. A "nay" was a vote in support of the president's position.

10. HR 3759. Fiscal 1994 Disaster Supplemental Appropriations/Full Offset. Nussle, R-Iowa, amendment to fully offset the $9.7 billion in the emergency funding in the bill by cutting spending for more than 70 federal programs, including a $1.8 billion reduction in agency overhead, a $1.6 billion savings by cutting 252,000 positions from the federal work force and a $400 million reduction in Community Development Block Grants. Rejected in the Committee of the Whole 178-240: R 144-26; D 34-213 (ND 18-151, SD 16-62); I 0-1, Feb. 3, 1994. A "nay" was a vote in support of the president's position.

11. HR 3759. Fiscal 1994 Disaster Supplemental Appropriations/Government Reform Offsets. Fazio, D-Calif., amendment to offset $2.56 billion of the disaster assistance in the bill by implementing most of the rescissions contained in the Government Reform and Savings bill (HR 3400). Adopted in the Committee of the Whole 415-2: R 170-1; D 244-1 (ND 168-0, SD 76-1); I 1-0, Feb. 3, 1994.

12. HR 3759. Fiscal 1994 Disaster Supplemental Appropriations/Recommit. Myers, R-Ind., motion to recommit the bill to the House Appropriations Committee with instructions to report it back after offsetting $7.5 billion of the $9.7 billion in disaster assistance with rescissions. Motion rejected 184-228: R 162-8; D 22-219 (ND 13-150, SD 9-69); I 0-1, Feb. 3, 1994.

13. HR 3759. Fiscal 1994 Disaster Supplemental Appropriations/Passage. Passage of the bill to provide $9,719,150,000 in new appropriations for the emergency expenses of the Los Angeles-area earthquake, humanitarian assistance and peacekeeping activities, Midwest flood assistance and highway reconstruction in San Francisco. Passed 337-74: R 111-59; D 225-15 (ND 152-10, SD 73-5); I 1-0, Feb. 3, 1994. A "yea" was a vote in support of the president's position.

KEY

Y   Voted for (yea).
Paired for.
+   Announced for.
N   Voted against (nay).
X   Paired against.
—   Announced against.
P   Voted "present."
C   Voted "present" to avoid possible conflict of interest.
?   Did not vote or otherwise make a position known.
D   Delegates ineligible to vote.

Democrats *Republicans*
Independent

	8	9	10	11	12	13
ALABAMA						
1 *Callahan*	N	Y	Y	Y	Y	N
2 *Everett*	N	Y	Y	Y	Y	N
3 Browder	N	Y	N	Y	N	Y
4 Bevill	N	N	N	Y	N	Y
5 Cramer	N	N	N	Y	N	Y
6 *Bachus*	N	Y	Y	Y	Y	Y
7 Hilliard	?	N	N	Y	N	Y
ALASKA						
AL *Young*	N	Y	N	Y	Y	Y
ARIZONA						
1 Coppersmith	Y	Y	Y	Y	N	Y
2 Pastor	N	N	N	Y	N	N
3 *Stump*	N	Y	Y	Y	Y	N
4 *Kyl*	N	Y	Y	Y	Y	Y
5 *Kolbe*	N	Y	Y	Y	Y	Y
6 English	Y	Y	Y	Y	N	Y
ARKANSAS						
1 Lambert	N	N	Y	Y	N	Y
2 Thornton	N	N	N	Y	N	Y
3 *Hutchinson*	N	Y	Y	Y	Y	Y
4 *Dickey*	N	N	Y	Y	Y	Y
CALIFORNIA						
1 Hamburg	Y	N	N	Y	N	Y
2 *Herger*	Y	Y	Y	Y	Y	Y
3 Fazio	N	N	N	Y	N	Y
4 *Doolittle*	N	Y	Y	Y	Y	Y
5 Matsui	N	N	N	Y	N	Y
6 Woolsey	Y	N	N	Y	N	Y
7 Miller	?	N	N	Y	N	Y
8 Pelosi	N	N	N	Y	N	Y
9 Dellums	Y	N	N	Y	N	Y
10 *Baker*	N	Y	Y	Y	Y	Y
11 *Pombo*	Y	Y	Y	Y	Y	Y
12 Lantos	N	N	N	Y	N	Y
13 Stark	?	N	N	Y	N	Y
14 Eshoo	N	N	N	Y	N	Y
15 Mineta	N	N	N	Y	N	Y
16 Edwards	Y	N	N	Y	N	Y
17 Farr	N	N	N	Y	N	Y
18 Condit	N	Y	Y	Y	Y	Y
19 Lehman	?	?	?	?	?	?
20 Dooley	N	N	N	Y	N	Y
21 *Thomas*	N	Y	Y	Y	Y	Y
22 *Huffington*	Y	Y	Y	Y	Y	Y
23 *Gallegly*	N	Y	Y	Y	Y	Y
24 Beilenson	N	N	N	Y	N	Y
25 *McKeon*	N	N	N	Y	N	Y
26 Berman	N	N	N	Y	N	Y
27 *Moorhead*	N	Y	Y	Y	?	Y
28 *Dreier*	Y	Y	Y	Y	Y	Y
29 Waxman	Y	N	N	Y	N	Y
30 Becerra	Y	N	N	Y	N	Y
31 Martinez	N	N	N	Y	N	Y
32 Dixon	N	N	N	Y	N	Y
33 Roybal-Allard	N	N	N	Y	N	Y
34 Torres	N	N	N	?	N	Y
35 Waters	N	N	N	Y	N	Y
36 Harman	N	N	N	Y	N	Y
37 Tucker	N	N	N	Y	N	Y
38 *Horn*	N	Y	N	Y	Y	Y
39 *Royce*	Y	Y	Y	Y	Y	Y
40 *Lewis*	N	N	N	Y	N	Y
41 *Kim*	Y	N	Y	Y	N	Y

	8	9	10	11	12	13
42 Brown	N	N	N	Y	N	?
43 *Calvert*	N	N	N	Y	N	Y
44 *McCandless*	N	N	N	Y	N	Y
45 *Rohrabacher*	Y	Y	Y	Y	Y	Y
46 *Dornan*	Y	Y	Y	Y	Y	Y
47 *Cox*	Y	Y	Y	Y	Y	Y
48 *Packard*	N	Y	Y	Y	Y	Y
49 Schenk	N	N	N	Y	N	Y
50 Filner	Y	N	N	Y	N	Y
51 *Cunningham*	N	Y	Y	Y	Y	Y
52 *Hunter*	N	Y	Y	Y	Y	Y
COLORADO						
1 Schroeder	Y	Y	N	Y	N	Y
2 Skaggs	N	N	N	Y	N	Y
3 *McInnis*	N	Y	Y	Y	Y	N
4 *Allard*	Y	Y	Y	Y	Y	N
5 *Hefley*	N	Y	Y	Y	Y	N
6 *Schaefer*	N	Y	N	Y	Y	N
CONNECTICUT						
1 Kennelly	N	N	N	Y	N	Y
2 Gejdenson	N	N	N	Y	N	Y
3 DeLauro	N	N	N	Y	N	Y
4 *Shays*	Y	Y	Y	Y	Y	N
5 *Franks*	N	Y	Y	Y	Y	N
6 *Johnson*	Y	Y	Y	Y	Y	N
DELAWARE						
AL *Castle*	Y	Y	Y	Y	Y	Y
FLORIDA						
1 Hutto	N	N	N	Y	Y	Y
2 Peterson	N	N	N	Y	N	Y
3 Brown	N	N	N	Y	N	Y
4 *Fowler*	N	Y	Y	Y	Y	Y
5 Thurman	N	N	N	Y	N	Y
6 *Stearns*	N	Y	Y	Y	Y	N
7 *Mica*	Y	Y	Y	Y	Y	N
8 *McCollum*	N	Y	Y	Y	Y	Y
9 *Bilirakis*	Y	Y	Y	Y	Y	Y
10 *Young*	N	Y	N	Y	Y	Y
11 Gibbons	N	N	N	Y	N	Y
12 *Canady*	N	Y	Y	Y	Y	Y
13 *Miller*	N	Y	Y	Y	Y	Y
14 *Goss*	Y	Y	Y	Y	Y	Y
15 Bacchus	N	Y	N	Y	N	Y
16 *Lewis*	?	?	?	?	?	?
17 Meek	N	N	N	Y	N	Y
18 *Ros-Lehtinen*	N	Y	N	Y	N	Y
19 Johnston	Y	N	N	?	?	#
20 Deutsch	Y	N	N	Y	N	Y
21 *Diaz-Balart*	N	Y	N	Y	N	Y
22 *Shaw*	N	Y	Y	Y	Y	Y
23 Hastings	?	?	?	?	?	?
GEORGIA						
1 *Kingston*	Y	Y	Y	Y	Y	N
2 Bishop	N	Y	N	Y	N	Y
3 *Collins*	Y	Y	Y	Y	Y	N
4 *Linder*	N	Y	Y	Y	Y	Y
5 Lewis	N	N	N	Y	N	Y
6 *Gingrich*	N	Y	Y	Y	Y	Y
7 Darden	N	N	N	Y	N	Y
8 Rowland	N	Y	N	Y	N	Y
9 Deal	Y	N	Y	N	N	Y
10 Johnson	N	Y	N	Y	Y	Y
11 McKinney	Y	N	N	Y	N	Y
HAWAII						
1 Abercrombie	Y	N	N	Y	N	Y
2 Mink	Y	N	N	Y	N	Y
IDAHO						
1 LaRocco	Y	Y	N	Y	N	Y
2 *Crapo*	Y	Y	Y	Y	Y	N
ILLINOIS						
1 Rush	Y	N	N	Y	N	Y
2 Reynolds	?	?	?	?	?	?
3 Lipinski	N	N	N	Y	N	Y
4 Gutierrez	N	N	N	N	N	N
5 Rostenkowski	N	N	N	Y	N	Y
6 *Hyde*	N	Y	Y	Y	Y	Y
7 Collins	#	X	X	?	?	?
8 *Crane*	?	?	?	?	?	X
9 Yates	Y	N	N	Y	N	Y
10 *Porter*	Y	Y	Y	Y	Y	Y
11 Sangmeister	N	N	N	Y	N	Y
12 Costello	N	N	N	Y	N	Y
13 *Fawell*	Y	Y	Y	Y	Y	Y
14 *Hastert*	N	Y	Y	Y	Y	N
15 *Ewing*	Y	Y	Y	Y	Y	Y
16 *Manzullo*	Y	Y	Y	Y	Y	Y
17 Evans	Y	N	N	Y	N	Y

ND Northern Democrats   SD Southern Democrats

	8	9	10	11	12	13
18 *Michel*	N	Y	?	?	?	?
19 Poshard	Y	Y	Y	Y	Y	Y
20 Durbin	N	N	N	Y	N	Y
INDIANA						
1 Visclosky	N	N	N	Y	N	Y
2 Sharp	N	N	N	Y	N	Y
3 Roemer	N	N	N	Y	N	Y
4 Long	N	Y	Y	Y	N	Y
5 *Buyer*	N	Y	Y	Y	Y	Y
6 *Burton*	Y	Y	Y	Y	Y	Y
7 *Myers*	Y	Y	Y	Y	Y	N
8 McCloskey	N	N	N	Y	N	Y
9 Hamilton	N	Y	N	Y	Y	Y
10 Jacobs	Y	Y	N	Y	Y	Y
IOWA						
1 *Leach*	Y	Y	Y	Y	Y	Y
2 *Nussle*	Y	Y	Y	Y	Y	Y
3 *Lightfoot*	N	Y	Y	Y	Y	Y
4 Smith	N	N	N	Y	N	Y
5 *Grandy*	Y	Y	Y	Y	Y	Y
KANSAS						
1 *Roberts*	N	Y	Y	Y	Y	Y
2 Slattery	N	Y	N	Y	Y	Y
3 *Meyers*	N	Y	Y	Y	Y	Y
4 Glickman	N	N	N	Y	N	Y
KENTUCKY						
1 Barlow	N	Y	Y	Y	N	Y
2 Natcher	N	N	N	Y	N	Y
3 Mazzoli	N	N	Y	Y	N	Y
4 *Bunning*	Y	Y	Y	Y	Y	N
5 *Rogers*	N	Y	N	Y	Y	Y
6 Baesler	N	N	Y	Y	N	Y
LOUISIANA						
1 *Livingston*	N	Y	Y	Y	Y	Y
2 Jefferson	N	N	N	Y	N	Y
3 Tauzin	N	N	Y	Y	N	Y
4 Fields	N	N	N	Y	N	Y
5 *McCrery*	N	Y	Y	Y	Y	Y
6 *Baker*	N	Y	Y	Y	Y	Y
7 Hayes	N	Y	Y	Y	N	Y
MAINE						
1 Andrews	Y	N	N	Y	N	Y
2 *Snowe*	Y	N	N	Y	N	Y
MARYLAND						
1 *Gilchrest*	N	Y	Y	Y	Y	Y
2 *Bentley*	?	?	?	?	?	?
3 Cardin	Y	N	N	Y	N	Y
4 Wynn	N	N	N	Y	N	Y
5 Hoyer	N	N	N	Y	N	Y
6 *Bartlett*	N	Y	Y	Y	Y	N
7 Mfume	—	—	N	Y	N	Y
8 *Morella*	Y	Y	N	Y	Y	Y
MASSACHUSETTS						
1 Olver	Y	N	N	Y	N	Y
2 Neal	Y	N	X	Y	N	Y
3 *Blute*	N	Y	Y	Y	Y	Y
4 Frank	Y	N	N	Y	N	N
5 Meehan	Y	Y	Y	Y	N	Y
6 *Torkildsen*	N	Y	Y	Y	Y	Y
7 Markey	?	?	?	?	?	?
8 Kennedy	Y	N	N	Y	N	Y
9 Moakley	N	N	N	Y	N	Y
10 Studds	Y	N	N	Y	N	Y
MICHIGAN						
1 Stupak	Y	N	N	Y	N	Y
2 *Hoekstra*	Y	Y	Y	Y	Y	Y
3 *Ehlers*	Y	Y	Y	Y	Y	N
4 *Camp*	N	Y	Y	Y	Y	Y
5 Barcia	Y	Y	N	Y	N	Y
6 *Upton*	N	Y	Y	Y	Y	Y
7 *Smith*	Y	Y	Y	Y	Y	N
8 Carr	N	N	N	Y	N	Y
9 Kildee	N	N	N	Y	N	Y
10 Bonior	N	N	N	Y	N	Y
11 *Knollenberg*	N	Y	Y	Y	Y	Y
12 Levin	N	N	N	Y	N	Y
13 Ford	N	?	N	Y	N	Y
14 Conyers	Y	N	N	Y	N	Y
15 Collins	Y	N	N	Y	N	Y
16 Dingell	N	N	N	Y	N	Y
MINNESOTA						
1 Penny	Y	Y	Y	Y	Y	Y
2 Minge	Y	Y	Y	Y	N	Y
3 *Ramstad*	Y	Y	Y	Y	Y	N
4 Vento	Y	N	N	?	N	Y

	8	9	10	11	12	13
5 Sabo	N	N	N	Y	N	Y
6 *Grams*	Y	Y	Y	Y	Y	N
7 Peterson	Y	Y	Y	Y	Y	N
8 Oberstar	N	N	N	Y	N	Y
MISSISSIPPI						
1 Whitten	?	N	N	Y	N	Y
2 Thompson	N	N	N	Y	N	Y
3 Montgomery	N	Y	N	Y	N	Y
4 Parker	N	N	N	Y	N	Y
5 Taylor	N	N	N	Y	N	Y
MISSOURI						
1 Clay	Y	N	N	Y	N	Y
2 *Talent*	N	Y	Y	Y	Y	Y
3 Gephardt	N	N	N	Y	N	Y
4 Skelton	N	N	N	Y	N	Y
5 Wheat	Y	N	N	Y	N	Y
6 Danner	Y	N	N	Y	N	Y
7 *Hancock*	Y	Y	Y	Y	Y	N
8 *Emerson*	N	Y	N	Y	Y	Y
9 Volkmer	N	N	N	Y	N	Y
MONTANA						
AL Williams	Y	N	N	Y	N	Y
NEBRASKA						
1 *Bereuter*	Y	Y	N	Y	Y	Y
2 Hoagland	N	Y	N	Y	Y	Y
3 *Barrett*	Y	Y	Y	Y	Y	Y
NEVADA						
1 Bilbray	Y	N	N	Y	N	Y
2 *Vucanovich*	N	Y	Y	Y	Y	Y
NEW HAMPSHIRE						
1 *Zeliff*	N	Y	Y	Y	Y	N
2 Swett	Y	Y	Y	Y	Y	Y
NEW JERSEY						
1 Andrews	N	N	Y	Y	N	N
2 Hughes	N	Y	N	Y	Y	Y
3 *Saxton*	N	Y	Y	Y	Y	Y
4 *Smith*	N	Y	Y	Y	Y	Y
5 *Roukema*	Y	Y	Y	Y	Y	Y
6 Pallone	Y	N	N	Y	N	Y
7 *Franks*	Y	Y	Y	Y	Y	Y
8 Klein	Y	N	N	Y	N	Y
9 Torricelli	N	N	N	Y	N	Y
10 Payne	Y	N	N	Y	N	Y
11 *Gallo*	N	Y	Y	Y	Y	Y
12 *Zimmer*	Y	Y	Y	Y	Y	N
13 Menendez	Y	N	N	Y	N	Y
NEW MEXICO						
1 *Schiff*	Y	Y	Y	Y	Y	Y
2 *Skeen*	N	Y	N	Y	N	Y
3 Richardson	N	N	N	Y	N	Y
NEW YORK						
1 Hochbrueckner	N	N	N	Y	N	Y
2 *Lazio*	Y	N	N	Y	Y	Y
3 *King*	N	Y	#	Y	Y	Y
4 *Levy*	N	Y	Y	Y	Y	Y
5 Ackerman	N	N	N	Y	N	Y
6 Flake	Y	N	N	Y	N	Y
7 Manton	N	N	N	Y	X	?
8 Nadler	Y	N	N	Y	N	Y
9 Schumer	Y	N	N	Y	N	Y
10 Towns	Y	N	N	Y	N	Y
11 Owens	Y	?	?	?	?	?
12 Velazquez	Y	N	N	Y	N	N
13 *Molinari*	N	Y	Y	Y	Y	Y
14 Maloney	Y	N	N	Y	N	Y
15 Rangel	Y	N	N	Y	N	Y
16 Serrano	Y	N	N	Y	N	N
17 Engel	N	N	N	Y	N	Y
18 Lowey	N	N	N	Y	N	Y
19 *Fish*	N	Y	Y	Y	Y	Y
20 *Gilman*	N	N	N	Y	Y	+
21 McNulty	N	N	N	Y	N	Y
22 *Solomon*	N	Y	Y	Y	Y	N
23 *Boehlert*	N	Y	N	Y	Y	Y
24 *McHugh*	N	Y	Y	Y	Y	Y
25 *Walsh*	N	N	N	Y	N	Y
26 Hinchey	N	N	N	Y	N	Y
27 *Paxon*	N	Y	Y	Y	Y	N
28 Slaughter	N	N	N	Y	N	Y
29 LaFalce	N	N	N	Y	N	Y
30 *Quinn*	Y	Y	Y	Y	Y	Y
31 *Houghton*	N	Y	Y	Y	Y	Y
NORTH CAROLINA						
1 Clayton	Y	N	N	Y	N	Y
2 Valentine	Y	Y	Y	Y	Y	Y

	8	9	10	11	12	13
3 Lancaster	N	N	N	Y	N	Y
4 Price	N	N	N	Y	N	Y
5 Neal	Y	Y	N	Y	N	Y
6 *Coble*	Y	Y	Y	Y	Y	N
7 Rose	N	N	N	Y	N	Y
8 Hefner	N	N	N	Y	N	Y
9 *McMillan*	N	Y	Y	Y	Y	Y
10 *Ballenger*	Y	Y	Y	Y	Y	Y
11 *Taylor*	Y	Y	N	Y	Y	N
12 Watt	Y	N	N	Y	N	Y
NORTH DAKOTA						
AL Pomeroy	?	N	?	?	?	?
OHIO						
1 Mann	Y	Y	Y	Y	N	Y
2 *Portman*	Y	Y	Y	Y	Y	N
3 Hall	N	N	N	Y	N	Y
4 *Oxley*	N	Y	Y	Y	Y	Y
5 *Gillmor*	N	Y	N	Y	Y	Y
6 Strickland	Y	N	N	Y	N	Y
7 *Hobson*	N	Y	Y	Y	Y	Y
8 *Boehner*	N	Y	Y	Y	Y	N
9 Kaptur	N	N	N	Y	N	Y
10 *Hoke*	Y	Y	Y	Y	Y	N
11 Stokes	N	N	N	Y	N	Y
12 *Kasich*	N	Y	Y	Y	Y	Y
13 Brown	Y	Y	Y	Y	N	Y
14 Sawyer	N	N	N	Y	N	Y
15 *Pryce*	N	Y	Y	Y	Y	Y
16 *Regula*	Y	Y	Y	Y	Y	Y
17 Traficant	N	N	N	Y	N	Y
18 Applegate	N	N	N	Y	N	Y
19 Fingerhut	Y	N	Y	Y	N	N
OKLAHOMA						
1 *Inhofe*	N	Y	Y	Y	Y	N
2 Synar	Y	N	N	Y	N	Y
3 Brewster	Y	N	N	N	N	N
4 McCurdy	N	Y	Y	Y	N	Y
5 *Istook*	N	Y	Y	Y	Y	N
6 Vacancy						
OREGON						
1 Furse	Y	Y	N	Y	N	Y
2 *Smith*	X	#	#	?	#	X
3 Wyden	Y	N	N	Y	N	Y
4 DeFazio	Y	N	N	Y	N	N
5 Kopetski	N	N	N	Y	N	Y
PENNSYLVANIA						
1 Foglietta	N	N	N	Y	N	Y
2 Blackwell	N	N	N	Y	N	Y
3 Borski	N	N	N	Y	N	Y
4 Klink	N	N	N	Y	N	Y
5 *Clinger*	N	Y	Y	Y	Y	N
6 Holden	N	N	N	Y	N	Y
7 *Weldon*	N	?	Y	Y	Y	N
8 *Greenwood*	N	Y	Y	Y	Y	Y
9 *Shuster*	N	Y	Y	Y	Y	N
10 *McDade*	N	Y	Y	Y	Y	Y
11 Kanjorski	N	N	N	Y	N	Y
12 Murtha	N	N	N	Y	N	Y
13 Margolies-Mezv.	Y	Y	Y	Y	Y	Y
14 Coyne	Y	N	N	Y	N	Y
15 McHale	N	N	N	Y	N	Y
16 *Walker*	N	Y	Y	Y	Y	N
17 *Gekas*	N	Y	N	Y	Y	Y
18 *Santorum*	Y	Y	Y	Y	Y	N
19 *Goodling*	N	Y	Y	Y	N	N
20 Murphy	?	?	?	?	?	?
21 *Ridge*	Y	Y	Y	Y	Y	Y
RHODE ISLAND						
1 *Machtley*	N	Y	N	Y	Y	Y
2 Reed	N	N	N	Y	N	Y
SOUTH CAROLINA						
1 *Ravenel*	N	Y	Y	Y	Y	Y
2 *Spence*	N	Y	Y	Y	Y	Y
3 Derrick	N	N	N	Y	N	Y
4 *Inglis*	Y	Y	Y	Y	Y	Y
5 Spratt	N	N	N	Y	N	Y
6 Clyburn	N	N	N	Y	N	Y
SOUTH DAKOTA						
AL Johnson	Y	N	N	Y	N	Y
TENNESSEE						
1 *Quillen*	N	Y	N	Y	Y	N
2 *Duncan*	Y	Y	Y	Y	Y	N
3 Lloyd	N	Y	N	Y	N	Y
4 Cooper	N	Y	Y	Y	N	Y
5 Clement	N	N	N	Y	N	Y

	8	9	10	11	12	13
6 Gordon	Y	N	Y	Y	N	Y
7 *Sundquist*	N	Y	Y	Y	Y	N
8 Tanner	N	Y	Y	Y	Y	Y
9 Ford	Y	N	N	Y	N	Y
TEXAS						
1 Chapman	?	?	?	?	?	?
2 Wilson	N	Y	N	Y	N	Y
3 *Johnson, Sam*	N	Y	Y	Y	Y	N
4 Hall	N	Y	N	Y	Y	Y
5 Bryant	Y	N	N	Y	N	Y
6 *Barton*	Y	Y	Y	Y	Y	N
7 *Archer*	Y	Y	Y	Y	Y	N
8 *Fields*	N	Y	Y	Y	Y	N
9 Brooks	N	N	?	?	N	Y
10 Pickle	N	Y	N	Y	Y	Y
11 Edwards	N	N	Y	Y	N	Y
12 Geren	N	Y	N	Y	Y	Y
13 Sarpalius	N	N	Y	Y	N	Y
14 Laughlin	N	N	N	Y	N	Y
15 de la Garza	N	N	N	Y	N	Y
16 Coleman	N	N	N	Y	N	Y
17 Stenholm	Y	Y	Y	Y	Y	N
18 Washington	Y	?	?	?	?	#
19 *Combest*	Y	Y	Y	Y	Y	N
20 Gonzalez	Y	N	N	Y	N	Y
21 *Smith*	N	Y	Y	Y	Y	Y
22 *DeLay*	Y	Y	Y	Y	Y	N
23 *Bonilla*	Y	Y	Y	Y	Y	N
24 Frost	N	N	N	Y	N	Y
25 Andrews	?	?	?	?	?	?
26 *Armey*	N	Y	Y	Y	Y	Y
27 Ortiz	N	N	N	Y	N	Y
28 Tejeda	N	N	N	Y	N	Y
29 Green	Y	?	?	?	?	?
30 Johnson, E.B.	N	N	N	Y	N	Y
UTAH						
1 *Hansen*	N	Y	Y	Y	Y	N
2 Shepherd	+	+	-	+	+	+
3 Orton	N	Y	Y	Y	Y	N
VERMONT						
AL *Sanders*	Y	N	N	Y	N	Y
VIRGINIA						
1 *Bateman*	N	Y	Y	Y	Y	Y
2 Pickett	N	N	N	Y	N	Y
3 Scott	N	N	N	Y	N	Y
4 Sisisky	N	N	N	Y	N	Y
5 Payne	Y	Y	Y	Y	Y	N
6 *Goodlatte*	Y	Y	Y	Y	Y	N
7 *Bliley*	N	Y	Y	Y	Y	N
8 Moran	N	N	N	Y	N	Y
9 Boucher	Y	N	N	Y	N	Y
10 *Wolf*	N	Y	Y	Y	Y	Y
11 Byrne	N	N	N	Y	N	Y
WASHINGTON						
1 Cantwell	Y	N	N	Y	N	Y
2 Swift	N	N	N	Y	N	Y
3 Unsoeld	Y	N	N	Y	N	Y
4 Inslee	Y	N	Y	Y	N	Y
5 Foley			N	Y		
6 Dicks	N	N	N	Y	N	Y
7 McDermott	Y	N	N	Y	N	Y
8 *Dunn*	N	Y	Y	Y	Y	Y
9 Kreidler	Y	Y	N	Y	N	Y
WEST VIRGINIA						
1 Mollohan	N	N	N	Y	N	Y
2 Wise	N	N	N	Y	N	Y
3 Rahall	N	N	N	Y	N	Y
WISCONSIN						
1 Barca	Y	Y	Y	Y	Y	Y
2 *Klug*	Y	Y	Y	Y	Y	Y
3 *Gunderson*	N	Y	Y	Y	Y	Y
4 Kleczka	Y	N	N	Y	N	Y
5 Barrett	Y	N	N	Y	N	Y
6 *Petri*	Y	Y	Y	Y	Y	N
7 Obey	N	N	N	Y	N	Y
8 *Roth*	Y	Y	Y	Y	Y	N
9 *Sensenbrenner*	Y	Y	Y	Y	Y	N
WYOMING						
AL *Thomas*	Y	Y	Y	Y	Y	Y
DELEGATES						
de Lugo, V.I.	N	N	N	Y	D	D
Faleomavaega, Am.S.	N	N	N	Y	D	D
Norton, D.C.	Y	N	N	Y	D	D
Romero-B., P.R.	N	N	N	Y	D	D
Underwood, Guam	?	?	N	Y	D	D

Southern states - Ala., Ark., Fla., Ga., Ky., La., Miss., N.C., Okla., S.C., Tenn., Texas, Va.
Omitted votes are quorum calls, which CQ does not include in its vote charts.

KEY

Y Voted for (yea).
\# Paired for.
\+ Announced for.
N Voted against (nay).
X Paired against.
− Announced against.
P Voted "present."
C Voted "present" to avoid possible conflict of interest.
? Did not vote or otherwise make a position known.
D Delegates ineligible to vote.

Democrats *Republicans*
Independent

14. Procedural Motion. Approval of the House Journal of Monday, Feb. 7. Approved 235-147: R 17-139; D 217-8 (ND 149-7, SD 68-1); I 1-0, Feb. 8, 1994.

15. Procedural Motion. Approval of the House Journal of Tuesday, Feb. 8. Approved 246-151: R 22-146; D 223-5 (ND 149-4, SD 74-1); I 1-0, Feb. 9, 1994.

16. HR 811. Independent Counsel Reauthorization/Previous Question. Derrick, D-S.C., motion to order the previous question (thus limiting debate and the possibility of amendment) on adoption of the rule (H Res 352) to provide for House floor consideration of the bill to reauthorize for five years provisions of law that provide for the appointment of independent counsels to investigate and prosecute allegations of criminal wrongdoing by high executive branch officials. Motion agreed to 249-174: R 0-173; D 248-1 (ND 170-1, SD 78-0); I 1-0, Feb. 9, 1994.

17. HR 811. Independent Counsel Reauthorization/Rule. Adoption of the rule (H Res 352) to provide for House floor consideration of the bill to reauthorize for five years provisions of law that provide for the appointment of independent counsels to investigate and prosecute allegations of criminal wrongdoing by high executive branch officials. Adopted 242-174: R 0-171; D 241-3 (ND 165-1, SD 76-2); I 1-0, Feb. 9, 1994.

18. HR 811. Independent Counsel Reauthorization/Grounds for Removal. Ramstad, R-Minn., amendment to establish that failure to comply with certain Justice Department policies regarding enforcement of criminal laws and the avoidance of conflicts of interest may be grounds for removing an independent counsel from office. Rejected in the Committee of the Whole 187-227: R 168-0; D 19-226 (ND 10-161, SD 9-65); I 0-1, Feb. 10, 1994.

19. HR 811. Independent Counsel Reauthorization/Congressional Coverage. Bryant, D-Texas, substitute amendment to Gekas, R-Pa., amendment to allow but not require the coverage of Congress under the bill. The Gekas amendment would require that independent counsels be used to examine or prosecute serious allegations involving members of Congress. Adopted in the Committee of the Whole 230-188: R 2-167; D 227-21 (ND 164-9, SD 63-12); I 1-0, Feb. 10, 1994. A "yea" was a vote in support of the president's position.

20. HR 811. Independent Counsel Reauthorization/Congressional Coverage. Gekas, R-Pa., amendment, as amended by the Bryant, D-Texas, amendment, to allow but not require the coverage of Congress under the bill. Adopted in the Committee of the Whole 339-76: R 97-71; D 241-5 (ND 166-3, SD 75-2); I 1-0, Feb. 10, 1994.

	14	15	16	17	18	19	20
ALABAMA							
1 *Callahan*	N	N	N	N	Y	N	N
2 *Everett*	Y	N	N	N	Y	N	Y
3 Browder	Y	Y	Y	Y	N	Y	Y
4 Bevill	Y	Y	Y	Y	N	Y	Y
5 Cramer	Y	Y	Y	Y	N	Y	Y
6 *Bachus*	N	N	N	N	Y	N	Y
7 Hilliard	Y	Y	Y	Y	N	Y	Y
ALASKA							
AL *Young*	N	N	N	N	Y	N	Y
ARIZONA							
1 Coppersmith	Y	Y	Y	Y	N	N	Y
2 Pastor	Y	Y	Y	Y	N	Y	Y
3 *Stump*	N	N	N	N	Y	N	N
4 *Kyl*	N	N	N	N	Y	N	N
5 *Kolbe*	N	N	N	N	Y	N	N
6 English	Y	Y	Y	Y	N	Y	Y
ARKANSAS							
1 Lambert	Y	Y	Y	Y	N	Y	Y
2 Thornton	Y	Y	Y	Y	N	Y	Y
3 *Hutchinson*	N	N	N	N	Y	N	Y
4 *Dickey*	N	N	N	N	Y	N	Y
CALIFORNIA							
1 Hamburg	?	Y	Y	Y	N	Y	Y
2 *Herger*	N	N	N	N	Y	N	Y
3 Fazio	Y	Y	Y	Y	N	Y	#
4 *Doolittle*	N	N	N	N	Y	N	N
5 Matsui	Y	Y	Y	Y	N	Y	Y
6 Woolsey	Y	Y	Y	Y	N	Y	Y
7 Miller	N	Y	Y	Y	N	Y	?
8 Pelosi	?	?	Y	Y	N	Y	Y
9 Dellums	Y	?	Y	Y	N	Y	Y
10 *Baker*	N	N	N	N	Y	N	N
11 *Pombo*	Y	Y	N	N	Y	N	N
12 Lantos	Y	Y	Y	Y	N	Y	Y
13 Stark	Y	Y	Y	Y	N	Y	Y
14 Eshoo	Y	Y	Y	Y	N	Y	Y
15 Mineta	Y	Y	Y	Y	N	Y	Y
16 Edwards	Y	Y	Y	Y	N	Y	Y
17 Farr	Y	Y	Y	Y	N	Y	Y
18 Condit	Y	Y	Y	Y	N	Y	Y
19 Lehman	Y	Y	Y	Y	N	Y	Y
20 Dooley	Y	Y	Y	Y	Y	Y	Y
21 *Thomas*	N	N	N	N	Y	N	N
22 *Huffington*	N	?	?	Y	N	N	N
23 *Gallegly*	?	N	N	N	Y	N	N
24 Beilenson	Y	Y	Y	Y	N	Y	Y
25 *McKeon*	N	Y	N	N	Y	N	Y
26 Berman	Y	Y	Y	Y	N	Y	Y
27 *Moorhead*	N	N	N	N	Y	N	N
28 *Dreier*	N	N	N	N	Y	N	N
29 Waxman	Y	Y	Y	Y	N	Y	Y
30 Becerra	Y	+	Y	?	N	Y	Y
31 Martinez	Y	Y	Y	Y	?	Y	Y
32 Dixon	Y	Y	Y	Y	N	Y	Y
33 Roybal-Allard	Y	Y	Y	Y	N	Y	Y
34 Torres	Y	Y	Y	Y	N	Y	Y
35 Waters	Y	Y	Y	Y	N	Y	Y
36 Harman	Y	Y	Y	Y	N	Y	Y
37 Tucker	Y	Y	Y	Y	?	Y	Y
38 *Horn*	N	N	N	N	Y	N	N
39 *Royce*	N	N	N	N	Y	N	?
40 *Lewis*	N	N	N	N	Y	N	Y
41 *Kim*	N	N	N	N	Y	N	Y

	14	15	16	17	18	19	20
42 Brown	?	?	Y	Y	N	Y	?
43 *Calvert*	N	N	N	N	Y	N	Y
44 *McCandless*	N	N	N	N	Y	N	Y
45 *Rohrabacher*	N	?	N	N	Y	N	N
46 *Dornan*	?	?	N	N	#	N	N
47 *Cox*	N	N	N	N	Y	N	N
48 *Packard*	N	N	N	N	Y	N	N
49 Schenk	Y	Y	Y	Y	N	Y	Y
50 Filner	Y	Y	Y	Y	N	Y	Y
51 *Cunningham*	N	N	N	N	Y	N	Y
52 *Hunter*	?	N	N	N	Y	N	Y
COLORADO							
1 Schroeder	N	N	Y	Y	N	Y	Y
2 Skaggs	Y	Y	Y	Y	N	Y	Y
3 *McInnis*	Y	Y	N	N	Y	N	Y
4 *Allard*	N	N	N	N	Y	N	Y
5 *Hefley*	N	N	N	N	Y	N	Y
6 *Schaefer*	?	N	N	N	Y	N	Y
CONNECTICUT							
1 Kennelly	Y	Y	Y	Y	N	Y	Y
2 Gejdenson	?	Y	Y	Y	N	Y	Y
3 DeLauro	Y	Y	Y	Y	N	Y	Y
4 *Shays*	N	N	N	N	Y	N	Y
5 *Franks*	N	N	N	N	Y	N	N
6 *Johnson*	N	N	N	N	Y	N	Y
DELAWARE							
AL *Castle*	N	N	N	N	Y	N	Y
FLORIDA							
1 Hutto	Y	Y	Y	Y	N	Y	Y
2 Peterson	Y	Y	Y	Y	Y	Y	Y
3 Brown	Y	Y	Y	Y	N	Y	Y
4 *Fowler*	N	N	N	N	Y	N	N
5 Thurman	Y	Y	Y	Y	N	Y	Y
6 *Stearns*	N	N	N	N	Y	N	N
7 *Mica*	N	N	N	N	Y	N	N
8 *McCollum*	N	Y	N	N	Y	N	N
9 *Bilirakis*	?	?	X	X	#	X	X
10 *Young*	N	N	N	N	Y	N	N
11 Gibbons	?	?	Y	Y	N	Y	Y
12 *Canady*	N	N	N	N	Y	N	N
13 *Miller*	N	N	N	N	Y	N	N
14 *Goss*	N	N	N	N	Y	N	N
15 *Bacchus*	Y	?	Y	Y	N	N	Y
16 *Lewis*	N	N	N	N	Y	N	Y
17 Meek	Y	Y	Y	Y	N	Y	Y
18 *Ros-Lehtinen*	?	N	N	N	Y	N	N
19 Johnston	Y	Y	Y	Y	Y	Y	Y
20 Deutsch	Y	Y	Y	Y	N	Y	Y
21 *Diaz-Balart*	N	N	N	N	Y	N	N
22 *Shaw*	N	N	N	N	Y	N	Y
23 Hastings	?	?	?	?	?	?	?
GEORGIA							
1 *Kingston*	?	Y	N	N	Y	N	N
2 Bishop	Y	Y	Y	Y	N	Y	Y
3 *Collins*	Y	Y	N	N	Y	N	Y
4 *Linder*	N	N	N	N	Y	N	Y
5 Lewis	Y	Y	Y	Y	N	Y	Y
6 *Gingrich*	N	N	N	N	Y	N	N
7 *Darden*	Y	Y	Y	Y	N	Y	Y
8 Rowland	Y	Y	Y	Y	N	N	Y
9 Deal	Y	Y	Y	Y	N	N	Y
10 Johnson	Y	Y	Y	Y	N	Y	Y
11 McKinney	Y	Y	Y	Y	N	Y	Y
HAWAII							
1 Abercrombie	Y	Y	Y	Y	N	Y	N
2 Mink	Y	Y	Y	Y	N	Y	Y
IDAHO							
1 LaRocco	Y	Y	Y	Y	N	Y	Y
2 *Crapo*	N	N	N	N	Y	N	N
ILLINOIS							
1 Rush	Y	Y	Y	Y	N	Y	Y
2 Reynolds	Y	Y	Y	Y	N	Y	Y
3 Lipinski	Y	Y	Y	Y	N	Y	Y
4 Gutierrez	?	Y	Y	Y	N	Y	?
5 Rostenkowski	Y	Y	Y	Y	N	Y	Y
6 *Hyde*	Y	Y	N	?	Y	N	N
7 Collins	Y	Y	Y	Y	N	Y	Y
8 *Crane*	N	N	N	N	Y	N	N
9 Yates	?	Y	Y	Y	N	Y	Y
10 *Porter*	N	N	N	N	Y	N	Y
11 Sangmeister	Y	Y	Y	Y	N	Y	Y
12 Costello	Y	Y	Y	Y	N	Y	Y
13 *Fawell*	N	N	N	N	Y	N	N
14 *Hastert*	N	N	N	−	+	−	−
15 *Ewing*	N	N	N	N	#	?	?
16 *Manzullo*	N	Y	N	N	Y	N	Y
17 Evans	Y	Y	Y	Y	N	Y	Y

ND Northern Democrats   SD Southern Democrats

	14	15	16	17	18	19	20
18 ***Michel***	N	N	N	N	Y	?	?
19 Poshard	Y	Y	Y	Y	N	Y	Y
20 Durbin	Y	Y	Y	?	N	Y	Y
INDIANA							
1 Visclosky	Y	Y	Y	Y	N	Y	Y
2 Sharp	?	Y	Y	Y	N	Y	Y
3 Roemer	Y	Y	Y	Y	N	Y	Y
4 Long	Y	Y	Y	Y	N	Y	Y
5 ***Buyer***	N	N	N	N	Y	N	N
6 ***Burton***	?	?	N	N	Y	N	N
7 ***Myers***	Y	Y	N	N	Y	N	N
8 McCloskey	Y	Y	Y	Y	N	Y	Y
9 Hamilton	Y	Y	Y	Y	N	Y	Y
10 Jacobs	N	N	N	N	N	N	Y
IOWA							
1 ***Leach***	N	N	N	N	Y	N	Y
2 ***Nussle***	N	N	N	N	Y	N	N
3 ***Lightfoot***	N	N	N	N	Y	N	Y
4 Smith	Y	?	Y	Y	N	Y	Y
5 ***Grandy***	N	N	N	N	Y	N	N
KANSAS							
1 ***Roberts***	N	N	N	N	?	N	Y
2 Slattery	?	Y	Y	Y	?	?	?
3 ***Meyers***	N	N	N	N	Y	N	Y
4 Glickman	Y	Y	Y	Y	N	Y	Y
KENTUCKY							
1 Barlow	Y	Y	Y	Y	N	Y	Y
2 Natcher	Y	Y	Y	Y	N	Y	Y
3 Mazzoli	Y	Y	Y	Y	N	N	Y
4 ***Bunning***	?	N	N	N	Y	N	Y
5 ***Rogers***	N	N	N	N	Y	N	Y
6 Baesler	Y	Y	Y	Y	N	Y	Y
LOUISIANA							
1 ***Livingston***	Y	Y	N	N	Y	N	Y
2 Jefferson	?	Y	Y	Y	N	Y	Y
3 Tauzin	Y	Y	Y	Y	N	N	Y
4 Fields	?	Y	Y	Y	N	Y	Y
5 ***McCrery***	N	N	N	N	Y	N	Y
6 ***Baker***	N	N	N	N	Y	N	Y
7 Hayes	?	Y	Y	Y	Y	Y	Y
MAINE							
1 Andrews	Y	Y	Y	Y	N	Y	Y
2 ***Snowe***	N	N	N	N	Y	N	Y
MARYLAND							
1 ***Gilchrest***	N	N	N	N	Y	N	Y
2 ***Bentley***	N	N	N	N	Y	N	Y
3 Cardin	Y	Y	Y	Y	N	Y	Y
4 Wynn	Y	?	Y	Y	N	Y	Y
5 Hoyer	Y	?	Y	Y	N	Y	Y
6 ***Bartlett***	N	N	N	N	Y	N	N
7 Mfume	+	Y	Y	Y	N	Y	Y
8 ***Morella***	N	N	N	N	Y	?	Y
MASSACHUSETTS							
1 Olver	Y	Y	Y	Y	N	Y	Y
2 Neal	Y	Y	Y	Y	N	Y	Y
3 ***Blute***	N	N	N	N	Y	N	Y
4 Frank	Y	?	Y	Y	N	Y	Y
5 Meehan	?	Y	Y	Y	N	Y	Y
6 ***Torkildsen***	N	N	N	N	Y	N	Y
7 Markey	Y	Y	Y	Y	N	Y	Y
8 Kennedy	Y	Y	Y	Y	N	Y	Y
9 Moakley	Y	Y	Y	Y	N	Y	Y
10 Studds	Y	Y	Y	Y	N	Y	Y
MICHIGAN							
1 Stupak	Y	Y	Y	Y	N	Y	Y
2 ***Hoekstra***	N	N	N	N	Y	N	Y
3 ***Ehlers***	N	N	N	N	Y	N	N
4 ***Camp***	N	N	N	N	Y	N	Y
5 Barcia	Y	?	Y	Y	N	Y	Y
6 ***Upton***	N	N	N	N	Y	N	Y
7 ***Smith***	N	N	N	N	Y	N	Y
8 Carr	Y	?	Y	Y	N	Y	Y
9 Kildee	Y	Y	Y	Y	N	Y	Y
10 Bonior	Y	Y	Y	Y	N	Y	Y
11 ***Knollenberg***	N	N	N	N	Y	N	Y
12 Levin	Y	Y	Y	Y	N	Y	Y
13 Ford	Y	?	Y	?	N	Y	Y
14 Conyers	Y	?	Y	Y	N	Y	Y
15 Collins	Y	Y	Y	Y	N	Y	Y
16 Dingell	Y	Y	Y	Y	N	Y	Y
MINNESOTA							
1 Penny	N	Y	Y	Y	Y	Y	Y
2 Minge	Y	Y	Y	Y	N	Y	Y
3 ***Ramstad***	N	N	N	N	Y	N	Y
4 Vento	Y	Y	Y	Y	N	Y	Y

	14	15	16	17	18	19	20
5 Sabo	Y	?	Y	Y	N	Y	Y
6 ***Grams***	N	N	N	N	Y	N	N
7 Peterson	Y	Y	Y	Y	Y	Y	Y
8 Oberstar	Y	Y	Y	Y	N	Y	Y
MISSISSIPPI							
1 Whitten	Y	Y	Y	Y	N	Y	Y
2 Thompson	?	Y	Y	Y	N	Y	Y
3 Montgomery	Y	Y	Y	Y	N	Y	Y
4 Parker	?	Y	Y	Y	Y	N	Y
5 Taylor	N	N	Y	Y	Y	N	N
MISSOURI							
1 Clay	N	N	Y	Y	N	?	?
2 ***Talent***	?	N	N	N	Y	N	Y
3 Gephardt	Y	Y	Y	Y	N	Y	Y
4 Skelton	Y	Y	Y	Y	N	N	Y
5 Wheat	Y	?	Y	Y	N	Y	Y
6 Danner	Y	Y	Y	Y	N	Y	Y
7 ***Hancock***	N	N	N	N	Y	N	N
8 ***Emerson***	N	N	N	N	Y	N	N
9 Volkmer	Y	Y	Y	Y	N	N	Y
MONTANA							
AL Williams	?	?	Y	Y	N	?	?
NEBRASKA							
1 ***Bereuter***	N	N	N	N	Y	N	Y
2 Hoagland	Y	?	Y	Y	N	Y	Y
3 ***Barrett***	N	N	N	N	Y	N	N
NEVADA							
1 Bilbray	Y	Y	Y	Y	Y	Y	Y
2 ***Vucanovich***	N	N	N	N	?	N	N
NEW HAMPSHIRE							
1 ***Zeliff***	N	N	N	N	Y	N	N
2 Swett	Y	Y	Y	Y	N	N	N
NEW JERSEY							
1 Andrews	Y	Y	Y	Y	Y	N	Y
2 Hughes	Y	Y	Y	Y	N	Y	Y
3 ***Saxton***	N	N	N	N	Y	N	Y
4 ***Smith***	Y	Y	N	N	Y	N	Y
5 ***Roukema***	?	?	X	X	Y	N	Y
6 Pallone	Y	Y	Y	Y	N	Y	Y
7 ***Franks***	N	N	N	N	Y	N	Y
8 Klein	Y	Y	Y	Y	N	Y	Y
9 Torricelli	?	Y	Y	Y	N	Y	Y
10 Payne	?	Y	Y	Y	N	Y	Y
11 ***Gallo***	N	N	N	N	Y	N	Y
12 ***Zimmer***	N	N	N	N	Y	N	Y
13 Menendez	Y	Y	Y	Y	N	Y	Y
NEW MEXICO							
1 ***Schiff***	N	N	N	N	Y	N	Y
2 ***Skeen***	N	N	N	N	Y	N	Y
3 Richardson	Y	Y	Y	Y	N	Y	Y
NEW YORK							
1 Hochbrueckner	Y	Y	Y	Y	N	Y	Y
2 ***Lazio***	N	N	N	N	Y	N	Y
3 ***King***	N	N	N	N	Y	N	N
4 ***Levy***	N	N	N	N	Y	N	N
5 Ackerman	Y	Y	Y	Y	N	Y	Y
6 Flake	Y	Y	Y	Y	N	Y	Y
7 Manton	Y	Y	Y	Y	X	Y	Y
8 Nadler	Y	Y	Y	Y	N	Y	Y
9 Schumer	Y	Y	Y	Y	N	Y	Y
10 Towns	Y	Y	Y	Y	N	Y	Y
11 Owens	Y	Y	Y	Y	N	Y	Y
12 Velazquez	Y	Y	Y	?	N	Y	Y
13 ***Molinari***	?	N	N	N	Y	N	Y
14 Maloney	Y	Y	Y	Y	N	Y	Y
15 Rangel	Y	?	#	#	N	Y	Y
16 Serrano	Y	Y	Y	Y	N	Y	Y
17 Engel	Y	Y	Y	Y	N	Y	Y
18 Lowey	Y	Y	Y	Y	N	Y	Y
19 ***Fish***	Y	Y	N	N	Y	N	Y
20 ***Gilman***	Y	Y	N	N	Y	N	Y
21 McNulty	Y	Y	Y	Y	N	Y	Y
22 ***Solomon***	N	N	N	N	Y	N	N
23 ***Boehlert***	N	N	N	N	Y	N	Y
24 ***McHugh***	N	N	N	N	Y	N	N
25 ***Walsh***	N	N	N	N	Y	N	Y
26 Hinchey	Y	Y	Y	Y	N	Y	Y
27 ***Paxon***	N	N	N	N	Y	N	N
28 Slaughter	Y	Y	Y	Y	N	Y	Y
29 LaFalce	Y	Y	Y	Y	N	Y	Y
30 ***Quinn***	N	N	N	N	Y	N	Y
31 ***Houghton***	Y	Y	N	N	Y	N	N
NORTH CAROLINA							
1 Clayton	Y	Y	Y	Y	N	Y	Y
2 Valentine	?	Y	Y	Y	N	N	Y

	14	15	16	17	18	19	20
3 Lancaster	Y	Y	Y	Y	?	Y	Y
4 Price	?	Y	Y	Y	N	Y	Y
5 Neal	?	?	?	?	?	?	?
6 ***Coble***	N	N	N	N	Y	N	N
7 Rose	Y	Y	Y	Y	N	Y	Y
8 Hefner	Y	Y	Y	Y	N	Y	Y
9 ***McMillan***	N	?	N	N	Y	?	?
10 ***Ballenger***	N	N	N	N	Y	N	Y
11 ***Taylor***	N	N	N	N	Y	N	N
12 Watt	Y	Y	Y	Y	N	Y	Y
NORTH DAKOTA							
AL Pomeroy	Y	Y	Y	Y	N	Y	Y
OHIO							
1 Mann	Y	Y	Y	Y	N	Y	Y
2 ***Portman***	?	—	N	N	Y	N	Y
3 Hall	Y	Y	Y	Y	N	Y	Y
4 ***Oxley***	N	N	N	N	Y	Y	Y
5 ***Gillmor***	Y	Y	N	N	Y	N	Y
6 Strickland	Y	Y	Y	Y	N	Y	Y
7 ***Hobson***	?	N	N	N	Y	N	Y
8 ***Boehner***	?	N	N	N	Y	N	N
9 Kaptur	?	Y	Y	Y	N	Y	Y
10 ***Hoke***	N	N	N	N	Y	N	N
11 Stokes	Y	Y	Y	Y	N	Y	Y
12 ***Kasich***	Y	Y	N	N	Y	N	Y
13 Brown	Y	Y	Y	Y	N	Y	Y
14 Sawyer	Y	Y	Y	Y	N	Y	Y
15 ***Pryce***	?	N	N	N	Y	N	Y
16 ***Regula***	N	N	N	N	Y	N	Y
17 Traficant	Y	Y	Y	Y	Y	Y	Y
18 Applegate	Y	Y	Y	Y	N	Y	Y
19 Fingerhut	Y	Y	Y	Y	N	Y	Y
OKLAHOMA							
1 ***Inhofe***	N	N	N	N	Y	N	Y
2 Synar	Y	Y	Y	Y	N	Y	Y
3 Brewster	Y	Y	Y	Y	N	Y	Y
4 McCurdy	Y	Y	Y	Y	Y	?	Y
5 ***Istook***	N	N	N	N	Y	N	Y
6 Vacancy							
OREGON							
1 Furse	Y	Y	Y	Y	N	N	N
2 ***Smith***	?	N	N	N	?	N	Y
3 Wyden	Y	Y	Y	Y	N	Y	Y
4 DeFazio	?	Y	Y	Y	Y	Y	Y
5 Kopetski	Y	Y	Y	Y	N	Y	Y
PENNSYLVANIA							
1 Foglietta	Y	Y	Y	Y	N	Y	Y
2 Blackwell	Y	?	Y	Y	X	Y	Y
3 Borski	Y	Y	Y	Y	N	Y	Y
4 Klink	Y	Y	Y	Y	N	Y	Y
5 ***Clinger***	Y	N	N	N	Y	N	Y
6 Holden	Y	Y	Y	Y	N	Y	Y
7 ***Weldon***	N	N	N	N	Y	N	N
8 ***Greenwood***	Y	Y	N	N	Y	N	Y
9 ***Shuster***	N	N	N	N	Y	N	Y
10 ***McDade***	N	N	N	N	Y	N	Y
11 Kanjorski	Y	Y	Y	Y	N	Y	Y
12 Murtha	Y	Y	Y	?	N	Y	Y
13 Margolies-Mezv.	Y	Y	Y	Y	Y	Y	Y
14 Coyne	Y	Y	Y	Y	N	Y	Y
15 McHale	Y	Y	Y	Y	Y	N	Y
16 ***Walker***	N	N	N	N	Y	N	N
17 ***Gekas***	N	N	N	N	Y	N	N
18 ***Santorum***	N	Y	N	N	Y	N	Y
19 ***Goodling***	N	N	N	N	Y	N	Y
20 Murphy	N	N	Y	Y	N	Y	Y
21 ***Ridge***	?	N	N	N	?	?	?
RHODE ISLAND							
1 ***Machtley***	N	N	N	N	Y	N	Y
2 Reed	Y	Y	Y	Y	N	Y	Y
SOUTH CAROLINA							
1 ***Ravenel***	N	N	N	N	Y	N	Y
2 ***Spence***	N	N	N	N	Y	N	N
3 Derrick	Y	Y	Y	Y	N	?	Y
4 ***Inglis***	Y	Y	N	N	Y	N	N
5 Spratt	Y	Y	Y	Y	N	Y	Y
6 Clyburn	Y	Y	Y	Y	N	Y	Y
SOUTH DAKOTA							
AL Johnson	Y	Y	Y	Y	N	Y	Y
TENNESSEE							
1 ***Quillen***	N	N	N	N	Y	N	N
2 ***Duncan***	N	N	N	N	Y	N	?
3 Lloyd	Y	?	Y	Y	N	Y	Y
4 Cooper	Y	Y	Y	N	Y	N	Y
5 Clement	Y	Y	Y	Y	N	Y	Y

	14	15	16	17	18	19	20
6 Gordon	Y	Y	Y	Y	N	Y	Y
7 ***Sundquist***	N	N	N	N	Y	N	N
8 Tanner	Y	Y	Y	Y	N	Y	Y
9 Ford	?	?	?	?	?	Y	Y
TEXAS							
1 Chapman	Y	Y	Y	Y	?	Y	Y
2 Wilson	Y	Y	Y	N	N	Y	Y
3 ***Johnson, Sam***	N	N	N	N	Y	N	N
4 Hall	Y	Y	Y	Y	N	N	Y
5 Bryant	Y	Y	Y	Y	N	Y	Y
6 ***Barton***	N	N	N	N	Y	N	N
7 ***Archer***	N	N	N	N	Y	N	N
8 ***Fields***	?	N	N	N	Y	N	N
9 Brooks	Y	Y	Y	Y	N	Y	Y
10 Pickle	Y	Y	Y	Y	N	Y	Y
11 Edwards	Y	Y	Y	Y	N	Y	Y
12 Geren	Y	Y	Y	Y	N	N	Y
13 Sarpalius	Y	Y	Y	Y	N	Y	Y
14 Laughlin	?	?	?	?	?	?	?
15 de la Garza	?	?	?	?	?	?	?
16 Coleman	Y	Y	Y	Y	?	?	?
17 Stenholm	Y	Y	Y	Y	N	N	Y
18 Washington	?	?	#	#	X	#	?
19 ***Combest***	Y	N	N	N	Y	N	Y
20 Gonzalez	Y	Y	Y	Y	N	Y	Y
21 ***Smith***	N	N	N	N	Y	N	N
22 ***DeLay***	N	N	N	N	Y	N	N
23 ***Bonilla***	N	N	N	N	Y	N	Y
24 Frost	Y	Y	Y	Y	Y	Y	Y
25 Andrews	Y	Y	Y	Y	?	?	?
26 ***Armey***	N	N	N	N	Y	N	N
27 Ortiz	Y	Y	Y	Y	N	Y	Y
28 Tejeda	Y	Y	Y	Y	N	Y	Y
29 Green	Y	Y	Y	Y	N	Y	Y
30 Johnson, E.B.	Y	Y	Y	Y	N	Y	Y
UTAH							
1 ***Hansen***	N	N	N	N	Y	N	N
2 Shepherd	Y	Y	Y	Y	N	Y	Y
3 Orton	Y	Y	Y	Y	Y	N	Y
VERMONT							
AL *Sanders*	Y	Y	Y	Y	N	Y	Y
VIRGINIA							
1 ***Bateman***	?	Y	N	N	Y	N	Y
2 Pickett	Y	Y	Y	Y	N	Y	Y
3 Scott	Y	Y	Y	Y	N	Y	Y
4 Sisisky	Y	Y	Y	Y	Y	Y	Y
5 Payne	Y	Y	Y	Y	N	Y	Y
6 ***Goodlatte***	N	N	N	N	Y	N	Y
7 ***Bliley***	N	N	N	N	Y	N	N
8 Moran	Y	Y	Y	Y	N	Y	Y
9 Boucher	?	Y	Y	Y	N	Y	Y
10 ***Wolf***	N	N	N	N	Y	N	Y
11 Byrne	Y	Y	Y	Y	N	Y	Y
WASHINGTON							
1 Cantwell	Y	Y	Y	Y	N	Y	Y
2 Swift	Y	Y	Y	Y	—	Y	Y
3 Unsoeld	Y	?	Y	Y	N	Y	Y
4 Inslee	Y	Y	Y	Y	N	Y	Y
5 Foley							
6 Dicks	Y	Y	Y	Y	N	Y	Y
7 McDermott	Y	Y	Y	Y	N	Y	Y
8 ***Dunn***	N	N	N	N	Y	N	N
9 Kreidler	N	Y	Y	Y	N	Y	Y
WEST VIRGINIA							
1 Mollohan	Y	Y	Y	Y	N	Y	Y
2 Wise	?	Y	Y	Y	N	Y	Y
3 Rahall	Y	Y	Y	Y	N	Y	Y
WISCONSIN							
1 Barca	Y	Y	Y	Y	N	Y	Y
2 ***Klug***	N	N	N	N	Y	N	Y
3 ***Gunderson***	N	N	N	N	Y	N	Y
4 Kleczka	Y	Y	Y	Y	N	Y	Y
5 Barrett	Y	Y	Y	Y	N	Y	Y
6 ***Petri***	N	N	N	N	Y	N	Y
7 Obey	Y	Y	Y	Y	N	Y	Y
8 ***Roth***	N	N	N	N	Y	N	Y
9 ***Sensenbrenner***	N	N	N	N	Y	N	Y
WYOMING							
AL ***Thomas***	N	N	N	N	Y	N	Y
DELEGATES							
de Lugo, V.I.	D	D	D	D	N	Y	Y
Faleomavaega, Am.S.	D	D	D	D	N	Y	Y
Norton, D.C.	D	D	D	D	N	Y	Y
Romero-B., P.R.	D	D	D	D	N	Y	Y
Underwood, Guam	D	D	D	D	N	Y	?

Southern states - Ala., Ark., Fla., Ga., Ky., La., Miss., N.C., Okla., S.C., Tenn., Texas, Va.
Omitted votes are quorum calls, which CQ does not include in its vote charts.

KEY

Y   Voted for (yea).
Paired for.
+   Announced for.
N   Voted against (nay).
X   Paired against.
—   Announced against.
P   Voted "present."
C   Voted "present" to avoid possible conflict of interest.
?   Did not vote or otherwise make a position known.
D   Delegates ineligible to vote.

Democrats *Republicans*
Independent

21. HR 811. Independent Counsel Reauthorization/Substitute. Hyde, R-Ill., substitute amendment to provide mandatory congressional coverage; provide cost controls; provide guidelines for the jurisdiction of an investigation and the treatment of classified information; set a threshold for the initiation of an investigation; limit the duration of an investigation and provide for the reimbursement of attorneys' fees for those found innocent. Rejected in the Committee of the Whole 181-238: R 167-1; D 14-236 (ND 2-173, SD 12-63); I 0-1, Feb. 10, 1994.

22. HR 811. Independent Counsel Reauthorization/Motion to Recommit. Gekas, R-Pa., motion to recommit the bill to the Judiciary Committee with instructions to report it back with an amendment providing for the mandatory coverage of members of Congress under the bill. Motion rejected 183-230: R 168-1; D 15-228 (ND 5-164, SD 10-64); I 0-1, Feb. 10, 1994.

23. HR 811. Independent Counsel Reauthorization/Passage. Passage of the bill to reauthorize for five years provisions of law that provide for the appointment of an independent counsel to investigate and prosecute criminal wrongdoing by high-ranking executive branch officials. Passed 356-56: R 112-54; D 243-2 (ND 169-2, SD 74-0); I 1-0, Feb. 10, 1994. A "yea" was a vote in support of the president's position.

24. HR 3345. Work Force Restructuring/Federal Work Force Reduction. Penny, D-Minn., amendment to codify the administration's plan for a federal work force reduction of 252,000 over the next six years and change rehiring rules. Adopted in the Committee of the Whole 409-1: R 165-0; D 243-1 (ND 169-1, SD 74-0); I 1-0, Feb. 10, 1994.

25. HR 3345. Work Force Restructuring/Passage. Passage of the bill to authorize financial incentives up to $25,000 to encourage voluntary retirements or resignations from the federal work force. Passed 391-17: R 148-17; D 242-0 (ND 167-0, SD 75-0); I 1-0, Feb. 10, 1994. A "yea" was a vote in support of the president's position.

26. HR 3759. Fiscal 1994 Disaster Supplemental Appropriations/Instruct Conferees. McDade, R-Pa., motion to instruct the House conferees to agree to the Senate amendment to extend the statute of limitations for Resolution Trust Corporation civil actions for fraud and gross negligence until Dec. 31, 1995. Motion agreed to 390-1: R 161-0; D 228-1 (ND 156-1, SD 72-0); I 1-0, Feb. 10, 1994.

27. HR 3759. Fiscal 1994 Disaster Supplemental Appropriations/Conference Report. Adoption of the conference report to provide $11,061,147,600 in new budget authority and $1.1 billion in direct loans for the emergency expenses of the Los Angeles-area earthquake, humanitarian assistance and peacekeeping activities, Midwest flood assistance, and highway reconstruction in San Francisco. The bill also includes $3.26 billion in rescissions of prior appropriations. The administration requested $11,598,848,000 in new budget authority, $1.1 billion in direct loans and $3.17 billion in rescissions. Adopted 245-65: R 76-48; D 168-17 (ND 121-12, SD 47-5); I 1-0, Feb. 11, 1994. A "yea" was a vote in support of the president's position.

	21	22	23	24	25	26	27
ALABAMA							
1 *Callahan*	Y	Y	N	Y	Y	Y	X
2 *Everett*	Y	Y	Y	Y	Y	Y	?
3 Browder	N	N	Y	Y	Y	Y	Y
4 Bevill	N	N	Y	Y	Y	Y	Y
5 Cramer	N	N	Y	Y	Y	Y	Y
6 *Bachus*	Y	Y	Y	Y	Y	Y	Y
7 Hilliard	N	?	?	Y	Y	Y	Y
ALASKA							
AL *Young*	Y	Y	N	?	?	?	?
ARIZONA							
1 Coppersmith	N	N	Y	Y	Y	Y	Y
2 Pastor	N	N	Y	Y	Y	Y	N
3 *Stump*	Y	Y	N	Y	N	Y	N
4 *Kyl*	Y	Y	N	Y	Y	Y	?
5 *Kolbe*	Y	Y	N	Y	Y	Y	N
6 English	N	N	Y	Y	Y	Y	N
ARKANSAS							
1 Lambert	N	N	Y	Y	Y	Y	N
2 Thornton	N	N	Y	Y	Y	Y	Y
3 *Hutchinson*	Y	Y	N	Y	Y	Y	N
4 *Dickey*	Y	Y	N	Y	Y	Y	N
CALIFORNIA							
1 Hamburg	N	N	Y	Y	Y	Y	Y
2 *Herger*	Y	Y	Y	Y	Y	Y	?
3 Fazio	N	N	Y	Y	Y	Y	Y
4 *Doolittle*	Y	Y	N	Y	Y	Y	Y
5 Matsui	N	?	Y	Y	Y	Y	Y
6 Woolsey	N	N	Y	Y	Y	Y	Y
7 Miller	N	N	Y	Y	Y	Y	Y
8 Pelosi	N	N	Y	Y	Y	Y	Y
9 Dellums	N	N	Y	Y	Y	Y	Y
10 *Baker*	Y	Y	—	Y	Y	Y	Y
11 *Pombo*	Y	Y	N	Y	Y	Y	Y
12 Lantos	N	N	Y	Y	Y	Y	#
13 Stark	N	N	Y	Y	Y	Y	Y
14 Eshoo	N	N	Y	Y	Y	Y	Y
15 Mineta	N	N	Y	Y	Y	Y	#
16 Edwards	N	N	Y	Y	Y	Y	Y
17 Farr	N	N	Y	Y	Y	Y	Y
18 Condit	N	N	Y	Y	Y	Y	Y
19 Lehman	N	N	Y	Y	Y	Y	?
20 Dooley	N	N	Y	Y	Y	Y	?
21 *Thomas*	Y	Y	N	Y	Y	Y	Y
22 *Huffington*	Y	Y	Y	Y	Y	Y	Y
23 *Gallegly*	Y	Y	Y	Y	Y	Y	Y
24 Beilenson	N	N	Y	Y	Y	Y	Y
25 *McKeon*	Y	Y	Y	Y	Y	Y	Y
26 Berman	N	N	Y	Y	Y	Y	Y
27 *Moorhead*	Y	Y	Y	Y	Y	Y	Y
28 *Dreier*	Y	Y	N	Y	Y	Y	Y
29 Waxman	N	N	Y	Y	Y	Y	?
30 Becerra	N	N	Y	Y	Y	Y	Y
31 Martinez	N	N	Y	Y	Y	Y	?
32 Dixon	N	N	Y	Y	Y	Y	Y
33 Roybal-Allard	N	N	Y	Y	Y	Y	Y
34 Torres	N	N	Y	Y	Y	Y	Y
35 Waters	N	N	Y	Y	Y	Y	Y
36 Harman	N	N	Y	Y	Y	Y	Y
37 Tucker	N	N	Y	Y	Y	Y	Y
38 *Horn*	Y	Y	Y	Y	Y	Y	Y
39 *Royce*	Y	Y	Y	Y	Y	Y	Y
40 *Lewis*	Y	Y	Y	Y	Y	Y	Y
41 *Kim*	Y	Y	N	Y	Y	Y	Y

	21	22	23	24	25	26	27
42 Brown	N	N	Y	Y	Y	Y	Y
43 *Calvert*	Y	Y	Y	Y	Y	Y	Y
44 *McCandless*	Y	Y	Y	Y	Y	Y	Y
45 *Rohrabacher*	Y	Y	Y	Y	Y	Y	Y
46 *Dornan*	Y	Y	N	Y	Y	Y	#
47 *Cox*	Y	Y	N	Y	Y	Y	Y
48 *Packard*	Y	Y	Y	Y	Y	Y	Y
49 Schenk	N	N	Y	Y	Y	Y	Y
50 Filner	N	N	Y	Y	Y	Y	Y
51 *Cunningham*	?	Y	Y	Y	Y	Y	Y
52 *Hunter*	Y	Y	Y	Y	Y	Y	Y
COLORADO							
1 Schroeder	N	N	Y	Y	Y	Y	Y
2 Skaggs	N	N	Y	Y	Y	Y	Y
3 *McInnis*	Y	Y	N	Y	Y	Y	N
4 *Allard*	Y	Y	Y	Y	Y	Y	N
5 *Hefley*	Y	Y	N	Y	Y	Y	N
6 *Schaefer*	Y	Y	N	Y	Y	Y	N
CONNECTICUT							
1 Kennelly	N	N	Y	Y	Y	Y	Y
2 Gejdenson	N	N	Y	Y	Y	?	Y
3 DeLauro	N	N	Y	Y	Y	Y	Y
4 *Shays*	Y	Y	Y	Y	Y	Y	N
5 *Franks*	Y	Y	Y	Y	Y	Y	Y
6 *Johnson*	Y	Y	Y	Y	Y	Y	N
DELAWARE							
AL *Castle*	Y	Y	Y	Y	Y	Y	Y
FLORIDA							
1 Hutto	Y	N	Y	Y	Y	?	?
2 Peterson	N	N	Y	Y	Y	Y	Y
3 Brown	N	Y	Y	Y	Y	Y	Y
4 *Fowler*	Y	Y	Y	Y	Y	Y	?
5 Thurman	N	N	Y	Y	Y	Y	Y
6 *Stearns*	Y	Y	Y	Y	Y	Y	X
7 *Mica*	Y	Y	Y	Y	Y	Y	Y
8 *McCollum*	Y	Y	Y	Y	Y	Y	#
9 *Bilirakis*	?	#	?	?	?	?	?
10 *Young*	Y	Y	Y	Y	Y	Y	Y
11 Gibbons	N	N	Y	Y	Y	?	?
12 *Canady*	Y	Y	Y	Y	Y	N	Y
13 *Miller*	Y	Y	Y	Y	Y	Y	Y
14 *Goss*	Y	Y	Y	Y	Y	Y	N
15 Bacchus	N	?	?	Y	Y	Y	Y
16 *Lewis*	Y	Y	Y	?	?	?	?
17 Meek	N	N	Y	Y	Y	Y	Y
18 *Ros-Lehtinen*	Y	Y	Y	Y	Y	Y	?
19 Johnston	N	N	Y	Y	Y	Y	Y
20 Deutsch	N	N	Y	Y	Y	Y	?
21 *Diaz-Balart*	Y	Y	Y	Y	Y	Y	N
22 *Shaw*	Y	Y	Y	Y	Y	Y	Y
23 Hastings	?	?	?	?	?	?	?
GEORGIA							
1 *Kingston*	Y	Y	Y	Y	Y	Y	?
2 Bishop	N	N	Y	Y	Y	Y	Y
3 *Collins*	Y	Y	Y	Y	Y	Y	N
4 *Linder*	Y	Y	N	Y	Y	Y	Y
5 Lewis	N	N	Y	Y	Y	Y	Y
6 *Gingrich*	Y	Y	N	Y	Y	Y	Y
7 Darden	N	N	Y	Y	Y	Y	Y
8 Rowland	N	N	Y	Y	Y	Y	Y
9 Deal	N	Y	N	Y	Y	Y	N
10 Johnson	N	N	Y	Y	Y	Y	Y
11 McKinney	N	N	Y	Y	Y	Y	Y
HAWAII							
1 Abercrombie	N	N	N	Y	Y	Y	Y
2 Mink	N	N	Y	Y	Y	Y	Y
IDAHO							
1 LaRocco	N	N	Y	Y	Y	Y	Y
2 *Crapo*	Y	Y	N	Y	Y	Y	N
ILLINOIS							
1 Rush	N	N	Y	Y	Y	Y	?
2 Reynolds	N	N	Y	Y	Y	Y	Y
3 Lipinski	N	N	Y	Y	Y	?	Y
4 Gutierrez	N	N	Y	?	Y	?	?
5 Rostenkowski	N	N	Y	Y	Y	Y	Y
6 *Hyde*	Y	Y	Y	Y	Y	C	Y
7 Collins	N	N	Y	Y	Y	Y	#
8 *Crane*	Y	Y	N	Y	N	Y	?
9 Yates	N	N	Y	Y	Y	Y	Y
10 *Porter*	Y	Y	Y	Y	N	Y	Y
11 Sangmeister	N	N	Y	Y	Y	Y	Y
12 Costello	N	N	Y	Y	Y	Y	Y
13 *Fawell*	Y	Y	Y	Y	Y	Y	Y
14 *Hastert*	+	+	+	+	+	+	—
15 *Ewing*	#	#	?	?	?	?	?
16 *Manzullo*	Y	Y	N	Y	Y	Y	Y
17 Evans	N	N	Y	Y	Y	Y	Y

ND Northern Democrats   SD Southern Democrats

	21	22	23	24	25	26	27
18 ***Michel***	?	?	?	?	?	?	?
19 Poshard	N	N	Y	Y	Y	Y	Y
20 Durbin	N	N	Y	Y	Y	Y	Y
INDIANA							
1 Visclosky	N	N	Y	Y	Y	Y	Y
2 Sharp	N	N	Y	?	Y	Y	Y
3 Roemer	N	N	Y	Y	Y	Y	Y
4 Long	N	N	Y	Y	Y	Y	Y
5 ***Buyer***	Y	Y	N	Y	Y	Y	Y
6 ***Burton***	Y	Y	Y	Y	Y	Y	?
7 ***Myers***	Y	Y	Y	Y	Y	Y	N
8 McCloskey	N	N	Y	Y	Y	Y	Y
9 Hamilton	N	N	Y	Y	Y	Y	Y
10 Jacobs	Y	Y	Y	Y	Y	?	?
IOWA							
1 ***Leach***	Y	Y	Y	Y	Y	Y	?
2 ***Nussle***	Y	Y	N	Y	Y	Y	Y
3 ***Lightfoot***	Y	Y	Y	Y	Y	Y	Y
4 Smith	N	N	Y	Y	Y	Y	Y
5 ***Grandy***	Y	Y	Y	Y	Y	Y	?
KANSAS							
1 ***Roberts***	Y	Y	Y	Y	Y	Y	?
2 Slattery	?	?	?	?	?	?	?
3 ***Meyers***	Y	Y	Y	Y	Y	Y	Y
4 Glickman	N	N	Y	Y	Y	Y	?
KENTUCKY							
1 Barlow	N	N	Y	Y	Y	Y	?
2 ***Lewis***							
3 Mazzoli	N	N	Y	Y	Y	Y	Y
4 ***Bunning***	Y	Y	N	Y	Y	Y	N
5 ***Rogers***	Y	Y	Y	Y	N	Y	Y
6 Baesler	N	N	Y	Y	Y	Y	Y
LOUISIANA							
1 ***Livingston***	Y	Y	Y	Y	Y	Y	Y
2 Jefferson	N	N	Y	Y	Y	Y	Y
3 Tauzin	Y	Y	Y	Y	Y	?	?
4 Fields	N	N	Y	Y	Y	Y	Y
5 ***McCrery***	Y	Y	Y	Y	Y	Y	?
6 ***Baker***	Y	Y	Y	Y	Y	Y	?
7 Hayes	N	N	Y	Y	Y	Y	Y
MAINE							
1 Andrews	N	N	Y	Y	Y	Y	Y
2 ***Snowe***	Y	Y	Y	Y	Y	Y	Y
MARYLAND							
1 ***Gilchrest***	Y	Y	Y	Y	Y	Y	N
2 ***Bentley***	Y	Y	Y	Y	Y	Y	Y
3 Cardin	N	N	Y	Y	Y	Y	?
4 Wynn	N	N	Y	Y	Y	Y	Y
5 Hoyer	N	N	Y	Y	Y	Y	Y
6 ***Bartlett***	Y	Y	N	Y	Y	Y	N
7 Mfume	N	N	Y	Y	Y	Y	Y
8 ***Morella***	Y	Y	Y	Y	Y	Y	Y
MASSACHUSETTS							
1 Olver	N	N	Y	Y	Y	Y	Y
2 Neal	N	N	Y	Y	Y	Y	?
3 ***Blute***	Y	Y	Y	Y	Y	Y	Y
4 Frank	N	N	Y	Y	Y	Y	N
5 Meehan	N	N	Y	Y	Y	Y	Y
6 ***Torkildsen***	Y	Y	Y	Y	Y	Y	Y
7 Markey	N	?	Y	Y	Y	Y	Y
8 Kennedy	?	N	Y	Y	Y	Y	Y
9 Moakley	N	N	Y	Y	Y	Y	Y
10 Studds	N	N	Y	Y	Y	Y	Y
MICHIGAN							
1 Stupak	N	N	Y	Y	Y	Y	Y
2 ***Hoekstra***	Y	Y	Y	Y	Y	Y	Y
3 ***Ehlers***	Y	Y	Y	Y	N	Y	N
4 ***Camp***	Y	Y	Y	Y	N	Y	Y
5 Barcia	N	N	Y	Y	Y	Y	Y
6 ***Upton***	Y	Y	Y	Y	Y	Y	Y
7 ***Smith***	Y	Y	Y	Y	N	Y	N
8 Carr	N	N	Y	Y	Y	Y	Y
9 Kildee	N	N	Y	Y	Y	Y	Y
10 Bonior	N	N	Y	Y	Y	Y	Y
11 ***Knollenberg***	Y	Y	Y	Y	Y	Y	Y
12 Levin	N	N	Y	Y	Y	Y	?
13 Ford	N	N	Y	Y	Y	Y	Y
14 Conyers	N	N	Y	Y	Y	Y	Y
15 Collins	N	N	Y	Y	Y	Y	?
16 Dingell	N	N	Y	?	?	?	?
MINNESOTA							
1 Penny	N	N	Y	Y	Y	Y	N
2 Minge	N	N	Y	Y	Y	Y	Y
3 ***Ramstad***	Y	Y	Y	Y	Y	Y	N
4 Vento	N	N	Y	Y	Y	Y	?

	21	22	23	24	25	26	27
5 Sabo	N	N	Y	Y	Y	Y	Y
6 ***Grams***	Y	Y	N	Y	Y	Y	N
7 Peterson	N	N	Y	Y	Y	Y	N
8 Oberstar	N	N	Y	Y	Y	Y	Y
MISSISSIPPI							
1 Whitten	N	N	Y	Y	Y	Y	?
2 Thompson	N	N	Y	Y	Y	Y	Y
3 Montgomery	Y	N	Y	Y	Y	Y	Y
4 Parker	Y	Y	Y	Y	Y	Y	Y
5 Taylor	Y	Y	Y	Y	Y	Y	Y
MISSOURI							
1 Clay	N	N	Y	Y	Y	N	?
2 ***Talent***	Y	Y	—	Y	Y	Y	Y
3 Gephardt	N	N	Y	Y	Y	Y	Y
4 Skelton	Y	Y	Y	Y	Y	Y	Y
5 Wheat	N	N	Y	Y	Y	Y	Y
6 Danner	N	N	Y	Y	Y	Y	Y
7 ***Hancock***	Y	Y	N	Y	N	Y	N
8 ***Emerson***	Y	Y	N	Y	Y	Y	Y
9 Volkmer	N	Y	Y	Y	Y	Y	Y
MONTANA							
AL Williams	N	N	Y	Y	Y	Y	?
NEBRASKA							
1 ***Bereuter***	Y	Y	Y	Y	Y	Y	N
2 Hoagland	N	N	Y	Y	Y	Y	Y
3 ***Barrett***	Y	Y	Y	Y	Y	Y	Y
NEVADA							
1 Bilbray	N	N	Y	Y	Y	Y	Y
2 ***Vucanovich***	Y	Y	Y	Y	Y	Y	Y
NEW HAMPSHIRE							
1 ***Zeliff***	Y	Y	Y	Y	Y	Y	?
2 Swett	N	Y	Y	Y	Y	Y	Y
NEW JERSEY							
1 Andrews	N	N	Y	Y	Y	Y	N
2 Hughes	N	N	Y	Y	Y	Y	?
3 ***Saxton***	Y	Y	Y	Y	Y	Y	Y
4 ***Smith***	Y	Y	Y	Y	Y	Y	Y
5 ***Roukema***	Y	Y	Y	Y	Y	Y	?
6 Pallone	N	N	Y	Y	Y	Y	Y
7 ***Franks***	Y	Y	Y	Y	Y	Y	Y
8 Klein	N	N	Y	Y	Y	Y	Y
9 Torricelli	N	N	Y	Y	Y	Y	?
10 Payne	N	N	Y	Y	Y	Y	Y
11 ***Gallo***	Y	Y	Y	Y	Y	Y	?
12 ***Zimmer***	Y	Y	Y	Y	Y	Y	N
13 Menendez	N	N	Y	Y	Y	Y	N
NEW MEXICO							
1 ***Schiff***	Y	Y	Y	Y	Y	Y	Y
2 ***Skeen***	Y	Y	Y	Y	Y	Y	Y
3 Richardson	N	N	Y	Y	Y	?	?
NEW YORK							
1 Hochbrueckner	N	N	Y	Y	Y	Y	Y
2 ***Lazio***	Y	Y	Y	Y	Y	Y	Y
3 ***King***	N	N	N	Y	Y	Y	N
4 ***Levy***	Y	Y	Y	Y	Y	Y	Y
5 Ackerman	N	N	Y	Y	Y	Y	?
6 Flake	N	N	Y	Y	Y	Y	?
7 Manton	N	N	Y	Y	Y	Y	Y
8 Nadler	N	N	Y	Y	Y	Y	Y
9 Schumer	N	N	Y	Y	Y	Y	?
10 Towns	N	N	Y	?	?	?	?
11 Owens	N	N	Y	?	?	?	?
12 Velazquez	N	N	Y	Y	Y	Y	N
13 ***Molinari***	Y	Y	Y	Y	Y	Y	Y
14 Maloney	N	N	Y	Y	Y	Y	Y
15 Rangel	N	N	Y	Y	Y	Y	Y
16 Serrano	N	N	Y	Y	Y	Y	N
17 Engel	N	N	Y	Y	Y	Y	Y
18 Lowey	N	N	Y	Y	Y	Y	Y
19 ***Fish***	Y	Y	Y	Y	Y	Y	Y
20 ***Gilman***	Y	Y	Y	Y	Y	Y	N
21 McNulty	N	N	N	Y	Y	Y	Y
22 ***Solomon***	Y	Y	N	Y	Y	Y	N
23 ***Boehlert***	Y	Y	Y	Y	Y	Y	?
24 ***McHugh***	Y	Y	Y	Y	Y	Y	Y
25 ***Walsh***	Y	Y	Y	Y	Y	Y	?
26 Hinchey	N	N	Y	Y	Y	Y	Y
27 ***Paxon***	Y	Y	N	Y	Y	Y	N
28 Slaughter	N	N	Y	Y	Y	Y	Y
29 LaFalce	N	N	Y	Y	Y	Y	?
30 ***Quinn***	Y	Y	Y	Y	Y	Y	Y
31 ***Houghton***	Y	Y	N	Y	Y	Y	Y
NORTH CAROLINA							
1 Clayton	?	?	?	Y	Y	Y	Y
2 Valentine	Y	Y	Y	Y	Y	Y	?

	21	22	23	24	25	26	27
3 Lancaster	N	N	Y	Y	Y	Y	Y
4 Price	N	N	Y	Y	Y	Y	Y
5 Neal	?	?	?	?	?	Y	?
6 ***Coble***	Y	Y	N	Y	Y	Y	N
7 Rose	N	N	Y	Y	Y	?	?
8 Hefner	N	N	Y	Y	Y	Y	Y
9 ***McMillan***	?	?	?	Y	Y	?	Y
10 ***Ballenger***	Y	Y	N	Y	Y	Y	N
11 ***Taylor***	Y	Y	N	Y	Y	Y	—
12 Watt	N	N	Y	Y	Y	Y	Y
NORTH DAKOTA							
AL Pomeroy	N	N	Y	Y	Y	Y	Y
OHIO							
1 Mann	N	N	Y	Y	Y	Y	Y
2 ***Portman***	Y	Y	Y	Y	Y	Y	X
3 Hall	N	N	Y	?	?	?	?
4 ***Oxley***	Y	Y	N	Y	Y	Y	N
5 ***Gillmor***	Y	Y	Y	Y	Y	Y	Y
6 Strickland	N	N	Y	Y	Y	Y	Y
7 ***Hobson***	Y	Y	Y	Y	Y	Y	Y
8 ***Boehner***	Y	Y	Y	?	?	?	?
9 Kaptur	N	N	Y	Y	Y	Y	Y
10 ***Hoke***	Y	Y	N	Y	Y	Y	X
11 Stokes	N	N	Y	Y	Y	Y	Y
12 ***Kasich***	Y	Y	Y	Y	N	Y	?
13 Brown	N	N	Y	Y	Y	Y	Y
14 Sawyer	N	N	Y	Y	Y	Y	Y
15 ***Pryce***	Y	Y	Y	Y	Y	Y	Y
16 ***Regula***	Y	Y	Y	Y	Y	Y	Y
17 Traficant	N	N	Y	Y	Y	Y	Y
18 Applegate	N	N	Y	Y	Y	Y	?
19 Fingerhut	N	N	Y	Y	Y	+	X
OKLAHOMA							
1 ***Inhofe***	Y	Y	Y	Y	Y	Y	?
2 Synar	N	N	Y	Y	Y	Y	#
3 Brewster	N	N	Y	Y	Y	Y	?
4 McCurdy	N	N	Y	Y	Y	Y	?
5 ***Istook***	Y	Y	Y	Y	Y	Y	N
6 ***Lucas***							
OREGON							
1 Furse	N	N	Y	Y	Y	Y	Y
2 ***Smith***	Y	Y	Y	Y	Y	?	?
3 Wyden	N	N	Y	Y	Y	Y	Y
4 DeFazio	N	N	Y	Y	Y	?	N
5 Kopetski	N	N	Y	Y	Y	Y	Y
PENNSYLVANIA							
1 Foglietta	N	N	Y	Y	Y	?	Y
2 Blackwell	N	N	Y	Y	Y	Y	Y
3 Borski	N	N	Y	Y	Y	Y	Y
4 Klink	N	N	Y	Y	Y	Y	Y
5 ***Clinger***	Y	Y	Y	Y	Y	Y	?
6 Holden	N	N	Y	Y	Y	Y	Y
7 ***Weldon***	Y	Y	Y	Y	Y	Y	X
8 ***Greenwood***	Y	Y	Y	Y	Y	Y	?
9 ***Shuster***	Y	Y	N	Y	Y	Y	?
10 ***McDade***	Y	Y	Y	Y	Y	Y	Y
11 Kanjorski	N	N	Y	N	Y	Y	Y
12 Murtha	N	N	Y	Y	Y	?	?
13 Margolies-Mezv.	N	N	Y	Y	Y	Y	N
14 Coyne	N	N	Y	Y	Y	Y	Y
15 McHale	N	N	Y	Y	Y	Y	Y
16 ***Walker***	Y	Y	N	Y	Y	Y	N
17 ***Gekas***	Y	Y	N	Y	Y	Y	N
18 ***Santorum***	Y	Y	Y	Y	Y	Y	?
19 ***Goodling***	Y	Y	N	Y	Y	Y	N
20 Murphy	N	N	Y	Y	Y	?	?
21 ***Ridge***	?	?	?	?	?	?	?
RHODE ISLAND							
1 ***Machtley***	Y	Y	Y	?	?	?	?
2 Reed	N	N	Y	Y	Y	Y	?
SOUTH CAROLINA							
1 ***Ravenel***	Y	Y	Y	Y	Y	Y	Y
2 ***Spence***	Y	Y	Y	Y	Y	Y	Y
3 Derrick	N	N	Y	Y	Y	Y	Y
4 ***Inglis***	Y	Y	N	Y	Y	Y	Y
5 Spratt	N	N	Y	Y	Y	Y	Y
6 Clyburn	N	N	Y	Y	Y	Y	Y
SOUTH DAKOTA							
AL Johnson	N	N	Y	Y	Y	Y	Y
TENNESSEE							
1 ***Quillen***	Y	Y	N	Y	Y	?	X
2 ***Duncan***	Y	Y	N	Y	N	Y	?
3 Lloyd	?	N	Y	Y	Y	Y	?
4 Cooper	Y	N	Y	Y	Y	Y	?
5 Clement	N	N	Y	Y	Y	Y	Y

	21	22	23	24	25	26	27
6 Gordon	N	N	Y	Y	Y	Y	?
7 ***Sundquist***	Y	Y	N	Y	Y	Y	?
8 Tanner	N	N	Y	Y	Y	Y	Y
9 Ford	N	N	Y	Y	Y	Y	Y
TEXAS							
1 Chapman	N	N	Y	Y	Y	Y	Y
2 Wilson	Y	N	Y	Y	Y	Y	?
3 ***Johnson, Sam***	Y	Y	N	Y	N	Y	N
4 Hall	Y	Y	Y	Y	Y	Y	Y
5 Bryant	N	N	Y	Y	Y	Y	?
6 ***Barton***	Y	Y	N	Y	N	Y	?
7 ***Archer***	Y	Y	N	Y	N	Y	N
8 ***Fields***	?	?	?	?	?	?	?
9 Brooks	N	N	Y	?	?	?	?
10 Pickle	Y	N	Y	Y	Y	Y	?
11 Edwards	N	N	Y	Y	Y	Y	Y
12 Geren	Y	Y	Y	Y	Y	Y	?
13 Sarpalius	N	N	Y	Y	Y	Y	Y
14 Laughlin	?	?	?	?	?	?	?
15 de la Garza	?	?	?	?	?	?	?
16 Coleman	?	?	?	?	?	?	?
17 Stenholm	Y	Y	Y	Y	Y	Y	N
18 Washington	X	X	?	?	?	?	?
19 ***Combest***	Y	Y	Y	Y	Y	Y	?
20 Gonzalez	N	N	Y	Y	Y	Y	N
21 ***Smith***	Y	Y	Y	Y	Y	Y	N
22 ***DeLay***	Y	Y	N	Y	N	Y	N
23 ***Bonilla***	Y	Y	N	Y	Y	Y	N
24 Frost	N	N	Y	Y	Y	Y	?
25 Andrews	?	X	?	?	?	?	?
26 ***Armey***	Y	Y	N	Y	N	Y	#
27 Ortiz	N	N	Y	?	?	?	?
28 Tejeda	N	N	Y	Y	Y	Y	Y
29 Green	N	N	Y	Y	Y	Y	#
30 Johnson, E.B.	N	N	Y	Y	Y	Y	Y
UTAH							
1 ***Hansen***	Y	Y	N	Y	Y	Y	?
2 Shepherd	N	Y	Y	Y	Y	Y	Y
3 Orton	N	N	Y	Y	Y	?	?
VERMONT							
AL *Sanders*	N	N	Y	Y	Y	Y	Y
VIRGINIA							
1 ***Bateman***	Y	Y	Y	Y	Y	Y	Y
2 Pickett	N	N	Y	Y	Y	Y	Y
3 Scott	N	N	Y	?	Y	Y	Y
4 Sisisky	N	N	Y	Y	Y	Y	Y
5 Payne	N	N	Y	Y	Y	Y	?
6 ***Goodlatte***	Y	Y	Y	Y	Y	Y	N
7 ***Bliley***	Y	Y	N	Y	Y	Y	N
8 Moran	N	N	Y	Y	Y	Y	Y
9 Boucher	N	N	Y	Y	Y	Y	?
10 ***Wolf***	Y	Y	Y	Y	Y	Y	Y
11 Byrne	N	Y	Y	Y	Y	Y	?
WASHINGTON							
1 Cantwell	N	N	Y	Y	Y	Y	Y
2 Swift	N	N	Y	Y	Y	Y	?
3 Unsoeld	N	N	Y	Y	Y	Y	Y
4 Inslee	N	N	Y	Y	Y	Y	Y
5 Foley							
6 Dicks	N	N	Y	Y	Y	Y	Y
7 McDermott	N	N	Y	Y	Y	Y	Y
8 ***Dunn***	Y	Y	Y	Y	Y	Y	Y
9 Kreidler	N	N	Y	Y	Y	Y	Y
WEST VIRGINIA							
1 Mollohan	N	N	Y	Y	Y	Y	Y
2 Wise	N	N	Y	Y	Y	Y	Y
3 Rahall	N	N	Y	Y	Y	Y	?
WISCONSIN							
1 Barca	N	N	Y	Y	Y	Y	Y
2 ***Klug***	Y	Y	Y	Y	Y	Y	Y
3 ***Gunderson***	Y	Y	Y	Y	Y	Y	Y
4 Kleczka	N	N	Y	Y	Y	Y	Y
5 Barrett	N	N	Y	Y	Y	Y	Y
6 ***Petri***	Y	Y	Y	Y	Y	Y	N
7 Obey	N	N	Y	Y	Y	Y	Y
8 ***Roth***	Y	Y	?	?	?	?	X
9 ***Sensenbrenner***	Y	Y	N	Y	N	Y	N
WYOMING							
AL ***Thomas***	Y	Y	Y	Y	Y	Y	?
DELEGATES							
de Lugo, V.I.	N	D	D	Y	D	D	D
Faleomavaega, Am.S.	N	D	D	Y	D	D	D
Norton, D.C.	N	D	D	Y	D	D	D
Romero-B., P.R.	N	D	D	Y	D	D	D
Underwood, Guam	N	D	D	Y	D	D	D

Southern states - Ala., Ark., Fla., Ga., Ky., La., Miss., N.C., Okla., S.C., Tenn., Texas, Va.
Omitted votes are quorum calls, which CQ does not include in its vote charts.

KEY

Y   Voted for (yea).
\#   Paired for.
\+   Announced for.
N   Voted against (nay).
X   Paired against.
–   Announced against.
P   Voted "present."
C   Voted "present" to avoid possible conflict of interest.
?   Did not vote or otherwise make a position known.
D   Delegates ineligible to vote.

Democrats   *Republicans*
Independent

---

28. Procedural Motion. Approval of the House Journal of Tuesday, Feb. 22. Approved 250-160: R 15-156; D 234-4 (ND 157-4; SD 77-0); I 1-0, Feb. 23, 1994.

29. H Res 343. Condemning Nation of Islam Spokesman's Speech/Adoption. Adoption of the resolution to express the sense of the House condemning the "hate-mongering" and "vicious" speech given by Khalid Abdul Muhammad at Kean College in Union, N.J., on Nov. 29, 1993, and condemn all anti-Semitic, anti-Catholic and racist forms of expression. Adopted 361-34: R 169-2; D 192-31 (ND 126-22, SD 66-9); I 0-1, Feb. 23, 1994.

30. HR 1804. Goals 2000: Educate America/School Prayer. Duncan, R-Tenn., motion to instruct the House conferees to accept the Senate provisions regarding school prayer. The Senate had voted to deny federal school aid to state or local agencies that prohibit constitutionally protected voluntary prayer in public schools. Motion agreed to 367-55: R 174-0; D 192-55 (ND 120-49, SD 72-6); I 1-0, Feb. 23, 1994.

31. HR 6. Elementary and Secondary Education Reauthorization/Home Schooling. Ford, D-Mich., amendment to strike provisions in the bill that impose teacher certification requirements on states seeking federal money and insert language providing that nothing in the bill shall affect home schooling. Adopted in the Committee of the Whole 424-1: R 176-0 (ND 169-1, SD 78-0); I 1-0, Feb. 24, 1994.

32. HR 6. Elementary and Secondary Education Reauthorization/Home Schooling. Armey, R-Texas, amendment to provide that nothing in the bill shall permit federal control over any aspect of a private, religious or home school, but that this section shall not be construed to bar such schools from participating in the bill's programs. Adopted in the Committee of the Whole 374-53: R 176-0; D 197-53 (ND 128-45, SD 69-8); I 1-0, Feb. 24, 1994.

33. HR 6. Elementary and Secondary Education Reauthorization/Opportunity to Learn. Kildee, D-Mich., en bloc amendment to make mostly technical changes to the bill. It also included a bipartisan compromise on opportunity-to-learn standards, clarifying that the standards are voluntary, not mandated, narrowing the list of standards, limiting the paperwork burden on schools and educational agencies, and barring lawsuits to enforce the standards. Adopted in the Committee of the Whole 422-1: R 175-0; D 246-1 (ND 169-1, SD 77-0); I 1-0, Feb. 24, 1994.

	28	29	30	31	32	33
ALABAMA						
1 *Callahan*	N	Y	Y	Y	Y	Y
2 Everett	Y	Y	Y	Y	Y	Y
3 Browder	Y	Y	Y	Y	Y	Y
4 Bevill	Y	Y	Y	Y	Y	Y
5 Cramer	Y	Y	Y	Y	Y	Y
6 *Bachus*	N	Y	Y	Y	Y	Y
7 Hilliard	Y	?	?	Y	N	Y
ALASKA						
AL *Young*	N	Y	Y	Y	Y	Y
ARIZONA						
1 Coppersmith	Y	Y	N	Y	Y	Y
2 Pastor	Y	P	Y	Y	Y	Y
3 *Stump*	N	Y	Y	Y	Y	Y
4 *Kyl*	N	Y	Y	Y	Y	Y
5 *Kolbe*	N	Y	Y	Y	Y	Y
6 English	Y	Y	Y	Y	Y	Y
ARKANSAS						
1 Lambert	Y	Y	Y	Y	Y	Y
2 Thornton	Y	?	Y	Y	Y	Y
3 *Hutchinson*	N	Y	Y	Y	Y	Y
4 *Dickey*	N	Y	Y	Y	Y	Y
CALIFORNIA						
1 Hamburg	Y	N	N	Y	N	Y
2 *Herger*	N	Y	Y	Y	Y	Y
3 Fazio	Y	P	Y	Y	Y	Y
4 *Doolittle*	N	Y	Y	Y	Y	Y
5 Matsui	Y	Y	Y	N	Y	N
6 Woolsey	Y	Y	Y	Y	Y	Y
7 Miller	Y	N	N	N	N	Y
8 Pelosi	Y	Y	N	Y	N	Y
9 Dellums	Y	N	N	Y	N	Y
10 *Baker*	N	Y	Y	Y	Y	Y
11 *Pombo*	Y	Y	Y	Y	Y	Y
12 Lantos	Y	Y	N	Y	N	Y
13 Stark	Y	N	Y	N	Y	N
14 Eshoo	Y	Y	N	Y	N	Y
15 Mineta	Y	Y	N	Y	N	Y
16 Edwards	Y	N	N	Y	N	Y
17 Farr	Y	Y	Y	Y	Y	Y
18 Condit	Y	P	Y	Y	Y	Y
19 Lehman	Y	Y	Y	Y	Y	Y
20 Dooley	Y	N	Y	Y	Y	Y
21 *Thomas*	N	P	Y	Y	Y	Y
22 *Huffington*	N	Y	Y	Y	Y	Y
23 *Gallegly*	N	Y	Y	Y	Y	Y
24 Beilenson	Y	P	N	Y	Y	Y
25 *McKeon*	N	Y	Y	Y	Y	Y
26 Berman	Y	Y	N	Y	Y	Y
27 *Moorhead*	N	Y	Y	Y	Y	Y
28 *Dreier*	N	Y	Y	Y	Y	Y
29 Waxman	Y	Y	N	Y	Y	Y
30 Becerra	Y	P	N	Y	N	Y
31 Martinez	Y	Y	Y	Y	Y	Y
32 Dixon	Y	Y	Y	Y	Y	Y
33 Royal-Allard	Y	Y	N	Y	N	Y
34 Torres	Y	Y	Y	Y	Y	Y
35 Waters	Y	N	N	?	N	Y
36 Harman	Y	Y	Y	Y	Y	Y
37 Tucker	Y	Y	Y	Y	Y	Y
38 *Horn*	N	Y	Y	Y	Y	Y
39 *Royce*	N	Y	Y	Y	Y	Y
40 *Lewis*	N	P	Y	Y	Y	Y
41 *Kim*	N	Y	Y	Y	Y	Y
42 Brown	?	Y	Y	Y	Y	Y
43 *Calvert*	N	Y	Y	Y	Y	Y
44 *McCandless*	N	Y	Y	Y	Y	Y
45 *Rohrabacher*	N	Y	Y	Y	Y	Y
46 *Dornan*	?	P	Y	Y	Y	Y
47 *Cox*	N	Y	Y	Y	Y	Y
48 *Packard*	N	Y	Y	Y	Y	Y
49 Schenk	Y	Y	Y	Y	Y	Y
50 Filner	Y	N	N	Y	Y	Y
51 *Cunningham*	N	Y	Y	Y	Y	Y
52 *Hunter*	N	Y	Y	Y	Y	Y
COLORADO						
1 Schroeder	?	P	Y	Y	Y	Y
2 Skaggs	Y	N	Y	Y	Y	Y
3 *McInnis*	Y	Y	Y	Y	Y	Y
4 *Allard*	N	Y	Y	Y	Y	Y
5 *Hefley*	N	Y	Y	Y	Y	Y
6 *Schaefer*	N	Y	Y	Y	Y	Y
CONNECTICUT						
1 Kennelly	Y	Y	Y	?	?	?
2 Gejdenson	Y	Y	N	+	+	+
3 DeLauro	Y	Y	Y	Y	Y	Y
4 *Shays*	N	Y	Y	Y	Y	Y
5 *Franks*	N	Y	Y	Y	Y	Y
6 *Johnson*	N	Y	Y	Y	Y	Y
DELAWARE						
AL *Castle*	N	Y	Y	Y	Y	Y
FLORIDA						
1 Hutto	Y	Y	Y	Y	Y	Y
2 Peterson	Y	Y	Y	Y	Y	Y
3 Brown	Y	Y	Y	Y	Y	Y
4 *Fowler*	N	Y	Y	Y	Y	Y
5 Thurman	Y	Y	Y	Y	Y	Y
6 *Stearns*	N	Y	Y	Y	Y	Y
7 *Mica*	N	Y	Y	Y	Y	Y
8 *McCollum*	N	Y	Y	Y	Y	Y
9 *Bilirakis*	N	Y	Y	Y	Y	Y
10 *Young*	N	Y	Y	Y	Y	Y
11 Gibbons	Y	Y	Y	Y	Y	Y
12 *Canady*	N	Y	Y	Y	Y	Y
13 *Miller*	N	Y	Y	Y	Y	Y
14 *Goss*	N	Y	Y	Y	Y	Y
15 Bacchus	Y	Y	Y	Y	Y	Y
16 *Lewis*	N	Y	Y	Y	Y	Y
17 Meek	Y	Y	Y	Y	N	Y
18 *Ros-Lehtinen*	N	Y	Y	Y	Y	Y
19 Johnston	Y	Y	Y	Y	Y	Y
20 Deutsch	Y	Y	Y	Y	Y	Y
21 *Diaz-Balart*	N	Y	Y	Y	Y	Y
22 *Shaw*	N	Y	Y	Y	Y	Y
23 Hastings	?	?	?	?	?	?
GEORGIA						
1 *Kingston*	Y	Y	Y	Y	Y	Y
2 Bishop	Y	Y	Y	Y	Y	Y
3 *Collins*	N	Y	Y	Y	Y	Y
4 *Linder*	N	Y	Y	Y	Y	Y
5 Lewis	Y	Y	Y	Y	N	Y
6 *Gingrich*	N	Y	Y	Y	Y	Y
7 Darden	Y	Y	Y	Y	Y	Y
8 Rowland	?	Y	Y	Y	Y	Y
9 Deal	Y	Y	Y	Y	Y	Y
10 Johnson	Y	Y	Y	Y	Y	Y
11 McKinney	Y	N	Y	Y	Y	Y
HAWAII						
1 Abercrombie	Y	N	N	Y	N	Y
2 Mink	Y	Y	N	Y	N	Y
IDAHO						
1 LaRocco	Y	P	Y	Y	Y	Y
2 *Crapo*	N	Y	Y	Y	Y	Y
ILLINOIS						
1 Rush	?	N	Y	Y	?	?
2 Reynolds	Y	Y	Y	N	Y	Y
3 Lipinski	Y	Y	Y	Y	Y	Y
4 Gutierrez	Y	Y	Y	Y	Y	Y
5 Rostenkowski	Y	Y	N	Y	Y	Y
6 *Hyde*	Y	Y	Y	Y	Y	?
7 Collins	Y	Y	N	Y	N	Y
8 *Crane*	N	Y	Y	Y	Y	Y
9 Yates	Y	Y	N	Y	N	Y
10 *Porter*	N	Y	Y	Y	Y	Y
11 Sangmeister	Y	Y	Y	Y	Y	Y
12 Costello	Y	Y	Y	Y	Y	Y
13 *Fawell*	N	Y	Y	Y	Y	Y
14 *Hastert*	N	Y	Y	Y	Y	Y
15 *Ewing*	N	Y	Y	Y	Y	Y
16 *Manzullo*	N	Y	Y	Y	Y	Y
17 Evans	Y	Y	Y	Y	Y	Y

ND   Northern Democrats   SD   Southern Democrats

	28	29	30	31	32	33
18 ***Michel***	N	Y	Y	Y	Y	Y
19 Poshard	Y	Y	Y	Y	Y	Y
20 Durbin	Y	N	N	Y	Y	N
INDIANA						
1 Visclosky	Y	Y	Y	Y	N	Y
2 Sharp	Y	Y	Y	Y	Y	Y
3 Roemer	Y	Y	Y	Y	Y	Y
4 Long	Y	Y	Y	Y	Y	Y
5 ***Buyer***	N	Y	Y	Y	Y	Y
6 ***Burton***	N	Y	Y	Y	Y	Y
7 ***Myers***	Y	Y	Y	Y	Y	Y
8 McCloskey	Y	P	Y	Y	Y	Y
9 Hamilton	Y	Y	Y	Y	Y	Y
10 Jacobs	N	Y	Y	Y	Y	Y
IOWA						
1 ***Leach***	N	Y	Y	Y	Y	Y
2 ***Nussle***	N	Y	Y	Y	Y	Y
3 ***Lightfoot***	N	Y	Y	Y	Y	Y
4 Smith	Y	Y	Y	Y	Y	Y
5 ***Grandy***	N	Y	Y	Y	Y	Y
KANSAS						
1 ***Roberts***	N	N	Y	Y	Y	Y
2 Slattery	Y	Y	Y	Y	Y	Y
3 ***Meyers***	N	Y	Y	Y	Y	Y
4 Glickman	Y	Y	Y	Y	Y	Y
KENTUCKY						
1 Barlow	Y	Y	Y	Y	Y	Y
2 Natcher	Y	Y	Y	Y	N	Y
3 Mazzoli	Y	N	Y	Y	Y	Y
4 ***Bunning***	N	Y	Y	Y	Y	Y
5 ***Rogers***	N	Y	Y	Y	Y	Y
6 Baesler	Y	Y	Y	Y	Y	Y
LOUISIANA						
1 ***Livingston***	N	Y	Y	Y	Y	Y
2 Jefferson	Y	Y	Y	Y	Y	Y
3 Tauzin	Y	Y	Y	Y	Y	Y
4 Fields	Y	N	Y	Y	Y	Y
5 ***McCrery***	N	Y	Y	Y	Y	Y
6 ***Baker***	N	Y	Y	Y	Y	Y
7 Hayes	Y	Y	Y	Y	Y	Y
MAINE						
1 Andrews	Y	Y	N	Y	Y	Y
2 ***Snowe***	N	Y	Y	Y	Y	Y
MARYLAND						
1 ***Gilchrest***	N	Y	Y	Y	Y	Y
2 ***Bentley***	N	Y	Y	Y	Y	Y
3 Cardin	Y	Y	N	Y	Y	Y
4 Wynn	Y	Y	Y	Y	Y	Y
5 Hoyer	Y	Y	Y	Y	Y	Y
6 ***Bartlett***	N	Y	Y	Y	Y	Y
7 Mfume	Y	P	N	Y	Y	Y
8 ***Morella***	N	Y	Y	Y	Y	Y
MASSACHUSETTS						
1 Olver	Y	Y	N	Y	N	Y
2 Neal	Y	Y	Y	Y	Y	Y
3 ***Blute***	N	Y	Y	Y	Y	Y
4 Frank	Y	Y	N	Y	N	Y
5 Meehan	Y	Y	Y	Y	Y	Y
6 ***Torkildsen***	N	Y	Y	Y	Y	Y
7 Markey	Y	Y	Y	Y	Y	?
8 Kennedy	?	?	?	?	?	?
9 Moakley	Y	Y	Y	Y	Y	Y
10 Studds	Y	P	Y	Y	Y	Y
MICHIGAN						
1 Stupak	Y	P	Y	Y	Y	Y
2 ***Hoekstra***	N	Y	Y	Y	Y	Y
3 ***Ehlers***	N	Y	Y	Y	Y	Y
4 ***Camp***	N	Y	Y	Y	Y	Y
5 Barcia	?	Y	Y	Y	Y	Y
6 ***Upton***	N	Y	Y	Y	Y	Y
7 ***Smith***	N	Y	Y	Y	Y	Y
8 Carr	Y	Y	Y	Y	N	Y
9 Kildee	Y	Y	Y	Y	N	Y
10 Bonior	Y	P	Y	Y	Y	Y
11 ***Knollenberg***	N	Y	Y	Y	Y	Y
12 Levin	Y	Y	Y	Y	Y	Y
13 Ford	Y	P	N	Y	N	Y
14 Conyers	Y	Y	N	Y	N	Y
15 Collins	Y	P	N	Y	N	Y
16 Dingell	Y	Y	N	Y	N	Y
MINNESOTA						
1 Penny	Y	N	Y	Y	Y	Y
2 Minge	Y	Y	Y	Y	Y	Y
3 ***Ramstad***	N	Y	Y	Y	Y	Y
4 Vento	Y	Y	N	Y	N	Y

	28	29	30	31	32	33
5 Sabo	Y	Y	N	Y	Y	Y
6 ***Grams***	N	Y	Y	Y	Y	Y
7 Peterson	Y	Y	Y	Y	Y	Y
8 Oberstar	Y	Y	Y	Y	Y	Y
MISSISSIPPI						
1 Whitten	?	Y	Y	Y	Y	Y
2 Thompson	Y	N	Y	Y	Y	Y
3 Montgomery	Y	Y	Y	Y	Y	Y
4 Parker	Y	Y	Y	Y	Y	Y
5 Taylor	Y	Y	Y	Y	Y	Y
MISSOURI						
1 Clay	N	N	N	Y	N	?
2 ***Talent***	N	Y	Y	Y	Y	Y
3 Gephardt	Y	Y	Y	Y	Y	Y
4 Skelton	Y	Y	Y	Y	Y	Y
5 Wheat	?	Y	Y	Y	Y	Y
6 Danner	Y	Y	Y	Y	Y	Y
7 ***Hancock***	N	Y	Y	Y	Y	Y
8 ***Emerson***	N	N	Y	Y	Y	Y
9 Volkmer	Y	Y	Y	Y	Y	Y
MONTANA						
AL Williams	Y	P	Y	Y	Y	Y
NEBRASKA						
1 ***Bereuter***	N	Y	Y	Y	Y	Y
2 Hoagland	Y	Y	Y	Y	Y	Y
3 ***Barrett***	N	Y	Y	Y	Y	Y
NEVADA						
1 Bilbray	Y	Y	Y	Y	Y	Y
2 ***Vucanovich***	N	Y	Y	Y	Y	Y
NEW HAMPSHIRE						
1 ***Zeliff***	N	Y	Y	Y	Y	Y
2 Swett	Y	Y	Y	Y	Y	Y
NEW JERSEY						
1 Andrews	Y	Y	Y	Y	Y	Y
2 Hughes	Y	P	Y	Y	Y	Y
3 ***Saxton***	N	Y	Y	Y	Y	Y
4 ***Smith***	N	Y	Y	Y	Y	Y
5 ***Roukema***	N	Y	Y	Y	Y	Y
6 Pallone	Y	Y	Y	Y	Y	Y
7 ***Franks***	N	Y	Y	Y	Y	Y
8 Klein	Y	Y	Y	Y	Y	Y
9 Torricelli	Y	Y	Y	Y	Y	Y
10 Payne	Y	N	N	Y	N	Y
11 ***Gallo***	N	Y	Y	Y	Y	Y
12 ***Zimmer***	N	Y	Y	Y	Y	Y
13 Menendez	Y	Y	Y	Y	Y	Y
NEW MEXICO						
1 ***Schiff***	N	Y	Y	Y	Y	Y
2 ***Skeen***	N	Y	Y	Y	Y	Y
3 Richardson	Y	Y	Y	Y	Y	Y
NEW YORK						
1 Hochbrueckner	Y	Y	Y	Y	Y	Y
2 ***Lazio***	N	Y	Y	Y	Y	Y
3 ***King***	N	Y	Y	Y	Y	Y
4 ***Levy***	N	Y	Y	Y	Y	Y
5 Ackerman	Y	Y	N	Y	N	Y
6 Flake	?	?	?	Y	Y	Y
7 Manton	?	Y	Y	Y	Y	Y
8 Nadler	Y	Y	N	Y	N	Y
9 Schumer	Y	Y	Y	Y	Y	Y
10 Towns	Y	N	N	Y	N	Y
11 Owens	Y	Y	N	Y	N	Y
12 Velazquez	Y	Y	N	Y	N	Y
13 ***Molinari***	N	Y	Y	Y	Y	Y
14 Maloney	Y	Y	Y	Y	Y	Y
15 Rangel	Y	Y	?	Y	N	Y
16 Serrano	Y	Y	N	Y	Y	Y
17 Engel	?	Y	Y	Y	Y	Y
18 Lowey	Y	Y	Y	Y	Y	Y
19 ***Fish***	?	Y	Y	Y	Y	Y
20 ***Gilman***	Y	Y	Y	Y	Y	Y
21 McNulty	Y	Y	Y	Y	Y	Y
22 ***Solomon***	N	Y	Y	Y	Y	Y
23 ***Boehlert***	N	Y	Y	Y	Y	Y
24 ***McHugh***	N	Y	Y	Y	Y	Y
25 ***Walsh***	N	Y	Y	Y	Y	Y
26 Hinchey	Y	Y	Y	Y	Y	Y
27 ***Paxon***	N	Y	Y	Y	Y	Y
28 Slaughter	Y	Y	Y	Y	Y	Y
29 LaFalce	Y	Y	Y	Y	Y	Y
30 ***Quinn***	N	Y	Y	Y	Y	Y
31 ***Houghton***	Y	Y	Y	Y	Y	Y
NORTH CAROLINA						
1 Clayton	Y	P	Y	Y	Y	Y
2 Valentine	Y	N	Y	Y	Y	Y

	28	29	30	31	32	33
3 Lancaster	Y	Y	Y	Y	Y	Y
4 Price	Y	Y	Y	Y	Y	Y
5 Neal	Y	Y	Y	Y	Y	Y
6 ***Coble***	N	Y	Y	Y	Y	Y
7 Rose	Y	P	Y	Y	Y	Y
8 Hefner	Y	Y	Y	Y	Y	Y
9 ***McMillan***	N	Y	Y	Y	Y	Y
10 ***Ballenger***	N	Y	Y	Y	Y	Y
11 ***Taylor***	N	Y	Y	Y	Y	Y
12 Watt	Y	N	N	Y	N	Y
NORTH DAKOTA						
AL Pomeroy	Y	Y	Y	Y	Y	Y
OHIO						
1 Mann	Y	Y	Y	Y	Y	Y
2 ***Portman***	N	Y	Y	Y	Y	Y
3 Hall	Y	Y	Y	Y	Y	Y
4 ***Oxley***	N	Y	Y	Y	Y	Y
5 ***Gillmor***	Y	Y	Y	Y	Y	Y
6 Strickland	Y	P	Y	Y	Y	Y
7 ***Hobson***	N	Y	Y	Y	Y	Y
8 ***Boehner***	N	Y	Y	Y	Y	Y
9 Kaptur	Y	Y	Y	Y	Y	Y
10 ***Hoke***	?	Y	Y	Y	Y	Y
11 Stokes	Y	Y	N	Y	N	Y
12 ***Kasich***	Y	Y	Y	Y	Y	Y
13 Brown	Y	Y	Y	Y	Y	Y
14 Sawyer	Y	P	Y	Y	N	Y
15 ***Pryce***	N	Y	Y	Y	Y	Y
16 ***Regula***	N	Y	Y	Y	Y	Y
17 Traficant	Y	P	Y	Y	Y	Y
18 Applegate	?	Y	Y	Y	Y	Y
19 Fingerhut	Y	Y	Y	Y	Y	Y
OKLAHOMA						
1 ***Inhofe***	N	Y	Y	Y	Y	Y
2 Synar	Y	N	N	?	X	?
3 Brewster	Y	Y	?	Y	Y	Y
4 McCurdy	Y	Y	Y	Y	Y	Y
5 ***Istook***	N	Y	Y	Y	Y	Y
6 Vacancy						
OREGON						
1 Furse	Y	Y	Y	Y	Y	Y
2 ***Smith***	?	?	?	Y	Y	Y
3 Wyden	Y	Y	Y	Y	Y	Y
4 DeFazio	Y	Y	Y	Y	Y	Y
5 Kopetski	Y	N	N	Y	N	Y
PENNSYLVANIA						
1 Foglietta	Y	Y	Y	Y	N	Y
2 Blackwell	?	Y	Y	Y	N	Y
3 Borski	Y	Y	Y	Y	Y	Y
4 Klink	Y	Y	Y	Y	Y	Y
5 ***Clinger***	Y	Y	Y	Y	Y	Y
6 Holden	Y	Y	Y	Y	Y	Y
7 ***Weldon***	N	Y	Y	Y	Y	Y
8 ***Greenwood***	Y	Y	Y	Y	Y	Y
9 ***Shuster***	N	Y	Y	Y	Y	Y
10 ***McDade***	N	Y	Y	Y	Y	Y
11 Kanjorski	Y	N	Y	Y	Y	Y
12 Murtha	Y	Y	Y	Y	?	?
13 Margolies-Mezv.	Y	Y	Y	Y	Y	Y
14 Coyne	Y	Y	N	Y	N	Y
15 McHale	Y	Y	Y	Y	Y	Y
16 ***Walker***	N	Y	Y	Y	Y	Y
17 ***Gekas***	N	Y	Y	Y	Y	Y
18 ***Santorum***	N	Y	Y	Y	Y	Y
19 ***Goodling***	—	+	+	Y	Y	Y
20 Murphy	N	P	Y	Y	Y	Y
21 ***Ridge***	N	Y	Y	Y	Y	Y
RHODE ISLAND						
1 ***Machtley***	N	Y	Y	Y	Y	Y
2 Reed	Y	Y	Y	Y	Y	Y
SOUTH CAROLINA						
1 ***Ravenel***	N	Y	Y	Y	Y	Y
2 ***Spence***	N	Y	Y	Y	Y	Y
3 Derrick	Y	Y	Y	Y	Y	Y
4 ***Inglis***	Y	Y	Y	Y	Y	Y
5 Spratt	Y	Y	Y	Y	Y	Y
6 Clyburn	Y	Y	Y	Y	Y	Y
SOUTH DAKOTA						
AL Johnson	Y	Y	Y	Y	Y	Y
TENNESSEE						
1 ***Quillen***	N	Y	Y	Y	Y	Y
2 ***Duncan***	N	Y	Y	Y	Y	Y
3 Lloyd	Y	Y	Y	Y	Y	Y
4 Cooper	Y	Y	Y	Y	Y	Y
5 Clement	Y	Y	Y	Y	Y	Y

	28	29	30	31	32	33
6 Gordon	Y	Y	Y	Y	Y	Y
7 ***Sundquist***	N	Y	Y	Y	Y	Y
8 Tanner	Y	P	Y	Y	Y	Y
9 Ford	Y	P	Y	Y	Y	Y
TEXAS						
1 Chapman	Y	Y	Y	Y	Y	Y
2 Wilson	?	?	?	?	#	?
3 ***Johnson, Sam***	N	Y	Y	Y	Y	Y
4 Hall	Y	Y	Y	Y	Y	Y
5 Bryant	Y	Y	Y	Y	Y	Y
6 ***Barton***	N	Y	Y	Y	Y	Y
7 ***Archer***	N	Y	Y	Y	Y	Y
8 ***Fields***	N	Y	Y	Y	Y	Y
9 Brooks	Y	Y	Y	Y	Y	Y
10 Pickle	Y	Y	Y	Y	Y	Y
11 Edwards	Y	Y	Y	Y	Y	Y
12 Geren	Y	Y	Y	Y	Y	Y
13 Sarpalius	Y	Y	Y	Y	Y	Y
14 Laughlin	Y	Y	Y	Y	?	?
15 de la Garza	?	Y	?	Y	Y	Y
16 Coleman	Y	Y	Y	Y	Y	Y
17 Stenholm	Y	Y	Y	Y	Y	Y
18 Washington	?	N	N	?	?	?
19 ***Combest***	Y	Y	Y	Y	Y	Y
20 Gonzalez	Y	N	N	Y	N	Y
21 ***Smith***	N	Y	Y	Y	Y	Y
22 ***DeLay***	N	Y	Y	Y	Y	Y
23 ***Bonilla***	N	Y	Y	Y	Y	Y
24 Frost	Y	Y	Y	Y	Y	Y
25 Andrews	?	?	?	?	?	?
26 ***Armey***	N	Y	Y	Y	Y	Y
27 Ortiz	Y	Y	Y	Y	Y	Y
28 Tejeda	Y	Y	Y	Y	Y	Y
29 Green	Y	Y	Y	+	+	+
30 Johnson, E.B.	Y	Y	Y	Y	Y	Y
UTAH						
1 ***Hansen***	N	Y	Y	Y	Y	Y
2 Shepherd	Y	Y	Y	Y	Y	Y
3 Orton	Y	P	Y	Y	Y	Y
VERMONT						
AL *Sanders*	Y	N	Y	Y	Y	Y
VIRGINIA						
1 ***Bateman***	Y	Y	Y	Y	Y	Y
2 Pickett	Y	Y	Y	Y	Y	Y
3 Scott	Y	Y	N	Y	Y	Y
4 Sisisky	Y	Y	Y	Y	Y	Y
5 Payne	Y	Y	Y	Y	Y	Y
6 ***Goodlatte***	N	Y	Y	Y	Y	Y
7 ***Bliley***	N	Y	Y	Y	Y	Y
8 Moran	Y	Y	Y	Y	N	Y
9 Boucher	Y	Y	Y	Y	Y	Y
10 ***Wolf***	N	Y	Y	Y	Y	Y
11 Byrne	Y	Y	Y	Y	Y	Y
WASHINGTON						
1 Cantwell	Y	Y	Y	Y	Y	Y
2 Swift	Y	N	N	Y	N	Y
3 Unsoeld	Y	N	N	Y	N	Y
4 Inslee	Y	N	Y	Y	Y	Y
5 Foley					Y	
6 Dicks	Y	Y	Y	Y	Y	Y
7 McDermott	Y	P	N	+	N	Y
8 ***Dunn***	N	Y	Y	Y	Y	Y
9 Kreidler	N	Y	Y	Y	Y	Y
WEST VIRGINIA						
1 Mollohan	Y	Y	Y	Y	Y	Y
2 Wise	Y	Y	Y	Y	Y	Y
3 Rahall	Y	Y	Y	Y	Y	Y
WISCONSIN						
1 Barca	Y	Y	Y	Y	Y	Y
2 ***Klug***	N	Y	Y	Y	Y	Y
3 ***Gunderson***	N	Y	Y	Y	Y	Y
4 Kleczka	Y	N	N	Y	Y	Y
5 Barrett	Y	Y	Y	Y	Y	Y
6 ***Petri***	N	Y	Y	Y	Y	Y
7 Obey	Y	Y	Y	Y	Y	Y
8 ***Roth***	N	Y	Y	Y	Y	Y
9 ***Sensenbrenner***	N	Y	Y	Y	Y	Y
WYOMING						
AL ***Thomas***	N	Y	Y	Y	Y	Y
DELEGATES						
de Lugo, V.I.	D	D	D	+	N	Y
Faleomavaega, Am.S.	D	D	D	?	Y	Y
Norton, D.C.	D	D	D	Y	N	Y
Romero-B., P.R.	D	D	D	Y	N	Y
Underwood, Guam	D	D	D	Y	Y	Y

Southern states - Ala., Ark., Fla., Ga., Ky., La., Miss., N.C., Okla., S.C., Tenn., Texas, Va.
Omitted votes are quorum calls, which CQ does not include in its vote charts.

34. Procedural Motion. Approval of the House Journal of Tuesday, March 1. Approved 262-154: R 22-149; D 239-5 (ND 162-4, SD 77-1); I 1-0, March 2, 1994.

35. HR 6. Elementary and Secondary Education Reauthorization/Excess Title I Money. Romero-Barceló, D/NPP-Puerto Rico, amendment to phase out over five years the cap on Title I money for Puerto Rico. Title I provides grants to school districts to help educationally disadvantaged students, who tend to come from high-poverty areas. Rejected in the Committee of the Whole 70-358: R 2-171; D 68-186 (ND 50-125, SD 18-61); I 0-1, March 2, 1994.

36. H Res 375. House Post Office Investigation/Gephardt Resolution. Adoption of the resolution to defer further House inquiry into alleged misconduct at the House Post Office and continue to consult with the U.S. attorney as to when such an inquiry no longer would interfere with any ongoing criminal investigation. Adopted 241-184: R 0-173; D 240-11 (ND 166-5, SD 74-6); I 1-0, March 2, 1994.

37. H Res 238. House Post Office Investigation/Istook Resolution. Gephardt, D-Mo., motion to table, and thus kill, the Istook, R-Okla., resolution to instruct the Committee on Standards of Official Conduct to immediately investigate all possible violations at the House Post Office in coordination with the Department of Justice so as to not jeopardize any ongoing criminal investigations. Motion agreed to 238-186: R 2-171; D 235-15 (ND 164-6, SD 71-9); I 1-0, March 2, 1994.

38. Procedural Motion. Approval of the House Journal of Wednesday, March 2. Approved 250-153: R 17-147; D 232-6 (ND 160-5, SD 72-1); I 1-0, March 3, 1994.

39. HR 6. Elementary and Secondary Education Reauthorization/Excess Title I Money. Romero-Barceló, D/NPP-Puerto Rico, amendment to increase the weighting factor from 1.62 to 2.5 for the distribution of excess Title I money to Puerto Rico. Title I provides grants to school districts, particularly high-poverty districts. Rejected in the Committee of the Whole 76-340: R 4-167; D 72-172 (ND 56-112, SD 16-60); I 0-1, March 3, 1994.

40. HR 6. Elementary and Secondary Education Reauthorization/Transition Projects. Boehner, R-Ohio, amendment to eliminate the innovative elementary school transition projects in the bill. Title I provides grants to school districts, particularly high-poverty districts. Rejected in the Committee of the Whole 128-292: R 114-57; D 14-234 (ND 10-163, SD 4-71); I 0-1, March 3, 1994.

41. HR 6. Elementary and Secondary Education Reauthorization/Illegal Aliens. Rohrabacher, R-Calif., amendment to require Title I schools to report on the number of enrolled students who are illegally in the United States or who do not have at least one parent who is a legal resident of the United States. Rejected in the Committee of the Whole 78-329: R 77-86; D 1-242 (ND 0-167, SD 1-75); I 0-1, March 3, 1994.

KEY

Y	Voted for (yea).
#	Paired for.
+	Announced for.
N	Voted against (nay).
X	Paired against.
−	Announced against.
P	Voted "present."
C	Voted "present" to avoid possible conflict of interest.
?	Did not vote or otherwise make a position known.
D	Delegates ineligible to vote.

Democrats *Republicans*
Independent

	34	35	36	37	38	39	40	41
ALABAMA								
1 Callahan	Y	N	N	N	N	N	Y	Y
2 *Everett*	Y	N	N	N	Y	N	N	Y
3 Browder	Y	N	Y	Y	Y	N	N	N
4 Bevill	Y	N	Y	Y	Y	N	N	N
5 Cramer	Y	N	Y	Y	Y	N	N	N
6 *Bachus*	N	N	N	N	N	N	Y	Y
7 Hilliard	Y	Y	Y	Y	?	N	Y	N
ALASKA								
AL *Young*	N	N	N	N	N	Y	N	N
ARIZONA								
1 Coppersmith	Y	N	Y	Y	Y	N	N	N
2 Pastor	Y	Y	Y	Y	Y	Y	N	N
3 *Stump*	N	N	N	N	N	N	Y	Y
4 *Kyl*	N	N	N	N	N	N	Y	N
5 *Kolbe*	N	N	N	N	N	N	Y	N
6 English	Y	N	Y	Y	Y	N	N	N
ARKANSAS								
1 Lambert	Y	N	Y	Y	Y	N	N	N
2 Thornton	Y	N	Y	Y	Y	?	N	N
3 *Hutchinson*	N	N	N	N	N	N	N	N
4 *Dickey*	N	N	N	N	N	N	Y	N
CALIFORNIA								
1 Hamburg	?	Y	Y	Y	Y	Y	N	N
2 *Herger*	N	N	N	N	N	N	Y	Y
3 Fazio	Y	N	Y	Y	Y	Y	N	N
4 *Doolittle*	N	N	N	N	N	N	Y	Y
5 Matsui	Y	N	Y	Y	Y	N	N	N
6 Woolsey	Y	Y	Y	Y	Y	N	N	N
7 Miller	Y	N	Y	Y	Y	N	N	X
8 Pelosi	Y	Y	Y	Y	Y	Y	N	N
9 Dellums	Y	Y	Y	Y	Y	?	N	?
10 *Baker*	N	N	N	N	N	N	N	Y
11 *Pombo*	Y	N	N	N	N	N	Y	Y
12 Lantos	Y	N	Y	Y	Y	N	N	N
13 Stark	Y	N	Y	Y	Y	Y	N	N
14 Eshoo	Y	N	Y	Y	Y	N	N	N
15 Mineta	Y	N	Y	Y	Y	N	N	N
16 Edwards	Y	N	Y	Y	Y	N	N	N
17 Farr	Y	N	Y	Y	Y	N	N	N
18 Condit	Y	N	Y	Y	Y	N	Y	N
19 Lehman	Y	N	Y	Y	Y	N	Y	N
20 Dooley	Y	N	Y	Y	Y	N	N	N
21 *Thomas*	N	N	N	N	N	N	Y	#
22 *Huffington*	N	N	N	N	N	N	N	N
23 *Gallegly*	N	N	N	N	N	N	N	Y
24 Beilenson	Y	N	Y	Y	Y	N	N	N
25 *McKeon*	N	N	N	N	N	N	Y	N
26 Berman	Y	N	Y	Y	Y	N	N	N
27 *Moorhead*	N	N	N	N	N	N	N	N
28 *Dreier*	N	N	N	N	N	N	Y	Y
29 Waxman	Y	Y	Y	Y	Y	N	N	N
30 Becerra	Y	Y	Y	Y	Y	Y	N	N
31 Martinez	Y	Y	Y	Y	Y	?	N	N
32 Dixon	Y	N	Y	Y	Y	N	N	N
33 Roybal-Allard	Y	Y	Y	Y	Y	N	N	N
34 Torres	Y	Y	Y	Y	Y	N	N	N
35 Waters	Y	Y	Y	Y	Y	N	N	N
36 Harman	Y	N	Y	Y	Y	N	N	?
37 Tucker	Y	Y	Y	Y	Y	N	N	N
38 *Horn*	N	N	N	N	N	N	N	N
39 *Royce*	N	N	N	N	N	N	Y	Y
40 *Lewis*	N	N	N	N	N	N	N	N
41 *Kim*	N	N	N	N	N	N	N	Y

	34	35	36	37	38	39	40	41
42 Brown	?	N	Y	Y	?	N	N	N
43 *Calvert*	N	N	N	N	N	N	N	N
44 *McCandless*	N	N	N	N	N	N	N	N
45 *Rohrabacher*	N	N	N	N	N	N	Y	Y
46 *Dornan*	N	N	N	N	N	N	Y	Y
47 *Cox*	N	N	N	N	N	N	Y	Y
48 *Packard*	N	N	N	N	N	N	Y	Y
49 Schenk	Y	N	Y	Y	Y	N	N	N
50 Filner	Y	Y	Y	Y	Y	Y	N	N
51 *Cunningham*	N	N	N	N	N	N	Y	Y
52 *Hunter*	N	N	N	N	N	N	Y	Y
COLORADO								
1 Schroeder	N	N	Y	Y	N	N	N	N
2 Skaggs	Y	N	Y	Y	Y	N	N	N
3 *McInnis*	N	N	N	N	?	N	Y	Y
4 *Allard*	N	N	N	N	N	N	Y	Y
5 *Hefley*	N	N	N	N	N	N	Y	Y
6 *Schaefer*	N	N	N	N	N	N	Y	Y
CONNECTICUT								
1 Kennelly	Y	N	Y	Y	Y	N	N	N
2 Gejdenson	Y	N	Y	Y	Y	N	N	N
3 DeLauro	Y	N	Y	Y	Y	N	N	N
4 *Shays*	N	N	N	N	N	N	N	N
5 *Franks*	N	N	N	N	N	N	N	Y
6 *Johnson*	N	N	N	N	N	N	N	?
DELAWARE								
AL *Castle*	N	N	N	N	N	N	N	N
FLORIDA								
1 Hutto	Y	N	Y	N	Y	N	N	N
2 Peterson	Y	N	Y	Y	Y	N	N	N
3 Brown	Y	N	Y	Y	Y	N	N	N
4 *Fowler*	N	N	N	N	N	N	N	Y
5 Thurman	Y	N	Y	Y	Y	N	N	N
6 *Stearns*	N	N	N	N	N	N	Y	Y
7 *Mica*	N	N	N	N	N	N	N	Y
8 *McCollum*	N	N	N	N	N	N	N	N
9 *Bilirakis*	N	N	N	N	N	N	N	N
10 *Young*	N	N	N	N	N	N	N	N
11 Gibbons	Y	N	Y	Y	Y	N	N	N
12 *Canady*	N	N	N	N	N	N	N	N
13 *Miller*	N	N	N	N	N	N	Y	Y
14 *Goss*	N	N	N	N	N	N	Y	Y
15 Bacchus	Y	N	Y	Y	Y	N	N	N
16 *Lewis*	N	N	N	N	N	N	N	N
17 Meek	Y	Y	Y	Y	Y	N	N	N
18 *Ros-Lehtinen*	N	Y	N	N	Y	N	N	N
19 Johnston	Y	N	Y	Y	Y	N	?	N
20 Deutsch	Y	Y	Y	Y	Y	N	N	N
21 *Diaz-Balart*	N	Y	N	N	Y	N	N	N
22 *Shaw*	N	N	N	N	N	N	Y	N
23 Hastings	?	?	?	?	?	?	?	?
GEORGIA								
1 *Kingston*	Y	N	N	N	N	N	Y	Y
2 Bishop	Y	Y	Y	Y	Y	N	N	N
3 *Collins*	N	N	N	N	N	N	Y	Y
4 *Linder*	N	N	N	N	N	N	Y	Y
5 Lewis	Y	Y	Y	Y	Y	N	N	N
6 *Gingrich*	N	N	N	N	N	N	Y	Y
7 Darden	Y	N	Y	Y	Y	N	N	N
8 Rowland	Y	N	Y	Y	Y	N	N	N
9 Deal	Y	N	N	Y	N	N	Y	Y
10 Johnson	Y	N	Y	Y	Y	N	N	N
11 McKinney	Y	Y	Y	Y	Y	Y	N	N
HAWAII								
1 Abercrombie	Y	Y	Y	Y	Y	Y	N	N
2 Mink	Y	Y	Y	Y	Y	Y	N	N
IDAHO								
1 LaRocco	Y	N	Y	Y	Y	N	N	N
2 *Crapo*	N	N	N	N	N	?	Y	Y
ILLINOIS								
1 Rush	Y	N	Y	Y	Y	N	N	N
2 Reynolds	Y	Y	Y	Y	Y	Y	N	N
3 Lipinski	Y	N	Y	Y	Y	N	N	N
4 Gutierrez	Y	Y	Y	Y	Y	Y	N	N
5 Rostenkowski	Y	N	Y	Y	?	?	?	?
6 *Hyde*	Y	N	N	N	Y	N	N	N
7 Collins	?	?	#	#	?	#	?	?
8 *Crane*	?	N	N	N	Y	N	N	N
9 Yates	Y	N	Y	#	Y	N	N	N
10 *Porter*	N	N	N	N	Y	N	N	N
11 Sangmeister	Y	N	Y	Y	Y	N	N	N
12 Costello	Y	N	Y	Y	Y	N	N	N
13 *Fawell*	N	N	N	N	N	N	N	N
14 *Hastert*	N	N	N	N	N	N	Y	Y
15 *Ewing*	N	N	N	N	N	N	Y	Y
16 *Manzullo*	Y	N	N	N	N	N	N	N
17 Evans	Y	N	Y	Y	Y	N	N	N

ND Northern Democrats   SD Southern Democrats

	34	35	36	37	38	39	40	41
18 ***Michel***	N	N	N	N	N	N	?	Y
19 Poshard	Y	N	Y	Y	Y	N	N	N
20 Durbin	Y	N	Y	Y	Y	N	N	N
INDIANA								
1 Visclosky	Y	N	Y	Y	Y	N	N	N
2 Sharp	Y	N	Y	Y	Y	?	N	N
3 Roemer	Y	N	Y	Y	Y	N	N	N
4 Long	Y	N	Y	Y	Y	N	N	N
5 ***Buyer***	?	N	N	N	N	N	Y	Y
6 ***Burton***	N	N	N	N	N	N	Y	Y
7 ***Myers***	Y	N	N	N	Y	N	Y	Y
8 McCloskey	Y	N	Y	Y	Y	N	N	N
9 Hamilton	Y	N	N	N	Y	N	N	N
10 Jacobs	N	N	Y	N	N	N	N	N
IOWA								
1 ***Leach***	N	N	N	N	N	N	N	N
2 ***Nussle***	N	N	N	N	N	N	Y	N
3 ***Lightfoot***	N	N	N	N	N	N	N	N
4 Smith	Y	Y	Y	Y	Y	Y	N	N
5 ***Grandy***	N	N	N	N	N	N	N	?
KANSAS								
1 ***Roberts***	N	N	N	N	N	N	Y	N
2 Slattery	Y	N	Y	Y	Y	N	N	N
3 ***Meyers***	N	N	N	N	N	N	N	Y
4 Glickman	Y	N	Y	Y	Y	N	Y	N
KENTUCKY								
1 Barlow	Y	N	Y	Y	Y	N	N	N
2 Natcher	Y	N	Y	Y	?	?	?	?
3 Mazzoli	Y	N	N	N	Y	N	N	N
4 ***Bunning***	N	N	N	N	N	N	Y	Y
5 ***Rogers***	N	N	N	N	N	N	N	Y
6 Baesler	Y	N	Y	Y	Y	N	N	N
LOUISIANA								
1 ***Livingston***	N	N	N	N	?	N	Y	N
2 Jefferson	Y	Y	Y	Y	?	Y	?	?
3 Tauzin	Y	N	Y	Y	Y	N	N	N
4 Fields	Y	Y	Y	Y	Y	Y	N	N
5 ***McCrery***	Y	N	N	N	?	N	Y	N
6 ***Baker***	N	N	N	N	N	N	Y	Y
7 Hayes	Y	N	Y	Y	Y	N	N	N
MAINE								
1 Andrews	Y	Y	Y	Y	Y	Y	N	N
2 ***Snowe***	Y	N	N	N	N	N	N	N
MARYLAND								
1 ***Gilchrest***	N	N	N	N	N	N	N	N
2 ***Bentley***	N	N	N	N	N	N	N	N
3 Cardin	Y	N	Y	Y	Y	N	Y	N
4 Wynn	Y	Y	Y	Y	Y	Y	N	N
5 Hoyer	Y	Y	Y	Y	Y	N	N	N
6 ***Bartlett***	N	N	N	N	N	N	Y	Y
7 Mfume	Y	Y	Y	Y	Y	Y	N	N
8 ***Morella***	N	N	N	N	N	N	N	N
MASSACHUSETTS								
1 Olver	Y	Y	Y	Y	Y	Y	N	N
2 Neal	Y	N	Y	Y	Y	N	N	N
3 ***Blute***	N	N	N	N	N	N	N	N
4 Frank	Y	N	Y	Y	Y	Y	N	N
5 Meehan	Y	N	Y	Y	Y	N	N	?
6 ***Torkildsen***	N	N	N	N	?	N	N	N
7 Markey	Y	N	Y	Y	Y	N	N	N
8 Kennedy	Y	Y	Y	Y	Y	Y	N	N
9 Moakley	Y	N	Y	Y	Y	N	N	N
10 Studds	Y	N	Y	Y	Y	N	N	N
MICHIGAN								
1 Stupak	Y	N	Y	Y	Y	N	N	N
2 ***Hoekstra***	N	N	N	N	N	N	Y	N
3 ***Ehlers***	N	N	N	N	N	N	N	N
4 ***Camp***	N	N	N	N	N	N	N	N
5 Barcia	Y	N	Y	Y	Y	N	N	N
6 ***Upton***	N	N	N	N	N	N	N	N
7 ***Smith***	N	N	N	N	N	N	Y	N
8 Carr	Y	N	Y	Y	Y	N	N	N
9 Kildee	Y	N	Y	Y	Y	N	N	N
10 Bonior	Y	N	Y	Y	?	X	?	N
11 ***Knollenberg***	N	N	N	N	N	N	Y	N
12 Levin	Y	N	Y	Y	Y	N	N	N
13 Ford	Y	N	Y	Y	?	N	N	N
14 Conyers	Y	Y	Y	Y	Y	Y	N	N
15 Collins	Y	N	Y	Y	Y	Y	N	N
16 Dingell	Y	N	Y	Y	Y	N	N	N
MINNESOTA								
1 Penny	Y	N	N	N	Y	N	Y	N
2 Minge	Y	N	Y	Y	Y	N	Y	N
3 ***Ramstad***	N	N	N	N	N	N	Y	N
4 Vento	Y	Y	Y	Y	Y	Y	N	N
5 Sabo	Y	N	Y	Y	?	N	N	N
6 ***Grams***	N	N	N	N	N	N	Y	Y
7 Peterson	Y	N	N	N	Y	N	Y	N
8 Oberstar	Y	N	Y	Y	Y	N	N	N
MISSISSIPPI								
1 Whitten	?	?	Y	Y	?	N	N	N
2 Thompson	Y	Y	Y	Y	Y	Y	N	N
3 Montgomery	Y	N	Y	Y	Y	N	N	N
4 Parker	Y	N	N	N	Y	N	N	N
5 Taylor	N	N	Y	Y	N	N	N	N
MISSOURI								
1 Clay	N	Y	Y	Y	N	Y	N	N
2 ***Talent***	N	N	N	N	N	N	Y	N
3 Gephardt	Y	N	Y	Y	Y	N	N	N
4 Skelton	Y	N	Y	Y	Y	N	N	N
5 Wheat	Y	N	Y	Y	Y	Y	N	N
6 Danner	Y	Y	Y	Y	Y	N	N	N
7 ***Hancock***	N	N	N	N	N	N	Y	Y
8 ***Emerson***	N	N	N	N	N	N	Y	N
9 Volkmer	Y	N	Y	Y	Y	N	N	N
MONTANA								
AL Williams	Y	N	Y	Y	Y	N	N	N
NEBRASKA								
1 ***Bereuter***	N	N	N	N	N	N	N	Y
2 Hoagland	Y	N	Y	Y	Y	N	N	N
3 ***Barrett***	N	N	N	N	N	N	Y	N
NEVADA								
1 Bilbray	Y	N	Y	Y	Y	N	Y	N
2 ***Vucanovich***	N	N	N	N	N	N	N	?
NEW HAMPSHIRE								
1 ***Zeliff***	N	N	N	N	N	N	Y	Y
2 Swett	Y	N	N	N	Y	N	N	N
NEW JERSEY								
1 Andrews	Y	N	Y	Y	Y	?	N	N
2 Hughes	Y	N	Y	Y	Y	N	N	N
3 ***Saxton***	N	N	N	N	N	N	N	N
4 ***Smith***	Y	N	N	N	N	N	N	N
5 ***Roukema***	N	N	N	N	N	N	Y	N
6 Pallone	Y	Y	Y	Y	Y	Y	N	N
7 ***Franks***	N	N	N	N	N	N	Y	Y
8 Klein	Y	N	Y	Y	Y	N	N	N
9 Torricelli	Y	N	Y	Y	Y	N	N	N
10 Payne	Y	N	Y	Y	Y	Y	N	N
11 ***Gallo***	N	?	X	X	?	?	?	?
12 ***Zimmer***	N	N	N	N	N	N	Y	Y
13 Menendez	Y	Y	Y	Y	Y	Y	N	N
NEW MEXICO								
1 ***Schiff***	?	?	X	X	?	?	?	?
2 ***Skeen***	N	N	N	N	N	N	N	N
3 Richardson	Y	Y	Y	Y	Y	Y	N	N
NEW YORK								
1 Hochbrueckner	Y	N	Y	Y	Y	N	N	N
2 ***Lazio***	N	N	N	N	N	N	N	N
3 ***King***	N	N	N	N	Y	N	Y	N
4 ***Levy***	N	N	N	N	N	N	N	N
5 Ackerman	Y	Y	Y	Y	Y	Y	N	N
6 Flake	Y	Y	Y	Y	Y	Y	N	N
7 Manton	Y	N	Y	Y	Y	N	N	N
8 Nadler	Y	Y	Y	Y	Y	Y	N	N
9 Schumer	Y	Y	Y	Y	Y	Y	N	N
10 Towns	Y	Y	Y	Y	Y	?	N	N
11 Owens	Y	Y	Y	Y	?	Y	N	N
12 Velazquez	Y	Y	Y	Y	Y	Y	N	N
13 ***Molinari***	N	N	N	N	N	N	N	Y
14 Maloney	Y	N	Y	Y	Y	N	N	N
15 Rangel	?	Y	Y	Y	Y	Y	N	N
16 Serrano	Y	Y	Y	Y	Y	Y	N	N
17 Engel	Y	Y	Y	Y	Y	Y	N	N
18 Lowey	Y	N	Y	Y	Y	N	N	N
19 ***Fish***	?	N	N	N	?	N	N	N
20 ***Gilman***	Y	N	N	N	Y	N	N	N
21 McNulty	Y	N	Y	Y	Y	N	N	?
22 ***Solomon***	N	N	N	N	N	N	Y	Y
23 ***Boehlert***	N	N	N	N	N	N	N	N
24 ***McHugh***	N	N	N	N	N	N	Y	Y
25 ***Walsh***	N	N	N	N	N	N	N	N
26 Hinchey	Y	N	Y	Y	Y	N	N	N
27 ***Paxon***	N	N	N	N	N	N	Y	Y
28 Slaughter	Y	N	Y	Y	Y	N	N	N
29 LaFalce	Y	N	Y	Y	Y	N	N	N
30 ***Quinn***	N	N	N	N	N	N	N	N
31 ***Houghton***	Y	N	N	Y	Y	?	N	N
NORTH CAROLINA								
1 Clayton	Y	Y	Y	Y	Y	Y	N	N
2 Valentine	Y	N	Y	Y	Y	N	N	N
3 Lancaster	Y	N	Y	Y	Y	N	N	N
4 Price	Y	N	Y	Y	Y	N	N	N
5 Neal	Y	N	Y	Y	Y	N	N	N
6 ***Coble***	N	N	N	N	N	N	Y	Y
7 Rose	Y	N	Y	Y	Y	N	N	N
8 Hefner	Y	N	Y	Y	Y	N	N	N
9 ***McMillan***	N	N	N	N	N	N	Y	N
10 ***Ballenger***	N	N	N	N	N	N	Y	Y
11 ***Taylor***	N	N	N	N	N	N	#	#
12 Watt	Y	Y	Y	Y	Y	Y	N	N
NORTH DAKOTA								
AL Pomeroy	Y	N	Y	Y	Y	N	N	N
OHIO								
1 Mann	Y	N	Y	Y	Y	N	N	N
2 ***Portman***	N	N	N	N	N	N	Y	N
3 Hall	Y	N	Y	Y	Y	N	N	N
4 ***Oxley***	N	N	N	N	Y	N	Y	Y
5 ***Gillmor***	Y	N	N	N	Y	N	N	N
6 Strickland	Y	N	Y	Y	Y	N	N	N
7 ***Hobson***	N	N	N	N	N	N	Y	N
8 ***Boehner***	N	N	N	N	N	N	Y	Y
9 Kaptur	?	N	Y	Y	Y	N	?	N
10 ***Hoke***	N	N	N	N	N	N	Y	N
11 Stokes	Y	N	Y	Y	Y	Y	N	N
12 ***Kasich***	Y	N	N	N	Y	N	N	N
13 Brown	Y	N	Y	Y	Y	N	N	N
14 Sawyer	Y	N	Y	Y	Y	N	N	N
15 ***Pryce***	N	N	N	N	N	N	Y	N
16 ***Regula***	N	N	N	N	N	N	N	N
17 Traficant	Y	N	Y	Y	Y	N	N	N
18 Applegate	Y	N	Y	Y	Y	N	N	?
19 Fingerhut	Y	N	Y	Y	Y	—	Y	N
OKLAHOMA								
1 ***Inhofe***	N	N	N	N	N	N	Y	N
2 Synar	Y	N	Y	Y	Y	N	N	N
3 Brewster	Y	N	Y	Y	Y	N	N	N
4 McCurdy	Y	N	Y	Y	Y	N	N	N
5 ***Istook***	N	N	N	N	N	N	N	Y
6 Vacancy								
OREGON								
1 Furse	Y	N	Y	Y	Y	N	N	?
2 ***Smith***	N	N	N	N	N	N	Y	Y
3 Wyden	Y	N	Y	Y	Y	N	N	N
4 DeFazio	Y	N	Y	Y	Y	N	N	N
5 Kopetski	Y	Y	Y	Y	Y	N	N	N
PENNSYLVANIA								
1 Foglietta	Y	Y	Y	Y	Y	Y	N	N
2 Blackwell	Y	N	Y	Y	Y	Y	N	N
3 Borski	Y	N	Y	Y	Y	N	N	N
4 Klink	Y	N	Y	Y	Y	N	N	N
5 ***Clinger***	Y	N	N	N	Y	N	Y	?
6 Holden	Y	N	Y	Y	Y	N	N	N
7 ***Weldon***	N	N	N	N	N	N	Y	N
8 ***Greenwood***	Y	N	N	N	Y	N	Y	?
9 ***Shuster***	N	N	N	N	N	N	Y	Y
10 ***McDade***	?	?	?	?	?	?	?	?
11 Kanjorski	Y	N	Y	Y	Y	N	Y	N
12 Murtha	Y	N	Y	Y	Y	N	N	N
13 Margolies-Mezv.	Y	N	N	N	Y	N	N	N
14 Coyne	Y	N	Y	Y	Y	N	N	N
15 McHale	Y	N	Y	Y	Y	N	N	N
16 ***Walker***	N	N	N	N	N	N	Y	Y
17 ***Gekas***	N	N	N	N	N	N	Y	N
18 ***Santorum***	Y	N	N	N	N	N	Y	N
19 ***Goodling***	N	N	N	N	N	N	N	N
20 Murphy	N	Y	Y	Y	N	Y	N	N
21 ***Ridge***	N	N	N	N	N	N	N	N
RHODE ISLAND								
1 ***Machtley***	N	N	N	N	N	N	N	N
2 Reed	Y	N	Y	Y	Y	N	N	N
SOUTH CAROLINA								
1 ***Ravenel***	Y	N	N	N	N	N	Y	Y
2 ***Spence***	N	N	N	N	N	N	N	Y
3 Derrick	Y	N	Y	Y	Y	N	N	N
4 ***Inglis***	Y	N	N	N	Y	N	Y	N
5 Spratt	Y	N	Y	Y	Y	N	N	N
6 Clyburn	Y	Y	Y	Y	Y	Y	N	N
SOUTH DAKOTA								
AL Johnson	Y	N	Y	Y	Y	N	N	N
TENNESSEE								
1 ***Quillen***	N	N	N	N	N	N	Y	?
2 ***Duncan***	N	N	N	N	N	N	Y	Y
3 Lloyd	Y	N	Y	Y	Y	N	N	N
4 Cooper	Y	N	N	N	Y	N	N	N
5 Clement	Y	N	Y	Y	Y	N	N	N
6 Gordon	Y	N	Y	Y	Y	N	N	N
7 ***Sundquist***	N	N	N	N	N	N	N	N
8 Tanner	Y	N	Y	Y	Y	N	N	N
9 Ford	Y	N	Y	Y	Y	?	N	N
TEXAS								
1 Chapman	Y	N	Y	Y	Y	N	N	N
2 Wilson	Y	N	Y	Y	Y	N	N	N
3 ***Johnson, Sam***	N	N	N	N	N	N	Y	Y
4 Hall	Y	N	N	N	Y	N	Y	N
5 Bryant	Y	N	Y	Y	Y	N	N	N
6 ***Barton***	N	N	N	N	Y	N	Y	N
7 ***Archer***	N	N	N	N	?	N	Y	Y
8 ***Fields***	N	N	N	N	?	N	Y	Y
9 Brooks	Y	N	Y	Y	Y	N	N	N
10 Pickle	Y	N	Y	Y	Y	N	N	N
11 Edwards	Y	N	Y	Y	Y	N	N	N
12 Geren	Y	N	Y	Y	Y	N	Y	N
13 Sarpalius	Y	N	Y	Y	Y	N	N	N
14 Laughlin	Y	N	Y	Y	Y	N	?	?
15 de la Garza	?	?	?	?	?	?	?	?
16 Coleman	?	N	Y	Y	Y	N	N	N
17 Stenholm	Y	N	N	N	Y	N	Y	N
18 Washington	?	?	?	?	?	?	?	?
19 ***Combest***	Y	N	N	N	Y	N	Y	Y
20 Gonzalez	Y	Y	Y	Y	Y	Y	N	N
21 ***Smith***	N	N	N	N	N	N	Y	Y
22 ***DeLay***	N	N	N	N	N	N	Y	Y
23 ***Bonilla***	N	N	N	N	N	N	Y	N
24 Frost	Y	N	Y	Y	Y	N	N	N
25 Andrews	?	?	#	?	?	?	?	?
26 ***Armey***	N	N	N	N	N	N	Y	Y
27 Ortiz	Y	Y	Y	Y	Y	Y	N	N
28 Tejeda	Y	Y	Y	Y	Y	Y	N	N
29 Green	Y	Y	Y	Y	?	?	X	X
30 Johnson, E.B.	Y	Y	Y	Y	Y	Y	N	N
UTAH								
1 ***Hansen***	N	N	N	N	?	N	Y	N
2 Shepherd	Y	N	Y	Y	Y	N	N	N
3 Orton	Y	N	Y	Y	Y	N	N	N
VERMONT								
AL *Sanders*	Y	N	Y	Y	Y	N	N	N
VIRGINIA								
1 ***Bateman***	Y	N	N	N	Y	N	Y	?
2 Pickett	Y	N	Y	Y	Y	N	N	N
3 Scott	Y	Y	Y	Y	?	Y	N	N
4 Sisisky	Y	N	Y	Y	Y	N	N	N
5 Payne	Y	N	Y	Y	Y	N	N	N
6 ***Goodlatte***	N	N	N	N	N	N	Y	Y
7 ***Bliley***	N	N	N	N	N	N	Y	?
8 Moran	Y	N	Y	Y	?	N	N	N
9 Boucher	Y	N	Y	Y	Y	N	N	N
10 ***Wolf***	N	N	N	N	N	N	N	N
11 Byrne	Y	N	Y	N	Y	N	N	N
WASHINGTON								
1 Cantwell	Y	N	Y	Y	Y	N	N	N
2 Swift	Y	N	Y	Y	Y	N	N	N
3 Unsoeld	Y	N	Y	Y	Y	Y	N	N
4 Inslee	?	N	Y	Y	Y	N	N	N
5 Foley								
6 Dicks	Y	N	Y	Y	Y	N	N	?
7 McDermott	Y	N	Y	Y	Y	Y	N	N
8 ***Dunn***	N	N	N	N	N	N	Y	Y
9 Kreidler	Y	N	Y	Y	N	N	N	N
WEST VIRGINIA								
1 Mollohan	Y	N	Y	Y	Y	Y	N	N
2 Wise	Y	?	Y	Y	Y	N	N	N
3 Rahall	Y	N	Y	Y	Y	N	N	N
WISCONSIN								
1 Barca	Y	N	Y	Y	Y	N	N	N
2 ***Klug***	N	N	N	N	N	N	N	N
3 ***Gunderson***	N	N	N	N	N	N	N	N
4 Kleczka	Y	N	Y	Y	Y	N	N	N
5 Barrett	Y	N	Y	Y	Y	N	N	N
6 ***Petri***	N	N	N	N	N	N	Y	Y
7 Obey	Y	Y	Y	Y	Y	Y	N	N
8 ***Roth***	N	N	N	N	N	N	Y	Y
9 ***Sensenbrenner***	N	N	N	N	N	N	Y	Y
WYOMING								
AL ***Thomas***	N	N	N	N	N	N	Y	N
DELEGATES								
de Lugo, V.I.	D	Y	D	D	D	Y	N	N
Faleomavaega, Am.S.	D	Y	D	D	D	Y	N	N
Norton, D.C.	D	Y	D	D	D	Y	N	N
Romero-B., P.R.	D	Y	D	D	D	Y	N	N
Underwood, Guam	D	Y	D	D	D	Y	N	N

Southern states - Ala., Ark., Fla., Ga., Ky., La., Miss., N.C., Okla., S.C., Tenn., Texas, Va.
Omitted votes are quorum calls, which CQ does not include in its vote charts.

KEY

Y Voted for (yea).
\# Paired for.
+ Announced for.
N Voted against (nay).
X Paired against.
− Announced against.
P Voted "present."
C Voted "present" to avoid possible conflict of interest.
? Did not vote or otherwise make a position known.
D Delegates ineligible to vote.

Democrats   ***Republicans***
Independent

42. Procedural Motion. Approval of the House Journal of Monday, March 7. Approved 211-132: R 19-128; D 191-4 (ND 134-3, SD 57-1); I 1-0, March 8, 1994.

43. HR 6. Elementary and Secondary Education Reauthorization/Hawaiian Education Programs Cut. Boehner, R-Ohio, amendment to cut $13.5 million for Hawaiian education programs, which were not part of the Clinton administration's reauthorization proposal. Rejected in the Committee of the Whole 203-213: R 166-5; D 37-207 (ND 15-154, SD 22-53); I 0-1, March 9, 1994.

44. HR 6. Elementary and Secondary Education Reauthorization/Territorial Education Improvement Cut. Boehner, R-Ohio, amendment to cut $5 million for education programs in the Virgin Islands, Guam and American Samoa. The Clinton administration's reauthorization proposal did not include this provision, which was inserted at the committee level. Rejected in the Committee of the Whole 202-220: R 168-4; D 34-215 (ND 16-156, SD 18-59); I 0-1, March 9, 1994.

45. HR 6. Elementary and Secondary Education Reauthorization/DARE. Kildee, D-Mich., amendment to the Owens, D-N.Y., substitute amendment, to preserve 10 percent of a governor's grant under the Drug-Free Schools and Communities program for the Drug Abuse Resistance Education Program (DARE). Adopted in the Committee of the Whole 425-0: R 172-0; D 252-0 (ND 174-0, SD 78-0); I 1-0, March 9, 1994.

46. HR 6. Elementary and Secondary Education Reauthorization/Substitute. Owens, D-N.Y., substitute amendment, as authorized by the Kildee amendment, to the Barrett, R-Neb., amendment, to authorize $100 million in fiscal 1995 and such sums as necessary in fiscal 1996-99 for the Drug-Free Schools and Communities program. The Barrett amendment would reserve 20 percent of a state's allotment and require governors to create a long-term plan for the use of the money with 10 percent of that money going to Drug Abuse Resistance Education (DARE) program for local police efforts in school drug education. Rejected in the Committee of the Whole 125-296: R 3-168; D 121-128 (ND 93-77, SD 28-51); I 1-0, March 9, 1994.

47. HR 6. Elementary and Secondary Education Reauthorization/Drug-Free Schools and Communities Program. Barrett, R-Neb., amendment to reserve 20 percent of a state's allotment under the Drug-Free Schools and Communities Program and require governors to create a long-term plan for the use of the money with 10 percent of that money going to Drug Abuse Resistance Education (DARE) program for local police efforts in school drug education. Adopted in the Committee of the Whole 418-1: R 171-0; D 246-1 (ND 168-1, SD 78-0); I 1-0, March 9, 1994.

*49. HR 6. Elementary and Secondary Education Reauthorization/Tobacco Classification. Durbin, D-Ill., amendment to classify tobacco similarly to illegal drugs and the illegal use of alcohol for consideration under the Drug-Free Schools and Communities program. Adopted in the Committee of the Whole 353-70: R 136-35; D 216-35 (ND 163-10, SD 53-25); I 1-0, March 9, 1994.

* Omitted votes are quorum calls, which CQ does not include in its vote charts.

	42	43	44	45	46	47	49
ALABAMA							
1 Callahan	Y	Y	Y	Y	N	Y	N
2 Everett	Y	Y	Y	Y	N	Y	Y
3 Browder	Y	Y	N	Y	N	Y	Y
4 Bevill	Y	Y	Y	Y	N	Y	Y
5 Cramer	?	Y	Y	Y	N	Y	Y
6 Bachus	N	Y	Y	Y	N	Y	Y
7 Hilliard	?	N	N	Y	Y	Y	N
ALASKA							
AL Young	N	N	N	Y	N	Y	N
ARIZONA							
1 Coppersmith	Y	Y	Y	Y	N	Y	Y
2 Pastor	Y	N	N	Y	N	Y	Y
3 Stump	N	Y	Y	Y	N	Y	N
4 Kyl	N	Y	Y	Y	N	Y	Y
5 Kolbe	N	Y	Y	Y	N	Y	Y
6 English	?	N	N	Y	N	Y	Y
ARKANSAS							
1 Lambert	Y	N	N	Y	N	Y	Y
2 Thornton	Y	N	N	Y	N	Y	Y
3 Hutchinson	N	Y	Y	Y	N	Y	Y
4 Dickey	N	Y	Y	Y	N	Y	Y
CALIFORNIA							
1 Hamburg	Y	N	N	Y	Y	Y	Y
2 Herger	N	Y	Y	Y	N	Y	Y
3 Fazio	Y	N	N	Y	N	Y	Y
4 Doolittle	N	Y	Y	Y	N	Y	Y
5 Matsui	Y	N	N	Y	?	Y	Y
6 Woolsey	Y	?	N	Y	Y	Y	Y
7 Miller	N	N	N	Y	Y	Y	Y
8 Pelosi	Y	N	N	Y	Y	Y	Y
9 Dellums	?	N	N	Y	Y	Y	Y
10 Baker	N	Y	Y	Y	N	Y	Y
11 Pombo	Y	Y	Y	Y	N	Y	Y
12 Lantos	Y	N	N	Y	N	Y	Y
13 Stark	Y	N	N	Y	Y	Y	Y
14 Eshoo	Y	N	N	Y	Y	Y	Y
15 Mineta	Y	N	N	Y	Y	Y	Y
16 Edwards	?	?	?	?	?	?	?
17 Farr	Y	N	N	Y	Y	Y	Y
18 Condit	Y	Y	Y	Y	N	Y	Y
19 Lehman	Y	N	N	Y	Y	Y	Y
20 Dooley	Y	?	N	Y	N	Y	Y
21 Thomas	N	Y	Y	Y	N	Y	Y
22 Huffington	?	Y	Y	Y	N	Y	Y
23 Gallegly	N	Y	Y	Y	N	Y	Y
24 Beilenson	Y	N	N	Y	Y	Y	Y
25 McKeon	N	Y	Y	Y	N	Y	Y
26 Berman	?	?	N	Y	Y	Y	Y
27 Moorhead	N	Y	Y	Y	N	Y	Y
28 Dreier	N	Y	Y	Y	N	Y	Y
29 Waxman	Y	N	N	Y	Y	Y	Y
30 Becerra	?	N	N	Y	Y	Y	Y
31 Martinez	Y	N	N	Y	Y	Y	Y
32 Dixon	Y	N	N	Y	Y	Y	Y
33 Roybal-Allard	Y	N	N	Y	Y	Y	Y
34 Torres	Y	N	N	Y	Y	Y	Y
35 Waters	Y	N	N	Y	Y	Y	Y
36 Harman	Y	Y	Y	Y	N	Y	Y
37 Tucker	Y	N	N	Y	Y	Y	Y
38 Horn	N	N	Y	Y	N	Y	Y
39 Royce	N	Y	Y	Y	N	Y	Y
40 Lewis	N	Y	Y	Y	N	Y	Y
41 Kim	N	Y	Y	Y	N	Y	Y

	42	43	44	45	46	47	49
42 Brown	?	N	N	Y	?	?	Y
43 Calvert	N	Y	Y	Y	N	Y	Y
44 McCandless	N	Y	Y	Y	N	Y	Y
45 Rohrabacher	N	Y	Y	Y	N	Y	Y
46 Dornan	?	Y	Y	Y	N	Y	Y
47 Cox	?	Y	Y	Y	N	Y	Y
48 Packard	N	Y	Y	Y	N	Y	Y
49 Schenk	Y	N	N	Y	N	Y	Y
50 Filner	Y	N	N	Y	Y	Y	Y
51 Cunningham	N	Y	Y	Y	N	Y	Y
52 Hunter	?	Y	Y	Y	N	Y	N
COLORADO							
1 Schroeder	N	N	N	Y	Y	Y	Y
2 Skaggs	Y	N	N	Y	N	Y	Y
3 McInnis	Y	Y	Y	Y	N	Y	Y
4 Allard	N	Y	Y	Y	N	Y	Y
5 Hefley	N	Y	Y	Y	N	Y	Y
6 Schaefer	N	Y	Y	Y	N	Y	N
CONNECTICUT							
1 Kennelly	Y	N	N	Y	Y	Y	Y
2 Gejdenson	Y	N	N	Y	Y	Y	Y
3 DeLauro	Y	N	N	Y	Y	Y	Y
4 Shays	N	Y	Y	Y	N	Y	Y
5 Franks	N	Y	Y	Y	N	Y	Y
6 Johnson	N	Y	Y	Y	N	Y	Y
DELAWARE							
AL Castle	N	Y	Y	Y	N	Y	Y
FLORIDA							
1 Hutto	Y	Y	Y	Y	N	Y	Y
2 Peterson	Y	Y	Y	Y	N	Y	Y
3 Brown	Y	N	N	Y	N	Y	Y
4 Fowler	N	Y	Y	Y	N	Y	Y
5 Thurman	Y	Y	Y	Y	N	Y	Y
6 Stearns	N	Y	Y	Y	N	Y	Y
7 Mica	N	Y	Y	Y	N	Y	Y
8 McCollum	N	Y	Y	Y	N	Y	Y
9 Bilirakis	?	Y	Y	Y	N	Y	Y
10 Young	?	Y	Y	Y	N	Y	Y
11 Gibbons	?	N	N	Y	Y	Y	Y
12 Canady	N	Y	Y	Y	N	Y	Y
13 Miller	N	Y	Y	Y	N	Y	Y
14 Goss	N	Y	Y	Y	N	Y	Y
15 Bacchus	?	N	N	Y	N	Y	Y
16 Lewis	N	Y	Y	Y	N	Y	Y
17 Meek	Y	N	N	Y	Y	Y	N
18 Ros-Lehtinen	N	N	N	Y	Y	Y	Y
19 Johnston	Y	N	N	Y	N	Y	Y
20 Deutsch	Y	N	N	Y	Y	Y	Y
21 Diaz-Balart	N	N	N	Y	Y	Y	Y
22 Shaw	?	Y	Y	Y	N	Y	Y
23 Hastings	?	?	?	?	?	?	?
GEORGIA							
1 Kingston	Y	Y	Y	Y	N	Y	N
2 Bishop	Y	N	N	Y	N	Y	Y
3 Collins	N	Y	Y	Y	N	Y	N
4 Linder	N	Y	Y	Y	N	Y	Y
5 Lewis	Y	N	N	Y	Y	Y	Y
6 Gingrich	N	Y	Y	Y	N	Y	Y
7 Darden	Y	N	N	Y	N	Y	Y
8 Rowland	Y	Y	Y	Y	N	Y	Y
9 Deal	Y	Y	Y	Y	N	Y	Y
10 Johnson	Y	N	N	Y	N	Y	Y
11 McKinney	Y	N	N	Y	Y	Y	Y
HAWAII							
1 Abercrombie	Y	X	N	Y	Y	Y	Y
2 Mink	Y	N	N	Y	Y	Y	Y
IDAHO							
1 LaRocco	Y	N	N	Y	N	Y	Y
2 Crapo	N	Y	Y	Y	N	Y	Y
ILLINOIS							
1 Rush	?	?	N	Y	Y	Y	Y
2 Reynolds	?	?	?	?	?	?	?
3 Lipinski	?	Y	Y	Y	N	Y	Y
4 Gutierrez	Y	N	N	Y	Y	Y	Y
5 Rostenkowski	?	N	N	Y	Y	Y	Y
6 Hyde	N	Y	Y	Y	N	Y	Y
7 Collins	Y	N	N	Y	Y	Y	Y
8 Crane	?	?	?	?	?	?	?
9 Yates	Y	N	N	Y	Y	Y	Y
10 Porter	N	Y	Y	Y	N	Y	Y
11 Sangmeister	Y	N	N	Y	N	Y	Y
12 Costello	Y	Y	Y	Y	Y	?	Y
13 Fawell	N	Y	Y	Y	N	Y	Y
14 Hastert	N	Y	Y	Y	N	Y	Y
15 Ewing	N	Y	Y	Y	N	Y	Y
16 Manzullo	N	Y	Y	Y	N	Y	Y
17 Evans	Y	N	N	Y	Y	Y	Y

ND   Northern Democrats   SD   Southern Democrats

	42	43	44	45	46	47	49
18 ***Michel***	N	Y	Y	Y	N	Y	?
19 Poshard	Y	Y	Y	Y	Y	Y	Y
20 Durbin	Y	N	N	Y	Y	Y	Y
INDIANA							
1 Visclosky	?	N	N	Y	N	Y	Y
2 Sharp	?	N	N	Y	N	Y	Y
3 Roemer	Y	N	N	Y	N	Y	Y
4 Long	Y	N	N	Y	N	Y	Y
5 ***Buyer***	N	Y	Y	Y	N	Y	Y
6 ***Burton***	?	Y	Y	Y	N	Y	Y
7 ***Myers***	Y	Y	Y	Y	N	Y	Y
8 McCloskey	?	N	N	Y	N	Y	Y
9 Hamilton	Y	N	N	Y	N	Y	Y
10 Jacobs	?	N	N	Y	N	Y	Y
IOWA							
1 ***Leach***	N	Y	Y	Y	N	Y	Y
2 ***Nussle***	Y	Y	Y	Y	N	Y	Y
3 ***Lightfoot***	N	Y	Y	Y	N	Y	Y
4 Smith	Y	N	N	Y	Y	Y	Y
5 ***Grandy***	?	Y	Y	Y	N	Y	Y
KANSAS							
1 ***Roberts***	N	Y	Y	Y	N	Y	Y
2 Slattery	Y	N	N	Y	N	Y	Y
3 ***Meyers***	N	Y	Y	Y	N	Y	Y
4 Glickman	Y	Y	N	Y	N	Y	Y
KENTUCKY							
1 Barlow	Y	N	N	Y	Y	Y	N
2 Natcher	?	?	?	?	?	?	?
3 Mazzoli	Y	Y	N	Y	N	Y	Y
4 ***Bunning***	N	Y	Y	Y	N	Y	N
5 ***Rogers***	N	Y	Y	Y	N	?	N
6 Baesler	Y	N	N	Y	Y	Y	N
LOUISIANA							
1 ***Livingston***	Y	Y	Y	Y	N	Y	Y
2 Jefferson	Y	N	N	Y	Y	Y	Y
3 Tauzin	Y	Y	Y	Y	N	Y	Y
4 Fields	Y	N	N	Y	Y	Y	Y
5 ***McCrery***	?	Y	Y	Y	N	Y	Y
6 ***Baker***	?	Y	Y	Y	N	Y	N
7 Hayes	Y	?	N	Y	N	Y	Y
MAINE							
1 Andrews	?	N	?	Y	Y	Y	Y
2 ***Snowe***	Y	Y	Y	Y	N	Y	Y
MARYLAND							
1 ***Gilchrest***	N	Y	Y	Y	N	Y	Y
2 ***Bentley***	N	Y	Y	Y	N	Y	N
3 Cardin	Y	N	N	Y	N	Y	Y
4 Wynn	Y	N	N	Y	Y	Y	Y
5 Hoyer	Y	N	N	Y	N	Y	Y
6 ***Bartlett***	N	Y	Y	Y	N	Y	Y
7 Mfume	Y	N	N	Y	Y	Y	Y
8 ***Morella***	?	Y	Y	Y	N	Y	Y
MASSACHUSETTS							
1 Olver	Y	N	N	Y	Y	Y	Y
2 Neal	?	N	N	Y	N	Y	Y
3 ***Blute***	N	Y	Y	Y	N	Y	Y
4 Frank	Y	N	N	Y	Y	Y	Y
5 Meehan	?	N	N	Y	Y	Y	Y
6 ***Torkildsen***	N	Y	Y	Y	N	Y	Y
7 Markey	Y	N	N	Y	Y	Y	Y
8 Kennedy	Y	N	N	Y	?	Y	Y
9 Moakley	?	N	N	Y	Y	Y	Y
10 Studds	Y	N	N	Y	Y	Y	Y
MICHIGAN							
1 Stupak	Y	N	N	Y	N	Y	Y
2 ***Hoekstra***	N	Y	Y	Y	N	Y	Y
3 ***Ehlers***	N	Y	Y	Y	N	Y	Y
4 ***Camp***	N	Y	Y	Y	N	Y	Y
5 Barcia	Y	N	N	Y	Y	Y	N
6 ***Upton***	N	Y	Y	Y	N	Y	Y
7 ***Smith***	N	Y	Y	Y	N	Y	Y
8 Carr	Y	N	N	Y	Y	Y	N
9 Kildee	Y	N	N	Y	Y	Y	Y
10 Bonior	Y	N	N	Y	Y	Y	N
11 ***Knollenberg***	N	Y	Y	Y	N	Y	Y
12 Levin	Y	N	N	Y	N	Y	Y
13 Ford	?	N	N	Y	Y	Y	Y
14 Conyers	?	N	N	Y	Y	Y	Y
15 Collins	Y	N	N	Y	Y	Y	Y
16 Dingell	?	N	N	Y	Y	Y	N
MINNESOTA							
1 Penny	Y	Y	Y	Y	N	?	Y
2 Minge	Y	Y	Y	Y	N	Y	Y
3 ***Ramstad***	N	Y	Y	Y	N	Y	Y
4 Vento	Y	N	N	Y	Y	Y	Y

	42	43	44	45	46	47	49
5 Sabo	Y	N	N	Y	Y	Y	Y
6 ***Grams***	N	Y	Y	Y	N	Y	Y
7 Peterson	Y	Y	Y	Y	N	Y	Y
8 Oberstar	Y	N	N	Y	Y	Y	Y
MISSISSIPPI							
1 Whitten	?	?	?	?	N	Y	Y
2 Thompson	Y	N	N	Y	Y	Y	N
3 Montgomery	Y	Y	N	Y	N	Y	Y
4 Parker	Y	Y	Y	Y	N	Y	Y
5 Taylor	N	Y	Y	Y	N	Y	Y
MISSOURI							
1 Clay	?	N	N	Y	Y	Y	Y
2 ***Talent***	N	Y	Y	Y	N	Y	Y
3 Gephardt	Y	N	N	Y	Y	Y	Y
4 Skelton	Y	N	Y	Y	N	Y	Y
5 Wheat	Y	N	N	Y	Y	Y	Y
6 Danner	Y	N	N	Y	Y	Y	N
7 ***Hancock***	N	Y	Y	Y	N	Y	N
8 ***Emerson***	N	Y	Y	Y	N	Y	N
9 Volkmer	Y	N	?	Y	N	Y	Y
MONTANA							
AL Williams	Y	N	N	Y	N	Y	N
NEBRASKA							
1 ***Bereuter***	N	Y	N	Y	N	Y	Y
2 Hoagland	Y	Y	Y	Y	N	Y	Y
3 ***Barrett***	N	Y	Y	Y	N	Y	Y
NEVADA							
1 Bilbray	Y	N	Y	Y	N	Y	Y
2 ***Vucanovich***	?	Y	Y	Y	N	Y	N
NEW HAMPSHIRE							
1 ***Zeliff***	N	Y	Y	Y	N	Y	Y
2 Swett	?	N	N	Y	N	Y	Y
NEW JERSEY							
1 Andrews	Y	N	N	Y	N	Y	Y
2 Hughes	Y	N	N	Y	N	Y	Y
3 ***Saxton***	N	Y	Y	Y	N	Y	N
4 ***Smith***	N	Y	Y	Y	N	Y	Y
5 ***Roukema***	?	Y	Y	Y	N	Y	Y
6 Pallone	Y	N	N	Y	N	Y	Y
7 ***Franks***	N	Y	Y	Y	N	Y	Y
8 Klein	?	N	N	Y	N	Y	Y
9 Torricelli	?	N	N	Y	N	Y	Y
10 Payne	?	N	N	Y	Y	Y	Y
11 ***Gallo***	?	?	?	?	?	?	?
12 ***Zimmer***	N	Y	Y	Y	N	Y	Y
13 Menendez	Y	N	N	Y	Y	Y	Y
NEW MEXICO							
1 ***Schiff***	N	Y	Y	Y	N	Y	Y
2 ***Skeen***	N	Y	Y	Y	N	Y	Y
3 Richardson	Y	N	N	Y	N	Y	Y
NEW YORK							
1 Hochbrueckner	Y	N	N	Y	N	Y	Y
2 ***Lazio***	N	Y	Y	Y	N	Y	Y
3 ***King***	N	Y	Y	Y	N	Y	Y
4 ***Levy***	N	Y	Y	Y	N	Y	Y
5 Ackerman	Y	N	N	Y	Y	Y	Y
6 Flake	?	N	N	Y	Y	Y	Y
7 Manton	Y	N	N	Y	Y	Y	N
8 Nadler	?	N	N	Y	N	Y	Y
9 Schumer	?	N	N	Y	Y	Y	Y
10 Towns	Y	N	N	Y	Y	Y	Y
11 Owens	Y	N	N	Y	Y	N	Y
12 Velazquez	Y	N	N	Y	Y	Y	Y
13 ***Molinari***	N	Y	Y	Y	Y	Y	Y
14 Maloney	Y	N	N	Y	N	Y	Y
15 Rangel	Y	N	N	Y	Y	?	Y
16 Serrano	Y	N	N	Y	Y	Y	Y
17 Engel	Y	N	N	Y	Y	Y	Y
18 Lowey	Y	N	N	Y	Y	Y	Y
19 ***Fish***	Y	Y	Y	Y	N	Y	Y
20 ***Gilman***	Y	N	Y	Y	N	Y	Y
21 McNulty	Y	N	N	Y	N	Y	Y
22 ***Solomon***	N	Y	Y	Y	N	Y	Y
23 ***Boehlert***	N	Y	Y	Y	N	Y	Y
24 ***McHugh***	N	Y	Y	Y	N	Y	Y
25 ***Walsh***	N	Y	Y	Y	N	Y	Y
26 Hinchey	Y	N	N	Y	N	Y	Y
27 ***Paxon***	N	Y	Y	Y	N	Y	N
28 Slaughter	Y	N	N	Y	N	Y	Y
29 LaFalce	Y	N	N	Y	N	Y	Y
30 ***Quinn***	?	Y	Y	Y	N	Y	Y
31 ***Houghton***	?	?	Y	Y	N	Y	N
NORTH CAROLINA							
1 Clayton	Y	N	N	Y	N	Y	N
2 Valentine	?	Y	Y	Y	N	Y	?

	42	43	44	45	46	47	49
3 Lancaster	Y	N	N	Y	N	Y	N
4 Price	Y	Y	N	Y	N	Y	N
5 Neal	Y	N	N	Y	N	Y	N
6 ***Coble***	N	Y	Y	Y	N	Y	N
7 Rose	Y	N	N	Y	Y	Y	N
8 Hefner	Y	N	N	Y	N	Y	N
9 ***McMillan***	N	Y	Y	Y	N	Y	N
10 ***Ballenger***	N	Y	Y	Y	N	Y	N
11 ***Taylor***	N	Y	Y	Y	N	Y	N
12 Watt	?	N	N	Y	Y	Y	N
NORTH DAKOTA							
AL Pomeroy	Y	N	N	Y	N	Y	Y
OHIO							
1 Mann	Y	Y	Y	Y	Y	Y	Y
2 ***Portman***	N	+	+	+	−	+	+
3 Hall	Y	N	N	Y	N	Y	Y
4 ***Oxley***	Y	Y	Y	Y	N	Y	Y
5 ***Gillmor***	Y	Y	Y	Y	N	Y	Y
6 Strickland	Y	N	N	Y	Y	Y	Y
7 ***Hobson***	N	Y	Y	Y	N	Y	Y
8 ***Boehner***	N	Y	Y	Y	N	Y	N
9 Kaptur	Y	N	N	Y	N	Y	Y
10 ***Hoke***	N	Y	Y	Y	N	Y	Y
11 Stokes	Y	N	N	Y	Y	Y	Y
12 ***Kasich***	Y	Y	Y	Y	N	Y	Y
13 Brown	Y	N	N	Y	Y	Y	Y
14 Sawyer	Y	N	N	Y	Y	Y	Y
15 ***Pryce***	N	Y	Y	Y	N	Y	Y
16 ***Regula***	N	Y	Y	Y	N	Y	Y
17 Traficant	Y	N	N	Y	N	Y	Y
18 Applegate	Y	N	N	Y	N	Y	P
19 Fingerhut	Y	Y	N	Y	N	Y	Y
OKLAHOMA							
1 ***Inhofe***	N	Y	Y	Y	N	Y	Y
2 Synar	Y	N	N	Y	Y	Y	Y
3 Brewster	Y	N	N	Y	N	Y	N
4 McCurdy	Y	?	N	Y	N	Y	Y
5 ***Istook***	N	Y	Y	Y	?	Y	Y
6 Vacancy							
OREGON							
1 Furse	Y	N	N	Y	N	Y	Y
2 ***Smith***	N	Y	Y	Y	N	Y	N
3 Wyden	Y	N	N	Y	N	Y	Y
4 DeFazio	?	N	N	Y	N	Y	Y
5 Kopetski	Y	N	N	Y	N	Y	N
PENNSYLVANIA							
1 Foglietta	?	N	N	Y	Y	Y	Y
2 Blackwell	?	N	N	Y	Y	Y	Y
3 Borski	Y	?	?	?	?	?	?
4 Klink	Y	N	N	Y	N	Y	Y
5 ***Clinger***	Y	Y	Y	Y	N	Y	Y
6 Holden	Y	N	N	Y	N	Y	Y
7 ***Weldon***	?	Y	Y	Y	N	Y	Y
8 ***Greenwood***	Y	Y	Y	Y	N	Y	Y
9 ***Shuster***	?	Y	Y	Y	N	Y	Y
10 ***McDade***	N	Y	Y	Y	N	Y	Y
11 Kanjorski	Y	Y	Y	Y	N	Y	N
12 Murtha	?	N	N	Y	N	Y	Y
13 Margolies-Mezv.	Y	N	N	Y	N	Y	Y
14 Coyne	Y	N	N	Y	Y	Y	Y
15 McHale	Y	N	N	Y	N	Y	Y
16 ***Walker***	N	Y	Y	Y	N	Y	N
17 ***Gekas***	N	Y	Y	Y	N	Y	N
18 ***Santorum***	?	Y	Y	Y	N	Y	Y
19 ***Goodling***	N	Y	Y	Y	N	Y	Y
20 Murphy	N	N	N	Y	Y	Y	Y
21 ***Ridge***	N	Y	Y	Y	N	Y	Y
RHODE ISLAND							
1 ***Machtley***	?	Y	Y	Y	N	Y	Y
2 Reed	Y	N	N	Y	Y	Y	Y
SOUTH CAROLINA							
1 ***Ravenel***	N	Y	Y	Y	N	Y	N
2 ***Spence***	N	Y	Y	Y	N	Y	N
3 Derrick	?	N	N	Y	Y	Y	Y
4 ***Inglis***	Y	Y	Y	Y	N	Y	Y
5 Spratt	Y	N	N	Y	N	Y	N
6 Clyburn	Y	N	N	Y	Y	Y	N
SOUTH DAKOTA							
AL Johnson	Y	Y	Y	Y	N	Y	Y
TENNESSEE							
1 ***Quillen***	?	Y	Y	Y	N	Y	N
2 ***Duncan***	N	Y	Y	Y	N	Y	Y
3 Lloyd	?	N	N	Y	N	Y	Y
4 Cooper	Y	Y	Y	Y	N	Y	Y
5 Clement	Y	N	N	Y	N	Y	Y

	42	43	44	45	46	47	49
6 Gordon	Y	N	N	Y	N	Y	N
7 ***Sundquist***	N	#	?	?	?	?	?
8 Tanner	?	Y	Y	Y	N	Y	N
9 Ford	?	N	N	Y	Y	Y	Y
TEXAS							
1 Chapman	Y	Y	Y	Y	N	Y	Y
2 Wilson	?	N	N	Y	N	Y	Y
3 ***Johnson, Sam***	?	Y	Y	Y	N	Y	N
4 Hall	?	N	N	Y	N	Y	Y
5 Bryant	?	N	N	Y	N	Y	Y
6 ***Barton***	?	Y	Y	Y	N	Y	N
7 ***Archer***	?	Y	Y	Y	N	Y	Y
8 ***Fields***	?	Y	Y	Y	N	Y	Y
9 Brooks	?	?	?	?	?	?	?
10 Pickle	Y	N	N	Y	Y	?	Y
11 Edwards	Y	N	N	Y	N	Y	Y
12 Geren	?	Y	Y	Y	N	Y	N
13 Sarpalius	Y	N	N	Y	N	Y	Y
14 Laughlin	Y	N	Y	Y	N	Y	Y
15 de la Garza	?	?	?	Y	N	Y	Y
16 Coleman	?	N	N	Y	Y	Y	Y
17 Stenholm	Y	Y	Y	Y	N	Y	Y
18 Washington	?	?	?	?	?	?	?
19 ***Combest***	Y	Y	Y	Y	N	Y	Y
20 Gonzalez	Y	N	N	Y	Y	Y	Y
21 ***Smith***	?	Y	Y	Y	N	Y	Y
22 ***DeLay***	N	Y	Y	Y	N	Y	Y
23 ***Bonilla***	N	Y	Y	Y	N	Y	Y
24 Frost	Y	N	N	Y	N	Y	Y
25 Andrews	?	?	?	?	?	?	?
26 ***Armey***	?	Y	Y	Y	N	Y	N
27 Ortiz	?	N	N	Y	N	Y	Y
28 Tejeda	?	N	N	Y	N	Y	Y
29 Green	?	N	N	Y	Y	Y	N
30 Johnson, E.B.	?	N	N	Y	Y	Y	Y
UTAH							
1 ***Hansen***	N	Y	Y	Y	N	Y	Y
2 Shepherd	Y	N	N	Y	N	Y	Y
3 Orton	Y	N	N	Y	N	Y	Y
VERMONT							
AL *Sanders*	Y	N	N	Y	Y	Y	Y
VIRGINIA							
1 ***Bateman***	Y	Y	Y	Y	N	Y	N
2 Pickett	Y	N	N	Y	Y	Y	N
3 Scott	Y	N	N	Y	Y	Y	N
4 Sisisky	Y	Y	N	Y	N	Y	N
5 Payne	Y	Y	Y	Y	N	Y	N
6 ***Goodlatte***	N	Y	Y	Y	N	Y	N
7 ***Bliley***	N	Y	Y	Y	N	Y	N
8 Moran	Y	N	N	Y	Y	Y	Y
9 Boucher	Y	N	N	Y	N	Y	N
10 ***Wolf***	N	Y	Y	Y	N	Y	Y
11 Byrne	Y	N	N	Y	Y	Y	Y
WASHINGTON							
1 Cantwell	Y	N	N	Y	N	Y	Y
2 Swift	Y	N	N	Y	Y	?	Y
3 Unsoeld	Y	N	N	Y	N	Y	Y
4 Inslee	Y	N	N	Y	N	Y	Y
5 Foley							
6 Dicks	?	N	N	Y	Y	Y	Y
7 McDermott	Y	N	N	Y	Y	Y	Y
8 ***Dunn***	N	Y	Y	Y	N	Y	Y
9 Kreidler	Y	N	N	Y	N	Y	Y
WEST VIRGINIA							
1 Mollohan	Y	N	N	Y	Y	Y	N
2 Wise	Y	N	N	Y	Y	Y	Y
3 Rahall	Y	N	N	Y	Y	Y	Y
WISCONSIN							
1 Barca	Y	N	Y	Y	N	Y	Y
2 ***Klug***	N	Y	Y	Y	N	Y	Y
3 ***Gunderson***	N	Y	Y	Y	N	Y	Y
4 Kleczka	Y	N	N	Y	N	Y	Y
5 Barrett	Y	N	N	Y	N	Y	Y
6 ***Petri***	N	Y	Y	Y	N	Y	Y
7 Obey	?	N	N	Y	Y	Y	Y
8 ***Roth***	N	Y	Y	Y	N	Y	Y
9 ***Sensenbrenner***	N	Y	Y	Y	N	Y	Y
WYOMING							
AL ***Thomas***	N	Y	Y	Y	N	Y	Y
DELEGATES							
de Lugo, V.I.	D	N	N	Y	Y	Y	Y
Faleomavaega, Am.S.	D	N	N	Y	Y	Y	Y
Norton, D.C.	D	N	N	Y	Y	Y	Y
Romero-B., P.R.	D	N	N	Y	?	Y	Y
Underwood, Guam	D	N	N	Y	Y	Y	Y

Southern states - Ala., Ark., Fla., Ga., Ky., La., Miss., N.C., Okla., S.C., Tenn., Texas, Va.
Omitted votes are quorum calls, which CQ does not include in its vote charts.

KEY

Y Voted for (yea).
Paired for.
+ Announced for.
N Voted against (nay).
X Paired against.
— Announced against.
P Voted "present."
C Voted "present" to avoid possible conflict of interest.
? Did not vote or otherwise make a position known.
D Delegates ineligible to vote.

Democrats *Republicans*
Independent

50. H Con Res 218. Fiscal 1995 Budget Resolution/Rule. Adoption of the rule (H Res 384) to provide for House floor consideration of the resolution to set budget levels for the fiscal year ending Sept. 30, 1995: budget authority, $1.541 trillion; outlays, $1.514 trillion; revenues, $1.338 trillion; and a deficit of $175.3 billion. Adopted 245-171: R 0-170; D 244-1 (ND 165-1, SD 79-0); I 1-0, March 10, 1994.

51. H Con Res 218. Fiscal 1995 Budget Resolution/Defense Cuts. Frank, D-Mass., substitute amendment to reduce the $263.3 billion in defense budget authority in the resolution by $2.4 billion. Rejected in the Committee of the Whole 105-313: R 12-160; D 92-153 (ND 82-85, SD 10-68); I 1-0, March 10, 1994. A "yea" was a vote in support of the president's position.

52. H Con Res 218. Fiscal 1995 Budget Resolution/$698 Billion Spending Cut. Solomon, R-N.Y. substitute amendment to balance the budget by 1999 through $698 billion in additional spending cuts. Rejected in the Committee of the Whole 73-342: R 56-114; D 17-227 (ND 11-156, SD 6-71); I 0-1, March 10, 1994.

	50	51	52
ALABAMA			
1 *Callahan*	N	N	Y
2 *Everett*	N	N	N
3 Browder	Y	N	N
4 Bevill	Y	N	N
5 Cramer	Y	N	N
6 *Bachus*	N	N	Y
7 Hilliard	Y	N	N
ALASKA			
AL *Young*	N	N	N
ARIZONA			
1 Coppersmith	N	N	N
2 Pastor	Y	N	N
3 *Stump*	N	N	N
4 *Kyl*	N	N	N
5 *Kolbe*	N	N	N
6 English	Y	Y	N
ARKANSAS			
1 Lambert	Y	Y	N
2 Thornton	Y	N	N
3 *Hutchinson*	N	N	N
4 *Dickey*	N	N	N
CALIFORNIA			
1 Hamburg	Y	Y	N
2 *Herger*	N	N	N
3 Fazio	Y	N	N
4 *Doolittle*	N	N	N
5 Matsui	Y	N	N
6 Woolsey	Y	Y	N
7 Miller	Y	?	?
8 Pelosi	Y	?	?
9 Dellums	?	Y	N
10 *Baker*	N	N	N
11 *Pombo*	N	N	N
12 Lantos	Y	N	N
13 Stark	Y	Y	N
14 Eshoo	Y	Y	N
15 Mineta	Y	N	N
16 Edwards	Y	?	?
17 Farr	Y	Y	N
18 Condit	Y	N	Y
19 Lehman	Y	N	N
20 Dooley	Y	?	X
21 *Thomas*	N	N	N
22 *Huffington*	N	N	N
23 *Gallegly*	N	N	N
24 Beilenson	Y	Y	N
25 *McKeon*	N	N	N
26 Berman	Y	Y	N
27 *Moorhead*	N	N	Y
28 *Dreier*	N	N	Y
29 Waxman	Y	Y	N
30 Becerra	Y	Y	N
31 Martinez	Y	N	N
32 Dixon	Y	N	N
33 Roybal-Allard	Y	Y	N
34 Torres	Y	N	N
35 Waters	Y	Y	N
36 Harman	Y	N	N
37 Tucker	Y	N	N
38 *Horn*	N	N	N
39 *Royce*	N	N	Y
40 *Lewis*	N	?	#
41 *Kim*	N	N	N

	50	51	52
42 Brown	Y	N	N
43 *Calvert*	N	N	N
44 *McCandless*	N	N	Y
45 *Rohrabacher*	N	N	Y
46 *Dornan*	N	N	Y
47 *Cox*	N	N	Y
48 *Packard*	N	N	Y
49 Schenk	Y	N	N
50 Filner	Y	Y	N
51 *Cunningham*	N	N	Y
52 *Hunter*	N	N	Y
COLORADO			
1 Schroeder	Y	Y	N
2 Skaggs	Y	N	N
3 *McInnis*	N	N	N
4 *Allard*	N	N	N
5 *Hefley*	N	N	N
6 *Schaefer*	N	N	Y
CONNECTICUT			
1 Kennelly	Y	N	N
2 Gejdenson	Y	N	N
3 DeLauro	Y	N	N
4 *Shays*	N	Y	N
5 *Franks*	N	N	N
6 *Johnson*	N	N	N
DELAWARE			
AL *Castle*	N	N	N
FLORIDA			
1 Hutto	Y	N	N
2 Peterson	Y	N	N
3 Brown	Y	N	N
4 *Fowler*	N	N	N
5 Thurman	Y	N	N
6 *Stearns*	N	N	N
7 *Mica*	N	N	Y
8 *McCollum*	N	N	N
9 *Bilirakis*	N	N	N
10 *Young*	N	N	N
11 Gibbons	Y	N	N
12 *Canady*	N	N	N
13 *Miller*	N	N	Y
14 *Goss*	N	N	Y
15 Bacchus	Y	N	N
16 *Lewis*	N	N	N
17 Meek	Y	N	N
18 *Ros-Lehtinen*	N	N	N
19 Johnston	Y	Y	N
20 Deutsch	Y	N	N
21 *Diaz-Balart*	N	N	N
22 *Shaw*	N	N	X
23 Hastings	?	?	?
GEORGIA			
1 *Kingston*	N	N	N
2 Bishop	Y	N	N
3 *Collins*	N	N	Y
4 *Linder*	N	N	N
5 Lewis	Y	Y	N
6 *Gingrich*	N	N	N
7 Darden	Y	N	N
8 Rowland	Y	N	N
9 Deal	Y	N	Y
10 Johnson	Y	N	N
11 McKinney	Y	Y	N
HAWAII			
1 Abercrombie	Y	Y	N
2 Mink	Y	Y	N
IDAHO			
1 LaRocco	Y	N	N
2 *Crapo*	?	N	N
ILLINOIS			
1 Rush	Y	Y	N
2 Reynolds	?	?	?
3 Lipinski	Y	N	N
4 Gutierrez	Y	?	?
5 Rostenkowski	Y	N	N
6 *Hyde*	N	N	N
7 Collins	Y	?	?
8 *Crane*	?	?	?
9 Yates	Y	Y	N
10 *Porter*	N	N	Y
11 Sangmeister	Y	Y	N
12 Costello	Y	N	N
13 *Fawell*	N	N	Y
14 *Hastert*	N	N	N
15 *Ewing*	N	N	N
16 *Manzullo*	N	N	N
17 Evans	Y	Y	N

ND Northern Democrats   SD Southern Democrats

	50	51	52
18 Michel	N	N	N
19 Poshard	Y	Y	N
20 Durbin	Y	Y	N
INDIANA			
1 Visclosky	Y	N	N
2 Sharp	Y	N	N
3 Roemer	Y	N	N
4 Long	Y	N	N
5 *Buyer*	N	N	N
6 *Burton*	N	N	Y
7 *Myers*	N	N	N
8 McCloskey	Y	N	N
9 Hamilton	Y	N	N
10 Jacobs	Y	Y	N
IOWA			
1 *Leach*	N	Y	N
2 *Nussle*	N	Y	N
3 *Lightfoot*	?	N	N
4 Smith	Y	N	N
5 *Grandy*	N	N	N
KANSAS			
1 *Roberts*	N	N	N
2 Slattery	Y	N	N
3 *Meyers*	N	N	N
4 Glickman	Y	N	N
KENTUCKY			
1 Barlow	Y	N	N
2 Natcher	?	?	?
3 Mazzoli	Y	N	N
4 *Bunning*	N	N	N
5 *Rogers*	N	N	N
6 Baesler	Y	N	N
LOUISIANA			
1 *Livingston*	N	N	N
2 Jefferson	Y	N	N
3 Tauzin	Y	N	Y
4 Fields	Y	Y	N
5 *McCrery*	N	N	N
6 *Baker*	N	N	Y
7 Hayes	Y	N	N
MAINE			
1 Andrews	Y	Y	N
2 *Snowe*	N	N	N
MARYLAND			
1 *Gilchrest*	N	N	Y
2 *Bentley*	N	N	N
3 Cardin	Y	Y	N
4 Wynn	Y	Y	N
5 Hoyer	Y	N	N
6 *Bartlett*	N	N	Y
7 Mfume	Y	Y	N
8 *Morella*	N	Y	N
MASSACHUSETTS			
1 Olver	Y	Y	N
2 Neal	Y	Y	N
3 *Blute*	N	N	N
4 Frank	Y	Y	?
5 Meehan	Y	Y	N
6 *Torkildsen*	N	N	N
7 Markey	Y	Y	N
8 Kennedy	Y	Y	N
9 Moakley	Y	Y	N
10 Studds	Y	Y	N
MICHIGAN			
1 Stupak	Y	N	N
2 *Hoekstra*	N	N	Y
3 *Ehlers*	N	N	N
4 *Camp*	N	N	N
5 Barcia	Y	N	Y
6 *Upton*	N	Y	N
7 *Smith*	N	N	Y
8 Carr	Y	N	N
9 Kildee	Y	Y	N
10 Bonior	Y	N	N
11 *Knollenberg*	N	N	Y
12 Levin	Y	N	N
13 Ford	Y	Y	N
14 Conyers	?	Y	N
15 Collins	Y	Y	N
16 Dingell	Y	N	N
MINNESOTA			
1 Penny	Y	Y	Y
2 Minge	Y	Y	Y
3 *Ramstad*	N	N	Y
4 Vento	Y	Y	N

	50	51	52
5 Sabo	Y	N	N
6 *Grams*	N	N	N
7 Peterson	Y	Y	N
8 Oberstar	Y	Y	N
MISSISSIPPI			
1 Whitten	Y	N	N
2 Thompson	Y	N	N
3 Montgomery	Y	N	N
4 Parker	Y	N	N
5 Taylor	Y	N	Y
MISSOURI			
1 Clay	Y	N	N
2 *Talent*	N	N	N
3 Gephardt	Y	N	N
4 Skelton	Y	N	N
5 Wheat	Y	N	N
6 Danner	Y	Y	N
7 *Hancock*	N	N	Y
8 *Emerson*	N	N	N
9 Volkmer	Y	N	N
MONTANA			
AL Williams	Y	N	N
NEBRASKA			
1 *Bereuter*	N	N	N
2 Hoagland	Y	N	N
3 *Barrett*	N	N	N
NEVADA			
1 Bilbray	Y	N	N
2 *Vucanovich*	N	N	N
NEW HAMPSHIRE			
1 *Zeliff*	N	N	Y
2 Swett	Y	N	Y
NEW JERSEY			
1 Andrews	?	?	N
2 Hughes	Y	N	N
3 *Saxton*	N	N	N
4 *Smith*	N	N	N
5 *Roukema*	N	Y	N
6 Pallone	Y	N	N
7 *Franks*	N	N	Y
8 Klein	Y	Y	N
9 Torricelli	Y	?	?
10 Payne	Y	Y	N
11 *Gallo*	?	?	?
12 *Zimmer*	N	Y	Y
13 Menendez	Y	N	N
NEW MEXICO			
1 *Schiff*	N	N	N
2 *Skeen*	N	N	N
3 Richardson	Y	N	N
NEW YORK			
1 Hochbrueckner	Y	N	N
2 *Lazio*	N	N	N
3 *King*	N	N	N
4 *Levy*	N	N	N
5 Ackerman	Y	Y	N
6 Flake	Y	N	N
7 Manton	Y	N	N
8 Nadler	Y	Y	N
9 Schumer	?	Y	N
10 Towns	Y	Y	N
11 Owens	Y	Y	N
12 Velazquez	Y	Y	N
13 *Molinari*	N	N	N
14 Maloney	Y	Y	N
15 Rangel	Y	Y	N
16 Serrano	Y	N	N
17 Engel	Y	Y	N
18 Lowey	Y	N	N
19 *Fish*	N	N	Y
20 *Gilman*	N	N	N
21 McNulty	Y	N	N
22 *Solomon*	N	N	Y
23 *Boehlert*	N	N	N
24 *McHugh*	N	N	N
25 *Walsh*	?	N	N
26 Hinchey	Y	Y	N
27 *Paxon*	N	N	Y
28 Slaughter	Y	Y	N
29 LaFalce	Y	Y	N
30 *Quinn*	N	N	N
31 *Houghton*	N	N	N
NORTH CAROLINA			
1 Clayton	Y	N	N
2 Valentine	Y	N	N

	50	51	52
3 Lancaster	Y	N	N
4 Price	Y	N	N
5 Neal	Y	N	N
6 *Coble*	N	N	Y
7 Rose	Y	N	N
8 Hefner	Y	N	N
9 *McMillan*	N	?	#
10 *Ballenger*	N	N	N
11 *Taylor*	N	N	N
12 Watt	Y	Y	N
NORTH DAKOTA			
AL Pomeroy	Y	N	N
OHIO			
1 Mann	Y	N	N
2 *Portman*	?	N	Y
3 Hall	Y	N	N
4 *Oxley*	N	N	N
5 *Gillmor*	N	N	N
6 Strickland	Y	N	N
7 *Hobson*	N	N	N
8 *Boehner*	N	N	N
9 Kaptur	Y	N	N
10 *Hoke*	N	Y	Y
11 Stokes	Y	Y	N
12 *Kasich*	N	N	N
13 Brown	Y	Y	N
14 Sawyer	Y	N	N
15 *Pryce*	N	N	Y
16 *Regula*	N	N	N
17 Traficant	N	N	N
18 Applegate	Y	N	N
19 Fingerhut	Y	N	Y
OKLAHOMA			
1 *Inhofe*	N	N	N
2 Synar	Y	Y	N
3 Brewster	Y	N	N
4 McCurdy	Y	N	N
5 *Istook*	N	N	Y
6 Vacancy			
OREGON			
1 Furse	Y	Y	N
2 *Smith*	N	N	N
3 Wyden	Y	Y	N
4 DeFazio	Y	Y	N
5 Kopetski	?	?	?
PENNSYLVANIA			
1 Foglietta	Y	Y	N
2 Blackwell	Y	Y	N
3 Borski	Y	N	N
4 Klink	Y	N	N
5 *Clinger*	N	N	N
6 Holden	Y	N	N
7 *Weldon*	N	N	Y
8 *Greenwood*	N	N	N
9 *Shuster*	N	N	N
10 *McDade*	N	N	N
11 Kanjorski	Y	N	N
12 Murtha	Y	N	N
13 Margolies-Mezv.	Y	Y	Y
14 Coyne	Y	N	N
15 McHale	Y	N	N
16 *Walker*	N	N	N
17 *Gekas*	N	N	N
18 *Santorum*	N	N	N
19 *Goodling*	N	N	Y
20 Murphy	Y	N	Y
21 *Ridge*	N	N	N
RHODE ISLAND			
1 *Machtley*	N	N	N
2 Reed	Y	N	N
SOUTH CAROLINA			
1 *Ravenel*	N	N	Y
2 *Spence*	N	N	N
3 Derrick	Y	N	N
4 *Inglis*	N	N	N
5 Spratt	Y	N	N
6 Clyburn	Y	N	N
SOUTH DAKOTA			
AL Johnson	Y	Y	N
TENNESSEE			
1 *Quillen*	N	N	Y
2 *Duncan*	N	Y	Y
3 Lloyd	Y	N	N
4 Cooper	Y	N	N
5 Clement	Y	N	N

	50	51	52
6 Gordon	Y	Y	N
7 *Sundquist*	N	N	Y
8 Tanner	Y	N	N
9 Ford	Y	?	?
TEXAS			
1 Chapman	Y	N	N
2 Wilson	Y	N	?
3 *Johnson, Sam*	N	N	N
4 Hall	Y	N	N
5 Bryant	Y	Y	N
6 *Barton*	N	N	Y
7 *Archer*	N	N	N
8 *Fields*	N	N	N
9 Brooks	?	?	?
10 Pickle	Y	N	N
11 Edwards	Y	N	N
12 Geren	Y	N	N
13 Sarpalius	Y	N	N
14 Laughlin	Y	N	N
15 de la Garza	Y	N	N
16 Coleman	Y	N	N
17 Stenholm	Y	N	Y
18 Washington	?	?	?
19 *Combest*	N	N	N
20 Gonzalez	Y	N	N
21 *Smith*	N	N	?
22 *DeLay*	N	N	Y
23 *Bonilla*	N	N	N
24 Frost	Y	N	N
25 Andrews	?	?	?
26 *Armey*	N	N	Y
27 Ortiz	Y	N	N
28 Tejeda	Y	N	N
29 Green	Y	N	N
30 Johnson, E.B.	Y	N	N
UTAH			
1 *Hansen*	N	N	N
2 Shepherd	Y	Y	N
3 Orton	Y	N	Y
VERMONT			
AL *Sanders*	Y	Y	N
VIRGINIA			
1 *Bateman*	N	N	N
2 Pickett	Y	N	N
3 Scott	Y	N	N
4 Sisisky	Y	N	N
5 Payne	Y	N	Y
6 *Goodlatte*	N	N	Y
7 *Bliley*	N	N	N
8 Moran	Y	N	N
9 Boucher	Y	N	N
10 *Wolf*	N	N	N
11 Byrne	Y	N	N
WASHINGTON			
1 Cantwell	Y	N	N
2 Swift	Y	N	N
3 Unsoeld	Y	Y	N
4 Inslee	Y	Y	Y
5 Foley			
6 Dicks	Y	N	N
7 McDermott	Y	Y	N
8 *Dunn*	N	N	N
9 Kreidler	Y	N	Y
WEST VIRGINIA			
1 Mollohan	Y	N	N
2 Wise	Y	N	N
3 Rahall	Y	Y	N
WISCONSIN			
1 Barca	Y	Y	N
2 *Klug*	N	Y	N
3 *Gunderson*	N	N	N
4 Kleczka	Y	Y	N
5 Barrett	Y	Y	N
6 *Petri*	N	Y	Y
7 Obey	Y	N	N
8 *Roth*	N	N	Y
9 *Sensenbrenner*	N	Y	Y
WYOMING			
AL *Thomas*	N	N	N
DELEGATES			
de Lugo, V.I.	D	Y	N
Faleomavaega, Am.S.	D	N	N
Norton, D.C.	D	Y	N
Romero-B., P.R.	D	N	N
Underwood, Guam	D	N	N

Southern states - Ala., Ark., Fla., Ga., Ky., La., Miss., N.C., Okla., S.C., Tenn., Texas, Va.
Omitted votes are quorum calls, which CQ does not include in its vote charts.

KEY

Y   Voted for (yea).
Paired for.
+   Announced for.
N   Voted against (nay).
X   Paired against.
—   Announced against.
P   Voted "present."
C   Voted "present" to avoid possible conflict of interest.
?   Did not vote or otherwise make a position known.
D   Delegates ineligible to vote.

Democrats   **Republicans**
Independent

53. Procedural Motion. Approval of the House Journal of Thursday, March 10. Approved 225-148: R 15-141; D 209-7 (ND 143-6, SD 66-1); I 1-0, March 11, 1994.

54. H Con Res 218. Fiscal 1995 Budget Resolution/Black Caucus Substitute. Mfume, D-Md., amendment incorporating the Congressional Black Caucus budget substitute to shift $16.8 billion in budget authority and $9 billion in outlays from defense to domestic programs in fiscal 1995 and a total of $175.1 billion in budget authority and $125.3 billion in outlays over five years. Rejected in the Committee of the Whole 81-326: R 3-164; D 77-162 (ND 61-102, SD 16-60); I 1-0, March 11, 1994.

55. H Con Res 218. Fiscal 1995 Budget Resolution/Tax Cut and Spending Cut Substitute. Kasich, R-Ohio, substitute amendment to provide an additional $147.5 billion in deficit reduction over five years. Over five years the amendment would cut taxes by $119.1 billion, including a $500-per-child tax credit for families earning up to $200,000 a year; cut domestic spending by $284.4 billion; cut foreign aid by $13.1 billion; and increase defense spending by $61.1 billion. Rejected in the Committee of the Whole 165-243: R 158-9; D 7-233 (ND 2-162, SD 5-71); I 0-1, March 11, 1994. A "nay" was a vote in support of the president's position.

56. H Con Res 218. Fiscal 1995 Budget Resolution/Adoption. Adoption of the resolution to set budget levels for the fiscal year ending Sept. 30, 1995: budget authority, $1.541 trillion; outlays, $1.514 trillion; revenues, $1.338 trillion; and a deficit of $175.3 billion. The resolution generally follows the guidelines of President Clinton's budget. Adopted 223-175: R 0-164; D 222-11 (ND 152-7, SD 70-4); I 1-0, March 11, 1994. A "yea" was a vote in support of the president's position.

57. HR 3345. Work Force Restructuring/Crime Trust Fund. Castle, R-Del., motion to instruct the House conferees to agree to the Senate amendment to use the savings from the bill to establish a Violent Crime Reduction Trust Fund within the Treasury Department. Motion agreed to 231-150: R 150-8; D 81-141 (ND 46-107, SD 35-34); I 0-1, March 11, 1994.

58. Procedural Motion. Approval of the House Journal of Tuesday, March 15. Approved 246-144: R 21-139; D 224-5 (ND 150-4, SD 74-1); I 1-0, March 16, 1994.

	53	54	55	56	57	58
ALABAMA						
1 *Callahan*	Y	N	Y	N	?	?
2 *Everett*	Y	N	Y	N	Y	Y
3 Browder	Y	N	Y	N	Y	N
4 Bevill	Y	N	N	Y	Y	Y
5 Cramer	Y	N	N	Y	Y	N
6 *Bachus*	N	N	Y	N	Y	N
7 Hilliard	Y	Y	N	Y	N	Y
ALASKA						
AL *Young*	N	N	Y	N	Y	N
ARIZONA						
1 Coppersmith	Y	N	N	Y	N	Y
2 Pastor	Y	Y	N	Y	N	Y
3 *Stump*	N	N	Y	N	Y	N
4 *Kyl*	N	N	Y	N	Y	N
5 *Kolbe*	N	N	Y	N	Y	N
6 English	Y	N	N	Y	Y	Y
ARKANSAS						
1 Lambert	Y	N	N	Y	Y	Y
2 Thornton	Y	N	N	Y	N	Y
3 *Hutchinson*	N	N	Y	N	Y	N
4 Dickey	N	N	Y	N	Y	N
CALIFORNIA						
1 Hamburg	Y	Y	N	Y	N	Y
2 *Herger*	?	N	Y	N	Y	N
3 Fazio	Y	N	N	Y	N	Y
4 *Doolittle*	N	N	Y	N	Y	N
5 Matsui	Y	N	N	Y	N	Y
6 Woolsey	Y	Y	N	Y	N	Y
7 Miller	?	?	?	?	?	Y
8 Pelosi	?	?	?	?	?	Y
9 Dellums	Y	Y	N	Y	N	Y
10 *Baker*	N	N	Y	N	Y	N
11 *Pombo*	Y	N	Y	N	Y	Y
12 Lantos	Y	N	N	Y	N	Y
13 Stark	Y	Y	N	Y	N	Y
14 Eshoo	Y	N	N	Y	N	Y
15 Mineta	Y	Y	N	Y	N	Y
16 Edwards	Y	Y	N	Y	N	Y
17 Farr	Y	Y	N	Y	N	?
18 Condit	Y	N	Y	N	Y	Y
19 Lehman	Y	N	N	Y	Y	Y
20 Dooley	?	X	X	#	?	Y
21 *Thomas*	N	N	Y	N	Y	N
22 *Huffington*	N	N	N	N	Y	?
23 *Gallegly*	N	N	Y	N	Y	N
24 Beilenson	Y	N	N	Y	N	Y
25 *McKeon*	N	N	Y	N	Y	N
26 Berman	Y	N	N	Y	Y	Y
27 *Moorhead*	?	N	Y	N	Y	N
28 *Dreier*	N	N	Y	N	Y	N
29 Waxman	Y	N	N	Y	Y	Y
30 Becerra	Y	Y	N	Y	N	Y
31 Martinez	Y	N	N	Y	N	Y
32 Dixon	?	Y	N	Y	N	?
33 Roybal-Allard	Y	Y	N	Y	N	Y
34 Torres	?	Y	N	Y	N	Y
35 Waters	Y	Y	N	Y	N	Y
36 Harman	Y	N	N	Y	Y	Y
37 Tucker	Y	Y	N	Y	N	Y
38 *Horn*	N	N	N	N	Y	N
39 *Royce*	N	N	Y	N	Y	N
40 *Lewis*	?	?	#	?	?	N
41 *Kim*	N	N	Y	N	Y	N
42 Brown	?	Y	N	Y	N	?
43 *Calvert*	N	N	Y	N	Y	N
44 *McCandless*	N	N	Y	N	Y	N
45 *Rohrabacher*	N	N	Y	N	Y	N
46 *Dornan*	N	N	Y	N	Y	?
47 *Cox*	N	?	?	N	Y	N
48 *Packard*	N	N	Y	N	Y	N
49 Schenk	Y	N	N	Y	Y	Y
50 Filner	Y	Y	N	Y	N	Y
51 *Cunningham*	N	N	Y	N	Y	N
52 *Hunter*	N	N	Y	N	Y	N
COLORADO						
1 Schroeder	N	Y	N	N	N	N
2 Skaggs	Y	N	N	Y	?	Y
3 *McInnis*	N	N	Y	N	Y	Y
4 *Allard*	N	N	Y	N	Y	N
5 *Hefley*	N	N	Y	N	Y	N
6 *Schaefer*	N	N	Y	N	Y	N
CONNECTICUT						
1 Kennelly	Y	N	N	Y	Y	Y
2 Gejdenson	Y	N	N	Y	Y	Y
3 DeLauro	Y	N	N	Y	Y	Y
4 *Shays*	N	Y	Y	N	N	N
5 *Franks*	N	N	Y	N	Y	N
6 *Johnson*	N	N	Y	N	Y	N
DELAWARE						
AL *Castle*	N	N	Y	N	Y	N
FLORIDA						
1 Hutto	Y	N	N	Y	Y	Y
2 Peterson	Y	N	N	Y	Y	Y
3 Brown	+	Y	N	Y	N	Y
4 Fowler	N	N	Y	N	Y	N
5 Thurman	Y	N	N	Y	Y	N
6 *Stearns*	N	N	Y	N	Y	N
7 *Mica*	N	N	Y	N	Y	N
8 *McCollum*	N	N	Y	N	Y	N
9 *Bilirakis*	N	N	Y	N	#	N
10 *Young*	N	N	Y	N	Y	N
11 Gibbons	?	?	?	?	?	?
12 *Canady*	N	N	Y	N	Y	N
13 *Miller*	N	N	Y	X	?	N
14 *Goss*	N	N	Y	N	Y	N
15 Bacchus	Y	N	N	Y	N	Y
16 *Lewis*	N	N	Y	N	Y	N
17 Meek	Y	Y	N	?	N	Y
18 *Ros-Lehtinen*	N	N	N	N	Y	N
19 Johnston	Y	N	N	Y	Y	Y
20 Deutsch	Y	N	Y	N	Y	Y
21 *Diaz-Balart*	N	N	N	N	Y	N
22 *Shaw*	?	?	?	X	?	N
23 Hastings	?	?	?	?	?	?
GEORGIA						
1 *Kingston*	Y	N	Y	N	?	Y
2 *Bishop*	?	Y	N	Y	Y	Y
3 *Collins*	N	N	Y	N	Y	N
4 *Linder*	N	N	Y	N	Y	N
5 Lewis	Y	Y	N	Y	N	Y
6 *Gingrich*	N	N	Y	N	Y	?
7 Darden	Y	N	N	Y	Y	Y
8 Rowland	Y	N	N	Y	?	Y
9 Deal	Y	N	Y	Y	Y	Y
10 Johnson	Y	N	N	Y	?	Y
11 McKinney	Y	Y	N	Y	N	?
HAWAII						
1 Abercrombie	?	#	X	#	?	Y
2 Mink	Y	Y	N	Y	N	Y
IDAHO						
1 LaRocco	Y	N	N	Y	Y	Y
2 *Crapo*	N	N	Y	N	Y	N
ILLINOIS						
1 Rush	Y	Y	N	Y	N	Y
2 Reynolds	?	?	?	?	?	?
3 Lipinski	Y	N	N	Y	?	Y
4 Gutierrez	?	?	?	?	?	?
5 Rostenkowski	?	?	?	#	?	?
6 *Hyde*	N	Y	N	Y	N	Y
7 Collins	?	#	X	#	?	Y
8 *Crane*	?	?	?	X	?	?
9 Yates	Y	Y	N	Y	N	Y
10 *Porter*	?	N	Y	N	Y	N
11 Sangmeister	Y	N	N	Y	Y	Y
12 Costello	Y	N	N	Y	Y	Y
13 *Fawell*	N	N	Y	N	N	N
14 *Hastert*	N	N	Y	N	Y	N
15 *Ewing*	N	N	Y	N	Y	N
16 *Manzullo*	?	N	Y	N	Y	N
17 Evans	Y	Y	N	Y	N	?

ND Northern Democrats   SD Southern Democrats

	53	54	55	56	57	58
18 *Michel*	N	N	Y	?	Y	?
19 Poshard	Y	N	N	Y	Y	Y
20 Durbin	Y	N	N	Y	N	Y
INDIANA						
1 Visclosky	Y	N	N	Y	N	Y
2 Sharp	Y	N	N	Y	N	Y
3 Roemer	Y	N	N	Y	Y	Y
4 Long	Y	N	N	Y	N	Y
5 *Buyer*	?	N	Y	N	Y	N
6 *Burton*	N	N	Y	N	Y	N
7 *Myers*	Y	N	Y	N	N	Y
8 McCloskey	?	N	N	Y	N	Y
9 Hamilton	Y	N	N	Y	N	Y
10 Jacobs	N	Y	N	N	N	N
IOWA						
1 *Leach*	N	N	Y	N	Y	N
2 *Nussle*	N	N	Y	N	Y	N
3 *Lightfoot*	?	?	#	X	?	N
4 Smith	Y	N	N	Y	Y	Y
5 *Grandy*	N	N	Y	N	Y	N
KANSAS						
1 *Roberts*	N	N	Y	N	Y	N
2 Slattery	?	X	X	#	?	Y
3 *Meyers*	N	N	Y	N	Y	N
4 Glickman	Y	N	N	Y	Y	Y
KENTUCKY						
1 Barlow	Y	N	N	Y	N	Y
2 *Lewis*						
3 Mazzoli	Y	N	N	Y	N	Y
4 *Bunning*	N	N	Y	N	Y	N
5 *Rogers*	N	N	Y	N	Y	N
6 Baesler	Y	N	N	Y	N	Y
LOUISIANA						
1 *Livingston*	N	N	Y	N	Y	Y
2 Jefferson	?	Y	N	Y	N	?
3 Tauzin	Y	N	Y	Y	Y	Y
4 Fields	Y	Y	N	Y	N	Y
5 *McCrery*	?	N	Y	N	Y	Y
6 *Baker*	N	N	Y	N	Y	?
7 Hayes	?	?	?	?	?	Y
MAINE						
1 Andrews	Y	Y	N	Y	N	Y
2 *Snowe*	N	N	Y	N	Y	N
MARYLAND						
1 *Gilchrest*	N	N	Y	N	Y	N
2 *Bentley*	?	N	N	N	Y	N
3 Cardin	Y	N	N	Y	N	Y
4 Wynn	Y	Y	N	Y	N	Y
5 Hoyer	Y	N	N	Y	N	Y
6 *Bartlett*	N	N	Y	N	Y	N
7 Mfume	Y	Y	N	Y	N	Y
8 *Morella*	?	N	N	N	N	N
MASSACHUSETTS						
1 Olver	Y	Y	N	Y	N	Y
2 Neal	Y	N	N	Y	N	Y
3 *Blute*	N	N	Y	N	Y	N
4 Frank	?	Y	N	Y	N	Y
5 Meehan	?	#	X	#	X	?
6 *Torkildsen*	N	N	Y	N	Y	N
7 Markey	Y	Y	N	Y	N	Y
8 Kennedy	Y	Y	N	Y	N	Y
9 Moakley	Y	N	N	Y	N	Y
10 Studds	Y	N	N	Y	N	Y
MICHIGAN						
1 Stupak	Y	N	N	Y	Y	Y
2 *Hoekstra*	N	N	Y	N	Y	N
3 *Ehlers*	N	Y	Y	N	N	Y
4 *Camp*	N	N	Y	N	Y	N
5 Barcia	Y	N	N	Y	Y	Y
6 *Upton*	N	N	Y	N	N	N
7 *Smith*	N	N	Y	?	Y	N
8 Carr	Y	N	N	Y	N	Y
9 Kildee	Y	N	N	Y	N	Y
10 Bonior	Y	Y	N	Y	N	Y
11 *Knollenberg*	N	N	Y	N	Y	N
12 Levin	Y	N	N	Y	Y	Y
13 Ford	Y	Y	N	Y	N	?
14 Conyers	Y	Y	N	Y	N	Y
15 Collins	Y	Y	N	Y	N	Y
16 Dingell	Y	N	N	Y	N	Y
MINNESOTA						
1 Penny	Y	N	N	N	N	Y
2 Minge	Y	N	N	Y	N	Y
3 *Ramstad*	N	N	Y	N	Y	N
4 Vento	N	Y	N	Y	N	Y
5 Sabo	Y	Y	N	Y	N	Y
6 *Grams*	N	N	Y	N	Y	N
7 Peterson	Y	N	N	Y	Y	Y
8 Oberstar	Y	N	N	Y	N	Y
MISSISSIPPI						
1 Whitten	?	N	N	Y	Y	?
2 Thompson	Y	Y	N	Y	N	Y
3 Montgomery	Y	N	N	Y	Y	Y
4 Parker	Y	N	N	Y	Y	Y
5 Taylor	N	N	N	N	Y	N
MISSOURI						
1 Clay	N	Y	N	Y	N	N
2 *Talent*	N	N	Y	N	Y	N
3 Gephardt	?	?	N	Y	N	Y
4 Skelton	Y	N	N	Y	Y	Y
5 Wheat	Y	Y	N	Y	N	Y
6 Danner	Y	N	N	Y	Y	Y
7 *Hancock*	N	N	Y	N	Y	N
8 *Emerson*	N	N	Y	N	Y	N
9 Volkmer	Y	N	N	Y	N	Y
MONTANA						
AL Williams	Y	N	N	Y	N	?
NEBRASKA						
1 *Bereuter*	N	N	Y	N	Y	N
2 Hoagland	Y	N	N	Y	N	Y
3 *Barrett*	N	N	Y	N	Y	N
NEVADA						
1 Bilbray	Y	N	N	Y	Y	Y
2 *Vucanovich*	N	N	Y	N	Y	N
NEW HAMPSHIRE						
1 *Zeliff*	N	N	Y	N	Y	N
2 Swett	Y	N	N	Y	N	Y
NEW JERSEY						
1 Andrews	Y	N	N	N	Y	Y
2 Hughes	Y	N	N	Y	Y	Y
3 *Saxton*	N	N	Y	N	Y	N
4 *Smith*	N	N	Y	N	Y	Y
5 *Roukema*	N	N	Y	N	Y	N
6 Pallone	Y	N	N	Y	Y	Y
7 *Franks*	N	N	Y	N	Y	N
8 Klein	Y	N	N	Y	Y	Y
9 Torricelli	Y	N	N	Y	Y	Y
10 Payne	Y	Y	N	Y	N	?
11 Vacancy						
12 *Zimmer*	N	N	Y	N	Y	N
13 Menendez	Y	Y	N	Y	N	Y
NEW MEXICO						
1 *Schiff*	N	N	Y	N	Y	N
2 *Skeen*	N	N	Y	N	Y	N
3 Richardson	Y	Y	N	Y	N	Y
NEW YORK						
1 Hochbrueckner	Y	N	N	Y	N	Y
2 *Lazio*	N	N	Y	N	Y	N
3 *King*	N	N	Y	N	Y	N
4 *Levy*	N	N	Y	N	Y	N
5 Ackerman	Y	N	N	Y	N	Y
6 Flake	Y	Y	N	Y	N	Y
7 Manton	Y	N	N	Y	N	Y
8 Nadler	Y	Y	N	Y	N	Y
9 Schumer	Y	N	N	Y	Y	Y
10 Towns	?	?	?	?	?	Y
11 Owens	?	Y	N	Y	?	Y
12 Velazquez	Y	Y	N	Y	N	Y
13 *Molinari*	N	N	Y	N	Y	N
14 Maloney	?	Y	N	Y	Y	Y
15 Rangel	Y	Y	N	Y	N	Y
16 Serrano	Y	Y	N	Y	N	Y
17 Engel	Y	Y	N	Y	Y	?
18 Lowey	Y	N	N	Y	Y	Y
19 *Fish*	?	N	Y	N	Y	?
20 *Gilman*	Y	N	N	N	N	Y
21 McNulty	Y	N	N	Y	?	Y
22 *Solomon*	?	N	Y	N	?	N
23 *Boehlert*	N	N	N	N	Y	N
24 *McHugh*	N	N	Y	N	Y	N
25 *Walsh*	N	N	Y	N	Y	N
26 Hinchey	Y	Y	N	Y	N	Y
27 *Paxon*	N	N	Y	N	Y	N
28 Slaughter	Y	N	N	Y	N	Y
29 LaFalce	Y	N	N	Y	?	Y
30 *Quinn*	N	N	Y	N	Y	?
31 *Houghton*	Y	N	Y	N	Y	Y
NORTH CAROLINA						
1 Clayton	Y	Y	N	Y	N	Y
2 Valentine	Y	N	N	Y	Y	Y
3 Lancaster	Y	N	N	N	Y	Y
4 Price	Y	N	N	Y	N	Y
5 Neal	?	?	N	Y	Y	Y
6 *Coble*	N	N	Y	N	Y	N
7 Rose	Y	N	N	Y	?	Y
8 Hefner	Y	N	N	Y	N	Y
9 *McMillan*	?	?	#	X	?	N
10 *Ballenger*	N	N	Y	X	+	N
11 *Taylor*	N	N	Y	N	?	?
12 Watt	Y	Y	N	Y	?	Y
NORTH DAKOTA						
AL Pomeroy	Y	N	N	Y	Y	Y
OHIO						
1 Mann	Y	N	N	N	N	Y
2 *Portman*	N	N	Y	N	Y	N
3 Hall	Y	N	N	Y	N	Y
4 *Oxley*	N	N	Y	N	Y	N
5 *Gillmor*	Y	N	Y	N	Y	Y
6 Strickland	Y	N	N	Y	N	Y
7 *Hobson*	N	N	Y	N	Y	N
8 *Boehner*	N	N	Y	N	?	N
9 Kaptur	Y	N	N	Y	Y	Y
10 *Hoke*	N	N	Y	N	Y	N
11 Stokes	Y	Y	N	Y	N	Y
12 *Kasich*	Y	N	Y	N	Y	Y
13 Brown	?	N	N	Y	N	Y
14 Sawyer	Y	N	N	Y	N	Y
15 *Pryce*	N	N	Y	N	Y	N
16 *Regula*	N	N	Y	N	Y	N
17 Traficant	Y	N	N	N	Y	Y
18 Applegate	Y	N	N	Y	N	Y
19 Fingerhut	Y	N	Y	Y	Y	Y
OKLAHOMA						
1 *Largent*						
2 Synar	Y	N	N	Y	N	Y
3 Brewster	Y	N	N	Y	Y	Y
4 McCurdy	Y	N	N	Y	Y	Y
5 *Istook*	N	N	Y	N	Y	N
6 *Lucas*						
OREGON						
1 Furse	Y	Y	N	Y	Y	Y
2 *Smith*	N	N	Y	N	Y	N
3 Wyden	Y	N	N	Y	Y	Y
4 DeFazio	Y	N	N	N	Y	Y
5 Kopetski	?	?	?	?	?	Y
PENNSYLVANIA						
1 Foglietta	Y	Y	N	Y	N	Y
2 Blackwell	Y	Y	N	Y	N	Y
3 Borski	Y	N	N	Y	N	Y
4 Klink	Y	N	N	Y	N	?
5 *Clinger*	N	N	Y	N	Y	N
6 Holden	Y	N	N	Y	N	Y
7 *Weldon*	N	N	Y	N	Y	N
8 *Greenwood*	?	N	Y	N	Y	Y
9 *Shuster*	N	N	Y	N	Y	N
10 *McDade*	N	N	Y	N	Y	N
11 Kanjorski	Y	N	N	Y	N	Y
12 Murtha	Y	N	N	Y	?	Y
13 Margolies-Mezv.	Y	N	N	N	N	Y
14 Coyne	Y	Y	N	Y	N	Y
15 McHale	Y	N	N	Y	Y	Y
16 *Walker*	N	N	Y	N	Y	N
17 *Gekas*	N	Y	Y	N	Y	N
18 *Santorum*	Y	N	Y	N	Y	N
19 *Goodling*	N	N	Y	N	Y	N
20 Murphy	N	N	N	Y	N	N
21 *Ridge*	N	N	Y	N	Y	?
RHODE ISLAND						
1 *Machtley*	N	N	N	N	Y	N
2 Reed	Y	N	N	Y	Y	Y
SOUTH CAROLINA						
1 *Ravenel*	N	N	Y	N	Y	N
2 *Spence*	N	N	Y	N	Y	Y
3 Derrick	Y	N	N	Y	?	Y
4 *Inglis*	Y	N	Y	N	Y	Y
5 Spratt	Y	N	N	Y	Y	Y
6 Clyburn	Y	Y	N	Y	N	Y
SOUTH DAKOTA						
AL Johnson	Y	N	N	Y	N	Y
TENNESSEE						
1 *Quillen*	N	N	Y	N	?	N
2 *Duncan*	N	N	Y	N	Y	N
3 Lloyd	Y	N	?	#	?	Y
4 Cooper	Y	N	Y	Y	Y	Y
5 Clement	Y	N	N	Y	Y	Y
6 Gordon	Y	N	N	Y	N	Y
7 *Sundquist*	N	N	Y	N	?	N
8 Tanner	Y	N	N	Y	Y	Y
9 Ford	?	?	?	?	?	?
TEXAS						
1 Chapman	?	N	N	Y	Y	Y
2 Wilson	Y	N	N	Y	Y	Y
3 *Johnson, Sam*	N	N	Y	N	Y	N
4 Hall	Y	N	N	N	Y	Y
5 Bryant	Y	N	N	Y	Y	Y
6 *Barton*	?	?	#	X	?	N
7 *Archer*	N	N	Y	N	Y	?
8 *Fields*	?	?	#	X	?	N
9 Brooks	?	?	?	#	?	Y
10 Pickle	Y	N	N	Y	Y	Y
11 Edwards	?	N	N	Y	Y	Y
12 Geren	Y	N	Y	Y	Y	Y
13 Sarpalius	Y	N	N	Y	Y	Y
14 Laughlin	Y	N	N	Y	N	Y
15 de la Garza	Y	N	N	Y	Y	Y
16 Coleman	Y	N	N	Y	N	Y
17 Stenholm	Y	N	Y	Y	Y	Y
18 Washington	?	Y	N	Y	N	?
19 *Combest*	Y	N	Y	N	Y	Y
20 Gonzalez	Y	N	N	?	N	Y
21 *Smith*	N	N	Y	N	Y	N
22 *DeLay*	N	N	Y	N	Y	N
23 *Bonilla*	N	N	Y	N	Y	?
24 Frost	Y	N	N	Y	Y	Y
25 Andrews	?	?	?	?	?	Y
26 *Armey*	N	N	Y	N	Y	N
27 Ortiz	Y	N	N	Y	N	Y
28 Tejeda	Y	N	N	Y	N	Y
29 Green	Y	Y	N	Y	?	?
30 Johnson, E.B.	Y	Y	N	Y	N	Y
UTAH						
1 *Hansen*	N	N	Y	N	Y	N
2 Shepherd	Y	N	N	Y	Y	Y
3 Orton	?	X	X	#	—	Y
VERMONT						
AL *Sanders*	Y	Y	N	Y	N	Y
VIRGINIA						
1 *Bateman*	Y	N	Y	N	Y	Y
2 Pickett	Y	N	N	N	N	Y
3 Scott	Y	Y	N	Y	N	Y
4 Sisisky	Y	N	N	Y	?	Y
5 Payne	Y	N	N	Y	Y	Y
6 *Goodlatte*	N	N	Y	N	Y	N
7 *Bliley*	N	N	Y	N	Y	N
8 Moran	?	N	N	Y	N	Y
9 Boucher	Y	N	N	Y	N	Y
10 *Wolf*	N	N	Y	N	N	N
11 Byrne	?	N	N	Y	N	Y
WASHINGTON						
1 Cantwell	Y	N	N	Y	Y	Y
2 Swift	Y	N	N	Y	N	Y
3 Unsoeld	Y	N	N	Y	N	Y
4 Inslee	Y	N	N	Y	N	Y
5 Foley						
6 Dicks	Y	N	N	Y	N	Y
7 McDermott	?	Y	N	Y	N	Y
8 *Dunn*	N	N	Y	N	Y	N
9 Kreidler	N	N	N	Y	N	Y
WEST VIRGINIA						
1 Mollohan	Y	N	N	Y	Y	Y
2 Wise	Y	N	N	Y	Y	Y
3 Rahall	Y	N	N	Y	Y	Y
WISCONSIN						
1 Barca	Y	N	N	Y	Y	Y
2 *Klug*	N	N	Y	N	Y	N
3 *Gunderson*	N	N	Y	N	Y	N
4 Kleczka	Y	N	N	Y	N	Y
5 Barrett	Y	Y	N	Y	N	?
6 *Petri*	N	N	Y	N	Y	N
7 Obey	Y	N	N	Y	N	Y
8 *Roth*	N	N	Y	N	Y	N
9 *Sensenbrenner*	N	N	Y	N	Y	N
WYOMING						
AL *Thomas*	?	N	Y	N	Y	Y
DELEGATES						
de Lugo, V.I.	D	Y	N	D	D	D
Faleomavaega, Am.S.	D	Y	N	D	D	D
Norton, D.C.	D	Y	N	D	D	D
Romero-B., P.R.	D	Y	N	D	D	D
Underwood, Guam	D	Y	N	D	D	D

Southern states - Ala., Ark., Fla., Ga., Ky., La., Miss., N.C., Okla., S.C., Tenn., Texas, Va.
Omitted votes are quorum calls, which CQ does not include in its vote charts.

59. H J Res 103. Balanced-Budget Constitutional Amendment/Rule. Adoption of the rule (H Res 331) to provide for House floor consideration of the joint resolution to propose a constitutional amendment to require a balanced budget and for floor consideration of four substitute amendments thereto. If more than one substitute was adopted, the last adopted was to take precedence. Adopted 387-22: R 167-0; D 219-22 (ND 142-20, SD 77-2); I 1-0, March 16, 1994.

60. H J Res 103. Balanced-Budget Constitutional Amendment/Outlay Limitation. Kyl, R-Ariz., substitute amendment to mandate a balanced budget by 2000 or the third fiscal year following ratification, authorize a presidential line-item veto and limit federal outlays in a given year to 19 percent of the gross national product unless three-fifths of Congress votes to waive the limitation. Rejected in the Committee of the Whole 179-242: R 164-10; D 15-231 (ND 9-156, SD 6-75); I 0-1, March 16, 1994.

* 62. H J Res 103. Balanced-Budget Constitutional Amendment/Revenue Growth Limitation. Barton, R-Texas, substitute amendment to mandate a balanced budget by 2000 or the second fiscal year following ratification and limit the growth in federal receipts to the rate of growth in national income in the previous calendar year, unless three-fifths of Congress votes to allow revenue to increase at a faster rate. Rejected in the Committee of the Whole 213-215: R 169-4; D 44-210 (ND 13-161, SD 31-49); I 0-1, March 17, 1994. (Subsequently, the amendment was adopted on an automatic revote in the full House, required when delegate votes provide the margin deciding an issue. See vote 63.)

63. H J Res 103. Balanced-Budget Constitutional Amendment/Revote on Revenue Growth Limitation. Revote as required when delegate votes provide the margin deciding an issue, as occurred on the Barton, R-Texas, substitute amendment to limit the growth in federal spending to no more than the growth in national income unless three-fifths of Congress approves the specific tax increase. Under House rules, such revotes occur automatically, requiring the Committee of the Whole to rise and the revote to occur in the full House, where delegates may not vote. Following the revote, the Committee of the Whole resumed consideration of the joint resolution. (See vote 62.) Adopted 211-204: R 166-4; D 45-199 (ND 14-152, SD 31-47); I 0-1, March 17, 1994.

64. H J Res 103. Balanced-Budget Constitutional Amendment/Capital Budget and Social Security Exclusion. Wise, D-W.Va., substitute amendment to mandate a balanced budget by 2001 or the second fiscal year following ratification, prohibit the use of surplus Social Security revenues in the deficit calculation, authorize Congress to create a separate capital budget in which borrowing would be permitted for highway improvements and other capital projects, and allow deficit spending during periods of recession, war or a serious military threat. Rejected in the Committee of the Whole 111-318: R 5-169; D 106-148 (ND 79-94, SD 27-54); I 0-1, March 17, 1994.

65. H J Res 103. Balanced-Budget Constitutional Amendment/Passage. Passage of the joint resolution to propose a constitutional amendment to require a balanced budget by 2001 or the second fiscal year after ratification by three-fourths of the states, whichever is later. Congress could waive the balanced-budget requirement if three-fifths of the House and Senate approve deficit spending. It also could waive the requirement when a declaration of war was in effect or when there was a declared military threat to national security. Rejected 271-153: R 172-1; D 99-151 (ND 47-122, SD 52-29); I 0-1, March 17, 1994. (A two-thirds majority vote of those present and voting, 283 in this case, is required to pass a joint resolution proposing an amendment to the Constitution.) A "nay" was a vote in support of the president's position.

* Omitted votes are quorum calls, which CQ does not include in its vote charts.

KEY

Y	Voted for (yea).
#	Paired for.
+	Announced for.
N	Voted against (nay).
X	Paired against.
—	Announced against.
P	Voted "present."
C	Voted "present" to avoid possible conflict of interest.
?	Did not vote or otherwise make a position known.
D	Delegates ineligible to vote.

Democrats **Republicans**
Independent

	59	60	62	63	64	65
ALABAMA						
1 Callahan	Y	Y	Y	Y	N	Y
2 Everett	Y	Y	Y	Y	N	Y
3 Browder	Y	N	Y	Y	N	Y
4 Bevill	Y	N	Y	Y	N	Y
5 Cramer	Y	N	Y	Y	N	Y
6 Bachus	Y	Y	Y	Y	N	Y
7 Hilliard	?	N	N	N	Y	N
ALASKA						
AL Young	Y	Y	Y	Y	N	Y
ARIZONA						
1 Coppersmith	Y	N	N	N	N	Y
2 Pastor	Y	N	N	Y	N	Y
3 Stump	Y	Y	Y	Y	N	Y
4 Kyl	Y	Y	Y	Y	N	Y
5 Kolbe	Y	Y	Y	Y	N	Y
6 English	Y	N	N	N	N	Y
ARKANSAS						
1 Lambert	Y	N	Y	Y	Y	Y
2 Thornton	Y	N	N	N	Y	N
3 Hutchinson	Y	Y	Y	Y	N	Y
4 Dickey	Y	Y	Y	Y	N	Y
CALIFORNIA						
1 Hamburg	Y	N	N	N	?	N
2 Herger	Y	Y	Y	Y	N	Y
3 Fazio	N	N	N	N	N	N
4 Doolittle	Y	Y	Y	Y	N	Y
5 Matsui	Y	N	N	N	N	N
6 Woolsey	Y	N	N	N	N	N
7 Miller	Y	N	N	N	N	N
8 Pelosi	Y	N	N	N	N	N
9 Dellums	N	N	N	N	N	N
10 Baker	Y	Y	Y	Y	N	Y
11 Pombo	Y	Y	Y	Y	N	Y
12 Lantos	Y	N	N	N	N	Y
13 Stark	N	N	N	N	N	N
14 Eshoo	Y	N	N	Y	N	Y
15 Mineta	Y	N	N	N	Y	N
16 Edwards	Y	N	N	N	N	N
17 Farr	?	?	?	?	?	?
18 Condit	Y	N	Y	Y	N	Y
19 Lehman	Y	N	N	N	N	N
20 Dooley	Y	N	N	N	N	Y
21 Thomas	Y	Y	Y	Y	N	Y
22 Huffington	?	Y	Y	Y	N	Y
23 Gallegly	Y	Y	Y	Y	N	Y
24 Beilenson	N	N	N	N	N	N
25 McKeon	Y	Y	Y	Y	N	Y
26 Berman	Y	N	N	Y	N	N
27 Moorhead	Y	Y	Y	Y	N	Y
28 Dreier	Y	Y	Y	Y	N	Y
29 Waxman	Y	N	N	N	N	N
30 Becerra	Y	N	N	N	N	N
31 Martinez	Y	N	N	?	N	Y
32 Dixon	?	?	N	N	N	N
33 Roybal-Allard	Y	N	N	N	N	N
34 Torres	N	N	N	N	Y	N
35 Waters	Y	N	N	N	N	N
36 Harman	Y	N	N	N	Y	Y
37 Tucker	Y	?	N	N	N	N
38 Horn	Y	Y	Y	Y	N	Y
39 Royce	Y	Y	Y	Y	N	Y
40 Lewis	Y	Y	Y	Y	N	Y
41 Kim	Y	Y	Y	Y	N	Y

	59	60	62	63	64	65
42 Brown	Y	N	N	N	N	N
43 Calvert	Y	Y	Y	Y	N	Y
44 McCandless	Y	Y	Y	Y	N	Y
45 Rohrabacher	Y	Y	Y	Y	N	Y
46 Dornan	Y	Y	Y	Y	N	Y
47 Cox	Y	Y	Y	Y	N	Y
48 Packard	Y	Y	Y	Y	N	Y
49 Schenk	Y	Y	Y	Y	N	Y
50 Filner	Y	N	N	N	N	N
51 Cunningham	?	Y	Y	Y	N	Y
52 Hunter	Y	Y	Y	Y	N	Y
COLORADO						
1 Schroeder	Y	N	N	N	Y	N
2 Skaggs	Y	N	N	N	N	N
3 McInnis	Y	Y	Y	Y	N	Y
4 Allard	Y	Y	Y	Y	N	Y
5 Hefley	Y	Y	Y	Y	N	Y
6 Schaefer	Y	Y	Y	Y	N	Y
CONNECTICUT						
1 Kennelly	Y	N	N	N	N	N
2 Gejdenson	Y	N	N	N	Y	N
3 DeLauro	Y	N	N	N	N	N
4 Shays	Y	Y	Y	Y	N	Y
5 Franks	Y	Y	Y	Y	N	Y
6 Johnson	?	Y	Y	Y	N	Y
DELAWARE						
AL Castle	Y	Y	Y	Y	N	Y
FLORIDA						
1 Hutto	Y	N	Y	Y	N	Y
2 Peterson	Y	N	N	N	N	Y
3 Brown	Y	N	N	N	N	N
4 Fowler	Y	Y	Y	Y	N	Y
5 Thurman	Y	N	N	N	Y	N
6 Stearns	Y	Y	Y	Y	N	Y
7 Mica	Y	Y	Y	Y	N	Y
8 McCollum	Y	Y	Y	Y	N	Y
9 Bilirakis	Y	Y	Y	Y	N	Y
10 Young	Y	N	Y	Y	N	Y
11 Gibbons	Y	N	N	N	Y	N
12 Canady	Y	Y	Y	Y	N	Y
13 Miller	Y	Y	Y	Y	N	Y
14 Goss	Y	Y	Y	Y	N	Y
15 Bacchus	Y	Y	Y	Y	N	Y
16 Lewis	Y	Y	Y	Y	N	Y
17 Meek	Y	N	N	N	N	N
18 Ros-Lehtinen	Y	Y	Y	Y	N	Y
19 Johnston	Y	N	N	N	N	N
20 Deutsch	Y	N	N	N	Y	Y
21 Diaz-Balart	Y	Y	Y	Y	N	Y
22 Shaw	Y	N	Y	Y	N	Y
23 Hastings	?	?	?	?	?	?
GEORGIA						
1 Kingston	Y	Y	Y	Y	N	Y
2 Bishop	Y	N	Y	Y	Y	Y
3 Collins	Y	Y	Y	Y	N	Y
4 Linder	Y	Y	Y	Y	N	Y
5 Lewis	Y	N	N	N	N	N
6 Gingrich	Y	Y	Y	Y	N	Y
7 Darden	Y	N	N	N	N	Y
8 Rowland	Y	N	Y	Y	N	Y
9 Deal	Y	N	Y	Y	N	Y
10 Johnson	Y	N	Y	Y	N	Y
11 McKinney	Y	N	N	N	N	N
HAWAII						
1 Abercrombie	Y	N	N	N	N	N
2 Mink	Y	N	N	N	Y	N
IDAHO						
1 LaRocco	Y	N	N	N	N	Y
2 Crapo	Y	Y	Y	Y	N	Y
ILLINOIS						
1 Rush	?	?	N	N	N	N
2 Reynolds	?	?	N	N	N	N
3 Lipinski	Y	N	N	N	N	Y
4 Gutierrez	?	N	N	N	N	N
5 Rostenkowski	?	?	N	N	N	N
6 Hyde	Y	Y	Y	Y	N	Y
7 Collins	Y	N	N	N	N	N
8 Crane	?	Y	Y	Y	N	Y
9 Yates	?	?	N	N	Y	N
10 Porter	?	Y	Y	?	N	Y
11 Sangmeister	Y	N	N	N	N	N
12 Costello	Y	N	N	Y	N	N
13 Fawell	Y	Y	Y	Y	N	Y
14 Hastert	Y	Y	Y	Y	N	Y
15 Ewing	Y	Y	Y	Y	N	Y
16 Manzullo	Y	Y	Y	Y	N	Y
17 Evans	?	N	N	N	N	N

ND Northern Democrats   SD Southern Democrats

	59	60	62	63	64	65
18 ***Michel***	Y	Y	Y	Y	N	#
19 Poshard	Y	Y	Y	Y	N	Y
20 Durbin	Y	N	N	N	Y	N
INDIANA						
1 Visclosky	Y	N	N	N	N	N
2 Sharp	Y	N	N	N	Y	Y
3 Roemer	Y	N	N	N	Y	Y
4 Long	Y	N	N	N	Y	Y
5 ***Buyer***	Y	Y	Y	Y	N	Y
6 ***Burton***	Y	Y	Y	Y	N	Y
7 ***Myers***	Y	N	Y	Y	N	Y
8 McCloskey	Y	N	N	N	Y	Y
9 Hamilton	Y	N	N	N	Y	N
10 Jacobs	Y	N	N	N	N	Y
IOWA						
1 ***Leach***	Y	Y	Y	Y	N	Y
2 ***Nussle***	Y	Y	Y	Y	N	Y
3 ***Lightfoot***	Y	Y	Y	Y	N	Y
4 Smith	Y	?	N	N	Y	N
5 ***Grandy***	?	#	#	?	?	#
KANSAS						
1 ***Roberts***	Y	Y	Y	Y	N	Y
2 Slattery	Y	N	Y	Y	N	N
3 ***Meyers***	Y	Y	Y	Y	N	Y
4 Glickman	Y	N	N	N	N	Y
KENTUCKY						
1 Barlow	Y	N	N	N	N	N
2 ***Lewis***						
3 Mazzoli	Y	N	N	N	N	Y
4 ***Bunning***	Y	Y	Y	Y	N	Y
5 ***Rogers***	Y	Y	Y	Y	Y	Y
6 Baesler	Y	N	N	N	N	Y
LOUISIANA						
1 ***Livingston***	Y	Y	Y	Y	N	Y
2 Jefferson	Y	N	N	N	Y	N
3 Tauzin	Y	Y	Y	Y	N	Y
4 Fields	Y	N	N	N	Y	N
5 ***McCrery***	Y	Y	Y	?	N	Y
6 ***Baker***	Y	Y	Y	Y	N	Y
7 Hayes	Y	N	Y	Y	N	Y
MAINE						
1 Andrews	Y	N	N	N	Y	N
2 ***Snowe***	Y	Y	Y	Y	N	Y
MARYLAND						
1 ***Gilchrest***	Y	Y	Y	Y	N	Y
2 ***Bentley***	Y	Y	Y	Y	N	Y
3 Cardin	Y	N	N	N	N	N
4 Wynn	Y	N	N	N	N	N
5 Hoyer	Y	N	N	N	Y	Y
6 ***Bartlett***	Y	Y	Y	Y	N	Y
7 Mfume	Y	N	N	N	N	N
8 ***Morella***	Y	N	N	N	N	Y
MASSACHUSETTS						
1 Olver	Y	N	N	N	Y	N
2 Neal	Y	N	N	N	Y	N
3 ***Blute***	Y	Y	Y	Y	N	Y
4 Frank	Y	N	N	N	N	N
5 Meehan	?	N	N	N	Y	Y
6 ***Torkildsen***	Y	Y	Y	Y	N	Y
7 Markey	Y	N	N	N	Y	N
8 Kennedy	Y	N	N	N	Y	Y
9 Moakley	N	?	N	N	N	N
10 Studds	N	N	N	N	N	N
MICHIGAN						
1 Stupak	Y	N	N	N	Y	N
2 ***Hoekstra***	Y	Y	Y	Y	N	Y
3 ***Ehlers***	Y	Y	Y	Y	N	Y
4 ***Camp***	Y	Y	Y	Y	N	Y
5 Barcia	Y	Y	Y	Y	Y	Y
6 ***Upton***	Y	Y	Y	Y	N	Y
7 ***Smith***	Y	Y	Y	Y	N	Y
8 Carr	Y	N	N	N	Y	Y
9 Kildee	Y	N	N	N	N	N
10 Bonior	N	N	N	N	Y	N
11 ***Knollenberg***	Y	Y	Y	Y	N	Y
12 Levin	Y	N	N	N	N	N
13 Ford	N	?	N	N	Y	N
14 Conyers	Y	N	N	N	N	N
15 Collins	Y	N	N	?	N	N
16 Dingell	Y	N	N	N	N	N
MINNESOTA						
1 Penny	Y	N	N	N	N	Y
2 Minge	Y	N	Y	Y	N	Y
3 ***Ramstad***	Y	Y	Y	Y	N	Y
4 Vento	Y	N	N	N	N	N

	59	60	62	63	64	65
5 Sabo	Y	N	N	N	N	N
6 ***Grams***	Y	Y	Y	Y	N	Y
7 Peterson	Y	N	Y	Y	Y	Y
8 Oberstar	Y	N	N	N	Y	N
MISSISSIPPI						
1 Whitten	Y	N	N	N	Y	Y
2 Thompson	Y	N	N	N	N	N
3 Montgomery	Y	N	Y	Y	N	Y
4 Parker	Y	N	Y	Y	N	Y
5 Taylor	Y	Y	Y	Y	N	Y
MISSOURI						
1 Clay	N	N	N	N	N	N
2 ***Talent***	Y	Y	Y	Y	N	Y
3 Gephardt	N	N	N	N	N	N
4 Skelton	Y	N	Y	Y	N	Y
5 Wheat	N	N	N	N	Y	N
6 Danner	Y	N	N	N	Y	Y
7 ***Hancock***	Y	Y	Y	Y	N	Y
8 ***Emerson***	Y	Y	Y	Y	N	Y
9 Volkmer	Y	N	N	N	Y	Y
MONTANA						
AL Williams	Y	N	N	N	Y	N
NEBRASKA						
1 ***Bereuter***	Y	Y	Y	Y	N	Y
2 Hoagland	Y	Y	N	N	Y	Y
3 ***Barrett***	Y	Y	Y	Y	N	Y
NEVADA						
1 Bilbray	Y	Y	N	N	Y	Y
2 ***Vucanovich***	Y	Y	Y	Y	N	Y
NEW HAMPSHIRE						
1 ***Zeliff***	Y	Y	Y	Y	N	Y
2 Swett	Y	Y	Y	Y	Y	Y
NEW JERSEY						
1 Andrews	Y	Y	Y	Y	Y	Y
2 Hughes	Y	N	N	N	N	N
3 ***Saxton***	Y	Y	Y	Y	N	Y
4 ***Smith***	Y	Y	Y	Y	N	Y
5 ***Roukema***	Y	N	N	N	N	Y
6 Pallone	Y	Y	Y	Y	Y	Y
7 ***Franks***	Y	Y	Y	Y	N	Y
8 Klein	Y	N	N	N	N	N
9 Torricelli	Y	N	N	N	Y	Y
10 Payne	Y	N	?	?	?	—
11 Vacancy						
12 ***Zimmer***	Y	Y	Y	Y	N	Y
13 Menendez	Y	N	N	N	N	N
NEW MEXICO						
1 ***Schiff***	Y	Y	Y	Y	N	Y
2 ***Skeen***	Y	Y	Y	Y	N	Y
3 Richardson	Y	N	N	N	Y	Y
NEW YORK						
1 Hochbrueckner	Y	N	N	N	Y	N
2 ***Lazio***	Y	Y	Y	Y	N	Y
3 ***King***	Y	Y	Y	Y	N	Y
4 ***Levy***	Y	Y	Y	Y	N	Y
5 Ackerman	Y	N	N	N	Y	N
6 Flake	Y	N	N	N	N	N
7 Manton	Y	?	?	?	?	?
8 Nadler	Y	N	N	N	N	N
9 Schumer	Y	N	N	N	Y	N
10 Towns	Y	N	N	N	N	N
11 Owens	N	N	N	N	N	N
12 Velazquez	Y	N	N	N	N	N
13 ***Molinari***	Y	Y	Y	Y	N	Y
14 Maloney	Y	N	N	N	N	N
15 Rangel	N	N	N	N	N	N
16 Serrano	Y	N	N	?	N	N
17 Engel	Y	N	N	N	Y	N
18 Lowey	Y	N	N	N	N	N
19 ***Fish***	Y	Y	Y	Y	N	Y
20 ***Gilman***	Y	N	—	—	N	N
21 McNulty	Y	N	N	N	Y	Y
22 ***Solomon***	Y	Y	Y	Y	N	Y
23 ***Boehlert***	Y	N	Y	Y	N	Y
24 ***McHugh***	Y	Y	Y	Y	N	Y
25 ***Walsh***	Y	Y	Y	Y	N	Y
26 Hinchey	N	N	N	N	N	N
27 ***Paxon***	Y	Y	Y	Y	N	Y
28 Slaughter	Y	N	N	N	N	N
29 LaFalce	Y	N	N	N	N	N
30 ***Quinn***	?	Y	Y	Y	N	Y
31 ***Houghton***	Y	Y	Y	Y	N	Y
NORTH CAROLINA						
1 Clayton	Y	N	N	N	N	N
2 Valentine	Y	N	N	N	N	Y

	59	60	62	63	64	65
3 Lancaster	Y	N	Y	Y	Y	Y
4 Price	Y	N	N	N	Y	N
5 Neal	Y	N	N	N	N	Y
6 ***Coble***	Y	Y	Y	Y	N	Y
7 Rose	Y	N	N	N	Y	N
8 Hefner	Y	N	Y	Y	Y	Y
9 ***McMillan***	Y	Y	Y	Y	N	Y
10 ***Ballenger***	Y	Y	Y	Y	N	Y
11 ***Taylor***	Y	Y	Y	Y	N	Y
12 Watt	Y	N	N	N	N	N
NORTH DAKOTA						
AL Pomeroy	Y	N	N	N	Y	N
OHIO						
1 Mann	Y	N	N	N	Y	Y
2 ***Portman***	Y	Y	Y	Y	N	Y
3 Hall	Y	N	N	N	Y	N
4 ***Oxley***	Y	Y	Y	?	N	Y
5 ***Gillmor***	Y	Y	Y	Y	N	Y
6 Strickland	Y	N	N	N	Y	N
7 ***Hobson***	Y	Y	Y	Y	N	Y
8 ***Boehner***	Y	Y	Y	Y	N	Y
9 Kaptur	Y	N	N	N	Y	N
10 ***Hoke***	Y	N	N	N	N	Y
11 Stokes	N	N	N	N	N	N
12 ***Kasich***	Y	Y	Y	Y	N	Y
13 Brown	Y	N	N	N	Y	Y
14 Sawyer	Y	?	N	N	Y	N
15 ***Pryce***	Y	Y	Y	Y	N	Y
16 ***Regula***	Y	Y	Y	Y	Y	Y
17 Traficant	Y	N	N	N	N	N
18 Applegate	Y	N	N	N	Y	N
19 Fingerhut	Y	N	Y	Y	Y	Y
OKLAHOMA						
1 ***Largent***						
2 Synar	Y	N	N	N	N	N
3 Brewster	Y	N	N	N	N	Y
4 McCurdy	Y	N	N	N	N	Y
5 ***Istook***	Y	Y	Y	Y	N	Y
6 ***Lucas***						
OREGON						
1 Furse	Y	N	N	N	Y	N
2 ***Smith***	Y	Y	Y	Y	N	Y
3 Wyden	Y	N	N	N	N	N
4 DeFazio	Y	N	N	N	N	Y
5 Kopetski	N	N	N	N	Y	N
PENNSYLVANIA						
1 Foglietta	Y	N	N	N	N	N
2 Blackwell	Y	N	N	N	N	N
3 Borski	Y	N	N	N	Y	N
4 Klink	N	N	N	N	N	N
5 ***Clinger***	Y	Y	Y	Y	Y	Y
6 Holden	Y	N	N	N	Y	N
7 ***Weldon***	Y	Y	Y	Y	N	Y
8 ***Greenwood***	Y	Y	Y	Y	N	Y
9 ***Shuster***	Y	Y	Y	Y	N	Y
10 ***McDade***	Y	N	Y	Y	N	Y
11 Kanjorski	Y	N	N	N	N	N
12 Murtha	?	N	N	N	N	N
13 Margolies-Mezv.	N	N	N	N	N	N
14 Coyne	Y	N	N	N	N	N
15 McHale	Y	N	N	N	N	Y
16 ***Walker***	Y	Y	Y	Y	N	Y
17 ***Gekas***	Y	Y	Y	Y	N	Y
18 ***Santorum***	Y	Y	Y	Y	N	Y
19 ***Goodling***	Y	Y	Y	Y	N	Y
20 Murphy	Y	N	N	N	Y	N
21 ***Ridge***	?	Y	Y	Y	N	Y
RHODE ISLAND						
1 ***Machtley***	Y	Y	Y	Y	N	Y
2 Reed	Y	N	N	N	Y	N
SOUTH CAROLINA						
1 ***Ravenel***	Y	Y	Y	Y	N	Y
2 ***Spence***	Y	Y	Y	Y	Y	Y
3 Derrick	Y	N	N	N	N	Y
4 ***Inglis***	Y	Y	Y	Y	N	Y
5 Spratt	Y	N	N	N	N	Y
6 Clyburn	Y	N	N	N	Y	N
SOUTH DAKOTA						
AL Johnson	Y	N	N	N	Y	Y
TENNESSEE						
1 ***Quillen***	Y	Y	Y	Y	N	Y
2 ***Duncan***	Y	Y	Y	Y	Y	Y
3 Lloyd	Y	N	Y	Y	N	Y
4 Cooper	Y	Y	Y	Y	Y	Y
5 Clement	Y	N	Y	Y	N	Y

	59	60	62	63	64	65
6 Gordon	Y	N	Y	Y	N	Y
7 ***Sundquist***	Y	Y	Y	Y	N	Y
8 Tanner	Y	N	Y	Y	N	Y
9 Ford	Y	N	N	N	N	N
TEXAS						
1 Chapman	?	N	N	N	Y	Y
2 Wilson	Y	N	Y	Y	N	Y
3 ***Johnson, Sam***	Y	Y	Y	Y	N	Y
4 Hall	Y	Y	Y	Y	N	Y
5 Bryant	Y	N	N	N	Y	Y
6 ***Barton***	Y	Y	Y	Y	N	Y
7 ***Archer***	Y	Y	Y	Y	N	Y
8 ***Fields***	Y	Y	Y	Y	N	Y
9 Brooks	Y	N	N	N	N	N
10 Pickle	Y	N	?	?	N	Y
11 Edwards	Y	N	Y	Y	N	Y
12 Geren	Y	Y	Y	Y	N	Y
13 Sarpalius	Y	N	Y	Y	N	Y
14 Laughlin	Y	N	N	N	N	Y
15 de la Garza	Y	N	Y	Y	N	Y
16 Coleman	Y	N	N	N	Y	N
17 Stenholm	Y	N	Y	Y	N	Y
18 Washington	N	N	N	?	Y	N
19 ***Combest***	Y	Y	Y	Y	N	Y
20 Gonzalez	Y	N	N	N	N	N
21 ***Smith***	Y	Y	Y	Y	N	Y
22 ***DeLay***	Y	Y	Y	Y	N	Y
23 ***Bonilla***	Y	Y	Y	Y	N	Y
24 Frost	Y	N	N	N	Y	Y
25 Andrews	Y	N	N	N	N	Y
26 ***Armey***	Y	Y	Y	Y	N	Y
27 Ortiz	Y	N	N	N	Y	Y
28 Tejeda	Y	N	N	N	Y	N
29 Green	?	X	X	?	?	X
30 Johnson, E.B.	Y	N	N	N	N	N
UTAH						
1 ***Hansen***	Y	Y	Y	Y	N	Y
2 Shepherd	Y	Y	Y	Y	Y	Y
3 Orton	Y	N	N	N	N	Y
VERMONT						
AL *Sanders*	Y	N	N	N	N	N
VIRGINIA						
1 ***Bateman***	Y	Y	Y	Y	N	Y
2 Pickett	N	N	N	N	N	N
3 Scott	Y	N	N	N	Y	N
4 Sisisky	Y	N	Y	Y	N	Y
5 Payne	Y	N	Y	Y	N	Y
6 ***Goodlatte***	Y	Y	Y	Y	N	Y
7 ***Bliley***	Y	Y	Y	Y	N	Y
8 Moran	Y	N	N	N	Y	Y
9 Boucher	Y	N	N	?	Y	N
10 ***Wolf***	Y	Y	Y	Y	N	Y
11 Byrne	Y	N	N	N	Y	N
WASHINGTON						
1 Cantwell	Y	N	N	N	Y	N
2 Swift	Y	N	N	N	N	N
3 Unsoeld	N	N	N	N	N	N
4 Inslee	Y	N	N	N	N	Y
5 Foley						
6 Dicks	Y	N	N	N	N	N
7 McDermott	Y	N	N	N	N	N
8 ***Dunn***	Y	Y	Y	Y	N	Y
9 Kreidler	Y	N	N	N	N	N
WEST VIRGINIA						
1 Mollohan	Y	N	N	N	N	N
2 Wise	Y	N	N	N	Y	N
3 Rahall	Y	N	N	N	N	N
WISCONSIN						
1 Barca	Y	N	N	N	Y	N
2 ***Klug***	Y	Y	Y	Y	N	Y
3 ***Gunderson***	Y	N	N	N	N	Y
4 Kleczka	Y	N	N	N	Y	N
5 Barrett	Y	N	N	N	Y	N
6 ***Petri***	Y	Y	Y	Y	N	Y
7 Obey	Y	N	N	N	Y	N
8 ***Roth***	Y	Y	Y	Y	N	Y
9 ***Sensenbrenner***	Y	Y	Y	Y	N	Y
WYOMING						
AL ***Thomas***	Y	Y	Y	Y	N	Y
DELEGATES						
de Lugo, V.I.	D	N	N	D	N	D
Faleomavaega, Am.S.	D	N	N	D	N	D
Norton, D.C.	D	N	N	D	N	D
Romero-B., P.R.	D	N	N	D	Y	D
Underwood, Guam	D	N	N	D	N	D

Southern states - Ala., Ark., Fla., Ga., Ky., La., Miss., N.C., Okla., S.C., Tenn., Texas, Va.
Omitted votes are quorum calls, which CQ does not include in its vote charts.

KEY

Y   Voted for (yea).
Paired for.
+   Announced for.
N   Voted against (nay).
X   Paired against.
—   Announced against.
P   Voted "present."
C   Voted "present" to avoid possible conflict of interest.
?   Did not vote or otherwise make a position known.
D   Delegates ineligible to vote.

Democrats   ***Republicans***
Independent

66. S 636. Clinic Access/Previous Question. Slaughter, D-N.Y., motion to order the previous question (thus ending debate and the possibility of amendment) on adoption of the rule (H Res 374) to request a conference with the Senate on the House amendment to the bill to establish federal criminal and civil penalties for people who use force, the threat of force or physical obstruction to block access to abortion clinics. Motion agreed to 248-168: R 26-144; D 221-24 (ND 150-15, SD 71-9); I 1-0, March 17, 1994.

67. S 636. Clinic Access/Rule. Adoption of the rule (H Res 374) to request a conference with the Senate on the House amendment to the bill to establish federal criminal and civil penalties for people who use force, the threat of force or physical obstruction to block access to abortion clinics. Adopted 244-171: R 29-141; D 214-30 (ND 144-20, SD 70-10); I 1-0, March 17, 1994.

68. S 636. Clinic Access/House Amendment. Smith, R-N.J., motion to table (kill) the House amendment (the text of HR 796) to the Senate bill to establish federal criminal and civil penalties for people who use force, the threat of force or physical obstruction to block access to abortion clinics. Motion rejected 175-240: R 140-31; D 35-208 (ND 21-144, SD 14-64); I 0-1, March 17, 1994. (The House amendment subsequently was adopted by voice vote.)

69. S 636. Clinic Access/Commit to Judiciary. Smith, R-N.J., motion to commit to the Judiciary Committee the bill to establish federal criminal and civil penalties for people who use force, the threat of force or physical obstruction to block access to abortion clinics. Motion rejected 168-233: R 135-32; D 33-200 (ND 19-137, SD 14-63); I 0-1, March 17, 1994.

70. S 636. Clinic Access/Passage. Passage of the bill to establish federal criminal and civil penalties for people who use force, the threat of force or physical obstruction to block access to abortion clinics. Passed 237-169: R 35-133; D 201-36 (ND 138-22, SD 63-14); I 1-0, March 17, 1994.

71. S 636. Clinic Access/Insist on Amendments. Schroeder, D-Colo., motion to insist on the House amendments and ask for a conference with the Senate on the bill to establish federal criminal and civil penalties for people who use force, the threat of force or physical obstruction to block access to abortion clinics. Motion agreed to 228-166: R 31-133; D 196-33 (ND 134-20, SD 62-13); I 1-0, March 17, 1994.

72. S 636. Clinic Access/Religious Places. Sensenbrenner, R-Wis., motion to instruct the House conferees to accept Senate provisions to extend the bill's protections for abortion clinics to places of religious worship. Motion agreed to 398-2: R 163-0; D 234-2 (ND 158-2, SD 76-0); I 1-0, March 17, 1994.

	66	67	68	69	70	71	72
ALABAMA							
1 *Callahan*	N	N	Y	N	N	N	Y
2 *Everett*	N	N	Y	Y	N	N	Y
3 Browder	Y	Y	Y	N	Y	Y	Y
4 Bevill	Y	Y	Y	N	Y	Y	Y
5 Cramer	Y	Y	N	N	Y	Y	Y
6 *Bachus*	N	N	Y	Y	N	N	Y
7 Hilliard	Y	Y	N	N	Y	Y	Y
ALASKA							
AL *Young*	N	N	Y	N	N	N	Y
ARIZONA							
1 Coppersmith	Y	Y	N	N	Y	Y	Y
2 Pastor	Y	Y	N	N	Y	Y	Y
3 *Stump*	N	N	Y	N	N	N	Y
4 *Kyl*	N	N	Y	Y	N	N	Y
5 *Kolbe*	Y	Y	N	N	Y	Y	Y
6 English	Y	Y	N	N	Y	Y	Y
ARKANSAS							
1 Lambert	Y	Y	N	N	Y	Y	Y
2 Thornton	Y	Y	N	N	Y	Y	Y
3 *Hutchinson*	N	N	Y	Y	N	N	Y
4 Dickey	N	N	Y	Y	N	N	Y
CALIFORNIA							
1 Hamburg	Y	Y	N	N	Y	Y	Y
2 *Herger*	N	N	Y	Y	N	N	Y
3 Fazio	Y	Y	N	?	Y	Y	Y
4 *Doolittle*	N	N	Y	Y	N	N	Y
5 Matsui	Y	Y	N	N	Y	Y	Y
6 Woolsey	Y	Y	N	N	Y	Y	Y
7 Miller	Y	Y	N	N	Y	Y	Y
8 Pelosi	Y	Y	N	N	Y	Y	Y
9 Dellums	Y	Y	N	N	Y	Y	Y
10 Baker	N	N	Y	N	N	Y	Y
11 *Pombo*	N	N	Y	N	N	N	Y
12 Lantos	Y	Y	N	N	Y	Y	Y
13 Stark	Y	Y	N	N	Y	Y	Y
14 Eshoo	Y	Y	N	N	Y	Y	Y
15 Mineta	Y	Y	N	N	Y	Y	Y
16 Edwards	Y	Y	N	N	Y	Y	Y
17 Farr	?	?	?	?	?	?	?
18 Condit	Y	Y	N	N	Y	Y	Y
19 Lehman	Y	Y	N	N	Y	Y	Y
20 Dooley	Y	Y	N	?	Y	Y	Y
21 *Thomas*	N	N	Y	Y	Y	Y	N
22 *Huffington*	N	N	N	N	Y	Y	Y
23 *Gallegly*	N	N	Y	Y	N	?	Y
24 Beilenson	Y	Y	N	N	Y	Y	Y
25 *McKeon*	N	N	Y	N	N	N	Y
26 Berman	Y	Y	N	N	Y	Y	Y
27 *Moorhead*	N	N	Y	N	N	N	Y
28 *Dreier*	N	N	Y	N	N	N	Y
29 Waxman	Y	Y	N	N	Y	Y	Y
30 Becerra	Y	Y	N	N	Y	Y	Y
31 Martinez	Y	Y	N	?	Y	?	?
32 Dixon	Y	Y	N	N	Y	Y	Y
33 Roybal-Allard	Y	Y	N	N	Y	Y	Y
34 Torres	Y	Y	N	?	Y	Y	Y
35 Waters	Y	Y	N	N	Y	Y	Y
36 Harman	Y	Y	N	N	Y	Y	Y
37 Tucker	?	?	?	?	?	?	?
38 *Horn*	Y	Y	N	N	Y	Y	Y
39 *Royce*	N	N	Y	N	N	N	Y
40 *Lewis*	N	N	Y	N	N	N	Y
41 *Kim*	N	N	Y	N	N	N	Y
42 Brown	?	?	?	?	?	?	Y
43 *Calvert*	N	N	Y	N	N	N	Y
44 *McCandless*	N	N	Y	N	Y	?	Y
45 *Rohrabacher*	N	N	Y	N	N	N	Y
46 *Dornan*	N	N	Y	N	N	N	Y
47 *Cox*	N	N	Y	Y	N	N	?
48 *Packard*	N	N	Y	N	N	N	Y
49 Schenk	Y	Y	N	N	Y	Y	Y
50 Filner	Y	Y	N	N	Y	Y	Y
51 *Cunningham*	N	N	Y	N	N	N	Y
52 *Hunter*	N	N	Y	N	N	N	Y
COLORADO							
1 Schroeder	Y	Y	N	N	Y	Y	Y
2 Skaggs	Y	Y	N	N	Y	Y	Y
3 *McInnis*	N	N	Y	N	Y	Y	Y
4 *Allard*	N	N	Y	N	N	N	Y
5 *Hefley*	N	N	Y	N	N	N	Y
6 *Schaefer*	N	N	Y	?	?	?	?
CONNECTICUT							
1 Kennelly	Y	Y	N	N	Y	Y	Y
2 Gejdenson	Y	Y	N	N	Y	Y	Y
3 DeLauro	Y	Y	N	N	Y	Y	Y
4 *Shays*	Y	Y	N	N	Y	Y	Y
5 *Franks*	Y	Y	N	N	Y	Y	Y
6 *Johnson*	Y	Y	N	N	Y	Y	?
DELAWARE							
AL *Castle*	Y	Y	N	N	Y	Y	Y
FLORIDA							
1 Hutto	N	N	Y	N	N	N	Y
2 Peterson	Y	Y	N	N	Y	Y	Y
3 Brown	Y	Y	N	N	Y	Y	Y
4 *Fowler*	?	?	?	?	?	?	?
5 Thurman	Y	Y	N	N	Y	Y	Y
6 *Stearns*	N	N	Y	N	N	N	Y
7 *Mica*	N	N	Y	N	N	N	Y
8 *McCollum*	N	N	Y	N	N	N	Y
9 *Bilirakis*	N	N	Y	N	N	N	Y
10 *Young*	N	N	Y	N	N	N	Y
11 Gibbons	Y	Y	N	N	Y	Y	Y
12 *Canady*	N	N	Y	Y	N	N	Y
13 *Miller*	N	N	Y	N	N	N	Y
14 *Goss*	N	N	Y	N	N	N	Y
15 *Bacchus*	Y	Y	N	N	Y	Y	Y
16 *Lewis*	N	N	Y	N	N	N	Y
17 Meek	?	#	?	?	?	?	?
18 *Ros-Lehtinen*	N	N	Y	N	N	N	Y
19 Johnston	Y	Y	?	?	?	?	?
20 Deutsch	Y	Y	N	N	Y	Y	Y
21 *Diaz-Balart*	N	N	Y	N	N	N	Y
22 *Shaw*	N	N	Y	N	N	N	Y
23 Hastings	?	?	?	?	?	?	?
GEORGIA							
1 *Kingston*	N	N	Y	N	N	N	Y
2 Bishop	Y	Y	N	N	Y	Y	Y
3 *Collins*	N	N	Y	N	N	N	Y
4 *Linder*	N	N	Y	+	—	—	+
5 Lewis	Y	Y	N	N	Y	Y	Y
6 *Gingrich*	N	N	Y	N	N	N	Y
7 Darden	Y	Y	N	N	Y	Y	Y
8 Rowland	Y	Y	N	N	Y	Y	Y
9 Deal	Y	Y	Y	N	Y	Y	Y
10 Johnson	Y	Y	N	N	Y	Y	Y
11 McKinney	Y	Y	N	N	Y	Y	Y
HAWAII							
1 Abercrombie	Y	Y	N	N	Y	Y	Y
2 Mink	Y	Y	N	N	Y	Y	Y
IDAHO							
1 LaRocco	Y	Y	N	N	Y	Y	Y
2 *Crapo*	N	N	Y	N	N	N	Y
ILLINOIS							
1 Rush	Y	Y	N	N	Y	Y	Y
2 Reynolds	Y	Y	N	N	Y	Y	Y
3 Lipinski	Y	N	N	N	N	N	Y
4 Gutierrez	Y	Y	N	N	Y	Y	Y
5 Rostenkowski	Y	Y	?	?	?	?	?
6 *Hyde*	N	N	Y	N	N	N	Y
7 Collins	?	#	?	?	?	?	?
8 *Crane*	N	N	Y	N	N	N	Y
9 Yates	Y	Y	N	N	Y	Y	?
10 *Porter*	Y	Y	N	N	Y	Y	Y
11 Sangmeister	Y	Y	N	Y	Y	Y	Y
12 Costello	N	N	Y	N	N	Y	Y
13 *Fawell*	Y	Y	N	N	Y	Y	Y
14 *Hastert*	N	N	Y	+	—	N	Y
15 *Ewing*	N	N	Y	N	N	N	Y
16 *Manzullo*	N	N	Y	N	N	N	Y
17 Evans	Y	Y	N	N	Y	Y	Y

ND Northern Democrats   SD Southern Democrats

	66	67	68	69	70	71	72
18 ***Michel***	?	?	?	?	?	?	?
19 Poshard	N	N	Y	Y	N	N	Y
20 Durbin	Y	Y	N	N	Y	Y	Y
INDIANA							
1 Visclosky	Y	Y	N	N	Y	Y	Y
2 Sharp	Y	Y	N	N	Y	Y	Y
3 Roemer	Y	Y	N	N	Y	Y	Y
4 Long	Y	Y	N	N	Y	Y	Y
5 ***Buyer***	N	N	Y	Y	N	N	Y
6 ***Burton***	N	N	Y	Y	N	N	Y
7 ***Myers***	N	N	Y	Y	N	N	Y
8 McCloskey	Y	Y	N	?	Y	Y	Y
9 Hamilton	Y	Y	N	N	Y	Y	Y
10 Jacobs	Y	Y	N	N	Y	Y	Y
IOWA							
1 ***Leach***	N	N	Y	Y	Y	Y	Y
2 ***Nussle***	N	N	Y	Y	N	N	Y
3 ***Lightfoot***	N	N	Y	Y	N	N	Y
4 Smith	Y	Y	N	N	Y	Y	Y
5 ***Grandy***	?	X	?	?	?	?	?
KANSAS							
1 ***Roberts***	N	N	Y	Y	N	N	Y
2 Slattery	Y	Y	N	N	Y	Y	Y
3 ***Meyers***	Y	Y	N	N	Y	?	Y
4 Glickman	Y	Y	N	N	Y	Y	Y
KENTUCKY							
1 Barlow	Y	Y	N	N	Y	Y	Y
2 Natcher	?	?	?	?	?	?	?
3 Mazzoli	Y	Y	N	N	Y	Y	Y
4 ***Bunning***	N	N	Y	Y	N	N	?
5 ***Rogers***	N	N	Y	Y	N	N	Y
6 Baesler	Y	Y	N	N	Y	?	?
LOUISIANA							
1 ***Livingston***	?	X	?	?	?	?	?
2 Jefferson	Y	Y	N	?	?	Y	Y
3 Tauzin	N	N	Y	Y	N	N	Y
4 Fields	Y	Y	N	N	Y	Y	Y
5 ***McCrery***	N	N	Y	Y	N	N	Y
6 ***Baker***	N	N	Y	Y	N	N	Y
7 Hayes	N	N	Y	Y	N	N	Y
MAINE							
1 Andrews	Y	Y	N	N	Y	Y	Y
2 ***Snowe***	Y	Y	N	N	Y	Y	Y
MARYLAND							
1 ***Gilchrest***	N	Y	Y	Y	N	Y	Y
2 ***Bentley***	N	N	Y	Y	N	N	Y
3 Cardin	Y	Y	N	N	Y	Y	Y
4 Wynn	Y	Y	N	N	Y	Y	Y
5 Hoyer	Y	Y	N	N	Y	?	Y
6 ***Bartlett***	N	N	Y	Y	N	N	Y
7 Mfume	Y	Y	N	–	+	+	+
8 ***Morella***	Y	Y	N	N	Y	Y	Y
MASSACHUSETTS							
1 Olver	Y	Y	N	N	Y	Y	Y
2 Neal	Y	Y	N	N	Y	Y	Y
3 ***Blute***	N	N	Y	Y	N	N	Y
4 Frank	Y	Y	N	N	Y	Y	Y
5 Meehan	Y	Y	N	N	Y	Y	Y
6 ***Torkildsen***	N	N	Y	Y	N	N	Y
7 Markey	Y	Y	N	N	Y	Y	Y
8 Kennedy	Y	Y	N	N	Y	Y	Y
9 Moakley	Y	Y	N	N	Y	Y	Y
10 Studds	Y	Y	N	N	Y	Y	Y
MICHIGAN							
1 Stupak	N	N	Y	Y	N	N	Y
2 ***Hoekstra***	N	N	Y	Y	N	N	Y
3 ***Ehlers***	N	N	Y	Y	N	N	Y
4 ***Camp***	N	N	Y	Y	N	N	Y
5 Barcia	N	N	Y	Y	N	N	Y
6 ***Upton***	N	N	Y	Y	N	N	Y
7 ***Smith***	N	N	Y	Y	N	N	Y
8 Carr	Y	Y	N	N	Y	Y	Y
9 Kildee	N	N	Y	Y	N	N	Y
10 Bonior	Y	Y	N	N	Y	Y	Y
11 ***Knollenberg***	N	N	Y	Y	N	N	Y
12 Levin	Y	Y	N	N	Y	Y	Y
13 Ford	Y	Y	N	N	Y	?	?
14 Conyers	Y	?	N	N	Y	Y	Y
15 Collins	Y	Y	N	N	Y	Y	Y
16 Dingell	Y	Y	N	N	Y	Y	Y
MINNESOTA							
1 Penny	N	N	Y	Y	N	N	N
2 Minge	Y	Y	N	N	Y	Y	Y
3 ***Ramstad***	Y	Y	N	N	Y	Y	Y
4 Vento	Y	Y	N	N	Y	Y	Y

	66	67	68	69	70	71	72
5 Sabo	Y	Y	N	N	Y	Y	Y
6 ***Grams***	N	N	Y	Y	N	N	Y
7 Peterson	N	N	Y	Y	N	N	Y
8 Oberstar	Y	N	Y	Y	N	N	Y
MISSISSIPPI							
1 Whitten	Y	Y	N	Y	Y	Y	Y
2 Thompson	Y	Y	N	N	Y	Y	Y
3 Montgomery	Y	Y	N	N	Y	Y	Y
4 Parker	N	N	Y	Y	N	N	Y
5 Taylor	N	N	Y	Y	N	N	Y
MISSOURI							
1 Clay	Y	Y	N	N	Y	Y	Y
2 ***Talent***	N	N	Y	Y	N	N	Y
3 Gephardt	Y	Y	N	N	Y	Y	Y
4 Skelton	N	N	Y	?	?	?	?
5 Wheat	Y	Y	N	N	Y	Y	Y
6 Danner	Y	Y	N	N	Y	Y	Y
7 ***Hancock***	N	?	Y	Y	N	N	Y
8 ***Emerson***	N	N	Y	Y	N	N	Y
9 Volkmer	N	N	Y	Y	N	N	Y
MONTANA							
AL Williams	Y	Y	?	N	Y	Y	Y
NEBRASKA							
1 ***Bereuter***	Y	Y	N	N	Y	Y	Y
2 Hoagland	Y	Y	N	N	Y	Y	Y
3 ***Barrett***	N	N	Y	Y	N	N	Y
NEVADA							
1 Bilbray	Y	Y	N	N	Y	Y	Y
2 ***Vucanovich***	N	N	Y	Y	N	N	Y
NEW HAMPSHIRE							
1 ***Zeliff***	Y	Y	N	N	Y	Y	Y
2 Swett	Y	Y	N	N	Y	Y	Y
NEW JERSEY							
1 Andrews	Y	Y	N	N	Y	Y	Y
2 Hughes	Y	Y	N	N	Y	Y	Y
3 ***Saxton***	N	N	Y	Y	N	N	Y
4 ***Smith***	N	N	Y	Y	N	N	Y
5 ***Roukema***	Y	Y	N	N	Y	?	Y
6 Pallone	Y	Y	N	N	Y	Y	Y
7 ***Franks***	N	N	N	N	Y	Y	Y
8 Klein	Y	Y	N	N	Y	?	Y
9 Torricelli	Y	Y	N	N	Y	Y	Y
10 Payne	Y	Y	N	N	Y	Y	Y
11 ***Gallo***	?	?	?	?	?	?	?
12 ***Zimmer***	Y	Y	N	N	Y	Y	Y
13 Menendez	Y	Y	N	N	Y	Y	Y
NEW MEXICO							
1 ***Schiff***	N	N	N	N	Y	Y	Y
2 ***Skeen***	N	N	Y	Y	N	N	Y
3 Richardson	Y	Y	N	N	Y	Y	Y
NEW YORK							
1 Hochbrueckner	Y	Y	N	N	Y	Y	Y
2 ***Lazio***	Y	Y	N	N	Y	Y	Y
3 ***King***	N	N	Y	Y	N	N	Y
4 ***Levy***	N	N	Y	Y	N	N	Y
5 Ackerman	Y	Y	N	N	Y	Y	Y
6 Flake	Y	Y	N	N	Y	Y	Y
7 Manton	?	?	?	?	?	?	?
8 Nadler	Y	Y	N	N	Y	Y	N
9 Schumer	Y	Y	N	N	Y	Y	Y
10 Towns	Y	Y	N	N	Y	Y	Y
11 Owens	Y	Y	N	N	Y	Y	Y
12 Velazquez	Y	Y	N	N	Y	Y	Y
13 ***Molinari***	Y	Y	N	N	Y	Y	Y
14 Maloney	Y	Y	N	N	Y	Y	Y
15 Rangel	Y	Y	N	N	Y	Y	Y
16 Serrano	Y	Y	N	N	Y	Y	Y
17 Engel	Y	Y	N	N	Y	Y	Y
18 Lowey	Y	Y	N	N	Y	Y	Y
19 ***Fish***	N	N	Y	Y	N	N	Y
20 ***Gilman***	Y	Y	N	N	Y	Y	Y
21 McNulty	Y	N	Y	Y	N	N	Y
22 ***Solomon***	N	N	Y	Y	N	N	Y
23 ***Boehlert***	Y	Y	N	N	Y	Y	Y
24 ***McHugh***	N	N	Y	Y	N	N	Y
25 ***Walsh***	N	N	Y	Y	N	N	Y
26 Hinchey	Y	Y	N	N	Y	?	Y
27 ***Paxon***	N	N	Y	Y	N	N	Y
28 Slaughter	Y	Y	N	N	Y	Y	Y
29 LaFalce	N	N	Y	Y	N	N	Y
30 ***Quinn***	N	N	Y	Y	N	N	Y
31 ***Houghton***	Y	Y	N	N	Y	Y	Y
NORTH CAROLINA							
1 Clayton	Y	Y	N	N	Y	Y	Y
2 Valentine	Y	Y	N	N	Y	Y	Y

	66	67	68	69	70	71	72
3 Lancaster	Y	Y	N	N	Y	Y	Y
4 Price	Y	Y	N	N	Y	Y	Y
5 Neal	Y	Y	N	N	Y	Y	Y
6 ***Coble***	N	N	Y	Y	N	N	Y
7 Rose	Y	Y	N	N	Y	Y	Y
8 Hefner	Y	Y	N	N	Y	Y	Y
9 ***McMillan***	N	N	Y	Y	N	N	Y
10 ***Ballenger***	N	N	Y	Y	N	N	Y
11 ***Taylor***	N	N	Y	Y	N	N	Y
12 Watt	Y	Y	?	?	?	?	?
NORTH DAKOTA							
AL Pomeroy	Y	Y	N	N	Y	Y	Y
OHIO							
1 Mann	Y	Y	N	N	Y	Y	Y
2 ***Portman***	N	N	Y	Y	N	N	Y
3 Hall	Y	N	Y	Y	N	N	Y
4 ***Oxley***	N	N	N	Y	N	?	Y
5 ***Gillmor***	N	N	Y	Y	N	N	Y
6 Strickland	Y	Y	N	N	Y	Y	Y
7 ***Hobson***	N	N	Y	Y	N	N	Y
8 ***Boehner***	N	N	Y	Y	N	N	Y
9 Kaptur	Y	?	Y	N	N	Y	Y
10 ***Hoke***	N	N	Y	Y	N	N	Y
11 Stokes	Y	Y	N	N	Y	Y	Y
12 ***Kasich***	N	N	Y	Y	N	N	Y
13 Brown	Y	Y	N	N	Y	Y	Y
14 Sawyer	Y	Y	N	N	Y	Y	Y
15 ***Pryce***	Y	Y	N	N	Y	Y	Y
16 ***Regula***	N	N	Y	Y	N	N	Y
17 Traficant	Y	Y	N	N	Y	Y	Y
18 Applegate	N	N	Y	Y	N	N	Y
19 Fingerhut	Y	Y	N	N	Y	Y	Y
OKLAHOMA							
1 ***Inhofe***	N	N	Y	Y	N	N	Y
2 Synar	Y	Y	N	N	Y	Y	Y
3 Brewster	Y	Y	N	N	Y	Y	Y
4 McCurdy	Y	Y	N	N	Y	Y	Y
5 ***Istook***	N	N	Y	Y	N	N	Y
6 Vacancy							
OREGON							
1 Furse	Y	Y	N	N	Y	Y	Y
2 ***Smith***	N	N	Y	Y	N	N	?
3 Wyden	Y	Y	N	N	Y	Y	Y
4 DeFazio	Y	Y	N	N	Y	Y	Y
5 Kopetski	Y	Y	N	N	Y	Y	Y
PENNSYLVANIA							
1 Foglietta	Y	Y	N	N	Y	?	Y
2 Blackwell	Y	Y	N	N	Y	Y	Y
3 Borski	Y	Y	N	N	Y	Y	Y
4 Klink	N	N	Y	Y	N	N	Y
5 ***Clinger***	N	N	Y	Y	N	N	Y
6 Holden	N	N	Y	Y	N	N	Y
7 ***Weldon***	?	N	Y	Y	N	N	Y
8 ***Greenwood***	Y	Y	N	N	Y	Y	Y
9 ***Shuster***	N	N	Y	Y	N	N	Y
10 ***McDade***	N	N	Y	Y	N	N	Y
11 Kanjorski	?	?	N	Y	N	N	Y
12 Murtha	Y	Y	N	Y	N	N	Y
13 Margolies-Mezv.	Y	Y	N	N	Y	Y	Y
14 Coyne	Y	Y	N	N	Y	Y	Y
15 McHale	Y	Y	N	N	Y	Y	Y
16 ***Walker***	N	N	Y	Y	N	N	Y
17 ***Gekas***	N	N	Y	Y	N	N	Y
18 ***Santorum***	N	N	Y	Y	N	N	Y
19 ***Goodling***	N	N	Y	Y	N	N	Y
20 Murphy	N	N	N	?	?	?	?
21 ***Ridge***	Y	Y	N	N	Y	Y	Y
RHODE ISLAND							
1 ***Machtley***	Y	Y	N	N	Y	Y	Y
2 Reed	Y	Y	N	N	Y	Y	Y
SOUTH CAROLINA							
1 ***Ravenel***	N	N	Y	Y	N	N	Y
2 ***Spence***	N	N	Y	Y	N	N	Y
3 Derrick	Y	Y	N	N	Y	Y	Y
4 ***Inglis***	N	N	Y	Y	N	N	Y
5 Spratt	Y	Y	N	N	Y	Y	Y
6 Clyburn	Y	Y	N	N	Y	Y	Y
SOUTH DAKOTA							
AL Johnson	Y	Y	N	N	Y	Y	Y
TENNESSEE							
1 ***Quillen***	N	N	Y	Y	N	N	Y
2 ***Duncan***	N	N	Y	Y	N	N	Y
3 Lloyd	Y	Y	N	N	Y	Y	Y
4 Cooper	Y	Y	N	N	Y	Y	Y
5 Clement	Y	Y	N	N	Y	Y	Y

	66	67	68	69	70	71	72
6 Gordon	Y	Y	N	N	Y	Y	Y
7 ***Sundquist***	N	N	Y	Y	N	N	?
8 Tanner	Y	Y	N	N	Y	Y	Y
9 Ford	Y	Y	N	N	Y	Y	Y
TEXAS							
1 Chapman	Y	Y	N	N	Y	Y	Y
2 Wilson	Y	Y	N	N	Y	Y	Y
3 ***Johnson, Sam***	N	N	Y	Y	N	N	Y
4 Hall	N	N	Y	Y	N	N	Y
5 Bryant	Y	Y	N	N	Y	Y	Y
6 ***Barton***	N	N	Y	Y	N	N	Y
7 ***Archer***	N	N	Y	Y	N	N	Y
8 ***Fields***	N	N	Y	Y	N	N	Y
9 Brooks	Y	Y	N	N	Y	Y	Y
10 Pickle	Y	Y	N	N	Y	?	?
11 Edwards	Y	Y	N	N	Y	Y	Y
12 Geren	Y	Y	N	N	Y	Y	Y
13 Sarpalius	Y	N	Y	Y	N	N	Y
14 Laughlin	Y	Y	N	N	Y	Y	Y
15 de la Garza	Y	Y	Y	Y	N	N	Y
16 Coleman	Y	Y	N	N	Y	Y	Y
17 Stenholm	N	N	Y	Y	N	N	Y
18 Washington	Y	Y	N	N	Y	Y	Y
19 ***Combest***	N	N	Y	Y	N	N	Y
20 Gonzalez	Y	Y	N	N	Y	Y	Y
21 ***Smith***	N	N	Y	Y	N	N	Y
22 ***DeLay***	N	N	Y	Y	N	N	Y
23 ***Bonilla***	N	N	Y	Y	N	N	Y
24 Frost	Y	Y	N	N	Y	Y	Y
25 Andrews	Y	Y	N	N	Y	Y	Y
26 ***Armey***	N	N	Y	Y	N	N	Y
27 Ortiz	N	N	Y	Y	N	N	Y
28 Tejeda	N	N	Y	Y	N	N	Y
29 Green	?	?	?	?	?	?	?
30 Johnson, E.B.	Y	Y	N	N	Y	Y	Y
UTAH							
1 ***Hansen***	N	N	Y	Y	N	N	Y
2 Shepherd	Y	Y	N	N	Y	Y	Y
3 Orton	Y	Y	N	N	Y	Y	Y
VERMONT							
AL *Sanders*	Y	Y	N	N	Y	Y	Y
VIRGINIA							
1 ***Bateman***	N	N	Y	Y	N	N	Y
2 Pickett	Y	Y	N	N	Y	Y	Y
3 Scott	Y	Y	N	N	Y	Y	Y
4 Sisisky	Y	Y	N	N	Y	Y	Y
5 Payne	Y	Y	N	N	Y	Y	Y
6 ***Goodlatte***	N	N	Y	Y	N	N	Y
7 ***Bliley***	N	N	Y	Y	N	N	Y
8 Moran	Y	Y	N	N	Y	?	Y
9 Boucher	Y	Y	N	N	Y	Y	Y
10 ***Wolf***	N	N	Y	Y	N	N	Y
11 Byrne	Y	Y	N	N	Y	Y	Y
WASHINGTON							
1 Cantwell	Y	Y	N	N	Y	Y	Y
2 Swift	Y	Y	N	N	Y	Y	Y
3 Unsoeld	Y	Y	N	N	Y	Y	Y
4 Inslee	Y	Y	Y	N	Y	Y	Y
5 Foley							
6 Dicks	Y	Y	N	N	Y	?	Y
7 McDermott	Y	Y	N	?	?	?	?
8 ***Dunn***	N	N	Y	Y	Y	N	Y
9 Kreidler	Y	Y	N	N	Y	Y	Y
WEST VIRGINIA							
1 Mollohan	?	N	Y	Y	N	N	Y
2 Wise	Y	Y	N	N	Y	Y	Y
3 Rahall	N	N	Y	Y	N	N	Y
WISCONSIN							
1 Barca	Y	Y	N	N	Y	Y	Y
2 ***Klug***	Y	Y	N	N	Y	Y	Y
3 ***Gunderson***	N	N	Y	Y	N	N	Y
4 Kleczka	Y	Y	N	N	Y	Y	Y
5 Barrett	Y	Y	N	N	Y	Y	Y
6 ***Petri***	N	N	Y	Y	N	N	Y
7 Obey	Y	Y	N	N	Y	Y	Y
8 ***Roth***	N	N	Y	Y	N	N	Y
9 ***Sensenbrenner***	N	N	Y	Y	N	N	Y
WYOMING							
AL ***Thomas***	N	N	Y	Y	N	N	Y
DELEGATES							
de Lugo, V.I.	D	D	D	D	D	D	D
Faleomavaega, Am.S.	D	D	D	D	D	D	D
Norton, D.C.	D	D	D	D	D	D	D
Romero-B., P.R.	D	D	D	D	D	D	D
Underwood, Guam	D	D	D	D	D	D	D

Southern states - Ala., Ark., Fla., Ga., Ky., La., Miss., N.C., Okla., S.C., Tenn., Texas, Va.
Omitted votes are quorum calls, which CQ does not include in its vote charts.

73. HR 6. Elementary and Secondary Education Reauthorization/Bilingual Education. Roth, R-Wis., amendment to eliminate the $215 million authorization in fiscal 1995 for a bilingual education program for students whose second language is English. Rejected in the Committee of the Whole 58-334: R 58-105; D 0-228 (ND 0-156, SD 0-72); I 0-1, March 21, 1994.

74. HR 6. Elementary and Secondary Education Reauthorization/School Prayer. Williams, D-Mont., amendment to the Johnson, R-Texas, amendment, to prohibit states or school districts from using money received under the bill to adopt policies that prohibit voluntary school prayer. The Johnson amendment would withhold federal money from states or school districts that prohibit voluntary, constitutionally protected school prayer. Rejected in the Committee of the Whole 171-239: R 7-161; D 163-78 (ND 132-35, SD 31-43); I 1-0, March 21, 1994.

75. HR 6. Elementary and Secondary Education Reauthorization/School Prayer. Johnson, R-Texas, amendment to withhold federal money from states or school districts that prohibit voluntary, constitutionally protected school prayer. Adopted in the Committee of the Whole 345-64: R 166-0; D 178-64 (ND 109-58, SD 69-6); I 1-0, March 21, 1994.

76. HR 6. Elementary and Secondary Education Reauthorization/Sex Education. Unsoeld, D-Wash., amendment to the Doolittle, R-Calif., amendment, to give local school systems discretion over whether sex education programs should teach abstinence as the only method that is completely effective as protection against unwanted pregnancy and sexually transmitted diseases. The Doolittle amendment would require schools receiving money under the bill to teach abstinence as the only completely effective protection. Adopted in the Committee of the Whole 262-166: R 53-119; D 208-47 (ND 156-19, SD 52-28); I 1-0, March 22, 1994.

77. HR 6. Elementary and Secondary Education Reauthorization/Sex Education. Doolittle, R-Calif., amendment, as amended, to give local school systems discretion over whether sex education programs should teach abstinence as the only method that is completely effective as protection against unwanted pregnancy and sexually transmitted diseases. Adopted in the Committee of the Whole 407-20: R 171-1; D 235-19 (ND 158-15, SD 77-4); I 1-0, March 22, 1994.

78. H Res 394. Whitewater Hearings. Gephardt, D-Mo., motion to suspend the rules and adopt the resolution to express the sense of the House that the Democratic and Republican leaders should meet to determine the time, procedures and forum for congressional oversight hearings on all matters related to Madison Guaranty Savings and Loan, Whitewater Development Co. and Capital Management Services Co. Inc. Motion agreed to 408-15: R 172-0; D 235-15 (ND 156-13, SD 79-2); I 1-0, March 22, 1994. A two-thirds majority of those present and voting (282 in this case) is required for adoption under suspension of the rules.

79. H Res 369. Committee Funding Resolution/Republican Substitute. Roberts, R-Kan., motion to recommit the resolution to the House Administration Committee with instructions to report it back amended to reduce the funding level to $47.2 million from $50.1 million and give one-third of the funds to the minority. Motion rejected 172-251: R 170-0; D 2-250 (ND 2-168, SD 0-82); I 0-1, March 22, 1994.

80. H Res 369. Committee Funding Resolution/Adoption. Adoption of the resolution to provide $50.1 million to 21 House committees to support investigative staff and other committee operations. Adopted 250-172: R 2-168; D 247-4 (ND 165-4, SD 82-0); I 1-0, March 22, 1994.

KEY

Y	Voted for (yea).
#	Paired for.
+	Announced for.
N	Voted against (nay).
X	Paired against.
−	Announced against.
P	Voted "present."
C	Voted "present" to avoid possible conflict of interest.
?	Did not vote or otherwise make a position known.
D	Delegates ineligible to vote.

Democrats *Republicans*
Independent

	73	74	75	76	77	78	79	80
ALABAMA								
1 Callahan	Y	N	Y	N	Y	Y	Y	N
2 Everett	Y	N	Y	N	Y	Y	Y	N
3 Browder	N	N	Y	N	Y	Y	N	Y
4 Bevill	N	N	Y	N	Y	Y	N	Y
5 Cramer	N	N	Y	N	Y	Y	N	Y
6 Bachus	Y	N	?	N	Y	Y	Y	N
7 Hilliard	N	Y	Y	Y	Y	Y	N	Y
ALASKA								
AL Young	N	N	Y	N	Y	N	Y	Y
ARIZONA								
1 Coppersmith	N	Y	N	Y	Y	Y	N	Y
2 Pastor	N	Y	Y	Y	Y	Y	N	Y
3 Stump	Y	N	Y	N	Y	Y	Y	N
4 Kyl	N	N	Y	N	Y	Y	Y	N
5 Kolbe	N	N	Y	N	Y	Y	Y	N
6 English	N	Y	Y	Y	Y	Y	N	Y
ARKANSAS								
1 Lambert	N	Y	Y	Y	Y	Y	N	Y
2 Thornton	N	Y	Y	Y	Y	Y	N	Y
3 Hutchinson	Y	N	Y	N	Y	Y	Y	N
4 Dickey	Y	N	Y	N	Y	Y	Y	N
CALIFORNIA								
1 Hamburg	?	Y	N	Y	Y	Y	N	Y
2 Herger	Y	N	Y	N	Y	Y	?	?
3 Fazio	N	Y	Y	Y	Y	Y	N	Y
4 Doolittle	Y	N	Y	N	Y	Y	Y	N
5 Matsui	N	Y	Y	Y	Y	N	N	Y
6 Woolsey	N	Y	N	Y	Y	Y	N	Y
7 Miller	?	Y	N	Y	Y	N	N	Y
8 Pelosi	?	Y	N	Y	Y	Y	N	Y
9 Dellums	N	Y	N	Y	N	N	N	Y
10 Baker	Y	N	Y	N	Y	Y	Y	N
11 Pombo	N	N	Y	N	Y	Y	Y	N
12 Lantos	N	Y	Y	Y	Y	Y	N	Y
13 Stark	N	Y	N	Y	N	Y	N	Y
14 Eshoo	N	Y	Y	Y	Y	N	N	Y
15 Mineta	N	Y	Y	Y	Y	N	N	Y
16 Edwards	N	Y	N	Y	N	Y	N	Y
17 Farr	N	Y	Y	Y	Y	N	N	Y
18 Condit	N	N	Y	N	Y	Y	N	Y
19 Lehman	?	N	Y	Y	Y	N	N	Y
20 Dooley	N	N	Y	Y	Y	N	N	Y
21 Thomas	N	N	Y	Y	Y	Y	Y	N
22 Huffington	N	N	Y	Y	Y	Y	Y	N
23 Gallegly	N	N	Y	N	Y	Y	Y	N
24 Beilenson	N	Y	N	Y	Y	Y	N	Y
25 McKeon	N	N	Y	N	Y	Y	Y	N
26 Berman	N	Y	Y	Y	Y	Y	N	Y
27 Moorhead	N	N	Y	N	Y	Y	Y	N
28 Dreier	Y	N	Y	Y	Y	Y	Y	N
29 Waxman	N	Y	Y	Y	Y	N	N	Y
30 Becerra	−	Y	N	Y	Y	Y	N	Y
31 Martinez	N	Y	Y	Y	Y	N	N	Y
32 Dixon	N	Y	Y	Y	Y	Y	N	Y
33 Roybal-Allard	N	Y	N	Y	Y	Y	N	Y
34 Torres	N	Y	N	Y	Y	+	N	Y
35 Waters	N	Y	N	N	N	N	N	+
36 Harman	N	N	Y	Y	Y	Y	N	Y
37 Tucker	N	Y	Y	Y	Y	N	N	Y
38 Horn	N	N	Y	N	Y	Y	Y	N
39 Royce	Y	N	Y	N	Y	Y	Y	N
40 Lewis	N	N	Y	N	Y	Y	Y	N
41 Kim	Y	N	Y	N	Y	Y	Y	N
42 Brown	N	Y	Y	Y	?	Y	N	Y
43 Calvert	N	N	Y	N	Y	Y	Y	N
44 McCandless	Y	N	Y	Y	Y	Y	Y	N
45 Rohrabacher	Y	N	Y	Y	Y	Y	Y	N
46 Dornan	N	N	Y	N	Y	Y	Y	N
47 Cox	+	−	+	Y	Y	Y	Y	N
48 Packard	Y	N	Y	N	Y	Y	Y	N
49 Schenk	N	Y	N	Y	Y	Y	N	Y
50 Filner	N	Y	N	Y	Y	Y	N	Y
51 Cunningham	N	N	Y	N	Y	Y	Y	N
52 Hunter	Y	N	Y	N	Y	Y	Y	N
COLORADO								
1 Schroeder	N	Y	Y	Y	Y	Y	N	Y
2 Skaggs	N	Y	N	Y	Y	Y	N	Y
3 McInnis	N	N	Y	Y	Y	Y	N	Y
4 Allard	N	N	Y	N	Y	Y	Y	N
5 Hefley	N	N	Y	N	Y	Y	Y	N
6 Schaefer	N	N	Y	N	Y	Y	Y	N
CONNECTICUT								
1 Kennelly	N	Y	Y	Y	Y	Y	N	Y
2 Gejdenson	N	Y	Y	Y	Y	Y	N	Y
3 DeLauro	N	Y	Y	Y	Y	Y	N	Y
4 Shays	N	Y	Y	Y	Y	Y	Y	N
5 Franks	N	N	Y	N	Y	Y	Y	N
6 Johnson	N	Y	Y	Y	Y	Y	N	Y
DELAWARE								
AL Castle	N	N	Y	Y	Y	Y	Y	N
FLORIDA								
1 Hutto	N	N	Y	N	Y	Y	N	Y
2 Peterson	N	Y	Y	Y	Y	Y	N	Y
3 Brown	N	Y	Y	Y	Y	Y	N	Y
4 Fowler	?	N	Y	N	Y	Y	Y	N
5 Thurman	N	Y	Y	Y	Y	Y	N	Y
6 Stearns	N	N	Y	N	Y	Y	Y	N
7 Mica	Y	N	Y	N	Y	Y	Y	N
8 McCollum	N	N	Y	N	Y	Y	Y	N
9 Bilirakis	N	N	Y	N	Y	Y	Y	N
10 Young	N	N	Y	N	Y	Y	Y	N
11 Gibbons	N	Y	Y	Y	Y	Y	N	Y
12 Canady	N	N	Y	N	Y	Y	Y	N
13 Miller	N	N	Y	Y	Y	Y	Y	N
14 Goss	N	N	Y	Y	Y	Y	Y	N
15 Bacchus	?	?	?	Y	Y	Y	N	Y
16 Lewis	N	N	Y	N	Y	Y	Y	N
17 Meek	?	?	?	?	?	?	N	Y
18 Ros-Lehtinen	N	N	Y	Y	Y	Y	Y	N
19 Johnston	?	?	?	Y	Y	Y	N	Y
20 Deutsch	X	?	?	Y	Y	Y	N	Y
21 Diaz-Balart	N	N	Y	Y	Y	Y	Y	N
22 Shaw	N	N	Y	N	Y	Y	Y	N
23 Hastings	?	?	?	?	?	?	?	?
GEORGIA								
1 Kingston	Y	N	Y	N	Y	Y	Y	N
2 Bishop	N	Y	Y	N	Y	Y	N	Y
3 Collins	Y	N	Y	N	Y	Y	Y	N
4 Linder	Y	N	Y	N	Y	Y	Y	N
5 Lewis	N	Y	N	Y	N	Y	N	Y
6 Gingrich	?	N	Y	N	Y	Y	Y	N
7 Darden	N	N	Y	Y	Y	Y	N	Y
8 Rowland	N	N	Y	N	Y	Y	N	Y
9 Deal	N	N	Y	N	Y	Y	N	Y
10 Johnson	N	N	Y	Y	Y	Y	N	Y
11 McKinney	N	Y	N	Y	N	N	N	Y
HAWAII								
1 Abercrombie	N	Y	N	Y	N	N	N	Y
2 Mink	N	Y	N	Y	N	Y	N	Y
IDAHO								
1 LaRocco	N	Y	Y	Y	Y	Y	N	Y
2 Crapo	N	N	Y	N	Y	Y	Y	N
ILLINOIS								
1 Rush	N	Y	N	Y	Y	Y	N	Y
2 Reynolds	N	Y	N	Y	Y	Y	N	Y
3 Lipinski	N	N	Y	N	Y	Y	N	Y
4 Gutierrez	−	Y	Y	Y	Y	Y	N	Y
5 Rostenkowski	?	?	?	Y	Y	Y	N	Y
6 Hyde	N	N	Y	N	Y	Y	Y	N
7 Collins	N	Y	N	Y	N	Y	N	Y
8 Crane	Y	N	Y	N	N	Y	Y	N
9 Yates	N	Y	N	Y	Y	Y	N	Y
10 Porter	N	Y	Y	Y	Y	Y	Y	N
11 Sangmeister	N	N	Y	Y	Y	Y	N	Y
12 Costello	N	N	Y	N	Y	Y	N	Y
13 Fawell	N	Y	N	Y	Y	Y	Y	N
14 Hastert	N	N	Y	N	Y	Y	Y	N
15 Ewing	Y	N	Y	N	Y	Y	Y	N
16 Manzullo	Y	N	Y	N	Y	Y	Y	N
17 Evans	N	Y	Y	Y	Y	Y	N	Y

	73	74	75	76	77	78	79	80
18 ***Michel***	N	N	Y	N	Y	Y	Y	N
19 Poshard	N	N	Y	N	Y	Y	N	Y
20 Durbin	N	Y	Y	Y	Y	Y	N	Y
INDIANA								
1 Visclosky	N	Y	N	Y	Y	Y	N	Y
2 Sharp	N	Y	Y	Y	Y	Y	N	Y
3 Roemer	N	N	Y	Y	Y	Y	N	Y
4 Long	N	N	Y	Y	Y	Y	N	Y
5 ***Buyer***	?	?	?	N	Y	Y	Y	N
6 ***Burton***	Y	N	Y	N	Y	Y	Y	N
7 ***Myers***	Y	N	Y	N	Y	Y	Y	N
8 McCloskey	?	N	Y	Y	Y	Y	N	Y
9 Hamilton	N	N	Y	Y	Y	Y	N	Y
10 Jacobs	N	N	Y	Y	Y	Y	Y	N
IOWA								
1 ***Leach***	N	Y	Y	Y	Y	Y	Y	N
2 ***Nussle***	N	N	?	N	Y	Y	Y	N
3 ***Lightfoot***	N	N	Y	N	Y	Y	Y	N
4 Smith	N	Y	Y	Y	Y	Y	N	Y
5 ***Grandy***	?	?	?	?	?	?	?	?
KANSAS								
1 ***Roberts***	N	N	Y	N	Y	Y	Y	N
2 Slattery	?	?	?	N	Y	Y	N	Y
3 ***Meyers***	N	Y	Y	N	Y	Y	Y	N
4 Glickman	N	Y	Y	N	Y	Y	N	Y
KENTUCKY								
1 Barlow	?	Y	Y	Y	Y	Y	N	Y
2 Natcher	?	?	?	?	?	?	?	?
3 Mazzoli	N	N	Y	Y	Y	Y	N	Y
4 ***Bunning***	Y	N	Y	N	Y	Y	Y	N
5 ***Rogers***	Y	N	Y	N	Y	Y	Y	N
6 Baesler	N	N	Y	Y	Y	Y	N	Y
LOUISIANA								
1 ***Livingston***	N	N	Y	N	Y	Y	Y	N
2 Jefferson	N	Y	Y	Y	Y	Y	N	Y
3 Tauzin	N	N	Y	N	Y	Y	N	Y
4 Fields	N	Y	Y	Y	Y	Y	N	Y
5 ***McCrery***	N	N	Y	N	Y	Y	Y	N
6 ***Baker***	Y	N	Y	N	Y	Y	Y	N
7 Hayes	N	N	Y	N	Y	Y	N	Y
MAINE								
1 Andrews	?	Y	N	Y	Y	Y	N	Y
2 ***Snowe***	N	N	Y	Y	Y	Y	Y	N
MARYLAND								
1 ***Gilchrest***	N	N	Y	Y	Y	Y	Y	N
2 ***Bentley***	Y	N	Y	Y	Y	Y	Y	N
3 Cardin	N	Y	N	Y	Y	Y	N	Y
4 Wynn	N	N	Y	Y	Y	Y	N	Y
5 Hoyer	N	?	?	Y	Y	Y	N	Y
6 ***Bartlett***	Y	N	Y	N	Y	Y	Y	N
7 Mfume	N	Y	Y	Y	Y	Y	N	Y
8 ***Morella***	N	N	Y	Y	Y	Y	Y	N
MASSACHUSETTS								
1 Olver	N	Y	N	?	Y	Y	N	Y
2 Neal	N	Y	Y	Y	Y	Y	N	Y
3 ***Blute***	N	N	Y	Y	Y	Y	Y	N
4 Frank	N	Y	N	Y	N	Y	N	Y
5 Meehan	?	Y	N	Y	Y	Y	N	Y
6 ***Torkildsen***	N	N	Y	Y	Y	Y	Y	N
7 Markey	N	Y	N	Y	Y	Y	N	Y
8 Kennedy	N	N	Y	N	Y	Y	N	Y
9 Moakley	N	Y	Y	Y	Y	Y	N	Y
10 Studds	N	Y	Y	Y	Y	Y	N	Y
MICHIGAN								
1 Stupak	N	Y	Y	Y	Y	N	N	Y
2 ***Hoekstra***	N	N	Y	N	Y	Y	Y	N
3 ***Ehlers***	N	N	Y	N	Y	Y	Y	N
4 ***Camp***	N	N	Y	N	Y	Y	Y	N
5 Barcia	N	N	Y	Y	Y	Y	N	Y
6 ***Upton***	N	N	Y	N	Y	Y	Y	N
7 ***Smith***	N	N	Y	N	Y	Y	Y	N
8 Carr	N	Y	Y	Y	Y	Y	N	Y
9 Kildee	N	Y	Y	Y	Y	Y	N	Y
10 Bonior	N	Y	N	Y	Y	Y	N	Y
11 ***Knollenberg***	Y	N	Y	N	Y	Y	Y	N
12 Levin	N	Y	Y	Y	Y	Y	N	Y
13 Ford	N	Y	N	Y	N	N	N	Y
14 Conyers	N	N	N	Y	Y	N	N	Y
15 Collins	N	Y	N	Y	N	N	N	Y
16 Dingell	N	Y	N	Y	N	Y	N	Y
MINNESOTA								
1 Penny	N	N	Y	Y	Y	Y	N	Y
2 Minge	N	Y	Y	Y	Y	Y	N	Y
3 ***Ramstad***	N	N	Y	N	Y	Y	Y	N
4 Vento	N	Y	N	Y	Y	Y	N	Y
5 Sabo	N	Y	N	Y	Y	Y	N	Y
6 ***Grams***	#	N	Y	N	Y	Y	Y	N
7 Peterson	N	N	Y	N	Y	Y	N	Y
8 Oberstar	N	Y	N	Y	Y	Y	N	Y
MISSISSIPPI								
1 Whitten	N	N	Y	Y	Y	Y	N	Y
2 Thompson	N	Y	Y	?	N	Y	N	Y
3 Montgomery	N	N	Y	N	Y	Y	N	Y
4 Parker	N	N	Y	N	Y	Y	N	Y
5 Taylor	N	N	Y	N	Y	Y	N	Y
MISSOURI								
1 Clay	?	?	?	?	?	?	?	?
2 ***Talent***	N	N	Y	N	Y	Y	Y	N
3 Gephardt	N	Y	Y	Y	Y	Y	N	Y
4 Skelton	N	N	Y	N	Y	Y	N	Y
5 Wheat	N	?	?	Y	Y	Y	N	Y
6 Danner	N	N	Y	N	Y	Y	N	Y
7 ***Hancock***	Y	N	Y	N	Y	Y	Y	N
8 ***Emerson***	N	N	Y	N	Y	Y	Y	N
9 Volkmer	N	N	Y	N	?	Y	N	Y
MONTANA								
AL Williams	N	Y	N	Y	Y	Y	N	Y
NEBRASKA								
1 ***Bereuter***	N	N	Y	Y	Y	Y	Y	N
2 Hoagland	N	Y	Y	Y	Y	Y	N	Y
3 ***Barrett***	Y	N	Y	Y	Y	Y	Y	N
NEVADA								
1 Bilbray	N	N	Y	Y	Y	Y	N	Y
2 ***Vucanovich***	N	N	Y	N	Y	Y	Y	N
NEW HAMPSHIRE								
1 ***Zeliff***	?	N	Y	N	Y	Y	Y	N
2 Swett	N	Y	Y	N	Y	Y	N	Y
NEW JERSEY								
1 Andrews	N	Y	Y	Y	Y	Y	N	Y
2 Hughes	N	Y	Y	Y	Y	Y	N	Y
3 ***Saxton***	N	N	Y	N	Y	Y	Y	N
4 ***Smith***	N	N	Y	N	Y	Y	Y	N
5 ***Roukema***	N	N	Y	Y	Y	Y	Y	N
6 Pallone	N	Y	Y	Y	Y	Y	N	Y
7 ***Franks***	N	N	Y	Y	Y	Y	Y	N
8 Klein	N	Y	Y	Y	Y	Y	N	Y
9 Torricelli	N	Y	Y	Y	Y	Y	N	Y
10 Payne	N	Y	N	Y	N	Y	N	Y
11 ***Gallo***	?	?	?	?	?	?	?	?
12 ***Zimmer***	N	N	Y	N	Y	Y	Y	N
13 Menendez	N	Y	Y	Y	Y	Y	N	Y
NEW MEXICO								
1 ***Schiff***	N	N	Y	Y	Y	Y	Y	N
2 ***Skeen***	N	N	Y	N	Y	Y	Y	N
3 Richardson	N	Y	Y	Y	Y	Y	N	Y
NEW YORK								
1 Hochbrueckner	N	Y	Y	Y	Y	Y	N	Y
2 ***Lazio***	N	N	Y	N	Y	Y	Y	N
3 ***King***	Y	N	Y	N	Y	Y	Y	N
4 ***Levy***	N	N	Y	N	Y	Y	Y	N
5 Ackerman	?	?	?	Y	Y	Y	N	Y
6 Flake	N	Y	Y	Y	Y	Y	N	Y
7 Manton	N	Y	Y	Y	Y	Y	N	Y
8 Nadler	N	Y	N	Y	N	Y	N	Y
9 Schumer	N	Y	Y	Y	Y	Y	N	Y
10 Towns	N	Y	N	Y	Y	N	N	Y
11 Owens	?	Y	N	Y	N	Y	N	Y
12 Velazquez	?	Y	N	Y	Y	Y	N	Y
13 ***Molinari***	N	N	Y	Y	Y	Y	Y	N
14 Maloney	N	Y	Y	Y	Y	?	X	?
15 Rangel	N	Y	Y	Y	Y	Y	N	Y
16 Serrano	N	Y	N	Y	Y	Y	N	Y
17 Engel	N	Y	N	Y	Y	Y	N	Y
18 Lowey	?	Y	Y	Y	Y	Y	N	Y
19 ***Fish***	N	N	Y	Y	Y	Y	Y	N
20 ***Gilman***	N	Y	Y	Y	Y	Y	Y	N
21 McNulty	N	N	Y	N	Y	Y	N	Y
22 ***Solomon***	Y	N	Y	N	Y	Y	Y	N
23 ***Boehlert***	?	Y	Y	Y	Y	Y	Y	N
24 ***McHugh***	N	N	Y	N	Y	Y	Y	N
25 ***Walsh***	N	N	Y	N	Y	Y	Y	N
26 Hinchey	N	Y	Y	Y	Y	Y	N	Y
27 ***Paxon***	Y	N	Y	N	Y	Y	Y	N
28 Slaughter	N	Y	Y	Y	Y	Y	N	Y
29 LaFalce	N	Y	Y	N	Y	Y	N	Y
30 ***Quinn***	N	N	Y	N	Y	Y	Y	N
31 ***Houghton***	N	N	Y	Y	Y	Y	Y	N
NORTH CAROLINA								
1 Clayton	N	Y	Y	Y	N	Y	N	Y
2 Valentine	N	N	Y	N	Y	Y	N	Y
3 Lancaster	N	N	Y	N	Y	Y	N	Y
4 Price	N	Y	Y	Y	Y	Y	N	Y
5 Neal	N	N	Y	Y	Y	Y	N	Y
6 ***Coble***	Y	N	Y	N	Y	Y	Y	N
7 Rose	N	N	Y	Y	Y	Y	N	Y
8 Hefner	N	N	Y	Y	Y	Y	N	Y
9 ***McMillan***	Y	N	Y	N	Y	Y	Y	N
10 ***Ballenger***	N	N	Y	N	Y	Y	Y	N
11 ***Taylor***	Y	N	Y	N	Y	Y	Y	N
12 Watt	N	Y	N	Y	N	Y	N	Y
NORTH DAKOTA								
AL Pomeroy	N	Y	Y	Y	Y	Y	N	Y
OHIO								
1 Mann	N	N	Y	Y	Y	Y	N	Y
2 ***Portman***	N	N	Y	N	Y	Y	Y	N
3 Hall	N	N	Y	Y	Y	Y	N	N
4 ***Oxley***	Y	N	Y	N	Y	Y	Y	N
5 ***Gillmor***	?	?	?	?	?	?	?	?
6 Strickland	N	Y	Y	Y	Y	Y	N	Y
7 ***Hobson***	N	N	Y	Y	Y	Y	Y	N
8 ***Boehner***	N	N	Y	N	Y	Y	Y	N
9 Kaptur	N	N	Y	Y	Y	Y	N	Y
10 ***Hoke***	?	?	?	Y	Y	Y	Y	N
11 Stokes	?	Y	Y	Y	Y	Y	N	Y
12 ***Kasich***	N	N	Y	N	Y	Y	Y	N
13 Brown	N	Y	Y	Y	Y	Y	N	Y
14 Sawyer	N	Y	Y	Y	Y	Y	N	Y
15 ***Pryce***	N	N	Y	Y	Y	Y	Y	N
16 ***Regula***	N	N	Y	N	Y	Y	Y	N
17 Traficant	N	N	Y	N	Y	Y	N	Y
18 Applegate	N	N	Y	N	Y	Y	N	Y
19 Fingerhut	N	Y	N	Y	Y	Y	N	Y
OKLAHOMA								
1 ***Inhofe***	N	N	Y	N	Y	Y	Y	N
2 Synar	N	Y	N	Y	Y	Y	N	Y
3 Brewster	N	N	Y	N	Y	Y	N	Y
4 McCurdy	N	N	Y	Y	Y	Y	N	Y
5 ***Istook***	N	N	Y	Y	Y	Y	Y	N
6 Vacancy								
OREGON								
1 Furse	N	Y	N	Y	Y	Y	N	Y
2 ***Smith***	Y	N	Y	N	Y	Y	Y	N
3 Wyden	N	Y	Y	Y	Y	Y	N	Y
4 DeFazio	N	Y	Y	Y	Y	Y	N	Y
5 Kopetski	N	Y	N	Y	N	N	N	Y
PENNSYLVANIA								
1 Foglietta	N	Y	Y	N	Y	N	N	Y
2 Blackwell	N	Y	Y	Y	Y	Y	N	Y
3 Borski	N	Y	Y	N	Y	Y	N	Y
4 Klink	N	N	Y	Y	Y	Y	N	Y
5 ***Clinger***	N	N	Y	Y	Y	Y	Y	N
6 Holden	N	N	Y	Y	Y	Y	N	Y
7 ***Weldon***	N	N	Y	Y	Y	Y	Y	N
8 ***Greenwood***	N	N	Y	Y	Y	Y	Y	N
9 ***Shuster***	Y	N	Y	N	Y	Y	Y	N
10 ***McDade***	N	N	Y	Y	Y	Y	Y	N
11 Kanjorski	N	N	Y	Y	Y	Y	N	Y
12 Murtha	N	Y	Y	Y	Y	Y	N	Y
13 Margolies-Mezv.	N	Y	N	Y	Y	Y	N	Y
14 Coyne	N	Y	N	Y	Y	Y	N	Y
15 McHale	N	N	Y	Y	Y	Y	N	Y
16 ***Walker***	N	N	Y	N	Y	Y	Y	N
17 ***Gekas***	Y	N	Y	Y	Y	Y	Y	N
18 ***Santorum***	N	?	?	Y	Y	Y	Y	N
19 ***Goodling***	N	N	Y	Y	Y	Y	Y	N
20 Murphy	?	?	?	Y	Y	Y	N	Y
21 ***Ridge***	?	?	?	Y	Y	Y	Y	N
RHODE ISLAND								
1 ***Machtley***	N	N	Y	Y	Y	Y	Y	N
2 Reed	N	Y	N	Y	Y	Y	N	Y
SOUTH CAROLINA								
1 ***Ravenel***	N	N	Y	N	Y	Y	Y	N
2 ***Spence***	Y	N	Y	N	Y	Y	Y	N
3 Derrick	N	Y	Y	Y	Y	Y	N	Y
4 ***Inglis***	N	N	Y	N	Y	Y	Y	N
5 Spratt	N	Y	Y	Y	Y	Y	N	Y
6 Clyburn	N	Y	Y	Y	Y	Y	N	Y
SOUTH DAKOTA								
AL Johnson	N	Y	Y	Y	Y	Y	N	Y
TENNESSEE								
1 ***Quillen***	N	N	Y	N	Y	Y	#	?
2 ***Duncan***	Y	N	Y	N	Y	Y	Y	N
3 Lloyd	N	N	Y	N	Y	Y	N	Y
4 Cooper	N	N	Y	N	Y	Y	N	Y
5 Clement	N	N	Y	Y	Y	Y	N	Y
6 Gordon	N	N	Y	Y	Y	Y	N	Y
7 ***Sundquist***	?	N	Y	?	?	?	?	?
8 Tanner	N	N	Y	Y	Y	Y	N	Y
9 Ford	?	Y	Y	Y	Y	Y	N	Y
TEXAS								
1 Chapman	N	N	Y	Y	Y	Y	N	Y
2 Wilson	N	N	Y	N	Y	Y	N	Y
3 ***Johnson, Sam***	Y	N	Y	N	Y	Y	Y	N
4 Hall	N	N	Y	N	Y	Y	N	Y
5 Bryant	N	Y	Y	N	Y	Y	N	Y
6 ***Barton***	N	N	Y	N	Y	Y	Y	N
7 ***Archer***	Y	N	Y	N	Y	Y	Y	N
8 ***Fields***	Y	N	Y	N	Y	Y	Y	N
9 Brooks	N	Y	Y	Y	Y	Y	N	Y
10 Pickle	?	?	?	Y	Y	Y	N	Y
11 Edwards	N	N	Y	Y	Y	Y	N	Y
12 Geren	N	N	Y	N	Y	Y	N	Y
13 Sarpalius	N	N	Y	N	Y	Y	N	Y
14 Laughlin	N	Y	Y	Y	Y	Y	N	Y
15 de la Garza	N	N	Y	Y	Y	Y	N	Y
16 Coleman	N	Y	Y	Y	Y	Y	N	Y
17 Stenholm	N	N	Y	N	Y	Y	N	Y
18 Washington	?	?	?	Y	Y	N	N	Y
19 ***Combest***	Y	N	Y	N	Y	Y	Y	N
20 Gonzalez	N	Y	N	Y	Y	Y	N	Y
21 ***Smith***	N	N	Y	N	Y	Y	Y	N
22 ***DeLay***	Y	N	Y	N	Y	Y	Y	N
23 ***Bonilla***	N	N	Y	Y	Y	Y	Y	N
24 Frost	N	Y	Y	Y	Y	Y	N	Y
25 Andrews	N	N	Y	N	Y	Y	N	Y
26 ***Armey***	Y	N	Y	N	Y	Y	Y	N
27 Ortiz	N	N	Y	N	Y	Y	N	Y
28 Tejeda	N	N	Y	N	Y	Y	N	Y
29 Green	N	Y	Y	Y	Y	Y	N	Y
30 Johnson, E.B.	?	?	?	Y	Y	Y	N	Y
UTAH								
1 ***Hansen***	Y	N	Y	N	Y	Y	Y	N
2 Shepherd	N	Y	Y	Y	Y	Y	N	Y
3 Orton	N	N	Y	Y	Y	Y	N	Y
VERMONT								
AL *Sanders*	N	Y	Y	Y	Y	Y	N	Y
VIRGINIA								
1 ***Bateman***	N	N	Y	Y	Y	Y	Y	N
2 Pickett	N	N	Y	N	Y	Y	N	Y
3 Scott	N	Y	N	Y	N	Y	N	Y
4 Sisisky	N	Y	Y	N	Y	Y	N	Y
5 Payne	N	N	Y	N	Y	Y	N	Y
6 ***Goodlatte***	Y	N	Y	N	Y	Y	Y	N
7 ***Bliley***	Y	N	Y	N	Y	Y	Y	N
8 Moran	N	Y	Y	Y	Y	Y	N	Y
9 Boucher	?	N	Y	Y	Y	Y	N	Y
10 ***Wolf***	N	N	Y	N	Y	Y	Y	N
11 Byrne	N	?	Y	Y	Y	Y	N	Y
WASHINGTON								
1 Cantwell	N	Y	Y	Y	Y	Y	N	Y
2 Swift	N	Y	N	Y	Y	Y	N	Y
3 Unsoeld	N	Y	N	Y	Y	Y	N	Y
4 Inslee	N	Y	Y	Y	Y	Y	N	Y
5 Foley								
6 Dicks	N	Y	Y	Y	Y	Y	N	Y
7 McDermott	N	Y	Y	Y	Y	Y	N	Y
8 ***Dunn***	N	N	Y	Y	Y	Y	Y	N
9 Kreidler	N	Y	Y	Y	Y	Y	N	Y
WEST VIRGINIA								
1 Mollohan	N	N	Y	Y	Y	Y	N	Y
2 Wise	N	N	Y	Y	Y	Y	N	Y
3 Rahall	N	Y	Y	N	Y	Y	N	Y
WISCONSIN								
1 Barca	N	Y	Y	Y	Y	Y	N	Y
2 ***Klug***	N	N	Y	Y	Y	Y	Y	N
3 ***Gunderson***	N	N	Y	Y	Y	Y	Y	N
4 Kleczka	N	Y	Y	Y	Y	Y	N	Y
5 Barrett	N	Y	Y	Y	Y	Y	N	Y
6 ***Petri***	Y	N	Y	N	Y	Y	Y	N
7 Obey	N	Y	Y	Y	Y	Y	N	Y
8 ***Roth***	Y	N	Y	N	Y	Y	Y	N
9 ***Sensenbrenner***	Y	N	Y	N	Y	Y	Y	N
WYOMING								
AL ***Thomas***	N	N	Y	Y	Y	Y	Y	N
DELEGATES								
de Lugo, V.I.	N	Y	Y	Y	?	D	D	D
Faleomavaega, Am.S.	?	?	?	Y	Y	D	D	D
Norton, D.C.	N	Y	Y	Y	Y	D	D	D
Romero-B., P.R.	?	?	?	Y	Y	D	D	D
Underwood, Guam	?	?	?	Y	N	D	D	D

Southern states - Ala., Ark., Fla., Ga., Ky., La., Miss., N.C., Okla., S.C., Tenn., Texas, Va.
Omitted votes are quorum calls, which CQ does not include in its vote charts.

HOUSE VOTES 81, 82, 83, 84, 85, 86, 87, 88

81. HR 4067. Multifamily Housing Property Disposal/Suspension. Gonzalez, D-Texas, motion to suspend the rules and pass the bill to provide the Department of Housing and Urban Development with greater flexibility to dispose of its inventory of multifamily properties acquired through defaults. Motion agreed to 413-9: R 170-0; D 243-8 (ND 162-8, SD 81-0); I 0-1, March 22, 1994. A two-thirds majority of those present and voting (282 in this case) is required for passage under suspension of the rules. A "yea" was a vote in support of the president's position.

82. HR 4034. Urban Recreation and At-Risk Youth/Suspension. Vento, D-Minn., motion to suspend the rules and pass the bill to improve facilities and expand park and recreation opportunities for at-risk youth in high-crime urban areas. Motion agreed to 361-59: R 112-56; D 248-3 (ND 167-3, SD 81-0); I 1-0, March 22, 1994. A two-thirds majority of those present and voting (280 in this case) is required for passage under suspension of the rules.

83. Procedural Motion. Approval of the House Journal of Tuesday, March 22. Approved 244-153: R 19-146; D 225-7 (ND 150-6, SD 75-1); I 0-0, March 23, 1994.

84. HR 4092. Omnibus Crime Bill/Rule. Adoption of the rule (H Res 395) to provide for House floor consideration of the bill to authorize more than $15 billion for fiscal 1994-99 to implement various proposals to combat crime, including $3 billion for new prisons and $7 billion in direct aid to needy communities, drug treatment, midnight sports programs and targeted community investment programs. The bill also would require life imprisonment for three-time violent offenders, expand the death penalty to apply to dozens of federal crimes, authorize grants to hire 50,000 additional police officers and overhaul the process for death row habeas corpus appeals. Adopted 240-175: R 0-173; D 239-2 (ND 166-1, SD 73-1); I 1-0, March 23, 1994.

85. HR 1804. Goals 2000: Educate America/School Prayer. Duncan, R-Tenn., motion to recommit the conference report on the bill to the conference committee with instructions to report it back with an amendment to deny federal aid to state or local school agencies that prohibit constitutionally protected voluntary prayer in public schools. Motion rejected 195-232: R 166-8; D 29-223 (ND 9-162, SD 20-61); I 0-1, March 23, 1994.

86. HR 1804. Goals 2000: Educate America/Conference Report. Adoption of the conference report on the bill to authorize $400 million in fiscal 1994 and such sums as necessary in fiscal 1995-98 for competitive grants for schools seeking to improve their performance, write into law national education goals, and establish tests and standards for elementary and secondary students. Adopted (thus sent to the Senate) 306-121: R 59-115; D 246-6 (ND 169-2, SD 77-4); I 1-0, March 23, 1994. A "yea" was a vote in support of the president's position.

87. HR 3345. Federal Work Force Restructuring/Rule. Adoption of the rule (H Res 388) to waive points of order against and provide for House floor consideration of the conference report on the bill to authorize financial incentives of up to $25,000 per worker to encourage voluntary retirements or resignations from the federal work force. Adopted 253-170: R 6-168; D 246-2 (ND 167-2, SD 79-0); I 1-0, March 23, 1994.

88. HR 3345. Federal Work Force Restructuring/Crime Trust Fund. Castle, R-Del., motion to recommit the conference report to the conference committee with instructions to report it back with an amendment to require establishment of a Violent Crime Reduction Trust Fund within the Treasury Department with $22 billion, the assumed savings from the work force reductions. Motion rejected 166-261: R 165-9; D 1-251 (ND 0-172, SD 1-79); I 0-1, March 23, 1994.

KEY

Y	Voted for (yea).
#	Paired for.
+	Announced for.
N	Voted against (nay).
X	Paired against.
−	Announced against.
P	Voted "present."
C	Voted "present" to avoid possible conflict of interest.
?	Did not vote or otherwise make a position known.
D	Delegates ineligible to vote.

Democrats *Republicans*
Independent

	81	82	83	84	85	86	87	88
ALABAMA								
1 *Callahan*	Y	Y	?	N	Y	N	N	Y
2 *Everett*	Y	Y	N	N	Y	N	N	Y
3 Browder	Y	Y	Y	Y	Y	Y	Y	N
4 Bevill	Y	Y	Y	Y	Y	Y	Y	N
5 Cramer	Y	Y	Y	N	Y	Y	N	N
6 *Bachus*	Y	N	N	N	Y	N	N	Y
7 Hilliard	Y	Y	Y	N	N	Y	Y	N
ALASKA								
AL *Young*	Y	Y	N	N	Y	N	Y	N
ARIZONA								
1 Coppersmith	Y	Y	Y	Y	N	Y	N	N
2 Pastor	Y	Y	Y	Y	N	Y	N	N
3 *Stump*	Y	N	N	N	Y	N	N	Y
4 *Kyl*	Y	Y	N	N	Y	N	N	Y
5 *Kolbe*	Y	Y	N	N	Y	Y	N	Y
6 English	Y	Y	Y	Y	N	Y	Y	N
ARKANSAS								
1 Lambert	Y	Y	Y	?	N	Y	Y	N
2 Thornton	Y	Y	Y	N	Y	Y	Y	N
3 *Hutchinson*	Y	N	N	N	Y	N	N	Y
4 Dickey	Y	Y	N	N	Y	N	N	Y
CALIFORNIA								
1 Hamburg	Y	Y	Y	Y	N	Y	Y	N
2 *Herger*	Y	N	N	N	Y	N	N	Y
3 Fazio	Y	Y	?	Y	N	Y	Y	N
4 *Doolittle*	Y	N	N	N	Y	N	N	Y
5 Matsui	Y	Y	Y	Y	N	Y	Y	N
6 Woolsey	Y	Y	Y	+	N	Y	Y	N
7 Miller	Y	Y	Y	Y	N	Y	Y	N
8 Pelosi	Y	Y	Y	?	?	Y	Y	N
9 Dellums	Y	Y	Y	N	N	Y	Y	N
10 *Baker*	Y	N	N	N	Y	N	N	Y
11 *Pombo*	Y	Y	?	N	Y	N	N	Y
12 Lantos	Y	Y	Y	Y	N	Y	Y	N
13 Stark	Y	Y	Y	N	Y	Y	Y	N
14 Eshoo	Y	Y	Y	Y	N	Y	Y	N
15 Mineta	Y	Y	Y	Y	N	Y	Y	N
16 Edwards	Y	Y	Y	N	Y	Y	Y	N
17 Farr	Y	Y	Y	Y	N	Y	Y	N
18 Condit	Y	Y	Y	N	Y	Y	Y	N
19 Lehman	Y	Y	Y	Y	N	Y	Y	N
20 Dooley	Y	Y	?	Y	N	Y	Y	N
21 *Thomas*	Y	Y	N	N	Y	N	Y	N
22 *Huffington*	Y	N	N	N	Y	N	Y	N
23 *Gallegly*	Y	Y	N	N	Y	N	N	Y
24 Beilenson	Y	Y	Y	Y	N	Y	Y	N
25 *McKeon*	Y	Y	N	N	Y	N	N	Y
26 Berman	Y	Y	Y	Y	N	Y	Y	N
27 *Moorhead*	Y	N	N	N	Y	N	N	Y
28 *Dreier*	Y	N	N	N	Y	N	N	Y
29 Waxman	Y	Y	Y	Y	N	Y	Y	N
30 Becerra	Y	Y	Y	Y	N	Y	Y	N
31 Martinez	Y	Y	Y	Y	N	Y	Y	N
32 Dixon	Y	Y	Y	Y	N	Y	Y	N
33 Roybal-Allard	Y	Y	Y	Y	N	Y	Y	N
34 Torres	Y	Y	Y	Y	N	Y	Y	N
35 Waters	Y	Y	Y	Y	N	Y	Y	N
36 Harman	Y	Y	Y	Y	N	Y	Y	N
37 Tucker	Y	Y	Y	Y	N	Y	Y	N
38 *Horn*	Y	N	N	N	Y	N	N	Y
39 *Royce*	Y	N	N	N	Y	N	N	Y
40 *Lewis*	Y	Y	N	N	Y	N	N	Y
41 *Kim*	Y	Y	N	N	Y	N	N	Y
42 Brown	Y	Y	?	Y	N	Y	Y	N
43 *Calvert*	Y	Y	N	N	Y	N	N	Y
44 *McCandless*	Y	Y	N	N	Y	N	N	Y
45 *Rohrabacher*	Y	N	N	N	Y	N	N	Y
46 *Dornan*	Y	N	?	N	Y	N	N	Y
47 *Cox*	Y	N	?	N	Y	N	N	Y
48 *Packard*	Y	N	N	N	Y	N	N	Y
49 Schenk	Y	Y	Y	Y	N	Y	Y	N
50 Filner	N	Y	Y	N	N	Y	Y	N
51 *Cunningham*	Y	Y	N	N	Y	N	N	Y
52 *Hunter*	Y	Y	?	N	Y	N	N	Y
COLORADO								
1 Schroeder	Y	Y	N	Y	N	Y	Y	N
2 Skaggs	Y	Y	Y	Y	N	Y	Y	N
3 *McInnis*	Y	Y	N	N	Y	N	N	Y
4 *Allard*	N	N	N	N	Y	N	N	Y
5 *Hefley*	Y	N	N	N	Y	N	N	Y
6 *Schaefer*	Y	Y	N	N	Y	N	N	Y
CONNECTICUT								
1 Kennelly	Y	Y	?	Y	N	Y	Y	N
2 Gejdenson	Y	Y	?	Y	N	Y	Y	N
3 DeLauro	Y	Y	?	Y	N	Y	Y	N
4 *Shays*	Y	Y	N	N	Y	N	Y	N
5 *Franks*	Y	Y	N	N	Y	N	Y	N
6 *Johnson*	Y	Y	N	N	Y	N	N	Y
DELAWARE								
AL *Castle*	Y	Y	N	N	Y	N	Y	N
FLORIDA								
1 Hutto	Y	Y	Y	Y	N	Y	Y	N
2 Peterson	Y	Y	Y	Y	N	Y	Y	N
3 Brown	Y	Y	Y	Y	N	Y	Y	N
4 *Fowler*	Y	Y	?	N	Y	N	N	Y
5 Thurman	Y	Y	Y	Y	N	Y	Y	N
6 *Stearns*	Y	N	N	N	Y	N	N	Y
7 *Mica*	Y	N	N	N	Y	N	N	Y
8 *McCollum*	Y	N	N	N	Y	N	N	Y
9 *Bilirakis*	Y	N	N	N	Y	N	N	Y
10 *Young*	Y	Y	N	N	Y	N	N	Y
11 Gibbons	Y	Y	Y	Y	N	Y	Y	N
12 *Canady*	Y	N	N	N	Y	N	N	Y
13 *Miller*	Y	N	N	N	Y	N	N	Y
14 *Goss*	Y	N	N	N	Y	N	N	Y
15 Bacchus	Y	Y	Y	Y	N	Y	Y	N
16 *Lewis*	Y	Y	N	N	Y	N	N	Y
17 Meek	Y	Y	Y	Y	N	Y	Y	N
18 *Ros-Lehtinen*	Y	Y	N	N	Y	N	N	Y
19 Johnston	Y	Y	Y	Y	N	Y	Y	N
20 Deutsch	Y	Y	Y	Y	N	Y	Y	N
21 *Diaz-Balart*	Y	Y	N	N	Y	N	N	Y
22 *Shaw*	Y	Y	N	N	Y	N	N	Y
23 Hastings	?	?	Y	Y	N	Y	Y	N
GEORGIA								
1 *Kingston*	Y	N	N	N	Y	N	N	Y
2 Bishop	Y	Y	Y	Y	N	Y	Y	N
3 *Collins*	Y	N	N	N	Y	N	N	Y
4 *Linder*	N	N	N	N	Y	N	N	Y
5 Lewis	Y	Y	Y	Y	N	Y	Y	N
6 *Gingrich*	Y	N	N	N	Y	N	N	Y
7 Darden	Y	Y	Y	Y	N	Y	Y	N
8 Rowland	Y	Y	Y	Y	N	Y	Y	N
9 Deal	Y	Y	Y	Y	N	Y	Y	N
10 Johnson	Y	Y	Y	Y	N	Y	Y	N
11 McKinney	Y	Y	Y	Y	N	Y	Y	N
HAWAII								
1 Abercrombie	Y	Y	Y	Y	N	Y	Y	N
2 Mink	Y	Y	Y	Y	N	Y	Y	N
IDAHO								
1 LaRocco	Y	Y	Y	?	N	Y	Y	N
2 *Crapo*	Y	N	N	N	Y	N	N	Y
ILLINOIS								
1 Rush	Y	Y	?	Y	N	Y	Y	N
2 Reynolds	Y	Y	Y	Y	N	Y	Y	N
3 Lipinski	Y	Y	Y	Y	N	Y	Y	N
4 Gutierrez	N	Y	Y	Y	N	Y	Y	N
5 Rostenkowski	Y	Y	Y	Y	N	Y	Y	N
6 *Hyde*	Y	Y	N	N	Y	N	Y	N
7 Collins	N	Y	Y	N	N	Y	Y	N
8 *Crane*	Y	N	N	N	Y	N	N	Y
9 Yates	N	Y	Y	Y	N	Y	Y	N
10 *Porter*	Y	Y	N	N	Y	N	N	Y
11 Sangmeister	Y	Y	Y	Y	N	Y	Y	N
12 Costello	Y	Y	Y	Y	N	Y	Y	N
13 *Fawell*	Y	N	N	N	Y	N	N	Y
14 *Hastert*	Y	Y	N	N	Y	N	N	Y
15 *Ewing*	Y	Y	N	N	Y	N	N	Y
16 *Manzullo*	Y	Y	N	N	Y	N	N	Y
17 Evans	Y	Y	Y	Y	N	Y	Y	N

ND Northern Democrats   SD Southern Democrats

	81	82	83	84	85	86	87	88
18 ***Michel***	Y	Y	N	N	Y	N	N	Y
19 Poshard	Y	Y	Y	Y	Y	Y	Y	N
20 Durbin	Y	Y	Y	Y	N	Y	Y	N
INDIANA								
1 Visclosky	Y	Y	Y	Y	N	Y	Y	N
2 Sharp	Y	Y	Y	Y	N	Y	Y	N
3 Roemer	Y	Y	Y	Y	N	Y	Y	N
4 Long	Y	Y	Y	Y	N	Y	Y	N
5 ***Buyer***	Y	Y	N	N	Y	N	N	Y
6 ***Burton***	Y	N	N	N	Y	N	N	Y
7 ***Myers***	Y	Y	Y	N	Y	N	N	N
8 McCloskey	Y	Y	Y	Y	N	Y	Y	N
9 Hamilton	N	Y	Y	Y	N	Y	Y	N
10 Jacobs	Y	Y	N	Y	Y	Y	N	N
IOWA								
1 ***Leach***	Y	?	N	N	N	Y	N	Y
2 ***Nussle***	Y	N	N	N	Y	Y	N	Y
3 ***Lightfoot***	Y	N	N	N	Y	N	N	Y
4 Smith	Y	Y	?	Y	N	Y	Y	N
5 ***Grandy***	?	?	N	N	Y	Y	N	Y
KANSAS								
1 ***Roberts***	Y	N	?	N	Y	N	N	Y
2 Slattery	Y	Y	Y	Y	N	Y	Y	N
3 ***Meyers***	Y	Y	N	N	N	Y	N	Y
4 Glickman	Y	Y	Y	Y	N	Y	Y	N
KENTUCKY								
1 Barlow	Y	Y	Y	Y	N	Y	Y	N
2 Natcher	?	?	?	?	?	?	?	?
3 Mazzoli	Y	Y	+	+	−	+	+	−
4 ***Bunning***	Y	N	N	N	Y	N	N	Y
5 ***Rogers***	Y	N	N	N	Y	Y	N	Y
6 Baesler	Y	Y	Y	Y	N	Y	Y	N
LOUISIANA								
1 ***Livingston***	Y	Y	Y	N	Y	N	N	Y
2 Jefferson	Y	Y	?	Y	N	Y	?	N
3 Tauzin	Y	Y	Y	Y	Y	Y	Y	N
4 Fields	Y	Y	Y	Y	N	Y	Y	N
5 ***McCrery***	Y	Y	Y	N	Y	N	N	Y
6 ***Baker***	Y	Y	N	N	Y	N	N	Y
7 Hayes	Y	Y	Y	Y	Y	Y	?	N
MAINE								
1 Andrews	Y	Y	Y	Y	N	Y	Y	N
2 ***Snowe***	Y	Y	N	N	Y	Y	N	Y
MARYLAND								
1 ***Gilchrest***	Y	Y	N	N	N	Y	N	Y
2 ***Bentley***	Y	Y	N	N	Y	Y	N	N
3 Cardin	Y	Y	Y	Y	N	Y	Y	N
4 Wynn	Y	Y	Y	Y	N	Y	Y	N
5 Hoyer	Y	Y	?	Y	N	Y	Y	N
6 ***Bartlett***	Y	Y	N	N	Y	N	N	Y
7 Mfume	Y	Y	Y	Y	N	Y	Y	N
8 ***Morella***	Y	Y	N	N	N	Y	Y	N
MASSACHUSETTS								
1 Olver	Y	Y	Y	Y	N	Y	Y	N
2 Neal	Y	Y	Y	Y	N	Y	Y	N
3 ***Blute***	Y	Y	N	N	Y	Y	N	Y
4 Frank	Y	Y	Y	Y	N	Y	Y	N
5 Meehan	Y	Y	Y	Y	N	Y	Y	N
6 ***Torkildsen***	Y	Y	N	N	Y	Y	N	Y
7 Markey	Y	Y	Y	Y	N	Y	Y	N
8 Kennedy	Y	Y	Y	Y	N	?	Y	N
9 Moakley	Y	Y	Y	Y	N	Y	Y	N
10 Studds	Y	Y	Y	Y	N	Y	Y	N
MICHIGAN								
1 Stupak	Y	Y	Y	Y	N	Y	Y	N
2 ***Hoekstra***	Y	N	N	N	Y	N	N	Y
3 ***Ehlers***	Y	Y	N	N	Y	N	N	N
4 ***Camp***	Y	N	N	N	Y	Y	N	Y
5 Barcia	Y	Y	Y	Y	N	Y	Y	N
6 ***Upton***	Y	Y	N	N	Y	Y	N	Y
7 ***Smith***	Y	N	N	N	Y	Y	N	Y
8 Carr	Y	Y	Y	Y	N	Y	Y	N
9 Kildee	Y	Y	Y	Y	N	Y	Y	N
10 Bonior	Y	Y	?	Y	N	Y	Y	N
11 ***Knollenberg***	Y	N	N	N	Y	N	N	Y
12 Levin	Y	Y	Y	Y	N	Y	Y	N
13 Ford	Y	Y	?	Y	N	Y	Y	N
14 Conyers	Y	Y	Y	Y	N	Y	Y	N
15 Collins	N	Y	Y	Y	N	Y	Y	N
16 Dingell	Y	Y	Y	Y	N	Y	Y	N
MINNESOTA								
1 Penny	Y	N	Y	Y	N	N	Y	N
2 Minge	Y	Y	Y	Y	N	Y	Y	N
3 ***Ramstad***	Y	N	N	N	Y	Y	N	Y
4 Vento	Y	Y	Y	Y	N	Y	Y	N
5 Sabo	Y	Y	Y	Y	N	Y	Y	N
6 ***Grams***	Y	Y	N	N	Y	N	N	Y
7 Peterson	Y	Y	Y	Y	Y	Y	Y	N
8 Oberstar	Y	Y	Y	Y	N	Y	Y	N
MISSISSIPPI								
1 Whitten	Y	Y	?	Y	N	Y	Y	N
2 Thompson	Y	Y	Y	Y	N	Y	Y	N
3 Montgomery	Y	Y	Y	Y	Y	Y	Y	N
4 Parker	Y	Y	Y	Y	Y	Y	Y	N
5 Taylor	Y	Y	N	?	Y	N	Y	N
MISSOURI								
1 Clay	?	?	N	Y	N	Y	Y	N
2 ***Talent***	Y	Y	N	N	Y	N	N	Y
3 Gephardt	Y	Y	?	Y	N	Y	Y	N
4 Skelton	Y	Y	Y	Y	Y	Y	Y	N
5 Wheat	Y	Y	?	Y	N	Y	Y	N
6 Danner	Y	Y	Y	Y	N	Y	Y	N
7 ***Hancock***	Y	N	N	N	Y	N	N	Y
8 ***Emerson***	Y	Y	N	N	Y	N	N	Y
9 Volkmer	Y	Y	N	Y	N	Y	Y	N
MONTANA								
AL Williams	Y	Y	Y	Y	N	Y	Y	N
NEBRASKA								
1 ***Bereuter***	Y	N	N	N	Y	Y	N	Y
2 Hoagland	Y	Y	Y	Y	N	Y	Y	N
3 ***Barrett***	Y	N	N	N	Y	Y	N	Y
NEVADA								
1 Bilbray	Y	Y	Y	Y	N	Y	Y	N
2 ***Vucanovich***	Y	Y	N	N	Y	N	N	Y
NEW HAMPSHIRE								
1 ***Zeliff***	Y	N	N	N	Y	N	N	Y
2 Swett	Y	Y	Y	Y	N	Y	Y	N
NEW JERSEY								
1 Andrews	Y	Y	Y	?	N	Y	Y	N
2 Hughes	Y	Y	Y	Y	N	Y	Y	N
3 ***Saxton***	Y	Y	N	N	Y	Y	N	Y
4 ***Smith***	Y	Y	Y	N	Y	N	N	Y
5 ***Roukema***	Y	Y	N	N	Y	N	N	Y
6 Pallone	Y	Y	Y	Y	N	Y	Y	N
7 ***Franks***	Y	Y	N	N	Y	N	N	Y
8 Klein	Y	Y	Y	Y	N	Y	Y	N
9 Torricelli	Y	Y	Y	Y	N	Y	Y	N
10 Payne	Y	Y	Y	Y	N	Y	Y	N
11 ***Gallo***	?	?	?	?	?	?	?	?
12 ***Zimmer***	Y	N	N	N	Y	N	N	Y
13 Menendez	Y	Y	Y	Y	N	Y	Y	N
NEW MEXICO								
1 ***Schiff***	Y	Y	N	N	Y	Y	N	Y
2 ***Skeen***	Y	Y	N	N	Y	N	N	Y
3 Richardson	Y	Y	Y	Y	N	Y	Y	N
NEW YORK								
1 Hochbrueckner	Y	Y	Y	Y	N	Y	Y	N
2 ***Lazio***	Y	Y	N	N	Y	Y	N	Y
3 ***King***	Y	N	N	N	Y	N	N	Y
4 ***Levy***	Y	Y	N	N	Y	N	N	Y
5 Ackerman	Y	Y	Y	Y	N	Y	Y	N
6 Flake	Y	Y	Y	Y	N	Y	?	N
7 Manton	Y	Y	Y	Y	N	Y	Y	N
8 Nadler	Y	Y	Y	Y	N	Y	Y	N
9 Schumer	Y	Y	Y	Y	N	Y	Y	N
10 Towns	Y	Y	?	?	N	Y	Y	N
11 Owens	Y	Y	Y	Y	N	Y	Y	N
12 Velazquez	Y	Y	Y	Y	N	Y	Y	N
13 ***Molinari***	Y	Y	N	N	Y	Y	N	Y
14 Maloney	?	?	Y	Y	N	Y	Y	N
15 Rangel	Y	Y	Y	Y	N	Y	Y	N
16 Serrano	Y	Y	Y	Y	N	Y	Y	N
17 Engel	Y	Y	Y	Y	N	Y	Y	N
18 Lowey	Y	Y	Y	Y	N	Y	Y	N
19 ***Fish***	Y	?	Y	N	Y	Y	N	Y
20 ***Gilman***	Y	Y	?	N	N	Y	Y	N
21 McNulty	Y	Y	Y	Y	Y	Y	Y	N
22 ***Solomon***	Y	N	N	N	Y	N	N	Y
23 ***Boehlert***	Y	Y	N	N	N	Y	N	Y
24 ***McHugh***	Y	N	N	N	Y	N	N	Y
25 ***Walsh***	Y	Y	N	N	Y	Y	Y	Y
26 Hinchey	N	Y	Y	Y	N	Y	Y	N
27 ***Paxon***	Y	N	N	N	Y	N	N	Y
28 Slaughter	Y	Y	Y	Y	N	Y	Y	N
29 LaFalce	Y	Y	Y	Y	N	Y	?	N
30 ***Quinn***	Y	Y	N	N	Y	Y	N	Y
31 ***Houghton***	Y	Y	Y	N	Y	Y	N	Y
NORTH CAROLINA								
1 Clayton	Y	Y	Y	Y	N	Y	Y	N
2 Valentine	Y	Y	Y	Y	Y	Y	Y	N
3 Lancaster	Y	Y	Y	Y	Y	Y	Y	Y
4 Price	Y	Y	Y	Y	N	Y	Y	N
5 Neal	Y	Y	?	Y	N	Y	Y	N
6 ***Coble***	Y	N	N	N	Y	N	N	Y
7 Rose	Y	Y	Y	Y	N	Y	Y	N
8 Hefner	Y	Y	Y	Y	N	Y	Y	N
9 ***McMillan***	Y	Y	N	?	Y	Y	N	Y
10 ***Ballenger***	?	?	N	N	Y	N	N	Y
11 ***Taylor***	Y	N	N	N	Y	N	N	Y
12 Watt	Y	Y	Y	Y	N	Y	Y	N
NORTH DAKOTA								
AL Pomeroy	Y	Y	?	Y	N	Y	Y	N
OHIO								
1 Mann	Y	Y	Y	Y	N	Y	Y	N
2 ***Portman***	Y	Y	N	N	Y	N	N	Y
3 Hall	Y	Y	Y	Y	N	Y	Y	N
4 ***Oxley***	Y	Y	N	N	Y	N	N	Y
5 ***Gillmor***	?	?	?	N	Y	Y	N	Y
6 Strickland	Y	Y	Y	Y	N	Y	Y	N
7 ***Hobson***	Y	Y	N	N	Y	Y	N	Y
8 ***Boehner***	Y	Y	N	N	Y	N	N	Y
9 Kaptur	Y	Y	Y	Y	N	Y	Y	N
10 ***Hoke***	Y	Y	Y	N	Y	N	N	Y
11 Stokes	Y	Y	Y	Y	N	Y	Y	N
12 ***Kasich***	Y	Y	Y	N	Y	N	N	Y
13 Brown	Y	Y	Y	Y	N	Y	Y	N
14 Sawyer	Y	Y	Y	Y	N	Y	Y	N
15 ***Pryce***	Y	Y	N	N	Y	N	N	Y
16 ***Regula***	Y	Y	N	N	Y	Y	N	Y
17 Traficant	N	Y	Y	Y	Y	Y	Y	N
18 Applegate	Y	N	Y	Y	Y	Y	Y	N
19 Fingerhut	Y	Y	Y	Y	N	N	Y	N
OKLAHOMA								
1 ***Inhofe***	Y	Y	N	N	Y	N	N	Y
2 Synar	Y	Y	Y	Y	N	Y	Y	N
3 Brewster	Y	Y	Y	Y	N	Y	Y	N
4 McCurdy	Y	Y	Y	Y	N	Y	Y	N
5 ***Istook***	Y	Y	N	N	Y	N	N	Y
6 Vacancy								
OREGON								
1 Furse	Y	Y	Y	Y	N	Y	Y	N
2 ***Smith***	Y	Y	N	N	Y	N	N	Y
3 Wyden	Y	Y	Y	Y	N	Y	Y	N
4 DeFazio	Y	Y	Y	Y	N	Y	Y	N
5 Kopetski	Y	Y	Y	Y	N	Y	Y	N
PENNSYLVANIA								
1 Foglietta	Y	Y	Y	Y	N	Y	Y	N
2 Blackwell	Y	Y	Y	Y	N	Y	Y	N
3 Borski	Y	Y	Y	Y	N	Y	Y	N
4 Klink	Y	N	Y	Y	N	Y	Y	N
5 ***Clinger***	Y	Y	N	N	Y	Y	N	Y
6 Holden	Y	Y	Y	Y	N	Y	Y	N
7 ***Weldon***	Y	Y	N	?	Y	Y	N	Y
8 ***Greenwood***	Y	Y	Y	N	Y	Y	N	Y
9 ***Shuster***	Y	N	N	N	Y	N	N	Y
10 ***McDade***	Y	Y	N	N	Y	Y	N	Y
11 Kanjorski	Y	Y	Y	Y	N	Y	Y	N
12 Murtha	Y	Y	Y	Y	N	Y	Y	N
13 Margolies-Mezv.	Y	Y	Y	Y	N	Y	Y	N
14 Coyne	Y	Y	Y	Y	N	Y	Y	N
15 McHale	Y	Y	Y	Y	N	Y	Y	N
16 ***Walker***	Y	N	N	N	Y	N	N	Y
17 ***Gekas***	Y	Y	N	N	Y	N	N	Y
18 ***Santorum***	Y	N	?	N	Y	Y	N	Y
19 ***Goodling***	Y	Y	N	N	Y	Y	N	Y
20 Murphy	Y	Y	N	Y	N	Y	Y	N
21 ***Ridge***	Y	Y	N	N	?	?	?	?
RHODE ISLAND								
1 ***Machtley***	Y	Y	N	N	Y	Y	N	Y
2 Reed	Y	Y	Y	Y	N	Y	Y	N
SOUTH CAROLINA								
1 ***Ravenel***	Y	Y	N	N	Y	N	Y	Y
2 ***Spence***	Y	N	Y	N	Y	N	N	Y
3 Derrick	Y	Y	Y	Y	N	Y	Y	N
4 ***Inglis***	Y	N	Y	N	Y	N	N	Y
5 Spratt	Y	Y	Y	?	N	Y	Y	N
6 Clyburn	Y	Y	?	Y	N	Y	Y	N
SOUTH DAKOTA								
AL Johnson	Y	Y	Y	Y	N	Y	Y	N
TENNESSEE								
1 ***Quillen***	?	?	N	N	Y	N	N	Y
2 ***Duncan***	Y	N	N	N	Y	N	N	Y
3 Lloyd	Y	Y	Y	Y	Y	Y	Y	N
4 Cooper	Y	Y	Y	Y	N	Y	Y	N
5 Clement	Y	Y	Y	Y	N	Y	Y	N
6 Gordon	Y	Y	Y	Y	N	Y	Y	N
7 ***Sundquist***	?	?	N	N	Y	N	N	Y
8 Tanner	Y	Y	Y	Y	Y	Y	Y	N
9 Ford	Y	Y	Y	Y	N	Y	Y	N
TEXAS								
1 Chapman	Y	Y	Y	Y	N	Y	Y	N
2 Wilson	Y	Y	Y	Y	Y	Y	Y	N
3 ***Johnson, Sam***	Y	N	N	N	Y	N	N	Y
4 Hall	Y	Y	Y	Y	Y	Y	Y	N
5 Bryant	Y	Y	Y	?	N	Y	Y	N
6 ***Barton***	Y	Y	Y	N	Y	N	N	Y
7 ***Archer***	Y	N	N	N	Y	N	N	Y
8 ***Fields***	Y	N	N	N	Y	N	N	Y
9 Brooks	Y	Y	Y	Y	N	Y	Y	N
10 Pickle	Y	Y	Y	Y	?	?	?	?
11 Edwards	Y	Y	Y	Y	N	Y	Y	N
12 Geren	Y	Y	Y	Y	Y	N	Y	N
13 Sarpalius	Y	Y	Y	Y	Y	Y	Y	N
14 Laughlin	Y	Y	Y	Y	N	Y	Y	N
15 de la Garza	Y	Y	?	Y	N	Y	Y	N
16 Coleman	Y	Y	Y	Y	N	Y	Y	N
17 Stenholm	Y	Y	Y	Y	Y	N	Y	N
18 Washington	?	?	?	?	N	Y	Y	?
19 ***Combest***	Y	N	Y	N	Y	N	N	Y
20 Gonzalez	Y	Y	Y	?	N	Y	Y	N
21 ***Smith***	Y	Y	N	N	Y	N	N	Y
22 ***DeLay***	Y	N	N	N	Y	N	N	Y
23 ***Bonilla***	Y	Y	N	N	Y	N	N	N
24 Frost	Y	Y	Y	Y	N	Y	Y	N
25 Andrews	Y	Y	Y	Y	N	Y	Y	N
26 ***Armey***	Y	N	N	N	Y	N	N	Y
27 Ortiz	Y	Y	Y	?	N	Y	Y	N
28 Tejeda	Y	Y	Y	Y	N	Y	Y	N
29 Green	Y	Y	Y	Y	N	Y	Y	N
30 Johnson, E.B.	Y	Y	Y	Y	N	Y	Y	N
UTAH								
1 ***Hansen***	Y	N	N	N	Y	N	N	Y
2 Shepherd	Y	Y	Y	Y	N	Y	Y	N
3 Orton	Y	Y	Y	Y	Y	Y	Y	N
VERMONT								
AL *Sanders*	N	Y	?	Y	N	Y	Y	N
VIRGINIA								
1 ***Bateman***	Y	Y	Y	N	Y	Y	N	Y
2 Pickett	Y	Y	Y	Y	N	Y	Y	N
3 Scott	Y	Y	Y	Y	N	Y	Y	N
4 Sisisky	Y	Y	Y	Y	N	Y	Y	N
5 Payne	Y	Y	Y	Y	Y	Y	Y	N
6 ***Goodlatte***	Y	N	N	N	Y	N	N	Y
7 ***Bliley***	Y	Y	N	N	Y	N	N	Y
8 Moran	Y	Y	Y	?	N	Y	Y	N
9 Boucher	Y	Y	Y	Y	N	Y	Y	N
10 ***Wolf***	Y	Y	N	N	Y	N	Y	N
11 Byrne	Y	Y	Y	Y	N	Y	Y	N
WASHINGTON								
1 Cantwell	Y	Y	Y	Y	N	Y	Y	N
2 Swift	Y	Y	Y	Y	N	Y	Y	N
3 Unsoeld	Y	Y	Y	Y	N	Y	Y	N
4 Inslee	Y	Y	Y	Y	N	Y	Y	N
5 Foley								
6 Dicks	Y	Y	Y	Y	N	Y	Y	N
7 McDermott	Y	Y	Y	Y	N	Y	Y	N
8 ***Dunn***	Y	Y	N	N	Y	N	N	Y
9 Kreidler	Y	Y	N	Y	N	Y	Y	N
WEST VIRGINIA								
1 Mollohan	Y	Y	Y	Y	N	Y	Y	N
2 Wise	Y	Y	?	Y	N	Y	Y	N
3 Rahall	Y	Y	Y	Y	N	Y	Y	N
WISCONSIN								
1 Barca	Y	Y	Y	Y	N	Y	Y	N
2 ***Klug***	Y	Y	N	N	Y	Y	N	Y
3 ***Gunderson***	Y	Y	N	N	Y	Y	N	Y
4 Kleczka	Y	Y	Y	Y	N	Y	?	N
5 Barrett	Y	Y	Y	Y	N	Y	Y	N
6 ***Petri***	Y	Y	N	N	Y	Y	N	Y
7 Obey	Y	Y	Y	Y	N	Y	Y	N
8 ***Roth***	Y	Y	N	N	Y	N	N	Y
9 ***Sensenbrenner***	Y	N	N	N	Y	N	N	Y
WYOMING								
AL ***Thomas***	Y	N	N	N	Y	N	N	Y
DELEGATES								
de Lugo, V.I.	D	D	D	D	D	D	D	D
Faleomavaega, Am.S.	D	D	D	D	D	D	D	D
Norton, D.C.	D	D	D	D	D	D	D	D
Romero-B., P.R.	D	D	D	D	D	D	D	D
Underwood, Guam	D	D	D	D	D	D	D	D

Southern states - Ala., Ark., Fla., Ga., Ky., La., Miss., N.C., Okla., S.C., Tenn., Texas, Va.
Omitted votes are quorum calls, which CQ does not include in its vote charts.

89. S 349. Lobbying Disclosure/Rule. Adoption of the rule (H Res 397) to waive the normal three-day layover for rules and allow a motion to suspend the rules and pass the bill to require the registration of all lobbyists and prohibit lobbyists from providing meals, entertainment, travel or gifts to members of Congress or their staff except under certain circumstances. Adopted 221-202: R 9-163; D 211-39 (ND 154-17, SD 57-22); I 1-0, March 24, 1994.

90. S 349. Lobbying Disclosure/Passage. Bryant, D-Texas, motion to suspend the rules and pass the bill to require the registration of all lobbyists and prohibit lobbyists from providing meals, entertainment, travel or gifts to members of Congress or their staff except under certain circumstances. Motion agreed to 315-110: R 111-60; D 203-50 (ND 149-23, SD 54-27); I 1-0, March 24, 1994. A two-thirds majority of those present and voting (284 in this case) is required for passage under suspension of the rules. A "yea" was a vote in support of the president's position.

91. HR 6. Elementary and Secondary Education Reauthorization/Obscene Material. Unsoeld, D-Wash., amendment to the Hancock, R-Mo., amendment, to prohibit education agencies from using money received under the bill to distribute obscene material to minors on school grounds. The amendment also prohibits federal control of school curriculums at the state and local levels. The Hancock amendment would prohibit local education agencies receiving money under the bill from carrying out programs that encourage or support homosexuality as a positive lifestyle alternative. Adopted in the Committee of the Whole 224-194: R 27-139; D 196-55 (ND 154-17, SD 42-38); I 1-0, March 24, 1994.

92. HR 6. Elementary and Secondary Education Reauthorization/Obscene Material. Hancock, R-Mo., amendment, as amended by the Unsoeld, D-Wash., amendment, to prohibit education agencies from using money in the bill to distribute material to students that encourages or supports homosexuality as a positive lifestyle. The amendment also prohibits the federal government from controlling the curriculums of state or local education agencies. Before being amended, the Hancock amendment would have prohibited local education agencies receiving money under the bill from carrying out programs that encourage or support homosexuality as a positive lifestyle alternative. Adopted in the Committee of the Whole 301-120: R 155-12; D 146-107 (ND 82-91, SD 64-16); I 0-1, March 24, 1994.

93. HR 6. Elementary and Secondary Education Reauthorization/School Construction. Miller, R-Fla., amendment to strike the $200 million authorization in fiscal 1995 for low-interest direct loans to poor school districts for construction and renovation projects. The program was not included in the Clinton administration's original proposal. Rejected in the Committee of the Whole 181-235: R 149-18; D 32-216 (ND 17-151, SD 15-65); I 0-1, March 24, 1994.

94. HR 6. Elementary and Secondary Education Reauthorization/Republican Substitute. Michel, R-Ill., substitute amendment to cut the bill's authorization by $400 million; eliminate the new programs authorized by the bill; eliminate the opportunity to learn standards; allow the use of Title I money for public school choice programs; and prohibit the use of money in the bill for family planning and reproductive services. Rejected in the Committee of the Whole 173-245: R 164-4; D 9-240 (ND 2-169, SD 7-71); I 0-1, March 24, 1994. A "nay" was a vote in support of the president's position.

95. HR 6. Elementary and Secondary Education Reauthorization/Passage. Passage of the bill to reauthorize the 1965 Elementary and Secondary Education Act for six years through fiscal 1999, and to authorize $12.7 billion in fiscal 1995 spending for federal elementary and secondary school programs. Passed 289-128: R 45-124; D 243-4 (ND 169-0, SD 74-4); I 1-0, March 24, 1994. A "yea" was a vote in support of the president's position.

KEY

Y	Voted for (yea).
#	Paired for.
+	Announced for.
N	Voted against (nay).
X	Paired against.
−	Announced against.
P	Voted "present."
C	Voted "present" to avoid possible conflict of interest.
?	Did not vote or otherwise make a position known.
D	Delegates ineligible to vote.

Democrats *Republicans*
Independent

	89	90	91	92	93	94	95
ALABAMA							
1 Callahan	N	N	N	Y	Y	Y	N
2 Everett	N	Y	N	Y	Y	Y	N
3 Browder	Y	Y	N	N	Y	N	Y
4 Bevill	Y	Y	N	Y	N	N	Y
5 Cramer	Y	Y	N	Y	N	N	Y
6 Bachus	N	N	Y	Y	Y	Y	N
7 Hilliard	Y	N	Y	N	N	N	Y
ALASKA							
AL Young	N	Y	N	Y	Y	Y	N
ARIZONA							
1 Coppersmith	Y	Y	Y	N	N	N	Y
2 Pastor	N	Y	Y	N	N	N	Y
3 Stump	N	N	N	Y	Y	Y	N
4 Kyl	N	Y	N	Y	Y	Y	N
5 Kolbe	N	Y	Y	Y	Y	Y	N
6 English	Y	Y	Y	N	N	N	Y
ARKANSAS							
1 Lambert	N	Y	Y	Y	N	N	Y
2 Thornton	Y	Y	Y	Y	N	N	Y
3 Hutchinson	Y	Y	N	N	Y	Y	N
4 Dickey	N	Y	N	N	Y	Y	N
CALIFORNIA							
1 Hamburg	Y	Y	Y	N	N	N	Y
2 Herger	N	Y	N	Y	Y	Y	N
3 Fazio	Y	Y	Y	N	N	N	Y
4 Doolittle	N	N	Y	Y	Y	Y	N
5 Matsui	Y	Y	Y	N	N	N	Y
6 Woolsey	Y	Y	Y	N	N	N	Y
7 Miller	Y	Y	Y	N	N	N	Y
8 Pelosi	Y	Y	Y	N	N	N	Y
9 Dellums	Y	Y	Y	N	N	N	Y
10 Baker	N	Y	N	Y	Y	Y	N
11 Pombo	N	Y	N	Y	Y	Y	N
12 Lantos	Y	Y	Y	N	N	N	Y
13 Stark	Y	Y	Y	N	N	N	Y
14 Eshoo	Y	Y	Y	N	N	N	Y
15 Mineta	Y	Y	Y	N	N	N	Y
16 Edwards	Y	Y	Y	N	N	N	Y
17 Farr	Y	Y	Y	N	N	N	Y
18 Condit	Y	N	Y	Y	N	N	Y
19 Lehman	Y	Y	Y	Y	?	N	Y
20 Dooley	N	N	Y	Y	N	N	Y
21 Thomas	N	Y	Y	N	Y	Y	N
22 Huffington	N	Y	Y	N	Y	N	Y
23 Gallegly	?	?	?	?	?	?	?
24 Beilenson	Y	Y	Y	N	N	N	Y
25 McKeon	N	Y	N	Y	Y	Y	N
26 Berman	Y	Y	?	?	N	N	Y
27 Moorhead	N	N	N	Y	Y	Y	N
28 Dreier	N	N	N	Y	Y	Y	N
29 Waxman	Y	Y	Y	N	N	N	Y
30 Becerra	Y	Y	Y	N	N	N	Y
31 Martinez	Y	Y	Y	N	N	N	Y
32 Dixon	Y	Y	Y	N	N	N	Y
33 Roybal-Allard	Y	Y	Y	N	N	N	Y
34 Torres	Y	N	Y	N	N	N	Y
35 Waters	Y	Y	Y	N	N	N	Y
36 Harman	Y	Y	Y	N	N	N	Y
37 Tucker	#	N	Y	N	N	N	Y
38 Horn	N	Y	Y	Y	N	Y	N
39 Royce	N	N	N	Y	Y	Y	N
40 Lewis	N	N	N	Y	Y	Y	N
41 Kim	N	Y	N	Y	Y	Y	N

	89	90	91	92	93	94	95
42 Brown	Y	Y	Y	Y	?	N	Y
43 Calvert	N	Y	N	Y	Y	Y	N
44 McCandless	N	N	N	Y	Y	Y	N
45 Rohrabacher	N	Y	Y	Y	Y	Y	N
46 Dornan	N	Y	N	Y	Y	Y	N
47 Cox	N	Y	N	Y	Y	Y	N
48 Packard	N	N	N	Y	Y	Y	N
49 Schenk	Y	Y	Y	N	N	N	Y
50 Filner	Y	Y	Y	N	N	N	Y
51 Cunningham	N	N	Y	Y	Y	Y	N
52 Hunter	N	Y	N	Y	Y	Y	N
COLORADO							
1 Schroeder	Y	Y	Y	N	N	N	Y
2 Skaggs	Y	Y	Y	N	N	N	Y
3 McInnis	N	Y	N	Y	Y	Y	N
4 Allard	N	N	N	Y	Y	Y	N
5 Hefley	N	N	Y	Y	Y	Y	N
6 Schaefer	N	N	Y	Y	Y	Y	N
CONNECTICUT							
1 Kennelly	Y	Y	Y	N	N	N	Y
2 Gejdenson	Y	Y	Y	N	N	N	Y
3 DeLauro	Y	Y	Y	N	N	N	Y
4 Shays	N	Y	Y	Y	Y	Y	Y
5 Franks	N	Y	N	Y	Y	Y	Y
6 Johnson	Y	Y	Y	N	Y	Y	Y
DELAWARE							
AL Castle	N	Y	N	Y	Y	Y	Y
FLORIDA							
1 Hutto	N	Y	N	Y	Y	Y	Y
2 Peterson	Y	Y	Y	Y	Y	N	Y
3 Brown	Y	N	Y	N	N	N	Y
4 Fowler	N	Y	N	Y	Y	Y	Y
5 Thurman	Y	Y	Y	N	N	N	Y
6 Stearns	N	Y	N	Y	Y	Y	N
7 Mica	N	N	N	Y	Y	Y	N
8 McCollum	N	N	N	Y	Y	Y	N
9 Bilirakis	N	Y	N	Y	Y	Y	Y
10 Young	N	Y	N	Y	Y	Y	N
11 Gibbons	Y	Y	Y	N	N	N	Y
12 Canady	N	N	Y	Y	Y	Y	N
13 Miller	N	Y	N	Y	Y	Y	N
14 Goss	N	Y	N	Y	Y	Y	N
15 Bacchus	Y	Y	Y	N	N	N	Y
16 Lewis	?	?	?	?	?	?	?
17 Meek	Y	N	Y	N	N	N	Y
18 Ros-Lehtinen	N	Y	N	Y	N	Y	N
19 Johnston	Y	Y	Y	N	N	N	Y
20 Deutsch	Y	Y	Y	N	N	N	Y
21 Diaz-Balart	N	Y	N	Y	N	Y	N
22 Shaw	N	Y	N	Y	Y	Y	Y
23 Hastings	Y	N	Y	N	N	N	Y
GEORGIA							
1 Kingston	N	Y	N	Y	Y	Y	N
2 Bishop	Y	Y	Y	N	N	N	Y
3 Collins	N	Y	N	Y	Y	Y	N
4 Linder	N	Y	N	Y	Y	Y	N
5 Lewis	Y	Y	N	N	N	N	Y
6 Gingrich	N	N	N	Y	Y	Y	N
7 Darden	Y	Y	N	Y	N	N	Y
8 Rowland	Y	Y	N	Y	N	N	Y
9 Deal	Y	Y	N	Y	N	N	Y
10 Johnson	Y	Y	Y	Y	N	N	Y
11 McKinney	Y	Y	Y	N	N	N	Y
HAWAII							
1 Abercrombie	N	N	Y	N	N	N	Y
2 Mink	Y	Y	Y	N	N	N	Y
IDAHO							
1 LaRocco	Y	Y	Y	Y	N	N	Y
2 Crapo	N	Y	N	Y	Y	Y	N
ILLINOIS							
1 Rush	Y	N	Y	N	N	N	Y
2 Reynolds	Y	Y	Y	N	N	N	Y
3 Lipinski	Y	Y	N	Y	N	N	Y
4 Gutierrez	Y	Y	Y	N	N	N	Y
5 Rostenkowski	N	N	Y	N	?	N	Y
6 Hyde	N	N	Y	Y	Y	Y	N
7 Collins	Y	N	Y	N	N	N	Y
8 Crane	N	N	N	Y	Y	Y	N
9 Yates	Y	N	Y	N	N	N	Y
10 Porter	N	N	N	Y	Y	Y	Y
11 Sangmeister	N	Y	N	Y	N	N	Y
12 Costello	N	Y	N	Y	N	N	Y
13 Fawell	N	Y	N	Y	Y	Y	Y
14 Hastert	N	N	N	Y	Y	Y	N
15 Ewing	N	Y	N	Y	Y	Y	N
16 Manzullo	N	Y	N	Y	Y	Y	N
17 Evans	Y	Y	Y	N	N	N	Y

ND Northern Democrats   SD Southern Democrats

	89	90	91	92	93	94	95
18 *Michel*	N	N	N	Y	Y	Y	N
19 Poshard	Y	Y	N	Y	Y	N	Y
20 Durbin	Y	Y	Y	Y	N	N	Y
INDIANA							
1 Visclosky	Y	Y	Y	N	N	N	Y
2 Sharp	Y	Y	Y	N	N	N	Y
3 Roemer	N	Y	Y	Y	N	N	Y
4 Long	Y	Y	Y	Y	N	N	Y
5 *Buyer*	N	Y	N	Y	Y	Y	N
6 *Burton*	N	N	N	Y	Y	Y	N
7 *Myers*	N	Y	N	Y	Y	Y	N
8 McCloskey	Y	Y	Y	Y	N	N	Y
9 Hamilton	N	Y	Y	Y	Y	N	Y
10 Jacobs	N	Y	Y	Y	N	N	Y
IOWA							
1 *Leach*	Y	Y	Y	Y	N	?	Y
2 *Nussle*	N	Y	N	Y	Y	Y	N
3 *Lightfoot*	N	Y	N	Y	Y	Y	N
4 Smith	Y	Y	Y	Y	N	N	Y
5 *Grandy*	X	?	?	?	?	?	?
KANSAS							
1 *Roberts*	N	N	N	Y	Y	Y	N
2 Slattery	Y	Y	Y	Y	N	N	Y
3 *Meyers*	Y	Y	N	Y	Y	Y	Y
4 Glickman	Y	Y	Y	Y	Y	N	Y
KENTUCKY							
1 Barlow	Y	Y	N	Y	N	N	Y
2 Natcher	?	?	?	?	?	?	?
3 Mazzoli	Y	Y	Y	Y	N	N	Y
4 *Bunning*	N	N	N	N	Y	Y	N
5 *Rogers*	N	Y	N	Y	N	Y	N
6 Baesler	Y	Y	N	Y	N	N	Y
LOUISIANA							
1 *Livingston*	N	N	N	Y	Y	Y	N
2 Jefferson	Y	Y	Y	Y	N	N	Y
3 Tauzin	?	N	N	Y	N	Y	N
4 Fields	Y	Y	Y	Y	N	N	Y
5 *McCrery*	N	Y	N	Y	N	Y	N
6 *Baker*	N	N	N	Y	Y	Y	N
7 Hayes	N	N	N	Y	N	N	N
MAINE							
1 Andrews	Y	Y	Y	N	N	N	Y
2 *Snowe*	N	Y	Y	Y	Y	Y	Y
MARYLAND							
1 *Gilchrest*	N	N	Y	Y	Y	Y	Y
2 *Bentley*	N	N	?	Y	Y	Y	Y
3 Cardin	Y	?	?	?	?	?	?
4 Wynn	Y	Y	Y	N	N	N	Y
5 Hoyer	Y	Y	Y	N	N	N	Y
6 *Bartlett*	N	Y	N	Y	Y	Y	N
7 Mfume	Y	N	Y	Y	N	N	Y
8 *Morella*	N	Y	Y	N	Y	N	Y
MASSACHUSETTS							
1 Olver	Y	Y	Y	N	N	N	Y
2 Neal	Y	Y	Y	Y	N	N	Y
3 *Blute*	N	Y	Y	Y	N	Y	Y
4 Frank	Y	Y	Y	N	N	N	Y
5 Meehan	Y	Y	Y	N	N	N	Y
6 *Torkildsen*	N	Y	Y	N	N	Y	Y
7 Markey	Y	Y	Y	N	N	N	Y
8 Kennedy	Y	Y	Y	Y	N	N	Y
9 Moakley	Y	Y	Y	Y	N	N	Y
10 Studds	Y	Y	Y	N	N	N	Y
MICHIGAN							
1 Stupak	Y	Y	Y	Y	N	N	Y
2 *Hoekstra*	N	N	N	Y	Y	Y	N
3 *Ehlers*	N	Y	N	Y	Y	Y	N
4 *Camp*	N	Y	N	Y	Y	Y	N
5 Barcia	Y	Y	Y	Y	N	N	Y
6 *Upton*	N	Y	N	Y	Y	Y	Y
7 *Smith*	N	Y	N	Y	Y	Y	N
8 Carr	Y	Y	Y	Y	N	N	Y
9 Kildee	Y	Y	Y	Y	N	N	Y
10 Bonior	Y	Y	Y	N	N	N	Y
11 *Knollenberg*	N	N	N	Y	Y	Y	N
12 Levin	Y	Y	Y	Y	N	N	Y
13 Ford	N	N	Y	N	N	N	Y
14 Conyers	Y	Y	Y	N	N	N	Y
15 Collins	Y	N	Y	N	N	N	Y
16 Dingell	N	N	Y	Y	N	N	Y
MINNESOTA							
1 Penny	Y	Y	Y	Y	Y	Y	Y
2 Minge	Y	Y	Y	Y	Y	N	Y
3 *Ramstad*	N	Y	N	Y	Y	Y	Y
4 Vento	Y	Y	Y	Y	N	N	Y

	89	90	91	92	93	94	95
5 Sabo	Y	Y	Y	N	N	N	Y
6 *Grams*	N	N	N	Y	Y	Y	N
7 Peterson	Y	Y	N	Y	Y	N	Y
8 Oberstar	Y	Y	Y	Y	N	N	Y
MISSISSIPPI							
1 Whitten	Y	N	N	Y	N	?	?
2 Thompson	Y	N	Y	N	N	N	Y
3 Montgomery	Y	Y	N	Y	N	N	Y
4 Parker	Y	Y	N	Y	N	Y	Y
5 Taylor	N	Y	N	Y	Y	Y	Y
MISSOURI							
1 Clay	N	N	Y	N	N	N	Y
2 *Talent*	N	Y	N	Y	Y	Y	N
3 Gephardt	Y	Y	Y	Y	N	N	Y
4 Skelton	Y	Y	N	Y	Y	N	Y
5 Wheat	Y	Y	Y	N	?	N	Y
6 Danner	Y	Y	N	Y	N	N	Y
7 *Hancock*	N	N	N	Y	Y	Y	N
8 *Emerson*	N	N	N	Y	Y	Y	N
9 Volkmer	N	Y	N	Y	N	N	Y
MONTANA							
AL Williams	Y	Y	Y	Y	N	N	Y
NEBRASKA							
1 *Bereuter*	N	Y	Y	N	Y	Y	N
2 Hoagland	Y	Y	Y	N	N	N	Y
3 *Barrett*	N	N	N	Y	+	Y	N
NEVADA							
1 Bilbray	Y	Y	Y	Y	N	N	Y
2 *Vucanovich*	N	Y	N	Y	Y	Y	N
NEW HAMPSHIRE							
1 *Zeliff*	N	Y	N	Y	Y	Y	N
2 Swett	Y	Y	Y	Y	N	N	Y
NEW JERSEY							
1 Andrews	Y	Y	?	Y	N	N	Y
2 Hughes	Y	Y	Y	Y	N	N	Y
3 *Saxton*	N	Y	N	Y	Y	Y	Y
4 *Smith*	N	Y	N	Y	Y	Y	N
5 *Roukema*	Y	Y	N	Y	Y	Y	Y
6 Pallone	Y	Y	Y	N	N	N	Y
7 *Franks*	N	Y	N	Y	Y	Y	N
8 Klein	Y	Y	Y	Y	N	N	Y
9 Torricelli	Y	Y	?	?	?	?	?
10 Payne	Y	Y	Y	N	N	N	Y
11 *Gallo*	?	?	?	?	?	?	?
12 *Zimmer*	N	Y	N	Y	Y	Y	N
13 Menendez	Y	Y	Y	Y	N	N	Y
NEW MEXICO							
1 *Schiff*	N	Y	N	Y	Y	Y	N
2 *Skeen*	N	N	N	Y	Y	Y	N
3 Richardson	Y	Y	Y	Y	N	N	Y
NEW YORK							
1 Hochbrueckner	Y	Y	Y	Y	N	N	Y
2 *Lazio*	N	Y	Y	Y	N	Y	Y
3 *King*	N	N	N	Y	Y	Y	N
4 *Levy*	N	Y	N	Y	Y	Y	N
5 Ackerman	Y	Y	Y	Y	N	N	Y
6 Flake	Y	Y	Y	N	N	N	Y
7 Manton	N	Y	Y	Y	N	N	Y
8 Nadler	Y	Y	Y	N	N	N	Y
9 Schumer	Y	Y	Y	N	N	N	Y
10 Towns	N	N	Y	N	N	N	Y
11 Owens	Y	Y	Y	N	N	N	Y
12 Velazquez	Y	Y	Y	N	N	N	Y
13 *Molinari*	N	Y	N	Y	N	Y	Y
14 Maloney	Y	Y	Y	N	N	N	Y
15 Rangel	N	N	Y	N	N	?	Y
16 Serrano	Y	Y	Y	N	N	N	Y
17 Engel	Y	Y	Y	N	N	N	Y
18 Lowey	Y	Y	Y	N	N	N	Y
19 *Fish*	N	N	Y	Y	Y	Y	Y
20 *Gilman*	N	N	Y	Y	N	N	Y
21 McNulty	Y	Y	N	Y	N	N	Y
22 *Solomon*	N	?	N	Y	Y	Y	N
23 *Boehlert*	N	N	Y	Y	N	N	Y
24 *McHugh*	N	Y	N	Y	N	Y	N
25 *Walsh*	N	Y	N	Y	N	Y	Y
26 Hinchey	Y	Y	Y	N	N	N	Y
27 *Paxon*	N	N	N	Y	Y	Y	N
28 Slaughter	Y	Y	Y	N	N	N	Y
29 LaFalce	Y	Y	N	Y	Y	?	?
30 *Quinn*	N	Y	N	Y	N	Y	Y
31 *Houghton*	N	N	Y	Y	Y	Y	Y
NORTH CAROLINA							
1 Clayton	Y	Y	Y	N	N	N	Y
2 Valentine	Y	Y	N	Y	Y	N	Y

	89	90	91	92	93	94	95
3 Lancaster	Y	Y	N	Y	N	N	Y
4 Price	Y	Y	Y	Y	N	N	Y
5 Neal	Y	Y	Y	Y	N	N	Y
6 *Coble*	N	N	N	Y	Y	Y	N
7 Rose	N	N	Y	Y	N	N	Y
8 Hefner	N	N	Y	Y	N	N	Y
9 *McMillan*	N	N	?	?	?	?	?
10 *Ballenger*	N	N	N	Y	Y	Y	N
11 *Taylor*	N	N	N	Y	Y	Y	N
12 Watt	Y	N	Y	N	N	N	Y
NORTH DAKOTA							
AL Pomeroy	Y	Y	Y	Y	N	N	Y
OHIO							
1 Mann	Y	Y	Y	Y	N	N	Y
2 *Portman*	N	Y	N	Y	Y	Y	N
3 Hall	Y	Y	N	Y	N	N	Y
4 *Oxley*	N	N	N	Y	Y	Y	N
5 *Gillmor*	N	N	N	Y	Y	Y	Y
6 Strickland	Y	Y	Y	N	N	N	Y
7 *Hobson*	N	N	Y	Y	Y	Y	N
8 *Boehner*	N	N	N	Y	Y	Y	N
9 Kaptur	Y	Y	Y	Y	N	N	Y
10 *Hoke*	N	Y	Y	?	Y	Y	N
11 Stokes	Y	N	Y	N	N	N	Y
12 *Kasich*	Y	Y	N	Y	Y	Y	N
13 Brown	Y	Y	Y	Y	N	N	Y
14 Sawyer	Y	Y	Y	N	N	N	Y
15 *Pryce*	N	Y	N	Y	Y	Y	N
16 *Regula*	Y	Y	N	Y	Y	Y	N
17 Traficant	Y	N	N	Y	N	N	Y
18 Applegate	Y	N	N	Y	?	N	Y
19 Fingerhut	Y	Y	Y	Y	N	N	Y
OKLAHOMA							
1 *Inhofe*	N	Y	N	Y	Y	Y	N
2 Synar	Y	Y	Y	N	N	N	Y
3 Brewster	N	N	N	Y	N	N	Y
4 McCurdy	Y	Y	Y	Y	N	N	Y
5 *Istook*	N	Y	N	Y	Y	Y	N
6 Vacancy							
OREGON							
1 Furse	Y	Y	Y	N	N	N	Y
2 *Smith*	N	N	N	Y	Y	Y	N
3 Wyden	Y	Y	Y	N	N	N	Y
4 DeFazio	Y	Y	Y	N	N	N	Y
5 Kopetski	Y	N	Y	N	N	?	Y
PENNSYLVANIA							
1 Foglietta	Y	Y	Y	N	N	N	Y
2 Blackwell	Y	Y	?	N	N	N	Y
3 Borski	Y	Y	Y	Y	N	N	Y
4 Klink	Y	Y	N	Y	N	Y	Y
5 *Clinger*	N	Y	N	Y	Y	Y	N
6 Holden	Y	Y	N	Y	Y	N	Y
7 *Weldon*	N	Y	?	Y	?	Y	Y
8 *Greenwood*	N	Y	?	Y	Y	Y	Y
9 *Shuster*	N	N	N	Y	Y	Y	N
10 *McDade*	N	Y	N	Y	Y	Y	Y
11 Kanjorski	Y	Y	Y	Y	Y	N	Y
12 Murtha	Y	N	Y	Y	?	N	Y
13 Margolies-Mezv.	Y	Y	Y	N	Y	N	Y
14 Coyne	Y	Y	Y	N	N	N	Y
15 McHale	Y	Y	Y	Y	N	N	Y
16 *Walker*	N	N	N	Y	Y	Y	N
17 *Gekas*	N	Y	N	?	Y	Y	N
18 *Santorum*	N	Y	N	Y	?	Y	N
19 *Goodling*	N	N	N	Y	Y	Y	Y
20 Murphy	N	Y	N	Y	N	N	Y
21 *Ridge*	N	Y	N	Y	Y	Y	N
RHODE ISLAND							
1 *Machtley*	N	Y	Y	Y	Y	Y	Y
2 Reed	Y	Y	Y	N	N	N	Y
SOUTH CAROLINA							
1 *Ravenel*	N	N	N	Y	Y	Y	N
2 *Spence*	N	Y	N	Y	Y	Y	N
3 Derrick	Y	Y	?	?	?	?	?
4 *Inglis*	Y	Y	N	Y	Y	Y	N
5 Spratt	Y	Y	N	Y	N	N	Y
6 Clyburn	Y	N	Y	Y	N	N	Y
SOUTH DAKOTA							
AL Johnson	Y	Y	Y	Y	N	N	Y
TENNESSEE							
1 *Quillen*	N	N	N	Y	Y	Y	N
2 *Duncan*	N	Y	N	Y	Y	Y	N
3 Lloyd	N	N	N	Y	N	N	Y
4 Cooper	N	N	N	Y	Y	N	Y
5 Clement	N	N	N	Y	N	N	Y

	89	90	91	92	93	94	95
6 Gordon	Y	Y	N	Y	N	N	Y
7 *Sundquist*	N	N	N	Y	Y	Y	N
8 Tanner	N	N	N	Y	N	N	Y
9 Ford	?	?	?	?	?	?	?
TEXAS							
1 Chapman	N	Y	N	Y	Y	N	Y
2 Wilson	?	N	N	Y	N	N	Y
3 *Johnson, Sam*	N	N	N	Y	Y	Y	N
4 Hall	Y	Y	N	Y	Y	Y	N
5 Bryant	Y	Y	Y	Y	N	N	Y
6 *Barton*	N	N	N	Y	Y	?	?
7 *Archer*	N	Y	N	Y	Y	Y	N
8 *Fields*	N	N	N	Y	Y	Y	N
9 Brooks	N	N	Y	Y	N	N	Y
10 Pickle	?	?	?	?	?	?	?
11 Edwards	N	N	N	Y	N	N	Y
12 Geren	N	Y	N	Y	Y	N	Y
13 Sarpalius	Y	Y	N	Y	N	Y	Y
14 Laughlin	N	N	N	Y	Y	N	Y
15 de la Garza	Y	Y	Y	Y	N	N	Y
16 Coleman	Y	Y	Y	Y	N	N	Y
17 Stenholm	N	Y	N	Y	Y	N	N
18 Washington	N	N	Y	N	N	?	?
19 *Combest*	N	Y	N	Y	Y	Y	N
20 Gonzalez	Y	Y	Y	N	N	N	Y
21 *Smith*	N	Y	?	?	?	?	?
22 *DeLay*	N	N	N	N	Y	Y	N
23 *Bonilla*	N	Y	N	Y	Y	Y	N
24 Frost	Y	Y	Y	Y	N	N	Y
25 Andrews	Y	Y	N	Y	Y	N	Y
26 *Armey*	N	N	N	Y	Y	Y	N
27 Ortiz	Y	Y	N	Y	N	N	Y
28 Tejeda	Y	Y	N	Y	N	N	Y
29 Green	Y	Y	Y	Y	N	N	Y
30 Johnson, E.B.	Y	N	Y	N	N	N	Y
UTAH							
1 *Hansen*	N	N	N	Y	Y	Y	N
2 Shepherd	Y	Y	Y	Y	N	N	Y
3 Orton	N	N	Y	Y	Y	N	Y
VERMONT							
AL *Sanders*	Y	Y	Y	N	N	N	Y
VIRGINIA							
1 *Bateman*	N	N	N	Y	Y	Y	Y
2 Pickett	N	N	N	Y	N	N	Y
3 Scott	Y	N	Y	N	N	N	Y
4 Sisisky	N	N	N	Y	N	N	Y
5 Payne	N	Y	N	Y	N	N	Y
6 *Goodlatte*	N	Y	N	Y	Y	Y	N
7 *Bliley*	N	N	N	Y	Y	Y	N
8 Moran	Y	N	Y	N	N	N	Y
9 Boucher	N	Y	Y	Y	N	N	Y
10 *Wolf*	N	Y	N	Y	Y	Y	N
11 Byrne	Y	Y	Y	Y	N	N	Y
WASHINGTON							
1 Cantwell	Y	Y	Y	Y	N	N	Y
2 Swift	Y	N	Y	N	?	N	Y
3 Unsoeld	Y	Y	Y	N	N	N	Y
4 Inslee	Y	Y	Y	Y	N	N	Y
5 Foley		Y					
6 Dicks	Y	Y	Y	N	N	N	Y
7 McDermott	Y	Y	Y	N	N	N	Y
8 *Dunn*	N	Y	N	N	Y	Y	N
9 Kreidler	Y	Y	Y	N	N	N	Y
WEST VIRGINIA							
1 Mollohan	Y	Y	Y	Y	N	N	Y
2 Wise	Y	Y	Y	Y	N	N	Y
3 Rahall	Y	Y	N	Y	N	N	Y
WISCONSIN							
1 Barca	Y	Y	Y	Y	Y	N	Y
2 *Klug*	N	Y	Y	Y	Y	Y	Y
3 *Gunderson*	N	Y	Y	Y	Y	Y	Y
4 Kleczka	Y	Y	Y	N	N	N	Y
5 Barrett	Y	Y	Y	N	N	N	Y
6 *Petri*	N	Y	N	Y	Y	Y	Y
7 Obey	Y	Y	Y	Y	?	N	Y
8 *Roth*	N	Y	N	Y	Y	Y	N
9 *Sensenbrenner*	N	Y	N	Y	Y	Y	N
WYOMING							
AL *Thomas*	N	Y	−	+	Y	Y	N
DELEGATES							
de Lugo, V.I.	D	D	Y	Y	N	N	D
Faleomavaega, Am.S.	D	D	Y	Y	N	N	D
Norton, D.C.	D	D	+	+	N	N	D
Romero-B., P.R.	D	D	Y	Y	N	N	D
Underwood, Guam	D	D	Y	N	N	N	D

Southern states - Ala., Ark., Fla., Ga., Ky., La., Miss., N.C., Okla., S.C., Tenn., Texas, Va.
Omitted votes are quorum calls, which CQ does not include in its vote charts.

96. HR 4066. International Sporting Event Duty Suspension/Passage. Rostenkowski, D-Ill., motion to suspend the rules and pass the bill to temporarily suspend the duty on equipment and personal effects brought to the United States by participants in several international sporting events. Motion agreed to 406-1: R 164-0; D 241-1 (ND 162-0, SD 79-1); I 1-0, April 12, 1994. A two-thirds majority of those present and voting (272 in this case) is required for passage under suspension of the rules.

97. HR 3693. Byron White United States Courthouse/Passage. Traficant, D-Ohio, motion to suspend the rules and pass the bill to designate the U.S. courthouse in Denver, Colo., as the Byron White United States Courthouse. Motion agreed to 408-0: R 163-0; D 244-0 (ND 164-0, SD 80-0); I 1-0, April 12, 1994. A two-thirds majority of those present and voting (272 in this case) is required for passage under suspension of the rules.

98. Procedural Motion. Approval of the House Journal of Tuesday, April 12. Approved 261-153: R 21-147; D 239-6 (ND 161-5, SD 78-1); I 1-0, April 13, 1994.

99. HR 3770. Edward J. Schwartz Courthouse/Passage. Traficant, D-Ohio, motion to suspend the rules and pass the bill to name the U.S. courthouse and federal building in San Diego, Calif., in honor of Edward J. Schwartz, who served as a U.S. District judge from 1969 to 1982. Motion agreed to 417-1: R 168-1; D 248-0 (ND 168-0, SD 80-0); I 1-0, April 13, 1994. A two-thirds majority of those present and voting (279 in this case) is required for passage under suspension of the rules.

100. HR 3498. Great Falls Historic District/Passage. Vento, D-Minn., motion to suspend the rules and pass the bill to establish the Great Falls Historic District in Paterson, N.J., near the Great Falls of the Passaic River and authorize federal grants for the project. Motion agreed to 288-130: R 50-120; D 237-10 (ND 161-6, SD 76-4); I 1-0, April 13, 1994. A two-thirds majority of those present and voting (279 in this case) is required for passage under suspension of the rules.

101. HR 2843. Wheeling National Heritage Area/Passage. Vento, D-Minn., motion to suspend the rules and pass the bill to establish the Wheeling National Heritage Area in West Virginia and authorize federal grants for the project. Motion rejected 264-154: R 34-136; D 229-18 (ND 156-11, SD 73-7); I 1-0, April 13, 1994. A two-thirds majority of those present and voting (279 in this case) is required for passage under suspension of the rules.

102. S 2004. College Loan Default Exemption/Passage. Ford, D-Mich., motion to suspend the rules and pass the bill to extend the existing exemption from student loan ineligibility based on a high default rate for historically black colleges and universities and tribally controlled community colleges from July 1, 1994, to July 1, 1998. Motion agreed to 283-136: R 56-114; D 226-22 (ND 154-14, SD 72-8); I 1-0, April 13, 1994. A two-thirds majority of those present and voting (280 in this case) is required for passage under suspension of the rules.

103. HR 4092. Omnibus Crime/Rule. Adoption of the rule (H Res 401) to provide for further House floor consideration of the bill to authorize more than $15 billion for fiscal 1994-99 to implement various proposals to combat crime, including $3 billion for new prisons and more than $7 billion for crime prevention programs. The bill would also require life imprisonment for three-time violent offenders, expand the death penalty to apply to dozens of federal crimes, authorize grants to hire 50,000 additional police officers, and overhaul the process for habeas corpus appeals for death row inmates. Adopted 244-176: R 0-170; D 243-6 (ND 168-2, SD 75-4); I 1-0, April 13, 1994.

¹ William H. Natcher, D-Ky., died March 29. The last vote for which he was eligible was vote 95.

KEY

Y	Voted for (yea).
#	Paired for.
+	Announced for.
N	Voted against (nay).
X	Paired against.
−	Announced against.
P	Voted "present."
C	Voted "present" to avoid possible conflict of interest.
?	Did not vote or otherwise make a position known.
D	Delegates ineligible to vote.

Democrats ***Republicans***
Independent

	96	97	98	99	100	101	102	103
ALABAMA								
1 *Callahan*	Y	Y	N	Y	N	Y	N	N
2 *Everett*	Y	Y	Y	Y	N	N	N	N
3 Browder	Y	Y	Y	Y	Y	Y	Y	Y
4 Bevill	Y	Y	Y	Y	Y	Y	Y	Y
5 Cramer	Y	Y	Y	Y	Y	Y	Y	Y
6 *Bachus*	Y	N	N	N	N	N	N	N
7 Hilliard	Y	Y	Y	Y	Y	Y	Y	Y
ALASKA								
AL *Young*	Y	Y	Y	Y	Y	Y	N	N
ARIZONA								
1 Coppersmith	Y	Y	Y	Y	Y	Y	Y	Y
2 Pastor	Y	Y	Y	Y	Y	Y	Y	Y
3 *Stump*	Y	Y	N	Y	N	N	N	N
4 *Kyl*	Y	Y	N	Y	N	Y	N	N
5 *Kolbe*	Y	Y	N	Y	N	Y	N	N
6 English	Y	Y	Y	Y	Y	Y	Y	Y
ARKANSAS								
1 Lambert	Y	Y	Y	Y	Y	N	Y	Y
2 Thornton	Y	Y	Y	Y	Y	Y	Y	Y
3 *Hutchinson*	?	?	N	Y	N	N	N	N
4 *Dickey*	Y	Y	N	Y	N	N	N	N
CALIFORNIA								
1 Hamburg	?	Y	Y	Y	Y	Y	Y	Y
2 *Herger*	Y	Y	N	Y	N	N	N	N
3 Fazio	Y	Y	Y	Y	Y	Y	Y	Y
4 *Doolittle*	Y	Y	N	Y	N	N	N	N
5 Matsui	Y	Y	Y	Y	Y	Y	Y	Y
6 Woolsey	Y	Y	Y	Y	Y	Y	Y	Y
7 Miller	Y	Y	Y	Y	Y	Y	Y	Y
8 Pelosi	Y	Y	Y	Y	Y	Y	Y	Y
9 Dellums	Y	Y	Y	Y	Y	Y	Y	Y
10 *Baker*	Y	Y	N	Y	N	N	N	N
11 *Pombo*	Y	Y	N	Y	N	N	N	N
12 Lantos	Y	Y	Y	Y	Y	Y	Y	Y
13 Stark	Y	Y	Y	Y	Y	Y	Y	Y
14 Eshoo	Y	Y	Y	Y	Y	Y	Y	Y
15 Mineta	Y	Y	Y	Y	Y	Y	Y	Y
16 Edwards	Y	Y	Y	Y	Y	Y	Y	Y
17 Farr	Y	Y	Y	Y	Y	Y	Y	Y
18 Condit	Y	Y	Y	Y	N	?	N	Y
19 Lehman	Y	Y	Y	Y	Y	Y	Y	Y
20 Dooley	Y	Y	Y	Y	Y	N	N	Y
21 *Thomas*	Y	N	N	N	N	N	N	N
22 *Huffington*	Y	N	N	N	N	N	N	N
23 *Gallegly*	?	?	N	N	N	N	N	N
24 Beilenson	Y	Y	Y	Y	Y	Y	Y	Y
25 *McKeon*	Y	Y	N	Y	N	N	N	N
26 Berman	?	Y	Y	Y	Y	Y	Y	Y
27 *Moorhead*	Y	N	N	N	N	N	N	N
28 *Dreier*	Y	N	N	Y	N	N	N	N
29 Waxman	Y	Y	Y	Y	Y	Y	Y	Y
30 Becerra	Y	Y	Y	Y	Y	Y	Y	Y
31 Martinez	Y	Y	Y	Y	Y	Y	Y	Y
32 Dixon	Y	Y	Y	Y	Y	Y	Y	Y
33 Roybal-Allard	?	?	Y	Y	Y	Y	Y	Y
34 Torres	Y	Y	Y	Y	Y	Y	Y	Y
35 Waters	Y	Y	Y	Y	Y	Y	Y	Y
36 Harman	Y	Y	Y	Y	Y	Y	Y	Y
37 Tucker	Y	Y	Y	Y	Y	Y	Y	Y
38 *Horn*	Y	Y	N	Y	N	Y	N	N
39 *Royce*	Y	N	N	N	N	N	N	N
40 *Lewis*	Y	N	N	Y	N	N	N	N
41 *Kim*	Y	Y	N	Y	N	N	N	N

	96	97	98	99	100	101	102	103
42 Brown	Y	Y	?	Y	Y	Y	Y	Y
43 *Calvert*	Y	Y	N	Y	N	N	N	N
44 *McCandless*	Y	Y	N	Y	N	N	N	?
45 *Rohrabacher*	Y	Y	N	Y	N	N	N	N
46 *Dornan*	Y	Y	N	Y	N	N	N	N
47 *Cox*	Y	Y	N	Y	N	N	N	N
48 *Packard*	Y	Y	N	Y	N	N	N	N
49 Schenk	Y	Y	Y	Y	Y	Y	Y	Y
50 Filner	Y	Y	Y	Y	Y	Y	Y	Y
51 *Cunningham*	Y	Y	N	N	N	N	N	N
52 *Hunter*	Y	Y	N	?	N	N	N	N
COLORADO								
1 Schroeder	Y	Y	N	Y	N	Y	Y	Y
2 Skaggs	Y	Y	Y	Y	Y	Y	Y	Y
3 *McInnis*	Y	Y	Y	Y	N	N	N	N
4 *Allard*	Y	Y	N	Y	N	N	N	N
5 *Hefley*	Y	Y	N	Y	N	N	N	N
6 *Schaefer*	Y	Y	N	Y	N	N	N	N
CONNECTICUT								
1 Kennelly	Y	Y	Y	Y	Y	Y	Y	Y
2 Gejdenson	Y	Y	Y	Y	Y	Y	Y	Y
3 DeLauro	Y	Y	Y	Y	Y	Y	Y	Y
4 *Shays*	Y	Y	N	Y	N	N	N	N
5 *Franks*	Y	Y	Y	Y	N	N	N	N
6 *Johnson*	Y	Y	Y	Y	Y	Y	Y	N
DELAWARE								
AL *Castle*	Y	Y	N	Y	N	N	N	N
FLORIDA								
1 Hutto	Y	Y	Y	Y	Y	N	N	Y
2 Peterson	Y	Y	Y	+	+	−	+	Y
3 Brown	Y	Y	Y	Y	Y	Y	Y	Y
4 *Fowler*	Y	Y	N	Y	N	N	N	Y
5 Thurman	Y	Y	Y	Y	Y	Y	Y	Y
6 *Stearns*	Y	Y	N	Y	N	N	N	N
7 *Mica*	Y	Y	N	Y	N	N	N	N
8 *McCollum*	Y	Y	N	Y	N	N	N	N
9 *Bilirakis*	Y	Y	N	Y	N	N	N	N
10 *Young*	Y	Y	N	Y	N	N	N	N
11 Gibbons	Y	Y	Y	Y	Y	Y	Y	Y
12 *Canady*	Y	Y	N	Y	N	N	N	N
13 *Miller*	Y	Y	N	Y	N	N	N	N
14 *Goss*	Y	Y	N	Y	N	N	N	N
15 *Bacchus*	Y	Y	?	?	?	#	?	#
16 *Lewis*	Y	Y	N	N	N	N	N	N
17 Meek	Y	Y	Y	Y	Y	Y	Y	Y
18 *Ros-Lehtinen*	Y	Y	N	Y	N	N	N	N
19 Johnston	Y	Y	Y	Y	Y	Y	Y	Y
20 Deutsch	Y	Y	Y	Y	Y	Y	Y	Y
21 *Diaz-Balart*	Y	Y	N	Y	Y	Y	Y	N
22 *Shaw*	Y	Y	N	N	N	N	N	N
23 Hastings	Y	Y	Y	Y	Y	Y	Y	Y
GEORGIA								
1 *Kingston*	Y	Y	N	Y	N	N	N	N
2 Bishop	Y	Y	Y	Y	Y	Y	Y	Y
3 *Collins*	Y	Y	N	Y	N	N	N	N
4 *Linder*	Y	Y	N	Y	N	N	N	N
5 Lewis	Y	Y	Y	Y	Y	Y	Y	Y
6 *Gingrich*	Y	Y	N	Y	N	N	N	Y
7 Darden	Y	Y	Y	Y	Y	Y	Y	Y
8 Rowland	Y	Y	Y	Y	Y	Y	N	Y
9 Deal	Y	Y	Y	Y	Y	Y	Y	Y
10 Johnson	Y	Y	Y	Y	Y	Y	Y	Y
11 McKinney	Y	Y	Y	Y	Y	Y	Y	Y
HAWAII								
1 Abercrombie	Y	Y	Y	Y	Y	Y	Y	Y
2 Mink	?	?	Y	Y	Y	Y	Y	Y
IDAHO								
1 LaRocco	Y	Y	Y	Y	Y	Y	Y	Y
2 *Crapo*	Y	Y	N	Y	N	N	N	N
ILLINOIS								
1 Rush	Y	Y	Y	Y	Y	Y	Y	Y
2 Reynolds	Y	Y	Y	Y	Y	Y	Y	Y
3 Lipinski	Y	Y	Y	Y	Y	Y	Y	Y
4 Gutierrez	Y	Y	Y	Y	Y	Y	Y	Y
5 Rostenkowski	Y	Y	Y	Y	Y	Y	Y	Y
6 *Hyde*	Y	Y	Y	Y	Y	Y	Y	Y
7 Collins	Y	Y	Y	Y	Y	Y	Y	Y
8 *Crane*	Y	Y	N	N	N	N	N	N
9 Yates	Y	Y	Y	Y	Y	Y	Y	Y
10 *Porter*	Y	Y	N	Y	N	N	N	N
11 Sangmeister	Y	Y	Y	Y	Y	Y	Y	Y
12 Costello	Y	Y	Y	Y	Y	Y	Y	Y
13 *Fawell*	Y	Y	N	N	N	N	N	N
14 *Hastert*	Y	Y	N	Y	N	N	N	N
15 *Ewing*	Y	Y	N	Y	N	N	N	N
16 *Manzullo*	Y	Y	N	Y	N	N	N	N
17 Evans	Y	Y	Y	Y	Y	Y	Y	Y

ND Northern Democrats   SD Southern Democrats

	96	97	98	99	100	101	102	103
18 ***Michel***	Y	Y	?	Y	N	N	N	N
19 Poshard	Y	Y	Y	Y	Y	Y	N	Y
20 Durbin	Y	Y	Y	Y	Y	Y	Y	Y
INDIANA								
1 Visclosky	Y	Y	Y	Y	Y	Y	Y	Y
2 Sharp	Y	Y	Y	Y	Y	Y	Y	Y
3 Roemer	Y	Y	Y	Y	Y	Y	Y	Y
4 Long	Y	Y	Y	Y	Y	Y	Y	Y
5 ***Buyer***	Y	Y	N	Y	N	N	N	N
6 ***Burton***	Y	Y	N	Y	N	N	N	N
7 ***Myers***	Y	Y	Y	Y	Y	Y	N	N
8 McCloskey	Y	Y	Y	?	?	Y	Y	Y
9 Hamilton	Y	Y	Y	Y	Y	Y	Y	Y
10 Jacobs	Y	Y	N	Y	N	N	Y	Y
IOWA								
1 ***Leach***	Y	Y	N	Y	Y	Y	Y	N
2 ***Nussle***	Y	Y	N	Y	N	N	N	N
3 ***Lightfoot***	Y	Y	N	Y	Y	Y	Y	N
4 Smith	Y	Y	Y	Y	Y	Y	Y	Y
5 ***Grandy***	?	?	?	?	?	?	?	?
KANSAS								
1 ***Roberts***	Y	Y	N	Y	N	N	N	N
2 Slattery	Y	Y	Y	Y	Y	N	Y	Y
3 ***Meyers***	Y	Y	N	Y	N	N	N	N
4 Glickman	Y	Y	?	Y	Y	Y	Y	Y
KENTUCKY								
1 Barlow	Y	Y	Y	Y	Y	Y	Y	Y
2 Vacancy [1]								
3 Mazzoli	Y	Y	Y	Y	Y	Y	Y	Y
4 ***Bunning***	Y	Y	N	Y	N	Y	N	N
5 ***Rogers***	Y	Y	N	Y	Y	Y	N	N
6 Baesler	Y	Y	Y	Y	Y	Y	Y	Y
LOUISIANA								
1 ***Livingston***	Y	Y	N	Y	N	Y	N	N
2 Jefferson	Y	Y	Y	Y	Y	Y	Y	Y
3 Tauzin	Y	Y	Y	Y	N	Y	Y	Y
4 Fields	Y	Y	Y	Y	Y	Y	Y	Y
5 ***McCrery***	Y	Y	Y	Y	Y	N	N	N
6 ***Baker***	Y	Y	N	Y	Y	N	N	N
7 Hayes	Y	Y	Y	Y	Y	Y	Y	N
MAINE								
1 Andrews	Y	Y	Y	Y	Y	N	Y	Y
2 ***Snowe***	Y	Y	N	Y	N	N	Y	N
MARYLAND								
1 ***Gilchrest***	Y	Y	N	Y	N	N	N	N
2 ***Bentley***	?	?	N	Y	N	N	N	N
3 Cardin	Y	Y	Y	Y	Y	Y	Y	Y
4 Wynn	Y	Y	Y	Y	Y	Y	Y	Y
5 Hoyer	Y	Y	Y	Y	Y	Y	Y	Y
6 ***Bartlett***	Y	Y	N	Y	N	N	N	N
7 Mfume	Y	Y	Y	Y	Y	Y	Y	Y
8 ***Morella***	Y	Y	N	Y	Y	N	N	N
MASSACHUSETTS								
1 Olver	Y	Y	Y	Y	Y	Y	Y	Y
2 Neal	Y	Y	Y	Y	Y	Y	Y	Y
3 ***Blute***	Y	Y	N	Y	Y	Y	N	N
4 Frank	?	?	Y	Y	Y	Y	Y	Y
5 Meehan	Y	Y	Y	Y	Y	Y	Y	Y
6 ***Torkildsen***	Y	Y	N	Y	N	Y	N	N
7 Markey	Y	Y	Y	Y	Y	Y	Y	Y
8 Kennedy	Y	Y	Y	Y	Y	Y	Y	Y
9 Moakley	Y	Y	Y	Y	Y	Y	Y	Y
10 Studds	Y	Y	Y	Y	Y	Y	Y	Y
MICHIGAN								
1 Stupak	Y	Y	Y	Y	Y	Y	Y	Y
2 ***Hoekstra***	Y	Y	N	Y	N	N	Y	N
3 ***Ehlers***	Y	Y	N	Y	Y	N	Y	N
4 ***Camp***	Y	Y	N	Y	Y	Y	Y	N
5 Barcia	Y	Y	Y	Y	Y	Y	Y	Y
6 ***Upton***	Y	Y	N	Y	Y	Y	Y	N
7 ***Smith***	Y	Y	N	Y	N	N	N	N
8 Carr	Y	Y	Y	Y	Y	Y	Y	Y
9 Kildee	Y	Y	Y	Y	Y	Y	Y	Y
10 Bonior	Y	Y	Y	Y	Y	Y	Y	Y
11 ***Knollenberg***	Y	Y	N	Y	N	N	N	N
12 Levin	Y	Y	Y	Y	Y	Y	Y	Y
13 Ford	Y	Y	Y	Y	Y	Y	Y	Y
14 Conyers	Y	Y	Y	Y	Y	Y	Y	Y
15 Collins	Y	Y	Y	Y	Y	Y	Y	Y
16 Dingell	Y	Y	Y	Y	Y	Y	Y	Y
MINNESOTA								
1 Penny	Y	Y	Y	Y	N	N	N	Y
2 Minge	Y	Y	Y	Y	Y	N	Y	Y
3 ***Ramstad***	Y	Y	N	Y	N	N	N	N
4 Vento	Y	Y	Y	Y	Y	Y	Y	Y

	96	97	98	99	100	101	102	103
5 Sabo	Y	Y	Y	Y	Y	Y	Y	Y
6 ***Grams***	Y	Y	N	Y	N	N	N	N
7 Peterson	Y	Y	Y	Y	N	N	N	Y
8 Oberstar	Y	Y	Y	Y	Y	Y	Y	Y
MISSISSIPPI								
1 Whitten	?	?	Y	Y	Y	Y	Y	Y
2 Thompson	Y	Y	Y	Y	Y	Y	Y	Y
3 Montgomery	Y	Y	Y	Y	Y	Y	Y	Y
4 Parker	Y	Y	Y	Y	Y	Y	Y	Y
5 Taylor	N	Y	N	Y	N	Y	N	Y
MISSOURI								
1 Clay	Y	Y	N	Y	Y	Y	Y	Y
2 ***Talent***	Y	Y	N	Y	Y	N	Y	N
3 Gephardt	?	?	Y	Y	Y	Y	Y	Y
4 Skelton	Y	Y	Y	?	?	#	?	Y
5 Wheat	Y	Y	Y	Y	Y	Y	Y	Y
6 Danner	Y	Y	?	Y	Y	Y	N	Y
7 ***Hancock***	Y	Y	N	Y	N	N	N	N
8 ***Emerson***	Y	Y	N	Y	Y	Y	N	N
9 Volkmer	Y	Y	Y	Y	Y	Y	Y	Y
MONTANA								
AL Williams	Y	Y	?	Y	Y	Y	Y	Y
NEBRASKA								
1 ***Bereuter***	Y	Y	N	Y	N	N	N	N
2 Hoagland	Y	Y	Y	Y	Y	Y	Y	Y
3 ***Barrett***	Y	Y	N	Y	N	N	N	N
NEVADA								
1 Bilbray	Y	Y	Y	Y	Y	Y	Y	Y
2 ***Vucanovich***	Y	Y	N	Y	N	Y	N	N
NEW HAMPSHIRE								
1 ***Zeliff***	?	?	N	Y	N	N	N	N
2 Swett	Y	Y	Y	Y	Y	N	N	Y
NEW JERSEY								
1 Andrews	Y	Y	Y	Y	Y	Y	Y	?
2 Hughes	Y	Y	Y	Y	Y	Y	Y	Y
3 ***Saxton***	Y	Y	N	Y	Y	N	N	N
4 ***Smith***	Y	Y	N	Y	Y	Y	Y	N
5 ***Roukema***	+	+	−	+	#	−	−	X
6 Pallone	Y	Y	Y	Y	Y	Y	Y	Y
7 ***Franks***	Y	Y	N	Y	Y	N	Y	N
8 Klein	Y	Y	Y	Y	Y	Y	Y	Y
9 Torricelli	Y	Y	Y	Y	Y	Y	Y	Y
10 Payne	Y	Y	Y	Y	Y	Y	Y	Y
11 ***Gallo***	?	?	?	?	?	?	?	?
12 ***Zimmer***	Y	Y	N	Y	Y	N	N	N
13 Menendez	Y	Y	Y	Y	Y	Y	Y	Y
NEW MEXICO								
1 ***Schiff***	?	?	N	Y	Y	N	Y	N
2 ***Skeen***	Y	Y	N	Y	Y	N	Y	N
3 Richardson	Y	Y	Y	Y	Y	Y	Y	Y
NEW YORK								
1 Hochbrueckner	Y	Y	Y	Y	Y	Y	Y	Y
2 ***Lazio***	Y	Y	N	Y	Y	N	Y	N
3 ***King***	Y	Y	N	Y	N	N	N	N
4 ***Levy***	Y	Y	N	Y	N	N	N	N
5 Ackerman	Y	Y	Y	Y	Y	Y	Y	Y
6 Flake	Y	Y	?	?	?	Y	Y	Y
7 Manton	Y	Y	Y	Y	Y	Y	Y	Y
8 Nadler	Y	Y	Y	Y	Y	Y	Y	Y
9 Schumer	Y	Y	Y	Y	Y	Y	?	Y
10 Towns	Y	Y	Y	Y	Y	Y	Y	Y
11 Owens	Y	Y	Y	Y	Y	Y	Y	Y
12 Velazquez	Y	Y	Y	Y	Y	Y	Y	Y
13 ***Molinari***	Y	Y	N	Y	Y	N	Y	N
14 Maloney	Y	Y	Y	Y	Y	Y	Y	Y
15 Rangel	Y	Y	Y	Y	Y	Y	Y	Y
16 Serrano	Y	Y	Y	Y	Y	Y	Y	Y
17 Engel	Y	Y	Y	Y	Y	Y	Y	Y
18 Lowey	Y	Y	Y	Y	Y	Y	Y	Y
19 ***Fish***	?	?	?	?	?	?	?	?
20 ***Gilman***	Y	Y	Y	Y	Y	Y	Y	N
21 McNulty	Y	Y	Y	Y	Y	Y	Y	Y
22 ***Solomon***	Y	Y	N	Y	N	N	Y	N
23 ***Boehlert***	Y	Y	N	Y	Y	Y	Y	N
24 ***McHugh***	Y	Y	?	Y	N	N	Y	N
25 ***Walsh***	Y	Y	N	Y	Y	Y	Y	N
26 Hinchey	Y	Y	Y	Y	Y	Y	Y	Y
27 ***Paxon***	Y	Y	N	Y	N	N	N	N
28 Slaughter	Y	Y	Y	Y	Y	Y	Y	Y
29 LaFalce	Y	Y	Y	Y	Y	Y	Y	Y
30 ***Quinn***	Y	Y	N	Y	Y	Y	Y	N
31 ***Houghton***	Y	Y	Y	Y	Y	Y	Y	N
NORTH CAROLINA								
1 Clayton	Y	Y	Y	Y	Y	Y	Y	Y
2 Valentine	Y	Y	Y	Y	Y	Y	N	Y

	96	97	98	99	100	101	102	103
3 Lancaster	Y	Y	Y	Y	Y	Y	Y	Y
4 Price	Y	Y	Y	Y	Y	Y	Y	Y
5 Neal	Y	Y	?	Y	Y	Y	Y	Y
6 ***Coble***	Y	Y	N	Y	N	N	N	N
7 Rose	Y	Y	Y	Y	Y	Y	Y	Y
8 Hefner	Y	Y	Y	Y	Y	Y	Y	Y
9 ***McMillan***	Y	Y	?	Y	N	N	N	N
10 ***Ballenger***	Y	Y	N	Y	N	N	N	N
11 ***Taylor***	Y	Y	N	Y	N	N	Y	N
12 Watt	Y	Y	Y	Y	Y	Y	Y	Y
NORTH DAKOTA								
AL Pomeroy	Y	Y	Y	Y	Y	Y	Y	Y
OHIO								
1 Mann	Y	Y	Y	Y	Y	Y	Y	Y
2 ***Portman***	Y	Y	N	Y	N	N	N	N
3 Hall	Y	Y	Y	Y	Y	Y	Y	Y
4 ***Oxley***	Y	Y	N	Y	N	N	N	N
5 ***Gillmor***	Y	Y	Y	Y	Y	N	Y	N
6 Strickland	Y	Y	Y	Y	Y	Y	Y	Y
7 ***Hobson***	Y	Y	N	Y	Y	N	Y	N
8 ***Boehner***	Y	Y	N	Y	N	N	N	N
9 Kaptur	Y	Y	Y	Y	#	Y	Y	Y
10 ***Hoke***	Y	Y	N	Y	N	N	N	N
11 Stokes	Y	Y	Y	Y	Y	Y	Y	Y
12 ***Kasich***	Y	Y	Y	Y	N	N	Y	N
13 Brown	Y	Y	Y	Y	Y	Y	Y	Y
14 Sawyer	Y	Y	Y	Y	Y	Y	Y	Y
15 ***Pryce***	Y	Y	N	Y	N	N	N	N
16 ***Regula***	Y	Y	N	Y	Y	Y	Y	N
17 Traficant	Y	Y	Y	Y	Y	Y	Y	Y
18 Applegate	Y	Y	Y	Y	Y	Y	N	Y
19 Fingerhut	Y	Y	Y	Y	Y	Y	Y	Y
OKLAHOMA								
1 ***Inhofe***	Y	Y	N	Y	N	N	N	N
2 Synar	Y	Y	Y	Y	Y	Y	Y	Y
3 Brewster	Y	Y	Y	Y	Y	N	Y	Y
4 McCurdy	Y	Y	Y	Y	Y	N	Y	?
5 ***Istook***	Y	Y	N	Y	N	N	N	N
6 Vacancy								
OREGON								
1 Furse	?	?	Y	Y	Y	Y	Y	Y
2 ***Smith***	?	?	?	?	X	X	?	?
3 Wyden	Y	Y	Y	Y	Y	Y	Y	Y
4 DeFazio	?	?	Y	Y	Y	Y	Y	Y
5 Kopetski	Y	Y	Y	Y	Y	Y	Y	Y
PENNSYLVANIA								
1 Foglietta	Y	Y	Y	Y	Y	Y	?	Y
2 Blackwell	?	?	?	?	?	?	?	?
3 Borski	Y	Y	Y	Y	Y	Y	Y	Y
4 Klink	Y	Y	Y	Y	Y	Y	Y	Y
5 ***Clinger***	?	?	Y	Y	N	Y	N	N
6 Holden	Y	Y	Y	Y	Y	N	N	Y
7 ***Weldon***	Y	Y	N	Y	Y	N	Y	N
8 ***Greenwood***	Y	Y	Y	Y	Y	N	N	N
9 ***Shuster***	Y	Y	N	Y	N	N	N	N
10 ***McDade***	Y	Y	N	Y	Y	Y	Y	N
11 Kanjorski	Y	Y	Y	Y	Y	Y	Y	Y
12 Murtha	Y	Y	Y	Y	Y	Y	Y	Y
13 Margolies-Mezv.	Y	Y	Y	Y	Y	Y	Y	Y
14 Coyne	Y	Y	Y	Y	Y	Y	Y	Y
15 McHale	Y	Y	Y	Y	Y	N	N	Y
16 ***Walker***	Y	Y	N	Y	N	N	Y	N
17 ***Gekas***	Y	Y	N	Y	N	N	Y	N
18 ***Santorum***	Y	Y	Y	Y	N	N	N	N
19 ***Goodling***	Y	Y	N	Y	N	N	N	N
20 Murphy	Y	Y	N	Y	Y	Y	Y	Y
21 ***Ridge***	?	?	N	Y	Y	N	Y	N
RHODE ISLAND								
1 ***Machtley***	Y	Y	N	Y	N	N	Y	N
2 Reed	Y	Y	Y	Y	Y	Y	Y	Y
SOUTH CAROLINA								
1 ***Ravenel***	Y	Y	N	Y	N	N	N	N
2 ***Spence***	Y	Y	N	Y	N	Y	Y	N
3 Derrick	Y	Y	Y	Y	Y	Y	Y	Y
4 ***Inglis***	Y	Y	Y	Y	N	N	N	N
5 Spratt	Y	Y	Y	Y	Y	Y	Y	Y
6 Clyburn	Y	Y	Y	Y	Y	Y	Y	Y
SOUTH DAKOTA								
AL Johnson	Y	Y	Y	Y	Y	Y	Y	Y
TENNESSEE								
1 ***Quillen***	Y	Y	N	Y	Y	Y	Y	N
2 ***Duncan***	Y	Y	N	Y	N	N	Y	N
3 Lloyd	Y	Y	Y	Y	Y	Y	Y	Y
4 Cooper	Y	Y	Y	Y	Y	Y	Y	N
5 Clement	Y	Y	Y	Y	Y	Y	Y	Y

	96	97	98	99	100	101	102	103
6 Gordon	Y	Y	Y	Y	Y	Y	Y	Y
7 ***Sundquist***	Y	Y	N	Y	N	Y	Y	N
8 Tanner	Y	Y	Y	Y	Y	Y	Y	?
9 Ford	?	?	Y	Y	Y	Y	Y	Y
TEXAS								
1 Chapman	Y	Y	Y	Y	Y	Y	Y	Y
2 Wilson	Y	Y	?	Y	Y	Y	Y	?
3 ***Johnson, Sam***	Y	Y	N	+	−	−	−	N
4 Hall	Y	Y	Y	Y	Y	N	Y	Y
5 Bryant	Y	Y	Y	Y	Y	Y	Y	Y
6 ***Barton***	Y	Y	N	Y	N	N	N	N
7 ***Archer***	Y	Y	N	Y	N	N	N	N
8 ***Fields***	Y	Y	N	Y	N	N	N	N
9 Brooks	Y	Y	Y	Y	Y	Y	Y	Y
10 Pickle	Y	Y	Y	Y	Y	Y	Y	Y
11 Edwards	Y	Y	Y	Y	Y	Y	Y	Y
12 Geren	Y	Y	Y	Y	Y	Y	N	Y
13 Sarpalius	Y	Y	Y	Y	Y	Y	N	Y
14 Laughlin	Y	Y	Y	Y	Y	Y	Y	Y
15 de la Garza	Y	Y	Y	Y	Y	Y	Y	Y
16 Coleman	Y	Y	Y	Y	Y	Y	Y	Y
17 Stenholm	Y	Y	Y	Y	N	N	N	Y
18 Washington	?	?	?	?	?	?	?	Y
19 ***Combest***	Y	Y	Y	Y	N	N	N	N
20 Gonzalez	Y	Y	Y	Y	Y	Y	Y	Y
21 ***Smith***	Y	Y	N	Y	N	N	N	N
22 ***DeLay***	Y	Y	N	Y	N	Y	N	N
23 ***Bonilla***	Y	Y	N	Y	N	N	N	N
24 Frost	Y	Y	Y	Y	Y	Y	Y	Y
25 Andrews	Y	Y	Y	Y	Y	Y	Y	Y
26 ***Armey***	Y	Y	N	Y	N	N	N	N
27 Ortiz	Y	Y	Y	Y	Y	Y	Y	Y
28 Tejeda	Y	Y	Y	Y	Y	Y	Y	Y
29 Green	Y	Y	Y	Y	Y	Y	Y	Y
30 Johnson, E.B.	Y	Y	Y	Y	Y	Y	Y	Y
UTAH								
1 ***Hansen***	Y	Y	N	Y	N	Y	N	N
2 Shepherd	Y	Y	Y	Y	Y	Y	Y	Y
3 Orton	Y	Y	Y	Y	Y	Y	N	N
VERMONT								
AL *Sanders*	Y	Y	Y	Y	Y	Y	Y	Y
VIRGINIA								
1 ***Bateman***	Y	Y	Y	Y	Y	N	Y	N
2 Pickett	Y	Y	Y	Y	Y	Y	Y	Y
3 Scott	Y	Y	Y	Y	Y	Y	Y	Y
4 Sisisky	Y	Y	Y	Y	Y	Y	Y	Y
5 Payne	Y	Y	Y	Y	Y	Y	Y	Y
6 ***Goodlatte***	Y	Y	N	Y	N	N	N	N
7 ***Bliley***	Y	Y	N	Y	N	N	Y	N
8 Moran	Y	Y	Y	Y	Y	Y	Y	Y
9 Boucher	Y	Y	Y	Y	Y	Y	Y	Y
10 ***Wolf***	Y	Y	N	Y	Y	Y	N	N
11 Byrne	Y	Y	Y	Y	Y	Y	Y	N
WASHINGTON								
1 Cantwell	Y	Y	Y	Y	Y	Y	Y	Y
2 Swift	Y	Y	Y	Y	Y	?	Y	Y
3 Unsoeld	Y	Y	Y	Y	Y	Y	Y	Y
4 Inslee	Y	Y	Y	Y	Y	Y	Y	Y
5 Foley								
6 Dicks	Y	Y	Y	Y	Y	Y	Y	Y
7 McDermott	Y	Y	Y	Y	Y	Y	Y	Y
8 ***Dunn***	Y	Y	N	Y	N	N	N	N
9 Kreidler	Y	Y	N	Y	Y	Y	Y	Y
WEST VIRGINIA								
1 Mollohan	Y	Y	Y	Y	Y	Y	Y	Y
2 Wise	?	?	Y	Y	Y	Y	Y	Y
3 Rahall	Y	Y	Y	Y	Y	Y	Y	Y
WISCONSIN								
1 Barca	Y	Y	Y	Y	N	N	Y	Y
2 ***Klug***	Y	Y	N	Y	N	N	N	N
3 ***Gunderson***	Y	Y	N	Y	Y	N	Y	N
4 Kleczka	Y	Y	Y	Y	Y	Y	Y	Y
5 Barrett	Y	Y	Y	Y	Y	Y	Y	Y
6 ***Petri***	Y	Y	N	Y	N	N	N	N
7 Obey	Y	Y	Y	Y	Y	?	Y	Y
8 ***Roth***	Y	Y	N	Y	N	N	N	N
9 ***Sensenbrenner***	Y	Y	N	Y	N	N	N	N
WYOMING								
AL ***Thomas***	Y	?	Y	Y	N	N	N	N
DELEGATES								
de Lugo, V.I.	D	D	D	D	D	D	D	D
Faleomavaega, Am.S.	D	D	D	D	D	D	D	D
Norton, D.C.	D	D	D	D	D	D	D	D
Romero-B., P.R.	D	D	D	D	D	D	D	D
Underwood, Guam	D	D	D	D	D	D	D	D

Southern states - Ala., Ark., Fla., Ga., Ky., La., Miss., N.C., Okla., S.C., Tenn., Texas, Va.
Omitted votes are quorum calls, which CQ does not include in its vote charts.

1994 CQ ALMANAC — 31-H

104. HR 4092. Omnibus Crime Bill/En Bloc Amendment.
Brooks, D-Texas, en bloc amendment incorporating 35 amendments allowed by the rule, including amendments to authorize $350 million for rural anti-crime and anti-drug initiatives, prevent violence against truck drivers, authorize $210 million in each of fiscal 1995-99 for Treasury Department law enforcement activities, strengthen penalties for passport and visa fraud, study converting military bases to prisons, and establish a new $100 million grant program to prevent and prosecute young violent offenders. Adopted in the Committee of the Whole 395-25: R 147-23; D 247-2 (ND 170-2, SD 77-0); I 1-0, April 14, 1994.

105. Procedural Motion. Approval of the House Journal of Wednesday, April 13. Approved 237-158: R 12-154; D 224-4 (ND 152-4, SD 72-0); I 1-0, April 14, 1994.

106. HR 4092. Omnibus Crime Bill/Death Penalty for Drug Kingpins. Watt, D-N.C., amendment to eliminate the bill's death penalty provisions for drug kingpins involved in non-fatal crimes. Rejected in the Committee of the Whole 108-316: R 5-164; D 102-152 (ND 82-90, SD 20-62); I 1-0, April 14, 1994.

107. HR 4092. Omnibus Crime Bill/Life in Prison. Kopetski, D-Ore., amendment to substitute a penalty of life in prison without parole where the bill would impose the death penalty. Rejected in the Committee of the Whole 111-314: R 6-165; D 104-149 (ND 89-86, SD 15-63); I 1-0, April 14, 1994. A "nay" was a vote in support of the president's position.

108. HR 4092. Omnibus Crime Bill/Death Penalty for Drug Kingpins. McCollum, R-Fla., amendment to establish factors for determining whether the death penalty should be implemented for drug kingpins in cases where no death occurs, including prior conviction, use of a firearm, distribution to people under 21 or near schools and the use of minors in trafficking. Adopted in the Committee of the Whole 340-87: R 169-2; D 171-84 (ND 104-70, SD 67-14); I 0-1, April 14, 1994.

KEY

Y Voted for (yea).
Paired for.
+ Announced for.
N Voted against (nay).
X Paired against.
− Announced against.
P Voted "present."
C Voted "present" to avoid possible conflict of interest.
? Did not vote or otherwise make a position known.
D Delegates ineligible to vote.

Democrats *Republicans*
Independent

	104	105	106	107	108
ALABAMA					
1 *Callahan*	Y	N	N	N	Y
2 *Everett*	Y	Y	N	N	Y
3 Browder	Y	Y	N	N	Y
4 Bevill	Y	Y	N	N	Y
5 Cramer	Y	Y	N	N	Y
6 *Bachus*	Y	N	N	N	Y
7 Hilliard	Y	Y	Y	Y	N
ALASKA					
AL *Young*	Y	N	Y	N	Y
ARIZONA					
1 Coppersmith	Y	Y	N	N	Y
2 Pastor	Y	Y	N	N	Y
3 *Stump*	N	N	N	N	Y
4 *Kyl*	Y	N	N	N	Y
5 *Kolbe*	Y	N	N	N	Y
6 English	Y	Y	N	N	Y
ARKANSAS					
1 Lambert	Y	Y	N	N	Y
2 Thornton	Y	Y	N	N	Y
3 *Hutchinson*	Y	N	N	N	Y
4 *Dickey*	Y	N	N	N	Y
CALIFORNIA					
1 Hamburg	Y	Y	Y	Y	N
2 *Herger*	Y	N	N	N	Y
3 Fazio	Y	Y	Y	Y	Y
4 *Doolittle*	Y	N	N	N	Y
5 Matsui	Y	Y	N	N	Y
6 Woolsey	Y	Y	Y	Y	N
7 Miller	Y	Y	Y	Y	N
8 Pelosi	Y	Y	Y	Y	N
9 Dellums	Y	?	Y	Y	N
10 *Baker*	Y	N	N	N	Y
11 *Pombo*	Y	N	N	N	Y
12 Lantos	Y	Y	N	N	Y
13 Stark	?	?	Y	Y	N
14 Eshoo	Y	Y	Y	Y	N
15 Mineta	Y	Y	Y	Y	N
16 Edwards	Y	Y	Y	Y	N
17 Farr	Y	Y	Y	Y	N
18 Condit	N	Y	N	N	Y
19 Lehman	Y	Y	N	N	Y
20 Dooley	Y	Y	N	N	Y
21 *Thomas*	Y	N	N	N	Y
22 *Huffington*	Y	N	N	N	Y
23 *Gallegly*	Y	N	N	N	Y
24 Beilenson	Y	Y	N	N	Y
25 *McKeon*	Y	N	N	N	Y
26 Berman	Y	?	Y	Y	Y
27 *Moorhead*	Y	N	N	N	Y
28 *Dreier*	Y	N	N	N	Y
29 Waxman	Y	?	?	Y	N
30 Becerra	Y	Y	Y	Y	N
31 Martinez	Y	Y	N	N	Y
32 Dixon	Y	Y	Y	Y	N
33 Roybal-Allard	Y	Y	Y	Y	N
34 Torres	Y	Y	N	N	Y
35 Waters	Y	?	Y	Y	N
36 Harman	Y	Y	N	N	Y
37 Tucker	Y	Y	Y	Y	N
38 *Horn*	Y	N	N	N	Y
39 *Royce*	Y	N	N	N	Y
40 *Lewis*	Y	N	N	N	Y
41 *Kim*	Y	N	N	N	Y

	104	105	106	107	108
42 Brown	?	?	Y	Y	N
43 *Calvert*	Y	N	N	N	Y
44 *McCandless*	Y	N	N	N	Y
45 *Rohrabacher*	N	N	N	N	Y
46 *Dornan*	Y	N	?	N	Y
47 *Cox*	N	N	N	N	Y
48 *Packard*	Y	N	N	N	Y
49 Schenk	Y	Y	N	N	Y
50 Filner	Y	Y	Y	Y	Y
51 *Cunningham*	Y	N	N	N	Y
52 *Hunter*	Y	N	N	N	Y
COLORADO					
1 Schroeder	Y	N	N	N	Y
2 Skaggs	Y	Y	Y	Y	Y
3 *McInnis*	Y	N	N	N	Y
4 *Allard*	Y	N	N	N	Y
5 *Hefley*	Y	N	N	N	Y
6 *Schaefer*	N	N	N	N	Y
CONNECTICUT					
1 Kennelly	Y	Y	N	N	Y
2 Gejdenson	Y	Y	N	Y	N
3 DeLauro	Y	Y	N	N	Y
4 *Shays*	Y	N	N	Y	Y
5 *Franks*	Y	N	N	N	Y
6 *Johnson*	Y	N	N	?	Y
DELAWARE					
AL *Castle*	Y	N	N	N	Y
FLORIDA					
1 Hutto	Y	?	N	N	Y
2 Peterson	Y	Y	N	N	Y
3 Brown	Y	Y	N	N	Y
4 *Fowler*	Y	N	N	N	Y
5 Thurman	Y	Y	N	N	Y
6 *Stearns*	N	N	N	N	Y
7 *Mica*	Y	N	N	N	Y
8 *McCollum*	Y	N	N	N	Y
9 *Bilirakis*	Y	N	N	N	Y
10 *Young*	Y	N	N	N	Y
11 Gibbons	Y	Y	N	N	Y
12 *Canady*	Y	N	N	N	Y
13 *Miller*	Y	N	N	N	Y
14 Goss	Y	N	N	N	Y
15 Bacchus	?	?	N	N	Y
16 Lewis	Y	N	N	N	Y
17 Meek	Y	Y	Y	Y	N
18 *Ros-Lehtinen*	Y	N	N	N	Y
19 Johnston	Y	Y	N	N	Y
20 Deutsch	Y	Y	N	N	Y
21 *Diaz-Balart*	Y	N	N	N	Y
22 *Shaw*	Y	N	N	N	Y
23 Hastings	Y	Y	Y	Y	N
GEORGIA					
1 *Kingston*	Y	N	N	N	Y
2 Bishop	Y	Y	N	N	Y
3 *Collins*	Y	N	N	N	Y
4 *Linder*	Y	N	N	N	Y
5 Lewis	Y	Y	Y	Y	N
6 *Gingrich*	Y	N	N	N	Y
7 Darden	Y	Y	N	N	Y
8 Rowland	Y	Y	N	N	Y
9 Deal	Y	Y	N	N	Y
10 Johnson	?	?	N	N	Y
11 McKinney	Y	Y	Y	Y	N
HAWAII					
1 Abercrombie	Y	Y	N	Y	Y
2 Mink	Y	Y	Y	Y	N
IDAHO					
1 LaRocco	Y	Y	N	N	Y
2 *Crapo*	Y	N	N	N	Y
ILLINOIS					
1 Rush	Y	Y	Y	Y	N
2 Reynolds	Y	Y	Y	Y	N
3 Lipinski	Y	Y	N	N	Y
4 Gutierrez	Y	Y	?	Y	N
5 Rostenkowski	Y	Y	N	N	Y
6 *Hyde*	Y	N	N	N	Y
7 Collins	Y	Y	Y	Y	N
8 *Crane*	N	N	N	N	Y
9 Yates	Y	Y	Y	Y	N
10 *Porter*	Y	N	N	N	Y
11 Sangmeister	Y	?	N	N	Y
12 Costello	Y	Y	N	N	Y
13 *Fawell*	Y	N	N	N	Y
14 *Hastert*	Y	N	N	N	Y
15 *Ewing*	Y	N	?	N	Y
16 *Manzullo*	Y	N	N	N	Y
17 Evans	Y	Y	Y	Y	N

ND Northern Democrats   SD Southern Democrats

	104	105	106	107	108
18 Michel	Y	N	N	N	Y
19 Poshard	Y	Y	N	N	Y
20 Durbin	Y	Y	N	N	Y
INDIANA					
1 Visclosky	Y	Y	Y	Y	N
2 Sharp	Y	Y	Y	Y	N
3 Roemer	Y	Y	N	N	Y
4 Long	Y	Y	N	N	Y
5 *Buyer*	Y	N	N	N	Y
6 *Burton*	N	N	N	N	Y
7 *Myers*	Y	Y	N	N	Y
8 McCloskey	Y	Y	N	N	Y
9 Hamilton	Y	Y	N	Y	Y
10 Jacobs	Y	N	Y	N	Y
IOWA					
1 *Leach*	Y	N	N	N	Y
2 *Nussle*	Y	N	N	N	Y
3 *Lightfoot*	Y	N	N	N	Y
4 Smith	Y	Y	Y	Y	Y
5 *Grandy*	?	?	X	?	?
KANSAS					
1 *Roberts*	Y	N	N	N	Y
2 Slattery	Y	Y	N	N	Y
3 *Meyers*	Y	N	N	N	Y
4 Glickman	Y	Y	N	N	Y
KENTUCKY					
1 Barlow	Y	N	N	N	Y
2 Vacancy					
3 Mazzoli	Y	Y	Y	N	Y
4 *Bunning*	Y	N	N	N	Y
5 *Rogers*	Y	N	N	N	Y
6 Baesler	Y	?	N	N	Y
LOUISIANA					
1 *Livingston*	Y	Y	N	N	Y
2 Jefferson	Y	Y	Y	Y	N
3 Tauzin	Y	Y	Y	Y	N
4 Fields	Y	Y	Y	Y	N
5 *McCrery*	Y	N	N	N	Y
6 *Baker*	Y	N	N	N	Y
7 Hayes	?	Y	N	N	Y
MAINE					
1 Andrews	Y	Y	Y	Y	N
2 *Snowe*	Y	N	N	N	Y
MARYLAND					
1 *Gilchrest*	Y	N	N	N	Y
2 *Bentley*	Y	N	N	N	Y
3 Cardin	Y	Y	Y	N	Y
4 Wynn	Y	Y	Y	N	N
5 Hoyer	Y	Y	Y	N	Y
6 *Bartlett*	Y	N	N	N	Y
7 Mfume	Y	Y	Y	N	Y
8 *Morella*	Y	N	N	N	Y
MASSACHUSETTS					
1 Olver	Y	Y	Y	Y	N
2 Neal	Y	Y	N	Y	Y
3 *Blute*	Y	N	N	N	Y
4 Frank	Y	Y	Y	Y	N
5 Meehan	Y	Y	Y	Y	N
6 *Torkildsen*	Y	N	N	N	Y
7 Markey	Y	Y	Y	Y	N
8 Kennedy	Y	Y	Y	Y	N
9 Moakley	Y	Y	Y	Y	N
10 Studds	Y	Y	Y	Y	N
MICHIGAN					
1 Stupak	Y	Y	N	N	Y
2 *Hoekstra*	Y	N	Y	N	Y
3 *Ehlers*	Y	N	Y	Y	Y
4 *Camp*	Y	N	N	N	Y
5 Barcia	Y	Y	N	N	Y
6 *Upton*	Y	N	N	N	Y
7 *Smith*	Y	?	N	N	Y
8 Carr	Y	?	N	Y	Y
9 Kildee	Y	Y	Y	N	Y
10 Bonior	Y	Y	Y	Y	N
11 *Knollenberg*	Y	N	N	N	Y
12 Levin	Y	Y	Y	Y	Y
13 Ford	Y	Y	Y	Y	?
14 Conyers	Y	Y	Y	Y	N
15 Collins	Y	Y	Y	Y	N
16 Dingell	Y	Y	N	N	Y
MINNESOTA					
1 Penny	N	Y	Y	Y	Y
2 Minge	Y	Y	Y	Y	Y
3 *Ramstad*	Y	N	N	N	Y
4 Vento	Y	?	Y	Y	N

	104	105	106	107	108
5 Sabo	Y	Y	Y	Y	N
6 *Grams*	Y	N	N	N	Y
7 Peterson	Y	Y	N	N	Y
8 Oberstar	Y	Y	Y	Y	N
MISSISSIPPI					
1 Whitten	?	?	N	?	?
2 Thompson	Y	Y	Y	Y	N
3 Montgomery	Y	Y	N	N	Y
4 Parker	Y	Y	N	N	Y
5 Taylor	Y	Y	N	N	Y
MISSOURI					
1 Clay	Y	N	Y	Y	N
2 *Talent*	Y	N	N	N	Y
3 Gephardt	Y	Y	N	N	Y
4 Skelton	Y	Y	N	N	Y
5 Wheat	Y	Y	N	Y	Y
6 Danner	Y	Y	N	N	Y
7 *Hancock*	N	N	N	N	Y
8 *Emerson*	Y	N	N	N	Y
9 Volkmer	Y	Y	N	N	Y
MONTANA					
AL Williams	Y	?	N	N	Y
NEBRASKA					
1 *Bereuter*	Y	N	N	N	Y
2 Hoagland	Y	Y	N	N	Y
3 *Barrett*	Y	N	N	N	Y
NEVADA					
1 Bilbray	Y	?	N	N	Y
2 *Vucanovich*	Y	N	N	N	Y
NEW HAMPSHIRE					
1 *Zeliff*	Y	N	N	N	Y
2 Swett	Y	Y	N	N	Y
NEW JERSEY					
1 Andrews	Y	Y	N	N	Y
2 Hughes	Y	Y	Y	N	Y
3 *Saxton*	Y	N	N	N	Y
4 *Smith*	Y	N	Y	N	Y
5 *Roukema*	-	-	X	-	#
6 Pallone	Y	Y	N	N	Y
7 *Franks*	Y	N	N	N	Y
8 Klein	Y	Y	N	N	Y
9 Torricelli	Y	Y	N	N	Y
10 Payne	Y	Y	Y	Y	N
11 *Gallo*	?	?	?	?	?
12 *Zimmer*	N	N	N	N	Y
13 Menendez	Y	Y	N	N	Y
NEW MEXICO					
1 *Schiff*	Y	N	N	N	Y
2 *Skeen*	Y	N	N	N	Y
3 Richardson	Y	Y	N	N	Y
NEW YORK					
1 Hochbrueckner	Y	?	N	N	Y
2 *Lazio*	Y	N	N	N	Y
3 *King*	Y	N	N	N	Y
4 *Levy*	Y	N	N	N	Y
5 Ackerman	Y	Y	#	Y	Y
6 Flake	Y	Y	Y	Y	N
7 Manton	Y	Y	N	N	Y
8 Nadler	Y	Y	Y	Y	N
9 Schumer	Y	Y	N	N	Y
10 Towns	Y	Y	Y	Y	N
11 Owens	Y	?	P	Y	N
12 Velazquez	Y	Y	Y	Y	N
13 *Molinari*	Y	N	N	N	Y
14 Maloney	Y	Y	Y	Y	N
15 Rangel	?	?	#	#	X
16 Serrano	Y	Y	Y	Y	N
17 Engel	Y	Y	Y	Y	N
18 Lowey	Y	?	Y	Y	N
19 *Fish*	?	?	?	?	?
20 *Gilman*	Y	Y	N	N	Y
21 McNulty	Y	Y	Y	Y	N
22 *Solomon*	Y	N	N	N	Y
23 *Boehlert*	Y	N	N	N	Y
24 *McHugh*	Y	N	N	N	Y
25 *Walsh*	Y	N	N	N	Y
26 Hinchey	+	Y	Y	Y	N
27 *Paxon*	Y	N	N	N	Y
28 Slaughter	Y	Y	Y	Y	Y
29 LaFalce	Y	Y	Y	Y	N
30 *Quinn*	Y	N	N	N	Y
31 *Houghton*	Y	Y	N	N	Y
NORTH CAROLINA					
1 Clayton	Y	Y	Y	Y	N
2 Valentine	Y	Y	N	N	Y

	104	105	106	107	108
3 Lancaster	Y	Y	N	N	Y
4 Price	Y	Y	N	N	Y
5 Neal	?	?	N	N	Y
6 *Coble*	N	N	N	N	Y
7 Rose	Y	Y	N	N	Y
8 Hefner	Y	Y	N	N	Y
9 *McMillan*	Y	?	N	N	Y
10 *Ballenger*	Y	?	N	N	Y
11 *Taylor*	N	N	N	N	Y
12 Watt	Y	Y	Y	Y	N
NORTH DAKOTA					
AL Pomeroy	Y	Y	N	N	Y
OHIO					
1 Mann	Y	Y	Y	N	Y
2 *Portman*	+	-	N	N	Y
3 Hall	Y	Y	N	N	Y
4 *Oxley*	Y	N	N	N	Y
5 *Gillmor*	Y	N	N	N	Y
6 Strickland	Y	Y	N	N	Y
7 *Hobson*	Y	N	N	N	Y
8 *Boehner*	Y	N	N	N	Y
9 Kaptur	Y	Y	N	N	Y
10 *Hoke*	Y	N	N	N	Y
11 Stokes	Y	Y	Y	Y	N
12 *Kasich*	Y	N	N	N	Y
13 Brown	?	Y	Y	Y	N
14 Sawyer	Y	Y	N	N	Y
15 *Pryce*	Y	N	N	N	Y
16 *Regula*	Y	N	N	N	Y
17 Traficant	Y	Y	N	N	Y
18 Applegate	Y	?	N	N	Y
19 Fingerhut	Y	Y	N	N	Y
OKLAHOMA					
1 *Inhofe*	Y	N	N	N	Y
2 Synar	Y	?	Y	?	N
3 Brewster	Y	Y	N	N	Y
4 McCurdy	Y	Y	N	N	Y
5 *Istook*	Y	N	N	N	Y
6 Vacancy					
OREGON					
1 Furse	Y	Y	Y	Y	N
2 *Smith*	Y	N	N	N	Y
3 Wyden	Y	Y	Y	N	Y
4 DeFazio	Y	Y	Y	Y	N
5 Kopetski	Y	Y	Y	Y	N
PENNSYLVANIA					
1 Foglietta	Y	Y	N	N	Y
2 Blackwell	Y	Y	Y	Y	N
3 Borski	Y	Y	N	N	Y
4 Klink	Y	Y	N	N	Y
5 *Clinger*	Y	N	N	N	Y
6 Holden	Y	Y	N	N	Y
7 *Weldon*	Y	N	N	N	Y
8 *Greenwood*	?	?	N	N	Y
9 *Shuster*	Y	N	N	N	Y
10 *McDade*	Y	N	N	N	Y
11 Kanjorski	Y	Y	N	N	Y
12 Murtha	Y	Y	N	N	Y
13 Margolies-Mezv.	Y	Y	Y	Y	N
14 Coyne	Y	Y	Y	Y	N
15 McHale	Y	Y	N	N	Y
16 *Walker*	N	N	N	N	Y
17 *Gekas*	N	?	N	N	Y
18 *Santorum*	Y	N	N	N	Y
19 *Goodling*	N	N	N	Y	P
20 Murphy	Y	N	N	X	#
21 *Ridge*	Y	N	N	N	Y
RHODE ISLAND					
1 *Machtley*	Y	N	N	N	Y
2 Reed	Y	Y	N	N	N
SOUTH CAROLINA					
1 *Ravenel*	Y	N	N	N	Y
2 *Spence*	Y	N	N	N	Y
3 Derrick	Y	Y	N	N	Y
4 *Inglis*	Y	Y	N	N	Y
5 Spratt	Y	Y	N	N	Y
6 Clyburn	Y	Y	Y	Y	N
SOUTH DAKOTA					
AL Johnson	Y	Y	N	N	Y
TENNESSEE					
1 *Quillen*	Y	N	N	N	Y
2 *Duncan*	N	N	N	N	Y
3 Lloyd	Y	Y	N	N	Y
4 Cooper	Y	Y	N	N	Y
5 Clement	Y	Y	N	N	Y

	104	105	106	107	108
6 Gordon	Y	Y	N	N	Y
7 *Sundquist*	Y	N	N	N	Y
8 Tanner	Y	Y	N	N	Y
9 Ford	Y	Y	N	Y	Y
TEXAS					
1 Chapman	Y	Y	N	N	Y
2 Wilson	Y	Y	N	N	Y
3 *Johnson, Sam*	N	N	N	N	Y
4 Hall	Y	Y	N	N	Y
5 Bryant	Y	?	N	N	Y
6 *Barton*	N	N	N	N	Y
7 *Archer*	N	N	N	N	Y
8 *Fields*	N	N	N	N	Y
9 Brooks	Y	Y	Y	N	Y
10 Pickle	Y	Y	N	?	Y
11 Edwards	Y	?	N	N	Y
12 Geren	Y	Y	N	N	Y
13 Sarpalius	Y	Y	N	N	Y
14 Laughlin	Y	Y	N	N	Y
15 de la Garza	Y	Y	N	N	Y
16 Coleman	Y	Y	N	N	Y
17 Stenholm	Y	Y	N	N	Y
18 Washington	?	?	?	#	X
19 *Combest*	Y	N	N	N	Y
20 Gonzalez	Y	Y	Y	Y	N
21 *Smith*	Y	N	N	N	Y
22 *DeLay*	N	?	N	N	Y
23 *Bonilla*	Y	N	N	N	Y
24 Frost	Y	Y	N	N	Y
25 Andrews	Y	Y	N	N	Y
26 *Armey*	N	N	N	N	Y
27 Ortiz	Y	Y	N	N	Y
28 Tejeda	Y	Y	N	N	Y
29 Green	Y	Y	N	X	Y
30 Johnson, E.B.	Y	Y	Y	Y	Y
UTAH					
1 *Hansen*	Y	N	N	N	Y
2 Shepherd	Y	Y	N	N	Y
3 Orton	Y	Y	N	N	Y
VERMONT					
AL *Sanders*	Y	Y	Y	Y	N
VIRGINIA					
1 *Bateman*	Y	N	N	N	Y
2 Pickett	Y	?	N	N	Y
3 Scott	Y	Y	Y	Y	N
4 Sisisky	Y	Y	N	N	Y
5 Payne	Y	Y	N	N	Y
6 *Goodlatte*	Y	N	N	N	Y
7 *Bliley*	Y	N	N	N	Y
8 Moran	Y	Y	N	N	Y
9 Boucher	Y	Y	Y	Y	N
10 *Wolf*	Y	N	N	N	Y
11 Byrne	Y	Y	N	N	Y
WASHINGTON					
1 Cantwell	Y	Y	N	N	Y
2 Swift	Y	Y	Y	Y	Y
3 Unsoeld	Y	Y	Y	Y	Y
4 Inslee	Y	Y	Y	N	Y
5 Foley					
6 Dicks	Y	Y	N	N	Y
7 McDermott	Y	Y	Y	Y	N
8 *Dunn*	Y	N	N	N	Y
9 Kreidler	Y	Y	N	N	Y
WEST VIRGINIA					
1 Mollohan	Y	Y	Y	Y	Y
2 Wise	Y	Y	Y	Y	Y
3 Rahall	Y	Y	N	Y	Y
WISCONSIN					
1 Barca	Y	Y	Y	Y	N
2 *Klug*	Y	N	Y	Y	Y
3 *Gunderson*	Y	N	N	N	Y
4 Kleczka	Y	Y	Y	Y	Y
5 Barrett	Y	Y	Y	Y	N
6 *Petri*	N	N	N	N	Y
7 Obey	Y	Y	Y	Y	N
8 *Roth*	Y	N	-	N	Y
9 *Sensenbrenner*	N	N	N	N	Y
WYOMING					
AL *Thomas*	Y	N	N	N	Y
DELEGATES					
de Lugo, V.I.	Y	D	N	N	Y
Faleomavaega, Am.S.	Y	D	N	N	Y
Norton, D.C.	Y	D	Y	N	N
Romero-B., P.R.	Y	D	N	Y	Y
Underwood, Guam	Y	D	Y	N	Y

Southern states - Ala., Ark., Fla., Ga., Ky., La., Miss., N.C., Okla., S.C., Tenn., Texas, Va.
Omitted votes are quorum calls, which CQ does not include in its vote charts.

KEY

Y   Voted for (yea).
Paired for.
+   Announced for.
N   Voted against (nay).
X   Paired against.
—   Announced against.
P   Voted "present."
C   Voted "present" to avoid possible conflict of interest.
?   Did not vote or otherwise make a position known.
D   Delegates ineligible to vote.

Democrats   *Republicans*
Independent

109. HR 4092. Omnibus Crime Bill/Death Penalty Instructions. Gekas, R-Pa., amendment to make it easier for juries or courts to impose the death penalty by establishing instructions concerning weighing aggravating factors against mitigating ones. Adopted in the Committee of the Whole 226-198: R 166-5; D 60-192 (ND 29-144, SD 31-48); I 0-1, April 14, 1994.

110. HR 4092. Omnibus Crime Bill/Strike Enacting Clause. McCollum, R-Fla., motion to rise and report the bill back to the Rules Committee with the enacting clause stricken. The motion was an effort to force the committee to consider an amendment to allow evidence seized illegally in good faith to be used in criminal trials. Motion rejected in the Committee of the Whole 170-257: R 170-1; D 0-255 (ND 0-175, SD 0-80); I 0-1, April 14, 1994.

111. HR 4092. Omnibus Crime Bill/Death Penalty Aggravating Factors. Watt, D-N.C., amendment to eliminate the bill's provisions that allow unspecified aggravating factors to be considered for imposing the death penalty and limit the consideration of aggravating factors to those specified in the bill. Rejected in the Committee of the Whole 116-308: R 2-168; D 113-140 (ND 96-79, SD 17-61); I 1-0, April 14, 1994.

112. H Con Res 218. Fiscal 1995 Budget Resolution/Instruct Conferees. Kasich, R-Ohio, motion to instruct the House conferees to agree to the Senate amendment to provide an additional $26.1 billion in deficit reduction over the next five years and to protect defense spending from further cuts. Motion rejected 202-216: R 159-6; D 43-209 (ND 29-141, SD 14-68); I 0-1, April 14, 1994. A "nay" was a vote in support of the president's position.

	109	110	111	112
ALABAMA				
1 *Callahan*	Y	Y	N	Y
2 *Everett*	Y	Y	N	Y
3 Browder	Y	N	N	Y
4 Bevill	Y	N	N	N
5 Cramer	Y	N	N	N
6 *Bachus*	Y	Y	N	Y
7 Hilliard	N	?	Y	N
ALASKA				
AL *Young*	Y	Y	N	Y
ARIZONA				
1 Coppersmith	N	N	N	N
2 Pastor	N	N	N	N
3 *Stump*	Y	Y	N	Y
4 *Kyl*	Y	Y	N	Y
5 *Kolbe*	Y	Y	N	Y
6 English	N	N	N	Y
ARKANSAS				
1 Lambert	N	N	N	N
2 Thornton	N	N	N	N
3 *Hutchinson*	Y	Y	N	Y
4 Dickey	Y	Y	N	Y
CALIFORNIA				
1 Hamburg	N	N	Y	N
2 *Herger*	Y	Y	N	Y
3 Fazio	N	N	N	N
4 *Doolittle*	Y	Y	N	?
5 Matsui	N	N	N	N
6 Woolsey	N	N	Y	N
7 Miller	N	N	Y	N
8 Pelosi	N	N	Y	N
9 Dellums	N	N	Y	N
10 *Baker*	Y	Y	N	Y
11 *Pombo*	Y	Y	N	Y
12 Lantos	N	N	N	N
13 Stark	N	N	Y	N
14 Eshoo	N	N	Y	N
15 Mineta	N	N	Y	N
16 Edwards	N	N	Y	N
17 Farr	N	N	Y	N
18 Condit	Y	N	N	Y
19 Lehman	Y	N	N	Y
20 Dooley	Y	N	Y	N
21 *Thomas*	Y	Y	N	?
22 *Huffington*	Y	Y	N	Y
23 *Gallegly*	Y	Y	N	Y
24 Beilenson	N	N	Y	N
25 *McKeon*	Y	Y	N	Y
26 Berman	N	N	N	N
27 *Moorhead*	Y	Y	N	Y
28 *Dreier*	Y	Y	N	Y
29 Waxman	?	?	Y	N
30 Becerra	N	N	#	N
31 Martinez	N	N	N	N
32 Dixon	N	N	Y	N
33 Roybal-Allard	N	N	Y	N
34 Torres	N	N	N	N
35 Waters	N	N	Y	N
36 Harman	N	N	N	N
37 Tucker	N	N	Y	N
38 *Horn*	Y	Y	N	Y
39 *Royce*	Y	Y	N	Y
40 *Lewis*	Y	Y	N	#
41 *Kim*	Y	Y	N	Y

	109	110	111	112
42 Brown	N	N	Y	N
43 *Calvert*	Y	Y	N	Y
44 *McCandless*	Y	Y	N	Y
45 *Rohrabacher*	Y	Y	N	Y
46 *Dornan*	Y	Y	N	Y
47 *Cox*	Y	Y	N	Y
48 *Packard*	Y	Y	N	Y
49 Schenk	N	N	N	Y
50 Filner	N	N	Y	N
51 *Cunningham*	Y	Y	N	Y
52 *Hunter*	Y	Y	N	Y
COLORADO				
1 Schroeder	N	N	N	N
2 Skaggs	N	N	Y	N
3 *McInnis*	Y	Y	N	Y
4 *Allard*	Y	Y	N	Y
5 *Hefley*	Y	Y	N	Y
6 *Schaefer*	Y	Y	N	Y
CONNECTICUT				
1 Kennelly	N	N	Y	N
2 Gejdenson	N	N	Y	N
3 DeLauro	N	N	N	N
4 *Shays*	N	N	Y	N
5 *Franks*	Y	Y	N	?
6 *Johnson*	Y	Y	N	Y
DELAWARE				
AL *Castle*	Y	Y	N	Y
FLORIDA				
1 Hutto	N	N	N	N
2 Peterson	N	N	N	N
3 Brown	N	N	N	N
4 *Fowler*	Y	Y	N	Y
5 Thurman	N	N	N	N
6 *Stearns*	Y	Y	N	Y
7 *Mica*	Y	Y	N	Y
8 *McCollum*	Y	Y	N	Y
9 *Bilirakis*	Y	Y	N	N
10 *Young*	Y	Y	N	N
11 Gibbons	N	N	N	N
12 *Canady*	Y	Y	N	Y
13 *Miller*	Y	Y	N	Y
14 *Goss*	Y	Y	N	N
15 Bacchus	N	N	N	N
16 *Lewis*	Y	Y	N	Y
17 Meek	N	N	Y	N
18 *Ros-Lehtinen*	Y	Y	N	Y
19 Johnston	N	N	Y	N
20 Deutsch	Y	N	Y	N
21 *Diaz-Balart*	Y	Y	N	Y
22 *Shaw*	Y	Y	N	Y
23 Hastings	N	N	Y	N
GEORGIA				
1 *Kingston*	Y	Y	N	Y
2 Bishop	N	N	Y	N
3 *Collins*	Y	Y	N	Y
4 *Linder*	Y	Y	N	Y
5 Lewis	N	N	Y	N
6 *Gingrich*	Y	Y	N	Y
7 Darden	Y	N	N	Y
8 Rowland	Y	N	N	N
9 Deal	Y	N	N	Y
10 Johnson	N	N	N	Y
11 McKinney	N	N	Y	N
HAWAII				
1 Abercrombie	N	N	Y	N
2 Mink	N	N	Y	N
IDAHO				
1 LaRocco	Y	N	N	Y
2 *Crapo*	Y	Y	N	Y
ILLINOIS				
1 Rush	N	N	Y	N
2 Reynolds	N	N	Y	N
3 Lipinski	Y	N	N	N
4 Gutierrez	N	N	Y	N
5 Rostenkowski	N	N	N	N
6 *Hyde*	Y	Y	N	Y
7 Collins	N	N	Y	N
8 *Crane*	Y	Y	N	Y
9 Yates	N	N	Y	N
10 *Porter*	Y	Y	N	Y
11 Sangmeister	N	N	N	N
12 Costello	Y	N	N	N
13 *Fawell*	Y	Y	N	Y
14 *Hastert*	Y	Y	N	Y
15 *Ewing*	Y	Y	N	Y
16 *Manzullo*	Y	Y	N	Y
17 Evans	N	N	Y	N

ND   Northern Democrats   SD   Southern Democrats

	109	110	111	112
18 ***Michel***	Y	Y	N	Y
19 Poshard	Y	N	N	Y
20 Durbin	N	N	N	N

INDIANA

	109	110	111	112
1 Visclosky	N	N	Y	N
2 Sharp	N	N	Y	N
3 Roemer	Y	N	N	Y
4 Long	N	N	N	N
5 ***Buyer***	Y	Y	N	Y
6 ***Burton***	Y	Y	N	Y
7 ***Myers***	Y	Y	N	Y
8 McCloskey	N	N	Y	N
9 Hamilton	N	N	N	Y
10 Jacobs	N	N	Y	N

IOWA

	109	110	111	112
1 ***Leach***	Y	Y	N	Y
2 ***Nussle***	Y	Y	N	Y
3 ***Lightfoot***	Y	Y	N	Y
4 Smith	N	N	N	N
5 ***Grandy***	#	?	X	?

KANSAS

	109	110	111	112
1 ***Roberts***	Y	Y	N	Y
2 Slattery	N	N	N	N
3 ***Meyers***	Y	Y	N	Y
4 Glickman	N	N	N	N

KENTUCKY

	109	110	111	112
1 Barlow	N	N	N	N
2 Vacancy				
3 Mazzoli	N	N	N	N
4 ***Bunning***	Y	Y	N	Y
5 ***Rogers***	Y	Y	N	Y
6 Baesler	N	N	N	N

LOUISIANA

	109	110	111	112
1 ***Livingston***	Y	Y	N	Y
2 Jefferson	N	N	Y	N
3 Tauzin	Y	N	N	Y
4 Fields	N	N	Y	N
5 ***McCrery***	Y	Y	N	Y
6 ***Baker***	Y	Y	N	Y
7 Hayes	?	N	N	Y

MAINE

	109	110	111	112
1 Andrews	N	N	Y	N
2 ***Snowe***	Y	Y	N	Y

MARYLAND

	109	110	111	112
1 ***Gilchrest***	Y	Y	N	Y
2 ***Bentley***	Y	Y	N	Y
3 Cardin	N	N	Y	N
4 Wynn	N	N	Y	N
5 Hoyer	N	N	Y	N
6 ***Bartlett***	Y	Y	N	Y
7 Mfume	N	N	Y	N
8 ***Morella***	Y	Y	N	N

MASSACHUSETTS

	109	110	111	112
1 Olver	N	N	Y	N
2 Neal	N	N	N	N
3 ***Blute***	Y	Y	N	Y
4 Frank	N	N	Y	N
5 Meehan	N	N	N	Y
6 ***Torkildsen***	Y	Y	N	Y
7 Markey	N	N	Y	N
8 Kennedy	N	N	Y	N
9 Moakley	N	N	N	N
10 Studds	N	N	Y	N

MICHIGAN

	109	110	111	112
1 Stupak	N	N	N	N
2 ***Hoekstra***	N	Y	N	Y
3 ***Ehlers***	N	Y	N	Y
4 ***Camp***	Y	Y	N	Y
5 Barcia	Y	N	N	N
6 ***Upton***	Y	Y	N	Y
7 ***Smith***	Y	Y	N	Y
8 Carr	Y	N	N	N
9 Kildee	N	N	Y	N
10 Bonior	N	N	Y	N
11 ***Knollenberg***	Y	Y	N	Y
12 Levin	N	N	Y	N
13 Ford	?	N	Y	N
14 Conyers	N	N	Y	N
15 Collins	N	N	Y	N
16 Dingell	N	N	N	N

MINNESOTA

	109	110	111	112
1 Penny	N	N	N	Y
2 Minge	N	N	N	Y
3 ***Ramstad***	Y	Y	N	Y
4 Vento	N	N	Y	N
5 Sabo	N	N	Y	N
6 ***Grams***	Y	Y	N	Y
7 Peterson	Y	N	N	Y
8 Oberstar	N	N	Y	N

MISSISSIPPI

	109	110	111	112
1 Whitten	?	?	?	N
2 Thompson	N	N	Y	N
3 Montgomery	Y	N	N	N
4 Parker	Y	N	N	N
5 Taylor	Y	N	N	N

MISSOURI

	109	110	111	112
1 Clay	N	N	Y	N
2 ***Talent***	Y	Y	N	Y
3 Gephardt	N	N	N	N
4 Skelton	Y	N	N	N
5 Wheat	N	N	Y	N
6 Danner	N	N	N	N
7 ***Hancock***	Y	Y	N	Y
8 ***Emerson***	Y	Y	N	Y
9 Volkmer	N	N	N	N

MONTANA

	109	110	111	112
AL Williams	N	N	N	N

NEBRASKA

	109	110	111	112
1 ***Bereuter***	Y	N	N	Y
2 Hoagland	N	N	N	Y
3 ***Barrett***	Y	Y	N	Y

NEVADA

	109	110	111	112
1 Bilbray	Y	N	N	N
2 ***Vucanovich***	Y	Y	N	Y

NEW HAMPSHIRE

	109	110	111	112
1 ***Zeliff***	Y	Y	N	Y
2 Swett	N	N	N	Y

NEW JERSEY

	109	110	111	112
1 Andrews	Y	N	N	Y
2 Hughes	N	N	Y	N
3 ***Saxton***	Y	Y	N	Y
4 ***Smith***	N	Y	Y	Y
5 ***Roukema***	+	+	X	+
6 Pallone	Y	N	N	Y
7 ***Franks***	Y	Y	N	Y
8 Klein	Y	N	N	N
9 Torricelli	Y	N	N	N
10 Payne	N	N	Y	N
11 ***Gallo***	?	?	?	?
12 ***Zimmer***	Y	Y	N	Y
13 Menendez	N	N	N	N

NEW MEXICO

	109	110	111	112
1 ***Schiff***	Y	Y	N	Y
2 ***Skeen***	Y	Y	N	Y
3 Richardson	Y	N	N	N

NEW YORK

	109	110	111	112
1 Hochbrueckner	N	N	Y	N
2 ***Lazio***	Y	Y	N	Y
3 ***King***	Y	Y	N	Y
4 ***Levy***	Y	Y	N	Y
5 Ackerman	N	N	Y	N
6 Flake	N	N	Y	N
7 Manton	Y	N	N	N
8 Nadler	N	N	Y	N
9 Schumer	N	N	Y	N
10 Towns	N	N	Y	N
11 Owens	N	N	Y	N
12 Velazquez	N	N	Y	N
13 ***Molinari***	Y	Y	N	Y
14 Maloney	N	N	Y	N
15 Rangel	N	N	Y	N
16 Serrano	N	N	Y	N
17 Engel	N	N	Y	N
18 Lowey	N	N	Y	N
19 ***Fish***	?	?	?	?
20 ***Gilman***	Y	Y	N	N
21 McNulty	N	N	Y	N
22 ***Solomon***	Y	Y	N	Y
23 ***Boehlert***	Y	Y	N	N
24 ***McHugh***	Y	Y	N	Y
25 ***Walsh***	Y	Y	N	Y
26 Hinchey	N	N	Y	N
27 ***Paxon***	Y	Y	N	Y
28 Slaughter	N	N	Y	N
29 LaFalce	N	N	N	N
30 ***Quinn***	Y	Y	N	Y
31 ***Houghton***	Y	Y	N	Y

NORTH CAROLINA

	109	110	111	112
1 Clayton	N	N	Y	N
2 Valentine	Y	N	?	N
3 Lancaster	Y	N	N	N
4 Price	N	N	N	N
5 Neal	N	N	?	N
6 ***Coble***	Y	Y	N	Y
7 Rose	N	N	N	N
8 Hefner	N	N	N	N
9 ***McMillan***	Y	Y	N	Y
10 ***Ballenger***	Y	Y	N	Y
11 ***Taylor***	Y	Y	N	Y
12 Watt	N	N	Y	N

NORTH DAKOTA

	109	110	111	112
AL Pomeroy	N	N	N	Y

OHIO

	109	110	111	112
1 Mann	N	N	Y	Y
2 ***Portman***	Y	Y	N	Y
3 Hall	N	N	N	N
4 ***Oxley***	Y	Y	N	Y
5 ***Gillmor***	Y	Y	N	Y
6 Strickland	N	N	Y	N
7 ***Hobson***	Y	Y	N	Y
8 ***Boehner***	Y	Y	N	Y
9 Kaptur	Y	N	N	?
10 ***Hoke***	Y	Y	N	Y
11 Stokes	N	N	Y	N
12 ***Kasich***	Y	Y	N	Y
13 Brown	N	N	Y	Y
14 Sawyer	N	N	Y	N
15 ***Pryce***	Y	Y	N	Y
16 ***Regula***	Y	Y	N	Y
17 Traficant	Y	N	N	N
18 Applegate	Y	N	N	N
19 Fingerhut	Y	N	N	Y

OKLAHOMA

	109	110	111	112
1 ***Inhofe***	Y	Y	N	Y
2 Synar	N	N	Y	N
3 Brewster	Y	N	N	Y
4 McCurdy	Y	N	N	N
5 ***Istook***	Y	Y	N	Y
6 Vacancy				

OREGON

	109	110	111	112
1 Furse	N	N	Y	N
2 ***Smith***	Y	Y	N	Y
3 Wyden	Y	N	N	N
4 DeFazio	N	N	N	Y
5 Kopetski	N	N	Y	N

PENNSYLVANIA

	109	110	111	112
1 Foglietta	N	N	Y	N
2 Blackwell	N	N	Y	?
3 Borski	N	N	N	N
4 Klink	Y	N	N	N
5 ***Clinger***	Y	Y	N	Y
6 Holden	Y	N	N	N
7 ***Weldon***	Y	Y	N	Y
8 ***Greenwood***	Y	Y	N	Y
9 ***Shuster***	Y	Y	N	Y
10 ***McDade***	Y	Y	N	Y
11 Kanjorski	N	N	N	N
12 Murtha	?	N	N	N
13 Margolies-Mezv.	Y	N	N	Y
14 Coyne	N	N	Y	N
15 McHale	Y	N	N	Y
16 ***Walker***	Y	Y	N	Y
17 ***Gekas***	Y	Y	N	Y
18 ***Santorum***	Y	Y	N	Y
19 ***Goodling***	P	Y	P	Y
20 Murphy	?	?	?	?
21 ***Ridge***	Y	Y	N	?

RHODE ISLAND

	109	110	111	112
1 ***Machtley***	Y	Y	N	Y
2 Reed	N	N	Y	N

SOUTH CAROLINA

	109	110	111	112
1 ***Ravenel***	Y	Y	N	Y
2 ***Spence***	Y	Y	N	Y
3 Derrick	N	N	N	N
4 ***Inglis***	Y	Y	N	Y
5 Spratt	N	N	N	N
6 Clyburn	N	N	Y	N

SOUTH DAKOTA

	109	110	111	112
AL Johnson	N	N	N	N

TENNESSEE

	109	110	111	112
1 ***Quillen***	Y	?	?	?
2 ***Duncan***	Y	Y	N	Y
3 Lloyd	Y	N	N	N
4 Cooper	Y	N	N	Y
5 Clement	Y	N	N	Y
6 Gordon	Y	N	N	Y
7 ***Sundquist***	Y	Y	N	Y
8 Tanner	Y	N	N	N
9 Ford	?	N	N	N

TEXAS

	109	110	111	112
1 Chapman	Y	N	N	N
2 Wilson	N	N	N	N
3 ***Johnson, Sam***	Y	Y	N	Y
4 Hall	Y	N	N	Y
5 Bryant	N	N	N	N
6 ***Barton***	Y	Y	N	?
7 ***Archer***	Y	Y	N	Y
8 ***Fields***	Y	Y	N	Y
9 Brooks	N	N	N	N
10 Pickle	N	N	N	N
11 Edwards	Y	N	N	N
12 Geren	Y	N	N	N
13 Sarpalius	N	N	N	N
14 Laughlin	N	N	?	N
15 de la Garza	N	N	N	N
16 Coleman	N	N	N	N
17 Stenholm	Y	N	N	Y
18 Washington	X	?	#	X
19 ***Combest***	Y	Y	N	Y
20 Gonzalez	N	N	Y	N
21 ***Smith***	Y	Y	N	Y
22 ***DeLay***	Y	Y	N	Y
23 ***Bonilla***	Y	Y	N	Y
24 Frost	Y	N	N	N
25 Andrews	N	N	N	Y
26 ***Armey***	Y	Y	N	Y
27 Ortiz	N	N	N	N
28 Tejeda	Y	N	N	N
29 Green	N	N	N	N
30 Johnson, E.B.	N	N	Y	N

UTAH

	109	110	111	112
1 ***Hansen***	Y	Y	N	Y
2 Shepherd	N	N	N	N
3 Orton	Y	N	N	Y

VERMONT

	109	110	111	112
AL *Sanders*	N	N	Y	N

VIRGINIA

	109	110	111	112
1 ***Bateman***	Y	Y	N	Y
2 Pickett	N	N	N	N
3 Scott	N	N	Y	N
4 Sisisky	Y	N	N	N
5 Payne	Y	N	N	Y
6 ***Goodlatte***	Y	Y	N	Y
7 ***Bliley***	Y	Y	N	Y
8 Moran	Y	N	N	N
9 Boucher	N	N	N	N
10 ***Wolf***	Y	Y	N	Y
11 Byrne	Y	N	N	N

WASHINGTON

	109	110	111	112
1 Cantwell	N	N	N	Y
2 Swift	N	N	Y	N
3 Unsoeld	N	N	Y	N
4 Inslee	N	N	Y	Y
5 Foley				N
6 Dicks	N	N	N	N
7 McDermott	N	N	Y	N
8 ***Dunn***	Y	Y	N	Y
9 Kreidler	N	N	N	N

WEST VIRGINIA

	109	110	111	112
1 Mollohan	N	N	Y	N
2 Wise	N	N	N	N
3 Rahall	N	N	N	N

WISCONSIN

	109	110	111	112
1 Barca	N	N	N	Y
2 ***Klug***	N	Y	Y	Y
3 ***Gunderson***	Y	Y	N	Y
4 Kleczka	N	N	Y	N
5 Barrett	N	N	Y	N
6 ***Petri***	Y	Y	N	Y
7 Obey	N	N	Y	N
8 ***Roth***	Y	Y	N	Y
9 ***Sensenbrenner***	Y	Y	N	Y

WYOMING

	109	110	111	112
AL ***Thomas***	Y	Y	N	Y

DELEGATES

	109	110	111	112
de Lugo, V.I.	N	N	Y	D
Faleomavaega, Am.S.	N	N	Y	D
Norton, D.C.	N	N	Y	D
Romero-B., P.R.	N	N	Y	D
Underwood, Guam	N	N	Y	D

Southern states - Ala., Ark., Fla., Ga., Ky., La., Miss., N.C., Okla., S.C., Tenn., Texas, Va.
Omitted votes are quorum calls, which CQ does not include in its vote charts.

113. HR 2333. State Department Authorization/Counter-terrorism. Gilman, R-N.Y., motion to instruct the House conferees to insist on the House language to maintain the Office of Counterterrorism in the State Department at the coordinator level. Motion agreed to 357-2: R 150-0; D 207-2 (ND 141-2, SD 66-0); I 0-0, April 18, 1994.

114. H Con Res 222. Raoul Wallenberg Capitol Bust/Passage. Rose, D-N.C., motion to suspend the rules and pass the concurrent resolution to authorize the placement in the Capitol of a bust of Raoul Wallenberg, who coordinated the rescue of 100,000 Jews from the Nazis during World War II. Motion agreed to 358-0: R 150-0; D 208-0 (ND 142-0, SD 66-0); I 0-0, April 18, 1994. A two-thirds majority of those present and voting (239 in this case) is required for passage under suspension of the rules.

115. Procedural Motion. Approval of the House Journal of Monday, April 18. Approved 246-155: R 19-149; D 226-6 (ND 153-5, SD 73-1); I 1-0, April 19, 1994.

116. S 1654. Indian Law Technical Corrections/Passage. Richardson, D-N.M., motion to suspend the rules and pass the bill to make corrections and clarifications to certain laws regarding Native Americans. Motion agreed to 414-2: R 167-2; D 246-0 (ND 166-0, SD 80-0); I 1-0, April 19, 1994. A two-thirds majority of those present and voting (278 in this case) is required for passage under suspension of the rules.

117. HR 3813. Environmental Export Promotion/Passage. Gejdenson, D-Conn., motion to suspend the rules and pass the bill to promote U.S environmental exports through various means, including directing the Commerce Department to guide companies in exporting environmental technologies. Motion agreed to 416-0: R 170-0; D 246-0 (ND 167-0, SD 79-0); I 0-0, April 19, 1994. A two-thirds majority of those present and voting (278 in this case) is required for passage under suspension of the rules.

118. S Con Res 31. Iranian Bahai Community Emancipation/Passage. Gejdenson, D-Conn., motion to suspend the rules and pass the concurrent resolution to condemn repressive treatment of the Bahai community by the Iranian government and call upon the Iranian government to guarantee human rights to the Bahai community. Motion agreed to 414-0: R 169-0; D 244-0 (ND 164-0, SD 80-0); I 1-0, April 19, 1994. A two-thirds majority of those present and voting (276 in this case) is required for passage under suspension of the rules.

119. HR 4092. Omnibus Crime Bill/Habeas Corpus. Hyde, R-Ill., amendment to eliminate the bill's provisions to overhaul the system for death row appeals in federal court, known as habeas corpus petitions. Adopted in the Committee of the Whole 270-159: R 172-0; D 98-158 (ND 54-120, SD 44-38); I 0-1, April 19, 1994.

120. HR 4092. Omnibus Crime Bill/Habeas Corpus. Derrick, D-S.C., amendment to overhaul the system for habeas corpus appeals. The amendment generally would restrict inmates to one habeas corpus petition to be filed within one year of exhausting state appeals, and would adjust the circumstances under which subsequent appeals can be filed. Compared with the original bill language, the amendment would make it more difficult to challenge a death sentence as unconstitutional based on the retroactive application of new rules announced by the Supreme Court; narrow second habeas appeals to cases where a new claim would undermine the court's confidence in the person's guilt or the imposition of the death penalty; and delay for one year the requirements regarding providing indigent death row prisoners with competent counsel at various stages of the legal process. Rejected in the Committee of the Whole 171-256: R 0-172; D 170-84 (ND 128-44, SD 42-40); I 1-0, April 19, 1994.

KEY

Y	Voted for (yea).
#	Paired for.
+	Announced for.
N	Voted against (nay).
X	Paired against.
−	Announced against.
P	Voted "present."
C	Voted "present" to avoid possible conflict of interest.
?	Did not vote or otherwise make a position known.
D	Delegates ineligible to vote.

Democrats   ***Republicans***
Independent

	113	114	115	116	117	118	119	120
ALABAMA								
1 Callahan	Y	Y	N	Y	Y	Y	Y	N
2 Everett	Y	Y	Y	Y	Y	Y	Y	N
3 Browder	Y	Y	Y	Y	Y	Y	Y	N
4 Bevill	Y	Y	Y	Y	Y	Y	Y	N
5 Cramer	Y	Y	Y	Y	Y	Y	Y	N
6 Bachus	Y	Y	N	Y	Y	Y	Y	N
7 Hilliard	Y	Y	Y	Y	Y	Y	N	Y
ALASKA								
AL Young	Y	Y	N	Y	Y	Y	Y	N
ARIZONA								
1 Coppersmith	Y	Y	Y	Y	Y	Y	Y	N
2 Pastor	Y	Y	Y	Y	Y	Y	Y	Y
3 Stump	Y	Y	N	Y	Y	Y	Y	N
4 Kyl	Y	Y	N	Y	Y	Y	Y	N
5 Kolbe	Y	Y	N	Y	Y	Y	Y	N
6 English	+	+	Y	Y	Y	Y	Y	Y
ARKANSAS								
1 Lambert	Y	Y	Y	Y	Y	Y	Y	N
2 Thornton	?	?	Y	Y	Y	Y	N	Y
3 Hutchinson	Y	Y	N	Y	Y	Y	Y	N
4 Dickey	Y	Y	N	Y	Y	Y	Y	N
CALIFORNIA								
1 Hamburg	Y	Y	?	Y	Y	Y	N	Y
2 Herger	Y	Y	N	Y	Y	Y	Y	N
3 Fazio	Y	Y	Y	Y	Y	Y	Y	Y
4 Doolittle	?	?	N	Y	Y	Y	Y	N
5 Matsui	Y	Y	Y	Y	Y	Y	N	Y
6 Woolsey	Y	Y	Y	Y	Y	Y	N	Y
7 Miller	Y	Y	Y	Y	Y	Y	N	Y
8 Pelosi	Y	Y	?	?	?	?	N	Y
9 Dellums	Y	Y	Y	Y	Y	Y	N	Y
10 Baker	Y	Y	N	Y	Y	?	Y	N
11 Pombo	Y	Y	N	Y	Y	Y	Y	N
12 Lantos	Y	Y	Y	Y	Y	Y	N	Y
13 Stark	?	?	Y	Y	Y	Y	N	Y
14 Eshoo	Y	Y	Y	Y	Y	Y	N	Y
15 Mineta	Y	Y	Y	Y	Y	Y	N	Y
16 Edwards	Y	Y	Y	Y	Y	Y	N	Y
17 Farr	Y	Y	Y	Y	Y	Y	N	Y
18 Condit	Y	Y	Y	Y	Y	Y	Y	N
19 Lehman	?	?	Y	Y	Y	Y	N	Y
20 Dooley	Y	Y	Y	Y	Y	Y	Y	N
21 Thomas	Y	Y	?	Y	Y	Y	Y	N
22 Huffington	Y	Y	N	Y	Y	Y	Y	N
23 Gallegly	?	?	N	Y	Y	Y	Y	N
24 Beilenson	Y	Y	Y	Y	Y	Y	N	Y
25 McKeon	Y	Y	N	Y	Y	Y	Y	N
26 Berman	Y	Y	Y	Y	Y	?	N	Y
27 Moorhead	Y	Y	N	Y	Y	Y	Y	N
28 Dreier	Y	Y	N	Y	Y	Y	Y	N
29 Waxman	Y	Y	Y	Y	Y	Y	N	Y
30 Becerra	+	+	Y	Y	Y	Y	N	Y
31 Martinez	Y	Y	Y	Y	Y	Y	N	Y
32 Dixon	Y	Y	Y	Y	Y	Y	N	Y
33 Roybal-Allard	Y	Y	Y	Y	Y	Y	N	Y
34 Torres	Y	Y	Y	Y	Y	Y	N	Y
35 Waters	Y	Y	Y	Y	Y	Y	N	Y
36 Harman	Y	Y	Y	Y	Y	Y	N	Y
37 Tucker	Y	Y	Y	Y	Y	Y	N	Y
38 Horn	Y	Y	N	Y	Y	Y	Y	N
39 Royce	Y	Y	N	N	Y	Y	Y	N
40 Lewis	Y	Y	Y	Y	Y	Y	Y	N
41 Kim	Y	Y	N	Y	Y	Y	Y	N

	113	114	115	116	117	118	119	120
42 Brown	Y	Y	?	Y	Y	?	N	Y
43 Calvert	Y	Y	N	Y	Y	Y	Y	N
44 McCandless	Y	Y	N	Y	Y	Y	Y	N
45 Rohrabacher	Y	Y	N	Y	Y	Y	Y	N
46 Dornan	Y	Y	N	Y	Y	Y	Y	N
47 Cox	Y	Y	N	?	?	?	Y	N
48 Packard	Y	Y	N	Y	Y	Y	Y	N
49 Schenk	Y	Y	Y	Y	Y	Y	Y	N
50 Filner	Y	Y	Y	Y	Y	Y	N	Y
51 Cunningham	Y	Y	N	Y	Y	Y	Y	N
52 Hunter	Y	Y	N	Y	Y	Y	Y	N
COLORADO								
1 Schroeder	Y	Y	N	Y	Y	Y	N	Y
2 Skaggs	Y	Y	Y	Y	Y	Y	N	Y
3 McInnis	Y	Y	Y	Y	Y	Y	Y	N
4 Allard	Y	Y	N	Y	Y	Y	Y	N
5 Hefley	Y	Y	Y	Y	Y	Y	Y	N
6 Schaefer	Y	Y	N	Y	Y	Y	Y	N
CONNECTICUT								
1 Kennelly	Y	Y	Y	Y	Y	Y	N	Y
2 Gejdenson	Y	Y	Y	Y	Y	Y	N	Y
3 DeLauro	Y	Y	Y	Y	Y	Y	N	Y
4 Shays	Y	Y	N	Y	Y	Y	Y	N
5 Franks	Y	Y	Y	Y	Y	Y	Y	N
6 Johnson	Y	Y	N	Y	Y	Y	Y	N
DELAWARE								
AL Castle	Y	Y	N	Y	Y	Y	Y	N
FLORIDA								
1 Hutto	Y	Y	Y	Y	Y	Y	Y	N
2 Peterson	+	+	+	+	+	+	+	−
3 Brown	Y	Y	Y	Y	Y	Y	N	Y
4 Fowler	Y	Y	N	Y	Y	Y	Y	N
5 Thurman	Y	Y	Y	Y	Y	Y	Y	N
6 Stearns	Y	Y	N	Y	Y	Y	Y	N
7 Mica	Y	Y	N	Y	Y	Y	Y	N
8 McCollum	?	?	N	Y	Y	Y	Y	N
9 Bilirakis	Y	Y	N	Y	Y	Y	Y	N
10 Young	?	?	N	Y	Y	Y	Y	N
11 Gibbons	Y	Y	Y	Y	Y	Y	N	Y
12 Canady	Y	Y	N	Y	Y	Y	Y	N
13 Miller	Y	Y	N	Y	Y	Y	Y	N
14 Goss	Y	Y	N	Y	Y	Y	Y	N
15 Bacchus	Y	Y	Y	Y	Y	Y	Y	N
16 Lewis	?	?	N	Y	Y	Y	Y	N
17 Meek	Y	Y	Y	Y	Y	Y	N	Y
18 Ros-Lehtinen	Y	Y	N	Y	Y	Y	Y	N
19 Johnston	Y	Y	Y	Y	Y	Y	N	Y
20 Deutsch	Y	Y	Y	Y	Y	Y	N	Y
21 Diaz-Balart	Y	Y	N	Y	Y	Y	Y	N
22 Shaw	Y	Y	N	Y	Y	Y	Y	N
23 Hastings	?	?	Y	Y	Y	Y	N	Y
GEORGIA								
1 Kingston	Y	Y	Y	Y	Y	Y	Y	N
2 Bishop	Y	Y	Y	Y	Y	Y	N	Y
3 Collins	Y	Y	Y	Y	Y	Y	Y	N
4 Linder	Y	Y	N	Y	Y	Y	Y	N
5 Lewis	Y	Y	Y	Y	Y	Y	N	Y
6 Gingrich	Y	Y	N	Y	Y	Y	Y	N
7 Darden	Y	Y	Y	Y	Y	Y	Y	N
8 Rowland	Y	Y	?	Y	Y	Y	Y	N
9 Deal	Y	Y	Y	Y	Y	Y	Y	N
10 Johnson	Y	Y	Y	Y	Y	Y	Y	N
11 McKinney	Y	Y	Y	Y	Y	Y	N	Y
HAWAII								
1 Abercrombie	Y	Y	?	?	?	?	N	Y
2 Mink	Y	Y	Y	Y	Y	Y	N	Y
IDAHO								
1 LaRocco	Y	Y	Y	Y	Y	Y	Y	N
2 Crapo	Y	Y	N	Y	Y	Y	Y	N
ILLINOIS								
1 Rush	Y	Y	Y	Y	Y	Y	N	Y
2 Reynolds	Y	Y	Y	Y	Y	Y	N	Y
3 Lipinski	?	?	Y	Y	Y	Y	Y	N
4 Gutierrez	Y	Y	Y	Y	Y	Y	N	Y
5 Rostenkowski	?	?	Y	Y	Y	Y	N	Y
6 Hyde	Y	Y	?	Y	Y	Y	Y	N
7 Collins	Y	Y	?	?	?	?	X	#
8 Crane	Y	Y	N	Y	Y	Y	Y	N
9 Yates	Y	Y	Y	Y	Y	Y	N	Y
10 Porter	Y	Y	N	Y	Y	Y	Y	N
11 Sangmeister	?	?	Y	Y	Y	Y	Y	N
12 Costello	Y	Y	Y	Y	Y	Y	Y	N
13 Fawell	Y	Y	N	Y	Y	Y	Y	N
14 Hastert	Y	Y	N	Y	Y	Y	Y	N
15 Ewing	Y	Y	Y	Y	Y	Y	Y	N
16 Manzullo	Y	Y	N	Y	Y	Y	Y	N
17 Evans	Y	Y	Y	Y	Y	Y	N	Y

ND Northern Democrats   SD Southern Democrats

	113	114	115	116	117	118	119	120
18 ***Michel***	Y	Y	N	Y	Y	Y	Y	N
19 Poshard	Y	Y	Y	Y	Y	Y	Y	N
20 Durbin	Y	Y	Y	Y	Y	Y	N	Y
INDIANA								
1 Visclosky	Y	Y	Y	Y	Y	Y	N	Y
2 Sharp	Y	Y	Y	Y	Y	Y	N	Y
3 Roemer	Y	Y	Y	Y	Y	Y	Y	N
4 Long	Y	Y	Y	Y	Y	Y	Y	N
5 ***Buyer***	Y	Y	N	Y	Y	Y	Y	N
6 ***Burton***	?	?	N	Y	Y	Y	Y	N
7 ***Myers***	Y	Y	Y	Y	Y	Y	Y	N
8 McCloskey	Y	Y	?	Y	Y	Y	N	Y
9 Hamilton	Y	Y	Y	Y	Y	Y	Y	N
10 Jacobs	Y	Y	N	Y	Y	Y	N	Y
IOWA								
1 ***Leach***	Y	Y	N	Y	Y	Y	Y	N
2 ***Nussle***	Y	Y	N	Y	Y	Y	Y	N
3 ***Lightfoot***	Y	Y	N	Y	Y	Y	Y	N
4 Smith	Y	Y	Y	Y	Y	Y	N	Y
5 ***Grandy***	?	?	?	?	?	?	#	X
KANSAS								
1 ***Roberts***	Y	Y	N	Y	Y	Y	Y	N
2 Slattery	?	?	Y	Y	Y	Y	Y	N
3 ***Meyers***	Y	Y	N	Y	Y	Y	Y	N
4 Glickman	Y	Y	Y	Y	Y	Y	Y	N
KENTUCKY								
1 Barlow	?	?	Y	Y	Y	Y	N	Y
2 Vacancy								
3 Mazzoli	Y	Y	Y	Y	Y	Y	N	N
4 ***Bunning***	Y	Y	N	Y	Y	Y	Y	N
5 ***Rogers***	Y	Y	N	Y	Y	Y	Y	N
6 Baesler	?	?	Y	Y	Y	Y	Y	N
LOUISIANA								
1 ***Livingston***	?	?	?	?	?	?	+	−
2 Jefferson	?	?	Y	Y	Y	Y	N	Y
3 Tauzin	?	?	Y	Y	Y	Y	Y	N
4 Fields	Y	Y	Y	Y	Y	Y	N	Y
5 ***McCrery***	Y	Y	Y	Y	Y	Y	Y	N
6 ***Baker***	?	?	N	Y	Y	Y	Y	N
7 Hayes	Y	Y	Y	Y	Y	Y	Y	N
MAINE								
1 Andrews	Y	Y	Y	Y	Y	Y	N	N
2 ***Snowe***	Y	Y	N	Y	Y	Y	Y	N
MARYLAND								
1 ***Gilchrest***	Y	Y	N	Y	Y	Y	Y	N
2 ***Bentley***	Y	Y	N	Y	Y	Y	Y	N
3 Cardin	Y	Y	Y	Y	Y	Y	N	Y
4 Wynn	Y	Y	+	+	+	+	N	Y
5 Hoyer	Y	Y	Y	Y	Y	Y	N	Y
6 ***Bartlett***	Y	Y	N	Y	Y	Y	Y	N
7 Mfume	+	+	Y	Y	Y	Y	N	Y
8 ***Morella***	Y	Y	N	Y	Y	Y	Y	N
MASSACHUSETTS								
1 Olver	Y	Y	Y	Y	Y	Y	N	Y
2 Neal	Y	Y	Y	Y	Y	Y	N	Y
3 ***Blute***	Y	Y	N	Y	Y	Y	Y	N
4 Frank	Y	Y	Y	Y	Y	Y	N	Y
5 Meehan	Y	Y	Y	Y	Y	Y	N	Y
6 ***Torkildsen***	Y	Y	N	Y	Y	Y	Y	N
7 Markey	Y	Y	Y	Y	Y	Y	N	Y
8 Kennedy	Y	Y	Y	Y	Y	Y	N	Y
9 Moakley	Y	Y	?	Y	Y	Y	N	Y
10 Studds	Y	Y	Y	Y	Y	Y	N	Y
MICHIGAN								
1 Stupak	Y	Y	Y	Y	Y	Y	Y	Y
2 ***Hoekstra***	Y	Y	N	Y	Y	Y	Y	N
3 ***Ehlers***	Y	Y	N	Y	Y	Y	Y	N
4 ***Camp***	Y	Y	N	Y	Y	Y	Y	N
5 Barcia	Y	Y	Y	Y	Y	Y	Y	N
6 ***Upton***	Y	Y	N	Y	Y	Y	Y	N
7 ***Smith***	Y	Y	N	Y	Y	Y	Y	N
8 Carr	Y	Y	Y	Y	Y	Y	Y	N
9 Kildee	Y	Y	Y	Y	Y	Y	N	Y
10 Bonior	Y	Y	Y	Y	Y	Y	N	Y
11 ***Knollenberg***	Y	Y	N	Y	Y	Y	Y	N
12 Levin	Y	Y	Y	Y	Y	Y	N	Y
13 Ford	Y	?	?	Y	Y	Y	N	Y
14 Conyers	Y	Y	?	Y	Y	Y	N	Y
15 Collins	Y	Y	Y	Y	Y	Y	N	Y
16 Dingell	Y	Y	Y	Y	Y	Y	N	Y
MINNESOTA								
1 Penny	N	Y	Y	Y	Y	Y	Y	Y
2 Minge	Y	Y	Y	Y	Y	Y	Y	N
3 ***Ramstad***	Y	Y	N	Y	Y	Y	Y	N
4 Vento	Y	Y	?	Y	Y	Y	N	Y

	113	114	115	116	117	118	119	120
5 Sabo	Y	Y	?	Y	Y	Y	N	Y
6 ***Grams***	Y	Y	N	Y	Y	Y	Y	N
7 Peterson	Y	Y	Y	Y	Y	Y	Y	N
8 Oberstar	Y	Y	Y	Y	Y	Y	N	Y
MISSISSIPPI								
1 Whitten	?	?	?	?	?	?	N	Y
2 Thompson	Y	Y	Y	Y	Y	Y	N	Y
3 Montgomery	Y	Y	Y	Y	Y	Y	Y	Y
4 Parker	Y	Y	Y	Y	Y	Y	Y	Y
5 Taylor	Y	Y	N	Y	Y	Y	Y	N
MISSOURI								
1 Clay	?	?	N	Y	Y	Y	N	Y
2 ***Talent***	?	?	N	Y	Y	Y	Y	N
3 Gephardt	Y	Y	Y	Y	Y	Y	N	Y
4 Skelton	Y	Y	Y	Y	Y	Y	Y	N
5 Wheat	?	?	Y	Y	Y	Y	N	Y
6 Danner	Y	Y	Y	Y	Y	Y	Y	Y
7 ***Hancock***	Y	Y	N	Y	Y	Y	Y	N
8 ***Emerson***	Y	Y	N	Y	Y	Y	Y	N
9 Volkmer	Y	Y	Y	Y	Y	Y	Y	N
MONTANA								
AL Williams	Y	Y	?	Y	Y	Y	Y	N
NEBRASKA								
1 ***Bereuter***	Y	Y	N	Y	Y	Y	Y	N
2 Hoagland	Y	Y	Y	Y	Y	Y	N	Y
3 ***Barrett***	Y	Y	N	Y	Y	Y	Y	N
NEVADA								
1 Bilbray	Y	Y	Y	Y	Y	Y	N	Y
2 ***Vucanovich***	Y	Y	N	Y	Y	Y	Y	N
NEW HAMPSHIRE								
1 ***Zeliff***	Y	Y	N	Y	Y	Y	Y	N
2 Swett	?	?	Y	Y	Y	Y	N	Y
NEW JERSEY								
1 Andrews	Y	Y	Y	Y	Y	Y	Y	N
2 Hughes	Y	Y	Y	Y	Y	Y	N	Y
3 ***Saxton***	Y	Y	N	Y	Y	Y	Y	N
4 ***Smith***	Y	Y	Y	Y	Y	Y	Y	N
5 ***Roukema***	Y	Y	N	Y	Y	Y	Y	N
6 Pallone	Y	Y	Y	Y	Y	Y	N	Y
7 ***Franks***	Y	Y	N	Y	Y	Y	Y	N
8 Klein	Y	Y	Y	Y	Y	Y	Y	N
9 Torricelli	?	?	Y	Y	Y	Y	N	Y
10 Payne	?	?	Y	Y	Y	Y	N	Y
11 ***Gallo***	?	?	?	?	?	?	?	?
12 ***Zimmer***	Y	Y	N	Y	Y	Y	Y	N
13 Menendez	Y	Y	Y	Y	Y	Y	N	Y
NEW MEXICO								
1 ***Schiff***	Y	Y	N	Y	Y	Y	Y	N
2 ***Skeen***	Y	Y	N	Y	Y	Y	Y	N
3 Richardson	Y	Y	Y	Y	Y	Y	Y	Y
NEW YORK								
1 Hochbrueckner	Y	Y	Y	Y	Y	Y	N	Y
2 ***Lazio***	Y	Y	N	Y	Y	Y	Y	N
3 ***King***	Y	Y	N	Y	Y	Y	Y	N
4 ***Levy***	Y	Y	N	Y	Y	Y	Y	N
5 Ackerman	?	?	Y	Y	Y	Y	N	Y
6 Flake	Y	Y	Y	Y	Y	Y	N	Y
7 Manton	Y	Y	Y	Y	Y	Y	N	Y
8 Nadler	+	+	Y	Y	Y	Y	N	Y
9 Schumer	Y	Y	Y	Y	Y	Y	N	Y
10 Towns	?	?	Y	Y	Y	Y	N	Y
11 Owens	?	?	Y	Y	Y	Y	N	Y
12 Velazquez	Y	Y	Y	Y	Y	Y	N	Y
13 ***Molinari***	Y	Y	N	Y	Y	Y	Y	N
14 Maloney	Y	Y	Y	Y	Y	Y	N	Y
15 Rangel	Y	Y	Y	Y	Y	Y	N	Y
16 Serrano	Y	Y	Y	Y	Y	Y	N	Y
17 Engel	?	?	?	Y	Y	Y	N	Y
18 Lowey	?	?	Y	Y	Y	Y	N	Y
19 ***Fish***	?	?	?	?	?	?	?	?
20 ***Gilman***	Y	Y	Y	Y	Y	Y	Y	N
21 McNulty	Y	Y	Y	Y	Y	Y	Y	N
22 ***Solomon***	Y	Y	N	Y	Y	Y	Y	N
23 ***Boehlert***	Y	Y	N	Y	Y	Y	Y	N
24 ***McHugh***	?	?	N	Y	Y	Y	Y	N
25 ***Walsh***	?	?	N	Y	Y	Y	Y	N
26 Hinchey	Y	Y	Y	Y	Y	Y	N	Y
27 ***Paxon***	Y	Y	N	Y	Y	Y	Y	N
28 Slaughter	Y	Y	Y	Y	Y	Y	N	Y
29 LaFalce	Y	Y	Y	Y	Y	Y	N	Y
30 ***Quinn***	Y	Y	N	Y	?	?	Y	N
31 ***Houghton***	?	?	Y	Y	Y	Y	Y	N
NORTH CAROLINA								
1 Clayton	Y	Y	Y	Y	Y	Y	N	Y
2 Valentine	?	?	?	Y	Y	Y	Y	N

	113	114	115	116	117	118	119	120
3 Lancaster	Y	Y	Y	Y	Y	Y	Y	N
4 Price	Y	Y	Y	Y	Y	Y	N	Y
5 Neal	Y	Y	?	Y	Y	Y	Y	Y
6 ***Coble***	Y	Y	N	Y	Y	Y	Y	N
7 Rose	?	?	?	Y	Y	Y	N	Y
8 Hefner	?	?	Y	Y	Y	Y	N	Y
9 ***McMillan***	Y	Y	?	Y	Y	Y	Y	N
10 ***Ballenger***	Y	Y	N	Y	Y	Y	Y	N
11 ***Taylor***	Y	Y	N	Y	Y	Y	Y	N
12 Watt	Y	Y	Y	Y	Y	Y	N	Y
NORTH DAKOTA								
AL Pomeroy	Y	Y	Y	Y	Y	Y	Y	N
OHIO								
1 Mann	Y	Y	Y	Y	Y	Y	N	Y
2 ***Portman***	+	+	N	Y	Y	Y	Y	N
3 Hall	Y	Y	Y	Y	Y	Y	N	Y
4 ***Oxley***	Y	Y	N	Y	Y	Y	Y	N
5 ***Gillmor***	Y	Y	Y	Y	Y	Y	Y	N
6 Strickland	Y	Y	Y	Y	Y	Y	N	Y
7 ***Hobson***	Y	Y	N	Y	Y	Y	Y	N
8 ***Boehner***	Y	Y	N	Y	Y	Y	Y	N
9 Kaptur	?	?	Y	Y	Y	Y	Y	N
10 ***Hoke***	Y	Y	Y	Y	Y	Y	Y	N
11 Stokes	?	?	Y	?	?	?	N	Y
12 ***Kasich***	Y	Y	Y	Y	Y	Y	Y	N
13 Brown	Y	Y	Y	Y	Y	Y	Y	Y
14 Sawyer	Y	Y	Y	Y	Y	Y	N	Y
15 ***Pryce***	?	?	N	Y	Y	Y	Y	N
16 ***Regula***	Y	Y	N	Y	Y	Y	Y	N
17 Traficant	Y	Y	Y	Y	Y	Y	Y	N
18 Applegate	Y	Y	Y	Y	Y	Y	N	N
19 Fingerhut	Y	Y	Y	Y	Y	Y	Y	N
OKLAHOMA								
1 ***Inhofe***	Y	Y	N	Y	Y	Y	Y	N
2 Synar	Y	Y	Y	Y	Y	Y	N	Y
3 Brewster	Y	Y	Y	Y	Y	Y	Y	N
4 McCurdy	Y	Y	Y	Y	Y	Y	Y	N
5 ***Istook***	Y	Y	N	Y	Y	Y	Y	N
6 Vacancy								
OREGON								
1 Furse	Y	Y	Y	Y	Y	Y	N	Y
2 ***Smith***	Y	Y	N	Y	Y	Y	Y	N
3 Wyden	Y	Y	Y	Y	Y	Y	Y	N
4 DeFazio	Y	Y	Y	Y	Y	Y	N	Y
5 Kopetski	Y	Y	Y	Y	Y	Y	N	Y
PENNSYLVANIA								
1 Foglietta	?	?	Y	Y	Y	Y	N	Y
2 Blackwell	?	?	Y	?	Y	Y	N	?
3 Borski	Y	Y	Y	Y	Y	Y	Y	N
4 Klink	Y	Y	Y	Y	Y	Y	Y	N
5 ***Clinger***	Y	Y	Y	?	Y	Y	Y	N
6 Holden	Y	Y	Y	Y	Y	Y	Y	N
7 ***Weldon***	Y	Y	N	Y	Y	Y	Y	N
8 ***Greenwood***	Y	Y	Y	Y	Y	Y	Y	N
9 ***Shuster***	Y	Y	N	Y	Y	Y	Y	N
10 ***McDade***	?	?	N	Y	Y	Y	Y	N
11 Kanjorski	N	Y	Y	Y	Y	Y	Y	N
12 Murtha	?	?	Y	Y	Y	Y	Y	N
13 Margolies-Mezv.	?	?	Y	Y	Y	Y	N	Y
14 Coyne	Y	Y	Y	Y	Y	Y	N	Y
15 McHale	Y	Y	Y	Y	Y	Y	Y	N
16 ***Walker***	Y	Y	N	Y	Y	Y	Y	N
17 ***Gekas***	Y	Y	N	Y	Y	Y	Y	N
18 ***Santorum***	?	?	N	Y	Y	Y	Y	N
19 ***Goodling***	+	+	N	Y	Y	Y	Y	N
20 Murphy	?	?	N	Y	Y	Y	N	N
21 ***Ridge***	?	?	?	Y	Y	Y	Y	N
RHODE ISLAND								
1 ***Machtley***	Y	Y	Y	Y	Y	Y	Y	N
2 Reed	Y	Y	Y	Y	Y	Y	N	Y
SOUTH CAROLINA								
1 ***Ravenel***	Y	Y	N	Y	Y	Y	Y	N
2 ***Spence***	Y	Y	N	Y	Y	Y	Y	N
3 Derrick	Y	Y	Y	Y	Y	Y	N	Y
4 ***Inglis***	Y	Y	Y	Y	Y	Y	Y	N
5 Spratt	Y	Y	Y	Y	Y	Y	Y	Y
6 Clyburn	Y	Y	Y	Y	Y	Y	N	Y
SOUTH DAKOTA								
AL Johnson	Y	Y	Y	Y	Y	Y	Y	Y
TENNESSEE								
1 ***Quillen***	Y	Y	N	Y	Y	Y	Y	N
2 ***Duncan***	Y	Y	N	Y	Y	Y	Y	N
3 Lloyd	Y	Y	?	Y	Y	Y	Y	N
4 Cooper	?	?	Y	Y	Y	Y	Y	N
5 Clement	?	?	Y	Y	Y	Y	Y	N

	113	114	115	116	117	118	119	120
6 Gordon	Y	Y	Y	Y	Y	Y	Y	N
7 ***Sundquist***	?	?	N	Y	Y	Y	Y	N
8 Tanner	Y	Y	Y	Y	Y	Y	Y	N
9 Ford	?	?	?	Y	Y	Y	N	Y
TEXAS								
1 Chapman	?	?	Y	Y	Y	Y	Y	N
2 Wilson	Y	Y	Y	Y	Y	Y	N	Y
3 ***Johnson, Sam***	Y	Y	N	Y	Y	Y	Y	N
4 Hall	Y	Y	Y	Y	Y	Y	Y	N
5 Bryant	Y	Y	Y	Y	Y	Y	N	Y
6 ***Barton***	Y	Y	N	Y	Y	Y	Y	N
7 ***Archer***	Y	Y	N	Y	Y	Y	Y	N
8 ***Fields***	?	?	N	Y	Y	Y	Y	N
9 Brooks	Y	Y	Y	Y	Y	Y	N	Y
10 Pickle	Y	Y	Y	Y	Y	Y	N	Y
11 Edwards	Y	Y	Y	Y	Y	Y	Y	N
12 Geren	Y	Y	Y	Y	Y	Y	Y	N
13 Sarpalius	Y	Y	Y	Y	Y	Y	Y	N
14 Laughlin	Y	Y	Y	Y	Y	Y	N	Y
15 de la Garza	Y	Y	Y	Y	Y	Y	Y	N
16 Coleman	?	?	Y	Y	Y	Y	N	Y
17 Stenholm	Y	Y	Y	Y	Y	Y	Y	N
18 Washington	?	?	?	?	?	?	N	Y
19 ***Combest***	Y	Y	Y	Y	Y	Y	Y	N
20 Gonzalez	Y	Y	Y	Y	Y	Y	N	Y
21 ***Smith***	Y	Y	N	Y	Y	Y	Y	N
22 ***DeLay***	?	?	N	Y	Y	Y	Y	N
23 ***Bonilla***	Y	Y	N	Y	Y	Y	Y	N
24 Frost	Y	Y	Y	Y	Y	Y	N	Y
25 Andrews	Y	Y	Y	Y	Y	Y	N	Y
26 ***Armey***	Y	Y	N	Y	Y	Y	Y	N
27 Ortiz	Y	Y	Y	Y	Y	Y	Y	N
28 Tejeda	Y	Y	Y	Y	Y	Y	Y	N
29 Green	Y	Y	Y	Y	Y	Y	Y	Y
30 Johnson, E.B.	Y	Y	Y	Y	Y	Y	N	Y
UTAH								
1 ***Hansen***	Y	Y	N	Y	Y	Y	Y	N
2 Shepherd	Y	Y	Y	Y	Y	Y	Y	Y
3 Orton	Y	Y	Y	Y	Y	Y	Y	N
VERMONT								
AL *Sanders*	?	?	Y	Y	?	Y	N	Y
VIRGINIA								
1 ***Bateman***	Y	Y	Y	Y	Y	Y	Y	N
2 Pickett	Y	Y	Y	Y	Y	Y	Y	N
3 Scott	Y	Y	Y	Y	Y	Y	N	Y
4 Sisisky	Y	Y	Y	Y	Y	Y	Y	N
5 Payne	Y	Y	Y	Y	?	Y	Y	N
6 ***Goodlatte***	Y	Y	N	Y	Y	Y	Y	N
7 ***Bliley***	Y	Y	N	Y	Y	Y	Y	N
8 Moran	Y	Y	Y	Y	Y	Y	Y	N
9 Boucher	Y	Y	Y	Y	Y	Y	N	Y
10 ***Wolf***	Y	Y	N	Y	Y	Y	Y	N
11 Byrne	Y	Y	Y	Y	Y	Y	Y	N
WASHINGTON								
1 Cantwell	Y	Y	Y	Y	Y	Y	Y	N
2 Swift	Y	Y	Y	Y	Y	Y	N	Y
3 Unsoeld	Y	Y	Y	Y	Y	Y	N	Y
4 Inslee	Y	Y	Y	Y	Y	Y	Y	N
5 Foley								
6 Dicks	Y	Y	Y	Y	Y	Y	Y	Y
7 McDermott	Y	Y	Y	Y	Y	Y	N	Y
8 ***Dunn***	Y	Y	N	Y	Y	Y	Y	N
9 Kreidler	Y	Y	N	Y	Y	Y	Y	N
WEST VIRGINIA								
1 Mollohan	Y	Y	Y	Y	Y	Y	N	Y
2 Wise	Y	Y	Y	Y	Y	Y	N	Y
3 Rahall	Y	Y	Y	Y	Y	Y	N	Y
WISCONSIN								
1 Barca	Y	Y	Y	Y	Y	Y	Y	N
2 ***Klug***	?	?	N	Y	Y	Y	Y	N
3 ***Gunderson***	?	?	N	Y	Y	Y	Y	N
4 Kleczka	?	?	Y	Y	Y	?	N	Y
5 Barrett	?	?	Y	Y	Y	Y	N	Y
6 ***Petri***	Y	Y	N	Y	Y	Y	Y	N
7 Obey	Y	Y	Y	Y	Y	Y	N	Y
8 ***Roth***	Y	Y	N	Y	Y	Y	Y	N
9 ***Sensenbrenner***	Y	Y	N	N	Y	Y	Y	N
WYOMING								
AL ***Thomas***	Y	Y	N	+	Y	Y	Y	N
DELEGATES								
de Lugo, V.I.	D	D	D	D	D	D	N	Y
Faleomavaega, Am.S.	D	D	D	D	D	D	?	?
Norton, D.C.	D	D	D	D	D	D	N	Y
Romero-B., P.R.	D	D	D	D	D	D	?	?
Underwood, Guam	D	D	D	D	D	D	N	?

Southern states - Ala., Ark., Fla., Ga., Ky., La., Miss., N.C., Okla., S.C., Tenn., Texas, Va.
Omitted votes are quorum calls, which CQ does not include in its vote charts.

121. HR 4092. Omnibus Crime Bill/Strike Enacting Clause. McCollum, R-Fla., motion to rise and report the bill back to the Rules Committee with the enacting clause stricken. The motion was an effort to offer amendments not made in order by the rule. Motion rejected in the Committee of the Whole 184-246: R 173-0; D 11-245 (ND 3-171, SD 8-74); I 0-1, April 19, 1994.

122. HR 4092. Omnibus Crime Bill/Three-Time Drug Offenders. Solomon, R-N.Y., amendment to allow a serious drug offense to count as a violent offense for the purpose of imprisoning three-time violent offenders for life. Adopted in the Committee of the Whole 303-126: R 172-1; D 131-124 (ND 75-100, SD 56-24); I 0-1, April 19, 1994. A "nay" was a vote in support of the president's position.

123. HR 4092. Omnibus Crime Bill/Strike Enacting Clause. McCollum, R-Fla., motion to rise and report the bill back to the Rules Committee with the enacting clause stricken. The motion was an effort to offer amendments not made in order by the rule. Motion rejected in the Committee of the Whole 180-245: R 171-0; D 9-244 (ND 4-169, SD 5-75); I 0-1, April 19, 1994.

124. HR 4092. Omnibus Crime Bill/Prison Construction Increase. Chapman, D-Texas, amendment to increase the authorization for grants to states for prison construction by $10.5 billion to $13.5 billion. The amendment would distribute 75 percent of the money based on a state's violent crime rate, and the other 25 percent would be distributed as an incentive for states to comply with "Truth in Sentencing Laws," which require long prison terms for violent offenders. Adopted in the Committee of the Whole 377-50: R 171-1; D 205-49 (ND 132-40, SD 73-9); I 1-0, April 19, 1994. A "yea" was a vote in support of the president's position.

125. HR 4092. Omnibus Crime Bill/Comprehensive Correctional Plan. Schiff, R-N.M., amendment to eliminate the bill's requirement that states have a comprehensive correctional plan that represents an integrated approach to the management and operation of correctional facilities and includes diversional programs. Rejected in the Committee of the Whole 205-216: R 162-9; D 43-206 (ND 14-155, SD 29-51); I 0-1, April 19, 1994.

126. HR 4092. Omnibus Crime Bill/Prison Construction. Hughes, D-N.J., substitute amendment to the McCollum, R-Fla., amendment, to authorize $3 billion over five years for state prison construction grants. The McCollum amendment would authorize $10 billion and condition the grants on the state enaction of "Truth in Sentencing Laws," which require long prison terms and pretrial detention for violent offenders. Adopted in the Committee of the Whole 215-206: R 2-170; D 212-36 (ND 153-16, SD 59-20); I 1-0, April 19, 1994. (Subsequently, the McCollum amendment as amended was adopted by voice vote.)

127. Procedural Motion. Approval of the House Journal of Tuesday, April 19. Approved 236-149: R 16-145; D 219-4 (ND 147-3, SD 72-1); I 1-0, April 20, 1994.

128. HR 2884. School-to-Work Opportunities/Conference Report. Adoption of the conference report to authorize $300 million for grant programs to help students make the transition from school to the workplace. Adopted 339-79: R 93-78; D 245-1 (ND 167-0, SD 78-1); I 1-0, April 20, 1994. A "yea" was a vote in support of the president's position.

	121	122	123	124	125	126	127	128
ALABAMA								
1 Callahan	Y	Y	Y	Y	Y	N	N	N
2 Everett	Y	Y	Y	Y	Y	N	Y	N
3 Browder	N	Y	N	Y	N	Y	N	Y
4 Bevill	N	Y	N	Y	N	Y	N	Y
5 Cramer	N	Y	N	Y	N	Y	N	Y
6 Bachus	Y	Y	Y	Y	Y	N	N	N
7 Hilliard	N	N	N	N	N	Y	Y	Y
ALASKA								
AL Young	Y	Y	Y	Y	Y	N	?	Y
ARIZONA								
1 Coppersmith	N	N	N	Y	N	Y	Y	Y
2 Pastor	N	Y	N	Y	N	Y	Y	Y
3 Stump	Y	Y	Y	Y	Y	N	N	N
4 Kyl	Y	Y	Y	Y	Y	N	N	N
5 Kolbe	Y	Y	Y	Y	Y	N	N	Y
6 English	N	Y	N	Y	N	Y	Y	Y
ARKANSAS								
1 Lambert	N	Y	N	Y	N	N	N	Y
2 Thornton	N	Y	N	Y	N	Y	Y	Y
3 Hutchinson	Y	Y	Y	Y	Y	N	Y	Y
4 Dickey	Y	Y	Y	Y	Y	N	N	N
CALIFORNIA								
1 Hamburg	N	N	N	Y	N	Y	Y	Y
2 Herger	Y	Y	Y	Y	Y	N	N	N
3 Fazio	N	N	N	Y	N	Y	Y	Y
4 Doolittle	Y	Y	Y	Y	Y	N	N	N
5 Matsui	N	N	N	Y	N	Y	Y	Y
6 Woolsey	N	N	N	Y	N	Y	Y	Y
7 Miller	N	N	N	N	N	Y	Y	Y
8 Pelosi	N	N	N	N	N	Y	Y	Y
9 Dellums	N	N	N	N	N	Y	?	Y
10 Baker	Y	Y	Y	Y	Y	N	N	N
11 Pombo	Y	Y	Y	Y	Y	N	Y	N
12 Lantos	N	Y	N	Y	N	Y	Y	Y
13 Stark	N	N	N	?	?	?	?	Y
14 Eshoo	N	N	N	Y	N	Y	Y	Y
15 Mineta	N	N	N	Y	N	Y	Y	Y
16 Edwards	N	N	N	Y	N	Y	Y	Y
17 Farr	N	N	N	Y	N	Y	Y	Y
18 Condit	N	Y	N	Y	N	Y	N	Y
19 Lehman	N	Y	N	Y	N	Y	Y	Y
20 Dooley	N	Y	N	Y	N	Y	N	Y
21 Thomas	Y	Y	Y	Y	Y	N	N	Y
22 Huffington	Y	Y	Y	Y	Y	N	?	Y
23 Gallegly	Y	Y	Y	Y	Y	N	N	Y
24 Beilenson	N	N	N	Y	N	Y	Y	Y
25 McKeon	Y	Y	Y	Y	Y	N	N	N
26 Berman	N	N	N	Y	N	Y	Y	Y
27 Moorhead	Y	Y	Y	Y	Y	N	N	N
28 Dreier	Y	Y	Y	Y	Y	N	N	N
29 Waxman	N	N	N	Y	N	Y	?	Y
30 Becerra	N	N	N	N	N	Y	Y	Y
31 Martinez	N	Y	N	Y	N	Y	Y	Y
32 Dixon	N	N	N	N	Y	N	?	Y
33 Roybal-Allard	N	N	N	Y	N	Y	Y	Y
34 Torres	N	Y	N	Y	N	Y	Y	Y
35 Waters	N	N	N	N	N	P	?	Y
36 Harman	N	Y	N	Y	N	Y	Y	Y
37 Tucker	N	N	N	N	N	Y	?	Y
38 Horn	Y	Y	Y	Y	Y	N	N	Y
39 Royce	Y	Y	Y	Y	Y	N	N	N
40 Lewis	Y	Y	Y	Y	Y	N	N	Y
41 Kim	Y	Y	Y	Y	Y	N	N	Y
42 Brown	N	N	N	Y	N	Y	?	Y
43 Calvert	Y	Y	Y	Y	N	N	N	Y
44 McCandless	Y	Y	Y	Y	Y	N	N	N
45 Rohrabacher	Y	N	Y	Y	Y	N	N	N
46 Dornan	Y	Y	Y	Y	Y	N	N	N
47 Cox	Y	Y	Y	Y	Y	N	N	N
48 Packard	Y	Y	Y	Y	Y	N	N	N
49 Schenk	N	Y	N	Y	N	Y	Y	Y
50 Filner	N	N	N	Y	N	Y	Y	Y
51 Cunningham	Y	Y	Y	Y	Y	N	N	N
52 Hunter	Y	Y	Y	Y	Y	N	N	N
COLORADO								
1 Schroeder	N	N	N	Y	N	Y	N	Y
2 Skaggs	N	N	N	N	Y	Y	Y	Y
3 McInnis	Y	Y	Y	Y	Y	N	?	N
4 Allard	Y	Y	Y	?	Y	Y	N	N
5 Hefley	Y	Y	Y	Y	Y	N	N	N
6 Schaefer	Y	Y	Y	Y	Y	N	N	N
CONNECTICUT								
1 Kennelly	N	N	N	Y	N	Y	Y	Y
2 Gejdenson	N	N	N	Y	N	Y	Y	Y
3 DeLauro	N	N	N	Y	N	Y	Y	Y
4 Shays	Y	Y	Y	Y	Y	N	N	Y
5 Franks	Y	Y	Y	Y	Y	N	N	Y
6 Johnson	Y	Y	Y	?	Y	N	?	Y
DELAWARE								
AL Castle	Y	Y	Y	Y	Y	N	N	Y
FLORIDA								
1 Hutto	Y	Y	Y	Y	Y	Y	Y	Y
2 Peterson	−	+	−	+	−	+	Y	Y
3 Brown	N	N	N	N	N	?	?	Y
4 Fowler	Y	Y	Y	Y	Y	N	N	Y
5 Thurman	N	Y	N	Y	N	Y	Y	Y
6 Stearns	Y	Y	Y	Y	Y	N	N	N
7 Mica	Y	Y	Y	Y	Y	N	N	N
8 McCollum	Y	Y	Y	Y	Y	N	N	N
9 Bilirakis	Y	Y	Y	Y	Y	N	N	Y
10 Young	Y	Y	Y	Y	Y	N	N	Y
11 Gibbons	N	Y	N	Y	Y	Y	Y	Y
12 Canady	Y	Y	Y	Y	Y	N	N	N
13 Miller	Y	Y	Y	Y	Y	N	N	Y
14 Goss	Y	Y	Y	Y	Y	N	N	?
15 Bacchus	N	Y	N	Y	N	Y	?	?
16 Lewis	Y	Y	Y	Y	Y	N	N	N
17 Meek	N	N	N	Y	N	Y	Y	Y
18 Ros-Lehtinen	Y	Y	Y	Y	Y	N	N	Y
19 Johnston	N	N	N	Y	N	Y	Y	Y
20 Deutsch	N	Y	N	Y	N	Y	Y	Y
21 Diaz-Balart	Y	Y	Y	Y	Y	N	N	Y
22 Shaw	Y	Y	Y	Y	Y	N	N	N
23 Hastings	N	N	N	Y	N	Y	Y	Y
GEORGIA								
1 Kingston	Y	Y	Y	Y	Y	N	Y	N
2 Bishop	N	Y	N	Y	N	Y	Y	N
3 Collins	Y	Y	Y	Y	Y	N	N	N
4 Linder	Y	Y	Y	?	Y	N	N	N
5 Lewis	N	N	N	Y	N	Y	Y	Y
6 Gingrich	Y	Y	Y	Y	Y	N	N	N
7 Darden	N	Y	N	Y	Y	Y	Y	Y
8 Rowland	N	Y	N	Y	Y	Y	Y	?
9 Deal	Y	Y	Y	Y	Y	N	N	Y
10 Johnson	N	Y	N	Y	Y	Y	Y	Y
11 McKinney	N	N	N	N	Y	Y	Y	Y
HAWAII								
1 Abercrombie	N	Y	N	Y	N	Y	Y	Y
2 Mink	N	N	N	Y	N	Y	Y	Y
IDAHO								
1 LaRocco	N	Y	N	Y	N	Y	Y	Y
2 Crapo	Y	Y	Y	Y	Y	N	N	N
ILLINOIS								
1 Rush	N	N	N	N	N	Y	Y	Y
2 Reynolds	N	Y	N	Y	N	Y	Y	Y
3 Lipinski	Y	Y	N	Y	N	Y	Y	Y
4 Gutierrez	N	N	N	Y	N	Y	Y	Y
5 Rostenkowski	N	Y	N	Y	N	Y	Y	Y
6 Hyde	Y	Y	Y	Y	Y	N	Y	N
7 Collins	?	X	X	?	X	#	?	Y
8 Crane	Y	Y	Y	Y	Y	N	N	N
9 Yates	N	N	N	N	Y	N	Y	Y
10 Porter	Y	Y	Y	Y	Y	N	N	Y
11 Sangmeister	N	Y	N	Y	N	Y	Y	Y
12 Costello	N	Y	N	Y	N	Y	Y	Y
13 Fawell	Y	Y	Y	Y	Y	N	N	N
14 Hastert	Y	Y	Y	Y	Y	N	N	N
15 Ewing	Y	Y	Y	Y	Y	N	N	Y
16 Manzullo	Y	Y	Y	Y	Y	N	N	N
17 Evans	N	N	N	Y	N	Y	Y	Y

ND   Northern Democrats   SD   Southern Democrats

	121	122	123	124	125	126	127	128
18 ***Michel***	Y	Y	Y	Y	Y	N	N	Y
19 Poshard	Y	Y	N	Y	N	Y	Y	Y
20 Durbin	N	Y	N	Y	N	Y	Y	Y
INDIANA								
1 Visclosky	N	N	N	Y	N	Y	Y	Y
2 Sharp	N	N	N	Y	?	Y	?	Y
3 Roemer	N	Y	N	Y	Y	N	Y	Y
4 Long	N	Y	N	Y	N	Y	Y	Y
5 ***Buyer***	Y	Y	?	Y	Y	N	N	Y
6 ***Burton***	Y	Y	Y	Y	Y	N	N	N
7 ***Myers***	Y	Y	Y	Y	Y	N	Y	Y
8 McCloskey	N	Y	N	Y	N	Y	Y	Y
9 Hamilton	N	Y	N	Y	N	Y	Y	Y
10 Jacobs	N	N	N	Y	N	Y	N	Y
IOWA								
1 ***Leach***	Y	Y	Y	Y	Y	N	?	Y
2 ***Nussle***	Y	Y	Y	Y	Y	N	N	Y
3 ***Lightfoot***	Y	Y	Y	Y	Y	N	N	N
4 Smith	N	N	N	Y	N	Y	Y	Y
5 ***Grandy***	?	#	?	?	#	X	?	?
KANSAS								
1 ***Roberts***	Y	Y	Y	Y	Y	N	N	N
2 Slattery	N	N	N	Y	N	Y	Y	Y
3 ***Meyers***	Y	Y	Y	Y	Y	N	?	Y
4 Glickman	N	N	N	Y	N	Y	Y	Y
KENTUCKY								
1 Barlow	N	Y	N	Y	N	Y	Y	Y
2 Vacancy								
3 Mazzoli	N	N	N	Y	N	Y	Y	Y
4 ***Bunning***	Y	Y	Y	Y	Y	N	N	N
5 ***Rogers***	Y	Y	Y	Y	Y	N	N	Y
6 Baesler	N	Y	N	Y	N	Y	Y	Y
LOUISIANA								
1 ***Livingston***	Y	Y	Y	Y	Y	N	Y	N
2 Jefferson	N	N	N	Y	N	Y	Y	Y
3 Tauzin	N	Y	N	Y	Y	N	Y	Y
4 Fields	N	N	N	N	N	Y	Y	Y
5 ***McCrery***	Y	Y	Y	Y	Y	N	?	Y
6 ***Baker***	Y	Y	Y	Y	Y	N	N	Y
7 Hayes	N	Y	N	Y	Y	N	Y	Y
MAINE								
1 Andrews	N	N	N	Y	N	Y	Y	Y
2 ***Snowe***	Y	Y	Y	Y	Y	N	Y	Y
MARYLAND								
1 ***Gilchrest***	Y	Y	Y	Y	Y	N	N	Y
2 ***Bentley***	Y	Y	Y	Y	Y	N	N	Y
3 Cardin	N	Y	N	N	N	Y	Y	Y
4 Wynn	N	N	N	Y	N	Y	Y	Y
5 Hoyer	N	Y	N	Y	N	Y	?	Y
6 ***Bartlett***	Y	Y	Y	Y	Y	N	N	N
7 Mfume	N	N	N	N	N	Y	Y	Y
8 ***Morella***	Y	Y	Y	Y	N	N	N	Y
MASSACHUSETTS								
1 Olver	N	N	N	N	N	Y	Y	Y
2 Neal	N	N	N	Y	N	Y	Y	Y
3 ***Blute***	Y	Y	Y	Y	Y	N	N	Y
4 Frank	?	N	N	N	N	Y	Y	Y
5 Meehan	N	N	N	Y	N	Y	Y	Y
6 ***Torkildsen***	Y	Y	Y	Y	Y	N	N	Y
7 Markey	N	N	N	Y	N	Y	Y	Y
8 Kennedy	N	N	N	Y	N	Y	Y	Y
9 Moakley	N	N	N	Y	N	Y	Y	Y
10 Studds	N	N	N	Y	N	Y	Y	Y
MICHIGAN								
1 Stupak	N	Y	Y	Y	N	Y	Y	Y
2 ***Hoekstra***	Y	Y	Y	Y	Y	N	N	Y
3 ***Ehlers***	Y	Y	Y	N	N	N	N	Y
4 ***Camp***	Y	Y	Y	Y	Y	N	N	Y
5 Barcia	N	Y	Y	Y	N	Y	Y	Y
6 ***Upton***	Y	Y	Y	Y	N	N	N	Y
7 ***Smith***	Y	Y	Y	Y	Y	N	N	Y
8 Carr	N	Y	N	Y	Y	Y	Y	Y
9 Kildee	N	N	N	Y	N	Y	Y	Y
10 Bonior	N	N	N	Y	N	Y	Y	Y
11 ***Knollenberg***	Y	Y	Y	Y	Y	N	N	N
12 Levin	N	N	N	Y	N	Y	Y	Y
13 Ford	N	N	N	N	?	?	Y	Y
14 Conyers	N	N	N	N	N	Y	Y	Y
15 Collins	N	N	N	N	N	Y	?	Y
16 Dingell	N	N	N	Y	N	Y	Y	Y
MINNESOTA								
1 Penny	N	Y	Y	N	N	Y	Y	Y
2 Minge	N	Y	N	N	N	Y	Y	Y
3 ***Ramstad***	Y	Y	Y	Y	Y	N	N	Y
4 Vento	N	N	N	Y	N	Y	Y	Y

	121	122	123	124	125	126	127	128
5 Sabo	N	N	N	N	N	Y	Y	Y
6 ***Grams***	Y	Y	Y	Y	Y	N	N	N
7 Peterson	N	Y	N	Y	Y	N	Y	Y
8 Oberstar	N	N	N	N	N	Y	Y	Y
MISSISSIPPI								
1 Whitten	N	Y	N	Y	N	Y	?	?
2 Thompson	N	N	N	Y	N	Y	Y	Y
3 Montgomery	N	Y	N	Y	N	N	Y	Y
4 Parker	N	Y	N	Y	N	N	Y	Y
5 Taylor	Y	Y	Y	Y	Y	N	N	N
MISSOURI								
1 Clay	N	N	N	N	N	Y	?	?
2 ***Talent***	Y	Y	Y	Y	Y	N	N	Y
3 Gephardt	N	N	N	Y	N	Y	Y	Y
4 Skelton	N	Y	N	Y	Y	Y	Y	Y
5 Wheat	N	Y	N	Y	N	Y	Y	Y
6 Danner	N	Y	N	Y	N	Y	Y	Y
7 ***Hancock***	Y	Y	Y	Y	Y	N	N	N
8 ***Emerson***	Y	Y	Y	Y	Y	N	N	Y
9 Volkmer	N	Y	N	Y	N	Y	Y	Y
MONTANA								
AL Williams	N	N	?	Y	N	Y	Y	Y
NEBRASKA								
1 ***Bereuter***	Y	Y	Y	Y	N	N	N	Y
2 Hoagland	N	Y	N	Y	N	Y	Y	Y
3 ***Barrett***	Y	Y	Y	Y	Y	N	N	N
NEVADA								
1 Bilbray	N	Y	N	Y	N	Y	?	Y
2 ***Vucanovich***	Y	Y	Y	Y	Y	N	N	Y
NEW HAMPSHIRE								
1 ***Zeliff***	Y	Y	Y	Y	Y	N	N	Y
2 Swett	N	Y	N	Y	Y	N	Y	Y
NEW JERSEY								
1 Andrews	N	Y	N	+	+	+	Y	Y
2 Hughes	N	N	N	Y	N	Y	Y	Y
3 ***Saxton***	Y	Y	Y	Y	Y	N	N	Y
4 ***Smith***	Y	Y	Y	Y	Y	N	Y	Y
5 ***Roukema***	Y	Y	Y	Y	Y	N	N	Y
6 Pallone	N	Y	N	Y	N	Y	Y	Y
7 ***Franks***	Y	Y	Y	Y	#	X	N	N
8 Klein	N	N	N	Y	N	Y	Y	Y
9 Torricelli	N	Y	N	Y	N	N	Y	Y
10 Payne	N	N	N	N	N	Y	Y	Y
11 ***Gallo***	?	?	?	?	?	?	?	?
12 ***Zimmer***	Y	Y	Y	Y	Y	N	N	N
13 Menendez	N	Y	N	Y	N	Y	Y	Y
NEW MEXICO								
1 ***Schiff***	Y	Y	Y	Y	Y	N	N	Y
2 ***Skeen***	Y	Y	Y	Y	Y	N	N	Y
3 Richardson	N	Y	N	Y	Y	N	Y	Y
NEW YORK								
1 Hochbrueckner	N	Y	N	Y	N	Y	Y	Y
2 ***Lazio***	Y	Y	Y	Y	Y	N	N	Y
3 ***King***	Y	Y	Y	Y	Y	N	N	N
4 ***Levy***	Y	Y	Y	Y	Y	N	N	Y
5 Ackerman	N	Y	N	Y	N	Y	Y	Y
6 Flake	N	N	N	N	N	Y	Y	Y
7 Manton	N	Y	N	Y	N	Y	?	Y
8 Nadler	N	N	N	N	N	Y	Y	Y
9 Schumer	N	N	N	Y	N	Y	Y	Y
10 Towns	N	N	N	N	N	Y	?	Y
11 Owens	N	N	N	N	N	Y	?	Y
12 Velazquez	N	N	N	N	N	Y	Y	Y
13 ***Molinari***	Y	Y	Y	Y	Y	N	N	Y
14 Maloney	N	N	N	Y	N	Y	Y	Y
15 Rangel	N	N	N	N	?	?	Y	Y
16 Serrano	N	N	N	N	N	Y	Y	Y
17 Engel	N	Y	N	Y	N	Y	?	?
18 Lowey	N	N	N	Y	N	Y	Y	Y
19 ***Fish***	?	?	?	?	?	?	?	?
20 ***Gilman***	Y	Y	Y	Y	N	N	N	Y
21 McNulty	N	N	N	Y	N	Y	?	?
22 ***Solomon***	Y	Y	Y	Y	Y	N	N	N
23 ***Boehlert***	Y	Y	Y	Y	Y	N	N	Y
24 ***McHugh***	Y	Y	Y	Y	Y	N	N	Y
25 ***Walsh***	Y	Y	Y	Y	Y	N	N	Y
26 Hinchey	N	N	N	Y	N	Y	Y	Y
27 ***Paxon***	Y	Y	Y	Y	Y	N	N	N
28 Slaughter	N	N	N	Y	N	Y	Y	Y
29 LaFalce	N	N	N	Y	N	Y	Y	Y
30 ***Quinn***	Y	Y	Y	Y	Y	N	N	Y
31 ***Houghton***	Y	Y	Y	Y	Y	N	Y	Y
NORTH CAROLINA								
1 Clayton	N	N	N	Y	N	Y	Y	Y
2 Valentine	Y	Y	Y	Y	Y	Y	Y	Y

	121	122	123	124	125	126	127	128
3 Lancaster	Y	Y	Y	Y	N	Y	Y	Y
4 Price	N	Y	N	Y	N	Y	Y	Y
5 Neal	N	N	?	Y	N	Y	?	Y
6 ***Coble***	Y	Y	Y	Y	Y	N	N	N
7 Rose	N	?	N	Y	?	Y	Y	Y
8 Hefner	N	Y	N	Y	N	Y	?	Y
9 ***McMillan***	Y	Y	Y	Y	Y	N	?	Y
10 ***Ballenger***	Y	Y	Y	Y	Y	N	N	N
11 ***Taylor***	Y	Y	Y	Y	Y	N	N	N
12 Watt	N	N	N	N	N	Y	Y	Y
NORTH DAKOTA								
AL Pomeroy	N	Y	N	Y	N	Y	Y	Y
OHIO								
1 Mann	N	N	N	Y	N	Y	Y	Y
2 ***Portman***	Y	Y	Y	Y	Y	N	N	Y
3 Hall	N	Y	N	Y	N	Y	Y	Y
4 ***Oxley***	Y	Y	Y	Y	Y	N	N	N
5 ***Gillmor***	Y	Y	Y	Y	Y	N	Y	Y
6 Strickland	N	Y	N	Y	N	Y	Y	Y
7 ***Hobson***	Y	Y	Y	Y	Y	N	N	Y
8 ***Boehner***	Y	Y	Y	Y	Y	N	N	N
9 Kaptur	N	Y	#	?	X	#	?	?
10 ***Hoke***	Y	Y	Y	Y	Y	N	N	N
11 Stokes	N	N	N	N	N	Y	Y	Y
12 ***Kasich***	Y	Y	Y	Y	Y	N	Y	Y
13 Brown	N	Y	N	Y	N	Y	Y	Y
14 Sawyer	N	N	N	Y	N	Y	Y	Y
15 ***Pryce***	Y	Y	Y	Y	Y	N	N	Y
16 ***Regula***	Y	Y	Y	Y	Y	N	N	Y
17 Traficant	Y	Y	Y	Y	N	N	Y	Y
18 Applegate	N	N	N	Y	N	Y	Y	Y
19 Fingerhut	N	Y	N	Y	N	Y	Y	Y
OKLAHOMA								
1 ***Inhofe***	Y	Y	Y	Y	Y	N	N	N
2 Synar	N	N	N	N	N	Y	Y	Y
3 Brewster	N	Y	N	Y	?	N	Y	Y
4 McCurdy	N	Y	N	Y	N	N	Y	Y
5 ***Istook***	Y	Y	Y	Y	Y	N	N	N
6 Vacancy								
OREGON								
1 Furse	N	N	N	Y	N	Y	?	Y
2 ***Smith***	Y	Y	Y	Y	Y	N	N	Y
3 Wyden	N	Y	N	Y	N	Y	Y	Y
4 DeFazio	N	N	N	Y	N	Y	Y	Y
5 Kopetski	N	N	N	Y	N	Y	?	Y
PENNSYLVANIA								
1 Foglietta	N	N	N	N	N	Y	Y	Y
2 Blackwell	N	N	N	N	N	Y	Y	Y
3 Borski	N	Y	N	Y	N	Y	Y	Y
4 Klink	N	Y	N	Y	N	N	Y	Y
5 ***Clinger***	Y	Y	Y	Y	N	N	?	Y
6 Holden	N	Y	N	Y	Y	N	Y	Y
7 ***Weldon***	Y	Y	Y	Y	Y	N	N	Y
8 ***Greenwood***	Y	Y	Y	Y	N	N	Y	Y
9 ***Shuster***	Y	Y	Y	Y	Y	N	?	N
10 ***McDade***	Y	Y	Y	Y	Y	N	?	?
11 Kanjorski	N	N	N	N	N	Y	Y	Y
12 Murtha	N	Y	N	Y	N	Y	Y	Y
13 Margolies-Mezv.	N	Y	N	Y	N	N	Y	Y
14 Coyne	N	N	N	Y	N	Y	Y	Y
15 McHale	N	Y	N	Y	N	N	Y	Y
16 ***Walker***	Y	Y	Y	Y	Y	N	N	N
17 ***Gekas***	Y	Y	Y	Y	Y	N	N	N
18 ***Santorum***	Y	Y	Y	Y	Y	N	N	Y
19 ***Goodling***	Y	Y	Y	Y	Y	N	N	Y
20 Murphy	N	Y	N	Y	Y	N	N	Y
21 ***Ridge***	Y	Y	Y	Y	Y	N	?	?
RHODE ISLAND								
1 ***Machtley***	Y	Y	Y	Y	Y	N	N	Y
2 Reed	N	N	N	Y	N	Y	Y	Y
SOUTH CAROLINA								
1 ***Ravenel***	Y	Y	Y	Y	Y	N	N	Y
2 ***Spence***	Y	Y	Y	Y	Y	N	N	Y
3 Derrick	N	N	N	Y	N	Y	Y	Y
4 ***Inglis***	Y	Y	Y	Y	Y	Y	Y	N
5 Spratt	N	Y	N	Y	N	Y	Y	Y
6 Clyburn	N	N	N	Y	N	Y	?	Y
SOUTH DAKOTA								
AL Johnson	N	Y	N	Y	N	Y	Y	Y
TENNESSEE								
1 ***Quillen***	Y	Y	Y	Y	Y	N	N	Y
2 ***Duncan***	Y	Y	Y	Y	Y	N	N	N
3 Lloyd	N	Y	N	Y	Y	Y	Y	Y
4 Cooper	Y	Y	N	Y	Y	Y	Y	Y
5 Clement	N	Y	N	Y	N	?	Y	Y

	121	122	123	124	125	126	127	128
6 Gordon	N	Y	N	Y	Y	Y	Y	Y
7 ***Sundquist***	Y	Y	Y	Y	Y	N	N	Y
8 Tanner	Y	Y	N	Y	Y	Y	Y	Y
9 Ford	N	N	N	Y	Y	Y	?	Y
TEXAS								
1 Chapman	N	Y	N	Y	N	Y	?	Y
2 Wilson	N	Y	N	Y	N	Y	Y	Y
3 ***Johnson, Sam***	Y	Y	Y	Y	Y	N	N	N
4 Hall	Y	Y	N	Y	Y	N	Y	Y
5 Bryant	N	Y	N	Y	N	Y	Y	Y
6 ***Barton***	Y	Y	Y	Y	Y	N	N	Y
7 ***Archer***	Y	Y	Y	Y	Y	N	N	N
8 ***Fields***	Y	Y	Y	Y	Y	N	N	N
9 Brooks	N	N	N	Y	N	Y	Y	Y
10 Pickle	N	N	N	Y	Y	?	Y	Y
11 Edwards	N	Y	N	Y	N	Y	Y	Y
12 Geren	N	Y	N	Y	Y	N	Y	Y
13 Sarpalius	N	Y	N	Y	N	Y	Y	Y
14 Laughlin	N	N	N	Y	N	Y	Y	Y
15 de la Garza	N	Y	N	Y	N	Y	Y	Y
16 Coleman	N	Y	N	Y	N	Y	Y	Y
17 Stenholm	N	Y	N	Y	Y	N	Y	Y
18 Washington	N	?	?	N	N	Y	?	?
19 ***Combest***	Y	Y	Y	Y	Y	N	Y	N
20 Gonzalez	N	N	N	Y	N	Y	Y	Y
21 ***Smith***	Y	Y	Y	Y	Y	N	N	Y
22 ***DeLay***	Y	Y	Y	Y	Y	N	N	N
23 ***Bonilla***	Y	Y	Y	Y	Y	N	N	Y
24 Frost	N	Y	N	Y	N	Y	?	Y
25 Andrews	N	Y	N	Y	Y	Y	Y	Y
26 ***Armey***	Y	Y	Y	Y	Y	N	N	N
27 Ortiz	N	Y	N	Y	Y	Y	Y	Y
28 Tejeda	N	Y	N	Y	Y	Y	Y	Y
29 Green	N	Y	N	Y	N	Y	Y	Y
30 Johnson, E.B.	N	N	N	Y	N	Y	Y	Y
UTAH								
1 ***Hansen***	Y	Y	Y	Y	Y	N	N	N
2 Shepherd	N	Y	N	Y	N	Y	Y	Y
3 Orton	N	Y	N	Y	Y	Y	Y	Y
VERMONT								
AL *Sanders*	N	N	N	Y	N	Y	Y	Y
VIRGINIA								
1 ***Bateman***	Y	Y	Y	Y	Y	N	Y	Y
2 Pickett	N	Y	N	Y	N	Y	Y	Y
3 Scott	N	N	N	N	N	Y	Y	Y
4 Sisisky	N	Y	N	Y	Y	N	Y	Y
5 Payne	N	Y	N	Y	Y	N	Y	Y
6 ***Goodlatte***	Y	Y	Y	Y	Y	N	N	N
7 ***Bliley***	Y	Y	Y	Y	Y	N	N	Y
8 Moran	N	Y	N	Y	Y	N	Y	Y
9 Boucher	N	Y	N	Y	N	Y	?	Y
10 ***Wolf***	Y	Y	Y	Y	N	N	N	Y
11 Byrne	N	Y	N	Y	N	Y	Y	Y
WASHINGTON								
1 Cantwell	N	Y	N	Y	N	Y	Y	Y
2 Swift	N	N	N	N	N	Y	?	?
3 Unsoeld	N	N	N	Y	N	Y	Y	Y
4 Inslee	N	Y	N	Y	N	Y	Y	Y
5 Foley								
6 Dicks	N	Y	N	Y	N	Y	Y	Y
7 McDermott	N	N	N	N	N	Y	Y	Y
8 ***Dunn***	Y	Y	Y	Y	Y	N	N	N
9 Kreidler	N	Y	N	Y	N	Y	Y	Y
WEST VIRGINIA								
1 Mollohan	N	Y	N	N	N	Y	Y	Y
2 Wise	N	Y	N	Y	N	Y	Y	Y
3 Rahall	N	Y	N	Y	N	Y	Y	Y
WISCONSIN								
1 Barca	N	Y	N	Y	N	N	Y	Y
2 ***Klug***	Y	Y	Y	Y	Y	N	N	N
3 ***Gunderson***	Y	Y	Y	Y	Y	N	N	Y
4 Kleczka	N	N	N	Y	Y	Y	Y	Y
5 Barrett	N	N	N	Y	N	Y	Y	Y
6 ***Petri***	Y	Y	Y	Y	Y	N	N	Y
7 Obey	N	N	N	N	N	Y	Y	Y
8 ***Roth***	Y	Y	Y	Y	Y	N	N	Y
9 ***Sensenbrenner***	Y	Y	Y	Y	Y	N	N	N
WYOMING								
AL ***Thomas***	Y	Y	Y	Y	Y	N	N	Y
DELEGATES								
de Lugo, V.I.	N	Y	N	Y	N	Y	D	D
Faleomavaega, Am.S.	?	?	?	?	?	?	D	D
Norton, D.C.	N	N	N	N	N	Y	D	D
Romero-B., P.R.	N	Y	N	Y	N	Y	D	D
Underwood, Guam	N	N	N	N	N	Y	D	D

Southern states - Ala., Ark., Fla., Ga., Ky., La., Miss., N.C., Okla., S.C., Tenn., Texas, Va.
Omitted votes are quorum calls, which CQ does not include in its vote charts.

129. H Res 329. O'Neill Year/Passage. Rose, D-N.C., motion to suspend the rules and pass the resolution to designate 1994 as a year to honor the memory and leadership qualities of Thomas P. O'Neill Jr., the late Speaker of the House. Motion agreed to 416-2: R 166-2; D 249-0 (ND 168-0, SD 81-0); I 1-0, April 20, 1994. A two-thirds majority of those present and voting (279 in this case) is required for passage under suspension of the rules.

130. HR 4092. Omnibus Crime Bill/En Bloc Amendment. Brooks, D-Texas, en bloc amendment to restrict the rights of prisoners to sue; restrict disclosure of motor vehicle records; require federal reimbursement for the cost of imprisoning undocumented criminal aliens; allow law enforcement officials access to criminal histories in cases of stalking and domestic violence; and prohibit prisoner strength-building programs. Adopted in the Committee of the Whole 402-22: R 169-1; D 232-21 (ND 160-14, SD 72-7); I 1-0, April 20, 1994.

131. HR 4092. Omnibus Crime Bill/Racial Justice. McCollum, R-Fla., amendment to delete the provisions that allow the use of statistical evidence to make a claim of racial discrimination by inmates seeking to overturn death sentences. The amendment would have substituted provisions banning the use of such statistics and required jurors to sign certificates in death penalty cases that race had not been a factor in their deliberations. Rejected in the Committee of the Whole 212-217: R 164-5; D 48-211 (ND 16-161, SD 32-50); I 0-1, April 20, 1994.

132. HR 4092. Omnibus Crime Bill/Strike Enacting Clause. McCollum, R-Fla., motion to rise and report the bill back to the Rules Committee with the enacting clause stricken. The motion was an effort to offer amendments not made in order by the rule. Motion rejected in the Committee of the Whole 179-250: R 172-0; D 7-249 (ND 4-171, SD 3-78); I 0-1, April 20, 1994.

133. HR 4092. Omnibus Crime Bill/Child Pornography. Smith, R-N.J., amendment to express the sense of the House that the Justice Department repudiate its interpretation of federal child pornography laws and vigorously prosecute sexual exploitation of children. Adopted in the Committee of the Whole 425-3: R 172-0; D 252-3 (ND 171-2, SD 81-1); I 1-0, April 20, 1994.

134. HR 4092. Omnibus Crime Bill/Border Patrols. Hunter, R-Calif., amendment to authorize the hiring of 6,000 Border Patrol agents and necessary support staff over the next five years. Adopted in the Committee of the Whole 417-12: R 172-0; D 244-12 (ND 167-8, SD 77-4); I 1-0, April 20, 1994.

135. HR 4092. Omnibus Crime Bill/Made in America. Traficant, D-Ohio, amendment to establish penalties for those convicted of fraudulently labeling products as "Made in America." Adopted in the Committee of the Whole 310-116: R 129-43; D 180-73 (ND 118-56, SD 62-17); I 1-0, April 20, 1994.

136. HR 4092. Omnibus Crime Bill/Pell Grants. Gordon, D-Tenn., amendment to prohibit awarding Pell grants to federal and state prisoners. Adopted in the Committee of the Whole 312-116: R 165-6; D 147-109 (ND 91-83, SD 56-26); I 0-1, April 20, 1994. A "nay" was a vote in support of the president's position.

KEY

Y	Voted for (yea).
#	Paired for.
+	Announced for.
N	Voted against (nay).
X	Paired against.
−	Announced against.
P	Voted "present."
C	Voted "present" to avoid possible conflict of interest.
?	Did not vote or otherwise make a position known.
D	Delegates ineligible to vote.

Democrats ***Republicans***
Independent

	129	130	131	132	133	134	135	136
ALABAMA								
1 *Callahan*	Y	Y	Y	Y	Y	Y	Y	Y
2 *Everett*	Y	Y	Y	Y	Y	Y	Y	Y
3 Browder	Y	Y	N	Y	Y	Y	Y	Y
4 Bevill	Y	Y	Y	N	Y	Y	Y	Y
5 Cramer	Y	Y	N	Y	Y	Y	Y	Y
6 *Bachus*	Y	Y	Y	Y	Y	Y	Y	Y
7 Hilliard	Y	N	N	N	Y	N	Y	N
ALASKA								
AL *Young*	Y	Y	?	Y	Y	Y	Y	Y
ARIZONA								
1 Coppersmith	Y	Y	N	N	Y	Y	N	Y
2 Pastor	Y	Y	N	N	Y	Y	N	Y
3 *Stump*	?	Y	Y	Y	Y	Y	N	Y
4 *Kyl*	Y	Y	Y	Y	Y	Y	N	Y
5 *Kolbe*	Y	Y	Y	Y	Y	Y	N	Y
6 English	Y	Y	N	Y	Y	Y	N	Y
ARKANSAS								
1 Lambert	Y	Y	N	N	Y	Y	Y	Y
2 Thornton	Y	Y	N	N	Y	Y	Y	Y
3 *Hutchinson*	Y	Y	Y	Y	Y	Y	Y	Y
4 *Dickey*	Y	Y	Y	Y	Y	Y	Y	Y
CALIFORNIA								
1 Hamburg	Y	Y	N	N	Y	Y	N	N
2 *Herger*	Y	Y	Y	Y	Y	Y	Y	Y
3 Fazio	Y	Y	N	N	Y	Y	Y	Y
4 *Doolittle*	Y	Y	Y	Y	Y	Y	Y	Y
5 Matsui	Y	Y	N	N	Y	Y	N	N
6 Woolsey	Y	Y	N	N	Y	Y	N	N
7 Miller	Y	Y	N	N	Y	Y	N	N
8 Pelosi	Y	Y	N	N	Y	Y	N	N
9 Dellums	Y	N	N	N	Y	N	N	N
10 *Baker*	Y	Y	Y	Y	Y	Y	Y	Y
11 *Pombo*	Y	Y	Y	Y	Y	Y	Y	Y
12 Lantos	Y	Y	N	N	Y	Y	Y	Y
13 Stark	Y	Y	N	N	Y	Y	N	N
14 Eshoo	Y	Y	N	N	Y	Y	Y	Y
15 Mineta	Y	Y	N	N	Y	Y	N	N
16 Edwards	Y	Y	N	N	N	Y	N	N
17 Farr	Y	Y	N	N	Y	Y	N	N
18 Condit	Y	Y	N	Y	Y	Y	Y	Y
19 Lehman	Y	Y	N	Y	Y	Y	N	Y
20 Dooley	Y	Y	N	Y	Y	Y	Y	Y
21 *Thomas*	Y	Y	Y	Y	Y	Y	N	Y
22 *Huffington*	Y	Y	Y	Y	Y	Y	Y	Y
23 *Gallegly*	Y	Y	Y	Y	Y	Y	Y	Y
24 Beilenson	Y	Y	N	N	Y	Y	N	N
25 *McKeon*	Y	Y	Y	Y	Y	Y	N	Y
26 Berman	Y	Y	N	N	Y	Y	N	N
27 *Moorhead*	Y	Y	Y	Y	Y	Y	Y	Y
28 *Dreier*	Y	Y	Y	Y	Y	Y	N	Y
29 Waxman	Y	Y	N	N	Y	Y	N	N
30 Becerra	Y	Y	N	N	Y	Y	N	N
31 Martinez	Y	Y	N	Y	Y	Y	?	N
32 Dixon	Y	Y	N	N	Y	Y	N	N
33 Roybal-Allard	Y	Y	N	N	Y	Y	N	N
34 Torres	Y	Y	N	N	Y	Y	N	N
35 Waters	Y	Y	N	N	Y	Y	Y	−
36 Harman	Y	Y	N	N	Y	Y	Y	Y
37 Tucker	Y	Y	N	N	Y	Y	N	N
38 *Horn*	Y	Y	Y	Y	Y	Y	Y	Y
39 *Royce*	Y	Y	Y	Y	Y	Y	N	Y
40 *Lewis*	Y	Y	Y	Y	Y	Y	N	Y
41 *Kim*	Y	Y	Y	Y	Y	Y	Y	Y

	129	130	131	132	133	134	135	136
42 Brown	Y	Y	N	N	Y	Y	N	N
43 *Calvert*	Y	Y	Y	Y	Y	Y	Y	Y
44 *McCandless*	Y	Y	Y	Y	Y	Y	N	Y
45 *Rohrabacher*	Y	Y	Y	Y	Y	Y	Y	Y
46 *Dornan*	Y	Y	Y	Y	Y	Y	Y	Y
47 *Cox*	Y	Y	Y	Y	Y	Y	N	Y
48 *Packard*	Y	Y	Y	Y	Y	Y	Y	Y
49 Schenk	Y	Y	N	N	Y	Y	Y	Y
50 Filner	Y	Y	N	N	Y	Y	N	N
51 *Cunningham*	Y	Y	Y	Y	Y	Y	N	Y
52 *Hunter*	Y	Y	Y	Y	Y	Y	Y	Y
COLORADO								
1 Schroeder	Y	Y	N	N	Y	Y	N	Y
2 Skaggs	Y	Y	N	N	Y	Y	N	N
3 *McInnis*	Y	Y	Y	Y	Y	Y	Y	Y
4 *Allard*	Y	Y	Y	Y	Y	Y	Y	Y
5 *Hefley*	N	Y	Y	Y	Y	Y	Y	Y
6 *Schaefer*	Y	Y	Y	Y	Y	Y	Y	Y
CONNECTICUT								
1 Kennelly	Y	Y	N	Y	Y	?	Y	Y
2 Gejdenson	Y	Y	N	N	Y	Y	N	N
3 DeLauro	Y	Y	N	N	Y	Y	N	N
4 *Shays*	Y	Y	N	Y	Y	Y	Y	Y
5 *Franks*	Y	Y	Y	Y	Y	Y	Y	Y
6 *Johnson*	Y	Y	Y	Y	Y	Y	Y	Y
DELAWARE								
AL *Castle*	Y	Y	Y	Y	Y	Y	N	Y
FLORIDA								
1 Hutto	Y	Y	N	Y	Y	Y	Y	Y
2 Peterson	Y	Y	N	Y	Y	Y	Y	Y
3 Brown	Y	Y	N	N	Y	Y	N	N
4 *Fowler*	Y	Y	Y	Y	Y	Y	Y	Y
5 Thurman	Y	Y	N	Y	Y	Y	N	Y
6 *Stearns*	Y	Y	Y	Y	Y	Y	Y	Y
7 *Mica*	Y	Y	Y	Y	Y	Y	Y	Y
8 *McCollum*	Y	Y	Y	Y	Y	Y	Y	Y
9 *Bilirakis*	Y	Y	Y	Y	Y	Y	Y	Y
10 *Young*	Y	Y	Y	Y	Y	Y	Y	Y
11 Gibbons	Y	Y	N	N	Y	Y	N	Y
12 *Canady*	Y	Y	Y	Y	Y	Y	N	Y
13 *Miller*	Y	Y	Y	Y	Y	Y	Y	Y
14 *Goss*	Y	Y	Y	Y	Y	Y	N	Y
15 Bacchus	?	?	?	?	?	?	Y	Y
16 *Lewis*	Y	Y	Y	Y	Y	Y	N	Y
17 Meek	Y	N	N	N	Y	N	N	N
18 *Ros-Lehtinen*	Y	Y	Y	Y	Y	Y	Y	Y
19 Johnston	Y	Y	N	N	Y	Y	N	Y
20 Deutsch	Y	Y	N	Y	Y	Y	N	Y
21 *Diaz-Balart*	Y	Y	Y	Y	Y	Y	Y	Y
22 *Shaw*	Y	Y	Y	Y	Y	Y	Y	Y
23 Hastings	Y	N	N	N	Y	Y	N	N
GEORGIA								
1 *Kingston*	Y	Y	Y	Y	Y	Y	N	Y
2 Bishop	Y	Y	N	Y	Y	Y	Y	Y
3 *Collins*	Y	Y	Y	Y	Y	Y	Y	Y
4 *Linder*	Y	Y	Y	Y	Y	Y	Y	Y
5 Lewis	Y	Y	N	N	Y	Y	N	N
6 *Gingrich*	Y	Y	Y	Y	Y	Y	N	Y
7 *Darden*	Y	Y	Y	N	Y	Y	Y	Y
8 Rowland	Y	Y	Y	N	Y	Y	Y	Y
9 Deal	Y	Y	N	Y	Y	Y	Y	Y
10 Johnson	Y	Y	Y	Y	Y	Y	N	Y
11 McKinney	Y	N	N	N	Y	N	N	N
HAWAII								
1 Abercrombie	Y	Y	N	N	Y	Y	N	N
2 Mink	Y	Y	N	N	Y	Y	N	N
IDAHO								
1 LaRocco	Y	Y	N	N	Y	Y	N	Y
2 *Crapo*	Y	Y	Y	Y	Y	Y	Y	Y
ILLINOIS								
1 Rush	Y	−	N	N	Y	Y	N	N
2 Reynolds	Y	Y	N	N	Y	Y	N	N
3 Lipinski	Y	Y	Y	Y	Y	Y	Y	Y
4 Gutierrez	Y	Y	N	N	Y	Y	Y	?
5 Rostenkowski	Y	Y	N	N	Y	Y	Y	Y
6 *Hyde*	Y	Y	Y	Y	Y	Y	N	Y
7 Collins	Y	N	N	N	+	Y	Y	N
8 *Crane*	Y	Y	Y	Y	Y	Y	Y	?
9 Yates	Y	N	N	N	Y	Y	N	N
10 *Porter*	Y	Y	Y	Y	Y	Y	N	Y
11 Sangmeister	Y	Y	N	Y	Y	Y	N	Y
12 Costello	Y	Y	N	N	Y	Y	Y	Y
13 *Fawell*	Y	Y	Y	Y	Y	Y	N	Y
14 *Hastert*	Y	Y	Y	Y	Y	Y	Y	Y
15 *Ewing*	Y	Y	Y	Y	Y	Y	Y	Y
16 *Manzullo*	Y	Y	Y	Y	Y	Y	N	Y
17 Evans	?	Y	N	N	Y	Y	N	Y

	129	130	131	132	133	134	135	136
18 ***Michel***	Y	Y	Y	Y	Y	Y	N	Y
19 Poshard	Y	Y	N	N	Y	Y	N	Y
20 Durbin	Y	Y	N	N	Y	Y	N	Y
INDIANA								
1 Visclosky	Y	Y	N	N	Y	Y	Y	Y
2 Sharp	Y	Y	N	N	Y	Y	Y	N
3 Roemer	Y	Y	N	N	Y	Y	Y	Y
4 Long	Y	Y	N	N	Y	Y	Y	Y
5 ***Buyer***	Y	Y	Y	Y	Y	Y	Y	Y
6 ***Burton***	Y	Y	Y	Y	Y	Y	Y	Y
7 ***Myers***	Y	Y	Y	Y	Y	Y	Y	Y
8 McCloskey	Y	Y	N	N	Y	Y	Y	N
9 Hamilton	Y	Y	N	N	Y	Y	Y	Y
10 Jacobs	Y	Y	N	N	Y	Y	Y	N
IOWA								
1 ***Leach***	Y	Y	Y	Y	Y	Y	Y	Y
2 ***Nussle***	Y	Y	Y	Y	Y	Y	Y	Y
3 ***Lightfoot***	Y	Y	Y	Y	Y	Y	Y	Y
4 Smith	Y	Y	N	N	Y	Y	N	Y
5 ***Grandy***	?	?	#	?	?	?	?	#
KANSAS								
1 ***Roberts***	Y	Y	Y	Y	Y	Y	N	Y
2 Slattery	Y	Y	N	N	Y	Y	Y	Y
3 ***Meyers***	Y	Y	Y	Y	Y	Y	Y	Y
4 Glickman	Y	Y	N	N	Y	Y	N	Y
KENTUCKY								
1 Barlow	Y	Y	N	?	Y	Y	Y	Y
2 Vacancy								
3 Mazzoli	Y	Y	Y	N	Y	Y	Y	Y
4 ***Bunning***	Y	Y	Y	Y	Y	Y	Y	Y
5 ***Rogers***	Y	Y	Y	Y	Y	Y	Y	Y
6 Baesler	Y	Y	Y	N	Y	Y	N	Y
LOUISIANA								
1 ***Livingston***	Y	Y	Y	Y	Y	Y	Y	Y
2 Jefferson	Y	Y	N	N	Y	Y	N	N
3 Tauzin	Y	Y	Y	N	Y	Y	Y	Y
4 Fields	Y	Y	N	N	Y	Y	Y	N
5 ***McCrery***	Y	Y	Y	Y	Y	Y	N	Y
6 ***Baker***	Y	Y	Y	Y	Y	Y	N	Y
7 Hayes	Y	Y	Y	Y	Y	Y	Y	Y
MAINE								
1 Andrews	Y	Y	N	N	Y	Y	Y	N
2 ***Snowe***	Y	Y	Y	Y	Y	Y	Y	Y
MARYLAND								
1 ***Gilchrest***	Y	Y	Y	Y	Y	Y	N	Y
2 ***Bentley***	Y	Y	Y	Y	Y	Y	Y	Y
3 Cardin	Y	Y	N	N	Y	Y	N	N
4 Wynn	Y	Y	N	N	Y	Y	N	N
5 Hoyer	Y	Y	N	N	Y	Y	Y	Y
6 ***Bartlett***	Y	Y	Y	Y	Y	Y	Y	Y
7 Mfume	Y	Y	N	N	Y	Y	Y	N
8 ***Morella***	Y	Y	N	Y	Y	Y	Y	Y
MASSACHUSETTS								
1 Olver	Y	Y	N	N	Y	Y	Y	N
2 Neal	Y	Y	N	N	Y	Y	Y	Y
3 ***Blute***	Y	Y	Y	Y	Y	Y	Y	Y
4 Frank	Y	N	N	N	Y	N	N	N
5 Meehan	Y	Y	N	N	Y	Y	Y	Y
6 ***Torkildsen***	Y	Y	Y	Y	Y	Y	Y	Y
7 Markey	Y	Y	N	N	Y	Y	Y	N
8 Kennedy	Y	Y	N	N	Y	Y	Y	N
9 Moakley	Y	Y	N	N	Y	Y	Y	Y
10 Studds	Y	Y	N	N	Y	Y	Y	N
MICHIGAN								
1 Stupak	Y	Y	N	Y	Y	Y	Y	Y
2 ***Hoekstra***	Y	Y	Y	Y	Y	Y	N	Y
3 ***Ehlers***	Y	Y	Y	Y	Y	Y	Y	Y
4 ***Camp***	Y	Y	Y	Y	Y	Y	Y	Y
5 Barcia	Y	Y	N	N	Y	Y	Y	Y
6 ***Upton***	Y	Y	Y	Y	Y	Y	Y	Y
7 ***Smith***	Y	Y	Y	Y	Y	Y	N	Y
8 Carr	Y	Y	N	N	?	Y	Y	Y
9 Kildee	Y	Y	N	N	Y	Y	Y	N
10 Bonior	Y	Y	N	N	Y	Y	Y	N
11 ***Knollenberg***	Y	Y	Y	Y	Y	Y	N	Y
12 Levin	Y	Y	N	N	Y	Y	Y	N
13 Ford	Y	Y	N	N	Y	Y	Y	N
14 Conyers	Y	N	N	N	Y	Y	Y	N
15 Collins	Y	N	N	N	Y	N	Y	N
16 Dingell	Y	Y	N	N	Y	Y	Y	Y
MINNESOTA								
1 Penny	Y	Y	N	N	Y	N	N	Y
2 Minge	Y	Y	N	Y	Y	Y	N	Y
3 ***Ramstad***	Y	Y	Y	Y	Y	Y	Y	Y
4 Vento	Y	Y	N	N	Y	Y	Y	N

	129	130	131	132	133	134	135	136
5 Sabo	Y	N	N	N	Y	N	N	N
6 ***Grams***	Y	Y	Y	Y	Y	Y	Y	Y
7 Peterson	Y	Y	Y	N	Y	N	Y	Y
8 Oberstar	Y	Y	N	N	Y	Y	Y	Y
MISSISSIPPI								
1 Whitten	Y	Y	N	N	Y	?	?	?
2 Thompson	Y	N	N	N	Y	Y	Y	N
3 Montgomery	Y	Y	Y	N	Y	Y	Y	Y
4 Parker	Y	Y	N	N	Y	Y	Y	Y
5 Taylor	Y	Y	Y	Y	Y	Y	Y	Y
MISSOURI								
1 Clay	Y	N	N	N	Y	Y	Y	N
2 ***Talent***	Y	Y	Y	Y	Y	Y	Y	Y
3 Gephardt	Y	Y	N	N	Y	Y	Y	N
4 Skelton	Y	Y	N	N	Y	Y	Y	Y
5 Wheat	Y	Y	N	N	Y	Y	Y	N
6 Danner	Y	Y	N	N	Y	Y	Y	Y
7 ***Hancock***	Y	Y	Y	Y	Y	Y	Y	Y
8 ***Emerson***	Y	Y	Y	Y	Y	Y	Y	Y
9 Volkmer	Y	Y	N	N	Y	Y	Y	Y
MONTANA								
AL Williams	Y	Y	N	N	Y	Y	?	Y
NEBRASKA								
1 ***Bereuter***	Y	Y	Y	Y	Y	Y	N	Y
2 Hoagland	Y	Y	N	N	Y	Y	Y	Y
3 ***Barrett***	Y	Y	Y	Y	Y	Y	Y	Y
NEVADA								
1 Bilbray	Y	Y	Y	N	Y	Y	Y	Y
2 ***Vucanovich***	Y	Y	Y	Y	Y	Y	N	Y
NEW HAMPSHIRE								
1 ***Zeliff***	Y	N	Y	Y	Y	Y	N	Y
2 Swett	Y	Y	N	N	Y	Y	Y	Y
NEW JERSEY								
1 Andrews	Y	Y	N	N	Y	Y	Y	Y
2 Hughes	Y	Y	N	N	Y	Y	N	N
3 ***Saxton***	Y	Y	Y	Y	Y	Y	Y	Y
4 ***Smith***	Y	Y	Y	Y	Y	Y	Y	Y
5 ***Roukema***	Y	Y	Y	Y	Y	Y	Y	Y
6 Pallone	Y	Y	N	N	Y	Y	Y	Y
7 ***Franks***	Y	Y	Y	Y	Y	Y	Y	Y
8 Klein	Y	Y	N	N	Y	Y	Y	Y
9 Torricelli	Y	Y	N	N	Y	Y	Y	Y
10 Payne	Y	N	N	N	Y	Y	Y	N
11 ***Gallo***	?	?	?	?	?	?	?	?
12 ***Zimmer***	Y	Y	Y	Y	Y	Y	N	Y
13 Menendez	Y	Y	N	N	Y	Y	Y	Y
NEW MEXICO								
1 ***Schiff***	Y	Y	Y	Y	Y	Y	Y	Y
2 ***Skeen***	Y	Y	Y	Y	Y	Y	Y	Y
3 Richardson	Y	Y	N	N	Y	Y	Y	Y
NEW YORK								
1 Hochbrueckner	Y	Y	N	N	Y	Y	Y	Y
2 ***Lazio***	Y	Y	Y	Y	Y	Y	Y	Y
3 ***King***	Y	Y	Y	Y	Y	Y	N	Y
4 ***Levy***	Y	Y	Y	Y	Y	Y	Y	Y
5 Ackerman	Y	Y	N	N	Y	Y	Y	Y
6 Flake	Y	Y	N	N	Y	Y	Y	N
7 Manton	Y	Y	N	N	Y	Y	Y	Y
8 Nadler	Y	Y	N	N	N	Y	N	N
9 Schumer	Y	Y	N	N	Y	Y	N	Y
10 Towns	Y	Y	N	N	Y	Y	N	N
11 Owens	Y	N	N	N	Y	Y	Y	N
12 Velazquez	Y	Y	N	N	Y	Y	Y	N
13 ***Molinari***	Y	Y	Y	Y	Y	Y	Y	Y
14 Maloney	Y	Y	N	N	Y	Y	Y	Y
15 Rangel	Y	Y	N	?	Y	Y	Y	N
16 Serrano	Y	Y	N	N	Y	Y	Y	N
17 Engel	?	Y	N	N	Y	Y	Y	N
18 Lowey	Y	Y	N	N	Y	Y	N	Y
19 ***Fish***	?	?	X	?	?	?	?	?
20 ***Gilman***	Y	Y	Y	Y	Y	Y	Y	Y
21 McNulty	?	?	?	?	?	?	?	X
22 ***Solomon***	Y	Y	Y	Y	Y	Y	Y	Y
23 ***Boehlert***	Y	Y	N	Y	Y	Y	Y	Y
24 ***McHugh***	Y	Y	Y	Y	Y	Y	Y	Y
25 ***Walsh***	Y	Y	N	Y	Y	Y	Y	N
26 Hinchey	Y	Y	N	N	Y	Y	Y	N
27 ***Paxon***	Y	Y	Y	Y	Y	Y	N	Y
28 Slaughter	Y	Y	N	N	Y	Y	N	N
29 LaFalce	Y	Y	N	N	Y	Y	N	Y
30 ***Quinn***	Y	Y	N	Y	Y	Y	Y	Y
31 ***Houghton***	?	?	?	Y	Y	Y	Y	N
NORTH CAROLINA								
1 Clayton	Y	N	N	N	Y	Y	Y	N
2 Valentine	Y	Y	N	N	Y	Y	N	Y

	129	130	131	132	133	134	135	136
3 Lancaster	Y	Y	Y	N	Y	Y	Y	Y
4 Price	Y	Y	N	N	Y	Y	Y	N
5 Neal	Y	Y	N	N	Y	Y	?	Y
6 ***Coble***	Y	Y	Y	Y	Y	Y	Y	Y
7 Rose	Y	Y	N	N	Y	Y	Y	Y
8 Hefner	Y	Y	N	N	Y	Y	Y	Y
9 ***McMillan***	Y	Y	Y	Y	Y	Y	Y	Y
10 ***Ballenger***	Y	Y	Y	Y	Y	Y	Y	Y
11 ***Taylor***	N	Y	Y	Y	Y	Y	Y	Y
12 Watt	Y	N	N	N	Y	N	N	N
NORTH DAKOTA								
AL Pomeroy	Y	Y	N	N	Y	Y	Y	Y
OHIO								
1 Mann	Y	Y	N	N	Y	Y	Y	N
2 ***Portman***	Y	Y	Y	Y	Y	Y	Y	Y
3 Hall	Y	Y	N	N	Y	Y	Y	N
4 ***Oxley***	Y	Y	Y	Y	Y	Y	N	Y
5 ***Gillmor***	Y	Y	Y	Y	Y	Y	Y	Y
6 Strickland	Y	Y	N	N	Y	Y	Y	N
7 ***Hobson***	Y	Y	Y	Y	Y	Y	Y	N
8 ***Boehner***	Y	Y	Y	Y	Y	Y	Y	Y
9 Kaptur	?	Y	N	N	Y	Y	Y	Y
10 ***Hoke***	Y	Y	Y	Y	Y	Y	Y	Y
11 Stokes	Y	N	N	N	Y	Y	Y	N
12 ***Kasich***	Y	Y	Y	Y	Y	Y	Y	Y
13 Brown	Y	Y	N	N	Y	Y	Y	Y
14 Sawyer	Y	Y	N	N	Y	Y	Y	N
15 ***Pryce***	Y	Y	Y	Y	Y	Y	Y	Y
16 ***Regula***	Y	Y	Y	Y	Y	Y	Y	Y
17 Traficant	Y	Y	N	Y	Y	Y	Y	Y
18 Applegate	Y	Y	N	N	Y	Y	Y	Y
19 Fingerhut	Y	Y	N	N	Y	Y	Y	Y
OKLAHOMA								
1 ***Inhofe***	Y	Y	Y	Y	Y	Y	Y	Y
2 Synar	Y	Y	N	N	Y	N	N	N
3 Brewster	Y	Y	Y	N	Y	Y	Y	Y
4 McCurdy	Y	Y	Y	N	Y	Y	N	Y
5 ***Istook***	?	Y	Y	Y	Y	Y	Y	Y
6 Vacancy								
OREGON								
1 Furse	Y	Y	N	N	Y	Y	Y	N
2 ***Smith***	Y	Y	Y	Y	Y	Y	Y	Y
3 Wyden	Y	Y	N	N	Y	Y	N	Y
4 DeFazio	Y	Y	N	N	Y	Y	Y	N
5 Kopetski	Y	N	N	N	Y	Y	N	N
PENNSYLVANIA								
1 Foglietta	Y	N	N	N	Y	Y	Y	N
2 Blackwell	Y	N	N	N	Y	Y	Y	N
3 Borski	Y	Y	Y	N	Y	Y	Y	Y
4 Klink	Y	Y	Y	N	Y	N	Y	Y
5 ***Clinger***	Y	Y	Y	Y	Y	Y	Y	Y
6 Holden	Y	Y	Y	N	Y	Y	Y	Y
7 ***Weldon***	Y	Y	Y	Y	Y	Y	Y	Y
8 ***Greenwood***	Y	Y	Y	Y	Y	Y	Y	N
9 ***Shuster***	Y	Y	Y	Y	Y	Y	Y	Y
10 ***McDade***	?	?	?	?	?	?	?	?
11 Kanjorski	Y	Y	Y	N	Y	Y	N	Y
12 Murtha	Y	Y	N	N	Y	Y	Y	Y
13 Margolies-Mezv.	Y	Y	Y	N	Y	Y	Y	Y
14 Coyne	Y	Y	N	N	Y	Y	Y	N
15 McHale	Y	Y	Y	N	Y	Y	Y	Y
16 ***Walker***	Y	Y	Y	Y	Y	Y	N	Y
17 ***Gekas***	Y	Y	Y	Y	Y	Y	Y	Y
18 ***Santorum***	Y	Y	Y	Y	Y	Y	Y	Y
19 ***Goodling***	Y	Y	Y	Y	Y	Y	Y	N
20 Murphy	Y	Y	Y	Y	Y	Y	Y	Y
21 ***Ridge***	?	?	?	Y	Y	Y	Y	Y
RHODE ISLAND								
1 ***Machtley***	Y	Y	Y	Y	Y	Y	Y	Y
2 Reed	Y	Y	N	N	Y	Y	N	N
SOUTH CAROLINA								
1 ***Ravenel***	Y	Y	Y	Y	Y	Y	Y	Y
2 ***Spence***	Y	Y	Y	Y	Y	Y	Y	Y
3 Derrick	Y	Y	N	N	Y	Y	Y	N
4 ***Inglis***	Y	Y	Y	Y	Y	Y	Y	Y
5 Spratt	Y	Y	N	N	Y	Y	Y	Y
6 Clyburn	Y	Y	N	N	Y	Y	Y	N
SOUTH DAKOTA								
AL Johnson	Y	Y	Y	N	Y	Y	Y	Y
TENNESSEE								
1 ***Quillen***	Y	Y	Y	Y	Y	Y	Y	N
2 ***Duncan***	Y	Y	Y	Y	Y	Y	Y	Y
3 Lloyd	Y	Y	Y	N	Y	Y	Y	Y
4 Cooper	Y	Y	N	N	Y	Y	Y	Y
5 Clement	Y	Y	Y	N	Y	Y	Y	Y

	129	130	131	132	133	134	135	136
6 Gordon	Y	Y	N	N	Y	Y	Y	Y
7 ***Sundquist***	Y	Y	Y	Y	Y	Y	Y	Y
8 Tanner	Y	Y	Y	N	Y	Y	Y	Y
9 Ford	Y	Y	N	N	Y	Y	Y	N
TEXAS								
1 Chapman	Y	Y	N	N	Y	Y	N	Y
2 Wilson	Y	Y	N	N	Y	Y	Y	N
3 ***Johnson, Sam***	Y	Y	Y	Y	Y	Y	N	Y
4 Hall	Y	Y	Y	Y	Y	Y	Y	Y
5 Bryant	Y	Y	N	N	Y	Y	?	Y
6 ***Barton***	Y	Y	Y	Y	Y	Y	N	Y
7 ***Archer***	Y	Y	Y	Y	Y	Y	N	Y
8 ***Fields***	Y	Y	Y	Y	Y	Y	Y	Y
9 Brooks	Y	Y	N	N	Y	Y	N	N
10 Pickle	Y	Y	N	N	Y	Y	N	N
11 Edwards	Y	Y	Y	N	Y	Y	Y	Y
12 Geren	Y	Y	Y	N	Y	Y	Y	Y
13 Sarpalius	Y	Y	Y	N	Y	Y	Y	Y
14 Laughlin	Y	?	Y	N	Y	Y	Y	Y
15 de la Garza	Y	Y	N	N	Y	Y	Y	Y
16 Coleman	Y	Y	N	N	Y	Y	N	Y
17 Stenholm	Y	Y	Y	N	Y	Y	Y	Y
18 Washington	?	?	N	N	N	?	?	N
19 ***Combest***	Y	Y	Y	Y	Y	Y	Y	Y
20 Gonzalez	Y	Y	N	N	Y	N	N	N
21 ***Smith***	Y	Y	Y	Y	Y	Y	Y	Y
22 ***DeLay***	Y	Y	Y	Y	Y	Y	N	Y
23 ***Bonilla***	Y	Y	Y	Y	Y	Y	Y	Y
24 Frost	Y	Y	N	N	Y	Y	Y	Y
25 Andrews	Y	Y	N	N	Y	Y	Y	Y
26 ***Armey***	Y	Y	Y	Y	Y	Y	N	Y
27 Ortiz	Y	Y	N	N	Y	Y	Y	Y
28 Tejeda	Y	Y	N	N	Y	Y	Y	Y
29 Green	Y	Y	N	N	Y	Y	Y	N
30 Johnson, E.B.	Y	Y	N	N	Y	Y	Y	N
UTAH								
1 ***Hansen***	Y	Y	Y	Y	Y	Y	Y	Y
2 Shepherd	Y	Y	N	N	Y	Y	Y	Y
3 Orton	Y	Y	Y	N	Y	Y	Y	Y
VERMONT								
AL *Sanders*	Y	Y	N	N	Y	Y	Y	N
VIRGINIA								
1 ***Bateman***	Y	Y	Y	Y	Y	Y	Y	Y
2 Pickett	Y	Y	Y	N	Y	Y	Y	Y
3 Scott	Y	Y	N	N	Y	Y	Y	N
4 Sisisky	Y	Y	Y	N	Y	Y	Y	Y
5 Payne	Y	?	Y	N	Y	Y	Y	Y
6 ***Goodlatte***	Y	Y	Y	Y	Y	Y	Y	Y
7 ***Bliley***	Y	Y	Y	Y	Y	Y	Y	Y
8 Moran	Y	Y	Y	N	Y	Y	Y	N
9 Boucher	Y	Y	N	N	Y	Y	Y	Y
10 ***Wolf***	Y	Y	Y	Y	Y	Y	Y	Y
11 Byrne	Y	Y	N	N	Y	Y	Y	Y
WASHINGTON								
1 Cantwell	Y	Y	N	N	Y	Y	N	Y
2 Swift	Y	Y	N	N	Y	N	N	N
3 Unsoeld	Y	Y	N	N	Y	Y	N	N
4 Inslee	Y	Y	N	N	Y	Y	Y	Y
5 Foley			N					
6 Dicks	Y	Y	N	N	Y	Y	N	Y
7 McDermott	Y	Y	N	N	Y	Y	N	N
8 ***Dunn***	Y	Y	Y	Y	Y	Y	Y	Y
9 Kreidler	Y	Y	N	N	Y	Y	Y	Y
WEST VIRGINIA								
1 Mollohan	Y	Y	N	N	Y	Y	Y	Y
2 Wise	Y	Y	N	N	Y	Y	Y	Y
3 Rahall	Y	Y	N	N	Y	Y	Y	Y
WISCONSIN								
1 Barca	Y	Y	N	N	Y	Y	Y	Y
2 ***Klug***	Y	Y	Y	Y	Y	Y	Y	Y
3 ***Gunderson***	Y	Y	Y	Y	Y	Y	N	Y
4 Kleczka	Y	Y	N	N	Y	Y	N	Y
5 Barrett	Y	Y	N	N	Y	Y	Y	Y
6 ***Petri***	Y	Y	Y	Y	Y	Y	Y	Y
7 Obey	Y	Y	N	N	Y	N	Y	Y
8 ***Roth***	Y	Y	Y	Y	Y	Y	Y	Y
9 ***Sensenbrenner***	Y	Y	Y	Y	Y	Y	N	Y
WYOMING								
AL ***Thomas***	Y	Y	Y	Y	Y	Y	N	Y
DELEGATES								
de Lugo, V.I.	D	?	N	N	Y	Y	Y	N
Faleomavaega, Am.S.	D	Y	N	N	Y	Y	Y	Y
Norton, D.C.	D	Y	N	N	Y	Y	Y	N
Romero-B., P.R.	D	Y	N	N	Y	Y	Y	N
Underwood, Guam	D	Y	N	N	?	Y	Y	N

Southern states - Ala., Ark., Fla., Ga., Ky., La., Miss., N.C., Okla., S.C., Tenn., Texas, Va.
Omitted votes are quorum calls, which CQ does not include in its vote charts.

137. HR 4092. Omnibus Crime Bill/Pell Grants. Wynn, D-Md., amendment to prohibit awarding Pell Grants to federal, state and local prisoners after Jan. 1, 1996, unless the secretary of Education certifies the grants reduce recidivism, are cost-effective, and the inmates make satisfactory progress toward completion of an education program. Rejected in the Committee of the Whole 162-263: R 15-154; D 146-109 (ND 105-68, SD 41-41); I 1-0, April 20, 1994.

138. HR 4092. Omnibus Crime Bill/Police Corps and Scholarships. McCurdy, D-Okla., amendment to authorize $100 million in fiscal 1995 and $250 million in fiscal 1996 for a police corps program that would provide up to $10,000 a year to individuals in return for a four-year commitment to serve in law enforcement, and authorize $30 million in each of fiscal 1995-99 for scholarships to current law enforcement personnel to further their education. Adopted in the Committee of the Whole 250-174: R 44-127; D 205-47 (ND 135-38, SD 70-9); I 1-0, April 20, 1994. A "yea" was a vote in support of the president's position.

139. HR 4092. Omnibus Crime Bill/Private Security Officers. Martinez, D-Calif., amendment to require states to establish minimum standards for background checks and training of private security officers. Rejected in the Committee of the Whole 80-340: R 4-165; D 76-174 (ND 61-110, SD 15-64); I 0-1, April 20, 1994.

140. Procedural Motion. Approval of the House Journal of Wednesday, April 20. Approved 256-161: R 18-154; D 237-7 (ND 161-6, SD 76-1); I 1-0, April 21, 1994.

141. HR 4092. Omnibus Crime Bill/Cocaine Penalty Study. Hughes, D-N.J., amendment to require the U.S. Sentencing Commission to submit a report on sentences with recommendations for the retention or modification of the different penalties for crack vs. powder cocaine. Adopted in the Committee of the Whole 424-0: R 169-0; D 254-0 (ND 174-0, SD 80-0); I 1-0, April 21, 1994.

142. HR 4092. Omnibus Crime Bill/Early Release Education Requirement. Franks, R-N.J., amendment to require prisoners to earn a high school diploma or an equivalent degree before they can be eligible for early release. Adopted in the Committee of the Whole 347-82: R 170-2; D 177-79 (ND 108-67, SD 69-12); I 0-1, April 21, 1994.

143. HR 4092. Omnibus Crime Bill/Motion to Recommit. McCollum, R-Fla., motion to recommit the bill to the Judiciary Committee with instructions to report it back with an amendment to delete the provisions of the bill that allow the use of statistical evidence to demonstrate a significant racially discriminatory pattern to overturn death sentences. Motion rejected 192-235: R 167-5; D 25-229 (ND 9-162, SD 16-67); I 0-1, April 21, 1994.

144. HR 4092. Omnibus Crime Bill/Passage. Passage of the bill to authorize more than $27.5 billion over six years for various anti-crime initiatives, including $13.5 billion for new prisons and more than $7 billion for crime prevention programs. The bill would require life imprisonment for three-time violent offenders, expand the death penalty to apply to dozens of federal crimes and authorize grants to hire 50,000 additional police officers. Passed 285-141: R 65-107; D 219-34 (ND 149-21, SD 70-13); I 1-0, April 21, 1994. A "yea" was a vote in support of the president's position.

KEY

Y   Voted for (yea).
Paired for.
+   Announced for.
N   Voted against (nay).
X   Paired against.
−   Announced against.
P   Voted "present."
C   Voted "present" to avoid possible conflict of interest.
?   Did not vote or otherwise make a position known.
D   Delegates ineligible to vote.

Democrats   *Republicans*   *Independent*

Member	137	138	139	140	141	142	143	144
ALABAMA								
1 *Callahan*	N	N	N	N	Y	Y	Y	N
2 *Everett*	N	N	N	N	Y	Y	Y	N
3 Browder	Y	Y	N	Y	Y	Y	Y	Y
4 Bevill	N	Y	N	Y	Y	Y	N	Y
5 Cramer	N	Y	N	Y	Y	Y	Y	N
6 *Bachus*	N	N	?	N	Y	Y	Y	N
7 Hilliard	Y	N	N	Y	Y	N	N	N
ALASKA								
AL *Young*	N	N	Y	N	Y	Y	Y	N
ARIZONA								
1 Coppersmith	N	Y	N	Y	Y	N	N	Y
2 Pastor	Y	Y	Y	Y	Y	N	N	Y
3 *Stump*	N	N	N	Y	Y	Y	Y	N
4 *Kyl*	N	N	N	Y	Y	Y	Y	N
5 *Kolbe*	N	N	N	Y	Y	Y	Y	N
6 English	Y	N	N	Y	Y	Y	N	Y
ARKANSAS								
1 Lambert	N	Y	N	Y	Y	Y	N	Y
2 Thornton	N	Y	N	Y	Y	Y	N	Y
3 *Hutchinson*	N	N	N	Y	Y	Y	Y	N
4 *Dickey*	N	N	N	N	?	Y	Y	N
CALIFORNIA								
1 Hamburg	Y	N	N	Y	Y	N	N	Y
2 *Herger*	N	N	N	Y	Y	Y	Y	N
3 Fazio	Y	Y	Y	Y	Y	Y	N	Y
4 *Doolittle*	N	N	N	Y	Y	Y	Y	N
5 Matsui	Y	?	?	Y	Y	Y	N	Y
6 Woolsey	Y	Y	Y	Y	Y	Y	N	Y
7 Miller	Y	Y	Y	Y	N	N	N	Y
8 Pelosi	Y	Y	N	Y	?	N	N	Y
9 Dellums	Y	N	N	Y	Y	N	N	Y
10 *Baker*	N	N	N	Y	Y	Y	Y	N
11 *Pombo*	N	Y	N	Y	Y	Y	Y	N
12 Lantos	N	Y	Y	Y	Y	Y	N	Y
13 Stark	Y	N	N	Y	Y	N	N	Y
14 Eshoo	N	Y	N	Y	Y	Y	N	Y
15 Mineta	Y	Y	N	Y	Y	Y	N	Y
16 Edwards	Y	N	N	Y	Y	N	N	Y
17 Farr	N	Y	Y	Y	Y	Y	N	Y
18 Condit	Y	Y	N	Y	Y	Y	Y	Y
19 Lehman	N	Y	N	Y	Y	Y	Y	Y
20 Dooley	N	N	N	Y	Y	Y	N	Y
21 *Thomas*	N	N	N	N	Y	Y	Y	N
22 *Huffington*	N	Y	N	N	Y	Y	Y	Y
23 *Gallegly*	N	Y	N	Y	Y	Y	Y	Y
24 Beilenson	Y	Y	N	Y	Y	Y	N	Y
25 *McKeon*	N	N	N	Y	Y	Y	Y	N
26 Berman	Y	Y	Y	Y	Y	N	N	Y
27 *Moorhead*	N	N	N	N	Y	Y	Y	N
28 *Dreier*	N	N	N	N	Y	Y	Y	N
29 Waxman	Y	Y	Y	Y	Y	N	N	Y
30 Becerra	Y	N	N	Y	Y	N	N	Y
31 Martinez	Y	Y	Y	Y	Y	Y	N	Y
32 Dixon	Y	Y	Y	Y	Y	N	N	Y
33 Roybal-Allard	Y	Y	Y	Y	Y	N	N	Y
34 Torres	?	Y	N	Y	Y	N	N	Y
35 Waters	+	+	+	Y	Y	N	N	N
36 Harman	Y	Y	N	Y	Y	Y	N	Y
37 Tucker	Y	Y	N	Y	Y	N	N	Y
38 Horn	N	Y	N	Y	Y	Y	N	Y
39 *Royce*	N	N	N	Y	Y	Y	Y	Y
40 *Lewis*	N	N	N	?	?	?	?	?
41 *Kim*	N	N	N	N	Y	Y	Y	N
42 Brown	?	Y	N	?	Y	N	N	Y
43 *Calvert*	N	Y	N	Y	Y	Y	Y	Y
44 *McCandless*	N	N	N	N	Y	Y	Y	Y
45 *Rohrabacher*	N	N	N	N	Y	Y	Y	N
46 *Dornan*	N	N	N	N	Y	Y	Y	N
47 *Cox*	N	N	N	Y	Y	Y	Y	N
48 *Packard*	N	N	N	N	Y	Y	Y	N
49 Schenk	N	Y	N	Y	Y	N	N	Y
50 Filner	Y	Y	N	Y	Y	N	N	Y
51 *Cunningham*	N	N	N	N	Y	Y	Y	N
52 *Hunter*	N	Y	N	N	Y	Y	Y	Y
COLORADO								
1 Schroeder	Y	Y	N	Y	Y	N	N	Y
2 Skaggs	Y	N	N	Y	Y	N	N	Y
3 *McInnis*	N	N	N	Y	Y	Y	Y	N
4 *Allard*	N	N	N	Y	Y	Y	Y	N
5 *Hefley*	N	N	N	Y	Y	Y	Y	N
6 *Schaefer*	N	N	N	Y	Y	Y	Y	N
CONNECTICUT								
1 Kennelly	Y	Y	Y	Y	Y	N	N	Y
2 Gejdenson	Y	Y	Y	Y	Y	N	N	Y
3 DeLauro	N	Y	Y	Y	Y	Y	N	Y
4 *Shays*	N	N	N	N	Y	Y	N	Y
5 *Franks*	N	N	N	N	Y	Y	Y	Y
6 *Johnson*	N	N	Y	N	Y	Y	Y	Y
DELAWARE								
AL *Castle*	Y	N	N	Y	Y	N	Y	N
FLORIDA								
1 Hutto	N	N	Y	N	Y	Y	Y	Y
2 Peterson	N	Y	N	Y	Y	Y	Y	Y
3 Brown	Y	Y	N	Y	Y	Y	Y	Y
4 *Fowler*	N	N	N	N	Y	Y	Y	N
5 Thurman	N	Y	N	Y	Y	Y	Y	Y
6 *Stearns*	N	N	N	N	Y	Y	Y	N
7 *Mica*	N	N	N	N	Y	Y	Y	N
8 *McCollum*	N	N	N	N	Y	Y	Y	N
9 *Bilirakis*	N	N	N	N	Y	Y	Y	N
10 *Young*	N	N	N	N	Y	Y	Y	N
11 Gibbons	N	?	?	Y	Y	Y	N	Y
12 *Canady*	N	N	N	N	Y	Y	Y	N
13 *Miller*	N	N	N	N	Y	Y	Y	N
14 *Goss*	N	N	N	N	Y	Y	Y	N
15 Bacchus	N	Y	Y	Y	Y	Y	Y	Y
16 *Lewis*	N	N	N	N	Y	Y	Y	N
17 Meek	Y	Y	N	Y	Y	N	N	Y
18 *Ros-Lehtinen*	N	N	N	N	Y	Y	Y	N
19 Johnston	Y	Y	Y	Y	?	Y	N	Y
20 Deutsch	N	Y	N	Y	Y	Y	N	Y
21 *Diaz-Balart*	N	Y	N	Y	Y	Y	Y	N
22 *Shaw*	N	N	N	N	Y	Y	Y	N
23 Hastings	Y	Y	N	Y	Y	N	N	N
GEORGIA								
1 *Kingston*	Y	N	N	Y	Y	Y	Y	N
2 Bishop	Y	Y	N	Y	Y	Y	Y	N
3 *Collins*	N	N	N	N	Y	Y	Y	N
4 *Linder*	N	N	N	N	Y	Y	Y	N
5 Lewis	Y	Y	Y	Y	Y	Y	N	Y
6 *Gingrich*	N	Y	N	N	Y	Y	Y	N
7 Darden	N	Y	N	Y	Y	Y	Y	N
8 Rowland	Y	Y	N	Y	Y	Y	Y	N
9 Deal	Y	Y	N	Y	Y	Y	Y	N
10 Johnson	Y	N	N	?	Y	Y	Y	N
11 McKinney	Y	Y	Y	Y	Y	Y	N	Y
HAWAII								
1 Abercrombie	Y	Y	Y	Y	Y	Y	N	Y
2 Mink	Y	Y	Y	Y	Y	Y	N	Y
IDAHO								
1 LaRocco	N	Y	N	Y	Y	Y	N	Y
2 *Crapo*	N	N	N	N	Y	Y	Y	N
ILLINOIS								
1 Rush	Y	Y	N	Y	Y	N	N	N
2 Reynolds	Y	Y	Y	Y	Y	Y	N	Y
3 Lipinski	N	Y	N	Y	Y	Y	Y	Y
4 Gutierrez	Y	Y	Y	Y	Y	N	N	Y
5 Rostenkowski	N	?	?	Y	Y	Y	N	Y
6 *Hyde*	N	Y	?	Y	Y	Y	N	Y
7 Collins	Y	N	Y	Y	Y	N	N	N
8 *Crane*	?	?	?	N	Y	Y	Y	N
9 Yates	Y	N	N	Y	Y	N	N	N
10 *Porter*	N	N	N	Y	Y	Y	N	Y
11 Sangmeister	Y	N	Y	Y	Y	Y	N	Y
12 Costello	N	Y	Y	Y	Y	Y	N	Y
13 *Fawell*	N	N	N	N	Y	Y	Y	N
14 *Hastert*	N	N	N	N	Y	Y	Y	N
15 *Ewing*	N	N	N	N	Y	Y	Y	N
16 *Manzullo*	N	N	N	N	Y	Y	Y	N
17 Evans	Y	Y	N	Y	Y	Y	N	Y

ND Northern Democrats   SD Southern Democrats

	137	138	139	140	141	142	143	144
18 ***Michel***	N	Y	N	N	Y	Y	Y	N
19 Poshard	N	Y	N	Y	Y	Y	N	Y
20 Durbin	N	Y	Y	Y	Y	Y	N	Y
INDIANA								
1 Visclosky	N	N	N	Y	Y	N	N	Y
2 Sharp	Y	Y	N	Y	Y	?	N	Y
3 Roemer	N	Y	N	Y	Y	Y	N	Y
4 Long	N	Y	N	Y	Y	Y	N	Y
5 ***Buyer***	N	N	N	N	Y	Y	Y	Y
6 ***Burton***	N	N	N	N	Y	Y	Y	N
7 ***Myers***	N	Y	N	Y	Y	Y	Y	N
8 McCloskey	N	Y	Y	Y	Y	Y	N	Y
9 Hamilton	N	Y	N	Y	Y	Y	N	Y
10 Jacobs	Y	N	N	N	Y	N	N	Y
IOWA								
1 ***Leach***	Y	Y	N	N	Y	Y	Y	Y
2 ***Nussle***	N	N	N	N	Y	Y	Y	N
3 ***Lightfoot***	N	Y	N	N	Y	Y	Y	N
4 Smith	N	N	N	Y	Y	Y	N	Y
5 ***Grandy***	X	X	?	?	?	?	?	?
KANSAS								
1 ***Roberts***	N	N	N	N	Y	Y	Y	N
2 Slattery	Y	N	?	Y	Y	Y	N	+
3 ***Meyers***	N	Y	N	N	Y	Y	Y	Y
4 Glickman	N	N	N	Y	Y	Y	N	Y
KENTUCKY								
1 Barlow	N	Y	N	Y	Y	Y	N	Y
2 Vacancy								
3 Mazzoli	N	Y	N	Y	Y	Y	N	Y
4 ***Bunning***	N	N	N	N	Y	Y	Y	N
5 ***Rogers***	N	N	N	N	Y	Y	Y	Y
6 Baesler	N	N	N	Y	Y	Y	N	Y
LOUISIANA								
1 ***Livingston***	N	N	N	N	Y	Y	Y	N
2 Jefferson	Y	Y	N	Y	Y	Y	N	Y
3 Tauzin	N	N	N	Y	Y	Y	Y	N
4 Fields	Y	Y	N	Y	Y	Y	N	Y
5 ***McCrery***	N	N	N	N	Y	Y	Y	N
6 ***Baker***	N	N	N	N	Y	Y	Y	N
7 Hayes	N	Y	N	Y	Y	Y	N	Y
MAINE								
1 Andrews	Y	Y	N	Y	Y	Y	N	N
2 ***Snowe***	N	N	N	N	Y	Y	Y	Y
MARYLAND								
1 ***Gilchrest***	N	N	N	N	Y	Y	Y	Y
2 ***Bentley***	N	Y	N	N	Y	Y	Y	Y
3 Cardin	Y	Y	N	Y	Y	N	N	Y
4 Wynn	Y	Y	N	Y	Y	Y	N	Y
5 Hoyer	Y	Y	N	Y	Y	Y	N	Y
6 ***Bartlett***	N	N	N	N	Y	Y	Y	N
7 Mfume	Y	Y	Y	Y	Y	N	N	Y
8 ***Morella***	N	Y	N	N	Y	Y	N	Y
MASSACHUSETTS								
1 Olver	Y	Y	N	Y	Y	N	N	Y
2 Neal	N	Y	N	Y	Y	Y	N	Y
3 ***Blute***	N	N	N	N	Y	Y	Y	Y
4 Frank	Y	Y	N	Y	Y	N	N	Y
5 Meehan	N	Y	N	Y	Y	Y	N	Y
6 ***Torkildsen***	N	N	N	N	Y	Y	Y	Y
7 Markey	Y	Y	N	Y	Y	Y	N	Y
8 Kennedy	Y	Y	Y	Y	Y	Y	N	Y
9 Moakley	N	Y	N	Y	Y	Y	N	Y
10 Studds	Y	Y	N	Y	Y	N	N	Y
MICHIGAN								
1 Stupak	N	Y	N	Y	Y	Y	N	Y
2 ***Hoekstra***	N	N	N	N	Y	Y	Y	N
3 ***Ehlers***	N	N	N	N	Y	Y	Y	N
4 ***Camp***	N	Y	N	N	+	Y	Y	Y
5 Barcia	N	Y	N	Y	Y	Y	Y	Y
6 ***Upton***	N	Y	N	N	Y	Y	Y	Y
7 ***Smith***	N	N	N	N	Y	Y	Y	N
8 Carr	N	Y	N	Y	Y	Y	N	Y
9 Kildee	Y	Y	N	Y	Y	Y	N	Y
10 Bonior	Y	Y	N	Y	Y	N	N	Y
11 ***Knollenberg***	N	N	N	N	Y	Y	Y	N
12 Levin	Y	Y	N	Y	Y	Y	N	Y
13 Ford	Y	N	Y	Y	Y	N	N	N
14 Conyers	Y	N	N	Y	Y	N	N	Y
15 Collins	Y	N	Y	Y	Y	N	N	N
16 Dingell	N	N	N	Y	Y	Y	N	Y
MINNESOTA								
1 Penny	N	Y	N	Y	Y	Y	N	N
2 Minge	N	N	N	Y	Y	Y	N	Y
3 ***Ramstad***	N	N	N	N	Y	Y	Y	Y
4 Vento	Y	Y	Y	Y	Y	Y	N	Y

	137	138	139	140	141	142	143	144
5 Sabo	Y	N	N	Y	Y	N	N	N
6 ***Grams***	N	N	N	N	Y	Y	Y	N
7 Peterson	N	Y	N	Y	Y	Y	N	Y
8 Oberstar	Y	N	N	Y	Y	N	N	N
MISSISSIPPI								
1 Whitten	?	?	?	?	?	?	N	Y
2 Thompson	Y	Y	N	Y	Y	Y	N	Y
3 Montgomery	Y	Y	N	Y	Y	Y	N	Y
4 Parker	N	Y	N	?	Y	Y	N	Y
5 Taylor	N	Y	N	N	Y	Y	Y	Y
MISSOURI								
1 Clay	Y	N	N	N	Y	N	N	N
2 ***Talent***	N	N	N	N	Y	Y	Y	Y
3 Gephardt	Y	Y	Y	Y	Y	Y	N	Y
4 Skelton	N	Y	N	Y	Y	Y	N	Y
5 Wheat	Y	Y	N	Y	Y	Y	N	Y
6 Danner	N	Y	N	Y	Y	Y	N	Y
7 ***Hancock***	N	N	N	N	Y	Y	Y	N
8 ***Emerson***	N	Y	N	N	Y	Y	Y	N
9 Volkmer	N	Y	N	N	Y	Y	N	Y
MONTANA								
AL Williams	Y	N	N	Y	Y	Y	N	Y
NEBRASKA								
1 ***Bereuter***	N	N	N	N	Y	Y	Y	N
2 Hoagland	N	N	N	Y	Y	Y	N	Y
3 ***Barrett***	N	N	N	N	Y	Y	Y	N
NEVADA								
1 Bilbray	N	Y	Y	Y	Y	Y	Y	Y
2 ***Vucanovich***	Y	Y	N	N	Y	Y	Y	N
NEW HAMPSHIRE								
1 ***Zeliff***	N	N	N	N	Y	Y	Y	N
2 Swett	Y	Y	N	Y	Y	Y	N	Y
NEW JERSEY								
1 Andrews	N	Y	Y	?		—	—	
2 Hughes	Y	N	N	Y	Y	N	N	Y
3 ***Saxton***	N	N	N	N	Y	Y	Y	N
4 ***Smith***	N	Y	N	Y	Y	Y	Y	Y
5 ***Roukema***	N	Y	Y	N	Y	Y	Y	Y
6 Pallone	N	Y	N	Y	Y	Y	N	Y
7 ***Franks***	N	N	N	N	Y	Y	Y	Y
8 Klein	N	Y	N	Y	Y	Y	N	Y
9 Torricelli	N	Y	Y	Y	Y	Y	N	Y
10 Payne	Y	Y	Y	Y	Y	N	N	N
11 ***Gallo***	?	?	?	?	?	?	?	?
12 ***Zimmer***	N	N	N	N	Y	Y	Y	N
13 Menendez	Y	Y	Y	Y	Y	Y	N	Y
NEW MEXICO								
1 ***Schiff***	N	Y	N	N	Y	Y	Y	N
2 ***Skeen***	N	Y	N	N	Y	Y	Y	N
3 Richardson	N	Y	N	Y	Y	Y	N	Y
NEW YORK								
1 Hochbrueckner	N	Y	Y	Y	Y	Y	N	Y
2 ***Lazio***	N	Y	N	N	Y	Y	Y	Y
3 ***King***	N	N	N	N	Y	Y	Y	N
4 ***Levy***	N	N	N	N	Y	Y	Y	Y
5 Ackerman	N	Y	?	Y	Y	Y	N	Y
6 Flake	Y	Y	N	Y	Y	N	N	Y
7 Manton	N	Y	N	Y	Y	Y	N	Y
8 Nadler	Y	Y	Y	Y	Y	N	N	Y
9 Schumer	Y	Y	N	Y	Y	N	N	Y
10 Towns	Y	Y	Y	Y	Y	N	N	Y
11 Owens	Y	Y	Y	Y	Y	N	N	N
12 Velazquez	Y	Y	Y	Y	Y	N	N	N
13 ***Molinari***	N	Y	N	N	Y	Y	Y	Y
14 Maloney	Y	Y	N	Y	Y	Y	N	Y
15 Rangel	Y	Y	Y	Y	Y	N	N	N
16 Serrano	Y	N	Y	Y	Y	N	N	N
17 Engel	Y	Y	Y	?	Y	N	N	Y
18 Lowey	Y	Y	N	Y	Y	Y	N	Y
19 ***Fish***	?	?	?	?	?	?	?	?
20 ***Gilman***	Y	Y	N	Y	Y	Y	Y	Y
21 McNulty	#	#	?	Y	Y	Y	N	Y
22 ***Solomon***	N	N	N	N	Y	Y	Y	N
23 ***Boehlert***	Y	N	N	N	Y	Y	N	Y
24 ***McHugh***	?	N	N	N	Y	Y	Y	Y
25 ***Walsh***	Y	N	N	N	Y	Y	N	Y
26 Hinchey	Y	Y	Y	Y	Y	Y	N	Y
27 ***Paxon***	N	N	N	N	Y	Y	Y	N
28 Slaughter	Y	Y	N	Y	Y	Y	N	Y
29 LaFalce	Y	Y	N	Y	Y	N	N	Y
30 ***Quinn***	N	N	N	N	Y	Y	N	Y
31 ***Houghton***	Y	Y	N	Y	Y	Y	Y	Y
NORTH CAROLINA								
1 Clayton	Y	Y	N	Y	Y	Y	N	Y
2 Valentine	N	Y	N	Y	Y	Y	N	Y

	137	138	139	140	141	142	143	144
3 Lancaster	N	Y	Y	Y	Y	Y	Y	Y
4 Price	Y	Y	N	Y	Y	Y	N	Y
5 Neal	N	Y	N	?	Y	Y	N	Y
6 ***Coble***	N	N	N	N	Y	Y	Y	N
7 Rose	Y	Y	N	Y	Y	Y	N	Y
8 Hefner	N	Y	N	Y	Y	Y	N	Y
9 ***McMillan***	N	Y	N	N	Y	Y	Y	N
10 ***Ballenger***	N	N	N	N	Y	Y	Y	N
11 ***Taylor***	N	N	N	N	Y	Y	Y	N
12 Watt	Y	Y	N	Y	Y	N	N	N
NORTH DAKOTA								
AL Pomeroy	Y	Y	N	Y	Y	Y	N	Y
OHIO								
1 Mann	Y	N	N	Y	Y	Y	N	Y
2 ***Portman***	N	N	N	N	Y	Y	Y	N
3 Hall	Y	Y	Y	Y	Y	Y	N	Y
4 ***Oxley***	N	Y	N	N	Y	Y	Y	N
5 ***Gillmor***	N	Y	N	Y	Y	N	Y	Y
6 Strickland	Y	Y	N	Y	Y	Y	N	Y
7 ***Hobson***	Y	Y	N	N	Y	Y	Y	Y
8 ***Boehner***	N	N	N	N	Y	Y	Y	N
9 Kaptur	N	Y	N	Y	Y	Y	N	Y
10 ***Hoke***	N	N	N	N	Y	Y	Y	N
11 Stokes	Y	N	N	Y	Y	N	N	N
12 ***Kasich***	N	N	N	Y	Y	Y	Y	Y
13 Brown	Y	Y	N	Y	Y	Y	N	Y
14 Sawyer	Y	Y	N	Y	Y	N	N	Y
15 ***Pryce***	N	N	N	N	Y	Y	Y	Y
16 ***Regula***	Y	Y	N	N	Y	Y	Y	Y
17 Traficant	N	N	Y	Y	Y	Y	N	Y
18 Applegate	N	Y	Y	Y	Y	Y	N	Y
19 Fingerhut	N	Y	N	Y	Y	Y	N	Y
OKLAHOMA								
1 ***Inhofe***	N	Y	N	N	Y	Y	Y	N
2 Synar	Y	N	N	Y	Y	N	N	Y
3 Brewster	N	Y	N	Y	Y	Y	N	Y
4 McCurdy	N	Y	N	Y	Y	Y	N	Y
5 ***Istook***	N	N	N	N	Y	Y	Y	N
6 Vacancy								
OREGON								
1 Furse	Y	Y	Y	Y	Y	Y	N	+
2 ***Smith***	N	Y	N	N	Y	Y	Y	N
3 Wyden	N	Y	N	Y	Y	Y	N	Y
4 DeFazio	N	Y	Y	Y	Y	N	N	Y
5 Kopetski	Y	N	Y	Y	Y	N	N	N
PENNSYLVANIA								
1 Foglietta	Y	Y	Y	Y	Y	N	N	Y
2 Blackwell	Y	Y	Y	Y	Y	N	N	Y
3 Borski	N	Y	Y	Y	Y	Y	N	Y
4 Klink	N	Y	Y	Y	Y	Y	Y	Y
5 ***Clinger***	N	Y	N	Y	Y	Y	Y	N
6 Holden	N	Y	Y	Y	Y	Y	Y	Y
7 ***Weldon***	N	Y	N	N	Y	Y	Y	Y
8 ***Greenwood***	Y	N	N	Y	Y	Y	Y	Y
9 ***Shuster***	N	Y	N	N	Y	Y	Y	N
10 ***McDade***	?	?	?	N	Y	Y	Y	Y
11 Kanjorski	N	Y	Y	Y	Y	Y	N	Y
12 Murtha	N	N	N	Y	Y	Y	N	Y
13 Margolies-Mezv.	N	Y	N	Y	Y	Y	Y	Y
14 Coyne	Y	N	N	Y	Y	N	N	Y
15 McHale	N	Y	Y	Y	Y	Y	N	Y
16 ***Walker***	N	N	N	N	Y	Y	Y	N
17 ***Gekas***	N	N	N	N	Y	Y	Y	N
18 ***Santorum***	N	Y	N	N	Y	Y	Y	Y
19 ***Goodling***	Y	N	N	N	Y	Y	Y	N
20 Murphy	N	Y	Y	N	Y	Y	N	Y
21 ***Ridge***	N	N	N	N	?	Y	Y	Y
RHODE ISLAND								
1 ***Machtley***	N	Y	N	N	Y	Y	Y	Y
2 Reed	Y	N	N	Y	Y	Y	N	Y
SOUTH CAROLINA								
1 ***Ravenel***	N	N	N	N	Y	Y	Y	Y
2 ***Spence***	N	N	N	N	Y	Y	Y	Y
3 Derrick	Y	Y	N	Y	Y	Y	N	Y
4 ***Inglis***	N	N	N	Y	Y	Y	Y	N
5 Spratt	Y	Y	N	Y	Y	Y	N	Y
6 Clyburn	Y	Y	N	Y	Y	N	N	Y
SOUTH DAKOTA								
AL Johnson	Y	Y	N	Y	Y	Y	N	Y
TENNESSEE								
1 ***Quillen***	Y	N	N	N	Y	Y	Y	Y
2 ***Duncan***	N	N	N	N	Y	Y	Y	N
3 Lloyd	N	Y	N	Y	Y	Y	Y	Y
4 Cooper	N	Y	N	Y	Y	Y	N	Y
5 Clement	N	Y	N	Y	Y	Y	N	Y

	137	138	139	140	141	142	143	144
6 Gordon	N	Y	N	Y	Y	Y	N	Y
7 ***Sundquist***	N	N	Y	N	Y	Y	Y	Y
8 Tanner	Y	Y	Y	Y	Y	Y	Y	Y
9 Ford	Y	?	Y	Y	Y	N	N	Y
TEXAS								
1 Chapman	N	Y	N	Y	Y	Y	N	Y
2 Wilson	Y	N	N	Y	Y	Y	N	Y
3 ***Johnson, Sam***	N	N	N	N	Y	Y	Y	N
4 Hall	N	N	N	Y	Y	Y	Y	N
5 Bryant	Y	Y	N	Y	Y	Y	N	Y
6 ***Barton***	N	N	N	N	Y	Y	Y	N
7 ***Archer***	N	N	N	N	Y	Y	Y	N
8 ***Fields***	N	N	N	N	Y	Y	Y	N
9 Brooks	Y	N	N	Y	Y	Y	N	Y
10 Pickle	Y	Y	Y	Y	Y	Y	N	Y
11 Edwards	Y	Y	N	Y	Y	Y	N	Y
12 Geren	N	Y	?	Y	Y	Y	Y	N
13 Sarpalius	N	Y	Y	Y	Y	Y	Y	N
14 Laughlin	N	Y	N	Y	Y	Y	N	Y
15 de la Garza	Y	Y	Y	Y	Y	Y	N	Y
16 Coleman	Y	Y	N	Y	Y	N	N	Y
17 Stenholm	Y	Y	N	Y	Y	Y	Y	N
18 Washington	Y	?	?	?	?	?	N	N
19 ***Combest***	N	N	N	Y	Y	Y	Y	N
20 Gonzalez	Y	Y	Y	Y	Y	N	N	N
21 ***Smith***	N	N	N	N	Y	Y	Y	N
22 ***DeLay***	N	N	N	N	Y	Y	Y	N
23 ***Bonilla***	N	N	N	N	Y	Y	Y	Y
24 Frost	Y	Y	N	Y	Y	Y	N	Y
25 Andrews	N	Y	N	Y	Y	Y	N	Y
26 ***Armey***	N	N	N	N	Y	Y	Y	N
27 Ortiz	N	Y	Y	Y	Y	N	N	Y
28 Tejeda	N	Y	Y	Y	Y	Y	N	Y
29 Green	Y	N	N	Y	Y	Y	N	Y
30 Johnson, E.B.	Y	N	N	Y	Y	Y	N	Y
UTAH								
1 ***Hansen***	N	N	N	N	Y	Y	Y	N
2 Shepherd	Y	Y	N	Y	Y	Y	N	Y
3 Orton	N	Y	N	Y	Y	Y	Y	Y
VERMONT								
AL *Sanders*	Y	Y	N	Y	Y	N	N	Y
VIRGINIA								
1 ***Bateman***	N	Y	N	Y	Y	Y	Y	N
2 Pickett	N	Y	N	Y	Y	Y	Y	Y
3 Scott	Y	Y	Y	Y	Y	N	N	N
4 Sisisky	N	Y	N	Y	Y	Y	Y	Y
5 Payne	Y	Y	N	Y	Y	Y	N	Y
6 ***Goodlatte***	N	N	N	N	Y	Y	Y	N
7 ***Bliley***	N	N	N	N	Y	Y	Y	N
8 Moran	Y	Y	Y	Y	Y	Y	N	Y
9 Boucher	N	Y	N	?	Y	Y	N	Y
10 ***Wolf***	Y	N	N	N	Y	Y	Y	N
11 Byrne	N	Y	N	Y	Y	Y	N	Y
WASHINGTON								
1 Cantwell	N	Y	N	Y	Y	Y	N	Y
2 Swift	Y	Y	Y	Y	Y	N	N	Y
3 Unsoeld	Y	Y	N	Y	Y	Y	N	Y
4 Inslee	N	Y	N	Y	Y	Y	N	Y
5 Foley								Y
6 Dicks	N	N	N	Y	Y	Y	N	Y
7 McDermott	Y	N	N	Y	Y	N	N	Y
8 ***Dunn***	N	N	N	N	Y	Y	Y	N
9 Kreidler	Y	Y	Y	N	Y	N	N	Y
WEST VIRGINIA								
1 Mollohan	Y	Y	Y	Y	Y	N	N	N
2 Wise	Y	Y	N	?	Y	Y	N	Y
3 Rahall	Y	Y	N	Y	Y	Y	N	Y
WISCONSIN								
1 Barca	N	Y	N	Y	Y	Y	N	Y
2 ***Klug***	N	N	N	N	Y	Y	Y	Y
3 ***Gunderson***	N	N	N	N	Y	Y	Y	N
4 Kleczka	N	Y	N	Y	Y	Y	N	Y
5 Barrett	N	Y	N	Y	Y	Y	N	Y
6 ***Petri***	?	Y	N	N	Y	Y	Y	N
7 Obey	N	Y	N	Y	?	Y	N	Y
8 ***Roth***	N	N	N	N	Y	Y	Y	Y
9 ***Sensenbrenner***	N	N	N	N	Y	Y	Y	N
WYOMING								
AL ***Thomas***	N	N	N	N	Y	Y	Y	N
DELEGATES								
de Lugo, V.I.	Y	Y	Y	D	Y	N	D	D
Faleomavaega, Am.S.	Y	Y	Y	D	Y	Y	D	D
Norton, D.C.	Y	Y	Y	D	Y	N	D	D
Romero-B., P.R.	Y	Y	N	D	Y	Y	D	D
Underwood, Guam	Y	N	Y	D	Y	N	D	D

Southern states - Ala., Ark., Fla., Ga., Ky., La., Miss., N.C., Okla., S.C., Tenn., Texas, Va.
Omitted votes are quorum calls, which CQ does not include in its vote charts.

KEY

Y   Voted for (yea).
\#   Paired for.
\+   Announced for.
N   Voted against (nay).
X   Paired against.
−   Announced against.
P   Voted "present."
C   Voted "present" to avoid possible conflict of interest.
?   Did not vote or otherwise make a position known.
D   Delegates ineligible to vote.

Democrats   *Republicans*
Independent

145. HR 3355. Omnibus Crime Bill/Instruct Conferees. McCollum, R-Fla., motion to instruct the House conferees to insist on the House provisions that authorize an additional $10.5 billion in new prison construction grants and on Senate provisions requiring that states make violent felons serve at least 85 percent of their sentences in order to qualify for federal aid in incarcerating such criminals. Motion rejected 191-222: R 162-4; D 29-217 (ND 12-152, SD 17-65); I 0-1, April 21, 1994.

146. HR 3221. Iraqi Claims/Passage. Passage of the bill to establish procedures and authorize the disbursement of about $1.2 billion in Iraqi assets frozen during the Persian Gulf War to businesses and U.S. soldiers and their relatives with claims against the Iraqi government. Passed 398-5: R 168-0; D 229-5 (ND 154-5, SD 75-0); I 1-0, April 28, 1994. A "yea" was a vote in support of the president's position.

147. HR 2333. State Department Authorization/Vietnam Embargo. Snowe, R-Maine, motion to recommit the bill to conference with instructions to the House conferees to disagree with the section expressing the sense of the Senate that to expand U.S. and Vietnamese cooperation in accounting for POW/MIAs, the president should expeditiously lift the U.S. trade embargo against Vietnam. Motion rejected 195-209: R 159-7; D 36-201 (ND 24-138, SD 12-63); I 0-1, April 28, 1994. A "nay" was a vote in support of the president's position.

148. HR 4013. VA Work Force Reduction Exemption/ Passage. Montgomery, D-Miss., motion to suspend the rules and pass the bill to postpone for five years the personnel reductions proposed by the administration in Veterans' Health Administration hospitals, outpatient clinics and nursing homes. Motion agreed to 282-118: R 120-44; D 161-74 (ND 100-61, SD 61-13); I 1-0, April 28, 1994. A two-thirds majority of those present and voting (267 in this case) is required for passage under suspension of the rules. A "nay" was a vote in support of the president's position.

	145	146	147	148
ALABAMA				
1 Callahan	Y	Y	Y	Y
2 Everett	Y	Y	Y	Y
3 Browder	N	Y	Y	Y
4 Bevill	N	Y	N	Y
5 Cramer	N	Y	N	Y
6 *Bachus*	Y	Y	Y	Y
7 Hilliard	N	Y	N	Y
ALASKA				
AL *Young*	Y	Y	Y	Y
ARIZONA				
1 Coppersmith	N	Y	N	Y
2 Pastor	N	Y	N	Y
3 *Stump*	Y	Y	Y	Y
4 *Kyl*	Y	?	?	?
5 *Kolbe*	Y	Y	N	N
6 English	N	+	−	?
ARKANSAS				
1 Lambert	N	Y	N	N
2 Thornton	N	Y	N	?
3 *Hutchinson*	Y	Y	Y	Y
4 *Dickey*	Y	Y	Y	N
CALIFORNIA				
1 Hamburg	N	Y	N	Y
2 *Herger*	Y	Y	Y	Y
3 Fazio	N	Y	N	N
4 *Doolittle*	Y	Y	Y	Y
5 Matsui	N	Y	N	N
6 Woolsey	N	Y	N	N
7 Miller	N	Y	N	N
8 Pelosi	N	?	N	N
9 Dellums	X	Y	N	N
10 *Baker*	Y	Y	Y	Y
11 *Pombo*	Y	Y	Y	Y
12 Lantos	N	Y	N	Y
13 Stark	N	Y	N	N
14 Eshoo	N	Y	N	N
15 Mineta	N	Y	N	N
16 Edwards	N	Y	N	Y
17 Farr	N	Y	N	Y
18 Condit	Y	?	?	?
19 Lehman	?	Y	Y	Y
20 Dooley	N	Y	N	N
21 *Thomas*	#	Y	Y	Y
22 *Huffington*	Y	?	?	?
23 *Gallegly*	Y	Y	Y	Y
24 Beilenson	N	Y	N	N
25 *McKeon*	Y	Y	Y	Y
26 Berman	N	Y	N	N
27 *Moorhead*	Y	Y	Y	Y
28 *Dreier*	Y	Y	N	N
29 Waxman	N	Y	N	N
30 Becerra	N	Y	N	N
31 Martinez	N	Y	N	Y
32 Dixon	N	Y	N	N
33 Roybal-Allard	N	Y	N	Y
34 Torres	N	Y	N	Y
35 Waters	N	Y	N	Y
36 Harman	Y	Y	N	Y
37 Tucker	N	Y	N	Y
38 *Horn*	Y	Y	Y	Y
39 *Royce*	Y	Y	Y	N
40 *Lewis*	?	Y	Y	N
41 *Kim*	Y	Y	Y	Y

	145	146	147	148
42 Brown	N	Y	N	Y
43 *Calvert*	?	?	?	?
44 *McCandless*	Y	Y	Y	Y
45 *Rohrabacher*	Y	Y	Y	N
46 *Dornan*	Y	Y	Y	N
47 *Cox*	Y	Y	N	N
48 *Packard*	Y	Y	Y	N
49 Schenk	Y	Y	N	Y
50 Filner	N	N	N	Y
51 *Cunningham*	Y	Y	Y	Y
52 *Hunter*	Y	Y	Y	Y
COLORADO				
1 Schroeder	N	Y	N	N
2 Skaggs	N	Y	N	N
3 *McInnis*	Y	Y	Y	Y
4 *Allard*	Y	Y	N	N
5 *Hefley*	Y	Y	Y	Y
6 *Schaefer*	Y	Y	Y	Y
CONNECTICUT				
1 Kennelly	N	Y	N	Y
2 Gejdenson	N	Y	N	Y
3 DeLauro	N	+	−	+
4 *Shays*	Y	Y	N	N
5 *Franks*	Y	Y	Y	Y
6 *Johnson*	Y	Y	N	N
DELAWARE				
AL *Castle*	Y	Y	Y	N
FLORIDA				
1 Hutto	Y	Y	N	Y
2 Peterson	N	Y	N	Y
3 Brown	N	Y	N	Y
4 *Fowler*	Y	Y	Y	Y
5 Thurman	N	Y	Y	Y
6 *Stearns*	Y	Y	Y	Y
7 *Mica*	Y	Y	Y	Y
8 *McCollum*	Y	Y	Y	Y
9 *Bilirakis*	Y	Y	Y	Y
10 *Young*	Y	Y	Y	Y
11 Gibbons	N	Y	N	Y
12 *Canady*	Y	Y	Y	Y
13 *Miller*	Y	Y	Y	N
14 *Goss*	Y	Y	Y	Y
15 *Bacchus*	Y	Y	N	Y
16 *Lewis*	Y	Y	Y	Y
17 Meek	N	Y	N	Y
18 *Ros-Lehtinen*	Y	Y	Y	Y
19 Johnston	N	Y	N	Y
20 Deutsch	N	Y	N	Y
21 *Diaz-Balart*	Y	Y	Y	Y
22 *Shaw*	Y	Y	Y	Y
23 Hastings	N	Y	N	Y
GEORGIA				
1 *Kingston*	Y	Y	Y	Y
2 Bishop	N	Y	N	Y
3 *Collins*	N	Y	Y	Y
4 *Linder*	Y	Y	Y	Y
5 Lewis	N	Y	N	N
6 *Gingrich*	Y	Y	Y	Y
7 *Darden*	N	Y	N	Y
8 Rowland	Y	Y	N	Y
9 Deal	Y	Y	Y	Y
10 Johnson	N	Y	N	Y
11 McKinney	N	Y	N	Y
HAWAII				
1 Abercrombie	N	Y	N	Y
2 Mink	N	Y	N	Y
IDAHO				
1 LaRocco	N	Y	N	N
2 *Crapo*	Y	Y	Y	Y
ILLINOIS				
1 Rush	N	?	?	?
2 Reynolds	N	Y	N	N
3 Lipinski	N	Y	N	Y
4 Gutierrez	N	Y	Y	Y
5 Rostenkowski	N	Y	N	N
6 *Hyde*	Y	Y	Y	Y
7 Collins	N	Y	N	Y
8 *Crane*	Y	Y	N	N
9 Yates	N	Y	N	N
10 *Porter*	Y	Y	Y	Y
11 Sangmeister	N	Y	N	Y
12 Costello	N	Y	Y	Y
13 *Fawell*	Y	Y	Y	N
14 *Hastert*	Y	Y	Y	Y
15 *Ewing*	Y	Y	Y	Y
16 *Manzullo*	Y	Y	Y	Y
17 Evans	N	Y	N	Y

ND   Northern Democrats   SD   Southern Democrats

Southern states - Ala., Ark., Fla., Ga., Ky., La., Miss., N.C., Okla., S.C., Tenn., Texas, Va.
Omitted votes are quorum calls, which CQ does not include in its vote charts.

	145	146	147	148
18 Michel	Y	Y	Y	N
19 Poshard	N	Y	Y	Y
20 Durbin	N	Y	N	N
INDIANA				
1 Visclosky	N	Y	N	N
2 Sharp	N	Y	N	N
3 Roemer	Y	Y	N	N
4 Long	N	Y	N	Y
5 *Buyer*	Y	Y	Y	Y
6 *Burton*	Y	Y	Y	Y
7 *Myers*	Y	Y	Y	Y
8 McCloskey	N	Y	N	N
9 Hamilton	N	Y	N	Y
10 Jacobs	N	Y	N	Y
IOWA				
1 *Leach*	Y	Y	Y	Y
2 *Nussle*	Y	Y	Y	N
3 *Lightfoot*	Y	Y	Y	Y
4 Smith	N	Y	N	N
5 *Grandy*	?	?	?	?
KANSAS				
1 *Roberts*	Y	Y	Y	N
2 Slattery	N	?	?	?
3 *Meyers*	Y	Y	Y	?
4 Glickman	N	Y	Y	N
KENTUCKY				
1 *Barlow*	N	+	-	+
2 *Lewis*				
3 Mazzoli	N	Y	N	N
4 *Bunning*	Y	Y	Y	N
5 *Rogers*	Y	Y	Y	Y
6 Baesler	N	Y	N	Y
LOUISIANA				
1 *Livingston*	Y	Y	Y	Y
2 Jefferson	N	Y	N	Y
3 Tauzin	Y	Y	Y	Y
4 Fields	N	Y	N	Y
5 *McCrery*	Y	Y	Y	Y
6 *Baker*	Y	Y	Y	Y
7 Hayes	Y	Y	Y	Y
MAINE				
1 Andrews	N	Y	N	Y
2 *Snowe*	Y	Y	Y	Y
MARYLAND				
1 *Gilchrest*	Y	Y	N	Y
2 *Bentley*	Y	Y	Y	Y
3 Cardin	N	Y	N	N
4 Wynn	N	Y	N	Y
5 Hoyer	N	Y	N	N
6 *Bartlett*	Y	Y	Y	Y
7 Mfume	N	Y	N	Y
8 *Morella*	Y	Y	Y	Y
MASSACHUSETTS				
1 Olver	N	Y	N	N
2 Neal	N	Y	N	Y
3 *Blute*	Y	Y	Y	Y
4 Frank	N	Y	N	Y
5 Meehan	N	Y	N	Y
6 *Torkildsen*	Y	Y	Y	Y
7 Markey	N	Y	N	Y
8 Kennedy	N	Y	N	Y
9 Moakley	N	Y	N	Y
10 Studds	N	Y	N	N
MICHIGAN				
1 Stupak	Y	Y	Y	Y
2 *Hoekstra*	Y	Y	Y	Y
3 *Ehlers*	N	Y	Y	Y
4 *Camp*	Y	Y	Y	Y
5 Barcia	Y	Y	Y	Y
6 *Upton*	Y	Y	Y	Y
7 *Smith*	N	Y	Y	Y
8 Carr	N	Y	N	Y
9 Kildee	N	Y	Y	Y
10 Bonior	N	Y	N	Y
11 *Knollenberg*	Y	Y	Y	Y
12 Levin	N	Y	N	Y
13 Ford	?	?	N	Y
14 Conyers	N	Y	N	Y
15 Collins	N	Y	N	Y
16 Dingell	N	Y	N	Y
MINNESOTA				
1 Penny	N	Y	N	N
2 Minge	N	Y	N	N
3 *Ramstad*	Y	Y	N	N
4 Vento	N	Y	N	N

	145	146	147	148
5 Sabo	N	Y	N	N
6 *Grams*	Y	Y	Y	N
7 Peterson	N	Y	Y	Y
8 Oberstar	N	Y	N	Y
MISSISSIPPI				
1 Whitten	N	Y	N	Y
2 Thompson	N	Y	N	Y
3 Montgomery	N	Y	N	Y
4 Parker	Y	Y	N	Y
5 Taylor	Y	Y	Y	Y
MISSOURI				
1 Clay	N	?	?	?
2 *Talent*	?	Y	Y	Y
3 Gephardt	N	Y	N	N
4 Skelton	N	Y	Y	Y
5 Wheat	N	Y	?	?
6 Danner	N	Y	N	Y
7 *Hancock*	Y	Y	Y	Y
8 *Emerson*	Y	Y	Y	Y
9 Volkmer	N	?	?	Y
MONTANA				
AL Williams	N	Y	Y	Y
NEBRASKA				
1 *Bereuter*	Y	Y	Y	Y
2 Hoagland	N	Y	N	Y
3 *Barrett*	Y	Y	Y	?
NEVADA				
1 Bilbray	N	Y	Y	Y
2 *Vucanovich*	Y	?	?	?
NEW HAMPSHIRE				
1 *Zeliff*	Y	Y	Y	N
2 Swett	N	Y	N	N
NEW JERSEY				
1 Andrews	?	Y	N	N
2 Hughes	N	Y	N	N
3 *Saxton*	Y	Y	Y	Y
4 *Smith*	Y	Y	Y	Y
5 *Roukema*	Y	Y	Y	Y
6 Pallone	N	Y	Y	Y
7 *Franks*	Y	Y	Y	N
8 Klein	N	Y	N	Y
9 Torricelli	Y	Y	N	Y
10 Payne	N	Y	N	Y
11 *Gallo*	?	Y	Y	N
12 *Zimmer*	Y	Y	Y	N
13 Menendez	N	Y	N	Y
NEW MEXICO				
1 *Schiff*	Y	Y	Y	Y
2 *Skeen*	Y	Y	Y	Y
3 Richardson	Y	Y	N	Y
NEW YORK				
1 Hochbrueckner	N	Y	N	Y
2 *Lazio*	Y	Y	Y	Y
3 *King*	Y	Y	Y	Y
4 *Levy*	Y	Y	Y	Y
5 Ackerman	N	Y	N	Y
6 Flake	N	Y	N	Y
7 Manton	N	Y	N	Y
8 Nadler	N	Y	N	Y
9 Schumer	N	Y	N	Y
10 Towns	N	Y	N	Y
11 Owens	N	Y	N	Y
12 Velazquez	N	Y	N	Y
13 *Molinari*	Y	Y	Y	Y
14 Maloney	N	Y	N	Y
15 Rangel	N	Y	N	Y
16 Serrano	N	Y	N	Y
17 Engel	N	Y	N	Y
18 Lowey	N	Y	N	Y
19 *Fish*	?	Y	Y	Y
20 *Gilman*	Y	Y	Y	Y
21 McNulty	?	Y	Y	Y
22 *Solomon*	Y	Y	Y	Y
23 *Boehlert*	Y	Y	Y	Y
24 *McHugh*	Y	Y	Y	Y
25 *Walsh*	Y	Y	Y	Y
26 Hinchey	N	Y	N	Y
27 *Paxon*	Y	Y	Y	Y
28 Slaughter	N	Y	N	Y
29 LaFalce	?	Y	N	N
30 *Quinn*	Y	?	#	?
31 *Houghton*	?	Y	N	N
NORTH CAROLINA				
1 Clayton	N	Y	N	N
2 Valentine	N	Y	N	N

	145	146	147	148
3 Lancaster	N	Y	Y	Y
4 Price	N	Y	N	Y
5 Neal	N	Y	N	Y
6 *Coble*	Y	Y	Y	Y
7 Rose	N	Y	N	Y
8 Hefner	N	Y	N	Y
9 *McMillan*	Y	Y	Y	Y
10 *Ballenger*	Y	Y	Y	N
11 *Taylor*	Y	Y	Y	Y
12 Watt	N	Y	N	N
NORTH DAKOTA				
AL Pomeroy	N	Y	Y	Y
OHIO				
1 Mann	N	Y	N	N
2 *Portman*	Y	Y	Y	Y
3 Hall	N	Y	N	?
4 *Oxley*	Y	Y	Y	Y
5 *Gillmor*	Y	Y	Y	Y
6 Strickland	N	Y	N	Y
7 *Hobson*	Y	Y	Y	Y
8 *Boehner*	Y	Y	Y	Y
9 Kaptur	N	Y	N	Y
10 *Hoke*	Y	Y	Y	Y
11 Stokes	N	?	N	N
12 *Kasich*	Y	Y	Y	Y
13 Brown	N	Y	N	Y
14 Sawyer	N	Y	N	N
15 *Pryce*	Y	Y	Y	Y
16 *Regula*	Y	Y	Y	Y
17 Traficant	N	Y	Y	Y
18 Applegate	?	Y	Y	Y
19 Fingerhut	N	Y	N	N
OKLAHOMA				
1 *Inhofe*	Y	Y	?	?
2 Synar	N	Y	N	Y
3 Brewster	Y	Y	N	Y
4 McCurdy	Y	Y	N	Y
5 *Istook*	Y	?	?	?
6 Lucas				
OREGON				
1 Furse	N	Y	N	N
2 *Smith*	Y	Y	Y	Y
3 Wyden	N	Y	N	N
4 DeFazio	N	X	?	?
5 Kopetski	N	Y	N	N
PENNSYLVANIA				
1 Foglietta	N	Y	N	Y
2 Blackwell	N	Y	N	Y
3 Borski	N	Y	N	Y
4 Klink	N	N	N	N
5 *Clinger*	Y	Y	Y	Y
6 Holden	N	N	Y	Y
7 *Weldon*	Y	Y	Y	Y
8 *Greenwood*	Y	Y	?	?
9 *Shuster*	Y	Y	N	N
10 *McDade*	Y	Y	Y	Y
11 Kanjorski	N	N	N	N
12 Murtha	N	?	?	?
13 Margolies-Mezv.	Y	Y	N	Y
14 Coyne	N	Y	N	Y
15 McHale	Y	N	N	Y
16 *Walker*	Y	Y	Y	N
17 *Gekas*	Y	Y	Y	Y
18 *Santorum*	Y	Y	Y	Y
19 *Goodling*	Y	Y	Y	Y
20 Murphy	?	?	?	?
21 *Ridge*	?	Y	N	Y
RHODE ISLAND				
1 *Machtley*	Y	Y	Y	Y
2 Reed	N	Y	N	N
SOUTH CAROLINA				
1 *Ravenel*	Y	Y	Y	Y
2 *Spence*	Y	Y	Y	Y
3 Derrick	N	?	?	?
4 *Inglis*	N	Y	Y	Y
5 Spratt	N	Y	N	Y
6 Clyburn	N	Y	N	Y
SOUTH DAKOTA				
AL Johnson	N	Y	N	Y
TENNESSEE				
1 *Quillen*	Y	Y	Y	Y
2 *Duncan*	Y	Y	Y	Y
3 Lloyd	N	?	?	?
4 Cooper	Y	Y	N	Y
5 Clement	Y	Y	N	Y

	145	146	147	148
6 Gordon	N	?	N	Y
7 *Sundquist*	Y	Y	Y	Y
8 Tanner	N	Y	N	Y
9 Ford	N	?	N	N
TEXAS				
1 Chapman	N	Y	Y	Y
2 Wilson	N	Y	Y	Y
3 *Johnson, Sam*	Y	Y	Y	Y
4 Hall	Y	Y	Y	Y
5 Bryant	N	?	?	?
6 *Barton*	?	Y	Y	N
7 *Archer*	Y	Y	Y	Y
8 *Fields*	Y	Y	Y	Y
9 Brooks	N	Y	N	Y
10 Pickle	N	Y	N	Y
11 Edwards	N	Y	N	Y
12 Geren	Y	Y	N	Y
13 Sarpalius	N	Y	N	Y
14 Laughlin	N	Y	?	?
15 de la Garza	N	Y	N	Y
16 Coleman	N	Y	N	Y
17 Stenholm	Y	Y	N	N
18 Washington	?	?	N	N
19 *Combest*	Y	Y	Y	N
20 Gonzalez	N	Y	N	Y
21 *Smith*	Y	Y	Y	N
22 *DeLay*	Y	Y	Y	N
23 *Bonilla*	Y	Y	Y	Y
24 Frost	N	?	?	?
25 Andrews	N	Y	N	N
26 *Armey*	Y	Y	Y	N
27 Ortiz	N	Y	N	Y
28 Tejeda	N	Y	Y	Y
29 Green	N	Y	?	?
30 Johnson, E.B.	N	Y	N	Y
UTAH				
1 *Hansen*	Y	Y	Y	Y
2 Shepherd	N	Y	Y	N
3 Orton	Y	Y	N	N
VERMONT				
AL *Sanders*	N	Y	N	Y
VIRGINIA				
1 *Bateman*	Y	Y	Y	Y
2 Pickett	N	Y	?	?
3 Scott	N	Y	N	Y
4 Sisisky	Y	Y	N	Y
5 Payne	N	Y	N	Y
6 *Goodlatte*	Y	?	?	?
7 *Bliley*	Y	Y	Y	Y
8 Moran	N	Y	N	Y
9 Boucher	N	Y	N	Y
10 *Wolf*	Y	Y	Y	N
11 Byrne	Y	Y	N	Y
WASHINGTON				
1 Cantwell	N	Y	N	N
2 Swift	N	Y	N	N
3 Unsoeld	N	Y	N	N
4 Inslee	N	Y	N	N
5 Foley		N		
6 Dicks	N	Y	N	Y
7 McDermott	N	Y	N	N
8 *Dunn*	Y	Y	Y	Y
9 Kreidler	N	Y	N	Y
WEST VIRGINIA				
1 Mollohan	N	Y	N	Y
2 Wise	N	Y	N	Y
3 Rahall	N	Y	Y	Y
WISCONSIN				
1 Barca	Y	Y	Y	N
2 *Klug*	Y	Y	Y	N
3 *Gunderson*	Y	Y	Y	Y
4 Kleczka	N	Y	N	N
5 Barrett	N	Y	N	N
6 *Petri*	Y	Y	Y	N
7 Obey	N	Y	N	N
8 *Roth*	Y	Y	Y	N
9 *Sensenbrenner*	Y	Y	Y	N
WYOMING				
AL *Thomas*	Y	Y	Y	Y
DELEGATES				
de Lugo, V.I.	D	D	D	D
Faleomavaega, Am.S.	D	D	D	D
Norton, D.C.	D	D	D	D
Romero-B., P.R.	D	D	D	D
Underwood, Guam	D	D	D	D

KEY

Y   Voted for (yea).
Paired for.
+   Announced for.
N   Voted against (nay).
X   Paired against.
—   Announced against.
P   Voted "present."
C   Voted "present" to avoid possible conflict of interest.
?   Did not vote or otherwise make a position known.
D   Delegates ineligible to vote.

Democrats   *Republicans*
Independent

149. HR 3191. Flood Insurance Reform/Passage. Kennedy, D-Mass., motion to suspend the rules and pass the bill to require mortgage lenders to ensure that borrowers in flood-prone areas purchase flood insurance as a condition of their loan. Motion agreed to 335-60: R 102-57; D 232-3 (ND 157-1, SD 75-2); I 1-0, May 3, 1994. A two-thirds majority of those present and voting (264 in this case) is required for passage under suspension of the rules.

150. Procedural Motion. Approval of the House Journal of Tuesday, May 3. Approved 257-154: R 20-148; D 236-6 (ND 159-5, SD 77-1); I 1-0, May 4, 1994.

151. HR 3254. National Science Foundation Authorization/Authorization Cut. Boehlert, R-N.Y., amendment to reduce the bill's fiscal 1995 authorization by $50 million and its fiscal 1996 authorization by $158 million, to reflect figures in the House-passed budget resolution for fiscal 1995 (H Con Res 218). Adopted in the Committee of the Whole 227-197: R 169-3; D 58-193 (ND 38-132, SD 20-61); I 0-1, May 4, 1994.

152. HR 3254. National Science Foundation Authorization/Military Recruiting. Separate vote at the request of Solomon, R-N.Y., on the amendment offered by Solomon and adopted in the Committee of the Whole to withhold National Science Foundation grants from institutions that prohibit military recruitment on campus. The amendment was revised on the floor to make it symbolic and without legal effect. Adopted 331-90: R 170-1; D 161-88 (ND 90-77, SD 71-11); I 0-1, May 4, 1994. (On separate votes, which may be demanded on an amendment adopted in the Committee of the Whole, the four delegates and the resident commissioner of Puerto Rico cannot vote.)

153. HR 3254. National Science Foundation Authorization/Passage. Passage of the bill to reauthorize the National Science Foundation at $3.15 billion in fiscal 1995 and $3.23 billion in fiscal 1996. Passed 396-22: R 148-22; D 247-0 (ND 167-0, SD 80-0); I 1-0, May 4, 1994. A "yea" was a vote in support of the president's position.

	149	150	151	152	153
ALABAMA					
1 *Callahan*	Y	N	Y	Y	Y
2 *Everett*	Y	Y	Y	Y	Y
3 Browder	Y	Y	N	Y	Y
4 Bevill	Y	Y	N	Y	Y
5 Cramer	Y	Y	N	Y	Y
6 *Bachus*	Y	N	Y	Y	Y
7 Hilliard	Y	Y	N	Y	Y
ALASKA					
AL *Young*	Y	N	Y	Y	Y
ARIZONA					
1 Coppersmith	Y	Y	Y	Y	Y
2 Pastor	Y	Y	N	Y	Y
3 *Stump*	N	N	Y	Y	N
4 *Kyl*	Y	N	Y	Y	Y
5 *Kolbe*	Y	N	Y	Y	Y
6 English	Y	Y	Y	Y	Y
ARKANSAS					
1 Lambert	Y	Y	N	Y	Y
2 Thornton	?	Y	N	N	Y
3 *Hutchinson*	N	N	Y	Y	Y
4 Dickey	N	N	Y	Y	Y
CALIFORNIA					
1 Hamburg	Y	Y	N	N	Y
2 *Herger*	Y	N	Y	N	Y
3 Fazio	Y	Y	N	Y	Y
4 *Doolittle*	?	?	?	?	?
5 Matsui	Y	Y	N	N	Y
6 Woolsey	Y	Y	N	N	Y
7 Miller	Y	Y	N	N	Y
8 Pelosi	Y	Y	N	N	Y
9 Dellums	?	?	N	N	Y
10 *Baker*	N	N	Y	Y	Y
11 *Pombo*	Y	Y	Y	Y	Y
12 Lantos	Y	Y	N	N	Y
13 Stark	Y	Y	N	N	Y
14 Eshoo	Y	Y	N	N	Y
15 Mineta	Y	Y	N	N	Y
16 Edwards	Y	Y	N	N	Y
17 Farr	Y	Y	N	N	Y
18 Condit	Y	Y	Y	Y	Y
19 Lehman	Y	Y	Y	Y	Y
20 Dooley	Y	Y	N	Y	Y
21 *Thomas*	Y	N	Y	Y	Y
22 *Huffington*	N	N	Y	Y	Y
23 *Gallegly*	?	N	Y	Y	Y
24 Beilenson	Y	Y	N	N	Y
25 *McKeon*	N	N	Y	Y	Y
26 Berman	Y	Y	N	N	Y
27 *Moorhead*	N	N	Y	Y	Y
28 *Dreier*	N	N	Y	Y	Y
29 Waxman	Y	Y	N	N	Y
30 Becerra	Y	Y	N	N	Y
31 Martinez	Y	Y	Y	Y	Y
32 Dixon	Y	Y	N	Y	Y
33 Roybal-Allard	Y	Y	N	N	Y
34 Torres	Y	Y	N	N	Y
35 Waters	Y	Y	N	N	Y
36 Harman	Y	Y	N	N	Y
37 Tucker	Y	Y	N	N	Y
38 *Horn*	Y	N	Y	Y	Y
39 *Royce*	N	N	Y	Y	N
40 *Lewis*	N	Y	Y	Y	Y
41 *Kim*	N	N	Y	Y	Y
42 Brown	Y	?	N	N	Y
43 *Calvert*	Y	Y	Y	Y	Y
44 *McCandless*	Y	N	Y	Y	Y
45 *Rohrabacher*	N	N	Y	Y	Y
46 *Dornan*	N	N	Y	Y	Y
47 *Cox*	N	N	Y	Y	Y
48 *Packard*	N	N	Y	Y	Y
49 Schenk	Y	Y	N	N	Y
50 Filner	Y	Y	N	N	Y
51 *Cunningham*	Y	N	Y	Y	Y
52 *Hunter*	Y	N	Y	Y	N
COLORADO					
1 Schroeder	N	N	Y	N	Y
2 Skaggs	Y	Y	N	N	Y
3 *McInnis*	N	N	Y	Y	Y
4 *Allard*	N	N	Y	Y	Y
5 *Hefley*	N	N	Y	Y	Y
6 *Schaefer*	?	N	Y	Y	Y
CONNECTICUT					
1 Kennelly	Y	Y	N	Y	Y
2 Gejdenson	Y	Y	N	N	Y
3 DeLauro	+	Y	N	N	Y
4 *Shays*	Y	N	Y	Y	Y
5 *Franks*	Y	N	Y	Y	Y
6 *Johnson*	Y	N	Y	Y	Y
DELAWARE					
AL *Castle*	Y	N	Y	Y	Y
FLORIDA					
1 Hutto	Y	Y	Y	Y	Y
2 Peterson	Y	Y	N	Y	Y
3 Brown	Y	Y	N	Y	Y
4 *Fowler*	N	N	Y	Y	Y
5 Thurman	N	Y	N	Y	Y
6 *Stearns*	N	N	Y	Y	Y
7 *Mica*	N	N	Y	Y	Y
8 *McCollum*	N	N	Y	Y	Y
9 *Bilirakis*	N	N	Y	Y	Y
10 *Young*	?	?	Y	Y	Y
11 Gibbons	N	Y	N	Y	Y
12 *Canady*	N	N	Y	Y	Y
13 *Miller*	N	Y	Y	Y	Y
14 *Goss*	N	N	Y	Y	Y
15 Bacchus	Y	Y	N	Y	Y
16 *Lewis*	N	N	Y	Y	Y
17 Meek	Y	Y	N	N	Y
18 *Ros-Lehtinen*	Y	N	Y	Y	Y
19 Johnston	Y	Y	N	N	Y
20 Deutsch	Y	Y	Y	Y	Y
21 *Diaz-Balart*	Y	N	Y	Y	Y
22 *Shaw*	N	N	Y	Y	Y
23 Hastings	Y	Y	N	N	Y
GEORGIA					
1 *Kingston*	Y	Y	Y	Y	Y
2 Bishop	Y	Y	N	Y	Y
3 *Collins*	?	?	?	?	?
4 *Linder*	Y	N	Y	Y	Y
5 Lewis	?	Y	N	N	Y
6 *Gingrich*	Y	N	Y	Y	Y
7 *Darden*	Y	N	Y	?	?
8 Rowland	Y	Y	Y	Y	Y
9 Deal	Y	Y	N	Y	Y
10 Johnson	Y	?	N	Y	Y
11 McKinney	Y	Y	N	N	Y
HAWAII					
1 Abercrombie	Y	Y	N	N	Y
2 Mink	Y	Y	N	N	Y
IDAHO					
1 LaRocco	Y	Y	N	Y	Y
2 *Crapo*	Y	N	Y	Y	Y
ILLINOIS					
1 Rush	Y	Y	N	N	Y
2 Reynolds	Y	Y	N	N	Y
3 Lipinski	Y	Y	Y	Y	Y
4 Gutierrez	Y	Y	N	N	Y
5 Rostenkowski	Y	Y	N	N	Y
6 *Hyde*	Y	N	Y	Y	Y
7 Collins	Y	Y	N	N	Y
8 *Crane*	N	N	Y	Y	N
9 Yates	Y	Y	N	N	Y
10 *Porter*	Y	N	Y	Y	Y
11 Sangmeister	?	Y	?	?	?
12 Costello	Y	Y	N	Y	Y
13 *Fawell*	Y	N	Y	Y	Y
14 *Hastert*	Y	N	Y	Y	Y
15 *Ewing*	Y	N	Y	Y	Y
16 *Manzullo*	Y	N	Y	Y	Y
17 Evans	Y	Y	N	N	Y

ND   Northern Democrats   SD   Southern Democrats

	149	150	151	152	153
18 Michel	Y	N	Y	Y	Y
19 Poshard	Y	Y	Y	Y	Y
20 Durbin	Y	Y	N	Y	Y
INDIANA					
1 Visclosky	?	Y	Y	Y	Y
2 Sharp	Y	Y	?	?	Y
3 Roemer	Y	Y	N	Y	Y
4 Long	?	?	?	?	?
5 *Buyer*	Y	N	Y	Y	Y
6 *Burton*	N	N	Y	Y	N
7 *Myers*	?	?	Y	Y	Y
8 McCloskey	Y	Y	N	Y	Y
9 Hamilton	Y	Y	N	Y	Y
10 Jacobs	Y	N	Y	Y	Y
IOWA					
1 *Leach*	Y	N	N	Y	Y
2 *Nussle*	Y	N	Y	Y	Y
3 *Lightfoot*	Y	N	Y	Y	Y
4 Smith	Y	Y	N	Y	Y
5 *Grandy*	?	?	?	?	?
KANSAS					
1 *Roberts*	N	N	Y	Y	N
2 Slattery	Y	Y	Y	Y	Y
3 *Meyers*	Y	N	Y	Y	Y
4 Glickman	Y	Y	Y	Y	Y
KENTUCKY					
1 Barlow	Y	Y	N	Y	Y
2 Vacancy					
3 Mazzoli	Y	Y	N	Y	Y
4 *Bunning*	N	N	Y	Y	Y
5 *Rogers*	Y	N	Y	Y	Y
6 Baesler	Y	Y	N	Y	Y
LOUISIANA					
1 *Livingston*	Y	Y	Y	Y	Y
2 Jefferson	Y	Y	N	Y	Y
3 Tauzin	Y	Y	Y	Y	?
4 Fields	Y	Y	N	Y	Y
5 *McCrery*	Y	Y	Y	Y	?
6 *Baker*	Y	N	Y	Y	Y
7 Hayes	Y	Y	N	Y	Y
MAINE					
1 Andrews	?	Y	N	?	Y
2 *Snowe*	Y	Y	Y	Y	Y
MARYLAND					
1 *Gilchrest*	Y	N	Y	Y	Y
2 *Bentley*	Y	N	Y	Y	Y
3 Cardin	Y	Y	Y	Y	Y
4 Wynn	Y	Y	N	Y	Y
5 Hoyer	Y	Y	N	Y	Y
6 *Bartlett*	Y	N	Y	Y	Y
7 Mfume	Y	Y	N	Y	Y
8 *Morella*	Y	N	Y	Y	Y
MASSACHUSETTS					
1 Olver	Y	Y	N	N	Y
2 Neal	?	Y	N	N	Y
3 *Blute*	Y	N	Y	N	Y
4 Frank	Y	Y	N	N	Y
5 Meehan	Y	Y	N	N	Y
6 *Torkildsen*	Y	N	Y	N	Y
7 Markey	Y	Y	N	N	Y
8 Kennedy	Y	Y	N	N	Y
9 Moakley	Y	Y	N	N	Y
10 Studds	Y	Y	N	N	Y
MICHIGAN					
1 Stupak	Y	Y	Y	Y	Y
2 *Hoekstra*	N	N	Y	Y	N
3 *Ehlers*	N	N	N	N	Y
4 *Camp*	N	N	Y	Y	Y
5 Barcia	Y	Y	Y	Y	Y
6 *Upton*	N	N	Y	Y	Y
7 *Smith*	N	N	Y	Y	Y
8 Carr	Y	N	Y	Y	Y
9 Kildee	Y	Y	N	Y	Y
10 Bonior	Y	Y	N	N	Y
11 *Knollenberg*	Y	N	Y	Y	Y
12 Levin	Y	Y	N	Y	Y
13 Ford	Y	Y	?	N	Y
14 Conyers	Y	Y	N	N	Y
15 Collins	Y	Y	N	N	Y
16 Dingell	Y	Y	N	Y	Y
MINNESOTA					
1 Penny	Y	Y	Y	Y	Y
2 Minge	Y	Y	Y	N	Y
3 *Ramstad*	Y	N	Y	N	Y
4 Vento	Y	Y	N	N	Y

	149	150	151	152	153
5 Sabo	Y	Y	N	Y	Y
6 *Grams*	Y	N	Y	Y	Y
7 Peterson	Y	Y	Y	Y	Y
8 Oberstar	Y	Y	N	N	Y
MISSISSIPPI					
1 Whitten	?	?	N	Y	Y
2 Thompson	Y	Y	N	N	Y
3 Montgomery	Y	Y	Y	Y	Y
4 Parker	Y	Y	N	Y	Y
5 Taylor	Y	N	Y	Y	Y
MISSOURI					
1 Clay	Y	N	N	N	Y
2 *Talent*	Y	N	Y	Y	Y
3 Gephardt	Y	Y	N	N	Y
4 Skelton	Y	Y	Y	Y	Y
5 Wheat	?	?	N	Y	?
6 Danner	Y	Y	Y	Y	Y
7 *Hancock*	N	N	Y	N	Y
8 *Emerson*	Y	N	Y	Y	Y
9 Volkmer	Y	Y	N	Y	Y
MONTANA					
AL Williams	?	Y	N	Y	Y
NEBRASKA					
1 *Bereuter*	Y	N	Y	Y	Y
2 Hoagland	Y	Y	Y	N	Y
3 *Barrett*	Y	N	Y	Y	Y
NEVADA					
1 Bilbray	Y	Y	Y	Y	Y
2 *Vucanovich*	N	N	Y	Y	Y
NEW HAMPSHIRE					
1 *Zeliff*	N	N	Y	Y	N
2 Swett	Y	Y	N	Y	Y
NEW JERSEY					
1 Andrews	Y	Y	Y	Y	N
2 Hughes	Y	Y	Y	Y	Y
3 *Saxton*	Y	N	Y	Y	Y
4 *Smith*	Y	N	Y	Y	Y
5 *Roukema*	Y	N	Y	Y	Y
6 Pallone	Y	Y	Y	Y	Y
7 *Franks*	Y	N	Y	Y	Y
8 Klein	Y	Y	Y	Y	Y
9 Torricelli	Y	Y	N	Y	Y
10 Payne	Y	Y	N	N	Y
11 *Gallo*	Y	N	Y	Y	Y
12 *Zimmer*	Y	N	Y	Y	Y
13 Menendez	Y	Y	Y	Y	Y
NEW MEXICO					
1 *Schiff*	Y	N	Y	Y	Y
2 *Skeen*	Y	N	Y	Y	Y
3 Richardson	Y	Y	N	Y	Y
NEW YORK					
1 Hochbrueckner	Y	Y	N	Y	Y
2 *Lazio*	Y	N	Y	Y	Y
3 *King*	Y	N	Y	Y	Y
4 *Levy*	Y	N	Y	Y	Y
5 Ackerman	Y	Y	N	Y	Y
6 Flake	Y	Y	N	Y	Y
7 Manton	Y	Y	N	Y	Y
8 Nadler	Y	Y	N	N	Y
9 Schumer	Y	Y	Y	Y	Y
10 Towns	Y	?	N	N	Y
11 Owens	Y	?	N	N	Y
12 Velazquez	Y	Y	N	N	Y
13 *Molinari*	Y	N	Y	Y	Y
14 Maloney	Y	Y	N	N	Y
15 Rangel	Y	?	N	N	Y
16 Serrano	Y	?	N	N	Y
17 Engel	Y	Y	?	N	Y
18 Lowey	Y	Y	N	N	Y
19 *Fish*	?	Y	Y	Y	?
20 *Gilman*	Y	Y	Y	Y	Y
21 McNulty	Y	Y	N	Y	Y
22 *Solomon*	N	N	Y	Y	N
23 *Boehlert*	Y	N	Y	Y	Y
24 *McHugh*	Y	N	Y	Y	Y
25 *Walsh*	Y	N	Y	Y	Y
26 Hinchey	Y	Y	N	N	?
27 *Paxon*	N	N	Y	Y	N
28 Slaughter	Y	Y	N	N	Y
29 LaFalce	Y	?	N	Y	Y
30 *Quinn*	Y	N	Y	N	Y
31 *Houghton*	Y	Y	Y	Y	Y
NORTH CAROLINA					
1 Clayton	Y	Y	N	N	Y
2 Valentine	Y	Y	N	Y	Y

	149	150	151	152	153
3 Lancaster	Y	Y	N	Y	Y
4 Price	Y	Y	N	Y	Y
5 Neal	Y	Y	?	Y	Y
6 *Coble*	Y	N	Y	N	Y
7 Rose	Y	Y	N	Y	Y
8 Hefner	?	Y	Y	Y	Y
9 *McMillan*	Y	?	Y	Y	Y
10 *Ballenger*	N	N	Y	Y	N
11 *Taylor*	?	N	Y	Y	N
12 Watt	Y	Y	N	N	Y
NORTH DAKOTA					
AL Pomeroy	Y	Y	N	Y	Y
OHIO					
1 Mann	?	Y	N	Y	Y
2 *Portman*	Y	N	Y	Y	Y
3 Hall	Y	Y	N	Y	Y
4 *Oxley*	Y	N	Y	Y	Y
5 *Gillmor*	N	Y	Y	Y	Y
6 Strickland	Y	Y	N	Y	Y
7 *Hobson*	Y	N	Y	Y	Y
8 *Boehner*	?	N	Y	Y	Y
9 Kaptur	Y	?	Y	Y	Y
10 *Hoke*	?	N	Y	Y	Y
11 Stokes	?	?	N	N	Y
12 *Kasich*	Y	Y	N	Y	Y
13 Brown	Y	Y	N	N	Y
14 Sawyer	Y	Y	N	Y	Y
15 *Pryce*	?	N	Y	Y	Y
16 *Regula*	Y	N	Y	Y	Y
17 Traficant	Y	Y	N	N	Y
18 Applegate	Y	Y	N	Y	Y
19 Fingerhut	+	Y	N	Y	Y
OKLAHOMA					
1 *Inhofe*	Y	N	Y	Y	Y
2 Synar	Y	Y	N	Y	Y
3 Brewster	Y	Y	Y	Y	Y
4 McCurdy	Y	Y	N	Y	Y
5 *Istook*	Y	N	Y	Y	Y
6 Vacancy					
OREGON					
1 Furse	Y	Y	N	N	Y
2 *Smith*	?	N	Y	Y	Y
3 Wyden	Y	Y	N	N	Y
4 DeFazio	Y	Y	Y	N	Y
5 Kopetski	Y	Y	N	Y	Y
PENNSYLVANIA					
1 Foglietta	Y	Y	N	N	Y
2 Blackwell	?	Y	?	?	?
3 Borski	Y	Y	N	Y	Y
4 Klink	Y	Y	N	Y	Y
5 *Clinger*	Y	Y	Y	Y	Y
6 Holden	Y	Y	Y	Y	Y
7 *Weldon*	?	N	Y	Y	Y
8 *Greenwood*	Y	Y	Y	Y	Y
9 *Shuster*	Y	N	Y	Y	Y
10 *McDade*	Y	N	Y	Y	Y
11 Kanjorski	Y	Y	N	Y	Y
12 Murtha	Y	N	Y	Y	Y
13 Margolies-Mezv.	Y	Y	Y	Y	Y
14 Coyne	Y	Y	N	Y	Y
15 McHale	Y	Y	N	Y	Y
16 *Walker*	N	N	Y	Y	Y
17 *Gekas*	N	N	Y	Y	Y
18 *Santorum*	?	N	Y	Y	Y
19 *Goodling*	Y	N	Y	N	N
20 Murphy	Y	N	N	Y	Y
21 *Ridge*	?	?	?	?	?
RHODE ISLAND					
1 *Machtley*	Y	N	Y	Y	Y
2 Reed	Y	Y	N	Y	Y
SOUTH CAROLINA					
1 *Ravenel*	Y	N	Y	Y	Y
2 *Spence*	N	N	Y	Y	Y
3 Derrick	Y	Y	N	Y	Y
4 *Inglis*	N	Y	Y	Y	N
5 Spratt	Y	Y	N	Y	Y
6 Clyburn	Y	Y	N	Y	Y
SOUTH DAKOTA					
AL Johnson	Y	Y	N	Y	Y
TENNESSEE					
1 *Quillen*	Y	N	Y	Y	Y
2 *Duncan*	N	N	Y	Y	N
3 Lloyd	Y	Y	N	Y	Y
4 Cooper	Y	Y	N	Y	Y
5 Clement	Y	Y	Y	Y	Y

	149	150	151	152	153
6 Gordon	Y	Y	N	Y	Y
7 *Sundquist*	Y	Y	Y	Y	Y
8 Tanner	Y	Y	N	Y	Y
9 Ford	Y	Y	N	Y	Y
TEXAS					
1 Chapman	Y	Y	N	Y	Y
2 Wilson	Y	Y	N	Y	Y
3 *Johnson, Sam*	N	N	Y	Y	Y
4 Hall	Y	Y	N	Y	Y
5 Bryant	Y	Y	N	N	Y
6 *Barton*	N	N	Y	Y	Y
7 *Archer*	N	N	Y	Y	Y
8 *Fields*	N	?	Y	Y	Y
9 Brooks	Y	?	N	Y	Y
10 Pickle	Y	Y	Y	Y	Y
11 Edwards	Y	Y	Y	Y	Y
12 Geren	Y	Y	Y	Y	Y
13 Sarpalius	Y	Y	N	Y	Y
14 Laughlin	Y	Y	N	Y	Y
15 de la Garza	Y	Y	N	Y	Y
16 Coleman	Y	Y	N	Y	Y
17 Stenholm	Y	Y	Y	Y	Y
18 Washington	?	?	?	?	?
19 *Combest*	Y	Y	N	Y	Y
20 Gonzalez	Y	Y	N	Y	Y
21 *Smith*	N	N	Y	Y	Y
22 *DeLay*	N	N	Y	Y	Y
23 *Bonilla*	Y	N	Y	?	Y
24 Frost	Y	Y	N	Y	Y
25 Andrews	Y	Y	Y	Y	Y
26 *Armey*	N	N	Y	Y	Y
27 Ortiz	Y	Y	Y	Y	Y
28 Tejeda	Y	Y	N	Y	Y
29 Green	Y	Y	N	Y	Y
30 Johnson, E.B.	Y	Y	N	N	Y
UTAH					
1 *Hansen*	N	N	Y	Y	Y
2 Shepherd	Y	Y	Y	Y	Y
3 Orton	Y	Y	Y	Y	Y
VERMONT					
AL *Sanders*	Y	Y	N	N	Y
VIRGINIA					
1 *Bateman*	?	Y	Y	Y	Y
2 Pickett	Y	Y	Y	Y	Y
3 Scott	Y	Y	N	Y	Y
4 Sisisky	Y	Y	Y	Y	Y
5 Payne	Y	Y	N	Y	Y
6 *Goodlatte*	Y	N	Y	Y	Y
7 *Bliley*	N	N	Y	Y	Y
8 Moran	?	?	N	Y	Y
9 Boucher	Y	Y	N	Y	Y
10 *Wolf*	Y	N	Y	Y	Y
11 Byrne	Y	Y	N	Y	Y
WASHINGTON					
1 Cantwell	Y	Y	N	Y	Y
2 Swift	Y	Y	N	N	Y
3 Unsoeld	Y	Y	N	N	Y
4 Inslee	Y	Y	N	Y	Y
5 Foley					
6 Dicks	?	Y	N	Y	Y
7 McDermott	Y	Y	N	N	Y
8 *Dunn*	N	N	Y	Y	Y
9 Kreidler	Y	N	Y	Y	Y
WEST VIRGINIA					
1 Mollohan	Y	Y	N	Y	Y
2 Wise	Y	Y	N	Y	Y
3 Rahall	Y	Y	N	Y	Y
WISCONSIN					
1 Barca	Y	Y	Y	Y	Y
2 *Klug*	Y	N	Y	Y	Y
3 *Gunderson*	Y	N	Y	Y	Y
4 Kleczka	Y	Y	N	Y	Y
5 Barrett	Y	Y	Y	N	Y
6 *Petri*	Y	N	Y	Y	Y
7 Obey	Y	Y	N	Y	Y
8 *Roth*	Y	N	Y	Y	Y
9 *Sensenbrenner*	N	N	Y	Y	N
WYOMING					
AL *Thomas*	Y	N	Y	Y	Y
DELEGATES					
de Lugo, V.I.	D	D	N	D	D
Faleomavaega, Am.S.	D	D	N	D	D
Norton, D.C.	D	D	N	D	D
Romero-B., P.R.	D	D	?	D	D
Underwood, Guam	D	D	N	D	D

Southern states - Ala., Ark., Fla., Ga., Ky., La., Miss., N.C., Okla., S.C., Tenn., Texas, Va.
Omitted votes are quorum calls, which CQ does not include in its vote charts.

KEY

Y Voted for (yea).
Paired for.
+ Announced for.
N Voted against (nay).
X Paired against.
− Announced against.
P Voted "present."
C Voted "present" to avoid possible conflict of interest.
? Did not vote or otherwise make a position known.
D Delegates ineligible to vote.

Democrats *Republicans*
Independent

154. Procedural Motion. Approval of the House Journal of Wednesday, May 4. Approved 248-160: R 15-155; D 232-5 (ND 156-4, SD 76-1); I 1-0, May 5, 1994.

155. HR 4296. Assault Weapons Ban/Rule. Adoption of the rule (H Res 416) to provide for House floor consideration of the bill to ban the manufacture and possession of 19 types of semi-automatic weapons and high-capacity ammunition clips but exempt existing guns and about 670 guns that are deemed to have a legitimate sporting purpose. Adopted 220-209: R 4-171; D 215-38 (ND 152-18, SD 63-20); I 1-0, May 5, 1994.

156. HR 4296. Assault Weapons Ban/Passage. Passage of the bill to ban the manufacture and possession of 19 types of semiautomatic weapons and high-capacity ammunition clips but exempt existing guns and about 670 guns that are deemed to have a legitimate sporting purpose. Passed 216-214: R 38-137; D 177-77 (ND 137-34, SD 40-43); I 1-0, May 5, 1994. A "yea" was a vote in support of the president's position.

157. S 636. Abortion Clinic Access/Rule. Adoption of the rule (H Res 417) to provide for House floor consideration of the conference report to establish federal criminal and civil penalties for persons who use force, the threat of force or physical obstruction to block access to abortion clinics. Adopted 236-181: R 21-151; D 214-30 (ND 149-17, SD 65-13); I 1-0, May 5, 1994.

158. S 636. Abortion Clinic Access/Defendant Attorneys' Fees. Sensenbrenner, R-Wis., motion to recommit the bill to conference with instructions to report the bill back with an amendment that allows the awarding of reasonable attorneys' fees whether the prevailing party is the plaintiff or the defendant. The conference report allows only plaintiffs to recoup fees. Motion rejected 193-222: R 151-20; D 42-201 (ND 27-138, SD 15-63); I 0-1, May 5, 1994.

159. S 636. Abortion Clinic Access/Conference Report. Adoption of the conference report to establish federal criminal and civil penalties for persons who use force, the threat of force or physical obstruction to block access to abortion clinics. Adopted 241-174: R 40-131; D 200-43 (ND 139-26, SD 61-17); I 1-0, May 5, 1994. A "yea" was a vote in support of the president's position.

160. H Con Res 160. Fiscal 1995 Budget Resolution/Rule. Adoption of the rule (H Res 418) to waive points of order against and provide for House floor consideration of the conference report to set budget levels for the fiscal year ending Sept. 30, 1995: budget authority, $1.541 trillion; outlays, $1.514 trillion; revenues, $1.338 trillion; and a deficit of $175.4 billion. The resolution calls for an additional $13 billion in cuts over five years below the spending caps established last year. Adopted 228-168: R 0-165; D 227-3 (ND 158-2, SD 69-1); I 1-0, May 5, 1994.

161. H Con Res 218. Fiscal 1995 Budget Resolution/Conference Report. Adoption of the conference report to set budget levels for the fiscal year ending Sept. 30, 1995: budget authority, $1.541 trillion; outlays, $1.514 trillion; revenues, $1.338 trillion; and a deficit of $175.4 billion. The resolution calls for an additional $13 billion in cuts over five years below the spending caps established last year. Adopted (thus cleared for the Senate) 220-183: R 0-166; D 219-17 (ND 149-11, SD 70-6); I 1-0, May 5, 1994.

	154	155	156	157	158	159	160	161
ALABAMA								
1 Callahan	N	N	N	Y	N	N	N	
2 Everett	Y	N	N	N	Y	N	N	N
3 Browder	Y	N	N	N	Y	N	Y	Y
4 Bevill	Y	Y	N	?	?	?	?	?
5 Cramer	Y	Y	N	Y	N	Y	Y	Y
6 Bachus	N	N	N	N	Y	N	N	N
7 Hilliard	Y	Y	N	Y	N	Y	Y	Y
ALASKA								
AL Young	N	N	N	N	Y	N	N	N
ARIZONA								
1 Coppersmith	Y	Y	Y	Y	N	Y	Y	Y
2 Pastor	Y	Y	Y	Y	N	Y	Y	Y
3 Stump	N	N	N	N	Y	N	N	N
4 Kyl	N	N	N	N	Y	N	N	N
5 Kolbe	N	N	N	Y	N	Y	N	N
6 English	Y	Y	Y	Y	N	Y	Y	N
ARKANSAS								
1 Lambert	Y	N	N	Y	N	Y	Y	Y
2 Thornton	Y	Y	N	Y	N	Y	Y	Y
3 Hutchinson	N	N	N	N	Y	N	N	N
4 Dickey	?	N	N	N	Y	N	N	N
CALIFORNIA								
1 Hamburg	Y	Y	Y	Y	N	Y	Y	Y
2 Herger	N	N	N	?	?	?	?	X
3 Fazio	Y	Y	Y	Y	N	Y	Y	Y
4 Doolittle	N	N	N	#	X	?	?	X
5 Matsui	Y	Y	Y	Y	N	Y	#	#
6 Woolsey	Y	Y	Y	Y	N	Y	Y	Y
7 Miller	Y	Y	Y	Y	Y	Y	Y	Y
8 Pelosi	Y	Y	Y	Y	N	Y	Y	Y
9 Dellums	?	Y	Y	Y	N	Y	Y	Y
10 Baker	N	N	N	N	Y	N	N	N
11 Pombo	Y	N	N	N	Y	N	N	N
12 Lantos	Y	Y	Y	Y	N	Y	Y	Y
13 Stark	Y	Y	Y	?	X	#	?	?
14 Eshoo	Y	Y	Y	Y	N	Y	Y	Y
15 Mineta	Y	Y	Y	Y	N	Y	Y	Y
16 Edwards	Y	Y	Y	Y	N	Y	Y	Y
17 Farr	Y	Y	Y	Y	N	Y	Y	Y
18 Condit	Y	N	Y	Y	N	Y	Y	Y
19 Lehman	Y	Y	Y	Y	N	Y	Y	Y
20 Dooley	Y	Y	Y	Y	N	Y	?	Y
21 Thomas	N	N	N	N	Y	N	N	N
22 Huffington	?	N	Y	N	Y	N	N	N
23 Gallegly	N	N	N	N	Y	N	N	N
24 Beilenson	Y	Y	Y	Y	N	Y	Y	Y
25 McKeon	N	N	N	N	Y	N	N	N
26 Berman	Y	Y	Y	Y	N	Y	Y	Y
27 Moorhead	N	N	N	N	Y	N	N	N
28 Dreier	N	N	N	N	Y	N	N	N
29 Waxman	Y	Y	Y	Y	N	Y	Y	Y
30 Becerra	Y	Y	Y	Y	N	Y	Y	Y
31 Martinez	Y	Y	Y	Y	N	Y	Y	Y
32 Dixon	Y	Y	Y	Y	N	Y	Y	Y
33 Royal-Allard	Y	Y	Y	Y	N	Y	Y	Y
34 Torres	Y	Y	Y	Y	N	Y	Y	Y
35 Waters	Y	Y	Y	Y	N	Y	Y	Y
36 Harman	Y	Y	Y	Y	N	Y	Y	Y
37 Tucker	Y	Y	Y	Y	N	Y	N	Y
38 Horn	N	N	Y	Y	Y	Y	N	N
39 Royce	N	N	N	N	Y	N	N	N
40 Lewis	N	N	N	Y	N	N	?	N
41 Kim	N	N	N	N	Y	N	N	N
42 Brown	?	Y	Y	Y	N	Y	Y	Y
43 Calvert	N	N	N	N	Y	N	N	N
44 McCandless	N	N	N	N	Y	Y	?	?
45 Rohrabacher	N	N	N	N	Y	N	N	N
46 Dornan	?	N	N	N	Y	N	N	N
47 Cox	N	N	N	N	Y	N	?	N
48 Packard	N	N	N	N	Y	N	N	N
49 Schenk	Y	Y	Y	Y	N	Y	Y	Y
50 Filner	Y	Y	Y	Y	N	Y	Y	Y
51 Cunningham	N	N	N	N	Y	N	N	N
52 Hunter	N	N	N	N	Y	N	N	N
COLORADO								
1 Schroeder	N	Y	Y	Y	N	Y	Y	Y
2 Skaggs	Y	Y	Y	Y	N	Y	Y	Y
3 McInnis	N	N	N	N	Y	N	N	N
4 Allard	N	N	N	Y	N	N	N	N
5 Hefley	N	N	N	N	Y	N	N	N
6 Schaefer	N	N	N	N	Y	N	N	N
CONNECTICUT								
1 Kennelly	Y	Y	Y	Y	N	Y	Y	Y
2 Gejdenson	Y	Y	Y	Y	N	Y	Y	Y
3 DeLauro	Y	Y	Y	Y	N	Y	Y	Y
4 Shays	N	N	Y	Y	N	Y	N	N
5 Franks	N	N	N	Y	Y	N	N	N
6 Johnson	N	N	Y	Y	Y	Y	N	N
DELAWARE								
AL Castle	N	N	Y	N	N	Y	N	N
FLORIDA								
1 Hutto	Y	N	N	Y	N	Y	N	Y
2 Peterson	Y	Y	N	Y	N	Y	Y	Y
3 Brown	Y	Y	Y	Y	N	Y	Y	Y
4 Fowler	N	N	N	Y	Y	N	N	N
5 Thurman	Y	N	N	Y	N	Y	Y	Y
6 Stearns	N	N	N	N	Y	N	N	N
7 Mica	N	N	N	Y	N	N	N	N
8 McCollum	Y	N	N	?	#	X	X	X
9 Bilirakis	N	N	N	N	Y	N	N	N
10 Young	N	N	Y	N	Y	N	N	N
11 Gibbons	Y	Y	Y	Y	N	Y	Y	Y
12 Canady	N	N	N	N	Y	N	N	N
13 Miller	N	N	Y	N	Y	N	N	N
14 Goss	N	N	N	N	Y	N	N	N
15 Bacchus	Y	Y	Y	Y	N	Y	Y	Y
16 Lewis	N	N	N	N	Y	N	N	N
17 Meek	Y	Y	Y	Y	N	Y	Y	Y
18 Ros-Lehtinen	N	N	Y	N	N	N	N	N
19 Johnston	Y	Y	Y	Y	N	Y	Y	Y
20 Deutsch	Y	Y	Y	Y	N	Y	Y	Y
21 Diaz-Balart	N	N	N	Y	N	N	N	N
22 Shaw	N	N	Y	N	N	Y	N	N
23 Hastings	Y	Y	Y	Y	N	Y	Y	Y
GEORGIA								
1 Kingston	Y	N	N	N	Y	N	N	N
2 Bishop	Y	N	Y	Y	N	Y	Y	Y
3 Collins	N	N	N	N	Y	N	?	N
4 Linder	N	N	N	N	Y	N	N	N
5 Lewis	Y	Y	Y	Y	N	Y	Y	Y
6 Gingrich	N	N	N	N	Y	N	N	N
7 Darden	Y	N	Y	Y	N	Y	?	Y
8 Rowland	Y	Y	Y	Y	N	Y	Y	Y
9 Deal	Y	N	N	Y	N	Y	N	N
10 Johnson	Y	N	Y	Y	N	Y	Y	Y
11 McKinney	Y	Y	Y	Y	N	Y	Y	Y
HAWAII								
1 Abercrombie	Y	Y	Y	Y	N	Y	Y	Y
2 Mink	Y	Y	Y	Y	N	Y	Y	Y
IDAHO								
1 LaRocco	Y	N	N	Y	N	Y	Y	Y
2 Crapo	N	N	N	N	Y	N	N	N
ILLINOIS								
1 Rush	Y	Y	Y	Y	N	Y	Y	Y
2 Reynolds	Y	Y	Y	Y	N	Y	Y	Y
3 Lipinski	Y	Y	N	Y	N	Y	Y	?
4 Gutierrez	Y	Y	Y	Y	N	Y	Y	Y
5 Rostenkowski	Y	Y	Y	Y	N	Y	Y	Y
6 Hyde	N	N	Y	N	Y	N	N	N
7 Collins	Y	Y	Y	Y	N	Y	Y	Y
8 Crane	N	N	N	N	Y	N	N	N
9 Yates	Y	Y	Y	Y	N	Y	Y	Y
10 Porter	N	N	Y	Y	N	Y	N	N
11 Sangmeister	?	Y	Y	Y	N	Y	?	#
12 Costello	Y	Y	N	Y	N	Y	Y	Y
13 Fawell	N	N	Y	Y	N	Y	N	N
14 Hastert	N	N	N	N	Y	N	N	N
15 Ewing	N	N	N	N	Y	N	N	N
16 Manzullo	N	N	N	Y	N	N	N	N
17 Evans	Y	Y	Y	Y	N	Y	Y	Y

ND Northern Democrats   SD Southern Democrats

	154	155	156	157	158	159	160	161
18 ***Michel***	N	N	Y	N	Y	N	N	N
19 Poshard	Y	N	N	N	Y	N	Y	Y
20 Durbin	Y	Y	Y	Y	N	Y	Y	Y
INDIANA								
1 Visclosky	Y	Y	Y	Y	N	Y	Y	Y
2 Sharp	Y	Y	Y	Y	N	Y	?	?
3 Roemer	Y	Y	Y	Y	N	Y	Y	Y
4 Long	?	?	—	?	X	#	?	Y
5 ***Buyer***	N	N	N	N	Y	N	N	N
6 ***Burton***	N	N	N	N	Y	N	N	N
7 ***Myers***	Y	N	N	N	Y	N	N	?
8 McCloskey	Y	Y	N	Y	N	Y	Y	Y
9 Hamilton	Y	N	N	Y	Y	Y	Y	Y
10 Jacobs	N	Y	Y	Y	N	Y	Y	N
IOWA								
1 ***Leach***	N	N	Y	Y	N	Y	N	N
2 ***Nussle***	N	N	N	N	Y	N	N	N
3 ***Lightfoot***	N	N	N	N	Y	N	N	N
4 Smith	Y	Y	N	Y	N	Y	Y	Y
5 ***Grandy***	N	N	N	N	Y	N	?	N
KANSAS								
1 ***Roberts***	N	N	N	N	Y	N	N	N
2 Slattery	Y	Y	Y	Y	N	Y	Y	Y
3 ***Meyers***	N	N	Y	N	Y	Y	N	N
4 Glickman	Y	Y	Y	Y	N	Y	Y	Y
KENTUCKY								
1 Barlow	Y	N	N	N	N	N	Y	Y
2 Vacancy								
3 Mazzoli	Y	Y	Y	Y	Y	N	Y	Y
4 ***Bunning***	N	N	N	N	Y	N	N	N
5 ***Rogers***	?	X	?	?	#	X	?	?
6 Baesler	Y	N	Y	Y	N	Y	Y	Y
LOUISIANA								
1 ***Livingston***	N	N	N	N	Y	N	N	N
2 Jefferson	?	Y	Y	Y	N	Y	?	Y
3 Tauzin	Y	N	N	N	Y	N	Y	Y
4 Fields	Y	Y	Y	Y	N	Y	Y	Y
5 ***McCrery***	N	N	N	N	Y	N	N	N
6 ***Baker***	N	N	N	N	Y	N	N	N
7 Hayes	Y	N	N	Y	Y	N	Y	Y
MAINE								
1 Andrews	Y	Y	Y	Y	N	Y	Y	Y
2 ***Snowe***	N	N	N	Y	N	Y	N	N
MARYLAND								
1 ***Gilchrest***	N	N	Y	N	Y	N	N	N
2 ***Bentley***	N	N	N	N	Y	N	N	N
3 Cardin	Y	Y	Y	Y	N	Y	Y	Y
4 Wynn	Y	Y	Y	Y	N	Y	Y	Y
5 Hoyer	Y	Y	Y	Y	N	Y	Y	Y
6 ***Bartlett***	N	N	N	N	Y	N	N	N
7 Mfume	Y	Y	Y	Y	N	Y	Y	Y
8 ***Morella***	N	Y	Y	Y	N	Y	N	N
MASSACHUSETTS								
1 Olver	?	Y	Y	Y	N	Y	Y	Y
2 Neal	Y	Y	Y	Y	N	Y	Y	?
3 ***Blute***	N	N	Y	N	Y	N	N	N
4 Frank	?	Y	Y	Y	N	Y	Y	Y
5 Meehan	Y	Y	Y	Y	N	Y	Y	Y
6 ***Torkildsen***	N	N	N	Y	Y	Y	N	N
7 Markey	Y	Y	Y	Y	N	Y	Y	Y
8 Kennedy	Y	Y	Y	Y	N	Y	Y	Y
9 Moakley	Y	Y	Y	Y	N	Y	Y	Y
10 Studds	Y	Y	Y	Y	N	Y	Y	Y
MICHIGAN								
1 Stupak	Y	Y	N	N	Y	N	Y	Y
2 ***Hoekstra***	N	N	N	N	Y	N	N	N
3 ***Ehlers***	N	N	N	N	Y	N	N	N
4 ***Camp***	N	N	N	N	Y	N	N	N
5 Barcia	Y	Y	N	N	Y	N	N	N
6 ***Upton***	N	N	N	N	Y	N	N	N
7 ***Smith***	N	N	N	N	Y	N	N	N
8 Carr	Y	Y	Y	Y	N	Y	Y	Y
9 Kildee	Y	Y	Y	N	Y	N	Y	Y
10 Bonior	Y	Y	Y	Y	N	Y	Y	Y
11 ***Knollenberg***	N	N	N	N	Y	N	N	N
12 Levin	Y	Y	Y	Y	N	Y	Y	Y
13 Ford	?	Y	Y	Y	N	Y	Y	?
14 Conyers	Y	Y	Y	Y	N	Y	Y	Y
15 Collins	Y	Y	Y	Y	N	Y	Y	Y
16 Dingell	Y	Y	N	Y	N	Y	Y	Y
MINNESOTA								
1 Penny	Y	N	Y	N	Y	N	Y	N
2 Minge	Y	N	Y	Y	Y	Y	Y	Y
3 ***Ramstad***	N	N	N	Y	N	Y	N	N
4 Vento	Y	Y	Y	Y	N	Y	Y	Y

	154	155	156	157	158	159	160	161
5 Sabo	Y	Y	Y	Y	N	Y	Y	Y
6 ***Grams***	N	N	N	N	Y	N	N	N
7 Peterson	Y	N	N	N	Y	N	Y	Y
8 Oberstar	Y	Y	N	Y	Y	N	Y	Y
MISSISSIPPI								
1 Whitten	?	Y	N	Y	N	N	Y	Y
2 Thompson	Y	Y	Y	Y	N	Y	Y	Y
3 Montgomery	Y	Y	N	N	N	N	Y	Y
4 Parker	Y	N	N	N	Y	N	Y	Y
5 Taylor	N	N	N	N	Y	N	N	N
MISSOURI								
1 Clay	N	Y	Y	Y	N	Y	?	?
2 ***Talent***	N	N	N	N	Y	N	N	N
3 Gephardt	Y	Y	Y	Y	N	Y	Y	Y
4 Skelton	Y	N	N	N	Y	N	N	N
5 Wheat	Y	Y	Y	Y	N	Y	Y	Y
6 Danner	Y	Y	N	Y	N	Y	Y	Y
7 ***Hancock***	N	N	N	N	Y	N	N	N
8 ***Emerson***	N	N	N	N	Y	N	N	N
9 Volkmer	Y	N	N	N	Y	N	Y	Y
MONTANA								
AL Williams	Y	N	N	Y	N	Y	Y	Y
NEBRASKA								
1 ***Bereuter***	N	N	Y	N	Y	Y	N	N
2 Hoagland	Y	Y	Y	Y	N	Y	Y	Y
3 ***Barrett***	N	N	N	N	Y	N	N	N
NEVADA								
1 Bilbray	Y	Y	N	Y	N	Y	Y	Y
2 ***Vucanovich***	N	N	N	N	Y	N	N	N
NEW HAMPSHIRE								
1 ***Zeliff***	N	N	N	Y	N	Y	N	N
2 Swett	?	N	Y	?	X	#	?	#
NEW JERSEY								
1 Andrews	Y	Y	Y	Y	N	Y	Y	N
2 Hughes	Y	Y	Y	Y	N	Y	?	Y
3 ***Saxton***	N	N	Y	N	Y	N	N	N
4 ***Smith***	Y	N	Y	N	Y	N	N	N
5 ***Roukema***	N	Y	Y	N	N	Y	N	N
6 Pallone	Y	Y	Y	Y	N	Y	Y	Y
7 ***Franks***	N	N	Y	N	N	Y	N	N
8 Klein	Y	Y	Y	Y	N	Y	Y	Y
9 Torricelli	Y	Y	Y	Y	N	Y	Y	Y
10 Payne	Y	Y	Y	Y	N	Y	Y	Y
11 ***Gallo***	N	N	N	Y	N	Y	N	N
12 ***Zimmer***	N	N	N	Y	N	Y	N	N
13 Menendez	Y	Y	Y	Y	N	Y	Y	Y
NEW MEXICO								
1 ***Schiff***	N	N	N	N	Y	Y	N	N
2 ***Skeen***	N	N	N	N	Y	N	N	N
3 Richardson	Y	Y	N	Y	?	?	Y	Y
NEW YORK								
1 Hochbrueckner	Y	Y	Y	Y	N	Y	Y	Y
2 ***Lazio***	N	N	Y	N	Y	Y	N	N
3 ***King***	N	N	Y	N	Y	N	N	N
4 ***Levy***	N	N	Y	N	Y	N	N	N
5 Ackerman	Y	Y	Y	Y	N	Y	Y	Y
6 Flake	Y	Y	Y	Y	N	Y	Y	Y
7 Manton	Y	Y	Y	N	Y	N	Y	Y
8 Nadler	Y	Y	Y	Y	N	Y	Y	Y
9 Schumer	Y	Y	Y	Y	N	Y	Y	Y
10 Towns	Y	Y	Y	Y	N	Y	Y	Y
11 Owens	Y	Y	Y	Y	N	Y	Y	Y
12 Velazquez	Y	Y	Y	Y	N	Y	Y	Y
13 ***Molinari***	N	N	Y	Y	N	Y	N	N
14 Maloney	?	Y	Y	Y	N	Y	Y	Y
15 Rangel	?	#	Y	Y	N	Y	Y	Y
16 Serrano	Y	Y	Y	?	?	?	?	?
17 Engel	Y	Y	Y	Y	N	Y	Y	Y
18 Lowey	Y	Y	Y	Y	N	Y	Y	Y
19 ***Fish***	Y	N	N	?	?	?	?	?
20 ***Gilman***	Y	N	N	Y	N	Y	N	N
21 McNulty	Y	Y	Y	Y	Y	N	Y	Y
22 ***Solomon***	N	N	N	N	Y	N	N	N
23 ***Boehlert***	N	N	Y	Y	N	Y	N	N
24 ***McHugh***	N	N	N	N	Y	Y	N	N
25 ***Walsh***	N	N	N	N	Y	N	N	N
26 Hinchey	Y	Y	N	Y	N	Y	Y	Y
27 ***Paxon***	N	N	N	N	Y	N	N	N
28 Slaughter	Y	Y	Y	Y	N	Y	Y	Y
29 LaFalce	Y	Y	Y	N	Y	N	Y	Y
30 ***Quinn***	N	N	Y	N	Y	N	N	N
31 ***Houghton***	Y	N	Y	Y	Y	Y	N	N
NORTH CAROLINA								
1 Clayton	Y	Y	Y	Y	N	Y	Y	Y
2 Valentine	Y	Y	Y	Y	N	Y	Y	Y

	154	155	156	157	158	159	160	161
3 Lancaster	Y	N	N	Y	N	Y	Y	Y
4 Price	Y	Y	Y	?	?	?	?	?
5 Neal	Y	Y	Y	Y	?	?	?	?
6 ***Coble***	N	N	N	N	Y	N	N	N
7 Rose	Y	Y	N	?	N	Y	Y	Y
8 Hefner	Y	Y	N	Y	N	Y	Y	Y
9 ***McMillan***	?	N	N	N	Y	Y	N	N
10 ***Ballenger***	N	N	N	N	Y	N	N	N
11 ***Taylor***	N	N	N	N	Y	N	N	N
12 Watt	Y	Y	Y	Y	N	Y	Y	Y
NORTH DAKOTA								
AL Pomeroy	Y	N	Y	Y	N	Y	Y	Y
OHIO								
1 Mann	Y	Y	Y	Y	N	Y	Y	N
2 ***Portman***	N	N	N	N	Y	N	N	N
3 Hall	Y	Y	Y	Y	Y	N	Y	Y
4 ***Oxley***	N	N	N	N	Y	N	N	?
5 ***Gillmor***	Y	N	N	N	Y	N	N	N
6 Strickland	?	Y	N	Y	N	Y	Y	Y
7 ***Hobson***	N	N	N	N	Y	N	N	N
8 ***Boehner***	N	N	N	N	Y	N	N	N
9 Kaptur	Y	Y	Y	Y	N	N	Y	Y
10 ***Hoke***	N	N	N	N	Y	N	N	N
11 Stokes	Y	Y	Y	Y	N	Y	Y	Y
12 ***Kasich***	Y	N	Y	N	Y	N	N	N
13 Brown	Y	Y	Y	Y	N	Y	Y	Y
14 Sawyer	Y	Y	Y	Y	N	Y	Y	Y
15 ***Pryce***	N	N	Y	Y	N	Y	?	?
16 ***Regula***	N	N	N	N	Y	N	N	N
17 Traficant	Y	Y	Y	Y	N	Y	Y	N
18 Applegate	Y	Y	Y	Y	Y	N	Y	Y
19 Fingerhut	Y	Y	Y	Y	N	Y	Y	N
OKLAHOMA								
1 ***Inhofe***	N	N	N	N	Y	N	N	N
2 Synar	Y	Y	Y	Y	N	Y	Y	Y
3 Brewster	Y	Y	N	Y	N	Y	Y	Y
4 McCurdy	Y	Y	Y	Y	N	Y	Y	Y
5 ***Istook***	N	N	N	N	Y	N	N	N
6 Vacancy								
OREGON								
1 Furse	Y	Y	Y	Y	N	Y	Y	Y
2 ***Smith***	N	N	N	N	Y	N	N	N
3 Wyden	Y	Y	Y	Y	N	Y	Y	Y
4 DeFazio	Y	Y	N	Y	N	Y	Y	N
5 Kopetski	Y	Y	N	Y	N	Y	Y	Y
PENNSYLVANIA								
1 Foglietta	Y	Y	Y	?	?	?	?	?
2 Blackwell	?	Y	Y	?	?	?	?	?
3 Borski	Y	Y	Y	Y	Y	N	Y	Y
4 Klink	Y	N	N	N	Y	N	Y	Y
5 ***Clinger***	N	N	N	N	Y	N	N	N
6 Holden	Y	N	N	N	Y	N	Y	Y
7 ***Weldon***	N	N	N	N	Y	N	N	N
8 ***Greenwood***	Y	N	Y	N	Y	Y	N	N
9 ***Shuster***	N	N	N	N	Y	N	N	N
10 ***McDade***	N	N	Y	N	Y	N	N	N
11 Kanjorski	Y	N	N	Y	Y	N	Y	Y
12 Murtha	Y	Y	N	Y	Y	N	Y	Y
13 Margolies-Mezv.	Y	Y	Y	Y	N	Y	Y	N
14 Coyne	Y	Y	Y	Y	N	Y	Y	Y
15 McHale	Y	Y	Y	Y	N	Y	Y	Y
16 ***Walker***	N	N	N	N	Y	N	N	N
17 ***Gekas***	N	N	N	N	Y	N	N	N
18 ***Santorum***	N	N	N	N	Y	N	N	?
19 ***Goodling***	N	N	N	N	Y	N	N	N
20 Murphy	N	Y	N	N	Y	N	Y	Y
21 ***Ridge***	?	Y	Y	N	Y	Y	N	N
RHODE ISLAND								
1 ***Machtley***	N	N	Y	Y	N	Y	N	N
2 Reed	Y	Y	Y	Y	N	Y	Y	Y
SOUTH CAROLINA								
1 ***Ravenel***	N	N	N	N	Y	N	N	N
2 ***Spence***	N	N	N	N	Y	N	N	N
3 Derrick	Y	Y	Y	Y	N	Y	Y	Y
4 ***Inglis***	Y	N	N	N	Y	N	N	N
5 Spratt	Y	Y	Y	Y	N	Y	Y	Y
6 Clyburn	Y	Y	Y	Y	N	Y	Y	Y
SOUTH DAKOTA								
AL Johnson	Y	Y	N	Y	N	Y	Y	Y
TENNESSEE								
1 ***Quillen***	N	Y	N	N	Y	N	N	N
2 ***Duncan***	N	N	N	N	Y	N	N	N
3 Lloyd	?	Y	Y	Y	N	Y	Y	Y
4 Cooper	Y	Y	N	Y	N	Y	Y	N
5 Clement	Y	Y	N	?	?	?	?	?

	154	155	156	157	158	159	160	161
6 Gordon	Y	Y	N	Y	N	Y	Y	Y
7 ***Sundquist***	N	N	N	N	Y	N	N	N
8 Tanner	Y	N	N	Y	N	Y	Y	Y
9 Ford	Y	Y	Y	Y	N	Y	Y	Y
TEXAS								
1 Chapman	?	Y	N	Y	N	Y	Y	Y
2 Wilson	Y	N	N	Y	N	Y	?	Y
3 ***Johnson, Sam***	N	N	N	N	Y	N	N	N
4 Hall	Y	N	N	N	Y	N	?	?
5 Bryant	Y	Y	Y	Y	N	Y	?	Y
6 ***Barton***	N	N	N	N	Y	N	N	N
7 ***Archer***	N	N	N	N	Y	N	N	N
8 ***Fields***	N	N	N	N	Y	N	N	N
9 Brooks	Y	Y	N	Y	N	Y	Y	Y
10 Pickle	Y	Y	Y	Y	N	Y	Y	Y
11 Edwards	Y	Y	Y	Y	N	Y	Y	Y
12 Geren	Y	N	N	Y	Y	Y	Y	Y
13 Sarpalius	Y	Y	N	N	Y	N	Y	Y
14 Laughlin	Y	Y	N	?	?	?	?	?
15 de la Garza	Y	Y	N	N	Y	N	Y	Y
16 Coleman	Y	Y	Y	Y	N	Y	Y	Y
17 Stenholm	Y	N	N	N	Y	N	Y	Y
18 Washington	?	Y	Y	Y	N	Y	?	?
19 ***Combest***	Y	N	N	N	Y	N	N	N
20 Gonzalez	Y	Y	Y	Y	N	Y	Y	Y
21 ***Smith***	N	N	N	N	Y	N	N	N
22 ***DeLay***	N	N	N	N	Y	N	N	N
23 ***Bonilla***	N	N	N	N	Y	N	N	N
24 Frost	Y	Y	N	Y	N	Y	Y	Y
25 Andrews	?	Y	Y	Y	N	Y	?	Y
26 ***Armey***	N	N	N	N	Y	N	N	N
27 Ortiz	Y	Y	N	N	Y	N	Y	Y
28 Tejeda	Y	Y	N	N	Y	N	Y	Y
29 Green	Y	N	N	Y	N	Y	Y	Y
30 Johnson, E.B.	Y	Y	Y	Y	N	Y	Y	Y
UTAH								
1 ***Hansen***	N	N	N	N	Y	N	N	N
2 Shepherd	Y	Y	Y	Y	N	Y	Y	Y
3 Orton	Y	N	N	Y	Y	Y	Y	Y
VERMONT								
AL *Sanders*	Y	Y	Y	Y	N	Y	Y	Y
VIRGINIA								
1 ***Bateman***	Y	N	Y	N	Y	N	N	N
2 Pickett	Y	Y	N	Y	N	Y	Y	N
3 Scott	Y	Y	Y	Y	N	Y	Y	Y
4 Sisisky	Y	Y	N	Y	N	Y	Y	N
5 Payne	Y	Y	N	Y	N	Y	Y	Y
6 ***Goodlatte***	N	N	N	N	Y	N	N	N
7 ***Bliley***	N	N	N	N	Y	N	N	N
8 Moran	Y	Y	Y	Y	N	Y	?	Y
9 Boucher	Y	Y	N	Y	N	Y	Y	Y
10 ***Wolf***	N	N	N	N	Y	N	N	N
11 Byrne	Y	Y	Y	Y	N	Y	Y	Y
WASHINGTON								
1 Cantwell	Y	Y	Y	Y	N	Y	Y	Y
2 Swift	Y	Y	Y	Y	N	Y	Y	Y
3 Unsoeld	Y	Y	N	Y	N	Y	Y	Y
4 Inslee	Y	Y	Y	Y	N	Y	Y	Y
5 Foley								
6 Dicks	Y	Y	Y	Y	N	Y	Y	Y
7 McDermott	Y	Y	Y	Y	N	Y	Y	Y
8 ***Dunn***	N	N	N	N	Y	Y	N	N
9 Kreidler	Y	Y	Y	Y	N	Y	Y	Y
WEST VIRGINIA								
1 Mollohan	Y	Y	N	N	Y	N	Y	Y
2 Wise	Y	Y	N	Y	N	Y	Y	Y
3 Rahall	Y	Y	N	N	Y	N	Y	Y
WISCONSIN								
1 Barca	Y	N	N	Y	N	Y	Y	Y
2 ***Klug***	N	N	Y	Y	N	Y	N	N
3 ***Gunderson***	N	N	N	N	Y	N	N	N
4 Kleczka	Y	Y	Y	Y	N	Y	Y	Y
5 Barrett	Y	Y	Y	Y	N	Y	Y	Y
6 ***Petri***	N	N	N	N	Y	N	N	N
7 Obey	Y	Y	N	Y	N	Y	Y	Y
8 ***Roth***	N	N	N	N	Y	N	N	N
9 ***Sensenbrenner***	N	N	N	N	Y	N	N	N
WYOMING								
AL ***Thomas***	N	N	N	N	Y	N	N	N
DELEGATES								
de Lugo, V.I.	D	D	D	D	D	D	D	D
Faleomavaega, Am.S.	D	D	D	D	D	D	D	D
Norton, D.C.	D	D	D	D	D	D	D	D
Romero-B., P.R.	D	D	D	D	D	D	D	D
Underwood, Guam	D	D	D	D	D	D	D	D

Southern states - Ala., Ark., Fla., Ga., Ky., La., Miss., N.C., Okla., S.C., Tenn., Texas, Va.
Omitted votes are quorum calls, which CQ does not include in its vote charts.

KEY

Y Voted for (yea).
Paired for.
+ Announced for.
N Voted against (nay).
X Paired against.
— Announced against.
P Voted "present."
C Voted "present" to avoid possible conflict of interest.
? Did not vote or otherwise make a position known.
D Delegates ineligible to vote.

Democrats *Republicans*
Independent

162. HR 2442. Economic Development Administration Reauthorization/Computer Data Base. Kanjorski, D-Pa., amendment to establish a computer data base within the Commerce Department for the transfer to small businesses of information on technologies and processes developed by the federal government. Adopted in the Committee of the Whole 270-135: R 43-129; D 227-6 (ND 159-3, SD 68-3); I 0-0, May 11, 1994.

163. HR 2442. Economic Development Administration Reauthorization/Appalachian Regional Commission. Goss, R-Fla., amendment to eliminate the authorization for the Appalachian Regional Commission. Rejected in the Committee of the Whole 143-261: R 126-45; D 17-216 (ND 12-148, SD 5-68); I 0-0, May 11, 1994.

164. HR 2442. Economic Development Administration Reauthorization/Termination. Hefley, R-Colo., amendment to terminate the Economic Development Administration by striking the authorization in the bill for it. Rejected in the Committee of the Whole 97-319: R 90-82; D 7-236 (ND 6-161, SD 1-75); I 0-1, May 12, 1994.

165. HR 2442. Economic Development Administration Reauthorization/Authorization Reduction. Hefley, R-Colo., amendment to reduce the authorization for the Economic Development Administration by $10 million to the level requested by the administration. Rejected in the Committee of the Whole 171-244: R 144-28; D 27-215 (ND 16-149, SD 11-66); I 0-1, May 12, 1994.

166. HR 2442. Economic Development Administration Reauthorization/Task Force Elimination. Boehner, R-Ohio, amendment to eliminate the provisions of the bill that establish a Regional Development Task Force to study the unique characteristics and contributions of the Appalachian Regional Commission to distressed rural areas. Rejected in the Committee of the Whole 184-239: R 161-13; D 23-225 (ND 16-152, SD 7-73); I 0-1, May 12, 1994.

167. HR 2442. Economic Development Administration Reauthorization/Federal Regulations. Walker, R-Pa., amendment to allow businesses adversely affected by federal regulations to petition the administrator to ask agencies to waive those regulations. Adopted in the Committee of the Whole 410-10: R 172-0; D 237-10 (ND 160-8, SD 77-2); I 1-0, May 12, 1994.

168. HR 2442. Economic Development Administration Reauthorization/Passage. Passage of the bill to reauthorize the Economic Development Administration at $1.1 billion and Appalachian Regional Commission at $623 million over the three years of fiscal 1994-96 to help promote development in economically distressed communities. Passed 328-89: R 88-84; D 239-5 (ND 162-3, SD 77-2); I 1-0, May 12, 1994. A "yea" was a vote in favor of the president's position.

	162	163	164	165	166	167	168
ALABAMA							
1 Callahan	N	N	N	Y	N	Y	Y
2 *Everett*	N	N	N	N	N	Y	Y
3 Browder	Y	N	N	N	N	Y	Y
4 Bevill	Y	N	N	N	N	Y	Y
5 Cramer	Y	N	N	N	N	Y	Y
6 *Bachus*	N	N	N	Y	N	Y	Y
7 Hilliard	?	?	N	N	N	Y	Y
ALASKA							
AL *Young*	N	Y	N	Y	Y	Y	Y
ARIZONA							
1 Coppersmith	N	N	N	N	N	Y	Y
2 Pastor	Y	N	N	N	N	Y	+
3 *Stump*	N	Y	Y	Y	Y	Y	N
4 *Kyl*	N	Y	Y	Y	Y	Y	N
5 *Kolbe*	N	Y	Y	Y	Y	Y	N
6 English	Y	—	N	Y	N	Y	Y
ARKANSAS							
1 Lambert	Y	N	N	N	Y	N	Y
2 Thornton	N	N	N	N	N	Y	Y
3 *Hutchinson*	N	Y	N	Y	Y	Y	Y
4 Dickey	N	Y	N	Y	N	Y	Y
CALIFORNIA							
1 Hamburg	Y	N	N	N	N	Y	Y
2 *Herger*	Y	Y	N	N	Y	Y	Y
3 Fazio	Y	N	N	N	N	Y	Y
4 *Doolittle*	N	Y	Y	Y	Y	Y	N
5 Matsui	Y	N	N	N	N	Y	Y
6 Woolsey	Y	N	N	N	N	Y	Y
7 Miller	?	N	Y	N	N	Y	Y
8 Pelosi	Y	N	N	N	N	Y	Y
9 Dellums	#	?	N	N	N	Y	Y
10 *Baker*	N	Y	Y	Y	Y	Y	Y
11 *Pombo*	N	Y	N	Y	Y	Y	Y
12 Lantos	Y	N	N	N	N	Y	Y
13 Stark	Y	N	N	N	N	N	Y
14 Eshoo	Y	N	N	N	N	Y	Y
15 Mineta	Y	N	N	N	N	Y	Y
16 Edwards	Y	N	N	N	N	Y	Y
17 Farr	Y	N	N	N	N	Y	Y
18 Condit	Y	Y	Y	Y	Y	Y	Y
19 Lehman	Y	N	Y	N	Y	Y	Y
20 Dooley	Y	N	N	N	N	Y	Y
21 *Thomas*	N	Y	N	Y	Y	Y	Y
22 *Huffington*	N	Y	N	Y	Y	Y	Y
23 *Gallegly*	N	Y	N	Y	Y	Y	Y
24 Beilenson	Y	N	N	N	N	Y	Y
25 *McKeon*	N	Y	Y	Y	Y	Y	N
26 Berman	Y	?	N	N	N	Y	Y
27 *Moorhead*	N	Y	Y	Y	Y	Y	N
28 *Dreier*	N	Y	Y	Y	Y	Y	N
29 Waxman	Y	N	N	N	N	Y	Y
30 Becerra	Y	N	?	?	X	?	?
31 Martinez	Y	N	N	N	N	Y	Y
32 Dixon	Y	N	N	N	N	Y	Y
33 Roybal-Allard	Y	N	N	N	N	Y	Y
34 Torres	Y	N	N	N	N	Y	Y
35 Waters	Y	N	N	N	N	Y	Y
36 Harman	Y	Y	N	Y	N	Y	Y
37 Tucker	Y	N	N	N	N	Y	Y
38 *Horn*	Y	Y	N	Y	Y	Y	Y
39 *Royce*	N	Y	Y	Y	Y	Y	N
40 *Lewis*	N	Y	Y	N	Y	N	Y
41 *Kim*	N	Y	Y	Y	Y	Y	N
42 Brown	Y	N	N	N	N	Y	Y
43 *Calvert*	N	Y	Y	Y	Y	Y	Y
44 *McCandless*	N	Y	Y	Y	Y	Y	N
45 *Rohrabacher*	N	Y	Y	Y	Y	Y	Y
46 *Dornan*	N	Y	Y	?	Y	Y	N
47 *Cox*	N	Y	Y	Y	Y	Y	Y
48 *Packard*	N	N	N	Y	Y	Y	Y
49 Schenk	Y	Y	N	Y	Y	Y	Y
50 Filner	Y	N	N	N	N	Y	Y
51 *Cunningham*	N	Y	N	Y	Y	+	Y
52 *Hunter*	N	N	Y	Y	Y	Y	Y
COLORADO							
1 Schroeder	Y	N	N	N	N	N	Y
2 Skaggs	Y	N	N	N	N	Y	Y
3 *McInnis*	N	Y	Y	Y	Y	Y	N
4 *Allard*	N	Y	Y	Y	Y	Y	N
5 *Hefley*	N	Y	Y	Y	Y	Y	N
6 *Schaefer*	N	Y	Y	Y	Y	Y	N
CONNECTICUT							
1 Kennelly	Y	N	N	N	N	Y	Y
2 Gejdenson	Y	N	N	N	N	Y	Y
3 DeLauro	Y	N	N	N	N	Y	Y
4 *Shays*	Y	Y	N	Y	Y	Y	Y
5 *Franks*	Y	Y	N	Y	Y	Y	Y
6 *Johnson*	N	Y	N	Y	Y	Y	Y
DELAWARE							
AL *Castle*	N	Y	Y	Y	Y	Y	N
FLORIDA							
1 Hutto	Y	N	N	N	Y	Y	Y
2 Peterson	Y	N	N	N	N	Y	Y
3 Brown	?	?	N	N	N	Y	Y
4 *Fowler*	N	Y	N	Y	Y	Y	Y
5 Thurman	Y	N	N	Y	N	Y	Y
6 *Stearns*	N	Y	Y	Y	Y	Y	N
7 *Mica*	N	Y	N	Y	Y	Y	Y
8 *McCollum*	N	Y	Y	Y	Y	Y	N
9 *Bilirakis*	N	Y	Y	Y	Y	Y	N
10 *Young*	N	Y	Y	Y	Y	Y	N
11 Gibbons	Y	N	?	N	N	Y	Y
12 *Canady*	Y	Y	N	Y	Y	Y	Y
13 *Miller*	N	Y	Y	Y	Y	Y	N
14 *Goss*	N	Y	Y	Y	Y	Y	N
15 Bacchus	Y	N	N	N	N	Y	Y
16 *Lewis*	N	?	?	Y	Y	Y	N
17 Meek	Y	N	N	N	N	?	Y
18 *Ros-Lehtinen*	N	Y	N	Y	Y	Y	Y
19 Johnston	Y	N	N	N	N	Y	Y
20 Deutsch	Y	N	N	N	N	Y	Y
21 *Diaz-Balart*	Y	Y	N	N	Y	Y	Y
22 *Shaw*	N	Y	Y	Y	Y	Y	Y
23 Hastings	Y	N	N	N	N	Y	Y
GEORGIA							
1 *Kingston*	N	Y	N	Y	Y	Y	Y
2 Bishop	Y	N	N	N	N	Y	Y
3 *Collins*	N	Y	N	Y	Y	Y	Y
4 *Linder*	N	Y	Y	Y	Y	Y	?
5 Lewis	Y	N	N	N	N	Y	Y
6 *Gingrich*	N	Y	Y	Y	Y	Y	N
7 Darden	Y	N	N	N	N	Y	Y
8 Rowland	Y	N	N	N	N	Y	Y
9 Deal	Y	N	N	N	N	Y	Y
10 Johnson	Y	N	N	N	N	Y	Y
11 McKinney	Y	N	N	N	N	N	Y
HAWAII							
1 Abercrombie	Y	N	N	N	N	Y	Y
2 Mink	Y	N	N	N	N	Y	Y
IDAHO							
1 LaRocco	Y	N	N	N	N	Y	Y
2 *Crapo*	N	Y	Y	Y	Y	Y	N
ILLINOIS							
1 Rush	+	—	N	N	N	Y	Y
2 Reynolds	Y	N	N	N	N	Y	Y
3 Lipinski	Y	N	N	N	N	Y	Y
4 Gutierrez	Y	N	N	N	N	Y	+
5 Rostenkowski	?	?	N	N	N	Y	Y
6 *Hyde*	N	Y	Y	Y	Y	Y	Y
7 Collins	Y	N	N	N	N	Y	Y
8 *Crane*	N	Y	Y	Y	Y	Y	N
9 Yates	Y	N	N	N	N	Y	Y
10 *Porter*	Y	Y	Y	Y	Y	?	X
11 Sangmeister	Y	N	N	N	N	Y	Y
12 Costello	Y	N	N	N	N	Y	Y
13 *Fawell*	N	Y	Y	Y	Y	Y	Y
14 *Hastert*	N	Y	Y	Y	Y	Y	N
15 *Ewing*	Y	Y	Y	Y	Y	Y	Y
16 *Manzullo*	N	Y	Y	Y	Y	Y	N
17 Evans	Y	N	N	N	N	Y	Y

ND Northern Democrats   SD Southern Democrats

	162	163	164	165	166	167	168
18 ***Michel***	N	Y	Y	Y	Y	Y	N
19 Poshard	Y	N	N	N	N	Y	Y
20 Durbin	Y	N	N	N	N	Y	Y
INDIANA							
1 Visclosky	Y	N	N	N	N	Y	Y
2 Sharp	?	?	?	?	?	?	?
3 Roemer	Y	N	N	N	N	Y	Y
4 Long	Y	N	N	N	N	Y	Y
5 ***Buyer***	Y	Y	N	N	Y	Y	Y
6 ***Burton***	N	Y	Y	Y	Y	Y	N
7 ***Myers***	Y	N	N	Y	Y	Y	N
8 McCloskey	Y	N	N	N	N	Y	Y
9 Hamilton	Y	N	N	N	N	Y	Y
10 Jacobs	Y	N	N	Y	N	Y	Y
IOWA							
1 ***Leach***	Y	N	N	Y	Y	Y	Y
2 ***Nussle***	N	Y	Y	Y	Y	Y	N
3 ***Lightfoot***	N	N	?	Y	Y	Y	Y
4 Smith	Y	N	N	N	N	Y	Y
5 ***Grandy***	?	#	?	?	#	?	?
KANSAS							
1 ***Roberts***	N	Y	N	Y	Y	Y	N
2 Slattery	Y	Y	N	N	N	Y	Y
3 ***Meyers***	N	Y	N	Y	Y	Y	Y
4 Glickman	Y	N	N	N	N	Y	Y
KENTUCKY							
1 Barlow	Y	N	N	N	N	Y	Y
2 Vacancy							
3 Mazzoli	Y	N	N	N	N	Y	Y
4 ***Bunning***	N	N	N	N	Y	Y	Y
5 ***Rogers***	N	N	N	N	N	Y	Y
6 Baesler	Y	N	N	N	N	Y	Y
LOUISIANA							
1 ***Livingston***	N	Y	Y	Y	Y	Y	Y
2 Jefferson	?	?	?	N	N	Y	Y
3 Tauzin	Y	Y	N	Y	Y	Y	Y
4 Fields	?	N	N	N	N	Y	Y
5 ***McCrery***	N	Y	N	Y	Y	Y	Y
6 ***Baker***	N	Y	Y	Y	Y	Y	N
7 Hayes	Y	N	N	N	N	Y	Y
MAINE							
1 Andrews	Y	N	N	N	N	Y	Y
2 ***Snowe***	Y	N	N	N	Y	Y	Y
MARYLAND							
1 ***Gilchrest***	N	Y	Y	Y	Y	Y	N
2 ***Bentley***	Y	N	N	N	N	Y	Y
3 Cardin	Y	N	N	N	N	Y	Y
4 Wynn	Y	N	N	N	N	Y	Y
5 Hoyer	Y	N	?	?	N	Y	Y
6 ***Bartlett***	N	N	Y	Y	N	Y	Y
7 Mfume	Y	N	—	—	N	Y	Y
8 ***Morella***	N	N	N	Y	Y	Y	Y
MASSACHUSETTS							
1 Olver	Y	N	N	N	N	Y	Y
2 Neal	Y	N	N	N	N	Y	Y
3 ***Blute***	Y	N	N	N	N	Y	Y
4 Frank	N	N	N	N	N	N	Y
5 Meehan	Y	Y	N	N	Y	Y	Y
6 ***Torkildsen***	Y	Y	N	N	Y	Y	Y
7 Markey	Y	N	N	N	N	Y	Y
8 Kennedy	Y	N	N	N	N	Y	Y
9 Moakley	Y	N	N	N	N	Y	Y
10 Studds	Y	N	N	N	N	Y	Y
MICHIGAN							
1 Stupak	Y	N	N	N	N	Y	Y
2 ***Hoekstra***	N	Y	N	Y	Y	Y	Y
3 ***Ehlers***	Y	Y	N	Y	Y	Y	N
4 ***Camp***	N	Y	N	Y	Y	Y	Y
5 Barcia	Y	N	N	N	N	Y	Y
6 ***Upton***	Y	Y	N	Y	Y	Y	Y
7 ***Smith***	Y	Y	N	Y	Y	Y	N
8 Carr	Y	N	N	N	N	Y	Y
9 Kildee	Y	N	N	N	N	Y	Y
10 Bonior	Y	N	N	N	N	Y	Y
11 ***Knollenberg***	N	Y	Y	Y	Y	Y	N
12 Levin	Y	N	N	N	N	Y	Y
13 Ford	?	N	N	N	N	Y	Y
14 Conyers	Y	N	N	N	N	Y	Y
15 Collins	Y	N	N	N	N	Y	Y
16 Dingell	?	X	N	N	?	?	Y
MINNESOTA							
1 Penny	Y	Y	Y	Y	Y	Y	N
2 Minge	Y	Y	N	Y	Y	Y	Y
3 ***Ramstad***	N	Y	Y	Y	Y	Y	N
4 Vento	Y	N	N	N	N	Y	Y

	162	163	164	165	166	167	168
5 Sabo	Y	N	N	N	N	N	Y
6 ***Grams***	N	Y	Y	Y	Y	Y	N
7 Peterson	N	Y	N	Y	Y	Y	Y
8 Oberstar	Y	N	N	N	N	N	Y
MISSISSIPPI							
1 Whitten	Y	N	N	?	?	?	?
2 Thompson	?	?	N	N	N	Y	Y
3 Montgomery	Y	N	N	N	N	Y	Y
4 Parker	Y	N	?	?	?	?	?
5 Taylor	Y	N	N	Y	Y	Y	Y
MISSOURI							
1 Clay	Y	N	N	N	N	Y	Y
2 ***Talent***	N	Y	N	Y	Y	Y	N
3 Gephardt	Y	N	N	N	N	Y	Y
4 Skelton	Y	N	N	N	N	Y	Y
5 Wheat	Y	N	N	N	N	Y	Y
6 Danner	Y	N	N	N	N	Y	Y
7 ***Hancock***	N	Y	Y	Y	Y	Y	N
8 ***Emerson***	N	N	N	N	Y	Y	Y
9 Volkmer	Y	N	N	N	N	Y	Y
MONTANA							
AL Williams	Y	N	N	?	Y	Y	Y
NEBRASKA							
1 ***Bereuter***	Y	Y	Y	Y	Y	Y	N
2 Hoagland	Y	N	N	X	?	?	#
3 ***Barrett***	X	#	Y	Y	Y	Y	N
NEVADA							
1 Bilbray	Y	N	N	N	Y	Y	Y
2 ***Vucanovich***	Y	N	N	N	Y	Y	Y
NEW HAMPSHIRE							
1 ***Zeliff***	N	Y	Y	Y	Y	Y	N
2 Swett	Y	Y	N	N	N	Y	Y
NEW JERSEY							
1 Andrews	Y	?	N	N	Y	Y	N
2 Hughes	Y	N	N	N	N	Y	Y
3 ***Saxton***	N	Y	N	Y	Y	Y	Y
4 ***Smith***	Y	N	N	Y	Y	Y	Y
5 ***Roukema***	Y	Y	Y	Y	Y	Y	Y
6 Pallone	Y	N	N	N	N	Y	Y
7 ***Franks***	Y	N	N	Y	Y	Y	Y
8 Klein	Y	Y	N	N	N	Y	Y
9 Torricelli	Y	N	N	N	N	Y	Y
10 Payne	Y	N	N	N	N	Y	Y
11 ***Gallo***	N	N	N	Y	Y	Y	Y
12 ***Zimmer***	N	Y	Y	Y	Y	Y	N
13 Menendez	Y	N	N	N	N	Y	Y
NEW MEXICO							
1 ***Schiff***	Y	N	N	Y	Y	Y	Y
2 ***Skeen***	N	N	N	N	Y	Y	Y
3 Richardson	Y	N	N	N	N	Y	Y
NEW YORK							
1 Hochbrueckner	Y	N	N	N	N	Y	Y
2 ***Lazio***	Y	Y	N	Y	Y	Y	Y
3 ***King***	N	Y	Y	Y	Y	Y	N
4 ***Levy***	Y	Y	Y	Y	Y	Y	N
5 Ackerman	Y	N	N	N	N	Y	Y
6 Flake	?	?	?	?	?	?	?
7 Manton	Y	N	N	N	N	Y	Y
8 Nadler	Y	N	N	N	N	N	Y
9 Schumer	Y	?	N	N	N	Y	Y
10 Towns	Y	N	?	?	?	Y	Y
11 Owens	?	?	N	N	N	Y	Y
12 Velazquez	?	?	N	N	N	Y	Y
13 ***Molinari***	N	N	N	N	N	Y	Y
14 Maloney	Y	N	N	N	N	Y	Y
15 Rangel	Y	N	N	N	N	Y	Y
16 Serrano	Y	N	N	N	N	Y	Y
17 Engel	?	?	N	N	N	N	Y
18 Lowey	Y	N	N	N	N	Y	Y
19 ***Fish***	Y	N	N	Y	N	Y	Y
20 ***Gilman***	Y	N	N	Y	Y	Y	Y
21 McNulty	?	?	N	N	N	Y	Y
22 ***Solomon***	N	Y	?	Y	Y	Y	N
23 ***Boehlert***	Y	N	N	N	Y	Y	Y
24 ***McHugh***	N	Y	N	N	N	Y	Y
25 ***Walsh***	N	N	N	N	N	Y	Y
26 Hinchey	Y	N	N	N	N	Y	Y
27 ***Paxon***	N	Y	Y	Y	Y	Y	N
28 Slaughter	Y	N	N	N	N	Y	Y
29 LaFalce	Y	N	N	N	N	Y	Y
30 ***Quinn***	Y	N	N	N	Y	Y	Y
31 ***Houghton***	?	?	N	N	Y	Y	Y
NORTH CAROLINA							
1 Clayton	?	?	N	N	N	Y	Y
2 Valentine	Y	N	N	N	N	Y	Y

	162	163	164	165	166	167	168
3 Lancaster	Y	N	N	N	N	Y	Y
4 Price	Y	N	N	N	N	Y	Y
5 Neal	Y	N	N	N	N	Y	Y
6 ***Coble***	N	Y	Y	Y	Y	Y	N
7 Rose	Y	N	N	N	N	Y	Y
8 Hefner	Y	N	N	N	N	Y	Y
9 ***McMillan***	N	Y	Y	Y	Y	Y	N
10 ***Ballenger***	N	Y	Y	Y	Y	Y	N
11 ***Taylor***	N	N	N	Y	Y	Y	Y
12 Watt	Y	N	N	N	N	Y	Y
NORTH DAKOTA							
AL Pomeroy	Y	N	N	N	N	Y	Y
OHIO							
1 Mann	Y	Y	Y	Y	N	Y	N
2 ***Portman***	N	N	Y	Y	Y	Y	N
3 Hall	Y	N	N	N	N	Y	Y
4 ***Oxley***	N	Y	Y	Y	Y	Y	N
5 ***Gillmor***	Y	N	N	N	Y	Y	Y
6 Strickland	Y	N	N	N	N	Y	Y
7 ***Hobson***	N	N	Y	Y	Y	Y	N
8 ***Boehner***	N	Y	Y	Y	Y	Y	N
9 Kaptur	Y	N	N	N	N	Y	Y
10 ***Hoke***	N	Y	Y	Y	Y	Y	N
11 Stokes	?	X	?	N	N	Y	Y
12 ***Kasich***	N	Y	Y	Y	Y	Y	N
13 Brown	Y	N	Y	Y	Y	Y	Y
14 Sawyer	Y	N	N	N	N	Y	Y
15 ***Pryce***	N	Y	Y	Y	Y	Y	N
16 ***Regula***	Y	N	N	Y	Y	Y	Y
17 Traficant	Y	N	N	N	N	Y	Y
18 Applegate	Y	N	N	N	N	N	Y
19 Fingerhut	Y	N	N	N	N	Y	Y
OKLAHOMA							
1 ***Inhofe***	N	Y	Y	Y	Y	Y	N
2 Synar	Y	N	N	N	N	Y	Y
3 Brewster	Y	N	N	N	N	Y	Y
4 McCurdy	Y	Y	?	?	Y	Y	Y
5 ***Istook***	N	Y	Y	Y	Y	Y	N
6 Vacancy							
OREGON							
1 Furse	Y	N	N	N	N	Y	Y
2 ***Smith***	N	N	N	Y	Y	Y	Y
3 Wyden	Y	N	N	N	N	Y	Y
4 DeFazio	Y	N	N	?	N	Y	Y
5 Kopetski	Y	N	N	N	N	Y	Y
PENNSYLVANIA							
1 Foglietta	Y	N	N	N	N	N	Y
2 Blackwell	?	?	?	?	?	?	?
3 Borski	Y	N	N	N	N	Y	Y
4 Klink	Y	N	N	N	N	Y	Y
5 ***Clinger***	N	N	N	N	N	Y	Y
6 Holden	Y	N	N	N	N	Y	Y
7 ***Weldon***	Y	Y	Y	Y	Y	Y	Y
8 ***Greenwood***	Y	Y	N	Y	Y	Y	Y
9 ***Shuster***	N	N	N	N	Y	Y	Y
10 ***McDade***	Y	N	N	N	N	Y	Y
11 Kanjorski	Y	N	N	N	N	Y	Y
12 Murtha	Y	N	N	?	N	Y	Y
13 Margolies-Mezv.	Y	Y	N	N	Y	Y	Y
14 Coyne	Y	N	N	N	N	Y	Y
15 McHale	Y	N	N	N	N	Y	Y
16 ***Walker***	N	Y	Y	Y	Y	Y	N
17 ***Gekas***	N	N	N	Y	Y	Y	N
18 ***Santorum***	Y	N	N	Y	Y	Y	Y
19 ***Goodling***	N	Y	N	Y	Y	Y	Y
20 Murphy	Y	N	N	Y	N	Y	Y
21 ***Ridge***	?	?	?	?	?	?	?
RHODE ISLAND							
1 ***Machtley***	Y	Y	N	Y	Y	Y	Y
2 Reed	Y	N	N	N	N	Y	Y
SOUTH CAROLINA							
1 ***Ravenel***	Y	Y	N	Y	Y	Y	Y
2 ***Spence***	N	N	N	Y	Y	Y	Y
3 Derrick	Y	N	N	N	N	Y	Y
4 ***Inglis***	N	Y	N	Y	Y	Y	Y
5 Spratt	Y	N	N	N	N	Y	Y
6 Clyburn	?	?	N	N	N	Y	Y
SOUTH DAKOTA							
AL Johnson	Y	N	N	N	N	Y	Y
TENNESSEE							
1 ***Quillen***	Y	N	N	N	Y	Y	Y
2 ***Duncan***	N	Y	Y	Y	Y	Y	N
3 Lloyd	N	N	N	N	N	Y	Y
4 Cooper	?	?	N	Y	N	Y	Y
5 Clement	Y	N	N	N	N	Y	Y

	162	163	164	165	166	167	168
6 Gordon	Y	N	N	N	N	Y	Y
7 ***Sundquist***	Y	N	N	N	Y	Y	Y
8 Tanner	Y	N	N	N	N	Y	Y
9 Ford	Y	N	N	N	N	Y	Y
TEXAS							
1 Chapman	Y	N	N	N	N	Y	Y
2 Wilson	?	N	N	N	N	Y	Y
3 ***Johnson, Sam***	N	Y	Y	Y	Y	Y	N
4 Hall	Y	Y	N	Y	Y	Y	N
5 Bryant	Y	N	N	N	N	Y	Y
6 ***Barton***	N	Y	Y	Y	Y	Y	N
7 ***Archer***	N	Y	Y	Y	Y	Y	N
8 ***Fields***	N	Y	Y	Y	Y	Y	N
9 Brooks	Y	N	N	N	N	Y	Y
10 Pickle	N	N	N	N	N	Y	Y
11 Edwards	Y	N	N	N	N	Y	Y
12 Geren	Y	N	N	N	N	Y	Y
13 Sarpalius	Y	N	N	N	N	Y	Y
14 Laughlin	Y	N	N	Y	N	Y	Y
15 de la Garza	Y	N	N	N	N	Y	Y
16 Coleman	Y	N	N	N	N	Y	Y
17 Stenholm	Y	Y	Y	Y	Y	Y	N
18 Washington	?	?	?	?	?	?	Y
19 ***Combest***	N	Y	Y	Y	Y	Y	N
20 Gonzalez	Y	N	N	N	N	N	Y
21 ***Smith***	N	Y	Y	Y	Y	Y	N
22 ***DeLay***	N	Y	Y	Y	Y	Y	N
23 ***Bonilla***	N	Y	Y	Y	Y	Y	N
24 Frost	?	?	?	?	N	Y	Y
25 Andrews	Y	N	N	?	N	Y	Y
26 ***Armey***	N	Y	Y	Y	Y	Y	N
27 Ortiz	Y	N	N	N	N	Y	Y
28 Tejeda	Y	N	N	N	N	Y	Y
29 Green	Y	N	N	N	N	Y	Y
30 Johnson, E.B.	?	?	N	N	N	Y	+
UTAH							
1 ***Hansen***	N	Y	Y	Y	Y	Y	?
2 Shepherd	Y	N	N	Y	Y	Y	Y
3 Orton	Y	N	N	N	N	Y	Y
VERMONT							
AL *Sanders*	?	?	N	N	N	Y	Y
VIRGINIA							
1 ***Bateman***	N	N	N	Y	Y	Y	Y
2 Pickett	Y	N	N	N	N	Y	Y
3 Scott	Y	N	N	N	N	Y	Y
4 Sisisky	Y	N	N	Y	N	Y	Y
5 Payne	Y	N	?	Y	N	Y	Y
6 ***Goodlatte***	N	N	Y	Y	Y	Y	Y
7 ***Bliley***	N	N	Y	Y	Y	Y	N
8 Moran	Y	N	N	N	N	Y	Y
9 Boucher	Y	N	N	N	N	Y	Y
10 ***Wolf***	N	Y	Y	Y	Y	Y	Y
11 Byrne	Y	N	N	N	N	Y	Y
WASHINGTON							
1 Cantwell	Y	N	N	N	N	Y	Y
2 Swift	Y	N	N	N	N	Y	Y
3 Unsoeld	Y	N	N	N	N	Y	Y
4 Inslee	Y	N	?	Y	Y	Y	Y
5 Foley							
6 Dicks	Y	N	N	N	N	Y	Y
7 McDermott	Y	N	N	N	—	+	Y
8 ***Dunn***	N	Y	N	Y	Y	Y	Y
9 Kreidler	Y	N	N	N	N	Y	Y
WEST VIRGINIA							
1 Mollohan	Y	N	N	N	N	Y	Y
2 Wise	Y	N	N	N	N	Y	Y
3 Rahall	Y	N	N	N	N	Y	Y
WISCONSIN							
1 Barca	Y	N	N	Y	N	Y	Y
2 ***Klug***	N	Y	Y	Y	Y	Y	N
3 ***Gunderson***	Y	Y	N	Y	Y	Y	Y
4 Kleczka	Y	N	N	N	N	Y	Y
5 Barrett	Y	N	N	Y	N	?	Y
6 ***Petri***	Y	Y	Y	Y	Y	Y	N
7 Obey	Y	N	N	N	N	Y	Y
8 ***Roth***	Y	Y	N	#	Y	Y	Y
9 ***Sensenbrenner***	N	Y	Y	Y	Y	Y	N
WYOMING							
AL ***Thomas***	N	Y	N	Y	Y	Y	N
DELEGATES							
de Lugo, V.I.	Y	N	N	N	N	Y	D
Faleomavaega, Am.S.	Y	N	N	N	N	Y	D
Norton, D.C.	Y	N	N	N	N	Y	D
Romero-B., P.R.	Y	N	N	N	N	Y	D
Underwood, Guam	?	?	?	?	?	?	D

Southern states - Ala., Ark., Fla., Ga., Ky., La., Miss., N.C., Okla., S.C., Tenn., Texas, Va.
Omitted votes are quorum calls, which CQ does not include in its vote charts.

KEY

Y Voted for (yea).
\# Paired for.
+ Announced for.
N Voted against (nay).
X Paired against.
— Announced against.
P Voted "present."
C Voted "present" to avoid possible conflict of interest.
? Did not vote or otherwise make a position known.
D Delegates ineligible to vote.

Democrats **Republicans**
Independent

169. HR 4278. Social Security for Domestic Workers/ Passage. Rostenkowski, D-Ill., motion to suspend the rules and pass the bill to raise the threshold at which individuals are required to pay Social Security taxes for their domestic workers from $50 per quarter to $1,200 annually in 1994 and $1,250 in 1995. The threshold would be indexed thereafter to the national average wage increase. Motion agreed to 420-0: R 173-0; D 246-0 (ND 166-0, SD 80-0); I 1-0, May 12, 1994. A two-thirds majority of those present and voting (280 in this case) is required for passage under suspension of the rules.

170. S 2000. Head Start Reauthorization/Conference Report. Adoption of the conference report on the bill to reauthorize Head Start through fiscal 1998, expanding the program for preschoolers and providing new performance standards for grantees. The bill also authorizes several other anti-poverty programs: the Community Services Block Grant Program, which primarily finances local community action agencies serving the poor; the Low-Income Home Energy Assistance Program, which helps low-income families pay heating and cooling bills and insulate their homes, and Community-Based Family Resource Programs, which are mainly designed to prevent child abuse. Adopted (thus cleared for the president) 393-20: R 149-20; D 243-0 (ND 166-0, SD 77-0); I 1-0, May 12, 1994. A "yea" was a vote in support of the president's position.

	169	170
ALABAMA		
1 *Callahan*	Y	N
2 *Everett*	Y	Y
3 Browder	Y	Y
4 Bevill	Y	Y
5 Cramer	Y	Y
6 *Bachus*	Y	Y
7 Hilliard	Y	Y
ALASKA		
AL *Young*	Y	Y
ARIZONA		
1 Coppersmith	Y	Y
2 Pastor	Y	Y
3 *Stump*	Y	N
4 *Kyl*	Y	Y
5 *Kolbe*	Y	Y
6 English	Y	Y
ARKANSAS		
1 Lambert	Y	Y
2 Thornton	Y	Y
3 *Hutchinson*	Y	Y
4 *Dickey*	Y	Y
CALIFORNIA		
1 Hamburg	Y	Y
2 *Herger*	Y	Y
3 Fazio	Y	Y
4 *Doolittle*	Y	N
5 Matsui	Y	Y
6 Woolsey	Y	Y
7 Miller	Y	Y
8 Pelosi	Y	Y
9 Dellums	Y	Y
10 *Baker*	Y	Y
11 *Pombo*	Y	Y
12 Lantos	Y	Y
13 Stark	Y	Y
14 Eshoo	Y	Y
15 Mineta	Y	Y
16 Edwards	Y	Y
17 Farr	Y	Y
18 Condit	Y	Y
19 Lehman	Y	Y
20 Dooley	Y	Y
21 *Thomas*	Y	?
22 *Huffington*	Y	Y
23 *Gallegly*	Y	?
24 Beilenson	Y	Y
25 *McKeon*	Y	Y
26 Berman	Y	Y
27 *Moorhead*	Y	Y
28 *Dreier*	Y	Y
29 Waxman	Y	Y
30 Becerra	?	+
31 Martinez	Y	Y
32 Dixon	Y	Y
33 Roybal-Allard	Y	Y
34 Torres	Y	Y
35 Waters	Y	Y
36 Harman	Y	Y
37 Tucker	Y	Y
38 *Horn*	Y	Y
39 *Royce*	Y	N
40 *Lewis*	Y	Y
41 *Kim*	Y	Y

	169	170
42 Brown	Y	Y
43 *Calvert*	Y	Y
44 *McCandless*	Y	Y
45 *Rohrabacher*	Y	N
46 *Dornan*	Y	N
47 *Cox*	Y	?
48 *Packard*	Y	Y
49 Schenk	Y	Y
50 Filner	Y	Y
51 *Cunningham*	Y	Y
52 *Hunter*	Y	N
COLORADO		
1 Schroeder	Y	Y
2 Skaggs	Y	Y
3 *McInnis*	Y	Y
4 *Allard*	Y	N
5 *Hefley*	Y	?
6 *Schaefer*	Y	Y
CONNECTICUT		
1 Kennelly	Y	Y
2 Gejdenson	Y	Y
3 DeLauro	Y	Y
4 *Shays*	Y	Y
5 *Franks*	Y	Y
6 *Johnson*	Y	Y
DELAWARE		
AL *Castle*	Y	Y
FLORIDA		
1 Hutto	Y	?
2 Peterson	Y	Y
3 Brown	Y	Y
4 *Fowler*	Y	Y
5 Thurman	Y	Y
6 *Stearns*	Y	Y
7 *Mica*	Y	Y
8 *McCollum*	Y	Y
9 *Bilirakis*	Y	Y
10 *Young*	Y	Y
11 Gibbons	Y	Y
12 *Canady*	Y	Y
13 *Miller*	Y	N
14 *Goss*	Y	Y
15 Bacchus	Y	Y
16 *Lewis*	Y	Y
17 Meek	Y	Y
18 *Ros-Lehtinen*	Y	Y
19 Johnston	Y	Y
20 Deutsch	Y	Y
21 *Diaz-Balart*	Y	Y
22 *Shaw*	Y	Y
23 Hastings	Y	?
GEORGIA		
1 *Kingston*	Y	Y
2 Bishop	Y	Y
3 *Collins*	Y	N
4 *Linder*	Y	Y
5 Lewis	?	?
6 *Gingrich*	Y	Y
7 Darden	Y	Y
8 Rowland	Y	Y
9 Deal	Y	Y
10 Johnson	Y	Y
11 McKinney	Y	Y
HAWAII		
1 Abercrombie	Y	Y
2 Mink	Y	Y
IDAHO		
1 LaRocco	Y	Y
2 *Crapo*	Y	Y
ILLINOIS		
1 Rush	Y	Y
2 Reynolds	Y	Y
3 Lipinski	Y	Y
4 Gutierrez	+	+
5 Rostenkowski	Y	Y
6 *Hyde*	Y	Y
7 Collins	Y	Y
8 *Crane*	Y	N
9 Yates	Y	Y
10 *Porter*	?	Y
11 Sangmeister	Y	Y
12 Costello	Y	Y
13 *Fawell*	Y	Y
14 *Hastert*	Y	Y
15 *Ewing*	Y	Y
16 *Manzullo*	Y	Y
17 Evans	Y	Y

ND Northern Democrats   SD Southern Democrats

	169	170
18 Michel	Y	Y
19 Poshard	Y	Y
20 Durbin	Y	Y
INDIANA		
1 Visclosky	Y	Y
2 Sharp	?	?
3 Roemer	Y	Y
4 Long	Y	Y
5 Buyer	Y	Y
6 Burton	Y	N
7 Myers	Y	Y
8 McCloskey	Y	Y
9 Hamilton	Y	Y
10 Jacobs	Y	Y
IOWA		
1 Leach	Y	Y
2 Nussle	Y	Y
3 Lightfoot	Y	Y
4 Smith	Y	Y
5 Grandy	?	?
KANSAS		
1 Roberts	Y	Y
2 Slattery	Y	Y
3 Meyers	Y	Y
4 Glickman	Y	Y
KENTUCKY		
1 Barlow	Y	Y
2 Vacancy		
3 Mazzoli	Y	Y
4 Bunning	Y	Y
5 Rogers	Y	Y
6 Baesler	Y	Y
LOUISIANA		
1 Livingston	Y	Y
2 Jefferson	Y	Y
3 Tauzin	Y	Y
4 Fields	Y	Y
5 McCrery	Y	Y
6 Baker	Y	Y
7 Hayes	Y	Y
MAINE		
1 Andrews	Y	Y
2 Snowe	Y	Y
MARYLAND		
1 Gilchrest	Y	Y
2 Bentley	Y	Y
3 Cardin	Y	Y
4 Wynn	Y	Y
5 Hoyer	Y	Y
6 Bartlett	Y	Y
7 Mfume	Y	Y
8 Morella	Y	Y
MASSACHUSETTS		
1 Olver	Y	Y
2 Neal	Y	Y
3 Blute	Y	Y
4 Frank	Y	Y
5 Meehan	Y	Y
6 Torkildsen	Y	Y
7 Markey	Y	Y
8 Kennedy	Y	Y
9 Moakley	Y	Y
10 Studds	Y	Y
MICHIGAN		
1 Stupak	Y	Y
2 Hoekstra	Y	Y
3 Ehlers	Y	Y
4 Camp	Y	Y
5 Barcia	Y	Y
6 Upton	Y	Y
7 Smith	Y	Y
8 Carr	Y	Y
9 Kildee	Y	Y
10 Bonior	Y	Y
11 Knollenberg	Y	Y
12 Levin	Y	Y
13 Ford	Y	Y
14 Conyers	Y	Y
15 Collins	Y	Y
16 Dingell	Y	Y
MINNESOTA		
1 Penny	Y	Y
2 Minge	Y	Y
3 Ramstad	Y	Y
4 Vento	Y	Y

	169	170
5 Sabo	Y	Y
6 Grams	Y	Y
7 Peterson	Y	Y
8 Oberstar	Y	Y
MISSISSIPPI		
1 Whitten	?	Y
2 Thompson	Y	Y
3 Montgomery	Y	Y
4 Parker	?	?
5 Taylor	Y	Y
MISSOURI		
1 Clay	Y	Y
2 Talent	Y	Y
3 Gephardt	Y	Y
4 Skelton	Y	Y
5 Wheat	Y	Y
6 Danner	Y	Y
7 Hancock	Y	N
8 Emerson	Y	Y
9 Volkmer	Y	Y
MONTANA		
AL Williams	Y	Y
NEBRASKA		
1 Bereuter	Y	Y
2 Hoagland	?	?
3 Barrett	Y	Y
NEVADA		
1 Bilbray	Y	Y
2 Vucanovich	Y	Y
NEW HAMPSHIRE		
1 Zeliff	Y	Y
2 Swett	Y	Y
NEW JERSEY		
1 Andrews	Y	Y
2 Hughes	Y	Y
3 Saxton	Y	Y
4 Smith	Y	Y
5 Roukema	Y	Y
6 Pallone	Y	Y
7 Franks	Y	Y
8 Klein	Y	Y
9 Torricelli	Y	Y
10 Payne	Y	Y
11 Gallo	Y	Y
12 Zimmer	Y	Y
13 Menendez	Y	Y
NEW MEXICO		
1 Schiff	Y	Y
2 Skeen	Y	Y
3 Richardson	Y	Y
NEW YORK		
1 Hochbrueckner	Y	Y
2 Lazio	Y	Y
3 King	Y	Y
4 Levy	Y	Y
5 Ackerman	Y	Y
6 Flake	?	?
7 Manton	Y	Y
8 Nadler	Y	Y
9 Schumer	Y	Y
10 Towns	Y	Y
11 Owens	Y	Y
12 Velazquez	Y	Y
13 Molinari	Y	Y
14 Maloney	Y	Y
15 Rangel	Y	Y
16 Serrano	Y	Y
17 Engel	Y	Y
18 Lowey	Y	Y
19 Fish	Y	Y
20 Gilman	Y	Y
21 McNulty	Y	Y
22 Solomon	Y	Y
23 Boehlert	Y	Y
24 McHugh	Y	Y
25 Walsh	Y	Y
26 Hinchey	Y	Y
27 Paxon	Y	Y
28 Slaughter	Y	Y
29 LaFalce	Y	Y
30 Quinn	Y	Y
31 Houghton	Y	Y
NORTH CAROLINA		
1 Clayton	Y	Y
2 Valentine	Y	Y

	169	170
3 Lancaster	Y	Y
4 Price	Y	Y
5 Neal	Y	?
6 Coble	Y	N
7 Rose	Y	Y
8 Hefner	Y	Y
9 McMillan	Y	Y
10 Ballenger	Y	Y
11 Taylor	Y	Y
12 Watt	Y	Y
NORTH DAKOTA		
AL Pomeroy	Y	Y
OHIO		
1 Mann	Y	Y
2 Portman	Y	Y
3 Hall	Y	Y
4 Oxley	Y	Y
5 Gillmor	Y	Y
6 Strickland	Y	Y
7 Hobson	Y	Y
8 Boehner	Y	Y
9 Kaptur	Y	Y
10 Hoke	Y	Y
11 Stokes	Y	Y
12 Kasich	Y	Y
13 Brown	Y	Y
14 Sawyer	Y	Y
15 Pryce	Y	Y
16 Regula	Y	Y
17 Traficant	Y	Y
18 Applegate	Y	Y
19 Fingerhut	Y	Y
OKLAHOMA		
1 Inhofe	Y	Y
2 Synar	Y	Y
3 Brewster	Y	Y
4 McCurdy	Y	Y
5 Istook	Y	Y
6 Vacancy		
OREGON		
1 Furse	Y	Y
2 Smith	Y	Y
3 Wyden	Y	Y
4 DeFazio	Y	Y
5 Kopetski	Y	Y
PENNSYLVANIA		
1 Foglietta	Y	Y
2 Blackwell	?	?
3 Borski	Y	Y
4 Klink	Y	Y
5 Clinger	Y	Y
6 Holden	Y	Y
7 Weldon	Y	Y
8 Greenwood	Y	Y
9 Shuster	Y	Y
10 McDade	Y	Y
11 Kanjorski	Y	Y
12 Murtha	Y	Y
13 Margolies-Mezv.	Y	Y
14 Coyne	Y	Y
15 McHale	Y	Y
16 Walker	Y	N
17 Gekas	Y	Y
18 Santorum	Y	?
19 Goodling	Y	Y
20 Murphy	Y	Y
21 Ridge	?	?
RHODE ISLAND		
1 Machtley	Y	Y
2 Reed	Y	Y
SOUTH CAROLINA		
1 Ravenel	Y	Y
2 Spence	Y	Y
3 Derrick	Y	Y
4 Inglis	Y	Y
5 Spratt	Y	Y
6 Clyburn	Y	Y
SOUTH DAKOTA		
AL Johnson	Y	Y
TENNESSEE		
1 Quillen	Y	Y
2 Duncan	Y	Y
3 Lloyd	Y	Y
4 Cooper	Y	Y
5 Clement	Y	Y

	169	170
6 Gordon	Y	Y
7 Sundquist	Y	Y
8 Tanner	Y	Y
9 Ford	Y	Y
TEXAS		
1 Chapman	Y	Y
2 Wilson	Y	Y
3 Johnson, Sam	Y	N
4 Hall	Y	Y
5 Bryant	Y	Y
6 Barton	Y	Y
7 Archer	Y	N
8 Fields	Y	Y
9 Brooks	Y	Y
10 Pickle	Y	Y
11 Edwards	Y	Y
12 Geren	Y	Y
13 Sarpalius	Y	Y
14 Laughlin	Y	Y
15 de la Garza	Y	Y
16 Coleman	Y	Y
17 Stenholm	Y	Y
18 Washington	Y	Y
19 Combest	Y	Y
20 Gonzalez	Y	Y
21 Smith	Y	Y
22 DeLay	Y	N
23 Bonilla	Y	Y
24 Frost	Y	Y
25 Andrews	Y	Y
26 Armey	Y	N
27 Ortiz	Y	Y
28 Tejeda	Y	Y
29 Green	Y	?
30 Johnson, E.B.	Y	Y
UTAH		
1 Hansen	Y	Y
2 Shepherd	Y	Y
3 Orton	Y	Y
VERMONT		
AL Sanders	Y	Y
VIRGINIA		
1 Bateman	Y	Y
2 Pickett	Y	Y
3 Scott	Y	Y
4 Sisisky	Y	Y
5 Payne	Y	Y
6 Goodlatte	Y	Y
7 Bliley	Y	Y
8 Moran	Y	Y
9 Boucher	Y	Y
10 Wolf	Y	Y
11 Byrne	Y	Y
WASHINGTON		
1 Cantwell	Y	Y
2 Swift	Y	Y
3 Unsoeld	Y	Y
4 Inslee	Y	Y
5 Foley		
6 Dicks	Y	Y
7 McDermott	Y	Y
8 Dunn	Y	Y
9 Kreidler	Y	Y
WEST VIRGINIA		
1 Mollohan	Y	Y
2 Wise	Y	Y
3 Rahall	Y	Y
WISCONSIN		
1 Barca	Y	Y
2 Klug	Y	Y
3 Gunderson	Y	Y
4 Kleczka	Y	Y
5 Barrett	Y	Y
6 Petri	Y	Y
7 Obey	Y	Y
8 Roth	Y	Y
9 Sensenbrenner	Y	N
WYOMING		
AL Thomas	Y	Y
DELEGATES		
de Lugo, V.I.	D	D
Faleomavaega, Am.S.	D	D
Norton, D.C.	D	D
Romero-B., P.R.	D	D
Underwood, Guam	D	D

Southern states - Ala., Ark., Fla., Ga., Ky., La., Miss., N.C., Okla., S.C., Tenn., Texas, Va.
Omitted votes are quorum calls, which CQ does not include in its vote charts.

KEY

Y	Voted for (yea).
#	Paired for.
+	Announced for.
N	Voted against (nay).
X	Paired against.
−	Announced against.
P	Voted "present."
C	Voted "present" to avoid possible conflict of interest.
?	Did not vote or otherwise make a position known.
D	Delegates ineligible to vote.

Democrats *Republicans*
Independent

171. Procedural Motion. Approval of the House Journal of Monday, May 16. Approved 238-158: R 17-154; D 220-4 (ND 151-4, SD 69-0); I 1-0, May 17, 1994.

172. HR 2473. Montana Wilderness/Montana Rockies Study. DeLay, R-Texas, amendment to delete the provisions that establish an independent scientific panel to study, report and make recommendations on the ecosystem and economics of the federal lands in the Montana Northern Rockies. Rejected in the Committee of the Whole 182-244: R 150-25; D 32-218 (ND 10-163, SD 22-55); I 0-1, May 17, 1994.

173. HR 2473. Montana Wilderness/Multiple Use of Released Lands. Bryant, D-Texas, amendment to require the Forest Service to preserve native biodiversity on lands used for timber purposes and released for multiple-use management, and to prohibit clear-cutting and road construction on released lands. Rejected in the Committee of the Whole 142-283: R 32-141; D 109-142 (ND 84-91, SD 25-51); I 1-0, May 17, 1994.

174. HR 2473. Montana Wilderness/Passage. Passage of the bill to designate 1.6 million acres of land in Montana's 10 national forests as wilderness; place 1 million acres in a less restrictive classification, limiting development; and release 3.4 million acres of roadless forest for multiple uses such as logging, mining and recreation. Passed 308-111: R 65-106; D 242-5 (ND 168-2, SD 74-3); I 1-0, May 17, 1994. A "yea" was a vote in support of the president's position.

175. HR 518. California Desert Protection/Previous Question. Beilenson, D-Calif., motion to order the previous question (thus ending debate and the possibility of amendment) on adoption of the rule (H Res 422) to provide for House floor consideration of the bill to designate about 8 million acres of California desert as wilderness and establish the Death Valley, Joshua Tree and Mojave national parks. Motion agreed to 245-172: R 1-171; D 243-1 (ND 167-1, SD 76-0); I 1-0, May 17, 1994.

176. HR 518. California Desert Protection/Rule. Adoption of the rule (H Res 422) to provide for House floor consideration of the bill to designate about 8 million acres of California desert as wilderness and establish the Death Valley, Joshua Tree and Mojave national parks. Adopted 248-165: R 7-165; D 240-0 (ND 165-0, SD 75-0); I 1-0, May 17, 1994.

177. HR 4277. Independent Social Security Administration/Passage. Rostenkowski, D-Ill., motion to suspend the rules and pass the bill to establish the Social Security Administration as an independent agency. The bill also would restrict some payments made under the Social Security disability and Supplemental Security Income programs. Motion agreed to 413-0: R 172-0; D 240-0 (ND 166-0, SD 74-0); I 1-0, May 17, 1994. A two-thirds majority of those present and voting (276 in this case) is required for passage under suspension of the rules.

178. HR 4301. Fiscal 1995 Defense Authorization/Rule. Adoption of the rule (H Res 429) to provide for House floor consideration of the bill to authorize $263.3 billion in fiscal 1995 for defense programs. Adopted 369-49: R 124-49; D 244-0 (ND 165-0, SD 79-0); I 1-0, May 18, 1994.

[1] *Frank D. Lucas, R-Okla., was sworn in May 17, 1994. The first vote for which he was eligible was vote 172.*

	171	172	173	174	175	176	177	178
ALABAMA								
1 *Callahan*	N	Y	N	N	N	N	Y	Y
2 *Everett*	Y	Y	N	N	N	N	Y	Y
3 Browder	Y	Y	N	Y	Y	Y	Y	Y
4 Bevill	?	N	N	Y	Y	Y	Y	Y
5 Cramer	Y	Y	N	Y	Y	Y	Y	Y
6 *Bachus*	N	Y	N	N	N	N	Y	Y
7 Hilliard	Y	N	Y	Y	Y	Y	Y	Y
ALASKA								
AL *Young*	N	Y	N	N	N	N	Y	Y
ARIZONA								
1 Coppersmith	Y	N	N	Y	Y	Y	Y	Y
2 Pastor	Y	N	Y	Y	Y	Y	Y	Y
3 *Stump*	N	Y	N	N	N	N	Y	N
4 *Kyl*	N	Y	N	N	N	N	Y	Y
5 *Kolbe*	N	Y	N	N	N	N	Y	Y
6 English	?	?	N	Y	Y	Y	Y	Y
ARKANSAS								
1 Lambert	Y	Y	N	Y	Y	Y	Y	Y
2 Thornton	Y	N	Y	Y	Y	Y	Y	Y
3 *Hutchinson*	N	Y	N	N	N	N	Y	Y
4 *Dickey*	N	Y	N	N	N	N	Y	Y
CALIFORNIA								
1 Hamburg	Y	N	Y	N	Y	Y	Y	Y
2 *Herger*	N	Y	N	N	N	N	Y	Y
3 Fazio	Y	N	Y	Y	Y	Y	Y	Y
4 *Doolittle*	N	Y	N	N	N	N	Y	Y
5 Matsui	Y	N	Y	Y	Y	Y	Y	Y
6 Woolsey	Y	N	Y	Y	Y	Y	Y	Y
7 Miller	Y	N	Y	Y	Y	Y	Y	Y
8 Pelosi	Y	N	Y	Y	Y	Y	Y	Y
9 Dellums	Y	N	Y	Y	Y	Y	Y	Y
10 *Baker*	N	Y	N	N	N	N	Y	Y
11 *Pombo*	Y	Y	N	N	N	N	Y	N
12 Lantos	Y	N	Y	Y	Y	Y	Y	Y
13 Stark	Y	N	Y	Y	Y	Y	Y	Y
14 Eshoo	Y	N	Y	Y	Y	Y	Y	Y
15 Mineta	Y	N	Y	Y	Y	Y	Y	Y
16 Edwards	?	N	Y	Y	Y	Y	Y	Y
17 Farr	?	N	Y	Y	Y	Y	Y	Y
18 Condit	Y	Y	N	Y	Y	Y	Y	Y
19 Lehman	Y	N	Y	Y	Y	Y	Y	Y
20 Dooley	Y	N	N	Y	Y	Y	Y	Y
21 *Thomas*	N	Y	N	N	N	N	Y	N
22 *Huffington*	N	Y	N	N	N	N	Y	N
23 *Gallegly*	N	Y	N	?	N	N	Y	Y
24 Beilenson	Y	N	Y	Y	Y	Y	Y	Y
25 *McKeon*	N	Y	N	N	N	N	Y	Y
26 Berman	Y	N	Y	Y	Y	Y	Y	Y
27 *Moorhead*	N	Y	N	N	N	N	Y	Y
28 *Dreier*	N	Y	N	N	N	N	Y	Y
29 Waxman	Y	N	Y	Y	Y	Y	Y	Y
30 Becerra	Y	N	Y	Y	Y	Y	Y	Y
31 Martinez	Y	N	Y	Y	Y	Y	Y	Y
32 Dixon	Y	N	Y	Y	Y	Y	Y	Y
33 Roybal-Allard	Y	N	Y	Y	Y	Y	Y	Y
34 Torres	Y	N	Y	Y	Y	Y	Y	Y
35 Waters	Y	N	Y	Y	Y	?	Y	Y
36 Harman	Y	Y	N	Y	Y	?	Y	Y
37 Tucker	?	X	?	#	#	#	?	Y
38 *Horn*	N	Y	N	Y	Y	N	Y	Y
39 *Royce*	N	Y	N	N	N	N	Y	N
40 *Lewis*	N	Y	N	N	N	N	Y	Y
41 *Kim*	N	Y	N	N	N	N	Y	N

	171	172	173	174	175	176	177	178
42 Brown	?	N	N	Y	?	?	?	Y
43 *Calvert*	N	Y	N	N	N	N	Y	Y
44 *McCandless*	N	Y	N	N	N	N	Y	N
45 *Rohrabacher*	N	Y	N	N	N	N	Y	Y
46 *Dornan*	Y	Y	N	N	N	N	Y	Y
47 *Cox*	N	Y	N	N	N	N	Y	Y
48 *Packard*	N	Y	N	N	N	N	Y	Y
49 Schenk	Y	Y	Y	Y	Y	Y	Y	Y
50 Filner	Y	N	Y	Y	Y	Y	Y	Y
51 *Cunningham*	N	Y	N	Y	N	N	Y	N
52 *Hunter*	N	Y	N	N	N	N	Y	N
COLORADO								
1 Schroeder	N	N	Y	Y	Y	Y	Y	Y
2 Skaggs	Y	N	N	Y	Y	Y	Y	Y
3 *McInnis*	Y	Y	N	N	N	N	Y	Y
4 *Allard*	N	Y	N	N	N	N	Y	N
5 *Hefley*	N	Y	N	N	N	N	Y	Y
6 *Schaefer*	N	Y	N	N	N	N	Y	Y
CONNECTICUT								
1 Kennelly	Y	N	N	Y	Y	Y	Y	Y
2 Gejdenson	Y	N	Y	Y	Y	Y	Y	Y
3 DeLauro	Y	N	Y	Y	Y	Y	Y	Y
4 *Shays*	N	N	Y	N	Y	N	Y	Y
5 *Franks*	N	N	Y	Y	N	N	Y	Y
6 *Johnson*	N	N	Y	N	N	N	Y	Y
DELAWARE								
AL *Castle*	N	Y	N	Y	N	N	Y	Y
FLORIDA								
1 Hutto	Y	N	N	Y	Y	Y	Y	Y
2 Peterson	Y	N	N	Y	Y	Y	Y	Y
3 Brown	Y	N	N	Y	Y	Y	Y	Y
4 *Fowler*	N	Y	N	N	N	N	Y	Y
5 Thurman	Y	N	N	Y	Y	Y	Y	Y
6 *Stearns*	N	Y	N	N	N	N	Y	N
7 *Mica*	N	Y	N	N	N	N	Y	Y
8 *McCollum*	Y	Y	?	N	N	N	Y	Y
9 *Bilirakis*	N	Y	N	N	N	N	Y	Y
10 *Young*	N	Y	Y	N	N	N	Y	Y
11 Gibbons	Y	N	Y	Y	Y	Y	Y	Y
12 *Canady*	N	Y	N	Y	N	N	Y	Y
13 *Miller*	N	Y	N	Y	N	Y	N	Y
14 *Goss*	N	Y	N	N	N	N	Y	Y
15 Bacchus	Y	N	Y	Y	Y	Y	Y	Y
16 *Lewis*	N	Y	N	N	N	N	Y	Y
17 Meek	Y	N	Y	Y	Y	Y	Y	Y
18 *Ros-Lehtinen*	N	N	Y	N	N	Y	Y	Y
19 Johnston	?	N	Y	Y	Y	Y	Y	Y
20 Deutsch	Y	N	Y	Y	Y	Y	Y	Y
21 *Diaz-Balart*	N	Y	Y	N	N	Y	Y	Y
22 *Shaw*	N	Y	N	N	N	N	Y	Y
23 Hastings	Y	N	N	Y	Y	Y	Y	Y
GEORGIA								
1 *Kingston*	N	Y	N	Y	N	N	Y	Y
2 Bishop	Y	N	N	Y	Y	Y	Y	Y
3 *Collins*	Y	Y	N	N	N	N	Y	Y
4 *Linder*	N	Y	N	N	N	N	Y	Y
5 Lewis	Y	N	Y	Y	Y	Y	Y	Y
6 *Gingrich*	N	Y	N	N	N	N	Y	Y
7 Darden	Y	N	N	Y	Y	Y	Y	Y
8 Rowland	Y	N	N	Y	Y	Y	Y	Y
9 Deal	Y	N	N	Y	Y	Y	Y	Y
10 Johnson	Y	N	N	Y	Y	Y	Y	Y
11 McKinney	Y	N	Y	Y	?	Y	Y	Y
HAWAII								
1 Abercrombie	Y	N	Y	Y	Y	Y	Y	Y
2 Mink	Y	N	N	Y	Y	Y	?	Y
IDAHO								
1 LaRocco	Y	N	N	Y	Y	Y	Y	Y
2 *Crapo*	N	Y	N	N	N	N	Y	N
ILLINOIS								
1 Rush	?	N	Y	Y	Y	Y	Y	Y
2 Reynolds	Y	Y	Y	Y	Y	?	Y	Y
3 Lipinski	Y	N	N	Y	Y	Y	Y	Y
4 Gutierrez	Y	N	Y	Y	Y	Y	Y	Y
5 Rostenkowski	Y	N	N	Y	Y	Y	Y	Y
6 *Hyde*	N	Y	N	N	N	N	Y	Y
7 Collins	Y	N	Y	Y	Y	Y	Y	Y
8 *Crane*	N	Y	N	N	N	N	Y	?
9 Yates	Y	N	Y	Y	Y	Y	Y	Y
10 *Porter*	N	N	Y	N	N	Y	Y	Y
11 Sangmeister	Y	N	Y	Y	Y	Y	Y	Y
12 Costello	Y	N	Y	Y	Y	Y	Y	Y
13 *Fawell*	N	Y	N	N	N	N	Y	Y
14 *Hastert*	N	Y	N	N	N	N	Y	Y
15 *Ewing*	N	Y	N	Y	N	N	Y	?
16 *Manzullo*	N	Y	N	N	N	N	Y	Y
17 Evans	Y	N	Y	Y	Y	Y	Y	Y

ND Northern Democrats   SD Southern Democrats

	171	172	173	174	175	176	177	178
18 ***Michel***	N	Y	N	N	N	N	Y	Y
19 Poshard	Y	N	Y	Y	Y	Y	Y	Y
20 Durbin	Y	N	Y	Y	Y	Y	Y	Y
INDIANA								
1 Visclosky	Y	N	N	Y	Y	Y	Y	Y
2 Sharp	?	N	Y	Y	?	?	?	Y
3 Roemer	Y	N	N	Y	Y	Y	Y	Y
4 Long	Y	N	N	Y	Y	Y	Y	Y
5 ***Buyer***	N	Y	N	N	N	N	Y	N
6 ***Burton***	N	Y	N	N	N	N	Y	N
7 ***Myers***	Y	Y	N	N	N	N	Y	Y
8 McCloskey	Y	N	Y	Y	Y	Y	Y	Y
9 Hamilton	Y	N	N	Y	Y	Y	Y	Y
10 Jacobs	N	Y	Y	Y	N	Y	Y	Y
IOWA								
1 ***Leach***	N	Y	N	Y	X	X	Y	Y
2 ***Nussle***	N	Y	N	N	N	N	Y	Y
3 ***Lightfoot***	N	Y	N	N	N	N	Y	Y
4 Smith	Y	N	N	Y	Y	Y	Y	Y
5 ***Grandy***	?	?	?	?	?	?	?	?
KANSAS								
1 ***Roberts***	N	Y	N	N	N	N	Y	N
2 Slattery	Y	N	Y	Y	Y	Y	Y	Y
3 ***Meyers***	N	N	Y	Y	N	N	Y	Y
4 Glickman	Y	N	Y	Y	Y	Y	Y	Y
KENTUCKY								
1 Barlow	+	–	–	+	+	+	+	Y
2 Vacancy								
3 Mazzoli	Y	N	N	Y	Y	Y	Y	Y
4 ***Bunning***	N	Y	N	N	N	N	Y	N
5 ***Rogers***	N	Y	N	?	N	N	Y	Y
6 Baesler	Y	N	Y	Y	Y	Y	Y	Y
LOUISIANA								
1 ***Livingston***	N	Y	N	N	N	N	Y	Y
2 Jefferson	?	N	Y	Y	Y	Y	Y	Y
3 Tauzin	Y	Y	N	Y	Y	Y	Y	Y
4 Fields	Y	N	N	Y	Y	Y	Y	Y
5 ***McCrery***	N	Y	N	Y	N	Y	Y	N
6 ***Baker***	N	Y	N	N	N	N	Y	Y
7 Hayes	Y	Y	N	Y	Y	Y	Y	Y
MAINE								
1 Andrews	Y	N	Y	Y	Y	Y	Y	Y
2 ***Snowe***	N	N	N	Y	N	N	Y	Y
MARYLAND								
1 ***Gilchrest***	N	N	Y	Y	N	N	Y	Y
2 ***Bentley***	N	Y	N	Y	N	N	Y	Y
3 Cardin	Y	N	Y	Y	Y	Y	Y	Y
4 Wynn	Y	N	Y	Y	Y	Y	Y	Y
5 Hoyer	?	N	N	Y	Y	Y	Y	Y
6 ***Bartlett***	N	Y	N	N	N	N	Y	Y
7 Mfume	Y	N	N	Y	Y	Y	Y	Y
8 ***Morella***	N	N	N	Y	N	N	Y	Y
MASSACHUSETTS								
1 Olver	Y	N	Y	Y	Y	Y	Y	Y
2 Neal	Y	N	Y	Y	Y	Y	Y	Y
3 ***Blute***	N	N	Y	N	N	N	Y	Y
4 Frank	Y	N	Y	Y	Y	Y	Y	Y
5 Meehan	Y	N	Y	Y	Y	Y	Y	Y
6 ***Torkildsen***	N	N	Y	Y	N	N	Y	Y
7 Markey	Y	N	Y	?	Y	Y	Y	Y
8 Kennedy	Y	N	Y	Y	Y	Y	Y	Y
9 Moakley	Y	N	Y	Y	Y	Y	Y	Y
10 Studds	Y	N	Y	Y	Y	Y	?	Y
MICHIGAN								
1 Stupak	?	N	N	Y	Y	Y	Y	Y
2 ***Hoekstra***	N	Y	N	N	N	N	Y	N
3 ***Ehlers***	N	N	Y	Y	N	N	Y	N
4 ***Camp***	N	Y	N	Y	N	N	Y	Y
5 Barcia	Y	Y	N	Y	Y	Y	Y	Y
6 ***Upton***	N	Y	N	Y	N	N	Y	Y
7 ***Smith***	N	Y	N	N	N	N	Y	Y
8 Carr	Y	N	Y	Y	Y	Y	Y	Y
9 Kildee	Y	N	N	Y	Y	Y	Y	Y
10 Bonior	Y	N	N	Y	Y	Y	Y	Y
11 ***Knollenberg***	N	Y	N	N	N	N	Y	Y
12 Levin	Y	N	N	Y	Y	Y	Y	Y
13 Ford	Y	N	N	Y	Y	Y	Y	Y
14 Conyers	Y	N	N	Y	Y	Y	Y	Y
15 Collins	Y	N	Y	Y	Y	Y	Y	Y
16 Dingell	Y	N	N	Y	Y	Y	Y	Y
MINNESOTA								
1 Penny	Y	Y	N	Y	Y	Y	Y	Y
2 Minge	Y	N	N	Y	Y	Y	Y	Y
3 ***Ramstad***	N	Y	N	Y	N	N	Y	N
4 Vento	?	N	N	Y	Y	Y	Y	Y
5 Sabo	Y	N	N	Y	Y	?	?	Y
6 ***Grams***	N	Y	N	N	N	N	Y	N
7 Peterson	Y	Y	N	Y	Y	Y	Y	Y
8 Oberstar	Y	N	N	Y	Y	Y	Y	Y
MISSISSIPPI								
1 Whitten	Y	?	?	Y	Y	Y	Y	?
2 Thompson	?	N	Y	Y	Y	Y	Y	Y
3 Montgomery	Y	Y	N	Y	Y	Y	Y	Y
4 Parker	Y	Y	N	Y	Y	Y	Y	Y
5 Taylor	?	Y	N	Y	Y	Y	Y	Y
MISSOURI								
1 Clay	N	N	N	Y	Y	Y	Y	Y
2 ***Talent***	N	Y	N	Y	N	N	Y	Y
3 Gephardt	Y	N	N	Y	Y	Y	Y	Y
4 Skelton	Y	Y	N	Y	Y	Y	Y	Y
5 Wheat	?	N	Y	Y	Y	Y	Y	Y
6 Danner	Y	Y	N	Y	Y	Y	Y	Y
7 ***Hancock***	N	Y	N	N	N	N	Y	N
8 ***Emerson***	N	Y	?	X	X	X	?	?
9 Volkmer	Y	N	N	Y	Y	Y	Y	Y
MONTANA								
AL Williams	Y	N	Y	Y	Y	Y	Y	Y
NEBRASKA								
1 ***Bereuter***	N	Y	N	N	N	N	Y	Y
2 Hoagland	Y	N	N	Y	Y	Y	Y	Y
3 ***Barrett***	N	Y	N	N	N	N	Y	Y
NEVADA								
1 Bilbray	Y	N	N	Y	Y	Y	Y	Y
2 ***Vucanovich***	N	Y	N	N	N	N	Y	Y
NEW HAMPSHIRE								
1 ***Zeliff***	N	Y	N	N	N	N	Y	Y
2 Swett	Y	N	N	Y	Y	Y	Y	Y
NEW JERSEY								
1 Andrews	Y	N	Y	Y	Y	Y	Y	Y
2 Hughes	Y	N	N	Y	Y	Y	Y	Y
3 ***Saxton***	N	N	Y	Y	N	N	Y	Y
4 ***Smith***	Y	Y	Y	Y	N	N	Y	Y
5 ***Roukema***	N	N	Y	Y	N	N	Y	Y
6 Pallone	Y	N	Y	Y	Y	Y	Y	Y
7 ***Franks***	N	N	Y	Y	N	N	Y	N
8 Klein	Y	N	Y	Y	Y	Y	Y	Y
9 Torricelli	Y	?	Y	Y	Y	Y	Y	Y
10 Payne	Y	N	Y	Y	Y	Y	Y	Y
11 ***Gallo***	N	N	Y	Y	N	N	Y	N
12 ***Zimmer***	N	N	Y	Y	N	Y	Y	N
13 Menendez	Y	N	Y	Y	Y	Y	Y	Y
NEW MEXICO								
1 ***Schiff***	N	Y	N	N	N	N	Y	Y
2 ***Skeen***	N	Y	N	N	N	N	Y	Y
3 Richardson	Y	N	Y	Y	Y	Y	Y	Y
NEW YORK								
1 Hochbrueckner	Y	N	N	Y	Y	Y	Y	?
2 ***Lazio***	N	Y	Y	Y	N	N	Y	Y
3 ***King***	N	Y	N	N	N	N	Y	Y
4 ***Levy***	N	Y	N	N	N	N	Y	Y
5 Ackerman	Y	N	N	Y	Y	Y	Y	?
6 Flake	Y	N	N	Y	Y	Y	Y	Y
7 Manton	Y	N	N	Y	Y	Y	Y	Y
8 Nadler	Y	N	Y	Y	Y	Y	Y	Y
9 Schumer	Y	N	Y	Y	Y	Y	Y	Y
10 Towns	Y	N	N	Y	Y	Y	Y	?
11 Owens	Y	N	N	Y	Y	Y	Y	Y
12 Velazquez	?	N	Y	Y	Y	Y	Y	Y
13 ***Molinari***	N	N	N	Y	N	N	Y	Y
14 Maloney	Y	N	Y	Y	Y	Y	Y	Y
15 Rangel	Y	N	N	Y	Y	Y	Y	?
16 Serrano	Y	N	Y	Y	Y	Y	Y	Y
17 Engel	?	N	Y	Y	Y	Y	Y	Y
18 Lowey	Y	N	Y	Y	Y	Y	Y	Y
19 ***Fish***	Y	N	N	Y	?	?	?	Y
20 ***Gilman***	Y	N	N	Y	N	Y	Y	Y
21 McNulty	Y	N	Y	Y	Y	Y	Y	Y
22 ***Solomon***	N	Y	N	N	N	N	Y	Y
23 ***Boehlert***	N	N	Y	Y	N	N	Y	Y
24 ***McHugh***	N	Y	N	N	N	N	Y	N
25 ***Walsh***	N	N	Y	Y	N	N	Y	Y
26 Hinchey	?	N	Y	Y	Y	Y	Y	Y
27 ***Paxon***	N	Y	N	N	N	N	Y	Y
28 Slaughter	Y	N	Y	Y	Y	Y	Y	Y
29 LaFalce	Y	N	Y	Y	Y	Y	Y	Y
30 ***Quinn***	N	Y	N	Y	N	N	Y	Y
31 ***Houghton***	Y	Y	N	Y	N	N	Y	Y
NORTH CAROLINA								
1 Clayton	Y	N	Y	Y	Y	Y	Y	Y
2 Valentine	Y	Y	Y	Y	?	?	?	Y
3 Lancaster	Y	N	Y	Y	Y	Y	Y	Y
4 Price	?	N	N	Y	Y	Y	Y	Y
5 Neal	?	?	?	?	?	?	?	?
6 ***Coble***	N	Y	N	N	N	N	Y	N
7 Rose	Y	N	N	Y	Y	Y	?	Y
8 Hefner	Y	N	N	Y	Y	Y	Y	Y
9 ***McMillan***	N	Y	Y	Y	N	N	Y	Y
10 ***Ballenger***	N	Y	N	N	N	N	Y	N
11 ***Taylor***	N	Y	N	N	N	N	Y	Y
12 Watt	Y	N	Y	Y	Y	Y	Y	Y
NORTH DAKOTA								
AL Pomeroy	Y	N	N	Y	Y	Y	Y	Y
OHIO								
1 Mann	Y	N	Y	Y	Y	Y	Y	Y
2 ***Portman***	N	Y	N	Y	N	N	Y	Y
3 Hall	Y	N	N	Y	Y	Y	Y	?
4 ***Oxley***	N	Y	N	N	N	N	Y	Y
5 ***Gillmor***	Y	N	N	Y	N	N	Y	Y
6 Strickland	Y	N	N	Y	Y	Y	Y	Y
7 ***Hobson***	N	Y	N	Y	N	N	Y	Y
8 ***Boehner***	N	Y	N	N	N	N	Y	Y
9 Kaptur	?	N	N	Y	Y	Y	Y	Y
10 ***Hoke***	N	Y	N	Y	N	N	Y	Y
11 Stokes	Y	N	N	Y	Y	Y	Y	Y
12 ***Kasich***	Y	Y	N	N	N	N	Y	N
13 Brown	?	N	Y	Y	Y	Y	Y	Y
14 Sawyer	Y	N	Y	Y	Y	Y	Y	Y
15 ***Pryce***	N	Y	N	N	N	N	Y	Y
16 ***Regula***	N	Y	N	Y	N	N	Y	Y
17 Traficant	Y	N	N	Y	Y	Y	Y	Y
18 Applegate	Y	N	N	Y	Y	Y	Y	Y
19 Fingerhut	Y	N	Y	Y	Y	Y	Y	Y
OKLAHOMA								
1 ***Inhofe***	N	Y	N	N	N	N	Y	Y
2 Synar	Y	N	Y	Y	Y	Y	Y	Y
3 Brewster	Y	N	N	Y	Y	Y	Y	Y
4 McCurdy	Y	N	N	Y	Y	Y	Y	Y
5 ***Istook***	N	Y	N	N	N	N	Y	Y
6 ***Lucas*** [1]		Y	N	N	N	N	Y	Y
OREGON								
1 Furse	Y	N	Y	Y	Y	Y	Y	Y
2 ***Smith***	?	#	?	X	X	X	?	Y
3 Wyden	Y	N	N	Y	Y	Y	Y	Y
4 DeFazio	Y	N	N	Y	Y	Y	Y	Y
5 Kopetski	Y	N	N	Y	Y	Y	Y	Y
PENNSYLVANIA								
1 Foglietta	?	N	Y	Y	Y	Y	Y	Y
2 Blackwell	Y	N	?	Y	?	Y	Y	Y
3 Borski	Y	N	N	Y	Y	Y	Y	Y
4 Klink	Y	N	N	Y	Y	Y	Y	Y
5 ***Clinger***	Y	Y	N	Y	N	N	Y	Y
6 Holden	Y	N	N	Y	Y	Y	Y	Y
7 ***Weldon***	N	Y	Y	Y	N	N	Y	Y
8 ***Greenwood***	?	Y	Y	Y	N	N	Y	Y
9 ***Shuster***	N	Y	N	N	N	N	Y	Y
10 ***McDade***	N	Y	N	Y	N	Y	Y	Y
11 Kanjorski	Y	N	N	Y	Y	Y	Y	Y
12 Murtha	Y	N	N	Y	Y	Y	Y	Y
13 Margolies-Mezv.	Y	N	Y	Y	Y	Y	Y	Y
14 Coyne	Y	N	Y	Y	Y	Y	Y	Y
15 McHale	Y	N	N	Y	Y	Y	Y	Y
16 ***Walker***	N	Y	N	N	N	N	Y	Y
17 ***Gekas***	N	Y	N	N	N	N	Y	N
18 ***Santorum***	?	Y	N	N	N	N	Y	Y
19 ***Goodling***	N	Y	N	N	N	N	Y	Y
20 Murphy	N	N	N	Y	Y	Y	Y	Y
21 ***Ridge***	N	Y	N	Y	N	N	Y	Y
RHODE ISLAND								
1 ***Machtley***	?	N	Y	?	N	N	Y	Y
2 Reed	Y	N	Y	Y	Y	Y	Y	Y
SOUTH CAROLINA								
1 ***Ravenel***	N	N	N	Y	Y	Y	Y	Y
2 ***Spence***	N	Y	N	Y	N	N	?	Y
3 Derrick	?	N	N	Y	Y	Y	Y	Y
4 ***Inglis***	Y	Y	N	Y	N	N	Y	Y
5 Spratt	Y	N	N	Y	Y	Y	Y	Y
6 Clyburn	Y	N	Y	Y	Y	Y	Y	Y
SOUTH DAKOTA								
AL Johnson	Y	N	N	Y	Y	Y	Y	Y
TENNESSEE								
1 ***Quillen***	N	Y	N	N	N	N	Y	Y
2 ***Duncan***	N	Y	N	N	N	N	Y	N
3 Lloyd	Y	Y	N	Y	Y	Y	Y	Y
4 Cooper	Y	Y	N	Y	Y	Y	Y	Y
5 Clement	Y	Y	N	Y	Y	Y	Y	Y
6 Gordon	Y	N	N	Y	Y	Y	Y	Y
7 ***Sundquist***	N	Y	N	N	N	N	Y	Y
8 Tanner	Y	Y	N	Y	Y	Y	Y	Y
9 Ford	?	?	?	?	?	?	?	Y
TEXAS								
1 Chapman	?	N	N	Y	Y	Y	Y	Y
2 Wilson	Y	N	Y	Y	Y	Y	Y	Y
3 ***Johnson, Sam***	N	Y	N	N	N	N	Y	Y
4 Hall	Y	Y	N	N	Y	Y	Y	Y
5 Bryant	Y	N	Y	Y	Y	Y	Y	Y
6 ***Barton***	N	Y	N	N	N	N	Y	N
7 ***Archer***	N	Y	N	N	N	N	Y	N
8 ***Fields***	N	Y	N	N	N	N	Y	N
9 Brooks	Y	N	N	Y	Y	Y	Y	Y
10 Pickle	Y	Y	N	Y	Y	Y	Y	Y
11 Edwards	Y	Y	N	Y	Y	Y	Y	Y
12 Geren	Y	Y	N	N	Y	Y	Y	Y
13 Sarpalius	Y	Y	N	Y	Y	Y	Y	Y
14 Laughlin	Y	Y	N	Y	Y	Y	Y	Y
15 de la Garza	?	?	?	?	?	?	?	Y
16 Coleman	Y	N	Y	Y	Y	Y	?	Y
17 Stenholm	Y	Y	N	N	Y	Y	Y	Y
18 Washington	?	?	?	#	#	#	?	?
19 ***Combest***	Y	Y	N	N	N	N	Y	N
20 Gonzalez	Y	N	Y	Y	Y	Y	Y	Y
21 ***Smith***	N	Y	N	Y	N	N	Y	Y
22 ***DeLay***	N	Y	N	N	N	N	Y	N
23 ***Bonilla***	N	Y	N	N	N	N	Y	Y
24 Frost	Y	N	Y	Y	Y	Y	Y	Y
25 Andrews	?	N	Y	Y	Y	Y	Y	Y
26 ***Armey***	N	Y	N	N	N	N	Y	N
27 Ortiz	Y	N	N	Y	Y	Y	Y	Y
28 Tejeda	Y	N	N	Y	Y	Y	Y	Y
29 Green	Y	N	Y	Y	Y	Y	Y	Y
30 Johnson, E.B.	Y	N	Y	Y	Y	Y	Y	Y
UTAH								
1 ***Hansen***	N	Y	N	N	N	N	Y	Y
2 Shepherd	Y	N	Y	Y	Y	Y	Y	Y
3 Orton	Y	N	N	N	Y	Y	Y	Y
VERMONT								
AL *Sanders*	Y	N	Y	Y	Y	Y	Y	Y
VIRGINIA								
1 ***Bateman***	Y	Y	N	N	N	N	Y	Y
2 Pickett	Y	N	N	Y	Y	Y	Y	Y
3 Scott	Y	N	N	Y	Y	Y	Y	Y
4 Sisisky	Y	N	N	Y	Y	Y	Y	Y
5 Payne	Y	N	N	Y	Y	Y	Y	Y
6 ***Goodlatte***	N	Y	N	N	N	N	Y	Y
7 ***Bliley***	N	Y	N	N	N	N	Y	Y
8 Moran	Y	N	Y	Y	Y	Y	Y	Y
9 Boucher	Y	N	N	Y	Y	Y	Y	?
10 ***Wolf***	N	Y	N	N	N	N	Y	Y
11 Byrne	Y	N	?	?	#	#	?	Y
WASHINGTON								
1 Cantwell	Y	N	N	Y	Y	Y	Y	Y
2 Swift	Y	N	N	Y	Y	Y	Y	Y
3 Unsoeld	Y	N	N	Y	Y	Y	Y	Y
4 Inslee	Y	N	N	Y	Y	Y	Y	Y
5 Foley								
6 Dicks	Y	N	N	Y	Y	Y	Y	?
7 McDermott	Y	N	N	Y	Y	Y	Y	?
8 ***Dunn***	N	Y	N	N	N	N	Y	Y
9 Kreidler	Y	N	N	Y	Y	Y	Y	Y
WEST VIRGINIA								
1 Mollohan	Y	N	N	Y	Y	Y	Y	Y
2 Wise	Y	N	N	Y	Y	Y	Y	Y
3 Rahall	Y	N	N	Y	Y	Y	Y	Y
WISCONSIN								
1 Barca	Y	N	Y	Y	Y	Y	Y	Y
2 ***Klug***	N	Y	Y	Y	N	N	Y	N
3 ***Gunderson***	N	Y	N	N	N	N	Y	Y
4 Kleczka	Y	N	Y	Y	Y	Y	Y	Y
5 Barrett	Y	N	Y	Y	Y	Y	Y	Y
6 ***Petri***	N	Y	Y	N	N	N	Y	N
7 Obey	Y	N	N	Y	Y	Y	Y	Y
8 ***Roth***	N	Y	Y	N	N	N	Y	N
9 ***Sensenbrenner***	N	Y	Y	N	N	N	Y	N
WYOMING								
AL ***Thomas***	N	Y	N	N	N	N	Y	Y
DELEGATES								
de Lugo, V.I.	D	N	N	D	D	D	D	D
Faleomavaega, Am.S.	D	N	N	D	D	D	D	D
Norton, D.C.	D	N	Y	D	D	D	D	D
Romero-B., P.R.	D	?	N	D	D	D	D	D
Underwood, Guam	D	N	N	D	D	D	D	D

Southern states - Ala., Ark., Fla., Ga., Ky., La., Miss., N.C., Okla., S.C., Tenn., Texas, Va.
Omitted votes are quorum calls, which CQ does not include in its vote charts.

KEY

Y   Voted for (yea).
\#   Paired for.
\+   Announced for.
N   Voted against (nay).
X   Paired against.
−   Announced against.
P   Voted "present."
C   Voted "present" to avoid possible conflict of interest.
?   Did not vote or otherwise make a position known.
D   Delegates ineligible to vote.

Democrats   ***Republicans***
Independent

179. HR 4301. Fiscal 1995 Defense Authorization/Ballistic Missile Defense Cut. Meehan, D-Mass., amendment to reduce the amount for the Ballistic Missile Defense Organization by $200 million to $2.7 billion. Rejected in the Committee of the Whole 155-271: R 15-160; D 139-111 (ND 121-50, SD 18-61); I 1-0, May 18, 1994. A "nay" was a vote in support of the president's position.

180. HR 4301. Fiscal 1995 Defense Authorization/Deficit Reduction from Burden-Sharing. Bryant, D-Texas, amendment to require the president over a three-year period to secure burdensharing agreements with NATO nations and Japan, with the savings applied to deficit reduction. Rejected in the Committee of the Whole 163-260: R 23-152; D 139-108 (ND 117-52, SD 22-56); I 1-0, May 18, 1994. A "nay" was a vote in support of the president's position.

181. HR 2108. Black Lung Benefits/Debt Limit. Boehner, R-Ohio, amendment to require the Black Lung Trust Fund to be less than $600 million in debt before changes made by the bill could take effect. Rejected in the Committee of the Whole 189-234: R 154-17; D 35-216 (ND 13-160, SD 22-56); I 0-1, May 19, 1994.

182. HR 2108. Black Lung Benefits/Limits on Evidence. Fawell, R-Ill., amendment to strike the section of the bill that would allow a claimant to submit up to three medical examinations, while an employer or the Black Lung Trust Fund could submit only one medical exam in defense of a claim. Rejected in the Committee of the Whole 181-238: R 156-15; D 25-222 (ND 9-158, SD 16-64); I 0-1, May 19, 1994.

183. HR 2108. Black Lung Benefits/Attorney's Fees. Armey, R-Texas, amendment to strike the section of the bill that would allow reimbursement of reasonable attorney's fees by a responsible operator or the Black Lung Trust Fund after each administrative order or judicial ruling granting benefits to a claimant. Rejected in the Committee of the Whole 176-250: R 162-11; D 14-238 (ND 1-171, SD 13-67); I 0-1, May 19, 1994.

184. HR 2108. Black Lung Benefits/Advisory Committee. Barrett, R-Neb., substitute amendment to eliminate all the provisions of the bill and instead establish a Federal Black Lung Advisory Committee to determine whether state worker compensation laws include black lung disease as a compensable occupational illness and whether there is a need to continue the federal black lung program. Rejected in the Committee of the Whole 162-265: R 160-15; D 2-249 (ND 2-170, SD 0-79); I 0-1, May 19, 1994.

185. HR 2108. Black Lung Benefits/Refiled Claims. Boehner, R-Ohio, amendment to eliminate the provisions of the bill that would allow people who filed claims after Jan. 1, 1982, to file new claims with full consideration on the merits. Rejected in the Committee of the Whole 166-258: R 158-14; D 8-243 (ND 4-168, SD 4-75); I 0-1, May 19, 1994.

186. HR 2108. Black Lung Benefits/Passage. Passage of the bill to allow claimants found to be ineligible to keep black lung benefits already provided, to limit the submission of medical evidence in black lung benefit cases to make it easier for coal miners suffering from black lung disease to get benefits, to enable survivors to continue to receive benefits after the death of the miner, to establish a more timely process for the payment of legal fees and to provide benefits to operators of coke ovens. Passed 252-166: R 23-148; D 228-18 (ND 162-4, SD 66-14); I 1-0, May 19, 1994.

	179	180	181	182	183	184	185	186
ALABAMA								
1 *Callahan*	N	N	Y	Y	Y	Y	Y	N
2 *Everett*	N	N	Y	N	Y	Y	Y	N
3 *Browder*	N	N	N	N	N	N	N	Y
4 Bevill	N	N	N	N	N	N	N	Y
5 Cramer	N	N	N	N	N	N	N	Y
6 *Bachus*	N	N	Y	N	Y	Y	Y	Y
7 Hilliard	N	N	N	N	N	N	N	Y
ALASKA								
AL *Young*	N	Y	N	N	Y	Y	Y	Y
ARIZONA								
1 Coppersmith	N	N	N	N	N	N	N	Y
2 Pastor	N	Y	N	N	N	N	N	Y
3 *Stump*	N	N	Y	Y	Y	Y	Y	N
4 *Kyl*	N	N	Y	Y	Y	Y	Y	N
5 *Kolbe*	N	N	Y	Y	Y	Y	Y	N
6 English	Y	N	N	N	N	N	N	Y
ARKANSAS								
1 Lambert	Y	Y	Y	N	N	N	N	N
2 Thornton	N	Y	N	N	N	N	N	Y
3 *Hutchinson*	N	N	Y	Y	Y	Y	Y	N
4 *Dickey*	N	N	Y	Y	Y	Y	Y	N
CALIFORNIA								
1 Hamburg	Y	Y	N	N	N	N	N	Y
2 *Herger*	N	N	Y	Y	Y	Y	Y	N
3 Fazio	N	N	N	N	N	N	N	Y
4 *Doolittle*	N	N	Y	Y	Y	Y	Y	N
5 Matsui	N	Y	N	N	N	N	N	Y
6 Woolsey	Y	Y	N	N	N	N	N	Y
7 Miller	Y	N	N	N	N	N	N	Y
8 Pelosi	Y	Y	N	?	?	N	N	Y
9 Dellums	Y	Y	N	N	N	N	N	Y
10 *Baker*	N	N	Y	Y	Y	Y	Y	N
11 *Pombo*	N	N	Y	Y	Y	Y	Y	N
12 Lantos	N	N	N	N	N	N	N	Y
13 Stark	Y	Y	N	N	N	N	N	Y
14 Eshoo	Y	Y	N	N	N	N	N	Y
15 Mineta	Y	Y	N	N	N	N	N	Y
16 Edwards	Y	Y	N	N	N	N	N	Y
17 Farr	Y	Y	N	N	N	N	N	Y
18 Condit	Y	Y	N	N	N	N	N	Y
19 Lehman	Y	Y	N	N	N	N	N	Y
20 Dooley	Y	N	Y	N	Y	N	N	N
21 *Thomas*	N	N	Y	Y	Y	Y	?	X
22 *Huffington*	N	N	Y	Y	Y	Y	Y	N
23 *Gallegly*	N	N	Y	Y	Y	Y	Y	N
24 Beilenson	Y	N	N	N	N	N	N	Y
25 *McKeon*	N	N	Y	Y	Y	Y	Y	N
26 Berman	Y	N	N	N	N	N	N	Y
27 *Moorhead*	N	N	Y	Y	Y	Y	Y	N
28 *Dreier*	N	N	Y	Y	Y	Y	Y	N
29 Waxman	Y	Y	N	N	N	N	N	Y
30 Becerra	Y	Y	N	N	N	N	N	Y
31 Martinez	N	Y	N	N	N	N	N	Y
32 Dixon	N	Y	?	?	?	?	?	?
33 Roybal-Allard	Y	N	N	N	N	N	N	Y
34 Torres	N	N	N	N	N	N	?	?
35 Waters	Y	N	N	N	N	N	N	Y
36 Harman	Y	N	N	N	N	N	N	Y
37 Tucker	Y	Y	N	N	N	N	N	Y
38 *Horn*	N	Y	Y	Y	Y	Y	Y	N
39 *Royce*	N	N	Y	Y	Y	Y	Y	N
40 *Lewis*	N	N	Y	Y	Y	Y	Y	N
41 *Kim*	N	N	Y	Y	Y	Y	Y	N

	179	180	181	182	183	184	185	186
42 Brown	N	N	N	?	N	N	N	Y
43 *Calvert*	N	N	Y	Y	Y	Y	Y	N
44 *McCandless*	N	N	Y	Y	Y	Y	Y	N
45 *Rohrabacher*	N	Y	Y	Y	Y	Y	Y	N
46 *Dornan*	N	N	Y	Y	Y	Y	Y	N
47 *Cox*	N	N	?	?	Y	Y	Y	N
48 *Packard*	N	N	Y	Y	Y	Y	Y	N
49 Schenk	Y	Y	N	N	N	N	N	Y
50 Filner	Y	Y	N	N	N	N	N	Y
51 *Cunningham*	N	N	Y	Y	Y	Y	Y	N
52 *Hunter*	N	Y	N	Y	Y	Y	Y	N
COLORADO								
1 Schroeder	Y	Y	N	N	N	N	N	Y
2 Skaggs	N	N	N	N	N	N	N	Y
3 *McInnis*	N	N	N	Y	Y	Y	Y	N
4 *Allard*	N	N	Y	Y	Y	Y	Y	N
5 *Hefley*	N	N	Y	Y	Y	Y	Y	N
6 *Schaefer*	N	N	Y	Y	Y	Y	Y	N
CONNECTICUT								
1 Kennelly	Y	N	N	N	N	N	N	Y
2 Gejdenson	Y	Y	N	N	N	N	N	Y
3 DeLauro	Y	N	N	N	N	N	N	Y
4 *Shays*	Y	Y	Y	Y	Y	Y	Y	N
5 *Franks*	N	N	Y	Y	Y	Y	Y	N
6 *Johnson*	N	N	Y	Y	Y	Y	Y	N
DELAWARE								
AL *Castle*	N	N	Y	Y	Y	Y	Y	N
FLORIDA								
1 Hutto	N	N	Y	Y	Y	N	?	Y
2 Peterson	N	N	Y	N	N	N	N	Y
3 Brown	N	N	N	N	N	N	N	Y
4 *Fowler*	N	N	Y	Y	Y	Y	Y	N
5 Thurman	Y	Y	N	N	N	N	N	Y
6 *Stearns*	N	N	Y	Y	Y	Y	Y	N
7 *Mica*	N	N	Y	Y	Y	Y	Y	N
8 *McCollum*	N	N	Y	Y	Y	Y	Y	N
9 *Bilirakis*	N	N	Y	Y	Y	Y	Y	N
10 *Young*	N	N	Y	Y	Y	Y	Y	N
11 Gibbons	N	N	N	N	N	?	N	Y
12 *Canady*	N	N	Y	Y	Y	Y	Y	N
13 *Miller*	N	N	Y	Y	Y	Y	Y	N
14 *Goss*	N	N	Y	Y	Y	Y	Y	N
15 Bacchus	?	N	N	N	N	N	N	Y
16 *Lewis*	N	N	Y	Y	Y	Y	?	X
17 Meek	Y	N	N	N	N	N	N	Y
18 *Ros-Lehtinen*	N	Y	Y	Y	Y	Y	N	Y
19 Johnston	Y	Y	N	N	N	N	N	Y
20 Deutsch	Y	N	N	N	N	N	N	Y
21 *Diaz-Balart*	N	N	N	N	N	N	N	Y
22 *Shaw*	N	N	Y	Y	Y	Y	Y	N
23 Hastings	Y	N	N	N	N	N	N	Y
GEORGIA								
1 *Kingston*	N	N	Y	Y	Y	Y	Y	N
2 Bishop	N	N	N	N	N	N	N	Y
3 *Collins*	N	N	Y	Y	Y	Y	Y	N
4 *Linder*	N	N	Y	Y	Y	Y	Y	N
5 Lewis	Y	Y	N	N	N	N	N	Y
6 *Gingrich*	N	N	Y	Y	Y	Y	Y	N
7 Darden	N	N	N	?	N	N	N	Y
8 Rowland	N	N	Y	Y	Y	N	N	Y
9 *Deal*	N	N	Y	Y	Y	N	N	Y
10 Johnson	N	N	Y	Y	Y	N	N	Y
11 McKinney	Y	Y	N	N	N	N	N	Y
HAWAII								
1 Abercrombie	Y	Y	N	N	N	N	N	Y
2 Mink	Y	Y	N	N	N	N	N	Y
IDAHO								
1 LaRocco	N	Y	N	N	N	N	N	Y
2 *Crapo*	N	N	Y	Y	Y	N	Y	N
ILLINOIS								
1 Rush	Y	Y	N	N	N	N	N	Y
2 Reynolds	Y	Y	N	N	N	N	N	Y
3 Lipinski	N	N	N	N	N	N	N	Y
4 Gutierrez	Y	Y	N	N	N	N	N	Y
5 Rostenkowski	Y	Y	N	N	N	N	N	Y
6 *Hyde*	N	N	Y	Y	Y	Y	Y	N
7 Collins	Y	Y	N	N	N	N	N	Y
8 *Crane*	N	Y	Y	Y	Y	Y	Y	N
9 Yates	Y	Y	N	N	N	N	N	Y
10 *Porter*	Y	N	Y	Y	Y	Y	Y	N
11 Sangmeister	Y	Y	N	N	N	N	N	Y
12 Costello	Y	Y	N	N	N	N	N	Y
13 *Fawell*	N	N	Y	Y	Y	Y	Y	N
14 *Hastert*	N	N	Y	Y	Y	Y	Y	N
15 *Ewing*	N	N	Y	Y	Y	Y	Y	N
16 *Manzullo*	N	N	Y	Y	Y	Y	Y	N
17 Evans	Y	Y	N	N	N	N	N	Y

ND   Northern Democrats   SD   Southern Democrats

	179	180	181	182	183	184	185	186
18 ***Michel***	N	N	Y	?	Y	Y	Y	N
19 Poshard	Y	Y	N	N	N	N	N	Y
20 Durbin	Y	Y	N	N	N	N	N	Y
INDIANA								
1 Visclosky	N	N	N	N	N	N	N	Y
2 Sharp	Y	N	N	N	N	N	N	Y
3 Roemer	Y	N	N	N	N	N	N	Y
4 Long	N	Y	N	N	N	N	N	Y
5 ***Buyer***	N	N	Y	Y	Y	Y	Y	N
6 ***Burton***	N	N	Y	Y	Y	Y	Y	N
7 ***Myers***	N	N	N	N	Y	N	N	Y
8 McCloskey	Y	N	N	N	N	N	N	Y
9 Hamilton	N	N	N	Y	N	N	N	Y
10 Jacobs	Y	Y	N	Y	N	N	N	Y
IOWA								
1 ***Leach***	Y	N	Y	Y	Y	Y	Y	N
2 ***Nussle***	Y	Y	Y	Y	Y	Y	Y	N
3 ***Lightfoot***	N	N	Y	Y	Y	Y	Y	N
4 Smith	N	N	N	N	N	N	N	Y
5 ***Grandy***	X	X	#	#	#	#	?	?
KANSAS								
1 ***Roberts***	N	N	Y	Y	Y	Y	Y	N
2 Slattery	N	N	N	N	N	N	N	#
3 ***Meyers***	N	N	Y	Y	Y	Y	Y	N
4 Glickman	N	N	N	N	N	N	N	Y
KENTUCKY								
1 Barlow	N	N	N	N	N	N	N	Y
2 Vacancy								
3 Mazzoli	N	N	N	N	N	N	N	Y
4 ***Bunning***	N	N	N	Y	Y	Y	Y	N
5 ***Rogers***	N	N	N	N	N	N	N	Y
6 Baesler	N	N	N	N	N	N	N	Y
LOUISIANA								
1 ***Livingston***	N	N	Y	Y	Y	Y	Y	?
2 Jefferson	N	?	N	N	N	N	N	Y
3 Tauzin	N	Y	Y	Y	Y	N	N	N
4 Fields	Y	Y	N	N	N	N	N	Y
5 ***McCrery***	N	N	Y	Y	Y	Y	Y	N
6 ***Baker***	N	N	Y	Y	Y	Y	Y	N
7 Hayes	N	Y	Y	Y	N	N	N	N
MAINE								
1 Andrews	Y	Y	N	N	N	N	N	Y
2 ***Snowe***	N	N	Y	Y	Y	Y	Y	N
MARYLAND								
1 ***Gilchrest***	N	N	Y	Y	Y	Y	Y	N
2 ***Bentley***	N	N	Y	N	Y	N	N	Y
3 Cardin	N	Y	N	N	N	N	N	Y
4 Wynn	Y	Y	N	N	N	N	N	Y
5 Hoyer	N	N	N	N	N	N	N	Y
6 ***Bartlett***	N	N	Y	Y	Y	Y	Y	N
7 Mfume	Y	Y	N	N	N	N	N	Y
8 ***Morella***	Y	N	Y	N	N	Y	Y	Y
MASSACHUSETTS								
1 Olver	Y	Y	N	N	N	N	N	Y
2 Neal	Y	Y	N	N	N	N	N	Y
3 ***Blute***	N	N	Y	Y	Y	Y	Y	Y
4 Frank	Y	Y	N	N	N	N	N	Y
5 Meehan	Y	Y	Y	Y	N	N	N	Y
6 ***Torkildsen***	N	N	?	?	?	Y	Y	N
7 Markey	Y	Y	N	N	N	N	?	?
8 Kennedy	Y	Y	?	N	N	N	N	Y
9 Moakley	Y	Y	N	N	N	N	N	Y
10 Studds	Y	Y	N	N	N	N	N	Y
MICHIGAN								
1 Stupak	Y	Y	N	N	N	N	N	Y
2 ***Hoekstra***	Y	N	Y	N	Y	Y	Y	N
3 ***Ehlers***	N	N	Y	Y	Y	Y	Y	N
4 ***Camp***	N	Y	Y	Y	Y	Y	Y	N
5 Barcia	N	Y	N	N	N	N	N	Y
6 ***Upton***	Y	Y	Y	Y	Y	Y	Y	N
7 ***Smith***	N	N	Y	Y	Y	Y	N	N
8 Carr	Y	Y	N	N	N	N	N	Y
9 Kildee	Y	N	N	N	N	N	N	Y
10 Bonior	Y	Y	N	N	N	N	N	Y
11 ***Knollenberg***	N	N	Y	Y	Y	Y	Y	N
12 Levin	Y	N	N	N	N	N	N	Y
13 Ford	Y	?	N	?	N	N	N	Y
14 Conyers	Y	Y	N	N	N	N	N	Y
15 Collins	Y	Y	?	N	N	N	N	Y
16 Dingell	Y	N	N	N	N	N	N	Y
MINNESOTA								
1 Penny	Y	Y	Y	Y	Y	Y	Y	N
2 Minge	Y	Y	Y	N	N	N	N	N
3 ***Ramstad***	Y	Y	Y	Y	Y	Y	Y	N
4 Vento	Y	Y	N	N	N	N	N	Y
5 Sabo	Y	N	N	N	N	N	N	Y
6 ***Grams***	N	N	Y	Y	Y	Y	Y	N
7 Peterson	Y	Y	Y	N	N	N	N	Y
8 Oberstar	Y	Y	N	N	N	N	N	Y
MISSISSIPPI								
1 Whitten	?	?	N	N	N	N	N	Y
2 Thompson	N	N	N	N	N	N	N	Y
3 Montgomery	N	N	Y	Y	N	N	N	N
4 Parker	N	N	?	?	?	?	?	?
5 Taylor	N	N	Y	Y	Y	N	N	N
MISSOURI								
1 Clay	Y	Y	N	N	N	N	N	Y
2 ***Talent***	N	N	Y	Y	Y	Y	Y	N
3 Gephardt	?	?	N	N	N	N	N	Y
4 Skelton	N	N	N	N	N	N	N	Y
5 Wheat	Y	Y	N	N	N	N	N	Y
6 Danner	N	Y	N	N	N	N	N	Y
7 ***Hancock***	N	N	Y	Y	Y	Y	Y	N
8 ***Emerson***	?	?	?	?	?	?	?	?
9 Volkmer	N	N	N	N	N	N	N	Y
MONTANA								
AL Williams	Y	N	N	?	N	N	N	Y
NEBRASKA								
1 ***Bereuter***	N	N	Y	Y	Y	Y	Y	N
2 Hoagland	N	N	Y	N	N	N	N	Y
3 ***Barrett***	N	N	Y	Y	Y	Y	Y	N
NEVADA								
1 Bilbray	N	N	N	N	N	N	N	Y
2 ***Vucanovich***	N	N	Y	Y	?	Y	Y	N
NEW HAMPSHIRE								
1 ***Zeliff***	N	N	Y	Y	Y	Y	Y	N
2 Swett	N	Y	Y	N	N	N	N	Y
NEW JERSEY								
1 Andrews	N	N	N	N	N	N	N	Y
2 Hughes	Y	Y	N	Y	N	N	N	Y
3 ***Saxton***	N	N	Y	Y	Y	Y	Y	N
4 ***Smith***	N	N	N	N	Y	Y	N	Y
5 ***Roukema***	Y	N	Y	Y	Y	Y	Y	N
6 Pallone	Y	Y	N	N	N	N	N	Y
7 ***Franks***	Y	Y	Y	Y	Y	Y	Y	N
8 Klein	Y	Y	N	N	N	N	N	Y
9 Torricelli	Y	Y	N	N	N	N	N	Y
10 Payne	Y	Y	N	N	N	N	N	Y
11 ***Gallo***	N	N	Y	Y	Y	Y	Y	N
12 ***Zimmer***	N	Y	Y	Y	Y	Y	Y	N
13 Menendez	Y	Y	N	N	N	N	N	Y
NEW MEXICO								
1 ***Schiff***	N	Y	Y	Y	Y	Y	Y	N
2 ***Skeen***	N	N	Y	Y	Y	Y	Y	N
3 Richardson	N	N	N	N	N	N	N	Y
NEW YORK								
1 Hochbrueckner	N	N	N	N	N	N	N	Y
2 ***Lazio***	N	N	Y	Y	N	Y	Y	N
3 ***King***	N	N	Y	Y	Y	Y	Y	N
4 ***Levy***	N	N	Y	Y	Y	Y	Y	N
5 Ackerman	?	?	N	N	N	N	N	Y
6 Flake	Y	Y	N	N	N	N	N	Y
7 Manton	Y	N	N	N	N	N	N	Y
8 Nadler	Y	N	N	—	—	—	—	#
9 Schumer	Y	Y	N	Y	N	N	N	Y
10 Towns	?	?	N	N	N	N	N	Y
11 Owens	?	?	N	N	N	N	N	Y
12 Velazquez	Y	Y	N	N	N	N	N	Y
13 ***Molinari***	N	N	Y	Y	Y	Y	Y	N
14 Maloney	Y	N	N	N	N	N	N	Y
15 Rangel	#	#	N	N	N	N	N	Y
16 Serrano	Y	Y	N	N	N	N	N	Y
17 Engel	Y	Y	N	N	N	N	N	Y
18 Lowey	N	Y	N	N	N	N	N	Y
19 ***Fish***	N	N	?	N	Y	Y	Y	Y
20 ***Gilman***	N	N	Y	N	N	N	N	Y
21 McNulty	N	Y	N	N	N	N	N	Y
22 ***Solomon***	N	N	Y	Y	Y	Y	Y	N
23 ***Boehlert***	N	N	Y	N	Y	Y	N	Y
24 ***McHugh***	N	N	Y	Y	Y	Y	Y	Y
25 ***Walsh***	N	N	Y	Y	Y	Y	Y	Y
26 Hinchey	Y	Y	N	N	N	N	N	Y
27 ***Paxon***	N	N	Y	Y	Y	Y	Y	N
28 Slaughter	Y	Y	N	N	N	N	N	Y
29 LaFalce	Y	N	N	N	N	N	N	Y
30 ***Quinn***	N	N	N	N	N	N	Y	Y
31 ***Houghton***	N	N	Y	Y	Y	Y	Y	N
NORTH CAROLINA								
1 Clayton	Y	N	N	N	N	N	N	Y
2 Valentine	Y	Y	Y	Y	Y	N	Y	N
3 Lancaster	N	N	N	N	N	N	N	Y
4 Price	Y	N	N	N	N	N	N	Y
5 Neal	?	?	?	?	?	?	?	?
6 ***Coble***	N	Y	Y	Y	Y	Y	Y	N
7 Rose	N	N	N	N	N	N	N	Y
8 Hefner	N	Y	?	N	N	N	N	Y
9 ***McMillan***	N	N	Y	Y	Y	Y	?	N
10 ***Ballenger***	N	N	?	Y	Y	Y	Y	N
11 ***Taylor***	N	N	Y	Y	Y	Y	Y	N
12 Watt	Y	Y	N	N	N	N	N	Y
NORTH DAKOTA								
AL Pomeroy	N	Y	Y	N	N	N	N	?
OHIO								
1 Mann	N	N	Y	N	N	N	Y	Y
2 ***Portman***	N	N	Y	Y	Y	Y	Y	N
3 Hall	Y	Y	N	N	N	N	N	Y
4 ***Oxley***	N	N	Y	Y	Y	Y	Y	N
5 ***Gillmor***	N	N	Y	Y	Y	N	Y	N
6 Strickland	Y	Y	N	N	N	N	N	Y
7 ***Hobson***	N	N	Y	N	Y	Y	Y	N
8 ***Boehner***	N	N	Y	Y	Y	Y	Y	N
9 Kaptur	Y	Y	N	N	N	N	N	Y
10 ***Hoke***	N	N	Y	Y	Y	N	Y	?
11 Stokes	Y	Y	N	?	N	X	N	Y
12 ***Kasich***	N	N	Y	N	Y	Y	Y	N
13 Brown	Y	Y	N	N	N	N	N	Y
14 Sawyer	Y	N	N	N	N	N	N	Y
15 ***Pryce***	N	N	Y	Y	Y	Y	Y	N
16 ***Regula***	N	Y	Y	Y	N	Y	N	N
17 Traficant	N	Y	N	N	N	N	N	Y
18 Applegate	N	Y	N	N	N	N	N	Y
19 Fingerhut	Y	+	N	N	N	Y	N	Y
OKLAHOMA								
1 ***Inhofe***	N	N	Y	Y	Y	Y	Y	N
2 Synar	Y	N	N	N	N	N	N	Y
3 Brewster	N	N	Y	Y	Y	N	N	Y
4 McCurdy	N	Y	Y	N	N	N	N	N
5 ***Istook***	N	N	Y	Y	Y	N	Y	N
6 ***Lucas***	N	N	Y	Y	Y	Y	Y	N
OREGON								
1 Furse	Y	Y	N	N	N	N	N	Y
2 ***Smith***	N	N	Y	Y	Y	Y	Y	N
3 Wyden	Y	Y	N	N	N	N	N	Y
4 DeFazio	Y	Y	N	N	N	N	N	Y
5 Kopetski	Y	Y	N	N	N	N	N	Y
PENNSYLVANIA								
1 Foglietta	Y	Y	N	N	N	N	N	Y
2 Blackwell	Y	Y	N	N	N	?	N	Y
3 Borski	N	Y	N	N	N	N	N	Y
4 Klink	N	Y	N	N	N	N	N	Y
5 ***Clinger***	N	N	Y	Y	N	Y	Y	Y
6 Holden	Y	Y	N	N	N	N	N	Y
7 ***Weldon***	N	N	Y	Y	Y	Y	Y	N
8 ***Greenwood***	N	Y	Y	Y	Y	Y	Y	N
9 ***Shuster***	N	N	Y	Y	Y	Y	Y	N
10 ***McDade***	N	N	N	N	N	N	N	Y
11 Kanjorski	Y	Y	N	N	N	N	N	Y
12 Murtha	N	N	N	N	N	N	N	Y
13 Margolies-Mezv.	Y	Y	Y	N	N	N	Y	Y
14 Coyne	Y	Y	N	N	N	N	N	Y
15 McHale	N	Y	N	N	N	N	N	Y
16 ***Walker***	N	N	Y	Y	Y	Y	Y	N
17 ***Gekas***	N	N	Y	Y	Y	Y	Y	N
18 ***Santorum***	N	N	N	Y	Y	N	Y	Y
19 ***Goodling***	N	N	N	?	Y	Y	N	N
20 Murphy	Y	Y	N	N	N	N	N	Y
21 ***Ridge***	N	N	Y	Y	Y	N	Y	Y
RHODE ISLAND								
1 ***Machtley***	N	N	Y	Y	Y	N	Y	N
2 Reed	Y	N	N	N	N	N	N	Y
SOUTH CAROLINA								
1 ***Ravenel***	N	N	Y	Y	Y	Y	Y	N
2 ***Spence***	N	N	Y	Y	Y	Y	Y	N
3 Derrick	Y	?	N	N	N	N	N	Y
4 ***Inglis***	N	N	Y	Y	Y	Y	Y	N
5 Spratt	N	N	N	N	N	N	N	Y
6 Clyburn	N	N	N	N	N	N	N	Y
SOUTH DAKOTA								
AL Johnson	N	Y	N	N	N	N	N	Y
TENNESSEE								
1 ***Quillen***	N	N	N	Y	Y	Y	N	Y
2 ***Duncan***	Y	Y	Y	Y	Y	Y	Y	N
3 Lloyd	N	N	N	N	N	N	N	Y
4 Cooper	N	N	Y	N	N	N	N	Y
5 Clement	N	N	N	N	N	N	N	Y
6 Gordon	Y	N	N	N	N	N	N	Y
7 ***Sundquist***	N	N	N	Y	Y	Y	N	Y
8 Tanner	N	N	N	N	N	N	N	Y
9 Ford	Y	N	N	N	N	N	N	Y
TEXAS								
1 Chapman	N	N	N	Y	N	N	N	Y
2 Wilson	N	N	?	N	N	N	N	Y
3 ***Johnson, Sam***	N	N	Y	Y	Y	Y	Y	N
4 Hall	N	N	Y	Y	Y	N	N	N
5 Bryant	Y	Y	N	N	N	N	N	Y
6 ***Barton***	N	N	Y	Y	Y	Y	Y	N
7 ***Archer***	N	N	Y	Y	Y	Y	Y	N
8 ***Fields***	N	N	Y	Y	Y	Y	Y	N
9 Brooks	N	Y	N	N	Y	N	N	Y
10 Pickle	N	N	N	N	N	N	N	Y
11 Edwards	N	N	Y	N	Y	N	N	Y
12 Geren	N	N	Y	Y	Y	N	Y	N
13 Sarpalius	N	N	N	N	N	N	N	Y
14 Laughlin	N	N	Y	Y	Y	N	N	Y
15 de la Garza	N	N	N	N	N	N	N	Y
16 Coleman	N	Y	N	N	N	N	N	Y
17 Stenholm	N	N	Y	Y	Y	N	Y	N
18 Washington	?	?	X	X	X	?	?	?
19 ***Combest***	N	N	Y	Y	Y	Y	Y	N
20 Gonzalez	N	N	N	N	N	N	N	Y
21 ***Smith***	N	N	Y	Y	Y	Y	Y	N
22 ***DeLay***	N	N	Y	Y	Y	Y	Y	N
23 ***Bonilla***	N	N	Y	Y	Y	Y	Y	N
24 Frost	N	Y	N	N	N	N	N	Y
25 Andrews	N	N	N	N	N	N	N	Y
26 ***Armey***	N	N	Y	Y	Y	Y	Y	N
27 Ortiz	N	N	N	N	N	N	N	Y
28 Tejeda	N	N	N	N	N	N	N	Y
29 Green	N	Y	N	N	N	N	N	Y
30 Johnson, E.B.	N	Y	N	N	N	N	N	Y
UTAH								
1 ***Hansen***	N	N	Y	Y	Y	Y	Y	N
2 Shepherd	Y	Y	N	N	N	N	N	Y
3 Orton	N	N	Y	Y	N	N	Y	N
VERMONT								
AL *Sanders*	Y	Y	N	N	N	N	N	Y
VIRGINIA								
1 ***Bateman***	N	N	Y	Y	Y	Y	Y	N
2 Pickett	N	N	Y	Y	N	N	N	N
3 Scott	N	N	N	N	N	N	N	Y
4 Sisisky	N	N	Y	N	N	N	N	Y
5 Payne	N	N	Y	N	N	N	N	N
6 ***Goodlatte***	N	N	Y	Y	Y	Y	Y	N
7 ***Bliley***	N	N	Y	Y	Y	Y	Y	N
8 Moran	N	N	N	N	N	N	N	Y
9 Boucher	N	Y	N	N	N	N	N	Y
10 ***Wolf***	N	N	Y	Y	Y	Y	Y	N
11 Byrne	N	Y	N	N	N	N	N	Y
WASHINGTON								
1 Cantwell	Y	N	N	N	N	N	N	Y
2 Swift	N	N	N	N	N	N	N	Y
3 Unsoeld	Y	Y	N	N	N	N	N	Y
4 Inslee	Y	Y	N	N	N	N	N	Y
5 Foley								
6 Dicks	N	N	N	N	N	N	N	Y
7 McDermott	N	Y	N	—	N	N	N	Y
8 ***Dunn***	N	N	Y	Y	Y	Y	Y	N
9 Kreidler	Y	Y	N	N	N	N	N	Y
WEST VIRGINIA								
1 Mollohan	N	N	N	N	N	N	N	Y
2 Wise	N	N	N	N	N	N	N	Y
3 Rahall	Y	Y	N	N	N	N	N	Y
WISCONSIN								
1 Barca	Y	Y	N	N	N	N	N	Y
2 ***Klug***	Y	N	Y	Y	Y	Y	Y	N
3 ***Gunderson***	N	N	Y	Y	Y	Y	Y	N
4 Kleczka	Y	Y	N	N	N	N	N	Y
5 Barrett	Y	Y	N	N	N	N	N	Y
6 ***Petri***	Y	Y	Y	Y	Y	Y	Y	N
7 Obey	Y	Y	N	N	N	N	N	Y
8 ***Roth***	Y	Y	Y	Y	Y	Y	Y	N
9 ***Sensenbrenner***	Y	Y	Y	Y	Y	Y	Y	N
WYOMING								
AL ***Thomas***	N	N	Y	Y	Y	Y	Y	N
DELEGATES								
de Lugo, V.I.	N	Y	N	N	N	N	N	D
Faleomavaega, Am.S.	?	?	?	?	?	?	?	D
Norton, D.C.	Y	Y	N	N	N	N	N	D
Romero-B., P.R.	Y	N	N	?	?	N	N	D
Underwood, Guam	Y	N	N	N	N	N	N	D

Southern states - Ala., Ark., Fla., Ga., Ky., La., Miss., N.C., Okla., S.C., Tenn., Texas, Va.
Omitted votes are quorum calls, which CQ does not include in its vote charts.

1994 CQ ALMANAC — 57-H

HOUSE VOTES 187, 188, 189, 190, 191, 192, 193, 194

187. HR 4301. Fiscal 1995 Defense Authorization/Burden-Sharing European Troop Reduction. Frank, D-Mass., amendment to pressure the president to seek increased burden-sharing through a formula to reduce troop levels in Europe by 1,000 troops for each percentage point that European host nations do not contribute to the non-personnel costs of U.S. military installations with a goal of a 75 percent contribution by Sept. 30, 1998. Adopted in the Committee of the Whole 268-144: R 78-92; D 189-52 (ND 146-19, SD 43-33); I 1-0, May 19, 1994. A "nay" was a vote in support of the president's position.

188. HR 4301. Fiscal 1995 Defense Authorization/Trident II (D-5) Missile. Dicks, D-Wash., amendment to allow the secretary of Defense to waive the prohibition against equipping Trident I submarines with Trident II (D-5) missiles. Adopted in the Committee of the Whole 226-169: R 135-26; D 91-142 (ND 39-117, SD 52-25); I 0-1, May 20, 1994. A "yea" was a vote in support of the president's position.

189. HR 4301. Fiscal 1995 Defense Authorization/Trident II (D-5) Missile Termination. Penny, D-Minn., amendment to terminate production of the Trident II (D-5) missile after fiscal 1994 and cut $696 million from the Navy's weapons procurement account. Rejected in the Committee of the Whole 166-229: R 35-128; D 130-101 (ND 107-46, SD 23-55); I 1-0, May 20, 1994. A "nay" was a vote in support of the president's position.

190. HR 4301. Fiscal 1995 Defense Authorization/School of the Americas. Kennedy, D-Mass., amendment to prohibit the Defense Department from using money authorized in the bill to operate the Army School of the Americas at Fort Benning, Ga. Rejected in the Committee of the Whole 175-217: R 25-136; D 149-81 (ND 125-33, SD 24-48); I 1-0, May 20, 1994.

191. HR 4301. Fiscal 1995 Defense Authorization/Military Recruiting. Solomon, R-N.Y., amendment to bar expenditure of money provided under the bill to colleges or universities that prohibit military recruitment on campus or deny recruiters access to student directory information. Adopted in the Committee of the Whole 271-126: R 162-1; D 109-124 (ND 55-101, SD 54-23); I 0-1, May 23, 1994.

192. HR 4301. Fiscal 1995 Defense Authorization/Selective Service. Dellums, D-Calif., amendment to eliminate the draft registration requirement under the Military Selective Service Act after Sept. 30, 1994. Rejected in the Committee of the Whole 125-273: R 20-143; D 104-130 (ND 87-70, SD 17-60); I 1-0, May 23, 1994. A "nay" was a vote in support of the president's position.

193. HR 4453. Fiscal 1995 Military Construction Appropriations/Passage. Passage of the bill to provide $8,816,672,000 in new budget authority for military construction, Defense Department family housing and base-closure activities in fiscal 1995. The administration requested $8,346,202,000. Passed 380-42: R 140-33; D 239-9 (ND 161-7, SD 78-2); I 1-0, May 24, 1994.

194. HR 4301. Fiscal 1995 Defense Authorization/Base Closure Delay. Hansen, R-Utah, amendment to delay the next round of military base closings from 1995 until 1997. Rejected in the Committee of the Whole 68-362: R 40-135; D 28-226 (ND 19-156, SD 9-70); I 0-1, May 24, 1994. A "nay" was a vote in support of the president's position.

KEY

Y	Voted for (yea).
#	Paired for.
+	Announced for.
N	Voted against (nay).
X	Paired against.
—	Announced against.
P	Voted "present."
C	Voted "present" to avoid possible conflict of interest.
?	Did not vote or otherwise make a position known.
D	Delegates ineligible to vote.

Democrats *Republicans*
Independent

	187	188	189	190	191	192	193	194
ALABAMA								
1 Callahan	Y	Y	N	N	Y	N	Y	N
2 Everett	N	Y	N	N	Y	N	Y	N
3 Browder	N	Y	N	N	Y	N	Y	N
4 Bevill	N	Y	N	N	Y	N	Y	N
5 Cramer	N	Y	N	N	Y	N	Y	N
6 Bachus	Y	Y	N	N	Y	N	Y	N
7 Hilliard	Y	Y	N	N	N	Y	Y	N
ALASKA								
AL Young	Y	Y	N	N	Y	N	Y	Y
ARIZONA								
1 Coppersmith	N	N	Y	N	Y	Y	Y	N
2 Pastor	Y	Y	N	Y	N	N	N	Y
3 Stump	N	Y	N	N	Y	N	Y	Y
4 Kyl	N	Y	N	N	Y	N	Y	N
5 Kolbe	N	#	X	X	Y	N	Y	N
6 English	Y	N	Y	Y	N	Y	Y	N
ARKANSAS								
1 Lambert	Y	N	Y	Y	Y	Y	Y	N
2 Thornton	Y	Y	N	?	N	N	Y	N
3 Hutchinson	Y	Y	N	N	Y	N	Y	N
4 Dickey	N	Y	N	N	Y	N	Y	N
CALIFORNIA								
1 Hamburg	Y	N	Y	Y	N	Y	Y	N
2 Herger	Y	?	N	N	Y	N	Y	N
3 Fazio	Y	N	N	Y	Y	Y	Y	N
4 Doolittle	Y	Y	N	N	Y	N	N	N
5 Matsui	?	Y	?	Y	?	?	?	?
6 Woolsey	Y	N	Y	Y	N	Y	Y	N
7 Miller	Y	X	#	#	N	Y	N	Y
8 Pelosi	Y	N	Y	Y	N	Y	Y	N
9 Dellums	Y	N	Y	Y	N	Y	Y	N
10 Baker	N	?	N	N	Y	N	Y	N
11 Pombo	Y	Y	N	N	Y	N	Y	N
12 Lantos	Y	N	Y	Y	N	Y	Y	N
13 Stark	Y	N	Y	Y	Y	Y	N	N
14 Eshoo	Y	N	Y	Y	N	Y	Y	N
15 Mineta	Y	Y	N	Y	X	#	Y	N
16 Edwards	Y	N	Y	Y	N	Y	Y	N
17 Farr	Y	?	?	?	N	Y	Y	Y
18 Condit	Y	N	Y	Y	N	Y	N	N
19 Lehman	Y	?	?	?	Y	Y	?	N
20 Dooley	Y	N	Y	Y	N	Y	Y	N
21 Thomas	X	#	X	X	Y	N	Y	N
22 Huffington	N	Y	N	N	?	?	Y	Y
23 Gallegly	Y	Y	N	N	Y	N	Y	Y
24 Beilenson	Y	N	Y	N	Y	N	Y	N
25 McKeon	N	Y	N	N	Y	N	Y	Y
26 Berman	Y	N	Y	Y	N	Y	Y	N
27 Moorhead	N	Y	N	N	Y	N	Y	N
28 Dreier	Y	Y	N	N	Y	N	N	N
29 Waxman	Y	N	Y	Y	N	Y	Y	N
30 Becerra	Y	X	#	#	N	Y	Y	N
31 Martinez	Y	N	Y	N	Y	N	Y	N
32 Dixon	?	?	?	Y	N	Y	Y	N
33 Roybal-Allard	Y	N	Y	Y	N	Y	Y	N
34 Torres	?	?	?	+	N	N	N	N
35 Waters	Y	N	Y	Y	N	Y	Y	N
36 Harman	#	Y	N	N	N	N	Y	N
37 Tucker	Y	N	Y	N	N	N	N	Y
38 Horn	Y	Y	N	N	?	?	?	?
39 Royce	Y	N	Y	N	Y	N	Y	N
40 Lewis	N	?	?	?	Y	N	Y	N
41 Kim	Y	Y	N	N	Y	N	Y	Y
42 Brown	Y	?	?	?	?	Y	Y	N
43 Calvert	Y	Y	N	X	Y	N	Y	Y
44 McCandless	N	Y	N	N	Y	N	Y	N
45 Rohrabacher	Y	N	Y	N	Y	N	Y	N
46 Dornan	N	Y	N	N	Y	N	Y	N
47 Cox	N	Y	N	Y	Y	N	Y	N
48 Packard	N	Y	N	N	Y	N	Y	N
49 Schenk	Y	Y	Y	N	?	?	Y	Y
50 Filner	Y	N	Y	Y	N	Y	Y	N
51 Cunningham	Y	Y	N	N	Y	N	Y	N
52 Hunter	N	Y	N	N	Y	N	Y	N
COLORADO								
1 Schroeder	Y	N	Y	Y	N	N	Y	N
2 Skaggs	N	N	Y	N	N	Y	Y	N
3 McInnis	Y	N	Y	N	?	?	Y	N
4 Allard	Y	Y	N	Y	Y	N	N	N
5 Hefley	N	Y	N	N	Y	N	Y	N
6 Schaefer	Y	Y	Y	N	Y	N	Y	N
CONNECTICUT								
1 Kennelly	Y	Y	N	N	Y	N	Y	N
2 Gejdenson	Y	Y	N	Y	N	N	Y	Y
3 DeLauro	Y	N	Y	N	Y	N	Y	Y
4 Shays	Y	N	Y	Y	Y	Y	Y	N
5 Franks	N	Y	N	N	Y	N	Y	N
6 Johnson	Y	N	Y	Y	Y	Y	Y	N
DELAWARE								
AL Castle	N	Y	N	N	Y	N	Y	N
FLORIDA								
1 Hutto	N	Y	N	N	Y	N	Y	N
2 Peterson	N	N	N	N	N	N	N	Y
3 Brown	Y	N	N	N	N	N	Y	N
4 Fowler	N	Y	N	N	Y	N	Y	Y
5 Thurman	Y	N	Y	Y	N	N	N	N
6 Stearns	N	Y	N	N	Y	N	Y	Y
7 Mica	Y	Y	N	N	Y	N	Y	N
8 McCollum	X	#	X	?	Y	N	Y	Y
9 Bilirakis	Y	Y	N	N	Y	N	Y	N
10 Young	Y	Y	N	N	?	?	Y	Y
11 Gibbons	N	N	Y	N	Y	N	Y	N
12 Canady	N	Y	N	N	Y	N	Y	Y
13 Miller	Y	Y	N	N	Y	N	Y	N
14 Goss	N	Y	N	N	Y	N	N	N
15 Bacchus	N	N	N	N	N	Y	Y	N
16 Lewis	?	+	—	—	Y	N	Y	N
17 Meek	Y	Y	N	N	N	Y	Y	N
18 Ros-Lehtinen	N	Y	N	N	Y	N	Y	N
19 Johnston	Y	Y	N	N	Y	N	Y	N
20 Deutsch	Y	Y	N	N	Y	N	Y	N
21 Diaz-Balart	N	Y	N	N	Y	N	Y	N
22 Shaw	Y	Y	N	N	Y	N	Y	N
23 Hastings	N	N	Y	N	Y	N	Y	N
GEORGIA								
1 Kingston	N	Y	N	N	N	Y	N	N
2 Bishop	N	N	N	N	Y	N	Y	N
3 Collins	N	Y	N	N	Y	N	Y	N
4 Linder	N	Y	N	N	Y	N	Y	N
5 Lewis	Y	N	Y	Y	N	Y	Y	N
6 Gingrich	N	N	N	N	Y	N	Y	N
7 Darden	N	N	Y	N	Y	N	Y	N
8 Rowland	N	Y	N	N	Y	N	Y	N
9 Deal	Y	Y	N	N	#	X	Y	N
10 Johnson	N	Y	N	N	Y	N	Y	N
11 McKinney	Y	Y	Y	N	N	Y	Y	N
HAWAII								
1 Abercrombie	Y	N	Y	N	Y	N	N	Y
2 Mink	Y	N	Y	N	Y	N	Y	Y
IDAHO								
1 LaRocco	Y	Y	N	Y	N	Y	N	N
2 Crapo	Y	Y	N	N	Y	N	Y	N
ILLINOIS								
1 Rush	Y	N	Y	N	N	Y	Y	N
2 Reynolds	Y	N	Y	N	N	N	Y	N
3 Lipinski	N	N	N	N	N	N	Y	N
4 Gutierrez	Y	N	Y	N	Y	N	Y	N
5 Rostenkowski	Y	N	?	?	Y	Y	Y	N
6 Hyde	N	Y	N	Y	N	N	Y	N
7 Collins	Y	?	Y	N	Y	N	Y	N
8 Crane	Y	?	?	?	Y	Y	Y	N
9 Yates	Y	N	Y	Y	N	Y	Y	N
10 Porter	N	N	Y	N	Y	N	Y	N
11 Sangmeister	Y	N	N	Y	?	?	Y	N
12 Costello	N	N	N	N	Y	N	Y	N
13 Fawell	Y	N	N	Y	N	N	Y	N
14 Hastert	N	N	N	N	Y	N	Y	N
15 Ewing	Y	N	Y	N	Y	N	Y	N
16 Manzullo	Y	N	N	N	Y	N	Y	N
17 Evans	Y	N	Y	N	N	Y	Y	N

ND Northern Democrats   SD Southern Democrats

	187	188	189	190	191	192	193	194
18 ***Michel***	N	Y	N	?	?	?	Y	N
19 Poshard	Y	N	Y	N	Y	N	Y	N
20 Durbin	Y	N	Y	Y	N	Y	Y	N
INDIANA								
1 Visclosky	N	N	N	N	Y	N	Y	N
2 Sharp	Y	N	Y	Y	N	Y	Y	N
3 Roemer	Y	N	Y	Y	N	N	Y	N
4 Long	Y	Y	Y	Y	N	Y	Y	N
5 ***Buyer***	N	Y	N	N	Y	N	N	N
6 ***Burton***	N	Y	N	N	Y	N	N	Y
7 ***Myers***	N	Y	N	N	Y	N	Y	Y
8 McCloskey	Y	Y	N	Y	N	N	Y	N
9 Hamilton	N	Y	N	N	Y	N	Y	N
10 Jacobs	Y	N	Y	Y	Y	Y	Y	Y
IOWA								
1 ***Leach***	Y	Y	Y	Y	Y	Y	Y	N
2 ***Nussle***	Y	Y	Y	Y	Y	N	N	N
3 ***Lightfoot***	Y	Y	N	N	Y	N	Y	N
4 Smith	?	?	?	?	Y	N	Y	N
5 ***Grandy***	?	#	?	?	?	?	?	?
KANSAS								
1 ***Roberts***	N	?	?	?	Y	N	Y	Y
2 Slattery	?	?	?	#	?	?	Y	N
3 ***Meyers***	Y	N	Y	Y	Y	N	Y	Y
4 Glickman	Y	Y	N	Y	Y	Y	Y	N
KENTUCKY								
1 Barlow	?	+	–	–	+	–	+	–
2 Vacancy								
3 Mazzoli	N	Y	N	N	Y	N	Y	N
4 ***Bunning***	N	N	Y	N	Y	N	N	N
5 ***Rogers***	Y	N	N	N	Y	N	Y	N
6 Baesler	N	Y	N	Y	Y	N	Y	N
LOUISIANA								
1 ***Livingston***	?	?	?	?	Y	N	Y	Y
2 Jefferson	Y	N	Y	N	N	Y	Y	N
3 Tauzin	Y	Y	N	N	Y	N	Y	N
4 Fields	Y	N	Y	Y	N	N	Y	N
5 ***McCrery***	N	Y	N	N	Y	N	Y	N
6 ***Baker***	N	Y	N	N	Y	N	Y	N
7 Hayes	Y	Y	N	N	Y	N	Y	Y
MAINE								
1 Andrews	Y	N	Y	Y	N	Y	Y	N
2 ***Snowe***	Y	N	Y	N	?	?	Y	Y
MARYLAND								
1 ***Gilchrest***	Y	Y	Y	N	Y	N	Y	N
2 ***Bentley***	Y	Y	N	N	Y	N	Y	N
3 Cardin	+	N	Y	Y	Y	Y	Y	N
4 Wynn	Y	N	Y	N	Y	Y	Y	N
5 Hoyer	Y	Y	N	N	Y	N	Y	N
6 ***Bartlett***	N	Y	N	N	Y	N	Y	Y
7 Mfume	Y	N	?	Y	N	Y	Y	N
8 ***Morella***	Y	N	Y	Y	+	N	Y	N
MASSACHUSETTS								
1 Olver	Y	N	Y	Y	N	Y	Y	N
2 Neal	Y	N	Y	Y	N	N	Y	N
3 ***Blute***	Y	Y	N	Y	Y	N	Y	N
4 Frank	Y	N	Y	Y	N	Y	Y	N
5 Meehan	Y	N	Y	Y	N	Y	Y	N
6 ***Torkildsen***	N	Y	N	Y	Y	N	Y	Y
7 Markey	?	N	Y	Y	N	Y	Y	N
8 Kennedy	Y	N	Y	Y	N	Y	Y	N
9 Moakley	Y	N	Y	Y	N	N	Y	N
10 Studds	Y	N	Y	Y	N	Y	Y	N
MICHIGAN								
1 Stupak	Y	N	Y	Y	Y	N	Y	N
2 ***Hoekstra***	Y	Y	Y	N	Y	N	Y	N
3 ***Ehlers***	Y	Y	Y	N	N	N	N	N
4 ***Camp***	Y	Y	N	N	Y	Y	N	N
5 Barcia	Y	N	Y	Y	Y	N	Y	N
6 ***Upton***	Y	N	Y	Y	Y	Y	N	N
7 ***Smith***	N	Y	N	N	Y	N	Y	N
8 Carr	Y	Y	N	Y	?	?	Y	N
9 Kildee	Y	N	Y	Y	Y	Y	Y	N
10 Bonior	Y	N	Y	Y	N	N	Y	N
11 ***Knollenberg***	N	Y	N	N	Y	N	Y	N
12 Levin	N	N	Y	Y	N	Y	Y	N
13 Ford	Y	?	?	?	N	Y	Y	N
14 Conyers	Y	N	Y	Y	X	#	Y	N
15 Collins	Y	N	Y	Y	N	Y	Y	N
16 Dingell	N	X	X	X	N	Y	Y	N
MINNESOTA								
1 Penny	Y	N	Y	Y	Y	Y	N	N
2 Minge	Y	N	Y	Y	Y	Y	N	N
3 ***Ramstad***	Y	Y	Y	Y	Y	N	N	N
4 Vento	Y	N	Y	Y	N	Y	Y	N

	187	188	189	190	191	192	193	194
5 Sabo	Y	N	Y	Y	N	Y	Y	N
6 ***Grams***	N	#	X	#	Y	N	Y	N
7 Peterson	Y	N	Y	Y	Y	Y	N	N
8 Oberstar	Y	N	Y	Y	N	Y	Y	N
MISSISSIPPI								
1 Whitten	?	?	N	N	N	N	Y	?
2 Thompson	Y	Y	N	Y	N	N	Y	N
3 Montgomery	N	Y	N	N	Y	N	Y	Y
4 Parker	?	Y	N	N	Y	N	Y	Y
5 Taylor	N	Y	N	N	Y	N	Y	Y
MISSOURI								
1 Clay	?	N	Y	Y	N	Y	Y	N
2 ***Talent***	N	Y	N	N	Y	N	Y	N
3 Gephardt	Y	N	?	?	?	?	Y	N
4 Skelton	N	Y	N	N	Y	N	Y	N
5 Wheat	Y	N	Y	Y	N	Y	Y	N
6 Danner	Y	N	Y	N	Y	N	Y	N
7 ***Hancock***	Y	N	Y	N	Y	N	N	N
8 ***Emerson***	?	?	X	X	Y	N	Y	N
9 Volkmer	Y	N	N	Y	Y	N	Y	N
MONTANA								
AL Williams	Y	N	Y	Y	N	Y	Y	Y
NEBRASKA								
1 ***Bereuter***	N	Y	N	N	Y	N	Y	N
2 Hoagland	Y	Y	N	N	N	N	Y	N
3 ***Barrett***	N	Y	N	N	Y	Y	Y	N
NEVADA								
1 Bilbray	N	N	N	N	Y	N	Y	N
2 ***Vucanovich***	N	Y	N	N	Y	N	Y	N
NEW HAMPSHIRE								
1 ***Zeliff***	N	Y	N	N	Y	N	Y	Y
2 Swett	Y	Y	Y	Y	Y	N	?	Y
NEW JERSEY								
1 Andrews	Y	N	N	N	Y	N	Y	Y
2 Hughes	Y	N	N	N	N	N	Y	Y
3 ***Saxton***	N	Y	N	N	Y	N	Y	Y
4 ***Smith***	Y	N	Y	N	Y	N	Y	Y
5 ***Roukema***	Y	N	Y	Y	Y	N	Y	N
6 Pallone	Y	N	Y	Y	Y	N	Y	Y
7 ***Franks***	Y	N	N	Y	Y	Y	Y	N
8 Klein	Y	Y	N	N	?	?	Y	N
9 Torricelli	Y	?	?	N	Y	N	Y	N
10 Payne	Y	N	Y	Y	N	Y	Y	N
11 ***Gallo***	N	Y	N	N	Y	N	Y	Y
12 ***Zimmer***	Y	N	Y	N	Y	Y	Y	N
13 Menendez	Y	N	Y	N	Y	N	Y	N
NEW MEXICO								
1 ***Schiff***	Y	Y	N	Y	Y	N	Y	N
2 ***Skeen***	N	Y	N	N	Y	N	Y	Y
3 Richardson	N	Y	N	Y	Y	N	Y	N
NEW YORK								
1 Hochbrueckner	Y	Y	N	Y	Y	N	Y	N
2 ***Lazio***	N	Y	N	N	Y	N	Y	N
3 ***King***	N	Y	N	N	Y	N	Y	N
4 ***Levy***	N	Y	N	N	Y	N	Y	N
5 Ackerman	Y	N	Y	Y	N	N	Y	N
6 Flake	Y	?	?	?	N	N	Y	N
7 Manton	Y	Y	N	Y	N	N	Y	N
8 Nadler	#	N	Y	Y	–	+	Y	N
9 Schumer	Y	N	N	N	N	N	Y	N
10 Towns	Y	?	?	?	?	?	Y	N
11 Owens	Y	N	Y	Y	?	?	Y	N
12 Velazquez	Y	N	Y	Y	N	Y	Y	N
13 ***Molinari***	N	Y	N	N	Y	N	Y	Y
14 Maloney	Y	N	Y	Y	N	Y	Y	N
15 Rangel	Y	X	#	Y	N	N	Y	N
16 Serrano	Y	N	Y	Y	N	Y	Y	N
17 Engel	Y	N	Y	Y	N	N	Y	N
18 Lowey	Y	N	Y	Y	N	Y	Y	N
19 ***Fish***	Y	Y	N	Y	?	?	Y	N
20 ***Gilman***	N	Y	N	N	Y	N	Y	N
21 McNulty	Y	Y	N	N	Y	N	Y	N
22 ***Solomon***	N	Y	N	N	Y	N	N	N
23 ***Boehlert***	Y	N	Y	N	Y	N	Y	Y
24 ***McHugh***	N	Y	N	N	Y	N	Y	N
25 ***Walsh***	N	Y	N	Y	Y	N	Y	N
26 Hinchey	Y	N	Y	Y	N	Y	Y	N
27 ***Paxon***	N	Y	N	N	Y	N	N	N
28 Slaughter	Y	N	Y	Y	N	Y	Y	N
29 LaFalce	N	X	#	X	Y	N	Y	N
30 ***Quinn***	Y	Y	N	N	Y	N	N	N
31 ***Houghton***	N	Y	N	N	?	?	?	N
NORTH CAROLINA								
1 Clayton	Y	N	Y	Y	N	Y	Y	N
2 Valentine	Y	N	N	Y	Y	Y	Y	N

	187	188	189	190	191	192	193	194
3 Lancaster	N	Y	N	N	Y	N	Y	Y
4 Price	N	N	Y	Y	Y	Y	Y	N
5 Neal	?	?	?	?	Y	N	Y	N
6 ***Coble***	Y	Y	N	Y	Y	N	N	Y
7 Rose	Y	Y	Y	?	?	?	Y	N
8 Hefner	Y	Y	Y	Y	Y	N	Y	N
9 ***McMillan***	N	Y	N	N	Y	N	Y	N
10 ***Ballenger***	N	N	Y	N	Y	N	Y	N
11 ***Taylor***	Y	Y	N	Y	Y	N	Y	N
12 Watt	Y	N	Y	Y	N	Y	Y	N
NORTH DAKOTA								
AL Pomeroy	Y	N	Y	Y	Y	Y	Y	N
OHIO								
1 Mann	N	N	N	N	N	N	Y	N
2 ***Portman***	Y	Y	N	N	Y	N	Y	N
3 Hall	Y	N	Y	Y	Y	Y	Y	N
4 ***Oxley***	N	Y	N	N	Y	N	Y	N
5 ***Gillmor***	Y	Y	N	N	Y	N	Y	N
6 Strickland	Y	N	Y	Y	N	Y	Y	N
7 ***Hobson***	Y	Y	Y	N	Y	N	Y	N
8 ***Boehner***	Y	Y	N	N	Y	N	Y	N
9 Kaptur	Y	Y	N	N	N	N	Y	N
10 ***Hoke***	Y	Y	N	Y	Y	Y	N	N
11 Stokes	Y	N	Y	Y	N	Y	Y	N
12 ***Kasich***	Y	Y	N	N	Y	N	Y	N
13 Brown	Y	N	Y	Y	Y	Y	Y	N
14 Sawyer	Y	X	#	#	N	N	Y	N
15 ***Pryce***	Y	Y	N	N	Y	N	Y	N
16 ***Regula***	Y	Y	N	N	Y	N	Y	N
17 Traficant	Y	N	Y	N	Y	N	Y	Y
18 Applegate	Y	Y	N	Y	Y	N	Y	Y
19 Fingerhut	Y	N	Y	Y	Y	N	Y	N
OKLAHOMA								
1 ***Inhofe***	N	Y	N	N	Y	N	Y	N
2 Synar	Y	N	Y	Y	N	Y	Y	N
3 Brewster	Y	Y	N	N	Y	N	Y	N
4 McCurdy	?	Y	N	N	Y	N	Y	N
5 ***Istook***	Y	Y	N	N	Y	N	Y	N
6 ***Lucas***	N	Y	N	N	Y	N	Y	N
OREGON								
1 Furse	Y	N	Y	Y	N	Y	Y	N
2 ***Smith***	N	Y	N	N	Y	N	Y	N
3 Wyden	Y	N	Y	Y	N	Y	N	N
4 DeFazio	Y	N	Y	Y	N	Y	N	N
5 Kopetski	Y	N	Y	Y	N	N	Y	N
PENNSYLVANIA								
1 Foglietta	Y	N	Y	Y	N	N	Y	Y
2 Blackwell	Y	?	Y	Y	?	?	Y	Y
3 Borski	Y	Y	N	Y	Y	Y	Y	N
4 Klink	Y	N	Y	Y	N	N	Y	N
5 ***Clinger***	N	Y	N	N	Y	X	Y	Y
6 Holden	Y	N	N	Y	Y	N	Y	N
7 ***Weldon***	N	Y	N	N	Y	N	Y	N
8 ***Greenwood***	N	Y	N	Y	Y	N	Y	N
9 ***Shuster***	N	Y	N	N	Y	N	Y	Y
10 ***McDade***	N	Y	N	N	Y	N	Y	Y
11 Kanjorski	N	N	N	Y	N	N	Y	N
12 Murtha	N	Y	N	N	Y	N	Y	Y
13 Margolies-Mezv.	Y	N	Y	Y	?	?	Y	N
14 Coyne	Y	N	Y	Y	?	?	Y	N
15 McHale	N	Y	Y	Y	Y	N	Y	N
16 ***Walker***	N	Y	N	N	Y	Y	N	N
17 ***Gekas***	Y	Y	N	N	Y	N	Y	N
18 ***Santorum***	?	Y	Y	N	?	?	Y	N
19 ***Goodling***	Y	Y	N	N	Y	N	Y	N
20 Murphy	N	?	?	?	Y	Y	Y	N
21 ***Ridge***	Y	N	N	N	?	?	Y	N
RHODE ISLAND								
1 ***Machtley***	Y	?	?	N	Y	N	Y	N
2 Reed	Y	Y	Y	N	N	N	Y	N
SOUTH CAROLINA								
1 ***Ravenel***	Y	Y	N	Y	Y	N	Y	Y
2 ***Spence***	N	Y	N	N	Y	N	Y	Y
3 Derrick	Y	N	Y	N	N	N	Y	N
4 ***Inglis***	N	Y	N	N	Y	N	Y	N
5 Spratt	Y	Y	N	N	Y	N	Y	N
6 Clyburn	N	Y	N	N	N	N	Y	N
SOUTH DAKOTA								
AL Johnson	Y	N	N	N	#	X	Y	N
TENNESSEE								
1 ***Quillen***	N	Y	N	N	Y	N	Y	N
2 ***Duncan***	Y	N	Y	Y	Y	N	N	N
3 Lloyd	N	Y	N	N	Y	N	Y	N
4 Cooper	Y	Y	N	Y	Y	N	Y	N
5 Clement	Y	Y	Y	?	Y	N	Y	N

	187	188	189	190	191	192	193	194
6 Gordon	Y	N	Y	?	Y	N	Y	N
7 ***Sundquist***	N	Y	N	?	?	?	Y	N
8 Tanner	N	Y	N	N	Y	N	Y	N
9 Ford	Y	N	Y	Y	?	?	Y	N
TEXAS								
1 Chapman	Y	Y	N	N	Y	Y	Y	Y
2 Wilson	?	?	?	?	Y	N	Y	N
3 ***Johnson, Sam***	N	Y	N	N	Y	N	Y	N
4 Hall	Y	Y	N	N	Y	N	Y	N
5 Bryant	Y	N	Y	Y	Y	N	Y	N
6 ***Barton***	N	Y	N	N	Y	N	Y	N
7 ***Archer***	N	Y	N	N	Y	Y	N	N
8 ***Fields***	N	Y	N	N	?	?	N	N
9 Brooks	Y	?	?	?	Y	N	Y	N
10 Pickle	Y	Y	N	?	Y	N	Y	N
11 Edwards	N	N	N	N	Y	N	Y	N
12 Geren	N	Y	N	N	Y	N	Y	N
13 Sarpalius	N	Y	N	N	Y	N	Y	Y
14 Laughlin	Y	Y	N	N	Y	N	Y	N
15 de la Garza	Y	Y	N	N	Y	N	Y	N
16 Coleman	Y	Y	N	N	Y	N	Y	N
17 Stenholm	N	Y	N	?	Y	N	Y	N
18 Washington	?	?	#	#	X	?	?	?
19 ***Combest***	N	Y	N	N	Y	N	Y	Y
20 Gonzalez	N	Y	N	Y	N	Y	Y	Y
21 ***Smith***	N	?	?	?	Y	N	Y	N
22 ***DeLay***	N	Y	N	N	Y	Y	?	Y
23 ***Bonilla***	N	Y	N	N	Y	N	Y	N
24 Frost	Y	Y	N	N	N	N	Y	N
25 Andrews	Y	N	N	N	Y	N	Y	N
26 ***Armey***	N	Y	N	N	Y	N	Y	N
27 Ortiz	N	Y	N	N	+	–	+	–
28 Tejeda	N	Y	N	N	Y	N	Y	Y
29 Green	Y	N	Y	N	Y	Y	Y	N
30 Johnson, E.B.	Y	Y	N	Y	N	Y	Y	N
UTAH	•							
1 ***Hansen***	N	Y	N	N	Y	N	Y	Y
2 Shepherd	Y	Y	N	Y	N	N	Y	Y
3 Orton	Y	Y	N	Y	Y	N	Y	Y
VERMONT								
AL *Sanders*	Y	N	Y	Y	N	Y	Y	N
VIRGINIA								
1 ***Bateman***	N	Y	N	N	Y	N	Y	N
2 Pickett	N	Y	N	N	Y	N	Y	N
3 Scott	N	Y	N	N	N	Y	Y	N
4 Sisisky	N	Y	N	N	Y	N	Y	N
5 Payne	N	Y	N	N	Y	N	Y	N
6 ***Goodlatte***	Y	N	Y	N	Y	N	Y	N
7 ***Bliley***	N	Y	N	N	Y	N	Y	N
8 Moran	N	Y	N	Y	N	N	Y	N
9 Boucher	Y	N	N	Y	Y	N	Y	N
10 ***Wolf***	N	Y	N	N	Y	N	Y	N
11 Byrne	Y	N	Y	Y	Y	N	Y	N
WASHINGTON								
1 Cantwell	Y	Y	N	Y	N	Y	Y	N
2 Swift	N	Y	N	Y	N	N	Y	N
3 Unsoeld	Y	N	Y	Y	N	Y	Y	N
4 Inslee	Y	Y	Y	Y	Y	Y	Y	N
5 Foley								
6 Dicks	N	Y	N	Y	Y	N	Y	N
7 McDermott	Y	N	Y	Y	?	?	Y	N
8 ***Dunn***	N	Y	N	N	Y	N	N	N
9 Kreidler	Y	N	Y	Y	Y	Y	Y	N
WEST VIRGINIA								
1 Mollohan	N	Y	N	N	N	Y	Y	N
2 Wise	Y	N	N	N	N	N	Y	N
3 Rahall	Y	N	Y	Y	N	Y	Y	N
WISCONSIN								
1 Barca	Y	N	Y	Y	?	N	N	N
2 ***Klug***	Y	N	Y	Y	Y	Y	N	N
3 ***Gunderson***	N	Y	Y	N	Y	N	Y	N
4 Kleczka	Y	Y	N	Y	#	#	Y	N
5 Barrett	Y	N	Y	Y	N	Y	?	?
6 ***Petri***	Y	N	Y	N	Y	N	Y	N
7 Obey	Y	N	Y	Y	N	Y	Y	N
8 ***Roth***	Y	N	Y	N	Y	Y	N	N
9 ***Sensenbrenner***	Y	N	Y	Y	Y	Y	N	N
WYOMING								
AL ***Thomas***	Y	#	?	?	Y	N	Y	N
DELEGATES								
de Lugo, V.I.	Y	Y	N	Y	Y	N	D	N
Faleomavaega, Am.S.	?	?	?	?	?	?	D	N
Norton, D.C.	Y	N	Y	Y	N	Y	D	N
Romero-B., P.R.	?	N	?	N	?	?	D	N
Underwood, Guam	N	N	Y	N	N	Y	D	N

Southern states - Ala., Ark., Fla., Ga., Ky., La., Miss., N.C., Okla., S.C., Tenn., Texas, Va.
Omitted votes are quorum calls, which CQ does not include in its vote charts.

KEY

Y   Voted for (yea).
Paired for.
+   Announced for.
N   Voted against (nay).
X   Paired against.
−   Announced against.
P   Voted "present."
C   Voted "present" to avoid possible conflict of interest.
?   Did not vote or otherwise make a position known.
D   Delegates ineligible to vote.

Democrats   *Republicans*
Independent

195. HR 4301. Fiscal 1995 Defense Authorization/C-17 Aircraft Increase. Harman, D-Calif., amendment to increase from four to six the number of C-17 transport aircraft authorized in fiscal 1995. Adopted in the Committee of the Whole 330-100: R 152-23; D 178-76 (ND 110-64, SD 68-12); I 0-1, May 24, 1994. A "yea" was a vote in support of the president's position.

196. HR 4301. Fiscal 1995 Defense Authorization/Haitian Policy. Dellums, D-Calif., substitute amendment to the Goss, R-Fla., amendment, to express the sense of Congress that the president should intensify economic pressure on Haiti's military; replace shipboard processing of Haitian migrants with land-based processing; and seek international cooperation in establishing refugee processing centers. The Goss amendment would express the sense of Congress that the United States, with the Organization of American States and the United Nations, should establish a safe haven for Haitian refugees on the Haitian island of Ile de la Gonave while assisting the legitimate Haitian government in establishing the long-term stability of democracy in Haiti. Rejected in the Committee of the Whole 191-236: R 6-167; D 184-69 (ND 143-31, SD 41-38); I 1-0, May 24, 1994.

197. HR 4301. Fiscal 1995 Defense Authorization/Haitian Policy. Goss, R-Fla., amendment to express the sense of Congress that the United States, with the Organization of American States and the United Nations, should establish a safe haven for Haitian refugees on the Haitian island of Ile de la Gonave while assisting the legitimate Haitian government in establishing the long-term stability of democracy in Haiti. Adopted in the Committee of the Whole 223-201: R 169-3; D 54-197 (ND 25-149, SD 29-48); I 0-1, May 24, 1994.

198. HR 4301. Fiscal 1995 Defense Authorization/U.N. Peacekeeping Costs. Spence, R-S.C., amendment to limit the amounts authorized for the U.S. assessed share of U.N. peacekeeping costs to only those spent by the Defense Department in direct or indirect support of U.N. peacekeeping operations. Rejected in the Committee of the Whole 191-221: R 164-6; D 27-214 (ND 16-152, SD 11-62); I 0-1, May 24, 1994. A "nay" was a vote in support of the president's position.

199. HR 4385. National Highway System Designation/Indianapolis-Houston Corridor. Clement, D-Tenn., amendment to strike the provisions in the bill that require a proposed highway between Indianapolis and Houston to go through six particular cities in Kentucky. Rejected in the Committee of the Whole 64-364: R 32-142; D 32-221 (ND 19-154, SD 13-67); I 0-1, May 25, 1994.

200. HR 4385. National Highway System Designation/Passage. Passage of the bill to designate roughly 160,000 miles of roadway as the National Highway System with priority for federal aid; authorize $2 billion for 352 road and transit projects; make technical corrections to the 1991 surface transportation law; and for other purposes. Passed 412-12: R 161-11; D 250-1 (ND 169-1, SD 81-0); I 1-0, May 25, 1994.

201. HR 4426. Fiscal 1995 Foreign Operations Appropriations/Rule. Adoption of the rule (H Res 441) to waive the two-thirds requirement for consideration of a rule filed the same day on the fiscal 1995 foreign operations appropriations bill without the two-thirds majority vote normally required for adoption of a rule reported the same day. Adopted 246-174: R 4-169; D 241-5 (ND 168-1, SD 73-4); I 1-0, May 25, 1994.

	195	196	197	198	199	200	201
ALABAMA							
1 Callahan	Y	N	Y	Y	N	Y	Y
2 Everett	Y	N	Y	Y	N	Y	Y
3 Browder	Y	N	Y	N	N	N	Y
4 Bevill	Y	N	Y	N	N	N	Y
5 Cramer	Y	N	Y	N	Y	Y	Y
6 *Bachus*	Y	N	Y	N	Y	?	N
7 Hilliard	Y	Y	N	N	N	Y	Y
ALASKA							
AL *Young*	Y	N	Y	Y	N	Y	N
ARIZONA							
1 Coppersmith	Y	Y	Y	N	Y	Y	Y
2 Pastor	Y	Y	N	N	N	Y	Y
3 *Stump*	Y	N	Y	Y	N	N	N
4 *Kyl*	Y	N	Y	Y	N	N	N
5 *Kolbe*	Y	Y	Y	N	Y	N	N
6 English	N	Y	N	N	N	Y	Y
ARKANSAS							
1 Lambert	Y	N	N	Y	Y	Y	Y
2 Thornton	Y	Y	N	N	N	Y	Y
3 *Hutchinson*	Y	N	Y	Y	N	Y	N
4 *Dickey*	Y	N	Y	Y	N	Y	N
CALIFORNIA							
1 Hamburg	N	Y	N	N	N	Y	Y
2 *Herger*	Y	N	Y	Y	Y	Y	N
3 Fazio	Y	Y	N	N	N	Y	Y
4 *Doolittle*	Y	N	Y	Y	N	N	N
5 Matsui	Y	Y	N	N	N	Y	Y
6 Woolsey	N	Y	N	N	N	Y	Y
7 Miller	N	Y	N	N	N	Y	Y
8 Pelosi	N	Y	N	N	N	Y	Y
9 Dellums	N	Y	N	N	N	Y	Y
10 *Baker*	Y	N	Y	N	Y	N	N
11 *Pombo*	Y	N	Y	Y	N	Y	N
12 Lantos	Y	Y	Y	N	N	Y	Y
13 Stark	N	?	?	?	N	Y	Y
14 Eshoo	N	Y	N	N	N	Y	Y
15 Mineta	Y	Y	N	N	N	Y	Y
16 Edwards	N	Y	N	N	N	Y	Y
17 Farr	Y	Y	N	N	N	Y	Y
18 Condit	Y	N	Y	N	Y	N	N
19 Lehman	Y	N	N	N	N	Y	N
20 Dooley	Y	Y	N	N	N	Y	Y
21 *Thomas*	Y	N	Y	Y	N	Y	N
22 *Huffington*	Y	N	Y	N	Y	N	Y
23 *Gallegly*	Y	N	Y	N	Y	N	N
24 Beilenson	Y	Y	Y	N	Y	Y	Y
25 *McKeon*	Y	N	Y	Y	N	Y	N
26 Berman	Y	Y	N	N	N	Y	Y
27 *Moorhead*	Y	N	Y	Y	Y	N	N
28 *Dreier*	Y	N	Y	Y	Y	N	N
29 Waxman	N	Y	N	N	N	Y	Y
30 Becerra	N	Y	N	N	N	Y	Y
31 Martinez	Y	N	Y	N	N	N	Y
32 Dixon	Y	Y	N	N	N	Y	Y
33 Roybal-Allard	Y	Y	N	N	N	Y	Y
34 Torres	Y	N	N	N	N	Y	Y
35 Waters	Y	Y	N	N	N	Y	Y
36 Harman	Y	Y	N	N	N	Y	Y
37 Tucker	Y	Y	N	N	N	Y	Y
38 *Horn*	?	?	?	?	?	?	?
39 *Royce*	Y	N	Y	Y	Y	N	N
40 *Lewis*	Y	N	Y	N	Y	N	N
41 *Kim*	Y	N	Y	Y	N	Y	N
42 Brown	Y	N	Y	?	N	Y	Y
43 *Calvert*	Y	N	Y	N	Y	N	N
44 *McCandless*	Y	N	Y	N	Y	N	N
45 *Rohrabacher*	Y	N	Y	Y	Y	Y	N
46 *Dornan*	Y	N	Y	Y	N	N	N
47 *Cox*	Y	N	Y	Y	N	Y	N
48 *Packard*	Y	N	Y	N	Y	N	N
49 Schenk	Y	Y	N	N	N	Y	Y
50 Filner	Y	Y	N	N	N	Y	Y
51 *Cunningham*	Y	N	Y	Y	N	Y	N
52 *Hunter*	Y	N	Y	Y	N	Y	N
COLORADO							
1 Schroeder	N	Y	N	N	N	Y	Y
2 Skaggs	Y	Y	N	N	N	Y	Y
3 *McInnis*	Y	N	Y	N	Y	N	Y
4 *Allard*	Y	N	Y	Y	Y	N	N
5 *Hefley*	Y	N	Y	Y	Y	Y	Y
6 *Schaefer*	N	N	Y	N	Y	N	N
CONNECTICUT							
1 Kennelly	Y	Y	N	N	N	Y	Y
2 Gejdenson	Y	Y	N	N	N	Y	Y
3 DeLauro	Y	Y	N	N	N	Y	Y
4 *Shays*	Y	N	Y	N	Y	N	Y
5 *Franks*	Y	N	Y	N	N	Y	Y
6 *Johnson*	Y	N	Y	N	Y	Y	Y
DELAWARE							
AL *Castle*	Y	N	Y	Y	N	Y	N
FLORIDA							
1 Hutto	Y	N	N	N	N	Y	Y
2 Peterson	Y	N	N	N	N	Y	Y
3 Brown	Y	Y	N	N	N	Y	Y
4 *Fowler*	Y	N	Y	N	Y	N	Y
5 Thurman	Y	N	N	N	N	Y	Y
6 *Stearns*	Y	N	Y	Y	Y	Y	N
7 *Mica*	Y	N	N	N	N	Y	N
8 *McCollum*	Y	N	Y	N	Y	N	N
9 *Bilirakis*	Y	N	Y	Y	Y	Y	N
10 *Young*	Y	N	Y	Y	N	Y	N
11 Gibbons	Y	N	?	?	N	Y	Y
12 *Canady*	Y	N	Y	N	Y	N	N
13 *Miller*	N	N	Y	N	Y	N	N
14 *Goss*	Y	N	Y	N	N	N	N
15 Bacchus	Y	N	Y	N	Y	Y	Y
16 *Lewis*	Y	N	Y	?	N	Y	N
17 Meek	Y	Y	N	N	N	Y	Y
18 *Ros-Lehtinen*	Y	Y	N	N	N	Y	N
19 Johnston	N	N	N	N	?	Y	Y
20 Deutsch	N	N	N	N	N	Y	Y
21 *Diaz-Balart*	Y	N	Y	N	N	Y	Y
22 *Shaw*	Y	N	Y	N	Y	N	N
23 Hastings	Y	Y	N	N	N	Y	Y
GEORGIA							
1 *Kingston*	N	N	Y	N	Y	N	N
2 Bishop	Y	Y	N	N	N	Y	Y
3 *Collins*	Y	N	Y	Y	N	Y	N
4 *Linder*	N	N	Y	N	Y	N	N
5 Lewis	N	Y	N	N	N	Y	Y
6 *Gingrich*	Y	N	Y	Y	N	Y	N
7 Darden	N	N	Y	N	N	N	Y
8 Rowland	Y	N	Y	N	N	Y	Y
9 *Deal*	N	N	Y	N	N	Y	Y
10 Johnson	N	N	N	N	N	Y	Y
11 McKinney	N	Y	N	N	N	Y	Y
HAWAII							
1 Abercrombie	N	Y	N	N	N	Y	Y
2 Mink	N	Y	N	N	N	Y	Y
IDAHO							
1 LaRocco	Y	Y	N	N	N	Y	Y
2 *Crapo*	Y	N	Y	Y	N	Y	N
ILLINOIS							
1 Rush	N	Y	N	N	N	Y	?
2 Reynolds	Y	Y	N	N	N	Y	Y
3 Lipinski	Y	N	Y	Y	Y	Y	Y
4 Gutierrez	N	Y	N	N	N	Y	Y
5 Rostenkowski	Y	Y	N	N	N	Y	?
6 *Hyde*	Y	N	Y	N	Y	N	Y
7 Collins	Y	Y	N	N	N	Y	Y
8 *Crane*	Y	N	Y	Y	Y	N	N
9 Yates	N	Y	N	N	N	Y	Y
10 *Porter*	N	N	Y	N	Y	N	N
11 Sangmeister	Y	Y	Y	Y	Y	Y	Y
12 Costello	Y	Y	N	N	N	Y	Y
13 *Fawell*	Y	N	Y	Y	N	N	N
14 *Hastert*	Y	N	Y	N	Y	N	Y
15 *Ewing*	Y	N	Y	N	Y	N	Y
16 *Manzullo*	Y	N	Y	N	Y	N	N
17 Evans	N	Y	N	N	N	Y	Y

ND Northern Democrats   SD Southern Democrats

	195	196	197	198	199	200	201
18 ***Michel***	Y	N	Y	?	N	Y	N
19 Poshard	N	Y	N	Y	N	Y	Y
20 Durbin	Y	Y	N	N	N	Y	Y
INDIANA							
1 Visclosky	Y	Y	N	N	N	Y	Y
2 Sharp	Y	Y	N	?	N	Y	Y
3 Roemer	Y	Y	N	N	N	Y	Y
4 Long	Y	Y	N	N	N	Y	Y
5 ***Buyer***	Y	N	Y	Y	N	Y	N
6 ***Burton***	Y	N	Y	Y	N	Y	N
7 ***Myers***	Y	N	Y	Y	Y	Y	N
8 McCloskey	Y	N	N	N	N	Y	Y
9 Hamilton	Y	Y	N	N	N	Y	Y
10 Jacobs	Y	Y	N	Y	N	Y	Y
IOWA							
1 ***Leach***	Y	N	Y	N	Y	Y	N
2 ***Nussle***	N	N	Y	Y	Y	Y	N
3 ***Lightfoot***	Y	N	Y	Y	N	Y	Y
4 Smith	N	N	Y	N	N	Y	Y
5 ***Grandy***	?	?	?	?	?	?	?
KANSAS							
1 ***Roberts***	Y	N	Y	Y	N	Y	N
2 Slattery	Y	Y	N	N	N	Y	Y
3 ***Meyers***	Y	N	Y	Y	N	Y	N
4 Glickman	Y	Y	N	N	N	Y	Y
KENTUCKY							
1 Barlow	+	+	–	–	N	Y	Y
2 Vacancy							
3 Mazzoli	Y	N	N	Y	N	Y	Y
4 ***Bunning***	Y	N	Y	Y	N	Y	N
5 ***Rogers***	Y	N	Y	Y	N	Y	N
6 Baesler	Y	N	Y	N	N	Y	Y
LOUISIANA							
1 ***Livingston***	Y	N	Y	Y	N	Y	Y
2 Jefferson	Y	Y	N	N	N	Y	Y
3 Tauzin	Y	N	Y	Y	Y	Y	Y
4 Fields	Y	Y	N	N	N	Y	Y
5 ***McCrery***	Y	N	Y	Y	N	Y	N
6 ***Baker***	Y	N	Y	Y	N	Y	N
7 Hayes	Y	N	Y	Y	Y	Y	N
MAINE							
1 Andrews	Y	Y	N	N	Y	?	Y
2 ***Snowe***	Y	N	Y	Y	N	Y	N
MARYLAND							
1 ***Gilchrest***	Y	Y	Y	N	N	Y	N
2 ***Bentley***	Y	N	Y	Y	N	Y	N
3 Cardin	Y	N	N	N	N	Y	Y
4 Wynn	Y	N	N	N	N	Y	Y
5 Hoyer	Y	N	N	N	N	Y	Y
6 ***Bartlett***	Y	N	Y	Y	Y	Y	N
7 Mfume	N	Y	N	N	N	Y	Y
8 ***Morella***	N	N	Y	N	N	Y	N
MASSACHUSETTS							
1 Olver	N	Y	N	N	N	Y	Y
2 Neal	N	Y	N	N	Y	Y	Y
3 ***Blute***	Y	N	Y	Y	N	Y	N
4 Frank	N	Y	N	N	N	Y	Y
5 Meehan	N	Y	N	N	N	Y	Y
6 ***Torkildsen***	Y	N	Y	Y	N	Y	N
7 Markey	N	Y	N	N	N	Y	Y
8 Kennedy	N	Y	N	N	Y	Y	Y
9 Moakley	N	Y	N	N	N	Y	Y
10 Studds	N	Y	N	N	N	Y	Y
MICHIGAN							
1 Stupak	Y	Y	N	N	N	Y	Y
2 ***Hoekstra***	N	N	Y	Y	N	Y	N
3 ***Ehlers***	Y	N	Y	Y	N	Y	N
4 ***Camp***	Y	Y	Y	Y	N	Y	N
5 Barcia	N	Y	Y	N	Y	Y	Y
6 ***Upton***	Y	Y	Y	Y	N	Y	N
7 ***Smith***	Y	N	Y	Y	N	Y	N
8 Carr	Y	N	N	N	Y	Y	Y
9 Kildee	N	Y	N	N	N	Y	Y
10 Bonior	Y	Y	N	N	N	Y	Y
11 ***Knollenberg***	Y	N	Y	Y	N	Y	N
12 Levin	Y	Y	N	N	N	Y	Y
13 Ford	Y	Y	N	?	?	Y	Y
14 Conyers	N	Y	N	?	N	Y	Y
15 Collins	Y	Y	N	N	N	Y	Y
16 Dingell	N	N	Y	N	N	Y	Y
MINNESOTA							
1 Penny	N	Y	N	N	Y	N	Y
2 Minge	Y	N	N	N	N	Y	Y
3 ***Ramstad***	Y	N	Y	Y	N	Y	N
4 Vento	N	Y	N	N	N	Y	Y

	195	196	197	198	199	200	201
5 Sabo	Y	Y	N	N	N	Y	Y
6 ***Grams***	Y	N	Y	Y	Y	Y	N
7 Peterson	Y	N	Y	N	Y	Y	Y
8 Oberstar	Y	Y	N	N	N	Y	Y
MISSISSIPPI							
1 Whitten	Y	?	?	?	N	Y	?
2 Thompson	Y	Y	N	N	N	Y	Y
3 Montgomery	Y	Y	N	N	N	Y	Y
4 Parker	Y	N	Y	N	N	Y	Y
5 Taylor	N	N	N	Y	N	Y	N
MISSOURI							
1 Clay	Y	Y	N	N	N	Y	Y
2 ***Talent***	Y	N	Y	Y	N	Y	N
3 Gephardt	Y	Y	N	N	N	Y	Y
4 Skelton	Y	Y	N	N	N	Y	Y
5 Wheat	Y	Y	N	N	N	Y	Y
6 Danner	Y	N	Y	N	N	Y	Y
7 ***Hancock***	Y	N	Y	Y	N	N	N
8 ***Emerson***	Y	N	Y	Y	N	Y	N
9 Volkmer	Y	N	N	Y	N	Y	Y
MONTANA							
AL Williams	Y	Y	N	N	N	Y	Y
NEBRASKA							
1 ***Bereuter***	Y	N	Y	Y	N	Y	N
2 Hoagland	Y	N	N	N	N	Y	Y
3 ***Barrett***	Y	N	Y	Y	N	Y	N
NEVADA							
1 Bilbray	Y	N	Y	Y	N	Y	Y
2 ***Vucanovich***	Y	N	Y	Y	N	Y	N
NEW HAMPSHIRE							
1 ***Zeliff***	Y	N	Y	Y	N	Y	N
2 Swett	Y	Y	Y	N	N	Y	Y
NEW JERSEY							
1 Andrews	Y	N	Y	Y	N	Y	Y
2 Hughes	Y	Y	N	N	N	Y	Y
3 ***Saxton***	Y	N	Y	Y	N	Y	N
4 ***Smith***	Y	N	Y	Y	N	Y	N
5 ***Roukema***	N	N	Y	N	N	Y	N
6 Pallone	N	Y	N	N	Y	Y	Y
7 ***Franks***	Y	N	Y	Y	N	Y	N
8 Klein	N	Y	Y	N	N	Y	Y
9 Torricelli	Y	N	Y	Y	N	Y	Y
10 Payne	N	Y	N	N	N	Y	Y
11 ***Gallo***	Y	N	Y	Y	N	Y	N
12 ***Zimmer***	N	N	Y	Y	N	Y	N
13 Menendez	Y	Y	N	N	N	Y	Y
NEW MEXICO							
1 ***Schiff***	Y	N	Y	Y	N	Y	N
2 ***Skeen***	Y	N	Y	Y	N	Y	N
3 Richardson	Y	Y	N	N	N	Y	Y
NEW YORK							
1 Hochbrueckner	Y	Y	N	N	N	Y	Y
2 ***Lazio***	Y	N	Y	Y	N	Y	N
3 ***King***	Y	N	Y	Y	N	Y	N
4 ***Levy***	Y	N	Y	Y	N	Y	N
5 Ackerman	Y	Y	N	N	N	Y	Y
6 Flake	Y	Y	N	N	N	Y	Y
7 Manton	Y	Y	Y	N	N	Y	Y
8 Nadler	N	Y	N	N	N	Y	Y
9 Schumer	Y	Y	N	N	N	Y	Y
10 Towns	Y	Y	N	N	N	Y	Y
11 Owens	Y	Y	N	N	N	Y	Y
12 Velazquez	N	Y	N	N	N	Y	Y
13 ***Molinari***	Y	N	Y	Y	N	Y	N
14 Maloney	N	Y	N	Y	N	Y	Y
15 Rangel	Y	Y	N	N	N	Y	Y
16 Serrano	Y	Y	N	N	N	Y	Y
17 Engel	Y	Y	N	N	N	Y	Y
18 Lowey	Y	Y	N	N	N	Y	Y
19 ***Fish***	Y	?	?	?	N	Y	N
20 ***Gilman***	Y	N	Y	Y	N	Y	N
21 McNulty	Y	Y	Y	N	N	Y	Y
22 ***Solomon***	Y	N	Y	Y	Y	N	N
23 ***Boehlert***	Y	N	Y	Y	N	Y	N
24 ***McHugh***	Y	N	Y	Y	N	Y	N
25 ***Walsh***	Y	N	Y	Y	N	Y	N
26 Hinchey	Y	Y	N	N	N	Y	Y
27 ***Paxon***	Y	N	Y	Y	N	Y	N
28 Slaughter	N	Y	N	N	Y	Y	Y
29 LaFalce	N	Y	N	N	N	Y	Y
30 ***Quinn***	Y	N	Y	Y	N	Y	N
31 ***Houghton***	Y	N	Y	Y	N	Y	?
NORTH CAROLINA							
1 Clayton	Y	Y	N	N	N	Y	Y
2 Valentine	Y	N	Y	?	N	Y	N

	195	196	197	198	199	200	201
3 Lancaster	Y	Y	Y	N	N	Y	Y
4 Price	N	N	N	N	N	Y	Y
5 Neal	Y	Y	?	N	N	Y	Y
6 ***Coble***	Y	N	Y	Y	Y	Y	N
7 Rose	N	Y	N	N	N	Y	Y
8 Hefner	Y	Y	Y	N	N	Y	Y
9 ***McMillan***	N	N	Y	Y	?	?	N
10 ***Ballenger***	Y	N	Y	Y	N	Y	N
11 ***Taylor***	Y	N	Y	Y	Y	Y	N
12 Watt	N	Y	N	N	N	Y	Y
NORTH DAKOTA							
AL Pomeroy	Y	Y	N	N	N	Y	Y
OHIO							
1 Mann	N	Y	N	N	N	Y	Y
2 ***Portman***	N	N	Y	Y	N	Y	N
3 Hall	Y	Y	N	N	N	Y	Y
4 ***Oxley***	Y	N	Y	Y	N	Y	N
5 ***Gillmor***	N	N	Y	Y	N	Y	N
6 Strickland	N	Y	N	N	N	Y	Y
7 ***Hobson***	Y	N	Y	Y	N	Y	N
8 ***Boehner***	Y	N	Y	Y	N	N	N
9 Kaptur	Y	N	Y	N	N	Y	Y
10 ***Hoke***	Y	N	Y	Y	N	?	N
11 Stokes	N	Y	N	N	N	Y	Y
12 ***Kasich***	N	N	Y	Y	N	Y	N
13 Brown	N	Y	N	N	N	Y	Y
14 Sawyer	Y	Y	N	N	N	Y	Y
15 ***Pryce***	N	N	Y	Y	N	Y	N
16 ***Regula***	N	N	Y	Y	N	Y	N
17 Traficant	Y	N	N	Y	N	Y	Y
18 Applegate	N	N	N	Y	N	Y	Y
19 Fingerhut	N	Y	N	N	N	Y	Y
OKLAHOMA							
1 ***Inhofe***	Y	N	Y	Y	N	Y	N
2 Synar	N	Y	N	N	N	Y	Y
3 Brewster	Y	N	Y	N	Y	Y	Y
4 McCurdy	Y	N	Y	N	N	Y	?
5 ***Istook***	Y	N	Y	Y	N	Y	N
6 ***Lucas***	Y	N	Y	Y	N	Y	N
OREGON							
1 Furse	N	Y	N	N	N	Y	Y
2 ***Smith***	Y	N	Y	Y	N	Y	N
3 Wyden	N	Y	N	N	N	Y	Y
4 DeFazio	N	Y	N	Y	N	Y	Y
5 Kopetski	Y	Y	N	N	N	Y	Y
PENNSYLVANIA							
1 Foglietta	N	Y	N	N	N	Y	Y
2 Blackwell	Y	Y	N	N	?	?	?
3 Borski	Y	Y	N	N	N	Y	Y
4 Klink	Y	N	N	N	N	Y	Y
5 ***Clinger***	Y	N	Y	Y	N	Y	N
6 Holden	Y	N	Y	N	N	Y	Y
7 ***Weldon***	Y	N	Y	Y	Y	Y	N
8 ***Greenwood***	Y	N	Y	Y	N	Y	N
9 ***Shuster***	Y	N	Y	Y	N	Y	N
10 ***McDade***	Y	N	Y	Y	N	Y	N
11 Kanjorski	Y	N	N	N	Y	Y	Y
12 Murtha	Y	N	N	N	N	Y	Y
13 Margolies-Mezv.	N	Y	N	N	Y	Y	Y
14 Coyne	N	Y	N	N	N	Y	Y
15 McHale	Y	Y	Y	Y	N	Y	Y
16 ***Walker***	N	N	Y	Y	Y	Y	N
17 ***Gekas***	N	N	Y	Y	N	Y	N
18 ***Santorum***	Y	?	?	?	N	Y	N
19 ***Goodling***	N	N	Y	Y	N	Y	N
20 Murphy	Y	Y	Y	N	Y	Y	Y
21 ***Ridge***	N	N	Y	Y	N	Y	N
RHODE ISLAND							
1 ***Machtley***	Y	N	Y	Y	N	Y	?
2 Reed	Y	N	N	N	N	Y	Y
SOUTH CAROLINA							
1 ***Ravenel***	Y	N	Y	Y	N	Y	N
2 ***Spence***	Y	N	Y	Y	N	Y	N
3 Derrick	Y	Y	N	N	N	Y	Y
4 ***Inglis***	Y	N	Y	Y	Y	N	N
5 Spratt	Y	Y	N	N	N	Y	Y
6 Clyburn	Y	Y	N	N	N	Y	Y
SOUTH DAKOTA							
AL Johnson	Y	Y	Y	N	N	Y	Y
TENNESSEE							
1 ***Quillen***	Y	N	Y	Y	Y	Y	N
2 ***Duncan***	Y	N	Y	Y	Y	Y	N
3 Lloyd	Y	N	Y	?	Y	Y	N
4 Cooper	Y	N	Y	Y	Y	Y	Y
5 Clement	Y	Y	N	N	Y	Y	Y

	195	196	197	198	199	200	201
6 Gordon	Y	N	N	N	Y	Y	Y
7 ***Sundquist***	Y	N	Y	Y	Y	Y	N
8 Tanner	Y	N	Y	N	Y	Y	Y
9 Ford	Y	Y	N	?	N	Y	Y
TEXAS							
1 Chapman	Y	N	N	Y	N	Y	?
2 Wilson	Y	N	N	N	N	Y	Y
3 ***Johnson, Sam***	Y	N	Y	Y	N	Y	N
4 Hall	Y	N	N	Y	N	Y	Y
5 Bryant	Y	N	N	N	N	Y	Y
6 ***Barton***	Y	N	Y	Y	Y	Y	N
7 ***Archer***	Y	N	Y	Y	Y	Y	N
8 ***Fields***	Y	N	Y	Y	N	Y	N
9 Brooks	Y	Y	N	N	N	Y	Y
10 Pickle	Y	Y	N	?	N	Y	Y
11 Edwards	Y	Y	N	N	Y	Y	Y
12 Geren	Y	N	N	N	N	Y	Y
13 Sarpalius	Y	N	Y	N	N	Y	?
14 Laughlin	Y	Y	Y	N	N	Y	Y
15 de la Garza	Y	N	N	N	N	Y	Y
16 Coleman	Y	Y	N	N	N	Y	Y
17 Stenholm	Y	N	N	Y	Y	Y	Y
18 Washington	?	?	?	?	?	?	?
19 ***Combest***	Y	N	Y	Y	Y	Y	N
20 Gonzalez	Y	Y	N	N	N	Y	Y
21 ***Smith***	Y	N	Y	Y	Y	Y	N
22 ***DeLay***	Y	N	?	Y	N	Y	N
23 ***Bonilla***	Y	N	Y	Y	Y	Y	N
24 Frost	Y	Y	Y	N	N	Y	Y
25 Andrews	Y	Y	N	N	N	Y	Y
26 ***Armey***	Y	N	Y	Y	Y	N	N
27 Ortiz	+	+	–	–	–	+	+
28 Tejeda	Y	Y	N	N	N	Y	Y
29 Green	Y	Y	N	Y	N	Y	Y
30 Johnson, E.B.	Y	Y	N	N	N	Y	Y
UTAH							
1 ***Hansen***	Y	N	Y	Y	N	Y	N
2 Shepherd	N	Y	N	N	N	Y	Y
3 Orton	Y	N	Y	Y	N	Y	Y
VERMONT							
AL *Sanders*	N	Y	N	N	N	Y	Y
VIRGINIA							
1 ***Bateman***	Y	N	Y	Y	N	Y	N
2 Pickett	Y	N	Y	N	N	Y	Y
3 Scott	Y	Y	N	N	N	Y	Y
4 Sisisky	Y	Y	N	N	N	Y	Y
5 Payne	Y	Y	N	N	N	Y	Y
6 ***Goodlatte***	Y	N	Y	Y	N	Y	N
7 ***Bliley***	Y	N	Y	Y	Y	Y	N
8 Moran	Y	Y	N	N	N	Y	Y
9 Boucher	Y	N	Y	?	N	Y	Y
10 ***Wolf***	Y	N	Y	?	N	Y	N
11 Byrne	Y	N	Y	N	N	Y	Y
WASHINGTON							
1 Cantwell	N	Y	N	N	N	Y	Y
2 Swift	N	Y	N	N	N	Y	Y
3 Unsoeld	N	Y	N	N	N	Y	Y
4 Inslee	N	Y	N	N	Y	Y	Y
5 Foley							
6 Dicks	Y	N	N	N	N	Y	Y
7 McDermott	N	Y	N	N	N	Y	Y
8 ***Dunn***	Y	N	Y	Y	N	Y	N
9 Kreidler	N	Y	N	N	Y	Y	Y
WEST VIRGINIA							
1 Mollohan	Y	N	N	N	N	Y	Y
2 Wise	Y	Y	N	N	N	Y	Y
3 Rahall	Y	Y	N	N	N	Y	Y
WISCONSIN							
1 Barca	N	Y	N	N	N	Y	Y
2 ***Klug***	N	N	Y	Y	N	Y	N
3 ***Gunderson***	Y	N	Y	Y	N	Y	N
4 Kleczka	Y	Y	N	N	N	Y	Y
5 Barrett	?	?	?	?	N	Y	Y
6 ***Petri***	Y	N	Y	Y	N	Y	N
7 Obey	Y	N	N	N	N	Y	Y
8 ***Roth***	N	N	Y	Y	N	Y	N
9 ***Sensenbrenner***	N	N	Y	Y	N	N	N
WYOMING							
AL ***Thomas***	Y	N	Y	Y	Y	Y	N
DELEGATES							
de Lugo, V.I.	Y	Y	N	?	N	D	D
Faleomavaega, Am.S.	?	?	?	?	?	D	D
Norton, D.C.	N	Y	N	N	N	D	D
Romero-B., P.R.	?	Y	N	N	N	D	D
Underwood, Guam	Y	Y	N	?	?	D	D

Southern states - Ala., Ark., Fla., Ga., Ky., La., Miss., N.C., Okla., S.C., Tenn., Texas, Va.
Omitted votes are quorum calls, which CQ does not include in its vote charts.

KEY

Y   Voted for (yea).
Paired for.
+   Announced for.
N   Voted against (nay).
X   Paired against.
—   Announced against.
P   Voted "present."
C   Voted "present" to avoid possible conflict of interest.
?   Did not vote or otherwise make a position known.
D   Delegates ineligible to vote.

Democrats   *Republicans*
Independent

202. HR 4426. Fiscal 1995 Foreign Operations Appropriations/Previous Question. Hall, D-Texas, motion to order the previous question (thus ending debate and the possibility of amendment) on adoption of the rule (H Res 443) to provide for House floor consideration of the bill to provide $13,635,449,750 in new budget authority for foreign operations, export financing and related programs in fiscal 1995. Motion agreed to 233-191: R 0-175; D 232-16 (ND 162-7, SD 70-9); I 1-0, May 25, 1994.

203. HR 4426. Fiscal 1995 Foreign Operations Appropriations/Rule. Adoption of the rule (H Res 443) to provide for House floor consideration of the bill to provide $13,635,449,750 in new budget authority for foreign operation, export financing and related programs in fiscal 1995. Adopted 244-181: R 1-173; D 242-8 (ND 166-3, SD 76-5); I 1-0, May 25, 1994.

204. HR 4426. Fiscal 1995 Foreign Operations Appropriations/Committee Substitute. Committee amendment in the nature of a substitute to reduce the administration's request by $389 million. Adopted in the Committee of the Whole 426-1: R 174-0; D 251-1 (ND 169-1, SD 82-0); I 1-0, May 25, 1994.

205. HR 4426. Fiscal 1995 Foreign Operations Appropriations/Russian Aid. Callahan, R-Ala., amendment to cut the amount of money provided in the bill for aid to the former Soviet republics from $900 million to $552 million and limit aid to Russia to humanitarian assistance programs only. Rejected in the Committee of the Whole 144-286: R 111-63; D 32-223 (ND 17-156, SD 15-67); I 1-0, May 25, 1994.

206. HR 4426. Fiscal 1995 Foreign Operations Appropriations/South African Aid. Burton, R-Ind., amendment to limit money for the South African Assistance Program to the fiscal 1994 level. Rejected in the Committee of the Whole 103-321: R 99-73; D 4-247 (ND 4-169, SD 0-78); I 0-1, May 25, 1994.

207. HR 4426. Fiscal 1995 Foreign Operations Appropriations/Population Development. Beilenson, D-Calif., amendment to provide an additional $100 million for population development assistance offset by an across the board cut of three-fourths of 1 percent. Rejected in the Committee of the Whole 54-371: R 7-166; D 46-205 (ND 34-136, SD 12-69); I 1-0, May 25, 1994.

208. HR 4426. Fiscal 1995 Foreign Operations Appropriations/Passage. Passage of the bill to provide $13.6 billion in new budget authority for foreign operations, export financing and related programs in fiscal 1995. The administration requested $14,024,957,094. Passed 337-87: R 112-61; D 225-25 (ND 156-13, SD 69-12); I 0-1, May 25, 1994.

	202	203	204	205	206	207	208
ALABAMA							
1 *Callahan*	N	N	Y	Y	Y	N	N
2 *Everett*	N	N	Y	Y	Y	N	N
3 Browder	Y	Y	Y	N	N	N	Y
4 Bevill	Y	Y	Y	N	N	N	Y
5 Cramer	Y	Y	Y	N	N	N	Y
6 *Bachus*	N	N	Y	Y	N	N	Y
7 Hilliard	Y	Y	Y	N	N	N	Y
ALASKA							
AL *Young*	N	N	Y	?	Y	N	Y
ARIZONA							
1 Coppersmith	Y	Y	Y	N	N	N	Y
2 Pastor	Y	Y	Y	N	Y	Y	Y
3 *Stump*	N	N	Y	Y	Y	N	N
4 *Kyl*	N	N	Y	Y	Y	N	Y
5 *Kolbe*	N	N	Y	N	N	N	Y
6 English	Y	Y	Y	N	Y	Y	Y
ARKANSAS							
1 Lambert	Y	Y	Y	N	N	Y	Y
2 Thornton	Y	Y	Y	N	N	N	Y
3 *Hutchinson*	N	N	Y	Y	N	N	N
4 *Dickey*	N	N	Y	Y	N	N	Y
CALIFORNIA							
1 Hamburg	Y	Y	Y	N	N	Y	Y
2 *Herger*	N	N	Y	Y	Y	N	N
3 Fazio	Y	Y	Y	N	N	?	Y
4 *Doolittle*	N	N	Y	Y	Y	N	N
5 Matsui	Y	Y	Y	N	N	N	Y
6 Woolsey	Y	Y	Y	N	N	N	Y
7 Miller	Y	Y	Y	N	N	N	Y
8 Pelosi	Y	Y	Y	N	N	N	Y
9 Dellums	Y	Y	Y	N	N	N	Y
10 *Baker*	N	N	Y	Y	Y	N	N
11 *Pombo*	N	N	Y	Y	Y	N	N
12 Lantos	Y	Y	Y	N	N	N	Y
13 Stark	Y	Y	Y	N	N	Y	N
14 Eshoo	Y	Y	Y	N	Y	Y	Y
15 Mineta	Y	Y	Y	N	N	N	Y
16 Edwards	Y	Y	Y	N	N	Y	Y
17 Farr	Y	Y	Y	N	Y	Y	Y
18 Condit	Y	Y	Y	Y	Y	N	N
19 Lehman	Y	Y	Y	N	N	N	Y
20 Dooley	Y	Y	Y	N	?	N	Y
21 *Thomas*	N	N	Y	N	N	N	Y
22 *Huffington*	N	N	Y	Y	N	N	Y
23 *Gallegly*	N	N	Y	Y	N	N	N
24 Beilenson	Y	Y	Y	N	N	Y	Y
25 *McKeon*	N	N	Y	Y	Y	N	N
26 Berman	Y	Y	Y	N	N	N	Y
27 *Moorhead*	N	N	Y	Y	Y	N	N
28 *Dreier*	N	N	Y	N	N	N	N
29 Waxman	Y	Y	?	N	N	N	Y
30 Becerra	Y	Y	Y	N	N	N	Y
31 Martinez	Y	Y	Y	N	N	N	Y
32 Dixon	Y	Y	Y	N	N	N	Y
33 Roybal-Allard	Y	Y	Y	N	N	N	Y
34 Torres	Y	Y	Y	N	N	N	Y
35 Waters	Y	Y	Y	N	N	Y	Y
36 Harman	Y	Y	Y	N	N	N	Y
37 Tucker	?	Y	Y	?	N	N	Y
38 *Horn*	?	?	?	?	?	?	?
39 *Royce*	N	N	Y	Y	N	N	Y
40 *Lewis*	N	N	Y	N	N	N	Y
41 *Kim*	N	N	Y	Y	Y	N	Y

	202	203	204	205	206	207	208
42 Brown	Y	Y	Y	N	N	N	Y
43 *Calvert*	N	N	Y	N	N	N	Y
44 *McCandless*	N	N	Y	Y	Y	N	N
45 *Rohrabacher*	N	N	Y	Y	Y	N	N
46 *Dornan*	N	N	Y	N	N	N	Y
47 *Cox*	N	N	Y	Y	Y	N	Y
48 *Packard*	N	N	Y	Y	Y	N	N
49 Schenk	Y	Y	Y	N	N	N	Y
50 Filner	Y	Y	Y	N	N	Y	Y
51 *Cunningham*	N	N	Y	Y	Y	N	N
52 *Hunter*	N	N	Y	Y	Y	N	Y
COLORADO							
1 Schroeder	Y	Y	Y	N	N	N	Y
2 Skaggs	Y	Y	Y	N	N	N	Y
3 *McInnis*	N	N	Y	Y	Y	N	Y
4 *Allard*	N	N	Y	Y	Y	Y	Y
5 *Hefley*	N	N	Y	Y	N	N	N
6 *Schaefer*	N	N	Y	Y	Y	N	N
CONNECTICUT							
1 Kennelly	Y	Y	Y	N	N	N	Y
2 Gejdenson	Y	Y	Y	N	N	N	Y
3 DeLauro	Y	Y	Y	N	N	N	Y
4 *Shays*	N	N	Y	N	N	N	Y
5 *Franks*	N	N	Y	Y	N	N	Y
6 *Johnson*	N	N	Y	N	N	N	Y
DELAWARE							
AL *Castle*	N	N	Y	N	N	N	Y
FLORIDA							
1 *Hutto*	N	N	Y	Y	N	N	Y
2 Peterson	Y	Y	Y	N	N	N	Y
3 Brown	Y	Y	Y	N	N	N	Y
4 *Fowler*	N	N	Y	Y	Y	N	Y
5 Thurman	Y	Y	Y	N	N	N	Y
6 *Stearns*	N	N	Y	Y	Y	N	N
7 *Mica*	N	N	Y	Y	Y	N	N
8 *McCollum*	N	N	Y	Y	N	N	Y
9 *Bilirakis*	N	N	Y	Y	N	N	Y
10 *Young*	N	N	Y	Y	Y	N	N
11 Gibbons	Y	Y	Y	N	N	N	Y
12 *Canady*	N	N	Y	Y	N	N	Y
13 *Miller*	N	N	Y	Y	Y	N	Y
14 *Goss*	N	N	Y	N	N	N	Y
15 Bacchus	Y	Y	Y	N	N	N	Y
16 *Lewis*	N	N	Y	Y	Y	N	N
17 Meek	Y	Y	Y	N	N	N	Y
18 *Ros-Lehtinen*	N	N	Y	N	N	N	Y
19 Johnston	Y	Y	Y	N	N	N	Y
20 Deutsch	Y	Y	Y	N	N	N	Y
21 *Diaz-Balart*	N	N	Y	N	N	N	Y
22 *Shaw*	N	N	Y	N	Y	N	Y
23 Hastings	Y	Y	Y	N	N	N	Y
GEORGIA							
1 *Kingston*	N	N	Y	Y	Y	N	Y
2 Bishop	Y	Y	Y	N	N	N	Y
3 *Collins*	N	N	Y	Y	Y	N	Y
4 *Linder*	N	N	Y	Y	Y	N	Y
5 Lewis	Y	Y	Y	N	N	N	Y
6 *Gingrich*	N	N	Y	N	N	N	Y
7 Darden	Y	Y	Y	N	N	N	Y
8 Rowland	N	?	Y	N	Y	N	Y
9 Deal	Y	N	Y	N	N	N	Y
10 Johnson	Y	Y	Y	N	N	N	Y
11 McKinney	Y	Y	Y	N	N	Y	Y
HAWAII							
1 Abercrombie	Y	Y	?	N	N	Y	Y
2 Mink	Y	Y	Y	N	N	Y	Y
IDAHO							
1 LaRocco	Y	Y	Y	N	N	N	Y
2 *Crapo*	N	N	Y	Y	Y	N	N
ILLINOIS							
1 Rush	Y	Y	Y	N	N	N	Y
2 Reynolds	Y	Y	Y	N	N	N	Y
3 Lipinski	Y	Y	Y	N	N	N	Y
4 Gutierrez	Y	Y	Y	N	N	N	Y
5 Rostenkowski	Y	Y	Y	N	N	N	Y
6 *Hyde*	N	N	Y	N	N	N	Y
7 Collins	Y	Y	Y	N	N	N	Y
8 *Crane*	N	N	Y	Y	Y	N	N
9 Yates	Y	Y	Y	N	N	N	Y
10 *Porter*	N	N	Y	N	N	N	Y
11 Sangmeister	Y	Y	Y	N	N	N	Y
12 Costello	Y	Y	Y	N	N	N	Y
13 *Fawell*	N	N	Y	N	N	N	Y
14 *Hastert*	N	N	Y	Y	Y	N	Y
15 *Ewing*	N	N	Y	Y	Y	N	Y
16 *Manzullo*	N	N	Y	Y	N	N	Y
17 Evans	Y	Y	Y	N	N	N	Y

ND   Northern Democrats   SD   Southern Democrats

	202	203	204	205	206	207	208
18 ***Michel***	N	N	Y	N	N	N	Y
19 Poshard	Y	Y	Y	Y	N	N	Y
20 Durbin	Y	Y	Y	N	N	N	Y
INDIANA							
1 Visclosky	Y	Y	Y	N	N	N	Y
2 Sharp	Y	Y	Y	N	N	Y	Y
3 Roemer	Y	Y	Y	N	N	N	N
4 Long	Y	Y	Y	N	N	N	Y
5 ***Buyer***	N	N	Y	Y	Y	N	N
6 ***Burton***	N	N	Y	Y	Y	N	Y
7 ***Myers***	N	N	Y	Y	Y	N	N
8 McCloskey	Y	Y	Y	N	N	N	Y
9 Hamilton	Y	Y	Y	N	N	N	Y
10 Jacobs	N	N	Y	Y	N	Y	N
IOWA							
1 ***Leach***	N	N	Y	N	N	Y	Y
2 ***Nussle***	N	N	Y	Y	Y	N	N
3 ***Lightfoot***	N	N	Y	N	N	N	Y
4 Smith	Y	Y	Y	N	N	N	Y
5 ***Grandy***	?	?	?	?	?	?	?
KANSAS							
1 ***Roberts***	N	N	Y	N	Y	N	N
2 Slattery	N	Y	Y	N	N	N	Y
3 ***Meyers***	N	N	Y	N	N	Y	Y
4 Glickman	Y	Y	Y	N	N	N	Y
KENTUCKY							
1 Barlow	Y	Y	Y	N	N	N	Y
2 Vacancy							
3 Mazzoli	Y	Y	Y	N	N	N	Y
4 ***Bunning***	N	N	Y	Y	Y	N	N
5 ***Rogers***	N	N	Y	Y	Y	N	N
6 Baesler	Y	Y	Y	N	N	N	Y
LOUISIANA							
1 ***Livingston***	N	N	Y	N	N	N	Y
2 Jefferson	Y	Y	Y	N	N	N	Y
3 Tauzin	N	Y	Y	Y	N	N	N
4 Fields	Y	Y	Y	N	N	N	Y
5 ***McCrery***	N	Y	Y	N	N	N	Y
6 ***Baker***	N	N	Y	Y	N	N	Y
7 Hayes	N	Y	Y	Y	N	N	N
MAINE							
1 Andrews	Y	Y	Y	N	N	N	Y
2 ***Snowe***	N	N	Y	Y	N	N	Y
MARYLAND							
1 ***Gilchrest***	N	N	Y	N	N	Y	Y
2 ***Bentley***	N	N	Y	N	N	N	Y
3 Cardin	Y	Y	Y	N	N	N	Y
4 Wynn	Y	Y	Y	N	N	N	Y
5 Hoyer	Y	Y	Y	N	N	N	Y
6 ***Bartlett***	N	N	Y	N	Y	N	Y
7 Mfume	Y	Y	Y	N	N	N	Y
8 ***Morella***	N	N	Y	N	N	Y	Y
MASSACHUSETTS							
1 Olver	Y	Y	Y	N	N	N	Y
2 Neal	Y	Y	Y	N	N	N	Y
3 ***Blute***	N	N	Y	Y	Y	N	Y
4 Frank	Y	Y	Y	N	N	N	Y
5 Meehan	Y	Y	Y	N	N	N	Y
6 ***Torkildsen***	N	N	Y	N	N	N	Y
7 Markey	Y	Y	Y	N	N	N	Y
8 Kennedy	Y	Y	Y	N	N	N	Y
9 Moakley	Y	Y	Y	N	N	N	Y
10 Studds	Y	Y	Y	N	N	Y	Y
MICHIGAN							
1 Stupak	Y	Y	Y	N	N	N	Y
2 ***Hoekstra***	N	N	Y	Y	Y	N	Y
3 ***Ehlers***	N	N	Y	N	N	N	Y
4 ***Camp***	N	N	Y	Y	N	N	Y
5 Barcia	Y	?	Y	Y	N	N	Y
6 ***Upton***	N	N	Y	N	N	N	Y
7 ***Smith***	N	N	Y	N	Y	N	N
8 Carr	Y	Y	Y	N	N	N	Y
9 Kildee	Y	Y	Y	N	N	N	Y
10 Bonior	Y	Y	Y	N	N	Y	Y
11 ***Knollenberg***	N	N	Y	N	N	N	Y
12 Levin	Y	Y	Y	N	N	N	Y
13 Ford	Y	Y	Y	N	?	?	?
14 Conyers	N	Y	Y	N	N	N	Y
15 Collins	Y	Y	Y	N	N	N	Y
16 Dingell	Y	Y	Y	N	N	?	Y
MINNESOTA							
1 Penny	Y	Y	Y	N	N	N	Y
2 Minge	Y	Y	Y	N	N	Y	N
3 ***Ramstad***	N	N	Y	Y	Y	N	Y
4 Vento	Y	Y	Y	N	N	N	Y

	202	203	204	205	206	207	208
5 Sabo	Y	Y	Y	N	N	N	Y
6 ***Grams***	N	N	Y	Y	Y	N	Y
7 Peterson	Y	Y	Y	Y	Y	N	Y
8 Oberstar	Y	Y	Y	N	N	N	Y
MISSISSIPPI							
1 Whitten	Y	Y	Y	N	?	?	?
2 Thompson	Y	Y	Y	N	N	N	Y
3 Montgomery	Y	Y	Y	N	N	N	N
4 Parker	Y	Y	Y	N	N	N	Y
5 Taylor	Y	N	Y	Y	N	N	N
MISSOURI							
1 Clay	Y	Y	Y	N	N	N	Y
2 ***Talent***	N	N	Y	N	Y	N	Y
3 Gephardt	Y	Y	Y	N	N	N	Y
4 Skelton	Y	Y	Y	N	N	N	Y
5 Wheat	Y	Y	Y	N	N	N	Y
6 Danner	Y	Y	Y	Y	Y	N	Y
7 ***Hancock***	N	N	Y	Y	Y	N	N
8 ***Emerson***	N	N	Y	N	N	N	N
9 Volkmer	Y	Y	Y	N	N	N	N
MONTANA							
AL Williams	Y	?	Y	N	N	N	Y
NEBRASKA							
1 ***Bereuter***	N	N	Y	N	N	N	Y
2 Hoagland	Y	Y	Y	N	N	Y	Y
3 ***Barrett***	N	N	Y	Y	Y	N	N
NEVADA							
1 Bilbray	Y	Y	Y	N	N	N	Y
2 ***Vucanovich***	N	N	Y	Y	N	N	Y
NEW HAMPSHIRE							
1 ***Zeliff***	N	N	Y	N	Y	N	Y
2 Swett	Y	Y	Y	N	N	N	Y
NEW JERSEY							
1 Andrews	N	N	Y	Y	Y	N	Y
2 Hughes	N	Y	Y	N	N	N	Y
3 ***Saxton***	N	N	Y	N	N	N	Y
4 ***Smith***	N	N	Y	N	N	N	Y
5 ***Roukema***	N	N	Y	Y	N	N	Y
6 Pallone	Y	Y	Y	N	N	N	Y
7 ***Franks***	N	N	Y	N	N	N	Y
8 Klein	Y	Y	Y	N	N	N	Y
9 Torricelli	Y	Y	Y	?	N	N	Y
10 Payne	Y	Y	Y	N	N	N	Y
11 ***Gallo***	N	N	Y	N	N	N	Y
12 ***Zimmer***	N	N	Y	Y	Y	N	Y
13 Menendez	Y	Y	Y	N	N	N	Y
NEW MEXICO							
1 ***Schiff***	N	N	Y	N	N	N	Y
2 ***Skeen***	N	N	Y	N	N	N	Y
3 Richardson	Y	Y	Y	N	N	N	Y
NEW YORK							
1 Hochbrueckner	N	Y	Y	N	N	N	Y
2 ***Lazio***	N	N	Y	N	N	N	Y
3 ***King***	N	N	Y	N	N	N	Y
4 ***Levy***	N	N	Y	N	N	N	Y
5 Ackerman	Y	Y	Y	N	N	N	Y
6 Flake	Y	Y	Y	N	N	N	Y
7 Manton	Y	Y	Y	N	N	N	Y
8 Nadler	Y	Y	Y	N	N	N	Y
9 Schumer	Y	Y	Y	N	N	N	Y
10 Towns	Y	Y	Y	N	N	N	Y
11 Owens	Y	Y	Y	N	N	N	Y
12 Velazquez	Y	Y	Y	N	N	Y	Y
13 ***Molinari***	N	N	Y	Y	N	N	Y
14 Maloney	Y	Y	Y	N	N	N	Y
15 Rangel	N	Y	Y	N	N	N	Y
16 Serrano	Y	Y	Y	N	N	N	Y
17 Engel	Y	Y	Y	N	N	N	Y
18 Lowey	Y	Y	Y	N	N	N	Y
19 ***Fish***	N	N	Y	N	N	?	?
20 ***Gilman***	N	N	Y	N	N	N	Y
21 McNulty	Y	Y	Y	N	N	N	Y
22 ***Solomon***	N	N	Y	Y	Y	N	N
23 ***Boehlert***	N	N	Y	N	N	Y	Y
24 ***McHugh***	N	N	Y	Y	Y	N	Y
25 ***Walsh***	N	N	Y	N	N	N	Y
26 Hinchey	Y	Y	Y	N	N	N	Y
27 ***Paxon***	N	N	Y	Y	Y	N	Y
28 Slaughter	Y	Y	+	N	N	Y	Y
29 LaFalce	Y	Y	Y	N	N	N	Y
30 ***Quinn***	N	N	Y	Y	N	N	Y
31 ***Houghton***	N	N	Y	N	N	N	Y
NORTH CAROLINA							
1 Clayton	Y	Y	Y	N	N	N	Y
2 Valentine	N	Y	Y	Y	N	Y	N

	202	203	204	205	206	207	208
3 Lancaster	Y	Y	Y	N	N	N	Y
4 Price	Y	Y	Y	N	N	Y	Y
5 Neal	Y	Y	Y	N	N	Y	N
6 ***Coble***	N	N	Y	Y	Y	N	Y
7 Rose	Y	Y	Y	N	N	N	Y
8 Hefner	Y	Y	Y	Y	N	N	N
9 ***McMillan***	N	N	Y	N	Y	N	Y
10 ***Ballenger***	N	N	Y	Y	Y	N	Y
11 ***Taylor***	N	N	Y	Y	Y	N	Y
12 Watt	Y	Y	Y	N	N	N	Y
NORTH DAKOTA							
AL Pomeroy	Y	Y	Y	N	N	N	Y
OHIO							
1 Mann	Y	Y	Y	N	N	N	Y
2 ***Portman***	N	N	Y	Y	N	N	Y
3 Hall	Y	Y	Y	N	N	N	Y
4 ***Oxley***	N	?	Y	N	N	N	N
5 ***Gillmor***	N	N	Y	Y	N	N	Y
6 Strickland	Y	Y	Y	N	N	Y	Y
7 ***Hobson***	N	N	Y	Y	N	N	Y
8 ***Boehner***	N	N	Y	N	Y	N	Y
9 Kaptur	Y	Y	Y	Y	N	N	N
10 ***Hoke***	N	N	Y	Y	Y	N	Y
11 Stokes	Y	Y	Y	N	N	N	Y
12 ***Kasich***	N	N	Y	Y	N	N	Y
13 Brown	Y	Y	Y	N	N	Y	Y
14 Sawyer	Y	Y	Y	N	N	Y	Y
15 ***Pryce***	N	N	Y	Y	N	N	Y
16 ***Regula***	N	N	Y	Y	N	N	Y
17 Traficant	Y	Y	N	Y	N	N	N
18 Applegate	Y	Y	Y	Y	N	N	N
19 Fingerhut	Y	Y	Y	N	N	N	Y
OKLAHOMA							
1 ***Inhofe***	N	N	Y	Y	Y	N	Y
2 Synar	Y	Y	Y	N	N	Y	Y
3 Brewster	Y	Y	Y	Y	N	N	Y
4 McCurdy	Y	Y	Y	N	—	N	Y
5 ***Istook***	N	N	Y	N	Y	N	Y
6 ***Lucas***	N	N	Y	Y	N	N	Y
OREGON							
1 Furse	Y	Y	Y	N	N	N	Y
2 ***Smith***	N	N	Y	Y	Y	N	N
3 Wyden	Y	Y	Y	N	N	N	Y
4 DeFazio	Y	Y	Y	Y	N	Y	N
5 Kopetski	Y	Y	Y	N	N	Y	Y
PENNSYLVANIA							
1 Foglietta	Y	Y	Y	N	N	N	Y
2 Blackwell	?	?	?	?	?	?	?
3 Borski	Y	Y	Y	N	N	N	Y
4 Klink	Y	Y	Y	Y	N	N	Y
5 ***Clinger***	N	N	Y	N	N	N	Y
6 Holden	Y	Y	Y	N	N	N	Y
7 ***Weldon***	N	N	Y	N	Y	N	N
8 ***Greenwood***	N	N	Y	N	N	N	Y
9 ***Shuster***	N	N	Y	Y	Y	N	N
10 ***McDade***	N	N	Y	N	?	?	?
11 Kanjorski	Y	Y	Y	N	N	N	Y
12 Murtha	Y	Y	Y	N	N	N	Y
13 Margolies-Mezv.	Y	Y	Y	N	N	N	Y
14 Coyne	Y	Y	Y	N	N	N	Y
15 McHale	Y	Y	Y	N	N	N	Y
16 ***Walker***	N	N	Y	Y	Y	N	N
17 ***Gekas***	N	N	Y	Y	N	N	N
18 ***Santorum***	N	N	Y	Y	N	N	Y
19 ***Goodling***	N	N	Y	Y	N	N	N
20 Murphy	Y	Y	Y	N	N	?	?
21 ***Ridge***	N	N	Y	N	N	N	Y
RHODE ISLAND							
1 ***Machtley***	N	N	Y	Y	Y	N	Y
2 Reed	Y	Y	Y	N	N	N	Y
SOUTH CAROLINA							
1 ***Ravenel***	N	N	Y	Y	N	N	Y
2 ***Spence***	N	N	Y	Y	?	N	N
3 Derrick	Y	Y	Y	N	N	Y	Y
4 ***Inglis***	N	N	Y	Y	Y	N	N
5 Spratt	Y	Y	Y	N	N	N	Y
6 Clyburn	Y	Y	Y	N	N	N	Y
SOUTH DAKOTA							
AL Johnson	Y	Y	Y	N	N	N	Y
TENNESSEE							
1 ***Quillen***	N	N	Y	Y	Y	N	N
2 ***Duncan***	N	N	Y	Y	Y	N	N
3 Lloyd	N	N	Y	N	N	Y	N
4 Cooper	Y	Y	Y	N	N	N	Y
5 Clement	Y	Y	Y	N	N	N	Y

	202	203	204	205	206	207	208
6 Gordon	Y	Y	Y	N	N	Y	Y
7 ***Sundquist***	N	N	Y	Y	N	N	Y
8 Tanner	Y	Y	Y	N	N	N	N
9 Ford	N	Y	Y	N	N	N	Y
TEXAS							
1 Chapman	Y	Y	Y	Y	N	N	Y
2 Wilson	Y	Y	Y	N	N	N	Y
3 ***Johnson, Sam***	N	N	?	Y	Y	N	N
4 Hall	N	N	Y	Y	?	N	N
5 Bryant	Y	Y	Y	N	N	Y	Y
6 ***Barton***	N	N	Y	Y	Y	N	N
7 ***Archer***	N	N	Y	Y	Y	N	N
8 ***Fields***	N	N	Y	Y	Y	N	N
9 Brooks	Y	Y	Y	N	N	N	N
10 Pickle	N	Y	Y	N	N	N	Y
11 Edwards	Y	Y	Y	N	N	N	Y
12 Geren	Y	Y	Y	Y	N	N	Y
13 Sarpalius	Y	Y	Y	Y	N	N	N
14 Laughlin	Y	Y	Y	Y	N	N	Y
15 de la Garza	?	Y	Y	N	N	N	Y
16 Coleman	Y	Y	Y	N	N	N	Y
17 Stenholm	Y	Y	Y	Y	N	N	Y
18 Washington	?	?	?	?	?	?	?
19 ***Combest***	N	N	Y	Y	Y	N	N
20 Gonzalez	Y	Y	Y	N	N	N	Y
21 ***Smith***	N	N	Y	Y	Y	N	N
22 ***DeLay***	N	N	Y	Y	Y	N	Y
23 ***Bonilla***	N	N	Y	Y	Y	N	N
24 Frost	Y	Y	Y	N	N	N	Y
25 Andrews	?	Y	Y	N	N	N	Y
26 ***Armey***	N	N	Y	Y	Y	N	N
27 Ortiz	+	Y	Y	N	N	N	Y
28 Tejeda	Y	Y	Y	N	N	N	Y
29 Green	Y	Y	Y	N	N	N	Y
30 Johnson, E.B.	Y	Y	Y	N	N	N	Y
UTAH							
1 ***Hansen***	N	N	Y	Y	Y	N	N
2 Shepherd	Y	Y	Y	N	N	N	Y
3 Orton	Y	Y	Y	N	N	N	N
VERMONT							
AL *Sanders*	Y	Y	Y	Y	N	Y	N
VIRGINIA							
1 ***Bateman***	N	N	Y	N	Y	N	Y
2 Pickett	Y	Y	Y	N	N	N	Y
3 Scott	Y	Y	Y	N	N	N	Y
4 Sisisky	Y	Y	Y	N	N	N	Y
5 Payne	Y	Y	Y	N	N	Y	Y
6 ***Goodlatte***	N	N	Y	Y	Y	N	Y
7 ***Bliley***	N	N	Y	N	N	N	Y
8 Moran	Y	Y	Y	N	?	Y	Y
9 Boucher	Y	Y	Y	N	N	N	Y
10 ***Wolf***	N	N	Y	N	Y	N	Y
11 Byrne	Y	Y	Y	N	N	N	Y
WASHINGTON							
1 Cantwell	Y	Y	Y	N	N	N	Y
2 Swift	Y	Y	Y	N	N	Y	Y
3 Unsoeld	Y	Y	Y	N	N	N	Y
4 Inslee	Y	Y	+	Y	N	Y	Y
5 Foley							
6 Dicks	Y	Y	Y	N	N	N	Y
7 McDermott	Y	Y	Y	N	N	Y	Y
8 ***Dunn***	N	N	Y	N	N	N	Y
9 Kreidler	Y	Y	Y	N	N	Y	Y
WEST VIRGINIA							
1 Mollohan	Y	Y	Y	N	N	N	Y
2 Wise	?	Y	Y	N	N	N	Y
3 Rahall	Y	N	Y	Y	N	N	N
WISCONSIN							
1 Barca	Y	Y	Y	N	N	N	Y
2 ***Klug***	N	N	Y	Y	N	N	Y
3 ***Gunderson***	N	N	Y	N	?	N	Y
4 Kleczka	Y	Y	Y	N	N	N	Y
5 Barrett	Y	Y	Y	N	N	N	Y
6 ***Petri***	N	N	Y	N	Y	N	N
7 Obey	Y	Y	Y	N	N	N	Y
8 ***Roth***	N	N	Y	Y	Y	N	N
9 ***Sensenbrenner***	N	N	Y	Y	Y	N	N
WYOMING							
AL ***Thomas***	N	N	Y	Y	Y	N	Y
DELEGATES							
de Lugo, V.I.	D	D	Y	N	N	N	D
Faleomavaega, Am.S.	D	D	?	?	?	?	D
Norton, D.C.	D	D	Y	N	N	N	D
Romero-B., P.R.	D	D	Y	N	N	N	D
Underwood, Guam	D	D	?	N	N	?	D

Southern states - Ala., Ark., Fla., Ga., Ky., La., Miss., N.C., Okla., S.C., Tenn., Texas, Va.
Omitted votes are quorum calls, which CQ does not include in its vote charts.

KEY

Y	Voted for (yea).
#	Paired for.
+	Announced for.
N	Voted against (nay).
X	Paired against.
−	Announced against.
P	Voted "present."
C	Voted "present" to avoid possible conflict of interest.
?	Did not vote or otherwise make a position known.
D	Delegates ineligible to vote.

Democrats *Republicans*
Independent

209. Procedural Motion. Approval of the House Journal of Wednesday, May 25. Approved 238-152: R 16-147; D 221-5 (ND 149-4, SD 72-1); I 1-0, May 26, 1994.

210. HR 4454. Fiscal 1995 Legislative Branch Appropriations/Rule. Adoption of the rule (H Res 444) to provide for House floor consideration of the bill to provide $1,880,670,600 in new budget authority for the legislative branch and related agencies in fiscal 1995, excluding the Senate. Adopted 249-177: R 0-174; D 248-3 (ND 169-2, SD 79-1); I 1-0, May 26, 1994.

211. HR 4454. Fiscal 1995 Legislative Branch Appropriations/Salary and Expense Cut. Thurman, D-Fla., amendment to cut the salaries and expenses for House officers and employees by $2,942,000. Adopted in the Committee of the Whole 383-46: R 175-0; D 207-46 (ND 136-37, SD 71-9); I 1-0, May 26, 1994.

212. HR 4454. Fiscal 1995 Legislative Branch Appropriations/House Franking Cut. Pomeroy, D-N.D., amendment to reduce the account House members use for official mailings by $4 million to $31 million. Adopted in the Committee of the Whole 375-48: R 170-2; D 204-46 (ND 134-38, SD 70-8); I 1-0, May 26, 1994.

213. HR 4454. Fiscal 1995 Legislative Branch Appropriations/General Accounting Office Cut. Bereuter, R-Neb., amendment to cut the amount provided for the General Accounting Office by $31 million to $408.7 million. Rejected in the Committee of the Whole 193-232: R 161-11; D 32-220 (ND 19-154, SD 13-66); I 0-1, May 26, 1994.

214. HR 4454. Fiscal 1995 Legislative Branch Appropriations/Fiscal 1994 Spending Level. Boehner, R-Ohio, amendment to reduce the total amount of new budget authority provided by the bill to the amount appropriated for fiscal 1994 by cutting $47 million from the General Accounting Office, $22 million from the Office of Technology Assessment, $9 million for maintenance and renovation of House office buildings, $7 million from congressional printing and $7 million from the Botanic Garden; by eliminating all money for joint committees; and by other smaller cuts. Rejected in the Committee of the Whole 187-238: R 156-18; D 31-219 (ND 21-151, SD 10-68); I 0-1, May 26, 1994.

215. HR 4454. Fiscal 1995 Legislative Branch Appropriations/Recommittal Motion. Young, R-Fla., motion to recommit the bill to the Appropriations Committee with instructions to report it back with an amendment cutting $13 million from the amount provided for House Information Systems. Motion rejected 177-241: R 172-0; D 5-240 (ND 4-162, SD 1-78); I 0-1, May 26, 1994.

216. HR 4454. Fiscal 1995 Legislative Branch Appropriations/Passage. Passage of the bill to provide $1,880,670,600 in new budget authority for the legislative branch and related agencies in fiscal 1995, excluding the Senate. The agencies covered by the bill requested $1,967,807,000. The Senate is expected to add more than $500 million for its expenses during consideration of the bill. Passed 210-205: R 2-170; D 207-35 (ND 141-23, SD 66-12); I 1-0, May 26, 1994.

[1] *Ron Lewis, R-Ky., was sworn in May 26, 1994. The first vote for which he was eligible was vote 210.*

	209	210	211	212	213	214	215	216
ALABAMA								
1 *Callahan*	N	N	Y	Y	Y	Y	Y	N
2 *Everett*	Y	N	Y	Y	Y	Y	Y	N
3 Browder	Y	Y	Y	Y	N	N	N	Y
4 Bevill	Y	Y	Y	Y	N	N	N	Y
5 Cramer	Y	Y	Y	Y	N	N	N	Y
6 *Bachus*	N	N	Y	?	Y	Y	?	N
7 Hilliard	Y	Y	Y	Y	N	N	N	Y
ALASKA								
AL *Young*	N	N	Y	Y	Y	Y	Y	N
ARIZONA								
1 Coppersmith	Y	N	Y	Y	Y	Y	N	Y
2 Pastor	Y	Y	Y	Y	N	Y	N	Y
3 *Stump*	N	N	Y	Y	Y	Y	Y	N
4 *Kyl*	N	N	Y	Y	Y	Y	Y	N
5 *Kolbe*	N	N	Y	Y	Y	Y	Y	N
6 English	Y	Y	Y	Y	N	Y	N	Y
ARKANSAS								
1 Lambert	Y	Y	Y	Y	N	N	N	Y
2 Thornton	Y	Y	Y	Y	N	N	N	Y
3 *Hutchinson*	N	N	Y	Y	Y	Y	Y	N
4 Dickey	N	N	Y	Y	Y	Y	Y	N
CALIFORNIA								
1 Hamburg	Y	Y	Y	Y	N	N	N	Y
2 *Herger*	?	N	Y	Y	Y	Y	Y	N
3 Fazio	Y	Y	Y	Y	N	N	N	Y
4 *Doolittle*	N	N	Y	Y	Y	Y	Y	N
5 Matsui	Y	Y	Y	Y	N	N	N	Y
6 Woolsey	?	Y	Y	Y	N	N	N	Y
7 Miller	?	Y	Y	Y	?	N	N	Y
8 Pelosi	Y	Y	N	N	N	N	N	Y
9 Dellums	?	Y	N	N	N	N	N	Y
10 *Baker*	N	N	Y	Y	Y	Y	Y	N
11 *Pombo*	Y	N	Y	Y	Y	Y	Y	N
12 Lantos	Y	Y	Y	Y	N	N	N	Y
13 Stark	Y	Y	Y	Y	N	?	N	Y
14 Eshoo	Y	Y	Y	Y	N	N	N	Y
15 Mineta	Y	Y	Y	Y	N	N	N	Y
16 Edwards	Y	Y	N	Y	N	N	N	Y
17 Farr	Y	Y	Y	N	N	N	N	Y
18 Condit	Y	Y	Y	Y	N	Y	N	N
19 Lehman	Y	Y	Y	Y	N	N	N	Y
20 Dooley	Y	Y	Y	Y	N	N	N	Y
21 *Thomas*	?	N	Y	Y	Y	Y	Y	N
22 *Huffington*	?	N	Y	Y	Y	Y	Y	N
23 *Gallegly*	N	N	Y	Y	Y	Y	Y	N
24 Beilenson	Y	Y	Y	Y	N	N	N	Y
25 *McKeon*	N	N	Y	Y	Y	Y	Y	N
26 Berman	?	Y	N	N	N	N	N	Y
27 *Moorhead*	N	N	Y	Y	Y	Y	Y	N
28 *Dreier*	N	N	Y	Y	Y	Y	Y	N
29 Waxman	Y	Y	N	N	N	N	N	Y
30 Becerra	Y	Y	Y	Y	N	N	N	Y
31 Martinez	Y	Y	N	N	N	N	N	Y
32 Dixon	?	Y	Y	N	N	N	N	Y
33 Roybal-Allard	Y	Y	Y	Y	N	N	N	Y
34 Torres	Y	Y	N	Y	N	N	N	Y
35 Waters	Y	Y	N	N	N	N	N	Y
36 Harman	Y	Y	Y	Y	N	Y	N	Y
37 Tucker	?	Y	Y	Y	N	N	N	Y
38 *Horn*	?	?	?	?	?	?	?	?
39 *Royce*	N	N	Y	Y	Y	Y	Y	N
40 *Lewis*	N	N	Y	Y	N	N	N	Y
41 *Kim*	N	N	Y	Y	Y	Y	Y	N

	209	210	211	212	213	214	215	216
42 Brown	?	Y	Y	Y	N	N	N	Y
43 *Calvert*	N	N	Y	Y	Y	Y	Y	N
44 *McCandless*	N	N	Y	Y	Y	Y	Y	N
45 *Rohrabacher*	N	N	Y	Y	Y	Y	Y	N
46 *Dornan*	N	N	Y	?	Y	Y	Y	N
47 *Cox*	?	?	?	?	#	#	#	X
48 *Packard*	N	N	Y	Y	Y	Y	Y	N
49 Schenk	Y	Y	Y	N	Y	N	Y	Y
50 Filner	Y	Y	Y	Y	N	N	N	Y
51 *Cunningham*	N	N	Y	Y	Y	Y	Y	N
52 *Hunter*	N	N	Y	Y	Y	Y	Y	N
COLORADO								
1 Schroeder	N	Y	Y	Y	N	N	N	Y
2 Skaggs	Y	Y	Y	Y	N	N	N	Y
3 *McInnis*	N	N	Y	Y	Y	Y	Y	N
4 *Allard*	N	N	Y	Y	Y	Y	Y	N
5 *Hefley*	N	N	Y	Y	Y	Y	Y	N
6 *Schaefer*	N	N	Y	Y	Y	Y	Y	N
CONNECTICUT								
1 Kennelly	Y	Y	Y	Y	N	N	N	Y
2 Gejdenson	?	Y	Y	Y	N	N	N	Y
3 DeLauro	Y	Y	Y	Y	N	N	N	Y
4 *Shays*	N	N	Y	Y	N	N	N	Y
5 *Franks*	N	N	Y	Y	+	+	+	−
6 *Johnson*	N	N	Y	Y	N	N	N	Y
DELAWARE								
AL *Castle*	N	N	Y	Y	Y	Y	Y	N
FLORIDA								
1 Hutto	Y	Y	Y	Y	N	N	N	N
2 Peterson	Y	Y	Y	Y	N	N	N	Y
3 Brown	Y	Y	Y	Y	N	N	N	Y
4 *Fowler*	N	N	Y	Y	Y	Y	Y	N
5 Thurman	Y	Y	Y	Y	N	N	N	Y
6 *Stearns*	N	N	Y	Y	Y	Y	Y	N
7 *Mica*	N	N	Y	Y	Y	Y	Y	N
8 *McCollum*	N	N	Y	Y	Y	Y	Y	N
9 *Bilirakis*	N	N	Y	Y	Y	Y	Y	N
10 *Young*	N	N	Y	Y	Y	Y	Y	N
11 Gibbons	Y	Y	Y	Y	N	N	N	Y
12 *Canady*	N	N	Y	Y	Y	Y	Y	N
13 *Miller*	N	N	Y	Y	Y	Y	Y	N
14 *Goss*	N	N	Y	Y	Y	Y	Y	N
15 Bacchus	?	Y	Y	Y	N	N	N	Y
16 *Lewis*	−	−	Y	Y	+	Y	Y	N
17 Meek	Y	Y	N	N	N	N	N	Y
18 *Ros-Lehtinen*	N	N	Y	Y	Y	Y	Y	N
19 Johnston	Y	Y	Y	?	N	N	N	Y
20 Deutsch	Y	Y	Y	N	N	N	N	Y
21 *Diaz-Balart*	N	N	Y	Y	Y	Y	Y	N
22 *Shaw*	N	N	Y	Y	Y	Y	Y	N
23 Hastings	Y	Y	N	N	N	N	N	Y
GEORGIA								
1 *Kingston*	Y	N	Y	Y	Y	Y	Y	N
2 Bishop	Y	Y	Y	Y	N	N	N	Y
3 *Collins*	Y	N	Y	Y	Y	Y	Y	N
4 *Linder*	N	N	Y	Y	Y	Y	Y	N
5 Lewis	Y	Y	Y	Y	N	N	N	Y
6 *Gingrich*	N	N	Y	Y	Y	Y	Y	N
7 Darden	Y	Y	Y	Y	N	N	N	Y
8 Rowland	Y	Y	Y	?	N	N	N	Y
9 Deal	Y	Y	Y	Y	N	N	N	Y
10 Johnson	Y	Y	Y	Y	N	Y	N	Y
11 McKinney	Y	Y	N	N	N	N	N	Y
HAWAII								
1 Abercrombie	Y	Y	N	N	N	N	N	Y
2 Mink	Y	Y	Y	Y	N	N	N	Y
IDAHO								
1 LaRocco	Y	Y	Y	Y	N	N	N	Y
2 *Crapo*	N	N	Y	Y	Y	Y	Y	N
ILLINOIS								
1 Rush	Y	Y	Y	N	Y	N	N	Y
2 Reynolds	Y	Y	N	N	N	N	N	Y
3 Lipinski	Y	Y	Y	Y	N	N	N	Y
4 Gutierrez	?	Y	Y	N	Y	N	N	Y
5 Rostenkowski	Y	Y	N	N	N	N	N	Y
6 *Hyde*	N	N	Y	Y	Y	Y	Y	N
7 Collins	Y	Y	N	N	N	N	N	Y
8 *Crane*	N	N	Y	Y	Y	Y	Y	N
9 Yates	Y	Y	N	N	N	N	N	Y
10 *Porter*	N	N	Y	Y	Y	Y	Y	N
11 Sangmeister	Y	Y	Y	Y	N	N	N	Y
12 Costello	Y	Y	Y	Y	N	N	N	Y
13 *Fawell*	N	N	Y	Y	Y	Y	Y	N
14 *Hastert*	N	N	Y	Y	Y	Y	Y	N
15 *Ewing*	N	N	Y	Y	Y	Y	Y	N
16 *Manzullo*	N	N	Y	Y	Y	Y	Y	N
17 Evans	Y	Y	Y	Y	N	N	N	Y

ND Northern Democrats SD Southern Democrats

	209	210	211	212	213	214	215	216
18 ***Michel***	N	N	Y	Y	N	Y	Y	N
19 Poshard	Y	Y	Y	Y	Y	Y	N	Y
20 Durbin	Y	Y	Y	Y	N	N	N	Y
INDIANA								
1 Visclosky	Y	Y	N	Y	N	N	N	Y
2 Sharp	Y	Y	Y	Y	N	N	N	Y
3 Roemer	Y	Y	Y	Y	Y	N	N	N
4 Long	Y	Y	Y	Y	N	N	N	Y
5 ***Buyer***	N	N	Y	Y	Y	Y	Y	N
6 ***Burton***	N	N	Y	Y	Y	Y	Y	N
7 ***Myers***	Y	N	Y	Y	Y	Y	Y	N
8 McCloskey	Y	Y	Y	Y	N	N	N	Y
9 Hamilton	Y	N	Y	Y	N	N	Y	Y
10 Jacobs	N	Y	Y	Y	N	N	Y	N
IOWA								
1 ***Leach***	N	N	Y	Y	N	N	Y	N
2 ***Nussle***	N	N	Y	Y	Y	Y	Y	N
3 ***Lightfoot***	N	N	Y	Y	Y	Y	Y	N
4 Smith	Y	Y	Y	Y	N	N	N	Y
5 ***Grandy***	?	?	?	?	#	#	#	X
KANSAS								
1 ***Roberts***	N	N	Y	Y	Y	Y	Y	N
2 Slattery	?	Y	?	?	X	X	X	?
3 ***Meyers***	N	N	Y	Y	Y	N	Y	N
4 Glickman	Y	Y	Y	Y	N	N	N	Y
KENTUCKY								
1 Barlow	Y	Y	Y	Y	N	N	N	Y
2 ***Lewis*** [1]		N	Y	Y	Y	Y	Y	N
3 Mazzoli	Y	Y	Y	Y	N	N	N	Y
4 ***Bunning***	N	N	Y	Y	Y	Y	Y	N
5 ***Rogers***	N	N	Y	Y	Y	Y	Y	N
6 Baesler	Y	Y	Y	Y	N	N	N	Y
LOUISIANA								
1 ***Livingston***	Y	N	Y	Y	Y	Y	Y	N
2 Jefferson	Y	Y	Y	Y	N	N	N	Y
3 Tauzin	Y	Y	Y	Y	?	Y	N	N
4 Fields	Y	Y	Y	Y	N	N	N	Y
5 ***McCrery***	Y	N	Y	Y	Y	Y	Y	N
6 ***Baker***	N	N	Y	Y	Y	Y	Y	N
7 Hayes	Y	Y	Y	Y	N	Y	N	N
MAINE								
1 Andrews	Y	Y	Y	Y	N	N	N	N
2 ***Snowe***	Y	N	Y	Y	Y	Y	Y	N
MARYLAND								
1 ***Gilchrest***	N	N	Y	Y	Y	N	Y	N
2 ***Bentley***	N	N	Y	Y	Y	Y	Y	N
3 Cardin	Y	Y	Y	Y	N	N	N	Y
4 Wynn	Y	Y	Y	Y	N	N	N	Y
5 Hoyer	Y	Y	Y	Y	N	N	N	Y
6 ***Bartlett***	N	N	Y	Y	Y	Y	Y	N
7 Mfume	Y	Y	Y	Y	Y	N	N	Y
8 ***Morella***	?	N	Y	Y	N	N	Y	Y
MASSACHUSETTS								
1 Olver	Y	Y	Y	Y	N	N	N	Y
2 Neal	Y	Y	Y	Y	N	N	N	Y
3 ***Blute***	N	N	Y	Y	Y	Y	Y	N
4 Frank	Y	Y	Y	Y	N	N	N	Y
5 Meehan	Y	Y	Y	Y	N	N	N	Y
6 ***Torkildsen***	N	N	Y	Y	Y	Y	Y	N
7 Markey	Y	Y	Y	Y	N	N	N	Y
8 Kennedy	Y	Y	Y	Y	N	N	N	Y
9 Moakley	Y	Y	Y	Y	N	N	N	Y
10 Studds	Y	Y	Y	Y	N	N	N	Y
MICHIGAN								
1 Stupak	Y	Y	Y	Y	N	N	N	Y
2 ***Hoekstra***	N	N	Y	Y	Y	Y	Y	N
3 ***Ehlers***	N	N	Y	Y	Y	N	Y	N
4 ***Camp***	N	N	Y	Y	Y	Y	Y	N
5 Barcia	Y	Y	Y	Y	Y	N	N	Y
6 ***Upton***	N	N	Y	Y	Y	Y	Y	N
7 ***Smith***	N	N	Y	Y	Y	Y	Y	N
8 Carr	Y	Y	Y	Y	N	N	N	Y
9 Kildee	Y	Y	Y	Y	N	N	N	Y
10 Bonior	Y	Y	N	N	N	N	N	Y
11 ***Knollenberg***	N	N	Y	Y	Y	Y	Y	N
12 Levin	Y	Y	Y	Y	N	N	N	Y
13 Ford	?	Y	Y	N	N	N	N	?
14 Conyers	Y	Y	N	N	N	N	N	Y
15 Collins	?	Y	N	N	N	N	N	Y
16 Dingell	Y	Y	N	N	N	N	N	Y
MINNESOTA								
1 Penny	Y	Y	Y	Y	Y	Y	N	N
2 Minge	Y	Y	Y	Y	Y	Y	N	N
3 ***Ramstad***	N	N	Y	Y	Y	Y	Y	N
4 Vento	Y	Y	Y	Y	N	N	N	Y

	209	210	211	212	213	214	215	216
5 Sabo	Y	Y	N	N	N	N	N	Y
6 ***Grams***	N	N	Y	Y	Y	Y	Y	N
7 Peterson	Y	Y	Y	Y	N	Y	Y	N
8 Oberstar	Y	Y	N	N	N	N	N	Y
MISSISSIPPI								
1 Whitten	?	Y	?	?	N	N	N	Y
2 Thompson	Y	Y	N	Y	N	N	N	Y
3 Montgomery	Y	Y	Y	Y	Y	N	N	Y
4 Parker	Y	Y	Y	Y	Y	N	N	Y
5 Taylor	N	Y	Y	Y	Y	Y	N	N
MISSOURI								
1 Clay	N	Y	N	N	?	?	?	?
2 ***Talent***	?	N	Y	Y	Y	Y	Y	N
3 Gephardt	Y	Y	Y	N	N	N	N	Y
4 Skelton	Y	Y	Y	Y	N	?	?	#
5 Wheat	Y	Y	Y	Y	N	N	N	Y
6 Danner	Y	Y	Y	Y	N	N	N	Y
7 ***Hancock***	N	N	Y	Y	Y	Y	Y	N
8 ***Emerson***	N	N	Y	Y	Y	Y	Y	N
9 Volkmer	Y	Y	Y	Y	Y	N	N	Y
MONTANA								
AL Williams	?	Y	Y	Y	Y	N	N	Y
NEBRASKA								
1 ***Bereuter***	?	N	Y	Y	Y	N	Y	N
2 Hoagland	Y	Y	Y	Y	Y	N	N	Y
3 ***Barrett***	N	N	Y	Y	Y	Y	Y	N
NEVADA								
1 Bilbray	Y	Y	Y	Y	N	N	N	Y
2 ***Vucanovich***	N	N	Y	Y	Y	Y	Y	N
NEW HAMPSHIRE								
1 ***Zeliff***	N	N	Y	Y	Y	Y	Y	N
2 Swett	Y	Y	Y	Y	Y	Y	N	N
NEW JERSEY								
1 Andrews	Y	Y	Y	Y	N	N	N	N
2 Hughes	Y	Y	Y	Y	N	N	N	Y
3 ***Saxton***	N	N	Y	Y	Y	Y	N	N
4 ***Smith***	?	N	Y	Y	Y	Y	Y	N
5 ***Roukema***	N	N	Y	Y	Y	N	Y	N
6 Pallone	Y	Y	Y	Y	Y	Y	N	N
7 ***Franks***	N	N	Y	Y	Y	Y	Y	N
8 Klein	Y	Y	Y	Y	Y	Y	N	Y
9 Torricelli	Y	Y	Y	Y	N	N	N	Y
10 Payne	Y	Y	N	N	N	N	N	Y
11 ***Gallo***	N	N	Y	Y	Y	N	Y	N
12 ***Zimmer***	N	N	Y	Y	Y	Y	Y	N
13 Menendez	Y	Y	Y	Y	N	N	N	Y
NEW MEXICO								
1 ***Schiff***	N	N	Y	Y	N	N	Y	N
2 ***Skeen***	N	N	Y	Y	Y	Y	Y	N
3 Richardson	Y	Y	Y	Y	N	N	N	Y
NEW YORK								
1 Hochbrueckner	Y	Y	Y	Y	N	N	N	Y
2 ***Lazio***	N	N	Y	Y	Y	Y	Y	N
3 ***King***	N	N	Y	N	Y	Y	Y	N
4 ***Levy***	N	N	Y	Y	Y	Y	Y	N
5 Ackerman	Y	Y	Y	N	N	N	N	Y
6 Flake	Y	Y	N	N	N	N	N	Y
7 Manton	Y	Y	Y	Y	N	N	?	?
8 Nadler	Y	Y	Y	Y	N	N	N	?
9 Schumer	Y	Y	Y	Y	?	?	?	?
10 Towns	Y	Y	N	N	N	N	N	Y
11 Owens	Y	Y	N	N	N	N	N	Y
12 Velazquez	Y	Y	Y	N	N	N	N	Y
13 ***Molinari***	N	N	Y	Y	Y	Y	Y	N
14 Maloney	Y	Y	Y	Y	N	N	N	Y
15 Rangel	Y	Y	N	N	N	N	N	Y
16 Serrano	Y	Y	N	N	N	N	N	Y
17 Engel	?	Y	Y	N	N	N	N	Y
18 Lowey	Y	Y	Y	Y	N	N	N	Y
19 ***Fish***	?	N	Y	Y	Y	Y	Y	?
20 ***Gilman***	Y	N	Y	Y	Y	Y	Y	N
21 McNulty	Y	Y	Y	Y	N	N	N	Y
22 ***Solomon***	N	N	Y	Y	Y	Y	Y	N
23 ***Boehlert***	N	N	Y	Y	Y	N	Y	N
24 ***McHugh***	N	N	Y	Y	Y	Y	Y	N
25 ***Walsh***	N	N	Y	Y	Y	N	Y	N
26 Hinchey	Y	Y	Y	Y	N	N	N	Y
27 ***Paxon***	N	N	Y	Y	Y	Y	Y	N
28 Slaughter	Y	Y	Y	Y	N	N	N	Y
29 LaFalce	Y	Y	Y	Y	N	N	N	Y
30 ***Quinn***	N	N	Y	Y	Y	Y	Y	N
31 ***Houghton***	Y	N	Y	Y	N	N	Y	Y
NORTH CAROLINA								
1 Clayton	Y	?	N	Y	N	N	N	Y
2 Valentine	Y	Y	Y	Y	Y	N	N	Y

	209	210	211	212	213	214	215	216
3 Lancaster	Y	Y	Y	Y	N	N	N	Y
4 Price	Y	Y	Y	Y	N	N	N	Y
5 Neal	?	?	Y	Y	N	?	?	?
6 ***Coble***	N	N	Y	Y	Y	Y	Y	N
7 Rose	Y	Y	Y	Y	N	N	N	Y
8 Hefner	Y	Y	Y	Y	N	N	N	Y
9 ***McMillan***	?	N	Y	Y	Y	Y	Y	N
10 ***Ballenger***	N	N	Y	Y	Y	Y	Y	N
11 ***Taylor***	N	N	Y	Y	Y	Y	Y	N
12 Watt	Y	Y	Y	Y	N	N	N	Y
NORTH DAKOTA								
AL Pomeroy	Y	Y	Y	Y	N	N	N	N
OHIO								
1 Mann	Y	Y	Y	Y	Y	Y	N	N
2 ***Portman***	N	N	Y	Y	Y	Y	Y	N
3 Hall	?	Y	Y	Y	N	N	N	Y
4 ***Oxley***	N	N	Y	N	Y	N	Y	N
5 ***Gillmor***	Y	N	Y	Y	Y	Y	Y	N
6 Strickland	Y	Y	Y	Y	N	N	N	N
7 ***Hobson***	N	N	Y	Y	Y	Y	Y	N
8 ***Boehner***	N	N	Y	Y	Y	Y	Y	N
9 Kaptur	Y	Y	Y	Y	N	N	N	Y
10 ***Hoke***	N	N	Y	?	Y	Y	Y	N
11 Stokes	Y	Y	N	N	N	N	N	Y
12 ***Kasich***	Y	N	Y	Y	Y	Y	Y	N
13 Brown	Y	Y	Y	Y	Y	N	N	N
14 Sawyer	Y	Y	Y	Y	N	N	N	Y
15 ***Pryce***	N	N	Y	Y	Y	Y	Y	N
16 ***Regula***	N	N	Y	Y	Y	Y	Y	N
17 Traficant	Y	Y	Y	Y	N	N	N	Y
18 Applegate	Y	Y	Y	N	N	N	N	Y
19 Fingerhut	Y	Y	Y	Y	N	Y	N	N
OKLAHOMA								
1 ***Inhofe***	N	N	Y	Y	Y	Y	Y	N
2 Synar	Y	Y	N	N	N	N	N	Y
3 Brewster	Y	Y	Y	Y	N	N	N	Y
4 McCurdy	Y	Y	Y	Y	N	N	N	Y
5 ***Istook***	N	N	Y	Y	Y	Y	Y	N
6 ***Lucas***	N	N	Y	Y	Y	Y	Y	N
OREGON								
1 Furse	Y	Y	Y	Y	N	N	N	Y
2 ***Smith***	N	N	Y	Y	Y	Y	Y	N
3 Wyden	Y	Y	Y	Y	N	N	N	Y
4 DeFazio	Y	Y	Y	Y	N	N	X	#
5 Kopetski	Y	Y	N	N	N	N	N	Y
PENNSYLVANIA								
1 Foglietta	Y	Y	N	N	N	N	N	Y
2 Blackwell	?	?	?	?	N	N	N	Y
3 Borski	Y	Y	Y	Y	N	N	N	Y
4 Klink	Y	Y	Y	Y	N	N	N	Y
5 ***Clinger***	N	N	Y	Y	Y	N	Y	N
6 Holden	Y	Y	Y	Y	N	N	N	Y
7 ***Weldon***	N	N	Y	Y	Y	Y	Y	N
8 ***Greenwood***	?	N	Y	Y	Y	Y	Y	N
9 ***Shuster***	N	N	Y	Y	Y	Y	Y	N
10 ***McDade***	N	N	Y	Y	N	Y	Y	N
11 Kanjorski	Y	Y	Y	Y	N	N	N	Y
12 Murtha	Y	Y	N	N	N	N	N	Y
13 Margolies-Mezv.	Y	Y	Y	Y	N	N	N	N
14 Coyne	Y	Y	N	N	N	N	N	Y
15 McHale	Y	Y	Y	Y	N	N	N	Y
16 ***Walker***	N	N	Y	Y	Y	Y	Y	N
17 ***Gekas***	N	N	Y	Y	Y	Y	Y	N
18 ***Santorum***	N	N	Y	Y	Y	Y	Y	N
19 ***Goodling***	N	N	Y	Y	N	Y	Y	N
20 Murphy	N	Y	Y	Y	N	N	N	Y
21 ***Ridge***	N	N	Y	Y	Y	Y	Y	N
RHODE ISLAND								
1 ***Machtley***	N	N	Y	Y	Y	Y	#	X
2 Reed	Y	Y	Y	Y	N	N	N	Y
SOUTH CAROLINA								
1 ***Ravenel***	N	N	Y	Y	Y	Y	Y	N
2 ***Spence***	N	N	Y	Y	Y	Y	Y	N
3 Derrick	Y	Y	Y	Y	N	N	N	Y
4 ***Inglis***	Y	N	Y	Y	Y	Y	Y	N
5 Spratt	Y	Y	Y	Y	N	N	N	Y
6 Clyburn	Y	Y	Y	Y	N	N	N	Y
SOUTH DAKOTA								
AL Johnson	Y	Y	Y	Y	N	N	N	Y
TENNESSEE								
1 ***Quillen***	N	N	Y	Y	Y	Y	Y	N
2 ***Duncan***	N	N	Y	Y	Y	Y	Y	N
3 Lloyd	?	Y	Y	Y	N	N	N	Y
4 Cooper	Y	N	Y	Y	Y	Y	Y	N
5 Clement	Y	Y	?	?	?	?	?	?

	209	210	211	212	213	214	215	216
6 Gordon	Y	Y	Y	Y	N	N	N	Y
7 ***Sundquist***	N	N	Y	Y	Y	N	Y	N
8 Tanner	Y	Y	Y	Y	N	N	N	N
9 Ford	?	Y	Y	Y	N	Y	N	Y
TEXAS								
1 Chapman	?	Y	Y	Y	N	N	N	Y
2 Wilson	?	?	?	?	X	X	X	#
3 ***Johnson, Sam***	N	N	Y	Y	Y	Y	Y	N
4 Hall	Y	Y	Y	Y	Y	Y	N	N
5 Bryant	Y	Y	Y	Y	N	N	N	Y
6 ***Barton***	N	N	Y	Y	Y	Y	Y	N
7 ***Archer***	N	N	Y	Y	Y	Y	Y	N
8 ***Fields***	N	N	Y	Y	Y	Y	Y	N
9 Brooks	Y	Y	Y	Y	N	N	N	Y
10 Pickle	Y	Y	N	Y	N	N	N	Y
11 Edwards	Y	Y	Y	Y	N	N	N	Y
12 Geren	Y	Y	Y	Y	Y	Y	N	N
13 Sarpalius	Y	Y	Y	Y	N	N	N	N
14 Laughlin	Y	Y	Y	Y	N	N	N	Y
15 de la Garza	Y	Y	Y	Y	Y	N	N	?
16 Coleman	Y	Y	Y	Y	N	N	N	Y
17 Stenholm	Y	Y	Y	Y	Y	Y	N	N
18 Washington	?	Y	N	N	?	?	?	?
19 ***Combest***	Y	N	Y	Y	Y	Y	Y	N
20 Gonzalez	Y	Y	Y	N	N	N	N	Y
21 ***Smith***	N	N	Y	Y	Y	Y	Y	N
22 ***DeLay***	N	N	Y	Y	Y	Y	Y	N
23 ***Bonilla***	N	N	Y	Y	Y	Y	Y	N
24 Frost	?	Y	Y	N	N	N	N	Y
25 Andrews	Y	Y	Y	Y	Y	N	N	Y
26 ***Armey***	N	N	Y	Y	Y	Y	Y	N
27 Ortiz	Y	Y	Y	Y	N	N	N	Y
28 Tejeda	Y	Y	Y	Y	N	N	N	Y
29 Green	Y	Y	Y	Y	N	N	N	Y
30 Johnson, E.B.	Y	Y	N	N	N	N	N	Y
UTAH								
1 ***Hansen***	N	N	Y	Y	Y	Y	Y	N
2 Shepherd	Y	Y	Y	Y	Y	N	N	N
3 Orton	Y	Y	Y	Y	Y	N	N	Y
VERMONT								
AL *Sanders*	Y	Y	Y	Y	N	N	N	Y
VIRGINIA								
1 ***Bateman***	Y	N	Y	Y	Y	N	Y	N
2 Pickett	Y	Y	Y	Y	N	?	N	Y
3 Scott	Y	Y	Y	Y	N	N	N	Y
4 Sisisky	Y	Y	Y	Y	N	N	N	Y
5 Payne	?	Y	Y	Y	N	N	N	Y
6 ***Goodlatte***	N	N	Y	Y	Y	Y	Y	N
7 ***Bliley***	N	N	Y	Y	Y	Y	Y	N
8 Moran	Y	Y	Y	Y	N	N	N	Y
9 Boucher	Y	Y	Y	Y	N	N	N	Y
10 ***Wolf***	N	N	Y	Y	Y	Y	Y	N
11 Byrne	Y	Y	Y	Y	N	N	N	Y
WASHINGTON								
1 Cantwell	?	Y	Y	Y	N	N	N	N
2 Swift	?	Y	N	N	N	N	N	Y
3 Unsoeld	Y	Y	N	N	N	N	N	Y
4 Inslee	Y	Y	Y	Y	N	Y	N	N
5 Foley								
6 Dicks	Y	Y	?	Y	N	N	N	Y
7 McDermott	Y	Y	N	+	N	N	N	Y
8 ***Dunn***	N	N	Y	Y	Y	Y	Y	N
9 Kreidler	Y	Y	Y	Y	N	N	N	Y
WEST VIRGINIA								
1 Mollohan	?	Y	N	N	N	N	N	Y
2 Wise	Y	Y	Y	Y	N	N	N	Y
3 Rahall	Y	Y	Y	Y	N	N	N	Y
WISCONSIN								
1 Barca	Y	Y	Y	Y	N	Y	N	N
2 ***Klug***	N	N	Y	Y	Y	Y	Y	N
3 ***Gunderson***	N	N	Y	Y	?	Y	Y	N
4 Kleczka	Y	Y	Y	Y	N	N	N	Y
5 Barrett	Y	Y	Y	Y	N	Y	N	Y
6 ***Petri***	N	N	Y	Y	Y	Y	Y	N
7 Obey	Y	Y	N	N	N	N	N	Y
8 ***Roth***	N	N	Y	Y	Y	Y	Y	N
9 ***Sensenbrenner***	N	N	Y	Y	Y	Y	Y	N
WYOMING								
AL ***Thomas***	Y	N	Y	Y	Y	Y	Y	N
DELEGATES								
de Lugo, V.I.	D	D	?	?	N	N	D	D
Faleomavaega, Am.S.	D	D	Y	Y	N	N	D	D
Norton, D.C.	D	D	Y	Y	N	N	D	D
Romero-B., P.R.	D	D	Y	Y	N	N	D	D
Underwood, Guam	D	D	Y	?	N	N	D	D

Southern states - Ala., Ark., Fla., Ga., Ky., La., Miss., N.C., Okla., S.C., Tenn., Texas, Va.
Omitted votes are quorum calls, which CQ does not include in its vote charts.

KEY

Y Voted for (yea).
Paired for.
+ Announced for.
N Voted against (nay).
X Paired against.
— Announced against.
P Voted "present."
C Voted "present" to avoid possible conflict of interest.
? Did not vote or otherwise make a position known.
D Delegates ineligible to vote.

————
Democrats   *Republicans*
Independent

217. HR 4301. Fiscal 1995 Defense Authorization/ North Korea Nuclear Inspections. Solomon, R-N.Y., amendment to express the sense of Congress that if North Korea does not allow international inspections of the Yongbyon nuclear facility, the United States should take actions indicating the severity of the situation, including seeking international sanctions and the resumption of the "Team Spirit" military exercises with South Korea. Adopted in the Committee of the Whole 415-1: R 171-0; D 243-1 (ND 166-1, SD 77-0); I 1-0, June 8, 1994.

218. HR 4301. Fiscal 1995 Defense Authorization/Nuclear Testing Moratorium. Kopetski, D-Ore., amendment to commend the president for maintaining the U.S. nuclear testing moratorium, encourage all nuclear powers to refrain from conducting nuclear explosions and urge the Conference on Disarmament to complete a comprehensive test ban treaty by the end of 1994. Adopted in the Committee of the Whole 263-156: R 30-141; D 232-15 (ND 168-2, SD 64-13); I 1-0, June 8, 1994.

219. HR 4301. Fiscal 1995 Defense Authorization/Medical Conditions Separation Requirement. Harman, D-Calif., amendment to modify the section of the bill that requires the services to discharge military personnel who are "permanently non-worldwide assignable" as a result of medical conditions such as cancer, heart disease, diabetes or HIV-positive status. The amendment would give the service secretaries discretion to retain individuals if doing so would not adversely affect the ability of the services to carry out their missions. Adopted in the Committee of the Whole 227-192: R 27-144; D 199-48 (ND 154-16, SD 45-32); I 1-0, June 8, 1994.

220. HR 4301. Fiscal 1995 Defense Authorization/Missing Japanese Plutonium. Markey, D-Mass., amendment to express the sense of Congress that the president should report to Congress on the progress of accounting for missing plutonium in Japan. Rejected in the Committee of the Whole 68-349: R 5-166; D 62-183 (ND 56-112, SD 6-71); I 1-0, June 8, 1994.

221. HR 4301. Fiscal 1995 Defense Authorization/South Korea Military Readiness. Kasich, R-Ohio, amendment to express the sense of Congress that the president should urge South Korea to improve its military capabilities and that the secretary of Defense should report to Congress by Dec. 1, 1994, on the military readiness of South Korea to defeat an attack by North Korea. Adopted in the Committee of the Whole 414-3: R 170-0; D 243-3 (ND 168-1, SD 75-2); I 1-0, June 8, 1994.

	217	218	219	220	221
ALABAMA					
1 *Callahan*	Y	N	N	N	Y
2 *Everett*	Y	N	N	N	Y
3 Browder	Y	Y	Y	N	Y
4 Bevill	Y	Y	Y	N	Y
5 Cramer	Y	Y	Y	N	Y
6 *Bachus*	Y	N	N	N	Y
7 Hilliard	Y	Y	Y	N	Y
ALASKA					
AL *Young*	Y	N	N	N	Y
ARIZONA					
1 Coppersmith	Y	Y	Y	N	Y
2 Pastor	Y	Y	Y	N	Y
3 *Stump*	Y	N	N	N	Y
4 *Kyl*	Y	N	Y	N	Y
5 *Kolbe*	Y	N	Y	N	Y
6 English	Y	Y	Y	N	Y
ARKANSAS					
1 Lambert	Y	Y	N	N	Y
2 Thornton	Y	Y	N	N	Y
3 *Hutchinson*	Y	N	N	N	Y
4 *Dickey*	Y	N	N	N	Y
CALIFORNIA					
1 Hamburg	Y	Y	Y	Y	Y
2 *Herger*	Y	N	N	N	Y
3 Fazio	Y	Y	Y	N	Y
4 *Doolittle*	Y	N	N	N	Y
5 Matsui	Y	Y	Y	N	Y
6 Woolsey	Y	Y	Y	Y	Y
7 Miller	?	?	?	?	?
8 Pelosi	Y	Y	Y	Y	Y
9 Dellums	Y	Y	Y	Y	Y
10 *Baker*	Y	N	N	N	Y
11 *Pombo*	Y	N	N	N	Y
12 Lantos	Y	Y	Y	N	Y
13 Stark	Y	Y	Y	Y	Y
14 Eshoo	Y	Y	Y	N	Y
15 Mineta	Y	Y	Y	N	Y
16 Edwards	Y	Y	Y	Y	Y
17 Farr	Y	Y	Y	N	Y
18 Condit	Y	Y	Y	N	Y
19 Lehman	Y	Y	Y	N	Y
20 Dooley	Y	Y	N	N	Y
21 *Thomas*	Y	N	N	N	Y
22 *Huffington*	?	?	?	?	?
23 *Gallegly*	Y	N	N	N	Y
24 Beilenson	Y	Y	Y	N	Y
25 *McKeon*	Y	N	N	N	Y
26 Berman	Y	Y	Y	?	?
27 *Moorhead*	Y	N	N	N	Y
28 *Dreier*	Y	N	N	N	Y
29 Waxman	Y	Y	Y	N	Y
30 Becerra	?	?	?	?	?
31 Martinez	?	?	?	?	?
32 Dixon	N	Y	Y	N	Y
33 Roybal-Allard	Y	Y	Y	N	Y
34 Torres	Y	Y	Y	Y	Y
35 Waters	Y	Y	Y	Y	Y
36 Harman	Y	Y	Y	N	Y
37 Tucker	?	#	#	#	?
38 *Horn*	Y	Y	Y	Y	Y
39 *Royce*	?	?	?	?	?
40 *Lewis*	Y	N	N	N	Y
41 *Kim*	Y	N	N	N	Y

	217	218	219	220	221
42 Brown	Y	Y	Y	N	Y
43 *Calvert*	?	?	?	?	?
44 *McCandless*	Y	N	N	N	Y
45 *Rohrabacher*	Y	N	N	N	Y
46 *Dornan*	Y	N	N	N	Y
47 *Cox*	Y	N	N	N	Y
48 *Packard*	Y	N	N	N	Y
49 Schenk	Y	Y	Y	N	Y
50 Filner	Y	Y	Y	Y	Y
51 *Cunningham*	Y	N	N	N	Y
52 *Hunter*	Y	N	N	N	Y
COLORADO					
1 Schroeder	Y	Y	Y	Y	Y
2 Skaggs	Y	Y	Y	N	Y
3 *McInnis*	Y	N	N	N	Y
4 *Allard*	Y	N	N	N	Y
5 *Hefley*	Y	N	N	N	Y
6 *Schaefer*	Y	N	N	N	Y
CONNECTICUT					
1 Kennelly	Y	Y	Y	N	Y
2 Gejdenson	Y	Y	Y	Y	Y
3 DeLauro	Y	Y	Y	N	Y
4 *Shays*	Y	Y	Y	N	Y
5 *Franks*	Y	N	N	N	Y
6 *Johnson*	Y	Y	Y	N	Y
DELAWARE					
AL *Castle*	Y	N	N	N	Y
FLORIDA					
1 Hutto	Y	N	N	N	Y
2 Peterson	Y	Y	N	N	Y
3 Brown	Y	Y	Y	N	Y
4 *Fowler*	Y	N	N	N	Y
5 Thurman	Y	Y	N	N	Y
6 *Stearns*	Y	N	N	N	Y
7 *Mica*	Y	N	N	N	Y
8 *McCollum*	Y	N	N	N	Y
9 *Bilirakis*	Y	N	N	N	Y
10 *Young*	Y	N	N	N	Y
11 Gibbons	Y	Y	N	N	Y
12 *Canady*	Y	N	N	N	Y
13 *Miller*	Y	N	N	N	Y
14 *Goss*	Y	N	N	N	Y
15 Bacchus	Y	Y	Y	N	Y
16 *Lewis*	Y	N	N	N	Y
17 Meek	Y	Y	Y	N	Y
18 *Ros-Lehtinen*	Y	N	N	N	Y
19 Johnston	Y	Y	Y	N	Y
20 Deutsch	Y	Y	Y	N	Y
21 *Diaz-Balart*	Y	N	N	N	Y
22 *Shaw*	Y	N	N	N	Y
23 Hastings	Y	Y	Y	N	Y
GEORGIA					
1 *Kingston*	Y	N	N	N	Y
2 Bishop	Y	Y	Y	N	Y
3 *Collins*	Y	N	N	N	Y
4 *Linder*	Y	N	N	N	Y
5 Lewis	Y	Y	Y	N	Y
6 *Gingrich*	Y	N	N	N	Y
7 Darden	Y	Y	N	N	Y
8 Rowland	Y	N	N	N	Y
9 Deal	Y	Y	Y	N	Y
10 Johnson	Y	Y	Y	N	Y
11 McKinney	Y	Y	Y	Y	N
HAWAII					
1 Abercrombie	Y	Y	Y	Y	Y
2 Mink	Y	Y	Y	N	Y
IDAHO					
1 LaRocco	Y	Y	Y	N	Y
2 *Crapo*	Y	N	N	N	Y
ILLINOIS					
1 Rush	Y	Y	Y	Y	Y
2 Reynolds	Y	Y	Y	N	Y
3 Lipinski	Y	Y	Y	N	Y
4 Gutierrez	Y	Y	Y	N	Y
5 Rostenkowski	Y	Y	Y	N	Y
6 *Hyde*	Y	N	N	N	Y
7 Collins	Y	Y	Y	Y	Y
8 *Crane*	Y	N	N	N	Y
9 Yates	Y	Y	Y	Y	Y
10 *Porter*	Y	Y	N	N	Y
11 Sangmeister	Y	Y	Y	N	Y
12 Costello	Y	Y	Y	N	Y
13 *Fawell*	Y	Y	N	N	Y
14 *Hastert*	Y	N	N	N	Y
15 *Ewing*	Y	N	N	N	Y
16 *Manzullo*	Y	N	N	N	Y
17 Evans	Y	Y	Y	Y	Y

ND Northern Democrats   SD Southern Democrats

	217	218	219	220	221
18 Michel	Y	N	N	N	Y
19 Poshard	Y	Y	Y	N	Y
20 Durbin	Y	Y	Y	N	Y
INDIANA					
1 Visclosky	Y	Y	N	N	Y
2 Sharp	Y	Y	Y	N	Y
3 Roemer	Y	Y	Y	N	Y
4 Long	Y	Y	Y	N	Y
5 *Buyer*	Y	N	N	N	Y
6 *Burton*	Y	N	N	N	Y
7 *Myers*	Y	N	N	N	Y
8 McCloskey	Y	Y	Y	N	Y
9 Hamilton	Y	Y	Y	N	Y
10 Jacobs	Y	Y	Y	N	Y
IOWA					
1 *Leach*	Y	Y	N	N	Y
2 *Nussle*	Y	N	N	N	Y
3 *Lightfoot*	Y	N	N	N	Y
4 Smith	Y	Y	Y	N	Y
5 *Grandy*	?	?	?	?	?
KANSAS					
1 *Roberts*	Y	N	N	N	Y
2 Slattery	Y	Y	Y	N	Y
3 *Meyers*	Y	Y	Y	N	Y
4 Glickman	Y	Y	Y	N	Y
KENTUCKY					
1 Barlow	Y	Y	Y	N	Y
2 *Lewis*	Y	N	N	N	Y
3 Mazzoli	Y	Y	Y	N	Y
4 *Bunning*	Y	N	N	N	Y
5 *Rogers*	Y	N	N	N	Y
6 Baesler	Y	N	Y	N	Y
LOUISIANA					
1 *Livingston*	Y	N	N	N	Y
2 Jefferson	?	?	?	?	?
3 Tauzin	Y	Y	Y	N	Y
4 Fields	Y	Y	Y	N	Y
5 *McCrery*	Y	N	N	N	Y
6 *Baker*	Y	N	N	N	Y
7 Hayes	Y	N	N	N	Y
MAINE					
1 Andrews	Y	Y	Y	Y	Y
2 *Snowe*	Y	N	Y	N	Y
MARYLAND					
1 *Gilchrest*	Y	Y	N	N	Y
2 *Bentley*	Y	N	N	Y	Y
3 Cardin	Y	Y	Y	N	Y
4 Wynn	Y	Y	Y	N	Y
5 Hoyer	Y	Y	Y	N	Y
6 *Bartlett*	Y	N	N	N	Y
7 Mfume	Y	Y	Y	N	Y
8 *Morella*	Y	Y	Y	N	Y
MASSACHUSETTS					
1 Olver	Y	Y	Y	Y	Y
2 Neal	Y	Y	Y	Y	Y
3 *Blute*	Y	Y	Y	N	Y
4 Frank	Y	Y	Y	Y	Y
5 Meehan	Y	Y	Y	Y	Y
6 *Torkildsen*	Y	Y	Y	N	Y
7 Markey	Y	Y	Y	Y	Y
8 Kennedy	Y	Y	Y	Y	Y
9 Moakley	Y	Y	Y	Y	Y
10 Studds	Y	Y	Y	Y	Y
MICHIGAN					
1 Stupak	Y	Y	Y	N	Y
2 *Hoekstra*	Y	Y	N	N	Y
3 *Ehlers*	Y	Y	N	N	Y
4 *Camp*	Y	N	N	N	Y
5 Barcia	Y	Y	N	N	Y
6 *Upton*	Y	Y	Y	N	Y
7 *Smith*	Y	N	N	N	Y
8 Carr	?	Y	N	Y	Y
9 Kildee	Y	Y	Y	Y	Y
10 Bonior	Y	Y	Y	Y	Y
11 *Knollenberg*	Y	N	N	N	Y
12 Levin	Y	Y	Y	N	Y
13 Ford	Y	Y	Y	Y	Y
14 Conyers	Y	Y	Y	Y	Y
15 Collins	Y	Y	Y	Y	Y
16 Dingell	Y	Y	Y	?	Y
MINNESOTA					
1 Penny	Y	Y	Y	N	Y
2 Minge	Y	Y	Y	Y	Y
3 *Ramstad*	Y	N	N	N	Y
4 Vento	Y	Y	Y	Y	Y

	217	218	219	220	221
5 Sabo	Y	Y	Y	N	Y
6 *Grams*	Y	N	N	N	Y
7 Peterson	Y	Y	Y	N	Y
8 Oberstar	+	+	+	-	+
MISSISSIPPI					
1 Whitten	?	?	?	?	?
2 Thompson	Y	Y	N	N	Y
3 Montgomery	Y	Y	N	N	Y
4 Parker	Y	Y	N	N	Y
5 Taylor	Y	N	N	N	Y
MISSOURI					
1 Clay	Y	Y	Y	Y	Y
2 *Talent*	Y	N	Y	N	Y
3 Gephardt	Y	Y	Y	N	Y
4 Skelton	Y	N	N	N	Y
5 Wheat	Y	Y	Y	N	Y
6 Danner	Y	Y	Y	N	Y
7 *Hancock*	Y	N	N	N	Y
8 *Emerson*	Y	N	N	N	Y
9 Volkmer	Y	Y	Y	N	Y
MONTANA					
AL Williams	?	Y	Y	N	Y
NEBRASKA					
1 *Bereuter*	Y	N	N	N	Y
2 Hoagland	Y	Y	N	N	Y
3 *Barrett*	Y	N	N	N	Y
NEVADA					
1 Bilbray	Y	N	Y	N	Y
2 *Vucanovich*	Y	N	N	N	Y
NEW HAMPSHIRE					
1 *Zeliff*	Y	N	N	N	Y
2 Swett	Y	Y	N	N	Y
NEW JERSEY					
1 Andrews	Y	Y	Y	N	Y
2 Hughes	Y	Y	Y	N	Y
3 *Saxton*	Y	N	N	N	Y
4 *Smith*	Y	N	N	N	Y
5 *Roukema*	Y	N	N	N	Y
6 Pallone	Y	Y	Y	N	Y
7 *Franks*	Y	Y	Y	N	Y
8 Klein	Y	Y	Y	N	Y
9 Torricelli	Y	Y	Y	N	Y
10 Payne	Y	Y	Y	Y	Y
11 *Gallo*	Y	N	N	N	Y
12 *Zimmer*	Y	N	N	N	Y
13 Menendez	Y	Y	Y	N	Y
NEW MEXICO					
1 *Schiff*	Y	N	N	N	Y
2 *Skeen*	Y	N	N	N	Y
3 Richardson	Y	Y	Y	N	Y
NEW YORK					
1 Hochbrueckner	Y	Y	Y	N	Y
2 *Lazio*	Y	N	N	N	Y
3 *King*	Y	N	N	N	Y
4 *Levy*	Y	N	N	N	Y
5 Ackerman	Y	Y	Y	N	Y
6 Flake	Y	Y	Y	N	Y
7 Manton	Y	Y	Y	N	Y
8 Nadler	Y	Y	Y	Y	N
9 Schumer	Y	Y	Y	Y	Y
10 Towns	Y	Y	Y	Y	Y
11 Owens	Y	Y	Y	Y	Y
12 Velazquez	Y	Y	Y	Y	Y
13 *Molinari*	Y	N	Y	N	Y
14 Maloney	Y	Y	Y	Y	Y
15 Rangel	Y	Y	Y	Y	Y
16 Serrano	Y	Y	Y	Y	Y
17 Engel	Y	Y	Y	N	Y
18 Lowey	Y	Y	Y	N	Y
19 *Fish*	Y	Y	Y	N	Y
20 Gilman	Y	Y	Y	N	Y
21 McNulty	Y	Y	N	N	Y
22 *Solomon*	Y	N	N	N	Y
23 *Boehlert*	Y	N	N	N	Y
24 *McHugh*	Y	N	N	N	Y
25 *Walsh*	Y	N	N	N	Y
26 Hinchey	Y	Y	Y	Y	Y
27 *Paxon*	Y	N	N	N	Y
28 Slaughter	Y	Y	Y	N	Y
29 LaFalce	Y	Y	Y	N	Y
30 *Quinn*	Y	N	N	N	Y
31 Houghton	Y	N	Y	N	Y
NORTH CAROLINA					
1 Clayton	Y	Y	Y	N	Y
2 Valentine	Y	Y	Y	N	Y

	217	218	219	220	221
3 Lancaster	Y	Y	Y	N	Y
4 Price	Y	Y	Y	N	Y
5 Neal	Y	Y	Y	N	Y
6 *Coble*	Y	N	N	N	Y
7 Rose	Y	Y	Y	N	Y
8 Hefner	Y	Y	Y	N	Y
9 *McMillan*	Y	N	N	N	Y
10 *Ballenger*	Y	N	N	N	Y
11 *Taylor*	Y	N	N	N	Y
12 Watt	Y	Y	Y	Y	Y
NORTH DAKOTA					
AL Pomeroy	Y	Y	Y	N	Y
OHIO					
1 Mann	Y	Y	Y	N	Y
2 *Portman*	Y	N	N	N	Y
3 Hall	Y	Y	Y	N	Y
4 *Oxley*	Y	N	N	N	Y
5 *Gillmor*	Y	N	N	N	Y
6 Strickland	Y	Y	Y	N	Y
7 *Hobson*	Y	N	N	N	Y
8 *Boehner*	Y	N	N	N	Y
9 Kaptur	Y	Y	Y	N	Y
10 *Hoke*	Y	N	N	N	Y
11 Stokes	Y	Y	Y	Y	Y
12 *Kasich*	Y	N	N	N	Y
13 Brown	Y	Y	Y	N	Y
14 Sawyer	Y	Y	Y	N	Y
15 *Pryce*	Y	N	N	N	Y
16 *Regula*	Y	N	N	N	Y
17 Traficant	Y	Y	Y	N	Y
18 Applegate	Y	Y	Y	N	Y
19 Fingerhut	Y	Y	Y	N	Y
OKLAHOMA					
1 *Inhofe*	Y	N	N	N	Y
2 Synar	Y	Y	Y	N	Y
3 Brewster	Y	Y	N	N	Y
4 McCurdy	?	?	?	?	?
5 *Istook*	Y	N	N	N	Y
6 *Lucas*	Y	N	N	N	Y
OREGON					
1 Furse	Y	Y	Y	Y	Y
2 *Smith*	?	X	?	?	?
3 Wyden	Y	Y	Y	N	Y
4 DeFazio	Y	Y	Y	Y	Y
5 Kopetski	Y	Y	Y	N	Y
PENNSYLVANIA					
1 Foglietta	?	?	?	?	?
2 Blackwell	Y	Y	Y	N	Y
3 Borski	Y	Y	Y	N	Y
4 Klink	Y	Y	Y	N	Y
5 *Clinger*	+	-	-	-	+
6 Holden	Y	Y	N	N	Y
7 *Weldon*	Y	N	N	N	Y
8 *Greenwood*	Y	Y	Y	N	Y
9 *Shuster*	Y	N	N	N	Y
10 *McDade*	Y	N	N	N	Y
11 Kanjorski	Y	Y	Y	N	Y
12 Murtha	Y	Y	N	N	Y
13 Margolies-Mezv.	Y	Y	Y	Y	Y
14 Coyne	?	Y	Y	Y	Y
15 McHale	Y	Y	Y	N	Y
16 *Walker*	Y	N	N	N	Y
17 *Gekas*	Y	N	N	N	Y
18 *Santorum*	Y	N	N	N	Y
19 *Goodling*	Y	N	N	N	Y
20 Murphy	Y	Y	N	N	Y
21 *Ridge*	Y	N	Y	N	Y
RHODE ISLAND					
1 *Machtley*	Y	Y	Y	N	Y
2 Reed	Y	Y	Y	N	Y
SOUTH CAROLINA					
1 *Ravenel*	Y	N	Y	N	Y
2 *Spence*	Y	N	N	N	Y
3 Derrick	Y	Y	Y	N	Y
4 *Inglis*	Y	N	N	N	Y
5 Spratt	Y	Y	Y	N	Y
6 Clyburn	Y	Y	Y	N	Y
SOUTH DAKOTA					
AL Johnson	Y	Y	Y	N	Y
TENNESSEE					
1 *Quillen*	Y	N	N	N	Y
2 *Duncan*	Y	N	N	N	Y
3 Lloyd	Y	Y	Y	N	Y
4 Cooper	?	?	?	?	?
5 Clement	Y	Y	N	N	Y

	217	218	219	220	221
6 Gordon	Y	Y	Y	N	Y
7 *Sundquist*	Y	N	N	N	Y
8 Tanner	Y	Y	Y	N	Y
9 Ford	Y	Y	N	N	Y
TEXAS					
1 Chapman	Y	Y	Y	N	Y
2 Wilson	Y	Y	Y	N	Y
3 *Johnson, Sam*	Y	N	N	N	Y
4 Hall	Y	N	N	N	Y
5 Bryant	Y	Y	Y	Y	Y
6 *Barton*	Y	N	N	N	Y
7 *Archer*	Y	N	N	N	Y
8 *Fields*	Y	N	N	N	Y
9 Brooks	Y	N	Y	N	Y
10 Pickle	Y	Y	Y	N	Y
11 Edwards	Y	Y	Y	N	Y
12 Geren	Y	N	N	N	Y
13 Sarpalius	Y	Y	Y	N	Y
14 Laughlin	Y	Y	Y	N	Y
15 de la Garza	Y	Y	Y	N	Y
16 Coleman	Y	Y	Y	N	Y
17 Stenholm	Y	N	N	N	Y
18 Washington	?	?	?	?	?
19 *Combest*	Y	N	N	N	Y
20 Gonzalez	Y	Y	Y	Y	N
21 *Smith*	Y	N	N	N	Y
22 *DeLay*	Y	N	N	N	Y
23 *Bonilla*	Y	N	N	N	Y
24 Frost	Y	Y	N	N	Y
25 Andrews	Y	Y	Y	N	Y
26 *Armey*	Y	N	N	N	Y
27 Ortiz	Y	Y	Y	N	Y
28 Tejeda	Y	Y	Y	N	Y
29 Green	Y	Y	Y	N	Y
30 Johnson, E.B.	Y	Y	Y	N	Y
UTAH					
1 *Hansen*	Y	N	N	N	Y
2 Shepherd	Y	Y	Y	Y	Y
3 Orton	Y	Y	Y	N	Y
VERMONT					
AL *Sanders*	Y	Y	Y	Y	Y
VIRGINIA					
1 *Bateman*	Y	N	N	N	?
2 Pickett	Y	N	N	N	Y
3 Scott	?	?	?	?	?
4 Sisisky	Y	N	N	N	Y
5 Payne	Y	Y	Y	N	Y
6 *Goodlatte*	Y	N	N	N	Y
7 *Bliley*	Y	N	N	N	Y
8 Moran	Y	Y	Y	Y	Y
9 Boucher	Y	Y	Y	N	Y
10 *Wolf*	Y	N	N	N	Y
11 Byrne	Y	Y	Y	N	Y
WASHINGTON					
1 Cantwell	Y	Y	Y	N	Y
2 Swift	Y	Y	Y	N	Y
3 Unsoeld	Y	Y	Y	N	Y
4 Inslee	Y	Y	Y	N	Y
5 Foley					
6 Dicks	Y	Y	Y	N	Y
7 McDermott	Y	Y	Y	Y	Y
8 *Dunn*	Y	N	N	N	Y
9 Kreidler	Y	Y	Y	N	Y
WEST VIRGINIA					
1 Mollohan	Y	Y	Y	N	Y
2 Wise	Y	Y	Y	N	Y
3 Rahall	Y	Y	Y	N	Y
WISCONSIN					
1 Barca	Y	Y	Y	N	Y
2 *Klug*	Y	Y	Y	N	Y
3 *Gunderson*	Y	Y	Y	N	Y
4 Kleczka	Y	Y	Y	N	Y
5 Barrett	Y	Y	Y	N	Y
6 *Petri*	Y	N	N	N	Y
7 Obey	Y	Y	Y	N	Y
8 *Roth*	Y	N	N	N	Y
9 *Sensenbrenner*	Y	N	N	N	Y
WYOMING					
AL *Thomas*	+	-	X	X	+
DELEGATES					
de Lugo, V.I.	Y	Y	Y	Y	Y
Faleomavaega, Am.S.	?	?	?	?	?
Norton, D.C.	Y	Y	Y	Y	Y
Romero-B., P.R.	Y	Y	Y	Y	Y
Underwood, Guam	Y	Y	Y	Y	Y

Southern states - Ala., Ark., Fla., Ga., Ky., La., Miss., N.C., Okla., S.C., Tenn., Texas, Va.
Omitted votes are quorum calls, which CQ does not include in its vote charts.

222. HR 4301. Fiscal 1995 Defense Authorization/Bosnia Arms Embargo Unilateral Termination. McCloskey, D-Ind., amendment to require the president to terminate unilaterally the arms embargo of Bosnia-Herzegovina upon receipt from that government of a request for assistance in its right of self-defense, authorizing the president to provide up to $200 million in defense articles and services. Adopted in the Committee of the Whole 244-178: R 127-45; D 117-132 (ND 84-87, SD 33-45); I 0-1, June 9, 1994. A "nay" was a vote in support of the president's position.

223. HR 4301. Fiscal 1995 Defense Authorization/Bosnia Arms Embargo Consultation. Hamilton, D-Ind., amendment to urge the president to work with NATO allies and the United Nations Security Council to seek measures to enhance the ability of the people of Bosnia to provide for their defense, including lifting the arms embargo. Rejected in the Committee of the Whole 181-242: R 37-136; D 143-106 (ND 94-75, SD 49-31); I 1-0, June 9, 1994. A "yea" was a vote in support of the president's position.

224. HR 4301. Fiscal 1995 Defense Authorization/Haitian Policy. Separate vote at the request of Dellums, D-Calif., on the amendment offered by Goss, R-Fla., and adopted in the Committee of the Whole to express the sense of Congress that military action should not be undertaken in Haiti unless the president certifies a danger to U.S. citizens or interests, and that the United States, with the Organization of American States and the United Nations, should establish a safe haven for Haitian refugees on the Haitian island of Ile de la Gonave while assisting the legitimate Haitian government in establishing the long-term stability of democracy in Haiti. Rejected 195-226: R 171-3; D 24-222 (ND 9-156, SD 15-66); I 0-1, June 9, 1994. (On separate votes, which may be demanded on an amendment adopted in the Committee of the Whole, the four delegates and the resident commissioner of Puerto Rico cannot vote. See vote 197.)

225. HR 4301. Fiscal 1995 Defense Authorization/U.S. Troops Under U.N. Control. Michel, R-Ill., motion to recommit the bill to the Armed Services Committee with instructions to report it back with an amendment to limit the use of more than 100 U.S. troops under the command of a United Nations foreign national unless the president certifies it is necessary for national security, an emergency exists, or the U.S. troops maintain the right to decline orders judged to be illegal, militarily imprudent or beyond the mandate of the mission. Rejected 185-237: R 173-1; D 12-235 (ND 6-160, SD 6-75); I 0-1, June 9, 1994.

226. HR 4301. Fiscal 1995 Defense Authorization/Passage. Passage of the bill to authorize $263.3 billion in fiscal 1995 for defense programs. Passed 260-158: R 31-143; D 229-14 (ND 150-13, SD 79-1); I 0-1, June 9, 1994.

227. HR 4539. Fiscal 1995 Treasury-Postal Service Appropriations/Rule. Adoption of the rule (H Res 447) to provide for House floor consideration of the bill to provide $23,363,318,000 in new budget authority for the Treasury Department, the Postal Service, the Executive Office of the President, and certain independent agencies for fiscal 1995. The administration requested $24,569,399,000. Adopted 236-177: R 0-171; D 235-6 (ND 159-3, SD 76-3); I 1-0, June 9, 1994.

228. H Res 450. House Post Office Documents. Adoption of the resolution to require public release of all transcripts and relevant documents from the House Administration Committee's 1992 investigation of the House Post Office. A provision of the resolution calls for a designated member from each party to review the material; if both agree, they can block the release of any document. Members said this provision would prevent the release of trivial or irrelevant documents, matters of personal privacy or information given under pledges of confidentiality. Adopted 399-2: R 168-0; D 230-2 (ND 155-2, SD 75-0); I 1-0, June 9, 1994.

KEY

Y Voted for (yea).
Paired for.
+ Announced for.
N Voted against (nay).
X Paired against.
– Announced against.
P Voted "present."
C Voted "present" to avoid possible conflict of interest.
? Did not vote or otherwise make a position known.
D Delegates ineligible to vote.

Democrats *Republicans*
Independent

	222	223	224	225	226	227	228
ALABAMA							
1 *Callahan*	Y	N	Y	Y	N	N	Y
2 *Everett*	Y	N	Y	Y	N	N	Y
3 Browder	N	Y	N	N	Y	Y	Y
4 Bevill	N	Y	N	N	Y	Y	Y
5 Cramer	N	Y	N	N	Y	Y	Y
6 *Bachus*	N	N	Y	Y	N	N	Y
7 Hilliard	N	Y	N	N	Y	Y	Y
ALASKA							
AL *Young*	Y	N	Y	Y	N	N	Y
ARIZONA							
1 Coppersmith	Y	N	Y	N	Y	Y	Y
2 Pastor	Y	N	N	N	Y	Y	Y
3 *Stump*	Y	N	Y	N	N	N	Y
4 *Kyl*	Y	N	Y	N	N	N	Y
5 *Kolbe*	Y	N	Y	Y	N	N	Y
6 English	Y	N	N	N	Y	Y	Y
ARKANSAS							
1 Lambert	Y	Y	N	N	Y	Y	?
2 Thornton	N	Y	N	N	Y	Y	Y
3 *Hutchinson*	Y	N	Y	Y	N	N	Y
4 *Dickey*	Y	N	Y	Y	N	N	Y
CALIFORNIA							
1 Hamburg	N	Y	N	N	Y	Y	Y
2 *Herger*	N	Y	Y	Y	N	N	Y
3 Fazio	Y	N	N	N	Y	Y	Y
4 *Doolittle*	Y	N	Y	Y	N	N	Y
5 Matsui	N	Y	N	N	Y	Y	Y
6 Woolsey	N	Y	N	N	Y	Y	Y
7 Miller	N	Y	N	N	Y	Y	Y
8 Pelosi	N	N	N	N	Y	Y	Y
9 Dellums	N	Y	N	N	Y	Y	Y
10 *Baker*	N	Y	Y	Y	N	N	Y
11 *Pombo*	Y	N	Y	Y	N	N	Y
12 Lantos	Y	N	N	N	Y	Y	Y
13 Stark	N	Y	N	N	Y	Y	Y
14 Eshoo	N	N	N	N	Y	Y	Y
15 Mineta	N	Y	N	N	Y	Y	Y
16 Edwards	N	Y	N	N	Y	Y	Y
17 Farr	N	Y	N	N	Y	Y	Y
18 Condit	N	?	N	Y	N	Y	Y
19 Lehman	N	Y	N	N	+	Y	Y
20 Dooley	Y	N	N	N	Y	Y	Y
21 *Thomas*	Y	N	Y	Y	N	N	Y
22 *Huffington*	?	?	?	?	?	?	?
23 *Gallegly*	Y	N	Y	Y	Y	N	Y
24 Beilenson	Y	N	Y	N	Y	Y	Y
25 *McKeon*	Y	N	Y	Y	N	N	Y
26 Berman	Y	N	N	N	Y	Y	Y
27 *Moorhead*	Y	N	Y	Y	N	N	Y
28 *Dreier*	Y	N	Y	Y	N	N	Y
29 Waxman	N	Y	N	N	Y	Y	Y
30 Becerra	Y	N	N	N	Y	Y	Y
31 Martinez	Y	N	N	N	Y	Y	Y
32 Dixon	N	Y	N	N	Y	Y	Y
33 Roybal-Allard	N	Y	N	N	Y	Y	Y
34 Torres	N	Y	N	N	Y	Y	Y
35 Waters	Y	Y	N	N	Y	Y	Y
36 Harman	N	N	N	N	Y	Y	Y
37 Tucker	X	#	?	?	?	?	?
38 *Horn*	Y	N	Y	Y	Y	N	Y
39 *Royce*	?	?	?	?	?	?	?
40 *Lewis*	Y	N	Y	N	N	N	Y
41 *Kim*	Y	N	Y	N	N	N	Y

	222	223	224	225	226	227	228
42 Brown	N	Y	N	N	Y	Y	Y
43 *Calvert*	Y	N	Y	Y	N	N	Y
44 *McCandless*	Y	N	Y	Y	N	N	Y
45 *Rohrabacher*	Y	N	Y	Y	N	N	Y
46 *Dornan*	Y	N	Y	Y	N	N	Y
47 *Cox*	Y	N	Y	Y	N	N	Y
48 *Packard*	Y	N	Y	Y	N	N	?
49 Schenk	Y	N	N	N	Y	Y	Y
50 Filner	N	Y	N	N	Y	Y	Y
51 *Cunningham*	Y	N	Y	Y	N	N	Y
52 *Hunter*	Y	N	Y	Y	N	N	Y
COLORADO							
1 Schroeder	N	Y	N	N	Y	Y	Y
2 Skaggs	N	Y	N	N	Y	Y	Y
3 *McInnis*	Y	N	Y	Y	N	N	Y
4 *Allard*	Y	N	Y	Y	N	N	Y
5 *Hefley*	N	?	Y	Y	N	N	Y
6 *Schaefer*	Y	N	Y	Y	N	N	Y
CONNECTICUT							
1 Kennelly	Y	N	N	N	Y	Y	Y
2 Gejdenson	N	Y	N	N	Y	Y	Y
3 DeLauro	Y	N	N	N	Y	Y	Y
4 *Shays*	Y	N	Y	N	N	N	Y
5 *Franks*	Y	N	Y	N	N	N	Y
6 *Johnson*	N	Y	Y	Y	N	N	Y
DELAWARE							
AL *Castle*	Y	N	Y	Y	Y	N	Y
FLORIDA							
1 Hutto	N	Y	N	N	Y	Y	Y
2 Peterson	N	Y	N	N	Y	Y	Y
3 Brown	N	Y	N	N	Y	Y	Y
4 *Fowler*	N	Y	Y	Y	Y	N	Y
5 Thurman	Y	N	N	N	Y	Y	Y
6 *Stearns*	Y	N	Y	Y	N	N	Y
7 *Mica*	Y	N	Y	N	N	N	Y
8 *McCollum*	N	Y	Y	Y	N	N	Y
9 *Bilirakis*	N	Y	Y	Y	N	N	Y
10 *Young*	Y	N	Y	Y	N	N	Y
11 Gibbons	N	Y	N	N	Y	Y	Y
12 *Canady*	N	Y	Y	Y	N	N	Y
13 *Miller*	Y	N	Y	Y	N	N	Y
14 *Goss*	Y	N	Y	Y	N	N	Y
15 Bacchus	N	Y	N	N	Y	Y	Y
16 *Lewis*	Y	Y	Y	N	N	N	Y
17 Meek	N	N	N	N	Y	Y	Y
18 *Ros-Lehtinen*	Y	N	N	N	Y	N	Y
19 Johnston	N	Y	N	N	Y	Y	Y
20 Deutsch	N	Y	N	N	Y	Y	Y
21 *Diaz-Balart*	Y	N	N	N	Y	N	Y
22 *Shaw*	Y	N	Y	Y	N	N	Y
23 Hastings	Y	N	N	Y	?	?	?
GEORGIA							
1 *Kingston*	Y	N	Y	Y	N	N	Y
2 Bishop	N	N	N	N	Y	Y	Y
3 *Collins*	Y	N	Y	N	N	N	Y
4 *Linder*	Y	N	Y	Y	N	N	Y
5 Lewis	Y	N	N	N	Y	Y	Y
6 *Gingrich*	Y	N	Y	Y	N	N	Y
7 Darden	N	Y	N	N	Y	Y	Y
8 Rowland	N	Y	N	Y	Y	Y	Y
9 Deal	N	Y	N	N	Y	Y	Y
10 Johnson	N	Y	N	Y	Y	Y	Y
11 McKinney	N	Y	N	N	Y	Y	Y
HAWAII							
1 Abercrombie	Y	Y	N	N	Y	Y	Y
2 Mink	Y	Y	N	N	Y	Y	Y
IDAHO							
1 LaRocco	N	Y	N	N	Y	Y	Y
2 *Crapo*	Y	N	Y	N	N	N	Y
ILLINOIS							
1 Rush	Y	N	N	N	Y	Y	Y
2 Reynolds	N	Y	N	N	Y	Y	Y
3 Lipinski	Y	N	Y	N	Y	Y	Y
4 Gutierrez	Y	N	N	N	Y	Y	Y
5 Rostenkowski	N	Y	N	N	Y	Y	Y
6 *Hyde*	Y	N	Y	N	N	N	Y
7 Collins	N	Y	N	N	N	Y	Y
8 *Crane*	N	N	Y	N	N	N	Y
9 Yates	Y	Y	N	N	Y	Y	Y
10 *Porter*	Y	N	Y	Y	N	N	Y
11 Sangmeister	N	Y	N	N	Y	Y	Y
12 Costello	N	Y	N	N	Y	Y	Y
13 *Fawell*	Y	N	Y	Y	N	N	Y
14 *Hastert*	N	Y	Y	Y	N	N	Y
15 *Ewing*	Y	N	Y	Y	N	N	Y
16 *Manzullo*	N	Y	Y	Y	Y	N	Y
17 Evans	N	Y	N	N	Y	Y	Y

ND Northern Democrats   SD Southern Democrats

	222	223	224	225	226	227	228
18 ***Michel***	N	N	Y	Y	N	N	Y
19 Poshard	N	Y	N	N	Y	Y	Y
20 Durbin	N	Y	N	N	Y	Y	Y
INDIANA							
1 Visclosky	N	Y	N	N	Y	Y	Y
2 Sharp	Y	N	N	N	Y	Y	Y
3 Roemer	N	Y	N	N	Y	Y	Y
4 Long	Y	Y	N	N	Y	Y	Y
5 ***Buyer***	N	Y	Y	Y	N	N	Y
6 ***Burton***	Y	N	Y	Y	N	N	Y
7 ***Myers***	Y	N	Y	Y	N	N	Y
8 McCloskey	Y	N	N	N	Y	Y	Y
9 Hamilton	N	Y	N	N	Y	N	Y
10 Jacobs	N	Y	N	Y	Y	Y	Y
IOWA							
1 ***Leach***	Y	Y	Y	N	N	N	?
2 ***Nussle***	N	Y	Y	Y	N	N	Y
3 ***Lightfoot***	N	Y	Y	Y	N	N	Y
4 Smith	N	Y	N	N	Y	Y	Y
5 ***Grandy***	?	?	?	?	?	?	?
KANSAS							
1 ***Roberts***	Y	N	Y	Y	N	N	Y
2 Slattery	Y	?	?	?	?	?	?
3 ***Meyers***	Y	N	Y	Y	N	N	Y
4 Glickman	Y	N	N	N	Y	Y	Y
KENTUCKY							
1 Barlow	—	Y	N	N	Y	Y	Y
2 ***Lewis***	Y	N	Y	Y	N	N	Y
3 Mazzoli	N	Y	N	N	Y	Y	Y
4 ***Bunning***	Y	N	Y	Y	N	N	Y
5 ***Rogers***	Y	N	Y	Y	N	N	Y
6 Baesler	N	Y	Y	N	Y	Y	Y
LOUISIANA							
1 ***Livingston***	Y	N	Y	Y	N	N	Y
2 Jefferson	?	?	?	?	?	?	?
3 Tauzin	?	N	Y	Y	Y	Y	Y
4 Fields	Y	Y	N	N	Y	Y	Y
5 ***McCrery***	N	Y	Y	Y	N	N	Y
6 ***Baker***	Y	N	Y	Y	N	N	Y
7 Hayes	Y	N	Y	N	Y	N	Y
MAINE							
1 Andrews	N	Y	N	N	Y	Y	Y
2 ***Snowe***	Y	N	Y	Y	Y	N	Y
MARYLAND							
1 ***Gilchrest***	Y	N	Y	Y	Y	N	Y
2 ***Bentley***	N	Y	Y	Y	N	N	Y
3 Cardin	Y	N	N	N	Y	Y	Y
4 Wynn	Y	N	N	N	Y	Y	Y
5 Hoyer	Y	N	N	N	Y	Y	Y
6 ***Bartlett***	Y	N	Y	Y	N	N	Y
7 Mfume	Y	N	N	N	Y	Y	Y
8 ***Morella***	?	N	Y	Y	Y	N	Y
MASSACHUSETTS							
1 Olver	Y	N	N	N	Y	Y	Y
2 Neal	Y	N	N	N	Y	Y	Y
3 ***Blute***	Y	N	Y	Y	N	N	Y
4 Frank	Y	N	N	N	Y	Y	Y
5 Meehan	Y	N	N	N	Y	Y	Y
6 ***Torkildsen***	N	Y	Y	Y	N	N	Y
7 Markey	Y	N	N	N	Y	Y	Y
8 Kennedy	N	Y	N	N	Y	Y	Y
9 Moakley	N	Y	N	N	Y	?	?
10 Studds	N	Y	N	N	Y	Y	Y
MICHIGAN							
1 Stupak	N	Y	N	N	Y	Y	Y
2 ***Hoekstra***	Y	N	Y	Y	N	N	Y
3 ***Ehlers***	N	Y	Y	Y	N	N	Y
4 ***Camp***	Y	N	Y	Y	N	N	Y
5 Barcia	Y	Y	N	N	Y	Y	Y
6 ***Upton***	Y	N	Y	Y	Y	N	Y
7 ***Smith***	N	Y	Y	Y	N	N	Y
8 Carr	Y	N	N	N	Y	Y	?
9 Kildee	N	Y	N	N	Y	Y	Y
10 Bonior	Y	N	N	N	Y	Y	Y
11 ***Knollenberg***	N	N	Y	Y	N	N	Y
12 Levin	Y	N	N	N	Y	Y	Y
13 Ford	Y	Y	N	N	Y	Y	N
14 Conyers	N	Y	N	N	Y	Y	Y
15 Collins	#	?	?	?	?	?	?
16 Dingell	Y	N	Y	N	Y	Y	Y
MINNESOTA							
1 Penny	N	Y	N	N	Y	N	Y
2 Minge	N	Y	N	N	Y	Y	Y
3 ***Ramstad***	Y	N	Y	Y	N	N	Y
4 Vento	Y	Y	N	N	N	Y	Y

	222	223	224	225	226	227	228
5 Sabo	N	Y	N	N	Y	Y	Y
6 ***Grams***	Y	N	Y	Y	N	N	Y
7 Peterson	Y	N	Y	N	Y	Y	Y
8 Oberstar	N	Y	N	N	Y	Y	Y
MISSISSIPPI							
1 Whitten	?	Y	N	N	Y	?	?
2 Thompson	Y	N	N	N	Y	Y	Y
3 Montgomery	N	Y	N	N	Y	Y	Y
4 Parker	Y	N	N	N	Y	Y	Y
5 Taylor	N	Y	N	N	Y	N	Y
MISSOURI							
1 Clay	N	Y	N	N	Y	Y	Y
2 ***Talent***	Y	N	Y	Y	N	N	Y
3 Gephardt	N	Y	N	N	Y	Y	Y
4 Skelton	N	Y	N	N	Y	Y	?
5 Wheat	Y	N	N	N	Y	Y	Y
6 Danner	Y	N	Y	N	Y	Y	Y
7 ***Hancock***	N	Y	Y	Y	N	N	Y
8 ***Emerson***	N	Y	Y	Y	Y	N	Y
9 Volkmer	Y	N	N	N	Y	Y	Y
MONTANA							
AL Williams	N	Y	N	N	Y	Y	Y
NEBRASKA							
1 ***Bereuter***	Y	N	Y	Y	N	N	Y
2 Hoagland	N	Y	N	Y	Y	Y	Y
3 ***Barrett***	Y	N	Y	Y	N	N	Y
NEVADA							
1 Bilbray	Y	N	Y	N	Y	Y	Y
2 ***Vucanovich***	N	Y	Y	Y	N	N	Y
NEW HAMPSHIRE							
1 ***Zeliff***	Y	N	Y	Y	N	N	Y
2 Swett	Y	N	N	N	Y	Y	Y
NEW JERSEY							
1 Andrews	Y	N	Y	N	Y	Y	Y
2 Hughes	N	Y	N	N	Y	Y	Y
3 ***Saxton***	Y	N	Y	Y	N	N	Y
4 ***Smith***	Y	N	Y	Y	N	Y	Y
5 ***Roukema***	N	Y	Y	Y	N	N	Y
6 Pallone	Y	N	N	N	Y	Y	Y
7 ***Franks***	Y	N	Y	Y	N	N	Y
8 Klein	Y	N	?	N	Y	Y	Y
9 Torricelli	Y	N	N	N	Y	Y	Y
10 Payne	Y	Y	N	N	Y	Y	Y
11 ***Gallo***	Y	N	Y	Y	N	N	Y
12 ***Zimmer***	Y	N	Y	Y	N	N	Y
13 Menendez	Y	N	N	N	Y	Y	Y
NEW MEXICO							
1 ***Schiff***	Y	N	Y	Y	N	N	Y
2 ***Skeen***	Y	N	Y	Y	N	N	Y
3 Richardson	N	Y	N	N	Y	Y	Y
NEW YORK							
1 Hochbrueckner	N	Y	N	N	Y	Y	Y
2 ***Lazio***	Y	N	Y	Y	Y	N	Y
3 ***King***	Y	N	Y	Y	N	N	Y
4 ***Levy***	Y	N	Y	Y	N	N	Y
5 Ackerman	Y	N	N	N	Y	Y	Y
6 Flake	N	N	N	N	Y	Y	Y
7 Manton	Y	N	N	N	Y	Y	Y
8 Nadler	Y	N	N	N	N	?	?
9 Schumer	Y	N	N	N	Y	Y	Y
10 Towns	?	X	?	?	?	?	?
11 Owens	Y	N	N	N	Y	?	?
12 Velazquez	N	Y	N	N	Y	Y	Y
13 ***Molinari***	Y	N	Y	Y	N	N	Y
14 Maloney	Y	N	N	N	N	Y	Y
15 Rangel	N	Y	N	N	Y	?	?
16 Serrano	Y	N	N	N	Y	Y	Y
17 Engel	Y	N	N	N	Y	Y	Y
18 Lowey	Y	N	N	N	Y	Y	Y
19 ***Fish***	Y	N	Y	Y	N	N	?
20 ***Gilman***	Y	N	Y	Y	Y	N	Y
21 McNulty	Y	N	Y	Y	Y	Y	Y
22 ***Solomon***	Y	N	Y	Y	N	N	Y
23 ***Boehlert***	Y	N	Y	Y	N	N	Y
24 ***McHugh***	Y	N	Y	Y	N	N	Y
25 ***Walsh***	Y	N	Y	Y	N	N	Y
26 Hinchey	N	Y	N	N	Y	Y	Y
27 ***Paxon***	Y	N	Y	Y	N	N	Y
28 Slaughter	Y	N	N	N	Y	Y	Y
29 LaFalce	Y	Y	N	N	Y	Y	Y
30 ***Quinn***	Y	N	Y	Y	Y	N	Y
31 ***Houghton***	N	Y	Y	Y	Y	N	Y
NORTH CAROLINA							
1 Clayton	Y	N	N	N	+	Y	Y
2 Valentine	N	Y	Y	N	Y	Y	?

	222	223	224	225	226	227	228
3 Lancaster	Y	N	N	N	Y	Y	Y
4 Price	Y	N	N	N	Y	Y	Y
5 Neal	Y	N	N	N	Y	Y	Y
6 ***Coble***	Y	N	Y	Y	N	N	Y
7 Rose	N	Y	N	N	Y	Y	Y
8 Hefner	N	Y	N	N	Y	Y	Y
9 ***McMillan***	Y	N	Y	Y	Y	N	Y
10 ***Ballenger***	Y	N	Y	Y	N	N	Y
11 ***Taylor***	Y	N	Y	Y	N	N	Y
12 Watt	N	Y	N	N	Y	Y	Y
NORTH DAKOTA							
AL Pomeroy	N	Y	N	N	Y	Y	Y
OHIO							
1 Mann	N	Y	N	N	Y	Y	Y
2 ***Portman***	+	N	Y	Y	N	N	Y
3 Hall	Y	N	N	N	Y	Y	Y
4 ***Oxley***	Y	N	Y	Y	N	?	?
5 ***Gillmor***	Y	N	Y	Y	N	N	Y
6 Strickland	N	Y	N	N	?	Y	Y
7 ***Hobson***	Y	N	Y	Y	Y	N	Y
8 ***Boehner***	Y	N	Y	Y	N	N	Y
9 Kaptur	Y	Y	N	N	?	Y	Y
10 ***Hoke***	Y	N	Y	Y	N	N	Y
11 Stokes	N	Y	N	N	Y	Y	Y
12 ***Kasich***	Y	N	Y	Y	N	N	Y
13 Brown	Y	N	N	N	Y	Y	Y
14 Sawyer	Y	Y	N	N	Y	Y	Y
15 ***Pryce***	Y	N	Y	Y	N	N	Y
16 ***Regula***	Y	N	Y	Y	N	N	Y
17 Traficant	Y	N	N	Y	Y	N	Y
18 Applegate	N	Y	N	Y	Y	Y	Y
19 Fingerhut	Y	N	N	N	Y	Y	Y
OKLAHOMA							
1 ***Inhofe***	Y	N	Y	Y	N	N	Y
2 Synar	N	Y	N	N	Y	Y	Y
3 Brewster	N	Y	Y	Y	Y	Y	Y
4 McCurdy	Y	N	Y	Y	Y	Y	Y
5 ***Istook***	Y	N	Y	Y	N	N	Y
6 ***Lucas***	Y	N	Y	Y	N	N	Y
OREGON							
1 Furse	N	Y	N	N	Y	Y	Y
2 ***Smith***	N	Y	Y	Y	N	N	Y
3 Wyden	N	Y	N	N	N	Y	Y
4 DeFazio	N	Y	N	N	N	Y	Y
5 Kopetski	+	+	—	—	+	+	+
PENNSYLVANIA							
1 Foglietta	?	?	?	?	?	?	?
2 Blackwell	N	Y	N	N	Y	Y	Y
3 Borski	N	Y	N	N	Y	Y	Y
4 Klink	Y	N	N	N	Y	Y	Y
5 ***Clinger***	N	Y	Y	Y	N	N	Y
6 Holden	Y	N	N	N	Y	Y	Y
7 ***Weldon***	Y	N	Y	Y	Y	?	?
8 ***Greenwood***	Y	N	Y	Y	N	N	Y
9 ***Shuster***	N	Y	Y	Y	Y	N	Y
10 ***McDade***	N	Y	Y	Y	Y	N	Y
11 Kanjorski	N	Y	N	N	Y	Y	Y
12 Murtha	N	Y	N	N	Y	Y	?
13 Margolies-Mezv.	Y	N	N	N	N	Y	Y
14 Coyne	Y	N	N	N	Y	Y	Y
15 McHale	Y	N	N	N	Y	Y	Y
16 ***Walker***	Y	N	Y	Y	N	N	Y
17 ***Gekas***	Y	N	Y	Y	N	N	Y
18 ***Santorum***	Y	N	Y	Y	N	N	Y
19 ***Goodling***	N	Y	Y	Y	N	N	Y
20 Murphy	N	Y	N	N	Y	Y	Y
21 ***Ridge***	Y	N	Y	Y	Y	?	?
RHODE ISLAND							
1 ***Machtley***	Y	N	Y	Y	Y	N	Y
2 Reed	N	Y	N	N	Y	Y	Y
SOUTH CAROLINA							
1 ***Ravenel***	Y	N	Y	Y	Y	N	Y
2 ***Spence***	N	N	Y	Y	N	N	Y
3 Derrick	N	Y	N	N	Y	Y	Y
4 ***Inglis***	N	Y	Y	Y	N	N	Y
5 Spratt	Y	Y	N	N	Y	Y	Y
6 Clyburn	Y	N	N	N	Y	Y	Y
SOUTH DAKOTA							
AL Johnson	N	Y	N	N	Y	Y	Y
TENNESSEE							
1 ***Quillen***	Y	N	Y	Y	Y	N	Y
2 ***Duncan***	N	N	Y	Y	N	N	Y
3 Lloyd	N	Y	Y	N	Y	Y	Y
4 Cooper	N	Y	Y	Y	Y	N	Y
5 Clement	N	Y	N	N	Y	Y	Y

	222	223	224	225	226	227	228
6 Gordon	N	Y	N	N	Y	Y	Y
7 ***Sundquist***	?	?	?	?	?	?	?
8 Tanner	Y	Y	Y	N	Y	Y	Y
9 Ford	Y	N	N	N	Y	Y	Y
TEXAS							
1 Chapman	N	Y	N	N	Y	Y	Y
2 Wilson	Y	N	N	N	Y	Y	Y
3 ***Johnson, Sam***	N	Y	Y	Y	N	N	Y
4 Hall	N	Y	N	N	Y	Y	Y
5 Bryant	Y	N	N	N	Y	Y	?
6 ***Barton***	Y	N	Y	Y	N	N	Y
7 ***Archer***	N	N	Y	Y	N	N	Y
8 ***Fields***	N	N	Y	Y	N	N	Y
9 Brooks	N	Y	N	N	Y	Y	Y
10 Pickle	Y	N	N	N	Y	Y	Y
11 Edwards	N	Y	N	N	Y	Y	Y
12 Geren	Y	N	N	N	Y	Y	Y
13 Sarpalius	N	Y	N	N	Y	Y	Y
14 Laughlin	Y	N	N	N	Y	Y	?
15 de la Garza	Y	N	N	N	Y	Y	Y
16 Coleman	Y	N	N	N	Y	Y	Y
17 Stenholm	Y	N	N	Y	Y	Y	Y
18 Washington	?	?	?	?	?	?	?
19 ***Combest***	N	Y	Y	Y	N	N	Y
20 Gonzalez	N	Y	N	N	Y	Y	Y
21 ***Smith***	Y	N	Y	Y	N	N	Y
22 ***DeLay***	N	N	Y	Y	N	N	Y
23 ***Bonilla***	Y	N	Y	Y	N	N	Y
24 Frost	Y	N	N	N	Y	Y	Y
25 Andrews	N	Y	N	N	Y	Y	Y
26 ***Armey***	N	Y	Y	Y	N	N	Y
27 Ortiz	Y	N	N	N	Y	Y	Y
28 Tejeda	Y	N	N	N	Y	Y	Y
29 Green	N	Y	N	N	Y	Y	Y
30 Johnson, E.B.	Y	N	N	N	Y	Y	Y
UTAH							
1 ***Hansen***	Y	N	Y	Y	N	N	Y
2 Shepherd	N	Y	N	N	Y	Y	Y
3 Orton	N	Y	N	Y	Y	Y	+
VERMONT							
AL *Sanders*	N	Y	N	N	N	Y	Y
VIRGINIA							
1 ***Bateman***	N	Y	Y	Y	Y	N	Y
2 Pickett	Y	N	Y	N	Y	Y	Y
3 Scott	N	Y	N	N	Y	Y	Y
4 Sisisky	N	Y	N	N	Y	Y	Y
5 Payne	N	Y	N	N	Y	Y	Y
6 ***Goodlatte***	Y	N	Y	Y	N	N	Y
7 ***Bliley***	Y	N	Y	Y	Y	N	Y
8 Moran	Y	N	N	N	Y	Y	Y
9 Boucher	Y	?	Y	N	Y	Y	Y
10 ***Wolf***	Y	N	Y	Y	N	N	Y
11 Byrne	Y	N	N	N	Y	Y	Y
WASHINGTON							
1 Cantwell	N	Y	N	N	Y	Y	Y
2 Swift	Y	N	N	N	Y	Y	N
3 Unsoeld	N	Y	N	N	Y	Y	Y
4 Inslee	N	Y	N	N	Y	Y	Y
5 Foley							
6 Dicks	N	Y	N	N	Y	Y	?
7 McDermott	Y	N	N	N	Y	Y	Y
8 ***Dunn***	Y	N	Y	Y	N	N	Y
9 Kreidler	N	Y	N	N	Y	Y	Y
WEST VIRGINIA							
1 Mollohan	Y	N	N	N	Y	Y	Y
2 Wise	N	Y	N	N	Y	Y	Y
3 Rahall	Y	N	N	N	Y	Y	Y
WISCONSIN							
1 Barca	N	Y	N	N	N	Y	Y
2 ***Klug***	Y	N	Y	Y	N	N	Y
3 ***Gunderson***	Y	N	Y	Y	N	N	Y
4 Kleczka	N	Y	N	N	Y	Y	Y
5 Barrett	N	Y	N	N	N	Y	Y
6 ***Petri***	N	Y	Y	Y	N	N	Y
7 Obey	Y	N	N	N	Y	Y	Y
8 ***Roth***	N	Y	Y	Y	N	N	Y
9 ***Sensenbrenner***	Y	N	Y	Y	N	N	Y
WYOMING							
AL ***Thomas***	Y	N	Y	Y	N	N	Y
DELEGATES							
de Lugo, V.I.	Y	N	D	D	D	D	D
Faleomavaega, Am.S.	?	?	D	D	D	D	D
Norton, D.C.	N	Y	D	D	D	D	D
Romero-B., P.R.	Y	N	D	D	D	D	D
Underwood, Guam	N	Y	D	D	D	D	D

Southern states - Ala., Ark., Fla., Ga., Ky., La., Miss., N.C., Okla., S.C., Tenn., Texas, Va.
Omitted votes are quorum calls, which CQ does not include in its vote charts.

229. HR 518. California Desert Protection/China Lake Laser Facility. Thomas, R-Calif., amendment to allow construction of a space energy laser facility by the Navy on the China Lake Naval Air Warfare Center by removing the wilderness designation for 640 acres of the Argus Range. Before being adopted, the Thomas amendment was amended by a Miller, D-Calif., amendment to allow the secretary of the Interior to grant a right-of-way through the Argus Range for 15 years for construction of a road to facilitate access to the laser facility. Adopted in the Committee of the Whole 396-1: R 165-0; D 231-1 (ND 158-0, SD 73-1); I 0-0, June 10, 1994.

230. HR 518. California Desert Protection/Law Enforcement Vehicles. Hunter, R-Calif., amendment to ensure that nothing in the bill would impede law enforcement agencies from carrying out their duties, including allowing the use of law enforcement vehicles and aircraft in designated wilderness areas. Adopted in the Committee of the Whole 389-0: R 164-0; D 225-0 (ND 157-0, SD 68-0); I 0-0, June 10, 1994.

231. HR 518. California Desert Protection/Motorized Vehicle Use. Pombo, R-Calif., amendment to allow the continued use of motorized vehicles on 200 roads and trails in areas designated as wilderness by the bill. Rejected in the Committee of the Whole 169-191: R 135-20; D 34-171 (ND 16-133, SD 18-38); I 0-0, June 10, 1994.

232. HR 518. California Desert Protection/State Motorized Vehicles. McCandless, R-Calif., amendment to the Hunter, R-Calif., amendment to allow the use of authorized state motor vehicles in designated wilderness areas. The Hunter amendment would state that nothing in the bill affects California's jurisdiction over fish and wildlife management on public lands within the state. Adopted in the Committee of the Whole 360-0: R 151-0; D 208-0 (ND 138-0, SD 70-0); I 1-0, June 13, 1994.

233. HR 518. California Desert Protection/Substitute. Vento, D-Minn., substitute amendment to the Hunter, R-Calif., amendment, to give the Bureau of Land Management equal authority over fish and wildlife management as the state of California on public lands. The Hunter amendment would state that nothing in the bill affects California's jurisdiction over fish and wildlife management on public lands within the state. Rejected in the Committee of the Whole 183-189: R 18-139; D 164-50 (ND 121-21, SD 43-29); I 1-0, June 13, 1994.

234. HR 4506. Fiscal 1995 Energy and Water Appropriations/Helium Reactor. Byrne, D-Va., amendment to cut the $12 million earmarked for the continued development of the Gas Turbine-Modular Helium Reactor, a passively safe nuclear reactor for electricity production. The administration had requested no money for the project. Rejected in the Committee of the Whole 188-241: R 67-109; D 120-132 (ND 102-68, SD 18-64); I 1-0, June 14, 1994. A "yea" was a vote in support of the president's position.

235. HR 4506. Fiscal 1995 Energy and Water Appropriations/Passage. Passage of the bill to provide $20,355,622,000 in new budget authority for energy and water development for fiscal 1995. The administration had requested $20,512,750,000. Passed 393-29: R 148-27; D 244-2 (ND 162-2, SD 82-0); I 1-0, June 14, 1994.

236. HR 4539. Fiscal 1995 Treasury-Postal Service Appropriations/Executive Office of the President. Goss, R-Fla., amendment to cut the discretionary account of the Executive Office of the President by 20 percent except for the Office of National Drug Control Policy and Federal Drug Control Programs. Rejected in the Committee of the Whole 168-262: R 160-16; D 8-245 (ND 3-169, SD 5-76); I 0-1, June 15, 1994.

KEY

Y	Voted for (yea).
#	Paired for.
+	Announced for.
N	Voted against (nay).
X	Paired against.
−	Announced against.
P	Voted "present."
C	Voted "present" to avoid possible conflict of interest.
?	Did not vote or otherwise make a position known.
D	Delegates ineligible to vote.

Democrats *Republicans*
Independent

		229	230	231	232	233	234	235	236
ALABAMA									
1	Callahan	Y	Y	Y	Y	N	N	Y	Y
2	Everett	Y	Y	Y	Y	N	N	Y	Y
3	Browder	Y	Y	N	Y	N	N	Y	N
4	Bevill	?	?	?	Y	Y	N	Y	N
5	Cramer	Y	Y	N	Y	N	N	Y	N
6	Bachus	Y	Y	Y	Y	N	N	Y	Y
7	Hilliard	Y	?	?	Y	Y	N	Y	N
ALASKA									
AL	Young	Y	Y	Y	Y	N	N	Y	Y
ARIZONA									
1	Coppersmith	Y	Y	N	+	+	Y	Y	N
2	Pastor	Y	Y	N	Y	Y	N	Y	N
3	Stump	Y	Y	Y	Y	N	N	N	Y
4	Kyl	Y	Y	Y	Y	N	N	Y	Y
5	Kolbe	Y	Y	Y	Y	N	N	Y	Y
6	English	Y	Y	N	?	#	Y	Y	N
ARKANSAS									
1	Lambert	Y	Y	Y	Y	N	N	Y	N
2	Thornton	Y	Y	N	?	?	N	Y	N
3	Hutchinson	Y	Y	Y	Y	N	N	Y	Y
4	Dickey	Y	Y	?	Y	N	Y	Y	N
CALIFORNIA									
1	Hamburg	Y	Y	?	Y	Y	Y	Y	N
2	Herger	Y	Y	Y	Y	N	N	Y	Y
3	Fazio	Y	Y	N	Y	Y	N	Y	N
4	Doolittle	Y	Y	Y	Y	N	N	Y	Y
5	Matsui	Y	Y	N	Y	Y	N	Y	N
6	Woolsey	Y	Y	N	Y	Y	Y	Y	N
7	Miller	Y	Y	N	Y	Y	Y	Y	?
8	Pelosi	Y	Y	N	?	?	Y	Y	N
9	Dellums	Y	Y	N	Y	Y	Y	Y	N
10	Baker	Y	Y	#	Y	N	N	Y	Y
11	Pombo	Y	Y	Y	N	N	Y	Y	Y
12	Lantos	Y	Y	N	Y	Y	Y	Y	N
13	Stark	Y	Y	N	Y	Y	Y	Y	N
14	Eshoo	Y	Y	N	Y	Y	Y	Y	N
15	Mineta	Y	Y	N	Y	Y	Y	Y	N
16	Edwards	Y	Y	N	Y	Y	Y	Y	N
17	Farr	Y	Y	N	Y	Y	Y	Y	N
18	Condit	Y	Y	Y	Y	N	Y	Y	Y
19	Lehman	Y	Y	N	?	?	N	Y	N
20	Dooley	Y	Y	N	Y	Y	Y	Y	N
21	Thomas	Y	Y	Y	Y	N	N	Y	Y
22	Huffington	Y	Y	Y	Y	N	N	Y	N
23	Gallegly	Y	Y	Y	Y	N	N	Y	Y
24	Beilenson	Y	Y	N	Y	N	Y	Y	N
25	McKeon	Y	Y	Y	Y	N	N	Y	Y
26	Berman	Y	Y	N	Y	Y	Y	Y	N
27	Moorhead	Y	Y	Y	Y	N	N	Y	Y
28	Dreier	Y	Y	Y	Y	N	N	N	Y
29	Waxman	Y	Y	N	Y	Y	Y	Y	?
30	Becerra	Y	Y	N	Y	Y	Y	Y	N
31	Martinez	Y	Y	N	N	Y	N	Y	N
32	Dixon	Y	Y	N	Y	Y	Y	Y	N
33	Roybal-Allard	Y	Y	N	Y	Y	Y	Y	N
34	Torres	Y	Y	Y	Y	Y	Y	Y	N
35	Waters	Y	Y	N	Y	Y	Y	?	N
36	Harman	Y	Y	N	Y	N	N	Y	N
37	Tucker	?	?	X	Y	Y	Y	Y	N
38	Horn	Y	Y	Y	Y	N	Y	Y	N
39	Royce	?	?	?	?	?	?	?	Y
40	Lewis	Y	Y	Y	Y	N	N	Y	Y
41	Kim	Y	Y	Y	Y	N	N	Y	Y

		229	230	231	232	233	234	235	236
42	Brown	Y	Y	N	Y	Y	N	Y	?
43	Calvert	Y	Y	Y	Y	N	N	Y	Y
44	McCandless	Y	Y	Y	Y	N	N	Y	Y
45	Rohrabacher	Y	Y	Y	Y	N	N	Y	Y
46	Dornan	Y	Y	Y	Y	N	N	Y	Y
47	Cox	?	Y	Y	Y	N	N	Y	Y
48	Packard	?	?	?	?	?	N	Y	Y
49	Schenk	Y	Y	N	Y	N	Y	Y	?
50	Filner	Y	Y	N	Y	N	N	Y	N
51	Cunningham	Y	Y	Y	Y	N	N	Y	Y
52	Hunter	Y	Y	Y	Y	N	N	Y	Y
COLORADO									
1	Schroeder	Y	Y	N	Y	Y	Y	Y	N
2	Skaggs	Y	Y	N	Y	Y	N	Y	N
3	McInnis	Y	Y	Y	Y	N	Y	Y	Y
4	Allard	Y	Y	Y	Y	N	N	N	Y
5	Hefley	Y	Y	Y	N	Y	Y	Y	Y
6	Schaefer	Y	Y	?	Y	N	Y	Y	Y
CONNECTICUT									
1	Kennelly	Y	Y	N	Y	Y	Y	Y	N
2	Gejdenson	+	+	−	Y	Y	Y	Y	N
3	DeLauro	Y	Y	N	Y	Y	Y	Y	N
4	Shays	Y	Y	N	Y	N	Y	Y	Y
5	Franks	Y	Y	N	Y	N	Y	Y	Y
6	Johnson	Y	Y	Y	?	N	N	Y	Y
DELAWARE									
AL	Castle	Y	Y	Y	Y	N	Y	Y	Y
FLORIDA									
1	Hutto	Y	Y	Y	Y	N	N	Y	N
2	Peterson	Y	Y	N	Y	N	N	Y	N
3	Brown	Y	Y	N	Y	Y	N	Y	N
4	Fowler	Y	Y	Y	Y	N	N	Y	Y
5	Thurman	Y	Y	Y	Y	N	N	Y	N
6	Stearns	Y	Y	Y	Y	N	Y	Y	Y
7	Mica	Y	Y	Y	Y	N	N	Y	Y
8	McCollum	Y	Y	Y	?	N	N	N	Y
9	Bilirakis	Y	Y	#	Y	Y	N	Y	Y
10	Young	Y	Y	Y	?	N	Y	Y	Y
11	Gibbons	Y	Y	N	Y	N	Y	Y	N
12	Canady	Y	Y	Y	Y	N	Y	Y	Y
13	Miller	Y	Y	Y	Y	N	Y	N	?
14	Goss	Y	Y	Y	Y	N	Y	Y	Y
15	Bacchus	Y	?	?	Y	Y	N	Y	N
16	Lewis	Y	Y	Y	?	?	N	Y	Y
17	Meek	?	?	X	Y	Y	N	Y	N
18	Ros-Lehtinen	Y	Y	N	Y	Y	Y	Y	Y
19	Johnston	Y	?	?	Y	Y	N	Y	N
20	Deutsch	Y	Y	N	Y	Y	N	Y	N
21	Diaz-Balart	Y	Y	Y	N	N	Y	Y	Y
22	Shaw	Y	Y	Y	Y	N	N	Y	Y
23	Hastings	?	?	?	Y	Y	N	Y	N
GEORGIA									
1	Kingston	Y	Y	Y	Y	N	Y	Y	Y
2	Bishop	Y	?	?	Y	Y	N	Y	N
3	Collins	Y	Y	Y	Y	N	Y	N	Y
4	Linder	Y	Y	Y	Y	N	N	Y	Y
5	Lewis	Y	Y	N	Y	Y	N	Y	N
6	Gingrich	Y	Y	Y	?	?	N	Y	Y
7	Darden	Y	Y	N	Y	Y	N	Y	N
8	Rowland	Y	Y	Y	Y	N	N	Y	N
9	Deal	Y	Y	X	N	Y	N	Y	N
10	Johnson	Y	Y	N	Y	Y	N	Y	N
11	McKinney	Y	Y	N	Y	Y	Y	Y	N
HAWAII									
1	Abercrombie	Y	Y	N	Y	N	Y	Y	N
2	Mink	Y	Y	N	Y	Y	Y	Y	N
IDAHO									
1	LaRocco	Y	Y	N	Y	N	N	Y	N
2	Crapo	Y	Y	Y	Y	N	N	N	Y
ILLINOIS									
1	Rush	Y	Y	N	?	Y	Y	Y	N
2	Reynolds	Y	Y	N	?	?	?	?	?
3	Lipinski	Y	Y	Y	Y	N	Y	Y	N
4	Gutierrez	Y	Y	N	?	Y	Y	Y	N
5	Rostenkowski	Y	Y	N	?	N	Y	Y	N
6	Hyde	Y	Y	Y	Y	N	N	Y	Y
7	Collins	Y	Y	N	Y	Y	?	?	N
8	Crane	Y	Y	Y	Y	N	N	N	Y
9	Yates	Y	Y	N	Y	Y	Y	Y	N
10	Porter	Y	Y	Y	Y	Y	Y	Y	Y
11	Sangmeister	Y	Y	?	N	N	Y	Y	N
12	Costello	Y	Y	N	Y	N	Y	Y	N
13	Fawell	Y	Y	Y	Y	N	Y	Y	Y
14	Hastert	+	Y	Y	+	N	N	Y	Y
15	Ewing	Y	Y	Y	Y	N	N	Y	Y
16	Manzullo	Y	Y	?	Y	N	N	Y	Y
17	Evans	Y	Y	N	Y	Y	Y	Y	N

ND Northern Democrats   SD Southern Democrats

Member	229	230	231	232	233	234	235	236
18 ***Michel***	Y	Y	Y	Y	N	N	Y	?
19 Poshard	Y	Y	Y	Y	N	Y	Y	N
20 Durbin	Y	Y	N	Y	Y	N	Y	N
INDIANA								
1 Visclosky	Y	Y	N	Y	Y	N	Y	N
2 Sharp	?	Y	N	Y	Y	Y	Y	N
3 Roemer	Y	Y	N	Y	Y	N	Y	N
4 Long	Y	Y	N	Y	Y	Y	Y	N
5 ***Buyer***	Y	Y	Y	Y	N	N	Y	Y
6 ***Burton***	Y	Y	Y	Y	N	N	Y	Y
7 ***Myers***	Y	Y	Y	Y	N	N	Y	Y
8 McCloskey	Y	Y	N	Y	Y	N	Y	N
9 Hamilton	Y	Y	Y	Y	Y	Y	Y	Y
10 Jacobs	Y	Y	N	Y	Y	Y	N	Y
IOWA								
1 ***Leach***	Y	Y	N	Y	N	N	Y	Y
2 ***Nussle***	Y	Y	Y	Y	N	Y	Y	Y
3 ***Lightfoot***	Y	Y	Y	Y	N	Y	Y	N
4 Smith	Y	Y	?	Y	N	N	Y	N
5 ***Grandy***	?	?	?	Y	N	Y	Y	Y
KANSAS								
1 ***Roberts***	Y	?	?	?	?	Y	Y	Y
2 Slattery	?	?	X	?	?	?	#	N
3 ***Meyers***	Y	?	?	Y	Y	Y	Y	Y
4 Glickman	Y	Y	N	Y	?	Y	Y	N
KENTUCKY								
1 Barlow	Y	Y	N	Y	Y	N	Y	N
2 ***Lewis***	Y	Y	Y	Y	N	Y	Y	Y
3 Mazzoli	Y	Y	N	Y	Y	N	Y	N
4 ***Bunning***	Y	Y	Y	Y	N	Y	Y	Y
5 ***Rogers***	Y	Y	Y	Y	N	N	Y	Y
6 Baesler	Y	Y	Y	Y	N	N	Y	N
LOUISIANA								
1 ***Livingston***	Y	Y	Y	Y	N	N	Y	N
2 Jefferson	Y	Y	X	Y	Y	N	Y	N
3 Tauzin	Y	Y	?	Y	N	N	Y	Y
4 Fields	Y	Y	N	Y	Y	N	Y	N
5 ***McCrery***	Y	Y	Y	Y	N	Y	Y	Y
6 ***Baker***	Y	Y	Y	?	?	N	Y	Y
7 Hayes	Y	Y	Y	?	?	N	Y	N
MAINE								
1 Andrews	Y	Y	N	Y	Y	Y	Y	N
2 ***Snowe***	Y	Y	N	?	?	Y	Y	Y
MARYLAND								
1 ***Gilchrest***	Y	Y	N	Y	Y	Y	Y	Y
2 ***Bentley***	Y	Y	Y	Y	N	N	Y	Y
3 Cardin	Y	Y	N	Y	Y	N	Y	N
4 Wynn	Y	Y	N	Y	Y	Y	Y	N
5 Hoyer	Y	Y	N	Y	Y	N	Y	N
6 ***Bartlett***	Y	Y	Y	Y	N	N	Y	Y
7 Mfume	Y	Y	N	Y	N	Y	Y	N
8 ***Morella***	Y	Y	N	Y	Y	N	Y	Y
MASSACHUSETTS								
1 Olver	Y	Y	N	Y	Y	Y	Y	N
2 Neal	Y	Y	N	Y	Y	Y	Y	N
3 ***Blute***	Y	Y	Y	Y	N	Y	Y	Y
4 Frank	Y	Y	N	Y	Y	Y	Y	N
5 Meehan	Y	Y	?	Y	Y	Y	Y	N
6 ***Torkildsen***	Y	Y	Y	Y	N	Y	Y	Y
7 Markey	Y	Y	N	Y	Y	Y	Y	N
8 Kennedy	Y	Y	N	?	?	Y	Y	N
9 Moakley	?	?	?	Y	Y	N	Y	N
10 Studds	Y	Y	N	Y	Y	Y	Y	N
MICHIGAN								
1 Stupak	Y	Y	Y	+	–	Y	Y	N
2 ***Hoekstra***	Y	Y	Y	Y	N	Y	Y	Y
3 ***Ehlers***	Y	Y	Y	N	N	N	Y	Y
4 ***Camp***	Y	Y	Y	Y	N	Y	Y	Y
5 Barcia	Y	Y	Y	Y	N	Y	Y	N
6 ***Upton***	Y	Y	Y	Y	N	Y	Y	Y
7 ***Smith***	Y	Y	Y	Y	N	Y	N	Y
8 Carr	Y	Y	Y	?	?	N	Y	N
9 Kildee	Y	Y	N	Y	Y	Y	Y	N
10 Bonior	Y	Y	N	Y	Y	N	Y	N
11 ***Knollenberg***	Y	Y	Y	Y	N	N	N	Y
12 Levin	Y	Y	N	Y	Y	Y	Y	N
13 Ford	Y	Y	N	?	?	N	Y	N
14 Conyers	Y	Y	?	Y	Y	?	?	N
15 Collins	?	?	X	?	?	N	Y	N
16 Dingell	Y	Y	Y	?	?	N	Y	N
MINNESOTA								
1 Penny	Y	Y	+	Y	N	Y	Y	N
2 Minge	Y	Y	N	Y	Y	Y	N	N
3 ***Ramstad***	Y	Y	N	Y	Y	Y	N	Y
4 Vento	Y	Y	N	Y	Y	Y	Y	N
5 Sabo	Y	Y	N	?	?	Y	Y	N
6 ***Grams***	Y	Y	?	?	N	N	N	Y
7 Peterson	Y	Y	N	Y	N	Y	Y	N
8 Oberstar	Y	Y	N	Y	Y	Y	Y	N
MISSISSIPPI								
1 Whitten	?	?	?	?	?	N	Y	?
2 Thompson	Y	?	?	Y	Y	N	Y	N
3 Montgomery	Y	Y	?	Y	N	N	Y	N
4 Parker	Y	Y	?	?	N	N	Y	N
5 Taylor	Y	Y	Y	Y	N	N	Y	Y
MISSOURI								
1 Clay	?	?	?	?	?	N	Y	N
2 ***Talent***	Y	Y	Y	Y	N	Y	Y	Y
3 Gephardt	Y	Y	?	Y	Y	N	Y	N
4 Skelton	?	?	?	Y	N	N	Y	N
5 Wheat	Y	?	?	?	?	?	?	N
6 Danner	Y	Y	Y	?	?	?	?	N
7 ***Hancock***	Y	Y	Y	Y	N	Y	N	Y
8 ***Emerson***	Y	Y	Y	Y	N	N	Y	Y
9 Volkmer	Y	Y	N	?	?	N	Y	N
MONTANA								
AL Williams	?	Y	N	Y	Y	Y	Y	N
NEBRASKA								
1 ***Bereuter***	Y	Y	Y	Y	N	N	Y	N
2 Hoagland	Y	Y	N	Y	Y	Y	Y	N
3 ***Barrett***	Y	Y	Y	Y	N	N	Y	Y
NEVADA								
1 Bilbray	Y	Y	N	Y	Y	N	Y	N
2 ***Vucanovich***	Y	Y	Y	Y	N	N	Y	Y
NEW HAMPSHIRE								
1 ***Zeliff***	Y	Y	Y	?	?	Y	N	Y
2 Swett	Y	Y	N	?	?	Y	Y	N
NEW JERSEY								
1 Andrews	Y	Y	N	Y	Y	Y	Y	N
2 Hughes	Y	Y	N	Y	Y	N	Y	N
3 ***Saxton***	Y	Y	N	Y	Y	N	Y	Y
4 ***Smith***	Y	Y	N	Y	N	N	Y	Y
5 ***Roukema***	Y	Y	N	Y	Y	N	Y	Y
6 Pallone	Y	Y	N	Y	Y	Y	Y	N
7 ***Franks***	Y	Y	N	Y	Y	N	Y	Y
8 Klein	Y	Y	N	Y	Y	Y	Y	N
9 Torricelli	Y	Y	N	?	?	N	Y	N
10 Payne	Y	Y	N	?	?	Y	Y	N
11 ***Gallo***	Y	Y	Y	Y	N	N	Y	Y
12 ***Zimmer***	Y	Y	N	Y	Y	N	Y	Y
13 Menendez	Y	Y	N	Y	Y	Y	Y	N
NEW MEXICO								
1 ***Schiff***	Y	Y	Y	Y	N	N	Y	N
2 ***Skeen***	Y	Y	Y	Y	N	N	Y	N
3 Richardson	Y	Y	N	Y	Y	Y	Y	N
NEW YORK								
1 Hochbrueckner	Y	Y	N	?	?	N	Y	N
2 ***Lazio***	Y	Y	Y	Y	N	N	Y	Y
3 ***King***	Y	Y	Y	Y	N	N	Y	Y
4 ***Levy***	Y	Y	Y	Y	N	N	Y	Y
5 Ackerman	Y	Y	N	Y	Y	N	Y	N
6 Flake	?	?	?	?	?	?	Y	N
7 Manton	Y	Y	N	Y	Y	N	Y	N
8 Nadler	Y	Y	N	Y	Y	Y	Y	N
9 Schumer	?	?	?	Y	Y	Y	Y	N
10 Towns	Y	Y	N	?	?	N	Y	N
11 Owens	Y	Y	N	?	?	N	Y	N
12 Velazquez	Y	Y	N	?	?	N	Y	N
13 ***Molinari***	Y	Y	Y	Y	N	N	Y	Y
14 Maloney	Y	Y	N	?	Y	Y	Y	N
15 Rangel	?	?	X	?	#	N	Y	N
16 Serrano	Y	Y	N	?	Y	N	Y	N
17 Engel	Y	Y	N	?	Y	Y	Y	N
18 Lowey	Y	Y	N	?	?	Y	Y	N
19 ***Fish***	Y	Y	N	Y	Y	Y	Y	Y
20 ***Gilman***	Y	Y	N	Y	Y	Y	Y	Y
21 McNulty	Y	Y	?	Y	Y	N	Y	N
22 ***Solomon***	?	?	?	Y	N	N	N	Y
23 ***Boehlert***	Y	Y	?	Y	Y	Y	Y	Y
24 ***McHugh***	Y	Y	Y	Y	N	Y	X	Y
25 ***Walsh***	Y	Y	?	Y	N	N	Y	N
26 Hinchey	Y	Y	N	Y	Y	Y	Y	N
27 ***Paxon***	Y	Y	Y	Y	N	Y	N	Y
28 Slaughter	Y	Y	N	Y	Y	Y	Y	N
29 LaFalce	Y	Y	N	Y	Y	Y	Y	N
30 ***Quinn***	Y	Y	Y	Y	N	Y	Y	Y
31 ***Houghton***	Y	Y	Y	Y	N	N	Y	Y
NORTH CAROLINA								
1 Clayton	Y	Y	N	Y	Y	N	Y	N
2 Valentine	Y	Y	Y	Y	Y	N	Y	N
3 Lancaster	Y	Y	N	Y	Y	Y	Y	N
4 Price	Y	Y	N	Y	Y	N	Y	N
5 Neal	Y	Y	N	?	?	N	Y	N
6 ***Coble***	Y	Y	Y	Y	Y	N	N	Y
7 Rose	Y	Y	N	Y	N	N	Y	N
8 Hefner	Y	Y	N	Y	Y	N	Y	N
9 ***McMillan***	Y	Y	Y	Y	N	N	Y	Y
10 ***Ballenger***	+	+	+	Y	N	N	Y	Y
11 ***Taylor***	Y	Y	#	Y	N	N	Y	Y
12 Watt	Y	Y	N	Y	Y	Y	Y	N
NORTH DAKOTA								
AL Pomeroy	Y	Y	N	Y	Y	N	Y	N
OHIO								
1 Mann	Y	Y	N	Y	Y	Y	Y	N
2 ***Portman***	Y	Y	Y	Y	N	Y	Y	Y
3 Hall	Y	Y	?	Y	Y	Y	Y	N
4 ***Oxley***	Y	Y	Y	Y	Y	Y	Y	Y
5 ***Gillmor***	Y	Y	Y	Y	N	Y	Y	N
6 Strickland	Y	Y	Y	Y	N	Y	Y	N
7 ***Hobson***	Y	Y	Y	Y	N	Y	Y	Y
8 ***Boehner***	Y	Y	Y	Y	N	Y	N	Y
9 Kaptur	Y	Y	Y	Y	Y	Y	Y	N
10 ***Hoke***	Y	Y	Y	Y	N	Y	Y	Y
11 Stokes	Y	Y	?	Y	Y	N	Y	N
12 ***Kasich***	Y	Y	Y	Y	N	Y	Y	Y
13 Brown	Y	Y	N	Y	Y	Y	Y	N
14 Sawyer	Y	Y	N	Y	Y	N	Y	N
15 ***Pryce***	Y	Y	Y	?	?	Y	Y	Y
16 ***Regula***	Y	Y	Y	Y	Y	N	Y	Y
17 Traficant	Y	Y	Y	Y	N	N	Y	N
18 Applegate	Y	Y	Y	Y	N	N	Y	N
19 Fingerhut	Y	Y	N	Y	Y	Y	Y	N
OKLAHOMA								
1 ***Inhofe***	Y	Y	Y	?	?	Y	Y	Y
2 Synar	Y	Y	N	Y	Y	Y	Y	N
3 Brewster	Y	Y	Y	Y	N	Y	Y	N
4 McCurdy	?	?	?	?	?	N	Y	N
5 ***Istook***	Y	Y	Y	Y	N	Y	Y	N
6 ***Lucas***	Y	Y	Y	Y	N	N	Y	Y
OREGON								
1 Furse	Y	Y	N	?	?	Y	Y	N
2 ***Smith***	Y	Y	Y	Y	N	N	Y	Y
3 Wyden	Y	Y	N	Y	Y	Y	Y	N
4 DeFazio	Y	Y	N	Y	Y	Y	Y	N
5 Kopetski	Y	Y	N	+	–	Y	Y	N
PENNSYLVANIA								
1 Foglietta	?	?	?	Y	Y	N	Y	N
2 Blackwell	?	?	?	?	?	Y	Y	N
3 Borski	Y	Y	N	Y	Y	N	Y	N
4 Klink	Y	Y	N	Y	Y	Y	Y	N
5 ***Clinger***	Y	Y	Y	Y	N	N	Y	Y
6 Holden	Y	Y	N	Y	Y	Y	Y	N
7 ***Weldon***	?	?	?	Y	N	Y	Y	Y
8 ***Greenwood***	Y	Y	Y	Y	N	Y	Y	Y
9 ***Shuster***	?	?	?	Y	N	N	Y	Y
10 ***McDade***	Y	Y	Y	Y	N	N	Y	N
11 Kanjorski	Y	Y	N	Y	Y	Y	Y	N
12 Murtha	?	?	?	Y	Y	N	?	N
13 Margolies-Mezv.	Y	Y	N	Y	Y	Y	Y	N
14 Coyne	Y	Y	N	Y	Y	Y	Y	N
15 McHale	Y	Y	N	Y	Y	Y	Y	N
16 ***Walker***	Y	Y	Y	Y	N	N	Y	Y
17 ***Gekas***	Y	Y	Y	Y	N	N	Y	Y
18 ***Santorum***	Y	Y	Y	?	?	N	Y	Y
19 ***Goodling***	Y	Y	Y	Y	N	Y	Y	Y
20 Murphy	Y	?	?	Y	Y	N	Y	N
21 ***Ridge***	?	?	?	?	?	N	Y	Y
RHODE ISLAND								
1 ***Machtley***	?	?	?	?	?	Y	Y	Y
2 Reed	Y	Y	N	Y	Y	Y	Y	N
SOUTH CAROLINA								
1 ***Ravenel***	Y	Y	N	?	?	Y	Y	Y
2 ***Spence***	Y	Y	Y	Y	N	N	Y	Y
3 Derrick	Y	Y	N	?	?	N	Y	N
4 ***Inglis***	Y	Y	Y	Y	N	N	N	Y
5 Spratt	Y	Y	?	Y	Y	N	Y	N
6 Clyburn	Y	Y	N	Y	Y	N	Y	N
SOUTH DAKOTA								
AL Johnson	Y	Y	N	Y	Y	Y	Y	N
TENNESSEE								
1 ***Quillen***	Y	Y	#	Y	N	N	Y	Y
2 ***Duncan***	Y	Y	Y	Y	N	Y	N	Y
3 Lloyd	Y	Y	?	Y	N	N	Y	N
4 Cooper	?	?	?	?	?	Y	Y	N
5 Clement	Y	Y	N	Y	Y	N	Y	N
6 Gordon	Y	Y	N	Y	Y	N	Y	N
7 ***Sundquist***	?	?	?	?	?	?	?	Y
8 Tanner	Y	Y	#	Y	N	Y	Y	N
9 Ford	Y	Y	N	?	?	N	Y	N
TEXAS								
1 Chapman	Y	Y	Y	Y	N	N	Y	N
2 Wilson	Y	Y	Y	Y	N	N	Y	N
3 ***Johnson, Sam***	Y	Y	Y	Y	N	N	Y	Y
4 Hall	Y	Y	Y	Y	N	Y	Y	Y
5 Bryant	Y	Y	N	Y	Y	Y	Y	N
6 ***Barton***	?	?	#	?	X	N	Y	Y
7 ***Archer***	Y	Y	Y	Y	N	N	Y	Y
8 ***Fields***	Y	?	?	?	N	N	Y	Y
9 Brooks	Y	Y	N	Y	Y	N	Y	N
10 Pickle	Y	?	?	Y	N	N	Y	N
11 Edwards	Y	Y	Y	Y	N	N	Y	N
12 Geren	Y	Y	Y	Y	N	N	Y	N
13 Sarpalius	Y	Y	?	Y	N	N	Y	N
14 Laughlin	?	?	?	Y	N	N	Y	N
15 de la Garza	Y	Y	N	Y	N	N	Y	Y
16 Coleman	Y	Y	?	Y	Y	N	Y	N
17 Stenholm	Y	Y	Y	Y	N	Y	Y	Y
18 Washington	?	?	?	?	?	?	?	?
19 ***Combest***	Y	Y	Y	Y	N	N	Y	Y
20 Gonzalez	N	Y	N	Y	Y	N	Y	N
21 ***Smith***	Y	Y	Y	Y	N	N	Y	Y
22 ***DeLay***	Y	Y	Y	?	?	N	Y	Y
23 ***Bonilla***	Y	Y	Y	Y	N	N	Y	Y
24 Frost	?	?	?	?	?	N	Y	N
25 Andrews	Y	Y	N	?	?	Y	Y	N
26 ***Armey***	Y	Y	Y	Y	N	N	N	Y
27 Ortiz	Y	Y	Y	Y	N	N	Y	N
28 Tejeda	Y	Y	Y	Y	N	N	Y	N
29 Green	Y	Y	Y	?	?	N	Y	N
30 Johnson, E.B.	Y	Y	N	Y	Y	N	Y	N
UTAH								
1 ***Hansen***	Y	Y	Y	?	?	N	Y	Y
2 Shepherd	Y	Y	N	Y	Y	Y	Y	N
3 Orton	+	+	#	Y	N	N	Y	N
VERMONT								
AL *Sanders*	?	?	?	Y	Y	Y	Y	N
VIRGINIA								
1 ***Bateman***	Y	Y	Y	Y	N	N	Y	N
2 Pickett	Y	Y	?	Y	N	N	Y	N
3 Scott	Y	Y	N	Y	Y	N	Y	N
4 Sisisky	Y	Y	?	Y	N	N	Y	N
5 Payne	Y	Y	N	Y	N	Y	Y	N
6 ***Goodlatte***	Y	Y	Y	Y	N	Y	Y	Y
7 ***Bliley***	Y	Y	Y	Y	N	N	Y	Y
8 Moran	Y	Y	N	Y	Y	N	Y	N
9 Boucher	Y	Y	N	Y	Y	N	Y	N
10 ***Wolf***	Y	Y	Y	Y	N	N	Y	Y
11 Byrne	Y	Y	N	Y	Y	Y	Y	N
WASHINGTON								
1 Cantwell	Y	Y	N	Y	Y	Y	Y	N
2 Swift	Y	Y	N	Y	Y	N	Y	N
3 Unsoeld	Y	Y	N	Y	Y	Y	Y	N
4 Inslee	Y	Y	N	Y	Y	N	Y	N
5 Foley								
6 Dicks	?	?	N	Y	N	N	Y	N
7 McDermott	Y	Y	N	Y	Y	N	Y	N
8 ***Dunn***	Y	Y	Y	Y	N	N	Y	Y
9 Kreidler	Y	Y	N	Y	Y	Y	Y	N
WEST VIRGINIA								
1 Mollohan	Y	Y	N	Y	Y	N	Y	N
2 Wise	Y	Y	N	?	?	N	Y	N
3 Rahall	Y	Y	N	Y	Y	N	Y	N
WISCONSIN								
1 Barca	Y	Y	N	Y	Y	Y	Y	N
2 ***Klug***	Y	Y	N	Y	Y	N	Y	Y
3 ***Gunderson***	Y	Y	Y	Y	N	N	Y	Y
4 Kleczka	Y	?	N	+	+	Y	Y	N
5 Barrett	Y	Y	N	Y	Y	Y	Y	N
6 ***Petri***	Y	Y	Y	Y	N	Y	N	Y
7 Obey	Y	Y	?	Y	Y	Y	Y	N
8 ***Roth***	Y	Y	Y	?	X	Y	N	Y
9 ***Sensenbrenner***	Y	Y	Y	Y	N	Y	N	Y
WYOMING								
AL ***Thomas***	Y	Y	Y	?	?	N	Y	Y
DELEGATES								
de Lugo, V.I.	Y	Y	N	Y	Y	N	D	N
Faleomavaega, Am.S.	?	?	?	Y	Y	Y	D	N
Norton, D.C.	Y	Y	N	Y	Y	N	D	N
Romero-B., P.R.	?	?	?	Y	Y	Y	D	N
Underwood, Guam	Y	Y	N	Y	Y	Y	D	N

Southern states - Ala., Ark., Fla., Ga., Ky., La., Miss., N.C., Okla., S.C., Tenn., Texas, Va.
Omitted votes are quorum calls, which CQ does not include in its vote charts.

KEY

Y Voted for (yea).
Paired for.
+ Announced for.
N Voted against (nay).
X Paired against.
— Announced against.
P Voted "present."
C Voted "present" to avoid possible conflict of interest.
? Did not vote or otherwise make a position known.
D Delegates ineligible to vote.

Democrats *Republicans*
Independent

---

237. HR 4539. Fiscal 1995 Treasury-Postal Service Appropriations/White House Salaries and Expenses. Burton, R-Ind., amendment to cut $5 million from the White House salaries and expenses account. Rejected in the Committee of the Whole 147-287: R 143-34; D 4-252 (ND 3-173, SD 1-79); I 0-1, June 15, 1994.

238. HR 4539. Fiscal 1995 Treasury-Postal Service Appropriations/Golf Helicopter Trip. Bartlett, R-Md., amendment to cut the appropriation for the Office of the White House by $13,129.66, the cost of an unauthorized trip by White House staff on a presidential helicopter to play golf. Rejected in the Committee of the Whole 195-236: R 174-2; D 21-233 (ND 16-159, SD 5-74); I 0-1, June 15, 1994.

239. HR 4539. Fiscal 1995 Treasury-Postal Service Appropriations/Executive Office of the President. Hefley, R-Colo., amendment to cut the appropriation for the Executive Office of the President except the Office of National Drug Control Policy and Federal Drug Control Programs by 5 percent or about $7 million. Rejected in the Committee of the Whole 200-236: R 174-3; D 26-232 (ND 14-162, SD 12-70); I 0-1, June 15, 1994.

240. HR 4539. Fiscal 1995 Treasury-Postal Service Appropriations/Intergovernmental Relations Commission. Istook, R-Okla., amendment to eliminate the $1 million in the bill for the Advisory Commission on Intergovernmental Relations. Adopted in the Committee of the Whole 223-210: R 158-20; D 64-190 (ND 47-126, SD 17-64); I 1-0, June 15, 1994.

241. HR 4539. Fiscal 1995 Treasury-Postal Service Appropriations/Federal Election Commission. Livingston, R-La., amendment to cut the appropriation for the Federal Election Commission by $3.5 million to the fiscal 1994 level. Adopted in the Committee of the Whole 231-197: R 172-4; D 59-192 (ND 33-138, SD 26-54); I 0-1, June 15, 1994.

242. HR 4539. Fiscal 1995 Treasury-Postal Service Appropriations/Courthouse Construction. Pomeroy, D-N.D., substitute amendment to the Istook, R-Okla., amendment to cut $5.6 million from the appropriation for the construction of 13 new courthouses. The Istook amendment would have cut $32 million from 19 projects. Adopted in the Committee of the Whole 302-120: R 67-107; D 234-13 (ND 163-7, SD 71-6); I 1-0, June 15, 1994.

243. HR 4539. Fiscal 1995 Treasury-Postal Service Appropriations/Courthouse Construction. Istook, R-Okla., amendment, as amended by the Pomeroy, D-N.D., amendment, to cut $5.6 million from the appropriation for the construction of 13 new courthouses. Before being amended the Istook amendment would have cut $32 million from 19 projects. Adopted in the Committee of the Whole 393-22: R 159-12; D 233-10 (ND 162-4, SD 71-6); I 1-0, June 15, 1994.

244. HR 4539. Fiscal 1995 Treasury-Postal Service Appropriations/New Courthouses. Fawell, R-Ill., amendment to eliminate $15.8 million for three new courthouse projects in Albany, Ga.; Steubenville, Ohio; and Corpus Christi, Texas. Rejected in the Committee of the Whole 145-271: R 132-40; D 13-230 (ND 11-155, SD 2-75); I 0-1, June 15, 1994.

	237	238	239	240	241	242	243	244
ALABAMA								
1 *Callahan*	N	Y	Y	N	Y	N	Y	N
2 *Everett*	N	Y	Y	N	Y	Y	Y	N
3 Browder	N	N	N	Y	N	Y	Y	N
4 Bevill	N	N	N	N	Y	Y	Y	N
5 Cramer	N	N	N	N	Y	Y	Y	N
6 *Bachus*	Y	Y	?	Y	Y	N	Y	Y
7 Hilliard	N	N	N	N	Y	Y	Y	N
ALASKA								
AL *Young*	Y	Y	Y	Y	Y	Y	Y	N
ARIZONA								
1 Coppersmith	N	N	N	N	N	Y	Y	N
2 Pastor	N	N	N	N	N	Y	Y	N
3 *Stump*	Y	Y	Y	Y	Y	N	Y	Y
4 *Kyl*	Y	Y	Y	Y	Y	N	Y	Y
5 *Kolbe*	N	Y	Y	Y	Y	Y	Y	N
6 English	N	N	N	N	N	Y	Y	N
ARKANSAS								
1 Lambert	N	N	Y	N	Y	N	Y	N
2 Thornton	?	?	N	N	Y	N	Y	N
3 *Hutchinson*	Y	?	N	Y	Y	Y	Y	Y
4 *Dickey*	?	?	N	Y	Y	Y	Y	Y
CALIFORNIA								
1 Hamburg	N	N	N	N	N	Y	Y	N
2 *Herger*	Y	Y	Y	Y	Y	N	Y	Y
3 Fazio	N	N	N	N	N	Y	Y	N
4 *Doolittle*	Y	Y	Y	Y	Y	N	Y	Y
5 Matsui	N	N	N	N	N	Y	Y	N
6 Woolsey	N	N	N	N	N	Y	Y	N
7 Miller	N	N	N	N	N	Y	Y	N
8 Pelosi	N	N	N	N	N	Y	Y	N
9 Dellums	N	N	N	N	N	Y	Y	N
10 *Baker*	Y	Y	Y	Y	Y	N	Y	Y
11 *Pombo*	Y	Y	Y	Y	Y	Y	Y	Y
12 Lantos	N	N	N	N	N	Y	Y	N
13 Stark	N	N	N	Y	N	Y	Y	N
14 Eshoo	N	N	N	N	N	Y	Y	N
15 Mineta	N	N	N	N	N	Y	Y	N
16 Edwards	N	N	N	N	N	?	?	N
17 Farr	N	N	N	N	N	Y	Y	N
18 Condit	N	N	Y	Y	Y	Y	Y	Y
19 Lehman	N	N	N	Y	Y	Y	Y	N
20 Dooley	N	N	N	N	N	Y	Y	?
21 *Thomas*	Y	Y	Y	Y	Y	Y	Y	?
22 *Huffington*	Y	Y	Y	Y	Y	Y	Y	Y
23 *Gallegly*	Y	Y	Y	Y	Y	N	Y	N
24 Beilenson	N	N	N	N	N	Y	Y	N
25 *McKeon*	Y	Y	Y	Y	Y	N	Y	N
26 Berman	N	N	N	N	N	Y	Y	?
27 *Moorhead*	Y	Y	Y	Y	Y	N	Y	Y
28 *Dreier*	Y	Y	Y	Y	Y	N	Y	Y
29 Waxman	N	N	N	N	N	Y	?	N
30 Becerra	N	N	N	N	N	Y	Y	N
31 Martinez	N	N	N	N	N	Y	Y	N
32 Dixon	N	N	N	N	N	Y	Y	N
33 Roybal-Allard	N	N	N	N	N	Y	Y	N
34 Torres	N	N	N	N	N	?	?	?
35 Waters	N	N	N	N	N	Y	Y	N
36 Harman	N	Y	N	N	N	Y	Y	N
37 Tucker	N	N	N	N	N	Y	Y	N
38 *Horn*	Y	Y	Y	Y	Y	Y	Y	N
39 *Royce*	Y	Y	Y	Y	Y	N	Y	Y
40 *Lewis*	Y	Y	Y	Y	Y	N	N	Y
41 *Kim*	Y	Y	Y	Y	Y	Y	Y	Y
42 Brown	N	N	N	N	Y	Y	Y	N
43 *Calvert*	Y	Y	Y	Y	Y	Y	Y	Y
44 *McCandless*	Y	Y	Y	Y	Y	?	?	Y
45 *Rohrabacher*	Y	Y	Y	Y	Y	Y	Y	Y
46 *Dornan*	Y	Y	Y	Y	Y	Y	Y	?
47 *Cox*	Y	Y	Y	Y	Y	Y	Y	Y
48 *Packard*	N	Y	Y	Y	Y	Y	Y	N
49 Schenk	N	N	N	Y	N	Y	Y	N
50 Filner	N	N	N	N	N	Y	Y	N
51 *Cunningham*	N	Y	Y	Y	Y	Y	?	N
52 *Hunter*	N	Y	Y	Y	Y	Y	?	Y
COLORADO								
1 Schroeder	N	N	N	N	Y	Y	Y	N
2 Skaggs	N	N	N	N	N	Y	Y	N
3 *McInnis*	Y	Y	Y	Y	Y	Y	Y	Y
4 *Allard*	Y	Y	Y	Y	Y	N	Y	Y
5 *Hefley*	N	Y	Y	Y	Y	N	Y	N
6 *Schaefer*	Y	Y	Y	Y	Y	N	Y	N
CONNECTICUT								
1 Kennelly	N	N	N	N	X	Y	Y	N
2 Gejdenson	N	N	N	N	N	Y	Y	N
3 DeLauro	N	N	N	N	N	Y	Y	N
4 *Shays*	Y	Y	Y	Y	Y	Y	Y	Y
5 *Franks*	Y	Y	Y	Y	Y	Y	Y	N
6 *Johnson*	N	Y	Y	N	Y	Y	Y	N
DELAWARE								
AL *Castle*	Y	Y	Y	N	Y	N	Y	Y
FLORIDA								
1 Hutto	N	Y	Y	N	Y	Y	Y	N
2 Peterson	N	N	N	N	N	Y	Y	N
3 Brown	N	N	N	N	N	N	N	N
4 *Fowler*	Y	Y	Y	N	Y	N	N	?
5 Thurman	N	Y	Y	N	Y	Y	Y	N
6 *Stearns*	Y	Y	Y	Y	Y	N	Y	N
7 *Mica*	Y	Y	Y	Y	Y	N	N	Y
8 *McCollum*	Y	Y	Y	Y	Y	N	Y	N
9 *Bilirakis*	N	Y	Y	N	Y	Y	Y	N
10 *Young*	Y	Y	Y	Y	Y	N	Y	N
11 Gibbons	N	N	N	N	N	Y	Y	N
12 *Canady*	Y	Y	Y	Y	Y	N	Y	Y
13 *Miller*	Y	Y	Y	Y	Y	N	Y	N
14 *Goss*	Y	Y	Y	Y	Y	N	Y	Y
15 Bacchus	N	N	N	N	N	Y	N	N
16 *Lewis*	Y	Y	Y	Y	Y	N	Y	Y
17 Meek	N	N	N	N	N	N	N	N
18 *Ros-Lehtinen*	Y	Y	Y	Y	Y	Y	Y	Y
19 Johnston	N	N	N	N	N	Y	Y	N
20 Deutsch	N	N	N	N	Y	Y	Y	N
21 *Diaz-Balart*	N	Y	Y	N	Y	Y	Y	Y
22 *Shaw*	Y	Y	Y	Y	Y	N	Y	N
23 Hastings	N	N	N	N	N	Y	Y	N
GEORGIA								
1 *Kingston*	Y	Y	Y	Y	Y	Y	Y	N
2 Bishop	N	N	N	N	N	N	N	N
3 *Collins*	Y	Y	Y	Y	Y	Y	Y	N
4 *Linder*	Y	Y	Y	Y	Y	N	Y	N
5 Lewis	N	N	N	N	N	Y	Y	N
6 *Gingrich*	Y	Y	Y	N	Y	N	?	?
7 Darden	N	N	N	N	N	Y	Y	N
8 Rowland	N	N	Y	Y	Y	Y	Y	N
9 Deal	N	N	N	Y	Y	Y	Y	N
10 Johnson	N	N	N	N	N	Y	Y	N
11 McKinney	N	N	N	N	N	N	N	N
HAWAII								
1 Abercrombie	N	N	N	N	Y	Y	Y	N
2 Mink	N	N	N	N	Y	Y	Y	N
IDAHO								
1 LaRocco	N	N	N	N	N	Y	Y	N
2 *Crapo*	Y	Y	Y	Y	Y	N	Y	Y
ILLINOIS								
1 Rush	N	N	N	?	Y	Y	Y	N
2 Reynolds	?	?	?	?	?	?	?	?
3 Lipinski	N	N	N	N	N	Y	Y	N
4 Gutierrez	N	N	N	N	N	Y	Y	N
5 Rostenkowski	N	N	N	?	N	Y	Y	N
6 *Hyde*	Y	Y	Y	Y	Y	N	Y	Y
7 Collins	N	N	N	N	N	Y	Y	N
8 *Crane*	Y	Y	Y	Y	Y	Y	Y	Y
9 Yates	N	N	N	N	N	Y	Y	N
10 *Porter*	N	Y	Y	Y	Y	Y	Y	N
11 Sangmeister	N	N	N	N	N	Y	Y	N
12 Costello	N	N	Y	N	Y	Y	Y	N
13 *Fawell*	Y	Y	Y	Y	Y	Y	Y	Y
14 *Hastert*	Y	Y	Y	Y	Y	N	Y	N
15 *Ewing*	Y	Y	Y	Y	Y	N	Y	N
16 *Manzullo*	Y	Y	Y	Y	Y	N	Y	Y
17 Evans	N	N	N	N	N	Y	Y	N

ND Northern Democrats SD Southern Democrats

	237	238	239	240	241	242	243	244
18 ***Michel***	Y	Y	Y	Y	Y	?	?	Y
19 Poshard	N	Y	Y	Y	Y	Y	Y	N
20 Durbin	N	N	N	N	N	Y	Y	N
INDIANA								
1 Visclosky	N	N	N	Y	N	Y	Y	N
2 Sharp	N	N	N	?	?	?	?	?
3 Roemer	N	Y	Y	Y	Y	Y	Y	N
4 Long	N	N	N	N	N	Y	Y	N
5 ***Buyer***	N	Y	Y	Y	Y	Y	Y	Y
6 ***Burton***	Y	Y	Y	Y	Y	N	Y	Y
7 ***Myers***	Y	Y	Y	Y	Y	N	Y	N
8 McCloskey	N	N	N	N	N	Y	Y	N
9 Hamilton	Y	Y	Y	N	Y	Y	Y	N
10 Jacobs	Y	N	Y	Y	Y	N	Y	N
IOWA								
1 ***Leach***	Y	Y	Y	Y	Y	N	Y	Y
2 ***Nussle***	Y	Y	Y	Y	Y	N	Y	Y
3 ***Lightfoot***	N	Y	Y	Y	Y	N	Y	N
4 Smith	N	N	N	N	N	Y	Y	N
5 ***Grandy***	Y	Y	Y	Y	Y	Y	Y	Y
KANSAS								
1 ***Roberts***	Y	Y	Y	Y	Y	Y	Y	Y
2 Slattery	N	Y	N	N	N	Y	Y	Y
3 ***Meyers***	Y	Y	Y	Y	N	Y	Y	Y
4 Glickman	N	Y	N	Y	N	Y	Y	?
KENTUCKY								
1 Barlow	N	N	N	N	N	Y	Y	N
2 ***Lewis***	Y	Y	Y	Y	Y	N	N	Y
3 Mazzoli	N	N	N	N	N	Y	Y	N
4 ***Bunning***	Y	Y	Y	Y	Y	N	N	Y
5 ***Rogers***	Y	Y	Y	Y	Y	N	N	N
6 Baesler	N	N	N	N	N	Y	Y	N
LOUISIANA								
1 ***Livingston***	Y	Y	Y	Y	Y	N	Y	N
2 Jefferson	N	N	N	N	N	Y	Y	N
3 Tauzin	N	N	Y	Y	Y	Y	Y	?
4 Fields	N	N	N	N	N	Y	Y	N
5 ***McCrery***	Y	Y	Y	Y	Y	N	Y	Y
6 ***Baker***	Y	Y	Y	Y	Y	Y	Y	Y
7 Hayes	N	N	Y	Y	Y	Y	Y	N
MAINE								
1 Andrews	N	N	N	Y	N	Y	Y	Y
2 ***Snowe***	Y	Y	Y	Y	Y	Y	Y	Y
MARYLAND								
1 ***Gilchrest***	N	Y	Y	Y	Y	N	Y	Y
2 ***Bentley***	Y	Y	Y	Y	Y	N	Y	Y
3 Cardin	N	N	N	N	N	Y	Y	N
4 Wynn	N	N	N	N	N	Y	Y	N
5 Hoyer	N	N	N	N	N	Y	Y	N
6 ***Bartlett***	Y	Y	Y	Y	Y	N	Y	Y
7 Mfume	N	N	N	N	N	Y	Y	N
8 ***Morella***	N	Y	Y	N	Y	Y	Y	Y
MASSACHUSETTS								
1 Olver	N	N	N	N	N	Y	Y	N
2 Neal	N	N	N	Y	N	Y	Y	N
3 ***Blute***	N	Y	Y	N	Y	Y	Y	Y
4 Frank	N	N	N	N	N	Y	Y	N
5 Meehan	N	Y	N	Y	Y	Y	Y	N
6 ***Torkildsen***	N	Y	Y	Y	Y	Y	Y	Y
7 Markey	N	N	N	Y	N	Y	Y	N
8 Kennedy	N	N	N	N	N	Y	Y	N
9 Moakley	N	N	N	N	N	Y	Y	N
10 Studds	N	N	N	Y	N	Y	Y	N
MICHIGAN								
1 Stupak	N	N	N	Y	N	Y	Y	N
2 ***Hoekstra***	Y	Y	Y	Y	Y	N	Y	Y
3 ***Ehlers***	N	Y	Y	Y	Y	Y	Y	Y
4 ***Camp***	Y	Y	Y	Y	Y	N	Y	Y
5 Barcia	N	Y	N	Y	Y	Y	Y	N
6 ***Upton***	Y	Y	Y	Y	Y	N	Y	Y
7 ***Smith***	N	Y	Y	Y	Y	N	Y	Y
8 Carr	N	N	N	N	N	Y	Y	N
9 Kildee	N	Y	N	N	N	Y	Y	N
10 Bonior	N	N	N	N	N	Y	?	N
11 ***Knollenberg***	Y	Y	Y	Y	Y	N	Y	Y
12 Levin	N	N	N	N	N	Y	Y	N
13 Ford	N	N	N	?	Y	?	?	?
14 Conyers	N	N	N	N	N	Y	Y	N
15 Collins	N	N	N	N	N	Y	Y	N
16 Dingell	N	N	N	N	N	Y	Y	N
MINNESOTA								
1 Penny	Y	N	Y	Y	Y	Y	Y	Y
2 Minge	N	N	Y	Y	N	Y	Y	N
3 ***Ramstad***	Y	Y	Y	Y	Y	N	Y	Y
4 Vento	N	N	N	N	N	Y	Y	N

	237	238	239	240	241	242	243	244
5 Sabo	N	N	N	N	N	Y	Y	N
6 ***Grams***	Y	Y	Y	N	Y	N	Y	Y
7 Peterson	N	N	Y	Y	Y	Y	Y	N
8 Oberstar	N	N	N	N	N	Y	Y	N
MISSISSIPPI								
1 Whitten	N	N	N	N	N	?	?	?
2 Thompson	N	N	N	N	N	Y	Y	N
3 Montgomery	N	N	N	N	Y	Y	Y	N
4 Parker	N	N	N	Y	Y	Y	Y	N
5 Taylor	N	Y	Y	Y	Y	Y	Y	N
MISSOURI								
1 Clay	N	N	N	N	N	Y	?	N
2 ***Talent***	Y	Y	Y	Y	Y	Y	Y	Y
3 Gephardt	N	N	N	N	N	Y	Y	N
4 Skelton	N	N	N	Y	Y	Y	Y	N
5 Wheat	N	N	N	N	N	Y	Y	N
6 Danner	N	N	N	Y	N	Y	Y	Y
7 ***Hancock***	Y	Y	Y	Y	Y	N	Y	Y
8 ***Emerson***	N	Y	Y	Y	Y	Y	Y	Y
9 Volkmer	N	N	N	Y	Y	Y	Y	N
MONTANA								
AL Williams	N	N	N	N	Y	Y	Y	N
NEBRASKA								
1 ***Bereuter***	Y	Y	Y	N	Y	N	Y	Y
2 Hoagland	N	Y	Y	Y	N	Y	Y	Y
3 ***Barrett***	Y	Y	Y	Y	Y	N	Y	Y
NEVADA								
1 Bilbray	N	N	N	N	Y	Y	Y	N
2 ***Vucanovich***	Y	Y	Y	Y	Y	N	N	N
NEW HAMPSHIRE								
1 ***Zeliff***	Y	Y	Y	Y	Y	N	Y	Y
2 Swett	N	N	N	N	N	Y	Y	N
NEW JERSEY								
1 Andrews	N	N	N	Y	N	N	Y	Y
2 Hughes	N	N	N	N	N	Y	Y	N
3 ***Saxton***	Y	Y	Y	Y	Y	N	Y	?
4 ***Smith***	Y	Y	Y	Y	Y	Y	Y	N
5 ***Roukema***	Y	Y	Y	Y	Y	Y	Y	Y
6 Pallone	N	N	N	Y	N	Y	Y	Y
7 ***Franks***	Y	Y	Y	Y	N	N	Y	Y
8 Klein	N	N	N	N	N	Y	Y	N
9 Torricelli	N	N	N	Y	Y	Y	?	N
10 Payne	N	N	N	N	N	Y	Y	N
11 ***Gallo***	Y	Y	Y	Y	Y	Y	Y	N
12 ***Zimmer***	Y	Y	Y	Y	Y	N	Y	Y
13 Menendez	N	N	N	N	N	Y	Y	N
NEW MEXICO								
1 ***Schiff***	N	Y	N	N	Y	Y	Y	Y
2 ***Skeen***	Y	Y	Y	Y	Y	Y	Y	N
3 Richardson	N	N	N	N	N	Y	Y	N
NEW YORK								
1 Hochbrueckner	N	N	N	N	N	Y	N	N
2 ***Lazio***	Y	Y	Y	N	Y	N	N	N
3 ***King***	Y	Y	Y	Y	Y	N	Y	Y
4 ***Levy***	Y	Y	Y	Y	Y	N	Y	Y
5 Ackerman	N	N	N	N	N	Y	N	X
6 Flake	N	N	N	N	N	Y	Y	N
7 Manton	N	N	N	N	Y	Y	Y	N
8 Nadler	N	N	N	N	N	Y	Y	N
9 Schumer	N	N	N	Y	N	Y	Y	N
10 Towns	N	N	N	N	N	N	Y	N
11 Owens	N	N	N	Y	N	Y	Y	N
12 Velazquez	N	N	N	N	N	Y	Y	N
13 ***Molinari***	Y	Y	Y	Y	Y	Y	Y	Y
14 Maloney	N	Y	N	N	N	Y	Y	Y
15 Rangel	N	N	N	N	N	Y	Y	N
16 Serrano	N	N	N	N	N	Y	N	N
17 Engel	N	N	N	N	N	Y	Y	N
18 Lowey	N	?	N	N	N	N	Y	N
19 ***Fish***	N	Y	Y	N	?	?	?	?
20 ***Gilman***	Y	Y	Y	Y	Y	Y	Y	N
21 McNulty	N	N	N	N	N	Y	Y	N
22 ***Solomon***	Y	Y	Y	Y	Y	N	Y	Y
23 ***Boehlert***	Y	Y	Y	Y	Y	Y	Y	Y
24 ***McHugh***	Y	Y	Y	Y	Y	N	Y	Y
25 ***Walsh***	Y	Y	Y	Y	Y	Y	Y	N
26 Hinchey	N	N	N	N	N	Y	Y	N
27 ***Paxon***	Y	Y	Y	Y	Y	N	Y	Y
28 Slaughter	N	N	N	N	N	Y	?	N
29 LaFalce	N	N	N	N	Y	Y	Y	Y
30 ***Quinn***	N	N	Y	Y	Y	Y	Y	Y
31 ***Houghton***	N	N	Y	Y	Y	Y	Y	N
NORTH CAROLINA								
1 Clayton	N	N	N	N	N	Y	Y	N
2 Valentine	N	N	N	Y	N	Y	Y	N

	237	238	239	240	241	242	243	244
3 Lancaster	N	N	N	N	N	Y	Y	N
4 Price	N	N	N	N	N	Y	Y	N
5 Neal	N	N	N	N	?	?	?	?
6 ***Coble***	Y	Y	Y	Y	Y	N	Y	Y
7 Rose	N	N	N	Y	N	Y	Y	N
8 Hefner	N	N	N	N	N	Y	Y	N
9 ***McMillan***	N	Y	Y	Y	Y	Y	Y	N
10 ***Ballenger***	Y	Y	Y	Y	Y	N	Y	Y
11 ***Taylor***	Y	Y	Y	Y	Y	N	Y	Y
12 Watt	N	N	N	N	Y	Y	Y	N
NORTH DAKOTA								
AL Pomeroy	N	N	N	Y	N	Y	Y	N
OHIO								
1 Mann	N	N	Y	Y	N	Y	Y	N
2 ***Portman***	Y	Y	Y	Y	Y	N	Y	Y
3 Hall	N	N	N	Y	Y	Y	Y	N
4 ***Oxley***	Y	Y	Y	Y	Y	N	Y	Y
5 ***Gillmor***	N	Y	Y	Y	N	Y	Y	N
6 Strickland	N	N	N	Y	N	Y	Y	N
7 ***Hobson***	Y	Y	Y	Y	Y	Y	Y	N
8 ***Boehner***	Y	Y	Y	Y	Y	N	Y	Y
9 Kaptur	N	N	Y	N	N	Y	Y	N
10 ***Hoke***	Y	Y	Y	Y	Y	N	N	N
11 Stokes	N	N	N	N	N	Y	Y	N
12 ***Kasich***	Y	Y	Y	Y	Y	Y	Y	Y
13 Brown	N	N	N	N	N	Y	Y	N
14 Sawyer	N	N	N	N	N	Y	Y	N
15 ***Pryce***	Y	Y	Y	Y	Y	Y	Y	Y
16 ***Regula***	N	Y	Y	Y	Y	Y	Y	N
17 Traficant	N	N	N	N	Y	Y	Y	N
18 Applegate	N	N	N	N	N	Y	Y	?
19 Fingerhut	N	Y	N	Y	N	Y	Y	N
OKLAHOMA								
1 ***Inhofe***	Y	Y	Y	Y	Y	N	Y	Y
2 Synar	N	N	N	N	N	Y	Y	N
3 Brewster	N	N	N	Y	Y	Y	Y	N
4 McCurdy	N	Y	Y	Y	Y	?	?	Y
5 ***Istook***	N	Y	Y	Y	Y	N	Y	Y
6 ***Lucas***	Y	Y	Y	Y	Y	N	Y	Y
OREGON								
1 Furse	N	Y	N	Y	Y	Y	Y	N
2 ***Smith***	Y	Y	Y	Y	Y	Y	Y	Y
3 Wyden	N	N	N	Y	Y	Y	Y	N
4 DeFazio	N	N	N	Y	N	Y	Y	N
5 Kopetski	N	N	N	N	N	Y	Y	N
PENNSYLVANIA								
1 Foglietta	N	N	N	N	N	Y	Y	N
2 Blackwell	N	N	N	N	?	Y	Y	N
3 Borski	N	N	N	N	N	Y	Y	N
4 Klink	N	N	N	N	Y	Y	Y	N
5 ***Clinger***	N	Y	Y	N	Y	Y	Y	Y
6 Holden	N	N	N	N	Y	Y	Y	N
7 ***Weldon***	Y	Y	Y	Y	Y	Y	Y	Y
8 ***Greenwood***	Y	Y	Y	Y	Y	N	Y	Y
9 ***Shuster***	Y	Y	Y	Y	Y	Y	Y	Y
10 ***McDade***	N	Y	Y	Y	Y	N	N	?
11 Kanjorski	N	N	N	N	N	?	Y	N
12 Murtha	N	N	N	N	N	N	Y	N
13 Margolies-Mezv.	N	N	Y	Y	Y	N	Y	Y
14 Coyne	N	N	N	N	N	Y	Y	N
15 McHale	N	Y	N	Y	Y	Y	Y	N
16 ***Walker***	Y	Y	Y	N	Y	N	Y	Y
17 ***Gekas***	Y	Y	Y	Y	Y	N	Y	Y
18 ***Santorum***	Y	Y	Y	Y	Y	Y	Y	Y
19 ***Goodling***	N	Y	Y	N	N	Y	Y	Y
20 Murphy	N	N	N	N	Y	Y	Y	N
21 ***Ridge***	Y	Y	Y	Y	Y	Y	Y	Y
RHODE ISLAND								
1 ***Machtley***	Y	Y	Y	Y	Y	Y	Y	N
2 Reed	N	N	N	N	N	Y	Y	N
SOUTH CAROLINA								
1 ***Ravenel***	Y	Y	Y	Y	Y	N	Y	Y
2 ***Spence***	Y	Y	Y	Y	Y	N	Y	N
3 Derrick	N	N	N	N	N	Y	Y	N
4 ***Inglis***	Y	Y	Y	Y	Y	N	Y	Y
5 Spratt	N	N	N	N	Y	Y	Y	N
6 Clyburn	N	N	N	N	N	N	N	N
SOUTH DAKOTA								
AL Johnson	N	N	N	Y	N	Y	Y	N
TENNESSEE								
1 ***Quillen***	Y	Y	Y	N	Y	N	N	N
2 ***Duncan***	Y	Y	Y	Y	Y	N	Y	Y
3 Lloyd	N	N	N	N	N	Y	Y	N
4 Cooper	N	N	Y	?	#	?	?	#
5 Clement	N	N	N	N	N	Y	Y	N

	237	238	239	240	241	242	243	244
6 Gordon	N	N	N	N	Y	Y	Y	N
7 ***Sundquist***	Y	Y	Y	N	Y	N	Y	N
8 Tanner	N	N	N	N	Y	Y	Y	N
9 Ford	N	N	N	N	N	Y	Y	?
TEXAS								
1 Chapman	N	N	N	Y	N	Y	Y	N
2 Wilson	?	?	N	N	N	?	?	N
3 ***Johnson, Sam***	Y	Y	Y	Y	Y	N	Y	Y
4 Hall	Y	Y	Y	Y	Y	Y	Y	N
5 Bryant	N	N	N	N	N	Y	Y	N
6 ***Barton***	Y	Y	Y	Y	Y	Y	Y	N
7 ***Archer***	Y	Y	Y	Y	Y	N	Y	Y
8 ***Fields***	Y	Y	Y	Y	Y	N	Y	Y
9 Brooks	N	?	N	N	N	Y	Y	N
10 Pickle	N	N	N	N	N	Y	Y	N
11 Edwards	N	N	N	Y	Y	Y	Y	N
12 Geren	N	N	N	N	N	Y	Y	N
13 Sarpalius	N	N	N	N	Y	Y	Y	N
14 Laughlin	N	N	N	Y	Y	Y	Y	N
15 de la Garza	N	N	N	N	Y	Y	Y	N
16 Coleman	N	N	N	N	N	Y	Y	N
17 Stenholm	N	N	Y	Y	Y	Y	Y	Y
18 Washington	?	?	?	?	?	?	?	?
19 ***Combest***	Y	Y	Y	Y	Y	Y	Y	Y
20 Gonzalez	N	N	N	N	N	Y	Y	N
21 ***Smith***	Y	Y	Y	Y	Y	N	Y	N
22 ***DeLay***	Y	Y	Y	Y	Y	N	Y	N
23 ***Bonilla***	Y	Y	Y	Y	Y	N	Y	N
24 Frost	N	N	N	N	N	Y	Y	N
25 Andrews	N	N	N	N	N	Y	Y	N
26 ***Armey***	Y	Y	Y	Y	Y	N	Y	Y
27 Ortiz	N	N	N	N	N	Y	Y	N
28 Tejeda	N	N	N	N	N	Y	Y	N
29 Green	N	N	Y	Y	Y	Y	Y	N
30 Johnson, E.B.	N	N	N	N	N	Y	Y	N
UTAH								
1 ***Hansen***	Y	Y	Y	Y	Y	N	Y	Y
2 Shepherd	N	N	N	Y	N	Y	Y	N
3 Orton	N	N	Y	N	Y	Y	Y	N
VERMONT								
AL *Sanders*	N	N	N	Y	N	Y	Y	N
VIRGINIA								
1 ***Bateman***	N	Y	Y	Y	Y	N	Y	N
2 Pickett	N	N	N	N	Y	Y	Y	N
3 Scott	N	N	N	N	N	Y	Y	N
4 Sisisky	N	N	N	N	Y	Y	Y	N
5 Payne	N	N	N	N	Y	Y	Y	N
6 ***Goodlatte***	Y	Y	Y	Y	Y	N	Y	Y
7 ***Bliley***	N	Y	Y	Y	Y	N	Y	Y
8 Moran	N	N	N	N	N	Y	Y	N
9 Boucher	N	N	N	N	N	Y	Y	N
10 ***Wolf***	Y	Y	Y	Y	?	?	?	N
11 Byrne	N	N	N	N	N	Y	Y	N
WASHINGTON								
1 Cantwell	N	N	N	Y	N	Y	Y	N
2 Swift	N	N	N	N	N	Y	Y	N
3 Unsoeld	N	N	N	N	N	Y	Y	N
4 Inslee	N	N	N	Y	Y	Y	Y	N
5 Foley								
6 Dicks	N	N	N	Y	N	Y	Y	N
7 McDermott	N	N	N	N	N	Y	Y	N
8 ***Dunn***	Y	Y	Y	Y	Y	Y	Y	Y
9 Kreidler	N	N	N	Y	N	Y	Y	N
WEST VIRGINIA								
1 Mollohan	N	N	N	N	N	Y	Y	N
2 Wise	N	N	N	N	N	Y	Y	N
3 Rahall	N	N	N	N	N	N	N	N
WISCONSIN								
1 Barca	N	Y	N	N	Y	Y	Y	N
2 ***Klug***	Y	Y	Y	Y	Y	N	Y	Y
3 ***Gunderson***	N	Y	Y	Y	Y	N	Y	Y
4 Kleczka	N	N	N	N	N	Y	Y	N
5 Barrett	N	Y	N	Y	Y	Y	Y	N
6 ***Petri***	Y	Y	Y	Y	Y	N	Y	Y
7 Obey	N	N	N	N	N	Y	Y	N
8 ***Roth***	Y	Y	Y	Y	Y	N	Y	Y
9 ***Sensenbrenner***	Y	Y	Y	Y	Y	N	Y	Y
WYOMING								
AL ***Thomas***	Y	Y	Y	N	Y	Y	Y	Y
DELEGATES								
de Lugo, V.I.	N	N	N	N	N	Y	Y	N
Faleomavaega, Am.S.	N	N	N	N	N	Y	Y	N
Norton, D.C.	N	N	N	N	N	Y	Y	N
Romero-B., P.R.	N	N	N	N	N	N	Y	?
Underwood, Guam	N	N	N	N	?	?	?	?

Southern states - Ala., Ark., Fla., Ga., Ky., La., Miss., N.C., Okla., S.C., Tenn., Texas, Va.
Omitted votes are quorum calls, which CQ does not include in its vote charts.

245. HR 4539. Fiscal 1995 Treasury-Postal Service Appropriations/Corps of Engineers Building and Courthouse. Fawell, R-Ill., amendment to eliminate $11.4 million for the Kennedy Plaza federal courthouse in Providence, R.I., and the Corps of Engineers building in Walla Walla, Wash. Rejected in the Committee of the Whole 136-276: R 129-45; D 7-230 (ND 5-158, SD 2-72); I 0-1, June 15, 1994.

246. HR 4539. Fiscal 1995 Treasury-Postal Service Appropriations/Motion to Rise. Hoyer, D-Md., motion to rise and report the bill back to the House, thus eliminating the possibility of further amendments. Motion agreed to in the Committee of the Whole 245-175: R 0-175; D 244-0 (ND 166-0, SD 78-0); I 1-0, June 15, 1994.

247. HR 4539. Fiscal 1995 Treasury-Postal Service Appropriations/Passage. Passage of the bill to provide $23.4 billion in new budget authority for the Treasury Department, the Postal Service, the Executive Office of the President and certain independent agencies for fiscal 1995. The administration had requested $24,569,399,000. Passed 276-139: R 51-123; D 224-16 (ND 154-10, SD 70-6); I 1-0, June 15, 1994.

248. HR 4556. Fiscal 1995 Transportation Appropriations/Previous Question. Gordon, D-Tenn., motion to order the previous question (thus ending debate and the possibility of amendment) on adoption of the rule (H Res 454) to waive certain points of order against and provide for House floor consideration of the bill to provide $14,194,848,371 in new budget authority and authorize the expenditure of $24.1 billion from various user-supported trust funds for the Transportation Department and related agencies in fiscal 1995. Motion agreed to 241-177: R 0-174; D 240-3 (ND 163-2, SD 77-1); I 1-0, June 16, 1994.

249. HR 4556. Fiscal 1995 Transportation Appropriations/Rule. Adoption of the rule (H Res 454) to provide for House floor consideration of the bill to provide $14,194,848,371 in new budget authority and authorize the expenditure of $24.1 billion from various user-supported trust funds for the Transportation Department and related agencies in fiscal 1995. Adopted 239-180: R 0-176; D 238-4 (ND 164-1, SD 74-3); I 1-0, June 16, 1994.

250. HR 4556. Fiscal 1995 Transportation Appropriations/Interstate Commerce Commission. Kasich, R-Ohio, amendment to terminate the Interstate Commerce Commission by eliminating $43 million provided for it in the bill. Adopted in the Committee of the Whole 234-192: R 168-8; D 66-183 (ND 34-136, SD 32-47); I 0-1, June 16, 1994. A "nay" was a vote in support of the president's position.

251. HR 4556. Fiscal 1995 Transportation Appropriations/Amtrak. Hefley, R-Colo., amendment to cut assistance to Amtrak by $77 million. Rejected in the Committee of the Whole 103-326: R 94-81; D 9-244 (ND 2-171, SD 7-73); I 0-1, June 16, 1994. A "nay" was a vote in support of the president's position.

252. HR 4556. Fiscal 1995 Transportation Appropriations/Passage. Passage of the bill to provide $14.2 billion in new budget authority and authorize the expenditure of $24.1 billion from various user-supported trust funds for the Transportation Department and related agencies in fiscal 1995. The administration had requested $13,813,438,000 in net new budget authority and $24,696,697,000 from the trust funds. Passed 363-59: R 122-51; D 240-8 (ND 160-8, SD 80-0); I 1-0, June 16, 1994.

KEY

Y	Voted for (yea).
#	Paired for.
+	Announced for.
N	Voted against (nay).
X	Paired against.
−	Announced against.
P	Voted "present."
C	Voted "present" to avoid possible conflict of interest.
?	Did not vote or otherwise make a position known.
D	Delegates ineligible to vote.

Democrats **Republicans** *Independent*

	245	246	247	248	249	250	251	252
ALABAMA								
1 Callahan	N	N	Y	N	N	Y	N	Y
2 Everett	N	N	Y	N	N	Y	N	Y
3 Browder	N	Y	Y	Y	Y	N	Y	Y
4 Bevill	N	Y	Y	Y	Y	N	N	Y
5 Cramer	N	Y	Y	Y	N	N	Y	Y
6 Bachus	Y	N	N	N	N	Y	N	?
7 Hilliard	N	Y	Y	Y	Y	?	?	?
ALASKA								
AL Young	N	N	Y	N	N	Y	N	Y
ARIZONA								
1 Coppersmith	N	Y	Y	Y	Y	N	N	Y
2 Pastor	N	Y	Y	Y	Y	N	N	Y
3 Stump	Y	N	N	N	N	Y	Y	N
4 Kyl	Y	N	Y	N	N	Y	Y	N
5 Kolbe	N	N	Y	N	N	Y	Y	Y
6 English	N	Y	Y	Y	Y	N	N	Y
ARKANSAS								
1 Lambert	N	Y	Y	Y	Y	N	N	Y
2 Thornton	N	Y	Y	Y	Y	N	N	Y
3 Hutchinson	Y	N	N	N	N	Y	Y	Y
4 Dickey	Y	N	N	N	N	Y	Y	Y
CALIFORNIA								
1 Hamburg	N	Y	Y	Y	Y	N	N	Y
2 Herger	Y	N	N	N	N	Y	Y	N
3 Fazio	N	Y	Y	Y	Y	N	N	Y
4 Doolittle	Y	N	N	N	N	Y	Y	N
5 Matsui	N	Y	Y	Y	Y	N	N	Y
6 Woolsey	N	Y	Y	Y	Y	N	N	Y
7 Miller	N	Y	Y	Y	Y	N	N	Y
8 Pelosi	?	Y	Y	Y	Y	N	N	Y
9 Dellums	N	Y	?	Y	Y	N	N	Y
10 Baker	Y	N	N	N	N	Y	Y	Y
11 Pombo	Y	N	N	N	N	Y	Y	N
12 Lantos	N	Y	Y	Y	Y	N	N	Y
13 Stark	?	Y	Y	Y	Y	N	N	Y
14 Eshoo	N	Y	Y	Y	Y	N	N	Y
15 Mineta	N	Y	Y	Y	Y	N	N	Y
16 Edwards	N	Y	Y	Y	Y	N	N	Y
17 Farr	N	Y	Y	Y	Y	N	N	Y
18 Condit	Y	Y	N	Y	N	N	N	Y
19 Lehman	N	Y	Y	Y	Y	N	N	Y
20 Dooley	N	Y	Y	Y	Y	N	N	Y
21 Thomas	Y	N	?	N	N	Y	Y	Y
22 Huffington	Y	N	N	N	N	Y	Y	Y
23 Gallegly	Y	N	N	N	N	Y	Y	N
24 Beilenson	N	Y	Y	Y	Y	N	N	Y
25 McKeon	Y	N	N	N	N	Y	Y	Y
26 Berman	?	?	?	Y	Y	N	N	Y
27 Moorhead	Y	N	N	N	N	Y	N	N
28 Dreier	Y	N	N	N	N	Y	Y	N
29 Waxman	N	Y	Y	Y	Y	N	N	Y
30 Becerra	N	Y	Y	Y	Y	N	N	Y
31 Martinez	N	Y	Y	Y	Y	N	N	Y
32 Dixon	N	Y	Y	Y	Y	N	N	Y
33 Roybal-Allard	N	Y	Y	Y	Y	N	N	Y
34 Torres	?	?	?	Y	Y	N	N	Y
35 Waters	N	Y	Y	Y	Y	N	N	Y
36 Harman	N	Y	Y	Y	Y	?	N	Y
37 Tucker	N	Y	Y	?	#	X	X	?
38 Horn	N	Y	Y	N	Y	Y	Y	Y
39 Royce	Y	N	N	N	N	Y	N	Y
40 Lewis	N	N	Y	N	N	Y	N	Y
41 Kim	Y	N	N	N	N	Y	Y	Y
42 Brown	N	Y	Y	Y	Y	?	N	Y
43 Calvert	Y	N	Y	N	N	Y	Y	Y
44 McCandless	N	N	N	N	N	Y	Y	Y
45 Rohrabacher	Y	N	N	N	Y	Y	Y	N
46 Dornan	Y	N	N	N	N	Y	Y	Y
47 Cox	Y	N	N	N	N	Y	Y	Y
48 Packard	N	N	Y	N	N	Y	Y	Y
49 Schenk	N	Y	Y	Y	N	N	N	Y
50 Filner	N	Y	Y	Y	Y	N	N	Y
51 Cunningham	N	N	N	N	N	Y	Y	Y
52 Hunter	N	N	N	N	N	Y	Y	Y
COLORADO								
1 Schroeder	N	Y	Y	Y	Y	N	N	Y
2 Skaggs	N	Y	Y	Y	Y	N	N	Y
3 McInnis	Y	N	N	N	N	Y	Y	N
4 Allard	Y	N	N	N	N	Y	Y	N
5 Hefley	Y	N	N	N	N	Y	Y	N
6 Schaefer	Y	N	N	N	N	Y	N	Y
CONNECTICUT								
1 Kennelly	N	Y	Y	Y	Y	N	N	Y
2 Gejdenson	N	Y	Y	Y	Y	N	N	Y
3 DeLauro	N	Y	Y	Y	Y	N	N	Y
4 Shays	Y	N	N	N	N	Y	N	Y
5 Franks	Y	N	N	N	N	Y	N	Y
6 Johnson	N	N	N	N	N	Y	N	Y
DELAWARE								
AL Castle	Y	N	N	N	N	Y	N	Y
FLORIDA								
1 Hutto	N	Y	N	Y	Y	N	N	Y
2 Peterson	N	Y	Y	Y	Y	N	N	Y
3 Brown	N	Y	Y	Y	Y	N	N	Y
4 Fowler	?	N	Y	N	N	Y	N	Y
5 Thurman	N	Y	Y	Y	Y	N	N	Y
6 Stearns	Y	N	N	N	N	Y	N	Y
7 Mica	Y	N	N	X	N	Y	Y	Y
8 McCollum	N	N	N	N	N	Y	Y	Y
9 Bilirakis	N	N	N	N	N	Y	Y	Y
10 Young	N	N	N	N	N	Y	Y	Y
11 Gibbons	N	Y	Y	Y	Y	N	N	Y
12 Canady	Y	N	N	N	N	Y	Y	Y
13 Miller	Y	N	N	N	N	Y	Y	N
14 Goss	Y	N	N	N	N	Y	Y	N
15 Bacchus	N	Y	Y	Y	Y	N	N	Y
16 Lewis	Y	N	N	N	N	Y	N	Y
17 Meek	N	Y	Y	Y	Y	N	N	Y
18 Ros-Lehtinen	N	N	N	N	N	Y	N	Y
19 Johnston	N	Y	Y	Y	Y	N	N	Y
20 Deutsch	N	Y	Y	Y	Y	N	N	Y
21 Diaz-Balart	N	N	N	N	N	Y	N	Y
22 Shaw	N	N	N	N	N	Y	N	Y
23 Hastings	N	Y	Y	Y	Y	N	N	Y
GEORGIA								
1 Kingston	Y	N	N	N	N	Y	Y	Y
2 Bishop	N	Y	Y	N	N	Y	Y	Y
3 Collins	Y	N	N	N	N	Y	Y	N
4 Linder	Y	N	N	N	N	Y	Y	Y
5 Lewis	N	Y	Y	Y	Y	?	N	Y
6 Gingrich	Y	N	N	N	N	Y	Y	Y
7 Darden	N	Y	Y	Y	Y	N	N	Y
8 Rowland	N	Y	Y	Y	Y	N	N	Y
9 Deal	N	Y	Y	Y	Y	N	N	Y
10 Johnson	N	Y	Y	Y	Y	N	N	Y
11 McKinney	N	Y	Y	Y	Y	N	N	Y
HAWAII								
1 Abercrombie	N	Y	Y	Y	Y	N	N	Y
2 Mink	N	Y	Y	Y	Y	N	N	Y
IDAHO								
1 LaRocco	N	Y	Y	Y	Y	Y	N	Y
2 Crapo	Y	N	N	?	N	Y	N	N
ILLINOIS								
1 Rush	N	Y	Y	Y	Y	N	−	+
2 Reynolds	?	?	?	?	?	?	?	?
3 Lipinski	N	Y	Y	Y	Y	N	N	Y
4 Gutierrez	N	Y	Y	Y	Y	N	N	Y
5 Rostenkowski	N	Y	Y	Y	Y	N	N	Y
6 Hyde	Y	N	N	N	Y	N	?	?
7 Collins	?	?	?	Y	Y	N	?	#
8 Crane	Y	N	N	N	N	Y	Y	N
9 Yates	N	Y	Y	Y	Y	N	N	Y
10 Porter	Y	N	N	N	Y	Y	N	Y
11 Sangmeister	N	Y	Y	Y	Y	N	N	Y
12 Costello	N	Y	Y	Y	Y	N	N	Y
13 Fawell	Y	N	N	N	N	Y	Y	N
14 Hastert	Y	N	N	N	N	Y	Y	N
15 Ewing	Y	N	N	N	N	Y	N	Y
16 Manzullo	Y	N	N	N	N	Y	Y	N
17 Evans	N	Y	Y	Y	Y	N	N	Y

ND Northern Democrats   SD Southern Democrats

	245	246	247	248	249	250	251	252
18 ***Michel***	Y	N	Y	N	N	?	?	?
19 Poshard	N	Y	Y	Y	Y	Y	N	Y
20 Durbin	N	Y	Y	Y	Y	N	N	Y
INDIANA								
1 Visclosky	N	Y	Y	Y	Y	N	N	Y
2 Sharp	?	?	?	Y	Y	N	N	Y
3 Roemer	N	Y	Y	Y	Y	Y	N	Y
4 Long	N	Y	Y	Y	Y	Y	N	Y
5 ***Buyer***	Y	N	N	N	N	Y	Y	Y
6 ***Burton***	Y	N	N	N	N	Y	Y	Y
7 ***Myers***	N	N	N	N	N	Y	N	Y
8 McCloskey	?	Y	Y	Y	Y	N	N	Y
9 Hamilton	N	Y	Y	Y	Y	N	N	Y
10 Jacobs	N	Y	N	N	N	Y	N	Y
IOWA								
1 ***Leach***	Y	N	Y	N	N	Y	N	N
2 ***Nussle***	Y	N	N	N	N	Y	Y	N
3 ***Lightfoot***	N	N	Y	N	N	Y	Y	Y
4 Smith	N	Y	Y	Y	Y	N	N	Y
5 ***Grandy***	Y	N	Y	N	N	Y	N	Y
KANSAS								
1 ***Roberts***	N	N	N	N	N	Y	Y	N
2 Slattery	N	Y	N	?	?	N	N	Y
3 ***Meyers***	N	N	N	N	N	N	N	Y
4 Glickman	?	?	?	Y	Y	Y	N	Y
KENTUCKY								
1 Barlow	N	Y	Y	Y	Y	N	N	Y
2 ***Lewis***	Y	N	Y	N	N	Y	N	Y
3 Mazzoli	N	Y	Y	Y	Y	N	N	Y
4 ***Bunning***	Y	N	Y	N	N	Y	Y	N
5 ***Rogers***	N	N	Y	N	N	Y	N	Y
6 Baesler	N	Y	Y	Y	Y	N	N	Y
LOUISIANA								
1 ***Livingston***	N	N	Y	N	N	Y	Y	Y
2 Jefferson	N	Y	Y	Y	Y	N	N	Y
3 Tauzin	?	Y	N	?	Y	Y	N	Y
4 Fields	N	Y	Y	Y	Y	N	N	Y
5 ***McCrery***	Y	N	Y	N	N	Y	Y	Y
6 ***Baker***	Y	N	N	N	N	Y	Y	Y
7 Hayes	N	Y	Y	Y	Y	Y	N	Y
MAINE								
1 Andrews	Y	Y	Y	Y	Y	N	N	Y
2 ***Snowe***	N	N	N	?	N	Y	N	Y
MARYLAND								
1 ***Gilchrest***	Y	N	Y	N	N	Y	N	Y
2 ***Bentley***	N	N	Y	?	X	Y	N	Y
3 Cardin	N	Y	Y	Y	Y	Y	N	N
4 Wynn	N	Y	Y	Y	Y	N	N	Y
5 Hoyer	N	Y	Y	Y	Y	N	N	Y
6 ***Bartlett***	Y	N	N	N	N	Y	Y	Y
7 Mfume	N	Y	Y	Y	Y	Y	N	Y
8 ***Morella***	Y	N	Y	N	N	N	N	Y
MASSACHUSETTS								
1 Olver	N	Y	Y	Y	Y	N	N	Y
2 Neal	N	Y	Y	Y	Y	Y	N	Y
3 ***Blute***	N	N	N	N	N	Y	N	Y
4 Frank	N	Y	Y	Y	Y	Y	N	Y
5 Meehan	N	Y	Y	Y	Y	Y	N	Y
6 ***Torkildsen***	Y	N	N	N	N	Y	N	Y
7 Markey	N	Y	Y	Y	Y	N	N	Y
8 Kennedy	N	Y	Y	Y	Y	Y	N	Y
9 Moakley	N	Y	Y	Y	Y	N	N	Y
10 Studds	N	Y	Y	Y	Y	N	N	Y
MICHIGAN								
1 Stupak	N	Y	Y	Y	Y	N	N	Y
2 ***Hoekstra***	Y	N	N	N	N	Y	Y	N
3 ***Ehlers***	Y	N	N	N	N	Y	N	Y
4 ***Camp***	Y	N	N	N	N	Y	Y	Y
5 Barcia	N	Y	Y	Y	Y	N	N	Y
6 ***Upton***	Y	N	N	N	N	Y	N	Y
7 ***Smith***	Y	N	N	N	N	Y	Y	N
8 Carr	N	Y	Y	Y	Y	N	N	Y
9 Kildee	N	Y	Y	Y	Y	N	N	Y
10 Bonior	N	Y	Y	Y	Y	N	N	Y
11 ***Knollenberg***	Y	N	N	N	N	Y	Y	Y
12 Levin	N	Y	Y	Y	Y	N	N	Y
13 Ford	?	?	?	Y	Y	?	N	Y
14 Conyers	N	Y	Y	Y	Y	N	N	Y
15 Collins	N	Y	Y	Y	Y	N	N	Y
16 Dingell	N	Y	Y	Y	Y	N	N	Y
MINNESOTA								
1 Penny	?	Y	N	Y	Y	Y	Y	Y
2 Minge	N	Y	N	Y	Y	Y	Y	Y
3 ***Ramstad***	Y	N	N	N	N	Y	Y	N
4 Vento	N	Y	Y	Y	Y	N	N	Y

	245	246	247	248	249	250	251	252
5 Sabo	N	Y	Y	Y	Y	N	N	Y
6 ***Grams***	Y	N	N	N	N	#	#	X
7 Peterson	N	Y	Y	Y	Y	Y	N	Y
8 Oberstar	N	Y	Y	Y	Y	N	N	Y
MISSISSIPPI								
1 Whitten	?	?	?	?	?	N	N	Y
2 Thompson	N	Y	Y	Y	Y	N	N	Y
3 Montgomery	N	Y	Y	Y	Y	Y	N	Y
4 Parker	N	Y	Y	Y	Y	Y	N	Y
5 Taylor	N	Y	N	Y	Y	Y	N	Y
MISSOURI								
1 Clay	N	Y	Y	Y	Y	N	N	Y
2 ***Talent***	Y	N	N	N	N	Y	Y	Y
3 Gephardt	N	Y	Y	Y	Y	N	N	Y
4 Skelton	N	Y	Y	Y	Y	Y	N	Y
5 Wheat	N	Y	Y	?	?	N	N	Y
6 Danner	Y	Y	Y	Y	Y	N	N	Y
7 ***Hancock***	Y	N	N	N	N	Y	Y	N
8 ***Emerson***	N	N	Y	N	N	Y	N	Y
9 Volkmer	N	Y	Y	Y	Y	N	N	Y
MONTANA								
AL Williams	?	Y	Y	Y	Y	N	N	Y
NEBRASKA								
1 ***Bereuter***	Y	N	N	N	N	Y	N	Y
2 Hoagland	N	Y	Y	Y	Y	Y	N	Y
3 ***Barrett***	Y	N	N	N	N	Y	Y	Y
NEVADA								
1 Bilbray	N	Y	Y	Y	Y	Y	N	Y
2 ***Vucanovich***	N	N	Y	N	N	Y	Y	Y
NEW HAMPSHIRE								
1 ***Zeliff***	Y	N	N	N	N	Y	N	N
2 Swett	N	Y	N	Y	Y	N	N	Y
NEW JERSEY								
1 Andrews	Y	Y	N	?	#	Y	N	N
2 Hughes	N	Y	Y	Y	Y	N	N	N
3 ***Saxton***	?	?	?	N	N	Y	N	N
4 ***Smith***	N	N	N	N	N	Y	N	N
5 ***Roukema***	Y	N	N	N	N	Y	N	N
6 Pallone	N	Y	N	Y	Y	N	N	N
7 ***Franks***	Y	N	N	N	N	Y	N	N
8 Klein	N	Y	Y	Y	Y	N	N	N
9 Torricelli	N	Y	Y	Y	Y	Y	N	N
10 Payne	N	Y	Y	Y	Y	N	N	N
11 ***Gallo***	N	N	Y	N	N	Y	N	N
12 ***Zimmer***	Y	N	N	N	N	Y	N	N
13 Menendez	N	Y	Y	Y	Y	N	N	N
NEW MEXICO								
1 ***Schiff***	Y	N	N	N	N	Y	N	Y
2 ***Skeen***	N	N	Y	N	N	Y	N	Y
3 Richardson	N	Y	Y	Y	Y	N	N	Y
NEW YORK								
1 Hochbrueckner	N	Y	Y	Y	Y	N	N	Y
2 ***Lazio***	N	N	Y	N	N	Y	N	Y
3 ***King***	Y	N	N	N	N	Y	N	Y
4 ***Levy***	Y	N	N	N	N	Y	N	Y
5 Ackerman	N	Y	Y	Y	Y	N	N	Y
6 Flake	N	Y	Y	Y	Y	N	N	Y
7 Manton	N	Y	Y	Y	Y	N	N	Y
8 Nadler	N	Y	Y	Y	Y	N	N	Y
9 Schumer	N	Y	Y	Y	Y	N	N	Y
10 Towns	N	Y	Y	Y	Y	N	N	Y
11 Owens	N	Y	Y	Y	Y	N	N	Y
12 Velazquez	N	Y	Y	Y	Y	N	N	Y
13 ***Molinari***	N	N	N	N	N	Y	N	Y
14 Maloney	N	Y	Y	Y	Y	N	N	Y
15 Rangel	N	Y	Y	Y	Y	N	N	Y
16 Serrano	N	Y	Y	Y	Y	N	N	Y
17 Engel	N	Y	Y	Y	Y	N	N	Y
18 Lowey	N	Y	Y	Y	Y	N	N	Y
19 ***Fish***	?	?	?	N	N	Y	N	Y
20 ***Gilman***	Y	N	Y	N	N	Y	N	Y
21 McNulty	N	Y	Y	Y	Y	N	N	Y
22 ***Solomon***	Y	N	Y	N	N	Y	N	N
23 ***Boehlert***	Y	N	Y	N	N	N	N	Y
24 ***McHugh***	Y	N	Y	N	N	Y	N	N
25 ***Walsh***	N	N	Y	N	N	Y	N	Y
26 Hinchey	N	Y	Y	Y	Y	N	N	Y
27 ***Paxon***	Y	N	N	N	N	Y	Y	N
28 Slaughter	N	Y	Y	?	?	N	N	Y
29 LaFalce	N	Y	Y	Y	Y	N	N	Y
30 ***Quinn***	Y	N	N	N	N	Y	N	Y
31 ***Houghton***	N	N	Y	N	N	Y	N	Y
NORTH CAROLINA								
1 Clayton	N	Y	Y	Y	Y	N	N	Y
2 Valentine	N	Y	Y	Y	Y	Y	N	Y

	245	246	247	248	249	250	251	252
3 Lancaster	N	Y	Y	Y	Y	N	N	Y
4 Price	N	Y	Y	Y	Y	N	N	Y
5 Neal	?	?	?	Y	Y	Y	N	Y
6 ***Coble***	Y	N	N	N	N	Y	Y	Y
7 Rose	N	Y	Y	Y	Y	N	N	Y
8 Hefner	N	Y	Y	Y	Y	N	N	Y
9 ***McMillan***	Y	N	Y	N	N	Y	N	Y
10 ***Ballenger***	Y	N	N	N	N	Y	Y	Y
11 ***Taylor***	Y	N	N	N	N	Y	N	Y
12 Watt	N	Y	Y	Y	Y	N	N	Y
NORTH DAKOTA								
AL Pomeroy	N	Y	Y	Y	Y	N	N	Y
OHIO								
1 Mann	N	Y	Y	Y	Y	Y	N	Y
2 ***Portman***	Y	N	N	N	N	Y	Y	N
3 Hall	N	Y	Y	Y	?	N	N	Y
4 ***Oxley***	Y	N	N	N	N	N	N	N
5 ***Gillmor***	N	N	N	N	N	Y	N	Y
6 Strickland	N	Y	Y	Y	Y	Y	N	Y
7 ***Hobson***	N	N	Y	N	N	Y	Y	Y
8 ***Boehner***	Y	N	N	N	N	Y	Y	N
9 Kaptur	N	Y	Y	Y	Y	N	N	Y
10 ***Hoke***	N	N	Y	N	N	Y	N	Y
11 Stokes	N	Y	Y	Y	Y	N	N	Y
12 ***Kasich***	Y	N	Y	N	N	Y	Y	Y
13 Brown	N	Y	Y	Y	Y	N	N	Y
14 Sawyer	N	Y	Y	Y	Y	N	N	Y
15 ***Pryce***	Y	N	N	N	N	Y	Y	Y
16 ***Regula***	N	N	Y	N	N	Y	N	Y
17 Traficant	N	Y	Y	N	Y	N	N	Y
18 Applegate	N	Y	Y	Y	Y	N	N	Y
19 Fingerhut	N	Y	Y	Y	Y	Y	N	Y
OKLAHOMA								
1 ***Inhofe***	Y	N	N	N	N	Y	Y	Y
2 Synar	N	Y	Y	Y	Y	N	Y	Y
3 Brewster	N	Y	Y	Y	Y	N	Y	Y
4 McCurdy	N	Y	N	?	?	?	?	?
5 ***Istook***	Y	N	Y	?	N	Y	Y	N
6 ***Lucas***	Y	N	N	N	N	Y	N	Y
OREGON								
1 Furse	N	Y	Y	Y	Y	N	N	Y
2 ***Smith***	Y	N	N	N	N	Y	N	Y
3 Wyden	N	Y	Y	Y	Y	N	N	Y
4 DeFazio	N	Y	Y	Y	Y	N	N	Y
5 Kopetski	N	Y	Y	Y	Y	N	N	Y
PENNSYLVANIA								
1 Foglietta	N	Y	Y	Y	Y	N	N	Y
2 Blackwell	N	?	?	Y	Y	?	N	Y
3 Borski	N	Y	Y	Y	Y	N	N	Y
4 Klink	N	Y	Y	Y	Y	N	N	Y
5 ***Clinger***	Y	N	N	N	N	N	N	Y
6 Holden	N	Y	Y	Y	Y	N	N	Y
7 ***Weldon***	Y	N	N	N	N	Y	N	Y
8 ***Greenwood***	Y	N	N	N	N	Y	N	N
9 ***Shuster***	Y	N	N	N	N	N	Y	Y
10 ***McDade***	?	?	?	N	N	Y	N	Y
11 Kanjorski	N	Y	Y	Y	Y	N	N	Y
12 Murtha	N	Y	Y	Y	Y	N	N	Y
13 Margolies-Mezv.	Y	Y	Y	Y	Y	Y	N	Y
14 Coyne	N	Y	Y	Y	Y	N	N	Y
15 McHale	N	Y	Y	Y	Y	Y	N	Y
16 ***Walker***	Y	N	N	N	N	Y	Y	N
17 ***Gekas***	Y	N	N	N	N	Y	N	Y
18 ***Santorum***	Y	N	N	N	N	Y	N	Y
19 ***Goodling***	Y	N	N	N	N	Y	N	Y
20 Murphy	N	Y	Y	Y	Y	N	N	Y
21 ***Ridge***	N	N	N	N	N	Y	?	?
RHODE ISLAND								
1 ***Machtley***	N	N	Y	N	N	Y	N	Y
2 Reed	N	Y	Y	Y	Y	N	N	Y
SOUTH CAROLINA								
1 ***Ravenel***	Y	N	N	N	N	Y	Y	Y
2 ***Spence***	Y	N	N	N	N	Y	N	Y
3 Derrick	N	Y	Y	Y	?	N	N	Y
4 ***Inglis***	Y	N	N	N	N	Y	Y	Y
5 Spratt	N	Y	Y	Y	Y	N	N	Y
6 Clyburn	N	Y	Y	Y	Y	N	N	Y
SOUTH DAKOTA								
AL Johnson	N	Y	Y	Y	Y	N	N	Y
TENNESSEE								
1 ***Quillen***	N	N	Y	N	N	Y	N	Y
2 ***Duncan***	Y	N	N	N	N	Y	Y	N
3 Lloyd	N	Y	Y	Y	Y	Y	N	Y
4 Cooper	?	?	?	Y	Y	Y	Y	Y
5 Clement	N	Y	Y	Y	Y	Y	N	Y

	245	246	247	248	249	250	251	252
6 Gordon	N	Y	Y	Y	Y	Y	N	Y
7 ***Sundquist***	N	N	Y	N	N	Y	N	Y
8 Tanner	N	Y	Y	Y	Y	Y	N	Y
9 Ford	?	Y	Y	Y	Y	N	N	Y
TEXAS								
1 Chapman	N	Y	?	?	?	Y	N	Y
2 Wilson	N	Y	?	Y	Y	N	N	Y
3 ***Johnson, Sam***	Y	N	N	N	N	Y	Y	Y
4 Hall	Y	Y	N	Y	?	Y	Y	Y
5 Bryant	N	Y	Y	Y	Y	N	N	Y
6 ***Barton***	Y	N	N	N	N	Y	Y	Y
7 ***Archer***	Y	N	N	N	N	Y	Y	N
8 ***Fields***	Y	N	N	N	N	N	Y	Y
9 Brooks	N	Y	Y	Y	Y	N	N	Y
10 Pickle	?	Y	Y	Y	Y	Y	N	Y
11 Edwards	N	Y	Y	Y	Y	Y	Y	Y
12 Geren	N	Y	Y	Y	Y	Y	N	Y
13 Sarpalius	N	Y	Y	Y	Y	N	N	Y
14 Laughlin	N	Y	Y	Y	Y	Y	N	Y
15 de la Garza	N	Y	Y	Y	Y	Y	N	Y
16 Coleman	N	Y	Y	Y	Y	N	N	Y
17 Stenholm	Y	Y	N	Y	Y	Y	Y	Y
18 Washington	?	?	?	?	?	?	?	?
19 ***Combest***	Y	N	N	N	N	Y	Y	Y
20 Gonzalez	N	Y	Y	Y	Y	N	N	Y
21 ***Smith***	Y	N	N	N	N	Y	Y	Y
22 ***DeLay***	N	N	N	N	N	Y	Y	Y
23 ***Bonilla***	N	N	Y	N	N	Y	Y	Y
24 Frost	N	Y	Y	Y	Y	N	N	Y
25 Andrews	N	Y	Y	Y	Y	Y	Y	Y
26 ***Armey***	Y	N	N	N	N	Y	Y	N
27 Ortiz	N	Y	Y	Y	Y	N	N	Y
28 Tejeda	N	Y	Y	Y	Y	Y	N	Y
29 Green	N	Y	Y	Y	Y	N	N	Y
30 Johnson, E.B.	N	Y	Y	Y	Y	N	N	Y
UTAH								
1 ***Hansen***	Y	N	Y	N	N	Y	Y	N
2 Shepherd	N	Y	Y	Y	Y	N	N	Y
3 Orton	N	Y	Y	Y	Y	Y	N	Y
VERMONT								
AL *Sanders*	N	Y	Y	Y	Y	N	N	Y
VIRGINIA								
1 ***Bateman***	N	N	Y	N	N	Y	N	Y
2 Pickett	N	Y	Y	Y	N	Y	N	Y
3 Scott	N	Y	Y	Y	Y	N	N	Y
4 Sisisky	N	Y	Y	Y	N	Y	N	Y
5 Payne	N	Y	Y	Y	Y	Y	N	Y
6 ***Goodlatte***	Y	N	N	N	N	Y	N	Y
7 ***Bliley***	Y	N	N	N	N	Y	N	Y
8 Moran	?	?	?	Y	Y	N	N	Y
9 Boucher	?	Y	Y	Y	Y	N	N	Y
10 ***Wolf***	N	N	N	N	N	Y	N	Y
11 Byrne	N	Y	Y	N	N	Y	N	Y
WASHINGTON								
1 Cantwell	N	Y	Y	Y	Y	N	N	Y
2 Swift	N	?	Y	Y	Y	N	N	Y
3 Unsoeld	N	Y	Y	Y	Y	N	N	Y
4 Inslee	N	Y	Y	Y	Y	N	N	Y
5 Foley								
6 Dicks	N	Y	Y	Y	Y	N	N	Y
7 McDermott	N	Y	Y	Y	Y	N	N	Y
8 ***Dunn***	Y	N	N	N	N	Y	N	Y
9 Kreidler	N	Y	Y	Y	Y	N	N	Y
WEST VIRGINIA								
1 Mollohan	N	Y	Y	Y	Y	N	N	Y
2 Wise	N	Y	Y	Y	Y	N	N	Y
3 Rahall	N	Y	Y	Y	Y	N	N	Y
WISCONSIN								
1 Barca	N	Y	N	Y	Y	Y	N	Y
2 ***Klug***	Y	N	N	N	N	Y	Y	Y
3 ***Gunderson***	N	N	N	N	N	Y	N	Y
4 Kleczka	N	Y	Y	Y	Y	N	N	Y
5 Barrett	N	Y	Y	Y	Y	Y	N	Y
6 ***Petri***	Y	N	N	N	N	Y	Y	Y
7 Obey	N	Y	Y	Y	Y	N	N	Y
8 ***Roth***	Y	N	N	N	N	Y	Y	N
9 ***Sensenbrenner***	Y	N	N	N	N	Y	Y	N
WYOMING								
AL ***Thomas***	Y	N	Y	N	N	Y	Y	N
DELEGATES								
de Lugo, V.I.	N	Y	D	D	D	N	N	D
Faleomavaega, Am.S.	N	Y	D	D	D	N	N	D
Norton, D.C.	N	Y	D	D	D	N	N	D
Romero-B., P.R.	?	?	D	D	D	N	N	D
Underwood, Guam	?	?	D	D	D	N	N	D

Southern states - Ala., Ark., Fla., Ga., Ky., La., Miss., N.C., Okla., S.C., Tenn., Texas, Va.
Omitted votes are quorum calls, which CQ does not include in its vote charts.

253. HR 3355. Omnibus Crime Bill/Instruct Conferees. McCollum, R-Fla., motion to instruct House conferees on the bill to strike House provisions that would allow the use of statistical evidence to make a claim of racial discrimination by inmates seeking to overturn death sentences. Motion agreed to 264-149: R 165-6; D 99-142 (ND 55-109, SD 44-33); I 0-1, June 16, 1994.

254. HR 4554. Fiscal 1995 Agriculture Appropriations/ Socially Disadvantaged Farmers. Burton, R-Ind., motion to eliminate the $3 million used to provide outreach and technical assistance to individuals whose livelihoods as farmers have been hindered by discrimination or economic circumstances. Rejected in the Committee of the Whole 139-264: R 129-35; D 10-228 (ND 8-156, SD 2-72); I 0-1, June 17, 1994.

255. HR 4554. Fiscal 1995 Agriculture Appropriations/ Motion to Rise. Durbin, D-Ill., motion to rise from the Committee of the Whole and report the bill, as amended, back to the House. Motion agreed to in the Committee of the Whole 232-146: R 12-146; D 219-0 (ND 152-0, SD 67-0); I 1-0, June 17, 1994. (The effect of the vote was to block an amendment to bar illegal immigrants from receiving money provided by the bill.)

256. HR 4554. Fiscal 1995 Agriculture Appropriations/ Passage. Passage of the bill to provide $67.9 billion in new budget authority for agriculture, rural development, the Food and Drug Administration, and related agencies in fiscal 1995. The administration had requested $68.4 billion. Passed 278-127: R 42-125; D 235-2 (ND 159-2, SD 76-0); I 1-0, June 17, 1994.

257. S 24. Independent Counsel Reauthorization/Rule. Adoption of the rule (H Res 439) to waive points of order against and provide for House floor consideration of the conference report to reauthorize for five years provisions that allow for the appointment of an independent counsel to investigate and prosecute criminal wrongdoing by high-ranking executive branch officials, and to give the attorney general discretion to apply the law to members of Congress and to eliminate a prohibition on the appointment of Whitewater special prosecutor Robert B. Fiske Jr. as an independent counsel. Adopted 243-171: R 0-170; D 242-1 (ND 163-1, SD 79-0); I 1-0, June 21, 1994.

258. S 24. Independent Counsel Reauthorization/Conference Report. Adoption of the conference report to reauthorize for five years provisions that allow for the appointment of an independent counsel to investigate and prosecute criminal wrongdoing by high-ranking executive branch officials, and to give the attorney general discretion to apply the law to members of Congress and to eliminate a prohibition on the appointment of Whitewater special prosecutor Robert B. Fiske Jr. as an independent counsel. Adopted (thus cleared for the president) 317-105: R 77-100; D 239-5 (ND 162-4, SD 77-1); I 1-0, June 21, 1994. A "yea" was a vote in support of the president's position.

259. HR 4568. Fiscal 1994 Housing Supplemental Appropriations/Passage. Passage of the bill to provide $18,080,000 in new budget authority to subsidize mortgages for purchase or construction of rental housing, allow the Federal Housing Administration to guarantee an additional $38 billion in mortgages, and allow the Government National Mortgage Association to guarantee an additional $55 billion in mortgage-backed securities. The bill matches the administration request. Passed 410-9: R 167-9; D 242-0 (ND 164-0, SD 78-0); I 1-0, June 21, 1994. A "yea" was a vote in support of the president's position.

260. HR 4602. Fiscal 1995 Interior Appropriations/Biological Survey. Allard, R-Colo., amendment to eliminate the $167.2 million in the bill for the National Biological Survey. Rejected in the Committee of the Whole 169-259: R 128-48; D 41-210 (ND 18-154, SD 23-56); I 0-1, June 22, 1994. A "nay" was a vote in support of the president's position.

KEY

Y	Voted for (yea).
#	Paired for.
+	Announced for.
N	Voted against (nay).
X	Paired against.
−	Announced against.
P	Voted "present."
C	Voted "present" to avoid possible conflict of interest.
?	Did not vote or otherwise make a position known.
D	Delegates ineligible to vote.

Democrats **Republicans** *Independent*

	253	254	255	256	257	258	259	260
ALABAMA								
1 *Callahan*	Y	N	N	N	N	N	Y	Y
2 *Everett*	Y	N	N	N	N	Y	Y	Y
3 Browder	Y	N	Y	Y	Y	Y	Y	Y
4 Bevill	Y	N	Y	Y	Y	Y	Y	N
5 Cramer	Y	N	Y	Y	Y	Y	Y	Y
6 *Bachus*	Y	N	N	N	N	Y	Y	Y
7 Hilliard	?	?	?	?	Y	Y	Y	N
ALASKA								
AL *Young*	Y	N	N	Y	N	Y	Y	Y
ARIZONA								
1 Coppersmith	Y	N	Y	Y	Y	Y	Y	N
2 Pastor	Y	N	Y	Y	Y	Y	Y	N
3 *Stump*	Y	Y	N	N	N	N	N	Y
4 *Kyl*	Y	Y	N	N	N	N	Y	Y
5 *Kolbe*	Y	Y	N	Y	N	N	Y	N
6 English	Y	N	Y	Y	Y	Y	Y	N
ARKANSAS								
1 Lambert	Y	N	Y	Y	Y	Y	Y	Y
2 Thornton	N	N	Y	Y	Y	Y	Y	N
3 *Hutchinson*	Y	Y	N	N	N	N	Y	Y
4 Dickey	Y	N	N	N	N	N	Y	Y
CALIFORNIA								
1 Hamburg	N	N	Y	Y	Y	Y	Y	N
2 *Herger*	Y	Y	−	N	N	Y	Y	Y
3 Fazio	Y	N	Y	Y	Y	Y	Y	N
4 *Doolittle*	Y	Y	N	N	N	N	Y	Y
5 Matsui	N	N	?	Y	Y	Y	Y	N
6 Woolsey	N	N	Y	Y	Y	Y	Y	N
7 Miller	N	?	Y	Y	Y	Y	Y	N
8 Pelosi	N	N	Y	Y	Y	?	Y	N
9 Dellums	N	N	Y	Y	Y	Y	Y	N
10 *Baker*	Y	Y	N	N	N	N	Y	Y
11 *Pombo*	Y	Y	N	N	N	N	Y	Y
12 Lantos	N	N	Y	Y	Y	Y	Y	N
13 Stark	N	N	?	Y	Y	Y	Y	N
14 Eshoo	N	N	Y	Y	Y	Y	Y	N
15 Mineta	N	N	Y	Y	#	?	?	N
16 Edwards	N	N	Y	Y	Y	Y	Y	N
17 Farr	N	N	Y	Y	Y	Y	Y	N
18 Condit	Y	Y	Y	Y	Y	Y	Y	Y
19 Lehman	Y	N	Y	Y	Y	Y	Y	Y
20 Dooley	Y	N	Y	Y	Y	Y	Y	Y
21 *Thomas*	Y	Y	−	Y	N	N	Y	Y
22 *Huffington*	Y	Y	N	N	N	N	Y	Y
23 *Gallegly*	Y	N	N	N	N	N	Y	Y
24 Beilenson	Y	N	Y	Y	Y	Y	Y	N
25 *McKeon*	Y	Y	N	N	N	Y	Y	Y
26 Berman	N	N	Y	Y	Y	Y	Y	N
27 *Moorhead*	Y	Y	N	N	N	N	Y	Y
28 *Dreier*	Y	Y	N	N	N	N	Y	Y
29 Waxman	N	N	Y	Y	Y	Y	Y	N
30 Becerra	N	N	Y	Y	Y	Y	Y	N
31 Martinez	N	N	Y	Y	Y	Y	Y	N
32 Dixon	N	N	Y	Y	Y	Y	Y	N
33 Roybal-Allard	N	N	Y	Y	Y	Y	Y	N
34 Torres	N	N	Y	Y	Y	Y	Y	N
35 Waters	N	N	Y	Y	Y	Y	Y	N
36 Harman	Y	Y	Y	Y	Y	Y	Y	N
37 Tucker	?	X	#	#	Y	Y	Y	N
38 *Horn*	Y	Y	N	Y	N	N	Y	Y
39 *Royce*	Y	Y	N	N	N	N	Y	Y
40 *Lewis*	Y	N	N	Y	N	Y	Y	Y
41 *Kim*	Y	Y	N	N	N	N	Y	Y

	253	254	255	256	257	258	259	260
42 Brown	N	?	?	?	Y	N	Y	N
43 *Calvert*	Y	Y	N	Y	N	Y	Y	Y
44 *McCandless*	Y	N	Y	N	Y	N	Y	Y
45 *Rohrabacher*	Y	Y	N	N	N	N	Y	Y
46 *Dornan*	Y	Y	N	N	?	Y	Y	Y
47 *Cox*	Y	Y	N	N	N	N	Y	Y
48 *Packard*	Y	Y	N	N	N	N	Y	Y
49 Schenk	Y	Y	Y	Y	Y	Y	Y	N
50 Filner	N	N	Y	Y	Y	Y	Y	N
51 *Cunningham*	Y	N	N	N	N	N	Y	Y
52 *Hunter*	Y	Y	N	Y	N	N	Y	Y
COLORADO								
1 Schroeder	?	N	Y	Y	Y	Y	Y	N
2 Skaggs	N	N	Y	Y	Y	Y	Y	N
3 *McInnis*	Y	Y	N	N	N	N	Y	Y
4 *Allard*	Y	Y	N	N	Y	N	Y	Y
5 *Hefley*	Y	Y	N	N	N	N	Y	Y
6 *Schaefer*	Y	Y	N	N	N	N	Y	Y
CONNECTICUT								
1 Kennelly	N	N	?	Y	Y	Y	Y	N
2 Gejdenson	N	N	Y	Y	Y	Y	Y	N
3 DeLauro	Y	N	Y	Y	Y	Y	Y	N
4 *Shays*	N	Y	N	N	Y	Y	Y	N
5 *Franks*	Y	N	N	Y	N	Y	Y	Y
6 *Johnson*	Y	Y	−	Y	N	Y	Y	Y
DELAWARE								
AL *Castle*	Y	Y	N	N	N	N	Y	Y
FLORIDA								
1 Hutto	Y	N	Y	Y	Y	Y	Y	Y
2 Peterson	Y	N	Y	Y	Y	Y	Y	Y
3 Brown	N	N	Y	Y	Y	Y	Y	N
4 *Fowler*	Y	Y	N	Y	N	N	Y	Y
5 Thurman	Y	N	Y	Y	Y	Y	Y	Y
6 *Stearns*	Y	N	N	N	N	N	Y	Y
7 *Mica*	Y	Y	N	N	N	Y	Y	Y
8 *McCollum*	Y	Y	N	N	?	N	Y	Y
9 *Bilirakis*	Y	Y	N	N	Y	Y	Y	Y
10 *Young*	Y	Y	N	N	Y	N	Y	Y
11 Gibbons	N	N	?	Y	Y	Y	Y	N
12 *Canady*	Y	Y	N	N	N	Y	Y	Y
13 *Miller*	?	Y	N	N	N	Y	N	Y
14 *Goss*	Y	Y	N	N	N	N	N	Y
15 *Bacchus*	Y	N	?	?	Y	Y	Y	N
16 *Lewis*	Y	Y	N	N	N	N	Y	Y
17 Meek	N	N	Y	Y	Y	Y	Y	N
18 *Ros-Lehtinen*	Y	Y	N	N	N	Y	Y	Y
19 Johnston	N	N	Y	Y	Y	Y	Y	N
20 Deutsch	Y	N	Y	Y	Y	Y	Y	N
21 *Diaz-Balart*	Y	N	Y	Y	Y	Y	Y	Y
22 *Shaw*	Y	Y	−	N	?	Y	Y	Y
23 Hastings	N	N	?	?	Y	Y	Y	N
GEORGIA								
1 *Kingston*	Y	N	N	N	N	N	Y	Y
2 Bishop	N	N	Y	Y	Y	Y	Y	Y
3 *Collins*	Y	Y	N	N	N	N	N	Y
4 *Linder*	Y	Y	Y	N	N	Y	Y	Y
5 Lewis	N	N	?	Y	Y	Y	Y	N
6 *Gingrich*	Y	Y	N	N	N	N	Y	Y
7 Darden	Y	N	Y	Y	Y	Y	Y	Y
8 Rowland	Y	N	Y	Y	Y	Y	Y	Y
9 Deal	Y	N	Y	Y	Y	Y	Y	Y
10 Johnson	Y	N	Y	Y	Y	Y	Y	Y
11 McKinney	N	N	Y	Y	Y	Y	Y	N
HAWAII								
1 Abercrombie	N	N	Y	Y	Y	N	Y	N
2 Mink	N	N	Y	Y	Y	Y	Y	N
IDAHO								
1 LaRocco	Y	N	Y	Y	Y	Y	Y	N
2 *Crapo*	Y	Y	N	N	N	N	Y	Y
ILLINOIS								
1 Rush	−	−	+	+	Y	Y	Y	N
2 Reynolds	?	?	?	?	Y	Y	Y	N
3 Lipinski	Y	?	?	?	Y	Y	Y	Y
4 Gutierrez	N	N	Y	Y	Y	Y	Y	N
5 Rostenkowski	N	N	?	Y	Y	Y	Y	N
6 *Hyde*	?	Y	N	N	Y	N	Y	Y
7 Collins	?	X	#	#	Y	Y	Y	N
8 *Crane*	Y	?	N	N	N	N	N	Y
9 Yates	?	N	Y	Y	Y	Y	Y	N
10 *Porter*	Y	Y	N	N	Y	Y	Y	N
11 Sangmeister	Y	N	Y	Y	Y	Y	Y	Y
12 Costello	Y	N	Y	Y	Y	Y	Y	Y
13 *Fawell*	Y	Y	N	N	N	N	Y	Y
14 *Hastert*	Y	Y	N	N	N	N	Y	Y
15 *Ewing*	Y	Y	N	N	N	N	Y	Y
16 *Manzullo*	Y	Y	N	N	N	N	Y	Y
17 Evans	N	N	Y	Y	Y	Y	Y	Y

ND Northern Democrats   SD Southern Democrats

	253	254	255	256	257	258	259	260
18 ***Michel***	?	?	?	?	?	N	Y	Y
19 Poshard	Y	N	Y	Y	Y	Y	Y	Y
20 Durbin	Y	N	Y	Y	Y	Y	Y	N
INDIANA								
1 Visclosky	N	N	Y	Y	Y	Y	Y	N
2 Sharp	N	N	Y	Y	Y	Y	?	?
3 Roemer	Y	N	Y	Y	Y	Y	Y	N
4 Long	N	N	Y	Y	Y	Y	Y	Y
5 ***Buyer***	Y	Y	N	N	N	N	N	Y
6 ***Burton***	Y	Y	N	N	N	N	N	Y
7 ***Myers***	Y	Y	Y	Y	N	N	Y	N
8 McCloskey	Y	N	Y	Y	Y	Y	Y	N
9 Hamilton	N	N	Y	Y	Y	Y	Y	N
10 Jacobs	N	N	Y	N	Y	Y	Y	N
IOWA								
1 ***Leach***	Y	Y	N	Y	N	Y	Y	N
2 ***Nussle***	Y	Y	N	N	N	N	Y	Y
3 ***Lightfoot***	Y	Y	N	N	Y	N	Y	Y
4 Smith	N	N	Y	Y	Y	Y	Y	N
5 ***Grandy***	N	Y	N	N	N	Y	Y	N
KANSAS								
1 ***Roberts***	Y	N	N	N	N	N	Y	Y
2 Slattery	N	?	?	?	?	?	?	N
3 ***Meyers***	Y	Y	N	N	N	Y	Y	N
4 Glickman	N	N	Y	Y	Y	Y	Y	N
KENTUCKY								
1 Barlow	N	N	Y	Y	Y	Y	Y	Y
2 ***Lewis***	Y	Y	N	N	N	N	Y	Y
3 Mazzoli	Y	N	Y	Y	Y	Y	Y	N
4 ***Bunning***	Y	Y	N	X	N	N	Y	Y
5 ***Rogers***	Y	Y	N	Y	N	N	Y	Y
6 Baesler	Y	N	Y	Y	Y	Y	Y	Y
LOUISIANA								
1 ***Livingston***	Y	?	?	?	N	N	Y	Y
2 Jefferson	N	N	?	Y	Y	Y	Y	N
3 Tauzin	Y	N	Y	Y	Y	Y	Y	Y
4 Fields	N	N	Y	Y	Y	Y	Y	N
5 ***McCrery***	Y	N	—	Y	N	Y	Y	Y
6 ***Baker***	Y	N	N	Y	N	Y	Y	Y
7 Hayes	Y	?	?	?	Y	Y	Y	P
MAINE								
1 Andrews	N	?	Y	Y	Y	Y	Y	N
2 ***Snowe***	Y	Y	N	N	N	Y	Y	N
MARYLAND								
1 ***Gilchrest***	Y	Y	N	N	N	Y	Y	N
2 ***Bentley***	Y	Y	N	Y	?	N	Y	Y
3 Cardin	N	N	?	Y	Y	Y	Y	N
4 Wynn	N	N	Y	Y	Y	Y	Y	N
5 Hoyer	Y	N	Y	Y	Y	Y	Y	N
6 ***Bartlett***	Y	Y	N	N	N	N	Y	Y
7 Mfume	N	N	Y	Y	+	Y	Y	N
8 ***Morella***	N	N	Y	Y	N	Y	Y	N
MASSACHUSETTS								
1 Olver	N	N	Y	Y	Y	Y	Y	N
2 Neal	N	N	?	Y	Y	Y	Y	N
3 ***Blute***	Y	Y	N	N	N	Y	Y	N
4 Frank	N	N	Y	Y	Y	Y	Y	N
5 Meehan	N	N	Y	Y	Y	Y	Y	N
6 ***Torkildsen***	Y	Y	N	N	N	Y	Y	N
7 Markey	N	N	Y	Y	Y	Y	Y	N
8 Kennedy	N	N	Y	Y	Y	Y	Y	N
9 Moakley	N	N	Y	Y	Y	Y	Y	N
10 Studds	N	N	Y	Y	Y	Y	Y	N
MICHIGAN								
1 Stupak	Y	N	Y	Y	Y	Y	Y	N
2 ***Hoekstra***	Y	Y	N	N	N	Y	Y	Y
3 ***Ehlers***	Y	N	N	N	N	Y	Y	N
4 ***Camp***	Y	Y	—	Y	N	Y	Y	Y
5 Barcia	Y	N	Y	Y	Y	Y	Y	N
6 ***Upton***	Y	Y	N	N	N	Y	Y	Y
7 ***Smith***	Y	Y	N	N	N	Y	Y	Y
8 Carr	N	N	Y	Y	?	?	?	N
9 Kildee	N	N	Y	Y	Y	Y	Y	N
10 Bonior	N	N	Y	Y	Y	Y	Y	N
11 ***Knollenberg***	Y	Y	N	N	N	Y	Y	Y
12 Levin	N	N	?	Y	Y	Y	Y	N
13 Ford	N	N	Y	Y	Y	Y	?	?
14 Conyers	N	N	Y	Y	Y	Y	Y	N
15 Collins	N	N	Y	Y	Y	Y	Y	N
16 Dingell	N	N	Y	Y	Y	Y	?	Y
MINNESOTA								
1 Penny	N	N	Y	Y	Y	Y	Y	Y
2 Minge	Y	N	Y	Y	Y	Y	Y	N
3 ***Ramstad***	Y	Y	N	N	N	Y	Y	Y
4 Vento	N	N	Y	Y	Y	Y	Y	N

	253	254	255	256	257	258	259	260
5 Sabo	N	N	Y	Y	Y	Y	Y	N
6 ***Grams***	?	#	X	X	X	N	Y	Y
7 Peterson	Y	N	Y	N	Y	Y	Y	Y
8 Oberstar	N	N	Y	Y	Y	Y	Y	N
MISSISSIPPI								
1 Whitten	Y	N	Y	Y	Y	Y	Y	N
2 Thompson	N	N	Y	Y	Y	Y	Y	N
3 Montgomery	Y	N	Y	Y	Y	Y	Y	Y
4 Parker	Y	N	Y	Y	Y	Y	Y	Y
5 Taylor	Y	Y	Y	Y	Y	Y	Y	Y
MISSOURI								
1 Clay	?	?	?	?	Y	Y	Y	N
2 ***Talent***	Y	?	N	N	N	N	Y	Y
3 Gephardt	N	N	Y	Y	Y	Y	Y	N
4 Skelton	Y	N	Y	Y	Y	Y	Y	N
5 Wheat	N	N	Y	Y	Y	Y	Y	N
6 Danner	Y	N	Y	Y	Y	Y	Y	Y
7 ***Hancock***	Y	Y	—	N	N	N	Y	Y
8 ***Emerson***	Y	Y	Y	N	N	N	Y	Y
9 Volkmer	Y	N	Y	Y	Y	Y	Y	Y
MONTANA								
AL Williams	N	N	Y	Y	Y	Y	Y	N
NEBRASKA								
1 ***Bereuter***	?	N	N	Y	N	Y	Y	Y
2 Hoagland	Y	N	?	Y	Y	Y	Y	N
3 ***Barrett***	Y	N	N	N	N	Y	Y	Y
NEVADA								
1 Bilbray	Y	N	Y	Y	Y	Y	Y	N
2 ***Vucanovich***	Y	Y	N	Y	N	N	Y	Y
NEW HAMPSHIRE								
1 ***Zeliff***	Y	Y	N	N	N	N	Y	Y
2 Swett	N	N	Y	Y	N	Y	Y	N
NEW JERSEY								
1 Andrews	N	N	Y	Y	Y	Y	Y	N
2 Hughes	Y	N	Y	Y	Y	Y	Y	N
3 ***Saxton***	Y	Y	N	Y	N	Y	Y	N
4 ***Smith***	Y	N	N	Y	N	Y	Y	N
5 ***Roukema***	Y	Y	N	N	N	Y	Y	N
6 Pallone	N	N	Y	Y	Y	Y	Y	N
7 ***Franks***	Y	Y	N	N	N	Y	Y	N
8 Klein	Y	N	Y	Y	Y	Y	Y	N
9 Torricelli	N	Y	Y	Y	Y	Y	Y	N
10 Payne	N	N	Y	Y	Y	Y	Y	N
11 ***Gallo***	Y	?	N	N	N	Y	Y	N
12 ***Zimmer***	Y	Y	N	N	N	Y	Y	N
13 Menendez	N	N	Y	Y	Y	Y	Y	N
NEW MEXICO								
1 ***Schiff***	Y	N	N	Y	N	Y	Y	N
2 ***Skeen***	Y	N	Y	Y	N	Y	Y	Y
3 Richardson	N	N	Y	Y	Y	Y	Y	N
NEW YORK								
1 Hochbrueckner	N	N	Y	Y	Y	Y	Y	N
2 ***Lazio***	Y	Y	N	N	N	Y	Y	N
3 ***King***	Y	Y	N	N	N	N	Y	Y
4 ***Levy***	Y	Y	N	N	N	Y	Y	Y
5 Ackerman	N	N	Y	Y	Y	Y	Y	N
6 Flake	N	?	?	?	Y	Y	Y	N
7 Manton	N	N	Y	Y	Y	Y	Y	N
8 Nadler	N	N	Y	Y	Y	Y	Y	N
9 Schumer	Y	N	Y	Y	?	Y	Y	?
10 Towns	N	N	Y	Y	?	Y	Y	N
11 Owens	N	N	Y	Y	Y	Y	Y	N
12 Velazquez	N	N	Y	Y	Y	Y	Y	N
13 ***Molinari***	Y	Y	N	N	N	Y	Y	N
14 Maloney	N	N	Y	Y	Y	Y	Y	N
15 Rangel	N	N	?	Y	Y	Y	Y	N
16 Serrano	N	N	Y	Y	Y	Y	Y	N
17 Engel	N	N	Y	Y	Y	Y	Y	N
18 Lowey	Y	N	Y	Y	Y	Y	Y	N
19 ***Fish***	?	N	N	N	N	Y	Y	N
20 ***Gilman***	Y	N	N	N	N	Y	Y	N
21 McNulty	N	N	?	Y	Y	N	Y	Y
22 ***Solomon***	Y	Y	N	N	?	?	?	?
23 ***Boehlert***	N	?	?	?	N	Y	Y	N
24 ***McHugh***	Y	Y	N	N	N	N	Y	Y
25 ***Walsh***	N	N	Y	Y	N	Y	Y	N
26 Hinchey	N	N	Y	Y	Y	Y	Y	N
27 ***Paxon***	Y	Y	N	N	N	N	Y	Y
28 Slaughter	N	Y	Y	Y	Y	Y	Y	N
29 LaFalce	N	N	Y	Y	Y	Y	Y	N
30 ***Quinn***	N	#	?	X	N	N	Y	Y
31 ***Houghton***	Y	Y	—	Y	N	N	Y	?
NORTH CAROLINA								
1 Clayton	N	N	Y	Y	Y	Y	Y	N
2 Valentine	?	N	Y	Y	?	?	?	N

	253	254	255	256	257	258	259	260
3 Lancaster	Y	N	Y	Y	Y	Y	Y	N
4 Price	Y	N	Y	Y	Y	Y	Y	N
5 Neal	Y	?	?	?	?	Y	Y	N
6 ***Coble***	Y	Y	N	N	N	N	N	Y
7 Rose	N	N	Y	Y	Y	Y	Y	N
8 Hefner	Y	N	Y	Y	Y	Y	Y	N
9 ***McMillan***	Y	?	?	?	N	N	Y	N
10 ***Ballenger***	Y	Y	N	N	N	N	Y	Y
11 ***Taylor***	Y	Y	N	N	N	N	Y	Y
12 Watt	N	N	Y	Y	Y	Y	Y	N
NORTH DAKOTA								
AL Pomeroy	Y	N	Y	Y	Y	Y	Y	Y
OHIO								
1 Mann	N	N	Y	Y	Y	Y	Y	N
2 ***Portman***	Y	Y	N	N	N	N	Y	Y
3 Hall	N	N	Y	Y	Y	Y	Y	N
4 ***Oxley***	Y	Y	N	N	N	Y	Y	Y
5 ***Gillmor***	Y	Y	N	N	N	Y	Y	N
6 Strickland	Y	N	Y	Y	Y	Y	Y	N
7 ***Hobson***	Y	Y	N	N	N	N	Y	N
8 ***Boehner***	Y	Y	N	N	N	N	Y	Y
9 Kaptur	N	N	Y	Y	Y	Y	Y	?
10 ***Hoke***	Y	Y	N	N	N	N	Y	Y
11 Stokes	N	N	Y	Y	Y	Y	Y	N
12 ***Kasich***	Y	Y	N	N	N	Y	Y	Y
13 Brown	N	N	Y	Y	Y	Y	Y	N
14 Sawyer	Y	N	Y	Y	Y	Y	Y	N
15 ***Pryce***	Y	?	?	?	N	N	Y	Y
16 ***Regula***	Y	N	N	Y	N	Y	Y	N
17 Traficant	Y	N	Y	Y	Y	Y	Y	N
18 Applegate	Y	N	Y	Y	Y	Y	Y	Y
19 Fingerhut	Y	Y	Y	Y	Y	Y	Y	N
OKLAHOMA								
1 ***Inhofe***	Y	Y	N	N	N	N	Y	Y
2 Synar	N	N	Y	Y	Y	Y	Y	N
3 Brewster	Y	N	?	Y	Y	Y	Y	Y
4 McCurdy	?	?	?	?	Y	Y	Y	N
5 ***Istook***	Y	Y	N	N	N	N	Y	Y
6 ***Lucas***	Y	N	N	N	N	N	Y	Y
OREGON								
1 Furse	N	N	Y	Y	?	Y	Y	N
2 ***Smith***	Y	?	X	X	N	N	Y	Y
3 Wyden	N	N	Y	Y	Y	Y	Y	N
4 DeFazio	N	N	Y	Y	?	?	?	N
5 Kopetski	N	N	+	Y	Y	Y	Y	N
PENNSYLVANIA								
1 Foglietta	N	N	Y	Y	Y	Y	Y	N
2 Blackwell	N	N	?	Y	Y	Y	Y	N
3 Borski	Y	N	Y	Y	Y	Y	Y	N
4 Klink	Y	N	Y	?	Y	Y	Y	Y
5 ***Clinger***	Y	Y	N	N	N	Y	Y	Y
6 Holden	Y	N	Y	Y	Y	Y	Y	N
7 ***Weldon***	Y	?	N	N	N	Y	Y	N
8 ***Greenwood***	Y	Y	N	N	N	Y	?	N
9 ***Shuster***	Y	Y	N	N	N	N	Y	Y
10 ***McDade***	Y	N	N	Y	N	Y	Y	N
11 Kanjorski	Y	N	Y	Y	Y	Y	Y	N
12 Murtha	Y	N	Y	Y	Y	Y	Y	N
13 Margolies-Mezv.	Y	N	Y	Y	Y	Y	Y	N
14 Coyne	N	N	?	Y	Y	Y	Y	N
15 McHale	Y	N	Y	Y	Y	Y	Y	N
16 ***Walker***	Y	Y	N	N	N	N	N	Y
17 ***Gekas***	Y	N	N	N	N	N	N	Y
18 ***Santorum***	Y	Y	—	N	N	Y	Y	Y
19 ***Goodling***	Y	N	N	N	N	N	Y	Y
20 Murphy	?	N	Y	?	Y	N	Y	N
21 ***Ridge***	?	?	?	?	N	Y	Y	N
RHODE ISLAND								
1 ***Machtley***	Y	?	?	?	N	N	Y	N
2 Reed	N	N	Y	Y	Y	Y	Y	N
SOUTH CAROLINA								
1 ***Ravenel***	Y	Y	N	Y	N	N	Y	N
2 ***Spence***	Y	Y	N	N	N	N	Y	Y
3 Derrick	N	?	Y	Y	Y	Y	Y	N
4 ***Inglis***	Y	Y	N	N	N	N	N	Y
5 Spratt	Y	N	Y	Y	Y	Y	Y	N
6 Clyburn	N	N	Y	Y	Y	Y	Y	N
SOUTH DAKOTA								
AL Johnson	Y	N	Y	Y	Y	Y	Y	N
TENNESSEE								
1 ***Quillen***	Y	N	Y	Y	N	N	Y	Y
2 ***Duncan***	Y	Y	N	N	N	N	Y	Y
3 Lloyd	Y	N	Y	Y	?	?	?	?
4 Cooper	Y	N	Y	Y	Y	Y	Y	N
5 Clement	Y	N	Y	Y	Y	Y	Y	N

	253	254	255	256	257	258	259	260
6 Gordon	Y	N	Y	Y	Y	Y	Y	N
7 ***Sundquist***	Y	N	Y	N	N	N	Y	Y
8 Tanner	Y	N	Y	Y	Y	Y	Y	Y
9 Ford	N	N	?	Y	Y	Y	Y	N
TEXAS								
1 Chapman	N	N	Y	Y	?	?	Y	N
2 Wilson	N	N	Y	Y	Y	N	Y	?
3 ***Johnson, Sam***	Y	Y	N	N	N	N	Y	Y
4 Hall	Y	Y	Y	Y	Y	Y	Y	Y
5 Bryant	N	N	Y	Y	Y	Y	Y	N
6 ***Barton***	Y	Y	N	Y	N	N	Y	Y
7 ***Archer***	Y	Y	—	N	N	N	Y	Y
8 ***Fields***	Y	Y	N	N	N	N	Y	Y
9 Brooks	?	?	?	#	Y	Y	Y	N
10 Pickle	N	N	?	Y	Y	Y	?	N
11 Edwards	Y	N	Y	Y	Y	Y	Y	Y
12 Geren	Y	N	Y	Y	Y	Y	Y	Y
13 Sarpalius	Y	N	Y	Y	Y	Y	Y	Y
14 Laughlin	Y	?	Y	Y	Y	Y	Y	Y
15 de la Garza	N	N	Y	Y	Y	Y	Y	N
16 Coleman	?	N	Y	Y	Y	Y	Y	N
17 Stenholm	Y	N	Y	Y	Y	Y	Y	Y
18 Washington	?	?	?	#	Y	?	?	?
19 ***Combest***	Y	Y	N	N	N	N	Y	Y
20 Gonzalez	N	N	Y	Y	Y	Y	Y	N
21 ***Smith***	Y	N	N	Y	N	N	Y	Y
22 ***DeLay***	Y	Y	N	N	?	N	Y	Y
23 ***Bonilla***	Y	N	N	Y	N	N	Y	Y
24 Frost	N	N	Y	Y	?	?	?	N
25 Andrews	N	N	?	Y	Y	Y	Y	N
26 ***Armey***	Y	Y	N	N	N	N	Y	Y
27 Ortiz	N	N	Y	Y	Y	Y	Y	Y
28 Tejeda	N	N	Y	Y	Y	Y	Y	Y
29 Green	N	N	Y	Y	Y	Y	Y	N
30 Johnson, E.B.	N	N	Y	Y	Y	Y	Y	N
UTAH								
1 ***Hansen***	Y	Y	N	N	N	N	Y	Y
2 Shepherd	Y	N	Y	Y	Y	Y	Y	N
3 Orton	Y	Y	Y	Y	Y	Y	Y	Y
VERMONT								
AL *Sanders*	N	N	Y	Y	Y	Y	Y	N
VIRGINIA								
1 ***Bateman***	Y	Y	N	N	N	N	Y	Y
2 Pickett	Y	N	Y	Y	Y	Y	Y	Y
3 Scott	N	N	Y	Y	Y	Y	Y	N
4 Sisisky	Y	N	Y	Y	Y	Y	Y	Y
5 Payne	Y	N	?	Y	Y	Y	Y	N
6 ***Goodlatte***	Y	Y	N	N	N	N	Y	Y
7 ***Bliley***	Y	Y	N	N	N	N	Y	Y
8 Moran	Y	?	Y	Y	Y	Y	Y	N
9 Boucher	Y	N	Y	Y	Y	Y	Y	N
10 ***Wolf***	Y	Y	N	N	N	Y	Y	Y
11 Byrne	Y	N	Y	Y	Y	Y	Y	N
WASHINGTON								
1 Cantwell	Y	N	Y	Y	Y	Y	Y	N
2 Swift	N	N	Y	Y	Y	Y	Y	N
3 Unsoeld	N	N	Y	Y	Y	Y	Y	N
4 Inslee	Y	N	Y	Y	Y	Y	Y	N
5 Foley								
6 Dicks	Y	N	Y	Y	Y	Y	Y	N
7 McDermott	N	N	?	Y	Y	Y	Y	N
8 ***Dunn***	Y	Y	N	N	N	Y	Y	Y
9 Kreidler	Y	N	Y	Y	Y	Y	Y	N
WEST VIRGINIA								
1 Mollohan	N	N	Y	Y	Y	Y	Y	N
2 Wise	N	N	Y	Y	Y	Y	Y	N
3 Rahall	N	N	Y	Y	Y	Y	Y	N
WISCONSIN								
1 Barca	Y	Y	Y	Y	Y	Y	Y	N
2 ***Klug***	Y	Y	N	N	N	Y	Y	N
3 ***Gunderson***	Y	N	N	N	N	Y	Y	N
4 Kleczka	Y	N	?	Y	Y	Y	Y	N
5 Barrett	N	N	Y	Y	Y	Y	Y	N
6 ***Petri***	Y	Y	N	N	N	N	Y	Y
7 Obey	N	N	Y	Y	Y	?	?	N
8 ***Roth***	Y	Y	N	N	N	N	Y	Y
9 ***Sensenbrenner***	Y	Y	N	N	N	N	Y	Y
WYOMING								
AL ***Thomas***	Y	Y	N	N	N	N	Y	Y
DELEGATES								
de Lugo, V.I.	D	N	Y	D	D	D	D	N
Faleomavaega, Am.S.	D	?	Y	D	D	D	D	N
Norton, D.C.	D	N	Y	D	D	D	D	N
Romero-B., P.R.	D	?	?	D	D	D	D	N
Underwood, Guam	D	N	Y	D	D	D	D	?

Southern states - Ala., Ark., Fla., Ga., Ky., La., Miss., N.C., Okla., S.C., Tenn., Texas, Va.
Omitted votes are quorum calls, which CQ does not include in its vote charts.

HOUSE VOTES 261, 262, 263, 264, 265, 266, 267

261. HR 4602. Fiscal 1995 Interior Appropriations/Presidio National Park. Duncan, R-Tenn., amendment to cut $14 million from the National Park Service's operational budget to reduce the operating expenses at the Presidio in San Francisco, which is being converted from a military base to a national park. Rejected in the Committee of the Whole 171-257: R 149-24; D 22-232 (ND 8-166, SD 14-66); I 0-1, June 22, 1994.

262. HR 4602. Fiscal 1995 Interior Appropriations/National Park Service Construction. Hefley, R-Colo., amendment to cut $6.3 million for National Park Service construction at the Fisher Peak Mountain Music Center on the Blue Ridge Parkway in Virginia and the Allegheny Portage Railroad in Pennsylvania. Rejected in the Committee of the Whole 146-282: R 121-54; D 25-227 (ND 19-153, SD 6-74); I 0-1, June 22, 1994.

263. HR 4602. Fiscal 1995 Interior Appropriations/National Endowment for the Arts. Crane, R-Ill., amendment to eliminate the $171.1 million appropriation for the National Endowment for the Arts. Rejected in the Committee of the Whole 113-313: R 97-78; D 16-234 (ND 5-165, SD 11-69); I 0-1, June 22, 1994. A "nay" was a vote in support of the president's position.

264. HR 3355. Omnibus Crime Bill/Motion to Instruct. McCollum, R-Fla., motion to instruct House conferees not to authorize less than $13.5 billion for prison construction, the amount approved by the House. Motion agreed to 338-81: R 173-1; D 165-79 (ND 100-66, SD 65-13); I 0-1, June 22, 1994.

265. HR 4602. Fiscal 1995 Interior Appropriations/National Endowment for the Arts. Bachus, R-Ala., amendment to cut the $171.1 million appropriation for the National Endowment for the Arts by $92.7 million to $78.4 million. Rejected in the Committee of the Whole 132-297: R 113-64; D 19-232 (ND 7-164, SD 12-68); I 0-1, June 23, 1994. A "nay" was a vote in support of the president's position.

266. HR 4602. Fiscal 1995 Interior Appropriations/National Endowment for the Arts. Dicks, D-Wash., amendment to the Stearns, R-Fla., amendment, to cut the $171.1 million appropriation for the National Endowment for the Arts (NEA) by 1.5 percent. The Stearns amendment would have cut NEA funding by 5 percent. Adopted in the Committee of the Whole 240-189: R 36-141; D 203-48 (ND 147-23, SD 56-25); I 1-0, June 23, 1994. (Subsequently, the Stearns amendment as modified by the amended Bachus amendment was adopted on vote 270; see vote 269.)

267. HR 4602. Fiscal 1995 Interior Appropriations/National Endowment for the Arts. Yates, D-Ill., amendment to the Bachus, R-Ala., substitute amendment to the Stearns, R-Fla., amendment to cut the $171.1 million appropriation for the National Endowment for the Arts (NEA) by 1 percent. The Bachus amendment provided for a 4.99 percent cut, and the Stearns amendment as modified by the Dicks amendment (see vote 266) called for a 1.5 percent cut. Adopted in the Committee of the Whole 218-214: R 14-163; D 203-51 (ND 149-25, SD 54-26); I 1-0, June 23, 1994. (Subsequently, the amendment was rejected on an automatic revote in the full House, required whenever delegate votes provide the margin deciding an issue. See vote 268.)

KEY

Y Voted for (yea).
\# Paired for.
+ Announced for.
N Voted against (nay).
X Paired against.
− Announced against.
P Voted "present."
C Voted "present" to avoid possible conflict of interest.
? Did not vote or otherwise make a position known.
D Delegates ineligible to vote.

Democrats **Republicans** *Independent*

	261	262	263	264	265	266	267
ALABAMA							
1 *Callahan*	Y	Y	Y	Y	Y	N	N
2 *Everett*	Y	Y	Y	Y	Y	N	N
3 Browder	N	N	N	Y	N	Y	N
4 Bevill	N	N	N	Y	N	Y	Y
5 Cramer	N	N	N	Y	N	Y	N
6 *Bachus*	?	Y	Y	Y	Y	N	N
7 Hilliard	N	N	N	N	N	Y	Y
ALASKA							
AL *Young*	Y	Y	Y	Y	N	Y	N
ARIZONA							
1 Coppersmith	N	N	N	Y	N	Y	Y
2 Pastor	N	N	N	Y	N	Y	Y
3 *Stump*	Y	Y	Y	Y	Y	N	N
4 *Kyl*	Y	Y	Y	Y	Y	N	N
5 *Kolbe*	Y	N	N	Y	N	N	N
6 English	N	N	N	Y	N	Y	Y
ARKANSAS							
1 Lambert	N	N	N	Y	N	Y	Y
2 Thornton	N	N	N	Y	N	Y	Y
3 *Hutchinson*	Y	Y	Y	Y	Y	N	N
4 Dickey	Y	Y	Y	Y	Y	N	N
CALIFORNIA							
1 Hamburg	N	N	N	Y	N	Y	Y
2 *Herger*	Y	Y	Y	Y	Y	N	N
3 Fazio	N	N	N	Y	N	Y	Y
4 *Doolittle*	Y	Y	Y	Y	Y	N	N
5 Matsui	N	N	N	Y	N	Y	Y
6 Woolsey	N	N	N	N	N	Y	Y
7 Miller	N	N	N	N	N	Y	Y
8 Pelosi	N	N	N	N	N	Y	Y
9 Dellums	N	N	N	N	N	Y	Y
10 *Baker*	N	Y	Y	Y	Y	N	N
11 *Pombo*	Y	Y	Y	Y	Y	N	N
12 Lantos	N	N	N	Y	N	Y	Y
13 Stark	N	N	N	N	N	Y	Y
14 Eshoo	N	N	N	Y	N	Y	Y
15 Mineta	N	N	N	Y	N	Y	Y
16 Edwards	N	N	N	Y	N	Y	Y
17 Farr	N	N	N	Y	N	Y	Y
18 Condit	N	Y	Y	Y	Y	N	N
19 Lehman	Y	N	N	Y	N	N	N
20 Dooley	N	N	Y	Y	N	Y	Y
21 *Thomas*	Y	Y	Y	Y	Y	N	N
22 *Huffington*	N	Y	Y	N	N	N	N
23 *Gallegly*	Y	Y	Y	Y	Y	N	N
24 Beilenson	N	N	N	N	N	Y	Y
25 *McKeon*	Y	Y	Y	Y	Y	N	N
26 Berman	N	N	N	N	N	Y	Y
27 *Moorhead*	Y	N	Y	Y	Y	N	N
28 *Dreier*	Y	Y	Y	Y	Y	N	N
29 Waxman	N	N	N	N	N	Y	Y
30 Becerra	N	N	N	N	N	Y	Y
31 Martinez	N	N	N	Y	N	Y	Y
32 Dixon	N	N	N	Y	N	Y	Y
33 Roybal-Allard	N	N	N	Y	N	Y	Y
34 Torres	N	N	N	N	N	Y	Y
35 Waters	N	N	N	N	N	N	Y
36 Harman	N	N	N	Y	N	?	Y
37 Tucker	N	N	N	Y	N	?	Y
38 *Horn*	N	N	N	Y	N	Y	N
39 *Royce*	Y	Y	Y	Y	Y	N	N
40 *Lewis*	Y	N	Y	Y	Y	N	N
41 *Kim*	Y	Y	Y	Y	Y	N	N

	261	262	263	264	265	266	267
42 Brown	N	N	N	N	N	Y	Y
43 *Calvert*	Y	N	Y	Y	Y	N	N
44 *McCandless*	Y	N	Y	Y	Y	N	N
45 *Rohrabacher*	Y	N	Y	Y	Y	N	N
46 *Dornan*	Y	Y	Y	Y	Y	N	N
47 *Cox*	N	Y	Y	Y	Y	N	N
48 *Packard*	N	N	N	N	N	N	N
49 Schenk	N	N	N	Y	N	Y	Y
50 Filner	N	N	N	N	N	Y	Y
51 *Cunningham*	N	Y	Y	Y	Y	N	N
52 *Hunter*	Y	N	Y	Y	Y	N	N
COLORADO							
1 Schroeder	N	N	N	N	N	Y	Y
2 Skaggs	N	N	N	N	N	Y	Y
3 *McInnis*	Y	N	Y	Y	Y	N	N
4 *Allard*	Y	Y	Y	Y	Y	N	N
5 *Hefley*	Y	Y	Y	Y	Y	N	N
6 *Schaefer*	Y	Y	Y	Y	Y	N	N
CONNECTICUT							
1 Kennelly	N	N	N	Y	N	Y	Y
2 Gejdenson	N	N	N	Y	N	Y	Y
3 DeLauro	N	N	N	Y	N	Y	Y
4 *Shays*	Y	Y	N	Y	N	Y	N
5 *Franks*	Y	Y	Y	N	N	Y	N
6 *Johnson*	Y	N	N	Y	N	Y	Y
DELAWARE							
AL *Castle*	Y	Y	N	Y	N	Y	N
FLORIDA							
1 Hutto	N	N	Y	Y	Y	N	N
2 Peterson	N	N	N	Y	N	Y	Y
3 Brown	N	N	N	N	N	Y	Y
4 *Fowler*	Y	N	N	Y	N	Y	N
5 Thurman	N	Y	N	Y	N	Y	Y
6 *Stearns*	Y	Y	Y	Y	Y	N	N
7 *Mica*	Y	N	Y	Y	Y	N	N
8 *McCollum*	Y	Y	Y	Y	Y	N	N
9 *Bilirakis*	Y	Y	Y	Y	Y	N	N
10 *Young*	Y	Y	Y	Y	Y	N	N
11 Gibbons	?	N	N	Y	N	Y	Y
12 *Canady*	Y	Y	Y	Y	Y	N	N
13 *Miller*	Y	Y	Y	Y	Y	N	N
14 *Goss*	Y	Y	N	Y	N	Y	N
15 Bacchus	N	N	N	Y	N	Y	Y
16 *Lewis*	Y	Y	Y	Y	Y	N	N
17 Meek	N	N	N	N	N	Y	Y
18 *Ros-Lehtinen*	Y	N	Y	Y	Y	N	N
19 Johnston	N	N	N	Y	N	Y	Y
20 Deutsch	N	N	N	Y	N	Y	Y
21 *Diaz-Balart*	Y	N	N	Y	Y	N	N
22 *Shaw*	Y	N	Y	Y	Y	N	N
23 Hastings	N	N	N	N	N	Y	Y
GEORGIA							
1 *Kingston*	Y	Y	Y	Y	Y	N	N
2 Bishop	N	N	N	Y	N	Y	Y
3 *Collins*	Y	Y	Y	Y	Y	N	N
4 *Linder*	Y	Y	Y	Y	Y	N	N
5 Lewis	N	N	N	N	N	Y	Y
6 *Gingrich*	Y	Y	Y	Y	Y	N	N
7 Darden	N	N	N	Y	N	Y	Y
8 Rowland	N	N	N	N	N	Y	Y
9 Deal	N	N	N	N	N	Y	Y
10 Johnson	N	N	N	Y	N	Y	Y
11 McKinney	N	N	N	Y	N	Y	Y
HAWAII							
1 Abercrombie	N	N	N	N	N	N	Y
2 Mink	N	N	N	N	N	Y	Y
IDAHO							
1 LaRocco	N	N	N	Y	N	Y	Y
2 *Crapo*	Y	Y	N	Y	N	N	N
ILLINOIS							
1 Rush	N	N	N	N	N	Y	Y
2 Reynolds	N	N	?	Y	N	Y	Y
3 Lipinski	N	N	N	Y	N	N	N
4 Gutierrez	N	N	N	N	N	Y	Y
5 Rostenkowski	N	N	N	?	N	Y	Y
6 *Hyde*	Y	Y	Y	Y	Y	N	N
7 Collins	N	N	N	N	N	Y	Y
8 *Crane*	Y	Y	Y	Y	Y	N	N
9 Yates	N	N	N	N	N	Y	Y
10 *Porter*	N	Y	N	Y	N	Y	Y
11 Sangmeister	N	N	N	Y	N	Y	Y
12 Costello	N	Y	N	Y	N	Y	Y
13 *Fawell*	Y	Y	N	Y	N	Y	Y
14 *Hastert*	Y	Y	N	Y	N	Y	N
15 *Ewing*	Y	N	N	Y	N	Y	N
16 *Manzullo*	Y	Y	Y	Y	Y	N	N
17 Evans	N	N	N	N	N	Y	Y

ND Northern Democrats   SD Southern Democrats

78-H — 1994 CQ ALMANAC

	261	262	263	264	265	266	267
18 ***Michel***	Y	N	N	Y	N	Y	N
19 Poshard	Y	Y	N	Y	N	N	N
20 Durbin	N	N	N	Y	N	Y	Y
INDIANA							
1 Visclosky	N	N	N	N	N	Y	Y
2 Sharp	?	?	?	?	N	Y	Y
3 Roemer	N	N	N	Y	N	Y	Y
4 Long	N	N	N	Y	N	N	N
5 ***Buyer***	Y	Y	Y	Y	Y	N	N
6 ***Burton***	Y	Y	Y	Y	Y	N	N
7 ***Myers***	Y	N	Y	Y	Y	N	N
8 McCloskey	N	N	N	Y	N	N	N
9 Hamilton	N	N	N	Y	N	N	N
10 Jacobs	N	N	N	Y	N	Y	Y
IOWA							
1 ***Leach***	Y	Y	N	Y	N	Y	Y
2 ***Nussle***	Y	Y	N	Y	Y	N	N
3 ***Lightfoot***	Y	N	Y	Y	Y	N	N
4 Smith	N	?	N	Y	N	Y	Y
5 ***Grandy***	Y	Y	N	Y	N	Y	Y
KANSAS							
1 ***Roberts***	Y	Y	Y	Y	Y	N	N
2 Slattery	N	N	N	Y	N	Y	Y
3 ***Meyers***	Y	Y	N	Y	N	N	N
4 Glickman	N	N	N	Y	N	Y	Y
KENTUCKY							
1 Barlow	N	N	N	N	N	Y	Y
2 ***Lewis***	Y	Y	Y	Y	Y	N	N
3 Mazzoli	N	N	N	Y	N	Y	Y
4 ***Bunning***	Y	Y	Y	Y	Y	N	N
5 ***Rogers***	Y	N	N	Y	N	N	N
6 Baesler	Y	N	N	Y	N	Y	Y
LOUISIANA							
1 ***Livingston***	Y	N	Y	Y	Y	N	N
2 Jefferson	N	N	N	Y	N	Y	Y
3 Tauzin	Y	Y	Y	Y	Y	N	N
4 Fields	N	N	N	N	N	Y	Y
5 ***McCrery***	Y	Y	Y	Y	Y	N	N
6 ***Baker***	Y	Y	Y	Y	Y	N	N
7 Hayes	N	N	Y	?	Y	N	N
MAINE							
1 Andrews	N	Y	N	Y	N	Y	Y
2 ***Snowe***	Y	Y	N	Y	N	N	N
MARYLAND							
1 ***Gilchrest***	N	N	Y	Y	Y	Y	N
2 ***Bentley***	Y	Y	N	Y	N	N	N
3 Cardin	N	N	N	Y	N	Y	Y
4 Wynn	N	N	N	Y	N	Y	Y
5 Hoyer	N	N	N	Y	N	Y	Y
6 ***Bartlett***	Y	Y	Y	Y	Y	N	N
7 Mfume	N	N	N	N	N	Y	Y
8 ***Morella***	N	N	N	Y	N	Y	Y
MASSACHUSETTS							
1 Olver	N	N	N	N	N	Y	Y
2 Neal	N	N	N	Y	N	Y	Y
3 ***Blute***	Y	Y	N	Y	N	Y	N
4 Frank	N	N	N	N	N	Y	Y
5 Meehan	N	N	N	N	N	Y	Y
6 ***Torkildsen***	Y	Y	N	Y	N	Y	N
7 Markey	N	N	N	N	N	Y	Y
8 Kennedy	N	N	N	N	N	Y	Y
9 Moakley	N	N	N	Y	N	Y	Y
10 Studds	N	N	N	N	N	Y	Y
MICHIGAN							
1 Stupak	N	N	N	Y	N	Y	Y
2 ***Hoekstra***	Y	Y	N	Y	N	N	N
3 ***Ehlers***	N	N	N	N	N	Y	Y
4 ***Camp***	Y	Y	N	Y	N	N	N
5 Barcia	N	Y	Y	Y	Y	Y	N
6 ***Upton***	Y	Y	N	Y	N	N	N
7 ***Smith***	Y	Y	Y	Y	Y	N	N
8 Carr	N	N	N	Y	N	Y	Y
9 Kildee	N	Y	N	Y	N	Y	Y
10 Bonior	N	N	N	N	N	Y	Y
11 ***Knollenberg***	Y	Y	Y	Y	Y	N	N
12 Levin	N	N	N	Y	N	Y	Y
13 Ford	N	N	N	?	N	Y	Y
14 Conyers	N	N	N	N	N	Y	Y
15 Collins	N	N	N	N	N	Y	Y
16 Dingell	N	N	N	N	N	Y	Y
MINNESOTA							
1 Penny	Y	Y	N	N	N	Y	N
2 Minge	Y	Y	N	N	N	N	N
3 ***Ramstad***	Y	Y	N	Y	N	N	N
4 Vento	N	N	N	N	N	Y	Y
5 Sabo	N	N	N	N	N	Y	Y
6 ***Grams***	Y	Y	Y	Y	Y	N	N
7 Peterson	N	Y	N	Y	N	Y	N
8 Oberstar	N	N	?	N	N	Y	Y
MISSISSIPPI							
1 Whitten	N	N	N	?	N	Y	Y
2 Thompson	N	N	N	Y	N	Y	Y
3 Montgomery	N	N	N	Y	N	N	N
4 Parker	Y	Y	Y	Y	Y	N	N
5 Taylor	Y	N	Y	Y	Y	N	N
MISSOURI							
1 Clay	N	N	N	N	N	Y	Y
2 ***Talent***	Y	Y	Y	Y	Y	N	N
3 Gephardt	N	N	N	Y	N	Y	Y
4 Skelton	N	N	Y	Y	Y	N	N
5 Wheat	N	N	N	Y	N	Y	Y
6 Danner	N	N	N	Y	N	Y	Y
7 ***Hancock***	Y	Y	Y	Y	Y	N	N
8 ***Emerson***	Y	Y	Y	Y	Y	N	N
9 Volkmer	N	N	N	Y	N	N	N
MONTANA							
AL Williams	Y	Y	N	Y	N	Y	Y
NEBRASKA							
1 ***Bereuter***	N	N	N	Y	Y	N	N
2 Hoagland	N	N	N	Y	N	Y	Y
3 ***Barrett***	Y	Y	Y	Y	Y	N	N
NEVADA							
1 Bilbray	N	N	N	Y	N	Y	Y
2 ***Vucanovich***	Y	N	Y	Y	Y	N	N
NEW HAMPSHIRE							
1 ***Zeliff***	Y	Y	N	Y	N	N	N
2 Swett	Y	Y	N	Y	N	N	N
NEW JERSEY							
1 Andrews	N	N	N	Y	N	N	N
2 Hughes	N	N	N	N	N	Y	Y
3 ***Saxton***	N	N	N	Y	N	N	N
4 ***Smith***	Y	N	Y	Y	Y	N	N
5 ***Roukema***	Y	Y	N	Y	N	N	N
6 Pallone	N	N	N	Y	N	Y	Y
7 ***Franks***	Y	Y	N	Y	N	N	N
8 Klein	N	Y	N	Y	N	Y	Y
9 Torricelli	N	N	N	Y	N	Y	Y
10 Payne	N	N	N	N	N	Y	Y
11 ***Gallo***	N	N	N	Y	N	Y	N
12 ***Zimmer***	Y	Y	N	Y	N	N	N
13 Menendez	N	N	N	Y	N	Y	Y
NEW MEXICO							
1 ***Schiff***	Y	N	N	Y	N	N	N
2 ***Skeen***	Y	N	N	Y	N	Y	N
3 Richardson	N	N	N	Y	N	Y	Y
NEW YORK							
1 Hochbrueckner	N	N	N	Y	N	?	Y
2 ***Lazio***	Y	N	N	Y	N	Y	N
3 ***King***	Y	N	Y	Y	Y	N	N
4 ***Levy***	Y	N	Y	Y	Y	N	N
5 Ackerman	?	?	?	?	N	N	Y
6 Flake	N	N	N	N	N	Y	Y
7 Manton	N	N	N	Y	N	Y	Y
8 Nadler	N	N	N	N	N	Y	Y
9 Schumer	N	N	N	?	?	?	#
10 Towns	N	N	N	N	?	?	?
11 Owens	N	N	N	N	N	N	Y
12 Velazquez	N	N	?	N	N	Y	Y
13 ***Molinari***	Y	Y	N	Y	Y	N	N
14 Maloney	N	N	N	Y	N	Y	Y
15 Rangel	N	N	N	N	N	Y	Y
16 Serrano	N	N	?	N	N	Y	Y
17 Engel	N	N	N	Y	?	N	Y
18 Lowey	N	N	N	Y	N	Y	Y
19 ***Fish***	Y	N	N	Y	N	Y	Y
20 ***Gilman***	N	N	N	Y	N	Y	Y
21 McNulty	N	N	N	Y	N	Y	N
22 ***Solomon***	?	?	?	?	Y	N	N
23 ***Boehlert***	N	N	N	Y	N	Y	Y
24 ***McHugh***	Y	Y	Y	Y	Y	N	N
25 ***Walsh***	N	N	N	Y	N	Y	N
26 Hinchey	N	N	N	N	N	Y	Y
27 ***Paxon***	Y	Y	Y	Y	Y	N	N
28 Slaughter	N	N	N	Y	N	Y	Y
29 LaFalce	N	N	N	N	N	Y	Y
30 ***Quinn***	Y	Y	Y	Y	Y	N	N
31 ***Houghton***	?	?	?	?	N	Y	Y
NORTH CAROLINA							
1 Clayton	N	N	N	Y	N	Y	Y
2 Valentine	N	N	N	Y	Y	Y	N
3 Lancaster	N	N	N	Y	N	Y	N
4 Price	N	N	N	Y	N	Y	Y
5 Neal	N	N	N	Y	N	Y	Y
6 ***Coble***	Y	Y	Y	Y	Y	N	N
7 Rose	N	N	N	Y	N	Y	Y
8 Hefner	N	N	N	Y	N	Y	Y
9 ***McMillan***	N	N	N	Y	N	Y	N
10 ***Ballenger***	Y	Y	N	Y	Y	N	N
11 ***Taylor***	Y	N	Y	Y	Y	N	N
12 Watt	N	N	N	N	N	Y	Y
NORTH DAKOTA							
AL Pomeroy	N	N	N	Y	N	Y	N
OHIO							
1 Mann	Y	Y	N	N	N	Y	N
2 ***Portman***	Y	Y	N	Y	Y	N	N
3 Hall	N	N	N	Y	N	N	N
4 ***Oxley***	?	Y	N	Y	Y	N	N
5 ***Gillmor***	Y	N	N	Y	Y	N	N
6 Strickland	N	N	N	Y	N	Y	Y
7 ***Hobson***	Y	N	N	Y	N	N	N
8 ***Boehner***	Y	Y	Y	Y	Y	Y	N
9 Kaptur	N	N	N	Y	N	Y	Y
10 ***Hoke***	Y	Y	N	Y	N	N	N
11 Stokes	N	N	N	N	N	Y	Y
12 ***Kasich***	Y	Y	N	Y	Y	Y	N
13 Brown	N	N	N	Y	Y	Y	Y
14 Sawyer	N	N	N	Y	N	Y	Y
15 ***Pryce***	Y	Y	N	Y	Y	N	N
16 ***Regula***	N	N	N	Y	N	Y	N
17 Traficant	N	N	N	Y	N	N	N
18 Applegate	N	N	N	Y	N	Y	Y
19 Fingerhut	N	Y	N	Y	N	Y	Y
OKLAHOMA							
1 ***Inhofe***	Y	Y	Y	Y	Y	N	N
2 Synar	N	N	N	N	N	Y	Y
3 Brewster	Y	N	N	Y	N	Y	Y
4 McCurdy	N	?	?	?	N	N	N
5 ***Istook***	Y	Y	Y	Y	Y	N	N
6 ***Lucas***	Y	Y	Y	Y	Y	N	N
OREGON							
1 Furse	N	N	N	Y	N	Y	Y
2 ***Smith***	Y	Y	Y	Y	Y	N	N
3 Wyden	N	N	N	Y	N	Y	Y
4 DeFazio	N	N	N	N	N	Y	Y
5 Kopetski	N	N	N	N	N	Y	Y
PENNSYLVANIA							
1 Foglietta	N	N	N	N	N	Y	Y
2 Blackwell	N	N	N	N	N	Y	Y
3 Borski	N	N	N	Y	N	Y	Y
4 Klink	N	N	N	Y	N	Y	N
5 ***Clinger***	Y	N	N	Y	N	Y	Y
6 Holden	N	N	Y	Y	Y	N	N
7 ***Weldon***	N	N	N	Y	N	N	N
8 ***Greenwood***	Y	Y	Y	Y	Y	N	N
9 ***Shuster***	Y	N	Y	Y	Y	N	N
10 ***McDade***	N	N	N	Y	N	N	N
11 Kanjorski	N	N	N	Y	N	N	N
12 Murtha	N	N	N	?	N	N	Y
13 Margolies-Mezv.	N	Y	N	Y	N	?	Y
14 Coyne	N	N	N	N	N	Y	Y
15 McHale	N	N	N	Y	N	Y	N
16 ***Walker***	Y	Y	Y	Y	Y	N	N
17 ***Gekas***	Y	Y	Y	Y	Y	N	N
18 ***Santorum***	?	N	N	Y	N	N	N
19 ***Goodling***	Y	N	N	Y	Y	N	N
20 Murphy	N	N	N	N	N	Y	Y
21 ***Ridge***	Y	N	N	Y	N	Y	Y
RHODE ISLAND							
1 ***Machtley***	Y	?	?	?	?	?	X
2 Reed	N	N	N	Y	N	Y	Y
SOUTH CAROLINA							
1 ***Ravenel***	N	Y	N	Y	N	Y	Y
2 ***Spence***	Y	Y	N	Y	N	N	N
3 Derrick	N	N	N	Y	N	Y	Y
4 ***Inglis***	Y	Y	Y	Y	Y	N	N
5 Spratt	N	N	N	Y	N	Y	Y
6 Clyburn	N	N	N	Y	N	Y	Y
SOUTH DAKOTA							
AL Johnson	N	N	N	Y	N	Y	Y
TENNESSEE							
1 ***Quillen***	Y	N	Y	Y	Y	N	N
2 ***Duncan***	Y	Y	Y	Y	Y	N	N
3 Lloyd	?	?	?	?	?	?	?
4 Cooper	Y	Y	N	Y	N	N	N
5 Clement	Y	N	N	Y	N	Y	Y
6 Gordon	N	N	N	Y	N	N	Y
7 ***Sundquist***	Y	N	N	Y	N	N	N
8 Tanner	Y	N	Y	Y	Y	N	N
9 Ford	N	N	N	N	N	Y	?
TEXAS							
1 Chapman	Y	N	N	Y	?	N	N
2 Wilson	N	N	N	Y	N	Y	Y
3 ***Johnson, Sam***	Y	Y	Y	Y	Y	N	N
4 Hall	N	Y	Y	Y	Y	N	N
5 Bryant	N	N	N	Y	N	Y	Y
6 ***Barton***	Y	Y	Y	Y	Y	N	N
7 ***Archer***	Y	Y	Y	Y	Y	N	N
8 ***Fields***	Y	Y	Y	Y	Y	N	N
9 Brooks	N	N	N	N	N	Y	Y
10 Pickle	N	N	N	Y	N	Y	Y
11 Edwards	N	N	N	Y	N	N	N
12 Geren	N	N	Y	Y	Y	N	N
13 Sarpalius	Y	N	Y	Y	Y	N	N
14 Laughlin	N	N	Y	Y	Y	N	N
15 de la Garza	N	N	N	Y	N	Y	Y
16 Coleman	N	N	N	Y	N	Y	Y
17 Stenholm	Y	Y	Y	Y	Y	N	N
18 Washington	?	?	?	?	?	?	?
19 ***Combest***	Y	Y	Y	Y	Y	N	N
20 Gonzalez	N	N	N	N	N	Y	Y
21 ***Smith***	Y	Y	Y	?	Y	N	N
22 ***DeLay***	Y	N	Y	Y	Y	N	N
23 ***Bonilla***	Y	Y	Y	Y	Y	N	N
24 Frost	N	N	N	Y	N	Y	Y
25 Andrews	N	N	N	Y	N	Y	Y
26 ***Armey***	Y	Y	Y	Y	Y	N	N
27 Ortiz	N	N	N	Y	N	N	N
28 Tejeda	N	N	N	Y	N	Y	Y
29 Green	Y	N	N	Y	N	Y	Y
30 Johnson, E.B.	N	N	N	N	N	Y	Y
UTAH							
1 ***Hansen***	Y	Y	N	Y	Y	N	N
2 Shepherd	N	N	N	Y	Y	Y	Y
3 Orton	N	N	Y	Y	Y	N	N
VERMONT							
AL *Sanders*	N	N	N	N	N	Y	Y
VIRGINIA							
1 ***Bateman***	N	N	N	Y	N	N	N
2 Pickett	Y	N	N	Y	N	N	N
3 Scott	N	N	N	N	N	Y	Y
4 Sisisky	Y	N	N	Y	N	N	N
5 Payne	N	N	N	Y	N	Y	Y
6 ***Goodlatte***	Y	N	Y	Y	Y	N	N
7 ***Bliley***	Y	N	Y	Y	N	N	N
8 Moran	N	N	N	Y	N	N	Y
9 Boucher	N	N	N	Y	N	Y	Y
10 ***Wolf***	N	N	N	Y	Y	N	N
11 Byrne	N	N	N	Y	N	Y	Y
WASHINGTON							
1 Cantwell	N	N	N	Y	N	Y	Y
2 Swift	N	N	N	Y	N	Y	Y
3 Unsoeld	N	N	N	Y	N	Y	Y
4 Inslee	N	Y	N	Y	N	Y	Y
5 Foley							
6 Dicks	N	N	N	Y	N	Y	Y
7 McDermott	N	N	N	N	N	Y	Y
8 ***Dunn***	Y	Y	N	Y	N	N	N
9 Kreidler	N	Y	N	Y	N	Y	Y
WEST VIRGINIA							
1 Mollohan	N	N	N	N	N	Y	Y
2 Wise	N	N	N	Y	N	Y	Y
3 Rahall	N	N	N	Y	N	Y	Y
WISCONSIN							
1 Barca	N	Y	N	Y	N	Y	Y
2 ***Klug***	Y	Y	N	Y	N	N	N
3 ***Gunderson***	N	Y	N	Y	N	Y	N
4 Kleczka	N	?	N	Y	N	Y	Y
5 Barrett	N	Y	N	Y	N	Y	Y
6 ***Petri***	Y	Y	Y	Y	Y	N	N
7 Obey	N	N	N	N	N	Y	Y
8 ***Roth***	Y	Y	Y	Y	Y	N	N
9 ***Sensenbrenner***	Y	Y	Y	Y	Y	N	N
WYOMING							
AL ***Thomas***	Y	Y	N	Y	N	N	N
DELEGATES							
de Lugo, V.I.	N	N	N	D	N	Y	Y
Faleomavaega, Am.S.	N	N	N	D	?	?	?
Norton, D.C.	N	N	N	D	N	Y	Y
Romero-B., P.R.	N	N	N	D	N	Y	Y
Underwood, Guam	?	?	?	D	?	?	Y

Southern states - Ala., Ark., Fla., Ga., Ky., La., Miss., N.C., Okla., S.C., Tenn., Texas, Va.
Omitted votes are quorum calls, which CQ does not include in its vote charts.

268. HR 4602. Fiscal 1995 Interior Appropriations/Revote on National Endowment for the Arts. Revote as required when delegate votes provide the margin deciding an issue, as occurred on the Yates, D-Ill., amendment to the Bachus, R-Ala., substitute amendment to the Stearns, R-Fla., amendment, to reduce NEA funding by 1 percent. The Bachus amendment provided for a 4.99 percent cut, and the Stearns amendment as modified by the Dicks, D-Wash., amendment called for a 1.5 percent cut. Rejected 210-216: R 11-165; D 198-51 (ND 146-25, SD 52-26); I 1-0, June 23, 1994. (Under House rules, such revotes occur automatically, requiring the Committee of the Whole to rise, and the revote to occur in the full House, where delegates may not vote. Following the revote, the Committee of the Whole resumed consideration of the bill. See vote 267.)

269. HR 4602. Fiscal 1995 Interior Appropriations/National Endowment for the Arts. Dicks, D-Wash., amendment to the Bachus, R-Ala., substitute amendment to the Stearns, R-Fla., amendment, to cut the National Endowment for the Arts by 2 percent. The Bachus amendment provided for a 4.99 percent cut; the original Stearns amendment provided for a 5 percent cut; the first Dicks amendment called for a 1.5 percent cut. Adopted in the Committee of the Whole 222-204: R 14-162; D 207-42 (ND 152-17, SD 55-25); I 1-0, June 23, 1994. (Subsequently, the Bachus amendment as amended by the second Dicks amendment was adopted by voice vote, and the Stearns amendment as modified by the amended Bachus amendment was adopted on vote 270.)

270. HR 4602. Fiscal 1995 Interior Appropriations/National Endowment for the Arts. Stearns, R-Fla., amendment, as amended, to cut the National Endowment for the Arts by 2 percent. Adopted in the Committee of the Whole 380-41: R 171-2; D 208-39 (ND 138-30, SD 70-9); I 1-0, June 23, 1994. A "nay" was a vote in support of the president's position.

271. HR 4602. Fiscal 1995 Interior Appropriations/Fossil Energy Research. Klug, R-Wis., amendment to cut the $428.5 million in new budget authority for fossil energy research by $27 million. Rejected in the Committee of the Whole 182-242: R 107-66; D 74-176 (ND 61-111, SD 13-65); I 1-0, June 23, 1994.

272. HR 4602. Fiscal 1995 Interior Appropriations/Passage. Passage of the bill to provide $13.2 billion in new budget authority for the Department of the Interior and related agencies for fiscal 1995. The administration had requested $13,424,299,000. Passed 338-85: R 95-78; D 242-7 (ND 166-3, SD 76-4); I 1-0, June 23, 1994.

273. HR 4603. Fiscal 1995 Commerce, Justice, State Appropriations/Rule. Adoption of the rule (H Res 461) to waive certain points of order against and provide for House floor consideration of the bill to provide $27,219,129,000 in new budget authority for the departments of Commerce, Justice and State, the Judiciary, and related agencies programs for fiscal 1995, of which $670,000,000 are supplemental appropriations for fiscal 1994. Adopted 243-177: R 0-174; D 242-3 (ND 165-1, SD 77-2); I 1-0, June 23, 1994.

274. HR 3355. Omnibus Crime Bill/Motion To Instruct. McCollum, R-Fla., motion to instruct the House conferees to strike the Local Partnership Act contained in the House bill, which authorizes $2 billion in formula grants to local governments in disadvantaged communities for education, substance abuse treatment and job programs. Motion rejected 143-247: R 141-27; D 2-219 (ND 0-144, SD 2-75); I 0-1, June 23, 1994.

KEY

Y	Voted for (yea).
#	Paired for.
+	Announced for.
N	Voted against (nay).
X	Paired against.
−	Announced against.
P	Voted "present."
C	Voted "present" to avoid possible conflict of interest.
?	Did not vote or otherwise make a position known.
D	Delegates ineligible to vote.

Democrats *Republicans*
Independent

	268	269	270	271	272	273	274
ALABAMA							
1 Callahan	N	N	Y	N	N	N	Y
2 Everett	N	N	Y	N	N	Y	Y
3 Browder	N	N	Y	N	N	Y	N
4 Bevill	Y	Y	Y	N	Y	Y	N
5 Cramer	N	N	Y	N	Y	Y	N
6 *Bachus*	N	N	Y	N	N	N	Y
7 Hilliard	Y	Y	N	?	Y	Y	N
ALASKA							
AL *Young*	N	N	Y	N	Y	N	N
ARIZONA							
1 Coppersmith	Y	Y	Y	Y	Y	Y	N
2 Pastor	Y	Y	Y	N	Y	Y	N
3 *Stump*	N	N	Y	N	Y	N	N
4 *Kyl*	N	N	Y	N	Y	N	Y
5 *Kolbe*	N	N	Y	N	Y	N	Y
6 English	Y	Y	Y	N	Y	Y	N
ARKANSAS							
1 Lambert	Y	Y	Y	Y	Y	Y	N
2 Thornton	Y	Y	Y	?	Y	Y	N
3 *Hutchinson*	N	N	Y	N	Y	Y	N
4 *Dickey*	N	N	Y	Y	N	N	Y
CALIFORNIA							
1 Hamburg	Y	Y	N	Y	Y	Y	N
2 *Herger*	N	N	Y	N	N	N	Y
3 Fazio	Y	Y	Y	N	Y	Y	N
4 *Doolittle*	N	N	Y	N	Y	N	N
5 Matsui	Y	Y	Y	N	Y	Y	N
6 Woolsey	Y	Y	Y	N	Y	Y	N
7 Miller	Y	Y	Y	N	Y	Y	N
8 Pelosi	Y	Y	N	Y	Y	Y	N
9 Dellums	Y	Y	N	?	Y	Y	N
10 *Baker*	N	N	Y	Y	N	N	Y
11 *Pombo*	N	N	Y	Y	N	N	N
12 Lantos	Y	Y	N	Y	Y	Y	N
13 Stark	Y	Y	N	Y	Y	Y	N
14 Eshoo	Y	Y	Y	N	Y	Y	N
15 Mineta	Y	Y	Y	N	Y	Y	N
16 Edwards	Y	Y	Y	N	Y	Y	N
17 Farr	Y	Y	Y	Y	Y	Y	N
18 Condit	N	N	Y	Y	N	?	N
19 Lehman	N	N	Y	N	Y	Y	N
20 Dooley	Y	Y	N	Y	Y	Y	N
21 *Thomas*	N	N	Y	N	Y	N	Y
22 *Huffington*	N	N	Y	Y	N	N	Y
23 *Gallegly*	N	N	Y	Y	Y	N	?
24 Beilenson	Y	Y	N	Y	Y	Y	N
25 *McKeon*	N	N	Y	Y	Y	Y	N
26 Berman	Y	Y	N	Y	Y	Y	?
27 *Moorhead*	N	N	Y	N	N	N	Y
28 *Dreier*	N	N	Y	Y	Y	N	Y
29 Waxman	Y	?	Y	Y	Y	Y	N
30 Becerra	Y	Y	Y	N	Y	Y	N
31 Martinez	Y	Y	Y	N	Y	Y	?
32 Dixon	Y	Y	N	Y	Y	Y	N
33 Roybal-Allard	Y	Y	Y	Y	Y	Y	N
34 Torres	Y	Y	N	Y	Y	Y	N
35 Waters	Y	Y	N	Y	Y	Y	N
36 Harman	Y	Y	N	Y	Y	Y	?
37 Tucker	Y	Y	?	N	Y	Y	N
38 *Horn*	Y	Y	Y	N	Y	Y	N
39 *Royce*	N	N	Y	N	Y	N	N
40 *Lewis*	N	N	Y	Y	Y	N	Y
41 *Kim*	N	N	Y	N	N	N	Y
42 Brown	Y	Y	Y	N	Y	Y	N
43 *Calvert*	N	N	Y	Y	Y	N	Y
44 *McCandless*	N	N	Y	Y	Y	N	Y
45 *Rohrabacher*	N	N	Y	Y	N	N	Y
46 *Dornan*	N	N	Y	Y	?	N	Y
47 *Cox*	N	N	Y	Y	N	N	Y
48 *Packard*	N	N	Y	N	Y	N	Y
49 Schenk	Y	Y	Y	Y	Y	Y	N
50 Filner	Y	Y	N	Y	Y	Y	N
51 *Cunningham*	N	N	Y	Y	N	N	Y
52 *Hunter*	N	N	Y	N	N	N	Y
COLORADO							
1 Schroeder	Y	Y	Y	Y	Y	Y	N
2 Skaggs	Y	Y	N	Y	Y	Y	N
3 *McInnis*	N	N	Y	N	N	N	N
4 *Allard*	N	N	Y	Y	N	N	Y
5 *Hefley*	N	N	Y	N	N	N	Y
6 *Schaefer*	N	N	Y	N	N	N	N
CONNECTICUT							
1 Kennelly	Y	Y	Y	Y	Y	Y	N
2 Gejdenson	Y	Y	Y	N	Y	Y	N
3 DeLauro	Y	Y	Y	Y	Y	Y	N
4 *Shays*	N	N	Y	Y	Y	Y	N
5 *Franks*	N	N	Y	Y	Y	N	?
6 *Johnson*	Y	Y	Y	?	Y	N	N
DELAWARE							
AL *Castle*	N	N	Y	Y	Y	N	Y
FLORIDA							
1 Hutto	N	N	Y	Y	Y	Y	N
2 Peterson	Y	Y	Y	N	Y	Y	N
3 Brown	Y	Y	Y	Y	Y	Y	N
4 *Fowler*	N	N	Y	Y	Y	N	N
5 Thurman	N	N	Y	Y	Y	Y	N
6 *Stearns*	N	N	Y	Y	N	N	Y
7 *Mica*	N	N	Y	N	Y	N	Y
8 *McCollum*	N	N	Y	N	N	N	Y
9 *Bilirakis*	N	N	Y	N	Y	N	Y
10 *Young*	N	N	Y	Y	Y	N	Y
11 Gibbons	Y	Y	Y	N	Y	Y	N
12 *Canady*	N	N	Y	N	Y	N	Y
13 *Miller*	N	N	Y	Y	N	N	Y
14 *Goss*	N	N	Y	Y	Y	N	Y
15 Bacchus	Y	Y	Y	N	Y	Y	N
16 *Lewis*	N	N	Y	Y	N	N	N
17 Meek	Y	Y	Y	N	Y	Y	N
18 *Ros-Lehtinen*	N	N	Y	Y	N	N	Y
19 Johnston	Y	Y	N	Y	Y	Y	N
20 Deutsch	Y	Y	Y	Y	Y	Y	N
21 *Diaz-Balart*	N	N	Y	Y	N	N	Y
22 *Shaw*	N	N	Y	Y	Y	N	Y
23 Hastings	Y	Y	N	N	Y	Y	N
GEORGIA							
1 *Kingston*	N	N	Y	Y	N	N	Y
2 Bishop	Y	Y	Y	N	Y	Y	N
3 *Collins*	N	N	Y	Y	N	N	Y
4 *Linder*	N	N	Y	Y	Y	N	Y
5 Lewis	Y	Y	N	Y	Y	Y	N
6 *Gingrich*	N	N	Y	N	Y	N	Y
7 Darden	Y	Y	Y	N	Y	Y	N
8 Rowland	N	N	Y	N	Y	Y	N
9 Deal	N	N	Y	N	Y	Y	N
10 Johnson	Y	Y	Y	N	Y	Y	N
11 McKinney	?	Y	N	Y	Y	Y	N
HAWAII							
1 Abercrombie	Y	Y	N	N	Y	Y	N
2 Mink	Y	Y	Y	N	Y	Y	N
IDAHO							
1 LaRocco	Y	Y	Y	N	Y	Y	N
2 *Crapo*	N	N	Y	N	N	N	Y
ILLINOIS							
1 Rush	Y	Y	+	N	Y	Y	N
2 Reynolds	Y	Y	Y	N	Y	Y	N
3 Lipinski	N	Y	Y	N	Y	Y	N
4 Gutierrez	Y	Y	Y	Y	Y	Y	N
5 Rostenkowski	Y	Y	Y	N	Y	Y	N
6 *Hyde*	N	N	Y	N	Y	N	?
7 Collins	Y	Y	N	Y	Y	Y	N
8 *Crane*	N	N	Y	N	N	Y	N
9 Yates	Y	Y	N	N	Y	Y	Y
10 *Porter*	N	N	Y	Y	Y	N	Y
11 Sangmeister	Y	Y	Y	N	Y	Y	N
12 Costello	Y	Y	Y	N	Y	Y	N
13 *Fawell*	N	−	Y	N	Y	N	Y
14 *Hastert*	N	N	Y	N	N	N	Y
15 *Ewing*	N	N	Y	N	Y	N	Y
16 *Manzullo*	N	N	Y	N	N	N	Y
17 Evans	Y	Y	N	Y	Y	Y	N

ND Northern Democrats   SD Southern Democrats

	268	269	270	271	272	273	274
18 ***Michel***	N	N	Y	N	Y	N	Y
19 Poshard	N	N	Y	N	Y	Y	N
20 Durbin	Y	Y	Y	N	Y	Y	N
INDIANA							
1 Visclosky	Y	Y	Y	N	Y	Y	N
2 Sharp	Y	Y	Y	Y	Y	Y	N
3 Roemer	Y	Y	Y	N	Y	Y	N
4 Long	N	N	Y	N	Y	Y	N
5 ***Buyer***	N	N	Y	N	N	N	N
6 ***Burton***	N	N	Y	Y	N	N	Y
7 ***Myers***	N	N	Y	N	Y	N	Y
8 McCloskey	N	N	Y	N	Y	Y	N
9 Hamilton	N	N	Y	N	Y	Y	N
10 Jacobs	Y	Y	Y	Y	N	N	N
IOWA							
1 ***Leach***	Y	Y	N	Y	Y	N	N
2 ***Nussle***	N	N	Y	Y	Y	N	Y
3 ***Lightfoot***	N	N	Y	N	Y	N	Y
4 Smith	Y	Y	Y	N	Y	Y	N
5 ***Grandy***	Y	Y	Y	Y	Y	N	N
KANSAS							
1 ***Roberts***	N	N	Y	N	N	N	Y
2 Slattery	Y	Y	Y	Y	Y	Y	?
3 ***Meyers***	N	N	Y	Y	Y	N	Y
4 Glickman	Y	Y	Y	N	Y	Y	N
KENTUCKY							
1 Barlow	Y	Y	Y	N	Y	Y	N
2 ***Lewis***	N	N	Y	N	N	N	Y
3 Mazzoli	Y	Y	Y	N	Y	Y	N
4 ***Bunning***	N	N	Y	N	N	N	Y
5 ***Rogers***	N	N	Y	N	Y	N	Y
6 Baesler	Y	Y	Y	Y	Y	Y	N
LOUISIANA							
1 ***Livingston***	?	N	Y	N	Y	N	Y
2 Jefferson	Y	Y	Y	Y	Y	Y	N
3 Tauzin	N	N	Y	N	N	Y	N
4 Fields	Y	Y	N	N	Y	Y	N
5 ***McCrery***	N	N	Y	Y	Y	N	Y
6 ***Baker***	N	N	Y	Y	N	N	Y
7 Hayes	N	N	Y	N	Y	Y	?
MAINE							
1 Andrews	Y	Y	Y	Y	Y	Y	N
2 ***Snowe***	N	N	Y	Y	Y	N	N
MARYLAND							
1 ***Gilchrest***	N	N	Y	Y	Y	N	Y
2 ***Bentley***	N	N	Y	N	Y	N	?
3 Cardin	Y	Y	Y	N	Y	Y	N
4 Wynn	Y	Y	Y	Y	Y	Y	N
5 Hoyer	Y	Y	Y	N	Y	Y	N
6 ***Bartlett***	N	N	Y	Y	N	N	Y
7 Mfume	Y	Y	Y	N	Y	Y	N
8 ***Morella***	Y	Y	N	Y	Y	N	N
MASSACHUSETTS							
1 Olver	Y	Y	N	Y	Y	Y	N
2 Neal	Y	Y	N	N	Y	Y	N
3 ***Blute***	N	N	Y	Y	Y	N	N
4 Frank	Y	Y	N	Y	Y	Y	?
5 Meehan	Y	Y	Y	Y	Y	Y	N
6 ***Torkildsen***	N	N	Y	N	Y	N	N
7 Markey	Y	?	Y	Y	Y	Y	N
8 Kennedy	Y	Y	Y	Y	Y	Y	N
9 Moakley	Y	Y	Y	N	Y	Y	N
10 Studds	Y	Y	N	Y	Y	Y	?
MICHIGAN							
1 Stupak	Y	Y	Y	Y	Y	Y	N
2 ***Hoekstra***	N	N	Y	Y	Y	N	Y
3 ***Ehlers***	Y	Y	Y	Y	N	N	Y
4 ***Camp***	N	N	Y	Y	N	N	Y
5 Barcia	N	Y	Y	N	N	Y	N
6 ***Upton***	N	N	Y	Y	N	N	N
7 ***Smith***	N	N	Y	Y	N	N	Y
8 Carr	Y	Y	Y	N	Y	Y	N
9 Kildee	Y	Y	Y	N	Y	Y	N
10 Bonior	Y	Y	Y	N	?	Y	N
11 ***Knollenberg***	N	N	Y	Y	N	N	Y
12 Levin	Y	Y	Y	Y	Y	Y	N
13 Ford	Y	Y	Y	N	Y	Y	?
14 Conyers	Y	Y	Y	N	Y	Y	N
15 Collins	Y	Y	Y	N	Y	#	?
16 Dingell	Y	Y	Y	N	Y	Y	N
MINNESOTA							
1 Penny	N	Y	Y	Y	Y	Y	?
2 Minge	N	?	Y	Y	Y	Y	N
3 ***Ramstad***	N	N	Y	Y	N	N	N
4 Vento	Y	Y	Y	Y	Y	Y	?
5 Sabo	Y	Y	N	N	Y	Y	N
6 ***Grams***	N	N	Y	Y	N	N	Y
7 Peterson	N	N	Y	N	Y	Y	N
8 Oberstar	Y	Y	Y	N	Y	Y	?
MISSISSIPPI							
1 Whitten	Y	Y	Y	?	Y	Y	?
2 Thompson	Y	Y	Y	N	Y	Y	N
3 Montgomery	N	N	Y	N	Y	Y	N
4 Parker	N	N	Y	N	Y	Y	N
5 Taylor	N	N	Y	N	N	N	N
MISSOURI							
1 Clay	Y	?	?	?	?	?	?
2 ***Talent***	N	N	Y	Y	N	N	Y
3 Gephardt	Y	Y	Y	N	Y	Y	N
4 Skelton	N	N	Y	N	Y	Y	N
5 Wheat	Y	Y	Y	N	Y	Y	?
6 Danner	Y	Y	Y	N	Y	Y	N
7 ***Hancock***	N	N	Y	Y	N	N	Y
8 ***Emerson***	N	N	Y	N	N	N	Y
9 Volkmer	N	N	Y	N	Y	Y	?
MONTANA							
AL Williams	Y	Y	Y	N	Y	Y	N
NEBRASKA							
1 ***Bereuter***	N	N	Y	Y	Y	N	Y
2 Hoagland	Y	Y	Y	Y	Y	Y	N
3 ***Barrett***	N	N	Y	Y	N	N	Y
NEVADA							
1 Bilbray	Y	Y	Y	Y	Y	Y	N
2 ***Vucanovich***	N	N	Y	Y	N	N	Y
NEW HAMPSHIRE							
1 ***Zeliff***	N	N	?	?	?	?	?
2 Swett	N	N	Y	Y	Y	Y	N
NEW JERSEY							
1 Andrews	N	N	Y	Y	Y	Y	N
2 Hughes	Y	Y	Y	N	Y	Y	?
3 ***Saxton***	N	N	Y	N	Y	N	Y
4 ***Smith***	N	N	Y	Y	Y	N	N
5 ***Roukema***	N	N	Y	N	Y	N	Y
6 Pallone	Y	Y	Y	Y	Y	Y	N
7 ***Franks***	N	N	Y	Y	N	N	N
8 Klein	Y	Y	Y	Y	Y	Y	N
9 Torricelli	Y	Y	Y	N	Y	Y	?
10 Payne	Y	Y	N	Y	Y	Y	N
11 ***Gallo***	N	N	Y	N	Y	N	Y
12 ***Zimmer***	N	N	Y	Y	N	N	Y
13 Menendez	Y	Y	Y	Y	Y	Y	N
NEW MEXICO							
1 ***Schiff***	N	N	Y	N	Y	N	Y
2 ***Skeen***	N	N	Y	N	Y	N	Y
3 Richardson	Y	Y	Y	Y	Y	Y	N
NEW YORK							
1 Hochbrueckner	Y	Y	Y	N	Y	Y	N
2 ***Lazio***	N	N	Y	Y	Y	N	Y
3 ***King***	N	N	Y	Y	N	N	Y
4 ***Levy***	N	N	Y	Y	N	N	Y
5 Ackerman	Y	Y	Y	N	Y	Y	N
6 Flake	Y	?	Y	N	Y	Y	N
7 Manton	Y	Y	Y	N	Y	Y	N
8 Nadler	Y	Y	N	Y	Y	Y	?
9 Schumer	Y	Y	Y	Y	Y	Y	?
10 Towns	?	?	?	?	?	?	?
11 Owens	Y	Y	Y	N	Y	Y	?
12 Velazquez	Y	Y	Y	N	Y	Y	N
13 ***Molinari***	N	N	Y	Y	N	N	N
14 Maloney	Y	Y	N	Y	Y	Y	?
15 Rangel	Y	Y	Y	N	Y	?	N
16 Serrano	Y	Y	?	N	Y	Y	N
17 Engel	Y	Y	N	Y	Y	Y	?
18 Lowey	Y	Y	N	N	Y	Y	N
19 ***Fish***	Y	Y	Y	Y	Y	N	?
20 ***Gilman***	Y	Y	Y	Y	Y	N	N
21 McNulty	N	Y	Y	Y	Y	Y	N
22 ***Solomon***	N	N	Y	Y	N	N	Y
23 ***Boehlert***	Y	Y	Y	Y	Y	N	Y
24 ***McHugh***	N	N	Y	Y	N	N	Y
25 ***Walsh***	N	Y	Y	Y	Y	N	Y
26 Hinchey	Y	Y	N	Y	Y	Y	N
27 ***Paxon***	N	N	Y	Y	N	N	Y
28 Slaughter	Y	Y	N	N	Y	Y	N
29 LaFalce	Y	Y	Y	Y	Y	Y	?
30 ***Quinn***	N	N	Y	?	X	X	?
31 ***Houghton***	Y	Y	Y	Y	Y	N	N
NORTH CAROLINA							
1 Clayton	Y	Y	N	N	Y	Y	N
2 Valentine	N	N	Y	N	Y	Y	N
3 Lancaster	N	Y	Y	N	Y	Y	N
4 Price	Y	Y	Y	N	Y	Y	N
5 Neal	Y	Y	Y	N	Y	Y	N
6 ***Coble***	N	N	Y	Y	N	N	Y
7 Rose	Y	Y	Y	N	Y	Y	N
8 Hefner	Y	Y	Y	N	Y	Y	N
9 ***McMillan***	N	N	Y	Y	Y	N	Y
10 ***Ballenger***	N	N	Y	Y	N	N	Y
11 ***Taylor***	N	N	Y	N	Y	N	Y
12 Watt	Y	Y	N	Y	Y	?	N
NORTH DAKOTA							
AL Pomeroy	N	Y	Y	N	Y	Y	N
OHIO							
1 Mann	N	N	Y	Y	Y	Y	N
2 ***Portman***	N	N	Y	Y	Y	N	Y
3 Hall	N	Y	Y	N	Y	Y	N
4 ***Oxley***	N	N	?	N	N	N	Y
5 ***Gillmor***	N	N	Y	N	Y	N	Y
6 Strickland	Y	Y	?	N	Y	Y	N
7 ***Hobson***	N	N	Y	N	Y	N	Y
8 ***Boehner***	N	N	Y	N	N	N	Y
9 Kaptur	Y	Y	Y	N	Y	?	N
10 ***Hoke***	N	N	Y	N	Y	N	N
11 Stokes	Y	Y	Y	N	Y	Y	N
12 ***Kasich***	N	N	Y	N	Y	N	Y
13 Brown	Y	N	Y	N	Y	Y	N
14 Sawyer	Y	Y	Y	N	Y	Y	N
15 ***Pryce***	N	N	Y	N	Y	N	Y
16 ***Regula***	N	N	Y	N	Y	N	Y
17 Traficant	N	N	Y	N	Y	Y	N
18 Applegate	Y	Y	Y	N	Y	Y	?
19 Fingerhut	Y	Y	Y	Y	Y	Y	N
OKLAHOMA							
1 ***Inhofe***	N	N	Y	N	Y	N	Y
2 Synar	Y	Y	Y	N	Y	Y	N
3 Brewster	Y	Y	Y	N	Y	Y	N
4 McCurdy	N	N	Y	N	?	?	?
5 ***Istook***	N	N	?	N	Y	N	Y
6 ***Lucas***	N	N	Y	N	Y	N	Y
OREGON							
1 Furse	Y	Y	Y	Y	Y	Y	N
2 ***Smith***	N	N	Y	Y	N	N	N
3 Wyden	Y	?	Y	Y	Y	Y	N
4 DeFazio	Y	Y	Y	Y	Y	Y	N
5 Kopetski	Y	Y	Y	N	Y	Y	N
PENNSYLVANIA							
1 Foglietta	Y	Y	N	N	Y	Y	N
2 Blackwell	Y	Y	Y	?	Y	Y	N
3 Borski	Y	Y	Y	N	Y	Y	N
4 Klink	N	Y	Y	N	Y	Y	N
5 ***Clinger***	Y	Y	Y	N	Y	N	N
6 Holden	N	N	Y	N	Y	Y	N
7 ***Weldon***	N	N	Y	Y	Y	N	Y
8 ***Greenwood***	N	N	Y	Y	Y	N	Y
9 ***Shuster***	N	N	Y	N	Y	N	Y
10 ***McDade***	N	N	Y	N	Y	N	Y
11 Kanjorski	N	N	Y	N	Y	Y	?
12 Murtha	Y	Y	N	N	Y	Y	?
13 Margolies-Mezv.	Y	Y	Y	Y	Y	Y	N
14 Coyne	Y	Y	Y	N	Y	Y	N
15 McHale	N	Y	Y	N	Y	Y	N
16 ***Walker***	N	N	Y	Y	N	N	Y
17 ***Gekas***	N	N	Y	Y	N	N	Y
18 ***Santorum***	N	N	Y	N	N	N	Y
19 ***Goodling***	N	N	Y	N	Y	N	Y
20 Murphy	Y	Y	Y	N	Y	Y	?
21 ***Ridge***	N	N	Y	N	Y	N	?
RHODE ISLAND							
1 ***Machtley***	?	?	?	?	?	?	?
2 Reed	Y	Y	Y	N	Y	Y	N
SOUTH CAROLINA							
1 ***Ravenel***	N	N	Y	Y	Y	N	Y
2 ***Spence***	N	N	Y	Y	N	N	Y
3 Derrick	Y	Y	Y	N	Y	Y	N
4 ***Inglis***	N	N	Y	Y	N	N	Y
5 Spratt	Y	Y	Y	N	Y	Y	N
6 Clyburn	Y	Y	Y	N	Y	Y	N
SOUTH DAKOTA							
AL Johnson	Y	Y	Y	Y	Y	Y	N
TENNESSEE							
1 ***Quillen***	N	N	Y	N	Y	N	Y
2 ***Duncan***	N	N	Y	Y	N	N	Y
3 Lloyd	?	?	?	X	#	?	?
4 Cooper	N	N	Y	N	Y	N	N
5 Clement	Y	Y	Y	N	Y	Y	N
6 Gordon	Y	Y	Y	Y	Y	Y	N
7 ***Sundquist***	N	N	Y	N	Y	N	?
8 Tanner	N	N	Y	N	Y	Y	N
9 Ford	?	?	?	N	Y	Y	N
TEXAS							
1 Chapman	N	N	Y	N	Y	Y	N
2 Wilson	Y	Y	Y	N	Y	Y	?
3 ***Johnson, Sam***	N	N	Y	Y	N	N	Y
4 Hall	N	N	Y	N	N	Y	N
5 Bryant	Y	Y	Y	N	Y	Y	N
6 ***Barton***	N	N	?	Y	N	N	Y
7 ***Archer***	N	N	Y	Y	N	N	Y
8 ***Fields***	N	N	Y	N	N	N	Y
9 Brooks	Y	Y	Y	N	Y	Y	N
10 Pickle	Y	Y	Y	N	Y	Y	N
11 Edwards	N	N	Y	N	Y	Y	N
12 Geren	N	N	Y	N	Y	Y	N
13 Sarpalius	N	N	Y	N	N	Y	N
14 Laughlin	N	N	Y	N	Y	Y	N
15 de la Garza	?	Y	Y	N	Y	Y	N
16 Coleman	Y	Y	Y	N	Y	Y	N
17 Stenholm	N	N	Y	N	Y	Y	N
18 Washington	?	?	?	?	?	?	?
19 ***Combest***	N	N	Y	N	N	N	Y
20 Gonzalez	Y	Y	?	N	Y	Y	N
21 ***Smith***	N	N	Y	N	N	N	Y
22 ***DeLay***	N	N	Y	N	N	N	Y
23 ***Bonilla***	N	N	Y	Y	Y	N	Y
24 Frost	Y	Y	Y	N	Y	Y	N
25 Andrews	Y	Y	Y	Y	Y	Y	N
26 ***Armey***	N	N	Y	Y	N	N	Y
27 Ortiz	N	N	Y	N	Y	Y	N
28 Tejeda	Y	Y	Y	N	Y	Y	N
29 Green	Y	Y	Y	Y	Y	Y	N
30 Johnson, E.B.	Y	Y	Y	N	Y	Y	N
UTAH							
1 ***Hansen***	N	N	Y	N	Y	N	Y
2 Shepherd	Y	Y	Y	Y	Y	Y	N
3 Orton	N	N	Y	N	Y	Y	N
VERMONT							
AL *Sanders*	Y	Y	Y	Y	Y	Y	N
VIRGINIA							
1 ***Bateman***	N	N	Y	N	Y	N	Y
2 Pickett	N	N	Y	N	Y	Y	N
3 Scott	Y	Y	Y	N	Y	Y	N
4 Sisisky	N	N	Y	N	Y	Y	N
5 Payne	Y	Y	Y	N	Y	Y	N
6 ***Goodlatte***	N	N	Y	N	Y	N	Y
7 ***Bliley***	N	N	Y	N	N	N	Y
8 Moran	Y	Y	N	N	Y	Y	N
9 Boucher	Y	Y	Y	N	Y	Y	N
10 ***Wolf***	N	N	Y	Y	Y	N	Y
11 Byrne	Y	Y	Y	N	Y	Y	N
WASHINGTON							
1 Cantwell	Y	Y	Y	Y	Y	Y	N
2 Swift	Y	Y	Y	N	Y	Y	N
3 Unsoeld	Y	Y	Y	N	Y	Y	N
4 Inslee	Y	Y	Y	Y	Y	Y	N
5 Foley							
6 Dicks	Y	Y	Y	N	Y	Y	N
7 McDermott	Y	Y	Y	Y	Y	Y	N
8 ***Dunn***	N	Y	Y	N	Y	N	Y
9 Kreidler	Y	Y	Y	Y	Y	Y	N
WEST VIRGINIA							
1 Mollohan	Y	Y	Y	N	Y	Y	N
2 Wise	Y	Y	Y	N	Y	Y	N
3 Rahall	Y	Y	Y	N	Y	Y	N
WISCONSIN							
1 Barca	Y	Y	Y	Y	Y	Y	N
2 ***Klug***	N	N	Y	Y	N	N	N
3 ***Gunderson***	N	N	Y	#	?	?	Y
4 Kleczka	Y	Y	Y	Y	Y	Y	N
5 Barrett	Y	Y	Y	Y	Y	Y	N
6 ***Petri***	N	N	Y	Y	N	N	Y
7 Obey	Y	Y	Y	N	Y	Y	N
8 ***Roth***	N	N	Y	Y	N	N	Y
9 ***Sensenbrenner***	N	N	Y	Y	N	N	Y
WYOMING							
AL ***Thomas***	N	N	Y	N	Y	N	Y
DELEGATES							
de Lugo, V.I.	D	Y	N	N	D	D	D
Faleomavaega, Am.S.	D	?	?	?	D	D	D
Norton, D.C.	D	Y	N	N	D	D	D
Romero-B., P.R.	D	Y	?	N	D	D	D
Underwood, Guam	D	Y	?	N	D	D	D

Southern states - Ala., Ark., Fla., Ga., Ky., La., Miss., N.C., Okla., S.C., Tenn., Texas, Va.
Omitted votes are quorum calls, which CQ does not include in its vote charts.

1994 CQ ALMANAC — 81-H

275. HR 4603. Fiscal 1995 Commerce, Justice, State Appropriations/General Administration Account. Smith, R-Texas, amendment to cut $925,000 from the general administration account of the Justice Department. Rejected in the Committee of the Whole 171-212: R 149-13; D 22-198 (ND 16-134, SD 6-64); I 0-1, June 24, 1994.

276. HR 4603. Fiscal 1995 Commerce, Justice, State Appropriations/Antitrust Division. Schiff, R-N.M., amendment to reduce the appropriation for the Antitrust Division of the Department of Justice by $5.5 million. Rejected in the Committee of the Whole 160-241: R 149-16; D 11-224 (ND 9-150, SD 2-74); I 0-1, June 24, 1994.

277. HR 4603. Fiscal 1995 Commerce, Justice, State Appropriations/GLOBE Program. Fields, R-Texas, amendment to cut $7 million from the budget for the National Oceanic and Atmospheric Administration. The amendment was intended to eliminate the GLOBE (Global Learning and Observation to Benefit the Environment) Program proposed in the president's budget, which would create a global network of schoolchildren collecting environmental data. Rejected in the Committee of the Whole 190-192: R 146-9; D 44-182 (ND 24-127, SD 20-55); I 0-1, June 24, 1994. (Subsequently, the amendment was rejected on an automatic revote in the full House, required when delegate votes provide the margin deciding an issue. See vote 278.)

278. HR 4603. Fiscal 1995 Commerce, Justice, State Appropriations/Revote GLOBE Program. Revote as required when delegate votes provide the margin deciding an issue, as occurred on the Fields, R-Texas, amendment to cut $7 million from the budget for the National Oceanic and Atmospheric Administration. The amendment was intended to eliminate the GLOBE (Global Learning and Observation to Benefit the Environment) Program proposed in the president's budget, which would create a global network of schoolchildren collecting environmental data. Rejected 184-184: R 144-5; D 40-178 (ND 23-125, SD 17-53); I 0-1, June 24, 1994. (Under House rules, such revotes occur automatically, requiring the Committee of the Whole to rise and the revote to occur in the full House, where delegates may not vote. Following the revote, the Committee of the Whole resumed consideration of the bill. See vote 277.)

279. HR 4603. Fiscal 1995 Commerce, Justice, State Appropriations/Public Broadcasting. Burton, R-Ind., amendment to cut the $26 million account for public broadcasting facilities, planning and construction by $2 million. Rejected in the Committee of the Whole 156-230: R 132-29; D 24-200 (ND 15-139, SD 9-61); I 0-1, June 27, 1994.

280. HR 4603. Fiscal 1995 Commerce, Justice, State Appropriations/Information Infrastructure Grants. Burton, R-Ind., amendment to cut the amount appropriated to the National Telecommunications and Information Administration for information infrastructure grants by $22 million. Rejected in the Committee of the Whole 161-227: R 139-22; D 22-204 (ND 17-138, SD 5-66); I 0-1, June 27, 1994.

281. HR 4603. Fiscal 1995 Commerce, Justice, State Appropriations/Economic Development Administration. Penny, D-Minn., amendment to cut the Economic Development Administration by $67.7 million or about 20 percent. Rejected in the Committee of the Whole 110-282: R 102-61; D 8-220 (ND 6-151, SD 2-69); I 0-1, June 27, 1994.

282. HR 4603. Fiscal 1995 Commerce, Justice, State Appropriations/National Oceanic and Atmospheric Administration. Goodlatte, R-Va., amendment to cut the appropriation for operations, research and facilities at the National Oceanic and Atmospheric Administration by $26 million. Rejected in the Committee of the Whole 128-272: R 109-58; D 19-213 (ND 13-147, SD 6-66); I 0-1, June 27, 1994.

KEY

Y	Voted for (yea).
#	Paired for.
+	Announced for.
N	Voted against (nay).
X	Paired against.
—	Announced against.
P	Voted "present."
C	Voted "present" to avoid possible conflict of interest.
?	Did not vote or otherwise make a position known.
D	Delegates ineligible to vote.

Democrats ***Republicans***
Independent

	275	276	277	278	279	280	281	282
ALABAMA								
1 *Callahan*	Y	Y	Y	Y	N	Y	N	N
2 *Everett*	Y	Y	Y	Y	Y	Y	N	N
3 Browder	N	N	N	N	Y	N	N	N
4 Bevill	N	N	N	?	?	?	?	?
5 Cramer	N	N	N	N	N	N	N	N
6 *Bachus*	Y	Y	Y	Y	Y	Y	Y	Y
7 Hilliard	X	X	?	X	?	?	?	?
ALASKA								
AL *Young*	?	Y	Y	Y	N	N	N	N
ARIZONA								
1 Coppersmith	N	N	Y	Y	Y	N	N	Y
2 Pastor	N	N	N	N	N	N	N	N
3 *Stump*	Y	Y	Y	Y	Y	Y	Y	Y
4 *Kyl*	Y	Y	Y	Y	Y	Y	Y	Y
5 *Kolbe*	N	Y	?	?	Y	N	Y	N
6 English	N	N	N	N	N	N	N	N
ARKANSAS								
1 Lambert	N	N	Y	?	?	?	?	N
2 Thornton	N	N	N	?	N	N	N	N
3 *Hutchinson*	Y	Y	?	?	Y	Y	N	Y
4 Dickey	Y	Y	Y	Y	Y	Y	N	Y
CALIFORNIA								
1 Hamburg	N	N	N	N	N	N	N	N
2 *Herger*	Y	Y	Y	Y	Y	N	N	N
3 Fazio	N	N	N	N	N	N	N	N
4 *Doolittle*	Y	Y	Y	Y	Y	Y	Y	Y
5 Matsui	N	N	?	?	N	N	N	N
6 Woolsey	N	N	?	N	N	N	N	N
7 Miller	N	Y	N	N	N	N	N	N
8 Pelosi	N	N	N	N	N	N	N	N
9 Dellums	N	N	N	N	N	N	N	N
10 *Baker*	Y	Y	Y	Y	Y	Y	Y	Y
11 *Pombo*	Y	Y	Y	Y	?	?	?	?
12 Lantos	N	N	N	N	N	N	N	N
13 Stark	N	N	N	N	N	N	Y	N
14 Eshoo	N	N	N	N	N	N	N	N
15 Mineta	N	N	N	N	N	N	N	N
16 Edwards	N	N	N	N	N	N	N	N
17 Farr	N	N	N	N	N	N	N	N
18 Condit	N	Y	Y	Y	N	Y	N	Y
19 Lehman	N	N	Y	?	?	?	N	Y
20 Dooley	N	N	Y	N	N	N	N	N
21 *Thomas*	Y	Y	Y	Y	N	N	N	Y
22 *Huffington*	Y	Y	Y	Y	N	Y	N	Y
23 *Gallegly*	?	?	?	?	N	Y	Y	Y
24 Beilenson	N	N	N	N	N	N	N	N
25 *McKeon*	Y	Y	Y	Y	Y	Y	Y	Y
26 Berman	?	X	?	X	N	N	N	N
27 *Moorhead*	Y	Y	Y	Y	Y	Y	Y	Y
28 *Dreier*	Y	Y	Y	Y	Y	Y	Y	Y
29 Waxman	?	?	?	?	N	N	N	N
30 Becerra	N	N	N	N	N	N	N	N
31 Martinez	N	N	N	N	N	N	N	N
32 Dixon	N	N	N	N	N	N	N	N
33 Roybal-Allard	N	N	N	N	N	N	N	N
34 Torres	N	N	N	—	—	—	—	—
35 Waters	N	N	?	N	?	?	N	N
36 Harman	?	N	Y	N	Y	N	N	Y
37 Tucker	X	N	N	N	N	N	N	N
38 *Horn*	Y	Y	Y	Y	N	Y	N	Y
39 *Royce*	Y	Y	?	Y	Y	Y	Y	Y
40 *Lewis*	N	N	Y	Y	Y	N	N	N
41 *Kim*	Y	Y	Y	Y	Y	Y	Y	Y

	275	276	277	278	279	280	281	282
42 Brown	N	N	N	N	N	N	N	N
43 *Calvert*	Y	#	?	#	Y	Y	Y	Y
44 *McCandless*	Y	Y	Y	Y	?	?	?	?
45 *Rohrabacher*	Y	Y	Y	Y	Y	Y	Y	Y
46 *Dornan*	Y	Y	Y	Y	Y	Y	Y	Y
47 *Cox*	Y	Y	Y	Y	?	?	Y	Y
48 *Packard*	Y	Y	Y	N	Y	N	Y	Y
49 Schenk	N	N	N	N	N	N	N	N
50 Filner	N	N	N	N	N	N	N	N
51 *Cunningham*	Y	Y	Y	Y	N	Y	N	Y
52 *Hunter*	Y	Y	Y	Y	#	?	?	Y
COLORADO								
1 Schroeder	N	N	N	N	N	N	N	N
2 Skaggs	N	N	N	N	N	N	N	N
3 *McInnis*	Y	Y	Y	Y	N	Y	Y	Y
4 *Allard*	Y	Y	Y	Y	Y	Y	Y	Y
5 *Hefley*	Y	Y	Y	Y	Y	Y	Y	Y
6 *Schaefer*	?	#	?	#	Y	Y	Y	Y
CONNECTICUT								
1 Kennelly	N	N	N	N	N	N	N	N
2 Gejdenson	N	N	N	N	N	N	N	N
3 DeLauro	N	N	N	N	N	N	N	N
4 *Shays*	Y	Y	Y	Y	Y	Y	Y	Y
5 *Franks*	?	?	?	?	Y	Y	N	Y
6 *Johnson*	N	Y	N	N	N	N	N	N
DELAWARE								
AL *Castle*	Y	Y	Y	Y	Y	Y	Y	Y
FLORIDA								
1 Hutto	N	N	Y	Y	Y	N	N	N
2 Peterson	N	N	N	N	N	N	N	N
3 Brown	N	N	N	?	?	?	?	?
4 *Fowler*	Y	Y	Y	Y	Y	Y	Y	Y
5 Thurman	N	N	Y	N	N	N	N	N
6 *Stearns*	Y	Y	Y	?	Y	Y	Y	Y
7 *Mica*	Y	Y	X	N	Y	Y	Y	Y
8 *McCollum*	?	X	?	#	X	?	?	?
9 *Bilirakis*	Y	N	Y	?	Y	Y	Y	N
10 *Young*	Y	Y	Y	?	Y	Y	Y	N
11 Gibbons	N	N	N	N	N	N	N	N
12 *Canady*	Y	Y	Y	Y	Y	Y	N	Y
13 *Miller*	Y	Y	Y	Y	#	Y	Y	Y
14 *Goss*	Y	Y	Y	Y	Y	Y	Y	Y
15 Bacchus	N	N	N	N	N	N	N	N
16 *Lewis*	Y	#	?	#	Y	Y	Y	N
17 Meek	N	N	N	N	N	N	N	N
18 *Ros-Lehtinen*	Y	Y	N	Y	N	Y	Y	N
19 Johnston	N	N	N	N	N	N	N	N
20 Deutsch	N	N	N	N	N	N	N	N
21 *Diaz-Balart*	N	Y	N	Y	Y	Y	N	N
22 *Shaw*	Y	Y	Y	Y	Y	N	N	N
23 Hastings	N	N	N	?	X	?	X	?
GEORGIA								
1 *Kingston*	Y	Y	Y	Y	Y	Y	N	Y
2 Bishop	N	N	N	N	?	?	?	?
3 *Collins*	Y	Y	Y	Y	Y	Y	Y	Y
4 *Linder*	Y	Y	Y	Y	Y	Y	Y	Y
5 Lewis	?	?	?	?	N	N	N	N
6 *Gingrich*	Y	Y	Y	Y	Y	Y	Y	Y
7 Darden	N	N	N	N	N	N	N	N
8 Rowland	N	N	N	N	N	N	N	N
9 Deal	N	N	?	#	#	?	X	#
10 Johnson	N	N	N	N	N	N	N	N
11 McKinney	N	N	N	N	N	N	N	N
HAWAII								
1 Abercrombie	N	N	N	N	N	N	N	N
2 Mink	N	N	N	N	N	N	N	N
IDAHO								
1 LaRocco	N	N	N	N	N	N	N	N
2 *Crapo*	Y	Y	Y	Y	Y	Y	Y	Y
ILLINOIS								
1 Rush	N	N	N	—	—	—	—	—
2 Reynolds	N	?	?	?	?	?	?	?
3 Lipinski	?	X	?	?	N	N	N	N
4 Gutierrez	?	?	?	?	?	?	?	?
5 Rostenkowski	N	N	N	?	?	?	?	?
6 *Hyde*	Y	Y	Y	Y	Y	Y	Y	Y
7 Collins	N	N	N	N	N	N	N	N
8 *Crane*	?	Y	Y	Y	Y	Y	Y	Y
9 Yates	N	N	N	N	N	N	N	N
10 *Porter*	+	Y	Y	Y	Y	Y	Y	Y
11 Sangmeister	N	N	N	N	N	N	N	N
12 Costello	?	?	?	?	N	N	N	N
13 *Fawell*	Y	Y	Y	Y	Y	Y	Y	Y
14 *Hastert*	Y	Y	Y	Y	Y	Y	N	Y
15 *Ewing*	Y	Y	Y	Y	Y	Y	N	Y
16 *Manzullo*	Y	Y	Y	Y	Y	Y	Y	Y
17 Evans	N	N	N	N	N	N	N	N

	275	276	277	278	279	280	281	282
18 ***Michel***	N	Y	?	?	N	Y	Y	Y
19 Poshard	Y	N	N	N	Y	Y	N	Y
20 Durbin	N	N	N	N	N	N	N	N
INDIANA								
1 Visclosky	N	N	N	N	N	N	N	N
2 Sharp	N	N	N	N	N	N	N	N
3 Roemer	N	N	Y	Y	N	N	N	N
4 Long	N	N	N	N	N	N	N	N
5 ***Buyer***	Y	Y	?	?	Y	Y	N	N
6 ***Burton***	Y	Y	Y	Y	Y	Y	Y	Y
7 ***Myers***	N	Y	Y	Y	Y	N	N	N
8 McCloskey	N	N	N	N	X	X	?	?
9 Hamilton	Y	N	Y	Y	N	N	N	N
10 Jacobs	N	N	?	?	N	Y	N	N
IOWA								
1 ***Leach***	Y	N	Y	Y	N	Y	Y	Y
2 ***Nussle***	Y	Y	Y	Y	Y	Y	Y	Y
3 ***Lightfoot***	N	N	?	?	Y	Y	N	N
4 Smith	N	N	N	N	N	N	N	N
5 ***Grandy***	Y	Y	Y	Y	Y	N	N	Y
KANSAS								
1 ***Roberts***	Y	Y	Y	Y	Y	Y	Y	Y
2 Slattery	?	?	?	?	Y	N	N	N
3 ***Meyers***	Y	Y	Y	Y	Y	Y	Y	Y
4 Glickman	N	N	N	N	Y	Y	N	N
KENTUCKY								
1 Barlow	N	N	N	N	N	N	N	N
2 ***Lewis***	Y	Y	Y	Y	Y	Y	Y	Y
3 Mazzoli	N	N	N	N	N	N	N	N
4 ***Bunning***	Y	Y	Y	Y	Y	Y	Y	Y
5 ***Rogers***	N	N	Y	Y	N	N	N	N
6 Baesler	N	N	Y	N	N	N	N	N
LOUISIANA								
1 ***Livingston***	Y	Y	Y	Y	Y	N	Y	N
2 Jefferson	N	N	N	N	N	N	N	N
3 Tauzin	Y	N	Y	Y	N	N	N	N
4 Fields	N	N	N	N	N	N	N	N
5 ***McCrery***	?	Y	Y	Y	Y	Y	N	Y
6 ***Baker***	Y	Y	Y	Y	?	?	?	Y
7 Hayes	N	N	Y	Y	?	N	N	N
MAINE								
1 Andrews	?	N	N	N	?	?	?	?
2 ***Snowe***	Y	Y	Y	Y	Y	Y	N	N
MARYLAND								
1 ***Gilchrest***	Y	Y	Y	Y	Y	Y	N	N
2 ***Bentley***	?	?	Y	Y	Y	Y	N	N
3 Cardin	N	N	N	N	N	N	N	N
4 Wynn	?	N	N	N	N	N	N	N
5 Hoyer	N	N	N	?	N	N	N	N
6 ***Bartlett***	Y	Y	Y	Y	Y	Y	Y	Y
7 Mfume	N	N	Y	Y	N	N	N	N
8 ***Morella***	Y	Y	Y	Y	N	Y	Y	N
MASSACHUSETTS								
1 Olver	N	N	N	N	N	N	N	N
2 Neal	N	N	N	N	N	N	N	N
3 ***Blute***	N	N	Y	Y	Y	N	N	N
4 Frank	N	N	N	N	N	N	N	N
5 Meehan	N	N	N	N	?	?	?	?
6 ***Torkildsen***	#	?	Y	Y	Y	Y	N	N
7 Markey	N	N	N	N	N	N	N	N
8 Kennedy	N	N	N	N	Y	N	N	N
9 Moakley	N	N	N	N	N	N	N	N
10 Studds	N	N	N	N	N	N	N	N
MICHIGAN								
1 Stupak	N	N	N	N	N	N	N	N
2 ***Hoekstra***	Y	Y	Y	Y	Y	Y	Y	Y
3 ***Ehlers***	Y	Y	?	?	Y	Y	Y	Y
4 ***Camp***	Y	Y	Y	Y	Y	Y	N	Y
5 Barcia	N	N	N	N	Y	Y	N	N
6 ***Upton***	Y	Y	Y	Y	Y	N	N	Y
7 ***Smith***	Y	Y	Y	Y	Y	Y	Y	Y
8 Carr	N	N	N	N	N	N	N	N
9 Kildee	N	N	N	N	N	N	N	N
10 Bonior	N	N	N	N	N	N	N	N
11 ***Knollenberg***	Y	Y	Y	Y	Y	Y	Y	Y
12 Levin	N	N	N	N	N	N	N	N
13 Ford	?	?	?	?	?	?	?	?
14 Conyers	N	N	N	N	N	N	N	N
15 Collins	?	X	?	X	?	?	N	N
16 Dingell	?	?	?	X	N	N	N	N
MINNESOTA								
1 Penny	N	N	Y	Y	Y	Y	Y	Y
2 Minge	N	N	Y	Y	N	Y	N	Y
3 ***Ramstad***	Y	Y	Y	Y	Y	Y	Y	Y
4 Vento	N	N	N	N	N	N	N	N

	275	276	277	278	279	280	281	282
5 Sabo	N	N	N	N	N	N	N	N
6 ***Grams***	#	#	?	#	Y	Y	Y	Y
7 Peterson	N	Y	Y	Y	N	Y	N	N
8 Oberstar	N	N	N	N	N	N	N	N
MISSISSIPPI								
1 Whitten	N	N	N	N	N	N	N	N
2 Thompson	N	N	N	N	?	?	?	N
3 Montgomery	N	N	Y	Y	Y	N	N	N
4 Parker	N	N	Y	Y	Y	N	N	N
5 Taylor	#	#	?	?	Y	Y	N	N
MISSOURI								
1 Clay	?	?	?	?	N	N	N	N
2 ***Talent***	Y	Y	Y	Y	Y	Y	Y	Y
3 Gephardt	?	?	?	?	N	N	N	N
4 Skelton	N	N	Y	Y	N	N	N	N
5 Wheat	?	?	?	?	N	N	N	N
6 Danner	N	N	N	N	N	N	N	N
7 ***Hancock***	Y	Y	Y	Y	Y	Y	Y	Y
8 ***Emerson***	Y	Y	Y	Y	Y	N	N	N
9 Volkmer	N	N	Y	N	N	N	N	N
MONTANA								
AL Williams	N	N	N	N	N	N	N	N
NEBRASKA								
1 ***Bereuter***	Y	N	Y	Y	Y	Y	Y	N
2 Hoagland	N	N	N	N	N	N	Y	Y
3 ***Barrett***	Y	Y	Y	Y	Y	Y	Y	N
NEVADA								
1 Bilbray	N	Y	N	N	N	N	N	N
2 ***Vucanovich***	Y	Y	Y	Y	N	Y	N	N
NEW HAMPSHIRE								
1 ***Zeliff***	Y	Y	?	?	?	?	?	?
2 Swett	Y	Y	Y	Y	Y	Y	N	Y
NEW JERSEY								
1 Andrews	Y	N	Y	Y	?	?	?	Y
2 Hughes	N	N	N	N	N	N	N	N
3 ***Saxton***	Y	Y	Y	Y	Y	Y	N	N
4 ***Smith***	Y	Y	Y	Y	Y	Y	N	N
5 ***Roukema***	Y	Y	?	#	#	#	#	N
6 Pallone	N	N	N	N	N	N	N	N
7 ***Franks***	Y	N	Y	Y	Y	Y	N	Y
8 Klein	Y	N	N	N	N	N	N	N
9 Torricelli	N	N	N	N	?	?	?	?
10 Payne	N	N	N	N	N	N	N	N
11 ***Gallo***	Y	Y	Y	Y	Y	Y	N	Y
12 ***Zimmer***	Y	Y	Y	Y	Y	Y	Y	Y
13 Menendez	Y	N	N	N	N	N	N	N
NEW MEXICO								
1 ***Schiff***	Y	Y	Y	Y	Y	Y	N	N
2 ***Skeen***	Y	Y	Y	Y	N	N	N	N
3 Richardson	N	N	N	N	?	?	?	N
NEW YORK								
1 Hochbrueckner	N	N	N	N	N	N	N	N
2 ***Lazio***	Y	Y	Y	Y	Y	Y	N	Y
3 ***King***	Y	Y	Y	Y	N	Y	Y	Y
4 ***Levy***	Y	Y	Y	Y	Y	Y	Y	Y
5 Ackerman	X	X	?	X	N	N	N	N
6 Flake	N	N	?	N	N	N	N	N
7 Manton	N	N	N	N	N	N	N	N
8 Nadler	?	N	N	N	N	N	N	N
9 Schumer	?	?	?	?	N	N	N	N
10 Towns	?	?	?	?	X	?	?	?
11 Owens	?	N	N	?	?	?	?	?
12 Velazquez	N	N	N	N	N	N	N	N
13 ***Molinari***	Y	Y	Y	Y	Y	Y	Y	Y
14 Maloney	?	N	N	N	N	N	N	N
15 Rangel	N	N	N	N	X	X	?	X
16 Serrano	N	N	N	N	N	N	N	N
17 Engel	?	N	N	N	N	N	N	N
18 Lowey	N	N	N	N	N	N	N	N
19 ***Fish***	N	N	N	N	Y	N	N	N
20 ***Gilman***	Y	N	N	N	N	Y	N	Y
21 McNulty	N	N	N	N	N	N	N	N
22 ***Solomon***	Y	?	?	?	Y	Y	Y	Y
23 ***Boehlert***	Y	Y	Y	Y	N	Y	N	Y
24 ***McHugh***	Y	Y	Y	Y	Y	Y	N	Y
25 ***Walsh***	Y	Y	Y	Y	N	N	N	N
26 Hinchey	N	N	N	N	N	N	N	N
27 ***Paxon***	Y	Y	Y	Y	Y	Y	Y	Y
28 Slaughter	N	N	N	N	N	N	N	N
29 LaFalce	N	Y	N	N	N	N	N	N
30 ***Quinn***	Y	Y	Y	Y	X	X	?	?
31 ***Houghton***	Y	Y	N	N	N	N	N	N
NORTH CAROLINA								
1 Clayton	?	N	N	N	N	N	N	N
2 Valentine	N	N	N	N	N	N	N	N

	275	276	277	278	279	280	281	282
3 Lancaster	N	N	N	N	N	N	N	N
4 Price	N	N	N	N	N	N	N	N
5 Neal	?	N	Y	Y	N	N	N	N
6 ***Coble***	Y	Y	Y	Y	Y	Y	Y	Y
7 Rose	N	N	N	N	?	?	?	?
8 Hefner	N	N	N	N	N	N	N	N
9 ***McMillan***	Y	Y	Y	?	?	?	?	?
10 ***Ballenger***	Y	Y	Y	+	Y	Y	Y	Y
11 ***Taylor***	Y	N	Y	Y	Y	Y	N	N
12 Watt	N	N	N	N	N	N	N	N
NORTH DAKOTA								
AL Pomeroy	N	N	Y	Y	N	N	N	N
OHIO								
1 Mann	N	N	Y	Y	N	Y	Y	Y
2 ***Portman***	Y	Y	Y	Y	Y	Y	Y	Y
3 Hall	Y	N	?	N	N	N	N	N
4 ***Oxley***	Y	Y	Y	Y	Y	Y	Y	Y
5 ***Gillmor***	N	Y	Y	Y	Y	Y	N	N
6 Strickland	Y	N	N	N	N	N	N	N
7 ***Hobson***	Y	Y	Y	Y	Y	Y	N	N
8 ***Boehner***	Y	Y	Y	Y	Y	Y	Y	Y
9 Kaptur	N	N	N	N	N	Y	N	N
10 ***Hoke***	Y	Y	Y	Y	?	?	?	?
11 Stokes	?	?	?	?	N	N	N	N
12 ***Kasich***	?	Y	Y	Y	Y	Y	Y	Y
13 Brown	N	N	N	N	N	N	Y	N
14 Sawyer	N	N	N	N	N	N	N	N
15 ***Pryce***	Y	Y	Y	Y	+	+	+	+
16 ***Regula***	Y	Y	Y	Y	N	Y	N	N
17 Traficant	N	N	Y	Y	N	N	N	N
18 Applegate	N	N	Y	Y	N	N	N	N
19 Fingerhut	Y	Y	N	N	+	—	—	—
OKLAHOMA								
1 ***Inhofe***	Y	Y	Y	Y	Y	Y	Y	Y
2 Synar	N	N	N	N	N	N	N	N
3 Brewster	N	N	Y	Y	?	?	?	?
4 McCurdy	?	?	?	?	N	N	N	N
5 ***Istook***	Y	Y	Y	Y	Y	Y	Y	Y
6 ***Lucas***	Y	Y	Y	Y	Y	Y	Y	N
OREGON								
1 Furse	N	N	N	N	N	N	N	N
2 ***Smith***	#	#	?	?	#	#	#	?
3 Wyden	N	N	N	N	N	N	N	N
4 DeFazio	Y	N	N	N	N	N	N	N
5 Kopetski	N	N	N	N	N	N	N	N
PENNSYLVANIA								
1 Foglietta	N	N	N	N	N	N	N	N
2 Blackwell	?	N	N	N	?	?	?	?
3 Borski	N	N	N	N	N	N	N	N
4 Klink	N	N	?	?	N	N	N	N
5 ***Clinger***	Y	N	Y	Y	N	N	N	N
6 Holden	N	N	Y	Y	N	N	N	N
7 ***Weldon***	Y	Y	N	?	Y	Y	Y	Y
8 ***Greenwood***	Y	Y	Y	Y	Y	Y	Y	Y
9 ***Shuster***	Y	Y	Y	Y	Y	Y	N	Y
10 ***McDade***	N	N	Y	Y	N	N	N	N
11 Kanjorski	Y	N	N	N	N	N	N	N
12 Murtha	N	N	N	N	N	N	N	N
13 Margolies-Mezv.	Y	N	Y	Y	N	N	Y	Y
14 Coyne	N	N	N	N	N	N	N	N
15 McHale	N	N	N	N	N	N	N	N
16 ***Walker***	Y	Y	N	N	Y	Y	Y	Y
17 ***Gekas***	N	Y	Y	N	Y	Y	N	N
18 ***Santorum***	Y	Y	Y	Y	Y	Y	N	Y
19 ***Goodling***	Y	Y	Y	Y	N	Y	N	Y
20 Murphy	N	N	N	N	?	?	?	?
21 ***Ridge***	?	?	?	?	?	?	?	?
RHODE ISLAND								
1 ***Machtley***	X	?	?	?	Y	Y	N	N
2 Reed	N	N	N	N	N	N	N	N
SOUTH CAROLINA								
1 ***Ravenel***	Y	Y	N	Y	Y	Y	N	N
2 ***Spence***	Y	Y	Y	?	Y	Y	N	N
3 Derrick	N	N	N	N	N	N	N	N
4 ***Inglis***	Y	Y	Y	Y	Y	Y	Y	Y
5 Spratt	N	N	Y	N	N	N	N	N
6 Clyburn	N	N	N	N	N	N	N	N
SOUTH DAKOTA								
AL Johnson	N	N	N	N	N	N	N	N
TENNESSEE								
1 ***Quillen***	Y	Y	?	?	Y	N	N	N
2 ***Duncan***	Y	Y	Y	Y	Y	Y	Y	Y
3 Lloyd	?	?	?	?	N	N	N	N
4 Cooper	Y	Y	N	N	Y	N	N	Y
5 Clement	N	N	N	N	N	N	N	N

	275	276	277	278	279	280	281	282
6 Gordon	N	Y	N	N	N	N	N	N
7 ***Sundquist***	Y	Y	?	?	Y	N	N	Y
8 Tanner	N	N	N	N	N	N	N	N
9 Ford	?	N	N	N	?	?	?	?
TEXAS								
1 Chapman	?	N	Y	Y	N	N	N	?
2 Wilson	N	N	N	N	N	N	N	Y
3 ***Johnson, Sam***	Y	Y	Y	Y	Y	?	?	Y
4 Hall	Y	N	Y	Y	N	N	N	N
5 Bryant	N	N	N	N	N	N	N	N
6 ***Barton***	?	Y	Y	Y	Y	Y	Y	Y
7 ***Archer***	Y	Y	Y	Y	Y	Y	Y	Y
8 ***Fields***	Y	N	Y	Y	+	—	+	—
9 Brooks	N	N	N	N	N	N	N	N
10 Pickle	N	N	N	N	N	N	N	N
11 Edwards	N	N	N	N	N	Y	N	Y
12 Geren	Y	N	Y	Y	Y	N	N	N
13 Sarpalius	Y	N	N	N	N	N	N	N
14 Laughlin	?	N	Y	Y	Y	N	N	N
15 de la Garza	?	N	N	N	N	N	N	N
16 Coleman	N	N	N	N	N	N	N	N
17 Stenholm	Y	N	Y	Y	Y	Y	Y	Y
18 Washington	?	?	?	?	?	?	?	?
19 ***Combest***	Y	Y	Y	Y	Y	Y	Y	Y
20 Gonzalez	N	N	N	N	N	N	N	N
21 ***Smith***	Y	Y	Y	Y	Y	Y	Y	Y
22 ***DeLay***	Y	Y	Y	Y	Y	Y	Y	Y
23 ***Bonilla***	Y	Y	Y	Y	Y	Y	Y	Y
24 Frost	N	N	N	?	N	N	N	N
25 Andrews	N	N	N	N	N	N	Y	Y
26 ***Armey***	Y	Y	Y	Y	Y	Y	Y	Y
27 Ortiz	N	N	N	N	N	N	N	N
28 Tejeda	N	N	N	N	N	N	N	N
29 Green	—	N	N	N	N	N	N	N
30 Johnson, E.B.	N	N	N	N	N	N	N	N
UTAH								
1 ***Hansen***	Y	Y	Y	Y	Y	Y	Y	Y
2 Shepherd	N	N	N	N	N	N	N	N
3 Orton	Y	Y	Y	Y	Y	N	N	Y
VERMONT								
AL *Sanders*	N	N	N	N	N	N	N	N
VIRGINIA								
1 ***Bateman***	Y	N	Y	Y	N	N	N	N
2 Pickett	N	N	Y	Y	N	N	N	N
3 Scott	N	N	N	N	N	N	N	N
4 Sisisky	N	N	Y	Y	N	N	N	N
5 Payne	N	N	Y	Y	N	N	N	Y
6 ***Goodlatte***	Y	Y	Y	Y	Y	Y	Y	Y
7 ***Bliley***	Y	Y	Y	Y	N	N	Y	Y
8 Moran	N	N	N	N	N	N	N	N
9 Boucher	N	?	?	?	N	N	N	N
10 ***Wolf***	Y	Y	Y	Y	Y	Y	Y	N
11 Byrne	N	N	Y	Y	N	N	N	N
WASHINGTON								
1 Cantwell	Y	N	N	N	N	N	N	N
2 Swift	N	N	N	N	N	N	N	N
3 Unsoeld	N	N	N	N	N	N	N	N
4 Inslee	Y	N	Y	Y	Y	Y	N	N
5 Foley								
6 Dicks	N	N	N	N	N	N	N	N
7 McDermott	N	N	N	N	N	N	N	N
8 ***Dunn***	Y	Y	Y	Y	Y	Y	Y	Y
9 Kreidler	Y	N	N	N	Y	Y	N	N
WEST VIRGINIA								
1 Mollohan	N	N	N	N	N	N	N	N
2 Wise	N	N	N	N	N	N	N	N
3 Rahall	N	N	?	?	N	N	N	N
WISCONSIN								
1 Barca	N	Y	Y	Y	Y	Y	N	N
2 ***Klug***	Y	Y	Y	Y	Y	Y	Y	Y
3 ***Gunderson***	Y	N	Y	Y	Y	Y	N	Y
4 Kleczka	N	N	N	N	N	N	N	N
5 Barrett	N	N	N	N	Y	Y	N	N
6 ***Petri***	Y	Y	Y	Y	Y	Y	Y	Y
7 Obey	N	N	N	N	N	N	N	N
8 ***Roth***	Y	Y	Y	Y	Y	Y	Y	Y
9 ***Sensenbrenner***	Y	Y	Y	Y	Y	Y	Y	Y
WYOMING								
AL ***Thomas***	Y	Y	Y	Y	Y	Y	Y	N
DELEGATES								
de Lugo, V.I.	?	N	N	D	N	N	N	N
Faleomavaega, Am.S.	?	?	?	D	?	?	?	?
Norton, D.C.	N	N	?	D	N	N	N	N
Romero-B., P.R.	N	N	N	D	N	N	N	N
Underwood, Guam	N	N	N	D	?	N	N	N

Southern states - Ala., Ark., Fla., Ga., Ky., La., Miss., N.C., Okla., S.C., Tenn., Texas, Va.
Omitted votes are quorum calls, which CQ does not include in its vote charts.

283. HR 4603. Fiscal 1995 Commerce, Justice, State Appropriations/National Endowment for Democracy. Hefley, R-Colo., amendment to eliminate the National Endowment for Democracy by cutting its $33 million appropriation. Rejected in the Committee of the Whole 89-317: R 49-118; D 39-199 (ND 28-137, SD 11-62); I 1-0, June 27, 1994.

284. HR 4603. Fiscal 1995 Commerce, Justice, State Appropriations/Iraqi POWs Resettlement. Stearns, R-Fla., amendment to cut $2.8 million from the State Department's general administration account, the estimated amount spent in previous years on resettling Iraqi prisoners of war. Adopted in the Committee of the Whole 284-122: R 157-11; D 127-110 (ND 78-86, SD 49-24); I 0-1, June 27, 1994.

285. HR 4603. Fiscal 1995 Commerce, Justice, State Appropriations/Overseas Buildings. Inslee, D-Wash., amendment to cut $15 million from the account for acquisition and maintenance of buildings abroad by the State Department. Adopted in the Committee of the Whole 268-139: R 152-16; D 115-123 (ND 68-97, SD 47-26); I 1-0, June 27, 1994.

286. HR 4603. Fiscal 1995 Commerce, Justice, State Appropriations/Radio Free Asia. Porter, R-Ill., amendment to transfer $10 million to Radio Free Asia from the radio construction account of the U.S. Information Agency. Adopted in the Committee of the Whole 318-89: R 155-13; D 162-76 (ND 120-45, SD 42-31); I 1-0, June 27, 1994.

287. HR 4603. Fiscal 1995 Commerce, Justice, State Appropriations/Illegal Aliens Incarceration. Condit, D-Calif., amendment to impose an across-the-board cut of 2.5 percent and transfer the $600 million resulting from the cut to reimburse state and local governments for costs associated with incarcerating illegal aliens. Rejected in the Committee the Whole 148-256: R 100-68; D 48-187 (ND 21-141, SD 27-46); I 0-1, June 27, 1994.

288. HR 4603. Fiscal 1995 Commerce, Justice, State Appropriations/U.N. Contribution. Rogers, R-Ky., amendment to cut the U.S. contribution for international peacekeeping activities at the United Nations from 30.4 percent to 25 percent and transfer the resulting $207 million to reimburse states for costs associated with incarcerating illegal aliens and to hire 1,600 additional police officers. Rejected in the Committee of the Whole 178-228: R 165-4; D 13-223 (ND 6-157, SD 7-66); I 0-1, June 27, 1994.

289. HR 4603. Fiscal 1995 Commerce, Justice, State Appropriations/EEOC Religious Guidelines. Taylor, R-N.C., amendment to prohibit money in the bill from implementing proposed guidelines from the Equal Employment Opportunity Commission concerning religious harassment in the workplace. Adopted in the Committee of the Whole 366-37: R 168-0; D 198-36 (ND 130-32, SD 68-4); I 0-1, June 27, 1994 (in the session that began and the Congressional Record dated June 27).

290. HR 4603. Fiscal 1995 Commerce, Justice, State Appropriations/Motion To Recommit. Lightfoot, R-Iowa, motion to recommit the bill to the House Appropriations Committee with instructions to report it back with an amendment cutting the peacekeeping contribution to the United Nations by $25 million, the amount for operations in Haiti in fiscal 1995. Motion rejected 185-214: R 166-3; D 19-210 (ND 10-147, SD 9-63); I 0-1, June 28, 1994 (in the session that began and the Congressional Record dated June 27).

KEY

Y	Voted for (yea).
#	Paired for.
+	Announced for.
N	Voted against (nay).
X	Paired against.
−	Announced against.
P	Voted "present."
C	Voted "present" to avoid possible conflict of interest.
?	Did not vote or otherwise make a position known.
D	Delegates ineligible to vote.

Democrats *Republicans*
Independent

	283	284	285	286	287	288	289	290
ALABAMA								
1 Callahan	Y	Y	Y	Y	Y	Y	Y	Y
2 Everett	N	Y	Y	Y	N	Y	Y	Y
3 Browder	N	Y	Y	N	Y	N	Y	N
4 Bevill	?	?	?	?	?	N	Y	N
5 Cramer	N	Y	Y	N	N	N	Y	N
6 Bachus	N	Y	Y	Y	?	Y	Y	Y
7 Hilliard	?	?	?	?	?	?	?	?
ALASKA								
AL Young	N	Y	Y	Y	Y	Y	Y	Y
ARIZONA								
1 Coppersmith	N	N	Y	N	N	N	Y	N
2 Pastor	N	N	N	N	N	N	Y	N
3 Stump	Y	Y	Y	Y	Y	Y	Y	Y
4 Kyl	N	Y	Y	N	Y	Y	Y	Y
5 Kolbe	N	N	N	Y	N	Y	Y	Y
6 English	N	N	Y	Y	N	N	Y	N
ARKANSAS								
1 Lambert	N	Y	Y	Y	N	N	Y	N
2 Thornton	N	N	Y	N	N	N	Y	N
3 Hutchinson	N	Y	Y	Y	N	Y	Y	Y
4 Dickey	N	Y	Y	N	Y	Y	Y	Y
CALIFORNIA								
1 Hamburg	Y	N	N	Y	N	N	N	N
2 Herger	N	Y	Y	Y	Y	Y	Y	Y
3 Fazio	N	N	N	N	N	N	Y	N
4 Doolittle	N	Y	Y	Y	Y	Y	Y	Y
5 Matsui	N	N	N	N	N	?	?	?
6 Woolsey	N	N	Y	N	N	N	Y	N
7 Miller	Y	Y	N	Y	N	N	Y	N
8 Pelosi	N	N	N	N	N	N	Y	N
9 Dellums	N	N	N	N	N	N	N	N
10 Baker	N	Y	Y	Y	Y	Y	Y	Y
11 Pombo	?	?	?	?	?	?	?	?
12 Lantos	N	Y	N	Y	Y	N	Y	N
13 Stark	N	N	N	Y	N	N	N	N
14 Eshoo	N	Y	N	Y	N	N	Y	N
15 Mineta	N	N	N	N	N	N	N	N
16 Edwards	N	N	N	N	N	N	N	N
17 Farr	N	Y	N	N	N	N	Y	N
18 Condit	Y	Y	Y	N	Y	N	Y	Y
19 Lehman	N	Y	Y	Y	N	N	Y	N
20 Dooley	N	Y	Y	Y	N	Y	N	N
21 Thomas	N	Y	Y	Y	Y	Y	Y	Y
22 Huffington	N	Y	Y	Y	Y	Y	Y	Y
23 Gallegly	N	Y	Y	Y	Y	Y	Y	Y
24 Beilenson	N	N	N	Y	N	N	Y	N
25 McKeon	N	Y	Y	Y	Y	Y	Y	Y
26 Berman	N	N	N	Y	N	N	N	N
27 Moorhead	N	Y	Y	Y	Y	Y	Y	Y
28 Dreier	N	Y	Y	Y	Y	Y	Y	Y
29 Waxman	N	N	N	Y	N	N	N	N
30 Becerra	N	N	N	Y	N	N	N	N
31 Martinez	N	Y	N	N	N	N	Y	N
32 Dixon	N	N	N	N	N	N	Y	N
33 Roybal-Allard	N	N	N	N	N	N	N	N
34 Torres	N	N	Y	N	N	N	N	N
35 Waters	N	N	N	N	N	N	N	N
36 Harman	N	Y	Y	Y	N	Y	N	N
37 Tucker	N	N	Y	N	N	N	N	N
38 Horn	N	Y	Y	Y	Y	Y	Y	Y
39 Royce	N	Y	Y	Y	Y	Y	Y	Y
40 Lewis	N	N	N	Y	Y	Y	N	Y
41 Kim	N	Y	Y	Y	Y	Y	Y	Y

	283	284	285	286	287	288	289	290
42 Brown	N	N	N	N	N	N	Y	N
43 Calvert	N	Y	Y	Y	Y	Y	Y	Y
44 McCandless	?	?	?	?	?	?	?	?
45 Rohrabacher	N	N	Y	Y	Y	Y	Y	Y
46 Dornan	N	Y	Y	Y	Y	Y	Y	Y
47 Cox	N	Y	Y	Y	Y	Y	?	Y
48 Packard	N	Y	Y	Y	Y	Y	Y	Y
49 Schenk	N	Y	Y	Y	N	Y	N	Y
50 Filner	N	Y	N	Y	N	N	N	N
51 Cunningham	N	Y	Y	Y	Y	Y	Y	Y
52 Hunter	N	Y	Y	Y	Y	Y	Y	Y
COLORADO								
1 Schroeder	Y	N	Y	N	N	N	Y	N
2 Skaggs	N	N	N	N	N	P	N
3 McInnis	Y	Y	Y	Y	Y	Y	Y	Y
4 Allard	Y	Y	Y	N	Y	Y	Y	Y
5 Hefley	Y	Y	N	Y	Y	Y	Y	Y
6 Schaefer	Y	Y	Y	Y	Y	Y	Y	Y
CONNECTICUT								
1 Kennelly	N	N	Y	Y	N	N	Y	N
2 Gejdenson	N	N	N	Y	N	N	N	N
3 DeLauro	N	Y	N	N	N	N	Y	N
4 Shays	Y	Y	Y	Y	Y	Y	Y	Y
5 Franks	N	Y	Y	Y	N	Y	Y	Y
6 Johnson	N	Y	N	Y	Y	N	Y	Y
DELAWARE								
AL Castle	N	Y	Y	Y	Y	Y	Y	Y
FLORIDA								
1 Hutto	N	Y	Y	N	Y	N	Y	N
2 Peterson	N	Y	N	Y	N	N	Y	N
3 Brown	?	?	?	?	?	?	?	?
4 Fowler	N	Y	Y	Y	Y	Y	Y	Y
5 Thurman	Y	Y	Y	N	Y	N	Y	N
6 Stearns	N	Y	Y	Y	Y	Y	Y	Y
7 Mica	Y	Y	Y	Y	Y	Y	Y	Y
8 McCollum	?	X	?	?	?	?	?	?
9 Bilirakis	N	Y	Y	Y	Y	Y	Y	Y
10 Young	N	Y	Y	Y	Y	Y	Y	Y
11 Gibbons	N	N	N	N	N	?	?	?
12 Canady	N	Y	Y	Y	Y	Y	Y	Y
13 Miller	N	Y	Y	Y	Y	Y	Y	Y
14 Goss	N	Y	Y	Y	Y	Y	Y	Y
15 Bacchus	N	Y	N	Y	N	N	Y	N
16 Lewis	Y	Y	Y	Y	Y	Y	Y	Y
17 Meek	N	N	N	Y	N	N	Y	N
18 Ros-Lehtinen	N	Y	Y	Y	Y	Y	Y	Y
19 Johnston	N	N	N	N	N	N	N	N
20 Deutsch	N	Y	Y	N	N	N	N	N
21 Diaz-Balart	N	Y	N	Y	Y	N	Y	Y
22 Shaw	N	Y	Y	Y	Y	Y	Y	Y
23 Hastings	?	?	?	X	?	?	?	?
GEORGIA								
1 Kingston	N	Y	Y	Y	Y	Y	Y	Y
2 Bishop	?	?	?	?	?	N	Y	N
3 Collins	Y	Y	Y	N	Y	Y	Y	Y
4 Linder	N	Y	Y	Y	Y	Y	Y	Y
5 Lewis	N	N	N	N	N	N	Y	N
6 Gingrich	N	Y	Y	Y	Y	Y	Y	Y
7 Darden	N	Y	N	N	N	N	Y	N
8 Rowland	N	Y	Y	N	N	N	Y	N
9 Deal	N	Y	Y	N	Y	N	Y	N
10 Johnson	N	Y	Y	Y	N	Y	N	Y
11 McKinney	Y	N	Y	N	Y	N	Y	N
HAWAII								
1 Abercrombie	N	N	N	Y	N	N	N	N
2 Mink	N	N	N	Y	N	N	N	N
IDAHO								
1 LaRocco	Y	Y	Y	Y	N	N	Y	N
2 Crapo	N	Y	Y	Y	Y	Y	Y	Y
ILLINOIS								
1 Rush	−	−	+	+	−	−	−	−
2 Reynolds	?	?	?	?	?	?	?	?
3 Lipinski	N	N	Y	Y	N	N	Y	N
4 Gutierrez	N	N	Y	N	N	N	N	N
5 Rostenkowski	?	?	?	?	?	?	?	?
6 Hyde	N	N	N	Y	Y	Y	Y	Y
7 Collins	N	N	Y	N	N	N	N	N
8 Crane	Y	Y	Y	Y	Y	Y	Y	Y
9 Yates	Y	N	N	N	N	N	N	N
10 Porter	N	Y	Y	Y	Y	Y	Y	Y
11 Sangmeister	N	Y	Y	Y	N	Y	N	Y
12 Costello	N	Y	Y	Y	N	N	Y	N
13 Fawell	Y	Y	Y	Y	Y	Y	Y	Y
14 Hastert	N	Y	Y	Y	Y	Y	Y	Y
15 Ewing	N	Y	Y	Y	Y	Y	Y	Y
16 Manzullo	Y	Y	Y	Y	N	Y	Y	Y
17 Evans	N	N	N	Y	N	N	N	N

ND Northern Democrats SD Southern Democrats

	283	284	285	286	287	288	289	290
18 ***Michel***	N	Y	N	Y	N	Y	Y	Y
19 Poshard	N	Y	Y	Y	N	Y	Y	N
20 Durbin	N	Y	N	Y	N	N	Y	N
INDIANA								
1 Visclosky	N	N	N	N	N	N	Y	N
2 Sharp	N	N	Y	Y	N	N	Y	N
3 Roemer	N	Y	Y	Y	N	N	Y	N
4 Long	N	Y	Y	Y	N	N	Y	N
5 ***Buyer***	N	Y	Y	Y	Y	Y	Y	Y
6 ***Burton***	N	Y	Y	Y	Y	Y	Y	Y
7 ***Myers***	Y	Y	Y	N	N	Y	Y	Y
8 McCloskey	?	?	?	?	X	?	?	?
9 Hamilton	N	Y	N	Y	N	N	Y	N
10 Jacobs	Y	Y	Y	Y	N	N	Y	Y
IOWA								
1 ***Leach***	N	N	Y	Y	N	N	Y	Y
2 ***Nussle***	N	Y	Y	Y	Y	Y	Y	Y
3 ***Lightfoot***	Y	Y	N	Y	N	Y	Y	Y
4 Smith	N	N	N	N	N	N	Y	N
5 ***Grandy***	N	Y	Y	Y	Y	Y	Y	Y
KANSAS								
1 ***Roberts***	N	Y	Y	Y	N	Y	Y	Y
2 Slattery	N	Y	Y	Y	N	N	Y	N
3 ***Meyers***	N	Y	Y	Y	N	Y	Y	Y
4 Glickman	N	Y	Y	Y	N	N	Y	N
KENTUCKY								
1 Barlow	N	Y	Y	N	N	N	Y	N
2 ***Lewis***	N	Y	Y	Y	Y	Y	Y	Y
3 Mazzoli	Y	N	N	Y	N	Y	Y	N
4 ***Bunning***	N	Y	Y	Y	Y	Y	Y	Y
5 ***Rogers***	N	N	N	N	N	Y	Y	Y
6 Baesler	N	Y	Y	N	N	N	Y	N
LOUISIANA								
1 ***Livingston***	N	Y	N	Y	N	Y	Y	Y
2 Jefferson	N	Y	N	Y	N	N	Y	N
3 Tauzin	Y	Y	Y	Y	Y	Y	Y	Y
4 Fields	N	Y	Y	Y	N	N	Y	N
5 ***McCrery***	N	Y	Y	Y	N	Y	Y	Y
6 ***Baker***	Y	Y	Y	Y	N	Y	Y	Y
7 Hayes	N	Y	Y	Y	Y	Y	Y	Y
MAINE								
1 Andrews	Y	Y	Y	Y	N	N	Y	N
2 ***Snowe***	Y	Y	Y	Y	N	Y	Y	Y
MARYLAND								
1 ***Gilchrest***	N	Y	Y	Y	N	Y	Y	Y
2 ***Bentley***	N	Y	Y	Y	Y	Y	Y	Y
3 Cardin	N	N	N	Y	N	N	Y	N
4 Wynn	N	Y	Y	N	N	N	Y	N
5 Hoyer	N	N	N	Y	N	N	Y	N
6 ***Bartlett***	N	Y	Y	Y	Y	Y	Y	Y
7 Mfume	N	Y	N	N	N	N	Y	N
8 ***Morella***	N	Y	N	Y	N	N	Y	Y
MASSACHUSETTS								
1 Olver	N	N	N	N	N	N	N	N
2 Neal	N	Y	N	Y	N	N	Y	N
3 ***Blute***	N	Y	Y	Y	Y	Y	Y	Y
4 Frank	Y	N	N	N	N	N	N	N
5 Meehan	?	?	?	?	?	?	?	?
6 ***Torkildsen***	N	Y	Y	Y	Y	Y	Y	Y
7 Markey	N	N	N	N	N	N	Y	N
8 Kennedy	N	N	N	Y	N	N	Y	N
9 Moakley	N	Y	N	N	N	N	Y	N
10 Studds	N	N	N	Y	N	N	Y	N
MICHIGAN								
1 Stupak	N	Y	Y	Y	N	N	Y	Y
2 ***Hoekstra***	Y	Y	Y	Y	N	Y	Y	Y
3 ***Ehlers***	N	Y	Y	Y	N	Y	Y	Y
4 ***Camp***	Y	Y	Y	Y	N	Y	Y	Y
5 Barcia	N	Y	Y	Y	Y	N	Y	Y
6 ***Upton***	Y	Y	Y	Y	N	Y	Y	Y
7 ***Smith***	Y	Y	Y	Y	N	Y	Y	Y
8 Carr	N	N	N	N	N	N	Y	N
9 Kildee	N	Y	Y	Y	N	N	Y	N
10 Bonior	N	N	N	Y	N	N	Y	N
11 ***Knollenberg***	Y	Y	Y	Y	N	Y	Y	Y
12 Levin	N	N	Y	Y	N	N	Y	N
13 Ford	?	?	?	?	?	?	?	?
14 Conyers	Y	N	N	Y	N	?	N	N
15 Collins	N	N	N	N	N	N	Y	N
16 Dingell	N	N	N	Y	N	N	Y	N
MINNESOTA								
1 Penny	N	Y	Y	Y	Y	N	Y	N
2 Minge	N	Y	Y	Y	Y	N	Y	Y
3 ***Ramstad***	Y	Y	Y	Y	Y	N	Y	Y
4 Vento	N	N	N	Y	N	N	Y	N

	283	284	285	286	287	288	289	290
5 Sabo	N	N	N	N	N	N	Y	N
6 ***Grams***	Y	Y	Y	Y	Y	Y	Y	Y
7 Peterson	N	Y	Y	N	Y	N	Y	Y
8 Oberstar	N	N	N	N	N	N	Y	N
MISSISSIPPI								
1 Whitten	?	?	?	?	?	?	?	?
2 Thompson	N	N	Y	Y	N	N	Y	N
3 Montgomery	N	Y	Y	Y	Y	N	Y	N
4 Parker	N	Y	Y	Y	Y	N	Y	N
5 Taylor	Y	Y	Y	Y	N	N	Y	Y
MISSOURI								
1 Clay	Y	N	N	N	?	N	N	N
2 ***Talent***	Y	Y	Y	Y	N	Y	Y	Y
3 Gephardt	N	N	N	Y	N	N	Y	?
4 Skelton	N	Y	Y	Y	N	N	Y	N
5 Wheat	N	?	N	Y	N	N	Y	N
6 Danner	N	Y	Y	Y	N	N	Y	N
7 ***Hancock***	Y	Y	Y	Y	Y	Y	Y	Y
8 ***Emerson***	Y	Y	Y	Y	N	Y	Y	Y
9 Volkmer	N	Y	N	Y	N	N	Y	N
MONTANA								
AL Williams	N	Y	Y	Y	N	Y	?	?
NEBRASKA								
1 ***Bereuter***	N	Y	N	Y	N	Y	Y	Y
2 Hoagland	N	Y	Y	Y	N	N	Y	N
3 ***Barrett***	Y	Y	Y	Y	N	Y	Y	Y
NEVADA								
1 Bilbray	N	Y	Y	Y	N	N	Y	N
2 ***Vucanovich***	N	Y	Y	Y	N	Y	Y	Y
NEW HAMPSHIRE								
1 ***Zeliff***	Y	Y	Y	Y	N	Y	Y	Y
2 Swett	Y	Y	Y	Y	Y	N	Y	Y
NEW JERSEY								
1 Andrews	Y	Y	Y	Y	Y	N	Y	N
2 Hughes	N	Y	N	N	N	N	Y	N
3 ***Saxton***	N	Y	Y	Y	Y	Y	Y	Y
4 ***Smith***	N	Y	Y	Y	N	Y	Y	Y
5 ***Roukema***	Y	Y	Y	N	Y	N	Y	Y
6 Pallone	N	Y	Y	Y	N	N	Y	N
7 ***Franks***	N	Y	Y	Y	Y	Y	Y	Y
8 Klein	N	Y	Y	Y	N	N	Y	N
9 Torricelli	?	?	?	?	?	?	?	?
10 Payne	N	N	N	N	N	N	N	N
11 ***Gallo***	N	Y	Y	Y	N	Y	Y	Y
12 ***Zimmer***	Y	Y	Y	Y	Y	Y	Y	Y
13 Menendez	N	Y	N	Y	N	N	Y	N
NEW MEXICO								
1 ***Schiff***	N	Y	Y	Y	N	Y	Y	Y
2 ***Skeen***	N	Y	Y	Y	N	Y	Y	Y
3 Richardson	N	N	N	Y	N	N	Y	N
NEW YORK								
1 Hochbrueckner	N	Y	Y	Y	Y	N	Y	N
2 ***Lazio***	Y	Y	Y	Y	N	Y	Y	Y
3 ***King***	N	N	Y	Y	Y	Y	Y	Y
4 ***Levy***	N	N	Y	Y	Y	Y	Y	Y
5 Ackerman	N	N	N	Y	Y	N	Y	N
6 Flake	N	N	N	N	N	N	Y	N
7 Manton	N	Y	N	Y	N	N	Y	N
8 Nadler	N	N	N	Y	N	N	N	N
9 Schumer	N	Y	Y	Y	N	N	Y	N
10 Towns	?	?	X	?	?	?	?	?
11 Owens	?	?	?	?	?	?	?	?
12 Velazquez	N	N	Y	Y	N	N	N	N
13 ***Molinari***	N	Y	Y	Y	Y	Y	Y	Y
14 Maloney	N	Y	N	Y	N	N	Y	N
15 Rangel	?	?	?	?	?	?	?	?
16 Serrano	N	N	N	N	N	N	Y	N
17 Engel	N	N	N	Y	Y	N	N	N
18 Lowey	N	Y	N	N	N	N	Y	N
19 ***Fish***	?	?	?	?	?	?	?	?
20 ***Gilman***	N	N	N	Y	Y	Y	Y	Y
21 McNulty	Y	Y	Y	Y	N	N	Y	N
22 ***Solomon***	Y	Y	Y	Y	Y	Y	Y	Y
23 ***Boehlert***	N	Y	Y	Y	N	Y	Y	Y
24 ***McHugh***	N	Y	Y	Y	Y	Y	Y	Y
25 ***Walsh***	N	Y	N	Y	Y	Y	Y	Y
26 Hinchey	N	N	N	Y	N	N	N	N
27 ***Paxon***	N	Y	Y	Y	N	Y	Y	Y
28 Slaughter	N	N	N	Y	N	N	Y	N
29 LaFalce	N	N	N	N	N	N	Y	N
30 ***Quinn***	Y	Y	Y	Y	N	Y	Y	Y
31 ***Houghton***	N	N	N	Y	N	Y	Y	Y
NORTH CAROLINA								
1 Clayton	N	Y	Y	Y	N	N	Y	N
2 Valentine	N	Y	N	Y	N	N	Y	N

	283	284	285	286	287	288	289	290
3 Lancaster	N	Y	N	Y	N	N	Y	N
4 Price	N	N	N	N	N	N	Y	N
5 Neal	N	N	Y	Y	N	N	Y	N
6 ***Coble***	Y	Y	Y	Y	N	Y	Y	Y
7 Rose	?	?	?	?	?	?	?	?
8 Hefner	N	Y	N	N	N	N	Y	N
9 ***McMillan***	?	?	?	?	?	?	?	?
10 ***Ballenger***	N	Y	Y	Y	Y	Y	Y	Y
11 ***Taylor***	N	Y	Y	Y	Y	Y	Y	Y
12 Watt	N	N	N	N	N	N	N	N
NORTH DAKOTA								
AL Pomeroy	N	Y	Y	Y	N	N	Y	Y
OHIO								
1 Mann	Y	N	Y	N	N	N	Y	N
2 ***Portman***	N	Y	Y	Y	N	Y	Y	Y
3 Hall	N	Y	N	Y	?	N	Y	?
4 ***Oxley***	?	Y	Y	Y	N	Y	Y	Y
5 ***Gillmor***	N	Y	Y	Y	N	Y	Y	Y
6 Strickland	Y	Y	Y	Y	N	N	Y	N
7 ***Hobson***	N	Y	Y	Y	N	Y	Y	Y
8 ***Boehner***	Y	Y	Y	Y	N	Y	Y	Y
9 Kaptur	Y	Y	N	Y	N	N	Y	N
10 ***Hoke***	N	Y	Y	Y	Y	Y	Y	Y
11 Stokes	N	N	N	N	N	N	N	N
12 ***Kasich***	N	Y	Y	Y	Y	Y	Y	Y
13 Brown	N	N	Y	Y	N	N	Y	N
14 Sawyer	N	N	N	Y	N	N	Y	N
15 ***Pryce***	+	+	+	+	−	+	+	+
16 ***Regula***	N	Y	Y	Y	N	Y	Y	Y
17 Traficant	N	Y	Y	N	N	Y	Y	N
18 Applegate	N	Y	Y	N	N	N	Y	Y
19 Fingerhut	Y	Y	Y	Y	N	N	Y	N
OKLAHOMA								
1 ***Inhofe***	N	Y	Y	Y	Y	Y	Y	Y
2 Synar	N	N	N	N	N	N	Y	N
3 Brewster	?	?	?	?	?	?	?	?
4 McCurdy	N	Y	Y	Y	N	N	Y	N
5 ***Istook***	N	Y	Y	Y	Y	Y	Y	Y
6 ***Lucas***	N	Y	Y	Y	N	Y	Y	Y
OREGON								
1 Furse	N	N	Y	Y	N	N	Y	N
2 ***Smith***	?	#	#	#	#	?	?	?
3 Wyden	Y	N	Y	Y	N	N	Y	N
4 DeFazio	Y	Y	N	Y	N	N	Y	N
5 Kopetski	N	N	N	Y	N	N	N	N
PENNSYLVANIA								
1 Foglietta	N	N	N	Y	N	N	Y	N
2 Blackwell	?	?	?	?	?	?	?	?
3 Borski	N	N	N	Y	N	N	Y	N
4 Klink	N	Y	N	N	N	N	Y	N
5 ***Clinger***	N	Y	Y	Y	N	Y	Y	Y
6 Holden	Y	Y	Y	N	N	N	Y	N
7 ***Weldon***	Y	Y	Y	Y	N	Y	Y	Y
8 ***Greenwood***	N	Y	Y	Y	Y	Y	Y	Y
9 ***Shuster***	Y	Y	Y	Y	Y	Y	Y	Y
10 ***McDade***	N	Y	Y	Y	N	Y	Y	Y
11 Kanjorski	Y	Y	N	N	N	N	Y	N
12 Murtha	N	N	N	N	N	N	Y	N
13 Margolies-Mezv.	Y	Y	Y	Y	N	N	Y	N
14 Coyne	N	N	N	Y	N	N	N	N
15 McHale	N	Y	Y	Y	N	N	Y	N
16 ***Walker***	Y	Y	Y	Y	Y	Y	Y	Y
17 ***Gekas***	Y	Y	Y	Y	Y	Y	Y	Y
18 ***Santorum***	Y	Y	Y	Y	Y	Y	Y	Y
19 ***Goodling***	N	Y	Y	Y	Y	Y	Y	Y
20 Murphy	N	Y	N	N	N	N	Y	N
21 ***Ridge***	?	?	?	?	?	?	?	?
RHODE ISLAND								
1 ***Machtley***	N	Y	Y	Y	Y	Y	Y	Y
2 Reed	N	N	Y	N	N	N	Y	N
SOUTH CAROLINA								
1 ***Ravenel***	N	Y	Y	Y	Y	Y	Y	Y
2 ***Spence***	N	Y	Y	Y	N	Y	Y	Y
3 Derrick	N	N	N	N	N	?	?	?
4 ***Inglis***	Y	Y	Y	Y	Y	Y	Y	Y
5 Spratt	N	Y	Y	Y	N	N	Y	N
6 Clyburn	N	N	Y	Y	N	N	Y	N
SOUTH DAKOTA								
AL Johnson	N	N	N	Y	N	N	Y	N
TENNESSEE								
1 ***Quillen***	Y	Y	Y	N	N	Y	Y	Y
2 ***Duncan***	Y	Y	Y	N	N	Y	Y	Y
3 Lloyd	N	Y	Y	Y	N	N	Y	Y
4 Cooper	N	Y	Y	Y	N	Y	Y	Y
5 Clement	N	Y	Y	Y	N	N	Y	N

	283	284	285	286	287	288	289	290
6 Gordon	N	Y	Y	Y	N	N	Y	N
7 ***Sundquist***	Y	Y	Y	Y	N	Y	Y	Y
8 Tanner	Y	Y	Y	Y	N	N	Y	N
9 Ford	?	?	?	?	?	?	?	?
TEXAS								
1 Chapman	N	Y	Y	N	Y	N	Y	?
2 Wilson	N	N	N	N	Y	N	Y	N
3 ***Johnson, Sam***	N	Y	Y	N	Y	Y	Y	Y
4 Hall	Y	Y	Y	Y	Y	Y	Y	Y
5 Bryant	N	N	N	N	Y	N	Y	N
6 ***Barton***	N	Y	Y	Y	Y	Y	Y	Y
7 ***Archer***	Y	Y	Y	N	Y	Y	Y	Y
8 ***Fields***	+	+	+	−	+	+	+	+
9 Brooks	N	Y	N	N	Y	N	Y	N
10 Pickle	N	N	Y	Y	Y	N	Y	N
11 Edwards	N	Y	Y	Y	Y	N	Y	N
12 Geren	N	Y	Y	N	N	N	Y	Y
13 Sarpalius	N	Y	Y	Y	Y	N	Y	N
14 Laughlin	N	Y	Y	N	Y	N	Y	N
15 de la Garza	N	Y	N	Y	Y	N	Y	N
16 Coleman	N	N	N	N	Y	N	Y	N
17 Stenholm	Y	Y	Y	N	Y	N	Y	Y
18 Washington	?	?	?	?	?	?	?	?
19 ***Combest***	N	Y	Y	Y	Y	Y	Y	Y
20 Gonzalez	Y	N	N	N	N	N	N	N
21 ***Smith***	N	Y	Y	Y	Y	Y	Y	Y
22 ***DeLay***	N	Y	Y	Y	Y	Y	Y	Y
23 ***Bonilla***	N	Y	Y	Y	Y	Y	Y	Y
24 Frost	N	Y	Y	Y	Y	N	Y	N
25 Andrews	N	N	Y	N	Y	N	?	N
26 ***Armey***	N	Y	Y	Y	Y	Y	Y	Y
27 Ortiz	N	Y	Y	Y	Y	Y	Y	N
28 Tejeda	N	Y	Y	Y	Y	N	Y	N
29 Green	Y	Y	Y	N	Y	Y	Y	N
30 Johnson, E.B.	N	N	N	Y	N	N	Y	N
UTAH								
1 ***Hansen***	Y	Y	Y	Y	N	Y	Y	Y
2 Shepherd	N	Y	Y	Y	N	N	Y	N
3 Orton	Y	Y	Y	Y	N	N	Y	Y
VERMONT								
AL *Sanders*	Y	N	Y	Y	N	N	N	N
VIRGINIA								
1 ***Bateman***	N	N	N	Y	N	Y	Y	Y
2 Pickett	N	Y	Y	Y	N	N	Y	N
3 Scott	N	N	N	Y	N	N	Y	N
4 Sisisky	Y	Y	Y	Y	N	N	Y	N
5 Payne	N	Y	Y	N	N	N	Y	N
6 ***Goodlatte***	N	Y	Y	Y	N	Y	Y	Y
7 ***Bliley***	?	?	?	?	N	Y	Y	Y
8 Moran	N	N	N	N	N	N	Y	N
9 Boucher	N	N	N	N	N	N	Y	N
10 ***Wolf***	N	Y	N	Y	N	Y	Y	Y
11 Byrne	N	Y	N	Y	N	N	Y	N
WASHINGTON								
1 Cantwell	N	Y	Y	Y	N	N	Y	N
2 Swift	N	N	N	N	?	N	Y	N
3 Unsoeld	N	N	Y	Y	N	N	Y	N
4 Inslee	N	Y	Y	Y	Y	N	Y	N
5 Foley								
6 Dicks	N	Y	Y	Y	N	N	Y	N
7 McDermott	N	N	N	Y	N	N	Y	N
8 ***Dunn***	N	Y	Y	Y	Y	Y	Y	Y
9 Kreidler	Y	Y	Y	Y	N	N	Y	N
WEST VIRGINIA								
1 Mollohan	N	N	N	N	N	N	Y	N
2 Wise	N	Y	N	N	N	N	Y	N
3 Rahall	N	Y	Y	N	N	N	Y	N
WISCONSIN								
1 Barca	Y	Y	Y	Y	N	N	Y	N
2 ***Klug***	Y	Y	Y	Y	N	Y	Y	Y
3 ***Gunderson***	N	Y	Y	Y	N	Y	Y	Y
4 Kleczka	Y	Y	Y	N	N	N	Y	N
5 Barrett	Y	Y	Y	Y	N	N	Y	N
6 ***Petri***	N	Y	Y	Y	Y	Y	Y	Y
7 Obey	N	N	N	N	N	N	Y	N
8 ***Roth***	Y	Y	Y	N	N	Y	Y	Y
9 ***Sensenbrenner***	Y	Y	Y	N	N	Y	Y	Y
WYOMING								
AL ***Thomas***	N	Y	Y	N	N	Y	Y	Y
DELEGATES								
de Lugo, V.I.	N	N	N	Y	N	N	Y	D
Faleomavaega, Am.S.	?	?	?	?	?	?	?	D
Norton, D.C.	N	N	N	Y	N	N	N	D
Romero-B., P.R.	N	N	N	Y	N	N	Y	D
Underwood, Guam	N	N	N	Y	N	N	Y	D

Southern states - Ala., Ark., Fla., Ga., Ky., La., Miss., N.C., Okla., S.C., Tenn., Texas, Va.
Omitted votes are quorum calls, which CQ does not include in its vote charts.

291. HR 4603. Fiscal 1995 Commerce, Justice, State Appropriations/Passage. Passage of the bill to provide $27.2 billion in new budget authority for the departments of Commerce, Justice and State, the Judiciary and related agencies for fiscal 1995, of which $670,000,000 is supplemental appropriations for fiscal 1994. The administration requested $28,400,581,000. Passed 286-112: R 68-101; D 217-11 (ND 147-8, SD 70-3); I 1-0, June 28, 1994 (in the session that began and the Congressional Record dated June 27).

292. HR 3626. Revising Restrictions on the Regional Bell Companies/Passage. Brooks, D-Texas, motion to suspend the rules and pass the bill to set conditions that would allow the regional Bell telephone companies to enter the long-distance, telecommunications equipment manufacturing, alarm service and electronic publishing markets. Motion agreed to 423-5: R 173-1; D 249-4 (ND 168-3, SD 81-1); I 1-0, June 28, 1994. A two-thirds majority of those present and voting (286 in this case) is required for passage under suspension of the rules. A "yea" was a vote in support of the president's position.

293. HR 3636. Promoting Competition in Local Telephone Services and Cable Television/Passage. Markey, D-Mass., motion to suspend the rules and pass the bill to allow local telephone companies to enter the cable television market and to allow cable companies to enter the local telephone market. Motion agreed to 423-4: R 174-1; D 248-3 (ND 168-2, SD 80-1); I 1-0, June 28, 1994. A two-thirds majority of those present and voting (285 in this case) is required for passage under suspension of the rules. A "yea" was a vote in support of the president's position.

294. HR 4606. Fiscal 1995 Labor, Health and Human Services Appropriations/Community Health Centers. Porter, R-Ill., amendment to increase spending on community health centers and rural health outreach grants by $100 million and offset the increased spending by a corresponding reduction in administrative and enforcement accounts. Adopted in the Committee of the Whole 224-205: R 171-2; D 53-202 (ND 17-157, SD 36-45); I 0-1, June 28, 1994.

295. HR 4606. Fiscal 1995 Labor, Health and Human Services Appropriations/Native Hawaiian Education. Boehner, R-Ohio, amendment to cut the $8 million in the bill for the Native Hawaiian Education Program. Rejected in the Committee of the Whole 188-233: R 162-8; D 26-224 (ND 18-153, SD 8-71); I 0-1, June 28, 1994.

* 297. HR 4606. Fiscal 1995 Labor, Health and Human Services Appropriations/Higher Education. Grams, R-Minn., amendment to reduce the amount provided for higher education programs by $15 million with the intent of eliminating the Law School Clinical Experience Program. Rejected in the Committee of the Whole 194-232: R 156-17; D 38-214 (ND 23-151, SD 15-63); I 0-1, June 28, 1994.

298. HR 4606. Fiscal 1995 Labor, Health and Human Services Appropriations/Bilingual and Immigrant Education. Mica, R-Fla., amendment to increase the amount provided for bilingual and immigrant education by $25 million. Rejected in the Committee of the Whole 35-393: R 23-150; D 12-242 (ND 8-167, SD 4-75); I 0-1, June 28, 1994.

299. HR 4606. Fiscal 1995 Labor, Health and Human Services Appropriations/Public Library Services. Baker, R-Calif., amendment to increase the amount provided for public library services by $1 million. Adopted in the Committee of the Whole 319-109: R 170-3; D 148-106 (ND 96-79, SD 52-27); I 1-0, June 28, 1994.

* Omitted votes are quorum calls, which CQ does not include in its vote charts.

KEY

Y	Voted for (yea).
#	Paired for.
+	Announced for.
N	Voted against (nay).
X	Paired against.
−	Announced against.
P	Voted "present."
C	Voted "present" to avoid possible conflict of interest.
?	Did not vote or otherwise make a position known.
D	Delegates ineligible to vote.

Democrats *Republicans* *Independent*

	291	292	293	294	295	297	298	299
ALABAMA								
1 Callahan	Y	Y	Y	?	Y	Y	N	Y
2 Everett	N	Y	Y	Y	Y	Y	N	Y
3 Browder	Y	Y	N	N	N	N	N	Y
4 Bevill	Y	Y	N	N	N	N	N	N
5 Cramer	Y	Y	N	N	N	N	N	Y
6 Bachus	N	Y	Y	Y	Y	Y	N	Y
7 Hilliard	?	?	?	X	?	?	?	?
ALASKA								
AL Young	N	Y	Y	Y	N	N	N	Y
ARIZONA								
1 Coppersmith	Y	Y	Y	N	Y	N	N	Y
2 Pastor	Y	Y	N	N	N	N	Y	Y
3 Stump	N	Y	Y	Y	Y	Y	N	Y
4 Kyl	Y	Y	Y	Y	Y	Y	N	Y
5 Kolbe	Y	Y	Y	Y	Y	Y	N	Y
6 English	Y	Y	N	N	N	N	N	Y
ARKANSAS								
1 Lambert	Y	Y	+	Y	Y	N	N	Y
2 Thornton	Y	Y	N	N	N	N	N	Y
3 Hutchinson	Y	Y	Y	Y	Y	Y	N	Y
4 Dickey	Y	Y	Y	Y	Y	Y	N	Y
CALIFORNIA								
1 Hamburg	Y	Y	Y	N	N	N	N	N
2 Herger	N	Y	Y	Y	Y	Y	N	Y
3 Fazio	Y	Y	N	N	N	N	N	N
4 Doolittle	N	Y	Y	Y	Y	Y	N	Y
5 Matsui	?	Y	Y	N	N	N	N	N
6 Woolsey	Y	Y	N	N	N	N	N	N
7 Miller	Y	Y	N	N	N	N	N	N
8 Pelosi	Y	Y	N	N	N	N	N	N
9 Dellums	Y	Y	N	N	N	N	N	N
10 Baker	N	Y	Y	Y	Y	Y	N	Y
11 Pombo	?	?	?	?	?	?	?	?
12 Lantos	Y	Y	Y	N	N	N	N	N
13 Stark	Y	Y	N	N	N	N	Y	N
14 Eshoo	Y	Y	Y	N	N	N	N	N
15 Mineta	Y	Y	N	N	N	N	N	N
16 Edwards	Y	Y	N	N	N	N	N	N
17 Farr	Y	Y	Y	N	Y	N	Y	Y
18 Condit	N	Y	Y	N	Y	N	Y	Y
19 Lehman	Y	Y	N	N	N	N	N	Y
20 Dooley	Y	Y	Y	N	N	N	N	Y
21 Thomas	Y	Y	Y	Y	Y	Y	N	Y
22 Huffington	N	Y	Y	Y	Y	Y	N	Y
23 Gallegly	Y	Y	Y	Y	Y	Y	N	Y
24 Beilenson	Y	Y	N	N	N	N	N	N
25 McKeon	Y	Y	Y	Y	Y	Y	N	Y
26 Berman	Y	Y	Y	N	N	N	N	N
27 Moorhead	N	Y	Y	Y	Y	Y	N	Y
28 Dreier	N	Y	Y	Y	Y	Y	N	Y
29 Waxman	Y	Y	N	N	N	N	N	N
30 Becerra	Y	Y	N	N	N	N	Y	N
31 Martinez	Y	Y	N	N	N	N	N	N
32 Dixon	Y	Y	N	N	N	N	N	N
33 Roybal-Allard	Y	Y	N	N	N	N	N	N
34 Torres	Y	Y	N	N	N	N	N	N
35 Waters	Y	Y	N	N	N	N	N	N
36 Harman	Y	Y	Y	N	?	N	Y	Y
37 Tucker	Y	Y	N	N	N	N	Y	N
38 Horn	Y	Y	Y	Y	N	Y	N	Y
39 Royce	N	Y	Y	Y	Y	Y	N	Y
40 Lewis	Y	Y	Y	Y	Y	Y	N	Y
41 Kim	N	Y	Y	Y	Y	Y	N	Y
42 Brown	Y	Y	Y	N	N	N	N	N
43 Calvert	N	Y	Y	Y	Y	Y	N	Y
44 McCandless	?	Y	Y	Y	Y	Y	N	Y
45 Rohrabacher	N	Y	Y	Y	Y	Y	N	Y
46 Dornan	N	?	?	Y	Y	Y	N	Y
47 Cox	N	Y	Y	Y	Y	Y	N	Y
48 Packard	Y	Y	Y	Y	Y	Y	N	Y
49 Schenk	Y	Y	Y	N	N	N	Y	Y
50 Filner	Y	Y	N	N	N	N	Y	N
51 Cunningham	Y	Y	Y	Y	Y	Y	N	Y
52 Hunter	Y	Y	Y	Y	Y	Y	N	Y
COLORADO								
1 Schroeder	Y	Y	Y	N	N	N	N	Y
2 Skaggs	Y	Y	N	N	N	N	N	N
3 McInnis	Y	Y	Y	Y	Y	Y	N	Y
4 Allard	N	Y	Y	Y	Y	Y	N	Y
5 Hefley	N	Y	Y	Y	Y	Y	N	Y
6 Schaefer	N	Y	Y	Y	Y	Y	N	Y
CONNECTICUT								
1 Kennelly	Y	Y	Y	N	N	N	N	Y
2 Gejdenson	Y	Y	Y	N	N	N	N	N
3 DeLauro	Y	Y	N	N	N	N	N	N
4 Shays	N	Y	Y	Y	N	Y	N	Y
5 Franks	Y	Y	Y	Y	Y	Y	N	Y
6 Johnson	N	Y	Y	Y	Y	N	Y	Y
DELAWARE								
AL Castle	Y	Y	Y	Y	Y	Y	N	Y
FLORIDA								
1 Hutto	Y	Y	Y	N	Y	N	Y	N
2 Peterson	Y	Y	Y	N	N	N	N	Y
3 Brown	?	Y	Y	N	N	N	N	Y
4 Fowler	Y	Y	Y	Y	Y	Y	Y	Y
5 Thurman	Y	Y	Y	N	Y	N	Y	Y
6 Stearns	Y	Y	Y	Y	Y	Y	N	Y
7 Mica	N	Y	Y	Y	Y	Y	N	Y
8 McCollum	?	Y	Y	Y	Y	Y	N	Y
9 Bilirakis	Y	Y	Y	Y	Y	Y	N	Y
10 Young	Y	Y	Y	N	N	N	N	Y
11 Gibbons	?	Y	Y	N	N	N	N	N
12 Canady	Y	Y	Y	Y	Y	Y	N	Y
13 Miller	N	Y	Y	Y	Y	Y	N	Y
14 Goss	N	Y	Y	Y	Y	Y	N	Y
15 Bacchus	Y	Y	Y	N	N	N	N	N
16 Lewis	N	Y	Y	Y	Y	Y	Y	Y
17 Meek	Y	Y	N	N	N	N	N	N
18 Ros-Lehtinen	N	Y	Y	Y	Y	Y	N	Y
19 Johnston	Y	Y	N	N	N	N	N	N
20 Deutsch	Y	Y	Y	N	N	N	N	N
21 Diaz-Balart	N	Y	Y	N	N	N	Y	Y
22 Shaw	Y	Y	Y	Y	Y	Y	Y	Y
23 Hastings	?	Y	Y	N	N	N	N	N
GEORGIA								
1 Kingston	N	Y	Y	Y	Y	Y	N	Y
2 Bishop	Y	Y	Y	N	N	N	N	Y
3 Collins	N	Y	Y	Y	Y	Y	N	Y
4 Linder	N	Y	Y	Y	Y	Y	N	Y
5 Lewis	Y	Y	N	N	N	N	N	N
6 Gingrich	Y	Y	Y	Y	Y	Y	N	Y
7 Darden	Y	Y	Y	N	N	N	N	Y
8 Rowland	Y	Y	Y	N	N	N	N	N
9 Deal	Y	Y	Y	N	N	N	N	Y
10 Johnson	Y	Y	N	N	N	N	N	N
11 McKinney	Y	Y	N	N	N	N	N	N
HAWAII								
1 Abercrombie	Y	Y	N	N	N	N	N	N
2 Mink	Y	Y	N	N	N	N	N	N
IDAHO								
1 LaRocco	Y	Y	Y	N	N	N	N	Y
2 Crapo	N	Y	Y	Y	Y	Y	N	Y
ILLINOIS								
1 Rush	+	Y	Y	N	N	N	N	Y
2 Reynolds	?	Y	Y	N	N	N	N	N
3 Lipinski	Y	Y	N	N	N	N	N	Y
4 Gutierrez	Y	Y	N	N	N	N	Y	Y
5 Rostenkowski	?	Y	Y	N	N	N	N	N
6 Hyde	Y	Y	Y	Y	Y	Y	N	Y
7 Collins	Y	Y	N	N	N	N	N	N
8 Crane	N	Y	Y	Y	Y	Y	N	Y
9 Yates	#	N	N	N	N	N	N	Y
10 Porter	Y	Y	Y	Y	N	Y	N	Y
11 Sangmeister	Y	Y	Y	N	Y	N	Y	Y
12 Costello	Y	Y	Y	N	N	N	N	Y
13 Fawell	N	Y	Y	Y	Y	Y	N	Y
14 Hastert	N	Y	Y	Y	Y	Y	N	Y
15 Ewing	Y	Y	Y	Y	Y	Y	N	Y
16 Manzullo	Y	Y	N	N	N	N	N	Y
17 Evans	N	Y	Y	N	N	N	N	N

ND Northern Democrats   SD Southern Democrats

	291	292	293	294	295	297	298	299
18 ***Michel***	Y	Y	Y	Y	?	?	?	?
19 Poshard	Y	Y	Y	N	Y	Y	N	Y
20 Durbin	Y	Y	Y	N	N	N	N	Y
INDIANA								
1 Visclosky	Y	Y	Y	N	N	N	N	N
2 Sharp	Y	Y	Y	N	N	N	N	Y
3 Roemer	Y	Y	Y	N	N	N	N	Y
4 Long	Y	Y	Y	N	N	N	N	Y
5 ***Buyer***	Y	Y	Y	Y	Y	Y	N	Y
6 ***Burton***	N	Y	Y	Y	Y	Y	N	Y
7 ***Myers***	N	Y	Y	Y	Y	Y	N	Y
8 McCloskey	?	Y	Y	N	N	N	N	N
9 Hamilton	Y	Y	Y	Y	N	Y	N	Y
10 Jacobs	N	Y	Y	N	N	N	N	Y
IOWA								
1 ***Leach***	Y	Y	Y	Y	Y	Y	N	Y
2 ***Nussle***	N	Y	Y	Y	Y	Y	N	Y
3 ***Lightfoot***	Y	Y	Y	Y	Y	Y	N	Y
4 Smith	Y	Y	Y	N	N	N	N	N
5 ***Grandy***	Y	Y	Y	Y	N	N	N	Y
KANSAS								
1 ***Roberts***	N	Y	Y	Y	Y	Y	N	Y
2 Slattery	Y	Y	Y	N	N	N	N	N
3 ***Meyers***	Y	Y	Y	Y	Y	Y	N	Y
4 Glickman	Y	Y	Y	N	N	Y	N	Y
KENTUCKY								
1 Barlow	Y	Y	Y	N	N	N	N	Y
2 ***Lewis***	N	Y	Y	Y	Y	Y	N	Y
3 Mazzoli	Y	Y	Y	N	N	N	N	Y
4 ***Bunning***	N	Y	Y	Y	Y	Y	N	Y
5 ***Rogers***	Y	Y	Y	Y	Y	N	N	Y
6 Baesler	Y	Y	Y	N	N	N	N	Y
LOUISIANA								
1 ***Livingston***	Y	Y	Y	Y	Y	Y	N	Y
2 Jefferson	Y	Y	Y	N	N	N	N	Y
3 Tauzin	Y	Y	Y	Y	Y	Y	N	Y
4 Fields	Y	Y	Y	N	N	N	N	Y
5 ***McCrery***	Y	Y	Y	Y	Y	Y	N	Y
6 ***Baker***	N	Y	Y	Y	Y	Y	N	Y
7 Hayes	Y	Y	Y	Y	Y	Y	N	Y
MAINE								
1 Andrews	Y	Y	Y	Y	N	N	N	Y
2 ***Snowe***	Y	Y	Y	Y	Y	Y	N	Y
MARYLAND								
1 ***Gilchrest***	Y	Y	Y	Y	Y	N	N	Y
2 ***Bentley***	Y	Y	Y	Y	Y	Y	N	N
3 Cardin	Y	Y	Y	N	N	N	N	N
4 Wynn	Y	Y	Y	N	N	N	N	Y
5 Hoyer	Y	Y	Y	N	?	N	N	N
6 ***Bartlett***	N	Y	Y	Y	Y	Y	N	Y
7 Mfume	Y	Y	Y	N	N	N	N	Y
8 ***Morella***	Y	Y	Y	Y	Y	N	N	Y
MASSACHUSETTS								
1 Olver	Y	Y	Y	?	N	N	N	N
2 Neal	Y	Y	Y	N	N	N	N	Y
3 ***Blute***	Y	Y	Y	Y	Y	Y	N	Y
4 Frank	Y	Y	Y	N	N	N	N	N
5 Meehan	?	Y	Y	Y	N	Y	N	Y
6 ***Torkildsen***	Y	Y	Y	Y	Y	Y	N	Y
7 Markey	Y	Y	Y	N	N	N	N	N
8 Kennedy	Y	Y	Y	N	N	N	N	N
9 Moakley	Y	Y	Y	N	N	N	N	Y
10 Studds	Y	Y	Y	N	N	N	N	Y
MICHIGAN								
1 Stupak	Y	Y	Y	Y	N	N	N	Y
2 ***Hoekstra***	N	Y	Y	Y	Y	Y	N	Y
3 ***Ehlers***	N	Y	Y	Y	Y	Y	N	Y
4 ***Camp***	N	Y	Y	Y	Y	Y	N	Y
5 Barcia	Y	Y	Y	N	N	N	N	Y
6 ***Upton***	Y	Y	Y	Y	Y	Y	N	Y
7 ***Smith***	N	Y	Y	Y	Y	Y	N	Y
8 Carr	Y	Y	?	N	?	?	N	N
9 Kildee	Y	Y	Y	N	N	N	N	Y
10 Bonior	Y	Y	Y	N	N	N	N	N
11 ***Knollenberg***	N	Y	Y	Y	Y	Y	Y	Y
12 Levin	Y	Y	Y	N	N	N	N	N
13 Ford	?	Y	Y	N	N	N	N	N
14 Conyers	Y	Y	Y	N	N	N	N	N
15 Collins	Y	Y	Y	N	N	N	N	N
16 Dingell	Y	Y	Y	N	N	N	N	N
MINNESOTA								
1 Penny	N	Y	Y	Y	Y	Y	N	N
2 Minge	N	Y	Y	N	Y	N	N	Y
3 ***Ramstad***	N	Y	Y	Y	Y	Y	N	Y
4 Vento	Y	Y	Y	N	N	N	N	N

	291	292	293	294	295	297	298	299
5 Sabo	Y	Y	Y	N	N	N	N	N
6 ***Grams***	N	Y	Y	Y	Y	Y	N	Y
7 Peterson	N	Y	Y	Y	N	Y	N	Y
8 Oberstar	Y	Y	Y	N	N	N	N	Y
MISSISSIPPI								
1 Whitten	?	Y	Y	N	?	?	?	?
2 Thompson	Y	Y	Y	N	N	N	N	N
3 Montgomery	Y	Y	Y	Y	N	Y	N	Y
4 Parker	Y	Y	Y	Y	N	N	N	Y
5 Taylor	N	Y	Y	Y	N	Y	N	N
MISSOURI								
1 Clay	Y	Y	Y	N	N	N	N	N
2 ***Talent***	N	Y	Y	Y	Y	Y	N	Y
3 Gephardt	?	Y	Y	N	N	N	N	N
4 Skelton	Y	Y	Y	Y	N	Y	N	Y
5 Wheat	Y	Y	Y	N	N	N	N	N
6 Danner	Y	Y	Y	N	N	N	N	N
7 ***Hancock***	N	Y	Y	Y	Y	Y	N	Y
8 ***Emerson***	Y	Y	Y	Y	Y	Y	N	Y
9 Volkmer	Y	Y	Y	Y	N	N	N	N
MONTANA								
AL Williams	?	Y	Y	Y	N	N	N	Y
NEBRASKA								
1 ***Bereuter***	Y	Y	Y	Y	Y	Y	N	Y
2 Hoagland	Y	Y	Y	Y	Y	Y	N	Y
3 ***Barrett***	Y	Y	Y	Y	Y	Y	N	Y
NEVADA								
1 Bilbray	Y	Y	Y	N	N	N	N	Y
2 ***Vucanovich***	Y	Y	Y	Y	Y	Y	N	Y
NEW HAMPSHIRE								
1 ***Zeliff***	N	Y	Y	Y	Y	Y	N	Y
2 Swett	N	Y	Y	Y	Y	Y	N	Y
NEW JERSEY								
1 Andrews	N	Y	Y	N	Y	Y	N	Y
2 Hughes	Y	Y	Y	N	N	N	N	N
3 ***Saxton***	N	Y	Y	Y	Y	N	N	Y
4 ***Smith***	Y	Y	Y	Y	Y	N	N	Y
5 ***Roukema***	Y	Y	Y	Y	Y	Y	N	Y
6 Pallone	Y	Y	Y	N	N	N	N	Y
7 ***Franks***	N	Y	Y	Y	Y	Y	Y	Y
8 Klein	Y	Y	Y	N	N	N	N	N
9 Torricelli	?	Y	Y	N	Y	N	N	Y
10 Payne	Y	Y	Y	N	N	N	N	Y
11 ***Gallo***	N	Y	Y	Y	Y	N	N	Y
12 ***Zimmer***	N	Y	Y	Y	Y	Y	N	Y
13 Menendez	Y	Y	Y	N	N	N	N	Y
NEW MEXICO								
1 ***Schiff***	Y	Y	Y	Y	Y	Y	N	Y
2 ***Skeen***	Y	Y	Y	Y	Y	Y	N	Y
3 Richardson	Y	Y	Y	N	N	N	N	N
NEW YORK								
1 Hochbrueckner	Y	Y	Y	N	N	N	N	Y
2 ***Lazio***	N	Y	Y	Y	Y	N	N	Y
3 ***King***	Y	Y	Y	Y	N	Y	N	Y
4 ***Levy***	Y	Y	Y	Y	Y	Y	N	Y
5 Ackerman	Y	Y	Y	N	N	N	N	N
6 Flake	Y	+	+	−	N	N	N	N
7 Manton	Y	Y	Y	N	N	N	N	N
8 Nadler	Y	Y	Y	N	N	N	N	Y
9 Schumer	Y	Y	Y	N	N	?	?	?
10 Towns	?	Y	Y	N	N	N	N	N
11 Owens	?	Y	Y	N	?	N	N	Y
12 Velazquez	Y	Y	Y	N	N	N	N	Y
13 ***Molinari***	N	Y	Y	Y	Y	Y	Y	Y
14 Maloney	Y	Y	Y	N	N	N	N	Y
15 Rangel	?	Y	Y	N	N	N	N	Y
16 Serrano	Y	Y	Y	N	N	N	N	N
17 Engel	Y	Y	Y	N	N	N	N	Y
18 Lowey	Y	Y	Y	N	N	N	N	N
19 ***Fish***	?	Y	Y	Y	?	?	?	?
20 ***Gilman***	Y	Y	Y	N	N	N	N	Y
21 McNulty	Y	Y	Y	N	N	Y	N	N
22 ***Solomon***	N	Y	Y	Y	Y	Y	N	Y
23 ***Boehlert***	Y	Y	Y	Y	N	N	N	Y
24 ***McHugh***	N	Y	Y	Y	Y	Y	N	Y
25 ***Walsh***	Y	Y	Y	Y	Y	N	N	Y
26 Hinchey	Y	Y	Y	N	N	N	N	Y
27 ***Paxon***	N	Y	Y	Y	Y	Y	N	Y
28 Slaughter	Y	Y	Y	N	N	N	N	Y
29 LaFalce	Y	Y	Y	N	Y	N	N	Y
30 ***Quinn***	Y	Y	Y	Y	Y	Y	N	Y
31 ***Houghton***	Y	Y	Y	Y	Y	Y	N	Y
NORTH CAROLINA								
1 Clayton	Y	Y	Y	N	N	N	N	N
2 Valentine	Y	Y	Y	Y	N	N	N	Y

	291	292	293	294	295	297	298	299
3 Lancaster	Y	Y	Y	Y	N	N	N	Y
4 Price	Y	Y	Y	N	Y	N	N	N
5 Neal	Y	Y	Y	Y	N	N	N	Y
6 ***Coble***	N	Y	Y	Y	Y	Y	N	Y
7 Rose	?	Y	Y	N	N	N	N	Y
8 Hefner	Y	Y	Y	N	N	N	N	N
9 ***McMillan***	?	Y	Y	Y	Y	Y	N	Y
10 ***Ballenger***	N	Y	Y	Y	Y	Y	N	Y
11 ***Taylor***	Y	Y	Y	Y	Y	Y	N	Y
12 Watt	Y	Y	Y	N	N	N	N	N
NORTH DAKOTA								
AL Pomeroy	Y	Y	Y	Y	N	N	N	Y
OHIO								
1 Mann	Y	Y	Y	N	Y	N	N	N
2 ***Portman***	N	Y	Y	Y	Y	Y	N	Y
3 Hall	?	Y	Y	N	N	N	N	Y
4 ***Oxley***	N	Y	Y	Y	Y	Y	Y	Y
5 ***Gillmor***	N	Y	Y	Y	Y	Y	N	Y
6 Strickland	Y	Y	Y	N	Y	N	N	N
7 ***Hobson***	N	Y	Y	Y	Y	Y	N	Y
8 ***Boehner***	N	Y	Y	Y	Y	Y	N	Y
9 Kaptur	Y	Y	Y	N	N	N	N	Y
10 ***Hoke***	N	?	Y	Y	Y	Y	N	Y
11 Stokes	Y	Y	Y	N	N	N	N	N
12 ***Kasich***	N	Y	Y	Y	Y	Y	N	Y
13 Brown	Y	Y	Y	N	N	N	N	Y
14 Sawyer	Y	Y	Y	N	N	N	N	N
15 ***Pryce***	−	Y	Y	#	Y	Y	N	Y
16 ***Regula***	N	Y	Y	Y	Y	Y	N	Y
17 Traficant	Y	Y	Y	N	N	N	N	N
18 Applegate	Y	Y	Y	N	N	N	N	Y
19 Fingerhut	Y	Y	Y	N	Y	Y	N	Y
OKLAHOMA								
1 ***Inhofe***	N	Y	Y	Y	Y	Y	N	Y
2 Synar	Y	Y	Y	N	N	N	N	N
3 Brewster	?	Y	Y	Y	N	Y	N	Y
4 McCurdy	Y	Y	Y	Y	Y	Y	N	Y
5 ***Istook***	N	Y	Y	Y	Y	Y	N	Y
6 ***Lucas***	N	Y	Y	Y	Y	Y	N	Y
OREGON								
1 Furse	Y	Y	Y	N	N	N	N	Y
2 ***Smith***	X	Y	Y	Y	Y	Y	N	Y
3 Wyden	Y	Y	Y	N	N	N	N	N
4 DeFazio	Y	Y	Y	N	?	N	N	Y
5 Kopetski	Y	Y	Y	N	N	N	N	N
PENNSYLVANIA								
1 Foglietta	Y	Y	Y	N	N	N	N	Y
2 Blackwell	?	Y	Y	N	N	N	N	N
3 Borski	Y	Y	Y	N	N	N	N	Y
4 Klink	Y	Y	Y	N	N	N	N	Y
5 ***Clinger***	Y	Y	Y	Y	Y	N	N	Y
6 Holden	Y	N	Y	N	Y	Y	N	Y
7 ***Weldon***	N	Y	Y	Y	?	Y	N	Y
8 ***Greenwood***	N	Y	Y	Y	?	Y	N	Y
9 ***Shuster***	N	Y	Y	Y	Y	Y	N	Y
10 ***McDade***	Y	Y	Y	Y	Y	Y	N	Y
11 Kanjorski	Y	Y	Y	N	N	Y	N	Y
12 Murtha	?	Y	Y	N	N	N	N	N
13 Margolies-Mezv.	Y	Y	Y	N	Y	Y	N	Y
14 Coyne	Y	Y	Y	N	N	N	N	Y
15 McHale	Y	Y	Y	N	N	Y	N	Y
16 ***Walker***	N	Y	Y	Y	Y	Y	N	Y
17 ***Gekas***	Y	Y	Y	Y	Y	Y	N	Y
18 ***Santorum***	N	Y	Y	Y	Y	Y	N	Y
19 ***Goodling***	N	Y	Y	Y	Y	Y	Y	Y
20 Murphy	Y	Y	Y	N	N	N	N	Y
21 ***Ridge***	?	?	?	?	?	?	?	?
RHODE ISLAND								
1 ***Machtley***	Y	Y	Y	Y	Y	Y	N	Y
2 Reed	Y	Y	Y	N	N	N	N	Y
SOUTH CAROLINA								
1 ***Ravenel***	Y	Y	Y	Y	Y	Y	N	Y
2 ***Spence***	N	Y	Y	Y	Y	Y	N	Y
3 Derrick	?	Y	Y	Y	N	N	N	Y
4 ***Inglis***	N	Y	Y	Y	Y	Y	N	Y
5 Spratt	Y	Y	Y	Y	N	N	N	N
6 Clyburn	Y	Y	Y	N	N	N	N	N
SOUTH DAKOTA								
AL Johnson	Y	Y	Y	N	Y	N	N	Y
TENNESSEE								
1 ***Quillen***	N	Y	Y	Y	Y	Y	N	Y
2 ***Duncan***	N	Y	Y	Y	Y	Y	N	Y
3 Lloyd	Y	Y	Y	Y	N	N	N	Y
4 Cooper	Y	Y	Y	Y	Y	Y	N	Y
5 Clement	Y	Y	Y	N	N	N	N	N

	291	292	293	294	295	297	298	299
6 Gordon	Y	Y	Y	Y	N	N	N	Y
7 ***Sundquist***	N	Y	Y	Y	Y	Y	N	Y
8 Tanner	Y	Y	Y	Y	N	Y	N	Y
9 Ford	?	Y	Y	N	N	N	N	N
TEXAS								
1 Chapman	Y	Y	Y	Y	?	?	?	?
2 Wilson	Y	Y	Y	N	N	N	N	Y
3 ***Johnson, Sam***	N	Y	Y	Y	Y	Y	N	Y
4 Hall	N	Y	Y	Y	N	Y	N	Y
5 Bryant	Y	Y	Y	N	N	N	N	Y
6 ***Barton***	N	Y	Y	Y	Y	Y	N	N
7 ***Archer***	N	Y	Y	Y	Y	Y	N	Y
8 ***Fields***	−	Y	Y	?	?	?	?	?
9 Brooks	Y	Y	Y	N	N	N	N	Y
10 Pickle	Y	Y	Y	Y	N	N	N	Y
11 Edwards	Y	Y	Y	Y	N	N	N	Y
12 Geren	Y	Y	Y	Y	N	N	N	Y
13 Sarpalius	Y	Y	Y	Y	N	Y	N	Y
14 Laughlin	Y	Y	Y	Y	N	Y	N	Y
15 de la Garza	Y	Y	Y	Y	N	N	Y	Y
16 Coleman	Y	Y	Y	N	N	N	N	N
17 Stenholm	N	Y	Y	Y	N	Y	N	Y
18 Washington	?	Y	Y	?	?	?	?	?
19 ***Combest***	N	Y	Y	Y	Y	Y	N	Y
20 Gonzalez	Y	N	N	N	N	N	N	Y
21 ***Smith***	N	Y	Y	Y	Y	Y	N	Y
22 ***DeLay***	N	Y	Y	Y	Y	Y	N	Y
23 ***Bonilla***	Y	Y	Y	Y	Y	Y	Y	Y
24 Frost	Y	Y	Y	N	N	N	N	Y
25 Andrews	Y	Y	Y	Y	N	N	N	Y
26 ***Armey***	N	Y	Y	Y	Y	Y	N	N
27 Ortiz	Y	Y	Y	Y	N	N	N	Y
28 Tejeda	Y	Y	Y	Y	N	N	N	Y
29 Green	Y	Y	Y	N	N	N	N	Y
30 Johnson, E.B.	Y	Y	Y	N	N	N	N	Y
UTAH								
1 ***Hansen***	N	Y	Y	Y	Y	Y	N	Y
2 Shepherd	Y	Y	Y	N	N	N	N	Y
3 Orton	N	Y	Y	Y	Y	Y	N	Y
VERMONT								
AL *Sanders*	Y	Y	Y	N	N	N	N	Y
VIRGINIA								
1 ***Bateman***	Y	Y	Y	Y	?	Y	N	Y
2 Pickett	Y	Y	Y	Y	N	Y	N	N
3 Scott	Y	Y	Y	N	N	N	N	N
4 Sisisky	Y	Y	Y	Y	N	N	N	Y
5 Payne	Y	Y	Y	Y	N	N	N	Y
6 ***Goodlatte***	N	Y	Y	Y	Y	Y	N	Y
7 ***Bliley***	Y	Y	Y	Y	Y	Y	N	Y
8 Moran	Y	Y	Y	N	N	?	N	Y
9 Boucher	Y	Y	Y	N	N	N	N	N
10 ***Wolf***	Y	Y	Y	Y	Y	Y	N	Y
11 Byrne	Y	Y	Y	N	N	N	N	Y
WASHINGTON								
1 Cantwell	Y	Y	Y	N	N	N	N	Y
2 Swift	Y	Y	Y	N	N	N	N	N
3 Unsoeld	Y	Y	Y	N	N	N	N	N
4 Inslee	Y	Y	Y	N	N	Y	N	N
5 Foley								
6 Dicks	Y	Y	Y	Y	N	N	N	Y
7 McDermott	Y	Y	Y	N	N	N	N	N
8 ***Dunn***	N	Y	Y	Y	Y	Y	N	Y
9 Kreidler	Y	Y	Y	Y	N	N	N	N
WEST VIRGINIA								
1 Mollohan	Y	Y	Y	N	N	N	N	N
2 Wise	Y	Y	Y	N	N	N	N	N
3 Rahall	Y	Y	Y	N	N	N	N	Y
WISCONSIN								
1 Barca	Y	Y	Y	N	N	Y	N	Y
2 ***Klug***	N	Y	Y	Y	Y	Y	N	Y
3 ***Gunderson***	N	Y	Y	Y	Y	Y	N	Y
4 Kleczka	Y	Y	Y	N	N	N	N	Y
5 Barrett	Y	Y	Y	N	Y	N	N	Y
6 ***Petri***	N	N	N	Y	Y	Y	N	Y
7 Obey	Y	N	N	N	N	N	N	N
8 ***Roth***	N	Y	Y	Y	Y	Y	N	Y
9 ***Sensenbrenner***	N	Y	Y	Y	Y	Y	N	Y
WYOMING								
AL ***Thomas***	N	Y	Y	Y	Y	Y	N	Y
DELEGATES								
de Lugo, V.I.	D	D	D	N	N	N	N	Y
Faleomavaega, Am.S.	D	D	D	?	?	?	?	?
Norton, D.C.	D	D	D	N	N	N	N	Y
Romero-B., P.R.	D	D	D	N	N	N	N	N
Underwood, Guam	D	D	D	N	N	N	N	Y

Southern states - Ala., Ark., Fla., Ga., Ky., La., Miss., N.C., Okla., S.C., Tenn., Texas, Va.
Omitted votes are quorum calls, which CQ does not include in its vote charts.

KEY

Y Voted for (yea).
Paired for.
+ Announced for.
N Voted against (nay).
X Paired against.
— Announced against.
P Voted "present."
C Voted "present" to avoid possible conflict of interest.
? Did not vote or otherwise make a position known.
D Delegates ineligible to vote.

Democrats *Republicans*
Independent

300. HR 4606. Fiscal 1995 Labor, Health and Human Services Appropriations/Corporation for Public Broadcasting. Crane, R-Ill., amendment to rescind an additional $273 million for the Corporation for Public Broadcasting, thereby terminating all federal money for the corporation. Rejected in the Committee of the Whole 42-384: R 41-132; D 1-251 (ND 0-173, SD 1-78); I 0-1, June 28, 1994.

301. HR 4606. Fiscal 1995 Labor, Health and Human Services Appropriations/Vocational Schools. Waters, D-Calif., amendment to eliminate the provision in the bill that delays until July 1, 1995, implementation of an Education Department regulation that prohibits for-profit trade schools from obtaining more than 85 percent of their revenue from financial aid programs. Rejected in the Committee of the Whole 63-365: R 12-163; D 50-202 (ND 41-133, SD 9-69); I 1-0, June 29, 1994.

302. HR 4606. Fiscal 1995 Labor, Health and Human Services Appropriations/Community Health Centers. Separate vote at the request of Smith, D-Iowa, on the amendment offered by Porter, R-Ill., and adopted in the Committee of the Whole to increase spending on community health centers and rural health outreach grants by $100 million and offset the increased spending by a corresponding reduction in the administrative and enforcement accounts of the bill. Rejected 211-217: R 173-3; D 38-213 (ND 7-163, SD 31-50); I 0-1, June 29, 1994. (On separate votes, which may be demanded on an amendment adopted in the Committee of the Whole, the four delegates and the resident commissioner of Puerto Rico cannot vote. See vote 294.)

303. HR 4606. Fiscal 1995 Labor, Health and Human Services Appropriations/Motion to Recommit. Lightfoot, R-Iowa, motion to recommit the bill to the House Appropriations Committee with instructions to report it back with an amendment to increase spending on community health centers in rural areas by $50 million. Motion rejected 206-224: R 177-0; D 29-223 (ND 6-164, SD 23-59); I 0-1, June 29, 1994.

304. HR 4606. Fiscal 1995 Labor, Health and Human Services Appropriations/Passage. Passage of the bill to provide $252.3 billion in new budget authority for the departments of Labor, Health and Human Services, Education and related agencies. The administration requested $254,265,983,000. Passed 339-89: R 92-85; D 246-4 (ND 166-3, SD 80-1); I 1-0, June 29, 1994.

	300	301	302	303	304
ALABAMA					
1 *Callahan*	N	N	Y	Y	Y
2 *Everett*	N	N	Y	Y	Y
3 Browder	N	N	N	N	Y
4 Bevill	N	N	N	N	Y
5 Cramer	N	N	N	N	Y
6 *Bachus*	N	Y	Y	N	Y
7 Hilliard	?	?	N	N	Y
ALASKA					
AL *Young*	N	N	Y	Y	Y
ARIZONA					
1 Coppersmith	N	N	N	N	Y
2 Pastor	N	N	N	N	Y
3 *Stump*	Y	N	Y	Y	N
4 *Kyl*	N	N	Y	Y	N
5 *Kolbe*	N	N	Y	Y	N
6 English	N	N	N	N	Y
ARKANSAS					
1 Lambert	N	Y	Y	N	Y
2 Thornton	N	N	N	N	Y
3 *Hutchinson*	N	Y	Y	Y	Y
4 *Dickey*	N	N	Y	Y	Y
CALIFORNIA					
1 Hamburg	N	N	N	N	Y
2 *Herger*	N	N	Y	Y	N
3 Fazio	N	N	N	N	Y
4 *Doolittle*	Y	N	Y	Y	N
5 Matsui	N	Y	N	N	Y
6 Woolsey	N	N	N	N	Y
7 Miller	N	Y	N	N	Y
8 Pelosi	N	Y	N	N	Y
9 Dellums	N	N	N	N	Y
10 *Baker*	N	Y	Y	Y	Y
11 *Pombo*	?	?	?	Y	N
12 Lantos	N	N	N	N	Y
13 Stark	N	Y	N	N	Y
14 Eshoo	N	Y	N	N	Y
15 Mineta	N	N	N	N	Y
16 Edwards	N	N	N	N	Y
17 Farr	N	Y	N	N	+
18 Condit	N	N	N	N	Y
19 Lehman	N	N	N	N	Y
20 Dooley	N	Y	Y	N	Y
21 *Thomas*	N	N	Y	Y	Y
22 *Huffington*	N	N	Y	Y	N
23 *Gallegly*	N	N	Y	Y	Y
24 Beilenson	N	Y	N	N	Y
25 *McKeon*	N	N	Y	Y	Y
26 Berman	N	N	N	N	Y
27 *Moorhead*	N	N	Y	Y	N
28 *Dreier*	Y	N	Y	Y	N
29 Waxman	N	N	N	N	Y
30 Becerra	N	N	N	N	Y
31 Martinez	N	N	N	N	Y
32 Dixon	N	N	N	N	Y
33 Roybal-Allard	N	N	N	N	Y
34 Torres	N	N	N	N	Y
35 Waters	N	Y	N	N	Y
36 Harman	N	Y	N	N	Y
37 Tucker	N	Y	N	N	Y
38 *Horn*	N	Y	Y	Y	Y
39 *Royce*	Y	Y	Y	Y	N
40 Lewis	N	N	Y	Y	Y
41 *Kim*	Y	N	Y	Y	N

	300	301	302	303	304
42 Brown	N	N	N	N	Y
43 *Calvert*	N	N	Y	N	Y
44 *McCandless*	Y	N	Y	Y	N
45 *Rohrabacher*	Y	N	Y	Y	N
46 *Dornan*	Y	N	Y	Y	N
47 *Cox*	Y	N	Y	Y	N
48 *Packard*	N	N	Y	Y	N
49 Schenk	N	Y	N	N	Y
50 Filner	N	N	N	N	Y
51 *Cunningham*	N	N	Y	Y	N
52 *Hunter*	Y	N	Y	Y	N
COLORADO					
1 Schroeder	N	N	N	N	Y
2 Skaggs	N	N	N	N	Y
3 *McInnis*	N	N	Y	N	Y
4 *Allard*	N	Y	Y	Y	N
5 *Hefley*	N	N	Y	N	Y
6 *Schaefer*	N	N	Y	Y	N
CONNECTICUT					
1 Kennelly	N	N	N	N	Y
2 Gejdenson	N	N	N	N	Y
3 DeLauro	N	N	N	N	Y
4 *Shays*	N	N	Y	Y	Y
5 *Franks*	N	N	Y	Y	Y
6 *Johnson*	N	N	Y	Y	Y
DELAWARE					
AL *Castle*	N	N	Y	Y	Y
FLORIDA					
1 Hutto	N	N	Y	Y	Y
2 Peterson	N	N	N	N	Y
3 Brown	N	N	N	N	Y
4 *Fowler*	N	Y	Y	Y	Y
5 Thurman	N	N	N	N	Y
6 *Stearns*	N	N	Y	Y	Y
7 *Mica*	N	N	Y	N	Y
8 *McCollum*	N	Y	Y	N	Y
9 *Bilirakis*	N	N	Y	Y	Y
10 *Young*	N	N	Y	Y	Y
11 Gibbons	N	N	N	N	Y
12 *Canady*	Y	N	Y	Y	Y
13 *Miller*	N	N	Y	Y	N
14 *Goss*	N	N	Y	Y	N
15 Bacchus	N	Y	N	N	Y
16 *Lewis*	N	Y	Y	N	Y
17 Meek	N	N	N	N	Y
18 *Ros-Lehtinen*	N	N	Y	Y	Y
19 Johnston	N	Y	N	N	Y
20 Deutsch	N	N	N	N	Y
21 *Diaz-Balart*	N	N	N	N	Y
22 *Shaw*	N	N	Y	Y	Y
23 Hastings	N	N	N	N	Y
GEORGIA					
1 *Kingston*	Y	N	Y	Y	N
2 Bishop	N	N	Y	N	Y
3 *Collins*	Y	N	Y	N	Y
4 *Linder*	Y	N	Y	Y	N
5 Lewis	N	N	N	N	Y
6 *Gingrich*	N	N	Y	Y	N
7 Darden	N	N	N	N	Y
8 Rowland	N	N	Y	Y	Y
9 Deal	N	N	N	N	Y
10 Johnson	N	N	Y	Y	Y
11 McKinney	N	Y	N	N	Y
HAWAII					
1 Abercrombie	N	N	N	N	Y
2 Mink	N	N	N	N	Y
IDAHO					
1 LaRocco	N	N	N	N	Y
2 *Crapo*	N	N	Y	Y	N
ILLINOIS					
1 Rush	N	N	N	N	Y
2 Reynolds	N	N	?	?	?
3 Lipinski	N	Y	N	N	Y
4 Gutierrez	N	N	N	N	Y
5 Rostenkowski	N	N	N	N	Y
6 *Hyde*	Y	N	Y	Y	Y
7 Collins	N	N	N	N	Y
8 *Crane*	Y	N	Y	Y	N
9 Yates	N	N	N	N	Y
10 *Porter*	N	N	Y	Y	Y
11 Sangmeister	N	Y	N	N	Y
12 Costello	N	Y	N	N	Y
13 *Fawell*	N	N	Y	Y	Y
14 *Hastert*	Y	N	Y	Y	Y
15 *Ewing*	N	N	Y	Y	Y
16 *Manzullo*	Y	N	Y	Y	N
17 Evans	N	Y	N	N	Y

ND Northern Democrats SD Southern Democrats

	300	301	302	303	304
18 *Michel*	?	N	Y	Y	Y
19 Poshard	N	Y	N	N	Y
20 Durbin	N	Y	N	N	Y
INDIANA					
1 Visclosky	N	N	N	N	Y
2 Sharp	N	N	N	N	Y
3 Roemer	N	N	N	N	Y
4 Long	N	Y	N	N	Y
5 *Buyer*	N	N	Y	Y	N
6 *Burton*	Y	N	Y	Y	N
7 *Myers*	N	N	Y	Y	Y
8 McCloskey	N	N	N	N	Y
9 Hamilton	N	N	Y	Y	Y
10 Jacobs	N	Y	N	N	Y
IOWA					
1 *Leach*	N	N	Y	Y	Y
2 *Nussle*	N	N	Y	Y	N
3 *Lightfoot*	N	N	Y	Y	N
4 Smith	N	N	N	N	Y
5 *Grandy*	N	N	Y	Y	Y
KANSAS					
1 *Roberts*	N	N	Y	Y	N
2 Slattery	N	N	N	N	Y
3 *Meyers*	N	N	Y	Y	Y
4 Glickman	N	N	N	N	Y
KENTUCKY					
1 Barlow	N	N	N	N	Y
2 *Lewis*	N	N	Y	Y	N
3 Mazzoli	N	N	N	N	Y
4 *Bunning*	Y	N	Y	Y	N
5 *Rogers*	N	Y	Y	Y	Y
6 Baesler	N	N	N	N	Y
LOUISIANA					
1 *Livingston*	N	N	Y	Y	Y
2 Jefferson	N	N	N	N	Y
3 Tauzin	N	N	Y	Y	Y
4 Fields	N	Y	N	N	Y
5 *McCrery*	N	N	Y	Y	Y
6 *Baker*	N	N	Y	Y	N
7 Hayes	N	Y	Y	Y	Y
MAINE					
1 Andrews	N	Y	Y	Y	Y
2 *Snowe*	N	N	Y	Y	Y
MARYLAND					
1 *Gilchrest*	N	N	Y	Y	Y
2 *Bentley*	N	N	Y	Y	N
3 Cardin	N	N	N	N	Y
4 Wynn	N	N	N	N	Y
5 Hoyer	N	Y	N	N	Y
6 *Bartlett*	Y	N	Y	Y	N
7 Mfume	N	N	N	N	Y
8 *Morella*	N	N	Y	Y	Y
MASSACHUSETTS					
1 Olver	N	Y	N	N	Y
2 Neal	N	N	N	N	Y
3 *Blute*	N	Y	Y	Y	N
4 Frank	N	Y	N	N	Y
5 Meehan	N	N	N	N	Y
6 *Torkildsen*	N	N	Y	Y	Y
7 Markey	N	N	N	N	Y
8 Kennedy	N	Y	N	N	Y
9 Moakley	N	N	N	N	Y
10 Studds	N	N	N	N	Y
MICHIGAN					
1 Stupak	N	N	N	N	Y
2 *Hoekstra*	N	N	Y	Y	Y
3 *Ehlers*	N	N	Y	Y	N
4 *Camp*	N	N	Y	Y	N
5 Barcia	N	N	N	N	Y
6 *Upton*	N	N	Y	Y	Y
7 *Smith*	N	?	Y	Y	N
8 Carr	N	N	N	N	Y
9 Kildee	N	N	N	N	Y
10 Bonior	N	N	N	N	Y
11 *Knollenberg*	N	N	Y	Y	N
12 Levin	N	N	N	N	Y
13 Ford	N	N	N	N	Y
14 Conyers	N	N	N	N	Y
15 Collins	N	N	N	N	Y
16 Dingell	N	N	N	N	Y
MINNESOTA					
1 Penny	N	Y	Y	N	Y
2 Minge	N	Y	N	N	N
3 *Ramstad*	N	N	Y	Y	N
4 Vento	N	Y	N	N	Y

	300	301	302	303	304
5 Sabo	N	Y	N	N	Y
6 *Grams*	Y	N	Y	Y	N
7 Peterson	N	Y	Y	Y	N
8 Oberstar	N	N	N	N	Y
MISSISSIPPI					
1 Whitten	?	N	N	N	Y
2 Thompson	N	N	N	N	Y
3 Montgomery	N	N	Y	N	Y
4 Parker	N	N	Y	N	Y
5 Taylor	N	N	Y	Y	N
MISSOURI					
1 Clay	N	N	N	N	Y
2 *Talent*	N	N	Y	Y	N
3 Gephardt	N	N	N	N	Y
4 Skelton	N	N	N	N	Y
5 Wheat	?	N	N	N	Y
6 Danner	N	N	N	N	Y
7 *Hancock*	Y	N	Y	Y	N
8 *Emerson*	Y	N	Y	Y	Y
9 Volkmer	N	N	N	N	Y
MONTANA					
AL Williams	N	N	N	N	Y
NEBRASKA					
1 *Bereuter*	N	N	Y	Y	Y
2 Hoagland	N	N	N	N	Y
3 *Barrett*	N	N	Y	Y	Y
NEVADA					
1 Bilbray	N	N	N	N	Y
2 *Vucanovich*	N	N	Y	Y	Y
NEW HAMPSHIRE					
1 *Zeliff*	N	N	Y	Y	N
2 Swett	N	N	Y	Y	Y
NEW JERSEY					
1 Andrews	N	N	N	N	Y
2 Hughes	N	N	N	N	Y
3 *Saxton*	N	N	Y	Y	Y
4 *Smith*	N	N	Y	Y	Y
5 *Roukema*	N	Y	Y	Y	Y
6 Pallone	N	Y	N	N	Y
7 *Franks*	N	Y	Y	Y	N
8 Klein	N	N	N	N	Y
9 Torricelli	N	Y	N	N	Y
10 Payne	N	N	N	N	Y
11 *Gallo*	N	Y	Y	Y	Y
12 *Zimmer*	Y	Y	Y	Y	N
13 Menendez	N	N	N	N	Y
NEW MEXICO					
1 *Schiff*	N	N	Y	Y	Y
2 *Skeen*	N	N	Y	Y	Y
3 Richardson	N	N	N	N	Y
NEW YORK					
1 Hochbrueckner	N	N	N	N	Y
2 *Lazio*	N	N	Y	Y	Y
3 *King*	N	N	Y	Y	N
4 *Levy*	N	N	Y	Y	Y
5 Ackerman	N	N	N	N	Y
6 Flake	N	N	N	N	Y
7 Manton	N	N	N	N	Y
8 Nadler	N	N	N	N	Y
9 Schumer	?	?	?	?	?
10 Towns	N	N	N	N	Y
11 Owens	?	N	N	N	Y
12 Velazquez	N	N	N	N	Y
13 *Molinari*	N	N	Y	Y	Y
14 Maloney	N	N	N	N	Y
15 Rangel	N	N	N	N	Y
16 Serrano	N	?	N	N	Y
17 Engel	N	N	N	N	Y
18 Lowey	N	N	N	N	Y
19 *Fish*	?	N	Y	Y	Y
20 Gilman	N	Y	N	Y	Y
21 McNulty	N	N	N	N	Y
22 *Solomon*	Y	N	Y	N	N
23 *Boehlert*	N	N	Y	Y	Y
24 *McHugh*	N	N	Y	Y	N
25 *Walsh*	N	N	Y	Y	Y
26 Hinchey	N	Y	N	N	Y
27 *Paxon*	Y	N	Y	Y	N
28 Slaughter	N	N	N	N	Y
29 LaFalce	N	N	N	N	Y
30 Quinn	N	N	Y	Y	Y
31 *Houghton*	N	N	Y	Y	Y
NORTH CAROLINA					
1 Clayton	N	N	N	N	Y
2 Valentine	N	?	?	Y	Y

	300	301	302	303	304
3 Lancaster	N	?	Y	Y	Y
4 Price	N	N	N	N	Y
5 Neal	N	N	N	N	Y
6 *Coble*	N	N	Y	Y	Y
7 Rose	N	N	N	N	Y
8 Hefner	N	N	N	N	Y
9 *McMillan*	N	N	Y	Y	Y
10 *Ballenger*	N	N	Y	Y	N
11 *Taylor*	N	N	Y	Y	Y
12 Watt	N	N	N	N	Y
NORTH DAKOTA					
AL Pomeroy	N	N	Y	Y	Y
OHIO					
1 Mann	N	N	N	N	Y
2 *Portman*	N	N	Y	Y	N
3 Hall	N	N	N	N	Y
4 *Oxley*	N	N	Y	Y	N
5 *Gillmor*	N	N	Y	Y	Y
6 Strickland	N	N	N	N	Y
7 *Hobson*	N	N	Y	Y	N
8 *Boehner*	Y	N	Y	Y	N
9 Kaptur	N	N	N	N	Y
10 *Hoke*	N	N	Y	Y	N
11 Stokes	N	N	N	N	Y
12 *Kasich*	N	N	Y	Y	Y
13 Brown	N	N	N	N	Y
14 Sawyer	N	N	N	N	Y
15 *Pryce*	N	N	Y	Y	Y
16 *Regula*	N	N	Y	Y	Y
17 Traficant	N	N	N	N	Y
18 Applegate	N	N	N	N	Y
19 Fingerhut	N	N	N	N	Y
OKLAHOMA					
1 *Inhofe*	N	N	Y	Y	N
2 Synar	N	Y	N	N	Y
3 Brewster	N	N	Y	Y	Y
4 McCurdy	N	N	Y	Y	Y
5 *Istook*	Y	N	Y	Y	N
6 Lucas	N	N	Y	Y	N
OREGON					
1 Furse	N	Y	N	N	Y
2 *Smith*	N	N	Y	Y	N
3 Wyden	N	N	N	N	Y
4 DeFazio	N	N	N	N	Y
5 Kopetski	N	N	N	N	Y
PENNSYLVANIA					
1 Foglietta	N	Y	N	N	Y
2 Blackwell	N	N	N	N	Y
3 Borski	N	N	N	N	Y
4 Klink	N	N	N	N	Y
5 *Clinger*	N	N	Y	Y	Y
6 Holden	N	N	N	N	Y
7 *Weldon*	N	N	Y	Y	Y
8 *Greenwood*	N	N	Y	Y	Y
9 *Shuster*	Y	N	Y	Y	N
10 *McDade*	N	N	Y	Y	Y
11 Kanjorski	N	Y	N	N	Y
12 Murtha	N	N	N	N	Y
13 Margolies-Mezv.	N	Y	N	N	Y
14 Coyne	N	N	N	N	Y
15 McHale	N	N	N	N	Y
16 *Walker*	Y	N	Y	Y	N
17 *Gekas*	N	N	Y	Y	N
18 *Santorum*	Y	N	Y	Y	Y
19 *Goodling*	N	N	Y	Y	Y
20 Murphy	N	N	N	N	Y
21 *Ridge*	?	N	Y	Y	Y
RHODE ISLAND					
1 *Machtley*	N	?	?	?	?
2 Reed	N	N	N	N	Y
SOUTH CAROLINA					
1 *Ravenel*	N	N	Y	Y	Y
2 *Spence*	N	N	Y	Y	N
3 Derrick	N	N	N	N	Y
4 *Inglis*	N	N	Y	Y	N
5 Spratt	N	N	N	N	Y
6 Clyburn	N	N	N	N	+
SOUTH DAKOTA					
AL Johnson	N	Y	N	N	Y
TENNESSEE					
1 *Quillen*	N	N	N	N	Y
2 *Duncan*	N	N	Y	Y	N
3 Lloyd	N	N	Y	Y	Y
4 Cooper	N	N	Y	Y	Y
5 Clement	N	N	N	N	Y

	300	301	302	303	304
6 Gordon	N	Y	N	N	Y
7 *Sundquist*	N	N	Y	Y	Y
8 Tanner	N	N	Y	Y	Y
9 Ford	N	Y	N	N	Y
TEXAS					
1 Chapman	?	?	?	?	?
2 Wilson	N	N	N	N	Y
3 *Johnson, Sam*	Y	N	Y	Y	N
4 Hall	N	N	Y	Y	Y
5 Bryant	N	N	N	N	Y
6 *Barton*	Y	Y	Y	Y	N
7 *Archer*	Y	N	Y	Y	N
8 *Fields*	?	N	Y	Y	N
9 Brooks	N	N	N	N	Y
10 Pickle	N	N	Y	Y	Y
11 Edwards	N	N	Y	Y	Y
12 Geren	N	N	Y	Y	N
13 Sarpalius	N	?	Y	Y	Y
14 Laughlin	Y	N	Y	Y	N
15 de la Garza	N	N	Y	Y	Y
16 Coleman	N	N	N	N	Y
17 Stenholm	N	N	Y	Y	Y
18 Washington	?	N	N	N	Y
19 *Combest*	Y	N	Y	Y	N
20 Gonzalez	N	Y	N	N	Y
21 *Smith*	Y	N	Y	Y	Y
22 *DeLay*	Y	N	Y	Y	N
23 *Bonilla*	N	N	Y	Y	N
24 Frost	N	N	N	N	Y
25 Andrews	N	N	N	N	Y
26 *Armey*	Y	N	Y	Y	N
27 Ortiz	N	N	Y	Y	Y
28 Tejeda	N	N	Y	Y	Y
29 Green	N	N	N	N	Y
30 Johnson, E.B.	N	N	N	N	Y
UTAH					
1 *Hansen*	N	N	Y	Y	N
2 Shepherd	N	N	N	N	Y
3 Orton	N	N	N	N	N
VERMONT					
AL *Sanders*	N	Y	N	N	Y
VIRGINIA					
1 *Bateman*	N	N	Y	Y	Y
2 Pickett	N	N	Y	Y	Y
3 Scott	N	N	N	N	Y
4 Sisisky	N	N	Y	Y	Y
5 Payne	N	N	Y	Y	Y
6 *Goodlatte*	N	N	Y	Y	N
7 *Bliley*	N	N	Y	Y	Y
8 Moran	N	N	N	N	Y
9 Boucher	N	N	N	N	Y
10 *Wolf*	N	N	Y	Y	Y
11 Byrne	N	N	N	N	Y
WASHINGTON					
1 Cantwell	N	?	N	N	Y
2 Swift	N	N	N	N	Y
3 Unsoeld	N	N	N	N	Y
4 Inslee	N	N	N	N	Y
5 Foley					
6 Dicks	N	N	N	N	Y
7 McDermott	N	N	N	N	Y
8 *Dunn*	N	N	Y	Y	N
9 Kreidler	N	N	N	N	Y
WEST VIRGINIA					
1 Mollohan	N	N	N	N	Y
2 Wise	N	N	N	N	Y
3 Rahall	N	N	N	N	Y
WISCONSIN					
1 Barca	N	N	N	N	Y
2 *Klug*	N	N	Y	Y	Y
3 *Gunderson*	N	N	Y	Y	Y
4 Kleczka	N	N	N	N	Y
5 Barrett	N	N	N	N	Y
6 *Petri*	N	N	Y	Y	N
7 Obey	N	Y	N	N	Y
8 *Roth*	Y	N	Y	Y	N
9 *Sensenbrenner*	Y	N	Y	Y	N
WYOMING					
AL *Thomas*	N	N	Y	Y	N
DELEGATES					
de Lugo, V.I.	N	N	D	D	D
Faleomavaega, Am.S.	?	N	D	D	D
Norton, D.C.	N	Y	D	D	D
Romero-B., P.R.	N	N	D	D	D
Underwood, Guam	N	N	D	D	D

Southern states - Ala., Ark., Fla., Ga., Ky., La., Miss., N.C., Okla., S.C., Tenn., Texas, Va.
Omitted votes are quorum calls, which CQ does not include in its vote charts.

KEY

Y   Voted for (yea).
Paired for.
+   Announced for.
N   Voted against (nay).
X   Paired against.
—   Announced against.
P   Voted "present."
C   Voted "present" to avoid possible conflict of interest.
?   Did not vote or otherwise make a position known.
D   Delegates ineligible to vote.

Democrats   *Republicans*
Independent

305. HR 4649. Fiscal 1995 District of Columbia Appropriations/Previous Question. Gordon, D-Tenn., motion to order the previous question (thus ending debate and the possibility of amendment) on adoption of the rule (H Res 466) to provide for House floor consideration of the bill to provide $720 million in federal funds for the District of Columbia in fiscal 1995 and approve the spending of $3,684,736,635 raised from local taxes. Motion agreed to 251-177: R 0-177; D 250-0 (ND 169-0, SD 81-0); I 1-0, June 29, 1994.

306. HR 4649. Fiscal 1995 District of Columbia Appropriations/Rule. Adoption of the rule (H Res 466) to provide for House floor consideration of the bill to provide $720 million in federal funds for the District of Columbia in fiscal 1995 and approve the spending of $3,684,736,635 raised from local taxes. Adopted 236-188: R 0-176; D 235-12 (ND 162-4, SD 73-8); I 1-0, June 29, 1994.

307. HR 4624. Fiscal 1995 VA, HUD Appropriations/Assisted Housing. Smith, R-Mich., amendment to cut the accounts for new construction and reconstruction of public housing by $448 million and increase the amount provided for rental assistance under the Section 8 existing housing certificate program and the housing voucher program by $179 million. Rejected in the Committee of the Whole 162-269: R 148-29; D 14-239 (ND 5-167, SD 9-72); I 0-1, June 29, 1994.

308. HR 4624. Fiscal 1995 VA, HUD Appropriations/CIESIN. Hefley, R-Colo., amendment to cut $12 million from the Science, Aeronautics and Technology account of NASA, intended to reduce to $6 million the money recommended in the report for the Consortium for International Earth Science Information Network (CIESIN) in Michigan. Rejected in the Committee of the Whole 169-264: R 148-28; D 21-235 (ND 18-156, SD 3-79); I 0-1, June 29, 1994.

309. HR 4624. Fiscal 1995 VA, HUD Appropriations/Space Station. Roemer, D-Ind., amendment to terminate the space station and reallocate the $2.1 billion to other NASA programs. Rejected in the Committee of the Whole 155-278: R 40-136; D 114-142 (ND 101-72, SD 13-70); I 1-0, June 29, 1994. A "nay" was a vote in support of the president's position.

	305	306	307	308	309
ALABAMA					
1 *Callahan*	N	N	Y	N	N
2 *Everett*	N	N	Y	Y	N
3 Browder	Y	Y	N	N	N
4 Bevill	Y	Y	N	N	N
5 Cramer	Y	Y	N	N	N
6 *Bachus*	N	N	Y	Y	N
7 Hilliard	Y	Y	N	N	N
ALASKA					
AL *Young*	N	N	Y	N	N
ARIZONA					
1 Coppersmith	Y	Y	N	Y	Y
2 Pastor	Y	Y	N	N	N
3 *Stump*	N	N	Y	N	N
4 *Kyl*	N	N	Y	Y	N
5 *Kolbe*	N	N	Y	Y	Y
6 English	Y	Y	N	Y	Y
ARKANSAS					
1 Lambert	Y	Y	N	N	Y
2 Thornton	Y	Y	N	N	N
3 *Hutchinson*	N	N	Y	Y	Y
4 Dickey	N	N	Y	Y	N
CALIFORNIA					
1 Hamburg	Y	Y	N	N	Y
2 *Herger*	N	N	Y	Y	Y
3 Fazio	Y	Y	N	N	N
4 *Doolittle*	N	N	Y	Y	N
5 Matsui	Y	Y	N	N	N
6 Woolsey	Y	Y	N	Y	Y
7 Miller	Y	Y	N	Y	N
8 Pelosi	Y	Y	N	N	Y
9 Dellums	Y	Y	N	Y	Y
10 *Baker*	N	N	Y	Y	N
11 *Pombo*	N	N	Y	Y	N
12 Lantos	Y	Y	N	N	N
13 Stark	Y	Y	N	Y	N
14 Eshoo	Y	Y	N	N	N
15 Mineta	Y	Y	N	N	N
16 Edwards	Y	Y	N	N	N
17 Farr	Y	Y	N	N	N
18 Condit	Y	Y	Y	N	Y
19 Lehman	Y	Y	N	N	Y
20 Dooley	Y	Y	N	N	N
21 *Thomas*	N	N	Y	Y	N
22 *Huffington*	N	N	Y	Y	N
23 *Gallegly*	N	N	Y	Y	N
24 Beilenson	Y	Y	N	N	N
25 *McKeon*	N	N	Y	Y	N
26 Berman	Y	Y	N	N	N
27 *Moorhead*	N	N	Y	Y	N
28 *Dreier*	N	N	Y	Y	N
29 Waxman	Y	Y	N	N	N
30 Becerra	Y	Y	N	Y	N
31 Martinez	Y	Y	N	N	N
32 Dixon	Y	Y	N	N	N
33 Roybal-Allard	Y	Y	N	N	N
34 Torres	Y	Y	N	N	N
35 Waters	Y	Y	N	N	N
36 Harman	Y	Y	N	N	N
37 Tucker	Y	Y	N	N	N
38 *Horn*	N	N	Y	Y	N
39 *Royce*	N	N	Y	Y	N
40 *Lewis*	N	N	N	N	N
41 *Kim*	N	N	Y	Y	N

	305	306	307	308	309
42 Brown	Y	Y	N	N	N
43 *Calvert*	N	N	Y	Y	N
44 *McCandless*	N	N	Y	Y	N
45 *Rohrabacher*	N	N	Y	Y	N
46 *Dornan*	N	N	Y	Y	N
47 *Cox*	N	N	Y	Y	N
48 *Packard*	N	N	Y	Y	N
49 Schenk	Y	Y	N	Y	Y
50 Filner	Y	Y	N	N	N
51 *Cunningham*	N	N	Y	Y	N
52 *Hunter*	N	N	Y	Y	N
COLORADO					
1 Schroeder	Y	Y	N	Y	Y
2 Skaggs	Y	Y	N	N	Y
3 *McInnis*	N	N	Y	Y	N
4 *Allard*	N	N	Y	Y	N
5 *Hefley*	N	N	Y	Y	N
6 *Schaefer*	N	N	Y	Y	Y
CONNECTICUT					
1 Kennelly	Y	Y	N	N	N
2 Gejdenson	Y	Y	N	N	N
3 DeLauro	Y	Y	N	N	N
4 *Shays*	N	N	Y	Y	Y
5 *Franks*	N	N	Y	Y	N
6 *Johnson*	N	N	Y	N	N
DELAWARE					
AL *Castle*	N	N	Y	N	N
FLORIDA					
1 Hutto	Y	N	N	N	N
2 Peterson	Y	Y	N	N	N
3 Brown	Y	Y	N	N	N
4 *Fowler*	N	N	Y	Y	N
5 Thurman	Y	Y	N	N	N
6 *Stearns*	N	N	Y	Y	N
7 *Mica*	N	N	Y	Y	N
8 *McCollum*	N	N	Y	Y	N
9 *Bilirakis*	N	N	Y	Y	N
10 *Young*	N	N	N	Y	N
11 Gibbons	Y	Y	N	N	N
12 *Canady*	N	N	Y	Y	N
13 *Miller*	N	N	Y	Y	N
14 *Goss*	N	N	Y	Y	N
15 Bacchus	Y	Y	N	N	N
16 *Lewis*	N	N	Y	Y	N
17 Meek	Y	Y	N	N	N
18 *Ros-Lehtinen*	N	N	N	Y	N
19 Johnston	Y	Y	N	N	N
20 Deutsch	Y	Y	N	N	N
21 *Diaz-Balart*	N	N	N	N	N
22 *Shaw*	N	N	Y	N	N
23 Hastings	Y	Y	N	N	N
GEORGIA					
1 *Kingston*	N	N	Y	Y	N
2 Bishop	Y	Y	N	N	N
3 *Collins*	N	N	Y	Y	Y
4 *Linder*	N	N	Y	Y	N
5 Lewis	Y	Y	N	N	N
6 *Gingrich*	N	N	Y	Y	N
7 Darden	Y	Y	N	N	N
8 Rowland	Y	N	N	N	N
9 Deal	Y	N	N	N	N
10 Johnson	Y	Y	N	N	Y
11 McKinney	Y	Y	N	N	Y
HAWAII					
1 Abercrombie	Y	Y	N	N	N
2 Mink	Y	Y	N	N	Y
IDAHO					
1 LaRocco	Y	Y	N	N	N
2 *Crapo*	N	N	Y	Y	N
ILLINOIS					
1 Rush	Y	Y	N	N	Y
2 Reynolds	?	?	?	?	N
3 Lipinski	Y	Y	N	N	N
4 Gutierrez	Y	Y	N	N	Y
5 Rostenkowski	Y	Y	N	N	N
6 *Hyde*	N	N	Y	N	N
7 Collins	Y	Y	N	N	Y
8 *Crane*	N	N	Y	N	N
9 Yates	Y	Y	N	N	Y
10 *Porter*	N	N	Y	Y	Y
11 Sangmeister	Y	Y	N	N	Y
12 Costello	Y	Y	N	N	N
13 *Fawell*	N	N	Y	Y	Y
14 *Hastert*	N	N	Y	Y	Y
15 *Ewing*	N	N	Y	N	N
16 *Manzullo*	N	N	Y	Y	Y
17 Evans	Y	Y	N	N	Y

ND   Northern Democrats   SD   Southern Democrats

	305	306	307	308	309
18 ***Michel***	N	N	Y	Y	N
19 Poshard	Y	Y	N	Y	Y
20 Durbin	Y	Y	N	N	Y
INDIANA					
1 Visclosky	Y	Y	N	N	Y
2 Sharp	Y	Y	N	N	N
3 Roemer	Y	Y	N	N	Y
4 Long	Y	Y	N	N	Y
5 ***Buyer***	N	N	Y	Y	N
6 ***Burton***	N	N	Y	Y	N
7 ***Myers***	N	N	Y	N	N
8 McCloskey	Y	Y	N	N	N
9 Hamilton	Y	Y	N	Y	Y
10 Jacobs	Y	Y	N	N	Y
IOWA					
1 ***Leach***	N	N	Y	N	Y
2 ***Nussle***	N	N	Y	Y	Y
3 ***Lightfoot***	N	N	Y	Y	N
4 Smith	Y	Y	N	N	N
5 ***Grandy***	N	N	Y	Y	?
KANSAS					
1 ***Roberts***	N	N	Y	Y	N
2 Slattery	Y	Y	N	Y	N
3 ***Meyers***	N	N	Y	Y	N
4 Glickman	Y	N	N	Y	N
KENTUCKY					
1 Barlow	Y	Y	N	N	Y
2 ***Lewis***	N	N	Y	Y	N
3 Mazzoli	Y	Y	N	N	N
4 ***Bunning***	N	N	Y	Y	Y
5 ***Rogers***	N	N	N	Y	N
6 Baesler	Y	Y	N	N	Y
LOUISIANA					
1 ***Livingston***	N	N	Y	N	N
2 Jefferson	Y	Y	N	N	N
3 Tauzin	Y	N	Y	N	Y
4 Fields	Y	Y	N	N	N
5 ***McCrery***	N	N	N	N	N
6 ***Baker***	N	N	N	N	N
7 Hayes	Y	N	N	N	N
MAINE					
1 Andrews	Y	Y	N	N	Y
2 ***Snowe***	N	N	Y	Y	Y
MARYLAND					
1 ***Gilchrest***	N	N	Y	N	N
2 ***Bentley***	N	N	Y	Y	N
3 Cardin	Y	Y	N	N	N
4 Wynn	Y	Y	N	N	N
5 Hoyer	Y	Y	N	N	N
6 ***Bartlett***	N	N	Y	?	N
7 Mfume	Y	Y	N	N	Y
8 ***Morella***	N	N	N	N	N
MASSACHUSETTS					
1 Olver	Y	Y	N	N	Y
2 Neal	Y	Y	N	N	N
3 ***Blute***	N	N	N	Y	Y
4 Frank	Y	Y	N	N	Y
5 Meehan	Y	Y	N	N	Y
6 ***Torkildsen***	N	N	N	Y	N
7 Markey	Y	Y	N	N	Y
8 Kennedy	Y	Y	N	N	Y
9 Moakley	Y	Y	N	N	Y
10 Studds	Y	Y	N	N	Y
MICHIGAN					
1 Stupak	Y	Y	N	N	Y
2 ***Hoekstra***	N	N	Y	N	Y
3 ***Ehlers***	N	N	Y	N	N
4 ***Camp***	N	N	Y	N	Y
5 Barcia	Y	Y	N	N	N
6 ***Upton***	N	N	Y	N	Y
7 ***Smith***	N	N	Y	Y	Y
8 Carr	Y	Y	N	N	N
9 Kildee	Y	Y	N	N	Y
10 Bonior	Y	Y	N	N	N
11 ***Knollenberg***	N	N	Y	N	Y
12 Levin	Y	Y	N	N	Y
13 Ford	Y	Y	N	N	?
14 Conyers	Y	Y	N	N	N
15 Collins	Y	Y	N	N	Y
16 Dingell	Y	Y	?	N	N
MINNESOTA					
1 Penny	Y	Y	Y	Y	Y
2 Minge	Y	Y	Y	Y	Y
3 ***Ramstad***	N	N	Y	Y	Y
4 Vento	Y	Y	N	N	Y

	305	306	307	308	309
5 Sabo	Y	Y	N	N	Y
6 ***Grams***	N	N	Y	Y	N
7 Peterson	Y	N	N	N	Y
8 Oberstar	Y	Y	N	N	Y
MISSISSIPPI					
1 Whitten	Y	Y	N	N	N
2 Thompson	Y	Y	N	N	N
3 Montgomery	Y	Y	Y	N	N
4 Parker	Y	Y	Y	N	N
5 Taylor	Y	Y	Y	N	N
MISSOURI					
1 Clay	Y	Y	N	N	N
2 ***Talent***	N	N	Y	Y	N
3 Gephardt	Y	Y	N	N	N
4 Skelton	Y	Y	N	Y	N
5 Wheat	Y	Y	N	N	Y
6 Danner	Y	Y	N	N	Y
7 ***Hancock***	N	N	Y	Y	N
8 ***Emerson***	N	N	Y	Y	N
9 Volkmer	Y	?	N	N	N
MONTANA					
AL Williams	Y	Y	N	N	Y
NEBRASKA					
1 ***Bereuter***	N	N	N	Y	Y
2 Hoagland	Y	Y	N	N	Y
3 ***Barrett***	N	N	Y	Y	N
NEVADA					
1 Bilbray	Y	Y	N	N	Y
2 ***Vucanovich***	N	N	Y	Y	N
NEW HAMPSHIRE					
1 ***Zeliff***	N	N	Y	Y	N
2 Swett	Y	Y	N	N	Y
NEW JERSEY					
1 Andrews	Y	Y	?	Y	N
2 Hughes	Y	Y	N	N	Y
3 ***Saxton***	N	N	Y	Y	N
4 ***Smith***	N	N	N	Y	N
5 ***Roukema***	N	N	N	Y	Y
6 Pallone	Y	Y	N	Y	Y
7 ***Franks***	N	N	Y	Y	Y
8 Klein	Y	Y	N	N	Y
9 Torricelli	Y	Y	N	N	N
10 Payne	Y	Y	N	N	Y
11 ***Gallo***	N	N	N	N	N
12 ***Zimmer***	N	N	Y	Y	Y
13 Menendez	Y	Y	N	N	Y
NEW MEXICO					
1 ***Schiff***	N	N	Y	Y	N
2 ***Skeen***	N	N	N	N	N
3 Richardson	Y	Y	N	N	N
NEW YORK					
1 Hochbrueckner	Y	Y	Y	N	N
2 ***Lazio***	N	N	N	Y	Y
3 ***King***	N	N	Y	Y	Y
4 ***Levy***	N	N	Y	Y	N
5 Ackerman	Y	Y	N	N	Y
6 Flake	Y	Y	N	N	N
7 Manton	Y	Y	N	N	N
8 Nadler	Y	Y	N	N	Y
9 Schumer	?	?	?	?	Y
10 Towns	Y	Y	N	N	N
11 Owens	Y	Y	N	N	Y
12 Velazquez	Y	Y	N	N	Y
13 ***Molinari***	N	N	Y	Y	N
14 Maloney	Y	+	N	Y	Y
15 Rangel	Y	Y	N	N	?
16 Serrano	Y	Y	N	N	Y
17 Engel	Y	Y	N	N	N
18 Lowey	Y	Y	N	N	Y
19 ***Fish***	N	N	Y	N	N
20 ***Gilman***	N	N	N	Y	N
21 McNulty	Y	Y	N	N	Y
22 ***Solomon***	N	N	Y	Y	Y
23 ***Boehlert***	N	N	N	N	N
24 ***McHugh***	N	N	Y	Y	Y
25 ***Walsh***	N	N	N	Y	N
26 Hinchey	Y	Y	N	N	N
27 ***Paxon***	N	N	Y	Y	Y
28 Slaughter	Y	Y	N	N	Y
29 LaFalce	Y	Y	N	N	Y
30 ***Quinn***	N	N	Y	Y	N
31 ***Houghton***	N	N	N	Y	N
NORTH CAROLINA					
1 Clayton	Y	Y	N	N	N
2 Valentine	Y	Y	N	N	N

	305	306	307	308	309
3 Lancaster	Y	Y	N	N	Y
4 Price	Y	Y	N	N	N
5 Neal	Y	Y	N	N	Y
6 ***Coble***	N	N	Y	Y	N
7 Rose	Y	Y	N	N	N
8 Hefner	Y	Y	N	N	N
9 ***McMillan***	N	N	Y	Y	N
10 ***Ballenger***	N	N	Y	Y	N
11 ***Taylor***	N	N	Y	Y	N
12 Watt	Y	Y	N	N	N
NORTH DAKOTA					
AL Pomeroy	Y	Y	N	N	Y
OHIO					
1 Mann	Y	Y	N	N	Y
2 ***Portman***	N	N	Y	Y	Y
3 Hall	Y	Y	N	N	N
4 ***Oxley***	N	N	Y	Y	N
5 ***Gillmor***	N	N	Y	N	N
6 Strickland	Y	Y	N	N	Y
7 ***Hobson***	N	N	Y	Y	N
8 ***Boehner***	N	N	Y	Y	N
9 Kaptur	Y	Y	N	N	Y
10 ***Hoke***	N	N	Y	Y	N
11 Stokes	Y	Y	N	N	N
12 ***Kasich***	N	N	Y	Y	Y
13 Brown	Y	Y	N	N	Y
14 Sawyer	Y	Y	N	N	N
15 ***Pryce***	N	N	Y	Y	N
16 ***Regula***	N	N	Y	Y	N
17 Traficant	Y	Y	N	N	N
18 Applegate	Y	Y	N	N	N
19 Fingerhut	Y	Y	N	N	N
OKLAHOMA					
1 ***Inhofe***	N	N	Y	Y	N
2 Synar	Y	Y	N	Y	Y
3 Brewster	Y	Y	N	N	N
4 McCurdy	Y	Y	N	Y	N
5 ***Istook***	N	N	Y	Y	Y
6 ***Lucas***	N	N	N	Y	N
OREGON					
1 Furse	Y	Y	N	N	Y
2 ***Smith***	N	N	Y	Y	N
3 Wyden	Y	Y	N	N	Y
4 DeFazio	Y	Y	N	N	Y
5 Kopetski	Y	Y	N	N	N
PENNSYLVANIA					
1 Foglietta	Y	Y	N	N	Y
2 Blackwell	Y	Y	N	N	Y
3 Borski	Y	Y	N	N	N
4 Klink	Y	Y	N	N	Y
5 ***Clinger***	N	N	Y	Y	N
6 Holden	Y	Y	N	N	Y
7 ***Weldon***	N	N	Y	Y	N
8 ***Greenwood***	N	N	Y	Y	N
9 ***Shuster***	N	N	Y	Y	Y
10 ***McDade***	N	N	N	N	N
11 Kanjorski	Y	Y	N	N	Y
12 Murtha	Y	Y	N	N	N
13 Margolies-Mezv.	Y	Y	N	Y	Y
14 Coyne	Y	Y	N	N	Y
15 McHale	Y	Y	N	N	N
16 ***Walker***	N	N	Y	Y	N
17 ***Gekas***	N	N	Y	Y	N
18 ***Santorum***	N	N	Y	Y	N
19 ***Goodling***	N	N	Y	Y	Y
20 Murphy	Y	Y	N	N	N
21 ***Ridge***	N	N	N	Y	N
RHODE ISLAND					
1 ***Machtley***	?	?	?	?	?
2 Reed	Y	Y	N	N	Y
SOUTH CAROLINA					
1 ***Ravenel***	N	N	Y	N	Y
2 ***Spence***	N	N	Y	Y	N
3 Derrick	Y	Y	N	N	Y
4 ***Inglis***	N	N	Y	Y	Y
5 Spratt	Y	Y	N	N	Y
6 Clyburn	Y	Y	N	N	N
SOUTH DAKOTA					
AL Johnson	Y	Y	N	N	Y
TENNESSEE					
1 ***Quillen***	N	N	N	N	N
2 ***Duncan***	N	N	Y	Y	Y
3 Lloyd	Y	Y	N	N	N
4 Cooper	Y	Y	N	N	N
5 Clement	Y	Y	N	N	N

	305	306	307	308	309
6 Gordon	Y	Y	N	N	Y
7 ***Sundquist***	N	N	N	N	N
8 Tanner	Y	Y	N	N	N
9 Ford	Y	Y	N	N	N
TEXAS					
1 Chapman	?	?	?	N	N
2 Wilson	Y	Y	N	N	N
3 ***Johnson, Sam***	N	N	N	Y	N
4 Hall	Y	N	Y	N	N
5 Bryant	Y	Y	N	N	N
6 ***Barton***	N	N	Y	Y	N
7 ***Archer***	N	N	Y	Y	N
8 ***Fields***	N	N	Y	Y	N
9 Brooks	Y	Y	N	N	N
10 Pickle	Y	Y	N	N	N
11 Edwards	Y	Y	N	N	N
12 Geren	Y	N	Y	N	N
13 Sarpalius	Y	Y	N	N	N
14 Laughlin	Y	Y	N	N	N
15 de la Garza	Y	Y	N	N	N
16 Coleman	Y	Y	N	N	N
17 Stenholm	Y	N	Y	N	N
18 Washington	?	?	?	?	N
19 ***Combest***	N	N	Y	Y	N
20 Gonzalez	Y	Y	N	N	N
21 ***Smith***	N	N	Y	Y	N
22 ***DeLay***	N	N	Y	Y	N
23 ***Bonilla***	N	N	Y	Y	N
24 Frost	Y	Y	N	N	N
25 Andrews	Y	Y	N	N	N
26 ***Armey***	N	?	Y	Y	N
27 Ortiz	Y	Y	N	N	N
28 Tejeda	Y	Y	N	N	N
29 Green	Y	Y	N	N	N
30 Johnson, E.B.	Y	Y	N	N	N
UTAH					
1 ***Hansen***	N	N	Y	Y	N
2 Shepherd	Y	Y	N	N	Y
3 Orton	Y	N	Y	Y	Y
VERMONT					
AL *Sanders*	Y	Y	N	N	Y
VIRGINIA					
1 ***Bateman***	N	N	Y	N	N
2 Pickett	Y	Y	N	N	N
3 Scott	Y	Y	N	N	N
4 Sisisky	Y	Y	N	N	N
5 Payne	Y	Y	Y	N	Y
6 ***Goodlatte***	N	N	Y	Y	Y
7 ***Bliley***	N	N	Y	Y	N
8 Moran	Y	Y	Y	N	N
9 Boucher	Y	Y	N	N	N
10 ***Wolf***	N	N	Y	Y	N
11 Byrne	Y	Y	N	N	N
WASHINGTON					
1 Cantwell	Y	Y	N	N	Y
2 Swift	Y	?	N	N	N
3 Unsoeld	Y	Y	N	N	N
4 Inslee	Y	Y	N	N	Y
5 Foley					
6 Dicks	?	?	N	N	N
7 McDermott	Y	Y	N	N	N
8 ***Dunn***	N	N	Y	Y	N
9 Kreidler	Y	Y	N	N	Y
WEST VIRGINIA					
1 Mollohan	Y	Y	N	N	N
2 Wise	Y	Y	N	N	N
3 Rahall	Y	Y	N	N	N
WISCONSIN					
1 Barca	Y	Y	N	N	Y
2 ***Klug***	N	N	Y	Y	N
3 ***Gunderson***	N	N	N	Y	N
4 Kleczka	Y	Y	N	N	Y
5 Barrett	Y	Y	N	Y	Y
6 ***Petri***	N	N	Y	Y	N
7 Obey	Y	Y	N	N	Y
8 ***Roth***	N	N	Y	Y	N
9 ***Sensenbrenner***	N	N	Y	Y	N
WYOMING					
AL ***Thomas***	N	N	Y	Y	Y
DELEGATES					
de Lugo, V.I.	D	D	N	N	Y
Faleomavaega, Am.S.	D	D	?	?	?
Norton, D.C.	D	D	N	N	Y
Romero-B., P.R.	D	D	N	N	?
Underwood, Guam	D	D	N	N	Y

Southern states - Ala., Ark., Fla., Ga., Ky., La., Miss., N.C., Okla., S.C., Tenn., Texas, Va.
Omitted votes are quorum calls, which CQ does not include in its vote charts.

1994 CQ ALMANAC — 91-H

KEY

Y Voted for (yea).
Paired for.
+ Announced for.
N Voted against (nay).
X Paired against.
— Announced against.
P Voted "present."
C Voted "present" to avoid possible conflict of interest.
? Did not vote or otherwise make a position known.
D Delegates ineligible to vote.

Democrats *Republicans*
Independent

310. HR 4624. Fiscal 1995 VA, HUD Appropriations/ Motion To Rise. Stokes, D-Ohio, motion to rise from the Committee of the Whole and report the bill back to the full House, thus eliminating the possibility of further amendments. Motion agreed to 261-163: R 12-161; D 248-2 (ND 167-1, SD 81-1); I 1-0, June 29, 1994. (The effect of the vote was to block an amendment to bar illegal immigrants from receiving money provided by the bill.)

311. HR 4624. Fiscal 1995 VA, HUD Appropriations/ Motion To Recommit. Kolbe, R-Ariz., motion to recommit the bill to the House Appropriations Committee with instructions to report it back with an amendment cutting about $900 million from the FSLIC Resolution Fund managed by the Federal Deposit Insurance Corporation, the FDIC Affordable Housing Program and the Office of the Inspector General of the Resolution Trust Corporation. Motion rejected 166-262: R 166-8; D 0-253 (ND 0-171, SD 0-82); I 0-1, June 29, 1994.

312. HR 4624. Fiscal 1995 VA, HUD Appropriations/ Passage. Passage of the bill to provide approximately $90.5 billion in new budget authority for the departments of Veterans Affairs and Housing and Urban Development, and for sundry independent agencies, boards, commissions, corporations and offices for fiscal 1995. The administration had requested $90.1 billion. Passed 344-84: R 102-73; D 241-11 (ND 159-11, SD 82-0); I 1-0, June 29, 1994.

313. HR 4650. Fiscal 1995 Defense Appropriations/ Passage. Passage of the bill to provide $243.6 billion in new budget authority for the Department of Defense in fiscal 1995. The administration had requested $244.4 billion. Passed 330-91: R 101-72; D 229-18 (ND 150-17, SD 79-1); I 0-1, June 29, 1994.

314. HR 3355. Omnibus Crime Bill/Motion To Instruct. Molinari, R-N.Y., motion to instruct the House conferees to agree to the Senate provisions that allow information about prior sex offenses by a defendant to be admitted as evidence in federal trials alleging sex offenses. Motion agreed to 348-62: R 171-1; D 177-60 (ND 112-49, SD 65-11); I 0-1, June 30, 1994 (in the session that began and the Congressional Record dated June 29).

	310	311	312	313	314
ALABAMA					
1 *Callahan*	N	Y	Y	Y	Y
2 *Everett*	N	Y	Y	Y	Y
3 Browder	Y	N	Y	Y	Y
4 Bevill	Y	N	Y	Y	Y
5 Cramer	Y	N	Y	Y	Y
6 *Bachus*	N	Y	N	N	Y
7 Hilliard	Y	N	Y	Y	Y
ALASKA					
AL *Young*	N	Y	Y	Y	Y
ARIZONA					
1 Coppersmith	Y	N	Y	Y	Y
2 Pastor	Y	N	Y	Y	Y
3 *Stump*	N	Y	N	N	Y
4 *Kyl*	N	Y	N	N	Y
5 *Kolbe*	N	Y	N	Y	Y
6 English	Y	N	Y	Y	Y
ARKANSAS					
1 Lambert	Y	N	Y	Y	Y
2 Thornton	Y	N	Y	Y	Y
3 *Hutchinson*	N	Y	Y	Y	Y
4 Dickey	N	Y	Y	Y	Y
CALIFORNIA					
1 Hamburg	Y	N	Y	N	N
2 *Herger*	N	Y	N	N	Y
3 Fazio	Y	N	Y	Y	Y
4 *Doolittle*	N	Y	N	N	Y
5 Matsui	Y	N	Y	Y	Y
6 Woolsey	Y	N	Y	N	N
7 Miller	Y	N	Y	Y	N
8 Pelosi	Y	N	Y	Y	N
9 Dellums	Y	N	Y	?	?
10 *Baker*	N	Y	Y	N	Y
11 *Pombo*	N	Y	N	N	Y
12 Lantos	Y	N	Y	Y	Y
13 Stark	Y	N	N	N	?
14 Eshoo	Y	N	Y	Y	Y
15 Mineta	Y	N	Y	Y	Y
16 Edwards	Y	N	Y	N	N
17 Farr	Y	N	Y	Y	Y
18 Condit	Y	N	Y	Y	Y
19 Lehman	Y	N	Y	Y	Y
20 Dooley	Y	N	Y	Y	Y
21 *Thomas*	N	Y	Y	Y	Y
22 *Huffington*	N	Y	N	N	Y
23 *Gallegly*	N	Y	Y	Y	Y
24 Beilenson	Y	N	Y	N	N
25 *McKeon*	N	Y	N	Y	Y
26 Berman	Y	N	Y	Y	N
27 *Moorhead*	N	Y	N	Y	Y
28 *Dreier*	N	Y	N	N	Y
29 Waxman	Y	N	Y	N	N
30 Becerra	Y	N	Y	Y	N
31 Martinez	Y	N	Y	Y	Y
32 Dixon	Y	N	Y	Y	N
33 Roybal-Allard	Y	N	Y	Y	N
34 Torres	?	N	Y	Y	Y
35 Waters	Y	N	Y	Y	N
36 Harman	Y	N	Y	Y	Y
37 Tucker	Y	N	Y	Y	N
38 *Horn*	N	Y	Y	Y	Y
39 *Royce*	N	Y	N	N	Y
40 *Lewis*	Y	N	Y	Y	Y
41 *Kim*	N	Y	N	Y	Y

	310	311	312	313	314
42 Brown	Y	N	Y	N	N
43 *Calvert*	N	Y	N	Y	Y
44 *McCandless*	N	Y	N	Y	Y
45 *Rohrabacher*	N	Y	N	Y	Y
46 Dornan	N	Y	N	N	Y
47 *Cox*	?	Y	N	N	Y
48 *Packard*	N	Y	N	Y	Y
49 Schenk	Y	N	Y	Y	Y
50 Filner	Y	N	Y	Y	Y
51 *Cunningham*	N	Y	N	N	Y
52 *Hunter*	N	Y	N	N	Y
COLORADO					
1 Schroeder	Y	N	N	Y	Y
2 Skaggs	Y	N	Y	Y	N
3 *McInnis*	N	Y	Y	N	Y
4 *Allard*	N	Y	N	N	Y
5 *Hefley*	N	Y	N	N	Y
6 *Schaefer*	Y	Y	N	N	Y
CONNECTICUT					
1 Kennelly	Y	N	Y	Y	Y
2 Gejdenson	Y	N	Y	Y	Y
3 DeLauro	Y	N	Y	Y	Y
4 *Shays*	N	Y	Y	N	Y
5 *Franks*	N	Y	Y	Y	Y
6 *Johnson*	N	Y	Y	Y	Y
DELAWARE					
AL *Castle*	N	Y	N	Y	Y
FLORIDA					
1 Hutto	Y	N	Y	Y	Y
2 Peterson	Y	N	Y	Y	Y
3 Brown	Y	N	Y	Y	Y
4 *Fowler*	N	Y	Y	Y	Y
5 Thurman	Y	N	Y	Y	Y
6 *Stearns*	N	Y	N	Y	N
7 *Mica*	N	Y	N	Y	Y
8 *McCollum*	N	Y	Y	Y	Y
9 *Bilirakis*	Y	Y	Y	Y	Y
10 *Young*	Y	Y	Y	Y	Y
11 Gibbons	Y	N	Y	?	?
12 *Canady*	N	Y	Y	Y	Y
13 *Miller*	N	Y	N	N	Y
14 *Goss*	N	Y	N	N	Y
15 Bacchus	Y	N	Y	Y	Y
16 *Lewis*	N	Y	Y	Y	?
17 Meek	Y	N	Y	N	N
18 *Ros-Lehtinen*	Y	Y	N	N	Y
19 Johnston	Y	N	Y	Y	Y
20 Deutsch	Y	N	Y	Y	Y
21 *Diaz-Balart*	Y	Y	N	Y	Y
22 *Shaw*	N	Y	Y	Y	Y
23 Hastings	Y	N	Y	Y	N
GEORGIA					
1 *Kingston*	N	Y	Y	Y	Y
2 Bishop	Y	N	Y	Y	Y
3 *Collins*	N	Y	Y	Y	Y
4 *Linder*	N	Y	N	N	Y
5 Lewis	Y	N	Y	N	N
6 *Gingrich*	N	Y	Y	Y	Y
7 Darden	Y	N	Y	Y	Y
8 Rowland	Y	N	Y	Y	Y
9 Deal	Y	N	Y	Y	Y
10 Johnson	Y	N	Y	Y	Y
11 McKinney	Y	N	Y	Y	N
HAWAII					
1 Abercrombie	Y	N	Y	Y	N
2 Mink	Y	N	Y	Y	Y
IDAHO					
1 LaRocco	Y	N	Y	Y	Y
2 *Crapo*	N	Y	N	N	Y
ILLINOIS					
1 Rush	?	N	Y	Y	N
2 Reynolds	Y	N	Y	Y	Y
3 Lipinski	Y	N	Y	Y	Y
4 Gutierrez	Y	N	Y	Y	Y
5 Rostenkowski	Y	N	Y	Y	Y
6 *Hyde*	N	C	Y	Y	Y
7 Collins	Y	N	Y	N	N
8 *Crane*	N	Y	N	N	Y
9 Yates	Y	N	Y	?	?
10 *Porter*	N	Y	N	Y	Y
11 Sangmeister	Y	N	Y	Y	Y
12 Costello	Y	N	Y	Y	Y
13 *Fawell*	N	Y	N	N	Y
14 *Hastert*	N	Y	Y	Y	Y
15 *Ewing*	N	Y	N	Y	Y
16 *Manzullo*	N	Y	N	Y	Y
17 Evans	Y	N	Y	Y	N

ND Northern Democrats   SD Southern Democrats

	310	311	312	313	314
18 Michel	N	Y	Y	Y	Y
19 Poshard	Y	N	Y	Y	Y
20 Durbin	Y	N	Y	Y	Y
INDIANA					
1 Visclosky	Y	N	Y	Y	N
2 Sharp	Y	N	Y	Y	Y
3 Roemer	Y	N	N	Y	Y
4 Long	Y	N	Y	Y	Y
5 *Buyer*	N	Y	Y	N	Y
6 *Burton*	N	Y	N	N	Y
7 *Myers*	N	N	N	N	Y
8 McCloskey	Y	N	Y	Y	Y
9 Hamilton	Y	N	Y	Y	Y
10 Jacobs	Y	N	N	N	Y
IOWA					
1 *Leach*	N	N	N	Y	Y
2 *Nussle*	N	Y	N	N	Y
3 *Lightfoot*	N	Y	N	Y	Y
4 Smith	Y	N	Y	Y	Y
5 *Grandy*	?	?	?	?	?
KANSAS					
1 *Roberts*	N	Y	N	Y	Y
2 Slattery	Y	N	Y	Y	Y
3 *Meyers*	N	N	Y	N	Y
4 Glickman	Y	N	Y	Y	Y
KENTUCKY					
1 Barlow	Y	N	Y	Y	Y
2 *Lewis*	N	Y	Y	Y	Y
3 Mazzoli	Y	N	Y	Y	Y
4 *Bunning*	N	Y	N	Y	Y
5 *Rogers*	N	Y	Y	Y	Y
6 Baesler	Y	N	Y	Y	Y
LOUISIANA					
1 *Livingston*	Y	Y	Y	Y	Y
2 Jefferson	Y	N	Y	Y	Y
3 Tauzin	Y	N	Y	Y	Y
4 Fields	Y	N	Y	Y	Y
5 *McCrery*	N	Y	Y	N	Y
6 *Baker*	N	Y	N	Y	N
7 Hayes	Y	N	Y	Y	Y
MAINE					
1 Andrews	Y	N	Y	Y	N
2 *Snowe*	N	Y	Y	Y	Y
MARYLAND					
1 *Gilchrest*	N	Y	Y	Y	Y
2 *Bentley*	N	Y	Y	N	Y
3 Cardin	Y	N	Y	Y	Y
4 Wynn	Y	N	Y	Y	Y
5 Hoyer	Y	N	Y	Y	Y
6 *Bartlett*	N	Y	Y	N	Y
7 Mfume	Y	N	Y	Y	Y
8 *Morella*	Y	Y	Y	Y	Y
MASSACHUSETTS					
1 Olver	Y	N	Y	Y	N
2 Neal	Y	N	Y	Y	Y
3 *Blute*	N	Y	Y	Y	Y
4 Frank	Y	N	Y	N	Y
5 Meehan	Y	N	Y	Y	Y
6 *Torkildsen*	N	Y	Y	Y	Y
7 Markey	Y	N	Y	Y	Y
8 Kennedy	Y	N	Y	Y	N
9 Moakley	Y	N	Y	Y	Y
10 Studds	Y	N	Y	Y	?
MICHIGAN					
1 Stupak	Y	N	Y	Y	Y
2 *Hoekstra*	N	N	N	N	Y
3 *Ehlers*	N	Y	N	N	Y
4 *Camp*	N	Y	N	Y	Y
5 Barcia	Y	N	Y	Y	Y
6 *Upton*	N	Y	Y	Y	Y
7 *Smith*	N	N	Y	N	Y
8 Carr	Y	N	Y	Y	Y
9 Kildee	Y	N	Y	Y	Y
10 Bonior	Y	N	Y	Y	Y
11 *Knollenberg*	Y	N	Y	Y	Y
12 Levin	Y	N	Y	Y	Y
13 Ford	?	?	?	?	?
14 Conyers	Y	N	Y	Y	N
15 Collins	Y	N	Y	Y	N
16 Dingell	Y	N	Y	Y	Y
MINNESOTA					
1 Penny	Y	N	N	N	Y
2 Minge	Y	N	N	N	Y
3 *Ramstad*	N	Y	N	N	Y
4 Vento	Y	N	Y	N	N

	310	311	312	313	314
5 Sabo	Y	N	Y	Y	Y
6 *Grams*	N	Y	N	N	Y
7 Peterson	Y	N	N	N	Y
8 Oberstar	Y	N	Y	N	Y
MISSISSIPPI					
1 Whitten	Y	N	Y	?	?
2 Thompson	Y	N	Y	Y	Y
3 Montgomery	Y	N	Y	Y	Y
4 Parker	Y	N	Y	Y	Y
5 Taylor	Y	N	Y	Y	Y
MISSOURI					
1 Clay	Y	N	Y	Y	?
2 *Talent*	N	Y	Y	Y	Y
3 Gephardt	Y	N	Y	Y	Y
4 Skelton	Y	N	Y	Y	Y
5 Wheat	?	N	Y	Y	Y
6 Danner	Y	N	Y	Y	Y
7 *Hancock*	N	Y	N	Y	N
8 *Emerson*	N	Y	Y	Y	Y
9 Volkmer	Y	N	Y	Y	Y
MONTANA					
AL Williams	?	N	Y	Y	Y
NEBRASKA					
1 *Bereuter*	N	Y	Y	Y	Y
2 Hoagland	Y	N	Y	Y	Y
3 *Barrett*	N	Y	Y	Y	Y
NEVADA					
1 Bilbray	Y	N	Y	Y	Y
2 *Vucanovich*	N	Y	Y	Y	Y
NEW HAMPSHIRE					
1 *Zeliff*	N	Y	N	N	Y
2 Swett	Y	N	N	Y	Y
NEW JERSEY					
1 Andrews	N	N	Y	Y	Y
2 Hughes	Y	N	N	Y	N
3 *Saxton*	N	Y	Y	Y	Y
4 *Smith*	N	Y	Y	Y	Y
5 *Roukema*	N	N	N	N	Y
6 Pallone	Y	N	Y	Y	Y
7 *Franks*	N	Y	N	N	Y
8 Klein	Y	N	Y	Y	Y
9 Torricelli	Y	N	Y	Y	Y
10 Payne	Y	N	Y	Y	N
11 *Gallo*	Y	N	Y	Y	Y
12 *Zimmer*	N	Y	N	N	Y
13 Menendez	Y	N	Y	Y	Y
NEW MEXICO					
1 *Schiff*	N	Y	Y	Y	Y
2 *Skeen*	Y	Y	Y	Y	Y
3 Richardson	Y	N	Y	Y	Y
NEW YORK					
1 Hochbrueckner	Y	N	Y	Y	Y
2 *Lazio*	N	N	Y	Y	Y
3 *King*	N	Y	Y	Y	Y
4 *Levy*	N	Y	Y	Y	Y
5 Ackerman	Y	N	Y	Y	Y
6 Flake	Y	N	Y	Y	N
7 Manton	Y	N	Y	Y	N
8 Nadler	Y	N	Y	Y	N
9 Schumer	Y	N	Y	Y	N
10 Towns	Y	N	Y	Y	N
11 Owens	Y	N	Y	N	N
12 Velazquez	Y	N	Y	Y	N
13 *Molinari*	N	Y	Y	Y	Y
14 Maloney	Y	N	Y	Y	Y
15 Rangel	Y	N	Y	Y	N
16 Serrano	Y	N	Y	Y	Y
17 Engel	Y	N	Y	Y	Y
18 Lowey	Y	N	Y	Y	N
19 *Fish*	?	?	?	?	?
20 Gilman	N	Y	Y	Y	Y
21 McNulty	Y	N	Y	Y	Y
22 *Solomon*	N	Y	N	N	Y
23 *Boehlert*	N	Y	Y	Y	Y
24 *McHugh*	N	Y	Y	N	Y
25 *Walsh*	N	Y	Y	Y	Y
26 Hinchey	Y	N	Y	Y	Y
27 *Paxon*	N	Y	N	N	Y
28 Slaughter	Y	N	Y	Y	Y
29 LaFalce	Y	N	Y	Y	Y
30 Quinn	N	Y	Y	Y	Y
31 *Houghton*	N	Y	Y	Y	Y
NORTH CAROLINA					
1 Clayton	Y	N	Y	Y	N
2 Valentine	Y	N	Y	Y	?

	310	311	312	313	314
3 Lancaster	Y	N	Y	Y	Y
4 Price	Y	N	Y	Y	Y
5 Neal	Y	N	Y	Y	Y
6 *Coble*	N	Y	N	Y	Y
7 Rose	Y	N	Y	Y	Y
8 Hefner	Y	N	Y	Y	Y
9 *McMillan*	N	Y	Y	Y	Y
10 *Ballenger*	N	Y	N	N	Y
11 *Taylor*	N	Y	Y	Y	Y
12 Watt	Y	N	Y	Y	N
NORTH DAKOTA					
AL Pomeroy	Y	N	Y	Y	Y
OHIO					
1 Mann	Y	N	Y	Y	N
2 *Portman*	N	Y	N	Y	Y
3 Hall	Y	N	Y	Y	?
4 *Oxley*	N	Y	N	Y	Y
5 *Gillmor*	N	Y	Y	Y	Y
6 Strickland	Y	N	Y	Y	Y
7 *Hobson*	N	Y	N	Y	Y
8 *Boehner*	N	Y	N	Y	Y
9 Kaptur	Y	N	Y	Y	Y
10 *Hoke*	N	Y	N	Y	N
11 Stokes	Y	N	Y	Y	N
12 *Kasich*	N	Y	Y	Y	Y
13 Brown	Y	N	Y	Y	Y
14 Sawyer	Y	N	Y	Y	Y
15 *Pryce*	N	Y	Y	Y	Y
16 *Regula*	N	Y	Y	Y	Y
17 Traficant	Y	N	Y	Y	Y
18 Applegate	Y	N	Y	Y	?
19 Fingerhut	Y	N	Y	Y	Y
OKLAHOMA					
1 *Inhofe*	N	Y	N	N	Y
2 Synar	Y	N	Y	Y	N
3 Brewster	Y	N	Y	Y	Y
4 McCurdy	Y	N	Y	Y	Y
5 *Istook*	?	N	Y	N	Y
6 *Lucas*	N	Y	Y	Y	Y
OREGON					
1 Furse	Y	N	Y	Y	N
2 *Smith*	N	Y	Y	?	?
3 Wyden	Y	N	Y	Y	Y
4 DeFazio	Y	N	Y	N	?
5 Kopetski	Y	N	Y	Y	N
PENNSYLVANIA					
1 Foglietta	Y	N	Y	Y	Y
2 Blackwell	Y	N	Y	Y	Y
3 Borski	Y	N	Y	Y	Y
4 Klink	Y	N	Y	Y	Y
5 *Clinger*	N	Y	Y	Y	Y
6 Holden	Y	N	Y	Y	Y
7 *Weldon*	N	Y	Y	Y	Y
8 *Greenwood*	N	Y	Y	Y	Y
9 *Shuster*	N	Y	N	Y	Y
10 *McDade*	N	Y	Y	Y	Y
11 Kanjorski	Y	N	Y	Y	N
12 Murtha	Y	N	Y	Y	?
13 Margolies-Mezv.	Y	N	?	Y	N
14 Coyne	Y	N	?	Y	N
15 McHale	Y	N	Y	Y	Y
16 *Walker*	N	Y	N	Y	Y
17 *Gekas*	N	Y	N	Y	Y
18 *Santorum*	N	Y	Y	Y	Y
19 *Goodling*	N	Y	Y	Y	Y
20 Murphy	Y	N	?	?	Y
21 *Ridge*	N	Y	Y	Y	Y
RHODE ISLAND					
1 *Machtley*	?	?	?	?	?
2 Reed	Y	N	Y	Y	Y
SOUTH CAROLINA					
1 *Ravenel*	N	Y	Y	Y	Y
2 *Spence*	N	Y	N	Y	Y
3 Derrick	Y	N	Y	N	Y
4 *Inglis*	N	N	Y	N	Y
5 Spratt	Y	N	Y	Y	Y
6 Clyburn	Y	N	Y	Y	Y
SOUTH DAKOTA					
AL Johnson	Y	N	Y	Y	Y
TENNESSEE					
1 *Quillen*	Y	N	Y	Y	Y
2 *Duncan*	N	N	N	Y	Y
3 Lloyd	Y	N	Y	Y	Y
4 Cooper	N	N	Y	Y	Y
5 Clement	Y	N	Y	Y	Y

	310	311	312	313	314
6 Gordon	Y	N	Y	Y	Y
7 *Sundquist*	N	Y	Y	Y	Y
8 Tanner	Y	N	Y	Y	Y
9 Ford	Y	N	Y	Y	Y
TEXAS					
1 Chapman	Y	N	Y	Y	Y
2 Wilson	Y	N	Y	Y	Y
3 *Johnson, Sam*	N	Y	N	N	Y
4 Hall	Y	N	Y	Y	Y
5 Bryant	Y	N	Y	Y	Y
6 *Barton*	N	Y	N	N	Y
7 *Archer*	N	Y	N	N	Y
8 *Fields*	N	Y	Y	N	Y
9 Brooks	Y	N	Y	Y	N
10 Pickle	Y	N	Y	Y	Y
11 Edwards	Y	N	Y	Y	Y
12 Geren	Y	N	Y	Y	Y
13 Sarpalius	Y	N	Y	Y	Y
14 Laughlin	Y	N	Y	Y	Y
15 de la Garza	Y	N	Y	Y	Y
16 Coleman	Y	N	Y	Y	Y
17 Stenholm	Y	N	Y	Y	Y
18 Washington	?	?	?	?	?
19 *Combest*	N	Y	N	N	Y
20 Gonzalez	Y	N	Y	Y	N
21 *Smith*	N	Y	Y	Y	Y
22 *DeLay*	N	Y	Y	?	Y
23 *Bonilla*	Y	Y	Y	Y	Y
24 Frost	Y	N	Y	Y	Y
25 Andrews	Y	N	Y	Y	?
26 *Armey*	N	Y	N	N	Y
27 Ortiz	Y	N	Y	Y	Y
28 Tejeda	Y	N	Y	Y	Y
29 Green	Y	N	Y	Y	Y
30 Johnson, E.B.	Y	N	Y	Y	Y
UTAH					
1 *Hansen*	N	Y	Y	N	Y
2 Shepherd	Y	N	Y	Y	Y
3 Orton	Y	N	Y	Y	Y
VERMONT					
AL *Sanders*	Y	N	Y	N	N
VIRGINIA					
1 *Bateman*	N	Y	Y	Y	?
2 Pickett	Y	N	Y	Y	?
3 Scott	Y	N	Y	Y	N
4 Sisisky	Y	N	Y	Y	Y
5 Payne	Y	N	Y	Y	Y
6 *Goodlatte*	N	Y	Y	Y	Y
7 *Bliley*	N	Y	Y	Y	Y
8 Moran	Y	N	Y	Y	Y
9 Boucher	Y	N	Y	Y	?
10 *Wolf*	N	Y	Y	Y	Y
11 Byrne	Y	N	Y	Y	Y
WASHINGTON					
1 Cantwell	Y	N	Y	Y	Y
2 Swift	?	N	Y	?	N
3 Unsoeld	Y	N	Y	Y	N
4 Inslee	Y	N	Y	Y	Y
5 Foley					
6 Dicks	Y	N	Y	Y	Y
7 McDermott	Y	N	Y	Y	N
8 *Dunn*	N	Y	Y	N	Y
9 Kreidler	Y	N	Y	Y	Y
WEST VIRGINIA					
1 Mollohan	?	N	Y	Y	N
2 Wise	Y	N	Y	Y	Y
3 Rahall	Y	N	Y	Y	Y
WISCONSIN					
1 Barca	Y	N	N	N	Y
2 *Klug*	N	Y	N	N	Y
3 *Gunderson*	N	Y	Y	Y	Y
4 Kleczka	Y	N	Y	Y	Y
5 Barrett	Y	N	N	N	Y
6 *Petri*	N	Y	N	N	Y
7 Obey	Y	N	Y	Y	Y
8 *Roth*	N	Y	N	N	Y
9 *Sensenbrenner*	N	Y	N	N	Y
WYOMING					
AL *Thomas*	N	Y	Y	N	Y
DELEGATES					
de Lugo, V.I.	Y	D	D	D	D
Faleomavaega, Am.S.	?	D	D	D	D
Norton, D.C.	Y	D	D	D	D
Romero-B., P.R.	?	D	D	D	D
Underwood, Guam	Y	D	D	D	D

Southern states - Ala., Ark., Fla., Ga., Ky., La., Miss., N.C., Okla., S.C., Tenn., Texas, Va.
Omitted votes are quorum calls, which CQ does not include in its vote charts.

KEY

Y Voted for (yea).
\# Paired for.
+ Announced for.
N Voted against (nay).
X Paired against.
− Announced against.
P Voted "present."
C Voted "present" to avoid possible conflict of interest.
? Did not vote or otherwise make a position known.
D Delegates ineligible to vote.

Democrats **Republicans**
Independent

315. HR 518. California Desert Protection/Livestock Grazing. Vento, D-Minn., amendment to strike the bill's provisions that allow grazing in the Death Valley and Mojave national parks to continue indefinitely at existing levels and insert provisions that would terminate grazing upon the expiration of current permits. Rejected in the Committee of the Whole 190-207: R 27-136; D 163-71 (ND 121-37, SD 42-34); I 0-0, July 12, 1994.

316. HR 518. California Desert Protection/Hunting Exception. LaRocco, D-Idaho, en bloc amendment to designate the East Mojave Scenic Area a national preserve rather than a national park, thus permitting hunting, fishing and trapping to continue in the East Mojave Scenic Area. Adopted in the Committee of the Whole 239-183: R 146-26; D 92-157 (ND 39-131, SD 53-26); I 1-0, July 12, 1994.

317. HR 518. California Desert Protection/Condemnation Prohibition. DeLay, R-Texas, amendment to prohibit the Department of the Interior from using condemnation to acquire lands within the Mojave National Park. Rejected in the Committee of the Whole 145-274: R 132-38; D 13-235 (ND 5-164, SD 8-71); I 0-1, July 12, 1994.

318. Procedural Motion. Approval of the House Journal of Tuesday, July 12. Approved 241-149: R 17-145; D 223-4 (ND 154-3, SD 69-1); I 1-0, July 13, 1994.

319. HR 518. California Desert Protection/Land Exchanges and Monetary Credits. Miller, D-Calif., amendment to make all owners of private land within parks and wilderness areas eligible for land exchanges and monetary credits. Adopted in the Committee of the Whole 419-0: R 172-0; D 246-0 (ND 170-0, SD 76-0); I 1-0, July 13, 1994.

320. HR 4649. Fiscal 1995 D.C. Appropriations/Motion To Rise. Dixon, D-Calif., motion to rise from the Committee of the Whole and report the bill back to the full House, thus prohibiting the possibility of further amendments being offered. Motion rejected 192-236: R 4-170; D 187-66 (ND 145-30, SD 42-36); I 1-0, July 13, 1994.

321. HR 4649. Fiscal 1995 D.C. Appropriations/Domestic Partners. Barton, R-Texas, amendment to ban the use of money to implement the District of Columbia's domestic partners ordinance, which allows unmarried couples registered as domestic partners to be eligible for certain benefits, such as health insurance, accorded to married couples. Adopted in the Committee of the Whole 251-176: R 160-15; D 91-160 (ND 44-130, SD 47-30); I 0-1, July 13, 1994.

	315	316	317	318	319	320	321
ALABAMA							
1 *Callahan*	N	Y	Y	N	Y	N	Y
2 *Everett*	N	Y	Y	Y	Y	N	Y
3 Browder	Y	Y	N	Y	Y	Y	N
4 Bevill	N	Y	N	Y	Y	Y	Y
5 Cramer	N	Y	N	Y	Y	N	Y
6 *Bachus*	N	Y	Y	N	Y	N	Y
7 Hilliard	Y	Y	N	Y	Y	Y	N
ALASKA							
AL *Young*	N	Y	Y	?	Y	N	Y
ARIZONA							
1 Coppersmith	−	N	N	Y	Y	Y	N
2 Pastor	N	N	N	Y	Y	Y	N
3 *Stump*	N	Y	Y	N	Y	N	Y
4 *Kyl*	N	Y	Y	N	Y	N	Y
5 *Kolbe*	N	Y	Y	N	Y	N	N
6 English	N	N	N	Y	Y	Y	N
ARKANSAS							
1 Lambert	Y	Y	N	Y	Y	Y	Y
2 Thornton	N	Y	N	Y	Y	Y	Y
3 *Hutchinson*	N	Y	Y	N	Y	N	Y
4 *Dickey*	N	Y	Y	N	Y	N	Y
CALIFORNIA							
1 Hamburg	Y	N	N	Y	Y	Y	N
2 *Herger*	N	?	Y	N	Y	N	Y
3 Fazio	N	N	N	Y	Y	Y	N
4 *Doolittle*	N	Y	Y	?	Y	N	Y
5 Matsui	N	N	N	Y	Y	Y	N
6 Woolsey	Y	N	N	Y	Y	Y	N
7 Miller	Y	N	N	Y	Y	Y	N
8 Pelosi	Y	N	N	Y	Y	Y	N
9 Dellums	Y	N	N	Y	Y	Y	N
10 *Baker*	N	Y	N	Y	Y	N	Y
11 *Pombo*	N	Y	Y	N	Y	N	Y
12 Lantos	Y	N	N	Y	Y	Y	N
13 Stark	Y	N	N	Y	Y	Y	N
14 Eshoo	Y	N	N	Y	Y	Y	N
15 Mineta	Y	N	N	Y	Y	Y	N
16 Edwards	N	N	N	Y	Y	Y	N
17 Farr	Y	N	N	Y	Y	Y	N
18 Condit	N	Y	N	?	Y	N	N
19 Lehman	N	N	N	Y	Y	Y	N
20 Dooley	N	N	N	Y	Y	Y	N
21 *Thomas*	N	Y	N	N	Y	N	Y
22 *Huffington*	?	?	?	?	?	?	?
23 *Gallegly*	N	Y	Y	N	Y	N	Y
24 Beilenson	Y	N	N	Y	Y	Y	N
25 *McKeon*	N	Y	Y	N	Y	N	Y
26 Berman	Y	N	N	Y	Y	Y	N
27 *Moorhead*	N	Y	Y	N	Y	N	Y
28 *Dreier*	N	Y	Y	N	Y	N	Y
29 Waxman	Y	N	N	Y	Y	Y	N
30 Becerra	Y	N	N	?	Y	Y	N
31 Martinez	N	Y	N	Y	Y	Y	Y
32 Dixon	N	N	N	Y	Y	Y	N
33 Roybal-Allard	Y	N	N	Y	Y	Y	N
34 Torres	N	N	N	Y	Y	Y	N
35 Waters	N	N	N	Y	Y	Y	N
36 Harman	N	N	N	Y	Y	Y	N
37 Tucker	Y	N	N	Y	Y	N	Y
38 *Horn*	N	N	Y	N	Y	N	Y
39 *Royce*	N	Y	Y	N	Y	N	Y
40 *Lewis*	N	Y	Y	Y	Y	N	Y
41 *Kim*	N	Y	Y	N	Y	N	Y

	315	316	317	318	319	320	321
42 Brown	Y	?	N	?	Y	Y	N
43 *Calvert*	N	Y	Y	N	Y	N	Y
44 *McCandless*	N	Y	Y	N	Y	N	Y
45 *Rohrabacher*	N	Y	Y	N	Y	N	Y
46 *Dornan*	N	Y	Y	?	Y	N	Y
47 *Cox*	N	Y	Y	N	Y	N	Y
48 *Packard*	N	Y	Y	N	Y	N	Y
49 Schenk	Y	N	N	Y	Y	Y	Y
50 Filner	Y	N	N	Y	Y	Y	N
51 *Cunningham*	N	Y	Y	N	Y	N	Y
52 *Hunter*	N	Y	Y	N	Y	N	Y
COLORADO							
1 Schroeder	Y	N	N	N	Y	Y	N
2 Skaggs	Y	N	N	Y	Y	Y	N
3 *McInnis*	X	Y	Y	N	Y	N	Y
4 *Allard*	N	Y	Y	N	Y	N	Y
5 *Hefley*	N	Y	N	Y	Y	N	Y
6 *Schaefer*	N	Y	Y	N	Y	N	Y
CONNECTICUT							
1 Kennelly	Y	N	N	Y	Y	Y	N
2 Gejdenson	+	N	N	Y	Y	Y	N
3 DeLauro	Y	N	N	Y	Y	Y	N
4 *Shays*	Y	N	N	N	Y	N	N
5 *Franks*	Y	N	N	N	Y	N	N
6 *Johnson*	N	Y	N	N	Y	Y	N
DELAWARE							
AL *Castle*	N	Y	Y	Y	Y	N	Y
FLORIDA							
1 Hutto	N	Y	N	Y	Y	N	Y
2 Peterson	N	Y	N	Y	Y	Y	Y
3 Brown	Y	N	N	Y	Y	Y	N
4 *Fowler*	N	Y	Y	N	Y	N	Y
5 Thurman	N	Y	N	+	Y	Y	N
6 *Stearns*	N	Y	N	Y	Y	N	Y
7 *Mica*	X	Y	Y	N	Y	N	Y
8 *McCollum*	N	Y	N	N	Y	N	Y
9 *Bilirakis*	N	Y	N	N	Y	N	Y
10 *Young*	N	Y	Y	N	Y	N	Y
11 Gibbons	Y	N	N	Y	Y	Y	N
12 *Canady*	N	Y	Y	N	Y	N	Y
13 *Miller*	N	Y	Y	N	Y	N	Y
14 *Goss*	Y	N	N	N	Y	N	Y
15 Bacchus	Y	N	N	Y	Y	Y	?
16 *Lewis*	N	Y	Y	N	Y	N	Y
17 Meek	Y	N	N	Y	Y	Y	N
18 *Ros-Lehtinen*	N	N	N	N	Y	N	Y
19 Johnston	Y	N	N	Y	Y	Y	N
20 Deutsch	Y	N	N	Y	Y	Y	N
21 *Diaz-Balart*	N	Y	N	N	Y	N	Y
22 *Shaw*	N	Y	N	N	Y	N	Y
23 Hastings	Y	N	N	Y	Y	Y	N
GEORGIA							
1 *Kingston*	N	Y	Y	Y	Y	N	Y
2 Bishop	N	Y	N	?	?	?	?
3 *Collins*	N	Y	Y	N	Y	N	Y
4 *Linder*	N	Y	N	Y	Y	N	Y
5 Lewis	Y	N	N	Y	Y	Y	N
6 *Gingrich*	N	Y	Y	N	Y	N	Y
7 Darden	Y	Y	N	Y	Y	Y	Y
8 Rowland	N	Y	N	?	?	?	?
9 Deal	N	Y	Y	Y	Y	Y	Y
10 Johnson	Y	Y	N	Y	Y	Y	Y
11 McKinney	Y	N	N	Y	Y	Y	N
HAWAII							
1 Abercrombie	Y	N	N	Y	Y	Y	N
2 Mink	Y	N	N	?	Y	Y	N
IDAHO							
1 LaRocco	N	Y	N	Y	Y	Y	N
2 *Crapo*	N	Y	Y	N	Y	N	Y
ILLINOIS							
1 Rush	Y	N	N	Y	Y	Y	N
2 Reynolds	Y	N	N	Y	Y	Y	N
3 Lipinski	N	Y	N	Y	Y	Y	Y
4 Gutierrez	N	N	N	Y	Y	Y	N
5 Rostenkowski	Y	N	N	Y	Y	Y	N
6 *Hyde*	N	Y	Y	N	Y	N	Y
7 Collins	?	N	N	Y	Y	Y	N
8 *Crane*	N	Y	Y	?	Y	N	Y
9 Yates	Y	N	N	Y	Y	Y	N
10 *Porter*	Y	N	N	?	Y	N	Y
11 Sangmeister	Y	Y	N	Y	Y	Y	Y
12 Costello	N	Y	N	Y	Y	Y	Y
13 *Fawell*	Y	N	N	N	Y	N	Y
14 *Hastert*	N	Y	Y	N	Y	N	Y
15 *Ewing*	N	Y	Y	?	Y	N	Y
16 *Manzullo*	N	Y	Y	N	Y	N	Y
17 Evans	Y	N	N	Y	Y	Y	N

ND Northern Democrats   SD Southern Democrats

	315	316	317	318	319	320	321
18 ***Michel***	N	Y	Y	N	Y	N	Y
19 Poshard	N	Y	N	Y	Y	N	Y
20 Durbin	Y	N	N	Y	Y	Y	N
INDIANA							
1 Visclosky	Y	Y	N	Y	Y	Y	N
2 Sharp	Y	N	N	Y	Y	Y	N
3 Roemer	Y	N	N	Y	Y	Y	Y
4 Long	N	N	N	Y	Y	Y	N
5 ***Buyer***	N	Y	Y	N	Y	N	Y
6 ***Burton***	N	Y	Y	N	Y	N	Y
7 ***Myers***	N	Y	Y	Y	Y	N	Y
8 McCloskey	#	N	N	Y	Y	Y	N
9 Hamilton	Y	N	N	Y	Y	N	Y
10 Jacobs	Y	N	N	N	Y	Y	N
IOWA							
1 ***Leach***	Y	Y	N	N	Y	N	N
2 ***Nussle***	N	Y	Y	N	Y	N	Y
3 ***Lightfoot***	N	Y	Y	N	Y	N	Y
4 Smith	N	Y	N	Y	Y	Y	N
5 ***Grandy***	Y	Y	Y	N	Y	N	Y
KANSAS							
1 ***Roberts***	N	Y	Y	N	Y	N	Y
2 Slattery	?	?	?	?	?	?	?
3 ***Meyers***	Y	N	N	N	Y	N	Y
4 Glickman	N	N	Y	Y	Y	Y	Y
KENTUCKY							
1 Barlow	Y	Y	N	Y	+	Y	Y
2 ***Lewis***	N	Y	Y	N	Y	N	Y
3 Mazzoli	N	Y	N	Y	Y	N	Y
4 ***Bunning***	N	Y	Y	N	Y	N	Y
5 ***Rogers***	N	Y	Y	N	Y	N	Y
6 Baesler	N	Y	N	Y	Y	Y	Y
LOUISIANA							
1 ***Livingston***	N	Y	Y	N	Y	N	Y
2 Jefferson	Y	N	N	Y	Y	Y	N
3 Tauzin	?	Y	N	Y	Y	N	Y
4 Fields	Y	N	N	Y	Y	Y	N
5 ***McCrery***	N	Y	N	?	Y	?	Y
6 ***Baker***	N	Y	Y	N	Y	N	Y
7 Hayes	N	Y	N	Y	Y	N	Y
MAINE							
1 Andrews	Y	N	N	Y	Y	Y	N
2 ***Snowe***	Y	Y	Y	N	Y	N	Y
MARYLAND							
1 ***Gilchrest***	Y	N	N	N	Y	N	N
2 ***Bentley***	N	Y	Y	?	Y	N	Y
3 Cardin	Y	N	N	Y	Y	Y	N
4 Wynn	Y	N	N	Y	Y	Y	N
5 Hoyer	Y	N	N	Y	Y	Y	N
6 ***Bartlett***	N	Y	Y	N	Y	N	Y
7 Mfume	Y	N	N	Y	Y	Y	N
8 ***Morella***	Y	N	N	N	Y	Y	N
MASSACHUSETTS							
1 Olver	Y	N	N	Y	Y	Y	N
2 Neal	Y	N	N	Y	Y	Y	N
3 ***Blute***	N	Y	Y	N	Y	Y	N
4 Frank	Y	N	N	Y	Y	Y	N
5 Meehan	?	N	N	Y	Y	Y	N
6 ***Torkildsen***	Y	N	N	N	Y	N	N
7 Markey	Y	N	N	Y	Y	Y	N
8 Kennedy	Y	N	N	Y	Y	Y	N
9 Moakley	Y	N	N	Y	Y	Y	N
10 Studds	Y	N	N	Y	Y	Y	N
MICHIGAN							
1 Stupak	Y	N	N	Y	Y	Y	Y
2 ***Hoekstra***	N	Y	Y	N	Y	N	Y
3 ***Ehlers***	Y	N	N	N	Y	N	Y
4 ***Camp***	N	Y	Y	N	Y	N	Y
5 Barcia	N	Y	N	?	Y	Y	Y
6 ***Upton***	Y	N	N	N	Y	N	Y
7 ***Smith***	N	Y	Y	N	Y	N	Y
8 Carr	Y	?	N	Y	Y	Y	N
9 Kildee	Y	N	N	Y	Y	Y	N
10 Bonior	Y	N	N	Y	Y	Y	N
11 ***Knollenberg***	N	Y	Y	N	Y	N	Y
12 Levin	Y	N	N	Y	Y	Y	N
13 Ford	Y	Y	N	?	Y	Y	?
14 Conyers	Y	N	N	Y	Y	Y	N
15 Collins	?	N	N	?	Y	Y	N
16 Dingell	N	N	N	Y	Y	Y	Y
MINNESOTA							
1 Penny	Y	N	Y	Y	Y	N	Y
2 Minge	Y	Y	N	Y	Y	N	Y
3 ***Ramstad***	Y	N	N	N	Y	N	Y
4 Vento	Y	N	N	Y	Y	Y	N
5 Sabo	Y	N	N	Y	Y	Y	N
6 ***Grams***	N	Y	Y	N	Y	N	Y
7 Peterson	Y	Y	N	Y	Y	N	Y
8 Oberstar	Y	Y	N	Y	Y	Y	N
MISSISSIPPI							
1 Whitten	?	?	?	?	Y	?	Y
2 Thompson	Y	N	N	Y	Y	Y	N
3 Montgomery	?	Y	N	Y	Y	N	Y
4 Parker	Y	Y	N	Y	Y	N	Y
5 Taylor	N	Y	Y	N	Y	N	Y
MISSOURI							
1 Clay	Y	N	N	N	Y	Y	N
2 ***Talent***	N	Y	Y	N	Y	N	Y
3 Gephardt	Y	N	N	Y	Y	Y	N
4 Skelton	N	Y	Y	Y	Y	N	Y
5 Wheat	?	?	?	Y	Y	Y	N
6 Danner	Y	Y	N	?	?	N	Y
7 ***Hancock***	N	Y	Y	?	Y	N	Y
8 ***Emerson***	N	Y	Y	N	Y	N	Y
9 Volkmer	Y	Y	N	Y	?	N	Y
MONTANA							
AL Williams	N	Y	N	Y	Y	N	N
NEBRASKA							
1 ***Bereuter***	N	Y	Y	N	Y	N	Y
2 Hoagland	Y	N	N	Y	Y	Y	N
3 ***Barrett***	N	Y	Y	N	Y	N	Y
NEVADA							
1 Bilbray	N	N	N	Y	Y	Y	N
2 ***Vucanovich***	N	Y	Y	N	Y	N	Y
NEW HAMPSHIRE							
1 ***Zeliff***	N	Y	?	N	Y	N	Y
2 Swett	?	N	N	Y	Y	N	Y
NEW JERSEY							
1 Andrews	Y	N	N	Y	Y	Y	N
2 Hughes	N	N	N	Y	Y	Y	N
3 ***Saxton***	Y	Y	Y	N	Y	N	Y
4 ***Smith***	N	Y	?	Y	Y	N	Y
5 ***Roukema***	N	N	N	N	Y	N	Y
6 Pallone	Y	N	N	Y	Y	Y	N
7 ***Franks***	?	N	Y	N	Y	N	Y
8 Klein	Y	N	N	Y	Y	Y	N
9 Torricelli	Y	N	N	Y	Y	Y	N
10 Payne	Y	N	N	Y	Y	Y	N
11 ***Gallo***	?	?	?	?	?	?	?
12 ***Zimmer***	Y	N	N	N	Y	N	Y
13 Menendez	Y	N	N	Y	Y	Y	N
NEW MEXICO							
1 ***Schiff***	?	Y	N	N	Y	N	N
2 ***Skeen***	N	Y	Y	N	Y	N	Y
3 Richardson	Y	N	N	Y	Y	Y	N
NEW YORK							
1 Hochbrueckner	?	N	N	Y	Y	Y	N
2 ***Lazio***	N	N	N	N	Y	Y	N
3 ***King***	N	Y	Y	N	Y	N	Y
4 ***Levy***	N	Y	Y	N	Y	N	Y
5 Ackerman	Y	N	N	Y	Y	Y	N
6 Flake	?	?	?	Y	Y	Y	N
7 Manton	N	N	N	?	Y	Y	Y
8 Nadler	Y	N	N	Y	Y	Y	N
9 Schumer	Y	N	N	Y	Y	Y	N
10 Towns	Y	N	N	Y	Y	Y	N
11 Owens	Y	N	N	Y	Y	Y	N
12 Velazquez	Y	N	N	Y	Y	Y	N
13 ***Molinari***	N	Y	Y	N	Y	N	Y
14 Maloney	Y	N	N	Y	Y	Y	N
15 Rangel	Y	N	?	Y	Y	Y	N
16 Serrano	Y	N	N	Y	Y	Y	N
17 Engel	?	N	N	?	Y	Y	N
18 Lowey	Y	N	N	Y	Y	Y	N
19 ***Fish***	Y	N	N	Y	Y	N	N
20 ***Gilman***	N	N	N	Y	Y	N	Y
21 McNulty	Y	Y	N	Y	Y	N	Y
22 ***Solomon***	N	Y	Y	N	Y	N	Y
23 ***Boehlert***	Y	N	N	N	Y	N	N
24 ***McHugh***	N	Y	Y	N	Y	N	Y
25 ***Walsh***	Y	Y	N	N	Y	N	Y
26 Hinchey	Y	N	N	Y	Y	Y	N
27 ***Paxon***	N	Y	Y	N	Y	N	Y
28 Slaughter	Y	N	N	Y	Y	Y	N
29 LaFalce	Y	N	N	Y	Y	N	Y
30 ***Quinn***	N	Y	Y	N	Y	N	Y
31 ***Houghton***	N	Y	N	Y	Y	N	N
NORTH CAROLINA							
1 Clayton	Y	N	N	Y	Y	Y	N
2 Valentine	Y	N	N	?	Y	N	Y
3 Lancaster	Y	Y	N	Y	Y	N	Y
4 Price	Y	N	N	Y	Y	Y	N
5 Neal	Y	Y	N	?	Y	Y	N
6 ***Coble***	N	Y	Y	N	Y	N	Y
7 Rose	N	N	N	Y	Y	Y	Y
8 Hefner	Y	Y	N	Y	Y	Y	Y
9 ***McMillan***	N	Y	Y	N	Y	N	Y
10 ***Ballenger***	N	Y	Y	N	Y	N	Y
11 ***Taylor***	N	Y	Y	N	Y	N	Y
12 Watt	Y	N	N	Y	Y	Y	N
NORTH DAKOTA							
AL Pomeroy	N	Y	N	Y	Y	Y	Y
OHIO							
1 Mann	Y	N	N	Y	Y	Y	N
2 ***Portman***	Y	Y	Y	N	Y	N	Y
3 Hall	Y	N	N	Y	Y	N	Y
4 ***Oxley***	?	Y	Y	?	Y	N	Y
5 ***Gillmor***	N	N	Y	Y	Y	N	Y
6 Strickland	Y	Y	N	Y	Y	Y	N
7 ***Hobson***	N	N	Y	N	Y	N	Y
8 ***Boehner***	N	Y	Y	N	Y	N	Y
9 Kaptur	?	N	N	Y	Y	N	Y
10 ***Hoke***	N	Y	Y	N	Y	N	Y
11 Stokes	?	N	N	Y	Y	Y	N
12 ***Kasich***	N	Y	Y	Y	Y	N	Y
13 Brown	Y	N	N	Y	Y	Y	N
14 Sawyer	Y	Y	N	Y	Y	Y	N
15 ***Pryce***	N	Y	Y	N	Y	N	Y
16 ***Regula***	Y	Y	Y	N	Y	N	Y
17 Traficant	N	Y	Y	Y	Y	Y	Y
18 Applegate	N	Y	N	Y	Y	Y	Y
19 Fingerhut	Y	N	N	Y	Y	Y	N
OKLAHOMA							
1 ***Inhofe***	N	Y	Y	N	Y	N	Y
2 Synar	Y	N	N	Y	Y	Y	N
3 Brewster	N	Y	N	Y	Y	N	Y
4 McCurdy	?	?	?	?	?	?	?
5 ***Istook***	?	?	Y	N	Y	N	Y
6 ***Lucas***	N	Y	Y	N	Y	N	Y
OREGON							
1 Furse	Y	N	N	Y	Y	Y	N
2 ***Smith***	N	Y	Y	N	Y	N	Y
3 Wyden	Y	N	N	Y	Y	Y	N
4 DeFazio	?	?	N	Y	Y	Y	N
5 Kopetski	Y	Y	N	Y	Y	Y	N
PENNSYLVANIA							
1 Foglietta	Y	N	N	Y	Y	Y	N
2 Blackwell	?	N	N	?	Y	Y	N
3 Borski	Y	N	?	Y	Y	Y	N
4 Klink	Y	N	N	Y	Y	N	Y
5 ***Clinger***	N	Y	N	?	Y	N	Y
6 Holden	Y	Y	N	Y	Y	N	Y
7 ***Weldon***	?	N	N	N	Y	N	Y
8 ***Greenwood***	Y	Y	Y	Y	Y	N	Y
9 ***Shuster***	N	Y	?	N	Y	N	Y
10 ***McDade***	?	?	?	?	?	?	?
11 Kanjorski	Y	Y	N	Y	Y	Y	Y
12 Murtha	N	Y	?	Y	Y	Y	Y
13 Margolies-Mezv.	Y	N	N	Y	Y	Y	N
14 Coyne	Y	N	N	Y	Y	Y	N
15 McHale	Y	N	N	Y	Y	N	Y
16 ***Walker***	N	Y	Y	N	Y	N	Y
17 ***Gekas***	N	Y	Y	N	Y	N	Y
18 ***Santorum***	N	Y	?	N	Y	N	Y
19 ***Goodling***	N	Y	N	N	Y	N	Y
20 Murphy	N	Y	?	?	?	Y	Y
21 ***Ridge***	?	?	?	?	?	N	Y
RHODE ISLAND							
1 ***Machtley***	?	Y	N	N	Y	N	Y
2 Reed	Y	N	N	?	Y	Y	N
SOUTH CAROLINA							
1 ***Ravenel***	?	N	N	N	Y	N	Y
2 ***Spence***	N	Y	Y	N	Y	N	Y
3 Derrick	Y	N	N	Y	Y	Y	N
4 ***Inglis***	N	Y	Y	Y	Y	N	Y
5 Spratt	Y	Y	N	Y	Y	N	Y
6 Clyburn	Y	Y	N	Y	Y	Y	N
SOUTH DAKOTA							
AL Johnson	N	Y	N	Y	Y	N	Y
TENNESSEE							
1 ***Quillen***	N	Y	Y	N	Y	N	Y
2 ***Duncan***	N	Y	Y	N	Y	N	Y
3 Lloyd	N	Y	N	Y	Y	N	Y
4 Cooper	Y	Y	N	Y	Y	N	Y
5 Clement	Y	N	N	Y	Y	N	Y
6 Gordon	Y	Y	N	Y	Y	N	Y
7 ***Sundquist***	N	Y	Y	N	Y	N	Y
8 Tanner	N	Y	N	Y	Y	N	Y
9 Ford	Y	Y	N	?	Y	Y	?
TEXAS							
1 Chapman	N	Y	Y	Y	Y	N	Y
2 Wilson	N	Y	N	Y	Y	N	Y
3 ***Johnson, Sam***	?	Y	Y	?	?	N	Y
4 Hall	N	Y	Y	Y	Y	N	Y
5 Bryant	N	N	N	Y	Y	Y	N
6 ***Barton***	N	Y	Y	N	Y	N	Y
7 ***Archer***	N	Y	Y	N	Y	N	Y
8 ***Fields***	?	Y	Y	N	Y	N	Y
9 Brooks	N	Y	N	Y	Y	Y	N
10 Pickle	N	Y	N	Y	Y	Y	Y
11 Edwards	N	Y	N	Y	Y	N	Y
12 Geren	N	Y	Y	?	Y	N	Y
13 Sarpalius	N	Y	Y	Y	Y	N	Y
14 Laughlin	?	?	?	?	?	?	?
15 de la Garza	N	Y	N	Y	Y	N	Y
16 Coleman	Y	Y	N	Y	Y	Y	N
17 Stenholm	N	Y	Y	Y	Y	N	Y
18 Washington	?	?	?	?	?	Y	N
19 ***Combest***	N	Y	Y	Y	Y	N	Y
20 Gonzalez	Y	N	N	Y	Y	Y	N
21 ***Smith***	N	Y	Y	N	Y	N	Y
22 ***DeLay***	N	Y	Y	N	Y	N	Y
23 ***Bonilla***	N	Y	Y	N	Y	N	Y
24 Frost	N	Y	N	Y	Y	N	Y
25 Andrews	Y	Y	N	Y	Y	Y	Y
26 ***Armey***	N	Y	Y	N	Y	N	Y
27 Ortiz	N	Y	N	Y	Y	N	Y
28 Tejeda	N	Y	N	?	Y	N	Y
29 Green	Y	Y	N	Y	Y	Y	N
30 Johnson, E.B.	N	N	N	Y	Y	Y	N
UTAH							
1 ***Hansen***	N	Y	Y	N	Y	N	Y
2 Shepherd	Y	N	N	Y	Y	Y	Y
3 Orton	N	Y	Y	Y	Y	N	Y
VERMONT							
AL *Sanders*	#	Y	N	Y	Y	Y	N
VIRGINIA							
1 ***Bateman***	N	Y	Y	Y	Y	N	Y
2 Pickett	N	Y	Y	Y	Y	N	Y
3 Scott	?	N	N	Y	Y	Y	N
4 Sisisky	N	Y	Y	Y	Y	N	Y
5 Payne	Y	Y	N	Y	Y	N	Y
6 ***Goodlatte***	N	Y	Y	N	Y	N	Y
7 ***Bliley***	N	Y	Y	N	Y	N	Y
8 Moran	Y	N	N	Y	?	Y	N
9 Boucher	Y	Y	N	?	Y	N	Y
10 ***Wolf***	N	Y	N	N	Y	N	Y
11 Byrne	Y	N	N	Y	Y	Y	N
WASHINGTON							
1 Cantwell	Y	N	N	Y	Y	Y	N
2 Swift	N	Y	N	Y	Y	Y	N
3 Unsoeld	Y	N	N	Y	Y	Y	N
4 Inslee	N	Y	N	Y	Y	N	Y
5 Foley							
6 Dicks	Y	Y	N	Y	?	Y	N
7 McDermott	Y	N	N	Y	Y	Y	N
8 ***Dunn***	N	Y	Y	N	Y	N	Y
9 Kreidler	Y	N	N	Y	Y	Y	N
WEST VIRGINIA							
1 Mollohan	?	Y	N	Y	Y	Y	Y
2 Wise	Y	Y	N	Y	?	N	Y
3 Rahall	Y	Y	N	Y	Y	N	Y
WISCONSIN							
1 Barca	Y	Y	N	Y	Y	N	Y
2 ***Klug***	Y	Y	N	N	Y	N	Y
3 ***Gunderson***	N	N	Y	N	Y	N	N
4 Kleczka	Y	Y	N	Y	Y	N	Y
5 Barrett	Y	N	N	Y	Y	N	Y
6 ***Petri***	Y	Y	Y	N	Y	N	Y
7 Obey	?	?	?	?	?	?	?
8 ***Roth***	Y	Y	Y	N	Y	N	Y
9 ***Sensenbrenner***	N	Y	Y	N	Y	N	Y
WYOMING							
AL ***Thomas***	N	Y	Y	N	Y	N	Y
DELEGATES							
de Lugo, V.I.	Y	N	N	D	Y	Y	N
Faleomavaega, Am.S.	Y	N	N	D	Y	Y	N
Norton, D.C.	Y	N	N	D	Y	Y	N
Romero-B., P.R.	?	N	N	D	Y	Y	Y
Underwood, Guam	Y	N	N	D	Y	Y	N

Southern states - Ala., Ark., Fla., Ga., Ky., La., Miss., N.C., Okla., S.C., Tenn., Texas, Va.
Omitted votes are quorum calls, which CQ does not include in its vote charts.

KEY

Y   Voted for (yea).
\#   Paired for.
\+   Announced for.
N   Voted against (nay).
X   Paired against.
–   Announced against.
P   Voted "present."
C   Voted "present" to avoid possible conflict of interest.
?   Did not vote or otherwise make a position known.
D   Delegates ineligible to vote.

Democrats   **Republicans**
Independent

322. HR 4649. Fiscal 1995 D.C. Appropriations/Passage.
Passage of the bill to appropriate $720 million for the District of Columbia in fiscal 1995 and approve the spending of $3,648,736,635 raised from local taxes. The administration requested $722 million and $3,690,438,635, respectively. The bill incorporated a compromise that requires the District to cut its budget by $150 million and requires that if the District incurs a deficit in fiscal 1995, it will face a corresponding reduction from its fiscal 1996 federal payment. Passed 213-210: R 14-161; D 198-49 (ND 142-26, SD 56-23); I 1-0, July 13, 1994.

323. HR 3355. Omnibus Crime Bill/Motion To Instruct.
Dunn, R-Wash., motion to instruct House conferees to insist on Senate provisions that call on states to track sexually violent offenders released from jail and allow law enforcement agencies acting in good faith — and with immunity from liability laws — to notify communities of their presence. Motion agreed to 407-13: R 173-0; D 233-13 (ND 161-7, SD 72-6); I 1-0, July 13, 1994.

324. HR 3355. Omnibus Crime Bill/Motion To Instruct.
Rohrabacher, R-Calif., motion to instruct the House conferees to insist on Senate provisions that prohibit federal programs from providing payments to people not lawfully present within the United States. Motion agreed to 289-121: R 164-4; D 125-116 (ND 79-86, SD 46-30); I 0-1, July 13, 1994.

325. HR 518. California Desert Protection/Land Appraisal.
Tauzin, D-La., amendment to require the government to ignore land-use restrictions and endangered species designations when appraising land under review to be designated wilderness. Adopted in the Committee of the Whole 281-148: R 160-16; D 121-131 (ND 66-106, SD 55-25); I 0-1, July 14, 1994.

	322	323	324	325
ALABAMA				
1 *Callahan*	N	Y	Y	Y
2 *Everett*	N	Y	Y	Y
3 Browder	N	Y	Y	Y
4 Bevill	Y	Y	Y	Y
5 Cramer	N	Y	Y	Y
6 *Bachus*	N	Y	Y	Y
7 Hilliard	Y	N	N	Y
ALASKA				
AL *Young*	N	Y	Y	Y
ARIZONA				
1 Coppersmith	Y	Y	Y	N
2 Pastor	Y	Y	N	Y
3 *Stump*	N	Y	Y	Y
4 *Kyl*	N	Y	Y	Y
5 *Kolbe*	N	Y	Y	Y
6 English	Y	Y	Y	N
ARKANSAS				
1 Lambert	Y	Y	Y	Y
2 Thornton	Y	Y	Y	Y
3 *Hutchinson*	N	Y	Y	Y
4 *Dickey*	N	Y	Y	Y
CALIFORNIA				
1 Hamburg	Y	Y	N	N
2 *Herger*	N	Y	Y	Y
3 Fazio	Y	Y	N	Y
4 *Doolittle*	N	Y	?	Y
5 Matsui	Y	Y	N	N
6 Woolsey	Y	Y	N	N
7 Miller	Y	Y	N	N
8 Pelosi	Y	Y	N	N
9 Dellums	Y	Y	N	N
10 *Baker*	N	Y	Y	Y
11 *Pombo*	N	Y	Y	Y
12 Lantos	Y	Y	N	N
13 Stark	Y	Y	N	N
14 Eshoo	Y	Y	N	N
15 Mineta	Y	Y	N	N
16 Edwards	Y	?	N	N
17 Farr	Y	Y	N	N
18 Condit	N	Y	Y	Y
19 Lehman	N	Y	Y	Y
20 Dooley	Y	Y	N	Y
21 *Thomas*	N	Y	Y	Y
22 *Huffington*	?	Y	Y	Y
23 *Gallegly*	N	Y	Y	Y
24 Beilenson	Y	Y	Y	N
25 *McKeon*	N	Y	Y	Y
26 Berman	Y	Y	N	N
27 *Moorhead*	N	Y	Y	Y
28 *Dreier*	N	Y	Y	Y
29 Waxman	Y	Y	N	N
30 Becerra	Y	Y	N	N
31 Martinez	Y	Y	N	Y
32 Dixon	Y	Y	N	N
33 Roybal-Allard	Y	Y	N	N
34 Torres	Y	Y	N	N
35 Waters	Y	N	N	N
36 Harman	Y	Y	Y	Y
37 Tucker	Y	Y	N	N
38 *Horn*	N	Y	Y	Y
39 *Royce*	N	Y	Y	Y
40 *Lewis*	N	Y	Y	Y
41 *Kim*	N	Y	Y	Y

	322	323	324	325
42 Brown	Y	Y	N	N
43 *Calvert*	N	Y	Y	Y
44 *McCandless*	N	Y	Y	Y
45 *Rohrabacher*	N	Y	Y	Y
46 *Dornan*	N	Y	Y	Y
47 *Cox*	N	Y	Y	Y
48 *Packard*	N	Y	Y	Y
49 Schenk	N	Y	Y	N
50 Filner	Y	Y	N	N
51 *Cunningham*	N	Y	Y	Y
52 *Hunter*	N	Y	Y	Y
COLORADO				
1 Schroeder	N	Y	N	N
2 Skaggs	Y	Y	N	N
3 *McInnis*	N	Y	Y	Y
4 *Allard*	N	Y	Y	Y
5 *Hefley*	N	Y	Y	Y
6 *Schaefer*	N	Y	Y	Y
CONNECTICUT				
1 Kennelly	Y	Y	Y	N
2 Gejdenson	Y	Y	Y	N
3 DeLauro	Y	Y	Y	N
4 *Shays*	N	Y	Y	N
5 *Franks*	Y	Y	Y	Y
6 *Johnson*	Y	Y	Y	Y
DELAWARE				
AL *Castle*	N	Y	Y	Y
FLORIDA				
1 Hutto	N	Y	Y	Y
2 Peterson	Y	Y	N	Y
3 Brown	Y	Y	N	N
4 *Fowler*	N	Y	Y	Y
5 Thurman	Y	Y	Y	Y
6 *Stearns*	N	Y	Y	Y
7 *Mica*	N	Y	Y	Y
8 *McCollum*	N	Y	Y	Y
9 *Bilirakis*	N	Y	Y	Y
10 *Young*	N	Y	Y	Y
11 Gibbons	Y	Y	N	N
12 *Canady*	N	Y	Y	Y
13 *Miller*	N	Y	Y	Y
14 *Goss*	N	Y	Y	N
15 Bacchus	Y	N	N	N
16 *Lewis*	N	Y	Y	Y
17 Meek	Y	N	N	N
18 *Ros-Lehtinen*	N	Y	N	N
19 Johnston	Y	Y	N	N
20 Deutsch	Y	Y	Y	N
21 *Diaz-Balart*	N	Y	N	Y
22 *Shaw*	N	Y	Y	Y
23 Hastings	Y	N	N	N
GEORGIA				
1 *Kingston*	N	Y	Y	Y
2 Bishop	?	?	?	?
3 *Collins*	N	Y	Y	Y
4 *Linder*	N	Y	Y	Y
5 Lewis	Y	Y	N	N
6 *Gingrich*	Y	Y	Y	Y
7 *Darden*	Y	Y	Y	Y
8 Rowland	X	?	?	Y
9 Deal	N	Y	Y	Y
10 Johnson	Y	Y	Y	Y
11 McKinney	Y	Y	N	N
HAWAII				
1 Abercrombie	Y	Y	N	N
2 Mink	Y	Y	N	N
IDAHO				
1 LaRocco	N	Y	Y	Y
2 *Crapo*	N	Y	Y	Y
ILLINOIS				
1 Rush	Y	Y	N	N
2 Reynolds	Y	Y	Y	N
3 Lipinski	N	Y	Y	Y
4 Gutierrez	Y	Y	N	N
5 Rostenkowski	Y	Y	N	N
6 *Hyde*	N	Y	Y	Y
7 Collins	Y	Y	N	N
8 *Crane*	N	Y	Y	Y
9 Yates	Y	Y	N	N
10 *Porter*	N	Y	Y	Y
11 Sangmeister	Y	Y	Y	Y
12 Costello	N	Y	Y	Y
13 *Fawell*	N	Y	Y	Y
14 *Hastert*	N	Y	Y	Y
15 *Ewing*	N	Y	Y	Y
16 *Manzullo*	N	Y	Y	Y
17 Evans	Y	Y	N	N

ND   Northern Democrats   SD   Southern Democrats

	322	323	324	325
18 ***Michel***	Y	Y	?	Y
19 Poshard	N	Y	Y	Y
20 Durbin	Y	Y	N	N
INDIANA				
1 Visclosky	Y	Y	N	N
2 Sharp	Y	Y	?	N
3 Roemer	N	Y	Y	Y
4 Long	N	Y	Y	Y
5 ***Buyer***	N	Y	Y	Y
6 ***Burton***	N	Y	Y	Y
7 ***Myers***	N	Y	Y	Y
8 McCloskey	Y	Y	Y	Y
9 Hamilton	N	Y	Y	Y
10 Jacobs	Y	Y	Y	Y
IOWA				
1 ***Leach***	N	Y	Y	Y
2 ***Nussle***	N	Y	Y	Y
3 ***Lightfoot***	N	Y	Y	Y
4 Smith	Y	Y	N	Y
5 ***Grandy***	N	Y	Y	Y
KANSAS				
1 ***Roberts***	N	Y	Y	Y
2 Slattery	?	?	?	?
3 ***Meyers***	N	Y	Y	Y
4 Glickman	Y	Y	Y	Y
KENTUCKY				
1 Barlow	Y	Y	Y	Y
2 ***Lewis***	N	Y	Y	Y
3 Mazzoli	Y	Y	Y	Y
4 ***Bunning***	N	Y	Y	Y
5 ***Rogers***	N	Y	Y	Y
6 Baesler	Y	Y	Y	Y
LOUISIANA				
1 ***Livingston***	N	Y	Y	Y
2 Jefferson	Y	Y	N	N
3 Tauzin	N	Y	Y	Y
4 Fields	Y	Y	N	N
5 ***McCrery***	N	Y	Y	Y
6 ***Baker***	N	Y	Y	Y
7 Hayes	N	Y	Y	Y
MAINE				
1 Andrews	Y	Y	N	N
2 ***Snowe***	N	Y	Y	N
MARYLAND				
1 ***Gilchrest***	N	Y	Y	N
2 ***Bentley***	N	Y	Y	Y
3 Cardin	Y	Y	N	N
4 Wynn	Y	Y	N	N
5 Hoyer	Y	Y	Y	Y
6 ***Bartlett***	N	Y	Y	Y
7 Mfume	Y	Y	N	N
8 ***Morella***	Y	Y	N	N
MASSACHUSETTS				
1 Olver	Y	Y	N	N
2 Neal	Y	Y	Y	N
3 ***Blute***	N	Y	Y	Y
4 Frank	Y	Y	?	N
5 Meehan	Y	Y	N	N
6 ***Torkildsen***	N	Y	Y	Y
7 Markey	Y	Y	N	N
8 Kennedy	?	Y	Y	N
9 Moakley	Y	Y	Y	N
10 Studds	Y	Y	N	N
MICHIGAN				
1 Stupak	N	Y	Y	Y
2 ***Hoekstra***	N	Y	Y	Y
3 ***Ehlers***	N	Y	Y	Y
4 ***Camp***	N	Y	Y	Y
5 Barcia	Y	Y	Y	Y
6 ***Upton***	N	Y	Y	Y
7 ***Smith***	N	Y	Y	Y
8 Carr	Y	Y	Y	?
9 Kildee	Y	Y	Y	N
10 Bonior	Y	Y	N	N
11 ***Knollenberg***	N	Y	Y	Y
12 Levin	Y	Y	Y	N
13 Ford	Y	Y	?	N
14 Conyers	Y	?	N	X
15 Collins	Y	Y	N	N
16 Dingell	Y	Y	Y	N
MINNESOTA				
1 Penny	Y	Y	Y	Y
2 Minge	Y	Y	Y	Y
3 ***Ramstad***	N	Y	Y	Y
4 Vento	Y	Y	N	N

	322	323	324	325
5 Sabo	Y	Y	N	N
6 ***Grams***	N	Y	Y	Y
7 Peterson	N	Y	Y	Y
8 Oberstar	Y	Y	N	N
MISSISSIPPI				
1 Whitten	Y	Y	?	Y
2 Thompson	Y	Y	N	N
3 Montgomery	N	Y	Y	Y
4 Parker	N	Y	Y	Y
5 Taylor	N	Y	Y	Y
MISSOURI				
1 Clay	Y	N	N	N
2 ***Talent***	N	Y	Y	Y
3 Gephardt	Y	Y	N	Y
4 Skelton	N	Y	Y	Y
5 Wheat	Y	Y	N	Y
6 Danner	N	Y	Y	Y
7 ***Hancock***	N	Y	Y	Y
8 ***Emerson***	N	Y	Y	Y
9 Volkmer	N	Y	Y	Y
MONTANA				
AL Williams	N	Y	Y	Y
NEBRASKA				
1 ***Bereuter***	N	Y	Y	Y
2 Hoagland	Y	Y	Y	N
3 ***Barrett***	N	Y	Y	Y
NEVADA				
1 Bilbray	Y	Y	Y	Y
2 ***Vucanovich***	N	Y	Y	Y
NEW HAMPSHIRE				
1 ***Zeliff***	N	Y	Y	Y
2 Swett	N	Y	Y	Y
NEW JERSEY				
1 Andrews	N	Y	Y	N
2 Hughes	Y	N	N	Y
3 ***Saxton***	N	Y	Y	N
4 ***Smith***	N	Y	N	N
5 ***Roukema***	N	Y	Y	Y
6 Pallone	Y	Y	Y	N
7 ***Franks***	N	Y	Y	N
8 Klein	Y	Y	Y	Y
9 Torricelli	N	Y	Y	N
10 Payne	Y	Y	N	N
11 ***Gallo***	?	?	?	?
12 ***Zimmer***	N	Y	Y	N
13 Menendez	Y	Y	N	N
NEW MEXICO				
1 ***Schiff***	N	Y	Y	Y
2 ***Skeen***	N	Y	Y	Y
3 Richardson	Y	Y	N	N
NEW YORK				
1 Hochbrueckner	Y	Y	Y	Y
2 ***Lazio***	N	Y	Y	Y
3 ***King***	N	Y	Y	Y
4 ***Levy***	N	Y	Y	Y
5 Ackerman	Y	Y	Y	Y
6 Flake	Y	Y	N	Y
7 Manton	Y	Y	N	N
8 Nadler	Y	N	N	N
9 Schumer	Y	Y	Y	N
10 Towns	Y	Y	N	N
11 Owens	Y	N	N	N
12 Velazquez	Y	Y	N	N
13 ***Molinari***	N	Y	Y	Y
14 Maloney	Y	Y	Y	N
15 Rangel	Y	N	N	N
16 Serrano	#	Y	N	N
17 Engel	Y	Y	N	N
18 Lowey	Y	Y	N	N
19 ***Fish***	Y	Y	?	Y
20 ***Gilman***	Y	Y	Y	Y
21 McNulty	Y	Y	N	Y
22 ***Solomon***	N	Y	Y	Y
23 ***Boehlert***	N	Y	Y	N
24 ***McHugh***	N	Y	Y	Y
25 ***Walsh***	Y	Y	Y	Y
26 Hinchey	Y	Y	N	N
27 ***Paxon***	N	Y	Y	Y
28 Slaughter	Y	Y	Y	N
29 LaFalce	Y	Y	Y	Y
30 ***Quinn***	N	Y	Y	Y
31 ***Houghton***	Y	Y	Y	Y
NORTH CAROLINA				
1 Clayton	Y	Y	N	N
2 Valentine	N	Y	Y	Y

	322	323	324	325
3 Lancaster	N	Y	Y	Y
4 Price	Y	Y	Y	Y
5 Neal	Y	Y	Y	Y
6 ***Coble***	N	Y	Y	Y
7 Rose	Y	Y	N	Y
8 Hefner	Y	Y	Y	Y
9 ***McMillan***	Y	Y	Y	Y
10 ***Ballenger***	Y	Y	Y	Y
11 ***Taylor***	N	Y	Y	Y
12 Watt	Y	N	N	N
NORTH DAKOTA				
AL Pomeroy	Y	Y	Y	Y
OHIO				
1 Mann	Y	Y	Y	N
2 ***Portman***	N	Y	Y	Y
3 Hall	Y	Y	Y	Y
4 ***Oxley***	N	Y	?	Y
5 ***Gillmor***	N	Y	Y	Y
6 Strickland	Y	Y	Y	Y
7 ***Hobson***	N	Y	Y	Y
8 ***Boehner***	N	?	?	Y
9 Kaptur	Y	Y	Y	Y
10 ***Hoke***	N	Y	Y	Y
11 Stokes	Y	Y	N	N
12 ***Kasich***	N	Y	Y	Y
13 Brown	Y	Y	Y	Y
14 Sawyer	Y	Y	N	Y
15 ***Pryce***	N	Y	Y	Y
16 ***Regula***	N	Y	Y	Y
17 Traficant	Y	Y	Y	Y
18 Applegate	Y	Y	?	Y
19 Fingerhut	N	Y	Y	N
OKLAHOMA				
1 ***Inhofe***	N	Y	Y	Y
2 Synar	Y	Y	N	N
3 Brewster	N	Y	Y	Y
4 McCurdy	?	?	?	?
5 ***Istook***	N	Y	Y	Y
6 ***Lucas***	N	Y	Y	Y
OREGON				
1 Furse	Y	Y	Y	N
2 ***Smith***	N	Y	?	Y
3 Wyden	Y	Y	Y	N
4 DeFazio	N	Y	Y	N
5 Kopetski	Y	N	N	N
PENNSYLVANIA				
1 Foglietta	Y	Y	N	N
2 Blackwell	Y	Y	N	N
3 Borski	Y	Y	N	N
4 Klink	Y	Y	Y	Y
5 ***Clinger***	N	Y	Y	Y
6 Holden	Y	Y	Y	Y
7 ***Weldon***	N	Y	Y	N
8 ***Greenwood***	N	Y	Y	N
9 ***Shuster***	N	Y	Y	Y
10 ***McDade***	?	?	?	Y
11 Kanjorski	Y	Y	Y	N
12 Murtha	Y	Y	?	Y
13 Margolies-Mezv.	Y	Y	Y	Y
14 Coyne	Y	Y	N	N
15 McHale	Y	Y	Y	Y
16 ***Walker***	N	Y	Y	Y
17 ***Gekas***	N	Y	Y	Y
18 ***Santorum***	N	Y	Y	Y
19 ***Goodling***	N	Y	Y	Y
20 Murphy	N	Y	N	Y
21 ***Ridge***	N	Y	Y	Y
RHODE ISLAND				
1 ***Machtley***	N	Y	Y	Y
2 Reed	Y	Y	N	Y
SOUTH CAROLINA				
1 ***Ravenel***	N	Y	Y	Y
2 ***Spence***	N	Y	Y	Y
3 Derrick	Y	Y	N	N
4 ***Inglis***	N	Y	Y	Y
5 Spratt	Y	Y	Y	Y
6 Clyburn	Y	Y	N	N
SOUTH DAKOTA				
AL Johnson	Y	Y	Y	N
TENNESSEE				
1 ***Quillen***	N	Y	Y	Y
2 ***Duncan***	N	Y	Y	Y
3 Lloyd	N	Y	Y	Y
4 Cooper	N	Y	Y	Y
5 Clement	Y	Y	Y	Y

	322	323	324	325
6 Gordon	Y	Y	Y	Y
7 ***Sundquist***	N	Y	Y	Y
8 Tanner	Y	Y	Y	Y
9 Ford	Y	Y	N	N
TEXAS				
1 Chapman	Y	Y	Y	Y
2 Wilson	Y	Y	?	Y
3 ***Johnson, Sam***	N	Y	Y	Y
4 Hall	N	Y	Y	Y
5 Bryant	Y	Y	Y	Y
6 ***Barton***	N	Y	Y	Y
7 ***Archer***	N	Y	Y	Y
8 ***Fields***	N	Y	Y	Y
9 Brooks	Y	N	N	Y
10 Pickle	Y	Y	N	N
11 Edwards	N	Y	Y	Y
12 Geren	N	Y	Y	Y
13 Sarpalius	N	Y	Y	Y
14 Laughlin	?	?	?	Y
15 de la Garza	N	Y	N	Y
16 Coleman	Y	Y	N	Y
17 Stenholm	N	Y	Y	Y
18 Washington	Y	?	?	?
19 ***Combest***	N	Y	Y	Y
20 Gonzalez	Y	N	N	N
21 ***Smith***	N	Y	Y	#
22 ***DeLay***	N	?	?	Y
23 ***Bonilla***	Y	Y	Y	Y
24 Frost	Y	Y	Y	Y
25 Andrews	Y	Y	Y	Y
26 ***Armey***	N	?	?	Y
27 Ortiz	N	Y	N	Y
28 Tejeda	N	Y	Y	Y
29 Green	Y	Y	N	Y
30 Johnson, E.B.	Y	Y	N	N
UTAH				
1 ***Hansen***	N	Y	Y	Y
2 Shepherd	N	Y	N	N
3 Orton	N	Y	Y	Y
VERMONT				
AL *Sanders*	Y	Y	N	N
VIRGINIA				
1 ***Bateman***	Y	Y	Y	Y
2 Pickett	N	Y	Y	Y
3 Scott	Y	Y	N	N
4 Sisisky	Y	Y	Y	Y
5 Payne	Y	Y	Y	Y
6 ***Goodlatte***	N	Y	Y	Y
7 ***Bliley***	Y	Y	Y	Y
8 Moran	Y	Y	N	N
9 Boucher	Y	Y	Y	N
10 ***Wolf***	N	Y	Y	Y
11 Byrne	Y	Y	Y	N
WASHINGTON				
1 Cantwell	Y	Y	Y	Y
2 Swift	Y	Y	N	Y
3 Unsoeld	Y	Y	N	N
4 Inslee	Y	Y	Y	Y
5 Foley				
6 Dicks	Y	Y	N	Y
7 McDermott	Y	Y	N	N
8 ***Dunn***	N	Y	Y	Y
9 Kreidler	Y	Y	Y	Y
WEST VIRGINIA				
1 Mollohan	Y	Y	Y	Y
2 Wise	Y	Y	Y	Y
3 Rahall	N	Y	Y	Y
WISCONSIN				
1 Barca	Y	Y	Y	Y
2 ***Klug***	N	Y	Y	N
3 ***Gunderson***	N	Y	Y	Y
4 Kleczka	Y	Y	N	Y
5 Barrett	Y	Y	Y	N
6 ***Petri***	N	Y	Y	Y
7 Obey	?	?	?	?
8 ***Roth***	N	Y	Y	Y
9 ***Sensenbrenner***	N	Y	Y	Y
WYOMING				
AL ***Thomas***	N	Y	Y	Y
DELEGATES				
de Lugo, V.I.	D	D	D	N
Faleomavaega, Am.S.	D	D	D	N
Norton, D.C.	D	D	D	N
Romero-B., P.R.	D	D	D	?
Underwood, Guam	D	D	D	N

Southern states - Ala., Ark., Fla., Ga., Ky., La., Miss., N.C., Okla., S.C., Tenn., Texas, Va.
Omitted votes are quorum calls, which CQ does not include in its vote charts.

KEY

Y   Voted for (yea).
\#   Paired for.
\+   Announced for.
N   Voted against (nay).
X   Paired against.
\-   Announced against.
P   Voted "present."
C   Voted "present" to avoid possible conflict of interest.
?   Did not vote or otherwise make a position known.
D   Delegates ineligible to vote.

Democrats   **Republicans**
Independent

326. HR 4600. Expedited Rescissions/Previous Question. Derrick, D-S.C., motion to order the previous question (thus ending debate and the possibility of amendment) on adoption of the rule (H Res 467) to provide for House floor consideration of the bill to strengthen the president's existing authority to propose to rescind any part of an appropriations bill by adding a new requirement that Congress vote on that rescission proposal within a specified period. Motion agreed to 240-185: R 0-175; D 239-10 (ND 161-7, SD 78-3); I 1-0, July 14, 1994.

327. HR 4600. Expedited Rescissions/Solomon Substitute. Solomon, R-N.Y., substitute amendment to the Stenholm, D-Texas, amendment, to make a presidential rescission package or targeted tax break repeal package automatically effective unless Congress passed a resolution of disapproval over a likely presidential veto. Rejected in the Committee of the Whole 205-218: R 173-0; D 32-217 (ND 20-150, SD 12-67); I 0-1, July 14, 1994.

328. HR 4600. Expedited Rescissions/Stenholm Substitute. Stenholm, D-Texas, substitute amendment to require Congress to vote on presidential proposals to cancel individual spending items in appropriations bills or targeted tax breaks in revenue bills. The substitute would make the procedures permanent, allow the president to utilize the procedures at any time, allow 50 representatives or 15 senators to offer a motion to strike from a rescissions package an individual proposal, and allow the president to specify that the savings go to deficit reduction. Adopted in the Committee of the Whole 298-121: R 170-0; D 128-120 (ND 76-92, SD 52-28); I 0-1, July 14, 1994.

329. HR 4600. Expedited Rescissions/Passage. Passage of the bill to require Congress to vote on presidential proposals to cancel individual spending items in appropriations bills or targeted tax breaks in revenue bills. Passed 342-69: R 169-0; D 173-68 (ND 109-53, SD 64-15); I 0-1, July 14, 1994.

330. HR 3937. Export Administration Act Reauthorization/Rule. Adoption of the rule (H Res 474) to provide for House floor consideration of the bill to reauthorize the Export Administration Act through 1998. Adopted 188-157: R 72-67; D 116-89 (ND 72-70, SD 44-19); I 0-1, July 14, 1994.

	326	327	328	329	330
ALABAMA					
1 *Callahan*	N	Y	Y	Y	N
2 *Everett*	N	Y	Y	Y	?
3 Browder	Y	N	Y	Y	Y
4 Bevill	Y	N	N	N	Y
5 Cramer	Y	N	Y	Y	Y
6 *Bachus*	N	Y	Y	Y	Y
7 Hilliard	Y	N	N	N	?
ALASKA					
AL *Young*	N	Y	Y	Y	Y
ARIZONA					
1 Coppersmith	N	Y	Y	Y	Y
2 Pastor	Y	N	N	Y	Y
3 *Stump*	N	Y	Y	Y	N
4 *Kyl*	N	Y	Y	Y	?
5 *Kolbe*	N	Y	Y	Y	Y
6 English	Y	N	Y	Y	N
ARKANSAS					
1 Lambert	Y	N	Y	Y	Y
2 Thornton	Y	N	Y	Y	Y
3 *Hutchinson*	N	Y	Y	Y	?
4 *Dickey*	N	Y	Y	Y	?
CALIFORNIA					
1 Hamburg	Y	N	N	N	N
2 *Herger*	N	Y	Y	Y	N
3 Fazio	Y	N	N	Y	Y
4 *Doolittle*	N	Y	Y	Y	N
5 Matsui	Y	N	N	N	N
6 Woolsey	Y	N	N	N	N
7 Miller	Y	N	N	N	N
8 Pelosi	Y	N	N	N	N
9 Dellums	Y	N	N	N	N
10 *Baker*	N	Y	Y	Y	N
11 *Pombo*	N	Y	Y	Y	N
12 Lantos	Y	N	Y	Y	Y
13 Stark	Y	N	N	N	?
14 Eshoo	Y	N	N	Y	Y
15 Mineta	Y	N	N	Y	Y
16 Edwards	Y	N	N	N	Y
17 Farr	Y	N	N	Y	N
18 Condit	Y	Y	Y	Y	N
19 Lehman	Y	N	Y	Y	Y
20 Dooley	Y	N	Y	Y	?
21 *Thomas*	N	Y	Y	Y	N
22 *Huffington*	N	Y	Y	Y	N
23 *Gallegly*	N	Y	Y	Y	?
24 Beilenson	Y	N	N	N	Y
25 *McKeon*	N	Y	Y	Y	N
26 Berman	Y	?	?	?	?
27 *Moorhead*	N	Y	Y	Y	N
28 *Dreier*	N	Y	Y	Y	N
29 Waxman	Y	N	N	N	?
30 Becerra	Y	N	N	N	Y
31 Martinez	Y	N	Y	Y	?
32 Dixon	Y	N	N	N	Y
33 Roybal-Allard	Y	N	N	N	Y
34 Torres	Y	N	N	N	N
35 Waters	Y	N	N	N	N
36 Harman	Y	N	Y	Y	Y
37 Tucker	Y	N	N	N	N
38 *Horn*	N	Y	Y	Y	N
39 *Royce*	N	Y	Y	Y	Y
40 *Lewis*	N	Y	Y	Y	N
41 *Kim*	N	Y	Y	Y	N

	326	327	328	329	330
42 Brown	Y	N	N	Y	Y
43 *Calvert*	N	Y	?	?	X
44 *McCandless*	N	Y	Y	Y	N
45 *Rohrabacher*	N	Y	Y	Y	Y
46 *Dornan*	N	Y	Y	Y	N
47 *Cox*	N	Y	Y	Y	N
48 *Packard*	N	Y	Y	Y	Y
49 Schenk	Y	Y	Y	Y	N
50 Filner	Y	N	N	N	N
51 *Cunningham*	N	Y	Y	Y	?
52 *Hunter*	N	Y	Y	Y	Y
COLORADO					
1 Schroeder	Y	N	Y	Y	Y
2 Skaggs	Y	N	Y	Y	Y
3 *McInnis*	N	Y	Y	Y	N
4 *Allard*	N	Y	Y	Y	N
5 *Hefley*	N	Y	Y	Y	N
6 *Schaefer*	N	Y	Y	Y	Y
CONNECTICUT					
1 Kennelly	Y	N	N	N	N
2 Gejdenson	Y	N	N	Y	N
3 DeLauro	Y	N	N	Y	N
4 *Shays*	N	Y	Y	Y	N
5 *Franks*	N	Y	Y	Y	Y
6 *Johnson*	N	Y	Y	Y	Y
DELAWARE					
AL *Castle*	N	Y	Y	Y	N
FLORIDA					
1 Hutto	Y	N	Y	Y	Y
2 Peterson	Y	N	Y	Y	Y
3 Brown	Y	N	N	N	Y
4 *Fowler*	N	Y	Y	+	-
5 Thurman	Y	N	Y	Y	N
6 *Stearns*	N	Y	Y	Y	Y
7 *Mica*	N	Y	Y	Y	?
8 *McCollum*	N	Y	Y	Y	?
9 *Bilirakis*	N	Y	Y	Y	Y
10 *Young*	N	Y	Y	Y	?
11 Gibbons	Y	N	N	N	Y
12 *Canady*	N	Y	Y	Y	Y
13 *Miller*	N	Y	Y	Y	Y
14 *Goss*	N	Y	Y	Y	Y
15 Bacchus	Y	Y	Y	Y	Y
16 *Lewis*	N	Y	Y	Y	?
17 Meek	Y	N	N	N	N
18 *Ros-Lehtinen*	N	Y	Y	Y	N
19 Johnston	Y	N	Y	Y	Y
20 Deutsch	Y	Y	Y	Y	N
21 *Diaz-Balart*	N	Y	Y	Y	N
22 *Shaw*	N	Y	Y	Y	Y
23 Hastings	Y	N	N	N	N
GEORGIA					
1 *Kingston*	N	Y	Y	Y	Y
2 Bishop	?	?	Y	Y	Y
3 *Collins*	N	Y	Y	Y	N
4 *Linder*	N	Y	Y	Y	Y
5 Lewis	Y	N	N	N	N
6 *Gingrich*	N	Y	Y	Y	Y
7 Darden	Y	N	Y	Y	Y
8 Rowland	Y	N	Y	Y	N
9 *Deal*	N	Y	Y	Y	N
10 Johnson	Y	N	Y	Y	?
11 McKinney	Y	N	N	N	N
HAWAII					
1 Abercrombie	Y	N	N	N	Y
2 Mink	Y	N	N	N	N
IDAHO					
1 LaRocco	Y	N	Y	Y	Y
2 *Crapo*	N	Y	Y	Y	Y
ILLINOIS					
1 Rush	Y	N	N	N	N
2 Reynolds	Y	N	N	N	Y
3 Lipinski	Y	N	N	Y	?
4 Gutierrez	Y	N	Y	Y	?
5 Rostenkowski	Y	N	N	N	?
6 *Hyde*	N	Y	Y	Y	N
7 Collins	Y	N	N	N	N
8 *Crane*	N	Y	Y	Y	N
9 Yates	Y	N	N	N	N
10 *Porter*	N	Y	Y	Y	N
11 Sangmeister	Y	N	Y	Y	?
12 Costello	Y	N	Y	Y	?
13 *Fawell*	N	Y	Y	Y	N
14 *Hastert*	N	Y	Y	Y	N
15 *Ewing*	N	Y	Y	Y	N
16 *Manzullo*	N	Y	Y	Y	N
17 Evans	Y	N	N	N	N

ND   Northern Democrats   SD   Southern Democrats

	326	327	328	329	330
18 Michel	N	Y	Y	Y	Y
19 Poshard	Y	Y	Y	Y	Y
20 Durbin	Y	N	N	Y	N
INDIANA					
1 Visclosky	Y	N	Y	Y	Y
2 Sharp	Y	N	Y	Y	?
3 Roemer	Y	N	Y	Y	Y
4 Long	Y	N	Y	Y	Y
5 *Buyer*	N	Y	Y	Y	N
6 *Burton*	N	Y	?	?	?
7 *Myers*	N	Y	Y	Y	Y
8 McCloskey	Y	N	N	Y	N
9 Hamilton	N	N	Y	Y	Y
10 Jacobs	N	N	Y	Y	Y
IOWA					
1 *Leach*	N	Y	Y	Y	Y
2 *Nussle*	N	Y	Y	Y	Y
3 *Lightfoot*	N	Y	Y	Y	N
4 Smith	Y	N	N	N	Y
5 *Grandy*	N	Y	Y	Y	N
KANSAS					
1 *Roberts*	N	Y	Y	Y	Y
2 Slattery	?	?	?	?	?
3 *Meyers*	N	Y	Y	Y	?
4 Glickman	N	N	Y	Y	Y
KENTUCKY					
1 Barlow	Y	N	Y	Y	N
2 *Lewis*	N	Y	Y	Y	Y
3 Mazzoli	Y	Y	Y	Y	Y
4 *Bunning*	N	Y	Y	Y	Y
5 *Rogers*	N	Y	Y	Y	Y
6 Baesler	Y	Y	Y	Y	Y
LOUISIANA					
1 *Livingston*	N	Y	Y	Y	Y
2 Jefferson	Y	N	N	N	?
3 Tauzin	Y	Y	Y	Y	Y
4 Fields	Y	N	N	Y	Y
5 *McCrery*	N	Y	Y	Y	?
6 *Baker*	N	Y	Y	Y	?
7 Hayes	Y	Y	Y	Y	N
MAINE					
1 Andrews	Y	N	Y	Y	N
2 *Snowe*	N	Y	Y	Y	N
MARYLAND					
1 *Gilchrest*	N	Y	Y	Y	N
2 *Bentley*	N	Y	Y	Y	?
3 Cardin	Y	N	Y	?	?
4 Wynn	Y	N	Y	Y	Y
5 Hoyer	Y	N	N	Y	Y
6 *Bartlett*	N	Y	Y	Y	Y
7 Mfume	Y	N	N	N	Y
8 *Morella*	N	Y	Y	Y	Y
MASSACHUSETTS					
1 Olver	Y	N	N	Y	N
2 Neal	Y	N	N	Y	N
3 *Blute*	N	Y	Y	Y	N
4 Frank	Y	N	Y	Y	N
5 Meehan	Y	Y	Y	Y	N
6 *Torkildsen*	N	N	Y	Y	N
7 Markey	Y	N	Y	Y	N
8 Kennedy	Y	N	Y	Y	N
9 Moakley	Y	N	N	Y	N
10 Studds	Y	N	N	Y	?
MICHIGAN					
1 Stupak	Y	N	Y	Y	N
2 *Hoekstra*	N	Y	Y	Y	N
3 *Ehlers*	N	Y	Y	Y	N
4 *Camp*	N	Y	Y	Y	N
5 Barcia	Y	Y	Y	Y	N
6 *Upton*	N	Y	Y	Y	N
7 *Smith*	N	Y	Y	Y	?
8 Carr	?	?	?	?	?
9 Kildee	Y	N	Y	Y	N
10 Bonior	Y	N	N	?	Y
11 *Knollenberg*	N	Y	Y	Y	N
12 Levin	Y	N	Y	Y	N
13 Ford	Y	?	?	?	?
14 Conyers	Y	N	N	N	?
15 Collins	Y	N	N	N	?
16 Dingell	Y	N	N	Y	N
MINNESOTA					
1 Penny	Y	Y	Y	Y	N
2 Minge	Y	Y	Y	Y	N
3 *Ramstad*	N	Y	Y	Y	N
4 Vento	Y	N	N	N	N

	326	327	328	329	330
5 Sabo	Y	N	N	N	?
6 *Grams*	N	Y	Y	Y	Y
7 Peterson	Y	Y	Y	Y	N
8 Oberstar	Y	N	N	N	N
MISSISSIPPI					
1 Whitten	Y	N	N	Y	Y
2 Thompson	Y	N	N	Y	?
3 Montgomery	Y	N	Y	Y	Y
4 Parker	Y	Y	Y	Y	?
5 Taylor	N	N	Y	Y	Y
MISSOURI					
1 Clay	Y	N	N	N	?
2 *Talent*	N	Y	Y	Y	Y
3 Gephardt	Y	N	N	N	Y
4 Skelton	Y	N	Y	Y	Y
5 Wheat	Y	N	?	?	N
6 Danner	Y	N	Y	Y	?
7 *Hancock*	N	Y	Y	Y	N
8 *Emerson*	N	Y	Y	Y	N
9 Volkmer	Y	N	Y	Y	?
MONTANA					
AL Williams	Y	N	Y	Y	N
NEBRASKA					
1 *Bereuter*	N	Y	Y	Y	Y
2 Hoagland	Y	N	Y	Y	Y
3 *Barrett*	N	Y	Y	Y	Y
NEVADA					
1 Bilbray	Y	N	Y	Y	N
2 *Vucanovich*	N	Y	Y	Y	N
NEW HAMPSHIRE					
1 *Zeliff*	?	?	?	?	?
2 Swett	N	Y	Y	Y	N
NEW JERSEY					
1 Andrews	N	Y	Y	Y	Y
2 Hughes	Y	N	Y	Y	N
3 *Saxton*	N	Y	Y	Y	N
4 *Smith*	N	Y	Y	Y	N
5 *Roukema*	N	Y	Y	Y	N
6 *Pallone*	Y	Y	Y	Y	N
7 *Franks*	N	Y	Y	Y	N
8 Klein	Y	N	Y	Y	Y
9 Torricelli	Y	N	Y	Y	N
10 Payne	Y	N	N	N	N
11 *Gallo*	?	?	?	?	?
12 *Zimmer*	N	Y	Y	Y	Y
13 Menendez	Y	N	N	N	N
NEW MEXICO					
1 *Schiff*	N	Y	Y	Y	?
2 *Skeen*	N	Y	Y	Y	Y
3 Richardson	Y	N	Y	Y	N
NEW YORK					
1 Hochbrueckner	Y	N	Y	Y	Y
2 *Lazio*	N	Y	Y	Y	N
3 *King*	N	Y	Y	Y	N
4 *Levy*	N	Y	Y	Y	N
5 Ackerman	Y	N	N	Y	Y
6 Flake	Y	N	N	Y	Y
7 Manton	Y	N	Y	Y	Y
8 Nadler	Y	N	N	N	N
9 Schumer	Y	N	Y	Y	Y
10 Towns	?	N	N	N	Y
11 Owens	Y	N	N	N	?
12 Velazquez	Y	N	N	Y	N
13 *Molinari*	N	Y	Y	Y	Y
14 Maloney	Y	N	Y	Y	N
15 Rangel	Y	N	N	N	N
16 Serrano	Y	N	N	N	Y
17 Engel	Y	N	N	N	Y
18 Lowey	Y	N	N	Y	N
19 Fish	N	Y	?	?	?
20 Gilman	N	Y	Y	Y	Y
21 McNulty	Y	N	N	Y	N
22 *Solomon*	N	Y	Y	Y	?
23 *Boehlert*	N	Y	Y	Y	?
24 *McHugh*	N	Y	Y	Y	Y
25 *Walsh*	N	Y	Y	Y	?
26 Hinchey	Y	N	N	Y	N
27 *Paxon*	N	Y	Y	Y	Y
28 Slaughter	Y	N	Y	Y	Y
29 LaFalce	Y	N	Y	Y	Y
30 *Quinn*	N	Y	Y	Y	Y
31 *Houghton*	N	Y	Y	Y	#
NORTH CAROLINA					
1 Clayton	Y	N	N	N	N
2 Valentine	Y	N	Y	Y	?

	326	327	328	329	330
3 Lancaster	Y	N	Y	Y	?
4 Price	Y	N	Y	Y	Y
5 Neal	Y	N	Y	Y	Y
6 *Coble*	N	Y	Y	Y	N
7 Rose	Y	N	Y	Y	?
8 Hefner	Y	?	?	?	?
9 *McMillan*	N	Y	Y	Y	?
10 *Ballenger*	N	Y	Y	Y	N
11 *Taylor*	N	Y	Y	Y	N
12 Watt	Y	N	N	N	N
NORTH DAKOTA					
AL Pomeroy	Y	N	Y	Y	N
OHIO					
1 Mann	Y	Y	Y	Y	Y
2 *Portman*	N	Y	Y	Y	Y
3 Hall	Y	N	N	Y	?
4 *Oxley*	N	Y	Y	Y	?
5 *Gillmor*	N	Y	Y	Y	?
6 Strickland	Y	N	Y	Y	N
7 *Hobson*	N	Y	Y	Y	N
8 *Boehner*	N	Y	Y	Y	N
9 Kaptur	Y	N	Y	Y	N
10 *Hoke*	N	Y	Y	Y	N
11 Stokes	Y	N	N	Y	N
12 *Kasich*	N	Y	Y	Y	N
13 Brown	Y	N	N	N	N
14 Sawyer	Y	N	Y	Y	N
15 *Pryce*	N	Y	Y	Y	N
16 *Regula*	N	Y	Y	Y	N
17 Traficant	Y	N	N	N	N
18 Applegate	Y	N	N	N	?
19 Fingerhut	Y	Y	Y	Y	Y
OKLAHOMA					
1 *Inhofe*	N	Y	Y	Y	?
2 Synar	Y	N	N	Y	?
3 Brewster	Y	N	N	Y	?
4 McCurdy	#	?	?	?	?
5 *Istook*	N	Y	Y	Y	Y
6 *Lucas*	N	Y	Y	Y	Y
OREGON					
1 Furse	Y	N	Y	Y	N
2 *Smith*	N	Y	Y	Y	?
3 Wyden	Y	N	Y	Y	Y
4 DeFazio	Y	N	Y	Y	N
5 Kopetski	Y	N	N	N	Y
PENNSYLVANIA					
1 Foglietta	Y	N	N	Y	?
2 Blackwell	Y	N	N	?	N
3 Borski	Y	N	N	N	N
4 Klink	Y	N	N	N	N
5 Clinger	Y	Y	Y	Y	?
6 Holden	Y	Y	Y	Y	Y
7 *Weldon*	N	Y	Y	Y	N
8 *Greenwood*	N	Y	Y	Y	?
9 *Shuster*	N	Y	Y	Y	N
10 *McDade*	N	Y	Y	Y	Y
11 Kanjorski	N	N	N	N	N
12 Murtha	Y	N	?	?	?
13 Margolies-Mezv.	Y	N	Y	Y	N
14 Coyne	Y	N	N	Y	N
15 McHale	Y	Y	Y	Y	N
16 *Walker*	N	Y	Y	Y	N
17 *Gekas*	N	Y	Y	Y	N
18 *Santorum*	N	Y	Y	Y	N
19 *Goodling*	N	Y	Y	Y	N
20 Murphy	Y	N	Y	Y	?
21 *Ridge*	N	Y	Y	Y	?
RHODE ISLAND					
1 *Machtley*	N	Y	Y	Y	Y
2 Reed	Y	N	N	N	Y
SOUTH CAROLINA					
1 *Ravenel*	N	Y	Y	Y	N
2 *Spence*	N	Y	Y	Y	Y
3 Derrick	Y	N	N	Y	N
4 *Inglis*	N	Y	Y	Y	N
5 Spratt	Y	N	Y	Y	Y
6 Clyburn	Y	N	N	Y	?
SOUTH DAKOTA					
AL Johnson	Y	N	Y	Y	N
TENNESSEE					
1 *Quillen*	X	?	?	?	?
2 *Duncan*	N	Y	Y	Y	N
3 Lloyd	Y	N	Y	Y	?
4 *Cooper*	N	Y	Y	Y	N
5 Clement	Y	N	Y	Y	Y

	326	327	328	329	330
6 Gordon	Y	N	Y	Y	Y
7 *Sundquist*	N	Y	Y	Y	Y
8 Tanner	Y	N	Y	Y	Y
9 Ford	Y	N	Y	?	Y
TEXAS					
1 Chapman	Y	N	Y	Y	Y
2 Wilson	Y	Y	Y	Y	?
3 *Johnson, Sam*	N	Y	Y	Y	N
4 Hall	Y	Y	Y	Y	N
5 Bryant	Y	N	Y	Y	N
6 *Barton*	N	Y	Y	Y	?
7 *Archer*	N	Y	Y	Y	N
8 *Fields*	N	+	+	+	?
9 Brooks	Y	N	N	Y	N
10 Pickle	Y	N	N	Y	Y
11 Edwards	Y	N	Y	Y	Y
12 Geren	Y	Y	Y	Y	Y
13 Sarpalius	Y	N	N	Y	Y
14 Laughlin	Y	N	Y	Y	Y
15 de la Garza	Y	N	Y	Y	N
16 Coleman	Y	N	Y	Y	N
17 Stenholm	Y	N	Y	Y	?
18 Washington	Y	?	?	?	?
19 *Combest*	N	Y	Y	Y	N
20 Gonzalez	Y	N	N	N	N
21 *Smith*	N	Y	Y	Y	Y
22 *DeLay*	N	Y	Y	Y	N
23 *Bonilla*	N	Y	Y	Y	Y
24 Frost	Y	N	Y	Y	Y
25 Andrews	Y	N	Y	?	Y
26 *Armey*	N	Y	Y	Y	N
27 Ortiz	Y	N	Y	Y	N
28 Tejeda	Y	N	Y	Y	Y
29 Green	Y	N	Y	?	Y
30 Johnson, E.B.	Y	N	N	Y	N
UTAH					
1 *Hansen*	N	Y	Y	Y	N
2 Shepherd	Y	N	Y	Y	N
3 Orton	Y	Y	Y	Y	N
VERMONT					
AL *Sanders*	Y	N	N	N	N
VIRGINIA					
1 *Bateman*	N	Y	Y	Y	Y
2 Pickett	Y	N	Y	Y	Y
3 Scott	Y	N	N	N	N
4 Sisisky	Y	N	Y	Y	Y
5 Payne	Y	N	Y	Y	Y
6 *Goodlatte*	N	Y	Y	Y	N
7 *Bliley*	N	Y	Y	N	N
8 Moran	Y	N	N	N	?
9 Boucher	Y	N	Y	Y	N
10 *Wolf*	N	Y	Y	Y	Y
11 Byrne	Y	N	Y	Y	N
WASHINGTON					
1 Cantwell	Y	Y	Y	Y	Y
2 Swift	Y	N	N	Y	N
3 Unsoeld	Y	N	N	Y	N
4 Inslee	Y	N	Y	Y	Y
5 Foley					
6 Dicks	Y	N	Y	Y	N
7 McDermott	Y	N	N	Y	N
8 *Dunn*	N	Y	Y	Y	Y
9 Kreidler	Y	N	Y	Y	N
WEST VIRGINIA					
1 Mollohan	Y	N	N	N	Y
2 Wise	Y	N	Y	Y	N
3 Rahall	Y	N	N	N	N
WISCONSIN					
1 Barca	Y	Y	Y	Y	N
2 *Klug*	N	Y	Y	Y	?
3 *Gunderson*	N	Y	Y	Y	N
4 Kleczka	Y	N	Y	Y	N
5 Barrett	Y	Y	Y	Y	N
6 *Petri*	N	Y	Y	Y	?
7 Obey	?	?	?	?	?
8 *Roth*	N	Y	Y	Y	N
9 *Sensenbrenner*	N	Y	Y	Y	Y
WYOMING					
AL *Thomas*	N	+	+	+	?
DELEGATES					
de Lugo, V.I.	D	N	N	D	D
Faleomavaega, Am.S.	D	?	?	D	D
Norton, D.C.	D	N	N	D	D
Romero-B., P.R.	D	N	N	D	D
Underwood, Guam	D	?	?	D	D

Southern states - Ala., Ark., Fla., Ga., Ky., La., Miss., N.C., Okla., S.C., Tenn., Texas, Va.
Omitted votes are quorum calls, which CQ does not include in its vote charts.

331. HR 820. National Competitiveness Bill/Motion To Instruct. Walker, R-Pa., motion to instruct the House conferees on the national competitiveness bill (HR 820) to allow judicial review of agency compliance with the Regulatory Flexibility Act (PL 96-354), which requires regulatory agencies to consider the impact of proposed regulations and rules on small businesses and local governments. Motion agreed to 380-36: R 172-0; D 207-36 (ND 132-32, SD 75-4); I 1-0, July 19, 1994.

332. HR 4299. Fiscal 1995 Intelligence Authorization/ Budgetary Disclosure. Glickman, D-Kan., amendment to require public disclosure of total budgetary requests, authorizations and appropriations for intelligence agencies. Rejected in the Committee of the Whole 194-221: R 17-155; D 176-66 (ND 142-25, SD 34-41); I 1-0, July 19, 1994. A "nay" was a vote in support of the president's position.

333. HR 4299. Fiscal 1995 Intelligence Authorization/ Spending Cut. Sanders, I-Vt., amendment to cut the bill's authorization by 10 percent below the fiscal 1994 level. Rejected in the Committee of the Whole 106-315: R 8-163; D 97-152 (ND 79-93, SD 18-59); I 1-0, July 19, 1994.

334. HR 8. Federal Nutrition Programs Reauthorization/Passage. Kildee, D-Mich., motion to suspend the rules and pass the bill to reauthorize through fiscal 1998 eight expiring nutrition programs, including the Women, Infants and Children program, under the National School Lunch Act and the Child Nutrition Act of 1966. The bill also is intended to reduce paperwork and increase flexibility in the programs. Motion agreed to 372-40: R 130-39; D 241-1 (ND 162-1, SD 79-0); I 1-0, July 19, 1994. A two-thirds majority of those present and voting (275 in this case) is required for passage under suspension of the rules.

335. HR 4299. Fiscal 1995 Intelligence Authorization/ Drug Interdiction Cut. Frank, D-Mass., amendment to cut the amount provided for counter-narcotics and drug interdiction activities by intelligence agencies by $100 million. Rejected in the Committee of the Whole 18-406: R 0-173; D 18-232 (ND 17-154, SD 1-78); I 0-1, July 20, 1994.

336. HR 4299. Fiscal 1995 Intelligence Authorization/ Passage. Passage of the bill to authorize a classified amount for the activities of the CIA, the Defense Intelligence Agency, the National Security Agency and other U.S. intelligence agencies and activities in fiscal 1995. The amount has been estimated to be about $28 billion. Passed 410-16: R 170-3; D 240-12 (ND 161-11, SD 79-1); I 0-1, July 20, 1994.

337. HR 1188. Insurance Anti-Redlining Disclosure/ HUD Jurisdiction. Kennedy, D-Mass., amendment to place the responsibility for collecting and disclosing information required by the bill with the Department of Housing and Urban Development (HUD) rather than the Department of Commerce and require that all reports be transmitted to the Banking, Finance and Urban Affairs Committee instead of to the Energy and Commerce Committee. Rejected in the Committee of the Whole 88-343: R 3-172; D 84-171 (ND 70-105, SD 14-66); I 1-0, July 20, 1994.

338. HR 1188. Insurance Anti-Redlining Disclosure/ Reporting Requirements. Roybal-Allard, D-Calif., amendment to increase from 25 to 75 the number of metropolitan areas in which insurers must provide the Commerce Department with data; require insurers to provide voluntarily supplied data from policy applicants and policyholders on their race, ethnicity and gender; require insurers to report the amount paid out in claims by five-digit ZIP code; allow reporting of information by nine-digit ZIP code or census tract; and exempt small insurance companies from the reporting requirements; Rejected in the Committee of the Whole 97-333: R 1-174; D 95-159 (ND 80-95, SD 15-64); I 1-0, July 20, 1994.

KEY

Y   Voted for (yea).
Paired for.
+   Announced for.
N   Voted against (nay).
X   Paired against.
−   Announced against.
P   Voted "present."
C   Voted "present" to avoid possible conflict of interest.
?   Did not vote or otherwise make a position known.
D   Delegates ineligible to vote.

Democrats **Republicans**
Independent

	331	332	333	334	335	336	337	338
ALABAMA								
1 *Callahan*	Y	N	N	N	N	Y	N	N
2 *Everett*	Y	N	N	Y	N	Y	N	N
3 Browder	Y	N	N	Y	N	Y	N	N
4 Bevill	Y	N	N	Y	N	Y	N	N
5 Cramer	Y	N	N	Y	N	Y	N	N
6 *Bachus*	Y	N	N	N	N	Y	N	N
7 Hilliard	Y	Y	Y	Y	N	Y	N	N
ALASKA								
AL *Young*	Y	N	N	Y	N	Y	N	N
ARIZONA								
1 Coppersmith	Y	Y	N	Y	N	Y	N	N
2 Pastor	Y	Y	Y	Y	N	Y	Y	Y
3 *Stump*	Y	N	N	N	N	Y	N	N
4 *Kyl*	Y	N	N	Y	N	Y	N	N
5 *Kolbe*	Y	N	N	Y	N	Y	N	N
6 English	Y	Y	Y	Y	N	Y	N	N
ARKANSAS								
1 Lambert	Y	Y	Y	Y	N	Y	N	N
2 Thornton	Y	Y	N	Y	N	Y	N	N
3 *Hutchinson*	Y	N	N	Y	N	Y	N	N
4 *Dickey*	Y	N	N	Y	N	Y	N	N
CALIFORNIA								
1 Hamburg	Y	Y	Y	Y	N	N	N	Y
2 *Herger*	Y	N	N	Y	N	Y	N	N
3 Fazio	Y	Y	N	Y	N	Y	N	N
4 *Doolittle*	Y	N	N	N	N	Y	N	N
5 Matsui	Y	Y	N	Y	N	Y	N	N
6 Woolsey	Y	Y	Y	Y	N	Y	N	N
7 Miller	N	Y	Y	Y	N	Y	Y	Y
8 Pelosi	N	Y	N	Y	N	Y	Y	Y
9 Dellums	N	Y	Y	Y	N	Y	Y	Y
10 *Baker*	Y	N	N	Y	N	Y	N	N
11 *Pombo*	Y	N	N	Y	N	Y	N	N
12 Lantos	Y	N	N	Y	N	Y	N	N
13 Stark	N	Y	Y	Y	?	N	Y	Y
14 Eshoo	N	Y	N	Y	N	Y	Y	Y
15 Mineta	N	Y	N	Y	N	Y	Y	Y
16 Edwards	?	?	Y	Y	Y	Y	Y	Y
17 Farr	Y	Y	Y	Y	N	Y	Y	Y
18 Condit	Y	N	N	Y	N	Y	N	N
19 Lehman	Y	Y	N	Y	N	Y	N	N
20 Dooley	Y	Y	N	Y	N	Y	N	N
21 *Thomas*	Y	N	N	Y	N	Y	N	N
22 *Huffington*	Y	N	N	Y	N	Y	N	N
23 *Gallegly*	Y	N	N	Y	N	Y	N	N
24 Beilenson	N	Y	N	Y	N	Y	Y	Y
25 *McKeon*	Y	N	N	Y	N	Y	N	N
26 Berman	?	Y	N	Y	N	Y	Y	Y
27 *Moorhead*	Y	N	N	Y	N	?	N	N
28 *Dreier*	Y	N	N	Y	N	Y	N	N
29 Waxman	Y	Y	N	Y	N	Y	N	Y
30 Becerra	N	Y	Y	Y	N	Y	Y	Y
31 Martinez	Y	?	N	Y	N	Y	N	Y
32 Dixon	Y	Y	N	Y	N	Y	N	Y
33 Roybal-Allard	N	Y	N	Y	N	Y	Y	Y
34 Torres	Y	Y	Y	Y	N	Y	Y	Y
35 Waters	N	Y	Y	Y	N	Y	Y	Y
36 Harman	Y	Y	N	Y	N	Y	N	Y
37 Tucker	Y	Y	Y	Y	N	Y	N	Y
38 *Horn*	Y	N	N	Y	N	Y	N	N
39 *Royce*	Y	?	N	N	N	Y	N	N
40 *Lewis*	Y	N	N	Y	N	Y	N	N
41 *Kim*	Y	N	N	Y	N	Y	N	N

	331	332	333	334	335	336	337	338
42 Brown	N	Y	Y	Y	N	N	Y	Y
43 *Calvert*	?	N	N	Y	N	Y	N	N
44 *McCandless*	Y	N	N	Y	N	Y	N	N
45 *Rohrabacher*	Y	Y	Y	N	Y	Y	N	N
46 *Dornan*	Y	N	N	Y	N	Y	N	N
47 *Cox*	?	N	N	Y	N	Y	N	N
48 *Packard*	Y	N	N	Y	N	Y	N	N
49 Schenk	Y	Y	N	Y	N	Y	N	N
50 Filner	Y	Y	Y	Y	N	Y	Y	Y
51 *Cunningham*	Y	N	N	Y	N	Y	N	N
52 *Hunter*	Y	N	N	N	N	Y	N	N
COLORADO								
1 Schroeder	N	Y	Y	Y	Y	N	Y	Y
2 Skaggs	Y	Y	N	Y	N	Y	N	N
3 *McInnis*	Y	N	N	Y	N	Y	N	N
4 *Allard*	Y	N	N	N	N	Y	N	N
5 *Hefley*	Y	N	N	N	N	Y	N	N
6 *Schaefer*	Y	N	N	N	N	Y	N	N
CONNECTICUT								
1 Kennelly	Y	Y	N	Y	N	Y	N	N
2 Gejdenson	Y	Y	Y	Y	N	Y	Y	N
3 DeLauro	Y	Y	Y	Y	N	Y	N	N
4 *Shays*	Y	Y	Y	Y	N	Y	N	N
5 *Franks*	Y	N	N	Y	N	Y	N	N
6 *Johnson*	Y	N	N	Y	N	Y	N	N
DELAWARE								
AL *Castle*	Y	N	N	Y	N	Y	N	N
FLORIDA								
1 Hutto	Y	N	N	Y	N	Y	N	N
2 Peterson	Y	N	N	Y	N	Y	N	N
3 Brown	Y	N	N	Y	N	Y	N	Y
4 *Fowler*	Y	N	N	Y	N	Y	N	N
5 Thurman	Y	Y	N	Y	N	Y	N	N
6 *Stearns*	Y	N	N	N	N	Y	N	N
7 Mica	Y	N	N	Y	N	Y	N	N
8 *McCollum*	Y	N	N	N	N	Y	N	N
9 *Bilirakis*	Y	Y	N	Y	N	Y	N	N
10 *Young*	Y	N	N	Y	N	Y	N	N
11 Gibbons	Y	Y	N	Y	N	Y	N	N
12 *Canady*	Y	N	N	Y	N	Y	N	N
13 *Miller*	Y	N	N	N	N	Y	N	N
14 *Goss*	Y	N	N	N	N	Y	N	N
15 Bacchus	Y	Y	N	Y	N	Y	Y	Y
16 *Lewis*	Y	N	N	Y	N	Y	N	N
17 Meek	Y	Y	N	Y	N	Y	Y	N
18 *Ros-Lehtinen*	?	?	?	?	?	?	?	?
19 Johnston	Y	Y	Y	Y	N	N	Y	Y
20 Deutsch	Y	N	N	Y	N	Y	N	N
21 *Diaz-Balart*	Y	N	N	Y	Y	Y	Y	Y
22 *Shaw*	Y	N	N	Y	N	Y	N	N
23 Hastings	Y	Y	N	Y	N	Y	N	N
GEORGIA								
1 *Kingston*	Y	N	N	Y	N	?	N	N
2 Bishop	?	?	?	?	N	Y	N	N
3 *Collins*	Y	N	N	N	N	Y	N	N
4 *Linder*	Y	N	N	N	N	Y	N	N
5 Lewis	Y	Y	Y	Y	N	Y	N	N
6 *Gingrich*	?	?	?	?	N	Y	N	N
7 Darden	Y	N	N	Y	N	Y	N	N
8 Rowland	Y	N	N	Y	N	Y	N	N
9 Deal	Y	N	N	Y	N	Y	N	N
10 Johnson	Y	N	N	Y	N	Y	N	N
11 McKinney	Y	Y	Y	Y	N	Y	Y	Y
HAWAII								
1 Abercrombie	N	Y	Y	Y	N	Y	N	Y
2 Mink	N	Y	Y	Y	N	Y	Y	Y
IDAHO								
1 LaRocco	Y	N	N	Y	N	Y	Y	Y
2 *Crapo*	Y	N	N	N	N	Y	N	N
ILLINOIS								
1 Rush	Y	Y	Y	Y	N	Y	Y	Y
2 Reynolds	Y	Y	N	Y	N	Y	N	N
3 Lipinski	Y	Y	Y	Y	N	Y	N	N
4 Gutierrez	N	Y	Y	Y	?	Y	Y	Y
5 Rostenkowski	Y	Y	N	Y	N	Y	N	N
6 *Hyde*	Y	N	N	Y	N	Y	N	N
7 Collins	N	Y	Y	Y	N	Y	N	N
8 *Crane*	Y	N	N	N	N	Y	N	N
9 Yates	N	Y	Y	Y	Y	Y	Y	Y
10 *Porter*	Y	N	N	Y	N	Y	N	N
11 Sangmeister	Y	Y	N	Y	N	Y	N	N
12 Costello	Y	Y	Y	Y	N	Y	N	N
13 *Fawell*	Y	N	N	Y	N	Y	N	N
14 *Hastert*	Y	N	N	Y	N	Y	N	N
15 *Ewing*	Y	N	N	Y	N	Y	N	N
16 *Manzullo*	Y	N	N	N	N	Y	N	N
17 Evans	Y	Y	Y	Y	N	Y	Y	Y

ND Northern Democrats   SD Southern Democrats

	331	332	333	334	335	336	337	338
18 ***Michel***	Y	N	N	Y	N	Y	N	N
19 Poshard	Y	Y	Y	Y	N	Y	N	N
20 Durbin	N	Y	Y	Y	N	Y	Y	N
INDIANA								
1 Visclosky	Y	N	N	Y	Y	Y	N	N
2 Sharp	Y	Y	N	Y	N	Y	N	N
3 Roemer	Y	Y	Y	Y	N	Y	N	N
4 Long	Y	Y	N	Y	N	Y	N	N
5 ***Buyer***	Y	N	N	Y	N	Y	N	N
6 ***Burton***	Y	N	N	N	N	Y	N	N
7 ***Myers***	Y	N	N	Y	N	Y	N	N
8 McCloskey	Y	Y	N	Y	N	Y	N	N
9 Hamilton	Y	Y	N	Y	N	Y	N	N
10 Jacobs	Y	?	Y	Y	Y	Y	N	Y
IOWA								
1 ***Leach***	Y	Y	N	Y	N	Y	N	N
2 ***Nussle***	Y	Y	N	Y	N	Y	N	N
3 ***Lightfoot***	Y	N	N	Y	N	Y	N	N
4 Smith	Y	Y	N	Y	N	Y	N	N
5 ***Grandy***	Y	N	N	Y	N	Y	N	N
KANSAS								
1 ***Roberts***	Y	N	N	Y	N	Y	N	N
2 Slattery	?	?	?	?	N	Y	N	N
3 ***Meyers***	Y	N	N	Y	N	Y	N	N
4 Glickman	Y	Y	N	Y	N	Y	N	N
KENTUCKY								
1 Barlow	Y	N	N	Y	N	Y	N	N
2 ***Lewis***	Y	N	N	Y	N	Y	N	N
3 Mazzoli	Y	Y	N	Y	N	Y	N	N
4 ***Bunning***	Y	N	N	Y	N	Y	N	N
5 ***Rogers***	Y	N	N	Y	N	Y	N	N
6 Baesler	Y	N	N	Y	N	Y	N	N
LOUISIANA								
1 ***Livingston***	Y	N	N	N	N	Y	N	N
2 Jefferson	N	N	N	Y	N	Y	N	N
3 Tauzin	Y	N	N	Y	N	Y	N	N
4 Fields	Y	Y	Y	Y	N	Y	Y	Y
5 ***McCrery***	Y	N	N	Y	N	Y	N	N
6 ***Baker***	Y	N	N	Y	N	Y	N	N
7 Hayes	Y	N	N	Y	N	Y	N	N
MAINE								
1 Andrews	Y	Y	Y	?	N	Y	Y	Y
2 ***Snowe***	Y	N	N	Y	N	Y	N	N
MARYLAND								
1 ***Gilchrest***	Y	N	N	Y	N	Y	N	N
2 ***Bentley***	Y	N	N	Y	N	Y	?	?
3 Cardin	Y	N	N	Y	N	Y	N	Y
4 Wynn	Y	Y	N	Y	N	Y	Y	Y
5 Hoyer	Y	N	N	Y	N	Y	N	N
6 ***Bartlett***	Y	N	N	N	N	Y	N	N
7 Mfume	Y	Y	Y	Y	N	Y	Y	Y
8 ***Morella***	Y	N	N	Y	N	Y	N	N
MASSACHUSETTS								
1 Olver	Y	Y	Y	Y	Y	Y	Y	Y
2 Neal	Y	Y	Y	Y	N	Y	Y	N
3 ***Blute***	Y	N	N	Y	N	Y	N	N
4 Frank	Y	Y	Y	Y	Y	N	Y	Y
5 Meehan	Y	Y	Y	Y	N	Y	Y	Y
6 ***Torkildsen***	Y	N	N	Y	N	Y	N	N
7 Markey	Y	Y	Y	Y	N	Y	N	N
8 Kennedy	Y	Y	N	Y	N	Y	Y	Y
9 Moakley	Y	Y	N	Y	N	Y	Y	Y
10 Studds	Y	Y	N	?	N	Y	N	N
MICHIGAN								
1 Stupak	Y	Y	Y	Y	N	Y	Y	N
2 ***Hoekstra***	Y	N	N	Y	N	Y	N	N
3 ***Ehlers***	Y	N	Y	Y	N	N	N	N
4 ***Camp***	Y	N	N	Y	N	Y	N	N
5 Barcia	Y	Y	N	Y	N	Y	N	N
6 ***Upton***	Y	N	N	Y	N	Y	N	N
7 ***Smith***	Y	N	?	?	N	Y	N	N
8 Carr	?	Y	N	Y	N	Y	N	Y
9 Kildee	Y	Y	N	Y	N	Y	N	Y
10 Bonior	Y	Y	Y	Y	N	Y	N	Y
11 ***Knollenberg***	Y	N	N	Y	N	Y	N	N
12 Levin	Y	Y	N	Y	N	Y	N	N
13 Ford	Y	N	N	Y	N	Y	N	N
14 Conyers	Y	Y	Y	?	Y	Y	N	N
15 Collins	N	Y	Y	Y	N	Y	N	Y
16 Dingell	N	N	N	Y	N	Y	N	N
MINNESOTA								
1 Penny	Y	Y	Y	N	Y	N	N	N
2 Minge	Y	Y	Y	Y	N	N	Y	N
3 ***Ramstad***	Y	N	N	Y	N	Y	N	N
4 Vento	N	Y	N	Y	N	Y	Y	Y
5 Sabo	N	Y	N	Y	N	Y	Y	Y
6 ***Grams***	Y	N	N	Y	N	Y	N	N
7 Peterson	Y	Y	Y	Y	N	Y	N	N
8 Oberstar	N	Y	Y	Y	N	Y	N	N
MISSISSIPPI								
1 Whitten	Y	Y	Y	Y	N	Y	?	?
2 Thompson	Y	N	Y	Y	N	Y	N	N
3 Montgomery	Y	N	N	Y	N	Y	N	N
4 Parker	Y	N	N	Y	N	Y	N	N
5 Taylor	Y	N	N	Y	N	Y	N	N
MISSOURI								
1 Clay	N	Y	Y	?	N	Y	N	N
2 ***Talent***	Y	N	N	Y	N	Y	N	N
3 Gephardt	Y	Y	N	Y	N	Y	N	N
4 Skelton	Y	N	N	Y	N	Y	N	N
5 Wheat	Y	Y	Y	Y	N	Y	N	N
6 Danner	Y	Y	N	Y	N	Y	N	N
7 ***Hancock***	Y	N	N	N	N	Y	N	N
8 ***Emerson***	Y	N	N	Y	N	Y	N	N
9 Volkmer	Y	N	N	Y	N	Y	N	N
MONTANA								
AL Williams	Y	Y	Y	Y	N	N	N	N
NEBRASKA								
1 ***Bereuter***	Y	N	N	Y	N	Y	Y	N
2 Hoagland	Y	N	N	Y	N	Y	N	N
3 ***Barrett***	Y	N	N	Y	N	Y	N	N
NEVADA								
1 Bilbray	Y	N	N	Y	N	Y	N	N
2 ***Vucanovich***	Y	N	N	?	N	Y	N	N
NEW HAMPSHIRE								
1 ***Zeliff***	Y	N	N	Y	N	Y	N	N
2 Swett	Y	Y	N	Y	N	Y	N	Y
NEW JERSEY								
1 Andrews	Y	Y	N	Y	N	Y	Y	N
2 Hughes	Y	N	N	Y	N	Y	Y	N
3 ***Saxton***	Y	Y	N	Y	N	Y	N	N
4 ***Smith***	Y	?	?	?	N	Y	N	N
5 ***Roukema***	Y	N	?	Y	N	Y	N	N
6 Pallone	Y	Y	N	Y	N	Y	N	N
7 ***Franks***	Y	N	N	Y	N	Y	N	N
8 Klein	Y	Y	N	Y	N	Y	Y	N
9 Torricelli	Y	Y	Y	Y	N	Y	Y	Y
10 Payne	N	Y	Y	Y	N	Y	N	Y
11 ***Gallo***	?	?	?	?	?	?	?	?
12 ***Zimmer***	Y	Y	N	Y	N	Y	N	N
13 Menendez	Y	Y	N	Y	N	Y	N	Y
NEW MEXICO								
1 ***Schiff***	Y	N	N	Y	N	Y	N	N
2 ***Skeen***	Y	N	N	Y	N	Y	N	N
3 Richardson	?	?	?	?	N	Y	N	N
NEW YORK								
1 Hochbrueckner	Y	N	N	Y	N	Y	N	N
2 ***Lazio***	Y	N	N	Y	N	Y	N	N
3 ***King***	Y	N	N	Y	N	Y	N	N
4 ***Levy***	Y	N	N	Y	N	Y	N	N
5 Ackerman	Y	Y	N	Y	N	Y	N	N
6 Flake	Y	Y	Y	Y	N	Y	Y	Y
7 Manton	Y	Y	N	Y	N	Y	N	N
8 Nadler	N	Y	Y	Y	Y	Y	N	Y
9 Schumer	Y	Y	N	Y	N	Y	Y	Y
10 Towns	Y	Y	Y	Y	N	Y	N	N
11 Owens	?	Y	Y	Y	?	N	Y	Y
12 Velazquez	N	Y	Y	Y	Y	Y	Y	Y
13 ***Molinari***	Y	Y	N	Y	N	Y	N	N
14 Maloney	Y	Y	Y	Y	N	Y	Y	Y
15 Rangel	?	Y	Y	Y	N	Y	N	N
16 Serrano	Y	Y	Y	Y	N	Y	Y	Y
17 Engel	Y	Y	Y	Y	N	Y	N	Y
18 Lowey	Y	Y	N	Y	N	Y	N	Y
19 ***Fish***	Y	N	N	Y	N	Y	N	N
20 ***Gilman***	Y	N	N	Y	N	Y	N	N
21 McNulty	Y	Y	N	Y	N	Y	N	N
22 ***Solomon***	Y	N	N	Y	N	Y	N	N
23 ***Boehlert***	Y	N	N	Y	N	Y	N	N
24 ***McHugh***	Y	N	N	Y	N	Y	N	N
25 ***Walsh***	Y	N	N	Y	N	Y	N	N
26 Hinchey	Y	Y	Y	Y	N	Y	Y	Y
27 ***Paxon***	Y	N	N	N	N	Y	N	N
28 Slaughter	Y	Y	Y	Y	N	Y	N	N
29 LaFalce	Y	N	N	Y	N	Y	Y	Y
30 ***Quinn***	Y	N	N	Y	N	Y	N	N
31 ***Houghton***	Y	N	N	Y	N	Y	N	N
NORTH CAROLINA								
1 Clayton	Y	Y	Y	Y	N	Y	N	Y
2 Valentine	Y	Y	Y	Y	N	Y	N	N
3 Lancaster	Y	Y	N	Y	N	Y	N	N
4 Price	Y	Y	N	Y	N	Y	N	N
5 Neal	Y	Y	N	Y	N	Y	Y	N
6 ***Coble***	Y	Y	Y	N	N	Y	N	N
7 Rose	Y	Y	N	Y	N	Y	N	Y
8 Hefner	Y	Y	N	Y	N	Y	N	N
9 ***McMillan***	Y	N	N	Y	N	Y	N	N
10 ***Ballenger***	Y	N	N	N	N	Y	N	N
11 ***Taylor***	Y	N	N	N	N	Y	N	N
12 Watt	N	Y	Y	Y	N	Y	Y	Y
NORTH DAKOTA								
AL Pomeroy	Y	Y	N	Y	N	Y	N	N
OHIO								
1 Mann	Y	Y	N	Y	N	Y	N	N
2 ***Portman***	Y	N	N	Y	N	Y	N	N
3 Hall	Y	N	N	Y	N	Y	N	N
4 ***Oxley***	Y	N	N	Y	N	Y	N	N
5 ***Gillmor***	Y	N	N	Y	N	Y	N	N
6 Strickland	Y	Y	Y	Y	N	Y	N	N
7 ***Hobson***	Y	N	N	Y	N	Y	N	N
8 ***Boehner***	Y	N	N	Y	N	Y	N	N
9 Kaptur	Y	N	N	Y	N	Y	Y	N
10 ***Hoke***	Y	N	N	Y	N	Y	N	N
11 Stokes	?	?	N	Y	?	Y	N	N
12 ***Kasich***	Y	N	N	Y	N	Y	N	N
13 Brown	Y	Y	Y	Y	N	Y	N	N
14 Sawyer	Y	Y	N	Y	N	Y	N	Y
15 ***Pryce***	Y	N	N	Y	N	Y	N	N
16 ***Regula***	Y	N	N	Y	N	Y	N	N
17 Traficant	Y	Y	Y	Y	N	Y	N	Y
18 Applegate	Y	N	N	Y	N	Y	N	N
19 Fingerhut	Y	Y	Y	Y	N	Y	Y	N
OKLAHOMA								
1 ***Inhofe***	Y	N	N	N	?	Y	N	N
2 Synar	N	Y	Y	Y	Y	Y	N	Y
3 Brewster	?	?	?	Y	N	Y	N	N
4 McCurdy	Y	N	N	Y	N	Y	?	?
5 ***Istook***	Y	Y	N	N	N	Y	N	N
6 ***Lucas***	Y	N	N	Y	N	Y	N	N
OREGON								
1 Furse	Y	Y	Y	Y	N	Y	Y	Y
2 ***Smith***	Y	N	N	?	N	Y	N	N
3 Wyden	Y	Y	Y	Y	N	Y	N	N
4 DeFazio	Y	Y	Y	Y	Y	N	Y	Y
5 Kopetski	N	N	N	Y	N	Y	Y	Y
PENNSYLVANIA								
1 Foglietta	N	Y	Y	Y	N	Y	Y	Y
2 Blackwell	Y	?	?	?	N	Y	Y	Y
3 Borski	Y	N	N	Y	N	Y	N	N
4 Klink	Y	N	Y	Y	N	Y	Y	N
5 ***Clinger***	Y	N	N	Y	N	Y	N	N
6 Holden	Y	N	N	Y	N	Y	N	N
7 ***Weldon***	Y	N	N	Y	N	Y	N	N
8 ***Greenwood***	Y	N	N	Y	N	Y	N	N
9 ***Shuster***	Y	N	N	N	N	Y	N	N
10 ***McDade***	Y	N	N	Y	?	?	N	N
11 Kanjorski	Y	Y	Y	Y	Y	Y	Y	N
12 Murtha	Y	N	N	?	N	Y	N	N
13 Margolies-Mezv.	Y	Y	N	Y	N	Y	N	N
14 Coyne	N	Y	Y	Y	N	Y	Y	Y
15 McHale	Y	Y	N	Y	N	Y	Y	Y
16 ***Walker***	Y	N	N	N	N	Y	N	N
17 ***Gekas***	Y	N	N	Y	N	Y	N	N
18 ***Santorum***	Y	N	N	Y	N	Y	N	N
19 ***Goodling***	Y	N	N	Y	N	Y	N	N
20 Murphy	Y	Y	Y	?	Y	Y	N	N
21 ***Ridge***	Y	N	N	Y	N	Y	N	N
RHODE ISLAND								
1 ***Machtley***	?	?	?	?	N	Y	N	N
2 Reed	Y	Y	N	Y	N	Y	Y	N
SOUTH CAROLINA								
1 ***Ravenel***	Y	Y	N	Y	N	Y	N	N
2 ***Spence***	Y	N	N	Y	N	Y	N	N
3 Derrick	Y	Y	Y	Y	N	Y	N	N
4 ***Inglis***	Y	N	N	N	N	Y	N	N
5 Spratt	Y	Y	N	Y	N	Y	N	N
6 Clyburn	Y	Y	Y	Y	?	Y	N	Y
SOUTH DAKOTA								
AL Johnson	Y	Y	N	Y	N	Y	N	N
TENNESSEE								
1 ***Quillen***	Y	N	N	Y	N	Y	N	N
2 ***Duncan***	Y	Y	Y	N	N	N	N	N
3 Lloyd	Y	N	N	Y	N	Y	N	N
4 Cooper	Y	N	N	Y	N	Y	N	N
5 Clement	Y	Y	N	Y	N	Y	N	N
6 Gordon	Y	N	N	Y	N	Y	N	N
7 ***Sundquist***	Y	N	N	Y	N	Y	N	N
8 Tanner	Y	N	N	Y	N	Y	N	N
9 Ford	?	?	?	?	N	Y	N	Y
TEXAS								
1 Chapman	Y	N	N	Y	N	Y	N	N
2 Wilson	Y	?	?	?	N	Y	N	N
3 ***Johnson, Sam***	Y	N	N	N	N	Y	N	N
4 Hall	Y	N	Y	Y	N	Y	N	N
5 Bryant	Y	?	N	Y	N	Y	N	N
6 ***Barton***	Y	N	N	N	N	Y	N	N
7 ***Archer***	Y	N	N	N	N	Y	N	N
8 ***Fields***	Y	N	N	N	N	Y	N	N
9 Brooks	Y	Y	N	Y	N	Y	Y	N
10 Pickle	Y	N	N	Y	N	Y	Y	N
11 Edwards	Y	N	N	Y	N	Y	N	N
12 Geren	Y	N	N	Y	N	Y	N	N
13 Sarpalius	Y	N	N	Y	N	Y	N	N
14 Laughlin	Y	N	N	Y	N	Y	N	N
15 de la Garza	Y	N	Y	Y	N	Y	Y	Y
16 Coleman	Y	N	N	Y	N	Y	Y	N
17 Stenholm	Y	N	N	Y	N	Y	N	N
18 Washington	?	?	?	?	?	?	?	?
19 ***Combest***	Y	N	N	N	N	Y	N	N
20 Gonzalez	Y	Y	N	Y	N	Y	Y	Y
21 ***Smith***	Y	N	N	Y	N	Y	N	N
22 ***DeLay***	Y	N	N	N	N	Y	N	N
23 ***Bonilla***	Y	N	N	Y	N	Y	N	N
24 Frost	Y	?	N	Y	N	Y	N	?
25 Andrews	Y	N	N	Y	N	Y	N	N
26 ***Armey***	Y	N	N	N	N	Y	N	N
27 Ortiz	Y	N	N	Y	N	Y	N	N
28 Tejeda	Y	N	N	Y	N	Y	N	N
29 Green	Y	Y	—	Y	N	Y	N	Y
30 Johnson, E.B.	N	N	Y	Y	N	Y	Y	Y
UTAH								
1 ***Hansen***	Y	N	N	Y	N	Y	N	N
2 Shepherd	Y	Y	N	Y	N	Y	N	Y
3 Orton	Y	Y	N	Y	N	Y	Y	N
VERMONT								
AL *Sanders*	Y	Y	Y	Y	N	N	Y	Y
VIRGINIA								
1 ***Bateman***	Y	N	N	?	?	Y	N	N
2 Pickett	Y	N	N	Y	?	?	N	N
3 Scott	Y	Y	N	Y	N	Y	N	N
4 Sisisky	Y	N	N	Y	?	?	N	N
5 Payne	Y	N	Y	Y	N	Y	N	N
6 ***Goodlatte***	Y	N	N	Y	N	Y	N	N
7 ***Bliley***	Y	N	N	Y	N	Y	N	N
8 Moran	Y	Y	N	Y	N	Y	Y	N
9 Boucher	Y	?	N	Y	N	Y	N	N
10 ***Wolf***	Y	N	N	Y	N	Y	N	N
11 Byrne	Y	N	N	Y	N	Y	N	N
WASHINGTON								
1 Cantwell	Y	Y	Y	Y	N	Y	N	N
2 Swift	Y	Y	N	Y	N	Y	N	N
3 Unsoeld	Y	Y	Y	Y	N	Y	Y	Y
4 Inslee	Y	Y	Y	Y	N	Y	N	N
5 Foley								
6 Dicks	Y	Y	N	Y	N	Y	N	N
7 McDermott	N	Y	Y	Y	Y	Y	Y	Y
8 ***Dunn***	Y	N	N	Y	N	Y	N	N
9 Kreidler	Y	Y	Y	Y	N	Y	N	N
WEST VIRGINIA								
1 Mollohan	Y	N	N	Y	N	Y	N	N
2 Wise	Y	?	N	Y	N	Y	N	N
3 Rahall	Y	Y	Y	Y	N	Y	N	N
WISCONSIN								
1 Barca	Y	Y	Y	Y	N	Y	N	N
2 ***Klug***	Y	Y	N	Y	N	Y	N	N
3 ***Gunderson***	Y	N	N	Y	N	Y	N	N
4 Kleczka	Y	Y	N	Y	N	Y	N	Y
5 Barrett	Y	Y	N	Y	N	Y	Y	Y
6 ***Petri***	Y	N	Y	Y	N	Y	N	N
7 Obey	N	Y	Y	Y	Y	Y	N	N
8 ***Roth***	Y	Y	Y	Y	N	Y	Y	N
9 ***Sensenbrenner***	Y	Y	Y	N	N	N	N	N
WYOMING								
AL ***Thomas***	Y	N	N	Y	N	Y	N	N
DELEGATES								
de Lugo, V.I.	D	Y	N	D	N	D	Y	Y
Faleomavaega, Am.S.	D	?	?	D	?	D	?	?
Norton, D.C.	D	Y	Y	D	Y	D	N	Y
Romero-B., P.R.	D	N	N	D	N	D	N	Y
Underwood, Guam	D	?	?	D	?	D	?	?

Southern states - Ala., Ark., Fla., Ga., Ky., La., Miss., N.C., Okla., S.C., Tenn., Texas, Va.
Omitted votes are quorum calls, which CQ does not include in its vote charts.

1994 CQ ALMANAC — **101-H**

KEY

Y Voted for (yea).
Paired for.
+ Announced for.
N Voted against (nay).
X Paired against.
− Announced against.
P Voted "present."
C Voted "present" to avoid possible conflict of interest.
? Did not vote or otherwise make a position known.
D Delegates ineligible to vote.

Democrats *Republicans*
Independent

339. HR 1188. Insurance Anti-Redlining Disclosure/Reasons for Denial. Fields, D-La., amendment to require that in addition to other reports made to the Commerce Department, insurers be required to report the reasons when they deny new insurance or decline to renew existing policies. Rejected in the Committee of the Whole 123-305: R 3-173; D 119-132 (ND 91-83, SD 28-49); I 1-0, July 20, 1994.

340. HR 3355. Omnibus Crime Bill/Motion to Instruct. McCollum, R-Fla., motion to instruct the House conferees to accept the Senate provisions that create a new federal crime with mandatory minimum sentences for the possession or discharge of a firearm during a state crime or during a state drug trafficking crime. Motion agreed to 291-128: R 160-12; D 131-115 (ND 85-83, SD 46-32); I 0-1, July 20, 1994.

341. Procedural Motion. Approval of the House Journal of Wednesday, July 20. Approved 235-161: R 17-154; D 217-7 (ND 147-5, SD 70-2); I 1-0, July 21, 1994.

	339	340	341
ALABAMA			
1 *Callahan*	N	Y	N
2 *Everett*	N	Y	Y
3 Browder	N	Y	Y
4 Bevill	N	Y	Y
5 Cramer	N	Y	Y
6 *Bachus*	N	Y	N
7 Hilliard	?	N	Y
ALASKA			
AL *Young*	N	Y	N
ARIZONA			
1 Coppersmith	N	N	Y
2 Pastor	Y	N	Y
3 *Stump*	N	Y	N
4 *Kyl*	N	Y	N
5 *Kolbe*	N	Y	N
6 English	N	Y	Y
ARKANSAS			
1 Lambert	N	Y	Y
2 Thornton	N	N	Y
3 *Hutchinson*	N	Y	N
4 *Dickey*	N	Y	N
CALIFORNIA			
1 Hamburg	N	N	Y
2 *Herger*	N	Y	N
3 Fazio	N	Y	Y
4 *Doolittle*	N	N	N
5 Matsui	N	Y	Y
6 Woolsey	N	N	Y
7 Miller	Y	N	Y
8 Pelosi	Y	N	Y
9 Dellums	Y	N	?
10 *Baker*	N	Y	N
11 *Pombo*	N	Y	Y
12 Lantos	Y	Y	Y
13 Stark	Y	?	Y
14 Eshoo	Y	N	Y
15 Mineta	Y	N	Y
16 Edwards	Y	N	Y
17 Farr	Y	N	Y
18 Condit	N	Y	Y
19 Lehman	N	Y	Y
20 Dooley	N	Y	Y
21 *Thomas*	N	Y	N
22 *Huffington*	N	Y	N
23 *Gallegly*	N	Y	N
24 Beilenson	Y	N	?
25 *McKeon*	N	Y	N
26 Berman	Y	N	Y
27 *Moorhead*	N	Y	N
28 *Dreier*	N	Y	N
29 Waxman	Y	N	Y
30 Becerra	Y	N	?
31 Martinez	N	N	Y
32 Dixon	Y	N	?
33 Roybal-Allard	Y	N	Y
34 Torres	Y	Y	Y
35 Waters	?	N	Y
36 Harman	N	Y	Y
37 Tucker	Y	Y	?
38 *Horn*	N	N	N
39 *Royce*	N	Y	N
40 *Lewis*	N	Y	N
41 *Kim*	N	Y	N
42 Brown	Y	N	N
43 *Calvert*	N	Y	N
44 *McCandless*	N	Y	N
45 *Rohrabacher*	N	N	N
46 *Dornan*	N	Y	N
47 *Cox*	N	N	N
48 *Packard*	N	Y	N
49 Schenk	N	Y	Y
50 Filner	Y	Y	Y
51 *Cunningham*	N	Y	N
52 *Hunter*	N	Y	?
COLORADO			
1 Schroeder	N	N	N
2 Skaggs	Y	N	Y
3 *McInnis*	N	Y	N
4 *Allard*	N	Y	N
5 *Hefley*	Y	Y	N
6 *Schaefer*	N	Y	N
CONNECTICUT			
1 Kennelly	N	Y	Y
2 Gejdenson	Y	Y	Y
3 DeLauro	N	N	Y
4 *Shays*	N	Y	N
5 *Franks*	N	Y	N
6 *Johnson*	N	Y	N
DELAWARE			
AL *Castle*	N	Y	N
FLORIDA			
1 Hutto	N	?	Y
2 Peterson	N	N	Y
3 Brown	Y	N	Y
4 *Fowler*	N	Y	N
5 Thurman	N	Y	Y
6 *Stearns*	N	Y	N
7 *Mica*	N	Y	N
8 *McCollum*	N	Y	N
9 *Bilirakis*	N	Y	N
10 *Young*	N	Y	N
11 Gibbons	N	Y	Y
12 *Canady*	N	Y	?
13 *Miller*	N	Y	N
14 *Goss*	N	Y	N
15 Bacchus	Y	N	Y
16 *Lewis*	N	Y	N
17 Meek	N	N	Y
18 *Ros-Lehtinen*	?	?	?
19 Johnston	Y	Y	Y
20 Deutsch	N	Y	Y
21 *Diaz-Balart*	Y	Y	N
22 *Shaw*	N	Y	N
23 Hastings	Y	N	Y
GEORGIA			
1 *Kingston*	N	Y	Y
2 Bishop	Y	Y	Y
3 *Collins*	N	Y	N
4 *Linder*	N	Y	N
5 Lewis	Y	N	Y
6 *Gingrich*	N	Y	N
7 Darden	N	Y	Y
8 Rowland	N	Y	Y
9 Deal	N	Y	Y
10 Johnson	N	Y	Y
11 McKinney	Y	N	Y
HAWAII			
1 Abercrombie	Y	N	Y
2 Mink	Y	N	Y
IDAHO			
1 LaRocco	Y	Y	Y
2 *Crapo*	N	Y	N
ILLINOIS			
1 Rush	Y	N	Y
2 Reynolds	Y	Y	Y
3 Lipinski	N	N	Y
4 Gutierrez	Y	N	Y
5 Rostenkowski	Y	N	Y
6 *Hyde*	N	N	N
7 Collins	N	N	Y
8 *Crane*	N	Y	N
9 Yates	Y	N	Y
10 *Porter*	N	N	?
11 Sangmeister	N	Y	Y
12 Costello	Y	Y	Y
13 *Fawell*	N	Y	N
14 *Hastert*	N	Y	N
15 *Ewing*	N	Y	N
16 *Manzullo*	N	Y	Y
17 Evans	Y	N	Y

ND Northern Democrats SD Southern Democrats

	339	340	341
18 *Michel*	N	?	N
19 Poshard	Y	Y	Y
20 Durbin	Y	Y	Y
INDIANA			
1 Visclosky	N	N	Y
2 Sharp	N	?	Y
3 Roemer	N	Y	Y
4 Long	N	Y	Y
5 *Buyer*	N	Y	N
6 *Burton*	N	Y	N
7 *Myers*	N	Y	Y
8 McCloskey	Y	N	Y
9 Hamilton	N	Y	Y
10 Jacobs	N	N	N
IOWA			
1 *Leach*	N	Y	N
2 *Nussle*	N	Y	N
3 *Lightfoot*	N	Y	N
4 Smith	N	N	?
5 *Grandy*	N	Y	N
KANSAS			
1 *Roberts*	N	Y	N
2 Slattery	N	Y	Y
3 *Meyers*	N	Y	N
4 Glickman	N	N	Y
KENTUCKY			
1 Barlow	N	N	Y
2 *Lewis*	N	Y	N
3 Mazzoli	N	Y	Y
4 *Bunning*	N	Y	N
5 *Rogers*	N	Y	N
6 Baesler	N	Y	Y
LOUISIANA			
1 *Livingston*	N	?	N
2 Jefferson	Y	N	Y
3 Tauzin	Y	Y	Y
4 Fields	Y	N	Y
5 *McCrery*	N	Y	N
6 *Baker*	N	Y	N
7 Hayes	Y	Y	Y
MAINE			
1 Andrews	Y	N	Y
2 *Snowe*	N	Y	Y
MARYLAND			
1 *Gilchrest*	N	Y	N
2 *Bentley*	N	N	N
3 Cardin	N	N	Y
4 Wynn	Y	N	Y
5 Hoyer	N	N	Y
6 *Bartlett*	N	Y	N
7 Mfume	Y	Y	Y
8 *Morella*	N	N	N
MASSACHUSETTS			
1 Olver	Y	N	Y
2 Neal	N	Y	Y
3 *Blute*	N	Y	N
4 Frank	Y	Y	N
5 Meehan	Y	Y	Y
6 *Torkildsen*	N	Y	N
7 Markey	N	Y	N
8 Kennedy	Y	Y	Y
9 Moakley	N	Y	Y
10 Studds	Y	N	Y
MICHIGAN			
1 Stupak	N	Y	N
2 *Hoekstra*	N	Y	N
3 *Ehlers*	N	Y	N
4 *Camp*	N	Y	N
5 Barcia	N	Y	Y
6 *Upton*	N	Y	N
7 *Smith*	N	N	N
8 Carr	Y	Y	?
9 Kildee	Y	Y	Y
10 Bonior	Y	N	Y
11 *Knollenberg*	N	Y	N
12 Levin	N	Y	Y
13 Ford	N	?	?
14 Conyers	Y	N	?
15 Collins	Y	N	Y
16 Dingell	N	N	Y
MINNESOTA			
1 Penny	N	N	Y
2 Minge	N	Y	Y
3 *Ramstad*	N	Y	N
4 Vento	Y	N	Y

	339	340	341
5 Sabo	Y	N	Y
6 *Grams*	N	Y	N
7 Peterson	N	Y	Y
8 Oberstar	Y	Y	Y
MISSISSIPPI			
1 Whitten	?	?	?
2 Thompson	Y	N	Y
3 Montgomery	Y	Y	Y
4 Parker	N	Y	N
5 Taylor	N	Y	N
MISSOURI			
1 Clay	Y	N	N
2 *Talent*	N	Y	N
3 Gephardt	Y	N	?
4 Skelton	N	Y	Y
5 Wheat	Y	N	Y
6 Danner	N	Y	Y
7 *Hancock*	N	Y	N
8 *Emerson*	N	Y	N
9 Volkmer	N	Y	Y
MONTANA			
AL Williams	N	N	?
NEBRASKA			
1 *Bereuter*	N	N	N
2 Hoagland	N	Y	Y
3 *Barrett*	N	Y	N
NEVADA			
1 Bilbray	N	Y	Y
2 *Vucanovich*	N	Y	N
NEW HAMPSHIRE			
1 *Zeliff*	N	Y	N
2 Swett	Y	Y	Y
NEW JERSEY			
1 Andrews	N	Y	Y
2 Hughes	N	N	Y
3 *Saxton*	N	Y	N
4 *Smith*	N	Y	N
5 *Roukema*	N	Y	N
6 Pallone	N	Y	Y
7 *Franks*	N	Y	N
8 Klein	Y	Y	Y
9 Torricelli	Y	Y	Y
10 Payne	Y	N	Y
11 *Gallo*	?	?	?
12 *Zimmer*	N	Y	N
13 Menendez	Y	Y	Y
NEW MEXICO			
1 *Schiff*	N	Y	N
2 *Skeen*	N	Y	N
3 Richardson	N	Y	Y
NEW YORK			
1 Hochbrueckner	N	Y	Y
2 *Lazio*	N	Y	N
3 *King*	N	Y	N
4 *Levy*	N	Y	N
5 Ackerman	Y	Y	Y
6 Flake	Y	N	Y
7 Manton	N	Y	?
8 Nadler	Y	N	Y
9 Schumer	Y	N	Y
10 Towns	N	N	?
11 Owens	Y	N	Y
12 Velazquez	Y	N	?
13 *Molinari*	N	Y	N
14 Maloney	Y	Y	?
15 Rangel	Y	N	Y
16 Serrano	Y	N	Y
17 Engel	Y	Y	?
18 Lowey	Y	Y	Y
19 *Fish*	N	Y	Y
20 *Gilman*	Y	Y	Y
21 McNulty	N	Y	Y
22 *Solomon*	N	Y	N
23 *Boehlert*	N	Y	N
24 *McHugh*	N	Y	N
25 *Walsh*	N	Y	N
26 Hinchey	Y	N	Y
27 *Paxon*	N	Y	N
28 Slaughter	Y	N	Y
29 LaFalce	N	N	Y
30 *Quinn*	N	Y	N
31 *Houghton*	N	Y	Y
NORTH CAROLINA			
1 Clayton	Y	N	Y
2 Valentine	N	N	Y

	339	340	341
3 Lancaster	N	Y	Y
4 Price	N	N	Y
5 Neal	?	N	Y
6 *Coble*	N	Y	N
7 Rose	Y	N	Y
8 Hefner	Y	N	Y
9 *McMillan*	N	?	Y
10 *Ballenger*	N	Y	N
11 *Taylor*	N	Y	N
12 Watt	Y	N	Y
NORTH DAKOTA			
AL Pomeroy	N	Y	Y
OHIO			
1 Mann	N	Y	Y
2 *Portman*	N	Y	N
3 Hall	N	Y	Y
4 *Oxley*	N	Y	N
5 *Gillmor*	N	Y	Y
6 Strickland	N	Y	Y
7 *Hobson*	N	Y	N
8 *Boehner*	N	Y	N
9 Kaptur	N	Y	?
10 *Hoke*	N	N	N
11 Stokes	Y	N	Y
12 *Kasich*	N	Y	Y
13 Brown	N	Y	Y
14 Sawyer	N	N	Y
15 *Pryce*	N	Y	N
16 *Regula*	N	Y	N
17 Traficant	Y	Y	Y
18 Applegate	N	Y	Y
19 Fingerhut	Y	Y	Y
OKLAHOMA			
1 *Inhofe*	N	Y	N
2 Synar	Y	N	Y
3 Brewster	N	Y	Y
4 McCurdy	?	?	Y
5 *Istook*	N	Y	?
6 *Lucas*	N	Y	N
OREGON			
1 Furse	Y	Y	Y
2 *Smith*	N	Y	N
3 Wyden	Y	Y	Y
4 DeFazio	N	N	Y
5 Kopetski	Y	N	Y
PENNSYLVANIA			
1 Foglietta	Y	N	Y
2 Blackwell	Y	N	?
3 Borski	N	N	Y
4 Klink	Y	Y	Y
5 *Clinger*	N	Y	N
6 Holden	N	Y	Y
7 *Weldon*	N	Y	N
8 *Greenwood*	N	Y	?
9 *Shuster*	N	Y	N
10 *McDade*	N	Y	N
11 Kanjorski	Y	N	Y
12 Murtha	Y	N	Y
13 Margolies-Mezv.	N	Y	Y
14 Coyne	Y	N	Y
15 McHale	Y	Y	Y
16 *Walker*	N	Y	N
17 *Gekas*	N	Y	N
18 *Santorum*	N	Y	N
19 *Goodling*	N	Y	N
20 Murphy	Y	N	Y
21 *Ridge*	N	Y	N
RHODE ISLAND			
1 *Machtley*	N	Y	N
2 Reed	N	N	Y
SOUTH CAROLINA			
1 *Ravenel*	N	Y	N
2 *Spence*	N	Y	N
3 Derrick	N	N	Y
4 *Inglis*	N	N	Y
5 Spratt	N	Y	Y
6 Clyburn	Y	N	Y
SOUTH DAKOTA			
AL Johnson	N	Y	Y
TENNESSEE			
1 *Quillen*	N	Y	N
2 *Duncan*	N	Y	N
3 Lloyd	N	Y	N
4 Cooper	Y	Y	Y
5 Clement	Y	Y	Y

	339	340	341
6 Gordon	N	Y	Y
7 *Sundquist*	N	Y	N
8 Tanner	N	Y	Y
9 Ford	Y	N	?
TEXAS			
1 Chapman	N	Y	?
2 Wilson	?	Y	?
3 *Johnson, Sam*	N	Y	N
4 Hall	N	Y	Y
5 Bryant	N	Y	Y
6 *Barton*	N	Y	N
7 *Archer*	N	Y	N
8 *Fields*	N	Y	N
9 Brooks	Y	N	Y
10 Pickle	N	N	Y
11 Edwards	N	Y	Y
12 Geren	N	Y	Y
13 Sarpalius	N	Y	Y
14 Laughlin	N	N	Y
15 de la Garza	Y	?	?
16 Coleman	N	Y	Y
17 Stenholm	N	Y	Y
18 Washington	?	?	?
19 *Combest*	N	Y	N
20 Gonzalez	Y	N	Y
21 *Smith*	N	Y	N
22 *DeLay*	N	Y	N
23 *Bonilla*	N	Y	N
24 Frost	Y	Y	Y
25 Andrews	N	Y	Y
26 *Armey*	N	Y	N
27 Ortiz	Y	Y	Y
28 Tejeda	N	Y	Y
29 Green	N	Y	Y
30 Johnson, E.B.	Y	N	Y
UTAH			
1 *Hansen*	N	Y	Y
2 Shepherd	N	Y	Y
3 Orton	N	Y	Y
VERMONT			
AL *Sanders*	Y	N	Y
VIRGINIA			
1 *Bateman*	N	?	Y
2 Pickett	N	N	Y
3 Scott	N	N	Y
4 Sisisky	N	Y	Y
5 Payne	N	N	Y
6 *Goodlatte*	N	Y	N
7 *Bliley*	N	Y	N
8 Moran	N	Y	Y
9 Boucher	N	Y	?
10 *Wolf*	N	Y	N
11 Byrne	N	Y	Y
WASHINGTON			
1 Cantwell	N	Y	Y
2 Swift	N	N	Y
3 Unsoeld	Y	Y	Y
4 Inslee	N	Y	Y
5 Foley			
6 Dicks	Y	?	Y
7 McDermott	Y	N	Y
8 *Dunn*	N	Y	N
9 Kreidler	N	Y	Y
WEST VIRGINIA			
1 Mollohan	N	N	Y
2 Wise	N	N	Y
3 Rahall	N	Y	Y
WISCONSIN			
1 Barca	N	Y	Y
2 *Klug*	N	Y	N
3 *Gunderson*	N	Y	N
4 Kleczka	Y	Y	Y
5 Barrett	Y	N	Y
6 *Petri*	N	Y	N
7 Obey	N	Y	Y
8 *Roth*	N	Y	N
9 *Sensenbrenner*	N	Y	N
WYOMING			
AL *Thomas*	N	Y	N
DELEGATES			
de Lugo, V.I.	Y	D	D
Faleomavaega, Am.S.	?	D	D
Norton, D.C.	Y	D	D
Romero-B., P.R.	N	D	D
Underwood, Guam	?	D	D

Southern states - Ala., Ark., Fla., Ga., Ky., La., Miss., N.C., Okla., S.C., Tenn., Texas, Va.
Omitted votes are quorum calls, which CQ does not include in its vote charts.

342. HR 4604. Entitlement Spending Control/Previous Question. Derrick, D-S.C., motion to order the previous question (thus ending debate and the possibility of amendment) on adoption of the rule (H Res 484) to provide for House floor consideration of the bill to require the Office of Management and Budget to set long-term entitlement spending targets that, if exceeded by more than 0.5 percent, would trigger a process whereby the president would have to recommend legislation to address the excess spending and Congress would have to vote on the proposals. Motion agreed to 245-180: R 0-176; D 244-4 (ND 165-3, SD 79-1); I 1-0, July 21, 1994.

343. HR 4604. Entitlement Spending Control/Kasich Substitute. Kasich, R-Ohio, substitute amendment to require the president and Congress to annually set a binding, overall cap on entitlement spending (except Social Security) by converting the budget resolution, which is now non-binding, into a measure that would require the president's signature and become law. Authorizing committees would be required to set individual limits on entitlement programs. If the committees failed to cut projected spending enough to prevent the overall cap from being breached, programs that exceeded their individual limits would automatically be cut back. Rejected in the Committee of the Whole 194-233: R 170-3; D 24-229 (ND 14-157, SD 10-72); I 0-1, July 21, 1994.

344. HR 4604. Entitlement Spending Control/Stenholm Substitute. Stenholm, D-Texas, substitute amendment to set caps on all entitlement spending (including Social Security) for fiscal 1996-2000 that would result in some $150 billion in cuts below current projections; require automatic cuts in all programs (including Social Security) if Congress failed to pass reconciliation legislation to prevent spending from exceeding the caps; and prohibit using tax increases or cuts in discretionary spending to offset excess entitlement spending. Rejected in the Committee of the Whole 37-392: R 9-165; D 28-226 (ND 15-157, SD 13-69); I 0-1, July 21, 1994.

345. HR 4604. Entitlement Spending Control/Motion to Recommit. Goss, R-Fla., motion to recommit the bill to the Rules Committee with instructions to report the bill back to the House with an amendment to prohibit any attempt to fix a breach in overall entitlement limits by cutting Social Security benefits, borrowing from the Social Security trust fund or raising the Social Security payroll tax. Motion agreed to 424-0: R 172-0; D 251-0 (ND 169-0, SD 82-0); I 1-0, July 21, 1994.

346. HR 4604. Entitlement Spending Control/Passage. Passage of the bill to require the Office of Management and Budget to set long-term spending targets for entitlement programs with the exception of Social Security that, if exceeded by more than 0.5 percent, would trigger a process whereby the president would have to recommend legislation to address the excess spending and Congress would have to vote on the proposals. Passed 316-107: R 79-95; D 237-11 (ND 161-7, SD 76-4); I 0-1, July 21, 1994. A "yea" was a vote in support of the president's position.

KEY

Y Voted for (yea).
Paired for.
+ Announced for.
N Voted against (nay).
X Paired against.
— Announced against.
P Voted "present."
C Voted "present" to avoid possible conflict of interest.
? Did not vote or otherwise make a position known.
D Delegates ineligible to vote.

Democrats *Republicans*
Independent

	342	343	344	345	346
ALABAMA					
1 *Callahan*	N	Y	N	Y	N
2 *Everett*	N	#	N	Y	Y
3 Browder	Y	N	Y	Y	Y
4 Bevill	Y	N	Y	Y	Y
5 Cramer	Y	N	N	Y	Y
6 *Bachus*	N	Y	N	Y	N
7 Hilliard	Y	?	N	Y	Y
ALASKA					
AL *Young*	N	Y	N	Y	Y
ARIZONA					
1 Coppersmith	N	Y	N	Y	Y
2 Pastor	Y	N	N	Y	Y
3 *Stump*	N	Y	N	Y	N
4 *Kyl*	N	Y	N	Y	N
5 *Kolbe*	N	Y	N	Y	N
6 English	Y	N	N	Y	Y
ARKANSAS					
1 Lambert	Y	N	Y	Y	Y
2 Thornton	Y	N	N	Y	Y
3 *Hutchinson*	N	Y	N	Y	N
4 *Dickey*	N	Y	N	Y	N
CALIFORNIA					
1 Hamburg	Y	N	N	Y	Y
2 *Herger*	N	Y	N	Y	N
3 Fazio	Y	N	N	Y	Y
4 *Doolittle*	N	Y	N	Y	N
5 Matsui	Y	N	N	Y	Y
6 Woolsey	Y	N	N	Y	Y
7 Miller	Y	N	N	Y	Y
8 Pelosi	Y	N	N	Y	Y
9 Dellums	Y	N	N	Y	Y
10 *Baker*	N	Y	N	Y	N
11 *Pombo*	N	Y	N	Y	N
12 Lantos	Y	N	N	Y	Y
13 Stark	Y	N	N	Y	Y
14 Eshoo	Y	N	N	Y	Y
15 Mineta	Y	N	N	Y	Y
16 Edwards	Y	N	N	Y	Y
17 Farr	Y	N	N	Y	Y
18 Condit	Y	Y	N	Y	Y
19 Lehman	Y	N	N	Y	Y
20 Dooley	Y	N	Y	N	Y
21 *Thomas*	N	Y	?	Y	N
22 *Huffington*	N	Y	?	?	?
23 *Gallegly*	N	Y	N	Y	N
24 Beilenson	Y	N	N	Y	Y
25 *McKeon*	N	Y	N	Y	N
26 Berman	Y	N	N	Y	Y
27 *Moorhead*	N	Y	N	Y	N
28 *Dreier*	N	Y	N	Y	N
29 Waxman	Y	N	N	Y	Y
30 Becerra	Y	N	N	Y	Y
31 Martinez	Y	N	N	Y	Y
32 Dixon	Y	N	N	Y	Y
33 Roybal-Allard	Y	N	N	Y	Y
34 Torres	Y	N	N	Y	Y
35 Waters	Y	N	N	Y	?
36 Harman	Y	Y	N	Y	Y
37 Tucker	?	X	?	?	?
38 *Horn*	N	Y	N	Y	Y
39 *Royce*	N	Y	N	Y	N
40 *Lewis*	N	N	N	Y	Y
41 *Kim*	N	Y	N	Y	Y

	342	343	344	345	346
42 Brown	Y	N	N	Y	Y
43 *Calvert*	N	Y	N	Y	Y
44 *McCandless*	N	Y	N	Y	Y
45 *Rohrabacher*	N	Y	N	Y	N
46 *Dornan*	N	Y	N	Y	N
47 *Cox*	N	Y	N	Y	N
48 *Packard*	N	Y	N	Y	N
49 Schenk	Y	Y	N	Y	Y
50 Filner	Y	N	N	Y	Y
51 *Cunningham*	N	Y	N	Y	N
52 *Hunter*	N	Y	N	Y	N
COLORADO					
1 Schroeder	Y	N	N	Y	Y
2 Skaggs	Y	N	Y	Y	Y
3 *McInnis*	N	Y	N	Y	Y
4 *Allard*	N	Y	N	Y	N
5 *Hefley*	N	Y	N	Y	N
6 *Schaefer*	N	Y	Y	Y	N
CONNECTICUT					
1 Kennelly	Y	N	N	Y	Y
2 Gejdenson	Y	N	N	Y	Y
3 DeLauro	Y	N	N	Y	Y
4 *Shays*	N	Y	Y	Y	Y
5 *Franks*	N	Y	N	Y	Y
6 *Johnson*	N	Y	Y	Y	N
DELAWARE					
AL *Castle*	N	Y	N	Y	Y
FLORIDA					
1 Hutto	Y	N	Y	Y	Y
2 Peterson	Y	N	N	Y	Y
3 Brown	Y	N	N	Y	?
4 *Fowler*	N	Y	N	Y	Y
5 Thurman	Y	N	N	Y	Y
6 *Stearns*	N	Y	N	Y	N
7 *Mica*	N	Y	N	Y	N
8 *McCollum*	N	Y	N	Y	N
9 *Bilirakis*	N	Y	N	Y	N
10 *Young*	N	Y	N	Y	Y
11 Gibbons	?	N	N	Y	Y
12 *Canady*	N	Y	N	Y	Y
13 *Miller*	N	Y	N	Y	N
14 *Goss*	N	Y	N	Y	Y
15 Bacchus	Y	N	Y	Y	Y
16 *Lewis*	N	Y	N	Y	Y
17 Meek	Y	N	N	Y	Y
18 *Ros-Lehtinen*	?	?	?	?	?
19 Johnston	Y	N	N	Y	Y
20 Deutsch	Y	N	N	Y	Y
21 *Diaz-Balart*	N	Y	N	Y	Y
22 *Shaw*	N	Y	N	Y	Y
23 Hastings	Y	N	N	Y	Y
GEORGIA					
1 *Kingston*	N	Y	N	Y	Y
2 Bishop	Y	N	N	Y	Y
3 *Collins*	N	Y	N	Y	N
4 *Linder*	N	Y	N	Y	Y
5 Lewis	Y	N	N	Y	Y
6 *Gingrich*	N	Y	N	Y	N
7 Darden	Y	N	N	Y	Y
8 Rowland	Y	N	N	Y	Y
9 Deal	Y	Y	Y	Y	Y
10 Johnson	Y	N	Y	Y	Y
11 McKinney	Y	N	N	Y	Y
HAWAII					
1 Abercrombie	Y	N	N	Y	N
2 Mink	Y	N	N	Y	N
IDAHO					
1 LaRocco	Y	N	Y	Y	Y
2 *Crapo*	N	Y	N	Y	Y
ILLINOIS					
1 Rush	Y	N	N	Y	Y
2 Reynolds	Y	N	N	Y	Y
3 Lipinski	Y	Y	N	Y	Y
4 Gutierrez	Y	N	N	Y	Y
5 Rostenkowski	Y	N	N	Y	Y
6 *Hyde*	N	Y	N	Y	Y
7 Collins	Y	N	N	Y	Y
8 *Crane*	N	Y	N	Y	N
9 Yates	Y	N	N	Y	Y
10 *Porter*	N	Y	N	Y	Y
11 Sangmeister	Y	N	N	Y	Y
12 Costello	Y	N	N	Y	Y
13 *Fawell*	N	Y	N	Y	Y
14 *Hastert*	N	Y	N	Y	N
15 *Ewing*	N	Y	N	Y	Y
16 *Manzullo*	N	Y	N	Y	N
17 Evans	Y	N	N	Y	Y

ND Northern Democrats SD Southern Democrats

Column headers for all tables: 342, 343, 344, 345, 346

	342	343	344	345	346
18 Michel	N	Y	N	Y	N
19 Poshard	Y	Y	N	Y	Y
20 Durbin	Y	N	N	Y	Y
INDIANA					
1 Visclosky	Y	N	Y	Y	Y
2 Sharp	Y	N	N	Y	Y
3 Roemer	Y	N	N	Y	Y
4 Long	Y	N	Y	Y	Y
5 *Buyer*	N	Y	N	Y	N
6 *Burton*	N	#	N	Y	N
7 *Myers*	N	Y	N	Y	N
8 McCloskey	Y	N	N	Y	Y
9 Hamilton	Y	N	N	Y	Y
10 Jacobs	N	N	N	Y	Y
IOWA					
1 *Leach*	N	Y	N	Y	Y
2 *Nussle*	N	Y	N	Y	N
3 *Lightfoot*	N	Y	N	Y	N
4 Smith	Y	N	N	Y	Y
5 *Grandy*	N	?	Y	Y	Y
KANSAS					
1 *Roberts*	N	Y	N	Y	Y
2 Slattery	Y	N	N	Y	Y
3 *Meyers*	N	Y	N	Y	Y
4 Glickman	Y	N	N	Y	Y
KENTUCKY					
1 Barlow	Y	N	N	Y	Y
2 *Lewis*	N	Y	N	Y	Y
3 Mazzoli	Y	N	N	Y	Y
4 *Bunning*	N	Y	N	Y	N
5 *Rogers*	N	Y	N	Y	Y
6 Baesler	Y	N	N	Y	Y
LOUISIANA					
1 *Livingston*	N	Y	N	Y	N
2 Jefferson	Y	N	N	Y	?
3 Tauzin	Y	N	N	Y	Y
4 Fields	Y	N	N	Y	Y
5 *McCrery*	N	Y	N	Y	Y
6 *Baker*	N	Y	N	Y	Y
7 Hayes	Y	N	N	Y	Y
MAINE					
1 Andrews	Y	N	N	Y	Y
2 *Snowe*	N	Y	N	Y	Y
MARYLAND					
1 *Gilchrest*	N	Y	N	Y	N
2 *Bentley*	N	Y	N	Y	N
3 Cardin	Y	N	Y	Y	Y
4 Wynn	Y	N	N	Y	Y
5 Hoyer	Y	N	N	Y	Y
6 *Bartlett*	N	Y	N	Y	Y
7 Mfume	Y	N	N	Y	Y
8 *Morella*	N	Y	N	Y	Y
MASSACHUSETTS					
1 Olver	Y	N	N	Y	Y
2 Neal	Y	N	N	Y	Y
3 *Blute*	N	Y	N	Y	Y
4 Frank	Y	N	N	Y	Y
5 Meehan	Y	N	Y	Y	Y
6 *Torkildsen*	N	Y	N	Y	Y
7 Markey	Y	N	N	Y	Y
8 Kennedy	Y	N	N	Y	Y
9 Moakley	Y	N	N	Y	Y
10 Studds	Y	N	N	Y	Y
MICHIGAN					
1 Stupak	Y	N	N	Y	Y
2 *Hoekstra*	N	Y	N	Y	N
3 *Ehlers*	N	Y	N	Y	Y
4 *Camp*	N	Y	N	Y	Y
5 Barcia	Y	N	N	Y	Y
6 *Upton*	N	Y	N	Y	Y
7 *Smith*	N	Y	N	Y	N
8 Carr	?	?	?	?	?
9 Kildee	Y	N	N	Y	Y
10 Bonior	Y	N	N	Y	Y
11 *Knollenberg*	N	Y	N	Y	N
12 Levin	Y	N	N	Y	Y
13 Ford	?	?	?	?	?
14 Conyers	Y	N	N	Y	Y
15 Collins	Y	N	N	Y	Y
16 Dingell	Y	N	N	Y	Y
MINNESOTA					
1 Penny	N	N	Y	Y	Y
2 Minge	Y	N	Y	Y	Y
3 *Ramstad*	N	Y	N	Y	Y
4 Vento	Y	N	N	Y	Y

	342	343	344	345	346
5 Sabo	Y	N	N	Y	Y
6 *Grams*	N	Y	N	Y	N
7 Peterson	Y	Y	N	Y	Y
8 Oberstar	Y	N	N	Y	Y
MISSISSIPPI					
1 Whitten	?	N	N	Y	Y
2 Thompson	Y	N	N	Y	Y
3 Montgomery	Y	N	Y	Y	Y
4 Parker	Y	N	N	Y	Y
5 Taylor	Y	Y	N	Y	Y
MISSOURI					
1 Clay	Y	N	N	Y	Y
2 *Talent*	N	Y	N	Y	Y
3 Gephardt	Y	N	N	Y	Y
4 Skelton	Y	N	N	Y	Y
5 Wheat	Y	N	N	Y	Y
6 Danner	Y	N	N	Y	Y
7 *Hancock*	N	Y	N	Y	N
8 *Emerson*	N	Y	N	Y	Y
9 Volkmer	Y	N	N	Y	Y
MONTANA					
AL Williams	Y	N	N	Y	Y
NEBRASKA					
1 *Bereuter*	N	Y	N	Y	N
2 Hoagland	Y	Y	N	Y	Y
3 *Barrett*	N	Y	N	Y	Y
NEVADA					
1 Bilbray	Y	N	N	Y	Y
2 *Vucanovich*	N	N	N	Y	Y
NEW HAMPSHIRE					
1 *Zeliff*	N	Y	N	Y	N
2 Swett	Y	Y	N	Y	Y
NEW JERSEY					
1 Andrews	Y	Y	Y	Y	Y
2 Hughes	Y	N	N	Y	Y
3 *Saxton*	N	Y	N	Y	Y
4 *Smith*	N	Y	N	Y	Y
5 *Roukema*	N	Y	N	Y	Y
6 Pallone	Y	N	N	Y	Y
7 *Franks*	N	Y	N	Y	N
8 Klein	Y	N	Y	Y	Y
9 Torricelli	Y	N	Y	Y	Y
10 Payne	Y	N	N	Y	Y
11 *Gallo*	?	?	?	?	?
12 *Zimmer*	N	Y	N	Y	Y
13 Menendez	Y	N	N	Y	Y
NEW MEXICO					
1 *Schiff*	N	Y	N	Y	Y
2 *Skeen*	N	Y	N	Y	Y
3 Richardson	Y	N	N	Y	Y
NEW YORK					
1 Hochbrueckner	Y	N	N	Y	Y
2 *Lazio*	N	Y	N	Y	Y
3 *King*	N	Y	N	Y	N
4 *Levy*	N	Y	N	Y	N
5 Ackerman	Y	N	N	Y	Y
6 Flake	Y	N	N	Y	Y
7 Manton	Y	N	N	Y	Y
8 Nadler	Y	N	N	Y	Y
9 Schumer	Y	N	N	Y	Y
10 Towns	Y	N	N	Y	Y
11 Owens	Y	N	N	Y	Y
12 Velazquez	?	X	N	Y	Y
13 *Molinari*	N	Y	N	Y	N
14 Maloney	Y	N	N	Y	Y
15 Rangel	Y	N	N	Y	Y
16 Serrano	Y	N	N	Y	Y
17 Engel	Y	N	N	Y	Y
18 Lowey	Y	N	N	Y	Y
19 *Fish*	N	Y	N	Y	N
20 *Gilman*	N	Y	N	Y	N
21 McNulty	Y	N	N	Y	Y
22 *Solomon*	N	Y	N	Y	N
23 *Boehlert*	N	Y	N	Y	Y
24 *McHugh*	N	Y	N	Y	Y
25 *Walsh*	N	Y	N	Y	Y
26 Hinchey	Y	N	N	Y	Y
27 *Paxon*	N	Y	N	Y	N
28 Slaughter	Y	N	N	Y	Y
29 LaFalce	Y	N	N	Y	Y
30 *Quinn*	N	Y	N	Y	Y
31 *Houghton*	N	Y	N	Y	Y
NORTH CAROLINA					
1 Clayton	Y	N	N	Y	Y
2 Valentine	Y	N	Y	Y	Y

	342	343	344	345	346
3 Lancaster	Y	N	N	Y	Y
4 Price	Y	N	N	Y	Y
5 Neal	Y	N	N	Y	Y
6 *Coble*	N	N	N	Y	N
7 Rose	Y	N	N	Y	Y
8 Hefner	Y	N	N	Y	Y
9 *McMillan*	N	Y	Y	Y	N
10 *Ballenger*	N	Y	N	Y	N
11 *Taylor*	N	Y	N	Y	N
12 Watt	Y	N	N	Y	Y
NORTH DAKOTA					
AL Pomeroy	Y	N	N	Y	Y
OHIO					
1 Mann	Y	Y	N	Y	Y
2 *Portman*	N	Y	N	Y	N
3 Hall	Y	N	N	Y	Y
4 *Oxley*	N	Y	N	Y	N
5 *Gillmor*	N	Y	N	Y	N
6 Strickland	Y	N	N	Y	Y
7 *Hobson*	N	Y	N	Y	N
8 *Boehner*	N	Y	N	Y	N
9 Kaptur	Y	N	N	Y	Y
10 *Hoke*	N	Y	N	Y	N
11 Stokes	Y	N	N	Y	Y
12 *Kasich*	N	Y	N	Y	N
13 Brown	Y	N	N	Y	Y
14 Sawyer	Y	N	N	Y	Y
15 *Pryce*	N	Y	N	Y	Y
16 *Regula*	N	Y	N	Y	N
17 Traficant	Y	N	N	Y	Y
18 Applegate	Y	N	N	Y	Y
19 Fingerhut	Y	Y	N	Y	Y
OKLAHOMA					
1 *Inhofe*	N	Y	N	Y	N
2 Synar	Y	N	N	Y	Y
3 Brewster	Y	N	N	Y	Y
4 McCurdy	Y	Y	N	Y	Y
5 *Istook*	N	Y	N	Y	N
6 *Lucas*	N	Y	N	+	N
OREGON					
1 Furse	Y	N	N	Y	Y
2 *Smith*	N	Y	N	Y	Y
3 Wyden	Y	N	N	Y	Y
4 DeFazio	Y	N	N	Y	Y
5 Kopetski	Y	N	N	Y	Y
PENNSYLVANIA					
1 Foglietta	Y	N	N	Y	Y
2 Blackwell	Y	N	N	Y	Y
3 Borski	Y	N	N	Y	Y
4 Klink	Y	N	N	Y	Y
5 *Clinger*	N	Y	N	Y	Y
6 Holden	Y	N	N	Y	Y
7 *Weldon*	N	Y	N	?	?
8 *Greenwood*	N	Y	N	Y	Y
9 *Shuster*	N	Y	N	Y	N
10 *McDade*	N	Y	N	?	Y
11 Kanjorski	Y	N	N	Y	Y
12 Murtha	Y	N	N	Y	Y
13 Margolies-Mezv.	Y	N	Y	Y	Y
14 Coyne	Y	N	N	Y	Y
15 McHale	Y	N	Y	Y	Y
16 *Walker*	N	Y	N	Y	N
17 *Gekas*	N	Y	N	Y	N
18 *Santorum*	N	Y	N	Y	Y
19 *Goodling*	N	Y	N	Y	Y
20 Murphy	Y	N	N	Y	Y
21 *Ridge*	N	Y	N	Y	Y
RHODE ISLAND					
1 *Machtley*	N	Y	N	Y	Y
2 Reed	Y	N	N	Y	Y
SOUTH CAROLINA					
1 *Ravenel*	N	Y	N	Y	Y
2 *Spence*	N	Y	N	Y	Y
3 Derrick	Y	N	N	Y	Y
4 *Inglis*	N	Y	N	Y	Y
5 Spratt	Y	N	N	Y	Y
6 Clyburn	Y	N	N	Y	Y
SOUTH DAKOTA					
AL Johnson	Y	N	N	Y	Y
TENNESSEE					
1 *Quillen*	N	Y	N	Y	N
2 *Duncan*	N	Y	N	Y	N
3 Lloyd	Y	N	Y	Y	Y
4 Cooper	N	Y	N	Y	Y
5 Clement	Y	Y	N	Y	Y

	342	343	344	345	346
6 Gordon	Y	Y	N	Y	Y
7 *Sundquist*	N	Y	N	Y	N
8 Tanner	Y	Y	N	Y	Y
9 Ford	Y	N	N	Y	Y
TEXAS					
1 Chapman	Y	N	N	Y	Y
2 Wilson	Y	N	N	Y	Y
3 *Johnson, Sam*	N	Y	N	Y	N
4 Hall	Y	Y	N	Y	Y
5 Bryant	Y	N	N	Y	Y
6 *Barton*	N	Y	Y	Y	Y
7 *Archer*	N	Y	N	Y	N
8 *Fields*	N	Y	N	Y	N
9 Brooks	?	N	N	Y	Y
10 Pickle	Y	N	Y	Y	Y
11 Edwards	Y	N	N	Y	Y
12 Geren	Y	Y	Y	Y	Y
13 Sarpalius	Y	N	N	Y	Y
14 Laughlin	Y	N	N	Y	Y
15 de la Garza	Y	N	N	Y	Y
16 Coleman	Y	N	N	Y	Y
17 Stenholm	Y	N	Y	N	N
18 Washington	Y	N	?	?	?
19 *Combest*	N	Y	N	Y	N
20 Gonzalez	Y	N	N	Y	N
21 *Smith*	N	Y	N	Y	N
22 *DeLay*	N	Y	N	Y	N
23 *Bonilla*	N	N	N	Y	Y
24 Frost	Y	N	N	Y	Y
25 Andrews	Y	N	N	Y	Y
26 *Armey*	N	Y	N	Y	N
27 Ortiz	Y	N	N	Y	Y
28 Tejeda	Y	N	N	Y	Y
29 Green	Y	N	N	Y	Y
30 Johnson, E.B.	Y	N	N	Y	Y
UTAH					
1 *Hansen*	N	Y	Y	Y	N
2 Shepherd	Y	N	N	Y	Y
3 Orton	Y	N	Y	Y	Y
VERMONT					
AL *Sanders*	Y	N	N	Y	N
VIRGINIA					
1 *Bateman*	N	Y	Y	Y	Y
2 Pickett	Y	Y	N	Y	Y
3 Scott	Y	N	N	Y	Y
4 Sisisky	Y	N	N	Y	Y
5 Payne	Y	N	N	Y	Y
6 *Goodlatte*	N	Y	N	Y	Y
7 *Bliley*	N	Y	N	Y	Y
8 Moran	Y	N	N	Y	Y
9 Boucher	Y	N	N	Y	Y
10 *Wolf*	N	Y	N	Y	Y
11 Byrne	Y	N	N	Y	Y
WASHINGTON					
1 Cantwell	Y	N	N	Y	Y
2 Swift	Y	N	N	Y	Y
3 Unsoeld	Y	N	N	Y	Y
4 Inslee	Y	Y	N	Y	Y
5 Foley					
6 Dicks	Y	N	N	Y	Y
7 McDermott	Y	N	N	Y	Y
8 *Dunn*	N	Y	N	Y	Y
9 Kreidler	Y	Y	N	Y	Y
WEST VIRGINIA					
1 Mollohan	Y	N	N	Y	Y
2 Wise	Y	N	N	Y	Y
3 Rahall	Y	N	N	Y	N
WISCONSIN					
1 Barca	Y	N	N	Y	Y
2 *Klug*	N	Y	N	Y	Y
3 *Gunderson*	N	Y	N	Y	Y
4 Kleczka	Y	N	N	Y	Y
5 Barrett	Y	N	N	Y	Y
6 *Petri*	N	Y	N	Y	Y
7 Obey	Y	N	N	Y	Y
8 *Roth*	N	Y	N	Y	Y
9 *Sensenbrenner*	N	Y	N	Y	Y
WYOMING					
AL *Thomas*	N	Y	N	Y	Y
DELEGATES					
de Lugo, V.I.	D	N	N	D	D
Faleomavaega, Am.S.	D	?	?	D	D
Norton, D.C.	D	N	N	D	D
Romero-B., P.R.	D	N	N	D	D
Underwood, Guam	D	?	?	D	D

Southern states - Ala., Ark., Fla., Ga., Ky., La., Miss., N.C., Okla., S.C., Tenn., Texas, Va.
Omitted votes are quorum calls, which CQ does not include in its vote charts.

*348. HR 3838. Fiscal 1995-96 Housing Reauthorization/Illegal Immigrant Benefits. Kim, R-Calif., amendment, as amended, to prohibit illegal immigrants from receiving benefits under the Food and Shelter Program of the Federal Emergency Management Agency, as contained in the Stewart B. McKinney Homeless Assistance Act of 1987 (PL 100-77). Before being adopted, the Kim amendment was modified by a Roukema, R-N.J., amendment (adopted by a standing vote of 235-0) to provide an exception when a national disaster is declared by the president. Adopted in the Committee of the Whole 220-176: R 158-3; D 62-172 (ND 28-133, SD 34-39); I 0-1, July 22, 1994.

349. HR 3838. Fiscal 1995-96 Housing Reauthorization/Passage. Passage of the bill to reauthorize the programs of the Department of Housing and Urban Development and the Farmers Home Administration at $31.5 billion in fiscal 1995 and $33.4 billion in fiscal 1996. Passed 345-36: R 117-35; D 227-1 (ND 153-1, SD 74-0); I 1-0, July 22, 1994. A "yea" was a vote in support of the president's position.

350. S 2182. Fiscal 1995 Defense Authorization/Close Portions of Conference. Dellums, D-Calif., motion to close portions of the conference to the public on grounds of national security. Motion agreed to 363-1: R 154-0; D 208-1 (ND 136-1, SD 72-0); I 1-0, July 25, 1994.

*352. HR 3870. Environmental Technologies/Risk Assessment. Brown, D-Calif., substitute amendment to the Walker, R-Pa., amendment, to require the director of the Office of Science and Technology Policy to develop a method for risk assessment and to determine which environmental problems will be addressed. (The Walker amendment would have defined specific criteria for assessing environmental risks and making comparisons among categories of risks. See vote 353.) Rejected in the Committee of the Whole 202-225: R 3-173; D 198-52 (ND 145-23, SD 53-29); I 1-0, July 26, 1994.

353. HR 3870. Environmental Technologies/Risk Assessment. Walker, R-Pa., amendment to establish specific criteria for assessing environmental risks and for making comparisons among categories of risks. Adopted in the Committee of the Whole 286-139: R 174-0; D 112-138 (ND 59-110, SD 53-28); I 0-1, July 26, 1994.

354. H Res 476. United Germany Congratulations/Adoption. Hamilton, D-Ind., motion to suspend the rules and adopt the resolution to congratulate the people of Germany and the citizens of Berlin on the occasion of the withdrawal of U.S. troops from Berlin, and to reaffirm the U.S. and Berlin friendship. Motion agreed to 425-0: R 176-0; D 248-0 (ND 166-0, SD 82-0); I 1-0, July 26, 1994. A two-thirds majority of those present and voting (284 in this case) is required for adoption under suspension of the rules.

355. HR 518. California Desert Protection/Effective Date. Calvert, R-Calif., amendment to delay the effective date of the bill until the National Park Service reduces the backlog of land acquisition, construction and park operations by 50 percent as determined by the Office of Management and Budget. Rejected in the Committee of the Whole 138-288: R 129-43; D 9-244 (ND 6-167, SD 3-77); I 0-1, July 27, 1994.

* Omitted votes are quorum calls, which CQ does not include in its vote charts.

KEY

Y	Voted for (yea).
#	Paired for.
+	Announced for.
N	Voted against (nay).
X	Paired against.
−	Announced against.
P	Voted "present."
C	Voted "present" to avoid possible conflict of interest.
?	Did not vote or otherwise make a position known.
D	Delegates ineligible to vote.

Democrats *Republicans* Independent

	348	349	350	352	353	354	355
ALABAMA							
1 Callahan	Y	Y	Y	N	Y	Y	Y
2 Everett	Y	Y	Y	N	Y	Y	Y
3 Browder	Y	Y	Y	Y	Y	Y	N
4 Bevill	Y	Y	Y	N	Y	Y	N
5 Cramer	Y	?	Y	Y	Y	Y	N
6 Bachus	Y	Y	Y	N	Y	Y	Y
7 Hilliard	N	Y	Y	Y	N	Y	N
ALASKA							
AL Young	Y	Y	Y	N	Y	Y	Y
ARIZONA							
1 Coppersmith	N	Y	Y	Y	Y	Y	N
2 Pastor	N	Y	Y	N	Y	N	Y
3 Stump	Y	N	Y	N	Y	Y	Y
4 Kyl	?	?	Y	N	Y	Y	Y
5 Kolbe	Y	Y	Y	N	Y	Y	Y
6 English	N	Y	Y	Y	N	Y	N
ARKANSAS							
1 Lambert	Y	Y	Y	N	Y	Y	N
2 Thornton	N	Y	Y	N	Y	Y	N
3 Hutchinson	Y	Y	Y	N	Y	Y	Y
4 Dickey	Y	Y	?	N	Y	Y	N
CALIFORNIA							
1 Hamburg	N	Y	Y	Y	N	Y	N
2 Herger	Y	Y	Y	N	Y	Y	N
3 Fazio	N	Y	Y	Y	Y	Y	N
4 Doolittle	Y	?	Y	N	Y	Y	?
5 Matsui	N	Y	Y	Y	Y	Y	N
6 Woolsey	N	Y	Y	Y	Y	Y	N
7 Miller	N	?	Y	N	Y	N	N
8 Pelosi	N	Y	Y	Y	N	Y	N
9 Dellums	N	Y	Y	N	Y	N	N
10 Baker	Y	?	Y	N	#	Y	Y
11 Pombo	Y	?	Y	N	Y	Y	Y
12 Lantos	N	Y	Y	Y	N	Y	N
13 Stark	N	?	Y	N	Y	N	N
14 Eshoo	N	Y	Y	Y	N	Y	N
15 Mineta	N	Y	Y	N	Y	Y	N
16 Edwards	N	Y	Y	Y	N	Y	N
17 Farr	N	Y	Y	Y	N	Y	N
18 Condit	Y	Y	Y	N	Y	Y	Y
19 Lehman	Y	Y	Y	N	Y	Y	Y
20 Dooley	N	Y	Y	N	Y	Y	N
21 Thomas	?	Y	Y	N	Y	Y	Y
22 Huffington	?	?	Y	N	Y	Y	Y
23 Gallegly	?	?	?	N	Y	Y	Y
24 Beilenson	N	Y	Y	Y	N	Y	N
25 McKeon	#	?	Y	N	Y	Y	Y
26 Berman	N	Y	Y	Y	N	Y	N
27 Moorhead	Y	N	Y	N	Y	Y	Y
28 Dreier	Y	N	Y	N	Y	Y	Y
29 Waxman	N	Y	Y	Y	N	Y	N
30 Becerra	N	Y	?	Y	N	Y	N
31 Martinez	N	Y	Y	Y	Y	Y	N
32 Dixon	N	Y	Y	Y	N	Y	N
33 Roybal-Allard	N	Y	Y	N	Y	Y	N
34 Torres	N	Y	Y	Y	N	Y	N
35 Waters	N	Y	Y	Y	N	Y	N
36 Harman	?	Y	Y	Y	Y	Y	N
37 Tucker	X	?	?	#	X	?	N
38 Horn	Y	Y	Y	N	Y	Y	Y
39 Royce	Y	N	Y	N	Y	Y	Y
40 Lewis	Y	Y	Y	N	Y	Y	Y
41 Kim	Y	Y	Y	N	Y	Y	Y

	348	349	350	352	353	354	355
42 Brown	?	?	?	Y	N	Y	Y
43 Calvert	Y	Y	Y	N	Y	Y	Y
44 McCandless	?	?	?	N	Y	Y	Y
45 Rohrabacher	?	?	Y	N	Y	Y	Y
46 Dornan	?	?	Y	N	Y	Y	Y
47 Cox	Y	N	Y	N	Y	Y	Y
48 Packard	Y	Y	Y	N	Y	Y	Y
49 Schenk	Y	Y	Y	Y	Y	Y	N
50 Filner	N	Y	Y	Y	N	Y	N
51 Cunningham	Y	Y	Y	N	Y	Y	Y
52 Hunter	Y	N	Y	N	Y	Y	Y
COLORADO							
1 Schroeder	N	Y	Y	Y	N	Y	N
2 Skaggs	N	Y	Y	Y	N	Y	N
3 McInnis	Y	Y	Y	N	Y	Y	N
4 Allard	Y	Y	Y	N	Y	Y	Y
5 Hefley	Y	N	Y	N	Y	Y	Y
6 Schaefer	Y	N	?	N	Y	Y	Y
CONNECTICUT							
1 Kennelly	N	Y	Y	Y	N	Y	N
2 Gejdenson	N	Y	Y	Y	N	Y	N
3 DeLauro	N	Y	Y	Y	N	Y	N
4 Shays	Y	Y	Y	N	Y	Y	N
5 Franks	Y	Y	Y	N	Y	Y	Y
6 Johnson	Y	Y	Y	N	Y	Y	N
DELAWARE							
AL Castle	Y	Y	Y	N	Y	Y	Y
FLORIDA							
1 Hutto	?	Y	Y	N	Y	Y	N
2 Peterson	N	Y	Y	N	Y	Y	N
3 Brown	N	Y	?	Y	N	Y	N
4 Fowler	Y	Y	Y	N	Y	Y	N
5 Thurman	Y	Y	Y	N	Y	Y	N
6 Stearns	Y	N	Y	N	Y	Y	Y
7 Mica	Y	?	?	N	Y	Y	Y
8 McCollum	#	?	Y	N	Y	Y	Y
9 Bilirakis	Y	Y	Y	N	Y	Y	Y
10 Young	Y	Y	Y	X	?	?	Y
11 Gibbons	N	Y	Y	N	Y	Y	N
12 Canady	Y	Y	Y	N	Y	Y	Y
13 Miller	Y	N	?	N	Y	Y	Y
14 Goss	Y	N	Y	N	Y	Y	Y
15 Bacchus	N	Y	Y	Y	N	Y	N
16 Lewis	Y	Y	Y	N	Y	Y	N
17 Meek	N	Y	Y	Y	?	Y	N
18 Ros-Lehtinen	?	?	Y	N	Y	Y	N
19 Johnston	N	Y	?	Y	N	Y	N
20 Deutsch	Y	Y	Y	N	Y	Y	N
21 Diaz-Balart	N	Y	Y	N	Y	Y	N
22 Shaw	Y	?	Y	N	Y	Y	N
23 Hastings	N	Y	?	Y	N	Y	N
GEORGIA							
1 Kingston	Y	Y	?	N	Y	Y	Y
2 Bishop	N	Y	Y	Y	N	Y	N
3 Collins	Y	Y	Y	N	Y	Y	Y
4 Linder	Y	Y	Y	N	Y	Y	Y
5 Lewis	N	Y	Y	Y	N	Y	N
6 Gingrich	Y	Y	?	N	Y	Y	?
7 Darden	Y	Y	Y	Y	Y	Y	N
8 Rowland	Y	Y	Y	N	Y	Y	N
9 Deal	Y	Y	Y	N	Y	Y	N
10 Johnson	Y	Y	Y	Y	Y	Y	N
11 McKinney	N	Y	Y	N	Y	Y	N
HAWAII							
1 Abercrombie	N	Y	Y	Y	N	Y	N
2 Mink	N	Y	Y	Y	N	Y	N
IDAHO							
1 LaRocco	N	Y	Y	Y	Y	Y	N
2 Crapo	Y	Y	Y	N	Y	Y	Y
ILLINOIS							
1 Rush	N	Y	Y	Y	N	Y	N
2 Reynolds	N	Y	Y	Y	N	Y	N
3 Lipinski	N	Y	Y	Y	N	Y	N
4 Gutierrez	N	Y	Y	Y	N	Y	N
5 Rostenkowski	N	Y	?	?	?	?	N
6 Hyde	Y	Y	Y	N	Y	Y	N
7 Collins	N	Y	Y	Y	N	Y	N
8 Crane	Y	N	Y	N	Y	Y	N
9 Yates	N	Y	Y	Y	N	Y	N
10 Porter	Y	Y	?	N	Y	Y	N
11 Sangmeister	N	Y	Y	Y	N	Y	N
12 Costello	N	Y	Y	Y	Y	Y	N
13 Fawell	Y	N	Y	N	Y	Y	N
14 Hastert	Y	Y	Y	N	Y	Y	N
15 Ewing	Y	N	Y	N	Y	Y	N
16 Manzullo	Y	Y	Y	N	Y	Y	N
17 Evans	N	Y	Y	Y	N	Y	N

ND Northern Democrats   SD Southern Democrats

	348	349	350	352	353	354	355
18 ***Michel***	Y	Y	Y	N	Y	Y	Y
19 Poshard	N	Y	Y	N	Y	Y	N
20 Durbin	N	Y	Y	Y	Y	Y	N
INDIANA							
1 Visclosky	N	Y	Y	Y	N	Y	N
2 Sharp	N	Y	Y	Y	Y	Y	N
3 Roemer	N	Y	Y	N	Y	Y	N
4 Long	N	Y	Y	Y	Y	Y	N
5 ***Buyer***	Y	Y	Y	N	Y	Y	Y
6 ***Burton***	Y	Y	?	N	Y	Y	Y
7 ***Myers***	Y	Y	Y	N	Y	Y	Y
8 McCloskey	N	Y	Y	Y	N	Y	N
9 Hamilton	N	Y	Y	N	Y	Y	N
10 Jacobs	Y	Y	?	Y	Y	Y	Y
IOWA							
1 ***Leach***	Y	Y	Y	N	Y	Y	N
2 ***Nussle***	Y	Y	Y	N	Y	Y	Y
3 ***Lightfoot***	Y	Y	Y	N	Y	Y	Y
4 Smith	N	?	Y	N	Y	Y	N
5 ***Grandy***	Y	Y	Y	N	Y	Y	Y
KANSAS							
1 ***Roberts***	Y	N	Y	N	Y	Y	Y
2 Slattery	?	?	?	?	?	?	?
3 ***Meyers***	Y	Y	Y	N	Y	Y	Y
4 Glickman	Y	Y	?	Y	Y	Y	N
KENTUCKY							
1 Barlow	N	Y	Y	Y	N	Y	N
2 ***Lewis***	Y	Y	Y	N	Y	Y	Y
3 Mazzoli	N	Y	Y	Y	Y	Y	N
4 ***Bunning***	Y	N	Y	N	Y	Y	Y
5 ***Rogers***	Y	Y	Y	N	Y	Y	Y
6 Baesler	N	Y	Y	N	Y	Y	N
LOUISIANA							
1 ***Livingston***	Y	Y	Y	N	Y	Y	Y
2 Jefferson	N	Y	Y	Y	N	Y	N
3 Tauzin	Y	Y	Y	N	Y	Y	N
4 Fields	N	Y	Y	Y	N	Y	N
5 ***McCrery***	Y	Y	Y	N	Y	Y	Y
6 ***Baker***	Y	Y	?	N	Y	Y	Y
7 Hayes	Y	Y	Y	N	Y	Y	N
MAINE							
1 Andrews	N	Y	Y	Y	N	Y	N
2 ***Snowe***	Y	Y	Y	N	Y	Y	N
MARYLAND							
1 ***Gilchrest***	Y	Y	Y	N	Y	Y	N
2 ***Bentley***	Y	N	Y	N	Y	Y	?
3 Cardin	N	Y	Y	Y	N	Y	N
4 Wynn	N	Y	Y	Y	N	Y	N
5 Hoyer	N	Y	Y	Y	Y	Y	?
6 ***Bartlett***	Y	Y	Y	N	Y	Y	Y
7 Mfume	N	Y	Y	Y	N	Y	N
8 ***Morella***	N	Y	Y	N	Y	Y	N
MASSACHUSETTS							
1 Olver	N	Y	Y	Y	N	Y	N
2 Neal	N	Y	Y	Y	N	Y	N
3 ***Blute***	Y	Y	Y	N	Y	Y	Y
4 Frank	N	Y	?	Y	N	Y	N
5 Meehan	N	Y	?	Y	N	Y	N
6 ***Torkildsen***	Y	Y	Y	N	Y	Y	Y
7 Markey	N	Y	Y	Y	N	Y	N
8 Kennedy	N	Y	Y	Y	N	Y	N
9 Moakley	N	Y	Y	Y	N	Y	N
10 Studds	N	Y	?	Y	N	Y	N
MICHIGAN							
1 Stupak	Y	Y	Y	N	Y	Y	N
2 ***Hoekstra***	Y	Y	Y	N	Y	Y	Y
3 ***Ehlers***	Y	N	Y	N	Y	Y	N
4 ***Camp***	Y	Y	Y	N	Y	Y	Y
5 Barcia	Y	Y	Y	?	Y	Y	N
6 ***Upton***	Y	Y	Y	N	Y	Y	N
7 ***Smith***	Y	?	Y	N	Y	Y	Y
8 Carr	?	?	?	?	?	?	Y
9 Kildee	N	Y	Y	Y	N	Y	N
10 Bonior	N	Y	Y	Y	N	Y	N
11 ***Knollenberg***	Y	Y	Y	N	Y	Y	Y
12 Levin	N	Y	Y	Y	Y	Y	N
13 Ford	?	?	?	Y	N	Y	N
14 Conyers	N	Y	?	Y	N	Y	N
15 Collins	N	Y	Y	Y	N	Y	N
16 Dingell	N	Y	Y	N	N	Y	N
MINNESOTA							
1 Penny	Y	N	Y	N	Y	Y	Y
2 Minge	Y	Y	?	Y	Y	Y	N
3 ***Ramstad***	Y	Y	+	N	Y	Y	N
4 Vento	N	Y	Y	Y	N	Y	N
5 Sabo	N	Y	Y	Y	N	Y	N
6 ***Grams***	Y	Y	Y	N	Y	Y	Y
7 Peterson	Y	Y	Y	N	Y	Y	Y
8 Oberstar	—	+	Y	Y	N	Y	N
MISSISSIPPI							
1 Whitten	?	Y	?	Y	N	Y	N
2 Thompson	N	Y	Y	Y	N	Y	N
3 Montgomery	N	Y	Y	N	Y	Y	N
4 Parker	?	?	Y	N	Y	Y	N
5 Taylor	Y	Y	Y	N	Y	Y	N
MISSOURI							
1 Clay	?	?	Y	Y	N	Y	N
2 ***Talent***	Y	Y	Y	N	Y	Y	Y
3 Gephardt	N	Y	Y	Y	N	Y	N
4 Skelton	Y	Y	Y	N	Y	Y	N
5 Wheat	N	?	?	?	?	?	?
6 Danner	N	Y	Y	N	Y	Y	N
7 ***Hancock***	Y	N	Y	N	Y	Y	Y
8 ***Emerson***	Y	Y	Y	N	Y	Y	Y
9 Volkmer	Y	Y	Y	Y	Y	Y	N
MONTANA							
AL Williams	N	Y	Y	Y	Y	Y	N
NEBRASKA							
1 ***Bereuter***	Y	Y	Y	N	Y	Y	N
2 Hoagland	Y	Y	+	Y	Y	Y	N
3 ***Barrett***	Y	Y	Y	N	Y	Y	Y
NEVADA							
1 Bilbray	N	Y	Y	Y	Y	Y	N
2 ***Vucanovich***	Y	Y	Y	N	Y	Y	N
NEW HAMPSHIRE							
1 ***Zeliff***	Y	Y	Y	N	Y	Y	Y
2 Swett	Y	Y	?	Y	Y	Y	N
NEW JERSEY							
1 Andrews	Y	Y	Y	Y	Y	Y	N
2 Hughes	N	Y	Y	Y	N	Y	N
3 ***Saxton***	Y	Y	Y	N	Y	Y	Y
4 ***Smith***	?	?	Y	N	Y	Y	N
5 ***Roukema***	Y	Y	Y	Y	Y	Y	N
6 Pallone	N	Y	Y	Y	N	Y	N
7 ***Franks***	Y	Y	Y	N	Y	Y	N
8 Klein	Y	Y	Y	Y	N	Y	N
9 Torricelli	N	Y	?	Y	N	Y	N
10 Payne	N	Y	Y	Y	N	Y	N
11 ***Gallo***	?	?	?	N	Y	Y	Y
12 ***Zimmer***	Y	Y	Y	N	Y	Y	N
13 Menendez	N	Y	Y	Y	N	Y	N
NEW MEXICO							
1 ***Schiff***	Y	Y	Y	N	Y	Y	Y
2 ***Skeen***	Y	Y	Y	N	Y	Y	Y
3 Richardson	N	Y	Y	Y	N	Y	N
NEW YORK							
1 Hochbrueckner	N	Y	Y	Y	Y	Y	N
2 ***Lazio***	Y	Y	Y	N	Y	Y	N
3 ***King***	Y	Y	Y	N	Y	Y	Y
4 ***Levy***	Y	Y	Y	N	Y	Y	Y
5 Ackerman	N	Y	?	N	Y	Y	N
6 Flake	N	Y	Y	Y	N	Y	N
7 Manton	N	Y	Y	N	Y	Y	N
8 Nadler	N	Y	?	Y	N	Y	N
9 Schumer	N	Y	Y	Y	N	Y	N
10 Towns	X	Y	Y	Y	N	Y	N
11 Owens	N	?	?	Y	N	Y	?
12 Velazquez	N	Y	?	Y	N	Y	N
13 ***Molinari***	Y	Y	Y	N	Y	Y	Y
14 Maloney	N	Y	Y	Y	N	Y	N
15 Rangel	X	?	?	#	X	?	N
16 Serrano	N	Y	?	Y	N	Y	N
17 Engel	N	Y	?	Y	N	Y	N
18 Lowey	N	Y	?	Y	N	Y	N
19 ***Fish***	N	Y	Y	N	Y	Y	?
20 ***Gilman***	Y	Y	Y	Y	Y	Y	N
21 McNulty	N	#	Y	Y	Y	Y	N
22 ***Solomon***	Y	N	Y	N	Y	Y	?
23 ***Boehlert***	Y	Y	Y	N	Y	Y	N
24 ***McHugh***	Y	Y	Y	N	Y	Y	Y
25 ***Walsh***	Y	Y	Y	N	Y	Y	N
26 Hinchey	N	Y	Y	Y	N	Y	N
27 ***Paxon***	Y	N	Y	N	Y	Y	Y
28 Slaughter	N	Y	?	Y	N	Y	N
29 LaFalce	N	Y	Y	Y	N	Y	N
30 ***Quinn***	Y	Y	Y	N	Y	Y	Y
31 ***Houghton***	Y	Y	Y	N	Y	Y	Y
NORTH CAROLINA							
1 Clayton	N	Y	Y	Y	N	Y	?
2 Valentine	Y	Y	Y	Y	N	Y	N
3 Lancaster	Y	Y	Y	Y	Y	Y	Y
4 Price	N	Y	Y	Y	Y	Y	N
5 Neal	N	Y	Y	Y	Y	Y	N
6 ***Coble***	Y	Y	Y	N	Y	Y	Y
7 Rose	Y	Y	?	Y	N	Y	N
8 Hefner	Y	Y	Y	Y	Y	Y	N
9 ***McMillan***	Y	Y	Y	N	Y	Y	N
10 ***Ballenger***	Y	+	Y	N	Y	Y	Y
11 ***Taylor***	Y	Y	?	N	Y	Y	Y
12 Watt	N	Y	Y	Y	N	Y	N
NORTH DAKOTA							
AL Pomeroy	N	Y	Y	N	Y	Y	N
OHIO							
1 Mann	N	Y	?	Y	N	Y	N
2 ***Portman***	Y	Y	Y	N	Y	Y	Y
3 Hall	N	Y	Y	Y	Y	Y	N
4 ***Oxley***	?	N	Y	N	Y	Y	Y
5 ***Gillmor***	Y	Y	?	N	Y	Y	N
6 Strickland	N	Y	Y	N	Y	Y	N
7 ***Hobson***	Y	Y	Y	N	Y	Y	N
8 ***Boehner***	Y	N	Y	N	Y	Y	Y
9 Kaptur	N	Y	Y	Y	Y	Y	N
10 ***Hoke***	Y	Y	Y	N	Y	Y	Y
11 Stokes	N	Y	Y	Y	N	Y	N
12 ***Kasich***	Y	Y	Y	N	Y	Y	Y
13 Brown	N	Y	Y	Y	Y	Y	N
14 Sawyer	N	Y	Y	Y	N	Y	N
15 ***Pryce***	Y	Y	Y	N	Y	Y	Y
16 ***Regula***	Y	Y	Y	N	Y	Y	N
17 Traficant	Y	Y	Y	Y	Y	Y	N
18 Applegate	Y	?	?	Y	Y	Y	N
19 Fingerhut	Y	Y	Y	Y	Y	Y	N
OKLAHOMA							
1 ***Inhofe***	Y	?	?	N	Y	Y	Y
2 Synar	—	+	Y	Y	N	Y	N
3 Brewster	Y	Y	Y	N	Y	Y	N
4 McCurdy	Y	?	Y	N	Y	Y	N
5 ***Istook***	Y	Y	Y	N	Y	Y	Y
6 ***Lucas***	Y	Y	Y	N	Y	Y	N
OREGON							
1 Furse	N	Y	Y	Y	N	Y	N
2 ***Smith***	Y	Y	Y	N	Y	Y	Y
3 Wyden	?	?	Y	Y	N	Y	N
4 DeFazio	?	?	N	Y	N	Y	N
5 Kopetski	N	?	Y	Y	N	Y	N
PENNSYLVANIA							
1 Foglietta	N	Y	Y	Y	N	Y	N
2 Blackwell	N	Y	?	Y	N	Y	N
3 Borski	N	Y	Y	Y	N	Y	N
4 Klink	Y	Y	Y	N	Y	Y	N
5 ***Clinger***	Y	Y	Y	N	Y	Y	Y
6 Holden	Y	Y	Y	Y	Y	Y	N
7 ***Weldon***	Y	Y	?	N	Y	Y	N
8 ***Greenwood***	Y	Y	Y	N	Y	Y	N
9 ***Shuster***	Y	N	Y	N	?	Y	Y
10 ***McDade***	Y	Y	Y	N	Y	Y	Y
11 Kanjorski	N	Y	Y	Y	N	Y	N
12 Murtha	N	Y	?	N	Y	Y	N
13 Margolies-Mezv.	Y	Y	Y	Y	N	Y	N
14 Coyne	N	Y	Y	Y	N	Y	N
15 McHale	Y	Y	Y	Y	Y	Y	N
16 ***Walker***	Y	N	Y	N	Y	Y	Y
17 ***Gekas***	Y	N	?	N	Y	Y	Y
18 ***Santorum***	Y	Y	?	N	Y	Y	N
19 ***Goodling***	Y	Y	Y	N	Y	Y	+
20 Murphy	N	Y	Y	Y	Y	Y	N
21 ***Ridge***	?	?	?	N	Y	Y	N
RHODE ISLAND							
1 ***Machtley***	Y	Y	?	N	Y	Y	N
2 Reed	N	Y	Y	Y	N	Y	N
SOUTH CAROLINA							
1 ***Ravenel***	Y	Y	Y	N	Y	Y	N
2 ***Spence***	Y	Y	Y	N	Y	Y	Y
3 Derrick	N	Y	Y	Y	Y	Y	N
4 ***Inglis***	Y	N	?	N	Y	Y	Y
5 Spratt	Y	Y	Y	Y	Y	Y	N
6 Clyburn	N	Y	Y	Y	N	Y	N
SOUTH DAKOTA							
AL Johnson	Y	Y	Y	Y	Y	Y	N
TENNESSEE							
1 ***Quillen***	Y	N	Y	N	Y	Y	N
2 ***Duncan***	Y	N	Y	N	Y	Y	Y
3 Lloyd	?	?	Y	Y	N	Y	N
4 Cooper	Y	Y	?	N	Y	Y	N
5 Clement	Y	Y	?	N	Y	Y	N
6 Gordon	Y	Y	?	N	Y	Y	N
7 ***Sundquist***	?	?	?	N	Y	Y	N
8 Tanner	Y	Y	Y	Y	Y	Y	N
9 Ford	N	Y	?	Y	N	Y	N
TEXAS							
1 Chapman	?	?	Y	Y	Y	Y	N
2 Wilson	N	Y	?	Y	Y	Y	N
3 ***Johnson, Sam***	Y	Y	Y	N	Y	Y	Y
4 Hall	Y	Y	Y	Y	Y	Y	Y
5 Bryant	?	?	Y	Y	N	Y	N
6 ***Barton***	#	?	Y	N	Y	Y	Y
7 ***Archer***	Y	N	Y	N	Y	Y	Y
8 ***Fields***	Y	N	Y	N	Y	Y	Y
9 Brooks	Y	Y	Y	Y	N	Y	N
10 Pickle	N	Y	Y	Y	Y	Y	N
11 Edwards	Y	Y	Y	N	Y	Y	N
12 Geren	Y	Y	Y	N	Y	Y	Y
13 Sarpalius	Y	Y	Y	N	Y	Y	N
14 Laughlin	N	Y	Y	N	Y	Y	N
15 de la Garza	N	Y	Y	Y	Y	Y	N
16 Coleman	N	Y	Y	Y	N	Y	N
17 Stenholm	Y	Y	Y	N	Y	Y	N
18 Washington	?	?	?	?	?	?	?
19 ***Combest***	Y	Y	Y	N	Y	Y	Y
20 Gonzalez	N	Y	Y	Y	N	Y	N
21 ***Smith***	Y	Y	Y	N	Y	Y	Y
22 ***DeLay***	Y	X	Y	X	#	?	Y
23 ***Bonilla***	Y	Y	Y	N	Y	Y	Y
24 Frost	?	?	Y	Y	Y	Y	?
25 Andrews	Y	Y	Y	N	Y	Y	N
26 ***Armey***	Y	N	Y	N	Y	Y	Y
27 Ortiz	N	Y	Y	Y	Y	Y	N
28 Tejeda	N	Y	Y	Y	Y	Y	N
29 Green	N	Y	Y	Y	Y	Y	N
30 Johnson, E.B.	N	Y	Y	Y	N	Y	N
UTAH							
1 ***Hansen***	?	?	?	N	Y	Y	Y
2 Shepherd	N	Y	+	N	N	Y	N
3 Orton	Y	Y	?	N	Y	Y	Y
VERMONT							
AL *Sanders*	N	Y	Y	Y	N	Y	N
VIRGINIA							
1 ***Bateman***	Y	Y	Y	N	Y	Y	Y
2 Pickett	Y	Y	Y	N	Y	Y	N
3 Scott	N	Y	Y	Y	N	Y	N
4 Sisisky	Y	Y	Y	N	Y	Y	N
5 Payne	Y	Y	Y	N	Y	Y	N
6 ***Goodlatte***	Y	Y	Y	N	Y	Y	Y
7 ***Bliley***	Y	Y	Y	N	Y	Y	Y
8 Moran	N	Y	Y	N	Y	Y	N
9 Boucher	?	Y	Y	Y	Y	Y	N
10 ***Wolf***	Y	Y	Y	N	Y	Y	N
11 Byrne	N	Y	Y	N	Y	Y	N
WASHINGTON							
1 Cantwell	N	Y	Y	Y	N	Y	N
2 Swift	N	Y	Y	Y	N	Y	N
3 Unsoeld	N	Y	Y	Y	N	Y	N
4 Inslee	Y	Y	Y	N	Y	Y	N
5 Foley							
6 Dicks	N	Y	Y	Y	N	Y	N
7 McDermott	N	Y	Y	Y	N	Y	N
8 ***Dunn***	Y	+	Y	N	Y	Y	Y
9 Kreidler	N	Y	Y	Y	N	Y	N
WEST VIRGINIA							
1 Mollohan	N	Y	Y	N	Y	Y	N
2 Wise	N	Y	?	Y	Y	Y	N
3 Rahall	Y	Y	Y	Y	Y	Y	N
WISCONSIN							
1 Barca	Y	Y	Y	Y	Y	Y	N
2 ***Klug***	Y	Y	Y	N	Y	Y	N
3 ***Gunderson***	Y	Y	Y	N	Y	Y	Y
4 Kleczka	N	Y	?	Y	N	Y	N
5 Barrett	N	Y	Y	Y	N	Y	N
6 ***Petri***	Y	N	Y	N	Y	Y	Y
7 Obey	N	Y	Y	Y	N	Y	N
8 ***Roth***	Y	N	Y	N	Y	Y	Y
9 ***Sensenbrenner***	Y	N	Y	N	Y	Y	Y
WYOMING							
AL ***Thomas***	Y	?	Y	N	Y	Y	Y
DELEGATES							
de Lugo, V.I.	?	D	D	Y	N	D	N
Faleomavaega, Am.S.	?	D	D	?	?	D	N
Norton, D.C.	N	D	D	Y	N	D	N
Romero-B., P.R.	?	D	D	?	?	D	N
Underwood, Guam	?	D	D	Y	N	D	N

Southern states - Ala., Ark., Fla., Ga., Ky., La., Miss., N.C., Okla., S.C., Tenn., Texas, Va.
Omitted votes are quorum calls, which CQ does not include in its vote charts.

KEY

Y Voted for (yea).
\# Paired for.
+ Announced for.
N Voted against (nay).
X Paired against.
— Announced against.
P Voted "present."
C Voted "present" to avoid possible conflict of interest.
? Did not vote or otherwise make a position known.
D Delegates ineligible to vote.

Democrats *Republicans*
Independent

356. HR 518. California Desert Protection/Limit Debate. Miller, D-Calif., motion to end all debate and amendments to the bill at 2 p.m. Motion agreed to 246-179: R 4-169; D 241-10 (ND 166-4, SD 75-6); I 1-0, July 27, 1994.

357. HR 518. California Desert Protection/Passage. Passage of the bill to designate nearly 8 million acres in southeastern California as wilderness and establish the Death Valley, Joshua Tree and Mojave National Parks. Passed 298-128: R 53-122; D 244-6 (ND 167-1, SD 77-5); I 1-0, July 27, 1994. A "yea" was a vote in support of the president's position.

358. HR 4649. Fiscal 1995 District of Columbia Appropriations/Motion to Instruct. Walsh, R-N.Y., motion to instruct House conferees to insist on the House provisions that require the District of Columbia to cut its fiscal 1995 budget by $150 million, and balance its fiscal 1995 budget or face a corresponding reduction in its federal payment for fiscal 1996. Motion agreed to 316-101: R 172-1; D 144-99 (ND 87-78, SD 57-21); I 0-1, July 28, 1994.

*360. HR 2448. Radon Gas Disclosure/Eliminate Disclosure Requirements. Oxley, R-Ohio, amendment to eliminate the bill's provisions that require property owners to provide pamphlets approved by the Environmental Protection Agency on radon hazards and disclose the results of any known radon tests when selling or renting their property and insert provisions that require the EPA to disseminate information about the hazards of radon and distribute pamphlets in high radon areas. Rejected in the Committee of the Whole 193-227: R 156-13; D 37-213 (ND 21-151, SD 16-62); I 0-1, July 28, 1994.

361. HR 2448. Radon Gas Disclosure/Passage. Passage of the bill to require property owners to provide pamphlets approved by the Environmental Protection Agency on radon hazards and disclose the results of any known radon tests when selling or renting property and to create programs to increase public awareness of the dangers of radon gas. Passed 255-164: R 29-143; D 225-21 (ND 158-9, SD 67-12); I 1-0, July 28, 1994.

362. S 208. National Park Service Concessions/Visitor Facilities. Murphy, D-Pa., amendment to strike the bill's provisions stating congressional policy that the development of visitors' facilities should not occur inside the park if it is feasible to build facilities outside park boundaries or if adequate facilities already exist. Rejected in the Committee of the Whole 148-274: R 131-43; D 17-230 (ND 11-157, SD 6-73); I 0-1, July 28, 1994.

363. S 208. National Park Service Concessions/Passage. Passage of the bill to repeal a 1965 law that allows private companies exclusive rights to renew contracts within national parks for operations ranging from snack bars to hotels and to establish a competitive bidding process for concession contracts in national parks. Passed 386-30: R 144-29; D 241-1 (ND 163-1, SD 78-0); I 1-0, July 28, 1994. A "yea" was a vote in support of the president's position.

* Omitted votes are quorum calls, which CQ does not include in its vote charts.

	356	357	358	360	361	362	363
ALABAMA							
1 *Callahan*	N	N	Y	Y	N	Y	N
2 *Everett*	N	N	Y	Y	N	Y	Y
3 Browder	Y	Y	N	N	Y	N	Y
4 Bevill	Y	Y	Y	N	Y	N	Y
5 Cramer	Y	Y	Y	N	Y	N	Y
6 *Bachus*	N	N	Y	?	N	Y	Y
7 Hilliard	?	Y	N	?	Y	N	Y
ALASKA							
AL *Young*	N	N	Y	Y	N	Y	N
ARIZONA							
1 Coppersmith	Y	Y	Y	N	Y	N	Y
2 Pastor	Y	Y	N	N	Y	N	Y
3 *Stump*	N	N	Y	Y	N	Y	N
4 *Kyl*	N	N	Y	Y	N	Y	Y
5 *Kolbe*	N	N	Y	N	Y	Y	Y
6 English	Y	Y	Y	N	Y	C	C
ARKANSAS							
1 Lambert	Y	Y	Y	N	Y	N	Y
2 Thornton	Y	Y	Y	N	Y	N	Y
3 *Hutchinson*	N	N	Y	Y	N	Y	Y
4 *Dickey*	N	N	Y	Y	N	Y	Y
CALIFORNIA							
1 Hamburg	Y	Y	N	N	Y	N	Y
2 *Herger*	?	N	Y	Y	N	Y	N
3 Fazio	Y	Y	N	N	Y	N	Y
4 *Doolittle*	N	N	?	Y	N	Y	Y
5 Matsui	Y	?	N	N	Y	N	Y
6 Woolsey	Y	Y	N	N	Y	N	Y
7 Miller	Y	Y	N	N	Y	N	Y
8 Pelosi	Y	Y	N	N	Y	N	Y
9 Dellums	?	Y	N	N	Y	N	Y
10 *Baker*	N	N	Y	Y	N	Y	N
11 *Pombo*	N	N	Y	Y	N	Y	Y
12 Lantos	Y	Y	N	N	Y	N	Y
13 Stark	Y	Y	N	N	Y	N	Y
14 Eshoo	Y	Y	N	N	Y	N	Y
15 Mineta	Y	Y	N	N	Y	N	Y
16 Edwards	Y	Y	N	N	Y	N	Y
17 Farr	Y	Y	N	N	Y	N	Y
18 Condit	Y	Y	Y	Y	Y	Y	Y
19 Lehman	Y	Y	N	N	Y	N	Y
20 Dooley	Y	Y	Y	Y	Y	Y	Y
21 *Thomas*	N	N	Y	N	Y	N	Y
22 *Huffington*	N	N	Y	N	Y	Y	Y
23 *Gallegly*	N	N	Y	Y	Y	Y	Y
24 Beilenson	N	Y	N	N	Y	N	Y
25 *McKeon*	N	N	Y	Y	N	Y	N
26 Berman	Y	Y	N	N	Y	N	Y
27 *Moorhead*	N	N	Y	Y	N	Y	Y
28 *Dreier*	N	N	Y	?	?	Y	Y
29 Waxman	Y	Y	N	N	Y	N	Y
30 Becerra	Y	Y	N	N	Y	N	Y
31 Martinez	Y	Y	Y	N	Y	N	Y
32 Dixon	Y	Y	N	N	Y	N	Y
33 Roybal-Allard	Y	Y	N	N	Y	N	Y
34 Torres	Y	Y	N	N	Y	N	Y
35 Waters	Y	Y	N	N	Y	N	Y
36 Harman	Y	Y	Y	N	Y	N	Y
37 Tucker	Y	Y	N	N	Y	N	Y
38 *Horn*	N	Y	Y	Y	Y	Y	Y
39 *Royce*	N	N	Y	Y	N	Y	Y
40 *Lewis*	N	N	Y	Y	N	Y	N
41 *Kim*	N	N	Y	Y	N	Y	Y

	356	357	358	360	361	362	363
42 Brown	Y	Y	N	N	Y	N	Y
43 *Calvert*	N	N	Y	Y	N	Y	Y
44 *McCandless*	N	N	Y	Y	N	Y	N
45 *Rohrabacher*	N	N	Y	Y	N	Y	Y
46 *Dornan*	N	N	Y	Y	N	Y	Y
47 *Cox*	N	N	Y	Y	N	Y	Y
48 *Packard*	N	N	Y	Y	N	Y	Y
49 Schenk	Y	Y	N	N	Y	N	Y
50 Filner	Y	Y	N	N	Y	N	Y
51 *Cunningham*	N	N	Y	Y	N	Y	Y
52 *Hunter*	N	N	Y	N	Y	N	Y
COLORADO							
1 Schroeder	Y	Y	N	N	Y	N	Y
2 Skaggs	Y	Y	N	N	Y	N	Y
3 *McInnis*	N	N	Y	N	N	N	Y
4 *Allard*	N	N	Y	Y	N	Y	Y
5 *Hefley*	N	N	Y	N	Y	N	Y
6 *Schaefer*	N	Y	Y	N	Y	N	Y
CONNECTICUT							
1 Kennelly	Y	Y	N	N	Y	N	Y
2 Gejdenson	Y	Y	Y	N	Y	N	Y
3 DeLauro	Y	Y	N	N	Y	N	Y
4 *Shays*	N	Y	N	N	Y	N	Y
5 *Franks*	N	Y	N	N	Y	N	Y
6 *Johnson*	N	Y	N	N	Y	N	Y
DELAWARE							
AL *Castle*	N	Y	Y	Y	N	Y	Y
FLORIDA							
1 Hutto	Y	Y	Y	Y	Y	N	?
2 Peterson	Y	Y	Y	N	Y	N	Y
3 Brown	Y	Y	N	N	Y	N	Y
4 *Fowler*	N	N	Y	Y	N	Y	Y
5 Thurman	Y	Y	Y	N	Y	N	Y
6 *Stearns*	N	N	Y	N	Y	Y	Y
7 *Mica*	N	N	Y	Y	N	Y	Y
8 *McCollum*	N	N	Y	Y	N	Y	Y
9 *Bilirakis*	N	N	Y	N	Y	Y	Y
10 *Young*	N	N	Y	?	?	?	?
11 Gibbons	Y	Y	N	N	Y	N	Y
12 *Canady*	N	N	Y	Y	N	Y	Y
13 *Miller*	N	N	Y	N	Y	Y	Y
14 *Goss*	N	Y	Y	N	Y	N	Y
15 Bacchus	Y	Y	N	N	Y	N	Y
16 *Lewis*	N	N	Y	N	Y	Y	Y
17 Meek	Y	Y	N	N	Y	N	Y
18 *Ros-Lehtinen*	N	Y	Y	N	Y	N	Y
19 Johnston	Y	Y	Y	Y	Y	Y	Y
20 Deutsch	Y	Y	N	N	Y	N	Y
21 *Diaz-Balart*	N	Y	Y	N	Y	N	Y
22 *Shaw*	N	N	Y	N	Y	N	Y
23 Hastings	Y	Y	N	N	Y	N	Y
GEORGIA							
1 *Kingston*	N	N	Y	Y	N	Y	Y
2 Bishop	Y	Y	N	N	Y	N	Y
3 *Collins*	N	N	Y	Y	N	Y	Y
4 *Linder*	N	N	Y	Y	N	Y	Y
5 Lewis	Y	Y	N	N	Y	N	Y
6 *Gingrich*	N	N	Y	Y	N	Y	Y
7 Darden	Y	Y	Y	N	Y	N	Y
8 Rowland	Y	Y	Y	N	Y	N	Y
9 Deal	Y	Y	N	N	Y	N	Y
10 Johnson	Y	Y	Y	N	Y	N	Y
11 McKinney	Y	Y	N	N	Y	N	Y
HAWAII							
1 Abercrombie	Y	Y	N	N	Y	N	Y
2 Mink	Y	Y	N	N	Y	N	Y
IDAHO							
1 LaRocco	Y	Y	Y	N	Y	N	Y
2 *Crapo*	N	N	Y	N	Y	N	N
ILLINOIS							
1 Rush	Y	Y	N	N	Y	N	Y
2 Reynolds	?	Y	N	N	Y	?	?
3 Lipinski	Y	Y	Y	Y	Y	N	Y
4 Gutierrez	Y	Y	N	N	Y	N	Y
5 Rostenkowski	Y	Y	N	N	Y	N	Y
6 *Hyde*	N	N	Y	N	Y	N	Y
7 Collins	Y	Y	N	N	Y	N	Y
8 *Crane*	N	N	Y	Y	N	Y	Y
9 Yates	Y	Y	N	N	Y	N	Y
10 *Porter*	N	Y	N	N	Y	N	Y
11 Sangmeister	Y	Y	Y	N	Y	N	Y
12 Costello	Y	Y	Y	N	Y	N	Y
13 *Fawell*	N	Y	N	Y	N	Y	Y
14 *Hastert*	N	N	Y	Y	N	Y	Y
15 *Ewing*	N	N	Y	Y	N	Y	Y
16 *Manzullo*	N	N	Y	Y	N	Y	Y
17 Evans	Y	Y	N	N	Y	N	Y

ND Northern Democrats   SD Southern Democrats

	356	357	358	360	361	362	363
18 ***Michel***	N	N	Y	?	?	Y	Y
19 Poshard	Y	Y	Y	Y	Y	N	Y
20 Durbin	Y	Y	N	N	Y	N	Y
INDIANA							
1 Visclosky	Y	Y	N	N	Y	N	Y
2 Sharp	Y	?	N	N	Y	N	Y
3 Roemer	Y	Y	Y	N	Y	N	Y
4 Long	Y	Y	Y	N	N	N	Y
5 ***Buyer***	N	N	Y	Y	N	Y	Y
6 ***Burton***	N	N	Y	Y	N	Y	Y
7 ***Myers***	N	N	Y	Y	N	Y	N
8 McCloskey	Y	Y	N	N	Y	N	Y
9 Hamilton	Y	Y	Y	Y	Y	N	Y
10 Jacobs	Y	Y	Y	N	Y	N	Y
IOWA							
1 ***Leach***	N	Y	Y	Y	Y	N	Y
2 ***Nussle***	N	—	Y	Y	Y	N	Y
3 ***Lightfoot***	N	N	Y	Y	N	Y	N
4 Smith	Y	Y	Y	Y	N	N	Y
5 ***Grandy***	N	N	?	Y	N	N	Y
KANSAS							
1 ***Roberts***	N	N	Y	Y	N	Y	Y
2 Slattery	?	?	?	?	?	?	?
3 ***Meyers***	N	Y	Y	Y	Y	N	Y
4 Glickman	Y	Y	Y	Y	Y	N	Y
KENTUCKY							
1 Barlow	Y	Y	Y	Y	N	N	Y
2 ***Lewis***	N	N	Y	Y	N	Y	Y
3 Mazzoli	N	Y	Y	Y	Y	N	Y
4 ***Bunning***	N	N	Y	Y	N	Y	N
5 ***Rogers***	N	N	Y	Y	N	N	N
6 Baesler	Y	Y	Y	Y	N	N	Y
LOUISIANA							
1 ***Livingston***	N	Y	Y	Y	N	Y	Y
2 Jefferson	Y	Y	N	N	Y	N	Y
3 Tauzin	N	Y	Y	N	Y	Y	Y
4 Fields	Y	Y	N	N	Y	N	Y
5 ***McCrery***	N	Y	Y	Y	N	N	Y
6 ***Baker***	N	N	Y	Y	N	Y	Y
7 Hayes	Y	Y	?	?	?	?	?
MAINE							
1 Andrews	Y	Y	Y	N	Y	N	Y
2 ***Snowe***	N	Y	Y	N	Y	N	Y
MARYLAND							
1 ***Gilchrest***	N	Y	Y	?	Y	N	Y
2 ***Bentley***	?	N	Y	N	Y	Y	Y
3 Cardin	Y	Y	N	N	Y	N	Y
4 Wynn	Y	Y	N	N	Y	N	Y
5 Hoyer	Y	Y	?	N	Y	N	Y
6 ***Bartlett***	N	N	Y	Y	N	N	Y
7 Mfume	Y	Y	N	N	Y	N	Y
8 ***Morella***	N	Y	Y	N	Y	N	Y
MASSACHUSETTS							
1 Olver	Y	Y	N	N	Y	N	Y
2 Neal	Y	Y	Y	N	Y	N	Y
3 ***Blute***	N	Y	Y	Y	N	N	Y
4 Frank	Y	Y	N	N	Y	N	Y
5 Meehan	Y	Y	Y	N	Y	N	Y
6 ***Torkildsen***	N	Y	Y	Y	N	N	Y
7 Markey	?	Y	N	N	Y	N	Y
8 Kennedy	Y	Y	Y	N	Y	N	Y
9 Moakley	Y	Y	Y	N	Y	N	Y
10 Studds	Y	Y	N	N	Y	N	Y
MICHIGAN							
1 Stupak	Y	Y	Y	N	Y	N	Y
2 ***Hoekstra***	N	N	Y	Y	N	Y	Y
3 ***Ehlers***	N	Y	Y	N	Y	Y	Y
4 ***Camp***	N	N	Y	Y	N	Y	Y
5 Barcia	N	Y	Y	N	Y	Y	Y
6 ***Upton***	N	Y	Y	Y	Y	N	Y
7 ***Smith***	N	N	Y	Y	N	N	Y
8 Carr	Y	Y	?	?	?	?	?
9 Kildee	Y	Y	Y	N	Y	N	Y
10 Bonior	Y	Y	N	N	Y	N	Y
11 ***Knollenberg***	N	N	Y	Y	N	N	Y
12 Levin	Y	Y	Y	N	Y	N	Y
13 Ford	Y	Y	N	N	Y	N	Y
14 Conyers	Y	Y	N	?	N	N	Y
15 Collins	Y	Y	N	N	Y	N	Y
16 Dingell	Y	Y	Y	N	Y	N	Y
MINNESOTA							
1 Penny	Y	Y	Y	Y	N	N	Y
2 Minge	Y	Y	Y	Y	Y	N	Y
3 ***Ramstad***	N	Y	Y	Y	Y	Y	Y
4 Vento	Y	Y	N	N	Y	N	Y

	356	357	358	360	361	362	363
5 Sabo	Y	Y	N	N	Y	N	Y
6 ***Grams***	N	N	Y	Y	N	Y	Y
7 Peterson	Y	Y	Y	Y	Y	N	Y
8 Oberstar	Y	Y	N	N	Y	N	Y
MISSISSIPPI							
1 Whitten	N	Y	N	?	?	N	?
2 Thompson	Y	Y	N	N	Y	N	Y
3 Montgomery	Y	Y	Y	N	Y	N	Y
4 Parker	Y	Y	Y	N	Y	N	Y
5 Taylor	Y	Y	Y	N	N	Y	Y
MISSOURI							
1 Clay	?	Y	N	N	Y	?	?
2 ***Talent***	N	N	Y	Y	N	N	Y
3 Gephardt	Y	Y	N	N	Y	N	Y
4 Skelton	Y	Y	Y	Y	N	N	Y
5 Wheat	?	?	?	?	?	?	?
6 Danner	Y	Y	Y	Y	N	N	Y
7 ***Hancock***	N	N	Y	Y	N	Y	N
8 ***Emerson***	N	N	Y	Y	N	Y	N
9 Volkmer	Y	Y	Y	Y	N	N	Y
MONTANA							
AL Williams	Y	Y	Y	Y	Y	Y	Y
NEBRASKA							
1 ***Bereuter***	N	Y	Y	Y	N	Y	Y
2 Hoagland	Y	Y	Y	N	Y	N	Y
3 ***Barrett***	N	N	Y	Y	N	Y	Y
NEVADA							
1 Bilbray	Y	Y	Y	N	Y	N	Y
2 ***Vucanovich***	N	N	Y	Y	N	Y	N
NEW HAMPSHIRE							
1 ***Zeliff***	N	N	Y	Y	N	Y	Y
2 Swett	Y	Y	Y	N	Y	N	Y
NEW JERSEY							
1 Andrews	Y	Y	Y	N	Y	N	Y
2 Hughes	Y	Y	Y	N	N	N	Y
3 ***Saxton***	N	Y	Y	Y	N	N	Y
4 ***Smith***	N	Y	Y	N	Y	N	Y
5 ***Roukema***	N	Y	Y	N	Y	N	Y
6 Pallone	Y	Y	Y	N	Y	N	Y
7 ***Franks***	N	Y	Y	Y	Y	N	Y
8 Klein	Y	Y	?	N	Y	N	Y
9 Torricelli	Y	Y	Y	N	Y	N	Y
10 Payne	Y	Y	Y	N	Y	N	Y
11 Vacancy							
12 ***Zimmer***	N	Y	Y	Y	N	N	Y
13 Menendez	Y	Y	Y	N	Y	N	Y
NEW MEXICO							
1 ***Schiff***	N	Y	Y	Y	N	Y	Y
2 ***Skeen***	N	N	Y	Y	N	Y	N
3 Richardson	Y	Y	N	N	Y	N	Y
NEW YORK							
1 Hochbrueckner	Y	Y	Y	N	Y	N	Y
2 ***Lazio***	N	Y	Y	Y	Y	Y	Y
3 ***King***	N	N	Y	Y	N	Y	Y
4 ***Levy***	N	N	Y	Y	N	Y	Y
5 Ackerman	Y	Y	N	N	Y	N	Y
6 Flake	Y	Y	N	N	Y	N	Y
7 Manton	Y	Y	Y	N	Y	N	Y
8 Nadler	Y	Y	N	N	Y	?	Y
9 Schumer	Y	Y	Y	N	Y	N	Y
10 Towns	Y	Y	N	N	Y	N	Y
11 Owens	Y	Y	N	N	Y	N	Y
12 Velazquez	Y	Y	N	N	Y	N	Y
13 ***Molinari***	?	N	Y	Y	N	Y	Y
14 Maloney	Y	Y	Y	N	Y	N	Y
15 Rangel	Y	Y	X	N	Y	N	Y
16 Serrano	Y	Y	N	N	?	N	Y
17 Engel	Y	Y	N	N	Y	N	Y
18 Lowey	Y	Y	Y	N	Y	N	Y
19 ***Fish***	N	Y	Y	?	?	N	Y
20 ***Gilman***	N	Y	Y	N	Y	N	Y
21 McNulty	Y	Y	Y	N	Y	N	Y
22 ***Solomon***	N	N	Y	Y	N	Y	Y
23 ***Boehlert***	N	Y	Y	N	Y	Y	Y
24 ***McHugh***	N	N	Y	Y	N	Y	Y
25 ***Walsh***	N	Y	Y	Y	N	Y	Y
26 Hinchey	Y	Y	N	N	Y	N	Y
27 ***Paxon***	N	N	Y	Y	N	Y	Y
28 Slaughter	Y	Y	Y	N	Y	N	Y
29 LaFalce	Y	Y	N	Y	Y	Y	Y
30 ***Quinn***	N	N	Y	Y	N	Y	Y
31 ***Houghton***	N	N	Y	Y	N	Y	Y
NORTH CAROLINA							
1 Clayton	Y	Y	N	N	Y	N	Y
2 Valentine	?	Y	Y	Y	N	N	Y

	356	357	358	360	361	362	363
3 Lancaster	Y	Y	Y	Y	N	Y	Y
4 Price	Y	Y	Y	N	Y	N	Y
5 Neal	Y	Y	Y	Y	Y	N	Y
6 ***Coble***	N	N	Y	Y	N	Y	Y
7 Rose	Y	Y	Y	N	Y	N	Y
8 Hefner	Y	Y	Y	N	Y	N	Y
9 ***McMillan***	N	N	Y	Y	N	Y	Y
10 ***Ballenger***	N	N	Y	Y	N	Y	Y
11 ***Taylor***	N	N	Y	Y	N	Y	N
12 Watt	Y	Y	N	N	Y	N	Y
NORTH DAKOTA							
AL Pomeroy	Y	Y	Y	N	Y	N	Y
OHIO							
1 Mann	Y	Y	Y	N	Y	N	Y
2 ***Portman***	N	Y	Y	Y	N	Y	Y
3 Hall	Y	Y	Y	N	Y	N	Y
4 ***Oxley***	N	N	Y	Y	N	Y	N
5 ***Gillmor***	N	Y	Y	Y	N	Y	Y
6 Strickland	Y	Y	Y	N	Y	N	Y
7 ***Hobson***	N	Y	Y	Y	N	Y	Y
8 ***Boehner***	N	N	Y	Y	N	Y	Y
9 Kaptur	Y	Y	Y	N	Y	N	Y
10 ***Hoke***	?	?	Y	Y	N	Y	Y
11 Stokes	Y	Y	N	N	Y	N	Y
12 ***Kasich***	N	N	Y	Y	N	Y	Y
13 Brown	Y	Y	Y	N	Y	N	Y
14 Sawyer	Y	Y	Y	N	Y	N	Y
15 ***Pryce***	N	Y	Y	Y	N	Y	Y
16 ***Regula***	N	Y	Y	Y	N	Y	Y
17 Traficant	Y	Y	Y	N	Y	N	Y
18 Applegate	Y	Y	Y	Y	Y	Y	Y
19 Fingerhut	Y	Y	Y	N	Y	N	Y
OKLAHOMA							
1 ***Largent***							
2 Synar	Y	Y	Y	N	Y	N	Y
3 Brewster	N	Y	Y	N	Y	N	Y
4 McCurdy	Y	Y	Y	N	Y	N	Y
5 ***Istook***	N	N	Y	Y	N	N	Y
6 ***Lucas***	N	N	Y	Y	N	N	Y
OREGON							
1 Furse	Y	Y	Y	N	Y	N	Y
2 ***Smith***	N	N	Y	Y	N	Y	N
3 Wyden	Y	Y	Y	N	Y	N	Y
4 DeFazio	Y	Y	Y	N	Y	N	Y
5 Kopetski	Y	Y	N	N	Y	N	Y
PENNSYLVANIA							
1 Foglietta	Y	Y	N	N	Y	N	Y
2 Blackwell	Y	Y	N	N	Y	?	?
3 Borski	Y	Y	N	N	Y	N	Y
4 Klink	Y	Y	Y	N	Y	N	Y
5 ***Clinger***	N	N	Y	Y	Y	Y	Y
6 Holden	Y	Y	Y	N	Y	Y	Y
7 ***Weldon***	N	Y	Y	Y	N	N	Y
8 ***Greenwood***	N	Y	Y	N	Y	Y	Y
9 ***Shuster***	N	N	Y	Y	N	Y	Y
10 ***McDade***	N	Y	#	?	N	Y	?
11 Kanjorski	Y	Y	Y	Y	Y	N	Y
12 Murtha	Y	Y	N	N	Y	Y	Y
13 Margolies	Y	Y	?	?	?	?	?
14 Coyne	Y	Y	N	N	Y	N	Y
15 McHale	Y	Y	Y	N	Y	N	Y
16 ***Walker***	N	N	Y	Y	N	Y	Y
17 ***Gekas***	N	N	Y	Y	N	Y	Y
18 ***Santorum***	N	Y	Y	Y	N	Y	Y
19 ***Goodling***	N	N	Y	Y	N	Y	Y
20 Murphy	Y	Y	Y	Y	Y	Y	N
21 ***Ridge***	Y	Y	Y	Y	Y	N	Y
RHODE ISLAND							
1 ***Machtley***	N	Y	Y	Y	Y	N	Y
2 Reed	Y	Y	Y	N	Y	N	Y
SOUTH CAROLINA							
1 ***Ravenel***	Y	Y	Y	Y	N	N	Y
2 ***Spence***	N	N	Y	Y	N	Y	Y
3 Derrick	Y	Y	Y	Y	Y	N	Y
4 ***Inglis***	N	N	Y	Y	N	N	Y
5 Spratt	Y	Y	Y	N	Y	N	Y
6 Clyburn	Y	Y	N	N	Y	N	Y
SOUTH DAKOTA							
AL Johnson	Y	Y	N	N	Y	Y	Y
TENNESSEE							
1 ***Quillen***	Y	Y	Y	Y	N	Y	Y
2 ***Duncan***	N	N	Y	Y	N	Y	Y
3 Lloyd	Y	Y	Y	N	Y	N	Y
4 Cooper	Y	Y	Y	N	Y	N	Y
5 Clement	Y	Y	Y	N	Y	N	Y

	356	357	358	360	361	362	363
6 Gordon	Y	Y	Y	N	Y	N	Y
7 ***Sundquist***	Y	Y	?	?	?	?	?
8 Tanner	Y	Y	Y	Y	N	N	Y
9 Ford	Y	Y	N	N	Y	N	Y
TEXAS							
1 Chapman	Y	N	?	Y	N	N	Y
2 Wilson	Y	Y	Y	Y	Y	N	Y
3 ***Johnson, Sam***	N	N	Y	Y	N	Y	Y
4 Hall	Y	N	Y	Y	Y	N	Y
5 Bryant	Y	Y	Y	N	Y	N	Y
6 ***Barton***	N	N	Y	Y	N	N	Y
7 ***Archer***	N	N	Y	Y	N	Y	Y
8 ***Fields***	?	N	Y	Y	N	Y	N
9 Brooks	Y	?	Y	N	Y	N	Y
10 Pickle	N	Y	Y	N	Y	N	Y
11 Edwards	Y	N	Y	N	Y	N	Y
12 Geren	Y	Y	Y	N	Y	N	Y
13 Sarpalius	Y	N	Y	N	N	N	Y
14 Laughlin	Y	Y	?	?	?	?	?
15 de la Garza	Y	Y	Y	N	Y	N	Y
16 Coleman	Y	Y	Y	N	Y	N	Y
17 Stenholm	Y	N	Y	Y	N	Y	Y
18 Washington	Y	Y	?	?	?	?	?
19 ***Combest***	N	N	Y	Y	N	Y	N
20 Gonzalez	Y	Y	N	N	Y	N	Y
21 ***Smith***	N	N	Y	Y	N	Y	Y
22 ***DeLay***	N	N	Y	Y	N	Y	N
23 ***Bonilla***	N	N	Y	Y	N	Y	Y
24 Frost	Y	Y	Y	N	Y	?	Y
25 Andrews	Y	Y	?	N	Y	N	Y
26 ***Armey***	N	N	Y	Y	N	Y	Y
27 Ortiz	Y	Y	Y	N	Y	N	Y
28 Tejeda	Y	Y	Y	N	Y	N	Y
29 Green	Y	Y	Y	N	Y	N	Y
30 Johnson, E.B.	N	Y	N	N	Y	N	Y
UTAH							
1 ***Hansen***	N	N	Y	Y	N	Y	N
2 Shepherd	Y	Y	Y	N	Y	N	Y
3 Orton	N	N	Y	Y	N	Y	Y
VERMONT							
AL *Sanders*	Y	Y	N	N	Y	N	Y
VIRGINIA							
1 ***Bateman***	N	N	Y	Y	N	Y	Y
2 Pickett	Y	Y	Y	Y	N	Y	Y
3 Scott	Y	Y	N	N	Y	N	Y
4 Sisisky	Y	Y	Y	Y	N	Y	Y
5 Payne	Y	Y	Y	N	Y	N	Y
6 ***Goodlatte***	N	N	Y	Y	N	Y	Y
7 ***Bliley***	N	N	Y	Y	N	Y	Y
8 Moran	Y	Y	Y	N	Y	N	Y
9 Boucher	Y	Y	N	N	Y	N	Y
10 ***Wolf***	N	Y	Y	Y	N	Y	Y
11 Byrne	Y	Y	Y	N	Y	N	Y
WASHINGTON							
1 Cantwell	Y	Y	Y	N	Y	N	Y
2 Swift	Y	Y	N	N	Y	N	Y
3 Unsoeld	Y	Y	N	N	Y	N	Y
4 Inslee	Y	Y	Y	N	Y	N	Y
5 Foley							
6 Dicks	Y	Y	Y	N	Y	Y	Y
7 McDermott	Y	Y	N	N	Y	N	Y
8 ***Dunn***	N	Y	Y	Y	N	Y	Y
9 Kreidler	Y	Y	Y	N	Y	N	Y
WEST VIRGINIA							
1 Mollohan	Y	Y	N	N	Y	N	Y
2 Wise	Y	Y	Y	N	Y	N	Y
3 Rahall	Y	Y	Y	N	Y	N	Y
WISCONSIN							
1 Barca	N	Y	Y	N	Y	N	Y
2 ***Klug***	N	Y	Y	Y	N	N	Y
3 ***Gunderson***	N	N	Y	Y	N	N	Y
4 Kleczka	Y	Y	Y	N	Y	N	Y
5 Barrett	Y	Y	Y	N	Y	N	Y
6 ***Petri***	N	Y	Y	Y	N	Y	Y
7 Obey	Y	Y	N	N	Y	N	Y
8 ***Roth***	N	N	Y	Y	N	Y	Y
9 ***Sensenbrenner***	N	N	Y	Y	N	Y	Y
WYOMING							
AL ***Thomas***	N	N	Y	Y	N	Y	N
DELEGATES							
AL de Lugo	Y	I	I	N	I	N	I
AL Faleomavaega	Y	I	I	N	I	N	I
AL Norton	+	I	I	N	I	N	I
AL Romero-B.	Y	I	I	N	I	N	I
AL Underwood	Y	I	I	Y	I	N	I

Southern states - Ala., Ark., Fla., Ga., Ky., La., Miss., N.C., Okla., S.C., Tenn., Texas, Va.
Omitted votes are quorum calls, which CQ does not include in its vote charts.

364. HR 4801. Small Business Administration Reauthorization/Rule. Moakley, D-Mass., motion to order the previous question (thus ending debate and the possibility of amendment) on adoption of the rule (H Res 494) to provide for House floor consideration of the bill to reauthorize the programs of the Small Business Administration for fiscal 1995-97. Motion agreed to 215-169: R 0-159; D 214-10 (ND 149-6, SD 65-4); I 1-0, July 29, 1994.

365. HR 4801. Small Business Administration Reauthorization/Rule. Adoption of the rule (H Res 494) to provide for House floor consideration of the bill to reauthorize the programs of the Small Business Administration for fiscal 1995-97. Adopted 221-161: R 0-155; D 220-6 (ND 154-1, SD 66-5); I 1-0, July 29, 1994.

366. HR 4506. Fiscal 1995 Energy and Water Appropriations/Previous Question. Motion to order the previous question (thus ending debate and the possibility of amendment) on the Myers, R-Ind., motion to instruct the House conferees to insist on the provisions providing $279 million for high-energy physics research. Motion rejected 171-209: R 108-53; D 63-156 (ND 31-116, SD 32-40); I 0-0, Aug. 1, 1994. (The motion subsequently was agreed to by voice vote after being amended by a Sharp, D-Ind., amendment to instruct conferees to terminate the Advanced Liquid Metal Reactor program.)

367. HR 4448. Lowell Historical Park/Passage. Vento, D-Minn., motion to suspend the rules and pass the bill to extend the Lowell National Historical Park Commission for five years and increase its authorization from $34 million to $44 million. Motion rejected 221-160: R 13-147; D 208-13 (ND 141-7, SD 67-6); I 0-0, Aug. 1, 1994. A two-thirds majority of those present and voting (254 in this case) is required for passage under suspension of the rules.

368. HR 4158. Lower East Side Tenement Historical Site/Passage. Vento, D-Minn., motion to suspend the rules and pass a bill to authorize $6 million to designate and preserve the tenement building located on Orchard Street in New York as a national historic site. Motion rejected 154-226: R 6-154; D 147-72 (ND 113-33, SD 34-39); I 1-0, Aug. 1, 1994. A two-thirds majority of those present and voting (254 in this case) is required for passage under suspension of the rules.

369. HR 4003. Maritime Administration Reauthorization/Rule. Adoption of the rule (H Res 500) to provide for House floor consideration of the bill to reauthorize the Maritime Administration in fiscal 1995 and subsidize U.S. shipping lines through increased tonnage duties on vessels calling at U.S. ports. Adopted 336-77: R 123-52; D 212-25 (ND 140-18, SD 72-7); I 1-0, Aug. 2, 1994.

370. HR 4003. Maritime Administration Reauthorization/Tonnage Duties. Studds, D-Mass., amendment to raise $1.35 billion over 10 years from increased tonnage duties on vessels calling at U.S. ports for operating assistance to U.S. flag ships. The bill as reported by the Ways and Means Committee would have raised $1 billion over 10 years through a combination of increased tonnage duties and excise taxes on diesel fuel and cruise ship tickets. Adopted 268-153: R 70-106; D 197-47 (ND 134-31, SD 63-16); I 1-0, Aug. 2, 1994.

371. HR 4003. Maritime Administration Reauthorization/Passage. Passage of the bill to reauthorize the Maritime Administration at $763 million in fiscal 1995 and subsidize U.S. shipping lines through increased tonnage duties on vessels calling at U.S. ports. Passed 294-122: R 76-98; D 217-24 (ND 145-17, SD 72-7); I 1-0, Aug. 2, 1994. A "yea" was a vote in support of the president's position.

KEY

Y	Voted for (yea).
#	Paired for.
+	Announced for.
N	Voted against (nay).
X	Paired against.
—	Announced against.
P	Voted "present."
C	Voted "present" to avoid possible conflict of interest.
?	Did not vote or otherwise make a position known.
D	Delegates ineligible to vote.

Democrats *Republicans*
Independent

	364	365	366	367	368	369	370	371
ALABAMA								
1 *Callahan*	N	N	Y	N	N	Y	Y	Y
2 *Everett*	N	N	Y	N	N	Y	Y	Y
3 Browder	Y	Y	Y	N	Y	N	Y	Y
4 Bevill	Y	Y	Y	N	Y	N	Y	N
5 Cramer	Y	Y	Y	N	Y	Y	Y	Y
6 *Bachus*	N	N	Y	N	N	Y	Y	Y
7 Hilliard	Y	Y	Y	Y	Y	Y	Y	Y
ALASKA								
AL *Young*	N	N	Y	N	N	Y	Y	Y
ARIZONA								
1 *Coppersmith*	Y	Y	N	Y	Y	Y	Y	Y
2 Pastor	Y	Y	Y	Y	Y	Y	Y	Y
3 *Stump*	N	N	Y	N	N	N	N	N
4 *Kyl*	?	?	Y	N	N	N	N	N
5 *Kolbe*	N	N	Y	N	N	N	N	N
6 English	Y	Y	N	Y	Y	Y	Y	Y
ARKANSAS								
1 Lambert	Y	Y	N	Y	N	Y	Y	Y
2 Thornton	?	?	Y	Y	Y	Y	Y	Y
3 *Hutchinson*	N	N	Y	N	N	N	N	N
4 Dickey	?	?	Y	N	N	N	N	N
CALIFORNIA								
1 Hamburg	Y	Y	?	?	?	Y	Y	Y
2 *Herger*	N	N	Y	N	N	N	N	N
3 Fazio	Y	Y	Y	Y	Y	Y	Y	Y
4 *Doolittle*	N	N	Y	N	N	N	N	N
5 Matsui	Y	Y	N	?	N	N	N	Y
6 Woolsey	Y	Y	N	Y	Y	Y	Y	Y
7 Miller	Y	Y	N	Y	N	Y	N	Y
8 Pelosi	Y	Y	N	Y	Y	Y	Y	Y
9 Dellums	Y	Y	N	Y	Y	Y	Y	Y
10 *Baker*	N	N	Y	N	N	N	N	N
11 *Pombo*	N	N	Y	N	N	N	Y	N
12 Lantos	Y	Y	N	Y	Y	Y	Y	Y
13 Stark	?	Y	N	Y	N	Y	Y	Y
14 Eshoo	Y	Y	N	Y	Y	Y	Y	Y
15 Mineta	Y	Y	N	Y	N	Y	Y	Y
16 Edwards	Y	Y	N	Y	Y	Y	N	Y
17 Farr	Y	Y	N	Y	N	Y	Y	Y
18 Condit	N	N	?	N	Y	N	Y	N
19 Lehman	Y	Y	N	Y	N	Y	Y	Y
20 Dooley	Y	Y	N	Y	N	Y	N	N
21 *Thomas*	N	N	Y	N	N	N	N	N
22 *Huffington*	N	N	Y	N	N	?	N	Y
23 *Gallegly*	?	?	Y	N	N	Y	N	N
24 Beilenson	Y	Y	N	Y	Y	Y	Y	Y
25 *McKeon*	X	X	Y	N	N	Y	N	N
26 Berman	Y	Y	N	Y	Y	Y	Y	Y
27 *Moorhead*	N	N	Y	N	N	N	N	N
28 *Dreier*	N	N	Y	N	N	N	N	N
29 Waxman	Y	Y	N	Y	Y	Y	Y	Y
30 Becerra	#	#	?	?	?	Y	Y	Y
31 Martinez	Y	Y	Y	Y	Y	Y	Y	Y
32 Dixon	Y	Y	Y	Y	Y	Y	Y	Y
33 Roybal-Allard	Y	Y	N	Y	Y	Y	Y	Y
34 Torres	Y	Y	Y	Y	Y	?	Y	Y
35 Waters	Y	Y	N	Y	N	Y	N	Y
36 Harman	Y	Y	N	?	?	Y	Y	Y
37 Tucker	Y	Y	Y	Y	Y	Y	Y	Y
38 *Horn*	N	N	Y	N	N	N	N	Y
39 *Royce*	N	N	N	N	N	N	N	N
40 *Lewis*	N	N	Y	N	Y	N	Y	Y
41 *Kim*	N	N	Y	N	N	Y	N	N

	364	365	366	367	368	369	370	371
42 Brown	Y	Y	N	Y	N	Y	Y	Y
43 *Calvert*	N	N	Y	N	N	Y	Y	Y
44 *McCandless*	N	N	Y	N	N	N	Y	N
45 *Rohrabacher*	N	N	Y	N	N	Y	N	N
46 *Dornan*	N	N	Y	N	N	Y	N	N
47 *Cox*	N	N	Y	N	N	Y	N	N
48 *Packard*	N	N	Y	N	N	N	N	N
49 Schenk	Y	Y	N	Y	Y	Y	Y	Y
50 Filner	Y	Y	N	Y	Y	Y	Y	Y
51 *Cunningham*	N	N	Y	N	N	Y	Y	Y
52 *Hunter*	N	N	?	?	?	Y	Y	Y
COLORADO								
1 Schroeder	Y	?	?	Y	Y	Y	N	Y
2 Skaggs	Y	Y	N	Y	Y	Y	N	Y
3 *McInnis*	N	N	N	N	N	Y	N	Y
4 *Allard*	N	N	N	N	N	N	N	N
5 *Hefley*	N	N	N	N	N	Y	N	N
6 *Schaefer*	N	N	Y	N	N	Y	Y	Y
CONNECTICUT								
1 Kennelly	Y	Y	N	Y	Y	N	N	Y
2 Gejdenson	Y	Y	N	Y	Y	Y	Y	Y
3 DeLauro	Y	Y	N	Y	Y	Y	Y	Y
4 *Shays*	N	N	N	N	N	N	N	N
5 *Franks*	N	N	N	N	Y	Y	Y	Y
6 *Johnson*	N	N	Y	N	N	N	N	Y
DELAWARE								
AL *Castle*	N	N	N	N	N	Y	Y	Y
FLORIDA								
1 Hutto	?	?	Y	Y	N	Y	Y	Y
2 Peterson	Y	Y	Y	Y	Y	Y	Y	Y
3 Brown	Y	Y	Y	Y	Y	Y	Y	Y
4 *Fowler*	N	N	Y	N	N	Y	N	N
5 Thurman	Y	Y	N	Y	Y	Y	Y	Y
6 *Stearns*	N	N	N	N	N	Y	N	N
7 *Mica*	?	?	Y	N	N	Y	N	N
8 *McCollum*	N	N	N	N	N	Y	Y	Y
9 *Bilirakis*	N	N	N	N	Y	Y	Y	Y
10 *Young*	N	N	Y	N	N	N	N	N
11 Gibbons	?	Y	Y	Y	N	N	N	N
12 *Canady*	N	N	N	N	N	N	N	N
13 *Miller*	N	N	N	N	N	Y	Y	Y
14 *Goss*	N	N	N	N	N	Y	N	Y
15 Bacchus	?	?	Y	Y	Y	Y	Y	Y
16 *Lewis*	N	N	Y	N	N	N	N	N
17 Meek	Y	Y	Y	Y	Y	Y	Y	Y
18 *Ros-Lehtinen*	N	N	N	N	N	Y	Y	Y
19 Johnston	Y	Y	N	Y	Y	Y	Y	Y
20 Deutsch	Y	Y	N	Y	N	Y	Y	Y
21 *Diaz-Balart*	N	N	N	N	N	Y	Y	Y
22 *Shaw*	?	?	Y	N	N	N	N	Y
23 Hastings	Y	Y	N	Y	Y	Y	Y	Y
GEORGIA								
1 *Kingston*	N	N	N	N	Y	N	N	N
2 Bishop	Y	Y	N	Y	Y	Y	Y	Y
3 *Collins*	N	N	N	N	N	N	N	N
4 *Linder*	N	N	N	N	N	N	N	Y
5 Lewis	Y	Y	N	Y	N	Y	N	Y
6 *Gingrich*	N	N	N	N	N	N	N	N
7 Darden	Y	Y	Y	Y	Y	Y	Y	Y
8 Rowland	?	?	Y	Y	Y	Y	Y	N	Y
9 Deal	Y	Y	N	Y	N	Y	Y	Y
10 Johnson	Y	Y	N	Y	N	Y	Y	Y
11 McKinney	Y	Y	N	Y	Y	Y	Y	Y
HAWAII								
1 Abercrombie	Y	Y	N	Y	Y	Y	Y	Y
2 Mink	Y	Y	N	Y	Y	Y	Y	Y
IDAHO								
1 LaRocco	Y	Y	Y	Y	Y	Y	N	N
2 *Crapo*	N	N	Y	N	N	Y	N	N
ILLINOIS								
1 Rush	Y	Y	Y	?	Y	Y	Y	Y
2 Reynolds	?	?	?	?	?	N	N	Y
3 Lipinski	Y	Y	Y	N	Y	Y	Y	Y
4 Gutierrez	Y	Y	Y	Y	Y	?	Y	Y
5 Rostenkowski	Y	Y	Y	Y	Y	Y	N	N
6 *Hyde*	N	N	Y	N	N	N	N	N
7 Collins	Y	Y	#	#	#	N	N	Y
8 *Crane*	N	N	Y	N	N	N	N	N
9 Yates	Y	Y	Y	Y	Y	Y	Y	Y
10 *Porter*	N	N	Y	N	N	N	N	N
11 Sangmeister	Y	Y	Y	Y	Y	Y	Y	Y
12 Costello	Y	Y	N	N	N	N	N	N
13 *Fawell*	N	N	Y	N	N	N	N	N
14 *Hastert*	N	N	Y	N	N	N	N	N
15 *Ewing*	N	N	Y	N	N	N	N	N
16 *Manzullo*	N	N	Y	N	N	N	N	N
17 Evans	Y	Y	N	Y	Y	Y	Y	Y

	364	365	366	367	368	369	370	371
18 ***Michel***	N	N	Y	N	N	N	N	Y
19 Poshard	Y	Y	N	N	N	N	N	N
20 Durbin	Y	Y	Y	Y	Y	N	N	N
INDIANA								
1 Visclosky	Y	Y	N	Y	Y	Y	Y	Y
2 Sharp	Y	Y	N	Y	Y	Y	?	?
3 Roemer	+	+	N	Y	N	Y	Y	Y
4 Long	Y	Y	N	N	N	Y	N	N
5 ***Buyer***	N	N	Y	N	N	Y	Y	Y
6 ***Burton***	N	N	Y	N	N	Y	N	N
7 ***Myers***	N	N	Y	N	N	Y	Y	Y
8 McCloskey	Y	Y	N	Y	?	Y	Y	Y
9 Hamilton	N	Y	N	Y	N	Y	N	Y
10 Jacobs	N	Y	N	N	N	Y	N	N
IOWA								
1 ***Leach***	N	N	Y	N	N	N	N	N
2 ***Nussle***	N	N	N	N	N	Y	N	N
3 ***Lightfoot***	N	N	Y	N	N	N	N	N
4 Smith	?	?	Y	Y	Y	Y	N	N
5 ***Grandy***	?	?	N	N	N	N	N	N
KANSAS								
1 ***Roberts***	N	N	Y	N	N	N	N	N
2 Slattery	?	?	?	?	?	?	?	?
3 ***Meyers***	N	N	N	N	N	Y	N	N
4 Glickman	?	?	?	?	?	Y	N	N
KENTUCKY								
1 Barlow	Y	Y	N	Y	Y	Y	Y	Y
2 ***Lewis***	N	N	Y	N	N	N	N	N
3 Mazzoli	Y	Y	Y	Y	N	Y	Y	Y
4 ***Bunning***	N	N	N	N	N	N	N	N
5 ***Rogers***	N	N	Y	N	N	N	N	N
6 Baesler	Y	Y	N	Y	N	Y	N	N
LOUISIANA								
1 ***Livingston***	?	?	Y	N	N	Y	Y	Y
2 Jefferson	Y	Y	X	#	#	N	Y	Y
3 Tauzin	N	N	N	Y	N	Y	Y	Y
4 Fields	Y	Y	N	Y	Y	Y	Y	Y
5 ***McCrery***	N	N	Y	Y	N	Y	Y	?
6 ***Baker***	N	N	?	?	?	N	Y	Y
7 Hayes	Y	N	Y	Y	N	Y	Y	Y
MAINE								
1 Andrews	Y	Y	N	Y	Y	Y	Y	Y
2 ***Snowe***	N	N	N	N	N	Y	Y	Y
MARYLAND								
1 ***Gilchrest***	N	N	N	N	N	Y	Y	Y
2 ***Bentley***	N	N	N	N	N	Y	Y	Y
3 Cardin	Y	Y	N	Y	Y	N	Y	Y
4 Wynn	Y	Y	N	Y	Y	Y	Y	Y
5 Hoyer	Y	Y	Y	Y	Y	Y	Y	Y
6 ***Bartlett***	N	N	Y	N	N	Y	N	N
7 Mfume	Y	Y	N	N	Y	Y	Y	Y
8 ***Morella***	N	N	N	Y	N	Y	Y	Y
MASSACHUSETTS								
1 Olver	Y	Y	N	Y	Y	?	Y	Y
2 Neal	Y	Y	?	?	?	Y	Y	Y
3 ***Blute***	N	N	N	Y	N	Y	Y	Y
4 Frank	Y	Y	N	Y	Y	Y	Y	Y
5 Meehan	Y	Y	N	Y	Y	Y	Y	Y
6 ***Torkildsen***	N	N	N	Y	Y	Y	Y	Y
7 Markey	Y	Y	N	Y	Y	Y	Y	Y
8 Kennedy	Y	Y	N	Y	Y	Y	Y	Y
9 Moakley	Y	Y	N	Y	Y	Y	Y	Y
10 Studds	Y	Y	N	Y	Y	Y	Y	Y
MICHIGAN								
1 Stupak	Y	Y	?	Y	N	Y	Y	Y
2 ***Hoekstra***	N	N	N	N	N	Y	N	N
3 ***Ehlers***	N	N	Y	N	N	N	N	N
4 ***Camp***	N	N	Y	N	N	Y	N	N
5 Barcia	N	Y	Y	Y	N	Y	Y	Y
6 ***Upton***	N	N	N	N	N	Y	Y	N
7 ***Smith***	N	N	—	—	—	Y	?	?
8 Carr	?	?	?	?	?	?	?	?
9 Kildee	Y	Y	N	Y	N	Y	Y	Y
10 Bonior	Y	Y	N	Y	Y	Y	Y	Y
11 ***Knollenberg***	N	N	?	?	?	Y	N	N
12 Levin	Y	Y	N	Y	Y	Y	Y	Y
13 Ford	Y	Y	N	Y	Y	Y	Y	Y
14 Conyers	Y	Y	?	?	?	?	?	?
15 Collins	?	?	?	?	?	?	?	?
16 Dingell	Y	Y	?	?	?	?	?	?
MINNESOTA								
1 Penny	N	Y	N	Y	N	Y	N	N
2 Minge	Y	Y	N	Y	N	Y	N	N
3 ***Ramstad***	N	N	N	N	N	N	N	N
4 Vento	Y	Y	N	Y	Y	Y	Y	Y

	364	365	366	367	368	369	370	371
5 Sabo	Y	Y	N	Y	Y	Y	Y	Y
6 ***Grams***	N	N	#	X	?	Y	N	N
7 Peterson	N	Y	?	?	?	Y	N	Y
8 Oberstar	Y	Y	N	Y	Y	Y	Y	Y
MISSISSIPPI								
1 Whitten	Y	Y	?	?	?	Y	Y	Y
2 Thompson	Y	Y	?	?	?	Y	Y	Y
3 Montgomery	Y	Y	Y	Y	N	?	?	?
4 Parker	Y	Y	Y	Y	N	Y	Y	Y
5 Taylor	Y	N	Y	Y	N	Y	Y	Y
MISSOURI								
1 Clay	?	?	?	?	?	?	?	?
2 ***Talent***	N	N	N	N	N	Y	N	N
3 Gephardt	?	Y	N	Y	Y	Y	Y	Y
4 Skelton	Y	Y	?	?	?	?	N	Y
5 Wheat	?	?	?	?	?	?	?	?
6 Danner	Y	Y	N	Y	Y	Y	Y	Y
7 ***Hancock***	N	N	Y	N	N	N	N	N
8 ***Emerson***	N	N	Y	N	N	Y	N	N
9 Volkmer	Y	Y	N	Y	N	Y	Y	Y
MONTANA								
AL Williams	Y	Y	N	Y	?	Y	N	N
NEBRASKA								
1 ***Bereuter***	N	N	Y	N	N	N	N	N
2 Hoagland	Y	Y	N	Y	Y	N	Y	Y
3 ***Barrett***	N	N	Y	N	N	Y	N	N
NEVADA								
1 Bilbray	Y	Y	Y	Y	Y	Y	Y	Y
2 ***Vucanovich***	N	N	Y	N	N	Y	Y	Y
NEW HAMPSHIRE								
1 ***Zeliff***	N	N	?	Y	N	Y	N	N
2 Swett	Y	Y	N	Y	N	Y	Y	Y
NEW JERSEY								
1 Andrews	Y	Y	N	N	N	Y	Y	Y
2 Hughes	Y	Y	N	Y	N	Y	Y	Y
3 ***Saxton***	N	?	Y	N	N	Y	Y	Y
4 ***Smith***	N	N	N	Y	N	Y	Y	Y
5 ***Roukema***	N	N	N	N	N	Y	Y	Y
6 Pallone	Y	Y	N	Y	Y	Y	Y	Y
7 ***Franks***	N	N	Y	Y	N	N	N	N
8 Klein	Y	Y	N	Y	Y	Y	Y	Y
9 Torricelli	Y	Y	Y	Y	N	Y	Y	Y
10 Payne	Y	Y	N	Y	Y	Y	Y	Y
11 ***Gallo***	?	?	?	?	?	Y	N	Y
12 ***Zimmer***	N	N	N	N	N	N	N	N
13 Menendez	Y	Y	N	Y	Y	Y	Y	Y
NEW MEXICO								
1 ***Schiff***	N	N	Y	N	N	Y	Y	Y
2 ***Skeen***	N	N	Y	N	N	Y	N	Y
3 Richardson	Y	Y	N	Y	Y	Y	Y	Y
NEW YORK								
1 Hochbrueckner	Y	Y	Y	Y	Y	Y	Y	Y
2 ***Lazio***	N	N	N	N	N	Y	Y	Y
3 ***King***	N	N	N	N	N	Y	Y	Y
4 ***Levy***	N	N	N	N	N	Y	Y	Y
5 Ackerman	Y	Y	?	?	?	?	?	?
6 Flake	?	?	N	Y	Y	Y	Y	Y
7 Manton	Y	Y	N	Y	Y	Y	Y	Y
8 Nadler	Y	Y	?	?	?	Y	Y	Y
9 Schumer	Y	Y	N	Y	Y	Y	Y	Y
10 Towns	?	?	N	Y	Y	Y	Y	Y
11 Owens	?	?	?	?	?	?	?	Y
12 Velazquez	Y	Y	N	Y	Y	Y	Y	Y
13 ***Molinari***	N	N	Y	N	Y	Y	Y	Y
14 Maloney	Y	Y	N	Y	Y	Y	Y	Y
15 Rangel	Y	Y	Y	Y	Y	N	Y	Y
16 Serrano	Y	Y	N	Y	Y	Y	Y	Y
17 Engel	Y	Y	N	Y	Y	Y	Y	Y
18 Lowey	Y	Y	N	Y	Y	Y	Y	Y
19 ***Fish***	N	N	?	?	?	Y	Y	Y
20 ***Gilman***	N	N	N	Y	Y	Y	Y	Y
21 McNulty	Y	Y	N	Y	Y	Y	Y	Y
22 ***Solomon***	N	N	Y	N	?	Y	Y	Y
23 ***Boehlert***	N	N	?	?	?	Y	Y	Y
24 ***McHugh***	N	N	N	N	N	Y	Y	Y
25 ***Walsh***	N	N	Y	N	N	Y	Y	Y
26 Hinchey	Y	Y	N	Y	Y	Y	Y	Y
27 ***Paxon***	N	N	N	N	N	Y	N	N
28 Slaughter	Y	Y	N	Y	Y	Y	?	Y
29 LaFalce	Y	Y	N	Y	N	Y	Y	Y
30 ***Quinn***	N	N	N	Y	N	Y	Y	Y
31 ***Houghton***	?	?	Y	Y	Y	N	N	N
NORTH CAROLINA								
1 Clayton	Y	Y	N	Y	Y	Y	Y	Y
2 Valentine	Y	Y	N	Y	N	Y	N	Y

	364	365	366	367	368	369	370	371
3 Lancaster	N	Y	N	Y	Y	Y	Y	Y
4 Price	Y	Y	N	Y	N	Y	Y	Y
5 Neal	Y	Y	N	N	Y	Y	Y	Y
6 ***Coble***	N	N	N	N	N	Y	Y	Y
7 Rose	Y	Y	?	?	?	Y	Y	Y
8 Hefner	Y	Y	N	Y	Y	Y	Y	Y
9 ***McMillan***	?	?	?	?	?	Y	N	N
10 ***Ballenger***	N	N	Y	N	N	Y	N	N
11 ***Taylor***	N	N	Y	N	N	Y	Y	Y
12 Watt	Y	Y	N	Y	Y	Y	Y	Y
NORTH DAKOTA								
AL Pomeroy	Y	Y	N	Y	N	Y	N	Y
OHIO								
1 Mann	Y	Y	?	?	?	Y	Y	Y
2 ***Portman***	N	N	—	—	—	Y	N	N
3 Hall	Y	Y	N	Y	N	Y	N	Y
4 ***Oxley***	N	N	Y	?	?	Y	N	N
5 ***Gillmor***	N	N	N	N	N	Y	Y	Y
6 Strickland	Y	Y	N	Y	Y	Y	Y	Y
7 ***Hobson***	N	N	N	N	N	Y	N	N
8 ***Boehner***	?	?	Y	N	N	N	N	N
9 Kaptur	Y	Y	N	Y	Y	Y	Y	Y
10 ***Hoke***	N	N	N	N	N	?	Y	Y
11 Stokes	Y	Y	N	Y	Y	Y	Y	Y
12 ***Kasich***	N	N	Y	N	N	Y	N	N
13 Brown	Y	Y	N	Y	Y	Y	Y	Y
14 Sawyer	Y	Y	N	Y	Y	Y	Y	Y
15 ***Pryce***	N	N	N	N	N	Y	Y	N
16 ***Regula***	N	N	N	N	N	Y	N	Y
17 Traficant	Y	Y	N	Y	Y	Y	Y	Y
18 Applegate	Y	Y	Y	Y	Y	Y	Y	Y
19 Fingerhut	Y	Y	N	Y	N	Y	Y	Y
OKLAHOMA								
1 ***Inhofe***	?	?	?	?	?	?	?	?
2 Synar	#	#	N	Y	Y	Y	Y	Y
3 Brewster	Y	Y	N	Y	N	N	N	Y
4 McCurdy	Y	Y	N	Y	N	Y	N	Y
5 ***Istook***	N	N	?	?	?	Y	N	N
6 ***Lucas***	N	N	Y	N	N	Y	N	N
OREGON								
1 Furse	Y	Y	N	Y	Y	Y	Y	Y
2 ***Smith***	N	N	Y	N	N	N	N	N
3 Wyden	Y	Y	N	Y	Y	Y	Y	Y
4 DeFazio	Y	Y	?	?	?	?	?	?
5 Kopetski	Y	Y	Y	Y	Y	N	N	N
PENNSYLVANIA								
1 Foglietta	Y	Y	?	?	?	Y	Y	Y
2 Blackwell	Y	Y	Y	Y	Y	Y	Y	Y
3 Borski	Y	Y	N	Y	Y	Y	Y	Y
4 Klink	Y	Y	N	Y	Y	Y	Y	Y
5 ***Clinger***	N	N	Y	N	N	Y	Y	Y
6 Holden	Y	Y	N	Y	N	Y	Y	Y
7 ***Weldon***	N	N	Y	N	N	Y	Y	Y
8 ***Greenwood***	N	N	N	N	N	Y	N	N
9 ***Shuster***	N	N	Y	N	N	N	N	Y
10 ***McDade***	?	?	Y	Y	N	Y	Y	Y
11 Kanjorski	Y	Y	N	Y	Y	Y	Y	Y
12 Murtha	Y	Y	?	?	?	Y	Y	Y
13 Margolies-Mezv.	Y	Y	N	Y	N	Y	N	Y
14 Coyne	Y	Y	N	Y	Y	N	Y	Y
15 McHale	Y	Y	N	Y	N	Y	Y	Y
16 ***Walker***	N	N	Y	N	N	Y	N	N
17 ***Gekas***	N	N	N	N	N	Y	Y	Y
18 ***Santorum***	N	N	?	?	?	Y	N	?
19 ***Goodling***	N	N	Y	N	N	Y	Y	Y
20 Murphy	?	?	Y	Y	Y	Y	Y	Y
21 ***Ridge***	?	?	?	?	?	?	Y	Y
RHODE ISLAND								
1 ***Machtley***	N	N	?	?	?	Y	Y	Y
2 Reed	Y	Y	N	Y	Y	Y	Y	Y
SOUTH CAROLINA								
1 ***Ravenel***	?	?	N	Y	N	Y	Y	Y
2 ***Spence***	N	N	Y	N	N	Y	Y	Y
3 Derrick	Y	Y	N	Y	N	Y	Y	Y
4 ***Inglis***	N	N	N	N	N	N	N	N
5 Spratt	Y	Y	N	Y	N	Y	Y	Y
6 Clyburn	Y	Y	?	Y	Y	Y	Y	Y
SOUTH DAKOTA								
AL Johnson	Y	Y	N	Y	Y	Y	Y	Y
TENNESSEE								
1 ***Quillen***	X	X	Y	N	N	Y	Y	Y
2 ***Duncan***	N	N	N	N	N	Y	N	Y
3 Lloyd	?	?	Y	Y	N	Y	Y	Y
4 Cooper	N	N	N	N	N	Y	N	N
5 Clement	?	?	Y	Y	Y	Y	Y	Y

	364	365	366	367	368	369	370	371
6 Gordon	Y	Y	N	Y	N	Y	N	Y
7 ***Sundquist***	?	?	Y	N	N	Y	N	Y
8 Tanner	Y	Y	N	N	N	Y	N	Y
9 Ford	?	?	?	?	?	?	?	?
TEXAS								
1 Chapman	Y	Y	Y	Y	N	Y	Y	Y
2 Wilson	Y	Y	Y	Y	N	Y	Y	Y
3 ***Johnson, Sam***	N	N	Y	N	N	Y	N	N
4 Hall	N	N	N	N	N	Y	Y	N
5 Bryant	Y	Y	Y	Y	N	Y	Y	Y
6 ***Barton***	N	N	Y	N	N	N	N	N
7 ***Archer***	N	N	Y	N	N	N	N	N
8 ***Fields***	N	N	Y	N	N	Y	Y	Y
9 Brooks	?	Y	Y	Y	Y	Y	Y	Y
10 Pickle	?	?	?	?	?	N	N	N
11 Edwards	Y	Y	N	Y	N	Y	N	Y
12 Geren	?	?	Y	Y	N	Y	Y	Y
13 Sarpalius	Y	Y	N	Y	N	Y	Y	Y
14 Laughlin	?	?	?	?	?	?	?	?
15 de la Garza	Y	Y	N	Y	Y	Y	Y	Y
16 Coleman	Y	Y	?	?	?	Y	Y	Y
17 Stenholm	Y	Y	N	Y	N	Y	N	N
18 Washington	?	?	?	?	?	?	?	?
19 ***Combest***	N	N	Y	N	N	Y	N	N
20 Gonzalez	Y	Y	Y	Y	Y	Y	Y	Y
21 ***Smith***	N	N	Y	N	N	Y	N	N
22 ***DeLay***	N	N	Y	?	N	N	N	N
23 ***Bonilla***	N	N	Y	N	N	Y	N	N
24 Frost	Y	Y	?	?	?	?	Y	Y
25 Andrews	Y	Y	Y	Y	Y	N	N	N
26 ***Armey***	N	N	Y	N	N	Y	N	N
27 Ortiz	Y	Y	Y	Y	Y	Y	Y	Y
28 Tejeda	Y	Y	Y	Y	Y	Y	Y	Y
29 Green	Y	Y	N	Y	Y	Y	Y	Y
30 Johnson, E.B.	Y	Y	Y	Y	Y	Y	Y	Y
UTAH								
1 ***Hansen***	?	?	Y	N	N	Y	N	N
2 Shepherd	Y	Y	N	Y	Y	Y	N	Y
3 Orton	Y	Y	N	Y	N	Y	N	Y
VERMONT								
AL *Sanders*	Y	Y	X	?	Y	Y	Y	Y
VIRGINIA								
1 ***Bateman***	N	?	Y	N	N	Y	Y	Y
2 Pickett	Y	Y	Y	Y	N	Y	Y	Y
3 Scott	Y	Y	N	Y	Y	Y	Y	Y
4 Sisisky	Y	Y	N	Y	N	Y	Y	Y
5 Payne	Y	Y	N	Y	N	N	N	Y
6 ***Goodlatte***	N	N	N	N	N	Y	N	N
7 ***Bliley***	N	N	Y	N	N	Y	Y	Y
8 Moran	Y	Y	N	N	N	Y	Y	Y
9 Boucher	Y	Y	Y	Y	N	Y	N	Y
10 ***Wolf***	N	N	Y	N	N	Y	Y	Y
11 Byrne	Y	Y	N	Y	Y	Y	Y	Y
WASHINGTON								
1 Cantwell	Y	Y	N	Y	Y	Y	Y	Y
2 Swift	Y	Y	Y	Y	Y	Y	Y	Y
3 Unsoeld	Y	Y	N	Y	Y	Y	Y	Y
4 Inslee	?	?	Y	Y	N	Y	Y	Y
5 Foley								
6 Dicks	Y	Y	N	Y	Y	Y	Y	Y
7 McDermott	Y	?	N	Y	Y	N	Y	Y
8 ***Dunn***	N	N	Y	N	N	Y	Y	Y
9 Kreidler	Y	Y	N	Y	Y	Y	Y	Y
WEST VIRGINIA								
1 Mollohan	Y	Y	Y	Y	Y	Y	Y	Y
2 Wise	Y	Y	Y	Y	Y	Y	Y	Y
3 Rahall	Y	Y	Y	Y	Y	N	Y	Y
WISCONSIN								
1 Barca	Y	Y	N	Y	N	N	N	N
2 ***Klug***	N	N	N	N	N	N	N	N
3 ***Gunderson***	N	N	Y	N	N	Y	N	N
4 Kleczka	Y	Y	N	Y	Y	Y	Y	Y
5 Barrett	Y	Y	N	Y	N	Y	Y	Y
6 ***Petri***	N	N	N	N	N	N	N	N
7 Obey	Y	Y	N	Y	N	Y	Y	Y
8 ***Roth***	N	?	N	N	N	Y	N	N
9 ***Sensenbrenner***	N	N	N	N	N	N	N	N
WYOMING								
AL ***Thomas***	N	?	?	?	X	N	N	N
DELEGATES								
de Lugo, V.I.	D	D	D	D	D	D	Y	D
Faleomavaega, Am.S.	D	D	D	D	D	D	Y	D
Norton, D.C.	D	D	D	D	D	D	Y	D
Romero-B., P.R.	D	D	D	D	D	D	Y	D
Underwood, Guam	D	D	D	D	D	D	?	D

Southern states - Ala., Ark., Fla., Ga., Ky., La., Miss., N.C., Okla., S.C., Tenn., Texas, Va.
Omitted votes are quorum calls, which CQ does not include in its vote charts.

KEY

Y Voted for (yea).
\# Paired for.
+ Announced for.
N Voted against (nay).
X Paired against.
− Announced against.
P Voted "present."
C Voted "present" to avoid possible conflict of interest.
? Did not vote or otherwise make a position known.
D Delegates ineligible to vote.

Democrats **Republicans**
Independent

372. S 1357. Recognition of Little Traverse Bay Bands of Odawa and Little River Band of Ottawa Indians/Passage. Passage of the bill to give federal recognition to the Little Traverse Bay Bands of Odawa Indians and Little River Band of Ottawa Indians, both in northern Michigan, making them eligible for social services provided through the Bureau of Indian Affairs. Passed 238-180: R 24-151; D 213-29 (ND 155-12, SD 58-17); I 1-0, Aug. 3, 1994.

373. S 1066. Recognition of Pokagon Band of Potawatomi Indians/Passage. Passage of the bill to give federal recognition to the Pokagon Band of Potawatomi Indians in Michigan, making them eligible for social services provided through the Bureau of Indian Affairs. Passed 248-174: R 33-143; D 214-31 (ND 154-13, SD 60-18); I 1-0, Aug. 3, 1994.

374. Procedural Motion. Approval of the House Journal of Wednesday, Aug. 3. Approved 228-151: R 16-145; D 211-6 (ND 144-5, SD 67-1); I 1-0, Aug. 4, 1994.

375. HR 3474. Community Development Banking/Conference Report. Adoption of the conference report to authorize $382 million for loans, grants, deposits and equity investments to be administered by a new government corporation, the Community Development Financial Institutions Fund, which would be responsible for providing financial and technical assistance to a network of community lenders in underserved and poor areas. The bill also would curb abusive practices by home equity lenders, boost a secondary market in small business and commercial real estate loans and shore up the federal flood insurance program. And it includes an extensive package of "regulatory relief" provisions sought by the banking industry. Adopted 410-12: R 165-10; D 244-2 (ND 169-1, SD 75-1); I 1-0, Aug. 4, 1994.

376. HR 4426. Fiscal 1995 Foreign Operations Appropriations/Conference Report. Adoption of the conference report to provide $13,679,235,750 for foreign aid, export financing and related programs in fiscal 1995. The administration had requested $14,024,957,094. Adopted 341-85: R 115-61; D 226-23 (ND 156-14, SD 70-9); I 0-1, Aug. 4, 1994.

	372	373	374	375	376
ALABAMA					
1 *Callahan*	N	Y	N	Y	N
2 *Everett*	N	N	Y	Y	N
3 Browder	Y	Y	Y	Y	Y
4 Bevill	Y	Y	Y	Y	Y
5 Cramer	Y	Y	Y	Y	Y
6 *Bachus*	N	N	N	Y	Y
7 Hilliard	Y	Y	Y	Y	Y
ALASKA					
AL *Young*	Y	N	N	Y	Y
ARIZONA					
1 Coppersmith	Y	Y	Y	Y	Y
2 Pastor	Y	Y	Y	Y	Y
3 *Stump*	N	N	N	N	N
4 *Kyl*	N	N	N	Y	Y
5 *Kolbe*	N	N	N	Y	Y
6 English	Y	Y	Y	Y	Y
ARKANSAS					
1 Lambert	Y	Y	Y	Y	Y
2 Thornton	Y	Y	Y	Y	Y
3 *Hutchinson*	N	N	N	N	N
4 Dickey	N	N	N	Y	Y
CALIFORNIA					
1 Hamburg	Y	Y	Y	Y	Y
2 *Herger*	N	N	?	Y	N
3 Fazio	Y	Y	Y	Y	Y
4 *Doolittle*	N	Y	N	Y	N
5 Matsui	Y	Y	Y	Y	Y
6 Woolsey	Y	Y	Y	Y	Y
7 Miller	Y	Y	Y	Y	Y
8 Pelosi	Y	Y	Y	Y	Y
9 Dellums	Y	Y	?	Y	Y
10 *Baker*	N	N	?	Y	N
11 *Pombo*	N	Y	N	Y	N
12 Lantos	Y	Y	Y	Y	Y
13 Stark	Y	Y	?	Y	Y
14 Eshoo	Y	Y	Y	Y	Y
15 Mineta	Y	Y	Y	Y	Y
16 Edwards	Y	Y	Y	Y	Y
17 Farr	Y	Y	Y	Y	Y
18 Condit	Y	Y	Y	Y	N
19 Lehman	Y	Y	Y	Y	Y
20 Dooley	Y	Y	Y	Y	Y
21 *Thomas*	N	N	N	Y	Y
22 *Huffington*	N	N	N	Y	Y
23 *Gallegly*	N	N	N	Y	N
24 Beilenson	Y	Y	Y	Y	Y
25 *McKeon*	N	N	N	Y	N
26 Berman	Y	Y	Y	Y	Y
27 *Moorhead*	N	N	N	Y	N
28 *Dreier*	N	N	N	Y	N
29 Waxman	Y	Y	Y	Y	Y
30 Becerra	Y	Y	Y	Y	Y
31 Martinez	Y	Y	Y	Y	Y
32 Dixon	Y	Y	?	Y	Y
33 Roybal-Allard	Y	Y	Y	Y	Y
34 Torres	Y	Y	Y	Y	Y
35 Waters	Y	Y	Y	Y	Y
36 Harman	Y	Y	Y	Y	Y
37 Tucker	Y	Y	?	Y	Y
38 *Horn*	N	Y	N	Y	Y
39 *Royce*	N	N	N	N	Y
40 *Lewis*	N	N	N	Y	Y
41 *Kim*	N	N	N	Y	Y

	372	373	374	375	376
42 Brown	Y	Y	?	Y	Y
43 *Calvert*	N	N	N	Y	Y
44 *McCandless*	?	N	N	Y	N
45 *Rohrabacher*	N	N	N	N	N
46 *Dornan*	N	N	?	Y	Y
47 *Cox*	N	N	N	?	Y
48 *Packard*	N	N	N	Y	N
49 Schenk	Y	Y	Y	Y	Y
50 Filner	Y	Y	Y	Y	Y
51 *Cunningham*	N	N	?	Y	Y
52 *Hunter*	Y	Y	?	Y	Y
COLORADO					
1 Schroeder	Y	Y	N	Y	N
2 Skaggs	Y	Y	Y	Y	Y
3 *McInnis*	N	N	N	Y	Y
4 *Allard*	N	Y	N	Y	Y
5 *Hefley*	N	N	N	Y	N
6 *Schaefer*	N	N	N	Y	N
CONNECTICUT					
1 Kennelly	N	Y	Y	Y	Y
2 Gejdenson	Y	Y	Y	Y	Y
3 DeLauro	N	N	Y	Y	Y
4 *Shays*	N	N	Y	Y	Y
5 *Franks*	Y	Y	N	Y	Y
6 *Johnson*	N	N	N	Y	Y
DELAWARE					
AL *Castle*	N	N	Y	Y	Y
FLORIDA					
1 Hutto	N	N	Y	Y	Y
2 Peterson	Y	Y	Y	Y	Y
3 Brown	Y	Y	Y	Y	Y
4 *Fowler*	N	N	?	Y	Y
5 Thurman	Y	Y	Y	Y	Y
6 *Stearns*	N	N	N	N	N
7 *Mica*	N	Y	N	Y	N
8 *McCollum*	N	Y	N	Y	Y
9 *Bilirakis*	N	N	N	Y	Y
10 *Young*	N	N	N	Y	N
11 Gibbons	Y	Y	Y	Y	Y
12 *Canady*	N	N	N	Y	N
13 *Miller*	N	N	N	Y	N
14 *Goss*	N	N	N	Y	N
15 Bacchus	Y	Y	Y	Y	Y
16 *Lewis*	N	N	N	Y	Y
17 Meek	Y	Y	Y	Y	Y
18 *Ros-Lehtinen*	N	N	N	Y	Y
19 Johnston	Y	Y	Y	Y	Y
20 Deutsch	Y	Y	Y	Y	Y
21 *Diaz-Balart*	N	N	N	Y	Y
22 *Shaw*	N	N	N	Y	Y
23 Hastings	Y	Y	Y	Y	Y
GEORGIA					
1 *Kingston*	N	N	Y	Y	Y
2 Bishop	Y	Y	Y	Y	Y
3 *Collins*	N	N	N	Y	N
4 *Linder*	N	N	N	Y	Y
5 Lewis	Y	Y	Y	Y	Y
6 *Gingrich*	N	N	N	Y	Y
7 Darden	Y	Y	Y	Y	Y
8 Rowland	N	N	Y	Y	Y
9 *Deal*	N	N	?	Y	Y
10 Johnson	Y	Y	Y	Y	Y
11 McKinney	Y	Y	Y	Y	Y
HAWAII					
1 Abercrombie	Y	Y	Y	Y	Y
2 Mink	Y	Y	Y	Y	Y
IDAHO					
1 LaRocco	Y	Y	Y	Y	Y
2 *Crapo*	N	N	N	Y	N
ILLINOIS					
1 Rush	Y	Y	Y	Y	Y
2 Reynolds	?	?	Y	Y	Y
3 Lipinski	Y	Y	Y	Y	Y
4 Gutierrez	Y	Y	Y	Y	Y
5 Rostenkowski	Y	Y	Y	Y	Y
6 *Hyde*	N	N	N	P	Y
7 Collins	Y	Y	?	?	?
8 *Crane*	N	N	N	N	N
9 Yates	Y	Y	Y	Y	Y
10 *Porter*	N	N	N	Y	Y
11 Sangmeister	Y	Y	Y	Y	Y
12 Costello	Y	Y	Y	Y	N
13 *Fawell*	N	N	N	Y	Y
14 *Hastert*	N	N	N	Y	Y
15 *Ewing*	N	N	N	Y	Y
16 *Manzullo*	N	N	N	Y	Y
17 Evans	Y	Y	Y	Y	Y

ND Northern Democrats   SD Southern Democrats

	372	373	374	375	376
18 Michel	N	N	Y	Y	Y
19 Poshard	N	N	Y	Y	Y
20 Durbin	Y	Y	Y	Y	Y
INDIANA					
1 Visclosky	Y	Y	Y	Y	Y
2 Sharp	Y	Y	Y	Y	Y
3 Roemer	Y	Y	Y	Y	N
4 Long	Y	Y	Y	Y	Y
5 *Buyer*	N	N	N	Y	Y
6 *Burton*	N	N	N	Y	Y
7 *Myers*	Y	Y	Y	Y	Y
8 McCloskey	Y	Y	?	Y	Y
9 Hamilton	Y	Y	?	Y	Y
10 Jacobs	Y	Y	N	Y	N
IOWA					
1 *Leach*	N	Y	N	Y	Y
2 *Nussle*	N	N	N	Y	N
3 *Lightfoot*	N	N	N	Y	Y
4 Smith	Y	Y	Y	Y	Y
5 *Grandy*	N	N	N	Y	N
KANSAS					
1 *Roberts*	N	N	N	Y	Y
2 Slattery	?	?	Y	Y	N
3 *Meyers*	N	N	N	Y	Y
4 Glickman	Y	Y	Y	Y	Y
KENTUCKY					
1 Barlow	Y	Y	?	Y	Y
2 *Lewis*	N	N	N	Y	Y
3 Mazzoli	Y	Y	Y	Y	Y
4 *Bunning*	N	N	N	Y	N
5 *Rogers*	N	N	N	Y	N
6 Baesler	Y	Y	Y	Y	Y
LOUISIANA					
1 *Livingston*	N	N	Y	Y	Y
2 Jefferson	Y	Y	Y	Y	Y
3 Tauzin	N	N	Y	Y	Y
4 Fields	Y	Y	Y	Y	Y
5 *McCrery*	N	N	N	Y	Y
6 *Baker*	N	Y	N	Y	N
7 Hayes	N	Y	Y	Y	Y
MAINE					
1 Andrews	Y	Y	Y	Y	Y
2 *Snowe*	N	N	N	Y	Y
MARYLAND					
1 *Gilchrest*	Y	Y	Y	Y	Y
2 *Bentley*	N	N	?	Y	Y
3 Cardin	Y	Y	Y	Y	Y
4 Wynn	Y	Y	Y	Y	Y
5 Hoyer	Y	Y	Y	Y	Y
6 *Bartlett*	N	N	N	Y	Y
7 Mfume	Y	Y	Y	Y	Y
8 *Morella*	Y	Y	N	Y	Y
MASSACHUSETTS					
1 Olver	Y	Y	Y	Y	Y
2 Neal	Y	Y	Y	Y	Y
3 *Blute*	N	N	Y	Y	Y
4 Frank	Y	Y	Y	Y	Y
5 Meehan	Y	Y	Y	Y	Y
6 *Torkildsen*	Y	Y	N	Y	Y
7 Markey	Y	Y	Y	Y	Y
8 Kennedy	Y	Y	?	Y	Y
9 Moakley	Y	Y	Y	Y	Y
10 Studds	Y	Y	Y	Y	Y
MICHIGAN					
1 Stupak	Y	Y	Y	Y	Y
2 *Hoekstra*	Y	Y	?	Y	Y
3 *Ehlers*	Y	Y	N	Y	Y
4 *Camp*	Y	Y	?	Y	Y
5 Barcia	Y	Y	Y	Y	Y
6 *Upton*	Y	Y	N	Y	Y
7 *Smith*	Y	Y	N	Y	N
8 Carr	?	?	Y	Y	Y
9 Kildee	Y	Y	Y	Y	Y
10 Bonior	Y	Y	Y	Y	Y
11 *Knollenberg*	Y	Y	N	Y	Y
12 Levin	Y	Y	Y	Y	Y
13 Ford	Y	Y	?	Y	Y
14 Conyers	Y	Y	P	Y	Y
15 Collins	Y	Y	Y	Y	Y
16 Dingell	Y	Y	Y	Y	Y
MINNESOTA					
1 Penny	N	N	Y	Y	Y
2 Minge	N	N	Y	Y	N
3 *Ramstad*	N	N	N	Y	Y
4 Vento	Y	Y	Y	Y	Y

	372	373	374	375	376
5 Sabo	Y	Y	Y	Y	Y
6 *Grams*	N	N	N	Y	Y
7 Peterson	Y	N	N	Y	Y
8 Oberstar	Y	Y	Y	Y	Y
MISSISSIPPI					
1 *Whitten*	?	Y	?	Y	Y
2 Thompson	?	N	Y	Y	Y
3 Montgomery	?	?	Y	Y	N
4 Parker	N	N	Y	Y	Y
5 Taylor	N	N	N	N	N
MISSOURI					
1 Clay	Y	Y	N	Y	Y
2 *Talent*	N	N	N	Y	Y
3 Gephardt	Y	Y	Y	Y	Y
4 Skelton	Y	Y	Y	Y	Y
5 Wheat	?	?	Y	Y	Y
6 Danner	Y	Y	Y	Y	Y
7 *Hancock*	N	N	?	N	N
8 *Emerson*	Y	Y	N	Y	Y
9 Volkmer	Y	Y	Y	Y	N
MONTANA					
AL Williams	Y	Y	Y	Y	Y
NEBRASKA					
1 *Bereuter*	N	N	N	Y	Y
2 Hoagland	Y	Y	Y	Y	Y
3 *Barrett*	N	N	N	Y	N
NEVADA					
1 Bilbray	N	N	Y	Y	Y
2 *Vucanovich*	N	N	N	Y	Y
NEW HAMPSHIRE					
1 *Zeliff*	N	N	N	Y	Y
2 Swett	Y	N	?	Y	Y
NEW JERSEY					
1 Andrews	Y	Y	?	Y	Y
2 Hughes	N	N	Y	Y	Y
3 *Saxton*	N	N	N	Y	Y
4 *Smith*	Y	Y	Y	Y	Y
5 *Roukema*	N	N	N	Y	Y
6 Pallone	Y	Y	Y	Y	Y
7 *Franks*	N	N	N	Y	Y
8 Klein	Y	Y	Y	Y	Y
9 Torricelli	N	Y	Y	Y	Y
10 Payne	Y	Y	Y	Y	Y
11 *Gallo*	N	N	N	Y	Y
12 *Zimmer*	N	N	?	Y	Y
13 Menendez	Y	Y	Y	Y	Y
NEW MEXICO					
1 *Schiff*	N	N	N	Y	Y
2 *Skeen*	N	N	N	Y	Y
3 Richardson	Y	Y	Y	Y	Y
NEW YORK					
1 Hochbrueckner	Y	Y	Y	Y	Y
2 *Lazio*	N	N	N	Y	Y
3 *King*	N	N	N	Y	Y
4 *Levy*	N	N	N	Y	Y
5 Ackerman	Y	Y	Y	Y	Y
6 Flake	Y	Y	Y	Y	Y
7 Manton	Y	Y	?	Y	Y
8 Nadler	Y	Y	Y	Y	Y
9 Schumer	Y	Y	Y	Y	Y
10 Towns	Y	Y	?	Y	Y
11 Owens	Y	Y	Y	Y	Y
12 Velazquez	Y	Y	?	Y	Y
13 *Molinari*	N	N	N	Y	Y
14 Maloney	Y	Y	Y	Y	Y
15 Rangel	Y	Y	Y	Y	N
16 Serrano	Y	Y	Y	Y	Y
17 Engel	Y	Y	?	Y	Y
18 Lowey	Y	Y	Y	Y	Y
19 *Fish*	N	Y	N	Y	Y
20 Gilman	Y	Y	Y	Y	Y
21 McNulty	Y	Y	Y	Y	Y
22 *Solomon*	Y	N	N	N	Y
23 *Boehlert*	Y	N	N	Y	Y
24 *McHugh*	N	N	N	Y	Y
25 *Walsh*	N	N	N	Y	Y
26 Hinchey	Y	Y	?	Y	Y
27 *Paxon*	N	N	?	Y	Y
28 Slaughter	Y	Y	Y	Y	Y
29 LaFalce	Y	Y	Y	Y	Y
30 Quinn	Y	Y	Y	Y	Y
31 *Houghton*	N	N	Y	Y	Y
NORTH CAROLINA					
1 Clayton	Y	Y	Y	Y	Y
2 Valentine	N	N	Y	Y	N

	372	373	374	375	376
3 Lancaster	Y	Y	Y	Y	Y
4 Price	Y	Y	Y	Y	Y
5 Neal	Y	Y	Y	Y	Y
6 *Coble*	N	N	N	Y	Y
7 Rose	Y	Y	Y	?	Y
8 Hefner	Y	Y	Y	Y	Y
9 *McMillan*	N	N	Y	Y	Y
10 *Ballenger*	N	N	N	Y	Y
11 *Taylor*	N	N	N	Y	Y
12 Watt	Y	Y	?	Y	Y
NORTH DAKOTA					
AL Pomeroy	N	N	Y	Y	Y
OHIO					
1 Mann	Y	Y	Y	Y	Y
2 *Portman*	N	N	N	Y	Y
3 Hall	Y	Y	?	Y	Y
4 *Oxley*	?	?	N	Y	N
5 *Gillmor*	N	N	Y	Y	Y
6 Strickland	Y	Y	Y	Y	Y
7 *Hobson*	N	N	N	Y	Y
8 *Boehner*	N	N	N	Y	Y
9 Kaptur	Y	Y	Y	Y	Y
10 *Hoke*	N	N	N	Y	Y
11 Stokes	Y	Y	Y	Y	Y
12 *Kasich*	N	N	Y	Y	Y
13 Brown	Y	Y	Y	Y	Y
14 Sawyer	Y	Y	Y	Y	Y
15 *Pryce*	N	N	N	Y	Y
16 *Regula*	N	N	N	Y	Y
17 Traficant	Y	Y	Y	Y	N
18 Applegate	Y	Y	Y	Y	Y
19 Fingerhut	N	N	Y	Y	Y
OKLAHOMA					
1 *Inhofe*	N	N	N	Y	Y
2 Synar	N	N	Y	Y	Y
3 Brewster	Y	Y	Y	Y	Y
4 McCurdy	?	N	Y	Y	Y
5 *Istook*	N	N	N	Y	Y
6 *Lucas*	N	N	N	Y	Y
OREGON					
1 Furse	Y	Y	Y	Y	Y
2 *Smith*	N	N	N	Y	N
3 Wyden	Y	Y	Y	Y	Y
4 DeFazio	?	?	?	?	?
5 Kopetski	Y	Y	Y	Y	Y
PENNSYLVANIA					
1 Foglietta	Y	Y	Y	Y	Y
2 Blackwell	Y	Y	?	Y	Y
3 Borski	Y	Y	Y	Y	Y
4 Klink	Y	Y	Y	Y	Y
5 *Clinger*	N	N	Y	Y	Y
6 Holden	Y	Y	Y	Y	Y
7 *Weldon*	N	N	N	Y	Y
8 *Greenwood*	N	N	Y	Y	Y
9 *Shuster*	N	Y	N	Y	N
10 *McDade*	N	Y	N	Y	Y
11 Kanjorski	Y	Y	Y	Y	Y
12 Murtha	Y	Y	Y	Y	Y
13 Margolies-Mezv.	Y	Y	Y	Y	Y
14 Coyne	Y	Y	Y	Y	Y
15 McHale	Y	Y	Y	Y	Y
16 *Walker*	N	N	N	Y	Y
17 *Gekas*	N	N	N	N	Y
18 *Santorum*	N	N	?	Y	Y
19 *Goodling*	N	N	N	Y	Y
20 Murphy	Y	Y	N	Y	Y
21 *Ridge*	Y	Y	N	Y	Y
RHODE ISLAND					
1 *Machtley*	?	?	N	Y	Y
2 Reed	Y	Y	Y	Y	Y
SOUTH CAROLINA					
1 *Ravenel*	Y	Y	N	Y	Y
2 *Spence*	N	Y	N	Y	N
3 Derrick	Y	Y	Y	Y	Y
4 *Inglis*	N	N	N	Y	Y
5 Spratt	Y	Y	Y	Y	Y
6 Clyburn	?	Y	Y	Y	Y
SOUTH DAKOTA					
AL Johnson	Y	Y	Y	Y	Y
TENNESSEE					
1 *Quillen*	Y	Y	N	Y	?
2 *Duncan*	N	N	N	Y	N
3 Lloyd	N	N	?	Y	N
4 Cooper	N	N	Y	Y	Y
5 Clement	Y	Y	Y	?	?

	372	373	374	375	376
6 Gordon	N	N	Y	Y	Y
7 *Sundquist*	Y	Y	?	?	?
8 Tanner	N	N	Y	Y	N
9 Ford	?	?	?	?	?
TEXAS					
1 Chapman	Y	Y	?	Y	Y
2 Wilson	Y	Y	?	Y	Y
3 *Johnson, Sam*	N	N	N	N	N
4 Hall	N	N	Y	Y	N
5 Bryant	Y	Y	Y	Y	Y
6 *Barton*	N	N	?	Y	Y
7 *Archer*	N	N	N	Y	Y
8 *Fields*	N	N	N	Y	Y
9 Brooks	Y	Y	?	P	N
10 Pickle	Y	Y	Y	Y	Y
11 Edwards	Y	?	?	Y	Y
12 Geren	Y	Y	Y	Y	Y
13 Sarpalius	Y	Y	Y	Y	N
14 Laughlin	?	?	?	?	?
15 de la Garza	Y	Y	Y	Y	Y
16 Coleman	Y	Y	Y	Y	Y
17 Stenholm	N	N	Y	Y	Y
18 Washington	?	?	?	?	?
19 *Combest*	N	N	N	Y	Y
20 Gonzalez	Y	Y	Y	Y	Y
21 *Smith*	N	N	N	Y	Y
22 *DeLay*	N	N	N	Y	Y
23 *Bonilla*	N	N	N	Y	Y
24 Frost	Y	Y	?	Y	Y
25 Andrews	Y	Y	?	Y	Y
26 *Armey*	N	N	N	N	N
27 Ortiz	Y	Y	Y	Y	Y
28 Tejeda	Y	Y	Y	Y	Y
29 Green	Y	Y	Y	Y	Y
30 Johnson, E.B.	Y	Y	Y	Y	Y
UTAH					
1 *Hansen*	N	N	N	Y	N
2 Shepherd	Y	Y	Y	Y	Y
3 Orton	N	N	Y	Y	N
VERMONT					
AL *Sanders*	Y	Y	Y	Y	N
VIRGINIA					
1 *Bateman*	N	N	?	Y	Y
2 Pickett	N	N	Y	Y	Y
3 Scott	Y	Y	Y	Y	Y
4 Sisisky	N	N	Y	Y	Y
5 Payne	Y	Y	Y	Y	Y
6 *Goodlatte*	N	N	N	Y	Y
7 *Bliley*	N	N	N	Y	Y
8 Moran	Y	Y	?	Y	Y
9 Boucher	Y	Y	Y	Y	Y
10 *Wolf*	N	N	N	Y	Y
11 Byrne	Y	Y	Y	Y	Y
WASHINGTON					
1 Cantwell	Y	Y	Y	Y	Y
2 Swift	Y	Y	Y	Y	Y
3 Unsoeld	Y	Y	Y	Y	Y
4 Inslee	N	N	Y	Y	Y
5 Foley					
6 Dicks	Y	Y	Y	Y	Y
7 McDermott	Y	Y	Y	Y	Y
8 *Dunn*	N	N	Y	Y	Y
9 Kreidler	Y	Y	N	Y	Y
WEST VIRGINIA					
1 Mollohan	Y	Y	?	Y	Y
2 Wise	Y	Y	Y	Y	Y
3 Rahall	Y	Y	Y	Y	N
WISCONSIN					
1 Barca	Y	Y	Y	Y	Y
2 *Klug*	N	N	N	Y	Y
3 *Gunderson*	Y	Y	N	Y	Y
4 Kleczka	Y	Y	Y	Y	Y
5 Barrett	Y	Y	Y	Y	Y
6 *Petri*	N	N	N	Y	Y
7 Obey	Y	Y	Y	Y	Y
8 *Roth*	N	N	N	Y	Y
9 *Sensenbrenner*	N	N	N	Y	Y
WYOMING					
AL *Thomas*	N	N	N	Y	Y
DELEGATES					
de Lugo, V.I.	D	D	D	D	D
Faleomavaega, Am.S.	D	D	D	D	D
Norton, D.C.	D	D	D	D	D
Romero-B., P.R.	D	D	D	D	D
Underwood, Guam	D	D	D	D	D

Southern states - Ala., Ark., Fla., Ga., Ky., La., Miss., N.C., Okla., S.C., Tenn., Texas, Va.
Omitted votes are quorum calls, which CQ does not include in its vote charts.

377. HR 4217. Farm Crop Insurance/Mandatory Spending. De la Garza, D-Texas, amendment to the Penny, D-Minn., amendment, to make the costs of reimbursing private crop insurers part of the mandatory spending process for fiscal 1995-97 and the discretionary process in fiscal 1998-99, and make various changes to produce $272 million in savings over five years through various changes in the crop insurance program to offset the spending in the bill. The amendment would replace provisions of the Penny amendment that permanently would make the cost of reimbursing private insurers mandatory spending and provide $608 million in offset savings. Such spending currently is considered discretionary spending; HR 4217 would make it mandatory spending for fiscal 1995 only. Adopted in the Committee of the Whole 253-156: R 118-50; D 135-105 (ND 74-94, SD 61-11); I 0-1, Aug. 5, 1994.

378. HR 4217. Farm Crop Insurance/Mandatory Spending. Penny, D-Minn., amendment, as amended by the de la Garza, D-Texas, amendment, to make the costs of reimbursing private insurers part of the mandatory spending process for fiscal 1995-97 and the discretionary process in fiscal 1998-99, and make various changes to produce $272 million in savings over five years through various changes in the crop insurance program to offset the spending in the bill. Such spending currently is considered discretionary spending; HR 4217 would make it mandatory spending for fiscal 1995 only. Adopted in the Committee of the Whole 401-1: R 165-0; D 235-1 (ND 165-1, SD 70-0); I 1-0, Aug. 5, 1994.

379. HR 4545. Federal Railroad Safety Authorization/Passage. Schenk, D-Calif., motion to suspend the rules and pass the bill to authorize $317 million over fiscal 1995-98 for the programs of the Federal Railroad Administration to inspect and ensure safety on railroads. Motion agreed to 395-0: R 162-0; D 232-0 (ND 157-0, SD 75-0); I 1-0, Aug. 8, 1994. A two-thirds majority of those present and voting (264 in this case) is required for passage under suspension of the rules.

380. Procedural Motion. Approval of the House Journal of Monday, Aug. 8. Approved 251-153: R 19-145; D 231-8 (ND 155-7, SD 76-1); I 1-0, Aug. 9, 1994.

381. H J Res 373. 1994 China MFN Disapproval/Passage. Passage of the joint resolution to disapprove President Clinton's May 26 waiver of the Jackson-Vanik amendment to the 1974 trade act in order to grant most-favored-nation (MFN) status to China from July 1994 through July 1995, allowing Chinese products to enter the United States at the lowest available tariff rate. Jackson-Vanik bars MFN status to communist countries that do not allow free emigration. Rejected 75-356: R 36-141; D 38-215 (ND 27-145, SD 11-70); I 1-0, Aug. 9, 1994. A "nay" was a vote in support of the president's position.

382. HR 4590. China MFN/Executive Order Codification. Hamilton, D-Ind., substitute amendment to codify President Clinton's May 26 executive order waiving the Jackson-Vanik amendment to the 1974 trade act and granting most-favored-nation (MFN) status to China from July 1994 through July 1995, allowing Chinese products to enter the United States at the lowest available tariff rate. Jackson-Vanik bars MFN status to communist countries that do not allow free emigration. The substitute also would prohibit Chinese armaments imports; authorize the U.S. Information Agency to promote human rights in China; authorize increased money for broadcasting in China; urge U.S. businesses in China to protect workers' rights; and authorize a commission to monitor human rights conditions in China. The bill would deny the Jackson-Vanik amendment with respect to products manufactured or exported by the Chinese army, Chinese defense industrial trading companies or state-owned enterprises, and require the Treasury Department to publish a list of such enterprises. Adopted in the Committee of the Whole 280-152: R 129-44; D 151-107 (ND 90-86, SD 61-21); I 0-1, Aug. 9, 1994. A "yea" was a vote in support of the president's position.

KEY

Y Voted for (yea).
Paired for.
+ Announced for.
N Voted against (nay).
X Paired against.
− Announced against.
P Voted "present."
C Voted "present" to avoid possible conflict of interest.
? Did not vote or otherwise make a position known.
D Delegates ineligible to vote.

Democrats *Republicans*
Independent

	377	378	379	380	381	382
ALABAMA						
1 *Callahan*	Y	Y	Y	N	N	Y
2 *Everett*	Y	Y	Y	Y	Y	N
3 Browder	Y	Y	?	Y	N	Y
4 Bevill	Y	Y	Y	Y	N	Y
5 Cramer	Y	Y	Y	Y	N	Y
6 *Bachus*	Y	Y	Y	N	N	Y
7 Hilliard	Y	Y	Y	Y	Y	N
ALASKA						
AL *Young*	Y	Y	Y	N	N	Y
ARIZONA						
1 Coppersmith	N	Y	Y	Y	N	Y
2 Pastor	N	Y	Y	N	Y	N
3 *Stump*	N	Y	Y	N	N	Y
4 *Kyl*	N	Y	Y	N	N	Y
5 *Kolbe*	N	Y	Y	N	N	Y
6 English	Y	Y	Y	Y	N	Y
ARKANSAS						
1 Lambert	Y	Y	Y	N	N	Y
2 Thornton	Y	Y	Y	?	N	Y
3 *Hutchinson*	Y	Y	Y	N	N	N
4 Dickey	Y	Y	Y	N	N	Y
CALIFORNIA						
1 Hamburg	Y	Y	Y	Y	Y	N
2 *Herger*	Y	Y	Y	N	N	?
3 Fazio	Y	Y	Y	Y	N	Y
4 *Doolittle*	Y	Y	Y	N	N	Y
5 Matsui	Y	Y	Y	Y	N	Y
6 Woolsey	Y	Y	Y	Y	N	N
7 Miller	N	?	Y	N	Y	N
8 Pelosi	N	Y	Y	Y	Y	N
9 Dellums	N	Y	Y	Y	Y	N
10 *Baker*	Y	Y	Y	N	Y	N
11 *Pombo*	Y	Y	Y	N	Y	Y
12 Lantos	N	Y	Y	Y	N	Y
13 Stark	N	Y	Y	Y	Y	N
14 Eshoo	N	Y	Y	Y	N	N
15 Mineta	N	Y	Y	Y	N	Y
16 Edwards	N	Y	Y	Y	N	N
17 Farr	N	Y	Y	Y	N	N
18 Condit	N	Y	Y	Y	N	Y
19 Lehman	Y	Y	?	Y	N	Y
20 Dooley	Y	Y	Y	Y	N	Y
21 *Thomas*	N	Y	Y	N	N	Y
22 *Huffington*	Y	Y	Y	?	N	Y
23 *Gallegly*	?	?	Y	?	N	Y
24 Beilenson	N	Y	Y	Y	N	Y
25 *McKeon*	Y	Y	Y	N	N	Y
26 Berman	?	?	Y	N	N	Y
27 *Moorhead*	N	Y	Y	N	N	Y
28 *Dreier*	Y	Y	Y	N	N	Y
29 Waxman	N	Y	Y	Y	N	N
30 Becerra	Y	Y	?	?	N	Y
31 Martinez	Y	Y	Y	Y	N	Y
32 Dixon	N	Y	Y	Y	N	Y
33 Roybal-Allard	N	Y	Y	Y	N	N
34 Torres	N	Y	Y	Y	N	Y
35 Waters	N	Y	Y	?	Y	N
36 Harman	N	Y	Y	Y	N	Y
37 Tucker	N	Y	Y	Y	Y	N
38 *Horn*	N	Y	Y	N	Y	N
39 *Royce*	N	Y	Y	N	N	Y
40 *Lewis*	Y	Y	Y	N	N	Y
41 *Kim*	Y	Y	Y	N	N	Y

	377	378	379	380	381	382
42 Brown	Y	Y	Y	?	N	Y
43 *Calvert*	?	?	Y	N	N	Y
44 *McCandless*	N	Y	Y	N	N	Y
45 *Rohrabacher*	N	Y	Y	N	N	Y
46 *Dornan*	Y	Y	Y	?	N	Y
47 *Cox*	N	Y	Y	N	N	Y
48 *Packard*	N	Y	Y	N	N	Y
49 Schenk	N	Y	Y	Y	N	Y
50 Filner	Y	Y	Y	Y	Y	N
51 *Cunningham*	N	Y	Y	N	N	Y
52 *Hunter*	Y	Y	Y	?	Y	N
COLORADO						
1 Schroeder	N	Y	Y	N	Y	N
2 Skaggs	N	Y	Y	Y	N	Y
3 *McInnis*	N	Y	Y	N	N	Y
4 *Allard*	Y	Y	Y	N	N	Y
5 *Hefley*	N	Y	?	?	Y	N
6 *Schaefer*	Y	Y	?	N	N	Y
CONNECTICUT						
1 Kennelly	Y	Y	Y	N	N	Y
2 Gejdenson	N	Y	Y	Y	N	N
3 DeLauro	N	Y	Y	Y	N	Y
4 *Shays*	N	Y	Y	N	N	Y
5 *Franks*	N	Y	Y	N	N	Y
6 *Johnson*	N	Y	Y	N	N	Y
DELAWARE						
AL *Castle*	Y	Y	Y	N	N	Y
FLORIDA						
1 Hutto	Y	Y	Y	Y	N	N
2 Peterson	N	Y	Y	Y	N	Y
3 Brown	Y	Y	Y	Y	N	Y
4 *Fowler*	Y	Y	Y	N	N	Y
5 Thurman	Y	Y	Y	Y	N	Y
6 *Stearns*	N	Y	Y	N	N	N
7 *Mica*	N	Y	Y	N	N	Y
8 *McCollum*	Y	Y	Y	N	N	Y
9 *Bilirakis*	Y	Y	Y	N	N	Y
10 *Young*	Y	Y	Y	N	N	N
11 Gibbons	Y	Y	Y	Y	N	Y
12 *Canady*	Y	Y	Y	N	N	Y
13 *Miller*	N	Y	Y	N	N	Y
14 *Goss*	N	Y	Y	N	N	Y
15 Bacchus	?	?	Y	Y	N	Y
16 *Lewis*	Y	Y	Y	N	Y	N
17 Meek	Y	Y	Y	Y	N	Y
18 *Ros-Lehtinen*	?	?	Y	N	Y	N
19 Johnston	N	Y	Y	Y	N	Y
20 Deutsch	N	Y	Y	Y	N	Y
21 *Diaz-Balart*	X	?	Y	?	Y	N
22 *Shaw*	?	?	Y	N	N	Y
23 Hastings	Y	Y	Y	?	N	Y
GEORGIA						
1 *Kingston*	Y	Y	Y	Y	N	Y
2 Bishop	Y	Y	Y	Y	N	Y
3 *Collins*	Y	Y	Y	N	N	Y
4 *Linder*	Y	Y	Y	N	N	Y
5 Lewis	N	Y	Y	Y	Y	N
6 *Gingrich*	Y	Y	Y	N	N	Y
7 Darden	#	?	Y	Y	N	Y
8 Rowland	Y	Y	Y	Y	N	Y
9 Deal	N	Y	Y	Y	N	Y
10 Johnson	Y	Y	Y	Y	N	Y
11 McKinney	N	Y	?	Y	Y	N
HAWAII						
1 Abercrombie	Y	Y	Y	Y	Y	N
2 Mink	Y	Y	Y	Y	N	N
IDAHO						
1 LaRocco	Y	Y	Y	Y	N	Y
2 *Crapo*	Y	Y	Y	Y	N	Y
ILLINOIS						
1 Rush	N	Y	?	Y	N	Y
2 Reynolds	N	Y	Y	Y	N	Y
3 Lipinski	?	?	Y	Y	N	N
4 Gutierrez	N	Y	Y	Y	N	Y
5 Rostenkowski	N	Y	Y	Y	N	Y
6 *Hyde*	Y	Y	Y	N	N	N
7 Collins	N	Y	Y	Y	Y	N
8 *Crane*	N	Y	Y	N	N	Y
9 Yates	N	Y	Y	Y	N	N
10 *Porter*	N	Y	Y	N	N	N
11 Sangmeister	N	Y	Y	Y	N	Y
12 Costello	N	Y	Y	Y	N	Y
13 *Fawell*	N	Y	Y	N	N	N
14 *Hastert*	Y	Y	Y	N	N	Y
15 *Ewing*	Y	Y	?	N	N	Y
16 *Manzullo*	Y	Y	Y	N	N	Y
17 Evans	N	Y	Y	Y	Y	N

ND Northern Democrats   SD Southern Democrats

	377	378	379	380	381	382
18 ***Michel***	Y	Y	?	?	N	Y
19 Poshard	N	Y	Y	Y	N	N
20 Durbin	N	Y	Y	Y	Y	N
INDIANA						
1 Visclosky	N	Y	Y	Y	N	Y
2 Sharp	N	Y	Y	Y	N	N
3 Roemer	Y	Y	Y	Y	N	Y
4 Long	Y	Y	Y	Y	N	Y
5 ***Buyer***	Y	Y	Y	N	N	Y
6 ***Burton***	Y	Y	?	N	Y	N
7 ***Myers***	N	Y	Y	Y	N	Y
8 McCloskey	N	Y	Y	Y	N	N
9 Hamilton	Y	Y	Y	Y	N	Y
10 Jacobs	N	Y	Y	N	N	Y
IOWA						
1 ***Leach***	Y	Y	Y	N	N	Y
2 ***Nussle***	Y	Y	Y	N	N	Y
3 ***Lightfoot***	Y	Y	?	N	N	Y
4 Smith	Y	Y	Y	Y	N	Y
5 ***Grandy***	Y	Y	Y	N	N	Y
KANSAS						
1 ***Roberts***	Y	Y	Y	N	N	Y
2 Slattery	Y	Y	Y	Y	N	Y
3 ***Meyers***	Y	Y	Y	N	N	Y
4 Glickman	Y	Y	Y	Y	N	Y
KENTUCKY						
1 Barlow	Y	Y	Y	Y	N	Y
2 ***Lewis***	Y	Y	Y	N	Y	N
3 Mazzoli	N	Y	Y	Y	N	N
4 ***Bunning***	Y	Y	Y	N	Y	N
5 ***Rogers***	Y	Y	Y	N	Y	N
6 Baesler	Y	Y	Y	Y	N	Y
LOUISIANA						
1 ***Livingston***	Y	Y	Y	N	N	Y
2 Jefferson	Y	Y	Y	?	N	Y
3 Tauzin	Y	Y	Y	Y	Y	N
4 Fields	Y	Y	Y	Y	Y	N
5 ***McCrery***	Y	Y	Y	Y	N	Y
6 ***Baker***	?	?	?	N	N	Y
7 Hayes	?	?	Y	Y	N	N
MAINE						
1 Andrews	N	Y	Y	Y	Y	N
2 ***Snowe***	Y	Y	Y	N	Y	N
MARYLAND						
1 ***Gilchrest***	Y	Y	Y	N	N	Y
2 ***Bentley***	Y	Y	Y	N	Y	?
3 Cardin	N	Y	Y	Y	N	N
4 Wynn	Y	Y	Y	Y	N	N
5 Hoyer	N	Y	Y	Y	N	N
6 ***Bartlett***	Y	Y	Y	N	N	Y
7 Mfume	N	Y	Y	?	N	N
8 ***Morella***	N	Y	Y	N	N	Y
MASSACHUSETTS						
1 Olver	Y	Y	Y	Y	N	N
2 Neal	Y	Y	?	Y	N	Y
3 ***Blute***	Y	Y	Y	Y	N	Y
4 Frank	N	Y	Y	Y	Y	N
5 Meehan	N	Y	?	Y	N	N
6 ***Torkildsen***	Y	?	Y	N	N	Y
7 Markey	N	Y	Y	Y	Y	N
8 Kennedy	Y	Y	Y	Y	N	N
9 Moakley	Y	Y	Y	Y	N	N
10 Studds	N	Y	Y	Y	N	N
MICHIGAN						
1 Stupak	Y	Y	Y	Y	N	N
2 ***Hoekstra***	N	Y	Y	N	N	Y
3 ***Ehlers***	Y	Y	Y	N	N	Y
4 ***Camp***	Y	Y	Y	N	N	Y
5 Barcia	Y	Y	Y	Y	N	Y
6 ***Upton***	N	Y	Y	N	Y	N
7 ***Smith***	N	Y	Y	N	N	Y
8 Carr	N	Y	Y	Y	N	Y
9 Kildee	N	Y	Y	Y	N	N
10 Bonior	?	?	Y	Y	Y	N
11 ***Knollenberg***	N	Y	Y	N	N	Y
12 Levin	Y	Y	Y	Y	N	Y
13 Ford	Y	Y	Y	Y	N	N
14 Conyers	Y	Y	Y	Y	N	N
15 Collins	N	Y	Y	Y	Y	N
16 Dingell	Y	Y	Y	Y	N	Y
MINNESOTA						
1 Penny	N	Y	Y	Y	N	Y
2 Minge	Y	Y	Y	Y	N	Y
3 ***Ramstad***	N	Y	Y	N	N	Y
4 Vento	N	Y	Y	Y	N	N

	377	378	379	380	381	382
5 Sabo	N	Y	Y	Y	N	Y
6 ***Grams***	Y	Y	Y	?	N	Y
7 Peterson	Y	Y	Y	Y	N	Y
8 Oberstar	N	Y	Y	Y	N	Y
MISSISSIPPI						
1 Whitten	Y	Y	Y	Y	N	Y
2 Thompson	Y	Y	Y	Y	N	Y
3 Montgomery	Y	Y	Y	Y	N	Y
4 Parker	Y	Y	Y	Y	N	Y
5 Taylor	Y	Y	Y	N	Y	N
MISSOURI						
1 Clay	N	Y	Y	N	N	N
2 ***Talent***	Y	Y	Y	N	N	Y
3 Gephardt	?	Y	Y	Y	N	N
4 Skelton	Y	Y	Y	Y	N	Y
5 Wheat	Y	?	Y	Y	N	Y
6 Danner	Y	Y	?	Y	N	Y
7 ***Hancock***	N	Y	Y	N	N	Y
8 ***Emerson***	Y	Y	Y	N	N	Y
9 Volkmer	Y	Y	Y	Y	N	Y
MONTANA						
AL Williams	Y	Y	Y	?	N	Y
NEBRASKA						
1 ***Bereuter***	Y	Y	Y	N	N	Y
2 Hoagland	Y	Y	Y	Y	N	Y
3 ***Barrett***	Y	Y	Y	N	N	Y
NEVADA						
1 Bilbray	N	Y	Y	Y	N	N
2 ***Vucanovich***	Y	Y	Y	N	N	Y
NEW HAMPSHIRE						
1 ***Zeliff***	Y	Y	Y	N	N	Y
2 Swett	Y	Y	Y	Y	N	N
NEW JERSEY						
1 Andrews	N	Y	Y	Y	N	Y
2 Hughes	Y	Y	Y	Y	N	Y
3 ***Saxton***	Y	Y	Y	N	N	Y
4 ***Smith***	Y	Y	Y	N	Y	N
5 ***Roukema***	N	Y	Y	N	N	?
6 Pallone	N	Y	Y	Y	Y	N
7 ***Franks***	Y	Y	Y	N	N	Y
8 Klein	N	Y	Y	Y	N	Y
9 Torricelli	Y	Y	Y	Y	N	N
10 Payne	N	Y	Y	Y	N	N
11 ***Gallo***	N	Y	?	N	N	?
12 ***Zimmer***	N	Y	Y	N	N	Y
13 Menendez	Y	Y	Y	Y	N	Y
NEW MEXICO						
1 ***Schiff***	Y	Y	Y	N	Y	N
2 ***Skeen***	Y	Y	Y	N	N	Y
3 Richardson	Y	Y	Y	Y	N	N
NEW YORK						
1 Hochbrueckner	Y	Y	?	?	N	N
2 ***Lazio***	N	Y	Y	N	N	Y
3 ***King***	Y	Y	Y	N	N	Y
4 ***Levy***	Y	Y	Y	N	N	Y
5 Ackerman	N	Y	Y	Y	N	Y
6 Flake	N	Y	Y	Y	N	Y
7 Manton	Y	Y	Y	Y	N	Y
8 Nadler	N	Y	?	Y	Y	N
9 Schumer	N	Y	Y	Y	N	Y
10 Towns	Y	Y	Y	Y	N	N
11 Owens	N	Y	?	?	N	N
12 Velazquez	N	Y	?	N	N	N
13 ***Molinari***	Y	Y	Y	N	Y	N
14 Maloney	N	Y	Y	Y	N	Y
15 Rangel	N	Y	?	Y	N	Y
16 Serrano	Y	Y	Y	Y	N	Y
17 Engel	N	Y	Y	?	N	N
18 Lowey	N	Y	Y	Y	N	N
19 ***Fish***	Y	Y	Y	?	Y	N
20 ***Gilman***	Y	Y	Y	Y	Y	N
21 McNulty	Y	?	Y	Y	N	Y
22 ***Solomon***	Y	?	Y	N	Y	N
23 ***Boehlert***	Y	Y	Y	N	N	N
24 ***McHugh***	Y	Y	Y	N	N	Y
25 ***Walsh***	Y	Y	Y	N	N	Y
26 Hinchey	Y	Y	Y	Y	N	N
27 ***Paxon***	Y	Y	Y	N	N	Y
28 Slaughter	N	Y	Y	Y	N	Y
29 LaFalce	Y	Y	Y	Y	N	Y
30 ***Quinn***	N	Y	Y	N	N	Y
31 ***Houghton***	Y	Y	Y	Y	N	Y
NORTH CAROLINA						
1 Clayton	Y	Y	Y	Y	N	N
2 Valentine	N	Y	Y	Y	N	Y

	377	378	379	380	381	382
3 Lancaster	Y	Y	Y	Y	Y	N
4 Price	Y	Y	Y	Y	N	Y
5 Neal	Y	Y	?	Y	N	Y
6 ***Coble***	N	Y	Y	N	N	Y
7 Rose	Y	Y	?	Y	Y	N
8 Hefner	Y	Y	Y	Y	Y	N
9 ***McMillan***	N	Y	Y	N	N	Y
10 ***Ballenger***	—	+	Y	N	N	Y
11 ***Taylor***	Y	Y	Y	N	N	Y
12 Watt	N	Y	Y	Y	Y	N
NORTH DAKOTA						
AL Pomeroy	Y	Y	Y	Y	N	Y
OHIO						
1 Mann	N	Y	Y	Y	N	Y
2 ***Portman***	Y	Y	Y	N	N	Y
3 Hall	N	Y	Y	Y	Y	N
4 ***Oxley***	Y	Y	Y	Y	N	Y
5 ***Gillmor***	Y	Y	Y	Y	N	Y
6 Strickland	Y	Y	Y	Y	N	N
7 ***Hobson***	Y	Y	Y	N	N	N
8 ***Boehner***	Y	Y	Y	N	N	Y
9 Kaptur	N	Y	Y	Y	Y	N
10 ***Hoke***	Y	Y	Y	N	N	Y
11 Stokes	N	Y	Y	Y	N	N
12 ***Kasich***	Y	Y	Y	Y	Y	N
13 Brown	Y	Y	Y	Y	Y	N
14 Sawyer	N	Y	Y	Y	N	Y
15 ***Pryce***	Y	Y	?	N	N	Y
16 ***Regula***	N	Y	Y	N	N	Y
17 Traficant	Y	Y	Y	Y	Y	N
18 Applegate	N	N	Y	Y	Y	N
19 Fingerhut	N	Y	Y	Y	N	Y
OKLAHOMA						
1 ***Inhofe***	Y	Y	?	?	N	Y
2 Synar	X	?	Y	Y	N	Y
3 Brewster	Y	Y	?	Y	N	Y
4 McCurdy	Y	Y	?	Y	N	Y
5 ***Istook***	Y	Y	Y	N	N	Y
6 ***Lucas***	Y	Y	Y	N	N	Y
OREGON						
1 Furse	Y	Y	Y	Y	N	Y
2 ***Smith***	Y	Y	Y	N	N	Y
3 Wyden	N	Y	Y	Y	N	Y
4 DeFazio	?	?	?	Y	N	N
5 Kopetski	Y	Y	Y	Y	N	Y
PENNSYLVANIA						
1 Foglietta	?	?	Y	Y	N	Y
2 Blackwell	Y	Y	?	?	N	Y
3 Borski	Y	Y	Y	Y	N	N
4 Klink	Y	Y	Y	Y	Y	N
5 ***Clinger***	Y	Y	Y	Y	N	Y
6 Holden	Y	Y	Y	Y	N	N
7 ***Weldon***	N	Y	Y	N	Y	N
8 ***Greenwood***	N	Y	Y	Y	N	Y
9 ***Shuster***	Y	Y	Y	?	N	Y
10 ***McDade***	Y	Y	Y	N	N	Y
11 Kanjorski	Y	Y	Y	Y	N	Y
12 Murtha	Y	Y	Y	Y	N	Y
13 Margolies-Mezv.	N	Y	Y	Y	N	N
14 Coyne	N	Y	Y	Y	N	N
15 McHale	Y	Y	Y	Y	N	N
16 ***Walker***	Y	Y	Y	N	Y	N
17 ***Gekas***	Y	Y	Y	N	N	Y
18 ***Santorum***	Y	Y	?	N	N	Y
19 ***Goodling***	—	+	Y	N	N	N
20 Murphy	?	?	Y	N	N	Y
21 ***Ridge***	Y	Y	?	N	Y	N
RHODE ISLAND						
1 ***Machtley***	?	?	?	N	N	Y
2 Reed	N	Y	Y	Y	N	Y
SOUTH CAROLINA						
1 ***Ravenel***	Y	Y	?	?	?	?
2 ***Spence***	Y	Y	Y	Y	N	Y
3 Derrick	Y	Y	Y	Y	N	Y
4 ***Inglis***	Y	Y	?	?	Y	N
5 Spratt	Y	?	Y	Y	Y	N
6 Clyburn	Y	Y	Y	?	?	?
SOUTH DAKOTA						
AL Johnson	Y	Y	Y	Y	N	Y
TENNESSEE						
1 ***Quillen***	Y	?	Y	N	Y	Y
2 ***Duncan***	N	Y	Y	N	Y	N
3 Lloyd	Y	?	Y	Y	N	Y
4 Cooper	Y	Y	Y	Y	N	Y
5 Clement	?	?	Y	Y	N	Y

	377	378	379	380	381	382
6 Gordon	?	?	Y	Y	N	Y
7 ***Sundquist***	?	?	Y	N	N	Y
8 Tanner	Y	Y	Y	Y	N	Y
9 Ford	?	?	Y	Y	N	N
TEXAS						
1 Chapman	Y	Y	Y	Y	N	Y
2 Wilson	Y	Y	Y	Y	N	Y
3 ***Johnson, Sam***	Y	Y	Y	N	N	Y
4 Hall	Y	Y	Y	Y	N	Y
5 Bryant	Y	Y	Y	Y	N	Y
6 ***Barton***	Y	Y	Y	N	Y	N
7 ***Archer***	N	Y	Y	N	N	Y
8 ***Fields***	Y	Y	Y	N	N	Y
9 Brooks	Y	Y	Y	Y	N	Y
10 Pickle	Y	Y	?	Y	N	Y
11 Edwards	Y	Y	Y	Y	N	Y
12 Geren	Y	Y	Y	Y	N	Y
13 Sarpalius	Y	Y	Y	Y	N	Y
14 Laughlin	Y	Y	Y	Y	N	Y
15 de la Garza	Y	Y	Y	Y	N	Y
16 Coleman	Y	Y	Y	Y	N	Y
17 Stenholm	Y	Y	Y	Y	N	Y
18 Washington	?	?	?	?	?	N
19 ***Combest***	Y	Y	Y	Y	N	Y
20 Gonzalez	Y	Y	Y	Y	N	N
21 ***Smith***	Y	Y	Y	N	Y	N
22 ***DeLay***	Y	Y	Y	N	N	Y
23 ***Bonilla***	Y	Y	?	N	N	Y
24 Frost	Y	Y	Y	Y	N	Y
25 Andrews	?	?	Y	Y	N	Y
26 ***Armey***	N	Y	Y	N	N	Y
27 Ortiz	Y	Y	Y	Y	N	Y
28 Tejeda	Y	Y	Y	Y	N	Y
29 Green	#	?	Y	Y	N	N
30 Johnson, E.B.	Y	Y	Y	Y	N	Y
UTAH						
1 ***Hansen***	Y	Y	Y	N	N	Y
2 Shepherd	N	Y	Y	Y	N	N
3 Orton	N	Y	Y	Y	N	Y
VERMONT						
AL *Sanders*	N	Y	Y	Y	Y	N
VIRGINIA						
1 ***Bateman***	Y	Y	Y	Y	N	Y
2 Pickett	Y	Y	Y	Y	N	Y
3 Scott	Y	Y	Y	Y	N	N
4 Sisisky	Y	Y	Y	Y	N	Y
5 Payne	Y	Y	Y	Y	N	Y
6 ***Goodlatte***	Y	Y	Y	N	N	Y
7 ***Bliley***	Y	Y	Y	N	N	Y
8 Moran	N	Y	Y	?	N	Y
9 Boucher	?	?	Y	Y	N	Y
10 ***Wolf***	Y	Y	Y	N	Y	N
11 Byrne	N	Y	Y	Y	N	N
WASHINGTON						
1 Cantwell	N	Y	Y	Y	N	Y
2 Swift	Y	Y	Y	Y	N	Y
3 Unsoeld	N	Y	Y	Y	N	N
4 Inslee	N	Y	Y	Y	N	Y
5 Foley						Y
6 Dicks	Y	Y	Y	Y	N	Y
7 McDermott	N	Y	Y	Y	N	N
8 ***Dunn***	Y	Y	Y	?	N	Y
9 Kreidler	N	Y	Y	Y	N	Y
WEST VIRGINIA						
1 Mollohan	Y	Y	Y	Y	N	?
2 Wise	Y	Y	Y	?	N	Y
3 Rahall	Y	Y	Y	Y	N	N
WISCONSIN						
1 Barca	N	Y	Y	Y	N	Y
2 ***Klug***	N	Y	Y	N	N	N
3 ***Gunderson***	N	Y	Y	N	N	N
4 Kleczka	N	Y	Y	Y	N	Y
5 Barrett	N	Y	Y	Y	N	N
6 ***Petri***	N	Y	Y	N	N	Y
7 Obey	N	Y	?	Y	N	N
8 ***Roth***	N	Y	Y	N	N	Y
9 ***Sensenbrenner***	N	Y	Y	N	Y	N
WYOMING						
AL ***Thomas***	Y	Y	Y	N	N	Y
DELEGATES						
de Lugo, V.I.	?	?	D	D	D	Y
Faleomavaega, Am.S.	Y	Y	D	D	D	Y
Norton, D.C.	N	Y	D	D	D	N
Romero-B., P.R.	?	?	D	D	D	?
Underwood, Guam	Y	Y	D	D	D	N

Southern states - Ala., Ark., Fla., Ga., Ky., La., Miss., N.C., Okla., S.C., Tenn., Texas, Va.
Omitted votes are quorum calls, which CQ does not include in its vote charts.

383. HR 4590. China MFN/State-Owned Enterprises. Pelosi, D-Calif., substitute amendment to deny President Clinton's waiver of the Jackson-Vanik amendment to the 1974 trade act with respect to products manufactured or exported by the Chinese army, Chinese defense industrial trading companies or state-owned enterprises in order to grant most-favored-nation (MFN) status, which allows those products to enter the United States at the lowest available tariff rate. Jackson-Vanik bars MFN status to communist countries that do not allow free emigration. The substitute also would require the Treasury Department to publish a list of enterprises owned by the Chinese military and Chinese defense industrial trading companies, and would urge U.S. businesses in China to protect worker and human rights. Rejected in the Committee of the Whole 158-270: R 46-125; D 111-145 (ND 91-84, SD 20-61); I 1-0, Aug. 9, 1994. A "nay" was a vote in support of the president's position.

384. HR 4603. Fiscal 1995 Commerce, Justice, State, Judiciary Appropriations/Motion To Instruct. Rogers, R-Ky., motion to instruct the House conferees to accept the Senate amendments to cut the U.S. contribution to the United Nations' general budget in arrears by $40 million and the U.S. contribution to U.N. peacekeeping operations by $33.3 million. Motion rejected 177-250: R 163-10; D 14-239 (ND 7-165, SD 7-74); I 0-1, Aug. 10, 1994.

385. HR 4506. Fiscal 1995 Energy and Water Appropriations/Conference Report. Adoption of the conference report to provide approximately $20.5 billion in new budget authority for energy and water development in fiscal 1995. The administration had requested $20.5 billion. Adopted (thus cleared for the Senate) 393-34: R 145-29; D 247-5 (ND 165-5, SD 82-0); I 1-0, Aug. 10, 1994.

386. HR 4822. Congressional Compliance/Previous Question. Beilenson, D-Calif., motion to order the previous question (thus ending debate and the possibility of amendment) on adoption of the rule (H Res 514) to provide for House floor consideration of the bill to bring Congress into compliance with federal labor laws, including the Americans With Disabilities Act, the Family Leave Act, the Occupational Safety and Health Act and the Fair Labor Standards Act. Motion agreed to 247-185: R 1-176; D 245-9 (ND 168-4, SD 77-5); I 1-0, Aug. 10, 1994. (Subsequently, the rule was adopted by voice vote.)

*388. HR 4822. Congressional Compliance/Health Care Package. Byrne, D-Va., amendment to require that the health care benefits package for members of Congress be the same as any benefits package Congress enacts as part of national heath care changes this year. Adopted in the Committee of the Whole 374-57: R 150-26; D 223-31 (ND 149-25, SD 74-6); I 1-0, Aug. 10, 1994.

389. HR 4822. Congressional Compliance/Executive Director. Fingerhut, D-Ohio, amendment to the Beilenson, D-Calif., amendment, to prohibit former members of Congress and former congressional aides or lobbyists from serving as executive director of the office that would oversee congressional compliance with various labor laws. The Beilenson amendment would prohibit ex-members or lobbyists from holding the position, and prohibit aides from holding it for at least four years. Rejected in the Committee of the Whole 216-220: R 131-45; D 85-174 (ND 56-121, SD 29-53); I 0-1, Aug. 10, 1994. (Subsequently, the Beilenson amendment was adopted by voice vote.)

390. HR 4822. Congressional Compliance/Passage. Passage of the bill to bring Congress into compliance with federal labor laws, including the Americans With Disabilities Act, the Family Leave Act, the Occupational Safety and Health Act and the Fair Labor Standards Act. Passed 427-4: R 175-0; D 251-4 (ND 170-3, SD 81-1); I 1-0, Aug. 10, 1994.

* Omitted votes are quorum calls, which CQ does not include in its vote charts.

KEY

Y	Voted for (yea).
#	Paired for.
+	Announced for.
N	Voted against (nay).
X	Paired against.
−	Announced against.
P	Voted "present."
C	Voted "present" to avoid possible conflict of interest.
?	Did not vote or otherwise make a position known.
D	Delegates ineligible to vote.

Democrats **Republicans**
Independent

	383	384	385	386	388	389	390
ALABAMA							
1 *Callahan*	N	Y	Y	N	Y	N	Y
2 *Everett*	Y	Y	Y	N	Y	Y	Y
3 Browder	Y	N	Y	Y	Y	Y	Y
4 Bevill	N	N	Y	Y	Y	N	Y
5 Cramer	N	N	Y	Y	Y	N	Y
6 *Bachus*	N	Y	Y	N	Y	Y	Y
7 Hilliard	Y	N	Y	Y	Y	N	Y
ALASKA							
AL *Young*	N	Y	Y	N	N	N	Y
ARIZONA							
1 Coppersmith	N	N	Y	Y	Y	Y	Y
2 Pastor	N	N	Y	Y	Y	N	Y
3 *Stump*	N	Y	N	N	Y	N	Y
4 *Kyl*	N	Y	Y	N	Y	Y	Y
5 *Kolbe*	N	Y	Y	N	Y	Y	Y
6 English	N	N	Y	Y	Y	N	Y
ARKANSAS							
1 Lambert	N	N	Y	Y	Y	Y	Y
2 Thornton	N	N	Y	Y	Y	N	Y
3 *Hutchinson*	Y	Y	Y	N	Y	Y	Y
4 *Dickey*	Y	Y	Y	N	Y	Y	Y
CALIFORNIA							
1 Hamburg	Y	N	Y	Y	Y	N	Y
2 *Herger*	?	?	?	?	?	?	?
3 Fazio	N	N	Y	Y	Y	N	Y
4 *Doolittle*	N	Y	N	Y	Y	Y	Y
5 Matsui	N	N	Y	Y	Y	N	Y
6 Woolsey	Y	N	Y	Y	Y	N	Y
7 Miller	Y	N	Y	Y	Y	N	Y
8 Pelosi	Y	N	Y	Y	Y	N	Y
9 Dellums	Y	N	?	Y	Y	N	Y
10 *Baker*	Y	Y	Y	N	Y	Y	Y
11 *Pombo*	N	Y	N	N	Y	Y	Y
12 Lantos	Y	N	Y	Y	Y	Y	Y
13 Stark	?	N	Y	Y	Y	N	Y
14 Eshoo	Y	N	Y	Y	Y	Y	Y
15 Mineta	N	N	Y	Y	Y	N	Y
16 Edwards	Y	N	Y	N	N	Y	Y
17 Farr	Y	N	Y	Y	Y	Y	Y
18 Condit	N	Y	Y	Y	Y	N	Y
19 Lehman	N	N	Y	Y	Y	N	Y
20 Dooley	N	N	Y	Y	Y	N	Y
21 *Thomas*	N	Y	Y	N	N	Y	Y
22 *Huffington*	N	Y	N	Y	Y	Y	Y
23 *Gallegly*	N	Y	Y	N	Y	Y	Y
24 Beilenson	Y	N	Y	Y	Y	N	Y
25 *McKeon*	N	Y	Y	N	Y	Y	Y
26 Berman	Y	N	Y	Y	Y	N	Y
27 *Moorhead*	N	Y	Y	N	Y	Y	Y
28 *Dreier*	N	Y	N	N	Y	Y	Y
29 Waxman	Y	N	Y	Y	Y	N	Y
30 Becerra	N	N	Y	Y	Y	Y	Y
31 Martinez	N	N	Y	Y	Y	N	Y
32 Dixon	Y	N	Y	Y	Y	N	Y
33 Roybal-Allard	N	N	Y	Y	N	N	Y
34 Torres	N	N	Y	Y	Y	N	Y
35 Waters	Y	N	Y	Y	Y	N	Y
36 Harman	N	N	Y	Y	Y	Y	Y
37 Tucker	N	N	N	Y	N	Y	Y
38 *Horn*	Y	Y	Y	N	Y	N	Y
39 *Royce*	N	Y	N	N	Y	Y	Y
40 *Lewis*	N	Y	Y	N	N	N	Y
41 *Kim*	N	Y	Y	N	Y	Y	Y

	383	384	385	386	388	389	390
42 Brown	N	N	Y	Y	N	Y	Y
43 *Calvert*	N	Y	Y	N	Y	Y	Y
44 *McCandless*	N	Y	Y	N	Y	N	Y
45 *Rohrabacher*	Y	Y	N	Y	Y	Y	Y
46 *Dornan*	Y	?	Y	N	Y	Y	Y
47 *Cox*	N	Y	Y	N	Y	N	Y
48 *Packard*	N	Y	N	N	N	N	Y
49 Schenk	N	N	Y	Y	Y	Y	Y
50 Filner	N	N	Y	Y	Y	N	Y
51 *Cunningham*	N	Y	Y	N	Y	Y	Y
52 *Hunter*	Y	Y	N	Y	N	Y	Y
COLORADO							
1 Schroeder	Y	N	Y	Y	Y	Y	Y
2 Skaggs	N	N	Y	Y	Y	N	Y
3 *McInnis*	N	Y	Y	N	Y	Y	Y
4 *Allard*	N	Y	N	N	Y	Y	Y
5 *Hefley*	Y	Y	N	N	Y	N	Y
6 *Schaefer*	N	Y	N	Y	Y	Y	Y
CONNECTICUT							
1 Kennelly	N	N	Y	Y	Y	N	Y
2 Gejdenson	Y	N	Y	Y	Y	N	Y
3 DeLauro	N	N	Y	Y	Y	N	Y
4 *Shays*	N	Y	N	Y	Y	Y	Y
5 *Franks*	N	Y	Y	Y	Y	Y	Y
6 *Johnson*	N	N	Y	Y	Y	N	Y
DELAWARE							
AL *Castle*	N	Y	Y	N	Y	Y	Y
FLORIDA							
1 Hutto	Y	N	Y	Y	Y	Y	Y
2 Peterson	N	N	Y	Y	Y	N	Y
3 Brown	N	N	Y	N	P	N	Y
4 *Fowler*	N	Y	Y	N	N	Y	Y
5 Thurman	N	N	Y	Y	Y	N	Y
6 *Stearns*	Y	Y	N	Y	Y	Y	Y
7 *Mica*	N	Y	N	N	Y	N	Y
8 *McCollum*	?	Y	?	N	N	Y	Y
9 *Bilirakis*	Y	Y	N	Y	Y	N	Y
10 *Young*	Y	Y	Y	N	N	N	Y
11 Gibbons	N	N	Y	Y	Y	Y	Y
12 *Canady*	N	Y	Y	N	Y	Y	Y
13 *Miller*	N	Y	N	N	Y	N	Y
14 *Goss*	N	Y	Y	N	Y	Y	Y
15 *Bacchus*	N	N	Y	Y	Y	Y	Y
16 *Lewis*	N	Y	N	N	Y	N	Y
17 Meek	N	N	Y	N	N	N	Y
18 *Ros-Lehtinen*	Y	Y	Y	N	Y	N	Y
19 Johnston	N	N	Y	Y	N	N	Y
20 Deutsch	N	N	Y	Y	Y	Y	Y
21 *Diaz-Balart*	Y	Y	Y	N	Y	N	Y
22 *Shaw*	N	Y	Y	N	Y	Y	Y
23 Hastings	N	N	Y	N	N	N	Y
GEORGIA							
1 *Kingston*	N	Y	N	N	Y	Y	Y
2 Bishop	N	N	Y	Y	N	Y	Y
3 *Collins*	Y	Y	Y	N	Y	Y	Y
4 *Linder*	N	Y	Y	N	N	Y	Y
5 Lewis	Y	N	Y	Y	Y	N	Y
6 *Gingrich*	N	Y	Y	N	N	N	Y
7 Darden	N	N	Y	N	Y	N	Y
8 Rowland	N	N	Y	Y	Y	N	Y
9 Deal	N	N	Y	Y	Y	N	Y
10 Johnson	N	N	Y	Y	Y	Y	Y
11 McKinney	Y	N	Y	Y	Y	N	Y
HAWAII							
1 Abercrombie	Y	N	N	N	N	N	Y
2 Mink	Y	N	Y	N	N	N	Y
IDAHO							
1 LaRocco	N	N	Y	Y	Y	N	Y
2 *Crapo*	N	Y	N	N	Y	Y	Y
ILLINOIS							
1 Rush	N	N	Y	Y	Y	N	Y
2 Reynolds	N	N	Y	Y	Y	N	Y
3 Lipinski	Y	N	Y	Y	Y	Y	Y
4 Gutierrez	Y	N	Y	Y	Y	Y	Y
5 Rostenkowski	N	N	Y	Y	N	N	Y
6 *Hyde*	Y	Y	N	N	N	Y	Y
7 Collins	Y	N	Y	N	Y	N	Y
8 *Crane*	N	Y	N	N	N	N	Y
9 Yates	Y	N	Y	Y	Y	N	Y
10 *Porter*	Y	N	Y	Y	Y	Y	Y
11 Sangmeister	N	N	Y	Y	Y	N	Y
12 Costello	Y	Y	Y	Y	Y	N	Y
13 *Fawell*	N	Y	N	Y	Y	Y	Y
14 *Hastert*	N	Y	Y	N	Y	N	Y
15 *Ewing*	N	Y	Y	N	Y	N	Y
16 *Manzullo*	N	Y	N	N	Y	Y	Y
17 Evans	Y	N	Y	Y	Y	N	Y

ND Northern Democrats   SD Southern Democrats

	383	384	385	386	388	389	390
18 ***Michel***	N	Y	Y	N	N	N	Y
19 Poshard	Y	Y	Y	Y	Y	Y	Y
20 Durbin	Y	N	Y	Y	Y	N	Y
INDIANA							
1 Visclosky	N	N	Y	Y	Y	N	Y
2 Sharp	Y	N	Y	Y	Y	N	Y
3 Roemer	N	N	Y	Y	Y	Y	Y
4 Long	N	N	Y	Y	Y	Y	Y
5 ***Buyer***	N	Y	Y	N	Y	N	Y
6 ***Burton***	Y	Y	N	N	Y	N	Y
7 ***Myers***	N	Y	Y	N	Y	N	Y
8 McCloskey	Y	N	Y	Y	N	N	Y
9 Hamilton	N	N	Y	Y	Y	Y	Y
10 Jacobs	N	Y	N	N	Y	Y	Y
IOWA							
1 ***Leach***	N	N	Y	N	Y	Y	Y
2 ***Nussle***	N	Y	Y	N	Y	Y	Y
3 ***Lightfoot***	N	Y	Y	N	Y	Y	Y
4 Smith	N	N	Y	Y	Y	Y	Y
5 ***Grandy***	N	Y	Y	N	N	Y	Y
KANSAS							
1 ***Roberts***	N	Y	Y	N	Y	N	Y
2 Slattery	N	N	Y	Y	Y	N	Y
3 ***Meyers***	N	Y	Y	N	Y	Y	Y
4 Glickman	N	N	Y	Y	Y	N	Y
KENTUCKY							
1 Barlow	N	N	Y	Y	Y	Y	Y
2 ***Lewis***	Y	Y	Y	N	Y	Y	Y
3 Mazzoli	Y	Y	Y	N	Y	N	Y
4 ***Bunning***	Y	Y	Y	N	Y	Y	Y
5 ***Rogers***	Y	Y	Y	N	Y	Y	Y
6 Baesler	N	N	Y	Y	Y	N	Y
LOUISIANA							
1 ***Livingston***	N	Y	Y	N	Y	Y	Y
2 Jefferson	N	N	Y	Y	Y	Y	Y
3 Tauzin	N	Y	Y	Y	Y	N	Y
4 Fields	Y	N	Y	Y	Y	Y	Y
5 ***McCrery***	N	Y	Y	N	Y	N	Y
6 ***Baker***	N	Y	Y	N	N	N	Y
7 Hayes	N	Y	Y	Y	Y	Y	Y
MAINE							
1 Andrews	Y	N	Y	Y	Y	N	Y
2 ***Snowe***	Y	Y	Y	N	Y	Y	Y
MARYLAND							
1 ***Gilchrest***	N	Y	Y	N	Y	Y	Y
2 ***Bentley***	?	Y	Y	N	Y	N	Y
3 Cardin	Y	N	Y	Y	Y	N	Y
4 Wynn	Y	N	Y	Y	Y	N	Y
5 Hoyer	Y	N	Y	Y	Y	N	Y
6 ***Bartlett***	N	Y	Y	N	Y	Y	Y
7 Mfume	Y	N	Y	Y	Y	N	Y
8 ***Morella***	N	N	Y	N	Y	N	Y
MASSACHUSETTS							
1 Olver	Y	N	Y	Y	Y	N	Y
2 Neal	Y	N	Y	Y	Y	N	Y
3 ***Blute***	N	Y	Y	N	Y	Y	Y
4 Frank	Y	N	Y	Y	Y	N	Y
5 Meehan	Y	N	Y	Y	Y	Y	Y
6 ***Torkildsen***	N	N	Y	N	Y	Y	Y
7 Markey	Y	N	Y	Y	Y	N	Y
8 Kennedy	Y	N	Y	Y	Y	N	Y
9 Moakley	Y	N	Y	Y	Y	N	Y
10 Studds	Y	N	Y	Y	Y	N	Y
MICHIGAN							
1 Stupak	Y	N	Y	Y	Y	Y	Y
2 ***Hoekstra***	N	Y	Y	N	Y	Y	Y
3 ***Ehlers***	N	Y	Y	N	Y	Y	Y
4 ***Camp***	N	Y	Y	N	Y	Y	Y
5 Barcia	N	N	Y	Y	Y	Y	Y
6 ***Upton***	Y	Y	Y	N	Y	Y	Y
7 ***Smith***	N	Y	Y	N	Y	Y	Y
8 Carr	N	N	Y	Y	Y	Y	Y
9 Kildee	Y	N	Y	Y	Y	Y	Y
10 Bonior	Y	N	Y	Y	Y	N	Y
11 ***Knollenberg***	N	Y	Y	N	Y	N	Y
12 Levin	Y	N	Y	Y	Y	Y	Y
13 Ford	Y	N	Y	N	N	N	N
14 Conyers	Y	N	Y	Y	Y	N	Y
15 Collins	Y	N	Y	N	N	N	N
16 Dingell	N	N	Y	Y	Y	N	Y
MINNESOTA							
1 Penny	N	N	N	Y	Y	Y	Y
2 Minge	N	N	N	Y	Y	Y	Y
3 ***Ramstad***	N	Y	N	N	Y	Y	Y
4 Vento	Y	N	Y	Y	Y	N	Y
5 Sabo	N	N	Y	Y	Y	N	Y
6 ***Grams***	N	Y	N	N	Y	Y	Y
7 Peterson	N	N	N	Y	Y	Y	Y
8 Oberstar	N	N	Y	Y	Y	N	Y
MISSISSIPPI							
1 Whitten	?	?	Y	Y	Y	N	Y
2 Thompson	N	N	Y	Y	Y	N	Y
3 Montgomery	N	N	Y	Y	Y	Y	Y
4 Parker	N	N	Y	Y	Y	Y	Y
5 Taylor	Y	Y	Y	N	Y	Y	Y
MISSOURI							
1 Clay	Y	N	Y	Y	N	N	N
2 ***Talent***	N	Y	Y	N	Y	Y	Y
3 Gephardt	Y	N	Y	Y	Y	N	Y
4 Skelton	N	N	Y	Y	Y	N	Y
5 Wheat	N	N	Y	Y	Y	N	Y
6 Danner	N	N	Y	Y	Y	Y	Y
7 ***Hancock***	N	Y	N	N	Y	N	Y
8 ***Emerson***	N	Y	Y	N	Y	N	Y
9 Volkmer	N	N	Y	Y	Y	N	Y
MONTANA							
AL Williams	N	N	?	Y	Y	N	Y
NEBRASKA							
1 ***Bereuter***	N	N	Y	N	Y	Y	Y
2 Hoagland	N	N	Y	Y	Y	N	Y
3 ***Barrett***	N	Y	Y	N	Y	Y	Y
NEVADA							
1 Bilbray	Y	N	Y	Y	Y	Y	Y
2 ***Vucanovich***	N	Y	Y	N	Y	N	Y
NEW HAMPSHIRE							
1 ***Zeliff***	N	Y	N	N	Y	Y	Y
2 Swett	Y	N	Y	Y	Y	Y	Y
NEW JERSEY							
1 Andrews	N	N	Y	Y	Y	Y	Y
2 Hughes	N	N	Y	Y	Y	N	Y
3 ***Saxton***	N	Y	Y	N	Y	Y	Y
4 ***Smith***	Y	Y	Y	N	Y	Y	Y
5 ***Roukema***	?	?	Y	N	Y	Y	Y
6 Pallone	Y	N	Y	Y	Y	Y	Y
7 ***Franks***	?	Y	Y	N	Y	Y	Y
8 Klein	N	N	Y	Y	Y	Y	Y
9 Torricelli	Y	Y	Y	Y	Y	N	Y
10 Payne	Y	N	Y	Y	Y	N	Y
11 ***Gallo***	?	Y	Y	N	Y	Y	?
12 ***Zimmer***	N	Y	Y	N	Y	Y	Y
13 Menendez	Y	N	Y	Y	Y	Y	Y
NEW MEXICO							
1 ***Schiff***	Y	Y	Y	N	Y	Y	Y
2 ***Skeen***	N	Y	Y	N	Y	N	Y
3 Richardson	Y	N	Y	Y	Y	Y	Y
NEW YORK							
1 Hochbrueckner	Y	N	Y	Y	Y	N	Y
2 ***Lazio***	N	Y	Y	N	Y	Y	Y
3 ***King***	Y	Y	Y	N	N	N	Y
4 ***Levy***	N	Y	Y	N	Y	Y	Y
5 Ackerman	N	N	Y	Y	N	N	Y
6 Flake	N	N	Y	Y	N	N	Y
7 Manton	N	N	Y	Y	N	N	Y
8 Nadler	Y	N	Y	Y	Y	Y	Y
9 Schumer	N	N	Y	Y	Y	N	Y
10 Towns	Y	N	Y	Y	Y	N	Y
11 Owens	Y	N	Y	Y	Y	N	Y
12 Velazquez	Y	N	Y	Y	Y	N	Y
13 ***Molinari***	Y	Y	Y	N	?	?	?
14 Maloney	N	N	Y	Y	Y	Y	Y
15 Rangel	Y	N	Y	Y	Y	N	Y
16 Serrano	N	N	Y	Y	N	N	Y
17 Engel	Y	N	Y	Y	Y	N	Y
18 Lowey	Y	N	Y	Y	Y	Y	Y
19 ***Fish***	Y	N	Y	N	Y	Y	Y
20 ***Gilman***	Y	N	Y	N	Y	Y	Y
21 McNulty	N	Y	Y	Y	Y	N	Y
22 ***Solomon***	Y	Y	N	N	Y	Y	Y
23 ***Boehlert***	Y	N	Y	N	Y	N	Y
24 ***McHugh***	N	Y	N	N	Y	Y	Y
25 ***Walsh***	N	Y	Y	N	Y	N	Y
26 Hinchey	Y	N	Y	Y	Y	N	Y
27 ***Paxon***	N	Y	N	N	Y	Y	Y
28 Slaughter	N	N	Y	Y	Y	N	Y
29 LaFalce	N	N	Y	Y	Y	N	Y
30 ***Quinn***	N	Y	Y	N	Y	Y	Y
31 ***Houghton***	N	N	Y	N	N	Y	Y
NORTH CAROLINA							
1 Clayton	Y	N	Y	Y	N	N	Y
2 Valentine	N	N	Y	Y	?	N	Y
3 Lancaster	Y	N	Y	Y	Y	Y	Y
4 Price	N	N	Y	Y	Y	Y	Y
5 Neal	N	N	Y	Y	Y	N	Y
6 ***Coble***	N	Y	N	N	Y	Y	Y
7 Rose	Y	N	Y	Y	N	N	Y
8 Hefner	Y	N	Y	Y	Y	N	Y
9 ***McMillan***	N	?	Y	N	N	N	Y
10 ***Ballenger***	N	Y	Y	N	Y	Y	Y
11 ***Taylor***	Y	Y	N	N	Y	Y	Y
12 Watt	Y	N	Y	Y	N	N	Y
NORTH DAKOTA							
AL Pomeroy	N	N	Y	Y	Y	N	Y
OHIO							
1 Mann	N	N	Y	Y	Y	N	Y
2 ***Portman***	N	Y	Y	N	Y	Y	Y
3 Hall	Y	N	Y	Y	Y	N	Y
4 ***Oxley***	N	Y	Y	N	N	N	Y
5 ***Gillmor***	N	Y	Y	N	Y	N	Y
6 Strickland	Y	N	Y	Y	Y	Y	Y
7 ***Hobson***	Y	Y	Y	N	Y	N	Y
8 ***Boehner***	N	Y	?	N	Y	N	Y
9 Kaptur	Y	N	Y	Y	P	N	Y
10 ***Hoke***	N	Y	Y	N	Y	N	Y
11 Stokes	Y	N	Y	Y	Y	N	Y
12 ***Kasich***	Y	Y	Y	N	Y	Y	Y
13 Brown	Y	N	Y	Y	Y	Y	Y
14 Sawyer	N	N	Y	Y	Y	N	Y
15 ***Pryce***	N	Y	Y	N	Y	Y	Y
16 ***Regula***	N	Y	Y	N	Y	N	Y
17 Traficant	Y	Y	Y	Y	Y	Y	Y
18 Applegate	Y	N	Y	Y	Y	N	Y
19 Fingerhut	N	N	Y	Y	Y	Y	Y
OKLAHOMA							
1 ***Inhofe***	N	Y	Y	N	Y	Y	Y
2 Synar	N	N	Y	Y	Y	N	Y
3 Brewster	N	N	Y	Y	Y	N	Y
4 McCurdy	N	N	Y	Y	Y	Y	Y
5 ***Istook***	N	Y	Y	N	Y	Y	Y
6 ***Lucas***	N	Y	Y	N	Y	Y	Y
OREGON							
1 Furse	N	N	Y	Y	Y	Y	Y
2 ***Smith***	N	Y	Y	N	N	N	Y
3 Wyden	N	N	Y	Y	Y	Y	Y
4 DeFazio	Y	N	Y	Y	Y	N	Y
5 Kopetski	N	N	Y	Y	Y	N	Y
PENNSYLVANIA							
1 Foglietta	Y	N	Y	Y	Y	N	Y
2 Blackwell	Y	N	Y	Y	Y	N	Y
3 Borski	Y	N	Y	Y	N	N	Y
4 Klink	Y	N	Y	Y	N	N	Y
5 ***Clinger***	N	Y	Y	N	Y	Y	Y
6 Holden	Y	N	Y	Y	Y	Y	Y
7 ***Weldon***	Y	Y	Y	N	Y	Y	Y
8 ***Greenwood***	N	Y	Y	N	Y	N	Y
9 ***Shuster***	N	Y	Y	N	Y	Y	Y
10 ***McDade***	N	Y	Y	N	N	N	Y
11 Kanjorski	N	N	Y	Y	Y	N	Y
12 Murtha	N	N	Y	Y	N	N	Y
13 Margolies-Mezv.	Y	N	Y	Y	Y	Y	Y
14 Coyne	Y	N	Y	Y	Y	N	Y
15 McHale	Y	N	Y	Y	Y	Y	Y
16 ***Walker***	N	Y	Y	N	Y	Y	Y
17 ***Gekas***	N	Y	Y	N	Y	Y	Y
18 ***Santorum***	N	Y	Y	N	Y	Y	Y
19 ***Goodling***	Y	Y	Y	N	Y	Y	Y
20 Murphy	N	N	Y	Y	Y	N	Y
21 ***Ridge***	N	Y	Y	N	Y	Y	Y
RHODE ISLAND							
1 ***Machtley***	N	Y	Y	N	Y	Y	Y
2 Reed	N	N	Y	Y	Y	N	Y
SOUTH CAROLINA							
1 ***Ravenel***	?	?	?	N	Y	Y	Y
2 ***Spence***	Y	Y	Y	N	Y	Y	Y
3 Derrick	N	N	Y	Y	Y	N	Y
4 ***Inglis***	Y	Y	N	N	Y	Y	Y
5 Spratt	Y	N	Y	Y	Y	Y	Y
6 Clyburn	?	N	Y	Y	Y	N	Y
SOUTH DAKOTA							
AL Johnson	N	N	Y	Y	Y	N	Y
TENNESSEE							
1 ***Quillen***	N	Y	Y	N	Y	N	Y
2 ***Duncan***	Y	Y	N	N	Y	Y	Y
3 Lloyd	N	N	Y	Y	Y	N	Y
4 Cooper	N	Y	Y	N	Y	Y	Y
5 Clement	N	N	Y	Y	Y	Y	Y
6 Gordon	N	N	Y	Y	Y	N	Y
7 ***Sundquist***	N	Y	Y	N	Y	Y	Y
8 Tanner	N	N	Y	Y	Y	N	Y
9 Ford	Y	N	Y	Y	Y	N	Y
TEXAS							
1 Chapman	N	N	Y	Y	Y	N	Y
2 Wilson	N	N	Y	Y	Y	N	Y
3 ***Johnson, Sam***	N	Y	Y	N	Y	Y	Y
4 Hall	N	Y	Y	Y	Y	Y	Y
5 Bryant	N	N	Y	Y	Y	Y	Y
6 ***Barton***	Y	Y	Y	N	N	N	Y
7 ***Archer***	N	Y	N	N	Y	Y	Y
8 ***Fields***	N	Y	Y	N	Y	Y	Y
9 Brooks	N	N	Y	Y	Y	N	Y
10 Pickle	N	N	Y	Y	Y	N	Y
11 Edwards	N	N	Y	Y	Y	Y	Y
12 Geren	N	N	Y	Y	Y	N	Y
13 Sarpalius	N	N	Y	Y	Y	N	Y
14 Laughlin	N	N	Y	Y	Y	N	Y
15 de la Garza	N	N	Y	Y	Y	N	Y
16 Coleman	N	N	Y	Y	Y	N	Y
17 Stenholm	N	N	Y	Y	Y	Y	Y
18 Washington	Y	?	?	?	?	?	?
19 ***Combest***	N	Y	Y	N	Y	Y	Y
20 Gonzalez	Y	N	Y	Y	N	N	N
21 ***Smith***	Y	Y	Y	N	Y	Y	Y
22 ***DeLay***	N	Y	Y	N	N	Y	Y
23 ***Bonilla***	N	Y	Y	N	Y	N	Y
24 Frost	N	N	Y	Y	Y	N	Y
25 Andrews	N	N	Y	Y	Y	Y	Y
26 ***Armey***	N	Y	N	N	Y	Y	Y
27 Ortiz	N	N	Y	Y	Y	N	Y
28 Tejeda	N	N	Y	Y	Y	N	Y
29 Green	Y	Y	Y	Y	Y	N	Y
30 Johnson, E.B.	N	N	Y	Y	Y	N	Y
UTAH							
1 ***Hansen***	N	Y	Y	N	N	N	Y
2 Shepherd	Y	N	Y	Y	Y	Y	Y
3 Orton	N	N	Y	Y	Y	Y	Y
VERMONT							
AL *Sanders*	Y	N	Y	Y	Y	N	Y
VIRGINIA							
1 ***Bateman***	N	Y	Y	N	N	N	Y
2 Pickett	N	N	Y	Y	Y	N	Y
3 Scott	Y	N	Y	Y	Y	N	Y
4 Sisisky	N	N	Y	Y	Y	Y	Y
5 Payne	N	N	Y	Y	Y	N	Y
6 ***Goodlatte***	N	Y	Y	N	Y	Y	Y
7 ***Bliley***	N	Y	Y	N	N	Y	Y
8 Moran	N	N	Y	Y	Y	N	Y
9 Boucher	N	N	Y	Y	Y	N	Y
10 ***Wolf***	Y	Y	Y	N	Y	Y	Y
11 Byrne	Y	N	Y	Y	Y	Y	Y
WASHINGTON							
1 Cantwell	N	N	Y	Y	Y	Y	Y
2 Swift	N	N	Y	Y	Y	N	Y
3 Unsoeld	Y	N	Y	Y	Y	Y	Y
4 Inslee	N	N	Y	Y	Y	N	Y
5 Foley							Y
6 Dicks	N	N	Y	Y	Y	N	Y
7 McDermott	N	N	Y	Y	Y	N	Y
8 ***Dunn***	N	Y	Y	N	Y	Y	Y
9 Kreidler	N	N	Y	Y	Y	Y	Y
WEST VIRGINIA							
1 Mollohan	N	N	Y	Y	Y	N	Y
2 Wise	N	N	Y	Y	Y	N	Y
3 Rahall	Y	N	Y	Y	Y	N	Y
WISCONSIN							
1 Barca	N	N	Y	Y	Y	Y	Y
2 ***Klug***	Y	Y	N	N	Y	Y	Y
3 ***Gunderson***	Y	Y	Y	N	Y	Y	Y
4 Kleczka	N	N	Y	Y	Y	Y	Y
5 Barrett	Y	N	Y	Y	Y	Y	Y
6 ***Petri***	N	Y	N	N	Y	N	Y
7 Obey	Y	N	Y	Y	?	N	Y
8 ***Roth***	N	Y	Y	N	Y	Y	Y
9 ***Sensenbrenner***	Y	Y	N	N	Y	Y	Y
WYOMING							
AL ***Thomas***	N	Y	Y	N	Y	N	Y
DELEGATES							
de Lugo, V.I.	Y	D	D	D	N	N	D
Faleomavaega, Am.S.	N	D	D	D	Y	N	D
Norton, D.C.	Y	D	D	D	P	Y	D
Romero-B., P.R.	?	D	D	D	N	Y	D
Underwood, Guam	Y	D	D	D	N	N	D

Southern states - Ala., Ark., Fla., Ga., Ky., La., Miss., N.C., Okla., S.C., Tenn., Texas, Va.
Omitted votes are quorum calls, which CQ does not include in its vote charts.

KEY

Y Voted for (yea).
\# Paired for.
+ Announced for.
N Voted against (nay).
X Paired against.
− Announced against.
P Voted "present."
C Voted "present" to avoid possible conflict of interest.
? Did not vote or otherwise make a position known.
D Delegates ineligible to vote.

Democrats **Republicans**
Independent

391. Procedural Motion. Approval of the House Journal of Wednesday, Aug. 10. Approved 251-160: R 15-154; D 235-6 (ND 158-4, SD 77-2); I 1-0, Aug. 11, 1994.

392. HR 4277. Independent Social Security Administration/Conference Report. Adoption of the conference report to make the Social Security Administration an independent agency by March 31, 1995. The legislation also would restrict Supplemental Security Income and disability payments to alcoholics and drug addicts. Adopted (thus cleared for the president) 431-0: R 178-0; D 252-0 (ND 172-0, SD 80-0); I 1-0, Aug. 11, 1994.

393. HR 4907. Baseline Budgeting/Rule. Adoption of the rule (H Res 512) to provide for House floor consideration of the bill to revise budgeting procedures to require that both the president's budget and the congressional budget resolution include two baselines in estimating discretionary spending, "current policy" that would adjust for inflation and "current funding" that would not adjust for inflation. Adopted 255-178: R 2-176; D 252-2 (ND 171-1, SD 81-1); I 1-0, Aug. 11, 1994.

394. HR 3355. Omnibus Crime Bill/Rule. Adoption of the rule (H Res 517) to waive points of order against and provide for House floor consideration of the $33 billion crime conference report to help hire 100,000 police officers through an $8.8 billion community policing program, build state and local prisons through an $8.7 billion state grant program, provide $7.6 billion for crime prevention programs such as after-school sports leagues and job training programs, create a crime trust fund directing $30.2 billion over six years to combat crime, ban 19 specific assault weapons and expand the death penalty to dozens of federal crimes. Rejected 210-225: R 11-167; D 198-58 (ND 148-25, SD 50-33); I 1-0, Aug. 11, 1994. A "yea" was a vote in support of the president's position.

	391	392	393	394
ALABAMA				
1 Callahan	N	Y	N	N
2 Everett	Y	Y	N	N
3 Browder	Y	Y	Y	N
4 Bevill	Y	Y	Y	Y
5 Cramer	Y	Y	Y	Y
6 Bachus	N	Y	N	N
7 Hilliard	Y	Y	Y	N
ALASKA				
AL Young	N	Y	N	N
ARIZONA				
1 Coppersmith	Y	Y	Y	Y
2 Pastor	Y	Y	Y	Y
3 Stump	N	Y	N	N
4 Kyl	N	Y	N	N
5 Kolbe	N	Y	N	N
6 English	Y	Y	Y	Y
ARKANSAS				
1 Lambert	Y	Y	Y	Y
2 Thornton	Y	Y	Y	Y
3 Hutchinson	N	Y	N	N
4 Dickey	N	Y	N	N
CALIFORNIA				
1 Hamburg	Y	Y	Y	Y
2 Herger	N	Y	N	N
3 Fazio	Y	Y	Y	Y
4 Doolittle	N	Y	N	N
5 Matsui	Y	Y	Y	Y
6 Woolsey	Y	Y	Y	Y
7 Miller	Y	Y	Y	Y
8 Pelosi	Y	Y	Y	Y
9 Dellums	Y	Y	Y	Y
10 Baker	N	Y	N	N
11 Pombo	Y	Y	N	N
12 Lantos	Y	Y	Y	Y
13 Stark	Y	Y	Y	Y
14 Eshoo	Y	Y	Y	Y
15 Mineta	Y	Y	Y	Y
16 Edwards	Y	Y	Y	Y
17 Farr	Y	Y	Y	Y
18 Condit	Y	Y	Y	Y
19 Lehman	Y	Y	Y	Y
20 Dooley	Y	Y	Y	Y
21 Thomas	N	Y	N	N
22 Huffington	N	Y	N	N
23 Gallegly	N	Y	N	N
24 Beilenson	Y	Y	Y	Y
25 McKeon	N	Y	N	N
26 Berman	Y	Y	Y	Y
27 Moorhead	N	Y	N	N
28 Dreier	N	Y	N	N
29 Waxman	Y	Y	Y	Y
30 Becerra	Y	Y	Y	Y
31 Martinez	Y	Y	Y	Y
32 Dixon	P	Y	Y	Y
33 Roybal-Allard	Y	Y	Y	Y
34 Torres	Y	Y	Y	Y
35 Waters	Y	Y	Y	N
36 Harman	Y	Y	Y	Y
37 Tucker	Y	Y	Y	Y
38 Horn	N	Y	N	N
39 Royce	N	Y	N	N
40 Lewis	N	Y	N	N
41 Kim	N	Y	N	N
42 Brown	Y	Y	Y	Y
43 Calvert	N	Y	N	N
44 McCandless	N	Y	N	N
45 Rohrabacher	N	Y	N	N
46 Dornan	?	Y	N	N
47 Cox	N	Y	N	N
48 Packard	N	Y	N	N
49 Schenk	Y	Y	Y	Y
50 Filner	Y	Y	Y	Y
51 Cunningham	N	Y	N	N
52 Hunter	N	Y	N	N
COLORADO				
1 Schroeder	N	Y	Y	Y
2 Skaggs	Y	Y	Y	Y
3 McInnis	N	Y	N	N
4 Allard	N	Y	N	N
5 Hefley	N	Y	N	N
6 Schaefer	N	Y	N	N
CONNECTICUT				
1 Kennelly	Y	Y	Y	Y
2 Gejdenson	Y	Y	Y	Y
3 DeLauro	Y	Y	Y	Y
4 Shays	N	Y	N	Y
5 Franks	N	Y	N	N
6 Johnson	N	Y	N	Y
DELAWARE				
AL Castle	N	Y	N	N
FLORIDA				
1 Hutto	Y	Y	Y	Y
2 Peterson	Y	Y	N	Y
3 Brown	Y	+	Y	Y
4 Fowler	N	Y	N	N
5 Thurman	Y	Y	N	Y
6 Stearns	N	Y	N	N
7 Mica	N	Y	N	N
8 McCollum	N	Y	N	N
9 Bilirakis	N	Y	N	N
10 Young	N	Y	N	N
11 Gibbons	Y	Y	Y	Y
12 Canady	N	Y	N	N
13 Miller	N	Y	N	N
14 Goss	N	Y	N	N
15 Bacchus	Y	Y	Y	Y
16 Lewis	N	Y	N	N
17 Meek	Y	Y	Y	Y
18 Ros-Lehtinen	N	Y	N	N
19 Johnston	Y	Y	Y	Y
20 Deutsch	Y	Y	Y	Y
21 Diaz-Balart	?	Y	N	N
22 Shaw	N	Y	N	N
23 Hastings	?	Y	Y	Y
GEORGIA				
1 Kingston	?	Y	N	N
2 Bishop	Y	Y	Y	Y
3 Collins	Y	Y	N	N
4 Linder	N	Y	N	N
5 Lewis	Y	Y	Y	N
6 Gingrich	N	Y	N	N
7 Darden	?	Y	Y	Y
8 Rowland	Y	Y	Y	Y
9 Deal	Y	Y	Y	N
10 Johnson	Y	Y	Y	Y
11 McKinney	Y	Y	Y	Y
HAWAII				
1 Abercrombie	?	Y	Y	Y
2 Mink	Y	Y	Y	Y
IDAHO				
1 LaRocco	Y	Y	Y	N
2 Crapo	N	Y	N	N
ILLINOIS				
1 Rush	?	Y	Y	Y
2 Reynolds	Y	Y	Y	Y
3 Lipinski	Y	Y	Y	Y
4 Gutierrez	Y	Y	Y	Y
5 Rostenkowski	Y	Y	Y	Y
6 Hyde	N	Y	N	N
7 Collins	Y	Y	Y	Y
8 Crane	N	Y	N	N
9 Yates	Y	Y	Y	Y
10 Porter	N	Y	N	N
11 Sangmeister	?	Y	Y	Y
12 Costello	Y	Y	Y	N
13 Fawell	N	Y	N	N
14 Hastert	N	Y	N	N
15 Ewing	N	Y	N	N
16 Manzullo	N	Y	N	N
17 Evans	Y	Y	Y	Y

ND Northern Democrats SD Southern Democrats

Member	391	392	393	394
18 *Michel*	N	Y	N	N
19 Poshard	Y	Y	Y	N
20 Durbin	Y	Y	Y	Y
INDIANA				
1 Visclosky	Y	Y	Y	Y
2 Sharp	Y	Y	Y	Y
3 Roemer	Y	Y	Y	Y
4 Long	Y	Y	Y	Y
5 *Buyer*	N	Y	N	N
6 *Burton*	N	Y	N	N
7 *Myers*	Y	Y	N	N
8 McCloskey	Y	Y	Y	Y
9 Hamilton	Y	Y	Y	Y
10 Jacobs	N	Y	Y	Y
IOWA				
1 *Leach*	N	Y	N	N
2 *Nussle*	N	Y	N	N
3 *Lightfoot*	N	Y	N	N
4 Smith	Y	Y	Y	N
5 *Grandy*	?	Y	N	Y
KANSAS				
1 *Roberts*	N	Y	N	N
2 Slattery	Y	Y	Y	Y
3 *Meyers*	?	Y	N	Y
4 Glickman	Y	Y	Y	Y
KENTUCKY				
1 Barlow	Y	Y	Y	Y
2 *Lewis*	N	Y	N	N
3 Mazzoli	Y	Y	Y	Y
4 *Bunning*	N	Y	N	N
5 *Rogers*	N	Y	N	N
6 Baesler	Y	Y	Y	Y
LOUISIANA				
1 *Livingston*	N	Y	N	N
2 Jefferson	Y	Y	Y	Y
3 Tauzin	Y	Y	Y	N
4 Fields	Y	Y	Y	N
5 *McCrery*	N	Y	N	N
6 *Baker*	N	Y	N	N
7 Hayes	Y	Y	Y	N
MAINE				
1 Andrews	Y	Y	Y	Y
2 *Snowe*	N	Y	N	N
MARYLAND				
1 *Gilchrest*	N	Y	N	N
2 *Bentley*	N	Y	N	N
3 Cardin	Y	Y	Y	Y
4 Wynn	Y	Y	Y	Y
5 Hoyer	Y	Y	Y	Y
6 *Bartlett*	N	Y	N	N
7 Mfume	Y	Y	Y	Y
8 *Morella*	N	Y	N	Y
MASSACHUSETTS				
1 Olver	Y	Y	Y	Y
2 Neal	Y	Y	Y	Y
3 *Blute*	N	Y	Y	Y
4 Frank	Y	Y	Y	Y
5 Meehan	Y	Y	Y	Y
6 *Torkildsen*	N	Y	N	N
7 Markey	Y	Y	Y	Y
8 Kennedy	Y	Y	Y	Y
9 Moakley	Y	Y	Y	Y
10 Studds	Y	Y	Y	Y
MICHIGAN				
1 Stupak	Y	Y	Y	N
2 *Hoekstra*	N	Y	N	N
3 *Ehlers*	N	Y	N	N
4 *Camp*	N	Y	N	N
5 Barcia	Y	Y	Y	N
6 *Upton*	N	Y	N	N
7 *Smith*	N	Y	N	N
8 Carr	Y	Y	Y	Y
9 Kildee	Y	Y	Y	Y
10 Bonior	Y	Y	Y	Y
11 *Knollenberg*	N	Y	N	N
12 Levin	Y	Y	Y	Y
13 Ford	Y	Y	Y	Y
14 Conyers	Y	Y	Y	Y
15 Collins	Y	Y	Y	Y
16 Dingell	?	Y	Y	Y
MINNESOTA				
1 Penny	Y	Y	Y	Y
2 Minge	Y	Y	Y	Y
3 *Ramstad*	N	Y	N	Y
4 Vento	Y	Y	Y	Y

Member	391	392	393	394
5 Sabo	Y	Y	Y	Y
6 *Grams*	N	Y	N	N
7 Peterson	Y	Y	Y	Y
8 Oberstar	Y	Y	Y	Y
MISSISSIPPI				
1 Whitten	Y	Y	Y	Y
2 Thompson	Y	Y	Y	Y
3 Montgomery	Y	Y	Y	Y
4 Parker	Y	Y	Y	N
5 Taylor	N	Y	Y	N
MISSOURI				
1 Clay	N	Y	N	N
2 *Talent*	N	Y	N	N
3 Gephardt	Y	Y	Y	Y
4 Skelton	Y	Y	Y	N
5 Wheat	Y	Y	Y	Y
6 Danner	Y	Y	Y	N
7 *Hancock*	N	Y	N	N
8 *Emerson*	N	Y	N	N
9 Volkmer	Y	Y	Y	N
MONTANA				
AL Williams	Y	Y	Y	N
NEBRASKA				
1 *Bereuter*	N	Y	N	N
2 Hoagland	Y	Y	Y	Y
3 *Barrett*	N	Y	N	N
NEVADA				
1 Bilbray	Y	Y	Y	Y
2 *Vucanovich*	N	Y	N	N
NEW HAMPSHIRE				
1 *Zeliff*	N	Y	N	N
2 Swett	Y	Y	Y	Y
NEW JERSEY				
1 Andrews	Y	Y	Y	Y
2 Hughes	Y	Y	Y	Y
3 *Saxton*	N	Y	N	N
4 *Smith*	Y	Y	N	N
5 *Roukema*	N	Y	N	Y
6 Pallone	Y	Y	Y	Y
7 *Franks*	N	Y	N	N
8 Klein	Y	Y	Y	Y
9 Torricelli	Y	Y	Y	Y
10 Payne	Y	Y	Y	Y
11 *Gallo*	?	Y	N	N
12 *Zimmer*	N	Y	N	N
13 Menendez	Y	Y	Y	Y
NEW MEXICO				
1 *Schiff*	?	Y	N	N
2 *Skeen*	N	Y	N	N
3 Richardson	Y	Y	Y	Y
NEW YORK				
1 Hochbrueckner	Y	Y	Y	Y
2 *Lazio*	N	Y	N	N
3 *King*	N	Y	N	N
4 *Levy*	N	Y	N	N
5 Ackerman	Y	Y	Y	Y
6 Flake	?	Y	Y	Y
7 Manton	Y	Y	Y	Y
8 Nadler	Y	Y	Y	Y
9 Schumer	Y	Y	Y	Y
10 Towns	Y	Y	Y	Y
11 Owens	Y	Y	Y	Y
12 Velazquez	Y	Y	Y	Y
13 *Molinari*	N	Y	N	N
14 Maloney	Y	Y	Y	Y
15 Rangel	Y	Y	Y	Y
16 Serrano	Y	Y	Y	Y
17 Engel	Y	Y	Y	Y
18 Lowey	Y	Y	Y	Y
19 *Fish*	Y	Y	N	N
20 *Gilman*	Y	Y	N	N
21 McNulty	Y	Y	Y	Y
22 *Solomon*	N	Y	N	N
23 *Boehlert*	N	Y	N	Y
24 *McHugh*	N	Y	N	N
25 *Walsh*	N	Y	N	N
26 Hinchey	Y	Y	Y	Y
27 *Paxon*	N	Y	N	N
28 Slaughter	Y	Y	Y	Y
29 LaFalce	Y	Y	Y	Y
30 *Quinn*	N	Y	N	Y
31 *Houghton*	Y	Y	N	Y
NORTH CAROLINA				
1 Clayton	Y	Y	Y	Y
2 Valentine	Y	Y	Y	Y

Member	391	392	393	394
3 Lancaster	Y	Y	Y	N
4 Price	Y	Y	Y	Y
5 Neal	Y	Y	Y	Y
6 *Coble*	N	Y	N	N
7 Rose	Y	Y	Y	Y
8 Hefner	Y	Y	Y	Y
9 *McMillan*	N	Y	N	N
10 *Ballenger*	N	Y	N	N
11 *Taylor*	?	Y	N	N
12 Watt	Y	Y	Y	N
NORTH DAKOTA				
AL Pomeroy	Y	Y	Y	Y
OHIO				
1 Mann	Y	Y	Y	Y
2 *Portman*	N	Y	N	N
3 Hall	?	Y	Y	Y
4 *Oxley*	N	Y	N	N
5 *Gillmor*	Y	Y	N	N
6 Strickland	Y	Y	Y	Y
7 *Hobson*	N	Y	N	N
8 *Boehner*	N	Y	N	N
9 Kaptur	Y	Y	Y	Y
10 *Hoke*	N	Y	N	N
11 Stokes	Y	Y	Y	Y
12 *Kasich*	N	Y	N	N
13 Brown	Y	Y	Y	Y
14 Sawyer	Y	Y	Y	Y
15 *Pryce*	N	Y	N	N
16 *Regula*	N	Y	N	N
17 Traficant	Y	Y	Y	Y
18 Applegate	Y	Y	Y	Y
19 Fingerhut	Y	Y	Y	Y
OKLAHOMA				
1 *Inhofe*	N	Y	N	N
2 Synar	Y	Y	Y	Y
3 Brewster	Y	Y	Y	Y
4 McCurdy	Y	Y	Y	Y
5 *Istook*	N	Y	N	N
6 *Lucas*	N	Y	N	N
OREGON				
1 Furse	Y	Y	Y	Y
2 *Smith*	N	Y	N	N
3 Wyden	Y	Y	Y	Y
4 DeFazio	?	Y	Y	N
5 Kopetski	Y	Y	Y	Y
PENNSYLVANIA				
1 Foglietta	Y	Y	Y	Y
2 Blackwell	?	Y	Y	Y
3 Borski	Y	Y	Y	Y
4 Klink	Y	Y	Y	N
5 *Clinger*	N	Y	N	N
6 Holden	Y	Y	Y	N
7 *Weldon*	N	Y	N	N
8 *Greenwood*	N	Y	N	N
9 *Shuster*	N	Y	N	N
10 *McDade*	N	Y	N	N
11 Kanjorski	Y	Y	Y	Y
12 Murtha	Y	Y	Y	Y
13 Margolies-Mezv.	Y	Y	Y	Y
14 Coyne	Y	Y	Y	Y
15 McHale	Y	Y	Y	Y
16 *Walker*	N	Y	N	N
17 *Gekas*	N	Y	N	N
18 *Santorum*	N	Y	N	N
19 *Goodling*	N	Y	N	N
20 Murphy	N	Y	Y	Y
21 *Ridge*	N	Y	N	N
RHODE ISLAND				
1 *Machtley*	N	Y	N	N
2 Reed	Y	Y	Y	Y
SOUTH CAROLINA				
1 *Ravenel*	N	Y	N	N
2 *Spence*	N	Y	N	N
3 Derrick	Y	Y	Y	Y
4 *Inglis*	Y	N	N	N
5 Spratt	Y	Y	Y	Y
6 Clyburn	Y	Y	Y	Y
SOUTH DAKOTA				
AL Johnson	Y	Y	Y	Y
TENNESSEE				
1 *Quillen*	N	Y	N	N
2 *Duncan*	N	Y	N	N
3 Lloyd	Y	Y	Y	Y
4 Cooper	Y	Y	N	N
5 Clement	Y	Y	Y	Y

Member	391	392	393	394
6 Gordon	Y	Y	Y	Y
7 *Sundquist*	N	Y	N	N
8 Tanner	Y	Y	Y	Y
9 Ford	Y	?	Y	Y
TEXAS				
1 Chapman	?	Y	Y	N
2 Wilson	Y	Y	Y	N
3 *Johnson, Sam*	N	Y	N	N
4 Hall	Y	Y	Y	Y
5 Bryant	Y	Y	Y	Y
6 *Barton*	N	Y	N	N
7 *Archer*	N	Y	N	N
8 *Fields*	N	Y	N	N
9 Brooks	Y	Y	Y	Y
10 Pickle	Y	Y	Y	Y
11 Edwards	Y	Y	Y	Y
12 Geren	Y	Y	Y	N
13 Sarpalius	Y	Y	Y	Y
14 Laughlin	Y	Y	Y	N
15 de la Garza	Y	Y	Y	N
16 Coleman	Y	Y	Y	Y
17 Stenholm	Y	Y	Y	N
18 Washington	?	?	?	N
19 *Combest*	Y	Y	N	N
20 Gonzalez	Y	Y	Y	Y
21 *Smith*	N	Y	N	N
22 *DeLay*	N	Y	N	N
23 *Bonilla*	N	Y	N	N
24 Frost	Y	Y	Y	Y
25 Andrews	Y	Y	Y	Y
26 *Armey*	N	Y	N	N
27 Ortiz	Y	Y	Y	N
28 Tejeda	Y	Y	Y	N
29 Green	Y	Y	Y	Y
30 Johnson, E.B.	Y	Y	Y	Y
UTAH				
1 *Hansen*	?	Y	N	N
2 Shepherd	Y	Y	Y	Y
3 Orton	Y	Y	Y	N
VERMONT				
AL *Sanders*	Y	Y	Y	Y
VIRGINIA				
1 *Bateman*	Y	Y	N	N
2 Pickett	Y	Y	Y	N
3 Scott	Y	Y	Y	Y
4 Sisisky	Y	Y	Y	N
5 Payne	Y	Y	Y	N
6 *Goodlatte*	N	Y	N	N
7 *Bliley*	N	Y	N	N
8 Moran	Y	Y	Y	Y
9 Boucher	Y	Y	Y	Y
10 *Wolf*	N	Y	N	N
11 Byrne	Y	Y	Y	Y
WASHINGTON				
1 Cantwell	Y	Y	Y	Y
2 Swift	Y	Y	Y	Y
3 Unsoeld	Y	Y	Y	N
4 Inslee	Y	Y	Y	
5 Foley				Y
6 Dicks	Y	Y		Y
7 McDermott	?	Y	Y	Y
8 *Dunn*	N	Y	N	N
9 Kreidler	Y	Y	Y	Y
WEST VIRGINIA				
1 Mollohan	Y	Y	Y	N
2 Wise	Y	Y	Y	N
3 Rahall	Y	Y	N	N
WISCONSIN				
1 Barca	Y	Y	Y	Y
2 *Klug*	N	Y	N	N
3 *Gunderson*	N	Y	N	N
4 Kleczka	Y	Y	Y	Y
5 Barrett	Y	Y	Y	Y
6 *Petri*	N	Y	N	N
7 Obey	Y	Y	Y	Y
8 *Roth*	N	Y	N	N
9 *Sensenbrenner*	N	Y	N	N
WYOMING				
AL *Thomas*	N	Y	N	N
DELEGATES				
de Lugo, V.I.	D	D	D	D
Faleomavaega, Am.S.	D	D	D	D
Norton, D.C.	D	D	D	D
Romero-B., P.R.	D	D	D	D
Underwood, Guam	D	D	D	D

Southern states - Ala., Ark., Fla., Ga., Ky., La., Miss., N.C., Okla., S.C., Tenn., Texas, Va.
Omitted votes are quorum calls, which CQ does not include in its vote charts.

395. HR 4907. Budget Baselines/Uninflated Baseline. Penny, D-Minn., substitute amendment to change existing budget practice by barring use of an inflation-adjusted baseline (which allows comparison of the forthcoming year's discretionary spending with an inflation-adjusted version of the previous year's spending) and requiring the use of a "freeze" baseline that would show only the previous year's spending level. Adopted in the Committee of the Whole 247-171: R 171-0; D 76-170 (ND 41-126, SD 35-44); I 0-1, Aug. 12, 1994.

396. HR 4907. Budget Baselines/Inflation Adjusted Baseline. Spratt, D-S.C., substitute amendment to change existing budget practice by allowing the use of two baselines against which to compare the forthcoming year's discretionary spending — the existing inflation-adjusted baseline and a "freeze" baseline showing the previous year's spending with no adjustment. Rejected in the Committee of the Whole 170-243: R 0-170; D 169-73 (ND 126-41, SD 43-32); I 1-0, Aug. 12, 1994.

397. HR 2947. D.C. Memorial Construction Permits. Vento, D-Minn., motion to suspend the rules and concur in the Senate amendments to the bill to extend for three years the seven-year deadline established in the Commemorative Works Act (PL 99-652) for construction permits for memorials in Washington, D.C., for the Black Revolutionary War Patriots Memorial, the Women in Military Service for America Memorial and the National Peace Garden. Motion agreed to (thus clearing the bill for the president) 378-0: R 154-0; D 223-0 (ND 152-0, SD 71-0); I 1-0, Aug. 16, 1994. A two-thirds majority of those present and voting (252 in this case) is required for passage under suspension of the rules.

398. HR 4867. High-Speed Rail Development/Passage. Schenk, D-Calif., motion to suspend the rules and pass the bill to authorize $184 million over fiscal 1995-97 for high-speed rail corridor planning and technology development activities. Motion agreed to 281-103: R 67-87; D 213-16 (ND 150-5, SD 63-11); I 1-0, Aug. 16, 1994. A two-thirds majority of those present and voting (256 in this case) is required for passage under suspension of the rules.

399. Procedural Motion. Approval of the House Journal of Aug. 12. Approved 237-147: R 15-140; D 221-7 (ND 148-6, SD 73-1); I 1-0, Aug. 16, 1994.

400. HR 4906. Emergency Spending Procedures/'Look Back' Offset. Johnson, R-Texas, amendment to repeal existing emergency spending procedures and require that any emergency spending above discretionary spending caps be offset by reductions in discretionary spending the following year. Rejected in the Committee of the Whole 160-258: R 142-27; D 18-230 (ND 13-156, SD 5-74); I 0-1, Aug. 17, 1994.

401. HR 4906. Emergency Spending Procedures/Budget Reserve Account. Castle, R-Del., substitute amendment to require appropriators to set aside adequate money each year in a Budget Reserve Account to pay for natural disasters or national security emergencies, with any money left over at the end of the fiscal year going to deficit reduction. Rejected in the Committee of the Whole 184-235: R 154-16; D 30-218 (ND 19-151, SD 11-67); I 0-1, Aug. 17, 1994.

402. HR 4906. Emergency Spending Procedures/Non-Emergency Spending Prohibition. Kasich, R-Ohio, amendment to prohibit the inclusion of non-emergency spending provisions in emergency spending bills and allow points of order in both chambers against any emergency spending legislation that contains non-emergency spending. The original bill would have changed existing law by lowering from 25 members to 10 members the number required to trigger a roll call vote when a member offers a motion to strike non-emergency spending in emergency spending bills. Adopted in the Committee of the Whole 322-99: R 166-4; D 155-95 (ND 96-75, SD 59-20); I 1-0, Aug. 17, 1994.

KEY

Y	Voted for (yea).
#	Paired for.
+	Announced for.
N	Voted against (nay).
X	Paired against.
−	Announced against.
P	Voted "present."
C	Voted "present" to avoid possible conflict of interest.
?	Did not vote or otherwise make a position known.
D	Delegates ineligible to vote.

Democrats **Republicans**
Independent

	395	396	397	398	399	400	401	402
ALABAMA								
1 *Callahan*	Y	N	Y	N	N	N	Y	Y
2 Everett	Y	N	Y	N	Y	N	N	Y
3 Browder	Y	N	Y	Y	Y	N	N	Y
4 Bevill	N	Y	Y	Y	Y	N	N	N
5 Cramer	N	N	?	?	N	N	N	Y
6 *Bachus*	Y	N	Y	N	Y	N	Y	Y
7 Hilliard	N	Y	Y	Y	Y	N	N	N
ALASKA								
AL *Young*	Y	N	Y	N	N	N	N	Y
ARIZONA								
1 Coppersmith	Y	N	Y	Y	Y	N	Y	Y
2 Pastor	N	Y	Y	Y	Y	N	N	N
3 *Stump*	Y	N	Y	N	N	Y	Y	Y
4 *Kyl*	Y	N	Y	N	N	Y	Y	Y
5 *Kolbe*	Y	N	Y	N	N	N	Y	Y
6 English	Y	N	Y	Y	Y	N	Y	Y
ARKANSAS								
1 Lambert	Y	N	Y	Y	Y	N	Y	Y
2 Thornton	N	Y	Y	Y	Y	N	N	N
3 *Hutchinson*	Y	N	Y	N	N	Y	Y	Y
4 Dickey	Y	N	Y	N	N	Y	Y	Y
CALIFORNIA								
1 Hamburg	N	Y	Y	Y	Y	N	N	Y
2 *Herger*	Y	N	Y	N	N	Y	Y	Y
3 Fazio	N	Y	Y	Y	Y	N	N	N
4 *Doolittle*	Y	N	Y	N	N	Y	Y	Y
5 Matsui	N	Y	Y	Y	Y	N	N	N
6 Woolsey	N	Y	?	Y	Y	N	N	N
7 Miller	N	Y	Y	Y	Y	N	N	Y
8 Pelosi	N	Y	Y	Y	Y	N	N	N
9 Dellums	N	Y	Y	Y	N	N	N	N
10 *Baker*	Y	N	?	N	Y	Y	Y	Y
11 *Pombo*	Y	N	Y	Y	Y	Y	Y	Y
12 Lantos	?	?	?	?	?	?	?	?
13 Stark	N	Y	Y	Y	Y	N	N	Y
14 Eshoo	N	Y	Y	Y	Y	N	N	N
15 Mineta	N	Y	Y	Y	Y	N	N	N
16 Edwards	?	Y	?	?	N	N	N	N
17 Farr	N	Y	Y	Y	Y	N	N	N
18 Condit	Y	N	Y	Y	Y	Y	Y	Y
19 Lehman	Y	N	Y	Y	Y	N	N	Y
20 Dooley	Y	N	Y	Y	Y	N	N	Y
21 *Thomas*	Y	N	Y	N	Y	Y	Y	Y
22 *Huffington*	Y	N	?	?	Y	Y	Y	Y
23 *Gallegly*	Y	N	Y	N	Y	Y	Y	Y
24 Beilenson	N	Y	Y	Y	Y	N	N	Y
25 *McKeon*	Y	N	?	?	Y	Y	Y	Y
26 Berman	N	Y	Y	Y	Y	N	N	N
27 *Moorhead*	Y	N	Y	N	Y	Y	Y	Y
28 *Dreier*	Y	N	?	?	Y	Y	Y	Y
29 Waxman	N	Y	Y	Y	Y	N	N	N
30 Becerra	N	Y	?	?	?	X	X	X
31 Martinez	N	Y	Y	Y	Y	N	N	N
32 Dixon	N	Y	Y	Y	Y	N	N	N
33 Roybal-Allard	N	Y	Y	Y	Y	N	N	N
34 Torres	N	Y	Y	Y	Y	N	N	N
35 Waters	N	Y	+	Y	Y	N	N	N
36 Harman	Y	N	Y	Y	Y	N	N	Y
37 Tucker	N	Y	Y	Y	Y	N	N	Y
38 *Horn*	Y	N	Y	Y	Y	N	Y	Y
39 *Royce*	Y	N	Y	N	N	Y	Y	Y
40 *Lewis*	Y	N	Y	N	Y	N	Y	N
41 *Kim*	Y	N	Y	Y	Y	Y	Y	Y

	395	396	397	398	399	400	401	402
42 Brown	N	Y	Y	Y	N	N	N	N
43 *Calvert*	Y	N	Y	N	Y	Y	Y	Y
44 *McCandless*	?	?	Y	Y	Y	Y	Y	Y
45 *Rohrabacher*	Y	N	Y	N	N	Y	Y	Y
46 *Dornan*	Y	N	N	Y	Y	Y	Y	Y
47 *Cox*	Y	N	Y	N	N	Y	Y	Y
48 *Packard*	Y	N	Y	N	N	N	Y	Y
49 Schenk	Y	N	Y	Y	Y	N	N	Y
50 Filner	N	Y	Y	Y	N	N	N	N
51 *Cunningham*	Y	N	N	N	Y	Y	Y	Y
52 *Hunter*	Y	N	?	?	?	?	?	?
COLORADO								
1 Schroeder	N	N	Y	N	N	Y	N	Y
2 Skaggs	N	Y	Y	Y	Y	N	N	N
3 *McInnis*	Y	N	Y	N	N	Y	Y	Y
4 *Allard*	Y	N	Y	N	N	Y	Y	Y
5 *Hefley*	Y	N	Y	N	N	Y	Y	Y
6 *Schaefer*	Y	N	?	?	?	Y	Y	Y
CONNECTICUT								
1 Kennelly	N	Y	Y	Y	Y	N	N	Y
2 Gejdenson	−	+	?	?	?	N	N	N
3 DeLauro	N	Y	Y	Y	Y	N	N	N
4 *Shays*	Y	N	Y	N	Y	Y	Y	Y
5 *Franks*	Y	N	Y	N	Y	Y	Y	Y
6 *Johnson*	Y	N	Y	Y	?	Y	Y	Y
DELAWARE								
AL *Castle*	Y	N	Y	N	Y	N	Y	Y
FLORIDA								
1 Hutto	Y	N	Y	Y	Y	N	N	Y
2 Peterson	N	Y	Y	Y	Y	N	N	N
3 Brown	N	Y	+	?	?	N	N	N
4 *Fowler*	Y	N	Y	Y	Y	N	Y	Y
5 Thurman	Y	Y	Y	Y	Y	N	N	Y
6 *Stearns*	Y	N	Y	N	N	Y	Y	Y
7 *Mica*	Y	N	Y	N	Y	Y	Y	Y
8 *McCollum*	Y	N	?	?	Y	Y	Y	Y
9 *Bilirakis*	Y	N	?	?	Y	Y	Y	Y
10 *Young*	Y	N	Y	N	N	N	Y	Y
11 Gibbons	N	Y	Y	Y	N	N	N	N
12 *Canady*	Y	N	Y	N	Y	Y	Y	Y
13 *Miller*	Y	N	Y	N	N	Y	Y	Y
14 *Goss*	Y	N	Y	N	N	Y	Y	Y
15 *Bacchus*	Y	?	?	Y	N	N	Y	Y
16 *Lewis*	#	?	Y	N	N	Y	Y	Y
17 Meek	N	Y	Y	Y	Y	N	N	N
18 *Ros-Lehtinen*	Y	N	Y	N	Y	Y	Y	Y
19 Johnston	N	Y	Y	Y	Y	N	N	N
20 Deutsch	Y	Y	Y	Y	Y	N	N	Y
21 *Diaz-Balart*	Y	N	Y	N	N	Y	Y	Y
22 *Shaw*	Y	N	Y	N	Y	N	Y	Y
23 Hastings	N	Y	Y	Y	Y	N	N	N
GEORGIA								
1 *Kingston*	Y	N	Y	N	Y	Y	Y	Y
2 Bishop	N	Y	Y	Y	Y	N	N	Y
3 *Collins*	Y	N	?	?	?	Y	Y	Y
4 *Linder*	Y	N	Y	N	Y	Y	Y	Y
5 Lewis	N	Y	Y	Y	Y	N	N	N
6 *Gingrich*	Y	N	Y	N	N	Y	Y	Y
7 *Darden*	Y	N	Y	Y	Y	N	N	Y
8 Rowland	Y	N	Y	Y	Y	N	N	Y
9 Deal	Y	N	Y	Y	Y	N	Y	Y
10 Johnson	Y	N	Y	Y	Y	N	N	Y
11 McKinney	N	Y	Y	Y	N	N	N	Y
HAWAII								
1 Abercrombie	N	Y	Y	Y	Y	N	N	N
2 Mink	N	Y	Y	Y	Y	N	N	N
IDAHO								
1 LaRocco	Y	N	Y	Y	Y	N	N	Y
2 *Crapo*	Y	N	Y	N	Y	Y	Y	Y
ILLINOIS								
1 Rush	N	Y	+	+	+	N	N	N
2 Reynolds	?	?	?	?	?	?	?	?
3 Lipinski	N	N	Y	Y	Y	N	N	N
4 Gutierrez	N	Y	Y	Y	N	N	N	N
5 Rostenkowski	N	?	?	Y	Y	N	N	N
6 *Hyde*	Y	N	Y	N	Y	N	N	Y
7 Collins	N	Y	Y	Y	N	N	N	N
8 *Crane*	Y	N	?	N	N	Y	Y	Y
9 Yates	N	Y	Y	Y	Y	N	N	N
10 *Porter*	Y	N	Y	N	Y	N	Y	Y
11 Sangmeister	N	Y	Y	Y	Y	N	N	Y
12 Costello	N	Y	Y	Y	Y	N	N	N
13 *Fawell*	Y	N	Y	N	Y	Y	Y	Y
14 *Hastert*	Y	N	Y	N	Y	Y	Y	Y
15 *Ewing*	Y	N	Y	N	Y	Y	Y	Y
16 *Manzullo*	Y	N	Y	N	N	Y	Y	Y
17 Evans	N	Y	Y	Y	N	N	N	N

ND Northern Democrats   SD Southern Democrats

	395	396	397	398	399	400	401	402
18 ***Michel***	?	?	?	?	?	?	?	?
19 Poshard	Y	N	Y	Y	Y	N	Y	Y
20 Durbin	N	Y	Y	Y	Y	N	N	N
INDIANA								
1 Visclosky	N	Y	?	?	?	N	N	N
2 Sharp	N	Y	Y	Y	Y	N	N	?
3 Roemer	Y	N	Y	Y	Y	N	N	Y
4 Long	Y	N	Y	N	Y	N	N	Y
5 ***Buyer***	Y	N	Y	N	N	Y	Y	Y
6 ***Burton***	Y	N	Y	N	N	Y	Y	Y
7 ***Myers***	Y	N	Y	N	Y	N	Y	Y
8 McCloskey	N	Y	Y	Y	Y	N	N	Y
9 Hamilton	N	Y	Y	Y	Y	N	N	Y
10 Jacobs	Y	N	Y	N	N	Y	N	Y
IOWA								
1 ***Leach***	Y	N	Y	Y	N	Y	Y	Y
2 ***Nussle***	Y	N	Y	N	N	Y	Y	Y
3 ***Lightfoot***	Y	N	Y	N	N	N	N	Y
4 Smith	N	Y	Y	Y	Y	N	N	N
5 ***Grandy***	Y	N	Y	N	N	Y	Y	Y
KANSAS								
1 ***Roberts***	Y	N	Y	N	N	Y	Y	Y
2 Slattery	?	?	?	?	?	?	?	?
3 ***Meyers***	Y	N	Y	N	N	Y	Y	Y
4 Glickman	Y	N	Y	Y	Y	N	N	Y
KENTUCKY								
1 Barlow	N	Y	Y	Y	Y	N	N	N
2 ***Lewis***	Y	N	Y	N	N	Y	Y	Y
3 Mazzoli	Y	N	Y	Y	Y	N	N	Y
4 ***Bunning***	Y	N	Y	N	N	Y	Y	Y
5 ***Rogers***	Y	N	Y	N	N	N	N	Y
6 Baesler	Y	N	Y	Y	Y	N	N	Y
LOUISIANA								
1 ***Livingston***	Y	N	Y	N	N	N	N	Y
2 Jefferson	N	Y	Y	Y	Y	N	N	N
3 Tauzin	Y	N	Y	Y	Y	Y	Y	Y
4 Fields	?	?	Y	Y	Y	N	N	N
5 ***McCrery***	Y	N	Y	N	N	Y	Y	Y
6 ***Baker***	Y	N	Y	N	N	Y	Y	Y
7 Hayes	Y	N	Y	Y	Y	Y	N	Y
MAINE								
1 Andrews	N	Y	Y	Y	Y	N	N	Y
2 ***Snowe***	Y	N	Y	Y	N	N	Y	Y
MARYLAND								
1 ***Gilchrest***	Y	N	Y	Y	N	Y	Y	Y
2 ***Bentley***	?	N	Y	Y	N	N	Y	Y
3 Cardin	N	Y	Y	Y	Y	N	N	Y
4 Wynn	N	Y	Y	Y	Y	N	N	N
5 Hoyer	N	Y	Y	Y	Y	N	N	N
6 ***Bartlett***	Y	N	Y	N	N	Y	Y	Y
7 Mfume	N	Y	Y	Y	Y	?	N	Y
8 ***Morella***	Y	N	Y	Y	N	N	Y	Y
MASSACHUSETTS								
1 Olver	N	Y	Y	Y	Y	N	N	N
2 Neal	N	Y	Y	Y	Y	N	N	Y
3 ***Blute***	Y	N	Y	Y	N	Y	Y	Y
4 Frank	N	Y	Y	Y	Y	N	N	N
5 Meehan	Y	N	?	?	?	N	Y	Y
6 ***Torkildsen***	Y	N	Y	Y	N	N	Y	Y
7 Markey	N	Y	Y	Y	Y	N	N	N
8 Kennedy	N	Y	Y	Y	Y	N	N	N
9 Moakley	N	Y	Y	Y	Y	N	N	N
10 Studds	N	Y	Y	Y	Y	N	N	N
MICHIGAN								
1 Stupak	N	Y	Y	Y	Y	N	N	Y
2 ***Hoekstra***	Y	N	Y	Y	N	Y	Y	Y
3 ***Ehlers***	Y	N	Y	Y	N	Y	Y	Y
4 ***Camp***	Y	N	Y	Y	N	Y	Y	Y
5 Barcia	Y	N	Y	Y	Y	N	N	Y
6 ***Upton***	Y	N	Y	Y	N	Y	Y	Y
7 ***Smith***	Y	N	Y	Y	N	Y	Y	Y
8 Carr	N	Y	Y	Y	?	N	N	Y
9 Kildee	N	Y	Y	Y	Y	N	N	Y
10 Bonior	N	Y	Y	Y	Y	N	N	N
11 ***Knollenberg***	Y	N	Y	Y	N	Y	Y	Y
12 Levin	N	Y	Y	Y	Y	N	N	Y
13 Ford	N	Y	Y	Y	Y	N	N	N
14 Conyers	N	Y	Y	Y	Y	N	N	N
15 Collins	N	Y	Y	Y	Y	N	N	N
16 Dingell	N	Y	Y	Y	Y	N	N	N
MINNESOTA								
1 Penny	Y	N	Y	Y	Y	Y	Y	Y
2 Minge	Y	N	Y	Y	Y	Y	Y	Y
3 ***Ramstad***	Y	N	Y	Y	N	Y	Y	Y
4 Vento	X	#	Y	Y	Y	N	N	N

	395	396	397	398	399	400	401	402
5 Sabo	N	Y	Y	Y	Y	N	N	N
6 ***Grams***	Y	N	?	?	?	#	#	#
7 Peterson	Y	N	Y	N	Y	Y	Y	Y
8 Oberstar	N	Y	Y	Y	Y	N	N	N
MISSISSIPPI								
1 Whitten	N	Y	?	?	?	N	N	N
2 Thompson	N	Y	Y	Y	Y	N	N	N
3 Montgomery	N	?	?	?	?	N	N	Y
4 Parker	Y	N	Y	Y	Y	Y	Y	Y
5 Taylor	Y	N	?	Y	N	N	Y	Y
MISSOURI								
1 Clay	N	Y	Y	Y	N	N	N	N
2 ***Talent***	Y	N	Y	N	N	Y	Y	Y
3 Gephardt	N	Y	Y	Y	Y	N	N	N
4 Skelton	N	Y	Y	Y	Y	N	N	Y
5 Wheat	N	Y	Y	Y	Y	N	N	Y
6 Danner	N	N	Y	Y	Y	N	N	Y
7 ***Hancock***	Y	N	Y	N	N	Y	Y	Y
8 ***Emerson***	Y	N	Y	Y	N	Y	N	Y
9 Volkmer	N	Y	Y	Y	Y	N	N	Y
MONTANA								
AL Williams	?	?	Y	Y	Y	N	N	Y
NEBRASKA								
1 ***Bereuter***	Y	N	Y	N	N	Y	N	Y
2 Hoagland	N	Y	Y	Y	Y	N	Y	Y
3 ***Barrett***	Y	N	Y	N	N	Y	Y	Y
NEVADA								
1 Bilbray	N	Y	Y	Y	Y	N	N	Y
2 ***Vucanovich***	Y	N	Y	N	N	N	N	Y
NEW HAMPSHIRE								
1 ***Zeliff***	Y	N	Y	Y	N	Y	Y	Y
2 Swett	Y	N	Y	Y	Y	Y	Y	Y
NEW JERSEY								
1 Andrews	Y	N	Y	Y	Y	Y	Y	Y
2 Hughes	N	Y	Y	Y	Y	N	N	Y
3 ***Saxton***	Y	N	Y	Y	N	Y	Y	Y
4 ***Smith***	Y	N	Y	Y	N	Y	Y	Y
5 ***Roukema***	Y	N	Y	Y	N	Y	Y	Y
6 Pallone	Y	N	Y	Y	Y	Y	Y	Y
7 ***Franks***	Y	N	Y	Y	N	Y	Y	Y
8 Klein	N	Y	Y	Y	Y	N	N	Y
9 Torricelli	N	Y	Y	Y	Y	N	N	Y
10 Payne	N	Y	Y	Y	Y	N	N	N
11 ***Gallo***	Y	N	?	?	?	N	N	N
12 ***Zimmer***	Y	N	Y	Y	N	Y	Y	Y
13 Menendez	Y	Y	?	?	?	N	N	Y
NEW MEXICO								
1 ***Schiff***	Y	N	Y	Y	N	Y	Y	Y
2 ***Skeen***	Y	N	Y	N	N	N	N	N
3 Richardson	N	Y	Y	Y	Y	N	N	Y
NEW YORK								
1 Hochbrueckner	N	Y	Y	Y	Y	N	N	Y
2 ***Lazio***	Y	N	Y	Y	N	Y	Y	Y
3 ***King***	Y	N	Y	Y	N	Y	Y	Y
4 ***Levy***	Y	N	Y	Y	N	Y	Y	Y
5 Ackerman	N	Y	Y	Y	Y	N	N	Y
6 Flake	N	Y	?	?	?	?	?	?
7 Manton	N	Y	Y	Y	Y	N	N	N
8 Nadler	N	Y	?	?	?	N	N	N
9 Schumer	N	Y	Y	Y	Y	Y	Y	Y
10 Towns	N	Y	Y	Y	Y	N	N	N
11 Owens	N	Y	Y	Y	Y	N	N	N
12 Velazquez	N	Y	Y	Y	Y	N	N	N
13 ***Molinari***	Y	N	Y	Y	N	Y	Y	Y
14 Maloney	N	Y	Y	Y	Y	Y	N	Y
15 Rangel	N	Y	Y	Y	Y	N	N	N
16 Serrano	N	Y	Y	Y	Y	N	N	N
17 Engel	N	Y	Y	Y	Y	N	N	N
18 Lowey	N	Y	Y	Y	Y	N	N	N
19 ***Fish***	Y	N	Y	Y	N	Y	Y	Y
20 ***Gilman***	Y	N	Y	Y	Y	N	Y	Y
21 McNulty	N	Y	Y	Y	Y	N	N	Y
22 ***Solomon***	Y	N	Y	N	N	Y	Y	Y
23 ***Boehlert***	Y	N	Y	Y	N	Y	Y	Y
24 ***McHugh***	Y	N	Y	Y	N	Y	Y	Y
25 ***Walsh***	?	?	Y	Y	N	N	N	N
26 Hinchey	N	Y	Y	Y	Y	N	N	Y
27 ***Paxon***	Y	N	Y	N	N	Y	Y	Y
28 Slaughter	N	Y	Y	Y	Y	N	N	N
29 LaFalce	N	Y	Y	Y	Y	?	N	Y
30 ***Quinn***	Y	N	Y	Y	N	Y	Y	#
31 ***Houghton***	Y	N	Y	Y	Y	Y	Y	Y
NORTH CAROLINA								
1 Clayton	N	Y	Y	Y	Y	N	N	Y
2 Valentine	Y	N	Y	Y	Y	N	Y	Y

	395	396	397	398	399	400	401	402
3 Lancaster	Y	N	Y	N	Y	N	N	Y
4 Price	N	Y	Y	Y	Y	N	N	Y
5 Neal	Y	N	Y	Y	Y	N	N	Y
6 ***Coble***	Y	N	Y	N	N	Y	Y	Y
7 Rose	N	Y	Y	Y	Y	N	N	Y
8 Hefner	N	Y	Y	Y	Y	N	N	Y
9 ***McMillan***	Y	N	?	?	?	?	?	?
10 ***Ballenger***	Y	—	Y	N	N	Y	Y	Y
11 ***Taylor***	Y	N	Y	N	N	Y	Y	Y
12 Watt	N	Y	Y	Y	Y	N	N	N
NORTH DAKOTA								
AL Pomeroy	Y	Y	Y	Y	Y	N	N	Y
OHIO								
1 Mann	Y	N	Y	Y	Y	N	N	Y
2 ***Portman***	Y	N	Y	N	N	Y	Y	Y
3 Hall	N	Y	Y	Y	Y	N	N	N
4 ***Oxley***	Y	N	Y	Y	N	Y	Y	Y
5 ***Gillmor***	Y	N	Y	Y	Y	Y	Y	Y
6 Strickland	N	Y	Y	Y	Y	N	N	Y
7 ***Hobson***	Y	N	Y	Y	N	N	N	Y
8 ***Boehner***	Y	N	?	?	?	Y	Y	Y
9 Kaptur	N	Y	Y	Y	Y	N	?	Y
10 ***Hoke***	Y	N	?	?	?	Y	Y	Y
11 Stokes	N	Y	Y	Y	Y	N	N	N
12 ***Kasich***	Y	N	Y	N	Y	Y	Y	Y
13 Brown	Y	N	Y	Y	Y	N	N	Y
14 Sawyer	N	Y	Y	Y	Y	N	N	Y
15 ***Pryce***	Y	N	Y	N	N	Y	Y	Y
16 ***Regula***	Y	N	Y	N	N	N	N	Y
17 Traficant	N	Y	Y	Y	Y	N	N	Y
18 Applegate	?	Y	Y	Y	Y	N	N	N
19 Fingerhut	Y	N	Y	Y	Y	N	Y	Y
OKLAHOMA								
1 ***Inhofe***	Y	N	Y	N	N	Y	Y	Y
2 Synar	N	?	Y	Y	Y	N	N	N
3 Brewster	?	?	Y	Y	Y	N	N	Y
4 McCurdy	Y	N	?	?	?	?	?	?
5 ***Istook***	Y	N	Y	N	N	Y	Y	Y
6 ***Lucas***	Y	N	Y	N	N	Y	Y	Y
OREGON								
1 Furse	Y	N	Y	Y	Y	N	N	Y
2 ***Smith***	Y	N	Y	N	N	Y	Y	Y
3 Wyden	N	Y	Y	Y	Y	N	N	Y
4 DeFazio	Y	N	Y	Y	Y	N	N	Y
5 Kopetski	N	Y	Y	Y	Y	N	N	N
PENNSYLVANIA								
1 Foglietta	N	Y	?	?	?	N	N	N
2 Blackwell	N	Y	?	?	?	N	N	N
3 Borski	N	Y	?	?	?	N	N	N
4 Klink	N	Y	Y	Y	Y	N	N	Y
5 ***Clinger***	Y	N	Y	N	N	Y	Y	Y
6 Holden	N	Y	Y	Y	Y	N	N	Y
7 ***Weldon***	Y	N	Y	Y	N	Y	Y	Y
8 ***Greenwood***	Y	N	Y	Y	Y	Y	Y	Y
9 ***Shuster***	Y	N	Y	N	N	Y	Y	Y
10 ***McDade***	Y	N	?	?	?	?	?	?
11 Kanjorski	N	Y	Y	Y	Y	N	N	Y
12 Murtha	N	Y	Y	Y	Y	N	N	N
13 Margolies-Mezv.	Y	N	Y	Y	Y	N	N	Y
14 Coyne	N	Y	Y	Y	Y	N	N	N
15 McHale	Y	N	Y	Y	Y	N	N	Y
16 ***Walker***	Y	N	Y	N	N	Y	Y	Y
17 ***Gekas***	Y	N	Y	N	N	Y	Y	Y
18 ***Santorum***	Y	N	?	?	?	Y	Y	Y
19 ***Goodling***	Y	N	Y	N	N	Y	Y	Y
20 Murphy	Y	N	Y	Y	N	N	N	Y
21 ***Ridge***	Y	N	?	?	?	Y	Y	Y
RHODE ISLAND								
1 ***Machtley***	Y	N	?	?	?	Y	Y	Y
2 Reed	N	Y	Y	N	Y	N	N	Y
SOUTH CAROLINA								
1 ***Ravenel***	Y	N	Y	Y	N	Y	Y	Y
2 ***Spence***	Y	N	Y	N	N	?	#	?
3 Derrick	N	Y	Y	Y	Y	N	X	X
4 ***Inglis***	Y	N	Y	N	Y	Y	Y	Y
5 Spratt	N	Y	Y	Y	Y	N	N	Y
6 Clyburn	N	Y	Y	Y	Y	N	N	Y
SOUTH DAKOTA								
AL Johnson	Y	N	Y	Y	Y	N	N	Y
TENNESSEE								
1 ***Quillen***	Y	N	Y	N	N	Y	N	Y
2 ***Duncan***	Y	N	Y	N	N	Y	Y	Y
3 Lloyd	?	?	Y	Y	Y	N	N	Y
4 Cooper	Y	N	?	?	?	N	Y	Y
5 Clement	Y	N	?	?	?	N	N	Y

	395	396	397	398	399	400	401	402
6 Gordon	Y	N	?	?	?	N	N	Y
7 ***Sundquist***	?	?	?	?	?	?	?	?
8 Tanner	Y	N	Y	Y	Y	N	N	Y
9 Ford	N	Y	Y	Y	Y	N	N	Y
TEXAS								
1 Chapman	N	Y	Y	N	Y	N	?	Y
2 Wilson	N	Y	Y	N	Y	N	N	N
3 ***Johnson, Sam***	Y	N	Y	N	N	Y	Y	Y
4 Hall	Y	N	Y	N	Y	Y	Y	Y
5 Bryant	N	Y	Y	N	Y	N	N	Y
6 ***Barton***	?	X	Y	N	N	Y	Y	Y
7 ***Archer***	Y	N	Y	N	N	?	Y	Y
8 ***Fields***	Y	N	Y	N	N	Y	Y	Y
9 Brooks	N	Y	Y	Y	Y	N	N	Y
10 Pickle	N	#	Y	Y	Y	N	N	N
11 Edwards	Y	N	Y	N	Y	N	N	Y
12 Geren	Y	N	Y	N	Y	N	N	Y
13 Sarpalius	Y	Y	Y	N	Y	N	N	Y
14 Laughlin	Y	N	Y	N	Y	N	N	Y
15 de la Garza	N	Y	Y	Y	Y	N	N	Y
16 Coleman	N	Y	Y	Y	Y	N	N	Y
17 Stenholm	Y	N	Y	N	Y	Y	Y	Y
18 Washington	?	?	?	?	?	?	?	?
19 ***Combest***	Y	N	Y	N	Y	Y	Y	Y
20 Gonzalez	N	Y	?	Y	Y	N	N	N
21 ***Smith***	Y	N	?	?	?	Y	Y	Y
22 ***DeLay***	Y	N	Y	N	N	Y	Y	Y
23 ***Bonilla***	Y	N	Y	N	N	Y	Y	Y
24 Frost	Y	N	Y	N	Y	N	N	Y
25 Andrews	Y	N	Y	Y	Y	?	Y	Y
26 ***Armey***	Y	N	Y	N	N	Y	Y	Y
27 Ortiz	N	Y	Y	Y	Y	N	N	Y
28 Tejeda	N	Y	Y	Y	Y	N	N	Y
29 Green	N	Y	Y	Y	Y	N	N	Y
30 Johnson, E.B.	N	Y	Y	Y	Y	N	N	N
UTAH								
1 ***Hansen***	Y	N	Y	N	N	Y	Y	Y
2 Shepherd	Y	N	Y	Y	Y	N	Y	Y
3 Orton	Y	N	Y	Y	Y	Y	Y	Y
VERMONT								
AL *Sanders*	N	Y	Y	Y	Y	N	N	Y
VIRGINIA								
1 ***Bateman***	Y	N	Y	N	Y	N	Y	Y
2 Pickett	Y	N	Y	Y	Y	N	N	Y
3 Scott	N	Y	Y	Y	Y	N	N	Y
4 Sisisky	Y	N	Y	Y	Y	N	N	Y
5 Payne	Y	N	Y	Y	Y	N	N	Y
6 ***Goodlatte***	Y	N	?	?	?	Y	Y	Y
7 ***Bliley***	Y	N	Y	N	N	N	Y	Y
8 Moran	N	Y	+	Y	Y	?	?	?
9 Boucher	N	Y	Y	Y	Y	N	N	N
10 ***Wolf***	Y	N	Y	N	N	N	Y	Y
11 Byrne	N	Y	Y	Y	Y	N	N	Y
WASHINGTON								
1 Cantwell	Y	N	Y	Y	Y	N	N	Y
2 Swift	N	Y	?	?	?	N	N	N
3 Unsoeld	N	Y	Y	Y	Y	N	N	N
4 Inslee	Y	N	Y	Y	Y	N	Y	Y
5 Foley								
6 Dicks	N	Y	Y	Y	Y	?	N	Y
7 McDermott	N	Y	Y	Y	Y	N	N	N
8 ***Dunn***	Y	N	Y	N	N	Y	Y	Y
9 Kreidler	Y	Y	Y	Y	N	N	Y	Y
WEST VIRGINIA								
1 Mollohan	N	Y	Y	Y	Y	N	N	N
2 Wise	N	Y	?	?	?	N	N	N
3 Rahall	N	Y	Y	Y	Y	N	N	N
WISCONSIN								
1 Barca	Y	N	Y	Y	Y	Y	Y	Y
2 ***Klug***	Y	N	Y	Y	N	Y	Y	Y
3 ***Gunderson***	Y	N	Y	N	N	Y	Y	Y
4 Kleczka	Y	N	Y	Y	Y	N	N	Y
5 Barrett	Y	N	Y	Y	Y	N	N	Y
6 ***Petri***	Y	N	Y	N	N	Y	Y	Y
7 Obey	N	Y	Y	Y	Y	N	N	N
8 ***Roth***	Y	N	Y	N	N	Y	Y	Y
9 ***Sensenbrenner***	Y	N	Y	N	N	Y	Y	Y
WYOMING								
AL ***Thomas***	Y	X	?	?	?	+	+	Y
DELEGATES								
de Lugo, V.I.	N	Y	D	D	D	N	N	N
Faleomavaega, Am.S.	?	?	D	D	D	N	N	N
Norton, D.C.	N	Y	D	D	D	N	N	Y
Romero-B., P.R.	N	?	D	D	D	N	?	N
Underwood, Guam	?	?	D	D	D	N	N	Y

Southern states - Ala., Ark., Fla., Ga., Ky., La., Miss., N.C., Okla., S.C., Tenn., Texas, Va.
Omitted votes are quorum calls, which CQ does not include in its vote charts.

403. HR 4906. Emergency Spending Procedures/Passage. Passage of the bill to prohibit the inclusion of non-emergency spending provisions in emergency spending bills and allow points of order in both chambers against any emergency spending legislation that contains non-emergency spending. Passed 406-6: R 167-0; D 238-6 (ND 161-5, SD 77-1); I 1-0, Aug. 17, 1994.

404. S 2182. Fiscal 1995 Defense Authorization/Conference Report. Adoption of the conference report to authorize $263.7 billion in fiscal 1995 for the programs of the Department of Defense. Adopted (thus sent to the Senate) 280-137: R 57-113; D 223-23 (ND 147-20, SD 76-3); I 0-1, Aug. 17, 1994. A "yea" was a vote in support of the president's position.

405. Procedural Motion. Approval of the House Journal of Tuesday, Aug. 16. Approved 228-154: R 17-145; D 210-9 (ND 141-7, SD 69-2); I 1-0, Aug. 17, 1994.

406. HR 4603. Fiscal 1995 Commerce, Justice, State Appropriations/Previous Question. Beilenson, D-Calif., motion to order the previous question (thus ending debate and the possibility of amendment) on adoption of the rule (H Res 523) to provide for House floor consideration of the conference report to provide $27,667,611,000 in new budget authority for the departments of Commerce, Justice, and State, the Judiciary and related agencies' programs for fiscal 1995. The administration had requested $28,434,837,000. The bill includes $795 million in supplemental fiscal 1994 money, including aid through the Small Business Administration loan program for disaster victims in the South and West. Motion agreed to 241-172: R 9-163; D 231-9 (ND 162-1, SD 69-8); I 1-0, Aug. 18, 1994.

407. HR 4603. Fiscal 1995 Commerce, Justice, State Appropriations/Rule. Adoption of the rule (H Res 523) to provide for House floor consideration of the conference report to provide $27,667,611,000 in new budget authority for the departments of Commerce, Justice, and State, the Judiciary and related agencies' programs for fiscal 1995. The administration had requested $28,434,837,000. The bill includes $795 million in supplemental fiscal 1994 money, including aid through the Small Business Administration loan program for disaster victims in the South and West. Adopted 235-175: R 6-165; D 228-10 (ND 161-2, SD 67-8); I 1-0, Aug. 18, 1994.

408. HR 4603. Fiscal 1995 Commerce, Justice, State Appropriations/Conference Report. Adoption of the conference report to provide $27,667,611,000 in new budget authority for the departments of Commerce, Justice, and State, the Judiciary and related agencies' programs for fiscal 1995. The administration had requested $28,434,837,000. The bill includes $795 million in supplemental fiscal 1994 money, including aid through the Small Business Administration loan program for disaster victims in the South and West. Adopted (thus cleared for the Senate) 322-98: R 89-87; D 232-11 (ND 158-8, SD 74-3); I 1-0, Aug. 18, 1994.

409. HR 3433. Presidio Management/Authorization Limit. Allard, R-Colo., amendment to limit the overall authorization for the development of the Presidio to $58 million as established in the Golden Gate National Recreation Area Act of 1972 (PL 92-589); limit federal participation in the management of visitor programs or the development of visitor facilities to a 50 percent share; and allow federal appropriations only for general public uses. Rejected in the Committee of the Whole 171-244: R 152-20; D 19-223 (ND 10-157, SD 9-66); I 0-1, Aug. 18, 1994.

410. HR 3433. Presidio Management/Budget Caps. Grams, R-Minn., amendment to establish specific budget caps for the operation and management for the Presidio. Rejected in the Committee of the Whole 190-227: R 166-6; D 24-220 (ND 10-158, SD 14-62); I 0-1, Aug. 18, 1994.

KEY

	403	404	405	406	407	408	409	410
ALABAMA								
1 *Callahan*	Y	N	N	Y	N	N	Y	Y
2 *Everett*	Y	Y	Y	N	Y	Y	Y	Y
3 Browder	Y	Y	Y	Y	Y	Y	N	Y
4 Bevill	Y	Y	Y	Y	Y	Y	N	N
5 Cramer	Y	Y	Y	Y	Y	Y	N	Y
6 *Bachus*	Y	N	N	N	N	N	Y	Y
7 Hilliard	Y	Y	Y	Y	Y	Y	N	N
ALASKA								
AL *Young*	Y	N	N	N	N	N	Y	Y
ARIZONA								
1 Coppersmith	Y	Y	Y	Y	Y	Y	N	N
2 Pastor	Y	Y	Y	Y	Y	Y	N	N
3 *Stump*	Y	N	N	N	N	N	Y	Y
4 *Kyl*	Y	N	N	N	N	Y	Y	Y
5 *Kolbe*	Y	N	N	Y	N	Y	N	Y
6 English	Y	Y	Y	Y	Y	Y	N	N
ARKANSAS								
1 Lambert	Y	Y	Y	Y	Y	Y	N	N
2 Thornton	Y	Y	Y	Y	Y	Y	N	N
3 *Hutchinson*	Y	N	?	N	N	Y	Y	Y
4 *Dickey*	Y	N	N	N	N	Y	Y	Y
CALIFORNIA								
1 Hamburg	Y	Y	Y	Y	Y	Y	N	N
2 *Herger*	Y	N	N	N	N	N	Y	Y
3 Fazio	Y	Y	Y	Y	Y	Y	N	N
4 *Doolittle*	Y	N	N	N	N	N	Y	Y
5 Matsui	Y	Y	Y	Y	Y	Y	N	N
6 Woolsey	Y	Y	Y	Y	Y	Y	N	N
7 Miller	Y	Y	Y	Y	Y	Y	N	N
8 Pelosi	Y	Y	Y	Y	Y	Y	N	N
9 Dellums	Y	Y	Y	Y	Y	Y	N	N
10 *Baker*	Y	N	N	N	N	N	Y	Y
11 *Pombo*	?	N	Y	N	N	Y	Y	Y
12 Lantos	?	?	?	?	?	?	?	?
13 Stark	Y	N	Y	Y	Y	Y	N	N
14 Eshoo	Y	Y	Y	Y	Y	Y	N	N
15 Mineta	Y	Y	Y	Y	Y	Y	N	N
16 Edwards	Y	N	?	Y	Y	Y	N	N
17 Farr	Y	Y	Y	Y	Y	Y	N	N
18 Condit	Y	N	Y	Y	Y	Y	N	N
19 Lehman	Y	Y	Y	Y	Y	Y	N	N
20 Dooley	Y	Y	Y	Y	Y	Y	N	N
21 *Thomas*	Y	N	N	N	N	Y	N	N
22 *Huffington*	Y	N	?	N	N	N	N	N
23 *Gallegly*	Y	N	N	N	Y	Y	Y	N
24 Beilenson	Y	Y	Y	Y	Y	Y	N	N
25 *McKeon*	Y	N	N	Y	N	N	Y	Y
26 Berman	Y	Y	Y	Y	Y	Y	N	N
27 *Moorhead*	Y	Y	?	N	N	N	N	Y
28 *Dreier*	Y	N	N	N	N	N	Y	Y
29 Waxman	Y	N	?	Y	Y	Y	N	N
30 Becerra	?	?	?	?	?	Y	N	N
31 Martinez	Y	Y	Y	Y	Y	Y	N	N
32 Dixon	Y	Y	Y	Y	Y	Y	N	N
33 Roybal-Allard	Y	Y	Y	Y	Y	Y	N	N
34 Torres	Y	Y	Y	Y	Y	Y	N	N
35 Waters	Y	Y	Y	Y	Y	Y	N	N
36 Harman	Y	Y	Y	Y	Y	Y	N	N
37 Tucker	Y	Y	Y	Y	Y	Y	N	N
38 *Horn*	Y	Y	N	N	N	Y	N	N
39 *Royce*	Y	N	N	N	N	N	Y	Y
40 *Lewis*	Y	Y	N	N	N	Y	N	N
41 *Kim*	Y	Y	N	N	N	N	Y	Y

	403	404	405	406	407	408	409	410
42 Brown	Y	Y	?	Y	N	Y	N	N
43 *Calvert*	Y	Y	N	N	N	Y	Y	Y
44 *McCandless*	N	N	N	N	N	N	Y	Y
45 *Rohrabacher*	Y	N	N	N	N	N	Y	Y
46 *Dornan*	Y	N	N	N	N	N	Y	Y
47 *Cox*	Y	?	N	N	N	N	Y	Y
48 *Packard*	Y	N	N	N	N	Y	Y	Y
49 Schenk	Y	Y	Y	Y	Y	Y	N	N
50 Filner	Y	Y	Y	Y	Y	Y	N	N
51 *Cunningham*	Y	Y	N	N	Y	N	Y	Y
52 *Hunter*	?	N	N	N	N	Y	Y	Y
COLORADO								
1 Schroeder	Y	N	N	Y	Y	Y	N	N
2 Skaggs	Y	Y	?	Y	Y	Y	N	N
3 *McInnis*	Y	N	N	N	Y	Y	Y	Y
4 *Allard*	Y	N	N	N	N	N	Y	Y
5 *Hefley*	Y	N	N	N	N	Y	Y	Y
6 *Schaefer*	Y	N	?	N	N	N	Y	Y
CONNECTICUT								
1 Kennelly	Y	Y	Y	Y	Y	Y	N	N
2 Gejdenson	Y	Y	?	Y	Y	Y	N	N
3 DeLauro	Y	Y	Y	Y	Y	Y	N	N
4 *Shays*	Y	N	N	N	Y	Y	N	N
5 *Franks*	Y	N	N	N	Y	Y	Y	Y
6 *Johnson*	Y	Y	N	N	?	Y	Y	Y
DELAWARE								
AL *Castle*	Y	Y	Y	N	N	Y	Y	Y
FLORIDA								
1 Hutto	Y	Y	N	Y	N	N	N	N
2 Peterson	Y	Y	Y	Y	Y	Y	N	N
3 Brown	Y	Y	Y	Y	Y	Y	N	N
4 *Fowler*	Y	Y	N	N	N	Y	Y	Y
5 Thurman	Y	Y	Y	N	Y	Y	N	N
6 *Stearns*	Y	N	N	N	N	N	Y	Y
7 *Mica*	Y	N	N	N	N	N	Y	Y
8 *McCollum*	Y	N	N	N	N	N	Y	Y
9 *Bilirakis*	Y	N	N	N	N	Y	Y	Y
10 *Young*	Y	Y	Y	Y	N	Y	Y	Y
11 Gibbons	Y	Y	Y	Y	Y	Y	N	N
12 *Canady*	Y	Y	?	N	N	Y	Y	Y
13 *Miller*	Y	N	N	N	N	N	Y	Y
14 *Goss*	Y	N	N	N	N	Y	Y	Y
15 Bacchus	Y	Y	Y	Y	Y	N	N	N
16 *Lewis*	Y	N	N	N	N	N	Y	Y
17 Meek	Y	Y	Y	Y	Y	Y	N	N
18 *Ros-Lehtinen*	Y	N	N	N	N	N	Y	Y
19 Johnston	Y	N	Y	Y	Y	Y	N	N
20 Deutsch	Y	Y	Y	Y	Y	?	N	N
21 *Diaz-Balart*	Y	N	N	N	N	N	Y	Y
22 *Shaw*	Y	N	N	N	N	Y	Y	Y
23 Hastings	Y	Y	Y	Y	Y	Y	N	N
GEORGIA								
1 *Kingston*	Y	N	N	N	N	Y	Y	Y
2 Bishop	Y	Y	Y	Y	Y	Y	N	N
3 *Collins*	Y	Y	Y	Y	Y	Y	N	N
4 *Linder*	Y	N	N	N	N	Y	Y	Y
5 Lewis	Y	Y	Y	Y	Y	Y	N	N
6 *Gingrich*	Y	N	N	N	N	Y	Y	Y
7 Darden	Y	Y	Y	Y	Y	Y	N	N
8 Rowland	Y	Y	Y	Y	Y	Y	N	N
9 Deal	Y	Y	Y	N	Y	Y	N	N
10 Johnson	Y	Y	Y	Y	Y	Y	N	N
11 McKinney	Y	Y	Y	Y	Y	Y	N	N
HAWAII								
1 Abercrombie	Y	Y	Y	Y	Y	Y	N	N
2 Mink	Y	Y	Y	Y	Y	Y	N	N
IDAHO								
1 LaRocco	Y	Y	Y	Y	Y	Y	N	N
2 *Crapo*	Y	N	N	N	N	N	Y	Y
ILLINOIS								
1 Rush	Y	Y	Y	Y	Y	?	N	N
2 Reynolds	?	?	?	?	?	?	?	?
3 Lipinski	Y	Y	Y	Y	Y	Y	N	N
4 Gutierrez	Y	Y	Y	Y	Y	Y	N	N
5 Rostenkowski	Y	Y	Y	Y	Y	Y	N	N
6 *Hyde*	?	Y	N	N	N	N	Y	Y
7 Collins	Y	N	Y	Y	Y	X	X	X
8 *Crane*	Y	N	N	N	N	N	Y	Y
9 Yates	N	Y	?	Y	Y	Y	N	N
10 *Porter*	Y	Y	N	N	N	Y	Y	Y
11 Sangmeister	Y	Y	?	Y	Y	Y	N	N
12 Costello	Y	Y	Y	Y	Y	Y	N	N
13 *Fawell*	Y	N	N	N	N	N	Y	Y
14 *Hastert*	Y	N	N	N	N	Y	Y	Y
15 *Ewing*	Y	Y	N	N	N	Y	Y	Y
16 *Manzullo*	Y	N	N	N	N	Y	Y	Y
17 Evans	Y	Y	Y	Y	Y	Y	N	N

ND Northern Democrats   SD Southern Democrats

	403	404	405	406	407	408	409	410
18 ***Michel***	?	?	?	N	N	Y	Y	Y
19 Poshard	Y	Y	Y	Y	Y	Y	Y	N
20 Durbin	Y	Y	Y	Y	Y	Y	N	N
INDIANA								
1 Visclosky	Y	Y	?	Y	Y	Y	N	N
2 Sharp	Y	Y	Y	Y	Y	Y	N	N
3 Roemer	Y	Y	Y	Y	Y	Y	N	N
4 Long	Y	Y	Y	Y	Y	Y	N	N
5 ***Buyer***	Y	N	N	N	N	Y	Y	Y
6 ***Burton***	Y	N	N	N	N	N	Y	Y
7 ***Myers***	Y	Y	Y	Y	Y	Y	Y	Y
8 McCloskey	Y	Y	Y	Y	Y	Y	N	N
9 Hamilton	Y	Y	Y	Y	Y	Y	N	N
10 Jacobs	Y	Y	N	N	Y	N	Y	Y
IOWA								
1 ***Leach***	Y	N	N	N	N	Y	Y	Y
2 ***Nussle***	Y	N	N	N	N	N	Y	Y
3 ***Lightfoot***	Y	N	N	N	N	Y	Y	Y
4 Smith	Y	Y	Y	Y	Y	Y	N	N
5 ***Grandy***	Y	N	N	N	N	Y	Y	Y
KANSAS								
1 ***Roberts***	Y	N	N	N	N	N	Y	Y
2 Slattery	?	?	?	?	?	?	?	?
3 ***Meyers***	Y	N	N	N	N	N	Y	Y
4 Glickman	?	Y	Y	Y	Y	Y	N	N
KENTUCKY								
1 Barlow	Y	Y	Y	Y	Y	Y	N	N
2 ***Lewis***	Y	Y	N	N	N	N	Y	Y
3 Mazzoli	Y	Y	Y	Y	Y	Y	N	N
4 ***Bunning***	Y	N	N	N	N	N	Y	Y
5 ***Rogers***	Y	N	N	Y	Y	Y	Y	Y
6 Baesler	Y	Y	Y	Y	Y	Y	N	N
LOUISIANA								
1 ***Livingston***	Y	Y	?	Y	?	Y	Y	Y
2 Jefferson	Y	Y	Y	Y	Y	Y	N	N
3 Tauzin	Y	Y	Y	Y	N	Y	Y	N
4 Fields	?	Y	Y	Y	Y	Y	N	N
5 ***McCrery***	Y	N	N	N	N	Y	Y	Y
6 ***Baker***	Y	N	N	N	N	Y	Y	Y
7 Hayes	Y	Y	?	N	N	Y	Y	N
MAINE								
1 Andrews	Y	Y	Y	Y	Y	Y	N	N
2 ***Snowe***	Y	Y	N	N	N	Y	Y	Y
MARYLAND								
1 ***Gilchrest***	Y	Y	N	N	N	Y	N	Y
2 ***Bentley***	Y	N	N	N	N	Y	Y	Y
3 Cardin	Y	Y	Y	Y	Y	Y	N	N
4 Wynn	Y	Y	Y	Y	Y	Y	N	N
5 Hoyer	Y	Y	Y	Y	Y	Y	N	N
6 ***Bartlett***	Y	N	N	N	N	N	Y	Y
7 Mfume	Y	Y	N	Y	Y	Y	N	N
8 ***Morella***	Y	Y	N	Y	Y	Y	N	N
MASSACHUSETTS								
1 Olver	Y	Y	Y	Y	Y	Y	N	N
2 Neal	Y	Y	Y	Y	Y	Y	N	N
3 ***Blute***	Y	Y	N	N	N	Y	Y	Y
4 Frank	Y	N	Y	Y	Y	Y	N	N
5 Meehan	Y	Y	Y	Y	Y	Y	N	N
6 ***Torkildsen***	Y	N	N	?	N	Y	Y	Y
7 Markey	Y	Y	Y	Y	Y	Y	N	N
8 Kennedy	Y	Y	Y	Y	Y	Y	N	N
9 Moakley	Y	Y	Y	Y	Y	Y	N	N
10 Studds	Y	Y	Y	Y	Y	Y	N	N
MICHIGAN								
1 Stupak	Y	Y	Y	Y	Y	Y	N	N
2 ***Hoekstra***	Y	N	N	N	N	N	Y	Y
3 ***Ehlers***	Y	N	N	N	N	N	Y	Y
4 ***Camp***	Y	N	N	N	N	N	Y	Y
5 Barcia	Y	Y	Y	Y	Y	Y	Y	Y
6 ***Upton***	Y	Y	N	N	N	Y	Y	Y
7 ***Smith***	Y	Y	N	—	—	N	Y	Y
8 Carr	Y	Y	Y	Y	Y	Y	N	N
9 Kildee	Y	Y	Y	Y	Y	Y	N	N
10 Bonior	N	Y	Y	Y	Y	Y	?	?
11 ***Knollenberg***	Y	N	N	N	N	N	Y	Y
12 Levin	Y	Y	Y	Y	Y	Y	N	N
13 Ford	Y	Y	?	Y	Y	Y	N	N
14 Conyers	Y	N	Y	Y	Y	Y	N	N
15 Collins	Y	Y	Y	Y	Y	Y	N	N
16 Dingell	Y	Y	Y	Y	Y	Y	N	N
MINNESOTA								
1 Penny	Y	N	Y	Y	Y	N	Y	Y
2 Minge	Y	N	Y	Y	Y	N	Y	Y
3 ***Ramstad***	Y	N	N	N	N	N	Y	Y
4 Vento	Y	N	Y	Y	Y	Y	N	N
5 Sabo	Y	Y	Y	Y	Y	Y	N	N
6 ***Grams***	?	X	?	N	?	N	Y	Y
7 Peterson	Y	Y	Y	Y	Y	N	Y	N
8 Oberstar	Y	Y	Y	Y	Y	Y	N	N
MISSISSIPPI								
1 Whitten	Y	?	?	Y	Y	Y	N	N
2 Thompson	Y	Y	Y	Y	Y	Y	N	N
3 Montgomery	Y	Y	Y	Y	Y	Y	N	N
4 Parker	Y	Y	Y	Y	Y	Y	N	N
5 Taylor	Y	Y	N	N	N	N	Y	Y
MISSOURI								
1 Clay	Y	Y	N	Y	Y	Y	N	N
2 ***Talent***	Y	N	N	N	N	N	Y	Y
3 Gephardt	Y	Y	Y	Y	Y	Y	?	?
4 Skelton	Y	Y	Y	Y	N	Y	N	N
5 Wheat	Y	Y	Y	Y	Y	Y	N	N
6 Danner	Y	Y	Y	Y	Y	Y	N	N
7 ***Hancock***	Y	N	N	N	N	N	Y	Y
8 ***Emerson***	Y	N	N	N	N	Y	Y	Y
9 Volkmer	Y	Y	Y	Y	Y	Y	N	N
MONTANA								
AL Williams	Y	Y	?	Y	Y	Y	N	N
NEBRASKA								
1 ***Bereuter***	Y	Y	N	N	N	Y	N	Y
2 Hoagland	Y	Y	Y	Y	Y	Y	N	N
3 ***Barrett***	Y	Y	N	N	N	Y	Y	Y
NEVADA								
1 Bilbray	Y	Y	Y	Y	Y	Y	N	N
2 ***Vucanovich***	Y	N	N	N	N	Y	Y	Y
NEW HAMPSHIRE								
1 ***Zeliff***	Y	N	N	N	N	N	Y	Y
2 Swett	Y	Y	Y	Y	Y	N	N	Y
NEW JERSEY								
1 Andrews	Y	Y	?	Y	Y	N	Y	N
2 Hughes	Y	Y	Y	Y	Y	Y	N	N
3 ***Saxton***	Y	N	N	N	N	Y	Y	Y
4 ***Smith***	Y	Y	Y	N	N	Y	Y	Y
5 ***Roukema***	Y	N	N	N	N	Y	N	Y
6 Pallone	Y	Y	Y	Y	Y	Y	N	N
7 ***Franks***	Y	N	N	N	N	N	Y	Y
8 Klein	Y	Y	Y	?	?	?	?	?
9 Torricelli	Y	Y	Y	Y	Y	Y	N	N
10 Payne	Y	Y	Y	Y	Y	Y	N	N
11 ***Gallo***	Y	?	?	?	N	Y	?	?
12 ***Zimmer***	Y	N	N	N	N	N	Y	Y
13 Menendez	Y	Y	Y	Y	Y	Y	N	N
NEW MEXICO								
1 ***Schiff***	Y	N	N	N	N	Y	Y	Y
2 ***Skeen***	Y	Y	N	?	N	Y	N	Y
3 Richardson	Y	Y	Y	Y	Y	Y	N	N
NEW YORK								
1 Hochbrueckner	Y	Y	Y	Y	Y	Y	N	N
2 ***Lazio***	Y	Y	N	N	N	N	Y	Y
3 ***King***	Y	N	N	N	N	N	Y	Y
4 ***Levy***	Y	N	N	N	N	N	Y	Y
5 Ackerman	Y	Y	Y	Y	Y	Y	N	N
6 Flake	?	?	?	?	?	Y	N	N
7 Manton	Y	Y	Y	Y	Y	Y	N	N
8 Nadler	N	N	Y	Y	Y	Y	N	N
9 Schumer	Y	Y	Y	Y	Y	Y	N	N
10 Towns	Y	Y	N	Y	Y	Y	N	N
11 Owens	Y	Y	Y	?	?	?	?	?
12 Velazquez	Y	Y	Y	Y	Y	Y	N	N
13 ***Molinari***	Y	N	N	N	N	Y	Y	Y
14 Maloney	Y	N	Y	Y	Y	Y	N	N
15 Rangel	Y	Y	Y	?	Y	Y	N	N
16 Serrano	Y	Y	Y	Y	Y	Y	N	N
17 Engel	Y	Y	Y	Y	Y	Y	N	N
18 Lowey	Y	Y	Y	Y	?	Y	N	N
19 ***Fish***	Y	Y	?	N	Y	Y	Y	Y
20 ***Gilman***	Y	Y	Y	N	N	Y	N	Y
21 McNulty	Y	N	Y	Y	Y	Y	N	N
22 ***Solomon***	Y	N	N	N	N	N	Y	Y
23 ***Boehlert***	Y	N	N	N	N	Y	N	Y
24 ***McHugh***	Y	N	N	N	N	Y	Y	Y
25 ***Walsh***	Y	N	N	N	N	Y	Y	Y
26 Hinchey	Y	Y	Y	Y	Y	Y	N	N
27 ***Paxon***	Y	N	N	N	N	N	Y	Y
28 Slaughter	Y	Y	Y	Y	Y	Y	N	N
29 LaFalce	Y	Y	Y	Y	Y	Y	N	N
30 ***Quinn***	?	#	?	N	N	Y	Y	Y
31 ***Houghton***	Y	Y	Y	N	N	Y	?	?
NORTH CAROLINA								
1 Clayton	Y	Y	N	Y	Y	Y	N	N
2 Valentine	Y	Y	?	Y	?	Y	N	N
3 Lancaster	Y	Y	Y	Y	Y	Y	N	N
4 Price	Y	Y	Y	Y	Y	Y	N	N
5 Neal	Y	Y	Y	Y	Y	Y	N	N
6 ***Coble***	Y	N	N	N	N	N	Y	Y
7 Rose	Y	Y	Y	?	?	?	?	?
8 Hefner	Y	Y	?	Y	Y	Y	N	N
9 ***McMillan***	?	Y	N	N	N	Y	Y	Y
10 ***Ballenger***	Y	N	N	N	N	Y	Y	Y
11 ***Taylor***	Y	N	N	N	N	Y	Y	Y
12 Watt	Y	Y	Y	Y	Y	Y	N	N
NORTH DAKOTA								
AL Pomeroy	Y	Y	Y	Y	Y	Y	N	N
OHIO								
1 Mann	Y	Y	Y	Y	Y	Y	N	N
2 ***Portman***	Y	N	N	N	N	N	Y	Y
3 Hall	Y	Y	?	Y	Y	Y	N	N
4 ***Oxley***	Y	Y	N	N	N	Y	Y	Y
5 ***Gillmor***	Y	Y	N	N	N	Y	N	Y
6 Strickland	Y	Y	Y	Y	Y	Y	N	N
7 ***Hobson***	Y	Y	N	N	N	Y	Y	Y
8 ***Boehner***	Y	N	N	N	N	N	Y	Y
9 Kaptur	Y	Y	Y	Y	Y	Y	N	Y
10 ***Hoke***	Y	Y	N	N	N	Y	Y	Y
11 Stokes	Y	Y	Y	Y	Y	Y	N	N
12 ***Kasich***	Y	N	Y	N	N	N	Y	Y
13 Brown	Y	Y	Y	Y	Y	Y	N	N
14 Sawyer	Y	Y	Y	Y	Y	Y	N	N
15 ***Pryce***	Y	N	N	N	N	N	Y	Y
16 ***Regula***	Y	Y	N	Y	N	Y	N	Y
17 Traficant	Y	Y	Y	Y	Y	Y	N	N
18 Applegate	Y	Y	?	Y	Y	Y	N	N
19 Fingerhut	Y	Y	Y	Y	Y	Y	N	N
OKLAHOMA								
1 ***Inhofe***	Y	Y	N	N	N	N	Y	Y
2 Synar	Y	Y	Y	Y	Y	Y	N	N
3 Brewster	Y	Y	Y	Y	Y	Y	?	Y
4 McCurdy	?	Y	?	N	N	Y	N	N
5 ***Istook***	Y	Y	N	N	N	N	Y	Y
6 ***Lucas***	Y	Y	N	N	N	N	Y	Y
OREGON								
1 Furse	Y	Y	Y	Y	?	Y	N	N
2 ***Smith***	Y	Y	?	N	N	N	Y	Y
3 Wyden	Y	N	Y	Y	Y	Y	N	N
4 DeFazio	Y	N	N	Y	Y	Y	N	N
5 Kopetski	Y	Y	Y	Y	Y	Y	N	N
PENNSYLVANIA								
1 Foglietta	Y	Y	Y	Y	Y	Y	N	N
2 Blackwell	Y	Y	?	Y	Y	Y	?	N
3 Borski	Y	Y	Y	Y	Y	Y	N	N
4 Klink	Y	Y	Y	?	Y	Y	N	N
5 ***Clinger***	Y	N	N	N	Y	Y	Y	Y
6 Holden	Y	Y	Y	Y	Y	Y	N	Y
7 ***Weldon***	Y	Y	N	N	N	N	Y	Y
8 ***Greenwood***	Y	Y	Y	N	N	N	Y	Y
9 ***Shuster***	Y	N	N	N	N	N	Y	Y
10 ***McDade***	?	?	?	?	?	?	?	?
11 Kanjorski	Y	Y	Y	Y	Y	Y	Y	Y
12 Murtha	Y	Y	?	Y	Y	Y	N	N
13 Margolies-Mezv.	Y	N	Y	Y	Y	Y	N	N
14 Coyne	Y	Y	?	Y	Y	Y	N	N
15 McHale	Y	Y	Y	Y	Y	Y	N	N
16 ***Walker***	Y	N	N	N	N	N	Y	Y
17 ***Gekas***	Y	N	N	N	N	N	Y	Y
18 ***Santorum***	Y	Y	N	N	N	N	Y	Y
19 ***Goodling***	Y	N	N	N	N	N	Y	Y
20 Murphy	Y	Y	?	Y	Y	N	N	N
21 ***Ridge***	Y	Y	N	N	N	N	Y	Y
RHODE ISLAND								
1 ***Machtley***	Y	Y	N	N	N	Y	Y	Y
2 Reed	Y	Y	Y	Y	Y	Y	N	N
SOUTH CAROLINA								
1 ***Ravenel***	Y	Y	N	N	N	Y	N	N
2 ***Spence***	#	?	?	N	N	N	Y	Y
3 Derrick	X	?	?	Y	Y	Y	N	N
4 ***Inglis***	Y	N	Y	N	N	N	Y	Y
5 Spratt	Y	Y	Y	Y	Y	Y	N	N
6 Clyburn	Y	Y	Y	Y	Y	Y	N	N
SOUTH DAKOTA								
AL Johnson	Y	Y	?	Y	Y	Y	N	N
TENNESSEE								
1 ***Quillen***	Y	Y	N	N	N	Y	Y	Y
2 ***Duncan***	Y	N	N	N	N	N	Y	Y
3 Lloyd	Y	Y	Y	Y	Y	Y	N	N
4 Cooper	Y	Y	Y	?	?	?	?	?
5 Clement	Y	Y	Y	?	?	?	?	?
6 Gordon	Y	Y	Y	Y	Y	Y	N	N
7 ***Sundquist***	?	?	?	?	?	?	?	?
8 Tanner	Y	Y	Y	Y	Y	Y	N	N
9 Ford	Y	Y	Y	?	?	?	?	?
TEXAS								
1 Chapman	Y	Y	Y	Y	Y	Y	N	Y
2 Wilson	Y	Y	Y	Y	Y	Y	N	N
3 ***Johnson, Sam***	Y	N	N	N	N	N	Y	Y
4 Hall	Y	N	Y	Y	Y	N	Y	Y
5 Bryant	Y	Y	Y	Y	Y	Y	N	N
6 ***Barton***	Y	N	N	N	N	N	#	#
7 ***Archer***	Y	N	N	N	N	N	Y	Y
8 ***Fields***	Y	N	N	N	N	N	Y	Y
9 Brooks	Y	Y	Y	Y	Y	Y	N	N
10 Pickle	Y	Y	Y	Y	Y	Y	N	N
11 Edwards	Y	Y	Y	Y	Y	Y	N	Y
12 Geren	Y	Y	Y	Y	Y	Y	Y	Y
13 Sarpalius	Y	Y	Y	N	N	Y	Y	Y
14 Laughlin	Y	Y	Y	Y	Y	Y	N	N
15 de la Garza	Y	Y	Y	Y	Y	Y	N	N
16 Coleman	Y	Y	?	Y	Y	Y	N	N
17 Stenholm	Y	Y	Y	N	N	N	Y	Y
18 Washington	?	?	?	?	?	?	?	?
19 ***Combest***	Y	N	Y	N	N	N	Y	Y
20 Gonzalez	N	Y	Y	Y	Y	Y	N	N
21 ***Smith***	Y	N	N	N	N	N	Y	Y
22 ***DeLay***	Y	N	N	N	N	N	Y	Y
23 ***Bonilla***	Y	N	N	N	N	Y	Y	Y
24 Frost	Y	Y	Y	Y	Y	Y	N	N
25 Andrews	Y	Y	?	Y	Y	?	N	N
26 ***Armey***	Y	N	N	N	N	N	Y	Y
27 Ortiz	Y	Y	Y	Y	Y	Y	N	N
28 Tejeda	Y	Y	Y	Y	Y	Y	N	N
29 Green	Y	Y	?	Y	Y	Y	N	N
30 Johnson, E.B.	Y	Y	Y	Y	Y	Y	N	N
UTAH								
1 ***Hansen***	?	N	N	N	N	N	Y	Y
2 Shepherd	Y	Y	Y	Y	Y	Y	N	N
3 Orton	Y	Y	Y	Y	Y	Y	Y	Y
VERMONT								
AL *Sanders*	Y	N	Y	Y	Y	Y	N	N
VIRGINIA								
1 ***Bateman***	Y	Y	Y	N	N	Y	Y	Y
2 Pickett	Y	N	Y	?	?	Y	Y	Y
3 Scott	Y	Y	Y	Y	Y	Y	N	N
4 Sisisky	Y	Y	?	Y	Y	Y	?	?
5 Payne	Y	Y	Y	Y	Y	Y	N	Y
6 ***Goodlatte***	Y	N	N	N	N	N	Y	Y
7 ***Bliley***	Y	Y	N	N	N	N	?	?
8 Moran	?	?	?	Y	Y	Y	?	?
9 Boucher	Y	Y	Y	Y	Y	Y	N	N
10 ***Wolf***	Y	N	N	N	N	Y	Y	Y
11 Byrne	Y	Y	Y	Y	Y	Y	N	N
WASHINGTON								
1 Cantwell	Y	Y	Y	Y	Y	Y	N	N
2 Swift	Y	Y	Y	Y	Y	Y	N	N
3 Unsoeld	Y	Y	Y	Y	Y	Y	N	N
4 Inslee	Y	Y	Y	Y	Y	Y	N	N
5 Foley								
6 Dicks	Y	Y	Y	Y	Y	Y	N	N
7 McDermott	Y	Y	Y	Y	Y	Y	N	N
8 ***Dunn***	Y	N	N	N	N	N	Y	Y
9 Kreidler	Y	Y	N	Y	Y	Y	N	N
WEST VIRGINIA								
1 Mollohan	Y	Y	Y	Y	Y	Y	N	N
2 Wise	Y	Y	Y	Y	Y	Y	N	N
3 Rahall	N	Y	Y	Y	Y	Y	N	N
WISCONSIN								
1 Barca	Y	N	Y	Y	Y	Y	N	Y
2 ***Klug***	Y	N	N	N	N	N	Y	Y
3 ***Gunderson***	Y	N	N	N	N	Y	N	Y
4 Kleczka	Y	Y	?	Y	Y	Y	N	N
5 Barrett	Y	N	Y	Y	Y	Y	N	N
6 ***Petri***	Y	N	?	N	N	N	Y	Y
7 Obey	N	Y	Y	Y	Y	Y	N	N
8 ***Roth***	Y	N	N	N	N	N	Y	Y
9 ***Sensenbrenner***	Y	N	N	N	N	N	Y	Y
WYOMING								
AL ***Thomas***	Y	N	N	N	?	Y	Y	Y
DELEGATES								
de Lugo, V.I.	D	D	D	D	D	D	N	N
Faleomavaega, Am.S.	D	D	D	D	D	D	?	?
Norton, D.C.	D	D	D	D	D	D	N	N
Romero-B., P.R.	D	D	D	D	D	D	N	N
Underwood, Guam	D	D	D	D	D	D	N	N

Southern states - Ala., Ark., Fla., Ga., Ky., La., Miss., N.C., Okla., S.C., Tenn., Texas, Va.
Omitted votes are quorum calls, which CQ does not include in its vote charts.

411. HR 3433. Presidio Management/Passage. Passage of the bill to provide for the management and operation of the Presidio, at the base of the Golden Gate Bridge in San Francisco, by the National Park Service after its transfer from the Army on Oct. 1, 1994. Passed 245-168: R 27-144; D 217-24 (ND 153-12, SD 64-12); I 1-0, Aug. 18, 1994. A "yea" was a vote in support of the president's position.

412. HR 4908. Hydrogen Fusion Research/Lobbying Prohibition. Walker, R-Pa., amendment to prohibit universities and laboratories from using money authorized by the bill for lobbying activities to promote public support or opposition for legislative proposals still before Congress. Rejected in the Committee of the Whole 187-239: R 173-2; D 14-236 (ND 13-159, SD 1-77); I 0-1, Aug. 19, 1994.

413. Procedural Motion. Approval of the House Journal of Saturday, Aug. 20. Approved 248-165: R 17-155; D 230-10 (ND 156-7, SD 74-3); I 1-0, Aug. 21, 1994.

414. HR 3355. Omnibus Crime Bill/Rule. Adoption of the rule (H Res 526) to waive points of order and provide for House floor consideration of the conference report making a series of changes in the original conference report, including a cut in the overall authorization level from $33.5 billion to $30.2 billion over six years, a requirement that all spending authorized by the bill come from a six-year, $30.2 billion crime trust fund realized from eliminating 270,000 federal jobs, a reduction from $8.9 billion to $6.9 billion in the amount for crime prevention programs, a provision to notify communities about violent sex offenders, and a provision to allow prior sex offenses to be admitted in federal trials. Adopted 239-189: R 42-134; D 196-55 (ND 147-24, SD 49-31); I 1-0, Aug. 21, 1994. Previously, the House had rejected a rule (H Res 517) providing for consideration of an original conference report Aug. 11 (see vote 394). A "yea" was a vote in support of the president's position.

415. HR 3355. Omnibus Crime Bill/Recommit. McCollum, R-Fla., motion to recommit the conference report to the conference with instructions to prioritize the authorizations to maximize programs for public safety and policing, prison construction and border patrol, after eliminating the crime prevention programs in the bill as outlined in a proposal made by Brewster, D-Okla., and Hunter, R-Calif. Motion rejected 197-232: R 146-30; D 51-201 (ND 19-153, SD 32-48); I 0-1, Aug. 21, 1994. A "nay" was a vote in support of the president's position.

416. HR 3355. Omnibus Crime Bill/Conference Report. Adoption of the conference report to authorize $30.2 billion over six years and to require that all spending authorized by the bill come from a six-year, $30.2 billion crime trust fund realized from eliminating 270,000 federal jobs. The bill would authorize $6.9 billion for crime prevention programs, such as after-school sports leagues and job training programs, $8.8 billion for community policing programs and the hiring of 100,000 new police officers, and a $7.9 billion grant program to build state and local prisons. The bill also would ban 19 specific assault weapons, expand the death penalty to dozens of new federal crimes, mandate life imprisonment without parole for three-time violent felons, provide for community notification of violent sex offenders, allow prior sex offenses to be considered at federal trials and require HIV testing when requested in federal rape trials. Adopted (thus sent to the Senate) 235-195: R 46-131; D 188-64 (ND 141-31, SD 47-33); I 1-0, Aug. 21, 1994. A "yea" was a vote in support of the president's position.

KEY

Y   Voted for (yea).
Paired for.
+   Announced for.
N   Voted against (nay).
X   Paired against.
−   Announced against.
P   Voted "present."
C   Voted "present" to avoid possible conflict of interest.
?   Did not vote or otherwise make a position known.
D   Delegates ineligible to vote.

Democrats *Republicans*
Independent

	411	412	413	414	415	416
ALABAMA						
1 Callahan	N	Y	?	?	?	?
2 Everett	N	Y	Y	N	Y	N
3 Browder	Y	N	Y	N	Y	Y
4 Bevill	Y	N	Y	Y	Y	N
5 Cramer	N	N	Y	Y	Y	Y
6 *Bachus*	N	Y	N	N	Y	N
7 Hilliard	Y	N	Y	N	N	N
ALASKA						
AL *Young*	N	Y	N	N	Y	N
ARIZONA						
1 Coppersmith	Y	N	Y	Y	N	Y
2 Pastor	Y	N	Y	Y	N	Y
3 *Stump*	N	Y	N	N	Y	N
4 *Kyl*	N	Y	N	N	Y	Y
5 *Kolbe*	Y	Y	N	N	Y	Y
6 English	Y	N	Y	Y	N	Y
ARKANSAS						
1 Lambert	Y	N	Y	Y	N	Y
2 Thornton	Y	N	Y	Y	N	Y
3 *Hutchinson*	N	Y	N	N	Y	N
4 *Dickey*	N	Y	N	N	Y	N
CALIFORNIA						
1 Hamburg	Y	N	Y	Y	N	Y
2 *Herger*	N	Y	?	N	+	N
3 Fazio	Y	N	Y	Y	N	Y
4 *Doolittle*	N	Y	N	N	Y	N
5 Matsui	Y	N	Y	Y	N	Y
6 Woolsey	Y	N	Y	Y	N	Y
7 Miller	Y	N	Y	Y	N	Y
8 Pelosi	Y	N	Y	Y	N	Y
9 Dellums	Y	N	Y	Y	N	Y
10 *Baker*	Y	Y	?	N	Y	N
11 *Pombo*	N	Y	Y	N	Y	N
12 Lantos	?	?	Y	Y	N	Y
13 Stark	Y	N	Y	Y	N	Y
14 Eshoo	Y	N	Y	Y	N	Y
15 Mineta	Y	N	Y	Y	N	Y
16 Edwards	Y	N	Y	Y	N	Y
17 Farr	Y	N	Y	Y	N	Y
18 Condit	Y	Y	Y	Y	Y	Y
19 Lehman	Y	N	Y	Y	N	Y
20 Dooley	Y	N	Y	Y	N	Y
21 *Thomas*	N	Y	N	N	Y	N
22 *Huffington*	Y	Y	Y	Y	Y	Y
23 *Gallegly*	N	Y	N	N	Y	Y
24 Beilenson	Y	N	Y	N	Y	Y
25 *McKeon*	N	Y	N	N	Y	N
26 Berman	Y	N	Y	Y	N	Y
27 *Moorhead*	N	Y	N	N	Y	N
28 *Dreier*	N	Y	N	N	Y	N
29 Waxman	Y	N	Y	Y	N	Y
30 Becerra	Y	N	Y	Y	N	Y
31 Martinez	Y	N	Y	Y	N	Y
32 Dixon	Y	N	Y	Y	N	Y
33 Roybal-Allard	Y	N	Y	Y	N	Y
34 Torres	Y	N	Y	Y	N	Y
35 Waters	Y	N	Y	N	N	N
36 Harman	Y	N	Y	Y	N	Y
37 Tucker	Y	N	?	?	?	?
38 *Horn*	Y	Y	N	Y	Y	Y
39 *Royce*	N	Y	N	N	Y	N
40 *Lewis*	N	Y	N	N	Y	N
41 *Kim*	Y	Y	N	N	Y	N

	411	412	413	414	415	416
42 Brown	Y	N	N	Y	N	Y
43 *Calvert*	N	Y	N	N	Y	N
44 *McCandless*	N	Y	N	N	Y	N
45 *Rohrabacher*	N	Y	N	N	Y	N
46 *Dornan*	N	Y	N	N	Y	N
47 *Cox*	Y	Y	N	N	Y	N
48 *Packard*	N	Y	N	N	Y	N
49 Schenk	Y	N	Y	N	Y	N
50 Filner	Y	N	Y	Y	N	Y
51 *Cunningham*	Y	Y	N	N	Y	N
52 *Hunter*	N	Y	N	N	Y	N
COLORADO						
1 Schroeder	N	N	N	Y	N	Y
2 Skaggs	Y	N	Y	N	Y	Y
3 *McInnis*	N	Y	N	N	Y	N
4 *Allard*	N	Y	N	N	Y	N
5 *Hefley*	N	Y	N	N	Y	N
6 *Schaefer*	N	Y	N	N	Y	N
CONNECTICUT						
1 Kennelly	Y	N	Y	Y	N	Y
2 Gejdenson	Y	N	Y	Y	N	Y
3 DeLauro	Y	N	Y	Y	N	Y
4 *Shays*	N	Y	N	Y	N	Y
5 *Franks*	N	Y	N	Y	N	Y
6 *Johnson*	N	Y	N	Y	N	Y
DELAWARE						
AL *Castle*	N	Y	N	Y	N	Y
FLORIDA						
1 Hutto	Y	N	N	Y	N	Y
2 Peterson	Y	N	Y	N	Y	N
3 Brown	Y	N	Y	N	Y	N
4 *Fowler*	N	Y	N	N	Y	N
5 Thurman	Y	N	Y	N	Y	N
6 *Stearns*	N	Y	N	N	Y	N
7 *Mica*	N	Y	N	N	Y	N
8 *McCollum*	N	Y	N	N	Y	N
9 *Bilirakis*	N	Y	N	N	Y	N
10 *Young*	N	Y	N	N	Y	N
11 Gibbons	Y	N	Y	Y	N	Y
12 *Canady*	N	Y	N	N	Y	Y
13 *Miller*	N	Y	N	N	Y	N
14 *Goss*	N	Y	N	N	Y	N
15 Bacchus	Y	N	Y	Y	N	Y
16 *Lewis*	N	Y	N	N	Y	N
17 Meek	Y	N	Y	Y	N	Y
18 *Ros-Lehtinen*	N	Y	N	Y	Y	Y
19 Johnston	Y	N	Y	Y	N	Y
20 Deutsch	Y	N	Y	Y	N	Y
21 *Diaz-Balart*	Y	Y	N	Y	Y	Y
22 *Shaw*	Y	Y	N	Y	N	Y
23 Hastings	Y	N	Y	Y	N	Y
GEORGIA						
1 *Kingston*	N	Y	N	N	Y	N
2 Bishop	Y	N	Y	Y	N	Y
3 *Collins*	N	Y	N	N	Y	N
4 *Linder*	N	Y	N	N	Y	N
5 Lewis	Y	N	Y	Y	N	Y
6 *Gingrich*	N	Y	N	N	Y	N
7 Darden	Y	N	Y	Y	Y	Y
8 Rowland	Y	N	?	?	+	Y
9 Deal	Y	N	Y	Y	N	Y
10 Johnson	Y	N	Y	Y	N	Y
11 McKinney	Y	N	Y	Y	N	Y
HAWAII						
1 Abercrombie	Y	N	Y	Y	N	Y
2 Mink	Y	N	Y	Y	N	Y
IDAHO						
1 LaRocco	Y	N	Y	N	Y	N
2 *Crapo*	N	Y	N	N	Y	N
ILLINOIS						
1 Rush	Y	N	Y	Y	N	Y
2 Reynolds	?	N	?	+	N	Y
3 Lipinski	Y	N	Y	Y	N	Y
4 Gutierrez	Y	N	Y	Y	N	Y
5 Rostenkowski	Y	N	Y	Y	N	Y
6 *Hyde*	N	Y	N	N	Y	N
7 Collins	#	N	Y	Y	N	Y
8 *Crane*	N	Y	?	N	Y	N
9 Yates	Y	N	Y	Y	N	Y
10 *Porter*	Y	Y	N	Y	N	Y
11 Sangmeister	Y	N	Y	Y	N	Y
12 Costello	Y	N	Y	Y	N	Y
13 *Fawell*	N	Y	N	N	Y	N
14 *Hastert*	N	Y	N	N	Y	N
15 *Ewing*	N	Y	N	N	Y	N
16 *Manzullo*	N	Y	N	N	Y	N
17 Evans	Y	N	Y	Y	N	Y

ND Northern Democrats   SD Southern Democrats

	411	412	413	414	415	416
18 ***Michel***	N	Y	N	Y	Y	N
19 Poshard	Y	N	Y	N	N	Y
20 Durbin	Y	N	Y	Y	N	Y
INDIANA						
1 Visclosky	Y	N	Y	Y	N	Y
2 Sharp	Y	N	Y	Y	N	Y
3 Roemer	Y	N	Y	Y	N	Y
4 Long	N	N	Y	Y	N	Y
5 ***Buyer***	N	Y	N	N	Y	N
6 ***Burton***	N	Y	N	N	Y	N
7 ***Myers***	N	Y	Y	N	Y	N
8 McCloskey	Y	N	Y	Y	N	Y
9 Hamilton	Y	N	Y	N	Y	Y
10 Jacobs	N	N	N	Y	N	Y
IOWA						
1 ***Leach***	N	Y	N	Y	N	Y
2 ***Nussle***	N	Y	N	N	Y	N
3 ***Lightfoot***	N	Y	N	N	Y	N
4 Smith	Y	Y	Y	Y	N	Y
5 ***Grandy***	N	Y	N	Y	N	Y
KANSAS						
1 ***Roberts***	N	Y	N	N	Y	N
2 Slattery	?	?	Y	Y	N	Y
3 ***Meyers***	N	Y	N	Y	N	Y
4 Glickman	Y	N	Y	Y	N	Y
KENTUCKY						
1 Barlow	Y	N	Y	Y	Y	N
2 ***Lewis***	N	Y	N	N	Y	N
3 Mazzoli	Y	N	Y	Y	N	Y
4 ***Bunning***	N	Y	N	N	Y	N
5 ***Rogers***	N	Y	N	N	Y	N
6 Baesler	Y	N	Y	Y	N	Y
LOUISIANA						
1 ***Livingston***	?	Y	N	N	Y	N
2 Jefferson	Y	N	Y	Y	N	Y
3 Tauzin	Y	N	N	N	Y	N
4 Fields	Y	N	Y	Y	N	N
5 ***McCrery***	N	Y	N	N	Y	N
6 ***Baker***	N	Y	N	N	Y	N
7 Hayes	Y	Y	Y	N	Y	N
MAINE						
1 Andrews	Y	N	Y	Y	N	Y
2 ***Snowe***	N	Y	Y	Y	Y	Y
MARYLAND						
1 ***Gilchrest***	Y	Y	N	Y	N	Y
2 ***Bentley***	N	Y	N	N	Y	N
3 Cardin	Y	N	Y	Y	N	Y
4 Wynn	Y	N	Y	Y	N	Y
5 Hoyer	Y	N	Y	Y	N	Y
6 ***Bartlett***	N	Y	N	N	Y	N
7 Mfume	Y	N	Y	Y	N	Y
8 ***Morella***	Y	Y	N	Y	N	Y
MASSACHUSETTS						
1 Olver	Y	N	Y	Y	N	Y
2 Neal	Y	N	Y	Y	N	Y
3 ***Blute***	N	Y	N	Y	N	Y
4 Frank	Y	N	?	Y	N	Y
5 Meehan	Y	N	N	Y	N	Y
6 ***Torkildsen***	Y	Y	N	Y	N	Y
7 Markey	Y	N	Y	Y	N	Y
8 Kennedy	Y	N	Y	Y	N	Y
9 Moakley	Y	N	Y	Y	N	Y
10 Studds	Y	N	Y	Y	N	Y
MICHIGAN						
1 Stupak	Y	N	Y	N	Y	N
2 ***Hoekstra***	N	Y	N	N	Y	N
3 ***Ehlers***	Y	Y	N	N	Y	N
4 ***Camp***	N	Y	N	N	Y	N
5 Barcia	N	N	Y	N	Y	N
6 ***Upton***	N	Y	N	N	Y	Y
7 ***Smith***	N	Y	N	N	Y	N
8 Carr	Y	Y	Y	Y	N	Y
9 Kildee	Y	N	Y	Y	N	Y
10 Bonior	Y	N	Y	Y	N	Y
11 ***Knollenberg***	N	Y	N	N	Y	N
12 Levin	Y	N	Y	Y	N	Y
13 Ford	Y	N	?	Y	N	Y
14 Conyers	Y	N	Y	Y	N	N
15 Collins	Y	N	Y	Y	N	Y
16 Dingell	Y	N	Y	Y	N	Y
MINNESOTA						
1 Penny	N	Y	Y	Y	N	N
2 Minge	N	N	Y	Y	N	Y
3 ***Ramstad***	N	Y	N	Y	N	Y
4 Vento	Y	N	Y	Y	N	Y

	411	412	413	414	415	416
5 Sabo	Y	N	Y	Y	N	N
6 ***Grams***	N	Y	N	N	Y	N
7 Peterson	N	N	Y	N	Y	N
8 Oberstar	Y	N	Y	Y	N	N
MISSISSIPPI						
1 Whitten	Y	?	?	Y	N	Y
2 Thompson	Y	N	Y	Y	N	Y
3 Montgomery	Y	N	Y	Y	Y	N
4 Parker	N	N	Y	N	Y	N
5 Taylor	N	N	Y	N	Y	N
MISSOURI						
1 Clay	Y	N	Y	N	N	N
2 ***Talent***	N	Y	N	N	Y	Y
3 Gephardt	Y	N	Y	Y	N	Y
4 Skelton	Y	N	Y	N	Y	N
5 Wheat	Y	N	Y	Y	N	Y
6 Danner	Y	Y	Y	N	Y	N
7 ***Hancock***	N	Y	N	N	Y	N
8 ***Emerson***	N	Y	N	N	Y	N
9 Volkmer	Y	N	Y	N	Y	N
MONTANA						
AL Williams	Y	N	Y	N	N	N
NEBRASKA						
1 ***Bereuter***	Y	Y	N	N	Y	N
2 Hoagland	Y	N	Y	Y	N	Y
3 ***Barrett***	N	Y	N	N	Y	N
NEVADA						
1 Bilbray	Y	N	Y	Y	N	Y
2 ***Vucanovich***	N	Y	N	N	Y	N
NEW HAMPSHIRE						
1 ***Zeliff***	N	Y	N	N	Y	N
2 Swett	N	Y	Y	Y	N	Y
NEW JERSEY						
1 Andrews	Y	Y	Y	Y	N	Y
2 Hughes	Y	N	Y	Y	N	Y
3 ***Saxton***	N	Y	N	Y	Y	Y
4 ***Smith***	N	Y	Y	Y	N	Y
5 ***Roukema***	Y	Y	N	Y	N	Y
6 Pallone	Y	N	Y	Y	N	Y
7 ***Franks***	N	Y	N	Y	N	Y
8 Klein	?	N	Y	Y	N	Y
9 Torricelli	Y	N	Y	Y	N	Y
10 Payne	Y	N	Y	Y	N	N
11 ***Gallo***	?	Y	?	?	Y	N
12 ***Zimmer***	N	Y	N	Y	Y	Y
13 Menendez	Y	N	Y	Y	N	Y
NEW MEXICO						
1 ***Schiff***	N	Y	N	N	Y	N
2 ***Skeen***	N	Y	N	N	Y	N
3 Richardson	Y	N	Y	Y	N	Y
NEW YORK						
1 Hochbrueckner	Y	N	Y	Y	N	Y
2 ***Lazio***	N	Y	N	Y	N	Y
3 ***King***	N	Y	N	Y	N	Y
4 ***Levy***	N	Y	N	Y	N	Y
5 Ackerman	Y	N	Y	Y	N	Y
6 Flake	Y	N	?	Y	N	Y
7 Manton	Y	N	Y	Y	N	Y
8 Nadler	Y	N	Y	Y	N	N
9 Schumer	Y	N	Y	Y	N	Y
10 Towns	Y	N	Y	Y	N	Y
11 Owens	?	N	Y	Y	N	Y
12 Velazquez	Y	N	Y	Y	N	Y
13 ***Molinari***	N	Y	N	Y	N	Y
14 Maloney	Y	N	Y	Y	N	Y
15 Rangel	Y	N	?	Y	N	N
16 Serrano	Y	N	Y	Y	N	Y
17 Engel	Y	?	?	Y	N	Y
18 Lowey	Y	N	Y	Y	N	Y
19 ***Fish***	N	Y	Y	N	Y	N
20 ***Gilman***	Y	Y	Y	N	Y	N
21 McNulty	Y	N	Y	Y	N	Y
22 ***Solomon***	N	Y	N	N	Y	N
23 ***Boehlert***	Y	Y	N	Y	N	Y
24 ***McHugh***	N	Y	N	N	Y	N
25 ***Walsh***	Y	Y	N	Y	Y	Y
26 Hinchey	Y	N	Y	Y	N	Y
27 ***Paxon***	N	Y	N	N	Y	N
28 Slaughter	Y	N	Y	Y	N	Y
29 LaFalce	Y	N	Y	Y	N	Y
30 ***Quinn***	N	Y	N	N	Y	Y
31 ***Houghton***	?	?	Y	Y	N	Y
NORTH CAROLINA						
1 Clayton	Y	N	N	Y	N	Y
2 Valentine	Y	N	?	?	?	?

	411	412	413	414	415	416
3 Lancaster	Y	N	Y	N	N	Y
4 Price	Y	N	Y	Y	N	Y
5 Neal	Y	?	Y	Y	N	Y
6 ***Coble***	N	Y	N	N	Y	N
7 Rose	?	N	?	Y	N	Y
8 Hefner	Y	N	Y	Y	N	Y
9 ***McMillan***	Y	Y	N	Y	Y	N
10 ***Ballenger***	N	Y	N	N	Y	N
11 ***Taylor***	N	Y	N	N	Y	N
12 Watt	Y	N	Y	N	N	N
NORTH DAKOTA						
AL Pomeroy	Y	N	Y	Y	N	Y
OHIO						
1 Mann	Y	N	Y	Y	N	Y
2 ***Portman***	N	Y	N	N	Y	N
3 Hall	?	N	Y	Y	N	Y
4 ***Oxley***	N	Y	N	N	Y	N
5 ***Gillmor***	Y	Y	Y	N	Y	N
6 Strickland	Y	N	Y	N	Y	N
7 ***Hobson***	Y	Y	N	Y	Y	Y
8 ***Boehner***	N	Y	N	N	Y	N
9 Kaptur	N	N	Y	Y	N	Y
10 ***Hoke***	N	Y	N	N	Y	N
11 Stokes	Y	N	N	N	N	N
12 ***Kasich***	N	Y	Y	Y	N	Y
13 Brown	Y	N	Y	Y	N	Y
14 Sawyer	Y	N	Y	Y	N	Y
15 ***Pryce***	N	Y	N	Y	N	Y
16 ***Regula***	Y	Y	N	N	Y	N
17 Traficant	Y	N	Y	Y	N	Y
18 Applegate	Y	N	?	Y	N	Y
19 Fingerhut	Y	N	Y	Y	N	Y
OKLAHOMA						
1 ***Inhofe***	N	Y	N	N	Y	N
2 Synar	Y	N	Y	N	N	N
3 Brewster	N	N	Y	N	Y	N
4 McCurdy	Y	N	Y	Y	Y	Y
5 ***Istook***	N	Y	N	N	Y	N
6 ***Lucas***	N	Y	N	N	Y	N
OREGON						
1 Furse	Y	N	Y	Y	N	Y
2 ***Smith***	N	Y	N	N	Y	N
3 Wyden	Y	N	Y	Y	N	Y
4 DeFazio	Y	N	Y	N	N	N
5 Kopetski	Y	N	Y	Y	N	N
PENNSYLVANIA						
1 Foglietta	Y	N	Y	Y	N	Y
2 Blackwell	Y	N	Y	Y	N	Y
3 Borski	Y	N	Y	Y	N	Y
4 Klink	Y	Y	Y	N	Y	N
5 ***Clinger***	Y	Y	Y	N	Y	N
6 Holden	Y	N	Y	N	Y	Y
7 ***Weldon***	Y	Y	N	Y	Y	Y
8 ***Greenwood***	N	Y	Y	Y	N	Y
9 ***Shuster***	N	Y	N	N	Y	N
10 ***McDade***	?	?	?	N	Y	N
11 Kanjorski	N	N	Y	Y	N	N
12 Murtha	Y	N	?	Y	Y	N
13 Margolies-Mezv.	Y	Y	Y	Y	N	Y
14 Coyne	Y	N	Y	Y	N	Y
15 McHale	Y	N	Y	Y	N	Y
16 ***Walker***	N	Y	N	N	Y	N
17 ***Gekas***	N	Y	N	N	Y	N
18 ***Santorum***	N	Y	Y	N	Y	N
19 ***Goodling***	N	Y	N	N	Y	N
20 Murphy	Y	N	N	N	Y	N
21 ***Ridge***	N	Y	Y	Y	N	Y
RHODE ISLAND						
1 ***Machtley***	N	Y	N	Y	N	Y
2 Reed	Y	N	Y	Y	N	Y
SOUTH CAROLINA						
1 ***Ravenel***	Y	Y	N	N	Y	N
2 ***Spence***	N	Y	N	N	Y	N
3 Derrick	Y	N	Y	Y	N	Y
4 ***Inglis***	N	Y	Y	N	Y	N
5 Spratt	Y	N	Y	Y	N	Y
6 Clyburn	Y	N	Y	Y	N	Y
SOUTH DAKOTA						
AL Johnson	Y	Y	Y	Y	N	Y
TENNESSEE						
1 ***Quillen***	N	Y	N	N	Y	N
2 ***Duncan***	N	Y	N	N	Y	N
3 Lloyd	Y	N	N	Y	N	Y
4 Cooper	?	N	Y	N	Y	N
5 Clement	?	N	Y	Y	N	Y

	411	412	413	414	415	416
6 Gordon	Y	N	Y	Y	Y	Y
7 ***Sundquist***	?	?	N	N	Y	N
8 Tanner	N	N	Y	N	Y	N
9 Ford	?	N	Y	Y	N	Y
TEXAS						
1 Chapman	N	N	Y	N	Y	Y
2 Wilson	Y	N	Y	N	Y	N
3 ***Johnson, Sam***	N	Y	N	N	Y	N
4 Hall	N	N	Y	N	Y	N
5 Bryant	Y	N	Y	Y	N	Y
6 ***Barton***	X	N	N	N	Y	N
7 ***Archer***	N	Y	N	N	Y	N
8 ***Fields***	N	Y	N	N	Y	N
9 Brooks	Y	N	Y	Y	N	Y
10 Pickle	Y	N	Y	Y	N	Y
11 Edwards	N	N	Y	Y	N	Y
12 Geren	N	N	Y	N	Y	N
13 Sarpalius	N	N	Y	N	Y	N
14 Laughlin	Y	N	Y	N	N	N
15 de la Garza	Y	N	Y	N	Y	N
16 Coleman	Y	?	Y	Y	N	Y
17 Stenholm	N	N	Y	N	Y	N
18 Washington	?	?	?	?	?	?
19 ***Combest***	N	Y	Y	N	Y	N
20 Gonzalez	Y	N	Y	Y	N	Y
21 ***Smith***	N	Y	N	N	Y	N
22 ***DeLay***	N	Y	N	N	Y	N
23 ***Bonilla***	N	Y	N	N	Y	N
24 Frost	Y	N	Y	Y	N	Y
25 Andrews	Y	N	Y	Y	N	Y
26 ***Armey***	N	Y	N	N	Y	N
27 Ortiz	Y	N	Y	N	Y	N
28 Tejeda	Y	N	Y	N	Y	N
29 Green	Y	N	Y	Y	N	Y
30 Johnson, E.B.	Y	N	Y	Y	N	Y
UTAH						
1 ***Hansen***	N	Y	N	N	Y	N
2 Shepherd	Y	Y	Y	Y	N	Y
3 Orton	N	Y	N	N	Y	N
VERMONT						
AL *Sanders*	Y	N	Y	Y	N	Y
VIRGINIA						
1 ***Bateman***	N	N	Y	N	Y	N
2 Pickett	N	N	Y	N	Y	N
3 Scott	Y	N	Y	N	N	N
4 Sisisky	?	N	Y	N	Y	N
5 Payne	Y	N	Y	N	Y	N
6 ***Goodlatte***	N	Y	N	N	Y	N
7 ***Bliley***	?	Y	N	N	Y	N
8 Moran	?	?	?	Y	N	Y
9 Boucher	Y	N	Y	N	Y	N
10 ***Wolf***	Y	Y	N	N	Y	N
11 Byrne	Y	N	Y	Y	N	Y
WASHINGTON						
1 Cantwell	Y	N	Y	Y	N	Y
2 Swift	Y	?	Y	Y	N	Y
3 Unsoeld	Y	N	Y	N	Y	N
4 Inslee	Y	N	Y	Y	N	Y
5 Foley				Y	N	Y
6 Dicks	Y	N	Y	Y	N	Y
7 McDermott	Y	N	Y	Y	N	Y
8 ***Dunn***	N	Y	N	N	Y	N
9 Kreidler	Y	Y	Y	Y	N	Y
WEST VIRGINIA						
1 Mollohan	Y	N	Y	N	Y	N
2 Wise	Y	N	Y	N	Y	N
3 Rahall	Y	N	Y	N	Y	N
WISCONSIN						
1 Barca	N	N	Y	Y	N	Y
2 ***Klug***	N	Y	N	Y	N	Y
3 ***Gunderson***	N	Y	N	N	Y	N
4 Kleczka	Y	N	Y	Y	N	Y
5 Barrett	Y	N	Y	Y	N	Y
6 ***Petri***	N	Y	N	N	Y	N
7 Obey	Y	N	Y	Y	N	Y
8 ***Roth***	N	Y	N	N	Y	N
9 ***Sensenbrenner***	N	Y	N	N	Y	N
WYOMING						
AL ***Thomas***	N	Y	N	N	Y	N
DELEGATES						
de Lugo, V.I.	D	N	D	D	D	D
Faleomavaega, Am.S.	D	?	D	D	D	D
Norton, D.C.	D	N	D	D	D	D
Romero-B., P.R.	D	N	D	D	D	D
Underwood, Guam	D	N	D	D	D	D

Southern states - Ala., Ark., Fla., Ga., Ky., La., Miss., N.C., Okla., S.C., Tenn., Texas, Va.
Omitted votes are quorum calls, which CQ does not include in its vote charts.

KEY

Y Voted for (yea).
Paired for.
+ Announced for.
N Voted against (nay).
X Paired against.
— Announced against.
P Voted "present."
C Voted "present" to avoid possible conflict of interest.
? Did not vote or otherwise make a position known.
D Delegates ineligible to vote.

Democrats *Republicans*
Independent

417. HR 4624. Fiscal 1995 VA, HUD Appropriations/ Conference Report. Adoption of the conference report to provide $90,118,186,061 in new budget authority for the departments of Veterans Affairs and Housing and Urban Development, and for sundry independent agencies, boards, commissions, corporations and offices for fiscal 1995. The administration had requested $90,318,793,061. Adopted (thus sent to the Senate) 313-61: R 103-55; D 209-6 (ND 138-5, SD 71-1); I 1-0, Sept. 12, 1994.

418. HR 4624. Fiscal 1995 VA, HUD Appropriations/ HUD Special Purpose Projects. Stokes, D-Ohio, motion to recede and concur in the amendment of the Senate with an amendment to provide $290 million for 266 Housing and Urban Development (HUD) special purpose projects. Motion agreed to 189-180: R 36-120; D 153-59 (ND 106-36, SD 47-23); I 0-1, Sept. 12, 1994.

419. HR 4624. Fiscal 1995 VA, HUD Appropriations/ Imported Reformulated Gasoline. Boehner, R-Ohio, motion to recede and concur in the Senate amendment to prohibit the Environmental Protection Agency from using money in the bill to implement proposed regulations that would allow foreign oil refiners to use their own 1990 pollution levels as a basis for manufacturing reformulated gasoline rather than the 1990 average U.S. levels. Motion agreed to 222-148: R 124-31; D 97-117 (ND 59-84, SD 38-33); I 1-0, Sept. 12, 1994.

420. Procedural Motion. Approval of the House Journal of Monday, Sept. 12. Approved 214-141: R 18-134; D 195-7 (ND 127-6, SD 68-1); I 1-0, Sept. 13, 1994.

421. HR 4602. Fiscal 1995 Interior Appropriations/ Motion to Instruct. Regula, R-Ohio, motion to instruct the House conferees to insist on the House provision that imposes a one-year moratorium on the granting of hard-rock mining patents under the 1872 Mining Law, which charges no more than $5 an acre to acquire title to federal land. Motion agreed to 318-64: R 102-58; D 215-6 (ND 143-3, SD 72-3); I 1-0, Sept. 13, 1994.

422. HR 4650. Fiscal 1995 Defense Appropriations/Close Conference. Murtha, D-Pa., motion to close portions of the conference to the public during consideration of national security issues. Motion agreed to 376-0: R 159-0; D 216-0 (ND 142-0, SD 74-0); I 1-0, Sept. 13, 1994.

423. HR 4308. Wetlands Conservation Act Amendments/ Passage. Studds, D-Mass., motion to suspend the rules and pass the bill to reauthorize the North American Wetlands Act (PL 101-233) through fiscal 1998 with grants of $20 million in fiscal 1995 and 1996 and grants of $30 million in fiscal 1997 and 1998 to protect migratory wetlands. The bill also loosens restrictions to allow funding for projects in Mexico and makes changes to ensure that money allocated for wetlands conservation projects is used for coastal state wetlands ecosystems. Motion agreed to 368-5: R 150-5; D 217-0 (ND 143-0, SD 74-0); I 1-0, Sept. 13, 1994. A two-thirds majority of those present and voting (249 in this case) is required for passage under suspension of the rules.

	417	418	419	420	421	422	423
ALABAMA							
1 Callahan	Y	N	Y	Y	Y	Y	?
2 Everett	Y	N	Y	Y	Y	Y	Y
3 Browder	Y	N	N	Y	Y	Y	Y
4 Bevill	Y	Y	N	Y	Y	Y	Y
5 Cramer	Y	Y	N	Y	Y	Y	Y
6 Bachus	N	N	Y	N	N	Y	Y
7 Hilliard	Y	Y	N	Y	Y	Y	Y
ALASKA							
AL Young	Y	Y	Y	N	N	Y	Y
ARIZONA							
1 Coppersmith	+	—	—	+	+	+	+
2 Pastor	Y	Y	N	Y	Y	Y	Y
3 Stump	Y	N	N	N	N	Y	N
4 Kyl	N	N	N	N	N	Y	Y
5 Kolbe	Y	N	N	N	N	Y	Y
6 English	Y	N	N	Y	Y	Y	Y
ARKANSAS							
1 Lambert	Y	N	N	Y	Y	Y	Y
2 Thornton	Y	Y	Y	Y	Y	Y	Y
3 Hutchinson	Y	N	N	N	Y	Y	Y
4 Dickey	?	?	?	?	?	?	?
CALIFORNIA							
1 Hamburg	Y	Y	N	Y	Y	Y	Y
2 Herger	N	N	N	N	N	Y	?
3 Fazio	Y	Y	Y	Y	Y	Y	Y
4 Doolittle	N	N	N	N	N	Y	Y
5 Matsui	Y	N	Y	Y	Y	Y	Y
6 Woolsey	Y	Y	Y	Y	Y	Y	Y
7 Miller	?	?	?	?	?	?	?
8 Pelosi	Y	Y	N	Y	Y	Y	Y
9 Dellums	Y	Y	N	Y	Y	Y	Y
10 Baker	Y	N	Y	N	N	Y	Y
11 Pombo	N	N	Y	N	Y	Y	Y
12 Lantos	Y	?	?	Y	Y	Y	Y
13 Stark	Y	?	?	Y	Y	Y	Y
14 Eshoo	Y	Y	N	Y	Y	Y	Y
15 Mineta	Y	Y	N	Y	Y	Y	Y
16 Edwards	Y	?	?	?	?	?	?
17 Farr	Y	Y	N	Y	Y	Y	Y
18 Condit	?	?	?	?	?	?	?
19 Lehman	Y	N	Y	Y	Y	Y	Y
20 Dooley	Y	N	Y	?	Y	?	Y
21 Thomas	Y	N	N	N	Y	Y	Y
22 Huffington	?	?	?	?	?	?	?
23 Gallegly	Y	N	N	Y	Y	Y	Y
24 Beilenson	Y	N	N	Y	Y	Y	Y
25 McKeon	Y	N	N	N	N	Y	Y
26 Berman	Y	Y	N	Y	Y	Y	?
27 Moorhead	N	N	N	N	Y	Y	Y
28 Dreier	?	?	?	?	?	?	?
29 Waxman	?	?	?	?	?	Y	Y
30 Becerra	?	?	?	?	?	?	?
31 Martinez	Y	Y	Y	Y	Y	Y	Y
32 Dixon	Y	Y	N	Y	Y	Y	Y
33 Roybal-Allard	Y	Y	Y	Y	Y	Y	Y
34 Torres	Y	Y	N	Y	Y	Y	Y
35 Waters	Y	Y	N	Y	Y	Y	Y
36 Harman	Y	N	Y	Y	Y	Y	Y
37 Tucker	Y	N	Y	Y	Y	Y	Y
38 Horn	Y	N	N	Y	N	Y	Y
39 Royce	N	N	N	N	Y	Y	Y
40 Lewis	Y	Y	Y	N	?	?	?
41 Kim	Y	N	Y	N	Y	Y	Y
42 Brown	Y	N	N	N	Y	Y	Y
43 Calvert	Y	Y	N	N	Y	Y	Y
44 McCandless	Y	Y	N	N	Y	Y	Y
45 Rohrabacher	N	N	Y	N	Y	Y	Y
46 Dornan	X	X	?	?	X	?	?
47 Cox	N	N	Y	N	N	Y	Y
48 Packard	Y	Y	Y	N	Y	Y	Y
49 Schenk	Y	Y	N	Y	Y	Y	Y
50 Filner	Y	Y	Y	Y	Y	Y	Y
51 Cunningham	Y	N	Y	N	Y	Y	Y
52 Hunter	Y	N	Y	N	N	Y	Y
COLORADO							
1 Schroeder	Y	N	N	Y	Y	Y	Y
2 Skaggs	Y	Y	N	Y	Y	Y	Y
3 McInnis	Y	N	Y	N	Y	Y	Y
4 Allard	N	N	Y	N	N	Y	Y
5 Hefley	N	N	Y	N	Y	Y	Y
6 Schaefer	N	N	Y	N	N	Y	Y
CONNECTICUT							
1 Kennelly	Y	Y	N	Y	Y	Y	Y
2 Gejdenson	Y	Y	N	Y	Y	Y	Y
3 DeLauro	Y	Y	N	Y	Y	Y	Y
4 Shays	Y	N	N	N	Y	Y	Y
5 Franks	Y	N	Y	N	Y	Y	Y
6 Johnson	Y	N	N	?	Y	Y	Y
DELAWARE							
AL Castle	N	N	Y	?	Y	Y	Y
FLORIDA							
1 Hutto	Y	N	Y	Y	Y	Y	Y
2 Peterson	Y	Y	N	Y	Y	Y	Y
3 Brown	Y	Y	Y	Y	Y	Y	Y
4 Fowler	Y	Y	N	Y	Y	Y	Y
5 Thurman	Y	Y	Y	Y	Y	Y	Y
6 Stearns	Y	N	N	N	Y	Y	Y
7 Mica	Y	N	Y	N	Y	Y	Y
8 McCollum	Y	N	Y	N	Y	Y	Y
9 Bilirakis	Y	N	Y	N	Y	Y	Y
10 Young	Y	N	N	N	Y	Y	Y
11 Gibbons	Y	N	Y	Y	Y	Y	?
12 Canady	Y	N	Y	N	Y	Y	Y
13 Miller	N	N	Y	N	N	Y	?
14 Goss	N	N	Y	N	Y	Y	Y
15 Bacchus	Y	Y	N	Y	Y	Y	Y
16 Lewis	?	X	?	?	#	?	?
17 Meek	Y	Y	N	Y	Y	Y	Y
18 Ros-Lehtinen	?	?	?	N	Y	Y	Y
19 Johnston	Y	Y	N	Y	Y	Y	Y
20 Deutsch	Y	N	Y	Y	Y	Y	Y
21 Diaz-Balart	Y	Y	Y	N	Y	Y	Y
22 Shaw	Y	N	Y	N	Y	Y	Y
23 Hastings	?	?	?	Y	Y	Y	Y
GEORGIA							
1 Kingston	Y	N	Y	N	N	Y	Y
2 Bishop	Y	Y	N	Y	Y	Y	Y
3 Collins	Y	Y	Y	Y	Y	Y	Y
4 Linder	N	N	Y	N	Y	Y	Y
5 Lewis	Y	Y	Y	Y	Y	Y	Y
6 Gingrich	N	N	Y	N	Y	Y	Y
7 Darden	Y	Y	N	Y	Y	Y	Y
8 Rowland	Y	Y	N	Y	Y	Y	Y
9 Deal	Y	N	?	Y	Y	Y	Y
10 Johnson	Y	N	Y	Y	Y	Y	Y
11 McKinney	Y	Y	N	Y	Y	Y	Y
HAWAII							
1 Abercrombie	Y	Y	N	?	Y	Y	Y
2 Mink	?	?	?	?	?	?	?
IDAHO							
1 LaRocco	Y	N	N	Y	N	Y	Y
2 Crapo	N	N	N	N	N	Y	Y
ILLINOIS							
1 Rush	Y	Y	N	Y	Y	Y	Y
2 Reynolds	?	?	?	Y	Y	Y	Y
3 Lipinski	Y	N	Y	Y	Y	Y	Y
4 Gutierrez	Y	Y	N	Y	Y	Y	Y
5 Rostenkowski	?	?	?	?	?	?	?
6 Hyde	Y	N	Y	Y	Y	Y	Y
7 Collins	Y	Y	N	Y	Y	Y	Y
8 Crane	N	N	N	N	N	Y	N
9 Yates	#	#	?	?	?	?	Y
10 Porter	Y	N	Y	N	Y	Y	Y
11 Sangmeister	Y	N	Y	Y	Y	Y	Y
12 Costello	Y	N	Y	Y	Y	Y	Y
13 Fawell	N	N	Y	N	Y	Y	Y
14 Hastert	Y	N	Y	N	Y	Y	Y
15 Ewing	Y	Y	Y	Y	Y	Y	Y
16 Manzullo	N	N	Y	N	N	Y	Y
17 Evans	Y	Y	Y	Y	Y	Y	Y

ND Northern Democrats   SD Southern Democrats

	417	418	419	420	421	422	423
18 ***Michel***	Y	N	Y	N	Y	Y	Y
19 Poshard	Y	N	Y	N	Y	Y	Y
20 Durbin	Y	Y	N	Y	Y	Y	Y
INDIANA							
1 Visclosky	Y	Y	N	Y	Y	Y	Y
2 Sharp	Y	Y	N	Y	Y	?	?
3 Roemer	N	N	N	Y	Y	Y	Y
4 Long	Y	N	N	Y	Y	Y	Y
5 ***Buyer***	N	N	Y	N	N	Y	Y
6 ***Burton***	N	N	Y	N	N	Y	Y
7 ***Myers***	N	Y	Y	Y	Y	Y	Y
8 McCloskey	Y	Y	N	Y	Y	Y	Y
9 Hamilton	Y	N	N	Y	Y	Y	Y
10 Jacobs	Y	Y	N	N	Y	Y	Y
IOWA							
1 ***Leach***	Y	N	Y	N	Y	Y	Y
2 ***Nussle***	Y	N	Y	N	Y	Y	Y
3 ***Lightfoot***	Y	N	Y	N	N	Y	Y
4 Smith	Y	Y	N	?	Y	Y	Y
5 ***Grandy***	Y	N	?	?	Y	Y	Y
KANSAS							
1 ***Roberts***	N	N	Y	N	Y	Y	Y
2 Slattery	?	?	?	?	?	?	?
3 ***Meyers***	Y	N	Y	N	Y	Y	Y
4 Glickman	?	N	Y	Y	Y	Y	Y
KENTUCKY							
1 Barlow	Y	Y	Y	Y	Y	Y	Y
2 ***Lewis***	Y	N	Y	N	N	Y	Y
3 Mazzoli	Y	Y	Y	Y	Y	Y	Y
4 ***Bunning***	N	N	Y	N	Y	Y	Y
5 ***Rogers***	Y	Y	Y	N	Y	Y	Y
6 Baesler	Y	N	Y	Y	Y	Y	Y
LOUISIANA							
1 ***Livingston***	Y	Y	Y	N	N	Y	Y
2 Jefferson	Y	Y	Y	Y	Y	Y	Y
3 Tauzin	Y	N	Y	Y	N	Y	Y
4 Fields	Y	Y	Y	Y	Y	Y	Y
5 ***McCrery***	Y	N	Y	N	N	Y	Y
6 ***Baker***	?	?	?	N	N	Y	Y
7 Hayes	Y	N	Y	?	?	?	?
MAINE							
1 Andrews	Y	N	N	Y	Y	Y	Y
2 ***Snowe***	Y	Y	N	N	Y	Y	Y
MARYLAND							
1 ***Gilchrest***	Y	N	Y	?	Y	Y	Y
2 ***Bentley***	Y	Y	Y	?	?	?	?
3 Cardin	Y	Y	Y	?	Y	Y	Y
4 Wynn	Y	?	?	+	+	+	+
5 Hoyer	Y	Y	Y	?	Y	Y	Y
6 ***Bartlett***	Y	N	Y	N	Y	Y	Y
7 Mfume	Y	Y	Y	+	+	+	+
8 ***Morella***	Y	Y	N	?	Y	Y	Y
MASSACHUSETTS							
1 Olver	Y	Y	N	Y	Y	Y	Y
2 Neal	Y	Y	N	Y	Y	Y	Y
3 ***Blute***	Y	Y	N	N	Y	Y	Y
4 Frank	Y	Y	N	Y	Y	Y	Y
5 Meehan	Y	Y	N	Y	Y	Y	Y
6 ***Torkildsen***	Y	Y	N	N	Y	Y	Y
7 Markey	Y	Y	N	Y	Y	Y	Y
8 Kennedy	Y	Y	N	Y	Y	Y	Y
9 Moakley	Y	Y	N	Y	Y	Y	Y
10 Studds	Y	Y	N	Y	Y	Y	Y
MICHIGAN							
1 Stupak	Y	Y	Y	Y	Y	Y	Y
2 ***Hoekstra***	N	N	Y	N	Y	Y	Y
3 ***Ehlers***	N	N	Y	N	Y	Y	Y
4 ***Camp***	?	?	?	?	?	?	?
5 Barcia	?	?	N	Y	Y	Y	Y
6 ***Upton***	N	N	Y	N	Y	Y	Y
7 ***Smith***	N	N	Y	N	Y	Y	Y
8 Carr	Y	Y	N	Y	Y	Y	Y
9 Kildee	Y	Y	Y	Y	Y	Y	Y
10 Bonior	Y	Y	N	Y	Y	Y	Y
11 ***Knollenberg***	N	N	Y	N	N	Y	Y
12 Levin	Y	N	N	Y	Y	Y	Y
13 Ford	?	?	?	?	?	?	?
14 Conyers	?	Y	N	Y	Y	Y	Y
15 Collins	Y	Y	N	?	Y	Y	Y
16 Dingell	Y	Y	N	Y	Y	Y	Y
MINNESOTA							
1 Penny	N	N	N	Y	Y	Y	Y
2 Minge	N	N	Y	Y	Y	Y	Y
3 ***Ramstad***	N	N	N	N	Y	Y	Y
4 Vento	Y	N	Y	Y	Y	Y	Y

	417	418	419	420	421	422	423
5 Sabo	Y	Y	N	Y	Y	Y	Y
6 ***Grams***	X	X	?	?	X	?	?
7 Peterson	Y	N	Y	Y	Y	Y	Y
8 Oberstar	Y	Y	N	Y	Y	Y	Y
MISSISSIPPI							
1 Whitten	Y	Y	N	?	Y	Y	Y
2 Thompson	Y	Y	Y	Y	Y	Y	Y
3 Montgomery	Y	Y	Y	Y	Y	Y	Y
4 Parker	Y	N	Y	Y	Y	Y	Y
5 Taylor	Y	N	Y	N	Y	Y	Y
MISSOURI							
1 Clay	Y	Y	N	N	Y	Y	Y
2 ***Talent***	Y	N	Y	N	N	Y	Y
3 Gephardt	Y	Y	N	Y	Y	Y	Y
4 Skelton	Y	Y	Y	Y	Y	Y	Y
5 Wheat	Y	Y	N	?	Y	Y	Y
6 Danner	Y	N	Y	Y	Y	Y	Y
7 ***Hancock***	N	N	Y	N	N	Y	N
8 ***Emerson***	Y	N	Y	N	N	Y	Y
9 Volkmer	Y	N	N	Y	Y	Y	Y
MONTANA							
AL Williams	Y	Y	Y	?	Y	Y	?
NEBRASKA							
1 ***Bereuter***	Y	N	Y	N	Y	Y	Y
2 Hoagland	Y	N	Y	Y	Y	Y	Y
3 ***Barrett***	Y	N	Y	N	N	Y	Y
NEVADA							
1 Bilbray	Y	Y	Y	?	N	Y	Y
2 ***Vucanovich***	Y	Y	Y	N	N	Y	Y
NEW HAMPSHIRE							
1 ***Zeliff***	N	N	Y	N	Y	Y	Y
2 Swett	?	?	?	?	?	?	?
NEW JERSEY							
1 Andrews	Y	N	Y	?	Y	Y	Y
2 Hughes	Y	Y	N	Y	Y	Y	Y
3 ***Saxton***	N	N	Y	N	Y	Y	Y
4 ***Smith***	Y	Y	Y	Y	Y	Y	Y
5 ***Roukema***	N	N	Y	N	Y	Y	Y
6 Pallone	Y	Y	Y	Y	Y	Y	Y
7 ***Franks***	N	N	Y	N	Y	Y	Y
8 Klein	Y	N	Y	Y	Y	Y	Y
9 Torricelli	?	?	?	Y	Y	Y	Y
10 Payne	Y	Y	N	Y	Y	Y	Y
11 ***Gallo***	?	?	?	?	?	?	?
12 ***Zimmer***	N	N	Y	N	Y	Y	Y
13 Menendez	Y	Y	Y	Y	Y	Y	Y
NEW MEXICO							
1 ***Schiff***	Y	Y	Y	N	Y	Y	Y
2 ***Skeen***	Y	Y	Y	N	N	Y	Y
3 Richardson	Y	Y	Y	Y	Y	Y	Y
NEW YORK							
1 Hochbrueckner	Y	Y	Y	Y	Y	Y	Y
2 ***Lazio***	Y	N	Y	N	Y	Y	Y
3 ***King***	Y	N	Y	N	Y	Y	Y
4 ***Levy***	Y	N	Y	N	Y	Y	Y
5 Ackerman	?	Y	N	?	?	?	?
6 Flake	Y	Y	N	Y	Y	Y	Y
7 Manton	Y	Y	N	Y	Y	Y	Y
8 Nadler	?	#	?	?	#	?	?
9 Schumer	Y	Y	N	Y	Y	Y	Y
10 Towns	?	#	?	?	?	?	?
11 Owens	?	?	?	?	?	?	?
12 Velazquez	?	?	?	?	#	?	?
13 ***Molinari***	Y	Y	Y	N	N	Y	Y
14 Maloney	Y	N	Y	?	#	?	?
15 Rangel	#	#	X	?	?	?	?
16 Serrano	?	?	?	?	?	?	?
17 Engel	?	?	?	?	?	?	?
18 Lowey	Y	Y	N	Y	Y	Y	Y
19 ***Fish***	Y	N	Y	Y	?	?	?
20 ***Gilman***	Y	Y	Y	Y	Y	Y	Y
21 McNulty	Y	Y	N	Y	Y	Y	Y
22 ***Solomon***	Y	?	N	N	Y	Y	Y
23 ***Boehlert***	Y	Y	N	N	Y	Y	Y
24 ***McHugh***	Y	N	N	N	Y	Y	Y
25 ***Walsh***	Y	Y	N	N	Y	Y	Y
26 Hinchey	Y	Y	Y	Y	Y	Y	Y
27 ***Paxon***	N	N	N	N	N	Y	Y
28 Slaughter	Y	Y	Y	Y	Y	Y	Y
29 LaFalce	Y	Y	Y	Y	Y	Y	Y
30 ***Quinn***	Y	Y	N	N	Y	Y	Y
31 ***Houghton***	Y	Y	N	Y	Y	Y	Y
NORTH CAROLINA							
1 Clayton	Y	Y	N	Y	Y	Y	Y
2 Valentine	Y	N	N	Y	Y	Y	Y

	417	418	419	420	421	422	423
3 Lancaster	Y	N	N	Y	Y	Y	Y
4 Price	Y	Y	N	Y	Y	Y	Y
5 Neal	Y	?	N	Y	Y	Y	Y
6 ***Coble***	N	N	Y	N	Y	Y	Y
7 Rose	Y	Y	Y	Y	Y	Y	Y
8 Hefner	?	?	?	?	Y	Y	Y
9 ***McMillan***	Y	?	?	?	Y	Y	Y
10 ***Ballenger***	N	N	Y	N	N	Y	Y
11 ***Taylor***	Y	Y	Y	N	Y	Y	Y
12 Watt	Y	Y	N	Y	Y	Y	Y
NORTH DAKOTA							
AL Pomeroy	Y	Y	Y	Y	Y	Y	Y
OHIO							
1 Mann	Y	N	Y	Y	Y	?	Y
2 ***Portman***	—	—	+	N	Y	Y	Y
3 Hall	Y	Y	?	Y	Y	Y	Y
4 ***Oxley***	Y	N	Y	N	Y	Y	Y
5 ***Gillmor***	Y	N	Y	N	N	Y	Y
6 Strickland	Y	Y	Y	Y	Y	Y	Y
7 ***Hobson***	Y	Y	Y	N	Y	Y	Y
8 ***Boehner***	N	N	Y	?	Y	Y	Y
9 Kaptur	?	?	Y	Y	Y	Y	Y
10 ***Hoke***	Y	Y	Y	?	N	Y	Y
11 Stokes	Y	Y	N	?	Y	Y	Y
12 ***Kasich***	Y	N	Y	Y	Y	Y	Y
13 Brown	Y	Y	Y	Y	Y	Y	Y
14 Sawyer	Y	Y	N	Y	Y	Y	Y
15 ***Pryce***	Y	N	Y	N	Y	Y	Y
16 ***Regula***	Y	Y	Y	N	Y	Y	Y
17 Traficant	Y	Y	Y	Y	Y	Y	Y
18 Applegate	Y	Y	N	Y	Y	Y	Y
19 Fingerhut	Y	N	Y	Y	+	+	+
OKLAHOMA							
1 ***Inhofe***	?	?	?	?	N	?	?
2 Synar	?	?	?	?	?	?	?
3 Brewster	Y	N	N	Y	Y	Y	Y
4 McCurdy	?	?	?	?	?	?	?
5 ***Istook***	N	N	Y	N	N	Y	Y
6 ***Lucas***	Y	N	Y	N	N	Y	Y
OREGON							
1 Furse	Y	Y	N	Y	Y	Y	Y
2 ***Smith***	?	X	#	?	X	?	?
3 Wyden	Y	Y	Y	Y	Y	Y	Y
4 DeFazio	?	?	?	?	?	?	?
5 Kopetski	?	?	?	?	?	?	?
PENNSYLVANIA							
1 Foglietta	Y	Y	N	Y	Y	Y	Y
2 Blackwell	?	?	?	?	Y	Y	Y
3 Borski	Y	Y	Y	Y	Y	Y	Y
4 Klink	Y	Y	Y	Y	Y	Y	Y
5 ***Clinger***	?	?	?	?	?	?	?
6 Holden	Y	Y	Y	Y	Y	Y	Y
7 ***Weldon***	Y	N	Y	N	Y	Y	Y
8 ***Greenwood***	Y	N	Y	Y	Y	Y	Y
9 ***Shuster***	Y	N	Y	N	Y	Y	Y
10 ***McDade***	Y	Y	N	N	Y	Y	Y
11 Kanjorski	Y	Y	Y	Y	Y	Y	Y
12 Murtha	Y	Y	N	Y	Y	Y	Y
13 Margolies-Mezv.	Y	Y	Y	Y	Y	Y	Y
14 Coyne	Y	Y	N	Y	Y	Y	Y
15 McHale	Y	Y	Y	Y	Y	Y	Y
16 ***Walker***	N	N	Y	N	Y	Y	Y
17 ***Gekas***	N	N	Y	N	Y	Y	Y
18 ***Santorum***	?	?	?	Y	Y	Y	Y
19 ***Goodling***	Y	N	Y	N	Y	Y	Y
20 Murphy	?	?	?	?	Y	Y	Y
21 ***Ridge***	?	?	?	?	Y	Y	Y
RHODE ISLAND							
1 ***Machtley***	?	?	?	?	?	?	?
2 Reed	Y	Y	N	Y	Y	Y	Y
SOUTH CAROLINA							
1 ***Ravenel***	Y	N	?	N	Y	Y	Y
2 ***Spence***	Y	Y	Y	N	Y	Y	Y
3 Derrick	?	?	?	?	?	?	?
4 ***Inglis***	N	N	Y	Y	Y	Y	Y
5 Spratt	Y	N	N	Y	Y	Y	Y
6 Clyburn	Y	Y	N	Y	Y	Y	Y
SOUTH DAKOTA							
AL Johnson	Y	N	N	Y	Y	Y	Y
TENNESSEE							
1 ***Quillen***	Y	Y	N	N	Y	Y	Y
2 ***Duncan***	N	N	N	N	Y	Y	Y
3 Lloyd	Y	N	N	Y	Y	Y	Y
4 Cooper	?	?	?	?	?	?	?
5 Clement	Y	N	N	Y	Y	Y	Y

	417	418	419	420	421	422	423
6 Gordon	Y	Y	N	Y	Y	Y	Y
7 ***Sundquist***	?	?	?	?	?	?	?
8 Tanner	Y	N	N	Y	Y	Y	Y
9 Ford	Y	Y	N	Y	Y	Y	Y
TEXAS							
1 Chapman	Y	Y	Y	?	Y	Y	Y
2 Wilson	Y	?	?	?	?	?	?
3 ***Johnson, Sam***	N	N	Y	N	N	Y	N
4 Hall	N	Y	Y	Y	N	Y	Y
5 Bryant	?	?	?	?	Y	Y	Y
6 ***Barton***	N	N	Y	N	N	Y	Y
7 ***Archer***	N	N	Y	N	N	Y	Y
8 ***Fields***	Y	N	Y	N	N	Y	Y
9 Brooks	Y	Y	Y	Y	Y	Y	Y
10 Pickle	Y	Y	Y	Y	Y	Y	Y
11 Edwards	Y	N	Y	Y	Y	Y	Y
12 Geren	Y	N	Y	Y	Y	Y	Y
13 Sarpalius	Y	N	Y	Y	Y	Y	Y
14 Laughlin	?	?	?	?	?	?	?
15 de la Garza	Y	Y	Y	Y	Y	Y	Y
16 Coleman	Y	Y	Y	Y	Y	Y	Y
17 Stenholm	?	?	?	Y	N	Y	Y
18 Washington	?	?	?	?	?	?	?
19 ***Combest***	N	N	Y	Y	N	Y	Y
20 Gonzalez	Y	Y	N	Y	Y	Y	Y
21 ***Smith***	Y	N	Y	N	Y	Y	Y
22 ***DeLay***	Y	N	Y	?	N	Y	N
23 ***Bonilla***	Y	N	Y	N	Y	Y	Y
24 Frost	Y	Y	Y	Y	Y	Y	Y
25 Andrews	Y	N	Y	Y	Y	Y	Y
26 ***Armey***	N	N	Y	N	N	Y	Y
27 Ortiz	Y	Y	Y	Y	Y	Y	Y
28 Tejeda	Y	Y	Y	Y	Y	Y	Y
29 Green	Y	Y	Y	Y	Y	Y	Y
30 Johnson, E.B.	Y	Y	Y	Y	Y	Y	Y
UTAH							
1 ***Hansen***	Y	Y	Y	N	N	Y	Y
2 Shepherd	Y	Y	Y	Y	Y	Y	Y
3 Orton	Y	Y	N	Y	N	Y	Y
VERMONT							
AL *Sanders*	Y	N	Y	Y	Y	Y	Y
VIRGINIA							
1 ***Bateman***	Y	Y	N	Y	Y	Y	Y
2 Pickett	?	?	?	Y	Y	Y	Y
3 Scott	Y	Y	N	Y	Y	Y	Y
4 Sisisky	Y	Y	N	Y	Y	Y	Y
5 Payne	Y	N	N	Y	Y	?	Y
6 ***Goodlatte***	Y	N	N	N	Y	Y	Y
7 ***Bliley***	Y	N	N	N	Y	Y	Y
8 Moran	Y	Y	Y	?	Y	Y	Y
9 Boucher	Y	Y	N	Y	Y	Y	Y
10 ***Wolf***	Y	N	Y	N	Y	Y	Y
11 Byrne	Y	Y	Y	Y	Y	Y	Y
WASHINGTON							
1 Cantwell	Y	N	Y	Y	Y	Y	Y
2 Swift	Y	Y	N	Y	Y	Y	Y
3 Unsoeld	Y	Y	N	Y	Y	Y	Y
4 Inslee	Y	N	Y	Y	Y	Y	Y
5 Foley							
6 Dicks	Y	Y	N	Y	Y	Y	Y
7 McDermott	Y	Y	N	Y	Y	?	?
8 ***Dunn***	Y	N	Y	N	N	Y	Y
9 Kreidler	Y	Y	Y	N	Y	Y	Y
WEST VIRGINIA							
1 Mollohan	Y	Y	N	?	?	?	?
2 Wise	Y	Y	Y	Y	Y	Y	Y
3 Rahall	Y	Y	Y	Y	Y	Y	Y
WISCONSIN							
1 Barca	N	N	Y	Y	Y	Y	Y
2 ***Klug***	N	N	Y	N	Y	Y	Y
3 ***Gunderson***	Y	N	Y	N	?	?	?
4 Kleczka	Y	N	Y	Y	Y	Y	Y
5 Barrett	N	N	Y	Y	Y	Y	Y
6 ***Petri***	N	N	Y	N	Y	Y	Y
7 Obey	Y	Y	N	?	Y	Y	Y
8 ***Roth***	?	?	?	?	?	?	?
9 ***Sensenbrenner***	N	N	Y	N	Y	Y	Y
WYOMING							
AL ***Thomas***	?	?	?	?	X	?	?
DELEGATES							
de Lugo, V.I.	D	D	D	D	D	D	D
Faleomavaega, Am.S.	D	D	D	D	D	D	D
Norton, D.C.	D	D	D	D	D	D	D
Romero-B., P.R.	D	D	D	D	D	D	D
Underwood, Guam	D	D	D	D	D	D	D

Southern states - Ala., Ark., Fla., Ga., Ky., La., Miss., N.C., Okla., S.C., Tenn., Texas, Va.
Omitted votes are quorum calls, which CQ does not include in its vote charts.

424. H Con Res 290. Commend and Support Actions in Haiti/Adoption. Gephardt, D-Mo., motion to suspend the rules and adopt the concurrent resolution to express the sense of Congress commending the president and the special delegation to Haiti, supporting U.S. armed forces in Haiti and supporting an orderly withdrawal of U.S. forces as soon as possible. Motion agreed to 353-45: R 120-45; D 232-0 (ND 157-0, SD 75-0); I 1-0, Sept. 19, 1994. A two-thirds majority of those present and voting (266 in this case) is required for passage under suspension of the rules.

425. S 1587. Federal Procurement Overhaul/Conference Report. Adoption of the conference report to accompany the bill to streamline the federal purchasing process by encouraging federal agencies to buy more items off the shelf and exempting commercial purchases that cost less than $100,000 from complex procedural requirements. Adopted (thus cleared for the president) 425-0: R 174-0; D 250-0 (ND 171-0, SD 79-0); I 1-0, Sept. 20, 1994. A "yea" was a vote in support of the president's position.

426. HR 6. Elementary and Secondary School Reauthorization/Motion to Instruct. Gunderson, R-Wis., motion to instruct House conferees on the bill to insist on the House provision that would withhold federal money from states or school districts that prohibit voluntary, constitutionally protected school prayer. Motion agreed to 369-55: R 174-0; D 195-54 (ND 121-49, SD 74-5); I 0-1, Sept. 20, 1994.

427. HR 4801. Small Business Administration Reauthorization/Recommit. Kim, R-Calif., motion to recommit the bill to the Small Business Committee with instructions to report it back with an amendment to authorize the transfer of $38 million from the State Department's fiscal 1995 appropriation to two Small Business Administration programs. Motion rejected 176-242: R 154-17; D 22-224 (ND 17-149, SD 5-75); I 0-1, Sept. 21, 1994.

428. HR 4801. Small Business Administration Reauthorization/Passage. Passage of the bill to reauthorize the Small Business Administration through fiscal 1997 and establish an office of Women's Business Ownership. Passed 370-48: R 127-46; D 242-2 (ND 163-2, SD 79-0); I 1-0, Sept. 21, 1994. A "yea" was a vote in support of the president's position.

429. HR 2866. California Redwood Forest Expansion/Previous Question. Hall, D-Ohio, motion to order the previous question (thus ending debate and the possibility of amendment) on adoption of the rule (H Res 536) to provide for House floor consideration of the bill to authorize the Forest Service to acquire 44,000 acres of privately owned redwood forest in Humboldt County, Calif., for addition to the Six Rivers National Forest. Motion agreed to 245-175: R 1-173; D 243-2 (ND 165-2, SD 78-0); I 1-0, Sept. 21, 1994.

430. HR 2866. California Redwood Forest Expansion/Rule. Adoption of the rule (H Res 536) to provide for House floor consideration of the bill to authorize the Forest Service to acquire 44,000 acres of privately owned redwood forest in Humboldt County, Calif., for addition to the Six Rivers National Forest. Adopted 246-174: R 1-172; D 244-2 (ND 167-1, SD 77-1); I 1-0, Sept. 21, 1994.

431. HR 2866. California Redwood Forest Expansion/Authorization Limitation. Doolittle, R-Calif., amendment to limit the amount authorized for land acquisition under the bill to $200 million rather than such sums as may be necessary. Adopted in the Committee of the Whole 240-188: R 172-1; D 68-186 (ND 38-136, SD 30-50); I 0-1, Sept. 21, 1994.

KEY

Y	Voted for (yea).
#	Paired for.
+	Announced for.
N	Voted against (nay).
X	Paired against.
−	Announced against.
P	Voted "present."
C	Voted "present" to avoid possible conflict of interest.
?	Did not vote or otherwise make a position known.
D	Delegates ineligible to vote.

Democrats *Republicans*
Independent

	424	425	426	427	428	429	430	431
ALABAMA								
1 *Callahan*	Y	Y	Y	N	Y	N	N	Y
2 *Everett*	Y	Y	Y	Y	Y	N	N	Y
3 Browder	Y	Y	Y	N	Y	Y	Y	Y
4 Bevill	Y	Y	Y	N	Y	Y	Y	N
5 Cramer	Y	Y	Y	N	Y	Y	N	Y
6 *Bachus*	Y	Y	Y	Y	N	N	N	Y
7 Hilliard	Y	Y	Y	N	Y	Y	Y	N
ALASKA								
AL *Young*	Y	Y	Y	N	Y	N	N	Y
ARIZONA								
1 Coppersmith	Y	Y	N	N	Y	Y	Y	Y
2 Pastor	Y	Y	Y	N	Y	Y	Y	N
3 *Stump*	N	Y	Y	Y	N	N	N	Y
4 *Kyl*	?	Y	Y	Y	Y	N	N	Y
5 *Kolbe*	Y	Y	Y	Y	Y	N	N	Y
6 English	Y	Y	Y	N	Y	Y	Y	Y
ARKANSAS								
1 Lambert	Y	Y	Y	N	Y	Y	Y	Y
2 Thornton	Y	Y	Y	N	Y	Y	Y	N
3 *Hutchinson*	Y	Y	N	Y	N	N	N	Y
4 *Dickey*	Y	Y	Y	Y	Y	N	N	Y
CALIFORNIA								
1 Hamburg	Y	Y	N	N	Y	Y	Y	N
2 *Herger*	N	Y	Y	Y	Y	N	N	Y
3 Fazio	Y	Y	Y	N	Y	Y	Y	N
4 *Doolittle*	N	Y	Y	Y	N	N	N	Y
5 Matsui	Y	Y	Y	N	Y	Y	Y	N
6 Woolsey	Y	Y	Y	N	Y	Y	Y	N
7 Miller	Y	Y	Y	N	Y	Y	Y	N
8 Pelosi	Y	Y	N	N	Y	Y	Y	N
9 Dellums	Y	Y	?	N	Y	Y	Y	N
10 *Baker*	Y	Y	Y	Y	Y	N	N	Y
11 *Pombo*	Y	Y	Y	Y	Y	N	N	Y
12 Lantos	Y	Y	Y	N	Y	Y	Y	N
13 Stark	Y	N	N	N	Y	Y	Y	N
14 Eshoo	Y	Y	N	N	Y	Y	Y	N
15 Mineta	Y	Y	N	N	Y	Y	Y	N
16 Edwards	Y	Y	N	N	Y	Y	Y	N
17 Farr	Y	Y	N	N	Y	Y	Y	N
18 Condit	Y	Y	Y	Y	Y	Y	Y	Y
19 Lehman	Y	Y	Y	N	Y	Y	Y	Y
20 Dooley	Y	Y	Y	N	Y	Y	Y	Y
21 *Thomas*	Y	Y	Y	Y	Y	N	N	Y
22 *Huffington*	?	Y	Y	Y	Y	N	N	Y
23 *Gallegly*	Y	Y	Y	Y	Y	N	N	Y
24 Beilenson	Y	Y	N	N	Y	Y	Y	N
25 *McKeon*	Y	Y	Y	N	Y	N	N	Y
26 Berman	Y	Y	N	N	Y	Y	Y	N
27 *Moorhead*	Y	Y	Y	Y	N	N	N	Y
28 *Dreier*	Y	Y	Y	Y	N	N	N	Y
29 Waxman	Y	Y	N	N	Y	Y	Y	N
30 Becerra	Y	Y	N	N	Y	Y	Y	N
31 Martinez	Y	Y	N	N	Y	Y	Y	N
32 Dixon	Y	Y	N	N	Y	Y	Y	N
33 Roybal-Allard	Y	Y	N	N	Y	Y	Y	N
34 Torres	Y	Y	Y	N	Y	Y	Y	N
35 Waters	?	Y	N	N	Y	Y	Y	N
36 Harman	Y	Y	N	N	Y	Y	Y	Y
37 Tucker	?	Y	N	N	Y	Y	Y	N
38 *Horn*	Y	Y	Y	N	Y	Y	N	Y
39 *Royce*	Y	Y	Y	Y	N	N	N	Y
40 *Lewis*	Y	Y	Y	N	Y	N	N	Y
41 *Kim*	Y	Y	Y	N	N	N	N	Y

	424	425	426	427	428	429	430	431
42 Brown	Y	Y	Y	N	Y	N	N	Y
43 *Calvert*	Y	Y	Y	?	Y	N	N	Y
44 *McCandless*	N	Y	Y	N	Y	N	N	N
45 *Rohrabacher*	N	Y	Y	N	N	N	N	Y
46 *Dornan*	N	Y	Y	N	N	N	N	Y
47 *Cox*	Y	Y	Y	N	Y	N	N	Y
48 *Packard*	N	Y	Y	N	N	N	N	Y
49 Schenk	Y	Y	N	Y	N	Y	Y	N
50 Filner	Y	Y	N	N	Y	Y	Y	N
51 *Cunningham*	Y	Y	Y	Y	Y	N	?	Y
52 *Hunter*	Y	Y	Y	N	Y	N	N	Y
COLORADO								
1 Schroeder	Y	Y	Y	N	Y	Y	Y	N
2 Skaggs	Y	Y	N	N	Y	Y	Y	N
3 *McInnis*	Y	Y	Y	Y	Y	N	N	Y
4 *Allard*	N	Y	Y	Y	N	N	N	Y
5 *Hefley*	Y	Y	Y	N	N	N	N	Y
6 *Schaefer*	Y	Y	Y	Y	Y	N	N	Y
CONNECTICUT								
1 Kennelly	Y	Y	Y	N	Y	Y	Y	N
2 Gejdenson	Y	Y	Y	N	Y	Y	Y	N
3 DeLauro	Y	Y	Y	N	?	Y	Y	N
4 *Shays*	Y	Y	Y	Y	Y	N	N	Y
5 *Franks*	Y	Y	Y	Y	Y	N	N	Y
6 *Johnson*	Y	Y	Y	Y	Y	N	N	Y
DELAWARE								
AL *Castle*	Y	Y	Y	Y	Y	N	N	Y
FLORIDA								
1 Hutto	Y	Y	Y	N	Y	Y	Y	Y
2 Peterson	Y	Y	Y	N	Y	Y	Y	Y
3 Brown	Y	Y	Y	N	Y	Y	Y	N
4 *Fowler*	Y	Y	Y	Y	Y	N	N	Y
5 Thurman	Y	Y	Y	N	Y	Y	Y	N
6 *Stearns*	Y	Y	Y	Y	N	N	N	Y
7 *Mica*	Y	Y	Y	N	Y	N	N	Y
8 *McCollum*	Y	Y	Y	Y	N	N	N	Y
9 *Bilirakis*	Y	Y	Y	Y	Y	N	N	Y
10 *Young*	Y	Y	Y	N	Y	N	N	Y
11 Gibbons	Y	Y	Y	N	Y	Y	Y	N
12 *Canady*	Y	Y	Y	Y	Y	N	N	Y
13 *Miller*	Y	Y	Y	N	Y	N	N	Y
14 *Goss*	Y	Y	Y	N	Y	N	N	Y
15 Bacchus	Y	Y	N	N	Y	?	?	N
16 *Lewis*	?	Y	Y	Y	N	Y	Y	N
17 Meek	Y	Y	N	?	Y	Y	Y	N
18 *Ros-Lehtinen*	?	Y	Y	Y	N	N	N	?
19 Johnston	Y	Y	N	Y	Y	Y	Y	N
20 Deutsch	Y	Y	Y	N	Y	Y	Y	N
21 *Diaz-Balart*	Y	Y	Y	?	N	N	N	Y
22 *Shaw*	Y	Y	Y	Y	N	N	N	Y
23 Hastings	Y	Y	Y	N	Y	Y	Y	N
GEORGIA								
1 *Kingston*	Y	Y	Y	Y	N	N	N	Y
2 Bishop	?	Y	Y	N	Y	Y	Y	Y
3 *Collins*	Y	Y	Y	Y	N	N	N	Y
4 *Linder*	Y	Y	Y	Y	N	N	N	Y
5 Lewis	Y	Y	Y	N	Y	Y	Y	N
6 *Gingrich*	Y	Y	Y	Y	Y	N	N	?
7 Darden	?	Y	Y	N	Y	Y	Y	Y
8 Rowland	Y	Y	Y	N	Y	Y	Y	Y
9 Deal	Y	Y	Y	N	Y	Y	Y	Y
10 Johnson	Y	Y	Y	N	Y	Y	Y	N
11 McKinney	Y	Y	Y	N	Y	Y	Y	N
HAWAII								
1 Abercrombie	Y	Y	N	?	Y	Y	Y	N
2 Mink	Y	Y	N	N	Y	Y	Y	N
IDAHO								
1 LaRocco	Y	Y	Y	N	Y	Y	Y	N
2 *Crapo*	N	Y	Y	Y	N	N	N	Y
ILLINOIS								
1 Rush	?	Y	N	N	Y	Y	Y	N
2 Reynolds	?	Y	N	N	Y	Y	Y	N
3 Lipinski	Y	Y	Y	N	Y	Y	Y	N
4 Gutierrez	+	Y	Y	N	Y	Y	Y	N
5 Rostenkowski	Y	Y	Y	N	Y	?	?	?
6 *Hyde*	Y	Y	Y	Y	N	Y	N	Y
7 Collins	Y	Y	N	N	Y	Y	Y	N
8 *Crane*	N	Y	Y	N	N	N	N	Y
9 Yates	?	Y	N	N	Y	Y	Y	N
10 *Porter*	Y	Y	Y	Y	Y	N	N	Y
11 Sangmeister	Y	Y	Y	N	Y	Y	Y	N
12 Costello	Y	Y	Y	N	Y	Y	?	Y
13 *Fawell*	Y	Y	Y	N	N	N	N	Y
14 *Hastert*	Y	Y	Y	Y	N	N	N	Y
15 *Ewing*	Y	Y	Y	N	Y	N	N	Y
16 *Manzullo*	Y	Y	Y	N	N	N	N	Y
17 Evans	Y	Y	Y	N	Y	Y	Y	N

ND Northern Democrats SD Southern Democrats

	424	425	426	427	428	429	430	431
18 ***Michel***	Y	?	?	Y	Y	N	N	Y
19 Poshard	Y	Y	Y	N	Y	Y	Y	Y
20 Durbin	Y	Y	Y	N	Y	Y	Y	N
INDIANA								
1 Visclosky	Y	Y	Y	N	Y	Y	Y	N
2 Sharp	?	Y	Y	N	Y	Y	Y	N
3 Roemer	Y	Y	Y	Y	Y	Y	Y	Y
4 Long	Y	Y	Y	N	Y	Y	Y	Y
5 ***Buyer***	P	Y	Y	Y	Y	N	N	Y
6 ***Burton***	Y	Y	Y	Y	N	N	N	Y
7 ***Myers***	Y	Y	Y	N	N	N	N	Y
8 McCloskey	Y	Y	Y	N	Y	Y	Y	Y
9 Hamilton	Y	Y	Y	N	Y	Y	Y	Y
10 Jacobs	Y	Y	Y	N	Y	N	N	Y
IOWA								
1 ***Leach***	Y	Y	Y	Y	Y	N	N	Y
2 ***Nussle***	Y	Y	Y	Y	Y	N	?	Y
3 ***Lightfoot***	Y	Y	Y	Y	Y	N	N	Y
4 Smith	Y	Y	Y	N	Y	Y	Y	N
5 ***Grandy***	Y	Y	Y	Y	Y	N	N	Y
KANSAS								
1 ***Roberts***	N	Y	Y	Y	Y	N	N	Y
2 Slattery	?	Y	Y	?	?	?	?	?
3 ***Meyers***	Y	Y	Y	Y	Y	N	N	Y
4 Glickman	Y	Y	Y	N	Y	Y	Y	Y
KENTUCKY								
1 Barlow	Y	Y	Y	N	Y	Y	Y	N
2 ***Lewis***	N	Y	Y	Y	Y	N	N	Y
3 Mazzoli	Y	Y	Y	N	Y	Y	Y	N
4 ***Bunning***	N	Y	Y	Y	Y	N	N	Y
5 ***Rogers***	Y	Y	Y	N	Y	N	N	Y
6 Baesler	Y	Y	Y	N	Y	Y	Y	N
LOUISIANA								
1 ***Livingston***	N	Y	Y	N	Y	N	N	Y
2 Jefferson	Y	Y	Y	N	Y	Y	Y	N
3 Tauzin	Y	Y	Y	N	Y	Y	Y	Y
4 Fields	Y	Y	Y	N	Y	Y	Y	N
5 ***McCrery***	Y	Y	Y	Y	Y	N	N	Y
6 ***Baker***	N	Y	Y	Y	Y	N	N	Y
7 Hayes	Y	Y	Y	N	Y	Y	Y	N
MAINE								
1 Andrews	Y	Y	N	Y	Y	Y	Y	N
2 ***Snowe***	Y	Y	Y	Y	Y	N	N	Y
MARYLAND								
1 ***Gilchrest***	Y	Y	Y	Y	Y	N	N	Y
2 ***Bentley***	Y	Y	Y	Y	Y	N	N	Y
3 Cardin	Y	Y	N	N	Y	?	Y	Y
4 Wynn	Y	Y	Y	N	Y	Y	Y	N
5 Hoyer	Y	Y	Y	N	Y	Y	Y	N
6 ***Bartlett***	Y	Y	Y	Y	Y	N	N	Y
7 Mfume	Y	Y	Y	N	Y	Y	Y	Y
8 ***Morella***	Y	Y	Y	Y	Y	N	N	Y
MASSACHUSETTS								
1 Olver	Y	Y	N	N	Y	Y	Y	N
2 Neal	Y	Y	Y	N	Y	Y	Y	N
3 ***Blute***	Y	Y	Y	Y	Y	N	N	Y
4 Frank	Y	Y	N	N	Y	Y	Y	N
5 Meehan	?	Y	N	?	Y	Y	Y	N
6 ***Torkildsen***	Y	Y	Y	Y	Y	N	N	Y
7 Markey	Y	Y	N	N	Y	Y	Y	N
8 Kennedy	Y	Y	Y	?	?	Y	Y	N
9 Moakley	Y	Y	Y	N	Y	Y	Y	N
10 Studds	Y	Y	Y	N	Y	Y	Y	N
MICHIGAN								
1 Stupak	Y	Y	Y	N	Y	Y	Y	Y
2 ***Hoekstra***	N	Y	Y	Y	N	N	N	Y
3 ***Ehlers***	Y	Y	Y	Y	N	N	N	Y
4 ***Camp***	Y	Y	Y	Y	Y	N	N	Y
5 Barcia	Y	Y	Y	Y	Y	Y	Y	N
6 ***Upton***	Y	Y	Y	Y	N	N	N	Y
7 ***Smith***	Y	Y	Y	Y	N	N	N	Y
8 Carr	Y	Y	Y	N	Y	Y	Y	N
9 Kildee	Y	Y	Y	N	Y	Y	Y	N
10 Bonior	Y	Y	N	N	Y	Y	Y	N
11 ***Knollenberg***	Y	Y	Y	Y	Y	N	N	Y
12 Levin	Y	Y	Y	N	Y	Y	Y	Y
13 Ford	?	Y	Y	N	?	?	Y	N
14 Conyers	Y	Y	N	N	Y	Y	Y	N
15 Collins	Y	Y	N	N	Y	Y	Y	N
16 Dingell	Y	Y	Y	N	Y	Y	Y	N
MINNESOTA								
1 Penny	Y	Y	Y	Y	N	Y	Y	Y
2 Minge	Y	Y	Y	Y	Y	Y	Y	Y
3 ***Ramstad***	N	Y	Y	Y	Y	N	N	Y
4 Vento	Y	Y	Y	?	?	Y	Y	N

	424	425	426	427	428	429	430	431
5 Sabo	Y	Y	N	N	Y	Y	Y	N
6 ***Grams***	N	Y	Y	Y	Y	N	N	Y
7 Peterson	Y	Y	Y	Y	Y	Y	Y	N
8 Oberstar	Y	Y	N	N	Y	Y	Y	N
MISSISSIPPI								
1 Whitten	?	Y	Y	N	Y	Y	Y	N
2 Thompson	Y	Y	Y	N	Y	?	?	?
3 Montgomery	Y	Y	Y	N	Y	Y	Y	Y
4 Parker	Y	Y	Y	N	Y	Y	Y	N
5 Taylor	Y	Y	Y	Y	Y	Y	Y	Y
MISSOURI								
1 Clay	Y	Y	N	N	Y	Y	Y	N
2 ***Talent***	Y	Y	Y	Y	Y	N	N	Y
3 Gephardt	Y	Y	Y	N	Y	Y	Y	N
4 Skelton	Y	Y	Y	N	Y	Y	Y	N
5 Wheat	Y	?	?	N	Y	Y	Y	N
6 Danner	Y	Y	Y	N	Y	Y	Y	N
7 ***Hancock***	Y	Y	Y	Y	N	N	N	Y
8 ***Emerson***	Y	Y	Y	Y	Y	N	N	Y
9 Volkmer	Y	Y	Y	N	Y	Y	Y	N
MONTANA								
AL Williams	Y	Y	N	N	Y	Y	Y	N
NEBRASKA								
1 ***Bereuter***	Y	Y	Y	Y	Y	N	N	Y
2 Hoagland	Y	Y	Y	N	Y	Y	Y	N
3 ***Barrett***	Y	Y	Y	Y	Y	N	N	Y
NEVADA								
1 Bilbray	Y	Y	Y	Y	Y	Y	Y	N
2 ***Vucanovich***	N	Y	Y	?	?	N	N	Y
NEW HAMPSHIRE								
1 ***Zeliff***	N	Y	Y	Y	Y	N	N	Y
2 Swett	Y	Y	Y	Y	Y	Y	Y	Y
NEW JERSEY								
1 Andrews	Y	Y	Y	Y	N	Y	Y	N
2 Hughes	Y	Y	N	N	Y	Y	Y	N
3 ***Saxton***	Y	Y	Y	Y	Y	N	N	Y
4 ***Smith***	Y	Y	Y	Y	Y	N	N	Y
5 ***Roukema***	N	Y	Y	Y	Y	N	N	Y
6 Pallone	Y	Y	Y	N	Y	Y	Y	N
7 ***Franks***	Y	Y	Y	Y	Y	N	N	Y
8 Klein	Y	Y	Y	N	Y	Y	Y	Y
9 Torricelli	Y	Y	Y	N	Y	Y	Y	N
10 Payne	Y	Y	Y	N	Y	Y	Y	N
11 ***Gallo***	?	?	?	?	?	?	?	?
12 ***Zimmer***	Y	Y	Y	Y	N	N	N	Y
13 Menendez	Y	Y	Y	N	Y	Y	Y	N
NEW MEXICO								
1 ***Schiff***	Y	Y	Y	Y	Y	N	N	Y
2 ***Skeen***	N	Y	Y	N	Y	N	N	Y
3 Richardson	Y	Y	Y	N	Y	Y	Y	N
NEW YORK								
1 Hochbrueckner	+	Y	Y	N	Y	Y	Y	Y
2 ***Lazio***	Y	Y	Y	Y	Y	N	N	Y
3 ***King***	Y	Y	Y	Y	Y	N	N	Y
4 ***Levy***	Y	Y	Y	Y	Y	N	N	Y
5 Ackerman	Y	Y	N	N	Y	Y	Y	Y
6 Flake	?	Y	Y	N	Y	Y	Y	N
7 Manton	Y	Y	Y	N	Y	Y	Y	N
8 Nadler	Y	Y	N	N	Y	Y	Y	N
9 Schumer	Y	Y	Y	N	Y	Y	Y	N
10 Towns	Y	Y	Y	N	Y	Y	Y	N
11 Owens	Y	Y	Y	N	Y	Y	Y	Y
12 Velazquez	Y	Y	Y	N	Y	Y	Y	N
13 ***Molinari***	Y	Y	Y	Y	Y	N	N	Y
14 Maloney	Y	Y	Y	?	?	Y	Y	N
15 Rangel	?	Y	Y	N	Y	Y	Y	N
16 Serrano	Y	Y	Y	N	Y	Y	Y	N
17 Engel	Y	Y	N	N	Y	Y	Y	N
18 Lowey	Y	Y	Y	N	Y	Y	Y	N
19 ***Fish***	Y	Y	Y	Y	Y	N	N	Y
20 ***Gilman***	Y	Y	Y	Y	Y	N	N	Y
21 McNulty	Y	Y	Y	N	Y	Y	Y	N
22 ***Solomon***	Y	Y	Y	Y	Y	N	N	Y
23 ***Boehlert***	Y	Y	Y	Y	Y	N	N	Y
24 ***McHugh***	Y	Y	Y	Y	Y	N	N	Y
25 ***Walsh***	Y	Y	Y	Y	Y	N	N	Y
26 Hinchey	Y	Y	Y	N	Y	Y	Y	N
27 ***Paxon***	Y	Y	Y	Y	N	N	N	Y
28 Slaughter	Y	Y	Y	N	Y	Y	Y	N
29 LaFalce	Y	Y	Y	N	Y	Y	Y	N
30 ***Quinn***	Y	Y	Y	N	Y	N	N	Y
31 ***Houghton***	Y	Y	Y	Y	Y	N	N	Y
NORTH CAROLINA								
1 Clayton	Y	Y	Y	N	Y	Y	Y	N
2 Valentine	Y	Y	Y	N	Y	Y	Y	N

	424	425	426	427	428	429	430	431
3 Lancaster	Y	Y	Y	N	Y	Y	Y	Y
4 Price	Y	Y	Y	N	Y	Y	Y	Y
5 Neal	Y	Y	Y	N	Y	Y	Y	N
6 ***Coble***	N	Y	Y	Y	N	N	N	Y
7 Rose	?	Y	Y	N	Y	Y	Y	N
8 Hefner	Y	Y	Y	N	Y	Y	Y	N
9 ***McMillan***	N	Y	Y	?	Y	N	N	Y
10 ***Ballenger***	N	Y	Y	Y	Y	N	N	Y
11 ***Taylor***	N	Y	Y	N	Y	N	N	Y
12 Watt	Y	Y	N	N	Y	Y	Y	N
NORTH DAKOTA								
AL Pomeroy	Y	Y	Y	Y	Y	Y	Y	Y
OHIO								
1 Mann	Y	Y	Y	N	Y	Y	Y	N
2 ***Portman***	Y	Y	Y	Y	Y	N	N	Y
3 Hall	Y	Y	Y	N	Y	Y	Y	Y
4 ***Oxley***	?	Y	Y	Y	Y	N	N	Y
5 ***Gillmor***	Y	Y	Y	Y	Y	N	N	Y
6 Strickland	Y	Y	Y	N	Y	Y	Y	Y
7 ***Hobson***	Y	Y	Y	Y	Y	N	N	Y
8 ***Boehner***	N	Y	Y	Y	Y	N	N	Y
9 Kaptur	Y	Y	Y	N	Y	Y	?	Y
10 ***Hoke***	P	Y	Y	Y	Y	N	N	Y
11 Stokes	Y	Y	N	N	Y	Y	Y	N
12 ***Kasich***	Y	Y	Y	Y	Y	N	N	Y
13 Brown	Y	Y	Y	N	Y	Y	Y	N
14 Sawyer	Y	Y	Y	N	Y	Y	Y	N
15 ***Pryce***	?	Y	Y	Y	Y	N	N	Y
16 ***Regula***	Y	Y	Y	N	Y	N	N	Y
17 Traficant	Y	Y	Y	N	Y	N	Y	N
18 Applegate	?	Y	Y	N	Y	?	Y	N
19 Fingerhut	Y	Y	N	Y	Y	Y	Y	N
OKLAHOMA								
1 ***Inhofe***	?	?	?	Y	Y	N	N	?
2 Synar	?	?	?	?	?	?	?	N
3 Brewster	Y	Y	Y	N	Y	Y	Y	N
4 McCurdy	Y	Y	Y	Y	Y	Y	Y	N
5 ***Istook***	N	Y	Y	Y	N	?	N	Y
6 ***Lucas***	N	Y	Y	Y	Y	N	N	Y
OREGON								
1 Furse	Y	Y	N	N	Y	Y	Y	Y
2 ***Smith***	N	Y	Y	Y	Y	N	N	Y
3 Wyden	Y	Y	Y	N	Y	Y	Y	N
4 DeFazio	Y	Y	N	N	Y	Y	Y	Y
5 Kopetski	Y	Y	N	N	Y	Y	Y	N
PENNSYLVANIA								
1 Foglietta	Y	Y	Y	N	Y	Y	Y	N
2 Blackwell	Y	Y	Y	N	Y	Y	Y	?
3 Borski	Y	Y	Y	N	Y	Y	Y	N
4 Klink	Y	Y	Y	N	Y	Y	Y	N
5 ***Clinger***	Y	Y	Y	Y	Y	N	N	Y
6 Holden	Y	Y	Y	N	Y	Y	Y	Y
7 ***Weldon***	Y	Y	Y	Y	Y	N	N	Y
8 ***Greenwood***	Y	Y	Y	Y	Y	N	N	Y
9 ***Shuster***	Y	Y	Y	Y	Y	N	N	Y
10 ***McDade***	Y	Y	Y	N	Y	N	N	Y
11 Kanjorski	Y	Y	Y	N	Y	Y	Y	N
12 Murtha	?	Y	Y	N	Y	Y	Y	N
13 Margolies-Mezv.	Y	Y	N	N	Y	Y	Y	N
14 Coyne	Y	Y	N	N	Y	Y	Y	N
15 McHale	Y	Y	Y	N	Y	Y	Y	N
16 ***Walker***	N	Y	Y	Y	Y	N	N	Y
17 ***Gekas***	Y	Y	Y	N	Y	N	N	Y
18 ***Santorum***	Y	Y	Y	Y	Y	N	N	Y
19 ***Goodling***	Y	Y	Y	Y	Y	N	N	Y
20 Murphy	?	Y	Y	N	Y	Y	Y	N
21 ***Ridge***	Y	Y	Y	?	?	N	N	Y
RHODE ISLAND								
1 ***Machtley***	?	Y	Y	Y	Y	N	N	Y
2 Reed	Y	Y	Y	N	Y	Y	Y	N
SOUTH CAROLINA								
1 ***Ravenel***	Y	Y	Y	Y	Y	Y	Y	N
2 ***Spence***	N	Y	Y	N	Y	N	N	Y
3 Derrick	Y	Y	Y	N	Y	Y	Y	Y
4 ***Inglis***	N	Y	Y	Y	Y	N	N	Y
5 Spratt	Y	Y	Y	N	Y	Y	Y	Y
6 Clyburn	?	Y	Y	N	Y	Y	Y	N
SOUTH DAKOTA								
AL Johnson	Y	Y	Y	Y	Y	Y	Y	N
TENNESSEE								
1 ***Quillen***	N	Y	Y	N	Y	N	N	Y
2 ***Duncan***	N	Y	Y	Y	N	N	N	Y
3 Lloyd	Y	Y	Y	N	Y	Y	Y	Y
4 Cooper	Y	Y	Y	Y	Y	Y	Y	Y
5 Clement	Y	Y	Y	N	Y	Y	Y	Y

	424	425	426	427	428	429	430	431
6 Gordon	Y	Y	Y	N	Y	Y	Y	N
7 ***Sundquist***	?	?	?	?	?	?	?	?
8 Tanner	Y	Y	Y	N	Y	Y	Y	Y
9 Ford	Y	Y	Y	N	Y	Y	Y	N
TEXAS								
1 Chapman	Y	Y	Y	N	Y	Y	Y	Y
2 Wilson	Y	?	Y	N	Y	Y	Y	N
3 ***Johnson, Sam***	N	Y	Y	Y	Y	N	N	Y
4 Hall	Y	Y	Y	N	Y	Y	N	Y
5 Bryant	Y	Y	Y	N	Y	Y	Y	N
6 ***Barton***	Y	Y	Y	Y	N	N	N	Y
7 ***Archer***	N	Y	Y	Y	N	N	N	Y
8 ***Fields***	N	Y	Y	Y	N	N	N	Y
9 Brooks	Y	Y	Y	N	Y	Y	Y	N
10 Pickle	Y	Y	Y	N	Y	Y	Y	Y
11 Edwards	Y	Y	Y	N	Y	Y	Y	Y
12 Geren	Y	Y	Y	N	Y	Y	Y	Y
13 Sarpalius	Y	Y	Y	N	Y	Y	Y	N
14 Laughlin	?	Y	Y	N	Y	Y	Y	N
15 de la Garza	Y	Y	Y	N	Y	Y	Y	N
16 Coleman	Y	Y	Y	N	Y	Y	Y	N
17 Stenholm	Y	Y	Y	Y	Y	Y	Y	Y
18 Washington	?	?	?	?	?	?	?	?
19 ***Combest***	Y	Y	Y	Y	Y	N	N	Y
20 Gonzalez	Y	Y	N	N	Y	Y	Y	N
21 ***Smith***	Y	Y	Y	Y	Y	N	N	Y
22 ***DeLay***	?	Y	Y	Y	N	N	N	Y
23 ***Bonilla***	N	Y	Y	Y	Y	N	N	Y
24 Frost	Y	Y	Y	?	?	?	?	?
25 Andrews	Y	Y	Y	N	Y	Y	Y	N
26 ***Armey***	N	Y	Y	Y	N	N	N	Y
27 Ortiz	Y	Y	Y	N	Y	Y	Y	N
28 Tejeda	Y	Y	Y	N	Y	Y	Y	N
29 Green	Y	+	+	N	Y	Y	Y	Y
30 Johnson, E.B.	Y	Y	Y	N	Y	Y	Y	N
UTAH								
1 ***Hansen***	Y	Y	Y	N	Y	N	N	Y
2 Shepherd	Y	Y	Y	N	Y	Y	Y	Y
3 Orton	Y	Y	Y	Y	Y	Y	Y	Y
VERMONT								
AL *Sanders*	Y	Y	N	N	Y	Y	Y	N
VIRGINIA								
1 ***Bateman***	Y	Y	Y	N	Y	N	N	Y
2 Pickett	Y	Y	Y	N	Y	Y	Y	Y
3 Scott	Y	Y	N	N	Y	Y	Y	N
4 Sisisky	Y	Y	?	N	Y	Y	Y	Y
5 Payne	Y	Y	Y	N	Y	Y	Y	Y
6 ***Goodlatte***	Y	Y	Y	Y	N	N	N	Y
7 ***Bliley***	Y	Y	Y	Y	N	?	?	Y
8 Moran	Y	Y	Y	N	Y	Y	Y	N
9 Boucher	Y	Y	Y	N	Y	Y	Y	N
10 ***Wolf***	Y	Y	Y	Y	Y	N	N	Y
11 Byrne	Y	Y	Y	N	Y	Y	Y	N
WASHINGTON								
1 Cantwell	Y	Y	Y	Y	Y	Y	Y	Y
2 Swift	Y	Y	N	N	Y	Y	Y	N
3 Unsoeld	Y	Y	Y	N	Y	Y	Y	N
4 Inslee	Y	Y	Y	N	Y	Y	Y	Y
5 Foley	Y							
6 Dicks	Y	Y	Y	N	?	Y	Y	N
7 McDermott	Y	Y	N	N	Y	Y	Y	N
8 ***Dunn***	Y	Y	Y	Y	Y	N	N	Y
9 Kreidler	Y	Y	Y	N	Y	Y	Y	N
WEST VIRGINIA								
1 Mollohan	Y	Y	Y	N	Y	Y	Y	N
2 Wise	Y	Y	Y	N	Y	Y	Y	N
3 Rahall	Y	Y	Y	N	Y	Y	Y	N
WISCONSIN								
1 Barca	Y	Y	Y	Y	Y	Y	Y	Y
2 ***Klug***	N	Y	Y	Y	Y	N	N	Y
3 ***Gunderson***	N	Y	Y	Y	Y	N	N	Y
4 Kleczka	Y	Y	Y	N	Y	Y	Y	N
5 Barrett	Y	Y	Y	Y	Y	Y	Y	Y
6 ***Petri***	N	Y	Y	Y	N	N	N	Y
7 Obey	Y	Y	Y	N	Y	Y	Y	N
8 ***Roth***	N	Y	Y	?	N	N	N	Y
9 ***Sensenbrenner***	N	Y	Y	Y	N	N	N	Y
WYOMING								
AL ***Thomas***	Y	Y	Y	Y	Y	N	N	Y
DELEGATES								
de Lugo, V.I.	D	D	D	D	D	D	D	N
Faleomavaega, Am.S.	D	D	D	D	D	D	D	N
Norton, D.C.	D	D	D	D	D	D	D	N
Romero-B., P.R.	D	D	D	D	D	D	D	N
Underwood, Guam	D	D	D	D	D	D	D	N

Southern states - Ala., Ark., Fla., Ga., Ky., La., Miss., N.C., Okla., S.C., Tenn., Texas, Va.
Omitted votes are quorum calls, which CQ does not include in its vote charts.

432. HR 2866. California Redwood Forest Expansion/ Expansion Study. Pombo, R-Calif., amendment to strike the provisions in the bill that require a study and report on the potential for adding 13,620 acres in the Headwaters Forest area to the Six Rivers National Forest. Rejected in the Committee of the Whole 170-253: R 149-24; D 21-228 (ND 8-161, SD 13-67); I 0-1, Sept. 21, 1994.

433. HR 2866. California Redwood Forest Expansion/ Passage. Passage of the bill to authorize the Forest Service to acquire 44,000 acres of privately owned redwood forest in Humboldt County, Calif., for addition to the Six Rivers National Forest. Passed 288-133: R 46-127; D 241-6 (ND 167-1, SD 74-5); I 1-0, Sept. 21, 1994.

434. HR 4606. Fiscal 1995 Labor, HHS Appropriations/ Conference Report. Adoption of the conference report to provide $250,610,477,000 in new budget authority for the Departments of Labor, Health and Human Services, and Education, and related agencies in fiscal 1995-97. The administration had requested a total of $251,555,092,000. Adopted (thus sent to the Senate) 331-89: R 89-85; D 241-4 (ND 162-3, SD 79-1); I 1-0, Sept. 22, 1994.

435. HR 4539. Fiscal 1995 Treasury-Postal Appropriations/Rule. Adoption of the rule (H Res 537) to waive points of order against and provide for House floor consideration of the conference report to provide $23,584,247,000 in new budget authority for the Treasury Department, the U.S. Postal Service, the Executive Office of the President and certain independent agencies for fiscal 1995. The administration had requested $24,571,817,000. Adopted 250-169: R 6-166; D 243-3 (ND 165-3, SD 78-0); I 1-0, Sept. 22, 1994.

436. HR 4539. Fiscal 1995 Treasury-Postal Appropriations/Recommit. Istook, R-Okla., motion to recommit the conference report to the conference committee with instructions to report the bill back after eliminating $218 million for new federal construction (thereby restoring the construction total to the House-passed amount) and striking Senate provisions that authorize the collection of $149.7 million in additional fees by the Internal Revenue Service. Motion agreed to 234-192: R 169-6; D 65-185 (ND 38-132, SD 27-53); I 0-1, Sept. 22, 1994.

437. HR 4422. Coast Guard Authorization/Passage. Passage of the bill to reauthorize the Coast Guard at $3.8 billion in fiscal 1995. Before passage the House added to the bill the text of six other bills: Recreational Boating Safety Improvements (HR 3786), U.S. Passenger Vessel Development (HR 3821), Towing Vessel Safety (HR 3282), Boating Improvement (HR 4477), Coast Guard Regulatory Reform (HR 4959), and Foreign-Flag Passenger Vessel Restrictions (HR 1250). Passed 402-13: R 163-7; D 238-6 (ND 162-6, SD 76-0); I 1-0, Sept. 22, 1994.

KEY

Y   Voted for (yea).
\#   Paired for.
\+   Announced for.
N   Voted against (nay).
X   Paired against.
−   Announced against.
P   Voted "present."
C   Voted "present" to avoid possible conflict of interest.
?   Did not vote or otherwise make a position known.
D   Delegates ineligible to vote.

Democrats   *Republicans*
Independent

	432	433	434	435	436	437
ALABAMA						
1 *Callahan*	Y	N	Y	N	Y	Y
2 *Everett*	Y	N	N	Y	N	Y
3 Browder	N	Y	Y	Y	Y	Y
4 Bevill	N	Y	Y	Y	N	Y
5 Cramer	N	Y	Y	Y	N	Y
6 *Bachus*	Y	N	N	N	Y	Y
7 Hilliard	N	Y	Y	Y	N	Y
ALASKA						
AL *Young*	Y	N	Y	Y	N	Y
ARIZONA						
1 Coppersmith	N	Y	Y	Y	N	Y
2 Pastor	N	Y	Y	Y	N	Y
3 *Stump*	Y	N	N	N	Y	N
4 *Kyl*	Y	N	N	Y	N	Y
5 *Kolbe*	Y	N	N	N	Y	Y
6 English	N	Y	Y	Y	Y	Y
ARKANSAS						
1 Lambert	Y	Y	Y	Y	Y	Y
2 Thornton	N	Y	Y	Y	N	Y
3 *Hutchinson*	Y	N	Y	N	Y	Y
4 *Dickey*	Y	N	Y	N	Y	Y
CALIFORNIA						
1 Hamburg	N	Y	Y	Y	N	Y
2 *Herger*	Y	N	N	N	Y	?
3 Fazio	N	Y	Y	Y	N	Y
4 *Doolittle*	Y	N	N	N	Y	Y
5 Matsui	?	Y	Y	Y	N	Y
6 Woolsey	N	Y	Y	Y	N	Y
7 Miller	N	Y	Y	Y	N	Y
8 Pelosi	?	Y	Y	Y	N	Y
9 Dellums	N	Y	Y	Y	N	Y
10 *Baker*	Y	N	Y	N	Y	Y
11 *Pombo*	Y	N	N	N	Y	Y
12 Lantos	N	Y	Y	Y	N	Y
13 Stark	N	Y	Y	Y	N	Y
14 Eshoo	N	Y	Y	Y	N	Y
15 Mineta	N	Y	Y	Y	N	Y
16 Edwards	N	Y	Y	?	N	Y
17 Farr	N	Y	Y	Y	N	Y
18 Condit	Y	Y	Y	Y	Y	Y
19 Lehman	Y	N	Y	Y	N	Y
20 Dooley	Y	Y	Y	Y	N	Y
21 *Thomas*	Y	N	Y	N	Y	Y
22 *Huffington*	Y	N	N	N	Y	Y
23 *Gallegly*	Y	N	Y	N	Y	Y
24 Beilenson	N	Y	Y	Y	N	Y
25 *McKeon*	Y	N	N	N	Y	Y
26 Berman	N	Y	Y	Y	N	Y
27 *Moorhead*	Y	N	N	N	Y	Y
28 *Dreier*	Y	N	N	N	Y	Y
29 Waxman	N	Y	Y	Y	N	Y
30 Becerra	N	Y	Y	Y	N	Y
31 Martinez	N	Y	Y	Y	N	Y
32 Dixon	N	Y	Y	Y	N	Y
33 Roybal-Allard	N	Y	Y	Y	N	Y
34 Torres	N	Y	Y	Y	N	Y
35 Waters	N	Y	Y	Y	N	Y
36 Harman	N	Y	Y	Y	Y	Y
37 Tucker	N	Y	Y	Y	N	Y
38 *Horn*	Y	Y	Y	Y	N	Y
39 *Royce*	Y	N	N	N	Y	Y
40 *Lewis*	Y	N	Y	N	Y	Y
41 *Kim*	Y	N	N	N	Y	Y

	432	433	434	435	436	437
42 Brown	N	Y	Y	Y	N	Y
43 *Calvert*	Y	N	Y	N	Y	Y
44 *McCandless*	Y	N	N	N	Y	Y
45 *Rohrabacher*	Y	N	N	N	Y	Y
46 *Dornan*	Y	N	N	N	Y	Y
47 *Cox*	Y	N	N	Y	Y	Y
48 *Packard*	Y	N	N	N	Y	Y
49 Schenk	N	Y	Y	Y	N	Y
50 Filner	N	Y	Y	Y	N	Y
51 *Cunningham*	Y	N	N	Y	N	Y
52 *Hunter*	Y	N	N	N	Y	Y
COLORADO						
1 Schroeder	N	Y	Y	Y	Y	Y
2 Skaggs	N	Y	Y	Y	N	Y
3 *McInnis*	Y	N	N	N	Y	Y
4 *Allard*	Y	N	N	Y	Y	Y
5 *Hefley*	Y	N	N	N	Y	Y
6 *Schaefer*	Y	N	N	N	Y	Y
CONNECTICUT						
1 Kennelly	N	Y	Y	Y	N	Y
2 Gejdenson	N	Y	Y	Y	N	Y
3 DeLauro	N	Y	Y	Y	N	Y
4 *Shays*	N	Y	Y	Y	N	Y
5 *Franks*	N	Y	Y	Y	N	Y
6 *Johnson*	N	Y	Y	N	Y	Y
DELAWARE						
AL *Castle*	Y	N	Y	N	Y	Y
FLORIDA						
1 Hutto	N	Y	Y	Y	Y	Y
2 Peterson	N	Y	Y	Y	N	Y
3 Brown	N	Y	Y	Y	N	Y
4 *Fowler*	Y	N	N	Y	N	Y
5 Thurman	N	Y	Y	Y	N	Y
6 *Stearns*	Y	N	N	Y	Y	Y
7 *Mica*	Y	N	N	N	Y	Y
8 *McCollum*	Y	N	N	N	Y	Y
9 *Bilirakis*	Y	N	N	Y	Y	Y
10 *Young*	Y	Y	Y	N	Y	Y
11 Gibbons	N	Y	Y	Y	N	?
12 *Canady*	Y	N	N	N	Y	Y
13 *Miller*	Y	N	N	N	Y	Y
14 *Goss*	Y	Y	N	N	Y	Y
15 Bacchus	N	Y	Y	Y	N	Y
16 *Lewis*	Y	N	N	N	Y	Y
17 Meek	N	Y	Y	Y	N	Y
18 *Ros-Lehtinen*	?	?	N	Y	Y	Y
19 Johnston	N	Y	Y	Y	N	Y
20 Deutsch	N	Y	Y	Y	Y	Y
21 *Diaz-Balart*	Y	Y	Y	Y	Y	Y
22 *Shaw*	Y	Y	Y	Y	Y	Y
23 Hastings	N	Y	Y	Y	N	Y
GEORGIA						
1 *Kingston*	Y	Y	N	N	Y	Y
2 Bishop	N	Y	Y	Y	N	Y
3 *Collins*	Y	N	N	N	Y	Y
4 *Linder*	Y	N	Y	N	Y	Y
5 Lewis	N	Y	Y	Y	N	Y
6 *Gingrich*	?	?	Y	?	Y	Y
7 Darden	N	Y	Y	Y	N	Y
8 Rowland	N	Y	Y	Y	N	Y
9 Deal	Y	Y	Y	Y	Y	Y
10 Johnson	N	Y	Y	Y	Y	Y
11 McKinney	N	Y	Y	Y	N	Y
HAWAII						
1 Abercrombie	N	Y	Y	Y	N	Y
2 Mink	N	Y	Y	Y	N	Y
IDAHO						
1 LaRocco	N	Y	Y	Y	N	Y
2 *Crapo*	Y	N	N	N	Y	Y
ILLINOIS						
1 Rush	N	Y	Y	Y	N	Y
2 Reynolds	N	Y	Y	Y	N	Y
3 Lipinski	N	Y	Y	Y	N	N
4 Gutierrez	N	Y	Y	Y	N	N
5 Rostenkowski	?	?	Y	Y	N	Y
6 *Hyde*	Y	N	Y	N	Y	Y
7 Collins	N	Y	Y	Y	N	Y
8 *Crane*	Y	N	N	N	Y	Y
9 Yates	N	Y	Y	Y	N	Y
10 *Porter*	N	Y	Y	N	Y	Y
11 Sangmeister	N	Y	Y	Y	N	Y
12 Costello	N	Y	Y	Y	N	N
13 *Fawell*	Y	Y	Y	N	Y	Y
14 *Hastert*	Y	Y	+	N	Y	Y
15 *Ewing*	Y	Y	Y	N	Y	N
16 *Manzullo*	Y	N	N	N	Y	Y
17 Evans	N	Y	Y	Y	N	Y

ND   Northern Democrats   SD   Southern Democrats

	432	433	434	435	436	437
18 ***Michel***	Y	N	Y	Y	Y	Y
19 Poshard	N	Y	Y	Y	Y	N
20 Durbin	N	Y	Y	Y	N	Y
INDIANA						
1 Visclosky	N	Y	Y	Y	N	Y
2 Sharp	N	Y	Y	Y	N	Y
3 Roemer	N	Y	Y	Y	Y	Y
4 Long	N	Y	Y	Y	Y	Y
5 ***Buyer***	Y	N	N	N	Y	Y
6 ***Burton***	Y	N	N	N	Y	Y
7 ***Myers***	Y	N	Y	N	Y	Y
8 McCloskey	N	Y	Y	Y	N	Y
9 Hamilton	N	Y	Y	Y	Y	Y
10 Jacobs	N	Y	Y	Y	Y	Y
IOWA						
1 ***Leach***	N	Y	Y	N	Y	Y
2 ***Nussle***	Y	N	Y	N	Y	Y
3 ***Lightfoot***	Y	N	N	N	Y	Y
4 Smith	N	Y	Y	Y	N	Y
5 ***Grandy***	Y	Y	Y	N	Y	Y
KANSAS						
1 ***Roberts***	Y	N	N	N	Y	Y
2 Slattery	?	?	?	?	?	?
3 ***Meyers***	N	Y	Y	Y	Y	Y
4 Glickman	N	Y	Y	Y	Y	Y
KENTUCKY						
1 Barlow	N	Y	Y	Y	Y	Y
2 ***Lewis***	Y	N	Y	N	Y	Y
3 Mazzoli	N	Y	Y	Y	N	Y
4 ***Bunning***	Y	N	N	N	Y	Y
5 ***Rogers***	Y	N	Y	N	N	Y
6 Baesler	N	Y	Y	Y	Y	Y
LOUISIANA						
1 ***Livingston***	Y	N	Y	N	Y	Y
2 Jefferson	N	Y	Y	Y	N	Y
3 Tauzin	Y	Y	Y	Y	Y	Y
4 Fields	N	Y	Y	Y	N	Y
5 ***McCrery***	Y	N	Y	N	Y	Y
6 ***Baker***	Y	N	N	N	Y	Y
7 Hayes	Y	Y	Y	Y	?	Y
MAINE						
1 Andrews	N	Y	Y	Y	Y	Y
2 ***Snowe***	N	Y	Y	N	Y	Y
MARYLAND						
1 ***Gilchrest***	N	Y	Y	N	Y	Y
2 ***Bentley***	Y	N	Y	N	Y	Y
3 Cardin	N	Y	Y	Y	N	Y
4 Wynn	N	Y	Y	Y	N	Y
5 Hoyer	N	Y	Y	Y	N	Y
6 ***Bartlett***	Y	N	N	N	Y	Y
7 Mfume	N	Y	Y	Y	N	Y
8 ***Morella***	N	Y	Y	Y	Y	Y
MASSACHUSETTS						
1 Olver	N	Y	Y	Y	N	Y
2 Neal	N	Y	Y	Y	N	Y
3 ***Blute***	Y	Y	Y	N	Y	Y
4 Frank	N	Y	Y	Y	N	Y
5 Meehan	N	Y	Y	Y	N	Y
6 ***Torkildsen***	Y	Y	Y	N	Y	Y
7 Markey	N	Y	Y	Y	N	Y
8 Kennedy	N	Y	Y	Y	N	Y
9 Moakley	N	Y	Y	Y	N	Y
10 Studds	N	Y	Y	Y	N	Y
MICHIGAN						
1 Stupak	Y	Y	Y	Y	N	Y
2 ***Hoekstra***	Y	N	Y	N	Y	Y
3 ***Ehlers***	N	Y	N	N	Y	Y
4 ***Camp***	Y	N	Y	N	Y	Y
5 Barcia	N	Y	Y	Y	Y	Y
6 ***Upton***	Y	N	Y	N	Y	Y
7 ***Smith***	Y	N	N	N	Y	Y
8 Carr	N	Y	Y	Y	N	?
9 Kildee	N	Y	Y	Y	N	Y
10 Bonior	N	Y	Y	Y	N	Y
11 ***Knollenberg***	Y	N	N	N	Y	Y
12 Levin	N	Y	Y	Y	N	Y
13 Ford	N	Y	Y	Y	N	Y
14 Conyers	N	Y	Y	Y	N	Y
15 Collins	N	Y	?	Y	N	Y
16 Dingell	N	Y	Y	Y	N	Y
MINNESOTA						
1 Penny	N	Y	N	N	Y	N
2 Minge	N	Y	N	Y	Y	Y
3 ***Ramstad***	Y	N	N	N	Y	Y
4 Vento	N	Y	Y	Y	N	Y

	432	433	434	435	436	437
5 Sabo	N	Y	Y	Y	N	Y
6 ***Grams***	#	N	N	N	Y	Y
7 Peterson	N	Y	N	N	Y	Y
8 Oberstar	N	Y	Y	Y	N	Y
MISSISSIPPI						
1 Whitten	N	Y	Y	Y	N	?
2 Thompson	?	?	?	Y	N	Y
3 Montgomery	N	Y	Y	Y	N	Y
4 Parker	N	N	Y	Y	Y	Y
5 Taylor	N	Y	N	Y	Y	Y
MISSOURI						
1 Clay	N	Y	Y	Y	N	Y
2 ***Talent***	Y	N	N	N	Y	Y
3 Gephardt	N	Y	Y	Y	N	Y
4 Skelton	N	Y	Y	Y	Y	Y
5 Wheat	N	Y	Y	Y	N	Y
6 Danner	N	Y	Y	Y	Y	Y
7 ***Hancock***	Y	N	N	N	Y	N
8 ***Emerson***	Y	N	N	N	Y	Y
9 Volkmer	N	Y	Y	Y	N	Y
MONTANA						
AL Williams	N	Y	Y	Y	Y	Y
NEBRASKA						
1 ***Bereuter***	N	Y	Y	N	Y	Y
2 Hoagland	N	Y	Y	Y	Y	Y
3 ***Barrett***	Y	N	Y	N	Y	Y
NEVADA						
1 Bilbray	N	Y	Y	Y	Y	Y
2 ***Vucanovich***	Y	N	Y	N	N	Y
NEW HAMPSHIRE						
1 ***Zeliff***	Y	N	N	N	Y	Y
2 Swett	N	Y	Y	Y	Y	Y
NEW JERSEY						
1 Andrews	N	Y	Y	Y	Y	Y
2 Hughes	N	Y	Y	Y	N	Y
3 ***Saxton***	Y	Y	Y	N	Y	Y
4 ***Smith***	N	Y	Y	N	Y	Y
5 ***Roukema***	N	Y	Y	N	Y	Y
6 Pallone	N	Y	Y	Y	Y	Y
7 ***Franks***	N	Y	N	N	Y	Y
8 Klein	N	Y	Y	Y	Y	Y
9 Torricelli	N	Y	Y	Y	N	Y
10 Payne	N	Y	Y	Y	N	Y
11 ***Gallo***	?	?	?	?	?	?
12 ***Zimmer***	N	Y	N	N	Y	Y
13 Menendez	N	Y	Y	Y	N	Y
NEW MEXICO						
1 ***Schiff***	Y	Y	Y	N	Y	Y
2 ***Skeen***	Y	N	Y	N	Y	Y
3 Richardson	N	Y	Y	Y	Y	Y
NEW YORK						
1 Hochbrueckner	N	Y	Y	Y	N	Y
2 ***Lazio***	N	Y	Y	N	N	Y
3 ***King***	Y	N	Y	N	Y	Y
4 ***Levy***	Y	N	Y	N	Y	?
5 Ackerman	N	Y	Y	Y	N	Y
6 Flake	N	Y	Y	Y	N	Y
7 Manton	N	Y	Y	Y	N	Y
8 Nadler	N	Y	Y	Y	N	Y
9 Schumer	N	Y	Y	Y	N	Y
10 Towns	N	Y	?	Y	N	Y
11 Owens	N	Y	Y	Y	N	Y
12 Velazquez	N	Y	Y	Y	N	Y
13 ***Molinari***	Y	N	Y	N	Y	Y
14 Maloney	N	Y	Y	Y	N	Y
15 Rangel	X	?	?	#	?	?
16 Serrano	N	Y	Y	Y	N	?
17 Engel	N	Y	?	N	N	Y
18 Lowey	N	Y	Y	Y	N	Y
19 ***Fish***	Y	Y	Y	N	Y	Y
20 ***Gilman***	N	?	Y	N	Y	Y
21 McNulty	N	Y	Y	Y	N	Y
22 ***Solomon***	Y	N	N	N	Y	Y
23 ***Boehlert***	N	Y	Y	N	Y	Y
24 ***McHugh***	Y	N	N	N	Y	Y
25 ***Walsh***	Y	N	Y	N	Y	Y
26 Hinchey	N	Y	Y	Y	N	Y
27 ***Paxon***	Y	N	N	N	Y	Y
28 Slaughter	N	Y	Y	Y	N	Y
29 LaFalce	N	Y	Y	Y	N	Y
30 ***Quinn***	Y	N	Y	N	Y	Y
31 ***Houghton***	Y	N	Y	N	Y	Y
NORTH CAROLINA						
1 Clayton	N	Y	Y	Y	N	Y
2 Valentine	N	Y	Y	Y	N	Y

	432	433	434	435	436	437
3 Lancaster	N	Y	Y	Y	N	Y
4 Price	N	Y	Y	Y	N	Y
5 Neal	N	Y	Y	Y	N	Y
6 ***Coble***	Y	N	N	N	Y	Y
7 Rose	N	?	Y	Y	N	Y
8 Hefner	N	Y	Y	Y	N	Y
9 ***McMillan***	Y	N	Y	N	Y	Y
10 ***Ballenger***	Y	N	N	X	Y	Y
11 ***Taylor***	Y	N	Y	N	Y	Y
12 Watt	N	Y	Y	Y	N	Y
NORTH DAKOTA						
AL Pomeroy	Y	Y	Y	Y	Y	Y
OHIO						
1 Mann	N	Y	Y	Y	Y	Y
2 ***Portman***	Y	N	N	N	Y	Y
3 Hall	N	Y	Y	Y	N	Y
4 ***Oxley***	Y	N	N	N	Y	Y
5 ***Gillmor***	N	Y	Y	N	Y	Y
6 Strickland	Y	Y	Y	Y	N	Y
7 ***Hobson***	Y	N	Y	N	Y	Y
8 ***Boehner***	Y	N	N	N	Y	Y
9 Kaptur	N	Y	Y	Y	N	Y
10 ***Hoke***	Y	N	N	N	Y	Y
11 Stokes	?	Y	Y	Y	N	Y
12 ***Kasich***	Y	N	Y	N	Y	Y
13 Brown	N	Y	Y	Y	N	Y
14 Sawyer	N	Y	Y	Y	N	Y
15 ***Pryce***	Y	N	Y	N	Y	Y
16 ***Regula***	Y	Y	Y	N	Y	Y
17 Traficant	N	Y	Y	Y	Y	Y
18 Applegate	N	Y	Y	Y	N	Y
19 Fingerhut	N	Y	Y	Y	Y	Y
OKLAHOMA						
1 ***Inhofe***	Y	N	N	?	?	?
2 Synar	N	Y	Y	?	N	Y
3 Brewster	Y	Y	Y	Y	Y	Y
4 McCurdy	Y	Y	Y	?	Y	?
5 ***Istook***	Y	N	N	N	Y	Y
6 ***Lucas***	Y	N	N	N	Y	Y
OREGON						
1 Furse	N	Y	Y	Y	N	Y
2 ***Smith***	Y	N	Y	N	Y	Y
3 Wyden	N	Y	Y	Y	N	Y
4 DeFazio	N	Y	Y	Y	N	Y
5 Kopetski	N	Y	?	Y	N	Y
PENNSYLVANIA						
1 Foglietta	N	Y	Y	Y	N	Y
2 Blackwell	?	?	Y	Y	N	Y
3 Borski	N	Y	Y	Y	N	Y
4 Klink	N	Y	Y	Y	Y	Y
5 ***Clinger***	Y	N	Y	N	Y	Y
6 Holden	Y	Y	Y	Y	Y	Y
7 ***Weldon***	N	Y	Y	N	Y	Y
8 ***Greenwood***	N	Y	N	N	Y	Y
9 ***Shuster***	Y	N	N	N	Y	Y
10 ***McDade***	Y	Y	Y	Y	Y	Y
11 Kanjorski	N	Y	Y	Y	N	Y
12 Murtha	N	Y	Y	Y	N	Y
13 Margolies-Mezv.	N	Y	Y	Y	Y	Y
14 Coyne	N	Y	Y	Y	N	Y
15 McHale	N	Y	Y	Y	N	Y
16 ***Walker***	Y	N	N	N	Y	Y
17 ***Gekas***	Y	N	N	N	Y	Y
18 ***Santorum***	Y	Y	Y	N	Y	Y
19 ***Goodling***	Y	N	N	N	Y	Y
20 Murphy	N	Y	Y	Y	N	Y
21 ***Ridge***	Y	Y	?	N	Y	?
RHODE ISLAND						
1 ***Machtley***	Y	Y	Y	N	Y	Y
2 Reed	N	Y	Y	Y	N	Y
SOUTH CAROLINA						
1 ***Ravenel***	N	Y	N	?	Y	Y
2 ***Spence***	Y	Y	N	N	Y	Y
3 Derrick	N	Y	Y	Y	N	Y
4 ***Inglis***	Y	N	N	N	Y	?
5 Spratt	N	Y	Y	Y	Y	Y
6 Clyburn	N	Y	Y	Y	N	Y
SOUTH DAKOTA						
AL Johnson	N	Y	Y	?	N	Y
TENNESSEE						
1 ***Quillen***	Y	N	Y	Y	N	?
2 ***Duncan***	Y	N	Y	N	Y	N
3 Lloyd	N	N	Y	Y	Y	Y
4 Cooper	N	Y	Y	?	?	?
5 Clement	N	Y	Y	Y	N	Y

	432	433	434	435	436	437
6 Gordon	Y	Y	Y	Y	N	Y
7 ***Sundquist***	?	?	?	?	?	?
8 Tanner	Y	Y	Y	Y	Y	?
9 Ford	N	Y	Y	Y	N	Y
TEXAS						
1 Chapman	N	Y	Y	Y	N	Y
2 Wilson	N	Y	Y	Y	N	Y
3 ***Johnson, Sam***	Y	N	N	N	Y	N
4 Hall	Y	N	Y	Y	Y	Y
5 Bryant	N	Y	Y	?	N	Y
6 ***Barton***	Y	N	N	N	Y	Y
7 ***Archer***	Y	N	N	N	Y	Y
8 ***Fields***	Y	Y	N	N	Y	Y
9 Brooks	N	Y	Y	Y	N	Y
10 Pickle	N	Y	Y	Y	N	Y
11 Edwards	Y	Y	Y	Y	Y	Y
12 Geren	Y	Y	Y	Y	Y	Y
13 Sarpalius	N	Y	Y	Y	Y	Y
14 Laughlin	Y	N	Y	Y	Y	Y
15 de la Garza	N	Y	?	Y	N	Y
16 Coleman	N	Y	Y	Y	N	Y
17 Stenholm	Y	N	Y	Y	Y	Y
18 Washington	?	?	?	?	?	?
19 ***Combest***	Y	N	N	N	Y	Y
20 Gonzalez	N	Y	Y	Y	N	Y
21 ***Smith***	Y	N	Y	N	Y	Y
22 ***DeLay***	Y	N	N	N	Y	Y
23 ***Bonilla***	Y	N	Y	N	Y	Y
24 Frost	?	?	Y	Y	N	Y
25 Andrews	N	Y	Y	Y	N	Y
26 ***Armey***	Y	N	N	N	Y	Y
27 Ortiz	N	Y	Y	Y	N	Y
28 Tejeda	N	Y	Y	Y	Y	Y
29 Green	N	Y	Y	Y	N	+
30 Johnson, E.B.	N	Y	Y	Y	N	Y
UTAH						
1 ***Hansen***	Y	N	N	N	Y	Y
2 Shepherd	N	Y	Y	Y	N	Y
3 Orton	Y	Y	?	Y	Y	Y
VERMONT						
AL *Sanders*	N	Y	Y	Y	N	Y
VIRGINIA						
1 ***Bateman***	Y	Y	Y	N	Y	Y
2 Pickett	N	Y	Y	Y	Y	Y
3 Scott	N	Y	Y	Y	N	Y
4 Sisisky	N	Y	Y	Y	Y	Y
5 Payne	N	Y	Y	Y	Y	Y
6 ***Goodlatte***	Y	N	N	N	Y	Y
7 ***Bliley***	Y	N	N	N	Y	Y
8 Moran	N	Y	Y	Y	N	Y
9 Boucher	N	Y	Y	Y	N	Y
10 ***Wolf***	Y	N	Y	N	Y	Y
11 Byrne	N	Y	Y	Y	N	Y
WASHINGTON						
1 Cantwell	N	Y	Y	Y	N	Y
2 Swift	N	Y	Y	Y	N	Y
3 Unsoeld	N	Y	Y	Y	N	Y
4 Inslee	N	Y	Y	Y	Y	Y
5 Foley						
6 Dicks	N	Y	Y	Y	N	Y
7 McDermott	N	Y	Y	Y	N	Y
8 ***Dunn***	Y	N	N	N	Y	Y
9 Kreidler	N	Y	Y	Y	N	Y
WEST VIRGINIA						
1 Mollohan	N	Y	Y	Y	N	Y
2 Wise	N	Y	Y	Y	N	Y
3 Rahall	N	Y	Y	Y	N	Y
WISCONSIN						
1 Barca	N	Y	Y	Y	Y	Y
2 ***Klug***	N	Y	Y	N	Y	Y
3 ***Gunderson***	Y	N	Y	N	Y	Y
4 Kleczka	N	Y	Y	Y	N	Y
5 Barrett	N	Y	Y	Y	Y	Y
6 ***Petri***	Y	N	N	N	Y	N
7 Obey	N	Y	Y	Y	N	Y
8 ***Roth***	Y	N	N	N	Y	Y
9 ***Sensenbrenner***	Y	N	N	N	Y	N
WYOMING						
AL ***Thomas***	Y	N	N	N	Y	Y
DELEGATES						
de Lugo, V.I.	N	D	D	D	D	D
Faleomavaega, Am.S.	N	D	D	D	D	D
Norton, D.C.	—	D	D	D	D	D
Romero-B., P.R.	N	D	D	D	D	D
Underwood, Guam	N	D	D	D	D	D

Southern states - Ala., Ark., Fla., Ga., Ky., La., Miss., N.C., Okla., S.C., Tenn., Texas, Va.
Omitted votes are quorum calls, which CQ does not include in its vote charts.

438. HR 4554. Fiscal 1995 Agriculture Appropriations/ Conference Report. Adoption of the conference report to provide $69,097,365,000 in new budget authority for agriculture, rural development, the Food and Drug Administration, and related agencies' programs for fiscal 1995. The administration had requested $68,428,191,000. Adopted (thus sent to the Senate) 287-107: R 61-105; D 225-2 (ND 151-2, SD 74-0); I 1-0, Sept. 23, 1994.

439. HR 4448. Lowell Historical Park/Authorization Cut. Allard, R-Colo., amendment to increase the authorization for the Lowell National Historical Park Commission from $34 million to $39 million, rather than the $44 million level recommended in the bill. Rejected in the Committee of the Whole 165-215: R 149-8; D 16-206 (ND 9-142, SD 7-64); I 0-1, Sept. 26, 1994.

440. HR 4448. Lowell Historical Park/Passage. Passage of the bill to extend the Lowell National Historical Park Commission for five years and increase its authorization from $34 million to $44 million. Passed 237-145: R 26-135; D 210-10 (ND 141-7, SD 69-3); I 1-0, Sept. 26, 1994.

441. HR 4539. Fiscal 1995 Treasury-Postal Appropriations/Conference Report. Adoption of the conference report to provide $23,454,806,000 in new budget authority for the Treasury Department, the U.S. Postal Service, the Executive Office of the President and certain independent agencies in fiscal 1995. The administration had requested $24,571,817,000. After being recommitted on Sept. 22, the conference report was amended to place a $119 million cap on Internal Revenue Service user fees and to cut $157 million from federal courthouse and office building construction (see vote 436). Adopted (thus sent to the Senate) 360-53: R 129-43; D 230-10 (ND 156-8, SD 74-2); I 1-0, Sept. 27, 1994.

442. HR 5044. American Heritage Areas Partnership Program/Passage. Vento, D-Minn., motion to suspend the rules and pass the bill to establish procedures within the Interior Department for designating and managing national heritage areas to preserve natural, historic and cultural resources. The bill also designates 10 areas as American Heritage Areas and provides for the study of other areas for possible designation. Motion rejected 273-150: R 62-112; D 210-38 (ND 158-9, SD 52-29); I 1-0, Sept. 27, 1994. A two-thirds majority of those present and voting (282 in this case) is required for passage under suspension of the rules.

443. HR 4779. Interstate Solid Waste Control/Passage. Passage of the bill to authorize state and local governments to restrict the receipt of out-of-state waste. Passed 368-55: R 145-28; D 222-27 (ND 142-26, SD 80-1); I 1-0, Sept. 28, 1994.

444. HR 4476. National Park System Planning/Passage. Vento, D-Minn., motion to suspend the rules and pass the bill to require within three years the Interior Department to establish a plan for the management and expansion of the National Park System by the National Park Service with congressional approval. The bill also would require a review of areas for possible inclusion in or removal from the system. Motion agreed to 421-0: R 172-0; D 248-0 (ND 168-0, SD 80-0); I 1-0, Sept. 28, 1994. A two-thirds majority of those present and voting (281 in this case) is required for passage under suspension of the rules.

445. HR 3171. Agriculture Department Reorganization/ Agricultural Service Agency. Allard, R-Colo., amendment to eliminate the Agricultural Service Agency, which the bill would establish by consolidating the Agricultural Stabilization and Conservation Service, which manages crop subsidy programs, with the Federal Crop Insurance Corporation and the Farmers Home Administration. Rejected in the Committee of the Whole 177-247: R 171-3; D 6-243 (ND 4-166, SD 2-77); I 0-1, Sept. 28, 1994.

	438	439	440	441	442	443	444	445
ALABAMA								
1 *Callahan*	Y	?	?	Y	N	Y	Y	Y
2 *Everett*	Y	Y	N	Y	N	Y	Y	Y
3 Browder	Y	N	Y	N	Y	Y	Y	N
4 Bevill	Y	N	Y	Y	Y	Y	Y	N
5 Cramer	Y	N	Y	N	Y	Y	Y	N
6 *Bachus*	N	Y	N	Y	N	Y	Y	Y
7 Hilliard	Y	N	Y	N	Y	Y	Y	N
ALASKA								
AL *Young*	Y	Y	N	Y	N	Y	Y	Y
ARIZONA								
1 Coppersmith	Y	N	Y	Y	Y	Y	Y	N
2 Pastor	Y	N	Y	Y	Y	Y	Y	N
3 *Stump*	N	Y	N	N	N	Y	Y	Y
4 *Kyl*	N	?	?	Y	N	Y	Y	Y
5 *Kolbe*	?	Y	N	Y	Y	Y	Y	Y
6 English	Y	?	#	+	Y	Y	Y	N
ARKANSAS								
1 Lambert	Y	Y	Y	Y	Y	Y	Y	N
2 Thornton	Y	N	Y	Y	Y	Y	Y	N
3 *Hutchinson*	N	Y	N	Y	N	Y	Y	Y
4 *Dickey*	N	Y	N	Y	N	Y	Y	Y
CALIFORNIA								
1 Hamburg	Y	N	Y	Y	Y	Y	Y	N
2 *Herger*	X	Y	N	Y	N	Y	Y	Y
3 Fazio	Y	N	Y	Y	#	Y	Y	N
4 *Doolittle*	N	Y	N	Y	N	Y	Y	Y
5 Matsui	?	N	Y	Y	Y	Y	Y	N
6 Woolsey	Y	N	Y	Y	Y	Y	Y	N
7 Miller	Y	N	Y	Y	Y	Y	Y	N
8 Pelosi	Y	N	Y	Y	Y	?	Y	N
9 *Dellums*	#	N	Y	Y	Y	Y	Y	N
10 *Baker*	N	Y	N	Y	N	N	Y	Y
11 *Pombo*	N	Y	N	Y	N	Y	Y	Y
12 Lantos	?	N	Y	?	Y	Y	Y	N
13 Stark	?	N	Y	Y	Y	Y	Y	N
14 Eshoo	Y	N	Y	Y	Y	Y	Y	N
15 Mineta	Y	X	?	Y	Y	Y	Y	N
16 Edwards	Y	?	?	Y	Y	Y	Y	N
17 Farr	Y	N	Y	Y	Y	Y	Y	N
18 Condit	Y	N	N	Y	Y	Y	Y	N
19 Lehman	Y	N	Y	Y	N	Y	Y	N
20 Dooley	?	N	Y	Y	Y	Y	Y	N
21 *Thomas*	Y	#	X	Y	N	Y	Y	Y
22 *Huffington*	N	?	?	Y	N	Y	Y	Y
23 *Gallegly*	+	?	?	Y	N	Y	Y	Y
24 Beilenson	Y	N	Y	?	Y	Y	Y	N
25 *McKeon*	X	Y	N	Y	N	Y	Y	Y
26 Berman	?	N	Y	Y	Y	Y	Y	N
27 *Moorhead*	N	Y	N	Y	N	Y	Y	Y
28 *Dreier*	N	Y	N	N	N	Y	Y	Y
29 Waxman	Y	N	Y	Y	Y	Y	Y	N
30 Becerra	Y	N	Y	Y	Y	Y	Y	N
31 Martinez	Y	N	Y	Y	Y	Y	Y	N
32 Dixon	Y	N	Y	Y	Y	Y	Y	N
33 Roybal-Allard	Y	N	Y	Y	Y	Y	Y	N
34 Torres	Y	N	Y	Y	Y	Y	Y	N
35 Waters	Y	N	Y	Y	Y	Y	Y	N
36 Harman	Y	?	?	Y	Y	Y	Y	N
37 Tucker	Y	N	Y	Y	Y	Y	Y	N
38 *Horn*	Y	Y	Y	Y	Y	Y	Y	Y
39 *Royce*	N	Y	N	N	N	Y	Y	Y
40 *Lewis*	Y	Y	Y	Y	Y	Y	Y	Y
41 *Kim*	N	Y	N	Y	N	Y	Y	Y

	438	439	440	441	442	443	444	445
42 Brown	Y	N	Y	Y	Y	Y	Y	N
43 *Calvert*	?	?	?	Y	N	Y	Y	Y
44 *McCandless*	N	Y	Y	Y	Y	Y	Y	Y
45 *Rohrabacher*	N	Y	N	N	N	Y	Y	Y
46 *Dornan*	N	#	X	N	Y	N	Y	Y
47 *Cox*	N	Y	N	N	N	Y	Y	Y
48 *Packard*	N	Y	N	N	Y	Y	Y	Y
49 Schenk	Y	N	Y	Y	Y	Y	Y	N
50 Filner	Y	N	Y	Y	Y	Y	Y	N
51 *Cunningham*	N	Y	N	Y	N	Y	Y	Y
52 *Hunter*	Y	Y	N	N	N	Y	Y	Y
COLORADO								
1 Schroeder	Y	N	Y	Y	Y	Y	Y	N
2 Skaggs	Y	N	Y	Y	Y	Y	Y	N
3 *McInnis*	N	?	N	Y	Y	Y	Y	Y
4 *Allard*	N	Y	N	Y	N	Y	Y	Y
5 *Hefley*	N	Y	N	Y	N	Y	Y	Y
6 *Schaefer*	N	Y	N	N	N	Y	Y	Y
CONNECTICUT								
1 Kennelly	Y	N	Y	Y	Y	Y	Y	N
2 Gejdenson	Y	N	Y	Y	Y	Y	Y	N
3 DeLauro	Y	N	Y	Y	Y	Y	Y	N
4 *Shays*	N	Y	N	N	Y	Y	Y	Y
5 *Franks*	Y	Y	Y	Y	Y	Y	Y	Y
6 *Johnson*	?	Y	N	Y	Y	Y	?	Y
DELAWARE								
AL *Castle*	N	Y	Y	N	Y	Y	Y	Y
FLORIDA								
1 Hutto	Y	Y	Y	Y	Y	Y	Y	N
2 Peterson	Y	N	Y	Y	Y	Y	Y	N
3 Brown	Y	N	Y	Y	Y	Y	Y	N
4 *Fowler*	N	Y	N	Y	N	Y	Y	Y
5 Thurman	Y	N	Y	Y	Y	Y	Y	N
6 *Stearns*	N	+	N	Y	N	Y	Y	Y
7 *Mica*	N	Y	N	Y	N	Y	Y	Y
8 *McCollum*	N	Y	N	N	Y	Y	Y	Y
9 *Bilirakis*	Y	Y	Y	N	N	Y	Y	Y
10 *Young*	Y	Y	N	Y	Y	Y	Y	Y
11 Gibbons	Y	N	Y	Y	Y	Y	Y	N
12 *Canady*	N	Y	N	Y	N	Y	Y	Y
13 *Miller*	N	Y	N	N	N	Y	Y	Y
14 *Goss*	N	Y	N	N	N	Y	Y	Y
15 Bacchus	Y	N	Y	Y	Y	Y	Y	N
16 *Lewis*	Y	Y	N	N	N	+	Y	Y
17 Meek	Y	N	Y	Y	Y	Y	Y	N
18 *Ros-Lehtinen*	Y	?	?	Y	Y	Y	Y	Y
19 Johnston	Y	?	?	Y	Y	Y	Y	?
20 Deutsch	Y	N	Y	Y	Y	Y	Y	N
21 *Diaz-Balart*	Y	Y	N	Y	Y	Y	Y	Y
22 *Shaw*	N	Y	N	Y	Y	Y	Y	Y
23 Hastings	Y	N	Y	Y	Y	Y	Y	N
GEORGIA								
1 *Kingston*	N	Y	N	Y	N	Y	Y	Y
2 Bishop	Y	N	Y	Y	Y	Y	Y	N
3 *Collins*	Y	Y	N	Y	N	Y	Y	Y
4 *Linder*	Y	Y	N	Y	N	Y	Y	Y
5 Lewis	?	N	Y	Y	Y	Y	Y	N
6 *Gingrich*	N	?	?	Y	N	Y	Y	Y
7 Darden	Y	?	?	Y	Y	Y	Y	N
8 Rowland	Y	N	Y	Y	Y	Y	Y	N
9 Deal	Y	N	Y	Y	Y	Y	Y	N
10 Johnson	Y	N	Y	Y	Y	Y	Y	N
11 McKinney	Y	N	Y	Y	Y	Y	Y	N
HAWAII								
1 Abercrombie	Y	N	Y	Y	Y	Y	Y	N
2 Mink	Y	N	Y	Y	Y	Y	Y	N
IDAHO								
1 LaRocco	Y	N	Y	Y	Y	Y	Y	N
2 *Crapo*	N	Y	N	Y	N	Y	Y	Y
ILLINOIS								
1 Rush	Y	N	Y	Y	Y	Y	Y	N
2 Reynolds	Y	N	Y	Y	Y	N	Y	N
3 Lipinski	Y	N	Y	Y	Y	Y	Y	N
4 Gutierrez	Y	N	Y	Y	Y	Y	Y	N
5 Rostenkowski	Y	?	?	Y	Y	Y	Y	N
6 *Hyde*	Y	Y	N	Y	Y	Y	Y	Y
7 Collins	Y	X	?	Y	Y	Y	Y	N
8 *Crane*	N	Y	N	N	N	N	Y	Y
9 Yates	Y	N	Y	Y	Y	Y	Y	N
10 *Porter*	N	Y	Y	Y	Y	Y	Y	Y
11 Sangmeister	Y	N	Y	Y	Y	Y	Y	?
12 Costello	Y	N	Y	Y	Y	Y	Y	N
13 *Fawell*	N	Y	N	N	Y	Y	Y	Y
14 *Hastert*	Y	Y	N	N	N	Y	Y	Y
15 *Ewing*	Y	Y	N	N	N	Y	Y	Y
16 *Manzullo*	N	Y	N	N	N	N	Y	Y
17 Evans	Y	N	Y	Y	Y	Y	Y	N

ND Northern Democrats   SD Southern Democrats

	438	439	440	441	442	443	444	445
18 ***Michel***	Y	Y	N	Y	Y	Y	Y	Y
19 Poshard	Y	Y	N	Y	Y	Y	Y	N
20 Durbin	Y	N	Y	Y	Y	Y	Y	N
INDIANA								
1 Visclosky	Y	N	Y	Y	Y	Y	Y	N
2 Sharp	Y	?	?	Y	Y	Y	Y	N
3 Roemer	Y	N	Y	Y	Y	Y	Y	N
4 Long	Y	Y	Y	Y	Y	Y	Y	N
5 ***Buyer***	N	Y	N	Y	N	Y	Y	Y
6 ***Burton***	N	Y	N	N	N	Y	Y	Y
7 ***Myers***	N	Y	N	N	Y	Y	Y	Y
8 McCloskey	Y	N	Y	Y	Y	Y	Y	N
9 Hamilton	Y	N	Y	Y	Y	Y	Y	N
10 Jacobs	N	Y	N	N	Y	Y	Y	N
IOWA								
1 ***Leach***	Y	Y	N	Y	N	Y	Y	Y
2 ***Nussle***	Y	Y	N	Y	N	Y	Y	Y
3 ***Lightfoot***	Y	Y	N	Y	N	Y	Y	Y
4 Smith	Y	?	?	?	N	Y	Y	N
5 ***Grandy***	N	Y	N	Y	N	Y	Y	?
KANSAS								
1 ***Roberts***	N	Y	N	Y	N	Y	Y	Y
2 Slattery	?	?	?	?	?	?	?	?
3 ***Meyers***	N	Y	N	N	Y	Y	Y	Y
4 Glickman	?	N	Y	Y	Y	Y	Y	N
KENTUCKY								
1 Barlow	Y	N	Y	Y	Y	Y	Y	N
2 ***Lewis***	N	Y	N	Y	N	Y	Y	Y
3 Mazzoli	Y	N	Y	Y	Y	Y	Y	N
4 ***Bunning***	N	Y	N	Y	N	Y	Y	Y
5 ***Rogers***	Y	Y	N	Y	N	Y	Y	Y
6 Baesler	Y	N	Y	Y	Y	Y	Y	N
LOUISIANA								
1 ***Livingston***	Y	Y	N	N	Y	Y	Y	Y
2 Jefferson	Y	N	Y	Y	Y	Y	Y	N
3 Tauzin	Y	Y	Y	?	N	Y	Y	N
4 Fields	Y	N	Y	Y	Y	Y	Y	N
5 ***McCrery***	Y	Y	Y	Y	Y	Y	Y	Y
6 ***Baker***	?	?	?	N	N	Y	Y	Y
7 Hayes	?	N	Y	Y	N	Y	?	N
MAINE								
1 Andrews	Y	?	?	Y	Y	Y	Y	N
2 ***Snowe***	Y	Y	N	Y	N	Y	Y	N
MARYLAND								
1 ***Gilchrest***	N	Y	N	Y	Y	Y	Y	Y
2 ***Bentley***	Y	Y	N	Y	N	Y	Y	Y
3 Cardin	Y	N	Y	Y	Y	Y	Y	N
4 Wynn	Y	N	Y	Y	Y	Y	Y	N
5 Hoyer	Y	N	Y	Y	Y	Y	Y	N
6 ***Bartlett***	N	Y	N	Y	N	Y	Y	Y
7 Mfume	Y	N	Y	+	Y	Y	Y	N
8 ***Morella***	Y	N	Y	Y	Y	Y	Y	N
MASSACHUSETTS								
1 Olver	Y	N	Y	Y	Y	Y	Y	N
2 Neal	Y	?	?	Y	Y	Y	Y	N
3 ***Blute***	Y	?	?	Y	Y	Y	Y	Y
4 Frank	?	N	Y	Y	Y	N	Y	N
5 Meehan	Y	N	Y	Y	Y	Y	Y	N
6 ***Torkildsen***	N	N	Y	Y	Y	Y	Y	Y
7 Markey	Y	N	Y	Y	Y	Y	?	N
8 Kennedy	Y	N	Y	Y	Y	Y	Y	N
9 Moakley	Y	N	Y	Y	Y	Y	Y	N
10 Studds	Y	N	Y	Y	Y	Y	Y	N
MICHIGAN								
1 Stupak	Y	N	Y	Y	N	Y	Y	N
2 ***Hoekstra***	N	Y	N	N	N	Y	Y	Y
3 ***Ehlers***	N	Y	N	N	N	Y	Y	Y
4 ***Camp***	Y	Y	N	N	N	Y	Y	Y
5 Barcia	Y	Y	N	Y	N	Y	Y	N
6 ***Upton***	Y	Y	N	N	N	Y	Y	Y
7 ***Smith***	N	?	N	N	N	Y	Y	Y
8 Carr	?	?	?	Y	?	Y	Y	Y
9 Kildee	Y	N	Y	Y	Y	Y	Y	N
10 Bonior	?	N	Y	Y	Y	Y	Y	N
11 ***Knollenberg***	N	Y	N	Y	N	Y	Y	Y
12 Levin	Y	N	Y	Y	Y	Y	Y	N
13 Ford	Y	N	Y	Y	Y	Y	Y	?
14 Conyers	Y	N	Y	Y	Y	Y	Y	N
15 Collins	Y	N	Y	Y	Y	Y	Y	N
16 Dingell	Y	?	#	Y	Y	Y	Y	N
MINNESOTA								
1 Penny	Y	N	Y	N	Y	Y	Y	N
2 Minge	Y	Y	N	N	Y	Y	Y	N
3 ***Ramstad***	N	Y	N	N	N	Y	Y	Y
4 Vento	Y	N	Y	Y	Y	Y	Y	N

	438	439	440	441	442	443	444	445
5 Sabo	Y	N	Y	Y	Y	Y	Y	N
6 ***Grams***	N	Y	N	Y	N	Y	Y	Y
7 Peterson	Y	Y	Y	N	Y	Y	Y	N
8 Oberstar	Y	?	?	Y	Y	Y	Y	N
MISSISSIPPI								
1 Whitten	Y	?	?	Y	Y	Y	Y	N
2 Thompson	Y	N	Y	Y	Y	Y	Y	N
3 Montgomery	Y	N	Y	Y	Y	Y	Y	N
4 Parker	Y	N	Y	N	N	Y	Y	N
5 Taylor	Y	Y	N	N	N	Y	Y	N
MISSOURI								
1 Clay	?	N	Y	Y	Y	Y	Y	N
2 ***Talent***	N	Y	N	Y	N	Y	Y	Y
3 Gephardt	Y	N	Y	Y	Y	Y	Y	N
4 Skelton	Y	N	Y	Y	N	Y	Y	N
5 Wheat	?	?	?	?	?	?	?	?
6 Danner	Y	N	Y	Y	N	Y	Y	N
7 ***Hancock***	N	Y	N	N	N	Y	Y	Y
8 ***Emerson***	Y	Y	N	Y	N	Y	Y	Y
9 Volkmer	Y	Y	Y	Y	N	Y	Y	N
MONTANA								
AL Williams	Y	N	Y	Y	Y	Y	Y	N
NEBRASKA								
1 ***Bereuter***	Y	Y	N	Y	Y	Y	Y	Y
2 Hoagland	Y	N	Y	Y	Y	Y	Y	N
3 ***Barrett***	Y	Y	N	Y	N	Y	Y	Y
NEVADA								
1 Bilbray	Y	N	Y	Y	Y	Y	Y	N
2 ***Vucanovich***	Y	Y	N	Y	Y	Y	Y	Y
NEW HAMPSHIRE								
1 ***Zeliff***	N	N	Y	Y	N	N	Y	Y
2 Swett	Y	N	Y	N	Y	Y	Y	N
NEW JERSEY								
1 Andrews	Y	Y	N	N	N	Y	Y	N
2 Hughes	Y	N	Y	Y	Y	N	Y	N
3 ***Saxton***	N	Y	N	Y	N	N	Y	Y
4 ***Smith***	Y	Y	Y	N	Y	N	Y	Y
5 ***Roukema***	N	Y	Y	Y	Y	N	Y	Y
6 Pallone	Y	N	Y	N	Y	N	Y	N
7 ***Franks***	N	N	Y	Y	Y	N	Y	Y
8 Klein	Y	N	Y	Y	Y	N	Y	N
9 Torricelli	Y	N	Y	Y	Y	N	Y	N
10 Payne	Y	?	?	?	Y	N	Y	N
11 ***Gallo***	?	?	?	?	?	?	?	?
12 ***Zimmer***	N	Y	N	N	Y	N	Y	Y
13 Menendez	Y	N	Y	Y	Y	N	Y	N
NEW MEXICO								
1 ***Schiff***	Y	Y	N	Y	N	Y	Y	Y
2 ***Skeen***	Y	Y	N	Y	Y	Y	Y	Y
3 Richardson	Y	N	Y	Y	Y	Y	Y	N
NEW YORK								
1 Hochbrueckner	Y	N	Y	Y	Y	N	Y	N
2 ***Lazio***	N	Y	N	Y	Y	N	Y	Y
3 ***King***	N	N	Y	Y	N	N	Y	Y
4 ***Levy***	N	Y	N	Y	Y	N	Y	Y
5 Ackerman	Y	N	Y	Y	Y	N	Y	N
6 Flake	Y	?	?	Y	Y	N	Y	N
7 Manton	?	N	Y	Y	Y	N	Y	N
8 Nadler	Y	?	?	Y	Y	N	Y	N
9 Schumer	Y	N	Y	Y	Y	N	Y	N
10 Towns	Y	N	Y	Y	Y	N	Y	N
11 Owens	Y	?	?	Y	Y	N	Y	N
12 Velazquez	Y	N	Y	Y	Y	N	Y	N
13 ***Molinari***	N	Y	N	Y	N	N	Y	Y
14 Maloney	Y	N	Y	Y	Y	N	Y	N
15 Rangel	?	N	Y	Y	Y	N	Y	N
16 Serrano	Y	N	Y	Y	Y	N	Y	N
17 Engel	Y	N	Y	N	Y	N	Y	N
18 Lowey	Y	N	Y	Y	Y	N	Y	N
19 ***Fish***	Y	Y	Y	Y	Y	N	Y	Y
20 ***Gilman***	Y	Y	Y	Y	Y	N	Y	Y
21 McNulty	Y	N	Y	Y	Y	?	?	?
22 ***Solomon***	N	Y	N	Y	N	N	Y	Y
23 ***Boehlert***	Y	Y	Y	Y	Y	N	Y	Y
24 ***McHugh***	N	Y	N	Y	N	N	Y	Y
25 ***Walsh***	Y	Y	N	Y	Y	N	Y	Y
26 Hinchey	?	N	Y	Y	Y	N	Y	N
27 ***Paxon***	N	N	N	N	N	N	Y	Y
28 Slaughter	Y	N	Y	Y	Y	N	Y	N
29 LaFalce	Y	N	Y	Y	Y	N	Y	Y
30 ***Quinn***	N	N	Y	Y	N	N	Y	Y
31 ***Houghton***	Y	?	?	Y	N	N	?	Y
NORTH CAROLINA								
1 Clayton	Y	N	Y	Y	Y	Y	Y	N
2 Valentine	Y	N	Y	Y	Y	Y	Y	N

	438	439	440	441	442	443	444	445
3 Lancaster	Y	N	Y	Y	N	Y	Y	N
4 Price	Y	N	Y	Y	Y	Y	Y	N
5 Neal	Y	?	?	Y	Y	Y	Y	N
6 ***Coble***	N	Y	N	Y	N	Y	Y	Y
7 Rose	Y	N	Y	Y	Y	Y	Y	N
8 Hefner	Y	N	Y	Y	Y	Y	Y	N
9 ***McMillan***	Y	Y	Y	Y	Y	?	?	Y
10 ***Ballenger***	N	Y	N	N	N	Y	Y	Y
11 ***Taylor***	N	+	N	N	N	Y	Y	Y
12 Watt	Y	N	Y	Y	Y	Y	Y	N
NORTH DAKOTA								
AL Pomeroy	Y	N	Y	Y	Y	Y	Y	N
OHIO								
1 Mann	Y	N	Y	Y	Y	Y	Y	N
2 ***Portman***	N	Y	N	Y	Y	Y	Y	Y
3 Hall	Y	?	?	Y	Y	Y	Y	N
4 ***Oxley***	N	Y	N	N	Y	Y	Y	Y
5 ***Gillmor***	Y	N	Y	Y	Y	Y	Y	Y
6 Strickland	Y	N	Y	Y	Y	Y	Y	N
7 ***Hobson***	N	Y	N	Y	Y	Y	Y	Y
8 ***Boehner***	N	Y	N	N	N	Y	Y	Y
9 Kaptur	Y	N	Y	Y	Y	Y	Y	N
10 ***Hoke***	N	Y	N	Y	Y	Y	Y	Y
11 Stokes	Y	N	Y	Y	Y	Y	Y	N
12 ***Kasich***	N	Y	N	Y	Y	Y	Y	Y
13 Brown	Y	N	Y	Y	Y	Y	Y	N
14 Sawyer	Y	N	Y	Y	Y	Y	Y	N
15 ***Pryce***	N	Y	N	Y	Y	Y	Y	Y
16 ***Regula***	Y	Y	Y	Y	Y	Y	Y	Y
17 Traficant	Y	N	Y	Y	Y	Y	Y	N
18 Applegate	?	N	Y	Y	Y	Y	Y	?
19 Fingerhut	N	N	Y	Y	Y	Y	Y	N
OKLAHOMA								
1 ***Inhofe***	?	?	?	?	?	?	?	?
2 Synar	Y	N	Y	Y	Y	Y	Y	N
3 Brewster	Y	N	Y	Y	N	Y	Y	N
4 McCurdy	?	?	?	Y	N	Y	Y	N
5 ***Istook***	N	Y	N	Y	N	Y	Y	Y
6 ***Lucas***	Y	Y	N	Y	N	Y	Y	Y
OREGON								
1 Furse	Y	N	Y	Y	Y	Y	Y	N
2 ***Smith***	N	Y	N	Y	N	Y	Y	Y
3 Wyden	Y	?	?	Y	Y	Y	Y	N
4 DeFazio	Y	N	Y	Y	Y	Y	Y	N
5 Kopetski	Y	N	Y	Y	Y	Y	Y	N
PENNSYLVANIA								
1 Foglietta	Y	N	Y	Y	Y	Y	Y	N
2 Blackwell	?	?	?	Y	Y	Y	Y	N
3 Borski	Y	N	Y	Y	Y	Y	Y	N
4 Klink	Y	N	Y	Y	Y	Y	Y	N
5 ***Clinger***	N	Y	N	Y	Y	Y	Y	Y
6 Holden	Y	N	Y	Y	Y	Y	Y	N
7 ***Weldon***	N	Y	Y	?	N	Y	Y	Y
8 ***Greenwood***	Y	Y	N	Y	Y	Y	Y	Y
9 ***Shuster***	N	Y	N	Y	Y	Y	Y	Y
10 ***McDade***	Y	Y	Y	Y	Y	Y	Y	Y
11 Kanjorski	Y	N	Y	Y	Y	Y	Y	N
12 Murtha	Y	N	Y	Y	Y	Y	Y	N
13 Margolies-Mezv.	Y	N	Y	Y	Y	Y	Y	N
14 Coyne	Y	N	Y	Y	Y	Y	Y	N
15 McHale	Y	N	Y	Y	Y	Y	Y	N
16 ***Walker***	N	Y	N	Y	N	Y	Y	Y
17 ***Gekas***	Y	Y	N	+	N	Y	Y	Y
18 ***Santorum***	Y	Y	N	Y	Y	Y	Y	Y
19 ***Goodling***	N	Y	N	Y	N	Y	Y	Y
20 Murphy	?	N	Y	Y	Y	Y	Y	N
21 ***Ridge***	Y	?	?	Y	N	Y	Y	Y
RHODE ISLAND								
1 ***Machtley***	?	Y	Y	Y	Y	Y	Y	Y
2 Reed	Y	N	Y	Y	Y	Y	Y	N
SOUTH CAROLINA								
1 ***Ravenel***	Y	Y	N	Y	Y	Y	Y	Y
2 ***Spence***	N	Y	N	Y	Y	Y	Y	Y
3 Derrick	Y	?	?	?	Y	Y	Y	N
4 ***Inglis***	N	Y	N	Y	N	Y	Y	Y
5 Spratt	Y	N	Y	Y	Y	Y	Y	N
6 Clyburn	Y	N	Y	Y	Y	Y	Y	N
SOUTH DAKOTA								
AL Johnson	Y	N	Y	Y	Y	Y	Y	N
TENNESSEE								
1 ***Quillen***	?	Y	Y	Y	Y	Y	Y	Y
2 ***Duncan***	N	Y	N	N	N	Y	Y	Y
3 Lloyd	?	N	Y	Y	Y	?	?	?
4 Cooper	?	?	?	Y	N	Y	Y	Y
5 Clement	Y	N	Y	Y	Y	Y	Y	N

	438	439	440	441	442	443	444	445
6 Gordon	Y	N	Y	Y	Y	Y	Y	N
7 ***Sundquist***	?	?	?	?	?	?	?	?
8 Tanner	?	N	Y	Y	Y	Y	Y	Y
9 Ford	Y	?	?	?	?	Y	Y	N
TEXAS								
1 Chapman	Y	N	Y	Y	N	Y	Y	N
2 Wilson	Y	?	?	Y	N	Y	Y	N
3 ***Johnson, Sam***	N	Y	N	N	N	Y	Y	Y
4 Hall	Y	Y	N	Y	N	Y	Y	N
5 Bryant	Y	N	Y	Y	Y	Y	Y	N
6 ***Barton***	Y	Y	N	Y	N	Y	Y	Y
7 ***Archer***	N	Y	N	N	N	Y	Y	Y
8 ***Fields***	N	Y	N	Y	N	Y	Y	Y
9 Brooks	Y	N	Y	Y	Y	Y	Y	?
10 Pickle	Y	N	Y	Y	Y	Y	Y	N
11 Edwards	Y	N	Y	Y	N	Y	Y	N
12 Geren	Y	N	Y	Y	N	Y	Y	N
13 Sarpalius	Y	Y	Y	Y	N	Y	Y	N
14 Laughlin	Y	?	?	Y	N	Y	Y	N
15 de la Garza	Y	N	Y	Y	N	Y	Y	N
16 Coleman	Y	N	Y	Y	Y	N	Y	N
17 Stenholm	Y	Y	N	Y	N	Y	Y	N
18 Washington	?	?	?	?	?	?	?	?
19 ***Combest***	Y	Y	N	Y	N	Y	Y	Y
20 Gonzalez	Y	N	Y	Y	Y	Y	Y	N
21 ***Smith***	Y	Y	N	Y	N	Y	Y	Y
22 ***DeLay***	N	Y	N	N	N	Y	Y	Y
23 ***Bonilla***	Y	Y	N	Y	N	Y	Y	Y
24 Frost	Y	?	Y	Y	N	Y	Y	N
25 Andrews	Y	N	Y	?	Y	Y	Y	N
26 ***Armey***	N	Y	N	N	X	N	Y	Y
27 Ortiz	Y	N	Y	Y	N	Y	Y	N
28 Tejeda	Y	N	Y	Y	N	Y	Y	N
29 Green	Y	N	Y	Y	N	Y	Y	N
30 Johnson, E.B.	Y	N	Y	Y	Y	Y	Y	N
UTAH								
1 ***Hansen***	N	Y	N	Y	Y	Y	Y	Y
2 Shepherd	Y	N	Y	Y	Y	Y	Y	Y
3 Orton	Y	Y	N	Y	N	Y	Y	Y
VERMONT								
AL *Sanders*	Y	N	Y	Y	Y	Y	Y	N
VIRGINIA								
1 ***Bateman***	Y	Y	N	Y	Y	Y	Y	Y
2 Pickett	Y	N	Y	Y	N	Y	Y	N
3 Scott	Y	N	Y	?	Y	Y	Y	N
4 Sisisky	Y	N	Y	Y	N	Y	Y	N
5 Payne	Y	N	Y	Y	N	Y	Y	N
6 ***Goodlatte***	N	Y	N	Y	N	Y	Y	Y
7 ***Bliley***	Y	Y	N	Y	N	Y	Y	Y
8 Moran	?	N	Y	Y	Y	Y	Y	N
9 Boucher	Y	N	Y	Y	Y	Y	Y	N
10 ***Wolf***	Y	Y	N	Y	Y	Y	Y	Y
11 Byrne	#	N	Y	?	Y	Y	Y	N
WASHINGTON								
1 Cantwell	Y	N	Y	Y	Y	Y	Y	N
2 Swift	Y	N	Y	Y	Y	Y	Y	N
3 Unsoeld	Y	N	Y	Y	Y	Y	Y	N
4 Inslee	Y	N	Y	Y	Y	Y	Y	N
5 Foley								
6 Dicks	Y	N	Y	Y	#	Y	Y	N
7 McDermott	Y	N	Y	Y	Y	Y	Y	N
8 ***Dunn***	N	Y	N	Y	N	Y	Y	Y
9 Kreidler	Y	N	Y	Y	Y	Y	Y	N
WEST VIRGINIA								
1 Mollohan	Y	?	?	Y	Y	Y	Y	N
2 Wise	Y	N	Y	Y	Y	Y	Y	N
3 Rahall	Y	?	?	Y	Y	Y	Y	N
WISCONSIN								
1 Barca	Y	N	Y	Y	Y	Y	Y	N
2 ***Klug***	N	?	?	?	N	Y	Y	Y
3 ***Gunderson***	N	Y	Y	Y	N	Y	Y	Y
4 Kleczka	Y	N	Y	Y	Y	Y	Y	N
5 Barrett	Y	N	Y	Y	Y	Y	Y	N
6 ***Petri***	N	Y	N	N	N	Y	Y	Y
7 Obey	Y	N	Y	Y	Y	Y	Y	N
8 ***Roth***	N	Y	N	Y	N	Y	Y	Y
9 ***Sensenbrenner***	N	Y	N	N	N	Y	Y	Y
WYOMING								
AL ***Thomas***	Y	Y	N	Y	N	Y	Y	Y
DELEGATES								
de Lugo, V.I.	D	?	D	D	D	D	D	N
Faleomavaega, Am.S.	D	N	D	D	D	D	D	N
Norton, D.C.	D	N	D	D	D	D	D	N
Romero-B., P.R.	D	?	D	D	D	D	D	N
Underwood, Guam	D	N	D	D	D	D	D	?

Southern states - Ala., Ark., Fla., Ga., Ky., La., Miss., N.C., Okla., S.C., Tenn., Texas, Va.
Omitted votes are quorum calls, which CQ does not include in its vote charts.

KEY

Y Voted for (yea).
Paired for.
+ Announced for.
N Voted against (nay).
X Paired against.
– Announced against.
P Voted "present."
C Voted "present" to avoid possible conflict of interest.
? Did not vote or otherwise make a position known.
D Delegates ineligible to vote.

Democrats *Republicans*
Independent

446. HR 4650. Fiscal 1995 Defense Appropriations/Conference Report. Adoption of the conference report to provide $243,724,188,000 in new budget authority for the Department of Defense for fiscal 1995 and $299,300,000 for fiscal 1994. The administration had requested $244,711,179,000 for fiscal 1995. Adopted (thus sent to the Senate) 327-86: R 107-66; D 220-19 (ND 151-16, SD 69-3); I 0-1, Sept. 29, 1994.

447. Procedural Motion. Approval of the House Journal of Wednesday, Sept. 28. Approved 249-163: R 17-156; D 231-7 (ND 160-5, SD 71-2); I 1-0, Sept. 29,1994.

* 449. S 349. Lobbying Disclosure/Rule. Adoption of the rule (H Res 550) to provide for House floor consideration of the conference report to expand the disclosure of lobbying activities and impose new restrictions on gifts to members of Congress and their staffs. Adopted 216-205: R 5-170; D 210-35 (ND 156-13, SD 54-22); I 1-0, Sept. 29, 1994.

450. S 349. Lobbying Disclosure/Motion to Recommit. Gekas, R-Pa., motion to recommit the bill to the conference committee with instructions to report it back after removing the reporting and registration requirements for grass-roots lobbying. Motion rejected 202-215: R 170-4; D 32-210 (ND 8-159, SD 24-51); I 0-1, Sept. 29, 1994.

451. S 349. Lobbying Disclosure/Conference Report. Adoption of the conference report to expand the disclosure of lobbying activities and impose new restrictions on gifts to members of Congress and their staffs. Adopted (thus sent to the Senate) 306-112: R 82-92; D 223-20 (ND 162-6, SD 61-14); I 1-0, Sept. 29, 1994. A "yea" was a vote in support of the president's position.

452. HR 4683. Municipal Solid Waste Flow Control/Restrictions. Richardson, D-N.M., substitute amendment to place greater restrictions than the bill on the ability of state and local governments to direct the disposal of solid municipal waste to specific waste management facilities. Rejected in the Committee of the Whole 161-244: R 89-79; D 71-165 (ND 44-118, SD 27-47); I 1-0, Sept. 29, 1994.

* Omitted votes are quorum calls, which CQ does not include in its vote charts.

	446	447	449	450	451	452
ALABAMA						
1 *Callahan*	Y	N	N	Y	N	Y
2 *Everett*	Y	Y	N	Y	N	N
3 Browder	Y	Y	Y	N	Y	N
4 Bevill	Y	Y	Y	N	Y	N
5 Cramer	Y	Y	Y	N	Y	Y
6 *Bachus*	N	N	N	Y	N	Y
7 Hilliard	?	?	Y	N	Y	N
ALASKA						
AL *Young*	Y	N	N	Y	N	Y
ARIZONA						
1 Coppersmith	Y	Y	Y	N	Y	Y
2 Pastor	Y	Y	Y	N	Y	Y
3 *Stump*	N	N	N	Y	N	Y
4 *Kyl*	N	N	N	Y	N	Y
5 *Kolbe*	Y	N	N	Y	N	Y
6 English	Y	Y	Y	N	Y	Y
ARKANSAS						
1 Lambert	Y	Y	Y	N	Y	N
2 Thornton	Y	Y	Y	N	Y	N
3 *Hutchinson*	Y	N	N	Y	Y	Y
4 *Dickey*	Y	N	N	Y	N	N
CALIFORNIA						
1 Hamburg	Y	Y	Y	N	Y	N
2 *Herger*	N	N	N	Y	N	N
3 Fazio	Y	Y	Y	N	Y	N
4 *Doolittle*	N	N	N	Y	N	Y
5 Matsui	Y	Y	Y	N	Y	N
6 Woolsey	N	Y	Y	N	Y	N
7 Miller	Y	Y	Y	N	Y	N
8 Pelosi	Y	Y	Y	N	Y	Y
9 Dellums	N	Y	Y	N	Y	N
10 *Baker*	X	N	Y	N	Y	N
11 *Pombo*	Y	Y	N	Y	N	Y
12 Lantos	Y	Y	Y	N	Y	N
13 Stark	Y	Y	Y	N	Y	?
14 Eshoo	Y	Y	Y	N	Y	Y
15 Mineta	Y	Y	Y	N	Y	Y
16 Edwards	N	Y	Y	N	Y	N
17 Farr	Y	Y	Y	N	Y	N
18 Condit	Y	Y	N	Y	N	Y
19 Lehman	Y	Y	N	Y	N	Y
20 Dooley	Y	Y	N	N	N	N
21 *Thomas*	Y	N	N	Y	N	N
22 *Huffington*	N	N	N	Y	Y	Y
23 *Gallegly*	Y	N	N	Y	N	Y
24 Beilenson	Y	Y	Y	N	Y	Y
25 *McKeon*	Y	N	N	Y	N	N
26 Berman	Y	Y	Y	?	Y	Y
27 *Moorhead*	Y	N	N	Y	N	Y
28 *Dreier*	N	N	N	Y	N	Y
29 Waxman	N	Y	Y	N	Y	Y
30 Becerra	N	Y	Y	N	Y	Y
31 Martinez	Y	Y	Y	N	Y	Y
32 Dixon	Y	Y	Y	N	Y	N
33 Roybal-Allard	Y	Y	Y	N	Y	Y
34 Torres	Y	Y	Y	N	Y	Y
35 Waters	Y	Y	Y	N	Y	Y
36 Harman	Y	Y	Y	N	Y	Y
37 Tucker	Y	Y	Y	N	Y	N
38 *Horn*	Y	N	N	Y	N	N
39 *Royce*	N	N	N	Y	N	Y
40 *Lewis*	Y	N	N	Y	N	Y
41 *Kim*	Y	N	N	Y	N	Y

	446	447	449	450	451	452
42 Brown	Y	Y	Y	N	Y	N
43 *Calvert*	Y	N	N	Y	Y	#
44 *McCandless*	Y	N	N	Y	N	N
45 *Rohrabacher*	N	N	N	Y	N	Y
46 *Dornan*	N	N	N	Y	N	N
47 *Cox*	N	N	N	Y	N	Y
48 *Packard*	Y	N	N	Y	N	N
49 Schenk	Y	Y	Y	N	Y	N
50 Filner	Y	Y	Y	N	Y	Y
51 *Cunningham*	Y	N	N	Y	N	Y
52 *Hunter*	Y	N	N	Y	N	Y
COLORADO						
1 Schroeder	Y	N	N	Y	N	N
2 Skaggs	Y	Y	Y	N	Y	N
3 *McInnis*	N	N	N	Y	N	N
4 *Allard*	N	N	N	Y	Y	Y
5 *Hefley*	N	N	N	Y	N	Y
6 *Schaefer*	N	N	N	Y	N	N
CONNECTICUT						
1 Kennelly	Y	Y	Y	N	Y	N
2 Gejdenson	Y	Y	Y	N	Y	N
3 DeLauro	Y	Y	Y	N	Y	N
4 *Shays*	N	N	N	Y	N	Y
5 *Franks*	Y	N	N	Y	Y	N
6 *Johnson*	Y	N	N	Y	Y	N
DELAWARE						
AL *Castle*	Y	N	N	Y	Y	N
FLORIDA						
1 Hutto	?	?	?	?	?	?
2 Peterson	Y	Y	Y	N	Y	N
3 Brown	Y	N	N	N	N	N
4 *Fowler*	Y	N	N	Y	N	Y
5 Thurman	Y	Y	Y	N	Y	N
6 *Stearns*	Y	N	N	Y	N	N
7 *Mica*	Y	N	N	Y	N	N
8 *McCollum*	Y	N	N	Y	N	Y
9 *Bilirakis*	Y	N	N	Y	N	N
10 *Young*	Y	N	N	Y	N	N
11 Gibbons	Y	Y	Y	N	Y	N
12 *Canady*	Y	N	Y	Y	Y	Y
13 *Miller*	N	N	N	Y	N	N
14 *Goss*	N	N	N	Y	N	N
15 Bacchus	?	?	N	Y	N	N
16 *Lewis*	Y	N	N	Y	N	N
17 Meek	Y	Y	N	N	N	N
18 *Ros-Lehtinen*	N	N	N	Y	N	N
19 Johnston	N	Y	Y	N	Y	N
20 Deutsch	Y	Y	Y	N	Y	N
21 *Diaz-Balart*	N	N	N	Y	N	N
22 *Shaw*	Y	N	N	Y	N	N
23 Hastings	Y	Y	Y	N	N	N
GEORGIA						
1 *Kingston*	Y	Y	N	Y	N	Y
2 Bishop	Y	Y	Y	N	Y	Y
3 *Collins*	Y	N	N	Y	N	N
4 *Linder*	N	N	N	Y	Y	N
5 Lewis	Y	Y	Y	N	Y	Y
6 *Gingrich*	Y	N	N	Y	N	Y
7 Darden	Y	Y	Y	N	Y	N
8 Rowland	Y	N	N	N	N	N
9 Deal	Y	Y	N	Y	N	N
10 Johnson	Y	Y	Y	N	Y	N
11 McKinney	Y	Y	Y	N	Y	N
HAWAII						
1 Abercrombie	Y	Y	Y	N	Y	N
2 Mink	Y	Y	Y	N	Y	N
IDAHO						
1 LaRocco	Y	Y	Y	N	Y	N
2 *Crapo*	N	N	N	Y	Y	Y
ILLINOIS						
1 Rush	Y	Y	Y	N	N	N
2 Reynolds	Y	Y	Y	N	Y	N
3 Lipinski	Y	Y	Y	N	Y	N
4 Gutierrez	Y	Y	Y	N	Y	N
5 Rostenkowski	Y	Y	N	N	Y	N
6 *Hyde*	Y	N	N	Y	Y	Y
7 Collins	N	N	N	Y	N	N
8 *Crane*	N	N	N	Y	N	Y
9 Yates	Y	Y	Y	N	Y	?
10 *Porter*	Y	N	N	Y	Y	Y
11 Sangmeister	Y	Y	Y	N	Y	N
12 Costello	Y	Y	Y	N	Y	N
13 *Fawell*	Y	N	N	Y	Y	Y
14 *Hastert*	Y	N	N	Y	N	N
15 *Ewing*	Y	N	N	Y	Y	Y
16 *Manzullo*	Y	N	N	Y	N	Y
17 Evans	Y	Y	Y	N	Y	N

ND Northern Democrats   SD Southern Democrats

	446	447	449	450	451	452
18 ***Michel***	Y	N	N	Y	N	Y
19 Poshard	Y	Y	Y	Y	Y	Y
20 Durbin	Y	Y	Y	N	Y	N
INDIANA						
1 Visclosky	Y	Y	Y	N	Y	N
2 Sharp	Y	Y	Y	N	Y	N
3 Roemer	Y	Y	Y	N	Y	N
4 Long	Y	Y	Y	N	Y	N
5 ***Buyer***	N	N	N	Y	N	N
6 ***Burton***	N	N	N	Y	N	N
7 ***Myers***	N	Y	N	Y	N	N
8 McCloskey	Y	Y	Y	N	Y	N
9 Hamilton	Y	Y	Y	N	Y	N
10 Jacobs	Y	N	Y	N	Y	N
IOWA						
1 ***Leach***	Y	N	N	Y	Y	Y
2 ***Nussle***	N	N	N	Y	Y	Y
3 ***Lightfoot***	Y	N	N	Y	Y	Y
4 Smith	?	Y	Y	Y	Y	N
5 ***Grandy***	Y	N	N	Y	N	Y
KANSAS						
1 ***Roberts***	N	N	N	Y	N	Y
2 Slattery	?	?	?	?	?	?
3 ***Meyers***	N	N	N	Y	Y	N
4 Glickman	Y	Y	Y	N	Y	Y
KENTUCKY						
1 Barlow	Y	Y	Y	N	Y	N
2 ***Lewis***	Y	N	N	Y	Y	N
3 Mazzoli	Y	Y	Y	N	Y	N
4 ***Bunning***	N	N	N	Y	N	Y
5 ***Rogers***	Y	N	N	Y	Y	N
6 Baesler	Y	Y	N	Y	Y	N
LOUISIANA						
1 ***Livingston***	Y	Y	N	Y	N	Y
2 Jefferson	?	Y	Y	N	Y	Y
3 Tauzin	Y	Y	N	Y	Y	N
4 Fields	?	?	?	?	?	?
5 ***McCrery***	#	?	?	?	?	?
6 ***Baker***	Y	N	N	Y	N	N
7 Hayes	?	?	?	?	?	?
MAINE						
1 Andrews	Y	Y	Y	N	Y	N
2 ***Snowe***	Y	Y	Y	N	Y	N
MARYLAND						
1 ***Gilchrest***	Y	N	N	Y	Y	Y
2 ***Bentley***	Y	N	N	Y	N	Y
3 Cardin	Y	Y	Y	N	Y	N
4 Wynn	Y	Y	Y	N	Y	N
5 Hoyer	Y	Y	Y	N	Y	?
6 ***Bartlett***	N	N	N	Y	N	Y
7 Mfume	Y	Y	Y	N	Y	Y
8 ***Morella***	Y	N	Y	N	Y	Y
MASSACHUSETTS						
1 Olver	Y	Y	Y	N	Y	N
2 Neal	Y	Y	Y	N	Y	N
3 ***Blute***	Y	N	N	Y	Y	Y
4 Frank	N	Y	Y	N	Y	N
5 Meehan	Y	Y	Y	N	Y	N
6 ***Torkildsen***	?	?	N	Y	Y	Y
7 Markey	Y	Y	Y	N	Y	N
8 Kennedy	Y	Y	Y	N	Y	Y
9 Moakley	Y	Y	Y	N	Y	N
10 Studds	Y	Y	Y	N	Y	N
MICHIGAN						
1 Stupak	Y	Y	Y	N	Y	N
2 ***Hoekstra***	N	N	N	Y	N	Y
3 ***Ehlers***	N	N	N	Y	Y	N
4 ***Camp***	Y	N	N	Y	N	Y
5 Barcia	Y	Y	Y	N	Y	Y
6 ***Upton***	Y	N	N	Y	Y	Y
7 ***Smith***	Y	N	N	Y	Y	Y
8 Carr	Y	Y	Y	N	Y	N
9 Kildee	Y	Y	Y	N	Y	N
10 Bonior	Y	Y	Y	N	Y	N
11 ***Knollenberg***	N	N	N	Y	N	N
12 Levin	Y	Y	Y	N	Y	N
13 Ford	Y	Y	Y	N	Y	?
14 Conyers	N	Y	Y	N	Y	Y
15 Collins	Y	Y	N	N	Y	N
16 Dingell	Y	Y	Y	N	Y	N
MINNESOTA						
1 Penny	N	Y	Y	N	Y	N
2 Minge	N	Y	Y	N	Y	N
3 ***Ramstad***	N	N	N	Y	Y	N
4 Vento	Y	Y	Y	N	Y	N
5 Sabo	Y	?	Y	N	Y	N
6 ***Grams***	N	N	N	Y	N	Y
7 Peterson	N	Y	Y	N	Y	N
8 Oberstar	Y	Y	Y	N	Y	N
MISSISSIPPI						
1 Whitten	Y	Y	Y	N	N	N
2 Thompson	?	?	?	?	?	?
3 Montgomery	Y	Y	Y	Y	Y	N
4 Parker	Y	Y	N	Y	N	Y
5 Taylor	Y	N	Y	N	Y	N
MISSOURI						
1 Clay	Y	N	N	N	Y	N
2 ***Talent***	Y	N	N	Y	N	Y
3 Gephardt	Y	Y	Y	N	Y	N
4 Skelton	Y	Y	Y	Y	Y	N
5 Wheat	?	?	?	?	?	?
6 Danner	Y	Y	Y	N	Y	N
7 ***Hancock***	N	N	N	Y	N	Y
8 ***Emerson***	Y	N	N	Y	N	N
9 Volkmer	Y	Y	Y	N	Y	N
MONTANA						
AL Williams	Y	?	N	N	Y	N
NEBRASKA						
1 ***Bereuter***	Y	N	N	Y	Y	Y
2 Hoagland	Y	Y	Y	N	Y	N
3 ***Barrett***	Y	N	N	Y	Y	Y
NEVADA						
1 Bilbray	Y	Y	Y	N	Y	N
2 ***Vucanovich***	Y	N	N	Y	N	Y
NEW HAMPSHIRE						
1 ***Zeliff***	N	N	N	Y	Y	Y
2 Swett	Y	Y	N	Y	Y	Y
NEW JERSEY						
1 Andrews	Y	Y	Y	N	Y	X
2 Hughes	Y	Y	Y	N	Y	N
3 ***Saxton***	N	N	N	Y	Y	N
4 ***Smith***	Y	Y	N	Y	Y	N
5 ***Roukema***	N	N	N	Y	Y	N
6 Pallone	Y	Y	Y	N	Y	N
7 ***Franks***	N	N	N	Y	Y	N
8 Klein	N	Y	Y	N	Y	N
9 Torricelli	Y	Y	Y	N	Y	N
10 Payne	Y	Y	Y	N	Y	N
11 ***Gallo***	?	?	?	?	?	?
12 ***Zimmer***	N	N	N	Y	Y	N
13 Menendez	Y	Y	Y	N	Y	N
NEW MEXICO						
1 ***Schiff***	Y	N	N	Y	Y	Y
2 ***Skeen***	Y	N	N	Y	N	Y
3 Richardson	Y	Y	Y	N	Y	Y
NEW YORK						
1 Hochbrueckner	Y	Y	Y	N	Y	N
2 ***Lazio***	Y	N	N	Y	Y	N
3 ***King***	Y	N	N	Y	N	?
4 ***Levy***	Y	N	N	Y	Y	N
5 Ackerman	Y	Y	Y	N	Y	N
6 Flake	Y	Y	Y	N	Y	N
7 Manton	Y	Y	Y	N	Y	Y
8 Nadler	N	Y	Y	N	Y	Y
9 Schumer	Y	Y	Y	N	Y	N
10 Towns	Y	Y	Y	N	Y	Y
11 Owens	Y	Y	Y	?	?	?
12 Velazquez	Y	Y	Y	N	Y	Y
13 ***Molinari***	Y	N	N	Y	N	N
14 Maloney	Y	Y	Y	N	Y	Y
15 Rangel	Y	Y	Y	N	Y	N
16 Serrano	Y	Y	Y	N	Y	Y
17 Engel	Y	Y	Y	N	Y	?
18 Lowey	Y	Y	Y	N	Y	N
19 ***Fish***	Y	Y	N	?	?	?
20 ***Gilman***	Y	Y	N	Y	Y	N
21 McNulty	?	?	?	?	?	?
22 ***Solomon***	N	N	N	Y	Y	Y
23 ***Boehlert***	Y	N	N	Y	Y	N
24 ***McHugh***	Y	N	N	Y	Y	N
25 ***Walsh***	Y	N	N	Y	Y	N
26 Hinchey	Y	Y	Y	N	Y	N
27 ***Paxon***	N	N	N	Y	N	N
28 Slaughter	Y	Y	Y	N	Y	N
29 LaFalce	Y	Y	Y	N	Y	Y
30 ***Quinn***	Y	N	N	Y	Y	Y
31 ***Houghton***	Y	Y	N	Y	N	N
NORTH CAROLINA						
1 Clayton	Y	N	Y	N	Y	N
2 Valentine	Y	Y	N	Y	Y	N
3 Lancaster	Y	Y	Y	Y	Y	N
4 Price	Y	Y	Y	N	Y	N
5 Neal	?	Y	Y	N	Y	N
6 ***Coble***	N	N	N	Y	N	N
7 Rose	Y	Y	N	N	Y	N
8 Hefner	Y	Y	Y	Y	Y	N
9 ***McMillan***	Y	N	N	Y	N	N
10 ***Ballenger***	Y	N	N	Y	N	N
11 ***Taylor***	Y	N	N	Y	N	N
12 Watt	N	Y	Y	N	Y	Y
NORTH DAKOTA						
AL Pomeroy	Y	Y	Y	N	Y	N
OHIO						
1 Mann	Y	Y	Y	N	Y	Y
2 ***Portman***	Y	N	N	Y	Y	N
3 Hall	Y	Y	Y	N	Y	N
4 ***Oxley***	Y	N	N	Y	N	N
5 ***Gillmor***	Y	Y	N	Y	Y	N
6 Strickland	Y	Y	Y	N	Y	N
7 ***Hobson***	Y	N	N	Y	Y	N
8 ***Boehner***	Y	?	N	Y	N	Y
9 Kaptur	Y	Y	Y	N	Y	N
10 ***Hoke***	N	N	N	Y	Y	N
11 Stokes	Y	Y	Y	N	Y	?
12 ***Kasich***	Y	Y	N	Y	Y	N
13 Brown	Y	Y	Y	N	Y	N
14 Sawyer	Y	Y	Y	N	Y	N
15 ***Pryce***	Y	N	N	Y	Y	Y
16 ***Regula***	Y	N	N	Y	Y	N
17 Traficant	Y	Y	N	N	N	N
18 Applegate	?	?	?	?	?	?
19 Fingerhut	Y	Y	Y	N	Y	N
OKLAHOMA						
1 ***Inhofe***	Y	N	N	Y	N	?
2 Synar	Y	?	Y	N	Y	N
3 Brewster	Y	Y	N	Y	N	N
4 McCurdy	?	?	?	?	?	?
5 ***Istook***	Y	N	N	Y	N	N
6 ***Lucas***	Y	N	N	Y	N	N
OREGON						
1 Furse	Y	Y	Y	N	Y	Y
2 ***Smith***	Y	N	N	Y	N	Y
3 Wyden	N	Y	Y	N	Y	N
4 DeFazio	N	Y	Y	N	Y	N
5 Kopetski	Y	Y	Y	N	Y	Y
PENNSYLVANIA						
1 Foglietta	Y	Y	Y	N	Y	N
2 Blackwell	Y	Y	Y	N	Y	N
3 Borski	Y	Y	Y	N	Y	N
4 Klink	Y	?	Y	N	Y	Y
5 ***Clinger***	Y	N	N	Y	N	N
6 Holden	Y	Y	N	Y	Y	N
7 ***Weldon***	Y	N	N	Y	Y	N
8 ***Greenwood***	Y	Y	N	Y	Y	N
9 ***Shuster***	Y	N	N	Y	N	N
10 ***McDade***	Y	N	?	?	?	?
11 Kanjorski	Y	Y	Y	N	Y	N
12 Murtha	Y	Y	N	N	N	?
13 Margolies-Mezv.	Y	Y	Y	N	Y	N
14 Coyne	Y	Y	Y	N	Y	N
15 McHale	Y	Y	Y	N	Y	Y
16 ***Walker***	N	N	N	Y	N	N
17 ***Gekas***	N	N	N	Y	Y	N
18 ***Santorum***	Y	Y	N	Y	Y	N
19 ***Goodling***	N	N	N	Y	Y	Y
20 Murphy	Y	N	Y	N	Y	N
21 ***Ridge***	Y	N	Y	N	Y	?
RHODE ISLAND						
1 ***Machtley***	Y	N	N	Y	Y	Y
2 Reed	Y	Y	Y	N	Y	Y
SOUTH CAROLINA						
1 ***Ravenel***	Y	N	N	Y	N	N
2 ***Spence***	Y	N	N	Y	N	Y
3 Derrick	Y	Y	Y	N	Y	N
4 ***Inglis***	N	Y	N	Y	N	Y
5 Spratt	Y	Y	Y	N	Y	N
6 Clyburn	Y	Y	Y	?	?	?
SOUTH DAKOTA						
AL Johnson	Y	Y	Y	N	Y	N
TENNESSEE						
1 ***Quillen***	Y	N	N	Y	N	?
2 ***Duncan***	N	N	N	Y	Y	Y
3 Lloyd	?	?	?	?	?	?
4 Cooper	Y	Y	Y	N	Y	N
5 Clement	N	Y	N	Y	Y	N
6 Gordon	Y	Y	Y	N	Y	N
7 ***Sundquist***	?	?	N	Y	Y	?
8 Tanner	Y	Y	N	Y	N	Y
9 Ford	Y	Y	Y	N	Y	N
TEXAS						
1 Chapman	Y	Y	N	Y	Y	Y
2 Wilson	Y	Y	N	Y	N	Y
3 ***Johnson, Sam***	N	N	N	Y	N	Y
4 Hall	Y	Y	N	Y	N	Y
5 Bryant	Y	Y	Y	N	Y	Y
6 ***Barton***	N	N	N	Y	N	Y
7 ***Archer***	N	N	N	Y	N	Y
8 ***Fields***	N	N	N	Y	N	Y
9 Brooks	Y	Y	Y	Y	N	N
10 Pickle	Y	Y	Y	N	Y	Y
11 Edwards	Y	Y	Y	N	Y	Y
12 Geren	Y	Y	N	Y	Y	Y
13 Sarpalius	Y	Y	N	Y	N	Y
14 Laughlin	Y	Y	N	Y	N	?
15 de la Garza	Y	Y	Y	N	Y	Y
16 Coleman	Y	Y	Y	N	Y	N
17 Stenholm	Y	Y	N	Y	Y	Y
18 Washington	?	?	?	?	?	?
19 ***Combest***	N	Y	N	Y	N	N
20 Gonzalez	Y	Y	Y	N	Y	Y
21 ***Smith***	Y	N	N	Y	Y	Y
22 ***DeLay***	N	N	N	Y	N	Y
23 ***Bonilla***	Y	N	N	Y	Y	Y
24 Frost	Y	Y	Y	N	Y	Y
25 Andrews	Y	Y	Y	N	Y	Y
26 ***Armey***	N	N	N	Y	N	Y
27 Ortiz	Y	Y	Y	Y	Y	Y
28 Tejeda	Y	Y	Y	Y	Y	Y
29 Green	Y	Y	Y	N	Y	Y
30 Johnson, E.B.	Y	Y	Y	N	Y	Y
UTAH						
1 ***Hansen***	N	N	N	Y	N	N
2 Shepherd	Y	Y	Y	N	Y	Y
3 Orton	Y	Y	N	N	N	N
VERMONT						
AL *Sanders*	N	Y	Y	N	Y	Y
VIRGINIA						
1 ***Bateman***	Y	Y	N	Y	N	N
2 Pickett	Y	Y	N	Y	Y	N
3 Scott	Y	Y	Y	N	Y	Y
4 Sisisky	Y	Y	N	Y	Y	N
5 Payne	Y	Y	N	Y	Y	Y
6 ***Goodlatte***	Y	N	N	Y	Y	Y
7 ***Bliley***	Y	N	N	Y	N	Y
8 Moran	Y	Y	Y	N	N	N
9 Boucher	Y	Y	Y	N	Y	Y
10 ***Wolf***	Y	N	N	Y	Y	N
11 Byrne	Y	Y	Y	N	Y	Y
WASHINGTON						
1 Cantwell	Y	Y	Y	N	Y	N
2 Swift	Y	Y	Y	N	Y	N
3 Unsoeld	Y	Y	Y	N	Y	N
4 Inslee	Y	Y	Y	N	Y	N
5 Foley			Y	N	Y	
6 Dicks	Y	Y	Y	N	Y	N
7 McDermott	Y	Y	Y	N	Y	N
8 ***Dunn***	N	N	N	Y	N	Y
9 Kreidler	Y	N	Y	N	Y	N
WEST VIRGINIA						
1 Mollohan	Y	Y	Y	N	Y	N
2 Wise	Y	Y	Y	N	Y	N
3 Rahall	Y	Y	Y	Y	Y	Y
WISCONSIN						
1 Barca	Y	Y	Y	N	Y	Y
2 ***Klug***	N	N	N	Y	Y	Y
3 ***Gunderson***	Y	N	N	Y	Y	Y
4 Kleczka	Y	Y	Y	N	Y	N
5 Barrett	N	Y	Y	N	Y	N
6 ***Petri***	N	N	N	Y	Y	N
7 Obey	Y	Y	Y	N	Y	Y
8 ***Roth***	N	N	N	Y	Y	Y
9 ***Sensenbrenner***	N	N	N	Y	Y	N
WYOMING						
AL ***Thomas***	N	N	N	Y	Y	Y
DELEGATES						
de Lugo, V.I.	D	D	D	D	D	Y
Faleomavaega, Am.S.	D	D	D	D	D	?
Norton, D.C.	D	D	D	D	D	Y
Romero-B., P.R.	D	D	D	D	D	Y
Underwood, Guam	D	D	D	D	D	?

Southern states - Ala., Ark., Fla., Ga., Ky., La., Miss., N.C., Okla., S.C., Tenn., Texas, Va.
Omitted votes are quorum calls, which CQ does not include in its vote charts.

453. Procedural Motion. Approval of the House Journal of Thursday, Sept. 29. Approved 212-136: R 15-130; D 196-6 (ND 140-4, SD 56-2); I 1-0, Sept. 30, 1994.

454. HR 6. Elementary and Secondary School Reauthorization/Rule. Adoption of the rule (H Res 556) to waive points of order against and provide for House floor consideration of the conference report to reauthorize for five years the Elementary and Secondary Education Act of 1965, providing $12.7 billion to help disadvantaged students. Adopted 230-168: R 0-162; D 229-6 (ND 160-2, SD 69-4); I 1-0, Sept. 30, 1994.

455. HR 6. Elementary and Secondary School Reauthorization/Motion to Recommit. Johnson, R-Texas, motion to recommit the bill to conference with instructions to report the bill back to the House after amending it to include House-passed provisions that would withhold federal money from states or school districts that prohibit voluntary, constitutionally protected school prayer. The conference report includes Senate provisions that withhold federal money from any state or school district that willfully violates a federal court order regarding a violation of a student's constitutional right to school prayer. Motion rejected 184-215: R 151-10; D 33-204 (ND 11-153, SD 22-51); I 0-1, Sept. 30, 1994.

456. HR 6. Elementary and Secondary School Reauthorization/Conference Report. Adoption of the conference report to reauthorize for five years the Elementary and Secondary Education Act of 1965, providing $12.7 billion to help disadvantaged students. Adopted (thus sent to the Senate) 262-132: R 31-128; D 230-4 (ND 161-2, SD 69-2); I 1-0, Sept. 30, 1994. A "yea" was a vote in support of the president's position.

457. HR 2129. Madrid Protocol Implementation/Passage. Brooks, D-Texas, motion to suspend the rules and pass the bill to implement the Madrid Protocol, which establishes an international system for registering trademarks through the World Intellectual Property Organization. Motion agreed to 387-3: R 161-2; D 225-1 (ND 153-1, SD 72-0); I 1-0, Oct. 3, 1994. A two-thirds majority of those present and voting (260 in this case) is required for passage under suspension of the rules.

458. HR 4608. Patent and Trademark Office Authorization/Passage. Brooks, D-Texas, motion to suspend the rules and pass the bill to authorize $107 million in fiscal 1995 for the Patent and Trademark Office and exempt the Patent and Trademark Office from the governmentwide work force reduction cuts. Motion rejected 146-251: R 56-112; D 89-139 (ND 63-92, SD 26-47); I 1-0, Oct. 3, 1994. A two-thirds majority of those present and voting (265 in this case) is required for passage under suspension of the rules.

459. S 1233. Arizona Wilderness Land Title Resolution/Passage. Brooks, D-Texas, motion to suspend the rules and pass the bill to settle a $3.8 million claim by Perrin Properties to land in the Prescott National Forest in Arizona, thus enabling the land to be acquired by the Forest Service. Motion agreed to 381-15: R 160-8; D 220-7 (ND 152-2, SD 68-5); I 1-0, Oct. 3, 1994. A two-thirds majority of those present and voting (264 in this case) is required for passage under suspension of the rules.

460. HR 4777. U.S. Code Technical Improvements/Passage. Brooks, D-Texas, motion to suspend the rules and pass the bill to revise the U.S. Code to reflect the current names of congressional committees. Motion agreed to 391-3: R 166-0; D 224-3 (ND 153-1, SD 71-2); I 1-0, Oct. 3, 1994. A two-thirds majority of those present and voting (263 in this case) is required for passage under suspension of the rules.

KEY

Y Voted for (yea).
Paired for.
+ Announced for.
N Voted against (nay).
X Paired against.
– Announced against.
P Voted "present."
C Voted "present" to avoid possible conflict of interest.
? Did not vote or otherwise make a position known.
D Delegates ineligible to vote.

Democrats **Republicans** *Independent*

	453	454	455	456	457	458	459	460
ALABAMA								
1 Callahan	?	?	?	?	?	?	?	?
2 Everett	Y	N	Y	N	Y	N	Y	Y
3 Browder	?	Y	Y	Y	Y	N	Y	Y
4 Bevill	Y	Y	Y	Y	Y	N	Y	Y
5 Cramer	?	Y	Y	Y	Y	N	Y	Y
6 Bachus	N	N	Y	N	Y	N	Y	Y
7 Hilliard	Y	Y	N	Y	?	?	?	?
ALASKA								
AL Young	?	N	Y	N	Y	Y	Y	Y
ARIZONA								
1 Coppersmith	Y	Y	N	Y	Y	N	Y	Y
2 Pastor	Y	Y	N	Y	+	?	+	+
3 Stump	N	N	Y	N	Y	N	Y	Y
4 Kyl	N	N	Y	N	?	?	?	?
5 Kolbe	N	N	Y	N	Y	N	Y	Y
6 English	Y	Y	N	Y	Y	N	Y	Y
ARKANSAS								
1 Lambert	Y	Y	N	Y	Y	N	Y	Y
2 Thornton	Y	Y	N	Y	Y	Y	Y	Y
3 Hutchinson	?	N	Y	N	Y	N	Y	Y
4 Dickey	N	N	Y	N	Y	Y	Y	Y
CALIFORNIA								
1 Hamburg	Y	Y	N	Y	Y	Y	Y	Y
2 Herger	N	N	Y	N	Y	N	Y	Y
3 Fazio	Y	Y	N	Y	Y	Y	Y	Y
4 Doolittle	N	N	Y	N	Y	N	Y	Y
5 Matsui	Y	Y	N	Y	Y	N	Y	Y
6 Woolsey	Y	Y	N	Y	Y	Y	Y	Y
7 Miller	Y	Y	N	Y	Y	Y	Y	Y
8 Pelosi	Y	Y	N	Y	Y	Y	Y	Y
9 Dellums	Y	Y	N	Y	Y	Y	Y	Y
10 Baker	?	N	Y	N	Y	N	Y	Y
11 Pombo	N	N	Y	N	Y	N	Y	Y
12 Lantos	Y	Y	N	?	?	N	Y	Y
13 Stark	Y	Y	N	Y	Y	Y	Y	Y
14 Eshoo	Y	Y	N	Y	Y	N	Y	Y
15 Mineta	Y	Y	X	#	Y	Y	Y	Y
16 Edwards	Y	Y	N	Y	Y	Y	Y	Y
17 Farr	Y	Y	N	Y	Y	N	Y	Y
18 Condit	Y	Y	Y	Y	Y	N	Y	Y
19 Lehman	Y	Y	N	Y	Y	N	Y	Y
20 Dooley	Y	Y	N	Y	Y	N	Y	Y
21 Thomas	N	N	Y	Y	Y	N	Y	Y
22 Huffington	?	N	Y	Y	Y	N	Y	Y
23 Gallegly	?	–	+	–	Y	Y	Y	Y
24 Beilenson	?	Y	N	Y	Y	N	Y	Y
25 McKeon	N	N	Y	N	Y	N	Y	Y
26 Berman	?	#	X	#	?	?	?	?
27 Moorhead	N	N	Y	N	Y	N	Y	Y
28 Dreier	N	N	Y	N	Y	N	Y	Y
29 Waxman	Y	Y	N	Y	Y	N	Y	Y
30 Becerra	Y	Y	N	Y	Y	Y	Y	Y
31 Martinez	?	Y	N	Y	Y	N	Y	Y
32 Dixon	Y	Y	N	Y	Y	N	Y	Y
33 Roybal-Allard	Y	Y	N	Y	Y	Y	Y	Y
34 Torres	Y	Y	N	Y	Y	Y	Y	Y
35 Waters	?	Y	N	Y	Y	N	Y	Y
36 Harman	Y	Y	N	Y	?	?	?	?
37 Tucker	?	Y	Y	Y	?	?	?	?
38 Horn	N	N	Y	N	Y	N	Y	Y
39 Royce	N	N	Y	N	Y	N	Y	Y
40 Lewis	N	N	Y	N	Y	N	Y	Y
41 Kim	N	N	Y	N	Y	N	Y	Y

	453	454	455	456	457	458	459	460
42 Brown	?	Y	N	Y	Y	Y	Y	Y
43 Calvert	?	X	#	?	?	?	?	?
44 McCandless	N	N	Y	N	Y	N	Y	Y
45 Rohrabacher	N	N	Y	N	Y	N	N	Y
46 Dornan	?	N	Y	N	Y	N	Y	Y
47 Cox	N	N	Y	N	?	N	Y	Y
48 Packard	N	N	Y	N	Y	N	Y	Y
49 Schenk	Y	Y	N	Y	Y	N	Y	Y
50 Filner	Y	Y	N	Y	Y	Y	Y	Y
51 Cunningham	N	N	Y	N	Y	N	Y	Y
52 Hunter	?	N	Y	N	N	Y	N	Y
COLORADO								
1 Schroeder	N	Y	N	Y	Y	N	N	Y
2 Skaggs	Y	Y	N	Y	Y	Y	Y	Y
3 McInnis	N	N	Y	N	Y	Y	Y	Y
4 Allard	N	N	Y	N	Y	N	Y	Y
5 Hefley	N	N	Y	N	Y	N	Y	Y
6 Schaefer	N	N	Y	N	Y	N	Y	Y
CONNECTICUT								
1 Kennelly	Y	Y	N	Y	Y	Y	Y	Y
2 Gejdenson	Y	Y	N	Y	Y	Y	Y	Y
3 DeLauro	Y	Y	N	Y	Y	N	Y	Y
4 Shays	N	N	Y	Y	Y	Y	Y	Y
5 Franks	N	N	N	Y	Y	Y	Y	Y
6 Johnson	N	N	Y	Y	Y	Y	Y	Y
DELAWARE								
AL Castle	N	N	Y	Y	Y	Y	Y	Y
FLORIDA								
1 Hutto	?	?	?	?	Y	N	Y	Y
2 Peterson	Y	Y	N	Y	Y	N	Y	Y
3 Brown	?	Y	N	Y	Y	Y	Y	Y
4 Fowler	N	N	Y	N	Y	N	Y	Y
5 Thurman	Y	Y	N	Y	Y	N	Y	Y
6 Stearns	N	N	Y	N	Y	N	Y	Y
7 Mica	N	N	Y	N	Y	N	Y	Y
8 McCollum	N	N	Y	N	?	N	Y	Y
9 Bilirakis	N	N	Y	N	Y	N	Y	Y
10 Young	N	N	Y	N	Y	N	Y	Y
11 Gibbons	?	Y	?	?	Y	Y	Y	Y
12 Canady	N	N	Y	N	Y	N	Y	Y
13 Miller	N	N	Y	N	Y	N	Y	Y
14 Goss	N	N	Y	N	Y	N	Y	Y
15 Bacchus	Y	Y	N	Y	?	?	Y	Y
16 Lewis	N	N	Y	N	Y	N	Y	Y
17 Meek	Y	Y	N	Y	Y	Y	Y	Y
18 Ros-Lehtinen	N	N	Y	N	Y	N	Y	Y
19 Johnston	Y	Y	N	?	?	?	?	?
20 Deutsch	Y	Y	N	Y	Y	N	Y	Y
21 Diaz-Balart	N	N	Y	N	Y	N	Y	Y
22 Shaw	N	N	?	?	Y	N	Y	Y
23 Hastings	Y	Y	N	Y	Y	N	Y	Y
GEORGIA								
1 Kingston	Y	N	Y	N	Y	N	Y	Y
2 Bishop	Y	Y	N	Y	Y	N	Y	Y
3 Collins	?	N	Y	N	Y	N	N	Y
4 Linder	N	N	Y	N	Y	N	Y	Y
5 Lewis	Y	Y	N	Y	Y	Y	Y	Y
6 Gingrich	?	?	?	?	Y	N	Y	Y
7 Darden	Y	Y	N	Y	?	?	?	?
8 Rowland	Y	Y	N	Y	Y	N	Y	Y
9 Deal	Y	N	Y	N	Y	N	Y	Y
10 Johnson	Y	Y	N	Y	Y	N	Y	Y
11 McKinney	Y	Y	Y	Y	Y	Y	Y	Y
HAWAII								
1 Abercrombie	Y	Y	N	Y	Y	Y	Y	Y
2 Mink	Y	Y	N	Y	Y	N	Y	Y
IDAHO								
1 LaRocco	Y	Y	N	Y	Y	N	Y	Y
2 Crapo	N	N	Y	N	Y	N	Y	Y
ILLINOIS								
1 Rush	Y	Y	N	Y	Y	Y	Y	Y
2 Reynolds	Y	Y	N	Y	Y	Y	Y	Y
3 Lipinski	?	?	?	?	Y	Y	Y	Y
4 Gutierrez	Y	Y	N	Y	Y	Y	Y	Y
5 Rostenkowski	Y	Y	N	Y	?	?	?	?
6 Hyde	N	N	Y	N	Y	N	Y	Y
7 Collins	Y	Y	N	Y	Y	Y	Y	Y
8 Crane	?	N	Y	N	Y	N	Y	Y
9 Yates	Y	Y	N	Y	Y	Y	Y	Y
10 Porter	?	N	Y	Y	Y	Y	Y	Y
11 Sangmeister	Y	Y	N	Y	Y	N	Y	Y
12 Costello	Y	Y	N	Y	Y	N	Y	Y
13 Fawell	N	N	Y	N	Y	Y	Y	Y
14 Hastert	N	N	Y	N	Y	N	Y	Y
15 Ewing	?	N	Y	N	Y	N	Y	Y
16 Manzullo	N	N	Y	N	Y	N	Y	Y
17 Evans	Y	Y	N	Y	Y	Y	Y	Y

ND Northern Democrats   SD Southern Democrats

	453	454	455	456	457	458	459	460
18 ***Michel***	N	N	Y	N	Y	Y	Y	Y
19 Poshard	Y	Y	Y	Y	Y	N	N	Y
20 Durbin	Y	Y	N	Y	Y	N	Y	Y
INDIANA								
1 Visclosky	Y	Y	N	Y	Y	N	Y	Y
2 Sharp	?	Y	N	Y	Y	N	Y	Y
3 Roemer	?	Y	N	Y	Y	N	Y	Y
4 Long	Y	Y	Y	Y	Y	N	Y	Y
5 ***Buyer***	N	N	Y	N	Y	N	Y	Y
6 ***Burton***	N	N	Y	N	Y	N	Y	Y
7 ***Myers***	Y	N	Y	N	Y	Y	Y	Y
8 McCloskey	Y	Y	N	Y	Y	N	Y	Y
9 Hamilton	Y	Y	Y	Y	Y	N	Y	Y
10 Jacobs	N	Y	N	Y	Y	N	Y	Y
IOWA								
1 ***Leach***	N	N	N	Y	Y	Y	Y	Y
2 ***Nussle***	N	N	Y	Y	Y	Y	Y	Y
3 ***Lightfoot***	N	N	Y	N	Y	Y	Y	Y
4 Smith	Y	Y	N	Y	Y	Y	Y	Y
5 ***Grandy***	?	N	?	?	?	?	?	?
KANSAS								
1 ***Roberts***	N	N	Y	N	Y	N	Y	Y
2 Slattery	?	?	?	?	?	?	?	?
3 ***Meyers***	N	N	N	Y	Y	N	Y	Y
4 Glickman	Y	Y	N	Y	Y	N	Y	Y
KENTUCKY								
1 Barlow	Y	Y	N	Y	Y	N	Y	Y
2 ***Lewis***	N	N	Y	N	Y	Y	Y	Y
3 Mazzoli	Y	Y	N	Y	Y	Y	Y	Y
4 ***Bunning***	N	N	Y	N	Y	Y	Y	Y
5 ***Rogers***	N	N	Y	Y	Y	Y	Y	Y
6 Baesler	Y	Y	N	Y	Y	N	Y	Y
LOUISIANA								
1 ***Livingston***	Y	N	Y	N	Y	N	N	Y
2 Jefferson	Y	Y	N	Y	Y	Y	Y	Y
3 Tauzin	?	Y	Y	Y	Y	Y	Y	Y
4 Fields	?	?	?	?	Y	Y	Y	Y
5 ***McCrery***	?	?	?	?	Y	Y	Y	Y
6 ***Baker***	?	?	?	?	?	?	?	?
7 Hayes	?	?	?	?	?	?	?	?
MAINE								
1 Andrews	Y	Y	N	Y	Y	N	Y	Y
2 ***Snowe***	N	N	N	Y	Y	N	Y	Y
MARYLAND								
1 ***Gilchrest***	N	N	Y	N	Y	Y	Y	Y
2 ***Bentley***	N	N	Y	N	N	N	Y	Y
3 Cardin	Y	Y	N	Y	Y	N	Y	Y
4 Wynn	?	Y	N	Y	Y	Y	Y	Y
5 Hoyer	Y	Y	N	Y	Y	N	Y	Y
6 ***Bartlett***	N	N	Y	N	Y	Y	Y	Y
7 Mfume	Y	Y	N	Y	Y	N	Y	Y
8 ***Morella***	N	N	N	Y	Y	N	Y	Y
MASSACHUSETTS								
1 Olver	Y	Y	N	Y	Y	N	Y	Y
2 Neal	Y	Y	N	Y	?	?	?	?
3 ***Blute***	N	N	Y	Y	Y	N	Y	Y
4 Frank	Y	Y	N	Y	Y	Y	Y	Y
5 Meehan	Y	Y	N	Y	Y	N	Y	Y
6 ***Torkildsen***	N	N	Y	Y	Y	N	Y	Y
7 Markey	Y	Y	N	Y	Y	Y	Y	Y
8 Kennedy	Y	Y	N	Y	Y	Y	Y	Y
9 Moakley	Y	Y	N	Y	Y	Y	Y	Y
10 Studds	Y	Y	N	Y	Y	Y	Y	Y
MICHIGAN								
1 Stupak	Y	Y	N	Y	Y	N	Y	Y
2 ***Hoekstra***	N	N	Y	N	Y	N	Y	Y
3 ***Ehlers***	N	N	Y	N	Y	Y	Y	Y
4 ***Camp***	N	N	Y	N	Y	N	Y	Y
5 Barcia	Y	Y	N	Y	Y	N	Y	?
6 ***Upton***	N	N	Y	N	Y	N	Y	Y
7 ***Smith***	N	N	Y	N	Y	N	Y	Y
8 Carr	Y	Y	N	Y	?	?	?	?
9 Kildee	Y	Y	N	Y	Y	Y	Y	Y
10 Bonior	Y	Y	N	Y	Y	Y	Y	Y
11 ***Knollenberg***	N	N	Y	N	Y	Y	Y	Y
12 Levin	Y	Y	N	Y	Y	N	Y	Y
13 Ford	?	Y	N	Y	Y	Y	Y	Y
14 Conyers	Y	Y	N	Y	Y	Y	Y	Y
15 Collins	?	Y	N	Y	Y	Y	Y	Y
16 Dingell	?	Y	N	Y	Y	Y	Y	Y
MINNESOTA								
1 Penny	Y	Y	N	Y	Y	N	Y	N
2 Minge	Y	Y	N	Y	Y	N	Y	Y
3 ***Ramstad***	N	N	Y	N	Y	N	Y	Y
4 Vento	Y	Y	N	Y	Y	Y	Y	Y

	453	454	455	456	457	458	459	460
5 Sabo	Y	Y	N	Y	Y	N	Y	Y
6 ***Grams***	?	?	#	X	?	N	Y	Y
7 Peterson	Y	Y	Y	Y	Y	N	Y	Y
8 Oberstar	Y	Y	N	Y	Y	Y	Y	Y
MISSISSIPPI								
1 Whitten	?	Y	N	Y	?	?	?	?
2 Thompson	?	?	?	?	Y	Y	Y	Y
3 Montgomery	Y	Y	Y	Y	Y	Y	Y	Y
4 Parker	Y	Y	Y	Y	Y	Y	Y	Y
5 Taylor	N	Y	Y	Y	Y	N	N	Y
MISSOURI								
1 Clay	N	N	Y	N	Y	N	Y	Y
2 ***Talent***	N	N	Y	N	Y	N	Y	Y
3 Gephardt	?	Y	N	Y	Y	Y	Y	Y
4 Skelton	Y	Y	Y	Y	Y	N	Y	Y
5 Wheat	?	#	X	#	?	?	?	?
6 Danner	Y	Y	Y	Y	Y	N	Y	Y
7 ***Hancock***	N	N	Y	N	Y	N	Y	Y
8 ***Emerson***	N	N	Y	N	Y	N	Y	Y
9 Volkmer	Y	Y	N	Y	Y	N	Y	Y
MONTANA								
AL Williams	?	Y	N	Y	Y	Y	Y	Y
NEBRASKA								
1 ***Bereuter***	N	N	Y	N	Y	Y	Y	Y
2 Hoagland	?	Y	N	Y	Y	N	Y	Y
3 ***Barrett***	N	N	Y	N	Y	Y	Y	Y
NEVADA								
1 Bilbray	Y	Y	Y	Y	Y	N	Y	Y
2 ***Vucanovich***	N	N	Y	Y	Y	N	Y	Y
NEW HAMPSHIRE								
1 ***Zeliff***	N	N	Y	N	Y	N	Y	Y
2 Swett	Y	Y	N	Y	Y	N	Y	Y
NEW JERSEY								
1 Andrews	Y	Y	N	Y	Y	Y	Y	Y
2 Hughes	Y	Y	N	Y	Y	Y	Y	Y
3 ***Saxton***	?	?	Y	N	Y	N	Y	Y
4 ***Smith***	Y	N	Y	Y	Y	Y	Y	Y
5 ***Roukema***	N	N	Y	?	Y	Y	Y	Y
6 Pallone	Y	Y	N	Y	Y	N	Y	Y
7 ***Franks***	N	N	Y	N	Y	N	Y	Y
8 Klein	Y	Y	N	Y	Y	N	Y	Y
9 Torricelli	Y	Y	N	Y	?	?	?	?
10 Payne	Y	Y	N	Y	Y	Y	Y	Y
11 ***Gallo***	?	?	?	?	?	?	?	?
12 ***Zimmer***	N	N	Y	N	Y	N	Y	Y
13 Menendez	?	Y	N	Y	Y	Y	Y	Y
NEW MEXICO								
1 ***Schiff***	N	N	Y	N	Y	Y	Y	Y
2 ***Skeen***	N	N	Y	N	Y	N	Y	Y
3 Richardson	Y	?	N	Y	?	?	?	?
NEW YORK								
1 Hochbrueckner	Y	Y	N	Y	Y	Y	Y	Y
2 ***Lazio***	N	N	Y	Y	Y	N	Y	Y
3 ***King***	?	N	Y	N	Y	N	Y	Y
4 ***Levy***	N	N	Y	N	Y	Y	Y	Y
5 Ackerman	Y	N	X	X	Y	N	Y	Y
6 Flake	Y	Y	N	Y	Y	N	Y	Y
7 Manton	?	Y	N	Y	Y	Y	Y	Y
8 Nadler	?	Y	N	Y	Y	Y	Y	Y
9 Schumer	Y	Y	N	Y	Y	Y	Y	Y
10 Towns	?	?	?	?	Y	Y	Y	Y
11 Owens	Y	Y	N	Y	?	?	?	?
12 Velazquez	Y	Y	N	Y	Y	Y	Y	Y
13 ***Molinari***	N	N	Y	Y	Y	Y	Y	Y
14 Maloney	Y	Y	N	Y	?	?	?	?
15 Rangel	Y	Y	N	Y	?	?	?	?
16 Serrano	Y	Y	N	Y	Y	Y	Y	Y
17 Engel	Y	+	N	Y	Y	Y	Y	Y
18 Lowey	Y	Y	N	Y	?	?	?	?
19 ***Fish***	Y	N	N	Y	Y	Y	Y	Y
20 ***Gilman***	Y	N	N	Y	Y	N	Y	Y
21 McNulty	?	?	?	?	Y	N	Y	Y
22 ***Solomon***	N	N	Y	X	Y	N	Y	Y
23 ***Boehlert***	N	N	N	Y	Y	N	Y	Y
24 ***McHugh***	N	N	Y	N	Y	N	Y	Y
25 ***Walsh***	N	N	Y	Y	Y	Y	Y	Y
26 Hinchey	?	Y	N	Y	Y	Y	Y	Y
27 ***Paxon***	N	N	Y	N	Y	N	Y	Y
28 Slaughter	Y	Y	N	Y	Y	Y	Y	Y
29 LaFalce	Y	Y	N	Y	Y	N	Y	Y
30 ***Quinn***	N	N	Y	Y	Y	Y	Y	Y
31 ***Houghton***	Y	N	Y	N	Y	Y	Y	Y
NORTH CAROLINA								
1 Clayton	Y	Y	N	Y	Y	Y	Y	Y
2 Valentine	Y	Y	N	Y	Y	N	N	Y

	453	454	455	456	457	458	459	460
3 Lancaster	Y	Y	Y	Y	Y	N	Y	Y
4 Price	Y	Y	N	Y	Y	N	Y	Y
5 Neal	?	?	N	Y	Y	N	Y	Y
6 ***Coble***	N	N	Y	N	Y	N	Y	Y
7 Rose	Y	Y	N	Y	Y	Y	Y	Y
8 Hefner	Y	Y	N	Y	Y	N	Y	Y
9 ***McMillan***	?	?	?	?	?	?	?	?
10 ***Ballenger***	N	N	Y	N	Y	Y	Y	Y
11 ***Taylor***	?	N	Y	N	?	N	Y	Y
12 Watt	Y	Y	N	Y	Y	Y	Y	Y
NORTH DAKOTA								
AL Pomeroy	Y	Y	N	Y	Y	N	Y	Y
OHIO								
1 Mann	Y	Y	N	Y	Y	N	Y	Y
2 ***Portman***	N	N	Y	N	Y	N	Y	Y
3 Hall	Y	Y	N	Y	Y	N	Y	Y
4 ***Oxley***	N	N	Y	N	Y	Y	Y	Y
5 ***Gillmor***	Y	N	Y	Y	Y	N	Y	Y
6 Strickland	?	Y	N	Y	Y	N	Y	Y
7 ***Hobson***	N	N	Y	N	Y	N	Y	Y
8 ***Boehner***	N	N	Y	N	Y	N	Y	?
9 Kaptur	Y	Y	N	Y	N	N	?	Y
10 ***Hoke***	N	N	Y	N	Y	Y	Y	Y
11 Stokes	Y	Y	N	Y	Y	N	Y	Y
12 ***Kasich***	Y	N	Y	N	Y	N	Y	Y
13 Brown	Y	Y	N	Y	Y	Y	Y	Y
14 Sawyer	Y	Y	N	Y	Y	Y	Y	Y
15 ***Pryce***	N	N	Y	N	Y	N	Y	Y
16 ***Regula***	N	N	Y	N	Y	N	Y	Y
17 Traficant	Y	Y	Y	Y	Y	N	Y	Y
18 Applegate	?	?	?	?	Y	Y	Y	Y
19 Fingerhut	Y	Y	N	Y	Y	N	Y	Y
OKLAHOMA								
1 ***Inhofe***	?	?	?	?	?	?	?	?
2 Synar	?	?	?	?	Y	N	Y	Y
3 Brewster	?	Y	N	Y	Y	N	Y	Y
4 McCurdy	?	?	?	?	?	?	?	?
5 ***Istook***	?	N	Y	N	Y	N	Y	Y
6 ***Lucas***	N	N	Y	N	Y	Y	Y	Y
OREGON								
1 Furse	Y	Y	N	Y	Y	N	Y	Y
2 ***Smith***	?	?	#	?	Y	Y	Y	Y
3 Wyden	Y	Y	N	Y	Y	N	Y	Y
4 DeFazio	?	Y	N	Y	Y	N	Y	Y
5 Kopetski	Y	Y	N	Y	Y	Y	Y	Y
PENNSYLVANIA								
1 Foglietta	Y	Y	N	Y	Y	Y	Y	Y
2 Blackwell	?	?	N	Y	?	?	?	?
3 Borski	Y	Y	N	Y	?	?	?	?
4 Klink	Y	Y	N	Y	Y	Y	Y	Y
5 ***Clinger***	N	N	Y	N	Y	Y	Y	Y
6 Holden	Y	Y	N	Y	Y	N	Y	Y
7 ***Weldon***	N	N	Y	N	Y	Y	Y	Y
8 ***Greenwood***	Y	–	Y	N	Y	N	Y	Y
9 ***Shuster***	N	N	Y	N	Y	Y	N	Y
10 ***McDade***	?	?	?	?	?	?	?	?
11 Kanjorski	Y	Y	N	Y	Y	Y	Y	Y
12 Murtha	Y	Y	N	Y	Y	Y	Y	Y
13 Margolies-Mezv.	Y	Y	N	Y	Y	N	Y	Y
14 Coyne	Y	Y	N	Y	Y	Y	Y	Y
15 McHale	Y	Y	N	Y	Y	N	Y	Y
16 ***Walker***	N	N	Y	N	Y	Y	Y	Y
17 ***Gekas***	N	N	Y	N	Y	Y	Y	Y
18 ***Santorum***	?	N	Y	N	Y	N	Y	Y
19 ***Goodling***	N	N	Y	N	Y	N	Y	?
20 Murphy	N	Y	N	Y	Y	Y	Y	Y
21 ***Ridge***	?	N	Y	N	Y	N	Y	Y
RHODE ISLAND								
1 ***Machtley***	N	N	Y	Y	Y	N	Y	Y
2 Reed	Y	Y	N	Y	Y	N	Y	Y
SOUTH CAROLINA								
1 ***Ravenel***	N	N	?	?	Y	Y	Y	Y
2 ***Spence***	N	N	Y	N	Y	Y	Y	Y
3 Derrick	?	Y	N	Y	Y	Y	Y	Y
4 ***Inglis***	Y	N	Y	N	Y	N	Y	Y
5 Spratt	?	?	?	?	Y	N	Y	Y
6 Clyburn	?	Y	N	Y	Y	Y	Y	Y
SOUTH DAKOTA								
AL Johnson	Y	Y	N	Y	Y	N	Y	Y
TENNESSEE								
1 ***Quillen***	?	X	#	X	Y	Y	Y	Y
2 ***Duncan***	N	N	Y	N	Y	N	N	Y
3 Lloyd	?	Y	Y	Y	Y	N	Y	Y
4 Cooper	Y	N	Y	Y	Y	N	Y	Y
5 Clement	Y	Y	N	Y	Y	N	Y	Y

	453	454	455	456	457	458	459	460
6 Gordon	Y	?	?	?	Y	N	Y	Y
7 ***Sundquist***	?	?	?	?	?	?	?	?
8 Tanner	Y	Y	Y	Y	Y	N	N	Y
9 Ford	Y	Y	N	Y	?	?	?	?
TEXAS								
1 Chapman	Y	Y	N	Y	Y	N	Y	Y
2 Wilson	Y	Y	N	Y	Y	N	Y	Y
3 ***Johnson, Sam***	N	N	Y	N	Y	N	Y	Y
4 Hall	?	N	Y	Y	Y	N	Y	Y
5 Bryant	?	Y	N	Y	Y	N	Y	Y
6 ***Barton***	N	N	Y	N	Y	N	Y	Y
7 ***Archer***	N	N	Y	N	Y	N	Y	Y
8 ***Fields***	N	N	Y	N	Y	N	Y	Y
9 Brooks	Y	Y	N	?	Y	Y	Y	Y
10 Pickle	Y	Y	N	Y	Y	Y	Y	Y
11 Edwards	?	Y	N	Y	Y	N	Y	Y
12 Geren	Y	Y	Y	Y	Y	N	Y	Y
13 Sarpalius	Y	Y	Y	Y	Y	N	Y	Y
14 Laughlin	Y	Y	Y	Y	?	?	?	?
15 de la Garza	?	Y	N	Y	Y	N	Y	Y
16 Coleman	?	Y	N	Y	Y	N	Y	Y
17 Stenholm	N	N	Y	N	Y	N	Y	N
18 Washington	?	?	?	?	?	?	?	?
19 ***Combest***	Y	N	Y	N	Y	N	Y	Y
20 Gonzalez	Y	Y	N	Y	Y	Y	N	Y
21 ***Smith***	N	N	Y	N	Y	N	Y	Y
22 ***DeLay***	?	N	Y	N	Y	N	Y	Y
23 ***Bonilla***	N	N	Y	N	Y	Y	N	Y
24 Frost	Y	Y	Y	Y	Y	N	Y	Y
25 Andrews	Y	Y	N	Y	Y	N	Y	Y
26 ***Armey***	N	N	Y	N	Y	N	Y	Y
27 Ortiz	Y	Y	N	Y	Y	N	Y	Y
28 Tejeda	Y	Y	N	Y	Y	N	Y	Y
29 Green	Y	Y	N	Y	+	–	+	+
30 Johnson, E.B.	Y	Y	N	Y	Y	Y	Y	Y
UTAH								
1 ***Hansen***	N	N	Y	N	Y	Y	Y	Y
2 Shepherd	Y	Y	N	Y	Y	N	Y	Y
3 Orton	Y	Y	N	Y	Y	N	Y	Y
VERMONT								
AL *Sanders*	Y	Y	N	Y	Y	Y	Y	Y
VIRGINIA								
1 ***Bateman***	Y	N	Y	N	Y	N	Y	Y
2 Pickett	Y	Y	Y	Y	Y	Y	N	Y
3 Scott	Y	Y	N	Y	Y	Y	Y	Y
4 Sisisky	Y	Y	Y	Y	Y	N	Y	Y
5 Payne	Y	Y	Y	Y	Y	N	Y	Y
6 ***Goodlatte***	N	N	Y	N	Y	N	Y	Y
7 ***Bliley***	N	N	Y	N	Y	N	Y	Y
8 Moran	?	Y	N	Y	Y	Y	Y	Y
9 Boucher	Y	Y	Y	Y	Y	Y	Y	Y
10 ***Wolf***	N	N	Y	N	Y	N	Y	Y
11 Byrne	Y	Y	N	Y	Y	N	Y	Y
WASHINGTON								
1 Cantwell	Y	Y	N	Y	Y	N	Y	Y
2 Swift	Y	Y	N	Y	Y	Y	Y	Y
3 Unsoeld	Y	Y	N	Y	Y	N	Y	Y
4 Inslee	Y	Y	N	Y	Y	N	Y	Y
5 Foley			N	Y				
6 Dicks	Y	Y	N	Y	Y	N	N	Y
7 McDermott	Y	Y	N	Y	Y	Y	Y	Y
8 ***Dunn***	N	N	Y	N	Y	N	Y	Y
9 Kreidler	Y	Y	N	Y	Y	Y	Y	Y
WEST VIRGINIA								
1 Mollohan	Y	Y	N	Y	Y	N	Y	Y
2 Wise	Y	Y	N	Y	Y	N	Y	Y
3 Rahall	Y	Y	N	Y	Y	N	Y	Y
WISCONSIN								
1 Barca	Y	Y	N	N	Y	N	Y	Y
2 ***Klug***	N	N	Y	Y	Y	N	Y	Y
3 ***Gunderson***	N	N	Y	N	Y	N	Y	Y
4 Kleczka	Y	Y	N	Y	Y	N	Y	Y
5 Barrett	Y	Y	N	Y	Y	N	Y	Y
6 ***Petri***	N	N	Y	N	Y	Y	Y	Y
7 Obey	Y	N	N	N	Y	N	Y	Y
8 ***Roth***	?	N	Y	N	?	N	Y	Y
9 ***Sensenbrenner***	N	N	Y	N	Y	N	Y	Y
WYOMING								
AL ***Thomas***	N	N	Y	N	Y	N	Y	Y
DELEGATES								
de Lugo, V.I.	D	D	D	D	D	D	D	D
Faleomavaega, Am.S.	D	D	D	D	D	D	D	D
Norton, D.C.	D	D	D	D	D	D	D	D
Romero-B., P.R.	D	D	D	D	D	D	D	D
Underwood, Guam	D	D	D	D	D	D	D	D

Southern states - Ala., Ark., Fla., Ga., Ky., La., Miss., N.C., Okla., S.C., Tenn., Texas, Va.
Omitted votes are quorum calls, which CQ does not include in its vote charts.

461. HR 4462. Indian Federal Recognition/Passage. Richardson, D-N.M., motion to suspend the rules and pass the bill to establish a Commission on Indian Recognition authorized at $1.5 million a year to administer a new process for granting federal recognition to Indian tribes for eligibility in federal benefit and service programs. Motion agreed to 337-54: R 126-37; D 210-17 (ND 142-12, SD 68-5); I 1-0, Oct. 3, 1994. A two-thirds majority of those present and voting (261 in this case) is required for passage under suspension of the rules.

462. HR 4833. American Indian Trust Fund Management/Passage. Richardson, D-N.M., motion to suspend the rules and pass the bill to create an Office of Special Trustee within the Interior Department to ensure that Indian Trust Fund accounts are properly managed and audited. Motion agreed to 353-39: R 129-36; D 223-3 (ND 153-1, SD 70-2); I 1-0, Oct. 3, 1994. A two-thirds majority of those present and voting (262 in this case) is required for passage under suspension of the rules.

463. S 21. California Desert Protection/Floor Consideration. Miller, D-Calif., motion to take from the Speaker's table the bill to protect about 7.7 million acres of California desert as wilderness areas and to establish the Death Valley, Joshua Tree and Mojave national parks. Motion agreed to 268-148: R 29-144; D 238-4 (ND 161-2, SD 77-2); I 1-0, Oct. 4, 1994. (The motion to take a bill from the Speaker's table is one of several procedural steps required in order to go to conference.)

464. S 21. California Desert Protection/Motion To Table. Richardson, D-N.M., motion to table (kill) the Miller, D-Calif., motion to reconsider the Miller motion to take from the Speaker's table the bill to protect about 7.7 million acres of California desert as wilderness areas and to establish the Death Valley, Joshua Tree and Mojave national parks. Motion agreed to 271-150: R 28-147; D 242-3 (ND 164-0, SD 78-3); I 1-0, Oct. 4, 1994.

465. S 21. California Desert Protection/Motion To Table. Lewis, R-Calif., motion to table (kill) the Miller, D-Calif., motion to order the previous question (thus ending debate and the possibility of amendment) on the Miller motion to go to conference on the bill to protect about 7.7 million acres of California desert as wilderness areas and to establish the Death Valley, Joshua Tree and Mojave National Parks. Motion rejected 144-259: R 142-32; D 2-226 (ND 1-154, SD 1-72); I 0-1, Oct. 4, 1994.

466. S 21. California Desert Protection/Previous Question. Miller, D-Calif., motion to order the previous question (thus ending debate and the possibility of amendment) on the Miller motion to go to conference on the bill to protect about 7.7 million acres of California desert as wilderness areas and to establish the Death Valley, Joshua Tree and Mojave national parks. Motion agreed to 265-144: R 32-143; D 232-1 (ND 158-0, SD 74-1); I 1-0, Oct. 4, 1994.

467. S 21. California Desert Protection/Table Motion To Reconsider. Miller, D-Calif., motion to table (kill) the Baker, R-Calif., motion to reconsider the Miller motion to order the previous question (thus ending debate and the possibility of amendment) on the Miller motion to go to conference on the bill to protect about 7.7 million acres of California desert as wilderness areas and to establish the Death Valley, Joshua Tree and Mojave national parks. Motion agreed to 273-143: R 34-141; D 238-2 (ND 163-0, SD 75-2); I 1-0, Oct. 4, 1994.

468. S 21. California Desert Protection/Commit to Committee. Cunningham, R-Calif., motion to commit to the Merchant Marine and Fisheries Committee the Miller, D-Calif., motion to go to conference on the bill to protect about 7.7 million acres of California desert as wilderness areas and to establish the Death Valley, Joshua Tree and Mojave national parks. Motion rejected 141-277: R 137-37; D 4-240 (ND 3-160, SD 1-80); I 0-0, Oct. 4, 1994.

KEY

Y	Voted for (yea).
#	Paired for.
+	Announced for.
N	Voted against (nay).
X	Paired against.
−	Announced against.
P	Voted "present."
C	Voted "present" to avoid possible conflict of interest.
?	Did not vote or otherwise make a position known.
D	Delegates ineligible to vote.

Democrats *Republicans* *Independent*

	461	462	463	464	465	466	467	468
ALABAMA								
1 *Callahan*	?	?	N	N	Y	N	N	Y
2 *Everett*	Y	N	N	N	Y	N	N	Y
3 Browder	Y	Y	Y	Y	N	Y	Y	N
4 Bevill	Y	Y	Y	Y	N	Y	Y	N
5 Cramer	Y	Y	Y	Y	N	Y	Y	N
6 *Bachus*	Y	Y	N	N	Y	N	N	Y
7 Hilliard	?	?	Y	Y	?	Y	Y	N
ALASKA								
AL *Young*	Y	Y	N	N	Y	N	N	Y
ARIZONA								
1 Coppersmith	Y	Y	Y	Y	N	Y	Y	N
2 Pastor	+	+	Y	Y	N	Y	Y	N
3 *Stump*	N	N	N	N	Y	N	N	Y
4 *Kyl*	?	?	N	N	Y	N	N	Y
5 *Kolbe*	Y	Y	N	N	Y	N	N	Y
6 English	Y	Y	Y	Y	N	Y	Y	N
ARKANSAS								
1 Lambert	Y	Y	Y	Y	N	Y	Y	N
2 Thornton	Y	Y	Y	Y	N	Y	Y	N
3 *Hutchinson*	Y	Y	N	N	Y	N	N	Y
4 Dickey	Y	N	N	N	Y	N	N	Y
CALIFORNIA								
1 Hamburg	Y	Y	Y	Y	N	Y	Y	N
2 *Herger*	Y	Y	N	N	Y	N	N	Y
3 Fazio	Y	Y	Y	Y	N	Y	Y	?
4 *Doolittle*	Y	N	N	N	Y	N	N	Y
5 Matsui	?	Y	Y	Y	N	Y	Y	?
6 Woolsey	Y	Y	Y	Y	N	Y	Y	N
7 Miller	Y	Y	Y	Y	N	Y	Y	N
8 Pelosi	Y	Y	?	Y	N	Y	Y	N
9 Dellums	Y	Y	?	?	N	Y	Y	N
10 *Baker*	Y	Y	N	N	Y	Y	N	Y
11 *Pombo*	Y	N	N	N	Y	N	N	Y
12 Lantos	Y	Y	Y	Y	?	?	Y	?
13 Stark	Y	Y	Y	Y	N	Y	Y	N
14 Eshoo	Y	Y	Y	Y	N	Y	Y	N
15 Mineta	Y	Y	Y	Y	N	Y	Y	N
16 Edwards	Y	Y	Y	Y	N	Y	Y	N
17 Farr	Y	Y	Y	Y	N	Y	Y	N
18 Condit	N	Y	Y	Y	N	Y	Y	N
19 Lehman	Y	Y	Y	Y	N	Y	Y	N
20 Dooley	Y	Y	Y	Y	N	Y	Y	N
21 *Thomas*	Y	Y	N	N	Y	N	N	Y
22 *Huffington*	Y	Y	N	N	Y	N	N	Y
23 *Gallegly*	Y	Y	N	N	Y	N	N	Y
24 Beilenson	Y	Y	Y	Y	N	Y	Y	N
25 *McKeon*	Y	Y	N	N	Y	N	N	N
26 Berman	?	?	Y	Y	N	Y	Y	N
27 *Moorhead*	Y	Y	N	N	Y	N	N	Y
28 *Dreier*	Y	N	N	N	Y	N	N	Y
29 Waxman	Y	Y	Y	Y	N	Y	?	?
30 Becerra	Y	Y	Y	Y	N	Y	Y	N
31 Martinez	Y	Y	Y	Y	N	Y	Y	N
32 Dixon	Y	Y	Y	Y	N	Y	Y	N
33 Roybal-Allard	Y	Y	Y	Y	N	Y	Y	N
34 Torres	Y	Y	?	?	N	Y	Y	N
35 Waters	Y	Y	Y	Y	N	Y	Y	N
36 Harman	?	?	Y	Y	N	Y	Y	N
37 Tucker	?	?	?	?	?	?	?	?
38 *Horn*	Y	Y	N	N	Y	N	N	N
39 *Royce*	N	N	N	N	Y	N	N	Y
40 *Lewis*	Y	Y	N	N	Y	N	N	Y
41 *Kim*	Y	Y	N	N	Y	N	N	Y

	461	462	463	464	465	466	467	468
42 Brown	Y	Y	Y	Y	N	Y	Y	N
43 *Calvert*	?	?	N	N	Y	N	N	Y
44 *McCandless*	Y	Y	N	N	Y	N	N	Y
45 *Rohrabacher*	Y	N	N	N	Y	N	N	Y
46 *Dornan*	Y	Y	N	N	Y	N	N	Y
47 *Cox*	N	Y	N	N	Y	N	N	Y
48 *Packard*	Y	Y	N	N	Y	N	N	Y
49 Schenk	Y	Y	Y	Y	N	Y	Y	N
50 Filner	Y	Y	Y	Y	N	Y	Y	N
51 *Cunningham*	Y	Y	N	N	Y	N	N	Y
52 *Hunter*	Y	Y	N	N	Y	N	N	Y
COLORADO								
1 Schroeder	Y	Y	Y	Y	N	Y	Y	N
2 Skaggs	Y	Y	Y	Y	N	Y	Y	N
3 *McInnis*	Y	Y	N	N	Y	N	N	Y
4 *Allard*	N	N	N	N	Y	N	N	Y
5 *Hefley*	Y	N	N	N	Y	N	N	Y
6 *Schaefer*	N	N	N	N	Y	N	N	Y
CONNECTICUT								
1 Kennelly	Y	Y	Y	Y	N	Y	Y	N
2 Gejdenson	Y	Y	Y	Y	N	Y	Y	N
3 DeLauro	Y	Y	Y	Y	N	Y	Y	N
4 *Shays*	Y	Y	Y	Y	N	Y	Y	N
5 *Franks*	Y	Y	Y	Y	N	Y	Y	N
6 *Johnson*	Y	Y	Y	Y	N	Y	Y	N
DELAWARE								
AL *Castle*	Y	Y	N	N	N	Y	Y	N
FLORIDA								
1 Hutto	Y	Y	Y	Y	N	Y	Y	N
2 Peterson	Y	Y	Y	Y	N	Y	Y	N
3 Brown	Y	Y	Y	Y	?	?	Y	N
4 *Fowler*	N	Y	N	N	Y	N	N	Y
5 Thurman	Y	Y	Y	Y	N	Y	Y	N
6 *Stearns*	N	N	N	N	Y	N	N	Y
7 *Mica*	Y	Y	N	N	Y	N	N	Y
8 *McCollum*	Y	Y	N	N	Y	N	N	Y
9 *Bilirakis*	N	N	N	N	Y	N	N	Y
10 *Young*	N	N	N	N	Y	N	N	Y
11 Gibbons	Y	Y	Y	Y	N	Y	Y	N
12 *Canady*	N	Y	N	N	Y	N	N	Y
13 *Miller*	Y	Y	N	N	Y	N	N	Y
14 *Goss*	Y	Y	N	N	Y	N	N	Y
15 *Bacchus*	Y	Y	Y	Y	N	Y	Y	N
16 *Lewis*	N	N	N	N	Y	N	N	Y
17 Meek	Y	Y	Y	Y	?	?	Y	N
18 *Ros-Lehtinen*	Y	Y	N	N	Y	N	N	Y
19 Johnston	?	?	?	?	N	Y	?	N
20 Deutsch	Y	Y	Y	Y	N	Y	Y	N
21 *Diaz-Balart*	Y	Y	N	N	Y	N	N	Y
22 *Shaw*	Y	Y	N	N	Y	N	N	Y
23 Hastings	Y	Y	Y	Y	?	?	Y	N
GEORGIA								
1 *Kingston*	N	N	N	N	Y	N	N	Y
2 Bishop	Y	Y	Y	Y	N	Y	Y	N
3 *Collins*	N	N	N	N	Y	N	N	Y
4 *Linder*	Y	N	N	N	Y	N	N	Y
5 Lewis	Y	Y	Y	Y	N	Y	Y	N
6 *Gingrich*	Y	Y	?	N	Y	N	N	?
7 *Darden*	?	?	Y	Y	N	Y	Y	N
8 Rowland	Y	Y	Y	Y	N	Y	Y	N
9 Deal	N	Y	N	N	Y	N	N	Y
10 Johnson	Y	Y	Y	Y	N	Y	Y	N
11 McKinney	Y	Y	Y	Y	N	Y	Y	N
HAWAII								
1 Abercrombie	Y	Y	Y	Y	N	Y	Y	N
2 Mink	Y	Y	Y	Y	N	Y	Y	N
IDAHO								
1 LaRocco	Y	Y	Y	Y	N	Y	Y	N
2 *Crapo*	Y	Y	N	N	Y	N	N	Y
ILLINOIS								
1 Rush	Y	Y	Y	Y	?	?	Y	N
2 Reynolds	Y	Y	Y	Y	N	Y	Y	N
3 Lipinski	Y	Y	Y	Y	N	Y	Y	N
4 Gutierrez	Y	Y	Y	Y	N	Y	Y	N
5 Rostenkowski	?	?	?	N	?	Y	N	N
6 *Hyde*	Y	Y	Y	Y	?	?	Y	N
7 Collins	Y	Y	Y	Y	?	?	Y	N
8 *Crane*	N	N	N	N	Y	N	N	Y
9 Yates	Y	Y	Y	Y	N	Y	Y	N
10 *Porter*	Y	Y	Y	Y	N	Y	Y	N
11 Sangmeister	Y	Y	Y	Y	N	Y	Y	N
12 Costello	N	Y	Y	Y	N	Y	Y	N
13 *Fawell*	Y	Y	Y	Y	N	Y	Y	N
14 *Hastert*	N	N	N	N	Y	N	N	Y
15 *Ewing*	Y	Y	N	N	Y	N	N	Y
16 *Manzullo*	N	N	N	N	Y	N	N	Y
17 Evans	Y	Y	Y	Y	N	Y	Y	N

ND Northern Democrats SD Southern Democrats

	461	462	463	464	465	466	467	468
18 ***Michel***	Y	Y	N	N	Y	N	N	Y
19 Poshard	N	Y	Y	Y	N	Y	Y	N
20 Durbin	Y	Y	Y	Y	N	Y	Y	N
INDIANA								
1 Visclosky	N	Y	Y	Y	N	Y	Y	N
2 Sharp	Y	Y	Y	?	N	?	Y	N
3 Roemer	N	Y	Y	Y	N	Y	Y	N
4 Long	Y	Y	Y	Y	N	Y	Y	N
5 ***Buyer***	Y	Y	N	N	Y	N	N	Y
6 ***Burton***	Y	N	?	N	Y	N	N	Y
7 ***Myers***	Y	Y	N	N	Y	N	N	Y
8 McCloskey	Y	Y	?	?	N	Y	Y	N
9 Hamilton	Y	Y	Y	Y	N	Y	Y	N
10 Jacobs	Y	Y	Y	Y	N	Y	Y	N
IOWA								
1 ***Leach***	Y	Y	Y	Y	N	Y	Y	N
2 ***Nussle***	Y	Y	N	N	Y	N	N	Y
3 ***Lightfoot***	Y	Y	N	N	Y	N	N	Y
4 Smith	Y	Y	Y	Y	N	Y	Y	N
5 ***Grandy***	?	?	N	N	Y	N	N	Y
KANSAS								
1 ***Roberts***	N	Y	N	N	Y	N	N	Y
2 Slattery	?	?	?	?	?	?	?	?
3 ***Meyers***	Y	Y	Y	Y	N	Y	Y	N
4 Glickman	Y	Y	Y	Y	N	Y	Y	N
KENTUCKY								
1 Barlow	Y	Y	Y	Y	N	Y	Y	N
2 ***Lewis***	Y	N	N	N	Y	N	N	Y
3 Mazzoli	Y	Y	Y	Y	N	Y	Y	N
4 ***Bunning***	Y	N	N	N	Y	N	N	Y
5 ***Rogers***	Y	N	N	N	Y	N	N	Y
6 Baesler	Y	Y	Y	Y	N	Y	Y	N
LOUISIANA								
1 ***Livingston***	Y	Y	N	N	Y	N	N	Y
2 Jefferson	Y	Y	Y	Y	?	Y	Y	N
3 Tauzin	Y	Y	Y	Y	N	Y	Y	N
4 Fields	Y	Y	Y	Y	N	Y	Y	N
5 ***McCrery***	Y	Y	N	N	Y	N	N	Y
6 ***Baker***	?	?	N	N	Y	N	N	Y
7 Hayes	?	?	Y	Y	N	Y	Y	N
MAINE								
1 Andrews	Y	Y	Y	Y	N	Y	Y	N
2 ***Snowe***	Y	Y	Y	Y	N	Y	Y	N
MARYLAND								
1 ***Gilchrest***	Y	Y	Y	Y	N	Y	Y	N
2 ***Bentley***	Y	Y	N	N	Y	N	N	Y
3 Cardin	Y	Y	Y	Y	N	Y	Y	N
4 Wynn	Y	Y	Y	Y	N	Y	Y	N
5 Hoyer	Y	Y	Y	Y	N	Y	Y	N
6 ***Bartlett***	Y	Y	N	N	Y	N	N	Y
7 Mfume	Y	Y	Y	Y	?	?	?	N
8 ***Morella***	Y	Y	Y	Y	N	Y	Y	N
MASSACHUSETTS								
1 Olver	Y	Y	Y	Y	N	Y	Y	N
2 Neal	?	?	Y	Y	N	Y	Y	N
3 ***Blute***	Y	Y	Y	Y	N	Y	Y	N
4 Frank	Y	Y	Y	Y	N	Y	Y	N
5 Meehan	Y	Y	Y	Y	N	Y	Y	N
6 ***Torkildsen***	?	Y	Y	Y	N	Y	Y	N
7 Markey	Y	Y	Y	Y	N	Y	Y	N
8 Kennedy	Y	Y	Y	Y	N	Y	Y	N
9 Moakley	Y	Y	Y	Y	N	Y	Y	N
10 Studds	Y	Y	?	?	N	Y	Y	N
MICHIGAN								
1 Stupak	Y	Y	Y	Y	N	Y	Y	N
2 ***Hoekstra***	Y	Y	N	N	Y	N	N	Y
3 ***Ehlers***	Y	Y	Y	Y	N	N	N	N
4 ***Camp***	Y	Y	N	N	Y	N	N	Y
5 Barcia	Y	Y	Y	Y	N	Y	Y	N
6 ***Upton***	Y	Y	N	N	Y	N	N	Y
7 ***Smith***	N	Y	N	N	Y	N	N	Y
8 Carr	?	?	Y	Y	N	Y	Y	N
9 Kildee	Y	Y	Y	Y	N	Y	Y	N
10 Bonior	Y	Y	Y	Y	N	Y	Y	N
11 ***Knollenberg***	Y	Y	N	N	Y	N	N	Y
12 Levin	Y	Y	Y	Y	N	Y	Y	N
13 Ford	Y	Y	Y	Y	?	Y	Y	N
14 Conyers	Y	Y	Y	Y	N	Y	Y	N
15 Collins	Y	Y	Y	Y	?	?	Y	N
16 Dingell	Y	Y	Y	Y	N	Y	Y	N
MINNESOTA								
1 Penny	N	?	Y	Y	N	Y	Y	Y
2 Minge	Y	Y	Y	Y	N	Y	Y	N
3 ***Ramstad***	Y	Y	Y	Y	N	Y	Y	N
4 Vento	Y	Y	Y	Y	N	Y	Y	N

	461	462	463	464	465	466	467	468
5 Sabo	Y	Y	Y	Y	N	Y	Y	N
6 ***Grams***	Y	Y	N	N	Y	N	N	Y
7 Peterson	Y	Y	Y	Y	N	Y	Y	N
8 Oberstar	Y	Y	Y	Y	N	Y	Y	N
MISSISSIPPI								
1 Whitten	?	?	?	?	?	?	?	?
2 Thompson	Y	Y	Y	Y	N	Y	Y	N
3 Montgomery	Y	Y	Y	Y	N	Y	Y	N
4 Parker	N	N	Y	Y	N	Y	Y	N
5 Taylor	N	Y	Y	Y	N	Y	Y	N
MISSOURI								
1 Clay	Y	Y	Y	Y	?	Y	Y	N
2 ***Talent***	Y	N	N	N	Y	N	N	Y
3 Gephardt	Y	Y	Y	Y	N	Y	Y	N
4 Skelton	N	Y	Y	Y	N	Y	Y	N
5 Wheat	?	?	Y	Y	N	Y	Y	N
6 Danner	N	N	Y	Y	N	Y	Y	N
7 ***Hancock***	N	N	N	N	Y	N	N	Y
8 ***Emerson***	N	N	N	N	Y	N	N	Y
9 Volkmer	N	Y	Y	Y	N	Y	Y	N
MONTANA								
AL Williams	Y	Y	Y	Y	N	?	?	?
NEBRASKA								
1 ***Bereuter***	Y	Y	Y	Y	N	Y	Y	N
2 Hoagland	Y	Y	Y	Y	N	Y	Y	N
3 ***Barrett***	Y	Y	N	N	Y	N	N	Y
NEVADA								
1 Bilbray	Y	Y	Y	Y	N	Y	Y	N
2 ***Vucanovich***	Y	Y	N	N	Y	N	N	Y
NEW HAMPSHIRE								
1 ***Zeliff***	N	Y	N	N	Y	N	N	Y
2 Swett	Y	Y	Y	Y	N	Y	Y	N
NEW JERSEY								
1 Andrews	Y	Y	Y	Y	N	Y	Y	N
2 Hughes	Y	Y	Y	Y	N	Y	Y	N
3 ***Saxton***	?	Y	Y	Y	N	Y	Y	N
4 ***Smith***	Y	Y	Y	Y	N	Y	Y	N
5 ***Roukema***	N	Y	Y	Y	N	Y	Y	N
6 Pallone	Y	Y	Y	Y	N	Y	Y	N
7 ***Franks***	Y	Y	Y	Y	N	Y	Y	N
8 Klein	Y	Y	Y	Y	N	Y	Y	N
9 Torricelli	?	?	Y	Y	N	Y	Y	N
10 Payne	Y	Y	Y	Y	?	?	Y	N
11 ***Gallo***	?	?	?	?	?	?	?	?
12 ***Zimmer***	N	Y	Y	Y	N	Y	Y	N
13 Menendez	Y	Y	Y	Y	N	Y	Y	N
NEW MEXICO								
1 ***Schiff***	Y	Y	Y	N	Y	N	N	Y
2 ***Skeen***	Y	Y	N	N	Y	N	N	Y
3 Richardson	?	?	Y	Y	N	Y	Y	N
NEW YORK								
1 Hochbrueckner	Y	Y	Y	Y	N	Y	Y	N
2 ***Lazio***	Y	N	N	N	N	N	N	N
3 ***King***	Y	Y	N	N	Y	N	N	Y
4 ***Levy***	Y	Y	N	N	Y	N	N	Y
5 Ackerman	Y	Y	Y	Y	N	Y	Y	N
6 Flake	Y	Y	Y	Y	?	Y	Y	N
7 Manton	Y	Y	Y	Y	N	Y	Y	N
8 Nadler	Y	Y	Y	Y	N	Y	Y	N
9 Schumer	Y	Y	Y	Y	N	Y	Y	N
10 Towns	Y	Y	Y	Y	N	Y	Y	N
11 Owens	?	?	Y	Y	?	?	?	N
12 Velazquez	Y	Y	Y	Y	N	Y	Y	N
13 ***Molinari***	Y	Y	N	N	Y	N	N	Y
14 Maloney	?	?	Y	Y	N	Y	Y	N
15 Rangel	?	?	Y	Y	?	?	Y	N
16 Serrano	Y	Y	Y	Y	N	Y	Y	N
17 Engel	Y	Y	Y	Y	N	Y	Y	N
18 Lowey	?	?	Y	Y	N	Y	Y	N
19 ***Fish***	?	?	Y	N	N	Y	Y	N
20 ***Gilman***	Y	Y	Y	Y	N	Y	Y	N
21 McNulty	N	Y	Y	Y	N	Y	Y	N
22 ***Solomon***	N	Y	N	N	?	N	N	Y
23 ***Boehlert***	Y	Y	Y	Y	N	Y	Y	N
24 ***McHugh***	N	Y	N	N	Y	N	N	Y
25 ***Walsh***	N	N	N	N	Y	N	N	Y
26 Hinchey	Y	Y	Y	Y	N	Y	Y	N
27 ***Paxon***	N	Y	N	N	Y	N	N	Y
28 Slaughter	Y	Y	Y	+	N	Y	Y	N
29 LaFalce	Y	Y	Y	Y	N	Y	Y	N
30 ***Quinn***	Y	Y	N	N	Y	N	N	Y
31 ***Houghton***	Y	Y	N	N	Y	N	N	Y
NORTH CAROLINA								
1 Clayton	Y	Y	Y	Y	N	Y	Y	N
2 Valentine	Y	Y	Y	Y	N	Y	?	?

	461	462	463	464	465	466	467	468
3 Lancaster	Y	Y	Y	Y	N	Y	?	N
4 Price	Y	Y	Y	Y	N	Y	Y	N
5 Neal	Y	Y	Y	Y	N	Y	Y	N
6 ***Coble***	N	Y	N	N	Y	N	N	Y
7 Rose	Y	Y	Y	Y	N	Y	N	N
8 Hefner	Y	Y	Y	Y	N	Y	Y	N
9 ***McMillan***	?	?	N	N	?	?	N	N
10 ***Ballenger***	N	N	?	N	Y	N	N	Y
11 ***Taylor***	N	N	N	N	Y	N	N	Y
12 Watt	Y	Y	Y	Y	N	Y	Y	N
NORTH DAKOTA								
AL Pomeroy	Y	Y	Y	Y	N	Y	Y	N
OHIO								
1 Mann	Y	Y	Y	Y	N	Y	Y	N
2 ***Portman***	Y	Y	N	N	Y	N	N	Y
3 Hall	Y	Y	Y	Y	?	Y	Y	N
4 ***Oxley***	Y	Y	N	N	Y	N	N	Y
5 ***Gillmor***	Y	Y	N	N	Y	N	N	N
6 Strickland	Y	Y	Y	Y	N	Y	Y	?
7 ***Hobson***	Y	Y	N	N	Y	N	N	Y
8 ***Boehner***	?	?	N	N	Y	N	N	Y
9 Kaptur	Y	Y	Y	Y	N	Y	Y	N
10 ***Hoke***	Y	Y	N	N	Y	N	N	Y
11 Stokes	Y	Y	?	Y	?	?	?	N
12 ***Kasich***	Y	Y	N	N	Y	N	N	Y
13 Brown	Y	Y	Y	Y	N	Y	Y	N
14 Sawyer	Y	Y	Y	Y	N	Y	Y	N
15 ***Pryce***	Y	Y	N	N	Y	N	N	Y
16 ***Regula***	N	Y	N	N	N	N	Y	N
17 Traficant	Y	Y	N	Y	N	Y	Y	N
18 Applegate	Y	Y	Y	Y	N	Y	Y	?
19 Fingerhut	N	Y	Y	Y	N	Y	Y	N
OKLAHOMA								
1 ***Inhofe***	?	?	N	N	Y	N	N	Y
2 Synar	Y	Y	Y	Y	N	Y	Y	N
3 Brewster	Y	Y	Y	Y	N	Y	Y	N
4 McCurdy	?	?	Y	Y	N	Y	Y	N
5 ***Istook***	Y	Y	N	N	Y	N	N	Y
6 ***Lucas***	Y	Y	N	N	Y	N	N	Y
OREGON								
1 Furse	Y	Y	Y	Y	N	Y	Y	N
2 ***Smith***	Y	Y	N	N	Y	N	N	Y
3 Wyden	Y	Y	Y	Y	N	Y	Y	N
4 DeFazio	Y	Y	Y	Y	N	Y	Y	N
5 Kopetski	Y	Y	Y	Y	N	Y	Y	N
PENNSYLVANIA								
1 Foglietta	Y	Y	Y	Y	N	Y	Y	N
2 Blackwell	?	?	Y	Y	?	Y	Y	N
3 Borski	?	?	Y	Y	N	Y	Y	N
4 Klink	Y	Y	Y	Y	N	Y	Y	N
5 ***Clinger***	Y	Y	N	N	Y	N	Y	Y
6 Holden	Y	Y	Y	Y	N	Y	Y	N
7 ***Weldon***	Y	Y	Y	Y	N	Y	Y	N
8 ***Greenwood***	Y	Y	Y	Y	N	Y	Y	N
9 ***Shuster***	Y	Y	N	N	Y	N	N	Y
10 ***McDade***	Y	?	N	N	Y	N	N	Y
11 Kanjorski	Y	Y	Y	Y	N	Y	Y	N
12 Murtha	Y	Y	Y	Y	N	Y	Y	N
13 Margolies-Mezv.	Y	Y	Y	Y	N	Y	Y	N
14 Coyne	Y	Y	Y	Y	N	Y	Y	N
15 McHale	Y	Y	Y	Y	N	Y	Y	N
16 ***Walker***	Y	Y	N	N	Y	N	N	Y
17 ***Gekas***	Y	Y	N	N	Y	N	N	Y
18 ***Santorum***	Y	Y	N	N	Y	N	Y	Y
19 ***Goodling***	?	?	N	N	Y	N	N	Y
20 Murphy	Y	Y	Y	Y	N	Y	?	N
21 ***Ridge***	Y	Y	N	Y	Y	N	Y	N
RHODE ISLAND								
1 ***Machtley***	Y	Y	Y	Y	N	Y	Y	N
2 Reed	Y	Y	Y	Y	N	Y	Y	N
SOUTH CAROLINA								
1 ***Ravenel***	Y	Y	Y	Y	N	Y	Y	N
2 ***Spence***	Y	Y	N	N	Y	N	N	Y
3 Derrick	Y	Y	Y	Y	N	Y	Y	N
4 ***Inglis***	Y	Y	N	N	Y	N	N	Y
5 Spratt	Y	Y	Y	Y	N	Y	Y	N
6 Clyburn	Y	Y	Y	Y	N	Y	Y	N
SOUTH DAKOTA								
AL Johnson	Y	Y	Y	Y	N	Y	Y	N
TENNESSEE								
1 ***Quillen***	Y	Y	N	N	N	Y	Y	N
2 ***Duncan***	N	N	N	N	Y	N	N	Y
3 Lloyd	Y	Y	Y	Y	?	?	Y	N
4 Cooper	Y	Y	Y	Y	N	Y	Y	N
5 Clement	Y	Y	Y	Y	N	Y	Y	N

	461	462	463	464	465	466	467	468
6 Gordon	Y	Y	Y	Y	N	Y	Y	N
7 ***Sundquist***	?	?	?	?	?	?	?	?
8 Tanner	Y	Y	Y	Y	N	Y	Y	N
9 Ford	?	?	Y	Y	N	Y	Y	N
TEXAS								
1 Chapman	Y	Y	Y	Y	N	Y	Y	N
2 Wilson	Y	Y	Y	Y	N	Y	Y	N
3 ***Johnson, Sam***	N	N	N	N	Y	N	N	Y
4 Hall	Y	Y	N	N	Y	N	N	Y
5 Bryant	Y	Y	Y	Y	N	Y	Y	N
6 ***Barton***	Y	N	N	N	Y	N	N	Y
7 ***Archer***	Y	N	N	N	Y	N	N	Y
8 ***Fields***	Y	N	N	N	Y	N	N	Y
9 Brooks	Y	Y	Y	Y	N	?	Y	N
10 Pickle	Y	Y	Y	Y	N	Y	Y	N
11 Edwards	Y	Y	Y	Y	?	?	Y	N
12 Geren	N	Y	Y	Y	N	Y	Y	N
13 Sarpalius	Y	Y	N	N	N	Y	Y	N
14 Laughlin	?	?	Y	Y	N	Y	Y	N
15 de la Garza	Y	Y	Y	Y	N	Y	Y	N
16 Coleman	Y	Y	Y	Y	N	Y	Y	N
17 Stenholm	N	Y	Y	N	N	Y	Y	N
18 Washington	?	?	?	Y	N	?	Y	N
19 ***Combest***	Y	Y	N	N	Y	N	N	Y
20 Gonzalez	Y	Y	Y	Y	N	Y	Y	N
21 ***Smith***	Y	Y	N	N	Y	N	N	Y
22 ***DeLay***	N	N	N	N	Y	N	N	Y
23 ***Bonilla***	Y	Y	N	N	Y	N	N	Y
24 Frost	Y	Y	Y	Y	N	Y	Y	N
25 Andrews	Y	Y	?	Y	N	Y	Y	N
26 ***Armey***	N	N	N	N	Y	N	N	Y
27 Ortiz	Y	Y	Y	Y	N	Y	Y	N
28 Tejeda	Y	Y	Y	Y	N	Y	Y	N
29 Green	+	+	Y	Y	N	Y	?	N
30 Johnson, E.B.	Y	Y	Y	Y	–	+	Y	N
UTAH								
1 ***Hansen***	N	N	N	N	Y	N	N	Y
2 Shepherd	Y	Y	Y	Y	N	Y	Y	N
3 Orton	N	Y	N	Y	Y	Y	Y	Y
VERMONT								
AL *Sanders*	Y	Y	Y	Y	N	Y	Y	?
VIRGINIA								
1 ***Bateman***	Y	Y	N	N	Y	N	?	?
2 Pickett	Y	N	Y	Y	N	Y	Y	N
3 Scott	Y	Y	Y	Y	?	Y	Y	N
4 Sisisky	Y	Y	Y	Y	N	Y	?	N
5 Payne	Y	Y	Y	Y	N	Y	Y	N
6 ***Goodlatte***	N	Y	N	N	Y	N	N	Y
7 ***Bliley***	Y	Y	N	N	Y	N	N	Y
8 Moran	Y	Y	Y	Y	N	Y	Y	N
9 Boucher	Y	Y	Y	Y	N	Y	Y	N
10 ***Wolf***	Y	Y	N	?	Y	N	N	Y
11 Byrne	Y	?	?	Y	N	Y	Y	N
WASHINGTON								
1 Cantwell	Y	Y	Y	Y	N	Y	Y	N
2 Swift	Y	Y	Y	Y	N	Y	Y	N
3 Unsoeld	Y	Y	Y	Y	N	Y	Y	N
4 Inslee	Y	Y	Y	Y	N	Y	Y	N
5 Foley								
6 Dicks	Y	Y	Y	Y	N	Y	Y	N
7 McDermott	Y	Y	Y	Y	N	Y	Y	N
8 ***Dunn***	Y	Y	N	N	Y	Y	N	Y
9 Kreidler	Y	Y	Y	Y	N	Y	Y	N
WEST VIRGINIA								
1 Mollohan	Y	Y	Y	Y	?	Y	Y	N
2 Wise	Y	Y	Y	Y	N	Y	Y	N
3 Rahall	Y	Y	Y	Y	N	Y	Y	N
WISCONSIN								
1 Barca	Y	Y	Y	Y	N	Y	Y	N
2 ***Klug***	Y	N	Y	Y	Y	Y	Y	N
3 ***Gunderson***	Y	Y	N	N	Y	N	N	Y
4 Kleczka	Y	Y	Y	Y	N	Y	Y	N
5 Barrett	Y	Y	Y	Y	N	Y	Y	N
6 ***Petri***	N	Y	N	N	Y	N	N	Y
7 Obey	Y	Y	Y	Y	N	Y	Y	N
8 ***Roth***	Y	Y	N	N	Y	N	N	Y
9 ***Sensenbrenner***	N	N	N	N	Y	N	N	Y
WYOMING								
AL ***Thomas***	Y	Y	N	N	Y	N	N	Y
DELEGATES								
de Lugo, V.I.	D	D	D	D	D	D	D	D
Faleomavaega, Am.S.	D	D	D	D	D	D	D	D
Norton, D.C.	D	D	D	D	D	D	D	D
Romero-B., P.R.	D	D	D	D	D	D	D	D
Underwood, Guam	D	D	D	D	D	D	D	D

Southern states - Ala., Ark., Fla., Ga., Ky., La., Miss., N.C., Okla., S.C., Tenn., Texas, Va.
Omitted votes are quorum calls, which CQ does not include in its vote charts.

469. S 21. California Desert Protection/Table Motion to Reconsider. Miller, D-Calif., motion to table (kill) the McKeon, R-Calif., motion to reconsider the Cunningham, R-Calif., motion to commit to the Merchant Marine and Fisheries Committee the motion to go to conference on the bill to protect about 7.7 million acres of California desert as wilderness areas and to establish the Death Valley, Joshua Tree and Mojave national parks. Motion agreed to 280-141: R 33-141; D 246-0 (ND 165-0, SD 81-0); I 1-0, Oct. 4, 1994.

470. S 21. California Desert Protection/Agree to a Conference. Miller, D-Calif., motion to insist on House amendments and agree to a conference on the bill to protect about 7.7 million acres of California desert as wilderness areas and to establish the Death Valley, Joshua Tree and Mojave national parks. Motion agreed to 283-140: R 37-138; D 245-2 (ND 165-1, SD 80-1); I 1-0, Oct. 4, 1994.

471. S 21. California Desert Protection/Table Motion to Reconsider. Miller, D-Calif., motion to table (kill) the Doolittle, R-Calif., motion to reconsider the Miller motion to insist on House amendments and agree to a conference on the bill to protect about 7.7 million acres of California desert as wilderness areas and to establish the Death Valley, Joshua Tree and Mojave national parks. Motion agreed to 282-140: R 37-139; D 244-1 (ND 163-0, SD 81-1); I 1-0, Oct. 4, 1994.

472. Procedural Motion/Adjournment. Crane, R-Ill., motion to adjourn. Motion rejected 87-330: R 79-93; D 8-237 (ND 6-158, SD 2-79); I 0-0, Oct. 4, 1994.

473. S 21. California Desert Protection/Table Motion to Instruct. Miller, D-Calif., motion to table (kill) the Lewis, R-Calif., motion to instruct the conferees to insist upon certain House provisions on the bill to protect about 7.7 million acres of California desert as wilderness areas and to establish the Death Valley, Joshua Tree and Mojave national parks. Motion agreed to 274-147: R 32-142; D 241-5 (ND 162-2, SD 79-3); I 1-0, Oct. 4, 1994.

474. S 21. California Desert Protection/Table Motion to Reconsider. Vento, D-Minn., motion to table (kill) the Miller, D-Calif., motion to reconsider the Miller motion to table (kill) the Lewis, R-Calif., motion to instruct the conferees to accept certain House provisions on the bill to protect about 7.7 million acres of California desert as wilderness areas and to establish the Death Valley, Joshua Tree and Mojave national parks. Motion agreed to 271-142: R 33-140; D 237-2 (ND 160-0, SD 77-2); I 1-0, Oct. 4, 1994.

475. HR 967. Minor-Use Crop Pesticides/Passage. De la Garza, D-Texas, motion to suspend the rules and pass the bill to provide incentives to manufacturers of minor-use crop pesticides to maintain their Environmental Protection Agency approval and to apply for approval of new types of pesticides. Motion agreed to 334-80: R 168-3; D 166-76 (ND 92-71, SD 74-5); I 0-1, Oct. 4, 1994. A two-thirds majority of those present and voting (276 in this case) is required for passage under suspension of the rules.

476. HR 1520. Petroleum Marketing Practices/Passage. Sharp, D-Ind., motion to suspend the rules and pass the bill to clarify state authority under federal standards set by the 1978 Petroleum Marketing Practices Act, which governs the franchise relationship between oil companies and independent service station operators who sell gasoline under franchise agreements. Motion agreed to 413-0: R 173-0; D 239-0 (ND 162-0, SD 77-0); I 1-0, Oct. 4, 1994. A two-thirds majority of those present and voting (276 in this case) is required for passage under suspension of the rules.

KEY

Y	Voted for (yea).
#	Paired for.
+	Announced for.
N	Voted against (nay).
X	Paired against.
−	Announced against.
P	Voted "present."
C	Voted "present" to avoid possible conflict of interest.
?	Did not vote or otherwise make a position known.
D	Delegates ineligible to vote.

Democrats *Republicans*
Independent

	469	470	471	472	473	474	475	476
ALABAMA								
1 *Callahan*	N	N	N	N	N	N	Y	Y
2 *Everett*	N	N	N	N	N	N	Y	Y
3 Browder	Y	Y	Y	N	Y	Y	Y	?
4 Bevill	Y	Y	Y	N	Y	Y	Y	Y
5 Cramer	Y	Y	Y	N	Y	Y	Y	Y
6 *Bachus*	N	N	N	?	N	N	Y	Y
7 Hilliard	Y	Y	Y	N	Y	Y	Y	Y
ALASKA								
AL *Young*	N	N	N	Y	N	N	Y	Y
ARIZONA								
1 Coppersmith	Y	Y	Y	N	Y	Y	Y	Y
2 Pastor	Y	Y	Y	N	Y	Y	Y	Y
3 *Stump*	N	N	N	N	N	N	N	Y
4 *Kyl*	N	N	N	N	N	N	N	Y
5 *Kolbe*	N	N	N	N	N	N	Y	Y
6 English	Y	Y	Y	N	Y	Y	Y	Y
ARKANSAS								
1 Lambert	Y	Y	Y	N	Y	Y	Y	Y
2 Thornton	Y	Y	Y	N	Y	Y	Y	Y
3 *Hutchinson*	N	N	N	N	N	N	N	Y
4 *Dickey*	N	N	N	Y	N	N	Y	Y
CALIFORNIA								
1 Hamburg	Y	Y	Y	N	Y	N	Y	Y
2 *Herger*	N	N	N	Y	N	N	Y	Y
3 Fazio	?	?	Y	N	Y	Y	Y	Y
4 *Doolittle*	N	Y	N	N	Y	N	N	Y
5 Matsui	Y	Y	Y	N	Y	Y	Y	Y
6 Woolsey	Y	Y	Y	N	Y	Y	N	Y
7 Miller	Y	Y	Y	N	Y	Y	Y	?
8 Pelosi	Y	Y	Y	N	Y	Y	N	?
9 Dellums	Y	Y	Y	N	Y	Y	N	Y
10 *Baker*	N	N	N	Y	N	N	Y	Y
11 *Pombo*	N	N	N	N	N	N	Y	Y
12 Lantos	?	?	?	?	?	?	?	?
13 Stark	Y	Y	Y	N	Y	Y	N	Y
14 Eshoo	Y	Y	Y	N	Y	Y	Y	Y
15 Mineta	Y	Y	Y	N	Y	Y	N	Y
16 Edwards	Y	Y	Y	N	Y	Y	?	Y
17 Farr	Y	Y	Y	N	Y	Y	N	Y
18 Condit	Y	Y	Y	Y	Y	Y	Y	Y
19 Lehman	Y	Y	Y	N	Y	Y	?	Y
20 Dooley	Y	Y	Y	N	Y	Y	Y	Y
21 *Thomas*	N	N	N	Y	N	N	Y	Y
22 *Huffington*	N	N	N	N	N	N	N	?
23 *Gallegly*	N	N	N	N	N	N	N	Y
24 Beilenson	Y	Y	Y	N	Y	Y	Y	N
25 *McKeon*	N	N	N	N	N	N	Y	Y
26 Berman	Y	Y	Y	N	Y	Y	Y	Y
27 *Moorhead*	N	N	N	N	N	N	N	Y
28 *Dreier*	N	N	N	Y	N	N	Y	Y
29 Waxman	Y	Y	Y	N	Y	Y	Y	Y
30 Becerra	Y	Y	Y	N	Y	Y	N	Y
31 Martinez	Y	Y	Y	N	Y	Y	N	Y
32 Dixon	Y	Y	Y	N	Y	Y	Y	Y
33 Roybal-Allard	Y	Y	Y	N	Y	Y	Y	Y
34 Torres	Y	Y	Y	N	Y	Y	N	Y
35 Waters	Y	Y	Y	N	Y	Y	N	Y
36 Harman	Y	Y	Y	N	Y	Y	N	Y
37 Tucker	?	?	?	?	?	?	?	?
38 *Horn*	Y	Y	Y	N	Y	Y	Y	Y
39 *Royce*	N	N	N	Y	N	N	N	Y
40 *Lewis*	N	N	N	Y	N	N	Y	Y
41 *Kim*	N	N	N	Y	N	N	Y	Y
42 Brown	Y	Y	Y	N	Y	?	N	Y
43 *Calvert*	N	N	N	Y	N	N	N	Y
44 *McCandless*	N	N	N	N	N	N	N	Y
45 *Rohrabacher*	N	N	N	Y	N	N	Y	Y
46 *Dornan*	N	N	N	Y	N	N	Y	Y
47 *Cox*	N	N	N	Y	N	N	Y	Y
48 *Packard*	N	N	N	Y	N	N	Y	Y
49 Schenk	Y	Y	Y	N	Y	Y	N	Y
50 Filner	Y	Y	Y	N	Y	Y	N	Y
51 *Cunningham*	N	N	N	N	N	N	Y	Y
52 *Hunter*	N	N	N	Y	N	N	Y	Y
COLORADO								
1 Schroeder	Y	Y	Y	N	Y	Y	N	Y
2 Skaggs	Y	Y	Y	N	Y	Y	N	Y
3 *McInnis*	N	N	N	Y	N	N	Y	Y
4 *Allard*	N	N	N	Y	N	N	Y	Y
5 *Hefley*	N	N	N	Y	N	N	Y	Y
6 *Schaefer*	N	N	N	Y	N	N	Y	Y
CONNECTICUT								
1 Kennelly	Y	Y	Y	N	Y	Y	N	Y
2 Gejdenson	Y	Y	Y	N	Y	Y	N	Y
3 DeLauro	Y	Y	Y	N	Y	Y	N	Y
4 *Shays*	Y	Y	Y	N	Y	Y	Y	Y
5 *Franks*	Y	Y	Y	Y	Y	Y	Y	Y
6 *Johnson*	Y	Y	Y	N	Y	Y	Y	Y
DELAWARE								
AL *Castle*	Y	Y	Y	N	Y	Y	Y	Y
FLORIDA								
1 Hutto	Y	Y	Y	N	Y	Y	Y	Y
2 Peterson	Y	Y	Y	N	Y	Y	Y	Y
3 Brown	Y	Y	Y	N	Y	Y	Y	Y
4 *Fowler*	N	N	N	N	N	N	Y	Y
5 Thurman	Y	Y	Y	N	Y	Y	Y	Y
6 *Stearns*	N	N	N	Y	N	N	Y	Y
7 *Mica*	N	N	N	Y	N	N	Y	Y
8 *McCollum*	N	N	N	N	N	N	Y	Y
9 *Bilirakis*	N	N	N	Y	N	N	Y	Y
10 *Young*	N	N	N	Y	N	N	Y	Y
11 Gibbons	Y	Y	Y	N	Y	Y	Y	Y
12 *Canady*	N	N	N	Y	N	N	Y	Y
13 *Miller*	N	N	N	Y	N	N	Y	Y
14 *Goss*	N	N	N	Y	N	N	Y	Y
15 Bacchus	Y	Y	Y	N	Y	Y	Y	Y
16 *Lewis*	N	N	N	?	N	?	Y	Y
17 Meek	Y	Y	Y	N	Y	Y	N	Y
18 *Ros-Lehtinen*	N	N	N	N	N	N	Y	Y
19 Johnston	Y	Y	Y	?	Y	Y	Y	Y
20 Deutsch	Y	Y	Y	N	Y	Y	Y	Y
21 *Diaz-Balart*	N	N	N	N	N	N	Y	Y
22 *Shaw*	N	N	N	Y	N	N	Y	Y
23 Hastings	Y	Y	Y	N	Y	Y	Y	Y
GEORGIA								
1 *Kingston*	N	N	N	Y	N	N	Y	Y
2 Bishop	Y	Y	Y	N	Y	Y	Y	Y
3 *Collins*	N	N	N	Y	N	N	Y	Y
4 *Linder*	N	N	N	Y	N	N	Y	Y
5 Lewis	Y	Y	Y	N	Y	Y	?	?
6 *Gingrich*	N	N	N	N	N	N	Y	Y
7 Darden	Y	Y	Y	N	Y	Y	Y	Y
8 Rowland	Y	Y	Y	N	Y	Y	Y	Y
9 Deal	Y	Y	Y	N	Y	Y	Y	Y
10 Johnson	Y	Y	Y	N	Y	Y	Y	Y
11 McKinney	Y	Y	Y	N	Y	Y	Y	?
HAWAII								
1 Abercrombie	Y	Y	Y	N	Y	Y	Y	Y
2 Mink	Y	Y	Y	N	Y	Y	Y	Y
IDAHO								
1 LaRocco	Y	Y	Y	N	Y	Y	Y	Y
2 *Crapo*	N	N	N	Y	N	N	Y	Y
ILLINOIS								
1 Rush	Y	Y	Y	N	Y	Y	N	Y
2 Reynolds	Y	Y	Y	N	Y	Y	N	Y
3 Lipinski	Y	Y	Y	N	Y	Y	N	Y
4 Gutierrez	Y	Y	Y	N	Y	Y	N	Y
5 Rostenkowski	Y	Y	Y	N	Y	Y	N	Y
6 *Hyde*	N	N	N	N	N	N	Y	Y
7 Collins	Y	Y	Y	Y	Y	Y	Y	Y
8 *Crane*	N	N	N	Y	N	N	Y	Y
9 Yates	Y	Y	Y	N	Y	Y	N	Y
10 *Porter*	Y	Y	Y	N	Y	Y	Y	Y
11 Sangmeister	Y	Y	Y	N	Y	Y	Y	Y
12 Costello	Y	Y	Y	N	Y	Y	Y	Y
13 *Fawell*	Y	Y	Y	N	Y	Y	Y	Y
14 *Hastert*	N	N	N	N	N	N	Y	Y
15 *Ewing*	N	N	N	N	N	N	N	Y
16 *Manzullo*	N	N	N	N	N	N	Y	Y
17 Evans	Y	Y	Y	N	Y	Y	N	Y

ND Northern Democrats SD Southern Democrats

	469	470	471	472	473	474	475	476
18 ***Michel***	N	N	N	N	N	N	Y	Y
19 Poshard	Y	Y	Y	N	Y	Y	Y	Y
20 Durbin	Y	Y	Y	N	Y	?	Y	Y
INDIANA								
1 Visclosky	Y	Y	Y	Y	Y	Y	Y	Y
2 Sharp	Y	Y	?	?	?	?	Y	Y
3 Roemer	Y	Y	Y	N	Y	Y	Y	Y
4 Long	Y	Y	Y	N	Y	Y	Y	Y
5 ***Buyer***	N	N	N	Y	N	N	Y	Y
6 ***Burton***	N	N	N	Y	N	N	Y	Y
7 ***Myers***	N	N	N	Y	N	N	Y	Y
8 McCloskey	Y	Y	Y	N	Y	Y	Y	Y
9 Hamilton	Y	Y	Y	N	Y	Y	Y	Y
10 Jacobs	Y	Y	Y	N	Y	?	N	Y
IOWA								
1 ***Leach***	Y	Y	Y	N	Y	Y	Y	Y
2 ***Nussle***	N	N	N	N	N	N	Y	Y
3 ***Lightfoot***	N	N	N	N	N	N	Y	Y
4 Smith	Y	Y	Y	N	Y	Y	Y	Y
5 ***Grandy***	N	N	N	Y	N	N	Y	Y
KANSAS								
1 ***Roberts***	N	N	N	Y	N	N	Y	Y
2 Slattery	?	?	?	?	?	?	?	?
3 ***Meyers***	Y	Y	Y	N	Y	Y	Y	Y
4 Glickman	Y	Y	Y	N	Y	Y	Y	Y
KENTUCKY								
1 Barlow	Y	Y	Y	N	Y	Y	Y	Y
2 ***Lewis***	N	N	N	N	N	N	Y	Y
3 Mazzoli	Y	Y	Y	N	Y	Y	Y	Y
4 ***Bunning***	N	N	N	N	N	N	Y	Y
5 ***Rogers***	N	N	N	N	N	N	Y	Y
6 Baesler	Y	Y	Y	N	Y	Y	Y	?
LOUISIANA								
1 ***Livingston***	N	N	N	?	N	N	Y	Y
2 Jefferson	Y	Y	Y	N	Y	Y	Y	Y
3 Tauzin	Y	Y	Y	N	N	N	Y	Y
4 Fields	Y	Y	Y	N	Y	Y	Y	Y
5 ***McCrery***	N	N	N	N	N	N	Y	Y
6 ***Baker***	N	N	N	N	N	N	Y	Y
7 Hayes	Y	Y	Y	N	Y	Y	Y	Y
MAINE								
1 Andrews	Y	Y	Y	N	Y	Y	N	Y
2 ***Snowe***	Y	Y	Y	N	Y	Y	Y	Y
MARYLAND								
1 ***Gilchrest***	Y	Y	Y	N	Y	Y	Y	Y
2 ***Bentley***	N	N	N	N	N	N	Y	Y
3 Cardin	Y	Y	Y	N	Y	Y	N	Y
4 Wynn	Y	Y	Y	N	Y	Y	Y	Y
5 Hoyer	Y	Y	Y	N	Y	Y	Y	Y
6 ***Bartlett***	N	N	N	Y	N	N	Y	Y
7 Mfume	Y	Y	Y	N	Y	Y	N	Y
8 ***Morella***	Y	Y	Y	N	Y	Y	Y	Y
MASSACHUSETTS								
1 Olver	Y	Y	Y	N	Y	Y	Y	Y
2 Neal	Y	Y	Y	N	Y	Y	N	Y
3 ***Blute***	Y	Y	Y	N	Y	Y	Y	Y
4 Frank	Y	Y	Y	N	Y	Y	Y	Y
5 Meehan	Y	Y	Y	N	Y	Y	N	Y
6 ***Torkildsen***	Y	Y	Y	N	Y	Y	Y	Y
7 Markey	Y	Y	Y	N	Y	Y	N	Y
8 Kennedy	Y	Y	Y	N	Y	Y	N	Y
9 Moakley	Y	Y	Y	N	Y	Y	N	Y
10 Studds	Y	Y	Y	N	Y	Y	N	Y
MICHIGAN								
1 Stupak	Y	Y	Y	N	Y	Y	Y	Y
2 ***Hoekstra***	N	N	N	Y	N	N	Y	Y
3 ***Ehlers***	Y	Y	Y	N	N	N	Y	Y
4 ***Camp***	N	N	N	N	N	N	Y	Y
5 Barcia	Y	Y	Y	N	Y	Y	Y	Y
6 ***Upton***	N	N	N	N	N	N	Y	Y
7 ***Smith***	N	N	N	N	N	N	Y	Y
8 Carr	Y	?	Y	N	?	?	?	Y
9 Kildee	Y	Y	Y	N	Y	Y	N	Y
10 Bonior	Y	Y	Y	N	Y	Y	N	Y
11 ***Knollenberg***	N	N	N	N	N	N	Y	Y
12 Levin	Y	Y	Y	N	Y	Y	N	Y
13 Ford	Y	Y	Y	N	Y	Y	?	?
14 Conyers	Y	Y	Y	N	Y	Y	N	Y
15 Collins	Y	Y	Y	N	Y	?	Y	Y
16 Dingell	Y	Y	Y	N	Y	Y	Y	Y
MINNESOTA								
1 Penny	Y	Y	Y	N	N	?	Y	Y
2 Minge	Y	Y	Y	N	Y	Y	Y	Y
3 ***Ramstad***	Y	Y	Y	N	Y	Y	Y	Y
4 Vento	Y	Y	Y	N	Y	Y	N	Y

	469	470	471	472	473	474	475	476
5 Sabo	Y	Y	Y	N	Y	Y	N	Y
6 ***Grams***	N	N	N	N	N	N	Y	Y
7 Peterson	Y	Y	Y	N	Y	Y	Y	Y
8 Oberstar	Y	Y	Y	N	Y	Y	Y	Y
MISSISSIPPI								
1 Whitten	?	?	Y	N	N	Y	Y	Y
2 Thompson	Y	Y	Y	N	Y	Y	Y	Y
3 Montgomery	Y	Y	Y	N	Y	Y	Y	Y
4 Parker	Y	Y	Y	N	Y	Y	Y	Y
5 Taylor	Y	Y	Y	Y	Y	Y	Y	Y
MISSOURI								
1 Clay	?	Y	Y	N	Y	Y	N	Y
2 ***Talent***	N	N	N	N	N	N	Y	Y
3 Gephardt	Y	Y	Y	N	Y	Y	Y	Y
4 Skelton	Y	Y	Y	N	Y	Y	Y	Y
5 Wheat	Y	Y	Y	Y	Y	Y	Y	Y
6 Danner	Y	Y	Y	N	Y	Y	Y	Y
7 ***Hancock***	N	N	N	Y	N	N	Y	Y
8 ***Emerson***	N	N	N	Y	N	N	Y	Y
9 Volkmer	Y	Y	Y	N	Y	Y	Y	Y
MONTANA								
AL Williams	?	Y	Y	N	Y	Y	Y	Y
NEBRASKA								
1 ***Bereuter***	Y	Y	Y	N	Y	Y	Y	Y
2 Hoagland	Y	Y	Y	N	Y	Y	Y	Y
3 ***Barrett***	N	N	N	N	N	N	Y	Y
NEVADA								
1 Bilbray	Y	Y	?	N	Y	Y	Y	Y
2 ***Vucanovich***	N	N	N	Y	N	N	Y	Y
NEW HAMPSHIRE								
1 ***Zeliff***	N	N	N	Y	N	N	Y	Y
2 Swett	Y	Y	Y	N	Y	Y	Y	Y
NEW JERSEY								
1 Andrews	Y	Y	Y	N	Y	Y	Y	Y
2 Hughes	Y	Y	Y	N	Y	Y	?	Y
3 ***Saxton***	Y	Y	N	Y	Y	N	Y	Y
4 ***Smith***	Y	Y	Y	Y	Y	Y	Y	Y
5 ***Roukema***	Y	Y	Y	N	Y	Y	?	Y
6 Pallone	Y	Y	Y	N	Y	Y	N	Y
7 ***Franks***	Y	Y	Y	N	Y	Y	?	Y
8 Klein	Y	Y	Y	N	Y	Y	?	Y
9 Torricelli	Y	Y	Y	N	Y	Y	N	Y
10 Payne	Y	Y	Y	N	Y	Y	N	Y
11 ***Gallo***	?	?	?	?	?	?	?	?
12 ***Zimmer***	Y	Y	Y	N	Y	Y	Y	Y
13 Menendez	Y	Y	Y	N	Y	Y	Y	Y
NEW MEXICO								
1 ***Schiff***	N	Y	Y	N	N	Y	Y	Y
2 ***Skeen***	N	N	N	Y	N	N	Y	Y
3 Richardson	Y	Y	Y	N	Y	Y	N	Y
NEW YORK								
1 Hochbrueckner	Y	Y	Y	N	Y	Y	N	Y
2 ***Lazio***	N	N	N	N	N	N	Y	Y
3 ***King***	N	N	N	N	N	N	Y	Y
4 ***Levy***	N	N	N	N	N	N	Y	Y
5 Ackerman	Y	Y	Y	N	Y	Y	N	Y
6 Flake	Y	Y	Y	N	Y	Y	Y	Y
7 Manton	Y	Y	Y	N	Y	Y	Y	Y
8 Nadler	Y	Y	Y	N	Y	Y	N	Y
9 Schumer	Y	Y	Y	N	Y	Y	N	Y
10 Towns	Y	Y	Y	N	Y	Y	N	Y
11 Owens	Y	Y	?	?	Y	Y	Y	Y
12 Velazquez	Y	Y	Y	N	Y	Y	N	Y
13 ***Molinari***	N	N	N	Y	N	N	Y	Y
14 Maloney	Y	Y	Y	N	Y	Y	N	Y
15 Rangel	Y	?	?	?	?	Y	N	Y
16 Serrano	Y	Y	Y	N	Y	Y	N	Y
17 Engel	Y	Y	Y	N	Y	Y	N	Y
18 Lowey	Y	Y	Y	N	Y	Y	N	Y
19 ***Fish***	?	Y	Y	N	Y	Y	Y	Y
20 ***Gilman***	Y	Y	Y	N	N	N	Y	Y
21 McNulty	Y	Y	Y	N	Y	Y	Y	Y
22 ***Solomon***	N	N	N	Y	N	N	Y	Y
23 ***Boehlert***	Y	Y	Y	N	Y	Y	Y	Y
24 ***McHugh***	N	N	N	N	N	N	Y	Y
25 ***Walsh***	N	N	N	N	N	N	Y	Y
26 Hinchey	Y	Y	Y	N	Y	Y	N	Y
27 ***Paxon***	N	N	N	Y	N	N	Y	Y
28 Slaughter	Y	Y	Y	N	Y	Y	Y	Y
29 LaFalce	Y	Y	Y	N	Y	Y	Y	Y
30 ***Quinn***	N	N	N	N	N	N	Y	Y
31 ***Houghton***	N	N	N	N	N	N	Y	Y
NORTH CAROLINA								
1 Clayton	Y	Y	Y	N	Y	Y	Y	Y
2 Valentine	Y	Y	Y	?	Y	Y	?	Y

	469	470	471	472	473	474	475	476
3 Lancaster	?	Y	Y	N	Y	Y	Y	Y
4 Price	Y	Y	Y	N	Y	Y	Y	Y
5 Neal	Y	Y	Y	N	Y	Y	Y	Y
6 ***Coble***	N	N	N	N	N	N	Y	Y
7 Rose	Y	Y	Y	N	Y	Y	Y	Y
8 Hefner	Y	Y	Y	N	Y	Y	Y	Y
9 ***McMillan***	N	N	N	Y	?	?	?	?
10 ***Ballenger***	N	N	N	Y	N	N	Y	Y
11 ***Taylor***	N	N	N	Y	N	N	Y	Y
12 Watt	Y	Y	Y	N	Y	Y	Y	Y
NORTH DAKOTA								
AL Pomeroy	Y	Y	Y	N	Y	Y	Y	Y
OHIO								
1 Mann	Y	Y	Y	N	Y	Y	N	?
2 ***Portman***	N	Y	Y	N	N	N	Y	Y
3 Hall	Y	Y	Y	Y	Y	Y	Y	Y
4 ***Oxley***	N	N	N	Y	N	N	Y	Y
5 ***Gillmor***	Y	Y	Y	N	Y	Y	Y	Y
6 Strickland	Y	Y	Y	N	Y	Y	Y	Y
7 ***Hobson***	N	Y	N	Y	N	Y	Y	Y
8 ***Boehner***	N	N	N	N	N	N	Y	Y
9 Kaptur	Y	Y	Y	N	Y	Y	Y	Y
10 ***Hoke***	N	N	N	Y	N	N	Y	Y
11 Stokes	Y	Y	Y	N	Y	Y	?	Y
12 ***Kasich***	N	N	N	N	N	N	Y	Y
13 Brown	Y	Y	Y	N	Y	Y	N	Y
14 Sawyer	Y	Y	Y	N	Y	Y	Y	Y
15 ***Pryce***	N	N	N	N	N	N	Y	Y
16 ***Regula***	Y	Y	Y	N	N	Y	Y	Y
17 Traficant	Y	Y	Y	N	Y	Y	Y	Y
18 Applegate	?	Y	Y	?	?	?	?	?
19 Fingerhut	Y	Y	Y	N	Y	Y	Y	Y
OKLAHOMA								
1 ***Inhofe***	N	N	N	Y	N	?	Y	Y
2 Synar	Y	Y	Y	N	Y	Y	N	Y
3 Brewster	Y	Y	Y	N	Y	Y	Y	Y
4 McCurdy	Y	Y	Y	N	?	?	?	?
5 ***Istook***	N	N	N	N	N	N	?	?
6 ***Lucas***	N	N	N	Y	N	N	Y	Y
OREGON								
1 Furse	Y	Y	Y	N	Y	Y	+	?
2 ***Smith***	N	N	N	Y	N	N	Y	Y
3 Wyden	Y	Y	Y	N	Y	Y	Y	Y
4 DeFazio	Y	Y	Y	N	Y	Y	Y	Y
5 Kopetski	Y	Y	Y	N	Y	Y	Y	Y
PENNSYLVANIA								
1 Foglietta	Y	Y	Y	N	Y	Y	N	Y
2 Blackwell	Y	Y	Y	?	Y	Y	N	Y
3 Borski	Y	Y	Y	N	Y	Y	N	Y
4 Klink	Y	Y	Y	N	Y	Y	Y	Y
5 ***Clinger***	N	N	Y	N	Y	N	Y	Y
6 Holden	Y	Y	Y	N	Y	Y	Y	Y
7 ***Weldon***	Y	Y	Y	N	Y	Y	Y	Y
8 ***Greenwood***	Y	Y	Y	N	N	Y	Y	Y
9 ***Shuster***	N	N	N	Y	N	N	Y	Y
10 ***McDade***	N	N	N	N	N	N	Y	Y
11 Kanjorski	Y	Y	Y	N	Y	Y	Y	Y
12 Murtha	Y	Y	Y	N	?	Y	Y	Y
13 Margolies-Mezv.	Y	Y	Y	N	Y	Y	Y	Y
14 Coyne	Y	Y	Y	N	Y	Y	N	Y
15 McHale	Y	Y	Y	N	Y	Y	Y	Y
16 ***Walker***	N	N	N	N	N	N	Y	Y
17 ***Gekas***	N	N	N	N	N	N	Y	Y
18 ***Santorum***	Y	N	Y	Y	N	N	Y	Y
19 ***Goodling***	N	N	N	Y	N	N	Y	Y
20 Murphy	Y	Y	?	Y	Y	Y	N	Y
21 ***Ridge***	N	N	N	N	?	Y	Y	Y
RHODE ISLAND								
1 ***Machtley***	Y	Y	Y	N	Y	Y	Y	Y
2 Reed	Y	Y	Y	N	Y	Y	N	Y
SOUTH CAROLINA								
1 ***Ravenel***	Y	Y	Y	N	Y	Y	?	Y
2 ***Spence***	N	N	N	Y	N	N	Y	Y
3 Derrick	Y	Y	Y	N	Y	Y	Y	Y
4 ***Inglis***	N	N	N	Y	N	N	Y	Y
5 Spratt	Y	Y	Y	N	Y	Y	Y	Y
6 Clyburn	Y	Y	Y	N	Y	Y	Y	Y
SOUTH DAKOTA								
AL Johnson	Y	Y	Y	N	Y	Y	Y	?
TENNESSEE								
1 ***Quillen***	Y	Y	Y	N	N	N	Y	Y
2 ***Duncan***	N	N	N	Y	N	N	Y	Y
3 Lloyd	Y	Y	Y	N	Y	Y	Y	Y
4 Cooper	Y	Y	Y	N	Y	Y	Y	Y
5 Clement	Y	Y	Y	N	Y	Y	Y	Y

	469	470	471	472	473	474	475	476
6 Gordon	Y	Y	Y	N	Y	Y	Y	Y
7 ***Sundquist***	?	?	?	?	?	?	?	?
8 Tanner	Y	Y	Y	N	Y	Y	Y	Y
9 Ford	Y	Y	Y	Y	Y	Y	Y	Y
TEXAS								
1 Chapman	Y	Y	Y	N	Y	Y	Y	Y
2 Wilson	Y	Y	Y	N	Y	Y	Y	Y
3 ***Johnson, Sam***	N	N	N	Y	N	N	Y	Y
4 Hall	Y	N	N	N	N	N	Y	Y
5 Bryant	Y	Y	Y	N	Y	Y	Y	Y
6 ***Barton***	N	N	N	N	N	N	Y	Y
7 ***Archer***	N	N	N	Y	N	N	Y	Y
8 ***Fields***	N	N	N	Y	N	N	Y	Y
9 Brooks	Y	Y	Y	N	Y	Y	Y	Y
10 Pickle	Y	Y	Y	N	Y	Y	Y	Y
11 Edwards	Y	Y	Y	N	Y	?	Y	Y
12 Geren	Y	Y	Y	N	Y	Y	Y	Y
13 Sarpalius	Y	Y	Y	N	Y	Y	Y	Y
14 Laughlin	Y	Y	Y	N	Y	Y	Y	Y
15 de la Garza	Y	Y	Y	N	Y	Y	Y	Y
16 Coleman	Y	Y	Y	N	Y	Y	Y	Y
17 Stenholm	Y	Y	Y	N	Y	Y	Y	Y
18 Washington	Y	Y	Y	N	Y	?	?	?
19 ***Combest***	N	N	N	Y	N	N	Y	Y
20 Gonzalez	Y	Y	Y	N	Y	Y	Y	Y
21 ***Smith***	N	N	N	Y	N	N	Y	Y
22 ***DeLay***	N	N	N	Y	N	N	Y	Y
23 ***Bonilla***	N	N	N	Y	N	N	Y	Y
24 Frost	Y	Y	Y	N	Y	Y	Y	Y
25 Andrews	Y	Y	Y	N	Y	?	Y	Y
26 ***Armey***	N	N	N	Y	N	N	Y	Y
27 Ortiz	Y	Y	Y	N	Y	Y	Y	Y
28 Tejeda	Y	Y	Y	N	Y	Y	Y	Y
29 Green	Y	Y	Y	N	Y	Y	Y	Y
30 Johnson, E.B.	Y	Y	Y	N	Y	Y	N	Y
UTAH								
1 ***Hansen***	N	N	N	Y	N	N	Y	Y
2 Shepherd	Y	Y	Y	N	Y	Y	N	Y
3 Orton	Y	N	Y	Y	N	Y	Y	Y
VERMONT								
AL *Sanders*	Y	Y	Y	?	Y	Y	N	Y
VIRGINIA								
1 ***Bateman***	?	?	Y	N	N	N	Y	Y
2 Pickett	Y	Y	Y	N	Y	Y	Y	Y
3 Scott	Y	Y	Y	N	Y	Y	N	Y
4 Sisisky	Y	Y	Y	N	Y	Y	Y	Y
5 Payne	Y	Y	Y	N	Y	Y	Y	Y
6 ***Goodlatte***	N	N	N	N	N	N	Y	Y
7 ***Bliley***	N	N	N	N	N	N	Y	Y
8 Moran	Y	Y	Y	N	Y	Y	Y	Y
9 Boucher	Y	?	?	N	Y	Y	Y	Y
10 ***Wolf***	N	N	N	Y	N	N	Y	Y
11 Byrne	Y	Y	Y	N	Y	Y	N	Y
WASHINGTON								
1 Cantwell	Y	Y	Y	N	Y	Y	Y	Y
2 Swift	Y	Y	Y	N	Y	Y	Y	Y
3 Unsoeld	Y	Y	Y	N	Y	Y	Y	Y
4 Inslee	Y	Y	Y	N	Y	Y	Y	Y
5 Foley							Y	
6 Dicks	Y	Y	Y	N	Y	Y	Y	Y
7 McDermott	Y	Y	Y	N	Y	Y	N	Y
8 ***Dunn***	N	N	N	?	Y	Y	Y	Y
9 Kreidler	Y	Y	Y	N	Y	Y	Y	Y
WEST VIRGINIA								
1 Mollohan	Y	Y	Y	N	Y	Y	Y	Y
2 Wise	Y	Y	Y	N	Y	Y	Y	Y
3 Rahall	Y	Y	Y	N	Y	Y	Y	Y
WISCONSIN								
1 Barca	Y	Y	Y	N	Y	Y	Y	Y
2 ***Klug***	Y	Y	Y	Y	Y	Y	Y	Y
3 ***Gunderson***	N	N	N	N	Y	N	Y	Y
4 Kleczka	Y	Y	Y	N	Y	Y	Y	Y
5 Barrett	Y	Y	?	N	Y	Y	N	Y
6 ***Petri***	N	N	N	N	N	N	Y	Y
7 Obey	Y	Y	Y	N	Y	Y	Y	Y
8 ***Roth***	N	N	N	N	N	N	Y	Y
9 ***Sensenbrenner***	N	N	N	Y	N	N	Y	Y
WYOMING								
AL ***Thomas***	N	N	N	Y	N	N	Y	Y
DELEGATES								
de Lugo, V.I.	D	D	D	D	D	D	D	D
Faleomavaega, Am.S.	D	D	D	D	D	D	D	D
Norton, D.C.	D	D	D	D	D	D	D	D
Romero-B., P.R.	D	D	D	D	D	D	D	D
Underwood, Guam	D	D	D	D	D	D	D	D

Southern states - Ala., Ark., Fla., Ga., Ky., La., Miss., N.C., Okla., S.C., Tenn., Texas, Va.
Omitted votes are quorum calls, which CQ does not include in its vote charts.

477. HR 5108. Export Administration Act Extension/Passage. Menendez, D-N.J., motion to suspend the rules and pass the bill to extend the Export Administration Act, which regulates the export of sensitive technologies to Sept. 30, 1995. Motion agreed to 407-4: R 167-2; D 239-2 (ND 161-2, SD 78-0); I 1-0, Oct. 4, 1994. A two-thirds majority of those present and voting (274 in this case) is required for passage under suspension of the rules.

478. H Con Res 279. Condemn Cuban Sinking of Tugboat/Adoption. Menendez, D-N.J., motion to suspend the rules and adopt the concurrent resolution condemning the July 18 sinking by the Cuban government of a tugboat carrying 72 Cubans attempting to emigrate to the United States. Motion agreed to 413-0: R 172-0; D 240-0 (ND 163-0, SD 77-0); I 1-0, Oct. 4, 1994. A two-thirds majority of those present and voting (276 in this case) is required for passage under suspension of the rules.

479. H Con Res 286. Cristiani's Peace in El Salvador/Adoption. Menendez, D-N.J., motion to suspend the rules and adopt the concurrent resolution expressing admiration for former El Salvador President Alfredo Cristiani for his contributions to the peace and reconciliation process in El Salvador. Motion agreed to 414-0: R 174-0; D 239-0 (ND 161-0, SD 78-0); I 1-0, Oct. 4, 1994. A two-thirds majority of those present and voting (276 in this case) is required for adoption under suspension of the rules.

480. S 1225. U.S.-Mexico Border Health Commission/Passage. Waxman, D-Calif., motion to suspend the rules and pass the bill to authorize the president to conclude an agreement with Mexico to establish the U.S.-Mexico Border Health Commission. Motion rejected 246-169: R 35-139; D 210-30 (ND 140-22, SD 70-8); I 1-0, Oct. 4, 1994. A two-thirds majority of those present and voting (277 in this case) is required for passage under suspension of the rules.

481. S 1919. Rio Puerco Watershed/Passage. Vento, D-Minn., motion to suspend the rules and pass the bill to direct the Interior Department to collect information and issue a report on ecological damage to the Rio Puerco watershed near Albuquerque, N.M. Motion rejected 233-180: R 32-141; D 200-39 (ND 146-16, SD 54-23); I 1-0, Oct. 4, 1994. A two-thirds majority of those present and voting (276 in this case) is required for passage under suspension of the rules.

482. HR 4533. National Park Service Entrepreneurial Management Reform/Passage. Vento, D-Minn., motion to suspend the rules and pass the bill to authorize the Interior Department to increase fees for national park system sites to be deposited into a fund for park projects, beginning in fiscal 1996. Motion rejected 238-174: R 47-126; D 190-48 (ND 134-27, SD 56-21); I 1-0, Oct. 4, 1994. A two-thirds majority of those present and voting (275 in this case) is required for passage under suspension of the rules.

483. H Con Res 301. Entitlement Spending/Rule. Adoption of the rule (H Res 563) to provide for House floor consideration of the concurrent resolution to express the sense of Congress that action must be taken to ensure that current unsustainable entitlement spending trends do not create an unfair debt burden on America's children. Rejected 83-339: R 1-175; D 82-163 (ND 54-111, SD 28-52); I 0-1, Oct. 5, 1994.

484. HR 5044. American Heritage Areas Partnership Program/Written Consent From Landowners. Regula, R-Ohio, amendment to the Tauzin, D-La., amendment to remove the requirement in the Tauzin amendment that requires written consent from landowners before their property can be included in a heritage management area. Adopted in the Committee of the Whole 222-202: R 43-130; D 178-72 (ND 141-32, SD 37-40); I 1-0, Oct. 5, 1994.

KEY

Y	Voted for (yea).
#	Paired for.
+	Announced for.
N	Voted against (nay).
X	Paired against.
—	Announced against.
P	Voted "present."
C	Voted "present" to avoid possible conflict of interest.
?	Did not vote or otherwise make a position known.
D	Delegates ineligible to vote.

Democrats *Republicans* *Independent*

	477	478	479	480	481	482	483	484
ALABAMA								
1 Callahan	Y	Y	Y	N	N	N	N	?
2 Everett	Y	Y	Y	N	N	N	N	N
3 Browder	Y	Y	Y	Y	?	?	Y	?
4 Bevill	Y	Y	Y	Y	N	N	N	?
5 Cramer	Y	Y	Y	N	N	N	N	?
6 Bachus	Y	Y	Y	N	N	N	N	—
7 Hilliard	Y	Y	Y	Y	Y	Y	N	?
ALASKA								
AL Young	N	Y	Y	N	Y	Y	N	N
ARIZONA								
1 Coppersmith	Y	Y	Y	Y	Y	Y	Y	Y
2 Pastor	Y	Y	Y	Y	Y	Y	N	Y
3 Stump	Y	Y	Y	N	N	N	N	N
4 Kyl	Y	Y	Y	N	Y	N	N	N
5 Kolbe	Y	Y	Y	Y	Y	Y	N	N
6 English	Y	Y	Y	Y	Y	Y	N	Y
ARKANSAS								
1 Lambert	Y	Y	Y	Y	N	N	N	N
2 Thornton	Y	Y	Y	N	N	N	N	N
3 Hutchinson	Y	Y	Y	N	N	N	N	N
4 Dickey	Y	Y	Y	Y	Y	N	N	N
CALIFORNIA								
1 Hamburg	Y	Y	P	Y	Y	Y	?	Y
2 Herger	Y	Y	Y	N	N	N	N	N
3 Fazio	Y	Y	Y	Y	Y	Y	Y	N
4 Doolittle	Y	Y	Y	N	N	N	N	N
5 Matsui	Y	Y	Y	Y	Y	Y	Y	Y
6 Woolsey	Y	Y	Y	Y	Y	Y	N	Y
7 Miller	Y	Y	Y	Y	Y	Y	Y	Y
8 Pelosi	Y	Y	Y	Y	Y	Y	N	Y
9 Dellums	Y	Y	Y	Y	?	?	N	Y
10 Baker	Y	Y	Y	N	N	N	N	N
11 Pombo	Y	Y	Y	N	N	N	N	N
12 Lantos	?	?	?	?	?	?	N	Y
13 Stark	Y	Y	Y	Y	Y	N	Y	Y
14 Eshoo	Y	Y	Y	Y	Y	Y	N	Y
15 Mineta	?	Y	Y	Y	Y	Y	Y	Y
16 Edwards	Y	Y	Y	Y	Y	Y	Y	Y
17 Farr	Y	Y	Y	Y	Y	Y	N	Y
18 Condit	Y	Y	Y	Y	N	N	N	N
19 Lehman	Y	Y	Y	Y	Y	N	N	N
20 Dooley	Y	Y	Y	Y	Y	Y	N	N
21 Thomas	Y	Y	Y	Y	N	N	N	N
22 Huffington	?	?	?	?	?	?	N	N
23 Gallegly	Y	Y	Y	N	N	N	N	N
24 Beilenson	Y	Y	Y	N	N	N	N	Y
25 McKeon	Y	Y	Y	N	N	N	N	N
26 Berman	Y	Y	Y	Y	Y	Y	Y	Y
27 Moorhead	Y	Y	Y	N	N	N	N	N
28 Dreier	Y	Y	Y	N	N	N	N	N
29 Waxman	Y	Y	Y	Y	Y	Y	N	Y
30 Becerra	Y	P	Y	Y	Y	Y	N	Y
31 Martinez	Y	P	Y	Y	Y	Y	Y	Y
32 Dixon	Y	Y	Y	Y	Y	Y	N	Y
33 Roybal-Allard	Y	Y	Y	Y	Y	Y	N	Y
34 Torres	Y	Y	Y	Y	Y	Y	Y	Y
35 Waters	Y	Y	Y	?	?	?	N	Y
36 Harman	Y	Y	Y	Y	Y	Y	N	N
37 Tucker	?	?	?	?	?	?	?	?
38 Horn	Y	Y	Y	N	N	N	N	N
39 Royce	Y	Y	Y	N	N	N	N	N
40 Lewis	N	Y	Y	N	N	N	N	N
41 Kim	Y	Y	Y	N	N	N	N	N
42 Brown	Y	Y	Y	Y	Y	Y	N	Y
43 Calvert	Y	Y	Y	N	N	N	N	N
44 McCandless	Y	Y	Y	N	N	N	N	N
45 Rohrabacher	Y	Y	Y	N	N	N	N	N
46 Dornan	Y	Y	Y	N	N	N	N	N
47 Cox	Y	Y	Y	N	N	N	N	N
48 Packard	Y	Y	Y	N	N	N	N	N
49 Schenk	Y	Y	Y	Y	Y	Y	N	Y
50 Filner	Y	Y	Y	Y	Y	Y	N	Y
51 Cunningham	Y	Y	Y	N	N	N	N	N
52 Hunter	Y	Y	Y	N	N	N	N	N
COLORADO								
1 Schroeder	Y	Y	Y	Y	Y	Y	N	Y
2 Skaggs	Y	Y	Y	Y	Y	Y	N	Y
3 McInnis	Y	Y	Y	N	N	N	N	N
4 Allard	Y	Y	Y	N	N	N	N	N
5 Hefley	Y	Y	Y	N	N	N	N	N
6 Schaefer	Y	Y	Y	N	N	N	N	N
CONNECTICUT								
1 Kennelly	Y	Y	Y	Y	Y	Y	N	Y
2 Gejdenson	Y	Y	Y	Y	Y	Y	N	Y
3 DeLauro	Y	Y	Y	Y	Y	Y	N	Y
4 Shays	Y	Y	Y	Y	Y	Y	N	Y
5 Franks	Y	Y	Y	N	N	N	N	N
6 Johnson	?	Y	Y	Y	Y	Y	N	Y
DELAWARE								
AL Castle	Y	Y	Y	N	N	N	N	N
FLORIDA								
1 Hutto	Y	Y	Y	N	N	N	N	N
2 Peterson	Y	Y	Y	Y	Y	Y	N	N
3 Brown	Y	Y	Y	Y	Y	Y	N	N
4 Fowler	Y	Y	Y	N	N	N	N	N
5 Thurman	Y	Y	Y	Y	Y	Y	N	N
6 Stearns	Y	Y	Y	N	N	N	N	N
7 Mica	Y	Y	Y	N	N	N	N	N
8 McCollum	Y	Y	Y	N	N	N	N	Y
9 Bilirakis	Y	Y	Y	N	N	N	N	N
10 Young	Y	Y	Y	N	N	N	N	N
11 Gibbons	Y	Y	Y	Y	Y	Y	Y	Y
12 Canady	Y	Y	Y	N	N	N	N	N
13 Miller	Y	Y	Y	N	N	N	N	N
14 Goss	Y	Y	Y	N	N	Y	N	N
15 Bacchus	Y	Y	Y	Y	Y	Y	Y	Y
16 Lewis	Y	Y	Y	N	N	N	N	N
17 Meek	Y	Y	Y	Y	Y	Y	N	Y
18 Ros-Lehtinen	Y	Y	Y	Y	Y	Y	N	Y
19 Johnston	?	?	?	?	?	?	Y	Y
20 Deutsch	Y	Y	Y	Y	Y	Y	Y	Y
21 Diaz-Balart	Y	Y	Y	Y	Y	Y	N	Y
22 Shaw	Y	Y	Y	N	N	N	N	N
23 Hastings	Y	Y	Y	Y	Y	Y	Y	Y
GEORGIA								
1 Kingston	Y	Y	Y	N	N	N	N	N
2 Bishop	Y	Y	Y	Y	Y	Y	N	N
3 Collins	Y	Y	Y	N	N	N	N	N
4 Linder	Y	Y	Y	N	—	N	N	N
5 Lewis	?	?	?	?	?	?	N	Y
6 Gingrich	Y	Y	Y	N	N	N	N	N
7 Darden	Y	Y	Y	Y	Y	Y	Y	Y
8 Rowland	Y	Y	Y	N	Y	N	N	Y
9 Deal	Y	Y	Y	Y	N	N	Y	Y
10 Johnson	Y	Y	Y	Y	N	N	N	Y
11 McKinney	Y	Y	Y	Y	N	Y	N	Y
HAWAII								
1 Abercrombie	N	Y	Y	Y	Y	Y	N	Y
2 Mink	Y	Y	Y	Y	Y	N	N	N
IDAHO								
1 LaRocco	Y	Y	Y	N	Y	Y	Y	Y
2 Crapo	Y	Y	Y	N	N	N	N	N
ILLINOIS								
1 Rush	Y	Y	Y	Y	Y	Y	N	Y
2 Reynolds	Y	Y	Y	Y	Y	Y	N	Y
3 Lipinski	Y	Y	Y	N	N	N	N	N
4 Gutierrez	Y	Y	Y	Y	Y	N	N	N
5 Rostenkowski	Y	Y	Y	Y	Y	Y	N	N
6 Hyde	Y	Y	Y	N	N	Y	N	Y
7 Collins	Y	Y	Y	Y	Y	Y	N	Y
8 Crane	Y	Y	Y	N	N	N	N	N
9 Yates	Y	Y	Y	Y	Y	Y	N	Y
10 Porter	Y	Y	Y	N	Y	N	Y	Y
11 Sangmeister	Y	Y	Y	N	N	N	Y	Y
12 Costello	Y	Y	Y	Y	N	N	N	Y
13 Fawell	Y	Y	Y	N	Y	N	Y	Y
14 Hastert	Y	Y	Y	N	N	N	N	N
15 Ewing	Y	Y	Y	N	N	N	N	N
16 Manzullo	Y	Y	Y	N	N	N	N	N
17 Evans	Y	Y	Y	Y	Y	Y	N	Y

ND Northern Democrats SD Southern Democrats

	477	478	479	480	481	482	483	484
18 ***Michel***	Y	Y	Y	N	N	N	N	Y
19 Poshard	Y	Y	Y	Y	Y	N	N	N
20 Durbin	Y	Y	Y	Y	Y	Y	N	Y
INDIANA								
1 Visclosky	Y	Y	Y	?	?	?	Y	Y
2 Sharp	Y	?	Y	Y	Y	Y	?	Y
3 Roemer	Y	Y	Y	N	Y	Y	N	N
4 Long	Y	Y	Y	Y	Y	Y	Y	N
5 ***Buyer***	Y	Y	Y	N	N	N	N	N
6 ***Burton***	Y	Y	Y	N	N	N	N	N
7 ***Myers***	Y	Y	Y	N	N	N	N	Y
8 McCloskey	Y	Y	Y	Y	Y	Y	N	Y
9 Hamilton	Y	Y	Y	Y	Y	Y	Y	N
10 Jacobs	Y	Y	Y	Y	N	N	Y	Y
IOWA								
1 ***Leach***	Y	Y	Y	Y	N	N	N	N
2 ***Nussle***	Y	Y	Y	N	N	N	N	N
3 ***Lightfoot***	Y	Y	Y	N	N	N	N	N
4 Smith	Y	Y	Y	N	Y	N	N	N
5 ***Grandy***	Y	Y	Y	N	N	N	N	N
KANSAS								
1 ***Roberts***	Y	Y	Y	N	N	Y	N	N
2 Slattery	?	?	?	?	?	?	?	?
3 ***Meyers***	Y	Y	Y	N	N	Y	N	N
4 Glickman	Y	Y	Y	Y	N	Y	N	N
KENTUCKY								
1 Barlow	Y	Y	Y	Y	Y	Y	N	Y
2 ***Lewis***	Y	Y	Y	N	Y	N	N	N
3 Mazzoli	Y	Y	Y	Y	Y	Y	Y	Y
4 ***Bunning***	Y	Y	Y	N	Y	N	N	N
5 ***Rogers***	Y	Y	Y	Y	Y	N	N	Y
6 Baesler	Y	Y	Y	Y	Y	Y	N	N
LOUISIANA								
1 ***Livingston***	Y	Y	Y	N	N	N	N	Y
2 Jefferson	Y	Y	Y	Y	Y	Y	N	Y
3 Tauzin	Y	Y	Y	Y	Y	Y	N	N
4 Fields	Y	Y	Y	Y	Y	Y	N	N
5 ***McCrery***	Y	Y	Y	N	N	N	N	N
6 ***Baker***	Y	Y	Y	N	N	N	N	N
7 Hayes	Y	Y	Y	Y	Y	Y	N	N
MAINE								
1 Andrews	Y	Y	Y	Y	Y	Y	N	Y
2 ***Snowe***	Y	Y	Y	Y	Y	Y	N	N
MARYLAND								
1 ***Gilchrest***	Y	Y	Y	N	Y	Y	N	Y
2 ***Bentley***	Y	Y	Y	N	N	Y	N	N
3 Cardin	Y	Y	Y	Y	Y	N	N	Y
4 Wynn	Y	Y	Y	Y	Y	Y	N	Y
5 Hoyer	Y	Y	Y	Y	Y	Y	Y	Y
6 ***Bartlett***	Y	Y	Y	N	N	N	N	N
7 Mfume	+	+	+	Y	Y	Y	N	Y
8 ***Morella***	Y	Y	Y	Y	Y	Y	N	Y
MASSACHUSETTS								
1 Olver	Y	Y	Y	Y	Y	Y	Y	Y
2 Neal	Y	Y	Y	Y	Y	Y	N	Y
3 ***Blute***	Y	Y	Y	Y	Y	Y	N	Y
4 Frank	Y	Y	Y	Y	Y	Y	Y	Y
5 Meehan	Y	Y	Y	Y	Y	Y	Y	Y
6 ***Torkildsen***	Y	Y	Y	Y	Y	Y	N	Y
7 Markey	Y	Y	Y	Y	Y	Y	N	Y
8 Kennedy	Y	Y	Y	Y	Y	Y	Y	Y
9 Moakley	Y	Y	Y	?	?	?	Y	Y
10 Studds	Y	Y	?	?	?	?	N	Y
MICHIGAN								
1 Stupak	Y	Y	Y	Y	Y	Y	N	N
2 ***Hoekstra***	Y	Y	Y	N	N	N	N	N
3 ***Ehlers***	Y	Y	Y	Y	Y	N	N	Y
4 ***Camp***	Y	Y	Y	N	N	N	N	N
5 Barcia	Y	Y	Y	Y	N	Y	—	N
6 ***Upton***	Y	Y	Y	N	N	Y	N	N
7 ***Smith***	Y	Y	Y	N	N	N	N	N
8 Carr	Y	Y	Y	Y	Y	Y	N	N
9 Kildee	Y	Y	Y	Y	Y	Y	N	Y
10 Bonior	Y	Y	Y	Y	Y	Y	Y	Y
11 ***Knollenberg***	Y	Y	Y	N	N	N	N	N
12 Levin	Y	Y	Y	Y	Y	Y	N	Y
13 Ford	?	?	Y	Y	Y	Y	?	Y
14 Conyers	Y	Y	Y	Y	Y	Y	Y	Y
15 Collins	Y	Y	Y	Y	Y	Y	N	Y
16 Dingell	Y	?	Y	Y	Y	Y	N	Y
MINNESOTA								
1 Penny	?	Y	Y	N	N	Y	Y	N
2 Minge	Y	Y	Y	Y	Y	Y	Y	N
3 ***Ramstad***	Y	Y	Y	N	N	N	N	N
4 Vento	Y	Y	Y	Y	Y	Y	Y	Y
5 Sabo	Y	Y	Y	Y	Y	Y	Y	Y
6 ***Grams***	Y	Y	Y	N	N	Y	N	N
7 Peterson	Y	Y	Y	Y	Y	N	N	N
8 Oberstar	Y	Y	Y	Y	Y	Y	Y	Y
MISSISSIPPI								
1 Whitten	Y	Y	Y	Y	Y	Y	?	?
2 Thompson	Y	Y	Y	Y	Y	Y	N	Y
3 Montgomery	Y	Y	Y	Y	Y	Y	Y	N
4 Parker	Y	Y	Y	N	N	Y	Y	N
5 Taylor	Y	Y	Y	N	N	N	Y	N
MISSOURI								
1 Clay	Y	Y	Y	Y	Y	Y	N	Y
2 ***Talent***	Y	Y	Y	N	N	N	N	N
3 Gephardt	Y	Y	Y	Y	Y	Y	Y	Y
4 Skelton	Y	Y	Y	Y	Y	N	N	N
5 Wheat	Y	Y	Y	Y	Y	Y	N	Y
6 Danner	Y	Y	Y	Y	Y	N	N	N
7 ***Hancock***	Y	Y	Y	N	N	N	N	N
8 ***Emerson***	Y	Y	Y	N	N	N	N	N
9 Volkmer	Y	Y	Y	N	N	N	N	N
MONTANA								
AL Williams	Y	Y	Y	Y	Y	Y	Y	Y
NEBRASKA								
1 ***Bereuter***	Y	Y	Y	Y	Y	Y	N	Y
2 Hoagland	Y	Y	Y	Y	Y	Y	Y	Y
3 ***Barrett***	Y	Y	Y	N	N	Y	N	N
NEVADA								
1 Bilbray	Y	Y	Y	?	Y	Y	N	Y
2 ***Vucanovich***	Y	Y	Y	N	N	N	N	N
NEW HAMPSHIRE								
1 ***Zeliff***	Y	Y	Y	N	N	N	N	N
2 Swett	Y	Y	Y	N	N	Y	N	N
NEW JERSEY								
1 Andrews	Y	Y	Y	N	Y	N	N	N
2 Hughes	Y	Y	Y	Y	Y	Y	N	Y
3 ***Saxton***	Y	Y	Y	N	?	N	N	N
4 ***Smith***	Y	Y	Y	N	N	N	N	N
5 ***Roukema***	?	Y	Y	N	N	Y	N	Y
6 Pallone	Y	Y	Y	Y	Y	N	N	Y
7 ***Franks***	Y	Y	Y	N	N	Y	N	Y
8 Klein	Y	Y	Y	N	Y	Y	N	Y
9 Torricelli	Y	Y	Y	Y	Y	Y	N	Y
10 Payne	Y	Y	Y	Y	Y	Y	N	Y
11 ***Gallo***	?	?	?	?	?	?	?	?
12 ***Zimmer***	Y	Y	Y	N	N	Y	N	Y
13 Menendez	Y	Y	Y	Y	Y	Y	N	Y
NEW MEXICO								
1 ***Schiff***	Y	Y	Y	Y	Y	N	N	N
2 ***Skeen***	Y	Y	Y	Y	Y	N	N	N
3 Richardson	Y	Y	Y	Y	Y	Y	N	Y
NEW YORK								
1 Hochbrueckner	Y	Y	Y	Y	Y	Y	N	N
2 ***Lazio***	Y	Y	Y	N	N	N	N	Y
3 ***King***	Y	Y	Y	N	N	N	N	Y
4 ***Levy***	Y	Y	Y	N	N	N	N	Y
5 Ackerman	Y	Y	Y	Y	Y	Y	N	Y
6 Flake	Y	Y	Y	Y	Y	Y	N	Y
7 Manton	Y	?	?	?	?	?	N	Y
8 Nadler	Y	Y	Y	Y	Y	N	N	Y
9 Schumer	Y	Y	Y	Y	Y	N	N	Y
10 Towns	Y	Y	Y	Y	Y	N	N	Y
11 Owens	Y	Y	Y	Y	Y	Y	N	Y
12 Velazquez	Y	Y	Y	Y	Y	N	N	Y
13 ***Molinari***	Y	Y	Y	Y	N	N	N	Y
14 Maloney	Y	Y	Y	Y	Y	Y	N	Y
15 Rangel	Y	Y	Y	Y	Y	Y	N	Y
16 Serrano	Y	Y	Y	Y	Y	Y	N	Y
17 Engel	Y	Y	Y	Y	Y	Y	N	Y
18 Lowey	Y	Y	Y	Y	Y	Y	N	Y
19 ***Fish***	?	Y	Y	N	N	N	N	?
20 ***Gilman***	Y	Y	Y	Y	Y	N	N	Y
21 McNulty	Y	Y	Y	N	Y	?	?	Y
22 ***Solomon***	Y	Y	Y	N	N	N	N	N
23 ***Boehlert***	Y	Y	Y	N	Y	Y	N	Y
24 ***McHugh***	Y	Y	Y	N	N	N	N	N
25 ***Walsh***	Y	Y	Y	N	N	N	N	N
26 Hinchey	Y	Y	Y	Y	Y	Y	N	Y
27 ***Paxon***	Y	Y	Y	N	N	N	N	N
28 Slaughter	Y	Y	Y	Y	Y	Y	N	Y
29 LaFalce	Y	Y	Y	Y	Y	Y	Y	Y
30 ***Quinn***	Y	Y	Y	N	N	N	N	N
31 ***Houghton***	Y	Y	Y	N	N	Y	N	N
NORTH CAROLINA								
1 Clayton	Y	Y	Y	Y	Y	Y	?	Y
2 Valentine	Y	Y	Y	Y	N	Y	Y	N
3 Lancaster	Y	Y	Y	Y	Y	Y	N	N
4 Price	Y	Y	Y	Y	Y	Y	N	Y
5 Neal	Y	Y	Y	Y	Y	Y	Y	Y
6 ***Coble***	Y	Y	Y	N	N	N	N	N
7 Rose	Y	?	Y	Y	N	Y	N	Y
8 Hefner	Y	Y	Y	Y	Y	Y	N	N
9 ***McMillan***	?	?	?	?	?	?	N	Y
10 ***Ballenger***	Y	Y	Y	N	N	N	N	N
11 ***Taylor***	Y	Y	Y	N	N	N	N	N
12 Watt	Y	Y	Y	Y	Y	Y	Y	Y
NORTH DAKOTA								
AL Pomeroy	Y	Y	Y	Y	Y	Y	N	N
OHIO								
1 Mann	Y	Y	Y	Y	Y	Y	Y	Y
2 ***Portman***	Y	Y	Y	N	N	Y	N	Y
3 Hall	Y	Y	Y	Y	Y	Y	N	Y
4 ***Oxley***	Y	Y	Y	N	N	N	N	Y
5 ***Gillmor***	Y	Y	Y	N	N	N	N	Y
6 Strickland	?	Y	Y	Y	Y	Y	N	N
7 ***Hobson***	Y	Y	Y	N	Y	Y	N	Y
8 ***Boehner***	Y	Y	Y	N	N	N	N	N
9 Kaptur	Y	Y	Y	N	Y	Y	N	Y
10 ***Hoke***	Y	Y	Y	N	N	Y	N	N
11 Stokes	Y	Y	Y	Y	Y	Y	N	Y
12 ***Kasich***	Y	Y	Y	N	N	Y	N	N
13 Brown	Y	Y	Y	Y	Y	Y	N	Y
14 Sawyer	Y	Y	Y	Y	Y	Y	Y	Y
15 ***Pryce***	Y	Y	Y	N	N	N	N	Y
16 ***Regula***	Y	Y	Y	N	Y	Y	N	Y
17 Traficant	Y	Y	Y	N	Y	Y	N	Y
18 Applegate	?	?	?	?	?	?	N	Y
19 Fingerhut	Y	Y	Y	N	Y	Y	N	Y
OKLAHOMA								
1 ***Inhofe***	?	?	Y	N	N	N	N	N
2 Synar	Y	Y	Y	Y	Y	Y	N	Y
3 Brewster	Y	Y	Y	Y	N	N	N	N
4 McCurdy	?	?	?	?	?	?	N	N
5 ***Istook***	?	Y	Y	N	N	N	N	N
6 ***Lucas***	Y	Y	Y	N	N	N	N	N
OREGON								
1 Furse	Y	Y	Y	Y	Y	Y	N	Y
2 ***Smith***	Y	Y	Y	N	N	Y	N	N
3 Wyden	Y	Y	Y	Y	Y	Y	N	Y
4 DeFazio	N	Y	P	Y	Y	N	N	Y
5 Kopetski	Y	Y	Y	Y	Y	Y	N	Y
PENNSYLVANIA								
1 Foglietta	Y	Y	Y	Y	Y	N	Y	Y
2 Blackwell	Y	Y	Y	Y	Y	Y	N	?
3 Borski	Y	Y	Y	Y	Y	N	N	Y
4 Klink	Y	Y	Y	N	N	N	Y	Y
5 ***Clinger***	Y	Y	Y	N	Y	N	N	Y
6 Holden	Y	Y	Y	N	N	N	N	N
7 ***Weldon***	Y	Y	Y	N	N	N	N	Y
8 ***Greenwood***	Y	Y	Y	N	N	Y	N	Y
9 ***Shuster***	Y	Y	Y	N	Y	N	N	N
10 ***McDade***	Y	Y	Y	N	N	N	N	N
11 Kanjorski	Y	Y	Y	Y	N	Y	Y	Y
12 Murtha	Y	Y	Y	Y	Y	Y	N	Y
13 Margolies-Mezv.	Y	Y	Y	N	N	Y	Y	Y
14 Coyne	Y	Y	Y	Y	Y	Y	Y	Y
15 McHale	Y	Y	Y	Y	N	N	N	Y
16 ***Walker***	Y	Y	Y	N	N	N	N	N
17 ***Gekas***	Y	Y	Y	N	N	N	N	N
18 ***Santorum***	Y	Y	Y	N	N	N	N	N
19 ***Goodling***	Y	Y	Y	N	N	N	N	N
20 Murphy	Y	Y	Y	Y	N	Y	Y	N
21 ***Ridge***	Y	Y	Y	N	Y	N	N	Y
RHODE ISLAND								
1 ***Machtley***	Y	Y	Y	Y	Y	Y	N	Y
2 Reed	Y	Y	Y	Y	Y	Y	N	Y
SOUTH CAROLINA								
1 ***Ravenel***	Y	Y	Y	N	N	N	N	Y
2 ***Spence***	Y	Y	Y	N	N	N	N	Y
3 Derrick	Y	Y	Y	Y	Y	Y	Y	Y
4 ***Inglis***	Y	Y	Y	N	N	N	N	N
5 Spratt	Y	Y	Y	Y	Y	Y	N	Y
6 Clyburn	Y	Y	Y	Y	Y	Y	N	Y
SOUTH DAKOTA								
AL Johnson	Y	Y	Y	Y	Y	Y	N	Y
TENNESSEE								
1 ***Quillen***	Y	Y	Y	N	N	N	N	Y
2 ***Duncan***	Y	Y	Y	N	N	N	N	N
3 Lloyd	Y	Y	Y	Y	Y	N	Y	Y
4 Cooper	Y	Y	Y	N	N	N	Y	N
5 Clement	Y	Y	Y	N	Y	N	Y	N
6 Gordon	Y	Y	Y	Y	Y	N	N	N
7 ***Sundquist***	?	?	?	?	?	?	?	?
8 Tanner	Y	Y	Y	N	N	Y	Y	N
9 Ford	Y	Y	Y	Y	Y	Y	N	Y
TEXAS								
1 Chapman	Y	Y	Y	Y	N	N	N	N
2 Wilson	Y	Y	Y	Y	Y	Y	N	N
3 ***Johnson, Sam***	Y	Y	Y	N	N	N	N	N
4 Hall	Y	Y	Y	Y	N	N	N	N
5 Bryant	Y	Y	Y	Y	Y	Y	Y	Y
6 ***Barton***	Y	Y	Y	Y	N	Y	N	N
7 ***Archer***	Y	Y	Y	N	N	N	N	N
8 ***Fields***	Y	Y	Y	Y	N	N	N	N
9 Brooks	Y	Y	Y	Y	Y	Y	N	N
10 Pickle	Y	Y	Y	Y	Y	Y	Y	Y
11 Edwards	Y	Y	Y	Y	Y	N	N	N
12 Geren	Y	Y	Y	Y	N	N	N	N
13 Sarpalius	Y	Y	Y	Y	N	N	N	N
14 Laughlin	Y	Y	Y	Y	N	N	N	N
15 de la Garza	Y	Y	Y	Y	Y	N	N	N
16 Coleman	Y	Y	Y	Y	Y	Y	N	Y
17 Stenholm	Y	Y	Y	Y	N	N	Y	N
18 Washington	?	?	?	?	?	?	?	?
19 ***Combest***	Y	Y	Y	Y	N	N	N	N
20 Gonzalez	Y	Y	Y	N	Y	Y	N	N
21 ***Smith***	Y	Y	Y	Y	N	Y	N	N
22 ***DeLay***	Y	Y	Y	N	N	N	N	N
23 ***Bonilla***	Y	Y	Y	Y	Y	N	N	N
24 Frost	Y	Y	Y	Y	N	Y	Y	N
25 Andrews	?	?	?	?	?	?	N	Y
26 ***Armey***	Y	Y	Y	N	N	N	N	N
27 Ortiz	Y	Y	Y	Y	Y	Y	N	N
28 Tejeda	Y	Y	Y	Y	Y	Y	N	N
29 Green	Y	Y	Y	Y	Y	Y	N	N
30 Johnson, E.B.	Y	Y	Y	Y	Y	Y	N	Y
UTAH								
1 ***Hansen***	Y	Y	Y	N	N	Y	Y	N
2 Shepherd	Y	Y	Y	Y	Y	Y	Y	Y
3 Orton	Y	Y	Y	N	N	Y	Y	N
VERMONT								
AL *Sanders*	Y	Y	Y	Y	Y	Y	N	Y
VIRGINIA								
1 ***Bateman***	Y	Y	Y	Y	Y	Y	N	Y
2 Pickett	Y	Y	Y	N	N	Y	N	N
3 Scott	Y	Y	Y	Y	Y	Y	N	Y
4 Sisisky	Y	Y	Y	Y	N	Y	N	N
5 Payne	Y	Y	Y	Y	Y	Y	Y	N
6 ***Goodlatte***	Y	Y	Y	N	N	Y	N	N
7 ***Bliley***	Y	Y	Y	Y	N	N	N	N
8 Moran	Y	Y	Y	Y	Y	Y	Y	Y
9 Boucher	Y	Y	Y	Y	Y	Y	N	Y
10 ***Wolf***	Y	Y	Y	N	N	Y	N	Y
11 Byrne	Y	Y	Y	Y	Y	Y	N	Y
WASHINGTON								
1 Cantwell	Y	Y	Y	Y	Y	Y	N	Y
2 Swift	Y	Y	Y	Y	Y	Y	Y	Y
3 Unsoeld	Y	Y	Y	Y	Y	Y	N	Y
4 Inslee	Y	Y	Y	N	Y	Y	N	N
5 Foley								
6 Dicks	Y	Y	Y	Y	Y	Y	N	Y
7 McDermott	Y	Y	Y	Y	Y	Y	Y	?
8 ***Dunn***	Y	?	Y	N	N	Y	N	N
9 Kreidler	Y	Y	Y	Y	Y	Y	N	Y
WEST VIRGINIA								
1 Mollohan	Y	Y	Y	Y	Y	Y	N	Y
2 Wise	Y	Y	Y	Y	Y	Y	N	Y
3 Rahall	Y	Y	Y	N	Y	Y	N	Y
WISCONSIN								
1 Barca	Y	Y	Y	N	Y	Y	Y	N
2 ***Klug***	Y	Y	Y	N	N	N	N	N
3 ***Gunderson***	Y	Y	Y	N	N	N	N	N
4 Kleczka	Y	Y	Y	Y	Y	Y	Y	Y
5 Barrett	Y	Y	Y	N	Y	Y	N	Y
6 ***Petri***	Y	Y	Y	N	N	N	N	N
7 Obey	Y	Y	Y	Y	Y	Y	N	Y
8 ***Roth***	Y	Y	Y	Y	N	N	N	N
9 ***Sensenbrenner***	Y	Y	Y	N	N	N	N	N
WYOMING								
AL ***Thomas***	Y	Y	Y	N	Y	Y	N	N
DELEGATES								
de Lugo, V.I.	D	D	D	D	D	D	D	Y
Faleomavaega, Am.S.	D	D	D	D	D	D	D	Y
Norton, D.C.	D	D	D	D	D	D	D	Y
Romero-B., P.R.	D	D	D	D	D	D	D	Y
Underwood, Guam	D	D	D	D	D	D	D	Y

Southern states - Ala., Ark., Fla., Ga., Ky., La., Miss., N.C., Okla., S.C., Tenn., Texas, Va.
Omitted votes are quorum calls, which CQ does not include in its vote charts.

485. HR 5044. American Heritage Areas Partnership Program/Property Values. Rahall, D-W.Va., amendment to the Tauzin, D-La., amendment, to establish procedures to inform property owners affected by heritage area purchases of their constitutional rights. The Tauzin amendment would have compensated persons whose land was devalued through the program. Adopted in the Committee of the Whole 234-187: R 46-126; D 187-61 (ND 146-26, SD 41-35); I 1-0, Oct. 5, 1994.

486. HR 5044. American Heritage Areas Partnership Program/Passage. Passage of the bill to establish procedures with the Interior Department for designating and managing national heritage areas to preserve natural, historic and cultural resources. The bill also designates 10 areas as American Heritage Areas and provides for the study of other areas for possible designation. Passed 281-137: R 61-111; D 219-26 (ND 160-8, SD 59-18); I 1-0, Oct. 5, 1994. (The House previously had attempted to pass the bill under suspension of the rules. See vote 442.)

487. S 986. Corinth, Miss., Battlefield/Passage. Vento, D-Minn., motion to suspend the rules and pass the bill to authorize $6 million for an interpretive center at the Corinth Battlefield in Mississippi. Motion agreed to 363-45: R 128-41; D 234-4 (ND 158-4, SD 76-0); I 1-0, Oct. 5, 1994. A two-thirds majority of those present and voting (272 in this case) is required for passage under suspension of the rules.

488. HR 5139. Postal Service Re-employment/Passage. Clay, D-Mo., motion to suspend the rules and pass the bill to provide re-employment procedures for persons involuntarily separated by the Postal Service for improper narcotics arrests. Motion agreed to 300-117: R 64-108; D 235-9 (ND 164-3, SD 71-6); I 1-0, Oct. 5, 1994. A two-thirds majority of those present and voting (278 in this case) is required for passage under suspension of the rules.

489. HR 4533. National Park Service Entrepreneurial Management Reform/Passage. Vento, D-Minn., motion to suspend the rules and pass the bill to authorize the Interior Department to increase fees for national park system sites to be deposited into a fund for park projects, beginning in fiscal 1996. Motion rejected 242-174: R 46-126; D 195-48 (ND 136-31, SD 59-17); I 1-0, Oct. 5, 1994. A two-thirds majority of those present and voting (278 in this case) is required for passage under suspension of the rules. (The House previously had attempted to pass the bill under suspension of the rules. See vote 482.)

490. S 1919. Rio Puerco Watershed/Passage. Vento, D-Minn., motion to suspend the rules and pass the bill to direct the Interior Department to collect information and issue a report on ecological damage to the Rio Puerco watershed near Albuquerque, N.M. Motion rejected 220-196: R 25-148; D 195-48 (ND 141-26, SD 54-22); I 0-0, Oct. 5, 1994. A two-thirds majority of those present and voting (278 in this case) is required for passage under suspension of the rules. (The House previously had attempted to pass the bill under suspension of the rules. See vote 481.)

491. S 1225. U.S.-Mexico Border Health Commission/Passage. Dingell, D-Mich., motion to suspend the rules and pass the bill to authorize the president to conclude an agreement with Mexico to establish the U.S.-Mexico Border Health Commission. Motion agreed to 308-103: R 77-94; D 231-9 (ND 157-7, SD 74-2); I 0-0, Oct. 5, 1994. A two-thirds majority of those present and voting (274 in this case) is required for passage under suspension of the rules. (The House previously had attempted to pass the bill under suspension of the rules. See vote 480.)

492. HR 5110. General Agreement on Tariffs and Trade Implementation Bill/Rule. Adoption of the rule (H Res 564) to provide for House floor consideration of the bill to make statutory changes to implement the new world trade agreement negotiated under the Uruguay Round of the General Agreement on Tariffs and Trade (GATT). Adopted 298-123: R 105-70; D 193-52 (ND 126-39, SD 67-13); I 0-1, Oct. 5, 1994.

KEY

Y	Voted for (yea).
#	Paired for.
+	Announced for.
N	Voted against (nay).
X	Paired against.
−	Announced against.
P	Voted "present."
C	Voted "present" to avoid possible conflict of interest.
?	Did not vote or otherwise make a position known.
D	Delegates ineligible to vote.

Democrats **Republicans**
Independent

	485	486	487	488	489	490	491	492
ALABAMA								
1 *Callahan*	?	?	?	?	?	?	?	N
2 Everett	N	N	Y	Y	N	N	N	Y
3 Browder	?	?	?	?	?	?	?	N
4 Bevill	?	?	?	?	?	?	?	Y
5 Cramer	?	?	?	?	?	?	?	N
6 *Bachus*	−	−	+	−	−	−	−	Y
7 Hilliard	?	?	?	?	?	?	?	N
ALASKA								
AL *Young*	N	N	Y	Y	Y	Y	N	N
ARIZONA								
1 Coppersmith	Y	Y	Y	Y	Y	Y	Y	Y
2 Pastor	Y	Y	?	Y	Y	Y	Y	Y
3 *Stump*	N	N	N	N	N	N	N	N
4 *Kyl*	N	N	N	Y	N	N	Y	Y
5 *Kolbe*	N	Y	N	Y	N	Y	Y	Y
6 English	Y	Y	Y	Y	Y	Y	Y	Y
ARKANSAS								
1 Lambert	N	N	Y	N	Y	N	Y	Y
2 Thornton	Y	Y	Y	Y	Y	Y	N	Y
3 *Hutchinson*	N	N	N	N	N	N	N	N
4 *Dickey*	N	N	Y	N	N	N	N	N
CALIFORNIA								
1 Hamburg	Y	Y	Y	Y	Y	Y	Y	N
2 *Herger*	N	N	N	N	N	N	N	Y
3 Fazio	N	Y	Y	Y	Y	Y	Y	Y
4 *Doolittle*	N	N	N	N	N	N	N	N
5 Matsui	Y	Y	Y	Y	Y	Y	Y	Y
6 Woolsey	Y	Y	Y	Y	Y	Y	Y	Y
7 Miller	Y	Y	Y	Y	Y	Y	Y	Y
8 Pelosi	Y	Y	Y	Y	Y	Y	Y	Y
9 Dellums	Y	Y	Y	Y	Y	Y	Y	Y
10 *Baker*	N	N	N	N	N	N	Y	Y
11 *Pombo*	N	N	Y	N	N	N	N	N
12 Lantos	Y	Y	Y	Y	Y	Y	Y	Y
13 Stark	Y	Y	Y	Y	Y	Y	Y	Y
14 Eshoo	Y	Y	Y	Y	Y	Y	Y	Y
15 Mineta	Y	Y	Y	Y	Y	Y	Y	Y
16 Edwards	Y	Y	Y	Y	Y	Y	Y	?
17 Farr	Y	Y	Y	Y	Y	Y	?	Y
18 Condit	N	N	Y	N	Y	N	N	N
19 Lehman	N	Y	Y	Y	Y	Y	Y	Y
20 Dooley	N	N	Y	Y	Y	Y	Y	Y
21 *Thomas*	N	N	Y	N	N	Y	N	Y
22 *Huffington*	N	N	N	N	N	N	Y	Y
23 *Gallegly*	N	Y	Y	Y	Y	Y	Y	Y
24 Beilenson	Y	Y	Y	Y	Y	Y	Y	Y
25 *McKeon*	N	N	Y	N	N	N	Y	Y
26 Berman	Y	Y	Y	Y	Y	Y	Y	Y
27 *Moorhead*	N	N	N	N	N	N	N	Y
28 *Dreier*	N	N	N	N	N	N	N	Y
29 Waxman	Y	Y	Y	Y	Y	Y	Y	Y
30 Becerra	Y	Y	Y	Y	Y	Y	?	Y
31 Martinez	Y	Y	Y	Y	Y	Y	Y	?
32 Dixon	Y	Y	Y	Y	Y	Y	Y	Y
33 Roybal-Allard	Y	Y	Y	Y	Y	Y	Y	Y
34 Torres	Y	Y	?	Y	Y	Y	Y	Y
35 Waters	Y	Y	Y	Y	Y	Y	Y	Y
36 Harman	Y	Y	Y	Y	Y	Y	Y	Y
37 Tucker	?	?	?	?	?	?	?	?
38 Horn	N	N	Y	N	N	N	Y	Y
39 *Royce*	N	N	N	N	N	N	N	N
40 *Lewis*	N	Y	?	N	N	N	N	Y
41 *Kim*	N	N	Y	N	N	N	N	Y

	485	486	487	488	489	490	491	492
42 Brown	Y	Y	Y	?	?	?	?	Y
43 *Calvert*	N	N	Y	N	N	N	Y	Y
44 *McCandless*	N	N	Y	N	N	N	Y	Y
45 *Rohrabacher*	N	N	N	N	N	N	N	N
46 *Dornan*	N	N	N	N	N	N	N	N
47 *Cox*	N	N	Y	N	N	N	N	N
48 *Packard*	N	Y	Y	N	N	N	N	Y
49 *Schenk*	N	Y	Y	Y	Y	Y	Y	Y
50 Filner	Y	Y	Y	Y	Y	Y	Y	Y
51 *Cunningham*	N	N	Y	N	N	N	Y	N
52 *Hunter*	N	N	Y	N	N	N	Y	Y
COLORADO								
1 Schroeder	Y	Y	Y	Y	Y	Y	Y	Y
2 Skaggs	Y	Y	Y	Y	Y	Y	Y	Y
3 *McInnis*	N	N	Y	N	N	N	Y	N
4 *Allard*	N	N	N	N	N	N	N	N
5 *Hefley*	N	Y	N	N	N	N	N	N
6 *Schaefer*	N	N	Y	N	N	N	Y	N
CONNECTICUT								
1 Kennelly	Y	Y	Y	Y	Y	Y	Y	Y
2 Gejdenson	Y	Y	Y	Y	Y	Y	Y	Y
3 DeLauro	Y	Y	Y	Y	Y	Y	Y	Y
4 *Shays*	Y	Y	Y	Y	Y	Y	Y	Y
5 *Franks*	Y	Y	Y	Y	N	N	N	Y
6 *Johnson*	Y	Y	Y	Y	Y	Y	Y	Y
DELAWARE								
AL *Castle*	N	N	Y	N	N	N	N	Y
FLORIDA								
1 Hutto	N	Y	Y	Y	Y	N	Y	Y
2 Peterson	N	Y	?	Y	Y	Y	Y	Y
3 Brown	Y	Y	Y	Y	Y	Y	Y	Y
4 *Fowler*	N	N	Y	N	Y	N	Y	Y
5 Thurman	N	N	Y	Y	Y	N	Y	N
6 *Stearns*	N	N	Y	N	N	N	N	N
7 *Mica*	N	N	N	N	N	N	?	N
8 *McCollum*	N	N	N	N	N	N	Y	Y
9 *Bilirakis*	N	N	Y	N	N	N	N	N
10 *Young*	Y	N	Y	N	N	Y	N	Y
11 Gibbons	Y	Y	Y	Y	Y	Y	Y	Y
12 *Canady*	N	N	Y	N	N	N	N	N
13 *Miller*	N	N	N	N	N	N	N	N
14 *Goss*	N	N	N	N	N	N	Y	N
15 Bacchus	Y	Y	Y	Y	Y	Y	Y	Y
16 *Lewis*	N	N	Y	N	N	N	N	N
17 Meek	Y	Y	Y	Y	Y	Y	Y	Y
18 *Ros-Lehtinen*	N	Y	Y	N	Y	N	Y	Y
19 Johnston	Y	Y	Y	Y	Y	Y	Y	Y
20 Deutsch	Y	Y	Y	Y	Y	Y	Y	Y
21 *Diaz-Balart*	N	Y	Y	N	Y	N	Y	Y
22 *Shaw*	N	N	Y	N	N	N	N	Y
23 Hastings	Y	Y	Y	Y	Y	Y	Y	N
GEORGIA								
1 *Kingston*	N	N	N	N	N	N	N	N
2 Bishop	N	Y	Y	Y	Y	Y	Y	Y
3 *Collins*	N	N	Y	N	N	N	N	N
4 *Linder*	N	N	N	N	N	N	N	N
5 Lewis	Y	Y	Y	Y	Y	Y	Y	Y
6 *Gingrich*	N	N	Y	N	N	N	Y	N
7 Darden	Y	Y	Y	Y	Y	Y	Y	Y
8 Rowland	Y	Y	Y	Y	Y	N	N	Y
9 Deal	Y	Y	Y	Y	Y	Y	Y	Y
10 Johnson	Y	Y	Y	Y	Y	Y	Y	Y
11 McKinney	Y	Y	Y	Y	Y	Y	Y	Y
HAWAII								
1 Abercrombie	Y	Y	Y	Y	Y	Y	Y	Y
2 Mink	Y	Y	Y	Y	N	Y	Y	Y
IDAHO								
1 LaRocco	Y	Y	Y	Y	N	Y	Y	Y
2 *Crapo*	N	N	Y	N	N	N	N	N
ILLINOIS								
1 Rush	Y	Y	Y	Y	Y	Y	Y	Y
2 Reynolds	Y	Y	Y	Y	Y	Y	Y	Y
3 Lipinski	N	Y	Y	Y	Y	N	Y	Y
4 Gutierrez	Y	Y	Y	Y	Y	Y	Y	Y
5 Rostenkowski	Y	Y	Y	Y	Y	Y	Y	Y
6 *Hyde*	N	N	Y	N	N	N	N	Y
7 Collins	Y	Y	Y	Y	Y	Y	Y	Y
8 *Crane*	N	N	N	N	N	N	N	Y
9 Yates	Y	Y	?	Y	Y	Y	Y	?
10 *Porter*	Y	N	Y	N	Y	N	Y	Y
11 Sangmeister	Y	Y	Y	Y	Y	Y	Y	Y
12 Costello	Y	Y	Y	Y	Y	Y	Y	N
13 *Fawell*	Y	Y	N	N	N	N	N	Y
14 *Hastert*	N	N	Y	N	N	N	N	Y
15 *Ewing*	N	N	Y	N	N	N	N	Y
16 *Manzullo*	N	N	N	N	N	N	N	N
17 Evans	Y	Y	Y	Y	N	Y	N	N

ND Northern Democrats   SD Southern Democrats

	485	486	487	488	489	490	491	492
3 ***Michel***	Y	Y	Y	N	N	N	?	Y
9 Poshard	N	Y	Y	Y	N	N	Y	Y
0 Durbin	Y	Y	Y	Y	Y	Y	Y	Y
INDIANA								
1 Visclosky	Y	Y	Y	Y	Y	Y	Y	Y
2 Sharp	Y	Y	Y	Y	Y	Y	Y	?
3 Roemer	N	Y	Y	Y	Y	N	Y	Y
4 Long	N	Y	Y	Y	Y	Y	Y	Y
5 ***Buyer***	Y	N	Y	N	N	N	Y	N
6 ***Burton***	?	N	Y	Y	?	N	N	N
7 ***Myers***	N	N	Y	Y	N	N	Y	N
8 McCloskey	Y	Y	Y	Y	Y	Y	Y	Y
9 Hamilton	N	Y	Y	Y	Y	Y	Y	Y
10 Jacobs	?	Y	Y	Y	Y	N	Y	Y
IOWA								
1 ***Leach***	N	Y	Y	N	N	N	Y	Y
2 ***Nussle***	N	N	Y	N	N	N	Y	Y
3 ***Lightfoot***	N	N	Y	N	N	N	Y	Y
4 Smith	N	N	Y	Y	N	Y	Y	Y
5 ***Grandy***	N	N	Y	Y	N	N	Y	Y
KANSAS								
1 ***Roberts***	N	N	Y	N	Y	N	Y	Y
2 Slattery	?	?	?	?	?	?	?	?
3 ***Meyers***	Y	Y	Y	N	Y	N	N	Y
4 Glickman	Y	Y	Y	Y	Y	N	Y	N
KENTUCKY								
1 Barlow	Y	Y	Y	Y	Y	Y	Y	Y
2 ***Lewis***	N	N	Y	N	N	N	N	N
3 Mazzoli	Y	Y	Y	Y	Y	Y	Y	Y
4 ***Bunning***	N	N	Y	N	N	N	N	Y
5 ***Rogers***	Y	Y	Y	N	N	N	N	N
6 Baesler	Y	Y	Y	Y	Y	Y	Y	Y
LOUISIANA								
1 ***Livingston***	N	Y	Y	Y	N	N	Y	N
2 Jefferson	Y	Y	Y	Y	N	N	Y	Y
3 Tauzin	N	Y	Y	Y	Y	N	Y	Y
4 Fields	N	Y	Y	Y	N	Y	Y	Y
5 ***McCrery***	N	Y	Y	Y	N	N	Y	Y
6 ***Baker***	N	Y	Y	N	N	N	N	Y
7 Hayes	N	N	Y	Y	N	N	Y	Y
MAINE								
1 Andrews	Y	Y	Y	Y	Y	Y	Y	N
2 ***Snowe***	Y	Y	Y	Y	Y	Y	Y	N
MARYLAND								
1 ***Gilchrest***	Y	Y	Y	Y	Y	Y	Y	Y
2 ***Bentley***	N	N	?	N	N	N	N	N
3 Cardin	Y	Y	Y	Y	N	Y	Y	Y
4 Wynn	Y	Y	Y	Y	Y	Y	Y	Y
5 Hoyer	Y	Y	Y	Y	Y	Y	Y	Y
6 ***Bartlett***	N	N	Y	N	N	N	N	N
7 Mfume	Y	Y	Y	Y	Y	Y	Y	Y
8 ***Morella***	Y	Y	Y	Y	Y	Y	Y	Y
MASSACHUSETTS								
1 Olver	Y	Y	Y	Y	Y	Y	Y	Y
2 Neal	Y	Y	Y	Y	Y	Y	Y	Y
3 ***Blute***	Y	Y	Y	?	Y	Y	Y	N
4 Frank	Y	Y	?	?	?	?	?	Y
5 Meehan	Y	Y	Y	Y	Y	Y	Y	Y
6 ***Torkildsen***	Y	Y	Y	Y	Y	Y	Y	N
7 Markey	Y	Y	Y	Y	Y	Y	Y	Y
8 Kennedy	Y	Y	Y	Y	Y	Y	Y	Y
9 Moakley	Y	Y	Y	Y	Y	Y	Y	Y
10 Studds	Y	Y	Y	Y	Y	Y	Y	Y
MICHIGAN								
1 Stupak	N	Y	Y	Y	Y	Y	Y	N
2 ***Hoekstra***	N	N	N	N	N	N	N	Y
3 ***Ehlers***	Y	Y	N	N	N	Y	Y	N
4 ***Camp***	N	N	N	N	N	N	N	Y
5 Barcia	N	N	Y	Y	N	N	Y	N
6 ***Upton***	N	N	N	N	Y	N	N	N
7 ***Smith***	N	N	Y	N	Y	N	Y	Y
8 Carr	?	?	?	?	?	?	?	?
9 Kildee	Y	Y	Y	Y	Y	Y	Y	N
10 Bonior	Y	Y	Y	Y	Y	Y	Y	Y
11 ***Knollenberg***	N	N	Y	N	N	N	N	Y
12 Levin	Y	Y	Y	Y	Y	Y	Y	Y
13 Ford	Y	Y	Y	Y	Y	Y	Y	?
14 Conyers	Y	Y	Y	Y	Y	Y	Y	N
15 Collins	Y	Y	Y	Y	Y	Y	Y	Y
16 Dingell	Y	Y	Y	Y	Y	Y	Y	Y
MINNESOTA								
1 Penny	N	Y	Y	N	Y	N	N	Y
2 Minge	N	Y	Y	Y	Y	N	Y	Y
3 ***Ramstad***	N	N	N	N	N	N	Y	Y
4 Vento	Y	Y	Y	Y	Y	Y	Y	Y

	485	486	487	488	489	490	491	492
5 Sabo	Y	Y	?	Y	Y	Y	Y	Y
6 ***Grams***	N	N	N	N	Y	N	N	Y
7 Peterson	N	Y	Y	Y	N	Y	Y	N
8 Oberstar	Y	Y	Y	Y	Y	Y	Y	Y
MISSISSIPPI								
1 Whitten	?	?	Y	Y	Y	Y	Y	?
2 Thompson	Y	Y	Y	Y	Y	Y	Y	Y
3 Montgomery	N	Y	Y	Y	Y	Y	Y	Y
4 Parker	N	N	Y	Y	Y	N	Y	Y
5 Taylor	N	N	Y	N	N	N	Y	N
MISSOURI								
1 Clay	Y	Y	Y	Y	N	Y	Y	Y
2 ***Talent***	N	N	Y	N	N	N	Y	Y
3 Gephardt	Y	Y	Y	Y	Y	Y	Y	Y
4 Skelton	N	N	Y	Y	Y	N	N	Y
5 Wheat	Y	Y	Y	Y	Y	Y	Y	Y
6 Danner	N	Y	Y	N	N	N	Y	N
7 ***Hancock***	N	N	N	N	N	N	N	Y
8 ***Emerson***	N	N	Y	N	N	N	N	N
9 Volkmer	N	Y	Y	Y	Y	N	Y	N
MONTANA								
AL Williams	Y	Y	N	Y	Y	Y	Y	Y
NEBRASKA								
1 ***Bereuter***	Y	Y	Y	N	Y	Y	Y	Y
2 Hoagland	Y	Y	Y	Y	Y	Y	Y	Y
3 ***Barrett***	N	N	Y	N	N	N	N	Y
NEVADA								
1 Bilbray	Y	Y	Y	Y	Y	Y	Y	N
2 ***Vucanovich***	N	N	Y	N	N	N	Y	N
NEW HAMPSHIRE								
1 ***Zeliff***	N	N	N	Y	N	N	N	N
2 Swett	Y	Y	Y	Y	Y	N	N	N
NEW JERSEY								
1 Andrews	N	N	Y	Y	N	N	Y	N
2 Hughes	Y	Y	Y	Y	Y	Y	Y	Y
3 ***Saxton***	N	N	Y	Y	N	N	Y	Y
4 ***Smith***	Y	Y	Y	N	N	N	N	N
5 ***Roukema***	Y	Y	Y	Y	Y	N	Y	Y
6 Pallone	Y	Y	Y	Y	N	Y	Y	N
7 ***Franks***	Y	Y	Y	Y	Y	N	N	Y
8 Klein	Y	Y	Y	Y	N	Y	Y	Y
9 Torricelli	Y	Y	Y	Y	N	Y	Y	Y
10 Payne	Y	Y	Y	Y	N	Y	?	Y
11 ***Gallo***	?	?	?	?	?	?	?	?
12 ***Zimmer***	Y	Y	Y	N	N	N	N	Y
13 Menendez	Y	Y	Y	Y	N	Y	Y	Y
NEW MEXICO								
1 ***Schiff***	N	N	Y	Y	N	Y	Y	N
2 ***Skeen***	N	N	Y	Y	N	Y	Y	Y
3 Richardson	Y	Y	Y	Y	Y	Y	Y	Y
NEW YORK								
1 Hochbrueckner	Y	Y	Y	Y	Y	Y	Y	N
2 ***Lazio***	Y	Y	N	Y	N	N	N	Y
3 ***King***	Y	Y	Y	Y	N	N	N	Y
4 ***Levy***	Y	Y	Y	Y	N	N	N	Y
5 Ackerman	Y	Y	Y	Y	Y	Y	Y	Y
6 Flake	Y	Y	Y	Y	Y	Y	Y	Y
7 Manton	Y	Y	Y	Y	Y	Y	Y	Y
8 Nadler	Y	Y	Y	Y	N	Y	Y	Y
9 Schumer	Y	Y	Y	Y	N	N	Y	Y
10 Towns	Y	Y	Y	Y	Y	Y	Y	Y
11 Owens	Y	Y	Y	Y	N	Y	Y	N
12 Velazquez	Y	Y	Y	Y	N	Y	Y	N
13 ***Molinari***	Y	Y	Y	N	N	N	Y	Y
14 Maloney	Y	+	Y	Y	N	Y	Y	Y
15 Rangel	Y	Y	Y	Y	Y	Y	Y	Y
16 Serrano	Y	Y	Y	Y	Y	Y	Y	Y
17 Engel	Y	Y	Y	Y	N	Y	Y	Y
18 Lowey	Y	Y	Y	Y	Y	Y	Y	Y
19 ***Fish***	Y	Y	Y	Y	N	N	Y	Y
20 ***Gilman***	Y	Y	Y	Y	N	Y	Y	N
21 McNulty	N	Y	Y	Y	Y	N	Y	Y
22 ***Solomon***	N	N	Y	N	N	N	N	Y
23 ***Boehlert***	Y	Y	Y	Y	Y	Y	Y	N
24 ***McHugh***	N	N	Y	N	N	N	N	N
25 ***Walsh***	N	Y	Y	Y	N	Y	Y	N
26 Hinchey	Y	Y	Y	Y	Y	Y	Y	N
27 ***Paxon***	N	N	Y	N	N	N	N	Y
28 Slaughter	Y	Y	Y	Y	Y	Y	Y	Y
29 LaFalce	N	Y	Y	Y	Y	Y	Y	Y
30 ***Quinn***	N	N	Y	Y	N	N	N	N
31 ***Houghton***	N	N	Y	Y	Y	N	N	Y
NORTH CAROLINA								
1 Clayton	Y	Y	Y	?	+	+	+	Y
2 Valentine	N	N	Y	N	N	N	N	Y

	485	486	487	488	489	490	491	492
3 Lancaster	N	Y	Y	Y	N	Y	Y	Y
4 Price	Y	Y	Y	Y	Y	Y	Y	Y
5 Neal	Y	Y	Y	Y	Y	Y	Y	Y
6 ***Coble***	N	N	N	N	N	N	N	N
7 Rose	Y	Y	Y	Y	Y	Y	Y	N
8 Hefner	Y	Y	Y	Y	Y	Y	Y	N
9 ***McMillan***	N	Y	Y	Y	Y	N	Y	Y
10 ***Ballenger***	N	N	Y	N	N	N	N	Y
11 ***Taylor***	N	N	N	Y	N	N	N	N
12 Watt	Y	Y	Y	Y	Y	Y	Y	Y
NORTH DAKOTA								
AL Pomeroy	N	Y	Y	Y	Y	Y	Y	Y
OHIO								
1 Mann	Y	Y	Y	Y	Y	Y	Y	Y
2 ***Portman***	Y	Y	Y	N	Y	N	N	Y
3 Hall	Y	Y	Y	Y	Y	Y	Y	Y
4 ***Oxley***	Y	Y	Y	N	N	N	N	Y
5 ***Gillmor***	Y	Y	Y	Y	Y	N	Y	N
6 Strickland	Y	Y	Y	Y	Y	Y	Y	N
7 ***Hobson***	Y	Y	Y	Y	Y	N	N	Y
8 ***Boehner***	N	N	N	N	N	N	N	Y
9 Kaptur	Y	Y	Y	Y	Y	N	Y	N
10 ***Hoke***	Y	Y	Y	Y	Y	N	N	Y
11 Stokes	Y	Y	?	Y	N	Y	Y	N
12 ***Kasich***	Y	Y	Y	Y	Y	N	N	Y
13 Brown	Y	Y	Y	Y	Y	Y	Y	N
14 Sawyer	Y	Y	Y	Y	Y	Y	Y	Y
15 ***Pryce***	Y	Y	N	N	N	N	N	Y
16 ***Regula***	Y	Y	Y	Y	Y	Y	N	Y
17 Traficant	Y	Y	Y	Y	Y	Y	Y	N
18 Applegate	Y	Y	Y	Y	N	Y	Y	N
19 Fingerhut	Y	Y	Y	Y	Y	Y	Y	N
OKLAHOMA								
1 ***Inhofe***	N	N	Y	N	N	N	N	N
2 Synar	Y	Y	Y	Y	Y	Y	Y	Y
3 Brewster	N	Y	Y	Y	N	N	Y	Y
4 McCurdy	N	Y	Y	Y	?	?	?	Y
5 ***Istook***	N	N	Y	N	N	N	N	N
6 ***Lucas***	N	N	Y	N	Y	N	Y	N
OREGON								
1 Furse	Y	Y	Y	Y	Y	Y	Y	Y
2 ***Smith***	N	N	Y	N	Y	N	N	Y
3 Wyden	Y	Y	Y	Y	Y	Y	Y	Y
4 DeFazio	Y	Y	N	Y	N	N	Y	N
5 Kopetski	Y	Y	Y	Y	Y	Y	Y	Y
PENNSYLVANIA								
1 Foglietta	Y	Y	Y	Y	Y	Y	Y	Y
2 Blackwell	?	Y	Y	Y	Y	Y	Y	Y
3 Borski	Y	Y	Y	Y	Y	Y	Y	Y
4 Klink	Y	Y	Y	Y	Y	Y	Y	N
5 ***Clinger***	Y	Y	Y	Y	N	Y	N	Y
6 Holden	Y	Y	Y	Y	N	N	N	N
7 ***Weldon***	Y	Y	Y	Y	N	N	N	Y
8 ***Greenwood***	Y	Y	N	N	N	N	N	Y
9 ***Shuster***	N	Y	Y	N	N	Y	N	N
10 ***McDade***	Y	Y	?	Y	N	N	Y	Y
11 Kanjorski	Y	Y	Y	Y	Y	Y	Y	Y
12 Murtha	Y	Y	Y	Y	Y	Y	Y	Y
13 Margolies-Mezv.	Y	Y	N	N	Y	N	N	Y
14 Coyne	Y	Y	Y	Y	Y	Y	Y	Y
15 McHale	Y	Y	Y	Y	N	N	Y	Y
16 ***Walker***	N	N	Y	N	N	N	N	Y
17 ***Gekas***	N	N	Y	N	N	N	N	Y
18 ***Santorum***	Y	Y	Y	N	N	N	N	Y
19 ***Goodling***	N	N	Y	N	N	N	N	N
20 Murphy	N	Y	Y	Y	N	N	Y	N
21 ***Ridge***	?	?	?	?	?	?	?	?
RHODE ISLAND								
1 ***Machtley***	Y	?	Y	Y	Y	Y	Y	Y
2 Reed	Y	Y	Y	Y	Y	Y	Y	Y
SOUTH CAROLINA								
1 ***Ravenel***	Y	Y	Y	N	Y	N	Y	N
2 ***Spence***	N	Y	Y	Y	Y	N	Y	N
3 Derrick	Y	Y	Y	Y	Y	Y	Y	Y
4 ***Inglis***	N	N	N	N	N	N	N	N
5 Spratt	Y	Y	Y	N	Y	Y	Y	N
6 Clyburn	Y	Y	Y	Y	Y	Y	Y	Y
SOUTH DAKOTA								
AL Johnson	Y	Y	Y	Y	Y	Y	Y	Y
TENNESSEE								
1 ***Quillen***	Y	Y	Y	Y	N	N	Y	N
2 ***Duncan***	N	N	N	N	N	N	N	N
3 Lloyd	Y	Y	Y	Y	Y	Y	Y	Y
4 Cooper	N	N	Y	Y	N	N	N	Y
5 Clement	N	Y	Y	Y	N	Y	Y	?

	485	486	487	488	489	490	491	492
6 Gordon	N	Y	Y	Y	N	Y	Y	Y
7 ***Sundquist***	?	?	?	?	?	?	?	?
8 Tanner	N	N	Y	N	Y	N	Y	Y
9 Ford	Y	Y	Y	Y	N	Y	Y	Y
TEXAS								
1 Chapman	?	N	Y	Y	Y	N	Y	Y
2 Wilson	N	N	?	Y	Y	Y	Y	Y
3 ***Johnson, Sam***	N	N	Y	Y	N	N	Y	Y
4 Hall	N	N	Y	N	N	N	Y	N
5 Bryant	Y	Y	Y	Y	Y	Y	Y	Y
6 ***Barton***	N	N	Y	N	Y	N	Y	Y
7 ***Archer***	N	N	N	N	N	N	Y	Y
8 ***Fields***	N	N	N	N	N	N	Y	Y
9 Brooks	N	N	Y	Y	Y	Y	Y	Y
10 Pickle	Y	Y	Y	Y	Y	Y	Y	Y
11 Edwards	N	N	Y	Y	N	Y	Y	Y
12 Geren	N	N	Y	Y	N	N	Y	Y
13 Sarpalius	N	N	Y	Y	Y	N	Y	Y
14 Laughlin	N	N	Y	Y	N	N	Y	Y
15 de la Garza	N	Y	Y	Y	Y	Y	Y	Y
16 Coleman	Y	Y	Y	Y	Y	Y	Y	Y
17 Stenholm	N	N	Y	Y	Y	N	Y	Y
18 Washington	?	?	?	?	?	?	?	?
19 ***Combest***	N	N	Y	N	Y	N	Y	Y
20 Gonzalez	Y	Y	Y	Y	Y	Y	Y	Y
21 ***Smith***	N	N	Y	N	Y	N	Y	N
22 ***DeLay***	N	N	N	N	N	N	Y	Y
23 ***Bonilla***	N	N	Y	N	Y	N	Y	N
24 Frost	N	Y	Y	Y	Y	Y	Y	Y
25 Andrews	Y	Y	Y	Y	Y	Y	Y	Y
26 ***Armey***	N	N	N	N	N	N	Y	Y
27 Ortiz	N	Y	Y	Y	Y	N	Y	Y
28 Tejeda	N	Y	Y	Y	Y	Y	Y	Y
29 Green	N	Y	Y	Y	N	Y	Y	Y
30 Johnson, E.B.	Y	Y	Y	Y	Y	Y	Y	Y
UTAH								
1 ***Hansen***	N	Y	N	N	Y	N	N	Y
2 Shepherd	Y	Y	Y	Y	Y	Y	Y	Y
3 Orton	N	N	N	Y	Y	N	N	Y
VERMONT								
AL *Sanders*	Y	Y	Y	Y	Y	?	?	N
VIRGINIA								
1 ***Bateman***	Y	Y	Y	Y	Y	Y	Y	Y
2 Pickett	N	N	Y	Y	Y	N	Y	Y
3 Scott	Y	Y	Y	Y	Y	Y	Y	N
4 Sisisky	N	N	Y	Y	Y	N	Y	Y
5 Payne	N	Y	Y	Y	Y	Y	Y	N
6 ***Goodlatte***	N	N	N	N	Y	N	N	Y
7 ***Bliley***	N	N	N	N	N	N	Y	Y
8 Moran	Y	Y	Y	Y	Y	Y	Y	Y
9 Boucher	Y	Y	Y	Y	Y	Y	Y	Y
10 ***Wolf***	Y	Y	?	Y	Y	N	N	Y
11 Byrne	Y	Y	Y	Y	Y	Y	Y	Y
WASHINGTON								
1 Cantwell	Y	Y	Y	Y	Y	Y	Y	Y
2 Swift	Y	Y	Y	Y	Y	Y	Y	Y
3 Unsoeld	Y	Y	Y	Y	Y	Y	Y	Y
4 Inslee	N	Y	Y	Y	Y	Y	N	Y
5 Foley								Y
6 Dicks	Y	Y	Y	Y	Y	Y	Y	Y
7 McDermott	Y	Y	Y	Y	Y	Y	Y	Y
8 ***Dunn***	N	Y	Y	N	Y	Y	Y	Y
9 Kreidler	Y	Y	Y	Y	Y	Y	Y	Y
WEST VIRGINIA								
1 Mollohan	Y	Y	Y	Y	Y	Y	Y	N
2 Wise	Y	Y	Y	Y	Y	Y	Y	N
3 Rahall	Y	Y	Y	Y	Y	N	Y	N
WISCONSIN								
1 Barca	Y	N	Y	Y	Y	Y	N	Y
2 ***Klug***	N	N	N	N	N	N	N	N
3 ***Gunderson***	N	N	Y	Y	N	N	Y	N
4 Kleczka	Y	Y	Y	Y	Y	Y	Y	Y
5 Barrett	Y	Y	Y	Y	Y	Y	Y	Y
6 ***Petri***	N	N	Y	N	N	N	N	Y
7 Obey	Y	Y	?	Y	Y	Y	Y	N
8 ***Roth***	N	N	Y	Y	N	N	Y	N
9 ***Sensenbrenner***	N	N	N	N	N	N	N	N
WYOMING								
AL ***Thomas***	N	N	N	N	Y	Y	N	Y
DELEGATES								
de Lugo, V.I.	Y	D	D	D	D	D	D	D
Faleomavaega, Am.S.	Y	D	D	D	D	D	D	D
Norton, D.C.	Y	D	D	D	D	D	D	D
Romero-B., P.R.	Y	D	D	D	D	D	D	D
Underwood, Guam	Y	D	D	D	D	D	D	D

Southern states - Ala., Ark., Fla., Ga., Ky., La., Miss., N.C., Okla., S.C., Tenn., Texas, Va.
Omitted votes are quorum calls, which CQ does not include in its vote charts.

KEY

Y Voted for (yea).
\# Paired for.
+ Announced for.
N Voted against (nay).
X Paired against.
– Announced against.
P Voted ''present.''
C Voted ''present'' to avoid possible conflict of interest.
? Did not vote or otherwise make a position known.
D Delegates ineligible to vote.

Democrats **Republicans**
Independent

493. S 455. Payments in Lieu of Taxes/Rule. Adoption of the rule (H Res 565) to provide for House floor consideration of the bill to increase federal payments to local governments to compensate for federally owned land, for which they cannot collect taxes, from the current authorization level of $105 million to $227 million by fiscal 1999 with payments in subsequent years indexed for inflation. Adopted 384-28: R 148-19; D 235-9 (ND 158-8, SD 77-1); I 1-0, Oct. 6, 1994.

494. HR 4278. Domestic Workers Tax Threshold/Conference Report. Adoption of the conference report to increase the threshold at which Social Security taxes must be paid for domestic workers from $50 per calendar quarter to $1,000 annually. Adopted (thus sent to the Senate) 423-0: R 175-0; D 247-0 (ND 166-0, SD 81-0); I 1-0, Oct. 6, 1994.

495. H J Res 416. U.S. Troops in Haiti/Rule. Adoption of the rule (H Res 570) to provide for House floor consideration of the joint resolution to authorize the presence of U.S. troops in Haiti until March 1, 1995, unless the president determines and certifies that a continued presence is essential to protect U.S. citizens or is vital to U.S. national security interests. Adopted 241-182: R 0-174; D 240-8 (ND 164-4, SD 76-4); I 1-0, Oct. 6, 1994.

*497. H J Res 416. U.S. Troops in Haiti/Immediate Withdrawal. Gilman, R-N.Y., substitute amendment to express the sense of Congress that the president should not have ordered U.S. troops to occupy Haiti and that the president should immediately commence "the safe and orderly withdrawal" of all U.S. forces from Haiti. The substitute also would provide for consideration of a joint resolution to be introduced Jan. 3, 1995, that if enacted would prohibit the continued use of U.S troops in Haiti within 30 days. Rejected in the Committee of the Whole 205-225: R 173-1; D 32-223 (ND 21-153, SD 11-70); I 0-1, Oct. 6, 1994. A "nay" was a vote in support of the president's position.

* Omitted votes are quorum calls, which CQ does not include in its vote charts.

	493	494	495	497
ALABAMA				
1 Callahan	Y	Y	N	Y
2 Everett	Y	Y	N	Y
3 Browder	Y	Y	Y	N
4 Bevill	Y	Y	Y	N
5 Cramer	Y	Y	Y	N
6 *Bachus*	Y	Y	N	Y
7 Hilliard	Y	Y	Y	N
ALASKA				
AL *Young*	Y	Y	N	Y
ARIZONA				
1 Coppersmith	Y	Y	Y	Y
2 Pastor	Y	Y	Y	N
3 *Stump*	Y	Y	N	Y
4 *Kyl*	Y	Y	N	Y
5 *Kolbe*	Y	Y	N	Y
6 English	Y	Y	Y	N
ARKANSAS				
1 Lambert	Y	Y	Y	Y
2 Thornton	Y	Y	Y	N
3 *Hutchinson*	Y	Y	N	Y
4 Dickey	Y	Y	N	N
CALIFORNIA				
1 Hamburg	Y	Y	Y	N
2 *Herger*	Y	Y	N	Y
3 Fazio	Y	Y	Y	N
4 *Doolittle*	Y	Y	N	Y
5 Matsui	Y	Y	Y	N
6 Woolsey	Y	Y	Y	N
7 Miller	N	Y	Y	N
8 Pelosi	Y	Y	Y	N
9 Dellums	Y	Y	Y	N
10 *Baker*	Y	Y	N	Y
11 *Pombo*	Y	Y	N	Y
12 Lantos	Y	Y	Y	N
13 Stark	Y	?	Y	N
14 Eshoo	Y	Y	Y	N
15 Mineta	Y	Y	Y	N
16 Edwards	Y	Y	Y	N
17 Farr	Y	Y	Y	N
18 Condit	Y	Y	N	Y
19 Lehman	Y	Y	Y	N
20 Dooley	Y	Y	Y	N
21 *Thomas*	Y	Y	N	Y
22 *Huffington*	Y	Y	N	?
23 *Gallegly*	Y	Y	N	Y
24 Beilenson	Y	Y	Y	N
25 *McKeon*	Y	Y	N	Y
26 Berman	Y	Y	Y	N
27 *Moorhead*	Y	Y	N	Y
28 *Dreier*	Y	Y	N	Y
29 Waxman	Y	Y	Y	N
30 Becerra	Y	Y	Y	N
31 Martinez	Y	Y	Y	N
32 Dixon	Y	Y	Y	N
33 Roybal-Allard	Y	Y	Y	N
34 Torres	Y	Y	Y	N
35 Waters	Y	Y	Y	N
36 Harman	Y	Y	Y	Y
37 Tucker	?	?	\#	
38 *Horn*	Y	Y	N	Y
39 *Royce*	N	Y	N	Y
40 *Lewis*	Y	Y	N	Y
41 *Kim*	Y	Y	N	Y

	493	494	495	497
42 Brown	Y	Y	Y	N
43 *Calvert*	Y	Y	N	Y
44 *McCandless*	?	Y	N	Y
45 *Rohrabacher*	?	Y	N	Y
46 *Dornan*	?	Y	N	Y
47 *Cox*	Y	Y	N	Y
48 *Packard*	Y	Y	N	Y
49 Schenk	Y	Y	Y	Y
50 Filner	Y	Y	Y	N
51 *Cunningham*	Y	Y	N	Y
52 *Hunter*	Y	Y	N	Y
COLORADO				
1 Schroeder	Y	Y	N	N
2 Skaggs	Y	Y	Y	N
3 *McInnis*	Y	Y	N	Y
4 *Allard*	Y	Y	N	Y
5 *Hefley*	N	Y	N	Y
6 *Schaefer*	N	Y	N	Y
CONNECTICUT				
1 Kennelly	Y	Y	Y	N
2 Gejdenson	Y	Y	Y	N
3 DeLauro	Y	Y	Y	N
4 *Shays*	Y	Y	N	N
5 *Franks*	Y	Y	N	N
6 *Johnson*	Y	Y	N	N
DELAWARE				
AL *Castle*	Y	Y	N	Y
FLORIDA				
1 Hutto	Y	Y	N	N
2 Peterson	Y	Y	Y	N
3 Brown	Y	Y	Y	N
4 *Fowler*	Y	Y	N	Y
5 Thurman	Y	Y	Y	N
6 *Stearns*	Y	Y	N	Y
7 *Mica*	Y	Y	N	Y
8 *McCollum*	Y	Y	N	Y
9 *Bilirakis*	Y	Y	N	Y
10 *Young*	Y	Y	N	Y
11 Gibbons	Y	Y	Y	N
12 *Canady*	Y	Y	N	Y
13 *Miller*	Y	Y	N	Y
14 *Goss*	Y	Y	N	Y
15 *Bacchus*	Y	Y	Y	N
16 *Lewis*	Y	Y	N	Y
17 Meek	Y	Y	Y	N
18 *Ros-Lehtinen*	Y	Y	N	Y
19 Johnston	Y	Y	Y	N
20 Deutsch	Y	Y	Y	N
21 *Diaz-Balart*	Y	Y	N	Y
22 *Shaw*	Y	Y	N	Y
23 Hastings	Y	Y	Y	N
GEORGIA				
1 *Kingston*	Y	Y	N	Y
2 Bishop	Y	Y	Y	N
3 *Collins*	Y	Y	N	Y
4 *Linder*	Y	Y	N	Y
5 Lewis	Y	Y	Y	N
6 *Gingrich*	Y	Y	N	Y
7 Darden	Y	Y	Y	N
8 Rowland	Y	Y	Y	N
9 Deal	Y	Y	Y	N
10 Johnson	Y	Y	Y	N
11 McKinney	Y	Y	Y	N
HAWAII				
1 Abercrombie	Y	Y	Y	N
2 Mink	Y	Y	Y	N
IDAHO				
1 LaRocco	Y	Y	Y	N
2 *Crapo*	Y	Y	N	Y
ILLINOIS				
1 Rush	Y	Y	Y	N
2 Reynolds	Y	Y	Y	N
3 Lipinski	Y	Y	Y	Y
4 Gutierrez	Y	Y	Y	N
5 Rostenkowski	Y	Y	Y	N
6 *Hyde*	Y	Y	N	Y
7 Collins	Y	Y	Y	N
8 *Crane*	?	Y	N	Y
9 Yates	N	Y	Y	N
10 *Porter*	N	Y	N	Y
11 Sangmeister	Y	Y	Y	N
12 Costello	Y	Y	Y	N
13 *Fawell*	N	Y	N	Y
14 *Hastert*	Y	Y	N	Y
15 *Ewing*	?	Y	N	Y
16 *Manzullo*	Y	Y	N	Y
17 Evans	Y	Y	Y	N

ND Northern Democrats   SD Southern Democrats

	493	494	495	497
18 *Michel*	Y	Y	N	Y
19 Poshard	Y	Y	Y	N
20 Durbin	Y	Y	Y	N
INDIANA				
1 Visclosky	Y	Y	Y	N
2 Sharp	Y	Y	Y	N
3 Roemer	Y	Y	Y	N
4 Long	Y	Y	Y	N
5 *Buyer*	Y	Y	N	Y
6 *Burton*	Y	Y	N	Y
7 *Myers*	Y	Y	N	Y
8 McCloskey	Y	Y	Y	N
9 Hamilton	Y	Y	Y	N
10 Jacobs	Y	Y	Y	N
IOWA				
1 *Leach*	Y	Y	N	Y
2 *Nussle*	Y	Y	N	Y
3 *Lightfoot*	Y	Y	N	Y
4 Smith	Y	Y	N	Y
5 *Grandy*	Y	Y	N	Y
KANSAS				
1 *Roberts*	Y	Y	N	Y
2 Slattery	?	?	#	?
3 *Meyers*	Y	Y	N	Y
4 Glickman	Y	Y	Y	N
KENTUCKY				
1 Barlow	Y	Y	Y	N
2 *Lewis*	Y	Y	N	Y
3 Mazzoli	Y	Y	Y	N
4 *Bunning*	Y	Y	N	Y
5 *Rogers*	Y	Y	N	Y
6 Baesler	Y	Y	Y	N
LOUISIANA				
1 *Livingston*	Y	Y	N	Y
2 Jefferson	Y	Y	Y	N
3 Tauzin	Y	Y	Y	N
4 Fields	Y	Y	Y	N
5 *McCrery*	Y	Y	N	Y
6 *Baker*	Y	Y	N	Y
7 Hayes	Y	Y	Y	N
MAINE				
1 Andrews	Y	Y	Y	N
2 *Snowe*	Y	Y	N	Y
MARYLAND				
1 *Gilchrest*	N	Y	N	Y
2 *Bentley*	?	?	X	Y
3 Cardin	Y	Y	Y	N
4 Wynn	Y	Y	Y	N
5 Hoyer	Y	Y	Y	N
6 *Bartlett*	Y	Y	N	Y
7 Mfume	Y	Y	Y	—
8 *Morella*	N	Y	N	Y
MASSACHUSETTS				
1 Olver	Y	Y	Y	N
2 Neal	Y	Y	Y	N
3 *Blute*	Y	Y	N	Y
4 Frank	Y	Y	Y	N
5 Meehan	Y	Y	Y	N
6 *Torkildsen*	N	Y	N	Y
7 Markey	Y	Y	Y	N
8 Kennedy	Y	Y	Y	N
9 Moakley	Y	Y	Y	N
10 Studds	Y	Y	Y	N
MICHIGAN				
1 Stupak	Y	Y	Y	N
2 *Hoekstra*	Y	Y	N	Y
3 *Ehlers*	Y	Y	N	Y
4 *Camp*	Y	Y	N	Y
5 Barcia	Y	Y	Y	Y
6 *Upton*	N	Y	N	Y
7 *Smith*	Y	Y	N	Y
8 Carr	?	Y	Y	Y
9 Kildee	Y	Y	Y	Y
10 Bonior	Y	Y	Y	N
11 *Knollenberg*	Y	Y	N	Y
12 Levin	Y	Y	Y	N
13 Ford	Y	Y	Y	N
14 Conyers	Y	Y	Y	N
15 Collins	Y	Y	Y	N
16 Dingell	Y	?	Y	N
MINNESOTA				
1 Penny	N	Y	Y	N
2 Minge	Y	Y	Y	N
3 *Ramstad*	N	Y	N	Y
4 Vento	N	Y	Y	N

	493	494	495	497
5 Sabo	N	Y	Y	N
6 *Grams*	Y	Y	N	Y
7 Peterson	Y	Y	Y	N
8 Oberstar	Y	Y	Y	N
MISSISSIPPI				
1 Whitten	?	?	?	?
2 Thompson	Y	Y	Y	N
3 Montgomery	Y	Y	Y	N
4 Parker	Y	Y	Y	Y
5 Taylor	N	Y	N	Y
MISSOURI				
1 Clay	Y	Y	Y	N
2 *Talent*	Y	Y	N	Y
3 Gephardt	Y	Y	Y	N
4 Skelton	Y	Y	Y	N
5 Wheat	Y	Y	?	N
6 Danner	Y	Y	Y	Y
7 *Hancock*	Y	Y	N	Y
8 *Emerson*	Y	Y	N	Y
9 Volkmer	Y	Y	Y	N
MONTANA				
AL Williams	Y	Y	Y	N
NEBRASKA				
1 *Bereuter*	Y	Y	N	Y
2 Hoagland	Y	Y	Y	N
3 *Barrett*	Y	Y	N	P
NEVADA				
1 Bilbray	Y	Y	Y	N
2 *Vucanovich*	Y	Y	N	Y
NEW HAMPSHIRE				
1 *Zeliff*	Y	Y	N	Y
2 Swett	Y	Y	Y	Y
NEW JERSEY				
1 Andrews	Y	Y	N	Y
2 Hughes	Y	Y	Y	N
3 *Saxton*	Y	Y	N	Y
4 *Smith*	Y	Y	N	Y
5 Roukema	Y	Y	Y	N
6 Pallone	Y	Y	Y	N
7 *Franks*	N	Y	N	Y
8 Klein	Y	Y	Y	N
9 Torricelli	Y	Y	Y	N
10 Payne	Y	Y	Y	N
11 *Gallo*	?	?	?	?
12 *Zimmer*	N	Y	N	Y
13 Menendez	Y	Y	Y	N
NEW MEXICO				
1 *Schiff*	Y	Y	N	Y
2 *Skeen*	Y	Y	N	Y
3 Richardson	Y	Y	Y	N
NEW YORK				
1 Hochbrueckner	Y	Y	Y	N
2 *Lazio*	Y	Y	N	Y
3 *King*	Y	Y	N	Y
4 *Levy*	Y	Y	N	Y
5 Ackerman	Y	Y	Y	N
6 Flake	Y	Y	Y	N
7 Manton	Y	Y	Y	N
8 Nadler	Y	Y	Y	N
9 Schumer	Y	Y	Y	N
10 Towns	?	Y	Y	N
11 Owens	Y	Y	Y	N
12 Velazquez	Y	Y	Y	N
13 *Molinari*	Y	Y	N	Y
14 Maloney	Y	Y	Y	N
15 Rangel	Y	Y	Y	N
16 Serrano	Y	Y	Y	N
17 Engel	Y	Y	Y	N
18 Lowey	Y	Y	Y	N
19 *Fish*	Y	Y	N	Y
20 *Gilman*	Y	Y	N	Y
21 McNulty	Y	Y	Y	N
22 *Solomon*	Y	Y	N	Y
23 *Boehlert*	Y	Y	N	Y
24 *McHugh*	Y	Y	N	Y
25 *Walsh*	Y	Y	N	Y
26 Hinchey	Y	Y	Y	N
27 *Paxon*	Y	Y	N	Y
28 Slaughter	Y	Y	Y	N
29 LaFalce	Y	Y	Y	N
30 *Quinn*	Y	Y	N	Y
31 *Houghton*	Y	Y	N	Y
NORTH CAROLINA				
1 Clayton	Y	Y	Y	N
2 Valentine	Y	Y	?	N

	493	494	495	497
3 Lancaster	Y	Y	Y	N
4 Price	Y	Y	Y	N
5 Neal	Y	Y	Y	N
6 *Coble*	Y	Y	N	Y
7 Rose	Y	Y	Y	N
8 Hefner	Y	Y	Y	N
9 *McMillan*	Y	Y	N	Y
10 *Ballenger*	N	Y	N	Y
11 *Taylor*	Y	Y	N	Y
12 Watt	Y	Y	Y	N
NORTH DAKOTA				
AL Pomeroy	Y	Y	Y	Y
OHIO				
1 Mann	Y	Y	Y	N
2 *Portman*	Y	Y	N	Y
3 Hall	Y	Y	Y	N
4 *Oxley*	?	Y	N	Y
5 *Gillmor*	Y	Y	N	Y
6 Strickland	Y	Y	Y	N
7 *Hobson*	Y	Y	N	Y
8 *Boehner*	Y	Y	N	Y
9 Kaptur	Y	Y	Y	N
10 *Hoke*	N	Y	N	Y
11 Stokes	Y	Y	Y	N
12 *Kasich*	Y	Y	N	Y
13 Brown	Y	Y	Y	N
14 Sawyer	Y	Y	Y	N
15 *Pryce*	Y	Y	N	Y
16 *Regula*	Y	Y	N	Y
17 Traficant	Y	Y	Y	Y
18 Applegate	?	?	?	?
19 Fingerhut	Y	Y	Y	N
OKLAHOMA				
1 *Inhofe*	Y	Y	N	Y
2 Synar	Y	Y	Y	N
3 Brewster	Y	Y	Y	N
4 McCurdy	?	Y	Y	N
5 *Istook*	?	Y	N	Y
6 *Lucas*	Y	Y	N	Y
OREGON				
1 Furse	Y	Y	Y	N
2 *Smith*	Y	Y	N	Y
3 Wyden	Y	Y	Y	N
4 DeFazio	Y	Y	Y	N
5 Kopetski	Y	Y	Y	N
PENNSYLVANIA				
1 Foglietta	Y	Y	Y	N
2 Blackwell	?	Y	Y	N
3 Borski	Y	Y	Y	N
4 Klink	Y	Y	Y	N
5 *Clinger*	Y	Y	N	Y
6 Holden	Y	Y	Y	N
7 *Weldon*	Y	Y	N	Y
8 *Greenwood*	Y	Y	N	Y
9 *Shuster*	Y	Y	N	Y
10 *McDade*	Y	Y	N	Y
11 Kanjorski	N	Y	Y	N
12 Murtha	Y	Y	Y	N
13 Margolies-Mezv.	Y	Y	Y	N
14 Coyne	Y	?	Y	N
15 McHale	Y	Y	Y	N
16 *Walker*	Y	Y	N	Y
17 *Gekas*	Y	Y	N	Y
18 *Santorum*	Y	Y	N	Y
19 *Goodling*	Y	Y	N	Y
20 Murphy	N	Y	Y	N
21 *Ridge*	?	Y	N	Y
RHODE ISLAND				
1 *Machtley*	Y	Y	N	Y
2 Reed	Y	Y	Y	N
SOUTH CAROLINA				
1 *Ravenel*	Y	Y	N	Y
2 *Spence*	Y	Y	N	Y
3 Derrick	Y	Y	Y	N
4 *Inglis*	Y	Y	N	Y
5 Spratt	Y	Y	Y	N
6 Clyburn	Y	Y	Y	N
SOUTH DAKOTA				
AL Johnson	Y	Y	Y	Y
TENNESSEE				
1 *Quillen*	Y	Y	X	Y
2 *Duncan*	Y	Y	N	Y
3 Lloyd	Y	Y	Y	N
4 Cooper	Y	Y	Y	N
5 Clement	Y	Y	Y	N

	493	494	495	497
6 Gordon	Y	Y	Y	N
7 *Sundquist*	?	?	?	?
8 Tanner	Y	Y	N	N
9 Ford	Y	Y	Y	N
TEXAS				
1 Chapman	Y	Y	Y	N
2 Wilson	Y	Y	Y	N
3 *Johnson, Sam*	Y	Y	N	Y
4 Hall	Y	Y	N	Y
5 Bryant	Y	Y	Y	N
6 *Barton*	Y	Y	N	Y
7 *Archer*	Y	Y	N	Y
8 *Fields*	Y	Y	N	Y
9 Brooks	?	Y	Y	N
10 Pickle	Y	Y	Y	N
11 Edwards	Y	Y	Y	N
12 Geren	Y	Y	Y	N
13 Sarpalius	Y	Y	Y	Y
14 Laughlin	Y	Y	Y	N
15 de la Garza	Y	Y	Y	N
16 Coleman	Y	Y	Y	N
17 Stenholm	Y	Y	Y	Y
18 Washington	?	?	?	?
19 *Combest*	Y	Y	N	Y
20 Gonzalez	Y	Y	Y	N
21 *Smith*	Y	Y	N	Y
22 *DeLay*	Y	Y	N	Y
23 *Bonilla*	Y	Y	N	Y
24 Frost	Y	Y	Y	N
25 Andrews	Y	Y	Y	N
26 *Armey*	Y	Y	N	Y
27 Ortiz	Y	Y	Y	N
28 Tejeda	Y	Y	Y	N
29 Green	Y	Y	Y	N
30 Johnson, E.B.	Y	Y	Y	N
UTAH				
1 *Hansen*	Y	Y	N	Y
2 Shepherd	Y	Y	Y	N
3 Orton	Y	Y	Y	N
VERMONT				
AL *Sanders*	Y	Y	Y	N
VIRGINIA				
1 *Bateman*	Y	Y	N	Y
2 Pickett	Y	Y	Y	N
3 Scott	Y	Y	Y	N
4 Sisisky	Y	Y	Y	N
5 Payne	Y	Y	Y	N
6 *Goodlatte*	Y	Y	N	Y
7 *Bliley*	Y	Y	N	Y
8 Moran	?	Y	Y	N
9 Boucher	Y	Y	Y	N
10 *Wolf*	Y	Y	N	Y
11 Byrne	Y	Y	Y	N
WASHINGTON				
1 Cantwell	Y	Y	Y	N
2 Swift	Y	Y	Y	N
3 Unsoeld	Y	Y	Y	N
4 Inslee	Y	Y	Y	N
5 Foley				N
6 Dicks	Y	Y	Y	N
7 McDermott	Y	Y	Y	N
8 *Dunn*	Y	Y	N	Y
9 Kreidler	Y	Y	Y	N
WEST VIRGINIA				
1 Mollohan	Y	Y	Y	N
2 Wise	Y	Y	Y	N
3 Rahall	Y	Y	Y	N
WISCONSIN				
1 Barca	Y	Y	Y	Y
2 *Klug*	N	Y	N	Y
3 *Gunderson*	N	Y	N	Y
4 Kleczka	Y	Y	Y	N
5 Barrett	N	Y	Y	N
6 *Petri*	N	Y	N	Y
7 Obey	Y	Y	Y	N
8 *Roth*	N	Y	N	Y
9 *Sensenbrenner*	N	Y	N	Y
WYOMING				
AL *Thomas*	Y	Y	N	Y
DELEGATES				
de Lugo, V.I.	D	D	D	N
Faleomavaega, Am.S.	D	D	D	N
Norton, D.C.	D	D	D	N
Romero-B., P.R.	D	D	D	N
Underwood, Guam	D	D	D	N

Southern states - Ala., Ark., Fla., Ga., Ky., La., Miss., N.C., Okla., S.C., Tenn., Texas, Va.
Omitted votes are quorum calls, which CQ does not include in its vote charts.

KEY

Y Voted for (yea).
\# Paired for.
+ Announced for.
N Voted against (nay).
X Paired against.
− Announced against.
P Voted "present."
C Voted "present" to avoid possible conflict of interest.
? Did not vote or otherwise make a position known.
D Delegates ineligible to vote.

Democrats **Republicans**
Independent

498. H J Res 416. U.S. Troops in Haiti/Prompt Withdrawal. Dellums, D-Calif., substitute amendment to express the sense of Congress that all U.S. troops should be promptly and orderly withdrawn from Haiti and that the president should have sought congressional approval before deploying troops. The substitute also requires the president to submit within seven days of enactment a statement on the national security objectives of Operation Uphold Democracy and various reports on the situation in Haiti. Adopted in the Committee of the Whole 258-167: R 34-136; D 224-30 (ND 151-22, SD 73-8); I 0-1, Oct. 6, 1994.

499. H J Res 416. U.S. Troops in Haiti/March Termination. Torricelli, D-N.J., substitute amendment to authorize the presence of U.S. troops in Haiti until March 1, 1995, unless the president determines and certifies that a continued presence is essential to protect U.S. citizens or is vital to U.S. national security interests. Rejected in the Committee of the Whole 27-398: R 0-170; D 26-228 (ND 21-152, SD 5-76); I 1-0, Oct. 7, in the session that began and the Congressional Record dated Oct. 6, 1994.

500. H J Res 416. U.S. Troops in Haiti/Passage. Passage of the joint resolution to express the sense of Congress that all U.S. troops should be promptly and orderly withdrawn from Haiti as soon as possible and that the president should have sought congressional approval before deploying troops. The substitute also requires the president to submit within seven days of enactment a statement of the national security objectives of Operation Uphold Democracy and various reports on the situation in Haiti. Passed 236-182: R 19-150; D 217-31 (ND 146-21, SD 71-10); I 0-1, Oct. 7, in the session that began and the Congressional Record dated Oct. 6, 1994.

501. S 21. California Desert Protection/Rule. Adoption of the rule (H Res 568) to waive points of order against and provide for House floor consideration of the conference report to designate about 7.5 million acres of California desert as wilderness and to establish the Death Valley, Joshua Tree and Mojave national parks. Adopted 242-140: R 16-137; D 225-3 (ND 156-2, SD 69-1); I 1-0, Oct. 7, in the session that began and the Congressional Record dated Oct. 6, 1994.

	498	499	500	501
ALABAMA				
1 *Callahan*	Y	N	Y	N
2 *Everett*	Y	N	Y	N
3 Browder	Y	N	Y	Y
4 Bevill	Y	N	Y	Y
5 Cramer	Y	N	Y	Y
6 *Bachus*	N	N	N	N
7 Hilliard	Y	N	Y	Y
ALASKA				
AL *Young*	N	N	N	N
ARIZONA				
1 Coppersmith	Y	N	Y	Y
2 Pastor	Y	N	Y	Y
3 *Stump*	N	N	N	N
4 *Kyl*	N	N	N	N
5 *Kolbe*	N	N	N	N
6 English	Y	N	Y	Y
ARKANSAS				
1 Lambert	N	Y	N	Y
2 Thornton	Y	N	Y	Y
3 *Hutchinson*	N	N	N	N
4 *Dickey*	Y	N	Y	N
CALIFORNIA				
1 Hamburg	Y	N	Y	Y
2 *Herger*	N	N	N	N
3 Fazio	Y	N	Y	Y
4 *Doolittle*	N	N	N	N
5 Matsui	Y	N	Y	Y
6 Woolsey	Y	N	Y	Y
7 Miller	Y	N	Y	Y
8 Pelosi	Y	N	+	Y
9 Dellums	Y	N	Y	Y
10 *Baker*	N	N	N	N
11 *Pombo*	N	N	N	N
12 Lantos	Y	N	Y	Y
13 Stark	Y	N	Y	Y
14 Eshoo	Y	N	Y	Y
15 Mineta	Y	N	Y	Y
16 Edwards	Y	N	Y	Y
17 Farr	Y	N	Y	Y
18 Condit	N	N	N	Y
19 Lehman	Y	N	Y	Y
20 Dooley	Y	N	Y	Y
21 *Thomas*	N	N	N	N
22 *Huffington*	?	?	?	N
23 *Gallegly*	N	N	N	N
24 Beilenson	Y	N	Y	Y
25 *McKeon*	N	N	N	N
26 Berman	Y	N	Y	Y
27 *Moorhead*	N	N	N	N
28 *Dreier*	N	N	N	N
29 Waxman	Y	N	Y	Y
30 Becerra	Y	N	Y	Y
31 Martinez	Y	N	Y	?
32 Dixon	Y	N	Y	Y
33 Roybal-Allard	Y	N	Y	Y
34 Torres	Y	N	Y	Y
35 Waters	Y	N	Y	Y
36 Harman	N	N	N	Y
37 Tucker	?	?	?	#
38 *Horn*	N	N	N	N
39 *Royce*	N	N	N	N
40 *Lewis*	Y	N	Y	N
41 *Kim*	N	N	N	N
42 Brown	Y	N	Y	Y
43 *Calvert*	N	N	N	N
44 *McCandless*	N	N	N	N
45 *Rohrabacher*	N	N	N	N
46 *Dornan*	−	N	N	N
47 *Cox*	N	N	N	N
48 *Packard*	N	N	N	N
49 Schenk	N	N	N	Y
50 Filner	N	N	Y	Y
51 *Cunningham*	N	N	N	N
52 *Hunter*	N	N	N	N
COLORADO				
1 Schroeder	Y	N	Y	Y
2 Skaggs	N	Y	N	Y
3 *McInnis*	N	N	N	N
4 *Allard*	N	N	N	N
5 *Hefley*	N	N	N	?
6 *Schaefer*	N	N	N	N
CONNECTICUT				
1 Kennelly	Y	N	Y	Y
2 Gejdenson	Y	N	Y	Y
3 DeLauro	Y	N	Y	Y
4 *Shays*	N	N	N	Y
5 *Franks*	N	N	N	Y
6 *Johnson*	Y	N	Y	Y
DELAWARE				
AL *Castle*	Y	N	Y	N
FLORIDA				
1 Hutto	Y	N	Y	?
2 Peterson	Y	N	Y	Y
3 Brown	Y	N	Y	Y
4 *Fowler*	N	N	N	?
5 Thurman	Y	N	Y	Y
6 *Stearns*	N	N	N	N
7 *Mica*	N	N	N	N
8 *McCollum*	Y	N	N	N
9 *Bilirakis*	Y	N	N	N
10 *Young*	N	N	N	N
11 Gibbons	Y	N	Y	Y
12 *Canady*	N	N	N	N
13 *Miller*	N	N	N	N
14 *Goss*	N	N	N	N
15 Bacchus	Y	N	Y	Y
16 *Lewis*	N	?	?	X
17 Meek	Y	N	Y	Y
18 *Ros-Lehtinen*	N	N	N	N
19 Johnston	Y	N	Y	Y
20 Deutsch	Y	Y	Y	Y
21 *Diaz-Balart*	N	N	N	N
22 *Shaw*	N	N	?	?
23 Hastings	Y	N	Y	Y
GEORGIA				
1 *Kingston*	N	N	N	N
2 Bishop	Y	N	Y	Y
3 *Collins*	N	N	N	N
4 *Linder*	N	N	N	N
5 Lewis	Y	N	Y	Y
6 *Gingrich*	N	N	N	N
7 Darden	Y	N	Y	Y
8 Rowland	Y	N	Y	?
9 Deal	Y	N	Y	Y
10 Johnson	Y	N	Y	Y
11 McKinney	Y	N	Y	Y
HAWAII				
1 Abercrombie	Y	N	Y	Y
2 Mink	Y	N	Y	Y
IDAHO				
1 LaRocco	Y	N	Y	Y
2 *Crapo*	N	N	N	N
ILLINOIS				
1 Rush	Y	N	Y	Y
2 Reynolds	Y	N	Y	Y
3 Lipinski	Y	N	Y	Y
4 Gutierrez	Y	N	Y	Y
5 Rostenkowski	Y	Y	Y	Y
6 *Hyde*	N	N	N	?
7 Collins	Y	N	Y	Y
8 *Crane*	N	N	N	N
9 Yates	Y	N	Y	?
10 *Porter*	Y	N	N	N
11 Sangmeister	Y	N	Y	Y
12 Costello	Y	N	Y	Y
13 *Fawell*	N	N	N	N
14 *Hastert*	N	N	N	N
15 *Ewing*	N	N	N	?
16 *Manzullo*	N	N	N	?
17 Evans	Y	N	Y	Y

ND Northern Democrats   SD Southern Democrats

1994 CQ ALMANAC — 149-H

	498	499	500	501
18 Michel	N	N	N	?
19 Poshard	Y	N	Y	Y
20 Durbin	Y	N	Y	Y
INDIANA				
1 Visclosky	Y	N	Y	Y
2 Sharp	Y	Y	Y	Y
3 Roemer	Y	N	Y	Y
4 Long	Y	N	Y	Y
5 *Buyer*	N	N	N	N
6 *Burton*	N	N	N	N
7 *Myers*	N	N	N	N
8 McCloskey	Y	N	Y	Y
9 Hamilton	N	Y	N	Y
10 Jacobs	Y	N	Y	Y
IOWA				
1 *Leach*	N	N	N	N
2 *Nussle*	N	N	N	N
3 *Lightfoot*	N	N	N	N
4 Smith	Y	N	Y	Y
5 *Grandy*	Y	N	N	?
KANSAS				
1 *Roberts*	N	N	N	?
2 Slattery	?	?	#	?
3 *Meyers*	N	N	N	Y
4 Glickman	Y	N	Y	Y
KENTUCKY				
1 Barlow	Y	N	Y	Y
2 *Lewis*	N	N	N	N
3 Mazzoli	N	N	N	Y
4 *Bunning*	N	N	N	?
5 *Rogers*	N	N	N	N
6 Baesler	N	N	N	Y
LOUISIANA				
1 *Livingston*	N	N	N	N
2 Jefferson	Y	N	Y	Y
3 Tauzin	Y	N	Y	Y
4 Fields	Y	N	Y	Y
5 *McCrery*	N	N	N	N
6 *Baker*	N	N	N	N
7 Hayes	Y	N	Y	?
MAINE				
1 Andrews	Y	N	Y	Y
2 *Snowe*	N	N	N	Y
MARYLAND				
1 *Gilchrest*	Y	N	Y	N
2 *Bentley*	N	N	N	N
3 Cardin	Y	N	Y	Y
4 Wynn	Y	N	Y	Y
5 Hoyer	Y	N	Y	Y
6 *Bartlett*	N	N	N	N
7 Mfume	Y	N	Y	Y
8 *Morella*	Y	N	N	Y
MASSACHUSETTS				
1 Olver	Y	N	Y	Y
2 Neal	Y	Y	Y	Y
3 *Blute*	Y	N	Y	N
4 Frank	Y	N	Y	Y
5 Meehan	Y	N	Y	Y
6 *Torkildsen*	Y	N	Y	N
7 Markey	Y	N	Y	Y
8 Kennedy	Y	N	Y	Y
9 Moakley	Y	N	Y	Y
10 Studds	Y	N	Y	Y
MICHIGAN				
1 Stupak	Y	Y	Y	Y
2 *Hoekstra*	N	N	N	N
3 *Ehlers*	Y	N	N	N
4 *Camp*	N	N	N	N
5 Barcia	Y	N	Y	Y
6 *Upton*	N	N	N	N
7 *Smith*	Y	N	N	N
8 Carr	Y	N	Y	?
9 Kildee	N	N	N	Y
10 Bonior	Y	N	Y	Y
11 *Knollenberg*	N	N	N	N
12 Levin	N	N	N	Y
13 Ford	Y	N	?	?
14 Conyers	Y	N	Y	Y
15 Collins	Y	N	Y	Y
16 Dingell	Y	N	Y	Y
MINNESOTA				
1 Penny	Y	Y	Y	N
2 Minge	Y	Y	Y	Y
3 *Ramstad*	N	N	N	Y
4 Vento	Y	N	Y	Y

	498	499	500	501
5 Sabo	Y	N	Y	Y
6 *Grams*	N	N	N	N
7 Peterson	N	N	N	N
8 Oberstar	Y	N	Y	Y
MISSISSIPPI				
1 Whitten	?	?	?	?
2 Thompson	Y	N	Y	Y
3 Montgomery	Y	N	Y	?
4 Parker	N	N	N	Y
5 Taylor	Y	N	N	Y
MISSOURI				
1 Clay	Y	N	Y	?
2 *Talent*	N	N	N	N
3 Gephardt	Y	N	Y	Y
4 Skelton	Y	N	Y	Y
5 Wheat	Y	N	Y	Y
6 Danner	Y	N	Y	Y
7 *Hancock*	N	N	N	N
8 *Emerson*	Y	N	Y	N
9 Volkmer	Y	N	Y	Y
MONTANA				
AL Williams	N	Y	Y	?
NEBRASKA				
1 *Bereuter*	N	N	N	Y
2 Hoagland	Y	N	Y	Y
3 *Barrett*	Y	N	Y	N
NEVADA				
1 Bilbray	Y	N	Y	Y
2 *Vucanovich*	Y	N	N	?
NEW HAMPSHIRE				
1 *Zeliff*	N	N	N	N
2 Swett	N	N	N	Y
NEW JERSEY				
1 Andrews	N	N	N	Y
2 Hughes	Y	N	Y	Y
3 *Saxton*	N	N	N	Y
4 *Smith*	N	N	N	Y
5 *Roukema*	N	N	N	N
6 Pallone	N	Y	N	Y
7 *Franks*	N	N	N	N
8 Klein	Y	N	Y	Y
9 Torricelli	N	Y	N	Y
10 Payne	Y	N	Y	Y
11 *Gallo*	?	?	?	?
12 *Zimmer*	N	N	N	Y
13 Menendez	N	Y	N	Y
NEW MEXICO				
1 *Schiff*	N	N	N	N
2 *Skeen*	Y	N	Y	N
3 Richardson	Y	Y	Y	Y
NEW YORK				
1 Hochbrueckner	Y	N	Y	Y
2 *Lazio*	N	N	N	N
3 *King*	N	N	N	N
4 *Levy*	N	N	N	N
5 Ackerman	Y	Y	Y	Y
6 Flake	Y	N	Y	Y
7 Manton	Y	N	Y	Y
8 Nadler	Y	N	Y	Y
9 Schumer	Y	N	Y	Y
10 Towns	Y	N	Y	Y
11 Owens	P	N	P	?
12 Velazquez	Y	N	Y	Y
13 *Molinari*	N	N	N	N
14 Maloney	Y	N	Y	Y
15 Rangel	Y	N	Y	Y
16 Serrano	Y	N	Y	Y
17 Engel	Y	N	Y	Y
18 Lowey	Y	N	Y	Y
19 *Fish*	?	?	?	?
20 *Gilman*	N	N	Y	Y
21 McNulty	N	N	N	Y
22 *Solomon*	N	N	N	N
23 *Boehlert*	Y	N	Y	N
24 *McHugh*	N	N	N	N
25 *Walsh*	Y	N	N	N
26 Hinchey	Y	N	Y	Y
27 *Paxon*	N	N	N	N
28 Slaughter	Y	N	Y	Y
29 LaFalce	Y	N	Y	?
30 *Quinn*	Y	N	Y	N
31 *Houghton*	N	N	N	?
NORTH CAROLINA				
1 Clayton	Y	N	Y	Y
2 Valentine	Y	N	Y	?

	498	499	500	501
3 Lancaster	N	Y	N	Y
4 Price	Y	N	Y	Y
5 Neal	Y	N	Y	Y
6 *Coble*	N	N	N	N
7 Rose	Y	N	Y	Y
8 Hefner	Y	N	Y	Y
9 *McMillan*	N	N	N	?
10 *Ballenger*	N	N	N	N
11 *Taylor*	N	N	N	N
12 Watt	Y	N	Y	Y
NORTH DAKOTA				
AL Pomeroy	Y	N	N	Y
OHIO				
1 Mann	Y	N	Y	Y
2 *Portman*	N	N	N	N
3 Hall	Y	N	Y	?
4 *Oxley*	N	N	N	?
5 *Gillmor*	N	N	N	N
6 Strickland	Y	N	Y	Y
7 *Hobson*	N	N	N	N
8 *Boehner*	N	N	N	N
9 Kaptur	Y	Y	Y	Y
10 *Hoke*	Y	N	N	N
11 Stokes	Y	N	Y	Y
12 *Kasich*	N	N	N	N
13 Brown	Y	N	Y	Y
14 Sawyer	Y	N	Y	Y
15 *Pryce*	N	N	N	N
16 *Regula*	N	N	N	N
17 Traficant	Y	N	Y	Y
18 Applegate	?	?	?	?
19 Fingerhut	Y	N	Y	Y
OKLAHOMA				
1 *Inhofe*	?	?	?	?
2 Synar	Y	Y	Y	?
3 Brewster	Y	N	Y	Y
4 McCurdy	N	N	N	?
5 *Istook*	N	N	N	?
6 *Lucas*	N	N	N	N
OREGON				
1 Furse	Y	N	Y	Y
2 *Smith*	?	?	X	?
3 Wyden	Y	N	Y	Y
4 DeFazio	Y	N	Y	Y
5 Kopetski	Y	Y	Y	Y
PENNSYLVANIA				
1 Foglietta	Y	N	Y	Y
2 Blackwell	Y	N	Y	?
3 Borski	Y	N	Y	Y
4 Klink	Y	N	Y	Y
5 *Clinger*	Y	N	Y	?
6 Holden	N	N	N	Y
7 Weldon	Y	N	N	Y
8 *Greenwood*	N	N	N	N
9 *Shuster*	N	N	N	N
10 *McDade*	Y	N	Y	?
11 Kanjorski	Y	N	Y	Y
12 Murtha	Y	N	Y	Y
13 Margolies-Mezv.	Y	N	Y	Y
14 Coyne	Y	N	Y	Y
15 McHale	Y	N	Y	Y
16 *Walker*	N	N	N	N
17 *Gekas*	N	N	N	N
18 *Santorum*	Y	N	N	N
19 *Goodling*	N	N	N	N
20 Murphy	Y	N	Y	?
21 *Ridge*	N	N	N	N
RHODE ISLAND				
1 *Machtley*	N	N	N	N
2 Reed	Y	N	Y	Y
SOUTH CAROLINA				
1 *Ravenel*	?	?	?	?
2 *Spence*	Y	N	Y	N
3 Derrick	Y	N	Y	Y
4 *Inglis*	Y	N	N	N
5 Spratt	Y	N	Y	Y
6 Clyburn	Y	N	Y	Y
SOUTH DAKOTA				
AL Johnson	N	N	N	Y
TENNESSEE				
1 *Quillen*	N	N	N	Y
2 *Duncan*	N	N	N	N
3 Lloyd	Y	N	Y	?
4 Cooper	Y	N	Y	Y
5 Clement	Y	Y	Y	Y

	498	499	500	501
6 Gordon	Y	N	Y	Y
7 *Sundquist*	?	?	?	?
8 Tanner	Y	N	Y	Y
9 Ford	Y	N	Y	Y
TEXAS				
1 Chapman	Y	N	N	Y
2 Wilson	Y	N	Y	Y
3 *Johnson, Sam*	N	N	N	N
4 Hall	N	N	N	N
5 Bryant	Y	N	Y	Y
6 *Barton*	N	N	N	N
7 *Archer*	N	N	N	N
8 *Fields*	N	N	N	N
9 Brooks	Y	N	Y	Y
10 Pickle	Y	N	Y	Y
11 Edwards	Y	N	Y	Y
12 Geren	Y	N	Y	Y
13 Sarpalius	Y	N	Y	Y
14 Laughlin	Y	N	Y	Y
15 de la Garza	Y	N	Y	Y
16 Coleman	Y	N	Y	Y
17 Stenholm	Y	N	Y	Y
18 Washington	?	?	?	?
19 *Combest*	N	N	N	N
20 Gonzalez	Y	N	Y	Y
21 *Smith*	N	N	N	N
22 *DeLay*	N	N	N	N
23 *Bonilla*	N	N	N	N
24 Frost	Y	N	Y	Y
25 Andrews	Y	N	Y	Y
26 *Armey*	N	N	N	N
27 Ortiz	Y	N	Y	Y
28 Tejeda	Y	N	Y	Y
29 Green	Y	N	Y	Y
30 Johnson, E.B.	Y	N	Y	Y
UTAH				
1 *Hansen*	N	N	N	N
2 Shepherd	Y	N	Y	Y
3 Orton	N	N	Y	N
VERMONT				
AL *Sanders*	N	Y	N	Y
VIRGINIA				
1 *Bateman*	Y	N	N	N
2 Pickett	Y	N	Y	N
3 Scott	Y	N	Y	?
4 Sisisky	Y	N	Y	?
5 Payne	Y	N	Y	Y
6 *Goodlatte*	N	N	N	N
7 *Bliley*	N	N	N	N
8 Moran	Y	N	Y	Y
9 Boucher	Y	N	Y	?
10 *Wolf*	Y	N	Y	N
11 Byrne	Y	N	Y	Y
WASHINGTON				
1 Cantwell	N	Y	N	Y
2 Swift	Y	N	Y	Y
3 Unsoeld	Y	N	Y	Y
4 Inslee	Y	N	Y	Y
5 Foley			Y	
6 Dicks	Y	N	Y	Y
7 McDermott	Y	Y	Y	Y
8 *Dunn*	N	N	N	N
9 Kreidler	Y	N	Y	Y
WEST VIRGINIA				
1 Mollohan	Y	N	Y	Y
2 Wise	Y	N	Y	Y
3 Rahall	Y	N	Y	Y
WISCONSIN				
1 Barca	Y	N	Y	Y
2 *Klug*	N	N	N	N
3 *Gunderson*	Y	N	N	N
4 Kleczka	N	Y	N	Y
5 Barrett	Y	N	Y	Y
6 *Petri*	N	N	N	N
7 Obey	Y	N	Y	Y
8 *Roth*	N	N	N	N
9 *Sensenbrenner*	N	N	N	N
WYOMING				
AL *Thomas*	N	N	N	N
DELEGATES				
de Lugo, V.I.	Y	N	D	D
Faleomavaega, Am.S.	N	Y	D	D
Norton, D.C.	Y	N	D	D
Romero-B., P.R.	Y	?	D	D
Underwood, Guam	Y	N	D	D

Southern states - Ala., Ark., Fla., Ga., Ky., La., Miss., N.C., Okla., S.C., Tenn., Texas, Va.
Omitted votes are quorum calls, which CQ does not include in its vote charts.

KEY

Y   Voted for (yea).
Paired for.
+   Announced for.
N   Voted against (nay).
X   Paired against.
—   Announced against.
P   Voted "present."
C   Voted "present" to avoid possible conflict of interest.
?   Did not vote or otherwise make a position known.
D   Delegates ineligible to vote.

Democrats   *Republicans*
Independent

502. S 455. Payment in Lieu of Taxes/Temporary Increase. Miller, D-Calif., substitute amendment to provide a temporary two-year increase in payments made by the federal government to local governments in lieu of taxes instead of the permanent increase provided by the bill. Rejected in the Committee of the Whole 160-262: R 55-113; D 105-148 (ND 87-87, SD 18-61); I 0-1, Oct. 7, 1994.

503. S 455. Payment in Lieu of Taxes/Indexing. Vento, D-Minn., amendment to strike the provisions in the bill that index for inflation payments in lieu of taxes to local governments after 1999. Rejected in the Committee of the Whole 195-223: R 74-92; D 121-130 (ND 97-75, SD 24-55); I 0-1, Oct. 7, 1994.

504. S 1569. Minority Health Improvement/Conference Report. Adoption of the conference report to create a number of new public health programs to improve access for minority and low-income individuals to heath care services and increase the participation of minorities in health care professions. Adopted 394-5: R 156-5; D 237-0 (ND 164-0, SD 73-0); I 1-0, Oct. 7, 1994.

505. H Res 578. House Labor Law Compliance/Rule. Adoption of the rule (H Res 579) to provide for the adoption of the resolution to change House rules to apply several major labor and civil rights laws to the House of Representatives. Under the resolution, employees of the House could take complaints to a newly established Office of Compliance but could not seek redress in court, which could only be possible through a statutory change. Adopted 348-3: R 138-3; D 209-0 (ND 146-0, SD 63-0); I 1-0, Oct. 7, 1994.

506. Procedural Motion. Approval of the House Journal of Friday, Oct. 7. Approved 223-152: R 24-142; D 198-10 (ND 136-8, SD 62-2); I 1-0, Nov. 29, 1994.

507. HR 5110. General Agreement on Tariffs and Trade/Passage. Passage of the bill to make statutory changes to implement the new world trade agreement negotiated under the Uruguay Round of the General Agreement on Tariffs and Trade (GATT). The agreement would reduce tariffs and trade barriers, ensure stricter enforcement of world trade rules through the newly established World Trade Organization (WTO), and expand GATT rules to cover such economic sectors as agriculture, services and intellectual property. The bill also would accelerate tax payment schedules, change eligibility standards for certain federal programs, and make other changes to offset lost revenues from tariff reductions in order to comply with pay-as-you-go budget rules. Passed 288-146: R 121-56; D 167-89 (ND 107-66, SD 60-23); I 0-1, Nov. 29, 1994. A "yea" was a vote in support of the president's position.

[1] Dean A. Gallo, R-N.J., died Nov. 6, 1994. Vote 505 was the last vote for which he was eligible.

[2] James M. Inhofe, R-Okla., resigned Nov. 15, 1994, to replace Sen. David L. Boren, D-Okla. Inhofe was eligible for 495 votes in 1994. Steve Largent, R-Okla., was sworn in Nov. 29, 1994, to replace Inhofe. Largent was eligible for one vote in 1994, vote 507.

	502	503	504	505	506	507
ALABAMA						
1 Callahan	N	N	Y	?	N	Y
2 Everett	N	N	Y	Y	Y	N
3 Browder	N	N	Y	Y	Y	N
4 Bevill	N	N	Y	Y	Y	Y
5 Cramer	N	N	Y	Y	Y	N
6 Bachus	N	N	Y	N	N	N
7 Hilliard	N	N	Y	Y	Y	N
ALASKA						
AL Young	N	N	Y	Y	N	N
ARIZONA						
1 Coppersmith	N	N	Y	Y	Y	Y
2 Pastor	N	N	Y	Y	Y	Y
3 Stump	N	N	N	Y	N	N
4 Kyl	N	N	Y	?	N	Y
5 Kolbe	N	N	Y	Y	N	Y
6 English	N	N	Y	Y	?	Y
ARKANSAS						
1 Lambert	Y	Y	Y	Y	Y	Y
2 Thornton	N	N	Y	Y	Y	Y
3 Hutchinson	N	N	Y	?	N	N
4 Dickey	N	N	Y	Y	N	N
CALIFORNIA						
1 Hamburg	N	N	Y	Y	Y	N
2 Herger	N	N	Y	Y	N	Y
3 Fazio	N	N	Y	Y	Y	Y
4 Doolittle	N	N	Y	N	N	N
5 Matsui	N	N	Y	Y	Y	Y
6 Woolsey	Y	Y	Y	Y	Y	N
7 Miller	Y	Y	Y	Y	Y	Y
8 Pelosi	Y	Y	Y	Y	Y	Y
9 Dellums	Y	Y	Y	Y	Y	N
10 Baker	N	N	Y	Y	N	Y
11 Pombo	N	N	Y	N	N	N
12 Lantos	N	N	Y	Y	?	N
13 Stark	Y	Y	Y	Y	?	N
14 Eshoo	N	N	Y	Y	Y	Y
15 Mineta	Y	Y	Y	Y	Y	Y
16 Edwards	Y	Y	Y	?	Y	Y
17 Farr	N	N	Y	Y	Y	Y
18 Condit	Y	Y	Y	N	N	N
19 Lehman	N	N	?	+	Y	Y
20 Dooley	N	N	Y	Y	Y	Y
21 Thomas	N	N	Y	N	N	Y
22 Huffington	N	N	Y	N	Y	N
23 Gallegly	N	N	Y	N	N	N
24 Beilenson	Y	Y	Y	Y	Y	Y
25 McKeon	N	N	Y	Y	N	Y
26 Berman	Y	Y	Y	Y	Y	Y
27 Moorhead	N	Y	N	Y	N	N
28 Dreier	Y	N	Y	N	N	Y
29 Waxman	Y	Y	Y	?	?	N
30 Becerra	Y	N	Y	Y	Y	Y
31 Martinez	N	N	Y	Y	Y	Y
32 Dixon	N	N	Y	Y	Y	Y
33 Roybal-Allard	N	N	Y	Y	Y	Y
34 Torres	N	Y	Y	Y	Y	Y
35 Waters	N	Y	Y	Y	Y	Y
36 Harman	N	N	Y	Y	Y	Y
37 Tucker	#	#	?	?	?	N
38 Horn	N	N	Y	Y	Y	N
39 Royce	Y	Y	Y	N	N	N
40 Lewis	N	N	Y	Y	Y	Y
41 Kim	N	N	Y	Y	N	Y
42 Brown	N	N	Y	?	?	Y
43 Calvert	N	N	Y	Y	N	Y
44 McCandless	N	?	Y	Y	N	Y
45 Rohrabacher	Y	Y	Y	N	N	N
46 Dornan	N	N	Y	Y	?	N
47 Cox	Y	Y	Y	Y	Y	Y
48 Packard	N	N	Y	?	Y	Y
49 Schenk	N	N	Y	Y	Y	Y
50 Filner	Y	Y	Y	Y	Y	Y
51 Cunningham	N	N	Y	?	N	Y
52 Hunter	N	N	Y	Y	N	N
COLORADO						
1 Schroeder	N	Y	Y	Y	?	Y
2 Skaggs	N	Y	Y	Y	Y	Y
3 McInnis	N	N	Y	Y	N	N
4 Allard	N	N	Y	N	N	Y
5 Hefley	N	N	Y	Y	N	N
6 Schaefer	N	N	Y	N	N	N
CONNECTICUT						
1 Kennelly	N	N	Y	Y	Y	Y
2 Gejdenson	Y	Y	Y	Y	Y	Y
3 DeLauro	N	N	Y	Y	Y	Y
4 Shays	Y	Y	Y	Y	Y	N
5 Franks	Y	Y	Y	Y	N	Y
6 Johnson	N	N	Y	Y	?	Y
DELAWARE						
AL Castle	Y	Y	Y	Y	N	Y
FLORIDA						
1 Hutto	N	Y	Y	?	Y	Y
2 Peterson	N	N	Y	Y	Y	Y
3 Brown	N	N	Y	Y	Y	Y
4 Fowler	N	Y	Y	Y	N	Y
5 Thurman	N	N	Y	Y	Y	N
6 Stearns	N	Y	Y	Y	N	N
7 Mica	N	N	Y	Y	N	N
8 McCollum	N	Y	Y	?	?	Y
9 Bilirakis	?	?	?	?	?	N
10 Young	N	Y	Y	Y	N	Y
11 Gibbons	N	N	Y	?	Y	Y
12 Canady	N	N	Y	Y	N	Y
13 Miller	Y	Y	Y	Y	N	Y
14 Goss	N	N	Y	N	N	Y
15 Bacchus	N	N	Y	?	?	Y
16 Lewis	?	?	?	?	N	Y
17 Meek	N	N	Y	Y	Y	Y
18 Ros-Lehtinen	Y	Y	Y	N	N	Y
19 Johnston	Y	Y	Y	?	Y	Y
20 Deutsch	Y	Y	Y	Y	Y	Y
21 Diaz-Balart	Y	Y	Y	N	N	Y
22 Shaw	N	N	Y	Y	Y	Y
23 Hastings	N	N	Y	N	N	Y
GEORGIA						
1 Kingston	N	N	Y	N	N	N
2 Bishop	N	N	Y	Y	Y	Y
3 Collins	Y	Y	Y	Y	Y	N
4 Linder	N	N	Y	N	N	Y
5 Lewis	Y	Y	Y	Y	Y	Y
6 Gingrich	N	N	Y	N	Y	N
7 Darden	N	N	Y	Y	Y	Y
8 Rowland	N	N	Y	Y	Y	N
9 Deal	N	N	Y	Y	Y	N
10 Johnson	N	Y	Y	Y	?	Y
11 McKinney	N	Y	Y	Y	N	N
HAWAII						
1 Abercrombie	Y	Y	Y	Y	Y	Y
2 Mink	Y	Y	Y	Y	Y	N
IDAHO						
1 LaRocco	N	N	Y	Y	Y	Y
2 Crapo	N	N	Y	Y	N	N
ILLINOIS						
1 Rush	Y	Y	Y	Y	Y	N
2 Reynolds	Y	Y	Y	Y	Y	Y
3 Lipinski	Y	Y	Y	?	Y	N
4 Gutierrez	Y	Y	Y	?	Y	N
5 Rostenkowski	N	Y	Y	Y	Y	N
6 Hyde	N	N	Y	Y	Y	Y
7 Collins	Y	Y	Y	Y	Y	Y
8 Crane	Y	Y	Y	N	N	Y
9 Yates	Y	Y	Y	Y	Y	Y
10 Porter	Y	Y	—	+	N	Y
11 Sangmeister	N	N	Y	Y	Y	Y
12 Costello	N	N	Y	Y	Y	Y
13 Fawell	Y	Y	Y	Y	Y	Y
14 Hastert	Y	Y	Y	N	N	Y
15 Ewing	Y	Y	Y	Y	N	Y
16 Manzullo	Y	Y	Y	Y	Y	Y
17 Evans	N	N	Y	Y	Y	N

ND Northern Democrats   SD Southern Democrats

	502	503	504	505	506	507
18 ***Michel***	Y	Y	Y	Y	N	Y
19 Poshard	N	N	Y	Y	Y	Y
20 Durbin	Y	Y	Y	Y	Y	Y
INDIANA						
1 Visclosky	Y	Y	Y	Y	Y	Y
2 Sharp	Y	Y	Y	Y	Y	Y
3 Roemer	Y	Y	Y	Y	?	Y
4 Long	N	N	Y	Y	?	Y
5 ***Buyer***	N	Y	Y	Y	N	Y
6 ***Burton***	N	N	N	Y	N	N
7 ***Myers***	N	N	Y	Y	Y	N
8 McCloskey	N	Y	Y	Y	?	Y
9 Hamilton	Y	Y	Y	Y	Y	Y
10 Jacobs	Y	Y	Y	Y	N	Y
IOWA						
1 ***Leach***	Y	Y	Y	Y	N	Y
2 ***Nussle***	N	N	Y	Y	N	Y
3 ***Lightfoot***	N	N	Y	Y	N	Y
4 Smith	N	N	Y	Y	N	Y
5 ***Grandy***	N	N	?	?	N	Y
KANSAS						
1 ***Roberts***	N	N	Y	Y	N	Y
2 Slattery	?	?	?	?	Y	Y
3 ***Meyers***	Y	Y	Y	Y	Y	Y
4 Glickman	Y	N	Y	Y	?	N
KENTUCKY						
1 Barlow	N	N	Y	Y	Y	N
2 ***Lewis***	N	N	Y	Y	N	N
3 Mazzoli	N	N	Y	Y	Y	Y
4 ***Bunning***	N	N	Y	?	N	Y
5 ***Rogers***	N	N	Y	Y	N	N
6 Baesler	N	Y	Y	Y	Y	Y
LOUISIANA						
1 ***Livingston***	N	N	Y	Y	Y	N
2 Jefferson	Y	Y	Y	Y	Y	Y
3 Tauzin	N	N	Y	Y	Y	Y
4 Fields	Y	Y	Y	Y	Y	N
5 ***McCrery***	Y	Y	Y	?	N	Y
6 ***Baker***	N	N	Y	?	N	Y
7 Hayes	N	N	Y	Y	Y	N
MAINE						
1 Andrews	N	N	Y	Y	Y	N
2 ***Snowe***	N	N	Y	Y	N	N
MARYLAND						
1 ***Gilchrest***	Y	Y	Y	Y	N	Y
2 ***Bentley***	N	N	?	Y	N	N
3 Cardin	Y	Y	Y	Y	Y	Y
4 Wynn	N	Y	Y	Y	Y	Y
5 Hoyer	N	N	Y	Y	Y	Y
6 ***Bartlett***	N	N	Y	Y	N	Y
7 Mfume	Y	Y	Y	Y	Y	N
8 ***Morella***	Y	Y	Y	Y	N	Y
MASSACHUSETTS						
1 Olver	Y	Y	Y	Y	Y	Y
2 Neal	Y	Y	Y	?	Y	Y
3 ***Blute***	N	Y	Y	Y	N	N
4 Frank	Y	Y	Y	Y	Y	N
5 Meehan	Y	Y	Y	?	Y	Y
6 ***Torkildsen***	N	N	Y	Y	N	Y
7 Markey	Y	Y	Y	Y	Y	Y
8 Kennedy	N	Y	Y	Y	Y	Y
9 Moakley	N	N	Y	Y	Y	N
10 Studds	Y	?	?	?	Y	Y
MICHIGAN						
1 Stupak	N	N	Y	Y	Y	N
2 ***Hoekstra***	N	Y	Y	Y	N	Y
3 ***Ehlers***	Y	Y	Y	Y	N	Y
4 ***Camp***	N	N	Y	Y	N	Y
5 Barcia	N	Y	Y	Y	Y	N
6 ***Upton***	Y	Y	Y	Y	N	Y
7 ***Smith***	N	N	Y	Y	N	Y
8 Carr	Y	Y	Y	Y	Y	Y
9 Kildee	Y	Y	Y	Y	Y	N
10 Bonior	Y	N	Y	Y	Y	N
11 ***Knollenberg***	N	N	Y	Y	N	Y
12 Levin	Y	Y	Y	Y	Y	Y
13 Ford	N	N	Y	Y	?	N
14 Conyers	Y	N	Y	Y	Y	N
15 Collins	Y	Y	Y	?	?	N
16 Dingell	N	Y	Y	Y	Y	Y
MINNESOTA						
1 Penny	Y	Y	Y	?	Y	Y
2 Minge	Y	Y	Y	Y	Y	Y
3 ***Ramstad***	N	Y	Y	Y	N	Y
4 Vento	Y	Y	Y	Y	Y	Y
5 Sabo	Y	Y	Y	Y	Y	N
6 ***Grams***	Y	Y	Y	Y	?	Y
7 Peterson	N	N	Y	Y	Y	N
8 Oberstar	N	N	Y	Y	N	N
MISSISSIPPI						
1 Whitten	?	?	?	?	Y	Y
2 Thompson	N	N	Y	Y	Y	N
3 Montgomery	N	N	Y	Y	Y	N
4 Parker	N	N	Y	?	Y	Y
5 Taylor	N	N	Y	Y	?	N
MISSOURI						
1 Clay	N	N	Y	?	Y	N
2 ***Talent***	N	N	Y	Y	N	Y
3 Gephardt	Y	Y	Y	Y	Y	Y
4 Skelton	N	N	Y	?	Y	Y
5 Wheat	N	N	Y	Y	Y	Y
6 Danner	N	Y	Y	Y	N	N
7 ***Hancock***	Y	N	N	Y	N	N
8 ***Emerson***	N	N	Y	Y	N	Y
9 Volkmer	Y	Y	Y	Y	Y	N
MONTANA						
AL Williams	N	N	Y	Y	Y	N
NEBRASKA						
1 ***Bereuter***	N	Y	Y	Y	N	Y
2 Hoagland	N	N	Y	Y	?	Y
3 ***Barrett***	N	N	Y	Y	N	Y
NEVADA						
1 Bilbray	N	N	Y	Y	Y	N
2 ***Vucanovich***	N	N	Y	Y	N	Y
NEW HAMPSHIRE						
1 ***Zeliff***	N	Y	Y	Y	N	Y
2 Swett	N	Y	Y	Y	?	N
NEW JERSEY						
1 Andrews	N	N	Y	Y	Y	N
2 Hughes	N	Y	Y	Y	?	Y
3 ***Saxton***	Y	Y	Y	Y	N	Y
4 ***Smith***	Y	Y	Y	Y	Y	N
5 ***Roukema***	Y	Y	?	?	N	Y
6 Pallone	Y	Y	Y	Y	Y	N
7 ***Franks***	Y	Y	Y	Y	N	Y
8 Klein	Y	Y	Y	Y	?	Y
9 Torricelli	Y	Y	?	?	Y	Y
10 Payne	N	N	Y	?	Y	N
11 Vacancy [1]						
12 ***Zimmer***	Y	Y	Y	Y	N	Y
13 Menendez	N	N	Y	Y	Y	Y
NEW MEXICO						
1 ***Schiff***	N	N	Y	Y	N	N
2 ***Skeen***	N	N	Y	Y	N	N
3 Richardson	N	N	Y	Y	Y	Y
NEW YORK						
1 Hochbrueckner	N	N	Y	Y	?	N
2 ***Lazio***	N	N	Y	Y	N	Y
3 ***King***	N	Y	Y	Y	N	Y
4 ***Levy***	?	?	?	?	N	Y
5 Ackerman	N	N	Y	?	Y	Y
6 Flake	N	N	Y	?	Y	Y
7 Manton	N	N	Y	Y	Y	Y
8 Nadler	Y	Y	Y	Y	Y	N
9 Schumer	Y	Y	Y	Y	Y	Y
10 Towns	N	Y	Y	Y	Y	N
11 Owens	Y	Y	Y	Y	Y	N
12 Velazquez	Y	Y	Y	Y	Y	N
13 ***Molinari***	N	N	Y	+	N	Y
14 Maloney	Y	Y	Y	Y	Y	Y
15 Rangel	Y	N	Y	?	Y	N
16 Serrano	N	Y	Y	Y	Y	Y
17 Engel	Y	Y	Y	Y	Y	N
18 Lowey	Y	Y	Y	Y	Y	Y
19 ***Fish***	N	N	Y	?	Y	Y
20 ***Gilman***	N	N	Y	Y	Y	Y
21 McNulty	N	Y	Y	Y	Y	Y
22 ***Solomon***	N	Y	Y	Y	N	N
23 ***Boehlert***	N	Y	Y	?	N	Y
24 ***McHugh***	Y	Y	Y	Y	N	N
25 ***Walsh***	Y	Y	Y	?	N	Y
26 Hinchey	Y	Y	Y	Y	Y	N
27 ***Paxon***	N	N	Y	Y	N	Y
28 Slaughter	Y	Y	+	Y	Y	Y
29 LaFalce	Y	N	Y	?	Y	Y
30 ***Quinn***	Y	Y	Y	Y	?	N
31 ***Houghton***	N	?	?	?	Y	Y
NORTH CAROLINA						
1 Clayton	N	N	Y	Y	Y	Y
2 Valentine	N	N	Y	Y	?	Y
3 Lancaster	N	N	Y	Y	?	Y
4 Price	N	Y	Y	Y	?	Y
5 Neal	Y	Y	Y	Y	?	Y
6 ***Coble***	N	Y	Y	Y	N	N
7 Rose	N	N	Y	?	Y	N
8 Hefner	N	N	Y	Y	?	N
9 ***McMillan***	N	Y	?	?	?	Y
10 ***Ballenger***	N	Y	Y	Y	N	Y
11 ***Taylor***	N	N	Y	?	N	N
12 Watt	Y	Y	Y	Y	Y	N
NORTH DAKOTA						
AL Pomeroy	N	N	Y	Y	Y	Y
OHIO						
1 Mann	Y	Y	Y	Y	?	Y
2 ***Portman***	Y	Y	Y	Y	N	Y
3 Hall	Y	Y	Y	Y	?	Y
4 ***Oxley***	N	Y	Y	Y	N	Y
5 ***Gillmor***	Y	Y	Y	Y	Y	Y
6 Strickland	N	N	Y	Y	?	N
7 ***Hobson***	Y	Y	Y	Y	N	Y
8 ***Boehner***	N	N	Y	Y	N	Y
9 Kaptur	Y	Y	Y	Y	?	N
10 ***Hoke***	Y	Y	Y	Y	N	Y
11 Stokes	N	N	Y	Y	Y	N
12 ***Kasich***	Y	Y	Y	Y	Y	Y
13 Brown	Y	N	Y	Y	N	N
14 Sawyer	Y	Y	Y	Y	Y	Y
15 ***Pryce***	Y	Y	Y	?	N	Y
16 ***Regula***	Y	Y	Y	Y	N	Y
17 Traficant	Y	Y	Y	Y	Y	N
18 Applegate	?	?	?	?	Y	N
19 Fingerhut	Y	Y	Y	Y	?	Y
OKLAHOMA						
1 ***Largent*** [2]						N
2 Synar	Y	Y	Y	Y	Y	Y
3 Brewster	N	N	?	Y	Y	Y
4 McCurdy	?	?	?	?	Y	Y
5 ***Istook***	?	?	?	?	N	N
6 ***Lucas***	N	N	Y	Y	N	N
OREGON						
1 Furse	N	N	Y	Y	Y	Y
2 ***Smith***	N	N	Y	?	?	Y
3 Wyden	N	N	Y	Y	Y	Y
4 DeFazio	N	N	Y	?	N	N
5 Kopetski	Y	Y	Y	Y	Y	Y
PENNSYLVANIA						
1 Foglietta	N	Y	?	?	Y	Y
2 Blackwell	N	N	Y	?	Y	Y
3 Borski	N	Y	Y	Y	Y	Y
4 Klink	Y	Y	Y	Y	Y	N
5 ***Clinger***	N	N	Y	Y	Y	Y
6 Holden	Y	Y	Y	Y	Y	N
7 ***Weldon***	Y	Y	Y	Y	N	Y
8 ***Greenwood***	Y	Y	Y	Y	Y	Y
9 ***Shuster***	Y	Y	Y	Y	N	Y
10 ***McDade***	N	N	Y	?	N	Y
11 Kanjorski	Y	Y	Y	Y	Y	N
12 Murtha	N	Y	Y	?	Y	Y
13 Margolies	Y	Y	Y	Y	?	Y
14 Coyne	N	Y	Y	Y	Y	Y
15 McHale	Y	Y	Y	Y	Y	Y
16 ***Walker***	N	Y	Y	Y	N	Y
17 ***Gekas***	N	Y	Y	Y	N	Y
18 ***Santorum***	Y	Y	Y	Y	Y	Y
19 ***Goodling***	N	Y	Y	+	N	Y
20 Murphy	Y	Y	Y	?	N	N
21 ***Ridge***	N	N	Y	Y	?	Y
RHODE ISLAND						
1 ***Machtley***	N	N	Y	Y	N	Y
2 Reed	Y	Y	Y	Y	Y	Y
SOUTH CAROLINA						
1 ***Ravenel***	?	?	?	?	N	N
2 ***Spence***	N	Y	Y	Y	N	N
3 Derrick	N	N	Y	Y	?	Y
4 ***Inglis***	Y	Y	Y	Y	?	N
5 Spratt	N	Y	?	?	Y	N
6 Clyburn	N	N	Y	Y	Y	Y
SOUTH DAKOTA						
AL Johnson	N	N	Y	Y	Y	Y
TENNESSEE						
1 ***Quillen***	N	N	Y	?	Y	Y
2 ***Duncan***	Y	Y	N	Y	N	N
3 Lloyd	N	N	Y	?	?	Y
4 Cooper	N	N	Y	Y	?	Y
5 Clement	N	N	Y	Y	Y	Y
6 Gordon	Y	Y	Y	Y	Y	Y
7 ***Sundquist***	?	?	?	?	N	Y
8 Tanner	N	N	Y	Y	Y	Y
9 Ford	N	?	?	?	?	Y
TEXAS						
1 Chapman	?	N	Y	?	Y	N
2 Wilson	N	N	Y	Y	Y	Y
3 ***Johnson, Sam***	Y	Y	N	Y	N	N
4 Hall	N	N	Y	?	Y	N
5 Bryant	Y	Y	Y	Y	?	Y
6 ***Barton***	?	X	?	?	N	Y
7 ***Archer***	N	N	Y	?	N	Y
8 ***Fields***	N	N	Y	Y	N	Y
9 Brooks	N	N	Y	Y	?	Y
10 Pickle	Y	Y	?	Y	?	Y
11 Edwards	N	N	Y	Y	Y	Y
12 Geren	N	Y	Y	Y	Y	Y
13 Sarpalius	Y	N	Y	Y	?	Y
14 Laughlin	N	N	?	?	Y	Y
15 de la Garza	N	N	Y	Y	Y	Y
16 Coleman	N	N	Y	Y	Y	Y
17 Stenholm	N	N	?	?	Y	Y
18 Washington	?	?	?	?	?	Y
19 ***Combest***	Y	Y	Y	Y	Y	N
20 Gonzalez	N	Y	Y	Y	Y	N
21 ***Smith***	N	Y	Y	Y	N	Y
22 ***DeLay***	X	?	?	?	N	Y
23 ***Bonilla***	N	N	Y	Y	N	Y
24 Frost	Y	N	Y	Y	Y	Y
25 Andrews	Y	Y	Y	Y	?	Y
26 ***Armey***	Y	Y	Y	?	N	Y
27 Ortiz	N	N	Y	Y	Y	Y
28 Tejeda	N	N	Y	Y	Y	Y
29 Green	Y	Y	Y	?	Y	Y
30 Johnson, E.B.	N	N	Y	Y	Y	Y
UTAH						
1 ***Hansen***	N	N	Y	Y	N	Y
2 Shepherd	N	N	Y	Y	?	Y
3 Orton	N	N	Y	Y	Y	Y
VERMONT						
AL *Sanders*	N	N	Y	Y	Y	N
VIRGINIA						
1 ***Bateman***	N	N	?	?	Y	Y
2 Pickett	N	N	Y	?	Y	Y
3 Scott	N	N	Y	Y	Y	Y
4 Sisisky	N	Y	Y	?	Y	N
5 Payne	N	Y	?	?	Y	N
6 ***Goodlatte***	N	N	Y	Y	N	Y
7 ***Bliley***	N	N	Y	Y	N	Y
8 Moran	Y	N	Y	Y	Y	Y
9 Boucher	Y	N	Y	Y	Y	Y
10 ***Wolf***	N	N	Y	Y	N	N
11 Byrne	N	N	Y	Y	?	Y
WASHINGTON						
1 Cantwell	N	N	Y	Y	Y	Y
2 Swift	N	N	Y	Y	Y	Y
3 Unsoeld	N	N	Y	Y	Y	N
4 Inslee	N	N	Y	Y	Y	Y
5 Foley	N	N		Y		Y
6 Dicks	N	N	Y	Y	Y	Y
7 McDermott	N	N	Y	Y	Y	Y
8 ***Dunn***	N	N	Y	Y	N	Y
9 Kreidler	Y	Y	Y	Y	?	Y
WEST VIRGINIA						
1 Mollohan	Y	Y	Y	Y	Y	N
2 Wise	N	N	Y	Y	Y	N
3 Rahall	Y	Y	Y	Y	Y	N
WISCONSIN						
1 Barca	Y	Y	Y	Y	?	N
2 ***Klug***	Y	Y	Y	Y	N	N
3 ***Gunderson***	N	N	Y	Y	N	N
4 Kleczka	Y	Y	Y	Y	Y	Y
5 Barrett	Y	Y	Y	Y	Y	Y
6 ***Petri***	Y	Y	Y	Y	Y	Y
7 Obey	N	N	Y	Y	Y	N
8 ***Roth***	N	N	Y	Y	N	N
9 ***Sensenbrenner***	Y	Y	Y	Y	N	N
WYOMING						
AL ***Thomas***	N	N	Y	Y	N	Y
DELEGATES						
AL de Lugo	Y	Y	I	I	I	I
AL Faleomavaega	Y	?	I	I	I	I
AL Norton	N	N	I	I	I	I
AL Romero-B.	?	?	I	I	I	I
AL Underwood	Y	N	I	I	I	I

Southern states - Ala., Ark., Fla., Ga., Ky., La., Miss., N.C., Okla., S.C., Tenn., Texas, Va.
Omitted votes are quorum calls, which CQ does not include in its vote charts.

CQ

SENATE ROLL CALL VOTES

KEY

	1	2	3	4	5	6	7
ALABAMA							
Heflin	Y	Y	N	Y	N	Y	Y
Shelby	Y	Y	N	Y	N	Y	N
ALASKA							
Murkowski	Y	Y	N	Y	Y	N	Y
Stevens	Y	Y	N	Y	Y	Y	Y
ARIZONA							
DeConcini	Y	Y	Y	Y	Y	N	N
McCain	Y	Y	N	Y	Y	N	Y
ARKANSAS							
Bumpers	Y	Y	Y	Y	Y	N	N
Pryor	Y	Y	Y	Y	Y	N	N
CALIFORNIA							
Boxer	Y	Y	Y	Y	Y	N	N
Feinstein	Y	Y	Y	Y	Y	N	N
COLORADO							
Campbell	Y	Y	Y	Y	N	Y	N
Brown	Y	Y	N	Y	N	Y	N
CONNECTICUT							
Dodd	Y	Y	Y	N	Y	N	N
Lieberman	Y	Y	Y	Y	Y	N	Y
DELAWARE							
Biden	Y	Y	Y	N	Y	N	Y
Roth	Y	Y	N	Y	N	Y	N
FLORIDA							
Graham	Y	Y	Y	Y	Y	N	Y
Mack	Y	Y	N	Y	N	Y	Y
GEORGIA							
Nunn	Y	Y	Y	?	Y	N	N
Coverdell	Y	Y	N	Y	N	Y	N
HAWAII							
Akaka	Y	Y	Y	Y	Y	N	Y
Inouye	Y	Y	Y	Y	Y	N	Y
IDAHO							
Craig	Y	Y	N	Y	N	Y	Y
Kempthorne	Y	Y	N	Y	N	Y	Y
ILLINOIS							
Moseley-Braun	Y	Y	Y	Y	N	Y	N
Simon	Y	Y	Y	N	Y	N	Y
INDIANA							
Coats	Y	Y	N	Y	N	Y	N
Lugar	Y	Y	N	Y	N	Y	Y
IOWA							
Harkin	Y	Y	Y	Y	Y	N	N
Grassley	Y	Y	N	Y	N	Y	N
KANSAS							
Dole	Y	Y	N	Y	N	Y	N
Kassebaum	Y	Y	N	Y	N	Y	N
KENTUCKY							
Ford	Y	Y	N	Y	N	Y	N
McConnell	Y	Y	Y	Y	Y	N	Y
LOUISIANA							
Breaux	Y	Y	Y	Y	Y	N	N
Johnston	Y	Y	Y	Y	Y	N	N
MAINE							
Mitchell	Y	Y	Y	Y	Y	N	Y
Cohen	Y	Y	N	Y	Y	Y	Y
MARYLAND							
Mikulski	Y	Y	Y	Y	Y	N	Y
Sarbanes	Y	Y	Y	Y	Y	N	Y
MASSACHUSETTS							
Kennedy	Y	Y	Y	Y	Y	N	Y
Kerry	Y	Y	Y	Y	Y	N	Y
MICHIGAN							
Levin	Y	Y	Y	Y	Y	N	Y
Riegle	Y	Y	Y	Y	N	Y	Y
MINNESOTA							
Wellstone	Y	Y	Y	N	N	Y	N
Durenberger	Y	Y	N	Y	N	Y	Y
MISSISSIPPI							
Cochran	Y	Y	N	Y	Y	N	N
Lott	Y	Y	N	Y	N	Y	Y
MISSOURI							
Bond	Y	Y	N	Y	N	Y	N
Danforth	Y	Y	N	Y	N	Y	N
MONTANA							
Baucus	Y	Y	Y	Y	Y	N	N
Burns	Y	Y	N	Y	N	Y	N
NEBRASKA							
Exon	Y	Y	Y	Y	Y	N	N
Kerrey	Y	Y	Y	Y	Y	N	Y
NEVADA							
Bryan	Y	Y	Y	Y	Y	Y	N
Reid	Y	Y	Y	Y	Y	Y	N
NEW HAMPSHIRE							
Gregg	Y	Y	N	Y	N	Y	N
Smith	Y	Y	N	Y	N	Y	N
NEW JERSEY							
Bradley	Y	Y	Y	Y	Y	N	N
Lautenberg	Y	Y	Y	Y	Y	N	N
NEW MEXICO							
Bingaman	Y	Y	Y	Y	Y	N	N
Domenici	Y	Y	N	Y	N	Y	N
NEW YORK							
Moynihan	Y	Y	N	Y	N	Y	N
D'Amato	Y	Y	N	Y	N	Y	N
NORTH CAROLINA							
Faircloth	Y	Y	N	Y	N	Y	N
Helms	Y	Y	N	Y	N	Y	N
NORTH DAKOTA							
Conrad	Y	Y	Y	Y	N	Y	N
Dorgan	Y	Y	Y	Y	N	Y	N
OHIO							
Glenn	Y	Y	Y	Y	Y	N	N
Metzenbaum	Y	Y	Y	Y	Y	N	N
OKLAHOMA							
Boren	Y	Y	Y	Y	Y	N	N
Nickles	Y	Y	N	Y	Y	Y	N
OREGON							
Hatfield	Y	Y	Y	Y	Y	N	Y
Packwood	Y	Y	N	Y	Y	N	Y
PENNSYLVANIA							
Wofford	Y	Y	Y	Y	N	N	Y
Specter	Y	Y	Y	Y	N	Y	N
RHODE ISLAND							
Pell	Y	+	Y	N	Y	N	Y
Chafee	Y	Y	Y	Y	Y	N	N
SOUTH CAROLINA							
Hollings	Y	Y	N	Y	N	Y	N
Thurmond	Y	Y	N	Y	N	Y	N
SOUTH DAKOTA							
Daschle	Y	Y	Y	Y	Y	N	N
Pressler	Y	Y	N	Y	N	Y	N
TENNESSEE							
Mathews	Y	Y	Y	Y	Y	N	N
Sasser	Y	Y	N	Y	N	Y	N
TEXAS							
Hutchison	Y	Y	N	Y	N	Y	N
Gramm	Y	Y	N	Y	N	Y	Y
UTAH							
Bennett	Y	Y	N	Y	Y	N	N
Hatch	Y	Y	N	Y	N	Y	Y
VERMONT							
Leahy	Y	Y	Y	Y	Y	N	N
Jeffords	Y	Y	Y	Y	Y	Y	Y
VIRGINIA							
Robb	Y	Y	Y	Y	Y	N	Y
Warner	Y	Y	N	Y	N	Y	N
WASHINGTON							
Murray	Y	Y	Y	Y	Y	N	N
Gorton	Y	Y	N	Y	N	Y	Y
WEST VIRGINIA							
Byrd	Y	Y	N	Y	N	Y	N
Rockefeller	Y	Y	Y	Y	Y	N	Y
WISCONSIN							
Feingold	Y	Y	Y	Y	N	N	N
Kohl	Y	Y	Y	Y	Y	N	N
WYOMING							
Simpson	Y	Y	N	Y	Y	N	Y
Wallop	Y	Y	N	Y	Y	Y	Y

ND Northern Democrats SD Southern Democrats

Southern states - Ala., Ark., Fla., Ga., Ky., La., Miss., N.C., Okla., S.C., Tenn., Texas, Va.

1. Procedural Motion. Mitchell, D-Maine, motion to instruct the sergeant at arms to request the attendance of absent senators. Motion agreed to 100-0: R 44-0; D 56-0 (ND 42-0, SD 14-0), Jan. 25, 1994.

2. S 1281. Fiscal 1994-95 State Department Authorization/Pedophilia-Endorsing Organizations. Helms, R-N.C., amendment to withhold U.S. contributions to U.N. international organizations unless the president certifies to Congress that no U.N. agency or affiliated agency grants recognition to an organization that condones pedophilia. Adopted 99-0: R 44-0; D 55-0 (ND 41-0, SD 14-0), Jan. 26, 1994.

3. S 1281. Fiscal 1994-95 State Department Authorization/International Criminal Court. Kerry, D-Mass., motion to table (kill) the Helms, R-N.C., amendment to strike language expressing the sense of Congress in support of establishing an international criminal court. Motion agreed to 55-45: R 5-39; D 50-6 (ND 41-1, SD 9-5), Jan. 26, 1994.

4. S 1281. Fiscal 1994-95 State Department Authorization/U.N. Inspector General. Pressler, R-S.D., amendment to withhold 10 percent in fiscal 1994 and 20 percent in fiscal 1995 and thereafter from U.S.-assessed contributions to the United Nations unless the president certifies that the U.N. has established an independent and objective Office of Inspector General. Adopted 93-6: R 44-0; D 49-6 (ND 36-6, SD 13-0), Jan. 26, 1994.

5. S 1281. Fiscal 1994-95 State Department Authorization/Relations With Vietnam. Kerry, D-Mass., amendment to express the sense of the Senate that in order to expand and maintain Vietnamese cooperation in resolving POW/MIA cases, the president should lift the U.S. trade embargo against Vietnam. Adopted 62-38: R 20-24; D 42-14 (ND 31-11, SD 11-3), Jan. 27, 1994.

6. S 1281. Fiscal 1994-95 State Department Authorization/Conditional Vietnam Relations. Smith, R-N.H., amendment to condition the lifting of the U.S. trade embargo against Vietnam on the president's determination that Vietnam has provided the fullest possible accounting of all U.S. POW/MIA cases. Rejected 42-58: R 29-15; D 13-43 (ND 10-32, SD 3-11), Jan. 27, 1994.

7. S 1281. Fiscal 1994-95 State Department Authorization/National Endowment for Democracy. Kerry, D-Mass., motion to table (kill) the Bumpers, D-Ark., amendment to reduce authorized fiscal 1994 spending for the National Endowment for Democracy from $50 million to $35 million, the amount already appropriated for fiscal 1994. Motion rejected 41-59: R 21-23; D 20-36 (ND 17-25, SD 3-11), Jan. 27, 1994. (Subsequently, the Bumpers amendment was adopted by voice vote.)

KEY

Y   Voted for (yea).
Paired for.
+   Announced for.
N   Voted against (nay).
X   Paired against.
—   Announced against.
P   Voted "present."
C   Voted "present" to avoid possible conflict of interest.
?   Did not vote or otherwise make a position known.

Democrats   *Republicans*

	8	9	10
ALABAMA			
Heflin	Y	Y	Y
Shelby	Y	Y	Y
ALASKA			
Murkowski	Y	Y	Y
Stevens	Y	N	N
ARIZONA			
DeConcini	Y	Y	Y
McCain	Y	Y	Y
ARKANSAS			
Bumpers	Y	Y	Y
Pryor	Y	Y	Y
CALIFORNIA			
Boxer	Y	Y	Y
Feinstein	Y	Y	+
COLORADO			
Campbell	Y	Y	N
Brown	Y	Y	Y
CONNECTICUT			
Dodd	Y	Y	Y
Lieberman	Y	Y	Y
DELAWARE			
Biden	Y	Y	Y
Roth	Y	Y	Y
FLORIDA			
Graham	Y	Y	Y
Mack	Y	Y	Y
GEORGIA			
Nunn	Y	Y	Y
Coverdell	Y	Y	Y
HAWAII			
Akaka	Y	Y	Y
Inouye	Y	Y	Y
IDAHO			
Craig	Y	Y	Y
Kempthorne	Y	Y	Y
ILLINOIS			
Moseley-Braun	Y	Y	Y
Simon	Y	Y	Y
INDIANA			
Coats	N	Y	Y
Lugar	Y	Y	Y

	8	9	10
IOWA			
Harkin	Y	Y	Y
Grassley	Y	Y	Y
KANSAS			
Dole	Y	Y	Y
Kassebaum	?	?	?
KENTUCKY			
Ford	Y	Y	Y
McConnell	Y	Y	Y
LOUISIANA			
Breaux	Y	Y	Y
Johnston	Y	Y	Y
MAINE			
Mitchell	Y	Y	Y
Cohen	Y	Y	Y
MARYLAND			
Mikulski	Y	Y	Y
Sarbanes	Y	Y	Y
MASSACHUSETTS			
Kennedy	Y	Y	Y
Kerry	Y	Y	Y
MICHIGAN			
Levin	Y	Y	Y
Riegle	Y	Y	Y
MINNESOTA			
Wellstone	Y	Y	Y
Durenberger	N	Y	?
MISSISSIPPI			
Cochran	Y	Y	Y
Lott	Y	Y	Y
MISSOURI			
Bond	Y	Y	Y
Danforth	N	Y	Y
MONTANA			
Baucus	+	Y	Y
Burns	N	Y	Y
NEBRASKA			
Exon	Y	Y	Y
Kerrey	Y	Y	Y
NEVADA			
Bryan	Y	Y	Y
Reid	Y	Y	?

	8	9	10
NEW HAMPSHIRE			
Gregg	N	Y	Y
Smith	Y	Y	Y
NEW JERSEY			
Bradley	Y	Y	Y
Lautenberg	Y	Y	Y
NEW MEXICO			
Bingaman	Y	Y	Y
Domenici	Y	Y	Y
NEW YORK			
Moynihan	Y	Y	Y
D'Amato	Y	Y	Y
NORTH CAROLINA			
Faircloth	N	Y	Y
Helms	Y	Y	Y
NORTH DAKOTA			
Conrad	Y	Y	Y
Dorgan	Y	Y	Y
OHIO			
Glenn	Y	Y	Y
Metzenbaum	Y	Y	N
OKLAHOMA			
Boren	Y	Y	Y
Nickles	Y	Y	Y
OREGON			
Hatfield	N	Y	Y
Packwood	Y	Y	Y
PENNSYLVANIA			
Wofford	Y	Y	Y
Specter	N	Y	Y
RHODE ISLAND			
Pell	N	Y	Y
Chafee	Y	Y	Y
SOUTH CAROLINA			
Hollings	Y	N	N
Thurmond	Y	Y	Y
SOUTH DAKOTA			
Daschle	Y	Y	Y
Pressler	?	?	?
TENNESSEE			
Mathews	Y	Y	Y
Sasser	Y	Y	Y

	8	9	10
TEXAS			
Hutchison	Y	Y	Y
Gramm	Y	Y	Y
UTAH			
Bennett	Y	Y	Y
Hatch	Y	Y	Y
VERMONT			
Leahy	Y	Y	Y
Jeffords	Y	Y	Y
VIRGINIA			
Robb	Y	Y	Y
Warner	Y	Y	Y
WASHINGTON			
Murray	?	?	?
Gorton	Y	Y	Y
WEST VIRGINIA			
Byrd	Y	Y	Y
Rockefeller	Y	Y	Y
WISCONSIN			
Feingold	Y	Y	Y
Kohl	Y	Y	Y
WYOMING			
Simpson	Y	Y	Y
Wallop	Y	N	Y

ND   Northern Democrats   SD   Southern Democrats   Southern states - Ala., Ark., Fla., Ga., Ky., La., Miss., N.C., Okla., S.C., Tenn., Texas, Va.

8. S 1281. Fiscal 1994-95 State Department Authorization/Bosnia Arms Embargo. Dole, R-Kan., amendment to express the sense of the Senate that the president should lift the U.S. arms embargo against the government of Bosnia and Herzegovina. Adopted 87-9: R 34-8; D 53-1 (ND 39-1, SD 14-0), Jan. 27, 1994.

9. S 1281. Fiscal 1994-95 State Department Authorization/NATO Expansion. McConnell, R-Ky., amendment to express the sense of the Senate that the United States should urge immediate admission to NATO for European nations that support collective defense requirements, free and fair elections, civilian control of the military, territorial integrity, individual liberties and other established democratic practices. Adopted 94-3: R 40-2; D 54-1 (ND 41-0, SD 13-1), Jan. 27, 1994.

10. S 1281. Fiscal 1994-95 State Department Authorization/International Criminal Court. Helms, R-N.C., amendment to prohibit the United States from ratifying a treaty to create an international criminal court unless the court would guarantee American citizens their First and Fourth Amendment rights. Adopted 91-3: R 41-0; D 50-3 (ND 37-2, SD 13-1), Jan. 27, 1994.

KEY

Y	Voted for (yea).
#	Paired for.
+	Announced for.
N	Voted against (nay).
X	Paired against.
−	Announced against.
P	Voted "present."
C	Voted "present" to avoid possible conflict of interest.
?	Did not vote or otherwise make a position known.

Democrats *Republicans*

	11	12	13	14	15	16	17	18
ALABAMA								
Heflin	Y	Y	Y	Y	Y	N	Y	Y
Shelby	Y	Y	?	Y	N	Y	N	Y
ALASKA								
Murkowski	N	Y	Y	N	N	N	N	Y
Stevens	N	Y	Y	N	N	N	N	Y
ARIZONA								
DeConcini	Y	Y	Y	Y	Y	Y	N	Y
McCain	?	+	Y	Y	N	N	N	Y
ARKANSAS								
Bumpers	Y	Y	Y	Y	Y	Y	Y	Y
Pryor	Y	Y	Y	Y	Y	Y	Y	Y
CALIFORNIA								
Boxer	Y	Y	Y	Y	Y	Y	Y	Y
Feinstein	Y	Y	Y	Y	Y	Y	Y	Y
COLORADO								
Campbell	N	Y	Y	Y	Y	Y	Y	Y
Brown	N	Y	Y	Y	N	N	N	Y
CONNECTICUT								
Dodd	Y	Y	Y	Y	Y	Y	Y	Y
Lieberman	Y	Y	Y	Y	Y	Y	Y	Y
DELAWARE								
Biden	Y	Y	Y	Y	Y	Y	Y	Y
Roth	N	Y	Y	Y	N	N	N	Y
FLORIDA								
Graham	Y	Y	Y	Y	Y	Y	Y	Y
Mack	N	Y	Y	Y	N	N	N	Y
GEORGIA								
Nunn	Y	Y	Y	Y	Y	Y	Y	Y
Coverdell	N	Y	Y	Y	N	N	N	Y
HAWAII								
Akaka	Y	Y	Y	Y	Y	Y	Y	Y
Inouye	?	?	Y	Y	Y	Y	Y	Y
IDAHO								
Craig	N	Y	Y	N	N	N	N	N
Kempthorne	N	Y	Y	N	N	N	N	N
ILLINOIS								
Moseley-Braun	Y	Y	?	Y	Y	Y	Y	Y
Simon	Y	Y	Y	Y	Y	Y	Y	Y
INDIANA								
Coats	Y	Y	Y	Y	N	N	Y	Y
Lugar	Y	Y	Y	N	N	N	N	Y

	11	12	13	14	15	16	17	18
IOWA								
Harkin	Y	Y	Y	Y	N	Y	Y	Y
Grassley	N	Y	Y	Y	N	N	N	Y
KANSAS								
Dole	N	Y	Y	Y	N	N	N	Y
Kassebaum	?	?	Y	N	N	N	Y	Y
KENTUCKY								
Ford	Y	Y	Y	Y	Y	Y	Y	Y
McConnell	Y	Y	Y	Y	N	N	N	Y
LOUISIANA								
Breaux	Y	Y	Y	Y	Y	Y	Y	Y
Johnston	Y	Y	Y	Y	Y	Y	Y	Y
MAINE								
Mitchell	Y	Y	Y	Y	Y	Y	Y	Y
Cohen	N	Y	Y	Y	N	N	N	Y
MARYLAND								
Mikulski	Y	Y	Y	Y	Y	Y	Y	Y
Sarbanes	Y	Y	Y	Y	Y	Y	Y	Y
MASSACHUSETTS								
Kennedy	Y	Y	Y	Y	Y	Y	Y	Y
Kerry	Y	Y	Y	Y	Y	Y	Y	Y
MICHIGAN								
Levin	Y	Y	Y	Y	Y	Y	Y	Y
Riegle	Y	Y	Y	Y	Y	Y	Y	Y
MINNESOTA								
Wellstone	Y	Y	Y	Y	Y	Y	Y	Y
Durenberger	N	Y	Y	Y	N	N	Y	Y
MISSISSIPPI								
Cochran	?	?	Y	N	N	N	N	Y
Lott	N	Y	Y	Y	N	N	N	N
MISSOURI								
Bond	N	Y	?	Y	N	N	N	Y
Danforth	Y	Y	N	Y	N	N	Y	Y
MONTANA								
Baucus	Y	Y	Y	Y	Y	Y	Y	Y
Burns	Y	Y	Y	Y	N	Y	N	Y
NEBRASKA								
Exon	Y	Y	Y	Y	Y	N	N	Y
Kerrey	Y	Y	Y	Y	Y	Y	Y	Y
NEVADA								
Bryan	Y	Y	Y	Y	Y	Y	Y	Y
Reid	?	?	Y	Y	Y	Y	Y	Y

	11	12	13	14	15	16	17	18
NEW HAMPSHIRE								
Gregg	N	Y	Y	N	N	N	Y	Y
Smith	N	Y	Y	N	N	N	N	N
NEW JERSEY								
Bradley	Y	Y	Y	Y	Y	Y	Y	Y
Lautenberg	Y	Y	Y	Y	Y	Y	Y	Y
NEW MEXICO								
Bingaman	Y	Y	Y	Y	Y	Y	Y	Y
Domenici	N	Y	Y	Y	N	N	N	Y
NEW YORK								
Moynihan	Y	Y	Y	Y	Y	Y	Y	Y
D'Amato	N	Y	Y	Y	N	N	N	Y
NORTH CAROLINA								
Faircloth	N	Y	Y	N	N	N	N	N
Helms	N	Y	Y	N	N	N	N	Y
NORTH DAKOTA								
Conrad	N	Y	Y	Y	Y	Y	Y	N
Dorgan	N	Y	Y	Y	N	Y	Y	N
OHIO								
Glenn	Y	Y	Y	Y	Y	Y	Y	Y
Metzenbaum	Y	Y	Y	Y	Y	Y	Y	Y
OKLAHOMA								
Boren	Y	Y	Y	Y	Y	Y	Y	Y
Nickles	N	Y	Y	Y	N	N	N	Y
OREGON								
Hatfield	Y	Y	Y	Y	Y	Y	Y	Y
Packwood	N	Y	Y	Y	N	N	N	Y
PENNSYLVANIA								
Wofford	Y	Y	Y	Y	Y	Y	Y	Y
Specter	N	Y	Y	Y	N	N	N	Y
RHODE ISLAND								
Pell	Y	Y	Y	Y	Y	Y	Y	Y
Chafee	Y	Y	Y	Y	N	N	Y	Y
SOUTH CAROLINA								
Hollings	N	Y	Y	Y	Y	Y	Y	Y
Thurmond	N	Y	Y	N	N	N	N	Y
SOUTH DAKOTA								
Daschle	Y	Y	Y	Y	Y	Y	Y	Y
Pressler	?	?	Y	N	N	N	N	Y
TENNESSEE								
Mathews	Y	Y	Y	Y	Y	Y	Y	Y
Sasser	Y	Y	Y	Y	Y	Y	Y	Y

	11	12	13	14	15	16	17	18
TEXAS								
Hutchison	N	Y	Y	Y	N	N	N	Y
Gramm	N	Y	Y	Y	N	N	N	Y
UTAH								
Bennett	N	Y	Y	N	Y	N	Y	Y
Hatch	N	Y	Y	N	Y	N	Y	Y
VERMONT								
Leahy	Y	Y	Y	Y	Y	Y	Y	Y
Jeffords	Y	Y	Y	Y	N	Y	Y	Y
VIRGINIA								
Robb	Y	Y	Y	Y	Y	Y	Y	Y
Warner	Y	Y	Y	Y	N	N	N	Y
WASHINGTON								
Murray	?	?	Y	Y	Y	Y	Y	Y
Gorton	Y	Y	Y	Y	N	N	N	Y
WEST VIRGINIA								
Byrd	Y	Y	Y	Y	Y	Y	N	Y
Rockefeller	Y	Y	Y	Y	Y	Y	Y	Y
WISCONSIN								
Feingold	Y	Y	Y	Y	N	Y	Y	Y
Kohl	Y	Y	Y	Y	N	Y	Y	Y
WYOMING								
Simpson	N	Y	N	N	N	N	N	Y
Wallop	Y	Y	Y	N	N	N	N	N

ND Northern Democrats SD Southern Democrats Southern states - Ala., Ark., Fla., Ga., Ky., La., Miss., N.C., Okla., S.C., Tenn., Texas, Va.

11. S 1281. Fiscal 1994-95 State Department Authorization/Former Soviet Union Collateral. Kerry, D-Mass., motion to table (kill) the Specter, R-Pa., amendment to require that bilateral and international loans to the independent states of the former Soviet Union be collateralized by petroleum products, minerals or other commodities. Motion agreed to 60-33: R 11-29; D 49-4 (ND 36-3, SD 13-1), Jan. 28, 1994.

12. S 1281. Fiscal 1994-95 State Department Authorization/Israeli Boycott. Brown, R-Colo., amendment to prohibit the sale of defense services or articles to countries that participate in the secondary and tertiary boycott of U.S. companies that do business with Israel unless the president certifies that it is in the interest of national security. Adopted 93-0: R 40-0; D 53-0 (ND 39-0, SD 14-0), Jan. 28, 1994.

13. S 1281. Fiscal 1994-95 State Department Authorization/German Military Participation. Cohen, R-Maine, amendment to express the sense of Congress to encourage the full and active participation of Germany in international military efforts to maintain and restore peace. Adopted 96-1: R 42-1; D 54-0 (ND 41-0, SD 13-0), Feb. 1, 1994.

14. S 1281. Fiscal 1994-95 State Department Authorization/Russian Immigrants. Lautenberg, D-N.J., amendment to extend certain provisions of the 1990 immigration law that assume Russian Jews and evangelical Christians are politically oppressed without their having to prove it on an individual basis, thus facilitating their immigration to the United States. Adopted 85-15: R 29-15; D 56-0 (ND 42-0, SD 14-0), Feb. 1, 1994.

15. S 1281. Fiscal 1994-95 State Department Authorization/Assistant Secretaries of State. Kerry, D-Mass., motion to table (kill) the Helms, R-N.C., amendment to delete the increase in the number of assistant secretaries of state made by the bill. Motion agreed to 51-49: R 0-44; D 51-5 (ND 38-4, SD 13-1), Feb. 1, 1994.

16. S 1281. Fiscal 1994-95 State Department Authorization/China MFN. Kerry, D-Mass., amendment to the Helms, R-N.C., amendment, to express the sense of the Senate that the president should use all opportunities to press the Chinese for further concrete progress toward meeting the standards for renewal of that country's most-favored-nation (MFN) trade status. The Helms amendment would have expressed the sense of the Senate that MFN should be discontinued until the president certifies that certain conditions on human rights, trade and nuclear non-proliferation have been met. Adopted 61-39: R 6-38; D 55-1 (ND 42-0, SD 13-1), Feb. 1, 1994. (Subsequently, the Helms amendment, as amended by the Kerry amendment, was adopted by voice vote.)

17. S 1281. Fiscal 1994-95 State Department Authorization/Security Assistance Prohibition. Kerry, D-Mass., motion to table (kill) the Lott, R-Miss., amendment to prohibit U.S. security assistance to countries that vote with the United States less than 25 percent of the time in the U.N. General Assembly unless the secretary of State determines that it is necessary to promote U.S. foreign policy objectives. Motion agreed to 66-34: R 14-30; D 52-4 (ND 39-3, SD 13-1), Feb. 2, 1994.

18. S 1281. Fiscal 1994-95 State Department Authorization/Passage. Passage of the bill to authorize $6.3 billion in fiscal 1994 and $6.1 billion in fiscal 1995 in spending for the State Department, the U.S. Information Agency and related agencies. Passed 92-8: R 38-6; D 54-2 (ND 40-2, SD 14-0), Feb. 2, 1994.

SENATE VOTES 19, 20, 21, 22, 23

	19	20	21	22	23
ALABAMA					
Heflin	Y	Y	Y	Y	Y
Shelby	Y	Y	Y	Y	Y
ALASKA					
Murkowski	Y	Y	Y	Y	Y
Stevens	?	?	?	?	?
ARIZONA					
DeConcini	Y	N	Y	Y	Y
McCain	?	?	?	?	?
ARKANSAS					
Bumpers	Y	N	Y	Y	Y
Pryor	Y	?	Y	Y	Y
CALIFORNIA					
Boxer	Y	N	Y	N	Y
Feinstein	Y	N	Y	N	Y
COLORADO					
Campbell	Y	Y	Y	Y	Y
Brown	Y	Y	Y	Y	Y
CONNECTICUT					
Dodd	Y	N	Y	Y	Y
Lieberman	Y	N	Y	Y	Y
DELAWARE					
Biden	Y	?	Y	Y	Y
Roth	Y	Y	Y	Y	Y
FLORIDA					
Graham	Y	N	Y	Y	Y
Mack	Y	Y	Y	Y	Y
GEORGIA					
Nunn	Y	N	Y	Y	Y
Coverdell	Y	Y	Y	Y	Y
HAWAII					
Akaka	Y	N	Y	Y	Y
Inouye	Y	N	Y	N	Y
IDAHO					
Craig	Y	Y	Y	Y	Y
Kempthorne	Y	Y	Y	Y	Y
ILLINOIS					
Moseley-Braun	Y	N	Y	Y	Y
Simon	Y	N	Y	N	Y
INDIANA					
Coats	Y	Y	Y	Y	Y
Lugar	Y	Y	Y	Y	Y

	19	20	21	22	23
IOWA					
Harkin	Y	N	Y	N	Y
Grassley	Y	Y	Y	Y	Y
KANSAS					
Dole	Y	Y	Y	Y	Y
Kassebaum	Y	Y	Y	N	Y
KENTUCKY					
Ford	Y	N	Y	Y	Y
McConnell	Y	Y	Y	Y	Y
LOUISIANA					
Breaux	Y	Y	Y	Y	Y
Johnston	Y	N	Y	Y	Y
MAINE					
Mitchell	Y	N	Y	Y	Y
Cohen	Y	Y	Y	Y	Y
MARYLAND					
Mikulski	Y	N	Y	Y	Y
Sarbanes	Y	N	Y	Y	Y
MASSACHUSETTS					
Kennedy	Y	N	Y	Y	Y
Kerry	Y	N	Y	Y	Y
MICHIGAN					
Levin	Y	N	Y	N	Y
Riegle	Y	N	Y	N	Y
MINNESOTA					
Wellstone	Y	N	Y	N	Y
Durenberger	Y	?	Y	Y	Y
MISSISSIPPI					
Cochran	Y	Y	Y	Y	Y
Lott	Y	Y	Y	Y	Y
MISSOURI					
Bond	Y	Y	Y	Y	Y
Danforth	Y	Y	Y	N	Y
MONTANA					
Baucus	Y	N	Y	Y	Y
Burns	Y	Y	Y	Y	Y
NEBRASKA					
Exon	Y	Y	Y	Y	Y
Kerrey	Y	N	Y	Y	Y
NEVADA					
Bryan	Y	N	Y	N	Y
Reid	Y	N	Y	Y	Y

	19	20	21	22	23
NEW HAMPSHIRE					
Gregg	Y	Y	Y	Y	Y
Smith	Y	Y	Y	Y	Y
NEW JERSEY					
Bradley	Y	N	Y	Y	Y
Lautenberg	Y	N	Y	Y	Y
NEW MEXICO					
Bingaman	Y	N	Y	Y	Y
Domenici	Y	Y	Y	Y	Y
NEW YORK					
Moynihan	Y	N	Y	N	Y
D'Amato	Y	Y	Y	Y	Y
NORTH CAROLINA					
Faircloth	Y	Y	Y	Y	Y
Helms	Y	Y	Y	Y	Y
NORTH DAKOTA					
Conrad	Y	N	Y	Y	Y
Dorgan	Y	N	Y	Y	Y
OHIO					
Glenn	Y	N	Y	N	Y
Metzenbaum	Y	N	Y	N	Y
OKLAHOMA					
Boren	Y	N	Y	Y	Y
Nickles	?	?	?	?	?
OREGON					
Hatfield	Y	N	Y	N	Y
Packwood	Y	Y	Y	Y	Y
PENNSYLVANIA					
Wofford	Y	N	Y	Y	Y
Specter	Y	N	Y	N	Y
RHODE ISLAND					
Pell	Y	N	Y	N	Y
Chafee	Y	N	Y	N	Y
SOUTH CAROLINA					
Hollings	Y	N	Y	Y	Y
Thurmond	Y	Y	Y	Y	Y
SOUTH DAKOTA					
Daschle	Y	N	Y	Y	Y
Pressler	Y	Y	Y	Y	Y
TENNESSEE					
Mathews	Y	N	Y	Y	Y
Sasser	Y	N	Y	Y	Y

	19	20	21	22	23
TEXAS					
Hutchison	Y	Y	Y	Y	Y
Gramm	Y	Y	Y	Y	Y
UTAH					
Bennett	Y	Y	Y	Y	Y
Hatch	Y	Y	Y	Y	Y
VERMONT					
Leahy	Y	N	Y	N	Y
Jeffords	Y	N	Y	N	Y
VIRGINIA					
Robb	Y	N	Y	Y	Y
Warner	Y	Y	Y	Y	Y
WASHINGTON					
Murray	Y	N	Y	N	Y
Gorton	Y	Y	Y	Y	Y
WEST VIRGINIA					
Byrd	Y	Y	Y	Y	Y
Rockefeller	Y	N	Y	Y	Y
WISCONSIN					
Feingold	Y	N	Y	N	Y
Kohl	Y	N	Y	Y	Y
WYOMING					
Simpson	Y	Y	Y	Y	Y
Wallop	Y	Y	Y	Y	Y

KEY

- Y   Voted for (yea).
- #   Paired for.
- +   Announced for.
- N   Voted against (nay).
- X   Paired against.
- −   Announced against.
- P   Voted "present."
- C   Voted "present" to avoid possible conflict of interest.
- ?   Did not vote or otherwise make a position known.

Democrats   *Republicans*

ND   Northern Democrats   SD   Southern Democrats   Southern states - Ala., Ark., Fla., Ga., Ky., La., Miss., N.C., Okla., S.C., Tenn., Texas, Va.

19. S 1150. Goals 2000: Educate America/Sense of the Senate Condemnation of Racism. Danforth, R-Mo., amendment to express the sense of the Senate condemning Khalid Abdul Muhammad's speech at Kean College in Union, N.J., on Nov. 29, 1993, as false, anti-Semitic, racist, divisive, repugnant and a disservice to all Americans. Adopted 97-0: R 41-0; D 56-0 (ND 42-0, SD 14-0), Feb. 2, 1994.

20. S 1150. Goals 2000: Educate America/Opportunity To Learn. Gregg, R-N.H., amendment to strike all references in the bill to opportunity-to-learn standards. Rejected 42-52: R 36-4; D 6-48 (ND 3-38, SD 3-10), Feb. 2, 1994.

21. S 1150. Goals 2000: Educate America/Demonstration Waivers. Hatfield, R-Ore., amendment to authorize the Department of Education to designate three larger states and three smaller states that would have broad authority to waive federal statutory or regulatory education requirements in order to try comprehensive education reforms. Adopted 97-0: R 41-0; D 56-0 (ND 42-0, SD 14-0), Feb. 3, 1994.

22. S 1150. Goals 2000: Educate America/School Prayer. Helms, R-N.C., amendment to deny federal aid from the Department of Education to state or local school agencies that prohibit constitutionally protected voluntary prayer in public schools. Adopted 75-22: R 35-6; D 40-16 (ND 26-16, SD 14-0), Feb. 3, 1994.

23. Perry Nomination. Confirmation of President Clinton's nomination of William J. Perry to be secretary of Defense. Confirmed 97-0: R 41-0; D 56-0 (ND 42-0, SD 14-0), Feb. 3, 1994. A "yea" was a vote in support of the president's position.

	24	25	26	27	28	29	30	31
ALABAMA								
Heflin	Y	N	Y	N	Y	Y	Y	Y
Shelby	N	N	Y	Y	Y	Y	Y	N
ALASKA								
Murkowski	Y	Y	Y	Y	Y	Y	Y	N
Stevens	?	Y	Y	Y	N	Y	Y	N
ARIZONA								
DeConcini	Y	N	Y	N	N	Y	Y	Y
McCain	?	Y	Y	Y	N	Y	Y	N
ARKANSAS								
Bumpers	Y	N	Y	N	N	Y	Y	Y
Pryor	Y	N	Y	N	N	N	Y	Y
CALIFORNIA								
Boxer	N	N	Y	N	N	Y	Y	Y
Feinstein	Y	N	Y	N	N	Y	Y	Y
COLORADO								
Campbell	Y	N	Y	N	N	Y	Y	Y
Brown	Y	Y	Y	Y	Y	Y	Y	N
CONNECTICUT								
Dodd	Y	N	Y	N	N	Y	Y	Y
Lieberman	Y	Y	Y	N	Y	Y	Y	Y
DELAWARE								
Biden	Y	N	Y	N	N	Y	Y	Y
Roth	Y	Y	Y	Y	Y	Y	Y	N
FLORIDA								
Graham	Y	N	Y	N	N	Y	Y	Y
Mack	Y	Y	Y	Y	Y	Y	Y	N
GEORGIA								
Nunn	Y	Y	Y	N	N	Y	N	Y
Coverdell	Y	Y	Y	Y	Y	Y	Y	N
HAWAII								
Akaka	Y	N	Y	N	N	Y	Y	Y
Inouye	Y	N	Y	N	N	Y	Y	Y
IDAHO								
Craig	Y	Y	Y	Y	Y	Y	Y	N
Kempthorne	Y	Y	Y	Y	Y	Y	Y	N
ILLINOIS								
Moseley-Braun	Y	?	?	?	?	?	?	?
Simon	N	N	Y	N	N	Y	Y	Y
INDIANA								
Coats	Y	Y	Y	Y	Y	Y	Y	N
Lugar	Y	Y	Y	Y	N	Y	Y	N

	24	25	26	27	28	29	30	31
IOWA								
Harkin	Y	N	Y	N	N	Y	Y	Y
Grassley	Y	Y	Y	Y	Y	Y	Y	N
KANSAS								
Dole	Y	Y	Y	Y	Y	Y	Y	N
Kassebaum	Y	Y	Y	Y	Y	Y	Y	N
KENTUCKY								
Ford	Y	N	Y	N	Y	Y	Y	Y
McConnell	Y	Y	Y	Y	Y	Y	Y	N
LOUISIANA								
Breaux	Y	?	?	?	?	?	?	?
Johnston	Y	?	?	?	?	?	?	?
MAINE								
Mitchell	Y	N	Y	N	N	Y	Y	Y
Cohen	?	N	Y	N	N	Y	Y	N
MARYLAND								
Mikulski	?	N	Y	N	N	Y	Y	Y
Sarbanes	Y	N	Y	N	N	Y	Y	Y
MASSACHUSETTS								
Kennedy	Y	N	Y	N	N	Y	Y	Y
Kerry	Y	N	Y	N	N	Y	Y	Y
MICHIGAN								
Levin	Y	N	Y	N	N	Y	Y	Y
Riegle	Y	N	Y	N	N	Y	Y	Y
MINNESOTA								
Wellstone	Y	N	Y	N	N	Y	Y	Y
Durenberger	?	Y	Y	N	N	Y	Y	N
MISSISSIPPI								
Cochran	?	Y	Y	N	Y	Y	Y	N
Lott	Y	Y	Y	Y	Y	Y	Y	N
MISSOURI								
Bond	?	Y	Y	N	N	Y	Y	Y
Danforth	Y	Y	Y	N	N	Y	Y	Y
MONTANA								
Baucus	Y	N	Y	N	N	Y	Y	Y
Burns	Y	N	Y	Y	Y	Y	Y	N
NEBRASKA								
Exon	Y	N	Y	N	Y	Y	Y	Y
Kerrey	Y	Y	Y	Y	N	Y	Y	Y
NEVADA								
Bryan	Y	N	Y	N	N	Y	Y	Y
Reid	Y	N	Y	N	N	Y	Y	Y

	24	25	26	27	28	29	30	31
NEW HAMPSHIRE								
Gregg	Y	Y	Y	N	Y	Y	Y	N
Smith	?	Y	Y	Y	Y	Y	Y	N
NEW JERSEY								
Bradley	Y	Y	Y	N	N	Y	Y	Y
Lautenberg	Y	N	Y	N	N	Y	Y	Y
NEW MEXICO								
Bingaman	Y	N	Y	N	N	Y	Y	Y
Domenici	Y	Y	Y	Y	Y	Y	Y	N
NEW YORK								
Moynihan	Y	N	Y	N	N	Y	Y	Y
D'Amato	Y	Y	Y	Y	Y	Y	Y	N
NORTH CAROLINA								
Faircloth	Y	Y	Y	Y	Y	N	Y	N
Helms	?	Y	Y	Y	Y	Y	Y	N
NORTH DAKOTA								
Conrad	Y	N	Y	N	N	Y	Y	Y
Dorgan	Y	N	Y	N	N	Y	Y	Y
OHIO								
Glenn	?	N	Y	N	N	Y	Y	Y
Metzenbaum	Y	N	Y	N	N	Y	Y	Y
OKLAHOMA								
Boren	Y	N	Y	N	N	Y	Y	Y
Nickles	?	Y	Y	Y	Y	Y	Y	N
OREGON								
Hatfield	N	N	Y	N	N	Y	Y	N
Packwood	Y	Y	Y	Y	N	Y	Y	Y
PENNSYLVANIA								
Wofford	?	N	Y	N	N	Y	Y	Y
Specter	?	N	Y	N	N	Y	Y	Y
RHODE ISLAND								
Pell	Y	N	Y	N	N	Y	Y	Y
Chafee	Y	?	?	?	?	?	?	?
SOUTH CAROLINA								
Hollings	Y	N	Y	N	N	Y	Y	Y
Thurmond	Y	Y	Y	Y	Y	Y	Y	N
SOUTH DAKOTA								
Daschle	Y	N	Y	N	N	Y	Y	Y
Pressler	Y	Y	Y	Y	Y	Y	Y	N
TENNESSEE								
Mathews	Y	N	Y	N	N	Y	Y	Y
Sasser	Y	N	Y	N	Y	Y	Y	Y

	24	25	26	27	28	29	30	31
TEXAS								
Hutchison	Y	?	?	?	?	?	?	?
Gramm	Y	?	?	?	?	?	?	?
UTAH								
Bennett	Y	Y	Y	N	Y	Y	Y	N
Hatch	+	Y	Y	Y	Y	Y	Y	N
VERMONT								
Leahy	N	N	Y	N	N	Y	Y	Y
Jeffords	Y	N	Y	N	N	Y	Y	Y
VIRGINIA								
Robb	Y	N	Y	N	N	Y	Y	Y
Warner	Y	Y	Y	N	Y	Y	Y	N
WASHINGTON								
Murray	N	N	Y	N	N	Y	Y	Y
Gorton	Y	Y	Y	Y	N	Y	Y	N
WEST VIRGINIA								
Byrd	N	Y	N	Y	Y	Y	Y	Y
Rockefeller	Y	?	?	?	?	?	?	?
WISCONSIN								
Feingold	N	N	Y	N	N	Y	Y	Y
Kohl	Y	N	Y	N	N	Y	Y	Y
WYOMING								
Simpson	Y	Y	Y	N	N	Y	N	Y
Wallop	Y	Y	Y	Y	Y	N	Y	N

KEY

Y Voted for (yea).
Paired for.
+ Announced for.
N Voted against (nay).
X Paired against.
− Announced against.
P Voted "present."
C Voted "present" to avoid possible conflict of interest.
? Did not vote or otherwise make a position known.

Democrats *Republicans*

ND Northern Democrats SD Southern Democrats Southern states - Ala., Ark., Fla., Ga., Ky., La., Miss., N.C., Okla., S.C., Tenn., Texas, Va.

24. S 1150. Goals 2000: Educate America/Moment of Silence. Danforth, R-Mo., amendment to express the sense of the Senate that schools should allow students a brief period of daily silence for introspection and reflection. Adopted 78-8: R 32-1; D 46-7; (ND 33-6, SD 13-1), Feb. 4, 1994.

25. S 1150. Goals 2000: Educate America/Low-Income School Choice Demonstration Programs. Coats, R-Ind., amendment to authorize $30 million for six low-income school choice demonstration programs. The amendment would have allowed some poor children to attend private schools at public expense. Rejected 41-52: R 36-5; D 5-47 (ND 4-36, SD 1-11), Feb. 8, 1994.

26. S 1150. Goals 2000: Educate America/Consent Surveys. Grassley, R-Iowa, amendment to require parental and student consent for surveys or evaluations that pertain to political affiliations, psychological problems, sexual behavior or other private matters. Adopted 93-0: R 41-0; D 52-0 (ND 40-0, SD 12-0), Feb. 8, 1994.

27. S 1150. Goals 2000: Educate America/Direct Grants. Mack, R-Fla., amendment to provide that the money in the bill go directly to local school boards for school reform and innovation. Rejected 32-61: R 30-11; D 2-50 (ND 1-39, SD 1-11), Feb. 8, 1994.

28. S 1150. Goals 2000: Educate America/Condom Distribution. Helms, R-N.C., amendment to prohibit distribution of condoms, contraceptives or drugs financed by federal aid without parental consent. Rejected 34-59: R 27-14; D 7-45 (ND 2-38, SD 5-7), Feb. 8, 1994.

29. S 1150. Goals 2000: Educate America/Family Participation in Condom Distribution. Kennedy, D-Mass., amendment to encourage family participation in all federally financed contraceptive distribution programs for minors. Adopted 91-2: R 39-2; D 52-0 (ND 40-0, SD 12-0), Feb. 8, 1994.

30. S 1150. Goals 2000: Educate America/Individuals With Disabilities. Jeffords, R-Vt., amendment to express the sense of the Senate that programs under the Individuals With Disabilities Education Act should be adequately financed within the current budget constraints. Adopted 93-0: R 41-0; D 52-0 (ND 40-0, SD 12-0), Feb. 8, 1994.

31. S 1361. School To Work Opportunities/Youth Private Employment. Simon, D-Ill., motion to table (kill) the Gorton, R-Wash., amendment to give priority to the placement of youths in private sector jobs under the Summer Youth Employment and Training Program. Motion agreed to 50-43: R 1-40; D 49-3 (ND 39-1, SD 10-2), Feb. 8, 1994.

	32	33	34	35	36	37	38
ALABAMA							
Heflin	Y	Y	Y	Y	Y	N	N
Shelby	Y	Y	Y	Y	Y	Y	Y
ALASKA							
Murkowski	N	N	N	Y	Y	Y	Y
Stevens	N	Y	Y	Y	Y	Y	Y
ARIZONA							
DeConcini	Y	Y	Y	N	Y	N	N
McCain	N	Y	N	N	Y	Y	Y
ARKANSAS							
Bumpers	Y	Y	Y	Y	Y	N	N
Pryor	Y	Y	Y	Y	Y	N	N
CALIFORNIA							
Boxer	Y	Y	Y	Y	Y	N	N
Feinstein	Y	Y	Y	Y	Y	N	N
COLORADO							
Campbell	Y	Y	Y	Y	Y	N	N
Brown	N	Y	N	N	Y	Y	Y
CONNECTICUT							
Dodd	Y	Y	Y	Y	Y	N	N
Lieberman	Y	Y	Y	N	Y	Y	N
DELAWARE							
Biden	Y	Y	Y	Y	Y	N	N
Roth	N	Y	Y	Y	Y	Y	Y
FLORIDA							
Graham	Y	Y	Y	N	Y	N	N
Mack	N	Y	N	N	Y	Y	Y
GEORGIA							
Nunn	Y	Y	Y	Y	Y	N	N
Coverdell	N	Y	N	N	Y	Y	Y
HAWAII							
Akaka	Y	Y	Y	Y	Y	N	N
Inouye	Y	Y	Y	Y	Y	N	N
IDAHO							
Craig	N	N	N	N	Y	Y	Y
Kempthorne	N	N	N	N	Y	Y	Y
ILLINOIS							
Moseley-Braun	+	?	+	Y	Y	N	N
Simon	Y	Y	Y	N	Y	N	N
INDIANA							
Coats	N	Y	N	Y	Y	Y	Y
Lugar	N	N	N	Y	Y	Y	Y

	32	33	34	35	36	37	38
IOWA							
Harkin	Y	Y	Y	Y	Y	N	N
Grassley	N	Y	N	N	Y	Y	Y
KANSAS							
Dole	N	N	N	Y	Y	Y	Y
Kassebaum	N	N	N	Y	N	Y	Y
KENTUCKY							
Ford	Y	Y	Y	Y	Y	N	N
McConnell	N	Y	N	Y	Y	Y	Y
LOUISIANA							
Breaux	?	?	Y	Y	Y	N	N
Johnston	?	?	?	Y	Y	N	N
MAINE							
Mitchell	Y	Y	Y	Y	Y	N	N
Cohen	Y	Y	Y	N	Y	Y	N
MARYLAND							
Mikulski	Y	Y	Y	+	+	N	N
Sarbanes	Y	N	Y	Y	Y	N	N
MASSACHUSETTS							
Kennedy	Y	Y	Y	Y	Y	N	N
Kerry	Y	Y	Y	Y	Y	N	N
MICHIGAN							
Levin	Y	Y	Y	Y	Y	N	N
Riegle	Y	Y	Y	Y	Y	N	N
MINNESOTA							
Wellstone	Y	N	Y	Y	Y	N	N
Durenberger	Y	Y	Y	N	Y	?	?
MISSISSIPPI							
Cochran	Y	Y	Y	Y	Y	Y	Y
Lott	N	Y	N	Y	Y	Y	Y
MISSOURI							
Bond	Y	Y	Y	Y	Y	Y	Y
Danforth	Y	Y	Y	N	Y	?	?
MONTANA							
Baucus	Y	Y	Y	N	Y	N	N
Burns	N	Y	N	Y	Y	Y	Y
NEBRASKA							
Exon	Y	Y	Y	N	Y	N	N
Kerrey	Y	Y	Y	N	Y	N	N
NEVADA							
Bryan	Y	Y	Y	Y	Y	N	N
Reid	Y	Y	Y	Y	Y	N	N

	32	33	34	35	36	37	38
NEW HAMPSHIRE							
Gregg	N	Y	N	N	Y	Y	Y
Smith	N	N	N	N	Y	Y	Y
NEW JERSEY							
Bradley	Y	Y	Y	?	?	?	?
Lautenberg	Y	Y	Y	N	Y	N	N
NEW MEXICO							
Bingaman	Y	Y	Y	Y	?	N	N
Domenici	N	Y	Y	Y	Y	Y	Y
NEW YORK							
Moynihan	Y	N	Y	Y	Y	N	N
D'Amato	Y	Y	N	Y	Y	Y	Y
NORTH CAROLINA							
Faircloth	N	Y	N	N	Y	Y	Y
Helms	N	N	N	Y	Y	Y	Y
NORTH DAKOTA							
Conrad	Y	Y	Y	Y	Y	N	N
Dorgan	Y	Y	Y	Y	Y	N	N
OHIO							
Glenn	Y	Y	Y	Y	Y	N	N
Metzenbaum	Y	N	Y	Y	Y	Y	N
OKLAHOMA							
Boren	Y	Y	Y	N	Y	N	N
Nickles	N	Y	N	N	Y	Y	Y
OREGON							
Hatfield	Y	Y	Y	Y	Y	N	N
Packwood	Y	Y	Y	N	Y	?	?
PENNSYLVANIA							
Wofford	Y	Y	Y	Y	Y	N	N
Specter	Y	N	Y	N	Y	Y	N
RHODE ISLAND							
Pell	Y	Y	Y	Y	Y	N	N
Chafee	?	Y	Y	N	Y	Y	Y
SOUTH CAROLINA							
Hollings	Y	Y	Y	Y	Y	N	N
Thurmond	Y	Y	Y	Y	Y	Y	Y
SOUTH DAKOTA							
Daschle	Y	Y	Y	Y	Y	N	N
Pressler	N	Y	N	Y	Y	Y	Y
TENNESSEE							
Mathews	Y	Y	Y	Y	Y	N	N
Sasser	Y	Y	Y	Y	Y	N	N

KEY

Y	Voted for (yea).
#	Paired for.
+	Announced for.
N	Voted against (nay).
X	Paired against.
—	Announced against.
P	Voted "present."
C	Voted "present" to avoid possible conflict of interest.
?	Did not vote or otherwise make a position known.

Democrats   *Republicans*

	32	33	34	35	36	37	38
TEXAS							
Hutchison	?	?	?	?	?	?	?
Gramm	?	?	—	?	?	Y	Y
UTAH							
Bennett	N	Y	N	Y	Y	Y	Y
Hatch	N	Y	N	Y	Y	Y	Y
VERMONT							
Leahy	Y	Y	Y	Y	Y	N	N
Jeffords	Y	Y	Y	Y	Y	Y	N
VIRGINIA							
Robb	Y	Y	Y	N	Y	N	N
Warner	N	Y	N	Y	Y	Y	Y
WASHINGTON							
Murray	Y	Y	Y	Y	Y	N	N
Gorton	N	Y	Y	Y	Y	Y	Y
WEST VIRGINIA							
Byrd	N	N	Y	N	Y	N	N
Rockefeller	?	Y	Y	Y	Y	N	N
WISCONSIN							
Feingold	Y	N	Y	N	Y	N	N
Kohl	Y	Y	Y	N	Y	N	N
WYOMING							
Simpson	N	Y	Y	N	Y	Y	Y
Wallop	N	N	N	Y	Y	Y	Y

ND Northern Democrats   SD Southern Democrats   Southern states – Ala., Ark., Fla., Ga., Ky., La., Miss., N.C., Okla., S.C., Tenn., Texas, Va.

32. HR 2884. School to Work Opportunities/Passage. Passage of the bill to authorize $300 million in fiscal 1995 and such sums as necessary through fiscal 2003 for a program to assist young people in the transition from school to the workplace. Passed 62-31: R 11-30; D 51-1 (ND 39-1, SD 12-0), Feb. 8, 1994. (Before passage the Senate struck all after the enacting clause and inserted the text of S 1361 as amended.) A "yea" was a vote in support of the president's position.

33. Lawrence Nomination. Confirmation of M. Larry Lawrence of California to be ambassador to Switzerland. Confirmed 79-16: R 32-10; D 47-6 (ND 35-6, SD 12-0), Feb. 8, 1994. A "yea" was a vote in support of the president's position.

34. HR 1804. Goals 2000: Educate America/Passage. Passage of the bill to authorize $422 million for competitive grants for schools seeking to improve their performance, write into law six national education goals and establish tests and standards for elementary and secondary students. Passed 71-25: R 17-25; D 54-0 (ND 41-0, SD 13-0), Feb. 8, 1994. (Before passage the Senate struck all after the enacting clause and inserted the text of S 1150 as amended.) A "yea" was a vote in support of the president's position.

35. HR 3759. Fiscal 1994 Disaster Supplemental Appropriations/Rescissions. Byrd, D-W.Va., motion to table (kill) the Kerrey, D-Neb., amendment to rescind $94 billion over five years from 54 programs. Motion agreed to 65-31: R 23-19; D 42-12 (ND 31-9, SD 11-3), Feb. 9, 1994. (The motion also killed a Hatfield, R-Ore., substitute amendment to the Kerrey amendment, with $18.6 billion in defense rescissions.) A "yea" was a vote in support of the president's position.

36. HR 3759. Fiscal 1994 Disaster Supplemental Appropriations/Statute of Limitations. D'Amato, R-N.Y., amendment to extend the statute of limitations for Resolution Trust Corporation civil actions for fraud and gross negligence until Dec. 31, 1995, or until the corporation goes out of existence, whichever is later. Adopted 95-0: R 42-0; D 53-0 (ND 39-0, SD 14-0), Feb. 9, 1994.

37. HR 3759. Fiscal 1994 Disaster Supplemental Appropriations/Electronic Records. Brown, R-Colo., amendment to delete the money in the bill for the electronic communication record management activities of the Executive Office of the President. Rejected 44-51: R 39-1; D 5-50 (ND 4-37, SD 1-13), Feb. 10, 1994.

38. HR 3759. Fiscal 1994 Disaster Supplemental Appropriations/Disaster Checkoff. Craig, R-Idaho, motion to waive the budget act with respect to the Boren, D-Okla., point of order against the Murkowski, R-Alaska, amendment for violating the Budget Act. The Murkowski amendment would express the sense of the Senate that the tax checkoff for presidential election funds should be replaced with a tax checkoff for federal disaster relief assistance. Motion rejected 37-58: R 36-4; D 1-54 (ND 0-41, SD 1-13), Feb. 10, 1994. (A three-fifths majority (60) of the total Senate is required to waive the Budget Act. Subsequently, the chair upheld the Boren point of order, and the Murkowski amendment fell.)

KEY

- Y Voted for (yea).
- # Paired for.
- + Announced for.
- N Voted against (nay).
- X Paired against.
- − Announced against.
- P Voted "present."
- C Voted "present" to avoid possible conflict of interest.
- ? Did not vote or otherwise make a position known.

Democrats *Republicans*

	39	40	41	42	43	44	45
ALABAMA							
Heflin	N	N	N	N	N	Y	Y
Shelby	N	N	Y	N	N	Y	Y
ALASKA							
Murkowski	N	N	Y	N	Y	N	Y
Stevens	N	N	Y	N	Y	N	Y
ARIZONA							
DeConcini	N	Y	Y	N	N	Y	Y
McCain	N	N	Y	Y	Y	N	Y
ARKANSAS							
Bumpers	Y	N	N	N	N	Y	Y
Pryor	Y	N	N	N	N	Y	Y
CALIFORNIA							
Boxer	N	Y	N	N	N	Y	Y
Feinstein	N	N	N	N	N	Y	Y
COLORADO							
Campbell	N	N	N	N	N	Y	Y
Brown	N	Y	Y	Y	Y	N	N
CONNECTICUT							
Dodd	N	N	N	N	N	Y	Y
Lieberman	N	N	N	N	Y	Y	Y
DELAWARE							
Biden	N	N	N	N	N	Y	Y
Roth	N	N	Y	Y	Y	N	Y
FLORIDA							
Graham	N	N	N	N	N	Y	Y
Mack	N	N	N	N	Y	N	Y
GEORGIA							
Nunn	N	N	N	N	N	Y	Y
Coverdell	N	N	Y	Y	Y	N	Y
HAWAII							
Akaka	N	N	N	N	N	Y	Y
Inouye	N	N	N	N	N	Y	Y
IDAHO							
Craig	N	N	Y	N	Y	N	Y
Kempthorne	N	N	Y	N	Y	N	Y
ILLINOIS							
Moseley-Braun	N	N	N	N	N	Y	Y
Simon	N	Y	N	N	N	Y	Y
INDIANA							
Coats	N	N	Y	N	Y	N	Y
Lugar	N	N	N	N	Y	N	Y

	39	40	41	42	43	44	45
IOWA							
Harkin	Y	Y	N	N	N	Y	Y
Grassley	Y	Y	Y	N	Y	N	Y
KANSAS							
Dole	N	N	Y	Y	Y	N	Y
Kassebaum	N	N	Y	Y	Y	N	Y
KENTUCKY							
Ford	N	N	N	N	N	Y	Y
McConnell	N	N	Y	N	Y	N	Y
LOUISIANA							
Breaux	N	N	N	N	N	Y	Y
Johnston	N	N	N	N	N	Y	Y
MAINE							
Mitchell	N	N	N	N	N	Y	Y
Cohen	N	N	Y	N	Y	N	Y
MARYLAND							
Mikulski	N	N	N	N	N	Y	Y
Sarbanes	N	N	N	N	N	Y	Y
MASSACHUSETTS							
Kennedy	N	N	N	N	N	Y	Y
Kerry	Y	Y	N	N	N	Y	Y
MICHIGAN							
Levin	Y	N	N	N	N	Y	Y
Riegle	N	N	N	N	N	Y	Y
MINNESOTA							
Wellstone	Y	Y	N	N	N	Y	Y
Durenberger	?	?	?	?	?	?	?
MISSISSIPPI							
Cochran	N	N	Y	N	Y	N	Y
Lott	N	N	Y	N	Y	N	Y
MISSOURI							
Bond	N	N	Y	N	Y	N	Y
Danforth	?	?	?	?	?	?	?
MONTANA							
Baucus	N	N	N	N	N	Y	Y
Burns	N	N	Y	N	Y	N	Y
NEBRASKA							
Exon	N	N	N	N	N	Y	Y
Kerrey	N	N	N	N	N	Y	Y
NEVADA							
Bryan	N	N	N	N	N	Y	Y
Reid	N	N	N	N	N	Y	Y

	39	40	41	42	43	44	45
NEW HAMPSHIRE							
Gregg	N	Y	Y	Y	Y	N	N
Smith	N	N	Y	Y	Y	N	N
NEW JERSEY							
Bradley	?	?	?	?	?	?	?
Lautenberg	Y	Y	N	N	N	Y	Y
NEW MEXICO							
Bingaman	N	Y	N	N	N	Y	Y
Domenici	N	N	N	N	N	Y	Y
NEW YORK							
Moynihan	N	N	N	N	N	Y	Y
D'Amato	N	N	Y	N	Y	N	Y
NORTH CAROLINA							
Faircloth	N	N	Y	N	Y	N	N
Helms	N	N	Y	Y	Y	N	N
NORTH DAKOTA							
Conrad	Y	N	N	N	N	Y	Y
Dorgan	Y	Y	N	N	N	Y	Y
OHIO							
Glenn	N	N	N	N	N	Y	Y
Metzenbaum	Y	Y	Y	N	N	Y	Y
OKLAHOMA							
Boren	Y	N	N	N	N	Y	Y
Nickles	N	N	N	N	Y	?	N
OREGON							
Hatfield	Y	Y	N	N	N	N	Y
Packwood	?	?	?	?	?	?	?
PENNSYLVANIA							
Wofford	Y	Y	N	N	N	Y	Y
Specter	N	N	Y	N	Y	N	Y
RHODE ISLAND							
Pell	Y	N	N	N	N	Y	Y
Chafee	N	N	Y	Y	Y	N	Y
SOUTH CAROLINA							
Hollings	Y	N	Y	N	N	Y	Y
Thurmond	N	N	Y	Y	Y	N	Y
SOUTH DAKOTA							
Daschle	N	N	N	N	N	Y	Y
Pressler	N	N	Y	Y	Y	N	N
TENNESSEE							
Mathews	N	Y	Y	N	N	Y	Y
Sasser	N	Y	Y	N	N	Y	Y

	39	40	41	42	43	44	45
TEXAS							
Hutchison	?	?	?	?	?	?	?
Gramm	N	N	Y	Y	Y	N	Y
UTAH							
Bennett	N	N	Y	N	Y	N	Y
Hatch	N	N	Y	N	Y	N	Y
VERMONT							
Leahy	Y	N	N	N	N	Y	Y
Jeffords	Y	N	Y	N	N	N	Y
VIRGINIA							
Robb	N	N	N	N	Y	Y	Y
Warner	N	N	Y	N	Y	N	Y
WASHINGTON							
Murray	N	N	N	N	N	Y	Y
Gorton	N	N	Y	N	Y	N	Y
WEST VIRGINIA							
Byrd	N	N	N	N	N	Y	Y
Rockefeller	N	N	N	N	N	Y	Y
WISCONSIN							
Feingold	Y	Y	N	N	N	Y	N
Kohl	Y	Y	Y	N	Y	Y	N
WYOMING							
Simpson	N	N	Y	Y	Y	N	Y
Wallop	N	N	Y	Y	Y	N	N

ND Northern Democrats   SD Southern Democrats   Southern states - Ala., Ark., Fla., Ga., Ky., La., Miss., N.C., Okla., S.C., Tenn., Texas, Va.

39. HR 3759. Fiscal 1994 Disaster Supplemental Appropriations/Rescissions. Kerry, D-Mass., amendment to rescind $3 billion for a savings of more than $43 billion over five years through changes in programs in agriculture, defense, foreign relations, intelligence, government employees and operations, energy, and commerce. Rejected 20-75: R 3-37; D 17-38 (ND 13-28, SD 4-10), Feb. 10, 1994.

40. HR 3759. Fiscal 1994 Disaster Supplemental Appropriations/Peacekeeping Funds. Feingold, D-Wis., amendment to eliminate the $1.2 billion in the bill for peacekeeping operations in Somalia, Bosnia, Iraq and Haiti. Rejected 19-76: R 4-36; D 15-40 (ND 13-28, SD 2-12), Feb. 10, 1994. A "nay" was a vote in support of the president's position.

41. HR 3759. Fiscal 1994 Disaster Supplemental Appropriations/Disaster Relief Trust. Dole, R-Kan., motion to waive the budget act with respect to the Byrd, D-W.Va., point of order against the Durenberger, R-Minn., amendment for violating the Budget Act. The Durenberger amendment would create a Natural Disaster Relief Trust Fund within the Treasury. Motion rejected 41-54: R 34-6; D 7-48 (ND 3-38, SD 4-10), Feb. 10, 1994.(A three-fifths majority (60) of the total Senate is required to waive the Budget Act. Subsequently, the chair upheld the Byrd point of order, and the Durenberger amendment fell.)

42. HR 3759. Fiscal 1994 Disaster Supplemental Appropriations/Highway Demonstration Projects. McCain, R-Ariz., amendment to rescind $2.2 billion for highway demonstration projects from the Federal Highway Administration. Rejected 23-72: R 19-21; D 4-51 (ND 1-40, SD 3-11), Feb. 10, 1994.

43. HR 3759. Fiscal 1994 Disaster Supplemental Appropriations/Offsetting Cuts. Nickles, R-Okla., motion to waive the budget act with respect to the Byrd, D-W.Va., point of order against the Dole, R-Kan., amendment for violating the Budget Act. The Dole amendment would delete the emergency designation language in the bill and pay for the bill through cuts in the World Bank, aid to the Commonwealth of Independent States, the Agency for International Development, federal administrative expenses, San Francisco highway relocation, peacekeeping contributions and the Economic Development Administration. Motion rejected 43-52: R 38-2; D 5-50 (ND 3-38, SD 2-12), Feb. 10, 1994.(A three-fifths majority (60) of the total Senate is required to waive the Budget Act. Subsequently, the chair upheld the Byrd point of order, and the Dole amendment fell.)

44. HR 3759. Fiscal 1994 Disaster Supplemental Appropriations/State Department Personnel Files. Byrd, D-W.Va., motion to table (kill) the McConnell, R-Ky., amendment to express the sense of the Senate that the State Department Inspector General's report on the White House's disclosure of State Department personnel files from the Bush administration should be given to Congress for confidential review. Motion agreed to 55-39: R 0-39; D 55-0 (ND 41-0, SD 14-0), Feb. 10, 1994.

45. HR 3759. Fiscal 1994 Disaster Supplemental Appropriations/Passage. Passage of the bill to provide $7.55 billion in new budget authority and $1.1 billion in direct loans for the emergency expenses of the Los Angeles earthquake, humanitarian assistance and peacekeeping activities, Midwest flood assistance and highway reconstruction in San Francisco. Passed 85-10: R 32-8; D 53-2 (ND 39-2, SD 14-0), Feb. 10, 1994. A "yea" was a vote in support of the president's position.

	46	47	48	49
ALABAMA				
Heflin	Y	N	Y	Y
Shelby	Y	N	Y	Y
ALASKA				
Murkowski	N	N	Y	N
Stevens	Y	N	N	N
ARIZONA				
DeConcini	Y	N	Y	Y
McCain	N	N	Y	N
ARKANSAS				
Bumpers	Y	N	N	Y
Pryor	?	N	N	?
CALIFORNIA				
Boxer	Y	Y	N	Y
Feinstein	Y	Y	Y	Y
COLORADO				
Campbell	Y	N	Y	Y
Brown	N	N	Y	N
CONNECTICUT				
Dodd	Y	N	N	Y
Lieberman	Y	N	N	Y
DELAWARE				
Biden	Y	Y	N	Y
Roth	N	Y	Y	N
FLORIDA				
Graham	Y	N	Y	Y
Mack	N	N	Y	N
GEORGIA				
Nunn	Y	N	Y	Y
Coverdell	Y	N	Y	N
HAWAII				
Akaka	Y	N	N	Y
Inouye	Y	N	N	Y
IDAHO				
Craig	N	N	Y	N
Kempthorne	N	N	Y	N
ILLINOIS				
Moseley-Braun	Y	Y	Y	Y
Simon	Y	N	Y	Y
INDIANA				
Coats	N	N	Y	N
Lugar	Y	N	Y	N
IOWA				
Harkin	Y	Y	N	Y
Grassley	N	N	Y	N
KANSAS				
Dole	N	N	Y	N
Kassebaum	Y	N	N	N
KENTUCKY				
Ford	Y	Y	Y	Y
McConnell	N	N	Y	N
LOUISIANA				
Breaux	Y	Y	Y	Y
Johnston	Y	N	N	Y
MAINE				
Mitchell	Y	N	N	Y
Cohen	N	N	Y	N
MARYLAND				
Mikulski	Y	N	N	?
Sarbanes	Y	N	N	Y
MASSACHUSETTS				
Kennedy	Y	N	N	Y
Kerry	Y	N	N	Y
MICHIGAN				
Levin	Y	N	N	Y
Riegle	Y	N	N	Y
MINNESOTA				
Wellstone	Y	N	N	Y
Durenberger	N	N	Y	?
MISSISSIPPI				
Cochran	N	N	Y	N
Lott	N	N	Y	N
MISSOURI				
Bond	N	N	Y	N
Danforth	Y	N	Y	N
MONTANA				
Baucus	Y	N	N	Y
Burns	N	N	Y	N
NEBRASKA				
Exon	Y	N	Y	Y
Kerrey	Y	N	N	Y
NEVADA				
Bryan	Y	Y	Y	Y
Reid	Y	Y	N	Y
NEW HAMPSHIRE				
Gregg	Y	N	Y	N
Smith	N	N	Y	N
NEW JERSEY				
Bradley	Y	N	N	Y
Lautenberg	Y	N	N	Y
NEW MEXICO				
Bingaman	Y	N	Y	Y
Domenici	Y	N	Y	N
NEW YORK				
Moynihan	Y	N	N	Y
D'Amato	N	N	Y	N
NORTH CAROLINA				
Faircloth	N	N	Y	N
Helms	N	N	Y	N
NORTH DAKOTA				
Conrad	Y	Y	N	Y
Dorgan	Y	Y	Y	Y
OHIO				
Glenn	Y	N	N	?
Metzenbaum	Y	N	N	Y
OKLAHOMA				
Boren	Y	N	Y	Y
Nickles	N	N	Y	N
OREGON				
Hatfield	Y	N	N	Y
Packwood	N	N	Y	Y
PENNSYLVANIA				
Wofford	Y	Y	Y	Y
Specter	N	Y	Y	Y
RHODE ISLAND				
Pell	Y	N	N	Y
Chafee	Y	Y	Y	Y
SOUTH CAROLINA				
Hollings	Y	N	Y	Y
Thurmond	N	N	Y	N
SOUTH DAKOTA				
Daschle	Y	Y	Y	Y
Pressler	Y	N	Y	N
TENNESSEE				
Mathews	Y	Y	N	Y
Sasser	Y	Y	Y	Y
TEXAS				
Hutchison	N	N	Y	N
Gramm	N	N	Y	N
UTAH				
Bennett	−	N	Y	N
Hatch	N	N	Y	N
VERMONT				
Leahy	Y	N	N	Y
Jeffords	Y	Y	Y	Y
VIRGINIA				
Robb	Y	N	Y	Y
Warner	Y	N	Y	N
WASHINGTON				
Murray	Y	N	N	Y
Gorton	N	Y	Y	N
WEST VIRGINIA				
Byrd	Y	N	N	Y
Rockefeller	?	N	N	Y
WISCONSIN				
Feingold	Y	Y	N	Y
Kohl	Y	Y	Y	Y
WYOMING				
Simpson	N	N	Y	N
Wallop	N	N	Y	N

ND Northern Democrats   SD Southern Democrats   Southern states - Ala., Ark., Fla., Ga., Ky., La., Miss., N.C., Okla., S.C., Tenn., Texas, Va.

46. Talbott Nomination. Confirmation of President Clinton's nomination of Strobe Talbott of Ohio to be deputy secretary of State. Confirmed 66-31: R 12-31; D 54-0 (ND 41-0, SD 13-0), Feb. 22, 1994. A "yea" was a vote in support of the president's position.

47. S J Res 41. Balanced-Budget Amendment/Substitute. Reid, D-Nev., substitute amendment to propose a constitutional amendment to require a balanced budget but to prohibit the use of Social Security surpluses to mask the deficit, allow Congress to authorize creation of a separate capital budget in which borrowing would be permitted for highway and other unspecified capital improvements, and allow deficit spending during periods of slow economic growth. Rejected 22-78: R 5-39; D 17-39 (ND 13-29, SD 4-10), March 1, 1994. (Although the Reid amendment was only an amendment to the resolution, under a unanimous consent agreement the amendment required a two-thirds majority vote of the Senate, 67 in this case, the same proportion required for final passage of a joint resolution proposing an amendment to the Constitution.)

48. S J Res 41. Balanced-Budget Amendment/Passage. Passage of the joint resolution to propose a constitutional amendment to require a balanced budget by 2001 or the second fiscal year after ratification by three-fourths of the states, whichever is later. Congress could waive the balanced-budget requirement if three-fifths of the House and Senate approved deficit spending, or by a simple majority when a declaration of war was in effect or when there was a threat to national security. The amendment would prohibit the courts from ordering tax increases or spending cuts unless specifically authorized by Congress. Rejected 63-37: R 41-3; D 22-34 (ND 12-30, SD 10-4), March 1, 1994. (A two-thirds majority vote, 67 in this case, is required to pass a joint resolution proposing an amendment to the Constitution.) A "nay" was a vote in support of the president's position.

49. Gould Nomination. Confirmation of President Clinton's nomination of William B. Gould IV of California to be a member of the National Labor Relations Board. Confirmed 58-38: R 5-38; D 53-0 (ND 40-0, SD 13-0), March 2, 1994. A "yea" was a vote in support of the president's position.

KEY

- **Y** Voted for (yea).
- **#** Paired for.
- **+** Announced for.
- **N** Voted against (nay).
- **X** Paired against.
- **−** Announced against.
- **P** Voted "present."
- **C** Voted "present" to avoid possible conflict of interest.
- **?** Did not vote or otherwise make a position known.

Democrats *Republicans*

	50	51	52	53	54	55
ALABAMA						
Heflin	N	Y	Y	N	Y	Y
Shelby	N	Y	Y	N	Y	Y
ALASKA						
Murkowski	N	N	N	N	Y	N
Stevens	N	N	N	N	Y	N
ARIZONA						
DeConcini	N	Y	Y	Y	Y	Y
McCain	N	N	N	N	Y	N
ARKANSAS						
Bumpers	N	Y	Y	N	Y	Y
Pryor	N	Y	Y	Y	Y	?
CALIFORNIA						
Boxer	Y	Y	Y	Y	Y	Y
Feinstein	Y	Y	Y	N	Y	Y
COLORADO						
Campbell	N	Y	?	?	?	?
Brown	N	N	N	N	Y	N
CONNECTICUT						
Dodd	Y	?	?	?	?	?
Lieberman	Y	Y	Y	Y	Y	Y
DELAWARE						
Biden	Y	Y	Y	Y	?	?
Roth	N	N	N	N	Y	N
FLORIDA						
Graham	Y	Y	Y	Y	Y	Y
Mack	N	N	N	N	Y	N
GEORGIA						
Nunn	N	Y	Y	N	Y	Y
Coverdell	N	N	N	N	Y	N
HAWAII						
Akaka	N	Y	Y	Y	Y	Y
Inouye	N	Y	Y	Y	Y	?
IDAHO						
Craig	N	N	N	N	Y	?
Kempthorne	N	N	N	N	Y	N
ILLINOIS						
Moseley-Braun	Y	Y	Y	N	Y	Y
Simon	Y	Y	Y	Y	Y	Y
INDIANA						
Coats	N	N	N	N	Y	N
Lugar	N	N	N	N	Y	N

	50	51	52	53	54	55
IOWA						
Harkin	Y	Y	Y	N	Y	Y
Grassley	N	N	N	N	Y	N
KANSAS						
Dole	N	N	N	N	Y	N
Kassebaum	N	N	N	N	?	N
KENTUCKY						
Ford	N	Y	Y	Y	Y	Y
McConnell	N	N	N	N	Y	N
LOUISIANA						
Breaux	N	Y	Y	N	Y	Y
Johnston	N	Y	Y	Y	Y	Y
MAINE						
Mitchell	Y	Y	Y	Y	Y	Y
Cohen	N	N	N	N	Y	N
MARYLAND						
Mikulski	Y	Y	Y	Y	Y	Y
Sarbanes	Y	Y	Y	Y	Y	Y
MASSACHUSETTS						
Kennedy	Y	Y	Y	Y	Y	Y
Kerry	Y	Y	Y	N	Y	Y
MICHIGAN						
Levin	Y	Y	Y	Y	Y	Y
Riegle	Y	Y	Y	Y	Y	Y
MINNESOTA						
Wellstone	Y	Y	Y	Y	Y	Y
Durenberger	N	N	N	N	?	?
MISSISSIPPI						
Cochran	N	N	N	N	Y	N
Lott	N	N	N	N	Y	N
MISSOURI						
Bond	N	N	N	N	Y	N
Danforth	N	N	N	N	Y	N
MONTANA						
Baucus	Y	Y	Y	N	Y	Y
Burns	N	Y	Y	N	Y	Y
NEBRASKA						
Exon	N	Y	Y	N	Y	Y
Kerrey	N	Y	Y	N	Y	Y
NEVADA						
Bryan	Y	Y	Y	N	Y	Y
Reid	Y	Y	Y	N	Y	Y

	50	51	52	53	54	55
NEW HAMPSHIRE						
Gregg	N	N	N	N	Y	N
Smith	N	N	N	N	Y	N
NEW JERSEY						
Bradley	Y	Y	Y	Y	Y	N
Lautenberg	Y	Y	Y	N	Y	Y
NEW MEXICO						
Bingaman	N	Y	Y	N	Y	Y
Domenici	N	N	N	N	Y	N
NEW YORK						
Moynihan	Y	Y	Y	Y	Y	Y
D'Amato	N	N	N	N	Y	N
NORTH CAROLINA						
Faircloth	N	N	N	N	Y	N
Helms	N	?	N	N	?	?
NORTH DAKOTA						
Conrad	N	Y	Y	N	Y	Y
Dorgan	N	Y	Y	Y	Y	Y
OHIO						
Glenn	Y	Y	Y	Y	Y	Y
Metzenbaum	Y	Y	Y	Y	Y	Y
OKLAHOMA						
Boren	N	Y	Y	N	Y	Y
Nickles	N	N	N	N	Y	N
OREGON						
Hatfield	N	N	N	N	Y	N
Packwood	N	N	N	N	Y	N
PENNSYLVANIA						
Wofford	Y	Y	Y	Y	Y	Y
Specter	N	N	N	N	Y	N
RHODE ISLAND						
Pell	Y	Y	Y	Y	Y	Y
Chafee	N	N	N	N	Y	N
SOUTH CAROLINA						
Hollings	Y	Y	Y	Y	Y	Y
Thurmond	N	N	N	N	Y	N
SOUTH DAKOTA						
Daschle	N	Y	Y	Y	Y	Y
Pressler	N	N	N	N	Y	N
TENNESSEE						
Mathews	N	Y	Y	N	Y	Y
Sasser	N	Y	Y	N	Y	Y

	50	51	52	53	54	55
TEXAS						
Hutchison	N	N	N	N	Y	N
Gramm	N	N	N	N	Y	N
UTAH						
Bennett	N	N	N	N	Y	N
Hatch	N	N	N	N	Y	N
VERMONT						
Leahy	Y	Y	Y	N	Y	Y
Jeffords	Y	Y	Y	N	Y	Y
VIRGINIA						
Robb	Y	Y	Y	Y	Y	Y
Warner	N	N	N	N	Y	N
WASHINGTON						
Murray	Y	Y	Y	Y	Y	Y
Gorton	N	N	N	N	Y	N
WEST VIRGINIA						
Byrd	N	Y	Y	N	Y	Y
Rockefeller	Y	Y	Y	Y	Y	Y
WISCONSIN						
Feingold	Y	Y	Y	Y	Y	N
Kohl	Y	Y	Y	N	Y	N
WYOMING						
Simpson	N	N	N	N	Y	N
Wallop	N	N	N	N	Y	N

ND Northern Democrats   SD Southern Democrats   Southern states - Ala., Ark., Fla., Ga., Ky., La., Miss., N.C., Okla., S.C., Tenn., Texas, Va.

50. S 4. National Competitiveness/Pesticide Safety. Hollings, D-S.C., motion to table (kill) the Cochran, R-Miss., amendment to delay the compliance dates for farmworker pesticide safety requirements until Oct. 23, 1995. (The amendment subsequently was withdrawn after the compliance dates were moved to January 1995.) Motion rejected 35-65: R 1-43; D 34-22 (ND 31-11, SD 3-11), March 9, 1994.

51. S 4. National Competitiveness/Research and Development Tax Credit. Hollings, D-S.C., motion to table (kill) the Danforth, R-Mo., amendment to strike the bill's authorization and direct the Senate Finance Committee to consider using the equivalent amount to make the research and development tax credit permanent. Motion agreed to 57-41: R 2-41; D 55-0 (ND 41-0, SD 14-0), March 9, 1994.

52. S 4. National Competitiveness/Economic Impact Analyses. Hollings, D-S.C., motion to table (kill) the Simpson, R-Wyo., amendment to require economic impact analyses and cost-benefit reports on new federal regulations and proposed legislation. Motion agreed to 56-42: R 2-42; D 54-0 (ND 40-0, SD 14-0), March 10, 1994.

53. S 4. National Competitiveness/Regulatory Flexibility Act. Glenn, D-Ohio, motion to table (kill) the Wallop, R-Wyo., amendment to amend the Regulatory Flexibility Act to strengthen the analysis of the regulatory burden on small businesses and municipalities. Motion rejected 31-67: R 0-44; D 31-23 (ND 25-15, SD 6-8), March 10, 1994.

54. S 4. National Competitiveness/Political Contributions. Brown, R-Colo., amendment to make it a felony for a federal official giving grants under the bill to solicit political contributions from a grant recipient for five years. Adopted 94-0: R 41-0; D 53-0 (ND 39-0, SD 14-0), March 10, 1994.

55. S 4. National Competitiveness/Authorization Reduction. Hollings, D-S.C., motion to table (kill) the Brown, R-Colo., amendment to reduce the authorization in the bill to $1.5 billion, the same level authorized by the House, from $2.8 billion. Motion agreed to 49-43: R 2-39; D 47-4 (ND 34-4, SD 13-0), March 10, 1994.

	56 57 58 59 60 61 62
ALABAMA	
Heflin	Y Y Y Y Y N Y
Shelby	Y Y Y N Y N Y
ALASKA	
Murkowski	Y Y N Y N Y Y
Stevens	Y Y N N Y Y Y
ARIZONA	
DeConcini	Y Y Y N Y Y Y
McCain	Y Y N Y N Y Y
ARKANSAS	
Bumpers	Y Y Y N Y Y Y
Pryor	Y Y Y N Y Y Y
CALIFORNIA	
Boxer	Y Y Y N Y Y Y
Feinstein	Y Y Y N Y Y Y
COLORADO	
Campbell	? ? Y N Y Y Y
Brown	Y Y N Y N Y Y
CONNECTICUT	
Dodd	? ? Y N Y Y Y
Lieberman	Y Y Y N Y Y Y
DELAWARE	
Biden	+ ? Y N Y N Y
Roth	Y Y N Y N Y Y
FLORIDA	
Graham	Y Y Y N Y Y Y
Mack	Y ? N Y N Y Y
GEORGIA	
Nunn	Y Y Y N Y Y Y
Coverdell	Y Y N Y N Y Y
HAWAII	
Akaka	Y Y Y N Y Y Y
Inouye	Y Y Y N Y Y Y
IDAHO	
Craig	Y Y N Y N Y Y
Kempthorne	Y Y N Y N Y Y
ILLINOIS	
Moseley-Braun	Y Y Y N Y Y Y
Simon	N Y Y N Y N Y
INDIANA	
Coats	Y Y N Y N Y Y
Lugar	Y Y N Y N Y Y

	56 57 58 59 60 61 62
IOWA	
Harkin	? ? Y N Y Y Y
Grassley	Y Y N Y N Y Y
KANSAS	
Dole	Y Y N Y N Y Y
Kassebaum	Y Y N Y Y Y Y
KENTUCKY	
Ford	Y Y Y N Y Y Y
McConnell	Y Y N Y N Y Y
LOUISIANA	
Breaux	Y Y Y N Y Y Y
Johnston	Y Y Y N Y Y Y
MAINE	
Mitchell	Y Y Y N Y Y Y
Cohen	Y ? N Y Y Y Y
MARYLAND	
Mikulski	? ? Y N Y Y Y
Sarbanes	Y Y Y N Y Y Y
MASSACHUSETTS	
Kennedy	? ? Y N Y Y Y
Kerry	Y Y Y N Y Y Y
MICHIGAN	
Levin	Y Y Y N Y Y Y
Riegle	Y Y Y N Y Y Y
MINNESOTA	
Wellstone	Y Y Y N Y N Y
Durenberger	? ? N Y N Y Y
MISSISSIPPI	
Cochran	Y Y N Y N Y Y
Lott	Y Y N Y N Y Y
MISSOURI	
Bond	Y Y N Y N Y Y
Danforth	Y Y N Y N Y Y
MONTANA	
Baucus	Y Y Y N Y Y Y
Burns	Y Y N N Y Y Y
NEBRASKA	
Exon	Y Y Y N Y Y Y
Kerrey	Y Y Y N Y Y Y
NEVADA	
Bryan	Y Y Y N Y Y Y
Reid	Y Y Y N Y Y Y

	56 57 58 59 60 61 62
NEW HAMPSHIRE	
Gregg	Y ? N N N Y Y
Smith	Y Y N Y N Y Y
NEW JERSEY	
Bradley	Y Y Y Y N N Y
Lautenberg	Y Y Y N Y Y Y
NEW MEXICO	
Bingaman	Y Y Y N Y Y Y
Domenici	Y ? N Y N Y Y
NEW YORK	
Moynihan	Y Y Y N Y Y Y
D'Amato	Y Y N Y N Y Y
NORTH CAROLINA	
Faircloth	Y Y N Y N Y Y
Helms	Y Y N Y N Y Y
NORTH DAKOTA	
Conrad	Y Y Y N Y Y Y
Dorgan	Y Y Y N Y Y Y
OHIO	
Glenn	Y Y Y N Y Y Y
Metzenbaum	Y ? Y N Y Y Y
OKLAHOMA	
Boren	Y Y ? ? ? + Y
Nickles	Y ? N Y N Y Y
OREGON	
Hatfield	N + ? Y Y Y Y
Packwood	Y Y N Y N Y Y
PENNSYLVANIA	
Wofford	Y ? Y N Y N Y
Specter	Y Y N Y N N Y
RHODE ISLAND	
Pell	Y Y Y N Y Y Y
Chafee	Y Y N Y N Y Y
SOUTH CAROLINA	
Hollings	Y Y Y N Y Y Y
Thurmond	Y Y N Y N Y +
SOUTH DAKOTA	
Daschle	Y Y Y N Y Y Y
Pressler	Y Y N Y N Y Y
TENNESSEE	
Mathews	Y Y Y N Y Y Y
Sasser	Y Y Y N Y Y Y

KEY

Y Voted for (yea).
Paired for.
+ Announced for.
N Voted against (nay).
X Paired against.
− Announced against.
P Voted "present."
C Voted "present" to avoid possible conflict of interest.
? Did not vote or otherwise make a position known.

Democrats *Republicans*

	56 57 58 59 60 61 62
TEXAS	
Hutchison	Y Y N Y N Y Y
Gramm	Y ? N Y N Y Y
UTAH	
Bennett	Y Y N Y N Y Y
Hatch	Y Y N Y N Y Y
VERMONT	
Leahy	Y Y Y N Y Y Y
Jeffords	Y ? Y Y Y Y Y
VIRGINIA	
Robb	Y Y Y N Y Y Y
Warner	Y Y N Y N Y Y
WASHINGTON	
Murray	Y Y Y N Y Y Y
Gorton	Y Y N Y N Y Y
WEST VIRGINIA	
Byrd	Y Y Y N Y Y Y
Rockefeller	Y Y Y N Y Y Y
WISCONSIN	
Feingold	Y Y Y N N Y Y
Kohl	Y Y Y Y Y Y Y
WYOMING	
Simpson	Y Y N Y N Y +
Wallop	? ? N Y N Y Y

ND Northern Democrats   SD Southern Democrats   Southern states - Ala., Ark., Fla., Ga., Ky., La., Miss., N.C., Okla., S.C., Tenn., Texas, Va.

56. S 4. National Competitiveness/Crime Trust Fund. Gramm, R-Texas, amendment to establish a Violent Crime Reduction Trust Fund within the Treasury Department. Adopted 90-2: R 41-1; D 49-1 (ND 35-1, SD 14-0), March 11, 1994.

57. S 4. National Competitiveness/Heroic Acts. Kempthorne, R-Idaho, amendment to exempt employers from penalties or citations under the Occupational Health and Safety Act for heroic actions taken by individual employees to rescue others. Adopted 82-0: R 34-0; D 48-0 (ND 34-0, SD 14-0), March 11, 1994.

58. S 4. National Competitiveness/Cloture. Motion to invoke cloture (thus limiting debate) on the bill to authorize $2.8 billion over fiscal 1995-96 for grants and loans to expand technology development and computer manufacturing programs through the Commerce Department. Motion rejected 56-42: R 1-42; D 55-0 (ND 42-0, SD 13-0), March 15, 1994. Three-fifths of the total Senate (60) is required to invoke cloture.

59. S 4. National Competitiveness/Venture Capital. Danforth, R-Mo., amendment to eliminate venture capital loan guarantees from the bill and reduce the bill's authorization by $100 million. Rejected 44-55: R 41-3; D 3-52 (ND 2-40, SD 1-12), March 16, 1994.

60. HR 820. National Competitiveness/Passage. Passage of the bill to authorize $1.9 billion over fiscal 1995-96 for grants and loans to expand technology development and computer manufacturing programs under the Commerce Department. The authorization level was reduced by unanimous consent on the floor from the committee-passed bill's level of $2.8 billion. Passed 59-40: R 6-38; D 53-2 (ND 40-2, SD 13-0), March 16, 1994. (Before passage, the Senate struck all after the enacting clause and inserted the text of S 4 as amended.) A "yea" was a vote in support of the president's position.

61. S 1458. General Aviation Revitalization/Passage. Passage of the bill to limit product liability lawsuits against the manufacturers of small planes. For crashes involving planes or parts more than 18 years old, the bill would bar injured passengers from claiming that design or manufacturing defects were to blame. Passed 91-8: R 43-1; D 48-7 (ND 37-5, SD 11-2), March 16, 1994.

62. S 1275. Community Development Banks/Whitewater Hearings. Mitchell, D-Maine, amendment to express the sense of the Senate that the majority and Republican leaders should meet to determine the time, procedures and forum for congressional oversight hearings on all matters related to Madison Guaranty Savings and Loan and Whitewater Development Corp. without granting witnesses immunity or interfering with the ongoing investigation of special counsel Robert B. Fiske Jr. Adopted 98-0: R 42-0; D 56-0 (ND 42-0, SD 14-0), March 17, 1994.

KEY

Y   Voted for (yea).
Paired for.
+   Announced for.
N   Voted against (nay).
X   Paired against.
—   Announced against.
P   Voted "present."
C   Voted "present" to avoid possible conflict of interest.
?   Did not vote or otherwise make a position known.

Democrats   *Republicans*

	63	64	65	66	67	68	69	70
ALABAMA								
Heflin	Y	N	Y	N	N	Y	N	Y
Shelby	N	N	Y	N	N	Y	N	?
ALASKA								
Murkowski	N	N	Y	Y	N	Y	N	Y
Stevens	N	N	Y	Y	N	Y	N	Y
ARIZONA								
DeConcini	Y	Y	Y	N	N	Y	N	?
McCain	Y	N	Y	Y	N	Y	N	Y
ARKANSAS								
Bumpers	Y	Y	Y	N	Y	N	N	Y
Pryor	Y	Y	Y	N	Y	N	Y	N
CALIFORNIA								
Boxer	Y	Y	Y	N	Y	N	Y	N
Feinstein	Y	N	Y	N	N	Y	N	Y
COLORADO								
Campbell	Y	N	Y	N	N	Y	N	Y
Brown	Y	N	Y	Y	N	Y	Y	N
CONNECTICUT								
Dodd	Y	Y	Y	N	N	Y	N	Y
Lieberman	Y	N	Y	N	N	Y	N	Y
DELAWARE								
Biden	Y	Y	Y	N	N	Y	N	?
Roth	Y	N	Y	Y	N	Y	Y	Y
FLORIDA								
Graham	Y	N	Y	N	N	Y	N	Y
Mack	Y	N	Y	Y	N	Y	Y	Y
GEORGIA								
Nunn	Y	N	Y	N	N	Y	N	?
Coverdell	Y	N	Y	Y	N	Y	Y	N
HAWAII								
Akaka	Y	Y	Y	N	N	Y	N	Y
Inouye	?	?	?	N	N	Y	N	Y
IDAHO								
Craig	Y	N	Y	N	N	Y	Y	N
Kempthorne	Y	N	Y	N	Y	Y	Y	N
ILLINOIS								
Moseley-Braun	Y	Y	Y	N	N	Y	N	Y
Simon	Y	Y	Y	N	N	Y	N	Y
INDIANA								
Coats	Y	N	Y	N	Y	N	N	N
Lugar	Y	N	Y	Y	N	Y	N	N
IOWA								
Harkin	Y	Y	Y	N	Y	Y	N	Y
Grassley	Y	N	Y	Y	N	Y	Y	N
KANSAS								
Dole	Y	N	Y	Y	N	Y	N	Y
Kassebaum	Y	N	Y	Y	N	N	Y	Y
KENTUCKY								
Ford	Y	N	Y	N	Y	Y	N	Y
McConnell	Y	N	Y	Y	N	Y	N	Y
LOUISIANA								
Breaux	Y	Y	Y	N	Y	N	Y	N
Johnston	Y	N	Y	N	N	Y	N	?
MAINE								
Mitchell	Y	Y	Y	N	Y	N	Y	N
Cohen	Y	N	Y	Y	N	Y	Y	Y
MARYLAND								
Mikulski	Y	Y	Y	N	Y	N	Y	N
Sarbanes	Y	Y	Y	N	Y	N	Y	N
MASSACHUSETTS								
Kennedy	Y	Y	Y	N	Y	N	Y	N
Kerry	Y	Y	Y	N	N	Y	N	Y
MICHIGAN								
Levin	Y	Y	Y	N	Y	N	Y	N
Riegle	Y	Y	Y	N	?	?	?	Y
MINNESOTA								
Wellstone	Y	Y	Y	N	Y	N	Y	N
Durenberger	Y	N	Y	Y	N	Y	N	Y
MISSISSIPPI								
Cochran	Y	N	Y	N	Y	N	Y	Y
Lott	Y	N	Y	Y	Y	Y	Y	N
MISSOURI								
Bond	Y	N	Y	N	Y	N	Y	Y
Danforth	Y	N	Y	Y	N	Y	Y	Y
MONTANA								
Baucus	Y	Y	Y	N	N	Y	N	Y
Burns	Y	N	Y	Y	N	Y	Y	N
NEBRASKA								
Exon	Y	N	Y	N	N	Y	N	Y
Kerrey	Y	N	Y	N	N	Y	N	Y
NEVADA								
Bryan	Y	N	Y	N	N	Y	N	Y
Reid	Y	Y	Y	N	Y	N	Y	N
NEW HAMPSHIRE								
Gregg	Y	N	Y	Y	Y	Y	Y	N
Smith	Y	N	Y	N	Y	Y	Y	N
NEW JERSEY								
Bradley	Y	Y	Y	N	N	Y	N	Y
Lautenberg	Y	Y	Y	N	N	Y	N	Y
NEW MEXICO								
Bingaman	Y	N	Y	N	N	Y	N	Y
Domenici	Y	N	Y	Y	N	Y	N	Y
NEW YORK								
Moynihan	Y	Y	Y	N	Y	N	Y	N
D'Amato	Y	N	Y	Y	N	Y	Y	?
NORTH CAROLINA								
Faircloth	N	N	Y	N	N	Y	N	N
Helms	N	N	Y	N	N	Y	N	N
NORTH DAKOTA								
Conrad	Y	N	Y	N	N	Y	N	Y
Dorgan	Y	Y	?	N	N	Y	N	Y
OHIO								
Glenn	Y	N	Y	N	N	Y	N	Y
Metzenbaum	Y	Y	Y	N	?	?	?	?
OKLAHOMA								
Boren	Y	Y	Y	N	N	Y	N	?
Nickles	Y	N	Y	Y	N	Y	Y	N
OREGON								
Hatfield	Y	Y	Y	Y	Y	Y	N	Y
Packwood	Y	N	Y	Y	N	Y	N	N
PENNSYLVANIA								
Wofford	Y	Y	Y	N	Y	N	Y	N
Specter	Y	N	Y	Y	Y	Y	N	Y
RHODE ISLAND								
Pell	Y	Y	Y	N	Y	N	Y	N
Chafee	Y	N	Y	N	Y	N	Y	N
SOUTH CAROLINA								
Hollings	N	Y	N	N	Y	N	Y	N
Thurmond	N	N	Y	Y	N	Y	Y	N
SOUTH DAKOTA								
Daschle	Y	Y	Y	N	Y	N	Y	N
Pressler	Y	N	Y	Y	N	Y	N	N
TENNESSEE								
Mathews	Y	Y	Y	N	Y	N	Y	N
Sasser	Y	Y	Y	N	Y	N	Y	N
TEXAS								
Hutchison	Y	N	Y	Y	N	Y	Y	N
Gramm	Y	N	Y	Y	N	Y	Y	N
UTAH								
Bennett	Y	N	Y	Y	N	Y	Y	N
Hatch	Y	N	Y	Y	N	Y	Y	N
VERMONT								
Leahy	Y	Y	Y	N	Y	N	Y	N
Jeffords	Y	Y	Y	N	Y	N	Y	N
VIRGINIA								
Robb	Y	N	Y	N	N	Y	N	Y
Warner	Y	N	Y	Y	N	Y	Y	N
WASHINGTON								
Murray	Y	Y	Y	N	Y	N	Y	N
Gorton	Y	N	Y	Y	Y	Y	Y	Y
WEST VIRGINIA								
Byrd	Y	N	Y	N	Y	N	Y	N
Rockefeller	Y	Y	Y	N	Y	N	Y	N
WISCONSIN								
Feingold	Y	Y	Y	N	N	Y	N	Y
Kohl	Y	Y	Y	N	N	Y	N	Y
WYOMING								
Simpson	N	N	Y	Y	N	Y	N	Y
Wallop	N	N	Y	Y	N	N	Y	?

ND Northern Democrats   SD Southern Democrats   Southern states - Ala., Ark., Fla., Ga., Ky., La., Miss., N.C., Okla., S.C., Tenn., Texas, Va.

63. S 208. National Park Service Concessions/Passage. Passage of the bill to repeal a 1965 law that allows private companies exclusive rights to renew contracts within national parks for operations ranging from snack bars to hotels and establish a competitive bidding process for concession contracts in national parks. Passed 90-9: R 37-7; D 53-2 (ND 41-0, SD 12-2), March 22, 1994.

64. S Con Res 63. Fiscal 1995 Budget Resolution/Strategic Defense Initiative Cut. Harkin, D-Iowa, amendment to transfer $513 million from the Ballistic Missile Defense program (formerly the Strategic Defense Initiative), with $423 million going to state and local drug enforcement and $90 million to deficit reduction. Rejected 40-59: R 2-42; D 38-17 (ND 31-10, SD 7-7), March 22, 1994.

65. S Con Res 63. Fiscal 1995 Budget Resolution/Drug Enforcement Increase. Gorton, R-Wash., amendment to transfer $423 million from the governmentwide account for furniture and furnishings to state and local drug enforcement. Adopted 97-1: R 44-0; D 53-1 (ND 40-0, SD 13-1), March 22, 1994.

66. S Con Res 63. Fiscal 1995 Budget Resolution/Republican Substitute. Domenici, R-N.M., substitute amendment to cut an additional $318 billion over five years, chiefly through a $180 billion cut in non-defense discretionary spending and by using savings from Medicare and Medicaid for deficit reduction and not to finance a health care overhaul. The substitute also would have provided a $500-per-child tax credit for families, indexed capital gains for inflation, saved $33 billion by overhauling the welfare system, created individual retirement accounts for homemakers and first-time home buyers, and increased defense spending by $18.5 billion over five years. Rejected 42-58: R 42-2; D 0-56 (ND 0-42, SD 0-14), March 23, 1994. A "nay" was a vote in support of the president's position.

67. S Con Res 63. Fiscal 1995 Budget Resolution/Special Education Programs. Dodd, D-Conn., amendment to increase education spending for individuals with disabilities by $6 billion in fiscal 1995 and $30.5 billion over five years, and offset the increases by cutting intelligence spending, canceling the Milstar backup military communications satellite system and preserving about half the $26.1 billion in additional five-year cuts from discretionary spending proposed by the Senate Budget Committee. Rejected 33-65: R 7-37; D 26-28 (ND 20-20, SD 6-8), March 23, 1994.

68. S Con Res 63. Fiscal 1995 Budget Resolution/Children's Programs. Boxer, D-Calif., amendment to transfer $1 billion to five children's programs from accounts for non-essential federal government travel. Adopted 93-5: R 40-4; D 53-1 (ND 40-0, SD 13-1), March 23, 1994.

69. S Con Res 63. Fiscal 1995 Budget Resolution/Non-Defense Cuts. Lott, R-Miss., amendment to require that $26.1 billion in five-year discretionary spending cuts, proposed by the Senate Budget Committee to reduce the deficit below the amount proposed by President Clinton, come from non-defense accounts and to require an additional $20 billion in five-year deficit reduction by cutting mandatory spending programs. Rejected 34-64: R 34-10; D 0-54 (ND 0-40, SD 0-14), March 23, 1994.

70. HR 1804. Goals 2000: Educate America/Motion To Proceed. Mitchell, D-Maine, motion to proceed to the conference report to authorize $400 million in fiscal 1994 and such sums as necessary in fiscal 1995-98 for competitive grants for schools seeking to improve their performance, write into law national education goals, and establish tests and standards for elementary and secondary students. Motion agreed to 60-31: R 11-31; D 49-0 (ND 39-0, SD 10-0), March 24, 1994 (in the session that began and the Congressional Record dated March 23).

	71	72	73	74	75	76	77	78
ALABAMA								
Heflin	Y	N	Y	Y	Y	Y	Y	Y
Shelby	?	?	Y	Y	Y	Y	Y	Y
ALASKA								
Murkowski	N	Y	N	Y	N	N	Y	Y
Stevens	Y	Y	N	N	Y	Y	Y	N
ARIZONA								
DeConcini	?	N	Y	N	Y	Y	Y	N
McCain	N	Y	Y	Y	N	N	Y	Y
ARKANSAS								
Bumpers	Y	N	N	N	Y	Y	Y	N
Pryor	Y	N	N	N	Y	Y	Y	N
CALIFORNIA								
Boxer	Y	N	N	N	Y	Y	Y	N
Feinstein	Y	N	N	N	Y	Y	Y	N
COLORADO								
Campbell	Y	N	N	Y	Y	Y	Y	N
Brown	N	N	Y	N	Y	N	N	Y
CONNECTICUT								
Dodd	Y	N	N	N	Y	Y	Y	N
Lieberman	Y	Y	Y	N	Y	Y	Y	N
DELAWARE								
Biden	?	?	?	?	?	?	Y	N
Roth	N	N	Y	Y	N	N	Y	Y
FLORIDA								
Graham	Y	N	N	Y	Y	Y	Y	N
Mack	N	N	Y	Y	N	N	Y	Y
GEORGIA								
Nunn	?	Y	Y	Y	Y	Y	Y	N
Coverdell	N	N	Y	Y	N	N	N	Y
HAWAII								
Akaka	Y	N	N	N	Y	Y	Y	N
Inouye	Y	N	N	N	Y	Y	Y	N
IDAHO								
Craig	N	Y	Y	Y	N	N	Y	Y
Kempthorne	N	Y	Y	Y	N	N	Y	Y
ILLINOIS								
Moseley-Braun	Y	N	Y	N	Y	Y	Y	N
Simon	Y	N	Y	N	Y	Y	Y	N
INDIANA								
Coats	N	Y	Y	Y	N	N	Y	Y
Lugar	N	Y	Y	Y	N	N	Y	N

	71	72	73	74	75	76	77	78
IOWA								
Harkin	Y	N	N	N	Y	Y	Y	N
Grassley	N	N	Y	Y	N	N	Y	Y
KANSAS								
Dole	Y	Y	Y	Y	N	N	Y	N
Kassebaum	Y	Y	Y	Y	N	Y	Y	N
KENTUCKY								
Ford	Y	N	N	N	Y	Y	Y	N
McConnell	N	Y	Y	Y	N	N	Y	Y
LOUISIANA								
Breaux	Y	N	Y	Y	Y	Y	Y	N
Johnston	?	Y	N	N	Y	Y	Y	N
MAINE								
Mitchell	Y	N	N	N	Y	Y	Y	N
Cohen	Y	Y	Y	N	N	Y	Y	N
MARYLAND								
Mikulski	Y	N	N	N	Y	Y	Y	N
Sarbanes	Y	N	N	N	Y	Y	Y	N
MASSACHUSETTS								
Kennedy	Y	N	N	N	Y	Y	Y	N
Kerry	Y	N	Y	N	Y	Y	Y	N
MICHIGAN								
Levin	Y	N	N	N	Y	Y	Y	N
Riegle	Y	N	N	N	Y	Y	Y	N
MINNESOTA								
Wellstone	Y	N	N	N	Y	Y	Y	N
Durenberger	Y	N	Y	Y	N	N	Y	N
MISSISSIPPI								
Cochran	N	Y	Y	N	N	Y	Y	N
Lott	N	N	Y	Y	N	N	Y	Y
MISSOURI								
Bond	N	Y	Y	Y	N	N	Y	Y
Danforth	N	Y	Y	Y	N	N	Y	Y
MONTANA								
Baucus	Y	N	N	N	Y	Y	Y	N
Burns	N	Y	Y	+	N	N	Y	Y
NEBRASKA								
Exon	Y	N	N	N	Y	Y	Y	N
Kerrey	Y	N	Y	Y	Y	Y	Y	N
NEVADA								
Bryan	Y	N	Y	N	Y	Y	Y	N
Reid	Y	N	N	N	Y	Y	Y	N

	71	72	73	74	75	76	77	78
NEW HAMPSHIRE								
Gregg	N	N	Y	Y	N	N	Y	Y
Smith	N	N	Y	Y	N	N	Y	Y
NEW JERSEY								
Bradley	Y	N	N	N	Y	Y	Y	N
Lautenberg	Y	N	Y	Y	Y	Y	Y	N
NEW MEXICO								
Bingaman	Y	Y	N	Y	Y	Y	Y	N
Domenici	Y	Y	Y	Y	N	Y	Y	N
NEW YORK								
Moynihan	Y	N	N	N	Y	Y	Y	N
D'Amato	?	N	Y	Y	N	N	Y	Y
NORTH CAROLINA								
Faircloth	N	N	Y	Y	N	N	Y	Y
Helms	N	Y	Y	Y	N	N	Y	Y
NORTH DAKOTA								
Conrad	Y	N	N	N	Y	Y	Y	N
Dorgan	Y	N	N	N	Y	Y	Y	N
OHIO								
Glenn	Y	Y	N	Y	Y	Y	Y	N
Metzenbaum	?	N	N	N	Y	Y	Y	N
OKLAHOMA								
Boren	?	Y	N	N	Y	Y	Y	N
Nickles	N	N	Y	Y	N	N	Y	Y
OREGON								
Hatfield	Y	N	N	Y	Y	Y	Y	N
Packwood	N	Y	Y	N	N	Y	Y	N
PENNSYLVANIA								
Wofford	Y	N	Y	N	Y	Y	Y	N
Specter	Y	Y	Y	N	Y	N	Y	N
RHODE ISLAND								
Pell	Y	N	Y	N	Y	Y	Y	N
Chafee	Y	N	Y	N	Y	N	Y	N
SOUTH CAROLINA								
Hollings	Y	Y	N	N	Y	Y	Y	N
Thurmond	Y	Y	Y	N	Y	Y	Y	N
SOUTH DAKOTA								
Daschle	Y	N	N	N	Y	Y	Y	N
Pressler	N	Y	Y	Y	N	N	Y	Y
TENNESSEE								
Mathews	Y	N	N	N	Y	Y	Y	N
Sasser	Y	N	N	N	Y	Y	Y	N

KEY

Y Voted for (yea).
Paired for.
+ Announced for.
N Voted against (nay).
X Paired against.
− Announced against.
P Voted "present."
C Voted "present" to avoid possible conflict of interest.
? Did not vote or otherwise make a position known.

Democrats   *Republicans*

	71	72	73	74	75	76	77	78
TEXAS								
Hutchison	N	N	Y	Y	N	N	Y	Y
Gramm	N	N	Y	Y	N	N	Y	Y
UTAH								
Bennett	N	Y	Y	N	N	N	Y	Y
Hatch	N	Y	Y	N	N	N	Y	Y
VERMONT								
Leahy	Y	N	N	Y	Y	Y	Y	N
Jeffords	Y	N	N	Y	N	N	Y	N
VIRGINIA								
Robb	Y	Y	Y	Y	Y	Y	Y	N
Warner	Y	Y	Y	Y	Y	Y	Y	N
WASHINGTON								
Murray	Y	N	N	N	Y	Y	Y	N
Gorton	Y	N	Y	N	N	N	Y	Y
WEST VIRGINIA								
Byrd	Y	Y	N	N	Y	Y	Y	N
Rockefeller	Y	N	N	N	Y	Y	Y	+
WISCONSIN								
Feingold	Y	N	N	N	Y	Y	Y	N
Kohl	Y	N	Y	Y	Y	Y	Y	N
WYOMING								
Simpson	N	Y	Y	Y	N	N	Y	Y
Wallop	?	N	Y	Y	N	N	Y	Y

ND Northern Democrats   SD Southern Democrats   Southern states - Ala., Ark., Fla., Ga., Ky., La., Miss., N.C., Okla., S.C., Tenn., Texas, Va.

71. HR 3345. Federal Work Force Restructuring/Motion to Proceed. Mitchell, D-Maine, motion to proceed to the conference report on the bill to authorize financial incentives of up to $25,000 per worker to encourage voluntary retirements or resignations from the federal work force. Motion agreed to 62-29: R 13-29; D 49-0 (ND 39-0, SD 10-0), March 24, 1994 (in the session that began and the Congressional Record dated March 23).

72. S Con Res 63. Fiscal 1995 Budget Resolution/Mandatory Spending Cuts. Domenici, R-N.M., amendment to cancel the $26.1 billion in five-year discretionary spending cuts proposed by the Senate Budget Committee below the levels proposed by President Clinton and instead cut $20 billion in mandatory spending and $6 billion in discretionary spending, with most cuts occurring in 1999. Rejected 35-63: R 26-18; D 9-45 (ND 4-37, SD 5-8), March 24, 1994.

73. S Con Res 63. Fiscal 1995 Budget Resolution/Spending Reduction Commission. Mack, R-Fla., amendment to express the sense of the Senate that a Spending Reduction Commission should be created to propose annual spending cuts to balance the budget. Adopted 57-42: R 40-4; D 17-38 (ND 12-29, SD 5-9), March 24, 1994.

74. S Con Res 63. Fiscal 1995 Budget Resolution/Legislative Branch Reduction. Hutchison, R-Texas, amendment to reduce legislative branch appropriations in fiscal 1995 by 7.5 percent and freeze them at that level through 1999, saving $200 million in 1995 and $2.4 billion by 1999. Rejected 48-50: R 37-6; D 11-44 (ND 5-36, SD 6-8), March 24, 1994.

75. HR 3345. Federal Work Force Restructuring/Cloture. Motion to invoke cloture (thus limiting debate) on the conference report on the bill to authorize financial incentives of up to $25,000 per worker to encourage voluntary retirements or resignations from the federal work force. Motion rejected 58-41: R 3-41; D 55-0 (ND 41-0, SD 14-0), March 24, 1994. Three-fifths of the total Senate (60) is required to invoke cloture. A "yea" was a vote in support of the president's position.

76. HR 3345. Federal Work Force Restructuring/Cloture. Motion to invoke cloture (thus limiting debate) on the conference report on the bill to authorize financial incentives of up to $25,000 per worker to encourage voluntary retirements or resignations from the federal work force. Motion agreed to 63-36: R 8-36; D 55-0 (ND 41-0, SD 14-0), March 24, 1994. Three-fifths of the total Senate (60) is required to invoke cloture. A "yea" was a vote in support of the president's position.

77. HR 3345. Federal Work Force Restructuring/Adoption. Adoption of the conference report on the bill to authorize financial incentives of up to $25,000 per worker to encourage voluntary retirements or resignations from the federal work force. Adopted (thus cleared for the president) 99-1: R 43-1; D 56-0 (ND 42-0, SD 14-0), March 24, 1994. A "yea" was a vote in support of the president's position.

78. S Con Res 63. Fiscal 1995 Budget Resolution/Spending Freeze. Gramm, R-Texas, amendment to accept all of President Clinton's discretionary spending cuts except those to law enforcement and then freeze discretionary spending authority for the next five years, and to reject all of Clinton's discretionary spending increases. Savings would go to reduce the deficit and to double the tax exemption for dependent children. Rejected 32-67: R 30-14; D 2-53 (ND 0-41, SD 2-12), March 24, 1994.

	79	80	81	82
ALABAMA				
Heflin	N	N	N	Y
Shelby	Y	Y	N	Y
ALASKA				
Murkowski	Y	Y	N	N
Stevens	Y	N	N	N
ARIZONA				
DeConcini	N	N	Y	Y
McCain	Y	Y	N	N
ARKANSAS				
Bumpers	N	N	Y	Y
Pryor	N	N	Y	Y
CALIFORNIA				
Boxer	N	Y	Y	Y
Feinstein	N	Y	Y	Y
COLORADO				
Campbell	N	N	Y	Y
Brown	Y	Y	N	N
CONNECTICUT				
Dodd	N	N	Y	Y
Lieberman	Y	N	N	Y
DELAWARE				
Biden	N	N	Y	Y
Roth	Y	N	N	N
FLORIDA				
Graham	N	Y	N	Y
Mack	Y	Y	N	N
GEORGIA				
Nunn	Y	N	N	Y
Coverdell	Y	Y	N	N
HAWAII				
Akaka	N	N	Y	Y
Inouye	N	N	Y	Y
IDAHO				
Craig	N	Y	N	N
Kempthorne	N	Y	N	N
ILLINOIS				
Moseley-Braun	N	N	Y	Y
Simon	N	N	Y	Y
INDIANA				
Coats	Y	Y	N	N
Lugar	Y	Y	N	N

	79	80	81	82
IOWA				
Harkin	N	N	Y	Y
Grassley	N	Y	N	N
KANSAS				
Dole	Y	Y	N	N
Kassebaum	N	N	N	N
KENTUCKY				
Ford	N	N	Y	Y
McConnell	Y	Y	N	N
LOUISIANA				
Breaux	N	N	Y	Y
Johnston	N	N	Y	Y
MAINE				
Mitchell	N	N	N	Y
Cohen	Y	?	?	?
MARYLAND				
Mikulski	N	N	Y	Y
Sarbanes	N	N	Y	Y
MASSACHUSETTS				
Kennedy	N	N	Y	Y
Kerry	N	N	Y	Y
MICHIGAN				
Levin	N	N	Y	Y
Riegle	N	N	Y	Y
MINNESOTA				
Wellstone	N	N	Y	Y
Durenberger	N	Y	N	N
MISSISSIPPI				
Cochran	N	Y	N	N
Lott	Y	Y	N	?
MISSOURI				
Bond	?	N	N	N
Danforth	Y	N	N	N
MONTANA				
Baucus	N	N	Y	Y
Burns	N	Y	N	N
NEBRASKA				
Exon	N	N	N	Y
Kerrey	N	N	N	Y
NEVADA				
Bryan	N	N	Y	Y
Reid	N	N	Y	Y

	79	80	81	82
NEW HAMPSHIRE				
Gregg	N	Y	N	N
Smith	Y	Y	N	N
NEW JERSEY				
Bradley	N	N	Y	Y
Lautenberg	N	N	Y	Y
NEW MEXICO				
Bingaman	N	N	N	Y
Domenici	N	Y	N	N
NEW YORK				
Moynihan	N	N	Y	Y
D'Amato	N	Y	N	N
NORTH CAROLINA				
Faircloth	N	Y	N	N
Helms	Y	Y	N	N
NORTH DAKOTA				
Conrad	N	N	Y	Y
Dorgan	N	N	Y	Y
OHIO				
Glenn	Y	N	Y	Y
Metzenbaum	N	N	Y	Y
OKLAHOMA				
Boren	N	N	N	Y
Nickles	N	Y	N	N
OREGON				
Hatfield	N	N	N	Y
Packwood	N	N	N	N
PENNSYLVANIA				
Wofford	N	N	Y	Y
Specter	N	N	N	N
RHODE ISLAND				
Pell	N	N	Y	Y
Chafee	N	N	N	N
SOUTH CAROLINA				
Hollings	N	?	?	?
Thurmond	Y	Y	N	N
SOUTH DAKOTA				
Daschle	N	N	Y	Y
Pressler	N	Y	N	N
TENNESSEE				
Mathews	N	N	Y	Y
Sasser	N	N	Y	Y

KEY

Y   Voted for (yea).
Paired for.
+   Announced for.
N   Voted against (nay).
X   Paired against.
−   Announced against.
P   Voted "present."
C   Voted "present" to avoid possible conflict of interest.
?   Did not vote or otherwise make a position known.

Democrats   *Republicans*

	79	80	81	82
TEXAS				
Hutchison	Y	Y	N	N
Gramm	?	Y	N	N
UTAH				
Bennett	Y	Y	N	N
Hatch	Y	Y	N	N
VERMONT				
Leahy	N	N	Y	Y
Jeffords	N	N	Y	Y
VIRGINIA				
Robb	Y	N	N	Y
Warner	Y	Y	N	N
WASHINGTON				
Murray	N	N	Y	Y
Gorton	Y	Y	N	N
WEST VIRGINIA				
Byrd	N	N	Y	Y
Rockefeller	N	N	Y	Y
WISCONSIN				
Feingold	N	N	Y	Y
Kohl	N	N	Y	Y
WYOMING				
Simpson	Y	Y	N	N
Wallop	N	Y	N	N

ND Northern Democrats   SD Southern Democrats   Southern states - Ala., Ark., Fla., Ga., Ky., La., Miss., N.C., Okla., S.C., Tenn., Texas, Va.

79. S Con Res 63. Fiscal 1995 Budget Resolution/Recommittal. Robb, D-Va., motion to recommit the resolution to the Senate Budget Committee with instructions to report it back with provisions protecting defense spending from additional cuts. Rejected 28-70: R 23-19; D 5-51 (ND 2-40, SD 3-11), March 24, 1994.

80. S Con Res 63. Fiscal 1995 Budget Resolution/Illegal Immigration. Gramm, R-Texas, amendment to take $5 billion a year for five years from all of President Clinton's "investment" spending proposals except criminal justice and to transfer the money to the states to help defray the costs of federally mandated spending on illegal immigrants. Rejected 37-61: R 33-10; D 4-51 (ND 2-40, SD 2-11), March 25, 1994.

81. S Con Res 63. Fiscal 1995 Budget Resolution/Deficit Reduction. Sasser, D-Tenn., amendment to the Nunn, D-Ga., amendment, to express the sense of the Congress in support of comprehensive health care reform that would control the growth of health care spending and use the savings to reduce the deficit and offset the cost of health care reform. The Nunn amendment would express the sense of the Senate in favor of placing enforceable caps on mandatory spending, but only after a comprehensive health care reform plan was enacted. Rejected 45-53: R 1-42; D 44-11 (ND 37-5, SD 7-6), March 25, 1994. The Nunn amendment subsequently was adopted by voice vote.

82. H Con Res 218. Fiscal 1995 Budget Resolution/Adoption. Adoption of the resolution to set budget levels for the fiscal year ending Sept. 30, 1995: budget authority, $1.537 trillion; outlays, $1.512 trillion; revenues, $1.338 trillion; and a deficit of $174 billion. The resolution called for an additional $26 billion in cuts over five years below the guidelines established in 1993 and in President Clinton's fiscal 1995 budget. Adopted 57-40: R 2-40; D 55-0 (ND 42-0, SD 13-0), March 25, 1994. (Before adoption, the Senate inserted the text of S Con Res 63.) A "yea" was a vote in support of the president's position.

KEY

Y Voted for (yea).
\# Paired for.
+ Announced for.
N Voted against (nay).
X Paired against.
− Announced against.
P Voted "present."
C Voted "present" to avoid possible conflict of interest.
? Did not vote or otherwise make a position known.

Democrats   *Republicans*

	83 84 85 86
ALABAMA	
Heflin	Y Y Y Y
Shelby	Y Y N Y
ALASKA	
Murkowski	Y ? ? ?
Stevens	Y ? ? ?
ARIZONA	
DeConcini	Y Y Y Y
McCain	Y ? ? ?
ARKANSAS	
Bumpers	Y Y Y Y
Pryor	Y Y Y Y
CALIFORNIA	
Boxer	Y Y Y Y
Feinstein	Y Y Y Y
COLORADO	
Campbell	Y Y Y Y
Brown	Y N N N
CONNECTICUT	
Dodd	Y Y Y Y
Lieberman	Y ? ? ?
DELAWARE	
Biden	Y Y Y Y
Roth	Y Y N Y
FLORIDA	
Graham	Y Y Y Y
Mack	Y N N N
GEORGIA	
Nunn	Y Y Y Y
Coverdell	N Y N N
HAWAII	
Akaka	Y Y Y Y
Inouye	Y Y Y Y
IDAHO	
Craig	N N N N
Kempthorne	N N N N
ILLINOIS	
Moseley-Braun	Y Y Y Y
Simon	Y Y Y Y
INDIANA	
Coats	N N N N
Lugar	Y Y N N

	83 84 85 86
IOWA	
Harkin	Y Y Y Y
Grassley	Y Y N N
KANSAS	
Dole	Y Y N N
Kassebaum	Y Y N N
KENTUCKY	
Ford	Y Y Y Y
McConnell	Y N N N
LOUISIANA	
Breaux	Y Y Y Y
Johnston	Y ? Y Y
MAINE	
Mitchell	Y Y Y Y
Cohen	? ? ? ?
MARYLAND	
Mikulski	Y Y Y Y
Sarbanes	Y Y Y Y
MASSACHUSETTS	
Kennedy	Y Y Y Y
Kerry	Y Y Y Y
MICHIGAN	
Levin	Y Y Y Y
Riegle	Y Y Y Y
MINNESOTA	
Wellstone	Y Y Y Y
Durenberger	Y Y Y Y
MISSISSIPPI	
Cochran	Y Y N N
Lott	? ? ? ?
MISSOURI	
Bond	Y N Y Y
Danforth	Y Y Y N
MONTANA	
Baucus	Y Y Y Y
Burns	Y Y N N
NEBRASKA	
Exon	Y Y Y Y
Kerrey	Y Y Y Y
NEVADA	
Bryan	Y Y Y Y
Reid	Y Y Y Y

	83 84 85 86
NEW HAMPSHIRE	
Gregg	N ? ? ?
Smith	N ? ? ?
NEW JERSEY	
Bradley	Y Y Y Y
Lautenberg	Y Y Y Y
NEW MEXICO	
Bingaman	Y Y Y Y
Domenici	Y Y Y Y
NEW YORK	
Moynihan	Y Y Y Y
D'Amato	Y Y N N
NORTH CAROLINA	
Faircloth	Y ? ? ?
Helms	Y ? ? ?
NORTH DAKOTA	
Conrad	Y Y Y Y
Dorgan	Y Y Y Y
OHIO	
Glenn	Y Y Y Y
Metzenbaum	Y Y Y Y
OKLAHOMA	
Boren	Y Y Y Y
Nickles	N N N N
OREGON	
Hatfield	Y Y Y Y
Packwood	N Y N Y
PENNSYLVANIA	
Wofford	Y Y Y Y
Specter	Y Y Y Y
RHODE ISLAND	
Pell	Y Y Y Y
Chafee	? Y Y Y
SOUTH CAROLINA	
Hollings	? ? ? ?
Thurmond	N Y N N
SOUTH DAKOTA	
Daschle	Y Y Y Y
Pressler	Y N N N
TENNESSEE	
Mathews	Y Y Y Y
Sasser	Y Y Y Y

	83 84 85 86
TEXAS	
Hutchison	N Y N N
Gramm	N ? ? ?
UTAH	
Bennett	Y ? − −
Hatch	N Y N N
VERMONT	
Leahy	Y Y Y Y
Jeffords	Y Y Y Y
VIRGINIA	
Robb	Y Y Y Y
Warner	Y Y N N
WASHINGTON	
Murray	Y Y Y Y
Gorton	Y Y Y Y
WEST VIRGINIA	
Byrd	Y Y Y N
Rockefeller	Y Y Y Y
WISCONSIN	
Feingold	Y Y Y Y
Kohl	Y Y Y Y
WYOMING	
Simpson	Y ? − −
Wallop	? ? ? ?

ND Northern Democrats   SD Southern Democrats   Southern states - Ala., Ark., Fla., Ga., Ky., La., Miss., N.C., Okla., S.C., Tenn., Texas, Va.

---

83. HR 1804. Goals 2000: Educate America/Motion To Proceed. Mitchell, D-Maine, motion to proceed to the conference report to authorize $400 million in fiscal 1994 and such sums as necessary in fiscal 1995-98 for competitive grants for schools seeking to improve their performance, write into law national education goals, and establish tests and standards for elementary and secondary students. Motion agreed to 83-12: R 28-12; D 55-0 (ND 42-0, SD 13-0), March 25, 1994.

84. Procedural Motion. Mitchell, D-Maine, motion to instruct the sergeant at arms to request the attendance of absent senators. Motion agreed to 75-9: R 22-9; D 53-0 (ND 41-0, SD 12-0), March 26, 1994 (in the session that began and the Congressional Record dated March 25).

85. HR 1804. Goals 2000: Educate America/Cloture. Motion to invoke cloture (thus limiting debate) on the conference report to authorize $400 million in fiscal 1994 and such sums as

necessary in fiscal 1995-98 for competitive grants for schools seeking to improve their performance, write into law national education goals, and establish tests and standards for elementary and secondary students. Motion agreed to 62-23: R 9-22; D 53-1 (ND 41-0, SD 12-1), March 26, 1994 (in the session that began and the Congressional Record dated March 25). Three-fifths of the total Senate (60) is required to invoke cloture.

86. HR 1804. Goals 2000: Educate America/Conference Report. Adoption of the conference report to authorize $400 million in fiscal 1994 and such sums as necessary in fiscal 1995-98 for competitive grants for schools seeking to improve their performance, write into law national education goals, and establish tests and standards for elementary and secondary students. Adopted (thus cleared for the president) 63-22: R 10-21; D 53-1 (ND 40-1, SD 13-0), March 26, 1994 (in the session that began and the Congressional Record dated March 25). A "yea" was a vote in support of the president's position.

	87	88	89	90	91	92
ALABAMA						
Heflin	N	N	Y	Y	Y	Y
Shelby	?	?	?	?	?	?
ALASKA						
Murkowski	Y	Y	N	Y	Y	N
Stevens	Y	Y	N	Y	Y	N
ARIZONA						
DeConcini	N	N	Y	Y	Y	Y
McCain	Y	Y	N	Y	Y	N
ARKANSAS						
Bumpers	N	N	Y	Y	Y	Y
Pryor	N	N	Y	Y	Y	Y
CALIFORNIA						
Boxer	N	N	Y	Y	Y	Y
Feinstein	N	N	Y	Y	Y	Y
COLORADO						
Campbell	N	N	Y	Y	Y	?
Brown	Y	Y	N	Y	Y	N
CONNECTICUT						
Dodd	N	N	Y	N	Y	Y
Lieberman	N	N	Y	N	Y	Y
DELAWARE						
Biden	N	N	+	N	Y	Y
Roth	N	N	Y	N	Y	N
FLORIDA						
Graham	N	N	Y	Y	Y	Y
Mack	Y	Y	N	Y	Y	Y
GEORGIA						
Nunn	N	N	Y	Y	Y	Y
Coverdell	Y	Y	N	N	Y	N
HAWAII						
Akaka	N	N	Y	Y	Y	Y
Inouye	N	N	Y	Y	Y	Y
IDAHO						
Craig	Y	Y	N	Y	Y	N
Kempthorne	Y	Y	N	Y	Y	N
ILLINOIS						
Moseley-Braun	N	N	Y	Y	Y	Y
Simon	N	N	Y	Y	Y	Y
INDIANA						
Coats	?	Y	N	Y	Y	N
Lugar	N	N	Y	Y	Y	N
IOWA						
Harkin	N	N	Y	N	Y	Y
Grassley	Y	Y	Y	N	Y	N
KANSAS						
Dole	Y	Y	N	Y	Y	N
Kassebaum	Y	N	Y	Y	Y	N
KENTUCKY						
Ford	N	N	Y	Y	Y	Y
McConnell	Y	Y	N	Y	Y	N
LOUISIANA						
Breaux	N	N	Y	Y	Y	Y
Johnston	N	N	Y	Y	Y	Y
MAINE						
Mitchell	N	N	Y	N	Y	Y
Cohen	N	N	Y	?	Y	Y
MARYLAND						
Mikulski	N	N	Y	Y	Y	Y
Sarbanes	N	N	Y	Y	Y	Y
MASSACHUSETTS						
Kennedy	N	N	Y	Y	Y	Y
Kerry	N	N	Y	Y	Y	Y
MICHIGAN						
Levin	N	N	Y	Y	Y	Y
Riegle	N	N	Y	N	Y	Y
MINNESOTA						
Wellstone	N	N	Y	Y	Y	Y
Durenberger	Y	N	Y	Y	Y	Y
MISSISSIPPI						
Cochran	Y	Y	N	Y	Y	N
Lott	Y	Y	N	Y	Y	N
MISSOURI						
Bond	?	?	Y	Y	Y	N
Danforth	Y	Y	Y	Y	Y	Y
MONTANA						
Baucus	N	N	Y	Y	Y	Y
Burns	Y	Y	N	Y	Y	N
NEBRASKA						
Exon	N	N	Y	Y	Y	Y
Kerrey	N	N	Y	Y	N	Y
NEVADA						
Bryan	N	N	Y	Y	Y	Y
Reid	N	N	Y	Y	Y	Y
NEW HAMPSHIRE						
Gregg	N	N	Y	Y	Y	N
Smith	Y	Y	N	Y	Y	N
NEW JERSEY						
Bradley	N	N	Y	N	Y	Y
Lautenberg	N	N	Y	N	Y	Y
NEW MEXICO						
Bingaman	N	N	Y	Y	Y	Y
Domenici	Y	Y	Y	Y	Y	N
NEW YORK						
Moynihan	N	N	Y	Y	Y	Y
D'Amato	Y	Y	N	Y	Y	N
NORTH CAROLINA						
Faircloth	Y	Y	N	N	Y	N
Helms	Y	Y	N	Y	Y	N
NORTH DAKOTA						
Conrad	N	N	Y	Y	Y	Y
Dorgan	N	N	Y	Y	Y	Y
OHIO						
Glenn	N	N	Y	N	Y	Y
Metzenbaum	N	N	Y	N	Y	Y
OKLAHOMA						
Boren	N	N	Y	Y	Y	Y
Nickles	Y	Y	N	N	Y	N
OREGON						
Hatfield	Y	Y	Y	Y	Y	Y
Packwood	Y	Y	N	Y	Y	Y
PENNSYLVANIA						
Wofford	N	N	Y	Y	Y	Y
Specter	N	N	Y	Y	Y	N
RHODE ISLAND						
Pell	N	N	Y	Y	Y	Y
Chafee	N	N	Y	N	Y	Y
SOUTH CAROLINA						
Hollings	N	N	Y	Y	Y	Y
Thurmond	Y	Y	N	Y	Y	N
SOUTH DAKOTA						
Daschle	N	N	Y	Y	Y	Y
Pressler	Y	Y	N	Y	Y	N
TENNESSEE						
Mathews	N	N	Y	Y	Y	Y
Sasser	N	N	Y	Y	Y	Y
TEXAS						
Hutchison	Y	Y	N	Y	Y	N
Gramm	Y	Y	N	Y	Y	N
UTAH						
Bennett	Y	Y	N	Y	Y	N
Hatch	Y	Y	N	Y	Y	N
VERMONT						
Leahy	N	N	Y	Y	Y	Y
Jeffords	N	N	Y	Y	Y	Y
VIRGINIA						
Robb	N	N	Y	Y	Y	Y
Warner	Y	Y	Y	Y	Y	N
WASHINGTON						
Murray	N	N	Y	Y	Y	Y
Gorton	N	Y	Y	Y	Y	N
WEST VIRGINIA						
Byrd	Y	N	N	N	Y	N
Rockefeller	N	N	Y	N	Y	Y
WISCONSIN						
Feingold	N	N	Y	Y	Y	Y
Kohl	N	N	Y	Y	Y	Y
WYOMING						
Simpson	Y	Y	N	Y	Y	N
Wallop	Y	Y	N	Y	Y	N

KEY

Y   Voted for (yea).
\#   Paired for.
\+   Announced for.
N   Voted against (nay).
X   Paired against.
−   Announced against.
P   Voted "present."
C   Voted "present" to avoid possible conflict of interest.
?   Did not vote or otherwise make a position known.

Democrats   *Republicans*

ND   Northern Democrats   SD   Southern Democrats   Southern states - Ala., Ark., Fla., Ga., Ky., La., Miss., N.C., Okla., S.C., Tenn., Texas, Va.

87. S 21. California Desert Protection/Mojave National Monument. Wallop, R-Wyo., amendment to change the designation for the proposed Mojave National Park to the Mojave National Monument, to be maintained by the Bureau of Land Management rather than the National Park Service. Rejected 35-62: R 34-8; D 1-54 (ND 1-41, SD 0-13), April 12, 1994.

88. S 21. California Desert Protection/Private Land Acquisition. Bennett, R-Utah, amendment to require that within 10 years, 90 percent of private lands within the California desert be acquired and paid for by the federal government and to withhold the national park designation until such purchases have occurred. Rejected 34-64: R 34-9; D 0-55 (ND 0-42, SD 0-13), April 12, 1994.

89. S 21. California Desert Protection/Passage. Passage of the bill to designate about 7.7 million acres of California desert as wilderness and to establish the Death Valley, Joshua Tree and Mojave National Parks. Passed 69-29: R 16-28; D 53-1 (ND 40-1, SD 13-0), April 13, 1994. A "yea" was a vote in support of the president's position.

90. S 455. Payments in Lieu of Taxes/Passage. Passage of the bill to increase federal payments to local governments by about $150 million over five years to compensate them for diminished opportunities to tax federal land within their jurisdictions. Passed 78-20: R 37-6; D 41-14 (ND 28-14, SD 13-0), April 13, 1994.

91. S 1970. Agriculture Department Reorganization/Passage. Passage of the bill to authorize the secretary of Agriculture to overhaul the Agriculture Department, including reducing the department's agencies from 43 to 28. Passed 98-1: R 44-0; D 54-1 (ND 41-1, SD 13-0), April 13, 1994.

92. Barkett Confirmation. Confirmation of Rosemary Barkett of Florida to be U.S. circuit judge for the 11th U.S. Circuit Court of Appeals. Confirmed 61-37: R 8-36; D 53-1 (ND 40-1, SD 13-0), April 14, 1994. A "yea" was a vote in support of the president's position.

SENATE VOTES 93, 94, 95, 96

KEY

Y   Voted for (yea).
\#   Paired for.
\+   Announced for.
N   Voted against (nay).
X   Paired against.
–   Announced against.
P   Voted "present."
C   Voted "present" to avoid possible conflict of interest.
?   Did not vote or otherwise make a position known.

Democrats   *Republicans*

	93	94	95	96
ALABAMA				
Heflin	Y	N	Y	Y
Shelby	?	?	?	?
ALASKA				
Murkowski	Y	N	N	Y
Stevens	Y	Y	N	Y
ARIZONA				
DeConcini	Y	N	N	Y
McCain	Y	Y	Y	Y
ARKANSAS				
Bumpers	Y	N	N	Y
Pryor	Y	N	N	Y
CALIFORNIA				
Boxer	N	Y	Y	Y
Feinstein	N	Y	N	Y
COLORADO				
Campbell	N	N	N	Y
Brown	Y	Y	N	Y
CONNECTICUT				
Dodd	Y	N	N	Y
Lieberman	Y	Y	N	Y
DELAWARE				
Biden	N	N	Y	Y
Roth	N	Y	N	Y
FLORIDA				
Graham	Y	Y	Y	Y
Mack	Y	Y	Y	Y
GEORGIA				
Nunn	Y	N	Y	Y
Coverdell	Y	Y	Y	Y
HAWAII				
Akaka	N	N	Y	Y
Inouye	Y	N	Y	?
IDAHO				
Craig	Y	Y	Y	Y
Kempthorne	Y	Y	Y	Y
ILLINOIS				
Moseley-Braun	N	N	N	Y
Simon	N	N	N	Y
INDIANA				
Coats	Y	N	N	Y
Lugar	Y	N	Y	Y

	93	94	95	96
IOWA				
Harkin	N	N	Y	Y
Grassley	N	Y	Y	Y
KANSAS				
Dole	Y	N	Y	Y
Kassebaum	N	N	Y	Y
KENTUCKY				
Ford	Y	N	Y	Y
McConnell	N	Y	Y	Y
LOUISIANA				
Breaux	N	N	Y	Y
Johnston	Y	N	Y	Y
MAINE				
Mitchell	Y	N	N	Y
Cohen	Y	Y	Y	Y
MARYLAND				
Mikulski	N	N	N	Y
Sarbanes	N	Y	Y	Y
MASSACHUSETTS				
Kennedy	Y	Y	Y	Y
Kerry	N	Y	N	Y
MICHIGAN				
Levin	Y	N	Y	Y
Riegle	?	?	?	?
MINNESOTA				
Wellstone	N	Y	Y	Y
Durenberger	Y	N	N	Y
MISSISSIPPI				
Cochran	Y	N	Y	Y
Lott	Y	N	Y	Y
MISSOURI				
Bond	Y	N	Y	Y
Danforth	Y	N	?	Y
MONTANA				
Baucus	N	N	?	Y
Burns	Y	Y	N	Y
NEBRASKA				
Exon	Y	N	N	Y
Kerrey	Y	Y	N	Y
NEVADA				
Bryan	Y	Y	N	Y
Reid	N	N	N	Y

	93	94	95	96
NEW HAMPSHIRE				
Gregg	Y	N	N	Y
Smith	Y	Y	Y	Y
NEW JERSEY				
Bradley	N	Y	?	Y
Lautenberg	N	Y	Y	Y
NEW MEXICO				
Bingaman	Y	Y	N	Y
Domenici	Y	N	Y	Y
NEW YORK				
Moynihan	N	Y	?	Y
D'Amato	N	Y	Y	Y
NORTH CAROLINA				
Faircloth	Y	N	Y	Y
Helms	Y	N	Y	Y
NORTH DAKOTA				
Conrad	N	Y	N	Y
Dorgan	N	N	N	Y
OHIO				
Glenn	?	?	Y	Y
Metzenbaum	N	N	N	Y
OKLAHOMA				
Boren	N	Y	Y	?
Nickles	Y	Y	N	Y
OREGON				
Hatfield	Y	N	N	Y
Packwood	N	N	Y	Y
PENNSYLVANIA				
Wofford	N	Y	Y	Y
Specter	N	N	Y	Y
RHODE ISLAND				
Pell	Y	N	Y	Y
Chafee	Y	Y	N	Y
SOUTH CAROLINA				
Hollings	Y	N	N	Y
Thurmond	Y	N	Y	Y
SOUTH DAKOTA				
Daschle	N	N	N	Y
Pressler	N	Y	N	Y
TENNESSEE				
Mathews	Y	N	Y	Y
Sasser	Y	Y	Y	Y

	93	94	95	96
TEXAS				
Hutchison	N	Y	Y	Y
Gramm	Y	Y	Y	Y
UTAH				
Bennett	N	N	Y	Y
Hatch	N	Y	Y	Y
VERMONT				
Leahy	N	N	Y	Y
Jeffords	N	N	Y	?
VIRGINIA				
Robb	Y	Y	Y	Y
Warner	Y	Y	N	Y
WASHINGTON				
Murray	N	N	Y	Y
Gorton	N	Y	Y	Y
WEST VIRGINIA				
Byrd	N	Y	Y	Y
Rockefeller	N	N	Y	Y
WISCONSIN				
Feingold	N	Y	Y	Y
Kohl	N	Y	Y	Y
WYOMING				
Simpson	Y	N	Y	+
Wallop	Y	N	N	Y

ND Northern Democrats   SD Southern Democrats   Southern states - Ala., Ark., Fla., Ga., Ky., La., Miss., N.C., Okla., S.C., Tenn., Texas, Va.

93. Kelso Retirement Star Confirmation. Confirmation of the nomination of Adm. Frank B. Kelso II to be placed on the retired list with the rank of a four-star admiral. Confirmed 54-43: R 31-13; D 23-30 (ND 12-28, SD 11-2), April 19, 1994. A "yea" was a vote in support of the president's position.

94. S 540. Bankruptcy Reform/Airport Parking. McCain, R-Ariz., amendment to express the sense of the Senate that free parking privileges for members of Congress, other government officials and foreign diplomats at Washington National Airport and Dulles International Airport should be eliminated. Rejected 44-53: R 22-22; D 22-31 (ND 18-22, SD 4-9), April 20, 1994.

95. S 540. Bankruptcy Reform/Chapter 13 Petitions. Heflin, D-Ala., motion to table (kill) the Reid, D-Nev., amendment to limit the number of petitions a debtor may make to one bankruptcy filing every three years under Chapter 13. Motion agreed to 60-34: R 30-13; D 30-21 (ND 20-18, SD 10-3), April 20, 1994.

96. S 540. Bankruptcy Reform/Passage. Passage of the bill to adopt numerous changes to the bankruptcy code to speed the process of bankruptcy negotiations and help clear court dockets, and to establish a National Bankruptcy Review Commission. Passed 94-0: R 42-0; D 52-0 (ND 40-0, SD 12-0), April 21, 1994.

KEY

Y Voted for (yea).
\# Paired for.
\+ Announced for.
N Voted against (nay).
X Paired against.
− Announced against.
P Voted "present."
C Voted "present" to avoid possible conflict of interest.
? Did not vote or otherwise make a position known.

Democrats *Republicans*

	97	98	99	100	101	102	103	104
ALABAMA								
Heflin	Y	Y	Y	Y	N	Y	Y	Y
Shelby	?	?	?	?	?	?	?	?
ALASKA								
Murkowski	Y	Y	Y	Y	Y	Y	Y	Y
Stevens	Y	Y	Y	Y	Y	Y	N	Y
ARIZONA								
DeConcini	Y	Y	Y	Y	Y	Y	N	N
McCain	Y	Y	Y	N	N	Y	Y	Y
ARKANSAS								
Bumpers	Y	Y	Y	Y	Y	Y	N	N
Pryor	Y	Y	N	Y	Y	?	?	?
CALIFORNIA								
Boxer	Y	Y	Y	N	Y	N	N	Y
Feinstein	Y	Y	Y	Y	N	Y	N	Y
COLORADO								
Campbell	Y	Y	Y	Y	Y	Y	N	Y
Brown	Y	Y	Y	Y	N	Y	Y	Y
CONNECTICUT								
Dodd	Y	Y	N	?	Y	Y	N	Y
Lieberman	Y	Y	Y	Y	N	Y	N	Y
DELAWARE								
Biden	Y	Y	Y	Y	N	Y	N	N
Roth	Y	Y	Y	Y	Y	Y	N	Y
FLORIDA								
Graham	Y	N	?	Y	N	Y	N	N
Mack	Y	Y	Y	N	Y	Y	Y	Y
GEORGIA								
Nunn	Y	Y	Y	Y	Y	Y	N	Y
Coverdell	Y	Y	Y	N	Y	Y	Y	Y
HAWAII								
Akaka	Y	Y	Y	Y	Y	N	N	N
Inouye	Y	Y	Y	Y	Y	Y	N	N
IDAHO								
Craig	Y	Y	Y	Y	Y	Y	Y	Y
Kempthorne	Y	Y	Y	Y	Y	Y	Y	Y
ILLINOIS								
Moseley-Braun	Y	Y	N	Y	N	Y	N	Y
Simon	Y	N	N	Y	N	Y	N	Y
INDIANA								
Coats	Y	Y	Y	Y	N	Y	N	Y
Lugar	Y	Y	Y	Y	N	Y	N	Y
IOWA								
Harkin	Y	Y	N	Y	N	Y	N	N
Grassley	Y	Y	Y	Y	N	Y	Y	Y
KANSAS								
Dole	Y	Y	Y	Y	Y	Y	Y	Y
Kassebaum	Y	Y	Y	N	N	?	?	?
KENTUCKY								
Ford	Y	Y	Y	Y	N	Y	N	N
McConnell	Y	Y	Y	Y	Y	Y	Y	Y
LOUISIANA								
Breaux	Y	Y	Y	Y	Y	Y	N	N
Johnston	Y	Y	N	Y	Y	Y	N	N
MAINE								
Mitchell	Y	N	Y	Y	N	Y	N	N
Cohen	Y	Y	Y	Y	N	?	?	Y
MARYLAND								
Mikulski	Y	Y	Y	Y	N	Y	N	N
Sarbanes	Y	Y	Y	Y	N	Y	N	N
MASSACHUSETTS								
Kennedy	?	Y	Y	Y	N	Y	N	Y
Kerry	Y	Y	Y	Y	N	Y	N	Y
MICHIGAN								
Levin	Y	N	Y	Y	N	N	N	Y
Riegle	Y	Y	Y	Y	N	Y	N	N
MINNESOTA								
Wellstone	Y	Y	N	Y	N	Y	Y	Y
Durenberger	Y	Y	N	Y	Y	?	?	?
MISSISSIPPI								
Cochran	?	?	Y	N	Y	Y	N	Y
Lott	Y	Y	Y	Y	Y	Y	Y	Y
MISSOURI								
Bond	Y	Y	Y	Y	Y	?	?	Y
Danforth	Y	Y	Y	Y	Y	Y	N	Y
MONTANA								
Baucus	Y	Y	Y	Y	N	Y	N	Y
Burns	Y	Y	Y	N	Y	Y	Y	Y
NEBRASKA								
Exon	Y	N	Y	Y	N	Y	N	Y
Kerrey	Y	Y	Y	Y	N	Y	N	Y
NEVADA								
Bryan	Y	Y	Y	Y	N	Y	N	Y
Reid	Y	Y	Y	Y	N	Y	N	Y
NEW HAMPSHIRE								
Gregg	Y	Y	Y	Y	N	Y	N	Y
Smith	Y	Y	Y	Y	Y	Y	Y	Y
NEW JERSEY								
Bradley	Y	Y	N	Y	N	Y	N	Y
Lautenberg	Y	Y	N	Y	N	Y	Y	Y
NEW MEXICO								
Bingaman	Y	Y	Y	Y	N	Y	N	Y
Domenici	Y	Y	Y	Y	N	Y	Y	Y
NEW YORK								
Moynihan	Y	Y	Y	Y	N	Y	N	N
D'Amato	Y	Y	Y	Y	Y	Y	N	Y
NORTH CAROLINA								
Faircloth	Y	Y	Y	N	Y	Y	Y	Y
Helms	Y	Y	Y	Y	Y	Y	Y	Y
NORTH DAKOTA								
Conrad	N	N	Y	N	Y	N	N	N
Dorgan	N	N	Y	N	Y	N	N	N
OHIO								
Glenn	Y	Y	Y	Y	N	Y	N	Y
Metzenbaum	?	?	N	Y	N	N	N	N
OKLAHOMA								
Boren	Y	N	Y	Y	N	Y	N	N
Nickles	Y	Y	Y	Y	Y	Y	Y	Y
OREGON								
Hatfield	Y	Y	N	Y	N	Y	N	Y
Packwood	Y	Y	N	Y	?	?	?	?
PENNSYLVANIA								
Wofford	Y	Y	N	?	N	Y	Y	Y
Specter	Y	Y	Y	Y	N	Y	Y	Y
RHODE ISLAND								
Pell	Y	Y	N	Y	Y	Y	N	N
Chafee	Y	Y	Y	Y	N	Y	N	Y
SOUTH CAROLINA								
Hollings	Y	Y	Y	Y	N	Y	N	N
Thurmond	Y	Y	Y	Y	Y	Y	Y	Y
SOUTH DAKOTA								
Daschle	Y	N	N	Y	N	Y	N	N
Pressler	Y	Y	Y	Y	N	Y	Y	Y
TENNESSEE								
Mathews	Y	Y	N	Y	Y	Y	N	N
Sasser	Y	Y	N	Y	N	Y	N	N
TEXAS								
Hutchison	Y	Y	Y	N	Y	Y	Y	Y
Gramm	Y	Y	Y	N	Y	N	Y	Y
UTAH								
Bennett	Y	Y	Y	N	Y	Y	Y	Y
Hatch	Y	Y	Y	N	Y	Y	Y	Y
VERMONT								
Leahy	Y	Y	N	Y	N	Y	N	Y
Jeffords	Y	Y	N	Y	N	Y	N	Y
VIRGINIA								
Robb	Y	Y	N	Y	N	Y	N	N
Warner	Y	Y	Y	Y	N	Y	Y	Y
WASHINGTON								
Murray	Y	Y	Y	Y	N	Y	N	N
Gorton	Y	Y	Y	N	Y	Y	Y	Y
WEST VIRGINIA								
Byrd	Y	Y	Y	Y	N	Y	N	N
Rockefeller	Y	Y	Y	Y	Y	Y	N	Y
WISCONSIN								
Feingold	Y	Y	Y	Y	N	Y	N	N
Kohl	Y	Y	Y	Y	N	Y	Y	Y
WYOMING								
Simpson	Y	Y	Y	Y	Y	Y	Y	Y
Wallop	Y	Y	Y	Y	Y	Y	Y	Y

ND Northern Democrats   SD Southern Democrats   Southern states - Ala., Ark., Fla., Ga., Ky., La., Miss., N.C., Okla., S.C., Tenn., Texas, Va.

97. S 783. Fair Credit Reporting Amendments/Financial Accounting Standards Board. Levin, D-Mich., amendment to the Lieberman, D-Conn., amendment to express the sense of the Senate that Congress should not interfere with the Financial Accounting Standards Board's (FASB) decision-making process. The Lieberman amendment would have expressed the sense of the Senate that the FASB should maintain current accounting principles for the treatment of stock options and stock purchase plans to encourage investment. Adopted 94-2: R 43-0; D 51-2 (ND 38-2, SD 13-0), May 3, 1994.

98. S 783. Fair Credit Reporting Amendments/Financial Accounting Standards Board. Lieberman, D-Conn., amendment as amended by the Levin, D-Mich., amendment, to express the sense of the Senate that Congress should not interfere with the Financial Accounting Standards Board's decision-making process by legislating accounting rules. Adopted 88-9: R 43-0; D 45-9 (ND 34-7, SD 11-2), May 3, 1994.

99. S 783. Fair Credit Reporting Amendments/Privacy Commission. Bryan, D-Nev., motion to table (kill) the Simon, D-Ill., amendment to authorize $6 million in fiscal 1995-97 to establish a three-member U.S. Privacy Protection Commission to ensure that privacy rights are not abused or violated in regard to electronic data and fair information practices. Motion agreed to 77-21: R 40-4; D 37-17 (ND 30-12, SD 7-5), May 4, 1994.

100. S 783. Fair Credit Reporting Amendments/Passage. Passage of the bill to amend the 1970 Fair Credit Reporting Act, by requiring, among other things, that credit reporting agencies reinvestigate disputed information within 30 days or delete it from a consumer's credit report and furnish reports to consumers for a $3 fee. The bill would place furnishers of credit information under the law and pre-empt certain state credit reporting laws. Passed 87-10: R 34-10; D 53-0 (ND 40-0, SD 13-0), May 4, 1994.

101. S 1935. Congressional Gift Limitations/Substitute. McConnell, R-Ky., substitute amendment to permit members of Congress and staff to accept unlimited gifts valued at less than $75 (down from the current $100); to cap bigger gifts at $150 (down from $250); to continue to allow virtually unlimited free meals; to require advance public disclosure of certain aspects of privately financed trips (but not the cost); to bar travel expenditures for recreational activities unless they are part of a charity fundraising event; and to require the Senate to vote on whether to expel members who are reprimanded three times and to bar them from lobbying the Senate for 10 years. Rejected 39-59: R 25-18; D 14-41 (ND 7-35, SD 7-6), May 5, 1994.

102. S 1935. Congressional Gift Limitations/Gift Ban. Bumpers, D-Ark., amendment to eliminate the provisions of the bill that would allow gifts of $20 or less from non-lobbyists, thereby prohibiting virtually all gifts from everyone but friends and relatives. Adopted 90-3: R 38-1; D 52-2 (ND 40-2, SD 12-0), May 5, 1994.

103. S 1935. Congressional Gift Limitations/Congressional Pay Cut. Burns, R-Mont., amendment to reduce immediately the pay of members of Congress by 15 percent. Rejected 34-59: R 28-11; D 6-48 (ND 5-37, SD 1-11), May 5, 1994.

104. S 1935. Congressional Gift Limitations/Political Contributions. Murkowski, R-Alaska, amendment to prohibit members from accepting political contributions from political action committees and lobbyists. Adopted 66-29: R 41-0; D 25-29 (ND 23-19, SD 2-10), May 5, 1994.

	105	106	107	108	109
ALABAMA					
Heflin	N	Y	Y	N	Y
Shelby	?	?	?	?	?
ALASKA					
Murkowski	Y	Y	N	N	Y
Stevens	Y	Y	Y	Y	Y
ARIZONA					
DeConcini	N	Y	Y	Y	Y
McCain	Y	Y	Y	Y	Y
ARKANSAS					
Bumpers	N	Y	Y	Y	Y
Pryor	?	Y	Y	Y	Y
CALIFORNIA					
Boxer	N	N	Y	Y	Y
Feinstein	N	Y	Y	Y	Y
COLORADO					
Campbell	Y	N	Y	Y	Y
Brown	N	Y	Y	N	Y
CONNECTICUT					
Dodd	Y	N	Y	Y	Y
Lieberman	N	Y	Y	Y	Y
DELAWARE					
Biden	N	N	Y	Y	Y
Roth	N	Y	Y	Y	Y
FLORIDA					
Graham	N	Y	Y	Y	Y
Mack	N	Y	Y	Y	Y
GEORGIA					
Nunn	Y	Y	Y	Y	Y
Coverdell	Y	Y	Y	Y	Y
HAWAII					
Akaka	N	N	Y	Y	Y
Inouye	Y	N	Y	Y	Y
IDAHO					
Craig	Y	Y	Y	Y	Y
Kempthorne	Y	Y	Y	Y	Y
ILLINOIS					
Moseley-Braun	N	N	Y	Y	Y
Simon	N	N	Y	Y	Y
INDIANA					
Coats	Y	Y	Y	Y	Y
Lugar	N	Y	Y	Y	Y

	105	106	107	108	109
IOWA					
Harkin	N	N	Y	Y	Y
Grassley	N	Y	Y	Y	Y
KANSAS					
Dole	Y	Y	Y	Y	Y
Kassebaum	?	Y	Y	Y	Y
KENTUCKY					
Ford	N	Y	Y	Y	Y
McConnell	Y	Y	Y	Y	Y
LOUISIANA					
Breaux	N	N	Y	Y	Y
Johnston	Y	Y	Y	Y	Y
MAINE					
Mitchell	N	N	Y	Y	Y
Cohen	N	N	Y	Y	Y
MARYLAND					
Mikulski	N	N	Y	Y	Y
Sarbanes	N	N	Y	Y	Y
MASSACHUSETTS					
Kennedy	N	N	Y	Y	Y
Kerry	N	N	Y	Y	Y
MICHIGAN					
Levin	N	N	Y	Y	Y
Riegle	N	N	Y	Y	Y
MINNESOTA					
Wellstone	N	N	Y	Y	Y
Durenberger	?	N	Y	Y	Y
MISSISSIPPI					
Cochran	Y	Y	Y	Y	Y
Lott	Y	Y	Y	Y	Y
MISSOURI					
Bond	Y	Y	Y	Y	Y
Danforth	Y	Y	Y	N	Y
MONTANA					
Baucus	N	Y	Y	Y	Y
Burns	N	Y	Y	Y	Y
NEBRASKA					
Exon	N	Y	Y	Y	Y
Kerrey	N	N	Y	Y	Y
NEVADA					
Bryan	N	Y	Y	Y	Y
Reid	N	Y	Y	Y	Y

	105	106	107	108	109
NEW HAMPSHIRE					
Gregg	Y	Y	Y	Y	Y
Smith	Y	Y	Y	N	Y
NEW JERSEY					
Bradley	N	N	Y	Y	Y
Lautenberg	N	N	Y	Y	Y
NEW MEXICO					
Bingaman	N	Y	Y	Y	Y
Domenici	Y	Y	Y	Y	Y
NEW YORK					
Moynihan	N	N	Y	Y	Y
D'Amato	Y	Y	Y	Y	Y
NORTH CAROLINA					
Faircloth	Y	Y	Y	N	Y
Helms	Y	Y	Y	N	N
NORTH DAKOTA					
Conrad	N	Y	Y	N	Y
Dorgan	Y	Y	Y	N	Y
OHIO					
Glenn	N	N	Y	N	Y
Metzenbaum	N	N	Y	Y	Y
OKLAHOMA					
Boren	N	N	Y	Y	Y
Nickles	N	Y	Y	N	Y
OREGON					
Hatfield	N	N	Y	Y	Y
Packwood	?	N	Y	Y	Y
PENNSYLVANIA					
Wofford	N	Y	Y	Y	Y
Specter	N	Y	Y	Y	Y
RHODE ISLAND					
Pell	Y	N	Y	Y	Y
Chafee	Y	N	Y	Y	Y
SOUTH CAROLINA					
Hollings	Y	Y	N	Y	Y
Thurmond	Y	Y	Y	Y	Y
SOUTH DAKOTA					
Daschle	N	N	Y	Y	Y
Pressler	N	Y	Y	N	Y
TENNESSEE					
Mathews	N	N	Y	Y	Y
Sasser	N	N	Y	Y	Y

	105	106	107	108	109
TEXAS					
Hutchison	N	Y	Y	Y	Y
Gramm	Y	Y	Y	N	Y
UTAH					
Bennett	Y	Y	N	Y	Y
Hatch	Y	Y	Y	Y	Y
VERMONT					
Leahy	N	N	Y	Y	Y
Jeffords	Y	N	Y	Y	Y
VIRGINIA					
Robb	N	N	Y	Y	Y
Warner	N	Y	Y	Y	Y
WASHINGTON					
Murray	N	N	Y	Y	Y
Gorton	N	Y	Y	Y	Y
WEST VIRGINIA					
Byrd	Y	Y	Y	Y	Y
Rockefeller	Y	N	Y	Y	Y
WISCONSIN					
Feingold	N	N	Y	Y	Y
Kohl	N	N	Y	Y	Y
WYOMING					
Simpson	Y	Y	Y	Y	Y
Wallop	Y	Y	N	N	Y

ND   Northern Democrats   SD   Southern Democrats   Southern states - Ala., Ark., Fla., Ga., Ky., La., Miss., N.C., Okla., S.C., Tenn., Texas, Va.

105. S 1935. Congressional Gift Limitations/Charity Travel Reimbursement. Murkowski, R-Alaska, amendment to allow reimbursement for travel and lodging at charity events, such as corporate-backed golf and tennis tournaments that raise money for needy causes. Rejected 37-58: R 27-14; D 10-44 (ND 7-35, SD 3-9), May 5, 1994.

106. S 1935. Congressional Gift Limitations/Racial Justice. D'Amato, R-N.Y., amendment to the committee substitute amendment, to express the sense of the Senate that the conferees on the omnibus crime bill (HR 3355) should reject the racial justice provisions in the House version of HR 3355 that would allow prisoners to use statistics to challenge a death penalty sentence as racially discriminatory. Adopted 58-41: R 38-6; D 20-35 (ND 12-30, SD 8-5), May 11, 1994.

107. S 1935. Congressional Gift Limitations/Passage. Passage of the bill to bar members of Congress from accepting virtually any gifts from anyone unless the gifts are from verifiable friends or relatives and to impose new restrictions on privately financed trips, including a ban on free recreational activities and on travel for charity events, such as golf and tennis tournaments. Passed 95-4: R 41-3; D 54-1 (ND 42-0, SD 12-1), May 11, 1994.

108. S 978. National Environmental Technology/Passage. Passage of the bill to encourage the development and commercialization of environmental technologies through a coordinated federal effort, including seed money for private sector research and development, a reduction in market barriers to the development and utilization of "green technologies," and the collection and dissemination of information on environmental technologies. Passed 85-14: R 34-10; D 51-4 (ND 39-3, SD 12-1), May 11, 1994. A "yea" was a vote in support of the president's position.

109. S 2000. Head Start Reauthorization/Conference Report. Adoption of the conference report on the bill to reauthorize Head Start through fiscal 1998, expanding the program for preschoolers and providing new performance standards for grantees. The bill also authorizes several other anti-poverty programs: the Community Services Block Grant Program, which primarily finances local community action agencies serving the poor; the Low-Income Home Energy Assistance Program, which helps low-income families pay heating and cooling bills and insulate their homes, and Community-Based Family Resource Programs, which are mainly designed to prevent child abuse. Adopted (thus cleared for the House) 98-1: R 43-1; D 55-0 (ND 42-0, SD 13-0), May 11, 1994. A "yea" was a vote in support of the president's position.

	110	111	112	113
ALABAMA				
Heflin	Y	N	Y	Y
Shelby	?	?	?	?
ALASKA				
Murkowski	N	Y	N	N
Stevens	N	Y	Y	N
ARIZONA				
DeConcini	Y	Y	Y	Y
McCain	N	Y	N	N
ARKANSAS				
Bumpers	Y	N	Y	Y
Pryor	Y	N	Y	Y
CALIFORNIA				
Boxer	Y	N	Y	Y
Feinstein	Y	N	Y	Y
COLORADO				
Campbell	Y	Y	Y	Y
Brown	N	Y	Y	N
CONNECTICUT				
Dodd	Y	N	Y	Y
Lieberman	N	Y	Y	Y
DELAWARE				
Biden	Y	N	Y	Y
Roth	N	Y	Y	N
FLORIDA				
Graham	Y	N	Y	Y
Mack	N	Y	N	N
GEORGIA				
Nunn	Y	N	Y	N
Coverdell	N	Y	N	N
HAWAII				
Akaka	Y	N	Y	Y
Inouye	Y	N	Y	Y
IDAHO				
Craig	N	Y	N	N
Kempthorne	N	Y	N	N
ILLINOIS				
Moseley-Braun	Y	Y	Y	Y
Simon	Y	N	Y	Y
INDIANA				
Coats	N	Y	N	N
Lugar	N	Y	N	N

	110	111	112	113
IOWA				
Harkin	Y	N	Y	Y
Grassley	N	Y	N	N
KANSAS				
Dole	N	Y	N	N
Kassebaum	N	N	Y	N
KENTUCKY				
Ford	Y	N	Y	Y
McConnell	N	Y	Y	N
LOUISIANA				
Breaux	Y	N	N	Y
Johnston	Y	N	N	Y
MAINE				
Mitchell	Y	N	Y	Y
Cohen	N	Y	Y	N
MARYLAND				
Mikulski	Y	N	Y	Y
Sarbanes	Y	N	Y	Y
MASSACHUSETTS				
Kennedy	Y	N	Y	Y
Kerry	Y	N	Y	N
MICHIGAN				
Levin	N	Y	Y	Y
Riegle	Y	N	Y	Y
MINNESOTA				
Wellstone	Y	N	Y	Y
Durenberger	N	Y	Y	N
MISSISSIPPI				
Cochran	N	Y	N	N
Lott	N	Y	N	N
MISSOURI				
Bond	N	Y	Y	N
Danforth	N	N	Y	N
MONTANA				
Baucus	Y	N	Y	Y
Burns	N	N	N	N
NEBRASKA				
Exon	Y	N	N	Y
Kerrey	Y	N	Y	Y
NEVADA				
Bryan	Y	Y	Y	Y
Reid	Y	Y	Y	Y

	110	111	112	113
NEW HAMPSHIRE				
Gregg	N	N	N	N
Smith	N	Y	N	N
NEW JERSEY				
Bradley	N	Y	Y	N
Lautenberg	Y	Y	Y	N
NEW MEXICO				
Bingaman	Y	N	Y	Y
Domenici	N	Y	Y	Y
NEW YORK				
Moynihan	Y	Y	Y	Y
D'Amato	N	Y	N	N
NORTH CAROLINA				
Faircloth	N	Y	N	N
Helms	N	Y	N	N
NORTH DAKOTA				
Conrad	Y	N	Y	Y
Dorgan	Y	N	Y	Y
OHIO				
Glenn	Y	N	Y	Y
Metzenbaum	Y	N	Y	Y
OKLAHOMA				
Boren	Y	N	Y	Y
Nickles	N	Y	N	N
OREGON				
Hatfield	N	N	N	Y
Packwood	N	Y	Y	N
PENNSYLVANIA				
Wofford	Y	N	Y	Y
Specter	N	Y	Y	N
RHODE ISLAND				
Pell	Y	N	Y	Y
Chafee	N	N	Y	N
SOUTH CAROLINA				
Hollings	Y	N	Y	Y
Thurmond	N	Y	N	N
SOUTH DAKOTA				
Daschle	Y	N	Y	Y
Pressler	N	Y	N	N
TENNESSEE				
Mathews	Y	N	Y	Y
Sasser	Y	N	Y	Y

	110	111	112	113
TEXAS				
Hutchison	N	Y	Y	N
Gramm	N	Y	N	N
UTAH				
Bennett	N	Y	N	N
Hatch	N	Y	N	N
VERMONT				
Leahy	Y	N	Y	Y
Jeffords	N	Y	Y	Y
VIRGINIA				
Robb	Y	Y	Y	Y
Warner	N	N	N	N
WASHINGTON				
Murray	Y	N	Y	Y
Gorton	N	Y	Y	N
WEST VIRGINIA				
Byrd	Y	N	Y	Y
Rockefeller	Y	N	Y	Y
WISCONSIN				
Feingold	N	Y	Y	Y
Kohl	N	Y	Y	Y
WYOMING				
Simpson	N	Y	Y	N
Wallop	N	Y	N	N

ND Northern Democrats   SD Southern Democrats   Southern states - Ala., Ark., Fla., Ga., Ky., La., Miss., N.C., Okla., S.C., Tenn., Texas, Va.

---

110. S 2042. Bosnia Arms Embargo/Allies Consultation. Mitchell, D-Maine, amendment to direct the president to seek the immediate agreement of NATO allies to terminate the arms embargo against Bosnia-Herzegovina, direct the president to seek a U.N. Security Council resolution to terminate the arms embargo and require the president to consult Congress within five days about unilateral termination of the embargo, if the U.N. Security Council resolution fails. The amendment also would authorize U.S. air power to implement NATO exclusion zones and to protect U.N. forces but prohibit the deployment of U.S. ground combat forces without congressional authorization. Adopted 50-49: R 0-44; D 50-5 (ND 37-5, SD 13-0), May 12, 1994. A "yea" was a vote in support of the president's position.

111. S 2042. Bosnia Arms Embargo/Unilateral Termination. Dole, R-Kan., amendment to require the president to terminate the U.S. arms embargo of Bosnia-Herzegovina upon receipt of a request from that government for assistance in its right of self-defense and to prohibit interference with the transfer of conventional arms by the executive branch. The amendment also states that nothing in the amendment shall be interpreted as an authorization for the deployment of U.S. forces. Adopted 50-49: R 37-7; D 13-42 (ND 12-30, SD 1-12), May 12, 1994. A "nay" was a vote in support of the president's position.

112. S 636. Abortion Clinic Access/Conference Report. Adoption of the conference report to establish federal criminal and civil penalties for people who use force, the threat of force or physical obstruction to block access to abortion clinics. Adopted (thus cleared for the president) 69-30: R 17-27; D 52-3 (ND 41-1, SD 11-2), May 12, 1994. A "yea" was a vote in support of the president's position.

113. H Con Res 218. Fiscal 1995 Budget Resolution/Conference Report. Adoption of the conference report to set budget levels for the fiscal year ending Sept. 30, 1995: budget authority, $1.541 trillion; outlays, $1.514 trillion; revenues, $1.338 trillion; and a deficit of $175.4 billion. The resolution calls for an additional $13 billion in cuts over five years below the spending caps established last year. Adopted (thus cleared) 53-46: R 2-42; D 51-4 (ND 39-3, SD 12-1), May 12, 1994.

	114	115	116	117	118	119	120	121
ALABAMA								
Heflin	N	N	N	Y	N	Y	N	N
Shelby	?	?	?	?	?	?	?	?
ALASKA								
Murkowski	Y	N	Y	Y	N	Y	N	Y
Stevens	Y	N	N	Y	Y	Y	N	Y
ARIZONA								
DeConcini	N	Y	N	Y	Y	N	Y	N
McCain	N	N	Y	Y	N	Y	N	Y
ARKANSAS								
Bumpers	Y	Y	Y	Y	N	Y	Y	N
Pryor	Y	Y	Y	Y	N	Y	Y	N
CALIFORNIA								
Boxer	N	Y	N	N	Y	N	Y	N
Feinstein	N	Y	N	Y	Y	N	Y	N
COLORADO								
Campbell	N	Y	N	Y	Y	N	Y	N
Brown	Y	N	Y	Y	N	Y	N	Y
CONNECTICUT								
Dodd	N	Y	N	Y	Y	N	Y	N
Lieberman	Y	Y	N	Y	Y	N	Y	N
DELAWARE								
Biden	Y	Y	N	Y	Y	N	Y	N
Roth	Y	Y	Y	N	N	Y	Y	?
FLORIDA								
Graham	Y	Y	N	Y	Y	N	Y	N
Mack	Y	N	Y	Y	N	Y	Y	Y
GEORGIA								
Nunn	Y	N	N	Y	N	Y	Y	N
Coverdell	Y	N	Y	Y	N	Y	N	N
HAWAII								
Akaka	Y	Y	N	Y	Y	N	N	N
Inouye	Y	Y	N	Y	Y	N	Y	N
IDAHO								
Craig	Y	N	Y	Y	N	Y	N	Y
Kempthorne	Y	N	Y	Y	N	Y	N	?
ILLINOIS								
Moseley-Braun	?	Y	N	Y	Y	N	Y	N
Simon	N	Y	N	Y	Y	N	Y	N
INDIANA								
Coats	Y	N	Y	Y	N	Y	Y	Y
Lugar	Y	N	Y	Y	N	Y	N	N

	114	115	116	117	118	119	120	121
IOWA								
Harkin	N	Y	N	Y	Y	N	Y	N
Grassley	Y	N	Y	Y	N	Y	Y	Y
KANSAS								
Dole	Y	N	Y	Y	N	Y	N	Y
Kassebaum	Y	N	Y	Y	N	Y	Y	N
KENTUCKY								
Ford	Y	Y	N	Y	Y	N	N	N
McConnell	Y	N	Y	Y	N	Y	N	Y
LOUISIANA								
Breaux	Y	N	N	Y	N	Y	N	N
Johnston	N	N	N	Y	Y	N	N	?
MAINE								
Mitchell	Y	Y	N	Y	Y	N	Y	N
Cohen	Y	Y	Y	Y	N	Y	Y	N
MARYLAND								
Mikulski	Y	Y	N	Y	Y	N	Y	N
Sarbanes	Y	Y	N	Y	Y	N	Y	N
MASSACHUSETTS								
Kennedy	Y	Y	N	Y	Y	N	Y	N
Kerry	Y	Y	N	Y	Y	N	Y	N
MICHIGAN								
Levin	Y	Y	N	Y	Y	N	Y	N
Riegle	N	Y	N	?	?	?	Y	N
MINNESOTA								
Wellstone	Y	Y	N	N	Y	N	Y	N
Durenberger	Y	Y	N	Y	Y	N	Y	N
MISSISSIPPI								
Cochran	Y	N	Y	Y	N	Y	N	Y
Lott	Y	N	Y	Y	N	Y	N	Y
MISSOURI								
Bond	Y	N	Y	Y	N	Y	N	N
Danforth	Y	N	Y	Y	N	Y	Y	N
MONTANA								
Baucus	Y	Y	N	Y	Y	N	Y	N
Burns	Y	N	N	Y	N	Y	N	Y
NEBRASKA								
Exon	N	Y	N	Y	N	Y	Y	N
Kerrey	N	Y	N	Y	N	Y	Y	N
NEVADA								
Bryan	N	Y	N	N	Y	N	Y	N
Reid	N	Y	N	Y	Y	N	Y	N

	114	115	116	117	118	119	120	121
NEW HAMPSHIRE								
Gregg	Y	N	Y	Y	N	Y	Y	Y
Smith	Y	N	Y	Y	N	Y	Y	Y
NEW JERSEY								
Bradley	N	Y	N	Y	Y	N	Y	N
Lautenberg	N	Y	N	Y	Y	N	Y	N
NEW MEXICO								
Bingaman	N	Y	N	Y	Y	N	Y	N
Domenici	N	N	Y	Y	N	Y	N	N
NEW YORK								
Moynihan	Y	Y	N	Y	Y	N	Y	N
D'Amato	N	N	N	Y	Y	N	N	Y
NORTH CAROLINA								
Faircloth	Y	N	Y	Y	N	Y	N	Y
Helms	Y	N	Y	Y	N	Y	N	Y
NORTH DAKOTA								
Conrad	Y	Y	N	Y	Y	N	Y	?
Dorgan	Y	Y	N	Y	Y	N	Y	N
OHIO								
Glenn	Y	Y	N	Y	Y	N	Y	N
Metzenbaum	Y	Y	N	N	Y	N	Y	N
OKLAHOMA								
Boren	N	Y	Y	Y	N	Y	N	N
Nickles	Y	N	Y	Y	N	Y	Y	Y
OREGON								
Hatfield	Y	N	N	Y	Y	N	N	N
Packwood	Y	Y	N	Y	N	N	Y	N
PENNSYLVANIA								
Wofford	Y	Y	N	Y	Y	N	Y	N
Specter	Y	N	N	Y	N	Y	N	N
RHODE ISLAND								
Pell	Y	Y	N	Y	Y	N	Y	N
Chafee	Y	Y	Y	N	N	Y	Y	N
SOUTH CAROLINA								
Hollings	Y	Y	N	Y	Y	N	Y	N
Thurmond	Y	N	Y	Y	N	Y	N	Y
SOUTH DAKOTA								
Daschle	Y	Y	N	Y	Y	N	Y	N
Pressler	Y	N	Y	Y	N	Y	N	Y
TENNESSEE								
Mathews	Y	N	N	Y	N	Y	Y	N
Sasser	Y	N	N	Y	N	N	Y	N

	114	115	116	117	118	119	120	121
TEXAS								
Hutchison	N	N	Y	Y	N	Y	N	Y
Gramm	N	N	Y	Y	N	Y	N	Y
UTAH								
Bennett	Y	N	Y	Y	N	Y	N	Y
Hatch	Y	N	Y	Y	N	Y	N	Y
VERMONT								
Leahy	Y	Y	N	Y	Y	N	Y	N
Jeffords	Y	Y	N	N	Y	N	Y	N
VIRGINIA								
Robb	Y	Y	N	Y	Y	N	Y	N
Warner	Y	Y	Y	Y	N	Y	Y	Y
WASHINGTON								
Murray	Y	Y	N	Y	Y	N	Y	N
Gorton	Y	N	Y	Y	N	Y	N	N
WEST VIRGINIA								
Byrd	Y	Y	N	Y	Y	N	Y	N
Rockefeller	Y	Y	N	Y	Y	N	Y	N
WISCONSIN								
Feingold	Y	Y	N	N	Y	N	Y	N
Kohl	Y	Y	N	Y	Y	N	Y	N
WYOMING								
Simpson	Y	N	Y	Y	N	Y	N	Y
Wallop	Y	N	Y	Y	N	Y	N	Y

ND Northern Democrats SD Southern Democrats Southern states - Ala., Ark., Fla., Ga., Ky., La., Miss., N.C., Okla., S.C., Tenn., Texas, Va.

---

114. S 2019. Safe Drinking Water Act Reauthorization/ Mexican Border Water Treatment Inadequacies. Baucus, D-Mont., motion to table (kill) the DeConcini, D-Ariz., amendment to authorize the Environmental Protection Agency administrator to transfer money to communities along the U.S.-Mexico border to facilitate wastewater treatment projects. Motion agreed to 75-23: R 39-5; D 36-18 (ND 26-15, SD 10-3), May 17, 1994.

115. S 2019. Safe Drinking Water Act Reauthorization/ Unfunded Federal Mandates. Baucus, D-Mont., motion to table (kill) the Gregg, R-N.H., amendment to prohibit penalties against communities that cannot afford to comply with the Safe Water Drinking Act. Motion agreed to 56-43: R 7-37; D 49-6 (ND 42-0, SD 7-6), May 17, 1994.

116. S 2019. Safe Drinking Water Act Reauthorization/ Davis-Bacon Standards. Faircloth, R-N.C. amendment to strike from the bill the Davis-Bacon provisions, which require contractors on federal projects to pay the locally prevailing wage. Rejected 39-60: R 36-8; D 3-52 (ND 0-42, SD 3-10), May 17, 1994.

117. S 2019. Safe Drinking Water Act Reauthorization/ Risk Assessment. Johnston, D-La., amendment to require an analysis of risk, costs and benefits for regulations issued by the Environmental Protection Agency to enforce the bill that would have an impact of $100 million or more. Adopted 90-8: R 41-3; D 49-5 (ND 36-5, SD 13-0), May 18, 1994.

118. S 2019. Safe Drinking Water Act Reauthorization/ Davis-Bacon Standards. Metzenbaum, D-Ohio, motion to table (kill) the Smith, R-N.H., amendment to exempt the state revolving loan fund from Davis-Bacon provisions, which require contractors on federal projects to pay the locally prevailing wage. Motion agreed to 52-46: R 6-38; D 46-8 (ND 40-1, SD 6-7), May 18, 1994.

119. S 2019. Safe Drinking Water Act Reauthorization/ Davis-Bacon Standards. Simpson, R-Wyo., amendment to exempt water construction projects in disadvantaged communities from Davis-Bacon provisions, which require contractors on federal projects to pay the locally prevailing wage. Rejected 45-53: R 38-6;

120. S 2019. Safe Drinking Water Act Reauthorization/ Royalty Suspension. Baucus, D-Mont., motion to table (kill) Johnston, D-La., amendment to allow the secretary of the Interior to suspend royalties on deep-water oil and natural gas leases until capital costs are recovered. Motion agreed to 65-34: R 17-27; D 48-7 (ND 40-2, SD 8-5), May 18, 1994.

121. S 2019. Safe Drinking Water Act Reauthorization/ State Determination. Wallop, R-Wyo, amendment to permit each state to determine its own drinking water regulations. Rejected 28-67: R 28-14; D 0-53 (ND 0-41, SD 0-12), May 18, 1994.

	122	123	124	125	126
ALABAMA					
Heflin	Y	N	N	Y	N
Shelby	?	?	?	?	?
ALASKA					
Murkowski	Y	Y	Y	Y	Y
Stevens	Y	Y	Y	Y	Y
ARIZONA					
DeConcini	Y	N	Y	Y	Y
McCain	Y	Y	Y	Y	Y
ARKANSAS					
Bumpers	Y	N	Y	Y	N
Pryor	Y	Y	Y	Y	N
CALIFORNIA					
Boxer	Y	Y	Y	Y	N
Feinstein	Y	Y	Y	Y	Y
COLORADO					
Campbell	Y	Y	Y	Y	N
Brown	Y	Y	Y	Y	Y
CONNECTICUT					
Dodd	Y	N	N	Y	Y
Lieberman	Y	Y	Y	Y	Y
DELAWARE					
Biden	Y	N	N	Y	N
Roth	Y	Y	Y	Y	Y
FLORIDA					
Graham	Y	Y	Y	Y	N
Mack	Y	Y	Y	Y	Y
GEORGIA					
Nunn	Y	Y	Y	Y	Y
Coverdell	Y	Y	Y	Y	Y
HAWAII					
Akaka	Y	Y	N	Y	N
Inouye	Y	Y	N	Y	N
IDAHO					
Craig	Y	Y	Y	Y	Y
Kempthorne	Y	Y	Y	Y	Y
ILLINOIS					
Moseley-Braun	Y	N	N	Y	N
Simon	Y	N	N	Y	N
INDIANA					
Coats	Y	Y	Y	Y	N
Lugar	Y	Y	Y	Y	Y

	122	123	124	125	126
IOWA					
Harkin	Y	Y	N	Y	N
Grassley	Y	Y	Y	Y	Y
KANSAS					
Dole	Y	Y	Y	Y	Y
Kassebaum	Y	Y	Y	Y	Y
KENTUCKY					
Ford	Y	Y	Y	Y	Y
McConnell	Y	Y	Y	Y	Y
LOUISIANA					
Breaux	Y	Y	Y	Y	Y
Johnston	Y	N	N	Y	N
MAINE					
Mitchell	Y	N	N	Y	N
Cohen	Y	Y	Y	Y	N
MARYLAND					
Mikulski	Y	Y	Y	Y	Y
Sarbanes	Y	Y	Y	Y	N
MASSACHUSETTS					
Kennedy	Y	?	?	?	?
Kerry	Y	N	N	Y	N
MICHIGAN					
Levin	Y	N	N	Y	N
Riegle	Y	Y	Y	Y	Y
MINNESOTA					
Wellstone	Y	N	N	Y	N
Durenberger	Y	N	N	Y	N
MISSISSIPPI					
Cochran	Y	Y	Y	Y	N
Lott	Y	Y	Y	Y	Y
MISSOURI					
Bond	Y	Y	Y	Y	N
Danforth	Y	Y	N	Y	N
MONTANA					
Baucus	Y	Y	Y	Y	Y
Burns	Y	Y	Y	Y	Y
NEBRASKA					
Exon	Y	Y	Y	Y	Y
Kerrey	Y	Y	Y	Y	Y
NEVADA					
Bryan	Y	Y	Y	Y	Y
Reid	Y	Y	Y	Y	N

	122	123	124	125	126
NEW HAMPSHIRE					
Gregg	Y	Y	Y	Y	N
Smith	Y	Y	Y	Y	Y
NEW JERSEY					
Bradley	Y	N	N	Y	N
Lautenberg	Y	Y	Y	Y	N
NEW MEXICO					
Bingaman	Y	Y	Y	Y	N
Domenici	Y	?	Y	Y	Y
NEW YORK					
Moynihan	Y	N	N	Y	N
D'Amato	Y	Y	Y	Y	Y
NORTH CAROLINA					
Faircloth	N	Y	Y	Y	Y
Helms	N	Y	Y	N	Y
NORTH DAKOTA					
Conrad	Y	Y	Y	Y	Y
Dorgan	Y	Y	N	Y	Y
OHIO					
Glenn	Y	N	N	Y	N
Metzenbaum	Y	N	N	Y	N
OKLAHOMA					
Boren	Y	N	N	Y	N
Nickles	Y	Y	Y	N	N
OREGON					
Hatfield	Y	N	N	N	N
Packwood	Y	N	N	Y	N
PENNSYLVANIA					
Wofford	Y	Y	Y	Y	N
Specter	Y	N	Y	N	N
RHODE ISLAND					
Pell	+	N	N	Y	N
Chafee	Y	Y	N	Y	N
SOUTH CAROLINA					
Hollings	Y	Y	Y	Y	Y
Thurmond	Y	Y	Y	Y	Y
SOUTH DAKOTA					
Daschle	Y	Y	N	Y	N
Pressler	N	Y	Y	Y	Y
TENNESSEE					
Mathews	Y	Y	N	Y	N
Sasser	Y	Y	Y	Y	Y

KEY

Y	Voted for (yea).	
#	Paired for.	
+	Announced for.	
N	Voted against (nay).	
X	Paired against.	
−	Announced against.	
P	Voted "present."	
C	Voted "present" to avoid possible conflict of interest.	
?	Did not vote or otherwise make a position known.	

Democrats *Republicans*

	122	123	124	125	126
TEXAS					
Hutchison	Y	Y	Y	Y	Y
Gramm	Y	Y	Y	Y	Y
UTAH					
Bennett	Y	Y	Y	Y	Y
Hatch	Y	Y	Y	Y	Y
VERMONT					
Leahy	Y	Y	N	Y	N
Jeffords	Y	N	N	Y	Y
VIRGINIA					
Robb	Y	?	Y	Y	Y
Warner	Y	Y	Y	Y	Y
WASHINGTON					
Murray	Y	N	N	Y	N
Gorton	Y	Y	Y	Y	N
WEST VIRGINIA					
Byrd	Y	Y	Y	Y	Y
Rockefeller	Y	Y	Y	Y	Y
WISCONSIN					
Feingold	Y	N	N	Y	N
Kohl	Y	Y	Y	Y	N
WYOMING					
Simpson	Y	Y	Y	Y	Y
Wallop	Y	Y	Y	N	Y

ND Northern Democrats   SD Southern Democrats   Southern states - Ala., Ark., Fla., Ga., Ky., La., Miss., N.C., Okla., S.C., Tenn., Texas, Va.

122. S 2019. Safe Drinking Water/Passage. Passage of the bill to reauthorize and update the 1974 Safe Drinking Water Act, giving local governments more flexibility to tailor safe drinking water programs. The bill also would establish a $6.6 billion revolving loan fund to help states build or modernize water treatment systems. Passed 95-3: R 41-3; D 54-0 (ND 41-0, SD 13-0), May 19, 1994. A "yea" was a vote in support of the president's position.

123. HR 3355. Omnibus Crime Bill/Conference Instructions. Conrad, D-N.D., motion to instruct the Senate conferees to insist on the Senate provisions that require states to provide for truth in sentencing — requiring violent felons to serve at least 85 percent of their sentences — in order to be eligible for federal prison funds. Motion agreed to 74-22: R 39-4; D 35-18 (ND 27-14, SD 8-4), May 19, 1994.

124. HR 3355. Omnibus Crime Bill/Conference Instructions. Gramm, R-Texas, motion to instruct the Senate conferees to insist on a Violent Crime Reduction Trust Fund of not less than $22.3 billion and mandatory minimum prison sentences for those who sell drugs to minors, use a minor in drug trafficking or use a firearm during a violent crime or drug trafficking crime. The instructions only allow mandatory minimum sentences to be suspended for first-time, non-violent offenders. Motion agreed to 66-32: R 37-7; D 29-25 (ND 20-21, SD 9-4), May 19, 1994.

125. HR 3355. Omnibus Crime Bill/Conference Instructions. Biden, D-Del., motion to instruct the Senate conferees to insist on a Violent Crime Reduction Trust Fund to support vital programs ranging from prevention to punishment; an additional 100,000 police officers; state and local crime prevention programs; secure prison facilities for violent offenders; boot camps; tough penalties for violent criminals; a Violence Against Women Act; a Senior Citizens Against Marketing Scams Act; rural crime provisions; and other provisions. Adopted 94-4: R 40-4; D 54-0 (ND 41-0, SD 13-0), May 19, 1994.

126. HR 3355. Omnibus Crime Bill/Conference Instructions. D'Amato, R-N.Y., motion to instruct the Senate conferees to insist on the Senate provisions to require mandatory prison terms for the use, possession or carrying of a firearm during a crime committed under state law. Adopted 51-47: R 31-13; D 20-34 (ND 14-27, SD 6-7), May 19, 1994.

SENATE VOTES 127, 128, 129, 130, 131, 132, 133

	127	128	129	130	131	132	133
ALABAMA							
Heflin	N	Y	Y	Y	Y	Y	Y
Shelby	?	?	?	?	?	?	?
ALASKA							
Murkowski	Y	N	N	N	N	N	Y
Stevens	N	Y	N	N	N	N	Y
ARIZONA							
DeConcini	N	Y	Y	Y	Y	Y	Y
McCain	Y	N	N	N	N	N	Y
ARKANSAS							
Bumpers	N	Y	Y	Y	Y	Y	Y
Pryor	?	?	?	?	?	Y	Y
CALIFORNIA							
Boxer	N	Y	Y	Y	Y	Y	Y
Feinstein	N	Y	Y	Y	Y	Y	Y
COLORADO							
Campbell	N	Y	Y	Y	N	N	Y
Brown	Y	Y	N	N	N	N	Y
CONNECTICUT							
Dodd	N	Y	Y	Y	Y	Y	Y
Lieberman	N	Y	Y	Y	Y	Y	Y
DELAWARE							
Biden	N	Y	Y	Y	Y	Y	Y
Roth	N	Y	N	Y	N	N	Y
FLORIDA							
Graham	N	Y	Y	Y	Y	Y	Y
Mack	N	Y	N	N	N	N	Y
GEORGIA							
Nunn	N	Y	Y	Y	N	N	Y
Coverdell	Y	N	N	N	N	N	Y
HAWAII							
Akaka	N	Y	Y	Y	Y	Y	Y
Inouye	N	Y	Y	Y	Y	Y	Y
IDAHO							
Craig	Y	Y	N	N	N	N	Y
Kempthorne	Y	Y	N	N	N	N	Y
ILLINOIS							
Moseley-Braun	N	Y	Y	Y	Y	Y	Y
Simon	N	Y	Y	Y	Y	Y	Y
INDIANA							
Coats	N	Y	N	N	N	N	Y
Lugar	N	Y	Y	Y	N	N	Y
IOWA							
Harkin	N	Y	Y	Y	Y	Y	Y
Grassley	Y	Y	N	N	Y	Y	Y
KANSAS							
Dole	Y	Y	N	N	N	N	Y
Kassebaum	Y	Y	Y	Y	Y	Y	Y
KENTUCKY							
Ford	N	Y	Y	Y	N	Y	Y
McConnell	Y	Y	N	N	N	N	Y
LOUISIANA							
Breaux	N	Y	Y	Y	Y	Y	Y
Johnston	N	Y	Y	Y	Y	Y	Y
MAINE							
Mitchell	N	Y	Y	Y	Y	Y	Y
Cohen	N	Y	N	N	N	N	Y
MARYLAND							
Mikulski	N	Y	Y	Y	Y	Y	Y
Sarbanes	N	Y	Y	Y	Y	Y	Y
MASSACHUSETTS							
Kennedy	N	Y	Y	Y	Y	Y	?
Kerry	N	Y	Y	Y	Y	Y	Y
MICHIGAN							
Levin	N	Y	Y	Y	Y	Y	Y
Riegle	N	Y	Y	Y	Y	Y	Y
MINNESOTA							
Wellstone	N	Y	Y	Y	Y	Y	Y
Durenberger	N	Y	Y	Y	N	N	Y
MISSISSIPPI							
Cochran	N	Y	N	N	N	N	Y
Lott	Y	Y	N	N	N	N	Y
MISSOURI							
Bond	Y	Y	N	N	N	N	Y
Danforth	N	Y	Y	Y	Y	Y	Y
MONTANA							
Baucus	Y	Y	Y	Y	Y	Y	Y
Burns	Y	Y	N	N	N	N	Y
NEBRASKA							
Exon	N	Y	Y	Y	N	Y	Y
Kerrey	N	Y	Y	Y	N	N	Y
NEVADA							
Bryan	N	Y	Y	Y	Y	Y	Y
Reid	N	Y	Y	Y	Y	Y	Y
NEW HAMPSHIRE							
Gregg	Y	Y	N	N	N	N	Y
Smith	Y	N	N	N	N	N	Y
NEW JERSEY							
Bradley	N	Y	Y	Y	Y	Y	Y
Lautenberg	N	Y	Y	Y	Y	Y	Y
NEW MEXICO							
Bingaman	N	Y	Y	Y	Y	Y	Y
Domenici	N	Y	N	Y	N	N	Y
NEW YORK							
Moynihan	N	Y	Y	Y	Y	Y	Y
D'Amato	N	Y	N	N	N	N	Y
NORTH CAROLINA							
Faircloth	Y	N	N	N	N	−	Y
Helms	Y	N	N	N	N	N	N
NORTH DAKOTA							
Conrad	N	Y	Y	Y	N	N	Y
Dorgan	N	Y	Y	Y	Y	Y	Y
OHIO							
Glenn	N	Y	Y	Y	Y	Y	Y
Metzenbaum	N	Y	Y	Y	Y	Y	Y
OKLAHOMA							
Boren	N	Y	Y	Y	Y	Y	Y
Nickles	Y	N	N	N	N	N	Y
OREGON							
Hatfield	N	Y	Y	Y	Y	Y	Y
Packwood	Y	Y	N	Y	N	N	Y
PENNSYLVANIA							
Wofford	N	Y	Y	Y	Y	Y	Y
Specter	N	Y	Y	Y	N	N	Y
RHODE ISLAND							
Pell	N	Y	Y	Y	Y	Y	Y
Chafee	N	Y	Y	Y	N	N	Y
SOUTH CAROLINA							
Hollings	N	Y	N	Y	N	N	Y
Thurmond	Y	Y	N	N	N	N	Y
SOUTH DAKOTA							
Daschle	N	Y	Y	Y	Y	Y	Y
Pressler	Y	Y	N	N	N	N	Y
TENNESSEE							
Mathews	N	Y	Y	Y	Y	Y	Y
Sasser	N	Y	Y	Y	Y	Y	Y
TEXAS							
Hutchison	Y	Y	N	N	N	N	Y
Gramm	Y	Y	N	N	N	N	Y
UTAH							
Bennett	Y	Y	N	Y	N	N	Y
Hatch	Y	Y	N	Y	N	N	Y
VERMONT							
Leahy	N	Y	Y	Y	Y	Y	Y
Jeffords	N	Y	Y	Y	Y	Y	Y
VIRGINIA							
Robb	N	Y	Y	Y	Y	Y	Y
Warner	N	Y	N	N	N	N	Y
WASHINGTON							
Murray	N	Y	Y	Y	Y	Y	Y
Gorton	Y	Y	Y	Y	N	N	Y
WEST VIRGINIA							
Byrd	N	Y	Y	Y	Y	Y	Y
Rockefeller	N	Y	Y	Y	Y	Y	Y
WISCONSIN							
Feingold	N	Y	Y	Y	Y	Y	Y
Kohl	N	Y	Y	Y	Y	Y	Y
WYOMING							
Simpson	N	Y	N	N	N	N	Y
Wallop	Y	N	N	N	N	N	Y

ND Northern Democrats   SD Southern Democrats   Southern states - Ala., Ark., Fla., Ga., Ky., La., Miss., N.C., Okla., S.C., Tenn., Texas, Va.

127. HR 1933. Martin Luther Jr. King Holiday Commission/Federal Financing Prohibition. Helms, R-N.C., amendment to prohibit federal financing for the Martin Luther King Jr. Federal Holiday Commission. Rejected 28-70: R 27-17; D 1-53 (ND 1-41, SD 0-12), May 24, 1994.

128. HR 1933. Martin Luther King Jr. Holiday Commission/Passage. Passage of the bill to authorize $2 million over five years from fiscal 1995-99 for the Martin Luther King Jr. Federal Holiday Commission and broaden the commission's legislative mandate to include promoting community service. Passed 94-4: R 40-4; D 54-0 (ND 42-0, SD 12-0), May 24, 1994.

129. Shearer Nomination/Cloture. Motion to invoke cloture (thus limiting debate) on the confirmation of President Clinton's nomination of Derek Shearer of California to be ambassador to Finland. Motion agreed to 63-35: R 9-35; D 54-0 (ND 42-0, SD 12-0), May 24, 1994. Three-fifths of the total Senate (60) is required to invoke cloture.

130. Shearer Nomination/Confirmation. Confirmation of President Clinton's nomination of Derek Shearer of California to be ambassador to Finland. Confirmed 67-31: R 14-30; D 53-1 (ND 42-0, SD 11-1), May 24, 1994. A "yea" was a vote in support of the president's position.

131. Brown Nomination/Cloture. Motion to invoke cloture (thus limiting debate) on the confirmation of President Clinton's nomination of Sam W. Brown Jr. of California for the rank of ambassador during his tenure as head of the delegation to the conference on Security and Cooperation in Europe. Motion rejected 54-44: R 5-39; D 49-5 (ND 39-3, SD 10-2), May 24, 1994. Three-fifths of the total Senate (60) is required to invoke cloture.

132. Brown Nomination/Cloture. Motion to invoke cloture (thus limiting debate) on the confirmation of President Clinton's nomination of Sam W. Brown Jr. of California for the rank of Ambassador during his tenure as Head of the Delegation to the conference on Security and Cooperation in Europe. Motion rejected 56-42: R 5-38; D 51-4 (ND 39-3, SD 12-1), May 25, 1994. Three-fifths of the total Senate (60) is required to invoke cloture. A "yea" was a vote in support of the president's position.

133. S 729. Lead Exposure Reduction/Passage. Passage of the bill to gradually ban lead in products such as paints, toys, pesticides and plumbing fixtures; require the Environmental Protection Agency to maintain an inventory of the uses of lead; establish a pre-manufacture notification program for new lead products; establish a mandatory recycling program for lead acid batteries; and through various other programs. Passed 97-1: R 43-1; D 54-0 (ND 41-0, SD 13-0), May 25, 1994.

	134	135	136	137	138	139	140
ALABAMA							
Heflin	Y	Y	Y	Y	Y	Y	Y
Shelby	Y	Y	Y	Y	Y	Y	Y
ALASKA							
Murkowski	N	N	N	N	N	N	N
Stevens	Y	Y	Y	N	N	N	N
ARIZONA							
DeConcini	Y	Y	Y	Y	Y	Y	Y
McCain	N	N	N	N	N	N	N
ARKANSAS							
Bumpers	Y	Y	Y	Y	Y	Y	Y
Pryor	Y	Y	Y	Y	Y	Y	Y
CALIFORNIA							
Boxer	Y	?	Y	Y	Y	Y	Y
Feinstein	Y	Y	Y	Y	Y	Y	Y
COLORADO							
Campbell	Y	Y	Y	Y	Y	Y	Y
Brown	Y	Y	Y	N	N	N	N
CONNECTICUT							
Dodd	Y	?	Y	Y	Y	Y	Y
Lieberman	Y	Y	Y	Y	Y	Y	Y
DELAWARE							
Biden	?	?	Y	Y	Y	Y	Y
Roth	Y	Y	Y	N	N	N	N
FLORIDA							
Graham	Y	Y	Y	Y	Y	Y	Y
Mack	Y	Y	Y	N	N	N	N
GEORGIA							
Nunn	Y	?	Y	Y	Y	Y	Y
Coverdell	Y	Y	Y	N	?	?	N
HAWAII							
Akaka	Y	Y	Y	Y	Y	Y	Y
Inouye	?	?	Y	Y	Y	Y	Y
IDAHO							
Craig	N	N	Y	N	N	N	N
Kempthorne	N	N	Y	N	N	N	N
ILLINOIS							
Moseley-Braun	Y	Y	Y	Y	Y	Y	Y
Simon	Y	Y	Y	Y	Y	Y	Y
INDIANA							
Coats	Y	Y	Y	N	N	N	N
Lugar	Y	Y	Y	N	N	N	N

	134	135	136	137	138	139	140
IOWA							
Harkin	Y	Y	Y	Y	Y	Y	Y
Grassley	Y	Y	Y	N	N	N	N
KANSAS							
Dole	Y	Y	Y	N	N	N	N
Kassebaum	Y	Y	Y	N	N	N	N
KENTUCKY							
Ford	Y	Y	Y	Y	Y	Y	Y
McConnell	N	?	N	N	N	N	N
LOUISIANA							
Breaux	Y	Y	N	Y	Y	Y	Y
Johnston	Y	Y	Y	Y	Y	Y	Y
MAINE							
Mitchell	Y	Y	Y	Y	Y	Y	Y
Cohen	Y	Y	Y	N	N	N	N
MARYLAND							
Mikulski	Y	Y	Y	Y	Y	Y	Y
Sarbanes	Y	Y	Y	Y	Y	Y	Y
MASSACHUSETTS							
Kennedy	Y	Y	Y	Y	Y	Y	Y
Kerry	Y	?	Y	Y	Y	Y	Y
MICHIGAN							
Levin	Y	Y	Y	Y	Y	Y	Y
Riegle	Y	Y	Y	Y	Y	Y	Y
MINNESOTA							
Wellstone	Y	Y	Y	Y	Y	Y	Y
Durenberger	Y	Y	Y	N	N	N	N
MISSISSIPPI							
Cochran	Y	?	Y	N	N	N	N
Lott	N	N	N	N	N	N	N
MISSOURI							
Bond	Y	N	Y	N	N	N	N
Danforth	Y	Y	Y	N	N	N	N
MONTANA							
Baucus	Y	Y	Y	Y	Y	Y	Y
Burns	N	N	Y	N	N	N	N
NEBRASKA							
Exon	Y	Y	Y	Y	Y	Y	Y
Kerrey	Y	Y	Y	Y	Y	Y	Y
NEVADA							
Bryan	Y	Y	Y	Y	Y	Y	Y
Reid	Y	Y	Y	Y	Y	Y	Y

	134	135	136	137	138	139	140
NEW HAMPSHIRE							
Gregg	Y	Y	Y	N	N	N	N
Smith	Y	N	N	N	N	N	N
NEW JERSEY							
Bradley	Y	Y	Y	Y	Y	Y	Y
Lautenberg	?	?	Y	Y	Y	Y	Y
NEW MEXICO							
Bingaman	Y	Y	Y	Y	Y	Y	Y
Domenici	Y	Y	Y	N	N	N	N
NEW YORK							
Moynihan	Y	Y	Y	Y	Y	Y	Y
D'Amato	N	N	N	N	N	N	N
NORTH CAROLINA							
Faircloth	?	?	N	N	N	N	N
Helms	N	N	N	N	N	N	N
NORTH DAKOTA							
Conrad	Y	Y	Y	Y	Y	Y	Y
Dorgan	Y	Y	Y	Y	Y	Y	Y
OHIO							
Glenn	Y	Y	Y	Y	Y	Y	Y
Metzenbaum	Y	Y	Y	Y	Y	Y	Y
OKLAHOMA							
Boren	?	?	Y	Y	Y	Y	Y
Nickles	N	N	N	N	N	N	N
OREGON							
Hatfield	Y	Y	Y	–	N	N	N
Packwood	Y	Y	Y	N	N	N	N
PENNSYLVANIA							
Wofford	Y	Y	Y	Y	Y	Y	Y
Specter	N	?	?	N	N	N	N
RHODE ISLAND							
Pell	Y	Y	Y	Y	Y	Y	Y
Chafee	Y	Y	Y	N	N	N	N
SOUTH CAROLINA							
Hollings	Y	?	Y	Y	Y	Y	Y
Thurmond	Y	Y	Y	N	N	N	N
SOUTH DAKOTA							
Daschle	Y	Y	Y	Y	Y	Y	Y
Pressler	Y	Y	Y	N	N	N	N
TENNESSEE							
Mathews	Y	Y	Y	Y	Y	Y	Y
Sasser	Y	Y	Y	Y	Y	Y	Y

KEY

Y	Voted for (yea).
#	Paired for.
+	Announced for.
N	Voted against (nay).
X	Paired against.
–	Announced against.
P	Voted "present."
C	Voted "present" to avoid possible conflict of interest.
?	Did not vote or otherwise make a position known.

Democrats *Republicans*

	134	135	136	137	138	139	140
TEXAS							
Hutchison	?	?	Y	N	N	N	N
Gramm	?	?	N	N	N	N	N
UTAH							
Bennett	?	?	Y	N	N	N	N
Hatch	Y	Y	Y	N	N	N	N
VERMONT							
Leahy	Y	Y	Y	Y	Y	Y	Y
Jeffords	Y	Y	N	N	N	N	N
VIRGINIA							
Robb	?	?	Y	Y	Y	Y	Y
Warner	N	N	Y	N	N	N	N
WASHINGTON							
Murray	Y	Y	Y	Y	Y	Y	Y
Gorton	Y	Y	Y	N	N	N	N
WEST VIRGINIA							
Byrd	Y	Y	Y	Y	Y	Y	Y
Rockefeller	Y	Y	Y	Y	Y	Y	Y
WISCONSIN							
Feingold	Y	Y	Y	Y	Y	Y	Y
Kohl	Y	Y	Y	Y	Y	Y	Y
WYOMING							
Simpson	Y	Y	Y	N	N	N	N
Wallop	N	N	N	N	N	N	N

ND Northern Democrats   SD Southern Democrats   Southern states - Ala., Ark., Fla., Ga., Ky., La., Miss., N.C., Okla., S.C., Tenn., Texas, Va.

134. Procedural Motion. Mitchell, D-Maine, motion to instruct the sergeant at arms to request the attendance of absent senators. Motion agreed to 78-13: R 27-13; D 51-0 (ND 39-0, SD 12-0), June 10, 1994.

135. Procedural Motion. Mitchell, D-Maine, motion to instruct the sergeant at arms to request the attendance of absent senators. Motion agreed to 70-13: R 24-13; D 46-0 (ND 36-0, SD 10-0), June 10, 1994.

136. Procedural Motion. Mitchell, D-Maine, motion to instruct the sergeant at arms to request the attendance of absent senators. Motion agreed to 86-13: R 31-12; D 55-1 (ND 42-0, SD 13-1), June 14, 1994.

137. S 1491. Airport Improvement Program Reauthorization/Whitewater Hearings. Mitchell, D-Maine, amendment to the D'Amato, R-N.Y., amendment, to set hearings into the "Washington phase" of Whitewater, beginning in the Banking Committee no later than July 29. The D'Amato amendment would have established a 20-member special subcommittee of the Banking Committee evenly split along party lines with much broader authority to probe President Clinton's role in the Whitewater affair. Adopted 56-43: R 0-43; D 56-0 (ND 42-0, SD 14-0), June 14, 1994. (Subsequently, the D'Amato amendment as amended by the Mitchell amendment was adopted by voice vote.)

138. S 1491. Airport Improvement Program Reauthorization/Whitewater Hearings. Mitchell, D-Maine, amendment to the D'Amato, R-N.Y., amendment to provide for hearings into President Clinton's investments in the Whitewater development project in a manner agreed upon by the majority and minority leaders so as not to interfere with the special counsel's investigation. The D'Amato amendment would have authorized the Bank-

ing Committee to conduct hearings into Madison Guaranty Savings and Loan Association and the alleged use of federally insured money as campaign contributions. Adopted 56-43: R 0-43; D 56-0 (ND 42-0, SD 14-0), June 14, 1994. (Subsequently, the D'Amato amendment as amended by the Mitchell amendment was adopted by voice vote.)

139. S 1491. Airport Improvement Program Reauthorization/Whitewater Hearings. Mitchell, D-Maine, amendment to the D'Amato, R-N.Y., amendment to provide for hearings into President Clinton's investments in the Whitewater development project in a manner agreed upon by the majority and minority leaders so as not to interfere with the special counsel's investigation. The D'Amato amendment would have authorized the Banking Committee to conduct hearings into the pursuit by the Resolution Trust Corporation of civil causes of action against potentially liable parties associated with Madison Guaranty Savings and Loan Association. Adopted 56-43: R 0-43; D 56-0 (ND 42-0, SD 14-0), June 14, 1994. (Subsequently, the D'Amato amendment as amended by the Mitchell amendment was adopted by voice vote.)

140. S 1491. Airport Improvement Program Reauthorization/Whitewater Hearings. Daschle, D-S.D., amendment to the D'Amato, R-N.Y., amendment, to provide for hearings into President Clinton's investments in the Whitewater development project in a manner agreed upon by the majority and minority leaders so as not to interfere with the special counsel's investigation. The D'Amato amendment would have authorized a special subcommittee of the Banking Committee to hold hearings into the circumstances surrounding Hillary Rodham Clinton's commodity futures trading activities. Adopted 56-44: R 0-44; D 56-0 (ND 42-0, SD 14-0), June 15, 1994. (Subsequently, the D'Amato amendment as amended by the Daschle amendment was adopted by voice vote.)

KEY

Y Voted for (yea).
Paired for.
+ Announced for.
N Voted against (nay).
X Paired against.
− Announced against.
P Voted "present."
C Voted "present" to avoid possible conflict of interest.
? Did not vote or otherwise make a position known.

Democrats *Republicans*

	141	142	143	144	145
ALABAMA					
Heflin	Y	Y	Y	Y	Y
Shelby	Y	Y	Y	Y	Y
ALASKA					
Murkowski	N	N	N	N	N
Stevens	N	N	N	N	N
ARIZONA					
DeConcini	Y	Y	Y	Y	Y
McCain	N	N	N	N	N
ARKANSAS					
Bumpers	Y	Y	Y	Y	Y
Pryor	Y	Y	Y	Y	Y
CALIFORNIA					
Boxer	Y	Y	Y	Y	Y
Feinstein	Y	Y	Y	Y	Y
COLORADO					
Campbell	Y	Y	Y	Y	Y
Brown	N	N	N	N	N
CONNECTICUT					
Dodd	Y	Y	Y	Y	Y
Lieberman	Y	Y	Y	Y	Y
DELAWARE					
Biden	Y	Y	Y	Y	Y
Roth	N	N	N	N	N
FLORIDA					
Graham	Y	Y	Y	Y	Y
Mack	N	N	N	N	N
GEORGIA					
Nunn	Y	Y	Y	Y	Y
Coverdell	N	N	N	N	N
HAWAII					
Akaka	Y	Y	Y	Y	Y
Inouye	Y	Y	Y	Y	Y
IDAHO					
Craig	N	N	N	N	N
Kempthorne	N	N	N	N	N
ILLINOIS					
Moseley-Braun	Y	Y	Y	Y	Y
Simon	Y	Y	Y	Y	Y
INDIANA					
Coats	N	N	N	N	N
Lugar	N	N	N	N	N
IOWA					
Harkin	Y	Y	?	?	Y
Grassley	N	N	N	N	N
KANSAS					
Dole	N	N	N	N	N
Kassebaum	N	N	N	N	N
KENTUCKY					
Ford	Y	Y	Y	Y	Y
McConnell	N	N	N	N	N
LOUISIANA					
Breaux	?	Y	Y	Y	Y
Johnston	Y	Y	Y	Y	Y
MAINE					
Mitchell	Y	Y	Y	Y	Y
Cohen	N	N	N	N	N
MARYLAND					
Mikulski	Y	Y	Y	Y	Y
Sarbanes	Y	Y	Y	Y	Y
MASSACHUSETTS					
Kennedy	Y	Y	Y	Y	Y
Kerry	Y	Y	Y	Y	Y
MICHIGAN					
Levin	Y	Y	Y	Y	Y
Riegle	Y	Y	Y	Y	Y
MINNESOTA					
Wellstone	Y	Y	Y	Y	Y
Durenberger	N	N	N	N	N
MISSISSIPPI					
Cochran	N	N	N	N	N
Lott	N	N	N	N	N
MISSOURI					
Bond	N	N	N	N	N
Danforth	N	N	N	N	N
MONTANA					
Baucus	Y	Y	Y	Y	Y
Burns	N	N	N	N	N
NEBRASKA					
Exon	Y	Y	Y	Y	Y
Kerrey	Y	Y	Y	Y	Y
NEVADA					
Bryan	Y	Y	Y	Y	Y
Reid	Y	Y	Y	Y	Y
NEW HAMPSHIRE					
Gregg	N	N	N	N	N
Smith	N	N	N	N	N
NEW JERSEY					
Bradley	Y	Y	Y	Y	Y
Lautenberg	Y	Y	Y	Y	Y
NEW MEXICO					
Bingaman	Y	Y	Y	Y	Y
Domenici	N	N	N	N	N
NEW YORK					
Moynihan	Y	Y	Y	Y	Y
D'Amato	N	N	N	N	N
NORTH CAROLINA					
Faircloth	N	N	N	N	N
Helms	N	N	N	N	N
NORTH DAKOTA					
Conrad	Y	Y	Y	Y	Y
Dorgan	Y	Y	Y	Y	Y
OHIO					
Glenn	Y	Y	Y	Y	Y
Metzenbaum	Y	Y	Y	Y	Y
OKLAHOMA					
Boren	Y	Y	Y	Y	Y
Nickles	N	N	N	N	N
OREGON					
Hatfield	N	N	N	N	N
Packwood	N	N	N	N	N
PENNSYLVANIA					
Wofford	Y	Y	Y	Y	Y
Specter	N	N	N	N	N
RHODE ISLAND					
Pell	Y	Y	Y	Y	Y
Chafee	N	N	N	N	?
SOUTH CAROLINA					
Hollings	Y	Y	Y	Y	Y
Thurmond	N	N	N	N	N
SOUTH DAKOTA					
Daschle	Y	Y	Y	Y	Y
Pressler	N	N	N	N	N
TENNESSEE					
Mathews	Y	Y	Y	Y	Y
Sasser	Y	Y	Y	Y	Y
TEXAS					
Hutchison	N	N	N	N	N
Gramm	N	N	N	N	N
UTAH					
Bennett	N	N	N	N	N
Hatch	N	N	N	N	N
VERMONT					
Leahy	Y	Y	Y	Y	Y
Jeffords	N	N	N	N	N
VIRGINIA					
Robb	Y	Y	Y	Y	Y
Warner	N	N	N	N	N
WASHINGTON					
Murray	Y	Y	Y	Y	Y
Gorton	N	N	N	N	N
WEST VIRGINIA					
Byrd	Y	Y	Y	Y	Y
Rockefeller	Y	Y	Y	Y	Y
WISCONSIN					
Feingold	Y	Y	Y	Y	Y
Kohl	Y	Y	Y	Y	Y
WYOMING					
Simpson	N	N	N	N	N
Wallop	N	N	N	N	N

ND Northern Democrats   SD Southern Democrats   Southern states - Ala., Ark., Fla., Ga., Ky., La., Miss., N.C., Okla., S.C., Tenn., Texas, Va.

141. S 1491. Airport Improvement Program Reauthorization/Whitewater Hearings. Daschle, D-S.D., amendment to the Murkowski, R-Alaska, amendment to provide for hearings into President Clinton's investments in the Whitewater development project in a manner agreed upon by the majority and minority leaders so as not to interfere with the special counsel's investigation. The Murkowski amendment would have authorized a special Banking subcommittee to hold hearings into the Resolution Trust Corporation's handling of the criminal referrals concerning Madison Guaranty Savings and Loan Association. Adopted 55-44: R 0-44; D 55-0 (ND 42-0, SD 13-0), June 15, 1994. (Subsequently, the Murkowski amendment as amended by the Daschle amendment was adopted by voice vote.)

142. S 1491. Airport Improvement Program Reauthorization/Whitewater Hearings. Mitchell, D-Maine, amendment to the Lott, R-Miss., amendment to provide that hearings into President Clinton's investments in the Whitewater development project shall begin no later than July 29, 1994, or within 30 days after the conclusion of the first phase of the special counsel's investigation. The Lott amendment would have provided that the hearings would begin no later than July 15, 1994. Adopted 56-44: R 0-44; D 56-0 (ND 42-0, SD 14-0), June 15, 1994. (Subsequently, the Lott amendment as amended by the Mitchell amendment was adopted by voice vote.)

143. S 1491. Airport Improvement Program Reauthorization/Whitewater Hearings. Mitchell, D-Maine, amendment to the Specter, R-Pa., amendment to provide for hearings into President Clinton's investments in the Whitewater development project in a manner agreed upon by the majority and minority leaders so as not to interfere with the special counsel's investigation. The Specter amendment would have widened the scope of hearings by the Banking Committee to include improper contacts by White House

officials with the Resolution Trust Corporation, the Treasury Department, the Office of Thrift Supervision and any other federal agency. Adopted 55-44: R 0-44; D 55-0 (ND 41-0, SD 14-0), June 15, 1994. (Subsequently, the Specter amendment as amended by the Mitchell amendment was adopted by voice vote).

144. S 1491. Airport Improvement Program Reauthorization/Whitewater Hearings. Mitchell, D-Maine, amendment to the Bond, R-Mo., amendment, to provide for hearings into President Clinton's investments in the Whitewater development project in a manner agreed upon by the majority and minority leaders so as not to interfere with the special counsel's investigation. The Bond amendment would have authorized hearings into the Justice Department's handling of the Resolution Trust Corporation's criminal referrals relating to Madison Guaranty Savings and Loan Association. Adopted 55-44: R 0-44; D 55-0 (ND 41-0, SD 14-0), June 15, 1994. (Subsequently, the Bond amendment as amended by the Mitchell amendment was adopted by voice vote.)

145. S 1491. Airport Improvement Program Reauthorization/Whitewater Hearings. Mitchell, D-Maine, amendment to the Bond, R-Mo., amendment to provide for hearings into President Clinton's investments in the Whitewater development project in a manner agreed upon by the majority and minority leaders so as not to interfere with the special counsel's investigation. The Bond amendment would have authorized hearings into the sources of financing and the lending practices of Capital Management Services Inc. and its supervision and regulation by the Small Business Administration, including loans to Susan McDougal and the alleged diversion of money to Whitewater Development Corp. Adopted 56-43: R 0-43; D 56-0 (ND 42-0, SD 14-0), June 15, 1994. (Subsequently, the Bond amendment as amended by the Mitchell amendment was adopted by voice vote.)

KEY

Y Voted for (yea).
Paired for.
+ Announced for.
N Voted against (nay).
X Paired against.
− Announced against.
P Voted "present."
C Voted "present" to avoid possible conflict of interest.
? Did not vote or otherwise make a position known.

Democrats *Republicans*

State / Senator	146	147	148	149	150	151	152
ALABAMA							
Heflin	Y	N	Y	Y	Y	Y	N
Shelby	Y	N	Y	Y	Y	Y	N
ALASKA							
Murkowski	N	Y	N	Y	Y	Y	N
Stevens	N	Y	Y	Y	Y	Y	N
ARIZONA							
DeConcini	Y	N	Y	Y	Y	Y	Y
McCain	N	N	Y	Y	Y	?	?
ARKANSAS							
Bumpers	Y	N	Y	Y	Y	Y	N
Pryor	Y	N	Y	Y	Y	Y	N
CALIFORNIA							
Boxer	Y	N	Y	N	Y	Y	Y
Feinstein	Y	N	Y	N	Y	Y	Y
COLORADO							
Campbell	Y	N	Y	Y	Y	Y	Y
Brown	N	Y	N	Y	Y	Y	N
CONNECTICUT							
Dodd	Y	N	Y	Y	Y	Y	Y
Lieberman	Y	N	Y	Y	Y	Y	Y
DELAWARE							
Biden	Y	N	Y	Y	Y	Y	Y
Roth	N	N	Y	Y	Y	Y	N
FLORIDA							
Graham	Y	N	Y	Y	Y	Y	N
Mack	N	Y	Y	Y	Y	Y	N
GEORGIA							
Nunn	Y	N	Y	Y	Y	Y	N
Coverdell	N	Y	N	Y	Y	Y	N
HAWAII							
Akaka	Y	N	Y	Y	Y	Y	Y
Inouye	Y	N	Y	Y	?	?	?
IDAHO							
Craig	N	Y	N	Y	Y	Y	N
Kempthorne	N	Y	N	Y	Y	Y	N
ILLINOIS							
Moseley-Braun	Y	N	Y	Y	Y	+	?
Simon	Y	N	Y	N	?	?	?
INDIANA							
Coats	N	Y	N	Y	Y	Y	?
Lugar	N	Y	N	Y	Y	Y	N
IOWA							
Harkin	Y	N	Y	Y	Y	?	Y
Grassley	N	Y	N	Y	Y	Y	N
KANSAS							
Dole	N	Y	N	Y	Y	Y	N
Kassebaum	N	Y	Y	Y	Y	Y	N
KENTUCKY							
Ford	Y	N	Y	Y	Y	Y	Y
McConnell	N	Y	N	Y	Y	Y	N
LOUISIANA							
Breaux	Y	N	Y	Y	Y	Y	N
Johnston	Y	N	Y	Y	Y	Y	N
MAINE							
Mitchell	Y	N	Y	Y	Y	Y	Y
Cohen	N	N	Y	Y	Y	Y	N
MARYLAND							
Mikulski	Y	N	Y	Y	Y	Y	N
Sarbanes	Y	N	Y	Y	Y	Y	Y
MASSACHUSETTS							
Kennedy	Y	N	Y	Y	Y	Y	Y
Kerry	Y	N	Y	Y	Y	Y	N
MICHIGAN							
Levin	Y	N	Y	Y	Y	Y	Y
Riegle	Y	N	Y	?	Y	Y	Y
MINNESOTA							
Wellstone	Y	N	Y	Y	Y	Y	Y
Durenberger	N	N	Y	Y	Y	Y	N
MISSISSIPPI							
Cochran	N	Y	N	Y	Y	Y	N
Lott	N	Y	Y	Y	Y	Y	N
MISSOURI							
Bond	N	Y	N	Y	Y	Y	N
Danforth	N	N	Y	Y	Y	Y	N
MONTANA							
Baucus	Y	N	Y	Y	Y	Y	N
Burns	N	Y	N	Y	Y	Y	N
NEBRASKA							
Exon	Y	N	Y	Y	N	Y	N
Kerrey	Y	N	Y	Y	Y	Y	N
NEVADA							
Bryan	Y	N	Y	Y	Y	Y	N
Reid	Y	N	Y	Y	Y	Y	N
NEW HAMPSHIRE							
Gregg	N	Y	N	Y	Y	Y	N
Smith	N	Y	N	Y	Y	Y	N
NEW JERSEY							
Bradley	Y	N	Y	Y	Y	Y	Y
Lautenberg	Y	N	Y	Y	Y	Y	Y
NEW MEXICO							
Bingaman	Y	N	Y	Y	Y	Y	N
Domenici	N	Y	Y	Y	Y	Y	N
NEW YORK							
Moynihan	Y	Y	N	N	Y	Y	Y
D'Amato	N	Y	N	Y	Y	Y	N
NORTH CAROLINA							
Faircloth	N	Y	N	Y	Y	Y	N
Helms	N	Y	N	Y	Y	Y	N
NORTH DAKOTA							
Conrad	Y	Y	N	Y	Y	Y	N
Dorgan	Y	Y	N	Y	N	Y	N
OHIO							
Glenn	Y	N	Y	Y	Y	Y	N
Metzenbaum	Y	N	Y	Y	Y	Y	Y
OKLAHOMA							
Boren	Y	?	Y	Y	?	Y	N
Nickles	N	Y	N	Y	Y	Y	N
OREGON							
Hatfield	N	N	Y	Y	N	Y	N
Packwood	N	Y	Y	Y	Y	Y	N
PENNSYLVANIA							
Wofford	Y	N	Y	Y	Y	Y	Y
Specter	N	Y	N	Y	Y	Y	N
RHODE ISLAND							
Pell	Y	N	Y	Y	Y	Y	N
Chafee	?	Y	Y	Y	Y	Y	N
SOUTH CAROLINA							
Hollings	Y	N	Y	Y	Y	Y	N
Thurmond	N	Y	N	Y	Y	Y	N
SOUTH DAKOTA							
Daschle	Y	N	Y	Y	Y	Y	Y
Pressler	N	N	Y	Y	Y	Y	N
TENNESSEE							
Mathews	Y	N	Y	Y	Y	Y	N
Sasser	Y	N	Y	Y	Y	Y	Y
TEXAS							
Hutchison	N	Y	N	Y	Y	Y	N
Gramm	N	Y	N	Y	?	?	?
UTAH							
Bennett	N	Y	N	Y	Y	Y	N
Hatch	N	Y	N	Y	Y	Y	N
VERMONT							
Leahy	Y	N	Y	Y	Y	Y	Y
Jeffords	N	N	Y	Y	Y	Y	Y
VIRGINIA							
Robb	Y	N	Y	Y	Y	Y	Y
Warner	N	?	?	Y	Y	Y	N
WASHINGTON							
Murray	Y	N	Y	Y	Y	Y	Y
Gorton	N	N	Y	Y	Y	Y	N
WEST VIRGINIA							
Byrd	Y	N	Y	Y	Y	Y	N
Rockefeller	Y	N	Y	Y	Y	Y	Y
WISCONSIN							
Feingold	Y	N	Y	Y	Y	Y	Y
Kohl	Y	N	Y	Y	Y	Y	N
WYOMING							
Simpson	N	Y	N	Y	Y	Y	N
Wallop	N	Y	N	Y	Y	Y	N

ND Northern Democrats SD Southern Democrats

Southern states - Ala., Ark., Fla., Ga., Ky., La., Miss., N.C., Okla., S.C., Tenn., Texas, Va.

146. S 1491. Airport Improvement Program Reauthorization/Whitewater Hearings. Mitchell, D-Maine, amendment to the McConnell, R-Ky., amendment, to provide for hearings into President Clinton's investments in the Whitewater development project in a structured and sequenced manner agreed upon by the majority and minority leaders so as not to interfere with the investigation of Special Counsel Robert B. Fiske Jr. The McConnell amendment would have authorized hearings into any issues developed during or arising out of the Whitewater oversight hearings. Adopted 56-43: R 0-43; D 56-0 (ND 42-0, SD 14-0), June 15, 1994. (Subsequently, the McConnell amendment as amended by the Mitchell amendment was adopted by voice vote.)

147. Fitz-Pegado Confirmation/Recommit. Faircloth, R-N.C., motion to recommit to the Banking, Housing and Urban Affairs Committee (thus killing) the nomination of Lauri Fitz-Pegado of Maryland to be assistant secretary of Commerce and director general of the United States and Foreign Commercial Service. Motion rejected 37-61: R 34-9; D 3-52 (ND 3-39, SD 0-13), June 16, 1994. A "nay" was a vote in support of the president's position.

148. Fitz-Pegado Nomination. Confirmation of President Clinton's nomination of Lauri Fitz-Pegado of Maryland to be assistant secretary of Commerce and director general of the United States and Foreign Commercial Service. Confirmed 69-30: R 16-27; D 53-3 (ND 39-3, SD 14-0), June 16, 1994. A "yea" was a vote in support of the president's position.

149. S 1491. Airport Improvement Program Reauthorization/Airline Toilets. Danforth, R-Mo., motion to table (kill) the Metzenbaum, D-Ohio, amendment, to require new planes built for 10 or more passengers to have toilets, and to require airlines to notify passengers if a plane does not have a restroom. Motion agreed to 93-6: R 44-0; D 49-6 (ND 35-6, SD 14-0), June 16, 1994. (A pending McCain, R-Ariz., amendment to the Metzenbaum amendment, to express the sense of the Senate that the United States should take all necessary steps to enhance preparation to repel an attack from North Korea, fell when the Metzenbaum amendment was tabled.)

150. S 1491. Airport Improvement Program Reauthorization/North Korea. McCain, R-Ariz., amendment to express the sense of the Senate that the United States should take all necessary and appropriate action to enhance U.S. and South Korean readiness to deter and, if necessary, repel an attack from North Korea. Adopted 93-3: R 42-1; D 51-2 (ND 38-2, SD 13-0), June 16, 1994.

151. S 1491. Airport Improvement Program Reauthorization/EEOC Religious Guidelines. Brown, R-Colo., amendment to express the sense of Congress that the Equal Employment Opportunity Commission should withdraw its proposed guidelines on religious harassment and draft new regulations that do not have the potential to infringe on the freedom of speech or religion. Adopted 94-0: R 42-0; D 52-0 (ND 38-0, SD 14-0), June 16, 1994.

152. S 1491. Airport Improvement Program Reauthorization/Air-Traffic Controllers. Metzenbaum, D-Ohio, amendment to require half of air-traffic controllers hired by the Federal Aviation Administration to be controllers fired by President Ronald Reagan in 1981. Rejected 29-65: R 1-40; D 28-25 (ND 25-14, SD 3-11), June 16, 1994.

	153	154	155	156	157	158	159	160
ALABAMA								
Heflin	N	Y	N	N	Y	N	Y	Y
Shelby	N	Y	N	N	Y	N	Y	N
ALASKA								
Murkowski	Y	N	N	Y	Y	Y	Y	N
Stevens	Y	N	N	Y	?	N	Y	Y
ARIZONA								
DeConcini	N	Y	Y	Y	Y	Y	N	Y
McCain	Y	N	N	N	Y	Y	Y	N
ARKANSAS								
Bumpers	N	Y	Y	Y	Y	Y	Y	Y
Pryor	N	Y	Y	Y	Y	Y	Y	Y
CALIFORNIA								
Boxer	N	Y	Y	Y	Y	N	Y	Y
Feinstein	N	Y	Y	Y	Y	N	Y	Y
COLORADO								
Campbell	N	Y	N	Y	Y	N	N	Y
Brown	Y	N	N	N	Y	N	Y	N
CONNECTICUT								
Dodd	?	?	?	?	?	?	?	?
Lieberman	N	Y	Y	Y	Y	Y	Y	Y
DELAWARE								
Biden	N	Y	Y	Y	Y	Y	Y	Y
Roth	Y	N	N	N	Y	N	Y	N
FLORIDA								
Graham	N	Y	Y	Y	Y	N	Y	Y
Mack	Y	N	N	N	Y	N	Y	Y
GEORGIA								
Nunn	N	Y	Y	Y	Y	N	Y	Y
Coverdell	Y	N	N	N	Y	Y	Y	N
HAWAII								
Akaka	N	Y	Y	Y	Y	N	Y	Y
Inouye	N	Y	Y	Y	Y	N	Y	Y
IDAHO								
Craig	Y	N	N	N	Y	N	Y	N
Kempthorne	Y	N	N	N	Y	N	Y	N
ILLINOIS								
Moseley-Braun	N	Y	Y	Y	Y	Y	N	Y
Simon	N	Y	Y	Y	Y	Y	N	Y
INDIANA								
Coats	Y	N	N	N	Y	Y	Y	N
Lugar	Y	N	N	Y	Y	N	Y	N
IOWA								
Harkin	N	Y	Y	?	Y	Y	N	Y
Grassley	Y	N	N	N	Y	N	Y	N
KANSAS								
Dole	Y	N	N	N	Y	N	Y	N
Kassebaum	Y	N	N	N	Y	N	Y	Y
KENTUCKY								
Ford	N	Y	Y	Y	Y	Y	Y	Y
McConnell	Y	N	N	N	Y	N	Y	N
LOUISIANA								
Breaux	N	Y	Y	Y	Y	N	Y	Y
Johnston	N	Y	Y	Y	Y	N	Y	Y
MAINE								
Mitchell	N	Y	Y	Y	Y	Y	Y	Y
Cohen	Y	N	N	Y	Y	Y	Y	N
MARYLAND								
Mikulski	N	Y	Y	Y	Y	Y	Y	Y
Sarbanes	N	Y	Y	Y	Y	Y	Y	Y
MASSACHUSETTS								
Kennedy	N	Y	Y	Y	Y	N	Y	Y
Kerry	N	Y	Y	Y	N	Y	N	Y
MICHIGAN								
Levin	N	Y	Y	Y	Y	Y	Y	Y
Riegle	N	Y	Y	Y	Y	N	Y	Y
MINNESOTA								
Wellstone	N	Y	Y	Y	Y	Y	N	Y
Durenberger	Y	N	N	?	Y	Y	Y	Y
MISSISSIPPI								
Cochran	Y	N	N	Y	Y	N	Y	Y
Lott	Y	N	N	N	Y	N	Y	N
MISSOURI								
Bond	Y	N	Y	Y	Y	Y	Y	Y
Danforth	Y	N	Y	N	Y	N	Y	Y
MONTANA								
Baucus	N	Y	N	N	Y	N	N	Y
Burns	Y	N	N	?	Y	N	Y	N
NEBRASKA								
Exon	N	Y	Y	Y	Y	N	Y	Y
Kerrey	N	Y	Y	Y	N	Y	N	Y
NEVADA								
Bryan	N	Y	Y	N	Y	N	Y	Y
Reid	?	?	?	?	Y	N	N	N

	153	154	155	156	157	158	159	160
NEW HAMPSHIRE								
Gregg	Y	N	N	N	Y	N	Y	N
Smith	Y	N	N	N	Y	N	Y	N
NEW JERSEY								
Bradley	N	Y	Y	N	Y	Y	N	Y
Lautenberg	N	Y	Y	Y	Y	N	Y	Y
NEW MEXICO								
Bingaman	N	Y	N	Y	Y	Y	Y	Y
Domenici	Y	N	N	Y	Y	Y	Y	Y
NEW YORK								
Moynihan	N	Y	Y	Y	Y	Y	N	Y
D'Amato	Y	N	N	Y	Y	Y	Y	Y
NORTH CAROLINA								
Faircloth	Y	N	N	N	Y	N	Y	N
Helms	Y	N	N	N	Y	N	Y	N
NORTH DAKOTA								
Conrad	N	Y	Y	Y	Y	Y	Y	N
Dorgan	N	Y	Y	Y	Y	Y	Y	N
OHIO								
Glenn	N	Y	Y	Y	Y	N	N	N
Metzenbaum	N	Y	Y	Y	Y	N	N	N
OKLAHOMA								
Boren	N	Y	?	Y	Y	Y	N	Y
Nickles	Y	N	N	N	Y	N	Y	N
OREGON								
Hatfield	Y	N	Y	N	Y	Y	Y	Y
Packwood	Y	N	Y	N	Y	Y	Y	Y
PENNSYLVANIA								
Wofford	N	Y	Y	Y	Y	N	Y	Y
Specter	Y	N	Y	Y	Y	N	Y	Y
RHODE ISLAND								
Pell	N	Y	Y	Y	Y	N	Y	Y
Chafee	Y	N	N	N	Y	Y	Y	Y
SOUTH CAROLINA								
Hollings	N	Y	Y	Y	Y	Y	Y	Y
Thurmond	Y	N	N	N	Y	N	Y	N
SOUTH DAKOTA								
Daschle	N	Y	Y	Y	Y	N	N	N
Pressler	Y	N	N	N	Y	N	Y	N
TENNESSEE								
Mathews	N	Y	N	Y	Y	Y	Y	N
Sasser	N	Y	Y	Y	Y	N	Y	Y

KEY

Y	Voted for (yea).
#	Paired for.
+	Announced for.
N	Voted against (nay).
X	Paired against.
−	Announced against.
P	Voted "present."
C	Voted "present" to avoid possible conflict of interest.
?	Did not vote or otherwise make a position known.

Democrats   *Republicans*

	153	154	155	156	157	158	159	160
TEXAS								
Hutchison	Y	N	N	N	Y	Y	Y	Y
Gramm	Y	N	N	N	Y	Y	Y	Y
UTAH								
Bennett	Y	N	N	N	Y	N	Y	N
Hatch	Y	N	N	N	Y	N	Y	N
VERMONT								
Leahy	N	Y	Y	Y	Y	Y	N	Y
Jeffords	Y	N	Y	Y	Y	Y	Y	N
VIRGINIA								
Robb	N	Y	Y	Y	Y	Y	N	Y
Warner	Y	N	Y	N	Y	N	Y	N
WASHINGTON								
Murray	N	Y	Y	Y	Y	Y	Y	Y
Gorton	Y	N	Y	N	Y	N	Y	N
WEST VIRGINIA								
Byrd	N	Y	Y	Y	Y	N	N	Y
Rockefeller	N	Y	Y	Y	Y	Y	Y	Y
WISCONSIN								
Feingold	N	Y	N	N	Y	N	N	N
Kohl	N	Y	N	N	Y	N	N	N
WYOMING								
Simpson	Y	N	N	−	Y	N	Y	N
Wallop	Y	N	N	N	Y	N	Y	N

ND   Northern Democrats   SD   Southern Democrats   Southern states - Ala., Ark., Fla., Ga., Ky., La., Miss., N.C., Okla., S.C., Tenn., Texas, Va.

---

153. S Res 229. Whitewater Hearings/Republican Substitute. D'Amato, R-N.Y., substitute amendment to start hearings by July 22, 1994, on any "illegal, improper, unauthorized or unethical" actions by Clinton administration officials on Whitewater-related matters that have occurred since Clinton became president. Rejected 44-54: R 44-0; D 0-54 (ND 0-40, SD 0-14), June 21, 1994.

154. S Res 229. Whitewater Hearings/Adoption. Adoption of the resolution to limit the scope of hearings on President Clinton's investments in the Whitewater land deal to the first phase of the independent counsel's investigation: concerning contacts between administration officials and regulators, the suicide of deputy White House counsel Vincent W. Foster and the handling by administration officials of Foster's files. Adopted 54-44: R 0-44; D 54-0 (ND 40-0, SD 14-0), June 21, 1994.

155. HR 4539. Fiscal 1995 Treasury-Postal Appropriations/IRS Compliance Initiative. DeConcini, D-Ariz., motion to table (kill) the Grassley, R-Iowa, amendment to strike $405 million for an Internal Revenue Service tax compliance initiative in fiscal 1995. Motion agreed to 54-43: R 9-35; D 45-8 (ND 35-5, SD 10-3), June 21, 1994.

156. HR 4539. Fiscal 1995 Treasury-Postal Appropriations/Fiscal 1994 Level. DeConcini, D-Ariz., motion to table (kill) the Smith, R-N.H., motion to recommit the bill to the Appropriations Committee with instructions to report it back within three days with an amendment cutting the bill by $1.1 billion to the fiscal 1994 level. Motion to table agreed to 56-38: R 11-30; D 45-8 (ND 33-6, SD 12-2), June 21, 1994.

157. HR 4539. Fiscal 1995 Treasury-Postal Appropriations/White House Drug Testing. Faircloth, R-N.C., amendment that in effect would require that the person responsible for the White House drug testing program not have a history of prior drug use. Adopted 98-0: R 43-0; D 55-0 (ND 41-0, SD 14-0), June 22, 1994.

158. HR 4539. Fiscal 1995 Treasury-Postal Appropriations/Border Crossing Fee. DeConcini, D-Ariz., motion to table (kill) the Reid, D-Nev., amendment to delete language in the bill that would have prohibited the Customs Service from charging border crossing fees along the U.S.-Mexico border. Motion rejected 44-55: R 18-26; D 26-29 (ND 21-20, SD 5-9), June 22, 1994. (Subsequently, the Reid amendment was adopted by voice vote.)

159. HR 4539. Fiscal 1995 Treasury-Postal Appropriations/Recreational Diesel Fuel. Gorton, R-Wash., motion to waive the budget act with respect to the DeConcini, D-Ariz., point of order against the Gorton amendment for violating the 1974 Congressional Budget Act. The Gorton amendment would allow marinas to sell dyed diesel fuel intended for tax-exempt commercial use to recreational boaters, provided that the marina collects taxes on the fuel when sold. Motion agreed to 79-20: R 42-2; D 37-18 (ND 24-17, SD 13-1), June 22, 1994. A three-fifths majority vote (60) of the total Senate is required to waive the budget act. (Subsequently, the point of order was waived, and the Gorton amendment was adopted by voice vote.)

160. HR 4539. Fiscal 1995 Treasury-Postal Appropriations/Employment Floors. DeConcini, D-Ariz., motion to table (kill) the McCain, R-Ariz., amendment to eliminate the full-time equivalent employment minimum staffing requirements from the bill. Motion agreed to 66-33: R 19-25; D 47-8 (ND 35-6, SD 12-2), June 22, 1994.

	161	162	163	164	165
ALABAMA					
Heflin	N	N	Y	Y	N
Shelby	N	N	Y	Y	N
ALASKA					
Murkowski	N	N	Y	Y	Y
Stevens	Y	N	N	Y	Y
ARIZONA					
DeConcini	Y	N	Y	N	N
McCain	Y	N	Y	Y	Y
ARKANSAS					
Bumpers	Y	Y	Y	N	N
Pryor	Y	Y	Y	N	N
CALIFORNIA					
Boxer	Y	N	N	N	N
Feinstein	Y	N	N	Y	N
COLORADO					
Campbell	Y	N	Y	Y	N
Brown	N	Y	Y	N	Y
CONNECTICUT					
Dodd	?	?	?	?	?
Lieberman	Y	N	Y	Y	N
DELAWARE					
Biden	Y	Y	N	Y	N
Roth	N	Y	Y	Y	Y
FLORIDA					
Graham	Y	Y	Y	Y	N
Mack	N	Y	Y	Y	Y
GEORGIA					
Nunn	Y	Y	Y	Y	N
Coverdell	Y	N	Y	Y	N
HAWAII					
Akaka	Y	N	Y	Y	N
Inouye	Y	N	Y	Y	?
IDAHO					
Craig	N	N	Y	Y	?
Kempthorne	N	N	Y	Y	Y
ILLINOIS					
Moseley-Braun	Y	N	Y	N	N
Simon	Y	Y	Y	N	N
INDIANA					
Coats	N	N	Y	Y	Y
Lugar	Y	N	Y	Y	Y

	161	162	163	164	165
IOWA					
Harkin	Y	Y	Y	N	N
Grassley	N	Y	N	Y	Y
KANSAS					
Dole	N	N	N	Y	Y
Kassebaum	Y	N	Y	Y	N
KENTUCKY					
Ford	Y	N	Y	Y	N
McConnell	N	N	N	Y	Y
LOUISIANA					
Breaux	Y	Y	Y	Y	N
Johnston	Y	N	Y	Y	N
MAINE					
Mitchell	Y	N	N	Y	N
Cohen	Y	N	N	Y	Y
MARYLAND					
Mikulski	Y	N	Y	Y	N
Sarbanes	Y	N	Y	Y	N
MASSACHUSETTS					
Kennedy	Y	N	Y	Y	N
Kerry	Y	N	Y	Y	N
MICHIGAN					
Levin	Y	N	Y	Y	N
Riegle	Y	N	N	Y	N
MINNESOTA					
Wellstone	Y	Y	Y	N	N
Durenberger	Y	N	Y	Y	N
MISSISSIPPI					
Cochran	Y	N	N	Y	Y
Lott	N	N	N	Y	Y
MISSOURI					
Bond	Y	N	Y	Y	Y
Danforth	Y	N	Y	Y	Y
MONTANA					
Baucus	N	Y	Y	N	N
Burns	N	N	N	Y	Y
NEBRASKA					
Exon	Y	N	Y	?	N
Kerrey	Y	N	Y	Y	N
NEVADA					
Bryan	Y	N	Y	Y	N
Reid	Y	N	Y	Y	N

	161	162	163	164	165
NEW HAMPSHIRE					
Gregg	N	Y	Y	N	Y
Smith	N	Y	Y	N	Y
NEW JERSEY					
Bradley	Y	Y	N	N	N
Lautenberg	Y	Y	N	N	N
NEW MEXICO					
Bingaman	Y	Y	Y	Y	N
Domenici	Y	N	N	?	Y
NEW YORK					
Moynihan	Y	N	N	N	N
D'Amato	Y	Y	N	Y	Y
NORTH CAROLINA					
Faircloth	N	N	N	Y	Y
Helms	N	N	Y	Y	Y
NORTH DAKOTA					
Conrad	Y	Y	Y	N	N
Dorgan	Y	Y	Y	N	N
OHIO					
Glenn	Y	Y	Y	Y	N
Metzenbaum	Y	Y	Y	N	N
OKLAHOMA					
Boren	Y	N	Y	Y	N
Nickles	N	N	Y	Y	Y
OREGON					
Hatfield	Y	Y	Y	Y	N
Packwood	Y	N	N	Y	N
PENNSYLVANIA					
Wofford	Y	Y	N	Y	N
Specter	Y	Y	N	N	N
RHODE ISLAND					
Pell	Y	N	Y	Y	N
Chafee	Y	N	Y	Y	N
SOUTH CAROLINA					
Hollings	Y	N	Y	Y	N
Thurmond	N	N	Y	Y	Y
SOUTH DAKOTA					
Daschle	Y	N	Y	Y	N
Pressler	N	Y	N	Y	Y
TENNESSEE					
Mathews	Y	Y	Y	Y	N
Sasser	Y	N	Y	N	N

	161	162	163	164	165
TEXAS					
Hutchison	N	N	Y	Y	Y
Gramm	Y	N	Y	Y	Y
UTAH					
Bennett	Y	N	N	Y	Y
Hatch	Y	N	N	Y	Y
VERMONT					
Leahy	Y	N	Y	Y	N
Jeffords	Y	N	N	N	N
VIRGINIA					
Robb	Y	N	Y	Y	Y
Warner	N	N	Y	Y	N
WASHINGTON					
Murray	Y	N	Y	Y	N
Gorton	Y	N	Y	Y	Y
WEST VIRGINIA					
Byrd	Y	Y	Y	N	N
Rockefeller	Y	N	Y	Y	N
WISCONSIN					
Feingold	N	Y	Y	N	N
Kohl	N	Y	Y	N	N
WYOMING					
Simpson	Y	N	N	Y	Y
Wallop	N	?	+	+	+

ND Northern Democrats   SD Southern Democrats   Southern states - Ala., Ark., Fla., Ga., Ky., La., Miss., N.C., Okla., S.C., Tenn., Texas, Va.

161. HR 4539. Fiscal 1995 Treasury-Postal Appropriations/Passage. Passage of the bill to provide $23.6 billion in new budget authority for the Treasury Department, the U.S. Postal Service, the Executive Office of the President and certain independent agencies for fiscal 1995. The administration had requested $24,570,064,000. Passed 72-27: R 22-22; D 50-5 (ND 38-3, SD 12-2), June 22, 1994.

162. S 2182. Fiscal 1995 Defense Authorization/C-17 Contract Dispute. Grassley, R-Iowa, amendment to delete authorization for modifications of the contract for the C-17 transport plane, pursuant to a compromise negotiated between the Defense Department and McDonnell Douglas Corp. Rejected 32-66: R 10-33; D 22-33 (ND 16-25, SD 6-8), June 22, 1994. A "nay" was a vote in support of the president's position.

163. S 2182. Fiscal 1995 Defense Authorization/Base Closure Appeal. Warner, R-Va., motion to table (kill) the Specter, R-Pa., amendment to allow people affected by base closures to obtain a judicial review if they can show relevant information was fraudulently concealed from the base closure commission. Motion agreed to 71-27: R 24-19; D 47-8 (ND 33-8, SD 14-0), June 23, 1994.

164. S 2182. Fiscal 1995 Defense Authorization/Aircraft Carrier. Robb, D-Va., motion to table (kill) the Feingold, D-Wis., amendment to delay until fiscal 2000 spending $3.7 billion for the construction of a new CVN-76 nuclear-powered aircraft carrier. Motion agreed to 72-24: R 38-4; D 34-20 (ND 23-17, SD 11-3), June 23, 1994.

165. S 2182. Fiscal 1995 Defense Authorization/U.N. Peacekeeping Costs. Kempthorne, R-Idaho, amendment to prohibit money authorized by the bill from paying for U.S. contributions to U.N. peacekeeping operations and transfer the $300 million to accounts for training U.S. troops. Rejected 35-61: R 34-8; D 1-53 (ND 0-40, SD 1-13), June 23, 1994. A "nay" was a vote in support of the president's position.

SENATE VOTES 166, 167, 168, 169, 170, 171, 172, 173

KEY

Y Voted for (yea).
Paired for.
+ Announced for.
N Voted against (nay).
X Paired against.
− Announced against.
P Voted "present."
C Voted "present" to avoid possible conflict of interest.
? Did not vote or otherwise make a position known.

Democrats *Republicans*

	166	167	168	169	170	171	172	173
ALABAMA								
Heflin	Y	Y	N	N	N	Y	N	Y
Shelby	Y	Y	N	N	N	N	N	Y
ALASKA								
Murkowski	N	N	Y	Y	Y	Y	Y	Y
Stevens	Y	N	Y	Y	Y	Y	Y	Y
ARIZONA								
DeConcini	?	?	N	#	#	N	N	Y
McCain	N	N	Y	Y	Y	Y	N	Y
ARKANSAS								
Bumpers	Y	Y	N	N	N	N	N	Y
Pryor	Y	Y	Y	Y	Y	Y	N	Y
CALIFORNIA								
Boxer	Y	Y	N	N	N	N	N	Y
Feinstein	Y	?	N	N	Y	N	N	Y
COLORADO								
Campbell	Y	Y	N	N	N	Y	N	Y
Brown	Y	Y	Y	Y	Y	Y	Y	Y
CONNECTICUT								
Dodd	Y	Y	Y	Y	Y	N	N	Y
Lieberman	Y	Y	Y	Y	Y	N	N	Y
DELAWARE								
Biden	Y	Y	N	N	N	N	N	Y
Roth	Y	Y	Y	N	N	Y	Y	Y
FLORIDA								
Graham	Y	Y	N	N	N	N	N	Y
Mack	Y	Y	Y	Y	Y	Y	N	Y
GEORGIA								
Nunn	Y	Y	Y	Y	Y	N	N	Y
Coverdell	Y	N	Y	Y	Y	N	Y	Y
HAWAII								
Akaka	Y	Y	N	N	N	N	N	Y
Inouye	?	Y	N	N	N	N	N	Y
IDAHO								
Craig	?	?	Y	Y	Y	Y	Y	Y
Kempthorne	N	N	Y	Y	Y	Y	Y	Y
ILLINOIS								
Moseley-Braun	Y	Y	N	N	N	N	N	Y
Simon	Y	Y	N	N	N	N	N	Y
INDIANA								
Coats	Y	Y	Y	Y	Y	N	Y	Y
Lugar	Y	Y	Y	Y	Y	N	Y	Y

	166	167	168	169	170	171	172	173
IOWA								
Harkin	Y	Y	N	N	N	N	N	Y
Grassley	Y	Y	Y	Y	Y	Y	Y	Y
KANSAS								
Dole	Y	Y	Y	Y	Y	Y	Y	Y
Kassebaum	Y	Y	Y	Y	Y	N	N	Y
KENTUCKY								
Ford	Y	Y	N	N	N	Y	N	Y
McConnell	N	N	Y	Y	Y	Y	Y	Y
LOUISIANA								
Breaux	Y	N	N	N	N	N	N	Y
Johnston	Y	Y	N	N	N	N	N	Y
MAINE								
Mitchell	Y	Y	N	N	N	N	N	Y
Cohen	Y	Y	N	N	N	N	N	Y
MARYLAND								
Mikulski	Y	Y	N	Y	N	Y	N	Y
Sarbanes	Y	Y	N	N	N	N	N	Y
MASSACHUSETTS								
Kennedy	Y	Y	N	N	N	N	N	Y
Kerry	Y	Y	N	N	N	N	N	Y
MICHIGAN								
Levin	Y	Y	N	N	N	N	N	Y
Riegle	Y	Y	N	Y	N	N	N	?
MINNESOTA								
Wellstone	Y	Y	N	N	N	N	N	Y
Durenberger	Y	Y	Y	Y	Y	N	N	Y
MISSISSIPPI								
Cochran	Y	Y	Y	N	Y	Y	Y	?
Lott	N	N	Y	Y	Y	Y	Y	Y
MISSOURI								
Bond	?	N	Y	Y	Y	N	Y	Y
Danforth	Y	Y	Y	Y	Y	N	Y	Y
MONTANA								
Baucus	Y	Y	N	N	N	N	N	Y
Burns	Y	Y	Y	Y	Y	Y	N	Y
NEBRASKA								
Exon	Y	Y	N	Y	N	Y	N	Y
Kerrey	Y	Y	N	N	N	N	N	Y
NEVADA								
Bryan	Y	Y	N	N	N	N	?	?
Reid	Y	Y	N	N	N	N	N	Y

	166	167	168	169	170	171	172	173
NEW HAMPSHIRE								
Gregg	Y	Y	Y	Y	Y	Y	Y	Y
Smith	N	N	Y	Y	Y	Y	Y	Y
NEW JERSEY								
Bradley	Y	Y	N	N	N	N	N	Y
Lautenberg	Y	Y	N	N	N	N	N	Y
NEW MEXICO								
Bingaman	Y	?	N	N	N	N	N	Y
Domenici	Y	Y	Y	Y	Y	N	Y	Y
NEW YORK								
Moynihan	Y	Y	N	N	N	N	N	Y
D'Amato	N	N	N	N	N	Y	Y	Y
NORTH CAROLINA								
Faircloth	N	N	Y	Y	Y	Y	Y	N
Helms	N	N	Y	Y	Y	Y	Y	Y
NORTH DAKOTA								
Conrad	Y	Y	N	N	Y	N	N	Y
Dorgan	Y	Y	Y	N	Y	N	N	Y
OHIO								
Glenn	?	?	Y	Y	Y	N	N	Y
Metzenbaum	Y	Y	N	X	X	N	N	Y
OKLAHOMA								
Boren	Y	?	Y	Y	Y	N	N	Y
Nickles	?	?	Y	Y	Y	Y	Y	Y
OREGON								
Hatfield	Y	Y	N	N	Y	N	Y	N
Packwood	Y	Y	N	Y	N	Y	Y	Y
PENNSYLVANIA								
Wofford	Y	?	N	N	N	N	N	Y
Specter	N	Y	N	N	Y	N	Y	Y
RHODE ISLAND								
Pell	Y	Y	Y	N	N	N	N	Y
Chafee	Y	Y	Y	Y	Y	N	N	Y
SOUTH CAROLINA								
Hollings	Y	Y	N	N	N	N	N	Y
Thurmond	Y	Y	Y	N	Y	Y	Y	Y
SOUTH DAKOTA								
Daschle	Y	Y	N	Y	N	Y	N	Y
Pressler	Y	Y	Y	Y	N	Y	Y	Y
TENNESSEE								
Mathews	Y	Y	Y	Y	N	Y	N	Y
Sasser	Y	Y	Y	Y	Y	N	N	Y

	166	167	168	169	170	171	172	173
TEXAS								
Hutchison	Y	Y	Y	Y	Y	Y	Y	Y
Gramm	?	?	Y	Y	Y	Y	N	Y
UTAH								
Bennett	N	N	Y	Y	Y	Y	Y	Y
Hatch	Y	Y	Y	Y	Y	Y	Y	Y
VERMONT								
Leahy	Y	Y	N	N	N	N	N	Y
Jeffords	?	Y	Y	Y	N	N	N	Y
VIRGINIA								
Robb	Y	Y	Y	N	N	N	N	Y
Warner	Y	Y	Y	Y	Y	Y	N	Y
WASHINGTON								
Murray	Y	Y	N	N	N	N	N	Y
Gorton	Y	Y	Y	Y	Y	Y	Y	Y
WEST VIRGINIA								
Byrd	Y	Y	Y	Y	Y	Y	N	N
Rockefeller	Y	Y	Y	Y	N	N	N	Y
WISCONSIN								
Feingold	Y	Y	N	N	N	N	N	Y
Kohl	Y	Y	N	Y	N	Y	N	Y
WYOMING								
Simpson	Y	Y	N	N	N	Y	N	Y
Wallop	?	?	Y	Y	Y	Y	Y	N

ND Northern Democrats   SD Southern Democrats   Southern states - Ala., Ark., Fla., Ga., Ky., La., Miss., N.C., Okla., S.C., Tenn., Texas, Va.

166. Procedural Motion. Mitchell, D-Maine, motion to instruct the sergeant at arms to request the attendance of absent senators. Motion agreed to 80-11: R 27-11; D 53-0 (ND 39-0, SD 14-0), June 24, 1994.

167. Procedural Motion. Mitchell, D-Maine, motion to instruct the sergeant at arms to request the attendance of absent senators. Motion agreed to 76-14: R 27-13; D 49-1 (ND 37-0, SD 12-1), June 24, 1994.

168. S 687. Product Liability/Sealed Court Records. Rockefeller, D-W.Va., motion to table (kill) the Kohl, D-Wis., amendment to prevent courts from sealing records relating to public health or safety hazards, unless there is a "specific and substantial interest" in keeping the records confidential, and to bar agreements in federal court lawsuits that would restrict the disclosure of information to federal or state agencies. Motion agreed to 51-49: R 38-6; D 13-43 (ND 7-35, SD 6-8), June 28, 1994.

169. S 687. Product Liability/Cloture. Motion to invoke cloture (thus limiting debate) on the bill to set standards for awarding punitive damages, encourage out-of-court settlements, bar product liability claims against most product sellers, set new time limits for such lawsuits, end joint liability for non-economic damages and hold injured parties responsible for their own use of alcohol or drugs. Motion rejected 54-44: R 37-7; D 17-37 (ND 11-29, SD 6-8), June 28, 1994. Three-fifths of the total Senate (60) is required to invoke cloture.

170. S 687. Product Liability/Cloture. Motion to invoke cloture (thus limiting debate) on the bill to set standards for awarding punitive damages, encourage out-of-court settlements, bar product liability claims against most product sellers, set new time limits for such lawsuits, end joint liability for non-economic damages and hold injured parties responsible for their own use of alcohol or drugs. Motion rejected 57-41: R 38-6; D 19-35 (ND 13-27, SD 6-8), June 29, 1994. Three-fifths of the total Senate (60) is required to invoke cloture.

171. HR 4426. Fiscal 1995 Foreign Operations Appropriations/International Development Association. Helms, R-N.C., amendment to eliminate the $1.2 billion in the bill for the International Development Association, a lending agency of the World Bank. Rejected 34-66: R 30-14; D 4-52 (ND 1-41, SD 3-11), June 29, 1994.

172. HR 4426. Fiscal 1995 Foreign Operations Appropriations/Congressional Approval for Action in Haiti. Gregg, R-N.H., amendment to prohibit military action in Haiti unless the operations are authorized in advance by Congress or the action is necessary to protect U.S. citizens or national security interests. Rejected 34-65: R 34-10; D 0-55 (ND 0-41, SD 0-14), June 29, 1994. A "nay" was a vote in support of the president's position.

173. HR 4426. Fiscal 1995 Foreign Operations Appropriations/Haiti Sense of Senate. Mitchell, D-Maine, amendment to express the sense of Congress that Congress should authorize all U.S. military operations in Haiti unless U.S. citizens are in the imminent need of protection and evacuation or the deployment is vital to national security interests. Adopted 93-4: R 40-3; D 53-1 (ND 39-1, SD 14-0), June 29, 1994.

	174	175	176	177	178
ALABAMA					
Heflin	Y	Y	Y	Y	Y
Shelby	Y	Y	Y	Y	Y
ALASKA					
Murkowski	N	Y	Y	N	Y
Stevens	Y	Y	Y	Y	Y
ARIZONA					
DeConcini	N	N	N	Y	Y
McCain	Y	N	Y	N	N
ARKANSAS					
Bumpers	Y	N	N	Y	Y
Pryor	?	N	X	Y	Y
CALIFORNIA					
Boxer	N	N	N	Y	Y
Feinstein	Y	N	N	Y	Y
COLORADO					
Campbell	Y	N	N	N	Y
Brown	Y	Y	Y	N	N
CONNECTICUT					
Dodd	N	Y	Y	Y	Y
Lieberman	N	N	N	Y	Y
DELAWARE					
Biden	N	N	N	Y	Y
Roth	Y	N	N	N	Y
FLORIDA					
Graham	Y	N	N	Y	Y
Mack	Y	Y	Y	Y	Y
GEORGIA					
Nunn	Y	Y	Y	N	Y
Coverdell	Y	Y	Y	N	Y
HAWAII					
Akaka	Y	N	N	Y	Y
Inouye	Y	Y	N	Y	Y
IDAHO					
Craig	Y	Y	N	Y	Y
Kempthorne	Y	Y	Y	N	Y
ILLINOIS					
Moseley-Braun	N	Y	N	Y	Y
Simon	N	Y	N	Y	Y
INDIANA					
Coats	Y	Y	Y	N	Y
Lugar	Y	Y	Y	N	Y

	174	175	176	177	178
IOWA					
Harkin	N	N	N	Y	Y
Grassley	N	Y	N	N	Y
KANSAS					
Dole	Y	Y	Y	Y	Y
Kassebaum	Y	N	Y	N	Y
KENTUCKY					
Ford	N	Y	Y	N	Y
McConnell	Y	Y	Y	Y	Y
LOUISIANA					
Breaux	Y	Y	Y	Y	Y
Johnston	Y	Y	Y	Y	Y
MAINE					
Mitchell	N	N	Y	Y	Y
Cohen	Y	N	N	N	Y
MARYLAND					
Mikulski	Y	Y	Y	Y	Y
Sarbanes	N	N	N	Y	Y
MASSACHUSETTS					
Kennedy	N	N	N	Y	Y
Kerry	N	N	N	Y	N
MICHIGAN					
Levin	N	N	N	Y	Y
Riegle	?	?	N	Y	Y
MINNESOTA					
Wellstone	N	N	N	Y	Y
Durenberger	N	Y	N	Y	Y
MISSISSIPPI					
Cochran	?	Y	Y	Y	Y
Lott	Y	Y	Y	N	Y
MISSOURI					
Bond	Y	Y	Y	Y	Y
Danforth	Y	Y	Y	Y	Y
MONTANA					
Baucus	Y	N	N	Y	Y
Burns	Y	Y	Y	N	Y
NEBRASKA					
Exon	Y	N	N	Y	Y
Kerrey	Y	N	N	Y	Y
NEVADA					
Bryan	?	?	#	?	?
Reid	Y	N	Y	N	Y

	174	175	176	177	178
NEW HAMPSHIRE					
Gregg	Y	N	Y	N	N
Smith	Y	Y	Y	N	N
NEW JERSEY					
Bradley	N	N	N	Y	Y
Lautenberg	N	N	N	Y	Y
NEW MEXICO					
Bingaman	N	N	Y	Y	Y
Domenici	Y	Y	Y	Y	Y
NEW YORK					
Moynihan	N	N	N	Y	Y
D'Amato	N	Y	Y	N	Y
NORTH CAROLINA					
Faircloth	Y	Y	Y	N	N
Helms	Y	Y	Y	N	N
NORTH DAKOTA					
Conrad	Y	N	Y	Y	Y
Dorgan	N	N	N	Y	Y
OHIO					
Glenn	Y	N	Y	Y	Y
Metzenbaum	N	N	N	Y	Y
OKLAHOMA					
Boren	Y	Y	N	Y	Y
Nickles	Y	Y	Y	N	Y
OREGON					
Hatfield	N	N	N	Y	Y
Packwood	Y	Y	Y	Y	Y
PENNSYLVANIA					
Wofford	N	N	N	Y	Y
Specter	N	N	Y	Y	Y
RHODE ISLAND					
Pell	N	N	N	Y	Y
Chafee	?	Y	Y	N	Y
SOUTH CAROLINA					
Hollings	Y	Y	Y	Y	Y
Thurmond	Y	Y	Y	N	Y
SOUTH DAKOTA					
Daschle	N	Y	N	Y	Y
Pressler	Y	Y	N	Y	Y
TENNESSEE					
Mathews	Y	N	Y	Y	Y
Sasser	N	Y	Y	Y	Y

KEY

Y Voted for (yea).
\# Paired for.
\+ Announced for.
N Voted against (nay).
X Paired against.
− Announced against.
P Voted "present."
C Voted "present" to avoid possible conflict of interest.
? Did not vote or otherwise make a position known.

Democrats   *Republicans*

	174	175	176	177	178
TEXAS					
Hutchison	Y	Y	Y	N	Y
Gramm	Y	Y	Y	N	Y
UTAH					
Bennett	Y	Y	Y	Y	Y
Hatch	Y	Y	Y	Y	Y
VERMONT					
Leahy	N	N	N	Y	Y
Jeffords	Y	N	N	N	Y
VIRGINIA					
Robb	Y	N	Y	N	Y
Warner	Y	Y	Y	N	Y
WASHINGTON					
Murray	N	N	N	Y	Y
Gorton	Y	Y	Y	Y	Y
WEST VIRGINIA					
Byrd	Y	Y	Y	Y	Y
Rockefeller	Y	N	N	N	Y
WISCONSIN					
Feingold	N	N	N	Y	Y
Kohl	N	N	N	Y	Y
WYOMING					
Simpson	Y	Y	Y	Y	Y
Wallop	?	Y	Y	N	N

ND Northern Democrats   SD Southern Democrats

Southern states - Ala., Ark., Fla., Ga., Ky., La., Miss., N.C., Okla., S.C., Tenn., Texas, Va.

174. HR 4426. Fiscal 1995 Foreign Operations Appropriations/East Timor. Johnston, D-La., motion to table (kill) the committee amendment that prohibits Indonesia from using U.S. military equipment in East Timor. Motion agreed to 59-35: R 35-6; D 24-29 (ND 13-27, SD 11-2), June 29, 1994.

175. HR 4506. Fiscal 1995 Energy and Water Appropriations/Liquid Metal Reactor. Johnston, D-La., motion to table (kill) the Kerry, D-Mass., amendment to terminate the Advanced Liquid Metal Reactor Program. Motion agreed to 52-46: R 36-8; D 16-38 (ND 7-33, SD 9-5), June 30, 1994. A "nay" was a vote in support of the president's position.

176. HR 4506. Fiscal 1995 Energy and Water Appropriations/Renewable Energy Research. Johnston, D-La., motion to table (kill) the Harkin, D-Iowa, amendment to transfer $33 million from nuclear weapons research to support renewable energy research. Motion agreed to 53-45: R 36-8; D 17-37 (ND 7-34, SD 10-3), June 30, 1994.

177. HR 4506. Fiscal 1995 Energy and Water Appropriations/Fusion Reactor. Lautenberg, D-N.J., amendment to provide $45 million to begin building the Tokamak Physics Experiment, an experimental fusion reactor, near Princeton, N.J., if authorizing legislation is enacted. Adopted 69-30: R 18-26; D 51-4 (ND 39-2, SD 12-2), June 30, 1994.

178. HR 4506. Fiscal 1995 Energy and Water Appropriations/Passage. Passage of the bill to provide $20.5 billion in new budget authority for energy and water development for fiscal 1995. The administration had requested $20,512,750,000. Passed 91-8: R 37-7; D 54-1 (ND 40-1, SD 14-0), June 30, 1994.

	179	180	181	182	183
ALABAMA					
Heflin	N	Y	N	Y	N
Shelby	N	N	Y	Y	Y
ALASKA					
Murkowski	N	N	Y	Y	Y
Stevens	N	N	Y	N	Y
ARIZONA					
DeConcini	Y	N	Y	Y	Y
McCain	Y	N	Y	Y	N
ARKANSAS					
Bumpers	Y	Y	N	Y	Y
Pryor	Y	Y	N	Y	Y
CALIFORNIA					
Boxer	Y	N	Y	Y	Y
Feinstein	N	Y	N	Y	Y
COLORADO					
Campbell	N	Y	N	Y	Y
Brown	Y	N	Y	Y	N
CONNECTICUT					
Dodd	N	Y	N	Y	Y
Lieberman	N	N	Y	Y	Y
DELAWARE					
Biden	Y	N	Y	Y	Y
Roth	Y	N	Y	Y	N
FLORIDA					
Graham	Y	Y	N	Y	Y
Mack	N	N	Y	Y	Y
GEORGIA					
Nunn	N	Y	N	N	Y
Coverdell	N	N	Y	Y	N
HAWAII					
Akaka	N	Y	N	Y	Y
Inouye	N	Y	N	N	Y
IDAHO					
Craig	N	N	Y	Y	N
Kempthorne	N	N	Y	Y	N
ILLINOIS					
Moseley-Braun	Y	N	Y	N	Y
Simon	Y	Y	N	Y	Y
INDIANA					
Coats	N	N	Y	N	N
Lugar	N	N	Y	Y	N
IOWA					
Harkin	Y	Y	N	Y	Y
Grassley	N	N	Y	Y	Y
KANSAS					
Dole	N	N	Y	Y	Y
Kassebaum	N	Y	N	Y	Y
KENTUCKY					
Ford	N	Y	N	Y	Y
McConnell	N	N	Y	Y	N
LOUISIANA					
Breaux	N	Y	N	Y	Y
Johnston	N	Y	N	Y	Y
MAINE					
Mitchell	Y	Y	N	Y	Y
Cohen	Y	Y	Y	Y	Y
MARYLAND					
Mikulski	Y	Y	N	Y	Y
Sarbanes	Y	Y	N	Y	Y
MASSACHUSETTS					
Kennedy	Y	Y	N	Y	Y
Kerry	Y	Y	N	Y	Y
MICHIGAN					
Levin	Y	N	Y	Y	Y
Riegle	Y	Y	N	Y	Y
MINNESOTA					
Wellstone	Y	Y	N	Y	Y
Durenberger	N	N	Y	Y	Y
MISSISSIPPI					
Cochran	N	N	Y	Y	Y
Lott	N	N	Y	Y	N
MISSOURI					
Bond	N	N	Y	Y	Y
Danforth	N	Y	N	N	Y
MONTANA					
Baucus	Y	Y	N	Y	N
Burns	N	Y	N	Y	Y
NEBRASKA					
Exon	N	Y	N	Y	Y
Kerrey	N	Y	N	Y	Y
NEVADA					
Bryan	Y	Y	N	Y	Y
Reid	Y	Y	N	Y	Y
NEW HAMPSHIRE					
Gregg	N	N	N	Y	N
Smith	N	N	Y	Y	N
NEW JERSEY					
Bradley	Y	N	Y	Y	Y
Lautenberg	Y	N	Y	Y	N
NEW MEXICO					
Bingaman	N	Y	N	Y	Y
Domenici	N	N	Y	Y	Y
NEW YORK					
Moynihan	Y	N	Y	N	Y
D'Amato	N	N	Y	Y	Y
NORTH CAROLINA					
Faircloth	N	Y	Y	Y	N
Helms	N	N	Y	Y	N
NORTH DAKOTA					
Conrad	N	Y	N	Y	N
Dorgan	N	Y	N	Y	Y
OHIO					
Glenn	Y	Y	N	Y	Y
Metzenbaum	Y	Y	N	Y	N
OKLAHOMA					
Boren	N	Y	N	N	Y
Nickles	N	N	Y	Y	N
OREGON					
Hatfield	Y	Y	N	N	Y
Packwood	Y	N	Y	Y	Y
PENNSYLVANIA					
Wofford	Y	Y	N	Y	Y
Specter	N	N	Y	Y	Y
RHODE ISLAND					
Pell	Y	Y	N	Y	Y
Chafee	Y	Y	N	Y	Y
SOUTH CAROLINA					
Hollings	Y	Y	N	Y	Y
Thurmond	N	N	Y	Y	Y
SOUTH DAKOTA					
Daschle	Y	Y	N	Y	Y
Pressler	N	N	Y	Y	N
TENNESSEE					
Mathews	Y	Y	N	Y	Y
Sasser	Y	Y	N	Y	Y
TEXAS					
Hutchison	N	N	Y	Y	N
Gramm	N	N	Y	Y	N
UTAH					
Bennett	N	N	Y	Y	Y
Hatch	N	N	Y	Y	N
VERMONT					
Leahy	Y	Y	N	Y	Y
Jeffords	Y	N	Y	Y	Y
VIRGINIA					
Robb	N	Y	Y	Y	Y
Warner	N	Y	N	Y	N
WASHINGTON					
Murray	Y	Y	N	Y	Y
Gorton	N	N	Y	Y	Y
WEST VIRGINIA					
Byrd	Y	Y	N	N	Y
Rockefeller	Y	Y	N	N	Y
WISCONSIN					
Feingold	Y	N	Y	N	Y
Kohl	Y	N	Y	N	Y
WYOMING					
Simpson	N	N	Y	Y	Y
Wallop	N	N	Y	Y	Y

ND   Northern Democrats   SD   Southern Democrats   Southern states - Ala., Ark., Fla., Ga., Ky., La., Miss., N.C., Okla., S.C., Tenn., Texas, Va.

179. S 2182. Fiscal 1995 Defense Authorization/B-2 Bomber. Levin, D-Mich., amendment to strike the $150 million appropriated to keep open the production line for the B-2 stealth bomber and transfer the money to pay for environmental cleanups at former military bases. Rejected 45-55: R 8-36; D 37-19 (ND 31-11, SD 6-8), July 1, 1994. A "yea" was a vote in support of the president's position.

180. S 2182. Fiscal 1995 Defense Authorization/ International Effort in Bosnia. Nunn, D-Ga., amendment to express the sense of Congress that the United States should work with NATO member nations and the U.N. Security Council to endorse the efforts of the contact group to bring about a peaceful settlement of the conflict in Bosnia-Herzegovina. Adopted 52-48: R 8-36; D 44-12 (ND 31-11, SD 13-1), July 1, 1994.

181. S 2182. Fiscal 1995 Defense Authorization/Unilateral Termination. Dole, R-Kan., amendment to require the president to terminate the U.S. arms embargo of Bosnia-Herzego-

vina upon receipt from that government of a request for assistance in its right of self-defense. Rejected 50-50: R 37-7; D 13-43 (ND 11-31, SD 2-12), July 1, 1994. A "nay" was a vote in support of the president's position.

182. S 2182. Fiscal 1995 Defense Authorization/Military Retiree COLAs. Warner, R-Va., amendment to shift the 1995 cost of living adjustment (COLA) for military retirees forward from Oct. 1 to April 1, thus eliminating the disparity between effective dates for military and civilian retiree COLAs created by the 1993 Omnibus Budget Reconciliation Act (PL 103-66). Adopted 88-12: R 40-4; D 48-8 (ND 36-6, SD 12-2), July 1, 1994.

183. HR 4454. Fiscal 1995 Legislative Branch Appropriations/Conference Report. Adoption of the conference report to provide $2,367,421,100 in new budget authority for the legislative branch in fiscal 1995. The agencies covered by the bill had requested $2,509,703,500. Adopted (thus cleared for the president) 73-27: R 24-20; D 49-7 (ND 36-6, SD 13-1), July 1, 1994.

	184 185 186 187			184 185 186 187			184 185 186 187
ALABAMA		**IOWA**		**NEW HAMPSHIRE**		**KEY**	
Heflin	Y Y Y N	Harkin	Y N N N	*Gregg*	Y Y Y ?		
Shelby	Y ? ? ?	*Grassley*	Y N N N	*Smith*	Y N Y N		

KEY

Y	Voted for (yea).
#	Paired for.
+	Announced for.
N	Voted against (nay).
X	Paired against.
−	Announced against.
P	Voted "present."
C	Voted "present" to avoid possible conflict of interest.
?	Did not vote or otherwise make a position known.

Democrats *Republicans*

	184 185 186 187
ALABAMA	
Heflin	Y Y Y N
Shelby	Y ? ? ?
ALASKA	
Murkowski	? ? ? ?
Stevens	Y Y Y N
ARIZONA	
DeConcini	N Y N N
McCain	Y ? ? ?
ARKANSAS	
Bumpers	Y N N N
Pryor	Y N Y N
CALIFORNIA	
Boxer	Y ? ? ?
Feinstein	Y Y N N
COLORADO	
Campbell	Y ? ? ?
Brown	Y ? ? ?
CONNECTICUT	
Dodd	Y ? ? ?
Lieberman	Y ? ? ?
DELAWARE	
Biden	Y N Y ?
Roth	Y N Y N
FLORIDA	
Graham	Y Y Y N
Mack	Y Y Y N
GEORGIA	
Nunn	Y Y Y N
Coverdell	Y Y Y N
HAWAII	
Akaka	Y Y Y N
Inouye	Y Y Y ?
IDAHO	
Craig	Y Y Y N
Kempthorne	Y Y Y N
ILLINOIS	
Moseley-Braun	Y Y N N
Simon	Y ? ? ?
INDIANA	
Coats	Y Y Y N
Lugar	Y Y Y N

	184 185 186 187
IOWA	
Harkin	Y N N N
Grassley	Y N N N
KANSAS	
Dole	Y Y Y N
Kassebaum	Y Y Y N
KENTUCKY	
Ford	Y ? ? ?
McConnell	Y Y Y N
LOUISIANA	
Breaux	Y Y Y N
Johnston	Y ? ? ?
MAINE	
Mitchell	Y Y N N
Cohen	Y ? ? ?
MARYLAND	
Mikulski	Y Y Y ?
Sarbanes	Y Y Y N
MASSACHUSETTS	
Kennedy	Y Y N ?
Kerry	Y Y N ?
MICHIGAN	
Levin	Y Y N N
Riegle	Y Y Y N
MINNESOTA	
Wellstone	Y N N ?
Durenberger	N Y Y N
MISSISSIPPI	
Cochran	Y Y Y N
Lott	Y Y Y N
MISSOURI	
Bond	Y Y ? ?
Danforth	Y Y Y N
MONTANA	
Baucus	Y Y N N
Burns	Y Y Y N
NEBRASKA	
Exon	Y Y Y N
Kerrey	N Y N ?
NEVADA	
Bryan	Y Y Y N
Reid	Y Y N N

	184 185 186 187
NEW HAMPSHIRE	
Gregg	Y Y Y ?
Smith	Y N Y N
NEW JERSEY	
Bradley	Y Y N N
Lautenberg	Y Y N N
NEW MEXICO	
Bingaman	Y Y Y N
Domenici	Y Y Y N
NEW YORK	
Moynihan	Y Y N N
D'Amato	Y ? ? ?
NORTH CAROLINA	
Faircloth	Y Y Y ?
Helms	? ? ? ?
NORTH DAKOTA	
Conrad	Y Y Y N
Dorgan	Y Y Y N
OHIO	
Glenn	Y Y Y N
Metzenbaum	Y ? ? ?
OKLAHOMA	
Boren	Y Y Y N
Nickles	Y Y N Y
OREGON	
Hatfield	? N N N
Packwood	Y Y N N
PENNSYLVANIA	
Wofford	Y Y N N
Specter	Y Y ? ?
RHODE ISLAND	
Pell	Y Y Y ?
Chafee	Y Y N N
SOUTH CAROLINA	
Hollings	Y Y Y N
Thurmond	Y Y Y Y
SOUTH DAKOTA	
Daschle	Y Y N N
Pressler	Y Y Y N
TENNESSEE	
Mathews	Y N N N
Sasser	Y N Y N

	184 185 186 187
TEXAS	
Hutchison	Y Y Y N
Gramm	? ? ? ?
UTAH	
Bennett	Y ? ? ?
Hatch	Y Y Y N
VERMONT	
Leahy	Y N N N
Jeffords	Y Y N N
VIRGINIA	
Robb	Y Y Y N
Warner	Y Y Y N
WASHINGTON	
Murray	Y Y N N
Gorton	Y Y Y N
WEST VIRGINIA	
Byrd	Y Y Y N
Rockefeller	Y Y Y N
WISCONSIN	
Feingold	Y N N N
Kohl	Y N N N
WYOMING	
Simpson	Y + + +
Wallop	Y Y Y Y

ND Northern Democrats   SD Southern Democrats

Southern states - Ala., Ark., Fla., Ga., Ky., La., Miss., N.C., Okla., S.C., Tenn., Texas, Va.

184. S 2182. Fiscal 1995 Defense Authorization/Military Sexual Misconduct. Nunn, D-Ga., substitute amendment to the DeConcini, D-Ariz., amendment to create an advisory unit to study the necessity of establishing a unit to investigate allegations of sexual misconduct in the military. The DeConcini amendment would establish a director of special investigations position to investigate each allegation of sexual misconduct regarding Department of Defense personnel and make it a federal crime to not report an act of sexual misconduct in the military. Adopted 93-3: R 39-1; D 54-2 (ND 40-2, SD 14-0), July 1, 1994.

185. S 2182. Fiscal 1995 Defense Authorization/Airborne Jammer. Nunn, D-Ga., motion to table (kill) the Pryor, D-Ark., amendment to prohibit sale of the Airborne Self-Protection Jammer or related software to any foreign country. Motion agreed to 68-14: R 31-4; D 37-10 (ND 30-6, SD 7-4), July 1, 1994.

186. S 2182. Fiscal 1995 Defense Authorization/Selective Service. Nunn, D-Ga., motion to table (kill) the Bradley, D-N.J., amendment to terminate registration for the draft under the Selective Service System. Motion agreed to 50-30: R 27-6; D 23-24 (ND 15-21, SD 8-3), July 1, 1994.

187. S 2182. Fiscal 1995 Defense Authorization/Golan Heights. Wallop, R-Wyo., amendment to prohibit the use of money in the bill to support the use of U.S. troops for peacekeeping operations in the Golan Heights between Syria and Israel until the secretary of Defense submits to Congress a report addressing certain issues surrounding such an operation. Rejected 3-67: R 3-28; D 0-39 (ND 0-28, SD 0-11), July 1, 1994. A "nay" was a vote in support of the president's position.

KEY

- Y Voted for (yea).
- # Paired for.
- + Announced for.
- N Voted against (nay).
- X Paired against.
- — Announced against.
- P Voted "present."
- C Voted "present" to avoid possible conflict of interest.
- ? Did not vote or otherwise make a position known.

Democrats   *Republicans*

State / Senator	188	189	190	191	192	193
ALABAMA						
Heflin	Y	Y	Y	Y	Y	Y
Shelby	Y	Y	Y	N	Y	Y
ALASKA						
Murkowski	N	N	Y	Y	Y	Y
Stevens	N	N	Y	N	Y	Y
ARIZONA						
DeConcini	Y	Y	Y	Y	Y	Y
McCain	N	N	Y	Y	Y	Y
ARKANSAS						
Bumpers	N	N	Y	N	Y	Y
Pryor	N	N	N	N	Y	Y
CALIFORNIA						
Boxer	Y	Y	Y	N	Y	Y
Feinstein	Y	Y	Y	N	Y	Y
COLORADO						
Campbell	Y	Y	Y	N	Y	Y
Brown	N	N	Y	Y	Y	Y
CONNECTICUT						
Dodd	Y	Y	Y	N	Y	Y
Lieberman	Y	Y	Y	N	Y	Y
DELAWARE						
Biden	Y	Y	Y	N	Y	Y
Roth	N	N	Y	Y	Y	Y
FLORIDA						
Graham	Y	Y	Y	N	Y	Y
Mack	N	N	Y	Y	Y	Y
GEORGIA						
Nunn	N	N	?	N	Y	Y
Coverdell	N	?	?	Y	Y	Y
HAWAII						
Akaka	Y	Y	Y	N	Y	Y
Inouye	Y	Y	Y	N	Y	Y
IDAHO						
Craig	N	N	Y	Y	Y	Y
Kempthorne	N	N	Y	Y	Y	Y
ILLINOIS						
Moseley-Braun	Y	Y	Y	N	Y	Y
Simon	Y	Y	N	N	Y	Y
INDIANA						
Coats	N	N	Y	Y	Y	Y
Lugar	N	N	Y	Y	Y	Y
IOWA						
Harkin	Y	Y	Y	N	Y	Y
Grassley	N	N	Y	Y	Y	Y
KANSAS						
Dole	N	N	Y	Y	Y	Y
Kassebaum	N	N	Y	N	Y	Y
KENTUCKY						
Ford	Y	Y	N	Y	Y	Y
McConnell	N	N	Y	Y	Y	Y
LOUISIANA						
Breaux	Y	Y	Y	Y	Y	Y
Johnston	Y	Y	Y	Y	Y	Y
MAINE						
Mitchell	Y	Y	Y	N	Y	Y
Cohen	N	N	Y	N	Y	Y
MARYLAND						
Mikulski	Y	Y	Y	N	Y	Y
Sarbanes	Y	Y	Y	N	Y	Y
MASSACHUSETTS						
Kennedy	Y	Y	Y	N	Y	Y
Kerry	Y	Y	Y	N	Y	Y
MICHIGAN						
Levin	Y	Y	Y	N	Y	Y
Riegle	Y	Y	Y	N	Y	Y
MINNESOTA						
Wellstone	Y	Y	Y	N	Y	Y
Durenberger	N	N	Y	Y	Y	Y
MISSISSIPPI						
Cochran	N	N	Y	Y	Y	Y
Lott	N	N	Y	Y	Y	Y
MISSOURI						
Bond	N	N	Y	Y	Y	Y
Danforth	N	N	Y	Y	Y	Y
MONTANA						
Baucus	Y	Y	Y	N	Y	Y
Burns	N	N	Y	Y	Y	Y
NEBRASKA						
Exon	Y	Y	Y	Y	Y	Y
Kerrey	Y	Y	Y	N	Y	Y
NEVADA						
Bryan	Y	Y	Y	N	Y	Y
Reid	Y	Y	Y	N	Y	Y
NEW HAMPSHIRE						
Gregg	N	N	Y	Y	Y	Y
Smith	N	N	Y	Y	Y	Y
NEW JERSEY						
Bradley	Y	Y	Y	N	Y	Y
Lautenberg	Y	Y	Y	N	Y	Y
NEW MEXICO						
Bingaman	Y	Y	Y	N	Y	Y
Domenici	N	N	Y	Y	Y	Y
NEW YORK						
Moynihan	Y	Y	Y	N	Y	Y
D'Amato	Y	Y	Y	Y	Y	Y
NORTH CAROLINA						
Faircloth	N	N	Y	Y	Y	Y
Helms	N	N	Y	Y	Y	Y
NORTH DAKOTA						
Conrad	Y	Y	Y	N	Y	Y
Dorgan	Y	Y	Y	N	Y	Y
OHIO						
Glenn	Y	Y	N	N	Y	Y
Metzenbaum	Y	Y	N	N	Y	Y
OKLAHOMA						
Boren	N	N	N	N	Y	Y
Nickles	N	N	Y	Y	Y	Y
OREGON						
Hatfield	Y	Y	Y	Y	Y	Y
Packwood	N	N	Y	N	Y	Y
PENNSYLVANIA						
Wofford	Y	Y	Y	N	Y	Y
Specter	Y	Y	Y	N	Y	Y
RHODE ISLAND						
Pell	Y	Y	N	N	Y	Y
Chafee	N	N	?	N	Y	Y
SOUTH CAROLINA						
Hollings	N	N	N	N	Y	Y
Thurmond	N	N	Y	Y	Y	Y
SOUTH DAKOTA						
Daschle	Y	Y	Y	N	Y	Y
Pressler	N	N	Y	Y	Y	Y
TENNESSEE						
Mathews	N	N	Y	N	Y	Y
Sasser	Y	Y	Y	N	Y	Y
TEXAS						
Hutchison	N	N	Y	Y	Y	Y
Gramm	N	N	Y	Y	Y	Y
UTAH						
Bennett	N	N	Y	Y	Y	Y
Hatch	N	N	Y	Y	Y	Y
VERMONT						
Leahy	Y	Y	Y	N	Y	Y
Jeffords	N	N	Y	N	Y	Y
VIRGINIA						
Robb	Y	Y	Y	N	Y	Y
Warner	N	N	Y	Y	Y	Y
WASHINGTON						
Murray	Y	Y	Y	N	Y	Y
Gorton	N	N	Y	Y	Y	Y
WEST VIRGINIA						
Byrd	Y	Y	Y	N	Y	Y
Rockefeller	Y	Y	Y	N	Y	Y
WISCONSIN						
Feingold	Y	Y	Y	N	Y	Y
Kohl	Y	Y	Y	N	Y	Y
WYOMING						
Simpson	N	N	Y	N	Y	Y
Wallop	N	N	Y	Y	Y	Y

ND Northern Democrats   SD Southern Democrats   Southern states - Ala., Ark., Fla., Ga., Ky., La., Miss., N.C., Okla., S.C., Tenn., Texas, Va.

188. S 55. Striker Replacement/Cloture. Motion to invoke cloture (thus limiting debate) on the motion to proceed to the bill to prohibit employers from permanently replacing striking workers. Motion rejected 53-47: R 3-41; D 50-6 (ND 42-0, SD 8-6), July 12, 1994. Three-fifths of the total Senate (60) is required to invoke cloture.

189. S 55. Striker Replacement/Cloture. Motion to invoke cloture (thus limiting debate) on the motion to proceed to the bill to prohibit employers from permanently replacing striking workers. Motion rejected 53-46: R 3-40; D 50-6 (ND 42-0, SD 8-6), July 13, 1994. Three-fifths of the total Senate (60) is required to invoke cloture.

190. HR 4426. Fiscal 1995 Foreign Operations/Russian Baltic Troops. McConnell, R-Ky., amendment to move up from Dec. 31, 1994, to Aug. 31, 1994, the date by which Russia must withdraw all troops from the Baltics in order to receive U.S. economic aid. Adopted 89-8: R 42-0; D 47-8 (ND 38-4, SD 9-4), July 13, 1994.

191. HR 4426. Fiscal 1995 Foreign Operations/Abortion Intervention Prohibition. Helms, R-N.C., amendment to prohibit money in the bill from being spent to engage in efforts to change abortion laws in foreign countries, including population control programs. Rejected 42-58: R 36-8; D 6-50 (ND 2-40, SD 4-10), July 14, 1994.

192. HR 4426. Fiscal 1995 Foreign Operations/Russian Organized Crime. D'Amato, R-N.Y., amendment to provide $15 million to the Federal Bureau of Investigation to help countries of the former Soviet Union and Eastern Europe combat organized crime. Adopted 100-0: R 44-0; D 56-0 (ND 42-0, SD 14-0), July 14, 1994.

193. HR 4426. Fiscal 1995 Foreign Operations/Russian Criminal Justice Training. McConnell, R-Ky., amendment to earmark $15 million for an International Criminal Investigative Training Assistance Program to support police training and a professional criminal justice system based on democratic and human rights principles in the states of the former Soviet Union. Adopted 100-0: R 44-0; D 56-0 (ND 42-0, SD 14-0), July 14, 1994.

KEY

Y	Voted for (yea).
#	Paired for.
+	Announced for.
N	Voted against (nay).
X	Paired against.
−	Announced against.
P	Voted "present."
C	Voted "present" to avoid possible conflict of interest.
?	Did not vote or otherwise make a position known.

Democrats *Republicans*

	194	195	196	197	198
ALABAMA					
Heflin	Y	Y	Y	Y	Y
Shelby	Y	Y	Y	Y	N
ALASKA					
Murkowski	N	N	Y	N	Y
Stevens	N	N	Y	Y	Y
ARIZONA					
DeConcini	Y	N	Y	Y	N
McCain	N	N	Y	N	Y
ARKANSAS					
Bumpers	Y	Y	Y	Y	N
Pryor	Y	Y	N	Y	N
CALIFORNIA					
Boxer	Y	Y	N	Y	N
Feinstein	Y	Y	Y	Y	Y
COLORADO					
Campbell	Y	Y	Y	Y	N
Brown	N	N	Y	Y	Y
CONNECTICUT					
Dodd	Y	Y	Y	N	N
Lieberman	Y	N	Y	N	N
DELAWARE					
Biden	Y	Y	N	Y	N
Roth	N	N	Y	Y	Y
FLORIDA					
Graham	Y	Y	Y	N	N
Mack	Y	N	Y	N	Y
GEORGIA					
Nunn	Y	Y	Y	Y	N
Coverdell	N	N	Y	N	Y
HAWAII					
Akaka	Y	Y	N	Y	N
Inouye	Y	Y	N	Y	N
IDAHO					
Craig	N	N	Y	N	Y
Kempthorne	N	N	Y	N	Y
ILLINOIS					
Moseley-Braun	Y	Y	Y	Y	N
Simon	Y	N	Y	Y	N
INDIANA					
Coats	N	N	Y	N	Y
Lugar	N	N	Y	N	N

	194	195	196	197	198
IOWA					
Harkin	Y	Y	N	Y	N
Grassley	N	N	Y	Y	Y
KANSAS					
Dole	N	N	Y	N	Y
Kassebaum	N	Y	Y	Y	N
KENTUCKY					
Ford	Y	Y	N	Y	Y
McConnell	N	N	Y	N	N
LOUISIANA					
Breaux	Y	Y	Y	Y	N
Johnston	Y	Y	N	Y	N
MAINE					
Mitchell	Y	Y	N	Y	N
Cohen	N	N	Y	N	Y
MARYLAND					
Mikulski	Y	N	Y	N	N
Sarbanes	Y	Y	Y	Y	Y
MASSACHUSETTS					
Kennedy	Y	Y	N	Y	N
Kerry	Y	Y	Y	Y	N
MICHIGAN					
Levin	Y	Y	Y	Y	N
Riegle	Y	?	Y	Y	N
MINNESOTA					
Wellstone	Y	Y	Y	Y	N
Durenberger	N	N	Y	N	N
MISSISSIPPI					
Cochran	N	N	Y	Y	Y
Lott	N	N	Y	Y	Y
MISSOURI					
Bond	N	N	Y	N	Y
Danforth	N	Y	Y	N	N
MONTANA					
Baucus	Y	Y	Y	Y	N
Burns	N	N	Y	N	Y
NEBRASKA					
Exon	N	Y	Y	Y	N
Kerrey	Y	Y	Y	Y	N
NEVADA					
Bryan	Y	Y	Y	Y	N
Reid	Y	Y	Y	Y	N

	194	195	196	197	198
NEW HAMPSHIRE					
Gregg	N	N	Y	Y	Y
Smith	N	N	Y	Y	Y
NEW JERSEY					
Bradley	Y	Y	Y	N	N
Lautenberg	Y	N	Y	N	N
NEW MEXICO					
Bingaman	Y	Y	Y	Y	N
Domenici	N	N	Y	Y	Y
NEW YORK					
Moynihan	Y	Y	Y	Y	N
D'Amato	N	N	Y	Y	Y
NORTH CAROLINA					
Faircloth	N	N	Y	N	Y
Helms	N	N	Y	Y	Y
NORTH DAKOTA					
Conrad	Y	Y	N	Y	N
Dorgan	Y	Y	N	Y	N
OHIO					
Glenn	Y	Y	N	Y	N
Metzenbaum	Y	Y	N	Y	N
OKLAHOMA					
Boren	Y	?	?	?	?
Nickles	N	N	Y	N	Y
OREGON					
Hatfield	N	Y	N	N	N
Packwood	N	Y	Y	N	N
PENNSYLVANIA					
Wofford	Y	Y	Y	Y	N
Specter	N	N	Y	N	Y
RHODE ISLAND					
Pell	Y	Y	N	Y	N
Chafee	N	Y	Y	N	N
SOUTH CAROLINA					
Hollings	Y	Y	N	N	N
Thurmond	N	N	Y	N	Y
SOUTH DAKOTA					
Daschle	Y	Y	N	Y	N
Pressler	N	N	Y	N	Y
TENNESSEE					
Mathews	Y	Y	N	Y	N
Sasser	Y	Y	N	Y	Y

	194	195	196	197	198
TEXAS					
Hutchison	N	N	Y	N	Y
Gramm	N	N	Y	N	Y
UTAH					
Bennett	N	N	Y	N	Y
Hatch	N	N	Y	N	Y
VERMONT					
Leahy	Y	Y	N	Y	N
Jeffords	Y	Y	Y	N	N
VIRGINIA					
Robb	Y	Y	Y	Y	Y
Warner	N	N	Y	Y	Y
WASHINGTON					
Murray	Y	Y	N	Y	N
Gorton	N	N	Y	N	Y
WEST VIRGINIA					
Byrd	Y	Y	Y	Y	Y
Rockefeller	Y	Y	N	N	N
WISCONSIN					
Feingold	Y	N	Y	N	N
Kohl	Y	N	Y	N	N
WYOMING					
Simpson	N	N	Y	N	Y
Wallop	−	?	+	−	+

ND Northern Democrats   SD Southern Democrats   Southern states - Ala., Ark., Fla., Ga., Ky., La., Miss., N.C., Okla., S.C., Tenn., Texas, Va.

194. HR 4426. Fiscal 1995 Foreign Operations/Haiti Commission. Pell, D-R.I., motion to table (kill) the Dole, R-Kan., amendment to establish a congressional commission to assess and report to Congress within 45 days on the conditions in Haiti and options available to the United States with respect to Haiti. Motion agreed to 57-42: R 2-41; D 55-1 (ND 41-1, SD 14-0), July 14, 1994. A "yea" was a vote in support of the president's position.

195. HR 4426. Fiscal 1995 Foreign Operations/NATO Admission. Leahy, D-Vt., motion to table (kill) the McConnell, R-Ky., amendment to require the president to submit a report clarifying standards and obligations for admission to NATO, including an assessment of steps necessary for the participation in NATO by certain East European nations. The amendment would also allow excess defense articles to be transferred to certain East European countries to facilitate their participation in NATO. Motion agreed to 53-44: R 6-37; D 47-7 (ND 34-7, SD 13-0), July 14, 1994.

196. HR 4426. Fiscal 1995 Foreign Operations/East European NATO Inclusion. Brown, R-Colo., amendment to make Poland, Hungary and the Czech Republic eligible for certain NATO benefits, including the transfer of defense articles. Adopted 76-22: R 42-1; D 34-21 (ND 26-16, SD 8-5), July 14, 1994.

197. HR 4426. Fiscal 1995 Foreign Operations/Chinese Democracy Training. Bumpers, D-Ark., amendment to delete the $600,000 for democracy training programs in China. Adopted 60-38: R 13-30; D 47-8 (ND 37-5, SD 10-3), July 14, 1994.

198. HR 4426. Fiscal 1995 Foreign Operations/U.N. Development Program. Helms, R-N.C., amendment to prohibit money in the bill from being appropriated for the U.N. Development Program. Rejected 39-59: R 34-9; D 5-50 (ND 1-41, SD 4-9), July 14, 1994.

	199	200	201	202	203	204	205	206
ALABAMA								
Heflin	Y	Y	Y	Y	Y	N	Y	Y
Shelby	Y	Y	Y	Y	Y	N	Y	Y
ALASKA								
Murkowski	Y	Y	Y	Y	Y	N	?	Y
Stevens	Y	Y	Y	Y	Y	N	Y	Y
ARIZONA								
DeConcini	Y	Y	Y	Y	Y	N	Y	Y
McCain	Y	Y	Y	Y	Y	?	?	N
ARKANSAS								
Bumpers	N	Y	Y	Y	Y	Y	Y	N
Pryor	Y	Y	Y	Y	Y	Y	Y	Y
CALIFORNIA								
Boxer	N	Y	N	Y	Y	N	Y	Y
Feinstein	N	Y	Y	Y	Y	N	Y	Y
COLORADO								
Campbell	?	?	?	?	?	?	?	Y
Brown	Y	Y	Y	Y	Y	N	N	N
CONNECTICUT								
Dodd	N	Y	N	Y	Y	N	Y	N
Lieberman	N	Y	Y	Y	Y	?	?	N
DELAWARE								
Biden	N	Y	N	Y	Y	N	Y	Y
Roth	Y	Y	Y	Y	N	N	N	N
FLORIDA								
Graham	Y	Y	Y	Y	Y	Y	Y	Y
Mack	Y	Y	Y	Y	Y	N	Y	N
GEORGIA								
Nunn	N	Y	Y	Y	Y	Y	Y	N
Coverdell	?	?	?	?	?	?	?	N
HAWAII								
Akaka	N	Y	Y	Y	Y	N	Y	Y
Inouye	N	Y	Y	Y	Y	N	Y	N
IDAHO								
Craig	Y	Y	Y	Y	N	N	Y	Y
Kempthorne	Y	Y	Y	Y	N	N	Y	Y
ILLINOIS								
Moseley-Braun	?	Y	N	Y	Y	N	Y	Y
Simon	N	Y	N	Y	Y	Y	Y	Y
INDIANA								
Coats	Y	Y	Y	Y	Y	N	Y	Y
Lugar	N	Y	Y	Y	Y	N	Y	N

	199	200	201	202	203	204	205	206
IOWA								
Harkin	N	Y	N	?	?	N	Y	N
Grassley	Y	Y	Y	Y	Y	N	Y	Y
KANSAS								
Dole	Y	Y	Y	Y	N	N	Y	Y
Kassebaum	N	Y	Y	Y	Y	N	Y	Y
KENTUCKY								
Ford	N	Y	N	Y	Y	N	Y	N
McConnell	Y	Y	N	Y	Y	N	Y	Y
LOUISIANA								
Breaux	N	Y	Y	Y	Y	N	Y	Y
Johnston	N	Y	N	Y	Y	N	Y	N
MAINE								
Mitchell	N	Y	N	Y	Y	N	Y	N
Cohen	N	Y	Y	Y	Y	N	Y	Y
MARYLAND								
Mikulski	N	Y	N	Y	Y	N	Y	N
Sarbanes	N	Y	N	Y	Y	N	Y	N
MASSACHUSETTS								
Kennedy	N	Y	N	Y	Y	Y	Y	Y
Kerry	N	Y	N	Y	Y	N	Y	N
MICHIGAN								
Levin	N	Y	N	Y	Y	Y	Y	N
Riegle	N	Y	Y	Y	Y	N	Y	N
MINNESOTA								
Wellstone	N	Y	N	Y	Y	Y	Y	N
Durenberger	N	Y	Y	Y	Y	N	Y	Y
MISSISSIPPI								
Cochran	Y	Y	Y	Y	Y	N	Y	Y
Lott	Y	Y	?	?	?	?	?	Y
MISSOURI								
Bond	Y	Y	Y	Y	Y	N	Y	Y
Danforth	N	Y	N	Y	Y	N	Y	Y
MONTANA								
Baucus	N	Y	N	Y	Y	N	Y	Y
Burns	Y	Y	Y	Y	Y	N	Y	Y
NEBRASKA								
Exon	N	Y	Y	Y	Y	N	Y	Y
Kerrey	N	Y	N	Y	Y	N	Y	Y
NEVADA								
Bryan	N	Y	N	Y	Y	N	Y	N
Reid	N	Y	N	Y	Y	?	?	N

	199	200	201	202	203	204	205	206
NEW HAMPSHIRE								
Gregg	Y	Y	Y	Y	Y	?	?	N
Smith	Y	Y	Y	Y	N	N	Y	N
NEW JERSEY								
Bradley	N	Y	?	Y	Y	Y	Y	N
Lautenberg	N	Y	N	Y	Y	Y	Y	N
NEW MEXICO								
Bingaman	N	Y	Y	Y	Y	N	Y	N
Domenici	N	Y	Y	Y	Y	N	Y	N
NEW YORK								
Moynihan	N	Y	N	Y	Y	Y	Y	Y
D'Amato	Y	Y	Y	Y	Y	N	Y	Y
NORTH CAROLINA								
Faircloth	Y	Y	Y	Y	N	N	Y	Y
Helms	Y	Y	Y	Y	N	N	Y	Y
NORTH DAKOTA								
Conrad	N	Y	N	Y	Y	N	Y	N
Dorgan	N	Y	N	Y	Y	?	?	N
OHIO								
Glenn	N	Y	N	Y	Y	Y	Y	N
Metzenbaum	N	Y	N	Y	Y	Y	Y	N
OKLAHOMA								
Boren	?	?	?	?	+	?	?	Y
Nickles	Y	Y	Y	Y	Y	N	Y	N
OREGON								
Hatfield	N	Y	N	Y	Y	N	Y	Y
Packwood	N	Y	N	Y	Y	N	Y	Y
PENNSYLVANIA								
Wofford	N	Y	N	Y	Y	N	Y	Y
Specter	N	Y	Y	Y	Y	N	Y	Y
RHODE ISLAND								
Pell	N	Y	N	Y	Y	+	+	Y
Chafee	N	Y	Y	Y	Y	?	?	N
SOUTH CAROLINA								
Hollings	N	Y	N	Y	Y	N	Y	Y
Thurmond	Y	Y	Y	Y	Y	N	Y	Y
SOUTH DAKOTA								
Daschle	N	Y	N	Y	Y	N	Y	Y
Pressler	Y	?	Y	Y	?	N	Y	Y
TENNESSEE								
Mathews	N	Y	N	Y	Y	N	Y	Y
Sasser	Y	Y	Y	Y	Y	N	Y	Y

KEY

Y	Voted for (yea).
#	Paired for.
+	Announced for.
N	Voted against (nay).
X	Paired against.
–	Announced against.
P	Voted "present."
C	Voted "present" to avoid possible conflict of interest.
?	Did not vote or otherwise make a position known.

Democrats *Republicans*

	199	200	201	202	203	204	205	206
TEXAS								
Hutchison	Y	Y	Y	Y	Y	N	Y	Y
Gramm	Y	Y	Y	Y	Y	N	Y	Y
UTAH								
Bennett	Y	Y	Y	Y	Y	N	Y	Y
Hatch	Y	Y	Y	Y	Y	N	Y	Y
VERMONT								
Leahy	N	Y	N	Y	Y	N	Y	N
Jeffords	N	Y	Y	Y	Y	N	Y	Y
VIRGINIA								
Robb	N	Y	Y	Y	Y	Y	Y	Y
Warner	Y	Y	Y	Y	Y	N	?	Y
WASHINGTON								
Murray	N	Y	N	Y	Y	N	Y	Y
Gorton	Y	Y	Y	Y	Y	N	Y	Y
WEST VIRGINIA								
Byrd	Y	Y	Y	Y	N	N	Y	N
Rockefeller	N	Y	N	Y	Y	N	Y	N
WISCONSIN								
Feingold	N	Y	N	Y	Y	Y	Y	N
Kohl	Y	Y	N	Y	Y	Y	Y	Y
WYOMING								
Simpson	N	Y	Y	Y	Y	N	Y	Y
Wallop	+	+	+	+	–	?	+	Y

ND Northern Democrats   SD Southern Democrats   Southern states - Ala., Ark., Fla., Ga., Ky., La., Miss., N.C., Okla., S.C., Tenn., Texas, Va.

199. HR 4426. Fiscal 1995 Foreign Operations/International Narcotics Control. McConnell, R-Ky., amendment to increase the amount provided for international narcotics control by $52.4 million and cut the amount of the U.S. contribution to the Global Environmental Facility by $48.8 million and to the International Development Association by $110.8 million. Rejected 38-57: R 30-12; D 8-45 (ND 3-37, SD 5-8), July 15, 1994.

200. HR 4426. Fiscal 1995 Foreign Operations/North Korea. McConnell, R-Ky., amendment to prohibit North Korea from receiving any U.S. money until the president certifies that North Korea does not possess nuclear weapons, has halted its nuclear weapons program and has not exported weapons grade plutonium. Adopted 95-0: R 41-0; D 54-0 (ND 41-0, SD 13-0), July 15, 1994.

201. HR 4426. Fiscal 1995 Foreign Operations/Russian Nuclear Weapons. McConnell, R-Ky., amendment to allow the president to use Russian aid from the bill to finance the Nunn-Lugar cooperative threat reduction program, which helps to dismantle nuclear weapons in the former Soviet Union. Adopted 56-38: R 37-4; D 19-34 (ND 10-30, SD 9-4), July 15, 1994.

202. HR 4426. Fiscal 1995 Foreign Operations/Colombian Aid Contingency. McConnell, R-Ky., amendment to prohibit aid to Colombia unless the president certifies that the Colombian government is fully investigating all cases of corruption by narcotic cartels involving senior government officials, implementing steps to eliminate public corruption and reducing illicit drug production to the maximum extent. Adopted 94-0: R 41-0; D 53-0 (ND 40-0, SD 13-0), July 15, 1994.

203. HR 4426. Fiscal 1995 Foreign Operations/Passage. Passage of the bill to provide $13.7 billion in new budget authority for foreign assistance and related programs in fiscal 1995. The administration had requested $14,024,957,094. Passed 84-9: R 33-7; D 51-2 (ND 39-1, SD 12-1), July 15, 1994.

204. HR 4453. Fiscal 1995 Military Construction Appropriations/Seattle Land Conveyance. Glenn, D-Ohio, amendment to establish an expedited screening process for the disposal of federal land at the Naval Reserve Center in Seattle, Wash., which would give executive agencies, state and local governments, or nonprofit organizations located in the vicinity an enhanced opportunity to obtain jurisdiction over any portion of the land at fair market value. Rejected 16-72: R 0-38; D 16-34 (ND 11-26, SD 5-8), July 15, 1994.

205. HR 4453. Fiscal 1995 Military Construction Appropriations/Passage. Passage of the bill to provide $8,836,724,000 in new budget authority for military construction by the Department of Defense in fiscal 1995. The administration had requested $8,346,202,000. Passed 84-2: R 34-2; D 50-0 (ND 37-0, SD 13-0), July 15, 1994.

206. HR 4554. Fiscal 1995 Agriculture Appropriations/Market Promotion Program. Appropriations Committee amendment to provide up to $90 million for the Market Promotion Program, which subsidizes overseas advertising of U.S. agricultural products. Adopted 62-38: R 34-10; D 28-28 (ND 19-23, SD 9-5), July 19, 1994.

	207	208	209	210	211	212	213	214
ALABAMA								
Heflin	Y	N	Y	Y	N	Y	Y	Y
Shelby	N	Y	Y	Y	N	Y	Y	Y
ALASKA								
Murkowski	N	Y	Y	Y	Y	Y	Y	N
Stevens	N	Y	Y	Y	N	Y	Y	Y
ARIZONA								
DeConcini	Y	N	Y	Y	N	Y	Y	N
McCain	N	Y	Y	N	Y	Y	Y	N
ARKANSAS								
Bumpers	Y	N	Y	Y	N	Y	Y	N
Pryor	Y	N	Y	Y	N	Y	Y	N
CALIFORNIA								
Boxer	Y	N	N	Y	N	N	N	N
Feinstein	Y	N	N	N	N	Y	Y	N
COLORADO								
Campbell	Y	N	Y	N	N	Y	Y	Y
Brown	N	Y	Y	N	Y	Y	Y	Y
CONNECTICUT								
Dodd	Y	N	Y	N	Y	Y	Y	N
Lieberman	N	Y	Y	Y	N	Y	Y	Y
DELAWARE								
Biden	Y	N	Y	Y	N	Y	Y	N
Roth	N	Y	Y	N	Y	Y	N	Y
FLORIDA								
Graham	N	Y	N	Y	N	Y	Y	Y
Mack	N	Y	N	Y	N	Y	N	Y
GEORGIA								
Nunn	Y	Y	Y	N	Y	Y	Y	Y
Coverdell	N	Y	Y	N	N	Y	Y	Y
HAWAII								
Akaka	Y	N	N	Y	N	Y	Y	N
Inouye	Y	?	?	Y	N	Y	Y	N
IDAHO								
Craig	N	Y	N	Y	N	Y	Y	Y
Kempthorne	N	Y	N	Y	N	Y	Y	Y
ILLINOIS								
Moseley-Braun	Y	Y	Y	N	Y	Y	Y	N
Simon	?	N	Y	N	Y	Y	Y	N
INDIANA								
Coats	N	Y	Y	N	Y	Y	N	Y
Lugar	N	Y	Y	N	Y	Y	N	Y

	207	208	209	210	211	212	213	214
IOWA								
Harkin	N	Y	Y	Y	N	Y	Y	N
Grassley	N	Y	Y	Y	N	Y	Y	Y
KANSAS								
Dole	N	Y	Y	N	Y	Y	Y	Y
Kassebaum	N	Y	Y	Y	N	Y	Y	Y
KENTUCKY								
Ford	Y	N	Y	N	Y	Y	Y	Y
McConnell	N	Y	Y	Y	N	Y	Y	Y
LOUISIANA								
Breaux	N	Y	N	Y	N	Y	Y	Y
Johnston	N	Y	N	Y	N	Y	Y	Y
MAINE								
Mitchell	Y	N	Y	N	Y	Y	Y	N
Cohen	N	Y	Y	N	Y	Y	N	N
MARYLAND								
Mikulski	N	Y	Y	Y	N	Y	Y	N
Sarbanes	Y	N	Y	N	Y	Y	Y	N
MASSACHUSETTS								
Kennedy	N	Y	Y	N	Y	N	N	N
Kerry	Y	N	Y	N	Y	N	N	N
MICHIGAN								
Levin	N	Y	Y	N	Y	Y	Y	N
Riegle	Y	N	Y	N	Y	Y	Y	N
MINNESOTA								
Wellstone	Y	N	N	N	Y	N	Y	N
Durenberger	N	Y	N	Y	N	Y	N	N
MISSISSIPPI								
Cochran	N	Y	Y	N	Y	Y	Y	Y
Lott	N	Y	Y	N	Y	Y	Y	Y
MISSOURI								
Bond	N	Y	Y	Y	N	Y	Y	Y
Danforth	N	Y	Y	N	Y	Y	N	N
MONTANA								
Baucus	N	Y	N	Y	N	Y	Y	Y
Burns	N	Y	Y	N	Y	Y	Y	Y
NEBRASKA								
Exon	N	Y	Y	N	Y	Y	Y	Y
Kerrey	N	Y	Y	Y	Y	Y	Y	Y
NEVADA								
Bryan	Y	N	Y	N	Y	Y	Y	N
Reid	Y	N	Y	N	Y	Y	Y	N

	207	208	209	210	211	212	213	214
NEW HAMPSHIRE								
Gregg	N	Y	Y	N	Y	Y	N	Y
Smith	N	Y	Y	N	Y	Y	N	Y
NEW JERSEY								
Bradley	N	?	Y	N	Y	Y	N	N
Lautenberg	N	Y	N	N	Y	Y	N	N
NEW MEXICO								
Bingaman	Y	N	Y	N	Y	Y	N	N
Domenici	N	Y	Y	Y	N	Y	Y	Y
NEW YORK								
Moynihan	N	Y	Y	N	N	N	Y	N
D'Amato	N	Y	Y	Y	N	Y	N	Y
NORTH CAROLINA								
Faircloth	N	Y	Y	N	Y	Y	Y	Y
Helms	N	Y	Y	Y	Y	Y	Y	Y
NORTH DAKOTA								
Conrad	Y	N	N	Y	N	Y	Y	Y
Dorgan	Y	N	N	Y	N	Y	Y	Y
OHIO								
Glenn	Y	N	Y	N	Y	Y	Y	N
Metzenbaum	Y	N	Y	N	Y	N	Y	N
OKLAHOMA								
Boren	Y	?	N	N	N	Y	Y	N
Nickles	N	Y	N	Y	N	Y	Y	Y
OREGON								
Hatfield	N	Y	Y	N	Y	Y	N	N
Packwood	N	Y	Y	N	Y	N	N	N
PENNSYLVANIA								
Wofford	N	Y	Y	N	Y	N	Y	N
Specter	N	Y	Y	N	Y	Y	N	N
RHODE ISLAND								
Pell	Y	N	Y	N	N	N	N	N
Chafee	N	Y	Y	N	Y	Y	N	N
SOUTH CAROLINA								
Hollings	Y	N	Y	N	Y	Y	Y	Y
Thurmond	N	Y	Y	Y	N	Y	Y	Y
SOUTH DAKOTA								
Daschle	N	Y	Y	Y	N	Y	Y	Y
Pressler	N	Y	Y	Y	Y	Y	Y	Y
TENNESSEE								
Mathews	Y	N	N	N	Y	Y	Y	Y
Sasser	Y	N	N	N	Y	Y	Y	Y

	207	208	209	210	211	212	213	214
TEXAS								
Hutchison	N	Y	N	Y	N	Y	N	Y
Gramm	N	Y	Y	N	Y	N	Y	Y
UTAH								
Bennett	N	Y	Y	N	N	Y	N	Y
Hatch	N	Y	Y	N	Y	N	Y	Y
VERMONT								
Leahy	Y	N	Y	N	Y	Y	Y	N
Jeffords	Y	N	Y	N	Y	Y	N	N
VIRGINIA								
Robb	N	Y	N	N	Y	Y	Y	Y
Warner	N	Y	Y	N	Y	Y	Y	Y
WASHINGTON								
Murray	Y	N	Y	N	N	Y	Y	N
Gorton	N	Y	Y	N	N	Y	N	Y
WEST VIRGINIA								
Byrd	Y	N	Y	N	Y	Y	Y	Y
Rockefeller	Y	N	Y	N	Y	N	Y	Y
WISCONSIN								
Feingold	Y	N	Y	N	Y	N	N	N
Kohl	N	Y	Y	N	Y	Y	Y	N
WYOMING								
Simpson	N	Y	Y	Y	N	Y	Y	Y
Wallop	N	Y	Y	N	Y	Y	Y	Y

ND   Northern Democrats   SD   Southern Democrats   Southern states - Ala., Ark., Fla., Ga., Ky., La., Miss., N.C., Okla., S.C., Tenn., Texas, Va.

207. HR 4554. Fiscal 1995 Agriculture Appropriations/ Food Stamps Demonstration Initiatives. Bumpers, D-Ark., motion to table (kill) the McCain, R-Ariz., amendment to eliminate the provisions in the bill that prohibit food stamp "cash out" demonstration initiatives, which would allow the secretary of Agriculture to authorize states to experiment with providing cash benefits rather than food stamps to low-income individuals. Motion rejected 37-62: R 1-43; D 36-19 (ND 27-14, SD 9-5), July 19, 1994. (Subsequently, the McCain amendment was adopted by a roll call vote. See vote 208.)

208. HR 4554. Fiscal 1995 Agriculture Appropriations/ Food Stamps Demonstration Initiatives. McCain, R-Ariz., amendment to eliminate the provisions in the bill that prohibit food stamp "cash out" demonstration initiatives, which would allow the secretary of Agriculture to authorize states to experiment with providing cash benefits rather than food stamps to low-income individuals. Adopted 63-34: R 43-1; D 20-33 (ND 14-26, SD 6-7), July 19, 1994.

209. HR 4554. Fiscal 1995 Agriculture Appropriations/ Research Facilities Closure. Leahy, D-Vt., amendment, as amended by the Lugar, R-Ind., amendment, to authorize the secretary of Agriculture to close 19 Agricultural Research Service facilities specified in the president's fiscal 1995 budget. Adopted 76-23: R 36-8; D 40-15 (ND 33-8, SD 7-7), July 19, 1994.

210. HR 4554. Fiscal 1995 Agriculture Appropriations/ Agriculture Research Buildings. Bumpers, D-Ark., motion to table (kill) the Bradley, D-N.J., amendment to cut the amount appropriated for construction and repairs of Agricultural Research Service buildings and facilities from $38.7 million to $25.7 million. Motion rejected 50-50: R 25-19; D 25-31 (ND 16-26, SD 9-5), July

19, 1994. (Subsequently, the Bradley amendment was rejected by a roll call vote. See vote 211.)

211. HR 4554. Fiscal 1995 Agriculture Appropriations/ Agriculture Research Buildings. Bradley, D-N.J., amendment to cut the amount appropriated for construction and repairs of Agriculture Research Service buildings and facilities from $38.7 million to $25.7 million. Rejected 46-54: R 18-26; D 28-28 (ND 24-18, SD 4-10), July 19, 1994.

212. HR 4554. Fiscal 1995 Agriculture Appropriations/ Homosexual Seminars. Helms, R-N.C. amendment to prohibit the Agriculture Department from carrying out seminars or financing any position that encourages its employees to recruit on the basis of homosexual orientation or to accept homosexuality as a legitimate lifestyle. Adopted 92-8: R 43-1; D 49-7 (ND 35-7, SD 14-0), July 19, 1994.

213. HR 4554. Fiscal 1995 Agriculture Appropriations/ Tobacco Tariffs. McConnell, R-Ky., motion to table (kill) the Brown, R-Colo., amendment to require tobacco producers to pay for compensation to foreign producers, required by the General Agreement on Tariffs and Trade, that could result from a U.S. tariff on imported tobacco. Motion agreed to 63-37: R 20-24; D 43-13 (ND 29-13, SD 14-0), July 20, 1994.

214. HR 4554. Fiscal 1995 Agriculture Appropriations/ Departmental Homosexual Policy. Helms, R-N.C., amendment to require a public hearing prior to the removal of an Agriculture Department employee from a job position because of remarks made by the employee outside of work in opposition to departmental policies regarding homosexuals. The amendment also would reinstate any person removed for such reasons prior to the date of enactment. Adopted 59-41: R 36-8; D 23-33 (ND 14-28, SD 9-5), July 20, 1994.

KEY

Y Voted for (yea).
Paired for.
+ Announced for.
N Voted against (nay).
X Paired against.
− Announced against.
P Voted "present."
C Voted "present" to avoid possible conflict of interest.
? Did not vote or otherwise make a position known.

Democrats   *Republicans*

	215	216	217	218	219
ALABAMA					
Heflin	Y	Y	N	N	Y
Shelby	Y	Y	N	N	Y
ALASKA					
Murkowski	Y	Y	Y	N	N
Stevens	Y	Y	Y	N	Y
ARIZONA					
DeConcini	Y	Y	N	N	Y
McCain	Y	N	N	Y	N
ARKANSAS					
Bumpers	Y	Y	Y	N	Y
Pryor	Y	Y	Y	N	Y
CALIFORNIA					
Boxer	Y	Y	Y	N	Y
Feinstein	Y	Y	Y	N	Y
COLORADO					
Campbell	Y	Y	N	N	N
Brown	Y	N	N	Y	N
CONNECTICUT					
Dodd	Y	Y	Y	N	Y
Lieberman	Y	Y	Y	N	N
DELAWARE					
Biden	Y	Y	Y	N	Y
Roth	Y	N	N	N	N
FLORIDA					
Graham	Y	Y	Y	N	N
Mack	Y	Y	Y	N	N
GEORGIA					
Nunn	Y	Y	Y	N	N
Coverdell	Y	Y	N	N	Y
HAWAII					
Akaka	Y	Y	Y	N	Y
Inouye	Y	Y	Y	N	Y
IDAHO					
Craig	Y	Y	N	Y	Y
Kempthorne	Y	Y	N	Y	Y
ILLINOIS					
Moseley-Braun	Y	Y	N	N	Y
Simon	Y	Y	Y	N	Y
INDIANA					
Coats	Y	Y	N	Y	N
Lugar	Y	Y	N	Y	N

	215	216	217	218	219
IOWA					
Harkin	Y	Y	Y	N	Y
Grassley	Y	Y	N	N	N
KANSAS					
Dole	Y	Y	N	Y	Y
Kassebaum	Y	Y	Y	N	N
KENTUCKY					
Ford	Y	Y	Y	N	Y
McConnell	Y	Y	N	N	Y
LOUISIANA					
Breaux	Y	Y	Y	N	Y
Johnston	Y	Y	Y	N	Y
MAINE					
Mitchell	Y	Y	Y	N	Y
Cohen	Y	Y	Y	N	N
MARYLAND					
Mikulski	Y	Y	Y	N	Y
Sarbanes	Y	Y	Y	N	Y
MASSACHUSETTS					
Kennedy	Y	Y	Y	N	Y
Kerry	Y	Y	Y	N	N
MICHIGAN					
Levin	Y	Y	Y	N	Y
Riegle	Y	Y	Y	N	Y
MINNESOTA					
Wellstone	Y	Y	Y	N	N
Durenberger	Y	Y	Y	N	N
MISSISSIPPI					
Cochran	Y	Y	Y	N	Y
Lott	Y	Y	N	N	Y
MISSOURI					
Bond	Y	Y	Y	N	N
Danforth	Y	Y	Y	N	Y
MONTANA					
Baucus	Y	Y	N	Y	Y
Burns	Y	Y	N	Y	Y
NEBRASKA					
Exon	Y	Y	Y	N	N
Kerrey	Y	Y	Y	N	Y
NEVADA					
Bryan	Y	Y	Y	N	Y
Reid	Y	Y	Y	N	Y

	215	216	217	218	219
NEW HAMPSHIRE					
Gregg	Y	N	N	Y	N
Smith	Y	N	N	Y	N
NEW JERSEY					
Bradley	Y	Y	Y	N	N
Lautenberg	Y	Y	Y	N	Y
NEW MEXICO					
Bingaman	Y	Y	Y	N	Y
Domenici	Y	Y	N	N	Y
NEW YORK					
Moynihan	Y	Y	Y	N	Y
D'Amato	Y	Y	Y	N	Y
NORTH CAROLINA					
Faircloth	Y	N	N	Y	Y
Helms	Y	N	N	Y	N
NORTH DAKOTA					
Conrad	Y	Y	Y	N	N
Dorgan	Y	Y	Y	N	N
OHIO					
Glenn	Y	Y	Y	Y	N
Metzenbaum	Y	Y	Y	N	N
OKLAHOMA					
Boren	Y	Y	Y	N	Y
Nickles	Y	N	N	Y	N
OREGON					
Hatfield	Y	Y	Y	N	Y
Packwood	Y	Y	Y	N	Y
PENNSYLVANIA					
Wofford	Y	Y	Y	N	Y
Specter	Y	Y	N	Y	Y
RHODE ISLAND					
Pell	Y	Y	Y	N	Y
Chafee	Y	Y	Y	N	Y
SOUTH CAROLINA					
Hollings	Y	Y	Y	N	N
Thurmond	Y	Y	N	Y	N
SOUTH DAKOTA					
Daschle	Y	Y	Y	N	Y
Pressler	Y	Y	N	N	N
TENNESSEE					
Mathews	Y	Y	Y	N	Y
Sasser	Y	Y	Y	N	Y

	215	216	217	218	219
TEXAS					
Hutchison	Y	Y	N	N	Y
Gramm	Y	Y	N	Y	N
UTAH					
Bennett	Y	Y	Y	Y	Y
Hatch	Y	Y	Y	Y	Y
VERMONT					
Leahy	Y	Y	N	N	Y
Jeffords	Y	Y	Y	Y	Y
VIRGINIA					
Robb	Y	Y	Y	N	Y
Warner	Y	Y	Y	Y	N
WASHINGTON					
Murray	Y	Y	Y	N	Y
Gorton	Y	Y	Y	N	N
WEST VIRGINIA					
Byrd	Y	Y	Y	N	Y
Rockefeller	Y	Y	Y	N	Y
WISCONSIN					
Feingold	Y	Y	Y	N	N
Kohl	Y	Y	Y	Y	N
WYOMING					
Simpson	Y	Y	Y	N	N
Wallop	Y	N	N	Y	N

ND   Northern Democrats   SD   Southern Democrats   Southern states - Ala., Ark., Fla., Ga., Ky., La., Miss., N.C., Okla., S.C., Tenn., Texas, Va.

215. HR 4554. Fiscal 1995 Agriculture Appropriations/ Disagreement With Departmental Policies. Bumpers, D-Ark., amendment to require a hearing prior to the removal of an Agriculture Department employee from a job position because of remarks made by the employee outside of work in opposition to any departmental policies. Adopted 100-0: R 44-0; D 56-0 (ND 42-0, SD 14-0), July 20, 1994.

216. HR 4554. Fiscal 1995 Agriculture Appropriations/Passage. Passage of the bill to provide $67.98 billion in new budget authority for the Department of Agriculture, Rural Development, Food and Drug Administration, and related agencies for fiscal 1995. The administration had requested $68,428,191,000. Passed 92-8: R 36-8; D 56-0 (ND 42-0, SD 14-0), July 20, 1994.

217. HR 4649. Fiscal 1995 District of Columbia Appropriations/Passage. Passage of the bill to provide $700 million in federal funds for the District of Columbia in fiscal 1995 and approve total city spending of $3,589,736,635. The administration requested $722 million and $3,690,438,635, respectively. Passed 68-32: R 19-25; D 49-7 (ND 37-5, SD 12-2), July 21, 1994.

218. HR 4556. Fiscal 1995 Transportation Appropriations/Pennsylvania Station Redevelopment. McCain, R-Ariz., motion to table (kill) the Appropriations Committee amendment to provide $40 million to start converting the James A. Farley Post Office in New York City to an Amtrak train station and commercial center. Motion rejected 23-77: R 20-24; D 3-53 (ND 3-39, SD 0-14), July 21, 1994. (The amendment subsequently was adopted by voice vote.)

219. HR 4556. Fiscal 1995 Transportation Appropriations/Specific Highway Projects. Lautenberg, D-N.J., motion to table (kill) the McCain, R-Ariz., amendment to express the sense of the Senate that Congress should refrain from directing money to specific highway and transit projects. Motion agreed to 63-37: R 22-22; D 41-15 (ND 30-12, SD 11-3), July 21, 1994.

	220	221	222	223
ALABAMA				
Heflin	Y	Y	Y	N
Shelby	Y	Y	Y	N
ALASKA				
Murkowski	N	Y	Y	N
Stevens	Y	Y	Y	N
ARIZONA				
DeConcini	Y	Y	Y	Y
McCain	N	N	Y	N
ARKANSAS				
Bumpers	Y	Y	Y	Y
Pryor	Y	Y	Y	Y
CALIFORNIA				
Boxer	Y	Y	Y	Y
Feinstein	Y	Y	Y	Y
COLORADO				
Campbell	Y	Y	Y	Y
Brown	N	N	Y	N
CONNECTICUT				
Dodd	Y	Y	Y	Y
Lieberman	Y	Y	Y	Y
DELAWARE				
Biden	Y	Y	Y	Y
Roth	N	N	Y	N
FLORIDA				
Graham	Y	Y	Y	Y
Mack	N	Y	Y	N
GEORGIA				
Nunn	Y	Y	Y	N
Coverdell	N	Y	Y	N
HAWAII				
Akaka	Y	Y	Y	Y
Inouye	Y	Y	Y	Y
IDAHO				
Craig	N	Y	Y	N
Kempthorne	N	Y	Y	N
ILLINOIS				
Moseley-Braun	Y	Y	Y	Y
Simon	Y	Y	Y	Y
INDIANA				
Coats	N	Y	Y	N
Lugar	N	Y	Y	N

	220	221	222	223
IOWA				
Harkin	Y	Y	Y	Y
Grassley	N	Y	Y	N
KANSAS				
Dole	N	Y	Y	N
Kassebaum	N	Y	Y	Y
KENTUCKY				
Ford	Y	Y	Y	N
McConnell	Y	Y	Y	N
LOUISIANA				
Breaux	Y	Y	Y	N
Johnston	Y	Y	Y	N
MAINE				
Mitchell	Y	Y	Y	Y
Cohen	Y	Y	Y	Y
MARYLAND				
Mikulski	Y	Y	Y	Y
Sarbanes	Y	Y	Y	Y
MASSACHUSETTS				
Kennedy	Y	Y	Y	Y
Kerry	Y	Y	Y	Y
MICHIGAN				
Levin	Y	Y	Y	Y
Riegle	Y	Y	Y	Y
MINNESOTA				
Wellstone	Y	Y	Y	Y
Durenberger	Y	Y	Y	Y
MISSISSIPPI				
Cochran	Y	Y	Y	N
Lott	Y	Y	Y	N
MISSOURI				
Bond	Y	Y	Y	N
Danforth	Y	Y	Y	Y
MONTANA				
Baucus	Y	Y	Y	Y
Burns	N	Y	Y	N
NEBRASKA				
Exon	Y	Y	Y	Y
Kerrey	Y	Y	Y	Y
NEVADA				
Bryan	Y	Y	Y	Y
Reid	Y	Y	Y	Y

	220	221	222	223
NEW HAMPSHIRE				
Gregg	N	N	Y	N
Smith	N	N	Y	N
NEW JERSEY				
Bradley	N	Y	Y	Y
Lautenberg	Y	Y	Y	Y
NEW MEXICO				
Bingaman	Y	Y	Y	Y
Domenici	Y	Y	Y	Y
NEW YORK				
Moynihan	Y	Y	Y	Y
D'Amato	Y	Y	Y	Y
NORTH CAROLINA				
Faircloth	N	N	Y	N
Helms	N	N	Y	N
NORTH DAKOTA				
Conrad	Y	Y	Y	Y
Dorgan	Y	Y	Y	Y
OHIO				
Glenn	Y	Y	Y	Y
Metzenbaum	Y	Y	Y	Y
OKLAHOMA				
Boren	Y	Y	Y	Y
Nickles	N	Y	Y	N
OREGON				
Hatfield	Y	Y	Y	Y
Packwood	N	Y	Y	Y
PENNSYLVANIA				
Wofford	Y	Y	Y	Y
Specter	Y	Y	Y	Y
RHODE ISLAND				
Pell	Y	Y	Y	Y
Chafee	Y	Y	Y	Y
SOUTH CAROLINA				
Hollings	Y	Y	Y	N
Thurmond	N	Y	Y	N
SOUTH DAKOTA				
Daschle	Y	Y	Y	Y
Pressler	N	Y	Y	N
TENNESSEE				
Mathews	Y	Y	Y	N
Sasser	Y	Y	Y	N

KEY

Y   Voted for (yea).
Paired for.
+   Announced for.
N   Voted against (nay).
X   Paired against.
—   Announced against.
P   Voted "present."
C   Voted "present" to avoid possible conflict of interest.
?   Did not vote or otherwise make a position known.

Democrats   *Republicans*

	220	221	222	223
TEXAS				
Hutchison	Y	Y	Y	N
Gramm	Y	Y	Y	N
UTAH				
Bennett	Y	Y	Y	N
Hatch	Y	Y	Y	N
VERMONT				
Leahy	Y	Y	Y	Y
Jeffords	N	Y	Y	Y
VIRGINIA				
Robb	Y	Y	Y	Y
Warner	N	Y	Y	Y
WASHINGTON				
Murray	Y	Y	Y	Y
Gorton	Y	Y	Y	N
WEST VIRGINIA				
Byrd	Y	Y	Y	N
Rockefeller	Y	Y	Y	Y
WISCONSIN				
Feingold	Y	Y	Y	Y
Kohl	N	N	Y	N
WYOMING				
Simpson	N	Y	Y	N
Wallop	N	N	Y	N

ND Northern Democrats   SD Southern Democrats   Southern states - Ala., Ark., Fla., Ga., Ky., La., Miss., N.C., Okla., S.C., Tenn., Texas, Va.

220. HR 4556. Fiscal 1995 Transportation Appropriations/Fiscal 1994 Level. Lautenberg, D-N.J., motion to table (kill) the Smith, R-N.H., motion to recommit the bill to the Senate Appropriations Committee with instructions to reduce the bill's total to a level not greater than the fiscal 1994 level. Motion agreed to 72-28: R 18-26; D 54-2 (ND 40-2, SD 14-0), July 21, 1994.

221. HR 4556. Fiscal 1995 Transportation Appropriations/Passage. Passage of the bill to provide approximately $14.3 billion in new budget authority for the Department of Transportation and related agencies for fiscal 1995. The administration had requested $13.6 billion. The bill also authorizes the expenditure of $24.4 billion from the Highway and Airport trust funds. Passed 91-9: R 36-8; D 55-1 (ND 41-1, SD 14-0), July 21, 1994.

222. HR 4603. Fiscal 1995 Commerce, Justice, State Appropriations/Child Support. Shelby, D-Ala., amendment to express the sense of the Senate that the attorney general should increase enforcement of federal child support laws to prosecute fathers who have crossed state lines to avoid child payments. Adopted 100-0: R 44-0; D 56-0 (ND 42-0, SD 14-0), July 21, 1994.

223. HR 4603. Fiscal 1995 Commerce, Justice, State Appropriations/Legal Services Corporation. Specter, R-Pa., motion to table (kill) the Gramm, R-Texas, amendment to prohibit the Legal Services Corporation from using federal money to raise legal challenges in behalf of the poor against welfare reform. Motion agreed to 56-44: R 10-34; D 46-10 (ND 41-1, SD 5-9), July 21, 1994.

	224 225 226 227 228 229 230 231
ALABAMA	
Heflin	N N N Y N Y Y Y
Shelby	N N N Y Y Y N Y
ALASKA	
Murkowski	N N N Y N Y N Y
Stevens	N N N Y Y N Y ?
ARIZONA	
DeConcini	Y N N N Y Y Y Y
McCain	N Y N Y N Y N Y
ARKANSAS	
Bumpers	Y N Y ? Y Y Y Y
Pryor	Y N Y ? Y Y Y Y
CALIFORNIA	
Boxer	Y N N N ? ? ? ?
Feinstein	Y ? N N Y ? ? ?
COLORADO	
Campbell	Y N N ? Y Y Y Y
Brown	Y Y N Y Y Y N Y
CONNECTICUT	
Dodd	N N Y N Y Y Y Y
Lieberman	N N N Y Y Y Y Y
DELAWARE	
Biden	N N Y N Y Y Y Y
Roth	Y Y N Y Y Y N Y
FLORIDA	
Graham	N N N N Y Y Y Y
Mack	N N N Y N Y N Y
GEORGIA	
Nunn	N N Y N Y Y N Y
Coverdell	N N N Y Y Y N Y
HAWAII	
Akaka	N N Y N Y Y Y Y
Inouye	N N Y N ? Y Y Y
IDAHO	
Craig	N Y N Y N Y N Y
Kempthorne	N Y N Y ? Y Y Y
ILLINOIS	
Moseley-Braun	N N Y N Y Y Y Y
Simon	N N Y N Y Y Y Y
INDIANA	
Coats	Y Y N Y Y Y N Y
Lugar	N N Y Y Y Y N Y

	224 225 226 227 228 229 230 231
IOWA	
Harkin	Y N Y N ? ? ? ?
Grassley	Y Y N Y Y Y N Y
KANSAS	
Dole	N Y N ? Y Y ? ?
Kassebaum	N N Y Y Y Y Y Y
KENTUCKY	
Ford	N N Y N Y Y N Y
McConnell	N N N Y ? Y N Y
LOUISIANA	
Breaux	Y N N N N Y N Y
Johnston	N N Y N Y Y N Y
MAINE	
Mitchell	N N Y N Y Y Y Y
Cohen	N N N N Y Y Y Y
MARYLAND	
Mikulski	N N N Y N Y Y ?
Sarbanes	N N Y N Y Y Y Y
MASSACHUSETTS	
Kennedy	N N Y N ? ? + Y
Kerry	N N Y N Y Y Y Y
MICHIGAN	
Levin	N N Y N Y Y Y Y
Riegle	N N Y ? Y Y Y Y
MINNESOTA	
Wellstone	N N Y N Y Y Y Y
Durenberger	? ? ? ? Y Y Y Y
MISSISSIPPI	
Cochran	N N N Y Y Y N Y
Lott	Y Y N Y N Y N Y
MISSOURI	
Bond	N N N Y Y Y N Y
Danforth	N N N N Y Y Y Y
MONTANA	
Baucus	Y N Y ? Y Y Y Y
Burns	Y N N Y Y Y N Y
NEBRASKA	
Exon	Y N Y N Y Y N Y
Kerrey	Y N Y N Y Y Y Y
NEVADA	
Bryan	Y N N N Y Y Y Y
Reid	Y N N N Y Y Y Y

	224 225 226 227 228 229 230 231
NEW HAMPSHIRE	
Gregg	Y Y N Y Y Y Y Y
Smith	Y Y N Y N Y N Y
NEW JERSEY	
Bradley	N Y N N Y Y Y Y
Lautenberg	N N N N Y Y Y Y
NEW MEXICO	
Bingaman	Y N N N Y Y Y Y
Domenici	N N Y Y Y Y N Y
NEW YORK	
Moynihan	N N Y N Y Y Y Y
D'Amato	N N N ? ? ? ? ?
NORTH CAROLINA	
Faircloth	Y Y N Y N Y N Y
Helms	Y Y N Y N Y N Y
NORTH DAKOTA	
Conrad	Y N Y N Y Y Y Y
Dorgan	Y N Y N Y Y Y Y
OHIO	
Glenn	N N Y N Y Y Y Y
Metzenbaum	? ? ? ? ? ? ? ?
OKLAHOMA	
Boren	? ? ? ? Y Y Y Y
Nickles	Y Y N Y N Y N Y
OREGON	
Hatfield	N N Y N Y Y N Y
Packwood	N N Y N Y Y Y Y
PENNSYLVANIA	
Wofford	N N N N Y Y N Y
Specter	N N Y Y ? ? ? ?
RHODE ISLAND	
Pell	N N Y N Y Y Y Y
Chafee	Y N Y N ? Y Y Y
SOUTH CAROLINA	
Hollings	N N Y N Y Y Y Y
Thurmond	Y N N Y ? Y N Y
SOUTH DAKOTA	
Daschle	Y N N N Y Y Y Y
Pressler	Y Y N Y N Y N Y
TENNESSEE	
Mathews	Y N N N Y Y Y Y
Sasser	Y N N N Y Y N Y

KEY

Y Voted for (yea).
\# Paired for.
\+ Announced for.
N Voted against (nay).
X Paired against.
— Announced against.
P Voted ''present.''
C Voted ''present'' to avoid possible conflict of interest.
? Did not vote or otherwise make a position known.

Democrats   *Republicans*

	224 225 226 227 228 229 230 231
TEXAS	
Hutchison	N Y N Y Y Y N Y
Gramm	? ? ? ? N Y N Y
UTAH	
Bennett	N Y N Y ? ? ? ?
Hatch	N Y N Y ? ? ? ?
VERMONT	
Leahy	Y N Y N Y Y Y Y
Jeffords	N N Y N Y Y Y Y
VIRGINIA	
Robb	N N N N Y Y Y Y
Warner	Y Y N Y Y Y Y Y
WASHINGTON	
Murray	Y N Y ? Y Y Y Y
Gorton	N N N N Y Y N Y
WEST VIRGINIA	
Byrd	Y N Y N Y Y N Y
Rockefeller	N N Y N Y Y Y Y
WISCONSIN	
Feingold	Y Y Y N Y Y Y Y
Kohl	Y Y Y N Y Y Y Y
WYOMING	
Simpson	N Y N Y Y Y N Y
Wallop	N Y N + N Y N +

ND Northern Democrats   SD Southern Democrats   Southern states - Ala., Ark., Fla., Ga., Ky., La., Miss., N.C., Okla., S.C., Tenn., Texas, Va.

224. HR 4603. Fiscal 1995 Commerce, Justice, State Appropriations/National Endowment for Democracy. Dorgan, D-N.D., amendment to reduce the amount for the National Endowment for Democracy from $35 million to $25 million. Rejected 39-57: R 15-27; D 24-30 (ND 19-22, SD 5-8), July 22, 1994.

225. HR 4603. Fiscal 1995 Commerce, Justice, State Appropriations/Motion to Recommit. Smith, R-N.H., motion to recommit the bill to the Appropriations Committee with instructions to report it back with an amendment reducing the total appropriation to an amount not greater than the fiscal 1994 level without cutting programs intended to reduce crime. Motion rejected 24-71: R 21-21; D 3-50 (ND 3-37, SD 0-13), July 22, 1994.

226. HR 4603. Fiscal 1995 Commerce, Justice, State Appropriations/Illegal Immigrants Incarceration Costs. Hollings, D-S.C., motion to table (kill) the Dole, R-Kan., amendment to transfer $350 million from the U.S. contribution to the United Nations for international peacekeeping operations to reimburse states for the incarceration of illegal aliens. Motion rejected 44-52: R 8-34; D 36-18 (ND 29-12, SD 7-6), July 22, 1994. (Subsequently, the Dole amendment was adopted by voice vote.) A "yea" was a vote in support of the president's position.

227. HR 4603. Fiscal 1995 Commerce, Justice, State Appropriations/Death Penalty Statistics. Hatch, R-Utah, amendment to the Dole, R-Kan., amendment, to prohibit the executive branch from implementing policies that permit officials to use evidence that race was a statistically significant factor in the decision to seek the death penalty. (The Hatch and Dole amend-

ments were essentially similar.) Rejected 33-54: R 32-7; D 1-47 (ND 0-37, SD 1-10), July 22, 1994.

228. Procedural Motion. Byrd, D-W.Va., motion to instruct the sergeant at arms to request the attendance of absent senators. Motion agreed to 74-13: R 24-12; D 50-1 (ND 37-0, SD 13-1), July 25, 1994.

229. HR 4602. Fiscal 1995 Interior Appropriations/Firefighters. Byrd, D-W.Va., amendment to allow the Interior Department to reimburse representatives of employees who died in the line of duty in the last quarter of fiscal 1994 and subsequent years for burial costs and related out-of-pocket expenses above $800. Adopted 92-0: R 40-0; D 52-0 (ND 38-0, SD 14-0), July 25, 1994.

230. HR 4602. Fiscal 1995 Interior Appropriations/National Endowment for the Arts. Dodd, D-Conn., motion to table (kill) the Helms, R-N.C., amendment to prohibit the National Endowment for the Arts from financing any activity or work that involves human mutilation, invasive bodily procedures on human beings dead or alive, or the drawing or letting of blood. Motion agreed to 49-42: R 8-31; D 41-11 (ND 34-4, SD 7-7), July 25, 1994.

231. HR 4602. Fiscal 1995 Interior Appropriations/Land Acquisition. McCain, R-Ariz., amendment to require the National Park Service, Fish and Wildlife Service, the Bureau of Land Management and the Forest Service to submit a prioritized list of proposed land acquisitions with the president's budget each year. Adopted 89-0: R 37-0; D 52-0 (ND 38-0, SD 14-0), July 25, 1994.

KEY

Y   Voted for (yea).
Paired for.
+   Announced for.
N   Voted against (nay).
X   Paired against.
—   Announced against.
P   Voted "present."
C   Voted "present" to avoid possible conflict of interest.
?   Did not vote or otherwise make a position known.

Democrats   *Republicans*

	232	233	234	235	236	237	238
ALABAMA							
Heflin	Y	N	Y	Y	Y	Y	N
Shelby	Y	N	Y	Y	Y	Y	N
ALASKA							
Murkowski	Y	Y	N	Y	Y	Y	Y
Stevens	Y	N	Y	Y	Y	Y	Y
ARIZONA							
DeConcini	Y	N	Y	Y	N	Y	?
McCain	N	Y	N	Y	Y	Y	Y
ARKANSAS							
Bumpers	Y	N	Y	Y	N	Y	Y
Pryor	Y	N	Y	Y	N	Y	N
CALIFORNIA							
Boxer	Y	N	Y	Y	N	Y	N
Feinstein	Y	N	Y	Y	N	Y	N
COLORADO							
Campbell	N	Y	Y	Y	N	Y	N
Brown	N	Y	N	Y	Y	Y	Y
CONNECTICUT							
Dodd	Y	N	?	Y	N	Y	N
Lieberman	N	N	Y	Y	N	Y	Y
DELAWARE							
Biden	N	N	Y	Y	N	Y	N
Roth	N	Y	Y	Y	Y	Y	N
FLORIDA							
Graham	Y	N	Y	Y	N	Y	N
Mack	N	Y	N	Y	Y	Y	Y
GEORGIA							
Nunn	Y	Y	Y	Y	Y	Y	Y
Coverdell	N	Y	Y	Y	Y	Y	Y
HAWAII							
Akaka	Y	N	Y	Y	N	Y	N
Inouye	Y	N	Y	Y	N	Y	N
IDAHO							
Craig	Y	Y	?	Y	Y	Y	Y
Kempthorne	Y	Y	N	Y	Y	Y	Y
ILLINOIS							
Moseley-Braun	Y	N	N	Y	N	Y	N
Simon	Y	N	Y	Y	N	N	N
INDIANA							
Coats	N	Y	Y	Y	Y	Y	Y
Lugar	Y	Y	Y	Y	Y	Y	Y

	232	233	234	235	236	237	238
IOWA							
Harkin	Y	N	?	?	N	Y	N
Grassley	Y	Y	N	Y	Y	Y	Y
KANSAS							
Dole	Y	Y	Y	Y	Y	Y	Y
Kassebaum	Y	Y	Y	Y	N	Y	Y
KENTUCKY							
Ford	Y	N	Y	Y	Y	Y	N
McConnell	Y	Y	N	Y	Y	Y	Y
LOUISIANA							
Breaux	Y	N	N	Y	N	Y	Y
Johnston	Y	N	Y	Y	Y	Y	Y
MAINE							
Mitchell	N	N	Y	Y	N	Y	N
Cohen	N	Y	Y	Y	N	Y	Y
MARYLAND							
Mikulski	Y	N	Y	?	N	Y	N
Sarbanes	Y	N	Y	Y	N	Y	N
MASSACHUSETTS							
Kennedy	Y	N	Y	Y	N	Y	N
Kerry	N	N	Y	Y	N	Y	N
MICHIGAN							
Levin	Y	N	Y	Y	N	Y	N
Riegle	Y	N	Y	Y	N	Y	N
MINNESOTA							
Wellstone	N	N	Y	Y	N	Y	N
Durenberger	N	Y	Y	Y	N	Y	Y
MISSISSIPPI							
Cochran	Y	Y	Y	Y	Y	Y	Y
Lott	Y	Y	N	Y	Y	Y	Y
MISSOURI							
Bond	Y	Y	Y	Y	Y	Y	Y
Danforth	N	N	Y	Y	N	N	Y
MONTANA							
Baucus	N	N	Y	Y	N	Y	N
Burns	Y	N	Y	Y	Y	Y	N
NEBRASKA							
Exon	Y	N	Y	Y	N	Y	N
Kerrey	N	N	Y	Y	N	Y	N
NEVADA							
Bryan	N	N	Y	Y	N	Y	N
Reid	Y	N	Y	Y	N	Y	N

	232	233	234	235	236	237	238
NEW HAMPSHIRE							
Gregg	N	Y	Y	Y	Y	Y	Y
Smith	N	Y	N	Y	Y	Y	Y
NEW JERSEY							
Bradley	N	N	Y	Y	N	Y	Y
Lautenberg	N	N	Y	Y	N	Y	N
NEW MEXICO							
Bingaman	Y	N	Y	Y	N	Y	N
Domenici	Y	Y	Y	Y	Y	Y	Y
NEW YORK							
Moynihan	Y	Y	Y	Y	N	Y	N
D'Amato	Y	Y	N	Y	Y	Y	Y
NORTH CAROLINA							
Faircloth	Y	Y	N	Y	Y	Y	Y
Helms	N	Y	N	Y	Y	Y	?
NORTH DAKOTA							
Conrad	Y	N	Y	Y	N	Y	N
Dorgan	Y	N	Y	Y	N	Y	N
OHIO							
Glenn	N	N	Y	Y	N	Y	N
Metzenbaum	N	N	Y	Y	N	Y	N
OKLAHOMA							
Boren	Y	?	Y	Y	Y	Y	Y
Nickles	Y	N	Y	Y	Y	Y	Y
OREGON							
Hatfield	Y	N	Y	Y	N	N	N
Packwood	N	Y	Y	Y	N	Y	Y
PENNSYLVANIA							
Wofford	Y	N	Y	Y	N	Y	N
Specter	N	Y	N	Y	N	N	N
RHODE ISLAND							
Pell	Y	N	Y	Y	N	Y	N
Chafee	N	N	Y	Y	N	N	N
SOUTH CAROLINA							
Hollings	Y	N	Y	Y	N	Y	N
Thurmond	Y	Y	Y	Y	Y	Y	Y
SOUTH DAKOTA							
Daschle	N	N	Y	Y	N	Y	N
Pressler	Y	Y	N	Y	Y	Y	Y
TENNESSEE							
Mathews	N	N	Y	Y	Y	Y	N
Sasser	N	N	Y	Y	Y	Y	N

	232	233	234	235	236	237	238
TEXAS							
Hutchison	Y	Y	Y	Y	Y	Y	Y
Gramm	Y	Y	N	Y	Y	Y	Y
UTAH							
Bennett	Y	Y	N	Y	Y	Y	Y
Hatch	Y	Y	Y	Y	Y	Y	Y
VERMONT							
Leahy	N	N	Y	Y	N	Y	N
Jeffords	Y	Y	Y	Y	N	Y	N
VIRGINIA							
Robb	N	N	Y	Y	N	Y	N
Warner	N	Y	Y	Y	Y	Y	Y
WASHINGTON							
Murray	Y	N	Y	Y	N	Y	N
Gorton	Y	Y	Y	Y	Y	N	Y
WEST VIRGINIA							
Byrd	Y	N	Y	Y	N	Y	N
Rockefeller	Y	N	Y	Y	N	Y	N
WISCONSIN							
Feingold	N	N	Y	Y	N	N	N
Kohl	N	Y	Y	Y	N	Y	N
WYOMING							
Simpson	Y	Y	Y	Y	Y	Y	Y
Wallop	N	Y	N	Y	Y	Y	Y

ND Northern Democrats   SD Southern Democrats   Southern states - Ala., Ark., Fla., Ga., Ky., La., Miss., N.C., Okla., S.C., Tenn., Texas, Va.

232. HR 4602. Fiscal 1995 Interior Appropriations/Fossil Energy Research. Byrd, D-W.Va., motion to table (kill) the Bradley, D-N.J., amendment to cut $10 million from the Fossil Energy Research and Development account at the Department of Energy. The reduction was intended to come from the amount provided for the Advanced Computational Technology Initiative. Motion agreed to 63-37: R 27-17; D 36-20 (ND 25-17, SD 11-3), July 26, 1994.

233. HR 4602. Fiscal 1995 Interior Appropriations/Ellis Island. McCain, R-Ariz., motion to table (kill) the Appropriations Committee amendment to allow the National Park Service to construct a foot bridge from New Jersey to Ellis Island. Motion rejected 43-56: R 39-5; D 4-51 (ND 3-39, SD 1-12), July 26, 1994. (Subsequently, the committee amendment was adopted by voice vote.)

234. Procedural Motion. Mitchell, D-Maine, motion to instruct the sergeant at arms to request the attendance of absent senators. Motion agreed to 77-20: R 25-18; D 52-2 (ND 39-1, SD 13-1), July 27, 1994.

235. S 1513. Elementary and Secondary Education Reauthorization/Motion to Proceed. Mitchell, D-Maine, motion to proceed to the bill to reauthorize for five years the Elementary and Secondary Education Act of 1965, providing $12.7 billion to help disadvantaged students. Motion agreed to 98-0: R 44-0; D 54-0 (ND 40-0, SD 14-0), July 27, 1994.

236. S 1513. Elementary and Secondary Education Reauthorization/School Prayer. Helms, R-N.C., amendment to deny federal aid to state or local school agencies that prohibit constitutionally protected voluntary prayer in public schools. The amendment also would prohibit any person from being required to participate in prayer and protect any person from having the form or content of their constitutionally protected prayer influenced. Rejected 47-53: R 35-9; D 12-44 (ND 3-39, SD 9-5), July 27, 1994.

237. S 1513. Elementary and Secondary Education Reauthorization/School Prayer. Kassebaum, R-Kan., amendment to withhold federal aid from state or local agencies that willfully violate a federal court order mandating a remedy to a violation of a student's constitutional right to prayer in public schools. Adopted 93-7: R 39-5; D 54-2 (ND 40-2, SD 14-0), July 27, 1994.

238. S 1513. Elementary and Secondary Education Reauthorization/School Choice. Dole, R-Kan., amendment to provide $30 million each year for fiscal 1995-97 for a demonstration project at 20 violence-prone schools to allow students at such institutions to obtain vouchers to attend a public or private school of their choice. Rejected 45-53: R 38-5; D 7-48 (ND 2-39, SD 5-9), July 27, 1994.

	239	240	241
ALABAMA			
Heflin	Y	Y	Y
Shelby	Y	Y	Y
ALASKA			
Murkowski	Y	Y	Y
Stevens	Y	Y	N
ARIZONA			
DeConcini	N	Y	Y
McCain	Y	Y	Y
ARKANSAS			
Bumpers	Y	Y	Y
Pryor	Y	Y	Y
CALIFORNIA			
Boxer	N	Y	N
Feinstein	Y	Y	N
COLORADO			
Campbell	Y	Y	N
Brown	Y	Y	N
CONNECTICUT			
Dodd	Y	Y	N
Lieberman	Y	Y	N
DELAWARE			
Biden	Y	Y	N
Roth	Y	Y	N
FLORIDA			
Graham	N	Y	N
Mack	Y	Y	N
GEORGIA			
Nunn	Y	Y	Y
Coverdell	Y	Y	Y
HAWAII			
Akaka	N	Y	N
Inouye	N	Y	N
IDAHO			
Craig	Y	Y	Y
Kempthorne	Y	Y	Y
ILLINOIS			
Moseley-Braun	N	Y	N
Simon	N	Y	N
INDIANA			
Coats	Y	Y	N
Lugar	Y	Y	N

	239	240	241
IOWA			
Harkin	N	Y	N
Grassley	Y	Y	N
KANSAS			
Dole	Y	Y	Y
Kassebaum	N	Y	N
KENTUCKY			
Ford	Y	Y	N
McConnell	Y	Y	Y
LOUISIANA			
Breaux	Y	Y	N
Johnston	Y	Y	Y
MAINE			
Mitchell	N	Y	N
Cohen	Y	Y	Y
MARYLAND			
Mikulski	N	Y	N
Sarbanes	N	Y	N
MASSACHUSETTS			
Kennedy	N	Y	N
Kerry	N	Y	N
MICHIGAN			
Levin	N	Y	Y
Riegle	N	Y	N
MINNESOTA			
Wellstone	N	Y	N
Durenberger	N	Y	N
MISSISSIPPI			
Cochran	Y	Y	Y
Lott	Y	Y	Y
MISSOURI			
Bond	Y	Y	Y
Danforth	Y	Y	Y
MONTANA			
Baucus	Y	Y	Y
Burns	Y	Y	Y
NEBRASKA			
Exon	N	Y	Y
Kerrey	N	Y	Y
NEVADA			
Bryan	Y	Y	N
Reid	Y	Y	N

	239	240	241
NEW HAMPSHIRE			
Gregg	Y	Y	N
Smith	Y	Y	N
NEW JERSEY			
Bradley	N	Y	N
Lautenberg	N	Y	N
NEW MEXICO			
Bingaman	N	Y	Y
Domenici	Y	Y	Y
NEW YORK			
Moynihan	N	Y	N
D'Amato	Y	Y	N
NORTH CAROLINA			
Faircloth	Y	Y	Y
Helms	Y	Y	N
NORTH DAKOTA			
Conrad	Y	Y	Y
Dorgan	Y	Y	Y
OHIO			
Glenn	N	Y	N
Metzenbaum	N	Y	N
OKLAHOMA			
Boren	Y	Y	Y
Nickles	Y	Y	Y
OREGON			
Hatfield	N	Y	N
Packwood	N	Y	Y
PENNSYLVANIA			
Wofford	N	Y	N
Specter	Y	Y	N
RHODE ISLAND			
Pell	N	Y	N
Chafee	N	Y	N
SOUTH CAROLINA			
Hollings	N	Y	Y
Thurmond	Y	Y	Y
SOUTH DAKOTA			
Daschle	N	Y	Y
Pressler	Y	Y	Y
TENNESSEE			
Mathews	N	Y	Y
Sasser	Y	Y	Y

KEY

Y Voted for (yea).
Paired for.
+ Announced for.
N Voted against (nay).
X Paired against.
— Announced against.
P Voted "present."
C Voted "present" to avoid possible conflict of interest.
? Did not vote or otherwise make a position known.

Democrats *Republicans*

	239	240	241
TEXAS			
Hutchison	Y	Y	Y
Gramm	Y	Y	Y
UTAH			
Bennett	Y	Y	Y
Hatch	Y	Y	Y
VERMONT			
Leahy	N	Y	N
Jeffords	N	Y	N
VIRGINIA			
Robb	Y	Y	N
Warner	Y	Y	N
WASHINGTON			
Murray	N	Y	N
Gorton	Y	Y	N
WEST VIRGINIA			
Byrd	Y	Y	N
Rockefeller	N	Y	N
WISCONSIN			
Feingold	N	Y	N
Kohl	N	Y	N
WYOMING			
Simpson	Y	Y	Y
Wallop	Y	Y	Y

ND Northern Democrats   SD Southern Democrats   Southern states - Ala., Ark., Fla., Ga., Ky., La., Miss., N.C., Okla., S.C., Tenn., Texas, Va.

239. S 1513. Elementary and Secondary Education Reauthorization/Local Control of School Violence. Gorton, R-Wash., amendment to allow local schools to set disciplinary policy for all students, including those with developmental disabilities, who bring weapons to school or demonstrate life-threatening behavior. (The federal Individuals With Disabilities Education Act prohibited disabled students from being removed from classrooms for more than 10 days, regardless of their actions.) The Gorton amendment would allow local schools to place disabled students in an alternative educational setting for up to 90 days for violent or disruptive behavior. Adopted 60-40: R 38-6; D 22-34 (ND 11-31, SD 11-3), July 28, 1994.

240. S 1513. Elementary and Secondary Education Reauthorization/Local Control of School Violence. Jeffords, R-Vt., amendment to allow local schools autonomy to place disabled students who bring weapons to school in an alternative educational setting for up to 90 days. (The federal Individuals With Disabilities Education Act prohibited disabled students from being removed from classrooms for more than 10 days, regardless of their actions.) Adopted 100-0: R 44-0; D 56-0 (ND 42-0, SD 14-0), July 28, 1994.

241. S 1513. Elementary and Secondary Education Reauthorization/County Poverty Rate Formula. Bumpers, D-Ark., amendment to replace the Chapter I funding formula in the committee bill with a distribution plan using per pupil income, county income and the total number of school age children as the primary factors. These elements would have replaced the "effort" and "equity" factors in the bill, which reward states for spending more than the national average on education while minimizing disparity between affluent and poor districts within states. Rejected 46-54: R 25-19; D 21-35 (ND 10-32, SD 11-3), July 28, 1994.

ALABAMA	242	243	244	245	246	247	248	249
Heflin	Y	N	Y	Y	Y	N	N	Y
Shelby	Y	N	Y	Y	Y	N	N	Y
ALASKA								
Murkowski	N	N	Y	Y	Y	Y	N	Y
Stevens	Y	N	Y	Y	Y	Y	N	Y
ARIZONA								
DeConcini	Y	N	Y	N	Y	Y	N	Y
McCain	Y	Y	Y	Y	Y	Y	Y	Y
ARKANSAS								
Bumpers	Y	N	Y	Y	Y	Y	Y	Y
Pryor	Y	N	Y	Y	Y	Y	Y	Y
CALIFORNIA								
Boxer	Y	N	N	N	Y	N	N	Y
Feinstein	Y	N	N	N	Y	N	N	Y
COLORADO								
Campbell	Y	N	N	N	Y	N	N	Y
Brown	Y	Y	Y	Y	Y	Y	Y	Y
CONNECTICUT								
Dodd	Y	N	N	N	Y	N	N	Y
Lieberman	Y	N	Y	N	Y	Y	N	Y
DELAWARE								
Biden	Y	N	Y	N	Y	N	N	Y
Roth	Y	Y	Y	Y	Y	Y	Y	Y
FLORIDA								
Graham	+	N	N	Y	Y	N	N	Y
Mack	Y	Y	Y	Y	Y	Y	Y	Y
GEORGIA								
Nunn	Y	N	Y	Y	Y	Y	Y	Y
Coverdell	N	Y	Y	Y	Y	Y	Y	Y
HAWAII								
Akaka	Y	N	N	N	Y	N	N	Y
Inouye	Y	N	N	N	Y	N	N	Y
IDAHO								
Craig	Y	Y	Y	Y	Y	Y	Y	Y
Kempthorne	Y	Y	Y	Y	Y	Y	Y	Y
ILLINOIS								
Moseley-Braun	Y	N	N	N	Y	N	N	Y
Simon	Y	N	N	N	Y	N	N	Y
INDIANA								
Coats	N	Y	Y	Y	Y	Y	Y	Y
Lugar	N	N	Y	Y	Y	Y	Y	Y

IOWA	242	243	244	245	246	247	248	249
Harkin	Y	N	N	N	Y	N	N	Y
Grassley	Y	Y	Y	Y	Y	Y	Y	Y
KANSAS								
Dole	Y	Y	Y	Y	Y	Y	Y	Y
Kassebaum	Y	Y	Y	N	Y	Y	Y	Y
KENTUCKY								
Ford	Y	N	Y	Y	Y	N	Y	Y
McConnell	Y	Y	Y	Y	Y	Y	Y	Y
LOUISIANA								
Breaux	Y	N	Y	Y	Y	Y	N	Y
Johnston	Y	N	Y	Y	Y	Y	N	Y
MAINE								
Mitchell	Y	N	N	N	Y	N	N	Y
Cohen	Y	Y	Y	Y	Y	Y	Y	Y
MARYLAND								
Mikulski	Y	N	N	N	Y	N	N	Y
Sarbanes	Y	N	N	N	Y	N	N	Y
MASSACHUSETTS								
Kennedy	Y	N	N	N	Y	N	N	Y
Kerry	Y	N	N	N	Y	N	N	Y
MICHIGAN								
Levin	Y	N	N	N	Y	N	N	Y
Riegle	Y	N	N	N	Y	N	N	Y
MINNESOTA								
Wellstone	Y	N	N	N	Y	N	N	Y
Durenberger	?	N	Y	Y	Y	Y	N	Y
MISSISSIPPI								
Cochran	Y	N	Y	Y	Y	Y	Y	Y
Lott	N	Y	Y	Y	Y	Y	Y	Y
MISSOURI								
Bond	Y	Y	Y	Y	Y	Y	Y	Y
Danforth	Y	N	Y	Y	Y	Y	Y	Y
MONTANA								
Baucus	Y	N	Y	Y	Y	Y	Y	Y
Burns	N	Y	Y	Y	Y	Y	Y	Y
NEBRASKA								
Exon	Y	N	Y	Y	Y	Y	Y	N
Kerrey	Y	N	Y	Y	Y	Y	Y	N
NEVADA								
Bryan	Y	N	Y	Y	Y	Y	Y	N
Reid	Y	N	Y	Y	Y	N	N	Y

NEW HAMPSHIRE	242	243	244	245	246	247	248	249
Gregg	Y	Y	Y	Y	Y	Y	Y	Y
Smith	N	Y	Y	Y	Y	Y	Y	Y
NEW JERSEY								
Bradley	Y	N	N	N	Y	N	N	Y
Lautenberg	Y	N	N	N	Y	N	N	Y
NEW MEXICO								
Bingaman	Y	N	N	N	Y	N	N	Y
Domenici	Y	N	Y	Y	Y	Y	Y	Y
NEW YORK								
Moynihan	Y	N	N	Y	Y	N	N	Y
D'Amato	Y	Y	Y	Y	Y	Y	N	Y
NORTH CAROLINA								
Faircloth	Y	Y	Y	Y	Y	Y	Y	Y
Helms	N	Y	Y	Y	Y	Y	Y	Y
NORTH DAKOTA								
Conrad	Y	N	Y	N	Y	Y	N	Y
Dorgan	Y	N	Y	N	Y	Y	N	Y
OHIO								
Glenn	Y	N	N	Y	Y	N	N	Y
Metzenbaum	Y	N	N	N	Y	N	N	Y
OKLAHOMA								
Boren	Y	N	N	N	Y	Y	Y	Y
Nickles	N	Y	Y	Y	Y	Y	Y	Y
OREGON								
Hatfield	Y	N	Y	N	Y	N	N	Y
Packwood	Y	Y	N	N	Y	Y	N	Y
PENNSYLVANIA								
Wofford	Y	N	N	N	Y	N	N	Y
Specter	Y	N	Y	Y	Y	Y	N	Y
RHODE ISLAND								
Pell	?	N	N	Y	Y	N	N	Y
Chafee	Y	N	N	Y	Y	Y	Y	Y
SOUTH CAROLINA								
Hollings	Y	N	Y	N	Y	Y	N	Y
Thurmond	Y	Y	Y	Y	Y	Y	Y	Y
SOUTH DAKOTA								
Daschle	Y	N	N	Y	Y	N	N	Y
Pressler	Y	Y	Y	Y	Y	Y	Y	Y
TENNESSEE								
Mathews	Y	N	Y	Y	Y	Y	Y	Y
Sasser	Y	N	Y	Y	Y	Y	Y	Y

KEY

Y	Voted for (yea).
#	Paired for.
+	Announced for.
N	Voted against (nay).
X	Paired against.
—	Announced against.
P	Voted "present."
C	Voted "present" to avoid possible conflict of interest.
?	Did not vote or otherwise make a position known.

Democrats *Republicans*

TEXAS	242	243	244	245	246	247	248	249
Hutchison	Y	Y	Y	Y	Y	Y	Y	Y
Gramm	Y	Y	Y	Y	Y	Y	Y	Y
UTAH								
Bennett	Y	Y	Y	Y	Y	Y	Y	Y
Hatch	Y	Y	Y	Y	Y	Y	Y	Y
VERMONT								
Leahy	Y	N	N	N	Y	N	N	Y
Jeffords	Y	N	N	Y	Y	Y	Y	Y
VIRGINIA								
Robb	Y	N	N	N	Y	N	N	Y
Warner	Y	Y	Y	Y	Y	Y	Y	Y
WASHINGTON								
Murray	Y	N	N	N	Y	N	N	Y
Gorton	Y	Y	Y	Y	Y	N	N	Y
WEST VIRGINIA								
Byrd	Y	N	Y	Y	Y	N	Y	N
Rockefeller	Y	N	N	Y	Y	N	N	Y
WISCONSIN								
Feingold	Y	N	N	N	Y	N	N	Y
Kohl	Y	N	Y	Y	Y	Y	N	Y
WYOMING								
Simpson	Y	Y	Y	Y	Y	Y	Y	Y
Wallop	+	+	+	+	+	Y	Y	Y

ND Northern Democrats   SD Southern Democrats   Southern states - Ala., Ark., Fla., Ga., Ky., La., Miss., N.C., Okla., S.C., Tenn., Texas, Va.

242. Breyer Nomination/Confirmation. Confirmation of President Clinton's nomination of Stephen G. Breyer of Massachusetts to be an associate justice of the Supreme Court. Confirmed 87-9: R 33-9; D 54-0 (ND 41-0, SD 13-0), July 29, 1994. A "yea" was a vote in support of the president's position.

243. S 1513. Elementary and Secondary Education Reauthorization/New Programs. Gregg, R-N.H., amendment to eliminate all new programs authorized by the bill. Rejected 32-67: R 32-11; D 0-56 (ND 0-42, SD 0-14), Aug. 1, 1994.

244. S 1513. Elementary and Secondary Education Reauthorization/Homosexual Lifestyle. Helms, R-N.C., amendment to the Smith, R-N.H., amendment to prohibit agencies receiving money under the bill from encouraging or supporting homosexuality as a positive lifestyle alternative. The Smith amendment was essentially the same as Helms'. Adopted 63-36: R 40-3; D 23-33 (ND 12-30, SD 11-3), Aug. 1, 1994.

245. S 1513. Elementary and Secondary Education Reauthorization/Single Sex Schooling. Danforth, R-Mo., amendment to allow the secretary of Education to waive certain federal civil rights laws in order to create up to 10 demonstration projects that would establish single-sex schooling environments. Adopted 66-33: R 40-3; D 26-30 (ND 15-27, SD 11-3), Aug. 1, 1994.

246. S 1513. Elementary and Secondary Education Reauthorization/Sexual Activity. Kennedy, D-Mass., amendment to prohibit money in the bill from being spent to promote or encourage sexual activity. Adopted 99-0: R 43-0; D 56-0 (ND 42-0, SD 14-0), Aug. 1, 1994.

247. S 1513. Elementary and Secondary Education Reauthorization/Perkins Act. Kassebaum, R-Kan., amendment to prohibit the secretary of Education from issuing new regulations to carry out the Perkins Vocational and Applied Technology Education Act of 1990 prior to 1995 when the Perkins Act is due to be reauthorized. Adopted 63-37: R 44-0; D 19-37 (ND 11-31, SD 8-6), Aug. 2, 1994.

248. S 1513. Elementary and Secondary Education Reauthorization/Davis-Bacon Act. Craig, R-Idaho, amendment to limit the application of the Davis-Bacon Act, which requires federal construction contractors to pay workers prevailing local wages on public works projects, to those contracts where the federal contribution exceeds 25 percent of the cost. Rejected 44-56: R 37-7; D 7-49 (ND 0-42, SD 7-7), Aug. 2, 1994.

249. S 1513. Elementary and Secondary Education Reauthorization/Bilingual Teachers. Pressler, R-S.D., amendment to require that bilingual teachers hired under Title VII of the bill are proficient in both written and spoken English. Adopted 100-0: R 44-0; D 56-0 (ND 42-0, SD 14-0), Aug. 2, 1994.

	250	251	252	253	254	255
ALABAMA						
Heflin	Y	Y	Y	N	Y	N
Shelby	Y	N	Y	N	Y	N
ALASKA						
Murkowski	Y	N	Y	N	Y	N
Stevens	Y	N	Y	N	Y	N
ARIZONA						
DeConcini	Y	Y	Y	Y	Y	Y
McCain	Y	N	Y	N	Y	N
ARKANSAS						
Bumpers	Y	Y	Y	Y	Y	Y
Pryor	Y	?	Y	Y	Y	Y
CALIFORNIA						
Boxer	N	Y	Y	N	Y	N
Feinstein	Y	Y	Y	N	Y	N
COLORADO						
Campbell	Y	N	Y	N	Y	Y
Brown	Y	N	N	N	Y	N
CONNECTICUT						
Dodd	Y	Y	Y	N	Y	Y
Lieberman	Y	Y	Y	N	Y	N
DELAWARE						
Biden	Y	Y	Y	N	Y	N
Roth	Y	N	Y	N	Y	N
FLORIDA						
Graham	Y	Y	Y	N	Y	N
Mack	Y	N	Y	N	Y	N
GEORGIA						
Nunn	Y	Y	Y	N	Y	N
Coverdell	Y	N	Y	N	Y	N
HAWAII						
Akaka	Y	Y	Y	N	Y	Y
Inouye	Y	Y	Y	N	Y	Y
IDAHO						
Craig	Y	N	Y	N	Y	Y
Kempthorne	Y	N	Y	N	Y	Y
ILLINOIS						
Moseley-Braun	N	Y	Y	N	Y	Y
Simon	Y	Y	Y	Y	Y	Y
INDIANA						
Coats	Y	N	Y	N	Y	Y
Lugar	Y	N	Y	Y	Y	Y
IOWA						
Harkin	Y	Y	Y	Y	Y	Y
Grassley	Y	N	Y	N	Y	Y
KANSAS						
Dole	Y	N	Y	N	Y	Y
Kassebaum	Y	N	Y	N	Y	Y
KENTUCKY						
Ford	Y	Y	Y	N	Y	Y
McConnell	Y	N	Y	N	Y	Y
LOUISIANA						
Breaux	Y	Y	Y	N	Y	N
Johnston	Y	Y	Y	N	Y	N
MAINE						
Mitchell	Y	Y	Y	Y	Y	N
Cohen	Y	N	Y	Y	Y	N
MARYLAND						
Mikulski	Y	Y	Y	N	Y	Y
Sarbanes	Y	Y	Y	N	Y	Y
MASSACHUSETTS						
Kennedy	Y	Y	Y	Y	Y	N
Kerry	Y	Y	Y	Y	Y	N
MICHIGAN						
Levin	Y	Y	Y	Y	Y	Y
Riegle	Y	Y	Y	N	Y	Y
MINNESOTA						
Wellstone	N	Y	Y	Y	Y	Y
Durenberger	Y	Y	Y	N	Y	Y
MISSISSIPPI						
Cochran	Y	N	Y	N	Y	N
Lott	Y	N	Y	N	Y	N
MISSOURI						
Bond	Y	N	Y	N	Y	Y
Danforth	Y	N	Y	N	Y	Y
MONTANA						
Baucus	Y	Y	Y	Y	Y	Y
Burns	Y	N	Y	N	Y	Y
NEBRASKA						
Exon	Y	Y	Y	Y	Y	Y
Kerrey	Y	Y	Y	Y	Y	Y
NEVADA						
Bryan	Y	Y	Y	Y	Y	Y
Reid	Y	Y	Y	N	Y	Y
NEW HAMPSHIRE						
Gregg	Y	N	Y	N	Y	N
Smith	Y	N	N	N	Y	N
NEW JERSEY						
Bradley	Y	Y	Y	Y	Y	N
Lautenberg	Y	N	Y	Y	Y	N
NEW MEXICO						
Bingaman	Y	Y	Y	N	Y	N
Domenici	Y	N	Y	N	Y	N
NEW YORK						
Moynihan	Y	Y	Y	Y	Y	N
D'Amato	Y	N	Y	N	Y	N
NORTH CAROLINA						
Faircloth	Y	N	N	N	Y	N
Helms	Y	N	N	N	Y	Y
NORTH DAKOTA						
Conrad	Y	Y	Y	Y	Y	N
Dorgan	Y	Y	Y	Y	Y	Y
OHIO						
Glenn	Y	Y	Y	N	Y	Y
Metzenbaum	N	Y	Y	Y	Y	Y
OKLAHOMA						
Boren	Y	Y	Y	N	Y	N
Nickles	Y	N	N	N	Y	N
OREGON						
Hatfield	Y	Y	Y	N	Y	N
Packwood	Y	N	Y	N	Y	N
PENNSYLVANIA						
Wofford	Y	Y	Y	N	Y	N
Specter	Y	N	Y	Y	Y	N
RHODE ISLAND						
Pell	Y	Y	Y	N	Y	N
Chafee	N	Y	Y	Y	Y	Y
SOUTH CAROLINA						
Hollings	Y	Y	Y	N	Y	N
Thurmond	Y	N	Y	N	Y	Y
SOUTH DAKOTA						
Daschle	Y	Y	Y	N	Y	Y
Pressler	Y	N	Y	N	Y	Y
TENNESSEE						
Mathews	Y	Y	Y	Y	Y	Y
Sasser	Y	N	Y	Y	Y	Y
TEXAS						
Hutchison	Y	N	Y	N	Y	N
Gramm	Y	N	Y	N	Y	N
UTAH						
Bennett	Y	N	Y	N	Y	N
Hatch	Y	N	Y	N	Y	N
VERMONT						
Leahy	Y	Y	Y	Y	Y	Y
Jeffords	N	Y	Y	Y	Y	Y
VIRGINIA						
Robb	Y	Y	Y	N	Y	N
Warner	Y	N	Y	Y	Y	N
WASHINGTON						
Murray	N	Y	Y	N	Y	N
Gorton	N	N	Y	N	Y	Y
WEST VIRGINIA						
Byrd	Y	Y	Y	N	Y	N
Rockefeller	Y	Y	Y	N	Y	N
WISCONSIN						
Feingold	N	Y	Y	Y	Y	Y
Kohl	Y	Y	Y	Y	Y	Y
WYOMING						
Simpson	Y	N	Y	N	Y	N
Wallop	Y	N	N	N	Y	N

ND Northern Democrats   SD Southern Democrats

Southern states - Ala., Ark., Fla., Ga., Ky., La., Miss., N.C., Okla., S.C., Tenn., Texas, Va.

250. S 1513. Elementary and Secondary Education Reauthorization/Homosexual Lifestyle. Smith, R-N.H., amendment, as amended, to prohibit agencies receiving money under the bill to use federal money to encourage or support homosexuality as a positive lifestyle alternative. Before being adopted, the Smith amendment was amended by a similar Helms, R-N.C., amendment (see vote 244) and by two Kennedy, D-Mass., amendments. The first Kennedy amendment would prohibit money in the bill from being spent to promote or encourage sexual activity (see vote 246), and the second Kennedy amendment, adopted by voice vote, would prohibit money in the bill from being used to distribute condoms in public schools unless the programs met certain local control criteria. Adopted 91-9: R 41-3; D 50-6 (ND 36-6, SD 14-0), Aug. 2, 1994.

251. S 1513. Elementary and Secondary Education Reauthorization/Crime Provisions. Biden, D-Del., motion to table (kill) the Gramm, R-Texas, amendment to insert provisions dropped by conferees on the omnibus crime bill (HR 3355) that would have required mandatory sentences for possession of firearms during commission of a violent crime or drug felony or for selling drugs to a minor, and to prevent the administration from implementing provisions of the Racial Justice Act by executive order. Motion agreed to 55-44: R 4-40; D 51-4 (ND 40-2, SD 11-2), Aug. 2, 1994.

252. HR 6. Elementary and Secondary Education Reauthorization/Passage. Passage of the bill to reauthorize for five years the Elementary and Secondary Education Act of 1965, providing $12.6 billion to help disadvantaged students. Passed 94-6: R 38-6; D 56-0 (ND 42-0, SD 14-0), Aug. 2, 1994. A "yea" was a vote in support of the president's position.

253. HR 4624. Fiscal 1995 VA, HUD Appropriations/Space Station. Bumpers, D-Ark., amendment to terminate the space station program, cutting $1.9 billion from the bill. Rejected 36-64: R 6-38; D 30-26 (ND 23-19, SD 7-7), Aug. 3, 1994. A "nay" was a vote in support of the president's position.

254. HR 4624. Fiscal 1995 VA, HUD Appropriations/Haiti. Dole, R-Kan., amendment to express the sense of the Senate that U.N. Security Council Resolution 940 of July 31, 1994, does not constitute authorization for the deployment of U.S. forces in Haiti under the U.S. Constitution or the War Powers Resolution (PL 93-148). Adopted 100-0: R 44-0; D 56-0 (ND 42-0, SD 14-0), Aug. 3, 1994.

255. HR 4624. Fiscal 1995 VA, HUD Appropriations/Ethanol Mandate. Mikulski, D-Md., motion to table (kill) the Johnston, D-La., amendment to prohibit the Environmental Protection Agency from implementing its renewable oxygenates rule for reformulated gasoline, which would require a minimum of 15 percent and eventually 30 percent of the oxygenates used in reformulated gasoline to come from renewable sources, such as ethanol. The amendment also would have cut NASA's procurement budget by $39.3 million. Motion agreed to 51-50: R 19-25; D 31-25 (ND 26-16, SD 5-9), with Vice President Gore casting a "yea" vote, Aug. 3, 1994. A "yea" was a vote in support of the president's position.

	256	257	258	259	260	261	262
ALABAMA							
Heflin	?	?	?	?	?	?	?
Shelby	Y	Y	N	Y	N	N	Y
ALASKA							
Murkowski	N	N	N	Y	N	N	Y
Stevens	N	N	N	Y	N	N	Y
ARIZONA							
DeConcini	Y	Y	N	N	N	N	Y
McCain	N	N	Y	Y	Y	Y	Y
ARKANSAS							
Bumpers	Y	Y	N	N	N	N	Y
Pryor	Y	Y	N	N	N	N	Y
CALIFORNIA							
Boxer	Y	Y	N	N	N	N	Y
Feinstein	Y	Y	N	N	N	N	Y
COLORADO							
Campbell	Y	Y	N	N	N	N	Y
Brown	N	N	Y	Y	Y	Y	N
CONNECTICUT							
Dodd	Y	Y	N	N	N	N	Y
Lieberman	Y	Y	N	Y	N	Y	Y
DELAWARE							
Biden	Y	Y	N	N	N	N	Y
Roth	N	N	Y	Y	Y	Y	N
FLORIDA							
Graham	Y	Y	N	Y	Y	Y	Y
Mack	Y	N	N	Y	N	N	Y
GEORGIA							
Nunn	Y	N	N	Y	N	N	Y
Coverdell	N	N	N	Y	Y	N	Y
HAWAII							
Akaka	Y	Y	N	Y	N	N	Y
Inouye	Y	Y	N	Y	N	N	Y
IDAHO							
Craig	N	N	N	Y	Y	Y	Y
Kempthorne	N	N	N	Y	Y	Y	Y
ILLINOIS							
Moseley-Braun	Y	Y	N	N	N	N	Y
Simon	Y	Y	N	Y	N	N	Y
INDIANA							
Coats	N	N	N	Y	Y	Y	Y
Lugar	N	N	N	Y	Y	Y	Y
IOWA							
Harkin	Y	Y	N	Y	N	N	Y
Grassley	N	N	Y	Y	N	N	Y
KANSAS							
Dole	N	N	N	Y	Y	Y	Y
Kassebaum	N	N	N	Y	N	Y	Y
KENTUCKY							
Ford	Y	Y	N	Y	N	N	Y
McConnell	N	N	N	Y	Y	Y	Y
LOUISIANA							
Breaux	Y	Y	N	Y	N	N	?
Johnston	Y	Y	N	Y	N	N	Y
MAINE							
Mitchell	Y	Y	N	Y	N	N	Y
Cohen	N	N	N	Y	N	Y	Y
MARYLAND							
Mikulski	Y	Y	N	Y	N	N	Y
Sarbanes	Y	Y	N	Y	N	N	Y
MASSACHUSETTS							
Kennedy	Y	Y	N	Y	N	N	Y
Kerry	Y	Y	N	Y	N	N	Y
MICHIGAN							
Levin	Y	Y	N	Y	N	N	Y
Riegle	Y	Y	N	Y	N	?	Y
MINNESOTA							
Wellstone	Y	Y	N	Y	Y	Y	Y
Durenberger	N	N	N	Y	Y	Y	Y
MISSISSIPPI							
Cochran	N	N	N	Y	N	N	Y
Lott	?	?	?	?	?	?	?
MISSOURI							
Bond	Y	Y	N	Y	N	N	Y
Danforth	N	N	N	Y	N	N	Y
MONTANA							
Baucus	Y	Y	N	Y	N	Y	Y
Burns	N	N	N	Y	N	Y	Y
NEBRASKA							
Exon	Y	Y	N	Y	N	N	Y
Kerrey	Y	Y	N	Y	N	N	Y
NEVADA							
Bryan	Y	Y	N	Y	N	N	Y
Reid	Y	Y	N	Y	N	N	Y
NEW HAMPSHIRE							
Gregg	N	N	Y	Y	Y	Y	N
Smith	N	N	Y	Y	Y	Y	N
NEW JERSEY							
Bradley	Y	Y	Y	Y	N	Y	Y
Lautenberg	Y	Y	N	Y	N	Y	Y
NEW MEXICO							
Bingaman	Y	Y	N	Y	N	N	Y
Domenici	Y	N	N	Y	N	N	Y
NEW YORK							
Moynihan	Y	Y	N	Y	N	N	Y
D'Amato	Y	Y	N	Y	N	N	Y
NORTH CAROLINA							
Faircloth	N	N	Y	Y	Y	Y	N
Helms	N	N	Y	Y	Y	Y	N
NORTH DAKOTA							
Conrad	Y	Y	N	Y	N	N	Y
Dorgan	Y	Y	N	Y	N	N	Y
OHIO							
Glenn	Y	N	N	Y	N	N	Y
Metzenbaum	Y	Y	N	Y	Y	Y	Y
OKLAHOMA							
Boren	Y	Y	N	Y	N	N	Y
Nickles	N	N	Y	N	Y	Y	Y
OREGON							
Hatfield	Y	Y	N	Y	N	N	Y
Packwood	N	N	N	Y	N	N	Y
PENNSYLVANIA							
Wofford	Y	Y	N	Y	N	N	Y
Specter	N	N	N	Y	N	Y	Y
RHODE ISLAND							
Pell	Y	Y	N	Y	N	N	Y
Chafee	N	N	N	Y	Y	Y	Y
SOUTH CAROLINA							
Hollings	Y	Y	N	Y	N	N	Y
Thurmond	N	N	N	Y	Y	Y	Y
SOUTH DAKOTA							
Daschle	Y	Y	N	Y	N	N	Y
Pressler	N	N	Y	N	Y	Y	Y
TENNESSEE							
Mathews	Y	Y	N	Y	N	Y	Y
Sasser	Y	Y	N	Y	N	Y	+
TEXAS							
Hutchison	N	Y	N	Y	N	Y	N
Gramm	Y	N	N	Y	Y	N	Y
UTAH							
Bennett	N	N	N	Y	N	Y	Y
Hatch	N	N	N	Y	N	Y	Y
VERMONT							
Leahy	Y	Y	N	Y	N	N	Y
Jeffords	Y	N	N	Y	N	N	?
VIRGINIA							
Robb	Y	Y	N	Y	N	N	Y
Warner	N	N	N	Y	Y	Y	Y
WASHINGTON							
Murray	Y	Y	N	Y	N	N	Y
Gorton	N	N	N	Y	N	N	Y
WEST VIRGINIA							
Byrd	Y	Y	N	Y	N	N	Y
Rockefeller	Y	Y	N	Y	N	N	Y
WISCONSIN							
Feingold	Y	N	Y	Y	Y	Y	N
Kohl	Y	N	Y	N	Y	N	N
WYOMING							
Simpson	N	N	N	Y	N	Y	Y
Wallop	N	N	Y	Y	Y	Y	N

ND Northern Democrats   SD Southern Democrats   Southern states - Ala., Ark., Fla., Ga., Ky., La., Miss., N.C., Okla., S.C., Tenn., Texas, Va.

256. HR 4624. Fiscal 1995 VA, HUD Appropriations/VA Inpatient Facilities. Rockefeller, D-W.Va., motion to table (kill) the Murkowski, R-Alaska, amendment to restrict the use of $87.7 million in the bill to build or modernize three inpatient facilities at veterans hospitals in Tennessee, California, and Hawaii. Motion agreed to 62-36: R 7-36; D 55-0 (ND 42-0, SD 13-0), Aug. 4, 1994.

257. HR 4624. Fiscal 1995 VA, HUD Appropriations/ Pension Fund Housing Investment. Mikulski, D-Md., motion to table (kill) the Cohen, R-Maine, amendment to eliminate the $350 million in the bill for a government subsidy program to encourage investment by pension funds in low-income housing. Motion agreed to 55-43: R 4-39; D 51-4 (ND 39-3, SD 12-1), Aug. 4, 1994.

258. HR 4624. Fiscal 1995 VA, HUD Appropriations/ Motion To Recommit. Smith, R-N.H., motion to recommit the bill to the Appropriations Committee with instructions to report it back after cutting the overall total to an amount not greater than that appropriated in fiscal 1994 (a cut of about $1.4 billion). Motion rejected 14-84: R 11-32; D 3-52 (ND 3-39, SD 0-13), Aug. 4, 1994.

259. HR 4624. Fiscal 1995 VA, HUD Appropriations/ Abortion Clinics Attack. Lautenberg, D-N.J., amendment to express the sense of the Senate condemning the July 29 murders outside an abortion clinic in Pensacola, Fla., and urging federal law enforcement agencies to use their full authority under the First Amendment to ensure safety at clinics. Adopted 98-0: R 43-0; D 55-0 (ND 42-0, SD 13-0), Aug. 4, 1994.

260. HR 4624. Fiscal 1995 VA, HUD Appropriations/ Community Development Block Grants. Smith, R-N.H., amendment to eliminate the $135 million in "special purpose grants" under the Department of Housing and Urban Development and to redistribute the money through the Community Development Block Grant Program. Rejected 27-71: R 23-20; D 4-51 (ND 3-39, SD 1-12), Aug. 4, 1994.

261. HR 4624. Fiscal 1995 VA, HUD Appropriations/ Clean Water Revolving Fund. Smith, R-N.H., amendment to eliminate $697.2 million earmarked for specific waste-water treatment construction projects and redistribute the money through the formula established in the Clean Water State Revolving Fund. Rejected 37-60: R 25-18; D 12-42 (ND 8-33, SD 4-9), Aug. 4, 1994.

262. HR 4624. Fiscal 1995 VA, HUD Appropriations/ Passage. Passage of the bill to provide approximately $89.8 billion in new budget authority for the departments of Veterans Affairs and Housing and Urban Development, and multiple independent agencies, boards, commissions, corporations and offices for fiscal 1995. The administration had requested $90,093,793,061. Passed 86-9: R 35-7; D 51-2 (ND 40-2, SD 11-0), Aug. 4, 1994.

KEY

Y Voted for (yea).
Paired for.
+ Announced for.
N Voted against (nay).
X Paired against.
— Announced against.
P Voted "present."
C Voted "present" to avoid possible conflict of interest.
? Did not vote or otherwise make a position known.

Democrats   *Republicans*

	263	264	265	266	267	268	269	270
ALABAMA								
Heflin	?	?	?	?	Y	Y	Y	Y
Shelby	Y	Y	Y	Y	Y	N	Y	Y
ALASKA								
Murkowski	Y	Y	Y	Y	Y	N	N	Y
Stevens	Y	Y	Y	Y	Y	N	Y	Y
ARIZONA								
DeConcini	?	N	Y	Y	Y	Y	N	Y
McCain	Y	N	Y	Y	Y	N	N	Y
ARKANSAS								
Bumpers	Y	?	?	?	Y	Y	Y	Y
Pryor	Y	?	?	?	Y	Y	Y	Y
CALIFORNIA								
Boxer	Y	Y	Y	?	Y	Y	N	Y
Feinstein	Y	Y	Y	Y	Y	Y	N	Y
COLORADO								
Campbell	Y	Y	Y	Y	Y	N	Y	Y
Brown	N	N	Y	Y	Y	N	N	N
CONNECTICUT								
Dodd	Y	Y	Y	Y	Y	Y	Y	Y
Lieberman	Y	Y	Y	Y	Y	Y	Y	Y
DELAWARE								
Biden	Y	Y	Y	Y	Y	Y	Y	Y
Roth	N	N	Y	Y	Y	N	Y	N
FLORIDA								
Graham	Y	Y	Y	Y	Y	Y	N	Y
Mack	Y	N	Y	Y	Y	N	N	Y
GEORGIA								
Nunn	Y	Y	Y	Y	Y	Y	Y	Y
Coverdell	N	N	Y	Y	Y	N	N	Y
HAWAII								
Akaka	Y	Y	Y	Y	Y	Y	Y	Y
Inouye	Y	Y	Y	Y	Y	Y	Y	Y
IDAHO								
Craig	N	N	Y	Y	Y	N	N	N
Kempthorne	N	N	Y	Y	Y	N	N	N
ILLINOIS								
Moseley-Braun	Y	Y	Y	Y	Y	N	Y	Y
Simon	Y	Y	Y	Y	Y	Y	Y	Y
INDIANA								
Coats	Y	Y	Y	Y	Y	N	Y	Y
Lugar	N	Y	Y	Y	Y	N	Y	Y

	263	264	265	266	267	268	269	270
IOWA								
Harkin	Y	Y	Y	Y	Y	Y	Y	Y
Grassley	N	N	Y	Y	Y	N	N	Y
KANSAS								
Dole	N	N	Y	Y	Y	N	N	Y
Kassebaum	Y	N	Y	Y	Y	N	Y	Y
KENTUCKY								
Ford	Y	Y	Y	Y	Y	Y	Y	Y
McConnell	N	N	Y	Y	Y	N	N	Y
LOUISIANA								
Breaux	?	?	?	?	Y	Y	Y	Y
Johnston	Y	Y	Y	Y	Y	Y	Y	Y
MAINE								
Mitchell	Y	Y	Y	Y	Y	Y	N	Y
Cohen	N	Y	Y	Y	Y	N	Y	Y
MARYLAND								
Mikulski	Y	Y	Y	Y	Y	Y	Y	Y
Sarbanes	Y	Y	Y	Y	Y	Y	Y	Y
MASSACHUSETTS								
Kennedy	Y	Y	Y	Y	Y	Y	N	Y
Kerry	Y	Y	Y	Y	Y	Y	Y	Y
MICHIGAN								
Levin	Y	Y	Y	Y	Y	Y	Y	Y
Riegle	Y	Y	Y	Y	Y	Y	Y	Y
MINNESOTA								
Wellstone	N	Y	Y	Y	Y	Y	Y	Y
Durenberger	N	Y	Y	Y	Y	N	N	Y
MISSISSIPPI								
Cochran	Y	Y	Y	Y	Y	N	Y	Y
Lott	N	N	Y	Y	Y	N	N	Y
MISSOURI								
Bond	Y	Y	Y	Y	Y	N	Y	Y
Danforth	N	N	Y	Y	Y	N	Y	Y
MONTANA								
Baucus	Y	Y	Y	Y	Y	Y	Y	Y
Burns	N	Y	Y	Y	Y	N	N	Y
NEBRASKA								
Exon	Y	Y	Y	Y	Y	Y	Y	Y
Kerrey	Y	Y	Y	Y	Y	Y	Y	Y
NEVADA								
Bryan	Y	Y	Y	Y	Y	Y	Y	Y
Reid	Y	Y	Y	Y	Y	Y	Y	Y

	263	264	265	266	267	268	269	270
NEW HAMPSHIRE								
Gregg	N	Y	Y	?	Y	N	Y	N
Smith	N	Y	Y	Y	Y	N	Y	N
NEW JERSEY								
Bradley	Y	N	Y	Y	Y	Y	N	Y
Lautenberg	Y	N	Y	Y	Y	Y	N	Y
NEW MEXICO								
Bingaman	Y	Y	Y	Y	Y	Y	Y	Y
Domenici	N	Y	Y	Y	Y	N	N	Y
NEW YORK								
Moynihan	Y	Y	Y	Y	Y	Y	N	Y
D'Amato	N	N	Y	Y	Y	N	N	Y
NORTH CAROLINA								
Faircloth	N	N	Y	Y	Y	N	N	N
Helms	N	N	Y	Y	Y	N	Y	N
NORTH DAKOTA								
Conrad	Y	Y	Y	Y	Y	Y	Y	N
Dorgan	Y	Y	Y	Y	Y	Y	Y	Y
OHIO								
Glenn	Y	Y	Y	Y	Y	Y	N	Y
Metzenbaum	Y	Y	Y	Y	Y	Y	Y	Y
OKLAHOMA								
Boren	Y	Y	Y	Y	Y	Y	Y	Y
Nickles	N	N	Y	Y	Y	N	N	Y
OREGON								
Hatfield	Y	Y	Y	Y	Y	N	Y	Y
Packwood	N	Y	Y	Y	Y	N	Y	Y
PENNSYLVANIA								
Wofford	Y	Y	Y	Y	Y	Y	Y	Y
Specter	N	N	Y	Y	Y	N	Y	Y
RHODE ISLAND								
Pell	Y	Y	Y	Y	Y	Y	N	Y
Chafee	Y	Y	Y	Y	Y	N	Y	Y
SOUTH CAROLINA								
Hollings	Y	Y	Y	Y	Y	Y	Y	Y
Thurmond	N	Y	Y	Y	Y	N	Y	Y
SOUTH DAKOTA								
Daschle	Y	Y	Y	Y	Y	Y	Y	Y
Pressler	N	N	Y	Y	Y	N	N	N
TENNESSEE								
Mathews	?	?	?	?	Y	Y	Y	Y
Sasser	Y	Y	Y	Y	Y	Y	Y	Y

	263	264	265	266	267	268	269	270
TEXAS								
Hutchison	N	N	Y	Y	Y	N	N	N
Gramm	Y	N	Y	Y	Y	N	N	N
UTAH								
Bennett	N	Y	Y	Y	Y	N	N	Y
Hatch	N	Y	Y	+	Y	N	N	Y
VERMONT								
Leahy	Y	Y	Y	Y	Y	Y	Y	Y
Jeffords	#	?	?	?	Y	N	Y	Y
VIRGINIA								
Robb	Y	Y	Y	Y	Y	Y	N	Y
Warner	Y	Y	Y	Y	Y	N	Y	Y
WASHINGTON								
Murray	Y	Y	Y	Y	Y	Y	Y	Y
Gorton	Y	Y	Y	Y	Y	N	Y	Y
WEST VIRGINIA								
Byrd	Y	Y	Y	Y	Y	Y	Y	Y
Rockefeller	Y	Y	Y	Y	Y	Y	Y	Y
WISCONSIN								
Feingold	N	N	Y	Y	Y	Y	Y	Y
Kohl	Y	Y	Y	Y	Y	Y	Y	Y
WYOMING								
Simpson	N	Y	Y	Y	Y	N	Y	Y
Wallop	X	N	Y	Y	Y	N	N	N

ND Northern Democrats   SD Southern Democrats   Southern states - Ala., Ark., Fla., Ga., Ky., La., Miss., N.C., Okla., S.C., Tenn., Texas, Va.

263. HR 4606. Fiscal 1995 Labor, HHS and Education Appropriations/Haiti. McCain, R-Ariz., motion to table (kill) the Specter, R-Pa., amendment to bar the president from deploying U.S. troops to restore the legitimately elected government in Haiti unless authorized by Congress, or unless it is vital to national security interests or to protect the lives of U.S. citizens. Motion agreed to 63-31: R 13-29; D 50-2 (ND 39-2, SD 11-0), Aug. 5, 1994. A "yea" was a vote in support of the president's position.

264. HR 4606. Fiscal 1995 Labor, HHS and Education Appropriations/AIDS Research. Inouye, D-Hawaii, motion to table (kill) the McCain, R-Ariz., amendment to transfer $37.4 million of the $330 million provided for the Corporation for Public Broadcasting to increase AIDS research and prevention programs. Motion agreed to 68-26: R 21-22; D 47-4 (ND 38-4, SD 9-0), Aug. 5, 1994.

265. HR 4606. Fiscal 1995 Labor, HHS and Education Appropriations/Taiwanese Visas. Brown, R-Colo., amendment to allow Taiwanese government officials to enter the United States for reasons pertaining to trade, the environment, threats to U.S. national security and other diplomatic and economic reasons. Adopted 94-0: R 43-0; D 51-0 (ND 42-0, SD 9-0), Aug. 5, 1994.

266. HR 4606. Fiscal 1995 Labor, HHS and Education Appropriations/Selling AIDS-Infected Blood. Helms, R-N.C., amendment to impose fines and prison terms on any person who tries to sell his or her blood or body parts if that person has the AIDS virus, unless it is for scientific research. Adopted 91-0: R 41-0; D 50-0 (ND 41-0, SD 9-0), Aug. 5, 1994.

267. HR 4606. Fiscal 1995 Labor, HHS, Education Appropriations/Health Care Timetable. Helms, R-N.C., motion to table (kill) the Helms, R-N.C., amendment to express the sense of the Senate that Congress should defer action on major health care reform until next year, giving ample time to consider alternatives. Motion agreed to 100-0: R 44-0; D 56-0 (ND 42-0, SD 14-0), Aug. 10, 1994.

268. HR 4650. Fiscal 1995 Defense Appropriations/Heath Care Timetable. Inouye, D-Hawaii, motion to table (kill) the Helms, R-N.C., amendment to express the sense of the Senate that Congress should defer action on major health care reform until next year, giving ample time to consider alternatives and make wise choices, unless the Senate has had the full opportunity to debate and amend the proposal after the Congressional Budget Office estimates have been made available. Motion agreed to 54-46: R 0-44; D 54-2 (ND 41-1, SD 13-1), Aug. 10, 1994.

269. HR 4606. Fiscal 1995 Labor, HHS and Education Appropriations/Immigrant Education. Inouye, D-Hawaii, motion to table (kill) the Graham, D-Fla., amendment to provide $100 million to carry out the Emergency Immigrant Education Act of 1984 to help educate legal immigrants. Motion agreed to 66-34: R 21-23; D 45-11 (ND 34-8, SD 11-3), Aug. 10, 1994.

270. HR 4606. Fiscal 1995 Labor, HHS and Education Appropriations/Passage. Passage of the bill to provide $252.9 billion for the departments of Labor, Health and Human Services, and Education and related agencies for fiscal 1995. The administration had requested $254,422,523,000. Passed 87-13: R 32-12; D 55-1 (ND 41-1, SD 14-0), Aug. 10, 1994.

KEY

- Y Voted for (yea).
- # Paired for.
- + Announced for.
- N Voted against (nay).
- X Paired against.
- — Announced against.
- P Voted "present."
- C Voted "present" to avoid possible conflict of interest.
- ? Did not vote or otherwise make a position known.

Democrats *Republicans*

	271	272	273	274	275	276	277	278
ALABAMA								
Heflin	Y	Y	N	N	N	N	N	Y
Shelby	Y	Y	N	N	N	N	N	Y
ALASKA								
Murkowski	N	Y	N	N	N	N	Y	Y
Stevens	Y	Y	N	N	N	N	Y	Y
ARIZONA								
DeConcini	Y	Y	N	Y	Y	Y	N	N
McCain	Y	N	N	N	N	Y	Y	N
ARKANSAS								
Bumpers	Y	Y	Y	Y	Y	N	N	Y
Pryor	Y	Y	Y	Y	Y	?	?	?
CALIFORNIA								
Boxer	Y	Y	N	Y	N	N	N	N
Feinstein	Y	Y	N	Y	N	N	N	N
COLORADO								
Campbell	Y	Y	N	N	N	N	N	N
Brown	Y	N	N	Y	N	N	N	Y
CONNECTICUT								
Dodd	Y	Y	N	Y	N	N	N	N
Lieberman	Y	Y	N	N	N	N	N	N
DELAWARE								
Biden	Y	Y	Y	Y	Y	Y	N	Y
Roth	N	N	Y	Y	N	N	Y	Y
FLORIDA								
Graham	Y	Y	N	Y	N	N	N	N
Mack	Y	Y	N	N	N	Y	Y	Y
GEORGIA								
Nunn	Y	Y	N	N	Y	N	N	Y
Coverdell	Y	Y	N	N	Y	N	N	Y
HAWAII								
Akaka	Y	Y	N	N	Y	N	N	N
Inouye	Y	Y	N	N	Y	N	N	N
IDAHO								
Craig	N	Y	N	N	N	N	Y	Y
Kempthorne	N	Y	N	N	N	N	Y	Y
ILLINOIS								
Moseley-Braun	Y	Y	Y	Y	Y	N	N	N
Simon	Y	Y	Y	Y	Y	N	N	N
INDIANA								
Coats	Y	Y	N	N	N	Y	Y	Y
Lugar	Y	Y	Y	N	Y	Y	Y	Y
IOWA								
Harkin	Y	Y	Y	Y	Y	N	N	N
Grassley	Y	Y	N	Y	N	N	Y	Y
KANSAS								
Dole	Y	Y	N	N	N	Y	N	Y
Kassebaum	Y	Y	Y	Y	N	Y	N	Y
KENTUCKY								
Ford	Y	Y	N	N	Y	N	N	Y
McConnell	Y	Y	N	N	N	N	Y	Y
LOUISIANA								
Breaux	Y	Y	N	Y	N	N	N	N
Johnston	Y	Y	N	Y	N	N	N	N
MAINE								
Mitchell	Y	Y	N	Y	N	N	N	N
Cohen	Y	Y	N	N	Y	N	Y	Y
MARYLAND								
Mikulski	Y	Y	N	N	Y	?	?	?
Sarbanes	Y	Y	Y	Y	Y	N	N	N
MASSACHUSETTS								
Kennedy	Y	Y	N	Y	N	N	N	N
Kerry	Y	Y	N	Y	N	N	N	N
MICHIGAN								
Levin	Y	Y	N	N	Y	N	N	N
Riegle	Y	Y	Y	Y	Y	N	N	N
MINNESOTA								
Wellstone	Y	Y	Y	Y	N	N	N	N
Durenberger	Y	Y	N	N	Y	N	N	N
MISSISSIPPI								
Cochran	Y	Y	N	N	N	Y	Y	Y
Lott	N	Y	N	N	N	N	Y	Y
MISSOURI								
Bond	Y	Y	N	N	N	Y	Y	Y
Danforth	Y	Y	N	N	Y	N	Y	N
MONTANA								
Baucus	Y	Y	N	Y	N	Y	N	Y
Burns	Y	Y	N	N	N	N	Y	Y
NEBRASKA								
Exon	Y	Y	N	N	Y	N	N	N
Kerrey	Y	Y	Y	Y	Y	N	N	N
NEVADA								
Bryan	Y	Y	N	Y	Y	Y	N	N
Reid	Y	Y	N	Y	Y	Y	Y	N
NEW HAMPSHIRE								
Gregg	Y	N	N	N	N	N	Y	Y
Smith	N	N	N	N	N	Y	Y	Y
NEW JERSEY								
Bradley	Y	Y	Y	Y	N	N	N	N
Lautenberg	Y	Y	Y	Y	Y	N	N	N
NEW MEXICO								
Bingaman	Y	Y	N	N	Y	N	N	N
Domenici	N	Y	N	N	N	N	N	Y
NEW YORK								
Moynihan	Y	Y	Y	Y	N	N	N	N
D'Amato	Y	Y	N	N	N	Y	Y	Y
NORTH CAROLINA								
Faircloth	N	Y	N	N	N	Y	Y	Y
Helms	N	Y	N	N	N	Y	Y	Y
NORTH DAKOTA								
Conrad	Y	Y	Y	Y	Y	N	N	N
Dorgan	Y	Y	Y	Y	Y	N	N	N
OHIO								
Glenn	Y	Y	N	Y	N	N	N	N
Metzenbaum	Y	Y	Y	Y	Y	Y	N	N
OKLAHOMA								
Boren	Y	Y	N	N	Y	N	N	N
Nickles	Y	Y	N	N	N	Y	Y	Y
OREGON								
Hatfield	Y	Y	N	N	Y	N	N	N
Packwood	Y	Y	N	N	N	Y	N	N
PENNSYLVANIA								
Wofford	Y	Y	Y	Y	Y	N	N	N
Specter	Y	Y	N	N	Y	N	Y	N
RHODE ISLAND								
Pell	Y	Y	Y	Y	Y	N	N	N
Chafee	Y	Y	N	N	Y	N	Y	N
SOUTH CAROLINA								
Hollings	N	Y	Y	N	N	N	N	Y
Thurmond	Y	Y	N	N	N	N	Y	Y
SOUTH DAKOTA								
Daschle	Y	Y	N	N	Y	N	N	N
Pressler	Y	Y	N	N	Y	Y	Y	Y
TENNESSEE								
Mathews	Y	Y	Y	Y	Y	N	N	Y
Sasser	Y	Y	Y	Y	Y	N	N	Y
TEXAS								
Hutchison	Y	Y	N	N	N	Y	Y	Y
Gramm	Y	Y	N	N	N	N	Y	Y
UTAH								
Bennett	Y	Y	N	N	Y	N	Y	Y
Hatch	Y	Y	N	N	N	N	Y	Y
VERMONT								
Leahy	Y	Y	Y	Y	Y	Y	N	Y
Jeffords	Y	Y	Y	Y	Y	N	N	N
VIRGINIA								
Robb	Y	Y	Y	N	Y	N	N	N
Warner	Y	Y	N	N	N	Y	N	Y
WASHINGTON								
Murray	Y	Y	Y	Y	N	N	N	N
Gorton	Y	Y	N	N	Y	Y	Y	Y
WEST VIRGINIA								
Byrd	N	Y	Y	N	Y	N	N	Y
Rockefeller	Y	Y	Y	Y	N	N	N	N
WISCONSIN								
Feingold	Y	Y	Y	Y	N	N	N	Y
Kohl	Y	Y	Y	Y	N	Y	N	Y
WYOMING								
Simpson	Y	Y	Y	N	N	N	Y	Y
Wallop	N	Y	N	N	N	Y	Y	Y

ND Northern Democrats SD Southern Democrats Southern states - Ala., Ark., Fla., Ga., Ky., La., Miss., N.C., Okla., S.C., Tenn., Texas, Va.

271. HR 4426. Fiscal 1995 Foreign Operations Appropriations/Conference Report. Adoption of the conference report to provide $13,828,236,000 for foreign aid, export financing and related programs in fiscal 1995. The administration had requested $14,074,957,094. Adopted (thus cleared for the president) 88-12: R 34-10; D 54-2 (ND 41-1, SD 13-1), Aug. 10, 1994.

272. HR 4453. Fiscal 1995 Military Construction Appropriations/Conference Report. Adoption of the conference report to provide $8,836,000,000 for military construction for the Department of Defense in fiscal 1995. The administration had requested $8,346,202,000. Adopted (thus cleared for the president) 95-5: R 39-5; D 56-0 (ND 42-0, SD 14-0), Aug. 10, 1994.

273. HR 4650. Fiscal 1995 Defense Appropriations/MILSTAR. Bumpers, D-Ark., amendment to restrict money in the bill from being used for the expansion of the MILSTAR program, a military satellite communications system. Rejected 38-62: R 6-38; D 32-24 (ND 24-18, SD 8-6), Aug. 10, 1994.

274. HR 4650. Fiscal 1995 Defense Appropriations/Trident II Missiles. Bumpers, D-Ark., amendment to cut $257 million for 18 new Trident II sea-launched ballistic missiles. Rejected 40-60: R 6-38; D 34-22 (ND 29-13, SD 5-9), Aug. 10, 1994.

275. HR 4650. Fiscal 1995 Defense Appropriations/Colombia Military Aid. Inouye, D-Hawaii, motion to table (kill) the Helms, R-N.C., amendment to prohibit military aid to Colombia until the president certifies that the Colombian government is taking certain actions to combat illegal drug trafficking. Motion agreed to 53-47: R 10-34; D 43-13 (ND 33-9, SD 10-4), Aug. 10, 1994.

276. HR 4650. Fiscal 1995 Defense Appropriations/Civilian Sporting Events. McCain, R-Ariz., amendment to require that the Department of Defense be reimbursed for expenses incurred in supporting profitable civilian sporting events such as the World Cup Soccer Games, the Goodwill Games or the Olympics. Rejected 21-77: R 16-28; D 5-49 (ND 5-36, SD 0-13), Aug. 10, 1994.

277. HR 4650. Fiscal 1995 Defense Appropriations/Navy Anti-Missile System. Wallop, R-Wyo., amendment to increase from $18 million to $102 million funding for a project to equip the Navy's Aegis cruisers with long-range anti-ballistic missile capabilities. Rejected 38-60: R 38-6; D 0-54 (ND 0-41, SD 0-13), Aug. 10, 1994.

278. HR 4650. Fiscal 1995 Defense Appropriations/Somalia. Kempthorne, R-Idaho, amendment to prohibit money in the bill from supporting the continued presence of troops in Somalia after Sept. 30, 1994. Adopted 54-44: R 38-6; D 16-38 (ND 8-33, SD 8-5), Aug. 10, 1994.

	279	280	281	282
ALABAMA				
Heflin	Y	N	Y	Y
Shelby	N	Y	Y	Y
ALASKA				
Murkowski	N	Y	Y	Y
Stevens	Y	Y	Y	Y
ARIZONA				
DeConcini	N	Y	Y	Y
McCain	N	Y	Y	N
ARKANSAS				
Bumpers	Y	N	Y	Y
Pryor	Y	N	Y	Y
CALIFORNIA				
Boxer	Y	Y	Y	Y
Feinstein	Y	N	Y	Y
COLORADO				
Campbell	Y	N	Y	Y
Brown	N	Y	N	N
CONNECTICUT				
Dodd	Y	N	Y	Y
Lieberman	Y	Y	Y	Y
DELAWARE				
Biden	N	Y	Y	Y
Roth	N	Y	Y	N
FLORIDA				
Graham	Y	N	Y	Y
Mack	N	Y	Y	Y
GEORGIA				
Nunn	Y	N	Y	Y
Coverdell	Y	Y	Y	Y
HAWAII				
Akaka	Y	N	Y	Y
Inouye	Y	N	Y	Y
IDAHO				
Craig	N	Y	Y	N
Kempthorne	N	Y	Y	N
ILLINOIS				
Moseley-Braun	Y	Y	Y	Y
Simon	Y	Y	Y	Y
INDIANA				
Coats	Y	Y	Y	Y
Lugar	Y	Y	Y	Y

	279	280	281	282
IOWA				
Harkin	Y	N	Y	Y
Grassley	N	Y	N	Y
KANSAS				
Dole	N	Y	Y	N
Kassebaum	Y	N	Y	Y
KENTUCKY				
Ford	Y	N	Y	Y
McConnell	N	Y	Y	Y
LOUISIANA				
Breaux	Y	N	Y	Y
Johnston	Y	N	Y	Y
MAINE				
Mitchell	Y	N	Y	Y
Cohen	N	Y	Y	Y
MARYLAND				
Mikulski	Y	N	Y	Y
Sarbanes	Y	N	Y	Y
MASSACHUSETTS				
Kennedy	Y	N	Y	Y
Kerry	Y	Y	Y	Y
MICHIGAN				
Levin	Y	Y	Y	Y
Riegle	Y	Y	Y	Y
MINNESOTA				
Wellstone	Y	Y	Y	N
Durenberger	N	Y	Y	Y
MISSISSIPPI				
Cochran	N	Y	Y	Y
Lott	N	Y	Y	Y
MISSOURI				
Bond	Y	Y	Y	Y
Danforth	N	N	Y	Y
MONTANA				
Baucus	Y	N	Y	Y
Burns	N	N	Y	Y
NEBRASKA				
Exon	Y	N	Y	Y
Kerrey	Y	N	Y	Y
NEVADA				
Bryan	Y	Y	Y	Y
Reid	Y	N	Y	Y

	279	280	281	282
NEW HAMPSHIRE				
Gregg	N	N	Y	N
Smith	N	Y	Y	N
NEW JERSEY				
Bradley	N	Y	Y	Y
Lautenberg	N	Y	Y	Y
NEW MEXICO				
Bingaman	Y	N	Y	Y
Domenici	N	Y	Y	Y
NEW YORK				
Moynihan	N	Y	Y	Y
D'Amato	N	Y	Y	Y
NORTH CAROLINA				
Faircloth	N	Y	N	Y
Helms	N	Y	N	Y
NORTH DAKOTA				
Conrad	Y	N	Y	Y
Dorgan	Y	N	Y	Y
OHIO				
Glenn	Y	N	Y	Y
Metzenbaum	Y	Y	Y	Y
OKLAHOMA				
Boren	Y	N	Y	Y
Nickles	N	Y	Y	Y
OREGON				
Hatfield	N	N	Y	N
Packwood	N	Y	Y	Y
PENNSYLVANIA				
Wofford	Y	Y	Y	Y
Specter	N	Y	Y	Y
RHODE ISLAND				
Pell	Y	N	Y	Y
Chafee	Y	N	Y	Y
SOUTH CAROLINA				
Hollings	Y	N	Y	Y
Thurmond	Y	Y	Y	Y
SOUTH DAKOTA				
Daschle	Y	N	Y	Y
Pressler	N	Y	N	N
TENNESSEE				
Mathews	Y	N	Y	Y
Sasser	Y	N	Y	Y

KEY

Y Voted for (yea).
Paired for.
+ Announced for.
N Voted against (nay).
X Paired against.
— Announced against.
P Voted "present."
C Voted "present" to avoid possible conflict of interest.
? Did not vote or otherwise make a position known.

Democrats   *Republicans*

	279	280	281	282
TEXAS				
Hutchison	Y	Y	Y	Y
Gramm	N	Y	Y	Y
UTAH				
Bennett	N	Y	Y	Y
Hatch	N	Y	Y	N
VERMONT				
Leahy	N	Y	Y	Y
Jeffords	N	Y	Y	Y
VIRGINIA				
Robb	Y	Y	Y	Y
Warner	Y	N	Y	Y
WASHINGTON				
Murray	Y	N	Y	Y
Gorton	N	Y	Y	Y
WEST VIRGINIA				
Byrd	N	N	Y	Y
Rockefeller	Y	N	Y	Y
WISCONSIN				
Feingold	N	Y	Y	N
Kohl	N	Y	Y	Y
WYOMING				
Simpson	N	Y	Y	Y
Wallop	N	Y	N	N

ND Northern Democrats   SD Southern Democrats   Southern states - Ala., Ark., Fla., Ga., Ky., La., Miss., N.C., Okla., S.C., Tenn., Texas, Va.

279. HR 4650. Fiscal 1995 Defense Appropriations/Bosnia Arms Embargo. Nunn, D-Ga., amendment to express the sense of Congress urging President Clinton to seek an international agreement to end the arms embargo in Bosnia and end U.S. participation in enforcing the embargo if it is not lifted within 15 days of introducing a U.N. resolution or by Nov. 15, 1994, whichever is earlier. Adopted 56-44: R 10-34; D 46-10 (ND 33-9, SD 13-1), Aug. 11, 1994. A "yea" was a vote in support of the president's position.

280. HR 4650. Fiscal 1995 Defense Appropriations/Bosnia Arms Embargo. Dole, R-Kan., amendment to terminate the Bosnia arms embargo no later than Nov. 15, 1994. Adopted 58-42: R 37-7; D 21-35 (ND 19-23, SD 2-12), Aug. 11, 1994. A "nay" was a vote in support of the president's position.

281. Yellen Confirmation. Confirmation of President Clinton's nomination of Janet L. Yellen of California to be a member of the board of governors of the Federal Reserve System. Confirmed 94-6: R 38-6; D 56-0 (ND 42-0, SD 14-0), Aug. 11, 1994. A "yea" was a vote in support of the president's position.

282. HR 4650. Fiscal 1995 Defense Appropriations/Passage. Passage of the bill to provide approximately $243.2 billion in new budget authority for the Department of Defense in fiscal 1995 and $170 million in new budget authority for fiscal 1994. The administration had requested $244,341,179,000 for fiscal 1995, plus $270 million for fiscal 1994 and a contingency fund of $100 million for relief operations in Rwanda. Passed 86-14: R 32-12; D 54-2 (ND 40-2, SD 14-0), Aug. 11, 1995.

	283	284	285	286	287
ALABAMA					
Heflin	Y	Y	Y	N	Y
Shelby	Y	Y	Y	N	Y
ALASKA					
Murkowski	Y	Y	Y	?	?
Stevens	Y	Y	Y	Y	Y
ARIZONA					
DeConcini	Y	Y	Y	N	Y
McCain	Y	Y	Y	?	N
ARKANSAS					
Bumpers	Y	Y	Y	N	Y
Pryor	Y	Y	Y	N	Y
CALIFORNIA					
Boxer	Y	Y	Y	N	Y
Feinstein	Y	Y	Y	N	Y
COLORADO					
Campbell	Y	Y	Y	N	Y
Brown	Y	Y	Y	Y	N
CONNECTICUT					
Dodd	Y	Y	Y	N	Y
Lieberman	Y	Y	Y	N	Y
DELAWARE					
Biden	Y	Y	Y	N	?
Roth	Y	Y	Y	?	Y
FLORIDA					
Graham	Y	Y	Y	N	Y
Mack	Y	Y	Y	Y	N
GEORGIA					
Nunn	Y	Y	Y	N	?
Coverdell	Y	Y	Y	Y	Y
HAWAII					
Akaka	Y	Y	Y	N	Y
Inouye	Y	Y	Y	N	N
IDAHO					
Craig	Y	Y	Y	Y	Y
Kempthorne	Y	Y	Y	Y	Y
ILLINOIS					
Moseley-Braun	Y	Y	Y	N	Y
Simon	Y	Y	Y	N	Y
INDIANA					
Coats	Y	Y	Y	Y	Y
Lugar	Y	Y	Y	Y	Y

	283	284	285	286	287
IOWA					
Harkin	Y	Y	Y	N	Y
Grassley	Y	Y	Y	Y	Y
KANSAS					
Dole	Y	Y	Y	Y	Y
Kassebaum	Y	Y	Y	Y	Y
KENTUCKY					
Ford	Y	Y	Y	N	Y
McConnell	Y	Y	Y	Y	N
LOUISIANA					
Breaux	Y	Y	Y	N	N
Johnston	Y	Y	Y	N	Y
MAINE					
Mitchell	Y	Y	Y	N	Y
Cohen	Y	Y	Y	Y	Y
MARYLAND					
Mikulski	Y	Y	Y	N	Y
Sarbanes	Y	Y	Y	N	Y
MASSACHUSETTS					
Kennedy	Y	Y	Y	N	Y
Kerry	Y	Y	Y	N	Y
MICHIGAN					
Levin	Y	Y	Y	N	Y
Riegle	Y	Y	N	N	Y
MINNESOTA					
Wellstone	+	+	+	N	Y
Durenberger	Y	Y	Y	N	Y
MISSISSIPPI					
Cochran	Y	Y	Y	Y	Y
Lott	Y	Y	Y	Y	N
MISSOURI					
Bond	Y	Y	Y	Y	Y
Danforth	Y	Y	Y	Y	Y
MONTANA					
Baucus	Y	Y	Y	N	Y
Burns	Y	Y	Y	Y	Y
NEBRASKA					
Exon	Y	Y	Y	N	Y
Kerrey	Y	Y	Y	N	Y
NEVADA					
Bryan	Y	Y	Y	N	Y
Reid	Y	Y	Y	N	Y

	283	284	285	286	287
NEW HAMPSHIRE					
Gregg	Y	Y	Y	Y	Y
Smith	Y	Y	Y	Y	N
NEW JERSEY					
Bradley	Y	Y	Y	N	Y
Lautenberg	Y	Y	Y	N	?
NEW MEXICO					
Bingaman	Y	Y	Y	N	Y
Domenici	Y	Y	Y	?	Y
NEW YORK					
Moynihan	Y	Y	Y	N	Y
D'Amato	Y	Y	Y	Y	?
NORTH CAROLINA					
Faircloth	Y	Y	Y	Y	N
Helms	Y	Y	Y	Y	N
NORTH DAKOTA					
Conrad	Y	Y	Y	N	Y
Dorgan	Y	Y	Y	N	N
OHIO					
Glenn	Y	Y	Y	N	Y
Metzenbaum	Y	Y	Y	N	Y
OKLAHOMA					
Boren	Y	Y	Y	N	Y
Nickles	Y	Y	Y	Y	N
OREGON					
Hatfield	Y	Y	N	N	Y
Packwood	Y	Y	Y	Y	Y
PENNSYLVANIA					
Wofford	Y	Y	Y	N	Y
Specter	Y	Y	Y	Y	N
RHODE ISLAND					
Pell	Y	Y	Y	N	Y
Chafee	Y	Y	Y	Y	Y
SOUTH CAROLINA					
Hollings	Y	Y	Y	N	Y
Thurmond	Y	Y	Y	Y	Y
SOUTH DAKOTA					
Daschle	Y	Y	Y	N	Y
Pressler	Y	Y	Y	Y	Y
TENNESSEE					
Mathews	Y	Y	Y	N	Y
Sasser	Y	Y	Y	N	Y

KEY

Y Voted for (yea).
\# Paired for.
\+ Announced for.
N Voted against (nay).
X Paired against.
— Announced against.
P Voted "present."
C Voted "present" to avoid possible conflict of interest.
? Did not vote or otherwise make a position known.

Democrats *Republicans*

	283	284	285	286	287
TEXAS					
Hutchison	Y	Y	Y	Y	Y
Gramm	Y	Y	Y	Y	N
UTAH					
Bennett	Y	Y	Y	Y	N
Hatch	Y	Y	Y	Y	Y
VERMONT					
Leahy	Y	Y	Y	N	Y
Jeffords	Y	Y	Y	N	Y
VIRGINIA					
Robb	Y	Y	Y	N	Y
Warner	Y	Y	Y	Y	Y
WASHINGTON					
Murray	Y	Y	Y	N	Y
Gorton	Y	Y	Y	Y	Y
WEST VIRGINIA					
Byrd	Y	Y	Y	N	Y
Rockefeller	Y	Y	Y	N	Y
WISCONSIN					
Feingold	Y	Y	Y	N	Y
Kohl	Y	Y	Y	N	Y
WYOMING					
Simpson	Y	Y	Y	+	?
Wallop	Y	Y	Y	Y	N

ND Northern Democrats   SD Southern Democrats

Southern states - Ala., Ark., Fla., Ga., Ky., La., Miss., N.C., Okla., S.C., Tenn., Texas, Va.

283. S 2082. Fiscal 1995 Intelligence Authorization/ National Reconnaissance Headquarters. DeConcini, D-Ariz., amendment to require a review of the National Reconnaissance Office Headquarters Building project before additional money can be spent on the project, and to cap the total cost of the project at $310 million. Adopted 99-0: R 44-0; D 55-0 (ND 41-0, SD 14-0), Aug. 12, 1994.

284. S 2082. Fiscal 1995 Intelligence Authorization/ Review Commission. Warner, R-Va., amendment to establish an independent commission to review the roles and capabilities of U.S. intelligence and to report by March 1, 1996, its recommendations on the missions, organizational structure and funding for intelligence activities in the post-Cold War world. Adopted 99-0: R 44-0; D 55-0 (ND 41-0, SD 14-0), Aug. 12, 1994.

285. HR 4299. Fiscal 1995 Intelligence Authorization/ Passage. Passage of the bill to authorize a classified amount for the activities of the CIA, the Defense Intelligence Agency, the National Security Agency and other U.S. intelligence agencies and activities in fiscal 1995. The amount has been estimated to be about $28 billion. Passed 97-2: R 43-1; D 54-1 (ND 40-1, SD 14-0), Aug. 12, 1994. (Before passage, the Senate struck out all after the enacting clause and inserted the text of S 2082 as amended.)

286. S 1614. Child Nutrition Programs Reauthorization/ 'Motor Voter' Registration. McConnell, R-Ky., amendment to exempt offices administering the food and nutrition program for Women, Infants and Children from requirements that they provide voter registration assistance under the motor voter National Voter Registration Act (PL 103-31). Rejected 36-59: R 36-3; D 0-56 (ND 0-42, SD 0-14), Aug. 12, 1994.

287. Procedural Motion. Mitchell, D-Maine, motion to instruct the sergeant at arms to request the attendance of absent senators. Motion agreed to 78-16: R 28-13; D 50-3 (ND 38-2, SD 12-1), Aug. 15, 1994.

	288	289	290	291
ALABAMA				
Heflin	Y	Y	Y	Y
Shelby	Y	Y	Y	Y
ALASKA				
Murkowski	N	Y	Y	Y
Stevens	N	Y	Y	Y
ARIZONA				
DeConcini	Y	Y	Y	Y
McCain	N	Y	Y	Y
ARKANSAS				
Bumpers	Y	Y	Y	Y
Pryor	Y	Y	Y	Y
CALIFORNIA				
Boxer	Y	Y	Y	Y
Feinstein	Y	Y	Y	Y
COLORADO				
Campbell	Y	Y	Y	Y
Brown	N	Y	Y	Y
CONNECTICUT				
Dodd	Y	Y	Y	Y
Lieberman	Y	Y	Y	Y
DELAWARE				
Biden	Y	Y	Y	Y
Roth	Y	Y	N	Y
FLORIDA				
Graham	Y	Y	Y	Y
Mack	N	Y	Y	Y
GEORGIA				
Nunn	?	Y	Y	Y
Coverdell	N	Y	Y	Y
HAWAII				
Akaka	Y	Y	Y	Y
Inouye	Y	Y	Y	Y
IDAHO				
Craig	N	Y	Y	Y
Kempthorne	N	Y	Y	Y
ILLINOIS				
Moseley-Braun	Y	Y	Y	Y
Simon	Y	Y	Y	Y
INDIANA				
Coats	N	Y	Y	Y
Lugar	N	Y	Y	Y

	288	289	290	291
IOWA				
Harkin	Y	Y	Y	Y
Grassley	N	Y	Y	Y
KANSAS				
Dole	N	Y	Y	Y
Kassebaum	N	Y	Y	Y
KENTUCKY				
Ford	Y	Y	Y	Y
McConnell	N	Y	Y	Y
LOUISIANA				
Breaux	Y	Y	Y	Y
Johnston	Y	Y	Y	Y
MAINE				
Mitchell	Y	Y	Y	Y
Cohen	N	Y	?	Y
MARYLAND				
Mikulski	Y	Y	?	Y
Sarbanes	Y	Y	Y	Y
MASSACHUSETTS				
Kennedy	Y	Y	Y	Y
Kerry	Y	Y	Y	Y
MICHIGAN				
Levin	Y	Y	Y	Y
Riegle	Y	Y	Y	Y
MINNESOTA				
Wellstone	Y	Y	Y	Y
Durenberger	N	Y	N	Y
MISSISSIPPI				
Cochran	N	Y	Y	Y
Lott	N	Y	Y	Y
MISSOURI				
Bond	N	Y	Y	Y
Danforth	N	Y	N	Y
MONTANA				
Baucus	Y	Y	Y	Y
Burns	N	Y	Y	Y
NEBRASKA				
Exon	Y	Y	Y	Y
Kerrey	N	Y	Y	Y
NEVADA				
Bryan	Y	Y	Y	Y
Reid	Y	Y	Y	Y

	288	289	290	291
NEW HAMPSHIRE				
Gregg	N	Y	N	Y
Smith	N	Y	Y	Y
NEW JERSEY				
Bradley	Y	Y	Y	Y
Lautenberg	Y	Y	Y	Y
NEW MEXICO				
Bingaman	Y	Y	Y	Y
Domenici	N	Y	Y	Y
NEW YORK				
Moynihan	Y	Y	Y	Y
D'Amato	N	Y	Y	Y
NORTH CAROLINA				
Faircloth	N	Y	Y	Y
Helms	N	Y	Y	Y
NORTH DAKOTA				
Conrad	Y	Y	Y	Y
Dorgan	Y	Y	Y	Y
OHIO				
Glenn	Y	Y	Y	Y
Metzenbaum	Y	Y	Y	Y
OKLAHOMA				
Boren	Y	Y	Y	Y
Nickles	N	Y	Y	Y
OREGON				
Hatfield	?	Y	Y	Y
Packwood	N	Y	Y	Y
PENNSYLVANIA				
Wofford	Y	Y	Y	Y
Specter	N	Y	Y	Y
RHODE ISLAND				
Pell	Y	Y	Y	Y
Chafee	N	Y	Y	Y
SOUTH CAROLINA				
Hollings	Y	Y	Y	Y
Thurmond	N	Y	Y	Y
SOUTH DAKOTA				
Daschle	Y	Y	Y	Y
Pressler	N	Y	Y	Y
TENNESSEE				
Mathews	Y	Y	Y	Y
Sasser	?	Y	Y	Y

	288	289	290	291
TEXAS				
Hutchison	N	Y	Y	Y
Gramm	N	Y	Y	Y
UTAH				
Bennett	N	Y	Y	Y
Hatch	N	Y	Y	Y
VERMONT				
Leahy	Y	Y	Y	Y
Jeffords	Y	Y	Y	Y
VIRGINIA				
Robb	Y	Y	Y	Y
Warner	N	Y	Y	Y
WASHINGTON				
Murray	Y	Y	Y	Y
Gorton	N	Y	Y	Y
WEST VIRGINIA				
Byrd	Y	Y	Y	Y
Rockefeller	Y	Y	Y	Y
WISCONSIN				
Feingold	Y	Y	Y	Y
Kohl	Y	Y	Y	Y
WYOMING				
Simpson	N	Y	Y	Y
Wallop	N	Y	Y	Y

ND Northern Democrats   SD Southern Democrats   Southern states - Ala., Ark., Fla., Ga., Ky., La., Miss., N.C., Okla., S.C., Tenn., Texas, Va.

288. S 2351. Health Care/Child Preventive Services. Dodd, D-Conn., amendment to the Mitchell, D-Maine, substitute amendment to require all insurance policies to cover preventive services for children, including prenatal care, well-baby care and immunization care for children and pregnant women at no additional cost by July 1, 1995, rather than by Jan. 1, 1997, as required by the bill. Adopted 55-42: R 2-41; D 53-1 (ND 41-1, SD 12-0), Aug. 16, 1994.

289. S 2351. Health Care/Standard Benefits Package Fines. Nickles, R-Okla., amendment to the Mitchell, D-Maine, substitute amendment to strike the provisions of the substitute that would allow the secretary of Labor to fine employers up to $10,000 for each employee not offered the standards benefits package defined in the bill. Adopted 100-0: R 44-0; D 56-0 (ND 42-0, SD 14-0), Aug. 17, 1994.

290. S 2351. Health Care/Rural Health Care. Daschle, D-S.D., amendment to the Mitchell, D-Maine, substitute amendment to increase rural health care services and establish an office of assistant secretary for rural health at the Department of Health and Human Services. Adopted 94-4: R 39-4; D 55-0 (ND 41-0, SD 14-0), Aug. 18, 1994.

291. S 2351. Health Care/Sunshine Act. Mack, R-Fla., amendment to the Mitchell, D-Maine, substitute amendment to require all boards, commissions and advisory panels within the bill to conduct their business in public and to not meet in secret, in compliance with the Federal Advisory Committee Act. Adopted 100-0: R 44-0; D 56-0 (ND 42-0, SD 14-0), Aug. 18, 1994.

	292	293	294	295
ALABAMA				
Heflin	Y	Y	Y	Y
Shelby	Y	N	N	N
ALASKA				
Murkowski	?	N	N	N
Stevens	Y	N	N	N
ARIZONA				
DeConcini	Y	Y	Y	Y
McCain	N	N	N	N
ARKANSAS				
Bumpers	Y	Y	Y	Y
Pryor	Y	Y	Y	Y
CALIFORNIA				
Boxer	Y	Y	Y	Y
Feinstein	Y	Y	Y	Y
COLORADO				
Campbell	Y	Y	Y	Y
Brown	N	N	N	N
CONNECTICUT				
Dodd	Y	Y	Y	Y
Lieberman	Y	Y	Y	Y
DELAWARE				
Biden	Y	Y	Y	Y
Roth	Y	Y	Y	Y
FLORIDA				
Graham	Y	Y	Y	Y
Mack	Y	N	N	N
GEORGIA				
Nunn	Y	Y	Y	Y
Coverdell	Y	N	N	N
HAWAII				
Akaka	Y	Y	Y	Y
Inouye	Y	Y	Y	Y
IDAHO				
Craig	Y	N	N	N
Kempthorne	Y	N	N	N
ILLINOIS				
Moseley-Braun	Y	Y	Y	Y
Simon	Y	Y	Y	Y
INDIANA				
Coats	N	N	N	N
Lugar	Y	N	N	N
IOWA				
Harkin	Y	Y	Y	Y
Grassley	Y	N	N	N
KANSAS				
Dole	Y	N	N	N
Kassebaum	Y	Y	Y	Y
KENTUCKY				
Ford	Y	Y	Y	Y
McConnell	Y	N	N	N
LOUISIANA				
Breaux	Y	Y	Y	Y
Johnston	Y	Y	Y	Y
MAINE				
Mitchell	Y	Y	Y	Y
Cohen	Y	N	N	Y
MARYLAND				
Mikulski	Y	Y	Y	Y
Sarbanes	Y	Y	Y	Y
MASSACHUSETTS				
Kennedy	Y	Y	Y	Y
Kerry	Y	Y	Y	Y
MICHIGAN				
Levin	Y	Y	Y	Y
Riegle	Y	Y	Y	Y
MINNESOTA				
Wellstone	Y	Y	Y	Y
Durenberger	Y	N	N	N
MISSISSIPPI				
Cochran	Y	N	N	N
Lott	Y	N	N	N
MISSOURI				
Bond	Y	N	N	N
Danforth	Y	Y	Y	Y
MONTANA				
Baucus	N	Y	Y	Y
Burns	Y	N	N	N
NEBRASKA				
Exon	Y	Y	Y	Y
Kerrey	Y	Y	Y	Y
NEVADA				
Bryan	Y	Y	Y	Y
Reid	Y	Y	Y	Y
NEW HAMPSHIRE				
Gregg	Y	N	N	N
Smith	N	N	N	N
NEW JERSEY				
Bradley	Y	Y	Y	Y
Lautenberg	Y	Y	Y	Y
NEW MEXICO				
Bingaman	Y	Y	Y	Y
Domenici	Y	N	N	N
NEW YORK				
Moynihan	Y	Y	Y	Y
D'Amato	Y	N	N	N
NORTH CAROLINA				
Faircloth	N	N	N	N
Helms	N	N	N	N
NORTH DAKOTA				
Conrad	Y	Y	Y	Y
Dorgan	Y	Y	Y	Y
OHIO				
Glenn	Y	Y	Y	Y
Metzenbaum	Y	Y	Y	Y
OKLAHOMA				
Boren	Y	Y	Y	Y
Nickles	N	N	N	N
OREGON				
Hatfield	Y	N	N	N
Packwood	Y	N	N	N
PENNSYLVANIA				
Wofford	Y	Y	Y	Y
Specter	Y	Y	Y	Y
RHODE ISLAND				
Pell	Y	Y	Y	Y
Chafee	Y	Y	Y	Y
SOUTH CAROLINA				
Hollings	Y	Y	Y	Y
Thurmond	Y	N	N	N
SOUTH DAKOTA				
Daschle	Y	Y	Y	Y
Pressler	Y	N	N	N
TENNESSEE				
Mathews	Y	Y	Y	Y
Sasser	Y	Y	Y	Y
TEXAS				
Hutchison	Y	N	N	N
Gramm	Y	N	N	N
UTAH				
Bennett	Y	N	N	N
Hatch	Y	N	N	N
VERMONT				
Leahy	Y	Y	Y	Y
Jeffords	Y	Y	Y	Y
VIRGINIA				
Robb	Y	Y	Y	Y
Warner	Y	N	Y	N
WASHINGTON				
Murray	Y	Y	Y	Y
Gorton	Y	N	N	N
WEST VIRGINIA				
Byrd	Y	Y	Y	Y
Rockefeller	Y	Y	Y	Y
WISCONSIN				
Feingold	N	Y	N	N
Kohl	Y	Y	Y	Y
WYOMING				
Simpson	+	N	N	N
Wallop	N	N	?	?

KEY

Y Voted for (yea).
Paired for.
+ Announced for.
N Voted against (nay).
X Paired against.
− Announced against.
P Voted "present."
C Voted "present" to avoid possible conflict of interest.
? Did not vote or otherwise make a position known.

Democrats *Republicans*

ND Northern Democrats   SD Southern Democrats   Southern states - Ala., Ark., Fla., Ga., Ky., La., Miss., N.C., Okla., S.C., Tenn., Texas, Va.

292. HR 4603. Fiscal 1995 Commerce, Justice, State Appropriations/Conference Report. Adoption of the conference report to provide $27,667,611,000 in new budget authority for the Departments of Commerce, Justice and State, the Judiciary and related agencies' programs for fiscal 1995. The administration had requested $28,434,837,000. The bill includes $795 million in supplemental fiscal 1994 money, including aid through the Small Business Administration loan program for disaster victims in the South and West. Adopted (thus cleared for the president) 88-10: R 34-8; D 54-2 (ND 40-2, SD 14-0), Aug. 19, 1994.

293. HR 3355. Omnibus Crime Bill/Budget Act Waiver. Mitchell, D-Maine, motion to waive the budget act with respect to the Domenici, R-N.M., point of order against the Crime Conference Report for violating Section 306 of the 1974 Congressional Budget Act and encroaching on the Budget Committee's jurisdiction by establishing a trust fund not considered by the committee. The conference report would authorize $30.2 billion over six years and require that all spending authorized by the bill come from a crime trust fund realized from eliminating 270,000 federal jobs. The bill would authorize $6.9 billion for crime prevention programs, $8.8 billion for community policing programs and the hiring of 100,000 new police officers, and a $7.9 billion grant program to build state and local prisons. The bill would also ban 19 specific assault weapons, expand the death penalty to dozens of new federal crimes, mandate life imprisonment without parole for three-time violent felons, provide for community notification of violent sex offenders, and allow prior sex offenses to be admitted in federal trials. Motion agreed to 61-39: R 6-38; D 55-1 (ND 42-0, SD 13-1), Aug. 25, 1994. A three-fifths majority vote (60) of the total Senate is required to waive the budget act. (Subsequently, the point of order fell.) A "yea" was a vote in support of the president's position.

294. HR 3355. Omnibus Crime Bill/Cloture. Motion to invoke cloture (thus limiting debate) on the conference report to authorize $30.2 billion over six years and to require that all spending authorized by the bill come from a crime trust fund. The bill would authorize $6.9 billion for crime prevention programs, $8.8 billion for community policing programs and the hiring of 100,000 new police officers, and a $7.9 billion grant program to build state and local prisons. The bill would also ban 19 specific assault weapons, expand the death penalty to dozens of new federal crimes, mandate life imprisonment without parole for three-time violent felons, provide for community notification of violent sex offenders, and allow prior sex offenses to be admitted in federal trials. Motion agreed to 61-38: R 7-36; D 54-2 (ND 41-1, SD 13-1), Aug. 25, 1994. Three-fifths of the total Senate (60) is required to invoke cloture. A "yea" was a vote in support of the president's position.

295. HR 3355. Omnibus Crime Bill/Conference Report. Adoption of the conference report to authorize $30.2 billion over six years and to require that all spending authorized by the bill come from a crime trust fund realized from eliminating 270,000 federal jobs. The bill would authorize $6.9 billion for crime prevention programs, such as after-school sports leagues and job training programs, $8.8 billion for community policing programs and the hiring of 100,000 new police officers, and a $7.9 billion grant program to build state and local prisons. The bill would also ban 19 specific assault weapons, expand the death penalty to dozens of new federal crimes, mandate life imprisonment without parole for three-time violent felons, provide for community notification of violent sex offenders, allow prior sex offenses to be admitted in federal trials and require HIV testing when requested in federal rape trials. Adopted (thus cleared for the president) 61-38: R 7-36; D 54-2 (ND 41-1, SD 13-1), Aug. 25, 1994. A "yea" was a vote in support of the president's position.

ALABAMA	296	297	298	299
Heflin	Y	Y	Y	Y
Shelby	Y	Y	Y	Y
ALASKA				
Murkowski	Y	Y	Y	N
Stevens	Y	Y	Y	N
ARIZONA				
DeConcini	Y	Y	N	Y
McCain	Y	N	Y	N
ARKANSAS				
Bumpers	Y	Y	Y	Y
Pryor	Y	Y	Y	Y
CALIFORNIA				
Boxer	Y	Y	Y	Y
Feinstein	Y	Y	Y	Y
COLORADO				
Campbell	Y	Y	Y	?
Brown	Y	N	N	N
CONNECTICUT				
Dodd	Y	Y	Y	Y
Lieberman	Y	Y	Y	Y
DELAWARE				
Biden	Y	Y	Y	Y
Roth	Y	Y	Y	Y
FLORIDA				
Graham	Y	Y	Y	Y
Mack	Y	N	Y	N
GEORGIA				
Nunn	Y	Y	Y	Y
Coverdell	Y	N	Y	Y
HAWAII				
Akaka	Y	Y	Y	Y
Inouye	Y	Y	Y	?
IDAHO				
Craig	Y	N	Y	N
Kempthorne	Y	N	Y	Y
ILLINOIS				
Moseley-Braun	Y	Y	Y	Y
Simon	Y	Y	Y	Y
INDIANA				
Coats	Y	Y	Y	Y
Lugar	Y	Y	Y	Y

IOWA	296	297	298	299
Harkin	Y	Y	Y	Y
Grassley	Y	Y	Y	N
KANSAS				
Dole	Y	N	Y	?
Kassebaum	Y	Y	Y	Y
KENTUCKY				
Ford	Y	Y	Y	Y
McConnell	Y	N	Y	N
LOUISIANA				
Breaux	Y	Y	Y	N
Johnston	Y	Y	Y	Y
MAINE				
Mitchell	Y	Y	Y	Y
Cohen	Y	Y	Y	Y
MARYLAND				
Mikulski	Y	Y	Y	Y
Sarbanes	Y	Y	Y	Y
MASSACHUSETTS				
Kennedy	Y	Y	Y	Y
Kerry	Y	Y	Y	Y
MICHIGAN				
Levin	Y	Y	Y	Y
Riegle	Y	Y	Y	Y
MINNESOTA				
Wellstone	Y	N	Y	?
Durenberger	Y	Y	Y	Y
MISSISSIPPI				
Cochran	Y	Y	Y	Y
Lott	Y	Y	Y	N
MISSOURI				
Bond	Y	Y	Y	N
Danforth	Y	Y	Y	Y
MONTANA				
Baucus	Y	Y	Y	Y
Burns	Y	Y	Y	Y
NEBRASKA				
Exon	Y	Y	Y	Y
Kerrey	Y	Y	Y	Y
NEVADA				
Bryan	Y	Y	Y	Y
Reid	Y	Y	Y	Y

NEW HAMPSHIRE	296	297	298	299
Gregg	Y	N	Y	Y
Smith	Y	N	Y	N
NEW JERSEY				
Bradley	Y	Y	Y	Y
Lautenberg	Y	Y	Y	Y
NEW MEXICO				
Bingaman	Y	Y	Y	Y
Domenici	Y	Y	Y	Y
NEW YORK				
Moynihan	Y	Y	Y	Y
D'Amato	Y	Y	Y	?
NORTH CAROLINA				
Faircloth	Y	Y	Y	N
Helms	Y	Y	Y	N
NORTH DAKOTA				
Conrad	Y	Y	Y	Y
Dorgan	Y	Y	N	Y
OHIO				
Glenn	Y	Y	Y	Y
Metzenbaum	Y	Y	Y	Y
OKLAHOMA				
Boren	N	Y	N	N
Nickles	Y	N	Y	N
OREGON				
Hatfield	+	−	+	?
Packwood	Y	Y	Y	Y
PENNSYLVANIA				
Wofford	Y	Y	Y	Y
Specter	Y	Y	Y	N
RHODE ISLAND				
Pell	Y	Y	Y	Y
Chafee	?	?	?	Y
SOUTH CAROLINA				
Hollings	Y	Y	Y	Y
Thurmond	Y	Y	Y	Y
SOUTH DAKOTA				
Daschle	Y	Y	Y	Y
Pressler	Y	Y	Y	Y
TENNESSEE				
Mathews	Y	Y	Y	Y
Sasser	Y	Y	Y	Y

TEXAS	296	297	298	299
Hutchison	Y	Y	Y	Y
Gramm	Y	N	Y	?
UTAH				
Bennett	Y	N	Y	Y
Hatch	Y	N	Y	Y
VERMONT				
Leahy	Y	Y	Y	Y
Jeffords	Y	Y	Y	Y
VIRGINIA				
Robb	Y	Y	Y	Y
Warner	Y	Y	Y	N
WASHINGTON				
Murray	Y	Y	Y	Y
Gorton	Y	N	Y	Y
WEST VIRGINIA				
Byrd	Y	Y	Y	Y
Rockefeller	Y	Y	Y	Y
WISCONSIN				
Feingold	Y	N	N	N
Kohl	Y	Y	Y	Y
WYOMING				
Simpson	Y	Y	Y	Y
Wallop	Y	N	Y	N

ND Northern Democrats   SD Southern Democrats   Southern states - Ala., Ark., Fla., Ga., Ky., La., Miss., N.C., Okla., S.C., Tenn., Texas, Va.

296. HR 3841. Interstate Banking and Branching/Motion to Proceed. Mitchell, D-Maine, motion to proceed to the consideration of the conference report to allow bank holding companies to merge multistate subsidiary operations into branches of a single bank and remove barriers to interstate purchases of whole banks. Motion agreed to 97-1: R 42-0; D 55-1 (ND 42-0, SD 13-1), Sept. 13, 1994.

297. S 2182. Fiscal 1995 Defense Authorization/Conference Report. Adoption of the conference report to authorize $263.8 billion in fiscal 1995 for the programs of the Department of Defense. Adopted (thus cleared for the president) 80-18: R 26-16; D 54-2 (ND 40-2, SD 14-0), Sept. 13, 1994. A "yea" was a vote in support of the president's position.

298. HR 3841. Interstate Banking and Branching/Conference Report. Adoption of the conference report to allow bank holding companies to merge multistate subsidiary operations into branches of a single bank and remove barriers to interstate purchases of whole banks. Adopted (thus cleared for the president) 94-4: R 42-0; D 52-4 (ND 39-3, SD 13-1), Sept. 13, 1994. A "yea" was a vote in support of the president's position.

299. Procedural Motion. Mitchell, D-Maine, motion to instruct the sergeant at arms to request attendance of absent senators. Motion agreed to 74-19: R 23-17; D 51-2 (ND 39-0, SD 12-2), Sept. 14, 1994.

	300	301	302	303
ALABAMA				
Heflin	Y	Y	N	Y
Shelby	Y	Y	N	Y
ALASKA				
Murkowski	Y	Y	Y	Y
Stevens	Y	Y	Y	Y
ARIZONA				
DeConcini	Y	Y	N	Y
McCain	Y	Y	N	Y
ARKANSAS				
Bumpers	Y	Y	Y	Y
Pryor	Y	Y	Y	Y
CALIFORNIA				
Boxer	N	Y	Y	Y
Feinstein	Y	Y	Y	Y
COLORADO				
Campbell	Y	Y	Y	Y
Brown	Y	Y	N	Y
CONNECTICUT				
Dodd	Y	Y	Y	Y
Lieberman	Y	Y	Y	Y
DELAWARE				
Biden	Y	Y	Y	Y
Roth	Y	Y	N	Y
FLORIDA				
Graham	Y	Y	Y	Y
Mack	Y	Y	Y	Y
GEORGIA				
Nunn	Y	Y	Y	Y
Coverdell	Y	Y	N	Y
HAWAII				
Akaka	Y	Y	Y	Y
Inouye	Y	Y	Y	Y
IDAHO				
Craig	Y	Y	N	Y
Kempthorne	Y	Y	N	Y
ILLINOIS				
Moseley-Braun	N	Y	N	Y
Simon	N	Y	Y	Y
INDIANA				
Coats	Y	Y	N	Y
Lugar	Y	Y	Y	Y

	300	301	302	303
IOWA				
Harkin	Y	Y	Y	Y
Grassley	Y	Y	N	Y
KANSAS				
Dole	Y	Y	Y	Y
Kassebaum	Y	Y	Y	Y
KENTUCKY				
Ford	Y	Y	Y	Y
McConnell	Y	Y	N	Y
LOUISIANA				
Breaux	Y	Y	Y	Y
Johnston	Y	Y	Y	Y
MAINE				
Mitchell	Y	Y	Y	Y
Cohen	Y	Y	Y	Y
MARYLAND				
Mikulski	Y	Y	Y	Y
Sarbanes	Y	Y	Y	Y
MASSACHUSETTS				
Kennedy	Y	Y	Y	Y
Kerry	Y	Y	Y	Y
MICHIGAN				
Levin	Y	Y	Y	Y
Riegle	Y	Y	Y	Y
MINNESOTA				
Wellstone	Y	Y	Y	Y
Durenberger	Y	Y	Y	Y
MISSISSIPPI				
Cochran	Y	Y	N	Y
Lott	Y	Y	N	Y
MISSOURI				
Bond	Y	Y	Y	N
Danforth	Y	N	Y	Y
MONTANA				
Baucus	Y	Y	N	Y
Burns	Y	Y	N	Y
NEBRASKA				
Exon	Y	Y	Y	Y
Kerrey	Y	Y	Y	Y
NEVADA				
Bryan	Y	Y	Y	Y
Reid	Y	Y	Y	Y

	300	301	302	303
NEW HAMPSHIRE				
Gregg	Y	Y	N	Y
Smith	Y	Y	N	Y
NEW JERSEY				
Bradley	Y	Y	Y	Y
Lautenberg	Y	Y	Y	Y
NEW MEXICO				
Bingaman	Y	Y	Y	Y
Domenici	Y	Y	N	Y
NEW YORK				
Moynihan	Y	Y	Y	Y
D'Amato	Y	Y	Y	Y
NORTH CAROLINA				
Faircloth	Y	N	N	Y
Helms	Y	Y	N	N
NORTH DAKOTA				
Conrad	Y	Y	Y	Y
Dorgan	Y	Y	Y	Y
OHIO				
Glenn	Y	Y	Y	Y
Metzenbaum	N	Y	Y	Y
OKLAHOMA				
Boren	Y	Y	Y	Y
Nickles	Y	Y	N	Y
OREGON				
Hatfield	Y	N	Y	Y
Packwood	Y	Y	Y	Y
PENNSYLVANIA				
Wofford	Y	Y	Y	Y
Specter	Y	Y	Y	Y
RHODE ISLAND				
Pell	Y	Y	Y	Y
Chafee	Y	Y	?	Y
SOUTH CAROLINA				
Hollings	Y	Y	Y	Y
Thurmond	+	+	—	+
SOUTH DAKOTA				
Daschle	Y	Y	Y	Y
Pressler	Y	N	Y	Y
TENNESSEE				
Mathews	Y	Y	Y	Y
Sasser	Y	Y	Y	Y

Y Voted for (yea).
Paired for.
+ Announced for.
N Voted against (nay).
X Paired against.
— Announced against.
P Voted "present."
C Voted "present" to avoid possible conflict of interest.
? Did not vote or otherwise make a position known.

Democrats *Republicans*

	300	301	302	303
TEXAS				
Hutchison	Y	Y	N	Y
Gramm	Y	Y	N	Y
UTAH				
Bennett	Y	Y	Y	Y
Hatch	Y	Y	N	Y
VERMONT				
Leahy	Y	Y	Y	Y
Jeffords	Y	Y	Y	Y
VIRGINIA				
Robb	Y	Y	Y	Y
Warner	Y	Y	Y	Y
WASHINGTON				
Murray	N	Y	Y	Y
Gorton	Y	Y	Y	Y
WEST VIRGINIA				
Byrd	Y	Y	Y	Y
Rockefeller	?	Y	Y	Y
WISCONSIN				
Feingold	N	Y	Y	Y
Kohl	Y	Y	Y	Y
WYOMING				
Simpson	Y	Y	Y	Y
Wallop	Y	N	N	+

ND Northern Democrats   SD Southern Democrats   Southern states - Ala., Ark., Fla., Ga., Ky., La., Miss., N.C., Okla., S.C., Tenn., Texas, Va.

300. Mauz Nomination/Confirmation. Confirmation of President Clinton's nomination of Adm. Henry H. Mauz Jr. to be retired at the rank of four stars. Confirmed 92-6: R 43-0; D 49-6 (ND 35-6, SD 14-0), Sept. 20, 1994. A "yea" was a vote in support of the president's position.

301. S Res 259. Haiti Resolution/Adoption. Adoption of the resolution to express the sense of the Senate supporting the U.S. forces in Haiti and commending the efforts of the special delegation led by former President Jimmy Carter in securing an agreement for the peaceful departure from power of the military regime. The resolution also supports the lifting of economic sanctions on Haiti and the prompt and orderly withdrawal of all U.S forces. Adopted 94-5: R 38-5; D 56-0 (ND 42-0, SD 14-0), Sept. 21, 1994.

302. HR 4649. Fiscal 1995 D.C. Appropriations/Conference Report. Adoption of the conference report to provide $712,070,000 in new budget authority for the District of Columbia in fiscal 1995 and to approve the spending of $3,356,806,635 raised from local taxes. The bill also requires the District to cut its budget by $140 million and requires that if the District incurs a deficit in fiscal 1995, it will face a corresponding reduction from its fiscal 1996 federal payment. The administration requested $722,000,000 in new budget authority, and the city estimated $3,690,438,635 in local taxes. Adopted 71-27: R 20-22; D 51-5 (ND 39-3, SD 12-2), Sept. 21, 1994.

303. S 3. Campaign Finance Reform/Cloture. Motion to invoke cloture (thus limiting debate) on the motion to disagree to the amendments of the House on the bill to establish a system for voluntary spending caps on congressional campaigns and for other purposes. Motion agreed to 96-2: R 40-2; D 56-0 (ND 42-0, SD 14-0), Sept. 22, 1994. Three-fifths of the total Senate (60) is required to invoke cloture. (A motion to disagree to the House amendments is the first of three procedural hurdles that the Senate must overcome in order to go to conference on the bill. In trying to block the bill, some Republican senators filibustered the motion, thus requiring the cloture vote.)

	304	305	306	307	308	309	310	311
ALABAMA								
Heflin	Y	Y	Y	N	N	Y	Y	Y
Shelby	Y	Y	Y	N	N	N	Y	Y
ALASKA								
Murkowski	Y	N	Y	N	Y	N	Y	N
Stevens	Y	N	Y	N	N	N	Y	Y
ARIZONA								
DeConcini	Y	Y	Y	N	N	Y	Y	Y
McCain	Y	Y	N	Y	Y	Y	Y	Y
ARKANSAS								
Bumpers	Y	Y	Y	N	N	Y	Y	Y
Pryor	Y	Y	Y	N	N	Y	Y	Y
CALIFORNIA								
Boxer	Y	Y	Y	N	N	Y	Y	Y
Feinstein	Y	Y	Y	N	Y	Y	Y	Y
COLORADO								
Campbell	Y	Y	Y	N	Y	N	Y	Y
Brown	Y	N	N	Y	Y	N	N	N
CONNECTICUT								
Dodd	Y	Y	Y	N	N	Y	Y	Y
Lieberman	Y	Y	Y	N	N	Y	?	Y
DELAWARE								
Biden	Y	Y	Y	N	N	Y	Y	Y
Roth	?	Y	N	Y	N	N	N	N
FLORIDA								
Graham	Y	Y	Y	Y	N	Y	Y	Y
Mack	Y	N	Y	N	Y	N	Y	Y
GEORGIA								
Nunn	Y	Y	Y	Y	Y	Y	N	Y
Coverdell	Y	N	Y	N	Y	N	Y	Y
HAWAII								
Akaka	Y	Y	Y	N	N	Y	Y	Y
Inouye	Y	Y	Y	N	N	Y	Y	Y
IDAHO								
Craig	Y	N	Y	Y	Y	N	N	N
Kempthorne	Y	N	Y	Y	Y	N	N	N
ILLINOIS								
Moseley-Braun	Y	Y	Y	N	N	Y	Y	Y
Simon	Y	Y	Y	N	N	Y	Y	Y
INDIANA								
Coats	Y	Y	Y	Y	Y	N	Y	Y
Lugar	Y	Y	Y	Y	Y	N	Y	Y
IOWA								
Harkin	Y	Y	Y	N	N	Y	Y	Y
Grassley	Y	Y	Y	N	Y	N	Y	Y
KANSAS								
Dole	Y	Y	Y	N	Y	N	N	Y
Kassebaum	Y	Y	Y	Y	Y	Y	Y	Y
KENTUCKY								
Ford	Y	Y	Y	N	Y	Y	Y	Y
McConnell	Y	N	Y	N	Y	N	Y	Y
LOUISIANA								
Breaux	Y	Y	Y	N	N	Y	Y	Y
Johnston	Y	Y	Y	N	N	N	Y	Y
MAINE								
Mitchell	Y	Y	Y	N	N	Y	Y	Y
Cohen	Y	Y	Y	N	Y	Y	Y	Y
MARYLAND								
Mikulski	Y	Y	Y	N	N	Y	Y	Y
Sarbanes	Y	Y	Y	N	N	Y	Y	Y
MASSACHUSETTS								
Kennedy	?	?	Y	N	N	Y	Y	Y
Kerry	Y	Y	Y	N	N	Y	Y	Y
MICHIGAN								
Levin	Y	Y	Y	N	N	Y	Y	Y
Riegle	Y	Y	Y	N	N	Y	Y	Y
MINNESOTA								
Wellstone	Y	Y	Y	N	Y	Y	Y	Y
Durenberger	Y	Y	Y	Y	Y	Y	Y	Y
MISSISSIPPI								
Cochran	Y	N	Y	N	N	N	N	Y
Lott	Y	?	Y	N	Y	N	N	Y
MISSOURI								
Bond	Y	Y	Y	N	N	N	N	Y
Danforth	Y	Y	Y	N	N	N	Y	Y
MONTANA								
Baucus	Y	Y	Y	N	Y	N	Y	Y
Burns	+	?	Y	N	Y	N	Y	Y
NEBRASKA								
Exon	Y	Y	Y	N	Y	Y	Y	Y
Kerrey	Y	Y	Y	N	N	N	Y	Y
NEVADA								
Bryan	Y	Y	Y	N	Y	Y	Y	Y
Reid	?	?	Y	N	N	Y	Y	Y
NEW HAMPSHIRE								
Gregg	Y	Y	N	Y	Y	N	N	N
Smith	Y	N	N	Y	Y	N	N	N
NEW JERSEY								
Bradley	Y	Y	?	Y	Y	Y	Y	Y
Lautenberg	Y	Y	Y	N	N	Y	Y	Y
NEW MEXICO								
Bingaman	Y	Y	Y	N	N	Y	Y	Y
Domenici	Y	Y	Y	N	N	Y	Y	Y
NEW YORK								
Moynihan	Y	Y	Y	N	N	Y	Y	Y
D'Amato	Y	Y	Y	N	N	N	Y	Y
NORTH CAROLINA								
Faircloth	Y	N	Y	Y	Y	N	N	N
Helms	?	–	N	Y	Y	N	N	N
NORTH DAKOTA								
Conrad	Y	Y	Y	N	N	Y	N	Y
Dorgan	Y	Y	Y	N	N	Y	Y	Y
OHIO								
Glenn	Y	Y	Y	N	N	Y	Y	Y
Metzenbaum	Y	Y	Y	N	Y	Y	Y	Y
OKLAHOMA								
Boren	Y	Y	Y	N	N	Y	Y	Y
Nickles	?	?	Y	N	Y	N	N	N
OREGON								
Hatfield	Y	Y	Y	N	N	N	Y	Y
Packwood	Y	N	Y	N	Y	N	Y	Y
PENNSYLVANIA								
Wofford	Y	Y	Y	N	Y	Y	Y	Y
Specter	Y	Y	?	N	N	N	Y	Y
RHODE ISLAND								
Pell	Y	Y	Y	N	N	Y	Y	Y
Chafee	Y	Y	Y	Y	Y	Y	Y	Y
SOUTH CAROLINA								
Hollings	Y	Y	Y	N	N	Y	Y	Y
Thurmond	Y	N	Y	Y	Y	N	Y	Y
SOUTH DAKOTA								
Daschle	Y	Y	Y	N	N	Y	Y	Y
Pressler	Y	N	Y	Y	Y	N	N	Y
TENNESSEE								
Mathews	Y	Y	Y	N	N	N	Y	Y
Sasser	Y	Y	Y	Y	Y	Y	Y	+
TEXAS								
Hutchison	Y	N	Y	N	Y	N	N	Y
Gramm	Y	N	Y	N	N	N	N	Y
UTAH								
Bennett	Y	N	Y	N	N	Y	N	Y
Hatch	Y	N	Y	Y	Y	N	Y	Y
VERMONT								
Leahy	Y	Y	Y	N	N	Y	Y	Y
Jeffords	Y	Y	Y	N	Y	Y	Y	Y
VIRGINIA								
Robb	Y	Y	Y	N	N	Y	Y	Y
Warner	Y	Y	Y	Y	Y	N	Y	Y
WASHINGTON								
Murray	Y	Y	Y	N	N	Y	Y	Y
Gorton	Y	N	Y	Y	Y	N	Y	Y
WEST VIRGINIA								
Byrd	Y	Y	Y	N	N	Y	Y	Y
Rockefeller	Y	Y	Y	N	N	Y	Y	Y
WISCONSIN								
Feingold	Y	Y	N	Y	Y	Y	Y	Y
Kohl	Y	Y	N	Y	Y	Y	Y	Y
WYOMING								
Simpson	Y	N	Y	N	N	N	N	Y
Wallop	?	–	N	Y	Y	N	N	Y

KEY

Y   Voted for (yea).
Paired for.
+   Announced for.
N   Voted against (nay).
X   Paired against.
–   Announced against.
P   Voted "present."
C   Voted "present" to avoid possible conflict of interest.
?   Did not vote or otherwise make a position known.

Democrats   *Republicans*

ND   Northern Democrats   SD   Southern Democrats   Southern states - Ala., Ark., Fla., Ga., Ky., La., Miss., N.C., Okla., S.C., Tenn., Texas, Va.

304. S3. Campaign Finance/Disagree to House Amendments. Motion to disagree to the amendments of the House on the bill to establish a system for voluntary spending caps on congressional campaigns. Motion agreed to 93-0: R 39-0; D 54-0 (ND 40-0, SD 14-0), Sept. 23, 1994. (The motion to disagree to the House amendments is one of several procedural steps required in order to go to conference.)

305. S 21. California Desert Protection/Cloture. Motion to invoke cloture (thus limiting debate) on the motion to disagree to the amendments of the House on the bill to designate about 7.7 million acres of California desert as wilderness and to establish the Death Valley, Joshua Tree and Mojave National Parks. Motion agreed to 73-20: R 19-20; D 54-0 (ND 40-0, SD 14-0), Sept. 23, 1994. Three-fifths of the total Senate (60) is required to invoke cloture. (The motion to disagree to the House amendments is one of several procedural steps required in order to go to conference.)

306. HR 4624. Fiscal 1995 VA-HUD Appropriations/ Conference Report. Adoption of the conference report to provide $90,118,186,061 in fiscal 1995 budget authority for the Veterans Affairs and the Housing and Urban Development departments, and for independent agencies such as the National Aeronautics and Space Administration and the Environmental Protection Agency. The administration had requested $90,318,793,061. Adopted (thus cleared for the president) 90-9: R 37-7; D 53-2 (ND 39-2, SD 14-0), Sept. 27, 1994.

307. HR 4624. Fiscal 1995 VA-HUD Appropriations/ Unauthorized Projects. McCain, R-Ariz., amendment to the amendment in disagreement to the Senate amendment, to prohibit any unauthorized project added in conference from receiving money under the bill. Rejected 28-72: R 21-23; D 7-49 (ND 4-38, SD 3-11), Sept. 27, 1994.

308. HR 4624. Fiscal 1995 VA-HUD Appropriations/ Earmarks. Smith, R-N.H., amendment to the amendment in disagreement to the Senate amendment, to require that the joint explanatory statement on appropriation conference reports specify the origin of earmarked expenditures. Rejected 45-55: R 34-10; D 11-45 (ND 9-33, SD 2-12), Sept. 27, 1994.

309. S 3. Campaign Finance Conference/Cloture. Motion to invoke cloture (thus limiting debate) on the motion to request a conference with the House on the bill to establish a system for voluntary spending caps on congressional campaigns. Motion rejected 57-43: R 6-38; D 51-5 (ND 40-2, SD 11-3), Sept. 27, 1994. Three-fifths of the total Senate (60) is required to invoke cloture.

310. HR 4606. Fiscal 1995 Labor, HHS, Appropriations/ Conference Report. Adoption of the conference report to provide $250,610,477,000 in new budget authority for the departments of Labor, Health and Human Services, and Education, and related agencies in fiscal 1995-97. The administration had requested a total of $251,555,092,000. Adopted (thus cleared for the president) 83-16: R 30-14; D 53-2 (ND 40-1, SD 13-1), Sept. 27, 1994.

311. HR 4602. Fiscal 1995 Interior Appropriations/Conference Report. Adoption of the conference report to provide $13,669,540,000 for the Department of the Interior and related agencies in fiscal 1995. The administration had requested $13,424,299,000. Adopted (thus cleared for the president) 92-7: R 37-7; D 55-0 (ND 42-0, SD 13-0), Sept. 28, 1994.

KEY

Y Voted for (yea).
Paired for.
+ Announced for.
N Voted against (nay).
X Paired against.
— Announced against.
P Voted "present."
C Voted "present" to avoid possible conflict of interest.
? Did not vote or otherwise make a position known.

Democrats *Republicans*

	312	313
ALABAMA		
Heflin	Y	N
Shelby	Y	Y
ALASKA		
Murkowski	Y	Y
Stevens	Y	N
ARIZONA		
DeConcini	Y	N
McCain	N	Y
ARKANSAS		
Bumpers	Y	Y
Pryor	Y	Y
CALIFORNIA		
Boxer	Y	N
Feinstein	Y	N
COLORADO		
Campbell	Y	N
Brown	N	Y
CONNECTICUT		
Dodd	Y	N
Lieberman	Y	Y
DELAWARE		
Biden	Y	Y
Roth	N	Y
FLORIDA		
Graham	N	Y
Mack	Y	Y
GEORGIA		
Nunn	Y	Y
Coverdell	Y	Y
HAWAII		
Akaka	Y	N
Inouye	Y	N
IDAHO		
Craig	Y	Y
Kempthorne	Y	Y
ILLINOIS		
Moseley-Braun	Y	N
Simon	Y	Y
INDIANA		
Coats	Y	Y
Lugar	Y	Y

	312	313
IOWA		
Harkin	Y	N
Grassley	Y	N
KANSAS		
Dole	Y	Y
Kassebaum	Y	Y
KENTUCKY		
Ford	Y	N
McConnell	Y	N
LOUISIANA		
Breaux	Y	N
Johnston	Y	N
MAINE		
Mitchell	Y	N
Cohen	Y	Y
MARYLAND		
Mikulski	Y	N
Sarbanes	Y	N
MASSACHUSETTS		
Kennedy	Y	Y
Kerry	Y	Y
MICHIGAN		
Levin	Y	Y
Riegle	Y	N
MINNESOTA		
Wellstone	Y	Y
Durenberger	Y	Y
MISSISSIPPI		
Cochran	Y	N
Lott	Y	Y
MISSOURI		
Bond	Y	N
Danforth	Y	Y
MONTANA		
Baucus	Y	N
Burns	Y	Y
NEBRASKA		
Exon	Y	N
Kerrey	Y	N
NEVADA		
Bryan	Y	Y
Reid	Y	Y

	312	313
NEW HAMPSHIRE		
Gregg	N	Y
Smith	N	Y
NEW JERSEY		
Bradley	Y	Y
Lautenberg	Y	Y
NEW MEXICO		
Bingaman	Y	Y
Domenici	Y	Y
NEW YORK		
Moynihan	Y	N
D'Amato	Y	Y
NORTH CAROLINA		
Faircloth	N	Y
Helms	N	N
NORTH DAKOTA		
Conrad	Y	N
Dorgan	Y	N
OHIO		
Glenn	Y	N
Metzenbaum	Y	N
OKLAHOMA		
Boren	Y	Y
Nickles	N	Y
OREGON		
Hatfield	Y	N
Packwood	Y	Y
PENNSYLVANIA		
Wofford	Y	Y
Specter	Y	Y
RHODE ISLAND		
Pell	Y	N
Chafee	Y	Y
SOUTH CAROLINA		
Hollings	Y	N
Thurmond	Y	Y
SOUTH DAKOTA		
Daschle	Y	N
Pressler	Y	Y
TENNESSEE		
Mathews	Y	N
Sasser	Y	Y

	312	313
TEXAS		
Hutchison	Y	Y
Gramm	N	N
UTAH		
Bennett	Y	Y
Hatch	Y	Y
VERMONT		
Leahy	Y	N
Jeffords	Y	Y
VIRGINIA		
Robb	Y	?
Warner	Y	Y
WASHINGTON		
Murray	Y	N
Gorton	Y	Y
WEST VIRGINIA		
Byrd	Y	N
Rockefeller	Y	N
WISCONSIN		
Feingold	Y	Y
Kohl	Y	Y
WYOMING		
Simpson	Y	Y
Wallop	N	Y

ND Northern Democrats   SD Southern Democrats   Southern states - Ala., Ark., Fla., Ga., Ky., La., Miss., N.C., Okla., S.C., Tenn., Texas, Va.

312. HR 4556. Fiscal 1995 Transportation Appropriations/Conference Report. Adoption of the conference report to provide $14,290,468,000 in new budget authority for the Department of Transportation and related agencies for fiscal 1995. The administration had requested $13,813,438,000. Adopted (thus cleared for the president) 89-11: R 34-10; D 55-1 (ND 42-0, SD 13-1), Sept. 29, 1994.

313. HR 4649. Fiscal 1995 D.C. Appropriations/Waive Budget Act. Domenici, R-N.M., motion to waive the budget act with respect to the Byrd, D-W.Va., point of order against the Domenici amendment for violating the budget act for encroaching on the Budget Committee's jurisdiction. The Domenici amendment would have instituted a series of institutional changes recommended by the Joint Committee on the Reorganization of Congress, including a reduction in the number of Senate subcommittees, a two-year budget cycle and a cut in congressional staff. Motion rejected 58-41: R 36-8; D 22-33 (ND 15-27, SD 7-6), Sept. 29, 1994. A three-fifths majority vote (60) of the total Senate is required to waive the budget act. (Subsequently, the chair upheld the Byrd point of order, and the Domenici amendment fell.)

SENATE VOTES 314, 315, 316, 317, 318, 319, 320, 321

	314	315	316	317	318	319	320	321
ALABAMA								
Heflin	N	Y	Y	Y	Y	Y	Y	?
Shelby	N	Y	Y	Y	N	N	N	?
ALASKA								
Murkowski	N	N	N	Y	Y	Y	Y	Y
Stevens	N	?	?	?	?	?	?	?
ARIZONA								
DeConcini	Y	Y	Y	Y	Y	Y	Y	Y
McCain	N	N	N	Y	N	N	N	N
ARKANSAS								
Bumpers	Y	Y	Y	Y	Y	Y	Y	Y
Pryor	Y	Y	Y	Y	Y	Y	Y	Y
CALIFORNIA								
Boxer	Y	Y	Y	Y	Y	Y	Y	Y
Feinstein	Y	Y	Y	Y	Y	Y	Y	Y
COLORADO								
Campbell	N	Y	Y	Y	Y	Y	Y	Y
Brown	N	N	N	N	Y	N	N	N
CONNECTICUT								
Dodd	Y	Y	Y	Y	Y	Y	Y	Y
Lieberman	Y	Y	Y	Y	Y	Y	Y	Y
DELAWARE								
Biden	Y	Y	Y	Y	Y	Y	Y	Y
Roth	N	?	?	Y	Y	N	Y	Y
FLORIDA								
Graham	Y	Y	Y	Y	Y	Y	Y	Y
Mack	N	N	N	Y	Y	N	N	N
GEORGIA								
Nunn	Y	Y	Y	Y	Y	Y	Y	Y
Coverdell	N	N	N	Y	N	N	N	N
HAWAII								
Akaka	Y	Y	Y	Y	Y	Y	Y	Y
Inouye	Y	Y	Y	Y	Y	Y	Y	Y
IDAHO								
Craig	N	N	N	Y	N	Y	N	N
Kempthorne	N	Y	N	Y	Y	N	N	Y
ILLINOIS								
Moseley-Braun	Y	Y	Y	Y	Y	Y	Y	Y
Simon	Y	Y	Y	Y	Y	Y	Y	Y
INDIANA								
Coats	N	N	N	Y	Y	N	N	N
Lugar	N	Y	N	Y	Y	Y	Y	Y
IOWA								
Harkin	Y	Y	Y	Y	Y	Y	Y	Y
Grassley	N	N	N	Y	Y	N	N	N
KANSAS								
Dole	N	Y	N	Y	Y	N	N	N
Kassebaum	N	Y	N	Y	Y	Y	Y	Y
KENTUCKY								
Ford	Y	Y	Y	Y	N	N	Y	Y
McConnell	N	N	N	Y	Y	N	N	N
LOUISIANA								
Breaux	Y	Y	Y	Y	Y	Y	Y	Y
Johnston	N	Y	Y	Y	Y	Y	Y	Y
MAINE								
Mitchell	Y	Y	Y	Y	Y	Y	Y	Y
Cohen	N	Y	Y	Y	Y	Y	Y	Y
MARYLAND								
Mikulski	Y	Y	Y	Y	Y	Y	Y	Y
Sarbanes	Y	Y	Y	Y	Y	Y	Y	Y
MASSACHUSETTS								
Kennedy	Y	Y	Y	?	?	?	Y	Y
Kerry	Y	Y	Y	Y	Y	Y	Y	Y
MICHIGAN								
Levin	Y	Y	Y	Y	Y	Y	Y	Y
Riegle	Y	Y	Y	Y	Y	Y	Y	Y
MINNESOTA								
Wellstone	Y	Y	Y	Y	Y	Y	Y	Y
Durenberger	N	Y	Y	Y	Y	Y	Y	Y
MISSISSIPPI								
Cochran	N	Y	N	Y	Y	N	N	Y
Lott	N	N	N	Y	Y	N	N	Y
MISSOURI								
Bond	N	?	?	?	?	N	N	N
Danforth	N	Y	Y	Y	Y	Y	N	N
MONTANA								
Baucus	Y	Y	Y	Y	Y	Y	Y	Y
Burns	N	N	Y	Y	Y	N	Y	Y
NEBRASKA								
Exon	Y	Y	Y	Y	Y	Y	Y	Y
Kerrey	N	Y	Y	Y	Y	Y	Y	Y
NEVADA								
Bryan	Y	Y	Y	Y	Y	Y	N	Y
Reid	Y	Y	Y	Y	Y	N	Y	Y
NEW HAMPSHIRE								
Gregg	N	Y	N	Y	Y	Y	Y	Y
Smith	N	N	N	N	Y	N	N	N
NEW JERSEY								
Bradley	Y	Y	Y	Y	Y	Y	Y	Y
Lautenberg	Y	Y	Y	Y	Y	Y	Y	Y
NEW MEXICO								
Bingaman	Y	Y	Y	Y	Y	Y	Y	Y
Domenici	N	Y	N	N	Y	N	Y	Y
NEW YORK								
Moynihan	Y	Y	Y	Y	Y	Y	Y	Y
D'Amato	N	N	N	N	N	N	Y	Y
NORTH CAROLINA								
Faircloth	N	N	N	Y	N	N	N	N
Helms	N	N	N	N	N	N	N	N
NORTH DAKOTA								
Conrad	Y	Y	Y	Y	Y	Y	Y	Y
Dorgan	Y	Y	Y	Y	Y	Y	Y	Y
OHIO								
Glenn	Y	Y	Y	Y	Y	Y	Y	Y
Metzenbaum	Y	Y	Y	Y	Y	Y	Y	Y
OKLAHOMA								
Boren	Y	Y	Y	Y	Y	Y	Y	Y
Nickles	?	N	N	N	N	N	N	N
OREGON								
Hatfield	N	Y	Y	Y	Y	Y	Y	Y
Packwood	N	Y	Y	Y	Y	Y	Y	Y
PENNSYLVANIA								
Wofford	Y	Y	Y	Y	Y	Y	Y	Y
Specter	N	?	?	Y	Y	Y	Y	Y
RHODE ISLAND								
Pell	Y	Y	Y	Y	Y	Y	Y	Y
Chafee	Y	Y	N	Y	Y	Y	Y	Y
SOUTH CAROLINA								
Hollings	Y	Y	Y	Y	Y	Y	Y	Y
Thurmond	N	Y	N	Y	N	N	N	N
SOUTH DAKOTA								
Daschle	Y	Y	Y	Y	Y	Y	Y	Y
Pressler	N	N	N	Y	Y	Y	Y	Y
TENNESSEE								
Mathews	N	Y	Y	Y	Y	Y	Y	Y
Sasser	Y	Y	Y	Y	N	N	Y	Y
TEXAS								
Hutchison	N	Y	N	Y	Y	N	Y	Y
Gramm	N	N	N	Y	N	N	N	N
UTAH								
Bennett	?	N	N	Y	N	Y	N	Y
Hatch	N	Y	N	Y	Y	N	Y	Y
VERMONT								
Leahy	Y	Y	Y	Y	Y	Y	Y	Y
Jeffords	Y	Y	Y	Y	Y	Y	Y	Y
VIRGINIA								
Robb	Y	Y	Y	Y	Y	Y	Y	Y
Warner	N	Y	N	Y	Y	N	Y	Y
WASHINGTON								
Murray	Y	Y	Y	Y	Y	Y	Y	Y
Gorton	N	Y	N	Y	N	N	N	N
WEST VIRGINIA								
Byrd	Y	Y	Y	Y	Y	Y	N	Y
Rockefeller	Y	Y	Y	Y	Y	Y	Y	Y
WISCONSIN								
Feingold	Y	Y	Y	Y	Y	Y	Y	Y
Kohl	Y	Y	Y	Y	Y	Y	Y	Y
WYOMING								
Simpson	N	Y	N	Y	Y	Y	N	N
Wallop	N	?	?	N	N	N	N	N

ND Northern Democrats   SD Southern Democrats

Southern states - Ala., Ark., Fla., Ga., Ky., La., Miss., N.C., Okla., S.C., Tenn., Texas, Va.

314. S 3. Campaign Finance/Cloture. Motion to invoke cloture (thus limiting debate) on the motion to request a conference with the House on the bill to establish a system for voluntary spending caps on congressional campaigns. Motion rejected 52-46: R 2-40; D 50-6 (ND 40-2, SD 10-4), Sept. 30, 1994. Three-fifths of the total Senate (60) is required to invoke cloture. A "yea" was a vote in support of the president's position.

315. Procedural Motion. Mitchell, D-Maine, motion to instruct the sergeant at arms to request the attendance of absent senators. Motion agreed to 76-19: R 20-19; D 56-0 (ND 42-0, SD 14-0), Oct. 3, 1994.

316. Tigert Nomination/Cloture. Motion to invoke cloture (thus limiting debate) on the confirmation of President Clinton's nomination of Ricki R. Tigert of Tennessee to be a member of the board of directors of the Federal Deposit Insurance Corporation. Motion agreed to 63-32: R 7-32; D 56-0 (ND 42-0, SD 14-0), Oct. 3, 1994. Three-fifths of the total Senate (60) is required to invoke cloture.

317. Tigert Nomination/Confirmation. Confirmation of President Clinton's nomination of Ricki R. Tigert of Tennessee to be a member of the board of directors of the Federal Deposit Insurance Corporation. Confirmed 90-7: R 35-7; D 55-0 (ND 41-0, SD 14-0), Oct. 4, 1994. A "yea" was a vote in support of the president's position.

318. Sarokin Nomination/Cloture. Motion to invoke cloture (thus limiting debate) on the confirmation of President Clinton's nomination of H. Lee Sarokin of New Jersey to be a judge on the 3rd U.S. Circuit Court of Appeals. Motion agreed to 85-12: R 33-9; D 52-3 (ND 41-0, SD 11-3), Oct. 4, 1994. Three-fifths of the total Senate (60) is required to invoke cloture.

319. Sarokin Nomination/Confirmation. Confirmation of President Clinton's nomination of H. Lee Sarokin of New Jersey to be a judge on the 3rd U.S. Circuit Court of Appeals. Confirmed 63-35: R 14-29; D 49-6 (ND 38-3, SD 11-3), Oct. 4, 1994. A "yea" was a vote in support of the president's position.

320. HR 6. Elementary and Secondary School Reauthorization/Cloture. Motion to invoke cloture (thus limiting debate) on the conference report to reauthorize for five years the Elementary and Secondary Education Act of 1965, providing $12.7 billion to help disadvantaged students. Motion agreed to 75-24: R 20-23; D 55-1 (ND 42-0, SD 13-1), Oct. 5, 1994. Three-fifths of the total Senate (60) is required to invoke cloture.

321. HR 6. Elementary and Secondary School Reauthorization/Conference Report. Adoption of the conference report to reauthorize for five years the Elementary and Secondary Education Act of 1965, providing $12.7 billion to help disadvantaged students. Adopted (thus cleared for the president) 77-20: R 23-20; D 54-0 (ND 42-0, SD 12-0), Oct. 5, 1994. A "yea" was a vote in support of the president's position.

KEY

Y Voted for (yea).
Paired for.
+ Announced for.
N Voted against (nay).
X Paired against.
– Announced against.
P Voted "present."
C Voted "present" to avoid possible conflict of interest.
? Did not vote or otherwise make a position known.

Democrats *Republicans*

	322	323	324
ALABAMA			
Heflin	N	Y	Y
Shelby	N	Y	Y
ALASKA			
Murkowski	N	Y	Y
Stevens	?	?	?
ARIZONA			
DeConcini	Y	Y	?
McCain	N	Y	Y
ARKANSAS			
Bumpers	Y	Y	Y
Pryor	Y	Y	?
CALIFORNIA			
Boxer	Y	N	Y
Feinstein	Y	Y	?
COLORADO			
Campbell	N	Y	?
Brown	Y	Y	Y
CONNECTICUT			
Dodd	Y	Y	Y
Lieberman	Y	Y	Y
DELAWARE			
Biden	Y	Y	?
Roth	Y	Y	Y
FLORIDA			
Graham	Y	Y	Y
Mack	N	Y	Y
GEORGIA			
Nunn	N	Y	Y
Coverdell	N	Y	Y
HAWAII			
Akaka	Y	Y	Y
Inouye	Y	Y	?
IDAHO			
Craig	N	Y	Y
Kempthorne	N	Y	Y
ILLINOIS			
Moseley-Braun	Y	Y	Y
Simon	Y	Y	Y
INDIANA			
Coats	N	Y	Y
Lugar	N	Y	Y

	322	323	324
IOWA			
Harkin	Y	Y	Y
Grassley	N	Y	Y
KANSAS			
Dole	N	Y	Y
Kassebaum	N	Y	Y
KENTUCKY			
Ford	Y	Y	Y
McConnell	N	Y	Y
LOUISIANA			
Breaux	N	Y	Y
Johnston	Y	Y	Y
MAINE			
Mitchell	Y	Y	Y
Cohen	Y	Y	Y
MARYLAND			
Mikulski	Y	Y	Y
Sarbanes	Y	Y	Y
MASSACHUSETTS			
Kennedy	Y	Y	?
Kerry	Y	Y	Y
MICHIGAN			
Levin	Y	Y	Y
Riegle	Y	Y	Y
MINNESOTA			
Wellstone	Y	Y	Y
Durenberger	N	Y	?
MISSISSIPPI			
Cochran	N	Y	Y
Lott	N	Y	Y
MISSOURI			
Bond	N	Y	Y
Danforth	N	Y	Y
MONTANA			
Baucus	Y	N	Y
Burns	N	Y	Y
NEBRASKA			
Exon	Y	Y	Y
Kerrey	Y	Y	Y
NEVADA			
Bryan	Y	Y	Y
Reid	Y	Y	Y

	322	323	324
NEW HAMPSHIRE			
Gregg	N	Y	Y
Smith	N	Y	Y
NEW JERSEY			
Bradley	Y	N	Y
Lautenberg	Y	Y	Y
NEW MEXICO			
Bingaman	N	Y	Y
Domenici	N	Y	Y
NEW YORK			
Moynihan	Y	Y	Y
D'Amato	N	Y	Y
NORTH CAROLINA			
Faircloth	N	Y	Y
Helms	N	Y	Y
NORTH DAKOTA			
Conrad	N	Y	Y
Dorgan	Y	Y	Y
OHIO			
Glenn	Y	Y	Y
Metzenbaum	Y	Y	Y
OKLAHOMA			
Boren	Y	Y	?
Nickles	N	Y	Y
OREGON			
Hatfield	Y	N	Y
Packwood	N	Y	Y
PENNSYLVANIA			
Wofford	Y	Y	Y
Specter	Y	Y	Y
RHODE ISLAND			
Pell	Y	Y	?
Chafee	Y	Y	Y
SOUTH CAROLINA			
Hollings	N	Y	Y
Thurmond	N	Y	Y
SOUTH DAKOTA			
Daschle	Y	Y	Y
Pressler	N	N	Y
TENNESSEE			
Mathews	N	Y	Y
Sasser	?	Y	Y

	322	323	324
TEXAS			
Hutchison	N	Y	Y
Gramm	N	Y	Y
UTAH			
Bennett	N	Y	Y
Hatch	N	Y	Y
VERMONT			
Leahy	Y	Y	Y
Jeffords	Y	Y	Y
VIRGINIA			
Robb	Y	Y	Y
Warner	N	Y	Y
WASHINGTON			
Murray	Y	Y	Y
Gorton	N	Y	Y
WEST VIRGINIA			
Byrd	N	N	Y
Rockefeller	Y	Y	Y
WISCONSIN			
Feingold	Y	N	Y
Kohl	Y	Y	Y
WYOMING			
Simpson	N	Y	Y
Wallop	N	N	?

ND Northern Democrats   SD Southern Democrats   Southern states - Ala., Ark., Fla., Ga., Ky., La., Miss., N.C., Okla., S.C., Tenn., Texas, Va.

322. S 349. Lobbying Disclosure/Cloture. Motion to invoke cloture (thus limiting debate) on the conference report to expand the disclosure of lobbying activities and impose new restrictions on gifts to members of Congress and their staffs. Motion rejected 52-46: R 7-36; D 45-10 (ND 38-4, SD 7-6), Oct. 6, 1994. Because the bill would change Senate rules, two-thirds of those present and voting (66 in this case) is required to invoke cloture.

323. S J Res 229. U.S. Troops in Haiti/Passage. Passage of the joint resolution to express the sense of Congress for a prompt and orderly withdrawal of all U.S. forces from Haiti as soon as possible and require reports on the scope and duration of the U.S. mission in Haiti. Passed 91-8: R 40-3; D 51-5 (ND 37-5, SD 14-0), Oct. 6, 1994.

324. S 993. Unfunded Mandates/Motion to Proceed. Motion to proceed to the bill to ease the burden of unfunded federal mandates on state and local governments by allowing a parliamentary point of order against any bill imposing more than $50 million in unfunded mandates, unless the committee reporting the bill identified offsets to cover the cost. Motion agreed to 88-0: R 41-0; D 47-0 (ND 35-0, SD 12-0), Oct. 6, 1994.

	325	326	327	328	329
ALABAMA					
Heflin	N	Y	Y	N	N
Shelby	N	Y	Y	N	N
ALASKA					
Murkowski	N	?	?	N	Y
Stevens	?	?	?	N	N
ARIZONA					
DeConcini	Y	Y	Y	Y	Y
McCain	Y	N	Y	Y	Y
ARKANSAS					
Bumpers	Y	Y	Y	N	Y
Pryor	Y	Y	N	Y	Y
CALIFORNIA					
Boxer	Y	Y	N	Y	Y
Feinstein	Y	Y	Y	Y	Y
COLORADO					
Campbell	N	Y	Y	N	N
Brown	Y	N	Y	N	N
CONNECTICUT					
Dodd	Y	Y	N	Y	Y
Lieberman	Y	Y	Y	Y	Y
DELAWARE					
Biden	?	Y	Y	Y	Y
Roth	Y	Y	N	Y	Y
FLORIDA					
Graham	Y	Y	Y	Y	Y
Mack	N	N	Y	Y	Y
GEORGIA					
Nunn	Y	Y	Y	Y	Y
Coverdell	N	N	Y	Y	Y
HAWAII					
Akaka	Y	Y	Y	Y	Y
Inouye	Y	Y	Y	N	Y
IDAHO					
Craig	N	N	N	N	N
Kempthorne	N	N	N	N	N
ILLINOIS					
Moseley-Braun	Y	Y	N	Y	Y
Simon	Y	Y	Y	Y	Y
INDIANA					
Coats	Y	N	Y	Y	Y
Lugar	N	Y	N	Y	Y
IOWA					
Harkin	Y	Y	?	N	Y
Grassley	N	Y	N	Y	Y
KANSAS					
Dole	N	N	Y	Y	Y
Kassebaum	N	Y	Y	Y	Y
KENTUCKY					
Ford	Y	Y	Y	N	Y
McConnell	N	?	?	Y	Y
LOUISIANA					
Breaux	N	Y	Y	Y	Y
Johnston	Y	Y	Y	Y	Y
MAINE					
Mitchell	Y	Y	Y	Y	Y
Cohen	Y	Y	Y	Y	Y
MARYLAND					
Mikulski	Y	Y	N	Y	Y
Sarbanes	Y	Y	N	Y	Y
MASSACHUSETTS					
Kennedy	Y	Y	N	Y	Y
Kerry	Y	Y	N	Y	Y
MICHIGAN					
Levin	Y	Y	N	Y	Y
Riegle	Y	Y	N	Y	Y
MINNESOTA					
Wellstone	Y	Y	N	N	N
Durenberger	N	Y	Y	Y	Y
MISSISSIPPI					
Cochran	N	N	Y	Y	Y
Lott	N	N	Y	Y	Y
MISSOURI					
Bond	N	?	Y	Y	Y
Danforth	N	Y	Y	Y	Y
MONTANA					
Baucus	Y	Y	N	N	N
Burns	N	?	?	N	N
NEBRASKA					
Exon	Y	Y	N	N	N
Kerrey	Y	Y	N	Y	Y
NEVADA					
Bryan	Y	Y	N	N	N
Reid	Y	Y	Y	N	N
NEW HAMPSHIRE					
Gregg	N	Y	N	Y	Y
Smith	N	N	Y	N	N
NEW JERSEY					
Bradley	?	?	?	Y	Y
Lautenberg	Y	Y	?	Y	Y
NEW MEXICO					
Bingaman	N	Y	Y	Y	Y
Domenici	N	Y	Y	Y	Y
NEW YORK					
Moynihan	Y	Y	Y	Y	Y
D'Amato	N	N	Y	Y	Y
NORTH CAROLINA					
Faircloth	N	N	Y	N	Y
Helms	N	–	+	N	N
NORTH DAKOTA					
Conrad	Y	Y	Y	Y	Y
Dorgan	Y	Y	Y	N	N
OHIO					
Glenn	Y	Y	N	Y	Y
Metzenbaum	Y	Y	N	N	N
OKLAHOMA					
Inhofe [1]				N	N
Nickles	N	N	Y	Y	Y
OREGON					
Hatfield	Y	Y	N	Y	Y
Packwood	N	?	?	Y	Y
PENNSYLVANIA					
Wofford	Y	Y	Y	Y	Y
Specter	Y	Y	Y	Y	Y
RHODE ISLAND					
Pell	Y	Y	Y	Y	Y
Chafee	Y	Y	Y	Y	Y
SOUTH CAROLINA					
Hollings	N	?	?	N	N
Thurmond	N	N	Y	N	N
SOUTH DAKOTA					
Daschle	Y	Y	Y	Y	Y
Pressler	N	N	N	N	Y
TENNESSEE					
Mathews	N	Y	Y	Y	Y
Sasser	Y	Y	+	Y	Y
TEXAS					
Gramm	N	N	Y	Y	Y
Hutchison	N	N	Y	Y	Y
UTAH					
Bennett	N	N	Y	Y	Y
Hatch	N	N	Y	Y	Y
VERMONT					
Leahy	Y	Y	N	N	N
Jeffords	Y	Y	N	N	N
VIRGINIA					
Robb	Y	Y	Y	N	N
Warner	N	Y	Y	Y	Y
WASHINGTON					
Murray	Y	Y	N	Y	Y
Gorton	N	N	Y	Y	Y
WEST VIRGINIA					
Byrd	N	Y	N	N	N
Rockefeller	Y	Y	Y	Y	Y
WISCONSIN					
Feingold	Y	Y	N	N	N
Kohl	Y	Y	Y	Y	Y
WYOMING					
Simpson	N	N	Y	Y	Y
Wallop	N	N	Y	N	Y

KEY

- Y Voted for (yea).
- # Paired for.
- + Announced for.
- N Voted against (nay).
- X Paired against.
- – Announced against.
- P Voted "present."
- C Voted "present" to avoid possible conflict of interest.
- ? Did not vote or otherwise make a position known.

Democrats *Republicans*

ND Northern Democrats SD Southern Democrats Southern states - Ala., Ark., Fla., Ga., Ky., La., Miss., N.C., Okla., S.C., Tenn., Texas, Va.

325. S 349. Lobbying Disclosure/Cloture. Motion to invoke cloture (thus limiting debate) on the conference report to expand the disclosure of lobbying activities and impose new restrictions on gifts to members of Congress and their staffs. Motion rejected 55-42: R 9-34; D 46-8 (ND 37-3, SD 9-5), Oct. 7, 1994. Because the bill would change Senate rules, two-thirds of those present and voting (65 in this case) is required to invoke cloture. A "yea" was a vote in support of the president's position.

326. S 21. California Desert Protection/Cloture. Motion to invoke cloture (thus limiting debate) on the conference report to designate about 7.5 million acres of California desert as wilderness and to establish the Death Valley and Joshua Tree national parks and the Mojave National Preserve. Motion agreed to 68-23: R 14-23; D 54-0 (ND 41-0, SD 13-0), Oct. 8, 1994. Three-fifths of the total Senate (60) is required to invoke cloture. A "yea" was a vote in support of the president's position.

327. Glosson Nomination. Confirmation of President Clinton's nomination of Lt. Gen. Buster C. Glosson to be retired at the rank of lieutenant general. Confirmed 59-30: R 29-9; D 30-21 (ND 19-20, SD 11-1), Oct. 8, 1994. A "yea" was a vote in support of the president's position.

328. HR 5110. General Agreement on Tariffs and Trade/Budget Waiver. Moynihan, D-N.Y., motion to waive the budget act with respect to the Byrd, D-W.Va., point of order against the bill to implement the General Agreement on Tariffs and Trade (GATT) for violating the budget act. The bill would make statutory changes to implement the new world trade agreement negotiated under the Uruguay Round of GATT. Motion agreed to 68-32: R 31-15; D 37-17 (ND 29-13, SD 8-4), Dec. 1, 1994. A three-fifths majority vote (60) of the total Senate is required to waive the budget act. (Subsequently, the budget act was waived and the point of order fell.) A "yea" was a vote in support of the president's position.

329. HR 5110. General Agreement on Tariffs and Trade/Passage. Passage of the bill to make statutory changes to implement the new world trade agreement negotiated under the Uruguay Round of the General Agreement on Tariffs and Trade (GATT). The agreement would reduce tariffs and trade barriers, ensure stricter enforcement of world trade rules through the newly established World Trade Organization (WTO), and expand GATT rules to cover such economic sectors as agriculture, services and intellectual property. The bill also would accelerate tax payment schedules, change eligibility standards for certain federal programs, and make other changes to offset lost revenues from tariff reductions in order to comply with pay-as-you-go budget rules. Passed (thus cleared for the president) 76-24: R 35-11; D 41-13 (ND 31-11, SD 10-2), Dec. 1, 1994. A "yea" was a vote in support of the president's position.

[1] *David L. Boren, D-Okla., resigned Nov. 15, 1994. He was eligible for 327 votes in 1994. James M. Inhofe, R-Okla., was sworn in Nov. 17, 1994, replacing Boren. Inhofe was eligible for the last two votes in 1994.*

INDEXES

Bill Number Index...................................... 3-I
Roll Call Vote Index.................................... 4-I
General Index 11-I

Bill Number Index

House Bills

H Con Res 160, 48-H
H Con Res 218, 16-H,
    18-H, 34-H, 48-H, 14-S, 20-S
H Con Res 222, 36-H
H Con Res 279, 142-H
H Con Res 286, 142-H
H Con Res 290, 128-H
H Con Res 301, 142-H

H J Res 103, 20-H
H J Res 373, 114-H
H J Res 416, 146-H, 148-H

H Res 238, 12-H
H Res 329, 40-H
H Res 343, 10-H
H Res 369, 24-H
H Res 375, 12-H
H Res 394, 24-H
H Res 450, 68-H
H Res 476, 106-H
H Res 578, 150-H

HR 6, 10-H, 12-H, 14-H, 24-H, 28-
    H, 128-H, 136-H, 43-S, 55-S
HR 8, 100-H
HR 518, 54-H, 70-H, 94-H, 96-H,
    106-H, 108-H
HR 811, 6-H, 8-H
HR 820, 100-H, 11-S
HR 967, 140-H
HR 1188, 100-H, 102-H
HR 1520, 140-H
HR 1804, 10-H, 26-H, 7-S, 12-S,
    15-S
HR 1933, 23-S
HR 2108, 56-H
HR 2129, 136-H
HR 2333, 36-H, 44-H
HR 2442, 50-H
HR 2448, 108-H
HR 2473, 54-H
HR 2843, 30-H
HR 2866, 128-H, 130-H
HR 2884, 38-H, 7-S
HR 2947, 120-H
HR 3171, 132-H
HR 3191, 46-H
HR 3221, 44-H
HR 3254, 46-H
HR 3345, 8-H, 18-H, 26-H, 13-S
HR 3355, 44-H, 76-H,

78-H, 80-H, 92-H, 96-H, 102-H,
    118-H, 124-H,
    22-S, 50-S
HR 3425, 2-H
HR 3433, 122-H, 124-H
HR 3474, 112-H
HR 3498, 30-H
HR 3626, 86-H
HR 3636, 86-H
HR 3693, 30-H
HR 3759, 2-H, 4-H, 8-H,
    7-S, 8-S
HR 3770, 30-H
HR 3813, 36-H
HR 3838, 106-H
HR 3841, 51-S
HR 3870, 106-H
HR 3937, 98-H
HR 4003, 110-H
HR 4013, 44-H
HR 4034, 26-H
HR 4066, 30-H
HR 4067, 26-H
HR 4092, 26-H, 30-H,
    32-H, 34-H, 36-H, 38-H, 40-H, 42-
    H
HR 4158, 110-H
HR 4217, 114-H
HR 4277, 54-H, 118-H
HR 4278, 52-H, 146-H
HR 4296, 48-H
HR 4299, 100-H, 48-S
HR 4301, 54-H, 56-H,
    58-H, 60-H, 66-H, 68-H
HR 4308, 126-H
HR 4385, 60-H
HR 4422, 130-H
HR 4426, 60-H, 62-H,
    112-H, 29-S, 30-S, 33-S, 34-S,
    35-S, 46-S
HR 4448, 110-H, 132-H
HR 4453, 58-H, 35-S, 46-S
HR 4454, 64-H, 31-S
HR 4462, 138-H
HR 4476, 132-H
HR 4506, 70-H, 110-H,
    116-H, 30-S
HR 4533, 142-H, 144-H
HR 4539, 68-H, 70-H,
    72-H, 74-H, 130-H, 132-H, 27-S,
    28-S
HR 4545, 114-H
HR 4554, 76-H, 132-H,
    35-S, 36-S, 37-S

HR 4556, 74-H, 37-S, 38-S, 54-S
HR 4568, 76-H
HR 4590, 114-H, 116-H
HR 4600, 98-H
HR 4602, 76-H, 78-H,
    80-H, 126-H, 39-S, 40-S, 53-S
HR 4603, 80-H, 82-H,
    84-H, 86-H, 116-H, 122-H, 38-S,
    39-S, 50-S
HR 4604, 104-H
HR 4606, 86-H, 88-H,
    130-H, 45-S, 53-S
HR 4608, 136-H
HR 4624, 90-H, 92-H,
    126-H, 43-S, 44-S, 53-S
HR 4649, 90-H, 94-H,
    96-H, 108-H, 37-S, 52-S, 54-S
HR 4650, 92-H, 126-H, 134-H, 45-
    S, 46-S, 47-S
HR 4683, 134-H
HR 4777, 136-H
HR 4779, 132-H
HR 4801, 110-H, 128-H
HR 4822, 116-H
HR 4833, 138-H
HR 4867, 120-H
HR 4906, 120-H, 122-H
HR 4907, 118-H, 120-H
HR 4908, 124-H
HR 5044, 132-H, 142-H, 144-H
HR 5108, 142-H
HR 5110, 144-H, 150-H, 57-S
HR 5139, 144-H

Senate Bills

S 3, 52-S, 53-S, 55-S
S 4, 10-S, 11-S
S 21, 138-H, 140-H, 148-H, 16-S,
    53-S, 57-S
S 24, 76-H
S 55, 33-S
S 208, 108-H, 12-S
S 349, 28-H, 134-H, 56-S, 57-S
S 455, 146-H, 150-H, 16-S
S 540, 17-S
S 636, 22-H, 48-H, 20-S
S 687, 29-S
S 729, 23-S
S 783, 18-S
S 978, 18-S
S 986, 144-H
S 993, 56-S
S 1066, 112-H
S 1150, 5-S, 6-S
S 1225, 142-H, 144-H
S 1233, 136-H
S 1275, 11-S
S 1357, 112-H
S 1361, 6-S
S 1458, 11-S
S 1491, 24-S, 25-S, 26-S
S 1513, 40-S, 41-S, 42-S, 43-S
S 1569, 150-H
S 1587, 128-H
S 1614, 48-S
S 1654, 36-H
S 1919, 142-H, 144-H
S 1935, 18-S
S 1970, 16-S
S 2000, 52-H, 18-S
S 2004, 30-H
S 2019, 21-S, 22-S
S 2042, 20-S
S 2082, 48-S
S 2182, 106-H, 122-H,
    28-S, 31-S, 32-S, 51-S
S 2351, 49-S

S Con Res 31, 36-H
S Con Res 63, 12-S, 13-S, 14-S

S J Res 41, 9-S
S J Res 229, 56-S

S Res 229, 27-S
S Res 259, 52-S

Roll Call Vote Index

A

Abortion
  access to clinics, 22-H, 48-H, 20-S
  funding to change foreign laws, 33-S
  Pensacola clinic attack, 44-S
Advanced Computational Technology Initiative, 40-S
Advanced Liquid Metal Reactor Program, 30-S
Advisory Commission on Intergovernment Relations, 72-H
After-school sports leagues, 118-H, 124-H
Agricultural Research Service, 36-S
Agricultural Service Agency, 132-H
Agricultural Stabilization and Conservation Service, 132-H
Agriculture
  farm crop insurance, 114-H
  livestock grazing, 94-H
  minor-use crop pesticides, 140-H
  pesticide safety requirements, 10-S
Agriculture Department
  appropriations, 76-H, 132-H, 35-S, 36-S, 37-S
  homosexual policy, 36-S, 37-S
  homosexual seminars, 36-S
  reorganization, 132-H, 16-S
AIDS
  fines on selling infected blood, 45-S
  research, 45-S
Airborne Self-Protection Jammer, 32-S
Aircraft carriers
  authorizations, 28-S
Airplanes
  C-17 contract dispute, 28-S
  C-17 increase, 60-H
  toilet regulations, 26-S
Airports
  parking privileges, 17-S
Air-traffic controllers, 26-S
Albany, Ga.
  courthouses, 72-H
Alcoholics
  SSI and disability payments, 118-H
Allegheny Portage Railroad, 78-H
Ambassadors
  Brown nomination, 23-S
  Lawrence confirmation, 7-S
  Shearer nomination, 23-S
American Heritage Areas Partnership Program, 132-H, 142-H, 144-H
American Samoa education programs, 14-H
Americans With Disabilities Act
  congressional compliance, 116-H
Amtrak, 74-H
Anti-crime initiatives, 32-H, 42-H
Anti-drug initiatives, 32-H
Appalachian Regional Commission, 50-H
Appropriations. *See also specific departments, agencies, programs, offices*
  legislative branch cuts, 13-S

presidential line-item veto, 98-H
  rescissions, 4-H, 98-H, 8-S
Argus Range, 70-H
Arizona
  Prescott National Forest, 136-H
Army Department. *See also Defense*
  Corps of Engineers Walla Walla, Wash., building, 74-H
  Glosson confirmation for retirement as lieutenant general, 57-H
  Presidio, 78-H, 122-H, 124-H
Army School of the Americas, 58-H
Assault weapons ban, 48-H, 118-H, 124-H, 50-S
ATF. *See Bureau of Alcohol, Tobacco and Firearms*
At-risk youth, 26-H
Attorney general
  enforcement of federal child support laws, 38-S
Authorizations. *See specific departments, agencies, programs, offices*
Aviation product liability lawsuits, 11-S

B

B-2 bomber, 31-S
Bahai community, 36-H
Balanced-budget amendment, 16-H, 20-H, 9-S
Ballistic Missile Defense Organization, 56-H
Ballistic Missile Defense program, 12-S
Baltics
  Russian troops, 33-S
Banking
  community development, 112-H
  interstate, 51-H
  Madison Guaranty Savings and Loan, 24-H, 11-S, 24-S, 25-S
  regulatory relief provisions, 112-H
Banking, Finance and Urban Affairs Committee, 100-H
Banking Committee, Senate
  Whitewater hearings, 24-S, 25-S
Bankruptcy
  Chapter 13 petitions, 17-S
  National Bankruptcy Review Commission, 17-S
  reform, 17-S
Barkett, Rosemary, 16-S
Base closures, 28-S
Berlin
  withdrawal of U.S. troops from, 106-H
Bilingual education program, 24-H
Bilingual teachers, 42-S
Birth control
  condom distribution, 6-S
Black Lung Trust Fund, 56-H
Black Revolutionary War Patriots Memorial, 120-H
Blood
  AIDS-infected, 45-S
Blue Ridge Parkway
  Fisher Peak Mountain Music Center, 78-H
Boating, 130-H

Border crossing fee, 27-S
Border patrol programs, 124-H
Bosnia-Herzegovina
  arms embargo, 68-H, 3-S, 20-S, 31-S, 47-S
  peacekeeping and assistance, 4-H, 8-S, 31-S
Botanic Garden, 64-H
Breyer, Stephen G., 42-S
Brown, Sam W. Jr., 23-S
Budget
  balanced-budget amendments, 16-H, 20-H, 9-S
  baselines, 118-H, 120-H
  capital, 20-H
  current funding, 118-H
  current policy, 118-H
  defense cuts, 16-H, 14-S
  deficit reduction, 34-H
  discretionary cuts, 13-S
  emergency spending procedures, 120-H, 122-H
  entitlement spending trends, 142-H
  House committee funding, 24-H
  investment spending proposals, 14-S
  legislative branch appropriation cuts, 13-S
  line-item veto, 98-H
  mandatory spending cuts, 13-S
  reform, 13-S
  Republican deficit reduction, 12-S
  rescissions, 8-S
  revenue growth limitations, 20-H
  spending levels, 18-H, 48-H, 64-H, 14-S, 20-S
  supplemental appropriations, 7-S, 8-S
Budget act waiver, 50-S, 54-S, 57-S
Budget Reserve Account, 120-H
Budget resolutions, 16-H, 18-H, 34-H, 48-H, 12-S, 13-S, 14-S, 20-S
Bureau of Alcohol, Tobacco and Firearms, 4-H
Bureau of Indian Affairs
  recognition of Little River Band of Ottawa Indians, 112-H
  recognition of Little Traverse Bay Bands of Odawa Indians, 112-H
  recognition of Pokagon Band of Potawatomi Indians, 112-H
Bureau of Land Management, 70-H, 39-S
Business. *See Small Business Administration*
Byron White United States Courthouse, 30-H

C

Cable television, 86-H
California
  desert protection, 54-H, 70-H, 94-H, 96-H, 106-H, 108-H, 138-H, 140-H, 148-H, 16-S, 53-S, 57-S
  Edward J. Schwartz Courthouse, 30-H
  Los Angeles-area earthquake disaster assistance, 2-H, 8-H, 8-S
  redwood forest expansion,

128-H, 130-H
  San Francisco highway reconstruction, 2-H, 8-H, 8-S
  veterans hospitals, 44-S
Campaign finance
  reform, 52-S
  tax checkoff for presidential election fund, 7-S
  voluntary spending caps on congressional campaigns, 52-S, 53-S
Capital Management Services Inc., 24-H, 25-S
Carter, Jimmy, 52-S
Central Intelligence Agency (CIA)
  authorizations, 100-H, 48-S
Chapter I funding formula, 41-S
Charity travel reimbursements, 19-S
Child Nutrition Act, 100-H
Child nutrition programs, 48-S
Child pornography, 40-H
Child support
  enforcement of, 38-S
Children's programs funding, 12-S
China
  democracy training programs, 34-S
  MFN status, 114-H, 116-H, 4-S
China Lake laser facility, 70-H
China Lake Naval Air Warfare Center, 70-H
CIA. *See Central Intelligence Agency*
CIESIN. *See Consortium for International Earth Science Information Network*
Clean Water State Revolving Fund, 44-S
Clinton, Bill
  China MFN executive order, 114-H
  discretionary spending cuts, 13-S
  investment spending proposals, 14-S
  Whitewater hearings, 24-S, 25-S, 27-S
Clinton, Hillary Rodham, 24-S
Coast Guard
  authorizations, 130-H
  regulatory reform, 130-H
Cocaine penalty study, 42-H
COLAs. *See Cost of living adjustments*
Colombia
  military aid, 35-S, 46-S
Colorado
  Byron White United States Courthouse, 30-H
Commemorative Works Act (PL 99-652), 120-H
Commerce Department
  appropriations, 80-H, 82-H, 84-H, 86-H, 116-H, 122-H, 38-S, 39-S, 50-S
  computer data base, 50-H
  environmental export promotion, 36-H
  Fitz-Pegado nomination, 26-S
  insurance anti-redlining disclosure, 100-H, 102-H
Commission on Indian Recognition, 138-H
Communications. *See Telecommunications*
Community development bank-

ing, 112-H
Community Development Block Grants, 4-H, 44-S
Community Development Financial Institutions Fund, 112-H
Community health centers, 86-H, 88-H
Community investment programs, 26-H
Community policing programs, 118-H, 124-H, 50-S
Community Services Block Grant Program, 52-H, 19-S
Community-Based Family Resource Programs, 52-H, 19-S
Competitiveness, 10-S
  authorization reduction, 10-S, 11-S
  economic impact analyses, 10-S
  heroic act penalties or citations, 11-S
  local telephone services and cable television, 86-H
  national bill, 100-H
  Regulatory Flexibility Act, 10-S
  research and development tax credits, 10-S
Condemnations
  of Cuban sinking of tugboat carrying Cubans attempting to emigrate, 142-H
  Interior Department prohibition, 94-H
  of Iranian treatment of Bahai community, 36-H
  of Khalid Abdul Muhammad, 10-H, 5-S
Conference on Disarmament, 66-H
Conference on Security and Cooperation in Europe, 23-S
Confirmations
  Barkett, 16-S
  Fitz-Pegado, 26-S
  Glosson, 57-S
  Kelso, 17-S
  Lawrence, 7-S
  Mauz, 52-S
  Sarokin, 55-S
  Tigert, 55-S
  Yellen, 47-S
Congress
  charity travel reimbursements, 19-S
  gift restrictions, 28-H, 134-H, 18-S, 19-S, 56-S, 57-S
  pay cut, 18-S
Congressional Black Caucus, 18-H
Congressional Budget Office, 45-S
Congressional compliance, 116-H
Consent for surveys, 6-S
Consortium for International Earth Science Information Network (CIESIN), 90-H
Constitution
  balanced-budget amendment, 16-H, 9-S, 20-H
Corinth Battlefield interpretive center, 144-H
Corporation for Public Broadcasting, 88-H, 45-S
Corps of Engineers
  Walla Walla, Wash., building, 74-H
Corpus Christi, Texas
  new courthouses, 72-H
Cost of living adjustments (COLAs)
  for military retirees, 31-S

Counterterrorism, 36-H
County poverty rate formula, 41-S
Court records
  sealing, 29-S
Courthouses
  budget cuts, 132-H
  Byron White United States Courthouse, 30-H
  construction appropriations, 72-H
  Edward J. Schwartz Courthouse, 30-H
  Kennedy Plaza federal courthouse, 74-H
Credit reporting
  agencies, 18-S
  Fair Credit Reporting Act amendments, 18-S
Crime. *See also Law enforcement*
  Russian organized crime, 33-S
Crime Conference Report, 50-S
Crime prevention programs, 42-H, 118-H, 124-H, 50-S
Crime trust fund, 118-H, 124-H, 50-S
Criminal court
  international, 2-S, 3-S
Criminal histories
  access to, 40-H
Cristiani, Alfredo, 142-H
Cuba
  condemnation of sinking of tugboat carrying Cubans trying to emigrate, 142-H
Customs Service
  border crossing fee, 27-S
  international sporting event duty suspension, 30-H
CVN-76 aircraft carrier, 28-S
Czech Republic
  NATO inclusion, 34-S

D

D-5 missiles. *See Trident II missiles*
DARE. *See Drug Abuse Resistance Education Program*
Davis-Bacon Act, 42-S
Death penalty, 26-H, 30-H, 42-H, 118-H, 50-S
  aggravating factors, 34-H
  for drug kingpins, 32-H
  instructions, 34-H
  statistics, 40-H, 76-H, 39-S
Death row habeas corpus appeals, 26-H, 30-H, 36-H
Death Valley national park, 54-H, 108-H, 138-H, 140-H, 148-H, 16-S, 53-S, 57-S
  livestock grazing, 94-H
Defense. *See also Army Department; Military; Navy*
  B-2 bomber, 31-S
  Ballistic Missile Defense Organization, 56-H
  burden-sharing European troop reduction, 58-H
  C-17 aircraft authorizations, 60-H
  C-17 contract dispute, 28-S
  CVN-76 aircraft carrier, 28-S
  spending cuts, 16-H, 34-H, 14-S
  Trident II (D-5) missiles, 58-H, 46-S
  U.S. troops under U.N. control, 68-H
Defense Department
  appropriations, 58-H, 92-H, 126-H, 134-H, 35-S, 45-S,

46-S, 47-S
  authorizations, 54-H, 56-H, 58-H, 60-H, 66-H, 68-H, 106-H, 122-H, 28-S, 31-S, 32-S, 35-S, 51-S
  Perry nomination, 5-S
Defense Intelligence Agency
  authorizations, 100-H, 48-S
Deficit. *See Budget*
Democracy training programs, 34-H
Denver, CO
  Byron White United States Courthouse, 30-H
Desert protection, 54-H, 70-H, 94-H, 96-H, 100-H, 108-H, 138-H, 140-H, 148-H, 16-S, 53-S, 57-S
Disability payments, 118-H
Disaster assistance
  Los Angeles-area earthquake, 2-H, 8-H, 8-S
  National Disaster Relief Trust Fund, 8-S
  SBA loan program, 122-H
  supplemental appropriations, 2-H, 4-H, 8-H, 7-S, 8-S
  tax checkoff, 7-S
District of Columbia
  appropriations, 90-H, 94-H, 96-H, 108-H, 37-S, 52-S, 54-S
  domestic partners ordinance, 94-H
  memorial construction permits, 120-H
Domestic partners ordinance, 94-H
Domestic violence
  access to criminal histories in cases of, 40-H
Domestic workers
  Social Security for, 52-H
Drinking water regulations, 21-S
Drug Abuse Resistance Education program (DARE), 14-H
Drug addicts
  SSI and disability payments, 118-H
Drug enforcement
  cocaine penalty study, 42-H
  death penalty for kingpins, 32-H
  international narcotics control, 35-S
  rural initiatives, 32-H
  state and local funds, 12-S
  three-time drug offenders, 38-H
  White House drug testing program, 27-S
Drug treatment programs, 26-H, 80-H
Drug-Free Schools and Communities program, 14-H
Dulles International Airport
  parking privileges, 17-S

E

Earthquakes
  Los Angeles-area assistance, 2-H, 8-H, 8-S
East Europe
  NATO inclusion, 34-S
East Mojave Scenic Area, 94-H
East Timor, 30-S
Economic Development Administration, 50-H, 82-H
Economic impact analyses, 10-S
Education. *See also Training*
  bilingual, 24-H, 86-H, 42-S
  college loan default exemptions, 30-H
  condom distribution in schools,

6-S
  consent for surveys, 6-S
  county poverty rate formula, 41-S
  demonstration projects, 5-S, 6-S, 40-S
  distribution of materials on school grounds, 28-H
  Drug-Free Schools and Communities program, 14-H
  early release requirement, 42-H
  Elementary and Secondary Education Act reauthorization, 28-H, 136-H, 40-S, 43-S, 55-S
  elementary and secondary standards, 26-H
  Emergency Immigrant Education Act, 45-S
  funding for reforms, 7-S, 12-S, 15-S
  GLOBE (Global Learning and Observation to Benefit the Environment) Program, 82-H
  grants, 26-H, 6-S
  Hawaiian programs, 14-H, 86-H
  Head Start, 19-S
  higher education programs, 86-H
  home schooling, 10-H
  for illegal aliens, 12-H
  immigrant, 86-H
  moment of silence, 6-S
  national goals, 26-H
  new programs, 42-S
  opportunity-to-learn standards, 10-H, 28-H, 5-S
  Perkins Vocational and Applied Technology Education Act, 42-S
  programs, 80-H
  reauthorizations, 128-H
  scholarships to law enforcement personnel, 42-H
  school choice, 6-2, 40-S
  school disciplinary policy, 41-S
  school prayer, 10-H, 24-H, 26-H, 128-H, 136-H, 5-S, 40-S
  sex, 24-H
  single-sex schooling, 42-S
  special education programs, 12-S
  territorial programs, 14-H
  Title I money for Puerto Rico, 12-H
  transition projects, 12-H
  vocational schools, 88-H
Education Department
  appropriations, 130-H, 45-S, 53-S
  authorizations, 28-H, 88-H, 40-S, 41-S, 42-S, 43-S
Edward J. Schwartz Courthouse, 30-H
EEOC. *See Equal Employment Opportunity Commission*
El Salvador
  expression of admiration for Cristiani's peace in, 142-H
Electronic records, 7-S
  Commerce computer data base, 50-H
Elementary and Secondary Education Act
  reauthorization, 28-H, 136-H, 40-S, 43-S, 55-S
Ellis Island, 40-S
Employment. *See also Federal employment; Workers' compensation*
  job programs, 80-H
  job training programs, 118-H
  minimum staffing requirements,

27-S
striker replacement, 33-S
Summer Youth Employment and Training Program, 6-S
transition from school to workplace program, 7-S
Energy and Commerce Committee, 100-H
Energy and water
Advanced Liquid Metal Reactor Program, 30-S
appropriations, 70-H, 110-H, 116-H, 30-S
China Lake laser facility, 70-H
deep-water oil leases, 21-S
fossil energy research, 80-H, 40-S
fusion reactors, 30-S
Gas Turbine-Modular Helium Reactor, 70-H
hydrogen fusion research, 124-H
renewable energy research, 30-S
renewable oxygenates rule for reformulated gasoline, 43-S
Tokamak Physics Experiment, 30-S
Energy Department
Fossil Energy Research and Development account, 40-S
Entitlements
spending control, 104-H
spending trends, 142-H
Environment
California desert protection, 94-H, 106-H, 108-H, 138-H, 140-H, 148-H, 16-S, 53-S, 57-S
California redwood forest expansion, 128-H, 130-H
GLOBE (Global Learning and Observation to Benefit the Environment) Program, 82-H
Rio Puerco watershed, 142-H, 144-H
wetlands conservation act amendments, 126-H
Environmental export promotion, 36-H
Environmental Protection Agency
appropriations, 53-S
Cabinet-level status, 2-H
imported reformulated gasoline regulations, 126-H
minor-use crop pesticides, 140-H
radon gas disclosure requirements, 108-H
renewable oxygenates rule for reformulated gasoline, 43-S
safe drinking water regulations, 21-S
wastewater treatment projects, 21-S
Environmental technology, 19-S
risk assessment, 106-H
Equal Employment Opportunity Commission (EEOC)
religious guidelines, 84-H, 26-S
Ethanol mandate, 43-S
Europe
burden-sharing troop reduction, 58-H
Executive Office of the President
appropriations, 68-H, 70-H, 72-H, 74-H, 130-H, 132-H, 28-S
electronic records, 7-S
Export Administration Act
extension, 142-H
reauthorization, 98-H

F

Fair Credit Reporting Act amendments, 18-S
Fair Labor Standards Act
congressional compliance, 116-H
Family Leave Act
congressional compliance, 116-H
Family planning services, 28-H
condom distribution, 6-S
Farm crop insurance, 114-H
Farmers
assistance to, 76-H
Farmers Home Administration, 106-H, 132-H
FASB. *See Financial Accounting Standards Board*
FDIC. *See Federal Deposit Insurance Corporation*
Federal Aviation Administration
air-traffic controllers, 26-S
Federal Black Lung Advisory Committee, 56-H
Federal Bureau of Investigations (FBI)
funding, 33-S
Federal courthouses. *See also Courthouses*
budget cuts, 132-H
Federal Crop Insurance Corporation, 132-H
Federal Deposit Insurance Corporation (FDIC)
Affordable Housing Program, 92-H
FSLIC Resolution Fund, 92-H
Tigert confirmation, 55-S
Federal Drug Control Programs, 70-H, 72-H
Federal Election Commission, 72-H
Federal Emergency Management Agency
Food and Shelter Program, 106-H
Federal employment. *See also Employment*
Davis-Bacon Act, 42-S
golf helicopter trips, 72-H
House salary and expense cuts, 64-H
incentives for voluntary retirements or resignations, 8-H, 26-H, 13-S
re-employment procedures, 144-H
White House salaries and expense accounts, 72-H
work force reduction, 8-H, 44-H, 136-H
Federal Highway Administration
highway demonstration projects, 8-S
Federal Housing Administration, 76-H
Federal nutrition programs
reauthorization, 100-H
Federal procurement overhaul, 128-H
Federal programs. *See also specific programs*
payments to people not lawfully present, 96-H
Federal Railroad Administration, 114-H
Federal regulations, 50-H
airplane toilets, 26-S
banking relief provisions, 112-H
Coast Guard reform, 130-H
drinking water, 21-S
economic impact analyses,

10-S
imported reformulated gasoline, 126-H
Federal Reserve System
Yellen confirmation, 47-S
Financial Accounting Standards Board (FASB), 18-S
Finland
Shearer nomination as ambassador to, 23-S
Firefighters, 39-S
Fish and Wildlife Service
land acquisitions, 39-S
Fisher Peak Mountain Music Center, 78-H
Fiske, Robert B. Jr., 76-H, 26-S
Fitz-Pegado, Lauri, 26-S
Flood assistance, 2-H, 8-H, 8-S
Flood insurance reform, 46-H
Food and Drug Administration
appropriations, 76-H, 132-H
Food stamps
demonstration initiatives, 36-H
Foreign operations. *See also Peacekeeping; Trade*
aid to former Soviet republics, 62-H
appropriations, 60-H, 62-H, 112-H, 29-S, 30-S, 46-S
authorization, 35-S
Bosnia arms embargo, 68-H, 3-S, 20-S, 31-S, 47-S
funding, 34-S, 35-S
in Haiti, 60-H, 68-H, 146-H, 148-H, 29-S, 43-S, 45-S, 52-S, 56-S
NATO expansion, 3-S
population development assistance, 62-H
Russian Baltic troops, 33-S
in Somalia, 46-S
South African Assistance Program, 62-H
withdrawal from Berlin, 106-H
Forest Service
California redwood forest expansion, 128-H, 130-H
land acquisitions, 136-H, 39-S
multiple use of released lands, 54-H
Prescott National Forest, 136-H
Former Soviet Union
aid to, 62-H
collateral, 4-S
Fossil energy research, 80-H, 40-S
Foster, Vincent W., 27-S
FSLIC Resolution Fund, 92-H
Fuel taxes, 27-S

G

Gas Turbine-Modular Helium Reactor, 70-H
Gasoline
imported reformulated regulations, 126-H
renewable oxygenates rule, 43-S
GATT. *See General Agreement on Tariffs and Trade*
Gays. *See Homosexuality*
General Accounting Office
budget cuts, 64-H
General Agreement on Tariffs and Trade (GATT)
budget waiver, 57-S
implementation, 144-H, 150-H, 57-S
tobacco tariffs, 36-S
Germany
congratulations on reunification, 106-H

military participation, 4-S
Global Environmental Facility, 35-S
GLOBE (Global Learning and Observation to Benefit the Environment) Program, 82-H
Glosson, Buster C., 57-S
Golan Heights
peacekeeping operations, 32-S
Golden Gate National Recreation Area Act (PL 92-589), 122-H
Golf helicopter trips, 72-H
Goodwill Games, 46-S
Gore, Al, 43-S
Gould, William B. IV, 9-S
Government National Mortgage Association, 76-H
Government Reform and Savings bills, 4-H
Grass-roots lobbying
reporting and registration requirements, 134-H
Great Falls Historic District, 30-H
Green technologies, 19-S
Guam education programs, 14-H
Gun control
assault weapons ban, 48-H, 118-H, 124-H, 50-S

H

Habeas corpus appeals, 26-H, 30-H, 36-H
Haiti
congressional commission, 34-S
peacekeeping and assistance, 4-H, 60-H, 68-H, 128-H, 8-S
U.S. troops in, 146-H, 148-H, 29-S, 43-S, 45-S, 52-S, 56-S
Hard-rock mining patents, 126-H
Hawaii
education programs, 14-H, 86-H
veterans hospitals, 44-S
Head Start, 52-H, 19-S
Health and Human Services Department (HHS)
appropriations, 86-H, 88-H, 130-H, 45-S, 53-S
authorizations, 88-H
Office of Assistant Secretary for Rural Health, 49-S
Health care. *See also Safety*
abortion, 20-S, 33-S
abortion clinics, 22-H, 48-H, 20-S, 44-S
child preventive services, 49-S
community health centers, 88-H
fines on selling AIDS-infected blood, 45-S
public health programs, 150-H
reform, 14-S, 45-S
rural, 49-S
rural health outreach grants, 86-H, 88-H
Sunshine Act, 49-S
U.S.-Mexico Border Health Commission, 142-H, 144-H
veterans hospitals, 44-H, 44-S
Health insurance
congressional compliance, 116-H
standard benefits package fines, 49-S
Helium
Gas Turbine-Modular Helium Reactor, 70-H
HHS. *See Health and Human Services Department*
Higher education programs, 86-H
High-speed rail development,

120-H
Highway projects, 37-S
   demonstration, 8-S
   Indianapolis-Houston corridor,
      60-H
   National Highway System, 60-H
   San Francisco reconstruction,
      2-H, 8-H, 8-S
HIV testing, 124-H, 50-S
Home schooling, 10-H
Homosexuality, 42-S, 43-S
   Agriculture Department policy,
      36-S, 37-S
   distribution of material that sup-
      ports or encourages, 28-H
   domestic partners ordinance,
      94-H
   seminars, 36-S
**House Administration
   Committee,** 68-H
**House Appropriations
   Committee,** 27-S
**House Banking, Finance and
   Urban Affairs Committee,** 100-H
House committee funding, 24-H
   See also specific committees
**House Journal approval (proce-
   dural motions),** 2-H, 6-H, 10-H,
   12-H, 14-H, 18-H, 26-H, 30-H, 32-H,
   36-H, 38-H, 42-H, 46-H, 48-H,
   54-H, 64-H, 94-H, 102-H, 112-H,
   114-H, 118-H, 120-H, 122-H, 124-H,
   126-H, 134-H, 136-H, 150-H
House of Representatives
   franking cut, 64-H
   motion to adjourn (procedural
      motion), 140-H
   office buildings, 64-H
   salary and expense cuts, 64-H
House Post Office
   documents, 68-H
   investigation, 12-H
Housing
   assisted, 90-H
   pension fund investment, 44-S
   supplemental appropriations,
      76-H
   voucher program, 90-H
**Housing and Urban Development
   Department (HUD)**
   appropriations, 90-H, 92-H,
      126-H, 43-S, 44-S, 53-S
   authorizations, 92-H, 106-H
   insurance anti-redlining disclo-
      sure jurisdiction, 100-H
   multifamily housing property
      disposal, 26-H
   special purpose grants, 44-S
   special purpose projects, 126-H
HUD. *See Housing and Urban
   Development Department*
Human rights
   to Bahai community, 36-H
   in China, 114-H
Hungary
   NATO inclusion, 34-S
Hunting
   East Mojave Scenic Area
      exception, 94-H
Hydrogen fusion research, 124-H

I

Immigration
   benefits to illegal aliens, 106-H,
      14-S
   Cuban sinking of tugboat carry-
      ing Cubans attempting to emi-
      grate, 142-H
   education for illegal aliens, 12-H
   education for immigrants, 12-H,
      86-H

Emergency Immigrant
   Education Act, 45-S
incarceration of illegal aliens,
   40-H, 84-H, 39-S
Russian immigrants, 4-S
Independent counsel, 6-H, 8-H,
   76-H
Indian law corrections, 36-H
Indian tribes
   federal recognition, 138-H
Indian Trust Fund, 138-H
Indianapolis-Houston highway,
   60-H
**Individuals with Disabilities
   Education Act,** 6-S, 41-S
Indonesia
   East Timor, 30-S
Information infrastructure grants,
   82-H
Insurance. *See also Health insur-
   ance*
   anti-redlining disclosure, 100-H,
      102-H
   farm crop, 114-H
   Federal Crop Insurance
      Corporation, 132-H
   flood, 46-H
Intelligence
   authorizations, 100-H, 48-S
   budget disclosure, 100-H
Interior Department
   American Heritage Areas
      Partnership Program, 132-H,
      142-H, 144-H
   appropriations, 76-H, 78-H, 80-H,
      126-H, 39-S, 40-S, 53-S
   condemnation prohibition, 94-H
   National Park System planning,
      132-H
   national park system site fees,
      142-H, 144-H
   Office of Special Trustee, 138-H
   report on ecological damage to
      Rio Puerco watershed, 142-H,
      144-H
Internal Revenue Service (IRS)
   authorizations, 130-H
   compliance initiative, 27-S
   user fees cap, 132-H
International criminal court, 2-S,
   3-S
**International Criminal
   Investigative Training
   Assistance Program,** 33-S
**International Development
   Association,** 29-S, 35-S
**International sporting event duty
   suspension,** 30-H
**Interstate Commerce
   Commission,** 74-H
Iran
   condemnation of treatment of
      Bahai community, 36-H
Iraq
   peacekeeping and humanitarian
      assistance, 4-H, 8-S
Iraqi assets disbursement, 44-H
Iraqi prisoners of war
   resettlement, 84-H
IRS. *See Internal Revenue Service*
Israeli boycott, 4-S

J

**James A. Farley Post Office, New
   York City (NY),** 37-S
Japan
   burden-sharing agreement, 56-H
   missing plutonium, 66-H
Job programs, 80-H
Job training programs, 118-H,
   124-H

**Joint Committee on the
   Reorganization of Congress,**
   54-S
Joint committees. *See also specific committees*
   budget cuts, 64-H
Joshua Tree national park, 54-H,
   108-H, 138-H, 140-H, 148-H, 16-S,
   53-S, 57-S
Judiciary appropriations, 86-H,
   116-H, 122-H
Justice Department
   Antitrust Division appropria-
      tions, 82-H
   appropriations, 80-H, 82-H, 84-H,
      86-H, 116-H, 122-H, 38-S, 39-S,
      50-S
   general administration account,
      82-H

K

Kelso, Frank B. II, 17-S
**Kennedy Plaza federal court-
   house,** 74-H

L

Labor Department
   appropriations, 86-H, 88-H,
      130-H, 45-S, 53-S
   authorizations, 88-H
   standard benefits package
      fines, 49-S
Land acquisition, 94-H, 126-H,
   136-H, 39-S
   American Heritage Areas
      Partnership Program, 142-H,
      144-H
   appraisal, 96-H
   California redwood forest
      expansion, 128-H, 130-H
   conveyance, 35-S
   exchanges, 94-H
   payments in lieu of taxes, 146-H,
      16-S
   use of released lands, 54-H
Law enforcement. *See also Drug
   enforcement*
   access to criminal histories,
      40-H
   assault weapons ban, 118-H,
      124-H, 50-S
   child pornography, 40-H
   community notification of sex
      offenders, 96-H, 124-H, 50-S
   community policing programs,
      118-H, 124-H, 50-S
   converting military bases to
      prisons, 32-H
   death penalty, 26-H, 30-H, 42-H,
      118-H, 50-S
   death penalty aggravating fac-
      tors, 34-H
   death penalty for drug kingpins,
      32-H
   death penalty instructions, 34-H
   death penalty statistics, 39-S
   death row habeas corpus
      appeals, 26-H, 30-H, 36-H
   early release education require-
      ment, 42-H
   en bloc amendment, 40-H
   of federal child support laws,
      38-S
   grant program to prevent and
      prosecute young violent
      offenders, 32-H
   HIV testing in rape trials, 124-H,
      50-S
   illegally seized evidence in

criminal trials, 34-H
incarceration of illegal aliens,
   40-H, 84-H, 39-S
international criminal court, 2-S,
   3-S
International Criminal
   Investigative Training
   Assistance Program, 33-S
life in prison penalty, 32-H
Made in America labels, 40-H
mandatory prison terms, 102-H,
   22-S, 43-S
omnibus crime legislation, 26-H,
   102-H, 118-H, 124-H, 19-S,
   22-S, 50-S
police officers, 26-H, 42-H,
   118-H, 50-S
prior sex offenses in federal
   trials, 92-H, 124-H
prison construction authorizations, 38-H, 78-H
prison construction programs,
   44-H, 118-H, 124-H
prisons, 30-H, 50-S
private security officers, 42-H
product liability lawsuits, 11-S,
   29-S
racial justice, 40-H, 19-S
rural initiatives, 32-H
scholarships to personnel, 42-H
state comprehensive correctional plans, 38-H
three-time drug offenders, 38-H
three-time violent offenders,
   26-H, 30-H, 42-H, 124-H, 50-S
truth in sentencing, 38-H, 44-H,
   22-S
vehicles in wilderness areas,
   70-H
violence against truck drivers,
   32-H
**Law School Clinical Experience
   Program,** 86-H
Lawrence, M. Larry, 7-S
Lawsuits. *See Product liability lawsuits*
Lead exposure, 23-S
Legal Services Corporation, 4-H,
   38-S
**Legislative branch appropria-
   tions,** 64-H, 31-S
Libraries
   public services, 86-H
Lifestyle
   domestic partners ordinance,
      94-H
Line-item veto, 98-H
**Little River Band of Ottawa
   Indians,** 112-H
**Little Traverse Bay Bands of
   Odawa Indians,** 112-H
Lobbying
   gift restrictions, 28-H, 134-H,
      18-S, 19-S, 56-S, 57-S
   political contributions, 18-S
   reporting and registration
      requirements, 28-H, 134-H,
      56-S, 57-S
Local governments
   payments in lieu of taxes,
      146-H, 150-H, 16-S
Local Partnership Act, 80-H
Local telephone services
   promoting competition in, 86-H
Los Angeles-area earthquake
   disaster assistance, 2-H, 8-H, 8-S
**Lowell National Historical Park
   Commission,** 110-H, 132-H
**Low-Income Home Energy
   Assistance Program,** 52-H, 19-S
Low-income housing
   pension fund investment, 44-S

M

Made in America labels, 40-H
Madison Guaranty Savings and Loan, 24-H, 11-S, 24-S, 25-S
Madrid Protocol, 136-H
Mandates
    unfunded, 56-S
Marinas
    recreational diesel fuel taxes, 27-S
Maritime Administration
    reauthorization, 110-H
Maritime affairs
    tonnage duties, 110-H
    towing vessel safety, 130-H
Market Promotion Program, 35-S
Martin Luther King Jr. Federal Holiday Commission, 23-S
Mauz, Henry H. Jr., 52-S
McDonnell Douglas Corp.
    C-17 contract dispute, 28-S
McDougal, Susan, 25-S
Memorials
    construction permits, 120-H
    Raoul Wallenberg bust, 36-H
Merchant Marine and Fisheries Committee, 138-H, 140-H
Mexican border
    border crossing fee, 27-S
    wastewater treatment projects, 21-S
MIAs
    Vietnam embargo, 44-H
Midnight sports programs, 26-H
Midwest flood assistance, 2-H, 8-H, 8-S
Military. see also Defense
    construction appropriations, 58-H, 35-S, 46-S
    medical conditions separation requirement, 66-H
    Operation Uphold Democracy, 148-H
    recruiting, 46-H, 58-H
    satellite communications, 46-S
    sexual misconduct, 32-S
    Team Spirit exercises, 66-H
    withdrawal of U.S. troops from Berlin, 106-H
Military bases
    closures, 58-H, 28-S
    converting to prisons, 32-H
Military retirements
    COLAs for retirees, 31-S
    Glosson confirmation, 57-S
    incentives for, 13-S
    Kelso confirmation, 17-S
    Mauz confirmation, 52-S
Military Selective Service Act, 58-H
Miners
    Black Lung Trust Fund, 56-H
    Federal Black Lung Advisory Committee, 56-H
Mining
    hard-rock patents, 126-H
Mining Law, 126-H
Minorities
    public health programs for, 150-H
Missiles
    Ballistic Missile Defense Organization, 56-H
    Navy anti-missile system, 46-S
    Trident II (D-5), 58-H, 46-S
Mississippi
    Corinth Battlefield interpretive center, 144-H
Mojave national park, 54-H, 108-H, 138-H, 140-H, 148-H, 16-S, 53-S, 57-S
    land acquisition, 94-H
    livestock grazing, 94-H

Montana Rockies study, 54-H
Montana wilderness, 54-H
Motor vehicle records disclosure, 40-H
Motor voter registration, 48-S
Muhammad, Khalid Abdul, 10-H, 5-S
Multifamily housing property disposal, 26-H

N

Narcotics. See also Drug enforcement
    international control, 35-S
NASA. See National Aeronautics and Space Administration
National Aeronautics and Space Administration (NASA)
    appropriations, 90-H, 53-S
    procurement budget, 43-S
National Bankruptcy Review Commission, 17-S
National Biological Survey, 76-H
National competitiveness bill, 100-H
National Disaster Relief Trust Fund, 8-S
National education goals, 26-H
National Endowment for Democracy, 84-H, 39-S
    appropriations, 2-S
National Endowment for the Arts (NEA), 39-S
    appropriations, 78-H, 80-H
National Highway System, 60-H
National Labor Relations Board (NLRB), 9-S
National Oceanic and Atmospheric Administration
    appropriations, 82-H
National Park Service, 106-H, 132-H
    concession contracts, 108-H
    construction cuts, 78-H
    Ellis Island, 40-S
    entrepreneurial management reform, 142-H, 144-H
    land acquisitions, 39-S
    Presidio national park, 78-H, 124-H
    visitors' facilities, 108-H
National Park System, 132-H
National parks
    Death Valley, 94-H, 108-H, 138-H, 140-H, 148-H, 16-S, 53-S, 57-S
    Joshua Tree national park, 54-H, 108-H, 138-H, 140-H, 148-H, 16-S, 53-S, 57-S
    land exchanges and monetary credits, 94-H
    Mojave national park, 54-H, 94-H, 108-H, 138-H, 140-H, 148-H, 16-S, 53-S, 57-S
    Presidio, 78-H, 122-H, 124-H
    service concessions, 12-S
National Peace Garden, 120-H
National Reconnaissance Office Headquarters Building, 48-S
National School Lunch Act, 100-H
National Science Foundation
    authorizations, 46-H
National Security Agency
    authorizations, 100-H, 48-S
National Telecommunications and Information Administration, 82-H
National Voter Registration Act (PL 103-31), 48-S
Native Americans. See under Indian
Native Hawaiian Education

Program, 86-H
NATO. See North Atlantic Treaty Organization
Natural gas leases
    royalty suspension, 21-S
Naval Reserve Center, Seattle (WA), 35-S
Navy
    anti-missile system, 46-S
    China Lake Naval Air Warfare Center, 70-H
    Kelso confirmation for retirement star, 17-S
    Mauz confirmation for retirement at rank of four stars, 52-S
    Trident II (D-5) missiles, 58-H, 46-S
NEA. See National Endowment for the Arts
New Jersey
    Great Falls Historic District, 30-H
New Mexico
    report on ecological damage to Rio Puerco watershed, 142-H, 144-H
New York City, NY
    lower east side tenement historical site, 110-H
NLRB. See National Labor Relations Board
Nominations
    Breyer, 42-S
    Brown, 23-S
    Gould, 9-S
    Perry, 5-S
    Shearer, 23-S
    Talbott, 9-S
North American Wetlands Act (PL 101-233)
    reauthorization, 126-H
North Atlantic Treaty Organization (NATO)
    Bosnia arms embargo, 68-H
    burden-sharing agreements, 56-H
    expansion, 3-S, 34-S
    presidential report clarifying standards and obligations for admission, 34-S
North Korea, 26-S, 35-S
    nuclear inspections, 66-H
Nuclear power
    missing Japanese plutonium, 66-H
    North Korea inspections, 66-H
    Nunn-Lugar cooperative threat reduction program, 35-S
    test ban treaty, 66-H
    U.S. moratorium on testing, 66-H
Nunn-Lugar cooperative threat reduction program, 35-S
Nutrition programs
    reauthorization, 100-H

O

Obscene materials
    distribution on school grounds, 28-H
Occupational Safety and Health Act
    congressional compliance, 116-H
Odawa Indians
    Little Traverse Bay Bands, 112-H
Office building construction
    budget cuts, 132-H
Office of Assistant Secretary for Rural Health, 49-S
Office of Counterterrorism, 36-H
Office of Management and Budget (OMB)
    entitlement spending targets,

104-H
Office of National Drug Control Policy, 70-H, 72-H
Office of Science and Technology Policy
    risk assessment, 106-H
Office of Special Trustee, 138-H
Office of Technology Assessment
    budget cuts, 64-H
Office of the White House
    golf helicopter trip, 72-H
Office of Thrift Supervision
    Whitewater hearings, 25-S
Office of Women's Business Ownership, 128-H
Olympics, 46-S
Omnibus crime legislation, 26-H, 30-H, 32-H, 34-H, 36-H, 38-H, 40-H, 42-H, 44-H, 76-H, 78-H, 80-H, 92-H, 96-H, 102-H, 118-H, 124-H, 19-S, 22-S, 50-S
O'Neill, Thomas P. Jr., 40-H
O'Neill Year, 40-H
Operation Uphold Democracy, 148-H
Organization of American States
    assistance to Haiti, 60-H, 68-H
Ottawa Indians
    Little River Band, 112-H

P, Q

PACs. See Political action committees
Passport fraud, 32-H
Patent and Trademark Office
    authorizations, 136-H
Patents
    hard-rock mining, 126-H
Paterson, NJ
    Great Falls Historic District, 30-H
Peacekeeping
    in Bosnia, 4-H, 8-S, 31-S
    commendation to Carter, 52-S
    expression of admiration for Cristiani's contributions, 142-H
    funds, 4-H, 8-S
    in Golan Heights, 32-S
    in Haiti, 4-H, 60-H, 68-H, 128-H, 8-S
    in Somalia, 4-H, 8-S
    U.N. costs, 60-H, 84-H
Pedophilia-endorsing organizations
    U.N. recognition of, 2-S
Pell grants, 40-H, 42-H
Pennsylvania
    Allegheny Portage Railroad, 78-H
Pensacola, Fla.
    abortion clinic attack, 44-S
Pension fund housing investment, 44-S
Perkins Vocational and Applied Technology Education Act, 42-S
Perrin Properties, 136-H
Perry, William J., 5-S
Persian Gulf War
    disbursement of Iraqi assets frozen during, 44-H
Personnel files, 8-S
Pesticides
    minor-use, 140-H
    safety requirements, 10-S
Petroleum marketing practices, 140-H
Physics
    Tokamak Physics Experiment, 30-S
Plutonium

missing Japanese, 66-H
Pokagon Band of Potawatomi Indians, 112-H
Poland
NATO inclusion, 34-S
Police corps program, 42-H
Police officers, 26-H, 118-H, 124-H, 50-S
community programs, 118-H, 124-H, 50-S
grants for, 30-H, 42-H
Political action committees
political contributions from, 18-S
Population control programs, 33-S
Population development, 62-H
Pornography
child, 40-H
Postal Service
appropriations, 68-H, 70-H, 72-H, 74-H, 130-H, 132-H, 27-S, 28-S
re-employment procedures, 144-H
Potawatomi Indians
Pokagon Band, 112-H
POWs. *See Prisoners of War*
Prescott National Forest, 136-H
President
line-item veto, 98-H
report clarifying standards and obligations for admission to NATO, 34-S
rescissions, 98-H
Presidential elections
tax checkoff for presidential election fund, 7-S
Presidio national park, 78-H, 122-H, 124-H
Prisoners
early release education requirement, 42-H
Pell grants, 40-H, 42-H
rights to sue, 40-H
strength-building programs, 40-H
Prisoners of war
Iraqi resettlement, 84-H
Vietnam embargo, 44-H
Prisons, 50-S
construction authorizations, 38-H, 78-H
construction programs, 44-H, 118-H, 124-H
converting military bases to, 32-H
funding, 30-H
Private security officers, 42-H
Procedural motions
to adjourn, 140-H
attendance of senators, 2-S, 15-S, 24-S, 29-S, 39-S, 40-S, 48-S, 51-S, 55-S
House Journal approval, 2-H, 6-H, 10-H, 12-H, 14-H, 18-H, 26-H, 30-H, 32-H, 36-H, 38-H, 42-H, 46-H, 48-H, 54-H, 64-H, 94-H, 102-H, 112-H, 114-H, 118-H, 120-H, 122-H, 124-H, 126-H, 134-H, 136-H, 150-H
Procurement overhaul, 128-H
Product liability lawsuits
aviation, 11-S
standards for, 29-S
Providence, RI
Kennedy Plaza federal courthouse, 74-H
Public broadcasting
appropriations, 82-H
Public health programs, 150-H
Public Law 92-589. *See Golden Gate National Recreation Area Act*

Public Law 96-354. *See Regulatory Flexibility Act*
Public Law 99-652. *See Commemorative Works Act*
Public Law 100-77. *See Stewart B. McKinney Homeless Assistance Act*
Public Law 101-233. *See North American Wetlands Act*
Public Law 103-31. *See National Voter Registration Act*
Public library services, 86-H
Public safety programs, 124-H
Public works projects
Davis-Bacon Act, 42-S
Puerto Rico
Title I money for, 12-H

R

Racial justice, 40-H, 76-H, 19-S
Racial Justice Act, 43-S
Radio Free Asia, 84-H
Radon gas disclosure requirements, 108-H
Rail transportation
Amtrak, 74-H
high-speed rail development, 120-H
Rape trials
HIV testing in, 124-H, 50-S
Recreation. *See Sports and recreation*
Regional Bell telephone companies
restrictions on, 86-H
Regional Development Task Force, 50-H
Regulations, 50-H
airplane toilets, 26-S
banking relief provisions, 112-H
Coast Guard reform, 130-H
drinking water, 21-S
economic impact analyses, 10-S
imported reformulated gasoline, 126-H
Regulatory Flexibility Act (PL 96-354), 100-H, 10-S
Religion
access to places of worship, 22-H
Bahai community emancipation, 36-H
EEOC guidelines, 84-H
moment of silence, 6-S
school prayer, 10-H, 24-H, 26-H, 128-H, 136-H, 5-S
Reproductive services, 28-H
Resignations
incentives for, 8-H, 26-H, 13-S
Resolution Trust Corporation
Office of the Inspector General, 92-H
statute of limitations, 8-H, 7-S
Whitewater hearings, 24-S, 25-S
Retirees
COLAs for, 31-S
Retirements
Glosson confirmation, 57-S
incentives for, 8-H, 26-H, 13-S
Kelso confirmation, 17-S
Mauz confirmation, 52-S
Rio Puerco watershed
ecological damage report, 142-H, 144-H
Rural anti-crime and anti-drug initiatives, 32-H
Rural development appropriations, 76-H, 132-H
Rural health outreach grants, 86-H, 88-H
Russia

aid to, 62-H
Baltic troops, 33-S
criminal justice training, 33-S
immigrants from, 4-S
nuclear weapons, 35-S
Nunn-Lugar cooperative threat reduction program, 35-S
organized crime, 33-S

S

Safe Water Drinking Act, 21-S
reauthorization, 22-S
Safety
pesticide requirements, 10-S
private security officers, 42-H
public programs, 124-H
recreational boating improvements, 130-H
towing vessel, 130-H
San Diego, CA
Edward J. Schwartz Courthouse, 30-H
San Francisco, CA
highway reconstruction, 2-H, 8-H, 8-S
Presidio management, 122-H, 124-H
Sarokin, H. Lee, 55-S
Satellite communications
MILSTAR program, 46-S
SBA. *See Small Business Administration*
Scholarships
to law enforcement personnel, 42-H
School choice programs, 28-H, 6-S, 40-S
School prayer, 10-H, 24-H, 26-H, 128-H, 136-H, 5-S, 40-S
School vouchers, 40-S
Schools. *See also Education*
competitive grants for, 26-H
construction, 28-H
disciplinary policy, 41-S
distribution of homosexual materials on school grounds, 28-H
distribution of obscene materials on school grounds, 28-H
local control of violence in, 41-S
moment of silence in, 6-S
single-sex, 42-S
vocational, 88-H
School-to-work grant programs
authorizations, 38-H
Sculpture
Raoul Wallenberg bust, 36-H
Seattle, WA
land conveyance, 35-S
Section 8 existing housing certificate program, 90-H
Security assistance
prohibition of, 4-S
Security officers
private, 42-H
Selective Service System, 32-S
Senate attendance (procedural motions), 2-S, 15-S, 24-S, 29-S, 39-S, 40-S, 48-S, 51-S, 55-S
Senate Banking Committee
Whitewater hearings, 24-S, 25-S
Senior Citizens Against Marketing Scams Act, 22-S
Sex education programs, 24-H
condom distribution, 6-S
Sex offenders
community notification of, 96-H, 124-H, 50-S
Sexual activity, 42-S
Sexual misconduct
in military, 32-S

Shearer, Derek, 23-S
Six Rivers National Forest, 128-H, 130-H
Small Business Administration
loan program for disaster victims, 122-H
Office of Women's Business Ownership, 128-H
reauthorizations, 110-H, 128-H
supplemental appropriations, 50-S
Whitewater hearings, 25-S
Social Security, 54-H
for domestic workers, 52-H
entitlement spending control, 104-H
exclusion from balanced-budget amendment, 20-H
Social Security Administration, 54-H, 118-H
Solid waste control
interstate, 132-H
municipal, 134-H
Somalia
peacekeeping and humanitarian assistance, 4-H, 8-S, 46-S
South African Assistance Program, 62-H
South Korea, 26-S
military readiness, 66-H
Team Spirit military exercises, 66-H
Space energy
China Lake laser facility, 70-H
Space exploration
NASA, 43-S, 53-S
Space station program, 90-H, 43-S
Special education programs
funding, 12-S
Spending Reduction Commission, 13-S
Sports and recreation
after-school sports leagues, 118-H, 124-H
boating safety improvements, 130-H
civilian events, 46-S
East Mojave Scenic Area hunting exception, 94-H
golf helicopter trips, 72-H
international sporting event duty suspension, 30-H
midnight sports programs, 26-H
Olympics, 46-S
recreational boating safety improvements, 130-H
recreational diesel fuel taxes, 27-S
urban, 26-H
World Cup Soccer Games, 46-S
Stalking violence
access to criminal histories in cases of, 40-H
State Department
appropriations, 80-H, 82-H, 84-H, 86-H, 116-H, 122-H, 2-S, 4-S, 38-S, 39-S, 50-S
assistant secretaries, 4-S
authorizations, 36-H, 44-H, 2-S, 3-S, 4-S
Office of Counterterrorism, 36-H
overseas buildings, 84-H
personnel files, 8-S
Talbott nomination, 9-S
Steubenville, Ohio
new courthouses, 72-H
Stewart B. McKinney Homeless Assistance Act (PL 100-77), 106-H
Strategic Defense Initiative. *See Ballistic Missile Defense program*
Strategic Petroleum Reserve, 4-H

Striker replacement, 33-S
Substance abuse treatment pro-
    grams, 80-H
Summer Youth Employment and
    Training Program, 6-S
Sunshine Act, 49-S
Supplemental Security Income,
    54-H, 118-H
Supreme Court
    Breyer nomination, 42-S
Surface transportation law, 60-H
Surveys
    consent for, 6-S
Switzerland
    Lawrence confirmation as
        ambassador to, 7-S

T

Taiwanese visas, 45-S
Talbott, Strobe, 9-S
Taxation
    checkoff for disaster relief, 7-S
    checkoff for presidential election
        fund, 7-S
    IRS compliance initiative, 27-S
    payments in lieu of taxes, 146-H,
        150-H, 16-S
    recreational diesel fuel taxes,
        27-S
    research and development
        credit, 10-S
    Social Security for domestic
        workers, 52-H
    targeted tax break repeal pack-
        age, 98-H
    tax cuts, 18-H
Teachers
    bilingual, 42-S
Technology
    environmental, 106-H, 19-S
Teen pregnancy
    condom distribution, 6-S
Telecommunications
    local telephone services and
        cable television, 86-H
    MILSTAR program, 46-S
    regional Bell companies, 86-H
Tennessee
    veterans hospitals, 44-S
Tennessee Valley Authority, 4-H
Three-time drug offenders, 38-H
Three-time violent offenders,
    26-H, 30-H, 42-H, 124-H, 50-S
Tigert, Ricki R., 55-S
Title I
    for public school choice pro-
        grams, 28-H
    for Puerto Rico, 12-H
Tobacco
    classification, 14-H
    tariffs, 36-S
Toilets
    airplane, 26-S
Tokamak Physics Experiment, 30-S
Towing vessel safety, 130-H
Trade
    environmental export promo-
        tion, 36-H
    Export Administration Act exten-
        sion, 142-H
    GATT, 144-H, 150-H, 36-S, 57-S
    imported reformulated gasoline
        regulations, 126-H
    Israeli boycott, 4-S
    MFN status to China, 114-H,

116-H, 4-S
    tobacco tariffs, 36-S
    tonnage duties, 110-H
    Vietnam embargo, 44-H, 2-S
    World Trade Organization,
        150-H, 57-S
Trademarks
    registering, 136-H
Training
    criminal justice, 33-S
    democracy programs, 34-S
    International Criminal
        Investigative Training
        Assistance Program, 33-S
    Summer Youth Employment
        and Training Program, 6-S
    transition from school to work-
        place program funding, 7-S
Transportation
    airplane toilets, 26-S
    airport parking privileges, 17-S
    air-traffic controllers, 26-S
    Amtrak, 74-H
    aviation product liability law-
        suits, 11-S
    Federal Railroad Administration,
        114-H
    funding, 60-H
    golf helicopter trips, 72-H
    high-speed rail development,
        120-H
    highway projects, 60-H, 8-S, 37-S
    highway reconstruction, 2-H,
        8-H, 8-S
    James A. Farley Post Office,
        New York City (NY), 37-S
    surface transportation law, 60-H
    vehicles in wilderness areas,
        70-H
    violence against truck drivers,
        32-H
Transportation Department
    appropriations, 74-H, 37-S,
        38-S, 54-S
    authorizations, 38-S
Travel
    charity reimbursements, 19-S
Treasury Department
    appropriations, 68-H, 70-H, 72-H,
        74-H, 130-H, 132-H, 27-S,
        28-S
    authorizations, 32-H
    National Disaster Relief Trust
        Fund, 8-S
    Violent Crime Reduction Trust
        Fund, 18-H, 26-H, 11-S, 22-S
    Whitewater hearings, 25-S
Trident II (D-5) missiles, 58-H,
    46-S
Truck drivers
    violence against, 32-H
Truth in sentencing, 44-H
Truth in Sentencing Laws, 38-H

U

U.N. See United Nations
Unfunded mandates, 56-S
United Nations
    assistance to Haiti, 60-H, 68-H
    Bosnia arms embargo, 68-H
    control of U.S. troops, 68-H
    Development Program, 34-S
    Office of Inspector General, 2-S
    peacekeeping costs, 60-H
    recognition of pedophilia-

endorsing organizations, 2-S
    Security Council Resolution
        940, 43-S
    U.S. contributions, 84-H, 116-H,
        2-S, 28-S
United States and Foreign
    Commercial Service
    Fitz-Pegado nomination, 26-S
U.S. Circuit Court of Appeals
    Barkett confirmation, 16-S
    Sarokin confirmation, 55-S
U.S. Code
    technical improvements, 136-H
U.S. Information Agency (USIA)
    appropriations, 4-S
    authorizations, 114-H
    Radio Free Asia, 84-H
U.S. Postal Service. See Postal
    Service
U.S. Privacy Protection
    Commission, 18-S
U.S.-Mexico border
    border crossing fee, 27-S
    wastewater treatment projects,
        21-S
U.S.-Mexico Border Health
    Commission, 142-H, 144-H
USIA. See U.S. Information Agency

V

VA. See Veterans Affairs Department
Venture capital loan guarantees,
    11-S
Veterans Affairs Department (VA)
    appropriations, 90-H, 92-H,
        126-H, 44-S, 53-S
    authorizations, 92-H
    hospitals, 44-H, 44-S
    work force reduction, 44-H
Vietnam embargo, 44-H, 2-S
Violence
    access to criminal histories, 40-H
    community notification of sex
        offenders, 96-H, 124-H, 50-S
    grant program to prevent and
        prosecute young offenders,
        32-H
    life imprisonment for three-time
        offenders, 26-H, 30-H, 42-H,
        124-H, 50-S
    school disciplinary policy, 41-S
    against truck drivers, 32-H
Violence Against Women Act,
    22-S
Violent Crime Reduction Trust
    Fund, 18-H, 26-H, 11-S, 22-S
Virgin Islands education pro-
    grams, 14-H
Virginia
    Fisher Peak Mountain Music
        Center, 78-H
Visas
    fraud, 32-H
    Taiwanese, 45-S
Vocational schools, 88-H
Voter registration
    motor, 48-S
Vouchers
    housing, 90-H
    school, 40-S

W

Wallenberg, Raoul, 36-H
Washington National Airport

parking privileges, 17-S
Wastewater treatment projects,
    21-S, 44-S
Water. See Energy and water
Water construction projects, 21-S
Weaponry
    assault weapons ban, 48-H,
        118-H, 124-H, 50-S
    B-2 bomber, 31-S
    Ballistic Missile Defense
        Organization, 56-H
    Navy anti-missile system, 46-S
    Nunn-Lugar cooperative threat
        reduction program, 35-S
    Trident II (D-5) missiles, 58-H,
        46-S
Wetlands conservation act
    amendments, 126-H
Wheeling National Heritage Area,
    30-H
White House
    drug testing program, 27-S
    golf helicopter trip, 72-H
    salaries and expenses account,
        72-H
Whitewater Development Co.,
    24-H, 11-S, 25-S
Whitewater hearings, 24-H, 24-S,
    25-S, 26-S, 27-S
Wilderness areas
    California desert, 138-H, 140-H,
        148-H
    land appraisal, 96-H
    land exchanges and monetary
        credits, 94-H
    law enforcement vehicles in,
        70-H
    Montana wilderness, 54-H
    state motorized vehicles in,
        70-H
Women
    Office of Women's Business
        Ownership, 128-H
Women, Infants, and Children
    program, 100-H, 48-S
Women in Military Service for
    America Memorial, 120-H
Workers' compensation
    Black Lung Trust Fund, 56-H
    Federal Black Lung Advisory
        Committee, 56-H
World Bank, 4-H
World Cup Soccer Games, 46-S
World Intellectual Property
    Organization, 136-H
World Trade Organization (WTO),
    150-H, 57-S
WTO. See World Trade
    Organization

X, Y, Z

Yellen, Janet L.
    confirmation to Federal Reserve
        System, 47-S
Youths
    at-risk, 26-H
    grant program to prevent and
        prosecute violent offenders,
        32-H
    Summer Youth Employment
        and Training Program, 6-S
    transition from school to
        workplace program funding,
        7-S   ■

General Index

A

Abortion. *See also: Family Planning.*
  Access to clinics - 311, 355, 357, 15-C, 16-C, 22-C, 23-C
  Federal workers health care payments for abortions - 536
  Foreign Aid - 511
  FY 1995 budget - 78
  Health care reform - 334, 337, 341, 342
  Justice Blackmun retires - 303, 304
  Legislation - 356
  Treaty on Women - 471
  Veterans Affairs Department - 414, 415
Abraham, Spencer, R-Mich. - 565
Accuracy in Media (AIM) - 52
Acquired Immune Deficiency Syndrome (AIDS) - 78, 80, 520 (chart), 522
Administration Committee (House) - 13, 28, 29, 43
Administrative Office of the U.S. Courts - 484 (chart)
Administrative Procedures Act - 245
Advanced Technology Program - 71
Advertising. *See: Federal Trade Commission*
African Development Fund - 453, 506 (chart)
Aged persons. *See also: Medicare, Social Security*
  Anti-crime legislation - 292
  Appropriations, Labor-HHS-Education - 520 (chart)
  Republicans' "Contract with America" - 25
Agency for International Development (AID) - 452, 453, 506, 554 (chart)
Agnew, Spiro T. - 579
Agricultural Marketing Service - 200
Agricultural price and income support - 365
Agricultural Stabilization and Conservation Service - 549 (box), 551
Agriculture and farming. *See also: Agricultural price and income supports; Agricultural trade; Agriculture Department; Federal Insecticide and Fungicide and Rodenticide Act; Food safety; Food stamps; Livestock; Pesticides and herbicides; Rural affairs; Tobacco*
  Crop insurance program - 191
  Dairy farming legislation - 197, 198
  FY 1994 disaster supplemental - 549 (box), 551
  GATT - 134, 135
  Plant Variety Protection Act - 190
  Vegetable Oil-Based Ink - 199
Agriculture Committee (House)
  Child nutrition programs - 374
  Department reorganization - 192, 193
  Environmental issues - 254
  Federal crop insurance - 195, 196
  Logging on Forest Service lands - 256, 257
  Minor-use pesticides - 198
  Montana wilderness bill - 246
  Plant Variety Protection Act - 190
Agriculture Committee (Senate)
  Department reorganization - 191, 193, 194
  Federal crop insurance - 196
Agriculture Department. *See also: Agricultural price and income supports; Agricultural trade; Agriculture Department; Child nutrition; Federal Insecticide, Fungicide and Rodenticide Act; Food and nutrition; Food safety; Food stamps, Livestock; Pesticides and herbicides; Rural affairs; Tobacco; Women, Infants and Children program (WIC).*
  Anti-crime legislation - 288
  Appropriations - 70, 477, 478, 482 (chart)
  Clinton budget - 71
  Consolidated Farm Service Agency - 143, 191, 194
  Cooperative State Research Service - 553
  Department reorganization - 143, 191, 194, 552
  Federal crop insurance - 194, 197
  Food and nutrition assistance - 365, 374
  Food stamp measure - 376
  FY 1994 disaster supplemental provisions - 551, 552, 553
  National Appeals Division - 191
  National parks - 251
  Natural Resources Conservation Service - 191, 194
  Nutrition programs - 197
  Soil and water conservation - 191
  Soil Conservation Service - 255
AID. *See: Agency for International Development.*
Aid to Families with Dependent Children (AFDC) - 79, 327, 365, 390, 519, 520 (chart)
AIDS. *See: Acquired Immune Deficiency Syndrome*
Aikens, Joan D. - 35
Air Force, U.S. *See also: Aircraft, military; Defense Department; Military bases; Military construction; Military personnel issues.*
  Appropriations - 488, 489, 496 (chart)
  Military construction - 528 (chart)
Air transportation. *See also: Aerospace industry; Aerospace industry, Aircraft, military; Aircraft, military; Airports; Federal Aviation Administration*
  Child restraints on airplanes - 168
  Drug testing airline employees - 168
  Gambling devices on international flights - 168
  Government-owned aircraft accident investigation - 173
  Small aircraft product liability, 222. *See also: Product liability.*
  Smoking ban on all international, Alaska, Hawaii flights - 174
  Toilets on small commercial planes - 169
Aircraft, military
  AWACS radar planes - 493, 495
  B-1 bombers - 425, 429, 439
  B-52 bombers - 425, 429, 439, 491, 496
  B-2 stealth bombers - 421, 425, 427, 428, 432, 433, 488, 494, 496, 497
  Bomber industrial base fund - 433
  C-17 cargo planes - 72, 421, 422, 423, 425, 426, 427, 430, 433, 434, 440, 441, 488, 492, 494, 496
  Combat jet prototypes - 496
  F-22 fighter - 72
  F/A-18 fighters - 72, 425, 429, 491, 494, 496
  F-14s - 429, 494, 496
  F-16s - 72, 422
  F-22s - 422, 425, 428, 429, 490, 491, 496
  F-111s - 496
  Harrier jets - 429, 491, 496
  Hawkeye radar planes - 492, 494
  Helicopters
    Apache - 422, 428, 491, 493, 494
    Arming older scouts with new electronics - 495
    Blackhawk - 72, 491
    Cobra - 491
    Comanche - 72, 422, 428, 490, 491, 493, 494, 495
    Equip Apaches with Longbow radar - 428, 495
    Huey - 491
    Kiowas - 428
    Osprey - 430, 490, 492, 494, 496
    Seahawks - 492
  Hercules cargo planes - 430
  JPATS - 429
  JSTARS radar planes - 429, 494
  SC-141 cargo planes - 434
  SR-71 high-speed reconnaissance jets - 425, 429, 494, 496, 497
Airlines. *See: Air transportation.*
Airports
  Airport grant program - 168, 169
  Airport improvement program - 168, 530
  Airport landing fees - 169
  Airport trust fund - 531(chart)
  Free parking privileges at D.C. area - 177
  FY 1994 disaster supplemental - 554, 555
Akaka, Daniel K., D-Hawaii
  1994 election - 570
  Disaster relief - 155
  Veterans' affairs - 417, 418
  Voting participation - 12-C
Alabama
  1994 election - 563, 572, 576, 579
  Conservative coalition - 9-C

FY 1995 budget - 80
  Logging on Forest Service lands - 257
  National forests - 247
Alaska
  1994 election - 563, 576, 589
  Ballot initiatives - 581
  Exxon Valdez oil spill - 190
  Moratorium on oil and natural gas leases - 515
  Term limits - 581
  Tongass National Forest - 517, 518
  Wards Cove Packing Co. - 298
  Wilderness areas - 247
Albright, Madeleine K. - 446
Alcohol, Tobacco and Firearms - *See: Bureau of Alcohol, Tobacco and Firearms*
Alcohol and alcohol abuse - *See: Drugs and drug abuse*
Aliens
  FY 1994 disaster supplemental - 549, 555
  Immigrant education programs - 387, 521, 522
  Reimburse states for illegal immigrant costs - 487
  Reimburse states for incarcerating illegals - 486
Alito, Samuel A. Jr. - 52
Allard, Wayne, R-Colo. (4)
  Agriculture Department reorganization - 192
  Environmental issues - 255
  Montana wilderness bill - 246
  National Endowment for the Arts - 515
  Presidio management - 253, 254
Allen, Gov. George, R-Va. - 533
Alliance of American Insurers - 184, 233
Almond, Gov. Lincoln C., R-R.I. - 579
Altman, Roger C. - 31
Ambassadors. *See also: Foreign embassies.*
  Brown (Conference on Security and Cooperation in Europe [CSCE]) - 472
  Pastor nomination (Panama) - 471, 472
  Shearer nomination (Finland) - 472
American Association of Retired Persons - 181
American Bankruptcy Institute - 175
American Bar Association - 301
American Civil Liberties Union - 42, 215
American Heritage areas - 252
American Insurance Association - 184, 233
American Legion - 362, 468
American Personal Communications Inc. - 129
American Veterinary Medical Association - 360
Americans for Limited Terms - 588
America's Leaders Fund - 46
Ameritech - 214
Ames, Aldrich H. - 458, 459, 463, 464 (box), 466
Ames, Maria Del Rosario Casas - 458, 459

Amoco Corporation - 468
Amtrak - See: Federal Railroad Administration; Railroads.
Andrews, Michael A., D-Texas (25)
　Federal Election Commission spending regulations - 36
　Gun control - 276
　Health care reform - 329, 331
　Social Security - 367
Andrews, Robert E., D-N.J. (1)
　Budget process - 88
　Health care reform - 327
Andrews, Thomas H., D-Maine (1)
　1994 election - 568, 576
　Defense authorization - 423
　Maritime exhibit grants - 164
Anti-crime bill - See: Crime and criminal justice, Anticrime legislation
Anti-Defamation League of B'nai B'rith - 63
Anti-poverty programs. See also: Aid to Families with Dependent Children; Food and nutrition; Welfare; Women, Infants and Children
　Housing - 408, 410
Antitrust and competition
　Breyer appointment - 309
　Health care reform - 344
　Insurance industry - 183, 184
　Professional baseball antitrust exemption - 523
　Congressional action - 182
Appropriations
　Earmarks academic research facilities - 220
　Foreign aid - 453, 505, 508, 511, 512
　FY 1995
　　Agriculture - 477, 478 , 482 (chart)
　　Appropriators complete work - 475, 476
　　Commerce-Justice-State - 483, 484 (chart), 487
　　Defense - 488, 489 (chart), 497
　　District of Columbia - 498, 499 (chart), 501
　　Energy and water - 502, 504
　　Foreign operations - 505, 506 (chart), 512
　　Interior Department - 513, 514 (chart), 518
　　Labor-HHS-Education - 519, 520 (chart), 523
　　Legislative branch - 524, 525 (chart), 526
　　Mileposts - 476 (chart)
　　Military construction - 527, 528 (chart), 529
　　Transportation - 530, 531 (chart), 535
　　Treasury-Postal Service - 526, 536, 537 (chart), 540
　　Veterans Affairs Department-Housing and Urban Development - 541, 542 (chart), 547
　FY 1994 emergency supplemental - 548, 549, 556 (chart), 557
Appropriations Committee (House)
　Appropriators complete work - 475, 476
　Balanced-budget amendment - 86
　Energy and water - 502, 504
　Export-Import Bank - 138

Federal home mortgage supplemental - 557
　Labor-HHS-Education - 519, 521
　Legislative branch - 524
　Treasury Department - 536
　VA-HUD - 543, 544
Appropriations Committee (Senate)
　Agricultural Marketing Service Fees - 200
　Appropriators complete work - 475, 476
　Budget process - 88
　Chairmanship - 8, 9
　Clinton budget - 79
　District of Columbia subcommittee, FY 1995 outlook - 498, 499
　Energy and water appropriations - 502, 504
　Export-Import Bank - 138
　Federal land payments to localities - 156
　FY 1994 disaster supplemental - 550
　Labor-HHS-Education - 522
　Legislative branch - 525
　National Endowment for the Arts - 517
　Russian aid policy - 466, 467
　VA-HUD - 544, 546
Archer, Bill, R-Texas (7)
　GATT - 127
　Health care reform - 333, 334
　Presidio management - 253
Archer-Daniels-Midland - 544
Architect of the Capitol - 525, 526, 555
Architectural and Transportation Barriers Compliance Board - 531 (chart)
Aristide, President Jean-Bertrand - 449, 451
Arizona
　1994 election - 565, 568, 574, 580, 589
　Anti-crime legislation - 288
　Colonias - 71
　Logging on Forest Service lands - 257
　National forests - 247
　New courthouse projects - 539
　Senate race - 565
　United States-Mexico Border Health Commission - 363
　VA medical facilities - 415
Arkansas
　1994 election - 572, 580
　Conservative coalition - 9-C
　Military construction - 528
　Supreme Court - 314
Armed Forces -
　See: Defense Department; Military personnel issues; Veterans Affairs Department; individual branches: Air Force; Army; Coast Guard; Marine Corps; National Guard; Navy; Reserves, military.
Armed Services Committee (House)
　Child support - 375
　Energy research laboratories - 223, 224
　Health care reform - 343
　Renamed - 18
Armed Services Committee (Senate)
　Budget resolution FY 1995 - 84
　Energy and water appropriations - 504
　Health care reform - 343

Procurement reform - 145, 147
Armenia - 466, 467
Armey, Dick, R-Texas (26)
　1994 election - 14, 570
　Black lung benefits - 406
　Elementary and secondary education authorization - 386
　Health care reform - 325, 327
　Vote studies, presidential support - 4-C
Arms control. See also: Chemical, biological weapons
　ABM treaty - 426
Arms Control and Disarmament Agency - 457, 484 (chart)
Arms sales - 449, 451
Army, U.S. See also: Defense Department; Military bases; Military construction; Military personnel issues
　Ammunition - 495
　Appropriations - 489, 490, 495 (chart)
　Medical research institute - 556
　Military construction - 528 (chart)
　Personnel, FY 1995 - 422
Army Corps of Engineers, U.S.
　Appropriations - 242, 502, 504, 549 (chart), 551, 554
　Drinking water authorization - 239
　Everglades protection - 254
　Clinton budget - 73
Arnold, Richard S. - 304
Ashcroft, John, R-Mo. - 565, 568
Ashe, Victor - 150
Asia - 431, 483, 485, 486
Asian Development Fund - 506 (chart)
Aspin, Les - 71, 463
Association of Boxing Commissioners - 189
Association of National Park Rangers - 248
Association of Trial Lawyers of America - 178
Atlanta Journal-Constitution - 54, 129
Atlantic States Marine Fisheries Commission - 260
Atomic Vapor Laser Isotope Separation program - 73
Atwood, J. Brian - 452, 453
Automobiles, automobile industry. See also: Highways and roads; Oil industry; Transportation Department.
　Bumper damage standards - 190
　Unsafe drivers bill - 174

B

B-2, B-1 bombers - See: Aircraft, military
Babbitt, Bruce
　Appropriations, Interior Department - 513
　California desert protection - 228
　Clinton budget - 73
　Mining law rewrite - 236
　National Endowment for the Arts - 515
　National parks - 247
　Park user fees - 251
　Possible court nomination - 303, 304
Bachus, Spencer, R-Ala. (6) - 516
Backus, Jan - 569
Baesler, Scotty, D-Ky. (6) - 327

Bailey, Pam G. - 339
Baird, Zoe - 368
Baker, Bill, R-Calif. (10)
　Appropriations, Labor-HHS-Education - 521
　Energy Department research laboratories - 223
Baker, Richard H., R-La. (6) - 584
Balanced-budget amendment (constitutional)
　Defeated - 85, 87
　House action - 85, 87, 14-C
　Republicans' "Contract with America"- 22
　Senate action - 85, 22-C
Baldacci, John, D-Maine - 576
Ballenger, Cass, R-N.C. (10)
　Davis-Bacon wage revision - 406
　Elementary and secondary education authorization - 387
　Health care reform - 326, 329
　OSHA overhaul legislation - 403
Ballistic Missile Defense - See: Missiles, Ballistic Missile Defense
Bane, Mary Jo - 370
Bank Enterprise Act - 101
Banking, Finance and Urban Affairs Committee (House)
　Banking law - 93, 100
　Community Development Banking - 101, 107
　Economic Development Administration - 188
　Export-Import Bank - 138
　Flood insurance bill - 411, 412
　Housing authorization - 409, 410 (box)
　Whitewater/Madison affair - 31
Banking, Housing and Urban Affairs Committee (Senate)
　Banking laws - 98, 107
　Commerce Department - 189
　Community Development Banking - 101
　Export-Import Bank - 138
　Whitewater/Madison affair - 31
Bankruptcy law
　National Bankruptcy Review Commission - 176
　U.S. bankruptcy code revisions - 175, 177, 376
Banks and banking. See also: Bankruptcy law; Credit; Federal Reserve; Mortgages and home loans; Resolution Trust Corporation; Savings Association Insurance Fund; Stocks, bonds and securities.
　Banking law revision - 93, 108
　Community development banks - 100, 106, 411, 412
　Community Development Financial Institutions Fund - 100
　Douglas Amendment - 95
　Fair trade in financial services - 101, 102, 107, 108
　Interstate Banking and Branching Act - 94, 100
　Regulation - 104
　Resolution Trust Corporation - 556
　Tax simplification - 93
　Thrift bailout - 70, 71
　Whitewater/Madison affair - 298
　　Background - 31
　　Congressional hearings - 101
　　FY 1994 disaster supplemental - 556
　　Independent counsel law - 295, 298

Baran, Jan - 36
Barca, Peter W., D-Wis. (1) - 573
Barcia, James A., D-Mich. (5) - 584
Barlow, Tom, D-Ky. (1)
　1994 election - 571
　East-West Transamerica Corridor - 167
Barr, Bob, R-Ga. - 571
Barr, William - 300
Barrett, Bill, R-Neb. (3)
　Agriculture Department reorganization - 193
　Elementary and secondary education authorization - 387
　Head Start - 373
Barrett, Thomas M., D-Wis. (5) - 409
Barrick Goldstrike Mines Inc. - 237
Barry, Edward P. Jr. - 441
Bartlett, Roscoe G., R-Md. (6) - 223
Barton, Joe L., R-Texas (6)
　Appropriations, District of Columbia - 499
　Balanced-budget amendment - 87
　Medical devices - 362
　U.S. communications law rewrite - 207
Basha, Eddie - 580
Bass, Charles, R-N.H. - 576
Bass, Perkins - 576
Bassler, William G. - 52
Bateman, Herbert H., R-Va. (1)
　Incentives to build U.S. ships - 160
　Shipyard subsidies - 160
Bath Iron Works - 429, 430
Batt, Gov. Phil, R-Idaho - 580
Baucus, Max, D-Mont.
　Clean water law - 241, 242
　Drinking water authorization - 238, 240
　Environmental technology - 264
　GATT - 127
　Health care reform - 339, 341, 342
　Interstate Transport of Solid Waste - 261
　Montana wilderness bill - 245
　National Endowment for the Arts - 518
　National Highway System - 168
　Superfund reauthorization - 235
Bauer, Robert - 36
Bayh, Gov. Evan, D-Ind. - 578
Beasley, Gov. David, R-S.C. - 580
Becerra, Xavier, D-Calif. (30) - 328
Beech Aircraft Corporation - 180, 181
Beilenson, Anthony C., D-Calif. (24)
　1994 election - 573
　Appropriations, foreign operations - 508
　Population programs - 508
　Quality work guarantee - 167
BellSouth - 214
Bennett, Richard A. - 576
Bennett, Robert F., R-Utah
　California desert protection - 227
　Lobbying disclosure and gift ban - 39
　National parks - 249
　Preservation of historic black college buildings - 401
Bennett, Robert S. - 43, 44, 45
Bentley, Helen Delich, R-Md. (2)
　Incentives to build U.S. ships - 160

Minimum compensation - 164
Bentsen, Ken, D-Texas - 572
Bentsen, Lloyd - 51
　Banking law - 94
　Gun control - 277
Berman, Howard L., D-Calif. (26)
　Pension benefits - 405
　State Department authorization bill - 457
Bevill, Tom, D-Ala. (4)
　1994 election - 563
　Appropriations, energy and water - 503, 504
Biden, Joseph R. Jr., D-Del.
　Bankruptcy law - 175
　Bosnia-Herzegovina - 447
　Breyer appointment - 309, 310
　Breyer nomination - 19-D, 20-D
　Crime bill - 273, 282, 283
　Nominations and appointees - 301, 302
　Professional baseball antitrust exemption - 183
　State Department authorization bill - 454, 455, 456, 457
Big Seven - 150
Bilbray, Brian P., R-Calif. - 573, 584
Bilbray, James, D-Nev. (1)
　1994 election - 573, 575
　House leadership position races - 14
　Procurement reform - 146
　Small Business Administration (SBA) - 187
Bilirakis, Michael, R-Fla. (9) - 186
Bingaman, Anne K. - 298
Bingaman, Jeff, D-N.M.
　1994 election - 569
　Elementary and secondary education authorization - 388
　Haitian crisis - 451
　Health care reform - 336, 338
　Procurement reform - 144
　Technology for education - 402, 407
　United States-Mexico Border Health Commission - 363
Biotechnology
　Marine - 162
Bishop, Sanford D. Jr., D-Ga. (2)
　Conservative coalition - 11-C
Black Americans. See also: Civil rights; Congressional Black Caucus; Minority groups
　1994 election - 569
　Minority health programs - 358
　Nation of Islam Redistricting - 591
Black caucus - 282
Black Lung Disability Trust Fund - 406
Blackmun, Harry A.
　J.E.B. v. Alabama - 312
　Retirement - 303, 305, 310
Blackwell, Lucien E., D-Pa. (2) - 584
Blanchard, Chuck - 584
Bliley, Thomas J. Jr., R-Va. (7)
　Added-nicotine controversy - 360
　Appropriations, District of Columbia - 499
　House committee chairmen - 15
　Orphan drugs - 363
　Smoking restrictions - 362
　U.S. communications law rewrite - 206
Blute, Peter I., R-Mass. (3) - 410
Board for International Broadcasting - 555
Boehlert, Sherwood, R-N.Y. (23)
　Energy Department research

laboratories - 223
　Gun control - 277
　National Science Foundation reauthorization - 220
　Superfund reauthorization - 233
　Whip election - 7
Boehner, John A., R-Ohio (8)
　Appropriations, Labor-HHS-Education - 521
　Black lung benefits - 406
　Congressional pay raise - 63, 64
　Davis-Bacon wage revision - 406
　Elementary and secondary education authorization - 385
　Health care reform - 325, 329
　House leadership position races - 14
　OSHA overhaul legislation - 403
Boeing - 429, 434, 493, 494, 495
Bolton, Claude M. Jr. - 441
Bombs
　JDAM (smart bombs) - 425, 427, 429, 433, 496
　JSOW glider bomb - 429, 496
Bond, Christopher S., R-Mo.
　Clean water law - 242
　Vegetable oil-based ink - 199
Bond, Jon R. - 3-C
Bonilla, Henry, R-Texas (23)
　Appropriations, Labor-HHS-Education - 519, 521
　Clinton's State of the Union address - 30
　House leadership races - 14
Bonior, David E., D-Mich. (10)
　Bosnia-Herzegovina - 448
　Gingrich ethics investigation - 54
　House committee assignments - 16
　House leadership position races - 15, 16
　MFN China - 137
Bono, Sonny, R-Calif. - 573
Border Patrol - 294, 483, 487
Boren, David L., D-Okla.
　1994 election - 13, 565
　Appropriations, Defense - 497
　Campaign finance reform - 33
　Congressional reform - 27
　Drinking water authorization - 239
　GATT - 127
　Health care reform - 339, 340, 343
　Lobbying disclosure and gift ban - 40
　Oklahoma special election - 592
　Republican control of Senate - 565
　Striker replacement - 402
Borski, Robert A., D-Pa. (3) - 584
Bosnia-Herzegovina - 445, 446, 449, 454, 455, 457, 497
　Arms control - 507, 508
　Arms embargo - 421, 423, 425, 427, 432, 16-C, 25-C
　Bosnian war - 446, 449
　Defense authorization - 431
　FY 1994 disaster supplemental - 548
Botanic Garden - 524, 526
Boucher, Rick, D-Va. (9)
　Disaster relief - 155
　Fire Prevention and Control Act of 1974 amendment - 299
　Gun control - 277
　Health care reform - 335
　Interstate Transport of Solid Waste - 261
　Science policy - 220

Small aircraft product liability - 181
　Superfund reauthorization - 233
Boxer, Barbara, D-Calif.
　Adm. Mauz Jr.'s retirement - 440
　California desert protection - 227
　Drinking water authorization - 239
　Elementary and secondary education authorization - 391
　FY 1994 disaster supplemental - 548, 556
　Retooling bridges to withstand earthquakes - 167 (box)
　Superfund reauthorization - 235
Boyd, C. Robert, D-W.Va. - 530
Bradley, Bill, D-N.J.
　Appropriations, agricultural - 481
　Bosnia-Herzegovina - 448
　Competitiveness programs - 222
　Defense authorization - 426
　Health care reform - 339, 341
　MFN China - 137
　Nominations and appointees - 301
Brand, Stanley M. - 47
Breaux, John B., D-La.
　1994 election - 6
　Health care reform - 339, 342
　Senate leadership for 104th Congress - 18
　Shipyard subsidies - 159, 160
　U.S. communications law rewrite - 203, 209, 210, 212
Bredesen, Phil - 579
Brennan, Gov. Joseph E., D-Maine - 579
Brewster, Bill, D-Okla. (3)
　Health care reform - 334
　Social Security - 367
　Tax code simplification - 93
Breyer, Stephen G.
　Profile - 305 (box)
　Supreme Court appointment - 303, 310
　Supreme Court nomination - 17-D, 25-D
Broadcasting. See: Corporation for Public Broadcasting; Federal Communications Commission (FCC); International broadcasting; Radio; Television.
Brock, Bill - 570
Brookings Institution - 3, 7, 30, 31
Brooks, Jack, D-Texas (9)
　1994 election - 4, 55, 570, 572
　Antitrust legislation - 298
　Bankruptcy law - 175, 177
　Crime Bill - 273, 279, 282, 284
　Federal employee - 149, 150
　Gun control - 276, 277
　Health care reform - 344
　Independent Counsel Law - 296, 297
　INSLAW, Inc. claims - 300
　Insurance antitrust exemption - 183, 184
　Product liability - 178
　Small aircraft product liability - 181
　U.S. communications law rewrite - 204, 207, 209
Browder, Glen, D-Ala. (3) - 83
Brown, Corrine, D-Fla. (3) - 556
Brown, George E. Jr., D-Calif. (42)
　1994 election - 573
　Appropriations, VA-HUD - 541,

544, 547
Disaster relief - 155
Energy Department research
laboratories - 223
Environmental technology -
263, 264
National Aeronautics and Space
Administration reauthorization
- 218, 219
Risk assessment program -
244, 245
Brown, Gerald P. - 315
Brown, Hank, R-Colo.
Appropriations, Defense - 497
Appropriations, Foreign opera-
tions - 510
Appropriations, FY 1994 disas-
ter supplemental - 550
Bankruptcy law - 177
Biodiversity treaty - 267
Brown nomination - 472
Budget Resolution FY 1995 -
68, 85
Competitiveness programs -
222
Defense authorization - 427
Foreign aid reform - 453
Immigration law - 295
Pastor nomination - 471, 472
Shipyard subsidies - 159, 160
State Department authorization
bill - 456
Brown, Jesse - 412, 414
Brown, Lynne P. - 56, 59
Brown, Robert - 361
Brown, Ronald H.
Competitiveness programs -
222
Economic Development
Administration - 187
Fishing legislation - 259
Brown, Sam - 472
Brown, Sherrod, D-Ohio (13) -
362
**Brown & Williamson Tobacco
Corp.** - 360
Brownback, Sam, R-Kan. - 572
Browner, Carol M. - 73, 150, 232,
243
Bryan, James E. - 571
Bryan, Richard H., D-Nev.
1994 election - 569, 579
Appropriations, agricultural -
481
Appropriations, Defense - 497
Fire Prevention and Control Act
of 1974 amendment - 299
Bryant, J. Winston - 314
Bryant, John, D-Texas (5)
Dairy legislation - 197
Defense authorization - 423
Independent Counsel Law - 296
Legal Services Corporation -
298
Lobbying disclosure and gift
ban - 37, 38, 40
Montana wilderness bill - 246
U.S. communications law
rewrite - 206
Buchanan, Patrick J. - 124
Buckley, James L. - 52
Budget, U.S. See also:
*Appropriations; Congressional
Budget Office (CBO); Economic
indicators; Taxes and taxation.*
Administration economic
assumptions 1993-1999 - 74
(chart)
Balanced-budget amendment
(constitutional) - see: Main
subject heading.
Baseline budgeting - 89
Budget Authority, Outlays by

Agency - 75 (chart)
Budget glossary - 69
Budget process - 87, 90
Budget process changes pro-
posed - 18-C
Budget reconciliation bill, 1993 -
365, 368
Budget resolution, FY 1995 -
81, 85
House action - 14-C, 15-C
Senate action - 23-C
Deficit reduction - 21-C, 22-C
Deficits - 85, 87
Discretionary spending - 67, 81,
83
Emergency spending - 89, 90
Entitlement spending - 81, 87,
89
Fiscal 1995 Budget by Function
- 76 (chart), 77 (chart)
FY 1995 budget cap on discre-
tionary spending - 68
Deficit forecasts - 68
Economic assumptions - 69
Entitlement spending - 68
Health care - 69
Highlights of President's Budget
- 70, 73, 78, 81
President's budget requests -
67, 68, 81
Revenues - 70
Interest on Federal debt - 82
Investment spending on social
programs - 82
Line-item veto - 22
Nixon's congressional legacy -
61
Rescissions - 87, 88
"A to Z" plan (box) - 88
Budget Committee (House)
Budget resolution FY 1995 - 82
Budget Committee (Senate)
Budget resolution FY 1995 - 81
Budget resolution, FY 1995
House action - 82, 83
Senate action - 83, 84
Bumpers, Dale, D-Ark.
Appropriations
Agriculture - 479, 481
Defense - 497
Foreign Aid - 511
Labor-HHS-Education - 522
VA-HUD - 546
Elementary and secondary edu-
cation authorization - 389
Food labels - 363
Lobbying disclosure and gift
ban - 39
Mining law rewrite - 237
National Endowment for the
Arts - 517
National parks - 249
Procurement reform - 145
Small Business Administration
(SBA) - 186
State Department authorization
bill - 456
Striker replacement - 402
Student loan defaults - 401
Bunn, Jim, R-Ore. - 584
Bunning, Jim, R-Ky. (4)
Health care reform - 334
Rostenkowski's reimbursement
- 44
**Bureau of Alcohol, Tobacco and
Firearms** - 537 (chart)
Bureau of Indian Affairs - 379,
514, 514 (chart), 515, 552
Bureau of Land Management -
513, 514 (chart), 584
Bureau of Mines - 230, 514 (chart)
Bureau of Prisons - 289
Bureau of Reclamation -73, 551,

554
Bureau of the Public Debt - 537
(chart)
Burke, Richard E. - 52
Burns, Conrad, R-Mont.
1994 election - 569
Appropriations
District of Columbia - 500
Legislative branch - 526
Breyer appointment - 310
Lobbying disclosure and gift
ban - 40
Montana wilderness bill - 245
U.S. communications law
rewrite - 212
Burr, Richard M. - 571
Burton, Dan, R-Ind. (6)
Appropriations
Agricultural - 479
Foreign operations - 508
Military construction - 528
Defense Department peace-
keeping operations - 550
Elementary and secondary edu-
cation authorization - 387
Burton, Donna - 46
Bush, Former President George -
468
Bush, Gov. George W., R-Texas -
579
Bush, Jeb - 580
Business interests
Commercial fishing - 33, 257
Ethanol - 543
Health care reform - 321, 322,
330, 342
Mining law rewrite - 236, 237
Montana wilderness bill - 245
Petroleum industry - 546
Product liability - 178, 179
Radon - 264, 265
Risk assessment program - 245
Small aircraft product liability -
180, 181
Small business - 250
Superfund reauthorization -
233, 234, 235, 236
Textile Industry - 132
Timber industry - 256, 257
U.S. Bankruptcy code revisions
- 175
Button, Randy - 571
Buy American - 556
Buyer, Steve, R-Ind. (5) - 343
Byrd, Robert C., D-W.Va.
1994 election - 570
Adm. Kelso's retirement - 440
Appropriations
Commerce-Justice-State -
483
Defense - 488, 493
District of Columbia - 501
Interior Department - 513
Transportation - 534
VA-HUD - 543
Balanced-budget amendment -
86
Budget process - 88
California desert protection -
228
Congressional reform - 27
Crime bill - 283
Defense authorization - 426
Economic Development
Administration - 187
Federal employees - 149, 153
Federal land payments to locali-
ties - 156
FY 1994 disaster supplemental
- 548, 556
National Endowment for the
Arts - 517
Senate leadership for 104th

Congress - 18
Vote studies, presidential sup-
port - 6-C
Byrne, Leslie L., D-Va. (11)
1994 election - 572
Appropriations, Energy and
water - 503
Congressional workplace law
exemptions - 28
Metric highway signs - 166

C

Cabinet, Members of the 103rd
Congress, 2nd Session - 7-B
**Cable Communications Policy
Act** - 204
Cable News Network - 45
**Cable Telcommunications
Association** - 211
Cable television - *See: Television*
California
1994 election - 562, 563, 565,
566, 568, 573, 574, 579, 580
Anti-crime legislation - 288
Banking - 94
California Desert Protection Act
- 227, 231
Colonias - 71
Crime legislation - 581
Dairy industry - 362
Death Valley National
Monument - 227, 228
Earthquake relief, FY 1994 dis-
aster supplemental - 548,
549, 551
FY 1994 mortgage supplemen-
tal - 557
FY 1994 disaster supplemental
- 548
GATT - 129
Helium reactor - 503
Joshua Tree National
Monument - 227, 228
Logging on Forest Service
lands - 256, 257
Military construction - 528
Mojave Desert park bill - 6, 228,
17-C, 18-C, 27-C, 28-C
National forests - 247
Oil fields - 73
Presidio management - 253
Proposition 187 - 581
Redistricting - 591
Senate Race - 565
Six Rivers National Forest - 254
United States-Mexico Border
Health Commission - 363
VA medical facilities - 415
California Desert Protection Act -
249
Callahan, Sonny, R-Ala. (1)
Appropriations, Foreign opera-
tions - 508
Russian aid policy - 466
Calvert, Ken, R-Calif. (43)
1994 election - 573
California desert protection -
230
Campaign finance. See also:
*Federal Election Commission;
Political action committees*
Nixon's congressional legacy -
61
Personal use of campaign
funds - 35, 36
Political action committees
(PACs) - 27-C
Reform - 32, 34, 26-C, 27-C
**Campbell, Ben Nighthorse, D-
Colo.** - 17
Campbell, Bonnie - 579

Campbell, Jim - 580
Campbell, Luther R. - 312
Canady, Charles T., R-Fla. (12) - 344
Cantwell, Maria, D-Wash. (1)
    1994 election - 573, 574
    Fishing legislation - 260
Capital punishment. See also: Racial Justice Act.
    Anti-crime legislation - 274, 280, 290, 487
    Breyer appointment - 309
Capitol Police - 526
Cardin, Benjamin L., D-Md. (3) - 330
Carl Albert Congressional Research and Studies Center - 60
Carlin, John - 572
Carlson, Gov. Arne, R-Minn. - 579
Carr, Bob, D-Mich. (8)
    1994 election - 566, 573
    Appropriations, Transportation - 530
Carroll, John - 576
Carter, President Jimmy - 450, 451, 471, 472, 27-D, 28-D
Casey, William J. - 465
Castle, Michael N., R-Del. (AL)
    Budget process - 90
    Crime bill - 285
    Health care reform - 328
Castro, Bernadette - 570
Cayetano, Gov. Benjamin J., D-Hawaii - 581
CCC export loan subsidy - 478
Cédras, Lt. Gen. Raoul - 450
Censorship - See: Freedom of speech.
Census Bureau - 484 (chart)
Center for Responsive Politics - 35
Center for Science in the Public Interest - 182
Center on Budget and Policy Priorities - 283
Centers for Disease Control and Prevention
    Appropriations, Labor-HHS-Education - 520 (chart), 522
    FY 1995 budget - 78
    Lead exposure - 266
    Minority health programs - 358
    Traumatic brain injuries - 361
Central Intelligence Agency (CIA)
    Ames spy case - 463, 466
    Authorization - 458, 463
    Secret document classification - 459, 462, 463
Cessna Aircraft Co. - 180, 181
Chabot, Steve - 572
Chafee, John H., R-R.I.
    1994 election - 6, 569
    Asphalt requiring crumb rubber - 167
    Breyer appointment - 304
    Clean water law - 241, 242
    Crime bill - 286, 287
    Drinking water authorization - 239
    GATT - 130
    Health care reform - 320, 324, 331, 338, 340, 343
    Interstate Transport of Solid Waste - 262
    Medicare select - 361
    Party unity - 7-C
    Solid waste disposal - 313
    Striker replacement - 402
    Superfund reauthorization - 235
    Vote studies, presidential support - 6-C
Chamber of Commerce, U.S. -

468
Chambliss, Saxby, R-Ga. - 571
Chapman, Jim, D-Texas (1)
    Appropriations, VA-HUD - 546
    Crime bill - 281
Chemical, biological weapons - 438, 439, 489 (chart)
Chemical Safety and Hazard Investigation Board - 555
Cheney, Dick - 430
Chenoweth, Helen, R-Idaho - 584
Chicago Sun-Times - 45, 47
Children. See also: Education; Elementary and secondary education; Food and nutrition; Head Start; Women, Infants and Children (WIC) program; Youth
    Anti-crime legislation - 288, 289, 292
    Child abuse - 370
    Child abuse payments - 376
    Child care assistance - 365, 520 (chart)
    Child support enforcement - 177, 365, 375, 376
    Child support payments - 376
    Crime bill - 292
    FY 1995 budget - 72, 73
    Illegitimate - 365
    International children's programs - 466
    Republicans' "Contract With America" - 23, 24
Chiles, Gov. Lawton, D-Fla. - 563, 580
China, People's Republic - See: People's Republic of China
China Lake Naval Weapons Center - 230
Chocolate Mountain Aerial Gunnery Range - 230
Christensen, Jon, R-Neb. - 20, 573
Christian Coalition - 42, 573
Christopher, Warren
    Bosnia-Herzegovina - 446, 447
    Defense authorization - 426
    Foreign aid reform - 452, 453
    Haitian crisis - 451
    Treaty on Women - 471
Chrysler, Dick, R-Mich. - 573
Chuvakhin, Sergey - 465
Cisneros, Henry G. - 409
Citizens for a Sound Economy - 213
Civil rights - 289, 314
Civil Rights Act of 1991 - 298
Civil Rights Commission - 299
Claremont McKenna College - 7, 60
Clay, William L., D-Mo. (1)
    Child nutrition programs - 374
    Federal employees - 147, 148, 150, 152
    Health care reform - 328
    House Appropriations Committee chairmanship - 8
    Postal Service - 155
    U.S. labor wage laws for foreign ships in U.S. waters - 158
Clayburgh, Ben - 570
Clean Air Act - 541
Clean water act - 546
Clement, Bob, D-Tenn. (5)
    East-West Transamerica Corridor - 167
    Preservation of historic black college buildings - 401
    Smoking ban on all international, Alaska, Hawaii flights - 174
Clinger, William F., R-Pa. (5)

Party unity - 7-C
Unfunded mandates - 152
Clinton, Hillary Rodham - 569
    Health care reform - 321, 322
    Whitewater/Madison affair - 298
Clinton, President Bill. See also: Ambassadors; Cabinet; Congressional-executive relations; Executive branch; Executive orders.
    1994 election, President campaigns for Rostenkowski - 44
    Agriculture Department reorganization - 191
    Anti-crime legislation - 26-D
    Antitrust legislation - 298
    Appropriations, VA-HUD - 541
    Bill Vetoes - 5 (box)
    Civil Rights Commission - 299
    Comments on House Speaker Thomas P. O'Neill - 59
    Defense, officer rank at retirement - 440, 441
    Disaster relief - 549 (box), 552
    Domestic workers tax laws - 368
    Earthquake relief - 167 (box)
    Education Chapter 1 (Title I) education program - 384
    School-to-work bill - 400, 401
    Election results 1994 - 33-D, 34-D
    Energy and Water appropriations - 502
    Environmental issues - 255
    Eulogy delivered for former President Richard M. Nixon - 16-D
    Federal courts - 300
    Federal crop insurance - 194
    Fire Prevention and Control Act of 1974 amendment - 299
    Flawed legislative strategy - 29, 32
    Foreign affairs
        Bosnia-Herzegovina - 446, 449
        Changing world order - 445, 446
        Haitian crisis - 449, 451, 27-D, 28-D, 29-D, 32-D
        South African economic aid - 470
        U.S. Russian aid policy - 466, 467
        Vietnam trade embargo - 467, 468, 12-D
    Grants
        Disabled individuals - 359
        Health care reform demise - 29, 32
    Home ownership - 408
    "Human investment" - 519
    Legislation
        Export-Import Bank - 138
        Food labels - 363
        Medicare select - 361
        Nutritional supplements - 357
        United States-Mexico Border Health Commission - 362, 363
        Veterinary medicine - 360
    Legislative setbacks - 31, 32
    Marine Mammal Protection Act reauthorization - 257
    Nominations and appointees
        Barkett, Rosemary - 300, 301
        Blinder, Alan S. - 139
        Gorelick, Jamie S. - 302
        Patrick, Deval L. - 302
        Rivlin, Alice M. - 138, 139

Sarokin, H. Lee - 301
Tigert, Ricki - 139
Overseas Private Investment Corporation - 266
Plant Variety Protection Act - 190
Presidential support - 3-C
Reaction to election - 32
State Department authorization bill - 454
State of the Union address - 30, 3-D, 7-D
Supreme Court
    Breyer appointment - 303, 305
Tax cuts to help middle class - 60-D, 61-D
Telemarketing fraud - 217
Welfare Reform - 364
Coalition on Smoking OR Health - 181
Coast Guard - 81
    Appropriations - 530, 531 (chart)
    Boating safety - 161, 163
    FY 1994 disaster supplemental - 552
    Maritime industry aid - 161, 163
    Reauthorization - 161, 162
Coats, Daniel R., R-Ind.
    1994 election - 572
    Breyer appointment - 310
    Elementary and secondary education authorization - 388, 390, 392
    Goals 2000 school improvement - 398
    Health care reform - 337
    Interstate Transport of Solid Waste - 261
    Perry nomination - 439
Coble, Howard, R-N.C. (6) - 5-C
Coburn, Tom, R-Okla. - 571
Cochran, Thad, R-Miss.
    Appropriations
        Agriculture - 480
        Foreign operations - 510
    Competitiveness programs - 222
    Congressional reform - 27
    Federal employees - 149, 150
    Federal Insecticide, Fungicide and Rodenticide Act (FIFRA) - 199
    Senate leadership for 104th Congress - 17
    Technology for education - 402
Cohen, Louis - 314
Cohen, William S., R-Maine
    Appropriations
        District of Columbia - 501
        Labor-HHS-Education - 523
        VA-HUD - 546
    Breyer nomination - 309, 23-D, 24-D
    Competitiveness programs - 222
    Federal employees - 150
    Haitian crisis - 451
    Independent counsel law - 297
    Lobbying disclosure and gift ban - 42
    Nominations and appointees - 301
    Social Security - 366
    State Department authorization bill - 455
Cole, James M. - 46
Coleman, Marshall - 568
Coleman, Ronald D., D-Texas (16) - 459
Colleges and universities -See: Postsecondary education

Collins, Barbara-Rose, D-Mich. (15) - 155
Collins, Cardiss, D-Ill. (7)
  Commerce Department - 189
  House committee assignments - 16
  Superfund reauthoriztion - 233
Colombia - 497, 511, 512
Colorado
  1994 election - 563, 579, 584
  Campaign reform - 581
  Term limits - 581
  Wilderness areas - 247
  Wilderness plans - 245
Combest, Larry, R-Texas (19)
  Ames spy case - 465
  Plant Variety Protection Act - 190
Commerce. *See also: Banks and banking; Business interests; Commerce Department; Communications and telecommunications; Consumer affairs; Federal Trade Commission; Fish and fishing; Foreign trade; Ships, shipping; Transportation.*
Commerce, Science and Transportation Committee (Senate)
  Added-nicotine controversy - 360
  Commerce Department - 189, 190
  Competitiveness programs - 221
  Disaster relief - 156
  Fishing vessel registration - 267
  GATT - 123, 128
  National Science Foundation reauthorization - 220
  Product liability - 178
  Small aircraft product liability - 180
Commerce Department. *See also: Communications and telecommunications; Computers; Economic Development Administration; Gross domestic product; National Institute of Standards and Technology; Small Business Administration.*
  Appropriations -187, 483, 484 (chart), 486
  Boxing Safety - 189
  Competitiveness programs - 221, 223
  Environmental technology - 263, 264
  Fishing vessel registration - 267
  FY 1994 disaster supplemental provisions - 553, 554
  Hazardous pipelines - 189
  Immigration law - 295
  Landsat satellite launches - 219
  Made in America Hotline - 189
  Office of Strategic Economic Development Planning and Policy - 188
  Patent and Trademark Office - 184
  Patent Office authorization - 184
  Russian aid policy - 467
  U.S. and Foreign Commercial Service - 189
Commission on the Roles and Capabilities of the United States Intelligence Community - 463
Committee on Standards of Official Conduct (House) - *See: Ethics Committee (House)*
Commodity Credit Corporation -

70, 197, 551
Common Cause - 32, 35, 38, 39, 41, 42
Commonwealth of Independent States (CIS). *See also: Names of other republics created from former Soviet Union.*
  Ames spy case - 458, 459, 463, 466, 508
  Mir space station - 544
  Most-Favored-Nation status - 467
  Russian aid - 510, 511
  State Department authorization bill - 456
  U.S. defense spending - 423, 489 (chart)
  U.S. foreign aid - 466, 467, 505, 508
  U.S. foreign aid for Jewish refugees - 466, 467
  U.S. Russian aid policy - 466, 467
  U.S. Space Station Project - 80
Communications Act (1934) - 204
Communications and telecommunications. *See also: Federal Communications Commission (FCC); Films; National Telecommunications and Information Administration; Radio; Television*
  Communications Act (1934) - 203
  Intellectual property
    Copyright legislation revisions sought - 216, 217
  Technology for Education Act Telemarketing fraud - 217, 218
  Telephones
    Allowing Baby Bells to offer long-distance service - 208, 209, 210, 16-C, 17-C
    Allowing Baby Bells to provide "incidental" services - 206
    Bell requirement to establish subsidiaries - 213, 214
    Congressional "Farm Team" raises concerns - 210, 211 "Dialing parity" - 210
    Electronic eavesdropping - 215, 216
    Local competition - 204, 205, 208, 210, 213 (box)
    Long-distance service - 209
    Network costs - 205, 206
    Pay phone industry - 212
    Rural telephone companies - 205, 210, 211, 213 (box)
    Universal service - 207, 208, 209, 213 (box)
    U.S. communications law rewrite bills
      Armstrong lawsuit - 553
      Bills declared dead for 103rd Congress - 214
      Breaux-Packwood bill - 208, 209, 210
      Brooks-Dingell bill - 204, 205, 206, 209
      Domestic (American-only) content provision - 211
      Hollings-Danforth-Inouye bill - 207, 208, 209
      Legislative action - 16-C, 17-C
      Markey-Fields bill - 204, 205, 206

      Provision of Senate bill - 213 (box)
      Senate committee action - 212, 214
      Standards of decency proposed - 212
      State and local governments express concern - 214
      U.S. communications law rewrite bills - 203, 214
    Video, phone services for disabled, schools, libraries, other groups - 209, 213 (box)
Communications Workers of America - 211
Community development
  Community development block grants - 71, 551, 553
  Community Partnerships Against Crime (COMPAC) - 408, 409
  Community Reinvestment Act - 95, 97
Community development banks - *See: Banks and banking.*
Community health centers - 521
Community Services Block Grants - 72, 369, 372, 373, 520 (chart)
Community-Based Family Resources Programs - 372
Competitiveness policy -*See: Commerce Department; Research and Development, U.S.; Science and Technology.*
Comprehensive Environmental Response, Compensation and Liability Act - *See: Superfund, EPA*
Computers
  Competitiveness programs - 223
  Electronic mail addresses obtained by subpoena - 215
  Electronic monitoring - 407
  Elementary and secondary education authorization - 389, 395
  High-performance computing - 223
  Intellectual property - 214
  Nationwide computer networks - 71
  Technology for Education Act - 401, 402, 407
Condit, Gary A., D-Calif. (18)
  Agriculture Department reorganization - 193
  Appropriations- Commerce-Justice-State - 486
  Disaster relief - 550
  Elementary and secondary education authorization - 387
  Unfunded mandates - 151
  Vegetable oil-based ink - 199
Conference of Mayors, U.S. - 150, 238
Conference on Security and Cooperation in Europe (CSCE) - 472
Congress. *See also: Campaign finance, Congressional caucuses and coalitions; Cogressional elections; Congressional employees; Congressional ethics; Congressional redistricting; Congressional votes; Congressional-executive relations; CQ Roundtable; Democratic leadership; Ex-Members of Congress; House of*

Representatives; Legislation (general); Lobbies, lobbying; Politics and elections; Republican leadership; Senate.
  Administrative changes - 13
  Appropriators complete work - 475, 476
  Committee funding - 13
  Committee staff cuts - 20
  Fast Track procedures, GATT - 124
  Filibusters and cloture votes - 9 (box)
  FY 1994 disaster supplemental provisions - 552, 554
  Income tax rate increase - 20
  Lame-duck session - 7
  Leadership changes - 7, 9, 12
  Legislative achievements, failures - 3, 13
  Map of Capitol Hill - 16-B
  Members of Congress
    Changes - 12, 13
    103rd Congress, 2nd Session - 6-B, 7-B
    104th Congress - 582, 583
  Overview of 103rd Congress - 3, 13
  Proxy voting - 18, 19, 20 (box)
  Republican era - 14, 21
  Republicans' "Contract With America" - 26
  Term limits - 18, 20, 21 (box), 314, 315
Congressional Black Caucus
  Budget resolution - 83
  Death penalty - 279, 280
  Delgate's voting - 61
  Federal contracts - 187
  Foreign aid reform - 453
  Foreign operations appropriations - 508
  Haiti occupation - 449, 451
  House leadership contests - 16
  Lobbying disclosure - 42
  National Endowment for Democracy - 487
  Patrick nomination - 302
Congressional Budget Office (CBO)
  Balanced-budget amendment - 86
  Black lung disease - 406
  Budget resolution - 82
  Budget resolution FY 1995 - 82
  Clinton budget - 68
  Environmental issues - 255
  Federal worker buyouts - 148
  Health care reform - 324, 331, 350, 355
  Holocaust survivors - 377
  Persian Gulf Syndrome - 412
  Superfund reauthorization - 232
  Unfunded federal mandates - 25, 151
Congressional caucuses and coalitions - 375
Congressional elections. *See also: Campaign finance, CQ Roundtable; Federal Election Commission; names of individual states; Politics and elections*
  1994 results - 571, 578
  Congressional changes - 12, 13
  Elections mean sea change on Hill - 14, 21
  GOP election mandate - 35-D, 37-D
  Results, 1994 - 33-D, 34-D
Congressional employees
  Congressional workplace law exemptions - 28, 29
  Pay raises - 63, 64

Congressional ethics. *See also: Campaign finance; Ex-members of Congress.*
  Congress's image suffers - 3
  Durenberger case - 51
  Frost case dismissed - 53
  "Ghost voting" - 53, 54
  Gingrich investigation - 54
  Hubbard pleads guilty - 53
  Hutchison case - 51
  Kennedy cleared - 52, 53
  Lawmakers under indictment - 50, 55
  Lobbying legislation
    Background - 36, 37
    Gift-giving limits - 5, 37, 42
    Gift-giving restrictions - 41 (box)
    Lobbying disclosure - 5, 19-C, 20-C, 27-C
  McDade indictment, appeal - 51, 52
  Packwood investigation - 49, 50
  Perkins pleads guilty - 53
  Reynolds indictment - 51
  Rose case - 52
  Rostenkowski indictment - 43, 48
  Tucker indictment - 51
Congressional Research Service - 524, 526
Congressional Sportsmen's Caucus - 229
Congressional votes
  "Ghost voting" - 53, 54
  Key House - 13-C, 20-C
  Key Senate - 21-C, 28-C
  Natcher's voting string - 58
  Roll call votes and quorum calls by chamber - 5 (box)
Congressional-executive relations
  White House relations - 29, 32
Connecticut
  1994 election - 564, 570, 576, 579, 584
  Dairy legislation - 197
  VA medical facilities - 415
Conrad, Kent, D-N.D.
  1994 election - 570
  Budget resolution, FY 1995 - 83
  GATT - 127
  Health care reform - 338, 340, 342
  Procurement reform - 145
Conservative coalition
  House voting - 42-C
  Senate voting - 44-C
  Votes - 40-C
Constitution, U.S. *See also: Supreme Court.*
  Equality value - 308, 309
  Rulemaking Clause - 48
  Speech or Debate Clause - 48
Consumer affairs - 98
Consumer Federation of America - 206
Consumer Product Safety Commission - 179, 180
Consumers Union - 180
Convention on the Elimination of All Forms of Discrimination on Women - 471
Conyers, John Jr., D-Mich. (14)
  Crime bill - 278, 282
  Federal employees - 149
  Kennedy assassination - 157
  Procurement reform - 145
  U.S. communications law rewrite - 207
Cook, Merrill - 584
Cooley, Wes, R-Ore. - 584
Cooper, Jim, D-Tenn. (4)
  1994 election - 565, 566, 571

  Health care reform - 324, 331, 335
  Party unity - 7-C
  Republican control of Senate - 565
Cooper, Virgil R. - 571
Cooperative State Research Service - 70, 477
Coppersmith, Sam, D-Ariz. (1)
  1994 election - 565, 568, 575
  Postal Service appropriations - 538
  Republican control of Senate - 565
Copyright - 135, 312
Copyright Royalty Tribunal - 525, 526
Corning Inc. - 205
Corporation for National and Community Service - 372, 543, 545
Corporation for Public Broadcasting (CPB) - 520 (chart), 522
Cost of Living Adjustments (COLA) - 63
Council of Chief State School Officers - 523
Council of Economic Advisers - 139
  GATT - 123
Council on Environmental Quality - 243
  FY 1994 disaster supplemental - 553
Courts. *See also: Courts of Appeals, U.S.; District Courts, U.S.; Judiciary; Supreme Court.*
  New courthouse projects - 539
  Nominations and appointees - 300, 302
  Republicans' "Contract With America" - 26
  Tax Courts, U.S. - 537 (chart)
Courts of Appeals, U.S.
  Anti-crime legislation - 290
  Appropriations
    Commerce-Justice-State - 484 (chart)
  Congressional pay raise - 63, 64
  Delegate voting - 61, 62
  Ethanol rule - 546
  Rostenkowski indictment - 48
Coverdell, Paul, R-Ga.
  1994 election - 561
  Appropriations
    Commerce-Justice-State - 487
    Defense - 497
  Biodiversity treaty - 267
  Breyer appointment - 310
  Election victory - 561
  Striker replacement - 402
Cox, C. Christopher, R-Calif. (47) - 14
Cox Enterprises Inc. - 129
Cracraft, George K. - 314
Craig, Larry E., R-Idaho
  Crime bill - 287
  Federal land payments to localities - 156
  Idaho wilderness bill - 247
  Mining law rewrite - 237
Cramer, Robert E. "Bud," D-Ala. (5) - 572
Crane, Philip M., R-Ill. (8)
  Appropriations, Labor-HHS-Education - 521, 522
  National Endowment for the Arts - 515
Crapo, Michael D., R-Idaho (2) - 247

Credit
  U.S. bankruptcy code revisions - 175, 177
Cremeans, Frank A., R-Ohio - 572
Crime and criminal justice. *See also: Drugs and drug abuse, Federal Bureau of Investigation (FBI); Gun controls; Judiciary; Law and justice; Law enforcement; Prisons and prisoners; Racial Justice Act*
  Anti-crime legislation
    Anti-crime trust fund - 79, 282, 283, 293, 483, 484 (chart), 486
    Boot camps for young offenders - 486
    Brady gun control law - *See: Gun controls, Brady law.*
    Child abuse - 279
    Congressional action - 273, 294
      Conference report - 281, 285, 19-C
      Final passage - 286, 287
      House action - 5, 275, 281, 18-C, 19-C
      Senate action - 6, 286, 26-C
    Crime bill provisions - 287, 294
    Crime prevention programs - 274, 278, 288, 289
    Federal sentencing guidelines - 274, 278
    Funding - 80, 274, 281 (box)
    Hate crimes - 290
    Insurance fraud - 279
    Juveniles - 274, 278, 279
    Sentencing - 290
    Sexual predators - 292
    Three strikes and you're out proposal - 278, 281, 290
    Victims - 279, 292
    Violence against women - 486
  Congressional action
    Crime prevention programs - 23
    House action - 15-C, 26-D
    Crime bill - 273, 294
  Crime prevention programs - 399, 499 (chart), 501
  Housing authorization - 409
  Property forfeiture of criminal suspect - 314
  Public housing - 408
  Republican view - 8-D, 9-D
  Violent crime and drug emergency areas - 290
Crime Trust Fund - 283
Croatia - 447
Cuba - 457, 483, 487
Cuban-American Foundation - 457
Cubin, Barbara, R-Wyo. - 584
Cullerton, John - 44
Cunningham, Randy "Duke," R-Calif. (51)
  Appropriations
    Energy and water - 503
    Treasury Department - 539
  Elementary and secondary education authorization - 385
  Health care reform - 328, 329
Cuomo, Gov. Mario, D-N.Y. - 570, 576, 584
Curry, William - 579
Customs Service, U.S. - 536, 537 (chart), 540

Cyprus - 470, 509, 512

D

Daley, Richard M. - 48, 572
D'Amato, Alfonse M., R-N.Y.
  1994 election - 575, 579
  Appropriations
    Foreign operations - 510
    Transportation - 534
    Treasury Department - 539
    VA-HUD - 544
  Banking laws - 107, 108
  Community Development Banking - 100, 101, 107
  Flood insurance bill - 411, 412
  FY 1994 disaster supplemental - 556
  Russian aid policy - 467
  Striker replacement - 402
Danforth, John C., R-Mo.
  1994 election - 565
  Competitiveness programs - 221, 222
  Crime bill - 286, 287
  Elementary and secondary education authorization - 390, 391
  Federal railroad safety programs - 173
  GATT - 127
  Goals 2000 school improvement - 399
  Health care reform - 340, 342
  Republican control of Senate - 565
  U.S. communications law rewrite - 203, 207, 209
Darden, George "Buddy," D-Ga. (7) - 571
Daschle, Tom, D-S.D.
  1994 election - 8
  Disaster aid tax relief - 200
  Federal Insecticide, Fungicide and Rodenticide Act (FIFRA) - 198, 199
  Health care reform - 338
  Persian Gulf Syndrome compensation - 414
  Senate leadership for 104th Congress - 17, 18
  Vote studies, presidential support - 4-C
Davidson, Roger H. - 12-C
Davis, Thomas M., III, R-Va. - 572
Davis, William P. - 51
Davis-Bacon (1934) - 144, 147, 232, 234, 235, 239, 242, 329, 406
Days, Drew S. III - 314, 436
de la Garza, E. "Kika," D-Texas (15)
  Agriculture Department reorganization - 192, 193
  Enviromental issues - 254
  Federal crop insurance - 196
  Federal Insecticide, Fungicide and Rodenticide Act (FIFRA) - 198, 199
  Plant Variety Protection Act - 190
Deal, Nathan, D-Ga. (9)
  1994 congressional election - 563
  House leadership position races - 15
Death penalty - *See: Capital punishment.*
Death row appeals - 275
DeConcini, Dennis, D-Ariz.
  1994 election - 565
  Ames spy case - 464
  Appropriations, Treasury

Department - 536, 539, 540
Breyer nomination - 22-D, 23-D
Defense authorization - 426
Drinking water authorization - 239
Environmental issues - 247
Holocaust survivors - 377
Intelligence authorization bill - 459, 461, 462
Logging on Forest Service lands - 257
National Reconnaissance Office - 461 (box)
Patent and Trademark Office - 184, 185
Product liability - 179
Republican control of Senate - 565
Television signal retransmission - 217
Deering, Christopher - 9-C
DeFazio, Peter A., D-Ore. (4) - 250
Defense Base Closure and Realignment Commission - 436
Defense Department. *See also: Air Force; Army; Army Corps of Engineers; Government contractors; Marine Corps, U.S.; Military personnel issues; Navy.*
Abortion - 343
Aid to Commonwealth of Independent States - 496
Airborne self-protection jammer
Appropriations - 71, 72, 488, 489 (chart), 527, 528, 529 (chart)
Authorization - 421, 432
Base closings commissions - 247
Budget resolution FY 1995 - 84
Burden sharing - 423
Child support enforcement - 375
Contractors merger reorganization costs - 432
Defense conversion projects - 489 (chart), 496
Defense Finance and Accounting Service - 493
Defense Logistics Agency - 493
Defense spending - 24, 13-C, 14-C
Digitization - 495
Economic conversion - 431, 492
Environmental issues - 255
FY 1995 budget - 79, 80
FY 1994 disaster supplemental - 489 (chart)
FY 1994 disaster supplemental provisions - 551, 554
Haiti - 424, 450, 451
Halperin withdraws his candidacy for defense position - 440
Health care
Persian Gulf War - 469, 470
Programs - 489 (chart), 496
Reform - 343
Humanitarian, disaster relief - 431, 549 (box)
Intelligence - 458, 460, 462, 463
Military readiness - 490, 491, 493
North Korean threat - 424
Nuclear, chemical weapons disposal in former Soviet states - 423, 431, 492, 497
Olympic Games, 1996 - 431, 497
Operations and maintenance - 493

298
Overhauls to be performed by government depots - 431
Pay raises -*See: Military personnel issues.*
Peacekeeping - 427, 440, 447, 489 (chart), 492, 493, 549 (box), 550, 551
Pentagon medical school - 431
Number of assistant secretaries of Defense - 432
School of the Americas military school funding - 424
Perry nomination - 439, 440
Personnel locator service - 375
Presidio - 253
Research and development - 496, 554, 557
Secret document classification - 459, 462, 463
Sexual harassment against women in military - 435, 440, 441
Special Olympic Games - 431
Transportation - 81
Women to serve in combat units - 435
DeLauro, Rosa, D-Conn. (3)
Appropriations, agricultural - 520
House committee assignments - 16
Delaware - 569, 576
DeLay, Tom, R-Texas (22)
Appropriations
Agriculture - 479
Foreign operations - 508
Labor-HHS-Education - 521
Transportation - 532
VA-HUD - 541
California desert protection - 230
House leadership position races - 14, 15
Lobbying disclosure and gift ban - 38
Montana wilderness bill - 246
Preparing for new Republican role - 20
Delegates, U.S. territories - *See: Trust territories, U.S.*
Dellums, Ronald V., D-Calif. (9)
Appropriations, Defense - 488
California desert protection - 229
Defense authorization - 422, 423, 424, 427, 429, 432, 433, 434, 435
Procurement reform - 145, 146
Democratic Governors' Association - 576
Democratic leadership
House committee assignments 104th Congress - 15, 16
House leadership contests for the 104th Congress - 15, 16
House leadership position races - 17 (box)
Lobbying disclosure and gift ban - 38
Rostenkowski indicted, defeated - 43
Senate leadership for 104th Congress - 17, 18
Titans pass from scene - 55, 59
Democratic National Committee - 5, 570
Democratic Party
1994 election - 3
Appropriations
Legislative branch - 524, 525
VA-HUD - 547
Legal Services Corporation -

Senate defeat - 565, 570
Derrick, Butler, D-S.C. (3)
1994 election - 571
Congressional reform - 28
Deutch, John M.
Defense authorization - 428, 430, 433, 434
Haitian crisis - 451
National Reconnaissance Office - 461 (box)
Deutsch, Peter, D-Fla. (20) - 258
DeWine, Mike, R-Ohio - 565, 566
Dickey, Jay, R-Ark. (4) - 572
Dicks, Norm, D-Wash. (6)
Defense authorization - 424
Logging on Forest Service lands - 256, 257
National Endowment for the Arts - 516
DiDonato, Greg - 572
Dingell, John D., D-Mich. (16)
Appropriations
Transportation - 533
Banking laws - 108
Committe chairmen's terms - 18
Community Development Banking - 102
Environmental Protection Agency - 243
Federal Trade Commission - 181
GATT - 129
Health care reform - 5, 335
High-speed rail - 172
Interstate transport of solid waste - 261, 262
Nutritional supplements - 358
Product liability - 178
Safe drinking water reauthorization - 240
Small Business Administration (SBA) - 187
Superfund reauthorization - 233
U.S. communications law rewrite - 204, 206, 207, 209
Wetlands protection - 265
DioGuardi, Joseph J. - 576
Disabled - 389
Disaster relief. *See also: Federal Emergency Management Agency.*
Appropriations - 149
Commerce-Justice-State - 483, 487
Defense - 489 (chart)
Disaster insurance proposal - 70
Earthquake preparedness - 155
Federal crop insurance - 195
Federal Emergency Management Agency (FEMA) - 101
Flood insurance - 101, 105, 106
Flood insurance bill - 411, 412
FY 1994 disaster supplemental - 487
Legislative action - 548, 550, 556, 557
Midwest flood damage - 548
Supplemental also covers floods, fires, peacekeeping - 548
Legislation - 155, 156
Retooling bridges to withstand earthquakes - 167 (box)
Robert T. Stafford Disaster Relief and Emergency Assistance Act - 156
Tax relief - 200
Discretionary spending - 67
Discrimination. *See also: Aged persons; Civil rights; Women.*
FY 1994 disaster supplemental

provisions - 553
Gender equity - 312
District Courts, U.S. - 64, 315, 484 (chart), 10-D, 11-D
District of Columbia
Appropriations - 183, 498, 499 (chart), 501
D.C. School of Law - 500
Domestic partners law - 498, 499
GATT - 129
HUD special purpose grants - 545
Pension retirement program fund - 498, 499, 500
Dixon, Alan J. - 435
Dixon, Julian C., D-Calif. (32)
Appropriations, District of Columbia - 498, 499
FY 1994 disaster supplemental - 557
Dodd, Christopher J., D-Conn.
1994 election - 8
Banking law - 94, 95, 98
Budget resolution FY 1995 - 84
Defense authorization - 427
Elementary and secondary education authorization - 388
Goals 2000 school improvement - 399
Haitian crisis - 449, 450
Health care reform - 337
National Endowment for the Arts - 517
Senate leadership for 104th Congress - 17
Small Business Administration (SBA) - 187
State Department authorization bill - 455
Dole, Bob, R-Kan.
1994 election - 3, 14, 565, 569, 570
Appropriations
Commerce-Justice-State - 487
Defense - 494
Foreign aid - 512
Foreign operations - 510
VA-HUD - 546
Bosnia-Herzegovina - 177, 445, 447, 448, 449
Campaign finance reform - 34
Clinton's State of the Union address - 30
Competitiveness programs - 222
Crime bill - 283, 284, 286
Defense authorization - 425, 427
Drinking water authorization - 239, 240
Elementary and secondary education authorization - 390
Federal crop insurance - 197
FY 1994 disaster supplemental - 556
General Agreement on Tariffs and Trade (GATT) - 127, 128, 53-D, 56-D
Haiti - 450, 510
Health care reform - 340, 341, 343
Independent counsel law - 296
Lobbying disclosure and gift ban - 39, 42
Majority leader news conference - 38-D
Minority health programs - 359
Preservation of historic black college buildings - 401
President Clinton's State of the Union address, Republican

response - 8-D
Republican attitude - 6
Republican control of Senate - 565
Senate leadership for 104th Congress - 17
Special elections - 592
State Department authorization bill - 455
Superfund reauthorization - 231, 235, 236
Talbott nomination - 471
U.S. communications law rewrite - 203, 211, 214
Vietnam trade embargo - 468
Welfare reform - 364
Working Groups - 21
Domenici, Pete V., R-N.M.
Appropriations
   Commerce-Justice-State - 486
   District of Columbia - 501
   Foreign aid - 510
   Treasury Department - 539
Budget resolution FY 1995 - 69, 83, 85
California desert protection - 231
Congressional reform - 27
Crime bill - 286
Defense authorization - 426
Drinking water authorization - 239
Elementary and secondary education authorization - 390
Federal employees - 150
National parks - 249
Reorganization of Senate committees - 21
Russian aid policy - 466, 467
Domestic Volunteer Service Programs - 520 (chart)
Dooley, Cal, D-Calif. (20)
Agriculture Department reorganization - 192
Dairy legislation - 197
Doolittle, John T., R-Calif. (4)
Elementary and secondary education authorization - 387
Environmental issues - 255
Dorgan, Byron L., D-N.D.
Banking law - 98
Senate leadership for 104th Congress - 18
Unfunded mandates - 151
U.S. communications law rewrite - 210
Dornan, Robert K., R-Calif. (46)
California toll road project - 166
Defense authorization - 424
Douglass, Brooks - 592
Doyle, Mike, D-Pa. - 576
Dreier, David, R-Calif. (28)
Congressional workplace law exemptions - 29
   Preparing for new Republican role - 20
Driegert, Robert - 53
Drug Enforcement Administration (DEA) - 292, 485, 486
Drugs and drug abuse. *See also: DEA; Food and Drug Administration; Office of National Drug Control Policy; Pharmaceuticals.*
Anti-crime legislation - 289
Anti-crime programs - 408
Anti-narcotics program - 509
Appropriations - 489 (chart); Labor-HHS-Education - 520 (chart)
Coast Guard authorization -

161, 163
Cocaine - 293
Driving safety - 174
Drug Elimination Grant Program - 408
Drug-free schools program - 387, 392, 394
International narcotics control - 506 (chart), 507, 508, 511
Medicare and Medicaid - 367
Social Security benefits - 366
Supplemental Security Income or disability insurance payments - 365
Dudzinski, Lucille - 46
Duncan, John J. "Jimmy" Jr., R-Tenn. (2)
California desert protection - 228
Goals 2000 school improvement - 399
National Endowment for the Arts - 517
Dunn, Jennifer, R-Wash. (8) - 234
Duran-Owens, Guale - 146
Durbin, Richard J., D-Ill. (20)
Added-nicotine controversy - 360
Appropriations, agricultural - 477
Appropriations, Labor-HHS-Education - 521
Appropriations, Transportation - 532
Elementary and secondary education authorization - 387
Federal crop insurance - 196
Durenberger, Dave, R-Minn.
1994 election - 565, 568
Appropriations District of Columbia - 501
Ethics case - 50
Health care reform - 337, 340, 342
Republican control of Senate - 565
Senate leadership for 104th Congress - 17
Superfund reauthorization - 235
Dutremble, Dennis L. - 576

E

Eagle Forum - 573
Earle, Ronnie - 51
Earthquake aid - *See: Disaster relief*
Eastern Europe - *See: Europe*
EBRD - *See: European Bank for Reconstruction and Development (EBRD)*
Echeverria, John D. - 244
EchoHawk, Larry - 580
Economic Development Administration (EDA) - 187, 483, 484 (chart), 486, 553
Economic indicators
Administration economic asumptions 1993-1999 - 74 (chart)
Effect of economy on the budget - 69
Gross Domestic Product (GDP) - 82
Economic Support Fund - 506 (chart)
Education. *See also: Education Department; Elementary and secondary education; Head Start; National service; Postsecondary education; Student aid.*
Bilingual education - 520

(chart), 390, 395
Chapter 1 (Title I) rewrite - *See: Elementary and secondary education.*
Drug-free schools program - 392, 394
Eisenhower grants - 383
FY 1995 budget - 72
FY 1994 disaster supplemental - 549 (box)
Global Learning and Observations to Benefit the Environment (GLOBE) - 219, 220
Goals 2000: Educate America Act - 384, 397, 399, 401, 402, 519, 522, 523, 4-C, 21-C
Guns in schools - 383, 390, 391, 392
Home schooling - 386, 387
Immigrant education -371, 387, 391, 520 (chart), 521, 522
National education standards - 398
Non-English-speaking children - 371
Opportunity-to-learn standards - 383, 385, 387, 389, 397, 398 (box), 399
School prayer - 383, 388, 389, 390, 391, 395, 396, 398, 399
School-to-work bill - 400, 401, 519, 522
School-to-work Opportunities Act - 72
Sex education - 383, 390, 391, 395, 396
Single-sex classes - 390, 391
Star Schools program - 402
Teacher training - 383, 391
Education and Labor Committee (House)
Child nutrition programs - 374
Commerce Department - 189
Davis-Bacon revision - 406
Elementary and secondary education - 385, 386
Federal employees - 153
Foreign-register vessel labor laws - 160
Head Start - 373
Health care reform - 324, 329
OSHA overhaul - 403
Professional baseball antitrust exemption - 183
Restructuring House committees - 18
'School to Work' Program - 400
Underfunded pension plans - 404
Education Department
Anti-crime legislation - 288
Appropriations - 72, 356, 369
Appropriations
   FY 1995 - 519, 520 (chart), 523,
   FY 1994 disaster supplemental provisions - 551, 554
Native Hawaiians education program - 522
Rehabilitiation services - 520 (chart)
Research programs - 520 (chart)
School lunch and school breakfast programs - 373, 375
Star Schools program - 402
Vocational schools - 390, 520
Edwards, Don, D-Calif. (16)
1994 election - 573
Crime bill - 276, 277

Electronic eavesdropping - 215, 216
Nation of Islam - 62
Egypt - 453, 505
Eisenach, Jeffrey A. - 54, 55
Elections, congressional - *See: Congressional elections*
Elections and politics - *See: Politics and elections*
Electronic eavesdropping - 215, 216
Electronic Privacy Information Center - 215
Electronic publishing - *See: Communications and telecommunications, U.S. communications law*
Elementary and secondary education. *See also: Education Department*
Appropriations, Labor-HHS-Education - 520 (chart)
Authorization - 383, 392
   Bill provisions - 392, 396
Bilingual education - 390, 395
Chapter 1 (Title I) rewrite
   Authorization - 383, 390, 391
   Funding - 386
   House legislative action - 384, 388
   Kennedy-Pell proposal - 388, 389
   Kildee-Petri II - 386
   Provisions - 392, 393
   Results demanded - 385
   Senate legislative action - 388, 390
Chapter 2 (Title II) education grant program - 384, 385, 391, 393, 394
Drug-free schools program - 387, 392, 394
Eisenhower grants - 383
Grant programs to provide equity for women and girls - 385, 394
Guns in schools - 383, 390, 391, 392, 395
Homosexual, heterosexual activities - 387
"Impact aid" programs for local school districts - 385, 395
Indian education - 395
Migrant students - 391
Opportunity-to-learn standards - 383, 385, 387, 389, 397, 398 (box), 399
Promoting equity - 394
Safe Schools Act of 1994 - *See: Education, Goals 2000 school improvement*
School choice - 385, 386, 387, 390, 398
School construction - 389, 391, 392, 396
School construction grants - 523, 392, 396
School prayer - 383, 388, 389, 390, 391, 395, 396, 398, 399
Sex education - 383, 390, 391, 395, 396
Technology for education - 389, 394, 395, 401, 402, 407
Technology initative - 522
Trade and proprietary schools - 519, 521
Elks Lodge - 362
Emergency Food Assistance Program - 70, 477, 480, 482
Emergency relief - *See: Disaster relief.*
Emerson, Bill, R-Mo. (8)

Employee Retirement Income Security Act (ERISA) - 403, 404, 405

Employment and training
Labor-HHS-Education appropriations - 520 (chart)
Reemployment Act of 1994 - 405, 406
School-to-work bill - 400, 401
Veterans Affairs Department - 416, 417
Welfare reform job training - 364

Employment and Training Administration
FY 1994 disaster supplemental - 552

Employment and unemployment - 79, 407

Employment Retirement Income Security Act (ERISA) - 342

Empower America - 20

Endangered Species Act - 227, 229, 230, 515

Energy - See also: Nuclear energy.
Biomass energy development - 555
BTU tax - 333
Ethanol - 542, 543
Foreign refiners - 543
Navy Petroleum reserves - 73, 514
Oil fields - 73
Petroleum industry - 546, 547
Renewable resources - 73
Uranium supply and enrichment programs - 554

Energy and Commerce Committee (House)
Drinking water authorization - 240
Electronic eavesdropping - 216
Energy Department research laboratories - 223
Energy research laboratories - 223
Environmental Protection Agency - 243
FCC funding increase - 218
Federal Trade Commission - 181
GATT - 129
Health care reform - 335, 336
Indoor air - 266
Interstate Transport of Solid Waste - 261
Medical devices - 362
Minority health programs - 358
Nutritional supplements - 358
Orphan drugs - 363
Product liability - 178
Radon disclosure - 264
Smoking restrictions - 362
Superfund reauthoriztion - 233
United States-Mexico Border Health Commission - 363
U.S. communications law rewrite - 206

Energy and Natural Resources Committee (Senate) - 378
California desert protection - 227, 228
Drinking water authorization - 239
Everglades protection - 254
Federal land payments to localities - 156
Guam - 157
Historic preservation fund - 401
Mining law rewrite - 236
National parks - 247, 249, 251
Presidio management - 254
Steamtown - 252

Energy Department. See also: Nuclear energy; Nuclear waste management; Superconducting super collider
Appropriations - 73, 502, 504, 514 (chart)
Defense-related programs - 71
FY 1995 budget - 78
FY 1994 disaster supplemental provisions - 552, 554
High-energy physics programs - 221
International Thermonuclear Experimental Reactor - 221
Nuclear fusion research - 221
Relativistic Heavy Ion Collider - 221
Research laboratories - 223
Tritium manufacturing - 427

Engel, Eliot L., D-N.Y. (17)
Cyprus conflict - 470
Health care reform - 325

English, Glenn, D-Okla.
1994 election - 12
Special elections - 592

English, Karan, D-Ariz. (6)
1994 election - 575
Congressional workplace law exemptions - 28

Enhanced Structural Adjustment Facility - 505, 509

Ensign, John, R-Nev. - 584

Environment. See also: Bureau of Land Management; Department of the Interior.; Endangered Species Act; Environmental Protection Agency; Forest Service; Hazardous waste management; Nuclear waste management; Pesticides and herbicides; Pollution; Public lands management; Superfund, EPA; Waste management; Water projects.
Beach and barrier island restoration projects - 255
Conservation programs, appropriations - 478 (chart)
Drinking water authorization - 238, 240
Drinking water safety - 244
Endangered species - 254
Energy and water appropriations - 502
Environmental restoration - 489 (chart)
Environmental technology - 263, 264
Ethanol - 541, 542
Everglades protection - 254
Flow-control legislation - 262
FY 1995 budget - 73
Headwaters Forest Act - 254
Indoor air - 265
Interstate Transport of Solid Waste - 261, 263
Landfills - 265
Lead exposure - 266
Mining law rewrite - 236, 237
Minor-use pesticides - 198
Ocean dumping - 162
Outer continental shelf - 255
Radioactive waste - 263
Requiring scrap tire use in road asphalt - 166, 167
Water bank extension - 265
Water issues - 238, 243
Water quality, Safe Drinking Water Reauthorization - 238, 240
Wetlands - 265, 477
Wilderness plans - 245, 246
Wildlife preservation - 255

Environment and Public Works Committee (Senate)
Clean water law - 241, 242
Drinking water authorization - 238, 240
Economic Development Administration - 188
Environmental issues - 255
Environmental technology - 264
Fishing legislation - 260
Interstate Transport of Solid Waste - 261
National Endowment for the Arts - 518
National Highway System (NHS) - 165
Superfund reauthorization - 235
Wetlands protection - 265

Environmental Insurance Resolution Fund - 232, 233, 234, 236

Environmental Protection Agency (EPA) - 379
Added-nicotine controversy - 359, 360
Appropriations - 541, 545, 547
Cabinet status - 243, 13-C
Drinking water authorization - 238, 240, 23-C, 24-C
Environmental technology - 263, 264
Flow-control legislation - 262
FY 1994 disaster supplemental - 555
FY 1994 disaster supplemental provisions - 553
Hazardous waste - 243
Indoor air - 265
Pesticide safety - 199
Risk assessments - 23-C, 24-C
Superfund - 231
Unfunded mandates - 150
Water management projects - 255

Equal Employment Opportunity Commission (EEOC) - 153, 484 (chart)

Erlich, Robert L., R-Md. - 576

Eshoo, Anna G., D-Calif. (14) - 223

Espy, Mike
Agriculture Department reorganization - 192
Federal crop insurance - 195, 197
Resignation - 194

Estonia - 467

Ethics Committee (House) - 44, 50, 52, 53, 54

Ethics Committee (Senate)
Kennedy case - 52, 53
Lobbying disclosure and gift ban - 39
Packwood case - 10-D, 11-D, 49, 50

Ethics in government. See also: Congressional ethics; Fraud and abuse in government; Office of Government Ethics.
Rose indictment - 52

Europe
Eastern Europe foreign operations - 509
FY 1995 budget - 507
Partnership for Peace - 510
U.S. foreign aid - 506 (chart), 510

European Bank for Reconstruction and Development - 507

European Development Bank - 506 (chart)

European Union - 185

Evans, Lane, D-Ill. (17) - 413

Ewing, Thomas W., R-Ill. (15) - 196

Executive branch. See also: Cabinet; Clinton, President Bill; Congressional-executive relations; Ethics in government; Executive Office of the President; Nominations and confirmations.
Officers, 103rd Congress, 2nd Session - 7-B

Executive Life Insurance Company - 404

Executive Office of the President - 536
Appropriations - 537 (chart)
FY 1994 disaster supplemental provisions - 553

Ex-Members of Congress
Brock, Sen. Bill - 12-C
Coehlo, Democratic Whip Tony - 6, 56
Cranston, Sen. Alan - 227
DeWine, Rep. Mike - 565
Hubbard, Rep. Carroll Jr. - 53
Jackson, Sen. Henry M. "Scoop" - 56, 467
Jones, Rep. Ben - 54
Kolter, Rep. Joe - 43, 53
Melcher, Sen. John - 245
O'Neill, Speaker Thomas P. Jr. - 12, 59, 60
Perkins, Rep. Carl C. - 53
Poage, Rep. W.R. - 56
Rudman, Sen. Warren B. - 463
Vanik, Rep. Charles A. - 467
Wirth, Sen.Timothy E. - 454
Wright, Democratic Speaker Jim - 54, 56

Exon, Jim, D-Neb.
Adm. Kelso's retirement - 440
Appropriations, Transportation - 534
Budget resolution FY 1995 - 83, 84
Federal crop insurance - 197
Federal railroad safety programs - 173
Interstate Commerce Commission - 170, 171
U.S. communications law rewrite - 210, 212

Export Enhancement Program - 126

Export-Import Bank - 138, 506 (chart), 509

F

Fair Trade in Financial Services Act - 107, 108

Faircloth, Lauch, R-N.C.
Appropriations, Treasury Department - 539
Clean water law - 242
Commerce Department - 189
Drinking water authorization - 239
Housing authorization - 410
Nominations and appointees - 139
Welfare reform - 364

Faleomavaega, Eni F.H., D-Am. Samoa (AL) - 62

Families and marital issues. See also: Children; Family planning; Head Start; Women.
Adoption - 520 (chart)
Foster care - 520 (chart)
Housing - 408, 410

Family planning
Elementary and secondary education authorization - 385,

386, 388
Foreign aid - 507
Fannie Mae - *See: Federal National Mortgage Association (Fannie Mae)*
Farenkopf, Frank J., Jr. - 562
Farm Credit System - 200
Farmers - *See: Agriculture.*
Farmers Home Administration (FmHA)
FY 1994 disaster supplemental - 553
Housing authorization - 408, 409, 410
Loans - 200
Farrakhan, Louis - 62, 63
Farris, Michael P. - 309
Fawell, Harris W., R-Ill. (13)
Appropriations, Treasury Department - 539
Black lung benefits - 406
Davis-Bacon wage revision - 406
Electronic monitoring of workers - 407
Health care reform - 319, 326, 329
Fazio, Vic, D-Calif. (3)
1994 election - 573
Appropriations
Energy and water - 503
Legislative branch - 524, 526
Disaster relief - 550
House leadership races - 15, 16
FBI - *See: Federal Bureau of Investigation (FBI)*
Federal aid to states and cities
Elementary and secondary education authorization - 391
National Highway System - 530
Federal Aviation Administration (FAA)
Airport Improvement Program - 168
Appropriations, Transportation - 531 (chart)
Authorization - 168, 169
Clinton budget - 81
Product liability - 179
Federal Bureau of Investigation (FBI)
Appropriations - 485, 486, 510
Budget - 292
Counterintelligence operations - 458, 463
Displaced FBI workers' new job preferences - 153, 483
Electronic eavesdropping - 215, 216
FY 1995 budget - 80
FY 1994 disaster supplemental - 552
Packwood diaries - 50
Russian aid - 467
Tucker indictment - 51
Federal Communications Commission (FCC) - 129
Appropriations - 484 (chart)
Authorization - 218
Cable television reregulation - 312, 313
Electronic eavesdropping - 215, 216
Federal Coordinating Council for Science, Engineering and Technology - 220
Federal crop insurance - 479
Federal Deposit Insurance Corporation (FDIC) - 96, 98, 99, 104, 154
Federal Disaster Insurance - 155
Federal Election Commission

(FEC)
Appropriations
Legislative branch - 524
Treasury-Postal - 537 (chart)
Candidates' personal use of campaign funds - 35, 36
GOPAC - 55
Perkins ethics case - 53
Rostenkowski indictment - 46
Spending regulations - 35, 36
Federal Emergency Management Agency (FEMA) - 71, 155, 411, 547, 548, 549 (box), 551, 555, 557
Federal employees. *See also: Congressional employees; Judiciary; Military personnel issues; Office of Personnel Management*
Child abuse by federal workers - 152, 153
Child support enforcement - 375
EEOC - 153, 154
Federal retirements - 371, 376
Federal workers buyouts - 143, 147, 150
Federal work force reduction - 148
Leave usage - 152
Occupational Safety and Health Administration standards - 152
Pay raises - 538, 539
Reduction - 191
Federal Food, Drug and Cosmetic Act of 1938 - 198
Federal government (general). *See also: Ethics in government; Federal employees; Fraud and waste in government; General Services Administration; Procurement; Regulation; Research and development, U.S.*
Appropriations, Treasury-Postal Service - 536
Federal spending cuts - 550, 551
Paperwork Reduction Act reauthorization - 154, 155
'Reinventing' government - 143, 147, 175
Unfunded federal mandates - 25, 150, 152, 391, 556
Federal Highway Administration (FHwA) - 531 (chart), 549 (box)
Federal Home Loan Mortgage Corporation (Freddie Mac) - 106
Federal Housing Administration (FHA) - 408, 409, 410, 411, 543, 546, 551, 557
Federal Insecticide, Fungicide and Rodenticide Act (FIFRA) - 198, 199, 244,
Federal lands - 156
Federal Maritime Commission - 164
Federal National Mortgage Association (Fannie Mae) - 106
Federal Parent Locator Service - 375, 376
Federal Railroad Administration (FRA) - 531 (chart)
Federal Register - 328
Federal Reserve - 96, 98, 100, 104, 107, 139
Federal Savings and Loan Insurance Corporation (FSLIC) - 547
Federal Trade Commission (FTC) - 181, 189, 217, 298, 484 (chart)
Federal Transit Administration

(FTA) - 81, 531 (chart), 534
Federal Water Pollution Control Act - 238, 241
Federation of Independent Business - 262
Fees - *See: User fees*
Feingold, Russell D., D-Wis.
Defense authorization - 426, 427
FY 1994 disaster supplemental - 556
Haitian crisis - 449, 450
Lobbying disclosure and gift ban - 39
State Department authorization bill - 456
Vote studies, presidential support - 6-C
Voting participation - 12-C
Feinstein, Dianne, D-Calif.
1994 election - 563, 565
Appropriations
Agriculture - 481
Labor-HHS-Education - 522
VA-HUD - 545
California desert protection - 6, 227
Crime bill - 274
Elementary and secondary education authorization - 389
FY 1994 disaster supplemental - 548, 556
Mitchell withdraws name from Supreme Court consideration - 8
Professional baseball antitrust exemption - 183
Feminist Majority Foundation - 311
Fiechter, Jonathan - 99
Fields, Cleo, D-La. (4)
Banking law - 95
Crime bill - 285
Fields, Jack, R-Texas (8)
Appropriations
Commerce-Justice-State - 486
Boating safety - 163
Coast Guard authorization - 163
Maritime industry aid - 159
National Oceanic and Atmospheric Administration reauthorization - 219
Recreational boating safety - 162
U.S. communications law rewrite - 204, 209
Filibusters and cloture votes
Anti-crime legislation - 287
Brown nomination - 472
California desert protection - 231
Democrats decry GOP filibuster - 9 (box)
Lobbying disclosure and gift ban - 36
Procurement reform - 149, 150
Product liability - 179
103rd Congress - 9 (box)
Striking workers' replacement bill - 402, 403
Filner, Bob, D-Calif. (50) - 12-C
Finance Committee (Senate)
Domestic workers tax laws - 369
GATT - 126, 127, 128
Health care reform - 320, 321, 338, 343
Superfund reauthorization - 235
Treasury Department appropriations - 539
Finance Office (House) - 47
Fingerhut, Eric D., D-Ohio (19)

1994 election - 572
Economic Development Administration - 188
Lobbying disclosure and gift ban - 37
Finland - 472
Finney, Gov. Joan, D-Kan. - 579
Fire Prevention and Control Act of 1974 - 299
Fish, Hamilton Jr., R-N.Y. (19)
1994 election - 576
Health care reform - 344
Lobbying disclosure and gift ban - 38
Professional baseball antitrust exemption - 183
Television signal retransmission - 217
Voting participation - 12-C
Fish and fishing. *See also: Marine mammals protection; Ships, shipping.*
Aquatic Nuisance Species Task Force - 162
California desert protection - 229
Commercial fishing industry - 160, 161, 162
Fisherman's Guarantee Fund - 161
Fisherman's Protection Act reauthorization - 160, 161, 162
Ocean dumping - 162
Pacific salmon - 161
Transit fee on Canadian fishing vessels - 160, 161
U.S.-Canadian salmon fishing dispute - 161
Zebra mussels - 162
Fish and Wildlife Service, U.S. - 514, 515, 518, 552, 554
Fisher, Richard - 569
Fiske, Robert B. Jr.
Independent counsel law - 296, 298
Whitewater/Madison affair - 31
Fitz-Pegado, Lauri - 189
Flake, Floyd H., D-N.Y. (6)
Community Development Banking - 101
Small Business Administration (SBA) - 187
Flanagan, Michael Patrick, R-Ill. - 44, 48, 572
Fletcher, Virginia C. - 46
Flood aid - *See: Disaster relief*
Florida
1994 election - 562, 563, 569, 571, 574, 579, 580
Anti-crime legislation - 288
Conservative coalition - 9-C
Ecosystem restoration project - 517, 518
Everglades protection - 254
FY 1995 budget - 80
VA medical facilities - 415
Florida State Athletic Commission - 189
Florio, Gov. James J., D-N.J. - 569, 579
Foglietta, Thomas M., D-Pa. (1) - 535
Foley, Mark, R-Fla. - 571
Foley, Thomas S., D-Wash. (5)
1994 election - 3, 14, 55, 56, 563, 570, 573, 574
Budget resolution FY 1995 - 82
Campaign finance - 32
Clinton's State of the Union address - 30
Congressional pay raise - 63
Congressional workplace law

exemptions - 29
Crime bill - 279, 280, 284, 285
Filibusters and cloture votes - 9
FY 1994 disaster supplemental - 548
General Agreement on Tariffs and Trade (GATT) - 7, 126, 128
"Ghost voting" - 52
Health care reform - 335
Lobbying disclosure and gift ban - 37, 40
Superfund reauthorization - 236
Veterans' Affairs staff cut exemption - 416
Voting participation - 12-C
Folsom, Gov. James E. Jr., D-Ala. - 576, 579
Food, Drug and Cosmetic Act of 1958 - 244
Food and Drug Administration (FDA)
Added-nicotine controversy - 360
FY 1994 budget - 70
FY 1995 budget - 478
FY 1994 disaster supplemental - 552
Medical devices - 362
Nutritional supplements - 357
Product liability - 179
Veterinary medicine - 360
Food and nutrition - *See also: Agriculture; Children; Antipoverty programs; Welfare; Women, Infants and Children program (WIC).*
Assistance - 553
Child nutrition funding - 78, 365, 373, 375
Children - 79
Dietary Guidelines for Americans - 373, 374
Food and Nutrition Service - 357, 358, 478 (chart), 553
Food labels - 363
Summer Food Service program - 374
Food Animal Concerns Trust (FACT) - 361
Food for Peace - 478
Food stamps - 79, 365, 376
Forbes, Michael P., R-N.Y. - 584
Ford, Harold E., D-Tenn. (9)
1994 election - 4
Elementary and secondary education authorization - 391
Goals 2000 school improvement - 399
OSHA overhaul legislation - 403
Ford, Wendell H., D-Ky.
Airport improvement programs - 169, 170
Appropriations
Agriculture - 520
Defense - 488
Banking law - 97, 98
Congressional reform - 27
Interstate Commerce Commission - 171
Senate leadership for 104th Congress - 17
Smoking ban on all international, Alaska, Hawaii flights - 174
Ford, William D., D-Mich. (13)
1994 election - 55
Elementary and secondary education authorization - 384
Health care reform - 326, 327, 328
Reemployment Act of 1994 - 406

Superfund reauthorization - 234
Foreign affairs. *See also: Name of individual countries*
Appointments - 471, 472
Appropriations, Commerce-Justice-State - 484 (chart)
Changing world order - 445, 446
Fair trade in financial services - 107, 108
FY 1995 budget - 79
Nixon's congressional legacy - 60, 61
Foreign Affairs Committee (House)
Environmental technology exports - 266
Foreign aid reform - 452
Haitian crisis - 451
Foreign aid. *See also: Agency for International Development; Arms sales; names of individual countries.*
Appropriations - 505, 506 (chart), 512
Appropriations, Foreign operations - 511
FY 1995 budget - 79
FY 1994 disaster supplemental provisions - 554
International military education and training - 506 (chart)
Military assistance - 506 (chart), 554
Reform - 452, 453
Foreign Claims Settlement Commission, U.S. - 469
Foreign operations - *See: Foreign aid*
Foreign Relations Committee (Senate)
Biodiversity treaty - 266, 267
Fishing vessel registration - 267
Pastor nomination - 471, 472
State Department authorization bill - 455
Talbott nomination - 471
Treaty on Women - 471
Foreign trade. *See also: Agricultural trade; Bureau of Export Administration; General Agreement on Tariffs and Trade (GATT); North American Free Trade Agreement (NAFTA); Trade Adjustment Assistance Program*
U.S. Russian aid policy - 467
Vietnam - 21-C, 12-D,
Forest Service, U.S. *See also: Agriculture Department*
Agriculture reorganization - 192
Appropriations, Interior - 513, 514 (chart), 515, 518
Logging ban - 31, 256
Montana wilderness bill - 246, 247
Fox, Jon D., R-Pa. - 576
Fox Broadcasting - 55, 217
Frank, Barney, D-Mass. (4)
Appropriations, Defense - 490
Budget resolution FY 1995 - 83
Child support enforcement - 376
Defense authorization - 423
Defense Department peacekeeping operations - 549, 550
Haitian crisis - 450
House Appropriations Committee chairmanship - 8
Interstate Commerce Commission - 533
Whip election - 7
Franks, Gary A., R-Conn. (5)

1994 congressional election - 571, 575
Crime bill - 280
Fraud and abuse in government. *See also: Procurement*
Office of Special Counsel reauthorization - 154
Rostenkowski indicted/defeated - 43, 48
SSI - 367
Freddie Mac - *See: Federal Home Loan Mortgage Corporation (Freddie Mac)*
Freedom of Information Act (FOIA) - 28, 299, 548
Freedom of religion - *See: Religion and religious organizations*
Freedom of speech - 182, 313, 314
Freeh, Louis J. - 215
Frelinghuysen, Rodney, R-N.J. - 576
Friedman, Charles Timothy Jr. - 46
Frisa, Daniel, R-N.Y. - 576
Frist, Bill - 565, 566
Frost, Martin, D-Texas (24)
Ethics case - 53
Gun control - 277
Fund for Animals - 258
Funderburk, David, R-N.C. - 571
Funk, Sherman M. - 457
Furman, Hal - 569
Furse, Elizabeth, D-Ore. (1)
1994 election - 575
Appropriations, Defense - 493

G

Galbraith, Peter - 456
Gallo, Dean A., R-N.J. (11)
1994 election - 12, 13, 576
Appropriations
Energy and water - 503, 504
VA-HUD - 544
Voting participation - 12-C
Ganske, Greg, R-Iowa - 572
Garin, Geoff - 47
Gasoline - *See: Oil industry.*
Gates, Robert M. - 465
GATT - *See: General Agreement on Tariffs and Trade.*
Gejdenson, Sam, D-Conn. (2)
1994 election - 575
Campaign finance reform - 33
Environmental technology exports - 266
State Department authorization bill - 457
Gekas, George W., R-Pa. (17)
Crime bill - 280
Independent counsel law - 296
General Accounting Office (GAO) - 44, 152, 154, 156, 191, 249, 253, 295, 297, 367, 402, 499, 525, 526, 554
General Agreement on Tariffs and Trade (GATT) - 5, 6, 7, 69, 85, 107, 123, 125, 129, 131, 136, 235, 403, 482, 3-C, 4-C, 20-C, 28-C, 53-D, 56-D
General Atomics - 503
General Authorities Act - 247
General Services Administration (GSA) - 536, 537 (chart), 538, 540
Geological Survey, U.S. - 514 (chart), 155
Georgia
1994 election - 561, 580, 581

Board of Regents - 54
Conservative coalition - 9-C
Redistricting - 591, 592
Georgia (Republic of) - 466, 467
Gephardt, Richard A., D-Mo. (3)
Budget process - 88
Campaign finance reform - 33
Elementary and secondary education authorization - 387
FY 1994 disaster supplemental - 548
GATT implementation - 124
Goals 2000 school improvement - 399
House leadership position races - 15, 16
MFN China - 137
Preparing for new Republican role - 20
Rostenkowski's reimbursement - 44
Ways and Means chairmanship - 9
Gerdano, Samuel - 175
Geringer, Gov. Jim, R-Wyo. - 580
Gibbons, Jim - 581
Gibbons, John H. - 80
Gibbons, Sam M., D-Fla. (11)
1994 election - 571
GATT - 127, 128
Health care reform - 329, 333
Pension funding - 404
Presidio management - 253
Ways and Means chairmanship - 9, 159
Gilman, Benjamin A., R-N.Y. (20)
Foreign aid reform - 452
Haitian crisis - 451
House committee chairmen - 15
Party unity - 7-C
State Department authorization bill - 457
Gingrich, Newt, R-Ga. (6)
1994 election - 4, 7, 14, 566, 570
Bosnia-Herzegovina - 449
Clinton's State of the Union address - 30
Congressional pay raise - 63
Crime bill - 285
Defense authorization - 424
Drinking water authorization - 240
Ethics investigation - 54
GATT - 130
"Ghost voting" - 53, 54
GOP election mandate - 35-D, 37-D
Health care reform - 323, 335
Lobbying disclosure and gift ban - 37, 42
Republicans' "Contract With America" - 22
Rostenkowski indictment - 47
Rostenkowski plea negotiation talks - 45
Rostenkowski's reimbursement - 44
Speaker of the House acceptance speech - 57-D, 59-D
Ushering in Republican rule - 18
Ginsburg, Ruth Bader - 303, 310
Giuliani, Rudolph - 274
Glendenning, Gov. Parris, D-Md. - 579
Glenn, John, D-Ohio
Bosnia-Herzegovina - 448
Drinking water authorization - 239
Environmental Protection Agency - 243
Federal employees - 148, 149

Haitian crisis - 450
Homeless aid - 411
Procurement reform - 145
'Reinventing' government effort - 143
State Department authorization bill - 455, 457, 458
Unfunded mandates - 150
Glickman, Dan, D-Kan. (4)
1994 election - 571, 572
Agriculture Department reorganization - 191
Gun control - 276
Health care reform - 320
Intelligence authorization bill - 459, 460, 462
National Reconnaissance Office - 461 (box)
Small aircraft product liability - 181
Global Environment Facility - 506 (chart), 507, 508
Global Learning and Observations to Benefit the Environment (GLOBE) - 219, 220
Glosson, Buster C. - 441
Goldfarb, Sally F. - 153
Goldin, Daniel S. - 544
Gonzalez, Henry B., D-Texas (20)
Banking law - 100
Community Development Banking - 101
Housing authorization - 409, 410 (box)
Goodlatte, Robert W., R-Va. (6)
Appropriations, Commerce-Justice-State - 486
U.S. communications law rewrite - 207
Goodling, Bill, R-Pa. (19)
Child nutrition programs - 374
Elementary and secondary education authorization - 207, 385
Goals 2000 school improvement - 399
Head Start - 370
Health care reform - 327, 328
House committee chairmen - 15
OSHA overhaul legislation - 403
GOPAC - *See: Political Action Committees (PACs), GOPAC*
Gordon, Bart, D-Tenn. (6) - 571
Gore, Vice President Al
1994 election - 584
Air-traffic control system proposal - 169
Appropriations, VA-HUD - 544, 546
Competitiveness programs - 223
Environmental Protection Agency - 244
Federal employees - 147
Mission to Planet Earth - 80
Procurement reform - 144
'Reinventing' government - 249, 192
'Reinventing' government effort - 143
Republican control of Senate - 565
Gorelick, Jamie S. - 459
Gorton, Slade, R-Wash.
1994 election - 569
Appropriations
Agriculture - 481
Treasury Department - 539
Elementary and secondary education authorization - 390, 392
Fire Prevention and Control Act

of 1974 amendment - 299
Intelligence authorization bill - 462
Product liability - 178, 179
School-to-work bill - 400
Small aircraft product liability - 180
U.S. communications law rewrite - 212
Goss, Porter J., R-Fla. (14)
Defense authorization - 424
Haitian crisis - 450
Government contractors - 144, 147, 187
Government National Mortgage Association (Ginnie Mae) - 557
Government Operations Committee (House)
Federal employees - 149
Freedom of Information Act (FOIA) - 299
Health care reform - 343, 344
Holocaust survivors - 377
Kennedy assassination - 157
Procurement reform - 145
Unfunded mandates - 151
Vegetable Oil-Based Ink - 200
Government Printing Office (GPO) - 525, 526
Governmental Affairs Committee (Senate) - 29
Disaster relief - 155
Environmental Protection Agency - 243
Federal employees - 148
Homeless aid - 411
Lobbying disclosure and gift ban - 38, 39
Office of Government Ethics - 154
Procurement reform - 145, 147
'Reinventing' government - 143
Unfunded mandates - 150
Governors. *See also: Individual states' names*
Members of the 103rd Congress, 2nd Session - 7-B
Graham, Bob, D-Fla.
Appropriations, Labor-HHS-Education - 522
Banking law - 99
Clean water law - 241, 243
Governorship - 301
Intelligence authorization bill - 462
Superfund reauthorization - 235
Graham, Lindsey, R-S.C. - 571
Gramm, Phil, R-Texas
1994 election - 569
Appropriations
Commerce-Justice-State - 487
District of Columbia - 500
Transportation - 534
Azerbaijan - 509
Banking laws - 100, 107, 108
Breyer appointment - 310
Clinton's legislative setbacks - 31
Federal employees - 149, 150
Health care reform - 324
Housing authorization - 410
Professional baseball antitrust exemption - 183
Senate leadership for 104th Congress - 17
Shearer nomination - 472
Unfunded mandates - 152
U.S. communications law rewrite - 211
Voting participation - 12-C
Grams, Rod, R-Minn. (6)
1994 election - 565, 568, 573

Appropriations, Labor-HHS-Education - 522
Economic Development Administration - 188
Energy Department research laboratories - 224
Housing authorization - 410
Presidio management - 254
Republican control of Senate - 565
Grandy, Fred, R-Iowa (5)
1994 election - 572
Clinton's legislative setbacks - 31
Federal Election Commission spending regulations - 35
Frost ethics case - 53
Gingrich ethics investigation - 54
Health care reform - 331, 333
Reemployment Act of 1994 - 405
Rostenkowski indictment - 47
Grassley, Charles E., R-Iowa
Appropriations
Treasury Department - 539
VA-HUD - 546
Bankruptcy law - 175, 177
Budget resolution FY 1995 - 83
Clean water law - 241
Congressional workplace law exemptions - 29
Defense authorization - 426, 434
Goals 2000 school improvement - 398
Health care reform - 342
Military officer rank nominations - 441
Preservation of historic black college buildings - 401
Procurement reform - 145
Shipyard subsidies - 159, 160
Superfund reauthorization - 236
Graves, Gov. Bill, R-Kan. - 579
Gray, William H. III, D-Pa. - 450
Greece - 505, 507, 509, 510, 512
Green, Gene, D-Texas (29) - 325, 326, 328
Greene, Harold H. - 62
Greenwood, James C., R-Pa. (8) - 261, 358
Gregg, Judd, R-N.H.
Drinking water authorization - 239
Elementary and secondary education authorization - 389, 391
Goals 2000 school improvement - 398
Haiti - 509
Health care reform - 337
Orphan drugs - 363
Pastor nomination - 471, 472
Group of Seven - 126
Grow, Galusha A. - 570
Guam - 156, 157
Guinier, Lani - 302
Gun Owners of America - 572
Gunderson, Steve, R-Wis. (3)
Child nutrition programs - 374
Dairy legislation - 197
Elementary and secondary education authorization - 207, 385
Goals 2000 school improvement - 399
Health care reform - 324, 329
Guns and gun control
Anti-crime legislation - 274, 276, 277, 284, 290, 291
Assault weapons ban - 15-C, 26-D

Brady bill - 80, 282, 284, 485, 486, 540
Housing authorization - 409
Gustitus, Linda J. - 39
Gutierrez, Luis V., D-Ill. (4) - 409
Gutknecht, Gil, R-Minn. - 573
Guzman, Rob - 573

H

Haiti
Appropriations
Commerce-Justice-State - 485
Labor-HHS-Education - 523
Defense authorization - 424, 431
Dictator agreement - 29-D, 32-D
FY 1994 disaster supplemental - 548
Haitian Restoration of Democracy Act of 1994 - 450
U.S. foreign policy - 445
U.S. intervention - 449, 451, 20-C, 24-C, 25-C
U.S. occupation - 449, 451
Hall, Ralph M., D-Texas (4)
Health care reform - 336
National Aeronautics and Space Administration reauthorization - 218
Hall, Tony P., D-Ohio (3) - 16
Halperin, Morton H. - 440
Hamburg, Dan, D-Calif. (1)
1994 election - 573
Environmental Protection Agency - 244
Tribal self-governance programs - 167
Hamilton, Alexander - 315
Hamilton, Lee H., D-Ind. (9)
Bosnia-Herzegovina - 448
Defense authorization - 423
Foreign aid reform - 452
Foreign policy - 445
Iraqi Claims Act - 470
Lobbying disclosure and gift ban - 38
MFN China - 137, 138
Russian aid policy - 466
State Department authorization bill - 457
Hancock, Mel, R-Mo. (7) - 387
Handgun Control Inc. - 277, 282
Hansen, James V., R-Utah (1)
California desert protection - 228
Defense authorization - 423, 424, 435, 436
Small aircraft product liability - 181
Harkin, Tom, D-Iowa
Appropriations
Energy and water - 504
Labor-HHS-Education - 519, 522, 523
VA-HUD - 545, 546
Balanced-budget amendment - 86
Commerce Department - 190
Crime bill - 286
Disabled individuals - 359
Elementary and secondary education authorization - 388
Haitian crisis - 449, 450
Mitchell Supreme Court nomination - 57
Nutritional supplements - 357
Harman, Jane, D-Calif. (36) - 434
Harper, Ken - 569
HarperCollins - 55

Harris, Stanley S. - 50
Harvard University - 21
Hastert, Dennis, R-Ill. (14) - 14
Hastings, Alcee L., D-Fla. (23) - 563
Hastings, Richard "Doc," R-Wash. - 588
Hatch, Orrin G., R-Utah
  1994 election - 569, 575
  Abortion clinic access - 356
  Balanced-budget amendment - 86
  Bankruptcy law - 177
  Breyer nomination - 19-D, 20-D, 24-D
  Crime bill - 274, 282, 284
  Elementary and secondary education authorization - 388, 389
  Health care reform - 321, 339, 342, 343
  Minority health programs - 359
  Nominations and appointees - 300, 301
  Pension benefits - 405
  Professional baseball antitrust exemption - 182
  Rural health care - 362
  Striker replacement - 402
  Superfund reauthorization - 236
  Supreme Court nominee to replace Blackmun - 303
Hatch Act - 153
Hatfield, Mark O., R-Ore.
  Appropriations
    Foreign Operations - 505
    Transportation - 534
    VA-HUD - 545
  Drinking water authorization - 239
  Federal land payments to localities - 156
  FY 1994 disaster supplemental - 556
  National parks - 249
  Party unity - 7-C
  Rare diseases - 363
  Striker replacement - 402
  Vote studies, presidential support - 6-C
Hawaii
  1994 election - 563, 570, 579, 584
  Exemption from health care reform bill - 328
  FY 1994 disaster supplemental - 551, 553
  Native Hawaiian education program - 521, 522
Hayes, Carnie - 523
Hayes, Jimmy, D-La. (7) - 243
Hays, Steele - 314, 315
Haytaian, Garabed "Chuck" - 569, 9-C
Hayworth, J.D., R-Ariz. - 584
Hazardous waste management - 71, 379
Head Start
  Appropriations, Labor-HHS-Education - 519, 520 (chart), 522
  Authorization - 369, 373
  Clinton budget - 72
Headlund, Elizabeth - 35
Health. *See also: Abortion, Acquired Immune Deficiency Syndrome (AIDS); Biomedical research; Budget, U.S.; Cancer; Community health centers; Drugs and drug abuse; Food and nutrition; Health and Human Services Department; Health care reform; Health professionals; Hospitals;* Medicaid; Medical devices; Medicare; Mental health; National Institutes of Health (NIH); Nursing homes; Pharmaceuticals; Physicians; Preventive medicine; Public health; Smoking bans; Veterans Affairs Department, health care; Women.
  Anti-crime legislation - 288, 289
  Black lung benefits - 406, 407
  FY 1995 budget - 78
  Nursing education - 363
  Organ transplants - 361
  Orphan drugs - 363
  Persian Gulf Syndrome - 412, 414
  Rare diseases - 363
  Rural health care - 361
  Traumatic brain injuries - 361, 362
Health and Human Services Department (HHS). *See also: Medicaid; Medicare; Social Security*
  Anti-crime legislation - 288
  Appropriations - 356, 369, 519, 520 (chart), 523
  Bureau of Indian Affairs - 379
  FY 1994 disaster supplemental provisions - 551, 552, 554
  Medical devices - 362
  Minority health programs - 358
  Organ transplants - 361
  Social Security programs - 366
Health care
  Low-income citizens in rural and urban areas - 521
  Vaccine distribution program - 522
Health care reform. *See also: Abortion; Congressional Budget Office; Individual committee names; Insurance industry; Pharmaceuticals; Prescription drugs; Taxes and taxation.*
  Abortion - 324, 325, 334, 337, 341, 342
  Benefits - 324, 327, 332, 337, 340, 343
  Bipartisan plan - 354
  Chronology - 321
  Clinton budget - 69
  Community rating - 330, 332, 343
  Congressional action committees (House) - 324, 329
  Committees (Senate) - 336, 345
  Institutional breakdown - 320
  Crackdown on abuse and fraud in programs - 501
  Dental benefits - 324, 325
  Employer mandate - 322, 329, 330, 332, 335, 336, 339, 341, 350, 351
  Federal Employees Health Benefits Program - 345
  Financing proposals
    Cost controls - 330, 333, 335, 337, 339, 340
    Other taxes - 323, 330, 332, 339, 342, 351
    Payroll taxes - 326, 330
    Tobacco tax - 323, 330, 333, 337, 340, 351, 353
  Health alliances - 319, 320, 322, 327, 328, 330, 335, 340, 351
  Long-term care - 322
  Malpractice - 323, 327, 330, 341, 354
  Mammograms - 334
  Medicaid - 323, 338, 354
  Medical personnel - 325, 328, 343
  Medicare - 323, 329, 330, 332, 333, 338, 339, 340, 343, 354
  Mental health - 325
  Mental health benefits - 324, 332
  Mitchell, George J. - 319
  Partisanship - 319, 321, 337
  Plan comparisons - 352
  Plans
    Alternative plans - 324
    Bipartisan plan - 338, 343, 354 (highlights)
    Chafee bill - 331
    Chafee-Breaux - 350, 351
    Clinton Plan
      Highlights - 322, 324
      Labor committee plan similarities - 336
    Clinton plan highlights - 322
    Comparison of major plans - 352, 353
    Cooper-Grandy bill - 331
    Dole's Republican alternative - 340, 8-D
    Gephardt bill - 348, 349, 350
    House Republican bill - 331
    Mainstream bill - 350, 351
    McCrery bill - 331
    McDermott bill - 331
    Mitchell bill - 350, 351
    Plans compared - 352, 353
    Republican plan - 340
    Single-payer system - 324, 326, 329, 354
    Ways and Means committee plan - 329, 332
  Pre-existing conditions - 325, 328
  Premium caps - 319, 326, 327
  Public health issues - 323
  Purchasing cooperatives - 328, 336, 340
  Standard benefits package - 319, 329, 332, 336, 338, 341, 343, 354
  State and local governments - 322, 331, 332, 342, 351
  Subsidies - 330, 332, 338, 339, 340, 343, 351, 354
  Task Force on National Health Care Reform - 321, 322
  Universal coverage - 319, 322, 331, 335, 339
Health Insurance Association of America - 320, 330, 334
Healthcare Leadership Council - 339
Hefley, Joel, R-Colo. (5)
  Appropriations
    Commerce-Justice-State - 486
    Labor-HHS-Education - 522
  Defense Authorization - 422
  Interstate Commerce Commission - 533
  National Endowment for the Arts - 517
  National parks - 247
  Steamtown - 252
Heflin, Howell, D-Ala.
  Bankruptcy law - 175, 177
  Clean water law - 241
  Competitiveness programs - 222
Hefner, W.G. "Bill," D-N.C. (8) - 527
Heineman, Fred, R-N.C. - 571
Helms, Jesse, R-N.C.
  1994 election - 571
  Appropriations
    Agriculture - 481, 482
    Defense - 497
    Foreign Aid - 511, 512
    Foreign operations - 510
    Labor-HHS-Education - 522
  Biodiversity treaty - 267
  Breyer appointment - 310
  Elementary and secondary education authorization - 390, 391
  GATT - 126
  Gay rights - 194, 196, 481, 482
  Goals 2000 school improvement - 398, 399
  Haitian crisis - 450
  Martin Luther King Federal Holiday Commission - 157
  National Endowment for the Arts - 517
  Pastor nomination - 6, 471, 472
  Russian aid policy - 466
  State Department authorization bill - 455, 456, 457
  U.S. communications law rewrite - 212
  Vote studies, presidential support - 6-C
Heritage Foundation - 20
Hershiser, Orel - 183
Heston, Charlton - 569
Heymann, Philip B. - 302
Highway Trust Fund - 165, 166, 531 (chart), 534, 555
Highways and roads
  Appropriations, Commerce-Justice-State - 484 (chart)
  FY 1994 disaster supplemental - 552, 553, 555
  Highway projects - 530
  National Highway System - *See: Main heading.*
Hill and Barlow - 302
Hill and Knowlton - 189
Hilleary, Van, R-Tenn. - 571
Hilliard, Earl F., D-Ala. - 571
Hinchey, Maurice D., D-N.Y. (26) - 575
Hispanic caucuses - 280
Hoagland, Peter, D-Neb. (2)
  1994 election - 573
  Health care reform - 333
Hobson, David L., R-Ohio (7) - 82
Hochbrueckner, George J., D-N.Y. (1)
  1994 election - 575
  Appropriations, Energy and water - 503
Hoekstra, Peter, R-Mich. (2)
  Electronic monitoring of workers - 407
  Health care reform - 325, 328
Hogsett, Joseph H. - 572
Holder, Eric H., Jr. - 44, 45, 47, 48, 53
Hollings, Ernest F., D-S.C.
  Appropriations, Commerce-Justice-State - 486, 487
  Coast Guard authorization - 164
  Commerce Department - 190
  Competitiveness programs - 221
  General Agreement on Tariffs and Trade (GATT) - 6, 123
  Nation of Islam - 63
  Striker replacement - 402
  Unsafe drivers bill - 174
  U.S. communications law rewrite - 203, 207, 209, 210, 214
Holocaust - 299, 300
Home School Legal Defense Association - 386
Homeless - 438
Horn, Steve, R-Calif. (38) - 434

Hostettler, John, R-Ind. - 572
Houghton, Amo, R-N.Y. (31) - 334
House committees (general)
    Committee assignments - 10-B,
    15-B
House of Representatives. *See
    also: Congressional elections;
    Congressional ethics;
    Congressional votes; Democratic
    Caucus (House); Democratic
    leadership; House committees;
    House Post Office probe;
    Republican leadership.*
    1994 election - 561, 562
    Administrative changes - 13
    Committee assignments - 6-B,
    15-B
    Conservative coalition - 42-C
    Delegate voting ok'd - 11-D
    House expense rules - 13-D
    Key votes - 48-C, 53-C
    Leadership - 14, 17
    Leadership position races - 16
    (box), 17 (box)
    Legislation
        Abortion clinic access - 355,
        356
        Balanced-budget amend-
        ment - 86
        Export-Import Bank - 138
        GATT - 123, 130
        Minority health programs -
        358
        Nutritional supplements -
        357
    Membership (103rd Congress,
    2nd Session) - 6-B, 7-B
    Membership (104th
    Congress) - 582, 583
    Partisanship - 38-C
    Presidential support - 32-C
    Republicans restructure House
    Committees - 18, 21
    Restaurant operations proposal
    - 13
    Rules changes - 18, 20, 21
    (box)
    Voting participation - 46-C
House Post Office probe - 43, 44,
    46, 53
Housing. *See also: Community
    development; Energy
    Department, Federal weatheriza-
    tion assistance program; Housing
    and Urban Development; Low-
    Income Home Energy Assistance
    Program; Mortgages and home
    loans*
    Authorization - 408, 410
    Fair housing programs - 78, 79
    HOME Investment Partnership
    programs - 78, 409, 411
    Homeless aid - 78, 408, 411
    Housing and Community
    Development Act of 1987 -
    408
    National Homeownership Trust
    - 78
    Public housing
        Anti-crime proposals - 408
        Appropriations FY 1995 - 78
        Government housing pro-
        grams - 555
        Homeownership and
        Opportunity for People
        Everywhere (HOPE)
        grants - 555
        Modernization funds - 408
        Regulatory relief - 408
        Rent ceilings - 408
        Replacement housing - 408
        Replacement rule - 409
        Section 8 programs - 408,

    410
    U.S. Housing Act (1937) -
    408, 409
    Stewart B. McKinney Homeless
    Assistance Act - 78, 408, 411
**Housing and Urban Development
    Department (HUD)**
    Anti-crime legislation - 288
    Apartment buildings - 410 (box),
    411
    Appropriations - 541, 547
    FY 1994 disaster supplemental
    provisions - 549 (box), 551,
    553
    Holocaust reparation payments
    - 377
    Homeless aid - 411
    Housing authorization - 408,
    410
    Special-purpose grants - 547
Howe, Allen T. - 250
Hoyer, Steny H., D-Md. (5)
    Appropriations
        Foreign operations - 508
        Transportation - 532
        Treasury Department - 536,
        538, 540
    Congressional pay raise - 63
    Federal employees - 149
    Federal work force reduction -
    549
Hubbard, Carol Brown - 53
Huffington, Michael, R-Calif. (22)
    1994 election - 563, 566, 568,
    573
    California desert protection -
    230
Hughes, William J., D-N.J. (2)
    1994 election - 576
    Crime bill - 275
    Federal prison inmate wages -
    300
    Patent and Trademark Office -
    184, 185
    Rostenkowski's reimbursement
    - 44
    Television signal retransmission
    - 217
Hulshof, Kenny - 573
Human Genome Project - 78
Human rights - 137
**Humane Society of the United
    States** - 42
Humanitarian aid - 489 (chart)
Hunter, Duncan, R-Calif. (52)
    Appropriations, Energy and
    water - 503
    California desert protection -
    229
    Defense authorization - 422
    Federal Election Commission
    spending regulations - 36
    House leadership races - 14
Hutchinson, Tim, R-Ark. (3) - 15
Hutchison, Kay Bailey, R-Texas
    1994 election - 561, 569
    Adm. Kelso's retirement - 440
    Appropriations
        Commerce-Justice-State -
        487
        Labor-HHS-Education - 522
    Elementary and secondary edu-
    cation authorization - 389
    Ethics case - 51
Hyatt, Joel - 566
Hyde, Henry J., R-Ill. (6)
    Abortion clinic access - 356,
    357
    Appropriations, Labor-HHS-
    Education - 519
    Crime bill - 277, 282
    Gun control - 277
    House committee chairmen - 15

    Independent counsel law - 296,
    297
    Republican rule - 21
    State Department authorization
    bill - 457

I

Idaho
    1994 election - 584, 580
    Ballot initiatives - 581
    Logging on Forest Service
    lands - 257
    Term limits - 581
    Unfunded mandates - 151
    Wilderness areas - 245, 247
Illinois
    1994 election - 570, 572, 579
    Anti-crime legislation - 288
    Archer-Daniels-Midland - 544
IMF - *See: International Monetary
    Fund*
Immigration. *See also: Aliens;
    Immigration and Naturalization
    Service*
    Anti-crime legislation - 80, 288,
    291
    Appropriations - 83
    Immigration law adjustments -
    294, 295
    Supplemental Security Income
    program - 365
**Immigration and Naturalization
    Service (INS)** - 80, 291, 294,
    483, 484 (chart), 485, 487
Independent Agencies
    Appropriations - 537 (chart)
Independent Counsel Provisions
    - 297
**Independent Insurance Agents of
    America** - 184
**Indian Affairs Committee
    (Senate)** - 345, 378
Indian Health Service - 513, 517
Indiana - 569, 572
Indians and Alaskan natives
    Anti-crime legislation - 289
    Appropriations - 377
    Education - 514 (chart)
    Elementary and secondary
    education authorization - 395
    Food Stamps - 376
    Health care reform - 344, 345
    Housing authorization - 410
    (box)
    Indian Health Service - 78, 377,
    513, 514 (chart), 515
    Indian lands transfer - 556
    Indian Self-Determination and
    Education Assistance Act -
    377
    Recognition of tribes - 378
    Religious freedom
        Native American prisoners
        allowed to worship - 378
        Peyote - 378
        Protected eagle feathers
        and plants - 378
        Sacred sights - 378
    Reparations - 377
    Tribal settlements - 379
Indonesia - 505, 509, 510, 512
Information Agency, U.S. - 454,
    458, 552, 554, 555
Inhofe, James M., R-Okla. (1)
    1994 election - 13, 565, 566,
    571
    Republican control of Senate -
    565
Initiatives - 581
Inman, Bobby Ray - 439
Inouye, Daniel K., D-Hawaii

    Appropriations, Defense - 488
    Congressional reform - 27
    Disaster relief - 156
    FCC funding increase - 218
    Federal Election Commission
    spending regulations - 36
    U.S. communications law
    rewrite - 203, 207, 212
INSLAW Inc. - 300
Inslee, Jay, D-Wash. (4)
    1994 election - 573, 574
    Agriculture Department reorga-
    nization - 192
    Appropriations, Commerce-
    Justice-State - 485
Insurance industry
    Antitrust exemption - 183, 184
    Banking law - 94
    Disaster insurance - 156
    Health care reform - 183, 328,
    333, 340, 351, 354
    Insurance agents' lobby - 94
    Superfund reauthorization -
    233, 234, 235, 236
Intelligence Committee (House)
    Ames spy case - 465, 466
    Intelligence authorization bill -
    460
Intelligence Committee (Senate)
    Intelligence authorization bill -
    460, 462
Intelligence programs. *See also:
    Central Intelligence Agency (CIA);
    National Reconnaissance Office
    (NRO)*
    Authorization - 458, 463
    Defense appropriations - 489
    (chart)
    Secret document classification -
    459, 462, 463
**Inter-American Development
    Bank** - 506 (chart)
Interior Department. *See also:
    National Park Service*
    Anti-crime legislation - 288
    Appropriations - 78, 513, 514
    (chart), 518
    FY 1994 disaster supplemental
    - 548
    FY 1994 disaster supplemental
    provisions - 551, 552, 554
    Indian trust funds - 377
    National parks - 251
    Pacific Northwest timber plan -
    515, 517, 518
Internal Revenue Service (IRS)
    Appropriations - 537 (chart)
    FY 1994 disaster supplemental
    - 555
    Health care reform - 341
    Holocaust survivors - 377, 536,
    538, 540
International Banking Act - 97
International broadcasting. *See
    also: Radio; Television.*
    Appropriations-Commerce-
    Justice-State - 484 (chart),
    485, 486
    Radio, TV Marti - 483, 485, 487
    Radio Free Asia - 483, 485, 486
**International Brotherhood of
    Teamsters** - 403
**International Civil Aviation
    Organization (ICAO)** - 174
**International Development
    Association** - 506 (chart), 510
**International Finance
    Corporation** - 506 (chart)
**International Monetary Fund
    (IMF)** - 79, 505, 506 (chart), 507
**International Trade
    Administration (ITA)** - 484
    (chart), 553

Interstate Commerce Commission (ICC) - 531 (chart)
Iowa - 570, 572, 579
Iran-contra probe - 295, 468, 469
Iraq
Claims against frozen Iraqi assets - 469, 470
FY 1994 disaster supplemental - 548
Iraqi Claims Act - 469, 470
U.S. foreign policy - 445
Ireland - 138
Irving, Larry - 213, 214
Israel
Appropriations, Foreign operations - 508, 512
Clinton budget - 79
Haiti occupation - 453
Middle East peace - 426
Foreign Aid - 505, 509
U.S. aid to West Bank/Gaza Strip - 507
Russian aid - 466, 467
Istook, Ernest Jim Jr., R-Okla. (5)
Appropriations
District of Columbia - 498
Treasury Department - 538, 540
Rostenkowski's reimbursement - 44

J

Jackson, Thomas Penfield - 49, 10-D, 11-D
Jackson-Lee, Sheila - *See: Lee, Sheila Jackson*
Jacob, Paul - 315
Jacobs, Andrew Jr., D-Ind. (10)
Domestic workers tax laws - 368
Gun control - 277
Social Security - 366, 367
Jacobson, Gary C. - 563
James, Gov. Fob, Jr., R-Ala. - 579
Jamison, Cy - 584
Janklow, Gov. William, D-S.D. - 576
Jansen, Bonnie L. - 182
Japan - 424
Jefferson, William J., D-La. (2)
Health care reform - 333
Maritime Administration Reauthorization - 159
Jeffords, James M., R-Vt.
1994 election - 569
Appropriations, Legislative branch - 526
Campaign finance reform - 34
Crime bill - 286
Elementary and secondary education authorization - 390
Goals 2000 school improvement - 399
Health care reform - 336, 337
National Endowment for the Arts - 517
Party unity - 7-C Striker replacement - 402
Vote studies, presidential support - 6-C
Jews. *See also: Israel*
Nation of Islam - 62, 63
Talbott nomination - 471
Job Corps - 72
Job Opportunities and Basic Skills Training Program (JOBS) - 72, 364
Jobs - *See: Employment and unemployment*
Jobs programs - *See: Employment and training pro-*

grams
Johnson, Don, D-Ga. (10)
1994 election - 571
Elementary and secondary education - 391
Johnson, Gov. Gary E., R-N.M. - 579
Johnson, Nancy L., R-Conn. (6)
Health care reform - 320, 331
House leadership position races - 14
Johnson, Sam, R-Texas (3)
Budget process - 90
Elementary and secondary education authorization - 388
Johnson, Tim, D-S.D. (AL) - 196
Johnston, J. Bennett, D-La.
Appropriations
Defense - 488
Energy and water - 502, 504
VA-HUD - 544, 546
Balanced-budget amendment - 86
California desert protection - 227
Competitiveness programs - 223
Defense authorization - 426
Drinking water authorization - 239, 240
Energy Department research laboratories - 223
Environmental Protection Agency - 244
Indonesia - 509
Lobbying disclosure and gift ban - 39
Mining law rewrite - 236
National Endowment for the Arts - 517
National parks - 250
Joint committees
Organization of Congress - 13, 27, 28
Taxation - 93, 236
Jonassaint, Judge Emile - 450
Jones, Charles O.
Vote studies, Presidential support - 3-C
Jones, Jan Laverty - 580
Jones, Walter B., Jr., D-N.C. - 260, 571
Jontz, Jim - 569
Jordan - 505, 511
Judiciary. *See also: Courts; Crime and criminal justice; Supreme Court*
Appropriations - 187
Budget - 292
Federal prosecutors - 486
FY 1994 disaster supplemental provisions - 554
Judiciary Committee (House)
Abortion clinic access - 356
Abortion legislation - 356
Bankruptcy law - 175
Crime bill - 273, 275
Federal courts - 300
Federal employees - 149
Federal prison inmate wages - 300
Gun control - 276
Health care reform - 344
Holocaust torture lawsuits - 299, 300
Immigration law - 294
Independent counsel law - 295
INSLAW, Inc. claims - 300
Insurance antitrust exemption - 183
Office of Government Ethics - 154

Patent and Trademark Office - 184
Pension-related legislation - 405
Product liability - 178
Professional baseball antitrust exemption - 183
Small aircraft product liability - 181
U.S. communications law rewrite - 206, 207
Wiretapping - 216, 217
Judiciary Committee (Senate)
Antitrust legislation - 298
Balanced-budget amendment - 86
Bankruptcy law - 175, 177
Breyer appointment - 305, 308, 310
Breyer nomination - 17-D, 25-D
Child support enforcement - 376
Crime bill - 273
Freedom of Information Act (FOIA) - 299
Holocaust torture lawsuits - 299, 300
Immigration law - 294
Nominations and appointees - 302
Professional baseball antitrust exemption - 183
Wiretapping - 216
Justice Department
Anti-crime legislation - 287
Antitrust legislation - 298
Appropriations - 187, 483, 484 (chart), 485, 486, 487
Congressional pay raise - 63, 64
Electronic eavesdropping - 215, 216
FY 1995 budget - 79, 80, 485
FY 1994 disaster supplemental provisions - 552
Holocaust torture lawsuits - 299, 300
Hubbard investigation - 53
Independent counsel - 297
Independent counsel law - 295, 297
Rose indictment - 52
Telemarketing fraud - 217

K

Kahn, Charles N. - 330
Kaiser Permanente - 342
Kamarck, Elaine - 148
Kanjorski, Paul E., D-Pa. (11)
Community Development Banking - 102, 107
Economic Development Administration - 188
Iraqi Claims Act - 470
State Department authorization bill - 455
Kansas
1994 election - 571, 572, 573, 579
Health care reform - 336
Kansas City Star - 191
Kantor, Mickey - 125
Kaptur, Marcy, D-Ohio (9) - 130
Kardasz, John - 46
Kardasz, Patricia - 46
Karpan, Kathy - 580
Kasich, John R., R-Ohio (12)
Appropriations, Transportation - 533
Budget process - 87, 89
Budget resolution FY 1995 - 67,

82, 83, 85
Defense authorization - 424, 432, 433
Disaster relief - 550
Kassapis, Andrew - 470
Kassebaum, Nancy Landon, R-Kan.
California desert protection - 231
Competitiveness programs - 222
Crime bill - 286, 287
Elementary and secondary education authorization - 389, 391
Federal employees - 150
Goals 2000 school improvement - 399
Head Start - 370
Health care reform - 336, 338
Orphan drugs - 363
Party unity - 7-C
Pension benefits - 404
School-to-work bill - 400
Senate leadership for 104th Congress - 1-C
Small aircraft liability - 169
Small aircraft product liability - 180, 181
South African economic aid - 470
Treaty on Women - 471
Vote studies, presidential support - 6-C
Wards Cove Packing Co. - 298
Workplace issues - 407
Kean College - 63
Kelly, Sue W., R-N.Y. - 576
Kelman, Steven - 146
Kelso, Frank B. II - 441
Kemp, Evan - 153
Kemp, Jack F. - 543
Kempthorne, Dirk, R-Idaho
Appropriations, Defense - 497
Defense authorization - 426
Idaho wilderness bill - 247
Unfunded mandates - 150
Kennedy, Anthony M. - 310, 311
Kennedy, Edward M., D-Mass.
1994 election - 565, 569, 576
Abortion clinic access - 356, 357
Breyer nomination - 20-D, 21-D
Defense authorization - 434
Elementary and secondary education authorization - 388, 390, 392
Ethics case - 52, 53
Federal Insecticide, Fungicide and Rodenticide Act (FIFRA) - 198, 199
Flood insurance bill - 412
Goals 2000 school improvement - 398
Head Start - 372
Health care reform - 320, 336, 338
Immigration law - 294
Medical devices - 362
Minority health programs - 359
Nursing education - 363
Nutritional supplements - 357
Organ transplants - 361
Rural health care - 362
Technology for education - 402
Traumatic brain injuries - 362
Workplace issues - 407
Kennedy, President John F. - 156, 157
Kennedy, Joseph P. II, D-Mass. (8)
Banking law - 98, 99
Defense authorization - 424

Flood insurance bill - 412
Haitian crisis - 449
Indoor air - 265, 266
Interstate Commerce
    Commission - 533
Persian Gulf Syndrome com-
    pensation - 414
Veterans Affairs staff cut
    exemption - 416
Kennedy, Joseph P., III - 138
Kennedy, Patrick J., D-R.I. - 576
Kennedy, Roger G. - 73, 248
Kennedy, William III - 368
Kennelly, Barbara B., D-Conn. (1)
Health care reform - 331
House leadership races - 15
Superfund reauthorization - 234
Kennesaw State College - 54
Kentucky
1994 election - 561, 571, 580
Conservative coalition - 9-C
Special elections - 592
Kerr, Richard J. - 465, 466
Kerrey, Bob, D-Neb.
1994 election - 569
Agriculture Department reorga-
    nization - 193
Appropriations
    Agriculture - 480
    VA-HUD - 545
Brown nomination - 472
Budget Resolution FY 1995 -
    68, 85
Deficit reduction - 68, 85
Drinking water authorization -
    239
Flood insurance bill - 412
FY 1994 disaster supplemental
    - 550
Intelligence authorization - 462
Plant Variety Protection Act -
    190
Senate leadership for 104th
    Congress - 17, 18
U.S. communications law
    rewrite - 210
Vietnam trade embargo - 468
Kerry, John, D-Mass.
Appropriations, Energy and
    water - 504
Bosnia-Herzegovina - 448
Brown nomination - 472
Community Development
    Banking - 101
Defense authorization - 427
Fishing legislation - 259
Fishing vessel registration - 267
Flood insurance bill - 411
FY 1994 disaster supplemental
    - 556
Haitian crisis - 449, 450
Marine Mammal Protection Act
    reauthorization - 257, 259
Radioactive waste - 263
Small Business Administration
    (SBA) - 187
State Department authorization
    bill - 455, 458
Vietnam trade embargo - 468,
    12-D
Kessler, David A. - 360
Kildee, Dale E., D-Mich. (9)
Child nutrition programs - 374
Elementary and secondary edu-
    cation authorization - 384,
    387
Health care reform - 328
Voting participation - 12-C
Kim, Jay C., R-Calif. (41)
California toll road project - 166
Housing authorization - 410
Immigration law - 294
Small Business Administration

(SBA) - 186
Voting participation - 12-C
King, Gov. Angus, I-Maine - 564,
    579
King, Gov. Bruce, D-N.M. - 581
King, James B. - 149
Kissinger, Henry A. - 16-D
Kitzhaber, Gov. John D-Ore. -
    564, 580
Kleczka, Gerald D., D-Wis. (4)
Health care reform - 330
Maritime Administration
    Reauthorization - 159
Social Security - 367
Klein, Herb, D-N.J. (8)
1994 election - 576
Housing authorization - 409,
    410
Risk assessment program - 244
Klink, Ron, D-Pa. (4)
Elementary and secondary edu-
    cation authorization - 385
Health care reform - 325, 328
OSHA overhaul legislation - 403
Klug, Scott L., R-Wis. (2)
Crime bill - 285
Defense authorization - 424
Energy Department research
    laboratories - 224
National Endowment for the
    Arts - 517
Knowles, Gov. Tony, D-Alaska -
    581
Kohl, Herb, D-Wis.
1994 election - 569
Appropriations, District of
    Columbia - 500
Competitiveness programs -
    222
Dairy legislation - 197
Drinking water authorization -
    239
Electronic eavesdropping - 216
Product liability - 179
Kolbe, Jim, R-Ariz. (5) - 14
Kopacz, Roger - 45, 46
Kopetski, Mike, D-Ore. (5)
1994 election - 575
Crime bill - 280
Defense authorization - 424
Korea - 510, 495. See also: North
    Korea; South Korea
Korean Readiness Account -
    489 (chart)
Koziol, Barbara - 46
Kreidler, Mike, D-Wash. (9)
1994 election - 574
Appropriations, Agriculture -
    479
Energy Department research
    laboratories - 223
Kristol, William - 350
Kushner, Linda - 569
Kuwait - 189
Kyl, Jon, R-Ariz. (4)
1994 election - 565, 568
Balanced-budget amendment -
    87
Defense authorization - 423
National Highway System - 167
Republican control of Senate -
    565

L

Labor, labor unions. See also:
    AFL-CIO; Employment and unem-
    ployment
Congressional workplace law
    exemptions - 28, 29
Davis-Bacon wage revision -
    406

Electronic monitoring - 407
Health care reform - 341
Pension plan funding - 403, 405
Procurement reform - 144
Professional boxing regulations
    - 407
Ships, minimum wage and
    overtime laws - 160
Striker replacement - 402, 403
Labor and Human Resources
    Committee (Senate)
Abortion clinic access - 356
Abortion legislation - 356
Elementary and secondary edu-
    cation authorization - 388,
    390
ERISA pre-emption - 405
Head Start - 370
Health care reform - 336, 338
Minority health programs - 359
National Science Foundation -
    220
Nursing education - 363
Nutritional supplements - 357,
    358
Organ transplants - 361
Orphan drugs - 363
Rare diseases - 363
Rural health care - 361
School technology - 401, 402
School-to-work bill - 400
Wards Cove Packing Co. - 298
Workplace technology - 407
Labor Department. See also:
    Employment and unemployment;
    Occupational Safety and Health
    Administration (OSHA);
    Unemployment compensation
Anti-crime legislation - 288
Appropriations - 356, 369, 519,
    520, 523 (chart)
FY 1994 disaster supplemental
    - 552, 548, 554
School-to-work bill - 72, 400,
    401
Smoking ban - 360
Technology for workplace - 407
Training programs - 72
Labriola, Gerald - 570
LaFalce, John J., D-N.Y. (29)
Procurement reform - 146
Small Business Administration
    (SBA) - 186, 187
LaHood, Ray, R-Ill. - 572
Lake, Anthony
Budget resolution FY 1995 - 85
Intelligence authorization bill -
    462
Lambert, Blanche, D-Ark. (1)
Health care reform - 336
Superfund reauthorization - 233
Lancaster, H. Martin, D-N.C. (3)
1994 election - 571
National parks - 252
Land and Water Conservation
    Fund - 251
Lantos, Tom, D-Calif. (12) - 62
Largent, Steve, R-Okla. - 13, 571
LaRocco, Larry, D-Idaho (1)
California desert protection -
    228
Idaho wilderness bill - 247
Logging on Forest Service
    lands - 257
Lasater, Dan - 539
LaTourette, Steven C., D-Ohio -
    572
Laughlin, Greg, D-Texas (14) -
    461 (box)
Lautenberg, Frank R., D-N.J.
1994 election - 569
Appropriations
    Energy and water - 504

Foreign operations - 510
    Transportation - 533
Budget resolution FY 1995 - 83
California desert protection -
    231
Child support enforcement -
    376
Lobbying disclosure and gift
    ban - 37, 39
National Endowment for the
    Arts - 517
Party unity - 9-C
Small Business Administration
    (SBA) - 186
State Department authorization
    bill - 456
Superfund reauthorization - 235
LaVelle, Avis
Child support enforcement -
    375
Law and justice - See: Civil rights;
    Courts; Crime and criminal jus-
    tice; Judiciary; Supreme Court.
Law enforcement
Anti-crime legislation - 273,
    294, 26-D
Appropriations, Commerce-
    Justice-State - 484 (chart),
    486
Community policing - 287, 486
Electronic eavesdropping - 215,
    216
Police hiring grants - 483, 485,
    486
Leach, Jim, R-Iowa (1)
Banking law - 95
Independent counsel law - 297
Party unity - 7-C
Leahy, Patrick J., D-Vt.
Agriculture Department reorga-
    nization - 193
Appropriations
    Agriculture - 481
    Foreign Aid - 511
    Foreign operations - 508
Breyer nomination - 21-D, 22-D
Child nutrition programs - 374
Competitiveness programs -
    222
Dairy legislation - 197
Electronic eavesdropping - 215,
    216
Farmers Home Administration
    loans - 200
Federal crop insurance - 196
Freedom of Information Act
    (FOIA) - 299
Greece - 510
Russian aid policy - 466
Learjet Inc. - 180, 181
Lee, Sheila Jackson - 572, 12-C
Lefever, Tim - 573
Legal Services Corporation (LSC)
    - 41 (box), 484 (chart), 487
Legislation (general). See also:
    Appropriations; Budget, U.S.;
    Congressional-executive rela-
    tions; Lobbies, lobbying
103rd Congress major legisla-
    tion - 10, 11
Republicans' "Contract With
    America" - 22, 26
Legislative branch - 524, 525
    (chart), 526
Legislative process
Glossary - 3-A, 12-A
Process in brief - 3-B, 5-B
Lehman, Richard H., D-Calif. (19)
1994 election - 573
California desert protection -
    228
Drinking water authorization -
    240

Health care reform - 335
Levin, Carl, D-Mich.
Bosnia-Herzegovina - 448
Defense authorization - 432
Goals 2000 school improvement - 399
Independent counsel law - 297
Lobbying disclosure and gift ban - 37, 38, 40, 42
State Department authorization bill - 456
Unfunded mandates - 151
Levin, Mark B. - 467
Levin, Sander M., D-Mich. (12)
Fraud and abuse in government - 154
Health care reform - 330
Reemployment Act of 1994 - 405
Levy, David A., R-N.Y. (4) - 576
Lewis, Jerry, R-Calif. (40)
Appropriations, VA-HUD - 543, 544
California desert protection - 229
Pay-as-you-go approach to disaster aid - 548, 549
Lewis, John, D-Ga. (5)
Crime bill - 285
Health care reform - 330, 331
House committee assignments - 16
Nation of Islam - 63
Smithsonian Museum - 157
Lewis, Ron, R-Ky. - 12, 592
Lewis, Tom, R-Fla. (16) - 571
Libraries - 385, 520 (chart)
Library of Congress - 189, 525, 526, 554
Lieberman, Joseph I., D-Conn.
1994 election - 570
Appropriations, Defense - 494
Bosnia-Herzegovina - 448
Competitiveness programs - 222
Congressional workplace law exemptions - 29
Defense authorization - 425, 427
Lightfoot, Jim Ross, R-Iowa (3)
Appropriations
Commerce-Justice-State - 485
Treasury Department - 539
Congressional pay raise - 63
Rostenkowski indictment - 47
Linder, John, R-Ga. (4) - 264
Lipinski, William O., D-Ill. (3)
Aquatic Nuisance Species Task Force - 162
Federal Maritime Commission - 164
Incentives to build U.S. ships - 160
Lipsen, Linda - 180
Livable Communities Initiative - 81
Livestock - 228
Livingston, Robert L., R-La. (1)
Appropriations
Commerce-Justice-State - 485
Defense - 488
Foreign operations - 507
Legislative branch - 524
Military construction - 527
Treasury Department - 538
Campaign finance reform - 34
House committee chairmen - 15
Lobbying disclosure and gift ban - 37, 40, 41
Russian aid policy - 466
Lloyd, Marilyn, D-Tenn. (3)

1994 election - 571
Energy Department research laboratories - 223
Lloyd's of London - 308
Lobbies, lobbying. *See also: Business interests, Labor, labor unions; Names of specific groups; Political action committees.*
Health care reform - 320, 330
Lobbying legislation
Background - 36, 37
Gift-giving limits - 38, 42, 41 (box)
Lobbying disclosure - 36, 37, 38, 40, 41, 42
Montana wilderness bill - 246
Superfund reauthorization - 233, 234, 236
LoBiondo, Frank A., R-N.J. - 576
Lockheed Corp. - 434
Logging industry - 254
Long, Jill L., D-Ind. (4)
1994 election - 572
Agriculture Department reorganization - 193
Longley, James B., Jr., R-Maine - 576
Loomis, Burdett - 320, 9-C
Lott, Trent, R-Miss.
1994 election - 569
Breyer appointment - 310
Budget resolution Fy 1995 - 84
Civil War battlefield park - 252
Congressional workplace law exemptions - 29
Crime bill - 286
Defense authorization - 426
Federal employees - 149
National parks - 249
Nominations and appointees - 301
Senate leadership for 104th Congress - 17
Shipyard subsidies - 159, 160
State Department authorization bill - 456
Talbott nomination - 471
U.S. communications law rewrite - 210
Vote studies, presidential support - 4-C
Louisiana
1994 election - 572, 563
Conservative coalition - 9-C
FY 1994 disaster supplemental - 553
Jean Lafitte National Historical Park - 517
Lower Mississippi Delta - 230
Natural gas - 545
New Orleans historic park - 230
Redistricting - 591, 592
Lowey, Nita M., D-N.Y. (18) - 512
Low-income assistance - *See: Anti-poverty programs; Welfare and social services.*
Low-Income Home Energy Assistance Program (LIHEAP) - 68, 79, 82, 84, 370, 372, 519, 520 (chart), 522, 523, 549 (box), 551
Lucas, Frank D., R-Okla.
1994 election - 12
Special elections - 592
Lugar, Richard G., R-Ind.
1994 election - 569
Agriculture Department reorganization - 191
Appropriations, Foreign aid - 510
Breyer appointment - 310
Russian aid policy - 467
Luksik, Peg - 579
Luque, Nancy - 46

Luther, William P. "Bill," D-Minn. - 573

M

Machtley, Ronald K., R-R.I. (1) - 576
Mack, Connie, R-Fla.
1994 election - 569, 575
Appropriations, Legislative branch - 526
Banking laws - 107, 108
Community development banking - 101
Goals 2000 school improvement - 398
Housing authorization - 410
Nominations and appointees - 301
Madigan, Edward R., R-Ill. - 7, 191
Madison Guaranty Savings and Loan - *See: Banks and banking, Whitewater/Madison affair*
Mahley, Don - 438
Mahoney, Michael C. - 50
Maine
1994 election - 564, 565, 568, 576, 579
Dairy legislation - 197
Logging on Forest Service lands - 257
National forests - 247
Senate Race - 565
Term limits - 581
Major League Baseball - 58, 501, 523
Major League Baseball Players Association - 183
Maloney, Carolyn B., D-N.Y. (14)
Abortion clinic access - 357
Appropriations
Defense - 492
VA-HUD - 544
Mandate Watch List - 150
Mandela, Nelson - 470
Mann, David, D-Ohio (1)
1994 election - 572
Insurance antitrust exemption - 184
Manton, Thomas J., D-N.Y. (7)
Competitiveness programs - 223
Federal Trade Commission - 182
Fishing legislation - 259
Interstate transport of solid waste - 261
Superfund reauthorization - 233
U.S.-Canadian salmon fishing dispute - 161
Manufacturing Extension Partnership Program - 222
Maps
Capitol Hill - 16-B
Margolies-Mezvinsky, Marjorie, D-Pa. (13)
1994 election - 576
Health care reform - 336
Marine Corps, U.S. *See also: Defense Department; Military bases; Military construction; Military personnel issues; Navy.*
AAAV amphibious tractor - 430
Appropriations - 489 (chart), 490, 492, 494, 495
Large helicopter carrier - 425, 426
Marine Mammal Protection Act reauthorization - 33, 257
Maritime Heritage program - 164
Maritime industry. *See also: Ships, shipping.*

Foreign shipbuilding subsidies - 159, 160, 163
Maritime Administration - 158, 164, 484 (chart), 552
Revitalization aid - 158, 160, 163
Market Promotion Program - 477, 482
Markey, Edward J., D-Mass. (7)
Defense authorization - 424
FCC funding increase - 218
Radon disclosure - 264
Small Business Administration (SBA) - 187
U.S. communications law rewrite - 204, 205, 209
Martin Luther King Jr. Federal Holiday Commission - 156, 157
Martinez, Matthew G., D-Calif. (31)
Federal employees - 153
Head Start - 373
Martini, Bill, R-N.J. - 576
Marty, John - 579
Maryland
1994 election - 570, 576, 579
Military construction - 528
Mass transit
Appropriations - 530
FY 1995 budget - 81
FY 1994 disaster supplemental - 555
Interstate Commerce Commission - 533
National Highway System - 166
Massachusetts
1994 election - 562, 565, 569, 574, 576, 579
Ballot initiatives - 581
Campaign reform - 581
Clean water grant - 545
Dairy legislation - 197
Senate election - 565
Term limits - 581
VA medical facilities - 415
Massachusetts Mutual Life Insurance - 333
Matheson, Michael J. - 470
Mathews, Harlan, D-Tenn.
1994 election - 565
Balanced-budget amendment - 86
Republican control of Senate - 565
Striker replacement - 402
Mathis, Craig - 571
Mathis, Dawson - 571
Matsui, Robert T., D-Calif. (5)
Appropriations, Treasury Department - 538
Banking laws - 108
GATT - 127
House Ways and Means chairmanship - 12
Vote studies, Presidential support - 6-C
Welfare reform - 364
Mauz, Henry H. Jr. - 440
Mayhew, David R. - 3-C
Mazzoli, Romano L., D-Ky. (3)
1994 election - 571
Crime bill - 275
Immigration law - 295
McCain, John, R-Ariz.
1994 election - 6
Airport programs - 169
Airports, free parking at D.C. area - 177
Appropriations
Agriculture - 480
Defense - 497
Labor-HHS-Education - 522, 523

Military construction - 529
Transportation - 534
VA-HUD - 547
Bosnia-Herzegovina - 448
Campaign finance reform - 34
Commerce Department - 189
Defense authorization - 422
Disaster relief - 155
FY 1994 disaster supplemental
- 556
Lobbying disclosure and gift
ban - 40
Native Americans - 379
Perry nomination - 440
State Department authorization
bill - 455
Talbott nomination - 471
Unfunded mandates - 151
U.S. communications law
rewrite - 211, 212, 214
Vietnam Trade embargo - 12-D
McCandless, Al, R-Calif. (44)
1994 election - 573
California desert protection -
229
McCarran-Ferguson Act - 184,
344
McCarthy, John F. - 44
McCarthy, Karen, D-Mo. - 573
McCloskey, Frank, D-Ind. (8)
1994 election - 572
Bosnia-Herzegovina - 447, 448
Child support enforcement -
375
Federal employees - 152, 153
Fraud and abuse in government
- 154
McCollum, Bill, R-Fla. (8)
Crime bill - 275, 280, 281, 286
House leadership position races
- 14
Term limits - 314
McConnell, Mitch, R-Ky.
Appropriations
Defense - 497
Foreign Aid - 511
Foreign operations - 508,
510
Campaign finance reform - 34
Haitian crisis - 450
Israel - 509
Lobbying disclosure and gift
ban - 39, 40
Russian aid policy - 466, 467
State Department authorization
bill - 456
McCrery, Jim, R-La. (5)
Health care reform - 330, 331
Social Security - 367
McCurdy, Dave, D-Okla. (4)
1994 election - 565, 566, 568,
571
Republican control of Senate -
565
Welfare reform - 364
McDade, Joseph M., R-Pa. (10)
Appropriations, Treasury
Department - 538
House committee chairmen - 15
Indictment case - 51, 52
Rostenkowski indictment - 48
McDermott, Jim, D-Wash. (7)
Frost ethics case - 53
Gingrich ethics investigation -
54
Health care reform - 330
Superfund reauthorization - 234
McDonnell Douglas - 421, 426,
427, 430, 433, 434,493, 494, 495
McHale, Paul, D-Pa. (15)
1994 election - 576
Iraqi Claims Act - 470
McIntosh, David M., D-Ind. - 572

McIntyre, Edward - 51
McKeon, Howard P. "Buck," R-
Calif. (25)
California desert protection -
229
Health care reform - 325, 328
McKinney, Cynthia A., D-Ga. (11)
Defense authorization - 424
House Appropriations
Committee chairmanship - 8
McMillan, Alex, R-N.C. (9) - 205
McMillan, Colin R. - 569
Medicaid
Abortion legislation - 356
Appropriations, Labor-HHS-
Education - 519, 520 (chart)
Budget resolution FY 1995 - 84
Disability payment recipients -
367
FY 1995 budget - 78
Health care reform - 323, 354,
338
Medicare
Appropriations, Labor-HHS-
Education - 519, 520 (chart)
Demonstration program provid-
ing supplemental benefits -
501
Disability payment recipients -
367
FY 1995 budget - 78
Health care reform - 323, 329,
330, 332, 333, 338, 339, 340,
343, 354
Medicare select - 361
Spending cuts - 550
Medlock, Randall - 13
Meehan, Martin T., D-Mass. (5) -
423
Meek, Carrie P., D-Fla. (17)
1994 election - 563
Appropriations
Labor-HHS-Education - 521
Treasury Department - 538
VA-HUD - 547
House committee assignments
- 16
Meese, Edwin III - 469
Meissner, Doris - 294, 295
Mental health - 418
Merchant Marine and Fisheries
Committee (House)
Endangered species - 258
Environmental issues - 255
Environmental Protection
Agency - 243
Fishing legislation - 260
Maritime reauthorization - 158,
164
National Endowment for the
Arts - 515
NOAA authorization - 219
Radioactive waste - 263
Wetlands protection - 265
Mertz, Karl - 197, 481
Metcalf, Jack, R-Wash. - 588
Metzenbaum, Howard M., D-Ohio
1994 election - 563, 565, 566
Airport improvement program -
169
Appropriations
District of Columbia - 501
Labor-HHS-Education - 523
Banking law - 99
Bankruptcy law - 177
Breyer appointment - 308, 309,
310
Breyer nomination - 21-D, 25-D
Competitiveness programs -
222
Crime bill - 282, 284
Electronic eavesdropping - 216
FY 1994 disaster supplemental

- 556
Pension benefits - 404, 405
Product liability - 178
Professional baseball antitrust
exemption - 183
Republican control of Senate -
565
Small aircraft product liability -
180
Striker replacement - 402
Talbott nomination - 471
U.S. communications law
rewrite - 213, 214
Mexico
GATT - 128
United States-Mexico Border
Health Commission - 363
Meyers, Jan, R-Kan. (3)
Party unity - 7-C
Small Business Administration
(SBA) - 186, 187
Small Business Committee
(House) - 18
Mfume, Kweisi, D-Md. (7)
Banking law - 95, 98, 99
Budget resolution FY 1995 - 83
Crime bill - 280
House committee assignments
- 16
House leadership races - 16
Interstate Commerce commis-
sion - 533
Lobbying disclosure and gift
ban - 42
Nation of Islam - 62, 63
Small Business Administration
(SBA) - 187
Mica, John L., R-Fla. (7)
Appropriations, Labor-HHS-
Education - 521
Environmental Protection
Agency - 244
Risk assessment program - 244
Superfund reauthorization - 235
Unfunded mandates - 151
Michel, Robert H., R-Ill. (18)
1994 election - 4, 55, 572
Appropriations, Labor-HHS-
Education - 521
Budget process - 88
Congressional pay raise - 63
Crime bill - 284
Delegate voting appeal - 11-D
Elementary and secondary edu-
cation authorization - 388
GATT - 130
"Ghost voting" - 53
Gun control - 277
Haitian crisis - 451
House committee chairmen - 15
Lobbying disclosure and gift
ban - 40, 41
O'Neill's death - 60
Senate leadership for 104th
Congress - 17
Welfare reform - 364
Michigan
1994 election - 565, 566, 573,
574, 579
Senate race - 565
Middle East - See: Individual coun-
tries' names.
Middle East peace - 426
Mideast - See: Middle East.
Mikulski, Barbara A., D-Md.
Appropriations
Legislative branch - 526
VA-HUD - 543, 545
Disaster relief - 155
GATT - 130
Health care reform - 337
Senate leadership for 104th
Congress - 17

Mildren, Jack - 579
Military bases
Authorization - 435, 438
Base closings - 327, 424, 425,
432, 527, 557
FY 1994 disaster supplemental
- 554
Supreme Court case on base
closings - 436
Use of closed bases - 438
Military construction
Appropriations - 527, 528
(chart), 529
FY 1994 disaster supplemental
- 554
Military facilities and family
housing - 527, 528
Military personnel issues. See
also: Military bases; Veterans
Affairs Department.
Adm. Kelso's retirement - 440
Appropriations - 489 (chart)
Benefits for survivors of ser-
vicemen who die - 431
Child care and family support
services - 495
Child support enforcement -
375
Civilian employees early-out
incentive programs - 495
Defense authorization - 424
FY 1995 budget - 71, 72
Health care Issues affecting
servicewomen - 431
Persian Gulf research - 431
Officer rank at retirement - 440,
441
Pay raises - 421, 425, 428, 430,
431, 490, 491, 493, 495, 497
Personnel levels, FY 1995 -
430, 431
POW-MIA cases - 467, 468
Retirees cost of living - 426,
430
Sexual harassment against
women in military - 426, 430,
435, 440, 441
Women to serve in combat
units - 435
Miller, Gov. Bob, D-Nev. - 581
Miller, Dan, R-Fla. (13)
Elementary and secondary edu-
cation authorization - 386,
387, 391
Goals 2000 school improve-
ment - 399
Head Start - 373
Health care reform - 328, 329
Miller, George, D-Calif. (7)
Agriculture Department reorga-
nization - 193
California desert protection -
228, 229
Child nutrition programs - 374
Elementary and secondary edu-
cation authorization - 385
Federal land payments to locali-
ties - 156
Health care reform - 325, 326,
328, 335
National Endowment for the
Arts - 518
Omnibus Crime bill - 254
Miller, Gov. Walter D., R-S.D. -
578
Miller, Gov. Zell, D-Ga. - 563, 580
Millner, Guy - 580
Milosevic, President Slobodan -
446
Minerals Management Service -
514 (chart)
Mines and mining. See also:
Bureau of Mines

Black lung benefits - 406, 407, 520 (chart)
Mining Law - 517
Mining law rewrite - 70, 236, 237, 513
Mining moratorium - 516
Moratorium on new mining patents - 516, 517
Mineta, Norman Y., D-Calif. (15)
Appropriations, Transportation - 530
Clean water law - 241, 242, 243
Disaster relief - 156
Interstate Commerce Commission - 170
National Highway System (NHS) - 165, 166, 167, 168
Retooling bridges to withstand earthquakes - 167 (box)
Small aircraft product liability - 181
Superfund reauthorization - 234
Minge, David, D-Minn. (2)
Mink, Patsy T., D-Hawaii (2)
Appropriations, Labor-HHS-Education - 521
Elementary and secondary education authorization - 385
Head Start - 373
Health care reform - 328
Minnesota
1994 election - 568, 573, 574, 579
Minority Business Development Agency - 553
Minority Business Enterprise Legal Defense and Education Fund - 147
Minority groups. *See also: Asian Americans; Black Americans; Civil rights; Congressional redistricting; Hispanics; Indians and Alaskan natives; Racial Justice Act; Women.*
Equity in schools - 394
Minority health programs - 358
Missiles
Aegis anti-aircraft system - 429, 430
Ballistic missiles defense - 24, 72, 422, 423, 425, 496, 497
BAT warheads - 428, 491, 494
ERINT - 430
Harpoon warheads - 494
Have Nap guided missile - 429
Hawk - 469
Hellfires - 428, 494
Javelin - 428, 494
Minuteman III - 439
MLRS - 428, 430
Patriot - 430
Popeye - 491
RAM - 430
Standard - 430, 492, 494
THAAD - 430
Tomahawk - 494
TOW - 428, 494
Trident II - 423, 424, 430, 492, 496, 497, 43931
TSSAM - 422, 425, 427, 428, 429, 433, 491
TSSAY - 494
Mississippi
1994 election - 563, 569, 571, 574
Conservative coalition - 9-C
Term limits - 581
Thiokol Corp. - 544
Missouri
1994 election - 568, 573, 574
Campaign reform - 581
Tax restrictions - 581
VA medical facilities - 415

Mitchell, Bob - 573
Mitchell, George J., D-Maine
1994 election - 3, 7, 8, 14, 55, 57, 565
Adm. Mauz Jr.'s retirement - 440
Appropriations, Defense - 494
Balanced-budget amendment - 86
Bosnia-Herzegovina - 448
California desert protection - 227, 230, 231
Campaign finance reform - 32, 34
Crime bill - 286
Elementary and secondary education authorization - 391
Filibusters and cloture votes - 6, 9 (box)
GATT - 128
Goals 2000 school improvement - 399
Health care reform - 319, 338, 342, 350, 354
Indoor air - 265
Lobbying disclosure and gift ban - 39, 42
MFN China - 137
Nominations and appointees - 301
Republican control of Senate - 565
Senate leadership for 104th Congress - 17, 18
Shipyard subsidies - 160
State Department authorization bill - 455
Supreme Court, possible nomination - 57, 58, 303, 14-D, 15-D
Vote studies, presidential support - 3-C, 4-C
Voting participation - 12-C
Wetlands protection - 265
Moakley, Joe, D-Mass. (9)
Appropriations, Transportation - 532
Congressional reform - 28
Congressional workplace law exemptions - 29
Mobil Corporation - 173, 468
Molinari, Susan, R-N.Y. (13)
Crime bill - 285
Head Start - 370
House leadership races - 15
Mollohan, Alan B., D-W.Va. (1)
Appropriations, Commerce-Justice-State - 483, 485, 486
Environmental issues - 255
Mondragon, Roberto - 580
Mongolia - 509
Montana
1994 election - 569, 584
Campaign reform - 581
Tax restrictions - 581
Wilderness areas - 247
Montgomery, G.V. "Sonny," D-Miss. (3)
Persian Gulf Syndrome compensation - 413, 414
Veterans' affairs
Board of Veterans Appeals claims process - 417
Employment oppotunities for veterans - 418
Moore, Richard H. - 571
Moorhead, Carlos J., R-Calif. (27)
1994 election - 573
Energy Department research laboratories - 224
House committee chairmen - 15
Moose, Richard M. - 453
Moppert, Bob - 584

Morella, Constance A., R-Md. (8) - 6-C
Mortgage Bankers Association of America - 264
Mortgages and home loans
Flood insurance bill - 411, 412
FY 1994 supplemental appropriations - 557
Housing authorization - 408, 410
VA home loans - 418
Moseley-Braun, Carol, D-Ill.
Adm. Mauz Jr.'s retirement - 440
Bosnia-Herzegovina - 448
California desert protection - 231
Child support enforcement - 376
Crime bill - 279
Defense authorization - 426
Haitian crisis - 449, 450
Martin Luther King Jr. Federal Holiday Commission - 157
Preservation of historic black college buildings - 401
Procurement reform - 145
Small Business Administration (SBA) - 186
Motion Picture Association of America - 217
Moynihan, Daniel Patrick, D-N.Y.
1994 election - 570
Appropriations, Treasury Department - 539
Bosnia-Herzegovina - 448
Clinton health care initiative - 29
Domestic workers tax laws - 368, 369
Drinking water authorization - 239
Federal railroad safety programs - 173
GATT - 126, 127
Health care reform - 320, 338, 339, 341
Social Security - 366
Superfund reauthorization - 235, 236
Mudd, Jack - 569
Muhammad, Khalid Abdul - 62, 63
Munster, Edward - 584
Murdoch, Rupert - 55
Murkowski, Frank H., R-Alaska
Appropriations
Foreign operations - 510
VA-HUD - 546
Breyer appointment - 310
FY 1994 disaster supplemental - 556
Lobbying disclosure and gift ban - 39, 40
National Endowment for the Arts - 517, 518
Persian Gulf Syndrome compensaton - 414
State Department authorization bill - 458
U.S.-Canadian salmon fishing dispute - 161
Murphy, Austin J., D-Pa. (20)
Black lung benefits bills - 406
Davis-Bacon wage revision - 406
"Ghost voting" - 53
Health care reform - 326
National parks - 250
OSHA overhaul legislation - 403
Professonal boxing regulation - 407
Murray, Patty, D-Wash.
Adm. Mauz Jr.'s retirement -

440
Defense authorization - 426
National Endowment for the Arts - 518
Wards Cove Packing Co. - 298
Murtha, John P., D-Pa. (12)
Appropriations
Defense - 490, 492
Foreign operations - 508
Bosnia-Herzegovina - 447
Defense Department peace-keeping operations - 550
House Appropriations Committee chairmanship - 9
Music - 312
Myers, John T., R-Ind. (7)
Appropriations, Energy and water - 503, 504
Disaster relief - 550
House committee chairmen - 15
Party unity - 7-C
Myrick, Sue, R-N.C. - 571

N

NAACP - 302
Nader, Ralph - 309
GATT - 126
Nadler, Jerrold, D-N.Y. (8)
Crime bill - 278
National Endowment for the Arts - 515
Nanny Tax - *See: Taxes and Taxation.*
Narcotics - *See: Drugs and Drug abuse.*
Natcher, William H., D-Ky. (2)
Death - 55
FY 1994 disaster supplemental - 549
House Appropriations Committee chairmanship - 8
Profile upon his death - 58, 59
Replaced by Ron Lewis - 12
Voting participation - 11-C, 12-C
Nation of Islam - 62, 63
National Academy of Sciences - 503
National Aeronautics and Space Administration (NASA)
Advanced Solid Rocket Motor Program - 80
Appropriations - 80, 541, 547 (chart)
Authorization - 218, 219
Commercial Space Transportation Act - 219
FY 1994 disaster supplemental provisions - 553, 555
Land Remote Sensing Policy Act of 1992 (Landsat) - 219, 556
Mars Surveyor program - 80
Mission to Planet Earth - 80, 218
Space shuttle program - 80, 218, 219
Space shuttle program savings - 219
Space station
Appropriations, FY 1995 - 80, 17-C
FY 1994 disaster supplemental provisions - 553
Technology development grants - 219
National African-American Museum - 157
National Archives - 537 (chart)
National Association of Counties - 262
National Association of

Homebuilders - 264
National Association of Mutual Insurance Companies - 234
National Association of Realtors - 264
National Association of State Attorneys General - 181
National Audubon Society - 244
National Biological Survey - 230, 514 (chart), 515
National Cable Television Association - 213
National Cancer Institute - 78
National Competitiveness Act - 187, 407
National Conference of State Legislatures - 150
National Conference on Soviet Jewry - 467
National Consumers League - 217
National Corn Growers Association - 542
National Counterintelligence Center - 459
National Counterintelligence Policy Board - 459, 462
National Empowerment Television - 54
National Endowment for Democracy - 455, 456, 457, 485, 486, 487
National Endowment for the Arts - 514 (chart), 515, 517
National Endowment for the Humanities - 514 (chart)
National Federation of Independent Business - 231, 334
National Fish and Wildlife Foundation - 260
National Flood Insurance - 71
National Forest Management Act - 518
National Governors' Association - 238, 239, 240, 342
National Guard - 417, 423, 425, 430, 431, 489 (chart), 491, 495, 527, 528, 529 (chart). *See also: Reserves, military.*
National Highway System
East-West Transamerica Corridor - 167
Legislative action - 165, 168
Requiring that scrap tire be added to road asphalt - 166, 167
National Highway Traffic Safety Administration - 81, 531 (chart), 534
National Homeownership Trust - 78
National Industrial Transportation League - 170
National Institute of Allergy and Infectious Diseases - 78
National Institute for Occupational Safety and Health (NIOSH) - 266
National Institute of Standards and Technology (NIST) - 71, 221, 223, 483, 484 (chart)
National Institute on Drug Abuse - 78
National Institutes of Health (NIH)
Appropriations, Labor-HHS-Education - 520 (chart), 521
FY 1995 budget - 78
Nutritional supplements - 358
Rare diseases - 363
Traumatic brain injuries - 361
National Jewish Coalition - 471
National League of Cities - 238,

214
National Marine Fisheries Service - 257, 259
National Oceanic and Atmospheric Administration (NOAA) - *See also: Global Learning and Observations to Benefit the Environment (GLOBE); National Undersea Research Program*
219, 220, 260, 483, 484 (chart), 486, 553
National Organization for Women (NOW) Legal Defense and Education Fund - 153
National Park Hospitality Association - 250
National Park Service - 247, 251, 514 (chart), 518. *See also: Parks and recreation; State names for individual parks.*
Appropriations - 513, 515, 517
Concessions - 249, 251
FY 1994 disaster supplemental - 552
Golden Gate National Recreation Area - 253
Grand Canyon - 251
Heritage areas - 255
Interior Appropriations - 248
Legislation - 247, 254
National parks - 73
Steamtown - 252
User fees - 143
Yellowstone - 251
National Parks and Conservation Association - 248
National Performance Review (1993) - 143, 152
National Railroad Corporation - *See: Railroads.*
National Reconnaissance Office (NRO) - 458, 497
National Republican Congressional Committee - 47, 570, 592
National Rifle Association (NRA) - 56, 274, 276, 283, 286, 492, 569, 570, 588, 26-D
National Right to Life Committee - 42, 311
National Rural Electric Cooperative Association - 592
National Safety Council - 403
National Science and Technology Council - 220
National Science Foundation (NSF) - 80, 220, 221, 223, 543, 547, 555
National Security Act - 465
National Security Agency (NSA) - 458, 460, 463
National Security Council - 459, 462, 463, 469, 537 (chart)
National service - 73, 545, 547, 555
National Taxpayers Union - 12-C
National Transportation Safety Board (NTSB) - 173, 181, 531 (chart)
National Treasury Employees Union - 349
National Undersea Research Program - 219, 220
National Youth Sports Program - 373
National Zoo - 513
NATO - *See: North Atlantic Treaty Organization (NATO).*
Natural gas - 515
Natural Resources Committee (House)
American Heritage areas - 252

California desert protection - 228, 229
Enviromental issues - 254
Everglades protection - 254
Federal land payments to localities - 156
Health care reform - 344, 345
Indians and Alaskan natives - 377, 379
Logging on Forest Service lands - 256, 257
Montana wilderness bill - 245
National Endowment for the Arts - 518
National parks - 250, 251
Presidio management - 253
Renamed - 18
Steamtown - 252
Urban recreation - 254
Natural Resources Defense Council - 239, 240
Navy, U.S.
Aegis destroyers - 492
Appropriations - 488, 489 (chart), 490, 491, 492, 494, 496
Arleigh-Burke-class destroyers - 422, 425, 429
Nuclear-powered aircraft carrier
Appropriations - 488, 490, 494, 496
FY 1995 defense authorization - 421, 422, 426, 427
Submarines
Seawolf class - 427, 440
Smaller nuclear-powered class - 488, 492, 494, 496, 497
Tailhook scandal
Chief of Naval Operations Kelso retires early - 440
Congressional hearing on Kelso retirement benefits - 440
Neal, Richard E., D-Mass. (2) - 331
Neal, Stephen L., D-N.C. (5) - 94
Nebraska
1994 election - 569, 573, 579
Term limits - 581
Nedza, James - 46
Neighborhood LIFT initiative - 71
Nelson, Gov. Ben, D-Neb. - 579
Nelson, Lisa B. - 54, 55
Nelson, Sheffield - 580
Nethercutt, George, R-Wash. - 56, 588
Neumann, Mark W., R-Wis. - 573
Nevada
1994 election - 563, 569, 579, 584
Campaign reform - 581
Nuclear Waste disposal - 73
Tax restrictions - 581
Term limits - 581
New Hampshire
1994 election - 576, 579
Dairy legislation - 197
Logging on Forest Service lands - 257
National forests - 247
New Jersey
1994 election - 561, 562, 569, 574, 576, 579
Anti-crime legislation - 288
Natural gas pipeline explosion - 189
Pinelands National Reserve - 517
Tokamak nuclear reactor - 502, 504
New Mexico
1994 election - 569, 576, 579,

580, 584
Colonias - 71
New courthouse projects - 539
United States-Mexico Border Health Commission - 363
New York
1994 election - 562, 564, 570, 574, 576, 579, 584
Anti-crime legislation - 288
FY 1994 disaster supplemental - 548
GATT - 129
HUD special-purpose grants - 545
Love Canal - 232
New courthouse projects - 539
New train station - 552
New York Daily News - 55
New York University - 56, 59
Nickles, Don, R-Okla.
Appropriations, Foreign Aid - 511
Breyer appointment - 310
Competitiveness programs - 223
Defense authorization - 426
Lobbying disclosure and gift ban - 42
School-to-work bill - 400
Senate leadership for 104th Congress - 17
Nissenbaum, Ellen - 283
NIST - *See: National Institute for Standards and Technology.*
Nixon, President Richard M.
Eulogies delivered - 16-D
Nixon's congressional legacy - 60, 61
NOAA - *See: National Oceanic and Atmospheric Administration.*
Nominations and confirmations - *See: Ambassadors; Cabinet; Judiciary; Names of executive branch agencies.*
North, Oliver L. - 469, 563, 565
North American Free Trade Agreement (NAFTA) - 108, 123, 128, 144, 211, 277
North American Man-Boy Love Association - 457
North Atlantic Treaty Organization (NATO)
Appropriations - 511
Bosnia-Herzegovina - 446, 449
Burden sharing - 431
Eastern Europe and NATO - 496, 497
Infrastructure fund - 431, 529
North Carolina - 95
1994 election - 562, 571, 574, 579, 580
Banking - 94, 95
Conservative coalition - 9-C
Redistricting - 591, 592
North Dakota - 570, 573
North Korea
Appropriations, Foreign operations - 511
Nuclear weapons program - 455
State Department authorization bill - 458
Northrop-Grumman Corp. - 432
Norton, Eleanor Holmes, D-D.C. (AL)
Appropriations, District of Columbia - 499, 500 (box)
Child support enforcement - 375
Crime bill - 280
Delegate voting - 62
Federal employees - 152, 153, 154

Norwood, Charlie, R-Ga. - 571
Nuclear arms - *See: Arms control; Nuclear weapons; Weapons, military.*
Nuclear energy. *See also: Nuclear waste management; Nuclear weapons; Radiation exposure.*
   Energy Department research - 73
   International Thermonuclear Experimental Reactor - 221
Nuclear Regulatory Commission (NRC) - 555
Nuclear waste management
   Nuclear Waste Fund - 73
Nuclear weapons. *See also: Arms control; Export Administration Act; India; North Korea; Nuclear waste management; Pakistan; Weapons, military.*
   Appropriations - 502, 504
   Defense authorization - 439
   Research funding - 223
   State Department authorization bill - 455, 457, 458
   Strategic Arms Reduction Treaty (START II) - 439
   Test ban, Nuclear test ban extended - 424, 425
   U.S. Russian aid policy - 467
Nunn, Sam, D-Ga.
   Adm. Kelso's retirement - 440
   Appropriations
      Commerce-Justice-State - 487
      Defense - 494, 497
      Energy and water - 504
      Foreign aid - 510
   Bosnia-Herzegovina - 448
   Brown nomination - 472
   Budget resolution FY 1995 - 84
   Defense authorization - 425, 426, 427, 431, 432, 433
   Fraud and abuse in government - 154
   Haitian crisis - 450
   Lobbying disclosure and gift ban - 39
   MFN China - 137
   Nunn-Lugar program - 510
   Perry nomination - 439
   Russian aid policy - 467
   Striker replacement - 402
   U.S. troops in Haiti - 29-D, 32-D
Nussle, Jim, R-Iowa (2)
   Disaster relief - 550
   Transition team - 18

O

Oberdorfer, Louis - 53
Oberly, Charles M., III - 569
Oberstar, James L., D-Minn. (8)
   Air-traffic control system proposal - 169
   Small aircraft product liability - 181
   Smoking ban on all international, Alaska, Hawaii flights - 174
   Truck-safety amendment - 167, 168
Obey, David R., D-Wis. (7)
   Appropriations
      Agriculture - 479
      Commerce-Justice-State - 483, 485
      Foreign Aid - 511
      Foreign operations - 505, 507
      Labor-HHS-Education - 521, 523

      Transportation - 535
      Treasury Department - 539, 540
   Budget process - 88, 90
   Congressional pay raise - 63
   Foreign aid reform - 452
   House Appropriations Committee chairmanship - 8, 9
   Russian aid policy - 467
Occupational Safety and Health Administration (OSHA) - 152, 403
O'Connor, Justice Sandra Day - 310
Office of Compliance - 28
Office of Construction Safety, Health and Education - 403
Office of Educational Technology - 401
Office of Fair Employment Practices - 526
Office of Government Ethics - 154
Office of Independent Counsel - 295, 298
Office of Information and Regulatory Affairs - 155
Office of Management and Budget (OMB)
   Appropriations - 537 (chart)
   Deficit calculations - 68
   Environmental spending - 73
   Payroll cuts - 149, 155
   Unfunded federal mandates - 25, 26
Office of National Drug Control Policy - 290, 537 (chart)
Office of Personnel Management (OPM)
   Appropriations - 536, 537 (chart)
   Child support enforcement - 375
   Federal employee buyouts - 148, 149
   Federal employee leave usage - 152
Office of Science and Technology Policy (OSTP) - 220, 244, 264, 553
Office of Special Counsel - 154
Office of Technology Assessment (OTA) - 21, 526
Office of the Comptroller of the Currency (OCC) - 99, 105
Office of the U.S. Trade Representative (USTR) - 107, 108, 553
Office of Thrift Supervision (OTS) - 99, 105
Ohio
   1994 election - 562, 563, 565, 566, 572, 574, 579
   Fishing legislation - 260
   Water pollution - 241
Oil industry - 515
   Deep-water drilling royalties - 239
   Ethanol use - 25-C, 26-C
   Leases - 518
Oil Pollution Act of 1990 - 190
Oklahoma
   1994 election - 561, 565, 568, 571, 574, 579, 580
   Conservative coalition - 9-C
   Special elections - 592
O'Leary, Hazel R. - 224, 503
Omnibus Budget-Reconciliation Act of 1993 - 251
Omnibus crime bill - 254
Omnibus Trade and Competitiveness Act (1988) -

222
Omnipoint Communications Inc. - 129
Oregon
   1994 election - 563, 564, 579, 584
   Ballot initiatives - 581
   Campaign reform - 581
   Crime legislation - 581
   Food stamps - 480
   HUD special-purpose grants - 545
   Logging on Forest Service lands - 256, 257
   Tax restrictions - 581
   VA medical facilities - 415
O'Rourke, Joanna G. - 46
Ortiz, Solomon P., D-Texas (27) - 219
Orton, Bill, D-Utah (3)
   Budget process - 88, 89
   Budget resolution FY 1995 - 83
   Economic Development Administration - 188
OSHA - *See: Occupational Safety and Health Administration (OSHA).*
Overgaard, Paul P. - 50
Overseas Private Investment Corporation - 138, 467, 506 (chart)
Owens, Major R., D-N.Y. (11)
   Disabled individuals - 359
   Elementary and secondary education authorization - 385, 387
   Goals 2000 school improvement - 399
   Health care reform - 326, 328
   Professional boxing regulations - 407
Oxley, Michael G., R-Ohio (4)
   High-speed rail - 172
   Radon disclosure - 264
   Superfund reauthorization - 232, 234
   U.S. communications law rewrite - 206

P

Pacelle, Wayne - 258
Pacific Lumber Company - 254
Pacific Telesis - 129, 213
Packard, Ron, R-Calif. (48)
   Aid for illegal aliens - 549
   Appropriations
      Agriculture - 479
      Energy and water - 503
      Labor-HHS-Education - 521
      Legislative branch - 524
      Military construction - 527
   California toll road project - 166
   Immigration law - 294
Packwood, Bob, R-Ore.
   Adm. Kelso's retirement - 440
   Ethics probe
      Packwood diaries - 49, 50
      Senate Ethics Committee Diary Subpoena - 10-D, 11-D Sexual misconduct - 49, 50
   Health care reform - 342
   Interstate Commerce Commission - 170
   Superfund reauthorization - 236
   U.S. communications law rewrite - 203, 209, 212, 214
Packwood, Georgie - 50
Pakistan - 453
Palasz, Sophie - 46
Palestine Liberation Organization

(PLO) - 79, 458, 511, 512
Pallone, Frank Jr., D-N.J. (6)
   Commerce Department - 189
   Interstate Transport of Solid Waste - 262
Panama - 471, 472
Panama Canal Commission - 531 (chart)
Panetta, Leon E. - 31
   Budget Resolution FY 1995 - 67, 85
   Crime bill - 284
   Veterans' Affairs, Staff cut exemption - 416
Panzke, Nancy - 46
Paperwork Reduction Act - 154
Parker, Mike, D-Miss. (4)
   Asphalt requiring crumb rubber - 167
   Budget resolution FY 1995 - 83
   Superfund reauthorization - 234
Parker, Wayne - 572
Parks and Recreation
   California Mojave National Park - 228, 229
   Death Valley National Monument - 227, 228
   Joshua Tree National Monument - 227, 228
Pastor, Robert - 471, 472
Pataki, Gov. George E., R-N.Y. - 576, 579
Patent and Trademark Office - 167, 185, 484 (chart)
Patents and trademarks - 184, 190
Paxon, Bill, R-N.Y. (27)
   1994 election - 570
   House leadership races - 14
   Rostenkowski indictment - 47
Payne, Donald M., D-N.J. (10)
   Elementary and secondary education authorization - 385
   Foreign aid reform - 453
   Health care reform - 325, 327
Payne, Lewis F. Jr., D-Va. (5)
   1994 election - 572
   Health care reform - 333
Payton, John - 302
Peace Corps - 506 (chart)
Pell, Claiborne, D-R.I.
   Balanced-budget amendment - 86
   Elementary and secondary education authorization - 388
   State Department authorization bill - 455
   Vote studies, presidential support - 6-C
Pelosi, Nancy, D-Calif. (8)
   GATT - 127
   MFN China - 137
   Presidio management - 253
Peña, Federico F.
   Air-traffic control system proposal - 169
   Airport improvement program - 169
   High-speed rail - 171
   National Highway System (NHS) - 165
Pennsylvania
   1994 election - 562, 564, 565, 566, 574, 576, 579
   Military construction - 528
   Risk assessment program - 244
   Steamtown National Historic Site - 247, 248
Penny, Timothy J., D-Minn. (1)
   1994 election - 573
   Appropriations
      Commerce-Justice-State - 486

Transportation - 533
Budget process - 87, 89
Budget resolution FY 1995 - 67, 83, 85
Crime bill - 279
Defense authorization - 424
Disaster relief - 550
Federal crop insurance - 196
Federal employees - 149
Veterans Affairs staff cut exemption - 416
Pension Benefit Guaranty Corporation (PBGC) - 126, 404
Pentagon - See: Defense Department.
People's Republic of China - 454, 511
MFN China - 137, 455, 456
Radio Free Asia - 454
State Department authorization bill - 458
Perot, Ross - 42, 124, 568, 579, 588, 592
Perry, William J. - 72, 422, 449, 459, 27-D, 28-D
Budget resolution FY 1995 - 85
Defense authorization - 429, 439
Perry nomination - 439
Procurement reform - 144
Perryman, David - 571
Peters, Ronald M. Jr. - 60
Petri, Tom, R-Wis. (6)
Elementary and secondary education authorization - 384, 386, 390
Federal employees - 154
Health care reform - 328
National Highway System (NHS) - 165, 166
Surface transportation law - 166
Petroleum Reserves - 73, 514 (chart)
Pharmaceuticals - 330, 334, 337, 339. See also: Chemical industry; individual company names.
Philadelphia Naval Shipyard - 436
Philip Morris - 360
Pickett, Owen B., D-Va. (2) - 572
Pickle, J.J., D-Texas (10)
Appropriations, Treasury Department - 540
Social Security - 367
Pioneer Seed Co. - 190
Pitney, John J. Jr. - 60
PLO - See: Palestine Liberation Organization (PLO).
Poindexter, John M. - 469
Police - See: Law enforcement.
Political action committees (PACs)
Campaign finance reform Legislative action - 32, 34
GOPAC - 54, 55
Senate action - 27-C
Politics and elections. See also: Campaign finance; Congressional elections; Democratic Party; Federal Election Commission (FEC); Political parties; Presidential elections; Public opinion polls; Republican Party.
1994 election - 14, 21, 563
"Contract With America" - 570, 573, 584
Defeated incumbents - 572
Governors after 1994 election (map) - 580
Governors and Governors-Elect - 579
House Delegations in the 104th Congress (map) - 576
Incumbent re-election rates,

1946-94 (graph) - 584
Midterm revolutions - 562
83rd Congress 1953-54 (map) - 580
Redistricting - 591, 592
Republican House victories - 570, 576
Republican landslide - 561, 564
Republican Senate victories - 565, 570
Republican share of House, Senate, governorships by region - 564
Republican vote increase - 564
Senate in the 104th Congress (map) - 566
Senate membership - 104th Congress - 567
Senate newcomers - 568
State elections - 576, 579
Voter turnout - 561
Voters' hostility reshapes Congress - 3, 13
Pombo, Richard W., R-Calif. (11)
California desert protection - 229
Enviromental issues - 254
"Ghost voting" - 53
National Endowment for the Arts - 516
Pomeroy, Earl, D-N.D. (AL)
Appropriations Legislative branch - 524, 525
Treasury Department - 538
Pork barreling - See: Regional issues and regionalism.
Porter, John Edward, R-Ill. (10)
Appropriations, Commerce-Justice-State - 485
Foreign operations - 507
Party unity - 7-C
Portman, Rob, R-Ohio (2) - 151
Post Office and Civil Service Committee (House)
Federal employees - 147, 149, 152, 153
Fraud and abuse in government - 154
Health care reform - 345
Martin Luther King Jr. Federal Holiday Commission - 157
Postal Service, U.S. - 536
Appropriations - 536, 537 (chart)
Child support enforcement - 375
Health care reform - 342
Postsecondary education. See also: Education Department; Student aid.
Academic research appropriation - 220
Military recruiters barred from campus recruiting - 424, 426
Preservation of historic black college buildings - 401
Potter, Trevor - 35, 36
Powell, Adam Clayton, Jr. - 315
Powell, Gen. Colin L. - 450, 451, 29-D, 32-D
POW/MIA affairs - See: Vietnam.
Prather, Joseph W. - 592
Presidential addresses, announcements, news conferences
Administration plans - 60-D, 61-D
Clinton election response - 33-D, 34-D
Crime bill - 26-D
Election results 1994 - 33-D, 34-D
Haiti agreement - 29-D, 32-D

Haiti invasion plan - 27-D, 28-D
Lifting of Vietnam embargo - 12-D
State of the Union address - 3-D, 7-D
Presidential success history - 4-C (chart)
Pressler, Larry, R-S.D.
Biodiversity treaty - 267
Food stamps - 376
Foreign aid reform - 453
National Transportation Safety Board authorization - 173
School-to-work bill - 400
Shipyard subsidies - 159, 160
Small Business Administration (SBA) - 186
State Department authorization bill - 457
U.S. communications law rewrite - 210
Price, David, D-N.C. (4)
1994 congressional election - 571
Balanced-budget amendment - 87
Budget process - 88
Price, Stuart - 571
Primus, Wendall E. - 367
Prisons and prisoners
Anti-crime legislation - 274, 275, 281, 282, 287
Appropriations, Commerce-Justice-State - 484 (chart), 486
Inmate wages - 300
Privacy - 215, 216
Procurement
"800 Panel" - 144
Defense, Appropriations - 72, 489 (chart)
Federal Acquisition Computer Network (FACNET) - 145
Reform - 528 (chart), 143, 144, 147
Product liability. See also: Air transportation, Small aircraft liability.
Legislative action - 178, 179, 24-C
Legislative history - 179
Republicans' "Contract with America" - 26
Professional Boxing Corp. - 407
Progress and Freedom Foundation - 54
Progressive Policy Institute - 31
Project for the Republican Future - 350
Property rights - 26, 252, 309, 310, 311
Pryor, David, D-Ark.
Balanced-budget amendment - 86
Defense authorization - 426
Health care reform - 339, 343
Procurement reform - 146
Senate leadership for 104th Congress - 17
Striker replacement - 402
Public Citizen - 42
Public Health Service - 78, 361, 479
Public Interest Research Group - 262
Public laws - 10, 11, 3-E, 20-E
Public Works and Transportation Committee (House)
Clean water law - 243
Commerce Department - 190
Disaster relief - 156
Drinking water authorization - 240

Economic Development Administration - 188
National Highway System (NHS) - 165
Small aircraft product liability - 181
Superfund reauthorization - 233, 234
Puerto Rico - 545, 7-B
Pyongyang - 511

R

Racial Justice Act - 277, 281
Racketeer Influenced and Corrupt Organizations Act (RICO) - 52
Radanovich, George P., R-Calif. - 573
Radio. See also: International broadcasting.
Radio, TV Marti - 483, 485, 487
Radio and TV Marti - 454
Radio Free Asia - 454, 456, 457, 483, 485, 486
Radio Free Europe - 454, 455, 456
Radio Liberty - 454, 455
U.S. communications law rewrite - 205
Voice of America - 454, 555
Rahall, Nick J. II, D-W.Va. (3)
American Heritage areas - 252
Commerce Department - 190
Interstate Commerce Commission - 170
Mining law rewrite - 237
National Highway System (NHS) - 165, 167
Road projects - 166
Superfund reauthorization - 234, 235
Tow truck regulations - 174
Truck-safety amendment - 168
Railroads. See also: Mass transit.
Amtrak funding - 81, 171
Amtrak reauthorizations - 171
Federal safety programs - 172, 173, 365
High-speed rail - 81, 171, 172, 173, 552, 553
Interstate Commerce Commission Magnetic levitation (Maglev) - 172, 555
Unemployment insurance for railroad workers - 407
Ramirez, Anthony - 46
Rand Corp. - 384
Rangel, Charles B., D-N.Y. (15)
Crime bill - 285
Health care reform - 331
House Ways and Means chairmanship - 12
Nation of Islam - 62
Rostenkowski indictment - 45
Social Security - 367
Ravenel, Arthur Jr., R-S.C. (1)
Reagan, President Ronald - 468
Reed, Jack, D-R.I. (2)
Elementary and secondary education authorization - 384, 386
Health care reform - 328
Regional issues and regionalism. See also: Congressional redistricting; Politics and elections; State and local government.
Appalachian Regional Commission - 187
Appalachian Regional Development Act - 188
Appropriations, VA-HUD - 544,

546
Guaranteed loans - 71
National parks - 252
Pork barrel projects - 529
Special-purpose housing grants
- 71
Regula, Ralph, R-Ohio (16)
American Heritage areas - 252
Appropriations Interior
Department - 513, 515
Transportation - 533
House committee chairmen - 15
Mining law rewrite - 237
Party unity - 7-C
**Rehnquist, Chief Justice William
H.** - 36, 49, 310, 311, 312, 436
Reich, Robert B. - 403
Reid, Harry, D-Nev.
1994 election - 579
Appropriations, Legislative
branch - 525
Balanced-budget amendment -
86
Bankruptcy law - 177
Clean water law - 242
Drinking water authorization -
239
FY 1994 disaster supplemental
- 556
Lead exposure - 266
Mining law rewrite - 237
National Highway System - 168
Senate leadership for 104th
Congress - 18
Reinhardt College - 54
'Reinventing' government - *See:
Gore, Al.*
Reischauer, Robert D. - 69, 151
**Religion and religious organiza-
tions**
1994 election - 572, 573, 576
Bosnian muslims - 446, 449
Breyer appointment - 309
Church-state separation - 313,
EEOC proposed guidelines on
religious harassment - 486
Lobbying disclosure and gift
ban - 42
School prayer - 389, 390, 399
Reno, Janet - 31, 79, 277, 295,
296
Republican leadership
Anti-crime legislation concerns -
26-D
Campaign finance - 32, 34
Committee funding - 13
Gingrich Speaker of the House
- 57-D, 59-D
House leadership position races
- 16 (box)
Intelligence authorization bill -
460
Leadership for the 104th
Congress - 14, 15
Republican Conference ratifies
slate of new committee chair-
men - 15, 17
Senate leadership for 104th
Congress - 16, 17
Transition team - 18
Ushering in Republican rule -
18, 20, 21
Republican National Committee -
48
Republican Party
Appropriations, VA-HUD - 547
Dole's majority leader view - 38-
D
Election victory 1994 - 561, 581
GOP descriptions of bills to
enact "Contract With America"
- 39-D, 52-D
GOP election mandate - 35-D,

37-D
GOP plans for change - 61-D
Legal Services Corporation -
298
Legislative branch
Appropriations - 524, 525
Presidio management - 253,
254
Republicans' campaign pledge:
"Contract With America" - 3,4,
18, 20, 21, 22, 26, 446
Republicans gain seats in '94 -
14, 21
Senate victory - 565, 570
Wilderness plans - 245
**Republican Policy Committee
(House)** - 37
Rescissions - 81
Research and development, U.S.
- See also: Energy Department,
71, 72, 502. Environment,
Environmental technologies, 162,
220, 221, 489 (chart).
Reserves, military - 417, 489
(chart), 495
**Resolution Trust Corporation
(RTC)** - 31, 99, 154, 547
**Resource Conservation and
Recovery Act (RCRA)** - 313
Retirement and pensions. See
also: Social Security
Administration.
Pension plan funding - 403, 405
Pension plan funding enforce-
ment - 177
Reynolds, Mel, D-Ill. (2) - 51
Rhode Island
1994 election - 564, 569, 576,
579
Dairy legislation - 197
Richards, Gov. Ann W., D-Texas -
576, 579
Richards, James R. - 249
Richardson, Bill, D-N.M. (3)
Energy Department research
laboratories - 224
Flow-control legislation - 262
House committee assignments
- 16
Native Americans - 377, 379
Nutritional supplements - 358
Professional boxing regulations
- 407
Tribal self-governance pro-
grams - 167
U.S. communications law
rewrite - 206
Ridge, Tom, R-Pa. (21) - 101, 579
Riegle, Donald W. Jr., D-Mich.
1994 election - 4, 55, 565
Banking laws - 94, 97, 98, 107,
108
Community Development
Banking - 101
Health care reform - 339, 341,
342
Republican control of Senate -
565
Riggs, Frank, R-Calif. - 573
Riley, Richard W. - 386
Riordan, Richard - 274
Rivers, Lynn, D-Mich. - 573
Rivlin, Alice M. - 31
Robb, Charles S., D-Va.
1994 election - 563, 565, 568
Bosnia-Herzegovina - 448
Budget resolution FY 1995 - 84
Defense authorization - 426
State Department authorization
bill - 455
U.S. communications law
rewrite - 212
Vietnam trade embargo - 12-D

Roberts, Pat, R-Kan. (1)
Agriculture Department reorga-
nization - 193
Appropriations
Agriculture - 479
Legislative branch - 525
Elementary and secondary edu-
cation authorization - 387
Plant Variety Protection Act -
190
Privatizing House's restaurants
- 13
Rostenkowski indictment - 47
Roberts, Thomas - 13
Rockefeller, John D. IV, D-W.Va.
Budget resolution FY 1995 - 84
Competitiveness programs -
221, 222
Health care reform - 319, 338,
343
National Aeronautics and Space
Administration reauthorization
- 219
Persian Gulf Syndrome com-
pensation - 414
Persion Gulf Syndrome com-
pensation - 412
Product liability - 178
Senate leadership for 104th
Congress - 18
U.S. communications law
rewrite - 210
Veterans' affairs
Board of Veterans Appeals
claims process - 417
Mental illness treatment -
418
Radiation lawsuits - 417
Staff cut exemption - 416
VA medical facilities - 415
Rockets
MLRS - 491, 495
Titan IV - 492, 496, 497
Rodham, Hugh - 569
Roemer, Tim, D-Ind. (3)
Appropriations, VA-HUD - 544
Elementary and secondary edu-
cation authorization - 385,
387
Health care reform - 327, 328
National Aeronautics and Space
Administration reauthorization
- 218
Rogers, Harold, R-Ky. (5) - 483
Rohrabacher, Dana, R-Calif. (45)
Aid for illegal aliens - 549
Elementary and secondary edu-
cation authorization - 387,
388
Immigration law - 294
Romer, Gov. Roy, D-Colo. - 580
**Romero-Barceló, Carlos, D-P.R.
(AL)**
Delegate voting - 62
Education and secondary edu-
cation authorization - 386
Romney, Mitt - 565, 569
Rose, Charlie, D-N.C. (7)
Ethics case - 52
House Administration
Committee - 13
House leadership position races
- 15
Rostenkowski's reimbursement
- 43, 44
Ross, Steven R. - 315
Rostenkowski, Dan, D-Ill. (5)
1994 election - 3, 48, 55, 570,
572
Campaign finance reform - 33
Committee chairmen's terms -
18
FY 1994 election - 44, 45

Government indictment - 43, 48
Health care reform - 330, 331,
333
House Post Office probe - 53
House Ways and Means chair-
manship - 12
Reimburses government - 13-D
Superfund reauthorization - 234
Tax code simplification - 93
Vote counting - 5
Ways and Means chairmanship
- 9
Rota, Robert V. - 43, 46, 47, 53
Roth, William V. Jr., R-Del.
1994 election - 569
Banking law - 99
California desert protection -
231
Crime bill - 286
Federal employees - 147, 149
Health care reform - 342, 343
Procurement law - 146
Superfund reauthorization - 236
Roukema, Marge, R-N.J. (5)
Child support - 375
Health care reform - 325, 327,
329
Housing authorization - 410
Rowland, Gov. John G., R-Conn. -
579
Rowland, J. Roy, D-Ga. (8)
Health care reform - 336
Product liability - 178
Veterans' Affairs
Expanded health care for
women veterans - 415
Staff cut exemption - 416
VA medical facilities - 415
Rules Committee (House)
Added-nicotine controversy -
360
Budget process - 87, 88, 89
Congressional workplace law
exemptions - 28, 29
Crime bill - 279
Independent counsel law - 296
Legislative branch
Appropriations - 525
Montana wilderness bill - 246
National parks - 251
Superfund reauthorization - 234
**Rural Development
Administration** - 256, 478
**Rural Electrification
Administration** - 73, 478, 553
Rural Utilities Service - 73
Russia - See: Commonwealth of
Independent States.
Russo, Robert - 46
Rwanda - 431, 487, 493, 494, 505,
511

S

Sabo, Martin Olav, D-Minn. (5) -
538
Safe Drinking Water Act of 1974 -
244
Saiki, Patricia F. - 580
Salmon, Matt, R-Ariz. - 584
Sandefur, Thomas E. - 360
Sanders, Bernard, I-Vt. (AL) - 95
Sands, A. P. "Sandy" - 571
Sanford, Mark, R-S.C. - 571
Sangmeister, George E., D-Ill. (11)
- 572
Santorum, Rick, R-Pa. (18)
1994 election - 564, 565, 566,
576
Appropriations, Labor-HHS-
Education - 521
Health care reform - 334

Re-employment Act of 1994 -
406
Republican control of Senate -
565
Social Security - 367
Welfare reform - 364
Sarbanes, Paul S., D-Md.
1994 election - 570
Federal employees - 150
Foreign aid reform - 453
Haitian crisis - 451
Iraqi Claims Act - 470
Treaty on Women - 471
Voting participation - 12-C
Sarpalius, Bill, D-Texas (13)
1994 election - 572
Landfills - 265
Sasser, Jim, D-Tenn.
1994 election - 4, 8, 14, 55,565,
566
Appropriations
Defense - 488
Military construction - 528
Budget resolution FY 1995 - 81,
83, 84
California desert protection -
231
Haitian crisis - 451
Republican control of Senate -
565
Senate leadership for 104th
Congress - 17
Satellites
Brilliant Eyes - 430, 496, 497
Land Remote Sensing Policy
Act of 1992 (Landsat) - 219
LANDSAT-7 - 556
Milstar - 497
Pentagon space operations -
492
Satellite Home Viewer Act of
1994 - 216, 217
Sauerbrey, Ellen - 579
Sawyer, Tom, D-Ohio (14) - 385
Scalia, Justice Antonin - 310, 311,
312, 314
Scarborough, Joe, R-Fla. - 571
Schaefer, Dan, R-Colo. (6) - 233
Schenk, Lynn, D-Calif. (49)
1994 election - 573, 575
Appropriations, Energy and
water - 503
Health care reform - 336
High-speed rail - 172
National Oceanic and
Atmospheric Administration
reauthorization - 219
Schiff, Steven H., R-N.M. (1)
Appropriations, Commerce-
Justice-State - 486
Crime bill - 278
Schiliro, Philip M. - 576
Schlesinger, Arthur M. Jr. - 60
Schroeder, Patricia, D-Colo. (1)
Child support enforcement -
375, 376
Federal employees - 152
Health care reform - 343
House committee assignments
- 16, 17
Schumer, Charles E., D-N.Y. (9)
Banking laws - 107, 108
Crime bill - 275, 282, 283, 284,
285
Gun control - 277
Housing authorization - 409
**Science, Space and Technology
Committee (House)**
Appropriations, VA-HUD - 541
Disaster relief - 155
Energy research laboratories -
223, 224
Environmental technology -

263, 264
National Aeronautics and Space
Administration reauthorization
- 218
National Science Foundation -
220
NOAA renewal - 219
Risk assessment program - 244
Science policy - 220
Science and technology. *See
also: Communications and
telecommunications; Computers;
Energy Department; Executive
Office of the President; National
Aeronautics and Space
Administration; National Institutes
of Health; National Science
Foundation; Office of Science and
Technology Policy; Satellites.*
Advanced Technology Program
- 223
Competitiveness programs -
221, 223
FY 1995 budget - 80
National Competitiveness Act -
407
Space Station - 545, 546
Technology transfer - 223
Scirica, Anthony - 52
Scott, Robert C., D-Va. (3) - 280
Seastrand, Andrea, R-Calif. - 573
Secret Service, U.S. - 536, 537
(chart)
**Securities and Exchange
Commission (SEC)**
Appropriations - 484 (chart),
486, 487
Community development bank-
ing - 101
Fair trade - 107, 108
Telemarketing fraud - 217
**Select Committee on Intelligence
(Senate)** - 463, 466
Selective Service, U.S. - 424, 426
Selective Service System - 547
Senate. *See also: Congressional
elections; Congressional ethics;
Congressional votes; Democratic
leadership; Nominations and con-
firmations; Republican leadership;
Senate committees.*
1994 election - 561, 570
Appropriations Chairman,
Federal employees - 153
Committee assignments - 8-B,
9-B
Conservative coalition - 44-C
Key votes - 54-C, 56-C
Legislation - 86
Export-Import Bank - 138
GATT - 3, 48, 55, 123, 130
Minority health programs -
358, 359
Nutritional supplements -
357
Members of the 103rd
Congress, 2nd Session - 7-B
Presidential support - 34-C, 37-
C
Voting participation - 45-C
Senate committees (general) -
*See also: Joint committees; indi-
vidual committee names, e.g.,
Appropriations Committee
(Senate).*
Committee assignments - 8-B,
9-B
Congressional reform - 27, 28
Organization for the 104th
Congress - 16, 18
Staff cuts - 21
Senior citizens - *See: Aged per-
sons.*

**Sensenbrenner, F. James Jr., R-
Wis. (9)**
Abortion clinic access - 357
Crime bill - 278
Vote studies, presidential sup-
port - 6-C
Sentencing Commission, U.S. -
290, 291, 293
Serrano, Jose E., D-N.Y. (16)
Appropriations, Labor-HHS-
Education - 521
House committee assignments
- 16
Housing authorization - 410
Seymour, John - 227
Shalala, Donna E - 366, 369. *See
also: Health and Human Services
Department.*
Shalikashvili, Gen. John M. - 85,
422
Sharp, Philip R., D-Ind. (2)
1994 election - 572
Democratic Caucus - 5
Sharpe, Mark - 571
Shaw, E. Clay Jr., R-Fla. (22)
Everglades protection - 254
Welfare reform - 364
Shays, Christopher, R-Conn. (4)
Congressional workplace law
exemptions - 29
Defense authorization - 423
Rostenkowski indictment - 47
Shea, Diane S. - 262
Shea, Pat - 569
Shearer. Derek - 472
Shelby, Richard C., D-Ala.
1994 election - 13, 14, 565, 579
Appropriations, Foreign Aid -
512
California desert protection -
227
Community Development
Banking - 101
Conservative coalition - 11-C
Crime bill - 286
Party switch - 565
Party unity - 7-C
Vote studies, presidential sup-
port - 6-C
Voting participation - 12-C
Shell Oil Co. - 173
Shepherd, Karen, D-Utah (2)
1994 election - 575
Lobbying disclosure and gift
ban - 37
Ships, shipping. *See also: Taxes
and Taxation.*
Aegis destroyers - 492
Arleigh-Burke-class destroyers -
422, 425, 429
Boat safety - 162, 163, 164
Cargo-preference laws - 160
Defense funding for cargo ships
- 496
FY 1995 budget - 72, 81, 158,
164
Incentives to build cruise ships
in U.S. - 158, 160, 163
Jones Act - 160
Maritime industry aid - 158,
159, 160, 163
Navigational safety for barges,
tow boats - 162, 163
Ocean dumping - 162
RO/RO military cargo ships -
430
Safety regulation for U.S. flag
ships Shipyard subsidies -
158, 160
U.S. labor/wage laws for foreign
ships in U.S. waters - 158,
159, 160
Shultz, George P. - 469

Shuster, Bud, R-Pa. (9)
Clean water law - 243
National Highway System
(NHS) - 165, 166
Superfund reauthorization - 234
Truck-safety amendment - 168
Sierra Club - 228
Silajdzic, Prime Minister Haris -
447
Silberman, Laurence H. - 62
Silverglade, Bruce - 182
Simon, Paul, D-Ill.
Balanced-budget amendment -
85, 86
Budget resolution FY 1995 - 83
Elementary and secondary edu-
cation authorization - 388
Goals 2000 school improve-
ment - 399
School-to-work bill - 400
Unfunded mandates - 152
Simpson, Alan K., R-Wyo.
1994 election - 7, 14
Adm. Kelso's retirement - 440
Clean water law - 242
Competitiveness programs -
222
Filibusters and cloture votes - 9
(box)
Immigration law - 294
National parks - 250
Nominations and appointees -
301
Senate leadership for 104th
Congress - 17
Simpson, Dick - 44
Sims, Ron - 569
Singel, Mike - 579
Sisisky, Norman, D-Va. (4) - 572
Skaggs, David E., D-Colo. (2)
Health care reform - 320
Intelligence authorization bill -
459
Skeen, Joe, R-N.M. (2) - 479
Skelton, Ike, D-Mo. (4)
Child support enforcement -
376
Defense Authorization - 422,
423
Slattery, Jim, D-Kan. (2)
1994 election - 573, 579
Health care reform - 335
Persian Gulf Syndrome com-
pensation - 413
Small aircraft product liability -
181
U.S. communications law
rewrite - 206
Slaughter, Louise M., D-N.Y. (28)
House committee assignments
- 16
House leadership races - 16
Small business. *See also:
Business interests; Lobbies, lob-
bying; Small Business
Administration*
Anti-crime legislation - 288
Banking - 100, 101
Child support enforcement -
376
Government contracts - 187
Health care reform - 329, 331,
333, 336, 341
Investment exemption - 187
Loans, capital and construction
- 186
Minority-owned business - 187
Procurement reform - 147
Small-business loans - 100
U.S. Bankruptcy Code revisions
- 177
**Small Business Administration
(SBA)**

Appropriations - 71, 483, 484
(chart), 485
Authorization - 185, 186
Child support enforcement -
376
FY 1995 budget - 71, 185, 552
FY 1994 disaster supplemental
- 483, 487, 551 (box), 555
Minority Small Business and
Capital Ownership
Development Progam - 187
Office of Women's Business
Ownership - 186
**Small Business Committee
(House)**
Abolishing plan - 18
Procurement reform - 145, 147
Small Business Administration
(SBA) - 186
**Small Business Committee
(Senate)**
Child support enforcement -
376
Small Business Administration
(SBA) - 186
Smith, Bob, R-Ore. (2)
1994 election - 575
Agriculture Department re-
organization - 193
Breyer appointment - 310
Montana wilderness bill - 246
Smith, Christopher H., R-N.J. (4)
Abortion clinic access - 356,
357
VA medical services - 415
Smith, Denny - 564, 580
Smith, James C. - 46
Smith, Jeffrey H. - 459
Smith, Lamar, R-Texas (21)
Appropriations Agriculture - 479
Commerce-Justice-State - 486
Smith, Linda, R-Wash. - 588
Smith, Neal, D-Iowa (4)
1994 election - 55, 570, 572
Appropriations
Agriculture - 479, 480
Commerce-Justice-State -
485
Labor-HHS-Education - 519
FY 1994 disaster supplemental
- 556
House Appropriations
Committee chairmanship - 8,
9
Smith, Nick, R-Mich. (7) - 544
Smith, Robert C., R-N.H.
Appropriations
Legislative branch - 526
Transportation - 534
Treasury Department - 539
VA-HUD - 546
Clean water law - 242
Elementary and secondary edu-
cation authorization - 390
Lead exposure - 266
Shearer nomination - 472
Superfund reauthorization - 235
Vietnam trade embargo - 468
Smithsonian Institution - 152, 157
513, 514 (chart)
Smock, Raymond W. - 56
Smoking bans. *See also: Tobacco.*
Push for smoking ban legisla-
tion - 538
Snowe, Olympia J., R-Maine (2)
1994 election - 565, 568, 576
National Highway System - 167
Republican control of Senate -
565
State Department authorization
bill - 457
Social Security
Balanced-budget amendment -

85, 86, 87
Drug addicts and alcoholics -
366
Old Age, Survivors and
Disability insurance program -
366
**Social Security Administration
(SSA)**
FY 1994 disaster supplemental
provisions - 554
As independent agency - 366,
367
Technology assessment - 367
**Social Security Administration
Independence Act** - 366
Sodini, Joseph J. - 46
Software publishing industry -
See: Computers.
Soil Conservation Service - 549
(box), 551, 553
**Solomon, Gerald B. H., R-N.Y.
(22)**
Budget process - 88
Budget resolution FY 1995 - 83
Crime bill - 279
Defense authorization - 424
House committee chairmen - 15
MFN China - 137
Somalia - 431, 445, 446, 497, 548
Souder, Mark E., R-Ind. - 572
Souter, David H. - 310, 311, 313
South Africa - 461, 463, 470
South Carolina
1994 election - 571, 580
Conservative coalition - 9-C
GATT - 128
VA medical facilities - 415
South Dakota
1994 election - 573, 576
South Korea
Military readiness - 424, 455
Space Station - *See: Technology.*
Spanel, Harriet - 588
Specter, Arlen, R-Pa.
Adm. Kelso's retirement - 440
Appropriations
Foreign Aid - 512
Labor-HHS-Education -
522, 523
Breyer appointment - 310
Crime bill - 286
Defense authorization - 436
Goals 2000 school improve-
ment - 399
Party unity - 7-C
Striker replacement - 402
Spence, Floyd D., R-S.C. (2)
Defense authorization - 423,
435
Energy Department research
laboratories - 223
Procurement reform - 145, 146
Spence, Gene - 579
Sporkin, Stanley - 64
Sports, professional - *See: Labor,
labor unions; names of individual
associations.*
Spratt, John M. Jr., D-S.C. (5) - 89
St. Lawrence Seaway - 531 (chart)
**Standards of Official Conduct
Committee (House)** - 43
Stark, Pete, D-Calif. (13)
Appropriations, District of
Columbia - 500 (box)
Health care reform - 329, 333
Medicare select - 361
Starr, Kenneth W. - 31, 50, 297
State and local government. *See
also: Community development;
Congressional redistricting;
District of Columbia; Federal aid
to states and cities; names of
individual states.*

Child support enforcement -
376
Elementary and secondary edu-
cation reauthorization - 391,
392, 395, 396
Employee Retirement Income
Security Act (ERISA) - 405
School-to-work bill - 400, 401
States' rights - 314
State Department. *See also: Arms
control; Foreign aid; International
broadcasting.*
Appropriations - 187, 483, 484
(chart), 485, 486, 506 (chart)
Authorization - 454, 458
Banking - 107
Cyprus conflict - 470
FY 1995 budget - 79
FY 1994 disaster supplemental
provisions - 554
Holocaust torture lawsuits -
299, 300
International drug control - 506
(chart)
International drug control pro-
grams funding - 508
International programs - 506
(chart)
Office of Counter-Terrorism -
458
Talbott nomination - 471
Treaty on Women - 471
**State Dependent Care
Development Grants** - 372
Stearns, Cliff, R-Fla. (6)
Appropriations
Commerce-Justice-State -
485
Interior Department - 515
House leadership position races
- 15
Steiger, Janet D. - 182
Stein, Jacob A. - 49
**Stenholm, Charles W., D-Texas
(17)**
Agriculture Department reorga-
nization - 192
Balanced-budget amendment -
85, 86
Budget process - 87, 88, 89
Budget resolution FY 1995 - 67,
82, 83, 85
Elementary and secondary edu-
cation authorization - 387
Federal Insecticide, Fungicide
and Rodenticide Act (FIFRA) -
198
House leadership position races
- 15, 16
Plant Variety Protection Act -
190
Vote studies, presidential sup-
port - 6-C
Stevens, John Paul - 311, 314
Stevens, Ted, R-Alaska
Appropriations
Labor-HHS-Education -
522, 523
Legislative branch - 526
Balanced-budget amendment -
86
Defense authorization - 426
Environmental technology - 264
Lobbying disclosure and gift
ban - 39
Marine Mammal Protection Act
reauthorization - 259
National Endowment for the
Arts - 517
Senate leadership for 104th
Congress - 17
U.S. communications law
rewrite - 210, 212

Stocks, bonds and securities
Secondary security market -
107
Securities transaction fee
increases - 70
Stokes, Louis, D-Ohio (11) - 541,
543, 546, 547
Stokes, Susan B. - 571
Stoney, Jan - 569
**Strategic Arms Reduction Treaty
(START II)** - 467
Strategic Petroleum Reserve -
514 (chart)
Strickland, Ted, D-Ohio (6) - 572
Studds, Gerry E., D-Mass. (10)
Coast Guard authorization -
163, 164
Drinking water authorization -
240
Environmental Protection
Agency - 243
Fishing legislation - 259
Marine Mammal Protection Act
reauthorization - 257
Maritime industry aid - 158, 159
National Endowment for the
Arts - 515
State boating safety grants -
162
Student aid - *See also: Education*
Appropriations - 521
Appropriations, Labor-HHS-
Education - 520 (chart)
FY 1994 disaster supplemental
provisions - 551
Pell grants - 520 (chart)
Perkins college loan program -
522
Student loan defaults - 401
Student loans - See: Student aid.
Stump, Bob, R-Ariz. (3) - 422
Stupak, Bart, D-Mich. (1)
Submarines - *See: Navy U.S.,
Submarines.*
**Sub-Saharan African develop-
ment aid** - 506 (chart), 507, 509
Sullivan, Gov. Mike, D-Wyo. - 565,
568
Sulski, Robert B. - 46
Sundlof, Stephen, Dr. - 361
Sundlun, Gov. Bruce, D-R.I. - 576
Sundquist, Don, R-Tenn. (7) - 580
Superfund, EPA
Love Canal - 232
Superfund Amendments and
Reauthorization Act of 1995 -
231, 236
**Supplemental Security Income
Program** - 79, 520 (chart)
Supreme Court
1993-1994 term issues - 310,
314
Abortion - 303, 304, 311
Anti-crime legislation - 290
Appropriations, Commerce-
Justice-State - 484 (chart)
Breyer appointment - 303, 310
Breyer nomination (text) - 17-D,
25-D
Cable television reregulation -
312, 313
Church-state separation - 313
Civil rights retroactivity - 313
Copyrights and parody - 312
Forfeitures - 313
Freedom of speech - 313, 314
Justice Blackmun retires - 303,
304
McDade appeal - 51, 52
Members of the 103rd
Congress, 2nd Session - 7-B
Mitchell nomination - 57, 58
Mitchell withdraws name from

justice consideration - 14-D, 15-D
Possible nominees to replace Blackmun - 303
Punitive damages - 313
Redistricting lawsuits, North Carolina - 312
Sex discrimination - 312
Solid waste disposal - 313
Supplemental Security Income recipients - 367
Voting rights - 312
Supreme Court cases
Shaw v. Reno - 591, 592
Batson v. Kentucky - 312
Board of Education of Kiryas Joel v. Grumet - 313
Boyd v. United States - 49
Bray v. Alexandria Women's Health Clinic - 355
Bryant v. Hill - 314
C & A Carbone v. Clarkstown - 313
City of Chicago v. Environmental Defense Fund - 313
Dalton v. Specter - 436
Dolan v. City of Tigard - 311
Dole v. United Steelworkers of America - 155
Employment Division v. Smith - 378
FEC v. the National Rifle Association Political Victory Fund - 36
Fort Gratiot Sanitary Landfill v. Michigan Department of Natural Resources - 261
Griggs v. Duke Power Co. - 299
Harris v. Forklift Systems Inc. - 312
Holder v. Hall - 312
Honda Motor Co. v. Oberg - 314
J.E.B. v. Alabama - 312
Johnson v. De Grandy - 312
Lemon v. Kurtzman - 313
Madsen v. Women's Health Center - 311
Madsen v. Women's Health Center, Inc. - 355
Meritor Savings Bank v. Vinson - 312
Mertens v. Hewitt Associates - 404
National Labor Relations Board v. Mackay Radio and Telegraph - 402
National Organization for Women Inc. v. Scheidler - 311
NOW v. Scheidler - 311
Oregon Waste Systems v. Department of Environmental Quality - 313
Powell v. McCormack - 315
Shaw v. Reno - 312
Thornburg v. Gingles - 312
Turner Broadcasting System Inc. v. Federal Communications Commission - 312
United States v. James Daniel Good Real Property - 314
U.S. Term Limits v. Thornton - 314
Wards Cove Packing Co. v. Atonio - 299
Swett, Dick, D-N.H. (2)
1994 election - 576
Appropriations, Energy and water - 503
Congressional workplace law exemptions - 29
Swift, Al, D-Wash. (2)
1994 election - 574
Amtrak funding - 171
Federal Trade Commission - 182
Interstate Transport of Solid Waste - 263
Lead exposure - 266
Rostenkowski indictment - 47
Superfund reauthorization - 231, 236
Telemarketing fraud - 217
Uemployment insurance for railroad workers - 407
Sybert, Richard - 573
Symington, Gov. Fife, R-Ariz. - 580
Synar, Mike, D-Okla. (2)
1994 congressional election - 571
Appropriations
Agriculture - 479
Treasury Department - 536, 540
Crime bill - 278, 283
Drinking water authorization - 240
Energy Department research laboratories - 224
Health care reform - 344
Professional baseball antitrust exemption - 182
Small aircraft product liability - 181
Television signal retransmission - 217
U.S. communications law rewrite - 205, 206
Syria - 426

T

Taiwan - 458, 497
Talbott, Stobe - 471
Talent, James M., R-Mo. (2) - 364
Tanks, military
A-2 tank - 494
Appropriations, Defense - 491
Bradley armored troop carrier - 72, 428
M-1 tank - 72, 428, 491, 495
Tariffs
GATT - 132
Tate, Randy, R-Wash. - 588
Tauzin, W. J. "Billy," D-La. (3)
1994 election - 563

American Heritage areas - 252
Balanced-budget amendment - 87
Barge and towboat safety - 162
Boating safety - 163
California desert protection - 227
Coast Guard - 161, 162
Coast Guard authorization - 163
Conservative coalition - 11-C
Health care reform - 336
Interstate Transport of Solid Waste - 261
Recreational boating safety - 162
Superfund reauthorization - 233
U.S. communications law rewrite - 205, 206
Taxes and taxation. *See also: Internal Revenue Service.*
BTU tax - 333
Budget resolution FY 1995 - 82, 84
Corporate income taxes - 70
Domestic workers tax laws - 368
Earned-income tax credits - 365
Excise taxes - 70
Federal Insurance Contributions Act (FICA) - 367
GATT - 127, 136
Health care reform - 323, 326, 330, 332, 333, 337, 339, 340, 342, 351, 353
Income tax - 175
Middle class "Bill of Rights" - 60-D, 61-D
Republican view - 9-D
Republicans' "Contract with America" - 24, 25, 26, 39-D, 52-D
Shipping taxes - 159, 488
Social Security - 369
Targeted jobs tax credit - 70
Tax code simplification - 93
Taylor, Charles H., R-N.C. (11) - 485, 486
Taylor, Gene, D-Miss. (5)
Coast Guard authorization - 163
Incentives to build U.S. ships - 160
Technology transfers - See: Science and technology.
Telecommunications - *See: Communications and telecommunications.*
Telephone Association, U.S. - 214
Telephones - *See: Communications and telecommunications.*
Television
Broadcasting industry
Broadcasters want less regulation, more protection - 208
Congressional committees required to allow radio and television broadcasts - 20 (box)
Extra radio spectrum could offer "ancillary" services - 205, 206
Television signal retransmission via satellite - 212, 216, 217
Cable television
Deregulation - 55, 204, 207, 208, 213 (box)
Reregulation - 312, 313
Standards of decency on cable television - 212
TV Marti - 454
U.S. communications law

rewrite - 203, 205, 214
Tennessee
1994 election - 565, 566, 571, 572, 579, 580
Conservative coalition - 9-C
Military construction - 528
Senate race - 565
Term limits - See: Congress, Term limits.
Terrorism - 291, 454, 458, 506 (chart)
Texaco - 173
Texas
1994 election - 561, 562, 563, 565, 569, 570, 572, 576, 579, 581
Anti-crime legislation - 288
Banking - 95, 97, 100
Colonias - 71
Conservative coalition - 9-C
Fishing legislation - 260
FY 1995 budget - 80
Military construction - 528, 529
Redistricting - 591, 592
Supercollider - 503, 504
United States-Mexico Border Health Commission - 363
Theodore, Nick - 580
Thiokol Corp. - 544
Thomas, Bill, R-Calif. (21)
California desert protection - 229
GATT - 127
Health care reform - 331, 333
House Administration Committee - 13
Rostenkowski indictment - 47
Thomas, Justice Clarence - 310, 311
Thomas, Craig, R-Wyo. (AL)
1994 election - 565, 568, 575
Banking law - 95
Housing authorization - 409
Native Americans - 379
Thomasson, Patsy
Appropriations, Treasury Department - 539
Thompson, Fred, R-Tenn. - 565, 566
1994 election - 61-D
Republican control of Senate - 565
Thornberry, William M. "Mac," R-Texas - 572
Thornburgh, Dick - 564, 565
Thornton, Ray, D-Ark. (2) - 479
Thurber, James A. - 3-C
Thurman, Karen L., D-Fla. (5)
Appropriations, Commerce-Justice-State - 486
Environmental Protection Agency - 244
Thurmond, Strom, R-S.C.
Breyer nomination - 20-D, 21-D
Federal employees - 150
Nominations and appointees - 301
Perry nomination - 439
School-to-work bill - 400
Tiahrt, Todd, R-Kan. - 572
Tierney, John F. - 576
Time Warner Inc. - 214
Tobacco. *See also: Smoking bans.*
Added-nicotine controversy - 359, 360
Elementary and secondary education authorization - 387, 399
GATT - 128
Research programs - 477, 481, 482
Smoking restrictions - 362
Tobias, Robert M. - 349

Toiv, Barry - 148
Tongass National Forest - 517
Torkildsen, Peter G., R-Mass. (6) - 576
Torres, Esteban E., D-Calif. (34) - 549
Torricelli, Robert G., D-N.J. (9) - 189
Towns, Edolphus, D-N.Y. (10)
    Health care reform - 344
    Medical devices - 362
    Unfunded mandates - 151
Trade - See: Foreign Trade
Trade Adjustment Assistance - 406
Traficant, James A. Jr., D-Ohio (17)
    Commerce Department - 189
    Truck-safety amendment - 168
Transportation. See also: Air transportation; Automobiles, automobile industry; Highways and road; Mass transit; National Highway System; National Transit Safety Board; Railroads, Transportation Department.
    1991 surface transportation law - 165
    Budget resolution FY 1995 - 84
    Federal government's role in funding state road projects - 170
    FY 1995 budget - 80, 81
    Hazardous materials transportation - 170
    Road asphalt using recycled tires - 166, 167
    Seat belt laws - 166
    State motorcycle helmet laws - 166
    Unsafe drivers bill - 174
Transportation Department
    Appropriations, FY 1995 - 530, 531, 535
    Defense-related programs - 71
    FY 1995 budget - 81
    FY 1994 disaster supplemental provisions - 551, 552, 553, 554
    Hazardous materials transportation - 170, 171
    Hazardous pipelines - 189
    Interstate Commerce Commission duties - 170
    License commercial re-entry vehicles - 219
    Metric Highway signs - 166
    National Highway System - 165, 168
Travel and Tourism Administration, U.S. - 486
Treasury Committee (House) - 536
Treasury Department. See also: Bureau of Alcohol, Tobacco and Firearms.
    Anti-crime legislation - 288
    Appropriations - 292, 536, 537 (chart)
    Budget resolution, FY 1995 - 85
    Community development banking - 100, 101
    FY 1994 disaster supplemental provisions - 553, 555
    Nominations and appointees - 139
    Office of the Comptroller of the Currency - 96, 98
    Securities - 100
    Superfund reauthorization - 234
Treaties and international agreements. See also: Arms control; General Agreement on Tariffs and Trade (GATT); North American Free Trade Agreement (NAFTA); North Atlantic Treaty Organization (NATO)
    Strategic Arms Reduction Treaty (START II) - 467
    Treaty on Women - 471
Trucks, trucking
    Appropriations, Transportation - 533
    Deregulation - 168, 169, 170
    National Highway System - 167, 168
    Package delivery services - 169, 170
    Tow truck regulation - 174
Trust territories, U.S.
    Court affirms delegate voting - 11-D
    Court upholds delegate voting - 61, 62
    Delegates 103rd Congress, 2nd Session - 7-B
Truth in Negotiations Act - 146
Tucker, Gov. Jim Guy, D-Ark. - 580
Tucker, Walter R. III, D-Calif. (37) - 51
Tudjman, President Franjo - 447
Turkey - 505, 507, 509, 510, 512

Ukraine - 466, 467, 511
U.N. - See: United Nations.
Underwood, Robert A., D-Guam (AL)
    Delegate voting - 62
    Guam - 157
United Nations
    Appropriations
        Commerce-Justice-State - 483, 484 (chart)
        Foreign Operations - 505
        Peacekeeping operations - 483, 484 (chart), 485, 487
    Bosnia-Herzegovina - 425
    Cyprus conflict - 470
    Haitian crisis - 450, 27-D, 28-D
    Peacekeeping operations - 24, 25, 79, 421, 423, 425, 426, 427, 428, 446, 447, 454, 455, 457
    State Department authorization bill - 457
    United Nations Development Program - 511
    United Nations Food and Agriculture Organization - 267
    United Nations Population Fund - 505, 507, 509
United We Stand America - 42, 124
Unity Coalition - 213
University of Oklahoma - 60
Unsoeld, Jolene, D-Wash. (3)
    1994 election - 574
    Elementary and secondary education authorization - 387
    Fisherman's Protective Fund - 161
    Fishing legislation - 260
    Foreign-built vessels - 162, 163
    Health care reform - 325
    Incentives to build cruise ships - 158
    Marine Mammal Protection Act reauthorization - 258
    Pension benefits - 405
Upton, Fred, R-Mich. (6)
    Appropriations, VA-HUD - 544
    Interstate Transport of Solid Waste - 261
    Superfund reauthorization - 233
Urbom, Warren K. - 50
U.S. Term Limits - 315
US West - 214
User fees. See also: Names of executive branch agencies.
    Franchise fees - 250
    Grazing fees - 518
    National park entrance fees - 143
Uslaner, Eric M.
    Voting participation - 12-C
U.S.S.R. - See: Commonwealth of Independent States.
Utah
    1994 election - 569, 581, 584
    Thiokol Corp. - 544

Valentine, Tim, D-N.C. (2)
Vaughan, Thomas, Dr. - 360
Vento, Bruce F., D-Minn. (4)
    American Heritage areas - 252
    California desert protection - 229
    Federal land payments to localities - 156
    Housing authorization - 409
    Idaho wilderness bill - 247
    Montana wilderness bill - 245, 246
    National parks - 247, 250, 251
    Presidio management - 253
    Steamtown - 252
Vermont
    1994 election - 569, 576, 579
    Dairy legislation - 197
    National forests - 247
Veterans' Affairs Committee (House) - 345, 413, 414, 416, 417
Veterans' Affairs Committee (Senate) - 414, 415, 417, 418
Veterans Affairs Department
    Advisory Committee on Minority Veterans - 417
    Appropriations - 411, 541, 547
    Appropriations, FY 1995 - 408
    Board of Veterans Appeals - 413, 417
    Cemetery benefits - 413 (box), 417
    Cost of living adjustments (COLA) - 413 (box), 416
    Cost of living adjustments (COLA) for pensions - 84
    Employment opportunities for veterans - 413 (box), 416, 417
    FY 1995 budget - 81
    FY 1994 disaster supplemental provisions - 548, 549 (box), 551, 553, 555
    Health care
        Agent Orange treatment - 413, 414
        Center for Women Veterans - 413 (box)
        Medical facilities repairs, construction - 415
        Medical services for women veterans - 415
        Mental illness treatment - 418
        Persian Gulf syndrome compensation - 412, 414, 417, 418
        Persian Gulf syndrome provisions - 413 (box)
        Veterans exposed to radi-ation during service - 417
    Home loans - 413 (box), 418
    Home ownership - 555
    Services for homeless vets - 413 (box), 417, 418
    Staff cut exemption - 413 (box), 416
    Veterans center services - 417
    Veterans exposed to radiation during service - 417
    Vocational assistance - 418
    Vocational flight training program - 413 (box)
    Whistleblower protection - 154
Veterans of Foreign Wars - 468
Veterinary medicine - 360, 361
Vietnam
    Trade embargo lifted - 454, 455, 467, 468, 21-C, 12-D
    U.S. aid - 505
Violence Against Women Act - 285
Virginia
    1994 election - 561, 563, 565, 568, 569, 572, 574
    Conservative coalition - 9-C
    Senate race - 565
    VA medical facilities - 415
Visa Waiver Bill - 294
Visclosky, Peter J., D-Ind. (1) - 538
Vocational education - See: Education.
Voinovich, Gov. George V. R-Ohio - 563
Volkmer, Harold L., D-Mo. (9)
    1994 election - 573
    Plant Variety Protection Act - 190
Vote studies
    Conservative coalition - 9-C, 11-C
    Partisan votes - 6-C, 9-C
    Presidential support - 3-C, 6-C
    Voting participation - 11-C, 12-C
Voting Rights Act (1965) - 311, 312, 592
Vucanovich, Barbara F., R-Nev. (2)
    California desert protection - 230
    House leadership position races - 15

Waldholtz, Enid Greene, R-Utah - 584
Walker, Robert S., R-Pa. (16) - 164
    Appropriations, Legislative branch - 525
    Energy Department research laboratories - 223
    Environmental technology - 264
    "Ghost voting" - 54
    House leadership races - 14
    National Oceanic and Atmospheric Administration reauthorization - 219
    Risk assessment program - 244, 245
Wall Street Journal - 544
Wallop, Malcolm, R-Wyo.
    1994 election - 565, 566
    Appropriations, Defense - 497
    California desert protection - 6, 227, 228, 231
    Competitiveness programs - 223
    Defense authorization - 426
    Drinking water authorization -

239
Electonic eavesdropping - 215
Lobbying disclosure and gift ban - 42
National Endowment for the Arts - 518
National parks - 248, 249
Pension benefits - 405
Superfund reauthorization - 236
Voting participation - 12-C
Walsh, James T., R-N.Y. (25)
Appropriations, District of Columbia - 498, 499
Party unity - 7-C
Walsh, Lawrence E. - 295, 468
Wamp, Zach, R-Tenn. - 571
Ward, Mike, D-Ky. - 571
Wards Cove Packing Co. - 298, 299
Warner, John W., R-Va.
1994 election - 568
Ames spy case - 464
Bosnia-Herzegovina - 448
California desert protection - 231
Defense authorization - 425, 426
Drinking water authorization - 239
Intelligence authorization bill - 459, 462
National Reconnaissance Office - 461 (box)
Senate leadership for 104th Congress - 17
Superfund reauthorization - 235
Washington
1994 election - 569, 573, 575
Ballot initiatives - 581
Federal District Court - 315
Logging on Forest Service lands - 256, 257
Washington, Craig, D-Texas (18)
Crime bill - 279
Voting participation - 11-C
Washington Policy Group - 54
Washington Post Co. - 129
Waste management. *See also: Hazardous waste management; Nuclear waste management.*
Court authorizes flow control ordinances - 313
Water issues *See: Environment.*
Waters, Maxine, D-Calif. (35)
Appropriations, Labor-HHS-Education - 521
Banking law - 95
Housing authorization - 410
Watkins, Wes - 579
Watt, Melvin, D-N.C. (12) - 280
Watts, J.C., R-Okla. - 571
Waxman, Henry A., D-Calif. (29)
Added-nicotine controversy - 359, 360
Drinking water authorization - 240
Federal Insecticide, Fungicide and Rodenticide Act (FIFRA) - 198, 199
Food stamps - 377
Health care reform - 5, 320, 335
Indoor air - 266
Medical devices - 362
Minority health programs - 358
Nutritional supplements - 358
Orphan drugs - 363
Radon disclosure - 264
Smoking restrictions - 362
Unfunded mandates - 151
Ways and Means Committee (House)
Chairmanship - 9, 12
Community Development

Banking - 102
Domestic workers tax laws - 368, 369
Fair trade in financial services - 107, 108, 404
GATT - 127, 128
Gibbons assumes gavel - 9
Health care reform - 320, 329, 334
Committee bill highlights - 333
Immigration law - 294
MFN China - 137
Presidio management - 253
Social Security - 366
Superfund reauthorization - 234
Tax code simplification - 93
Welfare reform - 364
Weapons, military. *See also: Bombs; Missiles; Tanks, military.*
AFAS cannon - 428
SADARM - 428
Weaver, Gerald W. II - 53
Webb, Dan K. - 45, 47
Webber, Dan, Jr. - 592
Webster, William H. - 465, 466
Weicker, Gov. Lowell P. Jr., I-Conn. - 564, 579
Weinberger, Caspar W. - 469
Welch, Robert T. - 569, 570
Weldon, Curt, R-Pa. (7)
Defense authorization - 428, 436
Federal Election Commission spending regulations - 36
Radioactive waste - 263
Weldon, Dave, R-Fla. - 571
Welfare and social services. *See also: Anti-poverty programs; Food and nutrition; Food stamps; Medicaid; Women, Infants and Children.*
Appropriations, Labor-HHS-Education - 520 (chart)
Food Stamps - 480
Highlights of Clinton Plan - 364
Illegitimate children - 365
Legal clinic centers for low-income people - 522
Republicans' "Contract With America" - 23
Welfare reform - 364, 365
Clinton reinforces commitment to health care reform - 3-D
Government-sponsored jobs - 364, 365
Women's Infants and Children supplemental food program (WIC) - 374, 481
Work program - 365
Weller, Jerry, R-Ill. - 572
Wellstone, Paul, D-Minn.
Appropriations, Energy and water - 504
Defense authorization - 427
Elementary and secondary education authorization - 389
Haitian crisis - 449, 450
Health care reform - 338
Lobbying disclosure and gift ban - 37, 39, 40
Procurement reform - 145
Wertheimer, Fred - 35, 38, 41
West Bank/Gaza Strip - 509, *See: Israel.*
West Virginia
1994 election - 570, 576
FBI Fingerprint center to relocate in West Virginia - 153
Harper's Ferry National Historical Park - 517
HUD special-purpose grants - 545

National Education and Training Center - 517
Water projects - 242
Wheeling Heritage area - 255
Wetlands - *See: Environment.*
Wheat, Alan, D-Mo. (5) - 568, 573
Wheeler, Bill - 571
Whistleblowing - *See: Fraud and abuse in government.*
White, Justice Byron R. - 304
White, Rick, R-Wash. - 588
White, Wallace H., Jr. - 565
White House Office of Administration - 539
White House Office of Federal Procurement Policy - 147
Whitewater Development Co. - *See: Banks and banking; Whitewater/Madison affair.*
Whitfield, Edward, R-Ky. - 571
Whitman, Gov. Christine Todd, R-N.J.
1994 election - 579
Party unity - 9-C
Senate races - 569
Whitten, Jamie L., D-Miss. (1)
1994 election - 4, 55, 571
Retirement - 59
Whorley, Jeff - 571
WIC - *See: Women, Infants and Children program (WIC).*
Wicker, Roger, R-Miss. - 59, 571
Wickett, Jamie - 231
Wilder, L. Douglas - 568
Wilderness Society - 228
Wildlife aid - *See: Disaster relief.*
Wilhelm, David - 570, 5
Williams, Pat, D-Mont. (AL)
1994 election - 575
Elementary and secondary education authorization - 386, 388
Health care reform - 324, 328
Congressional action - 5, 6
Montana wilderness bill - 245
National parks - 251
Pension funding - 404
Professional baseball antitrust exemption - 183
Wills, Harold Joseph - 46
Wil-Shore Motor Sales - 47
Wilson, Charles, D-Texas (2)
Appropriations, Foreign operations - 507
Crime bill - 285
Lobbying disclosure and gift ban - 42
Wilson, Pete
1994 election - 580
Aid for illegal aliens - 549
California desert protection - 227
Wiretapping - *See: Electronic eavesdropping.*
Wisconsin - 569, 570, 573, 579
Wise, Bob, D-W.Va. (2)
Balanced-budget amendment - 87
Economic Development Administration - 188
Wishart, Leonard P. III - 13
Wofford, Harris, D-Pa.
1994 election - 564, 565, 566
Clean water law - 242
Elementary and secondary education authorization - 389
Health care reform - 337
Martin Luther King Jr. Federal Holiday Commission - 157
Republican control of Senate - 565
Workplace issues - 407
Wojick, Mike - 44

Wolf, Frank R., R-Va. (10)
Appropriations, Military construction - 527
Transportation - 530
Treasury Department - 540
Women. *See also: Abortion; Civil rights; Family and marital issues.*
Convention on the Elimination of All Forms of Discrimination on Women (Treaty on Women) - 471
Defense Department
Sexual harassment against women in military - 435
Woment to serve in combat units - 435
Equity in schools - 394
Treaty on Women - 471
Veterans Affairs Department
Medical services for women veterans - 414, 415
Violence against women - 274, 289
Women, Infants and Children (WIC) - 196, 329, 374. *See also: Food and nutrition; Welfare*
Woolsey, Lynn, D-Calif. (6)
Elementary and secondary education authorization - 385
Health care reform - 328, 329
Woolsey, R. James
Ames spy case - 463, 466
Defense authorization - 438
Intelligence authorization bill - 459
National Reconnaissance Office - 461 (box)
Workers - *See: Employment and training; Employment and unemployment; Labor, labor unions.*
World Bank - 79, 505, 506 (chart), 507, 554
World Trade Organization - 123, 124, 125, 131
Wyden, Ron, D-Ore. (3)
Added-nicotine controversy - 360
Appropriations, agricultural - 479
Independent service stations - 173
U.S. communications law rewrite - 205, 206
White House relations - 31
Wynia, Ann - 568
Wynn, Albert R., D-Md. (4)
House Appropriations Committee chairmanship - 8
Housing authorization - 409
Wyoming
1994 election - 565, 568, 580, 584
Ballot initiatives - 581
Senate race - 565

Y

Yates, Sidney R., D-Ill. (9) - 513, 515
Yeltsin, Boris N. - 466, 510
York, Myrth - 576
Young, C.W. Bill, R-Fla. (10)
Appropriations, Legislative branch - 525
House committee chairmen - 15
Young, Don, R-Alaska (AL)
Canadian fishing vessel fee - 161
Fishing legislation - 259, 260
Marine Mammal Protection Act reauthorization - 258
Montana wilderness bill - 246

Youths. *See also: Children; Elementary and secondary education; Postsecondary education.*
    Anti-crime legislation - 289, 291
    FY 1995 budget - 72
Yugoslavia - *See: Bosnia-Herzegovina; Names of other republics created from former Yugoslavia.*

Z

Zeliff, Bill, R-N.H. (1)
    1994 election - 576
    Budget process - 88, 89
    Superfund reauthorization - 236
Zenkich, Elias R. "Non-Incumbent" - 44
Zenner, Patrick J. - 330
Zigler, Edward F. - 370
Zimmer, Dick, R-N.J. (12)
    Appropriations, VA-HUD - 541, 544
    Budget resolution FY 1995 - 83
    Risk assessment program - 244
Zionist Organization of America - 471, 512